GUIDE TO U.S. FOUNDATIONS, THEIR TRUSTEES, OFFICERS, AND DONORS

GUIDE TO U.S. FOUNDATIONS, THEIR TRUSTEES, OFFICERS, AND DONORS
Volume Two

2003 Edition

Compiled by
THE FOUNDATION CENTER

David G. Jacobs, Editor

The Foundation Center
New York • 2003

CONTRIBUTING STAFF

**Senior Vice President for
Information Resources and Publishing**   Rick Schoff

**Director of Foundation Database
Publishing**   Jeffrey A. Falkenstein

Senior Database Editor   Margaret Mary Feczko

Assistant Editor   Juanita M. Bernacet

Editorial Associates   Edita Birnkrant
Julie Buzzeo
Hope LaDue
Greg Torso

Editorial Consultants   Melissa R. Lunn
Jose L. Santiago

Publishing Database Administrator   Kathye Giesler

Database Operations Assistant   Emmy So

Director of Communications   Cheryl L. Loe

Production Coordinator, Publications   Christine Innamorato

Manager of Bibliographic Services   Sarah Collins

Public Services Assistant   Jimmy Tom

Coordinator of Information Control   Yinebon Iniya

The Editor gratefully acknowledge the many other Foundation Center staff members who contributed support, encouragement, and information that was indispensable to the preparation of this publication. Special mention should be made of the staff members of the New York, Washington, D.C., Cleveland, San Francisco, and Atlanta libraries who assisted in tracking changes in foundation information. The staff would also like to express its appreciation to the foundations that cooperated by providing verified and updated information prior to completion of the *Guide to U.S. Foundations, Their Trustees, Officers, and Donors.*

Copyright © 2003 by the Foundation Center
All rights reserved
Printed and bound in the United States of America.
ISBN 1-931923-40-X

VOLUME TWO CONTENTS

DESCRIPTIVE DIRECTORY
   SECTION 1. Independent, Corporate, and Community Foundations (New York–Wyoming) 1
   SECTION 2. Operating Foundations 2089

APPENDIXES
   A. Edition 10 Foundations Not Included in Edition 11 2565
   B. Foundations That Award Grants to Specified Beneficiaries 2593

INDEPENDENT, CORPORATE, AND COMMUNITY FOUNDATIONS
(New York–Wyoming)

INDEPENDENT, CORPORATE, AND COMMUNITY FOUNDATIONS
(New York–Wyoming)

INDEPENDENT, CORPORATE, AND COMMUNITY FOUNDATIONS

NEW YORK

32481
The Ford Foundation
320 E. 43rd St.
New York, NY 10017 (212) 573-5000
FAX: (212) 351-3677; E-mail: office-secretary@fordfoundation.org; URL: http://www.fordfound.org
Contact: Secy.

Incorporated in 1936 in MI.
Donor(s): Henry Ford,‡ Edsel Ford.‡
Financial data (yr. ended 09/30/01): Grants paid, $829,190,310; assets, $10,814,696,000 (M); expenditures, $1,002,239,844; qualifying distributions, $929,659,367; giving activities include $12,320,000 for program-related investments.
Limitations: Giving on an international basis, including the U.S., Eastern Europe, Africa and the Middle East, Asia, Russia, Latin America and the Caribbean.
Publications: Annual report (including application guidelines), occasional report, informational brochure (including application guidelines), informational brochure, newsletter.
Application information: Prospective applicants are advised to review the foundation's Web site for information or current funding guidelines. Foreign applicants should contact foundation for addresses of its overseas offices, through which they must apply. Application form not required.
Officers and Trustees:* Paul A. Allaire,* Chair.; Susan V. Berresford,* Pres.; Barron M. Tenny, Exec. V.P., Genl. Counsel, and Secy.; Barry D. Gaberman, Sr. V.P.; Linda B. Strumpf, V.P. and C.I.O.; Alison R. Bernstein, V.P., Education, Media, Arts and Culture; Melvin L. Oliver, V.P., Asset Bldg. and Community Devel.; Bradford K. Smith, V.P., Peace and Social Justice; Alexander Wilde, V.P., Comm.; Nicholas M. Gabriel, Treas. and Dir., Financial Svcs.; Nancy P. Feller, Assoc. Genl. Counsel; Alain J.P. Belda, Afsaneh M. Beschloss, Anke A. Ehrhardt, Kathryn S. Fuller, Wilmot G. James, Yolanda Kakabadse, Wilma P. Mankiller, Richard Moe, Yolanda T. Moses, Luis G. Nogales, Deval L. Patrick, Ratan N. Tata, Carl B. Weisbrod, W. Richard West.
EIN: 131684331
Codes: FD, FM, GTI

32482
The Starr Foundation
70 Pine St.
New York, NY 10270 (212) 770-6881
FAX: (212) 425-6261; E-mail: florence.davis@starrfdn.org; URL: http://fdncenter.org/grantmaker/starr
Contact: Florence A. Davis, Pres.

Incorporated in 1955 in NY.
Donor(s): Cornelius V. Starr.‡
Financial data (yr. ended 12/31/01): Grants paid, $245,469,098; assets, $4,781,056,809 (M); gifts received, $7,970; expenditures, $247,836,594; qualifying distributions, $245,469,098.
Application information: Application form not required.
Officers and Directors:* Maurice R. Greenberg,* Chair.; Florence A. Davis,* Pres.; Gladys Thomas, V.P. and Secy.; Marion I. Breen,* V.P.; H.I. Smith,* Treas.; T.C. Hsu, Edwin A.G. Manton, E.E. Matthews, John J. Roberts, Ernest E. Stempel, E.S. Tse.
EIN: 136151545
Codes: FD, FM, GTI

32483
The Andrew W. Mellon Foundation
140 E. 62nd St.
New York, NY 10021 (212) 838-8400
URL: http://www.mellon.org
Contact: Michele S. Warman, Secy. and Genl. Counsel

Trust established in 1940 in DE as Avalon Foundation; incorporated in 1954 in NY; merged with Old Dominion Foundation and renamed the Andrew W. Mellon Foundation in 1969.
Donor(s): Ailsa Mellon Bruce,‡ Paul Mellon.‡
Financial data (yr. ended 12/31/01): Grants paid, $182,321,993; assets, $4,135,567,000 (M); expenditures, $207,798,000; qualifying distributions, $182,321,993.
Publications: Annual report.
Application information: Application form not required.
Officers and Trustees:* Hanna Holborn Gray,* Chair.; William G. Bowen,* Pres.; Harriet Zuckerman, Sr. V.P.; Glenda Burkhart, V.P., Opers. and Plan.; Mary Patterson McPherson, V.P.; John E. Hull, V.P., Finance; Michele S. Warman, Secy. and Genl. Counsel; Eileen M. Scott, Treas.; Lewis W. Bernard, Charles E. Exley, Jr., Paul LeClerc, Walter E. Massey, Timothy Mellon, W. Taylor Reveley III, Anne M. Tatlock.
EIN: 131879954
Codes: FD, FM

32484
The New York Community Trust
2 Park Ave., 24th Fl.
New York, NY 10016-9385 (212) 686-0010
FAX: (212) 532-8528; URL: http://www.nycommunitytrust.org
Contact: Lorie A. Slutsky, Pres. and Dir.

Established in 1924 in NY by resolution and declaration of trust.
Financial data (yr. ended 12/31/01): Grants paid, $126,621,735; assets, $1,785,215,504 (M); gifts received, $114,811,645; expenditures, $200,257,027.
Limitations: Giving limited to the metropolitan New York, NY, area.
Publications: Annual report, newsletter, occasional report, financial statement, application guidelines, informational brochure (including application guidelines).
Application information: Accepts NYRAG Common Application Form. Applicants for support from the Long Island Community Foundation should call (516) 681-5085; those wishing to apply to the Westchester Community Foundation should call (914) 948-5166. Application form required.
Officers and Distribution Committee:* Anne Sidamon-Eristoff,* Chair.; Lorie A. Slutsky,* Pres. and Dir.; Karen Metcalf, V.P., Finance and Admin. and Treas.; Joyce M. Bove, V.P., Progs. and Projects; Jane L. Wilton, Secy. and Genl. Counsel; Kathryn Conroy, Cont.; Bruce L. Ballard, M.D., Barbara H. Block, William M. Evarts, Jr., Charlotte M. Fischman, Barry H. Garfinkel, Robert M. Kaufman, Samuel S. Polk, Toni Randolph, Carroll L. Wainwright, Jr., Lulu C. Wang.
Trustees: The Bank of New York, Bankers Trust Co. of New York, Bessemer Trust Co., N.A., Brown Brothers Harriman Trust Co., The Chase Manhattan Bank, N.A., Citibank, N.A., Fiduciary Trust Co., Fleet National Bank, HSBC Bank USA, IBJ Whitehall Bank and Trust Company, Morgan Guaranty Trust Co. of New York, Neuberger and Berman Trust Co., Rockefeller Trust Co., U.S. Trust, Winthrop Trust Co.
EIN: 133062214
Codes: CM, FD, FM

32485
The Rockefeller Foundation
420 5th Ave.
New York, NY 10018-2702 (212) 869-8500
URL: http://www.rockfound.org
Contact: Lynda Mullen, Corp. Secy.

Incorporated in 1913 in NY.
Donor(s): John D. Rockefeller, Sr.‡
Financial data (yr. ended 12/31/01): Grants paid, $126,564,668; assets, $3,211,126,000 (M);

IN THIS SECTION, WITHIN EACH STATE, FOUNDATIONS ARE LISTED IN DESCENDING ORDER BY TOTAL GRANTS PAID

32485—NEW YORK

expenditures, $179,712,911; qualifying distributions, $163,825,000; giving activities include $1,000,000 for program-related investments and $19,317,805 for programs.
Limitations: Giving on a national and international basis.
Publications: Annual report (including application guidelines), program policy statement, application guidelines, financial statement.
Application information: The foundation strongly discourages unsolicited grant proposals. Organizations should carefully review grantmaking guidelines on the foundation's Web site. Application form not required.
Officers and Trustees:* James F. Orr III,* Chair.; Gordon Conway,* Pres.; Denise A. Gray-Felder, V.P., Admin. and Comm.; Robert W. Herdt, V.P., Prog. Admin.; Julia I. Lopez, V.P., Prog. Admin.; Lynda Mullen, Corp. Secy.; Donna Dean, Treas. and C.I.O.; Charles J. Lang, Compt.; Ela R. Bhatt, David de Ferranti, William H. Foege, Antonia Hernandez, Linda Hill, David M. Lawrence, Yo-Yo Ma, Jessica Tuchman Mathews, Mamphela Ramphele, Rev. Cannon Frederick Boyd Williams, D. Min., D.C.L., Vo-Tong Xuan.
EIN: 131659629
Codes: FD, FM, GTI

32486
Doris Duke Charitable Foundation
650 5th Ave., 19th Fl.
New York, NY 10019 (212) 974-7000
Additional tel.: (212) 974-7100; FAX: (212) 974-7590; URL: http://fdncenter.org/grantmaker/dorisduke
Contact: Office of Grants Admin.

Established in 1996 in NY.
Donor(s): Doris Duke.‡
Financial data (yr. ended 12/31/01): Grants paid, $89,200,564; assets, $1,444,832,885 (M); gifts received, $675,833; expenditures, $106,811,370; qualifying distributions, $74,820,710.
Limitations: Giving on a national basis.
Application information: The foundation staff responds to all letters of inquiry, however, it should be noted that very few grants result from unsolicited letters of inquiry. Do not send binders, books, CDs, videotapes, or audiotapes.
Officers and Trustees:* James F. Gill,* Chair.; Marion Oates Charles,* Vice-Chair.; Joan E. Spero, Pres.; Alan Altschuler, C.F.O.; Harry B. Demopoulos, M.D., Anthony S. Fauci, M.D., Nannerl O. Keohane, John J. Mack, John H.T. Wilson.
EIN: 137043679
Codes: FD, FM

32487
The Freeman Foundation
1211 Ave. of the Americas, 38th Fl.
New York, NY 10036 (212) 789-5734
E-mail: wong_elizabeth@jpmorgan.com
Contact: Elizabeth Wong

Established in 1978 in VT.
Donor(s): Houghton Freeman, Mansfield Freeman,‡ members of the Freeman family.
Financial data (yr. ended 12/31/01): Grants paid, $86,714,475; assets, $1,619,093,718 (M); expenditures, $89,613,539; qualifying distributions, $87,121,945.
Limitations: Giving primarily in VT for environment and special interest grants; Asian studies grants awarded nationally.
Publications: Annual report.
Application information: Application form not required.
Officer: Graeme Freeman, Exec. Dir.

Trustees: Houghton Freeman, George B. Snell, JPMorgan Chase Bank.
EIN: 132965090
Codes: FD, FM

32488
Verizon Foundation
(also known as Bell Atlantic Foundation)
1095 Ave. of the Americas, Rm. 3200
New York, NY 10036 (800) 360-7955
Additional tel.: (212) 395-2295; FAX: (212) 398-0951; E-mail: suzanne.dubose@verizon.com; URL: http://foundation.verizon.com
Contact: Suzanne A. DuBose, Pres.

Established in 1985 in NY; name changed to Bell Atlantic Foundation in Feb. 1998 following the merger of NYNEX Foundation and Bell Atlantic Charitable Foundation; current name adopted in Apr. 2000.
Donor(s): NYNEX Corp., Bell Atlantic Corp., Verizon Communications Inc.
Financial data (yr. ended 12/30/01): Grants paid, $77,137,397; assets, $80,235,431 (M); gifts received, $53,914,344; expenditures, $81,049,509; qualifying distributions, $77,108,119.
Limitations: Giving primarily in areas of corporate sponsor's operations concentrated in New England, DE, NJ, NY, PA, WV, and the greater metropolitan Washington, DC, area.
Publications: Annual report (including application guidelines), informational brochure (including application guidelines).
Application information: Common Application Form available on foundation's Web site. Application form not required.
Officers and Directors:* Charles R. Lee,* Chair.; Mary Beth Bardin,* Vice-Chair. and Secy.; Suzanne A. DuBose, Pres.; Thomas J. Tauke,* Exec. V.P.; Neil D. Olson, V.P. and Treas.; Michael Morrell, V.P. and Cont.; T. Britton Harris IV, C.I.O.; Bruce S. Gordon,* Exec. Dir.; Oscar C. Gomez, Katherine J. Harless.
EIN: 133319048
Codes: CS, FD, CD, FM

32489
Alfred P. Sloan Foundation
630 5th Ave., Ste. 2550
New York, NY 10111-0242 (212) 649-1649
FAX: (212) 757-5117; URL: http://www.sloan.org
Contact: Ralph E. Gomory, Pres.

Incorporated in 1934 in DE.
Donor(s): Alfred P. Sloan, Jr.,‡ Irene Jackson Sloan,‡ New Castle Corp.
Financial data (yr. ended 12/31/01): Grants paid, $60,842,714; assets, $1,314,367,357 (M); expenditures, $65,896,556; qualifying distributions, $66,211,362.
Publications: Informational brochure (including application guidelines).
Application information: Nomination forms available for fellowship candidates; direct applications not accepted. Application form not required.
Officers and Trustees:* Harold T. Shapiro,* Chair.; Ralph E. Gomory,* Pres.; Stewart F. Campbell, Financial V.P. and Secy.; William B. Petersen, V.P. and C.I.O.; Christopher Sia, Cont.; Stephen L. Brown, S. Parker Gilbert, William E. Hoglund, Donald N. Langenberg, Sandra O. Moose, Phillip A. Sharp, Roger B. Smith, Roger M. Solow, Dennis Weatherstone, Sheila E. Widnall.
EIN: 131623877
Codes: FD, FM, GTI

32490
The J. P. Morgan Chase Foundation
(Formerly The Chase Manhattan Foundation)
1 Chase Manhattan Plz., 5th Fl.
New York, NY 10081 (212) 552-1112
URL: http://www.jpmorganchase.com/grants
Contact: Steven W. Gelston, Secy.-Treas.

Incorporated in 1969 in NY; name changed in 2001 as a result of the merger of the Chase Manhattan Corp. and J.P. Morgan & Co. Inc.
Donor(s): The Chase Manhattan Bank, J.P. Morgan Chase & Co.
Financial data (yr. ended 12/31/01): Grants paid, $60,115,841; assets, $83,071,014 (M); gifts received, $16,680,882; expenditures, $61,869,768; qualifying distributions, $62,026,601.
Limitations: Giving in the tri-state region of NY, NJ, and CT; the states of AZ, CA, DE, FL, IL, LA, MA, and OH; some national programs; and approximately 50 countries where J.P. Morgan Chase has a business presence.
Publications: Annual report, corporate giving report (including application guidelines), application guidelines.
Application information: See foundation's Web site for application information and application forms or call Grants Hotline at (212) 552-1112. In all cases, it is up to the J.P. Morgan Chase staff whether to recommend funding from the foundation or the firm itself. In situations where benefits may be derived to the firm, its subsidiaries, or its employees, grants must necessarily be made by the firm. Application form required.
EIN: 237049738
Codes: CS, FD, CD, FM

32491
Wallace-Reader's Digest Funds
2 Park Ave., 23rd Fl.
New York, NY 10016 (212) 251-9700
E-mail: wrdf@wallacefunds.org; URL: http://www.wallacefunds.org
Contact: Lucas Held, Dir., Comm.

Lila Wallace-Reader's Digest Fund and DeWitt Wallace-Reader's Digest Fund Inc., incorporated in NY in 1956 and 1965 respectively.
Donor(s): DeWitt Wallace,‡ Lila Acheson Wallace.‡
Financial data (yr. ended 12/31/01): Grants paid, $58,274,675; assets, $1,303,278,360 (M); gifts received, $239,178; expenditures, $65,977,612; qualifying distributions, $66,113,494.
Limitations: Giving on a national basis.
Publications: Annual report, newsletter, occasional report, annual report (including application guidelines).
Application information: Application form not required.
Officers and Directors:* George V. Grune,* Chair.; M. Christine DeVita,* Pres.; Rob D. Nagel, Treas. and Dir., Investments; Gordon Ambach, Don Cornwell, Peter Marzio, Laraine S. Rothenberg, Joseph Shenker, Walter V. Shipley, C.J. Silas.
Codes: FD, FM

32492
Carnegie Corporation of New York
437 Madison Ave.
New York, NY 10022 (212) 371-3200
FAX: (212) 754-4073; URL: http://www.carnegie.org
Contact: Edward Sermier, V.P.

Incorporated in 1911 in NY.
Donor(s): Andrew Carnegie.‡

Financial data (yr. ended 09/30/01): Grants paid, $56,363,235; assets, $1,711,510,640 (M); expenditures, $78,531,470; qualifying distributions, $69,020,818; giving activities include $1,895,291 for programs.
Limitations: Giving primarily in the U.S. Some grants in former Commonwealth Countries in Sub-Saharan Africa, South Africa.
Publications: Annual report (including application guidelines), informational brochure, grants list, occasional report, newsletter.
Application information: Proposals from libraries and cultural institutions are not accepted. Application form required.
Officers and Trustees:* Helene L. Kaplan,* Chair.; Martin L. Leibowitz,* Vice-Chair.; Vartan Gregorian,* Pres.; Edward Sermier, V.P., C.A.O., and Secy.; D. Ellen Shuman, V.P. and C.I.O.; Neil Grabois, V.P. and Dir. Strategic Planning and Prog. Coord.; Susan Robinson King, V.P., Public Affairs; Bruce Alberts, Geoffrey T. Boisi, James B. Hunt, William McDonaugh, Sam Nunn, Olara A. Otunnu, William A. Owens, Ruth J. Simmons, Raymond W. Smith, Shirin Tahir-Kheli, Marta Tienda, Judy Woodruff.
EIN: 131628151
Codes: FD, FM

32493
Citigroup Foundation
(Formerly Citicorp Foundation)
850 3rd Ave., 13th Fl.
New York, NY 10043 (212) 793-8451
FAX: (212) 793-5944; E-mail: citigroupfoundation@citi.com; URL: http://www.citigroup.com/citigroup/corporate/foundation/index.htm
Contact: Charles V. Raymond, C.E.O. and Pres.

Established in 1994 in NY.
Donor(s): Citicorp, Citibank, N.A., Citigroup Inc.
Financial data (yr. ended 12/31/01): Grants paid, $50,733,278; assets, $193,865,626 (M); gifts received, $62,934,584; expenditures, $51,936,351; qualifying distributions, $38,024,738.
Limitations: Giving on a national and international basis.
Publications: Annual report.
Application information: The foundation solicits proposals from pre-selected organizations; relatively few unsolicited proposals are considered.
Officers and Directors:* Charles V. Raymond,* C.E.O. and Pres.; Patricia R. Byrne, V.P., U.S. Domestic Progs.; Leslie Meek, V.P., Comm. Devel.; Alan Okada, V.P., Health/Human Svcs.; Anne Roberts, V.P., Finance and Admin.; Daria Sheehan, V.P., Pre K-12 Education; Charles O. Prince III, Sanford I. Weill.
EIN: 133781879
Codes: CS, FD, CD, FM

32494
AT&T Foundation
32 Ave. of the Americas, 6th Fl.
New York, NY 10013 (212) 387-4801
FAX: (212) 387-4882; E-mail: Mcclimon@att.com; URL: http://www.att.com/foundation
Contact: Timothy J. McClimon, Exec. Dir.

Established in 1984 in NY.
Donor(s): American Telephone and Telegraph Co., Western Electric Fund, AT&T Corp.
Financial data (yr. ended 12/31/01): Grants paid, $44,196,080; assets, $48,824,236 (M); gifts received, $25,199,987; expenditures, $43,160,785; qualifying distributions, $43,889,285.
Limitations: Applications not accepted. Giving on a national and international basis, primarily to Los Angeles and San Francisco, CA; Denver, CO; Washington, DC; Miami, FL; Chicago, IL; NJ; NY; Pittsburgh and Philadelphia, PA; and Seattle, WA.
Application information: Unsolicited applications not considered.
Officers and Trustees:* Richard J. Martin,* Chair.; Mirian Graddick-Weir,* Vice Chair.; Esther Silver-Parker,* Pres.; Marilyn Reznick, V.P., Education Prog.; Mitzi Vaimberg, V.P., Civic and Community Svc. Prog.; Vivian Nero, Secy. Opers., Dir.; Robert E. Angelica, Treas.; Timothy J. McClimon, Exec. Dir.; Adele Ambrose, Harold W. Burlingame, David Condit, Regina Egea, Curt Fields, David Grain, R. Reed Harrison, Rick Jenkinson, Barbara Peda, Steve Van Dorselaer, Constance Weaver.
EIN: 133166495
Codes: CS, FD, CD, FM

32495
The Henry Luce Foundation, Inc.
111 W. 50th St., Rm. 4601
New York, NY 10020 (212) 489-7700
FAX: (212) 581-9541; E-mail: hlf@hluce.org; URL: http://www.hluce.org
Contact: Michael Gilligan, Pres.

Incorporated in 1936 in NY.
Donor(s): Henry R. Luce,‡ Clare Boothe Luce.‡
Financial data (yr. ended 12/31/01): Grants paid, $43,514,883; assets, $905,305,357 (M); expenditures, $49,452,478; qualifying distributions, $43,514,883.
Limitations: Giving on a national and international basis; international activities limited to East and Southeast Asia.
Publications: Biennial report (including application guidelines), informational brochure, grants list.
Application information: Nominees for Luce Scholars Program accepted from invited institutions only; Clare Boothe Luce Program by invitation to institutions only, individual applications cannot be considered; American Art Program requires prior inquiry by Mar.1. Application form not required.
Officers and Directors:* Margaret Boles Fitzgerald,* Chair.; Michael Gilligan,* Pres.; Terrill E. Lautz, V.P. and Secy.; John C. Evans,* V.P. and Treas.; John P. Daley, V.P., Finance and Admin.; Helene E. Redell, V.P. and Prog. Dir.; Luce Scholars; Robert E. Armstrong, John Wesley Cook, Anne d'Harnoncourt, Claire L. Gaudiani, Kenneth T. Jackson, James T. Laney, H. Christopher Luce, Henry Luce III, Thomas L. Pulling, David V. Ragone.
EIN: 136001282
Codes: FD, FM, GTI

32496
The Atlantic Foundation of New York
125 Park Ave., 21st Fl.
New York, NY 10017-5581
Contact: Cynthia R. Richards, V.P.

Established in 1989 in NY.
Donor(s): Atlan Management Corp., Interpacific Holdings, Inc., General Atlantic Corp.
Financial data (yr. ended 12/31/00): Grants paid, $42,608,907; assets, $100,563,696 (M); gifts received, $26,000,000; expenditures, $42,892,008; qualifying distributions, $43,804,668; giving activities include $1,000,000 for loans.
Limitations: Applications not accepted. Giving on a national basis.
Application information: Contributes only to pre-selected organizations. Unsolicited requests for funds not considered.
Officers and Directors:* John R. Healy,* Pres.; Cynthia R. Richards, V.P.; Alan Ruby,* Secy.-Treas.; Harvey P. Dale, Elizabeth McCormack, Frederick A.O. Schwarz, Jr., Michael Sovern.
EIN: 133562971
Codes: FD, FM

32497
Horace W. Goldsmith Foundation
375 Park Ave., Ste. 1602
New York, NY 10152 (212) 319-8700
Contact: James C. Slaughter, C.E.O.

Incorporated in 1955 in NY.
Donor(s): Horace W. Goldsmith.‡
Financial data (yr. ended 12/31/01): Grants paid, $40,112,467; assets, $864,590,763 (M); expenditures, $42,109,763; qualifying distributions, $39,634,935.
Limitations: Applications not accepted. Giving primarily in AZ, MA, and New York, NY.
Application information: Foundation depends almost exclusively on internally initiated grants.
Managing Directors: James C. Slaughter, C.E.O.; Richard L. Menschel, Robert B. Menschel, Thomas R. Slaughter, William A. Slaughter.
EIN: 136107758
Codes: FD, FM

32498
Surdna Foundation, Inc.
330 Madison Ave., 30th Fl.
New York, NY 10017-5001 (212) 557-0010
FAX: (212) 557-0003; E-mail: request@surdna.org; URL: http://www.surdna.org
Contact: Edward Skloot, Exec. Dir.

Incorporated in 1917 in NY.
Donor(s): John E. Andrus.‡
Financial data (yr. ended 06/30/01): Grants paid, $39,531,216; assets, $639,962,016 (M); gifts received, $1,595,930; expenditures, $45,346,075; qualifying distributions, $42,805,726.
Publications: Annual report (including application guidelines).
Application information: Application form not required.
Officers and Directors:* Elizabeth H. Andrus,* Chair.; Christopher F. Davenport,* Vice.-Chair.; John J. Lynagh,* Secy.; Frederick F. Moon III,* Treas.; Marc de Venoge, C.F.O. and C.A.O.; Edward Skloot, Exec. Dir.; John E. Andrus III, Chair. Emeritus; Peter B. Benedict, Lawrence S.C. Griffith, M.D., John F. Hawkins, Sandra T. Kaupe, J. Michael Pakradooni, Michael S. Spensley, Edith D. Thorpe, Samuel S. Thorpe III.
EIN: 136108163
Codes: FD, FM

32499
Avon Foundation, Inc.
(Formerly Avon Products Foundation, Inc.)
1345 Ave. of the Americas
New York, NY 10105-0196 (212) 282-5000
FAX: (212) 282-6049; URL: http://www.avonfoundation.org
Contact: Denise L. C. Yap, Admin.

Incorporated in 1955 in NY.
Donor(s): Avon Products, Inc.
Financial data (yr. ended 12/31/00): Grants paid, $31,629,489; assets, $38,437,478 (M); gifts received, $50,667,895; expenditures, $31,724,297; qualifying distributions, $31,696,799.

32499—NEW YORK

Limitations: Giving limited to areas immediately surrounding company operations in Pasadena, CA; Newark, DE; Atlanta, GA; Morton Grove, IL; New York, Rye, and Suffern, NY; and Springdale, OH; some support for national programs, and PR.
Publications: Annual report, informational brochure (including application guidelines).
Application information: Application form required for scholarships only. Guidelines are available on the foundation's Web site or by telephone.
Officers and Directors:* Kathleen Walas,* Pres.; Brian Connolly,* V.P.; Jill Kavin-Lovers,* V.P.; Thomas Sarakatsannis,* Secy.; Robert Corti,* Treas.; Mary Quinn.
EIN: 136128447
Codes: CS, FD, CD, FM

32500
Soros Charitable Foundation
400 W. 59th St.
New York, NY 10019
Contact: Steve Gutmann

Established in 1992 in NY.
Donor(s): George Soros.
Financial data (yr. ended 11/30/01): Grants paid, $31,100,000; assets, $101,081,755 (M); expenditures, $31,317,288; qualifying distributions, $31,128,565; giving activities include $31,100,000 for programs.
Limitations: Applications not accepted. Giving primarily in New York, NY.
Application information: Contributes only to pre-selected organizations.
Trustees: Daneil R. Eule, George Soros, Jonathan Soros, Susan Weber Soros, William D. Zabel.
EIN: 137003532
Codes: FD

32501
The Edna McConnell Clark Foundation
250 Park Ave., Rm. 900
New York, NY 10177-0026 (212) 551-9100
FAX: (212) 986-4558; E-mail: info@emcf.org
URL: http://www.emcf.org
Contact: Mary Hall, Asst. to the Pres.

Incorporated in 1950 in NY and 1969 in DE; the NY corporation merged into the DE corporation in 1974.
Donor(s): Edna McConnell Clark,‡ W. Van Alan Clark.‡
Financial data (yr. ended 09/30/01): Grants paid, $30,405,842; assets, $634,990,723 (M); expenditures, $38,352,078; qualifying distributions, $35,203,997.
Limitations: Applications not accepted. Giving primarily in the Northeast corridor (from Boston, MA to Washington, DC).
Publications: Annual report, grants list, occasional report.
Application information: The foundation is not actively seeking or accepting unsolicited proposals, direct-service youth organizations working with youth during non-school hours are invited to share some information about their organizations by completing an online form on our Web site.
Officers and Trustees:* Edward C. Schmults,* Chair.; Michael A. Bailin,* Pres.; Patricia Barron, H. Lawrence Clark, James McConnell Clark, Jr., John M. Emery, Hon. Theodore A. McKee, James E. Preston.
EIN: 237047034
Codes: FD, FM

32502
William Randolph Hearst Foundation
888 7th Ave., 45th Fl.
New York, NY 10106-0057 (212) 586-5404
Address for applicants from west of the Mississippi River: c/o Thomas Eastham, V.P. and Western Dir., 90 New Montgomery St., Ste. 1212, San Francisco, CA 94105; tel.: (415) 543-0400; URL: http://www.hearstfdn.org
Contact: Robert M. Frehse, Jr., V.P. and Exec. Dir. (east of the Mississippi River); Thomas Eastham, V.P. and Western Dir. (west of the Mississippi River)

Incorporated in 1948 in CA.
Donor(s): William Randolph Hearst.‡
Financial data (yr. ended 12/31/01): Grants paid, $28,928,400; assets, $624,456,279 (M); expenditures, $33,695,698; qualifying distributions, $32,934,504; giving activities include $2,284,238 for programs.
Limitations: Giving limited to the U.S. and its territories.
Publications: Application guidelines, grants list.
Application information: Only fully documented appeals will be considered; accepts NYRAG Common Application Form. Application form not required.
Officers and Directors:* Robert M. Frehse, Jr., V.P. and Exec. Dir.; Thomas Eastham, V.P. and Western Dir.; Frank A. Bennack, Jr.,* V.P.; John G. Conomikes,* V.P.; Richard E. Deems,* V.P.; Victor F. Ganzi,* V.P.; George R. Hearst, Jr.,* V.P.; John R. Hearst, Jr.,* V.P.; William R. Hearst III,* V.P.; Harvey L. Lipton,* V.P.; Gilbert C. Maurer,* V.P.; Mark F. Miller,* V.P.; Raymond J. Petersen,* V.P.; Ralph J. Cuomo, Treas.; Virginia Randt.
EIN: 136019226
Codes: FD, FM

32503
Park Foundation, Inc.
P.O. Box 550
Ithaca, NY 14851 (607) 272-9124
FAX: (607) 272-6057
Contact: Joanne V. Florino, Exec. Dir.

Established in 1966.
Donor(s): RHP, Inc., Roy H. Park.‡
Financial data (yr. ended 12/31/01): Grants paid, $28,384,050; assets, $546,921,909 (M); expenditures, $32,702,351; qualifying distributions, $29,346,704.
Limitations: Giving limited to the East Coast (primarily in central NY) and the southeastern U.S.
Publications: Informational brochure (including application guidelines).
Application information: Application form required.
Officers and Board Members:* Dorothy D. Park,* Pres.; Roy H. Park, Jr., 1st V.P.; Adelaide P. Gomer,* 2nd V.P. and Secy.; Elizabeth Fowler,* Treas.; Joanne V. Florino, Exec. Dir.; Jerome Libin, Richard G. Robb.
Junior Advisors: Alicia P. Gomer, Roy H. Park III.
EIN: 166071043
Codes: FD, FM

32504
Rockefeller Brothers Fund, Inc.
437 Madison Ave., 37th Fl.
New York, NY 10022-7001 (212) 812-4200
FAX: (212) 812-4299; General E-mail: rock@rbf.org; E-mail for annual report: anreport@rbf.org; URL: http://www.rbf.org
Contact: Benjamin R. Shute, Jr., Secy.

Incorporated in 1940 in NY.
Donor(s): John D. Rockefeller, Jr.,‡ Martha Baird Rockefeller,‡ Abby Rockefeller Mauze,‡ David Rockefeller, John D. Rockefeller III,‡ Laurance S. Rockefeller, Nelson A. Rockefeller,‡ Winthrop Rockefeller.‡
Financial data (yr. ended 12/31/01): Grants paid, $25,615,438; assets, $684,464,383 (M); expenditures, $34,775,705; qualifying distributions, $35,400,000; giving activities include $3,696,148 for programs.
Limitations: Giving on a national basis, and in Central and Eastern Europe, East and Southeast Asia, and South Africa.
Publications: Annual report (including application guidelines), grants list, occasional report, informational brochure.
Application information: Application form not required.
Officers and Trustees:* Steven C. Rockefeller,* Chair.; Neva R. Goodwin, Vice-Chair.; Stephen B. Heintz,* Pres.; William F. McCalpin, Exec. V.P. and C.O.O.; Benjamin R. Shute, Jr., Secy.; Boris A. Wessely, Treas.; Geraldine F. Watson, Compt.; David J. Callard, Richard Chasin, Peggy Dulany, Jessica P. Einhorn, Jonathan F. Fanton, Advisory Tr.; William H. Luers, Advisory Tr.; James E. Moltz, John Morning, Abby M. O'Neill, Advisory Tr.; Robert B. Oxnam, Richard D. Parsons, Advisory Tr.; Joseph A. Pierson, David Rockefeller, Advisory Tr.; David Rockefeller, Jr., Laurance S. Rockefeller, Advisory Tr.; Richard Rockefeller, Edmond D. Villani, Frank G. Wisner, Tadataka Yamada.
EIN: 131760106
Codes: FD, FM, GTI

32505
The John A. Hartford Foundation, Inc.
55 E. 59th St., 16th Fl.
New York, NY 10022 (212) 832-7788
FAX: (212) 593-4913; E-mail: mail@jhartfound.org; URL: http://www.jhartfound.org
Contact: Corinne H. Rieder, Exec. Dir.

Established in 1929; incorporated in 1942 in NY.
Donor(s): John A. Hartford,‡ George L. Hartford.‡
Financial data (yr. ended 12/31/01): Grants paid, $24,305,339; assets, $587,895,434 (M); expenditures, $30,704,024; qualifying distributions, $27,475,351; giving activities include $594,661 for programs.
Limitations: Giving primarily on a national basis.
Publications: Annual report, program policy statement, application guidelines.
Application information: See foundation's Web site for exact guidelines; Do not send correspondence by fax or e-mail. Application form not required.
Officers and Trustees:* Norman H. Volk,* Chair.; Kathryn D. Wriston, Pres.; William B. Matteson, Secy.; Corrine H. Rieder, Treas. and Exec. Dir.; Samuel R. Gische, Cont. and Dir., Finance; Anson McCook Beard, Jr., William T. Comfort, Jr., James D. Farley, James G. Kenan III, Christopher T.H. Pell, Thomas A. Reynolds, Jr.
EIN: 131667057
Codes: FD, FM

32506
The Michael R. Bloomberg Family Foundation Trust
c/o Martin Geller, C.P.A.
800 3rd Ave., 19th Fl.
New York, NY 10022

Established in 1998 in NY.
Donor(s): Michael R. Bloomberg.
Financial data (yr. ended 12/31/00): Grants paid, $22,500,000; assets, $3,445,077 (M); expenditures, $22,500,941; qualifying distributions, $22,495,939.

Limitations: Applications not accepted. Giving primarily in New York, NY.
Application information: Contributes only to pre-selected organizations.
Trustees: Michael R. Bloomberg, Richard K. Descherer.
EIN: 137176798
Codes: FD, FM

32507
Skirball Foundation
767 5th Ave., 43rd Fl.
New York, NY 10153 (212) 832-8500
Contact: Martin Blackman, Pres.

Established in 1950 in OH.
Donor(s): Members of the Skirball family, Skirball Investment Co.
Financial data (yr. ended 12/31/01): Grants paid, $22,204,211; assets, $67,051,060 (M); gifts received, $32,164,023; expenditures, $24,101,634; qualifying distributions, $23,196,295.
Limitations: Applications not accepted. Giving primarily in CA.
Application information: Contributes primarily to pre-selected organizations.
Officers and Trustees:* Martin Blackman,* Pres.; Robert D. Goldfarb,* V.P.; Audrey Skirball-Kenis,* V.P.; George H. Heyman, Jr.,* Treas.; Robert M. Tanenbaum.
EIN: 346517957
Codes: FD, FM

32508
John M. Olin Foundation, Inc.
330 Madison Ave., 22nd Fl.
New York, NY 10017 (212) 661-2670
URL: http://www.jmof.org
Contact: James Piereson, Secy.

Incorporated in 1953 in DE.
Donor(s): John M. Olin.‡
Financial data (yr. ended 12/31/01): Grants paid, $20,486,946; assets, $71,196,916 (M); expenditures, $23,013,651; qualifying distributions, $22,297,720.
Publications: Annual report (including application guidelines), application guidelines.
Application information: The foundation will terminate at the end of 2003. Therefore, unsolicited requests for funds not accepted. Proposals are by invitation only.
Officers and Trustees:* Eugene F. Williams, Jr.,* Chair.; George J. Gillespie III,* Pres. and Treas.; James Piereson,* Secy. and Exec. Dir.; Peter M. Flanigan, Richard M. Furlaud, Charles F. Knight.
EIN: 376031033
Codes: TN

32509
Robert W. Wilson Foundation, Inc.
520 83rd St., Ste. 3R
Brooklyn, NY 11209

Established in 1992 in NY.
Donor(s): Robert Wilson.
Financial data (yr. ended 12/31/00): Grants paid, $20,471,051; assets, $150,113,233 (M); gifts received, $130,960,376; expenditures, $22,382,260; qualifying distributions, $20,480,922.
Limitations: Applications not accepted. Giving primarily in New York, NY.
Application information: Contributes only to pre-selected organizations.
Officer: Robert W. Wilson, Pres.
EIN: 133686884
Codes: FD

32510
Harriet Ford Dickenson Foundation
c/o Morgan Guaranty Trust Co. of New York
345 Park Ave.
New York, NY 10154 (212) 464-1937
Contact: James Largey, V.P., Morgan Guaranty Trust Co. of New York

Established about 1958 in NY.
Donor(s): Harriet Ford Dickenson.‡
Financial data (yr. ended 12/31/00): Grants paid, $20,123,500; assets, $46,339,506 (M); expenditures, $20,336,252; qualifying distributions, $20,089,220.
Limitations: Giving limited to Broome County, NY.
Application information: Application form required.
Trustee: Morgan Guaranty Trust Co. of New York.
Advisory Committee: Gillian Attfield, Ann Hubbard, David Hubbard, Tom Hubbard, John Keeler, Shirley Keeler.
EIN: 136047225
Codes: FD, FM

32511
The Nathan Cummings Foundation, Inc.
475 10th Ave., 14th Fl.
New York, NY 10018 (212) 787-7300
FAX: (212) 787-7377; E-mail: info@nathancummings.org; URL: http://www.nathancummings.org
Contact: Lance E. Lindblom, Pres.

Established in 1949 in IL.
Donor(s): Nathan Cummings.‡
Financial data (yr. ended 12/31/01): Grants paid, $19,018,154; assets, $386,400,687 (M); expenditures, $24,946,770; qualifying distributions, $23,181,637.
Limitations: Giving primarily in the U.S. and Israel.
Publications: Annual report, grants list, application guidelines.
Application information: Application form required.
Officers and Trustees:* James K. Cummings,* Chair.; Ruth Cummings Sorensen,* Vice-Chair.; Lance E. Lindblom,* Pres. and C.E.O.; Robert N. Mayer,* Treas.; Caroline Williams, C.F.O.; Adam N. Cummings, Stephen P. Durchslag, Bevis Longstreth, Beatrice Cummings Mayer, Sonia Simon-Cummings, Albert Sui.
EIN: 237093201
Codes: FD, FM

32512
American Express Foundation
World Financial Ctr.
200 Vesey St. 48th Fl.
New York, NY 10285-4804 (212) 640-5661
URL: http://www.americanexpress.com/corp/philanthropy
Contact: Terry Savage, Dir.; or Cornelia W. Higginson, V.P. (Intl. Contact)

Incorporated in 1954 in NY.
Donor(s): American Express Co., and its subsidiaries.
Financial data (yr. ended 12/31/01): Grants paid, $18,884,619; assets, $337,567 (M); gifts received, $14,930,324; expenditures, $19,096,037; qualifying distributions, $18,876,826.
Limitations: Giving primarily in AZ, CA, FL, GA, MA, MN, NC, NY, TX, and UT; and internationally in Asia/Pacific, Canada, Europe, Latin America, and Japan.
Publications: Grants list.
Application information: Application form not required.
Officers and Trustees:* Mary Beth Salerno,* Pres.; Cornelia W. Higginson, Secy. and V.P., Intl. Prog.; Kenneth I. Chenault, Harvey Golub, Jon Linen, Thomas Schick.
EIN: 136123529
Codes: CS, FD, CD, FM, GTI

32513
Frederick P. & Sandra P. Rose Foundation
200 Madison Ave., 5th Fl.
New York, NY 10016

Established in 1982 in DE.
Donor(s): Frederick P. Rose,‡ Samuel and David Rose Charitable Foundation.
Financial data (yr. ended 11/30/00): Grants paid, $18,764,193; assets, $20,960,856 (M); gifts received, $5,000,000; expenditures, $18,904,613; qualifying distributions, $18,746,871.
Limitations: Applications not accepted. Giving primarily in New York, NY.
Application information: Contributes only to pre-selected organizations.
Officers and Directors:* Sandra P. Rose,* Pres.; Jonathan F.P. Rose,* V.P.; Adam R. Rose,* Secy.-Treas.; Deborah Rose.
EIN: 133136740
Codes: FD, FM

32514
MetLife Foundation
(Formerly Metropolitan Life Foundation)
1 Madison Ave.
New York, NY 10010-3690 (212) 578-6272
FAX: (212) 685-1435; URL: http://www.metlife.org
Contact: Sibyl C. Jacobson, C.E.O. and Pres.

Incorporated in 1976 in NY.
Donor(s): Metropolitan Life Insurance Co.
Financial data (yr. ended 12/31/01): Grants paid, $18,659,853; assets, $181,570,141 (M); expenditures, $18,743,176; qualifying distributions, $18,725,320; giving activities include $133,333 for program-related investments and $188,250 for programs.
Publications: Corporate giving report, application guidelines, annual report (including application guidelines).
Application information: Application form required for special programs where requests for proposals are issued. Application form not required for other grants.
Officers and Directors:* Catherine A. Rein,* Chair.; Sibyl C. Jacobson,* C.E.O. and Pres.; A. Dennis White, V.P.; Joseph A. Reali, Secy. and Counsel; Timothy Schmidt,* Treas.; Robert C. Tarnok, Cont.; James M. Benson, C. Robert Henrikson, Vincent P. Reusing, William J. Toppeta, Lisa M. Weber.
EIN: 132878224
Codes: CS, FD, CD, FM, GTI

32515
The Clark Foundation
1 Rockefeller Plz., 31st Fl.
New York, NY 10020 (212) 977-6900
Contact: Charles H. Hamilton, Exec. Dir.

Incorporated in 1931 in NY; merged with Scriven Foundation, Inc. in 1973.
Donor(s): Members of the Clark family.
Financial data (yr. ended 06/30/02): Grants paid, $17,939,478; assets, $469,042,395 (M); gifts received, $400; expenditures, $23,757,434; qualifying distributions, $20,705,141.
Limitations: Giving primarily in upstate NY and New York City; scholarships restricted to students residing in the Cooperstown, NY, area.
Publications: Program policy statement, application guidelines.

32515—NEW YORK

Application information: Accepts NYRAG Common Application Form. Application form not required.
Officers and Directors:* Jane Forbes Clark,* Pres.; Edward W. Stack,* V.P.; Alexander F. Treadwell,* V.P.; Charles H. Hamilton, Secy. and Exec. Dir.; Kevin S. Moore,* Treas.; Kent L. Barwick, Felicia H. Blum, William M. Evarts, Gates Helms Hawn, Archie F. MacAllaster, Mrs. Edward B. McMenamin, Kevin S. Moore, Thomas Q. Morris, M.D., Anne L. Peretz, Edward W. Stack, John Hoyt Stookey, Clifton R. Wharton, Jr.
EIN: 135616528
Codes: FD, FM, GTI

32516
The Pfizer Foundation, Inc.
c/o Pfizer Inc.
235 E. 42nd St.
New York, NY 10017 (212) 733-4250
Additional tel.: (800) 733-4717 (for all Pfizer publications and philanthropic guidelines); URL: http://www.pfizer.com/pfizerinc/philanthropy
Contact: Paget Walker, Grants Assoc.

Incorporated in 1953 in NY.
Donor(s): Pfizer Inc.
Financial data (yr. ended 12/31/00): Grants paid, $17,227,882; assets, $392,848,756 (M); expenditures, $18,673,922; qualifying distributions, $17,771,643.
Limitations: Giving primarily in areas of company operations, with emphasis on New York, NY, and national organizations.
Publications: Corporate giving report (including application guidelines), multi-year report.
Officers and Directors:* Henry A. McKinnell,* Pres.; Chuck Hardwick, V.P. and Exec. Dir.; C.L. Clemente, V.P. and Genl. Counsel; William Robison, V.P.; Sarah Williams,* Secy.; David Shedlarz, Treas.
EIN: 136083839
Codes: CS, FD, CD

32517
The Bristol-Myers Squibb Foundation, Inc.
(Formerly The Bristol-Myers Fund, Inc.)
c/o Fdn. Coord.
345 Park Ave., 43rd Fl.
New York, NY 10154
URL: http://www.bms.com/aboutbms/founda/data

Trust established in 1953 in NY; successor fund incorporated in 1982 in FL as The Bristol-Myers Fund, Inc., and subsequently in 1990 as The Bristol-Myers Squibb Foundation, Inc.
Donor(s): Bristol-Myers Squibb Co., and its divisions and subsidiaries.
Financial data (yr. ended 12/31/00): Grants paid, $15,836,964; assets, $26,867,580 (M); gifts received, $39,091,700; expenditures, $15,862,375; qualifying distributions, $15,862,375.
Limitations: Giving primarily in Stamford and Wallingford, CT, Evansville, IN, New Brunswick, Princeton, and Skillman, NJ, and Buffalo and Syracuse, NY.
Publications: Annual report.
Application information: Employee-related scholarships for IN division only. Application form not required.
Officers and Directors:* Peter R. Dolan, Chair.; John L. Damonti,* Pres.; Sandra Leung, Secy.; Harrison M. Bains, Jr., Treas.; John McGoldrick, John Skule.
EIN: 133127947
Codes: CS, FD, CD, FM

32518
Charles Hayden Foundation
140 Broadway, 51st Fl.
New York, NY 10005 (212) 785-3677
FAX: (212) 785-3689; URL: http://www.fdncenter.org/grantmaker/hayden
Contact: Kenneth D. Merin, C.E.O. and Pres.

Incorporated in 1937 in NY.
Donor(s): Charles Hayden.‡
Financial data (yr. ended 06/30/00): Grants paid, $15,483,696; assets, $327,800,572 (M); expenditures, $18,214,564; qualifying distributions, $15,938,353.
Limitations: Giving limited to the metropolitan Boston, MA, and the metropolitan New York, NY (including northern NJ), areas.
Publications: Application guidelines, annual report.
Application information: Accepts NYRAG and AGM Common Grant Application forms; Boston area, 2 copies of proposal (one copy sent to NYC and one copy sent to Boston); NY and NJ, 1 copy of proposal. Application form not required.
Officers and Trustees:* Kenneth D. Merin,* C.E.O. and Pres.; Carol Van Atten, V.P., Progs.; Kristen J. McCormack,* V.P.; Dean H. Steeger,* Secy.; Robert Howitt,* Treas.; Howard G. Wachenfeld.
EIN: 135562237
Codes: FD, FM

32519
The Commonwealth Fund
1 E. 75th St.
New York, NY 10021-2692 (212) 606-3844
FAX: (212) 606-3500; E-mail: cmwf@cmwf.org; URL: http://www.cmwf.org
Contact: Andrea C. Landes, Dir., Grants Mgmt.

Incorporated in 1918 in NY.
Donor(s): Mrs. Stephen V. Harkness,‡ Edward S. Harkness,‡ Mrs. Edward S. Harkness.‡
Financial data (yr. ended 06/30/01): Grants paid, $15,349,829; assets, $550,680,215 (M); expenditures, $27,006,731; qualifying distributions, $24,702,696; giving activities include $987,458 for programs.
Publications: Annual report (including application guidelines), grants list, newsletter, occasional report, informational brochure, program policy statement, financial statement.
Application information: The fund acknowledges letters on receipt; applicants are typically advised of results of initial staff review within two months. Application form not required.
Officers and Directors:* Samuel O. Thier, M.D.,* Chair.; Helene L. Kaplan,* Vice-Chair.; Karen Davis,* Pres.; John E. Craig, Jr., Exec. V.P. and Treas.; Stephen C. Schoenbaum, M.D., Sr. V.P.; Cathy Schoen, V.P., Health Policy, Research, and Eval.; Gary M. Stehr, Cont.; William R. Brody, M.D., Jane E. Henny, M.D., Lawrence S. Huntington, Walter E. Massey, Robert M. O'Neil, Robert C. Pozen, James R. Tallon, Jr.
EIN: 131635260
Codes: FD, FM, GTI

32520
Beatrice P. Delany Charitable Trust
c/o JPMorgan Chase Bank
1211 Avenue of the Americas, 34th FL.
New York, NY 10036
Contact: John H.F. Enteman

Trust established about 1977 in NY.
Donor(s): Beatrice P. Delany.‡
Financial data (yr. ended 10/31/01): Grants paid, $13,900,000; assets, $143,431,113 (M); expenditures, $14,791,116; qualifying distributions, $14,061,710.
Limitations: Giving primarily in the metropolitan Chicago, IL, area.
Application information: Application form not required.
Trust Committee: Thomas A. Reynolds, Jr., Mrs. Thomas A. Reynolds, Jr., Andrew Thomson, M.D.
Trustee: JPMorgan Chase Bank.
EIN: 136748171
Codes: FD, FM

32521
The Dana Foundation
(Formerly The Charles A. Dana Foundation, Inc.)
745 5th Ave., Ste. 900
New York, NY 10151 (212) 223-4040
FAX: (212) 317-8721; E-mail: danainfo@dana.org; URL: http://www.dana.org
Contact: Burton M. Mirsky, V.P., Finance

Incorporated in 1950 in CT.
Donor(s): Charles A. Dana,‡ Eleanor Naylor Dana.‡
Financial data (yr. ended 12/31/00): Grants paid, $13,884,221; assets, $330,431,279 (M); expenditures, $21,430,530; qualifying distributions, $19,006,362; giving activities include $3,462,589 for programs.
Publications: Annual report (including application guidelines), newsletter, informational brochure (including application guidelines), financial statement, occasional report, application guidelines.
Application information: Application form not required.
Officers and Directors:* William L. Safire,* Chair.; Edward F. Rover,* Pres.; Francis Harper, Exec. V.P.; Barbara E. Gill, V.P., Public Affairs; Burton M. Mirsky, V.P., Finance; Jane Nevins, V.P.; Clark M. Whittemore, Jr.,* Secy.-Treas.; Edward Bleier, Wallace L. Cook, Charles A. Dana III, Ann McLaughlin Korologos, LaSalle D. Leffall, Jr., Hildegarde E. Mahoney, Donald B. Marron, L. Guy Palmer II, Herbert J. Siegel.
EIN: 066036761
Codes: FD, FM, GTI

32522
Goldman, Sachs Foundation
(Formerly Goldman, Sachs Fund)
375 Park Ave.
New York, NY 10152 (212) 902-5402

Established in 1968 in NY.
Donor(s): Goldman, Sachs & Co., Robert E. Rubin.
Financial data (yr. ended 01/30/01): Grants paid, $13,695,500; assets, $211,943,536 (M); gifts received, $10,000,000; expenditures, $16,966,504; qualifying distributions, $14,681,345.
Application information: Scholarships for employees and their dependents are determined by the Educational Testing Service.
Officers and Directors:* John C. Whitehead,* Chair.; Stephanie Bell-Rose, Pres.; Aida Bekele, Secy.; David A. Dechman, Thomas W. Payzant, Frank H.T. Rhodes, Esta E. Stecher, John L. Thornton.
EIN: 237000346
Codes: CS, FD, CD, FM

32523
The John R. Oishei Foundation
(Formerly Julia R. and Estelle L. Foundation, Inc.)
1 HSBC Ctr., Ste. 3650
Buffalo, NY 14203 (716) 856-9490
FAX: (716) 856-9493; *E-mail:* info@oisheifdt.org;
URL: http://www.oisheifdt.org
Contact: Thomas E. Baker, Exec. Dir.

Incorporated in 1941 in NY.
Donor(s): Peter C. Cornell Trust, John R. Oishei, R. John Oshei,‡ Jean R. Oshei.
Financial data (yr. ended 12/31/00): Grants paid, $13,677,689; assets, $237,843,647 (M); gifts received, $640,020; expenditures, $14,794,303; qualifying distributions, $13,677,689.
Limitations: Giving limited to the Buffalo, NY, area.
Publications: Annual report, informational brochure (including application guidelines), grants list.
Application information: Application form not required.
Officers and Directors:* Erland E. Kailbourne,* Chair. and Pres.; Allan R. Wiegley,* V.P. and Treas.; Thomas E. Baker,* Secy. and Exec. Dir.; Robert M. Bennett, Christopher T. Dunstan, Richard D. Fors, Mary Martino, Albert R. Mugel, James M. Wadsworth.
EIN: 160874319
Codes: FD, FM

32524
Robertson Foundation
c/o American Express TBS, Inc.
1185 Ave. of the Americas
New York, NY 10036-2602

Established in 1996 in NY.
Donor(s): Julian H. Robertson, Jr.
Financial data (yr. ended 11/30/00): Grants paid, $13,619,781; assets, $196,855,493 (M); gifts received, $106,459,124; expenditures, $13,812,275; qualifying distributions, $11,235,554.
Limitations: Applications not accepted.
Application information: Contributes only to pre-selected organizations.
Trustees: Josephine T. Robertson, Julian H. Robertson, Jr.
EIN: 137068398
Codes: FD, FM

32525
Rochester Area Community Foundation
(Formerly Rochester Area Foundation)
500 East Ave.
Rochester, NY 14607-1912 (716) 271-4100
FAX: (716) 271-4292; *E-mail:* jleonard@racf.org;
URL: http://www.racf.org
Contact: Deborah A. Ellwood, V.P.

Incorporated in 1972 in NY.
Financial data (yr. ended 03/31/01): Grants paid, $13,453,576; assets, $131,287,342 (M); gifts received, $45,450,651; expenditures, $15,741,337.
Limitations: Giving limited to Monroe, Livingston, Ontario, Orleans, Genesee, and Wayne counties, NY, except for donor-designated funds.
Publications: Annual report (including application guidelines), program policy statement, financial statement, newsletter, informational brochure.
Application information: Scholarship recipients chosen by institutions. Application form required.
Officers: Richard A. Schwartz, Chair.-Elect; Bruce B. Bates, Vice-Chair.; Harold S. Feinbloom, Vice-Chair.; Margaret A. Sanchez, Vice-Chair.; Robert C. Silver, Vice-Chair.; Jennifer Leonard, Pres. and Exec. Dir.; Deborah Ellwood, V.P., Community Programs; Bonita W. Hindman, V.P., Grants and Prog.; Jeffrey B. Leahy, V.P., Finance and Admin.; J. Charmaine Bennett, Secy.; Ray H. Hutch, Treas.; Michael J. Cooney, Counsel; G. Russell West, Dir., Donor Rel.
Board Members: Francis R. Antonelli, Ted Boucher, James B. Brush, Michael F. Buckley, and 25 additional board members.
EIN: 237250641
Codes: CM, FD

32526
The Hearst Foundation, Inc.
888 7th Ave., 45th Fl.
New York, NY 10106-0057 (212) 586-5404
Address for applicants from west of the Mississippi River: c/o Thomas Eastham, V.P. and Western Dir., 90 New Montgomery St., Ste. 1212, San Francisco, CA 94105; tel.: (415) 543-0400; *URL:* http://www.hearstfdn.org
Contact: Robert M. Frehse, Jr., V.P. and Exec. Dir. (east of the Mississippi River); Thomas Eastham, V.P. and Western Dir. (west of the Mississippi River)

Incorporated in 1945 in NY.
Donor(s): William Randolph Hearst.‡
Financial data (yr. ended 12/31/01): Grants paid, $13,385,000; assets, $271,400,000 (M); expenditures, $14,355,000; qualifying distributions, $14,835,000.
Limitations: Giving limited to the U.S. and its territories.
Publications: Application guidelines, grants list.
Application information: Only fully documented appeals will be considered; accepts NYRAG Common Application Form. Application form not required.
Officers and Directors:* George R. Hearst, Jr.,* Pres.; Robert M. Frehse, Jr.,* V.P. and Exec. Dir.; Thomas Eastham, V.P. and Western Dir.; Frank A. Bennack, Jr.,* V.P.; John G. Conomikes,* V.P.; Richard E. Deems,* V.P.; Victor F. Ganzi,* V.P.; John R. Hearst, Jr.,* V.P.; William R. Hearst III,* V.P.; Harvey L. Lipton,* V.P.; Gilbert C. Maurer,* V.P.; Mark F. Miller,* V.P.; Raymond J. Petersen,* V.P.; Ralph J. Cuomo, Treas.; Virginia Randt.
EIN: 136161746
Codes: FD, FM

32527
Deutsche Bank Americas Foundation
(Formerly BT Foundation)
31 W. 52nd St., NYC01-1407
New York, NY 10019 (646) 324-2901
FAX: (646) 324-7229; *E-mail:* Gary.S.Hattem@db.com; *URL:* http://www.db.com/community
Contact: Gary S. Hattem, Pres.

Established as the BT Foundation in 1986 in NY; changed to Deutsche Bank Americas Foundation in 1999.
Donor(s): Bankers Trust Co., BT Capital Corp., Deutsche Bank Americas Holding Corp.
Financial data (yr. ended 12/31/01): Grants paid, $13,134,679; assets, $1,767,338 (M); gifts received, $11,526,836; expenditures, $13,143,939; qualifying distributions, $13,133,467.
Limitations: Giving primarily in areas of company operations in the U.S., Canada and Latin America.
Publications: Application guidelines, annual report, newsletter, grants list.
Application information: Application form not required.
Officers and Directors:* Rose Tobin, C.O.O.and Treas.; Gary S. Hattem,* Pres.; Robyn Brady Ince, V.P.; Sandra West, Secy.; E. Robert Cotter, Michael Hoelz, Grant Kvalheim, Alexander Labak, John A. Ross, Seth Waugh.
EIN: 133321736
Codes: CS, FD, CD, FM

32528
Tisch Foundation, Inc.
655 Madison Ave., 8th Fl.
New York, NY 10021-8087 (212) 521-2930
Contact: Mark J. Krinsky, V.P.

Incorporated in 1957 in FL.
Donor(s): Hotel Americana, Tisch Hotels, Inc., members of the Tisch family, and closely held corporations.
Financial data (yr. ended 12/31/00): Grants paid, $13,087,409; assets, $127,128,138 (M); expenditures, $13,326,329; qualifying distributions, $12,906,086.
Limitations: Applications not accepted. Giving primarily in NY.
Application information: Contributes only to pre-selected organizations.
Officers and Directors:* Preston R. Tisch,* Pres.; Laurence A. Tisch,* Sr. V.P.; Mark J. Krinsky, V.P.; Thomas M. Steinberg, V.P.; Laurie Tisch Sussman, V.P.; Andrew H. Tisch, V.P.; Daniel R. Tisch, V.P.; James S. Tisch, V.P.; Jonathan M. Tisch, V.P.; Steven E. Tisch, V.P.; Thomas J. Tisch, V.P.; Barry L. Bloom, Secy.-Treas.; Joan H. Tisch, Wilma S. Tisch.
EIN: 591002844
Codes: FD, FM

32529
Irene Diamond Fund
375 Park Ave., Ste. 3303
New York, NY 10152-3399 (212) 838-9525
Contact: Jane Silver, Exec. Dir.

Established in 1994 in NY.
Donor(s): Irene Diamond.‡
Financial data (yr. ended 12/31/00): Grants paid, $12,780,000; assets, $36,416,600 (M); expenditures, $13,997,510; qualifying distributions, $13,729,211.
Limitations: Applications not accepted. Giving primarily in NY.
Application information: Contributes only to pre-selected organizations.
Officers and Board Members:* Peter Kimmelman,* Treas.; Jane Silver, Exec. Dir.; Joseph Polisi.
EIN: 132678431
Codes: FD, FM

32530
The Shubert Foundation, Inc.
234 W. 44th St.
New York, NY 10036 (212) 944-3777
FAX: (212) 944-3767
Contact: Vicki Reiss, Exec. Dir.

Incorporated in 1945 in DE.
Donor(s): Lee Shubert,‡ J.J. Shubert.‡
Financial data (yr. ended 05/31/01): Grants paid, $12,562,000; assets, $251,889,489 (M); gifts received, $188,797; expenditures, $15,578,733; qualifying distributions, $13,172,348; giving activities include $339,636 for programs.
Publications: Annual report (including application guidelines).
Application information: The foundation does not acknowledge receipt of proposals. Interviews with applicants are granted by appointment. Unaudited financial statements are not accepted. Application form required.
Officers and Directors:* Gerald Schoenfeld,* Chair.; Michael I. Sovern,* Pres.; John W. Kluge,* V.P.; Irving M. Wall,* Secy.; Lee J. Seidler,* Treas.; Vicki Reiss, Exec. Dir.; Philip J. Smith.

32530—NEW YORK

EIN: 136106961
Codes: FD, FM

32531
Dyson Foundation
25 Halcyon Rd.
Millbrook, NY 12545-9611 (845) 677-0644
FAX: (845) 677-0650; *E-mail:* info@dyson.org;
URL: http://www.dysonfoundation.org
Contact: Diana M. Gurieva, Exec. Dir.

Trust established in 1949 in NY; incorporated in 1957 in DE.
Donor(s): Charles H. Dyson,‡ Margaret M. Dyson.‡
Financial data (yr. ended 12/31/01): Grants paid, $12,503,211; assets, $296,534,202 (M); expenditures, $15,652,094; qualifying distributions, $13,738,717; giving activities include $192,000 for loans.
Limitations: Giving primarily in Dutchess County, NY, and organizations providing services in Dutchess County; limited grants to other Mid-Hudson Valley counties. National and other grants on a solicited basis.
Publications: Annual report (including application guidelines).
Application information: Unsolicited proposals are not accepted, but letter inquiries are welcomed. Application form not required.
Officers and Directors:* Robert R. Dyson,* Pres.; Diana M. Gurieva, Exec. V.P.; John S. FitzSimmons, Secy.; Marc Feldman, Treas.; Raymond A. Lamontagne, Timmian C. Massie, Michael P. Murphy, David G. Nathan.
EIN: 136084888
Codes: FD, FM

32532
The AVI CHAI Foundation
(Formerly AVI CHAI - A Philanthropic Foundation)
52 Vanderbilt Ave., Ste. 1007
New York, NY 10017-3808 (212) 396-8850
Contact: Yossi Prager, Exec. Dir., North America

Established in 1984 in NY.
Donor(s): Zalman Chaim Bernstein.‡
Financial data (yr. ended 12/31/00): Grants paid, $12,217,250; assets, $427,293,174 (M); gifts received, $242,195,811; expenditures, $14,899,047; qualifying distributions, $23,204,526; giving activities include $8,600,000 for program-related investments and $839,289 for programs.
Limitations: Applications not accepted. Giving primarily in North America and Israel.
Publications: Multi-year report.
Application information: Solicits proposals only in the context of self-initiated projects.
Officers and Trustees:* Arthur W. Fried,* Chair., Pres., and Treas.; Marlene Wasserman, Secy.; Yossi Prager, Exec. Dir.; Mem Bernstein, Meir Buzaglo, Avital Darmon, Alan R. Feld, Lauren K. Merkin, George Rohr, Lief Rosenblatt, David Tadmor, Henry Taub, Ruth Wisse.
EIN: 133252800
Codes: FD, FM

32533
The Judy and Michael Steinhardt Foundation
650 Madison Ave., 17th Fl
New York, NY 10022

Established in 1986 in NY.
Financial data (yr. ended 09/30/00): Grants paid, $12,144,007; assets, $23,845,957 (M); gifts received, $3,075; expenditures, $12,192,972; qualifying distributions, $12,175,960.
Limitations: Applications not accepted.

Application information: Contributes only to pre-selected organizations.
Trustees: Judith Steinhardt, Michael Steinhardt.
EIN: 133357500
Codes: FD, FM

32534
The F. B. Heron Foundation
100 Broadway, 17th Fl.
New York, NY 10005 (212) 404-1800
FAX: (212) 404-1805; *URL:* http://www.fdncenter.org/grantmaker/fbheron
Contact: Mary Jo Mullan, V.P., Progs.

Established in 1992 in DE.
Financial data (yr. ended 12/31/01): Grants paid, $12,034,860; assets, $255,959,796 (M); expenditures, $14,553,495; qualifying distributions, $16,457,073; giving activities include $2,652,500 for program-related investments.
Limitations: Giving on a national basis in both urban and rural areas.
Publications: Annual report (including application guidelines), application guidelines.
Application information: Information is also available on the foundation's Web site. Application form not required.
Officers and Directors:* Ira S. Hirschfield,* Chair.; Sharon B. King, Pres.; Mary Jo Mullan, V.P. Progs. and Secy.-Treas.; Wallace Cook, James Sligar.
EIN: 133647019
Codes: FD, FM

32535
The Ambrose Monell Foundation
c/o Fulton, Rowe, Hart & Coon
1 Rockefeller Plz., Ste. 301
New York, NY 10020-2002 (212) 586-0700
URL: http://www.monellvetlesen.org
Contact: George Rowe, Jr., Pres.

Incorporated in 1952 in NY.
Donor(s): Maude Monell Vetlesen.‡
Financial data (yr. ended 12/31/00): Grants paid, $11,822,500; assets, $228,536,489 (M); expenditures, $12,266,055; qualifying distributions, $11,917,919.
Application information: Application form not required.
Officers and Directors:* George Rowe, Jr.,* Pres.; Laura Naus, Secy.; Joseph T.C. Hart, Treas.; Eugene P. Grisanti, Ambrose K. Monell, Henry G. Walter, Jr.
EIN: 131982683
Codes: FD, FM

32536
Altman Foundation
521 5th Ave., 35th Fl.
New York, NY 10175 (212) 682-0970
FAX: (212) 682-1648; *URL:* http://www.fdncenter.org/grantmaker/altman
Contact: Karen L. Rosa, V.P. and Exec. Dir.

Incorporated in 1913 in NY.
Donor(s): Benjamin Altman,‡ Col. Michael Friedsam.‡
Financial data (yr. ended 12/31/01): Grants paid, $11,556,896; assets, $236,988,050 (M); expenditures, $14,439,262; qualifying distributions, $12,504,139.
Limitations: Giving limited to NY, with emphasis on the boroughs of New York City.
Publications: Application guidelines, annual report (including application guidelines).
Application information: Accepts but does not require NYRAG Common Application Form. Application form not required.

Officers and Trustees:* Jane B. O'Connell,* Pres.; Karen L. Rosa, V.P. and Exec. Dir.; John W. Townsend IV,* V.P.; Julia V. Shea,* Secy.; John P. Casey, Treas.; James M. Burke, Bernard Finkelstein, Sharon B. King, Maurice A. Selinger, Jr., Patricia J. Volland.
EIN: 131623879
Codes: FD, FM

32537
William T. Grant Foundation
570 Lexington Ave., 18th Fl.
New York, NY 10022-6837 (212) 752-0071
E-mail: info@wtgrantfdn.org; *URL:* http://www.wtgrantfoundation.org
Contact: Grants Coord.

Incorporated in 1936 in DE.
Donor(s): William T. Grant.‡
Financial data (yr. ended 12/31/01): Grants paid, $11,464,123; assets, $245,087,187 (M); expenditures, $16,636,290; qualifying distributions, $15,172,430.
Limitations: Giving internationally for research grants and William T. Grant Scholars; giving limited to NY, NJ, and CT for youth service grants.
Publications: Annual report, informational brochure (including application guidelines), financial statement, grants list, informational brochure, application guidelines.
Application information: Application to William T. Grant Scholars Program by nomination only. All applicants will be notified as to required copies of proposals. All recipients are expected to submit annual progress reports, budget, and financial accountings of their expenditures. Application form not required.
Officers and Directors:* Kenneth S. Rolland,* Chair.; Karen Hein, M.D.,* Pres.; Robert Granger, Ed.D., Sr. V.P., Prog.; Lawrence Giannino, Ph.D., V.P., Strategic Comm.; Larry Moreland, V.P., Finance and Admin.; Thomas C. Barry,* Treas.; Eileen Dorann, Cont.; Paula Allen-Meares, Ph.D., Robert F. Boruch, Ph.D., Ronald A. Feldman, Ph.D., Henry E. Gooss, Kathleen Hall-Jamieson, Bridget MacAskill, Richard H. Price, Ph.D., Marta Tienda, Ph.D., Gary Walker.
EIN: 131624021
Codes: FD, FM, GTI

32538
The Charles Engelhard Foundation
645 5th Ave., Ste. 712
New York, NY 10022 (212) 935-2433
Contact: Mary F. Ogorzaly, Secy.

Incorporated in 1940 in NJ.
Donor(s): Charles Engelhard,‡ Engelhard Hanovia, Inc., and others.
Financial data (yr. ended 12/31/00): Grants paid, $11,401,948; assets, $133,114,339 (M); expenditures, $12,154,024; qualifying distributions, $11,354,549.
Limitations: Applications not accepted. Giving on a national basis.
Application information: Giving only to organizations known to the trustees. Unsolicited requests for funds not considered.
Officers and Trustees:* Charlene B. Engelhard,* Pres.; Mary F. Ogorzaly, Secy.; Edward G. Beimfohr,* Treas.; Sophie Engelhard Craighead, Anne E. de la Renta, Jane B. Engelhard, Anthony J. Gostkowski, Susan O'Connor, Sally E. Pingree.
EIN: 226063032
Codes: FD, FM

32539
Gilder Foundation, Inc.
c/o Anchin, Block & Anchin, LLP
1375 Broadway
New York, NY 10018 (212) 765-2500
Contact: Daniella Muhling, Exec. Dir.

Established in 1965 in NY.
Donor(s): Richard Gilder.
Financial data (yr. ended 12/31/00): Grants paid, $11,322,673; assets, $65,640,347 (M); gifts received, $5,039,310; expenditures, $12,314,282; qualifying distributions, $11,516,245.
Limitations: Applications not accepted. Giving primarily in NY.
Application information: Contributes only to pre-selected organizations.
Officers: Richard Gilder, Jr., Pres.; Joseph J. Pinto, V.P.; Richard Schneidman, Secy.; David Howe, Treas.; Daniella Muhling, Exec. Dir.
EIN: 136176041
Codes: FD, FM

32540
Monterey Fund, Inc.
c/o Bear Stearns & Co.
1 Metrotech Ctr. N.
Brooklyn, NY 11201
Contact: Gilbert Sherman

Incorporated in 1967 in NY.
Donor(s): Employees of Bear Stearns & Co.
Financial data (yr. ended 04/30/01): Grants paid, $11,262,530; assets, $14,576,923 (M); gifts received, $12,656,273; expenditures, $11,324,966; qualifying distributions, $11,263,360.
Limitations: Applications not accepted.
Publications: Annual report.
Application information: Contributes only to pre-selected organizations.
Officers: Kenneth Edlow, Pres.; Robert Steinberg, V.P.; Marshall Levinson, Secy.; Samel L. Molinaro, Jr., Treas.
EIN: 136255661
Codes: FD, FM

32541
Joukowsky Family Foundation
410 Park Ave., Ste. 1610
New York, NY 10022
E-mail: info@joukowsky.org; *URL:* http://www.joukowsky.org
Contact: Ms. Nina J. Koprulu, Pres. and Dir.

Established in 1981 in NY.
Financial data (yr. ended 10/31/01): Grants paid, $11,230,590; assets, $100,892,337 (M); gifts received, $387,504; expenditures, $12,287,765; qualifying distributions, $12,687,954; giving activities include $940,000 for program-related investments.
Limitations: Applications not accepted. Giving primarily in the northeastern U.S.
Application information: The foundation does not accept unsolicited proposals. Please refer to Web site for future application changes.
Officers and Directors:* Nina J. Koprulu,* Pres.; Emily R. Kessler, Exec. Dir.; Randall G. Drain, Artemis A.W. Joukowsky, Martha S. Joukowsky.
EIN: 133242753
Codes: FD, FM, GTI

32542
The Teagle Foundation, Inc.
10 Rockefeller Plz., Rm. 920
New York, NY 10020-1903 (212) 373-1970
URL: http://fdncenter.org/grantmaker/teagle
Contact: Lillian S. Moore, Secy.

Incorporated in 1944 in CT.
Donor(s): Walter C. Teagle,‡ Rowena Lee Teagle,‡ Walter C. Teagle, Jr.‡
Financial data (yr. ended 05/31/01): Grants paid, $11,074,031; assets, $18,414,596 (M); expenditures, $13,851,978; qualifying distributions, $11,823,742.
Limitations: Giving limited to the U.S. No grants to community organizations outside New York City. No grants to U.S. organizations for foreign programmatic activities.
Publications: Annual report (including application guidelines).
Application information: Application form not required.
Officers and Directors:* John S. Chalsty,* Chair. and Interim Pres.; Lillian S. Moore, Secy.; Eli Weinberg, Treas. and Cont.; George Bugliarello, Kenneth P. Cohen, Peter O. Crisp, Richard W. Kimball, Richard L. Morrill, Anne M. Tatlock, Walter C. Teagle III, Stephen H. Weiss.
EIN: 131773645
Codes: FD, FM

32543
Booth Ferris Foundation
1211 Ave. of the Americas, 38th Fl.
New York, NY 10036 (212) 789-5690
E-mail: maurer_barbara@jpmorgan.com
Contact: Barbara Maurer

Trusts established in 1957 and 1958 in NY; merged in 1964.
Donor(s): Chancie Ferris Booth,‡ Willis H. Booth.‡
Financial data (yr. ended 12/31/01): Grants paid, $10,917,000; assets, $240,552,843 (M); expenditures, $11,710,089; qualifying distributions, $10,917,000.
Limitations: Giving limited to the New York, NY, metropolitan area for the arts, K-12 education, and civic and urban affairs; a broader geographic scope for higher education.
Publications: Annual report (including application guidelines).
Application information: Application form not required.
Trustees: Robert J. Murtagh, JPMorgan Chase Bank.
EIN: 136170340
Codes: FD, FM

32544
Samuel I. Newhouse Foundation, Inc.
c/o Paul Scherer & Co. LLP
335 Madison Ave., 15th Fl.
New York, NY 10017

Incorporated in 1945 in NY.
Donor(s): Samuel I. Newhouse,‡ Mitzi E. Newhouse,‡ The Conde Nast Publications, Advance Publications, Inc.
Financial data (yr. ended 10/31/00): Grants paid, $10,898,128; assets, $126,604,130 (M); gifts received, $5,440,938; expenditures, $11,441,026; qualifying distributions, $10,898,128.
Limitations: Applications not accepted.
Application information: Contributes only to pre-selected organizations. Unsolicited requests for funds not considered.
Officers and Directors:* Samuel I. Newhouse, Jr.,* Pres. and Treas.; Donald E. Newhouse,* V.P. and Secy.
EIN: 116006296

Codes: FD, FM

32545
The Vivendi Universal Foundation, Inc.
(Formerly The Samuel Bronfman Foundation, Inc.)
375 Park Ave.
New York, NY 10152-0192
Contact: Ms. Dorothy Basta, Coord., Grants Admin.; or Ms. Patricia Glazer, V.P., Public Affairs

Incorporated in 1951 in DE.
Donor(s): Joseph E. Seagram & Sons, Inc., Seagram Distillers Charitable Trust.
Financial data (yr. ended 06/30/01): Grants paid, $10,886,000; assets, $14,266,518 (M); gifts received, $7,391,000; expenditures, $10,892,845; qualifying distributions, $10,886,845.
Limitations: Giving primarily in New York, NY, and to national U.S. programs.
Publications: Corporate giving report.
Application information: Application form not required.
Officers and Trustees:* Jean-Marie Messier, Chair. and C.E.O.; Edgar M. Bronfman,* Vice-Chair.; Edgar Bronfman, Jr., Vice-Chair.; Patricia Glazer,* V.P., Public Affairs; Nancy Morgan, Secy.; Charles R. Bronfman, Catherine Gros.
EIN: 136084708
Codes: CS, FD, CD, FM

32546
Lewis B. & Dorothy Cullman Foundation, Inc.
c/o Lewis B. Cullman
767 3rd Ave., 36th Fl.
New York, NY 10017 (212) 751-6655

Established in 1958 in NY.
Donor(s): Dorothy F. Cullman, Lewis B. Cullman.
Financial data (yr. ended 11/30/01): Grants paid, $10,662,246; assets, $53,569,643 (M); gifts received, $17,000,000; expenditures, $11,162,829; qualifying distributions, $10,832,481.
Limitations: Applications not accepted. Giving primarily in NY.
Application information: Contributes only to pre-selected organizations.
Officers and Directors:* Lewis B. Cullman,* Pres.; Dorothy F. Cullman,* V.P.; John C. Emmert, Treas.; Joseph P. Kremer.
EIN: 510243747
Codes: FD, FM

32547
The PepsiCo Foundation, Inc.
700 Anderson Hill Rd.
Purchase, NY 10577 (914) 253-3153
URL: http://www.pepsico.com/citizenship/contributions.shtml
Contact: Mrs. Jacqueline R. Millan, V.P., Contribs.

Incorporated in 1962 in NY.
Donor(s): PepsiCo, Inc.
Financial data (yr. ended 12/31/00): Grants paid, $10,541,880; assets, $36,909,223 (M); gifts received, $11,000,000; expenditures, $10,563,740; qualifying distributions, $10,541,654.
Limitations: Giving primarily in communities where operating divisions are located, including Irvine, CA, Wichita, KS, Louisville, KY, Somers, NY, and Plano, TX.
Publications: Informational brochure (including application guidelines).
Officers and Directors:* Roger A. Enrico,* Chair.; Robert F. Sharpe, Jr.,* Pres.; Jacqueline R. Millan, V.P., Contribs.; Kathleen A. Luke, Secy.; Matthew

M. McKenna, Treas.; Ronald E. Harrison, Donald M. Kendall, Indra K. Nooyi, Steven S. Reinemund, Karl M. von derHeyden, Craig Weatherup.
EIN: 136163174
Codes: CS, FD, CD

32548
Christian A. Johnson Endeavor Foundation
1060 Park Ave.
New York, NY 10128-1033 (212) 534-6620
FAX: (212) 410-5909
Contact: Julie J. Kidd, Pres.

Incorporated in 1952 in NY.
Donor(s): Christian A. Johnson.‡
Financial data (yr. ended 09/30/01): Grants paid, $10,541,563; assets, $191,167,107 (M); gifts received, $421,864; expenditures, $12,066,904; qualifying distributions, $11,903,276; giving activities include $200,000 for program-related investments and $266,270 for programs.
Limitations: Giving limited to the eastern U.S.
Publications: Financial statement, program policy statement, application guidelines.
Application information: Arts proposals by invitation only. Application form not required.
Officers and Trustees:* Julie J. Kidd,* Pres. and Treas.; Christin Kidd, Secy.; Donald W. Harwood, Ann B. Spence.
EIN: 136147952
Codes: FD, FM

32549
G. Harold & Leila Y. Mathers Charitable Foundation
103 S. Bedford Rd., Ste. 101
Mount Kisco, NY 10549-3440 (914) 242-0465
Contact: James H. Handelman, Exec. Dir.

Established in 1975 in NY.
Donor(s): G. Harold Mathers,‡ Leila Y. Mathers.‡
Financial data (yr. ended 12/31/00): Grants paid, $10,539,461; assets, $177,728,323 (M); expenditures, $13,471,506; qualifying distributions, $10,990,049.
Application information: Application form not required.
Officers and Directors:* Donald E. Handelman,* Pres.; William R. Handelman,* V.P.; Don Fizer,* Secy.; Joseph W. Handelman,* Treas.; James H. Handelman, Exec. Dir.; John R. Young.
EIN: 237441901
Codes: FD, FM

32550
The Gerald J. & Dorothy R. Friedman New York Foundation for Medical Research
c/o GGK
1185 Avenue of the Americas
New York, NY 10036

Established in 1999 in NY.
Donor(s): Dorothy Friedman, Gerald Friedman.
Financial data (yr. ended 02/28/01): Grants paid, $10,200,096; assets, $3,964,409 (M); expenditures, $10,423,865; qualifying distributions, $10,348,123.
Limitations: Applications not accepted. Giving on a national basis.
Application information: Contributes only to pre-selected organizations.
Officers: Dorothy Friedman, Pres.; Jane Friedman, Secy. and C.O.O.; Peter Schmidt, Treas.
EIN: 134034562
Codes: FD

32551
IBM International Foundation
(Formerly IBM South Africa Projects Fund)
c/o International Business Machines Corp.
New Orchard Rd.
Armonk, NY 10504-1709 (914) 766-1900
URL: http://www.ibm.com/ibm/ibmgives
Contact: Prog. Mgr.

Established in 1985 in NY.
Donor(s): International Business Machines Corp.
Financial data (yr. ended 12/31/00): Grants paid, $10,148,618; assets, $146,630,946 (M); gifts received, $10,614,843; expenditures, $11,373,620; qualifying distributions, $10,936,076.
Limitations: Giving on an international basis.
Publications: Informational brochure, application guidelines.
Application information: Limited funding is available for unsolicited proposals that fall within the foundation's fields of interest. Priority is placed on projects that include a role for technology and offer a potential for replication. The foundation's grantmaking decisions are not controlled by the corporation. Application form not required.
Officers and Directors:* Louis V. Gerstner, Jr.,* Chair.; Abby F. Kohnstamm,* Vice-Chair.; Stanley S. Litow,* Pres.; Paula W. Baker, V.P.; A. Bonzani, Secy.; Gerard Vilcot, Treas.; Richard J. Carroll, Cont.; Robin G. Willner, Robert F. Woods.
EIN: 133267906
Codes: CS, FD, CD

32552
The Carson Family Charitable Trust
c/o U.S. Trust
114 W. 47th St.
New York, NY 10036

Established in 1990 in NY.
Donor(s): Russell L. Carson, Judith M. Carson.
Financial data (yr. ended 12/31/00): Grants paid, $10,058,333; assets, $37,078,530 (M); gifts received, $19,416,253; expenditures, $10,281,533; qualifying distributions, $9,858,400.
Limitations: Applications not accepted. Giving primarily in New York, NY.
Application information: Contributes only to pre-selected organizations.
Trustees: Cecily M. Carson, Edward S. Carson, Judith M. Carson, Russell L. Carson.
EIN: 136957038
Codes: FD, FM

32553
The Fan Fox and Leslie R. Samuels Foundation, Inc.
350 5th Ave., Ste. 4301
New York, NY 10118 (212) 239-3030
FAX: (212) 239-3039; *E-mail:* info@samuels.org;
URL: http://www.samuels.org
Contact: Joseph C. Mitchell, Pres.

Incorporated in 1959 in UT; reincorporated in 1981 in NY.
Donor(s): Leslie R. Samuels,‡ Fan Fox Samuels.‡
Financial data (yr. ended 07/31/02): Grants paid, $10,004,000; assets, $173,993,000 (M); expenditures, $12,819,000; qualifying distributions, $11,568,000.
Limitations: Giving limited to New York, NY.
Application information: Do not submit musical scores. Application form not required.
Officers and Directors:* Marvin A. Kaufman,* Chair.; Joseph C. Mitchell,* Pres. and Treas.; Robert Marx, V.P. and Secy.; Morton J. Bernstein, Carlos D. Moseley, Jacqueline M. Taylor.
EIN: 133124818
Codes: FD, FM

32554
Eastman Kodak Charitable Trust
c/o The Chase Manhattan Bank
P.O. Box 1412
Rochester, NY 14603 (716) 724-2434
Application address: 343 State St., Rochester, NY 14650
Contact: Essie Calhoun, Dir., Corp. Contribs. Prog.

Trust established in 1952 in NY.
Donor(s): Eastman Kodak Co.
Financial data (yr. ended 12/31/00): Grants paid, $9,919,373; assets, $1,086,216 (M); expenditures, $10,111,567; qualifying distributions, $9,916,588.
Limitations: Giving primarily in high employment locations, including Windsor, CO, Rochester, NY, and Kingsport, TN; giving nationally only for higher education.
Publications: Corporate giving report.
Application information: Application form not required.
Trustee: The Chase Manhattan Bank.
EIN: 166015274
Codes: CS, FD, CD, FM

32555
New York Life Foundation
51 Madison Ave., Ste. 604
New York, NY 10010-1655 (212) 576-7341
E-mail: NYLFoundation@newyorklife.com; *URL:* http://www.newyorklife.com/foundation
Contact: Peter Bushyeager, Pres.

Established in 1979 in NY.
Donor(s): New York Life Insurance Co.
Financial data (yr. ended 12/31/01): Grants paid, $9,663,615; assets, $72,616,739 (M); gifts received, $8,655,780; expenditures, $10,041,962; qualifying distributions, $9,620,460.
Limitations: Giving to organizations that focus on issues and problems in New York, NY; national multi-site programs in two or more of the following cities: San Francisco, CA, Tampa, FL, Atlanta, GA, Minneapolis, MN, Cleveland, OH, Dallas, TX, Leawood, KS.
Publications: Annual report, informational brochure (including application guidelines).
Application information: While grants may be renewed on a periodic basis, continued support is not automatic from year to year. All requests, including those from organizations that previously have received foundation support, will be evaluated annually. Application form not required.
Officers and Directors:* Sy Sternberg,* Chair.; Peter Bushyeager,* Pres.; George J. Trapp,* Secy.; Theodore J. Kohnen, Treas.; Carolyn M. Buscarino, Mike T. Delahaye.
EIN: 132989476
Codes: CS, FD, CD, FM

32556
Charles H. Revson Foundation, Inc.
55 E. 59th St., 23rd Fl.
New York, NY 10022 (212) 935-3340
FAX: (212) 688-0633; *URL:* http://www.revsonfoundation.org
Contact: Eli N. Evans, Pres.

Incorporated in 1956 in NY.
Donor(s): Charles H. Revson.‡
Financial data (yr. ended 12/31/00): Grants paid, $9,490,041; assets, $199,488,289 (M); expenditures, $11,630,717; qualifying distributions, $10,519,930.
Limitations: Giving primarily in New York, NY.
Publications: Biennial report (including application guidelines), occasional report, application guidelines.

Application information: Application form not required.
Officers and Directors:* Robert S. Rifkind,* Chair.; Eli N. Evans,* Pres.; Lisa E. Goldberg, Exec. V.P.; Charles H. Revson, Jr.,* Secy.-Treas.; Red Burns, Henry Louis Gates, Phillip Leder, Ruth Mandel, Martha Minow, Matthew Nimetz, Dir. Emeritus; Louis Perlmutter, Harold Tanner.
EIN: 136126105
Codes: FD, FM

32557
The Kohlberg Foundation, Inc.
111 Radio Cir.
Mount Kisco, NY 10549
FAX: (914) 241-1195
Contact: Nancy White McCabe, Exec. Dir.

Established in 1989 in NY.
Donor(s): The Kohlberg Foundation.
Financial data (yr. ended 12/31/00): Grants paid, $9,383,087; assets, $228,490,472 (M); gifts received, $22,469,476; expenditures, $11,327,611; qualifying distributions, $9,410,012.
Limitations: Applications not accepted. Giving primarily in the U.S.
Publications: Annual report.
Application information: Contributes only to pre-selected organizations.
Officers and Trustees:* Jerome Kohlberg,* Pres.; Walter J. Farley, V.P. and Treas.; Eileen Capone, Secy.; Nancy W. McCabe, Exec. Dir.; David Davis, Karen K. Davis, Andrew Kohlberg, Karen B. Kohlberg, Pamela Kohlberg, Alfred C. Viebranz.
EIN: 133496263
Codes: FD, FM

32558
Marty and Dorothy Silverman Foundation
150 E. 58th St., 29th Fl.
New York, NY 10155
Contact: Lorin Silverman, Secy.-Treas.

Established in 1986.
Donor(s): Marty Silverman.
Financial data (yr. ended 07/31/00): Grants paid, $9,374,999; assets, $319,240,306 (M); gifts received, $1,116,344; expenditures, $9,625,081; qualifying distributions, $13,525,530; giving activities include $4,325,000 for program-related investments.
Limitations: Applications not accepted. Giving primarily in NY.
Application information: Contributes only to pre-selected organizations.
Officers and Directors:* Marty Silverman,* Pres.; Joan Silverman,* V.P.; Lorin Silverman,* Secy.-Treas.
EIN: 222777449
Codes: FD, FM

32559
The Peter Jay Sharp Foundation
(Formerly Sharp Foundation)
545 Madison Ave., 11th Fl.
New York, NY 10022 (212) 397-6060
Contact: Barry Tobias, Treas.

Established in 1984 in NY.
Donor(s): Peter J. Sharp.‡
Financial data (yr. ended 12/31/00): Grants paid, $9,369,680; assets, $45,423,070 (M); gifts received, $12,500,000; expenditures, $10,075,038; qualifying distributions, $9,605,911; giving activities include $90,275 for programs.
Limitations: Applications not accepted. Giving primarily in New York, NY.
Application information: Contributes only to pre-selected organizations.

Officers: Norman Peck, Pres.; Barry Tobias, Treas.
EIN: 133253731
Codes: FD, FM

32560
The Altus One Fund, Inc.
c/o Randall R. Weisenburger
437 Madison Ave., 9th Fl.
New York, NY 10022-7001

Established in 1999 in NY.
Donor(s): Orchard, Stanwich & Pierce Trusts.
Financial data (yr. ended 12/31/00): Grants paid, $9,276,958; assets, $59,274,750 (M); expenditures, $11,965,060; qualifying distributions, $9,760,413.
Limitations: Applications not accepted. Giving primarily in NY.
Application information: Contributes only to pre-selected organizations.
Officers: Randall Weisenburger, Pres. and Secy.; John Wren, V.P.
EIN: 510388792
Codes: FD, FM

32561
Beldon Fund
(also known as Beldon II Fund)
99 Madison Ave. 8th fl.
New York, NY 10016 (800) 591-9595
Additional tel.: (212) 616-5600; *FAX:* (212) 616-5656; *E-mail:* info@beldon.org; *URL:* http://www.beldon.org
Contact: Holeri Faruolo, Grants Mgr.

Established in 1987 in MI.
Donor(s): John R. Hunting.
Financial data (yr. ended 12/31/00): Grants paid, $9,236,000; assets, $98,518,388 (M); expenditures, $12,159,342; qualifying distributions, $11,363,516.
Limitations: Giving on a national basis.
Publications: Annual report (including application guidelines).
Application information: Applications submitted through Beldon Fund; the foundation encourages applicants to use environmentally sensitive applications. See program guidelines and grant application procedures posted on Web site. Application form not required.
Officers and Directors*: John R. Hunting,* Chair. and Pres.; Azade Ardali, C.O.O.; William J. Roberts, Exec. Dir.; Patricia Bauman, Wade Greene, Gene Karpinski, Roger Milliken, Lael Stegall, Ann Fowler Wallace.
EIN: 382756784
Codes: FD

32562
The Andy Warhol Foundation for the Visual Arts
65 Bleecker St., 7th Fl.
New York, NY 10012 (212) 387-7555
FAX: (212) 387-7560; *URL:* http://www.warholfoundation.org
Contact: Pamela Clapp, Prog. Dir.

Established in 1987 in NY.
Donor(s): Andy Warhol.‡
Financial data (yr. ended 04/30/01): Grants paid, $8,972,102; assets, $169,345,457 (M); expenditures, $13,896,675; qualifying distributions, $10,295,617.
Publications: Multi-year report, biennial report, grants list, application guidelines, financial statement.
Application information: Application form not required.
Officers and Directors:* Werner H. Kramarsky, Chair.; Joel Wachs,* Pres.; John Warhola,* V.P.; Peter P. McN. Gates, Secy.; K.C. Maurer, C.F.O.

and Treas.; Patricia Cruz, Vishakha N. Desai, Sherri Geldin, Richard Gluckman, Barbara Kruger, Ann R. Leven, Elizabeth Murray, Ann Philbin, Robert Storr, Robert G. Wilmers.
EIN: 133410749
Codes: FD, FM

32563
Gladys and Roland Harriman Foundation
c/o Brown Brothers Harriman Trust Co.
63 Wall St., Ste. 3101
New York, NY 10005 (212) 493-8182
Contact: William F. Hibberd, Secy.

Established in 1966 in NY.
Donor(s): Roland Harriman,‡ Gladys Harriman.‡
Financial data (yr. ended 12/31/00): Grants paid, $8,321,772; assets, $134,317,723 (M); expenditures, $9,064,686; qualifying distributions, $8,295,788.
Application information: Application form not required.
Officers and Directors:* Elbridge T. Gerry, Jr.,* Pres.; Thomas F. Dixon,* V.P.; William F. Hibberd, Secy.; Anna T. Korniczky, Treas.; Crispin H. Connery, Anthony E. Enders, Terrence M. Farley, Wilhelm E. Northrop.
EIN: 510193915
Codes: FD, FM

32564
George D. Smith Fund, Inc.
c/o Lawrence W. Milas
805 3rd Ave., 20th Fl.
New York, NY 10022 (212) 702-5801

Incorporated in 1956 in DE.
Donor(s): George D. Smith, Sr.‡
Financial data (yr. ended 12/31/00): Grants paid, $8,230,100; assets, $154,368,024 (M); expenditures, $8,281,915; qualifying distributions, $8,056,167.
Limitations: Applications not accepted. Giving primarily in CA and UT.
Application information: Unsolicited requests for funds not considered.
Officers and Trustees:* George D. Smith, Jr.,* Pres. and Secy.-Treas.; Lawrence W. Milas, V.P.; Camilla M. Smith,* V.P.; Sarah A. Smith.
EIN: 136138728
Codes: FD, FM

32565
Mary Flagler Cary Charitable Trust
122 E. 42nd St., Rm. 3505
New York, NY 10168 (212) 953-7700
FAX: (212) 953-7720; *E-mail:* info@carytrust.org
URL: http://www.carytrust.org
Contact: Edward A. Ames, Tr. and Dir., Conservartion; Gayle Morgan, Prog. Dir., Music; Lois M. Regan, Prog. Dir., Urban Environment

Trust established in 1968 in NY.
Donor(s): Mary Flagler Cary.‡
Financial data (yr. ended 06/30/02): Grants paid, $8,140,089; assets, $102,635,915 (M); expenditures, $9,818,141; qualifying distributions, $9,155,542.
Limitations: Giving limited to New York, NY, for music and the urban environment; and the southeastern coastal states for conservation.
Publications: Grants list, financial statement, annual report.
Application information: Application form not required.
Trustees: Edward A. Ames, Prog. Dir., Conservation; Paul B. Guenther, Phyllis J. Mills.
EIN: 136266964
Codes: FD, FM

32566
The William H. Donner Foundation, Inc.
60 E. 42nd St., Ste. 1651
New York, NY 10165 (212) 949-5292
FAX: (212) 949-6022; E-mail: whdf@donner.org;
URL: http://www.donner.org
Contact: Rachel Gregg, Prog. Off.

Incorporated in 1961 in DC.
Donor(s): William H. Donner.‡
Financial data (yr. ended 10/31/00): Grants paid, $8,053,198; assets, $212,198,341 (M); gifts received, $9,119,575; expenditures, $11,630,204; qualifying distributions, $8,935,948.
Limitations: Applications not accepted.
Application information: Only applications invited by the foundation will be considered.
Officers and Trustees*: William Roosevelt,* Pres.; Hon. Curtin Winsor, Jr.,* V.P.; Joseph W. Donner, Jr.,* Secy.; Deborah Donner,* Treas.; Alexander B. Donner, Timothy E. Donner, Stephanie Hanson, Robert D. Spencer.
EIN: 231611346
Codes: FD, FM

32567
Leon Lowenstein Foundation, Inc.
126 E. 56th St., 28th Fl.
New York, NY 10022 (212) 319-0670
FAX: (212) 688-0134
Contact: Robert Bendheim, Pres.

Incorporated in 1941 in NY.
Donor(s): Leon Lowenstein.‡
Financial data (yr. ended 12/31/00): Grants paid, $7,918,650; assets, $181,026,560 (M); expenditures, $9,261,665; qualifying distributions, $8,433,675.
Limitations: Giving primarily in the metropolitan New York, NY, area.
Application information: Application form not required.
Officers and Directors:* Robert Bendheim,* Pres.; John M. Bendheim, V.P.; Bernard R. Rapoport,* Secy.-Treas.; John Van Gorder, Exec. Dir.; John M. Bendheim, Jr., Kim Bendheim, Thomas Bendheim, Lynn B. Thoman, Thomas Wright.
EIN: 136015951
Codes: FD, FM

32568
John Simon Guggenheim Memorial Foundation
90 Park Ave.
New York, NY 10016 (212) 687-4470
FAX: (212) 697-3248; E-mail: fellowships@gf.org; URL: http://www.gf.org
Contact: Joel Conarroe, Pres.

Incorporated in 1925 in NY.
Donor(s): Simon Guggenheim,‡ Mrs. Simon Guggenheim.‡
Financial data (yr. ended 12/31/01): Grants paid, $7,576,807; assets, $219,610,673 (M); gifts received, $386,751; expenditures, $12,354,780; qualifying distributions, $10,813,993.
Limitations: Giving to citizens and permanent residents of the U.S., Canada, Latin America, and the Caribbean.
Publications: Annual report, informational brochure (including application guidelines), financial statement.
Application information: Grants are awarded to individuals rather than institutions. Application form required.
Officers and Trustees:* Joseph A. Rice,* Chair.; Joel Conarroe,* Pres.; G. Thomas Tanselle, Sr. V.P. and Secy.; Peter F. Kardon, V.P.; Coleen P. Higgins-Jacob, C.F.O. and Treas.; Richard W. Hatter, Dir., Devel. and Public Rels.; Michael Hegarty, Leon Levy, Joyce Carol Oates, A. Alex Porter, Richard A. Rifkind, Charles Andrew Ryskamp, Charles P. Stevenson, Jr., Roger W. Straus, Jr., Tr. Emeritus; Jean Strouse, Wendy Wasserstein, Ellen Taaffe Zwilich.
EIN: 135673173
Codes: FD, FM, GTI

32569
Texaco Foundation
(Formerly Texaco Philanthropic Foundation Inc.)
2000 Westchester Ave.
White Plains, NY 10650 (914) 253-4000
URL: http://www.texaco.com/support/index.html
Contact: Anne T. Dowling, Pres.

Incorporated in 1979 in DE.
Donor(s): Texaco Inc.
Financial data (yr. ended 12/31/00): Grants paid, $7,323,718; assets, $10,432,360 (M); gifts received, $5,250,000; expenditures, $7,469,116; qualifying distributions, $7,366,881.
Limitations: Giving primarily in areas of company operations to local organizations; support also for national organizations that serve a large segment of the population.
Publications: Annual report (including application guidelines), informational brochure, application guidelines.
Application information: Receipt of proposals is acknowledged. If the project is of interest to the foundation, interviews are granted in the initial stage of the application process. Application form not required.
Officers and Directors:* F.G. Jenifer,* Chair.; Anne T. Dowling, Pres.; K.E. Murray, Secy.; Ira D. Hall, Treas.; Steve A. Carlson, Compt.; R.A. Brown, Exec. Dir.; A.C. Bailue, R. Moore, R.C. Oelkers, E.P. Smith.
EIN: 133007516
Codes: CS, FD, CD, FM

32570
The Overbrook Foundation
122 East 42nd St., Ste. 2500
New York, NY 10168-2500 (212) 661-8710
FAX: (212) 661-8664
Contact: M. Sheila McGoldrick

Incorporated in 1948 in NY.
Donor(s): Frank Altschul,‡ Helen G. Altschul,‡ Arthur G. Altschul, Margaret A. Lang.
Financial data (yr. ended 12/31/00): Grants paid, $7,242,178; assets, $173,691,040 (M); gifts received, $79,938; expenditures, $9,563,879; qualifying distributions, $7,487,714.
Limitations: Applications not accepted. Giving primarily in New York, NY.
Application information: Applications by invitation only.
Officers and Directors:* Arthur G. Altschul,* Pres.; Margaret A. Lang,* V.P.; Emily H. Altschul,* Secy.; Robert C. Graham, Jr.,* Treas.; Steven A. Foster, Exec. Dir.; Arthur G. Altschul, Jr., Stephen F. Altschul, Julie Graham, Kathryn G. Graham, Cecily Kooijman, Isaiah Lang, Vincent McGee.
EIN: 136088860
Codes: FD, FM

32571
AXA Foundation, Inc.
(Formerly The Equitable Foundation, Inc.)
1290 Ave. of the Americas, 13th Fl.
New York, NY 10104 (212) 314-2566
Contact: Kathleen A. Carlson, C.E.O. and Pres.

Established in 1986 in NY.
Donor(s): The Equitable Life Assurance Society of the U.S., AXA Financial, Inc.
Financial data (yr. ended 09/30/01): Grants paid, $7,171,804; assets, $41,530,119 (M); gifts received, $43,582,818; expenditures, $8,529,611; qualifying distributions, $7,727,897.
Limitations: Giving on a national basis, with some emphasis on New York, NY.
Application information: Application form not required.
Officers and Directors:* Kathleen A. Carlson,* Chair., C.E.O., and Pres.; Jan Goldstein, V.P. and Secy.; John C. Taroni, V.P. and Treas.; Christiann M. Bishop, V.P. and Cont.; Kevin R. Byrne, Michael S. Martin.
EIN: 131340512
Codes: CS, FD, CD, FM

32572
Huberfeld-Bodner Family Foundation, Inc.
152 W. 57th St.
New York, NY 10022
Contact: Murray Huberfeld, Secy.

Established in 1994.
Donor(s): David Bodner, Naomi Bodner, Laura Huberfeld, Murray Huberfeld.
Financial data (yr. ended 12/31/00): Grants paid, $7,000,000; assets, $21,081,500 (M); expenditures, $1,395,342; qualifying distributions, $1,000,000.
Limitations: Giving primarily in the New York, NY, area.
Application information: Application form not required.
Officers: Naomi Bodner, Pres.; Laura Huberfeld, V.P.; Murray Huberfeld, Secy.; David Bodner, Treas.
EIN: 133682951
Codes: FD, FM

32573
The Simons Foundation
126 E. 19th St., 1F
New York, NY 10003
Contact: Marilyn Simons, Pres.

Established in 1994 in NY.
Financial data (yr. ended 06/30/01): Grants paid, $7,000,000; assets, $80,000,000 (M); expenditures, $7,040,000; qualifying distributions, $7,000,000.
Limitations: Applications not accepted. Giving primarily in the New York City metropolitan area.
Officer: Marilyn Simons, Pres.
EIN: 133794889
Codes: FD

32574
The Weill Family Foundation
(Formerly Sanford I. Weill Charitable Foundation, Inc.)
399 Park Ave., 3rd Fl.
New York, NY 10022
Contact: Sanford I. Weill, Chair.

Established around 1967.
Donor(s): Sanford I. Weill.
Financial data (yr. ended 12/31/00): Grants paid, $6,942,511; assets, $203,339,618 (M); gifts received, $51,932,121; expenditures, $8,671,536; qualifying distributions, $6,942,511.
Limitations: Applications not accepted. Giving primarily in the metropolitan New York, NY, area.
Application information: Contributes only to pre-selected organizations.
Officers: Sanford I. Weill, Chair.; Joan H. Weill, Pres.; Jessica Weill, V.P. and Secy.; Marc Weill, V.P. and Treas.
Directors: Ken Bialkin, Charles Prince.
EIN: 136223609
Codes: FD, FM

32575
Paul and Irma Milstein Foundation
1271 Ave. of the Americas, Ste. 4200
New York, NY 10020

Established in 1995.
Donor(s): Paul Milstein, Irma Milstein.
Financial data (yr. ended 12/31/01): Grants paid, $6,928,364; assets, $3,565,904 (M); gifts received, $7,607,065; expenditures, $6,938,466; qualifying distributions, $6,928,419.
Limitations: Applications not accepted. Giving primarily in New York, NY.
Application information: Contributes only to pre-selected organizations.
Officer: Paul Milstein, Pres.
Directors: Roslyn M. Meyer, Edward Milstein, Howard Milstein, Irma Milstein, Barbara M. Zalaznick.
EIN: 133771891
Codes: FD, FM

32576
The Carl and Lily Pforzheimer Foundation, Inc.
650 Madison Ave., 23rd Fl.
New York, NY 10022 (212) 223-6500
Contact: Carl H. Pforzheimer III, Pres.

Incorporated in 1942 in NY.
Donor(s): members of the Pforzheimer family.
Financial data (yr. ended 12/31/01): Grants paid, $6,908,349; assets, $42,081,769 (M); expenditures, $7,168,550; qualifying distributions, $7,110,189; giving activities include $236,979 for programs.
Application information: Application form not required.
Officers and Directors:* Carl H. Pforzheimer III,* Pres. and Treas.; Nancy P. Aronson,* V.P.; Martin F. Richman, Secy.; Anthony L. Ferranti, Compt.; Edgar D. Aronson, George L.K. Frelinghuysen, Carol K. Pforzheimer, Elizabeth S. Pforzheimer, Gary M. Pforzheimer, Alison A. Sherman, Thomas Sobol.
EIN: 135624374
Codes: FD, FM

32577
The Nash Family Foundation, Inc.
c/o Ulysses Partners L.P.
280 Park Ave.
New York, NY 10017

Established in 1964 in NY.
Donor(s): Jack Nash, Leo Levy, Helen Nash.
Financial data (yr. ended 06/30/00): Grants paid, $6,907,496; assets, $82,862,907 (M); gifts received, $11,262,807; expenditures, $7,602,981; qualifying distributions, $7,063,862.
Limitations: Applications not accepted. Giving primarily in New York, NY.
Application information: Contributes only to pre-selected organizations.
Officers and Directors:* Jack Nash,* Pres.; Ludwig Bravmann,* V.P.; Joshua Nash, V.P.; Pamela Rohr, V.P.; Morris H. Rosenthal, Secy.; Helen Nash,* Treas.
EIN: 136168559
Codes: FD, FM

32578
Edward John Noble Foundation, Inc.
32 E. 57th St.
New York, NY 10022-2513 (212) 759-4212
Contact: June Noble Larkin, Chair.

Trust established in 1940 in CT; incorporated in 1982.
Donor(s): Edward John Noble.‡
Financial data (yr. ended 12/31/01): Grants paid, $6,638,855; assets, $140,885,069 (M); expenditures, $8,514,611; qualifying distributions, $6,638,855.
Limitations: Giving primarily in the metropolitan New York, NY, area for arts organizations; St. Catherine's Island, GA, and the eastern states for conservation projects and family planning; and the Northeast for private colleges and universities.
Publications: Biennial report (including application guidelines).
Application information: Application form not required.
Officers and Directors:* June Noble Larkin,* Chair.; Frank Y. Larkin,* Vice-Chair.; E.J. Noble Smith,* Pres. and Exec. Dir.; Deborah A. Menton, Secy.; E. Mary Heffernan, Treas.; William G. Conway, Ellen V. Futter, Harold B. Johnson, Howard Phipps, Jr., Frank P. Piskor, Joseph W. Polisi, Bradford D. Smith, David Smith, Jeremy T. Smith, Carroll L. Wainwright, Jr.
EIN: 061055586
Codes: FD, FM

32579
The Pinkerton Foundation
630 5th Ave., Ste. 1755
New York, NY 10111 (212) 332-3385
FAX: (212) 332-3399; *E-mail:* pinkfdn@mindspring.com; *URL:* http://fdncenter.org/grantmaker/pinkerton
Contact: Joan Colello, Exec. Dir.

Incorporated in 1966 in DE.
Donor(s): Robert A. Pinkerton.‡
Financial data (yr. ended 12/31/01): Grants paid, $6,630,610; assets, $141,531,849 (M); gifts received, $26,568; expenditures, $7,841,963; qualifying distributions, $7,132,610.
Limitations: Giving primarily in New York, NY.
Publications: Biennial report (including application guidelines).
Application information: Accepts NYRAG Common Application Form. Application form required.
Officers and Trustees:* George J. Gillespie III,* Pres.; Joan Colello,* Secy. and Exec. Dir.; Eugene C. Fey,* Treas.; Michael S. Joyce, Daniel L. Mosley, Richard M. Smith, Thomas J. Sweeney.
EIN: 136206624
Codes: FD, FM

32580
The J. M. Kaplan Fund, Inc.
261 Madison Ave., 19th Fl.
New York, NY 10016 (212) 767-0630
FAX: (212) 767-0639; Application address for publication program: Furthermore, P.O. Box 667, Hudson, NY 12534; tel.: (518) 828-8900; *URL:* http://www.jmkfund.org
Contact: William P. Falahee, Cont.

Incorporated in 1948 in NY as Faigel Leah Foundation, Inc.; The J.M. Kaplan Fund, Inc., a DE corporation, merged with it in 1975 and was renamed The J.M. Kaplan Fund, Inc.
Donor(s): Members of the J.M. Kaplan family.
Financial data (yr. ended 12/31/00): Grants paid, $6,606,219; assets, $160,118,875 (M); gifts received, $4,627,454; expenditures, $10,273,459; qualifying distributions, $8,257,495; giving activities include $500,000 for program-related investments.
Limitations: Giving primarily in NY, with emphasis on New York City.
Publications: Annual report (including application guidelines).
Application information: Proposals received by FAX not considered. Application form required.
Officers and Trustees:* Peter W. Davidson,* Chair.; William P. Falahee, Cont.; Conn Nugent, Exec. Dir.; Betsy Davidson, G. Bradford Davidson, J. Matthew Davidson, Joan K. Davidson, Caio Fonseca, Elizabeth K. Fonseca, Isabel Fonseca, Quina Fonseca, Richard D. Kaplan, Mary E. Kaplan.
EIN: 136090286
Codes: FD, FM

32581
The Florence Gould Foundation
c/o Cahill Gordon and Reindel
80 Pine St., Ste. 1736
New York, NY 10005-1702 (212) 701-3400
Contact: John R. Young, Pres.

Incorporated in 1957 in NY.
Donor(s): Florence J. Gould.‡
Financial data (yr. ended 12/31/01): Grants paid, $6,592,672; assets, $101,675,466 (M); expenditures, $6,886,350; qualifying distributions, $6,729,618.
Limitations: Giving primarily in the U.S. and France.
Application information: Application form not required.
Officers and Directors:* John R. Young,* Pres.; Daniel P. Davison,* V.P. and Treas.; Walter C. Cliff,* Secy.
EIN: 136176855
Codes: FD, FM

32582
The Janaki Foundation, Inc.
c/o Judy Cedeno
1 Computer Associates Plz.
Hauppauge, NY 11788

Established in 1997 in NY.
Financial data (yr. ended 12/31/00): Grants paid, $6,551,670; assets, $165,483,740 (M); expenditures, $6,919,609; qualifying distributions, $6,543,379.
Limitations: Applications not accepted.
Application information: Contributes only to pre-selected organizations.
Officers and Directors:* Charles B. Wang,* Pres.; Kimberly Wang,* V.P.; Judy Cedeno, Secy.; Nancy Li,* Treas.
EIN: 113375738
Codes: FD, FM

32583
The Esther A. & Joseph Klingenstein Fund, Inc.
787 7th Ave., 6th Fl.
New York, NY 10019-6016 (212) 492-6181
FAX: (212) 492-7007
Contact: John Klingenstein, Pres.

Incorporated in 1945 in NY.
Donor(s): Esther A. Klingenstein,‡ Joseph Klingenstein.‡
Financial data (yr. ended 09/30/01): Grants paid, $6,444,762; assets, $135,085,087 (M); expenditures, $8,392,349; qualifying distributions, $6,884,247.
Publications: Informational brochure.
Application information: Application forms are required for the Klingenstein Fellowship Awards, and are available from department heads or from the foundation.
Officers and Directors:* John Klingenstein,* Pres. and Treas.; Frederick A. Klingenstein,* 1st V.P. and Secy.; Patricia D. Klingenstein, Sharon L. Klingenstein.
EIN: 136028788
Codes: FD, FM, GTI

32584
The Camille and Henry Dreyfus Foundation, Inc.
555 Madison Ave., Ste. 1305
New York, NY 10022-3301 (212) 753-1760
FAX: (212) 593-2256; E-mail:
admin@dreyfus.org; URL: http://www.dreyfus.org
Contact: Robert L. Lichter, Ph.D., Exec. Dir.

Incorporated in 1946 in NY.
Donor(s): Camille Dreyfus.‡
Financial data (yr. ended 12/31/01): Grants paid, $6,444,117; assets, $120,713,650 (M); expenditures, $6,959,887; qualifying distributions, $6,380,225.
Limitations: Giving only on a national basis.
Application information: Candidates for awards must be nominated by applying academic institution; individual applications not accepted; nomination forms required for all programs. Application form required.
Officers and Directors:* Dorothy Dinsmoor,* Pres.; John R.H. Blum,* V.P.; Edward A. Reilly,* Secy.-Treas.; Robert L. Lichter, Ph.D., Exec. Dir.; Marye Anne Fox, Ph.D., Joshua Lederberg, Ph.D., H. Marshall Schwarz, Henry C. Walter, Harry H. Wasserman, Ph.D.
EIN: 135570117
Codes: FD, FM, GTI

32585
The Arthur and Rochelle Belfer Foundation, Inc.
(Formerly The Belfer Foundation, Inc.)
c/o Belco Oil & Gas Corp.
767 5th Ave., 46th Fl.
New York, NY 10153-0002
Contact: Robert A. Belfer, V.P.

Incorporated in 1951 in NY.
Donor(s): Members of the Belfer family, Belfer Corp.
Financial data (yr. ended 12/31/00): Grants paid, $6,379,441; assets, $34,422,098 (M); expenditures, $6,642,993; qualifying distributions, $6,337,435.
Limitations: Applications not accepted. Giving primarily in NY.
Officers and Directors:* Selma Ruben,* Pres.; Robert A. Belfer, V.P.; Lawrence Ruben,* V.P.; Jack Saltz,* V.P.; Laurence D. Belfer,* Secy.; Anita Saltz, Treas.; Norman Belfer, Renee E. Belfer, Richard Ruben, Leonard Saltz.
EIN: 136086711
Codes: FD, FM

32586
Jerome L. Greene Foundation, Inc.
450 Park Ave., Ste. 1802
New York, NY 10022 (212) 688-1550

Established in 1978.
Donor(s): Jerome L. Greene.‡
Financial data (yr. ended 11/30/00): Grants paid, $6,310,022; assets, $35,359,760 (M); gifts received, $16,865,000; expenditures, $6,583,727; qualifying distributions, $6,311,022.
Limitations: Applications not accepted. Giving primarily in NY.
Application information: Contributes only to pre-selected organizations.
Officers and Directors:* Dawn Greene,* Pres. and Treas.; Christina McInerney,* V.P. and Secy.; Margaret Williams.
EIN: 132960852
Codes: FD

32587
The Pincus Family Fund
466 Lexington Ave.
New York, NY 10017 (212) 878-9291
Contact: Evelyn Lipori, Fund Admin.

Established in 1961 in NY.
Donor(s): Lionel I. Pincus, Suzanne Pincus.‡
Financial data (yr. ended 12/31/01): Grants paid, $6,306,523; assets, $36,209,715 (M); gifts received, $310; expenditures, $6,397,395; qualifying distributions, $6,332,663.
Limitations: Giving primarily in NY.
Application information: Grants from the Institutional Fund are made only to pre-selected organizations; unsolicited applications not accepted. Application form not required.
Officers and Directors:* Lionel I. Pincus,* Pres.; Edwin Gustafson, Jr.,* Secy.-Treas.; Henry Pincus, Matthew Pincus.
EIN: 136089184
Codes: FD, FM

32588
The Lauder Foundation, Inc.
767 5th Ave., 40th Fl.
New York, NY 10153
Contact: J. Krupskas

Incorporated in 1962 in NY.
Donor(s): Estee Lauder, Joseph H. Lauder,‡ Leonard A. Lauder, Ronald S. Lauder, Evelyn Lauder, William Lauder, Estee Lauder, Inc., LWG Family Partners.
Financial data (yr. ended 11/30/01): Grants paid, $6,165,305; assets, $18,096,216 (M); gifts received, $2,400,000; expenditures, $6,227,596; qualifying distributions, $6,166,437.
Limitations: Giving primarily in the metropolitan New York, NY, area.
Publications: Financial statement.
Officers and Directors:* Estee Lauder,* Pres.; Ronald S. Lauder,* V.P.; Leonard A. Lauder,* Secy.-Treas.; Aerin Lauder, William Lauder.
EIN: 136153743
Codes: FD

32589
Helene Fuld Health Trust
c/o HSBC Bank USA
452 5th Ave., 17th Fl.
New York, NY 10018 (212) 525-2418
Additional address: FAX: (212) 525-2395; E-mail: marianne.caskran@us.hsbc.com; URL: http://www.fuld.org
Contact: Marianne Caskran, Grants Admin.

Trust established in 1951 in NJ; activated in 1969 as successor to Helene Fuld Health Foundation incorporated in 1935.
Donor(s): Leonhard Felix Fuld,‡ Florentine M. Fuld.‡
Financial data (yr. ended 09/30/01): Grants paid, $6,151,556; assets, $129,228,254 (M); expenditures, $7,300,761; qualifying distributions, $6,592,790.
Limitations: Applications not accepted. Giving on a national basis.
Trustee: HSBC Bank USA.
EIN: 136309307
Codes: FD, FM

32590
Eugene M. Lang Foundation
535 5th Ave., Ste. 906
New York, NY 10017 (212) 949-4100
Contact: Mary Sivak, Fiscal Mgr.

Established in 1968 in NY.
Donor(s): Eugene M. Lang.

Financial data (yr. ended 12/31/00): Grants paid, $6,150,759; assets, $50,156,012 (M); gifts received, $150,000; expenditures, $6,585,066; qualifying distributions, $6,158,538.
Limitations: Giving primarily in NY and neighboring areas, including PA.
Application information: Application form not required.
Trustees: Belinda Lang, David A. Lang, Eugene M. Lang, Jane Lang, Kristina Lang, Stephen Lang, Theresa Lang, Paul Sprenger.
EIN: 136153412
Codes: FD, FM

32591
Mertz Gilmore Foundation
(Formerly Joyce Mertz-Gilmore Foundation)
218 E. 18th St.
New York, NY 10003-3694 (212) 475-1137
FAX: (212) 777-5226; E-mail:
info@mertzgilmore.org; URL: http://www.mertzgilmore.org
Contact: Jay Beckner, Exec. Dir.

Incorporated in 1959 in NY.
Donor(s): Robert Gilmore,‡ Joyce Mertz.‡
Financial data (yr. ended 12/31/01): Grants paid, $6,124,212; assets, $104,952,751 (M); expenditures, $8,755,140; qualifying distributions, $7,760,479.
Limitations: Giving on a national and international basis, with the exception of the New York City Program.
Publications: Biennial report (including application guidelines), application guidelines.
Application information: The foundation prefers to receive all inquiries by regular mail. Grantseekers outside the United States may submit inquiry letters via E-mail. Do not submit videos, CDs, audiocassettes, press clippings, books, or other materials unless they are requested. Application form required.
Officers and Directors:* Larry E. Condon,* Chair.; Elizabeth Burke Gilmore,* Vice-Chair. and Secy.; Denise Nix Thompson,* Treas.; Jay Beckner, Exec. Dir.; Harlan Cleveland, Robert Crane, Hal Harvey, Patricia Ramsay, Peggy Saika, Mikki Shepard, Franklin W. Wallin.
EIN: 132872722
Codes: FD, FM

32592
The Scherman Foundation, Inc.
16 E. 52nd St., Ste. 601
New York, NY 10022-5306 (212) 832-3086
FAX: (212) 838-0154
Contact: Sandra Silverman, Pres. and Exec. Dir.

Incorporated in 1941 in NY.
Donor(s): Members of the Scherman family.
Financial data (yr. ended 12/31/01): Grants paid, $6,110,200; assets, $87,473,557 (M); expenditures, $7,209,473; qualifying distributions, $6,612,654.
Limitations: Giving in NY and nationally in all areas, except for the arts and social welfare, which are primarily in New York City.
Publications: Annual report (including application guidelines).
Application information: Application form not required.
Officers and Directors:* Karen R. Sollins, Chair.; Axel G. Rosin,* Chair, Emeritus; Sandra Silverman, Pres. and Exec. Dir.; Susanna Bergtold,* Secy.; Mitchell C. Pratt, Treas. and Prog. Off.; Hillary Brown, Gordon N. Litwin, John J. O'Neil, Katharine S. Rosin, Anthony M. Schulte, Marcia Thompson, John Wroclawski.
EIN: 136098464
Codes: FD, FM

32593
The Gordon Fund
(Formerly The Gordon/Rousmaniere/Roberts Fund)
c/o Sullivan & Cromwell
125 Broad St.
New York, NY 10004-2498
FAX: (212) 558-3064
Contact: James I. Black III

Established in 1985 in NY.
Donor(s): Albert H. Gordon.
Financial data (yr. ended 12/31/00): Grants paid, $6,046,045; assets, $14,442,536 (M); expenditures, $6,224,774; qualifying distributions, $5,055,207.
Limitations: Giving primarily in CA, CT, MA, and NY.
Trustee: Mary Gordon Roberts.
EIN: 133257793
Codes: FD, FM

32594
M & T Charitable Foundation
1 M & T Plz., 6th Fl.
Buffalo, NY 14203 (716) 848-3804
FAX: (716) 848-7318
Contact: Debbie Pringle

Established in 1993 in NY.
Donor(s): Manufacturers and Traders Trust Company.
Financial data (yr. ended 12/31/00): Grants paid, $6,029,534; assets, $36,068,633 (M); expenditures, $6,091,534; qualifying distributions, $6,029,534.
Limitations: Applications not accepted. Giving primarily in NY.
Application information: Contributes only to pre-selected organizations.
Officers and Directors:* Shelley C. Drake,* Chair. and Pres.; Edward L. Beideck, V.P.; Keith M. Belanger, V.P.; John A. Carmichael,* V.P.; Scott E. Dagenais, V.P.; Edward Gajewski, V.P.; Brian E. Hickey, V.P.; Jeffrey M. Levy, V.P.; Kevin J. Pearson, V.P.; Michael S. Piemonte, V.P.; Julia Primavera-McGlynn, V.P.; Howard W. Sharp, V.P.; Marie King, Secy.; Michael P. Pinto,* Treas.; Richard A. Lammert, Robert E. Sadler, Jr.
EIN: 161448017
Codes: CS, FD, CD, FM

32595
The Woods Foundation
(Formerly The Ward W. Woods Foundation)
c/o Bessemer Trust Co., N.A., Tax Dept.
630 5th Ave.
New York, NY 10111
Contact: Ward W. Woods, Jr., Pres.

Established in 1985 in NY.
Donor(s): Ward W. Woods, Jr.
Financial data (yr. ended 09/30/00): Grants paid, $5,949,925; assets, $3,331,427 (M); gifts received, $3,011,649; expenditures, $6,041,037; qualifying distributions, $5,941,851.
Limitations: Applications not accepted. Giving on a national basis.
Application information: Unsolicited requests for funds are not accepted.
Officers and Directors:* Ward W. Woods, Jr.,* Pres.; Priscilla B. Woods,* V.P.; Robert Roriston,* Secy.-Treas.; Katherine Woods Emerick, Alexandra Woods.
EIN: 133314966
Codes: FD

32596
The Markle Foundation
(Formerly The John and Mary R. Markle Foundation)
10 Rockefeller Plz., 16th Fl.
New York, NY 10020-1903 (212) 489-6655
FAX: (212) 765-9690; *E-mail:* info@markle.org;
URL: http://www.markle.org/index.stm
Contact: Zoe Baird, Pres.

Incorporated in 1927 in NY.
Donor(s): John Markle,‡ Mary Markle.‡
Financial data (yr. ended 06/30/00): Grants paid, $5,897,081; assets, $208,737,484 (M); expenditures, $11,128,735; qualifying distributions, $12,693,307.
Publications: Annual report.
Application information: Application form required.
Officers and Directors:* Joel L. Fleishman,* Chair.; Zoe Baird,* Pres.; Karen D. Byers, V.P. and Secy.-Treas.; Raymond C. Clevenger III, Lewis W. Bernard, Stephen W. Fillo, Stephen Friedman, Ellen Condliffe Lagemann, Diana T. Murray, Stanley S. Shuman.
EIN: 131770307
Codes: FD, FM

32597
The New York Times Company Foundation, Inc.
229 W. 43rd St.
New York, NY 10036-3959 (212) 556-1091
FAX: (212) 556-4450; *URL:* http://www.nytco.com/foundation
Contact: Jack Rosenthal, Pres.

Incorporated in 1955 in NY.
Donor(s): The New York Times Co.
Financial data (yr. ended 12/31/01): Grants paid, $5,859,668; assets, $2,110,418 (M); gifts received, $6,057,300; expenditures, $6,657,077; qualifying distributions, $5,859,668.
Limitations: Giving primarily in the New York, NY, metropolitan area and in localities served by business units of the company.
Publications: Annual report (including application guidelines).
Application information: Application form required.
Officers and Directors:* Jacqueline H. Dryfoos,* Chair.; Jack Rosenthal,* Pres.; Russell T. Lewis,* Exec. V.P.; Michael Golden,* Sr. V.P.; John M. O'Brien, Sr. V.P.; Solomon B. Watson IV, Sr. V.P.; Rhonda L. Brauer, Secy.; James Lessersohn, Treas.; Ellen R. Marram, Donald M. Stewart, Arthur O. Sulzberger, Jr.
EIN: 136066955
Codes: CS, FD, CD, FM, GTI

32598
Max Kade Foundation, Inc.
6 E. 87th St.
New York, NY 10128 (646) 672-4354
Contact: Hans G. Hachmann, Pres.

Incorporated in 1944 in NY.
Donor(s): Max Kade.‡
Financial data (yr. ended 12/31/00): Grants paid, $5,821,035; assets, $107,911,588 (M); expenditures, $6,589,603; qualifying distributions, $5,911,149.
Limitations: Giving primarily in the U.S. and Europe.
Publications: Occasional report.
Officers and Directors:* Hans G. Hachmann,* Pres.; Lya Friedrich Pfeifer, Treas.; Berteline Baier Dale,* Secy.; Guenter Blobel, Fritz Kade, Jr., M.D.
EIN: 135658082
Codes: FD, FM

32599
China Medical Board of New York, Inc.
750 3rd Ave., 23rd Fl.
New York, NY 10017-2701 (212) 682-8000
Contact: M. Roy Schwarz, M.D., Pres.

Incorporated in 1928 in NY.
Donor(s): The Rockefeller Foundation.
Financial data (yr. ended 06/30/01): Grants paid, $5,806,319; assets, $205,367,622 (M); expenditures, $8,875,374; qualifying distributions, $8,155,740; giving activities include $507,990 for programs.
Limitations: Applications not accepted. Giving limited to East and Southeast Asia, including the People's Republic of China, Hong Kong, Indonesia, Korea, Malaysia, the Philippines, Singapore, Taiwan, and Thailand.
Publications: Annual report.
Application information: Submit request through dean's office of Asian institution in which foundation has a program of support.
Officers and Trustees:* Dwight H. Perkins, Ph.D.,* Chair.; M. Roy Schwarz, M.D.,* Pres.; Jean Hogan, V.P., Admin.; Robert H.M. Ferguson, Secy.; Walter G. Ehlers,* Treas.; Mary Brown Bullock, Ph.D.,* Jordan J. Cohen, Don Eugene Detmer, M.D., Michael Duffy,* Thomas S. Inui, M.D., Tom G. Kessinger, Ph.D., Peter J. Robbins, Gloria H. Spivak.
EIN: 131659619
Codes: FD, FM

32600
Stephen and Tabitha King Foundation, Inc.
c/o Arthur B. Greene and Co. Inc.
101 Park Ave.
New York, NY 10178 (212) 661-8200
URL: http://www.stkfoundation.org
Contact: Arthur B. Greene, Secy.

Established in 1986 in ME.
Donor(s): Stephen E. King.
Financial data (yr. ended 12/31/00): Grants paid, $5,776,207; assets, $10,165,047 (M); gifts received, $7,083,867; expenditures, $5,792,087; qualifying distributions, $5,783,282.
Limitations: Giving primarily in ME.
Officers: Stephen E. King, Pres.; Tabitha King, V.P.; Arthur B. Greene, Secy.
EIN: 133364647
Codes: FD, FM

32601
Howard Gilman Foundation, Inc.
111 W. 50th St., 2nd Fl.
New York, NY 10020 (212) 307-1073
FAX: (212) 262-4108; *E-mail:* jamis@gilman.com; *URL:* http://www.howardgilman.org
Contact: Jen Amis, Prog. Admin.

Incorporated in 1981 in DE.
Donor(s): Gilman Investment Co., Gilman Paper Co., Gilman Securities Corp.
Financial data (yr. ended 12/31/01): Grants paid, $5,725,656; assets, $244,640,000 (M); expenditures, $7,802,656; qualifying distributions, $5,725,656.
Limitations: Giving primarily in the metropolitan New York, NY, area with emphasis on the arts.
Publications: Program policy statement, informational brochure.
Application information: Applicants must call before submitting letter of inquiry. Application form not required.
Officer: Arlene Shuler, Exec. Dir.
Directors: Norman Alexander, Pierre Apraxine, Gwendolyn Baker, Bernard D. Bergreen, Jeff Borer, M.D., Donald Bruce, J.D. Campbell,

32601—NEW YORK

Stephen Cropper, Justin Feldman, Marcello Guidi, John J. Kennedy, Harvey Lichtenstein, William H. Luers, John Lukas, Raymond McGuire, Natalie Moody, Isabella Rossellini.
EIN: 133097486
Codes: FD, FM

32602
United States-Japan Foundation
145 E. 32nd St., 12th Fl.
New York, NY 10016 (212) 481-8753
FAX: (212) 481-8762; E-mail: info@US-JF.org; Tokyo, Japan office address: Reinanzaka Bldg. 1F, 1-14-2 Akasaka, Minato-ku, Tokyo 107-0052, Japan, tel.: (03) 3586-0541; FAX: (03) 3586-1128; E-mail: JDU05456@nifty.ne.jp; URL: http://www.us-jf.org

Foundation incorporated in 1980 in NY.
Donor(s): The Nippon Foundation.
Financial data (yr. ended 12/31/00): Grants paid, $5,719,928; assets, $99,997,997 (M); expenditures, $9,139,480; qualifying distributions, $7,443,834.
Limitations: Giving primarily in the U.S. and Japan.
Publications: Annual report.
Application information: The foundation is reviewing its program areas. Application form not required.
Officers and Trustees:* Thomas S. Johnson, Chair.; Shinji Fukukawa,* Vice-Chair.; George R. Packard,* Pres.; Takeo Takuma,* V.P. and Dir., Tokyo office; Yusuke Saraya,* Board Secy.; Christine Manapat-Sims, Treas.; John Brademas, Gerald L. Curtis, Robin Chandler Duke, Thomas S. Foley, William Frenzel, Masakazu Soko Izumi, Yotaro Kobayashi, T. Timothy Ryan, Jr., Yohei Sasakawa, Jiro Ushio.
EIN: 133054425
Codes: FD, FM

32603
Community Foundation for Greater Buffalo
(Formerly The Buffalo Foundation)
712 Main St.
Buffalo, NY 14202-1720 (716) 852-2857
FAX: (716) 852-2861; E-mail: mail@cfgb.org; URL: http://www.cfgb.org
Contact: Myra Lawrence, V.P., Finance and Admin.

Established in 1919 in NY by resolution and declaration of trust; corporate version established in 1985.
Financial data (yr. ended 12/31/01): Grants paid, $5,528,600; assets, $113,327,275 (M); gifts received, $6,847,699; expenditures, $7,245,672.
Limitations: Giving limited to western NY; scholarships awarded to students primarily from Erie County.
Publications: Annual report (including application guidelines), application guidelines, informational brochure, newsletter, program policy statement.
Application information: Application forms required for scholarships, and must be requested in writing between Mar. 1 and May 1 and include a SASE. Application form required.
Officers and Directors:* Ruth D. Bryant,* Chair.; Joseph F. Crangle,* Vice-Chair.; Gail E. Johnstone, C.E.O. and Pres.; Myra Lawrence, V.P. Finance and Admin.; Richard Tobe, V.P., Prog.; Kathryn L. Chatmon, Compt.; Joseph J. Castiglia, Anthony J. Colucci, Jr., Clotilde Perez-Bode Dedecker, Sue Gardner, Robert D. Gioia, William G. Gisel, Jr., Andrew J. Rudnick, David Zebro, Howard Zemsky.
Trustee Banks: Fleet National Bank, HSBC Bank USA, KeyBank, N.A., Manufacturers & Traders Trust Co.

EIN: 160743935
Codes: CM, FD, FM, GTI

32604
Hess Foundation, Inc.
1185 Ave. of the Americas
New York, NY 10036 (212) 997-8500
Contact: Norma Hess, Pres.

Incorporated in 1954 in DE.
Donor(s): Leon Hess.‡
Financial data (yr. ended 11/30/00): Grants paid, $5,476,788; assets, $155,292,679 (M); expenditures, $5,655,729; qualifying distributions, $5,522,745.
Limitations: Applications not accepted. Giving on a national basis, with some emphasis on NY.
Application information: Contributes only to pre-selected organizations.
Officers and Directors:* Norma Hess,* Pres.; Steven Gutman,* V.P.; John B. Hess,* V.P.; Marlene Hess, V.P.; Constance Hess Williams, V.P.; John Y. Schreyer,* Secy.; Robert Conner, Treas.
EIN: 221713046
Codes: FD, FM

32605
Robert Lehman Foundation, Inc.
c/o Hertz, Herson, & Co., LLP
2 Park Ave., Ste. 1500
New York, NY 10016 (212) 808-7946
Contact: Paul C. Guth, Secy.

Incorporated in 1943 in NY.
Donor(s): Robert Lehman.‡
Financial data (yr. ended 09/30/01): Grants paid, $5,463,684; assets, $62,824,901 (M); expenditures, $6,279,075; qualifying distributions, $5,628,704.
Limitations: Giving primarily in the northeastern U.S., with emphasis on New York, NY.
Application information: Unsolicited applications generally not considered.
Officers and Directors:* Philip H. Isles,* Pres.; Edwin L. Weisl, Jr.,* V.P.; Paul C. Guth,* Secy.; Michael M. Thomas,* Treas.; Robert A. Bernhard, James M. Hester, Robert Owen Lehman.
EIN: 136094018
Codes: FD, FM

32606
New York Foundation
350 5th Ave., No. 2901
New York, NY 10118 (212) 594-8009
URL: http://www.nyf.org
Contact: Madeline Lee, Exec. Dir.

Incorporated in 1909 in NY.
Donor(s): Louis A. Heinsheimer,‡ Alfred M. Heinsheimer,‡ Lionel J. Salomon.‡
Financial data (yr. ended 12/31/01): Grants paid, $5,327,000; assets, $76,469,000 (M); gifts received, $500,000; expenditures, $6,407,000; qualifying distributions, $6,097,000.
Limitations: Giving limited to local programs in the New York, NY, metropolitan area.
Publications: Annual report (including application guidelines).
Application information: Accepts NYRAG Common Application Form. Application form not required.
Officers and Trustees:* A. Carleton Dukess,* Chair.; Thomas I. Acosta,* Vice-Chair.; Rose Dobrof, Ph.D.,* Secy.; Madeline Einhorn Glick,* Treas.; Madeline Lee, Exec. Dir.; Alan Altschuler, Margaret Booth, Gladys Carrion, Angela Diaz, M.D., Stephen D. Heyman, Chung-Wha Hong, David R. Jones, William M. Kelly, Peter Kwong, Myra Mahon, Elba Montalvo, Jason Worwin.
EIN: 135626345

Codes: FD, FM

32607
Josiah Macy, Jr. Foundation
44 E. 64th St.
New York, NY 10021 (212) 486-2424
FAX: (212) 644-0765; E-mail: jmacyinfo@josiahmacyfoundation.org; URL: http://www.josiahmacyfoundation.org
Contact: June E. Osborn, M.D., Pres. and Martha Wolfgang, V.P.

Incorporated in 1930 in NY.
Donor(s): Kate Macy Ladd.‡
Financial data (yr. ended 06/30/02): Grants paid, $5,308,894; assets, $139,825,416 (M); expenditures, $6,967,007; qualifying distributions, $5,308,894; giving activities include $67,920 for programs.
Publications: Annual report, occasional report, grants list.
Application information: Additional program information is available on the foundation's Web site. Application form not required.
Officers and Directors:* Clarence F. Michalis,* Chair.; June E. Osborn, M.D., Pres.; Martha Wolfgang, V.P. and Treas.; Rina Forlini, Secy.; Lawrence K. Altman, M.D., J. Carter Bacot, Jordan J. Cohen, M.D., E. Virgil Conway, John W. Frymoyer, M.D., S. Parker Gilbert, Patricia Albjerg Graham, Ph.D., Bernard W. Harleston, Ph.D., Arthur H. Hayes, Jr., M.D., Lawrence S. Huntington, John Jay Iselin, Ph.D., Mary Patterson McPherson, Ph.D., William H. Wright II.
EIN: 135596895
Codes: FD, FM

32608
The Norman and Rosita Winston Foundation, Inc.
c/o Paul Weiss, Rifkind, et al.
1285 Ave. of the Americas
New York, NY 10019-6064 (212) 373-3000
Contact: John J. O'Neil

Incorporated in 1954 in NY.
Donor(s): Norman K. Winston,‡ The N.K. Winston Foundation, Inc.
Financial data (yr. ended 06/30/00): Grants paid, $5,166,000; assets, $104,446,037 (M); expenditures, $5,710,849; qualifying distributions, $5,010,016.
Limitations: Giving primarily in NY.
Officers and Directors:* Richard A. Rifkind,* Pres.; Lauri Levitt Friedland,* Secy.; Jan Krukowski,* Treas.
EIN: 136161672
Codes: FD, FM

32609
Dolan Foundations
(Formerly Dolan Children's Foundation)
1 Media Crossways
Woodbury, NY 11797 (516) 803-9201
Application address: 340 Crossways Park Dr., Woodbury, NY 11797
Contact: Dr. Robert F. Vizza, Pres.

Established in 1986 in NY.
Donor(s): Charles F. Dolan, Helen Dolan.
Financial data (yr. ended 12/31/01): Grants paid, $5,106,684; assets, $70,174,806 (M); gifts received, $50,000; expenditures, $5,197,224; qualifying distributions, $5,195,572.
Limitations: Giving primarily in Long Island, NY.
Publications: Application guidelines.
Application information: Application form required.
Officers: Marianne Dolan Weber, Chair.; Robert F. Vizza, Pres.; William Frewin, V.P. and Treas.

EIN: 113379933
Codes: FD

32610
The Mosaic Fund
c/o Satterlee, Stephens Burke & Burke
230 Park Ave., Ste. 1130
New York, NY 10169-1599

Established in 1994 in NY.
Donor(s): Clattesad Trust.
Financial data (yr. ended 12/31/00): Grants paid, $5,082,781; assets, $355,624 (M); gifts received, $5,519,243; expenditures, $5,195,931; qualifying distributions, $5,082,781.
Limitations: Applications not accepted. Giving primarily in NY.
Application information: Contributes only to pre-selected organizations.
Trustees: Howard G. Seitz, Richard T. Watson.
EIN: 137045257
Codes: FD

32611
Independence Community Foundation
182 Atlantic Ave.
Brooklyn, NY 11201 (718) 722-2300
FAX: (718) 722-5757; E-mail: inquiries@icfny.org; URL: http://www.icfny.org
Contact: Marilyn Gelber, Exec. Dir.

Established in 1998 in NY.
Donor(s): Independence Community Bank Corp.
Financial data (yr. ended 12/31/00): Grants paid, $5,064,524; assets, $68,532,842 (M); expenditures, $6,159,213; qualifying distributions, $5,498,112; giving activities include $500,000 for program-related investments.
Limitations: Giving primarily in New York, NY.
Application information: Only applicants that have received a positive response to a letter of inquiry should submit proposals. Application form not required.
Officers: Alan H. Fishman, Pres.; Marilyn G. Gelber, Exec. Dir.
Board of Directors: Charles J. Hamm, Chair.; Steven Adubato, Willard N. Archie, Lilliam Barrios-Paoli, Fred W. Beaufait, Robert B. Catell, Donald H. Elliott, David R. Jones, Donald M. Karp, Donald E. Kolowsky, Malcolm MacKay, Joseph S. Morgano, Maria Fiorini Ramirez, Wesley D. Ratcliff, Victor M. Richel.
EIN: 113422729
Codes: CS, FD, CD

32612
The Heckscher Foundation for Children
17 E. 47th St.
New York, NY 10017 (212) 371-7775
FAX: (212) 371-7787
Contact: Virginia Sloane, Pres.

Incorporated in 1921 in NY.
Donor(s): August Heckscher.‡
Financial data (yr. ended 12/31/01): Grants paid, $5,047,581; assets, $123,533,690 (M); expenditures, $5,593,025; qualifying distributions, $5,368,946.
Limitations: Giving primarily in the greater New York, NY, area.
Publications: Application guidelines, informational brochure.
Application information: Application form not required.
Officers and Trustees:* Howard G. Sloane,* Chair.; Virginia Sloane,* Pres.; William D. Hart, Jr.,* Secy.; Phyllis Fannan, Carole S. Landman, Gail Meyers, Fred Obser, Howard Rosenbaum, Marlene Shyer, Arthur J. Smadbeck, Louis Smadbeck, Jr., Mina Smadbeck, Paul Smadbeck.

EIN: 131820170
Codes: FD, FM

32613
Robert Sterling Clark Foundation, Inc.
135 E. 64th St.
New York, NY 10021 (212) 288-8900
FAX: (212) 288-1033; URL: http://www.fdncenter.org/grantmaker/rsclark
Contact: Margaret C. Ayers, Exec. Dir.

Incorporated in 1952 in NY.
Donor(s): Robert Sterling Clark.‡
Financial data (yr. ended 10/31/00): Grants paid, $5,018,114; assets, $141,216,231 (M); expenditures, $7,236,265; qualifying distributions, $5,153,546.
Limitations: Giving primarily in New York State for the Public Institutions Program and in New York City for the Cultural Program; giving nationally for reproductive freedom projects.
Publications: Annual report (including application guidelines), application guidelines.
Application information: Application form not required.
Officers and Directors:* Winthrop R. Munyan,* Pres.; Miner D. Crary, Jr.,* Secy.; John Hoyt Stookey,* Treas.; Margaret C. Ayers, Exec. Dir.; Raymond D. Horton, Virginia Hayes Sibbison, Joanna D. Underwood.
EIN: 131957792
Codes: FD, FM

32614
The Andrea and Charles Bronfman Philanthropies, Inc.
375 Park Ave., 4th Fl.
New York, NY 10152-0192

Established in 1998 in DE and NY.
Financial data (yr. ended 12/31/01): Grants paid, $4,922,410; assets, $4,646,406 (M); gifts received, $12,794,088; expenditures, $11,669,674; qualifying distributions, $11,492,384; giving activities include $4,998,642 for programs.
Limitations: Applications not accepted. Giving in the U.S. and Israel.
Application information: Contributes only to pre-selected organizations.
Officers and Directors:* Charles R. Bronfman,* Chair.; Andrea M. Bronfman,* Dep.-Chair.; Jeffrey Solomon,* Pres.; Ann Dadson, Sr. V.P., Admin.; Janet Aviad, Sr. V.P., Israel Prog.; Nancy Rosenfeld, V.P., Canada; Barry Chazan, V.P., Ed.; Roger Bennett, V.P., Strategic Initiatives; Simon Klarfeld, V.P.; G.F. Craig, Secy.; Andrew Parsons, Treas.
EIN: 133984936
Codes: FD

32615
The Ira W. DeCamp Foundation
1211 Ave. of the Americas, 38th Fl.
New York, NY 10036 (212) 789-5715
E-mail: Philp_lisa@jpmorgan.com
Contact: Lisa Philp, V.P., JPMorgan Private Bank

Trust established in 1975 in NY.
Donor(s): Elizabeth DeCamp McInerny.‡
Financial data (yr. ended 10/31/01): Grants paid, $4,915,000; assets, $84,038,904 (M); expenditures, $5,693,094; qualifying distributions, $5,258,971.
Limitations: Giving primarily in New York City.
Publications: Application guidelines.
Application information: Application form not required.
Trustee: JPMorgan Chase & Co.
EIN: 510138577
Codes: FD, FM

32616
Smile Train, Inc.
245 5th Ave., Ste. 2201
New York, NY 10016-8728 (212) 689-9199
E-mail: info@smiletrain.org; URL: http://www.smiletrain.org
Contact: Dir. of Progs.

Established in 1998 in NY.
Donor(s): Operation Smile, Inc.
Financial data (yr. ended 06/30/01): Grants paid, $4,876,638; assets, $60,470,412 (M); gifts received, $56,645,072; expenditures, $7,431,752; qualifying distributions, $4,876,638.
Limitations: Giving in the U.S. and China; some giving also to India.
Application information: Application form required.
Officers: Baxter Urist, Pres.; Hana Fuchs, V.P., Fin.; DeLois Greenwood, V.P. Stategic Projects; Peter Wilderotter, V.P., Development.
Board Members: Brian Mullaney, Don Murphy, Charles B. Wang, Sherrie Rollins Westin, Ann Ziff.
EIN: 133661416
Codes: FD

32617
Samuel H. Kress Foundation
174 E. 80th St.
New York, NY 10021 (212) 861-4993
URL: http://www.kressfoundation.org
Contact: Lisa M. Ackerman, V.P.

Incorporated in 1929 in NY.
Donor(s): Samuel H. Kress,‡ Claude W. Kress,‡ Rush H. Kress.‡
Financial data (yr. ended 06/30/01): Grants paid, $4,873,012; assets, $103,530,599 (M); expenditures, $7,972,124; qualifying distributions, $5,790,404.
Limitations: Giving primarily in the U.S. and Europe.
Publications: Annual report (including application guidelines).
Application information: Application forms required for fellowships in art history and art conservation. Applications sent by FAX not considered. Application form not required.
Officers and Trustees:* John C. Fontaine,* Chair.; Daniel N. Belin,* Vice-Chair.; Marilyn Perry,* Pres.; Lisa M. Ackerman, V.P.; Frederick W. Beinecke,* Treas.; William B. Bader, Inmaculada de Habsburgo, Cheryl Hurley, Walter L. Weisman.
EIN: 131624176
Codes: FD, FM, GTI

32618
Eleanor Naylor Dana Charitable Trust
375 Park Ave., 38th Fl., Ste. 3807
New York, NY 10152 (212) 754-2890
Contact: The Trustees

Established in 1979 in CT.
Donor(s): Eleanor Naylor Dana.‡
Financial data (yr. ended 05/31/01): Grants paid, $4,830,825; assets, $8,186,119 (M); gifts received, $4,197,096; expenditures, $5,230,323; qualifying distributions, $5,067,999.
Limitations: Giving primarily in areas east of the Mississippi River.
Publications: Informational brochure.
Application information: Application form not required.
Trustees: Robert A. Good, M.D., Carlos D. Moseley, A.J. Signorile, Stephen A. Signorile, Robert E. Wise, M.D.
EIN: 132992855
Codes: FD, FM

32619
The G. Unger Vetlesen Foundation
c/o Fulton, Rowe, Hart & Coon
1 Rockefeller Plz., Ste. 301
New York, NY 10020-2002 (212) 586-0700
E-mail: info@monellvetlesen.org; URL: http://www.monellvetlesen.org
Contact: George Rowe, Jr., Pres.

Incorporated in 1955 in NY.
Donor(s): George Unger Vetlesen.‡
Financial data (yr. ended 12/31/01): Grants paid, $4,730,000; assets, $86,579,908 (M); expenditures, $5,255,421; qualifying distributions, $4,755,610.
Publications: Annual report, application guidelines.
Application information: Application form not required.
Officers and Directors:* George Rowe, Jr.,* Pres. and Treas.; Maurizio J. Morello, Secy.; Gary K. Beauchamp, Eugene P. Grisanti, Ambrose K. Monell.
EIN: 131982695
Codes: FD, FM

32620
Corning Incorporated Foundation
(Formerly Corning Glass Works Foundation)
MP-LB-02
Corning, NY 14831 (607) 974-8746
URL: http://www.corning.com/inside_corning/foundation.asp
Contact: Kristin A. Swain, Pres.

Incorporated in 1952 in NY.
Donor(s): Corning Inc.
Financial data (yr. ended 12/31/01): Grants paid, $4,718,947; assets, $22,686,811 (M); gifts received, $405,058; expenditures, $5,309,749; qualifying distributions, $5,199,289.
Limitations: Giving primarily in communities where Corning Incorporated has significant operations.
Publications: Application guidelines, biennial report, grants list.
Application information: Application form not required.
Officers and Trustees:* E. Marie McKee,* Chair.; Kristin A. Swain, Pres.; Denise A. Hauselt, Secy.; Mark S. Rogus, Treas.; Katherine A. Asbeck, Thomas S. Buechner, William D. Eggers, James B. Flaws, Kirk P. Gregg, James R. Houghton, Joseph A. Miller, Pamela C. Schneider, Peter F. Volanakis, Wendell P. Weeks.
EIN: 166051394
Codes: CS, FD, CD, FM

32621
The Moshe Isaac Foundation
c/o Max Wasser
132 Nassau St., Ste. 300
New York, NY 10038
Contact: Michael Konig, Dir.

Established in 1986 in NY.
Donor(s): Michael Konig, Esther Konig.
Financial data (yr. ended 09/30/00): Grants paid, $4,693,950; assets, $5,720,841 (M); gifts received, $4,217,825; expenditures, $4,769,343; qualifying distributions, $4,693,950.
Limitations: Applications not accepted. Giving primarily in NY.
Application information: Contributes only to pre-selected organizations.
Directors: Esther Konig, Michael Konig.
EIN: 133385009
Codes: FD

32622
Jon & Joanne Corzine Foundation
c/o Goldman Sachs & Co.
85 Broad St., Tax Dept.
New York, NY 10004 (212) 902-6897

Established in 1981 in NJ.
Donor(s): Jon S. Corzine.
Financial data (yr. ended 01/31/00): Grants paid, $4,612,220; assets, $14,192,469 (M); gifts received, $9,542,996; expenditures, $4,617,915; qualifying distributions, $4,506,935.
Limitations: Applications not accepted. Giving primarily in NJ, with emphasis on Summit, and NY.
Application information: Contributes only to pre-selected organizations.
Trustees: Joanne Corzine, Jon S. Corzine.
EIN: 133103160
Codes: FD, FM

32623
May and Samuel Rudin Family Foundation, Inc.
c/o Rudin
345 Park Ave.
New York, NY 10154 (212) 407-2512
Contact: Robin Dubin, Admin. and Prog. Dir.

Established in 1996 in NY.
Financial data (yr. ended 06/30/00): Grants paid, $4,605,451; assets, $55,301 (M); gifts received, $5,000,000; expenditures, $5,034,714; qualifying distributions, $5,034,320.
Limitations: Giving primarily in New York City.
Application information: Application form not required.
Officers and Directors:* Jack Rudin,* Chair.; Beth Rudin DeWoody,* Pres.; Eric C. Rudin,* V.P. and Secy.-Treas.; Madeleine Rudin Johnson,* V.P.; David B. Levy,* V.P.; Katherine L. Rudin,* V.P.; Lewis Rudin,* V.P.; William C. Rudin,* V.P.
EIN: 133875171
Codes: FD, FM

32624
Fred L. Emerson Foundation, Inc.
P.O. Box 276
Auburn, NY 13021 (315) 253-9621
Contact: Ronald D. West, Exec. Dir.

Incorporated in 1943 in DE.
Donor(s): Fred L. Emerson.‡
Financial data (yr. ended 12/31/01): Grants paid, $4,541,975; assets, $80,971,549 (M); expenditures, $4,977,935; qualifying distributions, $4,581,666.
Limitations: Giving primarily in Auburn, Cayuga County, and upstate NY.
Publications: Application guidelines.
Application information: Application form not required.
Officers and Directors:* W. Gary Emerson,* Pres.; Anthony D. Franceschelli,* V.P.; Ronald D. West,* Secy. and Exec. Dir.; J. David Hammond,* Treas.; William F. Allyn, Christopher S. Emerson, David L. Emerson, Heather A. Emerson, Peter J. Emerson, Lori E. Robinson, Kristen E. Rubacka, Sally E. Wagner.
EIN: 156017650
Codes: FD, FM

32625
The Jacob and Valeria Langeloth Foundation
521 5th Ave., Ste. 1612
New York, NY 10175-1699 (212) 687-1133
FAX: (212) 681-2628; E-mail: info@langeloth.org; URL: http://www.langeloth.org
Contact: George Labalme, Jr., Pres.

Incorporated in 1915 in NY as the Valeria Home; renamed in 1975.
Donor(s): Jacob Langeloth.‡
Financial data (yr. ended 11/30/01): Grants paid, $4,428,835; assets, $94,220,414 (M); expenditures, $5,854,257; qualifying distributions, $4,954,947.
Limitations: Giving limited to the state of NY, with emphasis on New York City and the greater metropolitan area; and for proposals that hold promise of national impact or extensive replication.
Publications: Application guidelines.
Application information: Applicants may write or call the foundation for a brochure or visit the Web site. Application form not required.
Officers and Directors:* Adam Hochschild,* Chair. and V.P.; George Labalme, Jr.,* Pres. and Exec. Dir.; Alexandra L. Driscoll, Secy.; Peter K. Loeb,* Treas.; Dominique Boillot, M.D., Harold Epstein, David R. Hochschild, John L. Loeb, Jr., Richard G. Poole, Harvey Weinstein, M.D.
EIN: 131773646
Codes: FD, FM

32626
Jessie Smith Noyes Foundation, Inc.
6 E. 39th St., 12th Fl.
New York, NY 10016-0112 (212) 684-6577
FAX: (212) 689-6549; E-mail: noyes@noyes.org; URL: http://www.noyes.org
Contact: Victor De Luca, Pres.

Incorporated in 1947 in NY.
Donor(s): Charles F. Noyes.‡
Financial data (yr. ended 12/31/01): Grants paid, $4,391,000; assets, $70,225,000 (M); expenditures, $6,108,000; qualifying distributions, $5,586,000.
Limitations: Giving primarily in the southeast, south central, southwest, western, and Rocky Mountain regions of the U.S.
Application information: Applications not accepted for discretionary or founder-designated funds. Accepts NNG Common Application Form. Application form required.
Officers and Directors:* Linda Singer,* Chair.; Steven Carbo,* Vice-Chair.; Victor De Luca, Pres.; Nicholas Jacangelo,* Treas.; Dorothy Anderson, Miriam Ballert, Peter Bedell, Jr., Stephen Falci, Heather Findlay, Jeffrey Golliher, Michael Hamm, Laurel Kearns, Fred Kirschenmann, Dorothy E. Muma, Edith N. Muma, Dorceta Taylor, Ann Wiener.
EIN: 135600408
Codes: FD, FM

32627
Central New York Community Foundation, Inc.
500 S. Salina St., Ste. 428
Syracuse, NY 13202 (315) 422-9538
FAX: (315) 471-6031; URL: http://www.cnycf.org
Contact: Margaret G. Ogden, Pres.

Incorporated in 1927 in NY; reorganized in 1951.
Financial data (yr. ended 03/31/02): Grants paid, $4,379,819; assets, $84,028,489 (M); gifts received, $4,823,912; expenditures, $5,431,735.
Limitations: Giving limited to Onondaga and Madison counties, NY, for general grants; giving in a wider area for donor-advised funds.

Publications: Annual report (including application guidelines), newsletter, informational brochure (including application guidelines).
Application information: Application form required.
Officers and Directors:* Ronald R. Young,* Chair.; Elaine Rubenstein,* Vice-Chair.; Margaret G. Ogden, C.E.O. and Pres.; Dorothy R. Irish, V.P. and Secy.; Lisa Moore, V.P.; Kimberly S. Scott, V.P.; Robert H. Linn,* Treas.; David Barclay, Sanford A. Belden, Sharon A. Brangman, M.D., Gail Cowley, Marion Hancock Fish, John M. Frantz, Jr., Gloria Hooper-Rasberry, Cydney M. Johnson, James E. Mackin, John B. McCabe, M.D., John C. Mott, Eric Mower, Michael E. O'Connor, Marilyn L. Pinsky, William L. Pollard, Ph.D., Dirk E. Sonneborn, Harold H. Wanamaker, M.D.
EIN: 150626910
Codes: CM, FD

32628
Leo and Julia Forchheimer Foundation
(Formerly The Forchheimer Foundation)
c/o Golenbock, Eiseman, Assor & Bell
437 Madison Ave., 35th Fl.
New York, NY 10022

Established about 1957 in NY.
Donor(s): Leo Forchheimer.‡
Financial data (yr. ended 12/31/00): Grants paid, $4,268,559; assets, $18,098,505 (M); expenditures, $4,474,344; qualifying distributions, $4,256,697.
Limitations: Applications not accepted. Giving primarily in New York, NY; giving also in Israel.
Application information: Contributes only to pre-selected charitable organizations.
Officers and Directors:* Rudolph Forchheimer,* Pres.; Barbara Kamen,* V.P.; Michael Jesselson,* Secy.-Treas.
EIN: 136075112
Codes: FD, FM

32629
The Greenwall Foundation
2 Park Ave., 24th Fl.
New York, NY 10016-5603 (212) 679-7266
FAX: (212) 679-7269; E-mail: admin@greenwall.org; URL: http://www.greenwall.org
Contact: Fredrica Jarcho, V.P., Progs.

Incorporated in 1949 in NY.
Donor(s): Anna A. Greenwall,‡ Frank K. Greenwall.‡
Financial data (yr. ended 12/31/01): Grants paid, $4,265,545; assets, $85,138,754 (M); expenditures, $5,484,619; qualifying distributions, $4,983,745.
Limitations: Giving primarily in New York, NY, for arts and humanities; giving nationally for bioethics.
Application information: 4 copies required for bioethics, 1 for arts and humanities. Application form not required.
Officers and Directors:* Christine K. Cassel, M.D.,* Chair.; Oscar M. Ruebhausen, Chair., Emeritus; Harvey J. Goldschmid,* Vice-Chair.; William C. Stubing,* Pres.; Fredrica Jarcho, V.P., Progs.; Carl B. Menges,* Treas.; Rosmarie E. Homberger, Corp. Secy.; Troyen A. Brennan, M.D., J.D., MPH, John E. Craig, Jr., Matina S. Horner, Ph.D., Gayle Pemberton, Ph.D., Joseph G. Perpich, M.D., J.D., Edgar A. Robinson, Roger Rosenblatt, Richard L. Salzer, Jr., M.D., Stephen Stamas, James A. Tulsky, M.D.
EIN: 136082277
Codes: FD, FM

32630
Unilever United States Foundation
390 Park Ave.
New York, NY 10022
Contact: John T. Gould, Jr., Dir., Corp. Affairs

Incorporated in 1952 in NY.
Donor(s): Unilever United States, Inc., Lever Bros. Co., Van den Bergh Foods Co., Unilever Research.
Financial data (yr. ended 12/31/99): Grants paid, $4,263,565; assets, $61,289 (L); gifts received, $3,717,525; expenditures, $4,334,560; qualifying distributions, $4,229,815.
Limitations: Giving primarily in areas of company operations in CA, GA, IN, MD, MO, NJ, and NY.
Application information: Application form not required.
Officers and Directors:* Paul W. Wood,* Pres.; John T. Gould, Jr., V.P.; John Lamantia, T.K. Rowland.
EIN: 136122117
Codes: CS, FD, CD

32631
The Elmer and Mamdouha Bobst Foundation, Inc.
c/o The Elmer Holmes Bobst Library, New York Univ.
70 Washington Sq. S.
New York, NY 10012
Contact: Mamdouha S. Bobst, Pres.

Incorporated in 1968 in NY.
Donor(s): Elmer H. Bobst.‡
Financial data (yr. ended 12/31/00): Grants paid, $4,209,530; assets, $59,982,765 (M); expenditures, $4,370,305; qualifying distributions, $4,204,557.
Limitations: Applications not accepted.
Publications: Annual report, informational brochure.
Application information: Contributes only to pre-selected organizations. Unsolicited applications not considered.
Officer and Directors:* Mamdouha S. Bobst,* Pres. and Treas.; Raja Kabbani, Mazen Kamen, Laurance Rockefeller, Milton Rose, Farouk as-Sayed, Robert J. Task.
EIN: 132616114
Codes: FD, FM

32632
John & Cynthia Reed Foundation
c/o U.S. Trust
114 W. 47th St., 8th Fl.
New York, NY 10036
Contact: Andrew Lane, V.P.

Established in 2000 in NY.
Donor(s): John S. Reed.
Financial data (yr. ended 12/31/02): Grants paid, $4,155,730; assets, $72,824,800 (M); expenditures, $4,291,610; qualifying distributions, $4,155,730.
Limitations: Applications not accepted. Giving on a national basis, with some emphasis on Princeton, NJ, and the greater metropolitan New York, NY, area.
Application information: Unsolicited requests for funds not accepted.
Trustees: Cynthia Reed, John S. Reed.
EIN: 137219392
Codes: FD

32633
J. Aron Charitable Foundation, Inc.
126 E. 56th St., Ste. 2300
New York, NY 10022 (212) 832-3405
Contact: Peter A. Aron, Exec. Dir.

Incorporated in 1934 in NY.
Donor(s): members of the Aron family.
Financial data (yr. ended 12/31/01): Grants paid, $4,151,678; assets, $39,357,855 (M); expenditures, $4,662,454; qualifying distributions, $4,288,088.
Limitations: Applications not accepted. Giving primarily in New Orleans, LA, and New York, NY.
Officers and Directors:* Peter A. Aron,* Pres. and Exec. Dir.; Robert Aron,* V.P.; Hans G. Jepson,* Secy.-Treas.; Jacqueline Aron, Ronald J. Stein, Martha Ward.
EIN: 136068230
Codes: FD, FM

32634
Morgan Stanley Foundation
(Formerly Morgan Stanley Dean Witter Foundation)
1601 Bdwy., 12th fl.
New York, NY 10012 (212) 259-1235
Toll free TL: 800 832-4985; FAX: (212) 259-1253; E-mail: whatadifference@msdw.com
Contact: Joan Steinberg, V.P., Community Affairs

Trust established in 1961 in NY.
Donor(s): Morgan Stanley Group Inc., Morgan Stanley Dean Witter & Co.
Financial data (yr. ended 12/31/99): Grants paid, $4,137,304; assets, $32,329,164 (M); gifts received, $5,545,313; expenditures, $4,137,317; qualifying distributions, $4,137,304.
Limitations: Giving primarily in communities with a significant employee presence including the metropolitan areas of Phoenix, AZ; Los Angeles and San Francisco, CA; Wilmington, DE; Chicago, IL; New York, NY; Dayton, OH; Philadelphia, PA; Houston, TX; and Salt Lake City, UT.
Publications: Informational brochure (including application guidelines), application guidelines.
Application information: In some cases organizations will be asked to fill out an additional application. A site visit is usually scheduled if the organization appears to fall within foundation guidelines. Application form not required.
Trustees: Brian Leach, Chair.; Eduardo Diaz-Perez, Frank English, Carla Harris, William M. Lewis, Jr., Elizabeth Lynch, Bill McMahon, Kelly McNamara-Corley, Jose Rivera, Kathy Roberts, Colette Saucedo, Rich Woolworth.
EIN: 136155650
Codes: CS, FD, CD

32635
The Edmond de Rothschild Foundation
1585 Broadway, 24th Fl.
New York, NY 10036
Contact: Paul H. Epstein, Pres.

Incorporated in 1963 in NY.
Donor(s): Edmond de Rothschild.‡
Financial data (yr. ended 02/28/01): Grants paid, $4,113,797; assets, $71,359,526 (M); expenditures, $4,469,254; qualifying distributions, $4,206,434.
Limitations: Applications not accepted. Giving primarily in New York, NY.
Application information: Contributes only to pre-selected organizations.
Officers and Directors:* Benjamin de Rothschild,* Chair.; Paul H. Epstein,* Pres.; Gabriel Brack, V.P.; Georges C. Karlweis,* V.P.; Stanley Komaroff,* Secy.; Nadine de Rothschild.
EIN: 136119422
Codes: FD, FM

32636
The Riggio Foundation
c/o Robinson, Silverman, Pearce, et al
1290 Ave. of the Americas
New York, NY 10104
Contact: J. Levin

Established in 1994 in NY.
Donor(s): Leonard Riggio.
Financial data (yr. ended 08/31/00): Grants paid, $4,089,232; assets, $27,643,316 (M); expenditures, $4,101,982; qualifying distributions, $4,089,232.
Limitations: Applications not accepted. Giving primarily in NY.
Application information: Contributes only to pre-selected organizations.
Trustees: Leonard Riggio, Louise Riggio.
EIN: 137039631
Codes: FD

32637
Peierls Foundation
c/o U.S. Trust
114 W. 47th St.
New York, NY 10036
Application address: 73 S. Holman Way, Golden, CO 80401
Contact: E. Jeffrey Peierls, Pres.

Incorporated in 1956 in NY.
Donor(s): Brian E. Peierls, Edgar S. Peierls,‡ Ethel F. Peierls, E. Jeffrey Peierls, and sons.
Financial data (yr. ended 10/31/01): Grants paid, $4,083,044; assets, $72,107,995 (M); gifts received, $1,618,084; expenditures, $4,267,302; qualifying distributions, $4,028,470.
Limitations: Giving on a national basis.
Application information: Application form not required.
Officers: E. Jeffrey Peierls, Pres.; Brian Eliot Peierls, V.P.; Malcolm A. Moore, Secy.
EIN: 136082503
Codes: FD

32638
The Diebold Foundation, Inc.
c/o Bessemer Trust Co., N.A., Tax Dept.
630 5th Ave.
New York, NY 10111
Application address: c/o Diebold Foundation, Inc., P.O. Box 550, Southbury, CT 06488
Contact: Olive Simpson

Established in 1963.
Donor(s): A. Richard Diebold,‡ Dorothy Diebold.
Financial data (yr. ended 10/31/00): Grants paid, $4,080,000; assets, $112,347,438 (M); expenditures, $5,155,722; qualifying distributions, $4,301,497.
Limitations: Giving primarily in CT.
Officers and Directors:* Dorothy R. Diebold,* Pres.; A. Richard Diebold, Jr., V.P.; Dudley G. Diebold, V.P.; Diane Terni, V.P.; Andrew W. Bisset,* Secy.-Treas.
EIN: 136146478
Codes: FD

32639
William S. Paley Foundation, Inc.
1 E. 53rd St., Rm. 1400
New York, NY 10022 (212) 888-2520
FAX: (212) 308-7845; E-mail: wspf@asan.com
Contact: Patrick S. Gallagher, Exec. Dir.

Incorporated in 1936 in NY.
Donor(s): William S. Paley.‡
Financial data (yr. ended 12/31/01): Grants paid, $4,071,000; assets, $118,512,400 (M); expenditures, $5,800,993; qualifying distributions, $4,181,691.

Application information: Application form not required.
Officers and Directors:* Henry A. Kissinger,* Chair.; Sidney W. Harl,* V.P.; William C. Paley,* V.P.; Daniel L. Mosley,* Secy.-Treas.; Patrick S. Gallagher,* Exec. Dir.; George J. Gillespie III.
EIN: 136085929
Codes: FD, FM

32640
Homeland Foundation, Inc.
c/o Amco
505 Park Ave., 20th Fl.
New York, NY 10022-1106
Application address: c/o Wethersfield, 214 Pugsley Hill Rd., Amenia, NY 12501
Contact: E. Lisk Wyckoff, Jr., Treas.

Incorporated in 1938 in NY.
Donor(s): Chauncey Stillman.‡
Financial data (yr. ended 04/30/01): Grants paid, $4,055,854; assets, $85,616,134 (M); gifts received, $738; expenditures, $7,247,761; qualifying distributions, $6,153,292; giving activities include $1,490,318 for programs.
Limitations: Giving on a national and international basis.
Application information: Application form not required.
Officers and Board Members:* E. Lisk Wyckoff, Jr.,* Pres. and Treas.; Msgr. Eugene V. Clark,* V.P. and Secy.; Robert B. MacKay,* V.P.; Rev. Rafael F. Caamano, Lucy Fleming-McGrath, Carl Schmitt, Charles Scribner III.
EIN: 136113816
Codes: FD, FM

32641
Helen & Martin Kimmel Foundation
445 Park Ave., Ste. 2100
New York, NY 10022

Established in 1989 in NY; funded in 1990.
Donor(s): Helen Kimmel, Martin Kimmel, Helen Kimmel Foundation.
Financial data (yr. ended 12/31/01): Grants paid, $4,039,136; assets, $1,200,378 (M); gifts received, $3,097,500; expenditures, $4,046,106; qualifying distributions, $4,042,156.
Limitations: Applications not accepted. Giving primarily in the greater metropolitan areas of New York, NY, and Washington, DC.
Application information: Contributes only to pre-selected organizations.
Trustees: Helen Kimmel, Martin Kimmel.
EIN: 136940423
Codes: FD, FM

32642
The Max and Victoria Dreyfus Foundation, Inc.
50 Main St., Ste. 1000
White Plains, NY 10606 (914) 682-2008
Contact: Ms. Lucy Gioia, Office Admin.

Incorporated in 1965 in NY.
Donor(s): Victoria Dreyfus,‡ Max Dreyfus.‡
Financial data (yr. ended 12/31/01): Grants paid, $4,022,150; assets, $73,609,046 (M); expenditures, $5,080,295; qualifying distributions, $4,320,328.
Limitations: Giving on a national basis.
Publications: Application guidelines.
Application information: Application form not required.
Officers and Directors:* David J. Oppenheim,* Chair.; Winifred Riggs Portenoy,* Pres.; Nancy E. Oddo,* V.P.; Norman S. Portenoy,* V.P.; Sara R. Surrey,* V.P.; Mary P. Surrey,* Secy.-Treas.
EIN: 131687573
Codes: FD, FM

32643
YLRY, Inc.
c/o Hertz, Herson & Co., LLP
2 Park Ave., Ste. 1500
New York, NY 10016

Established in 1992 in NY.
Financial data (yr. ended 12/31/00): Grants paid, $4,000,036; assets, $40,051,030 (M); expenditures, $4,223,291; qualifying distributions, $4,015,553.
Limitations: Applications not accepted. Giving primarily in NY.
Application information: Contributes only to pre-selected organizations.
Officer and Directors:* Susan R. Wexner,* Secy.-Treas.; Bertrand Agus.
EIN: 133722745
Codes: FD

32644
Irene & Mac Schwebel Foundation, Inc.
2 Leith Pl.
White Plains, NY 10605-3316

Established in 1959.
Donor(s): M. Mac Schwebel.
Financial data (yr. ended 12/31/01): Grants paid, $3,960,000; assets, $6,535,579 (M); gifts received, $4,122,060; expenditures, $3,965,491; qualifying distributions, $3,956,330.
Limitations: Applications not accepted. Giving primarily in Palm Beach, FL, and NY.
Application information: Contributes only to pre-selected organizations.
Officer: M. Mac Schwebel, Pres.
EIN: 136161504
Codes: FD

32645
Louis and Anne Abrons Foundation, Inc.
c/o First Manhattan Co.
437 Madison Ave.
New York, NY 10017 (212) 756-3376
Contact: Richard Abrons, Pres.

Incorporated in 1950 in NY.
Donor(s): Anne S. Abrons,‡ Louis Abrons.‡
Financial data (yr. ended 12/31/01): Grants paid, $3,909,410; assets, $37,742,486 (M); expenditures, $3,927,178; qualifying distributions, $3,905,318.
Limitations: Applications not accepted. Giving primarily in the metropolitan New York, NY, area.
Application information: Contributes only to pre-selected organizations. Telephone calls not accepted. Unsolicited applications not considered or acknowledged.
Officers and Directors:* Richard Abrons,* Pres.; Herbert L. Abrons,* V.P.; Rita Aranow,* V.P.; Anne Abrons,* Secy.-Treas.; Alix Abrons, Henry Abrons, John Abrons, Leslie Abrons, Peter Abrons, Judith Aranow, Stephanie DeChristina, Vicki Feiner, Jennifer Schwartz.
EIN: 136061329
Codes: FD, FM

32646
Peter & Cynthia K. Kellogg Foundation
c/o Spear, Leeds, & Kellogg
120 Broadway
New York, NY 10271-0093

Established in 1983 in NJ.
Donor(s): Charles K. Kellogg, Lee I. Kellogg, Peter R. Kellogg, IAT Syndicate, Inc.
Financial data (yr. ended 06/30/00): Grants paid, $3,856,850; assets, $97,549,294 (M); gifts received, $1,389,299; expenditures, $4,398,863; qualifying distributions, $3,857,081.

Limitations: Applications not accepted. Giving primarily in NJ.
Application information: Contributes only to pre-selected organizations.
Officers: Peter R. Kellogg, Pres.; Cynthia R. Kellogg, Secy.; Marguerite Gorman, Treas.
EIN: 222472914
Codes: FD

32647
The Trust for Mutual Understanding
30 Rockefeller Plz., Rm. 5600
New York, NY 10112 (212) 632-3405
FAX: (212) 632-3409; E-mail: tmu@tmuny.org; URL: http://www.tmuny.org
Contact: Richard S. Lanier, Dir.

Established in 1984 in NY.
Financial data (yr. ended 12/31/01): Grants paid, $3,837,807; assets, $64,089,842 (M); expenditures, $5,030,588; qualifying distributions, $4,539,283.
Limitations: Giving for exchanges between the U.S. and the countries of Central and Eastern Europe, primarily the Czech Republic, Hungary, Poland, Russia, and Slovakia. Support is also provided, to a lesser extent, for exchanges involving Albania, Belarus, Bosnia and Herzegovina, Bulgaria, Croatia, Georgia, Macedonia, Moldova, Mongolia, Romania, Serbia and Montenegro, Slovenia, and Ukraine.
Publications: Annual report (including application guidelines), grants list.
Application information: Grants are made only to tax-exempt organizations in the United States for exchange projects involving Eastern and Central Europe. Application form required.
Director and Trustees:* Richard S. Lanier,* Dir.; Elizabeth J. McCormack, Donal C. O'Brien, Jr.
Board of Advisors: Ruth Adams, Wade Greene, Julie Kidd, William H. Luers, Joseph Polisi, Blair Ruble, Isaac Shapiro.
EIN: 133212724
Codes: FD, FM

32648
Alan B. Slifka Foundation, Inc.
477 Madison Ave., 8th Fl.
New York, NY 10022 (212) 303-9409
Contact: Admin.

Established in 1963 in NY.
Donor(s): Alan B. Slifka, Abraham Slifka.‡
Financial data (yr. ended 11/30/00): Grants paid, $3,833,932; assets, $5,011,388 (M); gifts received, $5,300,000; expenditures, $3,868,578; qualifying distributions, $3,860,417.
Limitations: Applications not accepted. Giving primarily in NY.
Application information: Unsolicited requests not considered.
Officers: Alan B. Slifka, Pres.; Barbara Merson, Secy.; Andrea Cespedes, Admin.
EIN: 136192257
Codes: FD, FM

32649
Daniel and Joanna S. Rose Fund, Inc.
c/o Rose Assocs.
200 Madison Ave., 5th Fl.
New York, NY 10016

Established in 1988 in DE.
Donor(s): Daniel Rose, Samuel and David Rose Charitable Foundation.
Financial data (yr. ended 12/31/00): Grants paid, $3,817,723; assets, $8,913,514 (M); expenditures, $4,243,139; qualifying distributions, $3,822,218.
Limitations: Applications not accepted. Giving primarily in NY.

Application information: Contributes only to pre-selected organizations.
Officer and Director:* Daniel Rose,* Pres. and Secy.
EIN: 133484179
Codes: FD, FM

32650
Henry R. Kravis Foundation, Inc.
c/o KKR & Co.
9 W. 57th St.
New York, NY 10019 (212) 750-8300

Established in 1985 in NY.
Donor(s): Henry R. Kravis.
Financial data (yr. ended 11/30/00): Grants paid, $3,784,433; assets, $51,106,114 (M); gifts received, $6,285,001; expenditures, $3,870,519; qualifying distributions, $3,726,550.
Limitations: Applications not accepted.
Application information: Contributes only to pre-selected organizations.
Officers: Henry R. Kravis, Chair.; Leslie Harrison, Secy.; James M. Goldrick, Treas.
Director: Richard I. Beattie.
EIN: 133341521
Codes: FD

32651
Gebbie Foundation, Inc.
Hotel Jamestown Bldg., Rm. 308
110 W. 3rd St.
Jamestown, NY 14701 (716) 487-1062
FAX: (716) 484-6401
Contact: Dr. Thomas M. Cardman, Exec. Dir.

Incorporated in 1963 in NY.
Donor(s): Marion B. Gebbie,‡ Geraldine G. Bellinger.‡
Financial data (yr. ended 09/30/01): Grants paid, $3,756,141; assets, $70,252,260 (M); expenditures, $4,598,225; qualifying distributions, $4,076,411.
Limitations: Giving primarily in Chautauqua County in western NY, especially the Jamestown, NY, area.
Publications: Application guidelines.
Application information: Applicants will be contacted for further information after review of letter of inquiry. A signed grant agreement is required before approval of the grant. Application form not required.
Officers and Directors:* Charles T. Hall,* Pres.; George A. Campbell,* V.P.; Linda Swanson,* Secy.; Rhoe B. Henderson III,* Treas.; Thomas M. Cardman, Ph.D., Exec. Dir.; Martin Coyle, Daniel Kathman, Lillian V. Ney, Bertram Parker, Rebecca Robbins.
EIN: 166050287
Codes: FD, FM

32652
The Prospect Hill Foundation, Inc.
99 Park Ave., Ste. 2220
New York, NY 10016-1601 (212) 370-1165
FAX: (212) 599-6282; URL: http://fdncenter.org/grantmaker/prospecthill
Contact: Constance Eiseman, Exec. Dir.

Incorporated in 1960 in NY; absorbed The Frederick W. Beinecke Fund in 1983.
Donor(s): William S. Beinecke.
Financial data (yr. ended 06/30/02): Grants paid, $3,753,137; assets, $62,189,000 (M); expenditures, $5,115,000; qualifying distributions, $3,753,137.
Limitations: Giving primarily in the northeastern U.S., including NY and RI.
Publications: Grants list, informational brochure (including application guidelines).

Application information: Accepts NYRAG Common Application Form. Application form not required.
Officers and Directors:* William S. Beinecke,* Pres.; Elizabeth G. Beinecke,* V.P.; Frederick W. Beinecke,* V.P.; John B. Beinecke,* V.P.; Constance Eiseman, Secy. and Exec. Dir.; Robert J. Barletta, Treas.; Frances Beinecke Elston, Sarah Beinecke Richardson.
EIN: 136075567
Codes: FD

32653
The Gruss Lipper Foundation
(Formerly The Kenneth & Evelyn Lipper Foundation)
c\o Grusso & Co.
667 Madison Ave.
New York, NY 10021-8029
Contact: Evelyn Gruss Lipper, Tr., or Erika L. Aronson

Established about 1982 in NY.
Donor(s): Gruss Petroleum Corp., Evmar Oil Corp.
Financial data (yr. ended 08/31/01): Grants paid, $3,749,933; assets, $62,475,767 (M); gifts received, $9,368,707; expenditures, $12,306,148; qualifying distributions, $3,770,518.
Limitations: Applications not accepted. Giving primarily in New York, NY.
Application information: Unsolicited requests for funds not accepted.
Trustees: Evelyn Gruss Lipper, Joanna Lipper.
EIN: 133188873
Codes: FD

32654
The Community Foundation for the Capital Region, Inc.
Executive Park Dr.
Albany, NY 12203 (518) 446-9638
FAX: (518) 446-9708; E-mail: info@cfcr.org; URL: http://www.cfcr.org
Contact: Judith Lyons, Exec. Dir.

Incorporated in 1968 in NY.
Financial data (yr. ended 12/31/00): Grants paid, $3,739,333; assets, $22,106,334 (M); gifts received, $3,436,443; expenditures, $4,302,062.
Limitations: Giving primarily in the Capital Area region, including Albany, Rensselaer, Schenectady and Saratoga, NY.
Publications: Annual report, application guidelines, newsletter, informational brochure, financial statement.
Application information: Application form required.
Officers and Directors:* Charles M. Liddle,* Pres.; Barbara K. Hoehn,* 1st V.P.; Phoebe P. Bender,* 2nd V.P.; Robert Johnson II, Secy.; William G. Caster, Treas.; Judith Lyons, Exec. Dir.; and 17 additional directors.
EIN: 141505623
Codes: CM, FD, GTI

32655
Sidney J. Weinberg, Jr. Foundation
c/o BCRS Associates, LLC
67 Wall St., 8th Fl.
New York, NY 10005

Established in 1979 in NY.
Donor(s): Sidney J. Weinberg, Jr.
Financial data (yr. ended 05/31/00): Grants paid, $3,736,550; assets, $51,175,110 (M); gifts received, $2,549,543; expenditures, $4,154,097; qualifying distributions, $3,611,932.
Limitations: Applications not accepted. Giving primarily in the eastern U.S., with emphasis on New York, NY.

32655—NEW YORK

Application information: Contributes only to pre-selected organizations.
Trustees: Elizabeth W. Smith, Peter A. Weinberg, Sidney J. Weinberg, Jr., Sydney H. Weinberg.
EIN: 132998603
Codes: FD

32656
Lawrence J. & Florence A. DeGeorge Charitable Trust
c/o Deutsche Bank Trust Co. of NY
P.O. Box 1297, Church St. Sta.
New York, NY 10008 (212) 454-3931

Established in 1994 in FL.
Donor(s): Lawrence DeGeorge, Florence DeGeorge.
Financial data (yr. ended 01/31/01): Grants paid, $3,666,510; assets, $62,185,897 (M); expenditures, $3,948,126; qualifying distributions, $3,651,803.
Limitations: Applications not accepted. Giving primarily in FL.
Application information: Contributes only to pre-selected organizations.
Trustees: Florence DeGeorge, Lawrence DeGeorge, Deutsche Bank.
EIN: 137053836
Codes: FD

32657
Irving Goldman Foundation, Inc.
52 Vanderbilt Ave., 16th Fl.
New York, NY 10017 (212) 557-6700
Contact: Robyn Calisti, Exec. Dir.

Established in 1984 in NY.
Financial data (yr. ended 12/31/00): Grants paid, $3,610,307; assets, $196,290,302 (M); gifts received, $9,989,944; expenditures, $3,906,249; qualifying distributions, $3,656,946.
Limitations: Giving primarily in New York, NY.
Application information: Application form not required.
Officers: Dorian Goldman, Pres.; Robyn Calisti, Exec. Dir.
EIN: 133216152
Codes: FD

32658
Foundation for Child Development
145 E. 32nd St., 14th Fl.
New York, NY 10016-6055 (212) 213-8337
FAX: (212) 213-5897; E-mail: claudia@ffcd.org
URL: http://www.ffcd.org
Contact: Claudia Conner, Grants Assoc.

Incorporated as a voluntary agency in 1900 in NY and established as the Association for the Aid of Crippled Children in 1908; current name adopted in 1972, affirming a broader focus on children at risk.
Donor(s): Milo M. Belding,‡ Annie K. Belding,‡ and others.
Financial data (yr. ended 03/31/01): Grants paid, $3,602,172; assets, $101,462,405 (M); gifts received, $3,000; expenditures, $5,484,638; qualifying distributions, $4,857,239; giving activities include $677,223 for programs.
Limitations: Giving limited to research and policy grants related to foundation focus and restricted to the U.S.; program development grants in New York City only.
Publications: Annual report (including application guidelines), grants list, informational brochure (including application guidelines).
Application information: Accepts NYRAG Common Application Form. Application form not required.

Officers and Directors:* P. Lindsay Chase-Lansdale, Ph.D.,* Chair.; Ruby Takanishi, Ph.D.,* Pres.; Michael I. Cohen, M.D.,* Secy.; John L. Furth,* Treas.; Ruth Ann Burns, Nancy Folbre, Ph.D., Karen N. Gerard, Ellen Berland Gibbs, Arthur Greenberg, Ed.D., Donald J. Hernandez, Ph.D., E. Mavis Hetherington, Ph.D., Karen Hill-Scott, Ed.D., David Lawrence, Jr., Julius B. Richmond, M.D., Henry W. Riecken, Margaret Beale Spencer, Ph.D., Cathy Trost.
EIN: 131623901
Codes: FD

32659
Essel Foundation, Inc.
2500 Westchester Ave., 4th Fl.
Purchase, NY 10577 (914) 698-7133
Contact: Constance Lieber, Pres.

Established in 1966.
Donor(s): Stephen Lieber, Constance Lieber.
Financial data (yr. ended 11/30/01): Grants paid, $3,593,500; assets, $87,712,111 (M); gifts received, $486,000; expenditures, $4,174,457; qualifying distributions, $3,593,500.
Limitations: Applications not accepted. Giving on a national basis.
Application information: Contributes only to pre-selected organizations.
Officers: Constance Lieber, Pres.; Samuel Lieber, Secy.-Treas.
Trustee: Janice Lieber.
EIN: 136191234
Codes: FD, FM

32660
Henry & Elaine Kaufman Foundation, Inc.
660 Madison Ave., 15th Fl.
New York, NY 10021
Contact: Dr. Henry Kaufman, Pres., or Elaine Kaufman, V.P.

Established in 1969.
Donor(s): Elaine Kaufman, Henry Kaufman, Henry Kaufman Charitable Lead Trust.
Financial data (yr. ended 12/31/01): Grants paid, $3,589,798; assets, $37,509,341 (M); expenditures, $4,062,644; qualifying distributions, $3,574,707.
Limitations: Giving primarily in the metropolitan New York, NY, area, including portions of NJ.
Officers and Directors:* Henry Kaufman,* Pres. and Treas.; Elaine Kaufman,* V.P.; Daniel Kaufman,* Secy.; Craig S. Kaufman, Glenn D. Kaufman.
EIN: 237045903
Codes: FD

32661
Reader's Digest Foundation
Reader's Digest Rd.
Pleasantville, NY 10570-7000 (914) 244-5370
FAX: (914) 238-7642; URL: http://www.readersdigest.com/corporate/rd_foundation.html
Contact: Claudia L. Edwards, Exec. Dir.

Incorporated in 1938 in NY.
Donor(s): The Reader's Digest Association, Inc.
Financial data (yr. ended 06/30/00): Grants paid, $3,542,170; assets, $26,357,527 (L); expenditures, $4,163,656; qualifying distributions, $4,031,595.
Limitations: Giving primarily in Westchester County, NY.
Publications: Annual report (including application guidelines).
Application information: If request falls within the foundation's grant guidelines, a proposal will be required. Application form not required.

Officers and Directors:* Thomas O. Ryder,* Chair.; Mary L. Terry, Secy.; William H. Magill, Treas.; Claudia L. Edwards, Exec. Dir.; M. John Bohane, Elizabeth G. Chambers, Thomas D. Gardner, Gary S. Rich, George S. Scimone, Christopher P. Willcox.
EIN: 136120380
Codes: CS, FD, CD, FM, GTI

32662
The Margaret L. Wendt Foundation
40 Fountain Plz., Ste. 277
Buffalo, NY 14202-2220 (716) 855-2146
Contact: Robert J. Kresse, Secy.-Treas.

Trust established in 1956 in NY.
Donor(s): Margaret L. Wendt.‡
Financial data (yr. ended 01/31/00): Grants paid, $3,538,865; assets, $104,080,210 (M); expenditures, $5,176,331; qualifying distributions, $3,867,593; giving activities include $85,714 for program-related investments.
Limitations: Giving primarily in Buffalo and western NY.
Publications: Application guidelines.
Application information: Application form not required.
Officer and Trustees:* Robert J. Kresse,* Secy.-Treas.; Janet L. Day, Thomas D. Lunt.
EIN: 166030037
Codes: FD

32663
The Tikvah Fund
1345 Ave. of the Americas
New York, NY 10036 (212) 756-4385
Contact: Roger Hertog, Chair.

Established in 1992 in NY.
Donor(s): Zalman C. Bernstein.
Financial data (yr. ended 12/31/00): Grants paid, $3,524,433; assets, $98,843,230 (M); gifts received, $60,573,000; expenditures, $3,638,777; qualifying distributions, $3,533,184.
Limitations: Giving primarily in Israel.
Officers and Directors:* Roger Hertog,* Chair.; Christine A. Holly, Secy.; Arthur W. Fried,* C.F.O.; Kenneth A. Abramowitz, Mem Bernstein, Morris Smith, David Stone.
EIN: 133676152
Codes: FD, FM

32664
Rhodebeck Charitable Trust
c/o McLaughind Stern LLP
260 Madison Ave.
New York, NY 10016
Contact: Huyler C. Held, Tr.

Established in 1987 in AZ.
Donor(s): Mildred T. Rhodebeck.‡
Financial data (yr. ended 04/30/01): Grants paid, $3,506,670; assets, $46,684,924 (M); expenditures, $3,650,920; qualifying distributions, $3,532,562.
Limitations: Giving limited to the metropolitan New York, NY, area.
Application information: Unsolicited applications are discouraged.
Trustee: Huyler C. Held.
EIN: 133413293
Codes: FD, FM

32665
The Bodman Foundation
767 3rd Ave., 4th Fl.
New York, NY 10017-2023 (212) 644-0322
FAX: (212) 759-6510; E-mail:
main@achelis-bodman-fnds.org.; URL: http://
www.fdncenter.org/grantmaker/achelis-bodman
Contact: Joseph S. Dolan, Secy. and Exec. Dir.

Incorporated in 1945 in NJ.
Donor(s): George M. Bodman,‡ Louise C. Bodman.‡
Financial data (yr. ended 12/31/01): Grants paid, $3,505,000; assets, $65,761,931 (M); expenditures, $3,885,289; qualifying distributions, $3,505,000.
Limitations: Giving primarily in northern NJ and New York, NY.
Publications: Biennial report (including application guidelines), financial statement, grants list.
Application information: Unless requested, do not send CDs, DVDs, discs, tapes, or proposals through the internet. Application form not required.
Officers and Trustees:* John N. Irwin III,* Chair., C.E.O. and Treas.; Guy G. Rutherfurd,* Hon. Chair.; Russell P. Pennoyer,* Pres.; Peter Frelinghuysen,* V.P.; Mary S. Phipps,* V.P.; Joseph S. Dolan, Secy. and Exec. Dir.; Horace I. Crary, Hon. Walter J.P. Curley, Anthony Drexel Duke, Sarah Henry Lederman.
EIN: 136022016
Codes: FD, FM

32666
New York Fine Arts Support Trust
c/o Rockefeller Trust Co.
30 Rockefeller Plz.
New York, NY 10112
Contact: Brian J. Keeney

Established in 1995 in NY.
Donor(s): Agnes Gund, David Rockefeller.
Financial data (yr. ended 12/31/99): Grants paid, $3,503,347; assets, $1,133,001 (M); gifts received, $800,000; expenditures, $3,575,317; qualifying distributions, $3,503,663.
Limitations: Giving limited to the New York City metropolitan area.
Trustee: Rockefeller Trust Co.
EIN: 137082559
Codes: FD

32667
Raether 1985 Charitable Trust
c/o Kohlberg, Kravis, Roberts & Co.
9 W. 57th St.
New York, NY 10019

Established in 1985 in NY.
Donor(s): Paul E. Raether, Wendy S. Raether.
Financial data (yr. ended 11/30/01): Grants paid, $3,497,224; assets, $18,173,690 (M); gifts received, $4,902,593; expenditures, $3,563,915; qualifying distributions, $3,430,060.
Limitations: Applications not accepted. Giving primarily in CT and NY.
Application information: Contributes only to pre-selected organizations.
Trustees: Paul E. Raether, Wendy S. Raether.
EIN: 136855420
Codes: FD

32668
The Joseph & Trina Cayre Foundation, Inc.
(Formerly Jack & Grace Cayre Foundation)
16 E. 40th St.
New York, NY 10016 (212) 951-3057
Contact: Joseph Cayre, Pres.

Established in 1988 in DE.
Donor(s): Joseph Cayre, Kenneth Cayre, Stanley Cayre.
Financial data (yr. ended 12/31/00): Grants paid, $3,481,393; assets, $6,280,634 (M); expenditures, $3,062,107; qualifying distributions, $2,978,773.
Limitations: Giving primarily in NY, with strong emphasis on Brooklyn.
Officers: Joseph Cayre, Pres.; Trina Cayre, V.P.
EIN: 133494146
Codes: FD

32669
The Seth Sprague Educational and Charitable Foundation
c/o U.S. Trust
114 W. 47th St.
New York, NY 10036-1532
FAX: (212) 852-3377
Contact: Carolyn L. Larke, Asst. V.P., U.S. Trust, or Linda R. Franciscovich, V.P., U.S. Trust

Trust established in 1939 in NY.
Donor(s): Seth Sprague.‡
Financial data (yr. ended 12/31/00): Grants paid, $3,442,723; assets, $72,790,263 (M); expenditures, $4,105,534; qualifying distributions, $3,790,732.
Limitations: Giving primarily in MA and NY.
Publications: Application guidelines.
Application information: Application form not required.
Trustees: Patricia Dunnington, Arline Ripley Greenleaf, Jacqueline D. Simpkins, U.S. Trust.
EIN: 136071886
Codes: FD, FM

32670
The Tinker Foundation Inc.
55 E. 59th St., 21st Fl.
New York, NY 10022 (212) 421-6858
FAX: (212) 223-3326; E-mail: tinker@tinker.org;
URL: http://fdncenter.org/grantmaker/tinker
Contact: Renate Rennie, Pres.

Trust established in 1959 in NY; incorporated in 1975 in NY.
Donor(s): Edward Larocque Tinker.‡
Financial data (yr. ended 12/31/01): Grants paid, $3,430,445; assets, $74,589,872 (M); expenditures, $4,514,718; qualifying distributions, $4,230,252.
Limitations: Giving limited to projects related to Latin America, Spain, Portugal, and Antarctica.
Publications: Annual report, application guidelines.
Application information: Application form required.
Officers and Directors:* Martha T. Muse,* Chair.; Renate Rennie,* Pres.; Richard de J. Osborne,* Secy.; John A. Luke, Jr.,* Treas.; William R. Chaney, Sally Grooms Cowal, Richard A. Grasso, Charles McC. Mathias, Jr., Susan L. Segal, Alan Stoga.
EIN: 510175449
Codes: FD, FM

32671
Tiger Foundation
101 Park Ave., 48th Fl.
New York, NY 10178 (212) 984-2565
FAX: (212) 949-9778
Contact: Phoebe Boyer, Exec. Dir.

Established in 1989 in NY.
Donor(s): Tiger Management LLC employees.
Financial data (yr. ended 06/30/00): Grants paid, $3,374,389; assets, $7,075,451 (M); gifts received, $1,625,991; expenditures, $3,735,974; qualifying distributions, $3,725,983.
Limitations: Giving primarily in New York, NY.
Publications: Biennial report.
Application information: Application form required.
Officer: Phoebe Boyer, Exec. Dir.
Trustees: Charlie Anderson, Terry Brennan, Carter Brooks, Rob Butler, Gil Caffray, Trent Carmichael, Sherman Chao, Chase Coleman, Richard Davies, Rob Ellis, David Fear, Laurel FitzPatrick, Bill Goodell, John A. Griffin, Mike Hodge, Bill Hwang, James Lyle, Pat McCormack, Jerry Norris, Brian Olson, Jill Olson, Steven C. Olson, Hence Orme, David Ott, Alex Rafale, Shiva Sarram, Chris Shumway, Scott Sinclair, Paul Touradji, Andrew Warford, Robert Williamson, Teddy Wong, Hope Woodhouse.
EIN: 133555671
Codes: FD, FM

32672
The Maurice R. & Corinne P. Greenberg Foundation, Inc.
c/o Marks, Paneth and Shron, LLP
622 3rd Ave.
New York, NY 10017

Established around 1984.
Donor(s): Corinne P. Greenberg, Maurice R. Greenberg, Greenberg Charitable Trust No. 1.
Financial data (yr. ended 09/30/01): Grants paid, $3,362,573; assets, $20,658,716 (M); gifts received, $12,105,049; expenditures, $3,366,005; qualifying distributions, $3,362,573.
Limitations: Applications not accepted. Giving primarily in New York, NY.
Application information: Contributes only to pre-selected organizations.
Officers and Directors:* Maurice R. Greenberg,* Chair.; Corinne P. Greenberg,* Pres.; Jeffrey W. Greenberg, V.P. and Treas.; Evan G. Greenberg,* V.P.; Lawrence S. Greenberg,* V.P.
EIN: 133208725
Codes: FD, FM

32673
The Louis and Harold Price Foundation, Inc.
450 Park Ave., Ste. 1102
New York, NY 10022 (212) 753-0240
Additional tel.: (212) 752-9335; FAX: (212) 752-9338; E-mail:
grantinquiry@pricefoundation.org; URL: http://
www.pricefoundation.org
Contact: Timothy A. Jones, Pres.

Incorporated in 1951 in NY.
Donor(s): Louis Price,‡ Harold Price.
Financial data (yr. ended 12/31/01): Grants paid, $3,359,743; assets, $82,700,172 (M); expenditures, $4,579,260; qualifying distributions, $3,980,612.
Limitations: Giving primarily in Los Angeles, CA, the metropolitan New York, NY, area, and CO; support also for Israel.
Application information: Receipt of proposals is acknowledged. The foundation grants interviews with applicants when deemed necessary. Application form not required.

32673—NEW YORK

Officers and Trustees:* Pauline Price,* Chair.; Timothy A. Jones, Pres.; Rosemary L. Guidone,* Exec. V.P. and Secy.-Treas.; George Asch, Lisa Beshkov, Linda Vitti Herbst, Bonnie Vitti.
EIN: 136121358
Codes: FD, FM

32674
Daisy Marquis Jones Foundation
1600 South Ave., Ste. 250
Rochester, NY 14620 (716) 461-4950
E-mail: mail@dmjf.org; URL: http://www.dmjf.org
Contact: Roger L. Gardner, Pres.

Established in 1968 in NY.
Donor(s): Daisy Marquis Jones,‡ Leo M. Lyons.‡
Financial data (yr. ended 12/31/01): Grants paid, $3,356,324; assets, $48,200,000 (M); expenditures, $3,576,324; qualifying distributions, $3,476,324.
Limitations: Giving limited to Monroe and Yates counties, NY.
Publications: Annual report (including application guidelines), application guidelines.
Application information: The foundation accepts the Rochester Grantmakers Forum Common Application Form. Application form required.
Officers and Trustees:* Donald W. Whitney,* Chair.; Roger L. Gardner,* Pres.; HSBC Bank USA, M & T Bank.
Advisor: Pearl W. Rubin.
EIN: 237000227
Codes: FD

32675
J. E. & Z. B. Butler Foundation, Inc.
825 3rd Ave., 40th Fl.
122 E. 42nd St.
New York, NY 10022
Contact: Leon Glaser, Treas.

Established in 1958.
Donor(s): Zella B. Butler,‡ Jack E. Butler.‡
Financial data (yr. ended 12/31/01): Grants paid, $3,292,496; assets, $109,446,183 (M); expenditures, $4,432,532; qualifying distributions, $3,516,348.
Limitations: Applications not accepted. Giving primarily in New York, NY.
Application information: Contributes only to pre-selected organizations.
Officers and Directors:* Ruth Pearson,* Co-Chair. and V.P.; Beatrice Doniger,* Co-Chair.; Bruce Doniger,* C.E.O. and Pres.; Carol Parrish,* V.P.; Patricia Goldman,* Secy.; Leon Glaser, Treas.
EIN: 136082916
Codes: FD, FM

32676
Branta Foundation, Inc.
c/o Perelson Weiner
1 Dag Hammarskjold Plz., 42nd Fl.
New York, NY 10017-2286

Established in 1955 in NY.
Donor(s): Harvey Picker.
Financial data (yr. ended 05/31/01): Grants paid, $3,291,053; assets, $17,423,739 (M); expenditures, $3,438,934; qualifying distributions, $3,386,508.
Limitations: Applications not accepted.
Application information: Contributes only to pre-selected organizations.
Officers and Directors:* Harvey Picker,* Pres. and Treas.; Christine Beshar,* V.P. and Secy.
EIN: 136130955
Codes: FD, FM

32677
Gleason Foundation
(Formerly Gleason Memorial Fund, Inc.)
P.O. Box 22970
Rochester, NY 14692-2970 (585) 241-4030
FAX: (585) 241-4099; E-mail: gf@gleasonfoundation.org
Contact: Ralph E. Harper, Secy.-Treas.

Incorporated in 1959 in NY.
Financial data (yr. ended 12/31/01): Grants paid, $3,224,000; assets, $125,000,000 (M); expenditures, $4,400,000; qualifying distributions, $3,224,000.
Limitations: Giving primarily in Monroe County, NY.
Application information: Application form required.
Officers and Directors:* James S. Gleason,* Chair.; Tracy R. Gleason,* Pres.; Ralph E. Harper,* Secy.-Treas.; Edward C. Atwater, Janis F. Gleason, Gary Kimmet, Albert W. Moore.
EIN: 166023235
Codes: FD, FM

32678
The Dillon Fund
1330 Ave. of the Americas, 27th Fl.
New York, NY 10019
Contact: Crosby R. Smith, Pres.

Incorporated in 1922 in NY.
Donor(s): Clarence Dillon,‡ C. Douglas Dillon.
Financial data (yr. ended 12/31/00): Grants paid, $3,205,500; assets, $17,541,562 (M); gifts received, $5,986,551; expenditures, $3,382,715; qualifying distributions, $3,240,281.
Limitations: Applications not accepted.
Application information: Contributes only to pre-selected organizations. Unsolicited applications not considered.
Officers and Directors:* Crosby R. Smith,* Pres.; Squire N. Bozorth,* V.P.; James J. Ruddy, V.P. and Treas.; Dorothy Davis, Secy.; Douglas Collins, Mark M. Collins, Jr., Phyllis D. Collins, Susan S. Dillon, Joan M. Frost, Robert Luxembourg.
EIN: 136400226
Codes: FD, FM

32679
Allen Brothers Foundation
711 5th Ave.
New York, NY 10022
Contact: Howard Felson

Established about 1983 in NY.
Financial data (yr. ended 12/31/01): Grants paid, $3,200,000; assets, $40,258 (M); expenditures, $3,222,393; qualifying distributions, $3,201,340.
Limitations: Giving on a national basis, with some emphasis on NY.
Application information: Application form not required.
Officers and Directors:* Herbert A. Allen,* Pres.; Robert H. Cosgriff, V.P.; Paul A. Gould,* V.P.; Irwin H. Kramer, V.P.; Robert H. Werbel,* Secy.; Richard M. Crooks, James W. Quinn, Philip Scaturro, Enrique Senior, Stanley S. Shuman, John Simon, Harold Wit.
EIN: 133202281
Codes: FD

32680
Harold S. Geneen Charitable Trust
c/o U.S. Trust Co.
114 W. 47th St.
New York, NY 10036

Established in 1999 in NY.
Donor(s): Harold S. Geneen.‡

Financial data (yr. ended 12/31/00): Grants paid, $3,200,000; assets, $4,648,900 (M); gifts received, $100,000; expenditures, $3,285,442; qualifying distributions, $3,202,810.
Limitations: Applications not accepted. Giving on a national basis.
Application information: Contributes only to pre-selected organizations.
Trustees: June Geneen, Phil E. Gilbert, Jr., Allen Keesee, U.S. Trust Co.
EIN: 137163001
Codes: FD

32681
Charitable Leadership Foundation
747 Pierce Rd.
Clifton Park, NY 12065 (518) 877-6701
Application address: P.O. Box 777, Clifton Park, NY 12065; FAX: (518) 877-6260; E-mail: info@charitableleadership.org; URL: http://www.charitableleadership.org

Established in 1997 in NY.
Financial data (yr. ended 12/31/01): Grants paid, $3,199,448; assets, $48,161,440 (M); gifts received, $47,596,081; expenditures, $4,189,168; qualifying distributions, $4,246,969; giving activities include $134,723 for programs.
Limitations: Giving primarily in upstate NY.
Application information: See foundation Web site for application guidelines.
Officers: Richard C. Liebich, Pres. and C.E.O.; Jeanrae M. Benoit, Exec. Secy.
EIN: 161514887
Codes: FD

32682
The Ridgefield Foundation
c/o American Express Tax & Business Svc. of New York
1185 6th Ave.
New York, NY 10036-2602

Incorporated in 1956 in NY.
Donor(s): Henry J. Leir,‡ Erna D. Leir,‡ Continental Ore Corp., International Ore and Fertilizer Corp.
Financial data (yr. ended 02/28/00): Grants paid, $3,196,793; assets, $54,141,702 (M); gifts received, $20,800,422; expenditures, $3,982,838; qualifying distributions, $3,370,572.
Limitations: Applications not accepted. Giving primarily in NY for local services; giving in the U.S. and Israel for education.
Application information: The foundation contributes only to pre-selected organizations.
Officers: Arthur S. Hoffman, Pres. and Treas.; Fred M. Lowenfels, Secy.
Directors: Mary-Ann Fribourg, Margot Gibis, Jerome Shelby.
EIN: 136093563
Codes: FD

32683
CLRC, Inc.
c/o Hertz, Herson & Co., LLP
2 Park Ave., Ste. 1500
New York, NY 10016

Established in 1998 in DE and NY.
Donor(s): Bella Wexner Charitable Remainder Unitrust.
Financial data (yr. ended 03/31/01): Grants paid, $3,161,285; assets, $34,200,763 (M); expenditures, $3,407,165; qualifying distributions, $3,173,067.
Limitations: Applications not accepted. Giving primarily in New York, NY.
Application information: Contributes only to pre-selected organizations.

Officer and Directors:* Susan R. Wexner,* Secy.-Treas.; Bertrand Agus.
EIN: 133997365
Codes: FD

32684
LSR Fund
c/o The Rockefeller Trust Co.
30 Rockefeller Plz.
New York, NY 10112 (212) 649-5140

Established in 1994 in NY.
Donor(s): Laurance S. Rockefeller.
Financial data (yr. ended 12/31/00): Grants paid, $3,161,232; assets, $31,898,867 (M); expenditures, $3,340,194; qualifying distributions, $3,239,653.
Limitations: Giving on a national basis.
Trustees: Clayton W. Frye, Jr., Donal C. O'Brien, Jr., Ellen R.C. Pomeroy, Laurance S. Rockefeller, James S. Sligar.
EIN: 137039108
Codes: FD, FM

32685
Bernard F. and Alva B. Gimbel Foundation, Inc.
271 Madison Ave., Ste. 606
New York, NY 10016 (212) 895-8050
FAX: (212) 895-8052; URL: http://www.gimbelfoundation.org
Contact: Leslie Gimbel, Exec. Dir.

Incorporated in 1943 in NY.
Donor(s): Bernard F. Gimbel,‡ Alva B. Gimbel.‡
Financial data (yr. ended 12/31/00): Grants paid, $3,150,600; assets, $69,331,567 (M); expenditures, $4,752,839; qualifying distributions, $3,308,498.
Limitations: Giving primarily in New York, NY.
Publications: Informational brochure (including application guidelines).
Application information: Accepts NY/NJ Area Common Application Form or similar format. Application form not required.
Officers and Directors:* Caral G. Lebworth,* Hon. Chair.; Hope G. Solinger,* Hon. Chair.; Leslie Gimbel,* Pres. and Exec. Dir.; Lynn Stern,* V.P.; Stephen D. Greenberg,* Treas.; Peter Mendelsund, Nicholas Stern.
EIN: 136090843
Codes: FD

32686
AHBA, Inc.
c/o Hertz, Herson & Co., LLP
2 Park Ave., Ste. 1500
New York, NY 10016

Established in 1998 in DE and NY.
Donor(s): Bella Wexner Charitable Remainder Unitrust.
Financial data (yr. ended 03/31/01): Grants paid, $3,147,428; assets, $36,155,961 (M); expenditures, $3,367,483; qualifying distributions, $3,163,261.
Limitations: Applications not accepted. Giving primarily in New York, NY.
Application information: Contributes only to pre-selected organizations.
Officer and Directors:* Susan R. Wexner,* Secy.-Treas.; Bertrand Agus.
EIN: 133997367
Codes: FD

32687
BCHB, Inc.
c/o Hertz, Herson & Co., LLP
2 Park Ave., Ste. 1500
New York, NY 10016

Established in 1997 in DE and NY.
Donor(s): Bella Wexner Charitable Remainder Unitrust.
Financial data (yr. ended 03/31/01): Grants paid, $3,147,262; assets, $36,573,935 (M); expenditures, $3,346,364; qualifying distributions, $3,153,953.
Limitations: Applications not accepted. Giving primarily in New York, NY.
Application information: Contributes only to pre-selected organizations.
Officer and Directors:* Susan R. Wexner,* Secy.-Treas.; Bertrand Agus.
EIN: 133997366
Codes: FD

32688
Willard T. C. Johnson Foundation, Inc.
c/o The Johnson Co., Inc.
630 5th Ave., Ste. 1510
New York, NY 10111
Contact: Robert W. Johnson IV, Pres.

Incorporated in 1979 in NY.
Donor(s): Willard T.C. Johnson,‡ Keith W. Johnson.‡
Financial data (yr. ended 12/31/00): Grants paid, $3,143,000; assets, $69,923,368 (M); expenditures, $3,703,001; qualifying distributions, $3,108,495.
Limitations: Giving primarily in CT, NJ, and NY.
Application information: Application form not required.
Officers and Directors:* Betty W. Johnson,* Chair.; Robert W. Johnson IV,* Pres.; Robert J. Mortimer,* V.P. and Secy.
EIN: 132993310
Codes: FD

32689
H. van Ameringen Foundation
509 Madison Ave.
New York, NY 10022-5501 (212) 758-6221
Contact: Henry P. van Ameringen, Pres.

Established in 1972.
Donor(s): Henry P. van Ameringen.
Financial data (yr. ended 12/31/00): Grants paid, $3,142,340; assets, $15,291,516 (M); gifts received, $3,001,919; expenditures, $3,167,416; qualifying distributions, $3,145,653.
Limitations: Applications not accepted. Giving primarily in NY.
Officer and Trustee:* Henry P. van Ameringen,* Pres.
EIN: 136215329
Codes: FD, FM

32690
EMLE, Inc.
c/o Hertz, Herson & Co., LLP
2 Park Ave., Ste. 1500
New York, NY 10016

Established in 1998 in DE and NY.
Donor(s): Bella Wexner Charitable Remainder Unitrust.
Financial data (yr. ended 03/31/01): Grants paid, $3,132,465; assets, $30,835,237 (M); expenditures, $3,318,240; qualifying distributions, $3,138,220.
Limitations: Applications not accepted. Giving primarily in New York, NY.
Application information: Contributes only to pre-selected organizations.
Officers and Directors:* Bella Wexner, Pres.; Susan R. Wexner,* Secy.-Treas.; Bertrand Agus.
EIN: 133997362
Codes: FD

32691
van Ameringen Foundation, Inc.
509 Madison Ave.
New York, NY 10022-5501 (212) 758-6221
URL: http://www.vanamfound.org
Contact: Henry P. van Ameringen, Pres.

Incorporated in 1950 in NY.
Donor(s): Arnold Louis van Ameringen.‡
Financial data (yr. ended 12/31/01): Grants paid, $3,120,073; assets, $73,052,165 (M); gifts received, $91,606; expenditures, $3,550,821; qualifying distributions, $3,120,073.
Limitations: Giving primarily in metropolitan New York, NY, and Philadelphia, PA.
Publications: Annual report.
Application information: In 2002, the foundation will be awarding single-year grants of $25,000 or less. NYRAG Common Application Form required. Application form required.
Officers and Directors:* Henry P. van Ameringen,* Pres. and Treas.; George Rowe, Jr.,* V.P. and Secy.; Eleanor K. Sypher, Exec. Dir.; Claire M. Fagin, T. Eric Galloway, Alexandra Herzan, Kenneth A. Kind, Patricia Kind, Valerie Kind-Rubin, Andrew Kindfuller, Laura K. McKenna, Clarence J. Sundram.
EIN: 136125699
Codes: FD, FM

32692
The Gladys Krieble Delmas Foundation
521 5th Ave., Ste. 1612
New York, NY 10175-1699 (212) 687-0011
FAX: (212) 687-8877; E-mail: info@Delmas.org;
URL: http://www.delmas.org
Contact: Shirley Lockwood, Fdn. Admin.

Established in 1976 in NY.
Donor(s): Gladys Krieble Delmas,‡ Jean Paul Delmas.‡
Financial data (yr. ended 12/31/00): Grants paid, $3,119,179; assets, $66,326,848 (M); expenditures, $4,213,934; qualifying distributions, $3,380,253.
Limitations: Giving on a national basis to organizations, but only in New York, NY, for performing arts grants; giving for individual research projects conducted in Venice or the Veneto, Italy.
Publications: Informational brochure (including application guidelines), multi-year report.
Application information: Application form required for grants for independent research on Venetian history and culture.
Trustees: Patricia H. Labalme, Joseph C. Mitchell, David H. Stam.
EIN: 510193884
Codes: FD, FM, GTI

32693
DBID, Inc.
c/o Hertz, Herson & Co., LLP
2 Park Ave., Ste. 1500
New York, NY 10016

Established in 1998 in DE and NY.
Donor(s): Bella Wexner Charitable Remainder Unitrust.
Financial data (yr. ended 03/31/01): Grants paid, $3,098,701; assets, $32,871,483 (M); expenditures, $3,287,528; qualifying distributions, $3,105,531.
Limitations: Applications not accepted. Giving primarily in New York, NY.
Application information: Contributes only to pre-selected organizations.
Officers and Directors:* Bella Wexner, Pres.; Susan R. Wexner,* Secy.-Treas.; Bertrand Agus.
EIN: 133997364

32693—NEW YORK

Codes: FD

32694
Jacob L. and Lillian Holtzmann Foundation
c/o Howard M. Holtzmann
630 5th Ave., Ste. 2000
New York, NY 10111
FAX: (212) 332-7142; E-mail:
Holtzmann@cs.com

Trust established in 1958 in NY.
Donor(s): Jacob L. Holtzmann,‡ Lillian Holtzmann,‡ Howard M. Holtzmann.
Financial data (yr. ended 12/31/00): Grants paid, $3,095,459; assets, $11,026,064 (M); gifts received, $50,000; expenditures, $3,184,500; qualifying distributions, $3,077,476.
Limitations: Giving primarily in NY.
Application information: Application form not required.
Trustees: Howard M. Holtzmann, Susan H. Richardson.
EIN: 136174349
Codes: FD

32695
ABC, Inc. Foundation
(Formerly Capital Cities/ABC Foundation)
77 W. 66th St., Rm. 16-15
New York, NY 10023   (212) 456-7498
Additional tel.: (212) 456-7011
Contact: Bernadette Longford, Mgr., Corp. Giving

Incorporated in 1974 in DE.
Donor(s): ABC, Inc.
Financial data (yr. ended 12/31/00): Grants paid, $3,086,650; assets, $0 (M); expenditures, $3,086,900; qualifying distributions, $3,086,179.
Limitations: Applications not accepted. Giving primarily in areas where company properties are located.
Application information: Contributes only to pre-selected organizations.
Officers: Steve Bornstein, Pres.; Alan N. Braverman, V.P.; Griffith Foxley, V.P.; Laurie Younger, V.P.; Marsha Reed, Secy.; Allan Edelson, Treas.
EIN: 237443020
Codes: CS, FD, CD, FM

32696
Stephen & Barbara Friedman Foundation
c/o Marsh and McLennan
1166 6th Ave., 44th Fl.
New York, NY 10036

Established in 1979 in NY.
Donor(s): Stephen B. Friedman, Barbara Friedman.
Financial data (yr. ended 07/31/00): Grants paid, $3,081,228; assets, $24,229,695 (M); gifts received, $9,542,996; expenditures, $3,384,331; qualifying distributions, $3,082,078.
Limitations: Applications not accepted. Giving primarily in NY.
Application information: Contributes only to pre-selected organizations.
Trustees: H. Corbin Day, Barbara Friedman, Stephen B. Friedman.
EIN: 133025979
Codes: FD

32697
Solon E. Summerfield Foundation, Inc.
1270 Avenue of the Americas, Ste. 2114
New York, NY 10020   (212) 218-7640
Contact: William W. Prager, Jr., Pres.

Incorporated in 1939 in NY.
Donor(s): Solon E. Summerfield.‡
Financial data (yr. ended 12/31/00): Grants paid, $3,077,680; assets, $68,114,969 (M); expenditures, $3,652,604; qualifying distributions, $3,343,161.
Limitations: Applications not accepted. Giving on a national basis.
Application information: Contributes only to pre-selected organizations.
Officers and Trustees:* William W. Prager, Jr.,* Pres.; Clarence R. Treeger,* Pres. Emeritus; Thomas C. Treeger,* Secy.-Treas.
EIN: 131797260
Codes: FD

32698
John L. Vogelstein Charitable Trust
c/o Warburg Pincus
466 Lexington Ave., 10th Fl.
New York, NY 10017

Established in 1999 in NY.
Donor(s): John L. Vogelstein.
Financial data (yr. ended 11/30/00): Grants paid, $3,075,750; assets, $5,050,281 (M); gifts received, $3,762,838; expenditures, $3,117,804; qualifying distributions, $3,036,113.
Limitations: Applications not accepted. Giving primarily in NY.
Application information: Contributes only to pre-selected organizations.
Trustees: Andrew W. Vogelstein, Hans A. Vogelstein, John L. Vogelstein.
EIN: 137177278
Codes: FD

32699
The Litwin Foundation
1200 Union Tpke.
New Hyde Park, NY 11040
Contact: Leonard Litwin, Pres.

Established in 1989 in NY.
Donor(s): Leonard Litwin.
Financial data (yr. ended 12/31/01): Grants paid, $3,066,209; assets, $41,003,975 (M); gifts received, $10,000,000; expenditures, $3,066,209; qualifying distributions, $3,019,252.
Limitations: Giving primarily in New York, NY.
Officers and Directors:* Leonard Litwin,* Pres.; Diane Miller,* V.P.; Ruth Litwin,* Secy.; Carole Pittelman,* Treas.; Howard Kalka, Morton Sanders.
EIN: 133501980
Codes: FD

32700
The Ohrstrom Foundation, Inc.
c/o Curtis Mallet
101 Park Ave., 35th Fl.
New York, NY 10178-0061

Incorporated in 1953 in DE.
Donor(s): Members of the Ohrstrom family.
Financial data (yr. ended 05/31/01): Grants paid, $3,039,166; assets, $74,573,366 (M); expenditures, $3,601,464; qualifying distributions, $3,364,859.
Limitations: Applications not accepted. Giving primarily in NY and VA.
Application information: Contributes only to pre-selected organizations.
Officers and Directors:* George L. Ohrstrom, Jr.,* Pres.; George F. Ohrstrom,* Exec. V.P.; Magalen O. Bryant,* V.P.; Peter A. Kalat,* Secy.; Dorothy Barry, Treas.; Kristiane C. Graham, George L. Ohrstrom II, Mark J. Ohrstrom, Winifred E.A. Ohrstrom.
EIN: 546039966
Codes: FD, FM

32701
Golden Family Foundation
500 Fifth Ave., 50th Fl.
New York, NY 10110   (212) 391-8960
Contact: William T. Golden, Pres.

Incorporated in 1952 in NY.
Donor(s): William T. Golden, Sibyl L. Golden.‡
Financial data (yr. ended 12/31/01): Grants paid, $3,013,436; assets, $58,370,673 (M); expenditures, $3,434,373; qualifying distributions, $3,274,155.
Limitations: Applications not accepted. Giving primarily in NY.
Application information: Contributes only to pre-selected organizations.
Officers and Directors:* William T. Golden,* Pres.; Sibyl R. Golden,* V.P.; Helene L. Kaplan,* Secy.; Ralph E. Hansmann,* Treas.; Pamela P. Golden, M.D.
EIN: 237423802
Codes: FD

32702
Credit Suisse First Boston Foundation Trust
(Formerly CS First Boston Foundation Trust)
11 Madison Ave.
New York, NY 10010   (212) 325-2389
Additional tel.: (212) 325-2000; URL: http://www.csfb.com/company_info/html/company_foundation_trust.shtml
Contact: Ms. Casey Karel

Trust established in 1959 in MA.
Donor(s): Credit Suisse First Boston Corp.
Financial data (yr. ended 12/31/00): Grants paid, $3,004,136; assets, $1,731,437 (M); gifts received, $4,708,373; expenditures, $3,004,136; qualifying distributions, $3,004,136.
Limitations: Giving primarily in New York, NY; some giving in other areas of company operations.
Publications: Application guidelines, corporate giving report.
Application information: Do not send video tapes unless specifically requested. Application form not required.
Trustees: Gates Hawn, Managing Dir.; Joseph McLaughlin, Managing Dir.; Liza Bailey, Grace Koo, Art Mbanefo, Elizabeth Millard, Tom Nides, Robert O'Brien, David C. O'Leary, Douglas L. Paul, Michael Schmertzler, Richard Thornburgh.
EIN: 046059692
Codes: CS, FD, CD

32703
Lorraine J. McNally Trust
P.O. Box 643
16 Harlem St.
Glens Falls, NY 12801-0643

Established in 1991 in NY.
Donor(s): Lorraine J. McNally.‡
Financial data (yr. ended 12/31/01): Grants paid, $3,000,000; assets, $87,255 (M); expenditures, $3,012,533; qualifying distributions, $2,983,321.
Limitations: Giving primarily in NY.
Trustee: Thomas M. Lawson.
EIN: 146149662
Codes: FD

32704
The Anne and Eric Gleacher Foundation
c/o Gleacher & Co., LLC
660 Madison Ave.
New York, NY 10021
Contact: Eric J. Gleacher, Pres.

Established in 1990 in DE and NY.
Donor(s): Eric J. Gleacher.
Financial data (yr. ended 12/31/00): Grants paid, $2,981,880; assets, $25,581,019 (M); gifts

received, $3,257,593; expenditures, $3,754,195; qualifying distributions, $2,982,915.
Limitations: Giving primarily in NY.
Application information: Application form not required.
Officers: Eric J. Gleacher, Pres.; Anne G. Gleacher, V.P.
EIN: 133597695
Codes: FD

32705
Charles B. Wang Foundation, Inc.
c/o Judy Cedeno
1 Computer Associates Plz.
Hauppauge, NY 11788-7000

Established in 1994 in NY.
Donor(s): Charles B. Wang.
Financial data (yr. ended 12/31/00): Grants paid, $2,956,854; assets, $2,614,803 (M); expenditures, $3,030,530; qualifying distributions, $2,943,306.
Limitations: Giving primarily in NY.
Application information: Application form not required.
Officers: Charles B. Wang, Pres.; Nancy Li, V.P.; Francis S.L. Wang, Secy.-Treas.
EIN: 113221752
Codes: FD

32706
Arthur Ross Foundation, Inc.
20 E. 74th St., 4-C
New York, NY 10021 (212) 737-7311
Contact: Arthur Ross, Pres.

Incorporated in 1955 in NY.
Donor(s): Arthur Ross.
Financial data (yr. ended 12/31/01): Grants paid, $2,932,551; assets, $9,410,450 (M); gifts received, $1,643,858; expenditures, $3,171,983; qualifying distributions, $3,035,722.
Limitations: Giving primarily in NY.
Officers and Directors:* Arthur Ross,* Pres. and Treas.; Janet C. Ross,* Exec. V.P.; George J. Gillespie III,* Secy.; Gail Lloyd, Exec. Dir.; William T. Golden, Hon. William J. vanden Heuvel, Edgar Wachenheim III.
EIN: 136121436
Codes: FD

32707
Penzance Foundation
237 Park Ave., 21st Fl.
New York, NY 10017 (212) 551-3559
Contact: John M. Emery, V.P.

Established in 1981 in DE.
Donor(s): Edna McConnell Clark.‡
Financial data (yr. ended 04/30/01): Grants paid, $2,908,000; assets, $55,458,880 (M); expenditures, $3,227,291; qualifying distributions, $2,950,190.
Limitations: Applications not accepted.
Officers and Trustees:* Hays Clark,* Pres.; James McConnell Clark,* V.P. and Treas.; John M. Emery,* V.P. and Secy.
EIN: 133081557
Codes: FD, FM

32708
Richard Lounsbery Foundation, Inc.
128 E. 65th St., Ste. 1
New York, NY 10021 (212) 794-7106
FAX: (212) 794-7058; E-mail: richardlounsbery@aol.com
Contact: Marta G. Norman, Exec. Dir.

Incorporated in 1959 in NY.
Donor(s): Richard Lounsbery,‡ Richard Lounsbery Foundation Trust, Inc.
Financial data (yr. ended 12/31/01): Grants paid, $2,907,124; assets, $27,636,451 (M); gifts received, $2,356,856; expenditures, $3,406,239; qualifying distributions, $3,387,332.
Limitations: Giving nationally and internationally.
Application information: Funds mainly committed to projects developed by the director. The foundation does not print any material and has no mailing list. Application form not required.
Officers and Directors:* David Abshire, Ph.D.,* Pres.; William Happer, Ph.D.,* V.P.; Marta G. Norman, Secy. and Exec. Dir.; Florence F. Arwade, Treas.; Jesse Ausubel, Bruce McHenry, David Sabatini, Frederick Seitz, Ph.D.
EIN: 136081860
Codes: FD, FM

32709
Bernard & Irene Schwartz Foundation, Inc.
c/o Loral Corp.
600 3rd Ave.
New York, NY 10016-2065

Established in 1981 in NY.
Donor(s): Bernard L. Schwartz, Irene Schwartz.
Financial data (yr. ended 11/30/00): Grants paid, $2,904,928; assets, $9,716,758 (M); gifts received, $411,100; expenditures, $3,244,283; qualifying distributions, $2,973,363.
Limitations: Applications not accepted. Giving primarily in New York, NY.
Application information: Contributes only to pre-selected organizations.
Officers and Directors:* Irene Schwartz,* Pres.; Karen Schwartz Paddock,* V.P.; Francesca Schwartz,* V.P.; Judith Linksman, Secy.-Treas.; Robert B. Hodes, Peter W. Schmidt.
EIN: 133099518
Codes: FD

32710
Hasbro Children's Foundation
32 W. 23rd St.
New York, NY 10010 (917) 606-6226
FAX: (917) 606-6264; URL: http://www.hasbro.org
Contact: Jane S. Englebardt, Exec. Dir.

Established in 1985 in RI.
Donor(s): Hasbro, Inc.
Financial data (yr. ended 12/31/00): Grants paid, $2,891,533; assets, $4,888,727 (M); gifts received, $2,501,124; expenditures, $3,455,223; qualifying distributions, $3,443,708.
Publications: Annual report, application guidelines, informational brochure.
Application information: Application form not required.
EIN: 222570516
Codes: CS, FD, CD

32711
Mrs. Giles Whiting Foundation
1133 Ave. of the Americas, 22nd Fl.
New York, NY 10036-6710 (212) 336-2138
URL: http://www.whitingfoundation.org
Contact: Robin Krause, Secy.

Incorporated in 1963 in NY.
Donor(s): Mrs. Giles Whiting.‡
Financial data (yr. ended 11/30/01): Grants paid, $2,865,035; assets, $60,363,200 (M); expenditures, $3,916,345; qualifying distributions, $3,281,443.
Limitations: Applications not accepted. Giving on a national basis.
Publications: Multi-year report.
Officers and Trustees:* Robert M. Pennoyer,* Pres. and Treas.; Robert L. Belknap,* V.P.; Antonia M. Grumbach,* V.P.; John N. Irwin III,* V.P.; Kate Douglas Torrey,* V.P.; Robin Krause, Secy.
EIN: 136154484
Codes: FD, GTI

32712
The Sandra Atlas Bass & Edythe & Sol G. Atlas Fund, Inc.
185 Great Neck Rd.
Great Neck, NY 11021 (516) 487-9030
Contact: Sandra A. Bass, Pres.

Established in 1962 in NY.
Donor(s): Sol G. Atlas.
Financial data (yr. ended 12/31/00): Grants paid, $2,862,550; assets, $7,442,977 (M); gifts received, $1,666,586; expenditures, $2,883,808; qualifying distributions, $2,847,964.
Limitations: Applications not accepted. Giving primarily in the metropolitan New York, NY, area, with emphasis on Long Island.
Application information: Unsolicited requests for funds not accepted.
Officers: Sandra A. Bass, Pres.; Morton M. Bass, V.P.; Robert Zabelle, Secy.; Richard J. Cunningham, Treas.
EIN: 116036928
Codes: FD, FM

32713
Robert S. Kaplan Foundation
c/o Goldman Sachs & Co.
85 Broad St., Tax Dept.
New York, NY 10004

Established in 1991 in NY.
Donor(s): Robert S. Kaplan.
Financial data (yr. ended 03/31/01): Grants paid, $2,855,300; assets, $8,103,293 (M); gifts received, $5,683,178; expenditures, $2,911,593; qualifying distributions, $2,855,593.
Limitations: Applications not accepted. Giving on a national basis, with emphasis on New York, NY.
Application information: Contributes only to pre-selected organizations.
Trustee: Robert S. Kaplan.
EIN: 133637444
Codes: FD

32714
Albert A. List Foundation, Inc.
1328 Broadway, Ste. 524
P.O. Box 117
New York, NY 10001-2121
URL: http://fdncenter.org/grantmaker/listfdn
Contact: Viki Laura List, Pres.

Incorporated in 1953 in CT.
Donor(s): Albert A. List,‡ Vera G. List.
Financial data (yr. ended 12/31/01): Grants paid, $2,853,900; assets, $7,008,938 (M); expenditures, $3,324,172; qualifying distributions, $3,245,947.
Limitations: Giving on a national basis.
Publications: Grants list, informational brochure (including application guidelines).
Application information: The foundation will cease grantmaking in May, 2005. Unsolicited applications will not be accepted.
Officers and Directors:* Viki Laura List,* Pres.; Olga List Mack,* Secy.; Jo List, Treas.; Carol List Schwartz.
EIN: 510188408
Codes: TN

32715
VH1 Save The Music Foundation
(Formerly Viacom Foundation)
1515 Broadway, 20th Fl.
New York, NY 10036 (212) 846-7627
FAX: (212) 846-1827; E-mail:
Bob.morrison@vh1staff.com; URL: http://
www.vh1savethemusic.com
Contact: Robert B. Morrison, Exec. Dir.

Incorporated in 1954 in NY; Re-classified as a public charity in 2000.
Donor(s): Viacom Inc.
Financial data (yr. ended 10/31/00): Grants paid, $2,845,996; assets, $2,886,476 (M); gifts received, $3,546,851; expenditures, $3,652,594; qualifying distributions, $2,845,996; giving activities include $2,845,996 for programs.
Limitations: Giving primarily in areas of company operations and its subsidiaries.
Publications: Financial statement, newsletter, informational brochure, program policy statement, application guidelines.
Application information: Application form required.
Officers and Directors:* John Sykes,* Pres.; Robert Morrison,* Exec. Dir.; Larry Cohen,* Secy.-Treas.; Raymond Chambers.
EIN: 136089816
Codes: CS, TN

32716
Lawrence M. Gelb Foundation, Inc.
1585 Broadway, 22nd Fl.
New York, NY 10036-8299
Contact: Robert M. Kaufman, Asst. Secy.

Established in 1957 in NY.
Donor(s): Lawrence M. Gelb,‡ Richard L. Gelb, Bruce S. Gelb, Lawrence N. Gelb.
Financial data (yr. ended 12/31/00): Grants paid, $2,829,790; assets, $8,979,585 (M); gifts received, $897,365; expenditures, $2,895,722; qualifying distributions, $2,824,274.
Limitations: Giving on a national basis.
Application information: Application form not required.
Officers and Directors:* Richard L. Gelb,* Chair.; Bruce S. Gelb,* Pres.; Wilbur H. Friedman,* Secy.; John T. Gelb, Lawrence N. Gelb, Robert M. Kaufman.
EIN: 136113586
Codes: FD

32717
Gross Foundation, Inc.
1660 49th St.
Brooklyn, NY 11204 (718) 851-7724
Contact: Chaim Gross, Pres.

Established in 1991 in NY.
Donor(s): Chaim Gross, Arie Herzog, Pinchus Gross, Esther Gross.
Financial data (yr. ended 02/28/01): Grants paid, $2,829,019; assets, $40,639,233 (M); gifts received, $244,840; expenditures, $2,882,196; qualifying distributions, $2,775,253.
Limitations: Giving primarily in NY.
Application information: Application form not required.
Officer: Chaim Gross, Pres.
Directors: Dov Gross, Faigy Gross.
EIN: 113006419
Codes: FD

32718
Cleveland H. Dodge Foundation, Inc.
670 W. 247th St.
Bronx, NY 10471 (718) 543-1221
FAX: (718) 543-0737
Contact: Phyllis M. Criscuoli, Exec. Dir.

Incorporated in 1917 in NY.
Donor(s): Cleveland H. Dodge.‡
Financial data (yr. ended 12/31/00): Grants paid, $2,815,716; assets, $54,642,155 (M); expenditures, $3,505,540; qualifying distributions, $3,053,933.
Limitations: Giving primarily in New York, NY, the Near East, and to national organizations.
Publications: Annual report, program policy statement.
Application information: Application form not required.
Officers and Directors:* Cleveland E. Dodge, Jr.,* Pres.; William Dodge Rueckert,* V.P.; Gilbert Kerlin,* Secy.; Phyllis M. Criscuoli, Treas. and Exec. Dir.; Nancy Lee Coughlin, Bayard Dodge, Cornelia W. Dodge, David S. Dodge, Robert Garrett, Sally Dodge Mole, Bayard D. Rea, C. Cary Rea, Ingrid R. Warren, Mary Rea Weidlein.
EIN: 136015087
Codes: FD, FM

32719
Dr. G. Clifford & Florence B. Decker Foundation
8 Riverside Dr.
Binghamton, NY 13905 (607) 722-0211
E-mail: deckerfn@pronetisp.net; URL: http://
www.pronetisp.net/~deckerfn/index.html
Contact: Gerald E. Putman, Exec. Dir.

Established in 1979 in NY.
Donor(s): G. Clifford Decker.‡
Financial data (yr. ended 12/31/01): Grants paid, $2,814,034; assets, $41,084,733 (M); expenditures, $3,037,897; qualifying distributions, $2,925,596.
Limitations: Giving in the Broome County, NY, area.
Publications: Annual report, informational brochure (including application guidelines).
Application information: Submission of 1 copy of proposal required for funding requests under $5,000. Application form required.
Officers and Trustees:* Ferris G. Akel,* Chair.; Alice A. Wales,* Vice-Chair.; Mary Lou Faust, Secy.; Douglas R. Johnson,* Treas.; Gerald E. Putman, Exec. Dir.; James A. Carrigg.
EIN: 161131704
Codes: FD

32720
USA Networks Foundation, Inc.
152 W. 57th St., 42nd Fl.
New York, NY 10019
Contact: William Severance, Dir.

Established in 1998 in NY.
Donor(s): USA Networks, Inc.
Financial data (yr. ended 12/31/00): Grants paid, $2,807,408; assets, $6,363,564 (M); gifts received, $165,949; expenditures, $2,817,809; qualifying distributions, $2,798,629.
Limitations: Giving on a national basis.
Application information: Application form not required.
Officers: Victor Kaufman, Pres.; Julius Genachowski, Secy.
Director: William Severance.
EIN: 133994361
Codes: CS, FD, CD

32721
Mark and Anla Cheng Kingdon Fund
c/o Peter J. Cobos
152 W. 57th St., 50th Fl.
New York, NY 10019

Established in 1997 in NY.
Financial data (yr. ended 12/31/00): Grants paid, $2,799,300; assets, $14,283,368 (M); gifts received, $3,850,000; expenditures, $2,799,816; qualifying distributions, $2,799,300.
Limitations: Applications not accepted. Giving primarily in NY.
Application information: Contributes only to pre-selected organizations.
Officers: Mark Kingdon, Chair.; Peter J. Cobos, Secy.
EIN: 133948023
Codes: FD

32722
Perelman Family Foundation
c/o MacAndrews & Fornes Holdings, Inc.
35 E. 62nd St.
New York, NY 10021

Established in 1999 in NY.
Financial data (yr. ended 12/31/00): Grants paid, $2,765,795; assets, $1,180 (M); gifts received, $2,766,490; expenditures, $2,765,761; qualifying distributions, $0.
Limitations: Applications not accepted. Giving on a national basis.
Application information: Contributes only to pre-selected organizations.
Officers and Directors:* Ronald O. Perelman,* Chair. and C.E.O.; Donald G. Drapkin, Vice Chair.; Howard Gittis,* Vice Chair.; Bruce Slovin, Vice Chair.; Richard E. Halperin,* Pres.; Irwin Engelman, Exec. V.P. and C.F.O.; Barry F. Schwartz, Exec. V.P.; James T. Conroy, Senior V.P.; Glenn P. Dickes, V.P. and Secy.; Laurence Winoker, V.P. and Cont.; Gerry R. Kessel, V.P.; Debra G. Perelman, V.P.; Hope G. Perelman, V.P.; Joshua G. Perelman, V.P.; Steven G. Perelman, V.P.; Marvin Schaffer, V.P.
EIN: 134008528
Codes: FD

32723
The Jaffe Family Foundation
c/o Elliot S. Jaffe, The Dress Barn, Inc.
30 Dunnigan Dr.
Suffern, NY 10901

Established in 1986 in NY.
Donor(s): Elliot Jaffe, Roslyn Jaffe.
Financial data (yr. ended 12/31/00): Grants paid, $2,764,114; assets, $53,488,805 (M); expenditures, $3,445,740; qualifying distributions, $2,794,337.
Limitations: Applications not accepted. Giving on a national basis.
Application information: Contributes only to pre-selected organizations.
Officer and Directors:* Elliot S. Jaffe,* Pres.; David R. Jaffe, Elise P. Jaffe, Richard E. Jaffe, Roslyn Jaffe.
EIN: 222827692
Codes: FD

32724
Ernest E. Stempel Foundation
c/o Calvin P. Stempel, Tr.
150 Broadway, Ste. 1102
New York, NY 10038-4302

Established in 1994 in DE.
Donor(s): Ernest E. Stempel.
Financial data (yr. ended 12/31/99): Grants paid, $2,733,253; assets, $39,667,015 (M); gifts

received, $5,000; expenditures, $2,842,771; qualifying distributions, $2,818,052.
Limitations: Applications not accepted. Giving on a national basis.
Application information: Contributes only to pre-selected organizations.
Trustees: Diana S. Bergquist, Calvin P. Stempel, Ernest E. Stempel, Neil F. Stempel, Robert R. Stempel.
EIN: 510363381
Codes: FD

32725
John & Daniel Tishman Fund, Inc.
(Formerly Rose & John Tishman Fund, Inc.)
666 5th Ave.
New York, NY 10103-0001
Contact: John L. Tishman, Pres.

Established in 1957 in NY.
Donor(s): Rose F. Tishman, John Tishman, Daniel Tishman.
Financial data (yr. ended 12/31/01): Grants paid, $2,700,000; assets, $5,830,568 (M); gifts received, $750,000; expenditures, $2,761,108; qualifying distributions, $2,718,728.
Limitations: Giving primarily in NY.
Officers: John Tishman, Pres.; Daniel Tishman, V.P. and Treas.; Katherine Blacklock, V.P.; Kathleen E. Kotoun, Secy.
EIN: 136151766
Codes: FD

32726
Alfred Jurzykowski Foundation, Inc.
15 E. 65th St.
New York, NY 10021 (212) 535-8930
Contact: Mrs. Bluma D. Cohen, Exec. Dir.

Incorporated in 1960 in NY.
Donor(s): Alfred Jurzykowski.‡
Financial data (yr. ended 12/31/01): Grants paid, $2,650,243; assets, $39,202,860 (M); expenditures, $2,958,296; qualifying distributions, $2,699,729.
Limitations: Giving primarily in the metropolitan New York, NY, area.
Publications: Application guidelines.
Application information: Application form not required.
Officers and Trustees:* Yolande L. Jurzykowski,* Exec. V.P.; Bluma D. Cohen,* V.P. and Exec. Dir.; M. Christine Jurzykowski,* Secy.-Treas.; Karin Falencki.
EIN: 136192256
Codes: FD

32727
The William C. And Susan F. Morris Foundation
c/o J & W Seligman & Co.
100 Park Ave., 8th Fl.
New York, NY 10017

Established in 2000 in DE.
Donor(s): William Morris.
Financial data (yr. ended 12/31/01): Grants paid, $2,635,000; assets, $7,763,132 (M); expenditures, $2,753,793; qualifying distributions, $2,635,302.
Limitations: Applications not accepted. Giving primarily in NY.
Application information: Contributes only to pre-selected organizations.
Officers: William Morris, Chair., Pres. and Treas.; Susan Morris, V.P. and Secy.
EIN: 134128044
Codes: FD

32728
Tova Foundation
13 Schunnemunk Rd.
Monroe, NY 10950 (845) 783-0328
Contact: Abe Schwarz, Tr.

Financial data (yr. ended 12/31/00): Grants paid, $2,633,785; assets, $55,990 (M); gifts received, $2,633,785; expenditures, $2,655,671; qualifying distributions, $2,655,671.
Trustees: David Mendlowitz, Abe Schwarz.
EIN: 134016145
Codes: FD

32729
The Barker Welfare Foundation
P.O. Box 2
Glen Head, NY 11545 (516) 759-5592
FAX: (516) 759-5497
Contact: Mrs. Sarane H. Ross, Pres.

Incorporated in 1934 in IL.
Donor(s): Mrs. Charles V. Hickox.‡
Financial data (yr. ended 09/30/01): Grants paid, $2,627,607; assets, $60,278,364 (M); expenditures, $3,446,876; qualifying distributions, $2,925,252.
Limitations: Giving primarily in Chicago, IL, Michigan City, IN, and New York, NY.
Publications: Application guidelines, annual report (including application guidelines).
Application information: Proposals must be completed according to the foundation's guidelines and grants process in order to be considered for funding. Grants to Chicago agencies are by invitation only. Proposals sent by FAX not considered. Application form required.
Officers and Directors:* Mrs. Sarane H. Ross,* Pres.; Katrina H. Becker,* V.P. and Secy.; Thomas P. McCormick,* Treas.; Diane Curtis, Danielle A. Hickox, John B. Hickox, Mary Lou Linnen, Alline Matheson, Sarane R. O'Connor, Alexander B. Ross.
EIN: 366018526
Codes: FD

32730
George Link, Jr. Foundation, Inc.
c/o The Bank of New York
1290 Ave. of The Americas, 5th Fl.
New York, NY 10104 (212) 238-3000
Contact: Michael J. Catanzaro, V.P.

Incorporated in 1980 in NY.
Donor(s): George Link, Jr.‡
Financial data (yr. ended 12/31/00): Grants paid, $2,611,100; assets, $52,001,322 (M); expenditures, $3,023,200; qualifying distributions, $2,631,435.
Limitations: Giving primarily in MA, NJ, and NY.
Application information: Application form not required.
Officers and Directors: Newton P.S. Merrill,* Chair.; Robert Emmet Link,* Vice-Chair.; Michael J. Catanzaro, V.P.; Bernard F. Joyce, V.P.; Kevin J. Bannon, Secy.-Treas.
EIN: 133041396
Codes: FD

32731
Lily Auchincloss Foundation, Inc.
16 E. 79th St., Ste. 31
New York, NY 10021 (212) 737-9533
FAX: (212) 737-9578; *E-mail:* info@lilyauch.org;
URL: http://www.lilyauch.org
Contact: Alexandra A. Herzan, Pres. and Treas.

Established in 1985 in NY; incorporated in 1997.
Donor(s): Lily Auchincloss,‡ Hedwig A. van Amerigen.‡

Financial data (yr. ended 12/31/00): Grants paid, $2,604,500; assets, $59,809,623 (M); gifts received, $973,390; expenditures, $3,103,243; qualifying distributions, $2,708,673.
Limitations: Giving limited to New York, NY and its surrounding boroughs.
Publications: Annual report, application guidelines.
Application information: Application form not required.
Officers and Directors:* Alexandra A. Herzan,* Pres. and Treas.; Paul K. Herzan,* V.P.; Steadman H. Westergaard,* Secy.; Anne Faulconer Hurley, Lee Auchincloss Link, Michael Rosenwasser.
EIN: 133935995
Codes: FD

32732
Helena Rubinstein Foundation, Inc.
477 Madison Ave., 7th Fl.
New York, NY 10022-5802 (212) 750-7310
URL: http://fdncenter.org/grantmaker/rubinstein
Contact: Diane Moss, C.E.O. Pres.

Incorporated in 1953 in NY.
Donor(s): Helena Rubinstein Gourielli.‡
Financial data (yr. ended 05/31/01): Grants paid, $2,598,150; assets, $40,474,526 (M); expenditures, $3,699,484; qualifying distributions, $3,102,766.
Limitations: Giving primarily in New York, NY.
Publications: Biennial report (including application guidelines), application guidelines, grants list.
Application information: Accepts NYRAG Common Grant Application Form. Application form not required.
Officers and Directors:* Gertrude G. Michelson,* Chair.; Diane Moss,* C.E.O. and Pres.; Robert Moss,* V.P.; Louis E. Slesin,* Secy.-Treas.; Laurie Shapley, Exec. Dir.; Robin F. Grossman, Suzanne Slesin, Deborah A. Zoullas.
EIN: 136102666
Codes: FD

32733
The Ronald S. Lauder Foundation
767 5th Ave., 46th Fl.
New York, NY 10153 (212) 319-6300
URL: http://www.rslfoundation.org
Contact: Dr. George Ban, Exec. V.P. and C.E.O.

Established in 1987 in NY.
Donor(s): Estee Lauder, Ronald S. Lauder, Estee Lauder, Inc.
Financial data (yr. ended 12/31/99): Grants paid, $2,581,928; assets, $30,497,268 (M); gifts received, $5,569,153; expenditures, $9,411,601; qualifying distributions, $12,331,523; giving activities include $2,715,922 for programs.
Limitations: Applications not accepted. Giving primarily in Central and Eastern Europe.
Publications: Financial statement, informational brochure, newsletter.
Application information: Unsolicited requests for funds are not considered.
Officers and Directors:* Ronald S. Lauder,* Chair. and Pres.; George Ban, Exec. V.P. and C.E.O.; Joan Braunstein, V.P.; Rachel S. Laufer, V.P.; Jacob Z. Schuster, Treas.; Michael Berenbaum, Rabbi Chaskel Besser, Rabbi Jacob Biderman, Micki Edelsohn, Marjorie S. Federbush, Rabbi Pinchas Goldschmidt, Rabbi Irving Greenberg, Malcolm Hoenlein, Jo Carole Lauder, Richard D. Parsons, Menachem Z. Rosensaft, Steven Schwager, Israel Singer, Kalman Sultanik.
EIN: 133445910
Codes: FD, GTI

32734—NEW YORK

32734
Ralph E. Ogden Foundation, Inc.
Pleasant Hill Rd.
P.O. Box 290
Mountainville, NY 10953

Incorporated in 1947 in DE.
Donor(s): Ralph E. Ogden,‡ H. Peter Stern, Margaret H. Ogden.‡
Financial data (yr. ended 12/31/99): Grants paid, $2,560,500; assets, $42,739,652 (M); expenditures, $3,057,967; qualifying distributions, $2,474,917.
Limitations: Applications not accepted. Giving primarily in Mountainville and New York, NY.
Application information: Contributes only to pre-selected organizations.
Officers and Trustees:* H. Peter Stern,* Pres.; Leslie A. Jacobson,* V.P.; Georgene Zlock, Secy.; Eugene L. Cohan,* Treas.; Frederick Lubcher, Beatrice Stern, Elisabeth Ellen Stern, John Peter Stern.
EIN: 141455902
Codes: FD

32735
The Harold & Mimi Steinberg Charitable Trust
c/o Schulte Roth & Zabel
900 3rd Ave.
New York, NY 10022

Established in 1986 in NY.
Donor(s): Harold Steinberg.‡
Financial data (yr. ended 12/31/00): Grants paid, $2,549,666; assets, $26,540,206 (M); expenditures, $2,927,481; qualifying distributions, $2,605,834.
Limitations: Applications not accepted. Giving primarily in New York, NY.
Application information: Contributes only to pre-selected organizations. Unsolicited requests for funds not considered.
Trustees: Charles Benenson, Carole A. Krumland, James D. Steinberg, Michael A. Steinberg, Seth Weingarten, William D. Zabel.
EIN: 133383348
Codes: FD, FM

32736
New York Stock Exchange Foundation, Inc.
11 Wall St.
New York, NY 10005 (212) 656-5290
Contact: James E. Buck, Secy.

Incorporated in 1983 in NY.
Donor(s): New York Stock Exchange, Inc.
Financial data (yr. ended 12/31/00): Grants paid, $2,547,851; assets, $28,186,655 (M); gifts received, $1,500,000; expenditures, $2,579,817; qualifying distributions, $2,517,625.
Limitations: Giving primarily in New York, NY.
Publications: Annual report.
Officers and Directors:* Geoffrey C. Bible,* Chair.; James E. Buck, Secy.; Keith R. Helsby, Treas.; Alan Holzer, Cont.; William R. Johnston, Joseph A. Mahoney, Deryck C. Maughan, Leon E. Panetta.
EIN: 133203195
Codes: CS, FD, CD

32737
Helaine Heilbrunn Lerner Fund, Inc.
175 E. 74th St.
New York, NY 10021

Established in 1999 in DE and NY.
Donor(s): Robert Heilbrunn, Helaine Lerner.
Financial data (yr. ended 12/31/00): Grants paid, $2,546,836; assets, $66,189,975 (M); gifts received, $3,798,500; expenditures, $2,562,249; qualifying distributions, $2,549,273.

Limitations: Applications not accepted.
Application information: Contributes only to pre-selected organizations. Unsolicited requests for funds not accepted.
Officer: Helaine Lerner, Pres.
EIN: 134082873
Codes: FD

32738
The Chazen Foundation
P.O. Box 801
Nyack, NY 10960
Contact: Dennis J. Fleming, Consultant

Established in 1985 in NY.
Donor(s): Jerome A. Chazen, Simona A. Chazen.
Financial data (yr. ended 12/31/00): Grants paid, $2,540,845; assets, $39,000,886 (M); gifts received, $2,145,313; expenditures, $3,298,046; qualifying distributions, $2,566,405.
Limitations: Giving primarily in the northeastern U.S.; education grants limited to students of the Rockland County, NY, area.
Publications: Informational brochure, application guidelines.
Trustees: Jerome A. Chazen, Simona A. Chazen.
EIN: 133229474
Codes: FD, GTI

32739
The Sue Ann and John L. Weinberg Foundation
(Formerly The Sue and John L. Weinberg Foundation)
375 Park Ave., Ste. 1002
New York, NY 10152-1099
Contact: John L. Weinberg, Tr.

Established in 1959 in NY.
Donor(s): John L. Weinberg.
Financial data (yr. ended 04/30/01): Grants paid, $2,537,251; assets, $49,949,896 (M); gifts received, $10,927; expenditures, $2,589,484; qualifying distributions, $2,508,094.
Limitations: Applications not accepted. Giving primarily in Greenwich, CT, and New York, NY.
Application information: Contributes only to pre-selected organizations.
Trustees: Arthur G. Altschul, Jean Weinberg Rose, John L. Weinberg, John S. Weinberg, Sue Ann Weinberg.
EIN: 136028813
Codes: FD

32740
The Benjamin M. Rosen Family Foundation
c/o Kelley Drye & Warren, LLP
101 Park Ave., Ste. 3101
New York, NY 10178

Established in 1998 in NY.
Donor(s): Benjamin M. Rosen.
Financial data (yr. ended 12/31/01): Grants paid, $2,531,060; assets, $29,207,234 (M); gifts received, $32,109,000; expenditures, $3,076,219; qualifying distributions, $2,542,467.
Limitations: Applications not accepted. Giving primarily in NY.
Application information: Contributes only to pre-selected organizations.
Trustees: Alexandra Rosen, Benjamin M. Rosen, Frederic A. Rubinstein.
EIN: 134034465
Codes: FD

32741
Martin Family Foundation
c/o Goldman Sachs & Co.
85 Broad St., Tax Dept.
New York, NY 10004

Established in 1989 in CA.

Donor(s): Eff W. Martin.
Financial data (yr. ended 03/31/01): Grants paid, $2,527,930; assets, $3,438,115 (M); gifts received, $2,756,310; expenditures, $2,735,503; qualifying distributions, $2,535,062; giving activities include $106,138 for programs.
Limitations: Applications not accepted. Giving primarily in Palo Alto and San Francisco, CA.
Application information: Contributes only to pre-selected organizations.
Trustees: Eff W. Martin, Flora Deena Martin, Patricia M. Martin.
EIN: 133532032
Codes: FD

32742
Weeden Foundation
(Formerly Frank Weeden Foundation)
747 3rd Ave., 34th Fl.
New York, NY 10017 (212) 888-1672
FAX: (212) 888-1354; E-mail:
weedenfdn@weedenfdn.org; URL: http://www.weedenfdn.org
Contact: Donald A. Weeden, Exec. Dir.

Established 1963 in CA.
Donor(s): Frank Weeden,‡ Alan N. Weeden, Donald E. Weeden, John D. Weeden, William F. Weeden, M.D.
Financial data (yr. ended 06/30/02): Grants paid, $2,526,983; assets, $30,189,252 (M); expenditures, $2,873,650; qualifying distributions, $2,526,983; giving activities include $270,876 for program-related investments.
Limitations: Giving on a national and international basis, primarily in northern CA, the Pacific Northwest, Latin America (Chile and Bolivia), and Central Siberia.
Application information: Application form not required.
Officers and Directors:* Norman Weeden, Ph.D.,* Pres.; William F. Weeden, M.D.,* V.P.; John D. Weeden,* Secy.-Treas.; Donald A. Weeden, Exec. Dir.; David Davies, Christina Roux, Alan N. Weeden, Donald E. Weeden, Leslie Weeden.
EIN: 946109313
Codes: FD

32743
The Sulzberger Foundation, Inc.
229 W. 43rd St., Ste. 1031
New York, NY 10036 (212) 556-1755
Contact: Marian S. Heiskell, Pres.

Incorporated in 1956 in NY.
Donor(s): Arthur Hays Sulzberger,‡ Iphigene Ochs Sulzberger,‡ Marian S. Heiskell, Ruth S. Holmberg, Judith P. Sulzberger, Arthur Ochs Sulzberger.
Financial data (yr. ended 12/31/00): Grants paid, $2,526,735; assets, $49,793,952 (M); expenditures, $3,227,833; qualifying distributions, $2,642,424.
Limitations: Giving primarily in NY and Chattanooga, TN.
Application information: Application form not required.
Officers and Directors:* Marian S. Heiskell,* Pres.; Arthur Ochs Sulzberger,* V.P. and Secy.-Treas.; Ruth S. Holmberg,* V.P.; Judith P. Sulzberger,* V.P.
EIN: 136083166
Codes: FD

32744
Susan and Elihu Rose Foundation, Inc.
c/o Rose Assocs.
200 Madison Ave., 5th Fl.
New York, NY 10016

Established in 1988 in DE.
Donor(s): Elihu Rose, Samuel and David Rose Charitable Foundation.
Financial data (yr. ended 12/31/00): Grants paid, $2,522,951; assets, $29,955,195 (M); expenditures, $3,064,375; qualifying distributions, $2,540,251.
Limitations: Applications not accepted. Giving primarily in New York, NY.
Application information: Contributes only to pre-selected organizations.
Officer and Directors:* Elihu Rose,* Pres. and Secy.; Susan Rose.
EIN: 133484181
Codes: FD, FM

32745
A. Lindsay and Olive B. O'Connor Foundation
P.O. Box D
Hobart, NY 13788 (607) 538-9248
FAX: (607) 538-9136
Contact: Donald F. Bishop II, Exec. Dir.

Trust established in 1965 in NY.
Donor(s): Olive B. O'Connor.‡
Financial data (yr. ended 12/31/99): Grants paid, $2,515,845; assets, $74,707,970 (M); expenditures, $3,117,014; qualifying distributions, $2,728,256.
Limitations: Giving primarily in Delaware County, NY, and 7 contiguous rural counties in upstate NY.
Publications: Program policy statement, multi-year report.
Application information: Application form required.
Officers: Donald F. Bishop II, Pres. and Exec. Dir.; Pamela Hill, Secy.-Treas.
Advisory Committee: Robert L. Bishop II, Chair.; Charlotte Bishop Hill, Vice-Chair.; William J. Murphy, Eugene E. Peckham.
Trustee: BSB Bank & Trust.
EIN: 166063485
Codes: FD

32746
The Appleman Foundation, Inc.
c/o Bessemer Trust Co.
630 5th Ave.
New York, NY 10111 (212) 708-9216
Application address: 222 Royal Palm Way, Palm Beach, FL 33480; tel.: (561) 655-4030

Incorporated in 1952 in DE.
Donor(s): Nathan Appleman,‡ and members of the Appleman family.
Financial data (yr. ended 12/31/00): Grants paid, $2,502,700; assets, $18,567,637 (M); gifts received, $5,257,830; expenditures, $2,686,353; qualifying distributions, $2,538,410.
Limitations: Giving primarily in Palm Beach, FL, and NY.
Officers: David Roberts, Pres.; Susan A. Unterberg, V.P.
Directors: Ellen Unterberg Celli, Jill A. Roberts.
EIN: 136154978
Codes: FD, FM

32747
The Paul Tudor Jones Family Foundation
c/o Sullivan & Cromwell
125 Broad St.
New York, NY 10004-2498

Established in 2000 in CT.
Donor(s): Paul Tudor Jones II.
Financial data (yr. ended 12/31/01): Grants paid, $2,500,000; assets, $458,189 (M); gifts received, $1,458,628; expenditures, $2,553,909; qualifying distributions, $2,493,336.
Limitations: Applications not accepted. Giving on a national and international basis.
Application information: Contributes only to pre-selected organizations.
Trustee: Paul Tudor Jones II.
EIN: 061600826
Codes: FD

32748
The Edward S. Gordon Foundation
441 Lexington Ave., Ste. 805
New York, NY 10017

Established in 1997 in NY.
Donor(s): Edward S. Gordon.‡
Financial data (yr. ended 12/31/00): Grants paid, $2,497,972; assets, $2,162,631 (M); expenditures, $2,543,278; qualifying distributions, $359,771.
Limitations: Applications not accepted. Giving primarily in New York, NY.
Application information: Contributes only to pre-selected organizations.
Trustees: Robin Apple, A.M. Saytanides.
EIN: 137107378
Codes: FD

32749
Recanati Foundation
511 5th Ave.
New York, NY 10017 (212) 578-1857

Incorporated in 1956 in NY.
Donor(s): Israel Discount Bank Ltd., Jewish Communal Fund, Raphael Recanati,‡ Gertrud Stark.
Financial data (yr. ended 06/30/00): Grants paid, $2,483,906; assets, $12,060,471 (M); expenditures, $2,576,879; qualifying distributions, $2,460,418.
Limitations: Applications not accepted. Giving primarily in NY.
Application information: Contributes only to pre-selected organizations.
Officers and Directors:* Diane Recanati,* Chair.; Leon Recanati,* Vice-Chair.; Oudi Recanati,* Vice-Chair.; Morton P. Hyman,* Pres.; Michael A. Recanati,* V.P.; Yudith Recanati, V.P.; Robert N. Cowen, Secy.-Treas.; Eli Cohen, Ran Hettena.
EIN: 136113080
Codes: FD, FM

32750
Keren Keshet - The Rainbow Foundation
1015 5th Ave.
New York, NY 10028 (212) 756-4117
Contact: Linda Sakacs

Established in 1999 in NY.
Donor(s): Zalman C. Bernstein.
Financial data (yr. ended 12/31/00): Grants paid, $2,482,858; assets, $173,746,920 (M); gifts received, $140,377,416; expenditures, $3,930,158; qualifying distributions, $5,121,462.
Limitations: Giving primarily in Washington, DC.
Officers: Arthur W. Fried, Pres. and Treas.; Mem Dryan Bernstein, V.P.
EIN: 134069592
Codes: FD

32751
The Skadden Fellowship Foundation, Inc.
(Formerly Skadden, Arps, Slate, Meagher & Flom Fellowship Foundation)
4 Times Sq., Rm. 40-228
New York, NY 10036 (212) 735-2956
FAX: (917) 777-2956; *URL:* http://www.skadden.com/SkaddenFellowshipIndex.ihtml
Contact: Susan Butler Plum

Established in 1988 in NY.
Donor(s): Skadden, Arps, Slate, Meagher & Flom.
Financial data (yr. ended 12/31/00): Grants paid, $2,475,573; assets, $4,636,292 (M); gifts received, $2,846,829; expenditures, $2,715,424; qualifying distributions, $2,709,904.
Publications: Multi-year report, application guidelines, informational brochure.
Application information: Applicants must secure a potential position with a sponsoring public interest organization before applying for a fellowship. Application form required.
Officers and Directors:* Joseph H. Flom,* Chair.; Peter Mullen, Pres.; Michael Connery, V.P.; Barry H. Garfinkel, V.P.; Earle Yaffa, Secy.-Treas.; Judith Areen, Jeffrey S. Lehman, Jose Lozano, Kurt Schmoke, Robert C. Sheehan, Sargent Shriver, Solomon Watson IV.
EIN: 133455231
Codes: CS, FD, CD, FM, GTI

32752
The Felix and Elizabeth Rohatyn Foundation, Inc.
(Formerly Felix G. Rohatyn Foundation)
810 Fifth Ave.
New York, NY 10021
Contact: Felix G. Rohatyn, Pres.

Established in 1968.
Donor(s): Felix G. Rohatyn, Elizabeth Rohatyn.
Financial data (yr. ended 12/31/01): Grants paid, $2,447,221; assets, $8,403,323 (M); gifts received, $1,000,000; expenditures, $2,549,119; qualifying distributions, $2,533,531.
Limitations: Applications not accepted. Giving primarily in the New York, NY, area.
Officers and Directors:* Felix G. Rohatyn,* Pres.; Elizabeth Rohatyn,* V.P.; Nicolas Rohatyn,* Secy.-Treas.; Vivien Stiles Duffy, Exec. Dir.; Melvin L. Heineman.
EIN: 237015644
Codes: FD

32753
The Whitehead Foundation
65 E. 55th St.
New York, NY 10022 (212) 755-3131
Contact: Denise Emmett

Established in 1982 in NY.
Donor(s): John C. Whitehead.
Financial data (yr. ended 06/30/01): Grants paid, $2,444,646; assets, $4,636,800 (M); gifts received, $2,450,000; expenditures, $2,462,086; qualifying distributions, $2,447,761.
Limitations: Applications not accepted. Giving primarily in NY.
Application information: Unsolicited proposals are rarely approved.
Trustees: Anne Whitehead Crawford, Wade Greene, John C. Whitehead, John Gregory Whitehead.
EIN: 133119344
Codes: FD

32754
Education for Youth Society
c/o Spear, Leeds & Kellogg
120 Broadway, Ste. 840
New York, NY 10271 (212) 433-7723
Contact: Isaac Sarmark

Established around 1976.
Donor(s): James H. Lynch, Jr.
Financial data (yr. ended 12/31/00): Grants paid, $2,444,463; assets, $66,857,463 (M); gifts received, $57,459,973; expenditures, $2,905,083; qualifying distributions, $2,465,083.
Limitations: Applications not accepted.
Application information: Contributes only to pre-selected organizations.
Officers: Andrew Cader, Chair.; Gary Goldring, Pres.; Carl Hewitt, V.P. and Secy.; Stephen Balsamo, V.P. and Treas.
EIN: 222101578
Codes: FD

32755
The Stanley S. Shuman Foundation
711 5th Ave., 9th Fl.
New York, NY 10022-3111

Established in 1966 in NY.
Donor(s): Stanley S. Shuman.
Financial data (yr. ended 12/31/01): Grants paid, $2,432,860; assets, $1,694,673 (M); expenditures, $2,468,035; qualifying distributions, $2,433,503.
Limitations: Applications not accepted. Giving primarily in MA, and New York, NY.
Application information: Contributes only to pre-selected organizations.
Trustees: David Shuman, Michael Shuman, Stanley S. Shuman.
EIN: 136216917
Codes: FD

32756
The George Rohr Foundation, Inc.
c/o Ulysses Partners, LLC
280 Park Ave., 21st Fl.
New York, NY 10017

Established in 1986 in NY.
Donor(s): George Rohr.
Financial data (yr. ended 12/31/00): Grants paid, $2,430,658; assets, $5,859,159 (M); gifts received, $492,428; expenditures, $2,475,478; qualifying distributions, $2,410,586.
Limitations: Applications not accepted. Giving primarily in NY.
Application information: Contributes only to pre-selected organizations.
Officers and Directors:* George Rohr,* Pres.; Pamela Rohr,* V.P.; Salomon R. Sassoon.
EIN: 133267203
Codes: FD

32757
J. P. Morgan Chase Texas Foundation, Inc.
(Formerly Chase Texas Foundation, Inc.)
52 Broadway, 8th Fl.
New York, NY 10004
Application address: c/o J.P. Morgan Chase & Co., P.O. Box 2558, Houston, TX 77252, tel.: (713) 216-4004
Contact: Jana Gunter, Chair.

Incorporated in 1952 in TX.
Donor(s): Texas Commerce Bank, N.A., J.P. Morgan Chase & Co.
Financial data (yr. ended 12/31/00): Grants paid, $2,429,940; assets, $3,731,678 (M); expenditures, $2,553,351; qualifying distributions, $2,429,940.
Limitations: Giving limited to Houston, TX.
Publications: Application guidelines.
Application information: Application form not required.
Officers and Trustees:* Jana Gunter,* Chair. and Pres.; Yolanda Londono,* V.P.; Beverly McCaskill,* Secy.
EIN: 746036696
Codes: CS, FD, CD

32758
Samuel Freeman Charitable Trust
c/o U.S. Trust
114 W. 47th St.
New York, NY 10036-1532
FAX: (212) 852-3377
Contact: Linda R. Franciscovich, Sr. V.P., U.S. Trust, or Carolyn L. Larke, Asst. V.P., U.S. Trust

Established in 1981 in NY.
Donor(s): Samuel Freeman.‡
Financial data (yr. ended 12/31/00): Grants paid, $2,424,953; assets, $4,872,663 (M); expenditures, $2,786,667; qualifying distributions, $2,622,139.
Limitations: Giving on a national basis.
Publications: Application guidelines.
Application information: Application form not required.
Trustees: Daniel P. Kelly, William E. Murray, Hilton C. Smith, Jr., Pamela Stack, U.S. Trust.
EIN: 136803465
Codes: FD

32759
Nicholas Family Charitable Trust
c/o Nicholas J. Nicholas, Jr.
88 Central Park W.
New York, NY 10023-6028

Established in 1992 in NY.
Donor(s): Nicholas J. Nicholas, Jr., Llewellyn J. Nicholas.
Financial data (yr. ended 12/31/00): Grants paid, $2,424,798; assets, $3,729,913 (M); gifts received, $3,877,063; expenditures, $2,452,456; qualifying distributions, $2,388,232.
Limitations: Applications not accepted. Giving primarily in NY.
Application information: Contributes only to pre-selected organizations.
Trustees: Llewellyn J. Nicholas, Nicholas J. Nicholas, Jr.
EIN: 136990536
Codes: FD

32760
Parkview Foundation
2600 Nostrand Ave.
Brooklyn, NY 11210

Established in 2000 in NY.
Donor(s): Parkview Realty Co.
Financial data (yr. ended 06/30/01): Grants paid, $2,424,100; assets, $6,800,577 (M); gifts received, $8,619,400; expenditures, $2,607,752; qualifying distributions, $2,373,850.
Limitations: Applications not accepted. Giving primarily in Brooklyn, NY.
Application information: Contributes only to pre-selected organizations.
Trustees: Issack Bernstein, Emil Fischman.
EIN: 113544307
Codes: FD

32761
The Cameron Baird Foundation
120 Delaware Ave., 6th Fl.
Buffalo, NY 14202 (716) 845-6000
Contact: Brian D. Baird, Tr.

Trust established in 1960 in NY.
Donor(s): Members of the family of Cameron Baird.
Financial data (yr. ended 12/31/00): Grants paid, $2,403,585; assets, $46,464,922 (M); expenditures, $2,535,501; qualifying distributions, $2,412,845.
Limitations: Applications not accepted. Giving primarily in the Buffalo, NY, area.
Application information: Contributes only to pre-selected organizations. Unsolicited requests for funds not considered or acknowledged.
Trustees: Brian D. Baird, Bridget B. Baird, Bruce C. Baird, Jane D. Baird, Peter C. Clauson, Brenda Baird Senturia.
EIN: 166029481
Codes: FD

32762
Theresa and Edward O'Toole Foundation
c/o The Bank of New York, Tax Dept.
1 Wall St., 28th Fl.
New York, NY 10286 (212) 635-1622
Contact: Stella Lau, V.P., The Bank of New York

Established in 1971.
Donor(s): Theresa O'Toole.‡
Financial data (yr. ended 06/30/00): Grants paid, $2,400,000; assets, $67,001,071 (M); expenditures, $2,733,723; qualifying distributions, $2,295,668.
Limitations: Giving primarily in FL, NJ, and NY.
Application information: Application form not required.
Trustees: Bert Degheri, The Bank of New York.
EIN: 136350175
Codes: FD

32763
Lake Placid Education Foundation
157 Saranac Ave.
Lake Placid, NY 12946 (518) 523-4433
Application address: Crestview Plz., Lake Placid, NY 12946; FAX: (518) 523-4434; E-mail: jsccpa@northnet.org
Contact: John Lansing, Exec. Dir.

Established in 1922 in NY.
Donor(s): Melvil Dewey.‡
Financial data (yr. ended 06/30/01): Grants paid, $2,392,110; assets, $6,572,237 (M); gifts received, $1,000; expenditures, $2,469,543; qualifying distributions, $2,409,289.
Limitations: Giving primarily in the northern Adirondack region of NY.
Publications: Informational brochure (including application guidelines).
Application information: Application form not required.
Officers and Directors:* Frederick C. Calder,* Pres.; Meredith Prime,* V.P.; George Hart,* Secy.; Peter F. Roland,* Treas.
EIN: 510243919
Codes: FD

32764
Jac & Eva Feinberg Foundation, Inc.
c/o Schneider & Abrams
1333 Broadway, Rm. 516
New York, NY 10018

Established around 1946.
Donor(s): Elmsmere Assocs., Abraham Feinberg.
Financial data (yr. ended 08/31/01): Grants paid, $2,381,500; assets, $5,576 (M); gifts received, $2,360,000; expenditures, $2,389,369; qualifying distributions, $2,388,820.
Limitations: Applications not accepted. Giving primarily in Waltham, MA; some giving also in New York, NY.
Application information: Contributes only to pre-selected organizations.

Officers: Norbert Weissberg, Pres.; Stephen R. Abrams, Secy.-Treas.
EIN: 136103597
Codes: FD

32765
The David & Lois Shakarian Foundation
(Formerly D. B. Shakarian Foundation)
156 W. 56th St.
New York, NY 10019

Established in 1986 in DE.
Donor(s): Lois V. Shakarian Blackburn, Linda Lucas, Louise Urleja, David Lucas, Michael Urleja.
Financial data (yr. ended 12/31/00): Grants paid, $2,380,000; assets, $12,213,663 (M); gifts received, $222,241; expenditures, $2,506,154; qualifying distributions, $2,354,087.
Limitations: Applications not accepted. Giving primarily in FL.
Application information: Contributes only to pre-selected organizations.
Officers: Lois V. Shakarian Blackburn, Chair.; P. Michael Ukleja, Pres.; David Lucas, V.P.; Linda Lucas, V.P.; Louise Ukleja, V.P.; Edward Beimfohr, Secy.; Charles L. Potter, Jr., Treas.
EIN: 133047543
Codes: FD

32766
The Frances L. & Edwin L. Cummings Memorial Fund
501 5th Ave., Ste. 708
New York, NY 10017-6103 (212) 286-1778
FAX: (212) 682-9458
Contact: Elizabeth Costas, Admin. Dir.

Established in 1982 in NY.
Donor(s): Edwin L. Cummings,‡ Frances L. Cummings.‡
Financial data (yr. ended 07/31/01): Grants paid, $2,365,700; assets, $41,741,286 (M); expenditures, $2,786,386; qualifying distributions, $2,563,463.
Limitations: Giving primarily in the metropolitan New York, NY, area, with emphasis on New York City and northeastern NJ.
Publications: Biennial report (including application guidelines).
Application information: Proposals received by FAX not accepted. Application form not required.
Trustees: J. Andrew Lark, The Bank of New York.
Board of Advisors: Jean Crystal, Anne Nordeman, Sarah Rosen.
EIN: 136814491
Codes: FD

32767
The Reb Ephraim Chaim & Miriam Rochel Klein Charitable Foundation
c/o Brand, Sonnenschine & Co.
69-70 Grand Central Pkwy.
Forest Hills, NY 11375
Contact: Samuel Sonnenschine, Dir.

Established in 1989 in NY.
Donor(s): Abraham Klein, Sarah Dinah Klein, Fairview Nursing Care Center, Inc., L. Rubin.
Financial data (yr. ended 12/31/00): Grants paid, $2,361,634; assets, $36,962,861 (M); gifts received, $2,009,000; expenditures, $2,767,877; qualifying distributions, $2,342,628.
Limitations: Applications not accepted. Giving primarily in Brooklyn, NY. Some giving also in Canada and Jerusalem, Israel.
Application information: Contributes only to pre-selected organizations.
Directors: Abraham Klein, Sarah Dinah Klein, Samuel Sonnenschine.
EIN: 223000780

Codes: FD

32768
Evan Frankel Foundation
P.O. Box 5072
East Hampton, NY 11937 (631) 329-2833
FAX: (631) 329-7102; E-mail: frankelfound@hamptons.com
Contact: Nancy Wendell

Established in 1978.
Donor(s): Evan M. Frankel.‡
Financial data (yr. ended 09/30/01): Grants paid, $2,353,398; assets, $7,866,273 (M); expenditures, $2,560,425; qualifying distributions, $2,432,722.
Limitations: Applications not accepted. Giving limited to the U.S.
Officers and Directors:* Ernest Frankel,* Pres.; C. Leonard Gordon,* Secy.; Andrew E. Sabin,* Treas.
EIN: 132998402
Codes: FD

32769
The Stanley & Doris Tananbaum Foundation, Inc.
16 Pleasant Ridge Rd.
Harrison, NY 10528
Contact: Stanley Tananbaum, Secy.

Established in 1962.
Donor(s): Stanley Tananbaum, Century Business Credit Corp.
Financial data (yr. ended 12/31/99): Grants paid, $2,352,581; assets, $3,003,794 (M); gifts received, $128,875; expenditures, $2,405,227; qualifying distributions, $2,334,153.
Limitations: Giving primarily in NY.
Officers: Doris Tananbaum, Pres.; Riki Zuriff, V.P.; Stanley Tananbaum, Secy. and Mgr.
Directors: Bryan Zuriff, Laurence Zuriff.
EIN: 136183100
Codes: FD

32770
Peter B. & Adeline W. Ruffin Foundation, Inc.
240 Madison Ave., Ste 704
New York, NY 10016
Contact: Edward G. McAnaney, Pres.

Established in 1964 in NY.
Financial data (yr. ended 11/30/01): Grants paid, $2,344,000; assets, $38,209,725 (M); expenditures, $2,353,830; qualifying distributions, $2,346,137.
Limitations: Applications not accepted. Giving primarily in CT, Washington, DC, NJ, NY, PA, and VA.
Application information: Contributes only to pre-selected organizations.
Officers and Trustees:* Edward G. McAnaney,* Pres., Treas., and Mgr.; Brian T. McAnaney, Secy.; Sheila K. Kostanecki, Kevin G. McAnaney.
EIN: 136170484
Codes: FD

32771
The Alice Tully Foundation
(Formerly Maya Corporation)
317 Madison Ave., Rm. 1511
New York, NY 10017-5219
Contact: James McGarry, Pres.

Established in 1953.
Donor(s): Alice Tully.‡
Financial data (yr. ended 12/31/01): Grants paid, $2,327,516; assets, $49,779,659 (M); gifts received, $6,714,978; expenditures, $2,647,322; qualifying distributions, $2,361,610.
Limitations: Giving primarily in New York, NY.
Officers and Directors:* James McGarry,* Pres.; Ettie Butler, Secy.; William A. Simon,* Treas.; Robert N. Davies, Maisie Houghton, William T. Powers.
EIN: 136135056
Codes: FD

32772
The Steele-Reese Foundation
32 Washington Sq. W.
New York, NY 10011 (212) 505-2696
Application addresses: 3121 Grantham Way, Lexington, KY 40509, tel.: (859) 263-5313 (for Appalachia), and P.O. Box 249, Alberton, MT 59820, tel.: (406) 722-4564 (for Idaho and Montana)
Contact: William T. Buice III, Tr. (in NY for general matters), Ms. Jane B. Stephenson (for southern Appalachian applicants) or Ms. Jeanne E. Wolverton (for Idaho and Montana)

Trust established in 1955 in NY.
Donor(s): Eleanor Steele Reese,‡ Emmet P. Reese.‡
Financial data (yr. ended 08/31/00): Grants paid, $2,326,200; assets, $53,998,613 (M); expenditures, $2,927,233; qualifying distributions, $2,437,285.
Limitations: Giving primarily in ID, MT, and the Appalachian Mountain region of GA, KY, NC, and TN; scholarship program limited to students from Lemhi and Custer counties, ID.
Publications: Annual report (including application guidelines).
Application information: High school seniors in Lemhi and Custer counties, ID, should apply for scholarships through their schools. Application form not required.
Trustees: William T. Buice III, Patricia F. Davidson, J.P. Morgan & Co. Incorporated.
EIN: 136034763
Codes: FD

32773
Randolph Foundation
(Formerly H. Smith Richardson Charitable Trust)
255 E. 49th St., Ste. 23D
New York, NY 10017 (212) 752-7148
Contact: Heather R. Higgins, Dir.

Trust established in 1976 in NC.
Donor(s): H. Smith Richardson.‡
Financial data (yr. ended 12/31/99): Grants paid, $2,322,755; assets, $82,543,126 (M); expenditures, $6,911,728; qualifying distributions, $2,717,810.
Limitations: Giving limited to the U.S.
Directors: Heather R. Higgins, R. Randolph Richardson, James Q. Wilson.
EIN: 237245123
Codes: FD

32774
The William T. Morris Foundation, Inc.
230 Park Ave., Ste. 622
New York, NY 10169-0622
Contact: Edward A. Antonelli, Pres.

Trust established in 1937; incorporated in 1941 in DE.
Donor(s): William T. Morris.‡
Financial data (yr. ended 06/30/01): Grants paid, $2,315,000; assets, $55,924,424 (M); expenditures, $4,833,063; qualifying distributions, $3,509,920.
Limitations: Applications not accepted. Giving primarily in the northeastern states, especially NY and CT.
Officers and Directors:* Edward A. Antonelli,* Pres.; Wilmot Fitch Wheeler, Jr.,* V.P.; Bruce A. August,* Secy.; Arthur C. Laske, Jr.,* Treas.; E.W. Burns.
EIN: 131600908

32774—NEW YORK

Codes: FD

32775
AOL Time Warner Foundation
(Formerly AOL Foundation, Inc.)
75 Rockefeller Plz.
New York, NY 10019
E-mail: aoltwfoundation@aol.com; *URL:* http://www.aoltimewarnerfoundation.org
Contact: Kirsten Powers

Established in 1997 in VA; name changed in Mar. 2001.
Donor(s): America Online, Inc.
Financial data (yr. ended 12/31/00): Grants paid, $2,311,026; assets, $2,849,076 (M); gifts received, $5,728,971; expenditures, $7,587,610; qualifying distributions, $4,695,524.
Limitations: Giving on a national basis.
Application information: Application form and guidelines available on the foundation's Web site. Application form required.
Officers and Directors:* Steve Case,* Chair.; Kathy Bushkin,* Pres.; Betty Cohen, Gary Credle, Andrew Kaslow, Ken Lerer, Michael Lynton, Henry McGee, Ken Novack, Dick Parsons, Lisa Quiroz, Sylvia Rhone, Tom Rutledge, George Vradenburg III, Audrey Weil.
EIN: 541886827
Codes: CS, FD, CD

32776
The Fisher Brothers Foundation, Inc.
c/o Fisher Brothers
299 Park Ave.
New York, NY 10017

Established in 1981 in NY.
Donor(s): Fisher Brothers, Fisher Park Lane Co., Fisher Capital Assets, and other Fisher Brothers affiliates.
Financial data (yr. ended 12/31/00): Grants paid, $2,304,400; assets, $2,705,558 (M); gifts received, $2,382,804; expenditures, $2,361,392; qualifying distributions, $2,316,241.
Limitations: Applications not accepted. Giving primarily in New York, NY.
Application information: Contributes only to pre-selected organizations.
Directors: Arnold Fisher, Larry Fisher, M. Anthony Fisher, Richard Fisher.
EIN: 133118286
Codes: CS, FD, CD

32777
Jewish Foundation for Education of Women
135 E. 64 St.
New York, NY 10021 (212) 288-3931
FAX: (212) 288-5798; *E-mail:* fdnscholar@aol.com; *URL:* http://www.jfew.org
Contact: Marge Goldwater, Exec. Dir.

Incorporated in 1884 in NY.
Financial data (yr. ended 06/30/02): Grants paid, $2,303,575; assets, $49,821,810 (M); gifts received, $54,481; expenditures, $2,831,946; qualifying distributions, $2,499,676.
Limitations: Giving limited to female students whose permanent residence is within a 50-mile radius of New York City.
Publications: Application guidelines, informational brochure.
Application information: Telephone requests not accepted. Direct applications accepted only for emigres in the health sciences, and emigres pursuing careers in Jewish education programs, and financially needy Jewish women. All other scholarships are offered by institutional referral. Application form required.
Officers and Directors:* Susan J. Schatz,* Chair.; Jean Bronstein,* Pres.; Suzanne H. Keusch,* 1st V.P.; Marcy C. Russo,* V.P.; Jill W. Smith, Secy.; Alan R. Kahn,* Treas.; Marge Goldwater, Exec. Dir.; Jack R. Ackerman, Bernice Block, Alan D. Cohn, Marcia Goldsmith, Neil Grabois, Irving Kahn, Michael S. Katz, Reeva S. Mager, Hon. Ruth Messinger, Marlon H. Spanbock, Charles J. Tanenbaum, James Wood.
EIN: 131860415
Codes: FD, GTI

32778
Soros Fund Charitable Foundation
(Formerly SGM Scholarship Foundation)
888 7th Ave., 33rd Fl.
New York, NY 10106-0011

Established in 1986 in NY.
Donor(s): George Soros, Soros Charitable Foundation, Soros Foundation-Hungary, Centennial Foundation.
Financial data (yr. ended 12/31/01): Grants paid, $2,291,617; assets, $82,417,067 (M); expenditures, $2,471,724; qualifying distributions, $2,295,235.
Limitations: Applications not accepted. Giving primarily in CT, NJ, and NY.
Application information: Contributes only to pre-selected organizations.
Officers and Directors:* Gary Gladstein,* Pres.; Daniel R. Eule,* V.P.; Susanne Quattrochi, Secy.; Peter Streinger, Treas.; Jennifer Ternoey, Treas.; Susan C. Frunzi.
EIN: 133388177
Codes: FD

32779
Lillian Vernon Foundation
c/o Nathan Berkman & Co.
29 Broadway, Ste. 2900
New York, NY 10006-3207

Established in 1995 in CT.
Donor(s): Lillian Vernon.
Financial data (yr. ended 06/30/01): Grants paid, $2,284,110; assets, $2,604,898 (M); gifts received, $745,555; expenditures, $2,376,947; qualifying distributions, $2,274,098.
Limitations: Applications not accepted. Giving primarily in NY.
Application information: Contributes only to pre-selected organizations.
Trustee: Lillian Vernon.
EIN: 223390451
Codes: FD

32780
The George F. Baker Trust
477 Madison Ave., Ste., 1650
New York, NY 10022 (212) 755-1890
FAX: (212) 319-6316; *E-mail:* rocio@bakernye.com
Contact: Miss Rocio Suarez, Exec. Dir.

Trust established in 1937 in NY.
Donor(s): George F. Baker.‡
Financial data (yr. ended 12/31/01): Grants paid, $2,279,800; assets, $20,896,834 (M); expenditures, $3,230,504; qualifying distributions, $2,279,800.
Limitations: Giving primarily in the eastern U.S., with some emphasis on the New York, NY, area.
Publications: Annual report.
Application information: Application form not required.
Officer: Rocio Suarez, Exec. Dir.
Trustees: Anthony K. Baker, George F. Baker III, Kane K. Baker, Citibank, N.A.
EIN: 136056818

Codes: FD, FM

32781
Mariposa Foundation, Inc.
c/o Lewis W. Bernard, Pres.
1221 Ave. of the Americas, 30th Fl.
New York, NY 10020

Established around 1976.
Donor(s): Lewis W. Bernard.
Financial data (yr. ended 11/30/99): Grants paid, $2,279,665; assets, $25,686,210 (M); gifts received, $2,137,969; expenditures, $2,409,005; qualifying distributions, $2,267,116.
Limitations: Applications not accepted. Giving primarily in New York, NY.
Application information: Contributes only to pre-selected organizations.
Officers: Lewis W. Bernard, Pres. and Treas.; Jill V. Bernard, V.P. and Secy.
EIN: 510170409
Codes: FD

32782
PLM Foundation
c/o Eric Kaplan
1285 6th Ave. 21st Fl.
New York, NY 10019

Established in 1996 in NY.
Donor(s): Philip L. Milstein.
Financial data (yr. ended 12/31/00): Grants paid, $2,272,833; assets, $7,602,099 (M); gifts received, $2,341,646; expenditures, $2,276,141; qualifying distributions, $2,270,777.
Limitations: Applications not accepted. Giving primarily in NY.
Application information: Contributes only to pre-selected organizations.
Trustees: Philip L. Milstein, Vivian Milstein.
EIN: 137105558
Codes: FD

32783
The Pollock-Krasner Foundation, Inc.
863 Park Ave.
New York, NY 10021 (212) 517-5400
FAX: (212) 288-2836; *E-mail:* grants@pkf.org; *URL:* http://www.pkf.org
Contact: Caroline Black, Prog. Off.

Established in 1984 in DE.
Donor(s): Lee Krasner.
Financial data (yr. ended 06/30/00): Grants paid, $2,255,700; assets, $66,384,728 (M); expenditures, $3,881,186; qualifying distributions, $3,141,205.
Limitations: Giving on a national and international basis.
Publications: Informational brochure (including application guidelines), annual report, application guidelines.
Application information: Application form required.
Officers and Directors:* Charles C. Bergman,* Chair.; Eugene Victor Thaw,* Pres.; Kerrie Buitrago, Exec. V.P.
EIN: 133255693
Codes: FD, FM, GTI

32784
Drue Heinz Trust
(Formerly H. J. & Drue Heinz Trust)
P.O. Box 68, FDR Station
New York, NY 10150 (212) 371-5757
Contact: Julia V. Shea, Fdn. Mgr.

Established in 1954 in PA.
Financial data (yr. ended 12/31/00): Grants paid, $2,251,761; assets, $39,274,369 (M);

expenditures, $2,369,798; qualifying distributions, $2,310,505.
Limitations: Giving primarily in NY and PA.
Trustees: James F. Dolan, Drue Heinz, Mellon Bank, N.A.
EIN: 256018930
Codes: FD, FM

32785
The Robert Kravis and Kimberly Kravis Foundation
c/o Kohlberg Kravis Roberts & Co.
9 W. 57th St.
New York, NY 10019

Established in 1998 in NY.
Donor(s): Kimberly R. Kravis, Robert S. Kravis.
Financial data (yr. ended 11/30/01): Grants paid, $2,249,560; assets, $49,993,226 (M); expenditures, $2,583,087; qualifying distributions, $1,929,133.
Limitations: Applications not accepted. Giving primarily in NY.
Application information: Contributes only to pre-selected organizations.
Directors: Richard I. Beattie, Kimberly R. Kravis, Robert S. Kravis.
EIN: 134000922
Codes: FD

32786
Richmond County Savings Foundation
900 South Ave., No. 17
Staten Island, NY 10314   (718) 568-3516
Contact: Cesar Claro, Exec. Dir.

Established in 1998 in NY.
Donor(s): Richmond County Financial Corp.
Financial data (yr. ended 12/31/00): Grants paid, $2,235,953; assets, $47,333,377 (M); expenditures, $2,955,849; qualifying distributions, $2,474,319.
Limitations: Giving primarily in Staten Island, NY.
Officer: Cesar J. Claro, Exec. Dir.
Directors: Richard Addeo, Anthony E. Burke, Godfrey H. Carstens, Jr., Edward Cruz, Alfred B. Curtis, Jr., Richard E. Diamond, Robert S. Farrell, William C. Frederick, James L. Kelly, Michael F. Manzulli, Patrick F.X. Nilan, T. Ronald Quinlan, Jr., Maurice K. Shaw.
EIN: 061503051
Codes: CS, FD, CD

32787
The Leo and Karen Gutmann Foundation
c/o Lawrence Putterman
470 West End Ave., 8F
New York, NY 10024

Established in 2001 in NY.
Donor(s): Karen Gutmann.‡
Financial data (yr. ended 12/31/01): Grants paid, $2,229,411; assets, $3,166,168 (M); gifts received, $5,466,500; expenditures, $2,343,818; qualifying distributions, $2,286,615.
Limitations: Applications not accepted. Giving primarily in CT, DE, MA, NJ, and NY.
Application information: Contributes only to pre-selected organizations.
Officers: Lawrence Putterman, Pres.; Constance Lowenthal, V.P.
EIN: 311751468

32788
Leon Black Family Foundation, Inc.
1301 Ave. of the Americas, 38th Fl.
New York, NY 10019-6022

Established in 1997 in DE and NY.
Financial data (yr. ended 12/31/00): Grants paid, $2,227,004; assets, $141,930 (M); gifts received, $1,950,000; expenditures, $2,227,190; qualifying distributions, $2,226,896.
Limitations: Applications not accepted.
Application information: Contributes only to pre-selected organizations.
Officers: Leon D. Black, Pres. and Treas.; Debra R. Black, V.P.-Secy.
Director: Jeffrey Epstein.
EIN: 133947890
Codes: FD

32789
The Carl C. Icahn Foundation
c/o Icahn Assoc. Corp
767 5th Ave., 47th Fl.
New York, NY 10153-0023
Contact: Gail Golden, Secy.-Treas.

Established in 1980 in NY and DE.
Donor(s): Carl C. Icahn.
Financial data (yr. ended 11/30/01): Grants paid, $2,225,650; assets, $12,833,905 (M); expenditures, $2,265,537; qualifying distributions, $2,224,403.
Limitations: Giving primarily in NJ and New York, NY.
Application information: Include brief description of project.
Officers: Carl C. Icahn, Pres.; Gail Golden-Icahn, V.P.
EIN: 133091588
Codes: FD

32790
Geoffrey C. Hughes Foundation, Inc.
c/o Cahill Gordon & Reindel
80 Pine St., Ste. 1736
New York, NY 10005   (212) 701-3400
Contact: John R. Young, Pres.

Established in 1991 in NY.
Donor(s): Geoffrey C. Hughes.‡
Financial data (yr. ended 03/31/02): Grants paid, $2,220,512; assets, $34,106,925 (M); expenditures, $2,481,694; qualifying distributions, $2,285,774.
Application information: Application form not required.
Officers and Directors:* John R. Young,* Pres.; Ursula Cliff,* V.P. and Secy.; Walter C. Cliff,* V.P. and Treas.; Mary K. Young,* V.P.; June McCandless.
EIN: 133622255
Codes: FD

32791
The Generoso Pope Foundation
(Formerly The Pope Foundation)
700 White Plains Rd., Ste. 315
Scarsdale, NY 10583
Contact: Anthony Pope, Pres.

Incorporated in 1947 in NY.
Donor(s): Generoso Pope.‡
Financial data (yr. ended 12/31/99): Grants paid, $2,215,655; assets, $54,076,449 (M); expenditures, $2,779,151; qualifying distributions, $2,543,109.
Limitations: Giving primarily in the metropolitan New York, NY, area, including Westchester County.
Application information: Application form required for the foundation's Awards for the Arts program.
Officer: Anthony Pope, Pres.
EIN: 136096193
Codes: FD

32792
The CIT Group Foundation, Inc.
c/o The CIT Group, Inc.
1211 Ave. of the Americas
New York, NY 10036
NJ tel.: (973) 740-5638; *FAX:* (973) 740-5424
Contact: Corinne Taylor

Incorporated in 1955 in NY.
Donor(s): The CIT Group, Inc., and its subsidiaries, Tyco Capital Corp., CIT Group Inc.
Financial data (yr. ended 12/31/00): Grants paid, $2,209,917; assets, $14,172 (M); gifts received, $2,150,000; expenditures, $2,209,917; qualifying distributions, $2,209,917.
Limitations: Giving limited to areas of company operations.
Directors: Albert R. Gamper, Jr., J.M. Leone, S.P. Mitchell, William M. O'Grady, Thomas J. O'Rourke, E.D. Stein.
EIN: 136083856
Codes: CS, TN, CD, GTI

32793
J. T. Tai & Company Foundation, Inc.
18 E. 67th St.
New York, NY 10021
Contact: Mr. Yuan Tai, Treas.

Incorporated in 1983 in DE.
Donor(s): Jun Tsei Tai, J.T. Tai & Co.
Financial data (yr. ended 12/31/00): Grants paid, $2,204,471; assets, $37,079,592 (M); expenditures, $2,323,140; qualifying distributions, $2,177,897.
Limitations: Applications not accepted. Giving on a national basis.
Application information: Contributes only to pre-selected organizations.
Officers and Director:* F. Richard Hsu, Pres.; Y.C. Chen, Secy.; Yuan Tai,* Treas.
EIN: 133157279
Codes: FD, GTI

32794
Stella and Charles Guttman Foundation, Inc.
445 Park Ave., 19th Fl.
New York, NY 10022   (212) 371-7082
FAX: (212) 371-8936; *E-mail:* info@guttmanfdn.org; *URL:* http://fdncenter.org/grantmaker/guttman
Contact: Elizabeth Olofson, Exec. Dir.

Incorporated in 1959 in NY.
Donor(s): Charles Guttman,‡ Stella Guttman.‡
Financial data (yr. ended 12/31/00): Grants paid, $2,198,150; assets, $50,937,066 (M); expenditures, $3,074,328; qualifying distributions, $2,445,372.
Limitations: Giving primarily in the metropolitan New York, NY, area.
Publications: Grants list, informational brochure (including application guidelines), multi-year report.
Application information: Application form not required.
Officers and Directors:* Peter A. Herbert,* Pres.; Edgar H. Brenner,* V.P.; Ernest Rubenstein,* Secy.; Robert S. Gassman,* Treas.; Elizabeth Olofson, Exec. Dir.; Charles S. Brenner, Sonia Rosenberg.
EIN: 136103039
Codes: FD

32795
Mary J. Hutchins Foundation, Inc.
45 John St., Rm. 1212
New York, NY 10038
Contact: Richard J. Mirabella, Secy.-Treas.

Incorporated in 1935 in NY.

32795—NEW YORK

Donor(s): Mary J. Hutchins,‡ Caspar J. Voorhis,‡ Waldo H. Hutchins, Jr.‡
Financial data (yr. ended 12/31/00): Grants paid, $2,194,590; assets, $40,571,935 (M); gifts received, $744,562; expenditures, $2,469,647; qualifying distributions, $2,253,479.
Limitations: Applications not accepted. Giving primarily in the New York, NY, area.
Officers and Directors:* Waldo Hutchins III,* Pres.; Richard J. Mirabella,* V.P. and Secy.-Treas.; Anne R. Hutchins,* V.P.; Elizabeth E. Hutchins,* V.P.; John N. Huwer,* V.P.; Richard G. Mulholland,* V.P.; Sidney S. Whelan, Jr., V.P.
EIN: 136083578
Codes: FD, GTI

32796
Frances & Benjamin Benenson Foundation, Inc.
708 3rd Ave., 28th Fl.
New York, NY 10017-4298 (212) 867-0990
Contact: Charles B. Benenson, Pres.

Established in 1983 in NY.
Donor(s): Charles B. Benenson.
Financial data (yr. ended 11/30/00): Grants paid, $2,191,156; assets, $38,116,077 (M); gifts received, $2,050,000; expenditures, $2,207,588; qualifying distributions, $2,184,769.
Officers: Charles B. Benenson, Pres.; Anthony J. DiNome, Secy.-Treas.
Directors: Bruce W. Benenson, Frederick C. Benenson, Lawrence B. Benenson.
EIN: 133267113
Codes: FD

32797
Adolph & Ruth Schnurmacher Foundation, Inc.
155 E. 55th St., Ste. 302A
New York, NY 10002 (212) 838-7766
Contact: Ira J. Weinstein, Pres.

Established in 1977 in NY.
Donor(s): Adolph Schnurmacher,‡ Ruth Schnurmacher.‡
Financial data (yr. ended 12/31/01): Grants paid, $2,188,738; assets, $39,120,781 (M); gifts received, $750,000; expenditures, $2,866,960; qualifying distributions, $2,531,518.
Limitations: Giving on a national basis, with emphasis on CA, CT, and NY.
Application information: Application form not required.
Officers and Trustees:* Ira J. Weinstein,* Pres.; Fred Plotkin,* Secy.; Barbara Packer, Amanda Plotkin, Carolyn Plotkin, Janet Plotkin, Andrea Weinstein, Peter Weinstein.
EIN: 132938935
Codes: FD

32798
The Marvin and Donna Schwartz Foundation
c/o Neuberger & Berman
605 3rd Ave.
New York, NY 10158-3698

Established in 1997 in NY.
Donor(s): Donna Schwartz, Marvin C. Schwartz.
Financial data (yr. ended 04/30/00): Grants paid, $2,175,915; assets, $44,527,744 (M); expenditures, $2,689,368; qualifying distributions, $2,166,849.
Limitations: Applications not accepted.
Application information: Contributes only to pre-selected organizations.
Trustees: Donna Schwartz, Marvin C. Schwartz.
EIN: 137114848
Codes: FD

32799
Institute for the Study of Aging, Inc.
767 5th Ave., Ste. 4600
New York, NY 10153 (212) 572-4086
FAX: 9212) 572-4094; *E-mail:* tlee@rslmgmt.com; *URL:* http://www.aging-institute.org
Contact: Tanya Lee, Grants Mgr.

Established in 1998 in NY.
Financial data (yr. ended 12/31/00): Grants paid, $2,159,184; assets, $5,752,196 (M); gifts received, $7,271,806; expenditures, $3,668,476; qualifying distributions, $4,897,670; giving activities include $3,473,291 for programs.
Limitations: Giving on a national and international basis.
Publications: Annual report, financial statement, grants list, occasional report, informational brochure (including application guidelines).
Application information: Application form required.
Officers: Howard M. Fillit, M.D., Exec. Dir.; Susan Reynolds Foley, Sr. Oper. Off.
Directors: Estee Lauder, Hon. Dir.; Robert N. Butler, M.D., Lanny Edelsohn, M.D., Julia P. Gregory, Leonard A. Lauder, Ronald S. Lauder.
EIN: 134024149
Codes: FD

32800
Clarence and Anne Dillon Dunwalke Trust
1330 Ave. of the Americas, 27th Fl.
New York, NY 10019
Contact: Crosby R. Smith, Tr.

Trust established in 1969 in NY.
Donor(s): Clarence Dillon.‡
Financial data (yr. ended 06/30/01): Grants paid, $2,121,050; assets, $38,420,679 (M); expenditures, $2,529,029; qualifying distributions, $2,147,973.
Limitations: Applications not accepted. Giving primarily in FL, NJ and NY.
Application information: Contributes only to pre-selected organizations.
Officer and Trustees:* Phyllis Dillon Collins,* Chair.; Alexandra F. Allen, Andrew D. Allen, Christine Allen, Christopher D. Allen, Nicholas E. Allen, Philip D. Allen, Theodore Caplow, Douglas Collins, Frances Collins, Mark M. Collins, Jr., C. Douglas Dillon, Dorothy Dillon Eweson, Joan M. Frost, Robert Luxembourg, David H. Peipers, Crosby R. Smith, Martin C. Zetterberg.
EIN: 237043773
Codes: FD

32801
Emily Davie and Joseph S. Kornfeld Foundation
41 Schermerhorn St., Ste. 208
Brooklyn, NY 11201 (718) 624-7969
FAX: (718) 834-1204; *E-mail:* office@kornfeldfdn.org; *URL:* http://fdncenter.org/grantmaker/kornfeld
Contact: Bobye G. List, Exec. Dir.

Established in 1979.
Donor(s): Emily Davie Kornfeld.‡
Financial data (yr. ended 12/31/00): Grants paid, $2,113,287; assets, $43,193,243 (M); expenditures, $2,664,198; qualifying distributions, $2,323,057.
Limitations: Giving limited to the continental U.S., with emphasis on New York, NY, for educational grants.
Publications: Annual report, application guidelines.
Application information: Application form not required.

Officers and Directors:* Christopher C. Angell,* Pres.; Karen R. Berry, Secy.; Morris S. Roberts,* Treas.; Bobye G. List, Exec. Dir.; Peter E. Bokor, Emme L. Deland, Patricia Llosa, Barry Smith.
EIN: 133042360
Codes: FD

32802
The William and Mary Greve Foundation, Inc.
630 5th Ave., Ste. 1750
New York, NY 10111 (212) 307-7850
Contact: Anthony C.M. Kiser, Pres.

Incorporated in 1964 in NY.
Donor(s): Mary P. Greve.‡
Financial data (yr. ended 12/31/01): Grants paid, $2,113,155; assets, $41,813,754 (M); expenditures, $2,882,435; qualifying distributions, $2,358,473.
Limitations: Applications not accepted.
Officers and Directors:* John W. Kiser III,* Chair.; Anthony C.M. Kiser,* Pres.; Victoria B. Bjorklund, Secy.; Robert E. Cohen, James W. Sykes, Jr.
EIN: 136020724
Codes: FD

32803
The de Kay Foundation
c/o Morgan Guaranty Trust of NY
1 Chase Manhattan Plz., 5th Fl.
New York, NY 10081
Application address: 1211 6th Ave., 34th Fl., New York, NY 10036
Contact: John Boncada

Trust established in 1967 in CT.
Donor(s): Helen M. de Kay.‡
Financial data (yr. ended 02/28/01): Grants paid, $2,113,077; assets, $44,784,429 (M); expenditures, $2,525,915; qualifying distributions, $2,303,873.
Limitations: Giving limited to CT, NJ, and NY.
Application information: Direct submissions from individuals not considered or acknowledged. Application form required.
Trustees: The Chase Manhattan Bank, N.A., Morgan Guaranty Trust Co.
EIN: 136203234
Codes: FD, GTI

32804
Anna Maria & Stephen Kellen Foundation, Inc.
1345 Ave. of the Americas, 44th Fl.
New York, NY 10105

Established in 1984.
Donor(s): Stephen M. Kellen, Anna-Maria Kellen.
Financial data (yr. ended 04/30/00): Grants paid, $2,109,535; assets, $42,985,053 (M); gifts received, $25,719,657; expenditures, $2,130,602; qualifying distributions, $2,118,078.
Limitations: Applications not accepted. Giving primarily in New York, NY.
Application information: Contributes only to pre-selected organizations.
Officers and Directors:* Stephen M. Kellen,* Chair.; Anna-Maria Kellen,* Pres.; Marina K. French,* V.P.; Michael Kellen,* Secy.-Treas.
EIN: 133173593
Codes: FD

32805
The Eckburg Foundation
c/o U.S. Trust
114 W. 47th St.
New York, NY 10036 (212) 852-3834

Established in 1995 in PA.
Donor(s): Richard Eckburg, Montie Eckburg.
Financial data (yr. ended 12/31/00): Grants paid, $2,088,450; assets, $73,893 (M); gifts received,

$1,844,029; expenditures, $2,135,950; qualifying distributions, $2,071,555.
Limitations: Applications not accepted. Giving on a national basis.
Application information: Unsolicited requests for funds not accepted.
Officers: Richard Eckburg, Pres.; Montie Eckburg, V.P.
EIN: 237806132
Codes: FD

32806
The Morton Foundation, Inc.
c/o Rosalind Davidowitz
44 Wall St., 2nd Fl.
New York, NY 10005

Established in 1961.
Donor(s): J. Morton Davis.
Financial data (yr. ended 12/31/00): Grants paid, $2,074,129; assets, $2,931,617 (M); expenditures, $2,089,234; qualifying distributions, $2,070,163.
Limitations: Applications not accepted. Giving primarily in NY.
Application information: Contributes only to pre-selected organizations.
Officers and Directors:* Rosalind Davidowitz,* Pres. and Treas.; Ruki Renov,* Secy.; Esther Stahler,* Treas.
EIN: 136107817
Codes: FD

32807
Dobkin Family Foundation
c/o BCRS Assoc., LLC
100 Wall St., 11th Fl.
New York, NY 10005

Established in 1984 in NY.
Donor(s): Eric S. Dobkin.
Financial data (yr. ended 03/31/01): Grants paid, $2,073,232; assets, $23,061,328 (M); gifts received, $14,123,325; expenditures, $3,035,439; qualifying distributions, $2,215,242.
Limitations: Applications not accepted. Giving primarily in New York, NY.
Application information: Contributes only to pre-selected organizations.
Trustees: Barbara Dobkin, Eric S. Dobkin, Jessica L. Dobkin, Rachel L. Dobkin.
EIN: 133248042
Codes: FD

32808
A. C. Israel Foundation, Inc.
707 Westchester Ave., Ste. 405
White Plains, NY 10604-3102
Contact: Barry W. Gray, V.P.

Incorporated in 1967 in DE as successor to the foundation of the same name incorporated in 1946 in NY.
Donor(s): Adrian C. Israel,‡ Adrian & James, Inc.
Financial data (yr. ended 12/31/00): Grants paid, $2,069,420; assets, $36,873,313 (M); expenditures, $2,194,562; qualifying distributions, $2,045,964.
Limitations: Applications not accepted. Giving primarily in CT, MA, and NY.
Application information: Contributes only to pre-selected organizations.
Officers and Directors:* Thomas C. Israel,* Pres.; Barry W. Gray,* V.P.; Jay M. Howard, Secy.; Stanley D. Aberman, Treas.
EIN: 516021414
Codes: FD

32809
Norman Foundation, Inc.
147 E. 48th St.
New York, NY 10017 (212) 230-9830
FAX: (212) 230-9849; *URL:* http://www.normanfdn.org
Contact: Andrew E. Norman, Chair.

Incorporated in 1935 in NY.
Donor(s): Aaron E. Norman,‡ and directors of the foundation.
Financial data (yr. ended 12/31/99): Grants paid, $2,051,702; assets, $32,982,983 (M); expenditures, $2,554,102; qualifying distributions, $2,337,843.
Limitations: Giving on a national basis.
Application information: Accepts NYRAG Common Application Form. Updated guidelines available on web site. Application form not required.
Officers and Directors:* Andrew E. Norman,* Chair.; Frank A. Weil,* Pres.; Lucinda W. Bunnen,* V.P.; William S. Weil,* Treas.; Robert L. Bunnen, Jr., Andrew D. Franklin, Deborah W. Harrington, and 12 additional directors.
EIN: 131862694
Codes: FD

32810
Herman Goldman Foundation
61 Broadway, 18th Fl.
New York, NY 10006 (212) 797-9090
Contact: Richard K. Baron, Exec. Dir.

Incorporated in 1943 in NY.
Donor(s): Herman Goldman.‡
Financial data (yr. ended 02/28/00): Grants paid, $2,046,400; assets, $40,539,451 (M); expenditures, $2,988,140; qualifying distributions, $2,471,391.
Limitations: Giving primarily in the metropolitan New York, NY, area.
Publications: Annual report (including application guidelines).
Application information: Application form not required.
Officers and Directors:* David A. Brauner,* Pres.; Roy M. Sparber,* V.P.; David R. Kay,* Secy.; Alan Nisselson,* Treas.; Richard K. Baron, Exec. Dir.; Mel P. Barkan, Jules M. Baron, Robert N. Davies, Michael L. Goldstein, Alan Michigan, Elias Rosenzweig, Gail Schneider, Christopher C. Schwabacher, Howard L. Simon, Norman H. Sparber.
EIN: 136066039
Codes: FD

32811
The Louis and Rachel Rudin Foundation, Inc.
345 Park Ave.
New York, NY 10154 (212) 407-2512
Contact: Robin Dubin, Admin. and Prog. Dir.

Incorporated in 1968 in NY.
Financial data (yr. ended 12/31/00): Grants paid, $2,043,780; assets, $36,779,444 (M); expenditures, $3,372,916; qualifying distributions, $2,153,366.
Limitations: Giving primarily in New York, NY.
Officers and Directors:* Jack Rudin,* Chair.; Beth Rudin DeWoody,* Pres.; Stephen Lewin,* Exec. V.P.; John Lewin, V.P.; Eric C. Rudin,* V.P.; William C. Rudin,* V.P.; Jeffrey Steinman,* V.P.
EIN: 237039549
Codes: FD

32812
Josephine Bay Paul and C. Michael Paul Foundation, Inc.
P.O. Box 20218
Park W. Finance Sta.
New York, NY 10025 (212) 932-0408
FAX: (212) 932-0316
Contact: Frederick Bay, Chair. and Exec. Dir.

Incorporated in 1962 in NY.
Donor(s): Josephine Bay Paul.‡
Financial data (yr. ended 12/31/01): Grants paid, $2,039,850; assets, $50,418,380 (M); expenditures, $2,911,309; qualifying distributions, $2,458,462.
Limitations: Giving on a national basis.
Publications: Program policy statement.
Application information: Application form not required.
Officers and Directors:* Frederick Bay,* Chair. and Exec. Dir.; Synnova B. Hayes,* Pres. and Treas.; Hans A. Ege,* V.P.; Daniel A. Demarest,* Secy.; Corinne Steel.
EIN: 131991717
Codes: FD, GTI

32813
Milstein Family Foundation, Inc.
1271 Ave. of the Americas, Ste. 4200
New York, NY 10020 (212) 708-0800

Established in 1975 in NY.
Donor(s): Builtland Partners, Seymour Milstein,‡ Paul Milstein, Gloria M. Flanzer.
Financial data (yr. ended 09/30/00): Grants paid, $2,028,211; assets, $15,253,367 (M); gifts received, $3,000,000; expenditures, $2,041,308; qualifying distributions, $2,029,036.
Limitations: Giving primarily in NY.
Officers and Directors:* Paul Milstein,* Chair.; Philip L. Milstein,* Secy.-Treas.; Roslyn M. Meyer, Constance Milstein, Edward L. Milstein, Howard P. Milstein, Barbara M. Zalaznick.
EIN: 510190133
Codes: FD, FM

32814
The Zilkha Foundation, Inc.
767 5th Ave.
New York, NY 10153-0002 (212) 758-7750
Contact: Ezra K. Zilkha, Pres.

Incorporated in 1948 in NY.
Donor(s): Zilkha & Sons, Inc., Ezra K. Zilkha.
Financial data (yr. ended 08/31/01): Grants paid, $2,022,921; assets, $3,420,244 (M); gifts received, $2,281,817; expenditures, $2,046,780; qualifying distributions, $2,021,616.
Limitations: Applications not accepted. Giving on a national basis.
Application information: Grants awarded largely at the initiative of the officers.
Officers: Ezra K. Zilkha, Pres. and Treas.; Cecile E. Zilkha, V.P. and Secy.
EIN: 136090739
Codes: CS, FD, CD

32815
SI Bank & Trust Foundation
(Formerly SISB Community Foundation)
81 Water St.
Staten Island, NY 10304 (718) 556-1381
Application address: P.O. Box 41275, Staten Island, NY 10304; FAX: (718) 556-1732; E-mail: dubovskyb@SISB.com; URL: http://www.sibk.com/42557.html
Contact: Betsy Dubovsky, Exec. Dir.

Established in 1998 in DE and NY.
Donor(s): Staten Island Savings Bank, SI Bank & Trust.

32815—NEW YORK

Financial data (yr. ended 06/30/01): Grants paid, $2,005,966; assets, $53,756,266 (M); expenditures, $2,224,845; qualifying distributions, $2,121,912.
Limitations: Giving primarily in Staten Island, NY; some giving also in Brooklyn and Manhattan, NY.
Publications: Application guidelines, biennial report.
Application information: Application form required.
Officers and Directors:* Harry P. Doherty,* Chair. and Pres.; Allan Weissglass,* V.P.; Patricia Villani,* Secy.; John R. Morris,* Treas.; Elizabeth Dubovsky,* Exec. Dir.; Arthur W. Decker, Alice B. Diamond, John G. Hall, Dennis P. Kelleher.
EIN: 133993115
Codes: CS, FD, CD

32816
Sue and Edgar Wachenheim Foundation
3 Manhattanville Rd.
Purchase, NY 10577-2116
Contact: Edgar Wachenheim III, Pres.

Established in 1969 in NY.
Donor(s): Sue W. Wachenheim, Edgar Wachenheim III.
Financial data (yr. ended 10/31/01): Grants paid, $2,005,675; assets, $36,535,886 (M); gifts received, $1,056,247; expenditures, $2,127,351; qualifying distributions, $1,894,013.
Limitations: Applications not accepted. Giving primarily in NY.
Application information: Contributes only to pre-selected organizations.
Officers and Directors:* Edgar Wachenheim III,* Pres.; Sue W. Wachenheim, Exec. V.P.; Kenneth L. Wallach, Secy.; Irwin Markow, Treas.; Ira D. Wallach.
EIN: 237011002
Codes: FD

32817
The GreenPoint Foundation, Inc.
90 Park Ave., 4th Fl.
New York, NY 10016-1303 (212) 834-1215
FAX: (212) 834-1406; E-mail: gperry@greenpoint.com; URL: http://www.greenpoint.com
Scholarship application address: c/o GreenPoint Achievers Scholarship Prog., Citizens' Scholarship Foundation of America, Inc., 1505 Riverview Rd., P.O. Box 297, St. Peter, MN 56082, tel.: (507) 931-1682
Contact: Gwen Perry, V.P. and Fdn. Mgr.

Established in 1994 in NY.
Donor(s): GreenPoint Bank.
Financial data (yr. ended 09/30/00): Grants paid, $2,001,321; assets, $49,807,395 (M); gifts received, $17,551,000; expenditures, $2,628,261; qualifying distributions, $2,445,895.
Limitations: Giving primarily in NY.
Application information: Application form required for scholarships.
Officers and Directors:* Thomas S. Johnson,* Pres.; Gwen Perry, V.P. and Fdn. Mgr.; Bernadette Arias, V.P.; Martin S. Dash, V.P.; Howard Bluver, Secy.; Richard Humphrey, Treas.; Calvin Butts, Ann Reynolds, Bishop Joseph Sullivan.
EIN: 113276603
Codes: CS, FD, CD

32818
ZIIZ, Inc.
c/o Hertz, Herson & Co., LLP
2 Park Ave., Ste. 1500
New York, NY 10016

Established in 2000 in DE and NY.
Financial data (yr. ended 03/31/01): Grants paid, $2,000,018; assets, $38,369,559 (M); gifts received, $4,000,036; expenditures, $2,016,399; qualifying distributions, $6,381.
Limitations: Applications not accepted. Giving primarily in Jenkintown, PA.
Application information: Contributes only to pre-selected organizations.
Officers and Directors:* Bella Wexner,* Pres.; Susan Wexner,* Secy.-Treas.; Bernard Agus.
EIN: 134031038
Codes: FD

32819
HKH Foundation
521 5th Ave., Ste. 1612
New York, NY 10175-1699
E-mail: hkh@hkhfdn.org; URL: http://www.hkhfdn.org
Contact: Harriet Barlow

Foundation established in 1980 in NY.
Financial data (yr. ended 12/31/01): Grants paid, $1,991,032; assets, $35,798,575 (M); expenditures, $2,500,998; qualifying distributions, $1,991,032; giving activities include $125,000 for loans.
Limitations: Applications not accepted. Giving limited to the U.S.
Application information: Unsolicited requests for funds not accepted.
EIN: 136784950
Codes: FD, FM

32820
William Bingham 2nd Betterment Fund
c/o U.S. Trust
114 W. 47th St.
New York, NY 10036
FAX: (212) 852-3377; Application address: 330 Madison Ave., Rm. 3500, New York, NY 10017
Contact: Linda Franciscovich, Sr. V.P., U.S. Trust

Financial data (yr. ended 12/31/00): Grants paid, $1,989,775; assets, $43,615,890 (M); expenditures, $2,689,050; qualifying distributions, $2,278,224.
Limitations: Giving limited to ME.
Application information: Application form not required.
Trustees: William P. Clough, Carol Berg Geist, William M. Throop, Jr., William Winship, Carolyn S. Wollen, U.S. Trust.
EIN: 136072625
Codes: FD

32821
Tomorrow Foundation
650 Madison Ave.
New York, NY 10022

Established in 1997 in NY.
Donor(s): Robert F.X. Sillerman, Laura Baudo Sillerman.
Financial data (yr. ended 12/31/00): Grants paid, $1,985,535; assets, $25,928,068 (M); gifts received, $4,900,000; expenditures, $2,392,651; qualifying distributions, $1,985,816.
Limitations: Applications not accepted. Giving primarily in NY.
Application information: Contributes only to pre-selected organizations.
Officers and Directors:* Laura Baudo Sillerman,* Pres.; Robert F.X. Sillerman,* V.P. and Treas.; John Coughlan, Secy.; Richard A. Liese, Secy.; Mitchell Nelson.
EIN: 133930172
Codes: FD

32822
Ann L. Bronfman Foundation
c/o M.R. Weiser & Co., LLP
135 W. 50th St., 12th Fl.
New York, NY 10020-1299

Established in 1958.
Donor(s): Ann L. Bronfman.
Financial data (yr. ended 07/31/01): Grants paid, $1,968,500; assets, $23,984,400 (M); expenditures, $2,104,023; qualifying distributions, $1,966,916.
Limitations: Applications not accepted. Giving primarily in Washington, DC, and New York, NY.
Application information: Contributes only to pre-selected organizations.
Officers: Ann L. Bronfman, Pres.; Ron Stein, Secy.
EIN: 136085595
Codes: FD

32823
Georges Lurcy Charitable and Educational Trust
125 W. 55th St.
New York, NY 10019
Contact: Seth E. Frank, Tr.

Established in 1985.
Donor(s): Georges Lurcy.‡
Financial data (yr. ended 06/30/00): Grants paid, $1,968,100; assets, $34,995,748 (M); expenditures, $2,351,585; qualifying distributions, $2,107,496.
Limitations: Giving to residents of the U.S. and France.
Application information: Fellowship applicants from America must be recommended by their universities; applicants from France must apply to the Franco-American Commission for Educational Exchange. Applicants cannot apply directly to the foundation.
Trustees: Alan S. Bernstein, Daniel L. Bernstein, Georges Lurcy Bernstein, Seth E. Frank.
EIN: 136372044
Codes: FD, GTI

32824
John D. and Doreen Miller Foundation
65 Hilton Ave.
Garden City, NY 11530-1342

Established in 1996 in NY.
Donor(s): Doreen D. Miller, John D. Miller.
Financial data (yr. ended 09/30/00): Grants paid, $1,965,175; assets, $12,232,184 (M); gifts received, $10,800,000; expenditures, $872,924; qualifying distributions, $1,946,520.
Limitations: Applications not accepted. Giving primarily in CA and NY.
Application information: Contributes only to pre-selected organizations.
Trustees: Doreen D. Miller, John D. Miller.
EIN: 680392078
Codes: FD

32825
Henrietta B. & Frederick H. Bugher Foundation
(also known as Bugher Foundation)
c/o Davis, Polk and Wardwell.
450 Lexington Ave.
New York, NY 10017
Application Address: P.O. Box 226, Southfield, MA 01259
Contact: Daniel N. Adams, Tr.

Established in 1961 in DC.
Donor(s): Frederick McLean Bugher.‡
Financial data (yr. ended 08/30/00): Grants paid, $1,961,900; assets, $43,639,494 (M); expenditures, $2,636,198; qualifying distributions, $2,041,335.
Limitations: Giving on a national basis.

Application information: Applications should follow the format of the application used by the National Institute of Health.
Trustees: Camilla Adams, D. Nelson Adams, Daniel N. Adams, Jr., Robert A. Robinson, Gayllis Ward.
EIN: 526034266
Codes: FD

32826
Ramapo Trust
126 E. 56th St., 10th Fl.
New York, NY 10022 (212) 308-7355
E-mail: BkdlFdn@aol.com; URL: http://www.ewol.com
Contact: Prog. Off. by telephone, or Stephen L. Schwartz, Tr., by mail

Trust established in 1973 in NY.
Donor(s): Henry L. Schwartz,‡ Montebello Trust.
Financial data (yr. ended 06/30/00): Grants paid, $1,961,879; assets, $76,472,728 (M); expenditures, $3,597,373; qualifying distributions, $2,945,588.
Publications: Application guidelines.
Application information: Application form not required.
Trustees: Arthur Norman Field, Karen Schwartz Hart, Andrew M. Schreier, William Schreier, Stephen L. Schwartz, Rebecca Shaffer, Mary Ann Van Clief.
EIN: 136594279
Codes: FD

32827
The KeySpan Foundation
175 E. Old Country Rd.
Hicksville, NY 11801 (516) 545-6100
URL: http://www.keyspanenergy.com/community/index.cfm
Contact: David M. Okorn, Exec. Dir.

Established in 1998 in NY.
Donor(s): MarketSpan Corp., KeySpan Corp.
Financial data (yr. ended 12/31/00): Grants paid, $1,959,500; assets, $29,249,561 (M); gifts received, $10,000,000; expenditures, $2,308,916; qualifying distributions, $1,971,945.
Limitations: Giving primarily in Brooklyn, Queens, Staten Island, and Nassau and Suffolk counties, NY. Some giving also internationally in areas of company operations.
Publications: Annual report, application guidelines.
Application information: The foundation accepts the New York Area Common Application Form. Application guidelines available on foundation Web site. Application form not required.
Officers and Directors:* Vicki Fuller,* Chair.; Colin Watson,* V.P.; Ronald Jendras, Treas.; David Okorn, Exec. Dir.; Donald Elliot, Brian McCaffrey, Basil Paterson, Maurice Shaw, Diana Taylor.
EIN: 113466416
Codes: CS, FD, CD

32828
The Woodcock Foundation
c/o Rock & Co.
30 Rockefeller Plz., Rm. 5600
New York, NY 10112
Contact: Penny Willgerodt

Established in 1988 in NY.
Donor(s): Polly Guth, John H.J. Guth.
Financial data (yr. ended 11/30/01): Grants paid, $1,955,543; assets, $42,134,997 (M); expenditures, $2,988,220; qualifying distributions, $1,955,543.
Limitations: Giving primarily in NY.
Application information: Application form not required.
Trustees: John H.J. Guth, Polly Guth, Virginia Montgomery, Herschel Post, Richard T. Watson.
EIN: 341606085
Codes: FD

32829
The Whittemore Foundation
c/o Frederick B. Whittemore, Morgan Stanley and Co.
1221 Ave. of the Americas, 30th Fl.
New York, NY 10020

Established in 1988 in NY.
Donor(s): Frederick B. Whittemore.
Financial data (yr. ended 12/31/00): Grants paid, $1,953,800; assets, $7,419,824 (M); gifts received, $2,678; expenditures, $2,029,809; qualifying distributions, $1,953,800.
Limitations: Applications not accepted. Giving primarily in CT and NH.
Application information: Contributes only to pre-selected organizations.
Officers and Trustees:* Frederick B. Whittemore,* Pres.; Edward B. Whittemore,* V.P.; Lawrence F. Whittemore,* V.P.
EIN: 133527578
Codes: FD

32830
The Bobolink Foundation
(Formerly Henry M. & Wendy J. Paulson, Jr. Foundation)
85 Broad St., Tax Dept.
New York, NY 10004

Established in 1985 in IL.
Donor(s): Henry M. Paulson, Jr., Goldman Sachs and Co.
Financial data (yr. ended 03/31/01): Grants paid, $1,948,500; assets, $18,181,242 (M); gifts received, $3,708,995; expenditures, $2,205,825; qualifying distributions, $1,952,516.
Limitations: Applications not accepted. Giving on a national basis, with some emphasis on New York, NY, Washington, DC, Arlington, VA, and Boston, MA.
Application information: Contributes only to pre-selected organizations.
Trustees: Amanda Clark Paulson, Henry M. Paulson, Jr., Henry Merritt Paulson III, Wendy J. Paulson.
EIN: 942988627
Codes: FD

32831
Robinson-Broadhurst Foundation, Inc.
101 Main St.
P.O. Box 160
Stamford, NY 12167-0160 (607) 652-2508
FAX: (607) 652-2453; E-mail: rbfi@dmcom.net
Contact: Charles K. McKenzie, Pres. and Exec. Dir.

Established in 1984 in NY.
Donor(s): Anna Broadhurst,‡ R. Avery Robinson,‡ Winnie M. Robinson.‡
Financial data (yr. ended 04/30/02): Grants paid, $1,947,232; assets, $49,417,830 (M); expenditures, $2,433,362; qualifying distributions, $2,106,365.
Limitations: Giving limited to Winchendon, MA; and Stamford and Worcester, NY.
Application information: Application form required.
Officers and Trustees:* Charles K. McKenzie,* Pres. and Exec. Dir.; Martin A. Parks,* V.P.; Ralph Beisler,* Secy.; Ernest P. Fletcher, Jr.,* Treas.; William H. Lister.
EIN: 222558699
Codes: FD

32832
Marjorie & Clarence E. Unterberg Foundation, Inc.
c/o C.E. Unterberg Towbin
350 Madison Ave., 9th Fl.
New York, NY 10017

Established in 1994 in NY.
Donor(s): Mary A. Debare, Thomas I. Unterberg.
Financial data (yr. ended 12/31/00): Grants paid, $1,946,250; assets, $14,174,940 (M); gifts received, $6,143,750; expenditures, $2,034,757; qualifying distributions, $1,858,445.
Limitations: Applications not accepted. Giving primarily in NJ and NY.
Application information: Contributes only to pre-selected organizations.
Officers: Thomas I. Unterberg, Pres.; Mary A. Debare, V.P. and Secy.; Andrew Arno, Treas.
EIN: 133792809
Codes: FD

32833
Hugoton Foundation
900 Park Ave., Ste. 17E
New York, NY 10021 (212) 734-5447
Contact: Joan K. Stout, Pres.

Established in 1981 in DE.
Donor(s): Wallace Gilroy.‡
Financial data (yr. ended 12/31/01): Grants paid, $1,941,100; assets, $41,234,974 (M); expenditures, $2,184,099; qualifying distributions, $2,100,657.
Limitations: Giving primarily in Miami, FL, and New York, NY.
Officers and Directors:* Joan K. Stout,* Pres.; Ray E. Stout III, V.P.; Joan M. Stout,* Secy.; Jean C. Stout,* Treas.; Frank S. Fejes, John K. Stout.
EIN: 341351062
Codes: FD

32834
Dynamic Strategies Research Foundation, Inc.
c/o Landau, Arnold & Fusco
85 E. Hoffman Ave.
Lindenhurst, NY 11757
Contact: Ethel R. Wells, Tr.

Established in 1967 in NY.
Donor(s): Ethel R. Wells.
Financial data (yr. ended 08/31/01): Grants paid, $1,939,955; assets, $3,572,416 (M); gifts received, $6,334,871; expenditures, $1,940,469; qualifying distributions, $1,939,955.
Limitations: Applications not accepted. Giving on a national basis.
Publications: Annual report, financial statement.
Application information: Contributes only to pre-selected organizations.
Trustee: Ethel R. Wells.
EIN: 116103324
Codes: FD

32835
The Kenneth & Lillian Cayre Foundation, Inc.
16 E. 40th St.
New York, NY 10016 (212) 951-3007
Contact: Kenneth Cayre, Pres.

Established in 1993 in DE.
Donor(s): Jack Cayre, Kenneth Cayre, Nathan Cayre, Grace K. Cayre, Michelle Cayre, Raquel Cayre.
Financial data (yr. ended 12/31/00): Grants paid, $1,938,455; assets, $10,463,264 (M); gifts received, $1,462,159; expenditures, $2,202,776; qualifying distributions, $1,938,455.

32835—NEW YORK

Limitations: Giving on a national basis.
Officers: Kenneth Cayre, Pres.; Lillian Cayre, V.P.
EIN: 133746793
Codes: FD

32836
The M.A.C. Global Foundation
c/o Lilia Garcia-Leyva
767 5th Ave.
New York, NY 10153

Established in 2000 in NY.
Financial data (yr. ended 12/31/01): Grants paid, $1,935,191; assets, $1,500,880 (M); gifts received, $1,864,265; expenditures, $2,043,522; qualifying distributions, $2,041,973.
Limitations: Applications not accepted. Giving primarily in New York, NY.
Application information: Contributes only to pre-selected organizations.
Officers and Directors:* John D. Demsey,* Chair. and Pres.; Robert Charles Richards,* Treas.; Nancy M. Louden, Secy.; Lilia Garcia-Leyva, Exec. Dir.; Frank Doyle, Bruce Hunter, Ian Ness.
EIN: 134144722
Codes: FD

32837
Thomas B. Walker III Foundation
c/o Goldman Sachs & Co.
85 Broad St., Tax Dept.
New York, NY 10004

Established in 1991 in NY.
Donor(s): Thomas B. Walker III.
Financial data (yr. ended 04/30/01): Grants paid, $1,927,558; assets, $2,262,881 (M); gifts received, $3,750; expenditures, $2,005,058; qualifying distributions, $1,931,558.
Limitations: Applications not accepted. Giving primarily in New York, NY.
Application information: Contributes only to pre-selected organizations.
Trustees: John A. Thain, Thomas B. Walker III.
EIN: 133632752
Codes: FD

32838
The Union Square Fund, Inc.
c/o Marks Paneth & Shron, LLP
622 3rd Ave., 7th Fl.
New York, NY 10017-6701

Established in 1997 in NY.
Donor(s): Peter Ungerleider.‡
Financial data (yr. ended 12/31/01): Grants paid, $1,925,202; assets, $36,483,395 (M); expenditures, $2,452,024; qualifying distributions, $1,925,487.
Limitations: Applications not accepted. Giving primarily in New York, NY.
Application information: Contributes only to pre-selected organizations.
Officers: Kathrin Scheel Ungerleider, Vice-Chair.; Jeane Ungerleider Springer, Pres.; Adam Bartos, V.P.; Steven Baum, Secy.-Treas.
Director: Vincent McGee.
EIN: 311574700
Codes: FD

32839
The Achelis Foundation
767 3rd Ave., 4th Fl.
New York, NY 10017 (212) 644-0322
FAX: (212) 759-6510; E-mail: main@achelis-bodman-fnds.org; URL: http://fdncenter.org/grantmaker/achelis-bodman
Contact: Joseph S. Dolan, Secy. and Exec. Dir.

Incorporated in 1940 in NY.
Donor(s): Elisabeth Achelis.‡

Financial data (yr. ended 12/31/01): Grants paid, $1,919,100; assets, $37,872,270 (M); expenditures, $2,131,530; qualifying distributions, $1,919,100.
Limitations: Giving primarily in the New York, NY, area.
Publications: Biennial report (including application guidelines), financial statement, grants list.
Application information: Do not send CDs, DVDs, discs or tapes, or proposals through the internet unless requested. Application form not required.
Officers and Trustees:* John N. Irwin III,* Chair., C.E.O. and Treas.; Russell P. Pennoyer,* Pres.; Peter Frelinghuysen,* V.P.; Mary S. Phipps,* V.P.; Joseph S. Dolan, Secy. and Exec. Dir.; Guy G. Rutherfurd, Hon. Chair.; Horace I. Crary, Hon. Walter J.P. Curley, Anthony Drexel Duke, Sarah Henry Lederman.
EIN: 136022018
Codes: FD

32840
Toyota USA Foundation
9 W. 57th St., Ste. 4900
New York, NY 10019 (212) 715-7486
URL: http://www.toyota.com/foundation
Contact: Foundation Admin.

Established in 1987 in CA.
Donor(s): Toyota Motor Sales, U.S.A., Inc.
Financial data (yr. ended 06/30/00): Grants paid, $1,914,500; assets, $37,804,944 (M); gifts received, $5,000,000; expenditures, $2,023,839; qualifying distributions, $1,889,600.
Publications: Informational brochure (including application guidelines).
Application information: K-12 public and private schools may not apply directly to the foundation, but may be the beneficiary of an independent nonprofit agency's funding request. Application form required.
Officer and Director:* James Press,* Exec. V.P.
EIN: 953255038
Codes: CS, FD, CD

32841
Barry L. and Jan R. Zubrow Foundation
c/o Goldman Sachs & Co.
85 Broad St., Tax Dept.
New York, NY 10004

Established in 1989 in NY.
Donor(s): Barry L. Zubrow.
Financial data (yr. ended 06/30/01): Grants paid, $1,906,243; assets, $6,199,473 (M); gifts received, $2,504,681; expenditures, $2,025,253; qualifying distributions, $1,886,220.
Limitations: Applications not accepted. Giving primarily in NJ and New York, NY.
Application information: Contributes only to pre-selected organizations.
Trustees: Richard M. Hayden, Barry L. Zubrow, Jan R. Zubrow.
EIN: 133532026
Codes: FD

32842
The Morris and Alma Schapiro Fund
(Formerly M. A. Schapiro Fund)
c/o Kronish, Lieb, Weiner and Hellman, LLP
1145 Ave. of the Americas, 46th Fl.
New York, NY 10036-7798

Established in 1955 in NY.
Donor(s): Morris A. Schapiro.‡
Financial data (yr. ended 12/31/00): Grants paid, $1,905,000; assets, $28,105,492 (M); gifts received, $7,809,988; expenditures, $2,068,101; qualifying distributions, $1,975,034.
Limitations: Applications not accepted. Giving primarily in New York, NY.
Application information: Contributes only to pre-selected organizations.
Officers and Directors:* Linda S. Collins,* Pres.; Stephen J. Paluszek,* V.P.; Daniel E. Schapiro, Secy.-Treas.
EIN: 136089254
Codes: FD

32843
The Jack Adjmi Family Foundation, Inc.
34 W. 33rd St.
New York, NY 10001 (212) 239-8615
Contact: Jack Adjmi, Dir.

Established in 1983 in NY.
Donor(s): Eric Adjmi, Jack Adjmi, Mark Adjmi, Ronald Adjmi, Beluga, Inc., Consolidated Childrens Apparel, IFG Corp., Popsicle Playwear, Ltd.
Financial data (yr. ended 11/30/00): Grants paid, $1,904,288; assets, $72,408 (M); gifts received, $2,005,554; expenditures, $1,908,246; qualifying distributions, $1,908,240.
Limitations: Giving primarily in NY.
Application information: Application form not required.
Directors: Eric Adjmi, Jack Adjmi, Rachel Adjmi.
EIN: 133202295
Codes: FD

32844
The Spunk Fund, Inc.
780 3rd Ave., 24th Fl.
New York, NY 10017 (212) 980-8880
FAX: (212) 980-8976; E-mail: sfi@spunkfund.com
Contact: Marianne Gerschel, Pres.

Incorporated in 1981 in NY.
Donor(s): Marianne Gerschel.
Financial data (yr. ended 12/31/01): Grants paid, $1,904,263; assets, $19,975,043 (M); gifts received, $2,148,005; expenditures, $3,054,671; qualifying distributions, $2,688,826.
Limitations: Giving primarily in NY, with growing support for international grants.
Publications: Informational brochure (including application guidelines).
Application information: Fund will request proposals from organizations in which it is interested; unsolicited proposals not considered. Application form not required.
Officer: Marianne Gerschel, Pres.
EIN: 133116094
Codes: FD

32845
Chautauqua Region Community Foundation, Inc.
418 Spring St.
Jamestown, NY 14701 (716) 661-3390
FAX: (716) 488-0387; E-mail: crcf@crcfoline.org
URL: http://www.crcfonline.org
Contact: Randall J. Sweeney, Exec. Dir.

Incorporated in 1978 in NY.
Financial data (yr. ended 12/31/01): Grants paid, $1,901,503; assets, $41,442,032 (M); gifts received, $5,058,859; expenditures, $2,498,303.
Limitations: Giving limited to the southern Chautauqua County, NY, area.
Publications: Annual report (including application guidelines), informational brochure, newsletter, application guidelines.
Application information: Guidelines available on Web site. Application form required.

Officers and Directors:* Max R. Pickard,* Pres.; Kristy B. Zabrodsky,* V.P.; Katherine K. Burch, Secy.; Jeanette J. Carlson,* Treas.; Randall J. Sweeney, Exec. Dir.; Daniel A. Black, Lyman A. Buck III, Hon. Stephen W. Cass, Cristie L. Herbst, Anna Marie Jochum, Bridget B. Johnson, Michael D. Metzger.
EIN: 161116837
Codes: CM, FD, GTI

32846
The Joseph H. Wender Foundation
c/o BCRS Assocs., LLC
100 Wall St., 11th Fl.
New York, NY 10005
FAX: (212) 902-3000

Established in 1985 in NY.
Donor(s): Joseph H. Wender.
Financial data (yr. ended 04/30/01): Grants paid, $1,900,502; assets, $3,963,526 (M); expenditures, $1,904,940; qualifying distributions, $1,888,074.
Limitations: Applications not accepted. Giving primarily in CA, and New York, NY; some funding nationally.
Application information: Contributes only to pre-selected organizations.
Trustees: Jonathan L. Cohen, Joseph H. Wender, Sherri Wender.
EIN: 133318170
Codes: FD

32847
Pascucci Family Foundation
270 S. Service Rd., Ste. 45
P.O. Box 888
Melville, NY 11747-2339

Established in 1996 in NY.
Donor(s): Christopher S. Pascucci, Ralph P. Pascucci.
Financial data (yr. ended 09/30/00): Grants paid, $1,897,240; assets, $13,884,303 (M); expenditures, $1,938,771; qualifying distributions, $1,882,017.
Limitations: Applications not accepted.
Application information: Contributes only to pre-selected organizations.
Officers and Directors:* Michael C. Pascucci,* Pres.; Peter Cavallaro, V.P. and Counsel; Christopher S. Pascucci,* V.P.; Ralph P. Pascucci,* Secy.-Treas.
EIN: 113346466
Codes: FD

32848
The Davenport-Hatch Foundation, Inc.
c/o Deloitte & Touche, LLP
2200 Chase Sq.
Rochester, NY 14604
Application address: c/o Fleet Trust Co., 1 East Ave., Rochester, NY 14638
Contact: Bill McKee

Incorporated in 1952 in NY.
Donor(s): Augustus Hatch.‡
Financial data (yr. ended 05/31/00): Grants paid, $1,879,014; assets, $44,295,016 (M); expenditures, $2,039,488; qualifying distributions, $1,947,415.
Limitations: Giving primarily in the greater Rochester, NY, area.
Application information: Application form not required.
Officers: Austin E. Hildebrandt, Pres.; Helen H. Heller, Secy.
Directors: Robert J. Brinkman, William L. Ely, A. Thomas Hildebrandt, Mary Hildebrandt, Lindsey Knoble, John W. Ross, David H. Taylor, Douglas F. Taylor, Shirley Warren.

Trustee: Fleet National Bank.
EIN: 166027105
Codes: FD

32849
The Adjmi-Dwek Family Foundation, Inc.
34 W. 33rd St.
New York, NY 10001 (212) 239-8615
Contact: Joseph Dwek, Dir.

Established in 1994 in NY.
Donor(s): Sister Sister.
Financial data (yr. ended 12/31/00): Grants paid, $1,874,387; assets, $0 (M); gifts received, $1,884,500; expenditures, $1,874,798; qualifying distributions, $1,874,387.
Limitations: Giving on a national and international basis.
Directors: Jack Adjmi, Joseph Dwek, Terry Dwek.
EIN: 133782816
Codes: FD

32850
Norcross Wildlife Foundation, Inc.
Caller Box No. 611
250 W. 88th St., Ste. 806
New York, NY 10024 (212) 362-4831
Additional tel.: (718) 791-2094; Application address: Grants Admin., P.O. Box 269, Wales, MA 01081; URL: http://www.norcrossws.org
Contact: Richard S. Reagan, Pres., or John McMurray, Prog. Off.

Established in 1964 in NY.
Donor(s): Arthur D. Norcross,‡ June Norcross Webster.‡
Financial data (yr. ended 12/31/01): Grants paid, $1,869,461; assets, $67,553,653 (M); gifts received, $102,000; expenditures, $4,419,058; qualifying distributions, $5,892,376; giving activities include $699,000 for loans.
Limitations: Giving primarily in North America.
Publications: Annual report (including application guidelines), application guidelines, multi-year report.
Application information: FAX, express mail applications or proposals without an attached application form not accepted; no 990-PF forms or annual reports required; only 1 copy of IRS letter is required. Application form required.
Officers and Directors:* Richard S. Reagan,* Pres.; Joseph A. Catalano,* V.P. and Secy.; Karen Outlaw, Treas.; Warren Balgooyen, Albia Dugger, Edward Gallagher, Arthur D. Norcross, Jr., Michael D. Patrick, Denise Schlener, Christof von Strasser, Ted Williams.
EIN: 132041622
Codes: FD

32851
Liz Claiborne & Art Ortenberg Foundation
(Formerly The Ortenberg Foundation)
650 5th Ave., 15th Fl.
New York, NY 10019 (212) 333-2536
FAX: (212) 956-3531; E-mail: lcaof@fcc.net
Contact: James Murtaugh, Dir.

Established in 1984 in NY.
Donor(s): Arthur Ortenberg, Elisabeth Claiborne Ortenberg.
Financial data (yr. ended 12/31/01): Grants paid, $1,867,149; assets, $43,428,370 (M); gifts received, $200,000; expenditures, $2,856,654; qualifying distributions, $2,250,401.
Limitations: Giving primarily in Third World countries in the Tropics and in the Northern Rocky Mountain region of the U.S.
Publications: Informational brochure (including application guidelines).

Application information: Application form not required.
Directors: Robert Dewar, James Murtaugh, Arthur Ortenberg, Elisabeth Claiborne Ortenberg, Mary Pearl, David Quammen, Alison Richard, David Western.
EIN: 133200329
Codes: FD, FM

32852
Sheldon H. Solow Foundation, Inc.
9 W. 57th St., Ste. 4500
New York, NY 10019-2601 (212) 754-0284
Contact: Rosalie S. Wolff, V.P.

Incorporated in 1986 in DE.
Donor(s): Sheldon H. Solow.
Financial data (yr. ended 11/30/01): Grants paid, $1,866,050; assets, $6,244,815 (M); gifts received, $1,756,000; expenditures, $1,869,203; qualifying distributions, $1,864,996.
Limitations: Giving on a national basis.
Application information: Application form not required.
Officers: Sheldon H. Solow, Pres.; Steven Cherniak, V.P.; Margaret E. Hewitt, Secy.
EIN: 133386646
Codes: FD

32853
David Schwartz Foundation, Inc.
c/o Siegel, Sacks & Co.
630 3rd Ave.
New York, NY 10017

Incorporated in 1945 in NY.
Donor(s): David Schwartz, Jonathan Logan, Inc., and others.
Financial data (yr. ended 05/31/01): Grants paid, $1,856,482; assets, $16,621,841 (M); expenditures, $2,163,182; qualifying distributions, $1,898,961.
Limitations: Applications not accepted. Giving primarily in NY, with emphasis on New York City.
Application information: Contributes only to pre-selected organizations.
Officers and Directors:* Richard J. Schwartz,* Pres.; Sheila Schwartz,* V.P.; Stephen D. Gardner,* Secy.; Irene Schwartz.
EIN: 226075974
Codes: FD

32854
Solow Foundation
9 W. 57th St., Ste. 4500
New York, NY 10019-2601
Contact: Rosalie S. Wolff, V.P.

Established in 1978 in DE.
Donor(s): Sheldon H. Solow.
Financial data (yr. ended 10/31/01): Grants paid, $1,850,000; assets, $9,242,365 (M); expenditures, $1,880,927; qualifying distributions, $1,844,852.
Limitations: Giving primarily in New York, NY.
Application information: Application form not required.
Officers: Sheldon H. Solow, Pres.; Rosalie S. Wolff, V.P.; Leonard Lazarus, Secy.; Steven M. Cherniak, Treas.
EIN: 132950685
Codes: FD

32855
Milliken Foundation
c/o Citibank, N.A.
153 E. 53rd St.
New York, NY 10043

Trust established in 1945 in NY.
Donor(s): Milliken and Co., and others.

Financial data (yr. ended 12/31/00): Grants paid, $1,846,004; assets, $6,173,046 (M); gifts received, $2,800,000; expenditures, $1,862,864; qualifying distributions, $1,855,120.
Limitations: Applications not accepted.
Application information: Contributes only to pre-selected organizations.
Trustee: Citibank, N.A.
Advisory Committee: Lawrence Heagney, Thomas J. Malone, Gerrish H. Milliken, Roger Milliken, Sidney S. Nichols.
EIN: 136055062
Codes: CS, FD, CD

32856
The Hauser Foundation, Inc.
712 5th Ave.
New York, NY 10019-4102   (212) 956-3645
FAX: (212) 956-1413
Contact: Rita E. Hauser, Pres.

Established in 1989 in NY.
Donor(s): Gustave M. Hauser, Rita E. Hauser.
Financial data (yr. ended 11/30/01): Grants paid, $1,837,325; assets, $63,311,313 (M); gifts received, $722,225; expenditures, $2,311,840; qualifying distributions, $2,199,310.
Limitations: Applications not accepted.
Application information: Unsolicited requests for funds not accepted.
Officers and Directors:* Rita E. Hauser,* Pres.; Gustave M. Hauser, V.P. and Secy.-Treas.; Ronald J. Stein.
EIN: 110016142
Codes: FD

32857
Trace Foundation
31 Perry St.
New York, NY 10014

Established in 1993 in NY.
Donor(s): Andrea Soros.
Financial data (yr. ended 12/31/99): Grants paid, $1,836,714; assets, $1,076,703 (M); gifts received, $4,010,000; expenditures, $3,911,734; qualifying distributions, $2,709,038.
Limitations: Applications not accepted. Giving on a national and international basis.
Application information: Unsolicited requests for funds not considered.
Trustees: Katrina Morris, Andrea Soros, Jonathan Soros, Robert Soros.
EIN: 137008868
Codes: FD

32858
The Peter M. Sacerdote Foundation
c/o BCRS Assocs., LLC
67 Wall St., 8th Fl.
New York, NY 10005   (212) 902-6897

Established in 1981.
Donor(s): Peter M. Sacerdote, P.M. Sacerdote Charitable Lead Trust.
Financial data (yr. ended 02/28/01): Grants paid, $1,830,775; assets, $15,318,014 (M); expenditures, $1,965,325; qualifying distributions, $1,832,794.
Limitations: Applications not accepted. Giving primarily in New York, NY.
Application information: Contributes only to pre-selected organizations.
Trustee: Peter M. Sacerdote.
EIN: 133102940
Codes: FD

32859
Gladys Brooks Foundation
c/o Thomas Q. Morris, M.D.
630 W. 168th St.
New York, NY 10032   (516) 746-6103
URL: http://www.gladysbrooksfoundation.org
Contact: Jessica L. Rutledge

Established in 1981 in NY.
Donor(s): Gladys Brooks Thayer.‡
Financial data (yr. ended 12/31/00): Grants paid, $1,830,080; assets, $39,459,852 (M); expenditures, $2,265,950; qualifying distributions, $2,091,059.
Limitations: Giving limited to CT, Washington, DC, DE, IN, MA, MD, ME, NC, NH, NJ, NY, OH, PA, RI, SC, VA, VT, and WV.
Publications: Annual report (including application guidelines), program policy statement.
Application information: Application form available on Web site. Application form required.
Board of Governors: Harman Hawkins, Chair.; James J. Daly, Secy.; Thomas Q. Morris, M.D., U.S. Trust.
EIN: 132955337
Codes: FD

32860
Jane H. Booker Residuary Trust
c/o U.S. Trust
114 W. 47th St.
New York, NY 10036
FAX: (212) 852-3377
Contact: Linda R. Franciscovich, Sr. V.P., U.S. Trust, or Carolyn L. Larke, Asst. V.P., U.S. Trust

Established in 1995.
Financial data (yr. ended 12/31/00): Grants paid, $1,828,500; assets, $39,804,908 (M); expenditures, $2,105,132; qualifying distributions, $1,952,181.
Limitations: Applications not accepted.
Application information: Contributes only to pre-selected organizations.
Trustees: Milton A. Mausner, US Trust Co. of New York.
EIN: 137070825
Codes: FD

32861
Marion O. & Maximilian Hoffman Foundation
168 Forest Ave.
Locust Valley, NY 11560
Contact: Ursula C. Niarakis, Pres.

Established in 1984 in NY.
Donor(s): Marion O. Hoffman, Maximilian Hoffman.‡
Financial data (yr. ended 06/30/00): Grants paid, $1,816,700; assets, $30,041,533 (M); expenditures, $2,213,152; qualifying distributions, $1,963,099.
Limitations: Applications not accepted. Giving primarily in New York, NY.
Application information: Contributes only to pre-selected organizations.
Officers: Ursula C. Niarakis, Pres.; William Niarakis, V.P.
Director: Margareta Jackel.
EIN: 112697957
Codes: FD

32862
The Tang Fund
c/o Oscar Tang
600 5th Ave., 8th Fl.
New York, NY 10020

Established in 1984 in NY.
Donor(s): Oscar L. Tang, Reich & Tang, and members of the Tang family.
Financial data (yr. ended 11/30/00): Grants paid, $1,813,341; assets, $43,307,173 (M); expenditures, $1,895,817; qualifying distributions, $1,772,440.
Limitations: Applications not accepted. Giving on a national basis.
Application information: Contributes only to pre-selected organizations.
Officers and Directors:* Oscar L. Tang,* Pres. and Treas.; Lorraine C. Hysler,* Secy.; Tracy L. Tang.
EIN: 133256295
Codes: FD

32863
The New-Land Foundation, Inc.
1114 Ave. of the Americas
New York, NY 10036-7798   (212) 479-6162

Incorporated in 1941 in NY.
Donor(s): Muriel M. Buttinger.‡
Financial data (yr. ended 12/31/99): Grants paid, $1,810,698; assets, $38,502,796 (M); expenditures, $2,165,931; qualifying distributions, $1,886,960.
Publications: Application guidelines.
Application information: Application form required.
Officers and Directors:* Hal Harvey,* Pres.; Constance Harvey,* V.P.; Renee G. Schwartz,* Secy.-Treas.; Ann Harvey, Joan Harvey, Albert Solnit.
EIN: 136086562
Codes: FD

32864
The Edward W. Hazen Foundation, Inc.
309 5th Ave., Rm. 200-3
New York, NY 10016   (212) 889-3034
E-mail: hazen@hazenfoundation.org; *URL:* http://www.hazenfoundation.org
Contact: Barbara Taveras, Pres.

Incorporated in 1925 in CT.
Donor(s): Edward Warriner Hazen,‡ Helen Russell Hazen,‡ Lucy Abigail Hazen,‡ Mary Hazen Arnold.‡
Financial data (yr. ended 12/31/00): Grants paid, $1,810,426; assets, $43,160,106 (M); expenditures, $2,763,258; qualifying distributions, $2,341,460.
Limitations: Giving on a national basis, with emphasis on CA, Washington, DC, FL, IL, MD, MS, NY and PA.
Publications: Grants list, newsletter, application guidelines.
Application information: Request guidelines for detailed program and support limitations; foundation will respond with application materials if interested. Hazen application form required. Application form required.
Officers and Trustees:* Arlene Adler,* Chair.; Earl Durham,* Vice-Chair.; Barbara A. Taveras,* Pres. and Secy.; Marsha Bonner, Maddy Delone, Beverly Divers-White, Edward M. Sermier, Arturo Vargas.
EIN: 060646671
Codes: FD

32865
Adrian & Jessie Archbold Charitable Trust
c/o Arthur J. Mahon
401 E. 60th St., Ste. 36B
New York, NY 10022   (212) 371-1152

Trust established in 1976 in NY.
Donor(s): Jessie Archbold.‡
Financial data (yr. ended 11/30/01): Grants paid, $1,791,000; assets, $33,986,070 (M); expenditures, $2,151,390; qualifying distributions, $1,842,635.

Limitations: Giving primarily in the northeastern U.S.; some giving in GA.
Application information: Unsolicited proposals not encouraged. Application form not required.
Trustees: Arthur J. Mahon, JPMorgan Chase Bank.
EIN: 510179829
Codes: FD

32866
The Thomas & Agnes Carvel Foundation
35 E. Grassy Sprain Rd.
Yonkers, NY 10710 (914) 793-7300
Contact: William E. Griffin, Pres.

Established in 1976 in NY.
Donor(s): Thomas Carvel,‡ Agnes Carvel.‡
Financial data (yr. ended 11/30/01): Grants paid, $1,788,400; assets, $35,932,208 (M); gifts received, $142,000; expenditures, $3,120,084; qualifying distributions, $1,927,632.
Limitations: Giving primarily in Westchester County, NY.
Application information: Application form not required.
Officers and Directors:* William E. Griffin,* Pres.; Salvador Molella,* V.P. and Treas.; Ann McHugh,* V.P.; Lorraine Gerard, Secy.; Robert H. Abplanalp, Brendan Byrne, Lawrence F. Fay.
EIN: 132879673
Codes: FD

32867
A. L. Mailman Family Foundation, Inc.
707 Westchester Ave.
White Plains, NY 10604 (914) 683-8089
FAX: (914) 686-5519; *E-mail:* almf@mailman.org; *URL:* http://www.mailman.org
Contact: Luba H. Lynch, Exec. Dir.

Established in 1976 in FL as the Dr. Marilyn M. Segal Foundation, Inc.
Donor(s): Abraham L. Mailman,‡ The Mailman Foundation, Inc.
Financial data (yr. ended 12/31/00): Grants paid, $1,788,175; assets, $30,412,921 (M); expenditures, $2,238,057; qualifying distributions, $2,225,088; giving activities include $68,955 for programs.
Limitations: Giving on a national basis.
Publications: Annual report.
Application information: Application form not required.
Officers and Trustees:* Betty S. Bardige,* Chair.; Patricia S. Lieberman,* Vice-Chair.; Richard D. Segal,* Pres.; Wendy S. Masi, V.P.; Luba H. Lynch, Secy. and Exec. Dir.; Donna Tookmanian, Treas.; Jonathan R. Gordon, Jay B. Langner, Marilyn M. Segal.
EIN: 510203866
Codes: FD

32868
The Niagara Mohawk Foundation, Inc.
300 Erie Blvd. W.
Syracuse, NY 13202 (315) 474-1511
URL: http://www.niagaramohawk.com/nimotod/community/foundat.html
Contact: Carolyn A. May, Dir.

Established in 1992 in NY.
Donor(s): Niagara Mohawk Power Corp.
Financial data (yr. ended 12/31/00): Grants paid, $1,787,205; assets, $2,996,775 (M); gifts received, $1,517,477; expenditures, $1,811,114; qualifying distributions, $1,793,154; giving activities include $1,793,154 for program-related investments.
Limitations: Giving limited to areas of company operations in upstate NY.
Publications: Informational brochure (including application guidelines), annual report.
Application information: Application form required.
Officers and Directors:* Christina M. Moran,* Secy.; Ralph Modugno, Treas.; Carolyn A. May.
Trustees: William E. Davis, Chair.; David J. Arrington, Thomas H. Baron, Albert J. Budney, Jr., Edward J. Dienst, William F. Edwards, J. Philip Frazier, Darlene D. Kerr, Gary J. Lavine, John H. Mueller.
EIN: 223132237
Codes: CS, FD, CD

32869
Loews Foundation
c/o John J. Kenny
655 Madison Ave.
New York, NY 10021 (212) 521-2650
FAX: (212) 521-2634
Contact: Candace Leeds, V.P., Public Affairs

Trust established in 1957 in NY.
Donor(s): Loews Corp., and subsidiaries.
Financial data (yr. ended 12/31/99): Grants paid, $1,782,597; assets, $13,223 (M); gifts received, $1,735,000; expenditures, $1,782,781; qualifying distributions, $1,782,781.
Application information: Applications for employee-related scholarship program available from the foundation, otherwise no application form required.
Trustees: Peter W. Keegan, John J. Kenny, Andrew Tisch, Preston R. Tisch.
EIN: 136082817
Codes: CS, FD, CD

32870
The Community Foundation of Herkimer & Oneida Counties, Inc.
(Formerly Utica Foundation, Inc.)
270 Genesee St.
Utica, NY 13502 (315) 735-8212
FAX: (315) 735-9363; *E-mail:* commfdn@borg.com
Contact: Susan D. Smith, Sr. Prog. Off. or Margaret Anne O'Shea

Incorporated in 1952 in NY.
Financial data (yr. ended 12/31/01): Grants paid, $1,781,108; assets, $50,147,196 (L); gifts received, $2,621,630; expenditures, $2,443,194.
Limitations: Giving limited to Oneida and Herkimer counties, NY.
Publications: Annual report, application guidelines, newsletter.
Application information: Application form not required.
Officers and Directors:* Milton Bloch,* Pres.; Jane A. Halbritter,* V.P.; Richard Hanna,* V.P.; Camille T. Kahler,* Secy.; Lauren E. Bull,* Treas.; Gordon M. Hayes, Exec. Dir.; Harold T. Clark, Jr., Timothy Foley, Judith B. Gorman, Mary K. Griffith, Joseph H. Hobika, Sr., John Livingston, Grace McLaughlin, Mary Morse, Earle C. Reed, Faye Short, Sheila Smith, William Stevens.
Trustee Banks: Fleet National Bank, HSBC Bank USA.
EIN: 156016932
Codes: CM, FD

32871
The Panaphil Foundation
c/o U.S. Trust
114 W. 47th St.
New York, NY 10036
Contact: Barry Waldorf

Established in 1990 in PA and NY.
Donor(s): Frances A. Velay.
Financial data (yr. ended 12/31/99): Grants paid, $1,773,000; assets, $39,086,241 (M); expenditures, $1,968,250; qualifying distributions, $1,798,792.
Limitations: Giving primarily on the East Coast.
Trustees: Barbara Paul Robinson, Christophe J. Velay, Frances A. Velay.
EIN: 136959472
Codes: FD

32872
The Peter and Eaddo Kiernan Foundation
c/o BCRS Assoc., LLC
100 Wall St., 11th Fl.
New York, NY 10005

Established in 1991 in NY.
Donor(s): Peter D. Kiernan.
Financial data (yr. ended 05/31/01): Grants paid, $1,762,200; assets, $1,938,632 (M); gifts received, $97,313; expenditures, $1,794,530; qualifying distributions, $1,762,530.
Limitations: Applications not accepted. Giving primarily in New York, NY; some giving in CT.
Application information: Contributes only to pre-selected organizations.
Trustees: Eaddo H. Kiernan, Peter D. Kiernan.
EIN: 133637705
Codes: FD

32873
Oliver S. and Jennie R. Donaldson Charitable Trust
c/o U.S. Trust
114 W. 47th St.
New York, NY 10036-1530
FAX: (212) 852-3377
Contact: Linda R. Franciscovich, Sr. V.P., U.S. Trust; or Carolyn L. Larke, Asst. V.P., U.S. Trust

Trust established in 1969 in NY.
Donor(s): Oliver S. Donaldson.‡
Financial data (yr. ended 12/31/01): Grants paid, $1,760,250; assets, $28,833,712 (M); expenditures, $1,926,619; qualifying distributions, $1,837,083.
Limitations: Giving primarily in the Northeast, with emphasis on MA and NY.
Publications: Application guidelines.
Application information: NY Common Application Form required. Application form required.
Trustees: Marjorie Atwood, Elizabeth Lawrence, M.D., William E. Murray, John F. Sisk, Pamela C. Smith, U.S. Trust.
EIN: 046229044
Codes: FD

32874
The Helen Hay Whitney Foundation
450 E. 63rd St.
New York, NY 10021-7999 (212) 751-8228
FAX: (212) 688-6794; *E-mail:* hhwf@earthlink.net; *URL:* http://www.hhwf.org
Contact: Robert Weinberger, Admin. Dir.

Charitable trust established in 1943; established as a private foundation in 1947; incorporated in 1951 in NY.
Donor(s): Mrs. Charles S. Payson.‡
Financial data (yr. ended 06/30/01): Grants paid, $1,755,148; assets, $48,233,853 (M); gifts received, $305,560; expenditures, $2,339,821; qualifying distributions, $2,149,734.
Limitations: Giving limited to North America, including Canada and Mexico.
Publications: Annual report, informational brochure (including application guidelines), financial statement.

Application information: Application forms available Mar. 15. Application form required.
Officers and Trustees:* Mrs. Henry B. Middleton, Pres.; Maclyn McCarty, M.D.,* V.P. and Chair, Scientific Advisory Comm.; Thomas A. Melfe,* Secy.; W. Perry Welch, Treas.; Milton N. Allen, Jerome Gross, M.D., Lisa A. Steiner, M.D.
Scientific Advisory Committee: Stephen C. Harrison, Ph.D., V.P.; Gerald Fischbach, M.D., David S. Hogness, Ph.D., Douglas A. Melton, Ph.D., Barbara J. Meyer, Ph.D.; Gerald M. Rubin, Ph.D., Matthew D. Scharff, M.D.
EIN: 131677403
Codes: FD, GTI

32875
Wolfensohn Family Foundation
277 Park Ave., 49th Fl.
New York, NY 10172 (212) 207-5509
URL: http://www.wolfensohn.org
Contact: Bridget Batson, Asst. Dir.

Established in 1995 in NY.
Financial data (yr. ended 12/31/00): Grants paid, $1,753,536; assets, $24,415,843 (M); gifts received, $300,000; expenditures, $2,791,154; qualifying distributions, $1,753,536.
Limitations: Applications not accepted. Giving primarily on the East Coast, with emphasis on NY and Washington, DC. Giving for environmental programs in AK and WY. Giving for religious pluralism and Jewish-Arab coexistence in Israel; giving also in Australia and England.
Application information: Contributes only to pre-selected organizations.
Director and Trustees:* Sara R. Wolfensohn,* Dir.; Adam R. Wolfensohn, Elaine R. Wolfensohn, James D. Wolfensohn, Naomi R. Wolfensohn.
EIN: 133781581
Codes: FD

32876
Personality Disorder Research Corp.
c/o Dr. Marco Stoffel
650 Madison Ave., 18th Fl.
New York, NY 10022

Established in 1999 in NY.
Donor(s): Maytown Universal, S.A.
Financial data (yr. ended 12/31/00): Grants paid, $1,750,000; assets, $44,026 (M); expenditures, $2,000,994; qualifying distributions, $1,996,507.
Limitations: Applications not accepted. Giving primarily in New Haven, CT, and New York, NY.
Application information: Contributes only to pre-selected organizations.
Officers and Directors:* Marco Stoffel,* Pres.; James S. Sligar,* Secy.-Treas.; Eric Kandel, Torsten Wiesel.
EIN: 134069081
Codes: FD

32877
The C. J. Mack Foundation
91 Sunset Ln.
Rye, NY 10580

Established in 1993 in NY and DE.
Donor(s): Christy K. Mack, John J. Mack.
Financial data (yr. ended 12/31/99): Grants paid, $1,749,600; assets, $41,336,724 (M); gifts received, $10,769,350; expenditures, $1,934,432; qualifying distributions, $1,749,600.
Limitations: Giving on a national basis.
Application information: Contributes only to pre-selected organizations.
Officers: John J. Mack, Pres.; Christy K. Mack, Secy.-Treas.

Directors: Susan DeWilde, John C. Mack, Stephen K. Mack.
EIN: 133746731
Codes: FD

32878
Lucky Star Foundation
c/o Yohalem Gillman & Co.
477 Madison Ave.
New York, NY 10022
Contact: Sonja Lepkowski

Established in 1993.
Donor(s): Judith Gluckstern, Steven Gluckstern.
Financial data (yr. ended 12/31/01): Grants paid, $1,734,267; assets, $3,269,114 (M); gifts received, $2,000; expenditures, $1,812,758; qualifying distributions, $1,763,615.
Limitations: Applications not accepted. Giving on a national basis.
Application information: Contributes only to pre-selected organizations.
Officers: Judith O'Connor Gluckstern, Pres.; Steven Gluckstern, V.P.; David Prager, Secy.
EIN: 133710572
Codes: FD

32879
Edwin Gould Foundation for Children
23 Gramercy Park S.
New York, NY 10003 (212) 982-5200
Contact: Michael Osheowitz, C.E.O.

Incorporated in 1923 in NY.
Donor(s): Edwin Gould.‡
Financial data (yr. ended 12/31/01): Grants paid, $1,730,551; assets, $45,509,444 (M); gifts received, $48,033; expenditures, $4,484,210; qualifying distributions, $3,330,726.
Limitations: Giving primarily in New York, NY, and throughout the U.S. for special projects.
Publications: Multi-year report, financial statement, grants list.
Application information: Applications generally not encouraged; current giving limited to previous recipients; accepts NYRAG Common Grant Application Form. Application form not required.
Officers and Trustees:* Michael W. Osheowitz,* C.E.O. and Chair.; Paul L. Spivey,* Pres. and C.O.O.; Herschel E. Sparks, Jr.,* Secy.; Jose A. Alonso, Jr., Treas.; Mark Bieler, Steven Brown, Harold M. Davis, Richard Eaddy, Truda C. Jewett, Eddie A. Knowles, Edward A. Lesser, Jon D. Smith, Jr., Alan S. Weinstein, Cynthia Rivera Weissblum.
Advisory Trustees: Malcolm J. Edgerton, Jr., Hon. Daniel W. Joy, Newton P.S. Merrill, Aileen "Chuca" Meyer, George C. Seward, Richard H. Valentine.
EIN: 135675642
Codes: FD

32880
Larry Aldrich Foundation, Inc.
40 Central Park S.
New York, NY 10019
Contact: Larry Aldrich, Pres.

Established in 1994 in NY.
Donor(s): Larry Aldrich.
Financial data (yr. ended 03/31/01): Grants paid, $1,728,762; assets, $9,166,859 (M); expenditures, $1,768,761; qualifying distributions, $1,716,780.
Limitations: Giving primarily in CT.
Officers: Larry Aldrich, Pres.; Joel Mallin, V.P.; Peter L. Malkin, Secy.-Treas.
EIN: 133777483
Codes: GTI

32881
The William Rosenwald Family Fund, Inc.
666 3rd Ave., 29th Fl.
New York, NY 10017
Contact: David P. Steinmann, Pres.

Incorporated in 1938 in CT.
Donor(s): William Rosenwald,‡ and family.
Financial data (yr. ended 12/31/99): Grants paid, $1,728,094; assets, $21,776,436 (M); gifts received, $5,000; expenditures, $1,919,948; qualifying distributions, $1,730,998.
Limitations: Applications not accepted. Giving primarily in NY.
Application information: Contributes only to pre-selected organizations.
Officers: David P. Steinmann, Pres. and Treas.; Elizabeth R. Varet, V.P. and Secy.; Nina Rosenwald, V.P.; Alice R. Sigelman, V.P.
EIN: 131635289
Codes: FD

32882
Beatrice & Samuel A. Seaver Foundation
c/o Eisner & Lubin
444 Madison Ave.
New York, NY 10022
Contact: Hirschel E. Levine, Tr.

Established in 1986 in NY.
Donor(s): Beatrice Seaver.‡
Financial data (yr. ended 11/30/00): Grants paid, $1,727,872; assets, $76,777,624 (M); gifts received, $375,688; expenditures, $2,548,674; qualifying distributions, $2,306,575.
Limitations: Applications not accepted. Giving primarily in New York, NY.
Application information: Contributes only to pre-selected organizations.
Trustees: John Cohen, Hirschell E. Levine.
EIN: 133251432
Codes: FD

32883
Isaac H. Tuttle Fund
1155 Park Ave., Office D
New York, NY 10128-1209 (212) 831-0429
FAX: (212) 426-5684; *E-mail:* mailto:info@tuttlefund.org; *URL:* http://www.tuttlefund.org
Contact: Stephanie A. Raneri, Exec. Dir

Incorporated in 1872 as a public charity; status changed to a private foundation in 2001.
Financial data (yr. ended 12/31/01): Grants paid, $1,714,684; assets, $50,770,815 (M); gifts received, $440,063; expenditures, $2,414,769; qualifying distributions, $2,323,233.
Limitations: Giving limited to New York, NY.
Publications: Financial statement, application guidelines.
Application information: Contact Exec. Dir. for grants, or Stipendiary Prog. Dir. for stipends. Application form required for stipends. Application form required.
Officers and Trustees:* Molly O. Parkinson,* Pres.; Kenneth R. Page,* V.P.; Christine Valentine,* Secy.; Anne H. Lindgren,* Treas.; Stephanie A. Raneri, Exec. Dir.; Shirley B. Bresler, Susan P. Cole, William H. Forsyth, Jr., Martha V. Johns, Paul A. Legvold, Elizabeth McClintock, Edward D. Pardoe III, Carol Robinson, Tr. Emeritus; Oscar S. Straus III.
EIN: 135628325
Codes: FD

32884
Strypemonde Foundation
1384 Park Ln.
Pelham Manor, NY 10803

Established in 1999 in NY.
Donor(s): Paul Francis.
Financial data (yr. ended 06/30/01): Grants paid, $1,714,400; assets, $19,173,373 (M); gifts received, $17,444,775; expenditures, $1,934,415; qualifying distributions, $1,714,400.
Limitations: Applications not accepted.
Application information: Contributes only to pre-selected organizations.
Officers: Titia Hulst, Pres.; Paul Francis, V.P. and Secy.
EIN: 137204588
Codes: FD

32885
The Christopher Reynolds Foundation, Inc.
267 5th Ave., Ste. 1001
New York, NY 10016 (212) 532-1606
FAX: (212) 532-1403; *E-mail:* CRFNY@aol.com;
URL: http://www.creynolds.org
Contact: Andrea Panaritis, Exec. Dir.

Incorporated in 1952 in NY.
Donor(s): Libby Holman Reynolds.‡
Financial data (yr. ended 01/31/99): Grants paid, $1,713,307; assets, $37,000,275 (M); expenditures, $2,468,560; qualifying distributions, $2,050,483.
Limitations: Giving on a national and international basis.
Publications: Multi-year report (including application guidelines), financial statement.
Application information: Application form not required.
Officers and Directors:* Michael Kahn,* Pres.; John R. Boettiger,* V.P.; Suzanne Derrer,* V.P.; Andrea Panaritis,* Secy. and Exec. Dir.; Jack Clareman,* Treas.
EIN: 136129401
Codes: FD

32886
The Allwin Family Foundation
c/o Aetos Capital, LLC
375 Park Ave., Ste. 3401
New York, NY 10152
Contact: James M. Allwin, Tr.

Established in 1997 in NY.
Donor(s): James M. Allwin.
Financial data (yr. ended 12/31/00): Grants paid, $1,712,661; assets, $4,316,099 (M); gifts received, $1,136; expenditures, $1,721,876; qualifying distributions, $1,716,600.
Trustees: James M. Allwin, Robert F. Larson.
Committee Member: Maria Allwin.
EIN: 137088461
Codes: FD

32887
Leonard Wagner Trust
c/o Alexander Forger and Paul Eichler
404 Park Ave. S., Ste. 700
New York, NY 10016

Established in 1994.
Donor(s): Leonard Wagner.‡
Financial data (yr. ended 12/31/99): Grants paid, $1,705,000; assets, $10,895,246 (M); expenditures, $1,859,081; qualifying distributions, $1,697,013.
Limitations: Applications not accepted. Giving primarily in NY.
Application information: Contributes only to pre-selected organizations.
Trustees: Paul Eichler, Alexander Forger.

EIN: 137012051
Codes: FD

32888
Theodore H. Barth Foundation, Inc.
45 Rockefeller Plz., 20th Fl., Ste. 2037
New York, NY 10111 (212) 332-3466
E-mail: barthfoundation@earthlink.net
Contact: Ellen S. Berelson, Pres.

Incorporated in 1953 in DE.
Donor(s): Theodore H. Barth.‡
Financial data (yr. ended 12/31/00): Grants paid, $1,692,313; assets, $33,187,196 (M); expenditures, $2,028,651; qualifying distributions, $1,756,325.
Limitations: Giving limited to the northeastern U.S. and to MD, NJ, PA, and VA.
Publications: Application guidelines.
Application information: Telephone inquiries will not be accepted. Application form not required.
Officers and Directors:* Ellen S. Berelson,* Pres. and Treas.; Lois Herrmann, V.P.; Lawrence Franks,* Secy.
EIN: 136103401
Codes: FD

32889
Norma Sutton Charitable Foundation
c/o Middlegate Securities Ltd.
8 W. 40th St.
New York, NY 10018

Established in 1993 in NY.
Donor(s): Albert Sutton, Elliot Sutton, Isaac Sutton.
Financial data (yr. ended 03/31/01): Grants paid, $1,690,640; assets, $641,724 (M); gifts received, $1,425,500; expenditures, $1,737,878; qualifying distributions, $1,690,640.
Limitations: Applications not accepted. Giving primarily in NY.
Application information: Contributes only to pre-selected organizations.
Officers: Albert Sutton, Pres.; Isaac Sutton, Secy.; Elliot Sutton, Treas.
EIN: 133747098
Codes: FD

32890
The Limo Almi Foundation
1335 Chicken Valley Rd.
Oyster Bay, NY 11771
Application Address: 1 C.A. Plz., Islandia, NY 11722
Contact: Sanjay Kumar, Tr.

Established in 1997 in NY.
Financial data (yr. ended 12/31/00): Grants paid, $1,685,766; assets, $1,664,032 (M); expenditures, $1,689,866; qualifying distributions, $1,685,608.
Limitations: Giving primarily in NY, with emphasis on Nassau and Suffolk counties.
Trustee: Sanjay Kumar.
EIN: 116481695
Codes: FD

32891
Irma T. Hirschl Trust for Charitable Purposes
c/o The Chase Manhattan Bank, N.A.
270 Park Ave.
New York, NY 10017 (212) 270-9113
Contact: Uwe Linder, V.P., The Chase Manhattan Bank, N.A.

Trust established in 1973 in NY.
Donor(s): Irma T. Hirschl.‡
Financial data (yr. ended 10/31/00): Grants paid, $1,680,000; assets, $75,290,815 (M); expenditures, $2,037,649; qualifying distributions, $1,858,123.
Limitations: Giving primarily in New York, NY.

Application information: All applications submitted by designated medical schools. Application form required.
Trustees: Robert Todd Lang, Leo Schmolka, The Chase Manhattan Bank, N.A.
EIN: 136356381
Codes: FD, GTI

32892
Terumah Foundation, Inc.
160 Broadway, 1st Fl.
New York, NY 10038 (212) 349-2875
Contact: Phillipe Katz, Secy.

Established in 1993 in NY.
Donor(s): Moses Marx.
Financial data (yr. ended 12/31/99): Grants paid, $1,676,741; assets, $19,260,451 (M); gifts received, $17,200; expenditures, $1,902,237; qualifying distributions, $1,619,577.
Limitations: Applications not accepted. Giving primarily in NY.
Application information: Contributes only to pre-selected organizations.
Officers and Directors:* Moses Marx,* Pres.; Joseph Fink,* V.P.; Phillipe Katz,* Secy.; Magda Marx,* Treas.; Eva Fink, Esther Katz.
EIN: 133694180
Codes: FD

32893
James H. Cummings Foundation, Inc.
1807 Elmwood Ave., Rm. 112
Buffalo, NY 14207
Tel./FAX: (716) 874-0040
Contact: William J. McFarland, Exec. Dir.

Incorporated in 1962 in NY.
Donor(s): James H. Cummings.‡
Financial data (yr. ended 05/31/01): Grants paid, $1,675,271; assets, $34,573,099 (M); expenditures, $1,983,254; qualifying distributions, $1,673,938.
Limitations: Giving limited to the vicinity of the cities of Toronto, Ontario, Canada, Hendersonville, NC, and Buffalo, NY.
Publications: Annual report (including application guidelines).
Application information: Application form not required.
Officers and Directors:* John N. Walsh, Jr.,* Pres.; John P. Naughton, M.D.,* V.P.; William J. McFarland, Secy. and Exec. Dir.; Robert J.A. Irwin,* Treas.; Richard C. Bryan, Jr., Charles F. Kreiner, Jr., Theodore I. Putnam, M.D.
EIN: 160864200
Codes: FD

32894
Victor H. Potamkin Charitable Trust
798 11th Ave.
New York, NY 10019

Established in 1995 in NY.
Donor(s): Victor Potamkin.‡
Financial data (yr. ended 05/31/01): Grants paid, $1,673,540; assets, $13,588,297 (M); expenditures, $2,026,163; qualifying distributions, $1,669,869.
Limitations: Applications not accepted. Giving on a national basis, with emphasis on FL, and PA.
Application information: Contributes only to pre-selected organizations.
Trustees: Peter Paris, Alan Potamkin, Robert Potamkin.
EIN: 137066009
Codes: FD

32895
Arnhold Foundation, Inc.
c/o Joel E. Sammet & Co.
20 Exchange Pl.
New York, NY 10005 (212) 208-4600

Established in 1988 in NY.
Donor(s): Henry H. Arnhold, John P. Arnhold, Bruder-Stiftung.
Financial data (yr. ended 12/31/99): Grants paid, $1,669,637; assets, $22,533,646 (M); gifts received $486,096; expenditures, $1,769,231; qualifying distributions, $1,637,008.
Limitations: Applications not accepted. Giving primarily in New York, NY.
Application information: Contributes only to pre-selected organizations.
Officers: Henry H. Arnhold, Pres.; John P. Arnhold, Secy.-Treas.
EIN: 133456684
Codes: FD

32896
Charitable Venture Foundation
747 Pierce Rd.
Clifton Park, NY 12065 (518) 877-8454
Contact: William Dessingue, Exec. Dir.

Established in 1992 in NY.
Donor(s): Herbert K. Liebich,‡ Isabel C. Liebich.
Financial data (yr. ended 12/31/00): Grants paid, $1,658,248; assets, $8,738,898 (M); expenditures, $1,788,639; qualifying distributions, $1,696,878.
Limitations: Giving primarily in the Albany, NY, area.
Publications: Program policy statement.
Application information: Application form required.
Trustees: Arthur Bates, Donald Liebich, Kurt Liebich, Richard C. Liebich, Daniel P. Nolan.
EIN: 141751211
Codes: FD

32897
RTS Family Foundation
c/o The AYCO Co., LP
P.O. Box 8019
Ballston Spa, NY 12020-8019

Established in 1998 in NJ.
Donor(s): Richard T. Santulli.
Financial data (yr. ended 12/31/00): Grants paid, $1,655,034; assets, $22,405,469 (M); gifts received, $1,449,575; expenditures, $1,721,248; qualifying distributions, $1,637,209.
Limitations: Applications not accepted. Giving primarily in NY.
Application information: Contributes only to pre-selected organizations.
Trustees: Sr. Mary McGrory, Margaret Santulli, Richard T. Santulli, Richard V. Santulli.
EIN: 237997212
Codes: FD

32898
Ruth & Milton Steinbach Fund, Inc.
c/o Klingenstein, Fields & Co., LLC
787 7th Ave., 6th Fl.
New York, NY 10019-6016 (212) 492-6181
FAX: (212) 492-7007
Contact: John Klingenstein, Pres.

Incorporated in 1950 in NY.
Donor(s): Milton Steinbach.‡
Financial data (yr. ended 10/31/01): Grants paid, $1,650,000; assets, $24,591,533 (M); expenditures, $1,928,272; qualifying distributions, $1,701,045.
Limitations: Applications not accepted. Giving on a national basis.
Application information: Unsolicited requests for funds not accepted.
Officers and Directors:* John Klingenstein,* Pres. and Treas.; Frederick A. Klingenstein,* 1st V.P. and Secy.; Patricia D. Klingenstein, Sharon L. Klingenstein.
EIN: 136028785
Codes: FD, GTI

32899
The Boisi Family Foundation
c/o Dalessio, Millner & Leben, LLP
245 5th Ave., 16th Fl.
New York, NY 10016

Established in 1983.
Donor(s): Geoffrey T. Boisi, Norine I. Boisi.
Financial data (yr. ended 02/28/01): Grants paid, $1,643,630; assets, $2,995,630 (M); gifts received, $1,600,000; expenditures, $1,732,751; qualifying distributions, $1,720,397.
Limitations: Applications not accepted. Giving primarily in NY.
Application information: Contributes only to pre-selected organizations.
Trustees: Geoffrey T. Boisi, Norine I. Boisi.
EIN: 133165815
Codes: FD

32900
Francis Finlay Foundation
200 Park Ave.
New York, NY 10166

Established in 1997 in NY.
Donor(s): Francis Finlay.
Financial data (yr. ended 12/31/00): Grants paid, $1,636,429; assets, $6,733,765 (M); gifts received, $6,875,000; expenditures, $1,646,250; qualifying distributions, $1,645,277.
Limitations: Applications not accepted.
Application information: Contributes only to pre-selected organizations.
Officers: Francis Finlay, Pres.; Robert Wessley, Secy.
EIN: 133922229
Codes: FD

32901
The Statler Foundation
107 Delaware Ave., Ste. 680
Buffalo, NY 14202 (716) 852-1104
FAX: (716) 852-3928
Contact: Edward M. Flynn, Chair.

Trust established in 1934 in NY.
Donor(s): Ellsworth Milton Statler.‡
Financial data (yr. ended 12/31/01): Grants paid, $1,632,164; assets, $34,124,284 (M); expenditures, $2,111,650; qualifying distributions, $1,745,421.
Limitations: Giving primarily in western NY.
Application information: The scholarship program has been discontinued; prior commitments will be honored. Application form not required.
Officers and Trustees:* Edward M. Flynn,* Chair.; Robert Bennett, Marguerite Collesano, William J. Cunningham, Jr., Joseph DiNardo, Peter J. Fiorella, Jr., Ernestine R. Green, Arthur F. Musarra, Carlo M. Perfetto, Arthur V. Sabia, Herbert M. Siegel, Peter A. Vinolus.
EIN: 131889077
Codes: FD, GTI

32902
The Rosenstiel Foundation
c/o Maurice C. Greenbaum
575 Madison Ave.
New York, NY 10022-2511 (212) 940-8839

Incorporated in 1950 in OH.
Donor(s): Lewis S. Rosenstiel.‡
Financial data (yr. ended 12/31/01): Grants paid, $1,626,050; assets, $24,918,143 (M); expenditures, $1,871,126; qualifying distributions, $1,650,249.
Limitations: Applications not accepted. Giving primarily in FL and NY.
Application information: Contributes only to pre-selected organizations.
Officers: Elizabeth R. Kabler, Pres.; Robert I. Fisher, V.P.; Blanka A. Rosenstiel, V.P.; Maurice C. Greenbaum, Secy.-Treas.
EIN: 066034536
Codes: FD

32903
The Stephen and Suzanne Weiss Foundation, Inc.
1 New York Plz.
New York, NY 10004

Established in 1986 in NY.
Donor(s): Stephen Weiss, Suzanne Weiss.
Financial data (yr. ended 12/31/99): Grants paid, $1,625,819; assets, $4,984,740 (M); expenditures, $1,630,072; qualifying distributions, $1,615,423.
Limitations: Applications not accepted. Giving primarily in New York, NY.
Application information: Contributes only to pre-selected organizations.
Officers: Stephen Weiss, Pres.; Suzanne Weiss, V.P.; Roger J. Weiss, Secy.-Treas.
EIN: 133384021
Codes: FD

32904
Jesselson Foundation
450 Park Ave
New York, NY 10022 (212) 751-3666
Contact: Michael Jesselson, 1st V.P.

Incorporated in 1955 in NY.
Donor(s): Ludwig Jesselson.‡
Financial data (yr. ended 04/30/01): Grants paid, $1,617,951; assets, $39,675,848 (M); expenditures, $1,860,987; qualifying distributions, $1,653,776.
Limitations: Giving on a national basis, with emphasis on NY.
Officers: Erica Jesselson, Pres.; Michael Jesselson, 1st V.P. and Secy.; Benjamin Jesselson, 2nd V.P. and Treas.
EIN: 136075098
Codes: FD

32905
Philip Morris Fund, Inc.
120 Park Ave.
New York, NY 10017-5592

Established in 1998 in NY.
Donor(s): Philip Morris Cos. Inc.
Financial data (yr. ended 12/31/01): Grants paid, $1,617,200; assets, $706,000 (M); gifts received, $1,617,200; expenditures, $1,617,200; qualifying distributions, $1,617,200.
Limitations: Giving on a national and international basis.
Application information: Application form required.
Officers: Geoffrey C. Bible, Chair.; Murray H. Bring, Vice-Chair.; Steven C. Parrish, Vice-Chair.; Thomas J. Collamore, Treas.
EIN: 133896922

Codes: CS, FD, CD

32906
The Joseph Leroy and Ann C. Warner Fund, Inc.
233 Broadway, 38th Fl.
New York, NY 10279
E-mail: warnerfund@aol.com

Established in 1998 in NY.
Financial data (yr. ended 12/31/00): Grants paid, $1,613,379; assets, $32,225,220 (M); gifts received, $78,840; expenditures, $2,083,028; qualifying distributions, $1,716,079.
Limitations: Giving primarily in the metropolitan New York, NY, area.
Application information: NYRAG Common Application Form is preferred. Application form required.
Trustees: Barbara Fei, Jo Ann Ferdinand, Peter Sherman.
EIN: 113426508
Codes: FD

32907
The Marilyn and Barry Rubenstein Family Foundation
68 Wheatley Rd.
Glen Head, NY 11545

Established in 1992 in NY.
Donor(s): Barry Rubenstein, Marilyn Rubenstein.
Financial data (yr. ended 06/30/01): Grants paid, $1,610,238; assets, $4,525,602 (M); gifts received, $1,082,813; expenditures, $1,641,698; qualifying distributions, $1,607,782.
Limitations: Applications not accepted. Giving primarily in NY.
Application information: Contributes only to pre-selected organizations.
Trustees: Barry Rubenstein, Brian Rubenstein, Marilyn Rubenstein, Rebecca Rubenstein.
EIN: 116417671
Codes: FD

32908
Feinstein Family Foundation
c/o Bed Bath & Beyond
110 Bi-County Blvd., Ste. 114
Farmingdale, NY 11735

Established in 1992.
Donor(s): Leonard Feinstein.
Financial data (yr. ended 06/30/00): Grants paid, $1,609,868; assets, $63,059,008 (M); gifts received, $15,402,564; expenditures, $2,093,084; qualifying distributions, $1,609,868.
Limitations: Applications not accepted. Giving primarily in NY.
Application information: Contributes only to pre-selected organizations.
Officers: Susan Feinstein, Vice-Chair.; Leonard Feinstein, Pres.; Amy Feinstein, Secy.
EIN: 113131761
Codes: FD

32909
Rose M. Badgeley Residuary Charitable Trust
c/o HSBC Bank USA
452 Fifth Ave., 17th Fl.
New York, NY 10018-2706 (212) 525-2418
FAX: (212) 525-2395; *E-mail:* marianne.caskran@us.hsbc.com
Contact: Marianne Caskran, Grants Admin.

Trust established about 1977 in NY.
Donor(s): Rose Badgeley.‡
Financial data (yr. ended 12/31/01): Grants paid, $1,609,500; assets, $27,605,022 (M); expenditures, $217,428; qualifying distributions, $1,609,500.
Limitations: Giving limited to the greater metropolitan New York, NY, area.
Publications: Application guidelines.
Application information: Contact foundation for application guidelines. Application form required.
Trustee: HSBC Bank USA.
EIN: 136744781
Codes: FD

32910
Louis & Gertrude Feil Foundation, Inc.
370 7th Ave., Ste. 618
New York, NY 10001 (212) 563-6557

Established in 1977 in NY.
Donor(s): Louis Feil.‡
Financial data (yr. ended 06/30/01): Grants paid, $1,608,026; assets, $1,570,818 (M); gifts received, $150,000; expenditures, $1,614,756; qualifying distributions, $1,612,277.
Limitations: Giving primarily in NY.
Application information: Contributes mostly to pre-selected organizations.
Officers and Directors:* Jeffrey Feil,* Pres.; Gertrude Feil,* V.P.; Carole Feil, V.P. and Secy.; Jay Anderson, Treas.
EIN: 132958414
Codes: FD

32911
S. H. and Helen R. Scheuer Family Foundation, Inc.
350 5th Ave., Ste. 1413
New York, NY 10118 (212) 947-9009
Contact: Linda Ehrlich, Admin. Dir.

Incorporated in 1943 in NY.
Donor(s): Members of the Scheuer family.
Financial data (yr. ended 11/30/00): Grants paid, $1,603,241; assets, $13,781,585 (M); gifts received, $452,000; expenditures, $2,009,924; qualifying distributions, $1,671,304.
Limitations: Giving primarily in New York, NY.
Officers and Directors:* Richard J. Scheuer,* Pres.; Laura L. Scheuer,* V.P.; Elizabeth H. Scheuer,* Secy.; Sidney Silberman,* Treas.
EIN: 136062661
Codes: FD, FM

32912
Schlumberger Foundation, Inc.
c/o Schlumberger, Ltd.
277 Park Ave.
New York, NY 10172
Application address: c/o Arthur W. Alexander, 153 E. 53rd St., 57th Fl., New York, NY 10022, tel.: (212) 350-9400

Schlumberger Foundation established as a trust in 1954 in TX; terminated in 1982 and assets transferred to Schlumberger Horizons, Inc., a DE foundation; in 1982 name changed to Schlumberger Foundation, Inc.
Donor(s): Schlumberger, Ltd.
Financial data (yr. ended 12/31/00): Grants paid, $1,602,612; assets, $29,984,897 (M); expenditures, $1,674,424; qualifying distributions, $1,613,476.
Limitations: Giving limited to the North American continent.
Application information: Application form not required.
Officer: Arthur W. Alexander, Secy.
Directors: David S. Browning, Simone Crook, Arthur Lindenauer, Larry Schwartz.
EIN: 237033142
Codes: CS, FD, CD

32913
Mary W. Harriman Foundation
c/o Brown Brothers Harriman Trust Co.
63 Wall St., 31st Fl.
New York, NY 10005 (212) 493-8182
Contact: William F. Hibberd, Secy.

Trust established in 1925 in NY; incorporated in 1973.
Donor(s): Mary W. Harriman.‡
Financial data (yr. ended 12/31/00): Grants paid, $1,600,950; assets, $34,494,139 (M); expenditures, $1,796,831; qualifying distributions, $1,594,425.
Limitations: Giving primarily in the metropolitan New York, NY, and Washington, DC, areas.
Application information: Application form not required.
Officers and Directors:* David H. Mortimer,* Pres.; Kathleen L.F. Ames,* V.P.; William F. Hibberd, Secy.; Anna T. Korniczky, Treas.; Marjorie Northrop Friedman, Kathleen H. Mortimer.
EIN: 237356000
Codes: FD

32914
Helen A. Benedict Foundation, Inc.
330 Madison Ave., 30th Fl.
New York, NY 10017-6204

Established in 1997 in NY.
Donor(s): John E. Andres Memorial, Inc.
Financial data (yr. ended 12/31/00): Grants paid, $1,599,123; assets, $41,804,901 (M); expenditures, $1,941,188; qualifying distributions, $2,017,008.
Limitations: Applications not accepted. Giving limited to Hastings, NY.
Application information: Contributes only to pre-selected organizations.
Officers and Directors:* Peter B. Benedict,* Chair.; Frederick F. Moon III,* Vice-Chair.; John J. Lynagh, Secy.; Samuel S. Thorpe III,* Treas.; Marc De Venoge, Kate Downes, Josie Lowman.
EIN: 133940833
Codes: FD

32915
LaSalle Adams Fund
c/o Rockefeller Fin. Svcs.
30 Rockefeller Plz., 56th Fl.
New York, NY 10112
Contact: Chris Page, Philanthropic Advisor

Established in 1953 in IL; incorporated in 1999 in NY.
Donor(s): Sydney Stein, Jr.‡
Financial data (yr. ended 12/31/00): Grants paid, $1,595,000; assets, $39,475,029 (M); expenditures, $2,346,499; qualifying distributions, $1,665,306.
Limitations: Applications not accepted. Giving primarily in the Rocky Mountain States and the Grand Traverse Bay region, MI.
Application information: Contributes only to pre-selected organizations.
Officer and Directors:* Carol Stein,* Pres.; Craig Kennedy.
EIN: 161562907
Codes: FD

32916
KBRK, Inc.
c/o Hertz, Herson & Company, LLP
Two Park Ave., Ste. 1500
New York, NY 10016

Established in 1997 in NY and DE.
Financial data (yr. ended 06/30/01): Grants paid, $1,590,000; assets, $26,800,024 (M); gifts

32916—NEW YORK

received, $3,161,285; expenditures, $1,610,493; qualifying distributions, $11,494.
Limitations: Applications not accepted. Giving primarily in Jenkintown, PA.
Application information: Contributes only to pre-selected organizations.
Officers and Directors:* Bella Wexner,* Pres.; Susan Wexner,* Secy.-Treas.; Bertrand Agus.
EIN: 134077801
Codes: FD

32917
The Charles G. Phillips Family Foundation
775 Park Ave.
New York, NY 10021

Established in 1997 in NY.
Donor(s): Charles G. Phillips, Candace Phillips.
Financial data (yr. ended 10/31/00): Grants paid, $1,581,667; assets, $7,273,073 (M); gifts received, $3,000,017; expenditures, $1,586,117; qualifying distributions, $1,557,676.
Limitations: Applications not accepted. Giving primarily in New York, NY.
Application information: Contributes only to pre-selected organizations.
Trustees: Candace Phillips, Charles G. Phillips.
EIN: 133981242
Codes: FD

32918
IIMI, Inc.
c/o Hertz, Herson & Company, LLP
Two Park Ave., Ste. 1500
New York, NY 10016

Established in 1997 in NY.
Financial data (yr. ended 06/30/01): Grants paid, $1,580,000; assets, $25,882,513 (M); gifts received, $3,147,428; expenditures, $1,602,544; qualifying distributions, $11,634.
Limitations: Applications not accepted. Giving primarily in Jenkintown, PA.
Application information: Contributes only to pre-selected organizations.
Officers and Directors:* Bella Wexner,* Pres.; Susan Wexner,* Secy.-Treas.; Bertrand Agus.
EIN: 134077817
Codes: FD

32919
JLRJ, Inc.
c/o Hertz, Herson & Company, LLP
Two Park Ave., Ste. 1500
New York, NY 10016

Established in 1997 in NY and DE.
Financial data (yr. ended 06/30/01): Grants paid, $1,580,000; assets, $24,409,182 (M); gifts received, $3,147,262; expenditures, $1,602,433; qualifying distributions, $11,575.
Limitations: Applications not accepted. Giving primarily in Jenkintown, PA.
Application information: Contributes only to pre-selected organizations.
Officers and Directors:* Bella Wexner,* Pres.; Susan Wexner,* Secy.-Treas.; Bertrand Agus.
EIN: 134077806
Codes: FD

32920
MRHM, Inc.
c/o Hertz, Herson & Company, LLP
Two Park Ave., Ste. 1500
New York, NY 10016

Established in 1997 in NY and DE.
Financial data (yr. ended 06/30/01): Grants paid, $1,580,000; assets, $30,617,792 (M); gifts received, $3,132,465; expenditures, $1,601,798; qualifying distributions, $11,481.

Limitations: Applications not accepted. Giving primarily in Jenkintown, PA.
Application information: Contributes only to pre-selected organizations.
Officers and Directors:* Bella Wexner,* Pres.; Susan Wexner,* Secy.-Treas.; Bertrand Agus.
EIN: 134077880
Codes: FD

32921
CJM Foundation
c/o Eric Kaplan
1285 6th Ave. 21st Fl.
New York, NY 10019

Established in 1996 in NY.
Donor(s): Seymour Milstein,‡ Vivian Milstein.
Financial data (yr. ended 12/31/00): Grants paid, $1,579,987; assets, $2,445,692 (M); gifts received, $1,500,000; expenditures, $1,582,008; qualifying distributions, $1,579,485.
Limitations: Applications not accepted. Giving primarily in NY.
Application information: Contributes only to pre-selected organizations.
Trustees: Constance Milstein, Vivian Milstein.
EIN: 137105559
Codes: FD

32922
Michael R. Lynch & Susan Baker Foundation
c/o Goldman Sachs & Co.
85 Broad St., Tax Dept.
New York, NY 10004

Established in 1987 in NY.
Donor(s): Michael R. Lynch.
Financial data (yr. ended 07/31/01): Grants paid, $1,575,401; assets, $6,581,562 (M); gifts received, $2,436,563; expenditures, $1,575,481; qualifying distributions, $1,577,624.
Limitations: Applications not accepted. Giving primarily in CT and New York, NY.
Application information: Contributes only to pre-selected organizations.
Trustees: Susan L. Baker, Kevin W. Kennedy, Michael R. Lynch.
EIN: 133438049
Codes: FD

32923
The Alice M. & Thomas J. Tisch Foundation, Inc.
c/o Mark J. Krinsky, CPA
655 Madison Ave., 8th Fl.
New York, NY 10021-8043

Established in 1992 in NY and DE.
Donor(s): Laurence A. Tisch, Thomas J. Tisch.
Financial data (yr. ended 12/31/01): Grants paid, $1,572,385; assets, $35,989,744 (M); expenditures, $1,590,502; qualifying distributions, $1,578,452.
Limitations: Applications not accepted. Giving primarily in New York, NY.
Application information: Contributes only to pre-selected organizations.
Officers: Thomas J. Tisch, Pres.; Alice M. Tisch, Sr. V.P.; Mark J. Krinsky, V.P.; Barry L. Bloom, Secy.-Treas.
EIN: 133693582
Codes: FD

32924
Liz Claiborne Foundation
1440 Broadway
New York, NY 10018 (212) 626-5704
FAX: (212) 626-5304
Contact: Melanie Lyons, V.P., Philanthropic Progs.

Established in 1981 in NY.

Donor(s): Liz Claiborne, Inc.
Financial data (yr. ended 12/31/00): Grants paid, $1,571,645; assets, $30,274,909 (M); expenditures, $1,891,558; qualifying distributions, $1,571,645.
Limitations: Giving only in the four areas where the main operating facilities of Liz Claiborne, Inc. are located: Montgomery, AL, Hudson County, NJ, New York, NY, and Mount Pocono, PA.
Publications: Application guidelines.
Application information: Product donations are strictly limited and are made only in support of significant volunteer involvement by Liz Claiborne, Inc. employees. Application form not required.
Trustees: Paul R. Charron, Robert McKean, Michael Scarpa, Robert Vill.
EIN: 133060673
Codes: CS, FD, CD

32925
Silverweed Foundation, Inc.
c/o Yohalem Gillman & Co., LLP
477 Madison Ave.
New York, NY 10022-5802

Established in 1989.
Financial data (yr. ended 12/31/00): Grants paid, $1,569,340; assets, $22,630,469 (M); expenditures, $2,102,443; qualifying distributions, $1,619,930.
Limitations: Applications not accepted. Giving primarily in New York, NY.
Application information: Contributes only to pre-selected organizations.
Officers: Karen Freedman, Pres.; Susan K. Freedman, V.P. and Secy.; Nina P. Freedman, V.P. and Treas.
EIN: 133496446
Codes: FD

32926
LMCL, Inc.
c/o Hertz, Herson & Company, LLP
Two Park Ave., Ste. 1500
New York, NY 10016

Established in 1997 in NY.
Financial data (yr. ended 06/30/01): Grants paid, $1,560,000; assets, $27,372,825 (M); gifts received, $3,098,701; expenditures, $1,581,032; qualifying distributions, $11,494.
Limitations: Applications not accepted. Giving primarily in Jenkintown, PA.
Application information: Contributes only to pre-selected organizations.
Officers and Directors:* Bella Wexner,* Pres.; Susan Wexner,* Secy.-Treas.; Bertrand Agus.
EIN: 134077883
Codes: FD

32927
Patterson Family Foundation
c/o Brandywine Mgmt. Svcs.
880 3rd Ave., 3rd Fl.
New York, NY 10022
Application address: 3343 Pacific Ave., San Francisco, CA 94118
Contact: Louise M. Patterson, Pres.

Established in 1997 in CA.
Donor(s): Arthur C. Patterson.
Financial data (yr. ended 12/31/00): Grants paid, $1,556,000; assets, $1,519,044 (M); gifts received, $272,781; expenditures, $1,617,168; qualifying distributions, $1,555,321.
Limitations: Giving primarily in CA.
Application information: Application form not required.

Officers: Louise M. Patterson, Pres.; Arthur C. Patterson, Treas.
EIN: 943268717
Codes: FD

32928
John Ben Snow Memorial Trust
50 Presidential Plz., Ste. 106
Syracuse, NY 13202
Contact: Jonathan L. Snow, Tr., Rollan D. Melton, Tr. (NV), or Allen R. Malcom, Tr (MD)

Trust established in 1975 in NY.
Donor(s): John Ben Snow.‡
Financial data (yr. ended 12/31/00): Grants paid, $1,550,514; assets, $29,985,247 (M); expenditures, $1,907,067; qualifying distributions, $1,637,306.
Limitations: Giving primarily in MD, NV, and central NY.
Publications: Annual report (including application guidelines).
Application information: Contact closest regional office. Application form required.
Trustees: Allen R. Malcom, Rollan D. Melton, Jonathan L. Snow, The Bank of New York.
EIN: 136633814
Codes: FD

32929
The Diller-von Furstenberg Family Foundation
(also known as The Diller Foundation)
c/o Patricia Doudna, Ernst & Young
787 7th Ave.
New York, NY 10019

Established in 1986 in CA.
Donor(s): Barry Diller.
Financial data (yr. ended 12/31/00): Grants paid, $1,542,985; assets, $5,104,827 (M); expenditures, $1,545,391; qualifying distributions, $1,544,511.
Limitations: Applications not accepted. Giving primarily in CA and New York, NY.
Application information: Contributes only to pre-selected organizations.
Officer: Barry Diller, Pres. and C.F.O.
EIN: 954081892
Codes: FD

32930
The Marc Haas Foundation, Inc.
405 Lexington Ave., 14th Fl.
New York, NY 10174-0208
Contact: Robert H. Haines, Pres.

Established in 1985 in NY.
Financial data (yr. ended 12/31/00): Grants paid, $1,540,000; assets, $43,404,977 (M); expenditures, $2,701,203; qualifying distributions, $1,645,449.
Limitations: Giving primarily in NJ, and New York, NY.
Application information: Application form not required.
Officers and Directors:* Stanley S. Shuman,* Chair. and Secy.; Robert H. Haines,* Pres. and Treas.
EIN: 133073137
Codes: FD

32931
The Concordia Foundation
c/o JPMorgan Chase Bank
1211 Ave. of the Americas. 38th Fl.
New York, NY 10036 (212) 789-5682
E-mail: jones_ed_l@jpmorgan.com
Contact: Edward L. Jones, V.P.

Established in 1997 in MD.
Donor(s): John J. Roberts.
Financial data (yr. ended 12/31/01): Grants paid, $1,533,230; assets, $31,430,817 (M); expenditures, $1,718,673; qualifying distributions, $1,704,125.
Limitations: Giving primarily in MD and NJ; some funding also in NY.
Application information: Application form not required.
Trustees: Christopher L. Roberts, John J. Roberts, Nancy L. Roberts, Rebecca B. Roberts.
EIN: 311486126
Codes: FD

32932
Hagedorn Fund
c/o JPMorgan Chase Bank
1211 Ave. of the Americas, 38th Fl.
New York, NY 10036 (212) 789-5702
Contact: Ms. Monica J. Neal, V.P., JPMorgan Chase Bank

Trust established in 1953 in NY.
Donor(s): William Hagedorn.‡
Financial data (yr. ended 12/31/01): Grants paid, $1,530,500; assets, $31,167,003 (M); expenditures, $1,883,602; qualifying distributions, $1,679,950.
Limitations: Giving primarily in New York, NY.
Application information: More than 95 percent of grants represent renewed support for previous grantees; a small number of new grantees may be considered each year. Application form not required.
Trustees: John J. Kindred III, Charles B. Lauren, JPMorgan Chase Bank.
EIN: 136048718
Codes: FD

32933
Task Foundation, Inc.
(Formerly Consumer Action Council on Collective Purchasing, Inc.)
c/o Phil Weinper
20 S. Bayles Ave.
Port Washington, NY 11050 (516) 883-7711
Contact: Theodore W. Kheel, Pres.

Established around 1992.
Donor(s): Ann S. Kheel, Theodore W. Kheel.
Financial data (yr. ended 12/31/00): Grants paid, $1,529,949; assets, $10,542,816 (M); gifts received, $2,750; expenditures, $1,855,475; qualifying distributions, $1,823,066.
Limitations: Giving primarily in NY.
Application information: Application form not required.
Officers: Theodore W. Kheel, Pres.; Ann S. Kheel, V.P.; Robert Kheel, Secy.
EIN: 131968353
Codes: FD

32934
The Aaron Copland Fund for Music, Inc.
c/o Brown Raysman LLP
900 3rd Ave., 23rd Fl.
New York, NY 10022 (212) 895-2367
Application address: c/o American Music Ctr., 30 W. 26th St. Ste 1001, New York, NY 10010-2011, tel.: (212) 366-5260 (for performing ensemble and recording programs); FAX: (212) 366-5265; URL: http://www.amc.net/resources/grants
Contact: James M. Kendrick, Secy.

Established in 1991 in NY; funded in 1992.
Donor(s): Aaron Copland.‡
Financial data (yr. ended 06/30/01): Grants paid, $1,527,115; assets, $15,208,332 (M); expenditures, $2,073,309; qualifying distributions, $1,891,420.
Limitations: Giving on a national basis.
Publications: Informational brochure (including application guidelines).
Application information: Application form required.
Officers and Directors:* John Harbison,* Pres.; Vivian Perlis,* V.P.; James M. Kendrick, Secy.; Norman Feit, Treas.; Arthur Berger, Elliot Carter, John Corigliano, David Del Tredici, Lukas Foss, Ellis J. Freedman, Ursula Oppens, Christopher Rouse, Ellen Taaffe Zwilich.
EIN: 133620909
Codes: FD

32935
The Louis Marx Foundation, Inc.
645 Madison Ave., Ste. 500
New York, NY 10022 (212) 888-4004

Incorporated in 1953 in NY.
Donor(s): Wycombe Corp., Marline Co., Inc., Louis Marx, Sr.,‡ Louis Marx, Jr.
Financial data (yr. ended 02/28/01): Grants paid, $1,526,917; assets, $414,791 (M); expenditures, $1,527,400; qualifying distributions, $1,527,400.
Limitations: Applications not accepted. Giving on a national basis.
Application information: Contributes only to pre-selected organizations.
Officers and Trustees:* Louis Marx, Jr.,* Pres.; Seymour L. Wane,* Secy.; Jacqueline E. Barnett, Emmett Marx.
EIN: 136113640
Codes: FD

32936
The Allison Family Foundation, Inc.
50 Butler Rd.
Scarsdale, NY 10583-2238

Established in 1998 in NY.
Donor(s): Herbert M. Allison, Jr.
Financial data (yr. ended 05/31/01): Grants paid, $1,526,672; assets, $8,503,048 (M); gifts received, $5,009,228; expenditures, $1,620,130; qualifying distributions, $1,507,797.
Limitations: Applications not accepted.
Application information: Contributes only to pre-selected organizations.
Directors: Herbert M. Allison, Jr., John R. Allison, Simin Nazemi Allison.
EIN: 134011223
Codes: FD

32937
The James E. and Patricia D. Cayne Charitable Trust
245 Park Ave., 9th Fl.
New York, NY 10167

Established in 1996 in NY.
Donor(s): James E. Cayne.
Financial data (yr. ended 05/31/01): Grants paid, $1,523,890; assets, $17,693,853 (M); gifts received, $53,700; expenditures, $1,546,383; qualifying distributions, $1,523,890.
Limitations: Applications not accepted. Giving on a national basis; some giving also in Jerusalem, Israel.
Application information: Contributes only to pre-selected organizations.
Trustees: James E. Cayne, Patricia Cayne.
EIN: 137100859
Codes: FD

32938
The Carmel Hill Fund
(Formerly Ruane Family Fund)
767 5th Ave., Ste. 4701
New York, NY 10153-4798

Established in 1986 in NY.
Donor(s): William J. Ruane.
Financial data (yr. ended 12/31/00): Grants paid, $1,522,535; assets, $50,383,849 (M); gifts received, $500,000; expenditures, $1,652,863; qualifying distributions, $1,632,341.
Limitations: Applications not accepted. Giving primarily in NY.
Application information: Contributes only to pre-selected organizations.
Trustee: William J. Ruane.
EIN: 136881103
Codes: FD

32939
The Lillian Goldman Charitable Trust
c/o Anchin Block & Anchin, LLP
1375 Broadway
New York, NY 10018

Established in 1995 in NY.
Donor(s): Sol Goldman,‡ The Sol Goldman Charitable Trust.
Financial data (yr. ended 04/30/01): Grants paid, $1,518,400; assets, $46,327,055 (M); gifts received, $1,944,191; expenditures, $1,692,406; qualifying distributions, $1,521,989.
Limitations: Applications not accepted. Giving limited to NY.
Application information: Contributes only to pre-selected organizations.
Trustee: Amy Goldman.
EIN: 137048279
Codes: FD

32940
The MAT Charitable Foundation, Inc.
c/o Lutz & Carr
300 E. 42nd St.
New York, NY 10017
Contact: Samantha Tsao, Admin.

Established in 1992 in NY.
Donor(s): Ruth Uris.‡
Financial data (yr. ended 06/30/01): Grants paid, $1,514,894; assets, $20,627,482 (M); gifts received, $612,081; expenditures, $1,827,128; qualifying distributions, $1,730,840.
Limitations: Applications not accepted. Giving primarily in NY.
Application information: Contributes only to pre-selected organizations.
Officers: Timothy U. Nye, Pres.; Amy J. Nye, V.P.; Jane U. Bayard, Secy.-Treas.
EIN: 136991067
Codes: FD

32941
The B. Thomas Golisano Foundation
c/o Fishers Asset Mgmt.
1 Fishers Rd.
Pittsford, NY 14534 (585) 340-1203
FAX: (716) 340-1204; E-mail: acostello@golisanofoundation.org; URL: http://www.golisanofoundation.org
Contact: Ann Costello, Dir.

Established in 1985 in NY.
Donor(s): B. Thomas Golisano.
Financial data (yr. ended 10/31/01): Grants paid, $1,508,565; assets, $25,025,010 (M); expenditures, $1,753,616; qualifying distributions, $1,530,092.
Limitations: Giving primarily in Rochester, NY.

Publications: Program policy statement, application guidelines, annual report, grants list.
Application information: Application form required.
Trustees: Gloria Austin, G. Thomas Clark, B. Thomas Golisano, Nancy Koch, James Murray, Margaret Raymond.
EIN: 222692938
Codes: FD

32942
The Price Family Foundation, Inc.
25 E. 86th St.
New York, NY 10028
Contact: Robert Price, Dir.

Established in 1998 in NY.
Donor(s): Robert Price.
Financial data (yr. ended 12/31/01): Grants paid, $1,507,790; assets, $2,358,513 (M); expenditures, $1,557,710; qualifying distributions, $1,517,946.
Limitations: Giving primarily in NY.
Directors: Catherine Dana, Eileen Farbman, Robert Price.
EIN: 134003955

32943
The Sol Goldman Charitable Trust
640 5th Ave., 3rd Fl.
New York, NY 10019
Contact: Jane H. Goldman, Tr.

Established in 1988 in NY; funded in fiscal 1990.
Donor(s): Sol Goldman.‡
Financial data (yr. ended 01/31/01): Grants paid, $1,504,888; assets, $121,622,183 (M); gifts received, $7,221,721; expenditures, $1,863,060; qualifying distributions, $1,517,745.
Limitations: Giving primarily in New York, NY.
Application information: Application form not required.
Trustees: Allan H. Goldman, Jane H. Goldman, Louisa Little.
EIN: 133577310
Codes: FD

32944
The Betty & Norman F. Levy Foundation, Inc.
270 Park Ave., 38th Fl.
New York, NY 10017-2070

Established in 1965 in NY.
Donor(s): Norman F. Levy.
Financial data (yr. ended 09/30/01): Grants paid, $1,501,974; assets, $29,487,087 (M); expenditures, $1,528,724; qualifying distributions, $1,435,657.
Limitations: Applications not accepted. Giving primarily in New York, NY.
Application information: Contributes only to pre-selected organizations.
Officers and Directors:* Norman F. Levy,* Pres.; Francis N. Levy,* V.P.; Albert L. Maltz,* Secy.
EIN: 132553674
Codes: FD

32945
Louis & Emanuel G. Rosenblatt Foundation, Inc.
360 Central Ave., Ste. 111
Lawrence, NY 11559 (516) 295-2530
Contact: Edward W. Fox, Pres.

Established around 1966 in NY.
Donor(s): Master Equities Corp.
Financial data (yr. ended 06/30/01): Grants paid, $1,499,400; assets, $3,336,619 (M); gifts received, $3,500,000; expenditures, $1,523,911; qualifying distributions, $1,497,155.
Limitations: Applications not accepted. Giving primarily in FL and NY.

Application information: Contributes only to pre-selected organizations.
Officers: Edward W. Fox, Pres.; Bernice Selevan, V.P.; Lois Lustig, Secy.-Treas.
EIN: 136189436
Codes: FD

32946
Greentree Foundation
400 Madison Ave., Ste. 1001
New York, NY 10017 (212) 888-7755
Contact: George Patterson, Grants Mgr.

Established in 1982 in NY.
Donor(s): Betsey C. Whitney.‡
Financial data (yr. ended 12/31/00): Grants paid, $1,491,900; assets, $286,496,400 (M); gifts received, $157,880,676; expenditures, $7,797,989; qualifying distributions, $7,260,428.
Limitations: Giving primarily in the metropolitan New York, NY, area.
Application information: Application form not required.
Officers and Trustees:* Robert Curvin, Pres.; Kate R. Whitney,* V.P.; Sara R. Wilford,* V.P.; Robert Carswell,* Treas.; Franklin A. Thomas, Ronald A. Wilford.
EIN: 133132117
Codes: FD

32947
The Perkin Fund
c/o Morris & McVeigh
767 3rd Ave.
New York, NY 10017
Application address: 200 Connecticut Ave., 5th Fl., Norwalk, CT 06854
Contact: Robert S. Perkin, Tr.

Established in 1967 in NY.
Donor(s): Richard S. Perkin.‡
Financial data (yr. ended 12/31/01): Grants paid, $1,489,795; assets, $30,132,342 (M); expenditures, $1,952,668; qualifying distributions, $1,525,796.
Limitations: Giving primarily in CT, MA, and NY.
Publications: Annual report, informational brochure (including application guidelines), financial statement.
Application information: Application form not required.
Trustees: James G. Baker, Kristina P. Davison, John M. Gray, Matthew E.P. Gray, Winifred P. Gray, Peter W. Oldershaw, Christopher T. Perkin, Nicolas R. Perkin, Richard T. Perkin, Robert S. Perkin, Howard Phipps, Jr.
EIN: 136222498
Codes: FD

32948
Dow Jones Foundation
c/o U.S. Trust
114 W. 47th St.
New York, NY 10036
Application address: P.O. Box 300, Princeton, NJ 08543, tel.: (609) 520-5146; FAX: (212) 852-3377
Contact: Carolyn L. Larke, Asst. V.P., U.S. Trust; or Linda Franciscovich, Sr. V.P.

Trust established in 1954 in NY.
Donor(s): Dow Jones & Co., Inc.
Financial data (yr. ended 12/31/00): Grants paid, $1,488,244; assets, $311,324 (M); expenditures, $1,494,407; qualifying distributions, $1,488,609.
Limitations: Applications not accepted. Giving primarily in areas of company operations.
Advisory Committee: Nicole Bourgois, Leonard E. Doherty, Peter R. Kann, James H. Ottaway, Jr.
Trustee: U.S. Trust.

EIN: 136070158
Codes: CS, FD, CD

32949
Lemberg Foundation, Inc.
60 E. 42nd St., Rm. 1814
New York, NY 10165 (212) 682-9595
Contact: John Usdan, Pres.

Incorporated in 1945 in NY.
Donor(s): Samuel Lemberg.‡
Financial data (yr. ended 12/31/00): Grants paid, $1,485,877; assets, $31,227,340 (M); gifts received, $75,000; expenditures, $1,870,234; qualifying distributions, $1,457,255.
Limitations: Giving primarily in NY.
Officers: John Usdan, Pres.; Esme Usdan, V.P.; Adam Usdan, Treas.
EIN: 136082064
Codes: FD

32950
Betty & John A. Levin Fund
(Formerly Elisabeth & John Levin Fund)
c/o John A. Levine & Co., Inc.
1 Rockefeller Plz., 25th Fl.
New York, NY 10020
Contact: Betty Levin, Pres.

Established in 1964.
Donor(s): Elisabeth L. Levin, John Levin.
Financial data (yr. ended 11/30/00): Grants paid, $1,482,247; assets, $3,327,054 (M); gifts received, $7,592; expenditures, $1,568,784; qualifying distributions, $1,482,572.
Limitations: Applications not accepted. Giving primarily in New York, NY.
Application information: Contributes only to pre-selected organizations.
Officers: Elisabeth L. Levin, Pres.; John A. Levin, Secy.-Treas.
EIN: 136168345
Codes: FD

32951
The Sue and Eugene Mercy, Jr. Foundation, Inc.
c/o BCRS Assoc., LLC
67 Wall St., 8th Fl.
New York, NY 10005

Established in 1967 in NY.
Donor(s): Eugene Mercy, Jr.
Financial data (yr. ended 12/31/00): Grants paid, $1,482,088; assets, $7,764,703 (M); expenditures, $1,700,435; qualifying distributions, $1,469,695.
Limitations: Applications not accepted. Giving primarily in New York, NY.
Application information: Contributes only to pre-selected organizations.
Officers: Eugene Mercy, Jr., Pres.; Sue Mercy, V.P.; Robert E. Mnuchin, Secy.
Directors: Andrew Seth Mercy, Eugene Mercy III.
EIN: 136217050
Codes: FD

32952
The Rosamond Gifford Charitable Corporation
518 James St., Ste. 280
Syracuse, NY 13203 (315) 474-2489
FAX: (315) 475-4983; URL: http://www.giffordfd.org
Contact: Kathryn Goldfarb, Exec. Dir.

Incorporated in 1954 in NY.
Donor(s): Rosamond Gifford.‡
Financial data (yr. ended 12/31/00): Grants paid, $1,480,636; assets, $33,583,452 (M); expenditures, $2,087,748; qualifying distributions, $1,677,782.
Limitations: Giving limited to organizations located within and serving the residents of the town of Syracuse, and Onondaga, Oswego, and Madison counties, NY.
Publications: Program policy statement, application guidelines, annual report.
Application information: Application form not required.
Officers and Trustees:* Edward S. Green,* Pres.; Bethaida C. Gonzalez,* V.P.; Charles A. Chappell, Jr.,* Secy.; Patricia T. Civil,* Treas.; Kathy Goldfarb, Exec. Dir.; Richard Case, Robert F. Dewey, Amelia Greiner, Linda M. Hall, Bill Harper, Patrick A. Mannion, Judith C. Mower, Minister Mark Muhammad, Sharon Northrup, Joanne Reddick, Jack H. Webb.
EIN: 150572881
Codes: FD

32953
Roslyn Milstein Meyer Foundation
c/o Eric Kaplan
335 Madison Ave., 15th Fl.
New York, NY 10017

Established in 1996 in NY.
Donor(s): Irma Milstein, Paul Milstein, Roslyn Meyer.
Financial data (yr. ended 12/31/01): Grants paid, $1,479,845; assets, $2,426,170 (M); gifts received, $1,250,000; expenditures, $1,487,875; qualifying distributions, $1,479,671.
Limitations: Applications not accepted. Giving primarily in CT.
Application information: Contributes only to pre-selected organizations.
Trustees: Roslyn Meyer, Irma Milstein, Paul Milstein.
EIN: 133921828
Codes: FD

32954
Ralph C. Sheldon Foundation, Inc.
P.O. Box 417
Jamestown, NY 14702-0417 (716) 664-9890
Application address: 7 E. 3rd St., Jamestown, NY 14701; FAX: (716) 483-6116
Contact: Miles L. Lasser, Exec. Dir.

Incorporated in 1948 in NY.
Donor(s): Julia S. Livengood,‡ Isabell M. Sheldon.‡
Financial data (yr. ended 05/31/01): Grants paid, $1,477,190; assets, $10,152,667 (M); gifts received, $1,380,143; expenditures, $1,564,980; qualifying distributions, $1,501,871.
Limitations: Giving limited to southern Chautauqua County, NY.
Publications: Application guidelines.
Application information: Contact foundation for deadlines. Application form required.
Officers and Directors:* Jane E. Sheldon,* Pres.; Mark Hampton,* V.P.; Barclay O. Wellman,* V.P.; Miles L. Lasser,* Secy. and Exec. Dir.; Peter B. Sullivan,* Treas.
EIN: 166030502
Codes: FD

32955
Louis S. & Molly B. Wolk Foundation
1600 East Ave., Ste. 701
Rochester, NY 14610 (716) 442-6900
Contact: Grants Committee

Established in 1982.
Donor(s): Louis S. Wolk.
Financial data (yr. ended 12/31/00): Grants paid, $1,475,374; assets, $30,852,262 (M); expenditures, $1,935,706; qualifying distributions, $1,535,064.
Limitations: Giving primarily in Rochester, NY.
Application information: Application form required.
Trustees: Leon Germanow, Chair.; Michael B. Berger, Audrey P. Cooke, Harold Samloff, Alvin L. Ureles, M.D., David M. Wolk, Marvin L. Wolk.
EIN: 222405596
Codes: FD

32956
The Brownington Foundation
c/o Morris & McVeigh
767 3rd Ave.
New York, NY 10017

Established about 1970.
Donor(s): Mary J. Tweedy.‡
Financial data (yr. ended 12/31/00): Grants paid, $1,475,000; assets, $29,198,705 (M); gifts received, $703,809; expenditures, $1,558,040; qualifying distributions, $1,501,997.
Limitations: Applications not accepted. Giving primarily in NY.
Application information: Contributes only to pre-selected organizations.
Officers: Ann T. Savage, Pres.; Margot M. Tweedy, V.P.; Leonard B. Boehner, Secy.; Clare T. McMorris, Treas.
EIN: 237043230
Codes: FD

32957
The Lizbeth & Frank Newman Charitable Foundation
712 5th Ave., 20th Fl.
New York, NY 10019
Contact: Mary Reen, Treas.

Established in 1999 in NY.
Donor(s): Frank N. Newman, Lizabeth Newman.
Financial data (yr. ended 12/31/00): Grants paid, $1,454,550; assets, $3,551,118 (M); expenditures, $1,542,173; qualifying distributions, $1,452,955.
Limitations: Applications not accepted. Giving primarily in NY.
Application information: Contributes only to pre-selected organizations.
Officers: Frank Newman, Pres.; Lizabeth Newman, V.P. and Secy.; Mary Reen, Treas.
EIN: 134067790
Codes: FD

32958
Cody Family Foundation, Inc.
c/o BCRS Assocs., LLC, Att: Joseph DeMaio
100 Wall St., 11th Fl.
New York, NY 10005

Established in 1996 in NY.
Donor(s): Education for Youth, Matthew J. Cody.
Financial data (yr. ended 09/30/01): Grants paid, $1,446,667; assets, $183,270 (M); gifts received, $732,582; expenditures, $1,482,883; qualifying distributions, $1,482,498.
Limitations: Applications not accepted. Giving primarily in NY.
Application information: Contributes only to pre-selected organizations.
Officers: Matthew J. Cody, Pres. and Treas.; Debra Cody, V.P. and Secy.; John E. Cody, V.P.
EIN: 113365898
Codes: FD

32959
The Page and Otto Marx, Jr. Foundation
c/o Joseph W. Levy
3000 Marcus Ave., Ste. 3W10
New Hyde Park, NY 11042

Established in 1984 in NY.
Donor(s): Otto Marx, Jr., Page M. Marx.‡

32959—NEW YORK

Financial data (yr. ended 12/31/00): Grants paid, $1,444,500; assets, $34,504,339 (M); expenditures, $1,475,548; qualifying distributions, $1,403,278.
Limitations: Applications not accepted. Giving primarily in NY.
Application information: Contributes only to pre-selected organizations.
Officers and Directors:* Bruce J. Westcott,* Pres.; Joseph W. Levy,* V.P. and Treas.; Jeffrey S. Levin, Secy.; Jill S. Levy, Helen Westcott.
EIN: 133200783
Codes: FD

32960
Dorothy Jordan Chadwick Fund
c/o U.S. Trust of New York
114 W. 47th St.
New York, NY 10036
Application address: c/o Davidson Dawson & Clark, 36 Grove St., New Canaan, CT 06840; FAX: (203) 966-7894
Contact: Berkeley D. Johnson, Jr., Tr.

Trust established in 1957 in NY.
Donor(s): Dorothy J. Chadwick,‡ Dorothy R. Kidder.‡
Financial data (yr. ended 05/31/01): Grants paid, $1,443,600; assets, $27,077,858 (M); expenditures, $1,628,461; qualifying distributions, $1,485,749.
Limitations: Giving primarily along the Eastern Seaboard (Boston to Washington).
Publications: Application guidelines.
Application information: Application form not required.
Trustees: Berkeley D. Johnson, Jr., U.S. Trust.
EIN: 136069950
Codes: FD

32961
The Sharpe Family Foundation
c/o Fiduciary Trust Co.
600 5th Ave.
New York, NY 10020 (212) 466-4100
Contact: Henry D. Sharpe, Jr., Tr.

Established in 1966 in RI.
Donor(s): Mary Elizabeth Sharpe.‡
Financial data (yr. ended 12/31/00): Grants paid, $1,443,225; assets, $26,182,681 (M); gifts received, $6,000,029; expenditures, $1,607,978; qualifying distributions, $1,454,032.
Limitations: Giving primarily in RI.
Trustees: Henry B. Sharpe, Jr., Peggy B. Sharpe, Fiduciary Trust Co.
EIN: 136208422
Codes: FD

32962
The Humanitas Foundation
(Formerly Brencanda Foundation)
1114 Ave. of the Americas, 28th Fl.
New York, NY 10036 (212) 704-2300
Contact: Kathleen A. Mahoney, Pres.

Established in 1979.
Donor(s): American Retail Group, Inc.
Financial data (yr. ended 12/31/01): Grants paid, $1,434,750; assets, $157,832 (M); gifts received, $1,419,900; expenditures, $1,435,084; qualifying distributions, $1,434,666.
Limitations: Giving on a national basis.
Publications: Application guidelines, program policy statement.
Application information: Application form required.
Officer and Director:* Kathleen A. Mahoney,* Pres.
EIN: 133005012

Codes: FD

32963
The Peter and Elizabeth C. Tower Foundation
4232 Ridge Lea Rd., Ste. 28
Amherst, NY 14226-5100 (716) 862-4625
FAX: (716) 862-4642; E-mail: towerfdtn@att.net
Contact: Glenda M. Cadwallader, Exec. Dir.

Established in 1990.
Donor(s): Elizabeth C. Tower, Peter Tower, Peter Tower, Inc.
Financial data (yr. ended 12/31/00): Grants paid, $1,427,001; assets, $47,862,927 (M); gifts received, $25,190,130; expenditures, $2,005,944; qualifying distributions, $1,305,665.
Limitations: Giving primarily in MA, NY, and RI.
Publications: Application guidelines, grants list.
Application information: Application form required.
Officer: Glenda M. Cadwallader, Exec. Dir.
Trustees: John H. Byrnes, Mollie Tower Byrnes, Cynthia Tower Doyle, Robert M. Doyle, Todd M. Joseph, Elizabeth C. Tower, Peter Tower.
EIN: 166350753
Codes: FD

32964
Roy J. Zuckerberg Foundation
c/o BCRS Assocs., LLC
67 Wall St., 8th Fl.
New York, NY 10005

Established in 1980 in NY.
Donor(s): Roy J. Zuckerberg.
Financial data (yr. ended 09/30/00): Grants paid, $1,423,533; assets, $9,919,437 (M); gifts received, $1,230,000; expenditures, $1,424,710; qualifying distributions, $1,423,871.
Limitations: Applications not accepted. Giving primarily in the greater metropolitan New York, NY, area.
Application information: Contributes only to pre-selected organizations.
Trustees: James C. Kautz, Barbara Zuckerberg, Dina R. Zuckerberg, Lloyd P. Zuckerberg, Roy J. Zuckerberg.
EIN: 133052489
Codes: FD

32965
Morse Family Foundation, Inc.
(Formerly Enid & Lester S. Morse, Jr. Foundation, Inc.)
c/o Lester Morse Co.
60 E. 42nd St., Ste. 2446
New York, NY 10165-0015

Established in 1967 in NY.
Donor(s): Lester S. Morse, Jr.
Financial data (yr. ended 03/31/01): Grants paid, $1,422,396; assets, $4,671,547 (M); gifts received, $51,789; expenditures, $1,448,347; qualifying distributions, $1,407,787.
Limitations: Applications not accepted. Giving primarily in New York, NY.
Application information: Contributes only to pre-selected organizations.
Officers: Lester S. Morse, Jr., Pres.; Enid W. Morse, V.P.; Douglas A. Morse, Treas.
EIN: 136220174
Codes: FD

32966
Pinewood Foundation
c/o Rockefeller & Co.
30 Rockefeller Plz., Rm. 5600
New York, NY 10112

Incorporated in 1956 in NY as Celeste and Armand Bartos Foundation.

Donor(s): Celeste G. Bartos, D.S. and R.H. Gottesman Foundation.
Financial data (yr. ended 09/30/01): Grants paid, $1,420,050; assets, $2,412,673 (M); expenditures, $1,609,285; qualifying distributions, $1,553,924.
Limitations: Applications not accepted. Giving on a national basis, with some emphasis on the greater metropolitan New York, NY, area.
Application information: Contributes only to pre-selected organizations.
Officers and Directors:* Celeste G. Bartos,* Pres.; Jonathan Altman, V.P.; Kathleen Altman, V.P.; Adam Bartos, V.P.; Michael Lerner, V.P.; Marcia K. Townley, Secy.-Treas.
EIN: 136101581
Codes: FD

32967
Ross Family Charitable Foundation
c/o Starr & Co., LLC
350 Park Ave., Ste. 9
New York, NY 10022-6022 (212) 759-6556

Established in 1989 in NY.
Donor(s): Steven J. Ross.‡
Financial data (yr. ended 11/30/00): Grants paid, $1,418,268; assets, $8,861,360 (M); gifts received, $372,251; expenditures, $1,813,667; qualifying distributions, $1,422,016.
Limitations: Applications not accepted. Giving primarily in the greater metropolitan New York, NY, area, including Long Island.
Application information: Contributes only to pre-selected organizations.
Trustees: Bertram Fields, Elizabeth McCormack, Courtney S. Ross, Kenneth I. Starr.
EIN: 133552082
Codes: FD

32968
Joseph Rosen Foundation, Inc.
P.O. Box 334, Lenox Hill Sta.
New York, NY 10021

Incorporated in 1948 in NY.
Donor(s): Tranel, Inc.
Financial data (yr. ended 06/30/00): Grants paid, $1,415,958; assets, $23,810,760 (M); expenditures, $1,956,933; qualifying distributions, $1,342,161.
Limitations: Applications not accepted. Giving on a national basis.
Application information: Contributes only to pre-selected organizations.
Officers: Jonathan P. Rosen, Pres. and Secy.; Irving S. Bobrow, V.P.; Jeannette Rosen, V.P.; Miriam N. Rosen, Treas.
EIN: 136158412
Codes: FD

32969
Weil, Gotshal & Manges Foundation
767 5th Ave.
New York, NY 10153 (212) 310-8000
Contact: Jesse D. Wolff, Treas.

Established in 1983 in NY.
Donor(s): Weil, Gotshal & Manges LLP, Robert Todd Lang, Ira M. Millstein, Harvey R. Miller.
Financial data (yr. ended 12/31/99): Grants paid, $1,414,287; assets, $0 (M); gifts received, $1,515,000; expenditures, $1,416,052; qualifying distributions, $1,414,382.
Limitations: Giving primarily in NY.
Officers and Directors:* Robert Todd Lang,* Chair.; Ira M. Millstein,* Pres.; Harvey R. Miller,* Secy.; Jesse D. Wolff,* Treas.
EIN: 133158325
Codes: CS, FD, CD

32970
Miriam G. and Ira D. Wallach Foundation
3 Manhattanville Rd.
Purchase, NY 10577-2110

Incorporated in 1956 in NY.
Financial data (yr. ended 10/31/00): Grants paid, $1,413,209; assets, $17,634,120 (M); gifts received, $1,000,375; expenditures, $1,669,465; qualifying distributions, $1,458,757.
Limitations: Applications not accepted. Giving primarily in NY.
Application information: Contributes only to pre-selected organizations.
Officers and Directors:* Ira D. Wallach,* Chair.; Miriam G. Wallach,* Vice-Chair.; Kenneth L. Wallach,* Pres.; Edgar Wachenheim III,* V.P.; Peter C. Siegfried, Secy.; Reginald Reinhardt, Treas.; Kate W. Cassidy, Martin W. Cassidy, Sue W. Wachenheim, Mary K. Wallach, Susan S. Wallach.
EIN: 136101702
Codes: FD

32971
Abraham & Esther Hersh Foundation, Inc.
2310 Ave. R
Brooklyn, NY 11229

Established in 1994 in NY.
Donor(s): Ahron Hersh, Toby Hersh, Rosetti Handbags, Ltd.
Financial data (yr. ended 10/31/00): Grants paid, $1,410,001; assets, $1,467,568 (M); gifts received, $2,552,800; expenditures, $1,410,228; qualifying distributions, $1,410,001.
Limitations: Applications not accepted.
Application information: Contributes only to pre-selected organizations.
Directors: Ahron Hersh, Toby Hersh.
EIN: 113188332
Codes: FD

32972
Eugene and Emily Grant Family Foundation
277 Park Ave., 47th Fl.
New York, NY 10172 (212) 688-4700
Contact: Eugene M. Grant, Tr.

Established in 1998 in NY.
Donor(s): Eugene M. Grant, Terry E. Grant.
Financial data (yr. ended 12/31/01): Grants paid, $1,409,087; assets, $1,510,178 (M); gifts received, $1,050,000; expenditures, $1,414,161; qualifying distributions, $1,408,420.
Limitations: Giving in the U.S. and Israel.
Trustees: Emily Grant, Eugene M. Grant.
EIN: 133997005
Codes: FD

32973
The Icahn Family Foundation
c/o Icahn Assocs.
767 5th Ave., 47th Fl.
New York, NY 10153
Contact: Gail Golden Icahn, V.P.

Established in 1996 in DE and NY.
Donor(s): Carl C. Icahn.
Financial data (yr. ended 08/31/01): Grants paid, $1,408,000; assets, $28,547,009 (M); expenditures, $1,426,544; qualifying distributions, $1,397,764.
Limitations: Giving primarily in New York, NY; some funding also in Princeton, NJ.
Application information: Application form not required.
Officers: Carl C. Icahn, Pres. and Treas.; Gail Golden Icahn, V.P. and Secy.
EIN: 133906935
Codes: FD

32974
Miriam and Arthur Diamond Charitable Trust
c/o Cadwalader
100 Maiden Ln., Ste. 308
New York, NY 10038
Contact: Jay H. McDowell, Tr.; or Jack Adelman, Tr.

Established in 1996 in NY.
Financial data (yr. ended 12/31/01): Grants paid, $1,400,000; assets, $35,888,230 (M); expenditures, $1,930,505; qualifying distributions, $1,812,386.
Limitations: Giving primarily in New York, NY.
Trustees: Jack Adelman, Jay H. McDowell.
EIN: 137093689
Codes: FD

32975
The Laurie Tisch Sussman Foundation, Inc.
c/o Mark J. Krinsky, CPA
655 Madison Ave., 8th Fl.
New York, NY 10021-8043

Established in 1992 in NY.
Donor(s): Preston Robert Tisch, S. Donald Sussman, Joan H. Tisch.
Financial data (yr. ended 12/31/01): Grants paid, $1,398,374; assets, $13,125,528 (M); gifts received, $1,099,600; expenditures, $1,483,046; qualifying distributions, $1,464,315.
Limitations: Applications not accepted. Giving primarily in New York, NY.
Application information: Contributes only to pre-selected organizations.
Officers: Laurie Tisch Sussman, Pres.; Jonathan M. Tisch, Sr. V.P.; Mark J. Krinsky, V.P.; Thomas M. Steinberg, V.P.; Barry L. Bloom, Secy.-Treas.
EIN: 133693585
Codes: FD

32976
Ahavas Chesed Charitable Trust
c/o Abraham Trusts
200 W. 57th St., Ste. 1005
New York, NY 10019

Established in 1995 in NY.
Donor(s): Simona A. Ganz, Lionel "Aryeh" Ganz, Joshua Teitelbaum, Helene Teitelbaum, Reiss Charity Account, P & L Charity Foundation.
Financial data (yr. ended 06/30/01): Grants paid, $1,398,000; assets, $2,297,873 (M); gifts received, $346,165; expenditures, $1,433,727; qualifying distributions, $1,388,531.
Limitations: Applications not accepted.
Application information: Contributes only to pre-selected organizations.
Trustees: Lionel "Aryeh" Ganz, Simona A. Ganz.
EIN: 133780739
Codes: FD

32977
echoing green foundation
60 E. 42nd St., Ste. 2901
New York, NY 10165 (212) 689-1165
FAX: (212) 689-9010; *E-mail:* general@echoinggreen.org; *URL:* http://www.echoinggreen.org
Contact: Sandra K. Jones, V.P., Grants

Established in 1987 in DE.
Financial data (yr. ended 06/30/00): Grants paid, $1,397,389; assets, $1,469,454 (M); gifts received, $3,130,400; expenditures, $2,934,722; qualifying distributions, $2,878,012; giving activities include $930,243 for programs.
Limitations: Giving on a national and international basis.
Publications: Application guidelines.
Application information: Initial application available on website as of June 1, 2001. Application form required.
Officer and Directors:* Holland Hendrix,* Pres.; Carter Bayles, Cheryl Dorsey, Rosanne Haggerty, David C. Hodgson, Billy Shore.
EIN: 133424419
Codes: FD, GTI

32978
Nichols Foundation, Inc.
600 5th Ave.
New York, NY 10020 (212) 632-3000
E-mail: gscotto@ftcl.com
Contact: Peter Coxhead, Pres.

Incorporated in 1923 in NY.
Donor(s): Members of the Nichols family.
Financial data (yr. ended 12/31/01): Grants paid, $1,389,630; assets, $17,859,392 (M); gifts received, $270,000; expenditures, $1,640,796; qualifying distributions, $1,501,121.
Limitations: Applications not accepted. Giving primarily in Santa Barbara, CA, Hinsdale County, CO, FL, and the metropolitan New York, NY area.
Application information: Contributes only to pre-selected organizations. Unsolicited requests for funds not considered.
Officers and Directors:* Peter Coxhead,* Pres.; Peter C. Coxhead,* V.P.; Gina Scotto, Secy.; David H. Nichols,* Treas.; Marguerite D.R. Buttrick, Ralph N. Coxhead, Kathleen C. Moseley.
EIN: 136400615
Codes: FD

32979
Charles Henry Leach II Foundation
c/o The Bank of New York, Tax Dept.
1 Wall St., 28th Fl.
New York, NY 10286
Application address: 1290 Ave. of the Americas, New York, NY 10019
Contact: Willis J. Pruitt, V.P., The Bank of New York

Established in 1992 in NY.
Donor(s): Charles Henry Leach II.‡
Financial data (yr. ended 12/31/01): Grants paid, $1,389,500; assets, $16,728,541 (M); expenditures, $1,478,627; qualifying distributions, $1,421,179.
Limitations: Giving primarily in FL and NY.
Trustees: Jennifer B. Jordan, Philip E. Leone, The Bank of New York.
EIN: 133651713
Codes: FD

32980
The Fay J. Lindner Foundation
1161 Meadowbrook Rd.
North Merrick, NY 11566
Contact: Robert M. Goldberg, Pres.

Established in 1966.
Donor(s): Fay J. Lindner.‡
Financial data (yr. ended 08/31/00): Grants paid, $1,388,169; assets, $25,056,936 (M); gifts received, $3,350; expenditures, $1,462,103; qualifying distributions, $1,402,468.
Limitations: Applications not accepted. Giving primarily on Long Island, NY.
Application information: Contributes only to pre-selected organizations.
Officers and Directors:* Robert M. Goldberg,* Pres.; Robin Goldberg,* Co-Secy.; Norman Scheffer,* Co-Secy.; David Goldberg.
EIN: 116043320
Codes: FD

32981
Madeline and Kevin Brine Charitable Trust
c/o Sanford C. Bernstein & Co., Inc.
767 5th Ave.
New York, NY 10153-0185
Contact: Kevin R. Brine, Tr.

Established in 1989 in NY.
Donor(s): Madeline Brine, Kevin R. Brine.
Financial data (yr. ended 12/31/01): Grants paid, $1,386,300; assets, $30,218 (M); gifts received, $1,410,000; expenditures, $1,388,827; qualifying distributions, $1,386,300.
Limitations: Applications not accepted. Giving primarily in New York, NY.
Application information: Contributes only to pre-selected organizations.
Trustees: Kevin R. Brine, Madeline Brine.
EIN: 133549098
Codes: FD

32982
Eastern Star Hall and Home Foundation, Inc.
71 W. 23rd St.
New York, NY 10010-4102
Contact: Mrs. Pounder

Established in 1986 in NY.
Donor(s): Tucker Anthony, Elia Juchter,‡ Gladys Hart,‡ Ann Alsheimen,‡ John Cole,‡ J. Bleich Kolhmeir, Hilda Brooks,‡ Mildred Niley,‡ Althea Julson,‡ Geraldine Bear.‡
Financial data (yr. ended 06/30/01): Grants paid, $1,377,135; assets, $17,438,099 (M); gifts received, $326,462; expenditures, $1,550,274; qualifying distributions, $1,369,927.
Limitations: Applications not accepted. Giving primarily in NY.
Application information: Contributes only to pre-selected organizations.
Directors: William Dalgarno, Peggy Grupp, Walter Howe, Lawrence Unger, Wanda Williams.
EIN: 133458370
Codes: FD

32983
The American Friends of the Hebrew University Charitable Common Fund, Inc.
11 E. 69th St.
New York, NY 10021-4905

Established in 1989 in NY.
Donor(s): Ernest Bogan, Stanley Bogan, Robert Savin, John Steinhardt.
Financial data (yr. ended 09/30/01): Grants paid, $1,373,987; assets, $1,617,202 (M); gifts received, $906,327; expenditures, $1,376,959; qualifying distributions, $1,373,778.
Limitations: Applications not accepted. Giving primarily in New York, NY.
Application information: Contributes only to pre-selected organizations.
Trustees: Stanley Bogen, Adam B. Kahan, Keith Sachs, Ira Sorkin.
EIN: 133525587
Codes: FD

32984
The Moore Charitable Foundation, Inc.
1251 Ave. of the Americas, 53rd Fl.
New York, NY 10020
Contact: Ann Colley, Mgr.

Established in 1992 in NY; funded in 1993.
Donor(s): One to One Charitable Foundation.
Financial data (yr. ended 12/31/00): Grants paid, $1,372,414; assets, $1,314,151 (M); gifts received, $1,296,864; expenditures, $1,702,334; qualifying distributions, $1,672,533.
Limitations: Applications not accepted. Giving on a national basis.
Application information: Contributes only to pre-selected organizations. Unsolicited requests for funds not considered.
Officer: Ann Colley, Mgr.
Directors: Louis M. Bacon, Larry Noe.
EIN: 133741954
Codes: FD

32985
Joseph F. Stein Foundation, Inc.
30 Glenn St.
White Plains, NY 10603

Incorporated in 1954 in NY.
Donor(s): Joseph F. Stein,‡ Allen A. Stein,‡ Melvin M. Stein.‡
Financial data (yr. ended 12/31/01): Grants paid, $1,368,997; assets, $25,219,889 (M); gifts received, $307,241; expenditures, $1,652,626; qualifying distributions, $1,384,311.
Limitations: Applications not accepted. Giving primarily in FL and NY.
Application information: Contributes only to pre-selected organizations.
Managers: Roger H. Stein, Stuart M. Stein.
EIN: 136097095
Codes: FD

32986
Queensgate Foundation
c/o TAG Assocs., Ltd.
75 Rockefeller Plz., Ste. 900
New York, NY 10019
Contact: Mark Friedman, C.P.A.

Established in 1985 in NY.
Donor(s): Peter A. Joseph, Elizabeth H. Scheuer.
Financial data (yr. ended 11/30/00): Grants paid, $1,368,595; assets, $2,544,707 (M); gifts received, $1,679,688; expenditures, $1,379,809; qualifying distributions, $1,373,445.
Limitations: Applications not accepted. Giving primarily in NY.
Application information: Contributes only to pre-selected organizations.
Officers and Directors:* Peter A. Joseph,* Pres. and Treas.; Elizabeth H. Scheuer,* V.P. and Secy.; Carol Joseph.
EIN: 133336710
Codes: FD

32987
Harkness Foundation for Dance
145 E. 48th St., Ste. 26C
New York, NY 10017 (212) 755-5540
Contact: Theodore S. Bartwink, Exec. Dir.

William Hale Harkness Foundation established in 1936 in NY; Harkness Ballet Foundation established in 1959 in NY; adopted current name in 1973.
Donor(s): William Hale Harkness,‡ Rebekah Harkness.‡
Financial data (yr. ended 12/31/00): Grants paid, $1,366,075; assets, $26,318,345 (M); gifts received, $13,687; expenditures, $1,970,430; qualifying distributions, $1,630,305.
Limitations: Giving primarily in NY.
Application information: Application form not required.
Officers and Directors:* William A. Perlmuth,* Pres.; Etta Brandman, V.P.; Theodore S. Bartwink,* Secy.-Treas. and Exec. Dir.
EIN: 131926551
Codes: FD

32988
The Anita B. and Howard S. Richmond Foundation, Inc.
(Formerly Kings Piont Richmond Foundation, Inc.)
11 W. 19th St.
New York, NY 10011 (212) 627-4646
Contact: Howard S. Richmond, Pres.

Established in 1965 in NY.
Donor(s): Howard S. Richmond, Lawrence Richmond.
Financial data (yr. ended 12/31/01): Grants paid, $1,365,530; assets, $5,715,229 (M); gifts received, $414,868; expenditures, $1,407,545; qualifying distributions, $1,362,823.
Limitations: Giving on a national basis.
Application information: Application form not required.
Officers and Directors:* Howard S. Richmond, Pres. and Treas.; Frank Richmond,* V.P.; Lawrence Richmond,* V.P.; Philip Richmond,* V.P.; Robert Richmond,* V.P.; Elizabeth Richmond-Schulman,* V.P.; Bernard D. Gartlir, Secy.
EIN: 136180873
Codes: FD

32989
Jacob Burns Foundation, Inc.
c/o Barry Shenkman
427 Bedford Rd., Ste. 170
Pleasantville, NY 10570 (914) 769-3600

Incorporated in 1957 in NY.
Donor(s): Mary Elizabeth Hood,‡ Jacob Burns,‡ Rosalie A. Goldberg.
Financial data (yr. ended 12/31/01): Grants paid, $1,363,450; assets, $20,764,753 (M); gifts received, $410,000; expenditures, $1,926,621; qualifying distributions, $1,479,959.
Limitations: Applications not accepted. Giving primarily in NY.
Application information: Contributes only to pre-selected organizations.
Officers: Barry A. Shenkman, Pres. and Treas.; Rosalie A. Goldberg, V.P.; Jamie Shenkman, Secy.
EIN: 136114245
Codes: FD

32990
The Heller Foundation
745 5th Ave., Ste. 1250
New York, NY 10151

Established in 2001 in NY.
Financial data (yr. ended 12/31/01): Grants paid, $1,361,726; assets, $760 (M); gifts received, $1,362,486; expenditures, $1,361,726; qualifying distributions, $1,361,726.
Officers: Fanya Heller, Chair.; Benjamin Heller, Pres.; Jacqueline Heller, V.P.
EIN: 134150736
Codes: FD

32991
Rauch Foundation
229 7th St., Ste. 306
Garden City, NY 11530-0708 (516) 873-9808
FAX: (516) 873-0708; E-mail: info@rauchfoundation.org; URL: http://www.rauchfoundation.org
Contact: John McNally

Incorporated in 1960 in NY.
Donor(s): Philip Rauch, Louis J. Rauch,‡ Ruth T. Rauch, Philip J. Rauch, Nancy R. Douzinas.
Financial data (yr. ended 11/30/01): Grants paid, $1,354,620; assets, $39,446,311 (M); gifts received, $627,461; expenditures, $2,097,013; qualifying distributions, $1,932,597.

Limitations: Giving primarily in Nassau and Suffolk counties, NY; some giving also in MD.
Publications: Annual report (including application guidelines), grants list.
Application information: NYRAG Common Application form accepted. Application form not required.
Officers and Directors:* Nancy R. Douzinas,* Pres.; Philip Rauch, V.P. and Secy.-Treas.; Gerald I. Lustig,* V.P.; Philip J. Rauch, V.P.; Lance E. Lindblom, Brooke W. Mahoney, Ruth T. Rauch, John Wenzel.
EIN: 112001717
Codes: FD

32992
Jean and Louis Dreyfus Foundation, Inc.
420 Lexington Ave., Ste. 626
New York, NY 10170 (212) 599-1931
FAX: (212) 599-2956; E-mail: jldreyfusfdtn@hotmail.com
Contact: Edmee Firth

Incorporated about 1978 in NY.
Donor(s): Louis Dreyfus.‡
Financial data (yr. ended 12/31/01): Grants paid, $1,352,500; assets, $22,000,000 (M); expenditures, $1,700,000; qualifying distributions, $1,352,500.
Limitations: Giving primarily in the five boroughs of New York City.
Publications: Annual report.
Application information: The foundation uses its own application form provided at its discretion; NYRAG Common Application Form is not accepted. Application form required.
Officers and Directors:* Nicholas L.D. Firth,* Pres.; Katherine V. Firth,* V.P.; Thomas J. Hubbard,* Secy.; Thomas J. Sweeney,* Treas.; Edmee de M. Firth,* Exec. Dir.
EIN: 132947180
Codes: FD

32993
Aaron Ziegelman Foundation
250 W. 57th St., Ste. 530
New York, NY 10107 (212) 246-2915
Contact: Irwin Chanales, Tr.

Established in 1986 in NY.
Financial data (yr. ended 12/31/01): Grants paid, $1,352,348; assets, $120,658 (M); gifts received, $17,430; expenditures, $1,360,678; qualifying distributions, $1,359,771.
Limitations: Giving primarily in the metropolitan New York, NY, area.
Trustees: Irwin Chanales, Amy Ziegelman, Jane Ziegelman, Marjorie Ziegelman.
EIN: 133323659
Codes: FD

32994
The Alex Hillman Family Foundation
630 5th Ave., Rm. 2604
New York, NY 10111 (212) 265-3115
Contact: Rita K. Hillman, Pres.

Incorporated in 1966 in NY.
Donor(s): Alex L. Hillman,‡ Rita K. Hillman.
Financial data (yr. ended 12/31/01): Grants paid, $1,352,183; assets, $84,307,333 (M); expenditures, $1,766,962; qualifying distributions, $1,523,046.
Limitations: Applications not accepted. Giving primarily in the metropolitan New York, NY, area.
Application information: Contributes only to pre-selected organizations.
Officer and Directors:* Rita K. Hillman,* Pres. and Secy.; Dr. Polly Beere, Paul Garfinkle,

William M. Griffin, James Marcus, Ahrin Mishan, William Spiro, Henry Christensen III.
EIN: 132560546
Codes: FD

32995
The Gary Saltz Foundation, Inc.
600 Madison Ave., 20th Fl.
New York, NY 10022 (212) 980-0910
Additional address: 767 5th Ave., Ste. 4633, New York, NY 10153; additional tel.: (212) 508-9553

Incorporated in 1985 in NY.
Donor(s): Jack Saltz, Anita Saltz.‡
Financial data (yr. ended 04/30/01): Grants paid, $1,352,180; assets, $24,159,782 (M); expenditures, $1,532,712; qualifying distributions, $1,323,517.
Limitations: Applications not accepted. Giving primarily in New York, NY.
Application information: Contributes only to pre-selected organizations.
Officers: Ronald Saltz, V.P.; Susan Saltz, Secy.; Leonard Saltz, Treas.
EIN: 133267114
Codes: FD

32996
Everett Foundation
150 E. 69th St.
New York, NY 10021
Contact: Edith B. Everett, V.P. and Secy.

Incorporated in 1957 in NY.
Donor(s): Henry Everett, Edith B. Everett.
Financial data (yr. ended 12/31/01): Grants paid, $1,350,534; assets, $28,238,704 (M); expenditures, $2,093,362; qualifying distributions, $1,357,160.
Limitations: Applications not accepted. Giving primarily in the metropolitan New York, NY, area.
Application information: Contributes only to pre-selected organizations.
Officers: Henry Everett, Pres. and Treas.; Edith B. Everett, V.P. and Secy.
EIN: 116038040
Codes: FD

32997
Millbrook Tribute Garden, Inc.
c/o D'Arcangelo & Co., LLP
P.O. Box D, Franklin Ave.
Millbrook, NY 12545 (845) 677-6823
Contact: Kathy Shanks

Incorporated in 1943 in NY.
Financial data (yr. ended 09/30/00): Grants paid, $1,348,255; assets, $36,368,512 (M); expenditures, $1,621,842; qualifying distributions, $1,438,641.
Limitations: Giving primarily in Millbrook, NY.
Officers: Oakleigh B. Thorne, Pres.; Felicitas S. Thorne, V.P.; Vincent N. Turletes, Secy.; George T. Whalen, Jr., Treas.
Trustees: Oakleigh Thorne, Robert W. Whalen.
EIN: 141340079
Codes: FD

32998
The Donald C. McGraw Foundation, Inc.
c/o Deutsche Trust Co. of NY
P.O. Box 1297 Church St. Sta.
New York, NY 10008
Application address: 46 Summit Ave., Bronxville, NY 10708
Contact: John L. Cady, Secy.-Treas.

Incorporated in 1963 in NY.
Donor(s): Donald C. McGraw.‡

Financial data (yr. ended 01/31/02): Grants paid, $1,340,000; assets, $32,750,802 (M); gifts received, $91,000; expenditures, $1,372,869; qualifying distributions, $1,340,000.
Limitations: Giving on a national basis, with emphasis on FL, MA, RI, CT, and MD.
Application information: Available funds for new applicants are very limited.
Officers: Donald C. McGraw, Pres.; John L. McGraw, V.P.; John L. Cady, Secy.-Treas.
EIN: 136165603
Codes: FD

32999
Fuchsberg Family Foundation, Inc.
119 Haviland Rd.
Harrison, NY 10528 (914) 682-2228
Contact: Richard Kaufman, Exec. Dir.

Incorporated in 1954 in NY.
Donor(s): Jacob D. Fuchsberg,‡ Abraham Fuchsberg, Shirley Fuchsberg, Fuchsberg & Fuchsberg.
Financial data (yr. ended 12/31/00): Grants paid, $1,339,803; assets, $12,246,084 (M); expenditures, $1,460,248; qualifying distributions, $1,334,943.
Limitations: Giving primarily in NY.
Application information: Application form not required.
Officers: Shirley Fuchsberg, Chair.; Rosalind F. Kaufman, Pres.; Susan C. Raphaelson, V.P.; Alan L. Fuchsberg, Secy.; Janet Levine, Treas.; Richard Kaufman, Exec. Dir.
EIN: 136165600
Codes: FD

33000
Jack D. Cohen Foundation
c/o Carlton Assocs., Inc.
505 Park Ave., 5th Fl.
New York, NY 10022

Established in 1984 in NY.
Donor(s): Jack D. Cohen, Abraham J. Cohen, David J. Cohen.
Financial data (yr. ended 10/31/01): Grants paid, $1,338,332; assets, $19,618 (M); gifts received, $427,800; expenditures, $1,341,934; qualifying distributions, $1,338,332.
Limitations: Applications not accepted. Giving primarily in New York, NY.
Application information: Contributes only to pre-selected organizations.
Officer: Jack D. Cohen, Pres.
EIN: 112715275
Codes: FD

33001
The Lucius N. Littauer Foundation, Inc.
60 E. 42nd St., Ste. 2910
New York, NY 10165 (212) 697-2677
Contact: William Lee Frost, Pres., or Pamela Ween Brumberg, Prog. Dir.

Incorporated in 1929 in NY.
Donor(s): Lucius N. Littauer.‡
Financial data (yr. ended 12/31/01): Grants paid, $1,337,396; assets, $41,011,478 (M); gifts received, $3,332,084; expenditures, $1,774,535; qualifying distributions, $1,535,297.
Limitations: Giving primarily in NY for medical ethics and environmental projects.
Publications: Application guidelines.
Application information: Application form not required.
Officers and Directors:* William Lee Frost,* Pres. and Treas.; Henry A. Lowett,* V.P. and Secy.; Charles Berlin, Berthold Bilski, Mark A. Bilski,

33001—NEW YORK

Robert D. Frost, George Harris, Noah Perlman, Peter J. Solomon.
EIN: 131688027
Codes: FD

33002
J. M. R. Barker Foundation
530 5th Ave., 26th Fl.
New York, NY 10036-5101 (212) 398-8700
FAX: (212) 398-2042
Contact: Maureen Hopkins, Secy. and Admin.

Established in 1968 in NY.
Donor(s): James M. Barker,‡ Margaret R. Barker,‡ Robert R. Barker.
Financial data (yr. ended 12/31/01): Grants paid, $1,337,000; assets, $37,175,101 (M); expenditures, $1,455,891; qualifying distributions, $1,337,000.
Limitations: Giving primarily in the greater Boston, MA, area, and the greater New York, NY, area.
Application information: Application form not required.
Officers and Directors:* Margaret B. Clark,* Pres.; James R. Barker, V.P. and C.F.O.; Dr. W.B. Barker,* V.P.; Maureen A. Hopkins, Secy. and Admin.; Robert P. Connor,* Treas.; Ann S. Barker, Margaret S. Barker, Robert R. Barker, William S. Barker, John W. Holman, Jr., Richard D. Kahn, Troy Y. Murray.
EIN: 136268289
Codes: FD

33003
Ittleson Foundation, Inc.
15 E. 67th St., 5th Fl.
New York, NY 10021 (212) 794-2008
FAX: (212) 794-0351; URL: http://www.ittlesonfoundation.org
Contact: Anthony C. Wood, Exec. Dir.

Trust established in 1932 in NY.
Donor(s): Henry Ittleson,‡ Blanche F. Ittleson,‡ Henry Ittleson, Jr.,‡ Lee F. Ittleson,‡ Nancy S. Ittleson.‡
Financial data (yr. ended 12/31/00): Grants paid, $1,328,896; assets, $26,482,436 (M); gifts received, $3,000; expenditures, $1,919,342; qualifying distributions, $1,636,385.
Limitations: Giving on a national basis.
Publications: Annual report (including application guidelines).
Application information: Application form not required.
Officers and Directors:* H. Anthony Ittleson,* Chair. and Pres.; Pamela Lee Syrmis,* V.P.; Anthony C. Wood,* Secy. and Exec. Dir.; Lionel I. Pincus, Victor Syrmis, M.D.
EIN: 510172757
Codes: FD

33004
The Rice Family Foundation
P.O. Box 319
Bedford, NY 10506
FAX: (914) 234-3220
Contact: Eve. H. Rice, V.P. and Treas.

Established in 1989 in NY.
Donor(s): Henry Hart Rice.‡
Financial data (yr. ended 12/31/01): Grants paid, $1,327,219; assets, $31,198,616 (M); expenditures, $1,745,750; qualifying distributions, $1,327,537.
Limitations: Applications not accepted. Giving primarily in NY.
Application information: Contributes only to pre-selected organizations.
Officers: Margaret S. Rice, Pres.; Edward H. Rice, V.P. and Secy.; Eve H. Rice, V.P. and Treas.

EIN: 133542090
Codes: FD

33005
The Julia A. Whitney Foundation
c/o Thomas P. Whitney
210 E. 65th St., Apt. 19J
New York, NY 10021

Established in 1965 in NY.
Financial data (yr. ended 12/31/01): Grants paid, $1,325,000; assets, $1,588,072 (M); expenditures, $1,329,847; qualifying distributions, $1,326,128.
Limitations: Applications not accepted. Giving primarily in MA and NY.
Application information: Contributes only to pre-selected organizations.
Trustees: Louise Christofferson, Faye Dewitt, Julia F. Whitney, Thomas P. Whitney.
EIN: 136192314
Codes: FD

33006
The Rudin Foundation, Inc.
345 Park Ave.
New York, NY 10154 (212) 407-2512
Contact: Robin Dubin, Admin. and Prog. Dir.

Incorporated in 1960 in NY.
Financial data (yr. ended 12/31/99): Grants paid, $1,324,719; assets, $523,298 (M); gifts received, $1,970,300; expenditures, $1,510,123; qualifying distributions, $1,510,055.
Limitations: Giving primarily in New York, NY.
Officers and Directors:* Jack Rudin,* Chair.; Beth Rudin DeWoody,* Pres.; Jeffrey Steinman,* Exec. V.P.; John Lewin,* V.P.; Eric C. Rudin,* V.P.; William Rudin, V.P.; John L. Sills,* V.P.; Robert Steinman, V.P.; Richard C. Snider,* Secy.; David B. Levy,* Treas.
EIN: 136113064
Codes: FD

33007
Altman/Kazickas Foundation
c/o Dorian A. Vergos & Co., LLC
45 Rockefeller Plz., Ste. 2216
New York, NY 10111

Established in 1996 in NY.
Donor(s): Robert C. Altman, Roger C. Altman.
Financial data (yr. ended 04/30/01): Grants paid, $1,321,419; assets, $3,801,945 (M); gifts received, $1,536,687; expenditures, $1,325,534; qualifying distributions, $1,302,377.
Limitations: Applications not accepted. Giving on a national basis.
Application information: Contributes only to pre-selected organizations.
Trustees: Richard M. Altman, Roger C. Altman, Jurate Kazickas.
EIN: 133944577
Codes: FD

33008
American Friends of Meshivat Nefesh L'Bat Melech, Inc.
c/o Abraham Trusts
444 Madison Ave, 11th St.
New York, NY 10022

Established in 1999 in NY.
Donor(s): Estanne Abraham, Tamar Abraham, Martin Fawer.
Financial data (yr. ended 12/31/00): Grants paid, $1,319,454; assets, $1,938 (M); gifts received, $1,371,101; expenditures, $1,370,819; qualifying distributions, $1,334,554.
Limitations: Applications not accepted.
Application information: Contributes only to pre-selected organizations.

Officers and Directors:* Estanne Abraham,* Pres.; Tamar Abraham,* V.P.; Martin Fawer,* Secy.-Treas.
EIN: 134035508
Codes: FD

33009
The Swartz Foundation Trust
c/o Brandywine Mgmt. Svcs.
880 3rd Ave., 3rd Fl.
New York, NY 10022
Application address: c/o Accel Partners, 1 Palmer Sq., Princeton, NJ 08542, tel.: (609) 683-4500
Contact: James R. Swartz, Pres.

Donor(s): James R. Swartz.
Financial data (yr. ended 12/31/00): Grants paid, $1,311,258; assets, $25,043,270 (M); expenditures, $1,716,675; qualifying distributions, $1,168,139.
Limitations: Giving primarily in NJ and UT.
Application information: Application form not required.
Officer: James R. Swartz, Pres.
EIN: 226554026
Codes: FD

33010
New York Mercantile Exchange Charitable Foundation
(also known as NYMEX Charitable Foundation)
c/o Exec. Comm.
1 North End Ave.
New York, NY 10282

Established in 1989 in NY.
Donor(s): New York Mercantile Exchange.
Financial data (yr. ended 12/31/00): Grants paid, $1,308,274; assets, $1,435,000 (M); gifts received, $1,313,583; expenditures, $1,367,299; qualifying distributions, $1,324,068.
Limitations: Giving primarily in NJ and New York, NY.
Publications: Annual report, newsletter, application guidelines.
Application information: Application form required.
Officers: Daniel Rappaport, Chair.; Vincent Viola, Vice-Chair.
EIN: 133586378
Codes: CS, FD, CD

33011
Woodcock P Foundation
c/o Rockefeller & Co., Inc.
30 Rockefeller Plz., Ste. 5600
New York, NY 10112

Established in 2000 in NY.
Donor(s): Polly W. Guth.
Financial data (yr. ended 05/31/01): Grants paid, $1,306,467; assets, $64,900 (M); gifts received, $60; expenditures, $1,349,542; qualifying distributions, $1,306,467.
Limitations: Applications not accepted.
Application information: Contributes only to pre-selected organizations.
Trustees: John H.J. Guth, Polly W. Guth, Richard T. Watson.
EIN: 137248894
Codes: FD

33012
The John R. and Barbara A. Tormondsen Foundation
c/o Goldman Sachs & Co.
85 Broad St., Tax Dept.
New York, NY 10004

Established in 1996 in CT.
Donor(s): John R. Tormondsen.

Financial data (yr. ended 04/30/00): Grants paid, $1,305,095; assets, $871,066 (M); gifts received, $2,057,978; expenditures, $1,305,171; qualifying distributions, $1,292,439.
Limitations: Applications not accepted. Giving primarily in CT, with emphasis on Greenwich, MA, New York, NY, and Middlebury, VT.
Application information: Contributes only to pre-selected organizations.
Trustees: Roger Harper, Barbara A. Tormondsen, John R. Tormondsen.
EIN: 133921373
Codes: FD

33013
J. C. Kellogg Foundation, Inc.
c/o Spear, Leeds & Kellogg
120 Broadway
New York, NY 10271-0093
Contact: Isaac Jarmark, Tax Svcs.

Established in 1954 in NY.
Donor(s): Morris W. Kellogg, James C. Kellogg IV, Elizabeth I. Kellogg, Richard I. Kellogg, Peter R. Kellogg.
Financial data (yr. ended 08/31/00): Grants paid, $1,303,257; assets, $28,438,376 (M); gifts received, $463,066; expenditures, $1,400,200; qualifying distributions, $1,305,342.
Limitations: Applications not accepted. Giving primarily in MA, NJ, and NY.
Application information: Contributes only to pre-selected organizations.
Officers: James C. Kellogg IV, Pres. and Secy.; Peter R. Kellogg, V.P.
Trustees: Nancy K. Gifford, Morris W. Kellogg, Richard I. Kellogg.
EIN: 136092448
Codes: FD

33014
The Green Fund, Inc.
14 E. 60th St., Ste. 702
New York, NY 10022 (212) 755-2445
Contact: Cynthia Green Colin, Pres.

Incorporated in 1947 in NY.
Donor(s): Evelyn Green Davis,‡ Louis A. Green.‡
Financial data (yr. ended 01/31/02): Grants paid, $1,301,225; assets, $20,268,453 (M); gifts received, $240,980; expenditures, $1,524,765; qualifying distributions, $1,394,589.
Limitations: Applications not accepted. Giving primarily in the metropolitan New York, NY, area.
Application information: Grants initiated by the fund's members.
Officers and Directors:* Cynthia Green Colin,* Pres.; S. William Green,* Treas.; Patricia F. Green.
EIN: 136160950
Codes: FD

33015
The Robert Bowne Foundation, Inc.
c/o Bowne & Co., Inc.
345 Hudson St.
New York, NY 10014 (212) 229-7223
FAX: (212) 886-0400; URL: http://fdncenter.org/grantmaker/bowne
Contact: Lena Townsend, Exec. Dir.

Incorporated in 1968 in NY.
Donor(s): Edmund A. Stanley, Jr., and members of the Stanley family, Bowne & Co.
Financial data (yr. ended 12/31/01): Grants paid, $1,300,850; assets, $18,608,408 (M); gifts received, $100,000; expenditures, $1,625,278; qualifying distributions, $1,525,723.
Limitations: Giving limited to the New York, NY, area.

Publications: Informational brochure (including application guidelines), grants list, occasional report.
Application information: Accepts NYRAG Common Grant Application Form. Application form not required.
Officers and Trustees:* Edmund A. Stanley, Jr.,* Chair.; Jennifer Stanley, Pres.; Suzanne Carothers, 1st. V.P. and Treas.; Dianne Kangisser, 2nd. V.P.; Hali Hae Kyung Lee, Secy.; Lena Towsend, Exec. Dir.; Susan Cummiskey, Robert M. Johnson, Franz vonZiegesar.
EIN: 132620393
Codes: FD

33016
The Shoreland Foundation
1 Comac Loop
Ronkonkoma, NY 11779
Contact: Carol-Ann Mealy

Established in 1994 in NY.
Donor(s): Anthony W. Wang.
Financial data (yr. ended 12/31/00): Grants paid, $1,297,939; assets, $79,488,069 (M); expenditures, $1,463,099; qualifying distributions, $1,297,939.
Limitations: Applications not accepted. Giving primarily in NY.
Application information: Contributes only to pre-selected organizations.
Officers: Anthony W. Wang, Pres.; Lulu C. Wang, V.P.; Gary E. Martinelli, Secy.-Treas.
EIN: 113241828
Codes: FD

33017
Mel Karmazin Foundation
1 Central Park W., Ste. 48A
New York, NY 10023

Established in DE in 1998.
Donor(s): Melvin Karmazin.
Financial data (yr. ended 12/31/00): Grants paid, $1,296,500; assets, $2,474,872 (M); gifts received, $1,570,479; expenditures, $1,368,898; qualifying distributions, $1,296,500.
Limitations: Applications not accepted. Giving primarily in NY.
Trustees: Dina K. Elkins, Melvin Karmazin.
EIN: 311620186
Codes: FD

33018
Rita J. and Stanley H. Kaplan Family Foundation, Inc.
866 United Nations Plz., Ste. 306
New York, NY 10017 (212) 688-1047
FAX: (212) 688-6907
Contact: Rita J. Kaplan, Secy.

Incorporated in 1984 in NY.
Donor(s): Stanley H. Kaplan, Rita J. Kaplan.
Financial data (yr. ended 12/31/01): Grants paid, $1,293,937; assets, $22,811,229 (M); gifts received, $149,804; expenditures, $1,899,794; qualifying distributions, $1,532,060.
Limitations: Applications not accepted. Giving primarily in Boston, MA, and New York, NY; giving also in Israel.
Application information: Contributes only to pre-selected organizations.
Officers and Directors:* Stanley H. Kaplan,* Pres.; Nancy Kaplan Belsky, V.P.; Susan Beth Kaplan, V.P.; Rita J. Kaplan,* Secy.; Nancy W. Greenblatt, Exec. Dir.
EIN: 133221298
Codes: FD

33019
Barbara Lubin Goldsmith Foundation
(Formerly Goldsmith-Perry Philanthropies, Inc.)
c/o Hecht and Co., PC
111 W. 40th St.
New York, NY 10018

Established in 1969 in NY.
Donor(s): Barbara Lubin Goldsmith Charitable Trust, Joseph I. Lubin.‡
Financial data (yr. ended 12/31/00): Grants paid, $1,293,156; assets, $13,139,278 (M); expenditures, $1,519,636; qualifying distributions, $1,368,214.
Limitations: Applications not accepted. Giving primarily in New York, NY.
Application information: Contributes only to pre-selected organizations.
Officers and Directors:* Barbara L. Goldsmith,* Pres.; Alice Elgart,* Secy.
EIN: 237031986
Codes: FD

33020
The Reuben Y. & Susan Rosenberg Tzedokah Fund
8 Beechwood Dr.
Lawrence, NY 11559
Application address: c/o API Industries, Inc., Glenshaw St., Orangeburg, NY 10962
Contact: Reuben Rosenberg, Dir.

Established in 1987 in NY.
Donor(s): API Industries, Inc., Reuben Y. Rosenberg.
Financial data (yr. ended 10/31/00): Grants paid, $1,290,718; assets, $250 (L); gifts received, $1,312,000; expenditures, $1,296,104; qualifying distributions, $1,296,104.
Limitations: Giving primarily in NY.
Directors: Norman Rabenstein, Reuben Rosenberg, Susan Rosenberg.
EIN: 112778277
Codes: FD

33021
The Roslyn Savings Foundation
2 Seaview Blvd.
Port Washington, NY 11050-4634

Established in 1997 in NY.
Donor(s): Roslyn Bancorp, Inc.
Financial data (yr. ended 12/31/00): Grants paid, $1,290,417; assets, $29,593,375 (M); expenditures, $1,474,305; qualifying distributions, $1,437,142.
Limitations: Giving primarily in Nassau and Suffolk counties, NY.
Officers: Joseph L. Mancino, Pres.; John R. Bransfield, Jr., V.P.; R. Patrick Quinn, Secy.; Michael P. Puorro, Treas.; Sharon G. Grosser, Exec. Dir.
Directors: Victor C. McCuaig, Walter Mullins, Daniel L. Murphy, James E. Swiggert, Richard C. Webel.
EIN: 113354472
Codes: CS, FD, CD

33022
Theodore & Renee Weiler Foundation, Inc.
24 Rock St.
Brooklyn, NY 11206

Established in 1965 in NY.
Donor(s): Theodore R. Weiler.‡
Financial data (yr. ended 12/31/99): Grants paid, $1,290,100; assets, $19,914,111 (M); expenditures, $1,389,175; qualifying distributions, $1,301,957.
Limitations: Applications not accepted. Giving primarily in Palm Beach, FL, and New York, NY.

33022—NEW YORK

Application information: Contributes only to pre-selected organizations.
Officers and Directors:* Alan Safir,* Pres.; Richard Kandel,* Treas. and Mgr.; Rhoda Weiler.
EIN: 136181441
Codes: FD

33023
International Fund for Health & Family Planning
c/o Alan Dolinsky
9 Spruce Pl.
Great Neck, NY 11021

Incorporated in 1979.
Donor(s): Philip D. Harvey.
Financial data (yr. ended 12/31/01): Grants paid, $1,289,473; assets, $28,909,739 (M); expenditures, $1,344,770; qualifying distributions, $1,321,496.
Limitations: Applications not accepted. Giving on a national and international basis.
Application information: Contributes only to pre-selected organizations.
Officers and Directors:* Philip D. Harvey,* V.P.; Alan Dolinsky,* Treas.; Dr. Timothy Black, Robert Ciszewski, Richard Frank.
EIN: 133000463
Codes: FD, FM

33024
Henry and Lucy Moses Fund, Inc.
c/o Moses and Singer
1301 Ave. of the Americas
New York, NY 10019
Contact: Irving Sitnick, Esq.

Incorporated in 1942 in NY.
Donor(s): Henry L. Moses,‡ Lucy G. Moses.‡
Financial data (yr. ended 12/31/00): Grants paid, $1,277,838; assets, $2,040,374 (M); gifts received, $1,165,000; expenditures, $1,315,821; qualifying distributions, $121,207.
Limitations: Giving primarily in the New York, NY, area.
Application information: Support generally limited to previous grant recipients. Application form not required.
Officers and Directors:* Irving Sitnick,* Pres.; Joseph Fishman,* V.P. and Secy.; Jacqueline Schneider, V.P.
EIN: 136092967
Codes: FD

33025
The JKW Foundation
c/o Jean Stein
10 Gracie Sq., PH. N
New York, NY 10028

Established in 1997 in NY.
Financial data (yr. ended 12/31/00): Grants paid, $1,277,225; assets, $15,530,296 (M); gifts received, $980,277; expenditures, $1,395,657; qualifying distributions, $1,289,593.
Limitations: Applications not accepted.
Application information: Contributes only to pre-selected organizations.
Trustees: Jean Stein, Katrina Vanden Heuvel, Wendy Vanden Heuvel.
EIN: 137127165
Codes: FD

33026
Joseph E. & Norma G. Saul Foundation, Inc.
c/o Saul Partners
9 W. 57th St., Ste. 3405
New York, NY 10019

Established in 1984 in NY.
Donor(s): Joseph E. Saul, Norma G. Saul.

Financial data (yr. ended 09/30/01): Grants paid, $1,273,630; assets, $3,480,113 (M); expenditures, $1,277,205; qualifying distributions, $1,273,652.
Limitations: Applications not accepted. Giving primarily in New York, NY.
Application information: Contributes only to pre-selected organizations.
Officers: Joseph E. Saul, Pres.; Andrew M. Saul, V.P.; Norma G. Saul, Secy.
EIN: 133254180
Codes: FD

33027
The Barrington Foundation, Inc.
7-11 S. Broadway, Ste. 200
White Plains, NY 10601
Additional address: P.O. Box 750, Great Barrington, MA 01230
Contact: David H. Strassler, Pres.

Established in 1978 in DE.
Donor(s): Samuel A. Strassler.‡
Financial data (yr. ended 12/31/01): Grants paid, $1,271,700; assets, $1,247,006 (M); gifts received, $774,780; expenditures, $1,273,228; qualifying distributions, $1,258,141.
Limitations: Giving primarily in MA.
Application information: Application form not required.
Officers: David H. Strassler, Pres.; Robert B. Strassler, Secy.-Treas.
EIN: 132930849
Codes: FD

33028
William and Mildred Lasdon Foundation, Inc.
c/o Nanette L. Laitman
575 Madison Ave., 10th Fl.
New York, NY 10022-2588

Established in 1947 in DE.
Donor(s): Jacob S. Lasdon, William S. Lasdon, Mildred D. Lasdon,‡ Nanetta L. Leitman.
Financial data (yr. ended 12/31/99): Grants paid, $1,269,493; assets, $32,418,722 (M); expenditures, $1,393,652; qualifying distributions, $1,319,327.
Limitations: Giving primarily in New York, NY.
Trustees: Bonnie Eletz, Nanette L. Laitman, Cathy Seligman.
EIN: 237380362
Codes: FD

33029
Charles & Mildred Schnurmacher Foundation, Inc.
155 E. 55th St., Ste. 302A
New York, NY 10022 (212) 838-7766
Contact: Ira J. Weinstein, Pres.

Established in 1977 in NY.
Donor(s): Charles M. Schnurmacher.‡
Financial data (yr. ended 12/31/01): Grants paid, $1,264,200; assets, $22,036,506 (M); expenditures, $1,648,305; qualifying distributions, $1,450,521.
Limitations: Giving primarily in CA, CT, and NY.
Application information: Application form not required.
Officers and Directors:* Ira J. Weinstein, Pres.; Barbara Packer, Fred Plotkin, Secy.; Amanda Plotkin, Carolyn Plotkin, Janet Plotkin, Andrea Weinstein, Peter Weinstein.
EIN: 132937218
Codes: FD

33030
Joseph S. & Diane H. Steinberg 1992 Charitable Trust
c/o Leucadia National Corp.
315 Park Ave. S., 20th Fl.
New York, NY 10010-3607
Contact: Joseph S. Steinberg, Tr.

Established in 1992 in NY.
Donor(s): Joseph S. Steinberg, Diane H. Steinberg.
Financial data (yr. ended 06/30/00): Grants paid, $1,259,221; assets, $22,935,047 (M); gifts received, $2,226,251; expenditures, $1,372,195; qualifying distributions, $1,242,988.
Limitations: Giving primarily in NY.
Trustees: Diane H. Steinberg, Joseph S. Steinberg.
EIN: 137002791
Codes: FD

33031
Tanaka Memorial Foundation, Inc.
237 Park Ave., 21st Fl.
New York, NY 10017 (212) 551-3583
Contact: Kenji Tanaka, Chair.

Established in 1991 in NY.
Donor(s): Tanaka Ikubikai Educational Corp.
Financial data (yr. ended 06/30/01): Grants paid, $1,255,000; assets, $21,433,099 (M); expenditures, $1,580,854; qualifying distributions, $1,580,854.
Limitations: Giving on a national basis.
Application information: Application form not required.
Officers and Directors:* Kenji Tanaka,* Chair.; Taeko Tanaka,* Vice-Chair.; Makiko Tanaka,* Pres.; Kimiko Tanaka,* V.P.; Takeshi Hashimoto, Secy.; Tokiwa Morimoto, Treas.; Kiyoshi Okada, Yoshihiro Tajima, Takeshi Ueshima.
EIN: 110235010
Codes: FD

33032
Mary Jean & Frank P. Smeal Foundation
c/o Tom Burke, The Ayco Co., LP
P.O. Box 8019
Ballston Spa, NY 12020-8019

Established in 1985 in NY.
Donor(s): Frank P. Smeal.
Financial data (yr. ended 02/28/01): Grants paid, $1,254,889; assets, $2,433,905 (M); gifts received, $1,043,952; expenditures, $1,284,441; qualifying distributions, $1,246,416.
Limitations: Applications not accepted. Giving primarily in New York, NY.
Application information: Contributes only to pre-selected organizations.
Trustees: Frank P. Smeal, Henry F. Smeal, Mary Margaret Smeal.
EIN: 133318167
Codes: FD

33033
The FJJ Foundation, Inc.
c/o Stuart D. Baker
30 Rockefeller Plz., Ste. 3248
New York, NY 10112

Established in 1993 in DE.
Donor(s): Masham Corp.
Financial data (yr. ended 12/31/01): Grants paid, $1,254,433; assets, $1,881,958 (M); expenditures, $1,295,470; qualifying distributions, $1,265,676.
Limitations: Applications not accepted. Giving primarily in New York, NY.
Application information: Contributes only to pre-selected organizations.
Officers and Directors:* Roberto Constantiner,* Chair.; Stuart D. Baker,* Secy.; Arturo Constantiner.
EIN: 133693589

Codes: FD

33034
The Chasdei Yisroel Charitable Trust
P.O. Box 190-312
Brooklyn, NY 11219
Application address: 1446 42nd St., Brooklyn, NY 11219, tel. (718) 972-2440
Contact: Dov Rabinowitz, Tr.

Established in 2000 in NY.
Financial data (yr. ended 10/31/01): Grants paid, $1,254,300; assets, $8,315 (M); gifts received, $1,265,175; expenditures, $1,256,860; qualifying distributions, $1,254,300.
Trustees: Dov Rabinowitz, Goldy Rabinowitz.
EIN: 116552381

33035
Samuel Rubin Foundation, Inc.
777 United Nations Plz.
New York, NY 10017-3521 (212) 697-8945
FAX: (212) 682-0886; URL: http://www.samuelrubinfoundation.org
Contact: Cora Weiss, Pres.

Established in 1958 in NY.
Donor(s): Samuel Rubin Foundation, Inc.
Financial data (yr. ended 06/30/00): Grants paid, $1,253,935; assets, $15,680,280 (M); expenditures, $1,591,240; qualifying distributions, $1,408,788.
Limitations: Giving on a national and international basis.
Publications: Program policy statement, grants list.
Application information: Application form not required.
Officers and Directors:* Cora Weiss,* Pres.; Judy Weiss,* V.P.; Charles L. Mandelstam,* Secy.; Peter Weiss,* Treas.; Daniel Weiss, Tamara Weiss.
EIN: 136164671
Codes: FD

33036
The Woodheath Foundation, Inc.
c/o Barry M. Strauss Assocs., Ltd.
307 5th Ave., 8th Fl.
New York, NY 10016-6517

Incorporated in 1956 in NY.
Donor(s): Frederick L. Ehrman,‡ Edith K. Ehrman,‡ F. Warren Hellman.
Financial data (yr. ended 06/30/01): Grants paid, $1,253,263; assets, $10,660,816 (M); gifts received, $1,876,679; expenditures, $1,274,042; qualifying distributions, $1,242,832.
Limitations: Applications not accepted. Giving primarily in New York, NY.
Application information: Contributes only to pre-selected organizations.
Officers: F. Warren Hellman, Pres.; Nancy Bechtel, V.P.; Patricia C. Hellman, Secy.
Director: Joachim Bechtel.
EIN: 136094025
Codes: FD

33037
The David and Lyn Silfen Foundation
c/o BCRS Assocs., LLC
100 Wall St., 11th Fl.
New York, NY 10005 (212) 902-6697
Contact: David M. Silfen, Tr.

Established in 1981 in NY.
Donor(s): David M. Silfen.
Financial data (yr. ended 03/31/02): Grants paid, $1,251,650; assets, $1,906,246 (M); gifts received, $189,750; expenditures, $1,271,615; qualifying distributions, $1,250,149.
Limitations: Applications not accepted. Giving primarily in CT, New York, NY, and PA.

Application information: Contributes only to pre-selected organizations.
Trustees: Adam Gordon Silfen, David M. Silfen, Lyn Silfen.
EIN: 133103011
Codes: FD

33038
The Wachtell, Lipton, Rosen & Katz Foundation
51 W. 52nd St.
New York, NY 10019

Established in 1981 in NY.
Donor(s): Wachtell, Lipton, Rosen & Katz.
Financial data (yr. ended 09/30/99): Grants paid, $1,250,000; assets, $10,668,284 (M); gifts received, $3,000,000; expenditures, $1,330,280; qualifying distributions, $1,250,250.
Limitations: Applications not accepted. Giving primarily in New York, NY.
Application information: Contributes only to pre-selected organizations.
Officers: Martin Lipton, Pres.; Leonard M. Rosen, V.P. and Secy.; Herbert M. Wachtell, V.P. and Treas.; Constance Monte, Mgr.
EIN: 133099901
Codes: CS, FD, CD

33039
Chester & Dorris Carlson Charitable Trust
c/o Canandaigua National Bank and Trust
1150 Pittsford-Victor Rd.
Pittsford, NY 14534 (585) 419-0600
Contact: Anthony Figueiredo

Financial data (yr. ended 12/31/00): Grants paid, $1,246,441; assets, $12,022,430 (M); gifts received, $723,673; expenditures, $1,337,084; qualifying distributions, $1,246,441.
Limitations: Giving primarily in NY, with emphasis on Rochester.
Application information: Application form not required.
Trustees: Catherine B. Carlson, Canandaigua National Bank and Trust.
EIN: 136272334
Codes: FD

33040
The Bari Lipp Foundation, Inc.
c/o David Quinn
P.O. Box 15073
Albany, NY 12212-5073

Established in 1996 in NY.
Donor(s): Robert I. Lipp.
Financial data (yr. ended 12/31/01): Grants paid, $1,242,292; assets, $29,311,853 (M); gifts received, $13,880,242; expenditures, $1,526,751; qualifying distributions, $1,097,179.
Limitations: Applications not accepted. Giving primarily in MA and NY, some funding nationally.
Application information: Contributes only to pre-selected organizations.
Directors: Jeffrey D. Lipp, Robert I. Lipp, Wendy A. Lipp.
EIN: 133921302
Codes: FD

33041
F. Donald Kenney Foundation
c/o Christian R. Sonne
207 W. Lake Rd.
Tuxedo Park, NY 10987-4103

Established in 1963 in NY.
Donor(s): F. Donald Kenney.‡
Financial data (yr. ended 12/31/01): Grants paid, $1,237,000; assets, $1,322,067 (M); gifts received, $1,667,241; expenditures, $1,237,816; qualifying distributions, $1,237,000.

Limitations: Applications not accepted. Giving primarily in NY.
Application information: Contributes only to pre-selected organizations.
Trustees: Anne K. O'Neil, Christian R. Sonne.
EIN: 237002453
Codes: FD

33042
EHA Foundation, Inc.
c/o Kelley Drye & Warren, LLP
101 Park Ave., 30th Fl.
New York, NY 10178
Contact: Christin M. Mason, Secy.

Established in 1996 in NY.
Donor(s): Ruth Uris,‡ Linda M. Sanger.
Financial data (yr. ended 01/31/02): Grants paid, $1,236,440; assets, $25,257,386 (M); gifts received, $27,358; expenditures, $1,542,836; qualifying distributions, $1,238,531.
Limitations: Applications not accepted.
Application information: Contributes only to pre-selected organizations. Unsolicited requests for funds not accepted.
Officers: Linda M. Sanger, Pres.; Abbie W. Sanger, V.P.; Terence D. Sanger, V.P.; Victoria Sanger, V.P.; Christina M. Mason, Secy.; Michael S. Insel, Treas.
EIN: 133898642
Codes: FD

33043
Joseph Collins Foundation
c/o Willkie Farr & Gallagher
787 7th Ave., Rm. 3950
New York, NY 10019-6099
Contact: Augusta L. Packer, Secy.-Treas.

Incorporated in 1951 in NY.
Donor(s): Joseph Collins, M.D.‡
Financial data (yr. ended 06/30/01): Grants paid, $1,225,000; assets, $29,115,616 (M); expenditures, $1,671,151; qualifying distributions, $1,337,750.
Limitations: Giving limited to students attending accredited medical schools located east of the Mississippi River.
Publications: Annual report, program policy statement, application guidelines.
Application information: Application forms should be obtained from and submitted by medical schools on behalf of the students. Application form required.
Officers and Trustees:* Jack H. Nusbaum,* Pres.; Mark F. Hughes, Jr., V.P.; W. Graham Knox, M.D.,* V.P.; Nora Ann Wallace, V.P.; Augusta L. Packer,* Secy.-Treas.
EIN: 136404527
Codes: FD, GTI

33044
The Young & Rubicam Foundation
c/o WPP Group USA, Inc.
125 Park Ave.
New York, NY 10017 (212) 210-3000

Incorporated in 1955 in NY.
Donor(s): Young & Rubicam Inc.
Financial data (yr. ended 12/31/00): Grants paid, $1,222,084; assets, $137,065 (M); gifts received, $1,222,084; expenditures, $1,222,084; qualifying distributions, $1,222,084.
Limitations: Applications not accepted. Giving primarily in New York, NY, for general grants; giving on a national basis for matching gifts to education.
Application information: Contributes only to pre-selected organizations. Unsolicited requests for funds not accepted.
Directors: Peter Georgescu, Jacque Tortoroli.

33044—NEW YORK

EIN: 136156199
Codes: CS, FD, CD

33045
The Pepsi Bottling Group Foundation, Inc.
c/o The Pepsi Bottling Group
1 Pepsi Way
Somers, NY 10589-2201 (914) 767-7472
Contact: Angela Buonocore

Established in 1999 in NY.
Donor(s): The Pepsi Bottling Group, Inc., Bottling Group, LLC.
Financial data (yr. ended 12/31/01): Grants paid, $1,221,217; assets, $6,947,194 (M); gifts received, $5,008,422; expenditures, $1,221,217; qualifying distributions, $1,221,217.
Limitations: Giving on a national basis in areas of company operations.
Officers and Directors:* Craig E. Weatherup,* Chair.; L. Kevin Cox,* Vice-Chair.; Eric J. Foss,* Vice-Chair.; John T. Cahill, Pres.; Pamela C. McGuire, Secy.; Alfred H. Drewes,* Treas.
EIN: 134090130
Codes: CS, FD

33046
Maude Pritchard Charitable Trust
(Formerly William E. and Maude S. Pritchard Charitable Trust)
c/o JPMorgan Private Bank
1211 Ave. of the Americas, 38th Fl.
New York, NY 10036 (212) 789-5777
Contact: Lisa L. Philp

Established in 1983 in NY.
Financial data (yr. ended 12/31/01): Grants paid, $1,216,133; assets, $21,919,372 (M); expenditures, $1,389,494; qualifying distributions, $1,236,873.
Limitations: Applications not accepted. Giving primarily in Suffolk County, NY.
Application information: Unsolicited requests for funds not accepted.
Trustees: Herbert J. Wellington, Jr., JPMorgan Chase Bank.
EIN: 136824965
Codes: FD

33047
Arkell Hall Foundation, Inc.
P.O. Box 240
Canajoharie, NY 13317-0240
Contact: Joseph A. Santangelo, V.P. and Treas.

Incorporated in 1948 in NY.
Donor(s): Mrs. F.E. Barbour.‡
Financial data (yr. ended 11/30/01): Grants paid, $1,212,395; assets, $57,181,711 (M); expenditures, $2,325,523; qualifying distributions, $2,016,288; giving activities include $786,971 for programs.
Limitations: Giving limited to the Montgomery County, NY, area.
Publications: Application guidelines.
Application information: Application form not required.
Officers and Trustees:* Edward W. Shineman, Jr.,* Pres.; Ferdinand C. Kaiser,* V.P. and Secy.; Joseph A. Santangelo,* V.P. and Treas.; Robert H. Wille,* V.P.; Joyce G. Dresser, Frances L. Howard, Charles Tallent, Charles E. Wright.
EIN: 141343077
Codes: FD

33048
FIMF, Inc.
c/o Hertz, Herson & Company, LLP
2 Park Ave., Ste. 1500
New York, NY 10016

Established in 1995 in DE and NY.
Financial data (yr. ended 12/31/01): Grants paid, $1,210,000; assets, $25,387,556 (M); expenditures, $1,326,385; qualifying distributions, $1,236,164.
Limitations: Applications not accepted. Giving primarily in Jenkintown, PA.
Application information: Contributes only to pre-selected organizations.
Officers and Directors:* Susan Wexner,* Secy.-Treas.; Bernard Agus.
EIN: 134072661
Codes: FD

33049
GBRG, Inc.
c/o Hertz, Herson & Company, LLP
2 Park Ave., Ste. 1500
New York, NY 10016

Established in 1995 in DE and NY.
Financial data (yr. ended 12/31/01): Grants paid, $1,210,000; assets, $25,537,477 (M); expenditures, $1,326,592; qualifying distributions, $1,234,878.
Limitations: Applications not accepted. Giving primarily in Jenkintown, PA.
Application information: Contributes only to pre-selected organizations.
Officers and Directors:* Susan Wexner,* Secy.-Treas.; Bernard Agus.
EIN: 134072646
Codes: FD

33050
HLMH, Inc.
c/o Hertz, Herson & Company, LLP
2 Park Ave., Ste. 1500
New York, NY 10016

Established in 1995 in DE and NY.
Financial data (yr. ended 12/31/01): Grants paid, $1,210,000; assets, $25,472,729 (M); expenditures, $1,326,913; qualifying distributions, $1,235,298.
Limitations: Applications not accepted. Giving primarily in Jenkintown, PA.
Application information: Contributes only to pre-selected organizations.
Officers and Directors:* Susan Wexner,* Secy.-Treas.; Bernard Agus.
EIN: 134072644
Codes: FD

33051
The Wasily Family Foundation, Inc.
c/o JPMorgan Private Bank
1211 6th Ave., 34th Fl.
New York, NY 10036
Contact: Patrick N. Moloney, V.P.

Established in 1988 in NY.
Donor(s): Anne V. Wasily, H. Vira Kolisch.‡
Financial data (yr. ended 06/30/01): Grants paid, $1,210,000; assets, $38,462,178 (M); gifts received, $17,550,965; expenditures, $1,509,968; qualifying distributions, $1,333,309.
Limitations: Giving primarily in New York, NY.
Officers: Anne V. Wasily, Pres.; Patrick N. Moloney, V.P.; Margaret Moloney, Secy.; Frank Suchomel, Jr., Treas.
EIN: 133503227
Codes: FD

33052
The Leona M. and Harry B. Helmsley Charitable Trust
230 Park Ave., Ste. 659
New York, NY 10169

Established in 1999 in NY.
Donor(s): Leona M. Helmsley, Sierra Towers & Fresh Meadows, LLP, Eastdil Reality, Inc., LLC, Helmsley Enterprises, Inc.
Financial data (yr. ended 03/31/01): Grants paid, $1,208,000; assets, $47,017,807 (M); expenditures, $1,323,059; qualifying distributions, $1,187,873.
Limitations: Applications not accepted. Giving primarily in CT and NY.
Application information: Contributes only to pre-selected organizations.
Trustee: Leona M. Helmsley.
EIN: 137184401
Codes: FD

33053
Quarry Hill Foundation
c/o U.S. Trust Co.
114 W. 47th St.
New York, NY 10036

Established in 2000 in NY.
Donor(s): H. Marshall Schwarz.
Financial data (yr. ended 12/31/01): Grants paid, $1,207,000; assets, $5,005,792 (M); gifts received, $114,460; expenditures, $1,234,868; qualifying distributions, $1,206,378.
Limitations: Applications not accepted. Giving primarily in NY.
Application information: Contributes only to pre-selected organizations.
Trustees: H. Marshall Schwarz, Rae Paige Schwarz.
EIN: 134129864
Codes: FD

33054
The Kekst Family Foundation
895 Park Ave.
New York, NY 10021 (212) 521-4800
Contact: Gershon Kekst, Pres.

Established in 1986 in NY.
Donor(s): Gershon Kekst.
Financial data (yr. ended 12/31/01): Grants paid, $1,200,000; assets, $3,312,704 (M); gifts received, $1,000,075; expenditures, $1,205,482; qualifying distributions, $1,200,350.
Limitations: Giving primarily in NY.
Officers: Gershon Kekst, Pres.; Carol Kekst, Secy.-Treas.
EIN: 133382250
Codes: FD

33055
Olayan Charitable Trust
505 Park Ave., Ste. 1100
New York, NY 10022-1106
Contact: Richard Hobson, Jr.

Established in 1993 in NY.
Financial data (yr. ended 12/31/99): Grants paid, $1,197,130; assets, $3,029,501 (M); gifts received, $850,000; expenditures, $1,214,687; qualifying distributions, $1,206,630.
Limitations: Applications not accepted. Giving on an international basis.
Application information: Contributes only to pre-selected organizations.
Trustees: Nazeeh S. Habachy, Hutham S. Olayan.
EIN: 137031747
Codes: FD

33056
Huggy Bears, Inc.
c/o Forstmann Little & Co.
767 5th Ave., 44th Fl.
New York, NY 10153

Established in 1998 in NY.
Donor(s): Nicholas C. Forstmann, Theodore J. Forstmann.
Financial data (yr. ended 12/31/99): Grants paid, $1,196,500; assets, $0 (M); gifts received, $1,310,986; expenditures, $2,742,491; qualifying distributions, $1,997,063.
Limitations: Applications not accepted. Giving on a national basis, with some emphasis on NY.
Application information: Contributes only to pre-selected organizations.
Officers: Nicholas C. Forstmann, Pres.; Sarah Connell, Secy.; Kathleen Broderick, Treas.
EIN: 133998844
Codes: FD

33057
The G & P Foundation for Cancer Research, Inc.
(Formerly The G & P Charitable Foundation, Inc.)
770 Lexington Ave., 16th Fl.
New York, NY 10021

Established in 1996 in CA, DE, and NY.
Donor(s): Denise Rich.
Financial data (yr. ended 12/31/01): Grants paid, $1,194,406; assets, $2,439,118 (M); gifts received, $558,169; expenditures, $2,618,252; qualifying distributions, $555,953.
Limitations: Applications not accepted. Giving on a national basis.
Application information: Contributes only to pre-selected organizations.
Officers: Philip Aouad, Co-Chair., Pres. and Treas.; Denise Rich, Co-Chair., V.P. and Secy.; Charles Cohen, C.E.O. and Pres.; Kay Wright, Exec. V.P.; William Doescher, Sr. V.P. and Chief Comm. Off.; Deborah Dunsire, V.P., Oncology.
Directors: Francine Kittredge, Daniella Rich, Ilona Rich Schachter.
EIN: 133916689
Codes: FD

33058
The Beker Foundation
c/o The Millburn Corp.
1270 Ave. of the Americas, 11th Fl.
New York, NY 10020

Established in 1984 in NY.
Donor(s): Harvey Beker.
Financial data (yr. ended 12/31/00): Grants paid, $1,190,203; assets, $25,061,186 (M); gifts received, $491,275; expenditures, $1,994,367; qualifying distributions, $1,150,003.
Limitations: Applications not accepted. Giving primarily in New York, NY.
Application information: Contributes only to pre-selected organizations.
Officers: Harvey Beker, Pres.; Jayne Beker, Secy.
Director: George E. Crapple.
EIN: 133249239
Codes: FD

33059
Michael and Virginia Mortara Foundation
c/o BCRS Assocs., LLC
100 Wall St., 11th Fl.
New York, NY 10005

Established in 1987 in CT.
Donor(s): Michael P. Mortara.‡
Financial data (yr. ended 08/31/01): Grants paid, $1,177,550; assets, $8,743,550 (M); gifts received, $3,500; expenditures, $1,271,201; qualifying distributions, $1,179,300.
Limitations: Applications not accepted. Giving on a national basis, with some emphasis on Washington, DC.
Application information: Contributes only to pre-selected organizations.
Trustees: David F. Delucia, Steven T. Mnuchin, Virginia L. Mortara.
EIN: 133442300
Codes: FD

33060
Malkin Fund, Inc.
c/o Wien & Malkin, LLP
60 E. 42nd St.
New York, NY 10165

Established in 1994 in NY.
Donor(s): Peter L. Malkin.
Financial data (yr. ended 12/31/01): Grants paid, $1,168,023; assets, $2,705,246 (M); gifts received, $246,445; expenditures, $1,184,558; qualifying distributions, $1,158,628.
Limitations: Giving primarily in the Northeast, with emphasis on CT, MA, and NY.
Officers and Directors:* Peter L. Malkin,* Chair. and Secy.; Isabel W. Malkin,* Pres. and Treas.; Cynthia M. Blumenthal, Anthony E. Malkin, Scott D. Malkin.
EIN: 133749046
Codes: FD

33061
Greenhill Family Foundation
c/o Greenhill & Co., LLC
300 Park Ave., 23rd Fl.
New York, NY 10022

Established in 1997 in CT.
Donor(s): Robert F. Greenhill.
Financial data (yr. ended 12/31/01): Grants paid, $1,166,402; assets, $3,372,315 (M); expenditures, $1,185,153; qualifying distributions, $1,159,496.
Limitations: Applications not accepted. Giving primarily in CT, MA, and NY.
Application information: Contributes only to pre-selected organizations.
Trustees: Gayle G. Greenhill, Robert F. Greenhill.
EIN: 061488779
Codes: FD

33062
The Michael W. McCarthy Foundation
c/o Patrick C. McCarthy
400 Townline Rd., Ste. 155
Hauppauge, NY 11788

Trust established in 1958 in NY.
Donor(s): Michael W. McCarthy,‡ Margaret E. McCarthy.
Financial data (yr. ended 12/31/01): Grants paid, $1,165,000; assets, $30,378,282 (M); gifts received, $76,470; expenditures, $1,453,314; qualifying distributions, $1,213,335.
Limitations: Applications not accepted. Giving primarily in NY.
Application information: Contributes only to pre-selected organizations.
Trustees: Brian A. McCarthy, Patrick C. McCarthy, Patrick M. McCarthy.
EIN: 136150919
Codes: FD

33063
Riley Family Foundation
c/o Behan, Ling & Ruta
358 5th Ave., 9th Fl.
New York, NY 10001

Established in 1991 in NY.
Donor(s): James P. Riley, Jr.
Financial data (yr. ended 02/28/01): Grants paid, $1,164,300; assets, $5,859,638 (M); gifts received, $2,393,304; expenditures, $1,276,805; qualifying distributions, $1,141,572.
Limitations: Applications not accepted. Giving primarily in New York, NY.
Application information: Contributes only to pre-selected organizations.
Trustees: Ellen C. Riley, James P. Riley, Jr.
EIN: 133638509
Codes: FD

33064
The Reed Foundation, Inc.
444 Madison Ave., Ste. 2901
New York, NY 10022 (212) 223-1330
FAX: (212) 754-0078; E-mail:
trf@reedfoundation.org
Contact: David Latham, Prog. Admin.

Incorporated in 1949 in NY.
Donor(s): Samuel Rubin.‡
Financial data (yr. ended 12/31/00): Grants paid, $1,158,519; assets, $15,494,296 (M); expenditures, $1,391,632; qualifying distributions, $1,377,956.
Limitations: Giving primarily in the metropolitan New York, NY, area; some funding also in the Caribbean Basin.
Publications: Program policy statement.
Application information: Applications generally considered only from organizations that have been pre-selected or those with which the foundation has a funding history. Application form not required.
Officers and Directors:* Reed Rubin,* Pres.; Jane Gregory Rubin,* Secy.
EIN: 131990017
Codes: FD

33065
Tortuga Foundation
c/o Siegel, Sacks & Co.
630 3rd Ave., 22nd Fl.
New York, NY 10017

Established in 1979 in NY.
Donor(s): William C. Breed III, J.L. Tweedy.
Financial data (yr. ended 09/30/01): Grants paid, $1,155,000; assets, $19,453,182 (M); gifts received, $400,000; expenditures, $1,451,913; qualifying distributions, $1,268,424.
Limitations: Applications not accepted. Giving on a national basis.
Application information: Contributes only to pre-selected organizations.
Officers: Mildred Siceloff, Pres.; Patricia Livingston, Secy.
EIN: 510245279
Codes: FD

33066
Sarah K. deCoizart Perpetual Charitable Trust
c/o JPMorgan Chase Bank
1 Chase Manhattan Plz., 5th Fl.
New York, NY 10081
Application address: c/o JPMorgan Chase Bank, 1211 6th Ave., 34th Fl., New York, NY 10036, tel: (212) 789-5264
Contact: Philip DiMaulo

Established in 1995 in NY.
Financial data (yr. ended 01/31/01): Grants paid, $1,150,925; assets, $39,276,619 (M); gifts received, $10,000; expenditures, $1,478,586; qualifying distributions, $1,296,540.
Limitations: Giving primarily in New York, NY.
Application information: Application form not required.

33066—NEW YORK

Trustees: Carl S. Forsythe III, JPMorgan Chase Bank.
EIN: 137046581
Codes: FD

33067
The Charles Evans Hughes Memorial Foundation, Inc.
c/o Foundation Service
130 E. 59th St., 12th Fl.
New York, NY 10022-1302 (212) 836-1798
Contact: Lauren Katzowitz, Secy.

Incorporated in 1962 in NY.
Donor(s): Catherine Hughes Waddell,‡ Chauncey L. Waddell.‡
Financial data (yr. ended 07/31/01): Grants paid, $1,150,000; assets, $25,153,314 (M); expenditures, $1,421,013; qualifying distributions, $1,248,624.
Limitations: Applications not accepted. Giving primarily in New York, NY; some giving also in Washington, DC, MA, and NM.
Application information: Unsolicited requests for funds not accepted.
Officers and Directors:* Theodore H. Waddell,* Pres.; William G. Kirkland,* V.P. and Treas.; Lauren Katzowitz, Secy.; Christopher Angell, Anthony C. Howkins, Marjory Hughes Johnson, Karen A.G. Loud, Betty J. Stebman, Brewster Waddell, Wendy J. Williamson.
EIN: 136159445
Codes: FD

33068
Blue Ridge Foundation New York
(Formerly Rubicon Foundation)
660 Madison Ave.
New York, NY 10021
Application address: 150 Court St., 2nd Fl., Brooklyn, NY 11202; FAX: (718) 923-1400; E-mail: info@brfny.org; URL: http://www.brfny.org
Contact: Matthew Klein, Exec. Dir.

Established in 1993 in NY.
Donor(s): John A. Griffin.
Financial data (yr. ended 11/30/01): Grants paid, $1,149,135; assets, $8,664,627 (M); expenditures, $1,726,714; qualifying distributions, $1,157,376.
Limitations: Giving limited to New York City.
Application information: Application information available on Web site.
Trustee: John A. Griffin.
EIN: 137029270
Codes: FD

33069
St. Giles Foundation
(Formerly The House of St. Giles the Cripple)
420 Lexington Ave., Ste. 1641
New York, NY 10170 (212) 338-9001
Contact: Richard Crocker

Established around 1979.
Financial data (yr. ended 03/31/01): Grants paid, $1,148,677; assets, $27,995,630 (M); gifts received, $10,180; expenditures, $1,162,952; qualifying distributions, $875,350.
Limitations: Giving on a national basis.
Officers: Richard T. Arkwright, Pres.; John J. Bennett, Jr., Secy.
Trustees: Henry A. Brown, Hon. Edward R. Finch, Jr., Robert B. Mackay.
EIN: 111630806
Codes: FD

33070
The Lloyd and Laura Blankfein Foundation
c/o Goldman Sachs & Co.
85 Broad St., Tax Dept.
New York, NY 10004

Established in 1989 in NY.
Donor(s): Lloyd C. Blankfein.
Financial data (yr. ended 01/31/01): Grants paid, $1,147,215; assets, $6,782,610 (M); expenditures, $1,167,485; qualifying distributions, $1,147,485.
Limitations: Applications not accepted. Giving primarily in Cambridge, MA, and New York, NY.
Application information: Contributes only to pre-selected organizations.
Trustees: Laura Blankfein, Lloyd C. Blankfein, Gregory P. Ho.
EIN: 133557478
Codes: FD

33071
Third Millennium Charitable and Cultural Foundation
c/o Dr. Marco Stoffel
650 Madison Ave., 18th Fl.
New York, NY 10022

Established in 1999 in NY.
Financial data (yr. ended 12/31/01): Grants paid, $1,145,000; assets, $340,107 (M); expenditures, $1,255,077; qualifying distributions, $1,246,982.
Limitations: Applications not accepted. Giving primarily in New York, NY.
Application information: Contributes only to pre-selected organizations.
Officers and Directors:* Marco Stoffel,* Pres.; Raymond Merritt,* Secy.-Treas.
EIN: 134072609
Codes: FD

33072
The Morse Foundation
c/o Phillip H. Morse
44 Cunningham Ave.
Glens Falls, NY 12801

Established in 1998 in MA.
Donor(s): Phillip H. Morse, The Waterhouse Family Foundation.
Financial data (yr. ended 12/31/01): Grants paid, $1,140,421; assets, $8,165,265 (M); gifts received, $50,000; expenditures, $1,189,008; qualifying distributions, $1,134,786.
Limitations: Applications not accepted. Giving primarily in NY.
Application information: Contributes only to pre-selected organizations.
Trustees: Michael L. Brown, Katherine S. Morse, Lindsey A. Morse, Phillip H. Morse, Shelley H. Morse, Susan K. Morse.
EIN: 046868099
Codes: FD

33073
The Christopher D. Smithers Foundation, Inc.
P.O. Box 67
Oyster Bay Rd.
Mill Neck, NY 11765-0067 (516) 676-0067
FAX: (516) 676-0323; E-mail: smithers@concentric.net; URL: http://www.smithersfoundation.org
Contact: Adele C. Smithers-Fornaci, Pres.

Incorporated in 1952 in NY.
Donor(s): Christopher D. Smithers,‡ Mabel B. Smithers,‡ R. Brinkley Smithers,‡ Adele C. Smithers-Fornaci.
Financial data (yr. ended 12/31/01): Grants paid, $1,136,297; assets, $13,075,271 (M); gifts received, $148,803; expenditures, $1,813,949; qualifying distributions, $1,673,741.
Publications: Annual report.
Application information: Application form not required.
Officers and Directors:* Adele C. Smithers-Fornaci,* Pres.; M. Elizabeth Brothers,* V.P.; Henry S. Ziegler,* Secy.; Thomas D. Croci,* Treas.; Thomas D.A. Croci, Christopher B. Smithers.
EIN: 131861928
Codes: FD

33074
The Oliver & Elizabeth Stanton Foundation
c/o Transommonia Inc.
350 Park Ave.
New York, NY 10022

Established in 2000 in NY.
Donor(s): Transammonia, Inc.
Financial data (yr. ended 12/31/01): Grants paid, $1,135,714; assets, $4,345,230 (M); expenditures, $1,158,246; qualifying distributions, $1,136,203.
Limitations: Applications not accepted. Giving primarily in New York, NY.
Application information: Contributes only to pre-selected organizations.
Officers: Elizabeth Stanton, Pres.; Oliver K. Stanton, V.P.; Fred M. Lowenfels, Secy.; Edward G. Weiner, Treas.
EIN: 134138465
Codes: FD

33075
Louis Callmann Goldschmidt Family Foundation, Inc.
900 Park Ave., Apt. 3D
New York, NY 10021-0213 (212) 309-1000

Established in 1992 in NY.
Donor(s): Clifford H. Goldsmith.
Financial data (yr. ended 12/31/01): Grants paid, $1,134,781; assets, $1,876,279 (M); gifts received, $5,580; expenditures, $1,162,879; qualifying distributions, $1,139,948.
Limitations: Applications not accepted. Giving primarily in NY.
Application information: Contributes only to pre-selected organizations.
Directors: Alexandra Fallon, Clifford H. Goldsmith, Katherine W. Goldsmith, Audrey Kubie, James W. Shea.
EIN: 133691057
Codes: FD

33076
Charlotte Geyer Foundation
P.O. Box 1276
Williamsville, NY 14231 (716) 632-6448
Courier address: 9 Clarion Ct., Williamsville, NY 14221; FAX: (716) 632-6098; URL: http://www.charlottegeyer.org
Contact: Nancy Falletta, Exec. Dir.

Established in 1991 in FL.
Donor(s): Paul F. Eckel.
Financial data (yr. ended 12/31/01): Grants paid, $1,134,382; assets, $4,834 (M); gifts received, $1,140,000; expenditures, $1,186,022; qualifying distributions, $1,186,022.
Limitations: Giving on a national basis.
Application information: Application form not required.
Officer and Trustees:* Nancy E. Falletta,* Exec. Dir.; Charlotte E. Blaney, Joyce A. Eckel, Paul F. Eckel.
EIN: 650281614
Codes: FD

33077
Ellis A. Safdeye & Sons Foundation, Inc.
c/o E.S. Originals, Inc.
450 W. 33rd St.
New York, NY 10001
Contact: Alan J. Safdeye, Pres.

Established in 1982 in NY.
Donor(s): Ellis A. Safdeye.
Financial data (yr. ended 12/31/00): Grants paid, $1,133,972; assets, $643,100 (M); gifts received, $1,117,084; expenditures, $1,137,960; qualifying distributions, $1,130,953.
Limitations: Giving primarily in NY.
Officers: Alan J. Safdeye, Pres.; Joseph Safdeye, Secy.; Michael Safdeye, Treas.
EIN: 133091583
Codes: FD

33078
Sony USA Foundation Inc.
550 Madison Ave., 35th Fl.
New York, NY 10022-3211
Contact: Ann Morfogen, Pres.

Established in 1972 in NY.
Donor(s): Sony Corp. of America, Sony Electronics, Inc.
Financial data (yr. ended 12/31/00): Grants paid, $1,131,285; assets, $2,250,478 (M); gifts received, $880,000; expenditures, $1,137,137; qualifying distributions, $1,131,285.
Limitations: Giving on a national basis.
Application information: Employee-related scholarships are administered by the National Merit Scholarship Corp. Application form required.
Officers and Directors:* Tsunao Hashimoto,* Chair.; Ann Morfogen,* Pres.; H. Paul Burak,* Secy.
EIN: 237181637
Codes: CS, FD, CD

33079
Robert A. and Renee E. Belfer Family Foundation
767 5th Ave., 46th Fl.
New York, NY 10153

Established in 1990 in NY.
Donor(s): Robert A. Belfer, Jack Resnick & Sons, Inc.
Financial data (yr. ended 12/31/99): Grants paid, $1,130,338; assets, $22,003,406 (M); gifts received, $1,023,758; expenditures, $1,199,585; qualifying distributions, $1,111,816.
Limitations: Applications not accepted. Giving primarily in NY.
Application information: Contributes only to pre-selected organizations.
Officer: Robert A. Belfer, Pres. and Secy.
Trustees: Laurence D. Belfer, Renee E. Belfer.
EIN: 136935616
Codes: FD

33080
Chapman Family Fund
P.O. Box 194
Scarborough, NY 10510-0694
Contact: Max C. Chapman, Jr., Tr.

Established in 1987 in NY.
Donor(s): Max C. Chapman, Jr.
Financial data (yr. ended 12/31/01): Grants paid, $1,110,765; assets, $6,566,823 (M); expenditures, $1,159,482; qualifying distributions, $1,124,656.
Limitations: Applications not accepted. Giving primarily in NC and NY.
Application information: Contributes only to pre-selected organizations.
Trustees: Katharine M. Chapman, Max C. Chapman, Jr.
EIN: 133388410
Codes: FD

33081
The Sunrise Foundation Trust
c/o Nathan Low
135 E. 57th St., 11th Fl.
New York, NY 10022

Established in 1997 in NJ.
Donor(s): Nathan Low.
Financial data (yr. ended 12/31/01): Grants paid, $1,105,187; assets, $8,567,519 (M); gifts received, $105,552; expenditures, $1,189,307; qualifying distributions, $1,189,247.
Limitations: Applications not accepted. Giving primarily in New York, NY.
Application information: Contributes only to pre-selected organizations.
Trustees: Lisa Low, Nathan Low.
EIN: 226709496
Codes: FD

33082
Derby Foundation
c/o Eighteen Seventy Corp.
2 Manhattanville Rd.
Purchase, NY 10577
Application address: P.O. Box 1277, Orange, CT 06477
Contact: John J. Kennedy, V.P.

Established in 1980 in DE.
Donor(s): John S. Kennedy, Peter M. Kennedy.
Financial data (yr. ended 11/30/01): Grants paid, $1,104,374; assets, $2,420,501 (M); gifts received, $1,086,624; expenditures, $1,137,024; qualifying distributions, $1,122,440.
Limitations: Giving limited to the U.S.
Officers and Directors:* Peter M. Kennedy,* Pres.; John J. Kennedy, V.P.; John S. Kennedy, V.P.; Marie E. Kennedy,* V.P.; Paul L. Kennedy, V.P.; Peter M. Kennedy III, V.P.; Carol Lawrence,* Secy.
EIN: 133066903
Codes: FD

33083
The Grenfell Association of America
c/o Brown, Brothers, Harriman Trust Co.
63 Wall St.
New York, NY 10005

Donor(s): Seth N. Genung.
Financial data (yr. ended 12/31/99): Grants paid, $1,103,996; assets, $20,900,236 (M); expenditures, $1,394,435; qualifying distributions, $1,175,675.
Limitations: Applications not accepted.
Application information: Contributes only to pre-selected organizations.
Directors: Cecil S. Ashdown, Robert G. Brayton, Robert L. Collins, Charles W. Findlay, Jr., Joan Dobson Glazebrook, Julian Grenfell, R. Keating Hagmann, Lee F. Halla, William T. Heaney, Zaidee P. Laughlin, Carol M. Lynch, David C. Oxman, Robert T. Potter, Jackson Ream, Cynthia A. Roney, William T. Seed, Rosamond Grenfell Shaw, Patricia Simpson, Warren Sturgis, Judith Unis.
EIN: 136083942
Codes: FD

33084
The Walbridge Fund
c/o William S. Phillips, C.P.A.
26 Firemans Memorial Dr., Ste. 110
Pomona, NY 10970-3569

Established in 1997 in NY.
Financial data (yr. ended 12/31/01): Grants paid, $1,101,000; assets, $17,327,454 (M); expenditures, $1,246,582; qualifying distributions, $1,095,912.
Limitations: Applications not accepted. Giving primarily in NY and UT.
Application information: Contributes only to pre-selected organizations.
Officers: George W. Perkins, Jr., Pres.; Jennifer P. Speers, V.P.; Arthur V. Savage, Secy.; William S. Phillips, Treas.
Trustee: Randon W. Wilson.
EIN: 133936131
Codes: FD

33085
The Hilde L. Mosse Foundation
217 Broadway, Ste. 512B
New York, NY 10007-2941
Contact: Henry H. Muller, Secy.

Established in 1985 in NY.
Financial data (yr. ended 09/30/01): Grants paid, $1,100,000; assets, $15,524,681 (M); gifts received, $319,719; expenditures, $1,204,621; qualifying distributions, $1,187,491.
Limitations: Giving primarily in CA, MA, and NY.
Officers: Roger Strauch, Co-Pres. and Treas.; Hans Strauch, Co-Pres.; Henry H. Muller, Secy.
EIN: 133284797
Codes: FD

33086
Tommy Hilfiger Corporate Foundation, Inc.
25 W. 39th St., 11th Fl.
New York, NY 10018 (212) 840-8888

Established in 1996 in NY.
Donor(s): Tommy Hilfiger U.S.A., Inc.
Financial data (yr. ended 03/31/01): Grants paid, $1,099,004; assets, $157,328 (M); gifts received, $850,000; expenditures, $1,100,867; qualifying distributions, $1,098,974.
Limitations: Giving on a national basis.
Application information: Application form not required.
Directors: Steven R. Gursky, Joel H. Newman, Guy Vickers.
EIN: 133856562
Codes: CS, FD, CD

33087
McMullen Family Foundation
1 William St., 5th Fl.
New York, NY 10004

Established in 1993 in NY.
Donor(s): John J. McMullen, Sr.
Financial data (yr. ended 05/31/01): Grants paid, $1,096,384; assets, $21,234,739 (M); expenditures, $1,269,527; qualifying distributions, $1,101,927.
Limitations: Applications not accepted. Giving primarily in NJ; some giving also in Ireland.
Application information: Contributes only to pre-selected organizations.
Officers: Catherine McMullen-Blake, Pres.; John J. McMullen, Jr., V.P.; Peter McMullen, Treas.
Directors: Patrick J. Gilmartin, Jacqueline McMullen, John J. McMullen, Sr., Sanford E. Moore.
EIN: 133721747
Codes: FD

33088
The Glickenhaus Foundation
6 E. 43rd St.
New York, NY 10017 (212) 953-7867
Contact: Maddy Wehle

Incorporated in 1960 in NY.
Donor(s): Seth M. Glickenhaus.

33088—NEW YORK

Financial data (yr. ended 11/30/00): Grants paid, $1,096,185; assets, $9,588,685 (M); gifts received, $2,563,753; expenditures, $1,155,741; qualifying distributions, $1,096,185.
Limitations: Giving primarily in the greater metropolitan New York, NY, area, including Westchester County.
Application information: Application form not required.
Officers: Nancy G. Pier, Pres.; James Glickenhaus, V.P.; Alfred Feinman, Secy.-Treas.
EIN: 136160941
Codes: FD

33089
The Sherlund Family Foundation
85 Broad St., Tax Dept.
New York, NY 10004

Established in 1996 in NJ.
Donor(s): Richard G. Sherlund.
Financial data (yr. ended 04/30/01): Grants paid, $1,094,065; assets, $2,377,369 (M); gifts received, $1,445,629; expenditures, $1,162,983; qualifying distributions, $1,097,983.
Limitations: Applications not accepted. Giving primarily in NJ and NY.
Application information: Contributes only to pre-selected organizations.
Trustees: Janet Sherlund, Richard G. Sherlund.
EIN: 133918285
Codes: FD

33090
Lillian & H. Huber Boscowitz Charitable Trust
c/o Conner & Chopnick
500 5th Ave., Ste. 740
New York, NY 10110 (212) 768-0915
Contact: Paul Werner

Established in 1993.
Financial data (yr. ended 11/30/99): Grants paid, $1,093,500; assets, $4,262,918 (M); expenditures, $1,196,824; qualifying distributions, $1,093,500.
Trustees: Max Chopnick, Lester E. Degenstein, Anna Moffo Sarnoff.
EIN: 137028418
Codes: FD

33091
Martin and Toni Sosnoff Foundation
(Formerly Martin T. Sosnoff Foundation)
P.O. Box 135
Rhinebeck, NY 12572
Contact: Martin T. Sosnoff, Tr.

Established in 1978.
Donor(s): Martin T. Sosnoff.
Financial data (yr. ended 11/30/01): Grants paid, $1,090,962; assets, $2,299,785 (M); gifts received, $958,627; expenditures, $1,111,759; qualifying distributions, $1,087,503.
Limitations: Applications not accepted. Giving primarily in NY.
Application information: Contributes only to pre-selected organizations.
Trustees: Martin T. Sosnoff, Toni Sosnoff.
EIN: 222231640
Codes: FD

33092
Forbes Foundation
c/o Forbes, Inc.
60 5th Ave.
New York, NY 10011 (212) 620-2248
Contact: Leonard H. Yablon, Secy.

Established in 1979 in NJ.
Donor(s): Forbes, Inc.
Financial data (yr. ended 12/31/01): Grants paid, $1,089,221; assets, $1,848 (M); gifts received, $1,050,000; expenditures, $1,089,690; qualifying distributions, $1,089,217.
Limitations: Applications not accepted. Giving on a national basis.
Application information: Contributes only to pre-selected organizations.
Officers and Directors:* Timothy C. Forbes,* Pres.; Malcolm S. Forbes, Jr., V.P.; Leonard H. Yablon, Secy.-Treas.; Robert L. Forbes.
EIN: 237037319
Codes: CS, FD, CD

33093
The Chisholm Foundation
c/o U.S. Trust
114 W. 47th St.
New York, NY 10036

Established in 1960 in MS.
Donor(s): A.F. Chisholm.‡
Financial data (yr. ended 12/31/01): Grants paid, $1,086,471; assets, $25,309,443 (M); expenditures, $1,484,660; qualifying distributions, $1,158,581.
Limitations: Applications not accepted. Giving primarily in MS, and New York, NY.
Application information: Contributes only to pre-selected organizations. Unsolicited requests for funds not accepted.
Officers and Trustees:* John L. Lindsey,* Pres.; Alexander C. Lindsey,* Secy.; Nathan E. Saint-Amand, Treas.; Cynthia C. Saint-Amand.
EIN: 646014272
Codes: FD

33094
The Helen Hotze Haas Foundation, Inc.
c/o Blank Rome Tenzer Greenblatt LLP
405 Lexington Ave., 14th Fl.
New York, NY 10174 (212) 885-5000
Contact: Robert H. Haines, Pres.

Established in 1995 in DE and NY.
Financial data (yr. ended 12/31/00): Grants paid, $1,085,000; assets, $25,698,215 (M); expenditures, $2,076,175; qualifying distributions, $1,146,016.
Limitations: Giving primarily in NY.
Officers and Directors:* Stanley S. Shuman,* Chair.; Robert H. Haines,* Pres.
EIN: 133836626
Codes: FD

33095
Centennial Foundation
c/o Joel E. Sammet & Co.
20 Exchange Pl.
New York, NY 10005

Incorporated in 1965 in NY.
Donor(s): Henry H. Arnhold, Arnhold Ceramics, Inc., A.M. & S.M. Kellen Foundation, Arnhold Foundation, A. Bleichroeder, S. Bleichroeder, Stephen M. Kellen.
Financial data (yr. ended 12/31/01): Grants paid, $1,081,550; assets, $3,529,170 (M); gifts received, $40,000; expenditures, $1,097,946; qualifying distributions, $1,086,538.
Limitations: Applications not accepted. Giving primarily in New York, NY.
Application information: Contributes only to pre-selected organizations.
Officers and Trustees:* Stephen M. Kellen,* Chair.; Henry H. Arnhold,* Pres.; Michael Kellen,* Treas.; John P. Arnhold.
EIN: 136189397
Codes: FD

33096
Anne S. Richardson Fund
(Formerly Anne S. Richardson Charitable Trust)
c/o JPMorgan Chase Bank
1211 Ave. of the Americas, 38th Fl.
New York, NY 10036 (212) 789-5702
Contact: Monica Neal, V.P., JPMorgan Chase Bank

Trust established in 1965 in CT.
Donor(s): Anne S. Richardson.‡
Financial data (yr. ended 07/31/01): Grants paid, $1,079,000; assets, $13,734,294 (M); expenditures, $1,179,642; qualifying distributions, $1,076,811.
Limitations: Giving primarily in western CT; some giving in New York, NY.
Application information: Application form not required.
Trustee: JPMorgan Chase Bank.
EIN: 136192516
Codes: FD

33097
Bausch & Lomb Foundation, Inc.
c/o Bausch & Lomb Inc.
1 Bausch & Lomb Pl.
Rochester, NY 14604-2701 (585) 338-6000
Contact: Barbara M. Kelley, V.P.

Incorporated in 1927 in NY.
Donor(s): Bausch & Lomb Inc., and others.
Financial data (yr. ended 12/31/01): Grants paid, $1,075,784; assets, $1,987,200 (M); expenditures, $1,082,299; qualifying distributions, $1,075,853.
Limitations: Giving primarily in Rochester, NY.
Application information: Application form not required.
Officers and Directors:* Stephen C. McCluski,* Pres.; Barbara M. Kelley,* V.P.; Jean F. Geisel, Secy.; Alan H. Resnick,* Treas.; Robert Stiles.
EIN: 166039442
Codes: CS, FD, CD

33098
The JM Foundation
60 E. 42nd St., Rm. 1651
New York, NY 10165 (212) 687-7735
FAX: (212) 697-5495
Contact: Carl Helstrom, Assoc. Exec. Dir.

Incorporated in 1924 in NY.
Donor(s): Jeremiah Milbank,‡ Katharine S. Milbank.‡
Financial data (yr. ended 12/31/01): Grants paid, $1,072,270; assets, $24,972,000 (M); expenditures, $1,762,000; qualifying distributions, $1,072,270.
Publications: Annual report (including application guidelines), occasional report.
Application information: Application form not required.
Officers and Directors:* Jeremiah Milbank III,* Pres.; Margaret Milbank Bogert,* V.P.; Daniel G. Tenney, Jr.,* Secy.; William Lee Hanley, Jr.,* Treas.; Chris K. Olander, Exec. Dir.; Carl Helstrom, Assoc. Exec. Dir.; Jack Brauntuch, Special Counselor; Jeremiah M. Bogert, Peter C. Morse, Mary Caslin Ross, Michael Sanger.
EIN: 136068340
Codes: FD

33099
MRM Foundation, Inc.
100 Jericho Quadrangle, Ste. 212
Jericho, NY 11753 (516) 935-4200
Application address: 245 Middle Neck Rd., Sandspoint, NY 11050
Contact: Julia Greenblatt, Dir.

Established in 1994 in NY.

Donor(s): Joel N. Greenblatt.
Financial data (yr. ended 11/30/01): Grants paid, $1,071,300; assets, $797,597 (M); gifts received, $1,057,188; expenditures, $1,073,113; qualifying distributions, $1,069,338.
Limitations: Giving primarily in NY.
Application information: Application form not required.
Directors: Joel N. Greenblatt, Julia Greenblatt, Richard Greenblatt.
EIN: 113243133
Codes: FD

33100
Adler Foundation, Inc.
c/o Helen A. Potter
6 Windward Ln.
Scarsdale, NY 10583

Incorporated in 1951 in NY.
Donor(s): Morton M. Adler,‡ Helen R. Adler,‡ Harry Rosenthal,‡ John Adler.
Financial data (yr. ended 09/30/01): Grants paid, $1,067,250; assets, $8,608,921 (M); expenditures, $1,232,840; qualifying distributions, $1,129,410.
Limitations: Applications not accepted. Giving on a national basis.
Application information: Contributes only to pre-selected organizations.
Officers: John Adler, Pres.; Joel I. Berson, Secy.; Helen A. Potter, Treas.
EIN: 136087869
Codes: FD

33101
Michael E. Gellert Trust
122 E. 42nd St., 34th Fl.
New York, NY 10168-0001

Established in 1962 in NY.
Donor(s): Michael E. Gellert.
Financial data (yr. ended 06/30/01): Grants paid, $1,063,368; assets, $8,857,614 (M); expenditures, $1,263,973; qualifying distributions, $1,054,003.
Limitations: Applications not accepted. Giving primarily in CT and NY.
Application information: Contributes only to pre-selected organizations.
Trustees: Michael E. Gellert, Peter J. Gellert, Robert J. Gellert.
EIN: 136093842
Codes: FD

33102
Mortimer Levitt Foundation, Inc.
c/o Estelle Rubenstein
215 E. 68th St., Apt. 22B
New York, NY 10021-5728
Application address: 10 E. 82nd St., New York, NY 10028
Contact: Mortimer Levitt, Pres.

Established in 1966 in NY.
Donor(s): Mortimer Levitt, The Custom Shops.
Financial data (yr. ended 02/28/01): Grants paid, $1,060,494; assets, $18,327,245 (M); expenditures, $3,765,650; qualifying distributions, $1,051,540.
Limitations: Giving primarily in New York, NY.
Officers: Mortimer Levitt, Pres.; A. Levitt, V.P.; E. Rubenstein, Secy.-Treas.
EIN: 136204678
Codes: FD

33103
The Donald & Barbara Zucker Foundation, Inc.
103 W. 55th St.
New York, NY 10019

Established in 1998.
Donor(s): Donald Zucker, Barbara Zucker.
Financial data (yr. ended 09/30/01): Grants paid, $1,058,428; assets, $3,521 (M); gifts received, $1,055,000; expenditures, $1,058,528; qualifying distributions, $1,058,528.
Limitations: Applications not accepted. Giving primarily in NY.
Application information: Contributes only to pre-selected organizations.
Officers: Donald Zucker, Pres.; Barbara Zucker Albinder, V.P.; Laurie Zucker, V.P.; Barbara Hrbek Zucker, Secy.-Treas.
EIN: 134032142
Codes: FD

33104
The Vincent Camuto Charitable Trust
(Formerly The Kristen & Vincent Camuto Charitable Trust)
c/o Salibello & Broder
633 3rd Ave., 13th Fl.
New York, NY 10017

Established in 1994.
Financial data (yr. ended 12/31/99): Grants paid, $1,051,750; assets, $5,791,894 (M); gifts received, $4,167,225; expenditures, $1,066,016; qualifying distributions, $1,050,726.
Limitations: Applications not accepted.
Application information: Contributes only to pre-selected organizations.
Trustees: David J. Sweet, John Zampino.
EIN: 137051137
Codes: FD

33105
The Howard Bayne Fund
c/o Simpson Thacher & Bartlett
425 Lexington Ave.
New York, NY 10017-3909

Incorporated in 1960 in NY.
Donor(s): Louise Van Beuren Bayne Trust.
Financial data (yr. ended 12/31/00): Grants paid, $1,050,000; assets, $18,218,009 (M); expenditures, $1,231,853; qualifying distributions, $1,061,548.
Limitations: Applications not accepted. Giving primarily in CT, NJ, NY, with some emphasis on New York City, and RI.
Application information: Contributes only to pre-selected organizations.
Officers and Directors:* Gurdon B. Wattles,* Pres.; Daphne B. Shih,* V.P.; Victoria B. Bjorklund, Secy.-Treas.; Diana de Vegh, Pierre J. de Vegh, Daisy Paradis, Elizabeth W. Wilkes.
EIN: 136100680
Codes: FD

33106
John H. and Ethel G. Noble Charitable Trust
c/o Deutsche Bank Trust Co. of NY
P.O. Box 1297, Chruch St. Sta.
New York, NY 10008
Contact: Paul J. Bisset, V.P., Deutsche Bank Trust Co. of NY

Trust established in 1969 in CT.
Donor(s): Ethel G. Noble,‡ John H. Noble.‡
Financial data (yr. ended 05/31/01): Grants paid, $1,050,000; assets, $23,314,394 (M); expenditures, $1,178,237; qualifying distributions, $1,108,219.
Limitations: Giving limited to CT, FL, and NY.
Application information: Application form not required.
Trustee: Deutsche Bank.
EIN: 136307313
Codes: FD

33107
Oppenheimer & Haas Foundation
(Formerly Leo Oppenheimer and Flora Oppenheimer Haas Trust)
c/o JPMorgan Private Bank
1211 Ave. of the Americas, 38th Fl.
New York, NY 10036 (212) 789-5679
E-mail: elias_jacqueline@jpmorgan.com
Contact: Jacqueline Elias, V.P.

Trust established in 1950 in NY.
Donor(s): Flora Oppenheimer Haas.‡
Financial data (yr. ended 12/31/01): Grants paid, $1,050,000; assets, $19,709,346 (M); expenditures, $1,214,832; qualifying distributions, $1,102,744.
Limitations: Applications not accepted. Giving primarily in the New York, NY, metropolitan area.
Application information: Unsolicited requests for funds not accepted.
Trustee: JPMorgan Chase Bank.
EIN: 136013101
Codes: FD

33108
Jackson Hole Preserve, Inc.
30 Rockefeller Plz., Rm. 5600
New York, NY 10112 (212) 649-5819
Contact: Carmen Reyes, Treas.

Incorporated in 1940 in NY.
Donor(s): John D. Rockefeller, Jr.,‡ Laurance S. Rockefeller, Rockefeller Brothers Fund.
Financial data (yr. ended 12/31/00): Grants paid, $1,044,210; assets, $5,463,408 (M); expenditures, $1,402,828; qualifying distributions, $1,374,810; giving activities include $60,000 for programs.
Limitations: Giving primarily in the Hudson River Valley, NY, area and Jackson Hole, WY.
Application information: Application form not required.
Officers and Trustees:* Clayton W. Frye, Jr.,* Chair. and Pres.; Antonia M. Grumbach,* Secy.; Carmen Reyes, Treas.; Nash Castro, Henry L. Diamond, Donal C. O'Brien, Jr., Ellen R.C. Pomeroy, Laurance S. Rockefeller.
EIN: 131813818
Codes: FD

33109
The Harvey & Gloria Kaylie Foundation, Inc.
173 Hastings St.
Brooklyn, NY 11235

Established in 1999 in NY.
Donor(s): Scientific Components Corp.
Financial data (yr. ended 12/31/01): Grants paid, $1,043,575; assets, $11,591,432 (M); gifts received, $2,500,000; expenditures, $1,043,835; qualifying distributions, $1,037,724.
Limitations: Applications not accepted. Giving primarily in NY.
Application information: Contributes only to pre-selected organizations.
Officers and Directors:* Harvey Kaylie,* Pres.; Gloria Kaylie,* V.P.; Alicia Kaylie Yacoby,* Secy.-Treas.
EIN: 113502781
Codes: CS, FD, CD

33110
The Jane and Robert Katz Foundation
c/o Goldman Sachs & Co.
85 Broad St., Tax Dept.
New York, NY 10004

Established in 1989 in NY.
Donor(s): Robert J. Katz.
Financial data (yr. ended 02/28/01): Grants paid, $1,041,933; assets, $8,274,101 (M); gifts

33110—NEW YORK

received, $97,313; expenditures, $1,155,627; qualifying distributions, $1,042,187.
Limitations: Applications not accepted. Giving primarily in New York, NY.
Application information: Contributes only to pre-selected organizations.
Trustees: Jane L. Katz, Robert J. Katz.
EIN: 133534735
Codes: FD

33111
The Yablans Family Foundation
c/o Phyllis Yablans
4 Sycamore Dr.
Sands Point, NY 11050

Established in 2000 in NY.
Donor(s): Phyllis Yablans.
Financial data (yr. ended 12/31/01): Grants paid, $1,039,465; assets, $888,610 (M); expenditures, $1,044,061; qualifying distributions, $1,038,979.
Limitations: Applications not accepted.
Application information: Contributes only to pre-selected organizations.
Officers: Phyllis Yablans, Pres.; Bryan Yablans, V.P.; Robyn Levy, Secy.; Seth Yablans, Treas.
EIN: 113575904

33112
Albert & Barrie Zesiger Fund
c/o Albert & Barrie Zesiger
320 Park Ave.
New York, NY 10022

Donor(s): Albert L. Zesiger, Barrie R. Zesiger.
Financial data (yr. ended 08/31/01): Grants paid, $1,034,469; assets, $1,507,237 (M); expenditures, $1,046,591; qualifying distributions, $1,028,634.
Limitations: Applications not accepted. Giving on a national basis, with emphasis on New York, NY, and the greater Boston, MA, area.
Application information: Contributes only to pre-selected organizations.
Officer: Albert L. Zesiger,* Pres.
Directors: David Zesiger, Jeffrey Zesiger.
EIN: 133064459
Codes: FD

33113
American Friends of the Children's Day Nurseries & Children's Town in Israel
c/o Louis J. Septimus & Co.
120 W. 31st St.
New York, NY 10001-3407

Financial data (yr. ended 12/31/01): Grants paid, $1,023,292; assets, $71,354 (M); gifts received, $1,087,360; expenditures, $1,033,043; qualifying distributions, $1,032,520.
Limitations: Applications not accepted. Giving limited to Israel.
Application information: Contributes only to a pre-selected organization.
Officers: Menachem Porusch, Pres.; A.D. Davis, V.P.; Mel Heftler, Secy.; Eli Mendlowitz, Treas.
EIN: 237327778
Codes: TN

33114
Isak and Rose Weinman Foundation, Inc.
c/o BDO Seidman, LLP
330 Madison Ave.
New York, NY 10017-5001

Established in 1956.
Donor(s): Lilliana Teruzzi.‡
Financial data (yr. ended 12/31/01): Grants paid, $1,022,500; assets, $15,060,157 (M); expenditures, $1,160,569; qualifying distributions, $1,064,733.
Limitations: Applications not accepted. Giving primarily in NY, with emphasis on New York City.
Application information: Contributes only to pre-selected organizations.
Officers and Directors:* W. Loeber Landau,* Chair. and Secy.; Alexander E. Slater,* Pres. and Treas.; Donna Landau Hardiman, Barbara Landau, Frederick A. Terry, Blair Landau Trippe.
EIN: 136110132
Codes: FD

33115
Howard P. Milstein Foundation
335 Madison Ave., Ste. 1500
New York, NY 10017
Contact: Paul Milstein, Tr.

Established in 1998 in NY.
Donor(s): Irma Milstein, Howard P. Milstein.
Financial data (yr. ended 12/31/01): Grants paid, $1,019,625; assets, $842,879 (M); gifts received, $250,000; expenditures, $1,033,978; qualifying distributions, $1,019,955.
Limitations: Applications not accepted.
Application information: Contributes only to pre-selected organizations.
Trustees: Howard P. Milstein, Irma Milstein, Paul Milstein.
EIN: 133921824
Codes: FD

33116
Daniel P. and Nancy C. Paduano Family Foundation
c/o Daniel Paduano
19 E. 72nd St.
New York, NY 10021

Established in 1994 in NY.
Donor(s): Daniel P. Paduano, Nancy C. Paduano.
Financial data (yr. ended 11/30/99): Grants paid, $1,018,725; assets, $951,990 (M); gifts received, $784,564; expenditures, $1,022,090; qualifying distributions, $1,007,346.
Limitations: Applications not accepted. Giving primarily in New York, NY.
Application information: Contributes only to pre-selected organizations.
Directors: Daniel P. Paduano, James A. Paduano, Nancy C. Paduano.
EIN: 133796430
Codes: FD

33117
Steven L. Rattner and P. Maureen White Foundation, Inc.
c/o Quadrangle Group, LLC
375 Park Ave, 14th Fl.
New York, NY 10152

Established in 1989 in NY.
Donor(s): Steven L. Rattner.
Financial data (yr. ended 12/31/00): Grants paid, $1,018,665; assets, $3,050,309 (M); gifts received, $210,868; expenditures, $1,092,590; qualifying distributions, $1,013,672.
Limitations: Applications not accepted. Giving primarily in New York, NY.
Application information: Contributes only to pre-selected organizations.
Officers and Directors:* Steven L. Rattner,* Pres.; P. Maureen White,* V.P.; Howard Sontag, Secy.-Treas.
EIN: 133519099
Codes: FD

33118
The Sirus Fund
271 Madison Ave., Ste. 907
New York, NY 10016 (212) 252-8473
FAX: (212) 252-8476
Contact: Alice Paul, Exec. Dir.

Established in 1996 in NY.
Donor(s): Susan U. Halpern.
Financial data (yr. ended 06/30/01): Grants paid, $1,016,536; assets, $24,833,358 (M); gifts received, $313,480; expenditures, $1,385,349; qualifying distributions, $1,131,622; giving activities include $25,000 for loans.
Limitations: Giving primarily in New York City, with emphasis on the Red Hook area of Brooklyn.
Application information: NYRAG Common Application Form accepted. Application form not required.
Officers and Directors:* Susan U. Halpern,* Pres.; Alice Paul, Exec. Dir.; Robert Abrams, Robert Bachner, Bernard Fisher.
EIN: 137100236
Codes: FD

33119
The David B. & Virginia M. Ford Foundation
c/o Goldman Sachs & Co.
85 Broad St., Tax Dept.
New York, NY 10004-2456

Established in 1986 in PA.
Donor(s): David B. Ford.
Financial data (yr. ended 06/30/01): Grants paid, $1,012,942; assets, $11,956,181 (M); gifts received, $2,659,116; expenditures, $1,136,183; qualifying distributions, $981,719.
Limitations: Applications not accepted. Giving primarily in PA.
Application information: Contributes only to pre-selected organizations.
Trustees: David B. Ford, David B. Ford, Jr., James M. Ford, Virginia M. Ford.
EIN: 133385063
Codes: FD

33120
Brunckhorst Foundation
24 Rock St.
Brooklyn, NY 11206-3886

Established in 1968.
Donor(s): Barbara Brunckhorst.
Financial data (yr. ended 12/31/00): Grants paid, $1,012,500; assets, $27,655,262 (M); gifts received, $10,404,619; expenditures, $1,093,864; qualifying distributions, $934,747.
Limitations: Applications not accepted.
Application information: Contributes only to pre-selected organizations.
Trustees: Barbara Brunckhorst, Frank Brunckhorst III, Richard Todd Stravitz.
EIN: 237000850
Codes: FD

33121
Margaret Voorhies Haggin Trust in Memory of Her Late Husband, James Ben Ali Haggin
c/o The Bank of New York, Tax Dept.
1 Wall St., 28th Fl.
New York, NY 10286

Trust established in 1938 in NY.
Donor(s): Margaret Voorhies Haggin.‡
Financial data (yr. ended 12/31/01): Grants paid, $1,009,633; assets, $34,203,235 (M); expenditures, $1,112,028; qualifying distributions, $1,023,496.
Limitations: Applications not accepted. Giving limited to KY.

Application information: Contributes only to pre-selected organizations.
Trustee: The Bank of New York.
EIN: 136078494
Codes: FD

33122
Abe and Frances Lastfogel Foundation
c/o William Morris Agency, Inc.
1325 Ave. of the Americas, 15th Fl.
New York, NY 10019   (212) 586-5100
Contact: David Turi

Established in 1972 in CA.
Donor(s): Abe Lastfogel,‡ Frances Lastfogel,‡ Norman Brokaw, Walter Zifkin, William Morris Agency, Inc.
Financial data (yr. ended 12/31/00): Grants paid, $1,008,653; assets, $3,827,359 (M); gifts received, $1,005,730; expenditures, $1,011,276; qualifying distributions, $1,006,465.
Limitations: Giving primarily in the Los Angeles, CA, area and NY.
Officers: Walter Zifkin, Pres.; Steven Kram, Exec. V.P. and Secy.; Irving J. Weintraub, Exec. V.P. and C.F.O.; Norman Brokaw, Exec. V.P.; Alan Kannof, Exec. V.P.; Jerome F. Katzman, Exec. V.P.
EIN: 237146829
Codes: FD

33123
The Thomas & Janet Montag Family Foundation
c/o Goldman Sachs & Co.
85 Broad St., Tax Dept.
New York, NY 10004

Established in 1996 in NJ.
Donor(s): Thomas K. Montag.
Financial data (yr. ended 05/31/01): Grants paid, $1,007,700; assets, $3,964,749 (M); gifts received, $2,750; expenditures, $1,074,482; qualifying distributions, $1,000,159.
Limitations: Applications not accepted. Giving on a national basis.
Application information: Contributes only to pre-selected organizations.
Trustees: Janet Montag, Thomas K. Montag.
EIN: 137103239
Codes: FD

33124
MONY Foundation
(Formerly Mutual of New York Foundation)
1740 Broadway, 6-38
New York, NY 10019   (212) 708-2468
Additional contact: Lynn Stekas, Pres., tel.: (212) 708-2136, E-mail: lynn_stekas@mony.com; FAX: (212) 708-2001; E-mail: julie_white@mony.com; URL: http://www.mony.com/Foundation
Contact: Julie Schonberger White, Dir., Corp. Social Policy

Established in 1987 in NY.
Donor(s): The Mutual Life Insurance Co. of New York, MONY Life Insurance Co.
Financial data (yr. ended 12/31/01): Grants paid, $1,006,977; assets, $272,407 (M); gifts received, $1,032,500; expenditures, $1,038,785; qualifying distributions, $1,020,822.
Limitations: Giving only in communities where MONY maintains offices, including Syracuse and New York, NY.
Publications: Application guidelines.
Application information: Call before sending proposal. Accepts NYRAG Common Application Form. V.I.P. Award application form available on request. Prefers no multiple year requests as grant renewals are not automatic. Application form not required.

Officers: Lynn Stekas, Pres.; David S. Waldman, Secy.; Richard Daddario, C.F.O.; David V. Weigel, Treas.
Directors: Samuel Foti, Kenneth Levine, Michael Roth, Lee Smith.
EIN: 133398852
Codes: CS, FD, CD

33125
Northern New York Community Foundation, Inc.
(Formerly Watertown Foundation, Inc.)
120 Washington St.
Watertown, NY 13601   (315) 782-7110
FAX: (315) 782-0047; E-mail: nnycf@northnet.org
Contact: Alex C. Velto, Exec. Dir.

Incorporated in 1929 in NY.
Financial data (yr. ended 12/31/01): Grants paid, $1,006,890; assets, $22,009,442 (M); gifts received, $1,009,490; expenditures, $1,283,713.
Limitations: Giving limited to organizations and individuals in Jefferson and Lewis counties, NY.
Publications: Annual report, newsletter.
Application information: Application form not required.
Officers and Directors:* Janet L. George,* Pres.; Philip J. Sprague, V.P.; James R. Kanik,* Secy.-Treas.; Alex C. Velto, Exec. Dir.; Donald C. Alexander, Douglas Brodie, Lee Clary, Mary Mascott, Tony Morgia, Jan K. Turcotte, Anderson Wise, and 3 additional directors.
EIN: 156020989
Codes: CM, FD, GTI

33126
Emwiga Foundation
(Formerly Overlock Family Foundation)
c/o BCRS Associates, LLC
67 Wall St., 8th Fl.
New York, NY 10005

Established in 1984 in NY.
Donor(s): Willard J. Overlock.
Financial data (yr. ended 02/28/01): Grants paid, $1,003,500; assets, $5,111,688 (M); expenditures, $1,173,946; qualifying distributions, $1,005,350.
Limitations: Applications not accepted. Giving primarily in CT, MA, and New York, NY.
Application information: Contributes only to pre-selected organizations.
Trustees: Nicholas C. Forstman, Emily Phelps Overlock, Katherine Overlock, Willard J. Overlock.
EIN: 133247601
Codes: FD

33127
Schwartz Family Foundation
8 Laurel Way
Purchase, NY 10577
Contact: Alan Schwartz, Tr.

Established in 1997 in NY.
Donor(s): Alan Schwartz.
Financial data (yr. ended 12/31/01): Grants paid, $1,000,457; assets, $4,135,644 (M); gifts received, $1,640,900; expenditures, $1,022,529; qualifying distributions, $982,104.
Limitations: Applications not accepted. Giving primarily in NC.
Application information: Contributes only to pre-selected organizations.
Trustee: Alan Schwartz.
EIN: 137138217
Codes: FD

33128
Harold W. Siebens Charitable Foundation, Inc.
c/o Sullivan & Cromwell
125 Broad St.
New York, NY 10004-2498

Established in 2001 in NY.
Donor(s): Famsea Corporation, Seafam Corporation, Seacay Corporation.
Financial data (yr. ended 12/31/01): Grants paid, $1,000,000; assets, $229,450 (M); gifts received, $1,300,000; expenditures, $1,076,424; qualifying distributions, $1,000,000.
Limitations: Applications not accepted.
Application information: Contributes only to pre-selected organizations.
Directors: Henry Christensen III, Charles Dowling, Heather Rae Johnson, Clifford A. Rae, Stewart D. Siebens, William W. Siebens.
EIN: 133666768

33129
The Shalom and Rebecca Fogel Foundation, Inc.
18 Lord Ave.
Lawrence, NY 11559-1322

Established in 1971 in NY.
Donor(s): Shalom Fogel, Rebecca Fogel, Aaron Fogel, Esther Fogel.
Financial data (yr. ended 05/31/00): Grants paid, $998,430; assets, $22,222,706 (M); expenditures, $1,139,825; qualifying distributions, $998,430.
Limitations: Giving primarily in Brooklyn, NY.
Application information: Application form not required.
Officer: Rebecca Fogel, Pres.
EIN: 237323166
Codes: FD

33130
The Vidda Foundation
c/o Carter, Rupp & Roberts
10 E. 40th St., Ste. 3808
New York, NY 10016   (212) 696-4050
Contact: Gerald E. Rupp, Mgr.

Established in 1979 in NY.
Donor(s): Ursula Corning.
Financial data (yr. ended 05/31/01): Grants paid, $997,000; assets, $3,636,856 (M); expenditures, $1,213,949; qualifying distributions, $1,107,910.
Limitations: Giving primarily in NY.
Publications: Financial statement.
Application information: Application form not required.
Officer and Trustees:* Gerald E. Rupp,* Mgr.; John A. Downey, M.D., Helen C. Evarts, Ian Fraser.
EIN: 132981105
Codes: FD

33131
Alavi Foundation
500 5th Ave., 39th Fl.
New York, NY 10110-0397

Incorporated in 1973 in NY.
Financial data (yr. ended 03/31/01): Grants paid, $994,868; assets, $82,555,915 (M); gifts received, $14,573; expenditures, $2,348,469; qualifying distributions, $2,436,829; giving activities include $425,360 for program-related investments.
Limitations: Applications not accepted. Giving on a national basis.
Application information: Student scholarship program has been suspended.
Officers and Directors:* Mohammad Geramian, Pres.; Alireza Ebrahimi,* Secy.; Abbas Mirakhor,* Treas.; Hoshang Ahmadi, Mehdi Hodjat, Mohammad Pirayandeh.
EIN: 237345978
Codes: FD

33132
The David J. Greene Foundation, Inc.
599 Lexington Ave., No. 12
New York, NY 10022-6303 (212) 371-4200
Contact: Barbara A. McBride, Secy.

Incorporated in 1966 in NY.
Donor(s): David J. Greene,‡ and members of the Greene family.
Financial data (yr. ended 12/31/01): Grants paid, $994,407; assets, $18,568,737 (M); gifts received, $155,200; expenditures, $1,004,148; qualifying distributions, $990,131.
Limitations: Giving primarily in the metropolitan New York, NY, area.
Application information: Application form not required.
Officers and Directors:* Alan I. Greene,* Pres.; Robert J. Ravitz,* V.P.; Barbara A. McBride,* Secy.; James R. Greene,* Treas.; Michael C. Greene.
EIN: 136209280
Codes: FD

33133
The Conrad and Virginia Klee Foundation, Inc.
c/o M&T Bank
2 Court St.
Binghamton, NY 13901 (607) 754-2504
Application address: 700 Security Mutual Bldg., 80 Exchange St., Binghamton, NY 13901, tel.: (607) 754-2504
Contact: Clayton M. Axtell, Jr., Pres.

Incorporated in 1957 in NY.
Donor(s): Conrad C. Klee,‡ Virginia Klee.‡
Financial data (yr. ended 12/31/01): Grants paid, $992,318; assets, $18,289,283 (M); expenditures, $1,059,296; qualifying distributions, $992,601.
Limitations: Giving primarily in NY, with emphasis on Broome County and Guilford.
Application information: Application form not required.
Officers: Clayton M. Axtell, Jr., Pres.; David Birchenough, V.P. and Treas.; David Patterson, Secy.
Directors: Wells Allen, Jr., Clayton M. Axtell III, Linda Biemer, John E. Gwyn, Floyd Lawson, Robert Nash.
EIN: 156019821
Codes: FD

33134
The Popplestone Foundation
c/o JPMorgan Chase Bank
1211 Ave. of the Americas, 38th Fl.
New York, NY 10036 (212) 789-5715
E-mail: philp_lisa@JPMorgan.com
Contact: Lisa Philp, V.P., JPMorgan Chase Bank

Established in 2000 in MA.
Donor(s): Alan Dworsky, Suzanne Werber.
Financial data (yr. ended 12/31/01): Grants paid, $991,266; assets, $50,421,565 (M); gifts received, $6,900,484; expenditures, $1,446,016; qualifying distributions, $991,266.
Limitations: Applications not accepted. Giving on a national basis.
Application information: Contributes only to pre-selected organizations.
Trustees: Alan J. Dworsky, Suzanne E. Werber.
EIN: 043528004
Codes: FD

33135
Barry and Audrey Sullivan Foundation
11 Plateau Cir. W.
Bronxville, NY 10708

Established in 1986 in IL.
Donor(s): Barry F. Sullivan, Audrey M. Sullivan.
Financial data (yr. ended 12/31/01): Grants paid, $988,710; assets, $32,217 (M); expenditures, $989,611; qualifying distributions, $989,161.
Limitations: Applications not accepted. Giving primarily in Chicago, IL.
Application information: Contributes only to pre-selected organizations.
Officers: Barry F. Sullivan, Pres.; Audrey M. Sullivan, Secy.; Michael R. Leyden, Treas.
EIN: 363505831
Codes: FD

33136
Prudential Securities Foundation
1 Seaport Plz., 33rd Fl.
New York, NY 10292-0133 (212) 214-4884
FAX: (212) 214-5541; *E-mail:* liz_longley@prusec.com
Contact: Elizabeth Longley, V.P.

Incorporated in 1965 in NY.
Donor(s): Prudential Securities Inc., Bache Halsey Stuart Shields, Inc.
Financial data (yr. ended 01/31/02): Grants paid, $988,421; assets, $40,005 (M); gifts received, $1,016,986; expenditures, $988,446; qualifying distributions, $988,446.
Limitations: Applications not accepted. Giving limited to NY.
Publications: Annual report.
Application information: Unsolicited requests for funds not accepted.
Officers and Directors:* Elizabeth A. Longley,* V.P.; Paul Waldman, Secy.; William J. Horan,* Treas.
EIN: 136193023
Codes: CS, FD, CD

33137
Bernice and Milton Stern Foundation
1140 6th Ave., 18th Fl.
New York, NY 10036
Contact: Bernice Stern, Pres.

Established in 1982 in DE.
Financial data (yr. ended 04/30/01): Grants paid, $986,850; assets, $19,507,754 (M); expenditures, $1,415,171; qualifying distributions, $1,110,079.
Limitations: Giving primarily in NY.
Officers: Bernice Stern, Pres.; Wendy S. Pesky, V.P.
EIN: 510264122
Codes: FD

33138
The Paul and Karen Levy Family Foundation
c/o Schwartz & Co., LLP
2580 Sunrise Hwy.
Bellmore, NY 11710-3608
Contact: Paul Levy, Tr.

Established in 1997 in NY.
Donor(s): Paul Levy.
Financial data (yr. ended 11/30/01): Grants paid, $985,059; assets, $1,473,956 (M); expenditures, $1,002,997; qualifying distributions, $984,667.
Limitations: Giving on a national basis.
Application information: Application form not required.
Trustee: Paul Levy.
EIN: 133982379
Codes: FD

33139
Edward & Joan B. Steiniger Charitable Foundation
1 Court Sq., PBG Tax Dept., 22nd Fl.
Long Island City, NY 11120
Contact: Richard Monaghan

Established in 1990 in NY.
Donor(s): Pamela S. Saelzler Unitrust.
Financial data (yr. ended 12/31/00): Grants paid, $979,118; assets, $28,144,671 (M); gifts received, $28,715; expenditures, $1,113,080; qualifying distributions, $971,621.
Limitations: Applications not accepted. Giving primarily in the metropolitan New York, NY, area.
Application information: Contributes only to pre-selected organizations.
Trustee: Citibank, N.A.
EIN: 133585674
Codes: FD

33140
The Paul MacKall & Evanina MacKall Trust
c/o JPMorgan Guaranty Tr. Co.
345 Park Ave.
New York, NY 10154-1002 (212) 464-2590
Contact: James J. Watson, V.P., Morgan Guaranty Tr. Co.

Established in 1982 in NY.
Financial data (yr. ended 08/31/01): Grants paid, $978,137; assets, $17,729,531 (M); expenditures, $1,028,983; qualifying distributions, $967,586.
Limitations: Giving on a national basis.
Trustee: JPMorgan Guaranty Trust Co.
EIN: 136794686
Codes: FD

33141
Charina Foundation, Inc.
85 Broad St.
New York, NY 10004
Contact: Richard L. Menschel, Pres.

Incorporated in 1980 in NY.
Donor(s): Richard L. Menschel, The Menschel Foundation.
Financial data (yr. ended 08/31/01): Grants paid, $977,875; assets, $23,865,064 (M); gifts received, $1,216,087; expenditures, $1,084,251; qualifying distributions, $986,239.
Limitations: Applications not accepted. Giving primarily in NY.
Application information: Contributes only to pre-selected organizations.
Officers and Directors:* Richard L. Menschel,* Pres. and Treas.; Ronay Menschel,* Secy.; Eugene P. Polk.
EIN: 133050294
Codes: FD

33142
The Joelson Foundation
1780 Broadway, 10th Fl.
New York, NY 10019

Established in 1966 in NY.
Donor(s): Julius Joelson.‡
Financial data (yr. ended 03/31/01): Grants paid, $970,916; assets, $19,581,979 (M); gifts received, $183,384; expenditures, $1,181,401; qualifying distributions, $1,029,351.
Limitations: Applications not accepted. Giving primarily in New York, NY.
Application information: Contributes only to pre-selected organizations.
Officers: Barbara J. Fife, Pres.; Joseph C. Mitchell, Secy.-Treas.
Director: Stephen Fife.
EIN: 136220799
Codes: FD

33143
Abe and Barbara Chehebar Foundation, Inc.
c/o Accessory Network Group, Inc.
350 5th Ave., Ste. 400
New York, NY 10118

Established in 1997 in NY.

Donor(s): Abraham Chehebar, Barbara Chehebar, Morris Chehebar, Sam Hafif, Joseph Jack Sitt Foundation.
Financial data (yr. ended 12/31/01): Grants paid, $969,230; assets, $412,060 (M); gifts received, $609,432; expenditures, $969,614; qualifying distributions, $966,128.
Limitations: Applications not accepted. Giving primarily in NY.
Application information: Contributes only to pre-selected organizations.
Officers: Abraham Chehebar, Pres.; Barbara Chehebar, V.P.; Donald Hecht, Secy.-Treas.
EIN: 133980761
Codes: FD

33144
Waterhouse Family Foundation, Inc.
c/o L.M. Waterhouse & Co., Inc.
128 Todd Ln.
Briarcliff Manor, NY 10510

Established in 1996 in NY.
Donor(s): Lawrence M. Waterhouse, Jr.
Financial data (yr. ended 12/31/01): Grants paid, $968,625; assets, $1,281,046 (M); gifts received, $100,000; expenditures, $981,143; qualifying distributions, $967,454.
Limitations: Applications not accepted.
Application information: Contributes only to pre-selected organizations.
Officer: Lawrence M. Waterhouse, Jr., Pres.
Directors: Christine A. Waterhouse, Jennifer A. Waterhouse, Kevin C. Waterhouse, Lawrence M. Waterhouse III, Patrick R. Waterhouse.
EIN: 133914707
Codes: FD

33145
Harry Winston Research Foundation, Inc.
718 5th Ave.
New York, NY 10019 (212) 245-2000

Incorporated in 1964 in NY.
Donor(s): Harry Winston,‡ Ronald Winston.
Financial data (yr. ended 12/31/00): Grants paid, $964,518; assets, $1,123,687 (M); expenditures, $1,073,262; qualifying distributions, $1,056,322.
Limitations: Applications not accepted. Giving primarily in New York, NY, and Vesenaz, Switzerland.
Application information: Contributes only to pre-selected organizations.
Officers: Ronald Winston, Pres.; Robert Holtzman, V.P.; Richard Copaken, Secy.
EIN: 136168266
Codes: FD

33146
Cypress Foundation, Inc.
c/o Sandler O'Neill & Partners, LP
919 3rd Ave., 6th Fl.
New York, NY 10022
Contact: James Dunne

Established in 1992 in NY.
Donor(s): Herman Sandler, James Dunne III.
Financial data (yr. ended 12/31/01): Grants paid, $961,412; assets, $1,333,025 (M); gifts received, $501,250; expenditures, $1,000,745; qualifying distributions, $961,412.
Limitations: Applications not accepted. Giving primarily in the metropolitan New York, NY, area. Some giving also in Israel.
Application information: Contributes only to pre-selected organizations.
Officers: James Dunne, Chair.; Jonathan Doyle, V.P.; Fred D. Price, V.P.; May Della Pietra, Secy.-Treas.
EIN: 133667026

Codes: FD

33147
Billy Rose Foundation, Inc.
805 3rd Ave., 23rd Fl.
New York, NY 10022 (212) 407-7745
Contact: Terri C. Mangino, Asst. Secy.

Incorporated in 1958 in NY.
Donor(s): Billy Rose.‡
Financial data (yr. ended 12/31/00): Grants paid, $960,000; assets, $15,048,585 (M); expenditures, $1,167,777; qualifying distributions, $993,746.
Limitations: Giving primarily in New York, NY.
Application information: Application form not required.
Officers: Arthur Cantor, Chair.; James R. Cherry, Jr., Pres.; Edward J. Walsh, Jr., V.P.; John Wohlstetter, V.P.; Paul Silberberg, Treas.
EIN: 136165466
Codes: FD

33148
The Robert and Joyce Menschel Family Foundation
(Formerly The Robert and Joyce Menschel Foundation)
c/o Goldman Sachs & Co.
85 Broad St., Tax Dept.
New York, NY 10004

Established in 1958 in NY.
Donor(s): Robert B. Menschel.
Financial data (yr. ended 10/31/01): Grants paid, $949,256; assets, $14,664,843 (M); expenditures, $953,891; qualifying distributions, $953,891.
Limitations: Applications not accepted. Giving on a national basis.
Application information: All grants initiated by the foundation.
Officers and Directors:* Robert B. Menschel,* Pres. and Treas.; Joyce F. Menschel,* V.P. and Secy.; Henry Christensen III, David F. Menschel, Lauren E. Menschel.
EIN: 136098443
Codes: FD

33149
The Stanley & Frieda Cayre Foundation, Inc.
16 E. 40th St.
New York, NY 10016 (212) 951-3016
Contact: Stanley Cayre, Pres.

Established in 1993 in NY.
Donor(s): Stanley Cayre.
Financial data (yr. ended 12/31/00): Grants paid, $949,160; assets, $9,839,199 (M); gifts received, $2,697,983; expenditures, $1,290,366; qualifying distributions, $914,575.
Limitations: Giving primarily in NY.
Officers: Stanley Cayre, Pres.; Frieda Cayre, V.P.
EIN: 133746789
Codes: FD

33150
The Gorter Family Foundation
(Formerly Green Bay Foundation)
c/o BCRS Assocs., LLC
100 Wall St., 11th Fl.
New York, NY 10005 (212) 902-6897

Established in 1977 in IL.
Donor(s): James P. Gorter.
Financial data (yr. ended 12/31/01): Grants paid, $944,050; assets, $5,112,381 (M); gifts received, $428,655; expenditures, $1,031,235; qualifying distributions, $943,377.
Limitations: Applications not accepted. Giving primarily in IL and NC.
Application information: Contributes only to pre-selected organizations.

Trustee: James P. Gorter.
Directors: Audrey F. Gorter, David F. Gorter, James P. Gorter, Jr., Mary Gorter Krey.
EIN: 362950350
Codes: FD

33151
Chaim Mayer Foundation, Inc.
80 Broad St., 29th Fl.
New York, NY 10004
Contact: Hirsch Wulliger, Cont.

Established in 1981 in NY.
Donor(s): Joseph Neumann.
Financial data (yr. ended 04/30/01): Grants paid, $942,028; assets, $454 (M); gifts received, $942,365; expenditures, $942,028; qualifying distributions, $941,360.
Limitations: Giving on a national basis.
Application information: Application form not required.
Officers: Joseph Neumann, Pres.; Rachel Neumann, V.P.; Donald Press, V.P.; Rabbi J.A. Luria, Cont.; Hirsch Wulliger, Cont.
EIN: 133119407
Codes: FD, GTI

33152
Sam Spiegel Foundation
30 Wall St.
New York, NY 10005 (212) 269-6720
Contact: David N. Bottoms, Jr., Dir.

Established in 1958 in NY.
Donor(s): Sam Spiegel, Albatros Enterprises Trust.
Financial data (yr. ended 12/31/00): Grants paid, $941,500; assets, $12,281,995 (M); expenditures, $1,058,793; qualifying distributions, $949,485.
Limitations: Giving on a national and international basis, with some emphasis on NY.
Directors: David N. Bottoms, Jr., Raya Dreben, Alisa S. Freedman, Adam Spiegel.
EIN: 136163123
Codes: FD

33153
Riley J. and Lillian N. Warren and Beatrice W. Blanding Foundation
6 Ford Ave.
Oneonta, NY 13820 (607) 432-6720
Contact: Henry L. Hulbert, Mgr.

Trust established in 1972 in NY.
Donor(s): Beatrice W. Blanding.
Financial data (yr. ended 12/31/01): Grants paid, $940,850; assets, $21,571,075 (M); gifts received, $900,000; expenditures, $1,082,041; qualifying distributions, $1,052,951.
Limitations: Giving primarily in the Oneonta, NY, area.
Officer and Trustees:* Henry L. Hulbert,* Mgr.; Robert A. Harlem, Maureen P. Hulbert.
EIN: 237203341
Codes: FD

33154
The Liman Foundation, Inc.
c/o U.S. Trust Co. of NY, TAXVAS
114 W. 47th St.
New York, NY 10036 (212) 852-3629
Contact: Carolyn Lark, Tr. Off.

Established in 2000 in NY, as a result of a transfer of assets from the Joe and Emily Lowe Foundation.
Financial data (yr. ended 12/31/01): Grants paid, $940,000; assets, $8,753,351 (M); gifts received, $29,670; expenditures, $952,618; qualifying distributions, $945,559.
Limitations: Giving primarily in the New York, NY metropolitan area.

33154—NEW YORK

Application information: Foundation has limited ability to add new grantees and is unable to respond to unsolicited proposals.
Officers: Ellen Liman, Pres. and Treas.; Douglas Liman, V.P.; Emily Liman, V.P.; Lewis Liman, Secy.
EIN: 134062758
Codes: FD

33155
Selz Foundation, Inc.
230 Park Ave.
New York, NY 10169
Contact: Bernard T. Selz, Pres.

Established in 1983 in NY.
Donor(s): Bernard T. Selz.
Financial data (yr. ended 12/31/01): Grants paid, $938,547; assets, $19,232,423 (M); gifts received, $184,583; expenditures, $1,008,264; qualifying distributions, $984,399.
Limitations: Giving on a national basis.
Application information: Application form not required.
Officers and Directors:* Bernard T. Selz,* Pres.; Lisa Selz, Secy.-Treas.; Arnold Sytop.
EIN: 133180806
Codes: FD

33156
Daniel M. Neidich & Brooke Garber Foundation
c/o Goldman Sachs & Co.
85 Broad St., Tax Dept.
New York, NY 10004

Established in 1985 in NY.
Donor(s): Daniel M. Neidich.
Financial data (yr. ended 01/31/01): Grants paid, $937,700; assets, $9,212,989 (M); gifts received, $2,432,813; expenditures, $1,048,513; qualifying distributions, $937,950.
Limitations: Applications not accepted. Giving primarily in New York, NY.
Application information: Contributes only to pre-selected organizations.
Trustees: Brooke Garber, Daniel M. Neidich.
EIN: 133318126
Codes: FD

33157
Richard S. Fuld, Jr. Foundation, Inc.
c/o The Ayco Co., LP
P.O. Box 8019
Ballston Spa, NY 12020-8019
Contact: W. Michael Reickert

Established in 1994.
Donor(s): Richard S. Fuld, Jr.
Financial data (yr. ended 11/30/00): Grants paid, $936,964; assets, $145,647 (M); gifts received, $582,188; expenditures, $946,645; qualifying distributions, $931,560.
Limitations: Applications not accepted. Giving primarily in CT and NY.
Application information: Contributes only to pre-selected organizations.
Officers: Richard S. Fuld, Pres. and Treas.; Kathleen Bailey Fuld, V.P. and Secy.
EIN: 137042848
Codes: FD

33158
JCT Foundation
c/o Junction Advisors, Inc.
9 W. 57th St.
New York, NY 10019
Contact: Jeff C. Tarr, Dir.

Established in 1984 in NY.
Donor(s): Jeff C. Tarr.
Financial data (yr. ended 12/31/01): Grants paid, $934,500; assets, $19,800,605 (M); expenditures, $1,066,423; qualifying distributions, $933,148.
Limitations: Applications not accepted. Giving primarily in New York, NY.
Application information: Contributes only to pre-selected organizations.
Directors: Jeff C. Tarr, Patricia G. Tarr.
Trustees: Jeff Tarr, Jr., Jennifer Tarr.
EIN: 133237111
Codes: FD

33159
The Gloria & Sidney Danziger Foundation
c/o Wolf, Block, Schorr, et al.
250 Park Ave.
New York, NY 10177

Established in 1959 in NY.
Donor(s): Sidney Danziger.‡
Financial data (yr. ended 12/31/01): Grants paid, $928,990; assets, $6,043,766 (M); expenditures, $1,155,421; qualifying distributions, $1,046,967.
Limitations: Applications not accepted.
Application information: Contributes only to pre-selected organizations.
Officer: Rabbi B. Kreitman, Pres.
Directors: Robert E. Fischer, Stanley T. Miller.
EIN: 136124448
Codes: FD

33160
Doctoroff Family Foundation
c/o Oak Hill Partners, Inc.
65 E. 55th St., 32nd Fl.
New York, NY 10022

Established in 1997.
Donor(s): Daniel L. Doctoroff.
Financial data (yr. ended 12/31/00): Grants paid, $927,625; assets, $889,407 (M); gifts received, $1,146,369; expenditures, $929,131; qualifying distributions, $918,890.
Limitations: Applications not accepted. Giving primarily in NY.
Application information: Contributes only to pre-selected organizations.
Trustees: Alisa R. Doctoroff, Daniel L. Doctoroff.
EIN: 137137723
Codes: FD

33161
The Lita Annenberg Hazen Foundation
667 Madison Ave.
New York, NY 10021 (212) 751-4917

Established in 1996 in NY.
Financial data (yr. ended 12/31/00): Grants paid, $926,305; assets, $25,848,593 (M); gifts received, $215,748; expenditures, $1,050,387; qualifying distributions, $974,261.
Limitations: Applications not accepted. Giving primarily in NY.
Application information: Contributes only to pre-selected organizations.
Officers: Cynthia Polsky, Pres.; Adam Z. Cherry, V.P.; Alexander Polsky, V.P.; Nicholas Polsky, V.P.; Alison Cherry Zuber, V.P.; Leon Polsky, Secy. and Admin.
EIN: 137067727
Codes: FD

33162
HSBC in the Community USA Inc. Foundation
c/o HSBC Group Public Affairs
452 Fifth Ave.
New York, NY 10018 (212) 525-8239
URL: http://us.hsbc.com/inside/community/HSBCfoundation.asp
Contact: Kristen Alvanson

Established in 2000 in NY.
Donor(s): HSBC Bank USA.
Financial data (yr. ended 12/31/01): Grants paid, $924,165; assets, $4,109,877 (M); gifts received, $2,500,000; expenditures, $929,872; qualifying distributions, $929,394.
Limitations: Giving primarily in areas of company operations.
Officers: Linda Stryker, Pres.; Robert H. Muth, V.P., Treas.; Philip S. Toohey, Secy.
EIN: 161593742
Codes: CS, FD, CD

33163
Judith L. Chiara Charitable Fund, Inc.
61 Broadway, Ste. 2400
New York, NY 10006

Established in 1997 in NY.
Financial data (yr. ended 10/31/01): Grants paid, $921,183; assets, $19,516,633 (M); expenditures, $1,032,207; qualifying distributions, $915,783.
Limitations: Applications not accepted.
Application information: Contributes only to pre-selected organizations.
Trustees: John T. Beaty, Jr., Judith L. Chiara, Jerome Manning.
EIN: 311577990
Codes: FD

33164
Hettinger Foundation
c/o Oberfest & Assocs.
P.O. Box 318
Chappaqua, NY 10514

Trust established in 1961 in NY.
Donor(s): Albert J. Hettinger, Jr.,‡ John Hettinger.
Financial data (yr. ended 12/31/99): Grants paid, $915,000; assets, $18,262,001 (M); expenditures, $1,033,876; qualifying distributions, $909,958.
Limitations: Applications not accepted. Giving primarily in CT and New York, NY.
Application information: Contributes only to pre-selected organizations.
Trustees: Betty Hettinger, John Hettinger, William R. Hettinger.
EIN: 136097726
Codes: FD

33165
James J. McCann Charitable Trust and McCann Foundation, Inc.
(also known as McCann Foundation)
35 Market St.
Poughkeepsie, NY 12601 (845) 452-3085
Contact: John J. Gartland, Jr., Pres.

McCann Foundation, Inc. established in NY in l967; trust established in 1969 in NY; foundations function as single unit and financial data is combined.
Donor(s): James J. McCann.‡
Financial data (yr. ended 12/31/01): Grants paid, $914,766; assets, $33,308,891 (M); expenditures, $1,232,255; qualifying distributions, $1,032,045.
Limitations: Giving primarily in Poughkeepsie and Dutchess County, NY.
Publications: Annual report.
Application information: Application form not required.

Officers and Directors:* John J. Gartland, Jr.,* Pres.; Richard V. Corbally,* Secy.; Michael G. Gartland, Dennis J. Murray.
EIN: 146050628
Codes: FD

33166
Baisley Powell Elebash Fund
c/o JPMorgan Chase Bank
1211 Ave. of the Americas, 38th Fl.
New York, NY 10036 (212) 789-5682
E-mail: jones_ed_l@JPMorgan.com
Contact: Edward L. Jones, V.P., JPMorgan Chase Bank

Established in 1997.
Financial data (yr. ended 10/31/00): Grants paid, $914,000; assets, $11,521,885 (M); expenditures, $1,058,329; qualifying distributions, $924,696.
Limitations: Applications not accepted. Giving primarily in AL, AZ, and NY.
Application information: Contributes only to pre-selected organizations.
Trustee: JPMorgan Chase Bank.
EIN: 137125140

33167
Kraft Foods Fund
(Formerly Nabisco Foundation Trust)
c/o Deutsche Trust Co. of NY
P.O. Box 1297, Church St. Sta.
New York, NY 10008
Application address: c/o Henry A. Sandbach, Dir. Contribs., Nabisco Plz., 7 Campus Dr., Parsippany, NJ 07054

Incorporated in 1953 in NJ.
Donor(s): Nabisco Holdings Corp.
Financial data (yr. ended 12/31/01): Grants paid, $911,250; assets, $2,401,219 (M); expenditures, $931,745; qualifying distributions, $913,582.
Limitations: Giving on a national basis.
Publications: Occasional report.
Application information: Application form not required.
Trustee: Deutsche Bank.
EIN: 136042595
Codes: CS, FD, CD

33168
The Crisp Family Foundation
(Formerly The Peter O. Crisp Fund)
c/o U.S. Trust
114 W. 47th St.
New York, NY 10036
FAX: (212) 852-3377
Contact: Peter O. Crisp, Tr.; or Carolyn Larke, V.P., U.S. Trust

Established in 1993 in NY.
Donor(s): Peter O. Crisp.
Financial data (yr. ended 12/31/01): Grants paid, $910,850; assets, $6,858,697 (M); expenditures, $931,424; qualifying distributions, $911,723.
Limitations: Applications not accepted. Giving primarily in NY.
Application information: Contributes only to pre-selected organizations.
Trustee: Peter O. Crisp.
EIN: 137028080
Codes: FD

33169
Klingenstein Fund
(Formerly Clara Buttenwieser Unger Memorial Foundation)
31 Oxford Rd.
Scarsdale, NY 10583
Contact: Lee P. Klingenstein, Pres.

Established in 1940 in NY.
Donor(s): Alan Klingenstein, Lee Paul Klingenstein, Paul H. Klingenstein, Joanne Ziesing.
Financial data (yr. ended 12/31/01): Grants paid, $910,430; assets, $5,619,606 (M); gifts received, $540,490; expenditures, $1,036,751; qualifying distributions, $914,618.
Limitations: Giving primarily in CT and NY.
Officers: Lee Paul Klingenstein, Pres.; Paul H. Klingenstein, V.P.; Joanne K. Ziesing, Secy.; Alan Klingenstein, Treas.
EIN: 136077894
Codes: FD

33170
The Michel David-Weill Foundation
c/o Lazard, LLC
30 Rockefeller Plz.
New York, NY 10020
Contact: Michel David-Weill, Pres.

Established in 1984 in NY.
Donor(s): Michel David-Weill.
Financial data (yr. ended 06/30/01): Grants paid, $910,000; assets, $688,548 (M); gifts received, $1,012,894; expenditures, $939,620; qualifying distributions, $902,812.
Limitations: Giving primarily in the New York, NY, area.
Officers and Directors:* Michel David-Weill,* Pres.; Helene David-Weill,* V.P.; Melvin L. Heinemen,* Secy.-Treas.
EIN: 133240809
Codes: FD

33171
John L. Loeb, Jr. Foundation
c/o B. Strauss Assoc., Ltd.
307 5th Ave., 8th Fl.
New York, NY 10016-6517

Established in 1964.
Donor(s): John L. Loeb, Jr.
Financial data (yr. ended 12/31/01): Grants paid, $909,628; assets, $18,996,498 (M); expenditures, $941,191; qualifying distributions, $914,591.
Limitations: Applications not accepted. Giving primarily in NY.
Application information: Contributes only to pre-selected organizations.
Officer: John L. Loeb, Jr., Pres.
EIN: 136142345
Codes: FD

33172
Frederick & Sharon Klingenstein Fund
c/o Tanton & Co., LLP
37 W. 57th St., 5th Fl.
New York, NY 10019-3411
Application address: 787 7th Ave., 6th Fl., New York, NY 10019-6016
Contact: Frederick Klingenstein, Tr.

Established in 1997 in NY.
Donor(s): Frederick A. Klingenstein.
Financial data (yr. ended 12/31/00): Grants paid, $906,227; assets, $4,721,136 (M); gifts received, $1,500; expenditures, $949,199; qualifying distributions, $893,128.
Application information: Application form not required.
Trustees: Frederick A. Klingenstein, Sharon Klingenstein.
EIN: 061471980
Codes: FD

33173
The Daniele Agostino Foundation, Inc.
870 United Nations Plz., No. 35C
New York, NY 10017
FAX: (212) 752-1668; *E-mail:* da.found@verizon.net; *URL:* http://www.dafound.org
Contact: Flavia Robinson, Pres.

Established in 1991 in NY.
Donor(s): Flavia D. Robinson.
Financial data (yr. ended 06/30/02): Grants paid, $902,646; assets, $5,190,772 (M); expenditures, $958,000; qualifying distributions, $902,646.
Limitations: Giving primarily in Guatemala and Mexico; some giving also in New York, NY.
Publications: Informational brochure.
Application information: Application form not required.
Officers and Directors:* Flavia D. Robinson,* Pres.; Marshall A. Robinson,* V.P. and Secy.; Lorna Opatow,* Treas.; Peter De Janosi, Daniele DeRossi.
EIN: 133636541
Codes: FD

33174
Robert & Ardis James Foundation
80 Ludlow Dr.
Chappaqua, NY 10514
Application address: 475 5th Ave., Ste. 1700, New York, NY 10017
Contact: Catherine James Paglia, Tr.

Established in 1986 in NY.
Donor(s): Robert James.
Financial data (yr. ended 09/30/01): Grants paid, $902,255; assets, $14,177,296 (M); expenditures, $1,109,953; qualifying distributions, $910,421.
Trustees: Ardis James, Ralph M. James, Robert James, Catherine James Paglia.
EIN: 136880057
Codes: FD

33175
Robert L. and Kathrina H. MacLellan Foundation
c/o U.S. Trust, Tax Dept.
114 W. 47th St.
New York, NY 10036 (212) 852-3841
Contact: Debra A. Feeks

Established in 1972 in TN.
Donor(s): Kathrina H. MacLellan.
Financial data (yr. ended 12/31/00): Grants paid, $900,250; assets, $18,767,242 (M); gifts received, $900,029; expenditures, $1,045,159; qualifying distributions, $900,327.
Limitations: Giving primarily in TN.
Application information: Application form required.
Officers and Directors:* Kathrina H. MacLellan,* Pres. and Treas.; Thomas H. McCallie, Secy.; Lee S. Anderson, Lara Brindel, Douglas Daugherty, Robert H. MacLellan, Albert MacMillan.
EIN: 237159802
Codes: FD

33176
The Pamela Cole Charitable Trust
c/o Holland & Knight, LLP
195 Broadway, 24th Fl.
New York, NY 10007

Established in 1988 in NY.
Donor(s): Pamela Cole,‡ Augustine Properties.
Financial data (yr. ended 02/28/01): Grants paid, $900,000; assets, $596,292 (M); gifts received, $882; expenditures, $929,458; qualifying distributions, $899,202.

33176—NEW YORK

Limitations: Applications not accepted. Giving primarily in New York, NY and Philadelphia, PA.
Application information: Contributes only to pre-selected organizations.
Trustees: Charles Bernheim, Charles F. Gibbs.
EIN: 136901088
Codes: FD

33177
The Henry L. and Grace Doherty Charitable Foundation, Inc.
c/o McGrath, Doyle & Phair
150 Broadway
New York, NY 10038 (212) 571-2300
Contact: Walter R. Brown, Pres.

Incorporated in 1947 in DE.
Donor(s): Mrs. Henry L. Doherty,‡ Helen Lee Lassen.‡
Financial data (yr. ended 12/31/01): Grants paid, $897,275; assets, $19,024,391 (M); expenditures, $1,337,321; qualifying distributions, $978,979.
Limitations: Giving on a national basis, with some emphasis on MA and NY institutions.
Application information: Application form not required.
Officers and Directors:* Walter R. Brown,* Pres.; James R. Billingsley,* V.P. and Treas.; Helen Lee Billingsley, James R. Billingsley, Jr., Kiyoko O. Brown, Jacob C. Rardin, Jr.
EIN: 136401292
Codes: FD

33178
The Jockey Club Foundation
40 E. 52nd St.
New York, NY 10022-5911
Contact: Nancy Kelly, Secy.

Incorporated in 1943 in NY.
Donor(s): New York Racing Assn., Clark Foundation, and others.
Financial data (yr. ended 12/31/00): Grants paid, $895,621; assets, $10,612,821 (M); gifts received, $248,825; expenditures, $1,205,164; qualifying distributions, $889,621.
Limitations: Giving on a national basis.
Application information: Applicants must have been, at one time, associated with the thoroughbred industry.
Officers: Nancy Kelly, Secy. and Exec. Dir.; Alan Marzelli, Treas.
Trustees: John Hettinger, Managing Tr.; C. Steven Duncker, Daniel G. VanClef.
EIN: 136124094
Codes: FD, GTI

33179
The Pumpkin Foundation
c/o Joseph H. Reich & Co.
900 3rd Ave., Ste. 1801
New York, NY 10022
Contact: Joseph H. Reich, Tr.

Established in 1969.
Donor(s): Joseph H. Reich, Carol F. Reich, Janet Reich Elsbach.
Financial data (yr. ended 06/30/01): Grants paid, $892,025; assets, $25,707,666 (M); gifts received, $5,859,218; expenditures, $1,174,106; qualifying distributions, $893,235.
Limitations: Applications not accepted. Giving primarily in New York, NY; some giving also in MA.
Application information: Contributes only to pre-selected organizations.
Trustees: Janet Reich Elsbach, Carol F. Reich, Joseph H. Reich.
EIN: 136279814
Codes: FD

33180
Charles G. & Yvette Bluhdorn Charitable Trust
c/o Reminick, Aarons & Co., LLP
1430 Broadway
New York, NY 10018
Contact: Dominique Bluhdorn, Tr.

Established in 1967 in NY.
Donor(s): Paul Bluhdorn.
Financial data (yr. ended 12/31/01): Grants paid, $891,732; assets, $6,150,258 (M); expenditures, $1,058,635; qualifying distributions, $969,408.
Limitations: Applications not accepted. Giving primarily in NY, with emphasis on the greater metropolitan New York area.
Application information: Contributes only to pre-selected organizations.
Trustees: Dominique Bluhdorn, Paul Bluhdorn, Yvette Bluhdorn.
EIN: 136256769
Codes: FD

33181
Chehebar Family Foundation, Inc.
1000 Pennsylvania Ave.
Brooklyn, NY 11207-8417

Incorporated in 1985 in NY.
Donor(s): Albert Chehebar, Isaac Chehebar, Jack Chehebar, Joseph Chehebar, Rainbow Store, Inc., Rainbow Apparel Companies, Baraka Realty, Skiva International.
Financial data (yr. ended 08/31/01): Grants paid, $890,256; assets, $550,645 (M); gifts received, $1,100,000; expenditures, $890,817; qualifying distributions, $889,795.
Limitations: Applications not accepted. Giving primarily in the greater metropolitan New York, NY, area, with emphasis on Brooklyn.
Application information: Contributes only to pre-selected organizations.
Directors: Albert Chehebar, Isaac Chehebar, Jack Chehebar, Joseph Chehebar.
EIN: 133178015
Codes: FD

33182
Herman Lissner Foundation, Inc.
307 5th Ave., 13th Fl.
New York, NY 10016 (212) 532-6868
Contact: Edmund Badgley, Pres.

Established in 1947.
Donor(s): Gerda Lissner.
Financial data (yr. ended 12/31/01): Grants paid, $890,000; assets, $14,011,157 (M); expenditures, $970,714; qualifying distributions, $908,468.
Limitations: Giving primarily in New York, NY.
Application information: Application form not required.
Officers: Edmund W. Badgley, Pres. and Treas.; Betty Smith, V.P. and Secy.
EIN: 136106255
Codes: FD

33183
Barbara M. Zalaznick Foundation
c/o Eric Kaplan
335 Madison Ave., Ste. 1500
New York, NY 10017

Established in 1996 in NY.
Donor(s): Irma Milstein, Paul Milstein.
Financial data (yr. ended 12/31/01): Grants paid, $889,174; assets, $10,698,323 (M); gifts received, $5,014,706; expenditures, $890,635; qualifying distributions, $888,076.
Limitations: Applications not accepted. Giving primarily in New York, NY.
Application information: Contributes only to pre-selected organizations.

Trustees: Irma Milstein, Paul Milstein, Barbara Zalaznick, David Zalaznick.
EIN: 133921831
Codes: FD

33184
Donald A. Pels Charitable Trust
c/o Pelsco, Inc.
375 Park Ave., Ste. 3303
New York, NY 10152

Established in 1992 in NY.
Donor(s): Donald A. Pels.
Financial data (yr. ended 12/31/99): Grants paid, $888,850; assets, $30,548,850 (M); gifts received, $938,125; expenditures, $949,854; qualifying distributions, $900,236.
Limitations: Applications not accepted. Giving primarily in NY.
Application information: Contributes only to pre-selected organizations.
Trustee: Donald A. Pels.
EIN: 136998091
Codes: FD

33185
Universal Studios Foundation, Ltd.
(Formerly MCA Foundation, Ltd.)
P.O. Box 5023
New York, NY 10150
Application address: 100 Universal City Plz., Universal City, CA 91608, tel.: (818) 777-1208
Contact: Helene Giambone

Incorporated in 1956 in CA.
Donor(s): Universal Studios, Inc.
Financial data (yr. ended 06/30/01): Grants paid, $887,870; assets, $13,897,052 (M); expenditures, $887,870; qualifying distributions, $879,662.
Limitations: Giving primarily in the Los Angeles, CA, and New York, NY, areas.
Publications: Application guidelines.
Application information: Application form not required.
Officers and Directors:* Ron Meyer,* Pres.; Karen Randall,* Exec. V.P. and Secy.; Deborah S. Rosen,* Sr. V.P.; Kevin Conway, V.P.; H. Stephen Gorden, V.P.; Marc Palotay, V.P.; John R. Preston, V.P.
EIN: 136096061
Codes: CS, FD, CD

33186
The Swartz Foundation
199 Old Field Rd.
Setauket, NY 11733
URL: http://www.swartzneuro.org

Established in 1995 in NY.
Donor(s): Jerome Swartz.
Financial data (yr. ended 10/31/01): Grants paid, $885,917; assets, $9,340,131 (M); expenditures, $1,120,336; qualifying distributions, $934,662.
Limitations: Applications not accepted. Giving primarily in CA and NY.
Application information: Contributes only to pre-selected organizations.
Trustees: Andrew Schenker, Jerome Swartz.
EIN: 116447242
Codes: FD

33187
The Benjamin Jacobson & Sons Foundation
c/o Press Schonig & Co.
500 Bi-County Blvd., Ste 201
Farmingdale, NY 11735

Established in 1968 in NY and DE.
Donor(s): Benjamin Jacobson & Sons, Robert J. Jacobson, Jr., James A. Jacobson, Earl Ellis, Arthur Jacobson, Jr.

Financial data (yr. ended 06/30/01): Grants paid, $884,352; assets, $1,777,109 (M); gifts received, $1,200,470; expenditures, $893,949; qualifying distributions, $884,677.
Limitations: Applications not accepted. Giving primarily in the metropolitan New York, NY, area.
Application information: Contributes only to pre-selected organizations.
Officers: Robert J. Jacobson, Sr., Pres.; Benjamin Jacobson, Jr., V.P.; Robert J. Jacobson, Jr., Secy.; Arthur L. Jacobson, Treas.
Director: James A. Jacobson.
EIN: 132630862
Codes: CS, FD, CD

33188
The B. R. Thompson Charitable Trust
c/o Brown Brothers Harriman Trust Co.
63 Wall St.
New York, NY 10005
Application address: 4624 Chambliss Ave., Knoxville, TN 37919; FAX: (865) 588-2033
Contact: B. Ray Thompson, Jr., Tr.

Established in 1997 in TN.
Donor(s): The B.R. Charitable Foundation.
Financial data (yr. ended 08/31/01): Grants paid, $880,875; assets, $40,609,604 (M); expenditures, $1,056,514; qualifying distributions, $2,444,845.
Limitations: Applications not accepted. Giving primarily in TN.
Application information: Contributes only to pre-selected organizations.
Trustees: Rebekah T. Palmer, Sarah Thompson Tarver, Adella Sands Thompson, B. Ray Thompson, Jr., B. Ray Thompson III, Catherine Vance Thompson, Juanne J. Thompson.
EIN: 586350463
Codes: FD

33189
Ezra & Renee Dabah Charitable Foundation, Inc.
c/o Krusch & Modell
10 Rockefeller Plz.
New York, NY 10020

Established in 1998.
Donor(s): Ezra Dabah.
Financial data (yr. ended 12/31/00): Grants paid, $880,557; assets, $284,436 (M); gifts received, $1,128,813; expenditures, $885,776; qualifying distributions, $879,693.
Limitations: Applications not accepted. Giving on a national and international basis.
Application information: Contributes only to pre-selected organizations.
Officers: Ezra Dabah, Pres.; Eva Dabah, V.P.; Renee Dabah, Secy.-Treas.
EIN: 133986707
Codes: FD

33190
G.A.B.Y. Foundation
c/o David M. Rozen
400 W. 253rd St.
Bronx, NY 10471-2946

Financial data (yr. ended 12/31/00): Grants paid, $880,000; assets, $5,614 (M); gifts received, $20,000; expenditures, $891,107; qualifying distributions, $880,000.
Limitations: Applications not accepted. Giving primarily in New York, NY.
Application information: Contributes only to pre-selected organizations.
Trustee: David M. Rozen.
EIN: 137142970
Codes: FD

33191
The Harvey Silverman Foundation, Inc.
c/o BCRS Assocs., LLC, att.: Joseph De Maio
100 Wall St., 11th Fl.
New York, NY 10005

Established in 1985 in DE and NY.
Donor(s): Harvey Silverman.
Financial data (yr. ended 11/30/01): Grants paid, $879,854; assets, $6,842,597 (M); gifts received, $168,121; expenditures, $944,330; qualifying distributions, $874,178.
Limitations: Applications not accepted. Giving primarily in NJ and New York, NY.
Application information: Contributes only to pre-selected organizations.
Officers: Harvey Silverman, Pres.; Carl Hewitt, Secy.-Treas.
EIN: 133343289
Codes: FD

33192
Barrie A. & Dee Dee Wigmore Foundation
c/o BCRS Assocs., LLC
67 Wall St., 8th Fl.
New York, NY 10005

Established in 1978 in NY.
Donor(s): Barrie A. Wigmore.
Financial data (yr. ended 03/31/01): Grants paid, $872,485; assets, $9,025,713 (M); gifts received, $1,143,438; expenditures, $1,006,718; qualifying distributions, $882,876.
Limitations: Applications not accepted. Giving on a national basis, with emphasis on New York City and Saranac Lake, NY, and Washington, DC; giving also internationally in Moose Jaw, Canada, and London, England.
Application information: Contributes only to pre-selected organizations.
Trustees: Donald Lenz, Barrie A. Wigmore, DeeDee Wigmore.
EIN: 132967487
Codes: FD

33193
Fernleigh Foundation
1 Rockefeller Plz., 31st Fl.
New York, NY 10020
Contact: Charles H. Hamilton, Secy.

Established in 1993.
Donor(s): Jane F. Clark.
Financial data (yr. ended 12/31/01): Grants paid, $871,700; assets, $16,255,961 (M); expenditures, $937,786; qualifying distributions, $859,981.
Limitations: Applications not accepted. Giving on a national basis.
Officers and Directors:* Jane F. Clark,* Pres.; Edward W. Stack,* V.P.; Charles H. Hamilton,* Secy.; Kevin S. Moore,* Treas.
EIN: 137027378
Codes: FD

33194
Leo Model Foundation, Inc.
c/o Peter Model
500 E. 63rd St., No. 24K
New York, NY 10021

Established in 1970 in NY.
Donor(s): Model Charitable Lead Trust, Jane and Leo Model Foundation.
Financial data (yr. ended 12/31/01): Grants paid, $869,165; assets, $28,844,092 (M); expenditures, $1,005,650; qualifying distributions, $897,242.
Limitations: Applications not accepted. Giving primarily in New York, NY, and Philadelphia, PA.
Application information: Contributes only to pre-selected organizations.
Officers: Allen Model, Pres.; Pamela Model, V.P.; Peter H. Model, V.P.; John A. Nevins, Secy.-Treas.
Director: Marjorie Russel.
EIN: 237084119
Codes: FD

33195
Englander Foundation, Inc.
740 Park Ave.
New York, NY 10021 (212) 841-4148
Contact: Ada Mogavero

Established in 1991 in NY.
Donor(s): Israel A. Englander, Englander Capital Corp.
Financial data (yr. ended 11/30/01): Grants paid, $867,421; assets, $4,070,180 (M); gifts received, $2,052,450; expenditures, $897,475; qualifying distributions, $873,257.
Limitations: Applications not accepted. Giving primarily in the metropolitan New York, NY, area.
Publications: Financial statement, grants list.
Application information: Contributes only to pre-selected organizations.
Officers: Israel A. Englander, Pres.; Caryl S. Englander, V.P.; Allan S. Sexter, Secy.; Steven C. Weidman, Treas.
EIN: 133640833
Codes: FD

33196
Texaco Global Fund
c/o Texaco Foundation
2000 Westchester Ave.
White Plains, NY 10650
Contact: K.E. Murray, Secy.

Established in 1999 in NY.
Donor(s): Texaco Inc.
Financial data (yr. ended 12/31/01): Grants paid, $864,015; assets, $1,305,836 (M); gifts received, $1,800,000; expenditures, $1,496,193; qualifying distributions, $864,015.
Limitations: Giving on an international basis.
Officers: A.T. Dowling, Pres.; K.E. Murray, Secy.; I.D. Hall, Treas.; R.A. Brown, Exec. Dir.; E. Spencer, Compt.; J.E. Tuohy, Gen'l. Counsel.
Directors: J.E. Bethancourt, E.G. Celentano, R. Moore.
EIN: 311634478
Codes: CS, FD

33197
The Philip A. and Lynn Straus Foundation, Inc.
1037 Constable Dr. S.
Mamaroneck, NY 10543

Incorporated about 1957 in NY.
Donor(s): Lynn G. Straus, Philip A. Straus.
Financial data (yr. ended 03/31/01): Grants paid, $863,360; assets, $36,967,307 (M); gifts received, $2,182,353; expenditures, $997,738; qualifying distributions, $863,360.
Limitations: Applications not accepted. Giving primarily in NY.
Application information: Contributes only to pre-selected organizations.
Officers: Philip A. Straus, Pres.; Lynn G. Straus, V.P. and Treas.
EIN: 136161223
Codes: FD

33198
Eisenberg Family Charitable Trust
c/o JPMorgan Chase Bank
1211 Ave. of the Americas, 38th Fl.
New York, NY 10036 (212) 789-5679
E-mail: elias_jacqueline@jpmorgan.com
Contact: Jacqueline Elias, V.P., JPmorgan Chase Bank

Established in 2000 in NY.
Donor(s): Estelle Eisenberg.‡
Financial data (yr. ended 04/30/02): Grants paid, $860,000; assets, $7,414,037 (M); gifts received, $4,217,487; expenditures, $942,544; qualifying distributions, $880,421.
Trustee: JPMorgan Chase Bank.
EIN: 527091392
Codes: FD

33199
The Mark L. Serventi Family Foundation
93 N. Center St.
P.O. Box 88
Perry, NY 14530-0088

Donor(s): Mark L. Serventi, Michael J. Serventi.
Financial data (yr. ended 12/31/01): Grants paid, $860,000; assets, $656,601 (M); gifts received, $298,128; expenditures, $860,125; qualifying distributions, $859,422.
Limitations: Applications not accepted. Giving primarily in WY.
Application information: Contributes only to pre-selected organizations.
Directors: Lewis J. Serventi, Mark L. Serventi, Michael J. Serventi.
EIN: 311601563
Codes: FD

33200
MBIA Foundation, Inc.
113 King St.
Armonk, NY 10504 (914) 765-3832
Contact: Nancy Paulercio

Established in 2001 in NY.
Donor(s): MBIA Insurance Corp., John Caouette, Francie Heller, Kathleen Okenica, Kevin Silva, Kutak Rock LLP.
Financial data (yr. ended 12/31/01): Grants paid, $857,370; assets, $1,799,385 (M); gifts received, $266,279; expenditures, $866,274; qualifying distributions, $857,370.
Limitations: Giving primarily in CT, NY and PA.
Officers and Directors: Susan A. Voltz,* Pres.; Kevin D. Silva,* V.P.; Ethel Z. Geisinger, Secy.; Neil G. Budnick,* Treas.; Joseph W. Brown, Jr., Gary C. Dunton, Richard I. Weill, Harold Wagner.
EIN: 134163899
Codes: CS, FD

33201
Leopold Schepp Foundation
551 5th Ave., Ste. 3000
New York, NY 10176
Contact: Edythe Bobrow, Exec. Dir.

Incorporated in 1925 in NY.
Donor(s): Leopold Schepp,‡ Florence L. Schepp.‡
Financial data (yr. ended 02/28/01): Grants paid, $853,250; assets, $15,902,220 (M); gifts received, $51,205; expenditures, $1,255,787; qualifying distributions, $1,169,012.
Limitations: Giving on a national basis.
Publications: Informational brochure (including application guidelines).
Application information: Application form required.
Officers: Barbara McLendon, Pres.; William L.D. Barrett, V.P.; Kathryn Batchelder Cashman, V.P.; Sue Ann Dawson, V.P.; James G. Turino, Treas.; Edythe Bobrow, Exec. Dir.
Trustees: Louise M. Bozorth, Susan Brenner, Andrew Butterfield, Ph.D., Carvel H. Cartmell, Anne Coffin, Emily Crawford, Betty David, William G. Gridley, Jr., Diana P. Herrmann, Michele A. Paige, Elizabeth Stone Potter, Bruno A. Quinson, Robert F. Reder, M.D., Banning Repplier, George R. Walker.
EIN: 135562353
Codes: FD, GTI

33202
JJJ Charitable Foundation
c/o U.S. Trust
114 W. 47th St.
New York, NY 10036

Established in 1997 in CT.
Donor(s): Hillside Capital, Inc.
Financial data (yr. ended 12/31/00): Grants paid, $852,701; assets, $13,436,471 (M); gifts received, $839,612; expenditures, $966,409; qualifying distributions, $854,401.
Limitations: Applications not accepted. Giving primarily in NJ and NY.
Application information: Contributes only to pre-selected organizations.
Officers and Directors:* John N. Irwin III,* Pres. and Treas.; Robert H.M. Ferguson, Secy.; Jane W.I. Droppa, Jeanet E. Irwin, John N. Irwin II.
EIN: 133932002
Codes: FD

33203
The Lucille Lortel Foundation, Inc.
c/o Hecht & Co., PC
111 W. 40th St.
New York, NY 10018 (212) 924-2817
URL: http://www.lortel.org

Established in 1980 in NY.
Donor(s): Lucille Lortel Schweitzer.‡
Financial data (yr. ended 06/30/01): Grants paid, $850,076; assets, $26,376,911 (M); gifts received, $7,005,000; expenditures, $1,336,097; qualifying distributions, $1,128,769.
Limitations: Applications not accepted. Giving primarily in New York, NY.
Application information: Contributes only to pre-selected organizations.
Officers and Directors:* James J. Ross,* Pres.; George Forbes, V.P., Fin.; George Shaskan,* V.P.; Richard M. Ticktin,* Secy.; Michael Hecht,* Treas.
EIN: 133036521
Codes: FD

33204
The Goldie-Anna Charitable Trust
c/o Greenfield, Eisenberg, Stein & Senior
600 3rd Ave., 11th Fl.
New York, NY 10016
Contact: Kenneth L. Stein, Tr.

Established about 1977 in NY.
Financial data (yr. ended 12/31/01): Grants paid, $849,708; assets, $22,162,502 (M); expenditures, $1,075,748; qualifying distributions, $892,887.
Limitations: Applications not accepted. Giving primarily in the metropolitan New York, NY, area.
Trustees: Julius Greenfield, Kenneth L. Stein.
EIN: 132897474
Codes: FD

33205
The SDA Foundation
c/o Lindsay Goldberg & Bessemer, LLC
630 5th Ave.
New York, NY 10111

Established in 2000 in NY.
Donor(s): Alan E. Goldberg.
Financial data (yr. ended 12/31/01): Grants paid, $848,540; assets, $6,180,885 (M); gifts received, $1,086,099; expenditures, $848,540; qualifying distributions, $848,540.
Limitations: Applications not accepted. Giving primarily in NY.
Application information: Contributes only to pre-selected organizations.
Trustees: Alan E. Goldberg, Miriam P. Goldberg.
EIN: 137235530
Codes: FD

33206
The Einhorn Family Foundation
c/o BCRS Assocs., LLC
67 Wall St., 8th Fl.
New York, NY 10005

Established in 1989 in NJ.
Donor(s): Steven G. Einhorn.
Financial data (yr. ended 01/31/01): Grants paid, $847,850; assets, $4,643,432 (M); gifts received, $301,600; expenditures, $875,872; qualifying distributions, $849,050.
Limitations: Applications not accepted. Giving primarily in NY.
Application information: Contributes only to pre-selected organizations.
Trustees: Shelley Einhorn, Steven G. Einhorn.
EIN: 133531970
Codes: FD

33207
Marks Family Foundation
c/o Carl Marks & Co.
135 E. 57th St., 27th Fl.
New York, NY 10022 (212) 909-8400
Contact: Iris Rosken, Cont.

Established in 1986.
Donor(s): Edwin S. Marks, Nancy A. Marks.
Financial data (yr. ended 06/30/01): Grants paid, $844,572; assets, $6,278,299 (M); expenditures, $849,458; qualifying distributions, $844,822.
Limitations: Applications not accepted. Giving primarily in NY.
Application information: Contributes only to pre-selected organizations.
Officers: Edwin S. Marks, Pres. and Treas.; Nancy A. Marks, V.P. and Secy.
Directors: Linda Marks Katz, Carolyn Marks, Constance Marks.
EIN: 133385770
Codes: FD

33208
Arthur L. Loeb Foundation, Inc.
c/o Loeb Partners Corp.
61 Broadway, 24th Fl.
New York, NY 10006

Established around 1977.
Donor(s): Arthur L. Loeb.
Financial data (yr. ended 11/30/99): Grants paid, $840,924; assets, $25,344,483 (M); expenditures, $965,281; qualifying distributions, $846,099.
Limitations: Applications not accepted. Giving primarily in New York, NY.
Application information: Contributes only to pre-selected organizations.
Officers: Arthur L. Loeb, Pres.; William L. Bernhard, V.P.; Jerome P. Manning, Secy.-Treas.
EIN: 132933768
Codes: FD

33209
The Dorothy Schiff Foundation
c/o JPMorgan Chase Bank
53 E. 66th St.
New York, NY 10021
Contact: Adele Hall Sweet, Pres.

Incorporated in 1951 in NY.
Donor(s): Dorothy Schiff,‡ New York Post Corp.
Financial data (yr. ended 12/31/01): Grants paid, $840,000; assets, $12,304,777 (M); expenditures, $904,369; qualifying distributions, $838,996.
Limitations: Giving primarily in NY.
Officers: Adele Hall Sweet, Pres.; Sarah-Ann Kramarsky, Secy.; Mortimer W. Hall, Treas.
Trustee: JPMorgan Chase Bank.
EIN: 136018311
Codes: FD

33210
Louis Armstrong Educational Foundation, Inc.
c/o Present, Cohen, et al
40 Cuttermill Rd., Ste. 305
Great Neck, NY 11021-3213

Established in 1988 in NY.
Financial data (yr. ended 06/30/01): Grants paid, $835,500; assets, $4,375,224 (M); expenditures, $1,086,689; qualifying distributions, $833,429.
Limitations: Applications not accepted. Giving primarily in the greater metropolitan New York, NY, area.
Application information: Contributes only to pre-selected organizations.
Trustees: David Gold, Phoebe Jacobs.
EIN: 132659286
Codes: FD

33211
The Barry Friedberg and Charlotte Moss Family Foundation
c/o Merrill Lynch
225 Liberty St., 38th Fl.
New York, NY 10080-6131

Established in 1998 in NY.
Donor(s): Barry Friedberg.
Financial data (yr. ended 05/31/01): Grants paid, $835,171; assets, $2,304,299 (M); gifts received, $85,947; expenditures, $847,347; qualifying distributions, $821,630.
Limitations: Applications not accepted. Giving primarily in New York, NY.
Application information: Contributes only to pre-selected organizations.
Trustees: Barry S. Friedberg, Charlotte A. Moss.
EIN: 137154197
Codes: FD

33212
The Ritter Foundation, Inc.
1776 Broadway, Ste. 1700
New York, NY 10019 (212) 757-4646
FAX: (212) 489-6263
Contact: David Ritter, V.P. and Secy.

Incorporated in 1947 in NY.
Donor(s): Gladys Ritter Livingston,‡ Irene Ritter,‡ Lena Ritter,‡ Louis Ritter,‡ Sidney Ritter.‡
Financial data (yr. ended 11/30/01): Grants paid, $834,922; assets, $32,508,026 (M); expenditures, $2,425,617; qualifying distributions, $885,471.
Limitations: Applications not accepted. Giving on a national basis.
Publications: Annual report.
Application information: Contributes only to pre-selected organizations.
Officers and Trustees:* Toby G. Ritter,* Pres.; David Ritter,* V.P. and Secy.; Alan I. Ritter,* V.P. and Treas.; Frances Weisman,* V.P.
EIN: 136082276

Codes: FD

33213
The Starwood Foundation, Inc.
(Formerly The Sheraton Foundation, Inc.)
1111 Westchester Ave.
White Plains, NY 10604
Application address: 777 Westchester Ave., White Plains, NY 10604
Contact: Beth Shanholtz

Incorporated in 1950 in MA.
Donor(s): ITT Sheraton Corp., The Sheraton Corp.
Financial data (yr. ended 12/31/00): Grants paid, $831,000; assets, $6,034,297 (M); expenditures, $1,005,485; qualifying distributions, $846,873.
Limitations: Giving limited to the greater Boston, MA, area.
Officers: Barry F. Sternlicht, Pres.; James D. Latham, Clerk; Robyn Arnell, Treas.
Directors: Daniel Gibson, David Norton.
EIN: 046039510
Codes: CS, FD, CD

33214
Gilbert & Ildiko Butler Foundation, Inc.
(Formerly Butler Foundation, Inc.)
767 5th Ave.
New York, NY 10153

Established in 1988 in MA.
Donor(s): Gilbert Butler, Butler Capital Corp.
Financial data (yr. ended 12/31/00): Grants paid, $829,568; assets, $14,693,220 (M); gifts received, $2,872,731; expenditures, $859,876; qualifying distributions, $834,451.
Limitations: Applications not accepted. Giving on a national basis, with emphasis on NY and the New England region, primarily MA and ME.
Application information: Unsolicited requests for funds not considered.
Officers and Directors:* Gilbert Butler,* Pres. and Treas.; R. Bradford Malt, V.P. and Clerk; Ildiko Butler, Emily Rafferty, Winthrop Rutherford, Jr.
EIN: 043032409
Codes: CS, FD, CD, GTI

33215
Arnold D. Frese Foundation, Inc.
10 Rockefeller Plz., Ste. 916
New York, NY 10020 (212) 373-1960
Contact: James S. Smith, Pres.

Established in 1966.
Donor(s): Arnold D. Frese.‡
Financial data (yr. ended 12/31/01): Grants paid, $829,000; assets, $4,261,193 (M); expenditures, $1,196,832; qualifying distributions, $8,964,385.
Limitations: Giving primarily in Greenwich, CT, and New York, NY.
Officers and Trustees:* Ines Frese,* Chair.; James S. Smith, Pres. and Treas.; Hector G. Dowd, Secy.; Henry D. Mercer, Jr.
EIN: 136212507
Codes: FD

33216
The Bay Foundation, Inc.
(Formerly Charles Ulrick and Josephine Bay Foundation, Inc.)
17 W. 94th St., 1st Fl.
New York, NY 10025 (212) 663-1115
FAX: (212) 932-0316
Contact: Robert W. Ashton, Secy.

Incorporated in 1950 in NY.
Donor(s): Charles Ulrick Bay,‡ Josephine Bay.‡
Financial data (yr. ended 12/31/01): Grants paid, $826,221; assets, $20,252,858 (M); expenditures, $1,286,200; qualifying distributions, $1,124,389.

Limitations: Giving limited to the New England states, NJ, and NY for educational grants.
Publications: Annual report (including application guidelines).
Application information: New York Regional Common Application Form accepted (preferably by regular mail). Applications not accepted for Biodiversity Leadership Awards Program. Application form not required.
Officers and Directors:* Frederick Bay,* Chair.; Synnova B. Hayes,* Pres. and Treas.; Hans A. Ege,* V.P.; Robert W. Ashton,* Secy. and Exec. Dir.; Daniel A. Demarest, Corinne Steel.
EIN: 135646283
Codes: FD, GTI

33217
Taconic Foundation, Inc.
c/o JPMorgan Private Bank
1211 Avenue of the Americas, 38th Fl.
New York, NY 10036 (212) 789-5777
FAX: (212) 596-3712
Contact: Monica Neal, V.P., JPMorgan Private Bank

Incorporated in 1958 in DE.
Donor(s): Stephen R. Currier,‡ Mrs. Stephen R. Currier.‡
Financial data (yr. ended 12/31/00): Grants paid, $825,000; assets, $20,892,809 (M); expenditures, $1,173,772; qualifying distributions, $991,940.
Limitations: Giving primarily in the New York, NY, area.
Publications: Grants list, application guidelines.
Application information: Accepts New York/New Jersey area Common Application Form. Application form not required.
Trustees: L.F. Boker Doyle, Alan J. Dworsky, Jane Lee Eddy, William Green, Melvin A. Mister, John G. Simon, Hildy Simmons, Oliver Wesson.
Program Officers: Monica Neal, Lisa Philp.
EIN: 131873668
Codes: FD

33218
West Ferry Foundation
c/o Robert G. Wilmers
350 Park Ave., 6th Fl.
New York, NY 10022

Established in 1992 in NY.
Donor(s): Robert G. Wilmers.
Financial data (yr. ended 11/30/99): Grants paid, $823,491; assets, $10,041,957 (M); expenditures, $837,871; qualifying distributions, $814,943.
Limitations: Applications not accepted. Giving primarily in MA and Buffalo, NY.
Application information: Contributes only to pre-selected organizations.
Trustee: Robert G. Wilmers.
EIN: 133715532
Codes: FD

33219
Garofalo Foundation, Inc.
100 Horseshoe Rd.
Mill Neck, NY 11765

Established in 1999 in NY.
Donor(s): Stephen Garofalo.
Financial data (yr. ended 12/31/00): Grants paid, $822,500; assets, $8,391,371 (M); gifts received, $1,000,000; expenditures, $846,382; qualifying distributions, $974,776.
Limitations: Giving primarily in NY.
Officers and Trustees:* Stephen A. Garofalo,* Pres.; Lori Bianco,* V.P.; Frank Garofalo,* V.P.; Judith Garofalo,* Secy.; Ronald Balzano,* Treas.; Mark E. Brenner, John Garofalo.
EIN: 311693087

33219—NEW YORK

Codes: FD

33220
Florence V. Burden Foundation
10 E. 53rd St., 32nd Fl.
New York, NY 10022 (212) 872-1150
FAX: (212) 872-1149
Contact: Marjorie Lipkin, Exec. Dir.

Incorporated in 1967 in NY.
Donor(s): Florence V. Burden,‡ and members of her family.
Financial data (yr. ended 12/31/00): Grants paid, $821,298; assets, $18,269,634 (M); expenditures, $1,367,665; qualifying distributions, $962,773.
Limitations: Applications not accepted. Giving primarily in New England, Washington, DC, NJ, NY, and PA.
Application information: Unsolicited requests for funds not accepted.
Officers and Directors:* Edward P.H. Burden,* Co-Chair.; Margaret Burden Childs,* Co-Chair.; Ordway P. Burden,* V.P.; Susan L. Burden,* Secy.-Treas.; Marjorie Lipkin, Exec. Dir.; Charmaine S. Burden, Jean E.P. Burden, Norah P. Burden, Wendy L. Burden, Nicholas F. Childs, Flobelle Burden Davis, Constance C. Rosengarten.
EIN: 136224125
Codes: FD

33221
The Blue Ridge Foundation, Inc.
635 Madison Ave.
New York, NY 10022

Established in 1985 in NY.
Donor(s): Marcelle Halpern, Walter Scheuer, and members of the Scheuer family.
Financial data (yr. ended 10/31/99): Grants paid, $821,114; assets, $2,436,833 (M); expenditures, $830,541; qualifying distributions, $822,426.
Limitations: Applications not accepted. Giving primarily in New York, NY; some giving in Burlington, VT.
Application information: Contributes only to pre-selected organizations.
Officers and Directors:* Walter Scheuer, Pres.; David A. Scheuer,* V.P.; Jeffrey J. Scheuer,* V.P.; Judith Scheuer,* V.P.; Marge Scheuer,* V.P.; Susan Scheuer,* V.P.
EIN: 133282554
Codes: FD

33222
The Damial Foundation, Inc.
c/o Mark J. Krinsky, Acct.
655 Madison Ave., 8th Fl.
New York, NY 10021-8043

Established in 1992 in NY and DE.
Donor(s): Laurence A. Tisch, Daniel R. Tisch.
Financial data (yr. ended 12/31/01): Grants paid, $820,805; assets, $12,480,157 (M); expenditures, $834,840; qualifying distributions, $806,741.
Limitations: Applications not accepted. Giving primarily in NY.
Application information: Contributes only to pre-selected organizations.
Officers: Thomas M. Steinberg, V.P. and Secy.; Mark J. Krinsky, Treas.
EIN: 133693581
Codes: FD

33223
The Rodgers Family Foundation, Inc.
(Formerly Richard and Dorothy Rodgers Foundation)
575 Madison Ave.
New York, NY 10022
Contact: Milton Kain, Treas.

Established in 1952 in NY.
Donor(s): Richard Rodgers,‡ Dorothy F. Rodgers.‡
Financial data (yr. ended 12/31/01): Grants paid, $820,250; assets, $13,485,125 (M); gifts received, $200,682; expenditures, $974,169; qualifying distributions, $875,023.
Limitations: Applications not accepted. Giving primarily in New York, NY.
Application information: Contributes only to pre-selected organizations.
Officers: Linda Emory, Pres.; Mary Guettel, V.P.; Lawrence Buttenwieser, Secy.; Milton Kain, Treas.
EIN: 136062852
Codes: FD

33224
Ditmars Foundation, Inc.
c/o Irwin Kalmanowitz
60 E. 42nd St., Ste. 1760
New York, NY 10165

Established in 1995 in NY.
Donor(s): Tibor Klein, York Home Care, LLC.
Financial data (yr. ended 12/31/01): Grants paid, $817,979; assets, $66,519 (M); gifts received, $812,800; expenditures, $817,921; qualifying distributions, $817,979.
Limitations: Applications not accepted.
Application information: Contributes only to pre-selected organizations.
Officers: Tibor Klein, Pres.; Chaim Klein, V.P.; Gershon Klein, V.P.; Miriam Klein, Secy.-Treas.
EIN: 133861379
Codes: FD

33225
Marie C. and Joseph C. Wilson Foundation
160 Allens Creek Rd.
Rochester, NY 14618-3309 (716) 461-4699
Additional tel: (716) 461-4696; *FAX:* (716) 473-5206; *E-mail:* mcjc wilsonfdn@juno.com
Contact: Ruth H. Fleischmann, Exec. Dir.

Trust established in 1963 in NY.
Donor(s): Katherine M. Wilson,‡ Joseph C. Wilson.‡
Financial data (yr. ended 12/31/01): Grants paid, $815,705; assets, $16,915,144 (M); expenditures, $1,095,370; qualifying distributions, $957,410.
Limitations: Giving primarily in Rochester, NY.
Publications: Annual report (including application guidelines).
Application information: Telephone foundation for guidelines. Application form not required.
Officers and Board of Managers:* Joan D. Donahue, Co-Chair.; Scott R. Wilson,* Co-Chair.; Marie D. Tabah,* Chair, Nominating Comm.; Deirdre Wilson Garton, Secy.; Joseph R. Wilson,* Treas.; Ruth H. Fleischmann,* Exec. Dir.; Caitlin Cearton, R. Thomas Dalbey, Jr., Katherine Dalbey Ensign, Elenore Garton, Josie Garton, Breckenridge Kling, Christian G. Kling, Josh Kling, Jessa Martin, Judith W. Martin, Katherine W. Roby, J. Christine Wilson, J. Richard Wilson.
Trustee: JPMorgan Chase Bank.
EIN: 166042022
Codes: FD

33226
The Arnold Bernhard Foundation, Inc.
220 E. 42nd St., 6th Fl.
New York, NY 10017-5806 (212) 907-1620
Contact: Jean B. Buttner, Pres.

Established in 1976.
Donor(s): Arnold Bernhard Charitable Annuity Trust I, Arnold Bernhard Charitable Annuity Trust II.
Financial data (yr. ended 12/31/00): Grants paid, $815,300; assets, $9,918,475 (M); gifts received, $86,124; expenditures, $830,663; qualifying distributions, $815,754.
Limitations: Giving on a national basis, with some emphasis on CT, MA, and NY.
Officers and Directors:* Jean B. Buttner,* Pres.; Howard A. Brecher,* V.P.; David T. Henigson,* V.P.
EIN: 136100457
Codes: FD

33227
The Abraham Foundation, Inc.
c/o B. Strauss Assoc., Ltd.
307 5th Ave., 8th Fl.
New York, NY 10016-8775
Contact: Alexander Abraham, Pres.

Established in 1945.
Donor(s): Alexander Abraham.
Financial data (yr. ended 09/30/01): Grants paid, $812,200; assets, $1,995,828 (M); gifts received, $160,320; expenditures, $819,265; qualifying distributions, $813,839.
Limitations: Applications not accepted. Giving primarily in NY.
Application information: Contributes only to pre-selected organizations.
Officers: Alexander Abraham, Pres.; Nancy Abraham, V.P.; Helene Abraham, Secy.; James Abraham, Treas.
EIN: 136065944
Codes: FD

33228
The H. W. Wilson Foundation, Inc.
950 University Ave.
Bronx, NY 10452
Tel.: (718) 588-8400, ext. 2205
Contact: William V. Joyce, Pres.

Incorporated in 1952 in NY.
Donor(s): H.W. Wilson,‡ Mrs. H.W. Wilson,‡ The H.W. Wilson Co., Inc.
Financial data (yr. ended 11/30/01): Grants paid, $811,100; assets, $14,636,623 (M); expenditures, $847,075; qualifying distributions, $806,303.
Limitations: Giving on a national basis.
Application information: Application form not required.
Officers and Directors:* William V. Joyce,* Pres. and Treas.; James M. Matarazzo,* V.P.; William E. Stanton,* Secy.
EIN: 237418062
Codes: FD

33229
The McCarthy Charities, Inc.
P.O. Box 1090
Troy, NY 12181-1090
Contact: Robert P. McCarthy, Treas.

Incorporated in 1917 in NY.
Donor(s): Robert H. McCarthy,‡ Lucy A. McCarthy,‡ Peter F. McCarthy.‡
Financial data (yr. ended 12/31/01): Grants paid, $810,845; assets, $15,955,784 (M); expenditures, $864,046; qualifying distributions, $855,450.
Limitations: Giving primarily in the Albany Capital District, NY, area.
Application information: Application form not required.

Officers: Pamela McCarthy-Beauvais, Pres.; Denis McCarthy, V.P.; Roseanne M. Hall, Secy.; Robert P. McCarthy, Treas.
EIN: 146019064
Codes: FD

33230
The Raymond and Bessie Kravis Foundation
c/o Kohlberg, Kravis, Roberts & Co.
9 W. 57th St.
New York, NY 10019
Contact: James Goldrick

Established in 1992 in OK.
Donor(s): Bessie R. Kravis, Raymond F. Kravis.
Financial data (yr. ended 12/31/99): Grants paid, $809,850; assets, $31,343,183 (M); expenditures, $1,056,742; qualifying distributions, $9,775,770.
Limitations: Applications not accepted. Giving primarily in Tulsa, OK.
Application information: Contributes only to pre-selected organizations.
Trustees: George R. Kravis II, Henry R. Kravis, Kimberly R. Kravis, Robert S. Kravis.
EIN: 731393621
Codes: FD

33231
The Mayday Fund
c/o UBS AG
10 E. 50th St., 15th Fl.
New York, NY 10022 (212) 838-2904
FAX: (212) 838-2896; E-mail: maydyfnd@aol.com; URL: http://www.painandhealth.org/mayday/mayday-home.html
Contact: Christina Spellman, Exec. Dir.

Established in 1992 in NY.
Donor(s): Shirley S. Katzenbach,‡ John C. Beck.
Financial data (yr. ended 12/31/99): Grants paid, $809,171; assets, $26,907,327 (M); gifts received, $2,797; expenditures, $1,234,055; qualifying distributions, $1,128,838.
Limitations: Giving on a national basis.
Publications: Annual report.
Application information: Contact foundation for application deadlines. Application form not required.
Officer: Christina Spellman, Exec. Dir.
Trustees: John C. Beck, Robert D.C. Meeker, Jr., Caroline N. Sidnam, Pamela M. Thye.
EIN: 133645438
Codes: FD

33232
The Dolores Zohrab Liebmann Fund
c/o JPMorgan Chase Bank
1211 Ave. of the Americas, 38th Fl.
New York, NY 10036 (212) 789-5682
E-mail: jones_ed_l@jpmorgan.com
Contact: Edward L. Jones, V.P.

Established in 1995 in NY.
Financial data (yr. ended 12/31/01): Grants paid, $808,865; assets, $26,380,781 (M); expenditures, $1,507,381; qualifying distributions, $1,380,670.
Limitations: Giving on a national basis.
Application information: Application form required.
Trustee: JPMorgan Chase Bank.
EIN: 137060094
Codes: FD, GTI

33233
Anne & Harry J. Reicher Foundation
1173-A 2nd Ave.
Box 363
New York, NY 10021

Established in 1961 in PA.
Donor(s): Harry D. Reicher, Sydell Markelson.‡
Financial data (yr. ended 12/31/00): Grants paid, $807,500; assets, $558,632 (M); expenditures, $863,388; qualifying distributions, $807,500.
Limitations: Applications not accepted. Giving primarily in the metropolitan New York, NY, area.
Application information: Contributes only to pre-selected organizations.
Officers: Leonard Zalkin, V.P. and Treas.; Rabbi Balfour Brickner, Secy.
EIN: 136115086
Codes: FD

33234
The Eddie and Rachelle Betesh Family Foundation, Inc.
c/o Saramax Apparel Grp., Inc.
1372 Broadway, 7th Fl.
New York, NY 10018

Established in 1998 in DE and NY.
Donor(s): Eddie Betesh, Rachelle Betesh.
Financial data (yr. ended 12/31/99): Grants paid, $807,102; assets, $1,373 (M); gifts received, $783,350; expenditures, $809,497; qualifying distributions, $807,247.
Limitations: Applications not accepted. Giving primarily in NY.
Application information: Contributes only to pre-selected organizations.
Officers: Eddie Betesh, Pres.; Rachelle Betesh, Treas.
EIN: 133981963
Codes: FD

33235
The William Chinnick Charitable Foundation
c/o The Ayco Co., LP
P.O. Box 8019
Ballston Spa, NY 12020-8019
Contact: W. Michael Reickert

Established in 1992 in FL.
Donor(s): William C. Swaney.
Financial data (yr. ended 12/31/00): Grants paid, $806,266; assets, $14,709,260 (M); gifts received, $950,407; expenditures, $898,925; qualifying distributions, $782,433.
Limitations: Applications not accepted. Giving on a national basis.
Application information: Contributes only to pre-selected organizations.
Officers: William C. Swaney, Pres. and Treas.; Nancy C. Swaney, V.P.; Richard G. Swaney, Secy.
EIN: 650377446
Codes: FD

33236
The Fred & Rita Richman Foundation
261 5th Ave.
New York, NY 10016

Established in 1985 in NY.
Donor(s): Richloom Sales Corp.
Financial data (yr. ended 11/30/01): Grants paid, $806,000; assets, $23,199,293 (M); gifts received, $2,113,067; expenditures, $988,525; qualifying distributions, $789,183.
Limitations: Applications not accepted. Giving on a national basis.
Application information: Contributes only to pre-selected organizations.
Directors: Fred M. Richman, James Richman, Rita Richman.
EIN: 133332711
Codes: FD

33237
The Hill Family Foundation, Inc.
c/o Mahoney Cohen C.P.A.
111 W. 40th St.
New York, NY 10018

Established in 1987 in NY.
Donor(s): J. Tomilson Hill III, Janine W. Hill, Lehman Brothers.
Financial data (yr. ended 12/31/00): Grants paid, $805,000; assets, $2,646,073 (M); expenditures, $857,366; qualifying distributions, $802,008.
Limitations: Applications not accepted. Giving primarily in the northeastern U.S.
Application information: Contributes only to pre-selected organizations.
Officers: J. Tomilson Hill III, Pres. and Treas.; Janine W. Hill, V.P. and Secy.
EIN: 133436852
Codes: FD

33238
The Blood Family Foundation
c/o Goldman Sachs & Co.
85 Broad St., Tax Dept.
New York, NY 10004

Established in 1996 in NY.
Donor(s): David W. Blood.
Financial data (yr. ended 03/31/02): Grants paid, $804,075; assets, $5,169,361 (M); gifts received, $1,210,700; expenditures, $846,923; qualifying distributions, $807,423.
Limitations: Applications not accepted. Giving on an international basis, primarily in London, England; giving also in Washington, DC, MA, and NY.
Application information: Contributes only to pre-selected organizations.
Trustees: Alison Blood, David W. Blood.
EIN: 133919765
Codes: FD

33239
The Fredric B. & Anne G. Garonzik Foundation
c/o BCRS Associates, LLC
67 Wall St., 8th Fl.
New York, NY 10005

Established in 1985 in NY.
Donor(s): Frederic B. Garonzik.
Financial data (yr. ended 01/31/02): Grants paid, $802,722; assets, $2,017,706 (M); expenditures, $817,979; qualifying distributions, $803,971.
Limitations: Applications not accepted. Giving primarily in New York, NY.
Application information: Contributes only to pre-selected organizations.
Trustees: Anne G. Garonzik, Frederic B. Garonzik, Neil S. Garonzik.
EIN: 133350760
Codes: FD

33240
The Martin R. Lewis Charitable Foundation
c/o Martin R. Lewis
52 W. 11th St.
New York, NY 10011-8602

Established in 1996 in DE and NY.
Donor(s): Martin R. Lewis.
Financial data (yr. ended 12/31/01): Grants paid, $802,050; assets, $2,856,470 (M); expenditures, $821,620; qualifying distributions, $818,441.
Limitations: Applications not accepted. Giving on a national basis, with emphasis on the greater metropolitan areas of Washington, DC, including VA and MD, and New York, NY.
Application information: Contributes only to pre-selected organizations.

33240—NEW YORK

Officers and Directors:* Martin R. Lewis,* Pres.; Diance Carol Brandt, Secy.-Treas.; Lisa Lewis Cartolano, Wendy Lewis Kaye, Jeffrey S. Lewis.
EIN: 133877209
Codes: FD

33241
Lewis D. & John J. Gilbert Foundation
29 E. 64th St.
New York, NY 10021-7043 (212) 944-8811

Established in 1992 in NY.
Donor(s): John J. Gilbert, Lewis D. Gilbert.
Financial data (yr. ended 12/31/00): Grants paid, $801,261; assets, $1,811,224 (M); gifts received, $1,000,000; expenditures, $836,101; qualifying distributions, $814,988.
Limitations: Applications not accepted. Giving on a national basis.
Application information: Contributes only to pre-selected organizations.
Trustees: David Brown, John J. Gilbert, Margaret R. Gilbert, Margot R. Gilbert, Bernadette Liberti.
EIN: 133648972
Codes: FD

33242
Margaret & Richard Lipmanson Foundation, Inc.
c/o Miller, Ellin & Co., LLP
750 Lexington Ave., 23rd Fl.
New York, NY 10022-1200
Contact: Gerard Leeds, Chair.

Established in 1986 in DE.
Donor(s): Gerard G. Leeds, Liselotte J. Leeds.
Financial data (yr. ended 06/30/01): Grants paid, $800,000; assets, $22,960,465 (M); expenditures, $842,681; qualifying distributions, $813,473.
Limitations: Applications not accepted. Giving primarily in NY.
Application information: Contributes only to pre-selected organizations.
Officers: Gerard G. Leeds, Chair.; Greg Jobin-Leeds, Pres. and Secy.; Liselotte J. Leeds, V.P. and Treas.
EIN: 112856656
Codes: FD

33243
James and Cecilia Tse Ying Foundation
c/o The Bank of New York, Tax Dept.
1 Wall St., 28th Fl.
New York, NY 10286

Established in 2000 in NH.
Donor(s): James Ying, Cecilia Ying.
Financial data (yr. ended 12/31/01): Grants paid, $800,000; assets, $911,207 (M); gifts received, $1,010,460; expenditures, $834,694; qualifying distributions, $784,421.
Limitations: Applications not accepted. Giving primarily in New York, NY.
Application information: Contributes only to pre-selected organizations.
Trustee: The Bank Of New York.
EIN: 134149503
Codes: FD

33244
The IFF Foundation, Inc.
521 W. 57th St.
New York, NY 10019

Incorporated in 1963 in NY.
Donor(s): International Flavors & Fragrances, Inc.
Financial data (yr. ended 12/31/01): Grants paid, $797,421; assets, $176,688 (M); gifts received, $815,174; expenditures, $798,081; qualifying distributions, $797,421.
Limitations: Applications not accepted. Giving primarily in NJ and New York, NY.
Application information: Contributes only to pre-selected organizations.
Officers: R.A. Goldstein, Pres.; S.A. Block, Secy.; D.J. Wetmore, Treas.
EIN: 136159094
Codes: CS, FD, CD

33245
Heineman Foundation for Research, Educational, Charitable and Scientific Purposes, Inc.
c/o Brown Brothers Harriman Trust Co.
63 Wall St.
New York, NY 10005

Incorporated in 1947 in DE.
Donor(s): Dannie N. Heineman.‡
Financial data (yr. ended 12/31/01): Grants paid, $797,030; assets, $16,047,282 (M); expenditures, $910,918; qualifying distributions, $823,661.
Limitations: Giving on a national basis.
Application information: Application form not required.
Officers and Directors:* Ann R. Podlipny, Pres.; Maria Heineman Bergendahl, V.P.; Andrew Podlipny, Secy.; Agnes Gautier,* Treas.; Anders Bergendahl, Edith Fehr, Marilyn Heineman, June Heineman-Morris, Joan Heineman-Schur, Glen Morris, David Heineman Rose, James A. Rose, Marian Heineman Rose, Simon Rose.
EIN: 136082899
Codes: FD

33246
The Philip D. & Tammy S. Murphy Foundation
c/o Goldman Sachs & Co.
85 Broad St., Tax Dept.
New York, NY 10004

Established in 1993 in NY.
Donor(s): Philip D. Murphy.
Financial data (yr. ended 07/31/01): Grants paid, $796,750; assets, $6,627,190 (M); gifts received, $1,950,000; expenditures, $929,777; qualifying distributions, $800,777.
Limitations: Applications not accepted. Giving primarily in NJ, NY, and PA.
Application information: Contributes only to pre-selected organizations.
Trustees: Dorothy Murphy Egan, Kevin W. Kennedy, Philip D. Murphy, Tammy S. Murphy.
EIN: 133742910
Codes: FD

33247
The Dewar Foundation, Inc.
16 Dietz St.
Oneonta, NY 13820
Application address: P.O. Box 613, Oneonta, NY 13820
Contact: Frank W. Getman, Pres.

Incorporated in 1947 in NY.
Donor(s): Jessie Smith Dewar,‡ James A. Dewar.‡
Financial data (yr. ended 12/31/01): Grants paid, $796,550; assets, $14,450,416 (M); expenditures, $1,327,483; qualifying distributions, $795,271.
Limitations: Giving primarily in the greater Oneonta, NY, area.
Application information: Application form not required.
Officers and Directors:* Frank W. Getman,* Pres.; Sidney Levine, V.P.; Michael F. Getman,* Secy.-Treas.; Geoffrey A. Smith.
EIN: 166054329
Codes: FD

33248
The Peter and Kristen Gerhard Foundation
c/o Goldman Sachs & Co.
85 Broad St., Tax Dept.
New York, NY 10004

Donor(s): Peter C. Gerhard.
Financial data (yr. ended 08/31/01): Grants paid, $791,635; assets, $4,728,112 (M); gifts received, $2,059,810; expenditures, $902,218; qualifying distributions, $795,218.
Limitations: Applications not accepted. Giving primarily in Williamsport, PA; some giving also in NJ and NY.
Application information: Contributes only to pre-selected organizations.
Trustees: Kristen Gerhard, Peter C. Gerhard.
EIN: 133921375
Codes: FD

33249
The John R. and Kiendl Dauphinot Gordon Fund
(Formerly The John R. Gordon Fund)
c/o Sullivan & Cromwell
125 Broad St.
New York, NY 10004-2498
Contact: James I. Black III

Established in 1988 in NY.
Donor(s): Albert H. Gordon, John R. Gordon.
Financial data (yr. ended 12/31/01): Grants paid, $790,188; assets, $885,656 (M); gifts received, $185,000; expenditures, $797,480; qualifying distributions, $790,518.
Limitations: Applications not accepted. Giving primarily in New York, NY.
Application information: Contributes only to pre-selected organizations.
Trustees: John R. Gordon, Kiendl D. Gordon.
EIN: 136920431
Codes: FD

33250
Green Charitable Foundation, Inc.
14 E. 60th St., No. 702
New York, NY 10022

Established in 1999 in NY.
Donor(s): The Green Fund, Inc.
Financial data (yr. ended 01/31/02): Grants paid, $784,678; assets, $11,070,259 (M); gifts received, $290,000; expenditures, $924,152; qualifying distributions, $843,969.
Limitations: Applications not accepted. Giving primarily in NY.
Application information: Contributes only to pre-selected organizations.
Officers: S. William Green, Pres.; Patricia Green, Secy.
EIN: 134041346
Codes: FD

33251
Roy R. and Marie S. Neuberger Foundation, Inc.
605 3rd Ave., 41st Fl.
New York, NY 10158-0180 (212) 476-5866
Contact: Gloria Silverman

Incorporated in 1954 in NY.
Donor(s): Roy R. Neuberger, Marie S. Neuberger.‡
Financial data (yr. ended 12/31/01): Grants paid, $782,069; assets, $15,571,656 (M); expenditures, $930,385; qualifying distributions, $883,885.
Limitations: Giving primarily in NY.
Publications: Annual report.
Application information: Application form not required.
Officers and Directors:* Roy R. Neuberger,* Pres. and Treas.; Ann N. Aceves,* V.P.; James A. Neuberger,* V.P.; Roy S. Neuberger,* V.P.
EIN: 136066102

Codes: FD

33252
Little River Foundation
c/o Curtis, Mallet-Prevost, Colt, & Mosle
101 Park Ave., Ste.3500
New York, NY 10178-0061
Contact: Dale D. Hogoboom, Asst. Treas.

Established in 1972 in VA.
Donor(s): Ohrstrom Foundation.
Financial data (yr. ended 11/30/01): Grants paid, $781,877; assets, $731,729 (M); gifts received, $740,133; expenditures, $782,237; qualifying distributions, $782,058.
Limitations: Applications not accepted. Giving primarily in VA.
Application information: Contributes only to pre-selected organizations.
Officers: George L. Ohrstrom, Jr., Pres.; Magalen O. Bryant, V.P.; Peter A. Kalat, Secy.; Dorothy A. Barry, Treas.
EIN: 237218919
Codes: FD

33253
The Sperry Fund
99 Park Ave., Ste. 2220
New York, NY 10016-1601 (212) 370-1165
Application address: c/o Beinecke Scholarship Prog., 1200 Main St., Bethlehem, PA 18018, tel.: (610) 625-7830; FAX: (610) 625-7919; E-mail: BeineckeScholarship@moravian.edu
Contact: Dr. Thomas L. Parkinson, Prog. Dir.

Established in 1962 in NY.
Financial data (yr. ended 06/30/02): Grants paid, $781,325; assets, $16,616,000 (M); expenditures, $1,066,000; qualifying distributions, $781,325.
Limitations: Giving primarily in NY.
Publications: Informational brochure (including application guidelines).
Application information: College or university must be invited to nominate juniors for scholarship program; completion of application form required for nominees. Applications outside the nomination process not considered.
Officers and Directors:* Frederick W. Beinecke,* Pres.; John B. Beinecke,* V.P.; R. Scott Greathead,* Secy.; Robert J. Barletta, Treas.; William S. Beinecke, Melvyn L. Shaffir.
EIN: 136114308
Codes: FD, GTI

33254
Center for International Political Economy
c/o Kimmelman Asset Mgmt. Co.
800 Third Ave., Ste. 3100
New York, NY 10022

Established in 1995 in NY and WA.
Financial data (yr. ended 12/31/01): Grants paid, $781,156; assets, $596,502 (M); expenditures, $667,843; qualifying distributions, $1,153,798.
Limitations: Applications not accepted. Giving on a national basis.
Application information: Contributes only to pre-selected organizations.
Officers and Directors:* Eiji Ono,* Pres.; Catherine Wilkins,* Secy.; John Langlois, Exec. Dir.; William Clark, Peter Kimmelman.
EIN: 911695159
Codes: FD

33255
Hoffman Family Charitable Trust
1845 55th St.
Brooklyn, NY 11204

Established in 1993 in NY.
Donor(s): George Hoffman, Sarah Hoffman.
Financial data (yr. ended 12/31/00): Grants paid, $779,000; assets, $3,776,709 (M); gifts received, $1,000,000; expenditures, $799,002; qualifying distributions, $777,198.
Limitations: Applications not accepted. Giving primarily in Brooklyn, NY.
Application information: Contributes only to pre-selected organizations.
Trustees: George Hoffman, Sarah Hoffman.
EIN: 116436700
Codes: FD

33256
New York Jets Foundation, Inc.
c/o New York Jets Football Club, Inc.
1000 Fulton Ave.
Hempstead, NY 11550 (516) 560-8100
Contact: Steve Gutman, Pres.

Established in 1969.
Donor(s): New York Jets Football Club, Inc.
Financial data (yr. ended 12/31/01): Grants paid, $778,318; assets, $348,342 (M); gifts received, $949,572; expenditures, $900,201; qualifying distributions, $899,763.
Limitations: Giving primarily in NY.
Officers and Trustees:* Robert Wood Johnson IV,* Chair.; Loren J. Cross,* Pres. and Secy.; Neil Burmeister,* V.P.; Michael Gerstle,* Treas.
EIN: 237108291
Codes: CS, FD, CD

33257
Wasserstein Perella Foundation Trust
c/o Deutsche Trust Co. of NY
P.O. Box 1297, Church St. Sta.
New York, NY 10008
Application address: Edward Golden, Trust Off., c/o Deutsche Trust Co. of NY, 280 Park Ave., New York, NY 10017

Established in 1988 in NY.
Donor(s): Wasserstein Perella & Co., Inc.
Financial data (yr. ended 12/31/01): Grants paid, $777,000; assets, $36,037 (M); gifts received, $810,000; expenditures, $780,536; qualifying distributions, $778,700.
Limitations: Giving primarily in New York, NY.
Application information: Application form not required.
Trustee: Deutsche Bank.
EIN: 136916786
Codes: CS, FD, CD

33258
Joseph H. & Barbara I. Ellis Foundation
c/o BCRS Associates, LLC
100 Wall St., 11th Fl.
New York, NY 10005

Established in 1987 in NY.
Donor(s): Joseph H. Ellis.
Financial data (yr. ended 06/30/01): Grants paid, $776,699; assets, $6,225,731 (M); gifts received, $1,589,169; expenditures, $806,949; qualifying distributions, $760,662.
Limitations: Applications not accepted. Giving primarily in New York, NY.
Application information: Contributes only to pre-selected organizations.
Trustees: Leon Cooperman, Barbara I. Ellis, Joseph H. Ellis.
EIN: 133437916
Codes: FD

33259
H & M Charitable Fund, Inc.
1448 E. 8th St.
Brooklyn, NY 11230
Contact: Harry Muller, Tr.

Established in 1984 in NY.
Donor(s): Harry Muller, Hyman Muller.
Financial data (yr. ended 10/31/01): Grants paid, $774,800; assets, $3,443,461 (M); expenditures, $791,157; qualifying distributions, $769,313.
Limitations: Giving primarily in Brooklyn, NY.
Application information: Application form not required.
Trustees: Harry Muller, Hyman Muller.
EIN: 112720493
Codes: FD

33260
The Greeman Family Fund
c/o W.J. Handelman
1 N. Broadway, Ste. 1001
White Plains, NY 10601

Established in 1998 in NY.
Donor(s): Peter Greeman, Tamara Greeman.
Financial data (yr. ended 12/31/01): Grants paid, $773,000; assets, $723,083 (M); gifts received, $57,160; expenditures, $777,863; qualifying distributions, $773,720.
Limitations: Applications not accepted. Giving primarily in NY.
Application information: Contributes only to pre-selected organizations.
Officers and Directors:* Peter Greeman,* Pres. and Treas.; Tamara Greeman,* V.P.; Walter J. Handelman,* Secy.
EIN: 134003083
Codes: FD

33261
Carroll Petrie Foundation
834 5th Ave., Rm. 10B
New York, NY 10021
Contact: Carroll M. Petrie, Pres.

Established in 1996 in DE & NY.
Donor(s): Carroll M. Petrie.
Financial data (yr. ended 12/31/99): Grants paid, $773,000; assets, $2,762,322 (M); gifts received, $999,963; expenditures, $798,463; qualifying distributions, $765,896.
Limitations: Giving primarily in New York, NY.
Application information: Application form not required.
Officer and Director:* Carroll M. Petrie,* Pres.
EIN: 133912203
Codes: FD

33262
The Rosalind P. Walter Foundation
509 Madison Ave., Ste. 1216
New York, NY 10022

Established in 1951 as the Walter Foundation.
Donor(s): Henry G. Walter, Jr.,‡ Rosalind P. Walter.
Financial data (yr. ended 12/31/00): Grants paid, $772,383; assets, $2,400,108 (M); expenditures, $779,663; qualifying distributions, $773,883.
Limitations: Applications not accepted. Giving primarily in NY.
Application information: Contributes only to pre-selected organizations.
Trustee: Rosalind P. Walter.
EIN: 136177284
Codes: FD

33263
Krasnow Foundation
135 E. 57th St., Ste. 1100
New York, NY 10022

Donor(s): Maurice Krasnow.
Financial data (yr. ended 12/31/01): Grants paid, $771,204; assets, $153 (M); expenditures, $818,263; qualifying distributions, $771,204.
Limitations: Applications not accepted.
Application information: Contributes only to pre-selected organizations.
Officer and Trustees:* Maurice Krasnow,* Pres.; Debra Ann Krasnow Adler, Henry Kohn.
EIN: 136265101

33264
CBS Foundation
51 W. 52nd St.
New York, NY 10019 (212) 975-4073
FAX: (212) 975-3515; E-mail: CBSFoundation@cbs.com

Incorporated in 1953 in NY.
Donor(s): CBS Inc., Westinghouse Electric Corp., CBS Corp., Westinghouse Foundation.
Financial data (yr. ended 12/31/01): Grants paid, $770,651; assets, $3,155,957 (L); gifts received, $802,555; expenditures, $802,143; qualifying distributions, $795,727.
Limitations: Giving for national programs and in areas of major company operations.
Publications: Application guidelines.
Application information: Applications sent by FAX or E-mail not considered. Application form not required.
Officers and Directors:* Carl Folta,* Pres.; Karen Zatorski,* Secy.; Frank Tinghitella, Treas.; Dannell Suares, Genl. Counsel; Paulette Carpenter, G. Reynolds Clark, Cheryl Daly, Martin D. Franks, Joel Hollander, Matthew D. Margo, Martin P. Messinger, John D. Moran, Madeline Peerce, Josie J. Thomas, Leslie Anne Wade, David Zemelman.
EIN: 136099759
Codes: CS, FD, CD

33265
The Daniel K. Thorne Foundation, Inc.
c/o Stroock & Stroock
142 W. 57th St., 16th Fl.
New York, NY 10019

Established in 1996 in NY.
Donor(s): Daniel K. Thorne.
Financial data (yr. ended 12/31/00): Grants paid, $769,892; assets, $11,300,365 (M); expenditures, $842,426; qualifying distributions, $785,427.
Limitations: Applications not accepted. Giving on a national basis.
Application information: Unsolicited requests for funds not accepted.
Officers and Directors:* Daniel K. Thorne,* Pres. and Treas.; Theodore S. Lynn,* Secy.; Alexandra T. Thorne.
EIN: 133857951
Codes: FD

33266
Malcolm Gibbs Foundation, Inc.
14 E. 60th St., No. 702
New York, NY 10022

Established in 1999 in NY.
Donor(s): The Green Fund, Inc.
Financial data (yr. ended 01/31/02): Grants paid, $769,420; assets, $10,930,293 (M); gifts received, $200,000; expenditures, $903,530; qualifying distributions, $829,014.
Limitations: Applications not accepted. Giving primarily in NY.

Application information: Contributes only to pre-selected organizations.
Officers: Cynthia Green Colin, Pres.; Ann Colin Herbst, Secy.; Laura Colin Klein, Treas.
EIN: 134041340
Codes: FD

33267
Robert & Bethany Millard Charitable Foundation
(Formerly Robert B. Millard Charitable Foundation)
c/o Mahoney Cohen, C.P.A.
111 W. 40th St.
New York, NY 10018

Established in 1989 in NY.
Donor(s): Robert B. Millard.
Financial data (yr. ended 12/31/01): Grants paid, $768,834; assets, $7,834,518 (M); expenditures, $776,008; qualifying distributions, $769,210.
Limitations: Applications not accepted. Giving primarily in New York, NY.
Application information: Contributes only to pre-selected organizations.
Trustee: Robert B. Millard.
EIN: 133566723
Codes: FD

33268
B. & M. Steinmetz Foundation, Inc.
c/o David Soifer
24 Jackson N.E.
Spring Valley, NY 10977
Application address: 18 W. 33rd St., New York, NY 10001, tel.: (212) 563-5733
Contact: Bernat Steinmetz, Pres.

Established in 1969 in NY.
Donor(s): Bernat Steinmetz.
Financial data (yr. ended 05/31/01): Grants paid, $765,501; assets, $6,047,033 (M); gifts received, $693,858; expenditures, $777,927; qualifying distributions, $765,501.
Limitations: Giving primarily in New York, NY.
Application information: Application form not required.
Officer: Bernat Steinmetz, Pres.
EIN: 237048163
Codes: FD

33269
Sunny and Abe Rosenberg Foundation, Inc.
950 3rd Ave., 23rd Fl.
New York, NY 10022
Tel.: (212) 755-5390, Ext. 314; FAX: (212) 755-2310; E-mail: info@rosenbergfoundation.org; URL: http://www.rosenbergfoundation.org
Contact: Charles P. McLimans, Exec. Dir.

Incorporated in 1966 in NY.
Donor(s): Abraham Rosenberg,‡ Sonia Rosenberg.
Financial data (yr. ended 12/31/00): Grants paid, $762,400; assets, $16,818,882 (M); expenditures, $1,260,783; qualifying distributions, $685,182.
Limitations: Applications not accepted. Giving limited to the New York, NY, metropolitan area.
Application information: Unsolicited requests for funds not accepted.
Officers and Directors:* Susan R. Goldstein,* Pres.; Sonia Rosenberg, Pres. Emerita; Michael L. Rosenberg,* Sr. V.P.; Stuart D. Goldstein,* V.P. and Treas.; Robert Gassman, Secy.; Charles P. McLimans, Exec. Dir.
EIN: 136210591
Codes: FD

33270
The Elishis Family Foundation
c/o C. F. Burger, Esq.
405 Lexington Ave.
New York, NY 10174

Established in 1999 in NY.
Donor(s): Isser Elishis, Brenda Elishis, David Elishis.
Financial data (yr. ended 12/31/01): Grants paid, $758,661; assets, $548,543 (M); gifts received, $884,783; expenditures, $763,421; qualifying distributions, $753,761.
Limitations: Applications not accepted.
Application information: Contributes only to pre-selected organizations.
Officers and Directors:* Brenda Elishis,* Pres.; Sam Levin,* V.P. and Secy.; Wayne Coleson,* V.P. and Treas.; Isser Elishis, V.P.; David Elishis, V.P.
EIN: 113502742
Codes: FD

33271
The Chai X Four Charitable Trust
c/o Abraham Trusts
200 W. 57th St., Ste. 1005
New York, NY 10019

Established in 1990 in NY.
Donor(s): Rebecca Abraham Gridish, Tamar Abraham, Simona A. Ganz, Laurie Abraham Pinck, Martin Fawer, Estanne Abraham, Stephen Rudin.
Financial data (yr. ended 10/31/01): Grants paid, $758,095; assets, $217,867 (M); gifts received, $967,234; expenditures, $775,494; qualifying distributions, $759,262.
Limitations: Applications not accepted. Giving primarily in NY.
Application information: Contributes only to pre-selected organizations.
Trustees: Estanne Abraham, Tamar Abraham, Simona A. Ganz, Rebecca Abraham Gridish, Hirschell E. Levine, Laurie Abraham Pinck.
EIN: 136963182
Codes: FD

33272
Loewenberg Foundation, Inc.
450 Park Ave., Ste. 2700
New York, NY 10022 (212) 753-4100
Contact: Ralph E. Loewenberg, Pres.

Established in 1959 in NY.
Donor(s): Ralph E. Loewenberg, Kurt Loewenberg.‡
Financial data (yr. ended 10/31/01): Grants paid, $757,500; assets, $16,417,392 (M); gifts received, $812,001; expenditures, $1,035,510; qualifying distributions, $758,711.
Limitations: Giving primarily in New York, NY.
Officers and Directors:* Ralph E. Loewenberg,* Pres. and Treas.; Jeffry N. Grabel,* Secy.; Frederick Lubcher.
EIN: 136075586
Codes: FD

33273
Epstein Interests
(Formerly J. Epstein Foundation)
457 Madison Ave.
New York, NY 10022

Established in 1991 in NY.
Donor(s): Jeffrey E. Epstein.
Financial data (yr. ended 05/31/01): Grants paid, $757,357; assets, $2,038,563 (M); expenditures, $762,734; qualifying distributions, $760,986.
Limitations: Applications not accepted. Giving on a national basis.

Application information: Contributes only to pre-selected organizations.
Trustees: Jeffrey E. Epstein, Mark L. Epstein, Ira Zicherman.
EIN: 133643429
Codes: FD

33274
The Orentreich Family Foundation
909 5th Ave.
New York, NY 10021-1415

Established in 1986 in NY.
Donor(s): David Orentreich, Norman Orentreich, Orentreich Medical Group.
Financial data (yr. ended 09/30/01): Grants paid, $756,633; assets, $13,496,484 (M); expenditures, $813,114; qualifying distributions, $752,966.
Limitations: Applications not accepted. Giving primarily in New York, NY.
Application information: Contributes only to pre-selected organizations.
Trustees: David Orentreich, Norman Orentreich.
EIN: 136879797
Codes: FD

33275
Evelyn A. J. Hall Charitable Trust
c/o JPMorgan Chase Bank
345 Park Ave.
New York, NY 10154
Contact: Mary C. Dickens, V.P., JPMorgan Chase Bank

Trust established in 1952 in NY.
Donor(s): Evelyn A. Hall.
Financial data (yr. ended 12/31/01): Grants paid, $755,601; assets, $8,440,874 (M); expenditures, $812,577; qualifying distributions, $760,407.
Limitations: Applications not accepted. Giving primarily in FL and New York, NY.
Trustee: JPMorgan Chase Bank.
EIN: 236286760
Codes: FD

33276
Herman Frasch Foundation for Chemical Research
c/o U.S. Trust
114 W. 47th St.
New York, NY 10036-1532
FAX: (212) 852-3377; Address for requesting application forms: c/o American Chemical Society, 1155 16th St., N.W., Washington, DC 20036, tel.: (202) 872-4487
Contact: Andrew Lane, Asst. V.P.

Trust established in 1924 in NY.
Donor(s): Elizabeth Blee Frasch.‡
Financial data (yr. ended 12/31/01): Grants paid, $754,360; assets, $11,969,677 (M); expenditures, $833,736; qualifying distributions, $802,894.
Limitations: Giving limited to the U.S.
Publications: Application guidelines, program policy statement.
Application information: Application form required.
Trustee: U.S. Trust.
EIN: 136073145
Codes: FD

33277
The Bedminster Fund, Inc.
1330 Ave. of the Americas, 27th Fl.
New York, NY 10019-5490
Contact: Dorothy Davis, Secy.

Incorporated in 1948 in NY.
Financial data (yr. ended 06/30/01): Grants paid, $750,900; assets, $13,222,316 (M); expenditures, $805,739; qualifying distributions, $762,850.

Limitations: Applications not accepted. Giving on a national basis, with some emphasis on NJ and NY.
Application information: Contributes only to pre-selected organizations.
Officers and Directors:* Philip D. Allen,* Pres.; Martin C. Zetterberg,* V.P.; Dorothy Davis, Secy.; James J. Ruddy, Treas.; A. Christine Allen, Alexandra F. Allen, Andrew D. Allen, Christopher D. Allen, Douglas E. Allen, Elisabeth F. Allen, Nicholas E. Allen, Dorothy D. Caplow, Theodore Caplow, Dorothy Dillon Eweson, Judith S. Leonard, David H. Peipers.
EIN: 136083684
Codes: FD

33278
David and Katherine Moore Family Foundation
c/o D'Arcangelo Co.
3000 Westchester Ave.
Purchase, NY 10577 (914) 694-4600
E-mail: pwarner@darcangelo.com
Contact: Margaret Warner

Established in 1997 in NY.
Donor(s): David E. Moore, Sr.
Financial data (yr. ended 12/31/01): Grants paid, $749,500; assets, $20,621,000 (M); gifts received, $15,000; expenditures, $940,000; qualifying distributions, $689,247.
Limitations: Applications not accepted. Giving primarily in the northeastern U.S.
Application information: Unsolicited requests for funds not accepted.
Trustees: David E. Moore, Katherine C. Moore.
EIN: 137103979
Codes: FD

33279
The Bydale Foundation
11 Martine Ave.
White Plains, NY 10606 (914) 683-3519
Contact: Milton D. Solomon, V.P.

Incorporated in 1965 in DE.
Donor(s): James P. Warburg.‡
Financial data (yr. ended 12/31/01): Grants paid, $748,250; assets, $13,581,815 (M); expenditures, $862,046; qualifying distributions, $791,129.
Limitations: Giving on a national basis.
Application information: Application form not required.
Officers and Trustees:* Joan M. Warburg,* Pres.; Milton D. Solomon,* V.P. and Secy.; Frank J. Kick, Treas.; Sarah W. Bliumis, James P. Warburg, Jr., Jennifer Warburg, Philip N. Warburg.
EIN: 136195286
Codes: FD

33280
The Frog Rock Foundation
P.O. Box 865
Chappaqua, NY 10514 (914) 273-1375
FAX: (914) 273-5056; *E-mail:* info@frogrockfoundation.org; *URL:* http://www.frogrockfoundation.org
Contact: Libbie Naman Poppick, Exec. Dir.

Established in 2000 in NY.
Donor(s): Janet Inskeep Benton.
Financial data (yr. ended 12/31/01): Grants paid, $748,000; assets, $7,156,647 (M); gifts received, $7,140,937; expenditures, $755,006; qualifying distributions, $754,963.
Limitations: Giving primarily in Westchester County, NY.
Application information: Application information available on foundation website.
Officer and Trustees:* Janet Inskeep Benton,* Pres.; Elizabeth C. Namen.

EIN: 134127228
Codes: FD

33281
Ehrenkranz Family Foundation
c/o Joel S. Ehrenkranz
375 Park Ave., Ste. 2800
New York, NY 10152

Established in 1997 in NY.
Donor(s): Joel S. Ehrenkranz.
Financial data (yr. ended 12/31/00): Grants paid, $745,916; assets, $5,172,972 (M); gifts received, $3,794,978; expenditures, $797,061; qualifying distributions, $703,888.
Limitations: Applications not accepted. Giving primarily in New York, NY.
Application information: Contributes only to pre-selected organizations.
Trustees: Anne B. Ehrenkranz, Joel S. Ehrenkranz.
EIN: 133977888
Codes: FD

33282
Robison Family Foundation
(Formerly The Ellis H. and Doris B. Robison Foundation)
51 Collins Ave.
Troy, NY 12180

Trust established in 1980 in NY.
Donor(s): Ellis Robison.‡
Financial data (yr. ended 12/31/01): Grants paid, $745,750; assets, $13,705,302 (M); expenditures, $771,392; qualifying distributions, $740,605.
Limitations: Applications not accepted. Giving limited to western NY and Cincinnati, OH.
Application information: Contributes only to pre-selected organizations.
Officers: James A. Robison, Pres.; Richard G. Robison, V.P.; Elissa R. Prout, Secy.-Treas.
Director: Barbara R. Sporck.
EIN: 222470695
Codes: FD

33283
Sarita Kenedy East Foundation, Inc.
P.O. Box 604138
Bayside, NY 11360-4138
Contact: Margaret Devine

Established in 1962 in NY.
Donor(s): Sarita Kenedy East.‡
Financial data (yr. ended 12/31/00): Grants paid, $743,750; assets, $18,480,277 (M); expenditures, $937,219; qualifying distributions, $764,620.
Limitations: Giving on a national basis.
Application information: Contributes primarily to pre-selected organizations. Application form not required.
Officers and Directors:* Margaret F. Grace,* Pres.; Patrick P. Grace,* V.P. and Secy.-Treas.; Justine M. Carr, Thomas M. Doyle, Theresa G. Sears.
EIN: 136116447
Codes: FD

33284
William H. Kearns Foundation
c/o Milton Warshaw
45 E. 89th St.
New York, NY 10128

Established in 1965.
Financial data (yr. ended 12/31/01): Grants paid, $742,500; assets, $11,547,320 (M); expenditures, $1,110,964; qualifying distributions, $742,500.
Limitations: Applications not accepted. Giving primarily in NY.
Application information: Contributes only to pre-selected organizations.

33284—NEW YORK

Officers and Directors:* Milton Warshaw,* Pres. and Treas.; Maxine D. Prisyon,* V.P. and Secy.
EIN: 136199107
Codes: FD

33285
The Ferriday Fund Charitable Trust
c/o The Bank of New York, Tax Dept.
1 Wall St., 28th Fl.
New York, NY 10286
Application address: c/o The Bank of New York, 1290 Ave. of Americas, 5th Fl., New York, NY 10104
Contact: Douglas J. Boyle

Established in 1991 in NY.
Donor(s): Carolyn Ferriday.‡
Financial data (yr. ended 07/31/01): Grants paid, $741,750; assets, $11,816,927 (M); gifts received, $150,000; expenditures, $860,400; qualifying distributions, $780,026.
Limitations: Giving primarily in CT.
Trustees: Richard J. Carter, Jr., The Bank of New York.
EIN: 136967609
Codes: FD

33286
The Meyer Foundation
c/o Lazard Freres & Co., LLC
30 Rockefeller Plz.
New York, NY 10112-0002
Contact: Paul Cohen

Established in 1985 in NY.
Donor(s): George J. Ames.‡
Financial data (yr. ended 12/31/01): Grants paid, $740,750; assets, $13,194,836 (M); expenditures, $823,911; qualifying distributions, $736,871.
Limitations: Applications not accepted. Giving primarily in CA, MA, and NY.
Application information: Contributes to pre-selected organizations.
Officers and Directors:* Phillipe Meyer,* Pres.; Vincent Meyer,* V.P.; Charles M. Stieglitz, Secy.; Paul Cohen, Treas.
EIN: 133317912
Codes: FD

33287
The Dragomir Nicolitch Charitable Trust
c/o Kranz & Co.
145 E. 57th St.
New York, NY 10022
Application addresses: c/o Silas Mountsier, 205 Rutgers Pl., Nutley, NJ 07110, and Most Rev. Metropolitan Christopher, 32377 N. Milwaukee Ave., Libertyville, IL 60048

Established in 1996 in NY.
Donor(s): Dragomir Nicolitch.‡
Financial data (yr. ended 12/31/00): Grants paid, $740,500; assets, $8,916,257 (M); expenditures, $859,269; qualifying distributions, $751,368.
Limitations: Giving on a national basis.
Trustees: Most Rev. Metropolitan Christopher, Silas R. Mountsier III.
EIN: 137082276
Codes: FD

33288
The Edith & F. M. Achilles Memorial Fund
c/o JPMorgan Chase Bank
1211 Ave. of the Americas, 38th Fl.
New York, NY 10036 (212) 789-5682
E-mail: jones_ed_l@jpmorgan.com
Contact: Edward L. Jones, V.P.

Established in 1996 in NY.

Financial data (yr. ended 12/31/01): Grants paid, $740,000; assets, $14,475,092 (M); expenditures, $875,486; qualifying distributions, $761,872.
Limitations: Applications not accepted. Giving primarily in the metropolitan New York City area, and NC.
Application information: Contributes only to pre-selected organizations.
Trustee: JPMorgan Chase Bank.
EIN: 137102170
Codes: FD

33289
Frieda & Roy Furman Foundation, Inc.
770 Park Ave., Ste. 15D
New York, NY 10021
Additional address: c/o Pell Rudman, 3475 Piedmont Rd., Ste. 550, Atlanta, GA 30305, tel.: (404) 495-1600; E-mail: jmccolskey@pellrudman.com
Contact: John G. McColskey

Established in 1997 in NY.
Donor(s): Roy L. Furman.
Financial data (yr. ended 12/31/01): Grants paid, $738,800; assets, $2,945,203 (M); expenditures, $762,412; qualifying distributions, $734,724.
Limitations: Applications not accepted. Giving primarily in NY.
Application information: Contributes only to pre-selected organizations.
Officers: Frieda Furman, Pres.; Roy L. Furman, Secy.-Treas.
EIN: 133970732
Codes: FD

33290
Knafel Family Foundation
810 7th Ave., 41st Fl.
New York, NY 10019-5818

Established in 1994 in NY.
Financial data (yr. ended 12/31/00): Grants paid, $738,750; assets, $17,866,990 (M); expenditures, $763,723; qualifying distributions, $725,355.
Limitations: Applications not accepted. Giving primarily in MA and NY.
Application information: Contributes only to pre-selected organizations.
Officers: Sidney R. Knafel, Pres.; Andrew G. Knafel, Treas.
Director: Douglas R. Knafel.
EIN: 133779562
Codes: FD

33291
The Schulweis Family Foundation
c/o H. Schulweis, Schulweis Realty
9 W. 57th St., 50th Fl.
New York, NY 10019-2701

Established in 1989 in NY.
Donor(s): Harvey Schulweis, Carol Schulweis.
Financial data (yr. ended 12/31/99): Grants paid, $738,540; assets, $1,732,067 (M); gifts received, $1,102,520; expenditures, $738,945; qualifying distributions, $738,540.
Limitations: Applications not accepted. Giving primarily in New York, NY.
Application information: Contributes only to pre-selected organizations. Unsolicited requests for funds not considered.
Trustee: Harvey Schulweis.
EIN: 136930204
Codes: FD

33292
Jill & Marshall Rose Foundation, Inc.
c/o Georgetown Mgmt. Assn.
667 Madison Ave.
New York, NY 10021
Contact: Marshall Rose, Dir.

Established around 1980.
Donor(s): Marshall Rose, Alan R. Grossman.
Financial data (yr. ended 11/30/01): Grants paid, $738,415; assets, $2,690,505 (M); gifts received, $240,000; expenditures, $738,762; qualifying distributions, $738,415.
Limitations: Applications not accepted. Giving primarily in New York, NY.
Application information: Contributes only to pre-selected organizations.
Directors: Simeon Brinberg, Marshall Rose.
EIN: 133036439
Codes: FD

33293
The Greer Family Foundation
c/o Weiss, Peck & Greer
1 New York Plz., 30th Fl.
New York, NY 10004 (212) 908-9500
Contact: Philip Greer, Pres.

Established in 1985 in IL and NY.
Donor(s): Philip Greer.
Financial data (yr. ended 12/31/00): Grants paid, $737,742; assets, $5,680,175 (M); gifts received, $413,083; expenditures, $743,742; qualifying distributions, $733,392.
Limitations: Giving primarily in CA, CT, and NY.
Officers: Philip Greer, Pres. and Treas.; Norman M. Gold, V.P. and Secy.; Nancy Greer, V.P.; Stephen Weiss, V.P.
EIN: 133321858
Codes: FD

33294
Rich Family Foundation, Inc.
(Formerly Rich Foundation, Inc.)
1150 Niagara St.
P.O. Box 245
Buffalo, NY 14240-0245 (716) 878-8000
Contact: David A. Rich, Exec. Dir.

Established in 1961.
Donor(s): Rich Products Corp.
Financial data (yr. ended 12/31/00): Grants paid, $737,478; assets, $3,604,975 (M); gifts received, $660,000; expenditures, $782,677; qualifying distributions, $750,169.
Limitations: Giving primarily in Buffalo and western NY.
Officers: Robert E. Rich, Pres. and Treas.; Robert E. Rich, Jr., Secy.; David A. Rich, Exec. Dir.
EIN: 166026199
Codes: CS, FD, CD

33295
Elizabeth McGraw Foundation, Inc.
c/o Deutsche Bank Trust Co. of NY
P.O. Box 1297, Church St. Sta.
New York, NY 10008
Application address: c/o Donald C. McGraw, Jr., V.P., 1330 W. Ocean Blvd., Gulfstream, FL 33483

Established in 1990 in NY.
Donor(s): Donald C. McGraw Foundation, Inc.
Financial data (yr. ended 09/30/01): Grants paid, $737,000; assets, $11,126,029 (M); expenditures, $852,833; qualifying distributions, $741,636.
Limitations: Giving primarily in the northeastern U.S.
Officers: John L. McGraw, Pres.; Donald C. McGraw, Jr., V.P.; John L. Cady, Secy.-Treas.
EIN: 133591829

Codes: FD

33296
The Rosenkranz Foundation, Inc.
153 E. 53rd St., 49th Fl.
New York, NY 10022

Established in 1997 in DE and NY.
Donor(s): Robert Rosenkranz.
Financial data (yr. ended 10/31/01): Grants paid, $736,574; assets, $12,301,824 (M); expenditures, $845,863; qualifying distributions, $773,371.
Limitations: Applications not accepted. Giving primarily in New York, NY.
Application information: Contributes only to pre-selected organizations.
Officers and Directors:* Robert Rosenkranz,* Pres.; Linda Eike,* Secy.-Treas.; Nicholas Rosenkranz.
EIN: 133940017
Codes: FD

33297
Marion Esser Kaufmann Foundation
c/o A. Webber
2525 Palmer Ave.
New Rochelle, NY 10801 (914) 636-8400

Established in 1986 in NY.
Donor(s): Marion Esser Kaufmann.‡
Financial data (yr. ended 12/31/01): Grants paid, $735,000; assets, $12,295,438 (M); expenditures, $885,441; qualifying distributions, $734,496.
Limitations: Giving on a national basis, with some emphasis on New York, NY, CO, and Washington, DC.
Trustees: Frederick L. Bissinger, Richard Esser.
EIN: 133339941
Codes: FD

33298
The Jerome Robbins Foundation, Inc.
18 W. 21st St., 6th Fl.
New York, NY 10010 (212) 367-8956
FAX: (212) 367-8966; URL: http://www.jeromerobbins.org
Contact: Christopher Pennington

Established about 1959 in NY.
Donor(s): Jerome Robbins.‡
Financial data (yr. ended 09/30/01): Grants paid, $735,000; assets, $9,684,848 (M); expenditures, $1,261,171; qualifying distributions, $811,259.
Limitations: Giving primarily in New York, NY.
Application information: Application form not required.
Trustees: Allen Greenberg, Floria V. Lasky, Daniel Stern.
EIN: 136021425
Codes: FD

33299
The Alexandrine and Alexander L. Sinsheimer Fund
c/o JPMorgan Chase Bank
1211 6th Ave., 34th Fl.
New York, NY 10036

Trust established in 1959 in NY.
Donor(s): Alexander L. Sinsheimer,‡ Alexandrine Sinsheimer.‡
Financial data (yr. ended 04/30/01): Grants paid, $733,965; assets, $13,759,531 (M); expenditures, $879,034; qualifying distributions, $739,655.
Limitations: Giving limited to the metropolitan New York, NY, area.
Application information: Application form required.
Trustee: JPMorgan Chase Bank.
EIN: 136047421
Codes: FD

33300
The Cooper Family Foundation, Inc.
(Formerly Milton Cooper Foundation)
3333 New Hyde Park Rd., No. 100
New Hyde Park, NY 11042-0020

Established in 1987 in NY.
Donor(s): Milton Cooper.
Financial data (yr. ended 12/31/01): Grants paid, $729,140; assets, $8,063,879 (M); expenditures, $751,078; qualifying distributions, $717,741.
Limitations: Applications not accepted. Giving primarily in New York, NY.
Application information: Contributes only to pre-selected organizations.
Officers: Milton Cooper, Pres.; Arthur Friedman, Secy.; Todd Cooper, Treas.
EIN: 112831400
Codes: FD

33301
Roy & Marianne Smith Foundation
c/o BCRS Assocs., LLC
67 Wall St., 8th Fl.
New York, NY 10005

Established in 1980 in NJ.
Donor(s): Roy C. Smith, Marianne F. Smith.
Financial data (yr. ended 03/31/01): Grants paid, $728,191; assets, $2,887,864 (M); gifts received, $829,755; expenditures, $735,879; qualifying distributions, $728,809.
Limitations: Applications not accepted. Giving primarily in NJ and NY.
Application information: Contributes only to pre-selected organizations.
Trustees: Michael H. Coles, Marianne F. Smith, Roy C. Smith.
EIN: 133050754
Codes: FD

33302
Jerome & Kenneth Lipper Foundation
101 Park Ave.
New York, NY 10178
Contact: Kenneth Lipper, Tr.

Established in 1998 in NY.
Donor(s): Kenneth Lipper, Lipper Holdings, LLC.
Financial data (yr. ended 12/31/01): Grants paid, $727,907; assets, $2,182,259 (M); expenditures, $761,800; qualifying distributions, $726,865.
Limitations: Giving primarily in MA and NY.
Application information: Application form not required.
Trustee: Kenneth Lipper.
EIN: 137157260
Codes: FD

33303
The Elliot Laniado and Raymond Laniado Foundation, Inc.
1908 E. 7th St.
Brooklyn, NY 11223

Established in 2000 in NY.
Donor(s): Elliot Laniado, Raymond Laniado.
Financial data (yr. ended 12/31/00): Grants paid, $726,000; assets, $280,535 (M); gifts received, $1,019,471; expenditures, $726,068; qualifying distributions, $726,000.
Limitations: Applications not accepted. Giving primarily in Brooklyn, NY.
Application information: Contributes only to pre-selected organizations.
Officers and Directors:* Elliot Laniado,* Pres. and Treas.; Raymond Laniado,* V.P. and Secy.; Stephanie Laniado.
EIN: 113551760
Codes: FD

33304
The Isabelle and Leonard Goldenson Association, Inc.
(Formerly I. & L. Association)
100 Main St.
Tuckahoe, NY 10707

Established in 1946.
Financial data (yr. ended 12/31/99): Grants paid, $725,500; assets, $17,070,780 (M); expenditures, $849,901; qualifying distributions, $728,548.
Limitations: Applications not accepted. Giving primarily in CA; some giving also in NY.
Application information: Contributes only to pre-selected organizations.
Officers and Directors:* Martin Pompadur, Chair.; Loreen Arbus, Pres.; Isabelle W. Goldenson,* V.P.; Maxine Goldenson, V.P.; Maryellen Mastrogiorgio,* Secy.
EIN: 136115597
Codes: FD

33305
The Partridge Foundation
c/o Rock & Co.
30 Rockerfeller Plz., Rm. 5600
New York, NY 10112
Contact: Penny Willgerot

Established in 1992.
Donor(s): Polly Guth, PW Gath Char. Lead Unitrust.
Financial data (yr. ended 11/30/01): Grants paid, $725,000; assets, $22,641,972 (M); gifts received, $6,763,742; expenditures, $930,924; qualifying distributions, $725,000.
Limitations: Giving primarily in NY.
Application information: Application form not required.
Trustees: Virginia Montgomery, Richard T. Watson.
EIN: 341742512
Codes: FD

33306
Sondra & Charles Gilman, Jr. Foundation, Inc.
109 E. 64th St.
New York, NY 10021
Application address: P.O. Box 18925, Corpus Christi, TX 78480
Contact: Sondra Gilman Gonzalez-Falla, Chair.

Established in NY in 1981 as a successor to the Gilman Foundation.
Financial data (yr. ended 04/30/01): Grants paid, $724,000; assets, $10,008,148 (M); expenditures, $1,310,169; qualifying distributions, $906,583.
Limitations: Giving on a national basis, with some emphasis on New York, NY, NJ, and TX.
Publications: Program policy statement.
Application information: Application form not required.
Officers: Sondra Gilman Gonzalez-Falla, Chair.; Celso M. Gonzalez-Falla, Pres.; Jack Friedland, V.P.; John Mosler, Secy.; Walter Bauer, Treas.
Director: Myrna Schatz.
EIN: 133097485
Codes: FD

33307
The Julie and Michael Schwerin Foundation
c/o Pat Douda-Ernst & Young, LLP
787 7th Ave.
New York, NY 10019

Established in 1994 in NY.
Donor(s): Michael Schwerin.
Financial data (yr. ended 08/31/01): Grants paid, $722,700; assets, $417,174 (M); expenditures, $727,075; qualifying distributions, $720,781.
Limitations: Applications not accepted. Giving primarily in NY.

Application information: Contributes only to pre-selected organizations.
Trustees: Julie Schwerin, Michael Schwerin.
EIN: 133797380
Codes: FD

33308
The Dorothea L. Leonhardt Foundation, Inc.
c/o G. Gaylord
1 Chase Manhattan Plz., 47th Fl.
New York, NY 10005 (212) 530-5016

Incorporated in 1988 in NY.
Donor(s): Frederick H. Leonhardt.‡
Financial data (yr. ended 07/31/01): Grants paid, $721,800; assets, $13,791,067 (M); expenditures, $1,030,995; qualifying distributions, $804,341.
Limitations: Applications not accepted. Giving primarily in NY.
Application information: Contributes only to pre-selected organizations.
Officers and Directors:* Joanne L. Cassullo,* Pres.; Guilford W. Gaylord,* Secy.-Treas.; Alexander D. Forger, Richard A. Stark.
EIN: 133420520
Codes: FD

33309
Robert Saligman Charitable Trust
c/o Alice Saligman
830 Park Ave., Ste. 7B
New York, NY 10021-2757

Established in 1987 in PA.
Donor(s): Robert Saligman.‡
Financial data (yr. ended 12/31/99): Grants paid, $719,756; assets, $18,789,558 (M); expenditures, $866,104; qualifying distributions, $723,252.
Limitations: Giving primarily in New York, NY, and PA.
Application information: Application form not required.
Trustees: Herschel Cravitz, Alice Saligman, Carolyn Saligman.
EIN: 236875203
Codes: FD

33310
The Altschul Foundation
c/o Holland & Knight, LLP
195 Broadway
New York, NY 10007
Contact: Mary Ellen Sweeney, Legal Asst.

Incorporated in 1941 in NY.
Donor(s): Louis Altschul,‡ Jeanette Cohen Altschul.‡
Financial data (yr. ended 06/30/01): Grants paid, $719,500; assets, $14,119,687 (M); expenditures, $890,136; qualifying distributions, $723,917.
Limitations: Applications not accepted. Giving primarily in FL, New York, NY, and UT.
Application information: Contributes only to pre-selected organizations.
Officers and Trustees:* Susan Rothstein-Schwimmer,* Pres.; William Rothstein,* V.P. and Secy.; Valerie Aspinwall,* V.P.; Seth Schapiro,* Treas.; Daniel L. Kurtz.
EIN: 136400009
Codes: FD

33311
Arnold and Marie Schwartz Fund for Education and Health Research
465 Park Ave.
New York, NY 10022

Incorporated in 1971 in DE.
Donor(s): Arnold Schwartz Charitable Trust.
Financial data (yr. ended 03/31/01): Grants paid, $719,380; assets, $6,093,238 (M); expenditures, $827,546; qualifying distributions, $770,379.
Limitations: Giving on a national basis.
Application information: Application form not required.
Officers and Directors:* Marie D. Schwartz, Pres.; Ruth Kerstein,* Secy.; Sylvia Kassel, Nellie Jane McDonald.
EIN: 237115019
Codes: FD

33312
SMBC Global Foundation, Inc.
(Formerly Sumitomo Bank Global Foundation)
c/o Sumitomo Mitsui Banking Corp.
277 Park Ave.
New York, NY 10172
Additional address for international activities: c/o Sumitomo Mitsui Banking Corp., Plan. Dept., Intl. Banking Unit I-2, Yurakucho I-chome, Chiyoda-ku, Tokyo 100-0006
Contact: Naoyuki Kawamoto, Pres.

Established in 1994 in DE and NY.
Donor(s): Sumitomo Bank Capital Markets, Inc., SMBC Capital Markets, Inc.
Financial data (yr. ended 12/31/01): Grants paid, $718,968; assets, $14,450,422 (M); expenditures, $1,012,251; qualifying distributions, $761,381.
Limitations: Giving to citizens or residents of Asian countries, including but not limited to China, Thailand, Vietnam, Singapore, Indonesia, or Malaysia.
Application information: Scholarship recipients must be admitted and enrolled at an educational institution approved by the foundation. The foundation expects to pay the scholarships either directly to the individual recipient or the educational institution attended by the recipient. Application form required.
Officers and Directors:* Naoyuki Kawamoto,* Pres.; Jane Hutta,* Secy.; Yoshihiro Takami,* Treas.; Ryuzo Kodama, Robert A. Rabbino, Jr., Takao Umino.
EIN: 133766226
Codes: CS, FD, CD

33313
Harris Family Foundation
c/o BCRS Associates, LLC
67 Wall St., 8th Fl.
New York, NY 10005

Established in 1989 in CT.
Donor(s): Charles T. Harris III.
Financial data (yr. ended 02/28/01): Grants paid, $717,150; assets, $490,704 (M); expenditures, $721,960; qualifying distributions, $718,898.
Limitations: Applications not accepted. Giving primarily in the Northeast.
Application information: Contributes only to pre-selected organizations.
Trustees: Charles T. Harris III, Susan Harris, Charles Kaufmann III.
EIN: 133532019
Codes: FD

33314
The Herbert Allen Foundation
711 5th Ave.
New York, NY 10022-3194
Contact: Howard Felson, Asst. Treas.

Established in 1994 in NY.
Financial data (yr. ended 12/31/01): Grants paid, $711,000; assets, $13,765,518 (M); expenditures, $731,105; qualifying distributions, $709,070.
Limitations: Giving primarily in New York, NY.
Officers and Directors:* Susan K. Allen, Pres.; Bradley A. Roberts,* V.P. and Secy.; Herbert A. Allen III,* V.P. and Treas.
EIN: 133791176
Codes: FD

33315
Zedukah Vechesed Foundation, Inc.
c/o David Soifer
24 Jackson Ave.
Spring Valley, NY 10977-1908
Application address: 465 Bedford Ave., Brooklyn, NY 11211, tel.: (718) 387-7171
Contact: Clara Steinmetz

Established in 1967.
Donor(s): Emanuel Steinmetz, Yitzchak Steinmetz, Rita Wagschal, Solomon Steinmetz, Steinmetz Bros., Inc., Jrr Mgmt., Shoretown Mgmt., Sherman Mgmt.
Financial data (yr. ended 05/31/01): Grants paid, $710,038; assets, $2,218,454 (M); gifts received, $191,763; expenditures, $724,427; qualifying distributions, $710,038.
Application information: Application form not required.
Trustee: Clara Steinmetz.
EIN: 237057565
Codes: FD

33316
The Dreitzer Foundation, Inc.
330 Madison Ave., 35th Fl.
New York, NY 10017-5094 (212) 557-7700
FAX: (212) 286-8513
Contact: Alan D. Seget, Secy.

Established in 1958 in NY.
Donor(s): Albert J. Dreitzer,‡ Mildred H. Dreitzer.‡
Financial data (yr. ended 12/31/01): Grants paid, $710,000; assets, $11,568,444 (M); gifts received, $27,000; expenditures, $827,267; qualifying distributions, $705,090.
Limitations: Giving primarily in New York, NY.
Publications: Application guidelines.
Application information: Application form not required.
Officers: Judith Wallach, Pres.; Amy Halpen, V.P.; Sylvan Wallach, V.P.; Alan Seget, Secy.
EIN: 136162509
Codes: FD

33317
Sylvan and Ann Oestreicher Foundation, Inc.
c/o Marks Paneth & Shron, LLP
622 3rd Ave.
New York, NY 10017
Application address: Lenox Hill Sta., P.O. Box 2365, New York, NY 10021
Contact: Ann Oestreicher, Pres.

Incorporated in 1948 in NY.
Donor(s): Sylvan Oestreicher.‡
Financial data (yr. ended 04/30/01): Grants paid, $708,815; assets, $10,380,799 (M); expenditures, $785,036; qualifying distributions, $719,815.
Limitations: Giving primarily in Chicago, IL and NY.
Application information: Application form not required.
Officers: Ann Oestreicher, Pres.; Robert F. Welch, Secy.
EIN: 136085974
Codes: FD

NEW YORK—33327

33318
The Birkelund Fund
c/o B. Strauss Assoc., Ltd.
307 5th Ave., 8th Fl.
New York, NY 10016-6517

Established in 1989 in NY.
Donor(s): John P. Birkelund.
Financial data (yr. ended 04/30/01): Grants paid, $708,750; assets, $12,324,243 (M); gifts received, $1,195,940; expenditures, $780,203; qualifying distributions, $711,609.
Limitations: Applications not accepted. Giving primarily in NJ and NY.
Application information: Contributes only to pre-selected organizations.
Officer: John P. Birkelund, Pres.
Director: Immanuel Kohn.
EIN: 133539224
Codes: FD

33319
Glover-Crask Charitable Trust
c/o JPMorgan Chase Bank
P.O. Box 31412
Rochester, NY 14603 (716) 258-5169
Contact: Kate Noble, Tr. Off., JPMorgan Chase Bank

Established in 1998 in NY.
Financial data (yr. ended 11/30/01): Grants paid, $708,100; assets, $15,112,256 (M); expenditures, $819,679; qualifying distributions, $712,048.
Limitations: Applications not accepted. Giving primarily in NY.
Application information: Contributes only to pre-selected organizations.
Trustees: George F. Harris, JPMorgan Chase Bank.
EIN: 166478709
Codes: FD

33320
Levitt Foundation
c/o The Philanthropic Group
630 5th Ave., 20th Fl.
New York, NY 10111 (212) 501-7785
URL: http://fdncenter.org/grantmaker/levitt
Contact: Barbara R. Greenberg

Incorporated in 1949 in NY.
Donor(s): Levitt and Sons, Inc., Abraham Levitt,‡ Alfred Levitt,‡ William Levitt.
Financial data (yr. ended 04/30/01): Grants paid, $707,449; assets, $18,607,783 (M); expenditures, $1,065,269; qualifying distributions, $779,506.
Limitations: Applications not accepted. Giving limited to Long Island and New York, NY.
Application information: Applications accepted by invitation only.
Officers and Trustees:* Farrell Jones,* Pres.; Stephen J. Mathes,* Secy.; Robert J. Appel,* Treas.; Prudence Brown, Barbara R. Greenberg, May W. Newburger.
EIN: 136128226
Codes: FD

33321
JEHT Foundation
120 Wooster St.
New York, NY 10012

Established in 2000 in NY.
Donor(s): Jeanne Levy-Hinte.
Financial data (yr. ended 12/31/01): Grants paid, $705,975; assets, $351,620 (M); gifts received, $1,274,500; expenditures, $934,520; qualifying distributions, $934,513.
Limitations: Applications not accepted. Giving primarily in NY.
Application information: Contributes only to pre-selected organizations.
Trustees: Robert Crane, Jeanne Levy-Hinte, Jeffrey Levy-Hinte, William Zabel.
EIN: 137232160

33322
The Tilles Family Foundation
7600 Jericho Tpke.
Woodbury, NY 11797

Established in 1997 in NY.
Donor(s): Rose Tilles Revocable Trust.
Financial data (yr. ended 12/31/01): Grants paid, $705,258; assets, $3,821 (M); gifts received, $686,393; expenditures, $705,433; qualifying distributions, $705,433.
Limitations: Applications not accepted. Giving primarily in NY.
Application information: Contributes only to pre-selected organizations.
Officers and Directors:* Roger Tilles,* Pres.; Peter Tilles,* V.P.; Sol Wachtler,* Secy.-Treas.
EIN: 113372816
Codes: FD

33323
The Seymour H. Knox Foundation
1 HSBC Ctr., Ste. 3840
Buffalo, NY 14203

Incorporated in 1945 in NY.
Donor(s): Seymour H. Knox,‡ Marjorie K.C. Klopp,‡ Dorothy K.G. Rogers.‡
Financial data (yr. ended 12/31/01): Grants paid, $703,969; assets, $21,197,169 (M); expenditures, $1,142,463; qualifying distributions, $825,519.
Limitations: Giving primarily in the Buffalo, NY, area.
Officers and Directors:* Hazard K. Campbell, Chair.; Northrup R. Knox, Jr.,* Pres.; Seymour H. Knox IV,* V.P. and Secy.; Benjamin K. Campbell,* V.P. and Treas.; Charles W. Banta, Randolph A. Marks, Henry Z. Urban.
EIN: 160839066
Codes: FD

33324
The Schenker Family Foundation
c/o Curtis Schenker
1175 Park Ave., Apt. 8A
New York, NY 10128

Established in 1998 in NY.
Donor(s): Curtis Schenker, Leo Schenker.
Financial data (yr. ended 12/31/01): Grants paid, $701,783; assets, $923,315 (M); gifts received, $716,180; expenditures, $727,066; qualifying distributions, $701,783.
Limitations: Applications not accepted.
Application information: Contributes only to pre-selected organizations.
Officer: Livia Schenker, Secy.
Directors: Curtis Schenker, Leo Schenker, Jeffrey Schwarz.
EIN: 133992998
Codes: FD

33325
The Baron de Hirsch Fund
130 E. 59th St., 12th Fl.
New York, NY 10022 (212) 836-1358
Fellowship application address: c/o Fellowship Comm., Ministry of Agriculture, Tel Aviv, Israel
Contact: Lauren Katzowitz, Managing Dir.

Incorporated in 1891 in NY.
Donor(s): Baron Maurice de Hirsch,‡ Baroness Clara de Hirsch.‡
Financial data (yr. ended 08/31/01): Grants paid, $701,525; assets, $7,706,686 (M); expenditures, $998,701; qualifying distributions, $852,253.
Limitations: Giving on a national basis, with emphasis on the New York, NY area; support also in Israel.
Publications: Application guidelines, program policy statement.
Application information: Accepts NY/NJ Common Application Form from organizations; applications for fellowships not accepted. Application form required.
Officers: Seymour Zises, Pres.; Jenny Morgenthau, Exec. V.P.; Edwin H. Stern III, V.P.; Linda Gerstel, Secy.- Treas.
Trustees: Valerie Block, James A. Block, Martin Blumenthal, Beverly S. Coleman, Babeth Fribourg, Jerome W. Gottesman, Sally Gottesman, William M. Heineman, Abby Knopp, Ezra P. Mager, Ellen Merlo, George W. Naumburg, Jr., Misha Ratner, Francis F. Rosenbaum, Jr., Laura Scheuer, Christopher C. Schwabacher, Arthur D. Sporn.
EIN: 135562971
Codes: FD

33326
The Louis Comfort Tiffany Foundation
c/o American Federation of the Arts
41 E. 65th St.
New York, NY 10021
URL: http://www.tiffanyfoundation.org
Contact: Angela Westwater, Pres.

Association established in 1918 in NY.
Donor(s): Louis Comfort Tiffany.‡
Financial data (yr. ended 12/31/01): Grants paid, $700,000; assets, $8,045,085 (M); expenditures, $816,902; qualifying distributions, $751,203.
Limitations: Applications not accepted. Giving on a national basis.
Application information: Awards are by nomination only.
Officers and Trustees:* Angela Westwater,* Pres.; Robert Meltzer,* V.P.; Gerard Jones,* Secy.; Robert Shapiro,* Treas.; William Bailey, Amanda M. Burden, Chuck Close, Amanda Cruz, Arthur Danto, Carroll Dunham, Kerry James Marshall, David Pease, John Perreault, Judy Pfaff, Robert Shapiro, Cindy Sherman, Lowery Sims, Paul Smith, Robert Storr.
EIN: 131689389
Codes: FD, GTI

33327
The Spingold Foundation, Inc.
(Formerly Nate B. and Frances Spingold Foundation, Inc.)
c/o Holland & Knight, LLP
195 Broadway, 23rd Fl.
New York, NY 10007
Contact: Mary Ellen Sweeney, Legal Asst.

Incorporated in 1955 in NY.
Donor(s): Frances Spingold,‡ Nathan Breither Spingold.‡
Financial data (yr. ended 11/30/01): Grants paid, $698,500; assets, $10,981,279 (M); expenditures, $868,054; qualifying distributions, $737,842.
Limitations: Applications not accepted. Giving primarily in the metropolitan New York, NY, area.
Application information: Contributes only to pre-selected organizations. Unsolicited requests for funds not considered or acknowledged.
Officers: Daniel L. Kurtz, C.E.O. and Pres.; Lorance Hockert, V.P. and Treas.
Directors: Elizabeth Olofson, Ruth Rosenblatt, M.D.
EIN: 136107659
Codes: FD

33328
Mary A. H. Rumsey Foundation
c/o Brown Brothers Harriman Trust Co.
63 Wall St., 23rd Fl.
New York, NY 10005-3062

Established in 1984 in NY.
Donor(s): Mary A.H. Rumsey.‡
Financial data (yr. ended 09/30/00): Grants paid, $698,450; assets, $11,774,533 (M); expenditures, $814,549; qualifying distributions, $739,355.
Limitations: Applications not accepted. Giving primarily in the greater metropolitan New York, NY, area.
Application information: Contributes only to pre-selected organizations.
Officers and Directors:* Charles Cary Rumsey,* Pres.; Mary M. Rumsey,* V.P.; William F. Hibberd, Secy.; Anna T. Korniczky, Treas.; Edwin R. Ward, Douglas F. Williamson, Jr.
EIN: 133244314
Codes: FD

33329
Great Island Foundation
c/o US Trust Co.
114 W. 47th St., Ste. TAXVAS
New York, NY 10036

Established in 1994 in DE.
Donor(s): Eliot Chace Nolen, Wilson Nolen.
Financial data (yr. ended 12/31/99): Grants paid, $696,834; assets, $10,920,570 (M); gifts received, $194,080; expenditures, $702,408; qualifying distributions, $700,596.
Limitations: Giving primarily in New York, NY.
Application information: Unsolicited requests for funds not accepted.
Directors: Eliot Chace Nolen, Wilson Nolen.
EIN: 134049061
Codes: FD

33330
W. P. Stewart & Co. Foundation, Inc.
527 Madison Ave.
New York, NY 10022

Established in 1998 in NY and DE.
Donor(s): W.P. Stewart & Co., Inc.
Financial data (yr. ended 12/31/01): Grants paid, $696,525; assets, $508,325 (M); expenditures, $763,825; qualifying distributions, $698,263.
Limitations: Applications not accepted. Giving on a national and international basis.
Application information: Contributes only to pre-selected organizations.
Officers: William P. Stewart, Chair.; John C. Russell, Pres.; Lisa D. Levey, Secy.; Sandra Coleman, Treas.
Directors: Marilyn G. Breslow, Robert L. Rohn, Harry W. Segalas.
EIN: 134034704
Codes: CS, FD, CD

33331
Victorinox-Swiss Army Knife Foundation
645 Madison Ave., Ste. 500
New York, NY 10022

Established in 1993 in NY.
Donor(s): The Forschner Group, Inc., Victorinox Cutlery Co., Brae Group, Inc., Victorinox.
Financial data (yr. ended 12/31/01): Grants paid, $696,232; assets, $639,544 (M); gifts received, $250,000; expenditures, $707,067; qualifying distributions, $707,067.
Limitations: Applications not accepted. Giving on a national basis, with some emphasis on NY.
Application information: Contributes only to pre-selected organizations.
Officers and Directors:* Louis Marx, Jr.,* Pres.; Robert W. Lenthe, Secy.-Treas.; Alicia Munoz, Exec. Dir.; Herbert M. Friedman, M. Leo Hart, Lindsay Marx, Louis Marx III, Stanley R. Rawn, Jr., John Spencer.
EIN: 133692303
Codes: CS, FD, CD

33332
Waterfowl Research Foundation, Inc.
c/o Milbank, Tweed, Hadley & McCloy
1 Chase Manhattan Plz.
New York, NY 10005
Application address: c/o C.L. Wainwright, 57 Dunemere Ln., East Hampton, N.Y. 11937
Contact: Carroll L. Wainwright, Jr., Pres.

Established in 1955 in NY.
Donor(s): M.E. Davis.‡
Financial data (yr. ended 12/31/01): Grants paid, $696,000; assets, $10,108,140 (M); expenditures, $777,895; qualifying distributions, $698,522.
Limitations: Giving primarily in the U.S. and Canada.
Application information: Application form not required.
Officers: Carroll L. Wainwright, Jr., Pres.; Lincoln P. Lyman, Secy.
EIN: 136122167
Codes: FD

33333
Raymond & Beverly Sackler Fund for the Arts & Sciences
c/o Chadbourne & Parke
30 Rockefeller, Ste. 3218
New York, NY 10112-0129

Established in 2001 in DE.
Donor(s): Raymond R. Sackler.
Financial data (yr. ended 12/31/01): Grants paid, $695,000; assets, $25 (M); gifts received, $695,025; expenditures, $695,000; qualifying distributions, $695,000.
Limitations: Applications not accepted. Giving primarily in CT, MA, and NY.
Application information: Contributes only to pre-selected organizations.
Officers and Directors:* Beverly Sackler,* Chair.; Raymond R. Sackler,* Pres.; Richard S. Sackler,* V.P. and Secy.; Jonathan D. Sackler,* V.P. and Treas.
EIN: 134085037
Codes: FD

33334
Buddha Dharma Kyokai (Society), Inc.
c/o Thelen, Reid, & Priest
40 W. 57th St.
New York, NY 10019
Contact: K.W. Kolbe, Secy.

Established in 1997.
Financial data (yr. ended 12/31/00): Grants paid, $694,875; assets, $10,972,789 (M); expenditures, $980,099; qualifying distributions, $903,396.
Limitations: Applications not accepted.
Application information: Contributes only to pre-selected organizations.
Officers: Rev. Kenryu Tsuji, Pres.; K. William Kolbe, Secy.; Shigeru Yomamoto, Treas.
Trustees: Shosen Bando, Noboru Hanyu, Takamaro Shigaragi, Bishop Hirofumi Watanabe, Rev. Seishin Yamashita.
EIN: 222706437
Codes: FD

33335
Larsen Fund
c/o Condon, O'Meara, McGinty & Donnelly, LLP
300 E. 42nd St
New York, NY 10017-5947
Application address: 2537 Post Rd., Ste. 224, Southport, CT 06490
Contact: Patricia S. Palmer, Grants Admin.

Incorporated in 1941 in NY.
Donor(s): Roy E. Larsen.‡
Financial data (yr. ended 12/31/01): Grants paid, $693,233; assets, $12,869,339 (M); expenditures, $982,619; qualifying distributions, $791,803.
Limitations: Giving primarily in CT, MA, the Minneapolis, MN, area, and the New York, NY, area.
Publications: Annual report (including application guidelines).
Application information: Application form not required.
Officers and Directors:* Robert R. Larsen,* Pres.; Ann Larsen Simonson,* 1st V.P.; Christopher Larsen,* 2nd V.P.; Jonathan Z. Larsen,* Secy.; David L. Johnson,* Treas.
EIN: 136104430
Codes: FD

33336
The William and Estelle Golub Foundation, Inc.
501 Duanesburg Rd.
Schenectady, NY 12306-1058

Established in 1986 in NY.
Donor(s): William Golub,‡ Estelle Golub.‡
Financial data (yr. ended 12/31/01): Grants paid, $692,057; assets, $16,231,099 (M); gifts received, $429,703; expenditures, $775,079; qualifying distributions, $693,092.
Limitations: Applications not accepted. Giving primarily in Albany and Schenectady, NY.
Application information: Contributes only to pre-selected organizations.
Officers and Trustees:* Neil M. Golub,* Pres. and Treas.; Mona Golub, Secy.; Jane Golub.
EIN: 222809785
Codes: FD

33337
The Link Foundation
c/o Binghamton University Fdn.
P.O. Box 6005
Binghamton, NY 13902-6005
Contact: Thomas F. Kelly, Tr.

Trust established in 1953 in NY.
Donor(s): Edwin A. Link,‡ Mrs. Edwin A. Link,‡ Link Div. of CAE.
Financial data (yr. ended 06/30/01): Grants paid, $691,986; assets, $13,377,587 (M); gifts received, $275; expenditures, $730,029; qualifying distributions, $702,360.
Limitations: Giving primarily in FL and NY.
Publications: Informational brochure (including application guidelines).
Application information: Application form required.
Officers and Trustees:* David M. Gouldin,* Chair.; Thomas F. Kelly,* Secy.; Douglas R. Johnson, Treas.; Jon Forbes, Ronald N. Hendricks.
Special Advisors: Andrew Clark, Barry Kelly, Marilyn Link, Lee Lynd, Stuart McCarty, Richard Murray, Robert Sproull, Brian J. Thompson, William D. Turner.
EIN: 536011109
Codes: FD

33338
The Treetops Foundation
c/o Reminick Aarons & Co., LLP
1430 Broadway, 17th Fl.
New York, NY 10018

Established in 1999 in NY.
Donor(s): Lisa Belzberg, Matthew Bronfman.
Financial data (yr. ended 12/31/01): Grants paid, $689,912; assets, $103,292 (M); gifts received, $811,002; expenditures, $717,367; qualifying distributions, $685,904.
Limitations: Applications not accepted. Giving primarily in NY.
Application information: Contributes only to pre-selected organizations.
Trustees: Lisa Belzberg, Matthew Bronfman.
EIN: 134093466
Codes: FD

33339
The Wooden Nickel Foundation
466 Lexington Ave., 10th Fl.
New York, NY 10017

Established in 1997 in PA and NY.
Donor(s): Lionel I. Pincus.
Financial data (yr. ended 12/31/00): Grants paid, $688,780; assets, $7,437,797 (M); expenditures, $692,170; qualifying distributions, $687,264.
Limitations: Applications not accepted. Giving primarily in NY.
Application information: Contributes only to pre-selected organizations.
Officers: Lionel I. Pincus, Pres.; Edwin Gustafson, Jr., Secy.-Treas.
EIN: 232865370
Codes: FD

33340
The Afognak Foundation
c/o U.S. Trust
114 W. 47th St.
New York, NY 10036
FAX: (212) 852-3377
Contact: Linda Franciscovich, Managing Dir., or Carolyn Larke, V.P., U.S. Trust

Established in 1998 in MA.
Financial data (yr. ended 12/31/01): Grants paid, $688,100; assets, $14,921,494 (M); expenditures, $702,471; qualifying distributions, $687,497.
Limitations: Applications not accepted.
Application information: Contributes only to pre-selected organizations.
Trustee: Elizabeth King.
EIN: 061521981
Codes: FD

33341
Louis & Gloria Flanzer Charitable Trust
c/o E. Kaplan
335 Madison Ave., Ste. 1500
New York, NY 10017

Established in 1996 in FL.
Donor(s): Louis Flanzer, Gloria Flanzer.
Financial data (yr. ended 12/31/01): Grants paid, $686,890; assets, $10,468,420 (M); gifts received, $1,005,919; expenditures, $692,435; qualifying distributions, $686,990.
Limitations: Applications not accepted. Giving primarily in NY.
Application information: Contributes only to pre-selected organizations.
Trustees: Gloria Flanzer, Louis Flanzer.
EIN: 137080259
Codes: FD

33342
Valerie & Charles Diker Fund, Inc.
c/o Richard A. Eisner & Co.
575 Madison Ave.
New York, NY 10022

Established in 1961 in NY.
Donor(s): Charles Diker, Valerie Diker.
Financial data (yr. ended 11/30/01): Grants paid, $686,619; assets, $4,363,536 (M); expenditures, $750,465; qualifying distributions, $699,988.
Limitations: Applications not accepted. Giving primarily in New York, NY; some giving also in Cambridge, MA and Santa Fe, NM.
Application information: Contributes only to pre-selected organizations.
Directors: Charles Diker, Valerie Diker.
EIN: 136075504
Codes: FD

33343
Moshe Feldman Charitable Foundation
c/o Pincus Neiman
217 Havemeyer St., Ste. 505
Brooklyn, NY 11211
Contact: Dov Feldman, Tr.

Established in 1994 in NY.
Financial data (yr. ended 10/31/01): Grants paid, $686,263; assets, $1,109,462 (M); gifts received, $60,000; expenditures, $691,144; qualifying distributions, $685,447.
Limitations: Applications not accepted. Giving primarily in NY.
Application information: Contributes only to pre-selected organizations.
Trustees: Dov Feldman, Heni Haifetz, Evelyn Lefkowitz.
EIN: 113237941
Codes: FD

33344
The Landreth Family Foundation
(Formerly William C. Landreth Foundation)
c/o BCRS Assocs., LLP
100 Wall St., 11th Fl.
New York, NY 10005

Established in 1985 in NY.
Donor(s): William C. Landreth.
Financial data (yr. ended 05/31/01): Grants paid, $686,034; assets, $4,448,515 (M); expenditures, $698,007; qualifying distributions, $686,151.
Limitations: Applications not accepted. Giving primarily in CA.
Application information: Contributes only to pre-selected organizations.
Trustees: Keith Howard, Jeanne Murphy Landreth, Kerry Cathryn Landreth, Peter William Landreth, William C. Landreth.
EIN: 133318159
Codes: FD

33345
Sarah I. Schieffelin Residuary Trust
c/o The Bank of New York
1 Wall St., 28th Fl.
New York, NY 10286 (212) 635-1520
Application address: c/o The Bank of New York, 1290 6th Ave., New York, NY 10104
Contact: Grace Allen

Established in 1976.
Donor(s): Sarah I. Schieffelin.‡
Financial data (yr. ended 03/31/01): Grants paid, $683,711; assets, $14,692,378 (M); expenditures, $790,390; qualifying distributions, $714,731.
Limitations: Giving primarily in New York, NY.
Application information: Application form not required.
Trustees: Thomas B. Fenlon, The Bank of New York.
EIN: 136724459
Codes: FD

33346
Mary Woodard Lasker Charitable Trust
110 E. 42nd St., Ste. 1300
New York, NY 10017 (212) 286-0222
FAX: (212) 286-0924; *E-mail:*
nhunt@laskerfoundation.org; *URL:* http://www.laskerfoundation.org
Contact: Dr. Neen Hunt, Pres.

Established in 1994 in NY.
Donor(s): Mary W. Lasker.‡
Financial data (yr. ended 12/31/99): Grants paid, $683,671; assets, $28,018,938 (M); gifts received, $350,461; expenditures, $1,995,403; qualifying distributions, $1,511,595.
Limitations: Giving primarily in NY.
Officers and Trustees:* James W. Fordyce,* Chair.; Neen Hunt, Pres.; Christopher Brody, James E. Hughes.
EIN: 137049274
Codes: FD

33347
St. Faith's House Foundation
16 Crest Dr.
Tarrytown, NY 10591 (914) 631-6065
Additional address: P.O. Box 308, Ardsley-on-Hudson, NY 10503
Contact: Ann D. Phillips, Chair., Grants Comm.

Incorporated in 1901 in NY as St. Faith's House; reorganized in 1973 as a private foundation.
Financial data (yr. ended 06/30/01): Grants paid, $683,000; assets, $10,614,067 (M); expenditures, $825,476; qualifying distributions, $703,090.
Limitations: Giving restricted to Westchester County, NY.
Publications: Application guidelines.
Application information: Distributions awarded twice annually. Application form required.
Officers and Directors:* Mrs. C. Edward Midgley,* Pres.; Mrs. John C. Keenan, V.P.; Mrs. Joseph E. Rogers,* V.P.; Robert C. Myers,* Secy.; Daniel H. Childs,* Treas.; Mrs. William Bush, Bruce E. Clark, John A. Dimling, Mrs. Robert L. Huston, Michael H. Lowry, Mrs. Robert W. Lyman, Ann D. Phillips, Mrs. William Shore, Harvey J. Struthers, Jr., Mrs. Maarten van Hengel.
EIN: 131740123
Codes: FD

33348
Nicholas B. Ottaway Foundation, Inc.
P.O. Box 401
Campbell Hall, NY 10916-0401
(845) 294-4915
FAX: (914) 294-8591
Contact: Diane C. Massey, Secy.

Established in 1967 in NY.
Donor(s): Members of the Ottaway family.
Financial data (yr. ended 10/31/01): Grants paid, $682,100; assets, $2,504,096 (M); gifts received, $629,250; expenditures, $728,086; qualifying distributions, $711,579.
Application information: Application form not required.
Officers and Trustees:* Ruth O. Sherer,* Pres.; Jay W. Ottaway,* V.P.; Diane C. Massey,* Secy.; Christopher H. Ottaway,* Treas.; Alexandra H. Ottaway, David Ottaway, Eric B. Ottaway, James W. Ottaway, James H. Ottaway, Jr., Marina S. Ottaway, Robin Ottaway, Ruth B. Ottaway, Frank Alexei Sherer.
EIN: 141505939

33348—NEW YORK

Codes: FD, GTI

33349
Adelson Family Foundation
c/o Alliance Capital Mgmt.
1345 Ave. of the Americas
New York, NY 10105

Established in 2000 in NY.
Donor(s): Andrew Adelson, Nancy Adelson.
Financial data (yr. ended 12/31/01): Grants paid, $681,243; assets, $5,830,311 (M); gifts received, $1,000,000; expenditures, $687,738; qualifying distributions, $678,438.
Limitations: Applications not accepted. Giving primarily in NY.
Application information: Contributes only to pre-selected organizations.
Trustees: Andrew Adelson, Nancy Adelson.
EIN: 223769645
Codes: FD

33350
The Damaris Foundation
c/o U.S. Trust
114 W. 47th St.
New York, NY 10036

Established in 1992 in NY.
Donor(s): Gretchen K. Finch.
Financial data (yr. ended 12/31/01): Grants paid, $680,000; assets, $4,063,536 (M); expenditures, $695,774; qualifying distributions, $682,238.
Limitations: Applications not accepted. Giving on a national basis.
Application information: Contributes only to pre-selected organizations.
Trustee: U.S. Trust.
EIN: 133709363
Codes: FD

33351
Henry B. Plant Memorial Fund, Inc.
c/o U.S. Trust
114 W. 47th St., 8th Fl.
New York, NY 10036-1532
FAX: (212) 852-3377
Contact: Andrew D. Lane, V.P.

Incorporated in 1947 in NY.
Donor(s): Amy P. Statter.
Financial data (yr. ended 12/31/01): Grants paid, $680,000; assets, $12,377,433 (M); expenditures, $728,561; qualifying distributions, $674,914.
Limitations: Applications not accepted.
Application information: Contributes only to pre-selected organizations.
Officers and Directors:* Mrs. J. Phillip Lee,* Pres.; Mrs. David C. Oxman,* V.P.
Advisor: U.S. Trust.
EIN: 136077327
Codes: FD

33352
Beatrice Snyder Foundation
592 5th Ave., 6th Fl.
New York, NY 10036-4707

Established in 1998 in NJ.
Donor(s): Harold Snyder, Beryl Snyder, Jay Snyder.
Financial data (yr. ended 05/31/01): Grants paid, $678,610; assets, $3,949,089 (M); gifts received, $1,115,857; expenditures, $712,936; qualifying distributions, $679,714.
Limitations: Applications not accepted. Giving primarily in NY.
Application information: Contributes only to pre-selected organizations.
Trustees: Beryl L. Snyder, Brian S. Snyder, Harold Snyder, Jay T. Snyder.
EIN: 223595071

Codes: FD

33353
PBO Fund, Inc.
c/o American Express Tax Svcs.
1185 Ave. of the Americas
New York, NY 10036

Established in 1961.
Donor(s): William J. Oppenheim, Paula K. Oppenheim.
Financial data (yr. ended 08/31/01): Grants paid, $677,052; assets, $14,086,413 (M); expenditures, $868,387; qualifying distributions, $685,864.
Limitations: Applications not accepted. Giving primarily in Greenwich, CT, and New York, NY.
Application information: Contributes only to pre-selected organizations.
Officers: William J. Oppenheim, Pres. and Treas.; Paula K. Oppenheim, V.P. and Secy.
EIN: 136158857
Codes: FD

33354
The Dammann Fund, Inc.
c/o John P. Engel & Assocs.
1740 Broadway, 25th Fl.
New York, NY 10019 (212) 262-9154
FAX: (212) 489-8340
Contact: Penelope Johnston, Pres.

Incorporated in 1946 in NY.
Donor(s): Members of the Dammann family.
Financial data (yr. ended 11/30/01): Grants paid, $676,670; assets, $12,512,331 (M); expenditures, $926,795; qualifying distributions, $789,675.
Limitations: Giving primarily in the greater metropolitan New York, NY, area, including southern CT; giving also in Washington, DC, Boston, MA, and surrounding communities.
Application information: Application form required.
Officers and Directors:* Penelope D. Johnston,* Pres.; Christopher M. Kramer, V.P.; Daniel R. Kramer,* V.P.; Alistair D. Johnston,* Secy.-Treas.
EIN: 136089896
Codes: FD

33355
Youth Foundation, Inc.
36 W. 44th St., Ste. 716
New York, NY 10036-8144 (212) 840-6291
FAX: (212) 840-6747; E-mail: youthfdn@aol.com; URL: http://fdncenter.org/grantmaker/youthfdn
Contact: Johanna M. Lee

Incorporated in 1940 in NY.
Donor(s): Alexander M. Hadden,‡ Mrs. Alexander M. Hadden.‡
Financial data (yr. ended 12/31/01): Grants paid, $675,000; assets, $11,314,422 (M); gifts received, $14,825; expenditures, $851,847; qualifying distributions, $785,838.
Limitations: Giving on a national basis.
Publications: Application guidelines, program policy statement.
Application information: Applications limited to U.S. citizens. Application form required.
Officers and Directors:* Robert W. Radsch,* Pres.; Pamela S. Fulweiler,* V.P.; Guy N. Robinson,* Secy.; S. Scott Nicholls, Jr., Treas.; and 10 additional directors.
EIN: 136093036
Codes: FD

33356
The Stephen H. and Alida Brill Scheuer Foundation, Inc.
320 E. 54th St., Ste. 2A
New York, NY 10022 (212) 980-7945
FAX: (212) 644-3903
Contact: Patricia Dandonoli, Exec. Dir.

Established around 1993.
Donor(s): The S.H. and Helen R. Scheuer Family Foundation.
Financial data (yr. ended 12/31/99): Grants paid, $674,723; assets, $3,976,687 (M); expenditures, $1,084,627; qualifying distributions, $725,902.
Limitations: Applications not accepted. Giving on a national basis.
Application information: Contributes only to pre-selected organizations.
Officers: Alida Brill Scheuer, Pres. and Treas.; Daniel L. Kurtz, V.P. and Secy.
Directors: Loren D. Ross, Stephen H. Scheuer.
EIN: 133725704
Codes: FD

33357
The Hammerman and Fisch Foundation
(Formerly The Stephen & Eleanor Hammerman Foundation)
1806 Bay Blvd.
Atlantic Beach, NY 11509

Established in 1993 in NY.
Donor(s): Stephen Hammerman.
Financial data (yr. ended 12/31/00): Grants paid, $672,889; assets, $3,155,215 (M); gifts received, $2,082,400; expenditures, $707,484; qualifying distributions, $672,899.
Limitations: Applications not accepted. Giving primarily in NY.
Application information: Contributes only to pre-selected organizations.
Trustees: Eleanor Hammerman, Stephen Hammerman.
EIN: 116436649
Codes: FD

33358
Richard C. & Karen E. Penfold Family Foundation, Inc.
4588 S. Park Ave.
Blasdell, NY 14219

Established in 1995 in NY.
Donor(s): Karen E. Penfold, Richard C. Penfold, South Park Enterprises, Inc.
Financial data (yr. ended 06/30/01): Grants paid, $670,510; assets, $1,988,822 (M); gifts received, $8,602; expenditures, $697,559; qualifying distributions, $673,602.
Limitations: Applications not accepted. Giving on a national basis, with emphasis on NY.
Application information: Contributes only to pre-selected organizations.
Directors: Karen E. Penfold, Patrick R. Penfold, Richard C. Penfold.
EIN: 161490689
Codes: FD

33359
F. & J.S. Fund, Inc.
c/o Amex TBS, Inc.
1185 Ave. of the Americas
New York, NY 10036

Established in 1969.
Donor(s): David W. and Sadie Klau Foundation.
Financial data (yr. ended 12/31/01): Grants paid, $669,431; assets, $12,493,336 (M); expenditures, $793,937; qualifying distributions, $667,610.
Limitations: Applications not accepted. Giving primarily in NY.

Application information: Contributes only to pre-selected organizations.
Officers: Felice K. Shea, Pres. and Treas.; Steven J.C. Shea, V.P.
EIN: 237042425
Codes: FD

33360
The Godinger Lefkowitz Memorial Foundation, Inc.
63-15 Traffic Ave.
Ridgewood, NY 11385
Contact: William Lefkowitz, V.P.

Donor(s): Arnold Godinger, William Lefkowitz, Godindger Silver Art, Ltd.
Financial data (yr. ended 11/30/01): Grants paid, $669,237; assets, $37,385 (M); gifts received, $685,000; expenditures, $669,287; qualifying distributions, $669,237.
Officers: Arnold Godinger, Pres.; William Lefkowitz, V.P.; Rita Godinger, Secy.
EIN: 133800381
Codes: FD

33361
Theodore Luce Charitable Trust
c/o JPMorgan Chase Bank
1211 Ave. of the Americas, 38th Fl.
New York, NY 10036   (212) 789-5715
E-mail: philp_lisa@jpmorgan.com
Contact: Lisa Philp

Established in 1984 in NY.
Financial data (yr. ended 07/31/01): Grants paid, $667,000; assets, $13,204,054 (M); expenditures, $769,166; qualifying distributions, $673,327.
Limitations: Applications not accepted. Giving primarily in New York, NY.
Application information: Contributes only to pre-selected organizations. Grants made during the annual cycle in the summer. Because the 2002 RFP allowed for up to 3 years of funding, an open grant cycle will not occur until 2005.
Trustee: JPMorgan Chase Bank.
EIN: 136029703
Codes: FD

33362
The Daphne Foundation
419 E. 86th St.
New York, NY 10028   (212) 845-3845
FAX: (212) 831-1310; *E-mail:* daphnest@aol.com
Contact: Eloisa Gordon, Exec. Dir.

Established in 1990 in CA and NY.
Donor(s): Abigail E. Disney.
Financial data (yr. ended 06/30/01): Grants paid, $665,880; assets, $11,352,929 (M); expenditures, $840,506; qualifying distributions, $748,809.
Limitations: Giving primarily in the metropolitan New York, NY, area.
Publications: Application guidelines, grants list.
Officers: Abigail E. Disney, Pres.; Pierre Hauser II, Secy. and C.F.O.
EIN: 954288541
Codes: FD

33363
The M. J. A. Safdeye Foundation
c/o E.S. Originals, Inc.
450 W. 33rd St.
New York, NY 10001-3305   (212) 736-8124
Contact: Michael Safdeye, Pres.

Established in 1987 in DE.
Donor(s): Alan J. Safdeye, Joseph Safdeye, Michael Safdeye.
Financial data (yr. ended 12/31/99): Grants paid, $663,448; assets, $115 (M); gifts received, $580,496; expenditures, $666,042; qualifying distributions, $661,100.
Limitations: Giving primarily in NJ and NY.
Officers and Directors:* Michael Safdeye,* Pres.; Joseph Safdeye,* V.P.; Alan J. Safdeye,* Secy.-Treas.
EIN: 133446204
Codes: FD

33364
The Baird Foundation
P.O. Box 1210, Ellicott Sta.
Buffalo, NY 14205   (716) 883-2429
Contact: Catherine F. Schweitzer, Mgr.

Trust established in 1947 in NY.
Donor(s): Flora M. Baird,‡ Frank B. Baird, Jr.,‡ Cameron Baird,‡ William C. Baird.‡
Financial data (yr. ended 12/31/01): Grants paid, $659,461; assets, $11,127,368 (M); expenditures, $827,615; qualifying distributions, $742,624.
Limitations: Giving primarily in Erie County, NY.
Publications: Grants list.
Application information: Application form not required.
Trustees: Arthur W. Cryer, Robert J.A. Irwin, William Baird Irwin, Catherine F. Schweitzer.
EIN: 166023080
Codes: FD

33365
Donovan Foundation
c/o Michael Donovan
1040 Fifth Ave., Ste. 2A
New York, NY 10028-0137

Established in 1999 in NY.
Donor(s): Michael D.S. Donovan.
Financial data (yr. ended 12/31/01): Grants paid, $658,900; assets, $2,468,564 (M); gifts received, $950,000; expenditures, $666,888; qualifying distributions, $665,524.
Limitations: Giving primarily in NY and VA.
Trustees: Stephen Briganti, Linda Ramsey Donovan, Michael D.S. Donovan.
EIN: 137205869
Codes: FD

33366
White Flowers Foundation
c/o BCRS Assocs., LLC
100 Wall St., 11th Fl.
New York, NY 10005
Mailing address: 4 E. 70th St., No. 9A, New York, NY 10021
Contact: Mary H. White, Tr.

Established in 1989 in NY.
Donor(s): J. Christopher Flowers.
Financial data (yr. ended 05/31/01): Grants paid, $657,784; assets, $863,976 (M); gifts received, $1,156,080; expenditures, $659,684; qualifying distributions, $650,520.
Limitations: Applications not accepted. Giving primarily in New York, NY.
Application information: Contributes only to pre-selected organizations.
Trustees: J. Christopher Flowers, Mary H. White.
EIN: 133532030
Codes: FD

33367
Martin S. Kimmel Foundation
c/o Martin S. Kimmel
3333 New Hyde Park Rd., Ste. 100
New Hyde Park, NY 11042-1205

Established in 1994 in NY.
Donor(s): Martin S. Kimmel.
Financial data (yr. ended 12/31/01): Grants paid, $656,000; assets, $1,990,574 (M); expenditures, $663,884; qualifying distributions, $651,757.
Limitations: Applications not accepted. Giving primarily in New York, NY.
Application information: Contributes only to pre-selected organizations.
Trustee: Adam P. Kimmel, Martin S. Kimmel.
EIN: 137024058
Codes: FD

33368
The Robert K. Steel Family Foundation
c/o Goldman Sachs & Co.
85 Broad St., Tax Dept.
New York, NY 10004
Contact: Robert K. Steel, Tr.

Established in 1989 in NY.
Donor(s): Robert K. Steel Family.
Financial data (yr. ended 04/30/01): Grants paid, $656,000; assets, $8,895,892 (M); gifts received, $2,990,181; expenditures, $715,335; qualifying distributions, $656,275.
Limitations: Applications not accepted. Giving on a national basis, with some emphasis on CT and NY.
Application information: Contributes only to pre-selected organizations.
Trustees: Gillian V. Steel, Robert K. Steel.
EIN: 133531990
Codes: FD

33369
Amicus Foundation, Inc.
c/o Philip Mintz
29 W. 38th St.
New York, NY 10018

Established in 1976.
Financial data (yr. ended 10/31/01): Grants paid, $655,000; assets, $13,375,418 (M); expenditures, $707,956; qualifying distributions, $670,508.
Limitations: Applications not accepted. Giving primarily in FL, NH, and NY.
Application information: Contributes only to pre-selected organizations.
Officers and Directors:* Leigh Weiner,* Pres.; Sharyn Weiner, V.P.; Theodore Schiffman,* Treas.
EIN: 136075489
Codes: FD

33370
The Katzenberger Foundation, Inc.
200 Park Ave., S., Ste. 1700
New York, NY 10003   (212) 315-5575
Contact: Margaret Axelrod

Incorporated in 1952 in NY.
Donor(s): Walter B. Katzenberger,‡ Helen Katherine Katzenberger.‡
Financial data (yr. ended 11/30/01): Grants paid, $655,000; assets, $17,749,496 (M); expenditures, $906,313; qualifying distributions, $737,340.
Limitations: Giving primarily in AZ, Chicago, IL, NY, and OH.
Publications: Financial statement.
Application information: Application form not required.
Officers and Directors:* Abner J. Golieb,* Pres.; Edward Davis,* Secy.; Margaret Axelrod, Treas.; Richard Eason, George Haibloom, Earl Swanson.
EIN: 136094434
Codes: FD

33371
The Corey Foundation
c/o M. Corey
2 Columbus Ave., Ste. 35A
New York, NY 10023-6933

Established in 1998 in NY.
Donor(s): Emilie Corey, Michael Corey.

33371—NEW YORK

Financial data (yr. ended 12/31/01): Grants paid, $654,210; assets, $18,651,467 (M); gifts received, $9,500,000; expenditures, $704,878; qualifying distributions, $656,034.
Limitations: Applications not accepted.
Application information: Contributes only to pre-selected organizations.
Trustees: Emilie Corey, Michael Corey.
EIN: 113453820
Codes: FD

33372
Allene Reuss Memorial Trust
c/o The Bank of New York, Tax Dept.
1 Wall St., 28th Fl.
New York, NY 10286
Application address: c/o Leboeuf, Lamb, Greene and McRae, 125 W. 55th St. New York, NY 10019
Contact: Richard Pershan, Tr.

Established in 1996 in France.
Financial data (yr. ended 12/31/01): Grants paid, $652,003; assets, $13,907,326 (M); gifts received, $46,891; expenditures, $780,648; qualifying distributions, $678,330.
Limitations: Giving primarily in NY.
Application information: Application form not required.
Trustees: Richard Pershan, The Bank of New York.
EIN: 137086745
Codes: FD

33373
The Purchase Fund
c/o B. Strauss Assocs., Ltd.
307 5th Ave., 8th Fl.
New York, NY 10016-6517

Established in 1992 in NY.
Donor(s): Peter M. Flanigan.
Financial data (yr. ended 09/30/01): Grants paid, $651,750; assets, $1,096,137 (M); gifts received, $1,271,221; expenditures, $650,447; qualifying distributions, $636,321.
Limitations: Applications not accepted. Giving on a national basis, with emphasis on NY.
Application information: Contributes only to pre-selected organizations.
Trustees: Brigid S. Flanigan, Peter M. Flanigan, Robert W. Flanigan, Timothy P. Flanigan, Brigid S. Flanigan Lezak, Megan F. Skakel.
EIN: 137005756
Codes: FD

33374
Fludzinski Foundation
c/o Thales
140 Broadway, 45th Fl.
New York, NY 10005

Donor(s): Marek T. Fludzinski.
Financial data (yr. ended 12/31/02): Grants paid, $651,010; assets, $1,371,493 (L); expenditures, $651,010; qualifying distributions, $651,010.
Limitations: Giving primarily in NY.
Trustees: Marek T. Fludzinski, Laurel Galgano.
EIN: 134147622

33375
The Western New York Foundation
Main Seneca Bldg., Ste. 1402
237 Main St.
Buffalo, NY 14203 (716) 847-6440
FAX: (716) 847-6440
Contact: Welles V. Moot, Jr., Pres.

Incorporated in 1951 in NY as the Wildroot Foundation; present name adopted in 1958.
Donor(s): Welles V. Moot.‡

Financial data (yr. ended 07/31/01): Grants paid, $650,125; assets, $13,348,442 (M); expenditures, $932,588; qualifying distributions, $761,345.
Limitations: Giving limited to the 8th Judicial District of NY (Erie, Niagara, Genesee, Wyoming, Allegany, Cattaraugus, and Chautauqua counties).
Publications: Annual report (including application guidelines), informational brochure.
Application information: Application form required.
Officers and Trustees:* Welles V. Moot, Jr.,* Pres.; John R. Moot,* Secy.; Richard E. Moot,* Treas.; Theodore Buerger, Jennifer Johnson, Brenda McDuffie, Trudy A. Mollenberg, Andrew Moot, Andrew R. Moot, John N. Walsh III.
EIN: 160845962
Codes: FD

33376
The Lincoln Fund
295 Madison Ave., Ste. 700
New York, NY 10017 (212) 686-4797
Contact: Mrs. Duer McLanahan, Pres.

Incorporated in 1898 in NY.
Financial data (yr. ended 06/30/01): Grants paid, $650,000; assets, $10,028,225 (M); expenditures, $735,333; qualifying distributions, $659,907.
Limitations: Giving limited to the greater metropolitan New York, NY, area.
Application information: Application form not required.
Officers and Directors:* Mrs. Duer McLanahan,* Pres.; Phyllis Brown,* Secy.; Christian Melhado,* Treas.; Mrs. Paule R. Alexander, Richard Brown, E. Eldred Hill, Carmelina Price, Keith Thomas, Darren Walker.
EIN: 131740466
Codes: FD

33377
Marvin Azrak and Sons Foundation
10 W. 33rd St., Rm. 516
New York, NY 10001

Established in 1994 in NY.
Donor(s): Marvin Azrak, members of the Azrak family.
Financial data (yr. ended 12/31/01): Grants paid, $647,803; assets, $686,006 (M); gifts received, $307,707; expenditures, $647,064; qualifying distributions, $647,713.
Limitations: Applications not accepted. Giving primarily in NJ, and New York, NY.
Application information: Contributes only to pre-selected organizations.
Officer: Marvin Azrak, Mgr.
Trustees: Adam Azrak, Elliot Azrak, Victor Azrak.
EIN: 133771410
Codes: FD

33378
The Wendling Foundation
80 Broad St., 17th Fl.
New York, NY 10004
FAX: (212) 764-4298
Contact: Michelle Lord

Established in 1984 in FL.
Donor(s): Helen C. Vanderbilt.‡
Financial data (yr. ended 12/31/01): Grants paid, $646,000; assets, $10,265,356 (M); expenditures, $799,536; qualifying distributions, $797,440.
Limitations: Applications not accepted. Giving on a national basis, with emphasis on Washington, DC, and the New England states, especially ME.
Publications: Grants list.
Application information: Application process, initiated by the board of directors, includes completion of application in Apr. and Nov. (1 month prior to board meeting). Grantees must be invited to submit proposals; unsolicited requests not accepted.
Officers and Directors:* John Cook, Jr.,* Chair.; Heleny Cook,* Pres.; Averill Cook,* V.P. and Secy.; Willard Cook,* Treas.; Rebecca Cook, Warren C. Cook.
EIN: 133249448
Codes: FD

33379
Louise B. & Edgar M. Cullman Foundation
641 Lexington Ave., 29th Fl.
New York, NY 10022-4599
Application address: 387 Park Ave. S., New York, NY 10016
Contact: Edgar M. Cullman, Chair.

Established in 1956 in NY.
Donor(s): Edgar M. Cullman.
Financial data (yr. ended 12/31/01): Grants paid, $645,558; assets, $10,236,371 (M); gifts received, $2,500; expenditures, $666,480; qualifying distributions, $643,481.
Limitations: Giving primarily in CT and NY.
Application information: Application form required.
Officers: Edgar M. Cullman, Chair.; Louise B. Cullman, V.P.
EIN: 136100041
Codes: FD

33380
The Mailman Foundation, Inc.
150 E. 58th St., 14th Fl.
New York, NY 10155
FAX: (212) 421-3163
Contact: Joseph V. Hastings, Secy.-Treas.

Incorporated in 1943 in DE.
Donor(s): Joseph L. Mailman,‡ Joseph S. Mailman.‡
Financial data (yr. ended 12/31/00): Grants paid, $645,115; assets, $42,794,840 (M); expenditures, $1,154,768; qualifying distributions, $678,172.
Limitations: Applications not accepted. Giving on a national basis.
Application information: Contributes only to pre-selected organizations.
Officers and Trustees:* Phyllis Mailman,* Pres.; Joshua L. Mailman,* V.P.; Jody Wolfe,* V.P.; Judson A. Wolfe,* V.P.; Joseph V. Hastings, Secy.-Treas.
EIN: 136161556
Codes: FD

33381
The Banfi Vintners Foundation
(Formerly The Villa Banfi Foundation)
1111 Cedar Swamp Rd.
Glen Head, NY 11545
Contact: John G. Troiano, Exec. Dir.

Established in 1982 in NY.
Donor(s): Banfi Products Corp.
Financial data (yr. ended 12/31/01): Grants paid, $644,740; assets, $13,355,002 (M); expenditures, $721,465; qualifying distributions, $686,940.
Limitations: Giving primarily in, but not limited to, MA and NY.
Officers and Directors:* Joan C. Rupp, Secy.; Philip D. Calderone, Treas.; John G. Troiano,* Exec. Dir.; Cristina N. Mariani, Harry F. Mariani, James W. Mariani, John Mariani.
EIN: 112622792
Codes: FD

33382
Irving Langer Charitable Trust
1465A Flatbush Ave.
Brooklyn, NY 11210

Established in 1999 in NY.
Financial data (yr. ended 12/31/01): Grants paid, $644,432; assets, $54,385 (M); gifts received, $675,981; expenditures, $644,604; qualifying distributions, $644,432.
Director: Irving Langer.
EIN: 116449730
Codes: FD

33383
The Paul Rapoport Foundation, Inc.
220 E. 60th St., Ste. 3H
New York, NY 10022 (212) 888-6578
URL: http://fdncenter.org/grantmaker/rapoport
Contact: Jane D. Schwartz, Exec. Dir.

Established in 1987 in NY.
Donor(s): Paul Rapoport.‡
Financial data (yr. ended 06/30/02): Grants paid, $643,800; assets, $12,094,240 (M); expenditures, $957,589; qualifying distributions, $818,833.
Limitations: Giving primarily in the metropolitan New York, NY, area.
Publications: Grants list, application guidelines.
Application information: Proposals submitted without application form will not be accepted. Application form required.
Officers: Jed Mattes, Pres.; Jerry Rumain, Secy.; James M. Rosenberg, Treas.; Jane Schwartz, Exec. Dir.
Directors: Julio Dicent-Taillepierre, Laurie Goldberger, Bea Hanson, Richard T. Harris, Jessica Mates, Daniel Rapoport.
EIN: 136892333
Codes: FD

33384
Lawrence and Isabel Barnett Charitable Foundation
c/o RSM McGladrey, Inc.
106 Corporate Park Dr., Ste. 417
White Plains, NY 10604

Established in 1986 in CA.
Donor(s): Lawrence R. Barnett.
Financial data (yr. ended 09/30/01): Grants paid, $642,975; assets, $10,692,712 (M); expenditures, $691,212; qualifying distributions, $637,545.
Limitations: Applications not accepted. Giving on a national basis.
Application information: Contributes only to pre-selected organizations.
Officers and Directors:* Lawrence R. Barnett,* Pres.; Lawrence R. Barnett, Jr., V.P. and Secy.; Isabel Barnett,* V.P.; James Joseph Barnett, V.P.; Laurey J. Barnett, V.P.
EIN: 943031397
Codes: FD

33385
Tarnopol Family Foundation, Inc.
(Formerly Michael & Lynne Tarnopol Foundation, Inc.)
c/o Bear Stearns & Co.
383 Madison Ave.
New York, NY 10279

Established in 1969 in NY.
Donor(s): Michael Tarnopol, Lynne Tarnopol, The Monterey Fund, Inc.
Financial data (yr. ended 12/31/01): Grants paid, $642,671; assets, $401,346 (M); gifts received, $455,145; expenditures, $650,768; qualifying distributions, $649,078.
Limitations: Applications not accepted. Giving primarily in New York, NY, and PA.
Application information: Contributes only to pre-selected organizations. Unsolicited requests for funds not accepted.
Officers and Directors:* Michael Tarnopol,* Pres.; Lynne Tarnopol,* V.P.; Joel Ehrenkranz,* Secy.
EIN: 132626280
Codes: FD

33386
The Ernst C. Stiefel Foundation
c/o Coudert Bros.
1114 Ave. of the Americas, 4th Fl.
New York, NY 10036-7703
Contact: Kenneth R. Page

Established in 1997.
Donor(s): Ernst C. Stiefel.‡
Financial data (yr. ended 12/31/01): Grants paid, $642,500; assets, $10,028,274 (M); expenditures, $707,873; qualifying distributions, $638,301.
Limitations: Giving primarily in NY.
Application information: Application form not required.
Trustees: Robert J. Gellert, Kenneth R. Page.
EIN: 137117155
Codes: FD

33387
Hultquist Foundation, Inc.
c/o Price, Flowers, Malin & Westerberg
P.O. Box 1219
Jamestown, NY 14701-1219
Contact: Thomas I. Flowers, Pres.

Established in 1965 in NY.
Financial data (yr. ended 06/30/01): Grants paid, $640,145; assets, $16,299,991 (M); expenditures, $726,850; qualifying distributions, $645,957.
Limitations: Giving limited to Chautauqua County, NY, with emphasis on Jamestown, NY.
Application information: Application form required.
Officers: Thomas I. Flowers, Pres.; Charles H. Price, V.P.; William L. Wright, V.P.; Robert F. Rohm, Jr., Secy.-Treas.
EIN: 160907729
Codes: FD

33388
Coles Family Foundation
c/o BCRS Assocs., LLC
100 Wall St., 11th Fl.
New York, NY 10005

Established in 1980 in NY.
Donor(s): Michael H. Coles, Joan C. Coles.‡
Financial data (yr. ended 03/31/01): Grants paid, $639,695; assets, $4,180,904 (M); expenditures, $741,839; qualifying distributions, $642,991.
Limitations: Applications not accepted. Giving primarily in the greater metropolitan New York, NY, area.
Application information: Contributes only to pre-selected organizations.
Trustees: Alison Aldredge, Douglas M.C. Coles, Isobel Coles, Michael H. Coles, Richard Coles, Caroline Scudder, Roy C. Smith.
EIN: 133050747
Codes: FD

33389
Eileen W. Bamberger Foundation
c/o Deutsche Trust Co. of NY
P.O. Box 1297, Church St. Sta.
New York, NY 10008

Established in 1994 in NY.
Financial data (yr. ended 12/31/01): Grants paid, $638,917; assets, $12,357,847 (M); expenditures, $743,630; qualifying distributions, $673,731.
Limitations: Applications not accepted. Giving primarily in NY.
Application information: Contributes only to pre-selected organizations.
Trustee: Deutsche Bank.
EIN: 137053837
Codes: FD

33390
The James & Judith K. Dimon Foundation
c/o Popper, Seger & Popper, LLP
192 Lexington Ave., 11th Fl.
New York, NY 10016

Established in 1996 in NY.
Donor(s): James Dimon, Judith K. Dimon.
Financial data (yr. ended 11/30/99): Grants paid, $637,251; assets, $8,656,393 (M); gifts received, $3,531,250; expenditures, $717,741; qualifying distributions, $660,851.
Limitations: Applications not accepted.
Application information: Contributes only to pre-selected organizations.
Officers: James Dimon, Pres.; Theodore Dimon, Secy.; Judith K. Dimon, Treas.
EIN: 133922199
Codes: FD

33391
The Peter T. Joseph Foundation
c/o Wendy G. Joseph
500 Park Ave.
New York, NY 10022

Established in 1990 in NY.
Donor(s): Peter T. Joseph.
Financial data (yr. ended 12/31/00): Grants paid, $637,156; assets, $6,416,003 (M); expenditures, $551,162; qualifying distributions, $649,723.
Limitations: Applications not accepted. Giving primarily in NJ, NY, and OH.
Application information: Contributes only to pre-selected organizations.
Officers and Directors:* Wendy Evans Joseph,* Pres.; Evelyn C. Joseph,* V.P.; Richard L. Veron,* V.P.; Kathleen Joseph Reinhart,* Secy.; John A. Silberman,* Treas.; Robert Kasdin.
EIN: 133562511
Codes: FD

33392
The Jamie and Steve Tisch Foundation, Inc.
(Formerly The Steve Tisch Foundation, Inc.)
c/o Mark J. Krinsky, C.P.A.
655 Madison Ave., 8th Fl.
New York, NY 10021-8043

Established in 1992 in NY.
Donor(s): Preston Robert Tisch.
Financial data (yr. ended 12/31/01): Grants paid, $634,959; assets, $13,860,869 (M); gifts received, $1,099,600; expenditures, $658,476; qualifying distributions, $645,399.
Limitations: Applications not accepted. Giving primarily in CA.
Application information: Contributes only to pre-selected organizations.
Officers: Steven E. Tisch, Pres.; Jamie L. Tisch, Sr. V.P.; Mark J. Krinsky, V.P.; Thomas M. Steinberg, V.P.; Barry L. Bloom, Secy.-Treas.
EIN: 133693586
Codes: FD

33393
The Textor Family Foundation
c/o BCRS Assocs., LLC
100 Wall St., 11th Fl.
New York, NY 10005

Established in 1991 in NY.
Donor(s): Donald F. Textor, Elaine R. Textor.

33393—NEW YORK

Financial data (yr. ended 05/31/01): Grants paid, $634,500; assets, $5,849,657 (M); gifts received, $1,006,669; expenditures, $725,750; qualifying distributions, $634,750.
Limitations: Applications not accepted. Giving primarily in NY.
Application information: Contributes only to pre-selected organizations.
Trustees: Donald F. Textor, Elaine R. Textor.
EIN: 133637703
Codes: FD

33394
The Riedman Foundation
45 East Ave.
Rochester, NY 14604 (716) 232-4424
Contact: John R. Riedman, Mgr.

Established in 1980.
Donor(s): John R. Riedman, Riedman Corp.
Financial data (yr. ended 12/31/01): Grants paid, $634,400; assets, $11,068,106 (M); expenditures, $664,895; qualifying distributions, $653,928.
Limitations: Giving primarily in NY, with emphasis on Rochester.
Application information: Application form not required.
Officer: John R. Riedman, Mgr.
EIN: 222279168
Codes: FD

33395
Marvin & Susan Ostreicher Family Foundation
184 Wildacre Ave.
Lawrence, NY 11559-1413
Application address: c/o Zell & Ettinger, C.P.A., 3001 Ave. M, Brooklyn, NY 11210

Established in 1994 in NY.
Donor(s): Marvin Ostreicher.
Financial data (yr. ended 11/30/00): Grants paid, $633,875; assets, $0 (M); gifts received, $559,000; expenditures, $634,893; qualifying distributions, $633,875.
Officers: Marvin Ostreicher, Pres.; Susan Ostreicher, Secy.
EIN: 113241597
Codes: FD

33396
Sandler Capital Management Charitable Foundation
767 5th Ave., 45th Fl.
New York, NY 10153

Established in 1999 in NY.
Donor(s): John Kornreich, Harvey Sandler, Michael J. Marocco, Andrew Sandler, David Lee, Doug Schimmel, Hannah Stone.
Financial data (yr. ended 12/31/00): Grants paid, $633,000; assets, $15,529 (M); gifts received, $510,000; expenditures, $657,331; qualifying distributions, $634,421.
Limitations: Applications not accepted.
Application information: Contributes only to pre-selected organizations.
Officers and Directors:* John Kornreich,* Pres.; Andrew Sandler,* Secy.; Michael J. Marocco,* Treas.
EIN: 134092619
Codes: FD

33397
The Cody Foundation
c/o Hinman Straub, PC
121 State St.
Albany, NY 12207 (518) 436-0751
E-mail: JohnA.@HSPM.com or DebraH@HSPM.com
Contact: Debra Hamway

Established in 1992 in NY.
Financial data (yr. ended 12/31/01): Grants paid, $632,500; assets, $1,557,852 (M); gifts received, $591,925; expenditures, $637,888; qualifying distributions, $632,500.
Limitations: Applications not accepted. Giving limited to CT and NY.
Application information: Contributes only to pre-selected organizations.
Trustees: Frank Gifford, Kathie Lee Gifford.
EIN: 136992402
Codes: FD

33398
The Bank of New York Foundation
c/o The Bank of New York, Tax Dept.
1 Wall St., 28th Fl.
New York, NY 10286

Established in 1997 in NY.
Donor(s): The Bank of New York.
Financial data (yr. ended 12/31/01): Grants paid, $632,367; assets, $1,905 (L); gifts received, $597,214; expenditures, $639,057; qualifying distributions, $628,912.
Limitations: Applications not accepted. Giving primarily in NY.
Application information: Contributes only to pre-selected organizations.
Officers and Directors:* Charles E. Rappold,* Chair. and Pres.; Jacqueline R. McSwiggan, V.P. and Secy.; Dan S. Lazar, V.P. and Treas.; John M. Dowd, V.P.; John S. Lipori.
EIN: 311605320
Codes: CS, FD, CD

33399
Woodland Foundation
c/o White & Case, LLP
1155 6th Ave.
New York, NY 10036-2787
Contact: Stowe H. Tattersall

Incorporated in 1950 in DE.
Donor(s): William Durant Campbell.‡
Financial data (yr. ended 12/31/01): Grants paid, $632,000; assets, $3,725,607 (M); expenditures, $685,990; qualifying distributions, $629,944.
Limitations: Applications not accepted. Giving on a national basis.
Application information: Contributes only to pre-selected organizations.
Officers and Trustees:* Margot C. Bogert,* Pres.; Jeremiah M. Bogert,* V.P. and Treas.; Winthrop Rutherford, Jr.,* Secy.; Jeremiah M. Bogert, Jr., Milicient D. Bogert, Terence L. Elsberry.
EIN: 136018244
Codes: FD

33400
Amy Plant Statter Foundation
780 3rd Ave., 29th Fl.
New York, NY 10017-2024

Established in 1958 in NY.
Donor(s): Amy Plant Statter Clark.
Financial data (yr. ended 12/31/01): Grants paid, $630,000; assets, $4,828,128 (M); expenditures, $673,230; qualifying distributions, $625,484.
Limitations: Applications not accepted. Giving on a national basis, with some emphasis on the greater metropolitan New York, NY, area and Seattle, WA.
Application information: Contributes only to pre-selected organizations.
Trustees: Amy Plant Statter Clark, John H. Reilly, Jr.
EIN: 136152801
Codes: FD

33401
The Nina M. Ryan Foundation, Inc.
Box 321
Cold Spring, NY 10516

Incorporated in 1947 in NY.
Financial data (yr. ended 12/31/01): Grants paid, $628,357; assets, $14,303,229 (M); expenditures, $630,798; qualifying distributions, $629,944.
Limitations: Applications not accepted. Giving primarily in NY; some giving also in MA.
Application information: Contributes only to pre-selected organizations.
Officers: Leroy M. Parker, Pres.; Rosalie L. Parker, V.P. and Treas.; Katherine Parker, Secy.
EIN: 136111038
Codes: FD

33402
The Schiff Foundation
320 Park Ave., 10th Fl.
New York, NY 10022-6815

Incorporated in 1946 in NY.
Donor(s): John M. Schiff,‡ Edith B. Schiff,‡ David T. Schiff, Peter G. Schiff.
Financial data (yr. ended 12/31/01): Grants paid, $627,656; assets, $12,416,556 (M); expenditures, $705,990; qualifying distributions, $618,600.
Limitations: Applications not accepted. Giving primarily in NY.
Application information: Contributes only to pre-selected organizations.
Officers and Directors:* David T. Schiff,* Pres.; Peter G. Schiff,* V.P.; Sandra Frey Davies, Secy.; Andrew N. Schiff,* Treas.
EIN: 136088221
Codes: FD

33403
Mona Bismarck Charitable Trust
1133 Ave. of the Americas, 22nd Fl.
New York, NY 10036-6710
Application address: Attn: Mr. C. Rajakaruna, 5 rue Cambon, 75001 Paris, France
Contact: Russell M. Porter, Tr.

Established in 1986 in NY.
Donor(s): Russell M. Porter.
Financial data (yr. ended 12/31/00): Grants paid, $627,500; assets, $17,904,919 (M); expenditures, $837,263; qualifying distributions, $687,597.
Limitations: Giving primarily in France.
Trustee: Russell M. Porter.
EIN: 133244269
Codes: FD

33404
The Hilibrand Foundation
c/o Steven M. Loeb, Esq.
1 Liberty Plz.
New York, NY 10006

Established in 1991 in NY.
Donor(s): Deborah Z. Hilibrand, Lawrence E. Hilibrand.
Financial data (yr. ended 12/31/00): Grants paid, $626,650; assets, $15,489,615 (M); expenditures, $667,560; qualifying distributions, $588,319.
Limitations: Applications not accepted. Giving primarily in CT and New York, NY.
Application information: Contributes only to pre-selected organizations.

Trustees: Deborah Z. Hilibrand, Lawrence E. Hilibrand.
EIN: 133632625
Codes: FD

33405
The Coneway Family Foundation
(Formerly Lynn & Peter Coneway Foundation)
c/o Goldman Sachs & Co.
85 Broad St., Tax Dept.
New York, NY 10004
Additional address: c/o Natalie C. Page, 200 Riverside Blvd., Ste. 7D, New York, NY 10069
Contact: Peter R. Coneway, or Natalie C. Page, Trustees

Established in 1983.
Donor(s): Lynn M. Coneway, Peter R. Coneway, Peter R. Coneway Charitable Lead Trust.
Financial data (yr. ended 04/30/02): Grants paid, $623,731; assets, $10,097,378 (M); expenditures, $708,460; qualifying distributions, $682,404.
Limitations: Applications not accepted. Giving primarily in Houston, TX.
Application information: Contributes only to pre-selected organizations.
Trustees: Cecile L. Coneway, Lynn M. Coneway, Peter R. Coneway, Natalie Page, Steve Page.
EIN: 133188841
Codes: FD

33406
W. P. Carey Foundation
50 Rockefeller Plz., 2nd Fl.
New York, NY 10020

Established in 1991 in PA.
Donor(s): W.P. Carey.
Financial data (yr. ended 12/31/01): Grants paid, $621,604; assets, $6,382,405 (M); gifts received, $3,000,000; expenditures, $669,944; qualifying distributions, $665,382.
Limitations: Applications not accepted. Giving on a national basis.
Application information: Contributes only to pre-selected organizations.
Officers, Directors, and Trustees:* William P. Carey,* Chair.; Francis J. Carey,* Pres.; H. Augustus Carey,* V.P. and Secy.; Elizabeth P.C. Boden,* V.P.; Natalia A. Hooker,* V.P.; Elizabeth Shaw Willis,* V.P.; Claude Fernandez,* Treas.; Zachary J. Pack, Exec. Dir.; J. Samuel Armstrong IV, Gwendolen G. Bond, Francis J. Carey III, Anne R. Coolidge, V.P.; Gordon F. Dugan, Jan F. Karst, Lawrence R. Klein, Marcia M. Murray, A. Patterson Pendleton III, George E. Stoddard.
EIN: 133597510
Codes: FD

33407
The Lewis J. and Clelia M. Serventi Family Foundation
16 Prospect St.
P.O. Box 14
Perry, NY 14530-0014

Established in 1999 in NY.
Donor(s): Lewis J. Serventi, Debra Serventi Jones, Mary Michele Rechberger.
Financial data (yr. ended 12/31/01): Grants paid, $618,900; assets, $1,343,727 (M); expenditures, $619,152; qualifying distributions, $618,950.
Limitations: Applications not accepted. Giving primarily in Perry, NY.
Application information: Contributes only to pre-selected organizations.
Officers: Lewis J. Serventi, Pres.; Clelia M. Serventi, V.P.
Directors: Debra Serventi Jones, Mary Michele Rechberger.
EIN: 311585491
Codes: FD

33408
Reb Moishe Rosen Fund, Inc.
271 Madison Ave., 22nd Fl.
New York, NY 10016-1001

Donor(s): Charles Alpert, Joseph Alpert.
Financial data (yr. ended 06/30/02): Grants paid, $618,400; assets, $2,052,073 (M); gifts received, $2,650,000; expenditures, $618,515; qualifying distributions, $618,515.
Limitations: Applications not accepted. Giving primarily in NY.
Application information: Contributes only to pre-selected organizations.
Officers: Zelik Epstein, Pres.; Joseph Alpert, Secy.; Charles Alpert, Treas.
EIN: 116036649
Codes: FD

33409
Dextra Baldwin McGonagle Foundation, Inc.
P.O. Box 709
South Salem, NY 10590
Contact: Jonathan G. Spanier, Pres.

Incorporated in 1967 in NY.
Donor(s): Dextra Baldwin McGonagle.‡
Financial data (yr. ended 12/31/01): Grants paid, $617,028; assets, $12,375,372 (M); expenditures, $770,529; qualifying distributions, $676,210.
Limitations: Giving primarily in CA and NY.
Application information: Application form not required.
Officers and Directors:* Maury L. Spanier,* Chair.; David B. Spanier,* Vice-Chair.; Jonathan G. Spanier, Pres. and Treas.; Helen G. Spanier,* V.P. and Secy.
EIN: 136219236
Codes: FD

33410
Avalon Foundation
c/o BCRS Assocs., LLC
67 Wall St., 8th Fl.
New York, NY 10005

Established in 1987 in NY.
Donor(s): Michael D. McCarthy.
Financial data (yr. ended 01/31/01): Grants paid, $616,400; assets, $15,393,444 (M); expenditures, $686,159; qualifying distributions, $618,200.
Limitations: Applications not accepted. Giving primarily in New York, NY.
Application information: Contributes only to pre-selected organizations.
Trustees: Jonathan L. Cohen, Deborah Berg McCarthy, Michael D. McCarthy.
EIN: 133437931
Codes: FD

33411
Nina W. Werblow Charitable Trust
c/o Ehrenkranz and Ehrenkranz, LLP
375 Park Ave., Ste. 2800
New York, NY 10152 (212) 751-5959
Contact: Roger A. Goldman, Esq., Tr.

Trust established in 1977 in NY.
Donor(s): Nina W. Werblow.‡
Financial data (yr. ended 02/28/01): Grants paid, $616,000; assets, $12,553,580 (M); expenditures, $855,391; qualifying distributions, $651,535.
Limitations: Giving limited to New York, NY.
Trustees: Lillian Ahrens Carver, Joel S. Ehrenkranz, Roger A. Goldman.
EIN: 136742999
Codes: FD

33412
Emanuel & Riane Gruss Charitable Foundation, Inc.
74 Broad St.
New York, NY 10004

Established in 1978 in NY.
Donor(s): Emanuel Gruss, Riane Gruss.
Financial data (yr. ended 03/31/01): Grants paid, $615,287; assets, $11,486,563 (M); expenditures, $701,553; qualifying distributions, $617,803.
Limitations: Applications not accepted. Giving primarily in New York, NY.
Application information: Contributes only to pre-selected organizations.
Officers: Riane Gruss, Pres. and Treas.; Emanuel Gruss, V.P.
Directors: Brenda Gruss, Leslie Gruss.
EIN: 132969811
Codes: FD

33413
Herbert & Nell Singer Foundation, Inc.
745 5th Ave.
New York, NY 10151

Donor(s): Herbert M. Singer,‡ The Peter Singer Trust, The Steven Singer Trust.
Financial data (yr. ended 12/31/01): Grants paid, $614,750; assets, $19,581,908 (M); gifts received, $567,432; expenditures, $776,911; qualifying distributions, $645,986.
Limitations: Applications not accepted. Giving primarily in New York, NY.
Application information: Contributes only to pre-selected organizations.
Officers and Directors:* Nell Singer, Pres.; Richard Netter, V.P.; Jay Sandak, Eddie Singer.
EIN: 133151548
Codes: FD

33414
Joseph Alexander Foundation, Inc.
400 Madison Ave., Ste. 906
New York, NY 10017 (212) 355-3688
Contact: Robert Weintraub, Pres.

Established in 1960 in NY.
Donor(s): Joseph Alexander.‡
Financial data (yr. ended 10/31/01): Grants paid, $613,500; assets, $17,399,960 (M); expenditures, $803,181; qualifying distributions, $755,160.
Limitations: Giving primarily in the continental U.S., with emphasis on New York, NY; some giving also in Israel.
Publications: Financial statement.
Application information: Application form not required.
Officers and Directors:* Robert Weintraub,* Pres.; Arthur Alfert,* V.P.; Helen Mackler,* Secy.; Harvey Mackler, Randi Windheim.
EIN: 510175951
Codes: FD

33415
The Bernard & Anne Spitzer Foundation, Inc.
730 5th Ave.
New York, NY 10019
Contact: Bernard Spitzer, Pres., and Anne Spitzer, V.P.

Established around 1982.
Donor(s): Bernard Spitzer.
Financial data (yr. ended 12/31/01): Grants paid, $612,244; assets, $24,777,674 (M); gifts received, $1,975,000; expenditures, $1,052,812; qualifying distributions, $624,267.
Limitations: Giving primarily in NY.
Officers: Bernard Spitzer, Pres.; Anne Spitzer, V.P.
EIN: 133098005
Codes: FD

33416
Galasso Foundation
74 N. Aurora St.
Lancaster, NY 14086
E-mail: galasso@rdinet.net
Contact: Marta G. Carney, Admin.

Established in 1963 in NY.
Donor(s): Susquehanna Motel Corp., August J. Galasso.
Financial data (yr. ended 12/31/01): Grants paid, $612,205; assets, $10,696,198 (M); expenditures, $840,255; qualifying distributions, $638,818.
Limitations: Applications not accepted. Giving primarily in upstate NY.
Application information: Contributes only to pre-selected organizations.
Trustees: K.F. Burgin, Joseph R. Coppola, Martin A. Galasso, August J. Gillon, Paul M. Gonzalez, Michael J. Kelleher.
EIN: 166031447
Codes: FD

33417
A.P.W. Foundation, Inc.
1415 52nd St.
Brooklyn, NY 11219

Established in 1994 in NY.
Donor(s): Abraham Weiss.
Financial data (yr. ended 12/31/00): Grants paid, $611,501; assets, $6,102,182 (M); gifts received, $293,651; expenditures, $862,522; qualifying distributions, $607,640.
Limitations: Applications not accepted. Giving primarily in NY.
Application information: Contributes only to pre-selected organizations.
Officer: Abraham Weiss, Pres.
EIN: 113242355
Codes: FD

33418
The Iscol Family Foundation, Inc.
63 Lyndel Rd.
Pound Ridge, NY 10576 (914) 764-8479
FAX: (203) 972-5237
Contact: Jill W. Iscol, Pres.

Established in 1990 in NY.
Donor(s): Kenneth H. Iscol.
Financial data (yr. ended 06/30/01): Grants paid, $610,925; assets, $4,212,790 (M); expenditures, $973,070; qualifying distributions, $950,262.
Limitations: Giving primarily in CT and NY.
Officers and Directors:* Jill Iscol,* Pres. and Treas.; Kenneth Iscol,* V.P. and Secy.
EIN: 061314468
Codes: FD

33419
Lewis Schott Foundation
c/o A. Kozak and Co., LLP
192 Lexington Ave., Ste. 1100
New York, NY 10016-6823

Established in 1992 in DE and FL.
Donor(s): Lewis M. Schott.
Financial data (yr. ended 12/31/01): Grants paid, $610,400; assets, $2,905,740 (M); gifts received, $953,134; expenditures, $618,572; qualifying distributions, $602,826.
Limitations: Applications not accepted. Giving primarily in FL.
Application information: Contributes only to pre-selected organizations.
Officers and Directors:* Lewis M. Schott,* Pres.; Nash W. Schott,* Secy.-Treas.; Victoria de Rothschild, Steven G. Schott.
EIN: 581969908
Codes: FD

33420
The Manitoba Foundation
c/o First Spring Corp.
499 Park Ave., 26th Fl.
New York, NY 10022
Contact: Guido Goldman, Pres.

Established in 1996 in DE and NY.
Financial data (yr. ended 12/31/01): Grants paid, $610,008; assets, $11,731,054 (M); gifts received, $271,036; expenditures, $635,707; qualifying distributions, $610,017.
Limitations: Giving primarily in NY.
Application information: Application form not required.
Officers and Directors:* Guido Goldman,* Pres.; Mark O'Donnell, V.P. and Treas.; Kenneth M. Musen, Secy.; Jean De Gunzburg, Terry De Gunzburg, Avrom Udovitch.
EIN: 133775261
Codes: FD

33421
The Bachmann Foundation, Inc.
c/o The Ayco Co.
P.O. Box 8009
Clifton Park, NY 12065

Incorporated in 1949 in NY.
Donor(s): Louis Bachmann,‡ Thomas W. Strauss, B. Bachmann.
Financial data (yr. ended 12/31/99): Grants paid, $609,000; assets, $8,234,626 (M); gifts received, $101,250; expenditures, $639,111; qualifying distributions, $616,829.
Limitations: Applications not accepted. Giving primarily in NY.
Application information: Contributes only to pre-selected organizations.
Officers: Barbara Bachmann Strauss, Pres.; Thomas W. Strauss, V.P. and Treas.; Richard M. Danziger, Secy.
EIN: 136043497
Codes: FD

33422
Christian Humann Foundation
c/o Morris & McVeigh, LLP
767 Third Ave.
New York, NY 10017-2023

Established in 1999 in NY.
Financial data (yr. ended 03/31/01): Grants paid, $609,000; assets, $17,178,511 (M); expenditures, $737,680; qualifying distributions, $736,680.
Limitations: Applications not accepted.
Application information: Contributes only to pre-selected organizations.
Officers and Trustees:* Claus Virch,* Pres.; Edgar Humann,* V.P.; Alec Anderson, Secy.; Cummings V. Zuill,* Treas.; Michael Darling, Wm. Dev. Frith, Richard Griffith-Jones, Faith Low Humann.
EIN: 980055334
Codes: FD

33423
The Edouard Foundation, Inc.
c/o Phillips Nizer, et al.
666 5th Ave., 28th Fl.
New York, NY 10103-0084 (212) 977-9700
Contact: Morton Freilicher, Treas.

Established in 1987 in NY.
Financial data (yr. ended 12/31/01): Grants paid, $607,000; assets, $9,888,087 (M); expenditures, $729,203; qualifying distributions, $612,466.
Limitations: Applications not accepted. Giving on a national basis.
Application information: Contributes only to pre-selected organizations.
Officers and Directors:* Sandra Finch-Nguyen,* Pres.; Christopher Finch,* V.P.; Ronald Finch,* V.P.; Edwin A. Margolius,* Secy.; Morton Freilicher,* Treas.; Beatrice Phillipe.
EIN: 133446831
Codes: FD

33424
Grossman Family Foundation
1461 53rd St.
Brooklyn, NY 11219-3949

Established in 1989 in NY.
Donor(s): Marton Grossman.
Financial data (yr. ended 11/30/01): Grants paid, $606,856; assets, $1,608,527 (M); gifts received, $200,000; expenditures, $607,494; qualifying distributions, $606,231.
Limitations: Applications not accepted. Giving primarily in Brooklyn, NY.
Application information: Contributes only to pre-selected organizations.
Officers: Marton Grossman, Pres.; Sheila Grossman, V.P.; Isaac Grossman, Secy.
EIN: 112994863
Codes: FD

33425
Michael Chernow Trust
C Circle C
P.O. Box 197
Larchmont, NY 10538-0197 (914) 834-1900
Contact: Gordon S. Oppenheirner

Trust established in 1975 in NY.
Financial data (yr. ended 06/30/01): Grants paid, $605,500; assets, $8,028,162 (M); expenditures, $766,391; qualifying distributions, $642,249.
Limitations: Giving primarily in NY.
Application information: Application form not required.
Trustees: Martin P. Krasner, Ed Streim, Lynn Streim.
EIN: 136758226
Codes: FD

33426
The Kilian J. and Caroline F. Schmitt Foundation, Inc.
c/o HSBC Bank, USA
1 HSBC Plz.
Rochester, NY 14604 (585) 238-7721

Established in 1991 in NY as successor to Kilian J. and Caroline F. Schmitt Foundation.
Donor(s): Kilian J. Schmitt,‡ Caroline F. Schmitt.‡
Financial data (yr. ended 02/28/01): Grants paid, $605,400; assets, $11,885,828 (M); expenditures, $1,118,554; qualifying distributions, $644,765.
Limitations: Giving primarily in the metropolitan Rochester, NY, area.
Application information: Application form required.
Officers: Robert H. Fella, Pres.; Michael Walker, V.P.; Gary J. Lindsay, Secy.-Treas.
Directors: James R. Dray, Leon Fella, Alfred Hallenbeck, Roger D. Lathan.
EIN: 223087449
Codes: FD

33427
The Alice Pack Melly and L. Thomas Melly Foundation
(Formerly L. Thomas Melly Foundation)
c/o BCRS Assoc., LLC
100 Wall St., 11th Fl.
New York, NY 10005-3720

Established in 1969 in NY.
Donor(s): L. Thomas Melly, Alice Pack Melly.

Financial data (yr. ended 05/31/01): Grants paid, $605,015; assets, $10,303,514 (M); expenditures, $628,535; qualifying distributions, $600,009.
Limitations: Applications not accepted. Giving primarily in CT and NY.
Application information: Contributes only to pre-selected organizations.
Trustees: Alice P. Melly, David Randolph Melly, L. Thomas Melly, Laura A. Melly, Lee Scott Melly, Thomas L. Melly.
EIN: 237059703
Codes: FD

33428
The Raiff Foundation
Carnegie Hall Tower
152 W. 57th St., 38th Fl.
New York, NY 10019

Established in 1995 in NY.
Financial data (yr. ended 12/31/01): Grants paid, $605,000; assets, $11,700,000 (M); gifts received, $200,000; expenditures, $640,000; qualifying distributions, $605,000.
Limitations: Applications not accepted. Giving primarily in New York, NY, and Providence, RI.
Application information: Contributes only to pre-selected organizations.
Trustee: Robert M. Raiff.
EIN: 137070078
Codes: FD

33429
Edith C. Blum Foundation, Inc.
c/o KPMG, LLP
345 Park Ave.
New York, NY 10154
Application address: Frances M. Friedman c/o Bankers Trust Co., 280 Park Ave. 7th Fl. Mail stop 1071, New York, NY 10017
Contact: Frances M. Friedman, Dir.

Established in 1990 in NY as successor to the Edith C. Blum Foundation.
Donor(s): Edith C. Blum Foundation.
Financial data (yr. ended 09/30/01): Grants paid, $603,950; assets, $14,396,731 (M); expenditures, $810,429; qualifying distributions, $723,620.
Limitations: Giving primarily in New York, NY.
Application information: Application form not required.
Directors: Frances M. Friedman, Roy R. Friedman, Wilbur H. Friedman.
EIN: 133564317
Codes: FD

33430
His Will Foundation
(Formerly The Azariah Foundation)
c/o BCRS Associates, LLC
100 Wall St., 11th Fl.
New York, NY 10005

Established in 2000 in NJ.
Donor(s): John E. Urban.
Financial data (yr. ended 08/31/01): Grants paid, $601,000; assets, $2,166,002 (M); gifts received, $2,768,440; expenditures, $609,000; qualifying distributions, $597,130.
Limitations: Applications not accepted. Giving on a national basis.
Application information: Contributes only to pre-selected organizations.
Trustees: Carolyn L. Urban, John E. Urban.
EIN: 134043877
Codes: FD

33431
The L. Bravmann Foundation, Inc.
c/o L. Bravmann
3333-B Henry Hudson Pkwy., Apt. 6E
Riverdale, NY 10463-3241

Established in 1964 in NY.
Donor(s): Ludwig Bravmann, Lotte Bravmann.
Financial data (yr. ended 06/30/01): Grants paid, $600,982; assets, $15,536,019 (M); gifts received, $1,286,143; expenditures, $656,652; qualifying distributions, $590,448.
Limitations: Applications not accepted. Giving primarily in New York, NY.
Application information: Contributes only to pre-selected organizations.
Officers and Directors:* Ludwig Bravmann,* Pres.; Lotte Bravmann,* Secy.-Treas.; Carol Bravmann, Judith E. Kaufthal, Matthew Maryles, Jack Nash, Shimon Wolf.
EIN: 136168525
Codes: FD

33432
Bernard L. & Ruth Madoff Foundation
885 3rd Ave., 18th Fl.
New York, NY 10022-4834

Established in 1997 in NY.
Donor(s): Bernard L. Madoff, Ruth Madoff.
Financial data (yr. ended 12/31/01): Grants paid, $599,776; assets, $26,145,086 (M); expenditures, $604,656; qualifying distributions, $599,776.
Limitations: Applications not accepted. Giving primarily in NY.
Application information: Contributes only to pre-selected organizations.
Officers: Bernard L. Madoff, Pres.; Ruth Madoff, Secy.-Treas.
EIN: 133934626
Codes: FD

33433
The Hilda Mullen Foundation
c/o Simpson Thacher & Bartlett
425 Lexington Ave.
New York, NY 10017

Established in 1997 in NY.
Donor(s): Lois Q. Whitman, Martin J. Whitman.
Financial data (yr. ended 12/31/01): Grants paid, $599,500; assets, $7,770,674 (M); expenditures, $608,338; qualifying distributions, $606,463.
Limitations: Applications not accepted.
Application information: Contributes only to pre-selected organizations.
Trustees: Lois Q. Whitman, Martin J. Whitman.
EIN: 137120449
Codes: FD

33434
The Armand G. Erpf Fund, Inc.
c/o Condon, O'Meara, McGinty, and Donnelly, LLP
3 New York Plz., 18th Fl.
New York, NY 10004
Application address: c/o Grant Admin., 640 Park Ave., New York, NY 10021

Incorporated in 1951 in NY.
Donor(s): Armand G. Erpf.‡
Financial data (yr. ended 11/30/01): Grants paid, $597,592; assets, $12,145,233 (M); gifts received, $289,621; expenditures, $820,975; qualifying distributions, $692,902.
Limitations: Giving primarily in New York, NY; funding also in Washington, DC.
Application information: Application form not required.
Officers: Sue Erpf Van de Bovenkamp, Pres.; Gina Caimi, Secy.; Armand B. Erpf, Treas.

Directors: Louis Auchincloss, Douglas Campbell, Cornelia A. Erpf, Robert B. Oxnam, Roger D. Stone, Sophie Marr Verons.
EIN: 136085594
Codes: FD

33435
The Richard A. and Amelia Bernstein Foundation, Inc.
c/o P & E Properties, Inc.
444 Madison Ave.
New York, NY 10022-6903   (212) 688-4500
Contact: Richard A. Bernstein, Tr.

Established in 1981 in NY.
Donor(s): Richard A. Bernstein, Armand Lindenbaum.
Financial data (yr. ended 11/30/01): Grants paid, $597,275; assets, $331,829 (M); gifts received, $18; expenditures, $600,100; qualifying distributions, $598,992.
Limitations: Giving primarily in NY.
Directors: Mitchell Baron, Richard A. Bernstein, James A. Cohen.
EIN: 133147445
Codes: FD

33436
Keshet Foundation
c/o Abraham Trusts
444 Madison Ave., 11 Fl.
New York, NY 10022

Established in 1997 in NY.
Donor(s): Rebecca Gridish, Eli Gridish.
Financial data (yr. ended 11/30/99): Grants paid, $596,954; assets, $1,126,814 (M); gifts received, $1,338,180; expenditures, $605,432; qualifying distributions, $592,724.
Limitations: Applications not accepted.
Application information: Unsolicited requests for funds not accepted.
Trustees: Estanne Abraham, Eli Gridish, Rebecca Gridish.
EIN: 137132997
Codes: FD

33437
The Louis B. Mayer Foundation
67A E. 77th St.
New York, NY 10021-1813
Contact: Ann Brownell Sloane, Admin.

Trust established in 1947 in CA.
Donor(s): Louis B. Mayer.‡
Financial data (yr. ended 12/31/01): Grants paid, $595,001; assets, $11,771,880 (M); expenditures, $721,996; qualifying distributions, $595,001.
Limitations: Applications not accepted. Giving on a national basis.
Application information: Contributes only to pre-selected organizations.
Officers and Trustees:* Robert A. Gottlieb,* Pres.; Carol Farkas,* Secy.-Treas.; Elliot R. Cattarulla.
EIN: 952232340
Codes: FD

33438
The Arthur and Mae Orvis Foundation, Inc.
(Formerly The Arthur Emerton Orvis Foundation)
c/o Alston & Bird, LLP
90 Park Ave.
New York, NY 10016
Application address: 30 Rockefeller Plz., Rm. 5432, New York, NY 10016
Contact: Grover O'Neill, Jr., Pres.

Established in 1967 in NY.
Donor(s): Mae Zenke Orvis.‡

33438—NEW YORK

Financial data (yr. ended 09/30/01): Grants paid, $593,550; assets, $12,329,276 (M); expenditures, $814,330; qualifying distributions, $681,188.
Limitations: Giving limited to Honolulu, HI, Reno, NV, and New York, NY.
Application information: Application form not required.
Officers and Directors:* Grover O'Neill, Jr.,* Pres.; Roger M. Gerber,* V.P. and Treas.; Wallace L. Cook, V.P.; Paul M. Frank,* Secy.; Robert S. Hines, T.A. Nigro.
EIN: 136217675
Codes: FD

33439
The Townsend Family Foundation
c/o Goldman Sachs & Co.
85 Broad St., Tax Dept.
New York, NY 10004

Established in 1993 in NY.
Donor(s): John L. Townsend III.
Financial data (yr. ended 06/30/01): Grants paid, $593,335; assets, $4,989,114 (M); gifts received, $2,160,861; expenditures, $657,706; qualifying distributions, $598,706.
Limitations: Applications not accepted. Giving primarily in CT, NC, NY, and VA.
Application information: Contributes only to pre-selected organizations.
Trustees: John L. Townsend III, Marree S. Townsend.
EIN: 133748079
Codes: FD

33440
Jacob Hidary Foundation, Inc.
10 W. 33rd St.
New York, NY 10001
Contact: Isaac Hidary, Pres., or David J. Hidary, V.P.

Established in 1961.
Donor(s): M. Hidary Co., Inc., and members of the Hidary family.
Financial data (yr. ended 12/31/01): Grants paid, $593,053; assets, $419,584 (M); gifts received, $563,673; expenditures, $602,256; qualifying distributions, $594,145.
Limitations: Giving primarily in NY.
Officers: Isaac Hidary, Pres.; David J. Hidary, V.P.; Jacob I. Hidary, Secy.; Abraham B. Hidary, Treas.
EIN: 136125420
Codes: FD

33441
Atran Foundation, Inc.
23-25 E. 21st St., 3rd Fl.
New York, NY 10010 (212) 505-9677
Contact: Diane Fischer, Pres.

Incorporated in 1945 in NY.
Donor(s): Frank Z. Atran.‡
Financial data (yr. ended 11/30/01): Grants paid, $591,083; assets, $17,078,090 (M); expenditures, $819,522; qualifying distributions, $751,015.
Limitations: Giving on a national basis.
Publications: Application guidelines.
Application information: Application form not required.
Officers and Trustees:* Diane Fischer,* Pres.; William Stern,* V.P.; George Fraenkel,* Treas.
EIN: 135566548
Codes: FD

33442
The Timothy J. and Linda D. O'Neill Foundation
c/o Goldman Sachs & Co.
85 Broad St., Tax Dept.
New York, NY 10004

Established in 1991 in NY.
Donor(s): Timothy J. O'Neill.
Financial data (yr. ended 04/30/01): Grants paid, $590,805; assets, $6,203,133 (M); gifts received, $2,661,425; expenditures, $593,805; qualifying distributions, $593,805.
Limitations: Applications not accepted. Giving primarily in NY.
Application information: Contributes only to pre-selected organizations.
Trustees: Linda D. O'Neill, Timothy J. O'Neill.
EIN: 133642501
Codes: FD

33443
Charles R. Wood Foundation
499 Glen St.
Glens Falls, NY 12801-2205 (518) 792-8070

Established in 1978.
Donor(s): Charles R. Wood.
Financial data (yr. ended 12/31/01): Grants paid, $590,420; assets, $11,123,296 (M); gifts received, $369,486; expenditures, $853,113; qualifying distributions, $618,513; giving activities include $619,399 for programs.
Limitations: Applications not accepted. Giving primarily in NY.
Publications: Informational brochure, financial statement.
Application information: Contributes only to pre-selected organizations.
Officer: Charles R. Wood, Chair. and Pres.
Trustees: Dean Beckos, Georgia Beckos, Charlene Courtney, Edward Lewi, Barbara Beckos McDonald, Shirley Myott, Barbara Wages.
EIN: 222237193

33444
Kopf Family Foundation
(Formerly Kopf Foundation, Inc.)
c/o Kelley, Drye & Warren, LLP
101 Park Ave., Ste. 2936
New York, NY 10178

Incorporated in 1967 in NY.
Donor(s): R.C. Kopf.‡
Financial data (yr. ended 12/31/00): Grants paid, $589,800; assets, $15,824,143 (M); expenditures, $849,109; qualifying distributions, $620,718.
Limitations: Applications not accepted. Giving on a national basis.
Application information: Contributes only to pre-selected organizations.
Officers: Patricia Colagiuri, Pres.; Nancy Sue Mueller, V.P.; Michael S. Insel, Secy.; Brenda Helies, Treas.
EIN: 136228036
Codes: FD

33445
Phillips-Van Heusen Foundation, Inc.
200 Madison Ave., 10th Fl.
New York, NY 10016 (212) 381-3500
FAX: (212) 381-3960
Contact: Tiffany Vargas

Incorporated in 1969 in NY.
Donor(s): Phillips-Van Heusen Corp.
Financial data (yr. ended 12/31/01): Grants paid, $587,283; assets, $58,851 (M); gifts received, $83,786; expenditures, $587,283; qualifying distributions, $587,283.
Application information: Application form not required.

Officers: Bruce J. Klatsky, Chair.; Pamela N. Hootkin, V.P. and Secy.; Emanuel Chirico, V.P. and Treas.
EIN: 237104639
Codes: CS, FD, CD

33446
Thomas F. Staley Foundation
4 Chatsworth Ave., No. 3
Larchmont, NY 10538-2932 (914) 834-2669
Contact: Elizabeth D. Halliday

Trust established in 1943 in MI.
Donor(s): Thomas F. Staley,‡ Shirley H. Hunter.
Financial data (yr. ended 12/31/00): Grants paid, $586,580; assets, $7,924,515 (M); expenditures, $753,823; qualifying distributions, $667,608.
Limitations: Applications not accepted. Giving on a national basis.
Publications: Program policy statement, informational brochure.
Application information: Contributes only to pre-selected organizations.
Officers: Thomas F. Staley, Jr., Pres.; Diane Staley Bernard, Treas.; Robert G. Howard, Treas.; Stuart Staley, Treas.
Trustees: Susan H. Canada, Janet Howard, Catherine Staley, Sarah H. Wichert.
EIN: 136071888
Codes: FD

33447
Patrick A. Gerschel Foundation
720 5th Ave., 10th Fl.
New York, NY 10019-4107 (212) 399-4278

Established in 1986 in NY.
Donor(s): Patrick A. Gerschel.
Financial data (yr. ended 12/31/01): Grants paid, $584,000; assets, $6,182,863 (M); expenditures, $632,605; qualifying distributions, $581,022.
Limitations: Applications not accepted. Giving primarily in the New York, NY, area.
Application information: Unsolicited requests for funds not accepted.
Officer and Director:* Patrick A. Gerschel,* Pres.
EIN: 133317180
Codes: FD

33448
The M. & B. Weiss Family Foundation, Inc.
c/o Milberg, Weiss, et al.
1 Pennsylvania Plz.
New York, NY 10119

Established in 1996 in NY.
Donor(s): Melvyn I. Weiss.
Financial data (yr. ended 10/31/01): Grants paid, $583,886; assets, $358,461 (M); expenditures, $623,331; qualifying distributions, $580,080.
Limitations: Applications not accepted.
Application information: Contributes only to pre-selected organizations.
Officers: Melvyn I. Weiss, Pres.; Gary M. Weiss, V.P.; Leslie Weiss, V.P.; Stephen A. Weiss, V.P.; Barbara J. Weiss, Secy.
EIN: 133940345
Codes: FD

33449
The Yoreinu Foundation
(Formerly Laurence and Marsha Roth Charitable Foundation)
126 N. Salina St., Ste. 300
Syracuse, NY 13202-7067 (315) 234-5181
Application address: 24 Derech Beit Lechem, Apt. 25, Jerusalem, 93109 Israel; E-mail: dtroth@netvision.net.il
Contact: David M. Roth, Exec. Dir.

Established in 1991 in NY.

Donor(s): Laurence Roth, Marsha Roth.
Financial data (yr. ended 12/31/01): Grants paid, $583,000; assets, $4,483,691 (M); gifts received, $437,337; expenditures, $640,131; qualifying distributions, $593,132.
Application information: Application form required.
Officer: David M. Roth, Exec. Dir.
Trustees: Alexander S. Pasquale, Laurence N. Roth, Marsha Roth.
EIN: 161404154
Codes: FD

33450
Jephson Educational Trust No. 2
c/o JPMorgan Chase Bank
1211 Ave. of the Americas, 38th Fl.
New York, NY 10036
E-mail: jones_ed_l@JPmorgan.com
Contact: Edward L. Jones, V.P.

Trust established in 1979 in NY.
Donor(s): Lucretia Davis Jephson.‡
Financial data (yr. ended 09/30/01): Grants paid, $582,000; assets, $12,299,429 (M); expenditures, $765,666; qualifying distributions, $647,615.
Limitations: Applications not accepted. Giving on a national basis, with emphasis on NY.
Application information: Contributes only to pre-selected organizations.
Trustees: J. Stanley Parkin, Robert D. Taisey, JPMorgan Chase Bank.
EIN: 136777236
Codes: FD

33451
The B. L. Manger Foundation, Inc.
c/o U.S. Trust
114 W. 47th St., Ste. TAXVS
New York, NY 10036
Application address: 123 Prospect St., Stamford, CT 06901; FAX: (212) 852-3377
Contact: Harold Bernstein, V.P. and Treas., Linda Franciscovich, Senior V.P., US Trust, or Carolyn L. Larke, Asst. V.P., US Trust

Established in 1974 in CT.
Financial data (yr. ended 04/30/02): Grants paid, $581,500; assets, $9,163,620 (M); gifts received, $545,535; expenditures, $699,043; qualifying distributions, $585,741.
Limitations: Giving primarily in CT.
Officers: Joseph Lieberman, Pres.; Harold Bernstein, V.P. and Treas.; I.M. Mackler, Secy.
EIN: 237405994
Codes: FD

33452
Herman & Terese Cohn Foundation
c/o JPMorgan Chase Bank
P.O. Box 31412
Rochester, NY 14603
Contact: Patricia Burns, V.P., JPMorgan Chase Bank

Trust established in 1954 in NY.
Donor(s): Herman M. Cohn.‡
Financial data (yr. ended 12/31/01): Grants paid, $581,163; assets, $1,029,260 (M); expenditures, $598,313; qualifying distributions, $582,221.
Limitations: Applications not accepted. Giving on a national basis.
Application information: Contributes only to pre-selected organizations. Unsolicited requests for funds not accepted.
Trustee: JPMorgan Chase Bank.
EIN: 166015300
Codes: FD

33453
The Schenectady Foundation
c/o United Way of Schenectady County
P.O. Box 916
Schenectady, NY 12301
Contact: Robert A. Carreau, Secy.

Established in 1963 in NY.
Donor(s): Eleanor F. Green,‡ Mabel Birdsall,‡ Agnes Macdonald,‡ Laura Ayer,‡ S. Wells Corbin,‡ John N. Erbacher,‡ Kathryn Rice,‡ Martin Rice,‡ Willis R. Whitney,‡ Herman Blumer,‡ Patrick Garey,‡ Irving Handelman,‡ Sara Handelman,‡ Adelaide Parker,‡ Alice Stackpole,‡ Charles W. Carl, Jr.,‡ Edna Wood,‡ General Electric Foundation.
Financial data (yr. ended 12/31/01): Grants paid, $580,528; assets, $19,880,414 (M); gifts received, $438,000; expenditures, $1,286,695.
Limitations: Giving limited to Schenectady County, NY.
Publications: Annual report, application guidelines, informational brochure, grants list.
Application information: Contact foundation for current deadline. Application form required.
Officers: Joann E. Paulsen, Chair.; Robert A. Carreau, Secy.; Robert T. Cushing, Treas.
EIN: 146019650
Codes: CM, FD, GTI

33454
Hermione Foundation
c/o Sloate, Weisman, Murray & Co.
230 Park Ave., 7th Fl.
New York, NY 10169 (212) 499-2533
Contact: Donna Leone, Tr.

Established in 1992 in NY.
Donor(s): Laura J. Sloate.
Financial data (yr. ended 12/31/99): Grants paid, $580,213; assets, $483,366 (M); gifts received, $296,880; expenditures, $580,895; qualifying distributions, $580,213.
Application information: Application form required.
Officer and Trustees:* Laura J. Sloate,* Pres.; Jeffrey Cohen, Donna Leone, Michael Schwartz.
EIN: 133673826
Codes: FD

33455
Maurice R. Robinson Fund, Inc.
c/o JPMorgan Chase Bank
1211 Ave. of the Americas, 34th Fl.
New York, NY 10036 (212) 343-6731
FAX: (212) 343-6701
Contact: Marian Steffens, Secy.

Established in 1960 in NY.
Donor(s): Maurice R. Robinson,‡ Florence L. Robinson,‡ Scholastic Inc.
Financial data (yr. ended 06/30/01): Grants paid, $580,000; assets, $14,788,654 (M); expenditures, $667,475; qualifying distributions, $605,384.
Limitations: Giving limited to the U.S.
Publications: Informational brochure (including application guidelines).
Application information: Application form required.
Officers and Directors:* Barbara D. Sullivan,* Pres.; Ernie Fleishman,* Exec. V.P.; Katherine Carsky,* V.P.; Claudia Cohl,* V.P.; Marian I. Steffens, Secy.; John Quinn, Treas.; Michael R. Strickland.
EIN: 136161094
Codes: FD

33456
Fribourg Foundation, Inc.
277 Park Ave., 48th Fl.
New York, NY 10172 (212) 207-5879
Application address: 277 Park Ave., 50th Fl., New York, NY 10172
Contact: Susan McIntyre

Incorporated in 1953 in NY.
Donor(s): Michel Fribourg, Lucienne Fribourg, Arrow Steamship Co., Inc., Continental Grain Co.
Financial data (yr. ended 12/31/01): Grants paid, $577,400; assets, $99,197 (M); expenditures, $579,839; qualifying distributions, $576,037.
Limitations: Giving primarily in New York, NY.
Officers and Directors:* Paul Fribourg,* V.P.; Richard Anderson,* Treas.; Charles Fribourg, Mary Ann Fribourg.
EIN: 136159195
Codes: FD

33457
The Laurent and Alberta Gerschel Foundation, Inc.
P.O. Box 42 Planetarium Station
New York, NY 10024-0036
Contact: Laurent Gerschel, Pres.

Established in 1981.
Donor(s): Laurent Gerschel.
Financial data (yr. ended 12/31/99): Grants paid, $577,351; assets, $8,290,948 (M); expenditures, $715,934; qualifying distributions, $598,921.
Limitations: Giving primarily in NY.
Officers: Laurent Gerschel, Pres.; Alberta Gerschel, V.P.
EIN: 133098507
Codes: FD

33458
The Laura Pels Foundation
(Formerly The Pels Foundation)
200 W. 57th St., Ste. 803
New York, NY 10019 (212) 382-1404
E-mail: dmorrison@LauraPels.com
Contact: Diane Morrison, Exec. Dir.

Established in 1985 in NY; became The Laura Pels Foundation in 1992.
Donor(s): Laura J. Pels.
Financial data (yr. ended 12/31/00): Grants paid, $576,940; assets, $12,487,854 (M); expenditures, $840,359; qualifying distributions, $690,895.
Limitations: Applications not accepted. Giving primarily in New York, NY.
Application information: Unsolicited requests for funds not accepted. Grants are by invitation only.
Officers: Laura J. Pels, Pres.; Laurence Y. Pels, Secy.; Jeffrey S. Feinman, Treas.; Diane Morrison, Exec. Dir.
Director: Juliette Meeus.
EIN: 136865620
Codes: FD

33459
Grandison Foundation
c/o Kurzman & Eisenberg
1 N. Broadway, Ste. 1004
White Plains, NY 10601

Established in 1996 in NY.
Donor(s): Garry B. Trudeau, Jane P. Trudeau.
Financial data (yr. ended 12/31/01): Grants paid, $576,528; assets, $1,196,832 (M); gifts received, $330,000; expenditures, $597,208; qualifying distributions, $577,925.
Limitations: Giving primarily in NY.
Application information: Generally limits contributions to pre-selected organizations; the foundation occasionally makes grants to other

33459—NEW YORK

organizations based on unsolicited requests for funds. Application form not required.
Officers and Directors:* Jane P. Trudeau,* Chair. and Secy.; Garry B. Trudeau,* Pres. and Treas.; Lee Harrison Corbin, Ann Pauley.
EIN: 133883296
Codes: FD

33460
Dickler Family Foundation, Inc.
(Formerly Ruth & Gerald Dickler Foundation, Inc.)
130 E. 59th St., 12th Fl.
New York, NY 10022 (212) 836-1358
FAX: (212) 453-6512
Contact: Lauren Katzowitz, Exec. Dir.

Established in 1995 in DE and MA.
Donor(s): Gerald Dickler.
Financial data (yr. ended 12/31/01): Grants paid, $575,000; assets, $11,591,357 (M); expenditures, $858,787; qualifying distributions, $679,305.
Limitations: Giving primarily in New York, NY.
Application information: Application form required.
Officers and Directors:* Ruth Dickler,* Pres.; Susan Dickler,* Exec. V.P.; Jane Lebow,* V.P.; Fred Farkoun, Treas.; Lauren Katzowitz, Exec. Dir.; Willie Hoppe, Kate Lebow, Abby Pratt, Robert S. Pratt, Sam Pratt.
EIN: 133864553
Codes: FD

33461
The Grubman Compton Foundation
(Formerly Eric P. Grubman Foundation)
c/o BCRS Assocs., LLC
100 Wall St., 11th Fl.
New York, NY 10005

Established in 1996 in NJ.
Donor(s): Eric P. Grubman.
Financial data (yr. ended 07/31/01): Grants paid, $575,000; assets, $2,717,752 (M); gifts received, $1,692,938; expenditures, $646,052; qualifying distributions, $557,923.
Limitations: Applications not accepted. Giving primarily in MD, NJ and NY.
Application information: Contributes only to pre-selected organizations.
Trustees: Elizabeth K. Compton, Eric P. Grubman.
EIN: 133936474
Codes: FD

33462
The Marvin H. Davidson Foundation, Inc.
c/o M.H. Davidson & Co.
885 3rd Ave., Ste. 3300
New York, NY 10022

Established in 1967 in NY.
Donor(s): Marvin H. Davidson, Scott Davidson, Davidson Kempner Advisors, Inc.
Financial data (yr. ended 12/31/01): Grants paid, $574,979; assets, $6,666,360 (M); gifts received, $135,281; expenditures, $686,069; qualifying distributions, $580,479.
Limitations: Applications not accepted. Giving primarily in NY.
Application information: Contributes only to pre-selected organizations.
Officers and Directors:* Marvin H. Davidson,* Pres.; Scott Davidson,* Secy.; Seymour Hertz.
EIN: 136217756
Codes: FD

33463
Alpern Family Foundation, Inc.
c/o Weitzman & Rubin, PC
400 Jericho Tpke., Ste. 205
Jericho, NY 11753

Established in 1952.
Donor(s): Bernard E. Alpern.‡
Financial data (yr. ended 12/31/01): Grants paid, $574,500; assets, $11,866,436 (M); gifts received, $1,323,734; expenditures, $810,153; qualifying distributions, $654,537.
Limitations: Applications not accepted. Giving primarily in New York, NY.
Application information: Contributes only to pre-selected organizations.
Officers and Directors:* Lloyd J. Alpern,* Pres.; Martin H. Schneider,* Sr. V.P. and Secy.; Steven I. Rubin,* Treas.; Rochelle A. Rubin.
EIN: 136100302
Codes: FD

33464
Spirit Foundation, Inc.
c/o Sexter & Warmflash
115 Broadway
New York, NY 10006

Established in 1978 in NY.
Donor(s): John Lennon,‡ Yoko Ono Lennon, Bag One Arts, Inc., Fuji Films, Japan, Nike, Inc., Together Magazine.
Financial data (yr. ended 11/30/01): Grants paid, $571,709; assets, $1,421,938 (M); gifts received, $877,892; expenditures, $571,932; qualifying distributions, $571,709.
Limitations: Giving primarily in New York, NY, England and Hungary.
Officers and Directors:* Yoko Ono,* Pres.; David Warmflash,* Secy.-Treas.; Allan S. Sexter.
EIN: 132971714
Codes: FD

33465
Chesed Foundation of America
59 Maiden Ln., Plaza Level
New York, NY 10038
Contact: Henry Reinhold, Tr.

Donor(s): George Karfunkel, Michael Karfunkel, Karfunkel Family Foundation.
Financial data (yr. ended 06/30/01): Grants paid, $571,390; assets, $16,492,606 (M); gifts received, $4,000,000; expenditures, $691,093; qualifying distributions, $571,390.
Officers: Michael Karfunkel, Pres.; George Karfunkel, V.P.
Trustee: Henry Reinhold.
EIN: 133922068
Codes: FD

33466
The G. C. Andersen Family Foundation
c/o Sung Andersen
1050 Fifth Ave., Apt. 8F
New York, NY 10028-0140

Established in 1996 in DE and NJ.
Donor(s): G. Chris Andersen.
Financial data (yr. ended 12/31/01): Grants paid, $571,050; assets, $4,302,382 (M); expenditures, $592,676; qualifying distributions, $576,375.
Limitations: Applications not accepted. Giving primarily in NY.
Application information: Contributes only to pre-selected organizations.
Officers: G. Chris Andersen, Chair. and V.P.; Sung Han Andersen, Secy.-Treas.
EIN: 133921968
Codes: FD

33467
The Francois-Xavier Bagnoud U.S. Foundation
350 Madison Ave., 16th Fl.
New York, NY 10017-3700 (212) 849-8112
FAX: (212) 849-8113; *URL:* http://www.fxbfoundation.org/about.htm
Contact: Donald Casey, Exec. Dir.

Established in 1994.
Financial data (yr. ended 12/31/00): Grants paid, $569,983; assets, $593,739 (M); gifts received, $1,660,235; expenditures, $1,389,123; qualifying distributions, $1,144,971.
Limitations: Applications not accepted. Giving on an international basis.
Application information: Contributes only to pre-selected organizations.
Officers and Directors:* Alon E. Kasha,* Pres.; Robert J. Bertoldi,* Secy.-Treas.; Donald Casey, Exec. Dir.; Thomas Adamson, Jr., Harvey Fineberg, Robert S. Shriver.
EIN: 133772789
Codes: FD

33468
Hoerle Foundation
c/o Reich & Tang, LP
600 5th Ave.
New York, NY 10020 (212) 830-5353
Additional tel.: (212) 830-5357
Contact: Robert F. Hoerle, Pres.

Established in 1987 in NY.
Donor(s): Robert F. Hoerle, Sheila A. Hoerle.
Financial data (yr. ended 12/31/00): Grants paid, $569,181; assets, $10,456,813 (M); gifts received, $2,365,087; expenditures, $600,744; qualifying distributions, $562,782.
Limitations: Giving primarily in NY.
Application information: Application form not required.
Officers: Robert F. Hoerle, Pres.; Sheila A. Hoerle, V.P.; Pierre J. De Vegh, Treas.
EIN: 133419592
Codes: FD

33469
National Hockey League Foundation
c/o National Hockey League
1251 Ave. of the Americas, 47th Fl.
New York, NY 10020-1104 (212) 789-2000

Established in 1991 in NY.
Donor(s): National Hockey League.
Financial data (yr. ended 06/30/01): Grants paid, $569,086; assets, $3,487,648 (M); gifts received, $964,115; expenditures, $712,168; qualifying distributions, $688,221.
Limitations: Applications not accepted. Giving primarily in the U.S., Canada, and Europe; with some support in South Africa.
Application information: Contributes only to pre-selected organizations.
Officers: William Daly, Pres.; Bernadette Mansur, V.P. and Secy.; Craig C. Harnett, Treas.
Directors: Joseph DeSousa, David Zimmerman.
EIN: 133498589
Codes: FD

33470
The Blessing Way Foundation
c/o Carlin Ventures, Inc.
419 Lafayette St., 7th Fl.
New York, NY 10003 (646) 602-5770
Contact: Regina Durazzo, Pres.

Established in 1991 in DE.
Donor(s): Edwin C. Cohen.
Financial data (yr. ended 12/31/00): Grants paid, $568,795; assets, $6,755,840 (M); gifts received,

$14,132; expenditures, $726,016; qualifying distributions, $569,292.
Limitations: Giving to charitable organizations on a national basis, with emphasis on New York, NY, and Washington, DC; awards granted to students at Harvard University, Wellesley College, and Stanford University only.
Application information: Students should contact their university's coordinator for applications.
Directors: Edwin Cohen, Regina Durazzo.
EIN: 043138834
Codes: FD

33471
Milton F. & Rita C. Lewis Foundation, Inc.
c/o Skadden, Arps, et al.
4 Times Sq.
New York, NY 10036-6522

Financial data (yr. ended 05/31/02): Grants paid, $568,050; assets, $59,258 (M); expenditures, $579,674; qualifying distributions, $564,693.
Limitations: Applications not accepted. Giving on a national basis.
Application information: Contributes only to pre-selected organizations.
Director: Kenneth J. Bialkin.
EIN: 136220684
Codes: FD

33472
The Evelyn & Paul Robinson Family Foundation
c/o Bessemer Trust Co., N.A.
630 5th Ave., 34th Fl.
New York, NY 10111
Application address: 395 Bay Rd., Queensbury, NY 12804
Contact: Kathleen J. Fraher, Tr.

Established in 1999 in NY.
Donor(s): Evelyn M. Robinson Trust, E.M. Robinson Charitable Lead Annuity Trust.
Financial data (yr. ended 04/30/02): Grants paid, $567,900; assets, $249,247 (M); gifts received, $680,045; expenditures, $581,946; qualifying distributions, $578,768.
Limitations: Giving primarily in upstate NY, with emphasis on Amersterdam, Glens Falls, Albany, and Syracuse.
Trustees: Kathleen J. Fraher, Phillip K. Whittemore.
EIN: 141814054
Codes: FD

33473
Peer & Mary Pedersen Charitable Trust
c/o AMCO
505 Park Ave., 20th Fl.
New York, NY 10022-9306

Established in 1994 in NY.
Donor(s): Peer Pedersen, Mary Pedersen.
Financial data (yr. ended 11/30/01): Grants paid, $567,860; assets, $50,394 (M); expenditures, $578,662; qualifying distributions, $566,077.
Limitations: Applications not accepted. Giving primarily in CT and NY.
Application information: Contributes only to pre-selected organizations.
Officers: Peer Pedersen, Pres.; Mary Pedersen, Treas.
EIN: 133762413
Codes: FD

33474
Joseph & Sophia Abeles Foundation, Inc.
1055 Bedford Rd.
Pleasantville, NY 10570-3907
Contact: Lucille Werlinich, V.P.

Established in 1960 in NY.
Donor(s): Joseph Abeles, Sophia Abeles.‡

Financial data (yr. ended 12/31/01): Grants paid, $566,989; assets, $4,922,589 (M); gifts received, $226,900; expenditures, $570,409; qualifying distributions, $560,841.
Limitations: Applications not accepted. Giving primarily in New York, NY, and Westchester County, NY.
Application information: Contributes only to pre-selected organizations.
Officers: Joseph C. Abeles, Pres.; Lucille Werlinich, V.P.; Thomas A. Melfe, Secy.
EIN: 136259577
Codes: FD

33475
Carnahan-Jackson Foundation
c/o Not for Profit Institutions
1 East Ave., 3rd Fl.
Rochester, NY 14604
Application address: P.O. Box 3326, Jamestown, NY 14702-3326
Contact: Janet H. Schumacher, V.P.

Trust established in 1972 in NY.
Donor(s): Katharine J. Carnahan.‡
Financial data (yr. ended 07/31/01): Grants paid, $564,700; assets, $13,469,505 (M); expenditures, $744,957; qualifying distributions, $665,927.
Limitations: Giving primarily in western NY, particularly in the Jamestown area.
Publications: Application guidelines, grants list.
Application information: Application form required.
Trustee: Fleet National Bank.
EIN: 166151608
Codes: FD

33476
Shmuel Fuchs Foundation, Inc.
1271 60th St.
Brooklyn, NY 11219

Established in 1997 in NY.
Donor(s): Bernard Fuchs, Morris Fuchs.
Financial data (yr. ended 12/31/01): Grants paid, $564,622; assets, $77,479 (M); gifts received, $555,016; expenditures, $566,831; qualifying distributions, $566,831.
Limitations: Applications not accepted. Giving primarily in NY.
Application information: Contributes only to pre-selected organizations.
Officers: Bernard Fuchs, Pres.; Morris Fuchs, V.P.
Director: Serena Fuchs.
EIN: 113372438
Codes: FD

33477
The Boxer Foundation
c/o George Rothkopf
366 N. Broadway, Ste. 410
Jericho, NY 11753-2000

Established in 1985.
Donor(s): Leonard Boxer.
Financial data (yr. ended 11/30/01): Grants paid, $563,336; assets, $9,001,235 (M); expenditures, $611,885; qualifying distributions, $587,561.
Limitations: Applications not accepted. Giving primarily in the greater metropolitan New York, NY, area, including Long Island.
Application information: Contributes only to pre-selected organizations.
Officer: Leonard Boxer, Mgr.
Trustee: Steven Boxer.
EIN: 133345823
Codes: FD

33478
21st Century ILGWU Heritage Fund
275 7th Ave., 6th Fl.
New York, NY 10001 (212) 645-2740
FAX: (212) 645-2761
Contact: Muzaffar Chisti, Exec. Dir.

Established in 1999 in NY.
Donor(s): International Ladies Garment Workers Union.
Financial data (yr. ended 12/31/01): Grants paid, $563,250; assets, $13,310,553 (M); expenditures, $618,666; qualifying distributions, $597,629.
Publications: Application guidelines, program policy statement.
Application information: Applicants must submit one interim and one final report. Application form not required.
Officers and Directors:* Jay Mazur,* Pres.; Edgar Romney,* V.P.; Lloyd Goldenberg,* Treas.; Irwin Solomon,* Treas.; Muzaffar Chisti, Exec. Dir.; Ronald Alman, Theodore Bernstein, Susan Cowell, Hon. David Dinkins, Evelyn Dubrow, Joseph Fisher, Roy Goodson, Sol Hoffman, Christine Keiber, William T. Lee, David Melmon, Peter Nadash, and 11 additional directors.
EIN: 311593055
Codes: FD

33479
Louis V. Gerstner, Jr. Foundation, Inc.
c/o Bessemer Trust Co., N.A., Tax Dept.
630 5th Ave.
New York, NY 10111

Established in 1989 in NY.
Donor(s): Louis V. Gerstner, Jr.
Financial data (yr. ended 12/31/99): Grants paid, $561,262; assets, $31,811,761 (M); gifts received, $22,176,250; expenditures, $696,537; qualifying distributions, $590,816.
Limitations: Applications not accepted. Giving primarily in NY.
Application information: Contributes only to pre-selected organizations.
Officers and Directors:* Louis V. Gerstner, Jr.,* Pres.; Elizabeth R. Gerstner,* V.P.; Louis V. Gerstner III,* V.P.; Isabelle Cummins, Secy.; Preston Koster, Stan Litow.
EIN: 223045721
Codes: FD

33480
Filomena M. D'Agostino Foundation
950 3rd Ave., 32nd Fl.
New York, NY 10022 (212) 486-8615
Contact: David Malkin, V.P.

Established in 1990 in NY.
Donor(s): Filomena M. D'Agostino Greenberg.
Financial data (yr. ended 02/28/02): Grants paid, $561,000; assets, $8,151,988 (M); gifts received, $6,025,672; expenditures, $617,014; qualifying distributions, $567,428.
Limitations: Giving limited to New York, NY.
Application information: Application form not required.
Officers and Directors:* Max D'Agostino,* V.P.; David Malkin,* V.P.
EIN: 133548660
Codes: FD

33481
Novartis US Foundation
(Formerly Sandoz Foundation of America)
608 5th Ave.
New York, NY 10020
Washington, DC tel.: (202) 662-4371
Contact: Angelica Palacio

Incorporated in 1965 in DE; became Novartis US Foundation following a merger with Ciba educational foundation.
Donor(s): Sandoz Corp., Novartis Inc.
Financial data (yr. ended 12/31/01): Grants paid, $560,655; assets, $16,638,853 (M); gifts received, $174,943; expenditures, $631,151; qualifying distributions, $560,655.
Publications: Application guidelines.
Application information: Application form not required.
Trustees: Terry Barnett, Martin Henrich, Urs Nagelin, Burt Rosen, Erwin Schillinger.
EIN: 136193034
Codes: CS, FD

33482
The BTM Foundation, Inc.
c/o Bank of Tokyo-Mitsubishi, Ltd.
1251 Ave. of the Americas
New York, NY 10020-1104 (212) 782-4627
E-mail: bgilroy@btmna.com
Contact: Beth Gilroy, V.P.

Established in 1997 in NY.
Donor(s): Bank of Tokyo-Mitsubishi Trust Co.
Financial data (yr. ended 12/31/01): Grants paid, $560,500; assets, $4,992,328 (M); gifts received, $448,450; expenditures, $567,087; qualifying distributions, $560,500.
Limitations: Giving primarily in New York, NY.
Publications: Grants list, application guidelines.
Application information: Application form required.
Officers and Directors:* Nobuo Kuroyanagi,* Chair.; Saburo Sano,* Pres.; Robert Hand, Sr. V.P. and Secy.; Osamu Hida, Sr. V.P.; Beth Gilroy, V.P.; Thomas Greene, Treas.; Isaac Shapiro.
EIN: 133916201
Codes: CS, FD, CD

33483
Oscar and Regina Gruss Charitable and Educational Foundation, Inc.
74 Broad St.
New York, NY 10004

Incorporated in 1952 in NY.
Donor(s): Emanuel Gruss, Oscar Gruss,‡ Regina Gruss.‡
Financial data (yr. ended 03/31/01): Grants paid, $560,428; assets, $11,891,132 (M); expenditures, $576,763; qualifying distributions, $555,270.
Limitations: Applications not accepted. Giving primarily in New York, NY.
Application information: Contributes only to pre-selected organizations.
Officers: Riane Gruss, Pres.; Elizabeth Goldberg, V.P.; Emanuel Gruss, V.P.
Directors: Brenda Gruss, Donald Hamburg.
EIN: 136061333
Codes: FD

33484
Manfred R. & Anne Lehmann Foundation
910 5th Ave., Apt. 11A
New York, NY 10021
Contact: Sara Anne Lehmann, Pres.

Established in 1990 in NY.
Donor(s): Manfred R. Lehmann,‡ Sara A. Lehmann.
Financial data (yr. ended 09/30/01): Grants paid, $558,153; assets, $2,166,140 (M); gifts received, $216,000; expenditures, $749,456; qualifying distributions, $674,266.
Limitations: Giving primarily in NY.
Officer: Sara Anne Lehmann, Pres.
Directors: Karen Lehman Eisner, Barbara Lehmann Siegel.
EIN: 132918194
Codes: FD, GTI

33485
Hale Matthews Foundation
c/o Wormser, Kiely et al.
825 3rd Ave., 25th Fl.
New York, NY 10022 (212) 687-4900
Contact: Richard G. Hewitt, Dir.

Established in 1963.
Donor(s): Hale Matthews.‡
Financial data (yr. ended 12/31/01): Grants paid, $558,000; assets, $1,065,017 (M); expenditures, $582,617; qualifying distributions, $568,879.
Limitations: Applications not accepted. Giving primarily in NY.
Application information: Unsolicited requests for funds not accepted.
Officers and Directors:* William N. Ashbey,* Pres.; Helen Brann,* V.P.; Frances G. Scaife,* V.P.; Faith Stewart-Gordon, Secy.; Richard G. Hewitt.
EIN: 136157267
Codes: FD

33486
Point Gammon Foundation
c/o U.S. Trust Co.
114 W. 47th St.
New York, NY 10036

Established in 1994 in DE.
Financial data (yr. ended 12/31/01): Grants paid, $557,764; assets, $11,400,794 (M); gifts received, $137,547; expenditures, $568,551; qualifying distributions, $560,679.
Limitations: Applications not accepted. Giving primarily in New York, NY, and RI.
Application information: Unsolicited requests for funds not accepted.
Director: Jane Carroll.
EIN: 134049057
Codes: FD

33487
E. & H. Parnes Foundation, Inc.
c/o Parnes
P.O. Box 190620
Brooklyn, NY 11219-0620

Established in 1971 in NY.
Donor(s): Emanuel Parnes, Herschel Parnes.
Financial data (yr. ended 06/30/01): Grants paid, $557,633; assets, $7,455,351 (M); expenditures, $561,657; qualifying distributions, $556,835.
Limitations: Applications not accepted. Giving primarily in NY.
Application information: Contributes only to pre-selected organizations.
Managers: Emanuel Parnes, Herschel Parnes.
EIN: 237237932
Codes: FD

33488
The Peek Family Foundation, Inc.
2 World Financial Ctr., 38th Fl.
New York, NY 10281-6100

Established in 1999 in NY.
Donor(s): Elizabeth Peek, Jeffrey Peek.
Financial data (yr. ended 12/31/00): Grants paid, $557,423; assets, $2,428,604 (M); gifts received, $215,151; expenditures, $561,580; qualifying distributions, $554,534.
Limitations: Applications not accepted. Giving primarily in Princeton, NJ, and NY.
Application information: Contributes only to pre-selected organizations.
Officers: Jeffrey Peek, Pres.; Elizabeth Peek, V.P.
Director: Andrew Peek.
EIN: 134087127
Codes: FD

33489
Morris & Nellie L. Kawaler Foundation
c/o Zabelle, Shechter & Marks
P.O. Box 431
Millerton, NY 12546

Established in 1981.
Donor(s): Morris Kawaler.‡
Financial data (yr. ended 12/31/01): Grants paid, $557,000; assets, $10,181,852 (M); gifts received, $250,000; expenditures, $588,820; qualifying distributions, $553,617.
Limitations: Applications not accepted. Giving primarily in NY.
Application information: Contributes only to pre-selected organizations.
Officers: Robert Zabelle, Pres.; Justin Kawaler, Secy.; David J. Marks, Treas.
EIN: 133442495
Codes: FD

33490
Karen A. & Kevin W. Kennedy Foundation
c/o Goldman Sachs & Co.
85 Broad St., Tax Dept.
New York, NY 10004

Established 1985 in NY.
Donor(s): Kevin W. Kennedy.
Financial data (yr. ended 04/30/01): Grants paid, $556,563; assets, $1,542,759 (M); gifts received, $1,741,656; expenditures, $560,633; qualifying distributions, $556,633.
Limitations: Applications not accepted. Giving primarily in MA, NJ, and NY.
Application information: Contributes only to pre-selected organizations.
Trustees: Alfred C. Eckert III, Karen A. Kennedy, Kevin W. Kennedy.
EIN: 133318161
Codes: FD

33491
The Daniel and Florence Guggenheim Foundation
950 3rd Ave., 30th Fl.
New York, NY 10022 (212) 755-3199
FAX: (212) 755-4439
Contact: Oscar S. Straus II, Chair.

Incorporated in 1924 in NY.
Donor(s): Daniel M. Guggenheim,‡ Florence Guggenheim.‡
Financial data (yr. ended 12/31/01): Grants paid, $556,000; assets, $7,870,723 (M); expenditures, $796,428; qualifying distributions, $693,029.
Limitations: Giving primarily in CT, NJ, and NY.
Publications: Multi-year report.
Application information: Application form not required.
Officers and Directors:* Oscar S. Straus II,* Chair.; Oscar S. Schafer,* Pres.; Percy Preston, Jr.,* V.P. and Treas.; Anne Lindgren,* V.P.; Charles T. Locke III, Secy.; Powell M. Cabot, Michael B. Davies, Dana Draper, Daniel M. Guggenheim, Mrs. Max A. Hart, Mrs. Walter Metcalf III, Kristin Allyn Miller, Henry H. Patton, Susan H. Salomon, David A. Straus, Hon. Kenneth Taylor.
EIN: 135562232

Codes: FD

33492
Jean I. & Charles H. Brunie Foundation
21 Elm Rock Rd.
Bronxville, NY 10708

Established in 1986 in NY.
Donor(s): Charles H. Brunie, Jean I. Brunie.
Financial data (yr. ended 06/30/01): Grants paid, $553,908; assets, $1,008,122 (M); gifts received, $712,600; expenditures, $561,436; qualifying distributions, $555,294.
Limitations: Applications not accepted. Giving primarily in NY.
Application information: Contributes only to pre-selected organizations.
Trustees: Charles H. Brunie, Jean I. Brunie.
EIN: 133384777
Codes: FD

33493
The Summerhill Foundation
c/o BCRS Assoc., LLC
100 Wall St., 11th Fl.
New York, NY 10005

Established in 1954.
Donor(s): Peter G. Sachs, Eleanor B. Sachs,‡ Howard J. Sachs.‡
Financial data (yr. ended 11/30/01): Grants paid, $551,750; assets, $3,878,765 (M); expenditures, $559,186; qualifying distributions, $549,054.
Limitations: Applications not accepted. Giving primarily in CT, MA, and New York, NY.
Application information: Contributes only to pre-selected organizations.
Trustees: Katharine C. Sachs, Michael T. Sachs, Peter G. Sachs.
EIN: 136028811
Codes: FD

33494
Marianne Gaillard Faulkner Trust
c/o JPMorgan Chase Bank
1211 Ave. of the Americas, 38th Fl.
New York, NY 10036   (212) 789-5702
E-mail: neal_monica@jpmorgan.com
Contact: Monica Neal, V.P., JPMorgan Bank

Trust established in 1959 in VT.
Donor(s): Marianne Gaillard Faulkner.‡
Financial data (yr. ended 03/31/01): Grants paid, $551,544; assets, $10,266,131 (M); expenditures, $639,946; qualifying distributions, $581,253.
Limitations: Giving primarily in the Woodstock, VT, area.
Application information: Prefer matching or 1-time grants.
Trustee: JPMorgan Chase Bank.
EIN: 136047458
Codes: FD

33495
The Yacov and Rita Marmurstein Charitable Foundation Trust
5307 17th Ave.
Brooklyn, NY 11204

Established in 1999 in NY.
Donor(s): Yacov Marmurstein, Rita Marmurstein.
Financial data (yr. ended 12/31/00): Grants paid, $549,731; assets, $821,595 (M); gifts received, $720,219; expenditures, $552,532; qualifying distributions, $552,493.
Limitations: Applications not accepted. Giving primarily in Brooklyn, NY.
Application information: Contributes only to pre-selected organizations.
Trustees: Yacov Marmurstein, Rita Marmurstein.
EIN: 116532361

Codes: FD

33496
The Lookout Fund, Inc.
c/o Meyer Handelman Co.
P.O. Box 817
Purchase, NY 10577-0817

Established in 1966 in NY.
Donor(s): Fowler Merle-Smith, Annette C. Merle-Smith.
Financial data (yr. ended 12/31/01): Grants paid, $548,950; assets, $3,296,649 (M); expenditures, $562,185; qualifying distributions, $545,199.
Limitations: Applications not accepted. Giving primarily in NY.
Application information: Contributes only to pre-selected organizations.
Officers: Annette C. Merle-Smith, Pres.; William R. Handelman, V.P. and Treas.; Margaret F. Bergstrand, V.P.; Donald E. Handelman, V.P.; Russell J. Handelman, Secy.
EIN: 136213665
Codes: FD

33497
The Oncologic Foundation of Buffalo, Inc.
S. 5361 Fairgrounds Rd.
Hamburg, NY 14075-3008   (716) 648-3132
Contact: Kenneth R. Weishaupt, Treas.

Established in 1981 in NY.
Donor(s): Thomas J. Dougherty, Quadra Logic Technologies, Inc.
Financial data (yr. ended 04/30/01): Grants paid, $548,778; assets, $1,696,907 (M); expenditures, $596,368; qualifying distributions, $609,688.
Limitations: Giving primarily in Buffalo, NY.
Application information: Applicant must be a researcher employed by a research institute or university.
Officers: Thomas J. Dougherty, Ph.D., Pres.; John A. Buerk, V.P.; Raymond Reichert, Secy.; Kenneth R. Weishaupt, Treas.
EIN: 161183425
Codes: FD, GTI

33498
Reiss Family Foundation
c/o Georgica Advisors, LLC
152 W. 57th St., 46th Fl.
New York, NY 10019
Contact: Richard Reiss, Jr., Tr.

Established in 1987 in NY.
Donor(s): Richard Reiss.
Financial data (yr. ended 12/31/01): Grants paid, $547,016; assets, $2,363,464 (M); expenditures, $559,314; qualifying distributions, $553,165.
Limitations: Giving primarily in New York, NY.
Trustees: Bonnie Reiss, Richard Reiss, Jr.
EIN: 133383095
Codes: FD

33499
Richard Robinson & Helen Benham Charitable Fund
c/o JPMorgan Chase Bank
1211 Ave. of the Americas, 34th Fl.
New York, NY 10036

Established in 1992 in NY.
Donor(s): Richard Robinson.
Financial data (yr. ended 11/30/01): Grants paid, $546,773; assets, $6,123,378 (M); gifts received, $7,000; expenditures, $597,632; qualifying distributions, $549,084.
Limitations: Applications not accepted.
Application information: Contributes only to pre-selected organizations.
Trustee: JPMorgan Chase Bank.

EIN: 137005989
Codes: FD

33500
Leslie H. Wexner Charitable Fund
c/o George V. Delson Associates
110 E. 59th St., 28th Fl.
New York, NY 10022

Established in 1990 in OH.
Donor(s): Leslie H. Wexner.
Financial data (yr. ended 12/31/01): Grants paid, $546,666; assets, $332,609 (M); expenditures, $546,886; qualifying distributions, $546,886.
Limitations: Applications not accepted. Giving limited to Los Angeles, CA.
Application information: Contributes only to a pre-selected organization.
Officers and Directors:* Leslie H. Wexner,* Pres.; Jeffrey E. Epstein,* Secy.; Gideon Kaufman.
EIN: 311318013

33501
The Opatrny Family Foundation
(Formerly Donald C. and Judith T. Opatrny, Jr. Charitable Foundation)
c/o BCRS Assocs., LLC
100 Wall St., 11th Fl.
New York, NY 10005

Established in 1988 in NY.
Donor(s): Donald C. Opatrny, Jr.
Financial data (yr. ended 05/31/01): Grants paid, $546,050; assets, $5,264,647 (M); gifts received, $2,441,802; expenditures, $614,130; qualifying distributions, $548,630.
Limitations: Applications not accepted. Giving primarily in Greenwich, CT.
Application information: Contributes only to pre-selected organizations.
Trustees: Donald C. Opatrny, Jr., Judith T. Opatrny.
EIN: 133502411
Codes: FD

33502
The Wright Family Foundation, Inc.
P.O. Box 1046
Schenectady, NY 12301   (518) 347-4530
FAX: (518) 370-3105; *E-mail:* info@wrightfamilyfoundation.org; *URL:* http://www.wrightfamilyfoundation.org
Contact: Adeline W. Graham, Chair.

Established in 1997 in NY.
Donor(s): Schenectady International, Inc.
Financial data (yr. ended 09/30/99): Grants paid, $546,046; assets, $16,804,419 (M); expenditures, $546,046; qualifying distributions, $506,168.
Limitations: Giving limited to NY and Brazoria County, TX.
Application information: Application form available online. Application form required.
Officers: Adeline W. Graham, Chair.; A. Malcolm MacCormick, Vice-Chair.; Heather M. Ward, Secy.; Robert D. McQueen, Treas.
Trustees: Gregg W. Brown, Ashley G. Gardner.
EIN: 141792255
Codes: FD

33503
The Debs Foundation
1 Beekman Pl., Apt. 7A
New York, NY 10022
Contact: Richard A. Debs, Pres.

Established in 1991 in DE and CT.
Donor(s): Richard A. Debs.
Financial data (yr. ended 12/31/01): Grants paid, $545,875; assets, $6,999,291 (M); expenditures, $582,812; qualifying distributions, $551,779.

IN THIS SECTION, WITHIN EACH STATE, FOUNDATIONS ARE LISTED IN DESCENDING ORDER BY TOTAL GRANTS PAID

33503—NEW YORK

Limitations: Applications not accepted. Giving primarily in New York, NY.
Application information: Contributes only to pre-selected organizations.
Officers: Richard A. Debs, Pres.; Barbara K. Debs, V.P.
Directors: Elizabeth A. Debs, Nicholas A. Debs.
EIN: 133639449
Codes: FD

33504
Sweetgrass Foundation
170 Newell Rd.
Hammond, NY 13646
Contact: Allan P. Newell, Pres.

Established in 1992 in NY.
Donor(s): Allan P. Newell, Jean Newell.‡
Financial data (yr. ended 12/31/01): Grants paid, $545,683; assets, $8,223,837 (M); expenditures, $552,533; qualifying distributions, $547,132.
Limitations: Applications not accepted. Giving limited to St. Lawrence County and the St. Lawrence River Valley, NY, areas.
Application information: Contributes only to pre-selected organizations. Unsolicited requests for grants not accepted.
Officers and Directors:* Allan P. Newell,* Pres. and Treas.; Catherine B. Newell,* V.P. and Secy.; Mark Scarlett.
EIN: 161414871
Codes: FD

33505
The Albert Kunstadter Family Foundation
1035 5th Ave.
New York, NY 10028 (212) 794-3951
Additional tel.: (212) 249-1733; FAX: (212) 794-1273; E-mail: akff@aol.com
Contact: John W. Kunstadter, Pres., or Geraldine S. Kunstadter, Chair.

Incorporated in 1952 in IL.
Donor(s): Members of the Kunstadter family.
Financial data (yr. ended 12/31/01): Grants paid, $545,650; assets, $2,799,341 (M); expenditures, $630,793; qualifying distributions, $551,821.
Limitations: Giving in the U.S., primarily to organizations based in New York, NY, the Boston, MA, area, and Washington, DC; funding also in Hanoi, Vietnam, Vientiane, Laos, Phnom Penh, Cambodia, and Beijing, China.
Publications: Annual report (including application guidelines).
Application information: Accepts NYRAG Common Grant Application Form. Application form not required.
Officers and Directors:* Geraldine S. Kunstadter,* Chair.; John W. Kunstadter,* Pres. and Treas.; Lisa Kunstadter,* V.P. and Secy.; Christopher T.W. Kunstadter,* V.P.; Elizabeth Von Habsburg,* V.P.
EIN: 366047975
Codes: FD

33506
Dave H. & Reba W. Williams Foundation
1345 Ave. of the Americas, 38th Fl.
New York, NY 10105
Contact: Dave H. Williams, Tr.

Established in 1986 in NY.
Donor(s): Dave H. Williams, Reba W. Williams.
Financial data (yr. ended 06/30/01): Grants paid, $545,150; assets, $843,241 (M); gifts received, $600,000; expenditures, $562,350; qualifying distributions, $545,650.
Limitations: Applications not accepted. Giving primarily in New York, NY.
Application information: Contributes only to pre-selected organizations.

Trustees: Dave H. Williams, Reba W. Williams.
EIN: 133381821
Codes: FD

33507
Weissman Family Foundation, Inc.
81 Manursing Way
Rye, NY 10580
E-mail: weismg@idt.net
Contact: George Weissman, Chair.

Established in 1992 in NY.
Donor(s): George Weissman.
Financial data (yr. ended 12/31/01): Grants paid, $544,390; assets, $8,838,099 (M); gifts received, $477,650; expenditures, $581,392; qualifying distributions, $544,390.
Limitations: Applications not accepted. Giving primarily in New York, NY; some giving also in Israel.
Application information: Contributes only to pre-selected organizations.
Officers: George Weissman, Chair.; Mildred Weissman, Pres.; Daniel Weissman, V.P.; Ellen Weissman, Secy.; Paul Weissman, Treas.
EIN: 133688122
Codes: FD

33508
UJA-Federation Charitable Common Fund
c/o UJA-Federation of Jewish Philanthropies of NY
130 E. 59th St.
New York, NY 10022-1302

Established in 1996.
Financial data (yr. ended 12/31/01): Grants paid, $541,182; assets, $843,788 (M); gifts received, $249,610; expenditures, $554,910; qualifying distributions, $545,696.
Officers: James Tisch, Pres.; John S. Ruskay, V.P.; Charles B. Goldman, Secy.-Treas.
Directors: Richard L. Kay, Lynn Korda Kroll, Judith S. Peck, Peggy Tishman.
EIN: 061209895
Codes: FD

33509
Peter A. and Deborah L. Weinberg Family Foundation
c/o Goldman Sachs & Co.
85 Broad St., Tax Dept.
New York, NY 10004-2456

Established in 1996 in CT.
Donor(s): Peter A. Weinberg.
Financial data (yr. ended 07/31/01): Grants paid, $541,085; assets, $8,189,878 (M); gifts received, $2,639,627; expenditures, $627,229; qualifying distributions, $544,229.
Limitations: Applications not accepted. Giving in the U.S. and London, England.
Application information: Contributes only to pre-selected organizations.
Trustees: Deborah L. Weinberg, Peter A. Weinberg.
EIN: 133920469
Codes: FD

33510
Gimprich Family Foundation, Inc.
c/o Dr. Paul Steinberg
1 W. 4th St.
New York, NY 10012

Established in 1975.
Donor(s): Maryan Gimprich.‡
Financial data (yr. ended 05/31/01): Grants paid, $540,550; assets, $9,832,683 (M); expenditures, $689,482; qualifying distributions, $656,349.

Limitations: Giving primarily in the U.S.; some support for Israel.
Application information: Application form required.
Officers: Robert Satter, Pres.; Lila Gimprich, V.P.; Paul Steinberg, Secy.; Rosalie Dolmatch, Rec. Secy.; Max Nussbaum, Treas.
EIN: 510147095
Codes: FD

33511
The Kellner Foundation
c/o Kellner, Dileo, & Co.
900 3rd. Ave., 10th Fl.
New York, NY 10022

Established in 1996 in NY.
Donor(s): George Kellner, Martha Kellner.
Financial data (yr. ended 12/31/01): Grants paid, $539,840; assets, $4,040,420 (M); expenditures, $608,459; qualifying distributions, $539,840.
Limitations: Giving primarily in NY.
Trustees: Catherine Kellner, George Kellner, Martha Kellner, Peter Kellner.
EIN: 137084979
Codes: FD

33512
Priscilla & Richard J. Schmeelk Foundation, Inc.
c/o J. Anderson
1003 Park Blvd.
Massapequa Park, NY 11762
Contact: Richard J. Schmeelk, Pres. and Treas.

Established in 1983 in NY.
Donor(s): Richard J. Schmeelk.
Financial data (yr. ended 12/31/01): Grants paid, $539,743; assets, $4,688,232 (M); gifts received, $31,718; expenditures, $582,547; qualifying distributions, $539,743.
Limitations: Applications not accepted. Giving primarily in New York, NY.
Application information: Contributes only to pre-selected organizations.
Officers and Directors:* Richard J. Schmeelk,* Pres. and Treas.; Priscilla M. Schmeelk,* V.P. and Secy.
EIN: 133126387
Codes: FD

33513
The Dorothea Haus Ross Foundation
1036 Monroe Ave.
Rochester, NY 14620 (716) 473-6006
FAX: (716) 473-6007; E-mail: dhrossfnd@aol.com
Contact: Wayne S. Cook, Ph.D., Exec. Dir.

Established in 1979 in NY.
Donor(s): Dorothea Haus Ross.‡
Financial data (yr. ended 05/31/01): Grants paid, $539,460; assets, $18,438,162 (M); gifts received, $13,089,965; expenditures, $825,384; qualifying distributions, $725,929.
Limitations: Giving on a national and international basis.
Publications: Application guidelines.
Application information: 1 copy only of appendix material. Application form not required.
Trustees: Wayne S. Cook, Exec. Dir.; Charles C. Chamberlain, Kathryn C. Chamberlain, Edward C. Radin, Fleet National Bank.
EIN: 161080458
Codes: FD

33514
The Steinberg Family Fund, Inc.
c/o Bear Stearns & Co., Inc.
383 Madison Ave.
New York, NY 10179-0001

Established in 1984 in NY.
Donor(s): Robert Steinberg.
Financial data (yr. ended 11/30/01): Grants paid, $538,239; assets, $7,220,750 (M); expenditures, $540,989; qualifying distributions, $530,145.
Limitations: Applications not accepted. Giving primarily in CT, NJ, and NY.
Application information: Contributes only to pre-selected organizations.
Officers: Robert Steinberg, Pres.; Suzanne Steinberg, V.P. and Treas.
EIN: 133254493
Codes: FD

33515
Toshiba America Foundation
1251 Ave. of the Americas, 41st Fl.
New York, NY 10020 (212) 596-0620
FAX: (212) 588-0824; E-mail: foundation@tai.toshiba.com; URL: http://www.taf.toshiba.com
Contact: Laura Cronin, Fdn. Mgr.

Established in 1990 in NY.
Donor(s): Toshiba America, Inc.
Financial data (yr. ended 03/31/01): Grants paid, $536,140; assets, $11,224,269 (M); expenditures, $560,151; qualifying distributions, $546,495.
Limitations: Giving on a national basis, with some emphasis on areas of company operations in CA, NJ, NY, SD, TN, TX, and VA.
Publications: Annual report, grants list, occasional report, informational brochure (including application guidelines).
Application information: Applications received by FAX will not be considered. Requests in excess of $5,000 will be decided at the Mar. or Sept. board meeting. Application form required.
Officers and Board Member:* John Anderson,* Pres.; Laura Cronin, Fdn. Mgr.
EIN: 133596612
Codes: CS, FD, CD

33516
The Ted Snowdon Foundation
(Formerly The Snowdon Foundation)
50 Riverside Dr., No. 15-C
New York, NY 10024-6508
Tel./FAX: (212) 787-2413; E-mail: snowdonfound@aol.com
Contact: Edward W. Snowdon, Jr., Pres.

Established in 1997 in DE and NY.
Donor(s): Edward W. Snowdon, Jr.
Financial data (yr. ended 04/30/01): Grants paid, $535,500; assets, $6,627,163 (M); expenditures, $577,500; qualifying distributions, $577,500.
Limitations: Applications not accepted. Giving primarily in New York, NY.
Application information: Unsolicited requests for funds not accepted.
Officers and Directors:* Edward W. Snowdon, Jr.,* Pres. and Treas.; Richard W. Snowdon,* V.P.; Robert S. Blaustein, Secy.; Peter Boogaard.
EIN: 133948662
Codes: FD

33517
Marie Baier Foundation, Inc.
6 E. 87th St.
New York, NY 10128

Established about 1967.
Donor(s): John F. Baier.‡

Financial data (yr. ended 12/31/01): Grants paid, $534,950; assets, $16,251,889 (M); expenditures, $810,396; qualifying distributions, $704,553.
Limitations: Giving primarily in New York, NY.
Officers and Directors:* Berteline B. Dale,* Pres.; John F. Baier, Jr.,* V.P.; Irene Carr-Rollitt, Guenter F. Metsch, Sidney Sirkin.
EIN: 136267032
Codes: FD

33518
The Tokarz Foundation, Inc.
c/o Kohlberg, Kravis, Roberts & Co.
9 W. 57th St.
New York, NY 10019
Contact: Michael T. Tokarz, Pres.

Established in 1994 in NY.
Donor(s): Michael T. Tokarz.
Financial data (yr. ended 11/30/01): Grants paid, $534,432; assets, $4,392,181 (M); gifts received, $1,027,578; expenditures, $567,078; qualifying distributions, $540,307.
Limitations: Applications not accepted. Giving primarily in NY.
Application information: Contributes only to pre-selected organizations.
Officers: Michael T. Tokarz, Pres. and Treas.; Nancy C. Tokarz, V.P. and Secy.
EIN: 133797212
Codes: FD

33519
Kitov Foundation
c/o BCRS Assocs., LLC
100 Wall St., 11th Fl.
New York, NY 10005

Established in 1987 in NY.
Donor(s): Jacob Z. Schuster.
Financial data (yr. ended 06/30/01): Grants paid, $533,807; assets, $3,551,171 (M); expenditures, $583,432; qualifying distributions, $535,282.
Limitations: Applications not accepted. Giving primarily in NY.
Application information: Contributes only to pre-selected organizations.
Trustees: Diane T. Schuster, Jacob Z. Schuster.
EIN: 133437905
Codes: FD

33520
The P.S. Trust
(also known as The Healey Family Foundation)
c/o Thomas & Margaret Healey
32 Old Slip, 18th Fl.
New York, NY 10005

Established in 1989 in NJ.
Donor(s): Thomas J. Healey.
Financial data (yr. ended 04/30/01): Grants paid, $533,728; assets, $6,764,688 (M); gifts received, $2,182,125; expenditures, $618,275; qualifying distributions, $511,625.
Limitations: Applications not accepted. Giving primarily in NJ, NY, and PA.
Application information: Contributes only to pre-selected organizations.
Trustees: Megan H. Hagerty, Margaret S. Healey, Thomas J. Healey, Thomas Jeremiah Healey.
EIN: 133531967
Codes: FD

33521
The Community Foundation of Dutchess County
(Formerly The Area Fund)
80 Washington St., Ste. 201
Poughkeepsie, NY 12601 (845) 452-3077
Contact: Patricia A. Wright, Exec. Dir.

Established in 1969 in NY.

Donor(s): McCann Foundation, Lester Freer.‡
Financial data (yr. ended 06/30/00): Grants paid, $533,077; assets, $17,660,509 (M); gifts received, $5,247,796; expenditures, $916,101.
Limitations: Giving primarily in Dutchess County, NY.
Publications: Annual report, application guidelines.
Application information: Application form required.
Officers and Trustees:* Ira Effron,* Pres.; Thomas R.B. Campbell,* V.P., Devel.; John Cina,* V.P., Fin.; Susan Brown,* Secy.; Patricia A. Wright, Exec. Dir.; and 20 additional trustees.
EIN: 237026859
Codes: CM, FD, GTI

33522
Citibank Employees Foundation
(Formerly The National City Foundation)
c/o Corp. Tax Dept.
850 3rd Ave., 4th Fl.
New York, NY 10043
Scholarship application address: Scholarship Prog., c/o CSS Educational Testing Svc., P.O. Box 6730, Princeton, NJ 08541

Established in 1969.
Financial data (yr. ended 12/31/99): Grants paid, $532,300; assets, $1,906,718 (M); gifts received, $299,044; expenditures, $806,340; qualifying distributions, $804,730.
Limitations: Giving primarily in NY.
Publications: Annual report.
Application information: Scholarship recipients chosen by committee selected by College Scholarship Service. Application form required.
Officers: Paul Ostergard, Chair.; Paulette Samuels, Secy.; Elizabeth Ciaston, C.F.O.; Wilhelmena Kelly, Mgr.
Directors: Walter Kupferschmidt, Managing Dir.; Arlene Adler, Judith Fullmer, Alan Okada, Charlotte Overton.
EIN: 136097628
Codes: FD

33523
The Moshe and Frady Kalter Foundation, Inc.
c/o Moshe Kalter
1558 55th St.
Brooklyn, NY 11219

Established in 1995.
Donor(s): Moshe Kalter.
Financial data (yr. ended 12/31/00): Grants paid, $532,100; assets, $1,220,924 (M); gifts received, $1,525,000; expenditures, $751,526; qualifying distributions, $532,100.
Limitations: Giving primarily in Brooklyn, NY.
Officers: Moshe Kalter, Pres.; Frady Kalter, Secy.; Aryeh L. Kalter, Sheindy E. Saffer, Mindy L. Steger.
EIN: 113283510
Codes: FD

33524
Kissinger Family Foundation, Inc.
c/o Walter B. Kissinger
200 Broadhollow Rd., Ste. 402
Melville, NY 11747
Contact: Eugenie Kissinger, Tr.

Established in 1997 in NY.
Donor(s): The Kissinger Family.
Financial data (yr. ended 11/30/01): Grants paid, $530,050; assets, $5,104,686 (M); gifts received, $2,000; expenditures, $929,945; qualifying distributions, $270,624.
Limitations: Applications not accepted.
Application information: Contributes only to pre-selected organizations.

33524—NEW YORK

Trustees: Eugenie Kissinger, John Kissinger, Thomas Kissinger, Walter B. Kissinger, William Kissinger, Dana Kissinger-Matray.
EIN: 113397778
Codes: FD

33525
Chodron Foundation
112 Greene St., Ste. 5
New York, NY 10012
Contact: Leslie Sutton McGauley, Pres.

Established in 1999 in NY.
Donor(s): Mark McGauley, Leslie Sutton McGauley, Lava, LLC.
Financial data (yr. ended 12/31/01): Grants paid, $530,000; assets, $625,889 (M); gifts received, $1,073,087; expenditures, $543,046; qualifying distributions, $536,473.
Limitations: Applications not accepted.
Application information: Contributes only to pre-selected organizations.
Officers: Leslie McGauley, Pres.; Mark McGauley, Treas.
EIN: 134075603
Codes: FD

33526
Kautz Family Foundation
c/o BCRS Assocs., LLC
100 Wall St., 11th Fl.
New York, NY 10005
Contact: Caroline Kautz, Tr.

Established in 1981 in NY.
Donor(s): James C. Kautz, Peter Levy, Ron Tauber, Bob Friedman, Ann Brown Farrell, Martha Barnes Miller.
Financial data (yr. ended 02/28/01): Grants paid, $529,750; assets, $14,169,054 (M); gifts received, $742,639; expenditures, $643,117; qualifying distributions, $576,174.
Limitations: Applications not accepted. Giving primarily in NY.
Application information: Contributes only to pre-selected organizations.
Trustees: Caroline M. Kautz, Daniel P. Kautz, James C. Kautz, Leslie B. Kautz, Roy J. Zuckerberg.
EIN: 133103149
Codes: FD

33527
David Jaffe Charitable Trust
3904 15th Ave.
Brooklyn, NY 11218

Established in 1992 in NY.
Donor(s): David Jaffe.
Financial data (yr. ended 12/31/99): Grants paid, $528,500; assets, $0 (M); expenditures, $528,550; qualifying distributions, $532,448.
Limitations: Applications not accepted.
Directors: Rabbi Avrohom Ausband, Yerachmiel Barish, Rabbi Yaacov Horowitz.
EIN: 116414353
Codes: FD

33528
Schwartz Family Foundation
c/o Goldman Sachs & Co.
85 Broad St., Tax Dept.
New York, NY 10004

Established in 1991 in NY.
Donor(s): Mark Schwartz.
Financial data (yr. ended 04/30/01): Grants paid, $526,800; assets, $782,796 (M); expenditures, $526,888; qualifying distributions, $526,800.
Limitations: Applications not accepted. Giving primarily in MA and NY.
Application information: Contributes only to pre-selected organizations.
Trustees: Lisa H. Schwartz, Mark Schwartz.
EIN: 133632755
Codes: FD

33529
The Valentine Perry Snyder Fund
c/o JPMorgan Private Bank, Global Foundations Group
1211 Ave. of the Americas, 38th Fl.
New York, NY 10036 (212) 789-5715
Contact: Lisa L. Philp, V.P.

Trust established in 1942 in NY.
Donor(s): Sheba Torbert Snyder.‡
Financial data (yr. ended 12/31/01): Grants paid, $526,000; assets, $9,763,653 (M); expenditures, $594,425; qualifying distributions, $530,248.
Limitations: Giving limited to New York City.
Publications: Application guidelines, grants list.
Application information: Application form not required.
Officer: Lisa L. Philp, V.P.
Trustee: JPMorgan Chase Bank.
EIN: 136036765
Codes: FD

33530
Hagop Kevorkian Fund
1025 Northern Blvd., Ste. 209
Roslyn, NY 11576
Contact: Ralph D. Minasian, Pres. and Treas.

Trust established in 1950; incorporated in 1951 in NY.
Donor(s): Hagop Kevorkian.‡
Financial data (yr. ended 12/31/01): Grants paid, $525,250; assets, $7,218,042 (M); expenditures, $625,572; qualifying distributions, $374,423.
Limitations: Applications not accepted. Giving primarily in Cambridge, MA, New York, NY, and Philadelphia, PA.
Application information: Contributes only to pre-selected organizations.
Officers and Trustees:* Ralph D. Minasian,* Pres. and Treas.; Martin D. Polevoy,* V.P. and Secy.; Miriam Chan.
EIN: 131839686
Codes: FD

33531
Helen Hoffritz Charitable Trust
c/o JPMorgan Chase Bank
1211 6th Ave., 34th Fl.
New York, NY 10036 (212) 789-5679
E-mail: elias_jacqueline@jpmorgan.com
Contact: Jacqueline Elias, V.P., JPMorgan Chase Bank

Established in 1996 in NY.
Donor(s): Helen Hoffritz.‡
Financial data (yr. ended 12/31/01): Grants paid, $525,000; assets, $13,035,144 (M); gifts received, $497,339; expenditures, $668,448; qualifying distributions, $544,841.
Limitations: Applications not accepted. Giving primarily in NY.
Application information: Contributes only to pre-selected organizations.
Trustee: JPMorgan Chase Bank.
EIN: 136655406
Codes: FD

33532
The Lois Pope Life Foundation
c/o Winston & Strawn
200 Park Ave.
New York, NY 10166
Application address: 252 S. Ocean Blvd., Manalapan, FL 33462, tel.: (561) 547-9307
Contact: Robert C. Miller and Lois B. Pope, Trustees

Established in 1996 in FL.
Donor(s): Lois B. Pope.
Financial data (yr. ended 12/31/99): Grants paid, $524,850; assets, $404,016 (M); gifts received, $1,098,360; expenditures, $1,106,936; qualifying distributions, $1,007,697.
Application information: Application form not required.
Trustees: Robert C. Miller, Lois B. Pope.
EIN: 137086087
Codes: FD

33533
Peter C. Cornell Trust
c/o Fiduciary Svcs., Inc.
4050 Harlem Rd.
Snyder, NY 14226 (716) 839-3005

Established in 1949 in NY.
Donor(s): Peter C. Cornell, M.D.‡
Financial data (yr. ended 09/30/01): Grants paid, $523,746; assets, $7,144,694 (M); expenditures, $617,996; qualifying distributions, $518,066.
Limitations: Giving primarily in western NY, including Buffalo and the Niagara region.
Publications: Informational brochure.
Application information: Application form required.
Trustees: John A. Mitchell, J. Donald Schumacher, Susan Cornell Wilkes.
EIN: 951660344
Codes: FD

33534
Netzach Foundation
c/o Abraham Trusts
444 Madison Ave., 11th Fl.
New York, NY 10022

Established in 1992 in NY.
Donor(s): Laurie Pinck, Menachem Pinck, Jerry Solomon, Estanne Abraham, Bron Industries, Reliable Health Systems.
Financial data (yr. ended 03/31/01): Grants paid, $523,283; assets, $3,438,827 (M); gifts received, $292,017; expenditures, $551,404; qualifying distributions, $518,762.
Limitations: Applications not accepted. Giving primarily in NY.
Application information: Unsolicited requests for funds not accepted.
Trustees: Hirschell E. Levine, Laurie Pinck, Menachem Pinck.
EIN: 136967224
Codes: FD, GTI

33535
The Rosenthal Fund
784 Park Ave., Apt. 19B
New York, NY 10021

Established in 1996 in NY.
Donor(s): Charles Rosenthal.
Financial data (yr. ended 09/30/01): Grants paid, $523,215; assets, $2,845,489 (M); gifts received, $439,930; expenditures, $540,128; qualifying distributions, $518,900.
Limitations: Applications not accepted. Giving primarily in NY and RI.
Application information: Contributes only to pre-selected organizations.

Officers: Charles Rosenthal, Pres.; Phyllis Rosenthal, Secy.
EIN: 133919545
Codes: FD

33536
The Stone Foundation, Inc.
c/o Mariner Mgmt.
950 3rd Ave., 17th Fl.
New York, NY 10022-2705

Incorporated in 1985 in NY.
Donor(s): Donald Stone.
Financial data (yr. ended 11/30/99): Grants paid, $523,010; assets, $2,934,487 (M); gifts received, $35,276; expenditures, $560,924; qualifying distributions, $516,586.
Limitations: Applications not accepted. Giving primarily in New York, NY.
Application information: Contributes only to pre-selected organizations.
Directors: Donald Stone, James Stone, Jean Stone.
EIN: 136066290
Codes: FD

33537
Allyn Foundation, Inc.
P.O. Box 22
Skaneateles, NY 13152 (315) 685-9427
Contact: Meg M. O'Connell

Incorporated in 1956 in NY.
Donor(s): William N. Allyn,‡ Welch Allyn, Inc.
Financial data (yr. ended 12/31/01): Grants paid, $522,444; assets, $11,157,063 (M); expenditures, $588,869; qualifying distributions, $536,390.
Limitations: Giving primarily in Onondaga and Cayuga counties, NY.
Publications: Application guidelines.
Application information: Application form required.
Officers: William F. Allyn, Pres.; Lew F. Allyn, V.P.; Dawn N. Allyn, Secy.; Elsa A. Soderberg, Treas.; Meg O'Connel,* Exec. Dir.
Directors: Amy Allyn, David Allyn, Eric R. Allyn, Janet J. Allyn, Scott Allyn, M.D., Donald Nelson, Jon Soderberg, Libby Soderberg, Peer Soderberg, Peter Soderberg, Robert Soderberg, Wilbur Townsend, Charles S. Tracy, Sonya Weinfeld.
EIN: 156017723
Codes: FD

33538
The Selma Ruben Foundation
c/o Lawrence Ruben Co.
600 Madison Ave., 20th Fl.
New York, NY 10022-1615

Established in 1997 in NY.
Donor(s): Selma Ruben.
Financial data (yr. ended 12/31/00): Grants paid, $521,834; assets, $22,567,406 (M); expenditures, $602,422; qualifying distributions, $517,463.
Limitations: Applications not accepted. Giving primarily in NY.
Application information: Contributes only to pre-selected organizations.
Trustees: Rochelle Kivell, Lenore Ruben, Richard Ruben, Selma Ruben.
EIN: 137113807
Codes: FD

33539
The Irving Weinstein Foundation, Inc.
c/o Douglas F. Allen, Esq.
40 W. 57th St.
New York, NY 10019

Established in 1961.
Donor(s): Irving Weinstein.‡
Financial data (yr. ended 03/31/01): Grants paid, $521,001; assets, $10,669,852 (M); gifts received, $75,000; expenditures, $770,142; qualifying distributions, $650,862.
Limitations: Applications not accepted. Giving primarily in New York, NY; funding also in San Diego, CA.
Application information: Contributes only to pre-selected organizations.
Officers: Martin Lipkin, Chair.; Joan Lipkin, Treas.
Directors: Richard Lipkin, Steven M. Lipkin.
EIN: 136093068
Codes: FD

33540
The Mnuchin Foundation
c/o BCRS Assocs., LLC
67 Wall St., 8th Fl.
New York, NY 10005

Established in 1980 in NY.
Donor(s): Robert E. Mnuchin.
Financial data (yr. ended 04/30/01): Grants paid, $520,974; assets, $8,127,725 (M); gifts received, $700,000; expenditures, $546,764; qualifying distributions, $523,049.
Limitations: Applications not accepted. Giving primarily in New York, NY.
Application information: Contributes only to pre-selected organizations.
Trustees: Eugene Mercy, Jr., Adriana Mnuchin, Robert E. Mnuchin.
EIN: 133050751
Codes: FD

33541
The RJM Foundation
c/o Brown Brothers Harriman Trust. Co., LLC
63 Wall St.
New York, NY 10005

Donor(s): R. James MacAleer.
Financial data (yr. ended 07/31/01): Grants paid, $520,000; assets, $12,205,647 (M); expenditures, $702,887; qualifying distributions, $520,446.
Limitations: Applications not accepted. Giving primarily in Princeton, NJ, and West Chester, PA.
Application information: Contributes only to pre-selected organizations.
Trustee: R. James MacAleer.
EIN: 236953316
Codes: FD

33542
The Robert E. Keiter Charitable Trust
43 Taylor Rd., RFD-3
Mount Kisco, NY 10549

Established in 1984 in NY.
Donor(s): Robert E. Keiter.
Financial data (yr. ended 12/31/01): Grants paid, $519,670; assets, $484,249 (M); gifts received, $195,105; expenditures, $526,957; qualifying distributions, $520,299.
Limitations: Applications not accepted. Giving primarily in MA, NY, and PA.
Application information: Contributes only to pre-selected organizations.
Trustees: Jane Keiter, Robert E. Keiter.
EIN: 136847763
Codes: FD

33543
The Wickham Foundation, Inc.
7 Locust Ln.
Bronxville, NY 10708

Established in 1998 in NY.
Donor(s): Craig J. Foley, Judy M. Foley.
Financial data (yr. ended 05/31/02): Grants paid, $519,158; assets, $110,423 (M); expenditures, $524,535; qualifying distributions, $519,119.
Limitations: Applications not accepted. Giving primarily in Bronxville, NY, and Gambier, OH.
Application information: Contributes only to pre-selected organizations.
Officers and Directors:* Craig J. Foley,* Pres.; Judy M. Foley,* Secy.; Terrence C. Shea.
EIN: 134011572
Codes: FD

33544
Slovin Foundation
c/o Kraft Haiken & Bell, LLP
551 5th Ave.
New York, NY 10176

Established in 1988 in NY.
Donor(s): Bruce Slovin.
Financial data (yr. ended 02/28/01): Grants paid, $517,830; assets, $497,518 (M); gifts received, $197,156; expenditures, $527,515; qualifying distributions, $517,830.
Limitations: Applications not accepted. Giving primarily in NY.
Application information: Contributes only to pre-selected organizations.
Officer: Bruce Slovin, Pres.
EIN: 236912396
Codes: FD

33545
The Judy & Howard Berkowitz Foundation
c/o HPB Assocs., LLC
65 E. 55th St., 30th Fl.
New York, NY 10022

Established in 1987.
Donor(s): Howard P. Berkowitz.
Financial data (yr. ended 03/31/01): Grants paid, $517,620; assets, $1,694,190 (M); gifts received, $665,000; expenditures, $528,378; qualifying distributions, $517,870.
Limitations: Applications not accepted. Giving primarily in NY.
Application information: Contributes only to pre-selected organizations.
Trustees: Howard P. Berkowitz, Judith Berkowitz, Roger Berkowitz, Sandra Berkowitz.
EIN: 133371065
Codes: FD

33546
Horncrest Foundation, Inc.
6 Sleator Dr.
Ossining, NY 10562 (914) 941-5533
Contact: Lawrence Blau, Pres.

Established in 1960 in NY.
Financial data (yr. ended 09/30/01): Grants paid, $517,338; assets, $3,102,915 (M); gifts received, $2,852; expenditures, $527,616; qualifying distributions, $521,463.
Limitations: Applications not accepted. Giving primarily in the Twin Cities, MN, St. Louis, MO, and Madison, WI.
Application information: Unsolicited requests for funds not accepted.
Officers and Directors:* Lawrence Blau,* Pres.; Olivia Blau,* V.P. and Secy.
EIN: 136021261
Codes: FD

33547
The Lopatin Family Foundation
c/o BCRS Assocs., LLC
100 Wall St., 11th Fl.
New York, NY 10005

Established in 1994 in NY.

Donor(s): Jonathan M. Lopatin.
Financial data (yr. ended 08/31/01): Grants paid, $516,600; assets, $6,268,739 (M); gifts received, $4,478,675; expenditures, $655,338; qualifying distributions, $518,725.
Limitations: Applications not accepted. Giving primarily in New York, NY.
Application information: Contributes only to pre-selected organizations.
Trustees: Brenda Berry-Lopatin, Jonathan M. Lopatin.
EIN: 133797381
Codes: FD

33548
John & Patricia Klingenstein Fund
c/o Tanton & Co., LLP
37 W. 57th St., 5th Fl.
New York, NY 10019
Contact: Janet L. Mulligan, CPA

Established in 1999 in NY.
Donor(s): John Klingenstein.
Financial data (yr. ended 12/31/01): Grants paid, $516,351; assets, $9,931,029 (M); gifts received, $964,097; expenditures, $564,273; qualifying distributions, $514,632.
Limitations: Applications not accepted. Giving primarily in NY.
Trustees: Kenneth H. Fields, John Klingenstein, Patricia Klingenstein.
EIN: 134062589
Codes: FD

33549
The Dakota Foundation, Inc.
c/o Barragato
950 3rd Ave., 17th Fl.
New York, NY 10022
Application address: 17 N. Ward Ave., Rumson, NJ 07760
Contact: John A. and Nancy B. Mulheren

Established in 1984 in NJ.
Donor(s): John Mulheren, Nancy Mulheren, John Mulheren, Jr.
Financial data (yr. ended 10/31/01): Grants paid, $516,298; assets, $988,200 (M); gifts received, $1,084,000; expenditures, $517,328; qualifying distributions, $516,298.
Limitations: Giving primarily in NJ.
Application information: Application form not required.
Trustees: Arthur Aeder, John Mulheren, Nancy Mulheren.
EIN: 222621688
Codes: FD

33550
Adam R. Rose Foundation
200 Madison Ave., 5th Fl.
New York, NY 10016

Established in 1996 in DE.
Donor(s): Adam Rose.
Financial data (yr. ended 12/31/01): Grants paid, $515,575; assets, $54,261 (M); gifts received, $400,000; expenditures, $515,885; qualifying distributions, $515,569.
Limitations: Applications not accepted. Giving primarily in NY.
Application information: Contributes only to pre-selected organizations.
Officers: Adam M. Rose, Pres.; Michael D. Sullivan, Secy.
EIN: 137095495
Codes: FD

33551
Rosh Foundation
c/o Goldman Sachs & Co.
85 Broad St., Tax Dept.
New York, NY 10004

Established in 1991 in NY.
Donor(s): Robin Neustein.
Financial data (yr. ended 03/31/01): Grants paid, $515,150; assets, $7,689,993 (M); gifts received, $756,897; expenditures, $583,041; qualifying distributions, $515,980.
Limitations: Applications not accepted. Giving primarily in the metropolitan New York, NY, area.
Application information: Contributes only to pre-selected organizations.
Trustees: Robin Neustein, Shimon Neustein.
EIN: 133637441
Codes: FD

33552
The M. & M. Schwartz Family Foundation
78 Joseph Ave.
Staten Island, NY 10314-5002 (718) 494-7005
Contact: Moshe Schwartz, Tr.

Established in 1998 in NY.
Donor(s): Arie Schwartz, Francis Schwartz, Malka Schwartz, Moshe Schwartz.
Financial data (yr. ended 12/31/01): Grants paid, $515,000; assets, $553,241 (M); gifts received, $886,000; expenditures, $516,677; qualifying distributions, $516,677.
Limitations: Giving primarily in Brooklyn, NY.
Trustees: Malka Schwartz, Moshe Schwartz.
EIN: 134034456
Codes: FD

33553
The Robin Brown and Charles Seelig Family Foundation
c/o Goldman Sachs & Co.
85 Broad St., Tax Dept.
New York, NY 10004

Established in 1993 in NY.
Donor(s): Charles B. Seelig, Jr.
Financial data (yr. ended 05/31/01): Grants paid, $514,500; assets, $2,710,317 (M); gifts received, $3,750; expenditures, $573,500; qualifying distributions, $516,739.
Limitations: Applications not accepted. Giving primarily in NY.
Application information: Contributes only to pre-selected organizations.
Trustees: Robin D. Brown, Charles B. Seelig, Jr.
EIN: 133748044
Codes: FD

33554
Gasper & Irene Lazzara Charitable Foundation
c/o Franklin Montgomery
90 Broad St., 19th Fl.
New York, NY 10022
Application address: 129 Bristol Pl., Ponte Vedra Beach, FL 32082
Contact: Irene Lazzara, Pres.

Established in 1996 in FL.
Donor(s): Gasper Lazzara, Irene Lazzara.
Financial data (yr. ended 04/30/01): Grants paid, $514,451; assets, $13,950,509 (M); gifts received, $333,937; expenditures, $521,238; qualifying distributions, $514,451.
Limitations: Giving primarily in Jacksonville, FL.
Application information: Application form not required.
Officer: Irene Lazzara, Pres.
EIN: 597079426
Codes: FD

33555
The Robert J. Hurst Foundation
c/o Goldman Sachs & Co.
85 Broad St., Tax Dept.
New York, NY 10004

Established in 1997 in NY.
Donor(s): Robert J. Hurst.
Financial data (yr. ended 12/31/00): Grants paid, $512,488; assets, $21,808,837 (M); gifts received, $4,748,850; expenditures, $815,171; qualifying distributions, $513,308.
Limitations: Applications not accepted. Giving primarily in NY.
Application information: Contributes only to pre-selected organizations.
Trustees: Alexander B. Hurst, Robert J. Hurst.
EIN: 311568195
Codes: FD

33556
Ernst & Elfriede Frank Foundation, Inc
112-01 Queens Blvd., Apt. 11C
Forest Hills, NY 11375

Established around 1962.
Donor(s): Ernst L. Frank.
Financial data (yr. ended 08/31/01): Grants paid, $511,388; assets, $8,395,996 (M); expenditures, $550,632; qualifying distributions, $512,091.
Limitations: Applications not accepted. Giving on a national and international basis, with emphasis on Washington, DC, MA, and NY; some funding also in Canada and South America.
Application information: Contributes only to pre-selected organizations.
Officers: Ernst H. Frank, V.P. and Secy.; Sybil Ann Brennan, V.P.; Eva Maria Tausig, V.P.
EIN: 136106471
Codes: FD

33557
The Sullivan Family Foundation
c/o BCRS Associates, LLC
100 Wall St., 11th Fl.
New York, NY 10005-3720

Established in 1989 in MA.
Donor(s): Daniel J. Sullivan, Jr.
Financial data (yr. ended 05/31/01): Grants paid, $511,266; assets, $231,308 (M); gifts received, $259,063; expenditures, $518,541; qualifying distributions, $511,986.
Limitations: Applications not accepted. Giving primarily in Boston, MA and New York, NY.
Application information: Contributes only to pre-selected organizations.
Trustees: Daniel J. Sullivan, Jr., Marjorie O. Sullivan.
EIN: 133531989
Codes: FD

33558
The M. J. and Caral G. Lebworth Foundation
c/o Yohalem Gillman & Co., LLP
477 Madison Ave
New York, NY 10022-5802

Established in 1998 in NY.
Donor(s): Caral G. Lebworth, Marion J. Lebworth.
Financial data (yr. ended 12/31/01): Grants paid, $511,002; assets, $5,760,248 (M); expenditures, $639,649; qualifying distributions, $511,002.
Limitations: Applications not accepted. Giving primarily in New York, NY.
Application information: Contributes only to pre-selected organizations.
Trustees: Caral G. Lebworth, Marion J. Lebworth.
EIN: 134000723
Codes: FD

33559
James T. Lee Foundation, Inc.
c/o Grubb & Ellis New York Inc.
55 E. 59th St., 11th Fl.
New York, NY 10022
Contact: Raymond T. O'Keefe Jr., Pres.

Incorporated in 1958 in NY.
Donor(s): James T. Lee.‡
Financial data (yr. ended 11/30/01): Grants paid, $511,000; assets, $6,059,275 (M); expenditures, $554,744; qualifying distributions, $515,636.
Limitations: Applications not accepted. Giving primarily in NY.
Application information: Contributes only to pre-selected organizations.
Officers and Directors:* Raymond T. O'Keefe, Jr.,* Pres.; Delcour S. Potter,* V.P.; Thomas Appleby, Verne S. Atwater, Leelee D'Olier Brown, Paul Duffy, Stephen B. Siegel, Richard W. Wheeless, Vincent Ziccolella.
EIN: 131878496
Codes: FD

33560
The Troy Savings Bank Community Foundation
32 2nd St.
Troy, NY 12180
Application address: Hedley Park Pl., 433 River St., Troy, NY 12180, tel.: (518) 270-4932
Contact: Daniel J. Hogarty, Jr., Pres.

Established in 1999 in DE and NY.
Donor(s): Troy Financial Corp.
Financial data (yr. ended 12/31/01): Grants paid, $510,799; assets, $9,629,328 (M); expenditures, $554,027; qualifying distributions, $552,415.
Limitations: Giving primarily in NY.
Application information: Application form required.
Officers and Directors:* Daniel J. Hogarty, Jr.,* Pres.; Kevin M. O'Bryan,* Secy.; David Deluca,* Treas.; The Troy Savings Bank.
EIN: 141813866
Codes: CS, FD

33561
Charles M. & Mary D. Grant Foundation
c/o JPMorgan Chase Bank
1211 Ave. of the Americas, 38th Fl.
New York, NY 10036 (212) 789-5679
E-mail: elias_jacqueline@jpmorgan.com
Contact: Jacqueline E. Elias, V.P.

Established in 1967 in NY.
Donor(s): Mary D. Grant.‡
Financial data (yr. ended 12/31/01): Grants paid, $510,000; assets, $9,607,265 (M); expenditures, $581,045; qualifying distributions, $517,509.
Limitations: Giving limited to the southeastern U.S.
Publications: Grants list, application guidelines.
Application information: Application form not required.
Officer: Jacqueline E. Elias, V.P. and Senior Prog. Off.
Trustee: JPMorgan Chase Bank.
EIN: 136264329
Codes: FD

33562
Stowe Family Foundation
1088 Park Ave., No. 16F
New York, NY 10128-1132

Established in 1996.
Donor(s): Richard H. Stowe, Virginia K. Stowe.
Financial data (yr. ended 09/30/01): Grants paid, $509,624; assets, $1,301,874 (M); gifts received, $428,448; expenditures, $512,870; qualifying distributions, $509,106.
Limitations: Giving primarily in Brunswick, ME, New York, NY, and PA.
Trustees: Douglas Stowe, Richard H. Stowe, Virginia K. Stowe.
EIN: 137104307
Codes: FD

33563
Robert N. & Nancy A. Downey Foundation
c/o BCRS Assocs., LLC
67 Wall St, 8th Fl.
New York, NY 10005

Established in 1982.
Donor(s): Robert N. Downey.
Financial data (yr. ended 01/31/01): Grants paid, $509,359; assets, $551,091 (M); gifts received, $274,641; expenditures, $525,531; qualifying distributions, $506,377.
Limitations: Applications not accepted. Giving primarily in New York, NY.
Application information: Contributes only to pre-selected organizations.
Trustees: Nancy A. Downey, Robert N. Downey.
EIN: 133103213
Codes: FD

33564
The Central National-Gottesman Foundation
3 Manhattanville Rd.
Purchase, NY 10577-2110
Scholarship application address: 417 Riverside Dr., New York, NY 10025; Additional tels.: (914) 696-9153 (Joshua Eisenstein), or (914) 696-9062 (Geri Tolan)
Contact: Christine Royer

Established in 1981 in NY.
Donor(s): Central National-Gottesman, Inc.
Financial data (yr. ended 12/31/01): Grants paid, $508,729; assets, $14,518,870 (M); expenditures, $686,525; qualifying distributions, $546,407.
Limitations: Giving primarily in NY.
Application information: Scholarship application form required; applicants must be children of employees.
Officers: Kenneth Wallach, Pres; Ira Wallach, Exec. V.P.; Joshua J. Eisenstein, Treas.
EIN: 133047546
Codes: CS, FD, CD, GTI

33565
Ripplewood Foundation, Inc.
1 Rockefeller Plz., 32nd Fl.
New York, NY 10020

Established in 1997 in DE and NY.
Donor(s): Ripplewood Holdings LLC.
Financial data (yr. ended 12/31/00): Grants paid, $508,725; assets, $771,361 (M); expenditures, $540,903; qualifying distributions, $498,903.
Limitations: Applications not accepted. Giving on a national basis, with some emphasis on NY.
Application information: Contributes only to pre-selected organizations.
Officers: Timothy C. Collins, Pres.; John M. Duryea, Secy.
EIN: 522036080
Codes: CS, FD, CD

33566
Nelson B. Delavan Foundation
c/o JPMorgan Chase Bank
P.O. Box 1412
Rochester, NY 14603
Application address: 130 S. Main St., Canandaigua, NY 14424-1904, tel.: (315) 394-7675
Contact: Janis Mosher, Trust Off.

Established in 1983 in NY.
Financial data (yr. ended 12/31/01): Grants paid, $508,547; assets, $7,120,288 (M); expenditures, $576,540; qualifying distributions, $509,581.
Limitations: Giving primarily in NY, with emphasis on the Seneca Falls region.
Application information: Application form not required.
Trustee: JPMorgan Chase Bank.
EIN: 166260274
Codes: FD

33567
The Andrew & Ann Tisch Foundation, Inc.
c/o Mark J. Krinsky, C.P.A.
655 Madison Ave., 8th Fl.
New York, NY 10021-8043

Established in 1992 in NY.
Donor(s): Laurence A. Tisch.
Financial data (yr. ended 12/31/01): Grants paid, $508,236; assets, $6,626,848 (M); expenditures, $554,388; qualifying distributions, $504,640.
Limitations: Applications not accepted. Giving primarily in NY.
Application information: Contributes only to pre-selected organizations.
Officers: Andrew H. Tisch, Pres.; Ann R. Tisch, Sr. V.P.; Mark J. Krinsky, V.P.; Thomas M. Steinberg, V.P.; Barry L. Bloom, Secy.-Treas.
EIN: 133693583
Codes: FD

33568
Solomon and Clara Heisler Family Foundation
1661 53rd St.
Brooklyn, NY 11204
Contact: Solomon Heisler, Pres.

Established in 1992 in NY.
Donor(s): Solomon Heisler.
Financial data (yr. ended 12/31/01): Grants paid, $508,100; assets, $7,955,577 (M); gifts received, $666,188; expenditures, $611,106; qualifying distributions, $510,853.
Limitations: Giving primarily in Brooklyn, NY.
Application information: Application form not required.
Officers: Solomon Heisler, Pres.; Clara Heisler, V.P.; Rosemarie Weingarten, Secy.; Anna Schon, Treas.
EIN: 113133210
Codes: FD

33569
Kealy Family Foundation
c/o Goldman Sachs & Co.
85 Broad St., Tax Dept.
New York, NY 10004
Additional address: 120 N. Baum Trail, Duck, NC 27949, tel.: (252) 261-0233; E-mail: BEKRI@aol.com
Contact: William J. Kealy, Tr.

Established in 1985.
Donor(s): William F. Kealy, William J. Kealy, Ellen M. Kealy.
Financial data (yr. ended 05/31/01): Grants paid, $507,465; assets, $3,965,714 (M); expenditures, $541,333; qualifying distributions, $513,083.
Limitations: Applications not accepted. Giving primarily in the Outer Banks, NC area, and New York City.
Application information: Contributes only to pre-selected organizations.
Trustees: Maureen K. Jacquelin, Roger A. Jacquelin, Alexandra Kealy, Daniel M. Kealy, Ellen M. Kealy, Tracey E. Kealy, William J. Kealy, William K. Kealy.
EIN: 133318124
Codes: FD

33570
Sophia & William Casey Foundation
c/o Steven T. Rosenberg
201 Moreland Rd., Ste. 6
Hauppauge, NY 11788
Application address: Glenwood Rd., Roslyn Harbor, NY 11576, tel.: (516) 621-9332
Contact: Sophia Casey, Pres.

Established in 1974 in NY.
Donor(s): William J. Casey.‡
Financial data (yr. ended 11/30/01): Grants paid, $506,677; assets, $1,464,086 (M); expenditures, $526,677; qualifying distributions, $504,735.
Limitations: Giving on a national basis.
Officers: Sophia Casey, Pres. and Treas.; Bernadette Casey-Smith, V.P. and Secy.
EIN: 510153218
Codes: FD

33571
Pinky Foundation
c/o Ernst & Young LLP
787 7th Ave.
New York, NY 10019-6018
Contact: Pat Doudna

Established in 1997 in NY.
Donor(s): Cathy B. Graham, Stephen M. Graham.
Financial data (yr. ended 12/31/00): Grants paid, $506,670; assets, $23,733 (M); gifts received, $51,106; expenditures, $515,626; qualifying distributions, $508,770.
Limitations: Giving primarily in NY.
Trustees: Cathy B. Graham, Stephen M. Graham.
EIN: 137107821
Codes: FD

33572
Miles Hodsdon Vernon Foundation, Inc.
c/o Chadbourne, et al.
P.O. Box 701
Sleepy Hollow, NY 10591-0701
(914) 631-4226
Application address: 49 Beekman Ave., Sleepy Hollow, NY 10591
Contact: Robert C. Thomson, Jr., Pres.

Incorporated in 1953 in NY.
Donor(s): Miles Hodsdon Vernon,‡ Martha Hodsdon Kinney,‡ Louise Hodsdon.‡
Financial data (yr. ended 12/31/00): Grants paid, $506,100; assets, $10,163,429 (M); expenditures, $650,336; qualifying distributions, $524,150.
Limitations: Giving primarily in NY.
Officers and Directors:* Robert C. Thomson, Jr.,* Pres. and Treas.; Dennis M. Fitzgerald,* V.P. and Secy.; Linda T. Murray, Eloise T. Schundler, Gertrude Whalen.
EIN: 136076836
Codes: FD

33573
Robert H. and Janet C. Buescher Foundation
1400 Old Country Rd., Ste. 407
Westbury, NY 11590

Established in 1999 in NY.
Financial data (yr. ended 12/31/01): Grants paid, $506,000; assets, $127,767 (M); expenditures, $507,278; qualifying distributions, $507,111.
Limitations: Applications not accepted. Giving in the U.S., with emphasis on New York City and Long Island, NY.
Application information: Contributes only to pre-selected organizations.
Officer: Robert H. Buescher, Pres.
Trustees: Janet C. Buescher, Kurt A. Buescher, Kim L. Faass, Carol L. Maxwell.
EIN: 113497567
Codes: FD

33574
Michael Fuchs Charitable Foundation
c/o Michael Fuchs
9 W. 57th St., Ste. 4220
New York, NY 10019

Established in 1997 in NY.
Donor(s): Michael Fuchs.
Financial data (yr. ended 12/31/99): Grants paid, $505,833; assets, $5,956,097 (M); expenditures, $527,499; qualifying distributions, $503,482.
Limitations: Applications not accepted. Giving primarily in NY.
Application information: Contributes only to pre-selected organizations.
Trustee: Michael Fuchs.
EIN: 137068909
Codes: FD

33575
The Community Foundation of the Elmira-Corning Area
(Formerly The Community Foundation of the Chemung County Area and Corning Community Foundation)
307B, E. Water St.
Elmira, NY 14901-3402 (607) 734-6412
FAX: (607)734-7335; *E-mail:* info@communityfund.org; *URL:* http://www.communityfund.org
Contact: Suzanne H. Lee, Pres.

Established in 1977 in NY as Chemung County; Corning established in 1972 in NY; reincorporated in 1993 under current name after merger of Community Foundation of Chemung County Area and Corning Community Foundation.
Financial data (yr. ended 06/30/00): Grants paid, $505,712; assets, $9,929,602 (M); expenditures, $721,463.
Limitations: Giving only in Chemung and southeastern Steuben counties, NY.
Publications: Annual report (including application guidelines), newsletter, application guidelines.
Application information: Call or write for guidelines. Scholarship applications and guidelines (for residents of Chemung and southeastern Steuben counties only) available each year on Dec. 15; other grant applications available on Aug. 15. Application form required.
Officers and Trustees:* G. Thomas Tranter, Sr., Chair.; Suzanne H. Lee, Pres.; Richard Bessey,* V.P.; Linda J. Gudas,* V.P.; Clover M. Drinkwater, Secy.; Steve Albertalli,* Treas.; Dalton Cates, Jane H. Cadwallader, Thomas Connelly, Robert Crede, Elizabeth Dalrymple, Kevin Geoghan, John V. Goff, John Gough, Donald B. Beck, John Loose, Robert B. McKinnon, Patricia Powers, Mary Booth Roberts, Ginger Schirmer, Thomas Snow, Rowland Stebbins III, Ann Weiland.
EIN: 161100837
Codes: CM, FD, GTI

33576
Jerry and Emily Spiegel Family Foundation, Inc.
(Formerly Jerry Spiegel Foundation, Inc.)
2 E. 88th St.
New York, NY 10128-0555

Established in 1958 in NY.
Donor(s): Jerry Spiegel, Emily Spiegel.
Financial data (yr. ended 03/31/01): Grants paid, $505,662; assets, $9,395,701 (M); gifts received, $625,000; expenditures, $522,799; qualifying distributions, $518,146.
Limitations: Applications not accepted. Giving primarily in NY.
Application information: Contributes only to pre-selected organizations. Unsolicited requests for funds not accepted.
Officers: Jerry Spiegel, Pres.; Arthur D. Sanders, V.P.; Emily Spiegel, V.P.; Lise Spiegel, Secy.
EIN: 116006020
Codes: FD

33577
Ruth Bartsch Memorial Bank Trust
c/o JPMorgan Chase Bank, Tax Dept.
1211 6th Ave., 34th Fl.
New York, NY 10036-0001

Established in 1983 in NY.
Donor(s): Ruth Bartsch.‡
Financial data (yr. ended 11/30/01): Grants paid, $505,000; assets, $9,096,016 (M); expenditures, $610,700; qualifying distributions, $526,924.
Limitations: Applications not accepted. Giving primarily in NH.
Application information: Contributes only to pre-selected organizations.
Trustees: Theofore N. Richards, Vincent William Richards, Jr., JPMorgan Chase Bank.
EIN: 133188775
Codes: FD

33578
The LeBrun Foundation
200 Theater Pl.
Buffalo, NY 14202

Established in 1974.
Donor(s): Jennifer L. Jacobs, Jeremy Jacobs.
Financial data (yr. ended 06/30/01): Grants paid, $505,000; assets, $1,802,389 (M); gifts received, $26,066; expenditures, $547,249; qualifying distributions, $513,562.
Limitations: Giving on a national and international basis.
Publications: Application guidelines.
Application information: Grantseekers should submit a pre-application questionnaire prior to submitting a proposal. Application form not required.
Trustees: Thomas R. Beecher, Jr., Jennifer L. Jacobs.
EIN: 237408547
Codes: FD

33579
Loewy Family Foundation, Inc.
80 Wall St., No. 1018
New York, NY 10005
Contact: John P. Reiner, Secy.-Treas.

Established in 1966 in NY.
Donor(s): Alfred Loewy,‡ Edna Loewy Butler.‡
Financial data (yr. ended 06/30/01): Grants paid, $505,000; assets, $10,328,814 (M); expenditures, $607,201; qualifying distributions, $506,671.
Limitations: Giving primarily in New York, NY.
Application information: Application form required.
Officers and Directors:* Michael Green,* V.P.; Erik A. Hanson,* V.P.; Brigitte Linz,* V.P.; Mischa A. Zabotin,* V.P.; John P. Reiner,* Secy.-Treas.
EIN: 136225288
Codes: FD

33580
Ludwig W. Frohlich Charitable Trust
c/o Chadbourne & Parke, LLC
30 Rockefeller Plz.
New York, NY 10112

Trust established in 1969 in NY.
Donor(s): Ludwig W. Frohlich.‡
Financial data (yr. ended 12/31/01): Grants paid, $503,050; assets, $5,938,171 (M); expenditures, $672,739; qualifying distributions, $567,632.
Limitations: Applications not accepted. Giving primarily in New York, NY; some giving also in East Hampton.

Application information: Contributes only to pre-selected organizations.
Trustees: Kathleen B. Buddenhagen, Ingrid Lilly Burns, Madeleine D. Burns, Richard B. Leather.
EIN: 136288404
Codes: FD

33581
The Hurford Foundation
c/o Winston & Strawn
200 Park Ave.
New York, NY 10166-4193

Established in 1986.
Donor(s): John B. Hurford, BEA Assocs., Inc.
Financial data (yr. ended 12/31/00): Grants paid, $502,650; assets, $6,709,566 (M); gifts received, $126,500; expenditures, $582,209; qualifying distributions, $537,823.
Limitations: Applications not accepted. Giving primarily in NY.
Application information: Contributes only to pre-selected organizations.
Officers and Directors:* Robert C. Miller, Pres. and Treas.; Jayne M. Kurzman,* V.P.; William W. Priest, Jr.,* Secy.
EIN: 133394688
Codes: FD

33582
The Perry and Martin Granoff Family Foundation, Inc.
c/o Hogan & Hartson LLP, Att.: BJT
551 5th Ave.
New York, NY 10176

Established in 1993 in NJ.
Donor(s): Martin J. Granoff.
Financial data (yr. ended 12/31/01): Grants paid, $502,337; assets, $7,790,065 (M); gifts received, $902,760; expenditures, $619,196; qualifying distributions, $502,337.
Limitations: Applications not accepted. Giving primarily in Washington, DC, NJ and NY; some funding also in MA.
Application information: Contributes only to pre-selected organizations.
Officers and Trustees:* Martin J. Granoff,* Pres.; Perry Granoff,* V.P.; Michael Granoff,* Secy.
EIN: 521647009
Codes: FD

33583
Edward L. Milstein Foundation
355 Madison Ave., Ste. 1500
New York, NY 10017
Contact: Paul Milstein, Tr.

Established in 1996 in NY.
Donor(s): Irma Milstein, Paul Milstein, Edward L. Milstein.
Financial data (yr. ended 12/31/01): Grants paid, $501,672; assets, $1,478,653 (M); gifts received, $250,000; expenditures, $526,786; qualifying distributions, $511,737.
Limitations: Applications not accepted.
Application information: Contributes only to pre-selected organizations.
Trustees: Edward L. Milstein, Irma Milstein, Paul Milstein.
EIN: 133921821
Codes: FD

33584
Eric P. Sheinberg Foundation
c/o Goldman Sachs & Co.
85 Broad St., Tax Dept.
New York, NY 10004-2456

Established in 1971.
Donor(s): Eric P. Sheinberg.
Financial data (yr. ended 06/30/01): Grants paid, $500,550; assets, $10,730,185 (M); expenditures, $506,300; qualifying distributions, $498,744.
Limitations: Applications not accepted. Giving primarily in New York, NY.
Application information: Contributes only to pre-selected organizations.
Trustees: Eric P. Sheinberg, Michael Steinhardt.
EIN: 137004291
Codes: FD

33585
Marble Fund, Inc.
c/o Rosenberg Selsman and Co., LLP
655 3rd. Ave., Ste. 1610
New York, NY 10017
Contact: Marion H. Levy, Pres.

Established in 1952 in NY.
Donor(s): M. William Levy,‡ Marion H. Levy, Caryn L. Magid, William Guy Levy.
Financial data (yr. ended 12/31/01): Grants paid, $500,170; assets, $3,036,959 (M); expenditures, $517,512; qualifying distributions, $485,044.
Limitations: Giving primarily in NY.
Officers and Director:* Marion H. Levy,* Pres.; William Guy Levy, V.P.; Caryn L. Magid, V.P.
EIN: 136084387
Codes: FD

33586
Randolph L. Cowen & Phyllis Green Foundation
85 Broad St., Tax Dept.
New York, NY 10004

Established in 1996 in NY.
Donor(s): Randolph L. Cowen.
Financial data (yr. ended 05/31/01): Grants paid, $500,000; assets, $1,004,187 (M); gifts received, $540,668; expenditures, $532,330; qualifying distributions, $495,518.
Limitations: Applications not accepted. Giving primarily in MI.
Application information: Contributes only to pre-selected organizations.
Trustees: Randolph L. Cowen, Phyllis Green.
EIN: 137109419
Codes: FD

33587
The Aaron, Martha, Isidore & Blanche Rosansky Foundation
c/o Aronauer Goldfarb et al
444 Madison Ave., 17th Fl.
New York, NY 10022
Contact: Alan Sills, Dir.

Donor(s): B. Rosansky Trust.
Financial data (yr. ended 12/31/00): Grants paid, $500,000; assets, $3,752,409 (M); expenditures, $587,010; qualifying distributions, $523,329.
Limitations: Giving primarily in NY.
Directors: Zevulun Charlop, Jonathan I. Ginsberg, Betty Rifkin, Alan Sills, Leo N. Sokol.
EIN: 112594677
Codes: FD

33588
Meyer & Jean Steinberg Family Foundation, Inc.
(Formerly Meyer Steinberg Foundation, Inc.)
475 5th Ave., 12th Fl.
New York, NY 10017
Contact: Bonnie Englebardt, Dir.

Established in 1965 in NY.
Donor(s): Bonnie Englebardt, Susan Zizesgreen, Meyer Steinberg, Carol Weisman, Lois Zaro.
Financial data (yr. ended 12/31/01): Grants paid, $498,910; assets, $5,923,677 (M); gifts received, $200,884; expenditures, $532,293; qualifying distributions, $497,403.
Limitations: Giving primarily in NY.
Officers: Meyer Steinberg, Pres. and Treas.; Jean Steinberg, V.P. and Secy.
EIN: 136199973
Codes: FD

33589
Shamai & Richu Hartman Family Foundation
1639 52nd St.
Brooklyn, NY 11204

Established in 1993.
Donor(s): Alexander Hartman, Sima Hartman.
Financial data (yr. ended 11/30/01): Grants paid, $498,630; assets, $10,952,777 (M); gifts received, $959,490; expenditures, $507,178; qualifying distributions, $498,775.
Limitations: Applications not accepted.
Application information: Contributes only to pre-selected organizations.
Trustees: Alexander Hartman, Sima Hartman.
EIN: 113189198
Codes: FD

33590
The Reich Family Charitable Trust
131 Dover St.
Brooklyn, NY 11235

Established in 1993 in NY.
Donor(s): Raymond Reich.
Financial data (yr. ended 12/31/99): Grants paid, $498,493; assets, $542,348 (M); gifts received, $221,964; expenditures, $498,859; qualifying distributions, $496,208.
Limitations: Applications not accepted. Giving primarily in Brooklyn, NY.
Application information: Contributes only to pre-selected organizations.
Trustees: Raymond Reich, Sue Reich.
EIN: 137029481
Codes: FD

33591
The Jacobson Family Foundation
152 W. 57th St., 56th Fl.
New York, NY 10019

Established in 1997 in NY.
Donor(s): Mitchell Jacobson.
Financial data (yr. ended 12/31/00): Grants paid, $498,004; assets, $10,653,856 (M); gifts received, $7,404,688; expenditures, $515,290; qualifying distributions, $440,722.
Limitations: Applications not accepted. Giving primarily in Palm Beach, FL and New York, NY.
Application information: Contributes only to pre-selected organizations.
Officers and Directors:* Kathy Howard Jacobson,* Pres.; Mitchell Jacobson,* V.P.; Joseph L. Getraer,* Secy.
EIN: 133922461
Codes: FD

33592
J. & H. Gross Family Foundation
1224 E. 24th St.
Brooklyn, NY 11210
Contact: Jonathan Gross, Tr.

Established in 1996 in NY.
Donor(s): Jonathan Gross.
Financial data (yr. ended 06/30/01): Grants paid, $497,452; assets, $2,882,858 (M); gifts received, $5,000; expenditures, $590,160; qualifying distributions, $506,328.
Limitations: Giving primarily in NY.
Trustees: Ben Gross, Heddy Gross, Jonathan Gross.
EIN: 113344451
Codes: FD

33593
Virginia & Leonard Marx Foundation
18 Heathcote Rd.
Scarsdale, NY 10583-4418
Application address: 708 3rd Ave., New York, NY 10017, tel.: (212) 557-1400
Contact: Jennifer Gruenberg, Secy.

Established in 1959 in NY.
Donor(s): Leonard Marx,‡ Virginia Marx.
Financial data (yr. ended 12/31/01): Grants paid, $496,300; assets, $35,716,416 (M); gifts received, $1,233,768; expenditures, $541,985; qualifying distributions, $497,412.
Limitations: Giving primarily in New York, NY.
Application information: Application form not required.
Officers: John E. Tuchler, Pres.; Jennifer Gruenberg, Secy.; Leonard Marx, Jr., Treas.
EIN: 136162557
Codes: FD

33594
L and L Foundation
570 Park Ave.
New York, NY 10021
Contact: Mildred C. Brinn, Pres.

Incorporated in 1963 in NY.
Financial data (yr. ended 12/31/01): Grants paid, $495,850; assets, $9,628,975 (M); expenditures, $621,417; qualifying distributions, $546,635.
Limitations: Giving primarily in NY.
Application information: Application form not required.
Officers and Directors:* Mildred C. Brinn,* Pres. and Treas.; Peter F. De Gaetano,* Secy.
EIN: 136155758
Codes: FD

33595
Krueger Family Foundation
c/o Barry Strauss Assocs., Ltd.
307 5th Ave., 8th Fl.
New York, NY 10016-6517

Established in 1990 in NY.
Donor(s): Harvey M. Krueger.
Financial data (yr. ended 09/30/01): Grants paid, $495,600; assets, $16,117 (M); expenditures, $496,815; qualifying distributions, $495,626.
Limitations: Applications not accepted. Giving primarily in New York, NY.
Application information: Contributes only to pre-selected organizations.
Trustees: Abigail Krueger Bialer, Cathleen Krueger Cohen, Constance A. Krueger, Harvey M. Krueger, Elizabeth Krueger Seley.
EIN: 132696029
Codes: FD

33596
Gideon Charitable Trust Foundation
c/o U.S. Trust
114 W. 47th St.
New York, NY 10036-1510
Application address: c/o Duffy, Kekel, Jensen & Bernard, Attn.: Carolyn Wilson Miller, 1100 S.W. 6th Ave., Ste. 1200, Portland, OR 97204, tel.: (503) 226-1371

Established in 1994 in OR.
Donor(s): Charles Swindells.
Financial data (yr. ended 12/31/01): Grants paid, $494,500; assets, $554,658 (M); gifts received, $508,613; expenditures, $502,873; qualifying distributions, $491,531.
Limitations: Giving on a national basis.
Trustee: Charles Swindells, U.S. Trust.
EIN: 936279785
Codes: FD

33597
The Evelyn Sharp Foundation
c/o Peter Sharp & Co.
545 Madison Ave.
New York, NY 10022 (212) 977-1300
Contact: Mary Cronson, Pres.

Incorporated in 1952 in NY.
Donor(s): Evelyn Sharp.‡
Financial data (yr. ended 12/31/00): Grants paid, $493,844; assets, $15,492,320 (M); expenditures, $522,098; qualifying distributions, $504,146.
Limitations: Giving primarily in New York, NY.
Application information: Generally contributes to pre-selected organizations. Application form not required.
Officers and Trustees:* Mary Cronson,* Pres.; Paul Cronson,* Secy.; Barry Tobias,* Treas.; Claus Virch.
EIN: 136119532
Codes: FD

33598
The Mesdag Family Foundation
c/o BCRS Associates, LLC
100 Wall St., 11th Fl.
New York, NY 10005

Established in 1991 in NY.
Donor(s): T. Willem Mesdag.
Financial data (yr. ended 03/31/02): Grants paid, $493,105; assets, $5,240,032 (M); gifts received, $353,561; expenditures, $549,293; qualifying distributions, $495,227.
Limitations: Applications not accepted. Giving primarily in CA, with some giving in CO and Washington, DC.
Application information: Contributes only to pre-selected organizations.
Trustees: Lisa Ann Mesdag, T. Willem Mesdag, Mark Schwartz.
EIN: 133651269
Codes: FD

33599
A.E. Charitable Foundation
c/o U.S. Trust
114 W. 47th St.
New York, NY 10036 (212) 649-5971
Application address: 364 E. Middle Patent Rd., Greenwich, CT 06831
Contact: Anthony B. Evnin, Pres.

Established in 1986 in NY.
Donor(s): Anthony B. Evnin, Judith W. Evnin.
Financial data (yr. ended 12/31/00): Grants paid, $491,165; assets, $10,000,905 (M); gifts received, $706,729; expenditures, $577,345; qualifying distributions, $493,435.
Limitations: Giving primarily in Westchester County and New York, NY.
Application information: Application form not required.
Officers: Anthony B. Evnin, Pres.; Judith W. Evnin, Secy.
EIN: 133317246
Codes: FD

33600
Zena & Michael A. Wiener Foundation
c/o Lewis Braff & Co.
60 E. 42nd St., Ste. 850
New York, NY 10165

Established in 1993 in NH.
Donor(s): Michael A. Wiener, Zena Wiener.
Financial data (yr. ended 12/31/00): Grants paid, $491,037; assets, $3,077,268 (M); expenditures, $508,182; qualifying distributions, $486,967.
Limitations: Applications not accepted. Giving primarily in NY.
Application information: Contributes only to pre-selected organizations.
Officers and Directors:* Michael A. Wiener,* Pres.; Jennifer Wiener,* V.P.; Zena Wiener,* Secy.
EIN: 020468920
Codes: FD

33601
Andrea Frank Foundation, Inc.
c/o Yohalem Gillman and Co., LLP
477 Madison Ave., Ste. 900
New York, NY 10022-5802

Established in 1995 in NY.
Donor(s): Robert Frank.
Financial data (yr. ended 12/31/01): Grants paid, $489,800; assets, $468,210 (M); gifts received, $4,818; expenditures, $518,306; qualifying distributions, $500,443.
Officers: Jock Reynolds, Pres.; Paul M. Gulielmetti, Secy.; Clark B. Winter, Jr., Treas.
EIN: 133857299
Codes: FD

33602
David A. & Verna M. George Foundation
c/o BCRS Assocs., LLC
100 Wall St., 11th Fl.
New York, NY 10005

Established in 1986 in NY.
Donor(s): David A. George.
Financial data (yr. ended 05/31/01): Grants paid, $489,520; assets, $1,535,487 (M); expenditures, $511,156; qualifying distributions, $492,546.
Limitations: Applications not accepted. Giving primarily in Washington, DC and NY.
Application information: Contributes only to pre-selected organizations.
Trustees: Jonathan L. Cohen, David A. George, Verna M. George.
EIN: 133385061
Codes: FD

33603
MJPM Foundation
c/o McLaughlin & Stern LLP
260 Madison Ave.
New York, NY 10016

Established in 1999 in NY.
Donor(s): Mary J.P. Moore.
Financial data (yr. ended 12/31/01): Grants paid, $489,442; assets, $14,900,949 (M); gifts received, $4,859,754; expenditures, $546,399; qualifying distributions, $473,805.
Limitations: Applications not accepted.
Application information: Contributes only to pre-selected organizations.
Officers: Mary J.P. Moore, Pres.; Samuel F. Posey, Jr., V.P.; Nicholas J. Moore, Secy.; David W. Moore, Treas.
EIN: 134043598
Codes: FD

33604
J. Gurwin Foundation, Inc.
934 Middle Neck Rd.
Great Neck, NY 11024-1453
Contact: Joseph Gurwin, Pres.

Incorporated in 1959 in NY.
Donor(s): Joseph Gurwin, Kings Point Industries, Inc.
Financial data (yr. ended 07/31/01): Grants paid, $488,738; assets, $20,351,111 (M); expenditures, $531,697; qualifying distributions, $488,738.
Limitations: Applications not accepted. Giving primarily in NY.
Application information: Contributes only to pre-selected organizations.

Officers: Joseph Gurwin, Pres.; Laura Gurwin Flug, V.P.; Eric Gurwin, V.P.
EIN: 136059258
Codes: FD

33605
Chatterjee Charitable Foundation
888 7th Ave., Ste. 3000
New York, NY 10106

Established in 1995 in NY.
Donor(s): Purnendu Chatterjee, Sidhartha Maitra, Subir K. Sanyal.
Financial data (yr. ended 11/30/99): Grants paid, $487,880; assets, $15,510,851 (M); gifts received, $42,380; expenditures, $578,279; qualifying distributions, $483,887.
Limitations: Applications not accepted. Giving primarily in NY, with some giving in India.
Application information: Contributes only to pre-selected organizations.
Director: Purnendu Chatterjee.
EIN: 137072667
Codes: FD

33606
The Bahnik Foundation, Inc.
190 Pine Hollow Rd.
Oyster Bay, NY 11771
Contact: Roger L. Bahnik, Pres.

Established in 1994 in NY.
Donor(s): Roger L. Bahnik, Lore Bahnik.
Financial data (yr. ended 04/30/01): Grants paid, $487,500; assets, $9,050,381 (M); gifts received, $1,324,971; expenditures, $551,257; qualifying distributions, $470,819.
Limitations: Applications not accepted. Giving primarily in Long Island, NY.
Application information: Contributes only to pre-selected organizations.
Officers: Roger L. Bahnik, Pres.; Claude Bahnik, V.P.; Michele Bahnik, V.P.; Lore Bahnik, Secy.
EIN: 113216930
Codes: FD

33607
The Li Foundation, Inc.
57 Glen St.
Glen Cove, NY 11542 (516) 676-1315
FAX: (516) 676-2538
Contact: Edward Plumb

Established in 1944.
Financial data (yr. ended 12/31/01): Grants paid, $486,865; assets, $10,126,237 (M); expenditures, $663,951; qualifying distributions, $555,880.
Limitations: Giving primarily in China.
Application information: Grants are awarded to institutions for individuals. Application form required.
Officers and Directors:* Taie Li,* Pres.; Marie Chun,* V.P.; Mildred L. Distin,* Secy.; Eric W. Leong,* Treas.; Minfong Ho Dennis, William Distin, Carlos Koo, Linda Li, Ling Kuo Li, Sebastion Li, Taimin Li, Edward Plumb, Eric Leong Way.
EIN: 136098783
Codes: FD, GTI

33608
The Furth Family Foundation
c/o Klingenstein, Fields & Co., LLC
787 7th Ave.
New York, NY 10019

Established in 1986 in NY.
Donor(s): John L. Furth.
Financial data (yr. ended 11/30/01): Grants paid, $485,825; assets, $3,763,342 (M); gifts received,

$1,779,524; expenditures, $532,119; qualifying distributions, $473,556.
Limitations: Applications not accepted. Giving primarily in CT, and New York, NY.
Application information: Contributes only to pre-selected organizations.
Trustees: Hope L. Furth, John L. Furth.
EIN: 133401839
Codes: FD

33609
Marie and John Zimmermann Fund, Inc.
c/o U.S. Trust
114 W. 47th St.
New York, NY 10036-1532
FAX: (212) 852-3377
Contact: Carolyn L. Larke, Asst. V.P., or Linda Franciscovich, Sr. V.P.

Incorporated in 1942 in NY.
Donor(s): Marie Zimmermann.‡
Financial data (yr. ended 12/31/00): Grants paid, $485,000; assets, $10,291,704 (M); expenditures, $557,563; qualifying distributions, $501,159.
Limitations: Applications not accepted. Giving primarily in the Northeast.
Application information: Contributes only to pre-selected organizations.
Officers and Directors:* John C. Zimmermann III,* Pres.; Robert Perret, Jr.,* Secy.; J. Robert Buchanan, M.D., Anne C. Heller, Edward C. Kline.
EIN: 136158767
Codes: FD

33610
James A. Macdonald Foundation
1 N. Broadway
White Plains, NY 10601 (914) 428-9305
Contact: Walter J. Handelman, Secy.

Incorporated in 1966 in NY.
Donor(s): Flora Macdonald Bonney.‡
Financial data (yr. ended 12/31/01): Grants paid, $484,520; assets, $9,777,802 (M); expenditures, $586,354; qualifying distributions, $518,194.
Limitations: Giving primarily in NY.
Application information: Application form not required.
Officers and Directors:* Alice H. Model,* Pres.; Walter J. Handelman,* V.P. and Secy.; Alan L. Model,* Treas.
EIN: 136199690
Codes: FD

33611
The Burke Family Foundation
c/o Stonington Partners
767 5th Ave., 48th Fl.
New York, NY 10153
Contact: James J. Burke, Jr., Tr.

Established in 1994 in NJ.
Donor(s): James J. Burke, Jr.
Financial data (yr. ended 12/31/01): Grants paid, $483,590; assets, $5,634,197 (M); expenditures, $552,037; qualifying distributions, $488,545.
Limitations: Applications not accepted. Giving primarily in NJ and NY.
Application information: Contributes only to pre-selected organizations.
Trustees: James J. Burke, Jr., Jeanne J. Burke.
EIN: 223341317
Codes: FD

33612
The Calvin Klein Foundation
205 W. 39th St.
New York, NY 10018-3102 (212) 719-2600
Contact: Joel Semel, Mgr.

Established in 1981 in NY.

Donor(s): Calvin Klein, Inc.
Financial data (yr. ended 06/30/01): Grants paid, $483,270; assets, $27,802 (M); gifts received, $501,000; expenditures, $483,631; qualifying distributions, $483,224.
Limitations: Giving primarily in NY.
Application information: Application form not required.
Manager: Joel Semel.
Trustees: Robert DiPaola, Len Lasalandra.
EIN: 133094765
Codes: CS, FD, CD

33613
The Philip E. Potter Foundation
6 Ford Ave.
Oneonta, NY 13820
Contact: Henry L. Hulbert, Mgr.

Established in 1973.
Donor(s): Philip E. Potter, Mrs. Philip E. Potter, Lillian W. Potter.‡
Financial data (yr. ended 10/31/01): Grants paid, $482,915; assets, $11,529,214 (M); expenditures, $605,709; qualifying distributions, $592,405.
Limitations: Giving limited to residents of Otsego and Delaware counties, NY, with emphasis on residents of Oneonta.
Application information: Application forms available at local high schools or from foundation office. Application form required.
Officer and Trustees:* Henry L. Hulbert,* Mgr.; SueAnne T. De Bergh, Maureen P. Hulbert, Robert W. Moyer, Anne T. Wolek.
EIN: 166169167
Codes: FD, GTI

33614
The Canary Charitable Foundation
c/o First Spring Corp.
499 Park Ave., 26th Fl.
New York, NY 10022
Contact: Dr. Guido Goldman

Established in 1998 in DE.
Donor(s): Charles De Gunzburg.
Financial data (yr. ended 12/31/01): Grants paid, $482,014; assets, $4,128,689 (M); expenditures, $483,733; qualifying distributions, $483,424.
Limitations: Giving primarily in MA and NY.
Officer: Charles De Gunzburg, Pres.
EIN: 134005475
Codes: FD

33615
The Golub Foundation
c/o Scholarship Comm.
501 Duanesburg Rd.
Schenectady, NY 12306 (518) 356-9450
Additional tel.: (877) 877-0870; *FAX:* (518) 374-4259
Scholarship application address: c/o Price Chopper Scholarship Office, P.O. Box 1074, Mailbox 60, Schenectady, NY 12301

Established in 1981 in NY.
Donor(s): Jane Golub, Neil M. Golub, Golub Corp.
Financial data (yr. ended 03/31/01): Grants paid, $481,970; assets, $477,299 (M); gifts received, $962,265; expenditures, $576,415; qualifying distributions, $576,415.
Limitations: Giving limited to the Price Chopper Supermarket marketing area: Litchfield and Windham counties, CT; Berkshire, Hampden, Hampshire, Middlesex, and Worcester counties, MA; Grafton and Sullivan counties, NH; Albany, Broome, Chenango, Clinton, Columbia, Cortland, Delaware, Dutchess, Essex, Franklin, Fulton, Greene, Hamilton, Herkimer, Jefferson, Lewis,

33615—NEW YORK

Madison, Montgomery, Oneida, Onondaga, Oswego, Otego, Rensselaer, Schenectady, Schoharie, St. Lawrence, Tioga, Ulster, Warren, and Washington counties, NY; Lackawanna, Luzerne, Susquehanna, Wayne, and Wyoming counties, PA; Bennington, Caledonia, Chittenden, Franklin, Lamoille, Orange, Orleans, Rutland, Washington, Windham, and Windsor counties, VT.
Publications: Informational brochure.
Application information: Application form required for scholarships.
Trustees: Mona Golub-Ganz, Wesley Holloway, Sr., Barbara Page, Jean Simpson-Smith.
EIN: 222341421
Codes: CS, FD, CD, GTI

33616
Mildred Faulkner Truman Foundation
c/o M & T Trust, Tax Dept.
P.O. Box 22900
Rochester, NY 14692-2900
Application address: 195 Front St., P.O. Box 89, Owego, NY 13827-0089, tel.: (607) 687-0225; FAX: (607) 687-0268; E-mail: MFTF@clarityconnect.com
Contact: Irene C. Graven, Exec. Dir.

Established in 1985 in NY.
Donor(s): Mildred Faulkner Truman.‡
Financial data (yr. ended 08/31/01): Grants paid, $481,825; assets, $8,161,734 (M); expenditures, $604,929; qualifying distributions, $556,509.
Limitations: Giving primarily in Owego and Tioga counties, NY.
Publications: Annual report (including application guidelines).
Application information: Completed applications can be mailed or deposited in the drop box located in the basement lobby of M & T Bank at the corner of Front and Church Sts., Owego, NY, during normal banking hours. Application form required.
Officer: Irene C. Graven, Exec. Dir.
Trustee: M & T Bank.
EIN: 166271201
Codes: FD

33617
Engineering Information Foundation
(also known as EiF)
180 W. 80th St., Ste. 207
New York, NY 10024-6301 (212) 579-7596
FAX: (212) 579-7517; E-mail: info@eifgrants.org; URL: http://www.eifgrants.org
Contact: Thomas R. Buckman, Chair. and Pres.

Established in 1934 as a publisher of engineering information with the legal status of a public charity. Restructured in 1994 in NY as a private foundation; approved July 25, 1996, with first round of grants made in Aug. 1997.
Financial data (yr. ended 12/31/01): Grants paid, $481,519; assets, $8,165,575 (M); expenditures, $860,231; qualifying distributions, $587,584.
Limitations: Giving on a national and international basis.
Publications: Annual report (including application guidelines).
Application information: Application form not required.
Officers and Directors:* Thomas R. Buckman,* Chair. and Pres.; Anne M. Buck,* Vice-Chair. and V.P.; Hans Rutimann,* Secy.; John J. Regazzi, Julie A. Shimer.
EIN: 131679606
Codes: FD

33618
Patrina Foundation
P.O. Box 777
Manhasset, NY 11030 (516) 627-0172
FAX: (516) 627-5489; E-mail: patrina@ix.netcom.com; URL: http://www.patrinafoundation.org
Contact: Mary Jo McLoughlin, Exec. Dir.

Established in 1990 in NY.
Donor(s): Lorinda P. de Roulet.
Financial data (yr. ended 12/31/01): Grants paid, $481,380; assets, $9,803,541 (M); expenditures, $693,033; qualifying distributions, $542,679.
Limitations: Giving primarily in the Northeast.
Application information: Application form not required.
Officers and Trustees:* Lorinda P. de Roulet,* Pres.; Whitney Bullock,* Secy.; Daniel C. de Roulet,* Treas.; Elizabeth Rainoff.
EIN: 113035018
Codes: FD

33619
The Memton Fund, Inc.
515 Madison Ave., Ste. 3702
New York, NY 10022
Contact: Lillian I. Daniels, Exec. Dir.

Incorporated in 1936 in NY.
Donor(s): Albert G. Milbank,‡ Charles M. Cauldwell.‡
Financial data (yr. ended 12/31/01): Grants paid, $481,100; assets, $10,847,823 (M); expenditures, $707,086; qualifying distributions, $585,407.
Limitations: Applications not accepted. Giving limited to the U.S. and U.S. Pacific Islands.
Application information: Contributes only to pre-selected organizations.
Officers and Directors:* Samuel L. Milbank, Pres.; Elenita M. Drumwright,* V.P.; Lillian I. Daniels,* Secy.-Treas.; Elizabeth R.M. Drumwright, Robert V. Edgar, E. Shepard Farrar, Olivia Farrar-Wellman, Alexandra Giordano, Michelle R. Milbank, Thomas Milbank, Debbie Piccone, Karen M. Quackenbush, Pamela White.
EIN: 136096608
Codes: FD

33620
Keren Yud Memorial, Inc.
417 5th Ave., 3rd Fl.
New York, NY 10016

Established in 1997 in NY.
Financial data (yr. ended 09/30/99): Grants paid, $481,060; assets, $135,085 (M); gifts received, $610,000; expenditures, $481,060; qualifying distributions, $481,060.
Limitations: Applications not accepted.
Application information: Contributes only to pre-selected organizations.
Officer: Martin C. Sukenik, Mgr.
EIN: 133978009

33621
The Jack & Anita Saltz Foundation, Inc.
6 Martin Butler Ct.
Rye, NY 10580

Established in 1997 in NY.
Donor(s): Jack Saltz, Anita Saltz.‡
Financial data (yr. ended 12/31/01): Grants paid, $480,600; assets, $4,894,930 (M); expenditures, $490,363; qualifying distributions, $476,414.
Limitations: Applications not accepted. Giving primarily in New York, NY.
Application information: Contributes only to pre-selected organizations.
Officers: Jack Saltz, Pres.; Ronald I. Saltz, Secy.; Leonard B. Saltz, Treas.

Director: Susan Saltz.
EIN: 133914629
Codes: FD

33622
The RGI Group Foundation
(Formerly Revlon Group Foundation)
c/o MacAndrews & Forbes Holdings, Inc.
38 E. 63rd St.
New York, NY 10021

Incorporated in 1952 in PA.
Donor(s): Revlon Group Inc., Food Fair Stores, Inc., Pantry Pride, Inc.
Financial data (yr. ended 04/30/01): Grants paid, $480,500; assets, $498 (M); gifts received, $489,000; expenditures, $490,695; qualifying distributions, $490,500.
Limitations: Applications not accepted. Giving primarily in New York, NY, and Philadelphia, PA.
Application information: Contributes only to pre-selected organizations.
Officers: Debra Golding Perelman, Co-Pres.; Steven G. Perelman, Co-Pres.; Todd J. Slotkin, Exec. V.P. and C.F.O.; Glenn P. Dickes, V.P.; Marvin Schaffer, V.P.
Directors: Howard Gittis, Ronald O. Perelman.
EIN: 236259906
Codes: CS, FD, CD

33623
Northern Chautauqua Community Foundation, Inc.
212 Lake Shore Dr. W.
Dunkirk, NY 14048 (716) 366-4892
FAX: (716) 366-4276; E-mail: nccf@netsync.net; URL: http://www.nccfoundation.org
Contact: Diane Hannum, Exec. Dir.

Incorporated in 1986 in NY.
Financial data (yr. ended 12/31/01): Grants paid, $480,407; assets, $8,296,442 (M); expenditures, $624,645.
Limitations: Giving limited to northern Chautauqua County, NY.
Publications: Annual report (including application guidelines), application guidelines, newsletter.
Application information: Applications are considered in the spring and fall. Application form required.
Officers and Directors:* R. Bard Schaack,* Pres.; James H. Mintun, Jr.,* V.P.; Terry Clifton, Secy.; Susan Marsh,* Treas.; Rosemary Banach, Michael Brunecz, Andrew W. Dorn, Donald Eno, Wendy Heinz, George Pete Holt, Richard Ketcham, James Koch, David Larson, Kurt Maytum, Robert Miller, Jr., Jeffrey G. Passafaro, John Potter, Gerard Rocque, J. Carter Rowland, Ph.D., H.K. Williams IV.
EIN: 161271663
Codes: CM, FD, GTI

33624
Charitable Trust dated 4/28/83
c/o Cravath, Swaine & Moore
P.O. Box 825
New York, NY 10101-0825

Established in 1983 in NY.
Donor(s): George J. Gillespie III.
Financial data (yr. ended 03/31/01): Grants paid, $479,750; assets, $1,902,844 (M); gifts received, $360,600; expenditures, $500,075; qualifying distributions, $478,024.
Limitations: Applications not accepted. Giving primarily in the greater New York, NY, area.
Application information: Contributes only to pre-selected organizations.
Trustee: George J. Gillespie III.
EIN: 133183734

Codes: FD

33625
Lucien & Ethel Brownstone Foundation, Inc.
c/o Warshaw Burstein, et al.
555 5th Ave.
New York, NY 10017-2416

Established in 1953.
Financial data (yr. ended 02/28/01): Grants paid, $478,381; assets, $8,817,933 (M); gifts received, $500; expenditures, $660,283; qualifying distributions, $471,060.
Limitations: Applications not accepted. Giving primarily in NY.
Application information: Contributes only to pre-selected organizations.
Officers: Clyde Brownstone, Pres.; Diane Brownstone, Secy.
EIN: 136138834
Codes: FD

33626
The Swint Foundation
P.O. Box 1308
Southampton, NY 11969-1308
Contact: Samuel H. Swint, Jr., Chair.

Established in 1955 as a GA charitable foundation.
Financial data (yr. ended 12/31/01): Grants paid, $478,000; assets, $2,289,753 (M); expenditures, $498,767; qualifying distributions, $486,720.
Limitations: Applications not accepted. Giving primarily in GA, NY, and SC.
Publications: Annual report.
Officers and Trustees:* Samuel H. Swint, Jr.,* Chair.; Claire C. Avnyin, Secy.; Kit Carson Bennett, Thomas E. Oplinger.
EIN: 586032740
Codes: FD

33627
Rexford Fund, Inc.
c/o Marcus Schloss & Co., Inc.
1 Whitehall St.
New York, NY 10004

Established in 1967 in NY.
Donor(s): Marcus Schloss & Co., Inc.
Financial data (yr. ended 12/31/01): Grants paid, $477,795; assets, $5,730,900 (M); gifts received, $150,000; expenditures, $478,045; qualifying distributions, $477,993.
Limitations: Applications not accepted. Giving primarily in New York, NY; funding also in CT.
Application information: Contributes only to pre-selected organizations.
Officers and Directors:* Douglas Schloss,* Pres.; Richard Schloss,* Secy.; Irwin Schloss.
EIN: 136222049
Codes: CS, FD, CD

33628
Olive Bridge Fund, Inc.
500 5th Ave., 50th Fl.
New York, NY 10110 (212) 391-8960
Contact: Ralph E. Hansmann, Dir.

Incorporated in 1952 in NY.
Donor(s): Harold F. Linder,‡ Joshua Steiner, Susan E. Linder, Elizabeth Steiner, Daniel L. Steiner, Prudence L. Steiner.
Financial data (yr. ended 12/31/01): Grants paid, $477,460; assets, $36,599,191 (M); gifts received, $11,329; expenditures, $656,573; qualifying distributions, $651,573.
Limitations: Applications not accepted. Giving primarily in MA and NY.
Application information: Contributes only to pre-selected organizations.

Officers and Directors:* Daniel L. Steiner,* Pres.; Susan E. Linder,* V.P. and Secy.; William T. Golden,* V.P. and Treas.; Prudence L. Steiner,* V.P.; Anna Lou Dehavenon, Ralph E. Hansmann, William M. Kelly.
EIN: 136161669
Codes: FD

33629
Fred & Floy Willmott Foundation
c/o HSBC Bank USA
1 HSBC Ctr., 16th Fl.
Buffalo, NY 14203-2842
Application address: c/o Luther W. Miller, 1215 Alliance Bldg., 183 E. Main St., Rochester, NY 14604, tel.: (716) 232-7210

Established in 1984 in NY.
Financial data (yr. ended 12/31/01): Grants paid, $476,982; assets, $6,664,354 (M); expenditures, $578,528; qualifying distributions, $510,378.
Limitations: Giving primarily in Monroe County, NY.
Application information: Application form required.
Trustees: Rev. John D. Cooke, HSBC Bank USA.
EIN: 222587484
Codes: FD

33630
The Jacob Goldfield Foundation
85 Broad St., Tax Dept.
New York, NY 10004

Established in 1993 in NJ.
Donor(s): Jacob D. Goldfield.
Financial data (yr. ended 01/31/02): Grants paid, $476,108; assets, $11,246,505 (M); gifts received, $1,549,758; expenditures, $543,059; qualifying distributions, $486,408.
Limitations: Applications not accepted. Giving primarily in the New York, NY, area.
Application information: Contributes only to pre-selected organizations.
Trustee: Jacob D. Goldfield.
EIN: 133748049
Codes: FD

33631
J. D. Shatford Memorial Trust
c/o JPMorgan Chase Bank
1211 Ave. of the Americas, 38th Fl.
New York, NY 10036
E-mail: jones_ed_l@JPMorgan.com
Contact: Edward L. Jones, V.P.

Trust established in 1955 in NY.
Financial data (yr. ended 12/31/01): Grants paid, $475,890; assets, $7,841,630 (M); expenditures, $560,540; qualifying distributions, $472,962.
Limitations: Giving limited to Hubbards, Nova Scotia, Canada.
Application information: Application form available for scholarship grants.
Trustee: JPMorgan Chase Bank.
EIN: 136029993
Codes: FD, GTI

33632
The Abelard Foundation, Inc.
c/o White & Case
1155 Ave. of the Americas
New York, NY 10036

Incorporated in 1958 in NY as successor to Albert B. Wells Charitable Trust established in 1950 in MA.
Donor(s): Members of the Wells family.
Financial data (yr. ended 12/31/01): Grants paid, $475,000; assets, $5,484,888 (M); gifts received, $252,000; expenditures, $611,951; qualifying distributions, $590,883.
Limitations: Giving limited to New York, NY, the western states, and the southern states, including the Appalachia region.
Publications: Informational brochure (including application guidelines), grants list.
Application information: Application form not required.
Officers and Trustee:* Susan Collins, Pres.; Steven Bernhard, V.P.; Melissa Blessing, V.P.; Charles Schreck, V.P.; George B. Wells, V.P.; Malcolm J. Edgerton, Jr.,* Secy.; Charles R. Schreck, Treas.
EIN: 136064580
Codes: FD

33633
The James S. & Merryl H. Tisch Foundation, Inc.
c/o Mark J. Krinsky, C.P.A.
655 Madison Ave., 8th Fl.
New York, NY 10021-8043

Established in 1992 in NY.
Donor(s): Laurence A. Tisch, James S. Tisch.
Financial data (yr. ended 12/31/01): Grants paid, $474,969; assets, $7,225,454 (M); expenditures, $486,708; qualifying distributions, $474,086.
Limitations: Applications not accepted. Giving primarily in NY.
Application information: Contributes only to pre-selected organizations.
Officers and Directors:* James S. Tisch,* Pres.; Merryl H. Tisch,* Sr. V.P.; Mark J. Krinsky,* V.P.; Thomas M. Steinberg,* V.P.; Barry L. Bloom, Secy.-Treas.
EIN: 133693587
Codes: FD

33634
Chia Family Foundation, Inc.
298 Bedford-Banksville Rd.
Bedford, NY 10506

Established in 1996 in NY.
Donor(s): Pei-Yuan Chia, Frances T.C. Chia, Kitty S.H. Chia.
Financial data (yr. ended 03/31/01): Grants paid, $474,250; assets, $10,091,537 (M); gifts received, $623,953; expenditures, $538,421; qualifying distributions, $452,595.
Limitations: Applications not accepted. Giving primarily in NY.
Application information: Contributes only to pre-selected organizations.
Directors: Candice Chia, Douglas Chia, Frances T.C. Chia, Katherine Chia, Pei-Yuan Chia.
EIN: 133904882
Codes: FD

33635
Halcyon Hill Foundation
P.O. Box 506
Webster, NY 14580 (716) 442-6560
FAX: (315) 524-6240; *E-mail:* hhf@hhf.org; *URL:* http://www.hhf.org
Contact: Annette Weld

Established in 1991 in NY.
Donor(s): Anne G. Whitman.
Financial data (yr. ended 06/30/01): Grants paid, $473,360; assets, $11,250,218 (M); gifts received, $88,350; expenditures, $625,029; qualifying distributions, $532,353.
Limitations: Giving primarily in Rochester, NY.
Publications: Informational brochure.
Application information: Application form required.
Trustees: Renier Chaintreuil, JPMorgan Chase Bank.
EIN: 161553256

33635—NEW YORK

Codes: FD

33636
Rosenwald Foundation, Inc.
441 West End Ave., Apt. 8A
New York, NY 10024

Established in 1993 in NY.
Donor(s): Lindsay Rosenwald.
Financial data (yr. ended 11/30/01): Grants paid, $472,135; assets, $9,069,637 (M); gifts received, $10,226,933; expenditures, $482,495; qualifying distributions, $475,295.
Limitations: Giving on a national basis.
Officers and Directors:* Rivki Rosenwald,* Pres. and Treas.; Lindsay Rosenwald,* V.P.; Esther Stahler,* Secy.
EIN: 133746216
Codes: FD

33637
Lawrence and Dana Linden Family Foundation
c/o Goldman Sachs & Co.
85 Broad St., Tax Dept.
New York, NY 10004-2434

Established in 1993 in NY.
Donor(s): Lawrence H. Linden.
Financial data (yr. ended 02/28/01): Grants paid, $470,890; assets, $10,206,296 (M); gifts received, $4,768,313; expenditures, $616,151; qualifying distributions, $471,151.
Limitations: Applications not accepted. Giving primarily in NY.
Application information: Contributes only to pre-selected organizations.
Trustees: Dana Wechsler Linden, Lawrence H. Linden.
EIN: 133748063
Codes: FD

33638
The Brennan Charitable Foundation, Inc.
c/o T. Kwiatkowski
131 Tulip Ave.
Floral Park, NY 11001

Established in 1998 in NY.
Donor(s): John V. Brennan.
Financial data (yr. ended 12/31/01): Grants paid, $470,550; assets, $2,323,479 (M); expenditures, $475,707; qualifying distributions, $474,409.
Limitations: Applications not accepted. Giving primarily in New York, NY.
Application information: Contributes only to pre-selected organizations.
Officers and Directors:* John V. Brennan,* Pres.; John O. Brennan,* Secy.; Anita M. Brennan,* Treas.; Mary E. Brennan, Paul F. Brennan.
EIN: 113384432
Codes: FD

33639
Peter J. Solomon Foundation
(Formerly Peter J. & Linda N. Solomon Foundation)
c/o B. Strauss Assocs., Ltd.
307 5th Ave., 8th Fl.
New York, NY 10016-6517

Established in 1986 in NY.
Donor(s): Peter J. Solomon.
Financial data (yr. ended 03/31/01): Grants paid, $470,231; assets, $7,270,362 (M); gifts received, $391,821; expenditures, $558,311; qualifying distributions, $473,431.
Limitations: Applications not accepted. Giving on a national basis, with some emphasis on New York, NY.
Application information: Contributes only to pre-selected organizations.

Trustee: Peter J. Solomon.
EIN: 133384028
Codes: FD

33640
The Donald & Maria Cox Trust
c/o Fiduciary Trust Co. International
600 5th Ave.
New York, NY 10020 (212) 632-3000
Contact: Carl Scaturo

Established in 1985 in NY.
Donor(s): Donald M. Cox.
Financial data (yr. ended 12/31/01): Grants paid, $470,080; assets, $3,092,735 (M); expenditures, $500,894; qualifying distributions, $488,248.
Limitations: Giving primarily in New York, NY.
Trustees: Donald M. Cox, Maria R. Cox.
EIN: 136864749
Codes: FD

33641
The Mitsui U.S.A. Foundation
200 Park Ave.
New York, NY 10166-0130

Established in 1987 in NY.
Donor(s): Mitsui & Co. (U.S.A.), Inc.
Financial data (yr. ended 12/31/01): Grants paid, $470,035; assets, $696,545 (M); gifts received, $479,100; expenditures, $478,249; qualifying distributions, $478,220.
Limitations: Applications not accepted. Giving primarily in locations of company's main offices: Los Angeles, CA, Atlanta, GA, Chicago, IL, New York, NY, Houston, TX, and Seattle, WA.
Publications: Informational brochure.
Application information: Contributes only to pre-selected organizations. Unsolicited applications cannot be processed.
Officers and Directors:* K. Momii,* Chair.; S. Hirabayashi,* C.E.O. and Pres.; A. Getz,* Secy.-Treas.; L. Bruser, G. Clarke, Y. Ishida, Y. Kawashima, M. Nagahara, M. Nelson.
EIN: 133415220
Codes: CS, FD, CD

33642
Falconwood Foundation, Inc.
565 5th Ave.
New York, NY 10017 (212) 984-1444
Contact: Dr. Stanley Lefkowitz, V.P.

Established in 1987 in NY.
Donor(s): Henry G. Jarecki.
Financial data (yr. ended 12/31/01): Grants paid, $469,960; assets, $1,292,813 (M); gifts received, $6,000; expenditures, $475,891; qualifying distributions, $469,747.
Limitations: Giving on a national basis.
Application information: Application form not required.
Officers and Directors:* Henry G. Jarecki,* Pres. and Treas.; Stanley Lefkowitz, V.P. and Secy.; Andrew R. Jarecki, Earl Nemser.
EIN: 133456475
Codes: FD

33643
I.W. Foundation, Inc.
630 W. 246th St., Ste. 323
Riverdale, NY 10471

Established in 1997 in NY.
Financial data (yr. ended 12/31/00): Grants paid, $469,600; assets, $11,052,729 (M); expenditures, $679,050; qualifying distributions, $536,353.
Limitations: Applications not accepted.
Application information: Contributes only to pre-selected organizations.

Officers: Peter Seiden, Chair.; Judith Levi, Pres.; Mark Levi, V.P.; Joan Seiden, Secy.; Harold Seiden, Treas.
EIN: 133924347
Codes: FD

33644
The Pierpoint Foundation
186 21st St.
Brooklyn, NY 11232-1302

Established in 1994.
Donor(s): Jerrold Berger, HPI International, Inc.
Financial data (yr. ended 12/31/01): Grants paid, $469,340; assets, $10,247 (M); gifts received, $466,000; expenditures, $470,245; qualifying distributions, $470,245.
Limitations: Applications not accepted.
Application information: Contributes only to pre-selected organizations.
Trustees: Amy Berger, Jerrold Berger.
EIN: 113241151
Codes: FD

33645
Robert S. Harrison Foundation
c/o Goldman Sachs & Co., Tax Dept.
85 Broad St., Tax Dept.
New York, NY 10004-2456

Established in 1996 in NY.
Donor(s): Robert S. Harrison.
Financial data (yr. ended 07/31/01): Grants paid, $468,825; assets, $2,226,527 (M); gifts received, $587,625; expenditures, $504,760; qualifying distributions, $471,804.
Limitations: Applications not accepted. Giving primarily in New York, NY.
Application information: Contributes only to pre-selected organizations.
Trustees: Jane Hart Harrison, Robert S. Harrison, Robert S. Kaplan.
EIN: 137109420
Codes: FD

33646
Chana Sasha Foundation, Inc.
1 State St. Plz., 29th Fl.
New York, NY 10004
Contact: Morris Wolfson, Pres.

Established in 1995 in NY.
Financial data (yr. ended 08/31/01): Grants paid, $468,773; assets, $1,406,971 (M); gifts received, $502,618; expenditures, $508,818; qualifying distributions, $468,773.
Officer: Morris Wolfson, Pres.
EIN: 133739189
Codes: FD

33647
William Gundry Broughton Charitable Private Foundation, Inc.
133 Saratoga Rd., Ste. 6
Glenville, NY 12302-4162
Contact: James W. Pontius, Pres.

Established in 1995 in NY.
Donor(s): William Broughton Charitable Remainder Unitrust.
Financial data (yr. ended 12/31/01): Grants paid, $468,500; assets, $8,830,908 (M); gifts received, $780; expenditures, $539,242; qualifying distributions, $479,235.
Limitations: Giving primarily in Schenectady County, NY.
Application information: Application form not required.
Officers and Trustees:* James W. Pontius,* Pres.; Shirley M. Vogt,* V.P. and Secy.; Phyllis

Mrozkowski,* Treas.; Grace E. Golden, Ronald L. Lagasse.
EIN: 223122633
Codes: FD

33648
Charles & Constance Murcott Charitable Trust
10 Matinecock Farms Rd.
Glen Cove, NY 11542

Established in 1986 in NY.
Donor(s): Charles Murcott.
Financial data (yr. ended 08/31/01): Grants paid, $467,340; assets, $634,947 (M); expenditures, $469,949; qualifying distributions, $466,980.
Limitations: Applications not accepted. Giving primarily in the New York, NY, metropolitan area, including Long Island.
Application information: Contributes only to pre-selected organizations.
Trustees: Charles Murcott, Constance Murcott.
EIN: 112826619
Codes: FD

33649
The David Rockefeller Fund, Inc.
30 Rockefeller Plz., Rm. 5600
New York, NY 10112   (212) 649-5600
Contact: Marnie Pillsbury, Exec. Dir.

Established in 1989 in NY.
Donor(s): David Rockefeller.
Financial data (yr. ended 12/31/00): Grants paid, $464,850; assets, $10,839,421 (M); expenditures, $569,917; qualifying distributions, $484,065.
Limitations: Giving limited to Seal Harbor and Mount Desert Island, ME, the Pocantico communities in Westchester County, NY, and the Livingston communities of Columbia County.
Publications: Annual report.
Application information: Application form not required.
Officers and Directors:* Abby Rockefeller,* Pres.; Richard E. Salomon,* Secy.-Treas.; Marnie S. Pillsbury, Exec. Dir.; Colin G. Campbell, Christopher J. Kennan, David Rockefeller, Jr.
EIN: 133533359
Codes: FD

33650
The Meriwether Foundation
c/o Steven Loeb, Cleary Gottlieb et al.
1 Liberty Plz.
New York, NY 10006

Established in 1991 in NY.
Donor(s): John W. Meriwether, Mimi Murray Meriwether.
Financial data (yr. ended 12/31/00): Grants paid, $464,475; assets, $1,454,845 (M); gifts received, $102,300; expenditures, $467,336; qualifying distributions, $467,205.
Limitations: Applications not accepted. Giving on a national basis.
Application information: Contributes only to pre-selected organizations.
Trustees: John W. Meriwether, Mimi Murray Meriwether.
EIN: 133620935
Codes: FD

33651
H. Schaffer Foundation, Inc.
809 State St.
Schenectady, NY 12307
Contact: Sonya A. Stall, Pres.

Established in 1980 in NY.
Donor(s): Harry M. Schaffer,‡ Schaffer Stores Co., Inc.
Financial data (yr. ended 10/31/01): Grants paid, $464,000; assets, $5,592,265 (M); expenditures, $588,367; qualifying distributions, $551,449.
Limitations: Giving primarily in NY, with emphasis on Schenectady.
Application information: Application form not required.
Officers: Sonya A. Stall, Pres.; Adrienne Bieber, V.P.; Richard R. Bieber, V.P.; Jeffrey Stall, Secy.-Treas.
EIN: 222325485
Codes: FD

33652
Freeman Foundation
3115 Netherland Ave.
Bronx, NY 10463-3408

Established in 1968 in NY.
Donor(s): Alfred A. Freeman, Sara Lea Steinberg.
Financial data (yr. ended 12/31/01): Grants paid, $463,896; assets, $1,473,574 (M); gifts received, $223,631; expenditures, $467,104; qualifying distributions, $466,495.
Limitations: Applications not accepted. Giving primarily in the greater New York, NY, area.
Application information: Contributes only to pre-selected organizations.
Trustees: Alfred A. Freeman, Shoshana Freeman, Yaakov Freeman, Sara Lea Steinberg.
EIN: 237003467
Codes: FD

33653
Sanford C. Bernstein & Co. Foundation, Inc.
1345 Ave. of the Americas
New York, NY 10105

Established in 1968 in NY.
Donor(s): Sanford C. Bernstein & Co., Inc., Zalman C. Bernstein.‡
Financial data (yr. ended 12/31/01): Grants paid, $462,125; assets, $4,697,268 (M); expenditures, $266,170; qualifying distributions, $460,888.
Limitations: Giving on a national basis.
Application information: Generally contributes only to pre-selected organizations. Unsolicited requests for funds not accepted. Applications will only be accepted from employees on behalf of organizations with which they have direct involvement. Application form required.
Trustees: Andrew Adelson, Kevin R. Brine, Charles C. Cahn, Marilyn G. Fedak, Michael L. Goldstein, Roger Hertog, Jerry Lieberman, Lewis A. Sanders, Francis H. Trainer, Jr.
EIN: 136277976
Codes: CS, FD, CD

33654
Cyril F. and Marie E. O'Neil Foundation
c/o Siegal, Sacks & Co.
630 3rd Ave.
New York, NY 10017
Contact: Ralph O'Neil, Pres.

Incorporated in 1957 in OH.
Donor(s): Members of the O'Neil family.
Financial data (yr. ended 12/31/01): Grants paid, $461,900; assets, $7,062,705 (M); expenditures, $511,839; qualifying distributions, $461,900.
Limitations: Applications not accepted. Giving primarily in NY and OH.
Application information: Contributes only to pre-selected organizations.
Officers: Ralph M. O'Neil, Pres.; Priscilla O'Neil, V.P.
EIN: 346523819
Codes: FD

33655
Abe & Yvette Sutton Foundation, Inc.
c/o Bag Bazaar
1 E. 33rd St., 6th Fl.
New York, NY 10016

Established in 1996 in NY.
Donor(s): Bag Bazaar, Ltd.
Financial data (yr. ended 02/28/01): Grants paid, $461,502; assets, $348,640 (M); gifts received, $150,000; expenditures, $461,721; qualifying distributions, $461,629.
Limitations: Applications not accepted.
Application information: Contributes only to pre-selected organizations.
Officers: Solomon Sutton, Pres.; Alan Haber, V.P.; Jacob A. Sutton, Secy.
EIN: 133882767
Codes: FD

33656
Joshua L. Mailman Charitable Trust
c/o Hecht & Co.
111 W. 40th St.
New York, NY 10018

Established in 1987 in NY.
Donor(s): Joshua L. Mailman.
Financial data (yr. ended 12/31/01): Grants paid, $460,714; assets, $497,461 (M); expenditures, $460,894; qualifying distributions, $460,864.
Limitations: Applications not accepted. Giving primarily in CA, MA, and NY.
Application information: Contributes only to pre-selected organizations.
Trustee: Joshua L. Mailman.
EIN: 133450262
Codes: FD

33657
John Alfred & Oscar Johnson Memorial Trust
c/o JPMorgan Chase Bank
P.O. Box 92920
Rochester, NY 14692
Application address: 9-11 E. 4th St., P.O. Box 50, Jamestown, NY 14702-0050
Contact: Carole W. Sellstrom, Fdn. Coord.

Established in 1996 in NY.
Financial data (yr. ended 01/31/01): Grants paid, $460,092; assets, $9,312,213 (M); expenditures, $588,039; qualifying distributions, $520,948.
Limitations: Giving limited to Jamestown, NY.
Trustees: John L. Sellstrom, JPMorgan Chase Bank.
EIN: 166438291
Codes: FD

33658
Knight Vision Foundation, Inc.
c/o Schwartz & Co
2580 Sunrise Hwy.
Bellmore, NY 11710-3608
Contact: Peter Kleinknecht, V.P.

Established in 1998 in FL.
Donor(s): Peter Kleinknecht.
Financial data (yr. ended 12/31/99): Grants paid, $460,000; assets, $6,435,990 (M); expenditures, $619,187; qualifying distributions, $444,720.
Application information: Application form not required.
Officers: Maureen Kleinknecht, Pres.; Peter Kleinknecht, V.P. and Secy.
Trustees: Gavin Kleinknecht, Keir Kleinknecht, Sabrina Kleinknecht.
EIN: 650829583
Codes: FD

33659—NEW YORK

33659
Asmund S. Laerdal Foundation, Inc.
167 Myers Corners Rd.
Wappingers Falls, NY 12590

Established in 1977 in NY.
Donor(s): Laerdal Medical Corp.
Financial data (yr. ended 12/31/99): Grants paid, $459,983; assets, $9,173,958 (M); expenditures, $564,666; qualifying distributions, $446,159.
Limitations: Applications not accepted. Giving on a national basis.
Application information: Contributes only to pre-selected organizations.
Officers: Hans H. Dahll, Pres.; John Farrell, C.F.O.
EIN: 132885659
Codes: FD

33660
Charles Lawrence Keith and Clara Miller Foundation
217 Thompson St., No.7
New York, NY 10012

Established in 1976 as Clara Miller Foundation.
Donor(s): Charles L. Keith.‡
Financial data (yr. ended 01/31/01): Grants paid, $459,700; assets, $9,074,878 (M); gifts received, $1,439,097; expenditures, $679,748; qualifying distributions, $567,283.
Limitations: Giving limited to the greater metropolitan New York, NY, area.
Application information: Application form not required.
Directors: Linda Fisher, Brian O'Dwyer, Susan Ould, W.B. Richland, Gary Zucker.
EIN: 132918230
Codes: FD

33661
Michael Tuch Foundation, Inc.
122 E. 42nd St., Ste. 1003
New York, NY 10168 (212) 986-9082
Contact: Martha Tuck Rozett, Pres.

Incorporated in 1946 in NY.
Donor(s): Michael Tuch.‡
Financial data (yr. ended 12/31/01): Grants paid, $458,550; assets, $8,025,386 (M); gifts received, $56,023; expenditures, $572,976; qualifying distributions, $507,544.
Limitations: Giving primarily in New York, NY.
Application information: Application form not required.
Officers and Trustees:* Martha Tuck Rozett,* Pres. and Exec. Dir.; Jonathan S. Tuck, V.P. and Secy.-Treas.; Daniel H. Tuck, David A. Tuck.
EIN: 136002848
Codes: FD

33662
The O'Herron Family Foundation
(Formerly Jonathan & Shirley O'Herron Foundation)
c/o Lazard Freres & Co., LLC
30 Rockefeller Plz.
New York, NY 10020
Contact: Jonathan O'Herron, Pres.

Established in 1984 in NY.
Donor(s): Jonathan O'Herron, Shirley O'Herron.
Financial data (yr. ended 06/30/01): Grants paid, $457,700; assets, $382,990 (M); gifts received, $577,711; expenditures, $468,616; qualifying distributions, $459,800.
Limitations: Giving primarily in CT, MA, NY, and VT.
Application information: Application form not required.
Officers and Directors:* Jonathan O'Herron,* Pres.; Shirley O'Herron,* V.P.; Howard V. Sontag,* Secy.; Paul Cohen, Treas.
EIN: 133244207
Codes: FD

33663
Richard J. & Joan G. Scheuer Family Foundation, Inc.
c/o TAG Assocs., Ltd.
75 Rockefeller Plz., Ste. 900
New York, NY 10019-6908

Established in 1966 in NY.
Donor(s): Joan G. Scheuer, Richard J. Scheuer.
Financial data (yr. ended 10/31/01): Grants paid, $457,348; assets, $0 (M); gifts received, $375,169; expenditures, $462,578; qualifying distributions, $456,576.
Limitations: Applications not accepted. Giving primarily in MA, NY, and OH.
Application information: Contributes only to pre-selected organizations.
Officers and Directors:* Richard J. Scheuer,* Pres. and Treas.; Joan G. Scheuer,* V.P. and Secy.
EIN: 136197447
Codes: FD

33664
The Sandra and Howard Tytel Family Charitable Foundation, Inc.
100 Oyster Bay Rd.
Mill Neck, NY 11765

Established in 2000 in DE.
Donor(s): Howard Tytel, Sandra Tytel.
Financial data (yr. ended 12/31/01): Grants paid, $455,000; assets, $1,671,778 (M); gifts received, $2,055,475; expenditures, $511,104; qualifying distributions, $465,165.
Limitations: Applications not accepted.
Application information: Contributes only to pre-selected organizations.
Officers: Howard Tytel, Pres.; Sandra Tytel, Secy.
EIN: 113551535

33665
Jonathan Strasser Foundation
61-35 Dry Harbor Rd.
Middle Village, NY 11379-1528

Established in 1989 in NY.
Donor(s): Jonathan Strasser.
Financial data (yr. ended 10/31/99): Grants paid, $454,200; assets, $12,632,648 (M); gifts received, $1,000,000; expenditures, $523,306; qualifying distributions, $454,200.
Limitations: Applications not accepted. Giving primarily in NY.
Application information: Contributes only to pre-selected organizations.
Trustee: Jonathan Strasser.
EIN: 112993178
Codes: FD

33666
The Leslie & Roslyn Goldstein Foundation
c/o Nathan Berkman & Co., Inc.
29 Broadway, Rm. 2900
New York, NY 10006-3296

Established in 1980 in CT.
Donor(s): Leslie Goldstein, Roslyn Goldstein.
Financial data (yr. ended 11/30/01): Grants paid, $453,095; assets, $16,127,561 (M); expenditures, $492,806; qualifying distributions, $453,095.
Limitations: Applications not accepted. Giving primarily in Stamford, CT and New York, NY.
Application information: Contributes only to pre-selected organizations.
Trustees: Leslie Goldstein, Roslyn Goldstein.
EIN: 061035614
Codes: FD

33667
The Mindel Foundation
c/o Brand Sonnenschine, LLP
377 Broadway, 9th Fl.
New York, NY 10013

Established in 1998 in NY.
Donor(s): Morris Tuchman, Nelson Tuchman, Mitchell Adler.
Financial data (yr. ended 12/31/99): Grants paid, $452,610; assets, $505,021 (M); gifts received, $645,503; expenditures, $453,078; qualifying distributions, $452,693.
Limitations: Applications not accepted.
Application information: Contributes only to pre-selected organizations.
Trustees: Mitchell Adler, Morris Tuchman, Nelson Tuchman.
EIN: 066462625
Codes: FD

33668
Harbor Lights Foundation
c/o BCRS Assocs., LLC
100 Wall St., 11th Fl.
New York, NY 10005
Contact: J. Fred Weintz

Established in 1980 in CT.
Donor(s): J. Fred Weintz, Jr.
Financial data (yr. ended 04/30/01): Grants paid, $451,346; assets, $9,699,351 (M); gifts received, $968,998; expenditures, $501,662; qualifying distributions, $444,313.
Limitations: Applications not accepted. Giving on a national basis, primarily in CT, NY, and MA.
Application information: Contributes only to pre-selected organizations.
Trustees: Elizabeth Weintz Cerf, H. Frederick Krimendahl II, Polly Weintz Sanna, Elisabeth B. Weintz, Eric Cortelyou Weintz, J. Fred Weintz, Jr., Karl Fredrick Weintz.
EIN: 133052490
Codes: FD

33669
Simon and Eve Colin Foundation
1520 Northern Blvd.
Manhasset, NY 11030-3006
Application address: 8 Hickory Hill, Roslyn Estates, NY 11576
Contact: Fred Colin, Dir.

Established in 1984 in NY.
Donor(s): Fred Colin, Stephen Colin, Star Enterprises.
Financial data (yr. ended 10/31/01): Grants paid, $450,475; assets, $13,055,792 (M); gifts received, $155,882; expenditures, $585,352; qualifying distributions, $459,804.
Limitations: Giving primarily in the greater metropolitan New York, NY, area, including Long Island.
Application information: Application form not required.
Directors: Barbara Colin, Fred Colin, Rebecca Colin, Samuel F. Colin, Eva Usdan.
EIN: 112676434
Codes: FD

33670
The ASDA Foundation
c/o First Spring Corp.
499 Park Ave., 26th Fl.
New York, NY 10022

Established in 1983 in NY.

Financial data (yr. ended 12/31/01): Grants paid, $450,000; assets, $6,509,841 (M); expenditures, $497,375; qualifying distributions, $450,000.
Limitations: Applications not accepted. Giving primarily in the U.S.; some giving also in Quebec, Canada.
Application information: Contributes only to pre-selected organizations.
Officers: Guido Goldman, Pres.; Ken Musen, Secy.; Mark O'Donnell, Treas.
Directors: Stanley N. Bergman, Alain De Gunzburg, Charles De Gunzburg, Jean De Gunzburg, Leonard M. Nelson.
EIN: 521319624
Codes: FD

33671
Dixon-Comstock Scholarship Fund
c/o The Bank of New York
1 Wall St., Tax Dept., 28th Fl.
New York, NY 10286

Established in 1996 in NY.
Financial data (yr. ended 03/31/01): Grants paid, $450,000; assets, $7,461,412 (M); gifts received, $87,500; expenditures, $516,639; qualifying distributions, $459,159.
Limitations: Applications not accepted. Giving primarily in NY.
Application information: Contributes only to pre-selected organizations.
Trustee: The Bank of New York.
EIN: 137117658
Codes: FD

33672
Thomas and Jeanne Elmezzi Private Foundation
185 Great Neck Rd.
Great Neck, NY 11021-3312 (516) 498-2860
FAX: (516) 498-2859; E-mail:
jetfoundation@aol.com
Contact: Lynn Grossman, Pres.; or Nivia Pedroza, Admin.

Established in 1996 in NY.
Financial data (yr. ended 12/31/01): Grants paid, $450,000; assets, $6,531,298 (M); expenditures, $637,534; qualifying distributions, $508,220.
Limitations: Applications not accepted. Giving primarily in the New York tri-state region, with emphasis on New York City and Nassau County. Limited international giving primarily for disaster relief.
Application information: Contributes only to pre-selected organizations.
Officers: Thomas Elmezzi, Chair.; Lynn Grossman, Pres.
Directors: Jeanne Elmezzi, Carl Gallo, Arthur Nowak, Stephen J. Saft.
EIN: 113343740
Codes: FD

33673
Ellsworth Kelly Foundation, Inc.
c/o Ellsworth M. Kelly
P.O. Box 220
Spencertown, NY 12165
Contact: Jack Shear, Secy.-Treas.

Established in 1991 in NY.
Donor(s): Ellsworth Kelly.
Financial data (yr. ended 12/31/01): Grants paid, $450,000; assets, $11,448,191 (M); gifts received, $2,000,000; expenditures, $522,973; qualifying distributions, $452,810.
Limitations: Applications not accepted. Giving on a national basis, with some emphasis on the East Coast.
Application information: Contributes only to pre-selected organizations.

Officers: Ellsworth Kelly, Pres.; Jack Shear, Secy.-Treas.
Directors: Roberta Bernstein, Emily Pulitzer.
EIN: 223132379
Codes: FD

33674
Stern Family Philanthropic Foundation
15 Edgemont Rd.
Larchmont, NY 10538-1204
Contact: James Stern, Chair.

Established in 1997 in NY.
Donor(s): James Stern.
Financial data (yr. ended 11/30/01): Grants paid, $450,000; assets, $7,481,635 (M); gifts received, $353,700; expenditures, $504,093; qualifying distributions, $450,000.
Limitations: Applications not accepted.
Application information: Contributes only to pre-selected organizations.
Officers and Director:* Jane Stern, Pres. and Treas.; James Stern,* Secy.
EIN: 133949201
Codes: FD

33675
Edward and Adele Yedid Foundation, Inc.
1798 E. 5th St.
Brooklyn, NY 11223
Tel. for applications: (212) 695-3244
Contact: Edward Yedid, Dir.

Established in 1986 in NY.
Donor(s): Edward Yedid, Isaac Yedid, Jack Yedid.
Financial data (yr. ended 10/31/01): Grants paid, $449,951; assets, $59,207 (M); gifts received, $362,600; expenditures, $450,273; qualifying distributions, $449,951.
Limitations: Giving primarily in the greater metropolitan New York, NY, area.
Directors: Edward Yedid, Isaac Yedid, Jack Yedid.
EIN: 222766747
Codes: FD

33676
The Antz Foundation
c/o Goldman Sachs & Co.
85 Broad St., Tax Dept.
New York, NY 10004

Established in 1989 in NY.
Donor(s): John A. Thain.
Financial data (yr. ended 01/31/02): Grants paid, $449,762; assets, $10,232,291 (M); gifts received, $3,373,655; expenditures, $453,092; qualifying distributions, $453,092.
Limitations: Applications not accepted. Giving primarily in NY.
Application information: Contributes only to pre-selected organizations.
Trustees: Carmen M. Thain, John A. Thain.
EIN: 133536523
Codes: FD

33677
Robert Black Charitable Foundation
c/o U.S. Trust Co. of New York
P.O. Box 2004
New York, NY 10109-1910
Application address: c/o U.S. Trust Co. of New York, 114 W. 47th St., New York, NY 10036

Established in 1998 in NY.
Donor(s): Robert Black.‡
Financial data (yr. ended 12/31/01): Grants paid, $447,560; assets, $8,610,480 (M); expenditures, $507,055; qualifying distributions, $482,275.
Limitations: Giving on a national basis.
Trustee: U.S. Trust Co. of New York.
EIN: 137174452

Codes: FD

33678
Brokaw Family Foundation
c/o Starr & Co.
350 Park Ave.
New York, NY 10022

Established in 1990 in NY.
Donor(s): Thomas J. Brokaw, Fast Track Productions, Inc.
Financial data (yr. ended 12/31/01): Grants paid, $447,350; assets, $75,955 (M); gifts received, $460,000; expenditures, $447,428; qualifying distributions, $447,349.
Limitations: Applications not accepted. Giving on a national basis.
Application information: Contributes only to pre-selected organizations.
Trustee: Thomas J. Brokaw.
EIN: 133594435
Codes: FD

33679
The DuBose and Dorothy Heyward Memorial Fund
c/o The Bank of New York, Tax Dept.
1 Wall St., 28th Fl.
New York, NY 10286
Application address: c/o The Bank of New York, 1290 Ave. of the Americas, New York, NY 10104
Contact: Peter McDermott, Asst. V.P.

Established in 1985 in NY.
Donor(s): Jenifer Heyward.‡
Financial data (yr. ended 12/31/01): Grants paid, $445,500; assets, $8,188,559 (M); expenditures, $573,118; qualifying distributions, $483,567.
Limitations: Giving primarily in New York, NY.
Publications: Program policy statement.
Trustees: Albert J. Cardinali, The Bank of New York.
EIN: 136840999
Codes: FD

33680
The James Hilton Manning and Emma Austin Manning Foundation, Inc.
c/o Davidson Dawson & Clark
330 Madison Ave.
New York, NY 10017

Incorporated in 1958 in NY.
Donor(s): Beatrice Austin Manning,‡ Alfred M. Hoelzer.‡
Financial data (yr. ended 07/31/01): Grants paid, $445,000; assets, $6,178,928 (M); expenditures, $541,161; qualifying distributions, $442,532.
Limitations: Applications not accepted. Giving on a national basis.
Publications: Annual report.
Application information: Contributes only to pre-selected organizations.
Officers and Directors:* John H. Bell, Jr.,* Pres.; Juliet Alexander,* Secy.; Ann Kissel Grun,* Treas.; Ralph A. Baer, M.D., Martin R. Post, M.D.
EIN: 136123540
Codes: FD

33681
Irving A. Hansen Memorial Foundation
c/o JPMorgan Chase Bank
270 Park Ave., 23rd Fl.
New York, NY 10017
Contact: Diane McGuire

Established in 1983 in NY.
Donor(s): Irving A. Hansen.‡
Financial data (yr. ended 07/31/01): Grants paid, $444,000; assets, $7,189,813 (M); expenditures, $545,033; qualifying distributions, $463,934.

33681—NEW YORK

Application information: Recipients chosen at the discretion of the trustees. Application form not required.
Trustees: Louis B. Frost, William F. Hibberd, JPMorgan Chase Bank.
EIN: 133177338
Codes: FD

33682
Redbird Foundation
c/o Anna T. Korniczky, Brown Brothers Harriman Trust Co.
63 Wall St.
New York, NY 10005-3001
Application address: 4624 Chambliss Ave., Knoxville, TN 37919
Contact: Adella S. Thompson, Dir.

Established in 1995.
Donor(s): B. Ray Thompson Charitable Trust, Juanne Thompson Charitable Trust.
Financial data (yr. ended 12/31/00): Grants paid, $444,000; assets, $10,025,212 (M); expenditures, $483,740; qualifying distributions, $434,298.
Limitations: Giving primarily in Bell, Clay, Laurel, and Leslie counties, KY, Knox, Anderson, Scott, and Blount counties, TN, and Buchanan and Tazewell counties, VA.
Publications: Annual report.
Application information: Application form required.
Officers: B. Ray Thompson, Jr., Pres.; Juanne J. Thompson, Secy.
Directors: Sarah Thompson Tarver, Adella Sands Thompson, B. Ray Thompson III, Catherine Vance Thompson, Rebekah Lee-Isla Thompson.
EIN: 621591527
Codes: FD

33683
The Melville Straus Charitable Trust
c/o B. Strauss Assoc., Ltd.
307 5th Ave., 8th Fl.
New York, NY 10016-6517

Established in 1986 in NY.
Donor(s): Melville Straus.
Financial data (yr. ended 02/28/01): Grants paid, $443,559; assets, $224,606 (M); gifts received, $66,991; expenditures, $458,844; qualifying distributions, $442,824.
Limitations: Applications not accepted. Giving primarily in New York, NY.
Application information: Contributes only to pre-selected organizations.
Trustees: Richard Reiss, Melville Straus, Eugene Zuriff.
EIN: 136881724
Codes: FD

33684
The Sister Fund
(Formerly The Hunt Alternatives Fund)
116 E. 16th St., 7th Fl.
New York, NY 10003-2112 (212) 260-4446
FAX: (212) 260-4633; E-mail: sisterfund@aol.com
Contact: Kanyere Eaton, Exec. Dir.

Established in 1981 in NY; in Dec. 1992, the New York, NY, office officially became a private women's fund with the current name; the Denver, CO, office has become a separate entity called the Hunt Alternatives Fund.
Donor(s): Helen Hunt.
Financial data (yr. ended 11/30/00): Grants paid, $442,813; assets, $51,674 (M); gifts received, $940,922; expenditures, $972,064; qualifying distributions, $896,136.

Limitations: Giving primarily in the metropolitan New York, NY, area for local programs; national support for public education campaigns.
Publications: Informational brochure (including application guidelines), newsletter, occasional report.
Application information: Application form not required.
Officers and Trustees:* Helen LaKelly Hunt,* Pres.; Harville Hendrix,* V.P.; Vincent McGee,* Secy.; Suzette Loh,* Treas.; Kanyere Eaton, Exec. Dir.
Directors: Olivia Cousins, China Galland, Terrie Bad Hand, Karen Hessel, Pati Martinson, Linda Tarry-Chard.
EIN: 751763787
Codes: FD

33685
The Slant/Fin Foundation, Inc.
100 Forest Dr.
Greenvale, NY 11548 (516) 484-2600
Contact: Melvin Dubin, Pres.

Established in 1985 in NY.
Donor(s): M. Dubin, Slant/Fin Corp.
Financial data (yr. ended 06/30/01): Grants paid, $442,536; assets, $148,895 (M); gifts received, $447,000; expenditures, $442,736; qualifying distributions, $442,736.
Limitations: Giving primarily in NY.
Officers: Melvin Dubin, Pres.; Delcy Brooks, Secy.; Donald Brown, Treas.
EIN: 112752009
Codes: CS, FD, CD

33686
The Jon & Susan Rotenstreich Foundation, Inc.
770 Park Ave.
New York, NY 10021

Established in 1975.
Donor(s): Jon W. Rotenstreich, Glenda Susan Rotenstreich.
Financial data (yr. ended 06/30/01): Grants paid, $442,285; assets, $850,531 (M); expenditures, $460,274; qualifying distributions, $442,385.
Limitations: Applications not accepted. Giving primarily in NY.
Application information: Contributes only to pre-selected organizations.
Officers and Directors:* Jon W. Rotenstreich,* Pres.; Glenda Susan Rotenstreich,* Treas.; James I. Rotenstreich.
EIN: 510180076
Codes: FD

33687
Memorial Fund, Inc.
33 Downing Dr. S.
White Plains, NY 10607-2011
Contact: Grants Admin.

Established in 1937.
Donor(s): Beth Rosenthal, Doris Rosenthal, Edward Rosenthal,‡ Peter Rosenthal, Kenneth Sarnoff, Jelp Assocs.
Financial data (yr. ended 12/31/00): Grants paid, $441,122; assets, $6,491,301 (M); gifts received, $47,060; expenditures, $539,355; qualifying distributions, $444,041.
Limitations: Applications not accepted. Giving on a national basis.
Application information: Contributes only to pre-selected organizations.
Officers: Doris Rosenthal, Pres.; Peter Rosenthal, V.P. and Secy.; Carol Maslow, V.P. and Treas.; Pat Mann, Ellen Sarnoff.
EIN: 136185716
Codes: FD

33688
Towbin Fund
1010 5th Ave., Apt. 11B
New York, NY 10028

Trust established in 1955 in NY.
Donor(s): A. Robert Towbin, Belmont Towbin.
Financial data (yr. ended 06/30/01): Grants paid, $440,390; assets, $7,812 (M); gifts received, $372,866; expenditures, $441,037; qualifying distributions, $436,867.
Limitations: Applications not accepted. Giving primarily in NY.
Application information: Contributes only to pre-selected organizations.
Trustee: A. Robert Towbin.
EIN: 136158005
Codes: FD

33689
Jonathan M. Tisch Foundation, Inc.
c/o Mark J. Krinsky, C.P.A.
655 Madison Ave., 8th Fl.
New York, NY 10021

Established in 1995 in NY.
Financial data (yr. ended 12/31/00): Grants paid, $440,056; assets, $8,774,148 (M); gifts received, $5,332,900; expenditures, $462,057; qualifying distributions, $424,588.
Limitations: Applications not accepted. Giving primarily in NY.
Application information: Contributes only to pre-selected organizations.
Officers: Jonathan M. Tisch, Pres.; Mark J. Krinsky, V.P.; Thomas M. Steinberg, V.P.; Barry L. Bloom, Secy.-Treas.
EIN: 311641042
Codes: FD

33690
De La Cour Family Foundation
P.O. Box 94
Glen Cove, NY 11542

Established in 1999 in DE.
Donor(s): Willis S. De La Cour.
Financial data (yr. ended 12/31/01): Grants paid, $440,000; assets, $8,507,362 (M); expenditures, $523,243; qualifying distributions, $437,179.
Limitations: Applications not accepted. Giving primarily on the East Coast, with some emphasis on NY, PA, and the New England region.
Application information: Contributes only to pre-selected organizations.
Officers and Directors:* Willis S. De La Cour,* Pres.; Willis S. De La Cour, Jr.,* V.P. and Secy.-Treas.; Edmund P. De La Cour, Eleanore P. De La Cour, Lea De La Cour.
EIN: 233025610
Codes: FD

33691
Marion E. Kenworthy - Sarah H. Swift Foundation, Inc.
130 E. 67th St.
New York, NY 10021-6136 (212) 988-0473
FAX: (212) 988-2483; E-mail: ksfdtn@aol.com
Contact: Rosalind W. Harris, Admin.

Established in 1962 in NY.
Donor(s): Marion E. Kenworthy.‡
Financial data (yr. ended 12/31/01): Grants paid, $439,342; assets, $8,214,664 (M); expenditures, $484,661; qualifying distributions, $439,342.
Limitations: Giving primarily in New York City and the surrounding tri-state area.
Publications: Application guidelines, informational brochure (including application guidelines).

Application information: Application form not required.
Officers and Directors:* Michael G. Kalogerakis, M.D.,* Pres.; Trudy Festinger,* V.P.; Alice Lin,* V.P.; Stephen Wise Tulin,* Secy.-Treas.
EIN: 136140940
Codes: FD

33692
Steckler Family Foundation, Inc.
(Formerly Philip H. & Lois R. Steckler Foundation)
c/o M.R. Weiser & Co. LLP
35 W. 50th St.
New York, NY 10020-1299

Established in 1969 in NY.
Donor(s): Philip H. Steckler, Jr.‡
Financial data (yr. ended 07/31/01): Grants paid, $438,500; assets, $4,647,944 (M); expenditures, $479,655; qualifying distributions, $434,069.
Limitations: Applications not accepted. Giving primarily in NY.
Application information: Contributes only to pre-selected organizations.
Officers and Board Members:* Philip H. Steckler III,* Pres.; Allan Steckler,* Secy.; Donald H. Steckler,* Treas.
EIN: 132621420
Codes: FD

33693
Magen Ezra Foundation
c/o Jack Cattan
37 W. 37th St., Rm. 10
New York, NY 10018

Established in 1998 in NY.
Donor(s): Judah Cattan, Ezra Jack Cattan, Jack Cattan, Ezrasons, Inc.
Financial data (yr. ended 11/30/01): Grants paid, $437,666; assets, $814,943 (M); gifts received, $609,356; expenditures, $451,041; qualifying distributions, $451,041.
Limitations: Applications not accepted.
Application information: Contributes only to pre-selected organizations.
Officers: Ezra Jack Cattan, Jack Cattan, Joseph Cattan, Judah Cattan.
EIN: 133980258
Codes: FD

33694
Zeron Foundation
200 Theatre Pl.
Buffalo, NY 14202

Established in 1993 in NY.
Donor(s): Jessica Enstice, members of the Jacobs family.
Financial data (yr. ended 12/31/01): Grants paid, $436,539; assets, $3,017,746 (M); expenditures, $456,341; qualifying distributions, $433,214.
Limitations: Giving primarily in IN and western NY.
Trustees: Jessica H. Enstice, Matthew Enstice, Christopher L. Jacobs, Danielle Jacobs, Elizabeth R. Jacobs, Lawrence D. Jacobs, Lawrence D. Jacobs, Jr., Luke T. Jacobs, Pamela R. Jacobs.
EIN: 161429495
Codes: FD

33695
Robert and Teresa Lindsay Family Foundation
630 5th Ave., 39th Fl.
New York, NY 10111

Established in 1997 in NY.
Donor(s): Robert D. Lindsay.
Financial data (yr. ended 09/30/01): Grants paid, $436,050; assets, $321,087 (M); gifts received, $972,318; expenditures, $451,650; qualifying distributions, $436,050.
Limitations: Giving on a national basis, with emphasis on NY and CA.
Trustees: Robert D. Lindsay, Teresa Lindsay.
EIN: 137142605
Codes: FD

33696
The 1994 Christopher W. Johnson Charitable Trust No. 33
(Formerly The Christopher W. Johnson Charitable Trust)
c/o The Johnson Co., Inc.
630 5th Ave., Ste. 1510
New York, NY 10111

Established in 1994 in NY.
Donor(s): Betty W. Johnson, Christopher W. Johnson.
Financial data (yr. ended 12/31/01): Grants paid, $436,000; assets, $10,189,439 (M); expenditures, $443,710; qualifying distributions, $432,888.
Limitations: Applications not accepted. Giving primarily in New York, NY.
Application information: Contributes only to pre-selected organizations.
Trustees: Betty W. Johnson, Christopher W. Johnson.
EIN: 137046311
Codes: FD

33697
William M. & Miriam F. Meehan Foundation, Inc.
120 E. 87th St., Ste. R4L
New York, NY 10128 (212) 534-8607
FAX: (212) 426-7472
Contact: John D. O'Leary, Exec. Dir.

Established in 1951.
Donor(s): Terence S. Meehan, Miriam F. Meehan, Maureen M. O'Leary, Joanne Berghold.
Financial data (yr. ended 12/31/00): Grants paid, $435,540; assets, $10,771,862 (M); gifts received, $547,211; expenditures, $625,039; qualifying distributions, $435,540.
Limitations: Applications not accepted. Giving primarily in New York, NY.
Application information: Contributes only to pre-selected organizations.
Officers and Directors:* Miriam F. Meehan,* Pres.; Maureen Meehan O'Leary,* V.P.; Terence S. Meehan,* Treas.; John D. O'Leary,* Exec. Dir.; Elisabetta Berghold, Joanne M. Berghold, Wm. Mark Berghold, Emily Souvaine Meehan, William M. Meehan, Ph.D.; Laura Roebuck, M.D., Tad Sennott.
EIN: 136062834
Codes: FD

33698
The Friedman Family Charitable Foundation Trust
377 Broadway
New York, NY 10013

Established in 1993 in NY.
Donor(s): Elie Fried, Ari Friedman, Jack Friedman, Elissa Mermelstein.
Financial data (yr. ended 12/31/99): Grants paid, $434,975; assets, $1,067,612 (M); gifts received, $618,000; expenditures, $445,348; qualifying distributions, $435,241.
Limitations: Applications not accepted. Giving primarily in NY.
Application information: Contributes only to pre-selected organizations.
Trustees: Ari Friedman, David Friedman, Esther Friedman, Jack Friedman.
EIN: 116431495
Codes: FD

33699
Frank and Deenie Brosens Foundation
c/o Arthur J. Giglio
250 E. Hartsdale Ave., Ste. 34
Hartsdale, NY 10530

Established in 1989 in NY.
Donor(s): Frank P. Brosens, Deenie M. Brosens.
Financial data (yr. ended 01/31/02): Grants paid, $434,889; assets, $688,690 (M); expenditures, $435,059; qualifying distributions, $431,952.
Limitations: Applications not accepted. Giving primarily in Westchester County, NY.
Application information: Contributes only to pre-selected organizations.
Trustees: Deenie M. Brosens, Frank P. Brosens.
EIN: 133532018
Codes: FD

33700
David C. Clapp Foundation
c/o BCRS Assocs., LLC
100 Wall St., 11th Fl.
New York, NY 10005

Established in 1985 in NY.
Donor(s): David C. Clapp.
Financial data (yr. ended 06/30/01): Grants paid, $433,942; assets, $495,278 (M); expenditures, $451,729; qualifying distributions, $435,390.
Limitations: Applications not accepted. Giving primarily in New York, NY.
Application information: Contributes only to pre-selected organizations.
Trustees: Constance L. Clapp, David C. Clapp.
EIN: 133318134
Codes: FD

33701
Yvonne & Leslie Pollack Family Foundation, Inc.
8 Long Meadow Rd.
Bedford, NY 10506 (212) 476-5888
Contact: Leslie Pollack, Pres.

Established in 1998 in NY.
Donor(s): Leslie Pollack, Rae Pollack.‡
Financial data (yr. ended 12/31/01): Grants paid, $433,491; assets, $6,522,518 (M); expenditures, $464,364; qualifying distributions, $455,173.
Limitations: Giving primarily in New York, NY.
Application information: Application form not required.
Officers and Directors:* Leslie Pollack,* Pres.; Yvonne Pollack,* Secy.; Fredrica Pollack, Jonathan Pollack, Jennifer Pollack Reiner.
EIN: 133985619
Codes: FD

33702
Mathis-Pfohl Foundation
5-46 46th Ave.
Long Island City, NY 11101 (718) 784-4800
Contact: James M. Pfohl, Pres.

Incorporated in 1947 in IA.
Donor(s): Members of the Pfohl family and associated companies.
Financial data (yr. ended 11/30/99): Grants paid, $433,170; assets, $9,933,087 (M); expenditures, $445,234; qualifying distributions, $429,176.
Officer: James M. Pfohl, Pres.
EIN: 116013764
Codes: FD

33703
The Margaret M. Hill Foundation
c/o Lutz & Carr, LLP
300 E. 42nd St.
New York, NY 10017
Contact: Margaret M. Hill, Pres.

Established in 1997 in NY.
Donor(s): The Rosenkranz Foundation.
Financial data (yr. ended 12/31/00): Grants paid, $433,082; assets, $4,302,668 (M); expenditures, $478,227; qualifying distributions, $433,171.
Limitations: Applications not accepted. Giving primarily in IN and NY.
Application information: Contributes only to pre-selected organizations.
Officer: Margaret M. Hill, Pres.
EIN: 137088667
Codes: FD

33704
Elizabeth & Frank Ingrassia Foundation
c/o Goldman Sachs & Co.
85 Broad St., Tax Dept.
New York, NY 10004

Established in 1994 in NY.
Donor(s): Francis J. Ingrassia.
Financial data (yr. ended 09/30/01): Grants paid, $433,000; assets, $2,625,991 (M); gifts received, $1,502,059; expenditures, $490,127; qualifying distributions, $433,000.
Limitations: Applications not accepted.
Application information: Contributes only to pre-selected organizations.
Trustees: Francis J. Ingrassia, Elizabeth McCaul.
EIN: 133801229

33705
Frederick Loewe Foundation, Inc.
c/o Fitelson, Lasky, Aslan & Couture
551 5th Ave.
New York, NY 10176

Established in 1959.
Donor(s): Frederick Loewe.‡
Financial data (yr. ended 11/30/01): Grants paid, $432,500; assets, $6,343,175 (M); expenditures, $519,955; qualifying distributions, $439,705.
Limitations: Applications not accepted. Giving primarily in NY.
Application information: Contributes only to pre-selected organizations.
Officers: Floria V. Lasky, Pres.; Jerold L. Couture, V.P.; Robert A. Schlesinger, V.P.; Clifford Forster, Secy.; David S. Rhine, Treas.
EIN: 136111444
Codes: FD

33706
Max & Marian Farash Charitable Foundation
919 Winton Rd., S.
Rochester, NY 14618-1633
Contact: Max M. Farash, Tr.

Established in 1988 in NY.
Financial data (yr. ended 12/31/01): Grants paid, $431,600; assets, $4,115,068 (M); expenditures, $450,305; qualifying distributions, $429,697.
Limitations: Applications not accepted. Giving primarily in the Rochester, NY, area.
Application information: Unsolicited requests for funds not accepted.
Trustees: Marian M. Farash, Max M. Farash, Eric R. Fox.
EIN: 222948675
Codes: FD

33707
The Joan Mitchell Foundation, Inc.
P.O. Box 1902
New York, NY 10025-1902
Tel./FAX: (212) 865-8491; *URL:* http://fdncenter.org/grantmaker/joanmitchellfdn
Donor(s): Joan Mitchell.‡
Financial data (yr. ended 01/31/01): Grants paid, $431,500; assets, $1,543,185 (M); gifts received, $60,920; expenditures, $627,439; qualifying distributions, $526,966.
Limitations: Giving on a national basis.
Application information: Application form required.
Officers: Adrian Gaines, Pres.; Yolanda Shashaty, Treas.; Carolyn Somers, Secy. and Prog. Dir.; Dan Bergman, Exec. Dir.
Directors: Alejandro Anreus, Grace Hartigan, John Koos.
EIN: 113161054
Codes: FD

33708
W.S.P. & R. Charitable Trust Fund
c/o Pillsbury Winthrop, LLP
1 Battery Park Plz.
New York, NY 10004-1490

Established in 1940 in NY.
Donor(s): Winthrop, Stimson, Putnam & Roberts.
Financial data (yr. ended 12/31/01): Grants paid, $430,829; assets, $164,870 (M); expenditures, $431,145; qualifying distributions, $431,009.
Limitations: Giving primarily in New York, NY.
Trustees: Leo T. Crowley, Jane W. Stein, Robert D. Webster.
EIN: 510243782
Codes: CS, FD, CD

33709
Samuel Goldberg & Sons Foundation, Inc.
1 N. Broadway
White Plains, NY 10601
Contact: David Wechsler

Established in 1943.
Financial data (yr. ended 12/31/01): Grants paid, $430,202; assets, $4,960,381 (M); expenditures, $491,092; qualifying distributions, $429,171.
Limitations: Giving primarily in NY.
Trustees: Amy Eller, Robert Goldberg.
EIN: 136111269
Codes: FD

33710
Herdrich 1985 Charitable Trust
c/o Donald J. Herdrich
1 S. Greeley Ave., Ste. 3
Chappaqua, NY 10514

Established in 1986 in NY.
Donor(s): Donald J. Herdrich, Frances I. Herdrich.
Financial data (yr. ended 11/30/01): Grants paid, $429,500; assets, $7,799,451 (M); gifts received, $4,000; expenditures, $506,844; qualifying distributions, $431,500.
Limitations: Applications not accepted. Giving primarily in NY.
Application information: Contributes only to pre-selected organizations.
Trustee: Donald J. Herdrich.
EIN: 136855419
Codes: FD

33711
Nola Maddox Falcone Charitable Foundation
c/o Satterlee Stephens, et al.
230 Park Ave., Rm. 1130
New York, NY 10169

Established in 1993.
Donor(s): Nola Maddox Falcone.
Financial data (yr. ended 12/31/01): Grants paid, $429,330; assets, $1,103,402 (M); gifts received, $111,462; expenditures, $433,963; qualifying distributions, $427,072.
Limitations: Applications not accepted. Giving primarily in FL, GA, MA, NC, NY, and PA.
Application information: Contributes only to pre-selected organizations.
Trustee: Nola Maddox Falcone.
EIN: 133731865
Codes: FD

33712
The Anne Marie and Thomas B. Walker, Jr. Foundation
c/o BCRS Assocs., LLC
100 Wall St., 11th Fl.
New York, NY 10005

Established in 1996 in TX.
Donor(s): Thomas B. Walker, Jr.
Financial data (yr. ended 05/31/01): Grants paid, $428,500; assets, $5,152,747 (M); expenditures, $446,262; qualifying distributions, $426,433.
Limitations: Applications not accepted. Giving primarily in TN and TX.
Application information: Contributes only to pre-selected organizations.
Trustees: Anne Marie Walker, John Newton Walker, Thomas B. Walker, Jr., Thomas B. Walker III.
EIN: 137103237
Codes: FD

33713
Phalarope Foundation
(Formerly Raval Charitable Foundation)
c/o Rockefeller & Co.
30 Rockefeller Plz., Rm. 5600
New York, NY 10112-0002

Established in 1992 in MA.
Financial data (yr. ended 12/31/00): Grants paid, $428,200; assets, $6,406,030 (M); expenditures, $507,780; qualifying distributions, $428,200.
Limitations: Applications not accepted. Giving primarily in CA.
Application information: Contributes only to pre-selected organizations.
Trustees: Stuart P. Davidson, Richard T. Watson.
EIN: 046729068
Codes: FD

33714
The Joseph G. Goldring Foundation
100 Crossways Park W., Rm. 306
Woodbury, NY 11797-2084

Established about 1970 in NY.
Donor(s): Overseas Military Sales Corp., Military Car Sales, Inc., Chrysler Military Sales Corp., Allen A. Goldring.
Financial data (yr. ended 06/30/01): Grants paid, $426,755; assets, $329,455 (M); gifts received, $405,000; expenditures, $426,855; qualifying distributions, $426,755.
Limitations: Applications not accepted. Giving primarily in the metropolitan New York, NY, area, including the North Shore of Long Island.
Application information: Contributes only to pre-selected organizations. Unsolicited requests for funds not accepted.

Officers: Allen A. Goldring, Pres.; Lola A. Goldring, V.P.; Muriel W. Logan, Secy.; Leo Breittholz, Treas.
EIN: 116084103
Codes: FD

33715
Santa Maria Foundation, Inc.
P.O. Box 604138
Bayside, NY 11360-4138
Contact: Margaret Devine, Admin. Asst.

Established in 1978 in NY.
Donor(s): J. Peter Grace,‡ Margaret F. Grace.
Financial data (yr. ended 12/31/00): Grants paid, $426,500; assets, $9,378,255 (M); expenditures, $512,176; qualifying distributions, $430,615.
Limitations: Giving primarily in NY.
Application information: Organization must be listed in Kenedy's Official Catholic Directory. Application form not required.
Officers and Directors:* Margaret F. Grace,* Pres.; Theresa G. Sears,* Secy.; Patrick P. Grace,* Treas.; Mary Grace Benson.
EIN: 132938749
Codes: FD

33716
Morton & Carole Olshan Foundation
c/o Morton Olshan, Mall Properties, Inc.
654 Madison Ave.
New York, NY 10021

Established in 1991 in NY.
Donor(s): Morton Olshan.
Financial data (yr. ended 12/31/00): Grants paid, $426,130; assets, $6,462 (M); gifts received, $430,000; expenditures, $426,157; qualifying distributions, $426,129.
Limitations: Applications not accepted. Giving primarily in NY.
Application information: Contributes only to pre-selected organizations.
Directors: Carole Olshan, Morton Olshan, Robert Steinberg.
EIN: 133601794
Codes: FD

33717
Finneran Family Foundation
c/o Anchin, Block & Anchin
1375 Broadway
New York, NY 10017

Established in 1986 in NY.
Donor(s): William B. Finneran.
Financial data (yr. ended 11/30/00): Grants paid, $425,630; assets, $1,523,405 (M); expenditures, $457,044; qualifying distributions, $450,255.
Limitations: Applications not accepted. Giving primarily in NY.
Application information: Contributes only to pre-selected organizations.
Officer: William B. Finneran, Pres.
EIN: 133447863
Codes: FD

33718
Carl Marks Foundation, Inc.
135 E. 57th St., 27th Fl.
New York, NY 10022 (212) 909-8400
Contact: Iris Resken, Cont.

Established in 1986 in NY.
Donor(s): Members of the Boas family, Mark Claster, Susan Claster, Andrew Boas.
Financial data (yr. ended 06/30/01): Grants paid, $425,441; assets, $12,459,307 (M); expenditures, $450,966; qualifying distributions, $426,191.
Limitations: Applications not accepted. Giving primarily in New York, NY.
Application information: Contributes only to pre-selected organizations.
Officers: Andrew M. Boas, Pres. and Secy.; Mark Claster, V.P. and Treas.; Iris Reskin, Cont.
EIN: 136169215
Codes: FD

33719
Century 21 Associates Foundation, Inc.
(Formerly Gindi Associates Foundation, Inc.)
22 Cortlandt St.
New York, NY 10007

Established in 1982 in NJ.
Donor(s): Century 21, Inc.
Financial data (yr. ended 05/31/99): Grants paid, $424,355; assets, $545,951 (M); gifts received, $305,000; expenditures, $427,517; qualifying distributions, $423,948.
Limitations: Applications not accepted. Giving primarily in NJ, and Brooklyn and New York, NY.
Application information: Contributes only to pre-selected organizations.
Trustees: Abraham Gindi, Sam Gindi.
EIN: 212412138
Codes: CS, FD

33720
Joy Family Foundation
107-111 Goundry St.
North Tonawanda, NY 14120 (716) 695-0944
FAX: (716) 695-1074; *E-mail:* info@joyfamilyfoundation.org; *URL:* http://www.joyfamilyfoundation.org
Contact: Marsha J. Sullivan, Exec. Dir.

Established in 1989 in NY.
Donor(s): Paul W. Joy, H. Joan Joy.
Financial data (yr. ended 12/31/01): Grants paid, $423,826; assets, $6,124,317 (M); expenditures, $470,838; qualifying distributions, $361,674.
Limitations: Giving primarily in Erie and Niagara counties, NY.
Publications: Informational brochure (including application guidelines), application guidelines, grants list.
Application information: Application form required.
Officer and Trustees:* Marsha Joy Sullivan,* Exec. Dir.; H. Joan Joy, Lene Joy, Paul W. Joy, Stephen T. Joy, John Reinhold, Paula Joy Reinhold, Ian Sturdevant, Michael Sullivan.
EIN: 166335211
Codes: FD

33721
George Graham and Elizabeth Galloway Smith Foundation, Inc.
84 S. Davis St.
Orchard Park, NY 14127-2651
(716) 662-9749
Contact: Graham Wood Smith, Pres.

Established in 1960.
Donor(s): Elizabeth G. Smith, Beatrice Erlin,‡ George G. Smith.‡
Financial data (yr. ended 05/31/01): Grants paid, $423,505; assets, $5,426,084 (M); gifts received, $113,789; expenditures, $443,776; qualifying distributions, $428,697.
Limitations: Giving primarily in western NY.
Officers: Elizabeth G. Smith, Chair.; Graham Wood Smith, Pres. and Treas.; George G. Smith III, V.P.; Mary Jane C. Smith, Secy.
Directors: C. Schuyler Morehouse, Elizabeth S. Morehouse, Janet Smith.
EIN: 166031530
Codes: FD

33722
Albert Penick Fund
c/o JPMorgan Chase Bank
1211 6th Ave., 34th Fl.
New York, NY 10036
Application address: 65 S. Main St., Pennington, NJ 08534
Contact: K. Philip Dresdner, Tr.

Trust established in 1951 in NY.
Donor(s): A.D. Penick,‡ Mrs. Albert D. Penick.
Financial data (yr. ended 12/31/01): Grants paid, $423,000; assets, $4,741,628 (M); expenditures, $480,103; qualifying distributions, $431,677.
Limitations: Giving primarily in CT, MA, NJ, and NY.
Application information: Application form not required.
Trustees: K. Philip Dresdner, V. Susan Penick.
EIN: 136161137
Codes: FD

33723
Saunders Foundation
760 Brooks Ave.
Rochester, NY 14619-2259

Incorporated in 1986 in NY.
Financial data (yr. ended 12/31/01): Grants paid, $422,908; assets, $1,763,349 (M); expenditures, $440,046; qualifying distributions, $428,171.
Limitations: Applications not accepted. Giving primarily in upstate NY.
Application information: Contributes only to pre-selected organizations.
Officers: Carole M. Saunders, Pres.; William Burslem III, Treas.
Director: Max Stoner.
EIN: 161289330
Codes: FD

33724
The Alpert Family Foundation, Inc.
c/o Norman W. Alpert
17 Linden Dr.
Purchase, NY 10577-1438

Established in 1995 in NY.
Donor(s): Norman W. Alpert.
Financial data (yr. ended 11/30/01): Grants paid, $422,750; assets, $77,233 (M); gifts received, $275,596; expenditures, $427,155; qualifying distributions, $422,750.
Limitations: Applications not accepted. Giving primarily in MA and RI.
Application information: Contributes only to pre-selected organizations.
Officers and Directors:* Norman W. Alpert,* Pres.; Jane Alpert,* V.P. and Secy.; William Goldberg.
EIN: 133745910
Codes: FD

33725
Samuel C. & Sally T. Butler Charitable Trust
(Formerly Samuel C. Butler Charitable Trust)
c/o Cravath, Swaine & Moore
825 8th Ave., Ste. 4600
New York, NY 10019-7475

Established in 1985 in NY.
Donor(s): Samuel C. Butler, Sally T. Butler.
Financial data (yr. ended 12/31/01): Grants paid, $422,000; assets, $308,619 (M); gifts received, $184,420; expenditures, $422,000; qualifying distributions, $422,000.
Limitations: Applications not accepted. Giving primarily in MA and NY.
Application information: Contributes only to pre-selected organizations.
Trustees: Sally T. Butler, Samuel C. Butler.

EIN: 136870361
Codes: FD

33726
Bialkin Family Foundation
c/o Skadden, Arps, Slate, Meagher & Flom
4 Times Sq.
New York, NY 10036

Established in 1968 in NY.
Donor(s): Kenneth J. Bialkin, Ann E. Bialkin.
Financial data (yr. ended 12/31/00): Grants paid, $420,980; assets, $11,171,022 (M); expenditures, $448,759; qualifying distributions, $421,778.
Limitations: Applications not accepted. Giving primarily in New York, NY.
Application information: Contributes only to pre-selected organizations.
Officers and Directors:* Kenneth J. Bialkin,* Pres.; Ann E. Bialkin,* Sr. V.P.; Johanna Bialkin, V.P.; Lisa Bialkin, V.P.; Jonathan L. Koslow, Secy.
EIN: 237003181
Codes: FD

33727
The Katz Foundation
(Formerly Howard & Holly Katz Foundation)
c/o BCRS Assocs., LLC
100 Wall St., 11th Fl.
New York, NY 10005

Established in 1983 in NY.
Donor(s): Howard C. Katz.
Financial data (yr. ended 08/31/01): Grants paid, $420,437; assets, $1,789,719 (M); expenditures, $434,857; qualifying distributions, $422,390.
Limitations: Applications not accepted. Giving primarily in New York, NY.
Application information: Contributes only to pre-selected organizations.
Trustees: Ellen Katz, Howard C. Katz, Ronald S. Tauber.
EIN: 133199938
Codes: FD

33728
Blanche Enders Charitable Trust
c/o JPMorgan Chase Bank
1211 6th Ave., 34th Fl.
New York, NY 10036 (212) 789-4502
Contact: Raymond Zelin

Financial data (yr. ended 12/31/01): Grants paid, $420,000; assets, $7,220,451 (M); expenditures, $482,854; qualifying distributions, $422,941.
Limitations: Giving primarily in the tri-state NY, NJ, and CT area.
Application information: Application form not required.
Trustee: JPMorgan Chase Bank.
EIN: 136164229
Codes: FD

33729
The Francis Asbury Palmer Foundation
c/o The Bank of New York
1 Wall St., Tax Dept., 28th Fl.
New York, NY 10286

Incorporated in 1897 in NY.
Donor(s): Francis Asbury Palmer.‡
Financial data (yr. ended 04/30/01): Grants paid, $420,000; assets, $7,898,203 (M); expenditures, $445,522; qualifying distributions, $422,191.
Limitations: Applications not accepted. Giving on a national basis.
Application information: Contributes only to pre-selected organizations. Unsolicited requests for funds not accepted.
Officers: Diana L. Reed, Pres.; William Sword, Treas.

Directors: Allison C. Hansen, Page Hughes, E. Gayle McGuigan, Jr., Phillip P. McGuigan, Susan K. Reed.
EIN: 136400635
Codes: FD

33730
Samuel and Julia Bernstein Foundation
c/o Northville Industries Corp.
25 Melville Park Rd.
Melville, NY 11747

Trust established in 1946 in NY.
Donor(s): Northville Industries Corp.
Financial data (yr. ended 12/31/00): Grants paid, $419,254; assets, $1,133,955 (M); expenditures, $426,259; qualifying distributions, $417,325.
Limitations: Applications not accepted. Giving primarily in NY.
Application information: Contributes only to pre-selected organizations.
Trustees: Gene M. Bernstein, Harold P. Bernstein, Helen Bernstein, Jay Bernstein.
EIN: 116012498
Codes: CS, FD, CD

33731
Whispering Bells Foundation
c/o McLaughlin & Stern, LLP
260 Madison Ave., 18th Fl.
New York, NY 10016

Established in 1990 in NY.
Donor(s): Peter Workman, Carolan Workman, Workman Publishing Co.
Financial data (yr. ended 12/31/00): Grants paid, $419,165; assets, $1,259,262 (M); gifts received, $400,000; expenditures, $419,846; qualifying distributions, $419,165.
Limitations: Applications not accepted. Giving primarily in NY.
Application information: Contributes only to pre-selected organizations.
Officer and Trustees:* Peter Workman,* Pres.; Edward Klagsbrun, Carolan Workman.
EIN: 136962126
Codes: FD

33732
Alfiero Family Charitable Foundation
2150 Elmwood Ave.
Buffalo, NY 14207 (716) 689-4972
Contact: Salvatore H. Alfiero, Chair.

Established in 1989 in NY.
Financial data (yr. ended 12/31/01): Grants paid, $418,333; assets, $7,353,763 (M); expenditures, $567,482; qualifying distributions, $418,333.
Limitations: Giving limited to NY.
Officers: Salvatore H. Alfiero, Chair.; Victor S. Alfiero, Pres.; Charles C. Alfiero, V.P.; James J. Alfiero, Secy.
EIN: 110036051
Codes: FD

33733
The Beir Foundation
110 E. 59th St.
New York, NY 10022

Incorporated in 1944 in NY.
Donor(s): Robert L. Beir.
Financial data (yr. ended 12/31/01): Grants paid, $418,092; assets, $7,251,587 (M); expenditures, $488,633; qualifying distributions, $418,092.
Limitations: Applications not accepted. Giving primarily in the New York, NY, area.
Application information: Contributes only to pre-selected organizations.
Officers: Robert L. Beir, Pres.; Joan S. Beir, V.P.; Michael Katz, Secy.

EIN: 136084093
Codes: FD

33734
The Dirk E. Ziff Foundation
c/o Ziff Bros. Investments
153 E. 53rd St., 43rd Fl.
New York, NY 10022

Established in 2000 in DE.
Donor(s): Ziff Investment Partnership LP II.
Financial data (yr. ended 12/31/00): Grants paid, $417,661; assets, $3,367,759 (M); gifts received, $3,474,164; expenditures, $461,988; qualifying distributions, $379,600.
Limitations: Applications not accepted. Giving primarily in FL and NY.
Application information: Contributes only to pre-selected organizations.
Officers: Dirk E. Ziff, Pres.; David Moody, V.P. and Secy.; Mark Beaudoin, V.P.; Peter Cawley, V.P.; Timothy Mitchell, Treas.
EIN: 134083748
Codes: FD

33735
The Icahn Charitable Foundation
c/o Icahn Assoc. Corp.
767 5th Ave., 47th Fl.
New York, NY 10153
Contact: Gail Golden, V.P.

Established in 1995 in DE.
Financial data (yr. ended 11/30/01): Grants paid, $416,500; assets, $2,779,946 (M); expenditures, $426,402; qualifying distributions, $421,238.
Limitations: Giving on a national basis.
Application information: Application form not required.
Officers and Directors:* Carl C. Icahn,* Pres. and Treas.; Gail Golden,* V.P. and Secy.
EIN: 133863205
Codes: FD

33736
Stony Wold-Herbert Fund, Inc.
136 E. 57th St., Rm. 1705
New York, NY 10022 (212) 753-6565
FAX: (212) 753-6053; E-mail: director@stonywold-herbertfund.com; URL: http://www.stonywold-herbertfund.com
Contact: Cheryl S. Friedman, Exec. Dir.

Incorporated in 1974 in NY.
Financial data (yr. ended 12/31/00): Grants paid, $416,446; assets, $8,377,993 (M); gifts received, $2,150; expenditures, $547,005; qualifying distributions, $478,007.
Limitations: Giving limited to New York City.
Publications: Annual report, application guidelines, newsletter, informational brochure.
Application information: Application form required.
Officers and Board Members:* Anne Logan Davis, M.D.,* Pres.; Mrs. George C. Moore,* V.P.; Mrs. Ronald Carr,* Secy.; Adams H. Nickerson,* Treas.; Cheryl S. Friedman, Exec. Dir.; H. Kent Atkins, C. Redington Barrett, Jr., M.D., Mrs. James L. German III, Ashton Harvey, Milena Lewis, M.D., Lawrence L. Scharer, M.D., Henry M. Thomas III, M.D., Mrs. Charles S. Whitman, Jr.
EIN: 132784124
Codes: FD, GTI

33737
Daniel Rosenblum Family Foundation, Inc.
370 7th Ave., Ste. 1110
New York, NY 10001

Established in 1989 in NY.
Donor(s): Daniel Rosenblum.

Financial data (yr. ended 12/31/01): Grants paid, $415,638; assets, $5,063,806 (M); gifts received, $50,000; expenditures, $444,975; qualifying distributions, $422,285.
Limitations: Giving primarily in NY.
Officers and Directors:* Daniel Rosenblum,* Pres.; Leonard Rosenblum,* Secy.; N. Barry Ross,* Treas.
EIN: 133520602
Codes: FD

33738
Edward B. Osborn Charitable Trust
c/o U.S. Trust
114 W. 47th St.
New York, NY 10036-1532   (212) 852-1000

Trust established in 1961 in NY.
Donor(s): Edward B. Osborn.
Financial data (yr. ended 10/31/01): Grants paid, $415,600; assets, $7,303,416 (M); expenditures, $457,021; qualifying distributions, $423,092.
Limitations: Giving primarily in FL and NY.
Application information: Application form not required.
Trustee: U.S. Trust.
EIN: 136071296
Codes: FD

33739
Samalexa Charitable Foundation
c/o Starr & Co.
350 Park Ave., 9th Fl.
New York, NY 10022   (212) 759-6556
Contact: Ronald Starr, Secy.-Treas.

Established in 1997 in NY.
Donor(s): Kenneth I. Starr, Marisa Starr.
Financial data (yr. ended 12/31/00): Grants paid, $414,500; assets, $3,932 (M); gifts received, $445,000; expenditures, $416,578; qualifying distributions, $414,500.
Officers: Kenneth Starr, Pres.; Marisa Starr, V.P.; Ronald Starr, Secy.-Treas.
EIN: 133963669
Codes: FD

33740
John and Elaine Kanas Family Foundation
c/o North Fork Bancorp
275 Broadhollow Rd., 4th Fl.
Melville, NY 11747
Contact: John A. Kanas, Pres.

Established in 1998 in NY.
Donor(s): John Kanas, Elaine Kanas.
Financial data (yr. ended 12/31/01): Grants paid, $413,150; assets, $4,544,552 (M); gifts received, $150,000; expenditures, $447,885; qualifying distributions, $413,150.
Limitations: Giving primarily in NY.
Officers: John Kanas, Pres.; Elaine Kanas, V.P.
Director: Patricia Blake.
EIN: 113440709
Codes: FD

33741
The Klingenstein Third Generation Foundation
787 7th Ave., 6th Fl.
New York, NY 10019-6016   (212) 492-6179
FAX: (212) 492-7007; *URL:* http://www.ktgf.org
Contact: Sally Klingenstein, Exec. Dir.

Established in 1993 in NY.
Donor(s): Esther A. and Joseph Klingenstein Fund.
Financial data (yr. ended 09/30/01): Grants paid, $413,075; assets, $7,374,232 (M); expenditures, $538,635; qualifying distributions, $478,667.
Limitations: Giving on a national basis, with emphasis on the New York, NY, Chicago, IL, and Washington, DC, areas.

Publications: Informational brochure (including application guidelines).
Application information: E-mail proposals accepted. Application form not required.
Officers and Trustees:* Andrew Klingenstein,* Pres.; Susan Klingenstein,* V.P.; Nancy Simpkins,* Secy.; Thomas Klingenstein,* Treas.; Sally D. Klingenstein,* Exec. Dir.; Kathy Klingenstein, Amy Pollinger.
EIN: 133732439
Codes: FD

33742
Jane W. Nuhn Charitable Trust
c/o Van DeWater & Van DeWater
P.O. Box 112
Poughkeepsie, NY 12602
Contact: Noel De Cordova, Jr., Tr.

Established in 1988 in NY.
Financial data (yr. ended 12/31/01): Grants paid, $412,800; assets, $11,380,879 (M); expenditures, $424,479; qualifying distributions, $465,770.
Limitations: Applications not accepted. Giving primarily in Dutchess County, NY.
Publications: Annual report.
Application information: Unsolicited requests for funds not accepted.
Trustees: Edward V.K. Cunningham, Jr., Michael De Cordova, Noel De Cordova, Jr.
EIN: 146134057
Codes: FD

33743
The Raine & Stanley Silverstein Family Foundation, Inc.
c/o Krusch & Modell
10 Rockefeller Plz., Ste. 1212
New York, NY 10020-1966

Established in 1996 in NY.
Donor(s): Raine Silverstein, Stanley Silverstein.
Financial data (yr. ended 11/30/99): Grants paid, $412,155; assets, $1,382,298 (M); expenditures, $419,823; qualifying distributions, $419,823.
Limitations: Applications not accepted. Giving primarily in NY.
Application information: Contributes only to pre-selected organizations.
Officers: Stanley Silverstein, Pres.; Nina Miner, V.P. and Secy.; Raine Silverstein, V.P. and Treas.; Flori Silverstein, V.P.
EIN: 113353084
Codes: FD

33744
The Goldstein Family Foundation
c/o Bear Stearns Companies, Inc.
383 Madison Ave., 30th Fl.
New York, NY 10179
Contact: Jerome Goldstein, Pres.

Established in 1984 in NY.
Donor(s): Jerome Goldstein.
Financial data (yr. ended 11/30/01): Grants paid, $412,080; assets, $9,322,399 (M); expenditures, $467,865; qualifying distributions, $411,459.
Limitations: Applications not accepted. Giving primarily in New York, NY.
Application information: Contributes only to pre-selected organizations.
Officers and Directors:* Jerome Goldstein,* Pres.; Dorothy Goldstein,* V.P.; Veronica Blugerman, Secy.; Bettina Goldstein, Treas.
EIN: 133192220
Codes: FD

33745
J. Howard & Brenda LaCronge Johnson Family Fund
19 E. 72nd St.
New York, NY 10021-4145
Application address: 34 Stag Ln., Greenwich, CT 06831-3128
Contact: J. Howard Johnson, Admin.

Established in 1997 in NY.
Financial data (yr. ended 12/31/01): Grants paid, $409,841; assets, $1,113,224 (M); gifts received, $232,902; expenditures, $420,544; qualifying distributions, $409,841.
Officer: J. Howard Johnson, Admin.
Director: Brenda LaCronge Johnson.
EIN: 133952877
Codes: FD

33746
Viburnum Foundation, Inc.
111 Hicks St., Ste. 10L
Brooklyn, NY 11201
E-mail: mollyturner@earthlink.net
Contact: Molly L. Turner, Exec. Dir.

Established in 1989 in NY.
Financial data (yr. ended 09/30/01): Grants paid, $409,650; assets, $6,784,786 (M); gifts received, $49,976; expenditures, $409,603; qualifying distributions, $443,301.
Limitations: Applications not accepted. Giving on a national basis.
Publications: Occasional report.
Application information: Unsolicited requests for funds not accepted.
Officer and Director:* Molly L. Turner,* Exec. Dir.
EIN: 223019875
Codes: FD

33747
The Frank J. Antun Foundation
100 Crossways Park W., Ste. 205
Woodbury, NY 11797
Contact: Josephine Alex, Mgr.

Established in 1986 in NY.
Donor(s): Frank J. Antun.‡
Financial data (yr. ended 08/31/01): Grants paid, $409,500; assets, $13,310,513 (M); gifts received, $365,942; expenditures, $506,522; qualifying distributions, $448,473.
Limitations: Giving primarily in the greater New York, NY, area.
Application information: Application form required.
Officer: Josephine Alex, Mgr.
Trustees: I.J. La Surdo, Joseph P. Scanlon.
EIN: 112822395
Codes: FD

33748
The Naomi and Isaac Kaplan Family Foundation, Inc.
82 Magnolia Ave.
Larchmont, NY 10538-4010

Established in 1995 in NY.
Donor(s): Naomi Kaplan.
Financial data (yr. ended 07/31/01): Grants paid, $408,800; assets, $1,552,960 (M); gifts received, $809,827; expenditures, $428,366; qualifying distributions, $405,401.
Limitations: Applications not accepted. Giving primarily in NJ and NY.
Application information: Contributes only to pre-selected organizations.
Trustees: John Ferguson, Naomi Kaplan.
EIN: 133847359
Codes: FD

33749—NEW YORK

33749
The Alex J. Ettl Foundation
c/o U.S. Trust Co., Tax Dept.
114 W. 47th St.
New York, NY 10036

Established in 1989 in NY.
Donor(s): Alex J. Ettl.‡
Financial data (yr. ended 12/31/00): Grants paid, $408,500; assets, $6,431,996 (M); expenditures, $435,960; qualifying distributions, $406,110.
Limitations: Applications not accepted. Giving on a national basis, with emphasis on NY.
Application information: Contributes only to pre-selected organizations.
Trustees: Cordelia E. Clement, Judith E. Hazen, William H. Hazen.
EIN: 226503965
Codes: FD

33750
Cornpauw Foundation, Ltd.
c/o Strauss Assocs., Ltd.
307 5th Ave., 8th Fl.
New York, NY 10016-6517

Established in 1986 in NY.
Donor(s): Nelson Schaenen, Jr.
Financial data (yr. ended 03/31/01): Grants paid, $407,700; assets, $1,710,183 (M); gifts received, $274,247; expenditures, $412,270; qualifying distributions, $409,658.
Limitations: Applications not accepted. Giving primarily in NJ and NY.
Application information: Contributes only to pre-selected organizations.
Officers: Nelson Schaenen, Jr., Pres. and Treas.; Nancy Schaenen, V.P. and Secy.; Douglas K. Schaenen, V.P.
EIN: 133387939
Codes: FD

33751
David M. Leuschen Foundation
c/o BCRS Associates, LLC
100 Wall St., 11th Fl.
New York, NY 10005-3720

Established in 1988 in CT.
Donor(s): David M. Leuschen.
Financial data (yr. ended 04/30/01): Grants paid, $407,000; assets, $782,254 (M); expenditures, $408,750; qualifying distributions, $407,875.
Limitations: Applications not accepted. Giving limited to New York, NY.
Application information: Contributes only to pre-selected organizations.
Trustees: Jonathan L. Cohen, David M. Leuschen, Patricia A. Napoli.
EIN: 133501179
Codes: FD

33752
M.U.S.-J. R. Hyde, Jr. Scholarship Fund
c/o The Bank of New York, Tax Dept.
1 Wall St., 28th Fl.
New York, NY 10286
Scholarship application address: c/o D.E. Thorn, Headmaster, Memphis Univ. School, 6191 Park Ave., Memphis, TN 38119

Established in 1991 in NY.
Donor(s): Joseph R. Hyde, Jr.‡
Financial data (yr. ended 07/31/01): Grants paid, $406,676; assets, $14,611,616 (M); gifts received, $671,482; expenditures, $539,168; qualifying distributions, $417,062.
Limitations: Giving limited to Memphis, TN.
Application information: Application form required.
Trustee: The Bank of New York.

EIN: 136967610
Codes: FD

33753
The Salmon Foundation, Inc.
67A E. 77th St.
New York, NY 10021 (212) 737-1011
Contact: Ann Brownell Sloane, Admin.

Established in 1991 in NY.
Donor(s): Lois S. Duffey.
Financial data (yr. ended 12/31/01): Grants paid, $406,500; assets, $12,640,954 (M); gifts received, $1,000,000; expenditures, $537,469; qualifying distributions, $435,191.
Limitations: Giving primarily in CO, CT, MD, NH, and VT.
Publications: Application guidelines.
Application information: Application form required.
Officers and Directors:* Lois S. Duffey,* Pres.; Amanda D. Rutledge,* Secy.; Harry J. Duffey III,* Treas.; Jack Cortner, Diana Pedinielli, Peter L. Rutledge.
EIN: 133637630
Codes: FD

33754
Reis-Wein Family Charitable Foundation
c/o Sigmund Balaban & Co.
44 Wall St.
New York, NY 10005

Established in 1993 in NY.
Donor(s): David Reis, Dina Wein.
Financial data (yr. ended 12/31/01): Grants paid, $406,318; assets, $222,144 (M); gifts received, $246,350; expenditures, $406,535; qualifying distributions, $406,353.
Limitations: Applications not accepted. Giving primarily in NY.
Application information: Contributes only to pre-selected organizations.
Directors: David Reis, Dina Wein.
EIN: 521807458
Codes: FD

33755
Ross Family Fund
(Formerly Lynn & George M. Ross Foundation)
c/o BCRS Assoc., LLC
67 Wall St., 8th Fl.
New York, NY 10005

Established in 1977.
Donor(s): George M. Ross.
Financial data (yr. ended 02/28/01): Grants paid, $405,194; assets, $11,965,729 (M); gifts received, $6,985; expenditures, $466,447; qualifying distributions, $412,968.
Limitations: Applications not accepted. Giving primarily in Philadelphia, PA.
Application information: Contributes only to pre-selected organizations.
Trustees: George M. Ross, Lyn M. Ross.
EIN: 232049592
Codes: FD

33756
Francena T. Harrison Foundation Trust
c/o Deutsche Trust Co.
P.O. Box 1297, Church St. Sta.
New York, NY 10008
Application address: Stowe H. Tattersall, V.P., c/o Bankers Trust Co., 280 Park Ave., New York, NY 10017

Established in 1986 in NY.
Donor(s): Francena T. Harrison.‡

Financial data (yr. ended 04/30/01): Grants paid, $405,000; assets, $7,809,007 (M); expenditures, $535,889; qualifying distributions, $432,314.
Limitations: Giving primarily in NY.
Trustee: Deutsche Bank.
EIN: 136911262
Codes: FD

33757
New York Crohns Foundation
1200 Union Tpke.
New Hyde Park, NY 11040
Contact: Leonard Litwin, Pres.

Established in 1998 in NY.
Donor(s): Litwin Foundation.
Financial data (yr. ended 12/31/01): Grants paid, $405,000; assets, $59,563 (M); gifts received, $330,000; expenditures, $405,130; qualifying distributions, $405,000.
Limitations: Giving primarily in NY.
Application information: Application form required.
Officers and Directors:* Leonard Litwin,* Pres.; Michael Kerr,* V.P.; Carole Pittelman,* V.P.; Howard Swarzman,* Secy.-Treas.
EIN: 113437172

33758
Owen Cheatham Foundation
530 Park Ave., Ste. 16-C
New York, NY 10021 (212) 753-4733
E-mail: OCFound@aol.com
Contact: Celeste Wickliffe Cheatham, Pres.

Incorporated in 1957 in NY as successor to Owen R. Cheatham Foundation, a trust established in 1934 in GA.
Donor(s): Owen Robertson Cheatham,‡ Celeste W. Cheatham.‡
Financial data (yr. ended 12/31/01): Grants paid, $404,830; assets, $6,942,145 (M); expenditures, $766,714; qualifying distributions, $632,181.
Limitations: Applications not accepted. Giving on a national basis.
Officers and Directors:* Celeste Wickliffe Cheatham,* Pres.; Edward A. Reilly,* V.P. and Treas.; MacDonald Budd,* Secy.
EIN: 136097798
Codes: FD

33759
Joseph and Martha Melohn Tzedaka Fund
c/o Melohn
1995 Broadway, 14th Fl.
New York, NY 10023 (212) 787-2500
Contact: Leon Melohn, Tr.

Established in 1986 in NY.
Donor(s): Leon Melohn, Martha Melohn.
Financial data (yr. ended 11/30/01): Grants paid, $404,746; assets, $416,713 (M); gifts received, $375,000; expenditures, $430,986; qualifying distributions, $406,088.
Limitations: Giving primarily in the metropolitan New York, NY, area.
Trustee: Leon Melohn.
EIN: 133395219
Codes: FD

33760
The Nagle Family Foundation
19 Garden Ave.
Bronxville, NY 10708-3007
Contact: Arthur J. Nagle, Chair.

Established in 1987 in NY.
Donor(s): Arthur J. Nagle.
Financial data (yr. ended 12/31/00): Grants paid, $404,256; assets, $713,037 (M); gifts received,

$348,413; expenditures, $406,729; qualifying distributions, $402,205.
Limitations: Giving primarily in NY.
Officer: Arthur J. Nagle, Chair.
Director: Paige L. Nagle.
EIN: 133453422
Codes: FD

33761
The William Marx Foundation
c/o H.J. Behrman & Co., LLP
215 Lexington Ave., Ste. 202
New York, NY 10016-6023

Donor(s): Helen Schulman Marx, William Marx.
Financial data (yr. ended 10/31/01): Grants paid, $403,850; assets, $1,255,470 (M); expenditures, $412,242; qualifying distributions, $408,144.
Limitations: Applications not accepted. Giving primarily in NY.
Application information: Contributes only to pre-selected organizations.
Officers: Cynthia Marks, Pres.; Laurie Lederman, V.P.
EIN: 116020448
Codes: FD

33762
The Carwill Foundation
c/o Goldman Sachs & Co.
85 Broad St., Tax Dept.
New York, NY 10004
Contact: William C. Stutt, or Carolyn L. Stutt, Trustees

Established in 1985 in NY.
Donor(s): William C. Stutt.
Financial data (yr. ended 08/31/01): Grants paid, $402,790; assets, $1,438,628 (M); expenditures, $409,053; qualifying distributions, $403,380.
Limitations: Applications not accepted. Giving primarily in FL.
Application information: Contributes only to pre-selected organizations.
Trustees: Carolyn Stutt, David S. Stutt, William C. Stutt.
EIN: 133318130
Codes: FD

33763
Marjorie D. Kienzle Foundation, Inc.
c/o FUST, Charles Chambers, LLP
5786 Widewaters Pkwy.
Syracuse, NY 13214-0016 (315) 446-3600
Contact: Joseph L. Charles, Treas.

Established in 1978 in NY.
Donor(s): Lester C. Kienzle,‡ Marjorie D. Kienzle,‡ Terrence M. Foran.
Financial data (yr. ended 06/30/01): Grants paid, $402,445; assets, $1,047,511 (M); expenditures, $418,938; qualifying distributions, $401,725.
Limitations: Giving primarily in Onondaga County, NY.
Officers: Terrence M. Foran, Pres.; William F. Wein, V.P.; H.A. Kallusch, Jr., Secy.; Joseph L. Charles, Treas.
EIN: 222238115
Codes: FD

33764
The B & L Foundation
c/o Bernard Palitz
221 E. 70th St., Box 2520
New York, NY 10021

Established about 1963.
Donor(s): Bernard Palitz.
Financial data (yr. ended 12/31/01): Grants paid, $402,352; assets, $5,996,008 (M); expenditures, $477,386; qualifying distributions, $381,617.

Limitations: Giving primarily in MA and NY.
Trustee: Bernard Palitz.
EIN: 136064168
Codes: FD

33765
The Louis R. Cappelli Foundation, Inc.
115 Stevens Ave.
Valhalla, NY 10595 (914) 769-6500
Contact: Marylou Oliva, Secy.

Established in 1999 in NY.
Donor(s): Louis R. Cappelli.
Financial data (yr. ended 12/31/01): Grants paid, $402,075; assets, $2,141 (L); gifts received, $412,000; expenditures, $412,956; qualifying distributions, $402,075.
Limitations: Giving primarily in NY.
Officers and Directors:* Louis R. Cappelli,* Pres.; Marylou Oliva,* Secy.; Jeffrey Klein, Treas.; Celia Clark, Richard Ferrucci, Margaret Schneider.
EIN: 134048754
Codes: FD

33766
Bruce L. Crary Foundation, Inc.
c/o Hand House, River St.
P.O. Box 396
Elizabethtown, NY 12932 (518) 873-6496
Contact: Hanna Kissam, Exec. Dir.

Incorporated in 1973 in NY.
Donor(s): Crary Public Trust, Bruce L. Crary.‡
Financial data (yr. ended 06/30/02): Grants paid, $402,026; assets, $8,686,582 (M); gifts received, $5,270; expenditures, $553,246; qualifying distributions, $499,972; giving activities include $17,021 for programs.
Limitations: Giving limited to Clinton, Essex, Franklin, Hamilton, and Warren counties, NY, for undergraduate scholarships, and to Essex County, NY, for educational and social service agencies.
Application information: Scholarship application form is available through high school guidance offices in Clinton, Essex, Franklin, Hamilton, and Warren counties, NY. Application form required.
Officers and Governors:* Euphemia V. Hall,* Pres.; Arthur V. Savage,* V.P.; Meredith Prime,* Treas.; Janet Decker, Steven Engelhart, Sue Reaser, Gail Rogers-Rice.
EIN: 237366844
Codes: FD, GTI

33767
The Paul and Harriet Weissman Family Foundation, Inc.
(Formerly The Paul M. Weissman Family Foundation)
2 Oxford Rd.
White Plains, NY 10605

Established in 1969 in NY.
Donor(s): Paul M. Weissman.
Financial data (yr. ended 02/28/02): Grants paid, $401,848; assets, $8,531,959 (M); gifts received, $118,250; expenditures, $432,411; qualifying distributions, $401,765.
Limitations: Applications not accepted. Giving primarily in NY.
Application information: Contributes only to pre-selected organizations.
Officers and Directors:* Paul M. Weissman,* Pres. and Treas.; Harriet L. Weissman,* V.P. and Secy.; Michael A. Weissman,* V.P.; Peter A. Weissman,* V.P.; Stephanie T. Weissman,* V.P.
EIN: 237049744
Codes: FD

33768
Marcy and Leona Chanin Foundation, Inc.
50 E. 77th St., Ste. 11B
New York, NY 10021

Established in 1972.
Financial data (yr. ended 12/31/01): Grants paid, $401,426; assets, $6,434,208 (M); expenditures, $425,766; qualifying distributions, $411,626.
Limitations: Applications not accepted. Giving primarily in New York, NY.
Application information: Contributes only to pre-selected organizations.
Officer: Leona Chanin, Pres.
EIN: 237156719
Codes: FD

33769
U.S. Trust Corporation Foundation
(Formerly United States Trust Company of New York Foundation)
c/o United States Trust Co. of New York
114 W. 47th St.
New York, NY 10036 (212) 852-1400
FAX: (212) 852-1314; E-mail: foundation@ustrust.com; URL: http://www.ustrust.com/ustrust/html/aboutUs/community
Contact: Carol A. Strickland, Contrib. Comm. Chair., U.S. Trust Corporate Foundation

Trust established in 1955 in NY.
Donor(s): United States Trust Co. of New York.
Financial data (yr. ended 12/31/01): Grants paid, $401,345; assets, $1 (M); expenditures, $401,562; qualifying distributions, $401,450.
Limitations: Giving in the corporation's primary market areas, including Costa Mesa, Larkspur, Los Angeles, Palo Alto, and San Francisco, CA; Essex, Greenwich, Stamford, and West Hartford, CT; Wilmington, DE; Boca Raton, Naples, Palm Beach, and Vero Beach, FL; the Twin Cities, MN; Jersey City, Morristown, and Princeton, NJ; Garden City and New York, NY; Charlotte, Greensboro, and Raleigh, NC; Portland, OR; Wayne, PA; Dallas and Houston, TX; McLean, VA; Tacoma, WA; and Washington, DC.
Publications: Application guidelines, grants list.
Application information: Cultural and arts proposals reviewed in the spring; civic and community proposals reviewed in the fall; accepts NYRAG Common Application Form. Application form not required.
Corporate Contributions Committee: Carol A. Strickland, Chair.
EIN: 136072081
Codes: CS, FD, CD

33770
The Edlow Family Fund, Inc.
c/o Bear Stearns & Co., Inc.
383 Madison Ave., 6th Fl.
New York, NY 10179 (212) 272-4394
FAX: (212) 272-8239; E-mail: kedlow@bear.com
Contact: Kenneth L. Edlow, V.P. and Secy.

Established in 1983 in NY.
Donor(s): Kenneth Lewis Edlow.
Financial data (yr. ended 11/30/01): Grants paid, $401,000; assets, $8,803,860 (M); expenditures, $406,737; qualifying distributions, $403,200.
Limitations: Applications not accepted. Giving primarily in New York, NY.
Application information: Contributes only to pre-selected organizations.
Officers and Directors:* Mary Edlow,* Pres. and Treas.; Kenneth Lewis Edlow,* V.P. and Secy.; Brian Lewis Edlow, Donald William Edlow, Elizabeth Fielding Edlow.
EIN: 133190911

33770—NEW YORK

Codes: FD

33771
American Society of the French Legion of Honor, Inc.
22 E. 60th St.
New York, NY 10021 (212) 751-8537
Contact: Odile Duff

Established in 1949.
Donor(s): Guy Wildenstein.
Financial data (yr. ended 08/31/00): Grants paid, $400,000; assets, $8,424,797 (M); gifts received, $324,313; expenditures, $785,676; qualifying distributions, $556,502; giving activities include $187,305 for programs.
Limitations: Giving primarily in NY.
Application information: Application form not required.
Officers and Directors:* Guy N. Wildenstein,* Pres.; John H.F. Haskell, Jr.,* V.P. and Secy.; Ezra K. Zilkha,* V.P. and Treas.; Hon. Walter J.P. Curley,* V.P.; Edward Finch, Jr., V.P.; Nicole Hirsh, V.P.; Hon. Joseph Verner Reed,* V.P.; John R. Young,* V.P.; and 17 additional directors.
EIN: 130434237
Codes: FD

33772
Colombe Foundation
c/o Siegel, Sacks
630 3rd Ave.
New York, NY 10017

Established in 1996 in DE.
Donor(s): Edith W. Allen.
Financial data (yr. ended 06/30/01): Grants paid, $400,000; assets, $9,448,218 (M); gifts received, $440,853; expenditures, $432,202; qualifying distributions, $400,000.
Limitations: Applications not accepted.
Application information: Contributes only to pre-selected organizations.
Officers: Edith W. Allen, Pres.; Frederick Allen, Secy.
EIN: 137103356
Codes: FD

33773
The Cricket Island Foundation
c/o Jeffrey F. Welles
780 3rd Ave., Ste. 3400
New York, NY 10017

Established in 2000 in NY.
Donor(s): David K. Welles, Georgia E. Welles, Jeffrey F. Welles, David K. Welles, Jr., Peter C. Welles, Christopher S. Welles, Virginia W. Jordan.
Financial data (yr. ended 12/31/01): Grants paid, $400,000; assets, $36,278,510 (M); expenditures, $1,055,051; qualifying distributions, $400,000.
Officers and Directors:* Jeffrey F. Welles,* Pres.; Georgia E. Welles,* V.P.; Peter C. Welles,* Secy.; Christopher S. Welles,* Treas.; Virginia W. Jordan, David K. Welles, David K. Welles, Jr.
EIN: 341925915

33774
Herman Forbes Charitable Trust
c/o JPMorgan Chase Bank
1211 6th Ave., 34th Fl.
New York, NY 10036
Contact: John S. Jordan, V.P., JPMorgan Chase Bank

Incorporated in 1982 in NY.
Donor(s): Herman Forbes.‡
Financial data (yr. ended 03/31/01): Grants paid, $400,000; assets, $8,155,049 (M); expenditures, $523,297; qualifying distributions, $413,145.
Limitations: Giving on a national basis.

Application information: Application form not required.
Trustees: William H. Fleece, Jacob Silverman, JPMorgan Chase Bank.
EIN: 136814404
Codes: FD

33775
Karches Foundation
84 Feeks Ln.
Locust Valley, NY 11560-2022

Established in 1997 in DE.
Donor(s): Peter Karches, Susan Karches.
Financial data (yr. ended 12/31/01): Grants paid, $400,000; assets, $6,480,131 (M); gifts received, $862,121; expenditures, $702,026; qualifying distributions, $400,000.
Limitations: Applications not accepted. Giving primarily in NY.
Application information: Contributes only to pre-selected organizations.
Trustees: Charles Harris, Peter Karches, Susan Karches.
EIN: 137106278
Codes: FD

33776
Winley Foundation
2303 Salt Point Tpke.
Clinton Corners, NY 12514 (845) 266-3065
Contact: Anna M. Barone, Treas.

Financial data (yr. ended 12/31/01): Grants paid, $400,000; assets, $16,764,657 (M); gifts received, $335; expenditures, $489,924; qualifying distributions, $400,000.
Limitations: Giving primarily in Washington, DC and New York, NY.
Officers: Christine Stevens, Pres.; Marion Probst, V.P.; Edward J. Walsh, Jr., Secy.; Anna M. Barone, Treas.
Directors: Cathy Liss, Tatiana Nagro, Heidi Prescott.
EIN: 521230146
Codes: FD

33777
The Richard W. Rupp Foundation
1806 Liberty Bldg.
Buffalo, NY 14202 (716) 876-2129
Contact: William R. Rupp, Treas.

Established in 1998 in NY.
Donor(s): Richard W. Rupp.
Financial data (yr. ended 12/31/01): Grants paid, $399,450; assets, $11,063,941 (M); gifts received, $416,125; expenditures, $556,000; qualifying distributions, $415,775.
Officers: Frances O. Rupp, Pres.; Christina D. Rupp, V.P.; Susan S. Rupp, Secy.; William R. Rupp, Treas.
EIN: 161551594
Codes: FD

33778
Milton and Sally Avery Arts Foundation
c/o Radin, Glass & Co., LLP
360 Lexington Ave.
New York, NY 10017
Application address: 300 Central Park W., Apt. 16J, New York, NY 10024; FAX: (212) 595-2840
Contact: March Avery Cavanaugh, Pres.

Established in 1983.
Donor(s): Sally M. Avery.
Financial data (yr. ended 12/31/01): Grants paid, $399,250; assets, $4,822,398 (M); expenditures, $438,658; qualifying distributions, $398,554.
Limitations: Giving primarily in NY.

Application information: Application form not required.
Officers: March A. Cavanaugh, Pres.; Sean A. Cavanaugh, V.P.; Harvey S. Miller, Secy.; Philip G. Cavanaugh, Treas.
EIN: 133093638
Codes: FD

33779
The Cove Point Foundation
P.O. Box 1995
New York, NY 10021
Contact: William C. Morris, Tr.

Established in 1998 in DE.
Donor(s): The Morris Family Foundation.
Financial data (yr. ended 12/31/01): Grants paid, $398,200; assets, $7,521,720 (M); expenditures, $449,636; qualifying distributions, $388,614.
Application information: Application form required.
Trustees: David Lockhart Morris, Edward Follett Morris, Kenneth Van Avery Morris, Susan F. Morris, William C. Morris.
EIN: 311637257
Codes: FD

33780
Fred and Harriett Taylor Foundation
c/o JPMorgan Chase Bank
P.O. Box 31412
Rochester, NY 14603 (716) 258-5156
Contact: Dave Devries

Trust established in 1976 in NY.
Donor(s): Fred C. Taylor.‡
Financial data (yr. ended 12/31/01): Grants paid, $397,766; assets, $10,347,717 (M); expenditures, $441,874; qualifying distributions, $402,123.
Limitations: Giving limited to Steuben County, NY.
Trustee: JPMorgan Chase Bank.
EIN: 166205365
Codes: FD

33781
Tribune New York Foundation
220 E. 42nd St., 10th Fl.
New York, NY 10017 (212) 210-2604

Incorporated in 1958 in NY.
Donor(s): Daily News, L.P., WPIX, Inc.
Financial data (yr. ended 12/31/00): Grants paid, $397,096; assets, $6,743,877 (M); expenditures, $397,346; qualifying distributions, $371,315.
Limitations: Giving limited to the tri-state CT, NJ, and NY area, with emphasis on the five boroughs of New York.
Publications: Application guidelines.
Application information: Application form required.
Officers and Directors:* Michael Eigner,* Pres.; Betty Ellen Berlamino,* V.P.; Kathleen Shepherd,* Secy.; Patrick J. Austin,* Treas.; Steve Mulderrig, Kevin Murphy.
EIN: 136161525
Codes: FD

33782
The Rubin Family Foundation, Inc.
1466 59th St.
Brooklyn, NY 11219-5016

Established in 1991.
Donor(s): Liebel Rubin.
Financial data (yr. ended 12/31/99): Grants paid, $396,793; assets, $16,990,152 (M); gifts received, $2,967,500; expenditures, $556,658; qualifying distributions, $397,543.
Limitations: Applications not accepted. Giving primarily in Brooklyn, NY.

Application information: Contributes only to pre-selected organizations.
Officers: Liebel Rubin, Pres.; Dorothy Rubin, V.P.; Eugene Rubin, Secy.; Dina Rubin, Treas.
EIN: 113047773
Codes: FD

33783
Ahava Foundation
c/o Abraham Trusts
200 W. 57th St., Ste. 1005
New York, NY 10019

Established in 1998 in NY.
Donor(s): Tamar Abraham.
Financial data (yr. ended 06/30/01): Grants paid, $396,787; assets, $100,706 (M); gifts received, $376,943; expenditures, $401,254; qualifying distributions, $396,837.
Limitations: Applications not accepted. Giving primarily in NY.
Application information: Contributes only to pre-selected organizations.
Director: Tamar Abraham.
EIN: 133990332
Codes: FD

33784
Maleh-Shalom Foundation, Inc.
c/o Children's Apparel Network, Ltd.
112 W. 34th St.
New York, NY 10120
Contact: Murray Maleh, Mgr.

Established in 1967 in NY.
Donor(s): Cradle Togs, Inc.
Financial data (yr. ended 12/31/01): Grants paid, $396,680; assets, $798,173 (M); gifts received, $790,000; expenditures, $397,277; qualifying distributions, $396,680.
Limitations: Giving primarily in NJ and NY.
Officer: Murray Maleh, Mgr.
EIN: 136265282
Codes: FD

33785
Zenkel Foundation
15 W. 53rd St.
New York, NY 10019-5410
Contact: Lois Zenkel, Pres.

Established in 1987 in NY.
Financial data (yr. ended 12/31/01): Grants paid, $396,184; assets, $3,859,225 (M); expenditures, $478,339; qualifying distributions, $429,379.
Limitations: Applications not accepted.
Application information: Contributes only to pre-selected organizations.
Officers and Directors:* Lois S. Zenkel,* Pres.; Daniel R. Zenkel,* Secy.; Gary B. Zenkel,* Treas.; Lisa Z. Sheldon, Bruce L. Zenkel.
EIN: 133380631
Codes: FD

33786
The Sidney and Mildred Edelstein Foundation
(Formerly The Sidney M. Edelstein Foundation)
c/o American Express Tax & Business Svcs. of NY, Inc.
1185 Ave. of the Americas
New York, NY 10036

Established in 1986 in NY.
Donor(s): Sidney M. Edelstein,‡ Mildred Edelstein.
Financial data (yr. ended 12/31/99): Grants paid, $395,596; assets, $2,075,985 (M); gifts received, $5,209,573; expenditures, $398,957; qualifying distributions, $395,596.
Limitations: Applications not accepted. Giving primarily in New York, NY.

Application information: Contributes only to pre-selected organizations.
Directors: Mildred Edelstein, Richard Finkelstein, Leo Goldberg, Jeffrey Grossman, Roy Jacobs, Harvey Reich.
EIN: 133347784
Codes: FD

33787
The H. Frederick Krimendahl II Foundation
c/o BCRS Assocs., LLC
67 Wall St., 8th Fl.
New York, NY 10005

Established in 1968 in NY.
Donor(s): H. Frederick Krimendahl II.
Financial data (yr. ended 05/31/01): Grants paid, $395,233; assets, $9,645,966 (M); expenditures, $412,284; qualifying distributions, $396,693.
Limitations: Applications not accepted. Giving primarily in New York, NY.
Application information: Contributes only to pre-selected organizations.
Trustees: Elizabeth K. Krimendahl, H. Frederick Krimendahl II, Nancy C. Krimendahl, James S. Marcus, Emilia A. Saint-Amand.
EIN: 237000391
Codes: FD

33788
The O'Sullivan Children Foundation, Inc.
355 Post Ave.
Westbury, NY 11590 (516) 334-3209
FAX: (516) 334-3949

Established in 1981 in NY.
Donor(s): Kevin P. O'Sullivan, Carole O'Sullivan.
Financial data (yr. ended 09/30/01): Grants paid, $395,053; assets, $4,862,378 (M); gifts received, $64,043; expenditures, $670,248; qualifying distributions, $525,804.
Limitations: Applications not accepted. Giving primarily in the greater metropolitan New York, NY, area, with some emphasis on Long Island.
Application information: Contributes only to pre-selected organizations.
Officers and Directors:* Kevin P. O'Sullivan,* Pres.; Erin A. O'Sullivan, V.P.; Carole O'Sullivan,* V.P. and Treas.; Neil M. Delman,* Secy.
EIN: 133126389
Codes: FD

33789
John P. & Anne Welsh McNulty Foundation
c/o BCRS Assoc., LLC
100 Wall St., 11th Fl.
New York, NY 10005

Established in 1985 in FL.
Donor(s): John P. McNulty, Anne Welsh McNulty.
Financial data (yr. ended 11/30/01): Grants paid, $394,992; assets, $15,436,632 (M); gifts received, $7,398,820; expenditures, $663,173; qualifying distributions, $396,242.
Limitations: Applications not accepted. Giving primarily in NY and PA.
Application information: Contributes only to pre-selected organizations.
Trustees: Anne Welsh McNulty, John P. McNulty.
EIN: 521445003
Codes: FD

33790
Lee and Cynthia Vance Foundation
c/o BCRS Associates, LLC
100 Wall St., 11th Fl.
New York, NY 10005

Established in 1993 in NY.
Donor(s): Lee G. Vance.

Financial data (yr. ended 06/30/01): Grants paid, $393,560; assets, $12,072,377 (M); gifts received, $6,325,313; expenditures, $611,700; qualifying distributions, $393,837.
Limitations: Applications not accepted. Giving primarily in New York, NY.
Application information: Contributes only to pre-selected organizations.
Trustees: Cynthia King Vance, Lee G. Vance.
EIN: 133789060
Codes: FD

33791
The Regina Frankenberg Foundation
(Formerly The Regina Bauer Frankenberg Foundation)
c/o JPMorgan Chase Bank
1211 Ave. of the Americas, 38th Fl.
New York, NY 10036 (212) 789-5702
E-mail: neal_monica@JPMorgan.com
Contact: Monica Neal, V.P., JPMorgan Chase Bank

Established in 1994 in NY.
Donor(s): Regina Bauer Frankenberg.‡
Financial data (yr. ended 12/31/01): Grants paid, $393,500; assets, $23,807,529 (M); expenditures, $572,912; qualifying distributions, $408,873.
Limitations: Giving primarily in NY, with respect to companion animals; broader focus with respect to wildlife.
Application information: Application form not required.
Trustee: JPMorgan Chase Bank.
EIN: 133741659
Codes: FD

33792
Genetic Disease Foundation
(Formerly Associated Charitable Foundation, Inc.)
c/o Edward Isaacs & Co., LLP
380 Madison Ave., 15th Fl.
New York, NY 10017

Financial data (yr. ended 10/31/00): Grants paid, $393,061; assets, $287,905 (M); gifts received, $741,496; expenditures, $577,470; qualifying distributions, $577,314; giving activities include $32,950 for programs.
Limitations: Applications not accepted.
Application information: Contributes only to pre-selected organizations.
Officers: Stanley Michelman, Chair.; Tom Buckley, Pres.; Dennis Smiler, V.P.; Marion Yanovsky, Secy.; Jed Isaacs, Treas.
EIN: 136151644
Codes: TN

33793
Deo B. Colburn Education Foundation
P.O. Box 824
Lake Placid, NY 12946-0824
Contact: Margaret E. Doran, Treas.

Established in 1987 in NY.
Donor(s): Deo B. Colburn.
Financial data (yr. ended 06/30/01): Grants paid, $392,500; assets, $6,544,748 (M); gifts received, $44,131; expenditures, $457,455; qualifying distributions, $420,210.
Limitations: Giving limited to the Adirondack region of northern NY.
Application information: Application forms available after Feb. 1. Application form required.
Officers and Directors:* Craig Randall,* Pres.; Robert D. Clark,* Secy.; Margaret E. Doran,* Treas.
EIN: 222777121
Codes: FD, GTI

33794
The Petersmeyer Family Foundation, Inc.
332 Bleeker St., No. K84
New York, NY 10014
E-mail: petermeyerfnd@earthlink.net
Contact: Susan Petersmeyer, Tr.

Established in 1990 in FL.
Donor(s): C. Wrede Petersmeyer.‡
Financial data (yr. ended 12/31/01): Grants paid, $392,500; assets, $6,546,146 (M); expenditures, $452,691; qualifying distributions, $403,277.
Limitations: Applications not accepted.
Application information: Contributes only to pre-selected organizations.
Officers and Trustees:* Frances G. Petersmeyer,* Pres.; Susan C. Petersmeyer,* Secy.; Nancy Q. Petersmeyer,* Treas.; C. Gregg Petersmeyer.
EIN: 650194584
Codes: FD

33795
Mollie Parnis Livingston Foundation, Inc.
135 Madison Ave.
New York, NY 10016
Journalism award application address: c/o C.R. Eisendrath, Exec. Dir., 2098 Frieze Blvd., Univ. of Michigan, Ann Arbor, MI 48109, tel.: (734) 764-0420

Established in 1967 in NY.
Donor(s): Mollie Parnis Livingston,‡ Robert L. Livingston.‡
Financial data (yr. ended 12/31/01): Grants paid, $392,339; assets, $4,082,192 (M); expenditures, $435,014; qualifying distributions, $400,185.
Limitations: Giving primarily in New York, NY for organizations.
Application information: Application form required for journalism awards.
Officers and Directors:* Neal S. Hochman,* Pres. and Treas.; Eugene V. Kokot, Secy.; Cynthia Hochman, David P. Hochman, Sara B. Hochman, Mike Wallace.
EIN: 136265280
Codes: FD, GTI

33796
Martha Washington Straus & Harry H. Straus Foundation, Inc.
8 Sky Meadow Farm
Lincoln Ave.
Port Chester, NY 10573
Contact: Roger J. King, Treas.

Incorporated in 1949 in NC.
Donor(s): Harry H. Straus, Sr.,‡ Louise Straus King.
Financial data (yr. ended 12/31/01): Grants paid, $392,000; assets, $7,752,577 (M); expenditures, $403,230; qualifying distributions, $392,000.
Limitations: Applications not accepted. Giving primarily in the metropolitan Washington, DC, area, including MD, and New York, NY.
Application information: Contributes only to pre-selected organizations.
Officers: Louise Straus King, Pres.; David Straus, V.P.; Roger J. King, Treas. and Mgr.
EIN: 560645526
Codes: FD

33797
Mark Family Foundation
c/o American Express TBS of NY, Inc.
1185 Ave. of the Americas
New York, NY 10036-2601

Established in 1994 in NY.
Donor(s): Morris Mark, Susan Mark.
Financial data (yr. ended 11/30/01): Grants paid, $391,914; assets, $3,187,962 (M); expenditures, $397,031; qualifying distributions, $394,331.
Limitations: Applications not accepted.
Application information: Contributes only to pre-selected organizations.
Trustees: Morris Mark, Susan Mark.
EIN: 137052586
Codes: FD

33798
Jacob Bleibtreu Foundation, Inc.
c/o Grant Thornton, LLP
60 Broad St.
New York, NY 10004-2501

Incorporated in 1945 in NY.
Donor(s): Helen R. Bleibtreu,‡ Jacob Bleibtreu.‡
Financial data (yr. ended 09/30/01): Grants paid, $391,500; assets, $958,649 (M); expenditures, $400,952; qualifying distributions, $394,945.
Limitations: Applications not accepted. Giving primarily in New York, NY; some funding nationally.
Application information: Contributes only to pre-selected organizations.
Officers: Alexander Abraham, Pres. and Treas.; George H. Heyman, Jr., V.P. and Secy.
Directors: Nancy Abraham, William H. Heyman.
EIN: 136065942
Codes: FD

33799
Utopia Fund
c/o U.S. Trust of NY
114 W. 47th St.
New York, NY 10036

Established in 1952 in NY.
Financial data (yr. ended 12/31/00): Grants paid, $391,300; assets, $4,233,772 (M); expenditures, $418,161; qualifying distributions, $390,620.
Limitations: Applications not accepted. Giving primarily in CT and NY.
Application information: Contributes only to pre-selected organizations.
Trustee: Francis F. Randolph, Jr.
EIN: 131963929
Codes: FD

33800
The Riversville Foundation
1221 Ave. of the Americas
New York, NY 10020
Application address: 390 Riversville Rd., Greenwich, CT 06831, tel.: (212) 762-7344
Contact: Barton M. Biggs, Tr.

Established in 2000 in NY.
Donor(s): Barton M. Biggs.
Financial data (yr. ended 12/31/01): Grants paid, $391,285; assets, $13,326,002 (M); gifts received, $7,021,250; expenditures, $431,186; qualifying distributions, $391,285.
Trustee: Barton M. Biggs.
EIN: 066504128

33801
Marrus Family Foundation, Inc.
(Formerly David & Judith Marrus Foundation, Inc.)
c/o Levine & Seltzer
150 E. 52nd St., 19th Fl.
New York, NY 10022-6017

Established in 1994 in NY.
Donor(s): David Marrus, Judith Marrus.
Financial data (yr. ended 12/31/01): Grants paid, $390,397; assets, $5,054,358 (M); gifts received, $68,970; expenditures, $401,239; qualifying distributions, $398,952.
Limitations: Applications not accepted. Giving primarily in MA, NY, and RI.
Application information: Contributes only to pre-selected organizations.
Officers: David Marrus, Pres.; Judith Marrus, Secy.
EIN: 136279584
Codes: FD

33802
Friedman Family Foundation
c/o David M. Brickman
6 E. 43rd St., 19th Fl.
New York, NY 10017

Donor(s): Gerald L. Friedman.
Financial data (yr. ended 12/31/01): Grants paid, $390,250; assets, $2,535,768 (M); expenditures, $409,229; qualifying distributions, $390,154.
Limitations: Applications not accepted. Giving on a national basis.
Application information: Contributes only to pre-selected organizations.
Trustees: Gerald L. Friedman, Sheree A. Friedman.
EIN: 061474685
Codes: FD

33803
Ruth Turner Fund, Inc.
c/o Davidson, Dawson & Clark
330 Madison Ave.
New York, NY 10017

Established in 1973.
Donor(s): Ruth Turner.‡
Financial data (yr. ended 12/31/01): Grants paid, $390,000; assets, $6,451,497 (M); expenditures, $444,210; qualifying distributions, $405,086.
Limitations: Applications not accepted. Giving primarily in New York, NY.
Application information: Contributes only to pre-selected organizations.
Officer: Gloria S. Neuwirth, Pres.
EIN: 237240889
Codes: FD

33804
The Fred & Sharon Stein Foundation, Inc.
c/o Charles A. Barragato & Co., LLP
950 3rd Ave., 17th Fl.
New York, NY 10022
Contact: Fred Stein, Dir.

Established in 1985 in NY.
Donor(s): Fred Stein, Susan Haugh Stein.
Financial data (yr. ended 11/30/00): Grants paid, $388,633; assets, $443,469 (M); expenditures, $395,656; qualifying distributions, $387,517.
Limitations: Giving primarily in NY.
Directors: James Kaufman, Fred Stein, Sharon Haugh Stein.
EIN: 133389107
Codes: FD

33805
The Margot Marsh Biodiversity Foundation
c/o Trainer Wortham & Co.
845 3rd Ave.
New York, NY 10022

Established in 1996 in CA.
Financial data (yr. ended 12/31/01): Grants paid, $388,388; assets, $11,311,951 (M); expenditures, $5,745,760; qualifying distributions, $4,865,309.
Limitations: Applications not accepted. Giving on a national and international basis.
Application information: Contributes only to pre-selected organizations.
Officers: Russell Mittermeier, Pres.; Karl Zobell, V.P. and Secy.; H. Williamson Ghriskey, Jr., V.P. and C.F.O.
Director: William Konstant.
EIN: 330683174
Codes: FD

33806
Ruth and Jerome A. Siegel Foundation
1175 Old White Plains Rd.
Mamaroneck, NY 10543-1018

Incorporated in 1951 in NY.
Donor(s): Titan Industrial Corp., Jerome Siegel, Ruth Siegel.
Financial data (yr. ended 11/30/01): Grants paid, $388,229; assets, $1,451,360 (M); expenditures, $392,545; qualifying distributions, $388,417.
Limitations: Applications not accepted. Giving primarily in NY.
Application information: Contributes only to pre-selected organizations.
Officer: Jerome A. Siegel, Pres. and Treas.
EIN: 136066216
Codes: CS, FD, CD

33807
ILC Industries Foundation, Inc.
105 Wilbur Pl.
Bohemia, NY 11716

Established in 1995 in NY.
Donor(s): ILC Industries, Inc.
Financial data (yr. ended 12/31/00): Grants paid, $388,169; assets, $3,525,243 (M); gifts received, $1,114,905; expenditures, $403,121; qualifying distributions, $388,169.
Limitations: Applications not accepted. Giving primarily in NY.
Application information: Contributes only to pre-selected organizations.
Officers: Clifford Lane, Pres.; Stewart Lane, V.P.; Arlene Fisher, Secy.
EIN: 113219127
Codes: CS, FD, CD

33808
The Big Wood Foundation
c/o Yohalem Gillman & Co.
477 Madison Ave.
New York, NY 10022
Contact: Elizabeth Morin, Acct.

Established in 1987 in DE.
Donor(s): Marjorie Stern, Michael Stern.
Financial data (yr. ended 12/31/01): Grants paid, $388,161; assets, $7,494,506 (M); expenditures, $486,600; qualifying distributions, $406,542.
Limitations: Applications not accepted. Giving primarily in NY.
Application information: Contributes only to pre-selected organizations.
Officers: Michael Stern, Pres. and Treas.; Marjorie Stern, Secy.
Directors: Mark Stern, Ricki Stern.
EIN: 133440362
Codes: FD

33809
Sy Friedman Memorial Foundation
580 5th Ave., Ste. 617
New York, NY 10036-4701

Established in 2000 in NY.
Financial data (yr. ended 08/31/01): Grants paid, $387,700; assets, $1,301 (M); gifts received, $388,500; expenditures, $387,931; qualifying distributions, $387,693.
Officers: Morris Friedman, Pres.; Isaac Friedman, V.P.; Perl Friedman, Secy.-Treas.
EIN: 134139005
Codes: FD

33810
The Sokoloff Foundation, Inc.
200 E. 78th St.
New York, NY 10021-2004 (212) 744-5377
Contact: Stephen Sokoloff, Mgr.

Established in 1960.
Donor(s): Gertrude Sokoloff,‡ Stephen Sokoloff.
Financial data (yr. ended 12/31/01): Grants paid, $387,028; assets, $4,780,292 (M); gifts received, $36,160; expenditures, $397,696; qualifying distributions, $394,856.
Limitations: Giving primarily in New York, NY.
Application information: Application form not required.
Officer and Trustee:* Stephen Sokoloff,* Mgr.
EIN: 136155196
Codes: FD

33811
The Iris & Saul Katz Foundation, Inc.
111 Great Neck Rd., Ste. 408
Great Neck, NY 11021
Contact: Saul B. Katz, Pres.

Established in 1982 in DE and NY.
Donor(s): Saul B. Katz.
Financial data (yr. ended 12/31/00): Grants paid, $386,550; assets, $4,575,473 (M); gifts received, $694,550; expenditures, $469,874; qualifying distributions, $386,550.
Limitations: Giving primarily in NY, with some emphasis on Long Island.
Application information: Application form not required.
Officer and Directors:* Saul B. Katz,* Pres.; David M. Katz, Iris J. Katz.
EIN: 112626656
Codes: FD

33812
The Fanny V. W. Boos Trust
c/o Jeffery C. Richards
75 Washington St.
Poughkeepsie, NY 12601

Established in 1989 in NY.
Donor(s): Fanny V.W. Boos.‡
Financial data (yr. ended 12/31/99): Grants paid, $386,500; assets, $29,507 (M); expenditures, $411,802; qualifying distributions, $397,125.
Limitations: Applications not accepted. Giving limited to the Mid-Hudson Valley, NY, area, including Fishkill and Poughkeepsie.
Application information: Contributes only to pre-selected organizations.
Trustee: Jeffery C. Richards.
EIN: 226477634
Codes: FD

33813
The Kimmelman Family Foundation
c/o Goldman Sachs & Co.
85 Broad St., Tax Dept.
New York, NY 10004

Established in 1997 in NJ.
Donor(s): Douglas W. Kimmelman.
Financial data (yr. ended 08/31/01): Grants paid, $386,150; assets, $2,219,307 (M); gifts received, $894,743; expenditures, $431,814; qualifying distributions, $389,900.
Limitations: Applications not accepted. Giving primarily in CA and NJ.
Application information: Contributes only to pre-selected organizations.
Trustees: Carol Kimmelman, Douglas W. Kimmelman.
EIN: 133933319
Codes: FD

33814
Neve Shaanan Fund
(Formerly Alec & Tamar Gindis Charities)
c/o J. Popper
192 Lexington Ave.
New York, NY 10016-8823

Established in 1994 in NY.
Donor(s): Alec Gindis.
Financial data (yr. ended 10/31/99): Grants paid, $386,033; assets, $9,957,877 (M); expenditures, $404,091; qualifying distributions, $368,117.
Limitations: Applications not accepted. Giving primarily in NY.
Application information: Contributes only to pre-selected organizations.
Officers: Alec Gindis, Pres. and Treas.; Tamar Gindis, V.P. and Secy.; Willliam Kratenstein, V.P.
EIN: 133798548
Codes: FD

33815
Geller Family Religious Foundation
57 Wesley Chapel Rd.
Suffern, NY 10901

Established in 1998 in NY.
Donor(s): Moshe Geller.
Financial data (yr. ended 05/31/01): Grants paid, $386,022; assets, $3,220 (M); gifts received, $390,710; expenditures, $388,039; qualifying distributions, $386,022.
Limitations: Applications not accepted. Giving primarily in NY; some giving in NJ and Israel.
Application information: Contributes only to pre-selected organizations.
Trustees: Judith Geller, Moshe Geller, Shirley Preis.
EIN: 134029849
Codes: FD

33816
The Poznanski Family Foundation, Inc.
c/o Mendelsohn Kary Bell & Natoli
1633 Broadway, 20th Fl.
New York, NY 10019

Established in 1998 in NY.
Donor(s): Abraham Poznanski, Etty Poznanski.
Financial data (yr. ended 12/31/00): Grants paid, $385,960; assets, $902,924 (M); gifts received, $366,042; expenditures, $387,211; qualifying distributions, $385,695.
Limitations: Applications not accepted.
Application information: Contributes only to pre-selected organizations.
Directors: Robert T. Bell, Abraham Poznanski, Etty Poznanski.
EIN: 134023562
Codes: FD

33817
Charles and Lucille King Family Foundation, Inc.
366 Madison Ave., 10th Fl.
New York, NY 10017 (212) 682-2913
E-mail: info@Kingfoundation.org; *URL:* http://www.kingfoundation.org
Contact: Karen E. Kennedy, Asst. Educational Dir.

Established in 1988 in NJ.
Donor(s): Diana King.
Financial data (yr. ended 12/31/01): Grants paid, $385,762; assets, $5,366,741 (M); gifts received, $155,200; expenditures, $476,517; qualifying distributions, $475,993.
Limitations: Giving on a national basis.
Publications: Informational brochure (including application guidelines), application guidelines.
Application information: Application form for scholarships available on website. Application form required.

33817—NEW YORK

Officers and Directors:* Diana King,* Pres.; Charles J. Brucia,* V.P. and Treas.; Eugene V. Kokot,* Secy.; Michael Collyer.
EIN: 133489257
Codes: FD, GTI

33818
Klaus Family Foundation, Inc.
21-09 Borden Ave.
Long Island City, NY 11101
Contact: Mortimer Klaus, Tr.

Established in 1979 in NY.
Donor(s): Burma Bibas, Inc.
Financial data (yr. ended 11/30/01): Grants paid, $385,592; assets, $8,543,948 (M); gifts received, $250,000; expenditures, $425,536; qualifying distributions, $385,592.
Limitations: Applications not accepted. Giving primarily in NY.
Application information: Contributes only to pre-selected organizations.
Trustees: Arthur Klaus, Lester Klaus, Mortimer Klaus.
EIN: 133053197
Codes: FD

33819
Nazarian Family Foundation
c/o Marks Paneth Shron
88 Froehlich Farm Blvd., Ste. 200
Woodbury, NY 11797

Established in 1987 in NJ.
Donor(s): Nazar Nazarian, Artemis Nazarian, Seta Albrecht, Levon Nazarian.
Financial data (yr. ended 11/30/01): Grants paid, $385,460; assets, $4,622,681 (M); gifts received, $400,664; expenditures, $434,189; qualifying distributions, $385,460.
Limitations: Applications not accepted. Giving primarily in NY.
Application information: Contributes only to pre-selected organizations.
Directors: Seta Albrecht, Artemis Nazarian, Levon Nazarian, Nazar Nazarian.
EIN: 112889824
Codes: FD

33820
William and Mildred Levine Foundation
2921 Brighton-Henrietta Town Line Rd.
Rochester, NY 14623-2748

Established in 1987 in NY.
Donor(s): William Levine, Mildred Levine.
Financial data (yr. ended 12/31/01): Grants paid, $385,000; assets, $8,217,734 (M); gifts received, $370,732; expenditures, $436,123; qualifying distributions, $385,000.
Limitations: Applications not accepted. Giving primarily in NY.
Application information: Contributes only to pre-selected organizations.
Officers and Directors:* William Levine,* Pres.; Mildred Levine,* V.P.; Elena Oliveri,* Secy.-Treas.; Richard Levine, Barbara Slater.
EIN: 161310753
Codes: FD

33821
The Warburg Pincus Foundation
466 Lexington Ave., 10th Fl.
New York, NY 10017

Established in 2000 in NY.
Donor(s): Warburg Pincus Partners LLC.
Financial data (yr. ended 11/30/01): Grants paid, $385,000; assets, $140,407 (M); gifts received, $954,591; expenditures, $393,960; qualifying distributions, $385,000.

Limitations: Applications not accepted. Giving primarily in New York, NY.
Application information: Contributes only to pre-selected organizations.
Officers: Lionel I. Pincus, Pres.; Reuben S. Leibowitz, Secy.; Timothy J. Curt, Treas.
EIN: 134148834
Codes: CS, FD

33822
The Glens Falls Foundation
16 Maple St.
Glens Falls, NY 12801   (518) 761-7350
FAX: (518) 798-8620
Contact: G. Nelson Lowe, Admin.

Established in 1939 in NY by declaration of trust.
Financial data (yr. ended 12/31/00): Grants paid, $384,230; assets, $9,413,449 (M); gifts received, $185,875; expenditures, $414,603.
Limitations: Giving limited to Warren, Washington, and Saratoga counties, NY.
Publications: Annual report, application guidelines, informational brochure.
Application information: The foundation does not participate in the selection process for scholarship awards, except for scholarships to medical students. Application form not required.
Officer: G. Nelson Lowe, Admin.
Distribution Committee: Marilyn Cohen, Chair.; Katherine M. Barton, Franklin A. DePeters, Thomas H. Lapham, Donald A. Metivier, Floyd H. Rourke, Thomas R. Yole.
Trustee: Banknorth Investment Management Group, N.A.
EIN: 146036390
Codes: CM, FD, GTI

33823
Rukal Foundation, Inc.
c/o Renov
172 Broadway
Lawrence, NY 11559

Established in 1993 in NY.
Donor(s): Kalman M. Renov, Joseph Davdowitz, Rosalind Davdowitz.
Financial data (yr. ended 11/30/01): Grants paid, $383,343; assets, $1,777,062 (M); expenditures, $398,343; qualifying distributions, $383,625.
Limitations: Giving on a national basis.
Officers and Directors:* Ruki D. Renov,* Pres. and Treas.; Kalman M. Renov,* V.P.; Esther Stahler,* Secy.
EIN: 113189193
Codes: FD

33824
The Fatta Foundation, Inc.
1001 Admirals Walk
Buffalo, NY 14202

Established in 1998 in NY.
Donor(s): Angelo M. Fatta, Carol A. Fatta.
Financial data (yr. ended 12/31/01): Grants paid, $382,665; assets, $8,622,307 (M); expenditures, $450,995; qualifying distributions, $382,100.
Limitations: Applications not accepted. Giving primarily in Buffalo, NY.
Application information: Contributes only to pre-selected organizations.
Officers and Directors:* Carol A. Fatta,* Pres.; Angelo M. Fatta,* Secy.-Treas.; John D. Fatta, Suzanne E. Fatta.
EIN: 311617296
Codes: FD

33825
Isaacson Draper Foundation
c/o The Bank of New York
1 Wall St., 28th Fl.
New York, NY 10286
Application address: c/o Bank of New York, 1290 Avenue of the Americas, New York, NY 10104
Contact: Beth Camp

Established in 1999 in NY.
Donor(s): Robert L. Isaacson.‡
Financial data (yr. ended 12/31/01): Grants paid, $381,654; assets, $6,314,563 (M); gifts received, $72,100; expenditures, $517,570; qualifying distributions, $418,954.
Trustees: James D. Draper, Joshua Gold, The Bank of New York.
EIN: 137184851
Codes: FD

33826
Stephen C. & Katherine D. Sherrill Foundation
765 Park Ave.
New York, NY 10021
Contact: Stephen C. Sherrill, Mgr.

Established in 1995 in NY.
Donor(s): Katherine Sherrill, Stephen Sherrill.
Financial data (yr. ended 12/31/00): Grants paid, $381,031; assets, $2,075,135 (M); expenditures, $386,092; qualifying distributions, $382,063.
Limitations: Giving primarily in NY.
Managers: Katherine Sherrill, Stephen Sherrill.
EIN: 133789016
Codes: FD

33827
The Selma and Lawrence Ruben Foundation
(Formerly Ruben Family Foundation)
600 Madison Ave., 20th Fl.
New York, NY 10022

Established in 1982 in NY.
Donor(s): Lawrence Ruben, Selma Ruben.
Financial data (yr. ended 12/31/99): Grants paid, $380,500; assets, $11,795,703 (M); gifts received, $2,020,750; expenditures, $393,367; qualifying distributions, $366,714.
Limitations: Applications not accepted. Giving primarily in New York, NY.
Application information: Contributes only to pre-selected organizations.
Officers: Selma Ruben, Pres.; Richard Gordon Ruben, V.P.; Lawrence Ruben, Secy.-Treas.
EIN: 133124700
Codes: FD

33828
Providence Foundation, Inc.
1637 50th St.
Brooklyn, NY 11204

Established in 1997 in NY.
Donor(s): Michael Melnicke, Samuel Chmelnicki.
Financial data (yr. ended 06/30/01): Grants paid, $380,225; assets, $6,320,543 (M); gifts received, $3,425,000; expenditures, $420,749; qualifying distributions, $399,775.
Limitations: Applications not accepted. Giving primarily in Brooklyn, NY.
Application information: Contributes only to pre-selected organizations.
Officer and Directors:* Michael Melnicke,* Pres.; Cila Chmelnicki, Samuel Chmelnicki, Breindy Melnicke.
EIN: 113350828
Codes: FD

33829
Harley Street Foundation
c/o Morea Financial Svcs., FNC
120 Broadway, Ste. 1016
New York, NY 10271-1096

Established in 1964.
Donor(s): James F. Cleary.
Financial data (yr. ended 09/30/00): Grants paid, $380,200; assets, $1,391,272 (M); gifts received, $1,178,308; expenditures, $380,200; qualifying distributions, $368,779.
Limitations: Applications not accepted. Giving primarily in Boston, MA.
Application information: Contributes only to pre-selected organizations.
Trustees: Barbara M. Cleary, James F. Cleary.
EIN: 046060043
Codes: FD

33830
Bresnan Family Foundation Trust
c/o Bresnan Communications, Inc.
777 Westchester Ave.
White Plains, NY 10604

Established in 1999 in NY.
Donor(s): William J. Bresnan.
Financial data (yr. ended 12/31/01): Grants paid, $380,000; assets, $1,013,911 (M); gifts received, $306,455; expenditures, $400,363; qualifying distributions, $379,875.
Limitations: Applications not accepted.
Application information: Contributes only to pre-selected organizations.
Trustees: Daniel Bresnan, Maureen Bresnan, Michael Bresnan, Robert Bresnan, William J. Bresnan, Mary Cashman, Jeffrey Demond, Colleen Shelden.
EIN: 137203839
Codes: FD

33831
P. & C. Collins Fund
c/o U.S. Trust
114 W. 47th St., TaxVas
New York, NY 10036

Established in 2000 in DE.
Donor(s): Paul J. Collins.
Financial data (yr. ended 12/31/01): Grants paid, $379,250; assets, $8,272,286 (M); gifts received, $2,945,046; expenditures, $402,026; qualifying distributions, $379,250.
Limitations: Applications not accepted.
Directors: Carol H. Collins, Julia D. Collins, Paul J. Collins, Roland A. Collins.
EIN: 134112988

33832
The Merril & Dolores Halpern Foundation
c/o Charterhouse Group Int'l., Inc.
535 Madison Ave.
New York, NY 10022

Established in 1997 in NY.
Donor(s): Merril M. Halpern.
Financial data (yr. ended 03/31/01): Grants paid, $379,000; assets, $194,043 (M); gifts received, $150,000; expenditures, $381,610; qualifying distributions, $379,046.
Limitations: Applications not accepted. Giving in the U.S., primarily in New York, NY, and Rockport, ME; giving also in England.
Application information: Contributes only to pre-selected organizations.
Officers: Merril M. Halpern, Pres.; Myles W. Schumer, Secy.
Directors: Dolores M. Halpern, Joshua S. Rubenstein.
EIN: 133976461

33833
The Joseph H. & Miriam F. Weiss Foundation, Inc.
551 5th Ave., Ste. 1600
New York, NY 10176

Established in 1995 in NY.
Financial data (yr. ended 12/31/99): Grants paid, $378,818; assets, $322,897 (M); expenditures, $379,412; qualifying distributions, $378,818.
Limitations: Applications not accepted. Giving limited to NY.
Application information: Contributes only to pre-selected organizations.
Officers: Joseph H. Weiss, Pres.; Miriam F. Weiss, V.P.; Harold Weiser, Secy.
EIN: 133800609
Codes: FD

33834
The New Brook Charitable Foundation, Inc.
(Formerly Gerald David Neuman Foundation, Inc.)
1102 53rd St.
Brooklyn, NY 11219

Established in 1981 in NY.
Financial data (yr. ended 12/31/01): Grants paid, $378,601; assets, $7,151,557 (M); gifts received, $56,756; expenditures, $410,971; qualifying distributions, $378,601.
Limitations: Applications not accepted. Giving primarily in Brooklyn, NY.
Application information: Contributes only to pre-selected organizations.
Trustees: Rabbi Martin Laufer, Martin Leventhal, Vera Neuman.
EIN: 222979993
Codes: FD

33835
Nathan & Lena Seiler Family Foundation, Inc.
c/o Lenat Co.
315 Westchester Ave.
Port Chester, NY 10573

Established in 1981 in NY.
Donor(s): Lena Seiler, Nathan Seiler.
Financial data (yr. ended 12/31/01): Grants paid, $378,600; assets, $5,254,361 (M); expenditures, $439,773; qualifying distributions, $369,137.
Limitations: Applications not accepted. Giving primarily in the greater New York, NY, area.
Application information: Contributes only to pre-selected organizations.
Officers: Lena Seiler, Pres. and Treas.; Irving Kaplan, V.P. and Secy.
EIN: 133106906
Codes: FD

33836
Hochstein Foundation, Inc.
6 E. 45th St.
New York, NY 10017

Established in 1960.
Donor(s): Bernard Hochstein.
Financial data (yr. ended 12/31/00): Grants paid, $377,500; assets, $7,498,979 (M); gifts received, $2,600,000; expenditures, $379,595; qualifying distributions, $361,107.
Limitations: Applications not accepted. Giving primarily in NJ and NY.
Application information: Contributes only to pre-selected organizations.
Officer and Board Members:* Bernard Hochstein,* Pres.; Helen Fuss, Michael Hochstein, Miriam Hochstein, Richard Hochstein, Stephen Hochstein.
EIN: 136161765
Codes: FD

33837
Glen & Lynn Tobias Family Foundation, Inc.
22 Hampton Rd.
Scarsdale, NY 10583

Established in 1996 in NY.
Donor(s): Glen Tobias.
Financial data (yr. ended 11/30/01): Grants paid, $377,418; assets, $502,725 (M); expenditures, $397,644; qualifying distributions, $384,698.
Limitations: Applications not accepted. Giving primarily in New York, NY.
Application information: Contributes only to pre-selected organizations.
Officers: Glen Tobias, Pres.; Lynn Tobias, V.P.
EIN: 223487467
Codes: FD

33838
Jerome A. and Estelle R. Newman Assistance Fund, Inc.
925 Westchester Ave., Ste. 308
White Plains, NY 10604-3564   (914) 993-0777
Contact: Howard A. Newman, Chair.

Incorporated in 1954 in NY.
Donor(s): Howard A. Newman, Jerome A. Newman.‡
Financial data (yr. ended 06/30/01): Grants paid, $377,000; assets, $8,845,545 (M); expenditures, $413,505; qualifying distributions, $377,000.
Limitations: Giving primarily in NY.
Officers and Directors:* Howard A. Newman,* Chair.; William C. Newman,* Pres.; Patricia Nanon,* V.P.; Robert H. Haines,* Secy.; Michael Greenberg,* Treas.; Andrew H. Levy, Victoria Woolner Samuels, William C. Scott, Jerry I. Speyer.
EIN: 136096241
Codes: FD

33839
The Richardson Foundation
(Formerly Frank E. and Nancy M. Richardson Foundation)
245 Park Ave., 41st Fl.
New York, NY 10167

Established in 1987 in NY.
Donor(s): Frank E. Richardson III.
Financial data (yr. ended 12/31/01): Grants paid, $375,706; assets, $1,533,483 (M); gifts received, $358,809; expenditures, $387,488; qualifying distributions, $380,548.
Limitations: Applications not accepted. Giving primarily in NY; some giving also in MA and NJ.
Application information: Contributes only to pre-selected organizations.
Trustee: Frank E. Richardson.
EIN: 133440317
Codes: FD

33840
The ABS Charitable Foundation, Inc.
850 Piermont Ave.
Piermont, NY 10968
E-mail: desmdpc@creativeonline.com
Contact: Daniel E. Spitzer, Tr.

Established in 1999 in NY.
Donor(s): Daniel E. Spitzer, Heidi R. Spitzer.
Financial data (yr. ended 12/31/01): Grants paid, $375,520; assets, $267,309 (M); gifts received, $431,000; expenditures, $375,879; qualifying distributions, $375,830.
Limitations: Giving on a national basis.
Trustees: Daniel E. Spitzer, Heidi R. Spitzer.
EIN: 134088830
Codes: FD

33841
Metropolitan Philanthropic Fund, Inc.
(Formerly Jane P. & Charles D. Klein Foundation)
666 3rd Ave., 29th Fl.
New York, NY 10017-4011
Contact: Charles D. Klein, V.P.

Established in 1982.
Donor(s): Charles D. Klein, Laila Hafner.
Financial data (yr. ended 06/30/01): Grants paid, $375,380; assets, $6,806,411 (M); gifts received, $28,568; expenditures, $408,838; qualifying distributions, $376,380.
Limitations: Giving primarily in New York, NY.
Application information: Application form not required.
Officers and Directors:* Jane P. Klein,* Pres.; Charles D. Klein,* V.P.; David P. Steinmann,* Secy.-Treas.; Alex Anagnos.
EIN: 133128811
Codes: FD

33842
Thomas G. & Andrea Mendell Foundation
c/o Dalessio, Millner & Leben, LLP
245 5th Ave., 16th Fl.
New York, NY 10016

Established in 1987 in NY.
Donor(s): Thomas G. Mendell.
Financial data (yr. ended 07/31/01): Grants paid, $375,000; assets, $1,237,145 (M); gifts received, $1,237; expenditures, $378,928; qualifying distributions, $375,513.
Limitations: Applications not accepted. Giving primarily in Washington, DC, and New York, NY.
Application information: Contributes only to pre-selected organizations.
Trustees: Richard W. Herbst, Andrea Mendell, Thomas G. Mendell.
EIN: 133437893
Codes: FD

33843
The Meckler Foundation, Inc.
520 E. 86th St.
New York, NY 10028
Contact: Alan M. Meckler, Pres.

Established in 1994 in NY.
Donor(s): Alan M. Meckler.
Financial data (yr. ended 10/31/01): Grants paid, $374,950; assets, $2,171,489 (M); expenditures, $389,349; qualifying distributions, $374,889.
Limitations: Giving on a national basis.
Application information: Application form not required.
Officers: Alan M. Meckler, Pres.; Alan B. Abramson, V.P.; Ellen L. Meckler, Secy.-Treas.
EIN: 133802660
Codes: FD

33844
Epstein Philanthropies
907 5th Ave.
New York, NY 10021 (212) 879-0237
Application address: c/o Florence E. Teicher, V.P., 165 E. 65th St., New York, NY 10021, tel.: (212) 228-6128
Contact: Thomas Epstein, Pres.

Established in 1977 in NY.
Donor(s): Thomas Epstein, William A. Epstein, Florence E. Teicher.
Financial data (yr. ended 12/31/99): Grants paid, $372,813; assets, $2,506,488 (M); gifts received, $369,683; expenditures, $385,461; qualifying distributions, $382,687.
Limitations: Giving primarily in New York, NY.
Application information: Application form not required.

Officers: Thomas Epstein, Pres.; Florence E. Teicher, V.P.; Milton Teicher, Treas.
EIN: 132902852
Codes: FD

33845
The Stephen Muss Foundation, Inc.
30 Rockefeller Plz. 29th Fl.
New York, NY 10112

Donor(s): Stephen Muss.
Financial data (yr. ended 10/31/99): Grants paid, $372,807; assets, $3,645,702 (M); gifts received, $1,000,000; expenditures, $379,665; qualifying distributions, $375,665.
Limitations: Applications not accepted. Giving primarily in FL.
Application information: contributes only to pre-selected organizations.
Officers and Directors:* Stephen Muss,* Pres. and Treas.; Alan Rosebloom,* Secy.; Brian Bilzin.
EIN: 237424763
Codes: FD

33846
The Stephen D. Quinn Foundation
c/o Goldman Sachs & Co.
85 Broad St., Tax Dept.
New York, NY 10004

Established in 1993 in CT.
Donor(s): Stephen D. Quinn.
Financial data (yr. ended 07/31/01): Grants paid, $372,783; assets, $5,002,443 (M); gifts received, $2,387,321; expenditures, $373,883; qualifying distributions, $448,217.
Limitations: Applications not accepted. Giving primarily in CT and UT.
Application information: Contributes only to pre-selected organizations.
Trustees: Cydney P. Quinn, Stephen D. Quinn.
EIN: 133789066
Codes: FD

33847
Foundation for the Development of Humanity
57-03 48th St.
Maspeth, NY 11378-2015
Contact: David Teitler, Pres.

Established around 1988.
Donor(s): David Teitler.
Financial data (yr. ended 12/31/00): Grants paid, $372,300; assets, $1,223,445 (M); gifts received, $220,000; expenditures, $372,640; qualifying distributions, $372,350.
Limitations: Giving on a national basis.
Officer: David Teitler, Pres.
Trustee: Harvey Kitay.
EIN: 112933069
Codes: FD

33848
The Daniel M. Ziff Foundation
c/o Ziff Bros. Investments
153 E. 53rd St., 43rd Fl.
New York, NY 10022

Donor(s): Ziff Investment Partnership II.
Financial data (yr. ended 12/31/00): Grants paid, $372,211; assets, $3,415,004 (M); gifts received, $3,474,164; expenditures, $416,561; qualifying distributions, $334,132.
Limitations: Applications not accepted. Giving primarily in FL and NY.
Application information: Contributes only to pre-selected organizations.
Officers: Daniel M. Ziff, Pres.; David Moody, V.P. and Secy.; Mark Beaudoin, V.P.; Peter Cawley, V.P.; Timothy Mitchell, Treas.
EIN: 134083253

Codes: FD

33849
Zemsky Family Foundation
(Formerly Russer Foods/Zemsky Family Trust)
c/o Taurus Partners
70 W. Chippewa St., Rm. 500
Buffalo, NY 14202
Contact: Shirley Zemsky, Tr.; or Sam Zemsky, Tr.

Established in 1987 in NY.
Donor(s): Zemco Industries, Inc., Sam Zemsky, Mrs. Sam Zemsky.
Financial data (yr. ended 12/31/01): Grants paid, $372,170; assets, $3,150,851 (M); gifts received, $1,000,000; expenditures, $383,865; qualifying distributions, $372,170.
Limitations: Giving primarily in NY, with emphasis on Buffalo, and FL; some giving in western MA.
Application information: Application form not required.
Trustees: Howard Zemsky, Sam Zemsky, Shirley Zemsky.
EIN: 112867625
Codes: FD

33850
Fanny & Stephen Rosenak Foundation
945 5th Ave., Apt. 11C
New York, NY 10021
Contact: Rhoda Cohen, Secy.

Established in 1990 in DE.
Donor(s): Fanny Rosenak.
Financial data (yr. ended 12/31/00): Grants paid, $372,168; assets, $7,410,215 (M); gifts received, $322,443; expenditures, $534,329; qualifying distributions, $372,168.
Limitations: Giving primarily in New York, NY.
Officers: Herbert G. Cohen, Pres.; Rhoda Cohen, Secy.; Mark Cohen, Treas.
EIN: 133563950
Codes: FD

33851
Radio Drama Network, Inc.
285 Central Park W., No. 8N
New York, NY 10024 (212) 724-4333
Contact: Himan Brown, Pres.

Financial data (yr. ended 12/31/01): Grants paid, $371,199; assets, $12,356,794 (M); expenditures, $375,899; qualifying distributions, $372,699.
Limitations: Giving primarily in NY.
Officers and Directors:* Himan Brown,* Pres.; Arnold Sheiffer,* V.P.; Richard Kay,* Secy.
EIN: 133253712
Codes: FD

33852
The L.E. Charitable Trust
c/o Ludvik Hilman
1453 50th St.
Brooklyn, NY 11219

Established in 1992 in NY.
Donor(s): Ludvik Hilman, Eva Hilman.
Financial data (yr. ended 11/30/01): Grants paid, $370,458; assets, $5,503,848 (M); gifts received, $340,782; expenditures, $384,499; qualifying distributions, $367,780.
Limitations: Applications not accepted. Giving limited to Brooklyn, NY.
Application information: Contributes only to pre-selected organizations.
Trustees: Eva Hilman, Ludvik Hilman.
EIN: 113133027
Codes: FD

33853
Nomura American Foundation
2 World Financial Ctr., Bldg. B, 17th Fl.
New York, NY 10281-1198 (212) 667-1712
Contact: Chris Becker

Established in 1994 in NY.
Donor(s): Nomura (America) Corp.
Financial data (yr. ended 12/31/01): Grants paid, $370,255; assets, $3,429,630 (M); gifts received, $198,456; expenditures, $401,389; qualifying distributions, $367,177.
Limitations: Giving primarily in NY.
Application information: Application form not required.
Officer: Matthew Bromberg, Secy.
Directors: Peter Giacometti, Sam Herbstman.
EIN: 133772961
Codes: CS, FD, CD

33854
The Prince Family Foundation
c/o Goldman Sachs & Co.
85 Broad St., Tax Dept.
New York, NY 10004

Established in 1999 in NY.
Donor(s): Scott Prince.
Financial data (yr. ended 05/31/02): Grants paid, $368,500; assets, $1,229,559 (M); gifts received, $403,085; expenditures, $380,106; qualifying distributions, $368,500.
Limitations: Applications not accepted. Giving primarily in NY.
Application information: Contributes only to pre-selected organizations.
Trustees: Daniel Och, Scott Prince, Sharon Prince.
EIN: 134088759
Codes: FD

33855
Fortis Foundation
(Formerly AMEV Foundation)
1 Chase Manhattan Plz., 41st Fl.
New York, NY 10005 (212) 859-7000
Contact: Jacqueline Gentile

Established in 1982 in NY.
Donor(s): Time Insurance Co., Fortis Insurance Co., Fortis, Inc., Fortis Benefits Insurance Co.
Financial data (yr. ended 12/31/01): Grants paid, $368,439; assets, $1,010,405 (M); gifts received, $244; expenditures, $377,631; qualifying distributions, $376,872.
Application information: Application form not required.
Trustees: Kerry Clayton, Robert Pollock, Lesley Silvester.
EIN: 133156497
Codes: CS, FD, CD, GTI

33856
Saul & Gayfryd Steinberg Foundation, Inc.
c/o Reliance Group Holdings, Inc.
55 E. 52nd St.
New York, NY 10055

Established in 1991 in NY.
Donor(s): Saul Steinberg, Gayfryd Steinberg, Julius Steinberg Foundation.
Financial data (yr. ended 11/30/99): Grants paid, $366,940; assets, $2,570,034 (M); expenditures, $379,692; qualifying distributions, $366,940.
Limitations: Giving on a national basis.
Application information: Application form not required.
Officers: Saul Steinberg, Pres. and Treas.; Gayfryd Steinberg, Secy.
EIN: 133639426
Codes: FD

33857
Ann Parsons Memorial Foundation
c/o Jenkens & Gilchrist
405 Lexington Ave., 8th Fl
New York, NY 10174
Contact: Carol F. Burger

Established in 1994 in TX.
Financial data (yr. ended 12/31/01): Grants paid, $366,814; assets, $3,263,668 (M); gifts received, $1,907; expenditures, $370,582; qualifying distributions, $366,814.
Limitations: Applications not accepted. Giving on a national basis.
Application information: Contributes only to pre-selected organizations.
Officers and Directors:* Roger Parsons,* Pres. and Treas.; Sofia Kartsotis,* Secy.; Kathy Elliot, Cheri Friedman, Bill Kartsotis.
EIN: 752550555
Codes: FD

33858
The Grateful Foundation, Inc.
250 Park Ave., Ste. 2030
New York, NY 10177

Established in 1987 in DE.
Donor(s): Jordan Seaman.
Financial data (yr. ended 10/31/01): Grants paid, $366,544; assets, $5,895,678 (M); expenditures, $387,390; qualifying distributions, $357,452.
Limitations: Applications not accepted. Giving primarily in CA and NY.
Application information: Contributes only to pre-selected organizations.
Officers: Jordan Seaman, Pres.; Dana Manning, V.P.; Robert Krissoff, Secy.
EIN: 112897411
Codes: FD

33859
Catherine & Paul Buttenwieser Foundation
c/o B. Strauss Assoc., Ltd.
307 5th Ave., 8th Fl.
New York, NY 10016-6517

Established in 1993 in MA.
Donor(s): Paul A. Buttenwieser.
Financial data (yr. ended 09/30/01): Grants paid, $366,396; assets, $1,431,368 (M); gifts received, $337,467; expenditures, $391,039; qualifying distributions, $366,646.
Limitations: Applications not accepted. Giving primarily in Boston, MA.
Application information: Contributes only to pre-selected organizations.
Trustees: Catherine F. Buttenwieser, Paul A. Buttenwieser.
EIN: 043216632
Codes: FD

33860
Bodner Family Foundation Trust
1337 E. 9th St.
Brooklyn, NY 11230
Contact: Moshe Bodner, Pres.

Established in 1997 in NY.
Financial data (yr. ended 12/31/01): Grants paid, $365,509; assets, $0 (M); gifts received, $372,000; expenditures, $367,336; qualifying distributions, $367,336.
Limitations: Applications not accepted.
Application information: Contributes only to pre-selected organizations.
Officer: Moshe Bodner, Pres.
EIN: 116487149
Codes: FD

33861
Muriel F. Siebert Foundation, Inc.
885 3rd Ave., Ste. 1720
New York, NY 10022

Donor(s): Muriel F. Siebert.
Financial data (yr. ended 12/31/00): Grants paid, $364,592; assets, $9,176,526 (M); gifts received, $320; expenditures, $535,577; qualifying distributions, $433,227.
Limitations: Applications not accepted. Giving primarily in NY.
Application information: Contributes only to pre-selected organizations.
Officers: Muriel F. Siebert, Pres.; Patricia L. Francy, V.P.; Jane H. Macon, V.P.; June Jaffee, Secy.
EIN: 136266367
Codes: FD

33862
J.I. Foundation, Inc.
c/o Patterson, Belknap, Webb & Tyler, LLP
1133 Ave. of the Americas, Ste. 2200
New York, NY 10036-6710

Established in 1954.
Financial data (yr. ended 12/31/01): Grants paid, $364,125; assets, $5,397,275 (M); expenditures, $417,811; qualifying distributions, $376,085.
Limitations: Applications not accepted. Giving primarily in Baltimore, MD, and New York, NY; funding also in NJ.
Application information: Contributes only to pre-selected organizations.
Officers and Trustees:* Herbert H. Chaice,* Pres.; Jane W.I. Droppa,* V.P.; Larry D. Droppa,* V.P.; Antonia M. Grumbach,* Secy.; Stephen W. Schwarz,* Treas.
EIN: 136149199
Codes: FD

33863
Harding Charitable Trust
(Formerly The Harding Educational and Charitable Foundation)
c/o JPMorgan Chase Bank
1211 6th Ave., 34th Fl.
New York, NY 10036

Trust established in 1945 in NY.
Donor(s): Henry J. Harding, Robert L. Harding, Martha Harding.‡
Financial data (yr. ended 12/31/01): Grants paid, $364,000; assets, $6,710,756 (M); expenditures, $441,636; qualifying distributions, $376,210.
Limitations: Applications not accepted. Giving primarily in MA and NY.
Application information: Contributes only to pre-selected organizations.
Trustees: Timothy L. Thompson, JPMorgan Chase Bank.
EIN: 136083440
Codes: FD

33864
JNT Foundation
c/o JPMorgan Chase Bank
1211 6th Ave., 34th Fl.
New York, NY 10036

Established in 1999 in IA.
Donor(s): Vesta Hanson.
Financial data (yr. ended 08/31/01): Grants paid, $363,000; assets, $7,363,225 (M); expenditures, $660,753; qualifying distributions, $438,394.
Limitations: Applications not accepted. Giving primarily in IA.
Application information: Contributes only to pre-selected organizations.

33864—NEW YORK

Trustees: Carolyn R. Hansen, Lucy E. Hansen, Vesta Hansen, Walter E. Hansen, James E. Kasper, Robert W. Seery.
EIN: 421493980
Codes: FD

33865
Jacob L. Reiss Foundation
c/o The Bank of New York, Tax Dept.
1 Wall St., 28th Fl.
New York, NY 10286
Application address: 1290 Ave. of the Americas, 5th Fl., New York, NY 10104
Contact: Ken Houghton, V.P., The Bank of New York

Trust established in 1953 in NY.
Donor(s): Jacob L. Reiss.‡
Financial data (yr. ended 12/31/01): Grants paid, $363,000; assets, $6,058,713 (M); expenditures, $402,964; qualifying distributions, $367,250.
Limitations: Giving primarily in NJ and NY.
Trustee: The Bank of New York.
EIN: 136064123
Codes: FD

33866
Lane Family Foundation
622 3rd Ave.
New York, NY 10017

Established in 1987 in NY.
Donor(s): James N. Lane, Susan W. Lane.
Financial data (yr. ended 06/30/00): Grants paid, $362,250; assets, $2,575,099 (M); gifts received, $3,000; expenditures, $369,315; qualifying distributions, $364,800.
Limitations: Applications not accepted. Giving on a national basis.
Application information: Contributes only to pre-selected organizations.
Trustees: James N. Lane, Susan W. Lane.
EIN: 133437903
Codes: FD

33867
Charles D. Farber Memorial Foundation, Inc.
c/o National Bank of New York City
136-29 38th Ave.
Flushing, NY 11354-6500

Established in 1969 in NY.
Donor(s): Jack Farber, Lafayette College.
Financial data (yr. ended 12/31/00): Grants paid, $361,466; assets, $3,674,504 (M); expenditures, $361,466; qualifying distributions, $259,598.
Limitations: Giving primarily in FL and NY.
Application information: Must demonstrate financial need.
Directors: Gail Farber, Corey Gelman, Gary Gelman, Richard Gelman.
EIN: 237017599
Codes: FD

33868
Frank E. Clark Charitable Trust
(Formerly Clark Charitable Fund)
c/o JPMorgan Chase Bank
1211 Ave. of the Americas
New York, NY 10036 (212) 789-5702
E-mail: neal_monica@jpmorgan.com
Contact: Monica J. Neal, V.P., JPMorgan Chase Bank

Trust established in 1936 in NY.
Donor(s): Frank E. Clark.‡
Financial data (yr. ended 12/31/01): Grants paid, $361,000; assets, $7,802,000 (M); expenditures, $424,443; qualifying distributions, $365,466.
Limitations: Giving primarily in the metropolitan New York, NY, area.
Application information: Application form not required.
Trustee: JPMorgan Chase Bank.
EIN: 136049032
Codes: FD

33869
Thanksgiving Foundation
c/o Fiduciary Trust Co.
600 5th Ave.
New York, NY 10020
Application addresses: c/o Thomas H. Stine, 380 Claremont Rd., Bernardsville, NJ 07924; or c/o Marc C. Winmill, 672 Tower Hill Rd., Millbrook, NY 12545
Contact: Alexandra von Stackelberg

Established in 1985 in NJ.
Donor(s): Thomas M. Peters, Marion Post Peters.
Financial data (yr. ended 07/31/01): Grants paid, $360,870; assets, $10,924,611 (M); expenditures, $564,232; qualifying distributions, $460,066.
Limitations: Giving primarily in NJ and New York, NY.
Officers: Marc C. Winmill, Chair.; Thomas H. Stine, Pres.
Trustee: Fiduciary Trust Co.
EIN: 136861874
Codes: FD

33870
CZ Foundation, Inc.
(Formerly Charles Zarkin Memorial Foundation, Inc.)
c/o Wachtell, Lipton, Rosen & Katz
51 W. 52nd St.
New York, NY 10019-6150

Incorporated in 1969 in NY.
Donor(s): Fay Zarkin.‡
Financial data (yr. ended 12/31/99): Grants paid, $360,500; assets, $4,650,400 (M); expenditures, $372,602; qualifying distributions, $358,027.
Limitations: Applications not accepted. Giving primarily in New York, NY.
Application information: Contributes only to pre-selected organizations.
Officers and Trustees:* Martin Lipton,* Pres. and Treas.; Leonard M. Rosen,* V.P.; Katherine Lipton, Susan Lipton, Constance Monte.
EIN: 237149277
Codes: FD

33871
Joseph M. & Barbara Cohen Foundation, Inc.
410 E. 57th St.
New York, NY 10022

Established in 1990 in NY.
Donor(s): Joseph M. Cohen.
Financial data (yr. ended 10/31/01): Grants paid, $360,386; assets, $122,426 (M); gifts received, $247,588; expenditures, $377,507; qualifying distributions, $363,039.
Limitations: Applications not accepted. Giving primarily in New York, NY.
Application information: Contributes only to pre-selected organizations.
Officers: Joseph M. Cohen, Pres.; Jarrod Cohen, Secy.; Raymond Merritt, Treas.
EIN: 133636511
Codes: FD

33872
Wilson Foundation
(Formerly Elaine P. and Richard U. Wilson Foundation)
c/o JPMorgan Chase Bank
P.O. Box 31412
Rochester, NY 14603-1412

Established in 1963 in NY.
Donor(s): Katherine M. Wilson.‡
Financial data (yr. ended 12/31/01): Grants paid, $360,150; assets, $6,845,104 (M); expenditures, $415,229; qualifying distributions, $361,730.
Limitations: Applications not accepted. Giving primarily in NY.
Application information: Contributes only to pre-selected organizations.
Trustee: JPMorgan Chase Bank.
EIN: 166042023
Codes: FD

33873
RMF Family Fund, Inc.
c/o W. Michael Reickert, The Ayco Co. LP
P.O. Box 8019
Ballston Spa, NY 12020-8019

Established in 1997 in NY.
Donor(s): Richard M. Furlaud.
Financial data (yr. ended 12/31/01): Grants paid, $359,993; assets, $1,887,772 (M); expenditures, $362,331; qualifying distributions, $359,429.
Limitations: Applications not accepted. Giving primarily in FL and NY.
Application information: Contributes only to pre-selected organizations.
Officers: Richard M. Furlaud, Pres.; Isabel P. Furlaud, V.P.; Therese A. Ninesling, Secy.
Director: Tamsin Rachofsky.
EIN: 133931623
Codes: FD

33874
The Robert & Mary Litterman Foundation
c/o Goldman Sachs & Co.
85 Broad St., Tax Dept.
New York, NY 10004

Established in 1994 in NJ.
Donor(s): Robert Litterman.
Financial data (yr. ended 09/30/01): Grants paid, $359,000; assets, $5,376,798 (M); gifts received, $1,425,537; expenditures, $440,652; qualifying distributions, $361,905.
Limitations: Applications not accepted. Giving primarily in NJ and New York, NY.
Application information: Contributes only to pre-selected organizations.
Trustees: Mary Litterman, Robert Litterman.
EIN: 133805239
Codes: FD

33875
The Levick Family Foundation, Inc.
(Formerly The Sarah & Hannah Levick Foundation, Inc.)
c/o Spear, Leeds & Kellogg
120 Broadway, 8th Fl., Tax Dept.
New York, NY 10271-0093

Established in 1999 in NY.
Donor(s): Stephen Levick.
Financial data (yr. ended 09/30/01): Grants paid, $358,000; assets, $462,815 (M); gifts received, $645,063; expenditures, $359,236; qualifying distributions, $358,420.
Limitations: Applications not accepted.
Application information: Contributes only to pre-selected organizations.
Officers: Stephen Levick, Pres. and Treas.; Leslie Levick, V.P. and Secy.; David Horowitz, V.P.

IN THIS SECTION, WITHIN EACH STATE, FOUNDATIONS ARE LISTED IN DESCENDING ORDER BY TOTAL GRANTS PAID

EIN: 134097853
Codes: FD

33876
Dr. William O. Benenson Family Foundation
(Formerly Benenson Family Foundation)
35-15 Parsons Blvd.
Flushing, NY 11354-4236

Established in 1996 in NY.
Donor(s): Esther Benenson, Michael Benenson.
Financial data (yr. ended 06/30/01): Grants paid, $357,642; assets, $1,495,292 (M); gifts received, $519,548; expenditures, $362,861; qualifying distributions, $358,802.
Limitations: Applications not accepted. Giving primarily in NY.
Application information: Contributes only to pre-selected organizations.
Officers: Esther Benenson, Pres.; Amy Benenson, V.P.; Michael Benenson, V.P.; Sharon Benenson Sydney, V.P.; Blanche Benenson, Secy.
EIN: 113352088
Codes: FD

33877
Joseph and Martha Melohn Fund
1995 Broadway, 14th Fl.
New York, NY 10023
Contact: Alfons Melohn, Tr.

Established in 1986.
Donor(s): Alfons Melohn.
Financial data (yr. ended 11/30/01): Grants paid, $356,652; assets, $16,404 (M); gifts received, $440,000; expenditures, $359,237; qualifying distributions, $357,791.
Limitations: Giving primarily in New York, NY.
Trustee: Alfons Melohn.
EIN: 133395218
Codes: FD

33878
Milton and Miriam Handler Foundation
225 Broadway, Ste. 1806
New York, NY 10007 (212) 964-5485
Contact: Albert Kalter, Secy.-Treas.

Established in 1963.
Donor(s): Milton Handler.‡
Financial data (yr. ended 12/31/01): Grants paid, $356,500; assets, $10,974,236 (M); gifts received, $78,731; expenditures, $586,206; qualifying distributions, $486,585.
Limitations: Giving primarily in New York, NY.
Officers: Lawrence Newman, Pres.; Albert Kalter, Secy.-Treas.
Director: Mark Inowitz.
EIN: 136136957
Codes: FD

33879
The Melohn Foundation, Inc.
c/o Melohn Properties
1995 Broadway, 14th Fl.
New York, NY 10023-5882

Established in 1965 in NY.
Donor(s): Members of the Melohn family.
Financial data (yr. ended 07/31/01): Grants paid, $356,120; assets, $9,574,506 (M); expenditures, $927,893; qualifying distributions, $356,695.
Limitations: Giving primarily in New York and Brooklyn, NY.
Officers: Martha Melohn, Pres.; Leon Melohn, V.P.; Alfons Melohn, Secy.
EIN: 136197827

33880
The Lewy Family Foundation
c/o Robert Stein
29 W. 38th St., Ste. 14F
New York, NY 10018

Established in 1996 in NY.
Donor(s): Glen S. Lewy.
Financial data (yr. ended 12/31/01): Grants paid, $355,700; assets, $4,197,608 (M); gifts received, $1,466; expenditures, $384,743; qualifying distributions, $355,816.
Limitations: Applications not accepted. Giving primarily in Washington, DC, and NY.
Application information: Contributes only to pre-selected organizations.
Officer: Glen S. Lewy, Chair.
Directors: Cheryl Winter Lewy, Zachary Jason Lewy.
EIN: 133907886
Codes: FD

33881
The Koppelman Family Foundation
575 Lexington Ave., 7th Fl.
New York, NY 10022-6102
Contact: Murray Koppelman, Tr.

Established in 1989 in NY.
Donor(s): Murray Koppelman.
Financial data (yr. ended 10/31/01): Grants paid, $355,140; assets, $4,354,735 (M); gifts received, $365,531; expenditures, $367,178; qualifying distributions, $356,965.
Limitations: Giving primarily in NY.
Application information: Application form not required.
Trustees: Janet Koppelman, Lisa Koppelman, Murray Koppelman, Suzanne Koppelman.
EIN: 133543828
Codes: FD

33882
Samuel and Francine Klagsbrun Foundation
c/o Lehman, Newman & Flynn, CPAs
225 W. 34th St., Rm. 2220
New York, NY 10122-0049
Application address: 941 Park Ave., New York, NY 10028
Contact: Samuel C. Klagsbrun, Dir., and Francine Klagsbrun, Dir.

Established in 1987 in NY.
Donor(s): Samuel C. Klagsbrun, Francine Klagsbrun.
Financial data (yr. ended 12/31/01): Grants paid, $354,892; assets, $1,196,660 (M); expenditures, $387,703; qualifying distributions, $354,892.
Limitations: Giving primarily in New York, NY.
Application information: Application form not required.
Directors: Francine Klagsbrun, Samuel C. Klagsbrun.
EIN: 133452159
Codes: FD

33883
Emma A. Sheafer Charitable Trust
c/o JPMorgan Chase Bank
1211 6th Ave., 38th Fl.
New York, NY 10036 (212) 789-5777
Contact: Edward Jones, V.P.

Trust established in 1975 in NY.
Donor(s): Emma A. Sheafer.‡
Financial data (yr. ended 12/31/01): Grants paid, $354,802; assets, $6,496,882 (M); expenditures, $425,720; qualifying distributions, $373,017.
Limitations: Giving limited to New York, NY.
Publications: Grants list.

Application information: Organizations may not receive more than 1 grant every 3 years. Application form not required.
Trustee: JPMorgan Chase Bank.
EIN: 510186114
Codes: FD

33884
The Bernhill Fund
c/o Siegel, Sacks
630 3rd Ave.
New York, NY 10017
FAX: (212) 605-0222

Incorporated in 1977 in NY as partial successor to The Bernhard Foundation, Inc.
Donor(s): The Bernhard Foundation, Inc.
Financial data (yr. ended 10/31/01): Grants paid, $354,317; assets, $832,218 (M); expenditures, $371,293; qualifying distributions, $351,771.
Limitations: Applications not accepted. Giving primarily in New York, NY.
Application information: Contributes only to pre-selected organizations.
Officers: William L. Bernhard, Pres.; Catherine G. Cahill, V.P.
EIN: 132988599
Codes: FD

33885
Hebrew Technical Institute
c/o O'Connor, Davies & Co.
60 E. 42nd St.
New York, NY 10165-3698
Application address: c/o Rem Residential, 118 E. 17th St., New York, NY 10003
Contact: Anita Goldberg

Established in 1884.
Financial data (yr. ended 12/31/00): Grants paid, $354,000; assets, $3,532,429 (M); gifts received, $29,157; expenditures, $375,777; qualifying distributions, $353,604.
Limitations: Giving primarily in NY.
Application information: Application form not required.
Directors: Catherine H. Behrend, Lawrence A. Benenson, Andrew Berkman, Seth H. Dubin, Jay J. Meltzer, John R. Menke, Hyman B. Ritchin, Sandra Priest Rose, Robert Rosenthal, Bruce D. Schlechter, Russel O. Vernon, Charles S. Weilman.
EIN: 135562240
Codes: FD

33886
Sarah L. Boles and Joseph R. Zimmel Foundation
(Formerly Sarah B. and Joseph R. Zimmel Foundation)
c/o Goldman Sachs & Co., Tax Dept.
85 Broad St.
New York, NY 10004

Established in 1990 in NJ.
Donor(s): Joseph R. Zimmel.
Financial data (yr. ended 07/31/01): Grants paid, $353,500; assets, $6,346,518 (M); gifts received, $3,050,911; expenditures, $464,000; qualifying distributions, $356,000.
Limitations: Applications not accepted. Giving on a national basis, with emphasis on the East.
Application information: Contributes only to pre-selected organizations.
Trustees: David R. Boles, Sarah L. Boles, Joseph R. Zimmel.
EIN: 133596015
Codes: FD

33887
Richard A. and Susan P. Friedman Family Foundation
c/o Goldman Sachs & Co.
85 Broad St., Tax Dept.
New York, NY 10004

Established in 1991 in NY.
Donor(s): Richard A. Friedman.
Financial data (yr. ended 06/30/01): Grants paid, $353,448; assets, $5,153,163 (M); expenditures, $453,460; qualifying distributions, $353,778.
Limitations: Applications not accepted. Giving primarily in New York, NY.
Application information: Contributes only to pre-selected organizations.
Trustee: Richard A. Friedman.
EIN: 133634385
Codes: FD

33888
The Low Wood Fund, Inc.
(Formerly Lefteria Foundation, Inc.)
c/o 61 Assocs.
350 5th Ave., Ste. 1413
New York, NY 10118-0001

Established in 1984 in NY.
Donor(s): Eli S. Garber, Helen S. Cohen, Thomas Cohen, Amy Cohen, Gail Schorsch, Carolyn Cohen, Daniel Cohen.
Financial data (yr. ended 11/30/01): Grants paid, $353,100; assets, $124,777 (M); gifts received, $260,000; expenditures, $353,730; qualifying distributions, $353,449.
Limitations: Applications not accepted. Giving on a national basis.
Application information: Contributes only to pre-selected organizations.
Officer: David Zahner, Pres.
EIN: 133337436
Codes: FD

33889
The Wildwood Foundation
(Formerly The Morgens East Foundation)
c/o American Express Tax & Business Svcs.
1185 Ave. of the Americas
New York, NY 10036

Established in 1968.
Donor(s): Edwin H. Morgens, Howard J. Morgens.
Financial data (yr. ended 12/31/99): Grants paid, $352,500; assets, $5,396,732 (M); expenditures, $389,049; qualifying distributions, $352,500.
Limitations: Applications not accepted. Giving primarily in CT and NY.
Application information: Contributes only to pre-selected organizations.
Trustees: Edwin H. Morgens, Linda M. Morgens, John C. Waterfall.
EIN: 316090956
Codes: FD

33890
Roger L. VonAmelunxen Foundation, Inc.
83-21 Edgerton Blvd.
Jamaica, NY 11432-2207 (718) 641-4800
Contact: Karen Donnelly, V.P.

Established in 1982.
Financial data (yr. ended 07/31/01): Grants paid, $352,408; assets, $658,383 (M); gifts received, $284,159; expenditures, $368,316; qualifying distributions, $352,408.
Limitations: Giving primarily in NY.
Officers: George VonAmelunxen, Pres. and Treas.; Karen Donnelly, V.P.; Helen VonAmelunxen, Secy.
EIN: 112583014
Codes: FD, GTI

33891
The John L. Neu Family Foundation, Inc.
79 5th Ave., 18th Fl.
New York, NY 10003-3034

Established in 1990 in NY.
Donor(s): Hugo Neu Corp.
Financial data (yr. ended 12/31/01): Grants paid, $351,788; assets, $3,397,006 (M); expenditures, $353,807; qualifying distributions, $350,859.
Limitations: Applications not accepted. Giving primarily in NJ and NY.
Application information: Contributes only to pre-selected organizations.
Officers and Directors:* John L. Neu,* Pres.; Donald Hamaker, Secy.-Treas.; Robert T. Neu, Wendy K. Neu.
EIN: 133731089
Codes: FD

33892
The Cambr Charitable Foundation Trust
c/o George V. Delson Assocs.
110 E. 59th St.
New York, NY 10022

Established in 1996 in NY.
Donor(s): Allen Skolnick, Connie Skolnick, Cambr Company.
Financial data (yr. ended 01/31/01): Grants paid, $351,700; assets, $12,246,943 (M); gifts received, $90,099; expenditures, $398,902; qualifying distributions, $345,237.
Limitations: Applications not accepted.
Application information: Contributes only to pre-selected organizations.
Trustees: Allen Skolnick, Connie Skolnick.
EIN: 116462058
Codes: FD

33893
Jean Mauze Charitable Trust
c/o U.S. Trust
114 W. 47th St.
New York, NY 10036-1532 (212) 852-3377
Contact: Linda Franciscovich, Sr. V.P., or Carolyn Larke, Asst. V.P., U.S. Trust

Established in 1977 in NY.
Financial data (yr. ended 12/31/01): Grants paid, $351,471; assets, $4,932,774 (M); expenditures, $428,802; qualifying distributions, $379,838.
Limitations: Applications not accepted.
Application information: Contributes only to pre-selected organizations. Unsolicited requests for funds not accepted.
Trustee: U.S. Trust.
EIN: 136690071
Codes: FD

33894
Eugene V. Fife Family Foundation
c/o BCRS Assoc., LLC
67 Wall St., 8th Fl.
New York, NY 10005

Established in 1982 in CA.
Donor(s): Eugene V. Fife.
Financial data (yr. ended 01/31/01): Grants paid, $350,913; assets, $8,819,441 (M); expenditures, $354,101; qualifying distributions, $351,922.
Limitations: Applications not accepted. Giving primarily in VA and WV.
Application information: Contributes only to pre-selected organizations.
Trustees: Jonathan L. Cohen, Amy S. Fife, David Fife, Eugene V. Fife.
EIN: 133153715
Codes: FD

33895
Ohel Harav Yehoshua Boruch Foundation
1337 E. 7th St.
Brooklyn, NY 11230

Established in 1994 in NY.
Donor(s): Ben Landa.
Financial data (yr. ended 12/31/01): Grants paid, $350,800; assets, $2,814,986 (M); gifts received, $1,130,000; expenditures, $399,075; qualifying distributions, $350,800.
Limitations: Applications not accepted. Giving primarily in NY.
Application information: Contributes only to pre-selected organizations.
Officers: Ben Landa, Pres.; Judy Landa, V.P.
Director: Robert Bleier.
EIN: 113201774
Codes: FD

33896
Merlin Foundation
c/o Schulte, Roth & Zabel
919 3rd Ave.
New York, NY 10022
Contact: William D. Zabel, Pres.

Established in 1978 in NY.
Donor(s): Audrey Sheldon Poon.‡
Financial data (yr. ended 12/31/01): Grants paid, $350,700; assets, $4,091,817 (M); expenditures, $427,569; qualifying distributions, $365,197.
Limitations: Applications not accepted. Giving on a national basis.
Application information: Contributes only to pre-selected organizations. Unsolicited requests for funds not considered.
Officers: William D. Zabel, Pres. and Treas.; Roger C. Altman, V.P.; Thomas H. Baer, V.P.; John J. McLaughlin, Secy.
EIN: 237418853
Codes: FD

33897
Louis Greenspan Charitable Trust
12 Raymond Ave.
Poughkeepsie, NY 12603 (845) 483-7745

Established in 1998 in NY.
Donor(s): Louis Greenspan.‡
Financial data (yr. ended 12/31/01): Grants paid, $350,000; assets, $5,541,765 (M); expenditures, $451,000; qualifying distributions, $386,734.
Limitations: Giving primarily in Poughkeepsie, NY.
Trustees: Daniel F. Curtin, Gary Koch.
EIN: 146185658
Codes: FD

33898
Edelman Family Foundation, Inc.
c/o Jankoff & Gabe, PC
705 Empire Ave.
Far Rockaway, NY 11691-4832

Established in 1998.
Donor(s): Alex Edelman, Susan Edelman.
Financial data (yr. ended 12/31/01): Grants paid, $349,845; assets, $51,907 (M); gifts received, $350,000; expenditures, $351,425; qualifying distributions, $351,425.
Limitations: Applications not accepted.
Application information: Contributes only to pre-selected organizations.
Officers: Alex Edelman, Pres.; Jeffrey Edelman, V.P.; Michael Edelman, V.P.; Fay Greenberg, V.P.; Susan Edelman, Secy.-Treas.
EIN: 113455820
Codes: FD

33899
The Julien J. Studley Foundation
300 Park Ave.
New York, NY 10022

Established in 1992 in NY.
Donor(s): Julien J. Studley.
Financial data (yr. ended 12/31/01): Grants paid, $349,407; assets, $1,359,570 (M); gifts received, $400,000; expenditures, $371,548; qualifying distributions, $352,825.
Limitations: Applications not accepted. Giving primarily in NY.
Application information: Contributes only to pre-selected organizations.
Trustee: Julien J. Studley.
EIN: 133703530
Codes: FD

33900
The 1994 Robert W. Johnson IV Charitable Trust
c/o The Johnson Co., Inc.
630 5th Ave., Ste. 1510
New York, NY 10111

Established in 1994 in NY.
Donor(s): Betty W. Johnson.
Financial data (yr. ended 12/31/01): Grants paid, $349,200; assets, $8,005,968 (M); expenditures, $356,402; qualifying distributions, $347,480.
Limitations: Applications not accepted. Giving on a national basis.
Application information: Contributes only to pre-selected organizations.
Trustees: Betty W. Johnson, Robert W. Johnson IV.
EIN: 137046310
Codes: FD

33901
The 1994 Elizabeth R. Johnson Charitable Trust
c/o Tag Associates, Ltd.
75 Rockefeller Plz.
New York, NY 10019

Established in 1994 in NY.
Financial data (yr. ended 12/31/00): Grants paid, $349,000; assets, $7,460,282 (M); gifts received, $250; expenditures, $353,463; qualifying distributions, $346,455.
Limitations: Applications not accepted. Giving primarily in NY.
Application information: Contributes only to pre-selected organizations.
Trustees: Betty Wold Johnson, Elizabeth Ross Johnson.
EIN: 137046313
Codes: FD

33902
Edward & Sandra Meyer Foundation, Inc.
c/o Philip Pollak
432 Park Ave. S., Ste. 400
New York, NY 10016-8013

Established in 1966.
Donor(s): Edward H. Meyer.
Financial data (yr. ended 12/31/00): Grants paid, $348,820; assets, $2,913,468 (M); gifts received, $578,440; expenditures, $354,267; qualifying distributions, $346,383.
Limitations: Applications not accepted. Giving primarily in the New York, NY, area.
Application information: Contributes only to pre-selected organizations.
Officers: Edward H. Meyer, Pres. and Treas.; Sandra Meyer, Secy.
EIN: 136204325
Codes: FD

33903
Reuben & Rose Mattus Foundation, Inc.
c/o Janover Rubinroit, LLC
100 Quentin Roosevelt Blvd., Ste. 516
Garden City, NY 11530

Established in 1983 in NY.
Donor(s): Reuben Mattus,‡ Rose Mattus, Doris Mattus Hurley.
Financial data (yr. ended 06/30/01): Grants paid, $347,615; assets, $2,804,514 (M); gifts received, $110,000; expenditures, $351,226; qualifying distributions, $746,063.
Limitations: Applications not accepted. Giving primarily in NJ and NY.
Application information: Contributes only to pre-selected organizations.
Officers: Rose Mattus, Pres. and Treas.; Doris Mattus Hurley, V.P.
EIN: 133183976
Codes: FD

33904
The Lou and Harry Stern Family Foundation
c/o Tashlik, Kreutzer, Goldwyn & Crandell, P.C.
833 Northern Blvd.
Great Neck, NY 11021

Established in 1988 in NY.
Donor(s): Harry Stern, Lou Stern.
Financial data (yr. ended 12/31/01): Grants paid, $347,615; assets, $2,709,985 (M); gifts received, $302,755; expenditures, $354,545; qualifying distributions, $347,615.
Limitations: Applications not accepted. Giving primarily in NY.
Application information: Contributes only to pre-selected organizations.
Officers: Harry Stern, Pres.; Lou Stern, V.P.; Theodore W. Tashlik, Secy.; Russell Stern, Treas.
EIN: 112952489
Codes: FD

33905
The Kupferberg Foundation
131-38 Sanford Ave.
Flushing, NY 11352

Established in 1961 in NY.
Donor(s): Kepco, Inc., and members of the Kupferberg family.
Financial data (yr. ended 11/30/01): Grants paid, $347,150; assets, $8,750,254 (M); expenditures, $354,147; qualifying distributions, $348,935.
Limitations: Applications not accepted. Giving primarily in NY.
Application information: Contributes only to pre-selected organizations.
Officers: Max Kupferberg, Pres.; Jesse Kupferberg, V.P.
Trustees: Martin Kupferberg, Saul Kupferberg.
EIN: 116008915
Codes: CS, FD, CD

33906
The William Fox, Jr. Foundation
c/o Jo-Ann Fox Weingarten
885 Park Ave., Ste. 6B
New York, NY 10021

Established in 1992 in NY.
Donor(s): Belle Fox.‡
Financial data (yr. ended 12/31/01): Grants paid, $346,317; assets, $2,938,209 (M); expenditures, $380,695; qualifying distributions, $373,205.
Limitations: Applications not accepted. Giving primarily in New York, NY.
Application information: Contributes only to pre-selected organizations.
Officer and Trustees:* Jo-Ann Fox Weingarten,* Pres.; Barbara W. Fox, Susan Fox Rosellini.
EIN: 133631257
Codes: FD

33907
Taylor Family Foundation
c/o U.S. Trust
114 W. 47th St.
New York, NY 10036

Established in 1998 in NY.
Donor(s): Frederick B. Taylor.
Financial data (yr. ended 12/31/00): Grants paid, $346,000; assets, $1,219,730 (M); gifts received, $950,013; expenditures, $348,500; qualifying distributions, $337,100.
Limitations: Applications not accepted.
Application information: Unsolicited requests for funds not accepted.
Trustees: Carole L. Taylor, Frederick B. Taylor.
EIN: 137138118
Codes: FD

33908
The Kurz Family Foundation, Ltd.
69 Lydecker St.
Nyack, NY 10960-2103 (845) 358-2300
Contact: Herbert Kurz

Established in 1992 in NY.
Donor(s): Herbert Kurz.
Financial data (yr. ended 12/31/01): Grants paid, $345,463; assets, $13,702,394 (M); gifts received, $525,500; expenditures, $444,613; qualifying distributions, $442,848.
Limitations: Giving primarily in NY.
Directors: Ellen Kurz, Leonard Kurz, Brenda Neal, Lewis Wechsler.
EIN: 133680855
Codes: FD

33909
Fern Karesh Hurst Foundation
1060 5th Ave.
New York, NY 10128

Established in 1998 in NY.
Donor(s): Fern Karesh Hurst.
Financial data (yr. ended 12/31/00): Grants paid, $345,125; assets, $2,824,217 (M); expenditures, $435,343; qualifying distributions, $340,664.
Limitations: Applications not accepted.
Application information: Contributes only to pre-selected organizations.
Trustee: Fern Karesh Hurst.
EIN: 137127514
Codes: FD

33910
Mebane Charitable Foundation, Inc.
c/o Bessemer Trust Co., N.A.
630 5th Ave.
New York, NY 10111

Established in 1998 in NC.
Donor(s): G. Allen Mebane IV.
Financial data (yr. ended 12/31/01): Grants paid, $345,000; assets, $27,281,374 (M); gifts received, $22,857,480; expenditures, $483,291; qualifying distributions, $432,375.
Limitations: Applications not accepted. Giving primarily in NC.
Application information: Contributes only to pre-selected organizations.
Officers and Directors:* G. Allen Mebane IV,* Pres.; William Michael Mebane,* V.P.; Clifford Frazier, Jr.,* Secy.; John H. Minehan,* Treas.; Frank Helsom, John C. Lathrop, G. Allen Mebane V, Marianne Mebane, Edward C. Smith, Jr.
EIN: 561853390
Codes: FD

33911—NEW YORK

33911
The Patricia M. Hynes & Roy L. Reardon Foundation
1148 5th Ave.
New York, NY 10128

Established in 1997 in NY.
Donor(s): Patricia M. Hynes.
Financial data (yr. ended 12/31/01): Grants paid, $344,960; assets, $1,698,068 (M); gifts received, $168,168; expenditures, $351,960; qualifying distributions, $344,223.
Limitations: Applications not accepted.
Application information: Contributes only to pre-selected organizations.
Trustees: Patricia M. Hynes, Roy L. Reardon.
EIN: 133928432
Codes: FD

33912
Equinox Foundation, Inc.
c/o M.R. Weiser & Co.
20 Corporate Woods Blvd., Rm. 600
Albany, NY 12211

Established in 1990 in NY.
Donor(s): John D. Picotte.
Financial data (yr. ended 12/31/01): Grants paid, $344,923; assets, $7,432,862 (M); gifts received, $347,500; expenditures, $452,347; qualifying distributions, $370,544.
Limitations: Giving primarily in NY.
Officers: John D. Picotte, Pres.; Michelle R. Leclair, Secy.; Margaret P. MacClarence, Treas.
Directors: Brooke A. Picotte, Jeffrey P. Resnick, John O. Picotte, Jr.
EIN: 223109260
Codes: FD

33913
Irma & Abram Croll Foundation, Inc.
c/o Maxwell Shmerler & Co.
1 N. Lexington Ave.
White Plains, NY 10601

Established in 1969.
Donor(s): Irma L. Croll.
Financial data (yr. ended 12/31/99): Grants paid, $343,548; assets, $839,216 (M); expenditures, $343,996; qualifying distributions, $343,548.
Limitations: Applications not accepted. Giving primarily in the metropolitan New York, NY, area.
Application information: Contributes only to pre-selected organizations.
Officers: Irma L. Croll, Pres.; Edwin Shmerler, Treas.
EIN: 237037312

33914
Ivor Foundation
c/o Saunders, Karp & Megrue, LP
667 Madison Ave., 5th Fl.
New York, NY 10021

Established in 1989 in NY.
Donor(s): Thomas A. Saunders III.
Financial data (yr. ended 12/31/01): Grants paid, $343,331; assets, $4,960,506 (M); expenditures, $381,919; qualifying distributions, $355,625.
Limitations: Applications not accepted. Giving primarily in NY.
Application information: Contributes only to pre-selected organizations.
Officers: Thomas A. Saunders III, Pres. and Treas.; Mary Jordan Saunders, Secy.
Directors: Joanne Saunders Berkley, Calvert S. Griffin, Thomas A. Saunders IV.
EIN: 133506932
Codes: FD

33915
The Jack Gantz Foundation, Inc.
c/o RSM McGladrey, Inc.
106 Corporate Park Dr., Ste. 417
White Plains, NY 10604

Established in 1985 in NY.
Donor(s): Empire Brushes, Inc., The Gantz Investment Co.
Financial data (yr. ended 10/31/01): Grants paid, $343,329; assets, $4,363,122 (M); expenditures, $374,319; qualifying distributions, $348,880.
Limitations: Applications not accepted. Giving primarily in NY.
Application information: Contributes only to pre-selected organizations.
Officers and Directors:* Sarita Gantz, Pres.; Joseph Gantz,* Secy.-Treas.; Elaine Gantz Berman.
EIN: 133352396
Codes: FD

33916
Donald B. & Catherine C. Marron Foundation
1285 Ave. of the Americas, 14th Fl.
New York, NY 10019
Contact: Donald B. Marron, Tr.

Established in 1972 as the Mitchell, Hutchins, Inc. Foundation.
Donor(s): Donald B. Marron.
Financial data (yr. ended 12/31/99): Grants paid, $343,325; assets, $4,178,416 (M); gifts received, $618,750; expenditures, $347,268; qualifying distributions, $343,645.
Limitations: Giving primarily in New York, NY.
Trustees: Elaine Conte, Donald B. Marron.
EIN: 237243134
Codes: FD

33917
The Sullivan Family Foundation
(Formerly The Thomas Sullivan Family Foundation)
c/o Megan R. Sullivan
1100 Park Ave., Ste. 12C
New York, NY 10128

Established in 1984 in DE.
Donor(s): Thomas A. Sullivan.
Financial data (yr. ended 11/30/01): Grants paid, $342,030; assets, $3,127,556 (M); expenditures, $392,912; qualifying distributions, $341,297.
Limitations: Applications not accepted. Giving primarily in NY.
Application information: Contributes only to pre-selected organizations.
Trustee: Thomas A. Sullivan.
EIN: 133341262
Codes: FD

33918
The Celia and Isaac Sutton Foundation
c/o Celia and Isaac Sutton
463 Ave. S
Brooklyn, NY 11223-3024

Established in 2000 in NY.
Donor(s): Isaac Sutton, The Jack Sitt 1992 Charitable Trust.
Financial data (yr. ended 10/31/01): Grants paid, $341,835; assets, $3,772,712 (M); expenditures, $432,194; qualifying distributions, $341,835.
Limitations: Applications not accepted.
Application information: Contributes only to pre-selected organizations.
Trustees: Celia Sutton, Isaac Sutton.
EIN: 137200889
Codes: FD

33919
Ann Eden Woodward Foundation
c/o J. Lapatin
977 6th Ave., No. 810
New York, NY 10018

Established in 1963 in NY.
Donor(s): Ann Eden Woodward.‡
Financial data (yr. ended 05/31/01): Grants paid, $341,725; assets, $725,055 (M); gifts received, $395,000; expenditures, $353,829; qualifying distributions, $341,725.
Limitations: Applications not accepted. Giving primarily in New York, NY.
Application information: Grants awarded at discretion of managers.
Managers: J. Lapatin, J.A. Wood.
EIN: 136126021
Codes: FD

33920
The G. & B. Horowitz Family Foundation, Inc.
(Formerly Gedale B. and Barbara S. Horowitz Foundation)
c/o Cleary Gottlieb
1 Liberty Plz.
New York, NY 10006

Established in 1970 in NY.
Donor(s): Gedale B. Horowitz, Gedale B. Horowitz Charitable Lead Trust.
Financial data (yr. ended 06/30/01): Grants paid, $341,500; assets, $5,045,219 (M); expenditures, $343,850; qualifying distributions, $342,777.
Limitations: Applications not accepted. Giving primarily in New York, NY.
Application information: Contributes only to pre-selected organizations.
Officers: Gedale B. Horowitz, Pres.; Ruth Horowitz, V.P.; Seth Horowitz, V.P.; Steven M. Loeb, Secy.; Barbara Horowitz, Treas.
EIN: 237101730
Codes: FD

33921
The Wagner Family Foundation, Inc.
c/o Leon Wagner
8 Lincoln Woods
Purchase, NY 10577

Established in 1997 in NY.
Donor(s): Leon Wagner, Marsha Wagner.
Financial data (yr. ended 09/30/01): Grants paid, $340,789; assets, $741,671 (M); gifts received, $312,121; expenditures, $362,946; qualifying distributions, $345,917.
Limitations: Applications not accepted. Giving primarily in CA and NY.
Application information: Contributes only to pre-selected organizations.
Officers: Leon Wagner, Pres.; Harry Wagner, V.P.; Marsha Wagner, Secy.
EIN: 133980685
Codes: FD

33922
Howard A. Silverstein Foundation
c/o Goldman Sachs & Co.
85 Broad St., Tax Dept.
New York, NY 10004-2434

Established in 1986.
Donor(s): Howard A. Silverstein.
Financial data (yr. ended 07/31/01): Grants paid, $340,615; assets, $5,268,477 (M); gifts received, $490,063; expenditures, $351,365; qualifying distributions, $344,365.
Limitations: Applications not accepted. Giving primarily in New York, NY and Philadelphia, PA.
Application information: Contributes only to pre-selected organizations.

Trustees: Gary D. Rose, Howard A. Silverstein.
EIN: 133385065
Codes: FD

33923
A. & Z. Hasenfeld Foundation, Inc.
580 5th Ave.
New York, NY 10036 (212) 575-0290
Contact: Alexander Hasenfeld, Pres.

Established in 1969.
Donor(s): Alexander Hasenfeld, Zissy Hasenfeld.
Financial data (yr. ended 03/31/01): Grants paid, $340,357; assets, $265,127 (L); gifts received, $606,566; expenditures, $340,651; qualifying distributions, $340,357.
Limitations: Giving on a national basis.
Application information: Application form not required.
Officers and Trustees:* Alexander Hasenfeld,* Pres.; Zissy Hasenfeld,* Treas.
EIN: 237017589
Codes: FD

33924
The M & E Foundation
(Formerly Moric & Elsa Bistricer Foundation)
c/o Moric Bistricer
4611 12th Ave.
Brooklyn, NY 11219

Established in 1988 in NY.
Donor(s): Moric Bistricer, Elsa Bistricer.
Financial data (yr. ended 04/30/01): Grants paid, $340,087; assets, $6,589,706 (M); expenditures, $359,563; qualifying distributions, $337,134.
Limitations: Applications not accepted.
Application information: Contributes only to pre-selected organizations.
Officer: Moric Bistricer, Mgr.
EIN: 112914881
Codes: FD

33925
Adolph and Esther Gottlieb Foundation, Inc.
380 W. Broadway
New York, NY 10012-5115 (212) 226-0581
FAX: (212) 226-0584
Contact: Sheila Ross, Grants Mgr.

Established in 1976 in NY.
Donor(s): Adolph Gottlieb,‡ Esther Gottlieb.‡
Financial data (yr. ended 06/30/01): Grants paid, $340,000; assets, $25,802,914 (M); gifts received, $223,341; expenditures, $757,082; qualifying distributions, $705,274.
Limitations: Giving on a national basis.
Publications: Informational brochure, application guidelines.
Application information: Emergency grant applications may be submitted and reviewed year-round. Application form required.
Officers and Directors:* Dick Netzer,* Pres.; Sanford Hirsch,* Secy.-Treas.; Lynda Benglis, Charlotta Kotik, Robert Mangold.
EIN: 132853957
Codes: FD, GTI

33926
The Ottinger Foundation
80 Broad St., 17th Fl.
New York, NY 10004 (212) 764-3878
FAX: (212) 764-4298; E-mail: info@ottingerfoundation.org; URL: http://www.ottingerfoundation.org
Contact: Michele Lord, Exec. Dir.

Incorporated in 1945 in NY.
Donor(s): Lawrence Ottinger.‡
Financial data (yr. ended 12/31/99): Grants paid, $340,000; assets, $7,971,507 (M); gifts received, $2,310,344; expenditures, $485,316; qualifying distributions, $340,000.
Limitations: Giving on a national basis.
Application information: Guidelines available on website. Accepts NNG Common Grant Application Form. Proposals for the environment and democratic participation by solicitation only. Application form not required.
Officers and Trustees:* Lawrence Ottinger,* Chair.; Richard L. Ottinger,* V.P.; Kim Baptiste,* Secy.-Treas.; Michael Goldberg, Karen Heath, Jennifer Ottinger, June Godfrey Ottinger, LeaAnne Ottinger, Randy Ottinger, Ronald Ottinger, Cinthia Schuman, Peter Smith, Betsy Taylor.
EIN: 136118423
Codes: FD

33927
Franconia Foundation, Inc.
c/o Eli Robins
1333 Broadway, Ste. 730
New York, NY 10018

Established in 1991 in NY.
Donor(s): Willy Beer, Rachel Beer.
Financial data (yr. ended 10/31/01): Grants paid, $339,763; assets, $1,218,927 (M); expenditures, $470,248; qualifying distributions, $340,894.
Limitations: Applications not accepted. Giving primarily in NY.
Application information: Contributes only to pre-selected organizations.
Officer: Willy Beer, Mgr.
EIN: 133646294
Codes: FD

33928
Morris and Anna Propp Sons Fund, Inc.
405 Park Ave., Ste. 1103
New York, NY 10022

Incorporated in 1944 in NY.
Donor(s): Members of the Propp family.
Financial data (yr. ended 12/31/01): Grants paid, $339,530; assets, $6,662,859 (M); gifts received, $118,363; expenditures, $361,437; qualifying distributions, $349,369.
Limitations: Applications not accepted. Giving primarily in NY.
Application information: Contributes only to pre-selected organizations.
Directors: Ephraim Propp, M.J. Propp, Morris S. Propp.
EIN: 136099110
Codes: FD

33929
YSF Foundation
c/o Joseph Furst
1244 49th St.
Brooklyn, NY 11219

Established in 1995 in NY.
Donor(s): 1113 Walton Ave. Corp.
Financial data (yr. ended 12/31/99): Grants paid, $339,450; assets, $386,980 (M); gifts received, $308,000; expenditures, $340,910; qualifying distributions, $338,470.
Limitations: Applications not accepted.
Application information: Contributes only to pre-selected organizations.
Trustees: Samuel Finkelstein, Shaindel Finkelstein.
EIN: 113271689
Codes: FD

33930
East Hill Foundation
6500 Main St., Ste. 6
Williamsville, NY 14221 (716) 204-0204
FAX: (716) 204-0208; E-mail: easthill@easthillfdn.org
Contact: Michele R. Schmidt, Admin. Dir.

Established in 1986 in NY.
Donor(s): Wilson Greatbatch, Eleanor Greatbatch.
Financial data (yr. ended 12/30/01): Grants paid, $339,436; assets, $13,574,350 (M); gifts received, $191; expenditures, $564,249; qualifying distributions, $473,251; giving activities include $7,887 for programs.
Limitations: Giving primarily in western NY.
Publications: Informational brochure (including application guidelines).
Application information: Only 1 application per grant cycle. Application form required.
Directors: Ami Greatbatch, Eleanor Greatbatch, Warren Greatbatch, Stanton H. Hudson, Jr., Michele R. Schmidt, John E. Siegel.
EIN: 161441497
Codes: FD

33931
The Murray & Irene Pergament Foundation
14 St. Andrews Ct.
Old Westbury, NY 11568

Established in 1991 in NY.
Donor(s): Irene Pergament, Murray Pergament.
Financial data (yr. ended 12/31/99): Grants paid, $339,080; assets, $2,742,911 (M); expenditures, $360,455; qualifying distributions, $339,080.
Limitations: Applications not accepted. Giving primarily in NY.
Application information: Contributes only to pre-selected organizations.
Trustees: Irene Pergament, Murray Pergament.
EIN: 136980687
Codes: FD

33932
Joan & Alan Ades-Taub Foundation, Inc.
1095 Park Ave., Apt. 8D
New York, NY 10128

Established in 1997.
Donor(s): Alan M. Ades.
Financial data (yr. ended 12/31/01): Grants paid, $339,000; assets, $840,576 (M); gifts received, $339,000; expenditures, $339,057; qualifying distributions, $339,000.
Limitations: Applications not accepted. Giving on a national basis, with emphasis in NY.
Application information: Unsolicited requests for funds not accepted.
Officers: Joan Ades, Pres.; Alan M. Ades, V.P.
EIN: 113293314
Codes: FD

33933
The Rechler Family Foundation, Inc.
(Formerly Morton & Beverley Rechler Foundation, Inc.)
c/o Katzman, Weinstein & Co., LLP
131 Jericho Tpke., Ste. 400
Jericho, NY 11753 (516) 333-6881
Contact: Morton Rechler, Pres.

Established in 1986 in FL.
Donor(s): Morton Rechler, Beverley Rechler, Yvetta Rechler-Newman, Bennett Rechler, Hannah Rabinowitz.
Financial data (yr. ended 12/31/00): Grants paid, $338,633; assets, $6,521,963 (M); gifts received, $1,362,847; expenditures, $338,919; qualifying distributions, $338,633.

33933—NEW YORK

Limitations: Applications not accepted. Giving primarily in New York, NY.
Application information: Contributes only to pre-selected organizations.
Officers: Morton Rechler, Pres.; Beverley Rechler, Secy.; Bennett Rechler, Treas.
Directors: Hannah Rabinowitz, Yvetta Rechler-Newman.
EIN: 592828631
Codes: FD

33934
Neuwirth Foundation, Inc.
c/o Cummings & Carroll
175 Great Neck Rd., Ste. 405
Great Neck, NY 11021-3366

Established in 1991 in NY.
Donor(s): Marvin R. Neuwirth.
Financial data (yr. ended 08/31/01): Grants paid, $338,300; assets, $5,378,725 (M); expenditures, $347,161; qualifying distributions, $332,318.
Limitations: Applications not accepted. Giving primarily in NY.
Application information: Contributes only to pre-selected organizations.
Officers and Directors:* Marvin R. Neuwirth,* Pres.; Barbara Braun,* V.P.; Felice Neuwirth,* Secy.; Anthony Braun,* Treas.
EIN: 113048776
Codes: FD

33935
The Lindmor Foundation
(Formerly The Reimers Family Foundation)
c/o BCRS Assocs. LLC
100 Wall St., 11th Fl.
New York, NY 10005

Established in 1991 in NJ.
Donor(s): Arthur J. Reimers III.
Financial data (yr. ended 12/31/01): Grants paid, $337,580; assets, $6,000,481 (M); gifts received, $1,924,154; expenditures, $393,504; qualifying distributions, $330,212.
Limitations: Applications not accepted. Giving primarily in Greenwich, CT, and New York, NY.
Application information: Contributes only to pre-selected organizations.
Trustees: Arthur J. Reimers III, Lindsay Reimers.
EIN: 133636205
Codes: FD

33936
Virginia Cretella Mars Foundation
c/o Brown Brothers Harriman Trust Co.
63 Wall St.
New York, NY 10005 (212) 493-8000
FAX: (212) 493-8206
Contact: Anna T. Korniczky, Acct.

Established in 1994.
Financial data (yr. ended 12/31/01): Grants paid, $337,378; assets, $6,863,306 (M); gifts received, $472,254; expenditures, $372,697; qualifying distributions, $342,966.
Limitations: Applications not accepted. Giving primarily in NY.
Application information: Contributes only to pre-selected organizations.
Officers: Pamela M. Wright, Pres.; Marijke E. Mars, V.P.; Valerie A. Mars, Secy.; Victoria B. Mars, Treas.
EIN: 133798973
Codes: FD

33937
Daedalus Foundation, Inc.
c/o Starr & Co.
350 Park Ave.
New York, NY 10022

Established in 1988 in NY.
Donor(s): L. Diane Sawyer, Mike Nichols.
Financial data (yr. ended 12/31/00): Grants paid, $337,363; assets, $24,177 (M); gifts received, $340,000; expenditures, $337,502; qualifying distributions, $337,502.
Limitations: Applications not accepted. Giving on a national basis.
Application information: Contributes only to pre-selected organizations.
Officers: Mike Nichols, Chair.; L. Diane Sawyer, Pres.; Ed Bradley, Treas.
EIN: 133489057
Codes: FD

33938
Roger Kresge Foundation, Inc.
P.O. Box 8566
Endwell, NY 13762-8566 (607) 786-0968
Contact: Carol Kresge, Exec. Dir.

Established in 1970 in NY.
Donor(s): Roger L. Kresge.‡
Financial data (yr. ended 12/31/01): Grants paid, $337,284; assets, $4,159,621 (M); expenditures, $431,758; qualifying distributions, $391,904.
Limitations: Giving primarily in Broome County, NY.
Publications: Informational brochure (including application guidelines), application guidelines.
Application information: Application form required.
Officers and Directors:* Carol Kresge,* Pres. and Exec. Dir.; Darwin R. Wales,* Secy.; Robert W. Carey, James Lee, Robert Lindridge, John Spence.
EIN: 237081254
Codes: FD

33939
The Starker Family Foundation, Inc.
c/o Spear, Leeds & Kellogg
120 Broadway, 8th Fl.
New York, NY 10271

Donor(s): Steven Starker.
Financial data (yr. ended 09/30/01): Grants paid, $337,274; assets, $2,952,082 (M); gifts received, $2,881,138; expenditures, $368,024; qualifying distributions, $337,426.
Limitations: Applications not accepted.
Application information: Contributes only to pre-selected organizations.
Officers: Steven Starker, Pres. and Treas.; Farrel Starker, V.P.; Stuart Dix, Ray Starker.
EIN: 133986718
Codes: FD

33940
The Harold & Blanche Schechter Foundation, Inc.
2600 Nostrand Ave.
Brooklyn, NY 11210

Established in 1999 in NY.
Donor(s): Saul Schechter, Dov Schechter, Benjamin Brecher, Richard Schechter.
Financial data (yr. ended 06/30/01): Grants paid, $337,268; assets, $1,247,507 (M); gifts received, $433,601; expenditures, $347,492; qualifying distributions, $334,735.
Limitations: Applications not accepted. Giving primarily in Brooklyn, NY.
Application information: Contributes only to pre-selected organizations.

Officers: Saul Schechter, Pres.; Benjamin Brecher, V.P.; Richard Schechter, V.P.; Dov Schechter, Treas.
EIN: 113494145
Codes: FD

33941
Jandon Foundation
1114 Ave. of the Americas
New York, NY 10036-7703
Contact: Donald Cecil, Pres.

Established in 1966 in NY.
Donor(s): Donald Cecil.
Financial data (yr. ended 12/31/01): Grants paid, $337,040; assets, $7,445,849 (M); expenditures, $363,333; qualifying distributions, $332,167.
Limitations: Applications not accepted. Giving primarily in CT, MA, and Westchester County and New York, NY.
Application information: Contributes only to pre-selected organizations.
Officers and Directors:* Donald Cecil,* Pres.; Alec Cecil,* V.P.; Leslie Cecil,* Secy.; Jane Cecil,* Treas.
EIN: 136199442
Codes: FD

33942
Jerome L. Stern Family Foundation, Inc.
(Formerly Jerome L. and Jane Stern Foundation, Inc.)
331 Madison Ave., 8th Fl.
New York, NY 10017

Incorporated in 1944 in NY.
Donor(s): Jerome L. Stern, Ronald A. Stern, members of the Stern family.
Financial data (yr. ended 02/28/01): Grants paid, $336,769; assets, $9,761,371 (M); gifts received, $500,000; expenditures, $455,503; qualifying distributions, $327,792.
Limitations: Applications not accepted. Giving primarily in New York, NY.
Application information: Contributes only to pre-selected organizations.
Officers and Directors:* Jerome L. Stern, Pres. and Secy.; Geoffrey S. Stern,* Treas.; Ellen L. Stern, Ronald A. Stern.
EIN: 136127063

33943
Phaedrus Foundation
c/o Peyser & Alexander Mgmt.
500 5th Ave., Ste. 2700
New York, NY 10110
Contact: T. Buckner, Pres.

Established in 1991 in NY.
Donor(s): Foundation for the Needs of Others, Inc.
Financial data (yr. ended 12/31/01): Grants paid, $336,650; assets, $3,978,491 (M); expenditures, $393,701; qualifying distributions, $335,499.
Limitations: Applications not accepted. Giving primarily in New York, NY.
Application information: Unsolicited requests for funds not accepted.
Officers and Director:* Thomas W. Buckner,* Pres.; Kamala Cesar Buckner, Secy.
EIN: 223120375
Codes: FD

33944
Daniel J. and Estrellita Brodsky Foundation
c/o The Brodsky Organization
400 W. 59th St.
New York, NY 10019-1105
Contact: Daniel Brodsky, Tr.

Established in 1999 in NY.
Donor(s): Daniel Brodsky.

Financial data (yr. ended 12/31/01): Grants paid, $336,234; assets, $725,639 (M); gifts received, $500,000; expenditures, $336,234; qualifying distributions, $336,234.
Trustees: Daniel Brodsky, Estrellita Brodsky.
EIN: 134065150
Codes: FD

33945
Schulhof Family Foundation
c/o Michael Schulhof
375 Park Ave., Ste. 1506
New York, NY 10152

Established in 2000 in NY.
Donor(s): Michael P. Schulhof.
Financial data (yr. ended 11/30/01): Grants paid, $335,648; assets, $2,822,997 (M); gifts received, $500,000; expenditures, $430,935; qualifying distributions, $0.
Application information: Application form not required.
Trustees: Michael P. Schulhof, Paola Schulhof.
EIN: 134150938
Codes: FD

33946
Mostyn Foundation, Inc.
c/o James C. Edwards & Co., Inc.
570 Lexington Ave., 29th Fl.
New York, NY 10022
Contact: Arthur B. Choate, Pres.

Trust established in 1949 in NY; incorporated in 1965.
Donor(s): Harvey D. Gibson,‡ Mrs. Harvey D. Gibson,‡ Whitney Bourne Atwood.
Financial data (yr. ended 12/31/01): Grants paid, $335,375; assets, $6,142,149 (M); expenditures, $421,039; qualifying distributions, $330,876.
Limitations: Applications not accepted. Giving in the U.S., with emphasis on FL and NY.
Application information: Contributes only to pre-selected organizations.
Officers: Arthur B. Choate, Pres.; Rev. Charles Newbery, V.P.; Peter Megargee Brown, Secy.-Treas.
EIN: 136171217
Codes: FD

33947
Butlea Foundation
c/o Subaru
6 Ramland Rd.
Orangeburg, NY 10962

Established in 1986 in NY.
Financial data (yr. ended 12/31/01): Grants paid, $335,300; assets, $1,707,396 (M); expenditures, $342,721; qualifying distributions, $335,300.
Limitations: Applications not accepted. Giving primarily in the Northeast.
Application information: Contributes only to pre-selected organizations.
Trustees: Michael K. Lewis, C. David Sammons.
EIN: 133397690
Codes: FD

33948
Norman M. Morris Foundation, Inc.
106 Corporate Park Dr.
White Plains, NY 10604 (914) 694-2000

Incorporated in 1947 in NY.
Donor(s): Norman M. Morris.‡
Financial data (yr. ended 12/31/01): Grants paid, $334,826; assets, $9,746,229 (M); gifts received, $442,502; expenditures, $407,987; qualifying distributions, $334,826.
Limitations: Giving primarily in NY.
Application information: Application form not required.
Officers and Trustees:* Arline J. Lubin, Pres.; Marvin Lubin,* V.P.; Robert E. Morris,* Secy.-Treas.; Kenneth A. Lubin, Leland M. Morris.
EIN: 136119134
Codes: FD

33949
The Karetsky Family Memorial Fund & Seth Kahn Foundation, Inc.
(Formerly Seth Kahn Foundation, Inc.)
c/o Starr & Co.
350 Park Ave.
New York, NY 10022

Established in 1987 in NY; re-established in 1992 in CO.
Donor(s): Herman Kahn Foundation, F. Seth Kahn.‡
Financial data (yr. ended 03/31/01): Grants paid, $334,750; assets, $729,171 (M); expenditures, $334,223; qualifying distributions, $335,268.
Limitations: Applications not accepted.
Application information: Contributes only to pre-selected organizations.
Officers: S. Sidney Kahn, Pres.; Geraldine K. Karetsky, V.P. and Secy.-Treas.
EIN: 841193115
Codes: FD

33950
Babbitt Family Charitable Trust
c/o Davis & Graber
150 E. 58th St., 22nd Fl.
New York, NY 10155

Established in 1991 in NY.
Donor(s): Edward Babbitt.
Financial data (yr. ended 06/30/01): Grants paid, $334,650; assets, $6,772,062 (M); gifts received, $19,670; expenditures, $356,074; qualifying distributions, $333,273.
Limitations: Applications not accepted. Giving primarily in NY.
Application information: Contributes only to pre-selected organizations.
Trustee: Susan Babbitt.
EIN: 136975951
Codes: FD

33951
Fink Foundation, Inc.
501 5th Ave., Rm. 1600
New York, NY 10017-7853 (212) 687-8098
Contact: Romie Shapiro, Pres.

Incorporated in 1956 in NY.
Donor(s): David Fink, Nathan Fink.
Financial data (yr. ended 12/31/01): Grants paid, $334,500; assets, $1,479,658 (M); expenditures, $341,221; qualifying distributions, $339,760.
Limitations: Giving on a national basis.
Officers: Romie Shapiro, Pres.; David Levitan, V.P.; Harold Fink, Secy.; Stanley Dalnefoff, Treas.
Directors: Charles Shanok, Seymour Zises.
EIN: 136135438
Codes: FD

33952
The Weitz Family Charitable Foundation
1 Sydney Rd.
Huntington, NY 11743

Established in 1997 in DE.
Donor(s): Perry Weitz.
Financial data (yr. ended 12/31/01): Grants paid, $334,109; assets, $195,551 (M); gifts received, $385,991; expenditures, $337,470; qualifying distributions, $334,813.
Limitations: Applications not accepted. Giving primarily in NY.
Application information: Contributes only to pre-selected organizations.
Officer and Director:* Perry Weitz,* Pres.
EIN: 113375476
Codes: FD

33953
The Ira M. Resnick Foundation, Inc.
133 E. 58th St.
New York, NY 10022 (212) 223-1009
Contact: Ira M. Resnick, Pres.

Established in 1994.
Donor(s): Ira M. Resnick.
Financial data (yr. ended 05/31/02): Grants paid, $334,097; assets, $8,976 (M); gifts received, $369,365; expenditures, $366,105; qualifying distributions, $334,096.
Limitations: Giving primarily in NY.
Application information: Application form not required.
Officers: Ira M. Resnick, Pres.; Gilbert A. Wang, Secy.-Treas.
Director: Charles F. Crames.
EIN: 133775995
Codes: FD

33954
Beth Nash & Joshua Nash Charitable Trust
(Formerly Joshua Nash Charitable Foundation)
c/o Ulysses Partners, LP
280 Park Ave., 21st Fl.
New York, NY 10017

Established in 1989 in NY.
Donor(s): Joshua Nash.
Financial data (yr. ended 06/30/01): Grants paid, $334,054; assets, $2,756,267 (M); expenditures, $338,304; qualifying distributions, $334,662.
Limitations: Applications not accepted. Giving primarily in New York, NY.
Application information: Contributes only to pre-selected organizations.
Trustees: Jack Nash, Joshua Nash.
EIN: 133560261
Codes: FD

33955
The Furtherance Fund, Inc.
c/o Davidson, Dawson & Clark
330 Madison Ave.
New York, NY 10017

Established in 1965 in NY.
Donor(s): Robert G. Olmsted, Robert M. Olmsted, Louise Olmsted.‡
Financial data (yr. ended 03/31/01): Grants paid, $334,000; assets, $5,977,167 (M); expenditures, $360,234; qualifying distributions, $328,107.
Limitations: Applications not accepted. Giving on a national basis.
Application information: Contributes only to pre-selected organizations.
Officers: Robert M. Olmsted, Pres. and Treas.; Nancy Olmsted Kaehr, V.P.; Robert G. Olmsted, V.P.; William H. Miller, Jr., Secy.
EIN: 136195082
Codes: FD

33956
The Freedman Family Fund
(Formerly The Eisner Family Fund)
c/o Executive Monetary Mgmt.
220 E. 42nd St.
New York, NY 10017

Established in 1988 in NY.
Donor(s): Michael D. Eisner.
Financial data (yr. ended 12/31/01): Grants paid, $333,805; assets, $4,483,497 (M); expenditures, $381,069; qualifying distributions, $333,495.

Limitations: Applications not accepted. Giving on a national basis.
Application information: Contributes only to pre-selected organizations.
Trustees: Douglas M. Freedman, Margot E. Freedman, Amy F. Lieberman.
EIN: 133486425
Codes: FD

33957
The Shalom Ish Foundation
c/o Saul N. Friedman & Co.
6201 15th Ave., Apt. 4L
Brooklyn, NY 11219
Contact: Saul N. Friedman, Dir.

Established in 1998.
Donor(s): Ish Shalom,‡ Saul N. Friedman, Ish Shalom Trust, Maison Grande Assocs.
Financial data (yr. ended 09/30/01): Grants paid, $333,600; assets, $625,741 (M); gifts received, $74,931; expenditures, $338,692; qualifying distributions, $333,600.
Director: Saul N. Friedman.
EIN: 113405442
Codes: FD

33958
Chasanoff Foundation, Inc.
c/o Michael J. Chasanoff
2 Jericho Plz.
Jericho, NY 11753-1658

Established in 1989 in NY.
Donor(s): Chasco Co., Hubspot Co., Allan Chasanoff, Michael J. Chasanoff, Nancy Chasanoff, Robert Chasanoff, Judith Chasanoff, Stephen Chasanoff.
Financial data (yr. ended 06/30/02): Grants paid, $333,422; assets, $11,678 (M); gifts received, $369,500; expenditures, $361,188; qualifying distributions, $361,187.
Limitations: Applications not accepted. Giving primarily in NY.
Application information: Contributes only to pre-selected organizations.
Officers and Directors:* Michael Chasanoff,* Pres.; Nancy Chasanoff Butler,* V.P.; Judith Chasanoff,* V.P.; Robert Chasanoff,* V.P.; Stephen Chasanoff,* V.P.; Allan Chasanoff,* Secy.-Treas.
EIN: 112978524
Codes: FD

33959
N. S. Meyer-Raeburn Foundation, Inc.
42 E. 20th St.
New York, NY 10003-1381

Donor(s): Rebecca Goodman.
Financial data (yr. ended 12/31/01): Grants paid, $332,273; assets, $88,136 (M); expenditures, $332,820; qualifying distributions, $332,273.
Limitations: Applications not accepted. Giving on a national basis.
Application information: Contributes only to pre-selected organizations.
Officers and Trustee:* Robert A. Raeburn,* Pres.; Alex Navarro, Secy.
EIN: 136097247

33960
Plymouth Foundation
c/o I.W. Burnham II, Burnham Securities, Inc.
1325 Ave. of the Americas, 17th Fl.
New York, NY 10019-6026

Established in 1957 in NY.
Donor(s): members of the Burnham family.
Financial data (yr. ended 12/31/01): Grants paid, $332,090; assets, $246,119 (M); gifts received, $334,476; expenditures, $340,106; qualifying distributions, $334,090.
Limitations: Applications not accepted. Giving primarily in NY and PA.
Application information: Contributes only to pre-selected organizations.
Officers and Directors:* I.W. Burnham II,* Pres.; Jon Burnham,* V.P.
EIN: 136163070
Codes: FD

33961
Andrew L. Clark Family Charitable Trust
(Formerly Clark Family Charitable Trust)
c/o The Bank of New York, Tax. Dept.
1 Wall St., 28th Fl.
New York, NY 10286
Application address: c/o The Bank of New York, 1290 Ave. of the Americas, New York, NY 10104
Contact: Grace Allen

Established in 1989 in NJ.
Donor(s): Andrew L. Clark.
Financial data (yr. ended 08/31/01): Grants paid, $331,000; assets, $5,284,073 (M); expenditures, $382,323; qualifying distributions, $331,395.
Limitations: Giving primarily in Boston, MA, South Orange, NJ, and New York, NY.
Application information: Application form not required.
Trustee: The Bank of New York.
EIN: 136948420
Codes: FD

33962
The David Ekstein Foundation, Inc.
17 Hayes Ct., Unit 201
Monroe, NY 10950

Financial data (yr. ended 12/31/01): Grants paid, $331,000; assets, $822,524 (M); expenditures, $363,237; qualifying distributions, $331,000.
Limitations: Applications not accepted. Giving primarily in NY.
Application information: Contributes only to pre-selected organizations.
Directors: David Ekstein, Herman Gluck, David Weisz.
EIN: 133954105
Codes: FD

33963
George & Adele Klein Foundation
c/o Park Tower Realty Corp.
499 Park Ave.
New York, NY 10022

Established in 1968 in NY.
Donor(s): Adele Klein, George Klein.
Financial data (yr. ended 03/31/02): Grants paid, $329,224; assets, $1,458,038 (M); gifts received, $1,399,975; expenditures, $329,466; qualifying distributions, $329,224.
Limitations: Applications not accepted.
Application information: Contributes only to pre-selected organizations.
Officers: George Klein, Pres.; Adele Klein, V.P.
EIN: 136279924

33964
C. L. C. Kramer Foundation
P.O. Box 431
Millerton, NY 12546-0431

Established in 1966.
Donor(s): Catherine Kramer.‡
Financial data (yr. ended 09/30/01): Grants paid, $329,000; assets, $8,110,689 (M); expenditures, $400,829; qualifying distributions, $339,506.
Limitations: Applications not accepted. Giving primarily in New York, NY.
Application information: Contributes only to pre-selected organizations.
Officers: Robert Zabelle, Pres.; Charles Looker, Secy.; David Marks, Treas.
EIN: 136226513
Codes: FD

33965
Jeffrey and Nancy Lane Foundation
c/o W. Michael Reickert, The Ayco Co., LP
P.O. Box 8019
Ballston Spa, NY 12020-8019

Established in 1987 in NY.
Donor(s): Jeffrey B. Lane.
Financial data (yr. ended 12/31/01): Grants paid, $328,708; assets, $148,410 (M); gifts received, $509,688; expenditures, $333,037; qualifying distributions, $328,708.
Limitations: Applications not accepted. Giving primarily in NY.
Application information: Contributes only to pre-selected organizations.
Officers: Jeffrey B. Lane, Pres. and Treas.; Nancy Z. Lane, Secy.
EIN: 112842376
Codes: FD

33966
The Richard Mather Fund
4132 W. Shore Manor
Jamesville, NY 13078
Contact: Stephen E. Chase, Tr.

Trust established in 1955 in NY.
Donor(s): Flora Mather Hosmer,‡ R.C. Hosmer, Jr.,‡ Hosmer Descendants Trust.
Financial data (yr. ended 12/31/00): Grants paid, $328,600; assets, $4,896,597 (M); expenditures, $374,933; qualifying distributions, $328,600.
Limitations: Giving primarily in central NY, with emphasis on Syracuse.
Publications: Informational brochure (including application guidelines).
Application information: Funds substantially committed. Application form not required.
Trustees: Stephen E. Chase, S. Sterling McMillan III, Gay Pomeroy, Elizabeth H. Schaefer.
EIN: 156018423
Codes: FD

33967
May Ellen and Gerald Ritter Foundation
9411 Shore Rd.
Brooklyn, NY 11209-6755
Contact: Emma Daniels, Pres.

Foundation established in 1980 in NY.
Donor(s): Gerald Ritter,‡ May Ellen Ritter.‡
Financial data (yr. ended 12/31/00): Grants paid, $328,000; assets, $13,125,115 (M); expenditures, $578,515; qualifying distributions, $396,809.
Limitations: Giving primarily in NY.
Application information: Application form not required.
Officers: Emma Daniels, Pres.; Vincent Rohan, V.P.; Helen Rohan, Secy.; Sophie Distanovich, Treas.
EIN: 136114269
Codes: FD

33968
The Woodcock No. 3 Foundation
30 Rockefeller Plz., Rm. 5600
New York, NY 10112-0002
Application address: 19 Polhemus Pl., Brooklyn, NY 11215
Contact: Lindsay Davidson Shea, Tr.

Established in 1991 in NY.

Donor(s): P.W. Guth Charitable Lead Unitrust No. 3, P.W. Guth Charitable Lead Unitrust No. 4, P.W. Guth Charitable Lead Unitrust No. 5, Polly W. Guth.
Financial data (yr. ended 11/30/01): Grants paid, $327,663; assets, $63 (M); gifts received, $196,043; expenditures, $333,510; qualifying distributions, $326,069.
Limitations: Giving primarily in the New York, NY, area.
Application information: Application form required.
Trustees: Lindsay Davidson Shea, Richard T. Watson.
EIN: 133651420
Codes: FD

33969
Tatiana Piankova Foundation
570 Park Ave.
New York, NY 10021 (212) 758-7764
Contact: Mildred C. Brinn, Pres. and Treas.

Established about 1983 in NY.
Donor(s): Susan Polachek.
Financial data (yr. ended 07/31/01): Grants paid, $325,850; assets, $5,220,391 (M); expenditures, $378,522; qualifying distributions, $348,685.
Limitations: Giving primarily in New York, NY.
Officers and Directors:* Mildred C. Brinn,* Pres. and Treas.; Peter F. De Gaetano,* Secy.
EIN: 133142090
Codes: FD

33970
The D J McManus Foundation
106 W. 78th St.
New York, NY 10024

Established in 1999 in NY.
Donor(s): Deborah McManus.
Financial data (yr. ended 12/31/01): Grants paid, $325,265; assets, $8,121,875 (M); gifts received, $3,893,049; expenditures, $388,811; qualifying distributions, $315,650.
Limitations: Applications not accepted. Giving primarily in NY.
Application information: Unsolicited requests for funds not accepted.
Officers: Deborah McManus, Pres.; Sophie McManus, V.P.; Jason D. McManus, Secy.-Treas.
EIN: 134080144
Codes: FD

33971
The Lifebridge Foundation, Inc.
Times Sq. Station
P.O. Box 793
New York, NY 10108
E-mail: LB457@aol.com or lifebridgenyc@aol.com; URL: http://www.lifebridge.org
Contact: Larry Elwood Auld, Prog. Dir.

Established in 1992 in CT.
Donor(s): Paul M. Hancock.‡
Financial data (yr. ended 12/31/01): Grants paid, $325,119; assets, $5,832,941 (M); expenditures, $569,399; qualifying distributions, $567,923.
Limitations: Applications not accepted. Giving on a national and international basis.
Publications: Occasional report, newsletter.
Application information: Unsolicited applications not considered; applicants must be invited to submit proposal.
Officers and Directors:* Evelyn W. Hancock,* Chair.; Barbara L. Valocore,* Pres.; Jane A. Southall,* V.P.; Larry Elwood Auld,* Secy. and Prog. Dir.
EIN: 061356766

Codes: FD, GTI

33972
David B. Kriser Foundation, Inc.
c/o Singer, Netter, Dowd & Berman
745 5th Ave.
New York, NY 10151

Established around 1977 in NY.
Donor(s): David B. Kriser.‡
Financial data (yr. ended 12/31/01): Grants paid, $325,000; assets, $9,482,169 (M); expenditures, $429,962; qualifying distributions, $325,500.
Limitations: Applications not accepted. Giving primarily in NY.
Application information: Contributes only to pre-selected organizations.
Trustees: Steve Danson, Hector G. Dowd, Richard Netter.
EIN: 132932531
Codes: FD

33973
The Valentine Charitable Foundation, Inc.
61 Broadway, 18th Fl.
New York, NY 10006-2794

Established in 1998 in FL.
Donor(s): Audrey I. Clark Charitable Lead Trust.
Financial data (yr. ended 12/31/01): Grants paid, $324,380; assets, $395,304 (M); gifts received, $696,301; expenditures, $330,587; qualifying distributions, $324,380.
Limitations: Applications not accepted.
Application information: Contributes only to pre-selected organizations.
Officers: Audrey I. Clark, Pres.; Peter Clark, V.P. and Treas.; Sandra C. Moore, Secy.
Director: Reed Clark.
EIN: 223603584

33974
The Sherrill Foundation
c/o H.V. Sherrill
1 Sutton Pl. S.
New York, NY 10022

Established around 1980.
Donor(s): H. Virgil Sherrill, Betty S. Sherrill.
Financial data (yr. ended 10/31/01): Grants paid, $323,630; assets, $3,252,399 (M); expenditures, $328,893; qualifying distributions, $321,403.
Limitations: Applications not accepted. Giving primarily in Hobe Sound, FL, and NY.
Application information: Contributes only to pre-selected organizations.
Officers and Trustees:* H. Virgil Sherrill,* Pres.; Ann Sherrill Pyne, V.P.; Betty S. Sherrill,* V.P.; Stephen Sherrill, V.P.; Joan Wells, V.P.
EIN: 136112730
Codes: FD

33975
The Deane A. and John D. Gilliam Foundation
(Formerly John D. Gilliam Foundation)
c/o BCRS Assocs., LLC
67 Wall St., 8th Fl.
New York, NY 10001

Established in 1978 in NY.
Donor(s): John D. Gilliam, Deane A. Gilliam.
Financial data (yr. ended 03/31/01): Grants paid, $322,582; assets, $7,009,111 (M); gifts received, $380,519; expenditures, $405,696; qualifying distributions, $328,004.
Limitations: Applications not accepted. Giving primarily in the Mount Kisco and New York, NY areas.
Application information: Contributes only to pre-selected organizations.

Trustees: Peter M. Fahey, Donald R. Gant, Deane A. Gilliam, John D. Gilliam, Stephanae D. Lariviere.
EIN: 132967490
Codes: FD

33976
The Progress Education Foundation
c/o M&T Bank
1 M&T Plz., 8th Fl.
Buffalo, NY 14203
Application address: c/o Grant Mgr., P.O. Box 810, Carlisle, PA 17013

Established in 1978.
Donor(s): David E. Lutz, June B. Lutz.
Financial data (yr. ended 12/31/00): Grants paid, $322,500; assets, $916,577 (M); expenditures, $342,624; qualifying distributions, $318,412.
Limitations: Giving primarily in Carlisle, PA.
Application information: Application form not required.
Trustees: David E. Lutz, June B. Lutz, M & T Bank.
EIN: 232053536
Codes: FD

33977
The Park B. Smith and Carol Smith Family Foundation
295 5th Ave.
New York, NY 10016

Established in 1994 in NY.
Donor(s): Park B. Smith, Carol Smith.‡
Financial data (yr. ended 12/31/99): Grants paid, $322,295; assets, $7,887,961 (M); gifts received, $7,580,000; expenditures, $322,718; qualifying distributions, $322,295.
Limitations: Applications not accepted.
Application information: Contributes only to pre-selected organizations.
Trustee: Park B. Smith.
EIN: 237050320
Codes: FD

33978
The Zankel Fund
(Formerly The Arthur & Nancy Zankel Foundation)
16 Bayberry Rd.
Armonk, NY 10504
Application address: c/o Arthur Zankel, 535 Madison Ave., New York, NY 10022, tel.: (212) 421-7548

Established in 1969.
Donor(s): Arthur Zankel.
Financial data (yr. ended 12/31/01): Grants paid, $322,186; assets, $13,069,833 (M); gifts received, $1,163,557; expenditures, $349,264; qualifying distributions, $322,186.
Limitations: Applications not accepted. Giving primarily in NY.
Trustee: Arthur Zankel.
EIN: 136284496
Codes: FD

33979
Hemmerdinger Foundation
c/o Warshaw, Burstein, et al., LLP
555 5th Ave.
New York, NY 10017-2416

Established in 1959 in DE.
Donor(s): H. Dale Hemmerdinger, The Hemmerdinger Corp.
Financial data (yr. ended 12/31/01): Grants paid, $322,067; assets, $1,690 (M); gifts received, $316,000; expenditures, $322,760; qualifying distributions, $322,760.

33979—NEW YORK

Limitations: Applications not accepted. Giving primarily in New York, NY.
Application information: Contributes only to pre-selected organizations.
Officers: H. Dale Hemmerdinger, Pres.; Elizabeth C. Hemmerdinger, V.P. and Secy.
EIN: 136278506
Codes: FD

33980
Kenneth Cole Foundation
c/o TAG Assocs.
75 Rockefeller Plz., Ste. 900
New York, NY 10019

Established in 1994 in NY.
Donor(s): Kenneth Cole.
Financial data (yr. ended 04/30/01): Grants paid, $322,055; assets, $6,657,988 (M); expenditures, $322,845; qualifying distributions, $322,380.
Limitations: Applications not accepted. Giving primarily in NY.
Application information: Contributes only to pre-selected organizations.
Trustees: Kenneth Cole, Maria Cuomo Cole.
EIN: 133799161
Codes: FD

33981
The Palmer Foundation, Inc.
c/o Manchester Capital Corp.
635 Madison Ave., 17th Fl.
New York, NY 10022-1009
Contact: James R. Palmer, Pres.

Established in 1988 in PA.
Donor(s): James R. Palmer.
Financial data (yr. ended 12/31/01): Grants paid, $321,692; assets, $4,249,520 (M); gifts received, $119,439; expenditures, $343,588; qualifying distributions, $320,263.
Limitations: Giving primarily in NY and PA.
Application information: Application form not required.
Officers: James R. Palmer, Pres.; Barbara R. Palmer, V.P.; Fred Grossman, Secy.-Treas.
EIN: 251568606
Codes: FD

33982
The Hales Family Foundation, Inc.
66 Brookwood Dr.
Briarcliff Manor, NY 10510-2041

Established in 1994 in NY.
Donor(s): Thomas E. Hales.
Financial data (yr. ended 12/31/01): Grants paid, $320,265; assets, $2,600,450 (M); expenditures, $323,628; qualifying distributions, $319,713.
Limitations: Applications not accepted. Giving primarily in NY.
Application information: Contributes only to pre-selected organizations.
Directors: Alice Hales, Terrance Hales, Thomas E. Hales.
EIN: 133801701
Codes: FD

33983
The Richard & Iris Abrons Foundation, Inc.
(Formerly The Richard & Mimi Abrons Foundation)
c/o Richard Abrons
437 Madison Ave.
New York, NY 10017

Established in 1964 in NY.
Donor(s): Richard Abrons, Mimi Abrons.
Financial data (yr. ended 12/31/01): Grants paid, $320,018; assets, $1,250,478 (M); gifts received, $137,500; expenditures, $320,354; qualifying distributions, $319,833.
Limitations: Applications not accepted. Giving primarily in New York, NY.
Application information: Contributes only to pre-selected organizations. Unsolicited requests for funds not accepted.
Officers and Directors:* Richard Abrons,* Pres.; Iris Abrons,* Secy.; John Abrons, Leslie Abrons, Peter Abrons.
EIN: 136184029
Codes: FD

33984
Harry Dent Family Foundation, Inc.
755 Center St.
P.O. Box 506
Lewiston, NY 14092-0506 (716) 754-8276
Contact: Jane E. Gailey, Secy.

Incorporated in 1954 in NY.
Donor(s): Harry M. Dent.‡
Financial data (yr. ended 10/31/01): Grants paid, $320,000; assets, $6,255,948 (M); expenditures, $467,881; qualifying distributions, $353,991.
Limitations: Applications not accepted. Giving limited to western NY.
Application information: Unsolicited requests for funds not accepted.
Officers and Directors:* Harry M. Dent III,* Pres.; Max Becker, Jr.,* V.P.; Jane E. Gailey,* Secy.; Susan L. Kimberly,* Treas.; Heidi Dent Arthurs, Dale B. Demyanick, Gloria G. Dent, Peter H. Dent, Georgia D. Knisley, Christopher D. Lenahan, Helen Dent Lenahan, Scott Strausser, Lisbeth L. Walls.
EIN: 160849923
Codes: FD

33985
Louis & Rose Klosk Fund
c/o JPMorgan Chase Bank
P.O. Box 31412, S-5
Rochester, NY 14603 (716) 258-5330

Trust established in 1970 in NY.
Donor(s): Louis Klosk.‡
Financial data (yr. ended 12/31/01): Grants paid, $320,000; assets, $6,558,628 (M); expenditures, $432,646; qualifying distributions, $326,395.
Limitations: Applications not accepted. Giving primarily in NY.
Application information: Contributes only to pre-selected organizations.
Trustees: Barry C. Cooper, Nathan R. Cooper, JPMorgan Chase Bank.
EIN: 136328994
Codes: FD

33986
Rheinstrom Hill Community Foundation
502 Union St.
Hudson, NY 12534-2427 (518) 828-1565
Contact: Richard Koskey, Pres.

Established around 1986 in NY.
Donor(s): Carroll Rheinstrom, Marjorie Rheinstrom.
Financial data (yr. ended 05/31/01): Grants paid, $319,750; assets, $1,739,503 (M); gifts received, $132,914; expenditures, $336,579; qualifying distributions, $317,333.
Limitations: Giving limited to Columbia County, NY.
Officers: Richard Koskey, Pres.; Edmond Herrington, V.P.; Jean Howe Lossi, Secy.
EIN: 141683989
Codes: FD

33987
Sarah Tod Fund
c/o U.S. Trust
114 W. 47th St.
New York, NY 10036

Established in 1956.
Financial data (yr. ended 12/31/99): Grants paid, $319,590; assets, $6,055,391 (M); expenditures, $336,887; qualifying distributions, $323,499.
Limitations: Applications not accepted. Giving primarily in CT and NY.
Application information: Contributes only to pre-selected organizations.
Trustee: Francis F. Randolph, Jr.
EIN: 131963936
Codes: FD

33988
The Christopher J. Carrera Foundation
c/o Goldman Sachs & Co.
85 Broad St., Tax Dept.
New York, NY 10004

Established in 1999 in NY.
Donor(s): Christopher J. Carrera.
Financial data (yr. ended 12/31/01): Grants paid, $319,106; assets, $220,105 (M); gifts received, $3,000; expenditures, $322,626; qualifying distributions, $322,595.
Limitations: Applications not accepted. Giving primarily in NY and PA.
Application information: Contributes only to pre-selected organizations.
Trustees: Christopher J. Carrera, Michael A. Carrera.
EIN: 134085897
Codes: FD

33989
The Mayrock Foundation, Inc.
70 Charles Lindbergh Blvd.
Uniondale, NY 11553
Contact: Isidore Mayrock, V.P.

Established in 1975.
Donor(s): M. Fortunoff of Westbury Corp., Harry Mayrock,‡ Birdie Samson, Isidore Mayrock, Rachel Sands, Elliot Mayrock.
Financial data (yr. ended 05/31/01): Grants paid, $318,945; assets, $766,112 (M); gifts received, $400,000; expenditures, $321,952; qualifying distributions, $319,246.
Limitations: Applications not accepted. Giving primarily in NY.
Application information: Unsolicited requests for funds not accepted.
Officers: Isidore Mayrock, V.P.; Rachel Sands, Secy.; Elliot Mayrock, Treas.
EIN: 112646558
Codes: FD

33990
The Keren Zichron Aron Foundation
c/o Weiss & Co.
22 W. 38th St.
New York, NY 10018-6204
Application address: 3442 Bedford Ave., Brooklyn, NY 11210-5235, tel.: (212) 302-3400
Contact: Abraham Weiss, Tr.

Established in 1996 in NY.
Donor(s): Abraham Weiss.
Financial data (yr. ended 12/31/00): Grants paid, $318,715; assets, $2,951 (M); gifts received, $123,050; expenditures, $318,818; qualifying distributions, $318,658.
Limitations: Giving primarily in Brooklyn, NY.
Application information: Application form not required.
Trustees: Jeffry Hollander, Abraham Weiss.

EIN: 137101887
Codes: FD

33991
Sandy Hill Foundation
P.O. Box 30
Hudson Falls, NY 12839 (518) 792-9314
Contact: Floyd H. Rourke, Tr.

Established in 1953.
Donor(s): J. Walter Juckett.
Financial data (yr. ended 08/31/01): Grants paid, $318,110; assets, $9,271,864 (M); expenditures, $410,109; qualifying distributions, $359,107.
Limitations: Giving primarily in the greater Hudson Falls, NY, area.
Application information: Scholarships paid directly to educational institutions on behalf of named recipients; application form must be typed or printed in black ink. Application form required.
Trustees: Nancy Juckett Brown, Floyd H. Rourke.
EIN: 146018954
Codes: FD, GTI

33992
Virginia Hunt Trust for Episcopal Charitable Institutions
c/o JPMorgan Chase Bank
1211 Ave. of the Americas, 38th Fl.
New York, NY 10036 (212) 789-5702
E-mail: neal_monica@JPmorgan.com
Contact: Monica Neal, V.P., JPMorgan Chase Bank

Donor(s): Virginia Hunt.‡
Financial data (yr. ended 03/31/02): Grants paid, $318,000; assets, $6,365,253 (M); expenditures, $377,383; qualifying distributions, $326,440.
Limitations: Giving primarily in NY and VT.
Application information: Application form not required.
Trustee: JPMorgan Chase Bank.
EIN: 237426415
Codes: FD

33993
The Lindemann Foundation, Inc.
111 W. 40th St., 12th Fl.
New York, NY 10018

Incorporated in 1943 in NY.
Donor(s): Joseph S. Lindemann,‡ Lilyan S. Lindemann.
Financial data (yr. ended 12/31/01): Grants paid, $317,552; assets, $6,079,503 (M); gifts received, $27,413; expenditures, $329,289; qualifying distributions, $295,230.
Limitations: Applications not accepted. Giving on a national basis.
Application information: Contributes only to pre-selected organizations.
Officers: Carol Lindemann Abend, Pres.; Lilyan S. Lindemann, V.P.; Barbara T. Lindemann, Secy.; George L. Lindemann, Treas.
EIN: 136140249
Codes: FD

33994
The Nakdimen Family Foundation Trust
7 Carlton Ln.
Monsey, NY 10952

Established in 1999.
Financial data (yr. ended 12/31/99): Grants paid, $317,145; assets, $15 (M); gifts received, $317,100; expenditures, $317,145; qualifying distributions, $317,145.
Trustees: Kenneth Nakdimen, Sheely Nakdimen.
EIN: 116509185
Codes: FD

33995
Douglas G. Anderson - Leigh R. Evans Foundation
c/o Richard L. Simons
1 Hardinge Dr.
Elmira, NY 14902 (607) 734-2281
Contact: Robert G. Prochnow, Pres.

Incorporated in 1960 in NY.
Donor(s): Hardinge, Inc.
Financial data (yr. ended 10/31/01): Grants paid, $316,800; assets, $1,634,206 (M); gifts received, $135,000; expenditures, $329,697; qualifying distributions, $336,224.
Limitations: Giving primarily in Elmira, NY.
Application information: Application form not required.
Officers and Trustees:* Robert G. Prochnow,* Pres.; Richard R. Schwartz,* V.P.; J. Philip Hunter,* Secy.; Richard L. Simons, Treas.; Robert E. Agan, John W. Bennett, Richard J. Cole, James L. Flynn, E. Martin Gibson, Douglas A. Greenlee.
EIN: 166024690
Codes: FD

33996
Mac and Sally Sands Foundation, Inc.
c/o Constellation Brands, Inc.
300 Willowbrook Office Park
Fairport, NY 14450

Established in 1959 in NY.
Donor(s): Robert Sands, Richard Sands.
Financial data (yr. ended 12/31/01): Grants paid, $316,483; assets, $2,094,120 (M); expenditures, $335,535; qualifying distributions, $315,091.
Limitations: Applications not accepted. Giving primarily in NY.
Application information: Contributes only to pre-selected organizations.
Officers: Robert Sands, Pres. and Treas.; Richard Sands, V.P. and Secy.
EIN: 546052978
Codes: FD

33997
The Esta and Jamie Stecher Foundation
c/o Goldman Sachs & Co.
85 Broad St., Tax Dept.
New York, NY 10004

Financial data (yr. ended 07/31/00): Grants paid, $316,072; assets, $3,285,344 (M); expenditures, $316,072; qualifying distributions, $286,784.
Limitations: Applications not accepted.
Application information: Contributes only to pre-selected organizations.
Trustees: Esta Eiger Stecher, Jamie B.W. Stecher.
EIN: 133918278

33998
The SO Charitable Trust
c/o Oded Aboodi, Tr.
1285 Ave. of the Americas, 21st Fl.
New York, NY 10019

Established in 1980 in NJ.
Donor(s): Oded Aboodi, Summer Assocs.
Financial data (yr. ended 11/30/99): Grants paid, $316,069; assets, $2,952,612 (M); gifts received, $275,000; expenditures, $325,911; qualifying distributions, $316,317.
Limitations: Applications not accepted. Giving primarily in NY.
Application information: Contributes only to pre-selected organizations.
Trustees: Oded Aboodi, Solomon M. Weiss.
EIN: 133050892
Codes: FD

33999
The Murray Foundation, Inc.
(Formerly John P. Murray, Jr. Foundation, Inc.)
20 W. Main St.
Beacon, NY 12508
Contact: John P. Murray III, Pres.

Established in 1987.
Donor(s): John P. Murray.
Financial data (yr. ended 12/31/00): Grants paid, $316,000; assets, $5,351,246 (M); expenditures, $360,876; qualifying distributions, $345,605.
Limitations: Applications not accepted. Giving on a national basis.
Application information: Unsolicited requests for funds not accepted.
Officers and Directors:* John P. Murray III,* Pres.; W. Stephen Murray, Secy.; Elizabeth Hosea, Ellen Kelsey, Mary T. Murray, Matthew T. Murray, Robert S. Murray.
EIN: 133421590
Codes: FD

34000
Agrilink Foods/Pro-Fac Foundation
(Formerly Curtice-Burns/Pro-Fac Foundation)
90 Linden Oaks
P.O. Box 20670
Rochester, NY 14602-0670 (716) 383-1850
URL: http://www.agrilinkfoods.com/corp/about/community
Contact: Susan C. Riker, Secy.

Trust established in 1966 in NY.
Donor(s): Agrilink Foods, Inc.
Financial data (yr. ended 06/30/01): Grants paid, $315,725; assets, $38,583 (M); gifts received, $300,000; expenditures, $316,548; qualifying distributions, $316,278.
Limitations: Giving primarily in areas of company operations.
Application information: Application form not required.
Officers and Trustees:* Paul Roe,* Chair.; Susan C. Riker,* Secy.; Virginia Ford, William Rice.
EIN: 166071142
Codes: CS, FD, CD

34001
The William H. & Helen C. Vanderbilt Foundation
c/o U.S. Trust
114 W. 47th St., Ste. C-1
New York, NY 10036-1594
Contact: Andrew Lane, Asst. V.P.

Donor(s): William H. Vanderbilt Charitable Trust.
Financial data (yr. ended 02/28/01): Grants paid, $315,250; assets, $6,385,519 (M); gifts received, $35,000; expenditures, $381,949; qualifying distributions, $317,340.
Limitations: Applications not accepted. Giving on a national basis, with emphasis on the Northeast.
Application information: Contributes only to pre-selected organizations.
Trustees: Ellen F. Vanderbilt Aidnoff, Anne C. Vanderbilt Hartwell, William Henry Vanderbilt, Jr., Emily Vanderbilt Wade.
EIN: 042743143
Codes: FD

34002
OSG Foundation
511 5th Ave., 13th Fl.
New York, NY 10017-4093

Established in 1981.
Donor(s): Overseas Shipholding Group, Inc., Glander International, Inc.
Financial data (yr. ended 12/31/01): Grants paid, $315,206; assets, $11,401 (M); gifts received,

34002—NEW YORK

$300,000; expenditures, $315,311; qualifying distributions, $315,311.
Limitations: Applications not accepted. Giving primarily in NY.
Application information: Contributes only to pre-selected organizations.
Officers and Directors:* Morton P. Hyman,* Pres.; Myles R. Itkin,* V.P. and Secy.-Treas.; Robert N. Cowen.
EIN: 133099337
Codes: CS, FD, CD

34003
Margaret T. Biddle Foundation
c/o Cusack & Stiles, LLP
61 Broadway, Rm. 2100
New York, NY 10006

Incorporated in 1952 in NY.
Donor(s): Margaret T. Biddle.‡
Financial data (yr. ended 12/31/01): Grants paid, $315,000; assets, $5,301,947 (M); expenditures, $332,725; qualifying distributions, $321,085.
Limitations: Applications not accepted. Giving on a national basis.
Application information: Contributes only to pre-selected organizations.
Officers and Directors:* Christian C. Hohenlohe,* Pres.; Peter Boyce Schulze,* V.P. and Secy.; Richard A. Smith,* V.P. and Treas.; Catherine H. Jacobus,* V.P.; Charles T. Schulze.
EIN: 131936016
Codes: FD

34004
Beck Foundation
330 Madison Ave., 31st Fl.
New York, NY 10017-5001
FAX: (540) 258-1227
Contact: T. Edmund Beck, Jr.

Established in 1954 in NY.
Donor(s): T. Edmund Beck.‡
Financial data (yr. ended 12/31/01): Grants paid, $314,500; assets, $4,888,124 (M); gifts received, $40,000; expenditures, $332,990; qualifying distributions, $315,774.
Limitations: Applications not accepted. Giving on a national basis.
Application information: Contributes only to pre-selected organizations.
Directors: John C. Beck, T.E. Beck, Jr., Susan Beck Wasch.
EIN: 136082501
Codes: FD

34005
The Pioneer Fund, Inc.
954 Lexington Ave., Ste. 211
New York, NY 10176 (212) 459-4084
E-mail: pioneerfnd@aol.com; *URL:* http://www.pioneerfund.org
Contact: Harry F. Weyher, Pres.

Incorporated in 1937 in NY.
Financial data (yr. ended 12/31/01): Grants paid, $314,247; assets, $3,173,641 (M); gifts received, $388,964; expenditures, $535,938; qualifying distributions, $502,655.
Application information: Application form not required.
Officers and Directors:* Harry F. Weyher,* Pres.; Marion A. Parrott,* Treas.; Karl Schakel.
EIN: 510181036
Codes: FD

34006
Dorr Foundation
P.O. Box 281
Bedford, NY 10506 (212) 683-1370

Trust established in 1940 in CT.
Donor(s): John Dorr.‡
Financial data (yr. ended 12/31/01): Grants paid, $314,150; assets, $5,887,326 (M); expenditures, $377,216; qualifying distributions, $324,438.
Limitations: Giving on a national basis, with limited international grants.
Application information: Foundation does not respond to requests for guidelines or annual reports, except by telephone. Application form not required.
Trustees: Allen Hardon, Roger Hardon, Virginia Maxwell, Barbara McMillan, Kenneth Punzeit, Shirley M. Punzeit, Gina Sessler.
EIN: 136017294
Codes: FD

34007
The PKL Foundation, Inc.
c/o Richard A. Eisner & Co., LLP
750 3rd Ave.
New York, NY 10017-2703

Established in 1965 in NY.
Donor(s): Peter K. Loeb, Jeanette Loeb, Constance L. Cohn.
Financial data (yr. ended 11/30/01): Grants paid, $313,528; assets, $1,205,011 (M); gifts received, $134,656; expenditures, $359,515; qualifying distributions, $330,805.
Limitations: Applications not accepted. Giving primarily in New York, NY.
Application information: Contributes only to pre-selected organizations.
Officers: Peter K. Loeb, Pres.; Jeanette Loeb, V.P. and Treas.; Charles S. Guggenheimer, Secy.
EIN: 136178307
Codes: FD

34008
Ostrovsky Family Fund, Inc.
c/o Horowitz and Ullmann
275 Madison Ave., Ste. 902
New York, NY 10016

Established in 1987.
Donor(s): Vivian S. Ostrovsky.
Financial data (yr. ended 11/30/01): Grants paid, $313,100; assets, $624,306 (M); gifts received, $378,000; expenditures, $367,513; qualifying distributions, $313,100.
Limitations: Applications not accepted. Giving primarily in New York, NY; some giving also in Washington, DC and Jerusalem, Israel.
Application information: Contributes only to pre-selected organizations.
Officers and Directors:* Vivian S. Ostrovsky,* Pres.; Jacob Friedman,* Secy.; Anthony R. Ullmann,* Treas.; Rose Ostrovsky.
EIN: 133389580
Codes: FD

34009
Philips Electronics North American Foundation
(Formerly North American Philips Foundation)
c/o Scholarship Prog. Admin.
1251 Ave. of the Americas, 19th Fl.
New York, NY 10020-1104

Established in 1979 in NY.
Donor(s): Philips Electronics North America Corp.
Financial data (yr. ended 12/31/01): Grants paid, $312,750; assets, $39,268 (M); gifts received, $324,400; expenditures, $312,750; qualifying distributions, $312,750.
Limitations: Giving on a national basis.

Application information: Application form required.
Officers: Belinda W. Chew, Pres.; Robert N. Smith, V.P.; Warren T. Oates, Jr., Secy.; Raymond C. Fleming, Treas.
EIN: 132961300
Codes: CS, FD, CD, GTI

34010
The Balm Foundation, Inc.
11 E. 73rd St.
New York, NY 10021
Contact: Janet Stein, Pres.

Established in 1993.
Donor(s): Howard Stein.
Financial data (yr. ended 11/30/01): Grants paid, $312,452; assets, $11,020,373 (M); gifts received, $4,000,000; expenditures, $425,571; qualifying distributions, $413,884.
Limitations: Applications not accepted. Giving primarily in CA and NY.
Application information: Contributes only to pre-selected organizations.
Officer and Directors:* Janet Stein,* Pres.; Peggy Davis, Vincent McGee.
EIN: 133746421
Codes: FD

34011
Fund for Life Foundation, Inc.
1428 36th St., Ste. 200
Brooklyn, NY 11218

Established in 1996 in NY.
Donor(s): Harry Reichman.
Financial data (yr. ended 12/31/01): Grants paid, $311,929; assets, $4,177,890 (M); gifts received, $1,560,000; expenditures, $315,276; qualifying distributions, $315,276.
Limitations: Giving primarily in Brooklyn, NY.
Officers: Harry Reichman, Pres.; Joshua Assaf, Secy.; Chaya Reichman, Treas.
EIN: 113239215
Codes: FD

34012
The Irene and Carroll Rheinstrom Fund
c/o The Bank of New York, Tax Dept.
1 Wall St., 28th Fl.
New York, NY 10286

Established in 1998 in NY.
Donor(s): Marjorie Rheinstrom,‡ Carroll Rheinstrom Trust Foundation.
Financial data (yr. ended 12/31/99): Grants paid, $311,400; assets, $10,869,561 (M); gifts received, $367,088; expenditures, $439,703; qualifying distributions, $311,400.
Limitations: Applications not accepted.
Application information: Contributes only to pre-selected organizations.
Trustees: Walter H. Davis, Richard Koskey, The Bank of New York.
EIN: 137174711

34013
Harry and Jane Fischel Foundation
60 E. 42nd St., Ste. 1419
New York, NY 10165

Incorporated in 1932 in NY.
Donor(s): Harry Fischel.‡
Financial data (yr. ended 12/31/01): Grants paid, $310,285; assets, $8,549,260 (L); expenditures, $860,272; qualifying distributions, $478,970.
Limitations: Applications not accepted. Giving primarily in NY.
Application information: Contributes only to pre-selected organizations.

IN THIS SECTION, WITHIN EACH STATE, FOUNDATIONS ARE LISTED IN DESCENDING ORDER BY TOTAL GRANTS PAID

Officers and Directors:* Rabbi O. Asher Reichel,* Pres.; Michael D. Jaspan,* V.P. and Exec. Dir.; Ronald Jaspan,* Secy.; Frederic S. Goldstein,* Treas.; Rabbi Shear Yashuv Cohen, Seth M. Goldstein, Simeon H.F. Goldstein, Norman Jaspan, Rabbi Aaron I. Reichel, Rabbi Hillel Reichel, Jay Stepelman.
EIN: 135677832
Codes: FD

34014
Gustav and Irene Stern Foundation, Inc.
(Formerly Gustav Stern Foundation, Inc.)
c/o Braver, Stern Securities Corp.
641 Lexington Ave.
New York, NY 10022

Established in 1980.
Donor(s): Roy Stern, Steven Stern.
Financial data (yr. ended 03/31/01): Grants paid, $309,406; assets, $8,527,690 (M); expenditures, $483,215; qualifying distributions, $379,364.
Limitations: Giving primarily in New York, NY.
Application information: Application form not required.
Officers: Irene Stern, Pres.; Steven Stern, V.P.; Joyce Herland, Secy.; Roy Stern, Treas.
Director: Ralph Suskind.
EIN: 136121155
Codes: FD

34015
Sol E. Betesh & Sons Foundation, Inc.
1 E. 33rd St.
New York, NY 10016

Established in 1988 in NY.
Donor(s): Sol E. Betesh, Norma Betesh, Elliot Betesh, Michael Betesh, Steven Betesh.
Financial data (yr. ended 12/31/00): Grants paid, $309,302; assets, $1,926 (M); gifts received, $310,000; expenditures, $309,302; qualifying distributions, $309,302.
Limitations: Applications not accepted. Giving primarily in New York City, with emphasis on Brooklyn, NY.
Application information: Contributes only to pre-selected organizations.
Officers: Sol E. Betesh, Pres.; Elliot Betesh, V.P.; Michael Betesh, V.P.; Norma Betesh, Secy.
EIN: 133479984
Codes: FD

34016
Foster Charitable Trust
c/o The Bank of New York, Tax Dept.
1 Wall St., 28th Fl.
New York, NY 10286
Application address: 6100 Via Subida, Rancho Palos Verdes, CA 90275
Contact: Robert Foster, Tr.

Established in 1997 in CA.
Financial data (yr. ended 12/31/01): Grants paid, $309,230; assets, $2,034,562 (M); expenditures, $326,673; qualifying distributions, $313,785.
Limitations: Giving primarily in CA.
Trustees: Gina Dominique Foster, Robert Foster.
EIN: 336195828
Codes: FD

34017
The Mary A. and John M. McCarthy Foundation
c/o KCG Capital Advisors
880 3rd Ave., 8th Fl.
New York, NY 10022
Contact: Stephen J. McCarthy, Tr.

Established in 1985.
Donor(s): Mary A. McCarthy, John M. McCarthy.
Financial data (yr. ended 11/30/01): Grants paid, $309,000; assets, $5,165,524 (M); expenditures, $394,868; qualifying distributions, $341,239.
Limitations: Applications not accepted. Giving primarily in the Mid-Atlantic and Northeast regions, with emphasis on the greater Washington, DC, area, Boston, MA, and New York, NY.
Publications: Multi-year report.
Application information: Contributes only to pre-selected organizations.
Trustees: John M. McCarthy, Laurette E. McCarthy, Mary A. McCarthy, Neil M. McCarthy, Stephen J. McCarthy, Tara A. McCarthy.
EIN: 136863980
Codes: FD

34018
The Stony Point Foundation
c/o BCRS Assocs., LLC
67 Wall St., 8th Fl.
New York, NY 10005
E-mail: greenjn56@aol.com

Established in 1993 in NY.
Donor(s): John O. Downing.
Financial data (yr. ended 01/31/01): Grants paid, $308,980; assets, $6,277,810 (M); gifts received, $2,088,255; expenditures, $379,517; qualifying distributions, $309,248.
Limitations: Applications not accepted. Giving primarily in NJ.
Application information: Contributes only to pre-selected organizations.
Trustees: Frances V.S. Downing, John O. Downing.
EIN: 133766973

34019
The Howard and Bush Foundation, Inc.
2 Belle Ave.
Troy, NY 12180 (518) 271-1134
Contact: Deborah Byers

Incorporated in 1961 in CT.
Donor(s): Edith Mason Howard,‡ Julia Howard Bush.‡
Financial data (yr. ended 12/31/01): Grants paid, $308,780; assets, $4,063,371 (M); expenditures, $372,740; qualifying distributions, $353,355.
Limitations: Giving limited to programs that benefit residents of Rensselaer County, NY.
Publications: Application guidelines, grants list.
Application information: Application form required.
Officers and Trustees:* David S. Haviland,* Pres.; Margaret Mochan,* V.P.; Donald C. Bowes,* Secy.; David W. Parmelee,* Treas.; Judith A. Barnes.
EIN: 066059063
Codes: FD

34020
U.S.B. Foundation, Inc.
c/o Steven T. Sabatini
100 Dutch Hill Rd.
Orangeburg, NY 10962

Established in 1996 in NY.
Donor(s): Union State Bank.
Financial data (yr. ended 12/31/01): Grants paid, $308,370; assets, $432,472 (M); expenditures, $309,733; qualifying distributions, $308,248.
Limitations: Applications not accepted. Giving primarily in NY.
Application information: Contributes only to pre-selected organizations.
Directors: Lynne Allan, Raymond J. Crotty, Thomas E. Hales, Steven T. Sabatini.
EIN: 133886297
Codes: FD

34021
The Roger W. Follett Foundation, Inc.
c/o Lee, Emerson & Ferrarese, LLP
35 W. Main St.
Norwich, NY 13815 (607) 334-2247
Contact: Thomas C. Emerson, V.P.

Established in 1995 in NY.
Donor(s): Roger Follet.‡
Financial data (yr. ended 12/31/00): Grants paid, $308,245; assets, $4,864,973 (M); expenditures, $359,321; qualifying distributions, $308,245.
Limitations: Giving primarily in Chenango County, NY.
Application information: Application form required.
Officers: Peter V. Smith, Pres.; Thomas C. Emerson, V.P.; Edward J. Lee, Secy.-Treas.
EIN: 223270901
Codes: FD

34022
Roger Todd Trust
c/o M&T Bank
1 M&T Plz., 8th Fl.
Buffalo, NY 14203

Established in 1998 in PA.
Financial data (yr. ended 12/31/00): Grants paid, $308,186; assets, $5,159,182 (M); gifts received, $657; expenditures, $347,016; qualifying distributions, $304,874.
Limitations: Applications not accepted. Giving primarily in Carlisle, PA.
Application information: Contributes only to pre-selected organizations.
Trustee: M & T Bank.
EIN: 256630150
Codes: FD

34023
Thomas F. Judson, Jr. & Elisabeth W. Judson Foundation
P.O. Box 1010
Rochester, NY 14603
Contact: Elisabeth W. Judson, Dir.

Established in 1999 in NY.
Donor(s): Thomas F. Judson, Jr., Elisabeth W. Judson, The Pike Company, Inc.
Financial data (yr. ended 12/31/01): Grants paid, $307,978; assets, $533,689 (M); gifts received, $100,000; expenditures, $313,680; qualifying distributions, $307,828.
Limitations: Giving primarily in NY, with emphasis on Rochester, NY.
Application information: Application form not required.
Officer: Thomas F. Judson, Jr., Exec. Dir.
Directors: Thomas R. Burns, Elisabeth W. Judson.
EIN: 161578008
Codes: FD

34024
Music for the World Foundation, Inc.
635 Madison Ave., 18th Fl.
New York, NY 10022

Established in 1994 in NY.
Donor(s): F. Richard Matthews.
Financial data (yr. ended 12/31/99): Grants paid, $307,780; assets, $1,854 (M); gifts received, $1,500; expenditures, $313,129; qualifying distributions, $307,780.
Limitations: Giving primarily in New York, NY.
Officers: Walter Scheuer, Chair.; Allan Miller, Pres.
EIN: 133685446
Codes: FD

34025—NEW YORK

34025
The Beam Foundation, Inc.
c/o Grant Thornton, LLP
60 Broad St.
New York, NY 10004-2501

Established in 1986 in NJ.
Donor(s): Bernard Myerson.
Financial data (yr. ended 09/30/01): Grants paid, $307,685; assets, $4,616,077 (M); expenditures, $332,240; qualifying distributions, $309,818.
Limitations: Applications not accepted. Giving primarily in New York, NY.
Application information: Contributes only to pre-selected organizations.
Officers: Bernard Myerson, Pres. and Treas.; Muriel Myerson, V.P.
Trustees: Alan Myerson, Edward Myerson.
EIN: 222786271
Codes: FD

34026
The Ames-Amzalak Memorial Trust
610 Wilder Bldg.
Rochester, NY 14614
Contact: Myrl S. Gelb, Tr.

Established in 1997 in NY.
Financial data (yr. ended 04/30/01): Grants paid, $307,575; assets, $5,981,505 (M); expenditures, $367,205; qualifying distributions, $335,687.
Trustees: Jay Gelb, Myrl Gelb, Justin Vigdor, Robert Vigdor.
EIN: 161530490

34027
Jacques Asseoff Charitable Trust
c/o Arthur Muhlstock
305 Madison Ave., Ste. 5118
New York, NY 10165

Financial data (yr. ended 12/31/01): Grants paid, $307,542; assets, $5,818,386 (M); expenditures, $385,471; qualifying distributions, $307,542.
Limitations: Applications not accepted. Giving primarily in New York, NY.
Application information: Contributes only to pre-selected organizations.
Trustees: Harry Asseoff, Lola Asseoff, Isaac Calev, Ernest Hirsch.
EIN: 136817770
Codes: FD

34028
The Anchorage Charitable Fund
666 3rd Ave., 29th Fl.
New York, NY 10017-4011
Contact: M.A. Varet, Pres.

Established in 1982 in NY.
Donor(s): Elizabeth R. Varet.
Financial data (yr. ended 04/30/01): Grants paid, $307,400; assets, $7,264,885 (M); expenditures, $351,797; qualifying distributions, $306,435.
Limitations: Applications not accepted. Giving primarily in New York, NY.
Application information: Contributes only to pre-selected organizations.
Officers: Elizabeth R. Varet, Chair.; Michael A. Varet, Pres. and Treas.; David P. Steinmann, V.P. and Secy.
EIN: 133202345
Codes: FD

34029
The William C. and Cindy L. Scott Foundation
885 3rd Ave., Ste. 3020
New York, NY 10022
Contact: William C. Scott, Pres.

Established in 1997 in DE.
Donor(s): William C. Scott.
Financial data (yr. ended 04/30/01): Grants paid, $306,675; assets, $2,735,051 (M); expenditures, $329,246; qualifying distributions, $312,240.
Officers: William C. Scott, Pres.; Cindy L. Scott, Secy.
EIN: 133999250
Codes: FD

34030
The Sylvan C. Coleman Foundation
c/o The Bank of New York, Tax Dept.
1 Wall St., 28th Fl.
New York, NY 10286
Application address: 2401 Merced St., San Leandro, CA 94577
Contact: Clarence B. Coleman, Tr.

Established about 1956 in NY.
Donor(s): Sylvan C. Coleman.‡
Financial data (yr. ended 11/30/01): Grants paid, $306,500; assets, $4,360,319 (M); expenditures, $347,686; qualifying distributions, $311,080.
Limitations: Giving primarily in CA.
Application information: Foundation requires permission to contact references. Application form not required.
Trustees: Clarence B. Coleman, Joan F. Coleman.
EIN: 136091160
Codes: FD

34031
Albert and Bessie Warner Fund
P.O. Box 2580
Sag Harbor, NY 11963
Application address: 666 Broadway, Ste. 500, New York, NY 10012

Trust established in 1955 in NY.
Financial data (yr. ended 12/31/00): Grants paid, $306,500; assets, $4,811,941 (L); expenditures, $341,177; qualifying distributions, $301,830.
Limitations: Giving primarily in New York City and Suffolk County, NY.
Publications: Annual report.
Application information: Application form not required.
Trustees: John Steel, Kitty Steel, Lewis M. Steel, Ruth M. Steel.
EIN: 136095213
Codes: FD

34032
The Ganger Foundation, Inc.
c/o Ira Ganger
34 Herrick Dr.
Lawrence, NY 11559

Established in 1993 in NY.
Donor(s): Ira Ganger, Joe Ganger, AMEREX (USA), Inc.
Financial data (yr. ended 04/30/01): Grants paid, $306,416; assets, $468,271 (M); gifts received, $320,000; expenditures, $311,085; qualifying distributions, $306,516.
Limitations: Applications not accepted. Giving primarily in New York, NY.
Application information: Contributes only to pre-selected organizations.
Officer and Trustees:* Ira Ganger,* Mgr.; Aviva Ganger, Shoshana Ganger.
EIN: 113162524
Codes: FD

34033
Raymond Foundation
c/o The Raymond Corp.
P.O. Box 518
Greene, NY 13778
Application address: P.O. Box 1273E, Greene, NY 13778, tel.: (607) 656-8897
Contact: Terri Brant, Tr.

Trust established in 1964 in NY.
Donor(s): The Raymond Corp., George G. Raymond.‡
Financial data (yr. ended 12/31/00): Grants paid, $306,132; assets, $6,301,729 (M); expenditures, $370,442; qualifying distributions, $306,132.
Limitations: Giving limited to areas of company operations in CA and NY.
Publications: Annual report, application guidelines, program policy statement.
Officers and Trustees:* James F. Barton,* Chair.; Stephen S. Raymond, Vice-Chair.; Pete Raymond, Exec. Secy.; Patrick J. McManus, Treas.; Richard Najarian, John Pilkington, George G. Raymond, Jr., Jean C. Raymond, Jeanette L. Williamson.
EIN: 166047847
Codes: CS, FD, CD

34034
Mortimer J. Harrison Article 11(A) Trust
c/o Torys
237 Park Ave.
New York, NY 10017
Application address: 810 S. Springfield Ave., Springfield, NJ 07081
Contact: Arthur E. Lashinsky, Tr.

Established in 1996 in NY.
Donor(s): Mortimer J. Harrison.‡
Financial data (yr. ended 12/31/00): Grants paid, $305,601; assets, $6,448,346 (M); gifts received, $100,000; expenditures, $357,268; qualifying distributions, $305,601.
Limitations: Giving primarily in NY.
Trustee: Arthur E. Lashinsky.
EIN: 137075860
Codes: FD

34035
Bartner Family Foundation Trust
c/o Young & Moriwaki, LLP
777 3rd Ave., 19th Fl.
New York, NY 10017

Established in 2000 in CT.
Donor(s): Robert Bartner.
Financial data (yr. ended 12/31/01): Grants paid, $304,650; assets, $531,356 (M); gifts received, $500,000; expenditures, $312,950; qualifying distributions, $308,450.
Limitations: Applications not accepted. Giving primarily in CT and NY.
Application information: Contributes only to pre-selected organizations.
Trustees: Arabella D. Bartner, Beverly D.N. Bartner, Robert G. Bartner, Nicole Bartner Graff, Jennifer Bartner Indeck.
EIN: 137235081
Codes: FD

34036
The Robert and Kate Niehaus Foundation
105 Evergreen Ave.
Rye, NY 10580

Established in 1998 in NY.
Donor(s): Robert H. Niehaus.
Financial data (yr. ended 12/31/01): Grants paid, $304,000; assets, $5,668,807 (M); gifts received, $63,242; expenditures, $415,271; qualifying distributions, $410,893.
Limitations: Giving primarily in New York, NY.

Officers: Robert H. Niehaus, Pres.; Kate Niehaus, V.P.
Director: Jerome L. Levine.
EIN: 134007527
Codes: FD

34037
Fahey Family Foundation
c/o BCRS Assocs., LLC
100 Wall St., 11th Fl.
New York, NY 10005

Established in 1987 in NY.
Donor(s): Peter M. Fahey.
Financial data (yr. ended 05/31/01): Grants paid, $303,914; assets, $1,706,170 (M); expenditures, $322,622; qualifying distributions, $306,311.
Limitations: Applications not accepted. Giving primarily in Hanover, NH, and NY.
Application information: Contributes only to pre-selected organizations.
Trustees: Helen D. Fahey, Peter M. Fahey.
EIN: 133437921
Codes: FD

34038
The Jack and Billie Schwartz Foundation
39 Kenilworth Rd.
Rye, NY 10580

Established in 1997 in DE.
Donor(s): Pearl T. Schwartz.
Financial data (yr. ended 12/31/01): Grants paid, $303,824; assets, $55,706 (M); gifts received, $87,181; expenditures, $308,105; qualifying distributions, $303,824.
Limitations: Applications not accepted.
Application information: Contributes only to pre-selected organizations.
Officers: Harriet Johnson, Secy.; Deborah Raizes, Treas.
Director: Pearl T. Schwartz.
EIN: 133920688
Codes: FD

34039
Andrew and Irma Hilton Foundation, Inc.
c/o Berlin & Kolin
1790 Broadway, Rm. 705
New York, NY 10019

Established in 1988 in NY.
Donor(s): Andrew C. Hilton, Irma Hilton.
Financial data (yr. ended 12/31/01): Grants paid, $303,650; assets, $1,605,314 (M); expenditures, $320,150; qualifying distributions, $303,479.
Limitations: Applications not accepted. Giving primarily in New York, NY.
Application information: Contributes only to pre-selected organizations.
Officers: Andrew C. Hilton, Pres.; Irma Hilton, V.P.; Lester Dembitzer, Secy.-Treas.
EIN: 133472804
Codes: FD

34040
The Kingsberg Foundation
c/o Reminick, Aarons & Co., LLP
1430 Broadway
New York, NY 10018

Established in 1954 in NY.
Financial data (yr. ended 12/31/01): Grants paid, $303,465; assets, $6,333,350 (M); expenditures, $306,052; qualifying distributions, $301,673.
Limitations: Applications not accepted. Giving on a national basis, with emphasis on MA and NY.
Application information: Contributes only to pre-selected organizations.
Trustees: Alan D. Kingsberg, Harold J. Kingsberg, Ruth J. Kingsberg, Sally Anne Kingsberg.

EIN: 136151289
Codes: FD

34041
Schwarz Family Foundation
211 E. 70th St., Ste. 23A
New York, NY 10021

Established in 1998 in NY.
Financial data (yr. ended 12/31/01): Grants paid, $302,309; assets, $761,865 (M); expenditures, $306,492; qualifying distributions, $302,101.
Limitations: Giving primarily in New York, NY.
Trustees: Joel Greenblatt, Rabbi Irwin Kula, Jeffrey E. Schwarz, Sherwood Schwarz.
EIN: 226743828
Codes: FD

34042
The IBJ Foundation Inc.
1251 Ave. of the Americas, 31st Fl.
New York, NY 10020-1104 (212) 282-4192
FAX: (212) 282-3250
Contact: Ms. Lesley Harris Palmer, Exec. Dir.

Established in 1989 in NY.
Donor(s): The Industrial Bank of Japan Trust Co., The Industrial Bank of Japan, Ltd.
Financial data (yr. ended 12/31/01): Grants paid, $302,009; assets, $11,771,427 (M); expenditures, $500,786; qualifying distributions, $525,988.
Limitations: Giving limited to communities where IBJ employees live and work: Los Angeles and San Francisco, CA, Atlanta, GA, Chicago, IL, New York, NY, and Houston, TX.
Publications: Multi-year report, informational brochure (including application guidelines), grants list.
Application information: Concept paper preferred; NY/NJ Common Area Application accepted. Application form not required.
Officers and Directors:* Merlin E. Nelson,* Chair.; Hajime Nakai,* Pres.; Eric Tarlow, Secy.; Akio Kariya, Treas.; Lesley Harris Palmer, Exec. Dir.; John H. Higgs, Shoji Noguchi.
EIN: 133550008
Codes: CS, FD, CD

34043
The Robert S. Rifkind Charitable Foundation
c/o Cravath, Swaine & Moore
825 8th Ave.
New York, NY 10019

Established in 1986 in NY.
Donor(s): Robert S. Rifkind.
Financial data (yr. ended 12/31/01): Grants paid, $302,000; assets, $2,569,892 (M); gifts received, $101,260; expenditures, $319,337; qualifying distributions, $302,000.
Limitations: Applications not accepted. Giving primarily in the Northeast.
Application information: Contributes only to pre-selected organizations. Unsolicited requests for funds are not considered.
Trustee: Robert S. Rifkind.
EIN: 133374924
Codes: FD

34044
The DM Foundation
(Formerly Northeastern Pooled Common Fund for Education in the Social Sciences and the Arts)
149 E. 63rd St.
New York, NY 10021-7405

Established in 1973 in NY.
Donor(s): Georges F. de Menil.
Financial data (yr. ended 12/31/01): Grants paid, $301,750; assets, $3,782,392 (M); expenditures, $327,569; qualifying distributions, $311,156.

Limitations: Applications not accepted. Giving limited to the Northeast.
Application information: Contributes mostly to 10 pre-selected organizations specified in the governing instrument.
Trustees: Aston Hawkins, Joy A. de Menil, Kenworth Moffett, Susan T. Nitze, Abraham L. Udovitch, Peter Wolff.
EIN: 237345848
Codes: FD

34045
The Keith Wold Johnson Charitable Trust
c/o The Johnson Co., Inc.
630 5th Ave., Ste. 1510
New York, NY 10111
Contact: Robert W. Johnson, IV, Tr.

Established in 1986 in NY.
Donor(s): Betty Wold Johnson.
Financial data (yr. ended 12/31/01): Grants paid, $301,500; assets, $4,639,687 (M); expenditures, $309,205; qualifying distributions, $304,581.
Limitations: Giving primarily in New York, NY.
Application information: Application form not required.
Trustees: Christopher W. Johnson, Elizabeth Ross Johnson, Robert W. Johnson IV.
EIN: 112845826
Codes: FD

34046
The Abraham & Beverly Sommer Foundation
810 7th Ave.
New York, NY 10019

Established in 1977 in NY.
Donor(s): Beverly Sommer.
Financial data (yr. ended 12/31/99): Grants paid, $301,250; assets, $7,156,564 (M); gifts received, $48,077; expenditures, $322,539; qualifying distributions, $287,079.
Limitations: Applications not accepted. Giving primarily in NY.
Application information: Contributes only to pre-selected organizations.
Officers: Beverly Sommer, Pres.; Amy Sommer, V.P.; Frank Stella, Secy.-Treas.
EIN: 132960992
Codes: FD

34047
The Louis Feinberg Foundation
c/o Buchbinder Tunick and Co., LLP
1 Penn Plz., Ste. 5335
New York, NY 10119
Application address: c/o Carrera Casting Corp., 64 W. 48th St., New York, NY 10036
Contact: Joel Weiss, Dir.

Established in 1998 in NY.
Donor(s): Louis Feinberg.‡
Financial data (yr. ended 12/31/01): Grants paid, $301,040; assets, $6,542,169 (M); expenditures, $491,108; qualifying distributions, $299,775.
Application information: Application form not required.
Directors: Stuart Feldman, Owen Schwartz, Vicky Weiner, Joel Weiss.
EIN: 137135427
Codes: FD

34048
The Fred C. Gloeckner Foundation, Inc.
600 Mamaroneck Ave.
Harrison, NY 10528 (914) 698-2300
Contact: Joseph A. Simone, Secy.

Incorporated in 1960 in NY.
Donor(s): Frederick C. Gloeckner.‡

34048—NEW YORK

Financial data (yr. ended 10/31/01): Grants paid, $300,935; assets, $4,599,159 (M); gifts received, $6,050; expenditures, $352,145; qualifying distributions, $300,935.
Limitations: Giving on a national basis.
Publications: Annual report.
Application information: Application form required.
Officers: John G. Seeley, Pres.; Paul L. Daum, V.P.; Joseph A. Simone, Secy.; Martin D. Kortjohn, Treas.
EIN: 136124190
Codes: FD

34049
Swidler Berlin Shereff Friedman Foundation
405 Lexington Ave.
New York, NY 10174

Established in 2000 in NY.
Donor(s): Andrew D. Lipman.
Financial data (yr. ended 02/28/01): Grants paid, $300,809; assets, $13,116 (M); gifts received, $313,925; expenditures, $300,809; qualifying distributions, $300,809.
Limitations: Giving primarily in New York, NY.
Trustees: David Butler, Robert J. Jossen.
EIN: 134148795
Codes: FD

34050
Wunsch Foundation, Inc.
72 Madison Ave.
New York, NY 10016
Contact: Eric M. Wunsch, Pres.

Incorporated in 1943 in NY.
Donor(s): Joseph W. Wunsch, Eric M. Wunsch, Samuel Wunsch, WEA Enterprises Co., Inc.
Financial data (yr. ended 12/31/01): Grants paid, $300,550; assets, $7,223,290 (M); gifts received, $15,000; expenditures, $309,231; qualifying distributions, $299,898.
Limitations: Applications not accepted. Giving primarily in NY.
Application information: Contributes only to pre-selected organizations.
Officers: Eric M. Wunsch, Pres.; Ethel Wunsch, Secy.; Peter E. Wunsch, Treas.
EIN: 116006013
Codes: FD

34051
The Atticus Foundation
152 W. 57th St.
New York, NY 10019
Contact: Timothy R. Barakett, Tr.

Established in 1997 in NY.
Donor(s): Timothy R. Barakett, Nathaniel Rothschild.
Financial data (yr. ended 12/31/01): Grants paid, $300,095; assets, $38,558 (M); expenditures, $300,195; qualifying distributions, $299,452.
Limitations: Giving primarily in NY.
Trustees: Peter Barakett, Timothy R. Barakett.
EIN: 133981257
Codes: FD

34052
Elizabeth Christy Kopf Foundation
c/o Kelley, Drye & Warren, LLP
101 Park Ave.
New York, NY 10178-0062
Contact: Michael S. Insel, Secy.

Established in 1982 in NY.
Donor(s): R.C. Kopf.‡
Financial data (yr. ended 12/31/99): Grants paid, $300,050; assets, $7,296,958 (M); expenditures, $354,128; qualifying distributions, $293,037.
Application information: Application form not required.
Officers and Board Members:* Patricia Ann Colagiuri,* Pres.; Nancy Sue Mueller,* V.P.; Michael S. Insel,* Secy.; Brenda Christy Helies,* Treas.
EIN: 133127936
Codes: FD

34053
The Martin Paskus Foundation, Inc.
c/o Richard M. Danziger
720 5th Ave., 15th Fl.
New York, NY 10019

Established in 1950 in NY.
Donor(s): Elsie Paskus,‡ D. Danziger, Richard M. Danziger.
Financial data (yr. ended 12/31/01): Grants paid, $300,024; assets, $2,003,295 (M); expenditures, $304,808; qualifying distributions, $296,649.
Limitations: Applications not accepted. Giving primarily in CT, MA, and NY.
Application information: Contributes only to pre-selected organizations.
Officers: Richard M. Danziger, Pres.; Frederick M. Danziger, Treas.
EIN: 510166266
Codes: FD

34054
Axe-Houghton Foundation
919 3rd Ave., 2nd Fl.
New York, NY 10022 (212) 909-8304
Contact: Remington P. Patterson, Pres.

Incorporated in 1965 in NY.
Donor(s): Emerson W. Axe.‡
Financial data (yr. ended 02/28/01): Grants paid, $300,000; assets, $7,440,590 (M); expenditures, $400,128; qualifying distributions, $351,958.
Limitations: Giving primarily in the metropolitan New York, NY, area.
Publications: Program policy statement, application guidelines.
Application information: Application form not required.
Officers and Directors:* Remington P. Patterson,* Pres.; William A. Hance,* V.P.; Robert B. von Mehren,* V.P.; Karen L. Chun, Secy.-Treas.; Lynn F. Angelson, Claire Brook, Suzanne Schwartz Davidson, Bruce D. Haims, Joan S. McMenamin.
EIN: 136200200
Codes: FD

34055
Cranshaw Corporation
c/o White and Case, LLP
1155 Ave. of the Americas, Ste. 3436
New York, NY 10036-2787

Incorporated in 1954 in DE.
Donor(s): Helen Babbott Sanders.‡
Financial data (yr. ended 12/31/01): Grants paid, $300,000; assets, $4,604,173 (M); expenditures, $331,131; qualifying distributions, $300,152.
Limitations: Applications not accepted. Giving primarily in MO and NY.
Application information: Contributes only to pre-selected organizations.
Officers: Robert MacDonald, Pres.; Edward F. Rover, V.P.
EIN: 136110555
Codes: FD

34056
Eye Surgery Fund, Inc.
c/o Peter Mullen
4 Times Sq.
New York, NY 10036

Donor(s): Mary C. Higgins.‡
Financial data (yr. ended 07/31/01): Grants paid, $300,000; assets, $5,784,721 (M); expenditures, $352,026; qualifying distributions, $301,058.
Limitations: Applications not accepted. Giving primarily in New York, NY.
Application information: Contributes only to pre-selected organizations.
Officers and Directors:* J. Dukes Wooters, Jr.,* Pres.; Joan Kirby,* V.P.; Cecilia K. Mullen,* V.P.; Peter Mullen,* Secy.-Treas.; Pamela Chin, Elaine Peer, Frederick Sheppard, Kirby White.
EIN: 131992063
Codes: FD

34057
NEC Foundation of America
8 Corporate Center Dr.
Melville, NY 11747 (631) 753-7021
FAX: (516) 753-7096; E-mail: foundation@necusa.com; URL: http://www.necus.com/company/foundation/nsindex.htm
Contact: Sylvia Clark, Exec. Dir.

Established in 1991 in NY.
Donor(s): NEC Corp., NEC USA, Inc.
Financial data (yr. ended 03/31/01): Grants paid, $300,000; assets, $15,988,164 (M); expenditures, $645,918; qualifying distributions, $557,451.
Limitations: Giving for programs/groups with immediate national reach and impact.
Publications: Informational brochure (including application guidelines), grants list.
Application information: Accepts NYRAG Common Application Form. Grantseekers may only apply every 18 months whether proposal is accepted or not. Generally, multi-year grants or grants for more than 2 consecutive years are not awarded. Application form not required.
Officers and Board Members:* Hisashi Kaneko,* Pres.; Masakatsu Miwa,* Sr. Exec. V.P.; Timothy M. Donovan, Secy.; Takao Ono, Treas.; Sylvia Clark, Exec. Dir.; Hirokazu Hasnimoto, Masao Hibino, Satoshi Nakaichi, Jun Oyamada, Norio Tanoue.
EIN: 113059554
Codes: CS, FD, CD

34058
The 25th Anniversary Foundation, Inc.
(Formerly Arista Records Foundation, Inc.)
1540 Broadway, 24th Fl.
New York, NY 10036-4064

Financial data (yr. ended 06/30/00): Grants paid, $300,000; assets, $699,682 (M); expenditures, $5,582,665; qualifying distributions, $300,000.
Officers and Directors:* Antonio Reid,* Pres.; Lawrence Mestel,* Exec. V.P.; Matthew J. Flott, Sr. V.P. and Treas.; Steven Gawley, Sr. V.P.; Robert J. Sorrentino, V.P.
EIN: 133557201
Codes: FD

34059
Sansom Foundation, Inc.
c/o Sanford Becker
1430 Broadway, 6th Fl.
New York, NY 10018

Established in 1958.
Donor(s): Ira D. Glackens.‡
Financial data (yr. ended 12/31/01): Grants paid, $299,700; assets, $21,106,764 (M); expenditures, $575,950; qualifying distributions, $575,956.

Limitations: Applications not accepted. Giving primarily in FL.
Application information: Contributes only to pre-selected organizations.
Directors: Sanford E. Becker, Frank Buscaglia, Rev. Edward M. DePaoli, C. Richard Hilker, Donald G. Hilker, Jorge H. Santis, Lawrence Thompson.
EIN: 136136127
Codes: FD

34060
Susan & Morris E. Dweck Foundation
c/o Ambras Fine Jewelry
48 W. 37th St.
New York, NY 10018

Established in 1988 in DE.
Donor(s): Morris E. Dweck.
Financial data (yr. ended 12/31/01): Grants paid, $299,618; assets, $3,128,314 (M); gifts received, $433,354; expenditures, $302,603; qualifying distributions, $300,268.
Limitations: Applications not accepted. Giving primarily in NY.
Application information: Contributes only to pre-selected organizations.
Officers: Morris E. Dweck, Pres.; Susan Dweck, V.P.
EIN: 133496732
Codes: FD

34061
Jana Foundation, Inc.
(Formerly Aaron H. & Dorothy S. Rubin Foundation)
c/o Davidson, Dawson, and Clark, LLP
330 Madison Ave., Ste. 3500
New York, NY 10017-5094 (212) 557-1407
Contact: Allan D. Seget

Established in NY as the Aaron & Dorothy Rubin Foundation.
Donor(s): Andrew Auerbach, Arnold Auerbach, Justine Auerbach, Nina Auerbach.
Financial data (yr. ended 12/31/01): Grants paid, $299,367; assets, $89,907 (M); gifts received, $251,006; expenditures, $306,410; qualifying distributions, $304,756.
Limitations: Giving primarily in CT and NY.
Application information: Individual applicants should submit a brief resume.
Directors: J. Auerbach, N. Auerbach, D. Rosen, A. Seget.
EIN: 133574540
Codes: FD

34062
Edith and Herbert Lehman Foundation, Inc.
151 E. 79th St.
New York, NY 10021-0417
FAX: (212) 744-2065
Contact: Wendy Lehman Lash, Pres.

Incorporated in 1952 in NY.
Donor(s): Edith A. Lehman,‡ Herbert H. Lehman.‡
Financial data (yr. ended 09/30/01): Grants paid, $298,500; assets, $6,351,105 (M); expenditures, $394,390; qualifying distributions, $335,002.
Limitations: Applications not accepted. Giving primarily in NY.
Publications: Annual report.
Application information: Proposals are accepted by invitation only. Preference is given to organizations which historically have been of interest to the Lehman family and to those in which the family is personally involved.
Officers and Directors:* Wendy Lehman Lash,* Pres.; Stephanie Wise,* V.P. and Treas.; Camilla M. Rosenfeld,* V.P.; Robert C. Graham, Jr., Abigail S. Lash.
EIN: 136094015
Codes: FD

34063
The Mrs. Cheever Porter Foundation
c/o Adams & Becker, CPAs
22 Oakwood Rd.
Huntington, NY 11743
Contact: Clifford E. Starkins, Dir.

Established in 1962 in NY.
Financial data (yr. ended 06/30/01): Grants paid, $298,500; assets, $3,398,278 (M); expenditures, $370,432; qualifying distributions, $315,647.
Limitations: Giving primarily in NY.
Directors: George Marchese, Elizabeth Peters, Clifford E. Starkins.
EIN: 136093181
Codes: FD

34064
Yahad Foundation, Inc.
c/o Zell & Ettinger, CPAs
3001 Ave. M
Brooklyn, NY 11210-4744 (718) 692-1212

Established in 1996 in NY.
Donor(s): Barry Webster.
Financial data (yr. ended 12/31/00): Grants paid, $297,556; assets, $1,662,936 (M); gifts received, $606,375; expenditures, $301,407; qualifying distributions, $298,101.
Officers: Barry Webster, Pres.; Helen Webster, V.P.; Mark Ettinger, Secy.
EIN: 113136436
Codes: FD

34065
Kinney Memorial Foundation
c/o The Bank of New York, Tax Dept.
1 Wall St., 28th Fl.
New York, NY 10286
Application address: c/o The Bank of New York, 1290 Ave. of Americas, New York, NY 10104
Contact: Thomas W. Bindert, V.P., The Bank of New York

Established in 1991 in NY.
Financial data (yr. ended 12/31/01): Grants paid, $297,257; assets, $4,569,469 (M); expenditures, $342,498; qualifying distributions, $299,766.
Limitations: Giving primarily in NJ, NY, and PA.
Trustees: Edward Holloway, Jr., Josephine J. Kinney, The Bank of New York.
EIN: 136968427
Codes: FD

34066
Max, Rose and Anna Heller Foundation
(Formerly Lawrence Klosk Foundation)
1123 Broadway, Ste. 1011
New York, NY 10010

Established in 1947.
Donor(s): Tobias Heller,‡ Lawrence Klosk.
Financial data (yr. ended 12/31/99): Grants paid, $297,030; assets, $106,613 (M); gifts received, $440,000; expenditures, $398,263; qualifying distributions, $297,030.
Limitations: Giving primarily in NY; some giving also in Israel.
Directors: Nathan Bernstein, Rachel Heller Bernstein, Debbie Lipshitz, Moshe Lipshitz.
EIN: 136154543
Codes: FD

34067
Louis & Virginia Clemente Foundation, Inc.
c/o Kelley, Drye, & Warren LLP
101 Park Ave.
New York, NY 10178
Contact: C. Caufield

Established in 1975.
Financial data (yr. ended 12/31/01): Grants paid, $297,000; assets, $4,608,763 (M); expenditures, $370,852; qualifying distributions, $310,444.
Limitations: Applications not accepted. Giving primarily in NY.
Application information: Contributes only to pre-selected organizations.
Officers and Directors:* Harry A. LeBien,* Pres. and Treas.; Mary Ellen LeBien,* Secy.; Laurent C. LeBien, Michele LeBien, Thomas E. LeBien.
EIN: 510163549
Codes: FD

34068
Vain and Harry Fish Foundation, Inc.
66 E. 79th St.
New York, NY 10021 (212) 879-2520
Contact: Vivian F. Gentleman, Pres.

Incorporated in 1972 in NY.
Donor(s): Vain B. Fish,‡ Harry Fish.‡
Financial data (yr. ended 12/31/01): Grants paid, $297,000; assets, $5,460,187 (M); expenditures, $369,646; qualifying distributions, $338,043.
Limitations: Giving on a national basis.
Application information: Application form not required.
Officers and Board Member:* Vivian F. Gentleman, Pres.; Aurora Doherty,* V.P.; Joan Leegant, Treas.
EIN: 132723211
Codes: FD

34069
Gustave M. Berne Foundation, Inc.
c/o Timko Contract
20 W. 64th St.
New York, NY 10023
Contact: Robert Berne

Established in 1951 in NY.
Donor(s): Gustave M. Berne,‡ Robert Berne.
Financial data (yr. ended 02/28/01): Grants paid, $296,380; assets, $2,388,449 (M); gifts received, $296,962; expenditures, $312,521; qualifying distributions, $296,630.
Limitations: Applications not accepted. Giving primarily in New York, NY.
Application information: Contributes only to pre-selected organizations.
Officer: Robert Berne, Mgr.
EIN: 116014207
Codes: FD

34070
Charlotte & Joseph Gardner Foundation, Inc.
c/o Joseph H. Gardner
36 Sutton Place S.
New York, NY 10022-4166 (212) 929-4210

Established in 1981.
Donor(s): Joseph H. Gardner.
Financial data (yr. ended 11/30/01): Grants paid, $296,264; assets, $416,052 (M); gifts received, $137,500; expenditures, $297,353; qualifying distributions, $295,779.
Limitations: Giving primarily in New York, NY.
Officers: Joseph H. Gardner, Pres.; Danielle Gardner, V.P.; Douglas B. Gardner, V.P.; Charlotte Gardner, Secy.-Treas.
EIN: 133057951
Codes: FD

34071
The Pines Bridge Foundation
1114 Ave. of the Americas, Ste. 3400
New York, NY 10036

Established in 1986 in NY.
Donor(s): Alan G. Weiler, The Weiler-Arnow Investment Co.
Financial data (yr. ended 12/31/01): Grants paid, $296,250; assets, $939,756 (M); gifts received, $250,000; expenditures, $303,672; qualifying distributions, $295,986.
Limitations: Applications not accepted. Giving primarily in New York, NY.
Application information: Contributes only to pre-selected organizations.
Trustees: Alan G. Weiler, Elaine Weiler.
EIN: 136872045
Codes: FD

34072
Society of International Cultural Exchange (SICE), Inc.
150 E. 52nd St., 34th Fl.
New York, NY 10022

Established in 1994 in FL and NY.
Donor(s): Fujisankei Communications International, Inc.
Financial data (yr. ended 03/31/01): Grants paid, $295,860; assets, $1,268,265 (M); gifts received, $300,000; expenditures, $299,716; qualifying distributions, $297,942.
Limitations: Giving primarily in New York, NY.
Application information: Application form not required.
Officers and Directors:* Hisashi Hieda,* Chair. and C.E.O.; Takashi Hoga, Pres.; Atsuo Nakahara,* Sr. V.P.; Koichi Murakami, John J. Parker.
EIN: 133244953
Codes: CS, FD, CD

34073
Ralph & Jean Baruch Charitable Foundation
784 Park Ave.
New York, NY 10021
Contact: Ralph Baruch, Chair.

Established in 1986 in NY.
Donor(s): Jean Baruch, Ralph Baruch.
Financial data (yr. ended 06/30/01): Grants paid, $294,729; assets, $527,646 (M); gifts received, $120,275; expenditures, $300,038; qualifying distributions, $291,825.
Limitations: Giving primarily in New York, NY.
Officer: Ralph Baruch, Chair.
Trustees: Jean Baruch, Sondra Shalman.
EIN: 133392139
Codes: FD

34074
Switzer Foundation
c/o John A. Pileski, Pres.
1000 Franklin Ave.
Garden City, NY 11530

Incorporated in 1909 in NY.
Donor(s): Margaret Switzer,‡ Sarah Switzer.‡
Financial data (yr. ended 12/31/99): Grants paid, $294,500; assets, $8,058,617 (M); expenditures, $377,411; qualifying distributions, $311,270.
Limitations: Giving primarily in the metropolitan New York, NY, area, including NJ.
Publications: Informational brochure.
Application information: Application form not required.
Officers: John A. Pileski, Pres.; John J. Murphy, Treas.
EIN: 135596831
Codes: FD

34075
The Setton Foundation
85 Austin Blvd.
Commack, NY 11725

Established in 2000 in NY.
Donor(s): Setton International Foods of Brooklyn.
Financial data (yr. ended 12/31/01): Grants paid, $294,480; assets, $181,703 (M); gifts received, $69,000; expenditures, $298,327; qualifying distributions, $298,187.
Limitations: Applications not accepted.
Application information: Contributes only to pre-selected organizations.
Officers: Joshua Setton, Pres.; Morris Setton, V.P. and Secy.
EIN: 113577481
Codes: FD

34076
Abraham Fuchsberg Family Foundation, Inc.
100 Church St., 18th Fl.
New York, NY 10007
Contact: Abraham Fuchsberg, Pres.

Established in 1978.
Donor(s): Abraham Fuchsberg, Seymour Fuchsberg, Fuchsberg & Fuchsberg, Fuchsberg Family Foundation.
Financial data (yr. ended 10/31/01): Grants paid, $294,412; assets, $0 (M); gifts received, $383,000; expenditures, $302,682; qualifying distributions, $294,412.
Limitations: Giving primarily in Washington, DC and New York, NY.
Application information: Application form not required.
Officers: Abraham Fuchsberg, Pres.; Jonathan Minkoff, Secy.
EIN: 132966385
Codes: FD

34077
The Lichter & Schwartz Family Foundation
850 W. 176th St.
New York, NY 10033

Established in 1996 in NY.
Donor(s): Joseph Schwartz, Alfred Lichter.
Financial data (yr. ended 12/31/01): Grants paid, $294,104; assets, $100,195 (M); gifts received, $294,500; expenditures, $294,359; qualifying distributions, $294,184.
Application information: Application form not required.
Officer: Alfred Lichter, Pres.
Directors: Claire Lichter, Joseph Schwartz.
EIN: 133899800
Codes: FD

34078
Thomas L. Kempner, Jr. Foundation
885 3rd Ave., Ste. 3300
New York, NY 10022

Established in 1987 in NY.
Donor(s): Thomas L. Kempner, Jr.
Financial data (yr. ended 12/31/01): Grants paid, $294,009; assets, $9,452,664 (M); gifts received, $2,163,757; expenditures, $366,119; qualifying distributions, $297,009.
Limitations: Applications not accepted.
Application information: Contributes only to pre-selected organizations.
Officers: Thomas L. Kempner, Jr., Pres.; Dean C. Berry, Secy.; Katheryn C. Patterson, Treas.
EIN: 133407819
Codes: FD

34079
Cutco Foundation, Inc.
c/o James Stitt
1116 E. State St.
Olean, NY 14760
Contact: Peter H. Laine, Treas.

Established in 1995 in NY.
Donor(s): Cutco Cutlery Corp.
Financial data (yr. ended 12/31/01): Grants paid, $293,784; assets, $1,504,180 (M); gifts received, $300,000; expenditures, $296,221; qualifying distributions, $240,650.
Limitations: Applications not accepted. Giving primarily in Olean, NY.
Application information: Contributes only to pre-selected organizations.
Officers and Directors:* James E. Stitt,* Pres.; John Whelpley,* Secy.; Peter H. Laine,* Treas.; Brent A. Driscoll, Erick J. Laine, Creed Terry.
EIN: 161491450
Codes: CS, FD, CD

34080
The Robert D. Ziff Foundation
c/o Ziff Bros. Investments
153 E. 53rd St., 43rd Fl.
New York, NY 10022

Established in 2000 in DE.
Donor(s): Ziff Investment Partnership LP II.
Financial data (yr. ended 12/31/00): Grants paid, $293,711; assets, $3,495,627 (M); gifts received, $3,474,165; expenditures, $338,087; qualifying distributions, $255,610.
Limitations: Applications not accepted. Giving primarily in FL and NY.
Application information: Contributes only to pre-selected organizations.
Officers: Robert D. Ziff, Pres.; David Moody, V.P. and Secy.; Mark Beaudoin, V.P.; Peter Cawley, V.P.; Timothy Mitchell, Treas.
EIN: 134083712
Codes: FD

34081
The Hajim Family Foundation
c/o Mahoney, Cohen & Co.
111 W. 40th St.
New York, NY 10018-2506 (212) 790-5700
Contact: Linda McCarty

Established in 1987 in NY.
Donor(s): Edmund A. Hajim.
Financial data (yr. ended 12/31/01): Grants paid, $293,513; assets, $4,183,687 (M); gifts received, $100,189; expenditures, $312,694; qualifying distributions, $293,513.
Limitations: Applications not accepted. Giving primarily in CT, MA, and NY.
Application information: Contributes only to pre-selected organizations.
Trustees: Barbara Hajim, Edmund A. Hajim.
EIN: 136893956
Codes: FD

34082
The Paul J. Koessler Foundation, Inc.
100 Corporate Pkwy., Ste. 410
Amherst, NY 14226
Contact: Paul J. Koessler, Pres.

Established in 1991 in DE and NY.
Donor(s): Paul J. Koessler, John W. Koessler, Jr., Mary R. Koessler.‡
Financial data (yr. ended 12/31/01): Grants paid, $293,012; assets, $5,739,865 (M); expenditures, $354,015; qualifying distributions, $292,560.
Limitations: Giving primarily in Buffalo, NY.

Officers and Directors:* Paul J. Koessler,* Pres.; Eric Koessler,* V.P.; Paul J. Koessler, Jr.,* V.P.; Paul C. Hilbert,* Secy.-Treas.
EIN: 161406642
Codes: FD

34083
NSB Family Foundation
2264 Ocean Pkwy.
Brooklyn, NY 11223

Established in 1997 in NY.
Donor(s): Nesim Bildirici.
Financial data (yr. ended 11/30/01): Grants paid, $292,940; assets, $400,911 (M); gifts received, $55,000; expenditures, $298,318; qualifying distributions, $297,335.
Limitations: Applications not accepted. Giving limited to Brooklyn, NY.
Application information: Contributes only to pre-selected organizations.
Officers: Nesim Bildirici, Pres.; Sophia Bildirici, V.P.
EIN: 113411724
Codes: FD

34084
The Levitin Family Charitable Trust
1222 E. 22nd St.
Brooklyn, NY 11210

Established in 1998 in NY.
Financial data (yr. ended 12/31/99): Grants paid, $292,880; assets, $1,309,030 (M); gifts received, $773,860; expenditures, $293,784; qualifying distributions, $290,161.
Trustees: Eli Levitin, Raizy Levitin.
EIN: 116496569
Codes: FD

34085
The Basil H. Alkazzi Foundation, Ltd.
126 E. 56th St., 12th Fl.
New York, NY 10022
Contact: George J. Khouri, Board Member

Established in 1999 in NY.
Donor(s): Basil H. Alkazzi.
Financial data (yr. ended 06/30/01): Grants paid, $291,524; assets, $0 (M); expenditures, $291,648; qualifying distributions, $291,509.
Board Members: Basil H. Alkazzi, Christopher Frayling, George J. Khouri.
EIN: 134080858
Codes: FD

34086
JJG Foundation, Inc.
666 3rd Ave., 29th Fl.
New York, NY 10017-4011

Established in 1985 in NY.
Donor(s): David P. Steinmann.
Financial data (yr. ended 12/31/00): Grants paid, $291,383; assets, $4,882,341 (M); expenditures, $316,678; qualifying distributions, $291,633.
Limitations: Applications not accepted. Giving primarily in the metropolitan New York, NY, area.
Application information: Contributes only to pre-selected organizations.
Officers: David P. Steinmann, Pres. and Treas.; Catherine P. Steinmann, V.P. and Secy.
Director: Joel Hirschtritt.
EIN: 133266112
Codes: FD

34087
William & Sheila Konar Foundation
110 Commerce Dr.
Rochester, NY 14623-3504 (716) 334-4110
Contact: William B. Konar, Tr.

Established in 1982.
Donor(s): Sheila Konar, William B. Konar.
Financial data (yr. ended 12/31/01): Grants paid, $291,164; assets, $3,106,410 (M); gifts received, $373,790; expenditures, $296,210; qualifying distributions, $291,164.
Limitations: Giving primarily in NY.
Trustees: Rachel K. Guttenberg, Howard E. Konar, Sheila Konar, William B. Konar.
EIN: 222434846
Codes: FD

34088
Mars Foundation
c/o Goldstein
2610 Ave. N
Brooklyn, NY 11210

Established in 2000 in NY.
Donor(s): Aryeh Goldstein.
Financial data (yr. ended 12/31/01): Grants paid, $290,699; assets, $156,075 (M); gifts received, $217,000; expenditures, $290,786; qualifying distributions, $290,681.
Limitations: Applications not accepted. Giving primarily in NY.
Application information: Contributes only to pre-selected organizations.
Officer: Aryeh Goldstein, Pres.
EIN: 311743263
Codes: FD

34089
Leviton Foundation, Inc. - New York
59-25 Little Neck Pkwy.
Little Neck, NY 11362-2531

Incorporated in 1952 in NY.
Donor(s): Leviton Manufacturing Co., Inc., American Insulated Wire Corp.
Financial data (yr. ended 12/31/01): Grants paid, $289,075; assets, $235,500 (M); gifts received, $303,500; expenditures, $289,205; qualifying distributions, $289,075.
Limitations: Applications not accepted.
Application information: Contributes only to pre-selected organizations.
Officers: Harold Leviton, Pres.; Shirley Leviton, Treas.
EIN: 116006368
Codes: CS, FD, CD

34090
The Jeffrey Steiner Family Foundation
c/o David I. Faust
488 Madison Ave.
New York, NY 10022

Established in 1982 in NY.
Donor(s): Jeffrey Steiner.
Financial data (yr. ended 06/30/01): Grants paid, $288,767; assets, $34,591 (M); gifts received, $69,985; expenditures, $294,535; qualifying distributions, $288,679.
Limitations: Applications not accepted. Giving primarily in New York, NY.
Application information: Contributes only to pre-selected organizations.
Directors: David I. Faust, Eric Steiner, Jeffrey Steiner.
EIN: 133152349
Codes: FD

34091
The Roxe Foundation
450 Park Ave., 6th Fl.
New York, NY 10022 (212) 634-1186
Additional tel.: (212) 634-1185; FAX: (212) 634-1153
Contact: Maryann B. Tolan, V.P.

Established in 1997 in CT.
Donor(s): Joseph D. Roxe, Maureen L. Roxe.
Financial data (yr. ended 12/31/01): Grants paid, $288,601; assets, $6,551,259 (M); expenditures, $379,255; qualifying distributions, $319,724.
Limitations: Applications not accepted. Giving primarily in CT and NY.
Application information: Contributes only to pre-selected organization.
Officers and Trustees:* Joseph D. Roxe,* Chair.; Maureen L. Roxe, Pres.; Hilary A. Roxe, V.P.; Joseph L. Roxe, V.P.; Lesley E. Roxe, V.P.; Maryann B. Tolan,* V.P.
EIN: 061480884
Codes: FD

34092
Juliet Rosenthal Foundation, Inc.
1370 Broadway
New York, NY 10018

Established in 1958.
Donor(s): Rosenthal & Rosenthal, Inc.
Financial data (yr. ended 12/31/99): Grants paid, $288,590; assets, $7,732,123 (M); expenditures, $318,794; qualifying distributions, $288,590.
Limitations: Applications not accepted. Giving primarily in New York, NY.
Application information: Contributes only to pre-selected organizations.
Officers: Stephen Rosenthal, V.P.; Julie Sanjenis, V.P.; Eric Rosenthal, Treas.
EIN: 136161085
Codes: FD

34093
Tuft Family Foundation
c/o Goldman Sachs & Co.
85 Broad St., Tax Dept.
New York, NY 10004

Established in 1987 in NY.
Donor(s): Thomas E. Tuft.
Financial data (yr. ended 08/31/01): Grants paid, $288,223; assets, $8,284,575 (M); gifts received, $2,638,520; expenditures, $365,053; qualifying distributions, $292,053.
Limitations: Applications not accepted. Giving primarily in New York, NY.
Application information: Contributes only to pre-selected organizations.
Trustees: Lewis M. Eisenberg, Diane H. Tuft, Thomas E. Tuft.
EIN: 133437888
Codes: FD

34094
The Tierney Family Foundation, Inc.
c/o Paul Tierney, Pres., or Susan Tierney, Secy.
1133 5th Ave.
New York, NY 10128

Established around 1990.
Financial data (yr. ended 12/31/99): Grants paid, $288,157; assets, $7,439,260 (M); expenditures, $330,001; qualifying distributions, $287,438.
Limitations: Giving on a national basis.
Officers: Paul E. Tierney, Jr., Pres.; Michael P. Tierney, V.P.; Patricia E. Tierney, V.P.; Susan E. Tierney, Secy.
EIN: 133541596
Codes: FD

34095
The Garber Family Foundation
P.O. Box 997
Nyack, NY 10960
Contact: Adele Garber, Admin.

Established in 1999 in TX.
Donor(s): Ross B. Garber, Laurie A. Garber.
Financial data (yr. ended 12/31/01): Grants paid, $288,000; assets, $4,018,233 (M); expenditures, $296,804; qualifying distributions, $287,597.
Limitations: Giving primarily in Austin, TX.
Application information: Application form required.
Officers: Ross B. Garber, Pres.; Laurie A. Garber, V.P.
Trustee: Adele Garber.
EIN: 742940367
Codes: FD

34096
Peter and Helen Haje Foundation
44 W. 77th St., Ste. 14W
New York, NY 10024

Established in 2000 in NY.
Donor(s): Peter R. Haje.
Financial data (yr. ended 12/31/00): Grants paid, $288,000; assets, $8,922,016 (M); gifts received, $8,619,260; expenditures, $289,399; qualifying distributions, $289,163.
Limitations: Applications not accepted. Giving on a national basis.
Application information: Contributes only to pre-selected organizations.
Officers: Peter R. Haje, Chair.; Helen Haje, Pres. and Treas.; Michael Haje, V.P.; Katie Haje, V.P. and Secy.
EIN: 134112185
Codes: FD

34097
The Kaufman Family Foundation
455 E. 86th St., Ste. 35B
New York, NY 10028

Established in 1994.
Donor(s): Stephen P. Kaufman.
Financial data (yr. ended 12/31/01): Grants paid, $287,750; assets, $266,854 (M); expenditures, $292,602; qualifying distributions, $287,895.
Limitations: Applications not accepted. Giving primarily in NY.
Application information: Contributes only to pre-selected organizations.
Trustees: Jeremy S. Kaufman, Sharon K. Kaufman, Stephen P. Kaufman.
EIN: 137036137
Codes: FD

34098
SMF Foundation, Inc.
c/o Goldstein, Golub, Kessler & Co.
1185 Ave. of the Americas, 5th Fl.
New York, NY 10036 (212) 523-1200

Established in 1961.
Donor(s): D. Griffel, Joseph Mayer, Elfriede Mayer, Amalia Steinberger, B. Westreich, Jack Mayer, Esther M. Mayer.
Financial data (yr. ended 12/31/99): Grants paid, $287,585; assets, $170,722 (M); gifts received, $184,769; expenditures, $291,923; qualifying distributions, $286,629.
Limitations: Giving primarily in Brooklyn, NY.
Application information: Application form not required.
Officers: Elfriede Mayer, Pres.; Joseph Mayer, Secy.; Jack N. Mayer, Treas.
EIN: 136113805
Codes: FD

34099
The John Ben Snow Foundation, Inc.
50 Presidential Plz., Ste. 106
Syracuse, NY 13202
FAX: (315) 471-5256
Contact: Jonathan L. Snow, Treas.

Incorporated in 1948 in NY.
Donor(s): John Ben Snow.‡
Financial data (yr. ended 12/31/01): Grants paid, $287,550; assets, $7,006,249 (M); expenditures, $441,903; qualifying distributions, $361,630.
Limitations: Giving limited to central NY, with emphasis on Onondaga and Oswego counties.
Publications: Annual report (including application guidelines), financial statement.
Application information: All inquiries by mail. Application form required.
Officers and Directors:* David H. Snow,* V.P. and Secy.; Jonathan L. Snow,* V.P. and Treas.; Valerie A. Macfie, Allen R. Malcolm, Bruce Malcolm, Emelie Melton-Williams.
EIN: 136112704
Codes: FD

34100
Peter T. and Laura M. Grauer Foundation
c/o M. Blumenreich & Co.
295 Madison Ave., Ste. 1125
New York, NY 10017-8393
Contact: Peter T. Grauer, Pres. and Treas.

Established in 1989 in NY and DE.
Donor(s): Peter T. Grauer.
Financial data (yr. ended 12/31/00): Grants paid, $287,500; assets, $149,788 (M); gifts received, $350,941; expenditures, $291,135; qualifying distributions, $287,474.
Limitations: Giving on a national basis.
Officers: Peter T. Grauer, Pres. and Treas.; Laura M. Grauer, V.P. and Secy.
EIN: 521702126
Codes: FD

34101
Elster Foundation
c/o Sydney E. Goldstein
925 Delaware Ave., Apt. 6B
Buffalo, NY 14209-1843

Established in 1964 in NY.
Donor(s): Robert S. Elster.‡
Financial data (yr. ended 12/31/01): Grants paid, $286,900; assets, $7,227,101 (M); expenditures, $383,575; qualifying distributions, $284,869.
Limitations: Applications not accepted. Giving primarily in FL, Atlanta, GA, and Buffalo, NY.
Application information: Contributes only to pre-selected organizations.
Trustees: Amy Gerome-Acuff, Douglas R. Goldstein, Elizabeth Geer Goldstein, Jerome E. Goldstein, Sydney E. Goldstein.
EIN: 166054742
Codes: FD

34102
Fishbein Family Interstitial Cystitis Research Foundation
c/o Hertz, Herson & Co., LLP
2 Park Ave.
New York, NY 10016

Established in 1998 in NY.
Donor(s): Robert Fishbein.
Financial data (yr. ended 12/31/01): Grants paid, $286,762; assets, $1,248,891 (M); expenditures, $301,993; qualifying distributions, $289,133.
Limitations: Applications not accepted. Giving primarily in NY.
Application information: Contributes only to pre-selected organizations.
Officers: Laurie Fishbein, Pres.; Robert Fishbein, Treas.
Directors: Jan Fishbein Bernstein, Elisabeth Fishbein, Kara Fishbein, Steven Goldman.
EIN: 133967301
Codes: FD

34103
The Ungar Foundation
P.O. Box 752
Copake, NY 12516
Contact: Mrs. Aine Ungar, Tr.

Financial data (yr. ended 11/30/01): Grants paid, $285,482; assets, $2,249,953 (M); expenditures, $345,342; qualifying distributions, $334,484.
Limitations: Giving primarily in New York, NY.
Trustee: Mrs. Aine Ungar.
EIN: 136937282
Codes: FD

34104
Llewellyn Burchell Charitable Trust
c/o JPMorgan Private Bank
1211 Ave. of the Americas, 38th Fl.
New York, NY 10036 (212) 789-5679
FAX: (212) 596-3712; *E-mail:* elias_jacqueline@jpmorgan.com
Contact: Jacqueline Elias, V.P.

Established in 1991 in NY.
Financial data (yr. ended 12/31/01): Grants paid, $285,000; assets, $4,381,903 (M); gifts received, $11,000; expenditures, $355,052; qualifying distributions, $281,853.
Limitations: Applications not accepted. Giving primarily in New York, NY.
Application information: Proposals will be solicited by the trust. Unsolicited proposals will not be accepted.
Trustee: JPMorgan Chase Bank.
EIN: 136989806
Codes: FD

34105
Iroquois Avenue Foundation
c/o Sheehan & Co.
230 Park Ave., Ste. 416
New York, NY 10169-0124

Established in 1989 in DE.
Donor(s): Lydia B. Mann.‡
Financial data (yr. ended 12/31/01): Grants paid, $285,000; assets, $5,215,320 (M); expenditures, $324,557; qualifying distributions, $283,609.
Limitations: Applications not accepted. Giving primarily in Palm Beach, FL, and New York, NY.
Application information: Contributes only to pre-selected organizations.
Officers: Christian A. Melhado, Co-Pres. and Secy.; Peter A.B. Melhado, Co-Pres.; Kenneth J. Siegal, Treas.
Directors: Jill F. Melhado, Teresa S. Melhado.
EIN: 133562887
Codes: FD

34106
Louis Morin Charitable Trust
c/o Piper Rudnick LLP
1251 Ave. of the Americas
New York, NY 10020
E-mail: christine.kehoe@piperudnick.com
Contact: Thomas A. Melfe, Tr. and Christine A. Kehoe, Admin.

Established in 2000 in NY.
Donor(s): Lily Lewis.‡
Financial data (yr. ended 12/31/01): Grants paid, $285,000; assets, $4,899,581 (M); expenditures, $363,832; qualifying distributions, $302,312.
Limitations: Giving primarily in NY.

Trustee: Thomas A. Melfe.
EIN: 137216266
Codes: FD

34107
The Thornton Foundation
c/o Goldman Sachs, Tax Dept.
85 Broad St.
New York, NY 10004-2456

Established in 1989.
Donor(s): John L. Thornton.
Financial data (yr. ended 06/30/01): Grants paid, $285,000; assets, $9,395,627 (M); gifts received, $2,750; expenditures, $288,900; qualifying distributions, $288,500.
Limitations: Applications not accepted. Giving primarily in CT and NY.
Application information: Contributes only to pre-selected organizations.
Trustees: Robert S. Harrison, John L. Thornton, John V. Thornton.
EIN: 133543268
Codes: FD

34108
Eberstadt-Kuffner Fund, Inc.
(Formerly The Vera and Walter Eberstadt Foundation)
c/o Yohalem Gillman & Co, LLP
477 Madison Ave.
New York, NY 10022-5802

Established in 1967 in NY.
Donor(s): Vera Eberstadt, Walter Eberstadt, Helene Kuffner.‡
Financial data (yr. ended 12/31/01): Grants paid, $284,228; assets, $8,337,079 (M); gifts received, $124,915; expenditures, $352,188; qualifying distributions, $285,311.
Limitations: Applications not accepted. Giving primarily in NY.
Application information: Contributes only to pre-selected organizations.
Directors: Vera Eberstadt, Walter Eberstadt, Daniel L. Mosley.
EIN: 136225395
Codes: FD

34109
Spektor Family Foundation, Inc.
262 Central Park West, Ste. 14 E
New York, NY 10024 (212) 790-5724
Contact: Mira Spektor, Pres.

Established in 1968 in NY.
Donor(s): Eryk Spektor.‡
Financial data (yr. ended 06/30/01): Grants paid, $284,165; assets, $3,520,864 (M); expenditures, $328,609; qualifying distributions, $275,945.
Limitations: Giving primarily in NY.
Officer: Mira Spektor, Pres.
EIN: 136277982
Codes: FD

34110
The Gellman Foundation
4053 Maple Rd.
Amherst, NY 14226

Established in 1988 in FL.
Donor(s): Members of the Gellman family, Jack E. Gellman.
Financial data (yr. ended 12/31/01): Grants paid, $284,000; assets, $246,527 (M); expenditures, $286,406; qualifying distributions, $283,768.
Limitations: Applications not accepted. Giving primarily in Miami, FL, and NY.
Application information: Contributes only to pre-selected organizations.
Trustee: Jack E. Gellman.

EIN: 581765283
Codes: FD

34111
David A. and Shoshanna Wingate Foundation, Inc.
3333 New Hyde Park Rd.
New Hyde Park, NY 11042

Established in 1987 in NY.
Donor(s): David A. Wingate, Shoshanna Wingate.
Financial data (yr. ended 05/31/01): Grants paid, $283,525; assets, $2,952,724 (M); expenditures, $355,469; qualifying distributions, $281,403.
Limitations: Applications not accepted. Giving primarily in Palm Beach, FL, and the metropolitan New York, NY, area, including Long Island.
Application information: Contributes only to pre-selected organizations.
Officers: David A. Wingate, Pres.; Shoshanna Wingate, V.P.; Batsheva Ostrow, Co-Secy.-Treas.; Ealan J. Wingate, Co-Secy.-Treas.
EIN: 112863716
Codes: FD

34112
Utica National Group Foundation, Inc.
P.O. Box 530
Utica, NY 13503
Contact: John R. Zapisek, Treas.

Established in 1987 in NY.
Donor(s): Utica Mutual Insurance Co.
Financial data (yr. ended 12/31/01): Grants paid, $283,405; assets, $4,767,563 (M); gifts received, $2,803; expenditures, $305,353; qualifying distributions, $305,353.
Limitations: Giving primarily in the greater Utica, NY, area.
Application information: Application form required.
Officers and Directors:* J. Douglas Robinson,* Pres.; George P. Wardley III, Secy.; John R. Zapisek, Treas.; C. William Bachman, Alfred B. Calligaris, Jerry J. Hartman, W. Craig Heston, Herbert P. Ladds, Jr., Linda E. Romano.
EIN: 161313450
Codes: CS, FD, CD

34113
The Potts Memorial Foundation
12 S. 4th St.
Hudson, NY 12534 (518) 828-3365
Contact: Charles E. Inman, Secy.

Incorporated in 1922 in NY.
Financial data (yr. ended 12/31/01): Grants paid, $283,375; assets, $4,567,859 (M); expenditures, $324,701; qualifying distributions, $283,375.
Limitations: Giving on a national basis.
Application information: Application form not required.
Officers: Stanley Bardwell, M.D., Pres.; Richard Cappelletti, M.D., V.P.; Charles Inman, Secy.; Sid Richter, Treas.
EIN: 141347714
Codes: FD

34114
Jack H. Ashkenazie Foundation, Inc.
31 W. 34th St., 8th Fl.
New York, NY 10001

Established in 2001 in NY.
Donor(s): Almar Sales Company, Inc.
Financial data (yr. ended 12/31/01): Grants paid, $283,218; assets, $4,306 (M); gifts received, $279,068; expenditures, $283,374; qualifying distributions, $283,218.
Limitations: Applications not accepted.

Application information: Contributes only to pre-selected organizations.
Officer: Jack R. Ashkenazie, Treas.
Directors: Harry J. Ashkenazie, Raymond J. Ashkenazie.
EIN: 134161819

34115
Victor E. Perley Fund
c/o Lillian Fable
629 9th Ave.
New York, NY 10036

Established in 1967 in NY.
Financial data (yr. ended 12/31/01): Grants paid, $283,000; assets, $4,562,993 (M); expenditures, $320,547; qualifying distributions, $280,331.
Limitations: Giving primarily in New York, NY.
Trustees: Richard Basini, Herbert Block, Lillian Fable, Ed Lee.
EIN: 136219298
Codes: FD

34116
The Brand Foundation of New York, Inc.
(Formerly The Martha and Regina Brand Foundation, Inc.)
521 5th Ave., Ste. 1805
New York, NY 10175-1899 (212) 687-3505

Established in 1962 in NY.
Donor(s): Martha Brand,‡ Marjorie D. Kogan.
Financial data (yr. ended 12/31/00): Grants paid, $282,650; assets, $4,038,649 (M); expenditures, $333,056; qualifying distributions, $307,212.
Limitations: Applications not accepted. Giving primarily in CA, New York, NY and SC.
Application information: Contributes only to pre-selected organizations.
Officers: Marjorie D. Kogan, Pres.; Michael S. Kogan, V.P. and Secy.; Barton H. Kogan, V.P. and Treas.
EIN: 136159106
Codes: FD

34117
Richard & Elizabeth Witten Family Foundation
c/o BCRS Assocs., LLC
100 Wall St., 11th Fl.
New York, NY 10005

Established in 1991 in NY.
Donor(s): Richard E. Witten.
Financial data (yr. ended 05/31/01): Grants paid, $282,506; assets, $4,758,237 (M); expenditures, $364,408; qualifying distributions, $282,768.
Limitations: Applications not accepted. Giving primarily in Larchmont and New York, NY.
Application information: Contributes only to pre-selected organizations.
Trustees: Elizabeth H. Witten, Richard E. Witten.
EIN: 133632751
Codes: FD

34118
Harmon Foundation, Inc.
c/o Boyce, Hughes & Farrell
1025 Northern Blvd., Ste. 300
Roslyn, NY 11576-1587

Established in 1988 in NY.
Donor(s): William E. Harmon Trust Fund f/b/o the Harmon Foundation, Inc.
Financial data (yr. ended 12/31/01): Grants paid, $282,500; assets, $1,196,950 (M); gifts received, $479,366; expenditures, $330,343; qualifying distributions, $312,883.
Limitations: Applications not accepted. Giving on a national basis.

34118—NEW YORK

Application information: Contributes only to pre-selected organizations. Unsolicited requests for funds not accepted.
Officers and Directors:* Thomas C. Harmon,* Chair.; Robert J. Clawson, Jr.,* Pres.; James F. McNevin, V.P.; Michael B. Hollyday, Secy.; Mary Harmon Persson,* Treas.; Nora McNevin Brenneis, Douglas B. Harmon, James Harmon, James S. Harmon, John V. Harmon, William B. Harmon, William F. Harmon, Ellen D. Hollyday, James Hollyday, Jr., Mary H. Hollyday, A.C.B. McNevin, Jr., Katherine K. McNevin, Joan Harmon Slipp, Caroline Nason Whetstone.
EIN: 135562236
Codes: FD

34119
The Henry Cornell Foundation
c/o Goldman Sachs & Co.
85 Broad St., Tax Dept.
New York, NY 10004

Established in 1996 in NY.
Donor(s): Henry Cornell.
Financial data (yr. ended 08/31/01): Grants paid, $282,450; assets, $2,983,099 (M); gifts received, $2,500; expenditures, $303,073; qualifying distributions, $285,373.
Limitations: Applications not accepted. Giving primarily in NY.
Application information: Contributes only to pre-selected organizations.
Trustees: Henry Cornell, Rose Schindler.
EIN: 133921374
Codes: FD

34120
Keren M. Y. and C. B. Elias, Inc.
(Formerly Keren Mordechai Yaakov and Blima Chaya Elias, Inc.)
1548 50th St.
Brooklyn, NY 11219

Established in 1989 in NY.
Donor(s): Moses Elias, Zev Fishman, Mordechai J. Elias, Simcha Fishman, Khal Chasidim Bobov, Keren DERL Inc.
Financial data (yr. ended 02/28/01): Grants paid, $282,187; assets, $249,469 (M); gifts received, $169,072; expenditures, $282,861; qualifying distributions, $282,257.
Limitations: Giving primarily in Brooklyn, NY.
Officer: Moses Elias, Mgr.
EIN: 133534646
Codes: FD

34121
Northside Foundation
c/o David M. Rozen
400 W. 253 St.
Bronx, NY 10471

Donor(s): David M. Rozen.
Financial data (yr. ended 11/30/00): Grants paid, $281,353; assets, $282,109 (M); gifts received, $134,073; expenditures, $284,298; qualifying distributions, $281,353.
Limitations: Applications not accepted. Giving primarily in NY.
Application information: Contributes only to pre-selected organizations.
Trustee: David M. Rozen.
EIN: 137069686
Codes: FD

34122
Murray & Beatrice Sherman Foundation
c/o Citibank, N.A.
PBG Tax, Sort No. 4850
New York, NY 10043

Established in 1999 in NY.
Financial data (yr. ended 12/31/00): Grants paid, $281,000; assets, $5,591,772 (M); expenditures, $379,054; qualifying distributions, $281,326.
Limitations: Applications not accepted. Giving primarily in New York,NY.
Application information: Contributes only to pre-selected organizations.
Trustee: Citibank, N.A.
EIN: 116509309
Codes: FD

34123
Virgil Thompson Foundation, Ltd.
900 3rd Ave.St.
New York, NY 10022 (212) 895-2357
Contact: Wesley York

Financial data (yr. ended 12/31/00): Grants paid, $279,500; assets, $3,538,977 (M); expenditures, $360,426; qualifying distributions, $309,466.
Limitations: Giving primarily in New York, NY.
Officers: Richard Flender, Pres. and Treas.; Charles Fussell, V.P.
EIN: 133070033
Codes: FD

34124
Rofe Family Foundation
c/o Nathan Berkman & Co.
29 Broadway, Ste. 2900
New York, NY 10006-3296

Established in 1994 in NJ.
Donor(s): Rene Rofe, Elie Rofe, Double R. Holding, Inc., International Intimates, Inc.
Financial data (yr. ended 11/30/01): Grants paid, $279,432; assets, $150,896 (M); gifts received, $133,000; expenditures, $310,551; qualifying distributions, $279,388.
Limitations: Applications not accepted. Giving primarily in the metropolitan New York, NY, area.
Application information: Contributes only to pre-selected organizations.
Trustee: Rene Rofe.
EIN: 133798583
Codes: FD

34125
The Roger Stevens Family Fund
c/o Sandra Price, Ernst & Young
787 7th Ave.
New York, NY 10019
Application address: 1686 34th St., N.W., Washington, DC 20007
Contact: Christine G. Stevens, Pres.

Donor(s): Christine Stevens, Roger Stevens.‡
Financial data (yr. ended 12/31/00): Grants paid, $279,364; assets, $9,785 (M); expenditures, $281,837; qualifying distributions, $279,347.
Limitations: Giving primarily in Washington, DC.
Application information: Application form not required.
Officers and Trustees:* Christine G. Stevens,* Pres.; Christabel Gough, Secy.-Treas.; John Gleiber.
EIN: 521111963
Codes: TN

34126
Nelco Foundation, Inc.
164 W. 25th St.
New York, NY 10001 (212) 924-7604
Contact: Leon Jolson, Pres.

Incorporated in 1953 in NY.
Donor(s): Nelco Sewing Machine Sales Corp., Leon Jolson.
Financial data (yr. ended 05/31/01): Grants paid, $279,325; assets, $7,614,454 (M); gifts received, $265,740; expenditures, $345,103; qualifying distributions, $330,867.
Limitations: Giving primarily in the greater metropolitan New York, NY, area.
Officers: Leon Jolson, Pres.; Barbara Jolson Blumenthal, Secy.
EIN: 136089850
Codes: CS, FD, CD

34127
The Coleman Foundation
740 Park Ave.
New York, NY 10021
FAX: (212) 980-5308

Trust established in 1962 in NY.
Donor(s): Janet M. Coleman, Martin S. Coleman.‡
Financial data (yr. ended 11/30/01): Grants paid, $279,154; assets, $5,767,831 (M); expenditures, $389,502; qualifying distributions, $311,796.
Limitations: Applications not accepted. Giving primarily in Los Angeles, CA and New York, NY.
Application information: Contributes only to pre-selected organizations.
Trustee: Janet M. Coleman.
EIN: 136126040
Codes: FD

34128
The Kaplan Foundation, Inc.
450 Park Ave.
New York, NY 10022

Established in 1986 in NY.
Donor(s): Gilbert E. Kaplan.
Financial data (yr. ended 12/31/99): Grants paid, $278,900; assets, $232,190 (M); gifts received, $450,000; expenditures, $375,019; qualifying distributions, $372,730.
Limitations: Applications not accepted. Giving limited to New York, NY.
Application information: Contributes only to pre-selected organizations.
Directors: Gilbert E. Kaplan, Lena Kaplan.
EIN: 133284732
Codes: FD

34129
Bertha & Isaac Liberman Foundation
480 Park Ave.
New York, NY 10022
Contact: Jeffrey Klein, Pres.

Established in 1947 in NY.
Donor(s): Isaac Liberman.‡
Financial data (yr. ended 06/30/01): Grants paid, $278,550; assets, $7,225,857 (M); expenditures, $330,877; qualifying distributions, $299,609.
Limitations: Giving primarily in New York, NY.
Application information: Application form not required.
Officers: Jeffrey Klein, Pres.; Michelle Klein, V.P.; Jerome Tarnoff, Secy.; David B. Forer, Treas.
EIN: 136119056
Codes: FD

34130
Sharon Steel Foundation
c/o Arthur Y. Fox
126 E. 56th St., 12th Fl.
New York, NY 10022
Application address: c/o Hume R. Steyer, Seward & Kissel, 1 Battery Park Plz., New York, NY 10004

Established in 1953 in PA.
Donor(s): Sharon Steel Corp.
Financial data (yr. ended 12/31/00): Grants paid, $278,272; assets, $5,672,228 (M); expenditures, $347,137; qualifying distributions, $279,107.
Limitations: Giving primarily in eastern OH and western PA.
Application information: Application form not required.
Trustees: Christian L. Oberbeck, Malvin G. Sander, Hume R. Steyer.
EIN: 256063133
Codes: CS, FD, CD

34131
J. Weinstein Foundation, Inc.
Rockridge Farm, 961 Rte. 52
Carmel, NY 10512
FAX: (845) 225-0164
Contact: Sal Cappuzzo, Secy.-Treas.

Incorporated in 1948 in NY.
Donor(s): Joe Weinstein,‡ J.W. Mays, Inc.
Financial data (yr. ended 12/31/01): Grants paid, $278,154; assets, $4,973,143 (M); expenditures, $279,692; qualifying distributions, $278,154.
Limitations: Giving primarily in NY.
Officers and Directors:* Lloyd J. Shulman,* Pres.; Sylvia W. Shulman,* V.P.; Salvatore Cappuzzo,* Secy.-Treas.
EIN: 116003595
Codes: FD

34132
John S. Hilson Family Fund, Inc.
(Formerly Sonhil Fund, Inc.)
c/o Tanton and Co., LLP
37 W. 57th St., 5th Fl.
New York, NY 10019
Contact: John S. Pyne, Treas.

Established in 1963 in NY.
Donor(s): John S. Hilson.‡
Financial data (yr. ended 06/30/01): Grants paid, $278,050; assets, $5,873,003 (M); expenditures, $311,557; qualifying distributions, $278,980.
Limitations: Giving primarily in the tri-state CT, NJ, and NY, area.
Application information: Contributes mostly to pre-selected organizations.
Officers: William E. Hilson, Pres.; Dwight Hilson, V.P.; Richard J. Cunningham, Secy.; John S. Pyne, Treas.
EIN: 136135887
Codes: FD

34133
Betts Family Foundation
c/o Roland W. Betts
313 W. 102nd St.
New York, NY 10025

Established in 1998 in NY.
Donor(s): Roland W. Betts.
Financial data (yr. ended 12/31/00): Grants paid, $277,283; assets, $4,267,570 (M); expenditures, $338,807; qualifying distributions, $275,820.
Limitations: Applications not accepted. Giving primarily in NY.
Application information: Contributes only to pre-selected organizations.
Trustees: Jessica E. Betts, Lois P. Betts, Margaret W. Betts, Roland W. Betts.
EIN: 137152740

34134
Marden Family Foundation, Inc.
1125 Park Ave.
New York, NY 10128

Financial data (yr. ended 08/31/01): Grants paid, $277,051; assets, $1,955,199 (M); expenditures, $283,916; qualifying distributions, $281,777.
Limitations: Applications not accepted. Giving primarily in New York, NY.
Application information: Contributes only to pre-selected organizations.
Officers: James Marden, Pres.; Iris Marden, V.P. and Secy.
EIN: 133914405
Codes: FD

34135
The Kurtz Family Foundation, Inc.
c/o U.S. Trust
114 W. 47th St., Ste. C-1
New York, NY 10036-1594

Established in 1996 in NJ.
Donor(s): Ronald Kurtz, Carol Kurtz, Steven Levitt.
Financial data (yr. ended 12/31/00): Grants paid, $277,000; assets, $40,311,121 (M); expenditures, $335,117; qualifying distributions, $284,493.
Limitations: Applications not accepted. Giving primarily in MA.
Application information: Contributes only to pre-selected organizations.
Officers: Ronald Kurtz, Pres.; Carol Kurtz, Secy.
Trustee: Steven Levitt.
EIN: 223479749
Codes: FD

34136
Miller-Sweezy Charitable Trust
993 Park Ave.
New York, NY 10028

Established in 1986 in NY.
Donor(s): Kenneth H. Miller, Elizabeth Sweezy, Josh Fergenbaum.
Financial data (yr. ended 11/30/01): Grants paid, $276,631; assets, $895,975 (M); gifts received, $65,300; expenditures, $282,874; qualifying distributions, $278,117.
Limitations: Applications not accepted. Giving primarily in New York, NY.
Application information: Contributes only to pre-selected organizations.
Trustees: Kenneth H. Miller, Elizabeth Sweezy.
EIN: 133395958
Codes: FD

34137
Julie and Martin Franklin Charitable Foundation, Inc.
555 Theodore Fremd Ave., Ste. B-302
Rye, NY 10580

Established in 1994.
Donor(s): Julie Franklin, Martin E. Franklin.
Financial data (yr. ended 10/31/01): Grants paid, $276,412; assets, $363,060 (M); expenditures, $284,450; qualifying distributions, $276,387.
Limitations: Applications not accepted. Giving primarily in NY.
Application information: Contributes only to pre-selected organizations.
Officers: Martin E. Franklin, Pres. and Treas.; Julie Franklin, V.P. and Secy.
Director: Ian Ashken.
EIN: 133800643
Codes: FD

34138
Gollust Foundation
c/o Gollust, Tierney & Oliver, Inc.
500 Park Ave., 5th Fl.
New York, NY 10022

Established in 1989 in NY.
Donor(s): Keith R. Gollust.
Financial data (yr. ended 12/31/99): Grants paid, $276,276; assets, $1,087,359 (M); expenditures, $289,520; qualifying distributions, $275,684.
Limitations: Applications not accepted. Giving primarily in NJ and NY.
Application information: Contributes only to pre-selected organizations.
Trustee: Keith R. Gollust.
EIN: 136935600
Codes: FD

34139
O'Donnell Iselin Foundation, Inc.
c/o John F. Walsh
230 Park Ave, Ste. 1550
New York, NY 10169
Contact: Peter Iselin, Pres.

Established in 1946.
Donor(s): Peter Iselin, Emilie I. Wiggin.
Financial data (yr. ended 12/31/01): Grants paid, $276,250; assets, $4,431,514 (M); expenditures, $325,318; qualifying distributions, $274,578.
Limitations: Applications not accepted. Giving primarily in NY.
Officers: Peter Iselin, Pres. and Treas.; Emilie I. Wiggin, V.P.; John F. Walsh, Secy.
EIN: 516016471
Codes: FD

34140
Ruth & Seymour Klein Foundation, Inc.
16 Tallwoods Rd.
Armonk, NY 10504
Contact: Donald S. Klein, Pres.

Established in 1947.
Donor(s): Seymour M. Klein,‡ Ruth L. Klein.‡
Financial data (yr. ended 04/30/02): Grants paid, $276,000; assets, $5,719,024 (M); expenditures, $295,567; qualifying distributions, $276,000.
Limitations: Giving primarily in NY.
Application information: Application form not required.
Officers and Directors:* Donald S. Klein,* Pres.; Barbara G. Klein,* V.P.; Zoe S. Klein,* Secy.; Jason A. Klein,* Treas.
EIN: 136114763
Codes: FD

34141
The John M. and Mary A. Joyce Foundation
37 Seminary Rd.
Bedford, NY 10506
Contact: Timothy J. Joyce, Pres.

Incorporated in 1956 in IL.
Donor(s): John M. Joyce,‡ Mary McCann Joyce,‡ Seven-Up Bottling Co.
Financial data (yr. ended 07/31/01): Grants paid, $275,500; assets, $7,884,876 (M); gifts received, $374,568; expenditures, $336,143; qualifying distributions, $302,084.
Limitations: Applications not accepted. Giving primarily in NY.
Application information: Unsolicited requests for funds not accepted.
Officers and Trustees:* Timothy J. Joyce,* Pres.; Cathleen Joyce Egan, Secy.; Mary Catherine McCooey, Treas.
EIN: 366054112
Codes: FD

34142
Marjorie C. Adams Charitable Trust
c/o JPMorgan Private Bank
1211 Ave. of the Americas, 38th Fl.
New York, NY 10036 (212) 789-5679
FAX: (212) 596-3712; E-mail:
elias_jacqueline@jpmorgan.com
Contact: Jacqueline Elias, V.P.

Established in 1987 in NY.
Donor(s): Marjorie Carr Adams.
Financial data (yr. ended 08/31/01): Grants paid, $275,000; assets, $4,707,210 (M); expenditures, $328,722; qualifying distributions, $318,544.
Limitations: Giving primarily in NY.
Application information: Proposals will be solicited by the foundation. Unsolicited requests for funds not accepted. Application form not required.
Trustee: JPMorgan Chase Bank.
EIN: 136897539
Codes: FD

34143
Wild Wings Foundation
c/o AMCO
667 Madison Ave., 20th Fl.
New York, NY 10021 (212) 973-8219

Established in 1981.
Donor(s): Rockefeller Charitable Trust, Anna M. Rockefeller Charitable Trust.
Financial data (yr. ended 12/31/99): Grants paid, $275,000; assets, $9,393,601 (M); gifts received, $375,000; expenditures, $547,599; qualifying distributions, $431,726.
Limitations: Applications not accepted. Giving primarily in NY.
Publications: Annual report, financial statement.
Application information: Unsolicited requests for funds not accepted.
Trustees: Christopher Elliman, David D. Elliman, David M. McAlpin.
EIN: 133096074
Codes: FD

34144
The Murphy Charitable Foundation
c/o Marcum & Kliegman, LLP
130 Crossways Park Dr.
Woodbury, NY 11797

Established in 1999 in NY.
Donor(s): Thomas S. Murphy, Jr., Karen Murphy.
Financial data (yr. ended 10/31/01): Grants paid, $274,734; assets, $928,217 (M); gifts received, $217,081; expenditures, $281,562; qualifying distributions, $273,123.
Limitations: Applications not accepted. Giving primarily in CT, NJ, and NY.
Application information: Contributes only to pre-selected organizations.
Trustees: Karen Murphy, Thomas S. Murphy, Jr.
EIN: 134089717
Codes: FD

34145
ContiGroup Companies Foundation
(Formerly Continental Grain Foundation)
277 Park Ave.
New York, NY 10172-0003 (212) 207-5470
Contact: Susan McIntyre, Asst. Secy.

Incorporated in 1961 in NY.
Donor(s): Continental Grain Co., ContiGroup Cos., Inc.
Financial data (yr. ended 01/31/01): Grants paid, $274,620; assets, $142 (M); gifts received, $283,230; expenditures, $283,170; qualifying distributions, $283,170.
Limitations: Giving primarily in NY.
Officers: Michel Fribourg, Pres.; Paul J. Fribourg, V.P.; Mark R. Baker, Secy.; Richard Anderson, Treas.
EIN: 136160912
Codes: CS, FD, CD, GTI

34146
The John P. & Constance A. Curran Charitable Foundation
237 Park Ave., Ste. 900
New York, NY 10017 (212) 808-2400
Application address: 100 Scarborough Station Rd., Scarborough, NY 10510
Contact: Constance Curran, Tr.

Established in 1997 in NY.
Financial data (yr. ended 12/31/00): Grants paid, $274,420; assets, $2,599,661 (M); gifts received, $1,200,180; expenditures, $351,382; qualifying distributions, $310,223.
Limitations: Giving primarily in NY, especially New York, NY, with other areas of donor interest in Ossining and Briarcliff Manor.
Application information: Application form required.
Trustees: Constance A. Curran, John P. Curran, Sean Curran, Michael Hartigan, Anthony Rauhut, Meredith Rauhut.
EIN: 133923928
Codes: FD

34147
Rock River Foundation, Inc.
1500 Broadway, Ste. 2400
New York, NY 10036 (212) 382-0404
FAX: (212) 382-2686; E-mail:
sjhammer@akmcpa.com
Contact: Stuart J. Hammer, Treas.

Established in 1994 in MS.
Donor(s): Morgan Freeman.
Financial data (yr. ended 09/30/01): Grants paid, $274,372; assets, $1,517,638 (M); gifts received, $300,000; expenditures, $358,176; qualifying distributions, $275,457.
Limitations: Giving primarily in NY.
Officers and Trustees:* Morgan Freeman,* Pres.; George P. Cossar,* V.P.; Otey Sherman,* V.P.; Myrna Colley-Lee,* Secy.; Stuart J. Hammer,* Treas.
EIN: 640838346
Codes: FD

34148
The SPIA Foundation
(Formerly Dorinda Pell and Mark Winkelman Foundation)
780 3rd Ave., 16th Fl.
New York, NY 10017

Established in 1985 in NY.
Donor(s): Mark O. Winkelman, Dorinda Pell.
Financial data (yr. ended 02/28/01): Grants paid, $273,925; assets, $5,076,895 (M); gifts received, $1,000; expenditures, $382,479; qualifying distributions, $382,479.
Limitations: Applications not accepted. Giving primarily in NY.
Application information: Contributes only to pre-selected organizations.
Trustees: Dorinda Pell, Marius O. Winkelman.
EIN: 133318172
Codes: FD

34149
The Seligsohn Family Foundation, Inc.
10 Hillview Dr.
Scarsdale, NY 10583

Established in 1992 in NY.
Donor(s): Gerald Seligsohn.
Financial data (yr. ended 12/31/01): Grants paid, $273,660; assets, $2,188,379 (M); expenditures, $287,564; qualifying distributions, $273,740.
Limitations: Applications not accepted. Giving primarily in NY.
Application information: Contributes only to pre-selected organizations.
Directors: Joseph Leshkowitz, Gerald Seligsohn, Sandra Seligsohn.
EIN: 133683755
Codes: FD

34150
Sasco Foundation
67A E. 77th St.
New York, NY 10021-1813
Contact: Ann Brownell Sloane, Admin.

Trust established in 1951 in NY.
Donor(s): Leila E. Riegel,‡ Katherine R. Emory.‡
Financial data (yr. ended 12/31/01): Grants paid, $273,500; assets, $6,482,312 (M); expenditures, $381,555; qualifying distributions, $293,342.
Limitations: Giving primarily in CT, ME, and NY.
Application information: Currently supporting trustee-sponsored projects only.
Trustees: Lucy E. Ambach, Benjamin Riegel Emory, Katherine Emory Stookey.
EIN: 136046567
Codes: FD

34151
Hildegarde D. Becher Foundation, Inc.
P.O. Box 11
Hartsdale, NY 10530
Contact: Lawrence Dix, Treas.

Established in 1995 in NY.
Financial data (yr. ended 12/31/01): Grants paid, $272,300; assets, $4,928,876 (M); expenditures, $366,374; qualifying distributions, $272,300.
Limitations: Giving on a national basis.
Application information: Application form not required.
Officers: Herbert Kroner, Pres.; Jack Geoghegan, Secy.; Lawrence Dix, Treas.
EIN: 133744010
Codes: FD

34152
The Grodzins Fund
155 E. 77th St., Ste. 3F
New York, NY 10021

Established in 1998 in NY.
Financial data (yr. ended 06/30/01): Grants paid, $272,200; assets, $4,253,789 (M); expenditures, $320,835; qualifying distributions, $276,409.
Limitations: Applications not accepted. Giving primarily in New York, NY.
Application information: Contributes only to pre-selected organizations.
Officer: Louis Slesin, Pres.
Directors: Muffie Meyer, Lesli Rice.
EIN: 134022751
Codes: FD

34153
Cunniff Family Fund
c/o Ruane Cunniff & Co., Inc.
767 5th Ave., Ste. 4701
New York, NY 10153-4798

Established in 1996 in NY.
Donor(s): Marilyn P.F. Cunniff, Matthew A. Baxter, Jr., Carol Cunniff, Richard T. Cunniff.
Financial data (yr. ended 11/30/01): Grants paid, $272,150; assets, $2,127,706 (M); gifts received, $211,828; expenditures, $276,125; qualifying distributions, $272,475.

Limitations: Applications not accepted. Giving primarily in NY.
Application information: Contributes only to pre-selected organizations.
Trustee: Richard T. Cunniff.
EIN: 137105085
Codes: FD

34154
Philippe Foundation, Inc.
405 Lexington Ave., 35th Fl.
New York, NY 10174 (212) 687-3290
Contact: Alain Philippe, Pres.

Incorporated in 1953 in NY.
Donor(s): Pierre Philippe, Alain Philippe, Anne-Marie Philippe, Beatrice Philippe.
Financial data (yr. ended 12/31/01): Grants paid, $271,857; assets, $5,621,602 (M); gifts received, $46,765; expenditures, $274,081; qualifying distributions, $269,001.
Limitations: Giving to citizens of the U.S. and France.
Publications: Application guidelines.
Application information: Application form not required.
Officers and Directors:* Alain Philippe,* Pres.; Anne-Marie Philippe,* V.P.; Beatrice Philippe,* V.P.; Douglas Bean, Secy.; Bruce Pauls, Treas.; Helene P. Grenier, Marie-Josette Larrieu, Irving London, Dominique Meyer, Anne Philippe-Vaysse.
EIN: 136087157
Codes: FD, GTI

34155
Isaac and Carol Auerbach Family Foundation
(Formerly Auerbach Family Foundation)
930 Park Ave., Ste. 9S
New York, NY 10028-0209 (212) 744-8951
Contact: Carol B. Auerbach, Tr.

Established in 1981 in PA.
Donor(s): Isaac L. Auerbach,‡ Carol B. Auerbach.
Financial data (yr. ended 03/31/01): Grants paid, $271,524; assets, $1,721,681 (M); gifts received, $70,600; expenditures, $300,330; qualifying distributions, $284,603.
Limitations: Giving primarily in the East Coast states.
Application information: Accepts Delaware Valley Grantmakers Common Grant Application and Common Report Form. Application form not required.
Trustee: Carol B. Auerbach.
EIN: 232169951
Codes: FD

34156
Victor Elmaleh Foundation
c/o World Wide Holdings Corp.
150 E. 58th St.
New York, NY 10155-0002

Established about 1962 in NY.
Donor(s): Victor Elmaleh, World-Wide Volkswagen Corp.
Financial data (yr. ended 12/31/00): Grants paid, $271,350; assets, $4,110,874 (M); gifts received, $100,800; expenditures, $319,283; qualifying distributions, $271,641.
Limitations: Applications not accepted. Giving primarily in NY.
Application information: Contributes only to pre-selected organizations.
Trustees: Ernest Alson, Niko Elmaleh, Sono Elmaleh, Victor Elmaleh.
EIN: 136075674
Codes: FD

34157
SVM Foundation
c/o Eric Kaplan
1285 6th Ave., 21st Fl.
New York, NY 10019

Established in 1996 in NY.
Donor(s): Seymour Milstein,‡ Vivian Milstein.
Financial data (yr. ended 12/31/00): Grants paid, $271,035; assets, $29,290,479 (M); gifts received, $6,998,911; expenditures, $529,202; qualifying distributions, $271,785.
Limitations: Applications not accepted.
Application information: Contributes only to pre-selected organizations.
Trustee: Vivian Milstein.
EIN: 137105557
Codes: FD

34158
Glenn N. Howatt Foundation, Inc.
c/o McGrath, Doyle & Phair
150 Broadway, No. 1703
New York, NY 10038 (212) 571-2300
Contact: James E. Lawler, Pres.

Established in 1965 in NY.
Financial data (yr. ended 11/30/01): Grants paid, $270,000; assets, $3,789,985 (M); expenditures, $313,974; qualifying distributions, $277,108.
Limitations: Applications not accepted. Giving primarily in NJ.
Application information: Contributes only to pre-selected organizations.
Officers and Directors:* James E. Lawler,* Pres.; Megan J. Thorn,* Secy.; Nicholas Jacangelo,* Treas.
EIN: 136191670
Codes: FD

34159
John W. & Mary M. Koessler Foundation, Inc.
c/o Paul Hilbert Assocs.
100 Corporate Pkwy., Ste. 410
Amherst, NY 14226
Contact: Mary M. Koessler, Pres.

Established in 1991 in DE and NY.
Donor(s): Mary M. Koessler.
Financial data (yr. ended 12/31/01): Grants paid, $270,000; assets, $2,068,620 (M); expenditures, $303,446; qualifying distributions, $268,758.
Limitations: Giving primarily in Buffalo, NY.
Officers and Directors:* Mary M. Koessler,* Pres.; Mary C. Smith,* V.P.; Paul C. Hilbert, Secy.
EIN: 161406643
Codes: FD

34160
T-4 Foundation
c/o Goldman Sachs & Co.
85 Broad St., Tax Dept.
New York, NY 10004

Established in 1999 in NY.
Donor(s): John A. Thain.
Financial data (yr. ended 09/30/01): Grants paid, $270,000; assets, $2,750,985 (M); gifts received, $2,750; expenditures, $285,080; qualifying distributions, $272,480.
Limitations: Applications not accepted. Giving primarily in Washington, DC and NY.
Application information: Contributes only to pre-selected organizations.
Trustees: John A. Thain, Barry L. Zubrow.
EIN: 134085189
Codes: FD

34161
The Albert C. Bostwick Foundation
Hillside Ave. and Bacon Rd.
P.O. Box 440
Old Westbury, NY 11568
Contact: Eleanor P. Bostwick, Tr.

Established in 1958 in NY.
Donor(s): Albert C. Bostwick.‡
Financial data (yr. ended 12/31/01): Grants paid, $269,500; assets, $4,241,359 (M); expenditures, $318,212; qualifying distributions, $271,760.
Limitations: Giving primarily in NY.
Trustees: Albert C. Bostwick, Jr., Eleanor P. Bostwick, Andrew G.C. Sage III.
EIN: 116003740
Codes: FD

34162
The William R. and Virginia F. Salomon Family Foundation, Inc.
1301 Ave. of the Americas, 41st Fl.
New York, NY 10019-6022

Incorporated in 1954 in NY.
Donor(s): William R. Salomon.
Financial data (yr. ended 12/31/99): Grants paid, $269,027; assets, $1,836,500 (M); gifts received, $137,359; expenditures, $290,543; qualifying distributions, $271,597.
Limitations: Applications not accepted. Giving primarily in New York, NY.
Application information: Contributes only to pre-selected organizations.
Officers and Directors:* William R. Salomon,* Pres. and Treas.; Virginia F. Salomon,* V.P.; Susan S. Neiman, Peter F. Salomon.
EIN: 136088823
Codes: FD

34163
The Victor and Esther Rozen Foundation
c/o Mondorf & Fenwick
4104 Old Vestal Rd., Ste. 107
Vestal, NY 13850
Application address: 19 Chenango St., Press Bldg., Ste. 1211, Binghamton, NY 13901
Contact: Hillard H. Rozen, Tr.

Established in 1994 in NY.
Financial data (yr. ended 12/31/01): Grants paid, $268,967; assets, $3,427,597 (M); expenditures, $347,397; qualifying distributions, $281,940.
Limitations: Giving primarily in NY, primarily in Binghamton and Vestal.
Application information: Application form required.
Trustees: Hillard H. Rozen, Milton A. Rozen.
EIN: 166400449
Codes: FD

34164
Andrea and Michael Leeds Family Foundation
P.O. Box 718
Syosset, NY 11791-0718

Established in 1999 in NY.
Donor(s): Michael S. Leeds, Liselotte J. Leeds, Gerard G. Leeds.
Financial data (yr. ended 03/31/01): Grants paid, $268,804; assets, $13,195,705 (M); expenditures, $369,621; qualifying distributions, $278,883.
Limitations: Applications not accepted. Giving primarily in NY.
Application information: Contributes only to pre-selected organizations.
Trustees: Andrea R. Leeds, Michael S. Leeds.
EIN: 134055742
Codes: FD

34165
Diane Goldberg Foundation
c/o Robert M. Goldberg
1161 Meadowbrook Rd.
North Merrick, NY 11566

Established in 1992 in NY.
Donor(s): Diane Lindner Goldberg.‡
Financial data (yr. ended 09/30/01): Grants paid, $268,750; assets, $5,244,410 (M); gifts received, $8,190; expenditures, $272,293; qualifying distributions, $268,750.
Limitations: Applications not accepted. Giving primarily in NY.
Application information: Contributes only to pre-selected organizations.
Officer and Directors:* Robert M. Goldberg,* Pres.; Norman Gross, Beverly Pion.
EIN: 113092291

34166
Moses L. Parshelsky Foundation
26 Court St., Rm. 904
Brooklyn, NY 11242   (718) 875-8883
Contact: Tony B. Berk, Tr.

Trust established in 1949 in NY.
Donor(s): Moses L. Parshelsky.‡
Financial data (yr. ended 12/31/01): Grants paid, $268,600; assets, $7,785,175 (M); expenditures, $382,353; qualifying distributions, $306,350.
Limitations: Giving primarily in Brooklyn and Queens County, NY.
Application information: Application form not required.
Trustees: Tony B. Berk, Josephine B. Krinsky, Robert D. Krinsky.
EIN: 111848260
Codes: FD

34167
Mary P. Dolciani Halloran Foundation
825 3rd Ave.
New York, NY 10022-7519

Established in 1982.
Donor(s): Mary P. Dolciani Halloran.‡
Financial data (yr. ended 12/31/01): Grants paid, $268,500; assets, $7,551,309 (M); expenditures, $499,744; qualifying distributions, $490,397.
Limitations: Applications not accepted. Giving on a national basis.
Application information: Contributes only to pre-selected organizations.
Officers: James J. Halloran, Pres.; Eugene J. Callahan, V.P.; Antonio Gonzalez, V.P.; Concepcion G. Halloran, V.P.; Denise Lyn Halloran, V.P.
EIN: 133147449
Codes: FD

34168
Washington Square Fund
FDR Station
P.O. Box 7938
New York, NY 10150
Contact: Louise Chinn, Pres.

Established in 1969 in NY.
Financial data (yr. ended 06/30/01): Grants paid, $268,500; assets, $4,496,471 (M); expenditures, $323,756; qualifying distributions, $271,614.
Limitations: Giving limited to New York City.
Application information: Application form not required.
Officers and Directors:* Louise Chinn,* Pres.; Theresa R. Schaff,* V.P.; Anthony Newman,* Secy.; Charles W. Kraushaar,* Treas.; Mrs. De Gers Armstrong, Susan Baisley, Neil E. Botwinoff, Lesley Hermann, Theresa Thompson, Mary-Ellen Weinrib, Claire Whittaker.

EIN: 131624213
Codes: FD

34169
The Parsons Family Foundation
c/o Tag Assocs.
75 Rockefeller Plz., Ste. 900
New York, NY 10019

Established in 1995 in NY and DE.
Donor(s): Richard D. Parsons.
Financial data (yr. ended 12/31/00): Grants paid, $268,450; assets, $1,895,418 (M); expenditures, $280,836; qualifying distributions, $269,016.
Limitations: Applications not accepted.
Application information: Contributes only to pre-selected organizations.
Officers and Directors:* Laura A. Parsons,* Pres.; Richard D. Parsons,* Secy.-Treas.; Elisa Del Parsons, Gregory A. Parsons, Leslie J. Parsons, Rebecca L. Parsons.
EIN: 133864478
Codes: FD

34170
The Greater Norwich Foundation
c/o NBT Bank, N.A.
52 S. Broad St.
Norwich, NY 13815   (607) 337-6193
Contact: James I. Dunne, Chair., or James A. Hoy, Secy.-Treas.

Established in 1965 in NY.
Financial data (yr. ended 03/31/01): Grants paid, $268,140; assets, $4,788,726 (M); gifts received, $21,612; expenditures, $286,137; qualifying distributions, $276,820.
Limitations: Giving primarily in the Norwich, NY, area.
Publications: Informational brochure.
Application information: Application form required.
Officers: James I. Dunne, Chair.; James A. Hoy, Secy.-Treas.
Trustees: Jane E. Eaton, Esther C. Flanagan, Everett A. Gilmour, Edward J. Lee, Frederic B. Miers, H. William Smith, Jr., Jacob K. Weinman, NBT Bank, N.A.
EIN: 166064927
Codes: FD

34171
The Palisades Educational Foundation, Inc.
(Formerly The Pren-Hall Foundation, Inc.)
c/o Gibney, Anthony & Flaherty, LLP
665 5th Ave., 2nd Fl.
New York, NY 10022   (212) 688-5151
Contact: Gerald J. Dunworth, Treas.

Incorporated in 1949 in DE.
Donor(s): Prentice-Hall, Inc.
Financial data (yr. ended 12/31/99): Grants paid, $268,000; assets, $6,577,116 (M); expenditures, $357,062; qualifying distributions, $307,761.
Limitations: Giving primarily in CT, NJ, and NY.
Application information: Grants limited almost entirely to organizations associated with interests of present or former directors.
Officers and Directors:* Donald A. Schaefer,* Pres.; Frederick W. Anthony,* Secy.; Gerald J. Dunworth,* Treas.; Colin Gunn.
EIN: 516015053
Codes: FD

34172
Finch, Pruyn Foundation, Inc.
1 Glen St.
Glens Falls, NY 12801-4499
Contact: David P. Manny, Secy.-Treas.

Established in 1952.

Financial data (yr. ended 12/31/01): Grants paid, $267,778; assets, $21,642 (M); gifts received, $280,000; expenditures, $268,013; qualifying distributions, $267,778.
Limitations: Giving primarily in Glens Falls, NY.
Officers and Directors:* Samuel P. Hoopes,* Pres.; Byron J. Lapham,* V.P.; David P. Manny,* Secy.-Treas.; Richard J. Carota.
EIN: 146029907
Codes: FD

34173
The Corrigan Foundation
c/o Goldman Sachs & Co.
85 Broad St., Tax Dept.
New York, NY 10004

Established in 1996 in NY.
Donor(s): E. Gerald Corrigan.
Financial data (yr. ended 07/31/01): Grants paid, $267,050; assets, $4,223,895 (M); gifts received, $2,144,625; expenditures, $289,199; qualifying distributions, $271,130.
Limitations: Applications not accepted. Giving primarily in CT, MA, and NY.
Application information: Contributes only to pre-selected organizations.
Trustees: E. Gerald Corrigan, Elizabeth A. Corrigan, Karen B. Corrigan, Cathy E. Minehan.
EIN: 137109402
Codes: FD

34174
Mitsubishi International Corporation Foundation
c/o Mitsubishi International Corp.
520 Madison Ave.
New York, NY 10022

Established in 1992 in NY.
Donor(s): Mitsubishi Corp., Mitsubishi International Corp.
Financial data (yr. ended 12/31/01): Grants paid, $267,000; assets, $4,374,208 (M); gifts received, $300,000; expenditures, $184,228; qualifying distributions, $267,000.
Limitations: Applications not accepted. Giving primarily in NY.
Application information: Contributes only to pre-selected organizations.
Officers: Hironori Aihara, Chair.; James E. Brumm, Pres.; Tracy L. Austin, Secy.; Yoshiro Sato, Treas.; Stephen Wechselblatt, Exec. Dir.
EIN: 133676166
Codes: CS, FD, CD

34175
F. A. O. Schwarz Family Foundation
c/o U.S. Trust
114 W. 47th St.
New York, NY 10036
FAX: (212) 852-3377
Contact: Carolyn L. Larke, Asst. V.P., U.S. Trust, or Linda R. Francisovich, Sr. V.P., U.S. Trust

Established in 1991 in NY.
Financial data (yr. ended 04/30/01): Grants paid, $267,000; assets, $2,367,783 (M); expenditures, $285,877; qualifying distributions, $269,577.
Limitations: Applications not accepted. Giving primarily in Gainesville, FL, Boston, MA, and New York, NY.
Application information: Contributes only to pre-selected organizations.
Trustees: Dorothy S. Hines, Caroline Schwarz Schastny, Eliza Ladd Schwarz, Frederick A.O. Schwarz III, H. Marshall Schwarz, Elizabeth S. Wing.
EIN: 136986221
Codes: FD

34176
Yin-Shun Foundation
c/o I. Peidilato
600 Forest Ave.
Staten Island, NY 10310

Established in 1996.
Financial data (yr. ended 12/31/99): Grants paid, $266,864; assets, $10,246,492 (M); gifts received, $146,877; expenditures, $664,069; qualifying distributions, $3,983,614.
Limitations: Giving primarily in New York, NY.
Officers: Tsu-Ku Lee, Pres.; Ken Chen, Secy.; Steve Lue, Treas.
EIN: 223458312
Codes: FD

34177
The Steve and Anita Westly Foundation
c/o Deutsche Bank Trust Co. of NY
P.O. Box 1297, Church St. Sta., Ste. 7 W.
New York, NY 10008

Established in 2000 in CA.
Donor(s): Steve Westly, Anita Westly.
Financial data (yr. ended 12/31/01): Grants paid, $266,560; assets, $4,949,424 (M); gifts received, $303; expenditures, $493,924; qualifying distributions, $304,877.
Limitations: Applications not accepted.
Application information: Contributes only to pre-selected organizations.
Officers and Directors:* Steve Westly,* Chair.; Nicole Bergeron, Pres.; Anita Yu,* Secy.
EIN: 943368338
Codes: FD

34178
Baker Charitable Foundation
c/o JPMorgan Chase Bank, Trust Dept.
P.O. Box 31412
Rochester, NY 14603
Contact: Kate Noble

Established in 1986 in NY.
Financial data (yr. ended 01/31/02): Grants paid, $266,500; assets, $2,452,432 (M); expenditures, $289,486; qualifying distributions, $267,944.
Limitations: Giving limited to the Syracuse, NY, area.
Trustee: JPMorgan Chase Bank.
EIN: 166290586
Codes: FD

34179
The Lynton Foundation
33 W. 81st St.
New York, NY 10024

Established in 1993 in NY.
Donor(s): Marion Lynton.
Financial data (yr. ended 12/31/01): Grants paid, $266,481; assets, $3,781,232 (M); gifts received, $883,553; expenditures, $309,923; qualifying distributions, $266,481.
Limitations: Applications not accepted.
Application information: Contributes only to pre-selected organizations.
Trustees: Michael Lynton, Carol Smilow.
EIN: 133743511
Codes: FD

34180
Mae Stone Goode Trust
c/o HSBC, USA
1 HSBC Ctr., 16th Fl.
Buffalo, NY 14203

Financial data (yr. ended 09/30/01): Grants paid, $266,322; assets, $5,348,237 (M); expenditures, $322,646; qualifying distributions, $271,726.
Limitations: Applications not accepted. Giving primarily in Buffalo and Rochester, NY.
Application information: Contributes only to pre-selected organizations.
Trustee: HSBC Bank USA.
EIN: 237175053
Codes: FD

34181
Gerda Lissner Foundation, Inc.
135 E. 55th St., 8th Fl.
New York, NY 10022-4049 (212) 826-6100
FAX: (212) 826-0366
Contact: Betty Smith, Pres.

Established in 1994 in NY.
Donor(s): Gerda Lissner.‡
Financial data (yr. ended 12/31/01): Grants paid, $266,270; assets, $14,968,660 (M); expenditures, $763,673; qualifying distributions, $759,833.
Limitations: Giving primarily in New York, NY.
Publications: Application guidelines.
Application information: Application form required.
Officers: Betty Smith, Pres.; Lynn Barnett, V.P.
Directors: Edmund Badgley, Angelene Rasmussen.
EIN: 133566516
Codes: FD, GTI

34182
Strong Foundation of New York
30 E. 71st St.
New York, NY 10021-4956 (212) 249-1253
E-mail: vicki.lee@worldnet.att.net
Contact: Roger L. Strong, Pres.

Established in 1961 in NY.
Donor(s): Marguerite Strong,‡ Roger L. Strong, Jeffrey Strong, Lee Strong, Roger L. Strong, Jr., Thomas Strong.
Financial data (yr. ended 03/31/02): Grants paid, $266,122; assets, $5,471,620 (M); gifts received, $110,580; expenditures, $302,543; qualifying distributions, $266,625.
Limitations: Applications not accepted. Giving primarily in New York, NY.
Publications: Annual report.
Application information: Contributes only to pre-selected organizations.
Officers: Roger L. Strong, Pres.; Roger L. Strong, Jr., V.P.; Lee Strong, Secy.
Directors: Jeffrey Strong, Thomas Strong.
EIN: 136093147
Codes: FD

34183
Mahir A. & Helene Reiss Foundation, Inc.
444 Madison Ave., Ste. 1800
New York, NY 10022
Contact: Mahir A. Reiss, Dir.

Established in 1981 in NY.
Donor(s): Mahir A. Reiss, Helene Reiss.
Financial data (yr. ended 12/31/00): Grants paid, $266,058; assets, $15,352 (M); gifts received, $250,000; expenditures, $267,201; qualifying distributions, $266,058.
Limitations: Giving primarily in NY.
Directors: Helene Reiss, Mahir A. Reiss.
EIN: 133050322
Codes: FD

34184
The Lucelia Foundation, Inc.
630 Clinton Sq.
Rochester, NY 14604
Contact: Elizabeth Gosrell, Pres.

Established in 1998 in NY.

Financial data (yr. ended 12/31/01): Grants paid, $266,000; assets, $5,121,659 (M); expenditures, $272,619; qualifying distributions, $265,037.
Limitations: Applications not accepted.
Application information: Contributes only to pre-selected organizations.
Officer and Director:* Elizabeth Gosnell,* Pres. and Treas.
EIN: 134009608
Codes: FD

34185
The Jack and Pearl Resnick Foundation
c/o Jack Resnick & Sons, Inc.
110 E. 59th St., 37th Fl.
New York, NY 10022

Established in 1989 in NY.
Donor(s): Jack Resnick, Pearl Resnick.‡
Financial data (yr. ended 03/31/01): Grants paid, $266,000; assets, $3,740,251 (M); gifts received, $2,000,000; expenditures, $275,645; qualifying distributions, $266,000.
Limitations: Applications not accepted. Giving primarily in Palm Beach, FL and New York, NY.
Application information: Contributes only to pre-selected organizations.
Officer and Directors:* Burton P. Resnick,* V.P. and Secy.; Ira Resnick, Steven J. Rotter.
EIN: 133579145
Codes: FD

34186
The Lufkin Family Foundation
(Formerly The Dan W. Lufkin Foundation)
c/o Bingham Dana, LLP
399 Park Ave.
New York, NY 10022-4689 (212) 207-1234
Contact: Hugh J. Freund, Tr.

Established in 1998.
Donor(s): Dan Lufkin.
Financial data (yr. ended 12/31/01): Grants paid, $265,950; assets, $1,946,828 (M); gifts received, $500; expenditures, $286,448; qualifying distributions, $262,302.
Limitations: Giving primarily in NY.
Application information: Application form not required.
Trustees: Margaret L. Bishop, Andrew Carduner, Alison W. Lufkin Faber, Hugh J. Freund, Abigail F. Lufkin, Dan W. Lufkin, Elise G.B. Lufkin.
EIN: 133999095
Codes: FD

34187
The Jerome Levy Foundation
c/o Warshaw, Burstein, Cohen, Schlesinger & Kuh
555 5th Ave.
New York, NY 10017
Contact: S. Jay Levy, Tr.

Trust established in 1955 in NY.
Donor(s): Leon Levy, S. Jay Levy.
Financial data (yr. ended 10/31/01): Grants paid, $265,847; assets, $952,923 (M); gifts received, $1,636,356; expenditures, $272,206; qualifying distributions, $265,847.
Limitations: Applications not accepted. Giving primarily in the metropolitan New York, NY, area.
Application information: Contributes only to pre-selected organizations.
Trustees: Leon Levy, S. Jay Levy, Shelby White.
EIN: 136159573
Codes: FD

34188
The Randall & Kathryn Smith Foundation
c/o Smith Mgmt., LLC
885 3rd Ave., 34th Fl.
New York, NY 10022
Contact: John W. Adams

Established in 1982 in NJ.
Donor(s): John W. Adams, Randall Smith.
Financial data (yr. ended 12/31/00): Grants paid, $265,694; assets, $1,797,064 (M); expenditures, $320,627; qualifying distributions, $264,623.
Limitations: Giving primarily in NY.
Officers: Randall D. Smith, Pres.; Jeffrey A. Smith, Secy.
Trustee: Robert Haribson.
EIN: 222422965
Codes: FD

34189
Elroy and Terry Krumholz Foundation, Inc.
c/o Rosalind Sackoff
P.O. Box 640085
Oakland Gardens, NY 11364

Established in 1992 in NY.
Donor(s): Terry Krumholz,‡ Roy Krumholz.‡
Financial data (yr. ended 12/31/01): Grants paid, $265,650; assets, $4,479,981 (M); expenditures, $313,701; qualifying distributions, $313,701.
Limitations: Giving primarily in NY.
Publications: Application guidelines.
Application information: Application must be on Krumholz form only. Application form required.
Officers and Trustees:* Rosalind Sackoff,* Pres.; Richard S. Becker,* V.P.; Sanford E. Becker,* V.P.; Harriet Krantz,* V.P.; Diane Razzano,* V.P.
EIN: 133641606
Codes: FD

34190
Irving Berlin Charitable Fund, Inc.
211 Central Park W.
New York, NY 10024
Contact: A.E. Peters, Secy.

Incorporated in 1947 in NY.
Donor(s): Irving Berlin.‡
Financial data (yr. ended 12/31/01): Grants paid, $265,500; assets, $2,520,089 (M); expenditures, $294,399; qualifying distributions, $266,693.
Limitations: Applications not accepted. Giving primarily in NY.
Application information: Contributes only to pre-selected organizations. Unsolicited requests for funds not accepted.
Officers: Mary Ellin Barrett, Pres.; Linda Louise Emmet, V.P.; Elizabeth I. Peters, Treas.
EIN: 136092592
Codes: FD

34191
Stephen and Ruth Hendel Foundation
10 Dundee Rd.
Larchmont, NY 10538

Established in 1989 in NY.
Donor(s): Stephen Hendel.
Financial data (yr. ended 02/20/02): Grants paid, $265,344; assets, $96,287 (M); gifts received, $151,922; expenditures, $266,417; qualifying distributions, $264,669.
Limitations: Applications not accepted. Giving primarily in CT and NY.
Application information: Contributes only to pre-selected organizations.
Trustees: Myron Hendel, Ruth Hendel, Stephen Hendel.
EIN: 133532037
Codes: FD

34192
Peter A. and Elizabeth S. Cohn Foundation, Inc.
c/o John P. Engel & Assocs.
1740 Broadway, 25th Fl.
New York, NY 10019-4304
Contact: John P. Engel, V.P.

Established in 1955 in NY.
Donor(s): Peter A. Cohn,‡ Elizabeth S. Cohn.‡
Financial data (yr. ended 06/30/01): Grants paid, $265,000; assets, $4,360,907 (M); expenditures, $307,493; qualifying distributions, $283,117.
Limitations: Applications not accepted. Giving primarily in New York, NY.
Application information: Unsolicited requests for funds not accepted.
Officers and Directors:* John M. Angelo,* Pres.; John P. Engel, V.P.; Richard L. Grossman,* V.P.
EIN: 136117647
Codes: FD

34193
The Gant Family Foundation
(Formerly Donald R. & Jane T. Gant Foundation)
c/o Behan, Ling, and Ruta
358 5th Ave., 9th Fl.
New York, NY 10001

Established in 1968 in NY.
Donor(s): Donald R. Gant.
Financial data (yr. ended 05/31/01): Grants paid, $264,800; assets, $7,309,562 (M); expenditures, $272,756; qualifying distributions, $265,050.
Limitations: Applications not accepted. Giving primarily in NJ and NY.
Application information: Contributes only to pre-selected organizations.
Trustees: Alison A. Gant, Christopher T. Gant, Donald R. Gant, Jane T. Gant, Laura G. Lilienfield, Sarah G. Mandanis.
EIN: 237015091
Codes: FD

34194
Samson & Halina Bitensky Foundation, Inc.
200 Madison Ave.
New York, NY 10016

Financial data (yr. ended 12/31/01): Grants paid, $264,750; assets, $3,158,761 (M); expenditures, $266,651; qualifying distributions, $264,560.
Limitations: Applications not accepted. Giving primarily in New York, NY.
Application information: Contributes only to pre-selected organizations.
Officer: Samson Bitensky, Pres.
EIN: 237010472
Codes: FD

34195
Massry Charitable Foundation, Inc.
c/o Norman Massry
Executive Park, N.
Albany, NY 12203

Established in 1994.
Donor(s): Morris Massry.
Financial data (yr. ended 12/31/00): Grants paid, $264,450; assets, $4,601,535 (M); gifts received, $1,459,375; expenditures, $267,714; qualifying distributions, $263,273.
Limitations: Giving primarily in NY.
Officers: Morris Massry, Pres.; Esther Massry, V.P.; Norman Massry, Secy.-Treas.
EIN: 141777179
Codes: FD

34196
Joseph & Carson Gleberman Foundation
c/o Goldman Sachs & Co.
85 Broad St., Tax Dept.
New York, NY 10004

Established in 1991 in NY.
Donor(s): Joseph H. Gleberman.
Financial data (yr. ended 03/31/01): Grants paid, $264,063; assets, $5,876,178 (M); gifts received, $2,485,751; expenditures, $349,354; qualifying distributions, $264,393.
Limitations: Applications not accepted. Giving on a national basis, with some emphasis on New York, NY.
Application information: Contributes only to pre-selected organizations.
Trustees: Carson Gleberman, Joseph H. Gleberman.
EIN: 133632753
Codes: FD

34197
The Mary Jane & William J. Voute Foundation, Inc.
c/o Leonard Stahl
12 Ashington Dr.
Ossining, NY 10562

Established in 1977 in NY.
Donor(s): Mary Jane Voute-Arrigoni, William J. Voute.‡
Financial data (yr. ended 06/30/01): Grants paid, $264,000; assets, $108,028 (M); gifts received, $203,883; expenditures, $267,063; qualifying distributions, $261,767.
Limitations: Applications not accepted. Giving primarily in the metropolitan New York, NY, area, including Westchester County.
Application information: Contributes only to pre-selected organizations.
Officers: Mary Jane Voute-Arrigoni, Pres. and Treas.; Kathleen Gudmundsson, Secy.
Directors: Carolyn Murphy, Mary Ellen Sutherland, Jean Voute.
EIN: 510249510
Codes: FD

34198
Arnold & Arlene Goldstein Family Foundation
c/o Samson Mgmt.
97-77 Queens Blvd., Ste. 710
Rego Park, NY 11374

Established in 1996 in NY.
Donor(s): Arnold Goldstein.
Financial data (yr. ended 12/31/99): Grants paid, $263,757; assets, $5,384,413 (M); expenditures, $273,476; qualifying distributions, $265,114.
Limitations: Applications not accepted. Giving primarily in NY.
Application information: Contributes only to pre-selected organizations.
Trustees: Arlene Goldstein, Arnold Goldstein.
EIN: 137091014
Codes: FD

34199
Apfelbaum Family Foundation
c/o McLaughlin & Stern, LLP
260 Madison Ave.
New York, NY 10016

Established in 1996 in NY.
Donor(s): Bonnie Apfelbaum, William Apfelbaum.
Financial data (yr. ended 12/31/01): Grants paid, $263,250; assets, $3,914,663 (M); expenditures, $315,530; qualifying distributions, $268,419.
Limitations: Applications not accepted. Giving primarily in NY.

Application information: Contributes only to pre-selected organizations.
Officers: William Apfelbaum, Pres. and Treas.; Bonnie Apfelbaum, V.P.; Geoffry Handler, Secy.
EIN: 133907687
Codes: FD

34200
Jephson Educational Trust No. 1
c/o JPMorgan Chase Bank
1211 Ave. of the Americas, 38th Fl.
New York, NY 10036
E-mail: jones_ed_l@JPMorgan.com
Contact: Edward L. Jones, V.P.

Trust established in 1946 in NY.
Donor(s): Lucretia Davis Jephson.‡
Financial data (yr. ended 12/31/01): Grants paid, $262,500; assets, $6,016,811 (M); expenditures, $358,599; qualifying distributions, $314,010.
Limitations: Applications not accepted. Giving on a national basis.
Application information: Contributes only to pre-selected organizations.
Trustees: J. Stanley Parkin, Robert D. Taisey, JPMorgan Chase Bank.
EIN: 136023169
Codes: FD

34201
The Eugene and Estelle Ferkauf Foundation
67 Allenwood Rd.
Great Neck, NY 11023-2213 (516) 773-3269
Contact: The Trustees

Established in 1967 in NY.
Donor(s): Eugene Ferkauf, Estelle Ferkauf.
Financial data (yr. ended 12/31/01): Grants paid, $262,450; assets, $5,662,325 (M); expenditures, $457,918; qualifying distributions, $351,076.
Limitations: Giving limited to NY.
Publications: Application guidelines.
Application information: Application form not required.
Trustees: Lenore Bronstein, Robert Bronstein, Barbara Dor, Benny Dor, Estelle Ferkauf, Eugene Ferkauf, Amy Shapira, Israel Shapira.
EIN: 132621094
Codes: FD

34202
Children's Foundation of Erie County, Inc.
P.O. Box 560
Kenmore, NY 14217 (716) 877-0418
Contact: Anne M. Denman, Treas.

Incorporated in 1836 in NY.
Financial data (yr. ended 12/31/01): Grants paid, $262,400; assets, $4,818,865 (M); expenditures, $278,199; qualifying distributions, $244,506.
Limitations: Giving limited to Erie County, NY.
Application information: Application form not required.
Officers and Trustees:* Betsy Mitchell,* Pres.; Susan Russ,* V.P.; Charles J. Hahn,* Secy.; Anne M. Denman, Treas.; and 14 additional trustees.
EIN: 166000171
Codes: FD

34203
Barrow Foundation
c/o U.S. Trust
114 W. 47th St.
New York, NY 10036
Contact: Carolyn L. Larke, Asst. V.P., U.S. Trust; or Linda R. Franciscovich, Sr. V.P., U.S. Trust

Established in 1952 in TX.
Donor(s): Nellie Dell Barrow.‡

Financial data (yr. ended 11/30/01): Grants paid, $262,250; assets, $5,188,214 (M); expenditures, $353,895; qualifying distributions, $297,109.
Limitations: Applications not accepted. Giving primarily in TX.
Application information: Contributes only to pre-selected organizations.
Trustees: Randall E. Kemper, Marvin H. Seline, Sarah Barrow Seline, U.S. Trust.
EIN: 746041372
Codes: FD

34204
D. E. French Foundation, Inc.
120 Genesee St., Rm. 503
Auburn, NY 13021 (315) 253-9321
Contact: Walter M. Lowe, Exec. Dir.

Incorporated in 1955 in NY.
Donor(s): Clara M. French,‡ D.E. French.‡
Financial data (yr. ended 12/31/01): Grants paid, $262,000; assets, $4,999,820 (M); expenditures, $290,870; qualifying distributions, $275,804.
Limitations: Giving primarily in the Cayuga County, NY, area.
Application information: Application form not required.
Officers and Directors:* Ronald D. West,* Pres.; Caryl W. Adams, Secy.; Walter M. Lowe,* Exec. Dir.; Frederick J. Atkins, James P. Costello, John P. McLane.
EIN: 166052246
Codes: FD

34205
Combe Trust
1101 Westchester Ave.
White Plains, NY 10604-3597

Established around 1964.
Donor(s): Ivan D. Combe,‡ Mary E. Combe.
Financial data (yr. ended 12/31/01): Grants paid, $261,500; assets, $293,457 (M); expenditures, $261,928; qualifying distributions, $261,928.
Limitations: Applications not accepted. Giving primarily in CT and NY.
Application information: Contributes only to pre-selected organizations.
Trustees: Christopher Combe, Mary Elizabeth Combe, Willis Deming.
EIN: 136154769
Codes: FD

34206
The Dime Foundation
(Formerly Dime Savings Charitable Foundation)
c/o The Dime Savings Bank
589 5th Ave., 2nd Fl.
New York, NY 10017 (516) 596-3849

Established in 1987 in NY.
Donor(s): The Dime Savings Bank of New York, FSB.
Financial data (yr. ended 12/31/01): Grants paid, $261,500; assets, $10,070 (M); gifts received, $245,600; expenditures, $277,902; qualifying distributions, $277,902.
Limitations: Giving primarily in the greater metropolitan New York, NY, area, including Long Island, and Westchester and Rockland counties.
Publications: Application guidelines.
Application information: Application form required.
Officers: Lawrence J. Toal, Pres.; Elizabeth Knoerzer, Secy.; Franklin L. Wright, Jr., Treas.
Directors: Richard Dalrymple, James Fulton, Virginia M. Kopp, James M. Large, Jr., John Morning.
EIN: 112966463
Codes: CS, TN

34207
The William and Eva Fox Foundation
c/o U.S. Trust Co.
114 W. 47th St., 8th Fl.
New York, NY 10036 (212) 852-3294
FAX: (212) 852-3377; *E-mail:* alane@ustrust.com
Contact: Andrew Lane

Established in 1987 in DE; funded in 1994.
Donor(s): Belle Fox.‡
Financial data (yr. ended 06/30/01): Grants paid, $261,312; assets, $6,820,906 (M); expenditures, $341,011; qualifying distributions, $261,312.
Limitations: Applications not accepted. Giving on a national basis; giving also in Canada and England.
Application information: Unsolicited requests for funds not accepted.
Officers and Directors:* Robert P. Warren,* Pres. and Treas.; June W. Warren, V.P.; Claudia P. Flynn.
EIN: 133497192
Codes: FD, GTI

34208
Morris L. Levinson Foundation, Inc.
c/o M.R. Weiser & Co., LLP
3000 Marcus Ave.
New Hyde Park, NY 11042-1066

Incorporated in 1952 in NY.
Donor(s): Morris L. Levinson, Associated Products, Inc.
Financial data (yr. ended 06/30/01): Grants paid, $261,250; assets, $5,016,127 (M); expenditures, $306,242; qualifying distributions, $262,080.
Limitations: Applications not accepted. Giving primarily in FL and NY.
Application information: Contributes only to pre-selected organizations.
Officer and Director:* Barbara S. Levinson,* V.P.
EIN: 136132727
Codes: FD

34209
The Pratt-Northam Foundation
c/o D.M. Hunt
7686 N. State St.
Lowville, NY 13367
Application address: P.O. Box 104, Lowville, NY 13367
Contact: Donald J. Exford, Exec. Dir.

Incorporated in 1962 in NY.
Donor(s): Hazel Northam.‡
Financial data (yr. ended 12/31/00): Grants paid, $261,226; assets, $6,038,888 (M); gifts received, $24,195; expenditures, $339,403; qualifying distributions, $601,256.
Limitations: Giving limited to the Black River Valley region of NY.
Application information: Application form required.
Officers and Directors:* Edward Sieber,* Pres.; John A. Beach, Secy.; Donald M. Hunt, Treas.; Gordon Allen, Roy Hammecker, Sally Jackson, Chris Lorence, Susan Parker, Rev. "Mickey" Robinson, Tom Sauter, Randall Schell.
EIN: 166088207
Codes: FD

34210
The Paul D. Schurgot Foundation, Inc.
c/o William Butler
280 Madison Ave., Ste. 1102
New York, NY 10016

Financial data (yr. ended 12/31/01): Grants paid, $261,000; assets, $10,177,521 (M); gifts received, $10,077,680; expenditures, $320,096; qualifying distributions, $292,649.

Limitations: Applications not accepted. Giving primarily in New York, NY.
Application information: Contributes only to pre-selected organizations.
Officers: William Butler, Pres.; Jane Butler, Secy.
Board Member: Tom Sweeney.
EIN: 237137799
Codes: FD

34211
Naftali Zvi Leshkowitz Memorial Foundation
270 Madison Ave., 17th Fl.
New York, NY 10016
Contact: C.H. Leshkowitz, Tr.

Established in 1986 in NY.
Donor(s): C.H. Leshkowitz, Joseph Leshkowitz.
Financial data (yr. ended 11/30/01): Grants paid, $260,655; assets, $1,415,509 (M); gifts received, $325,035; expenditures, $272,211; qualifying distributions, $260,655.
Limitations: Applications not accepted. Giving primarily in NY.
Application information: Contributes only to pre-selected organizations.
Trustees: C.H. Leshkowitz, Joseph Leshkowitz.
EIN: 133394520
Codes: FD

34212
Arthur N. Hershaft Foundation
c/o Levene, Gouldin & Thompson, LLP
450 Plaza Dr.
Vestal, NY 13850

Established in 1988 in NY.
Donor(s): Arthur N. Hershaft, Carol H. Hershaft.‡
Financial data (yr. ended 12/31/01): Grants paid, $260,497; assets, $2,402,538 (M); expenditures, $262,055; qualifying distributions, $260,791.
Limitations: Applications not accepted. Giving primarily in CT.
Application information: Contributes only to pre-selected organizations.
Trustees: Arthur N. Hershaft, Michael H. Zuckerman.
EIN: 226462965
Codes: FD

34213
The Mercer Trust
c/o D. Greenwood
15 Glen St., Ste. 203
Glen Cove, NY 11542-2784

Established in 1989 in NJ.
Donor(s): John B. Elliott.‡
Financial data (yr. ended 12/31/00): Grants paid, $260,000; assets, $1,144,139 (M); gifts received, $598,765; expenditures, $264,062; qualifying distributions, $260,389.
Limitations: Applications not accepted. Giving primarily in Princeton, NJ.
Application information: Contributes only to pre-selected organizations.
Trustees: Maxwell Hearn, Michael L.K. Hwang, Frederick W. Mote.
EIN: 136940594
Codes: FD

34214
Leo Rosner Foundation, Inc.
6 Westway
White Plains, NY 10605
Contact: William D. Robbins, Pres.

Established in 1960.
Financial data (yr. ended 10/31/01): Grants paid, $259,500; assets, $11,837,302 (M); expenditures, $600,755; qualifying distributions, $319,792.
Limitations: Giving primarily in New York, NY.
Application information: Application form required.
Officers and Directors:* William D. Robbins,* Pres.; Mildred R. Caplow,* V.P.; June Rosner,* V.P.; Marcy Wachtel, V.P.; Amy H. Caplow Chan,* Secy.-Treas.
EIN: 136161637
Codes: FD

34215
J & AR Foundation
c/o Yohalem Gillman & Co.
477 Madison Ave.
New York, NY 10022-5802
Contact: Elizabeth Morin

Established in 1990 in NY.
Donor(s): Janet C. Ross, Arthur Ross.
Financial data (yr. ended 12/31/01): Grants paid, $259,050; assets, $7,929,733 (M); gifts received, $1,322,021; expenditures, $373,860; qualifying distributions, $246,607.
Limitations: Applications not accepted. Giving primarily in NY.
Application information: Contributes only to pre-selected organizations.
Trustees: George J. Gillespie III, Janet C. Ross.
EIN: 136962028
Codes: FD

34216
Samuel & Rae Eckman Charitable Foundation
c/o Brown Raysman Millstein, Felder, & Steiner, LLP
900 3rd Ave.
New York, NY 10022 (212) 895-2000
Contact: Stephen F. Selig, Pres.

Established in 1970 in NY.
Donor(s): Rae Eckman,‡ Samuel Eckman.‡
Financial data (yr. ended 12/31/01): Grants paid, $259,000; assets, $2,242,838 (M); expenditures, $289,305; qualifying distributions, $257,117.
Limitations: Giving primarily in New York, NY.
Publications: Application guidelines.
Application information: Application form not required.
Officers and Directors:* Stephen F. Selig,* Pres.; Abraham J. Briloff, V.P.; William B. Norden, Secy.-Treas.; Arthur W. Murphy.
EIN: 237051411
Codes: FD

34217
Fribourg Family Foundation
277 Park Ave., 50th Fl.
New York, NY 10172

Established in 2000 in NY.
Donor(s): Michel Fribourg.
Financial data (yr. ended 12/31/01): Grants paid, $258,850; assets, $2,572,294 (M); gifts received, $532,260; expenditures, $303,341; qualifying distributions, $253,544.
Limitations: Applications not accepted. Giving primarily in NY.
Application information: Contributes only to pre-selected organizations.
Trustees: Mark R. Baker, Mary Ann Fribourg, Michel Fribourg, Paul Jules Fribourg, Mary Greenebaum, Susan McIntyre.
EIN: 134148779
Codes: FD

34218
Peale Foundation, Inc.
11 Mizzentop Rd.
Pawling, NY 12564
Contact: Elizabeth P. Allen, Secy.-Treas.

Established in 1991 in NY and DE.
Donor(s): JME II Charitable Lead Trust, JME Charitable Lead Trust, Ruth S. Peale Trust, Schiff, Hardin & Waite.
Financial data (yr. ended 09/30/01): Grants paid, $258,500; assets, $5,070,571 (M); gifts received, $540,716; expenditures, $371,650; qualifying distributions, $336,896.
Limitations: Giving primarily in NY.
Application information: Application form not required.
Officers and Directors:* Margaret P. Everett,* Pres.; John Peale,* V.P.; Elizabeth P. Allen,* Secy.-Treas.
EIN: 141746478
Codes: FD

34219
The Sheila Johnson Brutsch Charitable Trust
c/o The Johnson Co., Inc.
630 5th Ave., Ste. 1510
New York, NY 10111

Established in 1994 in NY.
Donor(s): Betty W. Johnson.
Financial data (yr. ended 12/31/01): Grants paid, $258,400; assets, $6,045,207 (M); expenditures, $263,858; qualifying distributions, $256,946.
Limitations: Applications not accepted. Giving primarily in FL.
Application information: Contributes only to pre-selected organizations.
Trustees: Sheila Johnson Brutsch, Betty W. Johnson.
EIN: 137046312
Codes: FD

34220
R. D. Brown Trust B
c/o JPMorgan Chase Bank
1211 6th Ave., 34th Fl.
New York, NY 10036 (212) 789-4073
Contact: John Boncada, Trust Off.

Established in 1990 in NY.
Financial data (yr. ended 12/31/01): Grants paid, $257,831; assets, $1,991,508 (M); gifts received, $12,338; expenditures, $284,253; qualifying distributions, $268,494; giving activities include $257,831 for loans to individuals.
Limitations: Applications not accepted. Giving primarily in NY.
Trustee: JPMorgan Chase Bank.
EIN: 136030429
Codes: FD, GTI

34221
Educational Support Foundation, Inc.
(Formerly Leon & Irene Scharf Foundation, Inc.)
800 West End Ave.
New York, NY 10025 (212) 866-6008

Established in 1963 in NY.
Donor(s): Leon Scharf, Irene Scharf, S. Schoferig, Chada Foundation, Franconia Foundation, Scharf, Scharf, & Beer, Weinreb Management, Nazel Family Trust.
Financial data (yr. ended 05/31/01): Grants paid, $257,664; assets, $9,433,404 (M); gifts received, $278,065; expenditures, $371,817; qualifying distributions, $261,430.
Limitations: Applications not accepted. Giving primarily in NY.
Application information: Contributes only to pre-selected organizations.
Officers: Irene Scharf, Mgr.; Leon Scharf, Mgr.
EIN: 136159760
Codes: FD

34222
The Andrew Cader & Deborah Reich Foundation, Inc.
c/o Spear, Leeds & Kellogg
120 Broadway
New York, NY 10271

Established in 1995 in NY.
Donor(s): Education For Youth Society, Andrew Cader.
Financial data (yr. ended 09/30/01): Grants paid, $257,558; assets, $11,127,311 (M); gifts received, $500,000; expenditures, $492,772; qualifying distributions, $258,388.
Limitations: Applications not accepted. Giving primarily in NY.
Application information: Contributes only to pre-selected organizations.
Officers: Andrew Cader, Pres. and Treas.; Deborah Reich, V.P. and Secy.; Seth J. Lapidow, V.P.
EIN: 133860405
Codes: FD

34223
Nila B. Hulbert Foundation
6 Ford Ave.
Oneonta, NY 13820-1898 (607) 432-6720
Contact: Henry L. Hulbert, Tr.

Established about 1971.
Donor(s): Nila B. Hulbert.
Financial data (yr. ended 12/31/01): Grants paid, $257,358; assets, $7,149,132 (M); expenditures, $337,082; qualifying distributions, $311,666.
Limitations: Giving primarily in Oneonta, NY.
Trustees: Henry L. Hulbert, J. Burton Hulbert, William H. Hulbert.
EIN: 237039996
Codes: FD

34224
Mitchell and Karen Kuflik Charitable Foundation
14 Beverly Rd.
Purchase, NY 10577

Established in 1999 in NY.
Donor(s): Mitchell Kuflik.
Financial data (yr. ended 12/31/01): Grants paid, $256,543; assets, $73,913 (M); gifts received, $283,323; expenditures, $256,657; qualifying distributions, $256,174.
Limitations: Applications not accepted. Giving primarily in NY.
Application information: Contributes only to pre-selected organizations.
Officers: Mitchell Kuflik, Pres.; Karen Kuflik, V.P.
EIN: 137197004
Codes: FD

34225
The Howard Johnson Foundation
c/o U.S. Trust
114 W. 47th St.
New York, NY 10036
FAX: (212) 852-3377
Contact: Carolyn L. Larke, Asst. V.P., U.S. Trust or Linda Francisovich, Sr. V.P.

Trust established in 1961 in MA.
Donor(s): Howard D. Johnson,‡ Dorothy J. Henry.
Financial data (yr. ended 12/31/99): Grants paid, $256,450; assets, $5,942,779 (M); gifts received, $10,425; expenditures, $262,665; qualifying distributions, $257,949.
Limitations: Giving primarily in CT, MA, and NY.
Publications: Application guidelines.
Application information: Application form not required.
Trustees: Marissa J. Brock, Patricia Johnson Crawford, Dorothy J. Henry, Howard Bates Johnson, Howard Brennan Johnson, Joshua J. Weeks, William H. Weeks.
EIN: 046060965
Codes: FD

34226
Hickrill Foundation, Inc.
c/o Abacus & Assocs.
147 E. 48th St.
New York, NY 10017
Contact: Denie S. Weil, V.P.

Incorporated in 1946 in NY.
Donor(s): Frank A. Weil, The Norman Foundation.
Financial data (yr. ended 12/31/00): Grants paid, $256,302; assets, $6,834,005 (M); gifts received, $296,709; expenditures, $288,158; qualifying distributions, $256,302.
Limitations: Giving on a national basis.
Officers: Frank A. Weil, Pres.; Denie S. Weil, V.P.; Deborah W. Harrington, Secy.
EIN: 136002949
Codes: FD

34227
Edgar M. Leventritt Foundation, Inc.
Box 125
Cold Spring, NY 10516-0125

Established in 1939 in NY.
Donor(s): Curtiss Wright Corp.
Financial data (yr. ended 12/31/01): Grants paid, $256,075; assets, $5,790,874 (M); expenditures, $257,915; qualifying distributions, $257,051.
Limitations: Applications not accepted. Giving primarily in MA and NY.
Application information: Contributes only to pre-selected organizations.
Officers: Winifred B. Parker, Pres.; Rosalie L. Parker, V.P. and Treas.; Katherine L. Parker, Secy.
EIN: 136111037
Codes: FD

34228
The Lincoln Ellsworth Foundation
c/o Morris & McVeigh, LLP
767 3rd Ave.
New York, NY 10017-2023

Established in 1943.
Financial data (yr. ended 12/31/01): Grants paid, $256,000; assets, $4,861,990 (M); expenditures, $296,839; qualifying distributions, $294,382.
Limitations: Applications not accepted. Giving primarily in the metropolitan New York, NY, area.
Application information: Contributes only to pre-selected organizations.
Officers: MacDonald Budd, Pres. and Secy.; Guy G. Rutherfurd, V.P.
EIN: 136022017
Codes: FD

34229
Pyewacket Foundation
c/o Reminick, Aarons & Co.
1430 Broadway
New York, NY 10018

Established in 1997 in NY.
Donor(s): William H. Janeway.
Financial data (yr. ended 12/31/00): Grants paid, $255,950; assets, $8,315,930 (M); gifts received, $4,734,941; expenditures, $358,914; qualifying distributions, $191,082.
Limitations: Applications not accepted. Giving primarily in New York, NY.
Application information: Contributes only to pre-selected organizations.
Officer: William H. Janeway, Pres.
EIN: 137051522
Codes: FD

34230
Deeds Foundation, Inc.
c/o Amco
505 Park Ave., 20th Fl.
New York, NY 10022

Established in 1994 in NY.
Donor(s): Nan Allen Nixon 1982 Trust.
Financial data (yr. ended 12/31/01): Grants paid, $255,850; assets, $5,729,576 (M); gifts received, $764,462; expenditures, $314,189; qualifying distributions, $256,685.
Limitations: Applications not accepted. Giving primarily in NY.
Application information: Contributes only to pre-selected organizations.
Officers and Directors:* Diane A. Nixon,* Pres.; E. Lisk Wyckoff, Jr.,* V.P. and Secy.; Robert Cahill.
EIN: 133752427
Codes: FD

34231
The Gould Family Charitable Foundation of New York
60 Cuttermill Rd., Ste. 303
Great Neck, NY 11021

Established in 1995 in NY.
Donor(s): Fredric H. Gould.
Financial data (yr. ended 12/31/99): Grants paid, $255,211; assets, $497,433 (M); gifts received, $171,092; expenditures, $260,495; qualifying distributions, $253,647.
Limitations: Applications not accepted. Giving primarily in New York, NY.
Application information: Contributes only to pre-selected organizations.
Trustees: Fredric H. Gould, Helaine Gould, Jeffrey A. Gould, Matthew J. Gould, Wendy Shenfeld.
EIN: 113262391
Codes: FD

34232
The Wiegers Family Foundation
c/o Barry Strauss Assoc., Ltd.
307 5th Ave., 8th Fl.
New York, NY 10016-6517

Established in 1992 in CO.
Donor(s): George A. Wiegers.
Financial data (yr. ended 02/28/01): Grants paid, $255,198; assets, $4,349,543 (M); gifts received, $17,200; expenditures, $289,019; qualifying distributions, $263,623.
Limitations: Applications not accepted. Giving primarily in CO and NY.
Application information: Contributes only to pre-selected organizations.
Trustees: Hans P. Utsch, E. Alexander Wiegers, Elizabeth C. Wiegers, George A. Wiegers.
EIN: 841214070
Codes: FD

34233
Lostand Foundation, Inc.
c/o Jonathan F.P. Rose
33 Katonah Ave.
Katonah, NY 10536

Established in 1997 in NY.
Donor(s): Jonathan F.P. Rose.
Financial data (yr. ended 10/31/01): Grants paid, $255,006; assets, $3,003,422 (M); gifts received, $250,000; expenditures, $276,647; qualifying distributions, $259,306.
Limitations: Applications not accepted. Giving primarily in Brooklyn, NY.

34233—NEW YORK

Application information: Contributes only to pre-selected organizations.
Officers: Jonathan F.P. Rose, Pres.; Diana C. Rose, V.P.; Michael Sullivan, Treas.
Director: Charles L. Mandelstam.
EIN: 133945705
Codes: FD

34234
Enterprise Foundation Trust
c/o Daniel R. Eule
888 7th Ave., 33rd Fl.
New York, NY 10106-0001

Established in 1995 in NY.
Donor(s): Robert Soros.
Financial data (yr. ended 11/30/01): Grants paid, $255,000; assets, $62,469 (M); gifts received, $255,000; expenditures, $265,130; qualifying distributions, $265,130.
Limitations: Applications not accepted. Giving primarily in Garrison, NY.
Application information: Contributes only to pre-selected organizations.
Trustee: Robert Soros.
EIN: 137029291
Codes: FD

34235
The Penny McCall Foundation, Inc.
c/o Jennifer McSweeney Reuss
163 E. 81st St., Apt. 10A
New York, NY 10028
FAX: (212) 988-9714; E-mail: pennymccallfnd@aol.com

Established in 1987 in NY.
Donor(s): Mrs. James Mills, Joan McCall,‡ David McCall.‡
Financial data (yr. ended 12/31/01): Grants paid, $255,000; assets, $2,572,326 (M); gifts received, $961,552; expenditures, $356,808; qualifying distributions, $254,461.
Limitations: Applications not accepted. Giving limited to U.S. citizens.
Application information: Unsolicited requests for funds not accepted.
Officers: Jennifer McSweeney Reuss, Chair.; George Mills, Pres.; Tom Sokolowski, V.P.
EIN: 133376289
Codes: FD, GTI

34236
Schon Family Foundation
1534 53rd St.
Brooklyn, NY 11219
Contact: Henry A. Schon, Pres.

Established in 1992 in NY.
Donor(s): Henry A. Schon.
Financial data (yr. ended 12/31/01): Grants paid, $255,000; assets, $8,694,290 (M); gifts received, $300,000; expenditures, $321,417; qualifying distributions, $257,310.
Limitations: Giving primarily in Brooklyn, NY.
Officers: Henry Schon, Pres.; Heidi Gelley, V.P. and Secy.; Baron Schon, V.P. and Treas.; Anna Schon, V.P.
EIN: 113133066
Codes: FD

34237
Lucerne Foundation
(Formerly SLEN Foundation)
519 8th Ave.
New York, NY 10018 (212) 563-7800
Contact: Robert Rimsky, Tr.

Established in 1985 in NY.
Donor(s): Robert Rimsky, DLD Assocs.

Financial data (yr. ended 09/30/01): Grants paid, $254,450; assets, $5,557,657 (M); gifts received, $197,741; expenditures, $261,319; qualifying distributions, $243,970.
Limitations: Giving primarily in NY.
Trustee: Robert Rimsky.
EIN: 133316334
Codes: FD

34238
The Everett S. Bulkley, Jr. Trust
(Formerly The Bulkley Foundation Trust)
c/o JPMorgan Chase Bank
P.O. Box 31412
Rochester, NY 14603-1412
Application address: 999 Broad St., Bridgeport, CT 06604, tel.: (203) 382-6395
Contact: Pamela Detoro, V.P., JPMorgan Chase Bank

Established in 1989 in CT.
Donor(s): Everett S. Bulkley, Jr.‡
Financial data (yr. ended 12/31/01): Grants paid, $254,290; assets, $4,594,224 (M); expenditures, $287,932; qualifying distributions, $254,825.
Limitations: Giving limited to the greater Norwalk, CT, area.
Application information: Application form not required.
Trustee: JPMorgan Chase Bank.
EIN: 066332021
Codes: FD

34239
Martha Mertz Foundation, Inc.
60 E. 42nd St., Ste. 1760
New York, NY 10165

Incorporated in 1939 in NY.
Donor(s): DeWitt W. Mertz.‡
Financial data (yr. ended 12/31/01): Grants paid, $254,100; assets, $7,180,414 (M); expenditures, $473,201; qualifying distributions, $379,134.
Limitations: Applications not accepted. Giving primarily in New York, NY.
Application information: Contributes only to pre-selected organizations.
Officers: Jonathan B. Reilly, Pres.; Robert A.N. Cudd, V.P. and Treas.; Nancy H. Cudd, Secy.
EIN: 136129085
Codes: FD

34240
Jane Stern Family Foundation, Inc.
733 Park Ave., 11th Fl.
New York, NY 10021-5046

Established in 1986 in NY.
Donor(s): Jane Stern Lebell.
Financial data (yr. ended 02/28/01): Grants paid, $252,977; assets, $1,418,484 (M); gifts received, $26,425; expenditures, $284,951; qualifying distributions, $253,864.
Limitations: Applications not accepted. Giving primarily in New York, NY.
Application information: Contributes only to pre-selected organizations.
Officer: Jane Stern Lebell, Pres. and Treas.
Directors: Geoffrey S. Stern, Ronald A. Stern.
EIN: 133389567
Codes: FD

34241
The United Elenar Foundation
5223 15th Ave.
Brooklyn, NY 11219 (718) 851-4811
Contact: Efraim Landau, Dir.

Established in 1997 in NY.
Financial data (yr. ended 11/30/00): Grants paid, $252,900; assets, $3,259,896 (M); gifts received, $2,018,000; expenditures, $291,653; qualifying distributions, $252,900.
Directors: Chaim Landau, Efraim Landau, Naomi Rabinowicz.
EIN: 116496241
Codes: FD

34242
Louis & Martha Silver Foundation, Inc.
120 Bloomingdale Rd., 4th Fl.
White Plains, NY 10605 (914) 285-1430
Contact: Steven Gelles, Treas.

Established in 1964 in NY.
Donor(s): Louis Silver,‡ Martha Silver.‡
Financial data (yr. ended 12/31/01): Grants paid, $252,635; assets, $4,999,199 (M); gifts received, $15,000; expenditures, $257,646; qualifying distributions, $249,972.
Limitations: Giving primarily along the East Coast.
Application information: Application form not required.
Officers: Martha Silver, Pres.; Steven Gelles, Treas.
Directors: Phyllis Gelles, Martin Silver, Robert Silver.
EIN: 136165326
Codes: FD

34243
The Robert Mize & Isa White Trimble Family Foundation
c/o Allen and Brown
60 E. 42nd St., Ste. 1760
New York, NY 10165

Established in 1978 in NY.
Donor(s): Mary Ray Finneran.‡
Financial data (yr. ended 06/30/01): Grants paid, $252,500; assets, $6,673,839 (L); gifts received, $1,500,000; expenditures, $316,982; qualifying distributions, $289,519.
Limitations: Applications not accepted. Giving primarily in NY.
Application information: Contributes only to pre-selected organizations.
Officers: Daniel J. Ashley, Pres.; Gerard B. Finneran, V.P. and Treas.; Rita H. Rowan, Secy.
EIN: 132972532
Codes: FD

34244
Jacques & Emy Cohenca Foundation, Inc.
550 Park Ave.
New York, NY 10021-7369

Established in 1979 in NY.
Donor(s): Emy Cohenca, Jacques Cohenca,‡ Jason Industrial, Inc.
Financial data (yr. ended 12/31/01): Grants paid, $252,154; assets, $3,944,962 (M); gifts received, $93,333; expenditures, $278,482; qualifying distributions, $252,206.
Limitations: Applications not accepted. Giving primarily in the greater metropolitan New York, NY, area.
Application information: Contributes only to pre-selected organizations.
Officers: Emy Cohenca, Pres.; Philip Cohenca, Treas.
Director: Nevine Michaan.
EIN: 133022911
Codes: FD

34245
The Assael Foundation
580 5th Ave., 21st Fl.
New York, NY 10036
Contact: Esther Posin, Pres.

Established in 1992 in NY.
Donor(s): Salvador J. Assael.

Financial data (yr. ended 12/31/01): Grants paid, $252,107; assets, $2,813,303 (M); gifts received, $260,470; expenditures, $260,703; qualifying distributions, $260,702.
Limitations: Applications not accepted.
Application information: Contributes only to pre-selected organizations.
Officers: Salvador J. Assael, Chair.; Christina L. Assael, Vice-Chair.; Esther Posin, Pres.; Janet Ades, V.P.; Jale Turcihini, Secy.-Treas.
Trustees: Rabbi Marc D. Angel, John D. Block, Cyril S. Dwek, Aron Kahana, Ephraim Propp, Peter Saphier, Arthur Winard, Benjamin Zucker.
EIN: 133683069
Codes: FD

34246
Theresa A. and Thomas W. Berry Foundation
c/o BCRS Assocs., LLC
67 Wall St., 8th Fl.
New York, NY 10005

Established in 1987 in NJ.
Donor(s): Thomas W. Berry.
Financial data (yr. ended 03/31/01): Grants paid, $252,100; assets, $1,018,442 (M); gifts received, $487,789; expenditures, $262,830; qualifying distributions, $257,007.
Limitations: Applications not accepted. Giving primarily in NJ and Providence, RI; some giving also in New York, NY.
Application information: Contributes only to pre-selected organizations.
Trustees: Theresa A. Berry, Thomas W. Berry, Barrie A. Wigmore.
EIN: 133437930
Codes: FD

34247
Ellen Philips Schwarzman Katz Foundation, Inc.
(Formerly Ellen Philips Schwarzman Foundation, Inc.)
c/o BCRS Assocs., LLC
100 Wall St., 11th Fl.
New York, NY 10005

Established in 1996 in NY.
Donor(s): Ellen Philips Schwarzman Katz.
Financial data (yr. ended 04/30/01): Grants paid, $251,665; assets, $249,218 (M); gifts received, $255,019; expenditures, $269,965; qualifying distributions, $252,565.
Limitations: Applications not accepted. Giving primarily in New York, NY.
Application information: Contributes only to pre-selected organizations.
Officers: Ellen Philips Schwarzman Katz, Pres.; Elizabeth B. Schwarzman, Secy.; Howard Katz, Treas.
EIN: 133925902
Codes: FD

34248
The Meryl & Charles Witmer Charitable Foundation
237 Park Ave., Ste. 800
New York, NY 10017

Established in 2000 in NY.
Donor(s): Charles H. Witmer, Meryl B. Witmer.
Financial data (yr. ended 12/31/01): Grants paid, $251,575; assets, $80,717 (M); gifts received, $58,010; expenditures, $259,981; qualifying distributions, $251,601.
Limitations: Applications not accepted. Giving primarily in New York, NY.
Application information: Contributes only to pre-selected organizations.
Trustees: Charles H. Witmer, Meryl B. Witmer.
EIN: 134129627

Codes: FD

34249
Andrew M. Paul Family Foundation
283 Pondfield Rd.
Bronxville, NY 10708
Contact: Andrew M. Paul, Tr.

Established in 1997 in NY.
Donor(s): Andrew M. Paul.
Financial data (yr. ended 08/31/01): Grants paid, $251,375; assets, $522,933 (M); gifts received, $176,813; expenditures, $251,425; qualifying distributions, $251,189.
Limitations: Giving on a national basis, with emphasis on NY.
Trustees: Andrew M. Paul, Margaret B. Paul.
EIN: 137143442
Codes: FD

34250
The Spiritus Gladius Foundation
(Formerly D.C. Foundation, Inc.)
c/o Meyer Handelman Co.
P.O. Box 817
Purchase, NY 10577-0817

Established in 1959 in NY.
Donor(s): Nedenia H. Hartley.
Financial data (yr. ended 08/31/01): Grants paid, $251,346; assets, $4,839,061 (M); expenditures, $268,760; qualifying distributions, $249,372.
Limitations: Applications not accepted. Giving on a national basis.
Application information: Contributes only to pre-selected organizations.
Officers: Nedenia H. Hartley, Pres.; Donald E. Handelman, V.P. and Secy.-Treas.
Trustees: Joseph W. Handelman, Heather M. Robertson, Nedenia C. Rumbough, Stanley H. Rumbough.
EIN: 136113272
Codes: FD

34251
The Yvette and Joel Mallah Family Foundation
P.O. Box 1297
Bridgehampton, NY 11932

Established in 1999 in NY.
Donor(s): Joel Mallah.
Financial data (yr. ended 12/31/01): Grants paid, $251,250; assets, $399,333 (M); gifts received, $250,000; expenditures, $251,890; qualifying distributions, $251,250.
Limitations: Applications not accepted. Giving primarily in NY.
Application information: Contributes only to pre-selected organizations.
Trustees: Joel Mallah, Yvette Mallah.
EIN: 137172805
Codes: FD

34252
Rapaport Shallat Foundation
Bay Pl. and Forest Ct.
Huntington, NY 11743

Financial data (yr. ended 12/31/01): Grants paid, $251,159; assets, $3,680,574 (M); gifts received, $730,942; expenditures, $310,009; qualifying distributions, $251,159.
Limitations: Applications not accepted. Giving primarily in NY.
Application information: Contributes only to pre-selected organizations.
Officer: Rabbi Barton A. Shallat, Mgr.
EIN: 137027583
Codes: FD

34253
Hudson River Bancorp, Inc. Foundation
1 Hudson City Centre
P.O. Box 76
Hudson, NY 12534 (518) 828-4600
Contact: Holly Rappleyea

Established in 1998 in NY.
Donor(s): Hudson River Bank & Trust Co.
Financial data (yr. ended 03/31/01): Grants paid, $251,055; assets, $6,839,775 (L); expenditures, $259,239; qualifying distributions, $249,804.
Limitations: Giving primarily in upstate NY.
Application information: Application form not required.
Officers: Marilyn A. Herrington, Pres.; William H. Jones, V.P.; Stanley Bardwell, M.D., Treas.
Director: Earl Schram.
EIN: 223595668
Codes: CS, FD, CD

34254
Moses Ginsberg Family Foundation, Inc.
110 E. 59th St., 28th Fl.
New York, NY 10022

Incorporated in 1946 in NY.
Donor(s): Moses Ginsberg,‡ Sylvia G. Kaplan.
Financial data (yr. ended 12/31/01): Grants paid, $251,000; assets, $4,100,739 (M); gifts received, $250,000; expenditures, $265,273; qualifying distributions, $251,000.
Limitations: Applications not accepted. Giving primarily in NY.
Application information: Contributes only to pre-selected organizations.
Officers: Donald G. Ginsberg, V.P.; Sylvia G. Kaplan, Secy.; Simon C. Wolkenbrod, Treas.
EIN: 237418806
Codes: FD

34255
The Bessent-Trinkle Foundation, Inc.
c/o Bessent Capital
900 3rd Ave., 29th Fl.
New York, NY 10022

Established in 2000 in NY.
Donor(s): Scott Bessent.
Financial data (yr. ended 11/30/01): Grants paid, $250,667; assets, $1,265,773 (M); expenditures, $257,070; qualifying distributions, $249,123.
Limitations: Applications not accepted. Giving primarily in NY and VA.
Application information: Contributes only to pre-selected organizations.
Officers: Scott K.H. Bessent, Pres.; William Trinkle, V.P.; Ian Hoblyn, Secy.
EIN: 134076337
Codes: FD

34256
Balbach Family Foundation
369 Franklin St.
Buffalo, NY 14202

Established in 1998 in NY.
Donor(s): Charles E. Balbach, Margaret C. Balbach, Carl T. Balbach, Melissa T. Balbach, Harvard University.
Financial data (yr. ended 06/30/01): Grants paid, $250,605; assets, $351,778 (M); gifts received, $321,596; expenditures, $260,694; qualifying distributions, $250,605.
Limitations: Applications not accepted. Giving primarily in Buffalo, NY.
Application information: Contributes only to pre-selected organizations.
Trustees: Carl Teo Balbach, Charles E. Balbach, Margaret C. Balbach, Melissa Todd Balbach.
EIN: 161542054

34256—NEW YORK

Codes: FD

34257
Beaverkill Foundation, Inc.
P.O. Box 311
Liberty, NY 12754 (845) 295-2400
Contact: Darrell Supak

Established in 1998 in DE and NY.
Donor(s): Sandra Gerry.
Financial data (yr. ended 10/31/01): Grants paid, $250,352; assets, $2,729,846 (M); gifts received, $251,433; expenditures, $292,987; qualifying distributions, $292,232.
Limitations: Giving primarily in NY.
Officers and Directors:* Sandra Gerry,* Pres.; Louis J. Boyd, Secy.-Treas.; Adam Gerry, Robyn Gerry, Annelise Melchick.
EIN: 141800129
Codes: FD

34258
The Hartley Corporation
c/o St. Philip's Church
1101 Rte. 9D, P.O. Box 158
Garrison, NY 10524

Established in 1921 in CT.
Financial data (yr. ended 05/31/02): Grants paid, $250,250; assets, $2,551,923 (M); expenditures, $278,059; qualifying distributions, $246,666.
Limitations: Applications not accepted. Giving primarily in CT.
Application information: Contributes only to pre-selected organizations.
Officers: Robert H. Mead, Jr., Pres.; Nicholas W. Platt, Treas.
EIN: 066036296
Codes: FD

34259
The Arrison Family Charitable Foundation
35 Lincoln Pkwy.
Buffalo, NY 14222
Contact: Clement R. Arrison, Dir.

Established in 1989 in NY.
Financial data (yr. ended 12/31/01): Grants paid, $250,146; assets, $4,998,643 (M); expenditures, $258,212; qualifying distributions, $258,212.
Limitations: Giving primarily in Buffalo, NY.
Directors: Clement R. Arrison, Craig Arrison, Karen Arrison, Barbara Roger.
EIN: 223021980
Codes: FD

34260
Charles Lillian and Betty Neuwirth Foundation
308 E. 72nd St., Ste. 8E
New York, NY 10021
Contact: Betty Lee, Pres.

Established in 2001 in NY.
Donor(s): Betty Lee.
Financial data (yr. ended 12/31/01): Grants paid, $250,100; assets, $27,285 (M); gifts received, $297,740; expenditures, $255,070; qualifying distributions, $250,100.
Officers: Betty Lee, Pres.; Michael C. Cantor, V.P.; Lorraine Hefferman, V.P.; Marc Kursman, Secy.-Treas.
EIN: 134184885

34261
The Bovin Family Foundation
c/o Clearly, Gottlieb, Steen & Hamilton
1 Liberty Plz.
New York, NY 10006

Established in 1999 in NY.
Donor(s): Denis A. Bovin, Steven M. Loeb.
Financial data (yr. ended 12/31/01): Grants paid, $250,078; assets, $784,599 (M); gifts received, $330,595; expenditures, $270,903; qualifying distributions, $250,078.
Limitations: Applications not accepted. Giving primarily in NJ and NY.
Application information: Contributes only to pre-selected organizations.
Trustees: Denis A. Bovin, Steven M. Loeb.
EIN: 134107990
Codes: FD

34262
The Craig & Deborah Cogut Foundation, Inc.
c/o L.H. Frishkoff & Co.
529 5th Ave.
New York, NY 10017

Established in 1993 in DE and NY.
Donor(s): Craig Cogut, Deborah Cogut.
Financial data (yr. ended 12/31/01): Grants paid, $250,000; assets, $5,021,538 (M); gifts received, $721,215; expenditures, $356,281; qualifying distributions, $250,000.
Limitations: Applications not accepted. Giving on a national basis, including the greater metropolitan New York, NY, area and Washington, DC.
Application information: Contributes only to pre-selected organizations.
Officers: Craig Cogut, Pres.; Deborah Cogut, Secy.-Treas.
EIN: 133746440
Codes: FD

34263
Paul P. Dosberg Foundation, Inc.
1010 Times Sq. Bldg.
Rochester, NY 14614
Contact: Myron S. Lewis, Tr.

Established in 1956 in NY.
Donor(s): Paul P. Dosberg.‡
Financial data (yr. ended 12/31/01): Grants paid, $250,000; assets, $2,884,832 (M); expenditures, $308,757; qualifying distributions, $249,071.
Limitations: Giving primarily in NY and PA.
Application information: Application form not required.
Trustees: Charlotte Kramer, Mark Kramer, Myron S. Lewis, David Stiller.
EIN: 166030605
Codes: FD

34264
The Dorothy and Lillian Gish Prize
c/o JPMorgan Chase Bank
1211 Ave. of the Americas, 38th Fl.
New York, NY 10260 (212) 789-5682
E-mail: jones_ed_l@JPMorgan.com
Contact: Edward L. Jones, V.P.

Established in 1994 in NY.
Donor(s): Lillian D. Gish.‡
Financial data (yr. ended 06/30/01): Grants paid, $250,000; assets, $8,561,566 (M); gifts received, $5,000; expenditures, $471,540; qualifying distributions, $362,079.
Limitations: Applications not accepted. Giving on a national and international basis.
Application information: Recipients are selected by the prize committee.
Trustees: Nathan Hale, JPMorgan Chase Bank.
EIN: 133751413
Codes: FD, GTI

34265
LGR Foundation
c/o US Trust Company of America
114 W. 47th St.
New York, NY 10036-1532

Established in 2000 in TX.
Donor(s): Lawrence G. Rawl, LGR Charitable Lead Annuity Trust.
Financial data (yr. ended 12/31/01): Grants paid, $250,000; assets, $7,788,742 (M); gifts received, $194,270; expenditures, $327,272; qualifying distributions, $250,000.
Limitations: Applications not accepted.
Application information: Contributes only to pre-selected organizations.
Officers: Kelly R. Guziejka, Pres. and Treas.; Lawrence V. Rawl, V.P.; Kent H. McMahan, Secy.
Director: Gail W. Rawl.
EIN: 742955428

34266
National Mah Jongg League Foundation, Inc.
250 W. 57th St., Ste. 613
New York, NY 10107

Established in 1995.
Financial data (yr. ended 02/28/01): Grants paid, $250,000; assets, $284,265 (M); gifts received, $200,000; expenditures, $250,309; qualifying distributions, $250,000.
Limitations: Applications not accepted. Giving primarily in NY.
Application information: Contributes only to pre-selected organizations.
Officers: David Unger, Pres.; Larry Unger, V.P.; Ruth Unger, V.P.; Marilyn Starr, Secy.; Norman Greenberg, Treas.
EIN: 133791092
Codes: FD

34267
Alan & Katherine Stroock Fund
c/o Stroock & Stroock & Lavan
180 Maiden Ln.
New York, NY 10038-4982
Contact: Mariana S. Leighton, Pres.

Established in 1958 in NY.
Donor(s): Alan M. Stroock,‡ Katherine W. Stroock.
Financial data (yr. ended 12/31/00): Grants paid, $250,000; assets, $8,316,888 (M); expenditures, $327,010; qualifying distributions, $252,286.
Limitations: Giving primarily in NY.
Officers: Mariana S. Leighton, Pres.; Ronald J. Stein, V.P.; Judith Jahnke, Secy.
EIN: 136086102
Codes: FD

34268
Tortora Family Foundation
c/o Goldman Sachs & Co.
85 Broad St., Tax Dept.
New York, NY 10004

Established in 1999 in NY.
Donor(s): Leslie C. Tortora.
Financial data (yr. ended 03/31/01): Grants paid, $250,000; assets, $5,984,788 (M); gifts received, $2,559,027; expenditures, $381,750; qualifying distributions, $250,750.
Limitations: Applications not accepted. Giving primarily in Hartford, CT.
Application information: Contributes only to pre-selected organizations.
Trustee: Leslie C. Tortora.
EIN: 134088705
Codes: FD

34269
James H. & Candace Van Alen Foundation
c/o J. Kamerman
655 3rd Ave., 8th Fl.
New York, NY 10017

Donor(s): Candace Van Alen.
Financial data (yr. ended 12/31/01): Grants paid, $250,000; assets, $321,343 (M); gifts received, $1,600; expenditures, $262,905; qualifying distributions, $249,870.
Limitations: Applications not accepted. Giving primarily in FL, NY, and RI.
Application information: Contributes only to pre-selected organizations.
Trustees: Jerome Kamerman, Candace Van Alen.
EIN: 137113596
Codes: FD

34270
Samuel J. Bloomingdale Foundation
641 Lexington Ave., 29th Fl.
New York, NY 10022-4599 (212) 838-0211
Contact: Edgar M. Cullman, Chair.

Incorporated in 1951 in NY.
Donor(s): Samuel J. Bloomingdale,‡ Rita G. Bloomingdale,‡ Richard C. Ernst,‡ Susan B. Ernst,‡ Edgar M. Cullman, Louise B. Cullman.
Financial data (yr. ended 12/31/01): Grants paid, $249,906; assets, $874,459 (M); expenditures, $265,739; qualifying distributions, $250,115.
Limitations: Giving primarily in NY.
Publications: Annual report.
Application information: Application form required.
Officers: Edgar M. Cullman, Sr., Chair.; Louise B. Cullman, V.P.
EIN: 136099790
Codes: FD

34271
A. Williams Charitable Trust
(Formerly A. Williams Residuary Trust Charities)
c/o JPMorgan Chase Bank, Global Foundations Group
1211 Ave. of the Americas, 38th Fl.
New York, NY 10036
Contact: Edward L. Jones, V.P.

Established in 1941.
Donor(s): Arthur Williams.
Financial data (yr. ended 07/31/01): Grants paid, $248,900; assets, $1,347,442 (M); expenditures, $274,244; qualifying distributions, $246,623.
Limitations: Applications not accepted. Giving primarily in the metropolitan New York, NY, area.
Application information: Contributes only to pre-selected organizations.
Trustee: JPMorgan Chase Bank.
EIN: 136029337
Codes: FD

34272
The Kumble Foundation
c/o Waldman, Hirsch & Co.
855 Ave. of Americas, Rm. 623
New York, NY 10001-4115

Established in 1999 in NY.
Donor(s): Steven J. Kumble.
Financial data (yr. ended 12/31/01): Grants paid, $248,750; assets, $775 (M); gifts received, $249,580; expenditures, $249,665; qualifying distributions, $249,665.
Limitations: Applications not accepted.
Application information: Contributes only to pre-selected organizations.
Directors: Peggy Kumble, Roger Kumble, Steven J. Kumble, Todd Kumble.
EIN: 134013985

Codes: FD

34273
Chesed Israel Foundation, Inc.
9 Camelot Dr.
Goshen, NY 10924 (845) 294-0916
Contact: Kathryn A. Mallard, Secy.

Established in 1990 in NY.
Donor(s): Barry Klein.
Financial data (yr. ended 10/31/01): Grants paid, $248,250; assets, $4,925,035 (M); gifts received, $865,612; expenditures, $281,146; qualifying distributions, $251,417.
Limitations: Giving primarily in Israel.
Application information: Application form not required.
Officers and Directors:* Barry Klein,* Pres. and Treas.; Kathryn A. Mallard, Secy.
EIN: 133601284
Codes: FD

34274
The Grace Hidary Foundation, Inc.
c/o Jack A. Hidary
10 W. 33rd St., Ste. 900
New York, NY 10001

Established in 1994.
Donor(s): Abraham J. Hidary, Jack A. Hidary, Morris Hidary.
Financial data (yr. ended 12/31/01): Grants paid, $248,075; assets, $352,271 (M); gifts received, $279,300; expenditures, $251,926; qualifying distributions, $249,500.
Limitations: Applications not accepted.
Application information: Contributes only to pre-selected organizations.
Officers: Abraham J. Hidary, Pres.; Jack A. Hidary, V.P.; Morris Hidary, Secy.-Treas.
EIN: 133785660
Codes: FD

34275
Sergei S. Zlinkoff Fund for Medical Research and Education, Inc.
2 Wall St.
New York, NY 10005-2072
Contact: Jerome J. Cohen, Secy.

Incorporated in 1956 in NY.
Donor(s): Sergei S. Zlinkoff.‡
Financial data (yr. ended 10/31/01): Grants paid, $248,000; assets, $3,015,279 (M); expenditures, $288,718; qualifying distributions, $268,491.
Limitations: Applications not accepted. Giving primarily in New York, NY.
Application information: Contributes only to pre-selected organizations.
Officers: Mack Lipkin, Jr., M.D.,* Pres.; William M. Kelly,* V.P. and Treas.; Dennis W. Cope, M.D., V.P.; Deborah L. Goldsmith, V.P.; Robert Goldstein, M.D., V.P.; Irwin M. Freedberg, M.D., V.P.; Sandra Z. Hamolsky, V.P.; Ralph E. Hansmann, V.P.; Barbara Lipkin, V.P.; John O. Lipkin, M.D., V.P.; Ellen Parker, V.P.; Jerome J. Cohen, Secy.
EIN: 136094651
Codes: FD

34276
Charlotte & Arthur Zitrin Foundation
56 Ruxton Rd.
Great Neck, NY 11023
Application address: 32 Lockerman Sq., Ste. L-100, Dover, DE 19901

Established in 1991 in DE.
Donor(s): Arthur Zitrin, Charlotte Zitrin.
Financial data (yr. ended 10/31/00): Grants paid, $247,965; assets, $6,268,895 (M); gifts received,

$187,584; expenditures, $297,702; qualifying distributions, $250,439.
Limitations: Giving primarily in New York, NY.
Application information: Application form not required.
Officers: Arthur Zitrin, Pres.; Charlotte Zitrin, V.P.
EIN: 510337212
Codes: FD

34277
The Palm Foundation
c/o Goldman Sachs & Co.
85 Broad St., Tax Dept.
New York, NY 10004

Established in 1993 in NY.
Donor(s): Gregory K. Palm.
Financial data (yr. ended 04/30/01): Grants paid, $247,500; assets, $4,695,763 (M); gifts received, $1,100; expenditures, $325,080; qualifying distributions, $248,850.
Limitations: Applications not accepted. Giving limited to Cambridge, MA and Bryn Mawr, PA.
Application information: Contributes only to pre-selected organizations.
Trustee: Gregory K. Palm.
EIN: 133748059
Codes: FD

34278
Morris & Erika Herman Foundation
36 Merrall Dr.
Lawrence, NY 11559
Contact: Erika Herman, Secy.

Established in 1987 in NY.
Donor(s): Morris Herman.
Financial data (yr. ended 12/31/00): Grants paid, $247,350; assets, $625,593 (M); gifts received, $120,000; expenditures, $248,660; qualifying distributions, $248,437.
Officers: Morris Herman, Pres.; Erika Herman, Secy.
EIN: 112888434
Codes: FD

34279
Miller S. & Adelaide S. Gaffney Foundation
c/o BSB Bank and Trust
P.O. Box 1056
Binghamton, NY 13902-1056
Contact: Phillip W. Gaffney, Chair.

Established in 1968.
Donor(s): Miller S. Gaffney.
Financial data (yr. ended 12/31/01): Grants paid, $246,583; assets, $6,208,361 (M); gifts received, $74,246; expenditures, $281,014; qualifying distributions, $248,366.
Limitations: Giving primarily in Broome County, NY.
Publications: Informational brochure (including application guidelines).
Application information: Application form not required.
Officers and Advisory Committee:* Philip W. Gaffney,* Chair.; David M. Gouldin,* Vice-Chair.; Kent Turner,* Secy.; David Miller Gaffney, James T. Gaffney.
Trustee: BSB Bank and Trust.
EIN: 166101748
Codes: FD

34280
Jed David Satow Family Foundation, Inc.
c/o Phillip M. Satow
583 Broadway
New York, NY 10012

Established in 1999 in NY.
Donor(s): Phillip M. Satow.

Financial data (yr. ended 12/31/00): Grants paid, $246,193; assets, $1,552,940 (M); expenditures, $252,871; qualifying distributions, $238,199.
Limitations: Applications not accepted. Giving primarily in NY.
Application information: Contributes only to pre-selected organizations.
Officers and Directors:* Donna Satow,* Pres.; Julie Satow, Secy.-Treas.; Michael Satow, Phillip Satow.
EIN: 134067343
Codes: FD2

34281
CAL Foundation, Inc.
c/o Siegel, Sacks & Co.
630 3rd Ave.
New York, NY 10017

Established in 1957.
Donor(s): Linda L. Hackett.
Financial data (yr. ended 12/31/01): Grants paid, $246,000; assets, $3,900,511 (M); expenditures, $302,958; qualifying distributions, $245,954.
Limitations: Applications not accepted. Giving primarily in the metropolitan New York, NY, area.
Application information: Contributes only to pre-selected organizations.
Officers: Linda Hackett, Pres.; Melinda Hackett, V.P.; Montague H. Hackett, Jr., Secy.
EIN: 136083347
Codes: FD2

34282
The Buhl Foundation, Inc.
(Formerly The Buhl Family Foundation, Inc.)
c/o Speer & Fulvio, LLP
60 E. 42nd St.
New York, NY 10165-0006
FAX: (212) 274-0527

Established in 1989 in FL.
Donor(s): Henry M. Buhl, Bruce M. Kaplan.
Financial data (yr. ended 09/30/01): Grants paid, $245,720; assets, $5,436,428 (M); gifts received, $2,034,800; expenditures, $760,179; qualifying distributions, $635,625.
Limitations: Applications not accepted. Giving primarily in NJ and NY.
Officer: Henry M. Buhl, Pres.
Trustees: Raymond Merritt, Peter W. Schmidt.
EIN: 136937849
Codes: FD2

34283
Dash Family Foundation
c/o BCRS Assocs., LLC
67 Wall St., 8th Fl.
New York, NY 10005

Established in 1990 in NJ.
Donor(s): Marcus J. Dash.
Financial data (yr. ended 07/31/00): Grants paid, $245,650; assets, $1,147,439 (M); gifts received, $396,150; expenditures, $248,227; qualifying distributions, $242,380.
Limitations: Applications not accepted. Giving primarily in NY.
Application information: Contributes only to pre-selected organizations.
Trustees: Marcus J. Dash, Patricia B. Dash.
EIN: 133593422

34284
The Stephen and Cathy Weinroth Charitable Trust
700 W. 247th St.
Riverdale, NY 10471

Established in 1998 in NY.
Donor(s): Stephen D. Weinroth.
Financial data (yr. ended 12/31/00): Grants paid, $245,611; assets, $1,542,708 (M); gifts received, $775,000; expenditures, $255,311; qualifying distributions, $249,285.
Limitations: Applications not accepted. Giving primarily in New York, NY.
Application information: Contributes only to pre-selected organizations.
Trustee: Stephen D. Weinroth.
EIN: 137131559
Codes: FD2

34285
The Giant Steps Foundation
c/o Miller Ellin & Co., LLP
750 Lexington Ave.
New York, NY 10022
E-mail: gsf@giantsteps.org; *URL:* http://www.giantsteps.org

Established in 1997 in CA and DE.
Donor(s): Jennifer Leeds, Tides Foundation.
Financial data (yr. ended 11/30/01): Grants paid, $245,000; assets, $12,502,039 (M); expenditures, $284,786; qualifying distributions, $252,708.
Limitations: Applications not accepted. Giving primarily in San Francisco, CA.
Application information: Contributes only to pre-selected organizations.
Officers and Directors:* Jennifer Leeds,* Pres.; Richard L. Braunstein, Secy.; Jeffrey J. Sundheim,* Treas.; Lilo J. Leeds.
EIN: 522069841
Codes: FD2

34286
Gumpel-Lury Foundation
c/o Stroock & Stroock & Lavan
180 Maiden Ln.
New York, NY 10038-4982
Contact: Ronald J. Stein, Dir.

Established in 1977 in NY.
Donor(s): Helmut N. Friedlaender.
Financial data (yr. ended 10/31/01): Grants paid, $244,000; assets, $1,788,957 (M); gifts received, $166,275; expenditures, $251,756; qualifying distributions, $229,073.
Limitations: Giving primarily in the metropolitan New York, NY, area.
Application information: Application form not required.
Officers and Directors:* Judith G. Friedlaender,* Pres.; Thomas M. Franck,* V.P.; Edgar J. Nathan III,* V.P.; Helmut N. Friedlaender, Secy.-Treas.; Ronald J. Stein.
EIN: 132915655
Codes: FD2

34287
Irfan Kathwari Foundation, Inc.
1875 Palmer Ave.
Larchmont, NY 10538
Application address: 151 Elk Ave., New Rochelle, NY 10804
Contact: M. Farooq Kathwari, Dir.

Established in 1992 in NY.
Donor(s): IFO Enterprises, Ltd.
Financial data (yr. ended 06/30/01): Grants paid, $243,061; assets, $5,246,418 (M); expenditures, $246,849; qualifying distributions, $241,690.
Limitations: Giving on a national and international basis, with emphasis on Pakistan.
Application information: Application form not required.
Directors: Farida Kathwari, M. Farooq Kathwari, Rafique Kathwari, Faroque A. Khan.
EIN: 133681135
Codes: CS, FD2, CD, GTI

34288
Edward & Ellen Roche Relief Foundation
c/o U.S. Trust
114 W. 47th St.
New York, NY 10036-1532
FAX: (212) 852-3377
Contact: Carolyn L. Larke, Asst. V.P., U.S. Trust, or Linda R. Franciscovich, Sr. V.P., U.S. Trust

Established in 1930 in NY.
Donor(s): Edward Roche.‡
Financial data (yr. ended 12/31/01): Grants paid, $243,000; assets, $6,633,678 (M); expenditures, $323,764; qualifying distributions, $280,783.
Limitations: Giving primarily in CT, NJ, and NY.
Publications: Program policy statement, application guidelines.
Application information: Only written requests for guidelines are accepted. Application form not required.
Trustee: U.S. Trust.
EIN: 135622067
Codes: FD2

34289
The Howard Rubenstein Family Foundation, Inc.
1345 Ave. of the Americas
New York, NY 10105

Established in 1986.
Donor(s): Howard J. Rubenstein.
Financial data (yr. ended 12/31/01): Grants paid, $243,000; assets, $1,383,690 (M); gifts received, $133,123; expenditures, $263,844; qualifying distributions, $242,473.
Limitations: Applications not accepted. Giving primarily in New York, NY.
Application information: Contributes only to pre-selected organizations.
Officers: Howard J. Rubenstein, Pres.; Amy Rubenstein, Secy.-Treas.
EIN: 133384019
Codes: FD2

34290
Weingarten Family Foundation
1661 53rd St.
Brooklyn, NY 11204
Contact: Otto I. Weingarten, Pres.

Established in 1992 in NY.
Donor(s): Otto I. Weingarten.
Financial data (yr. ended 12/31/01): Grants paid, $243,000; assets, $4,431,633 (M); gifts received, $700,166; expenditures, $316,191; qualifying distributions, $245,750.
Limitations: Giving primarily in NJ and NY; giving also in Israel.
Officers: Otto I. Weingarten, Pres.; Rosemarie Weingarten, V.P.; Simone Krause, Secy.; Herchie Weingarten, Treas.
Director: Harold Feinberg.
EIN: 113133160
Codes: FD2

34291
The Edward and Deanne Spiegel Foundation
(Formerly The Edward Spiegel Foundation)
c/o BCRS Associates, LLC
100 Wall St., 11th Fl.
New York, NY 10005

Established in 1985 in NY.
Donor(s): Edward P. Spiegel.
Financial data (yr. ended 09/30/01): Grants paid, $242,050; assets, $5,309,883 (M); expenditures, $256,016; qualifying distributions, $244,388.
Limitations: Applications not accepted. Giving primarily in New York, NY.
Application information: Contributes only to pre-selected organizations.

Trustees: Deanne Spiegel, Edward P. Spiegel, Roy J. Zuckerberg.
EIN: 133318169
Codes: FD2

34292
Walter H. D. Killough Trust
c/o HSBC Bank USA
452 5th Ave., 17th Fl.
New York, NY 10018 (212) 525-2417
Contact: Stephen B. Boies, 1st V.P., HSBC Bank USA

Trust established in 1929 in NY.
Donor(s): Walter H.D. Killough.‡
Financial data (yr. ended 07/31/01): Grants paid, $241,599; assets, $3,441,560 (M); expenditures, $324,112; qualifying distributions, $260,944.
Limitations: Giving primarily in NJ and NY.
Application information: Application form required.
Trustees: Norman S. Fink, Rt. Rev. Robert C. Witcher, HSBC Bank USA.
EIN: 136063894
Codes: FD2

34293
Ittleson-Beaumont Fund
1211 Ave. of the Americas
New York, NY 10036
Application Address: c/o The CIT Group, Inc., 650 CIT Dr., Livingston, NJ, 07039, tel.: (973) 740-5000
Contact: Victor Amato

Established in 1932 in NY.
Financial data (yr. ended 12/31/00): Grants paid, $241,444; assets, $2,123,005 (M); expenditures, $248,325; qualifying distributions, $241,444.
Limitations: Giving on a national basis.
Application information: Application form not required.
Trustees: Albert R. Gamper, Jr., Joseph M. Leone, Susan P. Mitchell, William M. O'Grady, Thomas J. O'Rourke, Ernest D. Stein.
EIN: 136083909
Codes: FD2, GTI

34294
Harold & Ann Sorgenti Family Foundation
c/o U.S. Trust
114 W. 47th St.
New York, NY 10036

Established in 1998 in PA.
Financial data (yr. ended 12/31/00): Grants paid, $241,075; assets, $1,562,481 (M); expenditures, $259,495; qualifying distributions, $242,173.
Limitations: Applications not accepted. Giving primarily in Philadelphia, PA.
Application information: Contributes only to pre-selected organizations.
Trustees: Elizabeth S. Paterno, Lucille S. Reynolds, Ann R. Sorgenti, Harold A. Sorgenti.
EIN: 237978500
Codes: FD2

34295
The Ned and Emily Sherwood Family Foundation
54 Morris Ln.
Scarsdale, NY 10583
Contact: Ned Sherwood

Established in 1999.
Donor(s): Ned L. Sherwood, Emily Layzer Sherwood.
Financial data (yr. ended 05/31/02): Grants paid, $240,600; assets, $3,753,366 (M); gifts received, $2,505,670; expenditures, $273,754; qualifying distributions, $218,533.

Limitations: Applications not accepted. Giving primarily in Westchester, NY.
Application information: Contributes only to pre-selected organizations.
Officers and Directors:* Ned L. Sherwood,* Pres.; Emily Layzer,* V.P.; Matthew F. Sherwood,* Secy.; Richard I. Sherwood,* Treas.
EIN: 364273196
Codes: FD2

34296
Peter and Elisabetta Mallinson Foundation
c/o Goldman Sachs & Co.
85 Broad St., Tax Dept.
New York, NY 10004

Established in 1996 in NY.
Donor(s): Peter G.C. Mallinson.
Financial data (yr. ended 03/31/01): Grants paid, $240,500; assets, $1,265,599 (M); gifts received, $2,500; expenditures, $270,496; qualifying distributions, $243,250.
Limitations: Applications not accepted. Giving primarily in NC and NY.
Application information: Contributes only to pre-selected organizations.
Trustees: Elisabetta Mallinson, Peter G.C. Mallinson, Robert K. Steel.
EIN: 133933324
Codes: FD2

34297
Malcolm E. Smith, Jr. Foundation, Inc.
59 Smith Ln.
St. James, NY 11780

Established in 1996 in ME.
Financial data (yr. ended 12/31/00): Grants paid, $240,500; assets, $590,820 (M); gifts received, $269; expenditures, $243,890; qualifying distributions, $240,500.
Limitations: Giving primarily in MI, NH, and NY.
Officers and Directors:* Jennifer Huntley,* V.P.; Helen L. Brosseau,* Secy.
EIN: 113344933
Codes: FD2

34298
Tennenbaum Family Foundation Trust
c/o Breindy Melnicke
1637 50th St.
Brooklyn, NY 11204

Established in 1994 in NY.
Financial data (yr. ended 12/31/01): Grants paid, $240,130; assets, $593,495 (M); expenditures, $256,446; qualifying distributions, $252,099.
Limitations: Applications not accepted. Giving primarily in Brooklyn, NY.
Application information: Contributes only to pre-selected organizations.
Trustees: Breindy Melnicke, Morris Tennenbaum.
EIN: 116431567
Codes: FD2

34299
Hahn Family Foundation
1807 Elmwood Ave., Office 287
Buffalo, NY 14207 (716) 447-7828
Contact: Charles D. Hahn, Tr.

Established in 1965.
Donor(s): Charles Hahn,‡ Charles J. Hahn.
Financial data (yr. ended 12/31/01): Grants paid, $240,000; assets, $5,245,583 (M); gifts received, $25,620; expenditures, $334,711; qualifying distributions, $308,028.
Limitations: Giving primarily in Buffalo and Erie County, NY.
Publications: Application guidelines.

Application information: Application form not required.
Trustees: Anne H. Hahn-Baker, Charles D. Hahn, Charles J. Hahn, Eric S. Hahn.
EIN: 166128499
Codes: FD2

34300
The Gertrude Kaufman Silver Foundation
c/o David Silver
P.O. Box 720
Sagaponack, NY 11962

Established in 1988 in DE.
Donor(s): David Silver, Patricia Walton.
Financial data (yr. ended 09/30/01): Grants paid, $239,660; assets, $14,210 (M); gifts received, $120,500; expenditures, $246,336; qualifying distributions, $245,097.
Limitations: Applications not accepted. Giving primarily in NY.
Application information: Contributes only to pre-selected organizations.
Officers: David Silver, Pres. and Treas.; Patricia Walton Silver, V.P. and Secy.
EIN: 133496535
Codes: FD2

34301
The Powers Family Foundation
c/o Goldman Sachs & Co.
85 Broad St., Tax Dept.
New York, NY 10004

Established in 1991 in NY.
Donor(s): John J. Powers.
Financial data (yr. ended 06/30/01): Grants paid, $239,500; assets, $5,638,984 (M); gifts received, $2,162,478; expenditures, $335,500; qualifying distributions, $211,987.
Limitations: Applications not accepted. Giving primarily in Boston, MA, and New York, NY.
Application information: Contributes only to pre-selected organizations.
Trustees: Charles A. Davis, John J. Powers, Linda E. Powers.
EIN: 133637704
Codes: FD2

34302
The Reich Fund
c/o Seymour Reich
640 Park Ave.
New York, NY 10021-6126

Established in 1975 in NY.
Donor(s): Seymour Reich.
Financial data (yr. ended 10/31/01): Grants paid, $239,441; assets, $4,626,555 (M); expenditures, $252,928; qualifying distributions, $238,480.
Limitations: Applications not accepted. Giving primarily in NY.
Application information: Contributes only to pre-selected organizations.
Trustees: Charles Reich, Elizabeth Reich, Lilian Reich, Seymour Reich.
EIN: 510166322
Codes: FD2

34303
The Martin & Doris Payson Charitable Foundation
c/o TAG Assocs.
75 Rockefeller Plz., Ste. 900
New York, NY 10019

Established in 1989 in NY.
Donor(s): Doris L. Payson, Martin D. Payson.
Financial data (yr. ended 11/30/00): Grants paid, $239,300; assets, $788,098 (M); gifts received,

$140,100; expenditures, $258,376; qualifying distributions, $239,484.
Limitations: Applications not accepted. Giving primarily in New York, NY.
Application information: Contributes only to pre-selected organizations.
Trustees: Doris L. Payson, Martin D. Payson.
EIN: 133556497
Codes: FD2

34304
Michael and Paula Rantz Foundation
c/o BCRS Associates, LLC
100 Wall St., 11th Fl.
New York, NY 10005

Established in 1994 in CT.
Donor(s): Michael G. Rantz.
Financial data (yr. ended 05/31/01): Grants paid, $239,295; assets, $4,274,134 (M); gifts received, $1,306,810; expenditures, $315,799; qualifying distributions, $240,799.
Limitations: Applications not accepted. Giving primarily in New York, NY, and Royesford, PA.
Application information: Contributes only to pre-selected organizations.
Trustees: Michael G. Rantz, Paula Anne Rantz.
EIN: 133792291
Codes: FD2

34305
Goldman Sachs Charitable Fund
c/o Goldman Sachs & Co.
10 Hanover Sq., 22nd Fl.
New York, NY 10005
Application addresses for both the H.R. Young Graduate Scholarship Program and the Walter F. Blain Scholarship Program: c/o Citizens Scholarship Foundation of America, 1505 Riverview Rd., P.O. Box 297, Saint Peter, MN 56082, tel.: (507) 931-1682 and ask for the Goldman Sachs Walter F. Blain Prog. Mgr. For the George E. Doty Master's Degree Fellowship Program: c/o Gregg Bloom, Human Resources Dept., 180 Maiden Ln., 21st Fl., New York, NY 10038-4958

Established in 1999 in NY.
Financial data (yr. ended 06/30/01): Grants paid, $239,000; assets, $345,581 (M); gifts received, $17,200; expenditures, $297,350; qualifying distributions, $239,100.
Application information: Application form required.
Officers: Esta E. Stecher, Pres.; Robert J. Katz, V.P. and Secy.; Gregory K. Palm, V.P.; David Viniar, Treas.
EIN: 311678646
Codes: FD2

34306
Charles and Pauline Kautz Foundation
c/o Rouis and Co., LLP
P.O. Box 209
Wurtsboro, NY 12790
Application address: c/o Robert Curtis, Fleet National Bank, Bridge St., Callicoon, NY 12723

Established in 1976 in NY.
Donor(s): Charles P. Kautz.‡
Financial data (yr. ended 12/31/01): Grants paid, $238,827; assets, $5,460,824 (M); expenditures, $309,561; qualifying distributions, $236,478.
Limitations: Giving limited to the Delaware Valley, NY, area.
Application information: Applications available at Guidance Dept. of Delaware Valley High School, NY. Application form required.
Trustees: Ruth Burstman, Mary Curtis, Robert Curtis, Maurice Roche, Fred Stabberd.

EIN: 141579429
Codes: FD2, GTI

34307
William & Miriam Olsten Foundation, Inc.
P.O. Box 326
Old Westbury, NY 11568-1522
Contact: Miriam Olsten, Tr.

Established in 1983.
Donor(s): Miriam Olsten, William Olsten.
Financial data (yr. ended 12/31/01): Grants paid, $238,650; assets, $621,783 (M); gifts received, $100,000; expenditures, $248,430; qualifying distributions, $238,650.
Limitations: Giving primarily in NY.
Trustees: Miriam Olsten, Stuart N. Olsten.
EIN: 133206285

34308
Theodore & Ruth Baum Charitable Foundation
(Formerly Theodore B. Family Baum Foundation)
c/o Becker & Co., LLC
551 Madison Ave., 8th Fl.
New York, NY 10022

Established in 1967 in NJ.
Donor(s): Elizabeth Baum, Theodore B. Baum, Dana Baum Hopper, Ruth Baum.
Financial data (yr. ended 12/31/01): Grants paid, $238,201; assets, $2,202,237 (M); gifts received, $510,805; expenditures, $241,333; qualifying distributions, $238,201.
Limitations: Applications not accepted. Giving primarily in New York, NY.
Application information: Contributes only to pre-selected organizations.
Officers: Ruth Baum, Pres.; Theodore B. Baum, V.P. and Treas.; Dana Baum Hopper, Secy.
EIN: 226088058
Codes: FD2

34309
Ira M. and Diane G. Millstein Family Foundation
1240 Flagler Dr.
Mamaroneck, NY 10543-4601

Established in 1997 in NY.
Donor(s): Diane G. Millstein, Ira Millstein.
Financial data (yr. ended 11/30/01): Grants paid, $238,100; assets, $1,177,952 (M); gifts received, $493,009; expenditures, $240,395; qualifying distributions, $237,737.
Limitations: Applications not accepted. Giving primarily in New York, NY.
Application information: Contributes only to pre-selected organizations.
Trustees: Diane G. Millstein, Ira M. Millstein.
EIN: 137131232
Codes: FD2

34310
Ann M. Martin Foundation, Inc.
P.O. Box 430
Boiceville, NY 12412
FAX: (845) 657-8002; *URL:* http://www.scholastic.com/annmartin/ann/foundation.htm
Contact: Elisa Geliebter, Secy.

Established in 1991 in NY.
Donor(s): Ann M. Martin.
Financial data (yr. ended 12/31/01): Grants paid, $237,696; assets, $750,000 (M); expenditures, $245,192; qualifying distributions, $237,696.
Limitations: Giving on a national basis, with some emphasis on New York City.
Publications: Grants list, informational brochure (including application guidelines), occasional report.

Application information: Application form not required.
Officers and Directors:* Ann M. Martin, Pres.; Jane Reed Martin, V.P.; Elisa Geliebter,* Secy.; Catherine Gordon, Treas.; Laura Godwin.
EIN: 133620569
Codes: FD2

34311
Leland Trust for Charitable Purposes
c/o The Bank of New York, Tax Dept.
1 Wall St., 28th Fl.
New York, NY 10286

Financial data (yr. ended 12/31/01): Grants paid, $237,598; assets, $3,630,341 (M); expenditures, $256,754; qualifying distributions, $236,199.
Limitations: Applications not accepted. Giving primarily in NY.
Application information: Contributes only to pre-selected organizations.
Trustee: The Bank of New York.
EIN: 136136775
Codes: FD2

34312
Andrew J. Kirch Charitable Trust
c/o James G. Vazzana
5 S. Fitzhugh St., Ste. 230
Rochester, NY 14614-1413

Financial data (yr. ended 12/31/01): Grants paid, $237,300; assets, $1,819,881 (M); expenditures, $288,610; qualifying distributions, $236,659.
Limitations: Giving limited to Rochester, NY.
Application information: Application form not required.
Trustees: Michael S. Ray, James G. Vazzana, Patricia O. Vazzana.
EIN: 166396501
Codes: FD2

34313
Corlette Glorney Foundation, Inc.
c/o Kirkpatrick & Lockhart, LLP
1251 6th Ave., 45th Fl.
New York, NY 10020-1104
Application address: c/o The New York Academy of Medicine, 2 E. 103rd St., New York, NY 10029-5291

Financial data (yr. ended 12/31/00): Grants paid, $237,200; assets, $4,022,422 (M); expenditures, $290,360; qualifying distributions, $239,047.
Limitations: Giving limited to New York, NY.
Officer: Robert F. Ambrose, Secy.-Treas.
Directors: William H. Bienfield, Jeffrey Borer, Edward P. Fichter, Peter Lawson-Johnston, Carl F. Rogge, Jr., Pascal Wirz.
EIN: 136104151
Codes: FD2

34314
The Roger Weiss Family Foundation
c/o Barry M. Strauss Assoc., Ltd.
307 5th Ave., 8th Fl.
New York, NY 10016-6517

Established in 1986 in NY.
Donor(s): Roger J. Weiss.
Financial data (yr. ended 02/28/02): Grants paid, $237,025; assets, $361,382 (M); gifts received, $135,566; expenditures, $242,807; qualifying distributions, $239,075.
Limitations: Applications not accepted. Giving primarily in NY.
Application information: Contributes only to pre-selected organizations.
Officers: Roger J. Weiss, Pres. and Treas.; Caren Weiss, Secy.
Director: Stephen H. Weiss.

EIN: 133321869
Codes: FD2

34315
The Holborn Foundation
c/o U.S. Trust Co. of New York
114 W 47th St.
New York, NY 10036

Established in 1998 in IL.
Donor(s): Gillett A. Gilbert, John N. Gilbert.
Financial data (yr. ended 11/30/00): Grants paid, $236,989; assets, $4,167,864 (M); expenditures, $261,345; qualifying distributions, $240,340.
Limitations: Applications not accepted.
Application information: Contributes only to pre-selected organizations.
Trustees: Gillett A. Gilbert, John N. Gilbert, Jr.
EIN: 367213630
Codes: FD2

34316
The Arthur Kontos Foundation, Inc.
c/o BCRS Assocs., LLC
100 Wall St., 11th Fl.
New York, NY 10005
Contact: Joseph De Maio

Established in 1985 in NY and DE.
Donor(s): Arthur Kontos.
Financial data (yr. ended 11/30/01): Grants paid, $236,425; assets, $6,096,510 (M); gifts received, $250,000; expenditures, $307,061; qualifying distributions, $234,728.
Limitations: Applications not accepted. Giving on a national basis.
Application information: Contributes only to pre-selected organizations.
Officers: Arthur Kontos, Pres.; Carl Hewitt, Secy.-Treas.
EIN: 133339956
Codes: FD2

34317
Jonathan S. Patrick Foundation, Inc.
20 Exchange Pl.
New York, NY 10005

Established in 1966 in NY.
Donor(s): Joseph A. Patrick.
Financial data (yr. ended 12/31/01): Grants paid, $235,650; assets, $4,511,418 (M); expenditures, $238,107; qualifying distributions, $231,692.
Limitations: Applications not accepted. Giving on a national basis.
Application information: Contributes only to pre-selected organizations.
Officers: Joseph A. Patrick, Pres.; Stuart K. Patrick, V.P.; John J. Glynn, Secy.-Treas.
EIN: 136208825
Codes: FD2

34318
The Dobson Foundation, Inc.
4 E. 66th St., Ste. 1E
New York, NY 10021

Incorporated in 1961 in NY.
Donor(s): Walter M. Jeffords, Jr.‡
Financial data (yr. ended 12/31/00): Grants paid, $235,550; assets, $5,173,101 (M); expenditures, $253,434; qualifying distributions, $245,284.
Limitations: Applications not accepted. Giving primarily on the East Coast, with emphasis on New York and Saratoga Springs, NY.
Application information: Contributes only to pre-selected organizations.
Officers: Kathleen McLaughlin Jeffords, Pres.; George Jeffords, V.P.; Sarah Jeffords Radcliff, Secy.
EIN: 136168259
Codes: FD2

34319
Helen & Irving Schneider Foundation, Inc.
880 5th Ave., Ste. 17F
New York, NY 10021-4951

Donor(s): Irving Schneider, Helen Schneider.
Financial data (yr. ended 12/31/00): Grants paid, $235,000; assets, $5,551,097 (M); expenditures, $242,882; qualifying distributions, $241,081.
Limitations: Applications not accepted. Giving primarily in New York, NY.
Application information: Contributes only to pre-selected organizations.
Officers: Irving Schneider, Pres.; Helen Schneider, Secy.
EIN: 136165503
Codes: FD2

34320
TBF Charitable Trust
(Formerly The Berkowitz Family Charitable Trust)
1665 47th St.
Brooklyn, NY 11204-1142

Established in 1992 in NY and NJ.
Donor(s): Israel Berkowitz, Leopold Berkowitz, Morris Berkowitz.
Financial data (yr. ended 12/31/00): Grants paid, $234,760; assets, $7,635,286 (M); gifts received, $655,000; expenditures, $241,096; qualifying distributions, $234,840.
Limitations: Applications not accepted. Giving primarily in Brooklyn, NY.
Application information: Contributes only to pre-selected organizations.
Trustees: Israel Berkowitz, Leopold Berkowitz, Morris Berkowitz.
EIN: 226585269
Codes: FD2

34321
Mary S. Mulligan Charitable Trust
1 East Ave.
Rochester, NY 14604
Contact: William A. Mckee, V.P., Fleet National Bank

Established in 1967 in NY.
Donor(s): Mary S. Mulligan.‡
Financial data (yr. ended 05/31/01): Grants paid, $234,250; assets, $4,727,080 (M); expenditures, $286,152; qualifying distributions, $254,567.
Limitations: Giving primarily in Rochester, NY.
Application information: Application form required.
Trustee: Fleet National Bank.
EIN: 166076169
Codes: FD2

34322
Benjamin & Seema Pulier Charitable Foundation, Inc.
c/o Pulier & Freedman
342 Madison Ave., Ste. 1220
New York, NY 10173-1220
Contact: Edith Freedman, Pres.

Established in 1993 in NY.
Financial data (yr. ended 12/31/99): Grants paid, $233,700; assets, $5,367,606 (M); gifts received, $11,902; expenditures, $284,252; qualifying distributions, $233,700.
Limitations: Applications not accepted. Giving primarily in FL, MA, and NY.
Application information: Contributes only to pre-selected organizations.
Officers and Directors:* Edith Freedman,* Pres.; Joseph Tsinberg,* V.P. and Secy.; Klaus Scheve,* V.P. and Treas.
EIN: 133683886
Codes: FD2

34323
The Bogatin Family Foundation, Inc.
c/o Mahoney Cohen & Co.
111 W. 40th St.
New York, NY 10018

Established in 1996 in NY.
Donor(s): Jeffrey Bogatin.
Financial data (yr. ended 12/31/01): Grants paid, $233,622; assets, $3,315,212 (M); expenditures, $257,183; qualifying distributions, $232,036.
Limitations: Applications not accepted. Giving primarily in NJ and NY.
Application information: Contributes only to pre-selected organizations.
Officers and Directors:* Jeffrey Bogatin,* Pres.; Susan Bogatin,* Secy.; Rachel Bogatin.
EIN: 133922730
Codes: FD2

34324
Blinken Foundation, Inc.
466 Lexington Ave., 10th Fl.
New York, NY 10017
Contact: Donald Blinken, Pres.

Established in 1965 in NY.
Donor(s): Alan Blinken, Donald Blinken, Milt Blinken,‡ Robert Blinken.
Financial data (yr. ended 12/31/01): Grants paid, $233,500; assets, $3,180,312 (M); expenditures, $253,990; qualifying distributions, $236,324.
Limitations: Applications not accepted. Giving primarily in New York, NY.
Application information: Contributes only to pre-selected organizations. Unsolicited requests for funds not accepted.
Officers and Directors:* Donald M. Blinken,* Pres. and Treas.; Robert J. Blinken,* V.P. and Secy.; Alan J. Blinken,* V.P.
EIN: 136190153
Codes: FD2

34325
The Stanton Family Foundation
c/o Goldman Sachs & Co.
85 Broad St., Tax Dept.
New York, NY 10004

Established in 1996 in NJ.
Donor(s): Daniel W. Stanton.
Financial data (yr. ended 09/30/01): Grants paid, $233,200; assets, $4,050,506 (M); gifts received, $1,739,318; expenditures, $312,627; qualifying distributions, $237,041.
Limitations: Applications not accepted. Giving primarily in NJ and NY.
Application information: Contributes only to pre-selected organizations.
Trustees: Daniel W. Stanton, Mary B. Stanton.
EIN: 137103245
Codes: FD2

34326
The Vincent and Harriet Palisano Foundation
3400 HSBC Ctr.
Buffalo, NY 14203
Contact: James M. Beardsley, Tr.

Established in 1962 in NY.
Donor(s): Vincent H. Palisano,‡ Harriet A. Palisano.‡
Financial data (yr. ended 05/31/01): Grants paid, $233,000; assets, $3,879,505 (M); expenditures, $276,180; qualifying distributions, $252,554.
Limitations: Applications not accepted. Giving primarily in the Buffalo, NY, area.
Application information: Unsolicited requests for funds not considered.
Trustees: James M. Beardsley, Beverly A. Leek, Angeline D. Smith.

EIN: 166052186
Codes: FD2

34327
Ciba Specialty Chemicals Foundation
c/o Hugh Stuart-Buttle
540 White Plains Rd., Tax Dept.
Tarrytown, NY 10591 (914) 785-2365

Donor(s): Ciba Specialty Chemicals Corp.
Financial data (yr. ended 12/31/01): Grants paid, $232,977; assets, $5,082,260 (M); gifts received, $29,415; expenditures, $292,131; qualifying distributions, $285,827.
Limitations: Applications not accepted. Giving primarily in areas of company operations, with emphasis on NY, NC, AR, AL, and DE.
Application information: Contributes only to pre-selected organizations.
Officers and Directors:* Stan Sherman,* Chair. and Pres.; John J. McGraw, Vice-Chair. and V.P.; Hugh Stuart-Buttle, Secy.-Treas.; Marshall White.
EIN: 133940874
Codes: CS, FD2, CD

34328
Diamondston Foundation, Inc.
317 Madison Ave., Ste. 1410
New York, NY 10017
Contact: Jesse Margolin, Pres.

Established in 2000 in NY.
Financial data (yr. ended 12/31/01): Grants paid, $232,100; assets, $3,378,646 (M); expenditures, $249,220; qualifying distributions, $233,873.
Limitations: Giving primarily in NY.
Application information: Application form not required.
Officers: Jesse Margolin, Pres. and Treas.; David Margolin, V.P.; Michael Margolin, V.P.; Susan Smith, V.P.; Barbara Margolin, Secy.
EIN: 134112479
Codes: FD2

34329
Metzger-Price Fund, Inc.
230 Park Ave., Ste. 2300
New York, NY 10169
Contact: Isaac A. Saufer, Secy.-Treas.

Trust established in 1970 in NY.
Donor(s): Estelle Metzger,‡ Leonard Metzger.‡
Financial data (yr. ended 06/30/01): Grants paid, $232,000; assets, $853,503 (M); gifts received, $197,695; expenditures, $250,188; qualifying distributions, $286,783.
Limitations: Giving primarily in New York, NY.
Publications: Financial statement.
Application information: Application form not required.
Officers: Ronald B. Sobel, Pres.; Don Robert Johnson, V.P.; Isaac A. Saufer, Secy.-Treas.
EIN: 237072764
Codes: FD2

34330
The Jim and Linda Robinson Foundation, Inc.
c/o The Avco Co., LLP
P.O. Box 8019
Ballston Spa, NY 12020-8019

Financial data (yr. ended 12/31/00): Grants paid, $231,701; assets, $463,687 (M); expenditures, $249,908; qualifying distributions, $229,371.
Limitations: Applications not accepted. Giving on a national basis.
Application information: Contributes only to pre-selected organizations.
Officers: James D. Robinson III, Pres.; Linda G. Robinson, V.P. and Treas.; Karen Marshon, Secy.
EIN: 133981478

Codes: FD2

34331
Demarest Lloyd, Jr. Foundation
c/o Sheehan & Co., C.P.A.
230 Park Ave., Ste. 416
New York, NY 10169-0124
Application address: 150 Stanwich Rd., Greenwich, CT 06830
Contact: Tangley L. DeLaney, Pres.

Established in 1975.
Donor(s): Tangley L. DeLaney.
Financial data (yr. ended 12/31/01): Grants paid, $231,000; assets, $3,507,289 (M); expenditures, $251,862; qualifying distributions, $229,923.
Limitations: Giving primarily in NY.
Application information: Application form not required.
Officers: Tangley L. DeLaney, Pres.; M. Robert DeLaney, V.P.
EIN: 510190219
Codes: FD2

34332
The Ruth & Oliver Stanton Foundation
c/o Anchin, Block & Anchin, LLP
1375 Broadway
New York, NY 10018

Established in 1994 in NY.
Donor(s): Ruth S. Stanton.
Financial data (yr. ended 12/31/01): Grants paid, $230,250; assets, $5,722,546 (M); gifts received, $1,000,000; expenditures, $274,738; qualifying distributions, $230,250.
Limitations: Applications not accepted. Giving primarily in New York, NY.
Application information: Contributes only to pre-selected organizations.
Officer and Trustees:* Ruth S. Stanton,* Mgr.; Oliver K. Stanton.
EIN: 137031172

34333
John Golden Fund, Inc.
c/o Paul Weiss Rifkind Wharton & Garrison
1285 Ave. of the Americas
New York, NY 10019-6064 (212) 373-3391
FAX: (212) 373-2092
Contact: John Breglio, Dir.

Incorporated in 1944 in NY.
Donor(s): John Golden.‡
Financial data (yr. ended 12/31/01): Grants paid, $230,225; assets, $4,148,348 (M); expenditures, $272,625; qualifying distributions, $248,674.
Limitations: Giving primarily in the New York, NY metropolitan area.
Application information: Application form not required.
Directors: Jill Allgaeuer, Jorg E. Allgaeuer, John Breglio, Edwin Wilson.
EIN: 136065978
Codes: FD2

34334
Laurmarlyn Foundation
c/o Lichtenstein
224 W. 35th St., Ste. 508
New York, NY 10001

Established in 1998 in DE.
Donor(s): James P. Manning.
Financial data (yr. ended 12/31/01): Grants paid, $230,107; assets, $184,632 (M); gifts received, $563,878; expenditures, $395,386; qualifying distributions, $230,107.
Limitations: Applications not accepted.
Application information: Contributes only to pre-selected organizations.

Officers and Directors:* James P. Manning,* Pres.; Laurie Manning,* V.P. and Treas.; Lynn Satalino,* Secy.-Treas.
EIN: 134025863
Codes: FD2

34335
Berthe M. Cote Foundation, Inc.
c/o U.S. Trust
114 W. 47th St.
New York, NY 10036
FAX: (212) 852-3377
Contact: Linda Francisovich, Sr. V.P. or Carolyn Larke, U.S. Trust

Financial data (yr. ended 10/31/01): Grants paid, $230,000; assets, $3,734,975 (M); expenditures, $272,500; qualifying distributions, $230,874.
Limitations: Giving primarily in NY.
Publications: Application guidelines.
Application information: Application form not required.
Officers and Directors:* E. Michael DiFabio,* Pres. and Treas.; Mary Anne Tommaney,* 1st V.P. and Secy.; Linda R. Francisovich, 2nd V.P.
EIN: 141681452
Codes: FD2

34336
The Barry & Rochelle Kaplan Foundation
c/o Goldman Sachs
85 Broad St., Tax Dept.
New York, NY 10004

Established in 1996 in NY.
Donor(s): Barry A. Kaplan.
Financial data (yr. ended 05/31/01): Grants paid, $230,000; assets, $2,029,312 (M); gifts received, $901,458; expenditures, $265,110; qualifying distributions, $234,110.
Limitations: Applications not accepted. Giving primarily in NY and PA.
Application information: Contributes only to pre-selected organizations.
Trustees: Barry A. Kaplan, Rachelle L. Kaplan.
EIN: 137109403
Codes: FD2

34337
Reginald A. & Elizabeth S. Lenna Foundation, Inc.
P.O. Box 407
Lakewood, NY 14750
E-mail: lennacre@alltel.net
Contact: Elizabeth S. Lenna, Pres.

Established in 1985 in NY.
Donor(s): Reginald A. Lenna.‡
Financial data (yr. ended 12/31/01): Grants paid, $230,000; assets, $9,448,550 (M); expenditures, $259,406; qualifying distributions, $237,663.
Limitations: Giving primarily in southwestern NY.
Officers: Elizabeth S. Lenna, Pres.; Joseph Johnson, V.P.; Samuel P. Price, Secy.; Randy Ordines, Treas.
Director: Florence Cass.
EIN: 112800733
Codes: FD2

34338
Overhills Foundation
380 Madison Ave.
New York, NY 10017

Established in 2000 in DE.
Donor(s): Omnibus Charitable Trust, Underhill Foundation, Wild Wings Foundation.
Financial data (yr. ended 11/30/01): Grants paid, $230,000; assets, $6,426,334 (M); gifts received, $2,804,277; expenditures, $262,212; qualifying distributions, $228,753.

Limitations: Applications not accepted. Giving primarily in NY.
Application information: Contributes only to pre-selected organizations.
Officers and Directors:* Ann R. Elliman,* Pres.; Lucia R. Brown,* V.P.; Edward H. Elliman,* V.P.; Christopher J. Elliman,* Secy.-Treas.
EIN: 133922745
Codes: FD2

34339
Braka Philanthropic Foundation
450 7th Ave., 45th Fl.
New York, NY 10123
Contact: Michele Needle

Established in 1994 in NJ.
Donor(s): Ivor Braka, David Braka.
Financial data (yr. ended 12/31/00): Grants paid, $229,876; assets, $1,753,298 (M); gifts received, $19,555; expenditures, $233,532; qualifying distributions, $185,532.
Limitations: Applications not accepted. Giving primarily in FL, NJ, and NY.
Application information: Contributes only to pre-selected organizations.
Officers: David Braka, Chair.; Ivor Braka, Mgr.; Pauline Braka, Mgr.; Robin Braka, Mgr.; Ira Levy, Mgr.
EIN: 226643642
Codes: FD2

34340
The Hagedorn Family Foundation, Inc.
P.O. Box 888
Port Washington, NY 11050

Established in 1989 in NY.
Donor(s): Susan Hagedorn, Horace Hagedorn, James Hagedorn, Peter Hagedorn, Kate Hagedorn Littlefield, Paul Hagedorn, Robert Hagedorn.
Financial data (yr. ended 12/31/01): Grants paid, $229,532; assets, $1,520,963 (M); expenditures, $245,908; qualifying distributions, $240,352.
Limitations: Applications not accepted. Giving primarily in NJ and NY.
Application information: Contributes only to pre-selected organizations.
Directors: James Hagedorn, Paul Hagedorn, Peter Hagedorn, Robert Hagedorn, Susan Hagedorn, Kate Hagedorn Littlefield.
EIN: 112996648
Codes: FD2

34341
Gerald B. Cramer Family Foundation, Inc.
707 Westchester Ave.
White Plains, NY 10604-3102

Established in 1993 in NY.
Donor(s): Members of the Cramer family.
Financial data (yr. ended 12/31/00): Grants paid, $229,501; assets, $3,075,287 (M); gifts received, $367,500; expenditures, $262,399; qualifying distributions, $224,489.
Limitations: Applications not accepted. Giving primarily in NY.
Application information: Contributes only to pre-selected organizations.
Officers: Gerald B. Cramer, Pres.; Camille Parisi, V.P. and Secy.-Treas.
Directors: Daphna Cramer, Douglas Cramer, Kimberly Cramer, Lauren Cramer, Thomas Cramer, Roy Raskin, Shelley Raskin.
EIN: 133749869
Codes: FD2

34342
RZH Foundation
4510 16th Ave.
Brooklyn, NY 11204

Established in 1994 in NY.
Donor(s): Ralph Herzka.
Financial data (yr. ended 12/31/00): Grants paid, $229,292; assets, $3,562,642 (M); gifts received, $1,111,760; expenditures, $246,826; qualifying distributions, $229,292.
Limitations: Applications not accepted. Giving primarily in NY.
Application information: Contributes only to pre-selected organizations.
Trustees: Judy Herzka, Ralph Herzka.
EIN: 113242489
Codes: FD2

34343
Acorn Foundation, Inc.
c/o The Bank of New York
1 Wall St., 28th Fl., Tax Dept.
New York, NY 10286

Established in 1992 in NJ.
Donor(s): Grace K. Culbertson, John H. Culbertson, Jr., Marian V.C. Hvolbeck, Katherine C. Prentice.
Financial data (yr. ended 12/31/01): Grants paid, $229,200; assets, $5,355,172 (M); gifts received, $177,020; expenditures, $261,923; qualifying distributions, $228,335.
Limitations: Applications not accepted. Giving primarily in NJ, and New York, NY.
Application information: Contributes only to pre-selected organizations.
Officers: Grace Culbertson, Pres.; Marian V.C. Hvolbeck, V.P.; Katherine Prentice, Secy.; John Culbertson, Jr., Treas.
EIN: 223079659
Codes: FD2

34344
Seherr-Thoss Foundation
c/o Bessemer Trust Co., N.A.
630 5th Ave., 38th Fl.
New York, NY 10111
Contact: Mark Karlin

Established in 1990 in CT.
Donor(s): Sonia Seherr-Thoss.
Financial data (yr. ended 12/31/00): Grants paid, $229,060; assets, $4,746,351 (M); expenditures, $267,796; qualifying distributions, $222,897.
Limitations: Giving primarily in the Litchfield, CT area.
Distribution Committee: Bruce C. Farrell, Deborah C. Foord, Perley H. Grimes, Jr., Susan B. Magary, Roderic Oneglia, Mrs. Hans C. Seherr-Thoss, Henry W. Seherr-Thoss, Clayton B. Spencer.
Trustee: Bessemer Trust Co., N.A.
EIN: 136959146
Codes: FD2

34345
Constans Culver Foundation
c/o JPMorgan Chase Bank
1211 Ave. of the Americas, 38th Fl.
New York, NY 10036
E-mail: jones_ed_l@jpmorgan.com
Contact: Edward L. Jones, V.P.

Trust established in 1965 in NY.
Donor(s): Erne Constans Culver.‡
Financial data (yr. ended 12/31/01): Grants paid, $229,000; assets, $7,091,802 (M); expenditures, $323,547; qualifying distributions, $245,961.
Limitations: Giving primarily in NY and PA.
Application information: Application form not required.
Trustees: Pauline Hoffmann Herd, Pauline May Herd, Victoria Prescott Herd, JPMorgan Chase Bank.
EIN: 136048059
Codes: FD2

34346
Golden Family Foundation
c/o BCRS Assocs., LLC
100 Wall St., 11th Fl.
New York, NY 10005

Established in 1987 in NY.
Donor(s): John A. Golden.
Financial data (yr. ended 06/30/01): Grants paid, $228,760; assets, $4,182,795 (M); gifts received, $442,868; expenditures, $299,962; qualifying distributions, $224,747.
Limitations: Applications not accepted. Giving primarily in New York, NY.
Application information: Contributes only to pre-selected organizations.
Trustees: John A. Golden, Suzanne F. Golden.
EIN: 133438614
Codes: FD2

34347
B.E.L.T. Trust
c/o Joseph C. Hoopes, Jr.
19 W. 44th St., Ste. 1100
New York, NY 10036

Established in 1985 in NY.
Donor(s): Lesley B. Hoopes, Joseph C. Hoopes, Jr.
Financial data (yr. ended 12/31/01): Grants paid, $228,222; assets, $221,417 (M); gifts received, $339,718; expenditures, $229,410; qualifying distributions, $227,050.
Limitations: Applications not accepted. Giving primarily in New York, NY.
Application information: Contributes only to pre-selected organizations.
Trustees: Joseph C. Hoopes, Jr., Lesley B. Hoopes.
EIN: 136858074
Codes: FD2

34348
The Swyer Foundation, Inc.
(Formerly The Lewis A. Swyer Foundation)
c/o Stuyvesant Plz., Inc.
Executive Park, Admin. Bldg.
Albany, NY 12203
FAX: (518) 482-5190
Contact: Sandra L. Tatem

Established in 1986 in NY.
Financial data (yr. ended 11/30/01): Grants paid, $228,000; assets, $1,357,036 (M); gifts received, $130,574; expenditures, $242,714; qualifying distributions, $228,000.
Limitations: Applications not accepted. Giving primarily in the Albany, NY, area.
Application information: Contributes only to pre-selected organizations.
Officers: Edward P. Swyer, Pres.; Julius Oestreicher, Secy.; Ann Swyer, Treas.
Directors: Susan S. Earle, Carol S. Noble.
EIN: 141687630
Codes: FD2

34349
Irwin & Marjorie Guttag Foundation, Inc.
c/o Mentor Partners
500 Park Ave.
New York, NY 10022

Established in 1956 in NY.
Donor(s): Irwin Guttag, Marjorie Guttag, John Guttag.

34349—NEW YORK

Financial data (yr. ended 12/31/00): Grants paid, $227,895; assets, $6,352,965 (M); gifts received, $14,625; expenditures, $235,395; qualifying distributions, $230,145.
Limitations: Applications not accepted. Giving primarily in New York, NY.
Application information: Contributes only to pre-selected organizations.
Officers: Irwin Guttag, Pres. and Secy.; Marjorie Guttag, V.P. and Treas.
EIN: 136061339
Codes: FD2

34350
OBX, Inc.
P.O. Box 163
Glen Head, NY 11545-0163

Established in 1992 in NY.
Donor(s): Oliver R. Grace, Jr.
Financial data (yr. ended 11/30/00): Grants paid, $227,500; assets, $573,465 (M); gifts received, $497,250; expenditures, $227,810; qualifying distributions, $227,500.
Limitations: Applications not accepted. Giving on a national basis, with some emphasis on NY.
Application information: Contributes only to pre-selected organizations.
Director: Alexander Rutherford.
EIN: 113089277
Codes: FD2

34351
Reginald F. Lewis Foundation, Inc.
9 W. 57th St., 39th Fl.
New York, NY 10019

Established in 1987 in NY.
Donor(s): Reginald F. Lewis,‡ Loida N. Lewis, Leslie N. Lewis, Christina S.N. Lewis.
Financial data (yr. ended 06/30/01): Grants paid, $227,100; assets, $934,745 (M); expenditures, $325,777; qualifying distributions, $325,777.
Application information: Contributes primarily to pre-selected organizations; unsolicited requests for funds usually not considered.
Officers and Directors:* Loida N. Lewis,* Chair.; Beverly A. Cooper,* V.P.; Anthony S. Fugett,* Christina S.N. Lewis, Leslie N. Lewis.
EIN: 133429965
Codes: FD2

34352
Walter P. & Elizabeth M. Stern Foundation, Inc.
450 Fort Hill Rd.
Scarsdale, NY 10583
Contact: Walter P. Stern, Pres.

Established in 1963 in NY.
Donor(s): Elizabeth M. Stern, Walter P. Stern.
Financial data (yr. ended 12/31/01): Grants paid, $227,096; assets, $3,927,457 (M); gifts received, $41,333; expenditures, $229,504; qualifying distributions, $226,553.
Limitations: Applications not accepted. Giving primarily in Washington, DC, and New York and Westchester counties, NY.
Application information: Unsolicited requests for funds not accepted.
Officers and Directors:* Walter P. Stern,* Pres.; Elizabeth M. Stern,* Secy.
EIN: 136111129
Codes: FD2

34353
Arthur & Henrietta A. Sorin Charitable Trust
225 Broadway, Ste. 2400
New York, NY 10007 (212) 237-0744
Contact: Herbert H. Plever, Secy.

Established in 1992 in NY; funded in 1995.
Financial data (yr. ended 12/31/01): Grants paid, $227,000; assets, $546,440 (M); expenditures, $240,716; qualifying distributions, $240,716.
Limitations: Giving primarily in NY.
Officer and Trustees:* Herbert H. Plever,* Secy.; Morris Mitchell, Steven Plever.
EIN: 136992637
Codes: FD2

34354
Richard C. & Susan B. Ernst Foundation
c/o Bloomingdale Properties, Inc.
641 Lexington Ave., 29th Fl.
New York, NY 10022-4599 (212) 838-0211
Contact: John L. Ernst, Pres.

Established in 1957 in NY.
Financial data (yr. ended 12/31/01): Grants paid, $226,900; assets, $2,705,565 (M); gifts received, $2,500; expenditures, $266,873; qualifying distributions, $227,230.
Limitations: Giving on a national basis.
Officers: John L. Ernst, Pres.; John Fletcher, V.P.
EIN: 136153761
Codes: FD2

34355
Carlton Charitable Trust
5223 15th Ave.
Brooklyn, NY 11219 (718) 851-1848
Contact: Naomi Rabinowicz, Dir.

Established in 1998 in NY.
Financial data (yr. ended 11/30/01): Grants paid, $226,810; assets, $964,352 (M); expenditures, $235,569; qualifying distributions, $226,084.
Limitations: Giving primarily in NY.
Directors: Chaim Landau, Efraim Landau, Naomi Rabinowicz.
EIN: 116508167
Codes: FD2

34356
Jay & Hadasa Pomrenze Foundation
c/o American Express TBS, Inc.
1185 Ave. of the Americas
New York, NY 10036-2602

Established in 1986 in DE.
Donor(s): Hadasa Pomrenze, Jay Pomrenze.
Financial data (yr. ended 12/31/00): Grants paid, $226,650; assets, $1,524,415 (M); gifts received, $40,000; expenditures, $256,634; qualifying distributions, $233,448.
Limitations: Applications not accepted. Giving primarily in NJ and NY.
Application information: Contributes only to pre-selected organizations.
Officer: Jay Pomrenze, Pres.
Director: Hadasa Pomrenze.
EIN: 222905892
Codes: FD2

34357
The Stephanie and Carter McClelland Foundation
c/o American Express, Inc.
1185 Ave. of the Americas
New York, NY 10036

Established in 1997 in NY.
Donor(s): W. Carter McClelland.
Financial data (yr. ended 11/30/01): Grants paid, $226,600; assets, $2,964,486 (M); gifts received, $1,091,913; expenditures, $234,138; qualifying distributions, $226,850.
Limitations: Applications not accepted. Giving primarily in NY.
Application information: Contributes only to pre-selected organizations.
Trustees: Stephanie P. McClelland, W. Carter McClelland.
EIN: 137154217
Codes: FD2

34358
Renate, Hans & Maria Hofmann Trust
(Formerly Hofmann Article 5 Charitable Trust)
c/o JPMorgan Chase Bank
1211 Ave. of the Americas, 34th Fl.
New York, NY 10036

Established in 1996 in NY.
Financial data (yr. ended 06/30/01): Grants paid, $226,500; assets, $22,130,364 (M); expenditures, $495,577; qualifying distributions, $390,869.
Limitations: Applications not accepted. Giving on a national basis, primarily in New York, NY.
Application information: Contributes only to pre-selected organizations.
Trustees: Patricia A. Gallagher, Robert S. Warshaw, JPMorgan Chase Bank.
EIN: 137102172
Codes: FD2

34359
Wyman-Potter Foundation
c/o HSBC Bank USA
1 HSBC Plz., 4th Fl.
Rochester, NY 14639 (716) 238-7726
Contact: JoAnn Roberts, V.P. and Senior Trust Off., HSBC Bank USA

Established in 1965 in NY.
Financial data (yr. ended 01/31/02): Grants paid, $226,282; assets, $1,826,760 (M); expenditures, $260,729; qualifying distributions, $228,461.
Limitations: Giving primarily in Monroe County, NY.
Publications: Grants list.
Application information: Application form not required.
Trustee: HSBC Bank USA.
EIN: 166060015
Codes: FD2

34360
Bennett M. & Gertrude Berman Foundation, Inc.
1700 Broadway, 23rd Fl.
New York, NY 10019-5905
Contact: Bennett M. Berman, Pres.

Established about 1964.
Donor(s): Bennett M. Berman.
Financial data (yr. ended 09/30/01): Grants paid, $226,252; assets, $2,675,849 (M); expenditures, $238,094; qualifying distributions, $226,252.
Limitations: Applications not accepted. Giving primarily in FL and NY.
Application information: Contributes only to pre-selected organizations.
Officers: Bennett M. Berman, Pres.; Jeffrey A. Berman, Secy.; Helaine B. Finnegan, Treas.
EIN: 136163607
Codes: FD2

34361
The David M. & Barbara Baldwin Foundation, Inc.
c/o McGrath, Doyle & Phair
150 Broadway
New York, NY 10038-4499

Established in 1986 in NJ.
Donor(s): David M. Baldwin.
Financial data (yr. ended 11/30/01): Grants paid, $226,025; assets, $5,487,306 (M); expenditures, $282,522; qualifying distributions, $246,120.
Limitations: Applications not accepted. Giving primarily in NJ and NY.

Application information: Contributes only to pre-selected organizations.
Officers and Trustees:* David M. Baldwin,* Pres.; Barbara Baldwin,* V.P.; Charles Gengler, V.P.; Nicholas Jacangelo, Secy.-Treas.
EIN: 133391384
Codes: FD2

34362
AGB Fund, Inc.
c/o CPI Assocs., Inc.
32 E. 57th St., 14th Fl.
New York, NY 10022   (212) 421-6600
Contact: Lee R. Robins, Treas.

Established in 1992 in NY.
Financial data (yr. ended 12/31/01): Grants paid, $226,000; assets, $2,905,503 (M); expenditures, $265,260; qualifying distributions, $231,744.
Limitations: Giving limited to NY.
Officers: Elizabeth B. Nevin, Pres.; Stephen C. Nevin, V.P. and Secy.; Lee R. Robins, Treas.
EIN: 133632843
Codes: FD2

34363
Mashala Foundation, Inc.
1957 E. 4th St.
Brooklyn, NY 11223   (718) 695-4510
Contact: Max Shalom, Dir.

Donor(s): Max Shalom, Allura Imports, Inc.
Financial data (yr. ended 12/31/01): Grants paid, $225,889; assets, $745,102 (M); gifts received, $386,530; expenditures, $226,552; qualifying distributions, $225,893.
Directors: Max Shalom, Raymond Shalom.
EIN: 116100993
Codes: FD2

34364
The H. E. Lentz, Jr. Foundation
c/o Mahoney, Cohen & Co.
111 W. 40th St.
New York, NY 10018

Established in 1990 in NY.
Donor(s): Henry E. Lentz, Jr.
Financial data (yr. ended 12/31/01): Grants paid, $225,707; assets, $920,606 (M); gifts received, $157,916; expenditures, $243,220; qualifying distributions, $225,707.
Limitations: Applications not accepted. Giving primarily in New York, NY.
Application information: Contributes only to pre-selected organizations.
Trustee: Henry E. Lentz, Jr.
EIN: 133595689

34365
Robert and Maurine Rothschild Fund, Inc.
450 E. 52nd St.
New York, NY 10022

Incorporated in 1948 in NY.
Donor(s): Herbert M. Rothschild,‡ Nannette F. Rothschild.‡
Financial data (yr. ended 12/31/01): Grants paid, $225,560; assets, $1,838,413 (M); expenditures, $298,916; qualifying distributions, $266,358.
Limitations: Applications not accepted. Giving on a national basis, with some emphasis on national organizations in New York City, Washington, DC, and along the East Coast.
Application information: Contributes only to pre-selected organizations.
Directors: Katherine Jackson, Maurine Rothschild, Peter Rothschild, Robert F. Rothschild.
EIN: 136059064
Codes: FD2

34366
AKC Fund, Inc.
67A E. 77th St.
New York, NY 10021
Contact: Ann Brownell Sloane, Admin.

Incorporated in 1955 in NY.
Donor(s): Members of the Childs and Lawrence families.
Financial data (yr. ended 12/31/01): Grants paid, $225,500; assets, $5,927,377 (M); expenditures, $273,880; qualifying distributions, $256,197.
Limitations: Applications not accepted. Giving primarily in CT, Washington, DC, MA, NY and VA.
Application information: Currently supporting trustee-sponsored projects only.
Officers and Directors:* Elisabeth C. Gill, Pres.; Alice Childs Anderson,* V.P.; Starling A. Keene,* Secy.; Elizabeth Ransome Garside, Treas.; Carolyn S. Childs, Anne Childs Collins, J. Vinton Lawrence, Adair Mali, Susannah L. Wood.
EIN: 136091321
Codes: FD2

34367
James E. Robison Foundation
17 Greenbriar Cir.
Armonk, NY 10504-1353
Contact: James E. Robison, Pres.

Established in 1960 in NY.
Donor(s): James E. Robison.
Financial data (yr. ended 11/30/00): Grants paid, $225,500; assets, $3,932,096 (M); expenditures, $307,136; qualifying distributions, $249,618.
Limitations: Applications not accepted. Giving primarily in the eastern U.S.
Application information: Contributes only to pre-selected organizations.
Officers: Molly Danies, Pres.; Christine Beshar, V.P.; Doris Stanley, Secy.-Treas.
Trustee: Michael A. Foley.
EIN: 136075171
Codes: FD2

34368
Donald and Eleanor Taffner Charitable Trust
31 W. 56th St.
New York, NY 10019   (212) 245-4682
Contact: Martin B. Jaffe, Admin.

Established in 1994.
Financial data (yr. ended 12/31/00): Grants paid, $225,500; assets, $827,985 (M); gifts received, $416,000; expenditures, $230,920; qualifying distributions, $225,500.
Limitations: Giving primarily in NY.
Officer: Martin B. Jaffe, Admin.
Trustees: Karen Taffner Butler, Donald L. Taffner, Jr.
EIN: 133746374
Codes: FD2

34369
The Brent Family Foundation
c/o White & Case JLLP
1155 Ave. of the Americas, Ste., 2714
New York, NY 10036-2787

Established in 1999 in DE.
Donor(s): Douglas B. Brent.
Financial data (yr. ended 12/31/01): Grants paid, $225,200; assets, $1,200,626 (M); gifts received, $255,009; expenditures, $229,373; qualifying distributions, $225,200.
Limitations: Applications not accepted.
Application information: Contributes only to pre-selected organizations.
Officers and Directors:* Douglas B. Brent,* Pres.; Averil R. Brent,* V.P.; Andrew Auchincloss, V.P.
EIN: 510395364

34370
The Richard and Gertrude Weininger Foundation, Inc.
c/o Stroock, Stroock & Lavan
180 Maiden Ln.
New York, NY 10038-4982

Established in 1982 in NY.
Donor(s): Gertrude Weininger.‡
Financial data (yr. ended 11/30/01): Grants paid, $225,200; assets, $5,349,798 (M); expenditures, $345,040; qualifying distributions, $250,276.
Limitations: Applications not accepted. Giving primarily in NY.
Application information: Contributes only to pre-selected organizations.
Officers: Peter Simon, Pres.; William A. Perlmuth, V.P. and Secy.; Tom J. Stevenson, V.P. and Treas.
EIN: 133147339
Codes: FD2

34371
The Belle Fund, Inc.
200 Madison Ave., 5th Fl.
New York, NY 10016-3901

Established in 1988 in DE.
Financial data (yr. ended 12/31/00): Grants paid, $225,000; assets, $327,377 (M); expenditures, $229,989; qualifying distributions, $224,162.
Limitations: Applications not accepted. Giving primarily in New York, NY.
Application information: Contributes only to pre-selected organizations.
Officers and Directors:* Adam R. Rose,* V.P.; David S. Rose,* Treas.; Abigail Rose, Gideon Rose.
EIN: 133471825
Codes: FD2

34372
The Kleban Foundation, Inc.
345 E. 56th St., No. 10-J
New York, NY 10022
Contact: Alan J. Stein, Secy.

Established in 1988 in NY.
Donor(s): Edward L. Kleban.‡
Financial data (yr. ended 06/30/01): Grants paid, $225,000; assets, $2,187,576 (M); expenditures, $262,428; qualifying distributions, $259,304.
Limitations: Giving primarily in New York, NY.
Application information: Application form required.
Officers: Maury Yeston, Pres.; Alan Stein, Secy.; Frank Neuwirth, Treas.
Directors: Andre Bishop, Sheldon Harnick, Richard Maltby, Wendy Wasserstein.
EIN: 133490882
Codes: FD2, GTI

34373
Shaya Shabot Levy Foundation, Inc.
1411 Broadway
New York, NY 10018
Contact: Stephen M. Levy, Pres.

Established in 1943 in NY.
Donor(s): David M. Levy, Stephen M. Levy, Joseph Ades.‡
Financial data (yr. ended 12/31/01): Grants paid, $224,967; assets, $271,163 (M); gifts received, $13,044; expenditures, $226,599; qualifying distributions, $224,576.
Limitations: Applications not accepted. Giving primarily in the greater New York, NY, area.
Application information: Contributes only to pre-selected organizations.
Officers: Stephen M. Levy, Pres.; David M. Levy, V.P.
EIN: 136163084
Codes: FD2

34374
The Eppley Foundation for Research, Inc.
c/o McLaughlin & Stern, LLP
260 Madison Ave.
New York, NY 10016 (212) 448-1100
Contact: Huyler C. Held, Secy.-Treas.

Established in 1947 in RI.
Donor(s): Marion Eppley.‡
Financial data (yr. ended 12/31/01): Grants paid, $224,402; assets, $2,539,879 (M); gifts received, $331,601; expenditures, $250,958; qualifying distributions, $235,184.
Publications: Program policy statement, application guidelines, informational brochure, grants list.
Application information: Funding unavailable for independent research; grants are made only through recognized educational and research organizations. Application form required.
Officers: Rivington R. Winant, Pres.; Huyler C. Held, Secy.-Treas.
Directors: Timothy Selders, Joan O'Meara Winant.
EIN: 050258857
Codes: FD2, GTI

34375
Saul & Eleanor Lerner Foundation
1705 Broadway
Hewlett, NY 11557

Established around 1965 in NY.
Donor(s): Saul Lerner, Eleanor Lerner.
Financial data (yr. ended 12/31/01): Grants paid, $223,568; assets, $2,542,559 (M); expenditures, $236,271; qualifying distributions, $219,009.
Limitations: Applications not accepted. Giving primarily in NY.
Application information: Contributes only to pre-selected organizations.
Trustee: Eleanor Lerner.
EIN: 116042721
Codes: FD2

34376
The Isaac Sitt Foundation
501 Ave. S.
Brooklyn, NY 11223-3048

Established in 1999 in NY.
Financial data (yr. ended 09/30/01): Grants paid, $223,268; assets, $3,487,240 (M); gifts received, $51,294; expenditures, $320,108; qualifying distributions, $223,268.
Limitations: Applications not accepted.
Application information: Contributes only to pre-selected organizations.
Officer: Isaac J. Sitt, Pres.
EIN: 137200888
Codes: FD2

34377
The William H. and Cathy Brienza Ingram Family Foundation, Inc.
(Formerly The Ingram Family Foundation)
c/o William Ingram
32 E. 64th St.
New York, NY 10021

Established in 1998 in NY.
Donor(s): William H. Ingram.
Financial data (yr. ended 12/31/01): Grants paid, $222,900; assets, $307,383 (M); gifts received, $62,935; expenditures, $229,770; qualifying distributions, $223,638.
Limitations: Applications not accepted.
Application information: Contributes only to pre-selected organizations.
Directors: Cathy M. Brienza, William H. Ingram, Jonathan M. Wainwright.
EIN: 134037558

Codes: FD2

34378
The Betsy & Alan D. Cohn Foundation, Inc.
c/o Tanton & Co.
37 W. 57th St.
New York, NY 10019-6708
Application address: c/o Salomon Smith Barney, Inc., 787 7th Ave., New York, NY 10019-6018, tel.: (212) 492-6990
Contact: Alan D. Cohn, V.P.

Established in 1967 in NY.
Donor(s): Alan D. Cohn.
Financial data (yr. ended 09/30/01): Grants paid, $222,803; assets, $4,416,374 (M); gifts received, $1,190; expenditures, $225,583; qualifying distributions, $225,583.
Limitations: Giving primarily in New York, NY.
Application information: Application form not required.
Officers: Betsy Cohn, Pres.; Alan D. Cohn, V.P.; John Klingenstein, Secy.; Janet Mulligan, Treas.
EIN: 237046420
Codes: FD2

34379
The Grinberg Family Foundation
(Formerly The Grinberg Foundation)
c/o Reminick Aarons & Co.
1430 Broadway, 17th Fl.
New York, NY 10018

Established in 1982.
Financial data (yr. ended 11/30/01): Grants paid, $222,306; assets, $1,462,994 (M); expenditures, $230,305; qualifying distributions, $221,922.
Limitations: Applications not accepted. Giving primarily in New York, NY.
Application information: Contributes only to pre-selected organizations.
Directors: Gedalio Grinberg, Sonia Grinberg, Leonard Silverstein.
EIN: 521233811
Codes: FD2

34380
Osceola Foundation, Inc.
c/o Brooks & Cantor
3000 Marcus Ave., No. 2E4
New Hyde Park, NY 11042
Additional address: 408 Cove View Pt., Columbia, SC 29212
Contact: Ann B. Oliver, Pres.

Incorporated in 1963 in NY.
Donor(s): Katherine Sperry Beinecke Trust.‡
Financial data (yr. ended 12/31/01): Grants paid, $221,980; assets, $4,816,638 (M); expenditures, $293,637; qualifying distributions, $219,938.
Limitations: Applications not accepted. Giving primarily in MA, NY, OH, and SC.
Application information: Contributes only to pre-selected organizations.
Officers: Ann B. Oliver, Pres.; Perry Ashley, Secy.; Barbara B. Spitler, Treas.
Directors: Deborah B. Beale, Walter Beinecke, Jr., Walter Beinecke III.
EIN: 136094234
Codes: FD2

34381
The Sallie Foundation, Inc.
c/o Brahman Capital Corp.
277 Park Ave., 26th Fl.
New York, NY 10017

Established in 1995 in NY.
Donor(s): Braham Securities, Inc., Gary Gladstein, Jordan Seaman.

Financial data (yr. ended 12/31/99): Grants paid, $221,500; assets, $56,559 (M); gifts received, $210,082; expenditures, $222,875; qualifying distributions, $221,478.
Limitations: Applications not accepted. Giving primarily in NY.
Application information: Contributes only to pre-selected organizations.
Officers: Mitchell Kuflik, Pres.; Robert J. Sobel, V.P.; Peter Hochfelder, Secy.
Director: Alan Eisenberg.
EIN: 133842759
Codes: FD2

34382
S. & E. Steinmetz Foundation
352 Marcy Ave.
Brooklyn, NY 11206
Contact: Solomon Steinmetz, Tr.

Established in 1999 in NY.
Financial data (yr. ended 06/30/01): Grants paid, $221,486; assets, $373,940 (M); expenditures, $221,926; qualifying distributions, $219,190.
Application information: Application form not required.
Trustees: Esther Steinmetz, Solomon Steinmetz.
EIN: 113481171
Codes: FD2

34383
Jacob & Gloria Schonberger Charitable Trust
82-45 Grenfell St.
Kew Gardens, NY 11415

Established in 1994.
Donor(s): Jacob Schonberger.
Financial data (yr. ended 10/31/01): Grants paid, $221,472; assets, $23,234 (M); gifts received, $241,500; expenditures, $221,568; qualifying distributions, $221,472.
Limitations: Applications not accepted. Giving primarily in Brooklyn, NY.
Application information: Contributes only to pre-selected organizations.
Trustees: Gloria Schonberger, Jacob Schonberger, Joseph Schonberger, Philip Schonberger.
EIN: 116448507
Codes: FD2

34384
The Ed Lee and Jean Campe Foundation, Inc.
c/o U.S. Trust
114 W. 47th St.
New York, NY 10036
Application address: c/o Tanya DeSilva, Frankenthaler, Kohn, Schneider & Katz, 26 Broadway, Ste. 26, New York, NY 10004-1801, tel.: (212) 269-4310
Contact: Carolyn L. Larke, Asst. V.P., or Linda Franciscovich, Sr. V.P., U.S. Trust

Incorporated in 1944 in NY.
Donor(s): Ed Lee Campe,‡ Jean Campe.‡
Financial data (yr. ended 12/31/00): Grants paid, $221,350; assets, $1,125,694 (M); expenditures, $249,488; qualifying distributions, $233,327.
Limitations: Giving primarily in NY.
Application information: Application form not required.
Officers: Henry Kohn, Pres.; Anne F. Kohn, V.P.; Herbert A. Schneider, Secy.
EIN: 136123929
Codes: FD2

34385
Adco Foundation, Inc.
130 MacDougal St.
New York, NY 10012   (212) 674-7105
FAX: (212) 674-7100; E-mail:
adcofoundation@aol.com
Contact: Kelly Anderson, Exec. Dir.

Established in 1973 in NY.
Donor(s): Philip Katz,‡ Philbert Realty,
International Foodcraft.
Financial data (yr. ended 03/31/00): Grants paid,
$221,309; assets, $2,121,512 (M); expenditures,
$298,336; qualifying distributions, $255,783.
Limitations: Giving limited to the New York, NY,
area.
Publications: Application guidelines.
Application information: Application form not
required.
Officers and Directors:* David Nasaw,* Pres. and
Treas.; Leith Mullings,* V.P.; Kelly Anderson,*
Exec. Secy.; Emily Jane Goodman.
EIN: 237268285
Codes: FD2

34386
Neil A. McConnell Foundation, Inc.
183 Jerome Ave.
Staten Island, NY 10305   (718) 981-1949
Contact: C. Matranga, Exec. Dir.

Incorporated in 1960 in NY.
Donor(s): Neil A. McConnell.
Financial data (yr. ended 03/31/01): Grants paid,
$221,000; assets, $1,938,339 (M); expenditures,
$293,939; qualifying distributions, $273,236.
Limitations: Giving limited to the northeastern
U.S., with emphasis on the metropolitan New
York, NY, area.
Application information: Application form not
required.
Officers: B. Scott McConnell, Pres.; James G.
Niven, V.P. and Treas.; Peter Brimelow, V.P.;
Sandra McConnell, V.P.; Douglas F. Williamson,
Jr., Secy.
EIN: 136114121
Codes: FD2

34387
The Cain Brothers Foundation
452 5th Ave., 25th Fl.
New York, NY 10018

Established around 1993.
Donor(s): Daniel M. Cain, James E. Cain, Cain
Bros. and Co., Inc.
Financial data (yr. ended 12/31/99): Grants paid,
$220,959; assets, $1,176,870 (M); gifts received,
$423,700; expenditures, $220,959; qualifying
distributions, $220,959.
Limitations: Applications not accepted. Giving
primarily in MA and NY.
Application information: Contributes only to
pre-selected organizations.
Directors: Daniel M. Cain, James E. Cain, William
M. Cain.
EIN: 133692990
Codes: FD2

34388
The Joyce and Daniel Cowin Foundation, Inc.
640 Park Ave.
New York, NY 10021
Application address: c/o Justine D. Tenney, M.R.
Weiser & Co., LLP, 135 W. 50th St., New York,
NY 10020
Contact: Joyce B. Cowin, Pres.

Established in 1957 in NY.
Donor(s): Sylvia J. Berger, Daniel Cowin, Joyce B.
Cowin.
Financial data (yr. ended 12/31/01): Grants paid,
$220,750; assets, $3,739,334 (M); gifts received,
$239,832; expenditures, $230,409; qualifying
distributions, $224,503.
Limitations: Giving primarily in New York, NY.
Application information: Application form not
required.
Officer: Joyce B. Cowin, Pres.
EIN: 136154142
Codes: FD2

34389
The Aeroflex Foundation
c/o Hecht & Assocs.
10 E. 40th St., Ste. 710
New York, NY 10016   (212) 696-4235

Established in 1964 in NY.
Donor(s): The Aeroflex Corp.
Financial data (yr. ended 09/30/01): Grants paid,
$220,700; assets, $5,148,878 (M); expenditures,
$341,679; qualifying distributions, $255,749.
Limitations: Applications not accepted. Giving on
a national basis.
Application information: Contributes only to
pre-selected organizations.
Trustees: Kay Knight Clarke, Derrick M. Hussey,
William A. Perlmuth.
EIN: 136168635
Codes: FD2

34390
The Stefany and Simon Bergson Foundation
P.O. Box 695, Woods Rd.
Palisades, NY 10964

Established in 1999 in NY.
Donor(s): Stefany Bergson, Simon Bergson.
Financial data (yr. ended 12/31/01): Grants paid,
$220,665; assets, $328,091 (M); gifts received,
$500,000; expenditures, $223,846; qualifying
distributions, $223,548.
Limitations: Applications not accepted.
Application information: Contributes only to
pre-selected organizations.
Trustees: Simon Bergson, Stefany Bergson.
EIN: 134077237
Codes: FD2

34391
**The Richard and Susan Braddock Family
Foundation, Inc.**
c/o American Express, Tax Bus. Svcs.
1185 Ave. of the Americas
New York, NY 10036

Established in 1999 in NY.
Donor(s): Richard S. Braddock.
Financial data (yr. ended 11/30/01): Grants paid,
$220,581; assets, $523,120 (M); gifts received,
$235,644; expenditures, $223,306; qualifying
distributions, $220,525.
Limitations: Applications not accepted.
Application information: Contributes only to
pre-selected organizations.
Officer: Jennifer Braddock Gerber, Pres.
Directors: Richard S. Braddock, Susan Braddock.
EIN: 061565971
Codes: FD2

34392
Edna Bailey Sussman Fund
c/o Boyce, Hughes & Farrell, LLP
1025 Northern Blvd., Ste. 300
Roslyn, NY 11576-1587
Contact: Dorothy Bertine, Admin.

Established in 1984 in NY.
Donor(s): Arthur H. Dean,‡ Edward S. Miller.
Financial data (yr. ended 04/30/01): Grants paid,
$220,063; assets, $5,679,633 (M); expenditures,
$256,533; qualifying distributions, $237,544.
Limitations: Giving on a national basis.
Application information: The fund only accepts
applications from colleges and universities with
whom it has established relationships. It does not
accept applications from individuals. Stipends are
disbursed to institution on behalf of intern
selected by fund trustees. Application form
required.
Trustees: Robert H. Frey, Edward S. Miller.
EIN: 133187064
Codes: FD2, GTI

34393
The Aronovitz Family Foundation, Inc.
1114 Ave. of the Americas, Ste. 3400
New York, NY 10036

Donor(s): The Weiler-Arnow Investment Co.,
David Arnow, Joshua Arnow.
Financial data (yr. ended 09/30/01): Grants paid,
$220,050; assets, $308,622 (M); gifts received,
$150,000; expenditures, $223,280; qualifying
distributions, $219,929.
Limitations: Applications not accepted. Giving on
a national basis.
Application information: Contributes only to
pre-selected organizations.
Officers: Ruth Arnow, Pres.; Kathi Arnow, V.P.;
Joshua Arnow, Secy.
Directors: David Arnow, Rabbi Irving Greenberg,
Albert Schussler.
EIN: 133219383
Codes: FD2

34394
The Paestum Foundation, Inc.
c/o Yohalem Gilman & Company, LLP
477 Madison Ave.
New York, NY 10022-5802

Established in 2000 in DE and NY.
Financial data (yr. ended 09/30/01): Grants paid,
$220,000; assets, $9,898,291 (M); expenditures,
$444,511; qualifying distributions, $256,933.
Limitations: Applications not accepted. Giving
primarily in New York, NY.
Application information: Contributes only to
pre-selected organizations.
Director: Michael Rudell.
EIN: 134082016
Codes: FD2

34395
Minnie Parker Charitable Trust
c/o JPMorgan Chase Bank
1211 6th Ave., 34th Fl.
New York, NY 10036
Contact: Jonathan Miller, V.P., JPMorgan Chase
Bank

Financial data (yr. ended 12/31/01): Grants paid,
$220,000; assets, $4,005,422 (M); expenditures,
$271,486; qualifying distributions, $229,605.
Limitations: Applications not accepted. Giving
primarily in CT.
Application information: Contributes only to
pre-selected organizations.
Trustees: Edward S. Rimer, Jr., JPMorgan Chase
Bank.
EIN: 136025155
Codes: FD2

34396
C. William Trout Charitable Trust
c/o U.S. Trust Co. of NY
P.O. Box 2004
New York, NY 10109-1910

Established in 1996.
Donor(s): C. William Trout.‡
Financial data (yr. ended 12/31/01): Grants paid, $220,000; assets, $3,098,281 (M); gifts received, $2,811,523; expenditures, $271,735; qualifying distributions, $253,681.
Limitations: Applications not accepted. Giving primarily in FL.
Application information: Contributes only to pre-selected organizations.
Trustees: John B. Anderson, U.S. Trust Co. of New York.
EIN: 137102464
Codes: FD2

34397
Hip Hop Has Heart, Inc.
395 Hudson St., 7th Fl.
New York, NY 10014
Application address: 16 Cornell Pl., Rye, NY 10580
Contact: Rocco Macri, Pres.

Established in 1994 in NY.
Financial data (yr. ended 12/31/01): Grants paid, $219,592; assets, $81,330 (M); gifts received, $210,406; expenditures, $220,124; qualifying distributions, $219,592.
Limitations: Giving primarily in NY.
Application information: Application form required.
Officers: Rocco Macri, Pres.; Judith Ellis, Secy.; Robert Finley, Treas.
EIN: 133775021

34398
Mortimer J. Harrison Article 11(D) Trust
c/o Torys
237 Park Ave.
New York, NY 10017
Application address: c/o Arthur E. Lashinsky, 810 S. Springfield Ave., Springfield, NJ 07081

Established in 1996 in NY.
Donor(s): Mortimer J. Harrison.‡
Financial data (yr. ended 12/31/00): Grants paid, $219,500; assets, $13,431 (M); gifts received, $50,000; expenditures, $227,071; qualifying distributions, $219,480.
Limitations: Giving primarily in NY.
Trustee: Arthur E. Lashinsky.
EIN: 137075863
Codes: FD2

34399
The Deedy & David Goldstick Foundation
450 West End Ave., Apt. 6A
New York, NY 10024

Established in 1996 in NY.
Donor(s): Dorothy Goldstick.
Financial data (yr. ended 10/31/01): Grants paid, $219,423; assets, $223,903 (M); gifts received, $98,536; expenditures, $225,575; qualifying distributions, $219,423.
Limitations: Applications not accepted.
Application information: Contributes only to pre-selected organizations.
Officers: Dorothy Goldstick, Pres.; David T. Goldstick, V.P.
Directors: James P. Goldstick, Julie A. Haroun.
EIN: 133877598

34400
Keefe Family Foundation
375 Park Ave., Ste. 2301
New York, NY 10152

Established in 1989 in NY.
Donor(s): Harry V. Keefe, Jr.
Financial data (yr. ended 12/31/01): Grants paid, $219,332; assets, $3,912,616 (M); expenditures, $221,482; qualifying distributions, $220,857.
Limitations: Applications not accepted. Giving on a national basis.
Application information: Contributes only to pre-selected organizations. Unsolicited requests for funds not accepted.
Officers: Harry V. Keefe, Pres. and Treas.; Kathleen Keefe Raffel, V.P. and Secy.; Anita L. Keefe, V.P.; Harry V. Keefe, Jr., V.P.
EIN: 133520397
Codes: FD2

34401
United Armenian Charities, Inc.
168 Canal St., Ste. 600
New York, NY 10013 (212) 334-0990
Contact: Haig Dadourian, Pres.

Established in 1951 in NY.
Donor(s): Dadour Dadourian.
Financial data (yr. ended 12/31/99): Grants paid, $219,245; assets, $5,616,126 (M); expenditures, $300,241; qualifying distributions, $240,209.
Limitations: Giving primarily in NY.
Application information: Application form not required.
Officers: Haig Dadourian, Pres.; Alexander Dadourian, V.P.; Peter Dadourian, Treas.
EIN: 136125023
Codes: FD2

34402
Eileen & Peter Rhulen Family Foundation, Inc.
P.O. Box 1256
Monticello, NY 12701
E-mail: eprhulen@aol.com
Contact: Peter L. Rhulen, Dir.

Established in 1991 in NY.
Donor(s): Eileen Rhulen, Peter L. Rhulen.
Financial data (yr. ended 12/31/01): Grants paid, $219,121; assets, $1,357,506 (M); expenditures, $237,859; qualifying distributions, $219,066.
Limitations: Applications not accepted. Giving primarily in New York City and Sullivan County, NY.
Application information: Contributes only to pre-selected organizations.
Directors: Blake Rhulen, Eileen Rhulen, Peter L. Rhulen, Samantha Rhulen, Sloane Rhulen.
EIN: 133601281
Codes: FD2

34403
The Hansmann Family Foundation, Inc.
(Formerly Doris & Ralph E. Hansmann Foundation)
500 5th Ave., 50th Fl.
New York, NY 10110

Donor(s): Ralph E. Hansmann, Doris M. Hansmann.
Financial data (yr. ended 12/31/00): Grants paid, $218,800; assets, $225,589 (M); gifts received, $229,462; expenditures, $224,713; qualifying distributions, $219,802.
Limitations: Applications not accepted. Giving primarily in NY.
Application information: Contributes only to pre-selected organizations.
Officers: Robert E. Hansmann, Pres.; Doris M. Hansmann, V.P.; Ralph E. Hansmann, V.P.; Elizabeth M. Kennedy, Secy.; Jane C. McKean, Treas.
Directors: Phillip I. Blumberg, William T. Golden.
EIN: 237028516
Codes: FD2

34404
Media Development Loan Fund
(Formerly Fund for Independent Media)
45 W. 21st St., 4th Fl.
New York, NY 10011

Established in 1993 in NY.
Donor(s): Open Society Institute.
Financial data (yr. ended 12/31/00): Grants paid, $218,615; assets, $15,643,610 (M); gifts received, $5,770,072; expenditures, $2,818,615; qualifying distributions, $4,914,939; giving activities include $3,394,083 for program-related investments.
Limitations: Applications not accepted. Giving on an international basis.
Application information: Contributes only to pre-selected organizations.
Trustees: Kenneth Anderson, Stuart Auerbach, Annette Laborey, Aryeh Neier, Bernard Poulet, John Ryle, Sasa Vucinic.
EIN: 137024057
Codes: FD2

34405
The Kenney Family Foundation, Inc.
415 E. 54th St., Ste. 19M
New York, NY 10022 (212) 888-1115
Contact: William J. Kenney, Dir.

Established in 2000 in NY.
Donor(s): William J. Kenney.
Financial data (yr. ended 12/31/01): Grants paid, $218,600; assets, $738,869 (M); gifts received, $922,598; expenditures, $221,227; qualifying distributions, $218,600.
Directors: Diane Kenney, W. James Kenney, William J. Kenney.
EIN: 134114128

34406
The David and Roberta Olsen Family Foundation
c/o U.S. Trust Co.
114 W. 47th St.
New York, NY 10036

Established in 1997 in CT.
Donor(s): David A. Olsen.
Financial data (yr. ended 12/31/01): Grants paid, $218,000; assets, $2,791,313 (M); expenditures, $239,818; qualifying distributions, $220,000.
Limitations: Applications not accepted. Giving primarily in NY.
Application information: Contributes only to pre-selected organizations.
Trustees: David A. Olsen, Roberta G. Olsen.
EIN: 061485843
Codes: FD2

34407
Raphael Foundation, Inc.
c/o Babyfair, Inc.
112 W. 34th St., Ste. 1615
New York, NY 10120

Established in 1962 in NY.
Donor(s): Maurice Shamah, Steven Shamah.
Financial data (yr. ended 12/31/01): Grants paid, $217,791; assets, $1,973,573 (M); gifts received, $2,800; expenditures, $226,478; qualifying distributions, $217,038.
Limitations: Applications not accepted. Giving primarily in NY.
Application information: Contributes only to pre-selected organizations.

Officers: Maurice Shamah, Mgr.; Steven Shamah, Mgr.
EIN: 237185539
Codes: FD2

34408
Brant Foundation
c/o Perelson Weiner, LLC
1 Dag Hammarskjold Plz., 42nd Fl.
New York, NY 10017-2286

Established in 1996 in WA.
Donor(s): John L. Larsen, Gale Jean Picker, Harvey Picker.
Financial data (yr. ended 12/31/01): Grants paid, $217,500; assets, $3,143,833 (M); gifts received, $75,000; expenditures, $239,764; qualifying distributions, $218,533.
Limitations: Applications not accepted. Giving primarily in WA.
Application information: Contributes only to pre-selected organizations.
Trustees: John Larsen, Gale Jean Picker.
EIN: 911724951
Codes: FD2

34409
The Milton V. Brown Foundation
2000 Plaza Ave.
P.O. Box 148
New Hyde Park, NY 11040 (516) 328-1400
Contact: Linda M. Emhardt

Established in 1986 in DE.
Donor(s): Milton V. Brown.‡
Financial data (yr. ended 12/31/01): Grants paid, $217,500; assets, $5,930,445 (M); gifts received, $5,000; expenditures, $254,503; qualifying distributions, $223,400.
Limitations: Giving primarily in NY.
Application information: Application form required.
Officers and Directors:* Kalman I. Nulman,* Pres.; Bruce D. Brown,* V.P.; Allan G. Brown,* Treas.
EIN: 112775808
Codes: FD2

34410
Lillian Adjmi Foundation
1407 Broadway, 32nd Fl.
New York, NY 10018

Established in 1999 in NY.
Financial data (yr. ended 07/31/01): Grants paid, $216,300; assets, $53,064 (M); expenditures, $224,257; qualifying distributions, $223,993.
Limitations: Applications not accepted.
Application information: Contributes only to pre-selected organizations.
Trustee: Harry Adjmi.
EIN: 061532888
Codes: FD2

34411
The Mollylou Foundation
175 E. 74th St.
New York, NY 10021

Established in 1998 in NY and DE.
Donor(s): Sidney Lerner.
Financial data (yr. ended 12/31/01): Grants paid, $216,000; assets, $506,380 (M); expenditures, $218,326; qualifying distributions, $218,326.
Limitations: Applications not accepted.
Application information: Contributes only to pre-selected organizations.
Officers: Sidney Lerner, Pres.; Helaine Lerner, Secy.
EIN: 134011378
Codes: FD2

34412
Harry S. Black & Allon Fuller Fund
c/o U.S. Trust
114 W. 47th St., 8th Fl.
New York, NY 10036-1532 (212) 852-3294
FAX: (212) 852-3377
Contact: Andrew Lane, Asst. V.P.

Established in 1930 in NY.
Donor(s): Harry S. Black, Allon Fuller.
Financial data (yr. ended 12/31/01): Grants paid, $215,660; assets, $4,115,973 (M); expenditures, $286,514; qualifying distributions, $243,320.
Limitations: Giving limited to Chicago, IL, and New York, NY.
Publications: Application guidelines.
Application information: Telephone proposals will not be accepted. Application form not required.
Trustee: U.S. Trust.
EIN: 136072632
Codes: FD2

34413
Dean S. Edmonds Foundation
c/o The Bank of New York, Tax Dept.
1 Wall St., 28th Fl.
New York, NY 10286
Contact: Marjorie Thompson

Established in 1959 in NY.
Financial data (yr. ended 12/31/01): Grants paid, $215,500; assets, $2,790,567 (M); expenditures, $252,214; qualifying distributions, $231,650.
Limitations: Giving primarily on the East Coast.
Trustees: Dean S. Edmonds III, The Bank of New York.
EIN: 136161381
Codes: FD2

34414
The Park Foundation
500 5th Ave., Ste. 1710
New York, NY 10110-0002

Incorporated in 1949 in DC.
Donor(s): Eunice K. Shriver, Joseph P. Kennedy, Jr. Foundation.
Financial data (yr. ended 12/31/00): Grants paid, $215,472; assets, $427,605 (M); gifts received, $265,687; expenditures, $216,654; qualifying distributions, $215,472.
Limitations: Applications not accepted. Giving primarily in Washington, DC, MA, and NY.
Application information: Contributes only to pre-selected organizations.
Officers and Trustees:* Eunice K. Shriver,* V.P.; Robert W. Corcoran, Treas.; Patricia K. Lawford, Jean K. Smith.
EIN: 136163065
Codes: FD2

34415
Roch & Carol Hillenbrand Foundation
c/o Goldman Sachs & Co.
85 Broad St., Tax Dept.
New York, NY 10004
Contact: Michael R. Hillenbrand, Tr.

Established in 1999 in NJ.
Donor(s): Michael R. Hillenbrand.
Financial data (yr. ended 09/30/01): Grants paid, $214,783; assets, $2,150,813 (M); gifts received, $489,313; expenditures, $229,365; qualifying distributions, $214,476.
Limitations: Applications not accepted. Giving primarily in NJ and NY.
Application information: Contributes only to pre-selected organizations.
Trustees: Carol Hillenbrand, Michael R. Hillenbrand.

EIN: 134050660
Codes: FD2

34416
The Charles Evans Foundation
745 5th Ave., Ste. 1604
New York, NY 10151

Established in 1988 in NY as successor to the Charles Evans Foundation, Inc.
Donor(s): Charles Evans.
Financial data (yr. ended 12/31/01): Grants paid, $214,665; assets, $3,370,114 (M); gifts received, $197,000; expenditures, $264,636; qualifying distributions, $226,617.
Limitations: Applications not accepted. Giving primarily in New York, NY.
Application information: Contributes only to pre-selected organizations.
Trustee: Charles Evans.
EIN: 136914974
Codes: FD2

34417
The Zachary Gindi Foundation, Inc.
2322 Ave. N
Brooklyn, NY 11210

Established in 1997 in NY.
Donor(s): Zachary Gindi.
Financial data (yr. ended 12/31/01): Grants paid, $214,478; assets, $1,096,070 (M); gifts received, $276,128; expenditures, $214,493; qualifying distributions, $214,478.
Limitations: Applications not accepted.
Application information: Contributes only to pre-selected organizations.
Trustees: Debra Gindi, Ralph Gindi, Zachary Gindi.
EIN: 113368631
Codes: FD2

34418
The Kandell Fund
59 E. 54th St.
New York, NY 10022-4211

Established in 1952.
Donor(s): Leslie Friedberg, Alice Joseph, Florence Kandell, Leonard Kandell.‡
Financial data (yr. ended 12/31/01): Grants paid, $214,415; assets, $255,773 (M); gifts received, $200,000; expenditures, $214,853; qualifying distributions, $214,530.
Limitations: Applications not accepted. Giving primarily in New York, NY.
Application information: Contributes only to pre-selected organizations.
Officers and Directors:* Donald Gordon,* Pres. and Treas.; Debbie Fechter, Secy.; Alice Kandell, Florence Kandell, Leslie Kandell.
EIN: 136117648
Codes: FD2

34419
The Longhill Charitable Foundation
c/o M.R. Weiser & Co.
135 W. 50th St.
New York, NY 10020
Contact: Wilbur A. Cowett, Pres.

Established in 1971.
Donor(s): Wilbur A. Cowett.
Financial data (yr. ended 06/30/01): Grants paid, $214,171; assets, $5,824,622 (M); gifts received, $559,663; expenditures, $235,421; qualifying distributions, $214,707.
Limitations: Applications not accepted. Giving primarily in New York, NY.
Application information: Contributes only to pre-selected organizations.

Officers: Wilbur A. Cowett, Pres.; Leonard M. Leiman, V.P. and Secy.; Anne F. Cowett, V.P.; Frederick D. Cowett, V.P.; Margaret F. Cowett, Treas.
EIN: 237149847
Codes: FD2

34420
The Netter Foundation, Inc.
(Formerly Alice & Fred Netter Foundation)
350 Theodore Fremd Ave.
Rye, NY 10580 (914) 925-3425
Contact: K. Fred Netter, Pres.

Established in 1965 in NY.
Donor(s): K. Fred Netter, Alice D. Netter.
Financial data (yr. ended 12/31/01): Grants paid, $214,090; assets, $4,565,229 (M); gifts received, $8,345; expenditures, $231,012; qualifying distributions, $213,365.
Limitations: Applications not accepted. Giving primarily in NY.
Application information: Contributes only to pre-selected organizations.
Officers and Trustees:* K. Fred Netter,* Pres. and Treas.; Nadine Levy,* V.P.; Alfred E. Netter,* V.P.; Ronald A. Netter,* V.P.; Kenneth J. Bialkin,* Secy.; Alice Netter.
EIN: 136176542
Codes: FD2

34421
The Knapp Fund
c/o James C. Edwards & Co., Inc.
570 Lexington Ave.
New York, NY 10022

Incorporated in 1917 in NY.
Donor(s): George O. Knapp.‡
Financial data (yr. ended 08/31/01): Grants paid, $214,000; assets, $3,894,290 (M); expenditures, $274,662; qualifying distributions, $211,996.
Limitations: Applications not accepted. Giving primarily in CT, FL, NY and PA.
Application information: Contributes only to pre-selected organizations.
Officers: George O. Knapp III, Pres.; Frank Jared Sprole, V.P. and Treas.; David MacNeil, V.P.; Margaret Hanlon, Secy.
Directors: Wendy Sprole Bangs, Thomas R. Knapp, W. Jared Knapp III, Louise Knapp Page, Jared K. Sprole.
EIN: 136068384
Codes: FD2

34422
Garfinkle Family Charitable Trust
c/o U.S. Trust
114 W. 47th St.
New York, NY 10036-1532
FAX: (212) 852-3377
Contact: Carolyn L. Larke, Asst. V.P., or Linda R. Franciscovich, Sr. V.P., U.S. Trust

Established in 1987 in NY.
Donor(s): Sandor A. Garfinkle, Lorraine Garfinkle.
Financial data (yr. ended 12/31/00): Grants paid, $213,970; assets, $2,450,191 (M); expenditures, $238,039; qualifying distributions, $215,670.
Limitations: Applications not accepted. Giving primarily in FL, NJ, and NY.
Application information: Contributes only to pre-selected organizations.
Trustees: Lorraine Garfinkle, Sandor A. Garfinkle.
EIN: 133411139
Codes: FD2

34423
Abraham Krasne Foundation, Inc.
65 W. Red Oak Ln.
White Plains, NY 10604

Established around 1989.
Donor(s): Krasdale Foods, Inc.
Financial data (yr. ended 12/31/01): Grants paid, $213,500; assets, $2,967,181 (M); gifts received, $100,000; expenditures, $214,314; qualifying distributions, $212,403.
Limitations: Applications not accepted. Giving on a national basis.
Application information: Contributes only to pre-selected organizations.
Officer: Charles A. Krasne, Pres. and Secy.
EIN: 136112855
Codes: FD2

34424
The Laura B. Vogler Foundation, Inc.
P.O. Box 610508
Bayside, NY 11361-0508 (718) 423-3000
FAX: (718) 631-4808; *E-mail:* volger foundation@yahoo.com; *URL:* http://fdncenter.org/grantmaker/vogler
Contact: Lawrence L. D'Amato, Pres.

Incorporated in 1959 in NY.
Donor(s): Laura B. Vogler,‡ John J. Vogler.‡
Financial data (yr. ended 10/31/01): Grants paid, $213,400; assets, $4,655,110 (M); expenditures, $287,130; qualifying distributions, $253,594.
Limitations: Giving limited to New York City and Long Island, NY.
Publications: Annual report (including application guidelines).
Application information: Accepts NYRAG Common Application Form. Application form required.
Officers and Trustees:* Lawrence L. D'Amato,* C.E.O. and Pres.; Laraine Diamond, Secy.-Treas.; Max L. Kupferberg, I. Jerry Lasurdo, Rev. Stephen S. Schwander, Robert T. Waldbauer, Karen M. Yost.
EIN: 116022241
Codes: FD2

34425
The Sigety Family Foundation, Inc.
1760 3rd Ave.
New York, NY 10029
Contact: Elizabeth Sigety Marcus, Exec. Dir.

Established in 1994 in NJ.
Donor(s): Charles Sigety, Katharine Sigety.
Financial data (yr. ended 02/28/01): Grants paid, $213,135; assets, $1,989,185 (M); expenditures, $221,626; qualifying distributions, $210,575.
Limitations: Giving primarily in CA, NY, and PA.
Officers and Trustees:* Charles Sigety,* Co-Chair.; Katharine Sigety,* Co-Chair.; Elizabeth S. Marcus,* Secy. and Exec. Dir.; Cornelius Sigety,* Treas.
EIN: 223287292

34426
Norwood Foundation, Inc.
c/o Bessemer Trust Co., N.A.
630 5th Ave.
New York, NY 10111
Mailing address: P.O. Box 238, East Norwich, NY 11732
Contact: Thomas M. Bancroft, Jr., Pres.

Incorporated in 1952 in NY.
Financial data (yr. ended 12/31/01): Grants paid, $213,000; assets, $2,897,745 (M); expenditures, $239,506; qualifying distributions, $215,987.
Limitations: Giving primarily in NY.
Application information: Limited available funding. Application form not required.

Officers: Thomas M. Bancroft, Jr., Pres. and Treas.; William Bancroft, V.P. and Secy.
EIN: 136111530
Codes: FD2

34427
Joseph C. and Clare F. Goodman Memorial Foundation, Inc.
c/o Lipsky Goodkin & Co.
120 W. 45th St., 7th Fl.
New York, NY 10036

Incorporated in 1969 in NY.
Donor(s): Clare F. Goodman.‡
Financial data (yr. ended 09/30/01): Grants paid, $212,500; assets, $5,102,188 (M); expenditures, $277,852; qualifying distributions, $216,848.
Limitations: Applications not accepted. Giving primarily in New York, NY.
Application information: Contributes only to pre-selected organizations.
Officers: Joyce N. Eichenberg, Pres.; Joseph F. Seminara, V.P.
EIN: 237039999
Codes: FD2

34428
The KCIG Foundation
P.O. Box 765
14 Melnick Dr.
Monsey, NY 10952

Established in 1997 in NY.
Donor(s): Israel Grossman.
Financial data (yr. ended 12/31/01): Grants paid, $212,205; assets, $84,569 (M); gifts received, $228,500; expenditures, $213,687; qualifying distributions, $213,283.
Limitations: Giving primarily in NY.
Trustees: Israel Grossman, Molly Grossman.
EIN: 137103160
Codes: FD2

34429
Stuntz Family Foundation
c/o Reminick Aarons & Co., LLP
1430 Broadway, 17th Fl.
New York, NY 10018

Established in 1997 in NY.
Donor(s): Mayo Stuntz, Elizabeth Stuntz.
Financial data (yr. ended 11/30/01): Grants paid, $212,167; assets, $2,942,191 (M); gifts received, $393,720; expenditures, $236,998; qualifying distributions, $212,721.
Limitations: Applications not accepted. Giving primarily in NY.
Application information: Contributes only to pre-selected organizations.
Officer: Mayo S. Stuntz, Jr., Pres.
Director: Elizabeth Stuntz.
EIN: 133979253
Codes: FD2

34430
The Eli Salig Charitable Trust
c/o ASI Solutions, Inc.
780 3rd Ave., 6th Fl.
New York, NY 10017-2024

Established in 1998 in NY.
Donor(s): Eli Salig.
Financial data (yr. ended 12/31/01): Grants paid, $211,964; assets, $927,285 (M); gifts received, $694,200; expenditures, $211,979; qualifying distributions, $211,964.
Limitations: Applications not accepted.
Application information: Contributes only to pre-selected organizations.
Trustee: Eli Salig.
EIN: 137159406

34431
Associated Food Stores Charitable Foundation, Inc.
1800 Rockaway Ave., Ste. 200
Hewlett, NY 11557

Established in 1987 in NY.
Donor(s): Associated Food Stores, Inc.
Financial data (yr. ended 12/31/01): Grants paid, $211,910; assets, $536,067 (M); gifts received, $28,650; expenditures, $212,431; qualifying distributions, $211,977.
Limitations: Applications not accepted. Giving primarily in the metropolitan New York, NY, area.
Application information: Contributes only to pre-selected organizations.
Directors: Harvey Berg, Ira Gober, Harry Laufer.
EIN: 112866371
Codes: CS, FD2, CD

34432
The Roothbert Fund, Inc.
475 Riverside Dr., Rm. 252
New York, NY 10115 (212) 870-3116
URL: http://www.roothbertfund.org
Contact: Jacob van Rossum, Admin. Secy.

Incorporated in 1958 in NY.
Donor(s): Albert Roothbert,‡ Toni Roothbert.‡
Financial data (yr. ended 12/31/01): Grants paid, $211,365; assets, $4,930,961 (M); gifts received, $4,785; expenditures, $311,699; qualifying distributions, $271,306.
Limitations: Giving primarily in the northeastern U.S., with emphasis on New Haven, CT, Washington, DC, New York, NY, and Philadelphia, PA.
Publications: Annual report, application guidelines, informational brochure.
Application information: Interview with Scholarship Committee is a requirement in the application process; interviews take place in Mar. in New York, NY, Washington, DC, Philadelphia, PA, and New Haven, CT. Application form required.
Officers and Directors:* Blake T. Newton III,* Pres.; Susan S. Purdy,* V.P., Fellowships; Carl Solberg,* Secy.; Charles Van Horne,* Treas.; Jane F. Century, Diamond Cephus, Jr., John P. Devlin, Donna M. Johnson, Gilbert M. Joseph, Lowell W. Livezey, Cynthia P. Olsen, Grace A. Troisi, Stephen F. Wilder.
EIN: 136162570
Codes: FD2, GTI

34433
The Niemiec Family Fund
c/o Barry Strauss Assocs., Ltd.
307 5th Ave., 8th Fl.
New York, NY 10016-6517

Established in 1992 in NY.
Donor(s): David W. Niemiec.
Financial data (yr. ended 03/31/01): Grants paid, $211,300; assets, $675,528 (M); expenditures, $217,409; qualifying distributions, $211,891.
Limitations: Applications not accepted. Giving primarily in NY.
Application information: Contributes only to pre-selected organizations.
Trustees: David W. Niemiec, Melanie M. Niemiec.
EIN: 133689379
Codes: FD2

34434
Henry and Myrtle Hirsch Foundation
(Formerly Louis Hirsch Foundation)
c/o Lawrence Gross
18 York Dr.
Great Neck, NY 11021

Established in 1947.
Donor(s): Henry Hirsch,‡ Myrtle G. Hirsch,‡ Carole Friedman, S. Minotto, and members of the Hirsch family.
Financial data (yr. ended 12/31/00): Grants paid, $211,271; assets, $4,803,771 (M); expenditures, $223,056; qualifying distributions, $211,271.
Limitations: Applications not accepted. Giving primarily in NY.
Application information: Contributes only to pre-selected organizations.
Officers: Richard Hirsch, Pres.; David Hirsch, V.P.
EIN: 116035655
Codes: FD2

34435
The Joan L. & Julius H. Jacobson II Foundation, Inc.
c/o Reminick, Aarons & Co., LLP
1430 Broadway
New York, NY 10018

Established in 1997 in NY.
Donor(s): Julius H. Jacobson II, Joan L. Jacobson.
Financial data (yr. ended 12/31/01): Grants paid, $211,000; assets, $4,159,952 (M); gifts received, $325,000; expenditures, $225,738; qualifying distributions, $211,000.
Limitations: Applications not accepted. Giving primarily in NY; some funding also in MA.
Application information: Contributes only to pre-selected organizations.
Officers: Julius H. Jacobson II, Pres. and Treas.; Joan L. Jacobson, V.P. and Secy.
EIN: 133938814
Codes: FD2

34436
The Schloss Family Foundation, Inc.
c/o Walter J. Schloss
350 Park Ave., 9th Fl.
New York, NY 10022-6022

Established in 1997 in NY.
Donor(s): Walter J. Schloss.
Financial data (yr. ended 12/31/01): Grants paid, $210,500; assets, $4,831,248 (M); expenditures, $213,495; qualifying distributions, $210,500.
Limitations: Applications not accepted. Giving limited to Washington, DC, and NY.
Application information: Contributes only to pre-selected organizations.
Officers: Walter J. Schloss, Pres. and Treas.; Edwin W. Schloss, V.P.; Stephanie Cassel Scott, Secy.
EIN: 133935646
Codes: FD2

34437
The Jack & Ruth Wexler Charitable Trust
(Formerly The Jack & Ruth Wexler Foundation)
c/o Katzman, Weinstein & Co., LLP
131 Jericho Tpke., Ste. 400
Jericho, NY 11753

Established in 1991 in NY.
Donor(s): Jack Wexler, Ruth Wexler.‡
Financial data (yr. ended 12/31/01): Grants paid, $210,500; assets, $2,071,248 (M); expenditures, $210,900; qualifying distributions, $210,500.
Limitations: Applications not accepted. Giving primarily in NY and PA.
Application information: Contributes only to pre-selected organizations.
Trustees: Ann R. Fromer, G. Martin Wexler, Jack Wexler.
EIN: 116398412
Codes: FD2

34438
The Garson Rappaport Family Foundation
325 West End Ave., Apt 10-D
New York, NY 10023

Established in 2001 in DE.
Donor(s): Steven N. Rappaport.
Financial data (yr. ended 12/31/01): Grants paid, $210,000; assets, $455,861 (M); gifts received, $33,135; expenditures, $210,000; qualifying distributions, $210,000.
Limitations: Applications not accepted.
Application information: Contributes only to pre-selected organizations.
Officers: Judith A. Garson, Pres.; Steven N. Rappaport, V.P.
EIN: 522359342
Codes: FD2

34439
The Herbert J. Seligmann Charitable Trust
c/o Windels Marx, et al.
156 W. 56th St.
New York, NY 10019
Contact: John Kriz

Established in 1997 in NY.
Donor(s): Lise R. Seligmann.
Financial data (yr. ended 12/31/01): Grants paid, $210,000; assets, $805,817 (M); expenditures, $228,374; qualifying distributions, $212,981.
Limitations: Giving primarily in NY.
Trustees: Lise R. Seligmann, W. David Wister, Robert Nathaniel Zicht.
EIN: 137114871
Codes: FD2

34440
Michael Palm Foundation
162 5th Ave., 7th Fl.
New York, NY 10010 (212) 366-8753
FAX: (212) 366-8754; *E-mail:* canderson@palmfoundation.com, bkanter@palmfoundation.com
Contact: Craig Anderson, Pres.

Established in 1993 in NY.
Donor(s): Michael Palm.‡
Financial data (yr. ended 12/31/01): Grants paid, $209,575; assets, $38,736 (M); gifts received, $1,200; expenditures, $578,473; qualifying distributions, $461,932.
Limitations: Applications not accepted. Giving on a national basis, with emphasis on New York City.
Application information: The foundation does not accept unsolicited requests for funds.
Officers and Directors:* M. Melissa Jamula,* Chair.; Craig Anderson,* Pres.; David W. Prager, Treas.; Eugene D. Falk, Judith O'Connor Gluckstern, Steven M. Gluckstern.
EIN: 133745516
Codes: FD2

34441
The Stuart Foundation, Inc.
599 Lexington Ave., Ste. 4102
New York, NY 10022 (212) 750-0055

Incorporated in 1951 in NY.
Donor(s): Members of the Stuart family.
Financial data (yr. ended 12/31/01): Grants paid, $209,103; assets, $3,934,568 (M); expenditures, $267,105; qualifying distributions, $211,953.
Limitations: Applications not accepted. Giving primarily in NY and New England, with emphasis on CT, MA, and RI.

34441—NEW YORK

Application information: Contributes only to pre-selected organizations.
Officers and Directors:* Alan L. Stuart,* Chair.; John E. Stuart, Pres.; James M. Stuart, Jr., V.P.; Jacqueline B. Stuart, Secy.; Ronda H. Lubin, Treas.; Carolyn A. Stuart.
EIN: 136066191
Codes: FD2

34442
E&WG Foundation
(Formerly Eleanor and Wilson Greatbatch Foundation)
8975 Main St.
Clarence, NY 14031 (716) 634-3358
Contact: Richard K. Milewicz, Secy.

Donor(s): Wilson Greatbatch.
Financial data (yr. ended 12/31/01): Grants paid, $209,029; assets, $3,910,527 (M); gifts received, $279,529; expenditures, $214,134; qualifying distributions, $210,291.
Limitations: Giving primarily in NY.
Officers: Wilson Greatbatch, Pres. and Treas.; Eleanor Greatbatch, V.P.; Richard K. Milewicz, Secy.
EIN: 161065309
Codes: FD2

34443
Mark IV Industries Foundation, Inc.
c/o Mark IV Industries, Inc.
P.O. Box 810
Amherst, NY 14226-0810 (716) 689-4972
Contact: Joann Eckert

Established in 1976 in NY.
Donor(s): Mark IV Industries, Inc.
Financial data (yr. ended 04/30/01): Grants paid, $208,893; assets, $1,054,604 (M); expenditures, $209,000; qualifying distributions, $208,181.
Limitations: Giving primarily in Buffalo, NY.
Application information: Application form not required.
Officer: William P. Montague, Pres.
EIN: 161082605
Codes: CS, FD2, CD

34444
The Harmon Foundation
c/o Tanton & Co., LLP
37 W. 57th St., 5th Fl.
New York, NY 10019

Established in 1988 in DE.
Donor(s): James A. Harmon.
Financial data (yr. ended 08/31/01): Grants paid, $208,750; assets, $4,316,927 (M); expenditures, $263,818; qualifying distributions, $205,591.
Limitations: Applications not accepted. Giving primarily in FL, NY, and RI.
Application information: Contributes only to pre-selected organizations.
Officers: James Harmon, Pres.; Leonard M. Leiman, Secy.; Jane Harmon, Treas.
EIN: 061180560
Codes: FD2

34445
Cornell/Weinstein Family Foundation
50 Wilshire Rd.
Rochester, NY 14618
Contact: Linda Cornell Weinstein, Exec. Dir.

Established in 1985 in NY.
Donor(s): Members of the Cornell Family, and members of the Weinstein family.
Financial data (yr. ended 08/31/01): Grants paid, $208,050; assets, $4,595,667 (M); gifts received, $250; expenditures, $263,063; qualifying distributions, $207,815.

Limitations: Applications not accepted. Giving primarily in NY.
Application information: Unsolicited requests for funds not considered or acknowledged.
Officers: Sherwin Weinstein, Secy.; Harry Cornell, Treas.; Linda Cornell Weinstein, Exec. Dir.
Director: David Cornell.
EIN: 161264534
Codes: FD2

34446
Doris Warner Vidor Foundation, Inc.
c/o Starr & Co.
350 Park Ave.
New York, NY 10022

Established in 1972 in NY.
Financial data (yr. ended 11/30/00): Grants paid, $207,860; assets, $790,427 (M); expenditures, $213,364; qualifying distributions, $205,482.
Limitations: Applications not accepted. Giving primarily in the greater metropolitan New York, NY, area.
Application information: Contributes only to pre-selected organizations.
Officers: Linda Janklow, Pres. and Treas.; Quentin Vidor, V.P.; Lewis Brian Vidor, Secy.
EIN: 237252504
Codes: FD2

34447
The Sealark Foundation, Inc.
c/o Bessemer Trust Co., N.A.
630 5th Ave.
New York, NY 10111

Established in 1997 in DE.
Donor(s): James M. Clark.
Financial data (yr. ended 12/31/01): Grants paid, $207,500; assets, $3,975,161 (M); expenditures, $233,250; qualifying distributions, $209,630.
Limitations: Applications not accepted. Giving primarily in Woods Hole, MA, and NY.
Application information: Contributes only to pre-selected organizations.
Officers: James M. Clark, Pres.; James M. Clark, Jr., V.P. and Secy.; Mrs. James M. Clark, Treas.
EIN: 133747240
Codes: FD2

34448
Louis Skalny Foundation Trust
c/o HSBC Bank USA
1 HSBC Ctr., 16th Fl.
Buffalo, NY 14203-2885

Established in 1970 in NY.
Financial data (yr. ended 12/31/01): Grants paid, $207,500; assets, $1,558,217 (M); expenditures, $229,009; qualifying distributions, $209,065.
Limitations: Applications not accepted. Giving primarily in Rochester, NY.
Application information: Contributes only to pre-selected organizations.
Trustee: HSBC Bank USA.
EIN: 166119085
Codes: FD2

34449
Robert C. Baker Foundation, Inc.
c/o Natl. Realty and Devel. Corp.
3 Manhattanville Rd.
Purchase, NY 10577-2116 (914) 694-4444

Donor(s): Robert C. Baker.
Financial data (yr. ended 12/31/01): Grants paid, $206,650; assets, $204,607 (M); expenditures, $217,051; qualifying distributions, $206,650.
Limitations: Giving primarily in CT.
Officer: Robert C. Baker, Pres.
EIN: 237086645

34450
Alana & Lewis Frumkes Foundation, Inc.
c/o Exec. Monetary Mgmt., Inc.
220 E. 42nd St.
New York, NY 10017

Established in 1988 in NY.
Donor(s): Sylvia Martin Foundation, Inc.
Financial data (yr. ended 12/31/00): Grants paid, $206,535; assets, $1,639,342 (M); expenditures, $278,978; qualifying distributions, $241,688.
Limitations: Applications not accepted. Giving primarily in NY.
Application information: Contributes only to pre-selected organizations.
Officers: Alana Martin Frumkes, Pres.; Lewis Frumkes, V.P.
Trustees: Amber Frumkes, Timothy Frumkes.
EIN: 133433686
Codes: FD2

34451
Jonathan L. Cohen Foundation
(Formerly Jonathan L. & Carolyn B. Cohen Foundation)
c/o BCRS Associates, LLC
100 Wall St., 11th Fl.
New York, NY 10005

Established in 1985 in NY.
Donor(s): Jonathan L. Cohen.
Financial data (yr. ended 07/31/01): Grants paid, $206,500; assets, $1,164,387 (M); expenditures, $217,903; qualifying distributions, $207,500.
Limitations: Applications not accepted. Giving primarily in New York, NY.
Application information: Contributes only to pre-selected organizations.
Trustees: Gregory D. Cohen, Jonathan L. Cohen, Robert M. Freeman, David A. George.
EIN: 133318133
Codes: FD2

34452
Kedusha Foundation
5417 18th Ave.
Brooklyn, NY 11204 (718) 256-6977
Contact: Septimus & Epstein

Established in 1999 in NY.
Financial data (yr. ended 08/31/01): Grants paid, $206,401; assets, $177,254 (M); gifts received, $146,900; expenditures, $206,401; qualifying distributions, $206,372.
Limitations: Giving primarily in NY.
Directors: Ben Epstein, Judah Septimus, Rabbi Simon Tov.
EIN: 113451034
Codes: FD2

34453
The Dunn Family Foundation
(Formerly Edward B. Dunn Foundation)
Pine Island
Rye, NY 10580
Contact: Edward B. Dunn, Dir.

Established in 1989 in NY.
Donor(s): Edward B. Dunn.
Financial data (yr. ended 12/31/01): Grants paid, $206,400; assets, $3,800,301 (M); gifts received, $385; expenditures, $221,951; qualifying distributions, $205,540.
Limitations: Giving primarily in NY.
Officer: Giovannella G. Dunn, Secy.
Director: Edward B. Dunn.
EIN: 133525637
Codes: FD2

34454
The Anderson Foundation, Inc.
c/o Chemung Canal Trust Co.
P.O. Box 1522
Elmira, NY 14902 (607) 737-3711

Incorporated in 1960 in NY.
Donor(s): Jane G. Anderson, Douglas G. Anderson.‡
Financial data (yr. ended 04/30/01): Grants paid, $206,240; assets, $3,884,217 (M); expenditures, $225,191; qualifying distributions, $203,611.
Limitations: Giving primarily in Elmira, NY.
Officers and Trustees:* Jane G. Joralemon,* Pres.; Paul Greenlee, Jr.,* V.P.; J. Philip Hunter,* Secy.; E. William Whittaker,* Treas.; Elizabeth T. Dalrymple, Edwin P. Marosek, Margaret B. Streeter, Jeanne Whittaker Ward.
EIN: 166024689
Codes: FD2

34455
The Michael J. Charles Foundation, Inc.
c/o CF Partners
126 E. 56th St.
New York, NY 10022

Established in 1993 in NY.
Donor(s): Michael J. Charles.
Financial data (yr. ended 12/31/01): Grants paid, $206,094; assets, $11,527 (M); expenditures, $207,376; qualifying distributions, $206,575.
Limitations: Applications not accepted. Giving primarily in the metropolitan New York, NY, area.
Application information: Contributes only to pre-selected organizations.
Officer: Michael J. Charles, Pres.
EIN: 133746799
Codes: FD2

34456
The Schlanger Family Foundation, Inc.
48 Pembroke Dr.
Glen Cove, NY 11542

Established in 1997 in NY.
Donor(s): Norman Schlanger.
Financial data (yr. ended 09/30/01): Grants paid, $206,000; assets, $1,980,820 (M); gifts received, $1,475,244; expenditures, $208,727; qualifying distributions, $206,000.
Limitations: Applications not accepted.
Application information: Contributes only to pre-selected organizations.
Officers: Norman Schlanger, Pres. and Treas.; Craig Schlanger, V.P. and Secy.; Darren Schlanger, V.P.; Jill Schlanger, V.P.
EIN: 133986709
Codes: FD2

34457
Y. A. Istel Foundation, Inc.
c/o Barry M. Strauss Assocs., Ltd.
307 5th Ave., 8th Fl.
New York, NY 10016-6517

Established in 1989 in NY.
Donor(s): Yves-Andre Istel.
Financial data (yr. ended 04/30/01): Grants paid, $205,990; assets, $1,093,317 (M); gifts received, $219,000; expenditures, $214,199; qualifying distributions, $210,240.
Limitations: Applications not accepted. Giving primarily in New York, NY.
Application information: Contributes only to pre-selected organizations.
Officers: Yves-Andre Istel, Pres.; Kenneth B. Newman, Secy.
EIN: 133524729
Codes: FD2

34458
The Toffey Family Charitable Trust
c/o Carter, Ledyard & Milburn
2 Wall St.
New York, NY 10005

Established in 1990 in WA.
Donor(s): H. James Toffey, Mrs. H. James Toffey.
Financial data (yr. ended 06/30/01): Grants paid, $205,931; assets, $2,488,192 (M); gifts received, $624,081; expenditures, $210,613; qualifying distributions, $205,931.
Limitations: Applications not accepted. Giving primarily in Hanover, NH.
Application information: Contributes only to pre-selected organizations.
Trustees: Debora Toffey Puckette, H. James Toffey, James W. Toffey, Sally N. Toffey.
EIN: 136955166

34459
The Brad and Patty Wechsler Foundation, Inc.
784 Park Ave., Ste. 7B
New York, NY 10021

Established in 1994 in DE and NY.
Donor(s): Bradley J. Wechsler, Patty Wechsler.
Financial data (yr. ended 01/31/01): Grants paid, $205,900; assets, $411,152 (M); expenditures, $207,089; qualifying distributions, $205,900.
Limitations: Applications not accepted. Giving primarily in NY.
Application information: Contributes only to pre-selected organizations.
Officers and Directors:* Bradley J. Wechsler,* Pres.; Patty Wechsler,* Secy.
EIN: 133798248
Codes: FD2

34460
Frederick H. Bedford, Jr. and Margaret S. Bedford Charitable Foundation
2 Wall St.
New York, NY 10005

Established in 1989 in DE; funded in fiscal 1990.
Donor(s): Victaulic Co. of America.
Financial data (yr. ended 09/30/01): Grants paid, $205,450; assets, $3,074,894 (M); gifts received, $275,000; expenditures, $210,849; qualifying distributions, $208,658.
Limitations: Applications not accepted. Giving in the U.S., primarily in PA.
Application information: Contributes only to pre-selected organizations.
Officers and Directors:* J.M. Trachtenberg,* Pres.; Pierre D'Arenberg,* V.P.; Muffie B. Murray,* Secy.-Treas.; Thomas M. Bancroft, Jr., George Naumann.
EIN: 133544702
Codes: FD2

34461
Amy and James Haber Foundation
340 E. 64th St., Ste. 5K
New York, NY 10021

Established in 2000 in NY.
Donor(s): James Haber.
Financial data (yr. ended 12/31/01): Grants paid, $205,408; assets, $300,747 (M); gifts received, $250,000; expenditures, $205,408; qualifying distributions, $205,408.
Limitations: Applications not accepted.
Application information: Contributes only to pre-selected organizations.
Trustee: James Haber.
EIN: 134144231

34462
The Bernard and Toby Nussbaum Foundation
(Formerly The Bernard W. Nussbaum Family Foundation)
c/o Wachtell, Lipton, Rosen & Katz
51 W. 52nd St.
New York, NY 10019

Established in 1986 in NY.
Donor(s): Bernard W. Nussbaum.
Financial data (yr. ended 04/30/01): Grants paid, $205,355; assets, $1,215,829 (M); gifts received, $96,293; expenditures, $245,514; qualifying distributions, $213,482.
Limitations: Applications not accepted. Giving primarily in New York, NY.
Application information: Contributes only to pre-selected organizations.
Officers: Bernard W. Nussbaum, Pres.; Toby A. Nussbaum, V.P.; Martin Nussbaum, Treas.
EIN: 133374849
Codes: FD2

34463
Higgins Family Foundation
c/o Goldman Sachs & Co.
85 Broad St., Tax Dept.
New York, NY 10004-2456 (212) 902-6987

Established in 1991 in NY.
Donor(s): Robert E. Higgins.
Financial data (yr. ended 03/31/01): Grants paid, $205,250; assets, $2,099,785 (M); expenditures, $230,500; qualifying distributions, $205,500.
Limitations: Applications not accepted. Giving primarily in RI.
Application information: Contributes only to pre-selected organizations.
Trustees: Gail R. Higgins, Robert E. Higgins.
EIN: 133638510
Codes: FD2

34464
Charlotte & Harry Katz Foundation, Inc.
76-19 171st St.
Flushing, NY 11366

Established in 1995 in NY.
Donor(s): Harry Katz, Charlotte Katz.
Financial data (yr. ended 12/31/01): Grants paid, $205,237; assets, $545,643 (M); gifts received, $250,000; expenditures, $209,679; qualifying distributions, $209,679.
Limitations: Applications not accepted. Giving primarily in the New York, NY, area.
Application information: Contributes only to pre-selected organizations.
Officers: Harry Katz, Pres.; Charlotte Katz, V.P.
EIN: 113295712
Codes: FD2

34465
Edna and Monroe C. Gutman Foundation, Inc.
c/o Hertz, Herson & Co., LLP
2 Park Ave.
New York, NY 10016

Incorporated in 1947 in NY.
Donor(s): Edna C. Gutman,‡ Monroe C. Gutman,‡ Cyrus H. Nathan.
Financial data (yr. ended 06/30/01): Grants paid, $205,000; assets, $7,995,444 (M); expenditures, $259,031; qualifying distributions, $206,308.
Limitations: Applications not accepted. Giving primarily in New England, NY, and PA.
Application information: Contributes only to pre-selected organizations.
Officers: Margaret S. Nathan, Pres.; Bernard Finkelstein, V.P.; Cyrus H. Nathan, V.P.; Michael T. Incantalupo, Treas.
EIN: 136094013

34465—NEW YORK

Codes: FD2

34466
The Shapiro Family Foundation
c/o Clarendon Mgmt.
435 W. 23rd St.
New York, NY 10011

Established in 1998 in NJ.
Donor(s): Harris Shapiro, Shirley Shapiro.
Financial data (yr. ended 12/31/00): Grants paid, $204,964; assets, $385,176 (M); gifts received, $88,970; expenditures, $213,847; qualifying distributions, $204,216.
Limitations: Applications not accepted. Giving primarily in NJ and NY.
Application information: Contributes only to pre-selected organizations.
Trustees: Harris Shapiro, Shirley Shapiro.
Manager: Elaine Appeloff.
EIN: 226767630
Codes: FD2

34467
Joseph & Sylvia Slifka Foundation, Inc.
477 Madison Ave., 8th Fl.
New York, NY 10022-5802

Established in 1944 in NY.
Donor(s): Joseph Slifka, Sylvia Slifka.
Financial data (yr. ended 10/31/99): Grants paid, $204,900; assets, $2,958,569 (M); expenditures, $222,224; qualifying distributions, $206,540.
Limitations: Applications not accepted. Giving primarily in the metropolitan New York, NY, area.
Application information: Contributes only to pre-selected organizations.
Officers: Sylvia Slifka, V.P.; Barbara S. Slifka, Secy.; Alan B. Slifka, Treas.
EIN: 136106433
Codes: FD2

34468
The Waterwheel Foundation
c/o Burton Goldstein & Co., LLC
156 W. 56th St., Ste. 1803
New York, NY 10019
URL: http://www.phunky.com/twwsit/wwf.html

Established in 1997 in VT.
Financial data (yr. ended 12/31/99): Grants paid, $204,785; assets, $517,221 (M); gifts received, $317,684; expenditures, $305,407; qualifying distributions, $212,897.
Limitations: Applications not accepted. Giving on a national basis, with some emphasis on VT.
Application information: Contributes only to pre-selected organizations.
Officers: Ernest Anastasio, Pres.; Jonathan Fishman, V.P.; Page McConnel, Secy.; Michael Gordon, Treas.
EIN: 133948773
Codes: FD2

34469
Furman Foundation, Inc.
170 Sullivan St.
New York, NY 10012
Contact: Gail Furman, Pres.

Established in 2000 in NY.
Donor(s): Jason Furman, Gail Furman.
Financial data (yr. ended 12/31/01): Grants paid, $203,950; assets, $288,128 (M); gifts received, $212,050; expenditures, $210,716; qualifying distributions, $203,950.
Limitations: Giving primarily in NY.
Application information: Application form not required.
Officers: Gail Furman, Pres.; Ariela Dubler, V.P.; Jason Furman, Secy.; Jesse Furman, Treas.

EIN: 134094739
Codes: FD2

34470
Eggleston Foundation
c/o Levene, Gouldin & Thompson, LLP
P.O. Box F-1706
Binghamton, NY 13902-0106 (607) 763-9200
Contact: Michael H. Zuckerman

Established in 1984 in NY.
Donor(s): Edith E. Lewis.
Financial data (yr. ended 12/31/01): Grants paid, $203,900; assets, $2,520,039 (M); expenditures, $228,667; qualifying distributions, $203,900.
Limitations: Giving primarily in upstate NY.
Trustees: William E. Lewis, Mary L. Meltzer.
EIN: 133216256
Codes: FD2

34471
The Gramercy Park Foundation, Inc.
c/o Zemlock, Levy, Bick & Karnbad
225 Broadway
New York, NY 10007
Contact: Lawrence S. Karnbad

Incorporated in 1952 in NY.
Donor(s): Benjamin Sonnenberg, Helen Sonnenberg Tucker.
Financial data (yr. ended 12/31/01): Grants paid, $203,627; assets, $4,335,191 (M); expenditures, $240,341; qualifying distributions, $207,541.
Limitations: Giving primarily in the metropolitan New York, NY, area.
Application information: Application form not required.
Officers: Helen Sonnenberg Tucker, Pres.; Steven Tucker, Secy.; William Spears, Treas.
EIN: 132507282
Codes: FD2

34472
The Claire & Maurits Edersheim Foundation
(Formerly Edersheim Foundation)
927 5th Ave.
New York, NY 10021
Contact: Claire Edersheim, Secy.-Treas.

Established in 1955 in NY.
Donor(s): Claire Edersheim, Maurits E. Edersheim.
Financial data (yr. ended 12/31/00): Grants paid, $203,502; assets, $5,212,456 (M); gifts received, $42,284; expenditures, $211,304; qualifying distributions, $206,828.
Limitations: Applications not accepted. Giving primarily in NY.
Application information: Contributes only to pre-selected organizations.
Officers: Maurits E. Edersheim, Pres.; Judy Edersheim, V.P.; Claire Edersheim, Secy.-Treas.
EIN: 136075353
Codes: FD2

34473
The Glades Foundation
c/o Sullivan & Cromwell
125 Broad St.
New York, NY 10004-2400

Established in 1991 in NY.
Donor(s): Mark F. Dalton.
Financial data (yr. ended 12/31/01): Grants paid, $203,500; assets, $297,909 (M); gifts received, $175,000; expenditures, $206,508; qualifying distributions, $203,139.
Limitations: Applications not accepted. Giving primarily in the U.S.; some giving also on an international basis.
Application information: Contributes only to pre-selected organizations.

Trustees: James I. Black III, Mark F. Dalton.
EIN: 136986506
Codes: FD2

34474
The Joseph & Susan Gatto Foundation
c/o Goldman Sachs & Co.
85 Broad St., Tax Dept.
New York, NY 10004

Established in 1996 in CT.
Donor(s): Joseph D. Gatto.
Financial data (yr. ended 09/30/01): Grants paid, $203,480; assets, $3,078,064 (M); gifts received, $1,947,750; expenditures, $246,050; qualifying distributions, $205,050.
Limitations: Applications not accepted. Giving primarily in NJ and NY.
Application information: Contributes only to pre-selected organizations.
Trustees: Joseph D. Gatto, Susan Gatto.
EIN: 133921102
Codes: FD2

34475
The Denis P. and Carol A. Kelleher Charitable Foundation
17 Battery Pl., 11th Fl.
New York, NY 10004-1101

Established in 2000 in NY.
Donor(s): Denis P. Kelleher.
Financial data (yr. ended 10/31/01): Grants paid, $202,053; assets, $2,043,336 (M); gifts received, $1,599,828; expenditures, $215,457; qualifying distributions, $206,723.
Limitations: Applications not accepted. Giving primarily in NY.
Application information: Contributes only to pre-selected organizations.
Directors: Carol A. Kelleher, Denis P. Kelleher, Denis P. Kelleher, Jr., Sean M. Kelleher, Colleen P. Sorrentino.
EIN: 134149751
Codes: FD2

34476
Helen I. Graham Charitable Foundation
9 Hunts Ln.
P.O. Box 320
Chappaqua, NY 10514

Established in 1999 in NY.
Donor(s): Helen I. Graham Trust.
Financial data (yr. ended 12/31/01): Grants paid, $202,000; assets, $4,236,703 (M); gifts received, $60,283; expenditures, $244,043; qualifying distributions, $201,081.
Limitations: Applications not accepted. Giving primarily in NY, PA, and VA.
Application information: Contributes only to pre-selected organizations.
Trustees: Harvey Dann IV, Tyler Dann.
EIN: 134070185
Codes: FD2

34477
The Manning Family Foundation, Inc.
(Formerly The Linus Foundation, Inc.)
250 Park Ave., Ste. 2030
New York, NY 10177-2003

Established in 1987 in DE.
Donor(s): Dana Manning.
Financial data (yr. ended 10/31/01): Grants paid, $202,000; assets, $2,791,757 (M); expenditures, $207,848; qualifying distributions, $202,028.
Limitations: Applications not accepted. Giving primarily in CA and NY.
Application information: Contributes only to pre-selected organizations.

Officers: Dana Manning, Pres.; Harold Manning, V.P.; Jordan Seaman, V.P.; Robert Krissoff, Secy.
EIN: 112897410
Codes: FD2

34478
Morris J. and Betty Kaplun Foundation, Inc.
c/o Freeman & Davis, LLP
225 W. 34th St., Ste. 320
New York, NY 10122
Contact: Moshe Sheinbaum, V.P.

Incorporated in 1955 in NY.
Donor(s): Morris J. Kaplun.‡
Financial data (yr. ended 08/31/01): Grants paid, $201,912; assets, $3,722,445 (M); gifts received, $18; expenditures, $340,873; qualifying distributions, $272,938.
Limitations: Giving primarily in New York, NY.
Application information: Application form not required.
Officers: Glorie Isakower, V.P.; Lawrence Marin, V.P.; Aaron Seligson, V.P.; Moshe Sheinbaum, V.P.
EIN: 136096009
Codes: FD2

34479
Schwalbe Brothers Foundation, Inc.
185 Madison Ave.
New York, NY 10016-4325 (212) 751-5884

Established in 1945.
Donor(s): Members of the Schwalbe family.
Financial data (yr. ended 12/31/01): Grants paid, $201,734; assets, $2,643,902 (M); gifts received, $5,865; expenditures, $207,884; qualifying distributions, $207,884.
Limitations: Applications not accepted. Giving primarily in New York, NY.
Application information: Contributes only to pre-selected organizations.
Officer and Directors:* Peter Schwalbe,* Secy.-Treas.; Robert Schwalbe.
EIN: 136162779
Codes: FD2

34480
The Henshel Foundation
24 Murray Hill Rd.
Scarsdale, NY 10583-2828
Contact: Harry B. Henshel, Pres.

Established in 1986 in NY.
Donor(s): Emily B. Henshel.
Financial data (yr. ended 05/31/01): Grants paid, $201,695; assets, $5,023,875 (M); expenditures, $257,622; qualifying distributions, $256,682.
Limitations: Giving primarily in NY.
Application information: Application form not required.
Officers: Harry B. Henshel, Pres.; Joy A. Henshel, Secy.
EIN: 136094082
Codes: FD2

34481
The Marks Family Foundation
369 Franklin St., Ste. 100
Buffalo, NY 14202 (716) 854-0425
Contact: Josephine Cane and Debra Kull

Established in 1990 in NY.
Donor(s): Randolph A. Marks.
Financial data (yr. ended 06/30/01): Grants paid, $201,554; assets, $3,048,289 (M); gifts received, $235,027; expenditures, $254,090; qualifying distributions, $198,155.
Limitations: Giving primarily in Buffalo, NY.
Application information: Application form required.

Officer and Trustees:* Randolph A. Marks,* Mgr.; Wendelyn W. Duquette, Joshua R. Marks, Sally Marks, Theodore E. Marks, Heather M. Palmer.
EIN: 161385716
Codes: FD2

34482
Doran Family Charitable Trust
c/o U.S. Trust, Tax Dept.
114 W. 47th St.
New York, NY 10036

Established in 1986 in MA.
Donor(s): Robert W. Doran.
Financial data (yr. ended 12/31/01): Grants paid, $201,450; assets, $710,658 (M); gifts received, $407,552; expenditures, $283,541; qualifying distributions, $201,700.
Limitations: Applications not accepted. Giving primarily in MA.
Application information: Contributes only to pre-selected organizations.
Trustees: Evelyn H. Doran, Robert W. Doran.
EIN: 226424850
Codes: FD2

34483
Sequa Foundation of Delaware
(Formerly Sun Chemical Foundation)
200 Park Ave.
New York, NY 10166-0005 (212) 986-5500
Contact: Kenneth Drucker

Established in 1967.
Donor(s): Sequa Corp.
Financial data (yr. ended 12/31/00): Grants paid, $201,335; assets, $150,752 (M); gifts received, $150,000; expenditures, $201,658; qualifying distributions, $201,335.
Limitations: Giving primarily in NY.
Application information: Application form not required.
Officers and Trustees:* Norman E. Alexander,* Pres.; S.Z. Krinsly,* V.P. and Secy.; Gerald S. Gutterman,* V.P.; K.A. Drucker, Treas.
EIN: 237000821
Codes: CS, FD2, CD

34484
The Jack & Muriel Seiler Foundation, Inc.
c/o Lenat Co.
315 Westchester Ave.
Port Chester, NY 10573

Established in 1981 in FL.
Donor(s): Jack M. Seiler.
Financial data (yr. ended 12/31/01): Grants paid, $201,188; assets, $3,880,376 (M); expenditures, $230,761; qualifying distributions, $201,188.
Limitations: Applications not accepted. Giving on a national basis.
Application information: Contributes only to pre-selected organizations.
Officers: John Heffer, Pres.; Jane H. Julius, V.P.; Elaine A. Seiler, V.P.; Lewis Seiler, V.P.
EIN: 581473401
Codes: FD2

34485
Herman Auerbach Memorial Fund Trust No. 2
c/o Deutsche Trust Co.
P.O. Box 1297, Church St. Sta., 7 W.
New York, NY 10008

Established in 1960 in NY.
Financial data (yr. ended 12/31/01): Grants paid, $201,150; assets, $3,631,560 (M); expenditures, $247,318; qualifying distributions, $221,677.
Limitations: Applications not accepted. Giving on a national basis.

Application information: Contributes only to pre-selected organizations.
Trustees: Ralph Smallberg, Victor Smallberg, Deutsche Bank.
EIN: 136307278
Codes: FD2

34486
Morse Hill Foundation, Inc.
20 Corporate Woods Blvd.
Albany, NY 12211

Established in 1990 in NY.
Donor(s): Kathleen M. Picotte, Michael B. Picotte.
Financial data (yr. ended 12/31/01): Grants paid, $201,100; assets, $5,840,190 (M); gifts received, $597,510; expenditures, $260,179; qualifying distributions, $210,616.
Limitations: Applications not accepted. Giving primarily in FL, NY, and PA.
Application information: Contributes only to pre-selected organizations.
Officers: Michael B. Picotte, Pres.; Margaret L. Picotte, V.P.; Margaret Ryhanych, Secy.-Treas.
EIN: 223083890
Codes: FD2

34487
The Kresevich and Marc A. Zambetti Foundation, Inc.
(Formerly The Kresevich Foundation, Inc.)
c/o Kresevich Capital Mgmt., LLC
221 Stanley Ave.
Mamaroneck, NY 10543

Incorporated in 1953 in NY.
Donor(s): Stella D'Oro Biscuit Co., Inc.
Financial data (yr. ended 11/30/01): Grants paid, $200,600; assets, $367,361 (M); expenditures, $203,304; qualifying distributions, $200,333.
Limitations: Applications not accepted. Giving primarily in NM.
Application information: Contributes only to pre-selected organizations.
Officers: Jonathan P. Zambetti, Pres.; Ada G. Zambetti, V.P.; Claudia V. Zambetti, Secy.; Audrey A. Zinman, Treas.
EIN: 136082003
Codes: FD2

34488
The Neisloss Family Foundation, Inc.
300 Corporate Plz., Ste. 301
Islandia, NY 11749 (631) 234-1600

Established in 1991 in NY.
Donor(s): Stanley Neisloss.‡
Financial data (yr. ended 07/31/01): Grants paid, $200,402; assets, $4,271,511 (M); gifts received, $502,095; expenditures, $213,004; qualifying distributions, $200,402.
Limitations: Giving primarily in New York, NY.
Application information: Application form not required.
Officer: Irma Neisloss, V.P. and Secy.
Director: Martin Mones.
EIN: 113086865
Codes: FD2

34489
The Frank A. Fusco and Nelly Goletti Foundation, Inc.
(Formerly The Frank A. and Nelly Fusco Foundation, Inc.)
c/o Teahan & Constantino
2780 South Rd., P.O. Box 1969
Poughkeepsie, NY 12601

Established in 1990 in NY.
Donor(s): Frank A. Fusco.‡

34489—NEW YORK

Financial data (yr. ended 12/31/00): Grants paid, $200,000; assets, $1,460,244 (M); gifts received, $384,278; expenditures, $237,660; qualifying distributions, $200,000.
Limitations: Applications not accepted. Giving primarily in Poughkeepsie, NY.
Application information: Contributes only to pre-selected organizations.
Officers: John M. Kennedy, Chair.; Frank J. Giumarra, Pres.; Charles J. Maneri, Jr., Secy.-Treas.
Directors: John V. Esposito, Shaileen Kopec, Judy Vasti.
EIN: 222983710
Codes: FD2

34490
Ann & Jules Gottlieb Foundation, Inc.
4 Nancy Ct.
Manhasset, NY 11030

Established in 1993 in NY.
Donor(s): Jules Gottlieb,‡ Ann Gottlieb.
Financial data (yr. ended 08/31/01): Grants paid, $200,000; assets, $1,712,759 (M); expenditures, $203,950; qualifying distributions, $200,250.
Limitations: Applications not accepted. Giving primarily in NY.
Application information: Contributes only to pre-selected organizations.
Officer: Ann Gottlieb, Pres.
Director: Richard Klinghoffer.
EIN: 133738495
Codes: FD2

34491
The David S. Howe Foundation
200 E. 69th St., Ste. PHG
New York, NY 10021

Donor(s): David S. Howe.
Financial data (yr. ended 11/30/01): Grants paid, $200,000; assets, $2,302,699 (M); gifts received, $118,224; expenditures, $222,700; qualifying distributions, $203,448.
Limitations: Applications not accepted. Giving primarily in NY.
Application information: Contributes only to pre-selected organizations.
Officer: David S. Howe, Pres.
Director: Benjamin Howe.
EIN: 134010543
Codes: FD2

34492
The Kurr Foundation
c/o Norma Pane
2057 63rd St.
Brooklyn, NY 11204-3071
Contact: Sara Zock, Secy.-Treas.

Established in 1992 in NJ.
Donor(s): Sara Zock.
Financial data (yr. ended 12/31/00): Grants paid, $200,000; assets, $5,218,403 (M); gifts received, $540,260; expenditures, $238,434; qualifying distributions, $216,335.
Limitations: Applications not accepted. Giving primarily in PA.
Application information: Contributes only to pre-selected organizations.
Officer and Trustees:* Sara Zock,* Secy.-Treas.; Robert J. Gaughran, Norma R. Pane, John H. Rogicki.
EIN: 223176150
Codes: FD2

34493
The Walter Levy Benevolent Trust
c/o Fried, Frank, Harris, & Lebetkin
1 New York Plz.
New York, NY 10004

Established in 1998.
Donor(s): Walter J. Levy.
Financial data (yr. ended 08/31/01): Grants paid, $200,000; assets, $4,082,413 (M); gifts received, $66,698; expenditures, $213,435; qualifying distributions, $211,445.
Limitations: Applications not accepted.
Application information: Contributes only to pre-selected organizations.
Trustee: Estafida Treuhand.
EIN: 137205508
Codes: FD2

34494
Maher Family Foundation
775 Park Ave., Ste. 10C
New York, NY 10021-4253

Established in 1999.
Donor(s): James Maher.
Financial data (yr. ended 12/31/01): Grants paid, $200,000; assets, $1,364,539 (M); gifts received, $1,000; expenditures, $210,728; qualifying distributions, $200,000.
Limitations: Applications not accepted. Giving primarily in MA.
Application information: Unsolicited requests for funds not accepted.
Trustees: Elizabeth Maher, James Maher.
EIN: 134082818
Codes: FD2

34495
The Milstein Brothers Foundation
c/o Kevin Buckley-Douglas Elliman
575 Madison Ave., 3rd Fl.
New York, NY 10022

Established in 1999 in DC.
Donor(s): Howard F. Milstein, Edward L. Milstein.
Financial data (yr. ended 12/31/00): Grants paid, $200,000; assets, $427,400 (M); expenditures, $222,481; qualifying distributions, $222,159.
Limitations: Applications not accepted.
Application information: Contributes only to pre-selected organizations.
Directors: Robert Linowes, Edward L. Milstein, Howard P. Milstein, Robert Mrazek, David M. Seldin, Carolyn Young.
EIN: 522198556
Codes: FD2

34496
Charlotte Palmer Phillips Foundation, Inc.
c/o Walter, Conston, Alexander
90 Park Ave.
New York, NY 10016

Incorporated in 1958 in NY.
Donor(s): Charlotte Palmer Phillips.‡
Financial data (yr. ended 12/31/01): Grants paid, $200,000; assets, $3,446,119 (M); expenditures, $269,136; qualifying distributions, $237,077.
Limitations: Applications not accepted. Giving primarily in NY.
Application information: Contributes only to pre-selected organizations.
Officers and Trustees:* Robert L. Strong,* Pres. and Treas.; James R. Cogan,* V.P. and Secy.; Marjorie J. Cook, Paul M. Frank, Stevens L. Frost, Louise H. Kerr, Charles E. Rogers, M.D.; Mary S. Strong.
EIN: 136100994
Codes: FD2

34497
Lawrence I. & Blanche H. Rhodes Memorial Fund
P.O. Box 7
Wynantskill, NY 12198

Established in 1994 in NY.
Financial data (yr. ended 07/31/01): Grants paid, $200,000; assets, $3,263,494 (M); expenditures, $259,768; qualifying distributions, $222,899.
Limitations: Applications not accepted. Giving primarily in NY and PA.
Application information: Contributes only to pre-selected organizations.
Officers: William J. Dwyer, Pres.; Barbara Egnot, Secy.; Joan K. Murphy, Exec. Dir.
EIN: 222159155
Codes: FD2

34498
Micol Schejola Foundation
250 E. 54th St., Ste. 10A
New York, NY 10022
Application address: 688 Cumberland Cir., Atlanta, GA 30306, tel.: (404) 607-8607
Contact: Michael K. Szalkowski

Established in 2000 in NY.
Donor(s): Linda Schejola.
Financial data (yr. ended 12/31/01): Grants paid, $200,000; assets, $175,991 (M); expenditures, $230,138; qualifying distributions, $199,963.
Limitations: Giving primarily in GA and TN.
Trustee: Linda Schejola.
EIN: 137257959
Codes: FD2

34499
Tai-Ping Foundation, Inc.
c/o Market St. Trust Co.
80 E. Market St., Ste. 300
Corning, NY 14830-2722

Donor(s): Gratia R. Montgomery.
Financial data (yr. ended 12/31/00): Grants paid, $200,000; assets, $2,132,311 (M); expenditures, $210,011; qualifying distributions, $197,915.
Limitations: Applications not accepted. Giving on a national basis.
Application information: Contributes only to pre-selected organizations.
Officers and Trustees:* Gratia R. Montgomery,* Chair. and Pres.; Richard G. Garrett,* Secy.-Treas.; Peter J.D. Allatt, Jr.,* Treas.; George D. Grice, Gordon E. Montgomery.
EIN: 237416887
Codes: FD2

34500
Andre & Elizabeth Kertesz Foundation, Inc.
450 7th Ave., Rm. 1802
New York, NY 10123-1802 (212) 594-7520
Contact: Jose Fernandez, Treas.

Established in 1982 in NY.
Financial data (yr. ended 12/31/01): Grants paid, $199,607; assets, $3,795,449 (M); expenditures, $344,079; qualifying distributions, $307,961.
Limitations: Giving primarily in New York, NY.
Officers: Alex Hollender, Pres.; Jose Fernandez, Treas.
EIN: 133136378
Codes: FD2

34501
Kenner Foundation, Inc.
437 Madison Ave., No. 2001
New York, NY 10021 (212) 319-2300
Contact: Jeffrey L. Kenner, Dir.

Established in 1996 in NY.

Donor(s): Jeffrey L. Kenner.
Financial data (yr. ended 12/31/99): Grants paid, $199,550; assets, $569,508 (M); expenditures, $200,810; qualifying distributions, $199,550.
Directors: Jeffrey L. Kenner, Patricia Kenner.
EIN: 133928876
Codes: FD2

34502
The Judith and Donald Rechler Foundation, Inc.
225 Broadhollow Rd., CS 5341
Melville, NY 11747

Established in 1998 in NY.
Donor(s): Donald Rechler, Judith Rechler.
Financial data (yr. ended 12/31/00): Grants paid, $199,550; assets, $1,550,556 (M); expenditures, $212,490; qualifying distributions, $205,095.
Directors: Donald Rechler, Judith Rechler, Mitchell Rechler.
EIN: 113430161
Codes: FD2

34503
Yellow Hat Fund
70A Greenwich Ave.
New York, NY 10011

Established in 1997 in NY and MA.
Donor(s): Jonathan Soros.
Financial data (yr. ended 11/30/01): Grants paid, $199,310; assets, $132,533 (M); expenditures, $210,777; qualifying distributions, $199,310.
Limitations: Applications not accepted.
Application information: Contributes only to pre-selected organizations.
Trustees: Jennifer Allan, Jonathan Soros.
EIN: 043403641

34504
The Mary Gordon Roberts Fund
c/o Sullivan & Cromwell
125 Broad St.
New York, NY 10004-2498
Contact: Mary G. Roberts, Tr.

Established in 1988 in NY.
Donor(s): Mary Gordon Roberts.
Financial data (yr. ended 12/31/01): Grants paid, $199,161; assets, $1,449,308 (M); expenditures, $193,106; qualifying distributions, $188,161.
Limitations: Giving primarily in New York, NY.
Application information: Application form not required.
Trustee: Mary G. Roberts.
EIN: 133007488
Codes: FD2

34505
Mab Foundation
c/o Meridian
4510 16th Ave.
Brooklyn, NY 11204

Established in 1997.
Financial data (yr. ended 11/30/99): Grants paid, $199,100; assets, $130,089 (M); gifts received, $91,594; expenditures, $199,275; qualifying distributions, $199,029.
Limitations: Applications not accepted.
Application information: Contributes only to pre-selected organizations.
Trustees: Aaron Birnbaum, Alisa Birnbaum.
EIN: 113409995
Codes: FD2

34506
The Young Family Charitable Foundation
c/o EOS Partners, LP
320 Park Ave., 22nd Fl.
New York, NY 10022-6838

Established in 1991 in NY.
Donor(s): Brian D. Young, Anne Young.
Financial data (yr. ended 06/30/01): Grants paid, $199,100; assets, $1,160,476 (M); gifts received, $21,804; expenditures, $206,384; qualifying distributions, $197,963.
Limitations: Applications not accepted. Giving primarily in Bridgeport, CT.
Application information: Contributes only to pre-selected organizations.
Trustee: Brian D. Young.
EIN: 136976453
Codes: FD2

34507
Agnus Noster Foundation
232 Madison Ave.
New York, NY 10016

Established in 1997 in DE.
Financial data (yr. ended 02/28/01): Grants paid, $198,750; assets, $3,615,976 (M); expenditures, $264,605; qualifying distributions, $210,466.
Limitations: Applications not accepted. Giving on a national basis, with some emphasis on Washington, DC.
Application information: Contributes only to pre-selected organizations.
Officers: Gayle Susan Marra, Pres.; Vincenzo R. Marra, Secy.
EIN: 133936959
Codes: FD2

34508
The Rose Family Foundation
(Formerly Karen & Gary Rose Foundation)
c/o BRCS Assocs.
67 Wall St., 8th Fl.
New York, NY 10005

Established in 1985 in NJ.
Donor(s): Gary D. Rose.
Financial data (yr. ended 01/31/01): Grants paid, $198,727; assets, $3,048,555 (M); expenditures, $235,451; qualifying distributions, $200,093.
Limitations: Applications not accepted. Giving primarily in NJ and NY.
Application information: Contributes only to pre-selected organizations.
Trustees: Gary D. Rose, Karen A. Rose, Howard A. Silverstein.
EIN: 133318165
Codes: FD2

34509
Robert and Jodi Rosenthal Family Foundation
c/o First Long Island Investors, Inc.
1 Jericho Plz.
Jericho, NY 11753
Contact: Robert D. Rosenthal, Tr.

Established in 1996.
Financial data (yr. ended 12/31/01): Grants paid, $198,650; assets, $767,766 (M); gifts received, $92,478; expenditures, $199,213; qualifying distributions, $198,282.
Limitations: Giving primarily in NY.
Trustees: Jodi Rosenthal, Robert D. Rosenthal.
EIN: 113357219
Codes: FD2

34510
Alper Family Foundation
c/o Goldman Sachs & Co.
85 Broad St., Tax Dept.
New York, NY 10004

Established in 1991 in NY.
Donor(s): Andrew M. Alper.
Financial data (yr. ended 02/28/01): Grants paid, $198,000; assets, $7,023,625 (M); gifts received, $2,411,445; expenditures, $270,788; qualifying distributions, $198,250.
Limitations: Applications not accepted. Giving primarily in New York, NY.
Application information: Contributes only to pre-selected organizations.
Trustees: Andrew M. Alper, Sharon Sadow Alper.
EIN: 133634384
Codes: FD2

34511
The Morris P. Leibovitz Foundation
c/o Radin, Glass & Co., LLP
360 Lexington Ave., 22nd Fl.
New York, NY 10017

Established in 1988 in NY.
Donor(s): Morris P. Leibovitz.‡
Financial data (yr. ended 12/31/01): Grants paid, $198,000; assets, $1,716,926 (M); expenditures, $249,365; qualifying distributions, $202,354.
Limitations: Applications not accepted. Giving primarily in NY.
Application information: Contributes only to pre-selected organizations.
Trustees: Albert Marston, Carole Anne McLeod.
EIN: 133442686
Codes: FD2

34512
The Gloria F. Ross Foundation
c/o Baron Bergstein & Weinberg, P.C.
450 7th Ave., Ste. 2906
New York, NY 10123-0086

Donor(s): Gloria F. Bookman.
Financial data (yr. ended 06/30/01): Grants paid, $197,450; assets, $831,952 (M); gifts received, $158,000; expenditures, $208,920; qualifying distributions, $199,070.
Limitations: Applications not accepted. Giving primarily in NY.
Application information: Contributes only to pre-selected organizations.
Officers: Michael I. Katz, Pres. and Treas.; Henry Kohn, V.P. and Secy.; Barbara K. Katz, V.P.
EIN: 237055699
Codes: FD2

34513
MYM Charitable Trust
c/o Israel Minzer
5223 19th Ave.
Brooklyn, NY 11204

Established in 1992 in NY.
Donor(s): Israel Minzer.
Financial data (yr. ended 12/31/99): Grants paid, $197,023; assets, $576,532 (M); gifts received, $125,563; expenditures, $197,494; qualifying distributions, $197,158.
Limitations: Applications not accepted. Giving primarily in Brooklyn, NY.
Application information: Contributes only to pre-selected organizations.
Trustees: Allan C. Bell, Israel Minzer, Miriam Minzer.
EIN: 223196450
Codes: FD2

34514
The Joseph & Anna Gartner Foundation
P.O. Box 226
Buffalo, NY 14226-0226

Established in 1981 in NY.
Donor(s): Carol N. Hirsh, Sanford M. Nobel.
Financial data (yr. ended 01/31/02): Grants paid, $197,000; assets, $4,192,646 (M); gifts received, $120,000; expenditures, $200,177; qualifying distributions, $194,633.
Limitations: Applications not accepted. Giving primarily in Buffalo and Rochester, NY.
Application information: Contributes only to pre-selected organizations.
Trustees: Carol N. Hirsh, Michael G. Hirsh, Margery S. Nobel, Sanford M. Nobel.
EIN: 222400456
Codes: FD2

34515
Faith Home Foundation
77 Carmen Pl.
Amityville, NY 11701 (631) 264-7161
Contact: M. Peterson

Incorporated in 1878 in NY.
Financial data (yr. ended 11/30/01): Grants paid, $196,500; assets, $4,269,125 (M); expenditures, $297,986; qualifying distributions, $233,161.
Limitations: Giving primarily in the metropolitan New York, NY, area, with emphasis on Brooklyn and Staten Island.
Application information: Application form required.
Officers: Henry A. Braun, Pres.; George C. Schaefer, V.P.; Alexander Pearson, Secy.; George E. Lawrence, Treas.
Trustees: Robert T. Arkwright, Owen E. Brooks, Gordon M. Brown, William F. deNeergaard, Kenneth S. Heiberg, Allan Larsen, Eugene H. Luntey, William F. Tucker.
EIN: 111776032
Codes: FD2

34516
The Goodman Family Foundation
c/o Roy M. Goodman
1035 5th Ave.
New York, NY 10028

Trust established in 1970 in NY as one of two successor trusts to the Matz Foundation.
Donor(s): Israel Matz.‡
Financial data (yr. ended 06/30/01): Grants paid, $196,278; assets, $5,018,845 (M); expenditures, $245,382; qualifying distributions, $203,183.
Limitations: Giving primarily in New York, NY.
Application information: Application form not required.
Trustees: Barbara F. Goodman, Roy M. Goodman.
EIN: 136355553
Codes: FD2

34517
Astar Foundation, Inc.
10 Lakeside Dr.
Lawrence, NY 11559

Established in 1994 in NY.
Donor(s): Alan Stahler.
Financial data (yr. ended 11/30/01): Grants paid, $196,210; assets, $2,212,946 (M); gifts received, $857,820; expenditures, $210,286; qualifying distributions, $199,042.
Limitations: Giving on a national basis.
Officers and Directors:* Esther Stahler,* Pres. and Treas.; Alan Stahler,* V.P.; Ruki Renov,* Secy.
EIN: 113189200
Codes: FD2

34518
Esther Simon Charitable Trust
c/o JPMorgan Chase Bank
345 Park Ave.
New York, NY 10154
Contact: Mary C. Dickens, V.P.

Trust established in 1952 in NY.
Donor(s): Esther Simon.‡
Financial data (yr. ended 12/31/01): Grants paid, $196,000; assets, $8,571,125 (M); expenditures, $270,134; qualifying distributions, $210,177.
Limitations: Applications not accepted. Giving primarily in Washington, DC, and New York, NY.
Application information: Contributes only to pre-selected organizations. Unsolicited requests for funds not accepted.
Trustees: Stephen Simon, JPMorgan Chase Bank.
EIN: 236286763
Codes: FD2

34519
Adirondack Community Trust
105 Saranac Ave.
Lake Placid, NY 12946 (518) 523-9904
E-mail: info@generousact.org; *URL:* http://www.generousact.org
Contact: Cali Brooks, Exec. Dir.

Established in 1997 in NY.
Financial data (yr. ended 06/30/02): Grants paid, $195,980; assets, $3,805,797 (L); gifts received, $1,199,920; expenditures, $375,176.
Limitations: Giving focused in the Adirondack region of NY.
Publications: Newsletter, informational brochure, annual report.
Officers and Trustees:* Meredith Prime, Chair.; David Johnson,* Vice-Chair.; Ann Merkel,* Secy. and Exec. Dir.; Roderic Giltz, Treas.; Cali Brooks, Exec. Dir.; Gary Benware, Adele Connors, Janet Decker, Craig Randall, Carol Ann Young.
EIN: 161535724
Codes: CM

34520
The Stefano La Sala Foundation, Inc.
141 Parkway Rd., Ste. 28
Bronxville, NY 10708-3605
Contact: A. Stephen La Sala, Dir.

Incorporated in 1956 in NY.
Donor(s): Members of the La Sala family, La Sala Contracting Co., Inc.
Financial data (yr. ended 12/31/00): Grants paid, $195,900; assets, $3,412,838 (M); expenditures, $275,671; qualifying distributions, $190,142.
Limitations: Applications not accepted. Giving primarily in the New York, NY, area.
Publications: Annual report.
Application information: Contributes only to pre-selected organizations.
Directors: A. Stephen La Sala, Andrew La Sala, Jr., Anthony J. La Sala, Kenneth La Sala, Sr.
EIN: 136110920
Codes: FD2

34521
Henfield Foundation
c/o Patterson, Belknap, Webb & Tyler, LLP
1133 Ave. of the Americas, Ste. 2200
New York, NY 10036-6710

Established in 1960.
Donor(s): Joseph F. McCrindle.
Financial data (yr. ended 12/31/01): Grants paid, $195,350; assets, $2,735,170 (M); expenditures, $220,406; qualifying distributions, $207,680.
Limitations: Applications not accepted. Giving primarily in New York, NY.
Application information: Contributes only to pre-selected organizations.
Officers and Directors:* Joseph F. McCrindle,* Pres. and Treas.; John Birmingham,* Sr. V.P.; John T. Rowe, Jr.,* V.P.; Antonia M. Grumbach,* Secy.; Sheila Biddle, Robert Frear, Andrew Roger Martindale.
EIN: 136112779
Codes: FD2

34522
The Swanson Foundation
122 E. 42nd St., Rm. 4400
New York, NY 10168 (212) 687-8360
Contact: Arthur Richenthal, Dir.

Incorporated in 1952 in NY.
Financial data (yr. ended 12/31/01): Grants paid, $195,125; assets, $3,916,475 (M); expenditures, $200,734; qualifying distributions, $195,125.
Limitations: Giving primarily in New York, NY.
Director: Arthur Richenthal.
EIN: 136108509
Codes: FD2

34523
George P. Wakefield Residuary Trust
c/o The Bank of New York, Tax Dept.
1 Wall St., 28th Fl.
New York, NY 10286
Application address: c/o Samuel Weinberg, Tr., 600 3rd Ave., New York, NY 10016-2088

Financial data (yr. ended 06/30/01): Grants paid, $195,000; assets, $3,550,277 (M); expenditures, $235,793; qualifying distributions, $202,898.
Limitations: Giving primarily in New York, NY.
Trustees: Samuel Weinberg, The Bank of New York.
EIN: 136079388
Codes: FD2

34524
The Obernauer Foundation, Inc.
60 E. 42nd St., Ste. 1912
New York, NY 10165
Contact: Donna McNairy, Secy.

Incorporated in 1966 in NY as the Marne and Joan Obernauer Foundation.
Donor(s): Marne Obernauer, Marne Obernauer, Jr., Harold Obernauer,‡ Joan S. Obernauer, Marion Gislason Obernauer.‡
Financial data (yr. ended 12/31/01): Grants paid, $194,997; assets, $3,013,365 (M); expenditures, $232,631; qualifying distributions, $194,811.
Limitations: Applications not accepted. Giving primarily in FL, New York, NY, and PA.
Application information: Contributes only to pre-selected organizations. Unsolicited requests for funds not considered or acknowledged.
Officers and Directors:* Marne Obernauer,* Pres.; Joan S. Obernauer,* V.P.; Marne Obernauer, Jr.,* V.P.; Donna McNairy, Secy.
EIN: 956149147
Codes: FD2

34525
Isidor Wiesbader Foundation, Inc.
c/o S.H. Bernstein & Assocs., CPA, PC
85 W. Hawthorne Ave.
Valley Stream, NY 11580

Established in 1987 in NY.
Financial data (yr. ended 06/30/01): Grants paid, $194,500; assets, $2,513,458 (M); expenditures, $210,829; qualifying distributions, $207,859.
Limitations: Giving primarily in NY.
Officers: Peter Diamond, Pres.; Richard Diamond, V.P.
EIN: 112849212

Codes: FD2

34526
Mitchell J. Blutt & Margo K. Blutt Family Foundation
57 E. 90th St.
New York, NY 10128
Contact: Mitchell J. Blutt, Dir.

Established in 1999 in NY.
Donor(s): Mitchell J. Blutt.
Financial data (yr. ended 11/30/02): Grants paid, $194,472; assets, $30,067 (M); gifts received, $65,000; expenditures, $195,737; qualifying distributions, $194,458.
Directors: Margo K. Blutt, Mitchell J. Blutt.
EIN: 134053216
Codes: FD2

34527
First Niagara Bank Foundation
(Formerly Lockport Savings Bank Foundation)
6950 S. Transit Rd.
P.O. Box 514
Lockport, NY 14095-0514 (716) 625-7503
E-mail: patricia.barry@firstniagarabank.com
Contact: Patricia D. Barry, Admin.

Established in 1998 in NY.
Donor(s): Niagara Bancorp, Inc., Lockport Savings Bank, First Niagara Financial Group, Inc., First Niagra Bank.
Financial data (yr. ended 03/31/01): Grants paid, $194,164; assets, $7,155,634 (M); expenditures, $255,720; qualifying distributions, $198,791.
Limitations: Giving primarily in western NY.
Publications: Application guidelines.
Application information: Application form required.
Officers: William Swan, Pres.; Christa Caldwell, V.P.; Robert Murphy, Secy.; Dan Dintino, Treas.
Directors: Gary Fitch, James Miklinski, Kathleen Monti.
EIN: 161549641
Codes: CS, FD2, CD

34528
John N. Blackman, Sr. Foundation
10 E. 40th St., Ste. 2710
New York, NY 10016-0340 (212) 679-0380
Contact: Howard Schain, Pres.

Established in 1988 in NY.
Donor(s): Mutual Marine Office, Inc.
Financial data (yr. ended 08/31/01): Grants paid, $194,000; assets, $3,065,063 (M); expenditures, $197,820; qualifying distributions, $194,000.
Limitations: Giving primarily in NY.
Officer: Howard Schain, Pres.
Trustees: John N. Blackman, Jr., Mark Blackman.
EIN: 222938619

34529
Lovell Family, Ltd.
125 Maiden Ln., 11th Fl.
New York, NY 10038-4912 (212) 709-8600
Contact: Stephen J. Lovell, Pres.

Established in 1962 in NY.
Donor(s): Stephen J. Lovell, Lowell Safety Mgmt. Co., Inc.
Financial data (yr. ended 06/30/01): Grants paid, $194,000; assets, $1,276,868 (M); gifts received, $329,213; expenditures, $268,917; qualifying distributions, $194,550.
Limitations: Applications not accepted. Giving primarily in New York, NY.
Application information: Contributes only to pre-selected organizations.
Officer: Stephen J. Lovell, Pres.

Directors: Barry S. Lovell, Diane P. Lovell, Hope S. Lovell, Wendy S. Lovell.
EIN: 136149611
Codes: FD2

34530
Robert & Lois Pergament Foundation, Inc.
17 W. John St.
Hicksville, NY 11801-1011

Established in 1994 in NY.
Financial data (yr. ended 12/31/00): Grants paid, $194,000; assets, $961,723 (M); expenditures, $201,372; qualifying distributions, $194,000.
Limitations: Applications not accepted. Giving primarily in Boca Raton, FL and NY.
Application information: Contributes only to pre-selected organizations.
Officer: Robert Pergament, Pres.
Directors: Arthur J. Pergament, Fred C. Weisberg.
EIN: 650541786
Codes: FD2

34531
Ushkow Foundation, Inc.
c/o Bama Equities, Inc.
220 E. 63rd St., No. LH
New York, NY 10021
Contact: Maurice A. Deane, Secy.-Treas.

Incorporated in 1956 in NY.
Donor(s): Joseph Ushkow.
Financial data (yr. ended 12/31/01): Grants paid, $193,975; assets, $2,755,731 (M); expenditures, $218,720; qualifying distributions, $204,841.
Limitations: Applications not accepted. Giving primarily in NY, with some emphasis on Nassau County.
Application information: Contributes only to pre-selected organizations.
Officers: Barbara Deane, Pres.; Maurice A. Deane, Secy.-Treas.
EIN: 116006274
Codes: FD2

34532
Pine Level Foundation, Inc.
c/o Ernst & Young
787 7th Ave.
New York, NY 10019
Contact: Terry Eyberg

Incorporated in 1968 in CT as a successor to the Stetson Foundation, a trust established in 1936 in CT.
Donor(s): Iola Wise Stetson.
Financial data (yr. ended 12/31/00): Grants paid, $193,944; assets, $2,072,229 (M); expenditures, $220,154; qualifying distributions, $193,216.
Limitations: Giving primarily in the Northeast.
Application information: Application form not required.
Officers and Directors:* Elizabeth Kratovil,* V.P.; S. Alexander Haverstick,* Secy.
EIN: 237008912
Codes: FD2

34533
The George W. & Patricia A. Wellde Foundation
c/o Goldman Sachs & Co.
85 Broad St., Tax Dept.
New York, NY 10004

Established in 1993 in NY.
Donor(s): George W. Wellde, Jr.
Financial data (yr. ended 07/31/01): Grants paid, $193,717; assets, $5,819,282 (M); gifts received, $1,945,329; expenditures, $297,217; qualifying distributions, $197,717.
Limitations: Applications not accepted. Giving primarily in New York, NY; funding also in VA.

Application information: Contributes only to pre-selected organizations.
Trustees: George W. Wellde, Jr., Patricia A. Wellde.
EIN: 133749673
Codes: FD2

34534
Druckenmiller Foundation
c/o Duquesne Capital Mgmt.
900 3rd Ave., 29th Fl.
New York, NY 10022

Established in 1993 in NY.
Donor(s): Stanley F. Druckenmiller.
Financial data (yr. ended 11/30/01): Grants paid, $193,700; assets, $4,129,889 (M); expenditures, $196,805; qualifying distributions, $196,805.
Limitations: Giving primarily in NY and PA.
Application information: Scholarship applicant must supply transcript and letters of recommendation. Application form required.
Trustees: Fiona Druckenmiller, Stanley F. Druckenmiller.
EIN: 133735187
Codes: FD2, GTI

34535
The Ralph S. Gindi Private Foundation
c/o Reji Gindi, LLC
1430 Broadway, Ste. 308
New York, NY 10118

Donor(s): Jeffrey Gindi, Eli Gindi, Irwin Gindi.
Financial data (yr. ended 12/31/99): Grants paid, $193,675; assets, $630,817 (M); gifts received, $749,697; expenditures, $193,812; qualifying distributions, $193,770.
Limitations: Applications not accepted. Giving primarily in New York, NY.
Application information: Contributes only to pre-selected organizations.
Officers: Jeffrey Gindi, Pres.; Irwin Gindi, V.P.; Eli Gindi, Secy.
EIN: 113431763
Codes: FD2

34536
Abraham and Yvonne Cohen Foundation, Inc.
100 United Nations Plz.
New York, NY 10017-1713

Established in 2000 in NY.
Donor(s): Abraham E. Cohen.
Financial data (yr. ended 11/30/01): Grants paid, $193,600; assets, $835,455 (M); gifts received, $1,033,000; expenditures, $219,326; qualifying distributions, $193,600.
Limitations: Applications not accepted. Giving primarily in New York, NY; some giving also in Quebec, Canada.
Application information: Contributes only to pre-selected organizations.
Officers: Yvette C. Pomerantz, Pres.; Denise A. Cohen, Secy.; Daniel H. Cohen, Treas.
EIN: 522283127
Codes: FD2

34537
The Rainis Family Foundation
c/o Brown, Brothers, Harriman & Co.
59 Wall St.
New York, NY 10005

Established in 1998 in NY.
Donor(s): Eugene C. Rainis.
Financial data (yr. ended 12/31/00): Grants paid, $193,250; assets, $27,334 (M); gifts received, $200,613; expenditures, $193,950; qualifying distributions, $193,950.
Limitations: Applications not accepted.

34537—NEW YORK

Application information: Contributes only to pre-selected organizations.
Officers: Eugene C. Rainis, Chair.; Jane M. Rainis, Pres.; Ellen Rainis Peters, V.P.; Mark E. Rainis, Secy.; David G. Rainis, Treas.
EIN: 133941787
Codes: FD2

34538
The Fascitelli Family Foundation
c/o Elizabeth Cogan
25 East End Ave., Ste. 11G
New York, NY 10028

Established in 1993 in NY.
Donor(s): Michael D. Fascitelli, Elizabeth Cogan Fascitelli.
Financial data (yr. ended 01/31/01): Grants paid, $192,817; assets, $64,370 (M); gifts received, $175,000; expenditures, $193,142; qualifying distributions, $192,808.
Limitations: Applications not accepted. Giving primarily in New York, NY.
Application information: Contributes only to pre-selected organizations.
Trustees: Elizabeth Cogan Fascitelli, Michael D. Fascitelli.
EIN: 133748071
Codes: FD2

34539
Leo & Trude Lemle Family Foundation
c/o Leo K. Lemle
232 E. 83rd St., Ste. 1FW
New York, NY 10028

Established in 1994 in NY.
Donor(s): Leo K. Lemle, Gertrude B. Lemle.
Financial data (yr. ended 11/30/01): Grants paid, $192,675; assets, $1,547,875 (M); gifts received, $99,800; expenditures, $211,872; qualifying distributions, $195,702.
Limitations: Applications not accepted. Giving primarily in New York, NY.
Application information: Contributes only to pre-selected organizations.
Trustees: Gertrude B. Lemle, Laura C. Lemle, Robert S. Lemle.
EIN: 137053800
Codes: FD2

34540
The Forty-Five Foundation
c/o Leslie Gordon Glass
333 E. 57th St.
New York, NY 10022

Established in 1991 in NY.
Donor(s): Leslie Gordon Glass.
Financial data (yr. ended 12/31/01): Grants paid, $192,517; assets, $2,142,409 (M); expenditures, $242,134; qualifying distributions, $200,945.
Limitations: Applications not accepted. Giving limited to NY.
Application information: Contributes only to pre-selected organizations.
Trustee: Leslie Gordon Glass.
EIN: 133586150
Codes: FD2

34541
The Shelley & Donald Rubin Foundation, Inc.
115 5th Ave., 7th Fl.
New York, NY 10003 (212) 780-2035
FAX: (212) 995-1575; E-mail: erich@sdrubin.org; URL: http://www.sdrubin.org
Contact: Evelyn Jones Rich, Exec. Dir.

Established in 1991 in NY.
Donor(s): Donald Rubin, Shelley Rubin, Medical Art Ctr. Hospital.
Financial data (yr. ended 06/30/01): Grants paid, $192,225; assets, $10,042,548 (M); expenditures, $357,825; qualifying distributions, $356,325.
Limitations: Giving limited to the U.S. and PR, with emphasis on New York, NY.
Publications: Application guidelines, grants list.
Application information: The range of funding is between $5000-$60000 maximum, with most grants falling between $5000 and $15000. Application form not required.
Officers: Donald Rubin, Pres.; Shelley Rubin, Secy.; Evelyn Jones Rich, Exec. Dir.
Director: Harvey Sigelbaum.
EIN: 133639542
Codes: FD2

34542
The Robert Z. Greene Foundation
c/o Jenkens & Gilchrist
405 Lexington Ave., 8th Fl.
New York, NY 10174
Contact: Seymour Levine, Tr.

Established in 1947 in NY.
Donor(s): Robert Z. Greene.‡
Financial data (yr. ended 12/31/01): Grants paid, $192,024; assets, $271,055 (M); expenditures, $204,052; qualifying distributions, $199,874.
Limitations: Applications not accepted. Giving primarily in FL and NY.
Application information: Contributes only to pre-selected organizations.
Trustee: Seymour Levine.
EIN: 136121751
Codes: FD2

34543
Picotte Family Foundation Trust
20 Corporate Woods Blvd., Ste. 600
Albany, NY 12211-2370

Established in 1987 in NY.
Donor(s): Kathleen M. Picotte, Picotte Charitable Lead Trusts.
Financial data (yr. ended 12/31/01): Grants paid, $191,850; assets, $2,991,123 (M); gifts received, $112,500; expenditures, $212,333; qualifying distributions, $200,518.
Limitations: Applications not accepted. Giving primarily in the Albany, NY, area.
Application information: Contributes only to pre-selected organizations.
Trustees: Rhea P. Clark, Marcia P. Floyd, John D. Picotte, Michael B. Picotte.
EIN: 141699412
Codes: FD2

34544
Dramatists Guild Fund, Inc.
1501 Broadway
New York, NY 10036 (212) 391-8384
Contact: Susan Drury

Established in 1962 in NY.
Donor(s): Charlotte Kesselring,‡ Sidney S. Kingsley Fund.
Financial data (yr. ended 12/31/00): Grants paid, $191,695; assets, $2,763,552 (M); gifts received, $343,453; expenditures, $338,977; qualifying distributions, $317,871; giving activities include $25,580 for loans to individuals.
Limitations: Giving on a national basis.
Application information: Application form required.
Officers and Directors:* Romulus Linney,* Pres.; Carol Hall,* V.P.; Tina Howe,* Secy.; Susan Birkenhead,* Treas.; Lee Adams, Betty Comden, Charles Fuller, Sheldon Harnick, Herbert Mitgang, Neil Simon.
EIN: 136144932
Codes: FD2, GTI

34545
Maurice & Carol Feinberg Family Foundation
895 Park Ave.
New York, NY 10021

Established in 1993 in NY.
Donor(s): Carol J. Feinberg, Maurice Feinberg.‡
Financial data (yr. ended 11/30/01): Grants paid, $191,500; assets, $2,633,360 (M); expenditures, $195,147; qualifying distributions, $191,677.
Limitations: Applications not accepted. Giving primarily in MA and NY.
Application information: Contributes only to pre-selected organizations.
Officers and Directors:* David Feinberg,* V.P.; Hope Feinberg Schroy,* V.P.; Nancy Feinberg Tobin,* V.P.; Carol J. Feinberg, Secy.-Treas.
EIN: 133746078
Codes: FD2

34546
Eva & Jason Yagoda Charitable Foundation
c/o Krusch & Modell
10 Rockefeller Plz.
New York, NY 10020

Established in 2000.
Donor(s): Eva Yagoda.
Financial data (yr. ended 06/30/01): Grants paid, $191,131; assets, $18,618 (M); gifts received, $197,272; expenditures, $191,246; qualifying distributions, $191,006.
Limitations: Applications not accepted.
Application information: Contributes only to pre-selected organizations.
Trustees: Eva Yagoda, Jason Yagoda.
EIN: 113531503
Codes: FD2

34547
C. D. Shiah Charitable Foundation
c/o Oded Aboodi, Tr.
1700 Broadway, 17th Fl.
New York, NY 10019

Established in 1981 in NY.
Donor(s): Thomas Shiah, Vivien Shiah, Elizabeth Shiah.
Financial data (yr. ended 06/30/01): Grants paid, $191,100; assets, $736,128 (M); gifts received, $250,000; expenditures, $191,662; qualifying distributions, $190,970.
Limitations: Applications not accepted. Giving on a national basis, with emphasis on New York, NY.
Application information: Contributes only to pre-selected organizations.
Trustee: Oded Aboodi.
EIN: 133076929
Codes: FD2

34548
William & Marion Littleford Foundation, Inc.
c/o Citibank, N.A.
1 Court Sq., 22nd Fl.
Long Island City, NY 11120

Established in 1991 in NY.
Donor(s): William D. Littleford, Marian Littleford.
Financial data (yr. ended 12/31/99): Grants paid, $191,071; assets, $1,709,900 (M); expenditures, $211,329; qualifying distributions, $192,992.
Limitations: Applications not accepted. Giving primarily in NY.
Application information: Contributes only to pre-selected organizations.
Officers: William D. Littleford, Pres.; John F. Walsh, Jr., Secy.; Marian Littleford, Treas.
EIN: 133633150
Codes: FD2

34549
The Bradley L. Goldberg Charitable Trust
466 Lexington Ave., 18th Fl.
New York, NY 10017-3140

Established in 1984 in NY.
Donor(s): Jennison Assocs. Capital Corp., Bradley L. Goldberg.
Financial data (yr. ended 12/31/01): Grants paid, $191,000; assets, $5,714,781 (M); gifts received, $2,118,750; expenditures, $198,349; qualifying distributions, $191,330.
Limitations: Applications not accepted. Giving primarily in New York, NY.
Application information: Contributes only to pre-selected organizations.
Trustee: Bradley L. Goldberg.
EIN: 136847767
Codes: FD2

34550
S. Z. & P. R. Zedakah Fund
c/o Pauline Gutfreund
P.O. Box 16
Far Rockaway, NY 11691

Established in 1995 in NY.
Financial data (yr. ended 11/30/99): Grants paid, $190,766; assets, $5,782 (M); gifts received, $194,119; expenditures, $191,510; qualifying distributions, $191,510.
Limitations: Applications not accepted.
Application information: Contributes only to pre-selected organizations.
Trustees: Pauline Gutfruend, S. Gutfruend.
EIN: 113335250
Codes: FD2

34551
The Abby and Mitch Leigh Foundation
49 E. 68th St.
New York, NY 10021-5012

Established in 1987 in NY.
Donor(s): Milton A. Kimmelman.
Financial data (yr. ended 12/31/01): Grants paid, $190,730; assets, $9,329,029 (M); expenditures, $270,406; qualifying distributions, $201,210.
Limitations: Applications not accepted. Giving primarily in New York, NY.
Application information: Contributes only to pre-selected organizations.
Trustees: Abby Leigh, Mitch Leigh.
EIN: 133398045
Codes: FD2

34552
JJC Foundation, Inc.
c/o U.S. Trust
114 W. 47th St.
New York, NY 10036

Established in 1997 in DE.
Donor(s): John Peter Clay.
Financial data (yr. ended 10/31/00): Grants paid, $190,450; assets, $10,039,306 (M); gifts received, $2,500,000; expenditures, $321,427; qualifying distributions, $223,668.
Limitations: Applications not accepted. Giving primarily in London, England.
Application information: Unsolicited requests for funds not accepted.
Officers: Jennifer Mary Ellen Clay, Chair.; Jack Kaplan, Secy.
Director: John Peter Clay.
EIN: 133922180
Codes: FD2

34553
Normandie Foundation, Inc.
c/o Abacus & Assoc.
147 E. 48th St.
New York, NY 10017 (212) 230-9830
Contact: Andrew E. Norman, Pres.

Incorporated in 1966 in NY.
Donor(s): Andrew E. Norman, The Aaron E. Norman Fund, Inc.
Financial data (yr. ended 12/31/99): Grants paid, $190,317; assets, $4,937,423 (M); gifts received, $309,068; expenditures, $223,273; qualifying distributions, $191,049.
Limitations: Giving limited to Barnstable County, MA, and Rockland County and New York, NY.
Application information: Generally, grants are only to organizations with which the officers are personally familiar. Application form not required.
Officers: Andrew E. Norman, Pres. and Treas.; Nancy N. Lassalle, V.P. and Secy.; Abigail Norman, V.P.
EIN: 136213564
Codes: FD2

34554
The George B. & Elizabeth Reese Foundation
c/o Lazard Freres & Co.
30 Rockefeller Plz.
New York, NY 10020
Contact: George B. Reese, Pres.

Established in 1986 in NY.
Donor(s): George B. Reese.
Financial data (yr. ended 06/30/01): Grants paid, $190,000; assets, $5,960 (M); expenditures, $192,580; qualifying distributions, $192,481.
Limitations: Giving primarily in CT.
Application information: Application form not required.
Officers: George B. Reese, Pres.; Elizabeth Reese, V.P.; Howard Sontag, Secy.-Treas.
EIN: 133393532
Codes: FD2

34555
Ruth & Samuel J. Rosenwasser Charitable Trust
c/o JPMorgan Chase Bank
1211 6th Ave., 34th Fl.
New York, NY 10036

Established in 1999 in NY.
Donor(s): S. Rosenwasser.‡
Financial data (yr. ended 12/31/01): Grants paid, $190,000; assets, $1,536,247 (M); expenditures, $220,918; qualifying distributions, $190,000.
Limitations: Applications not accepted.
Application information: Contributes only to pre-selected organizations.
Trustees: Eugene L. Reiser, JPMorgan Chase Bank.
EIN: 526952137

34556
Uphill Foundation
c/o U.S. Trust
114 W. 47th St., (TAXVAS)
New York, NY 10036
Contact: Barry Waldorf

Established in 2000 in PA.
Donor(s): Frances A. Velay.
Financial data (yr. ended 12/31/01): Grants paid, $190,000; assets, $4,087,541 (M); expenditures, $245,559; qualifying distributions, $190,000.
Trustees: Dan McCarthy, Barbara Paul Robinson, Frances A. Velay.
EIN: 137196672
Codes: FD2

34557
Hilliard Foundation, Inc.
100 W. 4th St.
Elmira, NY 14901-2190 (607) 733-7121
Contact: Nelson Mooers van den Blink, Pres.

Donor(s): The Hilliard Corp.
Financial data (yr. ended 04/30/02): Grants paid, $189,800; assets, $1,134,803 (M); expenditures, $194,183; qualifying distributions, $190,855.
Limitations: Giving primarily in Elmira, NY.
Officers and Trustees:* Nelson Mooers van den Blink,* Pres.; Mary Welles Mooers Smith,* V.P.; Gordon Webster,* Treas.; George L. Howell, Gerald F. Schichtel, Paul H. Schweizer, Allen C. Smith, Finley M. Steele, Richard W. Swan, Jan van den Blink.
EIN: 161176159
Codes: CS, FD2, CD

34558
Henry M. Blackmer Foundation, Inc.
c/o JPMorgan Chase Bank
1211 Ave. of the Americas, 34th Fl.
New York, NY 10036

Incorporated in 1952 in DE.
Donor(s): Henry M. Blackmer.‡
Financial data (yr. ended 12/31/01): Grants paid, $189,500; assets, $3,570,970 (M); expenditures, $227,475; qualifying distributions, $195,800.
Limitations: Applications not accepted. Giving on a national basis.
Application information: Contributes only to pre-selected organizations.
Officer: Morton Moskin, Pres.
Trustee: JPMorgan Chase Bank.
EIN: 136097357
Codes: FD2

34559
Joseph & Claire Flom Foundation
c/o Skadden, Arps, Slate, Meagher & Flom
4 Times Sq., 40-132
New York, NY 10036 (212) 735-3222
FAX: (917) 510-1717; *E-mail:*
NLaing7007@aol.com
Contact: Nancy Laing, Exec. Dir.

Established in 1988 in NY.
Donor(s): Claire Flom, Joseph H. Flom.
Financial data (yr. ended 12/31/01): Grants paid, $189,500; assets, $1,078,989 (M); gifts received, $727,694; expenditures, $296,315; qualifying distributions, $289,376.
Limitations: Giving primarily in New York, NY.
Publications: Grants list, program policy statement, application guidelines.
Application information: Application form not required.
Officers and Directors:* Joseph H. Flom,* Pres.; Claire Flom,* Secy.-Treas.; Nancy Laing,* Exec. Dir.; Jason Flom, Peter Flom, Stuart A. Hersch, Raymond McGuire, Susan Butler Plum, Edwin Robbins.
EIN: 133499384
Codes: FD2

34560
Kalkin Family Foundation, Inc.
c/o Saul L. Klaw & Co., P.C.
275 Madison Ave., Ste. 1914
New York, NY 10016-1101
Application address: 5965 Mine Brook Rd., Bernardsville, NJ 07924, tel.: (908) 696-1999
Contact: Eugene Kalkin, Tr.

Established in 1983 in NJ.
Financial data (yr. ended 12/31/01): Grants paid, $189,265; assets, $3,255,119 (M); expenditures, $193,561; qualifying distributions, $189,266.

34560—NEW YORK

Limitations: Giving primarily in NY and VT.
Trustees: Adam Kalkin, Eugene W. Kalkin, Joan Kalkin, Nancy Kalkin, Saul L. Klaw, Stanley Lesser.
EIN: 133185333
Codes: FD2

34561
The Carbetz Foundation, Inc.
c/o U.S. Trust
114 W. 47th St.
New York, NY 10036
Application address: 650 Madison Ave., 23rd Fl., New York, NY 10022
Contact: Carl H. Pforzheimer III, Pres.

Established in 1987.
Donor(s): Elizabeth S. Pforzheimer, Carl H. Pforzheimer III.
Financial data (yr. ended 12/31/00): Grants paid, $189,250; assets, $12,647 (M); gifts received, $180,197; expenditures, $191,558; qualifying distributions, $189,535.
Limitations: Giving primarily in New York, NY.
Officers: Carl H. Pforzheimer III, Pres.; Elizabeth S. Pforzheimer, V.P.; Martin F. Richman, Secy.
EIN: 133431027
Codes: FD2

34562
K.W. Charitable Foundation
4706 18th Ave.
Brooklyn, NY 11204

Established in 1998 in NY.
Financial data (yr. ended 12/31/99): Grants paid, $189,211; assets, $1,233,995 (M); gifts received, $391,760; expenditures, $195,606; qualifying distributions, $189,211.
Limitations: Applications not accepted.
Application information: Contributes only to pre-selected organizations.
Trustee: Robert Wolf.
EIN: 113366771
Codes: FD2

34563
Curtis Family Foundation
c/o Barry Strauss Assocs., Ltd.
307 5th Ave., 8th Fl.
New York, NY 10016-6517

Established in 1993 in NY and FL.
Donor(s): Alan Curtis.
Financial data (yr. ended 10/31/01): Grants paid, $189,097; assets, $1,721,434 (M); expenditures, $209,448; qualifying distributions, $189,167.
Limitations: Applications not accepted. Giving primarily in Palm Beach, FL.
Application information: Contributes only to pre-selected organizations.
Officers: Alan Curtis, Pres.; Christine W. Curtis, Secy.-Treas.
Directors: Bryan Curtis, Linda Curtis, Roberta Curtis, Mark Ginsberg.
EIN: 650441571
Codes: FD2

34564
The Picheny Charitable Trust
322 Central Park West, Ste. 6B
New York, NY 10025-7629

Established in 1997 in NY.
Donor(s): Stanley Picheny, Vivian Picheny.
Financial data (yr. ended 12/31/00): Grants paid, $189,010; assets, $888,103 (M); expenditures, $189,359; qualifying distributions, $188,989.
Limitations: Applications not accepted.
Application information: Contributes only to pre-selected organizations.

Trustees: Lonn Berney, Stanley Picheny, Vivian Picheny.
EIN: 137114720
Codes: FD2

34565
Max A. Adler Charitable Foundation, Inc.
1010 Times Sq. Bldg.
Rochester, NY 14614 (585) 232-7290
Contact: David M. Gray, Pres.

Established in 1969 in NY.
Donor(s): Max A. Adler.‡
Financial data (yr. ended 12/31/01): Grants paid, $189,000; assets, $568 (L); gifts received, $195,000; expenditures, $195,411; qualifying distributions, $189,000.
Limitations: Giving primarily in Monroe County, NY.
Application information: Application form not required.
Officers: David M. Gray, Pres.; Beatrice Schonfeld Rapoport, V.P.; John F. Liebschutz, Treas.
EIN: 160961112
Codes: FD2

34566
The Lucille and Paul Maslin Foundation, Inc.
61 Broadway, 19th Fl.
New York, NY 10006-2794

Established in 2000 in NY.
Financial data (yr. ended 12/31/01): Grants paid, $189,000; assets, $188,777 (M); gifts received, $298,383; expenditures, $198,788; qualifying distributions, $189,456.
Limitations: Applications not accepted.
Application information: Contributes only to pre-selected organizations.
Officers and Directors:* Janet Cheever,* Pres.; Benjamin Cheever,* V.P. and Secy.; Stephen Katz,* Treas.
EIN: 137230954

34567
The K Foundation
555 Madison Ave., Ste. 1105
New York, NY 10022-3301

Established in 1999.
Financial data (yr. ended 12/31/01): Grants paid, $188,850; assets, $67,672 (M); gifts received, $257,255; expenditures, $189,600; qualifying distributions, $188,850.
Directors: Amran Kass, Miriam Kass, Naftali Kass.
EIN: 133780167

34568
Salomon Family Foundation, Inc.
97 Summit Dr.
Hastings-on-Hudson, NY 10706
URL: http://fdncenter.org/grantmaker/salomon
Contact: Bernice Kurchin, Pres.

Established in 1996 in FL.
Donor(s): Samuel Salomon.
Financial data (yr. ended 04/30/01): Grants paid, $188,500; assets, $798,796 (M); gifts received, $392,752; expenditures, $238,509; qualifying distributions, $231,574.
Limitations: Giving primarily in the eastern U.S.
Publications: Financial statement, informational brochure, application guidelines.
Application information: Application form required.
Officers and Trustees:* Bernice Kurchin,* Pres.; Eve LaBelle,* V.P.; Patricia Salomon,* Secy.; Morton Salomon,* Treas.; Julio Rodriguez.
EIN: 656232937
Codes: FD2

34569
Jacques and Natasha Gelman Trust
c/o McLaughlin & Stern, LLP
260 Madison Ave., 18th Fl.
New York, NY 10016-2401 (212) 448-1100
Contact: Janet C. Neschis, Tr.

Established in 1998 in NY.
Financial data (yr. ended 11/30/00): Grants paid, $188,360; assets, $12,117,439 (M); gifts received, $140,125; expenditures, $570,621; qualifying distributions, $235,573.
Trustees: Marylin G. Diamond, Janet C. Neschis.
EIN: 137166150
Codes: FD2

34570
REBNY Foundation, Inc.
c/o The Real Estate Board of New York, Inc.
570 Lexington Ave.
New York, NY 10022 (212) 532-3100
Contact: Marolyn Davenport

Incorporated in 1985 in NY.
Donor(s): The Real Estate Board of New York, Inc.
Financial data (yr. ended 06/30/01): Grants paid, $188,122; assets, $213,751 (M); gifts received, $427,971; expenditures, $410,803; qualifying distributions, $382,274.
Limitations: Giving limited to New York, NY.
Officers: Bernard M. Mendik, Pres.; Daniel Brodsky, V.P.; Jerry Cohen, V.P.; James Digney, V.P.; Dan J. Gronich, V.P.; Samuel Lindenbaum, V.P.; Burton Resnick, V.P.; Edward Riguardi, V.P.; William Rudin, V.P.; Steven Spinola, V.P.; Elizabeth Stribling, V.P.; Fred Wilpon, V.P.; Leonard Litwin, Secy.
EIN: 133317104
Codes: FD2

34571
The Quincy Jones Listen Up Foundation
(Formerly Listen Up Foundation)
c/o Ann Burke, Time Warner, Inc.
75 Rockefeller Plz., Ste. 533
New York, NY 10019 (212) 484-6401
Contact: Toni Fay, V.P.

Donor(s): Clarence Avant, Bernard Beiser, Wendy Beiser.
Financial data (yr. ended 12/31/00): Grants paid, $188,102; assets, $40,926 (M); gifts received, $234,718; expenditures, $325,738; qualifying distributions, $320,626.
Limitations: Giving primarily in Los Angeles, CA and New York, NY.
Officers and Directors:* Quincy Jones,* Pres.; Toni G. Fay, V.P. and Secy.; Lisette Derouaux, V.P. and Exec. Dir.; Joseph Morello, Treas.; Marilyn Bergman, Clint Eastwood, Gloria Estefan, Richard Parsons.
EIN: 133586397
Codes: FD2

34572
Chitrik Family Charitable Foundation
590 5th Ave.
New York, NY 10036

Established in 1999 in NY.
Donor(s): Citra Trading Corp.
Financial data (yr. ended 12/31/01): Grants paid, $188,044; assets, $19,216 (M); gifts received, $199,510; expenditures, $188,146; qualifying distributions, $188,146.
Limitations: Giving primarily in Brooklyn, NY.
Officer: Hirsch Chitrik, Pres.
EIN: 137167506
Codes: FD2

34573
N. S. Goldstein Foundation, Inc.
c/o Willikie, Farr and Gallagher
787 7th Ave., Ste. 3950
New York, NY 10019-6099
Application address: 150 E. 69th St., New York, NY 10021
Contact: Marjorie Doniger, Pres.

Incorporated in 1956 in NY.
Donor(s): Nathan S. Goldstein,‡ Rosalie W. Goldstein.‡
Financial data (yr. ended 10/31/01): Grants paid, $188,037; assets, $3,358,513 (M); expenditures, $192,268; qualifying distributions, $183,160.
Limitations: Giving primarily in NY.
Officers: Marjorie Doniger, Pres. and Treas.; Burt J. Goldstein, V.P.; Alan Doniger, Secy.-Treas.
EIN: 136127750
Codes: FD2

34574
The Lagemann Foundation
c/o Diamond, Wohl, Fried, & Leonard
1775 Broadway, Ste. 419
New York, NY 10019-1903

Established in 1944 in NY.
Financial data (yr. ended 12/31/01): Grants paid, $188,000; assets, $2,260,615 (M); expenditures, $205,619; qualifying distributions, $194,180.
Limitations: Applications not accepted. Giving primarily in NY.
Application information: Contributes only to pre-selected organizations.
Officers: Peter J. Lagemann, Pres.; Carter S. Bacon, Jr., Secy.; Franklyn E. Parker, Treas.
EIN: 136115306
Codes: FD2

34575
Howard and Bess Chapman Charitable Corporation
c/o Alliance Bank, N.A., Trust Dept.
160 Main St.
Oneida, NY 13421
Application address: c/o Peter Dunn, 109 Farrier Ave., P.O. Box 58, Oneida, NY 13421-0058, FAX: (315) 363-4195
Contact: Peter M. Dunn, Secy.

Established in 1989 in NY.
Financial data (yr. ended 10/31/01): Grants paid, $187,552; assets, $3,419,453 (M); expenditures, $231,682; qualifying distributions, $198,445.
Limitations: Giving primarily in Oneida, NY.
Application information: Application form not required.
Officers and Directors:* John G. Haskell,* Pres.; Robert H. Fearon, Jr.,* V.P.; Peter M. Dunn,* Secy. and Genl. Counsel; Steven Schneeweiss,* Treas.; Rowland Stevens.
EIN: 161373396
Codes: FD2

34576
The Hope & Norman Hope Foundation
c/o Cadwalader
100 Maiden Ln.
New York, NY 10038 (212) 504-6926
Contact: Jennifer B. Jordan, Tr.

Established in 1996 in NY.
Donor(s): Hope D. Douglas.‡
Financial data (yr. ended 12/31/01): Grants paid, $187,500; assets, $1,973,888 (M); expenditures, $330,369; qualifying distributions, $294,651.
Limitations: Giving primarily in NY.
Trustee: Jennifer B. Jordan.
EIN: 137099599
Codes: FD2

34577
Melvin & Sylvia Kafka Foundation, Inc.
200 E. 66th St.
New York, NY 10021-6703
Application address: c/o Wiener, Frushtick & Straub, 500 5th Ave., New York, NY 10110

Financial data (yr. ended 12/31/99): Grants paid, $187,355; assets, $743,112 (M); expenditures, $193,915; qualifying distributions, $185,882.
Limitations: Giving primarily in New York, NY.
Officers: Sylvia Kafka, Pres.; Elaine Suchman, V.P.
EIN: 136134569

34578
The Trott Family Foundation
c/o Goldman Sachs & Co.
85 Broad St., Tax Dept.
New York, NY 10004

Established in 1996 in IL.
Donor(s): Byron D. Trott.
Financial data (yr. ended 08/31/01): Grants paid, $187,311; assets, $4,513,215 (M); gifts received, $1,234,379; expenditures, $241,381; qualifying distributions, $189,881.
Limitations: Applications not accepted. Giving primarily in IL and MO.
Application information: Contributes only to pre-selected organizations.
Trustees: Byron D. Trott, Tina L. Trott.
EIN: 133919816
Codes: FD2

34579
Ralph and Lucy Palleschi Family Foundation
c/o FLII
1 Jericho Plz.
Jericho, NY 11753
Contact: Ralph F. Palleschi, Tr.

Established in 1999 in NY.
Donor(s): Ralph F. Palleschi.
Financial data (yr. ended 12/31/00): Grants paid, $187,000; assets, $310,671 (M); gifts received, $208,438; expenditures, $187,675; qualifying distributions, $186,735.
Limitations: Giving primarily in Long Island, NY.
Application information: Application form not required.
Trustees: Lucy Palleschi, Ralph F. Palleschi.
EIN: 113507211
Codes: FD2

34580
Isidore Stern Foundation
60 E. 42nd St., Rm. 1148
New York, NY 10165-0033

Established in 1943 in NY.
Financial data (yr. ended 12/31/01): Grants paid, $186,950; assets, $2,332,088 (M); expenditures, $196,128; qualifying distributions, $186,163.
Limitations: Applications not accepted. Giving primarily in NY.
Application information: Contributes only to pre-selected organizations.
Trustees: James A. Stern, Richard M. Stern, Theodore L. Stern.
EIN: 136113256
Codes: FD2

34581
The East West Management Institute
575 Madison Ave., 25th Fl.
New York, NY 10022
E-mail: info@ewmi.org

Established in 1998 in NY.
Donor(s): Open Society Fund, Inc.

Financial data (yr. ended 12/31/00): Grants paid, $186,857; assets, $5,660,953 (M); gifts received, $101,047; expenditures, $12,883,483; qualifying distributions, $186,857; giving activities include $8,281,940 for programs.
Limitations: Giving primarily in Eastern Europe.
Application information: Application form not required.
Officer and Directors:* Adrian Hewryk,* Pres.; Stewart Paperin, Nina Rosenwald, Walter Weiner, Byron Wien.
EIN: 133586432
Codes: FD2

34582
The RDM Foundation
992 E. 15th St.
Brooklyn, NY 11230

Established in 1996 in NY.
Donor(s): Rosenthal Family Charitable Lead Annuity Trust.
Financial data (yr. ended 12/31/00): Grants paid, $186,630; assets, $583,398 (M); gifts received, $340,000; expenditures, $187,312; qualifying distributions, $186,624.
Limitations: Applications not accepted.
Application information: Contributes only to pre-selected organizations.
Trustee: Judy Rosenthal.
EIN: 116472758
Codes: FD2

34583
The Emory and Ilona E. Ladanyi Foundation, Inc.
P.O. Box 6
Merrick, NY 11566-0006
Contact: Andrew S. Erdelyi, Pres.

Established in 1987 in NY.
Donor(s): Ilona Ladanyi.‡
Financial data (yr. ended 10/31/01): Grants paid, $186,150; assets, $512,018 (M); expenditures, $253,292; qualifying distributions, $186,001.
Limitations: Giving on a national basis.
Application information: Applicants must submit sample portfolio.
Officer: Andrew S. Erdelyi,* Pres. and Treas.
Directors: Elizabeth Hogan, Edward Kowalcyk.
EIN: 133448832
Codes: FD2, GTI

34584
The Fred and Suzan Ehrman Foundation
115 Central Park West, No. 6A
New York, NY 10023

Established in 1968 in NY.
Donor(s): Fred Ehrman.
Financial data (yr. ended 12/31/01): Grants paid, $185,716; assets, $5,229,744 (M); gifts received, $15,000; expenditures, $194,702; qualifying distributions, $185,716.
Limitations: Applications not accepted. Giving primarily in NY.
Application information: Contributes only to pre-selected organizations.
Officers and Directors:* Fred Ehrman,* Pres. and Treas.; Suzan Ehrman,* V.P.; Lawrence Kobrin.
EIN: 136271584
Codes: FD2

34585
The Hultquist Foundation
c/o Morgan Stanley & Co.
1221 Ave. of the Americas
New York, NY 10020
Contact: Timothy Hultquist, Pres.

Established in 1991 in DE.

Donor(s): Timothy Hultquist.
Financial data (yr. ended 12/31/01): Grants paid, $185,000; assets, $2,411,276 (M); expenditures, $190,303; qualifying distributions, $186,270.
Limitations: Applications not accepted. Giving primarily in Fairfield County, CT, and the metropolitan New York, NY, area.
Officers: Timothy Hultquist, Pres.; Cynthia M. Hultquist, V.P.
Director: Wayne B. Hultquist.
EIN: 980120582
Codes: FD2

34586
The Wildes Family Foundation, Inc.
c/o Winkler & Co.
345 7th Ave., 21st Fl.
New York, NY 10001

Established in 200 in NY.
Donor(s): Leon Wildes.
Financial data (yr. ended 12/31/00): Grants paid, $185,000; assets, $57,044 (M); gifts received, $213,150; expenditures, $188,046; qualifying distributions, $186,648.
Limitations: Giving primarily in NY.
Officer: Leon Wildes, Pres.
EIN: 134049917
Codes: FD2

34587
WJS Foundation, Inc.
c/o JPMorgan Chase Bank
1211 6th Ave., 34th Fl.
New York, NY 10036

Established in 1997 in NJ.
Donor(s): Walter J. Shipley.
Financial data (yr. ended 12/31/00): Grants paid, $185,000; assets, $2,847,614 (M); expenditures, $265,507; qualifying distributions, $169,207.
Limitations: Applications not accepted. Giving primarily in NJ and NY.
Application information: Contributes only to pre-selected organizations.
Officers and Directors:* Walter J. Shipley,* Pres.; Judith L. Shipley,* V.P. and Secy.; Allison P. Shipley, Treas.; Barbara S. Pandoli, John P. Shipley, Pamela J. Shipley, Dorothy S. Stabolepszy.
EIN: 223514762
Codes: FD2

34588
Kenneth L. and Katherine G. Koessler Family Foundation, Inc.
c/o Stephen Juhasz, Jr.
124 Brantwood Rd.
Snyder, NY 14226

Established in 1991 in NY.
Donor(s): Members of the Brosnahan family, and members of the Koessler family, Anne Laura K. Brosnahan, Katherine K. Juhasz, Kenneth L. Koessler, Jr.
Financial data (yr. ended 12/31/01): Grants paid, $184,500; assets, $6,032,744 (M); gifts received, $136,445; expenditures, $237,243; qualifying distributions, $184,500.
Limitations: Giving limited to the western NY area.
Officers: Anne Laura K. Brosnahan, Pres.; Katherine K. Juhasz, Secy.; Stephen G. Juhasz, Jr., Treas.
Directors: William P. Brosnahan, Jr., Kenneth L. Koessler, Jr., Paula K. Koessler.
EIN: 223137752
Codes: FD2

34589
The Steven T. Mnuchin Foundation
c/o Goldman Sachs & Co.
85 Broad St., Tax Dept.
New York, NY 10004

Established in 1996 in NY.
Donor(s): Steven T. Mnuchin.
Financial data (yr. ended 11/30/01): Grants paid, $184,460; assets, $5,036,442 (M); gifts received, $1,220,156; expenditures, $280,865; qualifying distributions, $188,577.
Limitations: Applications not accepted.
Application information: Contributes only to pre-selected organizations.
Trustees: Heather C. Mnuchin, Robert E. Mnuchin, Steven T. Mnuchin.
EIN: 133990500
Codes: FD2

34590
Pearson-Rappaport Foundation
c/o The Ayco Co., LP
P.O. Box 15014
Albany, NY 12212-5014

Established in 1997 in CT.
Donor(s): Andrall E. Pearson, Jill P. Rappaport, Joanne P. Pearson.
Financial data (yr. ended 12/31/01): Grants paid, $184,385; assets, $2,330,614 (M); gifts received, $196,350; expenditures, $192,527; qualifying distributions, $183,743.
Limitations: Applications not accepted. Giving on a national basis.
Application information: Contributes only to pre-selected organizations.
Trustees: Andrall E. Pearson, Joanne P. Pearson, Alan H. Rappaport, Jill P. Rappaport.
EIN: 061484929
Codes: FD2

34591
Rare Breeds Survival Foundation of America
c/o Hyman L. Battle, Jr.
75 E. 55th St.
New York, NY 10022 (212) 856-6800

Established in 1977 in DE.
Donor(s): Michael M. Rosenberg.
Financial data (yr. ended 12/31/99): Grants paid, $184,347; assets, $6,972 (M); gifts received, $189,950; expenditures, $185,334; qualifying distributions, $185,334.
Limitations: Giving on a national and international basis.
Officers and Directors:* Hyman L. Battle, Jr.,* Pres. and Treas.; Robert P. Belnap,* V.P.; Edward L. Peck,* Secy.
EIN: 132909879
Codes: FD2

34592
The Geri & Lester Pollack Family Foundation, Inc.
(Formerly The Pollack Family Foundation, Inc.)
30 Rockefeller Plz.
New York, NY 10020
Contact: Lester Pollack, Pres.

Established in 1986 in NY.
Donor(s): Lester Pollack.
Financial data (yr. ended 09/30/01): Grants paid, $184,126; assets, $1,240,225 (M); gifts received, $224,973; expenditures, $184,456; qualifying distributions, $184,456.
Limitations: Giving primarily in New York, NY.
Officers and Directors:* Lester Pollack,* Pres.; Geri Pollack,* V.P.; Howard Sontag,* Secy.-Treas.
EIN: 133384943
Codes: FD2

34593
Davidowitz Foundation, Inc.
220 W. 19th St., Ste. 2A
New York, NY 10011
Application address: Line and Grove St., Nanticoke, PA 18634, tel.: (717) 735-3200
Contact: Jeff Davidowitz, Pres.

Established in 1957 in NY.
Donor(s): William Davidowitz, Penn Footwear Co., Jibs Equities, Columbia Footwear Co.
Financial data (yr. ended 12/31/99): Grants paid, $183,294; assets, $998,713 (M); gifts received, $202,938; expenditures, $210,188; qualifying distributions, $180,624.
Limitations: Giving primarily in PA.
Application information: Application form not required.
Officer: Jeff Davidowitz, Pres.
EIN: 136102755
Codes: FD2

34594
The Houghton Foundation, Inc.
c/o Market Street Trust Co.
80 E. Market St., Ste. 300
Corning, NY 14830

Incorporated in 1955 in NY.
Donor(s): Arthur A. Houghton, Jr.,‡ Amory Houghton.‡
Financial data (yr. ended 12/31/01): Grants paid, $183,103; assets, $2,377,517 (M); expenditures, $208,208; qualifying distributions, $182,656.
Limitations: Applications not accepted. Giving primarily in Corning, NY.
Application information: Contributes only to pre-selected organizations.
Officers and Trustees:* Amory Houghton, Jr.,* Pres.; Alanson B. Houghton II,* V.P.; James R. Houghton,* V.P.; Rowland Stebbins III, Secy.-Treas.; Laura R. Houghton.
EIN: 166028719
Codes: FD2

34595
The Chesed Global Foundation, Inc.
c/o Eli Robins
1333 Broadway, Rm. 730
New York, NY 10018

Established in 1991 in NY.
Donor(s): Esther Scharf.
Financial data (yr. ended 10/31/01): Grants paid, $182,984; assets, $1,748,791 (M); gifts received, $173,423; expenditures, $189,135; qualifying distributions, $181,269.
Limitations: Applications not accepted.
Application information: Contributes only to pre-selected organizations.
Officers: Esther Scharf, Pres.; Samuel Offen, V.P. and Secy.
Director: Charles Scharf.
EIN: 133648412
Codes: FD2

34596
The William G. Walters Foundation
c/o Sand Bros. & Co., Ltd.
90 Park Ave.
New York, NY 10016

Established in 1986.
Donor(s): William G. Walters.
Financial data (yr. ended 11/30/01): Grants paid, $182,870; assets, $770,917 (M); gifts received, $151,742; expenditures, $192,369; qualifying distributions, $182,945.
Limitations: Applications not accepted. Giving primarily in New York, NY.

Application information: Contributes only to pre-selected organizations.
Officers: William G. Walters, Pres.; Elliot J. Smith, V.P. and Treas.
EIN: 133387377
Codes: FD2

34597
Max & Clara Fortunoff Foundation
70 Charles Lindbergh Blvd.
Uniondale, NY 11553
Contact: Helene Fortunoff, Pres.

Established in 1959 in NY.
Donor(s): Max Fortunoff, Alan Fortunoff,‡ Marjorie Mayrock.‡
Financial data (yr. ended 12/31/01): Grants paid, $182,600; assets, $74,595 (M); gifts received, $114,394; expenditures, $182,743; qualifying distributions, $182,743.
Limitations: Giving primarily in NY.
Officer: Helene Fortunoff, Pres.
EIN: 116036903
Codes: FD2

34598
Suzanne M. Nora Johnson and David G. Johnson Foundation
c/o Goldman Sachs & Co.
85 Broad St., Tax Dept.
New York, NY 10004

Established in 1993 in NY.
Donor(s): Suzanne M. Nora Johnson.
Financial data (yr. ended 01/31/01): Grants paid, $182,575; assets, $4,382,848 (M); gifts received, $2,425,806; expenditures, $185,599; qualifying distributions, $182,585.
Limitations: Applications not accepted.
Application information: Contributes only to pre-selected organizations.
Trustees: David G. Johnson, Suzanne M. Nora Johnson.
EIN: 133748062
Codes: FD2

34599
Isaac Gordon Foundation, Inc.
c/o Robert Gordon
1530 First Federal Plz.
Rochester, NY 14614-1974

Incorporated in 1951 in NY.
Financial data (yr. ended 09/30/01): Grants paid, $182,260; assets, $281,687 (M); expenditures, $185,910; qualifying distributions, $181,914.
Limitations: Applications not accepted. Giving primarily in NY.
Application information: Contributes only to pre-selected organizations.
Officers: Robert Gordon, Pres.; Donald Sasso, V.P.; Beryl Nusbaum, Secy.
EIN: 237425361
Codes: FD2

34600
The Persepolis Foundation
c/o Goldman Sachs & Co.
85 Broad St., Tax Dept.
New York, NY 10005

Established in 1999 in NY.
Donor(s): Sharmin Mossavar-Rahmani.
Financial data (yr. ended 12/31/01): Grants paid, $182,187; assets, $4,046,883 (M); gifts received, $2,500; expenditures, $219,665; qualifying distributions, $200,505.
Limitations: Applications not accepted. Giving primarily in Washington, DC, MA, and NY.
Application information: Contributes only to pre-selected organizations.

Trustees: Bijan Mossavar-Rahmani, Sharmin Mossavar-Rahmani.
EIN: 134093707
Codes: FD2

34601
J. Homer Butler Foundation
30 W. 16th St.
New York, NY 10011
FAX: (718) 442-5088
Contact: Dorothy Montalto, Grant Admin.

Incorporated in 1961 in NY.
Donor(s): Mabel A. Tod.‡
Financial data (yr. ended 12/31/01): Grants paid, $182,000; assets, $5,162,409 (M); expenditures, $262,069; qualifying distributions, $234,403.
Limitations: Giving to domestic organizations for programs in the U.S., Central and South America, Africa, and Asia.
Publications: Informational brochure (including application guidelines).
Application information: Application form required.
Officers and Directors:* Rev. Henry Zenorini,* Pres.; Rev. James F. Keenan,* V.P.; Nicholas Montalto,* Secy.; Bro. John J. Campbell, Rev. David Casey, Daniel H. Coleman, M.D., Rev. Francis P. Golden, Rev. James P. Higgins, Joan MacLean, Dorothy Montalto, Rev. John Replogle, F. Patrick Rogers, Michael Ross.
EIN: 136126669
Codes: FD2

34602
Crosswicks Foundation, Ltd.
924 West End Ave.
New York, NY 10025
CT tel.: (860) 626-0523

Established in 1972 in NY.
Financial data (yr. ended 11/30/01): Grants paid, $182,000; assets, $3,635,375 (M); expenditures, $223,752; qualifying distributions, $179,940.
Limitations: Giving on a national basis.
Application information: Application form not required.
Officers: Madeleine L'Engle Franklin, Pres.; Josephine Jones, V.P.; Laurie Franklin, Secy.
EIN: 132732197
Codes: FD2

34603
Theodore & Cashmere Mendick Foundation, Inc.
468 Ridge Rd. E.
Rochester, NY 14621-1222

Established in 1986 in NY.
Donor(s): Theodore Mendick.‡
Financial data (yr. ended 07/31/01): Grants paid, $181,849; assets, $3,803,281 (M); expenditures, $233,407; qualifying distributions, $195,585.
Limitations: Applications not accepted. Giving primarily in NY.
Application information: Contributes only to pre-selected organizations.
Officers: John Mendick, Pres.; Peter Mendick, V.P. and Secy.; A. Michael Mendick, Treas.
EIN: 161289406
Codes: FD2

34604
Louis Berkowitz Family Foundation, Inc.
1 Huntington Quad., Ste. 2S12
Melville, NY 11747 (631) 420-4370
FAX: (631) 420-4372
Contact: John E. Tuchler, Pres.

Established in 1983 in NY.
Donor(s): Louis Berkowitz.‡

Financial data (yr. ended 12/31/01): Grants paid, $181,000; assets, $7,225,000 (M); expenditures, $201,000; qualifying distributions, $181,000.
Limitations: Giving primarily in the metropolitan New York, NY, area.
Application information: Application form not required.
Officers and Directors:* John E. Tuchler,* Pres.; Mollie Auerbach,* V.P.; Herbert Cohen,* V.P.; Blanche Heiling,* V.P.; Ruth Martin,* V.P.; Frederick Siegmund,* Secy.; Louis Katz,* Treas.; Gail Hoeffner, Michael Martin, Lynn Schor, Helen Sherman.
EIN: 133190334
Codes: FD2

34605
Geraldine S. Violet Charitable Foundation
c/o JPMorgan Chase Bank
1211 Avenue of The Americas, 34th Fl.
New York, NY 10036

Established in 1996 in NY.
Financial data (yr. ended 08/31/01): Grants paid, $181,000; assets, $3,646,330 (M); expenditures, $278,719; qualifying distributions, $190,847.
Limitations: Applications not accepted.
Application information: Contributes only to pre-selected organizations.
Trustees: Eugene E. Ressler, JPMorgan Chase Bank.
EIN: 136952499
Codes: FD2

34606
Keren D.E.R.L., Inc.
c/o Zev Fishman
4600 14th Ave.
Brooklyn, NY 11219

Established in 1989 in NY.
Donor(s): Zev Fishman, David Ben Mayer, Nachum Fishman, Simcha Fishman.
Financial data (yr. ended 02/28/01): Grants paid, $180,850; assets, $96,646 (M); gifts received, $49,500; expenditures, $182,146; qualifying distributions, $180,900.
Limitations: Applications not accepted. Giving limited to Brooklyn, NY.
Application information: Contributes only to pre-selected organizations.
Officer: Zev Fishman, Mgr.
EIN: 133533229
Codes: FD2

34607
William Nelson Cromwell Foundation for the Research of the Law and Legal History of the Colonial Period of the U.S.A.
c/o Sullivan & Cromwell
125 Broad St.
New York, NY 10004-2498 (212) 558-4000
Contact: Henry Christensen, III, Tr.

Established in 1930 in NY.
Financial data (yr. ended 11/30/01): Grants paid, $180,807; assets, $3,746,051 (M); expenditures, $319,581; qualifying distributions, $201,530.
Limitations: Giving primarily in NY.
Trustees: Henry Christensen III, Hon. Jose Cabranes, Merrell Clark, Jr., Robert B. Fiske, John D. Gordan III, Conrad Harper, Hon. Judith S. Kaye, Robert MacCrate, Hon. Michael Mukasey, Hon. James L. Oakes, Barbara P. Robinson, Frederick A.O. Schwarz, Jr., Leon Silverman, Hon. Harold R. Tyler, Jr.
EIN: 136068485
Codes: FD2, GTI

34608
The Stanley & Nancy Grossman Family Foundation
100 Park Ave., 26th Fl.
New York, NY 10017-5516

Established in 1994 in DE and NY.
Donor(s): Stanley Grossman, Nancy Grossman.
Financial data (yr. ended 12/31/00): Grants paid, $180,776; assets, $329,539 (M); gifts received, $107,843; expenditures, $187,745; qualifying distributions, $181,175.
Limitations: Applications not accepted. Giving primarily in New York, NY.
Application information: Contributes only to pre-selected organizations.
Officers: Stanley Grossman, Pres. and Secy.; Nancy Grossman, V.P. and Treas.
EIN: 133800204
Codes: FD2

34609
Heathcote Art Foundation, Inc.
c/o Condon, O'Meara, McGinty & Donnelly, LLP
3 New York Plz., 18th Fl.
New York, NY 10004 (212) 661-7777
Contact: Mercy Bona Pavelic, Pres.

Incorporated in 1964 in NY.
Donor(s): Josephine Mercy Heathcote Haskell.‡
Financial data (yr. ended 10/31/00): Grants paid, $180,600; assets, $2,821,429 (M); expenditures, $400,337; qualifying distributions, $366,852.
Limitations: Giving primarily in the metropolitan New York, NY, area.
Publications: Grants list, informational brochure (including application guidelines).
Application information: Renewal grants not considered for 3 fiscal years. Application guidelines available on website. Application form required.
Officers and Directors:* Mercy Bona Pavelic,* Pres. and Treas.; Lorraine Miles,* V.P.; Josephine P. Newsome,* Secy.; Marie Therese Droutskoy, Richard Mason, Patricia Newsome.
EIN: 510201123
Codes: FD2

34610
Rose and Sherle Wagner Foundation
250 W. 57th St., Ste. 820
New York, NY 10107 (212) 581-6922
FAX: (212) 245-1889; E-mail: wagnerfund@aol.com
Contact: Amy Wagner

Established in 1994 in NY.
Donor(s): Rose Wagner, Sherle Wagner.‡
Financial data (yr. ended 12/31/01): Grants paid, $180,600; assets, $6,153,640 (M); gifts received, $278,876; expenditures, $286,942; qualifying distributions, $238,685.
Limitations: Applications not accepted. Giving primarily in NY.
Application information: Contributes only to pre-selected organizations.
Trustee: Rose Wagner.
EIN: 133738106
Codes: FD2

34611
Beryl H. Doft Foundation, Inc.
124 Fulton St.
Lawrence, NY 11559

Established in 1947 in NY.
Donor(s): Barry Escott, Emanuel Doft, Avrom Doft, Doft & Co., Inc., Arlene Doft, David Doft.
Financial data (yr. ended 12/31/00): Grants paid, $180,550; assets, $66,396 (M); gifts received, $30,580; expenditures, $183,075; qualifying distributions, $182,262.
Limitations: Applications not accepted. Giving primarily in NY.
Application information: Contributes only to pre-selected organizations.
Officers: Emanuel Doft, Pres.; Avrom Doft, V.P.; Barry Escott, Secy.
Directors: Arlene Doft, David Doft, Jacob Doft.
EIN: 116035628
Codes: FD2

34612
Spaulding Family Foundation Trust
251 Elm St.
Buffalo, NY 14203-1603

Established in 1991 in NY.
Donor(s): Anne W. Spaulding.
Financial data (yr. ended 11/30/00): Grants paid, $180,500; assets, $2,981,387 (M); expenditures, $225,011; qualifying distributions, $180,500.
Limitations: Applications not accepted. Giving primarily in Buffalo, NY.
Application information: Contributes only to pre-selected organizations.
Trustees: Anne S. Rose, Allen P. Spaulding, Jr., Anne W. Spaulding, Frederick A. Spaulding, William V.R. Spaulding.
EIN: 166363027
Codes: FD2

34613
Harold L. Wyman Foundation, Inc.
c/o C. Jerry Ploss and Co.
111 Bowmon Ave., Ste. C
Rye Brook, NY 10573-1065
E-mail: WGK10@earthlink.net
Contact: Walter G. Korntheuer, Fdn. Mgr.

Established in 1965 in NY.
Financial data (yr. ended 09/30/01): Grants paid, $180,500; assets, $3,244,777 (M); expenditures, $193,994; qualifying distributions, $183,458.
Limitations: Applications not accepted. Giving primarily in CA, CT, FL, MA and NY.
Application information: Contributes only to pre-selected organizations. Unsolicited requests for funds not accepted.
Officers: Otto Korntheuer,* Pres.; Barbara M. Korntheuer, V.P.; Diane Korntheuer, V.P.; Walter G. Korntheuer, Secy.-Treas.
EIN: 136201289
Codes: FD2

34614
The Jim Jacobs Charitable Foundation
450 Park Ave., Ste. 1001
New York, NY 10022

Established in 1998 in NY.
Donor(s): Loraine Jacobs.
Financial data (yr. ended 12/31/01): Grants paid, $180,000; assets, $2,826,098 (M); expenditures, $234,558; qualifying distributions, $189,730.
Limitations: Applications not accepted. Giving primarily in NY.
Application information: Contributes only to pre-selected organizations.
Officers: Loraine Jacobs, Pres.; Timothy M. Costello, Secy.-Trea.
Directors: James Brady, Martin H. Lager.
EIN: 134008195
Codes: FD2

34615
The Tebil Foundation, Inc.
c/o Edward I. Speer, CPA
550 Mamaroneck Ave., Ste. 504
Harrison, NY 10528

Established in 1959 in NY.
Donor(s): William K. Jacobs.‡
Financial data (yr. ended 12/31/01): Grants paid, $180,000; assets, $3,702,619 (M); expenditures, $183,961; qualifying distributions, $181,530.
Limitations: Applications not accepted. Giving primarily in New York, NY.
Application information: Contributes only to pre-selected organizations.
Officers: George DeSipio, Pres.; Steve Loeb, V.P.
Director: Bernard Kahn.
EIN: 136082546
Codes: FD2

34616
The Reba Judith Sandler Foundation, Inc.
c/o Yohalem Gillman & Co., LLP
477 Madison Ave.
New York, NY 10022-5802
Contact: Sheri C. Sandler, Pres.

Established in 1996 in NY.
Donor(s): Reba Sandler Charitable Lead Trust, Sheri C. Sandler.
Financial data (yr. ended 12/31/01): Grants paid, $179,925; assets, $1,505,861 (M); gifts received, $342,746; expenditures, $191,859; qualifying distributions, $185,665.
Limitations: Applications not accepted. Giving primarily in NY.
Application information: Contributes only to pre-selected organizations.
Officers: Sheri C. Sandler, Pres.; Barry W. Silverstein, Secy.-Treas.
EIN: 133919640
Codes: FD2

34617
Blythmour Corporation
c/o Winston & Strawn
200 Park Ave., 28th Fl.
New York, NY 10166 (212) 351-3000
Contact: David F. Kroenlein, Secy.-Treas.

Established in 1951 in NY.
Donor(s): Lloyd S. Gilmour, Jr.
Financial data (yr. ended 12/31/01): Grants paid, $179,500; assets, $779,865 (M); expenditures, $192,840; qualifying distributions, $186,990.
Limitations: Giving primarily in NY.
Officers and Directors:* Blyth G. Gilmour,* V.P.; Lloyd S. Gilmour, Jr.,* V.P.; David F. Kroenlein, Secy.-Treas.
EIN: 136157750
Codes: FD2

34618
The Himmel Foundation
(Formerly The Himmel Family Foundation)
c/o Himmel Equities
450 Park Ave., Ste. 501
New York, NY 10022

Donor(s): Jeffrey S. Himmel.
Financial data (yr. ended 12/31/00): Grants paid, $179,357; assets, $698,797 (M); gifts received, $105,776; expenditures, $186,400; qualifying distributions, $182,088.
Limitations: Applications not accepted.
Application information: Contributes only to pre-selected organizations.
Trustee: Jeffrey S. Himmel.
EIN: 133916501
Codes: FD2

34619
The Roy & Niuta Titus Foundation, Inc.
1000 Park Ave., Ste. 2A
New York, NY 10028 (212) 734-2776
E-mail: titusfoundation@mindspring.com
Contact: Jane Creech, Exec. Dir.

Established in 1998 in NY.
Financial data (yr. ended 06/30/01): Grants paid, $179,200; assets, $4,405,140 (M); expenditures, $315,093; qualifying distributions, $246,260.
Limitations: Giving primarily in NY.
Application information: Application form not required.
Officers: Suzanne Slesin, Pres.; Michael Steinberg, Secy.-Treas.; Jane Creech, Exec. Dir.
EIN: 134027009
Codes: FD2

34620
The Freund Family Foundation
620 5th Ave., 7th Fl.
New York, NY 10020

Established in 1999 in NY.
Donor(s): Henry I. Freund, Harry I. Freund.
Financial data (yr. ended 12/31/01): Grants paid, $179,120; assets, $330,764 (M); gifts received, $327,300; expenditures, $179,446; qualifying distributions, $179,446.
Limitations: Applications not accepted.
Application information: Contributes only to pre-selected organizations.
Officers: Harry I. Freund, Pres.; Matta Freund, V.P.
EIN: 061549441
Codes: FD2

34621
Joseph and Margot Ganger Foundation, Inc.
c/o Ira Ganger
34 Herrick Dr.
Lawrence, NY 11559

Established in 1990 in NY.
Donor(s): Joseph Ganger,‡ AMEREX (USA), Inc.
Financial data (yr. ended 12/31/99): Grants paid, $178,967; assets, $2,336,346 (M); expenditures, $187,963; qualifying distributions, $180,037.
Limitations: Applications not accepted. Giving primarily in NY.
Application information: Contributes only to pre-selected organizations.
Trustees: Ira Ganger, Margot Ganger.
EIN: 113002962
Codes: FD2

34622
DLR Cohen Foundation
c/o EDC Assocs., Ltd.
3501 Bedford Ave.
Brooklyn, NY 11210
Contact: Leon E. Cohen, Secy.

Established in 1991 in NY.
Donor(s): Eli D. Cohen, David E. Cohen, Leon E. Cohen, Ronald E. Cohen.
Financial data (yr. ended 12/31/01): Grants paid, $178,813; assets, $149,295 (M); expenditures, $178,953; qualifying distributions, $178,893.
Limitations: Applications not accepted. Giving primarily in NY.
Application information: Contributes only to pre-selected organizations.
Officers and Directors:* Eli D. Cohen, Pres.; David E. Cohen,* V.P.; Leon E. Cohen,* Secy.; Ronald E. Cohen,* Treas.
EIN: 113085524
Codes: FD2

34623
Peter K. Barker Foundation
c/o BCRS Assocs., LLC
100 Wall St., 11th Fl.
New York, NY 10005

Established in 1983 in CA.
Donor(s): Peter K. Barker.
Financial data (yr. ended 12/31/01): Grants paid, $178,800; assets, $3,153,529 (M); expenditures, $190,457; qualifying distributions, $178,025.
Limitations: Applications not accepted. Giving primarily in Pasadena and Los Angeles, CA.
Application information: Contributes only to pre-selected organizations.
Trustees: Peter K. Barker, Robin B. Barker.
EIN: 133198247
Codes: FD2

34624
The Gutfreund Foundation, Inc.
c/o John Gutfreund
1 Rockefeller Plz.
New York, NY 10020

Incorporated in 1967 in NY.
Donor(s): John H. Gutfreund.
Financial data (yr. ended 04/30/01): Grants paid, $178,500; assets, $361,120 (M); expenditures, $185,830; qualifying distributions, $182,073.
Limitations: Applications not accepted. Giving primarily in New York, NY.
Publications: Annual report.
Application information: Contributes only to pre-selected organizations.
Officers: John H. Gutfreund, Pres.; Lawrence B. Buttenwieser, Secy.-Treas.
EIN: 136227515
Codes: FD2

34625
The Fredric E. Steck Family Foundation
c/o Goldman Sachs & Co.
85 Broad St., Tax Dept.
New York, NY 10004

Established in 1999 in NY.
Donor(s): Fredric E. Steck.
Financial data (yr. ended 05/31/01): Grants paid, $178,500; assets, $3,720,837 (M); gifts received, $978,360; expenditures, $222,670; qualifying distributions, $171,828.
Limitations: Applications not accepted. Giving primarily in CA, Washington, DC, and NY.
Application information: Contributes only to pre-selected organizations.
Trustees: Abigail B. Steck, Amanda B. Steck, Fredric E. Steck.
EIN: 134073097
Codes: FD2

34626
Lucille and Carl Loeb, Jr. Foundation, Inc.
c/o Richard A. Eisner & Co.
759 3rd Ave.
New York, NY 10017-2703

Established in 1950 in NY.
Donor(s): Carl M. Loeb, Jr.,‡ Lucille H. Loeb.‡
Financial data (yr. ended 11/30/01): Grants paid, $178,090; assets, $227,582 (M); expenditures, $197,358; qualifying distributions, $192,964.
Limitations: Applications not accepted. Giving primarily in MA and New York, NY.
Application information: Contributes only to pre-selected organizations.
Officers: Charles Guggenheimer, Pres. and Secy.-Treas.; Peter K. Loeb, V.P.
EIN: 136085599
Codes: FD2

34627
Abramson Family Foundation, Inc.
355 Meadowview Ave.
Hewlett, NY 11557

Established in 1997 in NY.
Donor(s): Richard Abramson, Lorraine Abramson.
Financial data (yr. ended 04/30/01): Grants paid, $178,000; assets, $766,697 (M); gifts received, $174,254; expenditures, $178,512; qualifying distributions, $177,243.
Limitations: Applications not accepted. Giving primarily in NY.
Application information: Contributes only to pre-selected organizations.
Officers: Richard Abramson, Pres.; Gregg Abramson, V.P. and Treas.; Jill Abramson, V.P.; Lorraine Abramson, V.P.
Director: Lauren Abramson.
EIN: 113374949
Codes: FD2

34628
Seneca Foods Foundation
1162 Pittsford-Victor Rd.
Pittsford, NY 14534 (716) 385-9500
E-mail: foundation@senecafoods.com
Contact: Kraig H. Kayser, Pres.

Established in 1988 in NY.
Donor(s): Seneca Foods Corp.
Financial data (yr. ended 03/31/02): Grants paid, $177,953; assets, $3,132,580 (M); gifts received, $24,699; expenditures, $211,112; qualifying distributions, $173,779.
Limitations: Giving primarily in communities where Seneca Foods Corporation has a processing facility.
Application information: Application form required.
Officers and Directors:* Arthur S. Wolcott,* Chair.; Kraig H. Kayser,* C.E.O. and Pres.; Jeffrey L. Van Riper, Secy.
EIN: 222996324
Codes: CS, FD2, CD

34629
Leff Foundation, Inc.
c/o National Spinning Co., Inc.
111 W. 40th St.
New York, NY 10018-2506

Incorporated in 1942 in NY.
Donor(s): Carl Leff,‡ Phillip Leff, National Spinning Co., Inc.
Financial data (yr. ended 12/31/01): Grants paid, $177,891; assets, $700,879 (M); expenditures, $184,488; qualifying distributions, $174,634.
Limitations: Applications not accepted. Giving primarily in NY.
Application information: Contributes only to pre-selected organizations.
Officers and Directors:* Marjorie Miller,* V.P.; Joseph Leff,* Treas.; Julie Satinover.
EIN: 116007845
Codes: FD2

34630
Julia O. Wells Memorial Educational Foundation, Inc.
P.O. Box 1931
Albany, NY 12201-1931

Financial data (yr. ended 12/31/00): Grants paid, $177,750; assets, $2,177,879 (M); expenditures, $208,335; qualifying distributions, $188,277.
Limitations: Applications not accepted. Giving limited to NY.
Officers and Directors:* Arthur F. Young, Jr.,* Pres.; Sharon Carpinello,* V.P.; Paul A. Levine,* Secy.; Gloria LaForte,* Treas.; Susan Wright,*

Admin.; Chris Ball, Bonita Bazyk, R.N., Laura Heidelmark, Barbara H. Sippel, Ann Yetman.
EIN: 222921430
Codes: FD2

34631
Perry & Donna Golkin Family Foundation
c/o Kohlberg Kravis Roberts & Co.
9 W. 57th St.
New York, NY 10019

Established in 1997 in NY.
Donor(s): Perry Golkin.
Financial data (yr. ended 11/30/01): Grants paid, $177,704; assets, $1,657,683 (M); gifts received, $611,400; expenditures, $188,424; qualifying distributions, $181,413.
Limitations: Applications not accepted.
Application information: Contributes only to pre-selected organizations.
Officers: Perry Golkin, Pres. and Treas.; Donna Golkin, V.P.
EIN: 133928587
Codes: FD2

34632
The Davidson Krueger Foundation
5002 2nd Ave.
Brooklyn, NY 11232

Incorporated in 1955 in NY.
Donor(s): Philip Davidson, Davidson Pipe Co., Inc.
Financial data (yr. ended 11/30/01): Grants paid, $177,703; assets, $1,782,656 (M); gifts received, $20,000; expenditures, $179,537; qualifying distributions, $178,956.
Limitations: Applications not accepted. Giving primarily in FL and NY.
Officers: H. Peter Davidson, Pres.; Stuart Krueger, Secy.-Treas.
EIN: 116005674
Codes: FD2, GTI

34633
Ravenel B. Curry III Foundation
435 E. 52nd St., Ste. 4C
New York, NY 10022

Established in 1974 in NY.
Donor(s): Elizabeth R. Curry, Ravenel B. Curry III.
Financial data (yr. ended 11/30/01): Grants paid, $177,700; assets, $3,155,033 (M); gifts received, $238,174; expenditures, $196,277; qualifying distributions, $194,774.
Limitations: Applications not accepted. Giving on a national basis.
Application information: Contributes only to pre-selected organizations.
Officers: Ravenel B. Curry III, Pres.; Elizabeth R. Curry, Secy.
EIN: 237411083
Codes: FD2

34634
Artists Fellowship, Inc.
c/o Salmagundi Club
47 5th Ave.
New York, NY 10003
URL: http://www.artistsfellowship.com
Contact: Richard Pionk, Tr.

Established in 1859.
Financial data (yr. ended 10/31/01): Grants paid, $177,660; assets, $3,718,066 (M); gifts received, $11,942; expenditures, $220,953; qualifying distributions, $197,514.
Limitations: Giving limited to U.S. residents and organizations.

Application information: Application form can be downloaded from foundation Web site. Application form required.
Officers: Marc Mellon, Pres.; Morton Kaish, V.P.; Robert J. Riedinger, Corr. Secy.; Kim Butwell, Recording Secy.; Pamela Singleton, Treas.
Trustees: Joan Brandt, Raoul Carranza, Maria Chatzinakis, Elisa Coleman, Gary Erbe, Richard Pionk, Marion Roller, Claire Romano, John Ross, Immi Storrs.
EIN: 136122134
Codes: FD2, GTI

34635
J. W. Heller Foundation
15 Maiden Ln., Ste. 1300
New York, NY 10038-4003

Donor(s): Melvin S. Heller, Helen A. Heller.
Financial data (yr. ended 11/30/01): Grants paid, $177,545; assets, $555,167 (M); gifts received, $93,414; expenditures, $179,542; qualifying distributions, $176,805.
Limitations: Applications not accepted. Giving primarily in New York, NY.
Application information: Contributes only to pre-selected organizations.
Trustee: Melvin S. Heller.
EIN: 237003624
Codes: FD2

34636
Zwerling Family Foundation
c/o BCRS Associates, LLC
100 Wall St., 11th Fl.
New York, NY 10005-3702

Established in 1989 in NJ.
Donor(s): Gary L. Zwerling.
Financial data (yr. ended 06/30/01): Grants paid, $177,475; assets, $604,922 (M); expenditures, $179,762; qualifying distributions, $178,576.
Limitations: Applications not accepted. Giving primarily in NJ and NY.
Application information: Contributes only to pre-selected organizations.
Trustees: Gary L. Zwerling, Marie Rose Zwerling.
EIN: 133532036
Codes: FD2

34637
The Frank & Roslyn Grobman Foundation, Inc.
c/o Dans Supreme Supermarkets, Inc.
474 Fulton Ave.
Hempstead, NY 11550 (516) 483-2400
Contact: Frank Grobman, Dir.

Established in 1994 in NY.
Financial data (yr. ended 12/31/00): Grants paid, $177,310; assets, $1,698,361 (M); expenditures, $177,707; qualifying distributions, $176,191.
Limitations: Giving primarily in NY.
Directors: Frank Grobman, Richard Grobman, Roslyn Grobman.
EIN: 113241420
Codes: FD2

34638
Dr. Roberts C. Atkins Foundation, Inc.
150 E. 55th St.
New York, NY 10022 (212) 457-9300
Contact: Greg Schraer, Treas.

Established in 1999 in NY.
Donor(s): Atkins Nutritionals, Inc.
Financial data (yr. ended 12/31/00): Grants paid, $176,680; assets, $1,787,378 (M); gifts received, $1,000,000; expenditures, $231,926; qualifying distributions, $176,680.
Application information: Application form not required.

Officers: Robert C. Atkins, M.D., Chair.; Veronica Atkins, Vice-Chair.; Paul D. Wolff, Pres.; Scott W. Kaback, V.P.; Paul Puskas, Secy.; Gregory K. Schraer, Treas.
EIN: 134089952
Codes: FD2

34639
The Fifth Floor Foundation
560 Broadway, Ste. 507A
New York, NY 10012
Contact: Werner H. Kramarsky, Pres.

Established in 1995 in NY.
Donor(s): Werner H. Kramarsky, Sarah Kramarsky.
Financial data (yr. ended 12/31/01): Grants paid, $176,528; assets, $351,933 (M); gifts received, $392,500; expenditures, $360,640; qualifying distributions, $373,821.
Limitations: Giving on a national basis.
Officers: Werner H. Kramarsky, Pres.; Lesley J. Spector, Secy.-Treas.
Director: David P. Lasry.
EIN: 133833077
Codes: FD2

34640
Yoel & Chaya Sarah Aronson Foundation
12 Jeffrey Pl.
Monsey, NY 10952

Established in 1997 in NY.
Donor(s): Eileen Aronson, Joel Aronson.
Financial data (yr. ended 12/31/01): Grants paid, $176,420; assets, $13,809 (M); gifts received, $66,183; expenditures, $178,341; qualifying distributions, $176,420.
Limitations: Applications not accepted. Giving primarily in NY.
Application information: Contributes only to pre-selected organizations.
Officers: Joel Aronson, Pres. and Secy.; Eileen Aronson, V.P. and Treas.
Board Member: Miriam Klein.
EIN: 133769478
Codes: FD2

34641
The Laurance H. & Mindy B. Friedman Family Foundation
225 W. 34th St., Ste. 400
New York, NY 10122-0490

Established in 1968.
Donor(s): Laurance H. Friedman.
Financial data (yr. ended 06/30/01): Grants paid, $176,250; assets, $61,094 (M); gifts received, $241,415; expenditures, $176,290; qualifying distributions, $176,250.
Limitations: Applications not accepted.
Application information: Contributes only to pre-selected organizations.
Officers: Laurance H. Friedman, Pres.; Mindy Beth Friedman, V.P. and Secy.; Jeffrey L. Saltzer, Treas.
EIN: 133953958
Codes: FD2

34642
Charles J. & Burton S. August Family Foundation
c/o Monro Muffler Brake Inc.
200 Holleder Pkwy.
Rochester, NY 14615-3808
Tel.: (585) 647-6400, ext. 315 or 302
Contact: Charles J. August, Tr.; or Burton S. August, Tr.

Established in 1989 in NY.
Donor(s): Burton S. August, Charles J. August.
Financial data (yr. ended 06/30/02): Grants paid, $176,130; assets, $3,400,000 (M); gifts received,

$450,000; expenditures, $191,000; qualifying distributions, $173,200.
Limitations: Giving limited to Rochester and Monroe County, NY.
Application information: Application form not required.
Officers and Trustees:* Charles J. August,* Chair.; Burton S. August,* Vice-Chair.; Elizabeth August,* Secy.; Andrew August, Burton Stuart August, Jan August, Jean B. August, John August, Robert August, Susan Eastwood, David C. Mitchell, Hon. Michael Telesea.
EIN: 161355601
Codes: FD2

34643
Rosenblatt Family Foundation, Inc.
155 Riverside Dr.
New York, NY 10024

Incorporated in 1956 in NY.
Donor(s): Marcus Retter, Betty Retter,‡ C. Rosenblatt.
Financial data (yr. ended 11/30/01): Grants paid, $176,097; assets, $3,640,214 (M); expenditures, $179,023; qualifying distributions, $176,097.
Limitations: Giving primarily in NY.
Application information: Application form not required.
Officers: Marcus Retter, Pres.; Mary Schreiber, Secy.-Treas.
EIN: 136145385
Codes: FD2

34644
The Thorne Foundation
435 E. 52nd St.
New York, NY 10022 (212) 758-2425
Contact: Miriam Thorne Gilpatric, Pres.

Incorporated in 1930 in NY.
Donor(s): Landon K. Thorne,‡ Julia L. Thorne.‡
Financial data (yr. ended 12/31/01): Grants paid, $176,050; assets, $1,317,358 (M); expenditures, $190,186; qualifying distributions, $176,050.
Limitations: Applications not accepted. Giving primarily in NY.
Application information: Contributes only to pre-selected organizations.
Officers: Miriam Thorne Gilpatric, Pres.; John B. Jessup, V.P.; David H. Thorne, V.P.
EIN: 136109955
Codes: FD2

34645
Suzanne T. and Irving D. Karpas, Jr. Foundation, Inc.
(Formerly Karpas Family Foundation, Inc.)
c/o Polakoff & Michaelson
225 W. 34th St., Ste. 1703
New York, NY 10122
Contact: Arnold Beiles, Secy.

Incorporated in 1945 in DE.
Donor(s): Irving D. Karpas, Jr., Suzanne T. Karpas.
Financial data (yr. ended 12/31/01): Grants paid, $175,713; assets, $2,081,845 (M); gifts received, $37,380; expenditures, $200,894; qualifying distributions, $178,863.
Limitations: Applications not accepted. Giving primarily in NY.
Application information: Contributes only to pre-selected organizations.
Officers and Directors:* Irving D. Karpas, Jr.,* Pres.; Suzanne T. Karpas,* Sr. V.P.; Bruce T. Karpas,* V.P.; Matthew P. Karpas, V.P.; Patricia E. Karpas, V.P.; Arnold Beiles, Secy.; Theodore R. Shiffman, Treas.
EIN: 136116217
Codes: FD2

34646
Cohoes Savings Foundation
60 Remsen St.
P.O. Box 230
Cohoes, NY 12047 (518) 233-6568
Contact: Harry L. Robinson, Chair.

Established in 1998.
Donor(s): Cohoes Savings Bank, Hudson River Bank & Trust Co.
Financial data (yr. ended 12/31/01): Grants paid, $175,381; assets, $5,157,115 (M); gifts received, $165,498; expenditures, $236,712; qualifying distributions, $192,493.
Limitations: Giving limited to communities in and around Cohoes, NY.
Application information: Application form required.
Officers: Harry L. Robinson, C.E.O. and Pres.; Walter H. Speidel, Secy.; Chester C. DeLaMater, Treas.
Directors: Frank D. Colaruotolo, Duncan S. MacAffer.
EIN: 141809837
Codes: CS, FD2

34647
The Hyde Foundation, Inc.
11 Summer St.
Buffalo, NY 14209-2256
Contact: George H. Hyde, Jr., V.P.

Established around 1964 in NY.
Financial data (yr. ended 12/31/01): Grants paid, $175,255; assets, $1,929,301 (M); expenditures, $198,022; qualifying distributions, $182,780.
Limitations: Giving limited to NY.
Officers: George H. Hyde, Pres.; George H. Hyde, Jr., V.P.
Trustees: Donald Egan, William I. Magavern.
EIN: 166035220
Codes: FD2

34648
Good Neighbor Foundation, Inc.
c/o Grey Advertising, Inc.
777 3rd Ave., Rm. 1217
New York, NY 10017 (212) 546-2000
FAX: (212) 546-2332
Contact: Ilene P. Meiseles, Secy.

Incorporated in 1952 in NY.
Financial data (yr. ended 12/31/01): Grants paid, $175,151; assets, $40,510 (M); gifts received, $175,000; expenditures, $176,220; qualifying distributions, $176,217.
Limitations: Applications not accepted. Giving primarily in CA, and New York, NY.
Application information: Grants only to public foundations and institutions.
Officers: Edward H. Meyer, Pres.; Robert L. Berenson, V.P.; Ilene P. Meiseles, Secy.; Steven G. Felsher, Treas.
EIN: 136161259
Codes: FD2

34649
Ernst & Paula Deutsch Foundation
c/o Blank, Rome, Tenzer, Greenblatt, LLP
405 Lexington Ave.
New York, NY 10174

Established in 1954 in NY.
Financial data (yr. ended 12/31/01): Grants paid, $175,000; assets, $3,244,439 (M); expenditures, $253,980; qualifying distributions, $174,555.
Limitations: Applications not accepted. Giving primarily in New York, NY.
Application information: Contributes only to pre-selected organizations.
Officers: Laurence S. Rogers, Pres.; John D. Cohen, V.P.; Ira J. Greenblatt, Secy.-Treas.
EIN: 136112579
Codes: FD2

34650
Ross Foundation, Inc.
6 E. 45th St., Ste. 209
New York, NY 10017
Additional address: 50 W. Broad St., Ste. 3300, Columbus, OH 43215, tel.: (614) 889-1969; FAX: (614) 224-6221; E-mail: rlovelan@columbus.rr.com
Contact: Catherine Ross Loveland, Pres.

Established in 1950 in NY.
Donor(s): William E. Ross,‡ Catherine Ross Loveland, Richard L. Loveland, Susan R. Hughson.
Financial data (yr. ended 12/31/00): Grants paid, $174,988; assets, $3,399,063 (M); expenditures, $180,103; qualifying distributions, $174,771.
Limitations: Giving on a national basis.
Publications: Application guidelines.
Application information: Application form not required.
Officers and Trustees:* Catherine Ross Loveland,* Chair. and Pres.; William L. Loveland,* V.P.; Daniel Ross Loveland,* Secy.; Richard L. Loveland,* Treas.; Susan R. Hughson, James R. Loveland, Susan G. Loveland, Bernice Lyon, Catherine L. Vowell.
EIN: 136106681
Codes: FD2

34651
Marina P. and Stephen E. Kaufman Foundation
c/o Stephen E. Kaufman, PC
277 Park Ave., Ste. 3604
New York, NY 10172-3699
Contact: Marina P. Kaufman, Tr.

Established in 1996 in NY.
Donor(s): Marina P. Kaufman, Stephen E. Kaufman.
Financial data (yr. ended 12/31/01): Grants paid, $174,870; assets, $523,125 (M); gifts received, $132,628; expenditures, $183,784; qualifying distributions, $174,870.
Trustees: Marina P. Kaufman, Stephen E. Kaufman.
EIN: 133922035
Codes: FD2

34652
Chada Foundation, Inc.
c/o Eli Robins
1333 Broadway, Ste. 730
New York, NY 10018-7204

Established in 1991 in NY.
Donor(s): Esther Reichman.
Financial data (yr. ended 11/30/01): Grants paid, $174,860; assets, $1,844,241 (M); gifts received, $453,000; expenditures, $178,074; qualifying distributions, $175,646.
Limitations: Applications not accepted. Giving primarily in NY.
Application information: Contributes only to pre-selected organizations.
Officers: Esther Reichman, Pres.; Joseph Reichman, V.P. and Secy.
Trustee: Alfred I. Scherzer.
EIN: 133650373
Codes: FD2

34653
The Dannon Research Institute, Inc.
120 White Plains Rd.
Tarrytown, NY 10591-5536

Established in 1996 in DE and NY.
Donor(s): The Dannon Co., Inc.

Financial data (yr. ended 12/31/00): Grants paid, $174,759; assets, $43,299 (M); gifts received, $1,005,622; expenditures, $1,011,417; qualifying distributions, $1,011,417; giving activities include $755,637 for programs.
Limitations: Applications not accepted. Giving on a national basis.
Application information: Contributes only to pre-selected organizations.
Officers and Directors:* Barbara O. Schneeman, Ph.D.,* Pres.; Richard L. Atkinson, M.D.,* V.P.; Thomas Kunz,* V.P.; Rick Lees,* Secy.-Treas.; Cheryl Achterberg, Ph.D., Anna Moses, Ellen Rohrer, Virginia A. Stallings, M.D.
EIN: 133889717
Codes: FD2

34654
A. & B. Stein Family Foundation
57 Henry St.
Merrick, NY 11566

Established in 2000 in NY.
Donor(s): Aaron M. Stein.
Financial data (yr. ended 12/31/00): Grants paid, $174,613; assets, $38,723 (M); gifts received, $213,289; expenditures, $175,163; qualifying distributions, $174,613.
Limitations: Applications not accepted. Giving primarily in New York, NY.
Application information: Contributes only to pre-selected organizations.
Trustees: Aaron M. Stein, Abraham Stein, Betsy Stein.
EIN: 113567653
Codes: FD2

34655
Ralph B. Post Trust
c/o HSBC Bank, USA
P.O. Box 4888
Syracuse, NY 13221

Established in 1985 in NY.
Financial data (yr. ended 09/30/01): Grants paid, $174,027; assets, $3,024,078 (M); expenditures, $250,233; qualifying distributions, $189,354.
Limitations: Applications not accepted. Giving primarily to residents of small towns in upstate NY.
Application information: Unsolicited requests for funds not accepted.
Trustee: HSBC Bank USA.
EIN: 146052967
Codes: GTI

34656
Lindau Foundation, Inc.
59 Holden Rd.
Pine City, NY 14871 (607) 734-0440

Established in 1973 in NY.
Financial data (yr. ended 04/30/01): Grants paid, $174,000; assets, $3,002,501 (M); gifts received, $2,091; expenditures, $178,386; qualifying distributions, $174,000.
Limitations: Giving primarily in Elmira, NY.
Application information: Application form not required.
Officers and Trustees:* Whitney S. Powers, Jr.,* Pres.; Patricia L. Powers,* V.P.; Bela C. Tifft,* Secy.; J. Philip Hunter.
EIN: 166020704
Codes: FD2

34657
The Taub Family Foundation
c/o Miller, Ellen & Co.
750 Lexington Ave., 23rd Fl.
New York, NY 10022-1200

Established in 1996 in NY.
Donor(s): Israel Taub.
Financial data (yr. ended 11/30/00): Grants paid, $173,700; assets, $1,341,705 (M); gifts received, $461,000; expenditures, $180,689; qualifying distributions, $173,243.
Limitations: Applications not accepted.
Application information: Contributes only to pre-selected organizations.
Trustees: Mark C. Peltz, Israel Taub.
EIN: 137106040
Codes: FD2

34658
Adam Sender Charitable Trust
101 W. 67th St., Ste. 48D
New York, NY 10023

Established in 1999 in NY.
Donor(s): Adam Sender.
Financial data (yr. ended 12/31/00): Grants paid, $173,623; assets, $4,678 (M); gifts received, $171,576; expenditures, $175,823; qualifying distributions, $173,648.
Limitations: Applications not accepted.
Application information: Contributes only to pre-selected organizations.
Trustees: David Gerber, Adam Sender, Jared Sender.
EIN: 137187854
Codes: FD2

34659
The Alex J. Weinstein Foundation, Inc.
285 Peachtree Dr.
East Norwich, NY 11732 (516) 922-6859

Established in 1953 in NY.
Financial data (yr. ended 11/30/01): Grants paid, $173,300; assets, $4,209,510 (M); expenditures, $195,457; qualifying distributions, $185,955.
Limitations: Applications not accepted. Giving primarily in CT and NY.
Application information: Contributes only to pre-selected organizations.
Trustees and Directors:* Herbert D. Feinberg,* Ruth Fernberg,* Barrie J. Solesko,* Donald Selesko.*
EIN: 136160964
Codes: FD2

34660
Spitzer Trust
c/o David Rubin
1600 Hillside Ave., Ste. 203
New Hyde Park, NY 11040-2680

Established in 1976 in NY.
Donor(s): Albert Spitzer.
Financial data (yr. ended 10/31/00): Grants paid, $172,922; assets, $5,418,521 (M); expenditures, $175,141; qualifying distributions, $173,922.
Limitations: Applications not accepted. Giving primarily in Brooklyn, NY.
Application information: Contributes only to pre-selected organizations.
Trustees: Albert Spitzer, Eli Spitzer, Erica Spitzer, Michael Spitzer.
EIN: 112419181
Codes: FD2

34661
Paul D. and Joyce B. Rheingold Family Foundation
5 Manursing Way
Rye, NY 10580
Application address: 113 E. 37th St., New York, NY 10018, tel.: (212) 684-1880
Contact: Joyce B. Rheingold, Tr.

Established in 1993 in NY.
Donor(s): Paul D. Rheingold, Joyce B. Rheingold.
Financial data (yr. ended 11/30/00): Grants paid, $172,515; assets, $1,384,281 (M); gifts received, $198,750; expenditures, $172,515; qualifying distributions, $172,515.
Limitations: Giving primarily in New York, NY.
Trustees: Joyce B. Rheingold, Paul D. Rheingold.
EIN: 133744605
Codes: FD2

34662
The Irving & Geraldine Schaffer Foundation, Inc.
43 Hampton Rd.
Scarsdale, NY 10583 (914) 899-3500
Contact: Irving Schaffer, Pres.

Established in 1968.
Donor(s): Irving Schaffer, Geraldine Schaffer.‡
Financial data (yr. ended 12/31/01): Grants paid, $172,279; assets, $3,037,954 (M); gifts received, $143,291; expenditures, $205,003; qualifying distributions, $172,279.
Officers and Directors:* Irving Schaffer,* Pres.; Peter Schaffer,* V.P.; S. Andrew Schaffer, V.P.; Frederick P. Schaffer.
EIN: 132626706
Codes: FD2

34663
The Concannon Family Foundation
101 Park Ave., 30th Fl.
New York, NY 10178

Established in 1997 in NY.
Donor(s): Richard S. Concannon.
Financial data (yr. ended 12/31/00): Grants paid, $172,250; assets, $2,642,247 (M); expenditures, $202,378; qualifying distributions, $174,300.
Limitations: Applications not accepted.
Application information: Contributes only to pre-selected organizations.
Trustee: Richard J. Concannon.
EIN: 137119731
Codes: FD2

34664
John McEnroe Foundation
c/o Burton Goldstein & Co., LLC
156 W. 56th St.
New York, NY 10019

Established in 1986 in NY.
Donor(s): John McEnroe.
Financial data (yr. ended 12/31/01): Grants paid, $172,200; assets, $744,375 (M); gifts received, $42,285; expenditures, $173,396; qualifying distributions, $172,410.
Limitations: Applications not accepted. Giving primarily in NY.
Application information: Contributes only to pre-selected organizations.
Officers: John McEnroe, Pres. and Treas.; John P. McEnroe, V.P.; Mark T. McEnroe, V.P. and Secy.
EIN: 133389114
Codes: FD2

34665
Leo Cox Beach Philanthropic Foundation
P.O. Box 187
Hartford, NY 12838-0187
Contact: Barbara Velsini, Dir.

Established in 1989 in NY.
Donor(s): Thomas C. Beach, Jr.
Financial data (yr. ended 07/31/01): Grants paid, $172,000; assets, $3,667,520 (M); expenditures, $222,285; qualifying distributions, $170,623.
Limitations: Giving limited to Glens Falls, NY.
Application information: A major portion of funding (90 percent) committed; remainder of

giving limited to Washington County, NY. Application form required.
Directors: Thomas C. Beach, Jr., Deborah Burnham, A. Desmond Fitzgerald, Dorothy Jackson, Michael F. Massiano, Pauline E. Palmer, John T. Snell, Barbara Velsini.
EIN: 141732259
Codes: FD2

34666
Romenesa Foundation
600 Madison Ave., 23rd Fl.
New York, NY 10022

Established in 1997 in NY.
Donor(s): Meryl Meltzer, Robert Meltzer.
Financial data (yr. ended 12/31/01): Grants paid, $172,000; assets, $199,558 (M); expenditures, $177,102; qualifying distributions, $172,000.
Limitations: Applications not accepted. Giving primarily in NY.
Application information: Contributes only to pre-selected organizations.
Officers: Robert Meltzer, Chair. and Treas.; Meryl Meltzer, Pres. and Secy.; Neal Meltzer, V.P.; Sara Meltzer, V.P.
EIN: 133971081

34667
The Louise and Henry Epstein Family Foundation, Inc.
137 Kilbourn Rd.
Rochester, NY 14618

Established in 1994 in NY.
Donor(s): Henry P. Epstein,‡ Louise W. Epstein.
Financial data (yr. ended 03/31/01): Grants paid, $171,951; assets, $561,182 (M); expenditures, $184,302; qualifying distributions, $173,932.
Limitations: Applications not accepted. Giving primarily in Rochester, NY.
Application information: Contributes only to pre-selected organizations.
Officer: Louise W. Epstein, Pres. and Secy-Treas.
Directors: Geoffrey Epstein, Laurie Epstein, Linda Epstein, Neil Epstein, Steven Epstein.
EIN: 161459717
Codes: FD2

34668
The Edward H. Benenson Foundation
(Formerly RNB Foundation, Inc.)
445 Park Ave., Ste. 1902
New York, NY 10022-2638
Contact: Edward H. Benenson, Pres.

Established in 1955 in NY.
Financial data (yr. ended 11/30/01): Grants paid, $171,750; assets, $2,444,701 (M); gifts received, $10,825; expenditures, $172,000; qualifying distributions, $171,750.
Limitations: Giving primarily in NY.
Officers: Edward H. Benenson, Pres.; Gladys S. Benenson, V.P.; Lisa Benenson Quattrocchi, Secy.; Albert Fleischman, Treas.
EIN: 136162730
Codes: FD2

34669
Lynford Family Charitable Trust
c/o Wellsford Real Properties, Inc.
535 Madison Ave., 26th Fl.
New York, NY 10022

Established in 1985 in NY.
Donor(s): Jeffrey Lynnford.
Financial data (yr. ended 06/30/01): Grants paid, $171,700; assets, $907,365 (M); gifts received, $10,000; expenditures, $173,375; qualifying distributions, $171,244.

Application information: Application form not required.
Trustees: Jeffrey H. Lynford, Lance K. Lynford, Leslye A. Williams.
EIN: 133327503
Codes: FD2

34670
Weiksner Family Foundation
(Formerly The Sandra & George Weiksner Foundation)
c/o Cleary Gottlieb
1 Liberty Plz., 43rd Fl.
New York, NY 10006

Established in 1986 in NY.
Donor(s): George B. Weiksner, Jr.
Financial data (yr. ended 12/31/01): Grants paid, $171,700; assets, $514,283 (M); expenditures, $171,985; qualifying distributions, $171,647.
Limitations: Applications not accepted. Giving primarily in New York, NY.
Application information: Contributes only to pre-selected organizations.
Trustees: George B. Weiksner, Sandra S. Weiksner.
EIN: 133398052
Codes: FD2

34671
Max & Rika Knopf Foundation
1362 51st St.
Brooklyn, NY 11219

Established in 1988 in NY.
Donor(s): Max Knopf, Rika Knopf.
Financial data (yr. ended 11/30/01): Grants paid, $171,361; assets, $1,022,086 (M); gifts received, $521,749; expenditures, $181,831; qualifying distributions, $171,361.
Limitations: Applications not accepted.
Application information: Contributes only to pre-selected organizations.
Managers: Max Knopf, Rika Knopf.
EIN: 133523504
Codes: FD2

34672
The Artur Walther Foundation
c/o BCRS Assocs., LLC
100 Wall St., 11th Fl.
New York, NY 10005

Established in 1993 in NY.
Donor(s): Artur Walther.
Financial data (yr. ended 07/31/01): Grants paid, $171,333; assets, $1,405,664 (M); gifts received, $870,625; expenditures, $173,409; qualifying distributions, $167,011.
Limitations: Applications not accepted.
Application information: Contributes only to pre-selected organizations.
Trustee: Artur Walther.
EIN: 133748078
Codes: FD2

34673
Schlosstein Hartley Foundation
c/o B. Strauss Assoc. Ltd.
307 5th Ave., Ste. 8th Fl.
New York, NY 10016-6517

Established in 2000 in NY.
Donor(s): Ralph L. Schlosstein.
Financial data (yr. ended 09/30/01): Grants paid, $171,312; assets, $636,968 (M); gifts received, $860,000; expenditures, $171,312; qualifying distributions, $171,312.
Limitations: Applications not accepted.
Application information: Contributes only to pre-selected organizations.
Trustees: Jane Hartley, Ralph L. Schlosstein.

EIN: 137268307
Codes: FD2

34674
Clingman Family Foundation
c/o Centennial International, LLC
230 Park Ave.
New York, NY 10169

Established in 1997 in NY.
Donor(s): Alan Clingman.
Financial data (yr. ended 04/30/01): Grants paid, $171,293; assets, $6,716 (M); gifts received, $173,000; expenditures, $171,351; qualifying distributions, $171,351.
Limitations: Applications not accepted. Giving primarily in NY.
Application information: Contributes only to pre-selected organizations.
Trustee: Alan Clingman.
EIN: 137115455
Codes: FD2

34675
James S. Marcus Foundation
c/o BCRS Assocs., LLC
100 Wall St., 11th Fl.
New York, NY 10005-3101

Established in 1969 in NY.
Donor(s): James S. Marcus.
Financial data (yr. ended 05/31/01): Grants paid, $171,117; assets, $6,059,595 (M); gifts received, $65,557; expenditures, $177,231; qualifying distributions, $172,785.
Limitations: Applications not accepted. Giving primarily in New York, NY.
Application information: Contributes only to pre-selected organizations.
Trustees: H. Frederick Krimendahl II, Ellen F. Marcus, James S. Marcus.
EIN: 237044611
Codes: FD2

34676
Morgenthaler Family Foundation
c/o U.S. Trust
114 W. 47th St.
New York, NY 10036

Established in 1997 in OH.
Financial data (yr. ended 11/30/01): Grants paid, $171,000; assets, $1,578,753 (M); expenditures, $198,664; qualifying distributions, $173,200.
Limitations: Applications not accepted. Giving primarily in CA and OH.
Application information: Contributes only to pre-selected organizations.
Trustees: David T. Morgenthaler, Lindsay J. Morgenthaler.
EIN: 347065666
Codes: FD2

34677
The Marcello Lotti Foundation
c/o American Capital Partners
45 Rockefeller Plz., Ste. 2000
New York, NY 10111

Established in 2000 in NY.
Donor(s): Diane Britz Lotti, The Norfolk Trust.
Financial data (yr. ended 12/31/01): Grants paid, $170,968; assets, $162,945 (M); gifts received, $335,947; expenditures, $173,053; qualifying distributions, $173,053.
Limitations: Giving primarily in New York, NY.
Officers and Directors:* Diane Britz Lotti,* Pres.; Biance Maria Orlando,* Secy.; Nicolo Caiola, Ariane E. Lotti.
EIN: 134009807
Codes: FD2

34678
Peter & Stacy Hochfelder Charitable Foundation, Inc.
2 Lincoln Ln.
Purchase, NY 10577

Established in 1994 in NY.
Donor(s): Peter Hochfelder, Stacy Hochfelder.
Financial data (yr. ended 12/31/00): Grants paid, $170,862; assets, $1,630 (M); gifts received, $168,000; expenditures, $171,062; qualifying distributions, $171,060.
Limitations: Applications not accepted. Giving primarily in NY.
Application information: Contributes only to pre-selected organizations.
Officers: Peter Hochfelder, Pres.; Mitchell Kuflik, V.P.; Stacy Hochfelder, Secy.
EIN: 133799164
Codes: FD2

34679
Wainscott Charitable Trust
c/o Argonaut Capital Management
780 3rd Ave., 9th Fl.
New York, NY 10017-2024

Established in 1997 in NY.
Donor(s): David E. Gerstenhaber.
Financial data (yr. ended 12/31/01): Grants paid, $170,750; assets, $76,409 (M); gifts received, $15,000; expenditures, $170,750; qualifying distributions, $170,750.
Limitations: Applications not accepted. Giving primarily in New York, NY.
Application information: Contributes only to pre-selected organizations.
Trustee: David E. Gerstenhaber.
EIN: 137135370

34680
Elizabeth Wakeman Henderson Foundation
c/o Fiduciary Trust Co. International
600 5th Ave.
New York, NY 10020
Application address: 209 McKee Ave., Oxford, OH 45056
Contact: George Kataudella

Established in 1997 in OH.
Donor(s): William H. Eshbaugh, E.W. Henderson.‡
Financial data (yr. ended 12/31/01): Grants paid, $170,500; assets, $3,498,937 (M); gifts received, $30,000; expenditures, $234,549; qualifying distributions, $210,510.
Trustees: Stephen H. Eshbaugh, William H. Eshbaugh, Margaret E. Van Coller.
EIN: 656234202
Codes: FD2

34681
Mack Goldner Memorial Foundation
7 Indian Trail
Harrison, NY 10528 (914) 835-4848
Contact: Philip A. Marraccini, M.D., Pres.

Established in 1977 in NY.
Financial data (yr. ended 03/31/01): Grants paid, $170,375; assets, $3,669,598 (M); expenditures, $211,963; qualifying distributions, $196,941.
Limitations: Giving primarily in the greater New York, NY, area.
Officers: Philip A. Marraccini, M.D., Pres.; Philip A. Marraccini, Jr., Secy.; Leonard Yablon, Treas.
EIN: 132915664
Codes: FD2

34682
Maheras Foundation
24 Gramercy Pk. S., Ste. 5
New York, NY 10003

Established in 2000 in NY.
Donor(s): Thomas G. Maheras.
Financial data (yr. ended 12/31/01): Grants paid, $170,260; assets, $129,735 (M); gifts received, $1,080; expenditures, $171,940; qualifying distributions, $170,260.
Limitations: Applications not accepted.
Application information: Contributes only to pre-selected organizations.
Trustees: Leslie L. Maheras, Thomas G. Maheras.
EIN: 134150699

34683
Leiter's Landing Foundation, Inc.
c/o KRT Business Management
500 5th Ave., Ste. 3000
New York, NY 10110-3099

Established in 2000.
Donor(s): Alois Lieter, Lori Leiter.
Financial data (yr. ended 01/31/01): Grants paid, $170,200; assets, $406,093 (M); gifts received, $363,203; expenditures, $181,582; qualifying distributions, $170,200.
Officers: Alois Leiter, Pres.; Prentice Chevalier, V.P.; Lori Leiter, V.P.; Steve Forrest, Secy.; Robert Raiola, Treas.
EIN: 650708062
Codes: FD2

34684
The Carroll & Percy Klingenstein Foundation, Inc.
c/o Lipsky, Goodkin & Co., PC
120 W. 45th St., 7th Fl.
New York, NY 10036-4041

Established in 1975 in NY.
Donor(s): Percy Klingenstein.‡
Financial data (yr. ended 02/28/02): Grants paid, $170,050; assets, $2,651,577 (M); expenditures, $204,079; qualifying distributions, $169,974.
Limitations: Applications not accepted. Giving primarily in New York, NY.
Application information: Contributes only to pre-selected organizations.
Officers and Directors:* William P. Klingenstein,* Pres.; Richard Klingenstein,* V.P.; Jean Klingenstein,* Secy.; Philip P. Goodkin,* Treas.
EIN: 132850138
Codes: FD2

34685
Robert Goelet Foundation
c/o Davidson, Dawson & Clark
330 Madison Ave.
New York, NY 10017
Contact: Louis B. Frost

Established in 1964.
Financial data (yr. ended 01/31/02): Grants paid, $170,000; assets, $2,765,334 (M); expenditures, $201,492; qualifying distributions, $179,261.
Limitations: Giving primarily in New York, NY.
Application information: Application form not required.
Trustees: Louis B. Frost, JPMorgan Chase Bank.
EIN: 136146654
Codes: FD2

34686
Miriam T. and Howard N. Stern Foundation, Inc.
P.O. Box 947
Remsenburg, NY 11960

Established in 1998 in NY.
Donor(s): Howard N. Stern, Miriam T. Stern.
Financial data (yr. ended 11/30/01): Grants paid, $170,000; assets, $924,156 (M); gifts received, $2,000; expenditures, $184,876; qualifying distributions, $169,296.
Limitations: Applications not accepted. Giving primarily in New York, NY.
Application information: Contributes only to pre-selected organizations.
Officers: Miriam T. Stern, Pres.; Howard N. Stern, Secy.-Treas.
Director: Mark Stern.
EIN: 113407299
Codes: FD2

34687
The Julian J. Leavitt Family Charitable Trust
c/o Peter Leavitt
1976 Espirit Glade
Radison, NY 13027

Established in 1991 in MA.
Donor(s): Julian J. Levitt.
Financial data (yr. ended 12/31/01): Grants paid, $169,770; assets, $5,012,871 (M); expenditures, $183,353; qualifying distributions, $163,942.
Limitations: Applications not accepted. Giving primarily in Longmeadow, MA.
Application information: Contributes only to pre-selected organizations.
Directors: Susan Cohn, Clementine Leavitt, Peter M. Leavitt, S. Robert Leavitt.
EIN: 046657085
Codes: FD2

34688
Holland Lodge Foundation, Inc.
71 W. 23rd St.
New York, NY 10010-4102 (212) 675-0323
FAX: (212) 675-8730; E-mail: office@holland8.org

Established in 1929 in NY.
Financial data (yr. ended 09/30/01): Grants paid, $169,225; assets, $2,091,646 (M); gifts received, $2,751; expenditures, $170,199; qualifying distributions, $193,450.
Limitations: Giving primarily in New York, NY.
Officers and Directors:* Byam K. Stevens, Jr., Pres.; Jonathan Bitting, V.P.; Henry C.B. Lindh, Secy.; Edgar P.E. White, Treas.; Harvey G. Kemp, E. Timothy McAuliffe, Stephen W. Spencer, Donald L. Twiss.
EIN: 136126132
Codes: FD2, GTI

34689
Emma J. Adams Memorial Fund, Inc.
862 Park Ave.
New York, NY 10021
FAX: (212) 327-0593
Contact: Edward R. Finch, Jr., Pres.

Incorporated in 1932 in NY.
Donor(s): Emma J. Adams.‡
Financial data (yr. ended 12/31/01): Grants paid, $169,030; assets, $3,442,923 (M); gifts received, $19,400; expenditures, $321,575; qualifying distributions, $247,503.
Limitations: Giving primarily in the greater metropolitan New York, NY, area.
Publications: Application guidelines, multi-year report.

Application information: Application form required.
Officer: Edward R. Finch, Jr., Pres.
Directors: Martin D. Finch, M.D., Pauline Swayze Finch, Rev. Bruce Forbes, Mary D.F. Haskell, Rev. Elizabeth Jacks, Elizabeth Rowe, Henry Weldon.
EIN: 136116503
Codes: FD2, GTI

34690
The Daphne Seybolt Culpeper Foundation, Inc.
230 Park Ave., Ste. 625
New York, NY 10169

Established in 1973 in NY.
Financial data (yr. ended 10/31/00): Grants paid, $169,000; assets, $3,293,863 (M); expenditures, $218,018; qualifying distributions, $191,772.
Limitations: Applications not accepted. Giving primarily in, but not limited to, NY.
Application information: Contributes only to pre-selected organizations.
Manager: Kalman I. Nulman.
EIN: 237227846
Codes: FD2

34691
The Hadar Foundation
200 E. 69th St.
New York, NY 10021 (212) 832-9797
Contact: Richard Hadar, Pres.

Established in 1993 in FL.
Donor(s): Richard Hadar.
Financial data (yr. ended 12/31/00): Grants paid, $168,944; assets, $1,267,733 (M); gifts received, $50,000; expenditures, $199,400; qualifying distributions, $167,248.
Limitations: Giving primarily in NY.
Application information: Application form required.
Officer: Richard Hadar, Pres.
EIN: 133721350
Codes: FD2

34692
The Grossman Foundation
45 Clubside Dr.
Woodmere, NY 11598-1365

Established in 1954 in NY.
Donor(s): Lester Grossman,‡ Anna Grossman.
Financial data (yr. ended 12/31/01): Grants paid, $168,793; assets, $3,512,312 (M); expenditures, $191,089; qualifying distributions, $172,293.
Limitations: Giving primarily in FL.
Trustees: Carl C. Grossman, Glen Grossman, Peter Grossman.
EIN: 136097346
Codes: FD2

34693
Vinmont Foundation, Inc.
888 E. 19th St.
Brooklyn, NY 11230
Contact: William R. Nye, Pres.

Incorporated in 1947 in NY.
Donor(s): Lily H. Weinberg,‡ Robert C. Weinberg,‡ Ruth Weinberg.‡
Financial data (yr. ended 12/31/01): Grants paid, $168,000; assets, $727,902 (M); expenditures, $173,014; qualifying distributions, $168,000.
Limitations: Giving primarily in the metropolitan New York, NY, area; support for national African-American agencies.
Publications: Program policy statement.
Application information: Rarely funds unsolicited proposals. Application form not required.
Officers and Directors:* William R. Nye,* Pres.; Carolyn L. Whittle,* V.P.; Paul S. Byard,* Secy.; Bruce L. Bozeman, L. Franklyn Lowenstein.
EIN: 131577203

34694
Eli Mason Charitable Trust
400 Park Ave., Ste. 1200
New York, NY 10022-4406

Established in 1986 in NY.
Donor(s): Eli Mason.
Financial data (yr. ended 11/30/00): Grants paid, $167,695; assets, $1,002 (M); gifts received, $1,000; expenditures, $168,060; qualifying distributions, $167,707.
Limitations: Applications not accepted. Giving primarily in New York, NY.
Application information: Unsolicited requests for funds not accepted.
Trustees: Claire Mason, Eli Mason.
EIN: 133389027
Codes: FD2

34695
The Jonathan Sobel and Marcia Dunn Foundation
c/o Goldman Sachs & Co.
85 Broad St., Tax Dept.
New York, NY 10004-2456

Established in 1999 in NY.
Donor(s): Jonathan Sobel.
Financial data (yr. ended 11/30/01): Grants paid, $167,672; assets, $1,290,109 (M); gifts received, $197,125; expenditures, $176,502; qualifying distributions, $168,044.
Limitations: Applications not accepted. Giving primarily in New York, NY.
Application information: Contributes only to pre-selected organizations.
Trustees: Marcia Dunn, Jonathan Sobel.
EIN: 134050663
Codes: FD2

34696
TNG Charitable Trust
378 Crown St.
Brooklyn, NY 11225

Established in 1997 in NY.
Donor(s): Eli Itzinger Irrevocable Trust, Chmvel Labkowski Irrevocable Trust.
Financial data (yr. ended 12/31/01): Grants paid, $167,558; assets, $268,936 (M); gifts received, $317,437; expenditures, $167,680; qualifying distributions, $167,680.
Limitations: Applications not accepted.
Application information: Contributes only to pre-selected organizations.
Directors: Nathan Gurary, Tema Gurary.
EIN: 116482383
Codes: FD2

34697
Howard and Susan Finkelstein Foundation, Inc.
350 5th Ave., Ste. 1000
New York, NY 10118
Contact: Robert Braunschweig, Dir.

Established in 2000 in NY.
Donor(s): Howard Finkelstein, Susan Finkelstein.
Financial data (yr. ended 11/30/01): Grants paid, $167,406; assets, $38,313 (M); gifts received, $100,000; expenditures, $167,471; qualifying distributions, $167,381.
Application information: Application form not required.
Officers and Directors:* Howard Finkelstein,* Pres.; Susan Finkelstein,* Secy.; Robert S. Braunschweig.
EIN: 134092400
Codes: FD2

34698
La Rue Foundation
20 W. 33rd St.
New York, NY 10001-3305 (212) 563-1414
Contact: Jack Hafif, Mgr.

Donor(s): Jack Hafif, La Rue Distributors, Inc.
Financial data (yr. ended 04/30/01): Grants paid, $167,406; assets, $640,292 (M); gifts received, $166,600; expenditures, $167,516; qualifying distributions, $167,516.
Limitations: Giving primarily in NJ and the metropolitan New York, NY, area.
Officer: Jack Hafif, Mgr.
EIN: 132776277
Codes: FD2

34699
The Abby and David Cohen Family Foundation
c/o Goldman Sachs & Co.
85 Broad St., Tax Dept.
New York, NY 10004

Established in 1999 in NY.
Donor(s): Abby J. Cohen.
Financial data (yr. ended 03/31/02): Grants paid, $167,258; assets, $1,970,435 (M); gifts received, $502,901; expenditures, $169,088; qualifying distributions, $168,468.
Limitations: Applications not accepted. Giving primarily in Ithaca and New York, NY.
Application information: Contributes only to pre-selected organizations.
Trustees: Abby J. Cohen, David M. Cohen, Ellen M. Cohen.
EIN: 134090442
Codes: FD2

34700
Elmar Fund
45 E. 85th St., Rm. 3B
New York, NY 10028
Contact: Susan Lerner, Pres.

Established in 1993 in NY.
Financial data (yr. ended 09/30/01): Grants paid, $167,050; assets, $2,324,666 (M); expenditures, $206,301; qualifying distributions, $170,182.
Limitations: Giving primarily in NY.
Officers: Susan Lerner, Pres.; Laurence Lerner, V.P.; Kathleen B. Lipkins, Secy.-Treas.
EIN: 133635649
Codes: FD2

34701
Suskind Family Foundation
c/o BCRS Assocs., LLC
67 Wall St., 8th Fl.
New York, NY 10005

Established in 1984.
Donor(s): Dennis A. Suskind.
Financial data (yr. ended 04/30/01): Grants paid, $167,025; assets, $70,376 (M); expenditures, $169,100; qualifying distributions, $168,018.
Limitations: Applications not accepted. Giving primarily in NY.
Application information: Contributes only to pre-selected organizations.
Trustees: Carl B. Leverenz, Cynthia A. Suskind, Dennis A. Suskind.
EIN: 133203197

34702—NEW YORK

34702
The A. Woodner Fund, Inc.
c/o Teitler & Teitler
1114 Ave. of the Americas, 45th Fl.
New York, NY 10036

Established in 2000 in NY.
Financial data (yr. ended 12/31/01): Grants paid, $166,500; assets, $1,840,463 (M); gifts received, $1,985,395; expenditures, $175,323; qualifying distributions, $166,500.
Officers: Andrea Woodner, Pres.; Beth D. Tractenberg, V.P., Secy.; Claudia Slacik, Treas.
EIN: 134092338

34703
The Zarb Family Fund, Inc.
c/o W. Michael Reickert, The Ayco Co., LP
P.O. Box 8019
Ballston Spa, NY 12020-8019

Established in 1996 in NY.
Donor(s): Frank G. Zarb, Patricia K. Zarb.
Financial data (yr. ended 12/31/01): Grants paid, $166,500; assets, $2,718,869 (M); expenditures, $168,337; qualifying distributions, $165,934.
Limitations: Applications not accepted. Giving primarily in NY.
Application information: Contributes only to pre-selected organizations.
Officers: Patricia K. Zarb, Pres.; Frank G. Zarb, V.P.; Frank G. Zarb, Jr., Secy.-Treas.
EIN: 113353618
Codes: FD2

34704
EMSA Fund, Inc.
c/o Norman Foundation, Inc.
147 E. 48th St.
New York, NY 10017
Contact: Alice Franklin, Pres.

Incorporated in 1962 in GA.
Donor(s): Phoebe Weil Lundeen,‡ and members of the Franklin family.
Financial data (yr. ended 12/31/99): Grants paid, $166,288; assets, $3,377,077 (M); gifts received, $49,965; expenditures, $197,607; qualifying distributions, $167,667.
Limitations: Giving primarily in CO.
Publications: Grants list.
Application information: Application form not required.
Officers and Trustees:* Alice Franklin,* Pres.; Audrey Franklin, V.P.; Andrew D. Franklin,* Secy.
EIN: 586043282
Codes: FD2

34705
Barry K. Schwartz Family Foundation, Inc.
205 W. 39th St.
New York, NY 10018

Established in 1987 in DE.
Donor(s): Barry K. Schwartz.
Financial data (yr. ended 10/31/01): Grants paid, $166,000; assets, $35,884 (M); gifts received, $114,900; expenditures, $166,333; qualifying distributions, $165,553.
Limitations: Applications not accepted. Giving primarily in NY and Providence, RI.
Application information: Contributes only to pre-selected organizations.
Officers: Barry K. Schwartz, Pres.; Sheryl R. Schwartz, V.P.
EIN: 133472786
Codes: FD2

34706
The Victor Herbert Foundation, Inc.
45 E. 85th St.
New York, NY 10028 (212) 935-6000
Contact: Herbert P. Jacoby, Chair.

Established in 1969 in NY.
Financial data (yr. ended 04/30/01): Grants paid, $165,850; assets, $3,522,773 (M); expenditures, $218,858; qualifying distributions, $159,394.
Limitations: Giving primarily in New York, NY.
Application information: Application form not required.
Officers and Directors:* Herbert P. Jacoby,* Chair.; Carolyn B. Jacoby-Gabay,* Pres.; Lois C. Schwartz, Secy.
EIN: 237044623
Codes: FD2

34707
The Faith Golding Foundation, Inc.
900 3rd Ave., 35th Fl.
New York, NY 10022

Established in 1984 in NY.
Donor(s): Faith Golding, First Sterling Corp., Modern Properties, Inc.
Financial data (yr. ended 11/30/01): Grants paid, $165,750; assets, $2,279,553 (M); gifts received, $390,000; expenditures, $199,527; qualifying distributions, $173,314.
Limitations: Applications not accepted. Giving primarily in New York, NY.
Application information: Contributes only to pre-selected organizations.
Trustees: Faith Golding, Bernard Greene, Ira W. Krauss.
EIN: 133260491
Codes: FD2

34708
Alan B. and Barbara Mirken Foundation
805 3rd Ave., 22nd Fl.
New York, NY 10022
Contact: Alan B. Mirken, Tr., and Barbara Mirken, Tr.

Established in 1989 in NY.
Donor(s): Alan B. Mirken.
Financial data (yr. ended 12/31/01): Grants paid, $165,700; assets, $2,893,888 (M); gifts received, $150,170; expenditures, $200,827; qualifying distributions, $192,241.
Limitations: Giving primarily in New York, NY.
Application information: Application form not required.
Trustees: Alan B. Mirken, Barbara Mirken.
EIN: 136916436
Codes: FD2

34709
Pollack Family Foundation
c/o CSAM
466 Lexington Ave., Ste. 17
New York, NY 10017-3140

Established in 1998 in NY.
Donor(s): Leon Pollack.
Financial data (yr. ended 12/31/01): Grants paid, $165,527; assets, $2,807,157 (M); expenditures, $182,632; qualifying distributions, $165,326.
Limitations: Applications not accepted. Giving primarily in NJ and NY.
Application information: Contributes only to pre-selected organizations.
Trustees: Andrea Gabay, Michael Gabay, Leon Pollack, Marsha Pollack, Robin Pollack.
EIN: 137157336
Codes: FD2

34710
Simon and Annie Davis Foundation
c/o Davis Gilbert
1740 Broadway, 3rd Fl.
New York, NY 10019-4315

Incorporated in 1946 in NY.
Donor(s): Abraham M. Davis,‡ Meyer Davis,‡ Ruth Davis.
Financial data (yr. ended 12/31/01): Grants paid, $165,307; assets, $1,767,841 (M); expenditures, $171,762; qualifying distributions, $165,593.
Limitations: Applications not accepted. Giving primarily in NY.
Application information: Contributes only to pre-selected organizations.
Officers: Leonard Schwartz, Pres. and Treas.; Howard J. Rubin, Secy.
EIN: 136069454
Codes: FD2

34711
AAAA Foundation, Inc.
405 Lexington Ave.
New York, NY 10174-1801
URL: http://www.aaaa.org

Established in 1997 in NY.
Donor(s): American Association of Advertising Agencies, Inc., AAAA, Inc.
Financial data (yr. ended 12/31/99): Grants paid, $165,000; assets, $776,491 (M); gifts received, $412,108; expenditures, $450,981; qualifying distributions, $201,608.
Limitations: Applications not accepted.
Officers: Edward Wax, Chair.; O. Burtch Drake, Pres.; James C. Martucci, Jr., Secy.-Treas.
Trustees: David Bell, Jay Chiat, Micael Donahue, Daisy Exposito, Shelly Lazarus, Leland T. Lynch, Burt Manning, Patrick J. McGrath, Sally Minard, Ralph W. Rydholm.
EIN: 133949950
Codes: FD2

34712
Cornelius N. Bliss Memorial Fund
c/o Boyce, Hughes & Farrell, LLP
1025 Northern Blvd., Ste. 300
Roslyn, NY 11576

Incorporated in 1917 in NY.
Donor(s): Cornelius N. Bliss,‡ Elizabeth M. Bliss, Lizzie P. Bliss, William B. Markell.
Financial data (yr. ended 12/31/01): Grants paid, $165,000; assets, $2,599,956 (M); expenditures, $195,095; qualifying distributions, $170,032.
Limitations: Applications not accepted. Giving primarily in NY.
Application information: Contributes only to pre-selected organizations.
Officers: John Parkinson III, Pres.; Barbara B. Mestre, V.P.; Cornelius N. Bliss III, Treas.
EIN: 136400075
Codes: FD2

34713
Wilhelm Worth Charitable Foundation
c/o Davidson Dawson & Clark
330 Madison Ave.
New York, NY 10017

Established in 1998 in NY.
Donor(s): Ann Osborne Daniels.
Financial data (yr. ended 12/31/01): Grants paid, $165,000; assets, $583,571 (M); expenditures, $180,544; qualifying distributions, $164,875.
Limitations: Applications not accepted. Giving primarily in MD.
Application information: Contributes only to pre-selected organizations.

Trustees: Ann Osborne Daniels, Jane D. January Daniels, Jane Wilhelm Daniels.
EIN: 137154978
Codes: FD2

34714
Josef Fischer and Elaine Fischer Foundation, Inc.
6 Hilltop Pl.
Monsey, NY 10952-2403

Donor(s): Josef Fischer.
Financial data (yr. ended 11/30/01): Grants paid, $164,800; assets, $1,215,140 (M); expenditures, $189,415; qualifying distributions, $189,415.
Limitations: Applications not accepted.
Application information: Contributes only to pre-selected organizations.
Officers: Josef Fischer, Pres.; Ariel Fischer, Secy.-Treas.
EIN: 237303546
Codes: FD2

34715
Alexis Gregory Foundation
c/o Vendome Press
1370 Ave. of the Americas, No. 2003
New York, NY 10019-4602
Contact: Alexis Gregory, Pres.

Established in 1986 in NY.
Donor(s): Alexis Gregory.
Financial data (yr. ended 12/31/99): Grants paid, $164,740; assets, $3,260,823 (M); gifts received, $74,876; expenditures, $200,165; qualifying distributions, $179,992.
Limitations: Giving primarily in NY.
Application information: Application form not required.
Officers: Alexis Gregory, Pres.; Peter Gregory, V.P.; Larry Levett, Secy.
EIN: 133201280
Codes: FD2

34716
The James Harper Marshall Foundation, Inc.
c/o M.R. Weiser & Co., LLP
3000 Marcus Ave.
New Hyde Park, NY 11042-1066

Established in 1982 in NY and DE.
Donor(s): James Harper Marshall, John H. Peace.
Financial data (yr. ended 12/31/01): Grants paid, $164,700; assets, $3,047,852 (M); gifts received, $5,000; expenditures, $170,071; qualifying distributions, $162,702.
Limitations: Applications not accepted. Giving primarily in NY.
Application information: Contributes only to pre-selected organizations.
Officers and Director:* James Harper Marshall, Chair.; Lee Harper Marshall, Pres.; Edward G. Beimfohr,* Secy.-Treas.
EIN: 133157280
Codes: FD2

34717
Otto Sussman Trust
1025 Northern Blvd., Ste. 300
Roslyn, NY 11576
Application address: P.O. Box 1374, Trainsmeadow Sta., Flushing, NY 11370-0998
Contact: Edward S. Miller, Tr.

Trust established in 1947 in NY.
Donor(s): Otto Sussman.‡
Financial data (yr. ended 12/31/01): Grants paid, $164,491; assets, $4,766,344 (M); expenditures, $2,252,467; qualifying distributions, $209,953.
Limitations: Giving limited to residents of NJ, NY, OK and PA.

Application information: Applicants must be recommended by agencies known to the trustees. Application form required.
Trustees: Edward S. Miller, Alice M. Ullmann, Erwin A. Weil.
EIN: 136075849
Codes: FD2, GTI

34718
Tompkins County Foundation, Inc.
P.O. Box 97
Ithaca, NY 14851
Contact: Janet Hewitt, Recording Secy.

Established in 1945 in NY.
Financial data (yr. ended 12/31/01): Grants paid, $164,037; assets, $1,993,570 (M); gifts received, $140,887; expenditures, $192,138; qualifying distributions, $163,732.
Limitations: Giving limited to the Tompkins County, NY, area.
Publications: Application guidelines, informational brochure, annual report.
Application information: Application form not required.
Officers and Directors:* Larry Baum,* Pres.; Arthur W. Pearce,* V.P.; James Byrnes,* Secy.-Treas.; James Brown, R. Davis Cutting, Anthony C. Digiacomo, Bonnie Howell, Patricia Johnson, Bruce Kane, Charles W. Treman, Jr.
EIN: 156018481
Codes: FD2

34719
Nathan & Louise Goldsmith Foundation, Inc.
c/o Davis & Davis
333 West End Ave., No. 4B
New York, NY 10023

Established in 1986 in NY.
Donor(s): Nathan Goldsmith.‡
Financial data (yr. ended 06/30/01): Grants paid, $164,000; assets, $2,625,540 (M); expenditures, $175,306; qualifying distributions, $172,315.
Limitations: Applications not accepted. Giving primarily in New York, NY; some giving also in Israel.
Application information: Contributes only to pre-selected organizations.
Officers and Directors:* Rabbi Haskel Lookstein,* Pres.; Arthur C. Silverman,* V.P. and Treas.; Andrew P. Davis,* Secy.; Ahuvah Keller, Michael H. Klein, Bernice Reisman.
EIN: 133367816
Codes: FD2

34720
The Society of the Friendly Sons of Saint Patrick in the City of New York
80 Wall St., Ste. 712
New York, NY 10005-3601

Established in 1945 in NY.
Financial data (yr. ended 03/31/01): Grants paid, $163,950; assets, $2,111,639 (M); expenditures, $767,602; qualifying distributions, $401,596.
Limitations: Applications not accepted. Giving primarily in New York, NY.
Application information: Contributes only to pre-selected organizations.
Officers: Timothy G. Reynolds, Pres.; John H. Fitzsimons, 1st V.P.; Robert J. Reilly, 2nd V.P.; Raymond C. Teatum, Secy.; John M. Queenan, Treas.
EIN: 136164757
Codes: FD2

34721
Realty Foundation of New York
551 5th Ave., Ste. 415
New York, NY 10176
Contact: Scholarship and Aid Comm.

Established in 1956 in NY.
Financial data (yr. ended 06/30/01): Grants paid, $163,750; assets, $1,845,368 (M); gifts received, $160,100; expenditures, $338,638; qualifying distributions, $280,287.
Limitations: Giving limited to the five boroughs of New York City.
Publications: Informational brochure.
Application information: Application form required.
Officers: Larry Silverstein, Chair.; Jerry Cohen, Pres.; Charles Borrok, Exec. V.P.; H. Dale Hemmerdinger, Exec. V.P.; John Avlon, V.P.; David Baldwin, V.P.; Charles Benenson, V.P.; James Digney, V.P.; Richard Fisher, V.P.; Edward Gordon, V.P.; Joseph Grotto, V.P.; Aaron Gural, V.P.; Peter Kalikow, V.P.; Peter Malkin, V.P.; Burton Resnick, V.P.; Stephen Ross, V.P.; Irving Schneider, V.P.; Alvin Schwartz, V.P.; Sheldon Solow, V.P.; Jerry Speyer, V.P.; Alan Weiler, V.P.; Fred Wilpon, V.P.; William Zeckendorf, V.P.; Daniel Rose, Secy.; Eugene Grant, Treas.; Patricia Frank, Exec. Dir.
Directors: Lawrence Ackman, and 47 additional directors.
EIN: 136016622
Codes: FD2, GTI

34722
The Sitt Family Foundation
(Formerly Morris & Eddie Sitt Family Foundation)
1375 Broadway
New York, NY 10018 (212) 947-4111
Contact: Morris Sitt, Dir.

Established in 1977.
Donor(s): Morris Sitt, and members of the Sitt family.
Financial data (yr. ended 06/30/01): Grants paid, $163,665; assets, $223,718 (M); expenditures, $166,169; qualifying distributions, $164,916.
Limitations: Giving primarily in NY.
Directors: David Sitt, Jeffrey Sitt, Morris Sitt.
EIN: 132886778
Codes: FD2

34723
Glyndebourne Association America, Inc.
c/o Torys
237 Park Ave.
New York, NY 10017

Established in 1971.
Financial data (yr. ended 12/31/99): Grants paid, $163,530; assets, $605,830 (M); gifts received, $166,429; expenditures, $191,426; qualifying distributions, $177,238.
Limitations: Applications not accepted. Giving primarily in Sussex, England.
Application information: Contributes only to pre-selected organizations.
Officers and Trustees:* Paul Collins,* Pres.; Sir George Christie, V.P.; Roger H. Lloyd,* Secy.; Mark Waldstein,* Treas.; John Botts, Robert Conway, Robert Montgomery Scott.
EIN: 237174079
Codes: FD2

34724
The Julius Ada Foundation, Inc.
250 Park Ave., Ste. 2030
New York, NY 10177

Established in 1987 in NY.
Donor(s): Carl Seaman.

Financial data (yr. ended 10/31/01): Grants paid, $163,500; assets, $3,659,301 (M); expenditures, $163,976; qualifying distributions, $163,855.
Limitations: Applications not accepted. Giving primarily in NY.
Application information: Contributes only to pre-selected organizations.
Officers: Carl Seaman, Pres.; Linda Seaman, V.P.; Robert Krissoff, Secy.
EIN: 112897412
Codes: FD2

34725
The Mendelow Family Foundation, Inc.
88 Central Park West
New York, NY 10023

Established in 1986 in NY.
Donor(s): Steven Mendelow, Nancy Mendelow.
Financial data (yr. ended 12/31/01): Grants paid, $163,456; assets, $746,272 (M); gifts received, $161,000; expenditures, $165,424; qualifying distributions, $162,900.
Limitations: Applications not accepted.
Application information: Contributes only to pre-selected organizations.
Directors: Steven Green, Nancy Mendelow, Steven Mendelow.
EIN: 133382034
Codes: FD2

34726
The Pevaroff Cohn Family Foundation
c/o Goldman Sachs & Co.
85 Broad St., Tax Dept.
New York, NY 10004

Donor(s): Gary D. Cohn.
Financial data (yr. ended 08/31/01): Grants paid, $163,392; assets, $4,952,597 (M); gifts received, $2,750; expenditures, $262,624; qualifying distributions, $166,472.
Limitations: Applications not accepted. Giving primarily in NY.
Application information: Contributes only to pre-selected organizations.
Trustees: Gary D. Cohn, Lisa Pevaroff Cohn, James Riley, Jr.
EIN: 133797393
Codes: FD2

34727
Peckham Family Foundation
29 Old Aspetong Rd.
Katonah, NY 10536
Contact: John R. Peckham, Tr.

Established in 1999 in NY.
Financial data (yr. ended 12/31/00): Grants paid, $163,325; assets, $533,508 (M); gifts received, $265,000; expenditures, $175,190; qualifying distributions, $162,102.
Trustees: Amy Peckham, John R. Peckham.
EIN: 141814765
Codes: FD2

34728
The Charitable Foundation of the Burns Family, Inc.
c/o Allen & Brown
60 E. 42nd St., Ste. 1760
New York, NY 10165-0006

Established in 1962 in NY.
Donor(s): Randal B. Borough.
Financial data (yr. ended 11/30/01): Grants paid, $163,100; assets, $3,476,736 (M); expenditures, $265,184; qualifying distributions, $211,435.
Limitations: Applications not accepted. Giving primarily in Charlotte, NC, NJ, NY, and Sheridan, WY.

Application information: Contributes only to pre-selected organizations.
Officers: Randal B. Borough, Pres.; D. Bruce Burns, V.P.; William J. Ennis, Secy.; Jeremiah E. Brown, Treas.
Director: John B. Goldsborough.
EIN: 136114052
Codes: FD2

34729
Yaron Foundation, Inc.
201 E. 37th St., Lobby Ste.
New York, NY 10016-3142
Contact: Norman Horowitz, Exec. Dir.

Established in 1984.
Donor(s): Isaac Steven Herschkopf, Debrah Lee Charatan, Robert Durst, Martin L. Markowitz, Leon Miller, Charles Ramat, Jay Susman, Charles Yassky.
Financial data (yr. ended 12/31/00): Grants paid, $163,079; assets, $579,217 (M); gifts received, $107,879; expenditures, $166,351; qualifying distributions, $162,904.
Limitations: Giving primarily in New York, NY.
Application information: Academic qualifications required for individual applicants; proposal required for research grants. Application form not required.
Officers: Isaac Steven Herschkopf, Pres.; Norman Horowitz, Exec. Dir.
EIN: 133209791
Codes: FD2

34730
Kibel Foundation, Inc.
c/o The Kibel Companies, LLC
300 E. 34th St.
New York, NY 10016
Contact: Henry Kibel, Pres.

Established in 1964 in NY.
Donor(s): Henry Kibel, Lillian Kibel.
Financial data (yr. ended 12/31/01): Grants paid, $163,000; assets, $143,504 (M); gifts received, $100,000; expenditures, $163,130; qualifying distributions, $163,055.
Limitations: Giving primarily in the New York, NY, area.
Officer: Henry Kibel, Pres.
EIN: 136167907
Codes: FD2

34731
Hawley Foundation for Children
19 Underwood Dr.
Saratoga Springs, NY 12866
Application address: P.O. Box 1017, Saratoga Springs, NY 12866; E-mail: sheila.c.oconnell@gte.net
Contact: Sheila O'Connell, Tr.

Established in 1955.
Financial data (yr. ended 10/31/01): Grants paid, $162,925; assets, $2,751,390 (M); gifts received, $341; expenditures, $211,837; qualifying distributions, $162,158.
Limitations: Giving limited to Saratoga County, NY.
Application information: Scholarship applications available through high school guidance offices after Feb. 1. Application form required.
Officers and Trustees:* Jane Corrou, Mgr.; Mary Ellen D'Andrea, Mgr.; Sharon Gallagher, Mgr.; Anita Dunn, Mgr.; Mary Gecewicz, Mgr.; Eleanor Hutchins, Mgr.; Scott Johnson, Mgr.; Cheryl Lesniak, Mgr.; Darlene Newey, Mgr.; Carol Obloy, Mgr.; Lois Radke,* Mgr.; Katie Richman, Mgr.; Julie Rodriguez, Mgr.; Harry D. Snyder,* Mgr.; Betsy Sutton, Mgr.; Judy Thorsland, Mgr.; Harold

A. Burnham, Eleanor Hutchins, Sheila O'Connell, Walter M. Stroup, Robert Tarrant, John Wise.
EIN: 141340069
Codes: FD2, GTI

34732
LSK Foundation
(Formerly Charitable Trust dated 8/12/87)
61 E. 8th St., No. 114
New York, NY 10003
Contact: Sonja K. Binkhorst, Tr.

Established in 1987 in NY.
Donor(s): Sonja K. Binkhorst.
Financial data (yr. ended 12/31/00): Grants paid, $162,630; assets, $716,237 (M); gifts received, $169,266; expenditures, $163,348; qualifying distributions, $160,624.
Limitations: Giving primarily in CT and VT.
Trustees: Audrey Binkhorst, Gordon Binkhorst, Mark Binkhorst, Sonja K. Binkhorst.
EIN: 133427131
Codes: FD2

34733
Meadows Charitable Trust
c/o Market St. Trust Co.
80 E. Market St., Ste. 300
Corning, NY 14830-2666
Contact: Rowland Stebbins III

Established in 1970.
Financial data (yr. ended 12/31/01): Grants paid, $162,500; assets, $1,954,480 (M); expenditures, $187,646; qualifying distributions, $162,158.
Limitations: Applications not accepted. Giving primarily along the East Coast, with emphasis on Washington, DC, FL, GA, NY, and SC.
Application information: Contributes only to pre-selected organizations; does not accept unsolicited applications.
Trustees: Adelaide C. Griswold, Alanson B. Houghton II, Amory Houghton, Jr.
EIN: 166093057
Codes: FD2

34734
Menemsha Fund, Inc.
c/o Walter Scheuer
635 Madison Ave., 18th Fl.
New York, NY 10022-0000

Established in 1985 in NY.
Donor(s): Blue Ridge Foundation, Marcelle Halpern Trust, Jeffrey J. Scheuer, Judith Scheuer.
Financial data (yr. ended 11/30/00): Grants paid, $162,380; assets, $506,696 (M); expenditures, $162,698; qualifying distributions, $162,379.
Limitations: Applications not accepted. Giving primarily in New York, NY.
Application information: Contributes only to pre-selected organizations.
Officers and Directors:* Jeffrey Scheuer,* Pres.; Ruth Scheuer,* Exec. V.P.; David Scheuer,* V.P.; Susan Scheuer,* V.P.; Walter Scheuer,* V.P.
EIN: 133334205
Codes: FD2

34735
Zachary & Elizabeth Fisher Armed Services Foundation
c/o Intrepid Museum
W. 46th St. and 12th Ave.
New York, NY 10036
Contact: Lisa Clark

Established in 1987 in NY.
Donor(s): Zachary Fisher.‡
Financial data (yr. ended 09/30/01): Grants paid, $162,270; assets, $114,544 (M); gifts received,

$188,057; expenditures, $162,520; qualifying distributions, $162,520.
Limitations: Giving on a national basis.
Application information: Application form required.
Trustees: M. Anthony Fisher, Peter Haas, Jim Kallstrom, Leonard Marks, VADM. Edward Martin, RADM. Robert Rosen.
EIN: 136894054
Codes: FD2, GTI

34736
Samuel Carson Foundation, Inc.
150 White Plains Rd., Ste. 300
Tarrytown, NY 10591-5521
Contact: Samuel Carson, Pres.

Donor(s): Samuel Carson.‡
Financial data (yr. ended 12/31/00): Grants paid, $162,175; assets, $100,935 (M); gifts received, $25,000; expenditures, $162,508; qualifying distributions, $162,175.
Limitations: Applications not accepted. Giving primarily in NY.
Application information: Contributes only to pre-selected organizations.
Officers: Carol Johnson, Pres.; Harry Dean, V.P.
EIN: 139191380
Codes: FD2

34737
Higgins Family Foundation
P.O. Box 13085
Albany, NY 12212

Established in 1997 in NY.
Donor(s): Robert J. Higgins.
Financial data (yr. ended 12/31/01): Grants paid, $162,000; assets, $1,851,408 (M); expenditures, $189,397; qualifying distributions, $157,534.
Limitations: Applications not accepted. Giving primarily in Albany, NY.
Application information: Contributes only to pre-selected organizations.
Trustee: Robert J. Higgins.
EIN: 146187206
Codes: FD2

34738
Martha R. Gerry Townley Foundation
c/o Brown Brothers Harriman Trust Co.
63 Wall St.
New York, NY 10005

Established in 1996 in MA.
Donor(s): Martha R. Gerry Townley.
Financial data (yr. ended 12/31/01): Grants paid, $162,000; assets, $109,371 (M); gifts received, $561; expenditures, $170,899; qualifying distributions, $166,031.
Limitations: Applications not accepted. Giving on a national and international basis.
Application information: Contributes only to pre-selected organizations.
Trustees: Mark A. Nowak, F. Bradford Townley, Martha R. Gerry Townley.
EIN: 043340006
Codes: FD2

34739
Shirley G. Benerofe Foundation, Inc.
c/o Benerofe Properties Corp.
P.O. Box 339, 4 New King St.
Purchase, NY 10577 (914) 681-5100
Contact: Andrew Benerofe, Tr.

Established in 1999 in FL.
Financial data (yr. ended 05/31/01): Grants paid, $161,601; assets, $2,135,200 (M); expenditures, $194,560; qualifying distributions, $161,601.
Limitations: Giving primarily in NY.

Trustees: Andrew Benerofe, James Benerofe, Mitchell Benerofe.
EIN: 134031176
Codes: FD2

34740
Dean Foundation, Inc.
150 White Plains Rd., Ste. 300
Tarrytown, NY 10591-5535
Contact: Harry Dean, Pres.

Established in 1954 in NY.
Donor(s): Harry Dean, Samuel Carson, Samuel Carson Foundation, Inc.
Financial data (yr. ended 12/31/01): Grants paid, $161,312; assets, $2,615,000 (M); gifts received, $57,561; expenditures, $181,953; qualifying distributions, $164,196.
Limitations: Applications not accepted. Giving on a national basis.
Application information: Contributes only to pre-selected organizations.
Officer: Harry Dean, Pres.
EIN: 136161380
Codes: FD2

34741
The Bernard Bergreen Foundation
1060 5th Ave.
New York, NY 10128

Established in 1998 in NY.
Donor(s): Bernard Bergreen.
Financial data (yr. ended 12/31/99): Grants paid, $161,150; assets, $2,125,919 (M); expenditures, $179,336; qualifying distributions, $168,727.
Limitations: Giving primarily in New York, NY.
Officers: Bernard D. Bergreen, Pres.; Barbara R. Bergreen, V.P.
Directors: Karen Bergreen, Thomas Kevin Bergreen, Timothy Scott Bergreen.
EIN: 510386251

34742
Joe A. Esses & Sons Foundation, Inc.
c/o E.S. Originals, Inc.
450 W. 33rd St.
New York, NY 10001-3305
Contact: Joe A. Esses, Pres.

Incorporated in 1984 in DE.
Donor(s): Joe A. Esses, Abraham Esses, Ezra Esses, and members of the Esses family.
Financial data (yr. ended 12/31/01): Grants paid, $161,150; assets, $42,426 (M); gifts received, $159,800; expenditures, $162,543; qualifying distributions, $161,083.
Limitations: Giving primarily in Brooklyn, NY.
Officers: Joe A. Esses, Pres.; Abraham Esses, V.P. and Secy.; Ezra Esses, V.P. and Treas.
EIN: 133252542
Codes: FD2

34743
Gioconda & Joseph H. King Foundation
c/o U.S. Trust
P.O. Box 2004
New York, NY 10109-1910

Established in 1992 in NY.
Donor(s): Gioconda King.
Financial data (yr. ended 12/31/01): Grants paid, $161,150; assets, $3,794,410 (M); expenditures, $192,952; qualifying distributions, $180,148.
Limitations: Applications not accepted. Giving primarily in MA.
Application information: Contributes only to pre-selected organizations.
Trustees: Diana Barrett, Gioconda King, U.S. Trust.
EIN: 133679578
Codes: FD2

34744
Odyssey Partners Foundation, Inc.
280 Park Ave., 21st Fl.
New York, NY 10017
Contact: Jack Nash, Pres.

Established in 1965 in NY.
Donor(s): Odyssey Partners.
Financial data (yr. ended 01/31/02): Grants paid, $161,125; assets, $1,164,237 (M); expenditures, $167,538; qualifying distributions, $164,455.
Limitations: Applications not accepted. Giving primarily in New York, NY.
Application information: Contributes only to pre-selected organizations.
Officers: Jack Nash, Pres.; Ludwig Bravmann, V.P.; Lawrence Levitt, Secy.-Treas.
EIN: 136186566
Codes: CS, FD2, CD

34745
Falconhead Foundation
c/o Brown Brothers Harriman Trust Co.
63 Wall St.
New York, NY 10005

Established in 1997 in DE.
Donor(s): Rodney D. Day III.
Financial data (yr. ended 12/31/01): Grants paid, $161,000; assets, $3,191,044 (M); expenditures, $187,718; qualifying distributions, $163,912.
Limitations: Applications not accepted. Giving primarily in NY and PA.
Application information: Contributes only to pre-selected organizations.
Officers: Rodney D. Day III, Pres.; Evelyn S. Day, V.P. and Secy.-Treas.; Allison Day Lanni, V.P.; Evelyn Day Lasry, V.P.; Hilary Day Maner, V.P.
EIN: 133946281
Codes: FD2

34746
The Berger Mittlemann Family Foundation
P.O. Box 522
Locust Valley, NY 11560-0522

Established in 1983.
Donor(s): Marion W. Berger, Richard W. Berger, Josef Mittlemann, Marsy B. Mittlemann.
Financial data (yr. ended 08/31/01): Grants paid, $160,920; assets, $237,108 (M); gifts received, $62,500; expenditures, $161,598; qualifying distributions, $160,920.
Limitations: Giving primarily in NY and on the East Coast.
Application information: Applications accepted for research grants in the areas of human development and community-based school reform. Application form not required.
Managers: Richard W. Berger, Josef Mittlemann, Marsy B. Mittlemann.
EIN: 113158539
Codes: FD2

34747
Holmberg Foundation, Inc.
519 Washington St.
Jamestown, NY 14701
Contact: Dr. Robert F. Wettingfeld, Pres.

Established in 1992 in NY.
Financial data (yr. ended 07/31/01): Grants paid, $160,500; assets, $3,632,816 (M); gifts received, $500; expenditures, $200,034; qualifying distributions, $169,324.
Limitations: Giving primarily in Chautauqua County, NY.
Application information: Application form not required.

34747—NEW YORK

Officers and Directors:* Robert F. Wettingfeld,* Pres.; William J. Kelly,* V.P.; Leslie Johnson,* Secy.; Joseph C. Johnson,* Treas.
EIN: 161426226
Codes: FD2

34748
The Frank J. McGuire Family Foundation
100 Seneca St., Ste. 500
Buffalo, NY 14203 (716) 826-2010
Contact: Donna McGuire, Tr.

Established in 1998 in NY.
Financial data (yr. ended 12/31/00): Grants paid, $160,200; assets, $333,880 (M); gifts received, $240,000; expenditures, $169,047; qualifying distributions, $159,668.
Trustees: Jacquelyn M. Gurney, Donna M. McGuire, Kathleen M. McGuire.
EIN: 161547973
Codes: FD2

34749
Victor R. Wright Foundation
c/o BCRS Associates, LLC
100 Wall St., 11th Fl.
New York, NY 10005

Established in 1985 in NY.
Donor(s): Victor R. Wright.
Financial data (yr. ended 07/31/01): Grants paid, $160,192; assets, $3,338,183 (M); expenditures, $188,186; qualifying distributions, $159,904.
Limitations: Applications not accepted. Giving primarily in New York, NY.
Application information: Contributes only to pre-selected organizations.
Trustees: Raymond E. Worsdale, Joann Wright, Victor R. Wright.
EIN: 133318173
Codes: FD2

34750
The Stevens Kingsley Foundation, Inc.
c/o Sullivan & Cromwell
125 Broad St.
New York, NY 10004-2498 (212) 558-3845
Contact: Charles T. Dowling

Established in 1960 in NY.
Financial data (yr. ended 12/31/01): Grants paid, $160,095; assets, $3,005,171 (M); expenditures, $178,678; qualifying distributions, $166,670.
Limitations: Giving limited to the Rome, NY, area.
Application information: Application form not required.
Officers and Directors:* Donald R. Osborn,* Pres.; Henry Christensen III,* Secy.-Treas.; F. Paul Cataldo II, Charles T. Dowling, David C. Grow, Mark F. Hinman, George B. Waters.
EIN: 136150722
Codes: FD2

34751
New York Society for the Relief of Widows & Orphans of Medical Men
c/o O'Connor, Davies et al
60 E. 42nd St.
New York, NY 10165
Contact: Walter Wichern, Jr., Secy.

Established in 1939 in NY.
Financial data (yr. ended 03/31/02): Grants paid, $160,000; assets, $2,912,011 (M); expenditures, $209,133; qualifying distributions, $170,416.
Limitations: Giving primarily in New York, NY.
Officers: Charles Schetlin, Pres.; Walter Wichern, Jr., Secy.; Chin B. Yeoh, Treas.
EIN: 237156733
Codes: FD2, GTI

34752
The Warren and Augusta Hume Foundation, Inc.
c/o RSN McGladrey, Inc.
106 Corporate Park Dr., Ste. 417
White Plains, NY 10604-3818

Established in 1993 in NY.
Donor(s): Warren C. Hume.
Financial data (yr. ended 12/31/01): Grants paid, $159,785; assets, $3,648,948 (M); expenditures, $171,453; qualifying distributions, $162,206.
Limitations: Applications not accepted.
Application information: Contributes only to pre-selected organizations.
Officers and Directors:* Warren C. Hume, Chair. and Pres.; Augusta Hume,* Vice-Chair.; Harold A. Ward III,* Secy.; G. Russell Creighton,* Treas.; Elizabeth Brothers.
EIN: 133675579
Codes: FD2

34753
H.R.C. Foundation, Inc.
c/o John M. Emery
237 Park Ave., 21st Fl.
New York, NY 10017

Donor(s): Hays Clark, H. Lawrence Clark.
Financial data (yr. ended 12/31/01): Grants paid, $159,540; assets, $400,823 (M); gifts received, $399,966; expenditures, $170,804; qualifying distributions, $264,004.
Limitations: Applications not accepted. Giving on a national basis, with some emphasis on the greater metropolitan Washington, DC, area, including MD and VA.
Application information: Contributes only to pre-selected organizations.
Officers and Directors:* Rosamund S. Clark,* Chair.; H. Lawrence Clark,* Pres. and Treas.; Harris W. Clark,* V.P.; Valerie C. McNeely,* V.P.; Edward H. Hein, Secy.
EIN: 132962149
Codes: FD2

34754
The Pace Foundation
2200 Smithtown Ave.
Ronkonkoma, NY 11779-7329

Established in 1995 in NY.
Donor(s): Ben Pace.
Financial data (yr. ended 12/31/00): Grants paid, $159,500; assets, $3,838,121 (M); gifts received, $350,000; expenditures, $170,843; qualifying distributions, $159,500.
Limitations: Applications not accepted. Giving primarily in NY.
Application information: Contributes only to pre-selected organizations.
Trustees: Carol Gbur, Kerry A. Pace, Meghan E. Pace.
EIN: 116458173
Codes: FD2

34755
Louis and Bessie Adler Foundation, Inc.
654 Madison Ave., 14th Fl.
New York, NY 10021
Contact: Robert Liberman, Chair.

Incorporated in 1946 in NY.
Donor(s): Louis Adler,‡ Louis Adler Realty Co., Inc.
Financial data (yr. ended 12/31/00): Grants paid, $159,125; assets, $2,260,983 (M); expenditures, $184,320; qualifying distributions, $161,845.
Limitations: Applications not accepted. Giving primarily in New York, NY.
Application information: Contributes only to pre-selected organizations.
Officers: Robert Liberman, Chair. and Secy.; Louise Grunwald, Pres. and Treas.; Barbara Liberman, V.P.; Robert Savitt, V.P.
EIN: 131880122
Codes: FD2

34756
Abraham, David & Solomon Sutton Family Foundation
1 E. 33rd St., 6th Fl.
New York, NY 10016-5011

Established in 1979 in NY.
Donor(s): Bag Bazaar, Inc.
Financial data (yr. ended 12/31/00): Grants paid, $159,088; assets, $44,684 (M); gifts received, $130,000; expenditures, $159,088; qualifying distributions, $159,088.
Limitations: Applications not accepted. Giving primarily in NY.
Application information: Contributes only to pre-selected organizations.
Trustees: David Sutton, Solomon Sutton.
EIN: 132984908
Codes: FD2

34757
The Edward H. Butler Foundation
P.O. Box 115
Athol Springs, NY 14010 (716) 649-4960
FAX: (716) 648-1908
Contact: Eleanor J. Baldelli, Secy.

Established in 1957 in NY.
Donor(s): Kate Butler Wickham.
Financial data (yr. ended 12/31/01): Grants paid, $159,000; assets, $3,560,303 (M); expenditures, $194,140; qualifying distributions, $162,215.
Limitations: Applications not accepted. Giving primarily in the Buffalo, NY, area.
Application information: Contributes only to pre-selected organizations.
Officer: Eleanor J. Baldelli, Secy.
Trustees: Kate R. Gardner, Edward B. Righter, Kate Butler Wickham.
EIN: 166019785
Codes: FD2

34758
The Waldo Trust
c/o The Bank of New York
1 Wall St., Tax Dept., 28th Fl.
New York, NY 10286
Contact: Jill Cook

Established in 1996 in CT.
Donor(s): Disney Shares.
Financial data (yr. ended 10/31/01): Grants paid, $159,000; assets, $2,227,987 (M); expenditures, $181,921; qualifying distributions, $167,665.
Limitations: Applications not accepted. Giving primarily in CT.
Application information: Contributes only to pre-selected organizations.
Trustee: The Bank of New York.
EIN: 137102854
Codes: FD2

34759
The Leigh Foundation, Inc.
(Formerly The N. J. Leigh Foundation)
1125 Park Ave., Apt. 15E
New York, NY 10128
Contact: Jonathan Leigh

Established in 1963 in NY.
Donor(s): Ameden Leigh, David I. Leigh, Jonathan W. Leigh, Josephine Leigh, Roberta Leigh.

Financial data (yr. ended 08/31/01): Grants paid, $158,700; assets, $823,981 (M); gifts received, $174,668; expenditures, $172,523; qualifying distributions, $159,056.
Limitations: Applications not accepted. Giving primarily in NY.
Application information: Contributes only to pre-selected organizations.
Trustee: Jonathan W. Leigh.
EIN: 136169780
Codes: FD2

34760
Hayden Family Foundation
c/o Marilyn Callister, Andersen, LLP
1345 Ave. of the Americas, Ste. 1107
New York, NY 10105

Established in 1984 in NY.
Donor(s): Richard M. Hayden.
Financial data (yr. ended 02/28/01): Grants paid, $158,588; assets, $8,752,547 (M); expenditures, $245,575; qualifying distributions, $158,838.
Limitations: Applications not accepted. Giving primarily in the U.S. and London, England.
Application information: Contributes only to pre-selected organizations.
Trustees: Richard M. Hayden, Susan F. Hayden, Peter M. Sacerdote, Anthony Verdecchia.
EIN: 133248046
Codes: FD2

34761
The Christine and Jaime Yordan Foundation
c/o BCRS Assocs., LLC
100 Wall St., 11th Fl.
New York, NY 10005

Established in 1993 in CT.
Donor(s): Jaime E. Yordan.
Financial data (yr. ended 07/31/01): Grants paid, $158,500; assets, $534,207 (M); gifts received, $280,356; expenditures, $163,471; qualifying distributions, $159,620.
Limitations: Applications not accepted. Giving primarily in New Canaan, CT, Cambridge, MA, New York, NY, and Middlebury, VT.
Application information: Contributes only to pre-selected organizations.
Trustees: Kevin W. Kennedy, Michael R. Lynch, Jaime E. Yordan.
EIN: 133755228
Codes: FD2

34762
Jan and Betka Papanek Foundation
500 5th Ave., Ste. 4810
New York, NY 10110-4899 (212) 382-3357
Contact: Jiri Brotan, Tr.

Established in 1992.
Donor(s): Betka Papanek.
Financial data (yr. ended 12/31/01): Grants paid, $158,243; assets, $474,748 (M); expenditures, $204,768; qualifying distributions, $191,412.
Limitations: Giving in New York, NY, the Czech Republic, and Slovakia.
Application information: Application form not required.
Trustees: Jiri Brotan, Anne E. Lesak Scott.
EIN: 133694358
Codes: FD2

34763
Elizabeth & Robert Rosenman Charitable Foundation
Worldwide Plz.
825 8th Ave., Ste. 4350
New York, NY 10019

Established in 1985 in NY.
Donor(s): Elizabeth F. Rosenman, Robert Rosenman.
Financial data (yr. ended 12/31/00): Grants paid, $158,166; assets, $600,145 (M); gifts received, $155,906; expenditures, $158,602; qualifying distributions, $158,166.
Limitations: Applications not accepted. Giving primarily in Boston, MA, and New York, NY.
Application information: Contributes only to pre-selected organizations.
Trustees: Elizabeth F. Rosenman, Robert Rosenman.
EIN: 066290408
Codes: FD2

34764
The Dow Foundation
Renamor Ridge Rd.
Tuxedo Park, NY 10987
Contact: Robert Dow, Tr.

Established in 1986 in NY.
Financial data (yr. ended 11/30/99): Grants paid, $158,046; assets, $1,084,259 (M); gifts received, $128,360; expenditures, $162,896; qualifying distributions, $159,858.
Limitations: Applications not accepted. Giving primarily in NY.
Application information: Contributes only to pre-selected organizations.
Trustees: Christina Dow, Robert S. Dow.
EIN: 136879648
Codes: FD2

34765
The Donald J. Trump Foundation, Inc.
c/o M.R. Weiser
3000 Marcus Ave.
New Hyde Park, NY 11042
Application address: c/o The Trump Organization, 725 5th Ave., New York, NY 10022
Contact: Donald J. Trump, Pres.

Established in 1987 in NY.
Donor(s): Donald J. Trump.
Financial data (yr. ended 12/31/99): Grants paid, $157,950; assets, $2,282 (M); gifts received, $161,480; expenditures, $160,133; qualifying distributions, $160,133.
Limitations: Giving primarily in New York, NY.
Application information: Application form not required.
Officers: Donald J. Trump, Pres.; Norma Forederer, Secy.; Allen Weisselberg, Treas.
EIN: 133404773
Codes: FD2

34766
The Marvin & Annette Lee Foundation, Inc.
543 Cayuga Heights Rd.
Ithaca, NY 14850
Contact: David M. Lee, Tr.

Established in 1959 in NY.
Donor(s): Marvin Lee,‡ Annette Lee.
Financial data (yr. ended 12/31/01): Grants paid, $157,850; assets, $2,978,171 (M); expenditures, $171,652; qualifying distributions, $158,615.
Limitations: Applications not accepted. Giving primarily in Ithaca and Tompkins County, NY.
Application information: Contributes only to pre-selected organizations.
Officers: David M. Lee, Pres. and Treas.; Annette Lee, Secy.
EIN: 066034414
Codes: FD2

34767
The Alisa & Peter Savitz Foundation
(Formerly HPS Foundation)
c/o BCRS Assocs., LLC
100 Wall St., 11th Fl.
New York, NY 10005

Established in 1993 in NY.
Donor(s): Peter Savitz.
Financial data (yr. ended 05/31/01): Grants paid, $157,659; assets, $3,713,022 (M); gifts received, $1,088,440; expenditures, $221,663; qualifying distributions, $159,263.
Limitations: Applications not accepted. Giving primarily in CT, MA, and NY.
Application information: Contributes only to pre-selected organizations.
Trustees: Alisa B. Savitz, Peter Savitz.
EIN: 133748074
Codes: FD2

34768
Rostrust Foundation
5411 15th St.
Brooklyn, NY 11219
Application address: 7077 Ave. du Pare, Montreal, Quebec, Canada

Established in 1998 in NY.
Donor(s): NY Life Insurance.
Financial data (yr. ended 04/30/01): Grants paid, $157,623; assets, $0 (M); gifts received, $2,461,447; expenditures, $187,280; qualifying distributions, $157,623.
Limitations: Giving primarily in Brooklyn and New York, NY.
Trustees: Chanie Rosenberg, Martin Rosenberg, Michael Rosenberg, Thomas Rosenberg.
EIN: 137111711
Codes: FD2

34769
The Nelkin Foundation
111 Great Neck Rd., Ste. 304
Great Neck, NY 11021

Established in 1968 in NY.
Donor(s): Harold Nelkin, Leslie Andrew Nelkin.
Financial data (yr. ended 04/30/02): Grants paid, $157,510; assets, $902,220 (M); gifts received, $33,500; expenditures, $167,990; qualifying distributions, $157,510.
Limitations: Applications not accepted. Giving primarily in the greater metropolitan New York, NY, area, including Long Island.
Application information: Contributes only to pre-selected organizations.
Officers: Harold Nelkin, Pres.; Ruth Nelkin, V.P. and Secy.
EIN: 136261501
Codes: FD2

34770
Leffell Family Foundation
c/o M.H. Davidson Co.
885 3rd Ave.
New York, NY 10022

Established in 1999 in NY.
Donor(s): Michael Leffell.
Financial data (yr. ended 12/31/00): Grants paid, $157,493; assets, $408,163 (M); gifts received, $549,436; expenditures, $160,587; qualifying distributions, $156,223.
Limitations: Applications not accepted. Giving primarily in Westchester County, NY.
Application information: Contributes only to pre-selected organizations.
Trustees: Lisa Leffell, Michael Leffell.
EIN: 316633021
Codes: FD2

34771
The Resource Foundation, Inc.
(Formerly Simpson Family Foundation, Inc.)
c/o A.J. Signorile
10 Park Ave.
New York, NY 10016

Established in 1987 in CT.
Donor(s): Members of the Simpson family.
Financial data (yr. ended 12/31/01): Grants paid, $157,402; assets, $2,337,483 (M); expenditures, $172,856; qualifying distributions, $162,672.
Limitations: Applications not accepted. Giving primarily in Greenwich, CT.
Application information: Contributes only to pre-selected organizations.
Officers and Directors:* Roy B. Simpson,* Chair.; Edith J. Simpson,* Pres.; Roy B. Simpson, Jr.,* Treas.
EIN: 222870501
Codes: FD2

34772
Stephen, Charles & Nettie Grosberg Foundation, Inc.
601 E. 20th St., Ste. 8C
New York, NY 10010-7625

Established in 2000 in NY.
Financial data (yr. ended 12/31/01): Grants paid, $157,295; assets, $636,214 (M); expenditures, $158,207; qualifying distributions, $156,918.
Limitations: Giving primarily in New York, NY.
Officers: Stephen Grosberg, Pres.; Amelia Grosberg, V.P.
EIN: 132886469
Codes: FD2

34773
Josephine Goodyear Foundation
50 Fountain Plz., Ste. 301
Buffalo, NY 14202 (716) 856-0911
FAX: (716) 856-0990; *E-mail:* ewdstevens@hiscockbarclay.com
Contact: E.W. Dann Stevens, Pres.

Incorporated in 1913 in NY.
Donor(s): Josephine L. Goodyear.‡
Financial data (yr. ended 12/31/01): Grants paid, $157,278; assets, $6,957,894 (M); expenditures, $231,695; qualifying distributions, $188,544.
Limitations: Giving limited to the Buffalo, NY, area.
Application information: Application form not required.
Officers and Directors:* E.W. Dann Stevens,* Pres.; Edward F. Walsh, Jr.,* V.P.; Bradley Wyckoff, Secy.; Jean G. Bowen,* Treas.; William J. Gisil, Jr., Frank H. Goodyear, Robert M. Goodyear, Karen Magee, Elizabeth A. Mitchell, Ellen M. Montgomery.
EIN: 160755234
Codes: FD2

34774
Menche Family Charitable Trust
241 Viola Rd.
Monsey, NY 10952-1732

Established in 2000 in NY.
Donor(s): Solomon Menche.
Financial data (yr. ended 12/31/00): Grants paid, $157,190; assets, $70,924 (M); gifts received, $793,799; expenditures, $157,199; qualifying distributions, $157,190.
Limitations: Applications not accepted.
Application information: Contributes only to pre-selected organizations.
Trustees: Pinchus Menche, Rochelle Menche, Solomon Menche.
EIN: 137224566

Codes: FD2

34775
Ernest & Rose Samuels Foundation, Inc.
c/o Feldheim
8 Hillcrest Ln.
Woodbury, NY 11797

Established around 1977 in FL.
Donor(s): Ernest Samuels.
Financial data (yr. ended 12/31/01): Grants paid, $157,000; assets, $2,903,989 (M); expenditures, $251,126; qualifying distributions, $175,602.
Limitations: Applications not accepted.
Application information: Contributes only to pre-selected organizations.
Officers: Herbert D. Feldheim, Pres.; Deborah Feldheim, Secy.
EIN: 591733119
Codes: FD2

34776
Spencer Charitable Fund
P.O. Box 197
Larchmont, NY 10538-0197 (914) 834-1900
Contact: Gordon S. Oppenheimer, Tr.

Established in 1985 in NY.
Financial data (yr. ended 07/31/01): Grants paid, $157,000; assets, $3,097,077 (M); expenditures, $174,200; qualifying distributions, $164,350.
Limitations: Giving primarily in NY.
Application information: Application form not required.
Trustees: Karen Frader, Gordon S. Oppenheimer, Jason R. Oppenheimer.
EIN: 136855911
Codes: FD2

34777
The Bouncer Foundation, Inc.
30 Rockefeller Plz., Ste. 3218
New York, NY 10112

Established in 2000 in DE.
Donor(s): Jonathan D. Sackler.
Financial data (yr. ended 12/31/01): Grants paid, $156,500; assets, $85,518 (M); gifts received, $33,280; expenditures, $159,503; qualifying distributions, $156,500.
Limitations: Applications not accepted.
Application information: Contributes only to pre-selected organizations.
Officers and Directors:* Jonathan D. Sackler,* Pres.; Mary Corson,* V.P. and Secy.-Treas.; Lauren D. Kelly,* V.P.; Deborah L. Guider, Anthony M. Roncalli.
EIN: 134119735

34778
Newstead Foundation
(Formerly The Catoctin Creek Foundation)
c/o Grant Thornton, LLP
60 Broad St.
New York, NY 10004

Trust established in 1963 in NJ.
Donor(s): John Seward Johnson.‡
Financial data (yr. ended 12/31/00): Grants paid, $156,375; assets, $398,147 (M); expenditures, $164,163; qualifying distributions, $156,272.
Limitations: Applications not accepted. Giving primarily in the greater Washington, DC, area, including surrounding MD and VA.
Application information: Contributes only to pre-selected organizations.
Director: Diana J. Firestone.
Trustees: Phillip C. Broughton, Bertram R. Firestone, Richard F. Pappalardo.
EIN: 226054885
Codes: FD2

34779
John J. Flemm Foundation, Inc.
1010 Franklin Ave., Ste. 400
Garden City, NY 11530

Established in 1974 in NY.
Donor(s): John J. Flemm.‡
Financial data (yr. ended 01/31/01): Grants paid, $156,350; assets, $2,917,473 (M); expenditures, $183,388; qualifying distributions, $178,659.
Limitations: Applications not accepted. Giving on a national basis.
Application information: Contributes only to pre-selected organizations.
Officers and Trustees:* Daniel Harris,* Pres.; Judith Post,* V.P. and Secy.; Michael Harris,* Treas.; Avery Harris, Leona Post.
EIN: 237348789
Codes: FD2

34780
The Neuberg Family Foundation
7 Manor Ln.
Lawrence, NY 11559

Established in 1999 in DE and NY.
Donor(s): David Neuberg, Dave Neuberg.
Financial data (yr. ended 06/30/01): Grants paid, $156,290; assets, $907,593 (M); gifts received, $630,000; expenditures, $159,040; qualifying distributions, $157,290.
Limitations: Applications not accepted. Giving primarily in NY, with emphasis on Brooklyn, Lawrence, and New York City.
Application information: Contributes only to pre-selected organizations.
Directors: David Neuberg, Ira Neuberg, Malkie Neuberg.
EIN: 113505413
Codes: FD2

34781
Zichron Kedoshim Foundation
165 Hooper St.
Brooklyn, NY 11211-7911
Contact: Beno I. Donath, Tr.

Established in 1999 in NY.
Financial data (yr. ended 09/30/01): Grants paid, $156,201; assets, $15,369 (M); gifts received, $56,000; expenditures, $156,886; qualifying distributions, $156,201.
Limitations: Giving primarily in Brooklyn, NY.
Trustees: Beno I. Donath, Judith Donath.
EIN: 137171861

34782
The Equipart Foundation
2323 Eastchester Rd.
Bronx, NY 10469-5910

Established in 1986 in NY.
Donor(s): Arnold Berkowitz, Joseph Brachfeld, Isaac Goldbrenner, Israel Hartman, Equipart Assocs., BHC Co.
Financial data (yr. ended 06/30/00): Grants paid, $156,151; assets, $4,052 (M); gifts received, $163,667; expenditures, $156,442; qualifying distributions, $156,151.
Limitations: Applications not accepted. Giving primarily in NY.
Application information: Contributes only to pre-selected organizations.
Directors: Joseph Brachfeld, Isaac Goldbrenner, Israel Hartman.
EIN: 133355056
Codes: FD2

34783
Burdette E. Snyder Foundation
c/o JPMorgan Chase Bank
1211 Ave. of the Americas, 34th Fl.
New York, NY 10036 (212) 789-5329
Contact: Gregory Braithwaite or Jeffrey Johns

Established in 1951.
Financial data (yr. ended 12/31/01): Grants paid, $156,125; assets, $1,365,064 (M); expenditures, $176,463; qualifying distributions, $158,152.
Limitations: Giving on a national basis.
Trustees: Deborah C. Damon, JPMorgan Chase Bank.
EIN: 136023212
Codes: FD2

34784
Josephine Lawrence Hopkins Foundation
61 Broadway, Ste. 2100
New York, NY 10006 (212) 480-0400
Contact: William P. Hurley, V.P.

Incorporated in 1968 in NY.
Donor(s): Josephine H. Graeber.‡
Financial data (yr. ended 12/31/01): Grants paid, $156,000; assets, $3,947,217 (M); expenditures, $203,885; qualifying distributions, $165,157.
Limitations: Applications not accepted. Giving primarily in New York, NY.
Application information: Contributes only to pre-selected organizations.
Officers and Directors:* Ivan Obolensky,* Pres. and Treas.; William P. Hurley,* V.P. and Secy.; Vera L. Colage,* V.P.; Lee Harrison Corbin, John G. Ledes, Gerald C. Tobin.
EIN: 136277593
Codes: FD2

34785
The Marc and Micheline Ratzersdorfer Foundation, Inc.
15 W. 47th St., Rm. 705
New York, NY 10024 (212) 869-5424
Contact: Marc Ratzersdorfer, Pres.

Established in 1993 in NY.
Donor(s): Marc Ratzersdorfer, Micheline Ratzersdorfer, Naftali Ratzersdorfer.
Financial data (yr. ended 12/31/00): Grants paid, $155,990; assets, $190,401 (M); gifts received, $78,350; expenditures, $156,369; qualifying distributions, $156,175.
Limitations: Giving primarily in NY.
Officers: Marc Ratzersdorfer, Pres.; Micheline Ratzersdorfer, V.P.; Naftali Ratzersdorfer, Secy.
EIN: 133746899
Codes: FD2

34786
Marilyn and Marshall Butler Foundation
c/o AVX Corp.
750 Lexington Ave., 27th Fl.
New York, NY 10022-1282
Contact: Marshall D. Butler, Mgr.

Established in 1990 in NY.
Donor(s): Marshall D. Butler.
Financial data (yr. ended 12/31/01): Grants paid, $155,804; assets, $2,107,396 (L); gifts received, $127,000; expenditures, $176,387; qualifying distributions, $156,054.
Limitations: Giving limited to NY.
Officer: Marshall D. Butler, Mgr.
EIN: 133591664
Codes: FD2

34787
Plymouth Hill Foundation
P.O. Box 687
Millbrook, NY 12545
Contact: Robert Goodstein, Pres.

Established in 1993 in NY.
Financial data (yr. ended 09/30/01): Grants paid, $155,500; assets, $2,737,296 (M); expenditures, $211,180; qualifying distributions, $157,906.
Limitations: Applications not accepted. Giving primarily in Dutchess County, NY.
Application information: Unsolicited requests for funds not accepted.
Officers and Directors:* Robert Goodstein,* Pres.; Gillian Goodwin,* V.P. and Secy.; Jeanne Goodwin,* V.P.; Andrew Goodwin,* Treas.
EIN: 223136685
Codes: FD2

34788
Schafer Family Foundation
c/o Executive Monetary Mgmt.
220 E. 42nd St., 32nd Fl.
New York, NY 10017 (212) 536-9700

Established in 1986 in NY.
Donor(s): Oscar S. Schafer.
Financial data (yr. ended 12/31/01): Grants paid, $155,458; assets, $1,029,151 (M); gifts received, $460; expenditures, $184,347; qualifying distributions, $154,525.
Limitations: Applications not accepted. Giving primarily in the metropolitan New York, NY, area.
Application information: Contributes only to pre-selected organizations.
Officers: Oscar S. Schafer, Pres.; Ann E. Carmel, Treas.
Director: Michael Stein.
EIN: 133382931
Codes: FD2

34789
Shanahan Family Foundation, Inc.
300 Park Ave.
New York, NY 10022

Established in 1997 in CT.
Financial data (yr. ended 12/31/01): Grants paid, $155,400; assets, $139,699 (M); expenditures, $156,694; qualifying distributions, $155,400.
Limitations: Giving primarily in CT and New York, NY.
Officer: William Shanahan, Pres.
EIN: 133979302
Codes: FD2

34790
Janklow Foundation
445 Park Ave.
New York, NY 10022-2606
Contact: Maria Aydin

Established in 1986 in NY.
Donor(s): Morton L. Janklow.
Financial data (yr. ended 06/30/02): Grants paid, $155,250; assets, $3,648,451 (M); expenditures, $195,468; qualifying distributions, $158,415.
Limitations: Applications not accepted. Giving primarily in New York, NY.
Application information: Contributes only to pre-selected organizations.
Trustees: Angela Janklow Harrington, Linda LeRoy Janklow, Lucas Janklow, Morton L. Janklow.
EIN: 133357111
Codes: FD2

34791
The David Berg Foundation, Inc.
16 E. 73rd St.
New York, NY 10021 (212) 517-8634
E-mail: mtocci@bergfoundation.org
Contact: Michele Tocci, Pres.

Established in 1994 in NY.
Donor(s): David Berg Settlor Trust.
Financial data (yr. ended 12/31/00): Grants paid, $155,000; assets, $177,072 (M); gifts received, $416,330; expenditures, $295,167; qualifying distributions, $269,084.
Limitations: Giving primarily in New York, NY.
Application information: Application form not required.
Officers: Michele Tocci, Pres.; William D. Zabel, V.P.; Jerome Zoffer, Secy.-Treas.
EIN: 133753217
Codes: FD2

34792
Georges and Claire Mabardi Foundation, Inc.
c/o Marc Devenoge
45 Combes Dr.
Manhasset, NY 11030

Established in 1998 in NY.
Financial data (yr. ended 12/31/01): Grants paid, $155,000; assets, $3,348,943 (M); expenditures, $175,797; qualifying distributions, $168,011.
Limitations: Applications not accepted. Giving primarily in the greater metropolitan New York, NY, area, including Long Island.
Application information: Contributes only to pre-selected organizations.
Officers and Directors:* Marc DeVenoge,* Pres.; Burt Lewis,* Secy.; Noemie DeVenoge,* Treas.
EIN: 132918244
Codes: FD2

34793
Mex-Am Cultural Foundation, Inc.
c/o Grant, Herrmann, Schwartz & Klinger
675 3rd Ave.
New York, NY 10017 (212) 759-2400
Contact: Andrew M. Klinger

Established in 1985 in NY.
Donor(s): The Wolfgang Schoenborn Trust.
Financial data (yr. ended 09/30/01): Grants paid, $155,000; assets, $2,017,022 (M); expenditures, $243,488; qualifying distributions, $216,236.
Limitations: Giving to domestic organizations to aid and benefit Mexico.
Application information: Application form not required.
Officer: William J. Brown, Pres.
EIN: 133328723
Codes: FD2

34794
Pluta Family Foundation, Inc.
20 Office Park Way
Pittsford, NY 14534-1718

Incorporated in 1966 in NY.
Donor(s): James Pluta, Helen Pluta, Peter Pluta, Mrs. Peter Pluta, General Circuits, Inc., Pluta Manufacturing Corp.
Financial data (yr. ended 12/31/01): Grants paid, $155,000; assets, $5,863,739 (M); expenditures, $211,511; qualifying distributions, $190,065.
Limitations: Giving limited to Rochester, NY.
Director: Andrew Pluta.
EIN: 510176213
Codes: FD2

34795
Soybelman Family Foundation
360 Loretto St.
Staten Island, NY 10307

Established in 2000 in NY.
Donor(s): Michael Soybelman.
Financial data (yr. ended 12/31/01): Grants paid, $155,000; assets, $307 (M); gifts received, $155,500; expenditures, $156,210; qualifying distributions, $155,600.
Limitations: Applications not accepted. Giving limited to Brooklyn, NY.
Application information: Contributes only to pre-selected organizations.
Trustees: Alla Soybelman, Jacob Soybelman, Michael Soybelman.
EIN: 134137977
Codes: FD2

34796
The Norio Ohga Foundation
550 Madison Ave., 35th Fl.
New York, NY 10022
Contact: Kenneth L. Nees, V.P.

Established in 1991 in NY.
Donor(s): Sony Corp. of America.
Financial data (yr. ended 12/31/00): Grants paid, $154,950; assets, $7,795,155 (M); gifts received, $7,276,000; expenditures, $156,860; qualifying distributions, $156,860.
Limitations: Applications not accepted.
Application information: Contributes only to pre-selected organizations.
Officers and Directors:* Norio Ohga,* Pres.; Kenneth L. Nees,* V.P. and Secy.; N. Paul Burak,* V.P.; Midori Ohga,* V.P.
EIN: 133617866
Codes: FD2

34797
Patricia Quick Charitable Trust
c/o AMCO
505 Park Ave., 20th Fl.
New York, NY 10022-9306

Established in 1996 in FL.
Donor(s): Patricia Quick.
Financial data (yr. ended 12/31/99): Grants paid, $154,924; assets, $43,559 (M); gifts received, $101,933; expenditures, $156,957; qualifying distributions, $154,193.
Limitations: Applications not accepted.
Application information: Contributes only to pre-selected organizations.
Officer: Patricia Quick, Pres.
EIN: 656228829
Codes: FD2

34798
Meehan Foundation
c/o M.J. Meehan & Co.
39 Broadway, 36th Fl.
New York, NY 10006

Established in 1996 in NY.
Donor(s): Emily Souvaine Meehan, Terence Meehan.
Financial data (yr. ended 12/31/00): Grants paid, $154,865; assets, $2,484,753 (M); gifts received, $1,364,689; expenditures, $165,275; qualifying distributions, $156,415.
Limitations: Applications not accepted. Giving limited to New York, NY.
Application information: Contributes only to pre-selected organizations.
Trustees: Emily Souvaine Meehan, Terence S. Meehan.
EIN: 137099577
Codes: FD2

34799
Albert and Pearl Ginsberg Foundation, Inc.
64-35 Yellowstone Blvd.
Forest Hills, NY 11375

Established in 1980 in NY.
Donor(s): Albert Ginsberg,‡ Pearl Ginsberg.
Financial data (yr. ended 12/31/01): Grants paid, $154,795; assets, $2,893,509 (M); expenditures, $159,991; qualifying distributions, $159,991.
Limitations: Applications not accepted. Giving primarily in FL and NY.
Application information: Contributes only to pre-selected organizations.
Officers: Laurence T. Ginsberg, V.P.; Pearl Ginsberg, V.P.; Liane Ginsburg, Secy.; Hilary Feshbach, Treas.
EIN: 061039627
Codes: FD2

34800
Mary & Roy Anderson Charitable Foundation, Inc.
11 Martine Ave., 12th Fl.
White Plains, NY 10606-1934

Established in 1999 in NY.
Donor(s): Mary E. Anderson.
Financial data (yr. ended 12/31/01): Grants paid, $154,764; assets, $83,860 (M); gifts received, $209,585; expenditures, $169,969; qualifying distributions, $169,867.
Limitations: Applications not accepted.
Application information: Contributes only to pre-selected organizations.
Officers: Mary E. Anderson, Pres.; John J. Parker, V.P.; Kim Marie Parker, Treas.
EIN: 134067288
Codes: FD2

34801
Port Charitable Foundation
26 Harbor Pk. Dr.
Port Washington, NY 11050 (516) 484-4400
Contact: Hugh Freund, Pres.

Established in 1997.
Financial data (yr. ended 12/31/99): Grants paid, $154,696; assets, $15,676 (M); gifts received, $179,848; expenditures, $162,049; qualifying distributions, $154,696.
Limitations: Giving primarily in NY.
Officers: Hugh Freund, Pres.; Carol Freund, Secy.
Director: Gary Stoller.
EIN: 113298376
Codes: FD2

34802
Oliver B. Merlyn Foundation
P.O. Box 159
Victor, NY 14564
Contact: Thomas Kubiak, Tr.

Established in 1999 in NY.
Donor(s): Thomas Kubiak.
Financial data (yr. ended 12/31/01): Grants paid, $154,618; assets, $2,016,594 (M); expenditures, $177,492; qualifying distributions, $154,304.
Limitations: Giving limited to NY and RI.
Publications: Grants list.
Application information: Application form required.
Trustees: Christopher Kubiak, Elizabeth Ann Kubiak, Jennifer Elisa Kubiak, Kelly Kubiak, Paullette Kubiak, Rebecca Gene Kubiak, Thomas Kubiak, Thomas Kubiak II.
EIN: 161563802
Codes: FD2

34803
Irving & Adele Rosenberg Foundation, Inc.
c/o Aaron Halper & Co.
331 Madison Ave., 8th Fl.
New York, NY 10017 (212) 293-5100
Contact: Adele Rosenberg, Pres.

Established in 1977 in NY.
Donor(s): Haigro Fabrics, Inc.
Financial data (yr. ended 12/31/01): Grants paid, $154,462; assets, $1,075,202 (M); expenditures, $155,265; qualifying distributions, $155,083.
Limitations: Applications not accepted. Giving primarily in New York, NY.
Application information: Contributes only to pre-selected organizations.
Officer: Adele Rosenberg, Pres.
EIN: 510139277
Codes: FD2

34804
White Family Charitable Foundation, Inc.
118 E. 70th St.
New York, NY 10021-5007

Established in 1997 in NY.
Donor(s): Martin A. White.
Financial data (yr. ended 12/31/01): Grants paid, $154,138; assets, $2,644,349 (M); expenditures, $176,666; qualifying distributions, $154,138.
Limitations: Applications not accepted. Giving primarily in New York City.
Application information: Contributes only to pre-selected organizations.
Officer: Martin A. White, Pres.
Directors: Brian McConell, Laura Nagler.
EIN: 133946733
Codes: FD2

34805
The Burch Foundation
c/o Robert L. Burch, III
1 Rockefeller Plz.
New York, NY 10020

Established in 2000 in NY.
Donor(s): Robert L. Burch III.
Financial data (yr. ended 12/31/01): Grants paid, $154,000; assets, $2,048,335 (M); gifts received, $403,920; expenditures, $155,525; qualifying distributions, $154,000.
Limitations: Applications not accepted.
Application information: Contributes only to pre-selected organizations.
Director: Robert L. Burch III.
EIN: 134144134

34806
Koussevitzky Music Foundation, Inc.
c/o Brown Raysman, LLP
900 3rd Ave.
New York, NY 10022 (212) 895-2367
FAX: (212) 895-2900; *E-mail:* info@koussevitzky.org; *URL:* http://www.koussevitzky.org
Contact: James M. Kendrick, Secy.

Established in 1942 in NY.
Donor(s): Olga Koussevitzky,‡ Serge Koussevitzky.‡
Financial data (yr. ended 03/31/01): Grants paid, $153,750; assets, $1,986,359 (M); expenditures, $200,914; qualifying distributions, $190,136.
Publications: Application guidelines, informational brochure (including application guidelines).
Application information: Commission procedure will be provided upon request. Application form can be downloaded from foundation website. Application form required.

Officers and Directors:* Gunther Schuller,* Chair. and Pres.; Fred Lerdahl,* V.P.; James M. Kendrick, Secy.; George Newlin,* Treas.; Phyllis Bryn-Julson, Mario Davidovsky, John Harbison, Andrew Imbrie, Ursula Oppens, Shulamit Ran, Fred Sherry, Olly Wilson.
EIN: 046128361
Codes: FD2, GTI

34807
Ninah & Michael Lynne Foundation
c/o Michael Lynne
770 Park Ave., Apt. 18A
New York, NY 10021

Established in 1993 in NY.
Donor(s): Michael Lynne.
Financial data (yr. ended 12/31/01): Grants paid, $153,740; assets, $106,225 (M); gifts received, $50,000; expenditures, $166,898; qualifying distributions, $156,316.
Limitations: Applications not accepted. Giving primarily in NY.
Application information: Contributes only to pre-selected organizations.
Trustees: Michael Lynne, Ninah Lynne.
EIN: 133798596
Codes: FD2

34808
Dolan Family Foundation
c/o William A. Frewin, Jr.
340 Media Crossways Park Dr.
Woodbury, NY 11797 (516) 803-9210
Contact: Marianne Dolan Weber, Pres.

Established in 1987 in NY.
Donor(s): Charles F. Dolan, Helen A. Dolan.
Financial data (yr. ended 11/30/01): Grants paid, $153,503; assets, $40,133,462 (M); gifts received, $50,000; expenditures, $242,843; qualifying distributions, $238,800.
Limitations: Giving on a national basis.
Officers: Marianne Dolan Weber, Pres.; William A. Frewin, Jr., V.P.
Directors: Charles F. Dolan, Helen A. Dolan.
EIN: 113129948
Codes: FD2

34809
Jon and Abby Winkelried Foundation
(Formerly The Winkelried Family Foundation)
c/o Goldman Sachs & Co.
85 Broad St., Tax Dept.
New York, NY 10004

Established in 1991 in NJ.
Donor(s): Jon Winkelried.
Financial data (yr. ended 05/31/01): Grants paid, $153,267; assets, $5,693,639 (M); gifts received, $1,100; expenditures, $187,683; qualifying distributions, $154,555.
Limitations: Applications not accepted. Giving primarily in NJ and NY; some giving also in London, England.
Application information: Contributes only to pre-selected organizations.
Trustees: Mark Schwartz, Abby Winkelried, Jon Winkelried.
EIN: 133634388
Codes: FD2

34810
Friends of Sapient Charitable Foundation, Inc.
498 7th Ave., 10th Fl.
New York, NY 10018

Established in 1999 in MA.
Financial data (yr. ended 12/31/01): Grants paid, $152,890; assets, $133,467 (M); gifts received, $302,208; expenditures, $174,866; qualifying distributions, $152,890.
Limitations: Applications not accepted. Giving primarily in MD and NY.
Application information: Contributes only to pre-selected organizations.
Officers and Directors:* Michael D. Odell, Pres.; J. Stuart Moore,* Clerk; Christopher Marksky.
EIN: 043468866

34811
Floyd J. Reinhart Memorial Scholarship Foundation
256 Locust Ave.
Amsterdam, NY 12010
Contact: Frances Allen, Tr.

Financial data (yr. ended 06/30/01): Grants paid, $152,500; assets, $3,300,086 (M); expenditures, $182,278; qualifying distributions, $168,532.
Limitations: Giving limited to residents of Montgomery County, NY.
Application information: Application form not required.
Trustee: Frances Allen.
EIN: 141605307
Codes: FD2, GTI

34812
The William Ewing Foundation
c/o U.S. Trust, Tax Dept.
114 W. 47th St.
New York, NY 10036
Application address: c/o Isabelle Fitzpatrick, 342 Madison Ave., Ste. 702, New York, NY 10173-0799; FAX: (212) 852-3377
Contact: William Ewing, Jr.

Established in 1957 in NY.
Donor(s): Moore P. Huffman.
Financial data (yr. ended 12/31/01): Grants paid, $152,375; assets, $2,736,583 (M); expenditures, $187,877; qualifying distributions, $170,358.
Limitations: Giving primarily in the greater metropolitan New York, NY, area, including Long Island.
Trustees: Grace E. Huffman, Jessie E. Phillips, U.S. Trust.
EIN: 136065580
Codes: FD2

34813
Charlotte Cuneen Hackett Charitable Trust
c/o HSBC Bank USA
452 5th Ave., 17th Fl.
New York, NY 10018 (212) 525-2417
Contact: Stephen B. Boies, V.P., HSBC Bank USA

Established in 1971 in NY.
Donor(s): Charlotte Cuneen Hackett.‡
Financial data (yr. ended 12/31/01): Grants paid, $152,250; assets, $3,153,941 (M); expenditures, $207,072; qualifying distributions, $156,590.
Limitations: Applications not accepted. Giving limited to Dutchess County, NY.
Application information: Contributes only to pre-selected organizations.
Trustees: John J. Gartland, Jr., HSBC Bank USA.
EIN: 237215233
Codes: FD2

34814
The Bradford & Lauren Koenig Foundation
c/o Goldman Sachs & Co.
85 Broad St., Tax Dept.
New York, NY 10004

Established in 1997 in CA.
Donor(s): Bradford Koenig.
Financial data (yr. ended 12/31/01): Grants paid, $152,219; assets, $2,742,875 (M); gifts received, $570,884; expenditures, $157,754; qualifying distributions, $153,754.
Limitations: Applications not accepted. Giving primarily in CA.
Application information: Contributes only to pre-selected organizations.
Trustees: Bradford Koenig, Lauren Koenig, Mark R. Tercek.
EIN: 133993307
Codes: FD2

34815
Stephen & May Cavin Leeman Foundation, Inc.
471 W. 22nd St.
New York, NY 10011-2548
Contact: Gina Holland Waldo, Admin.

Established in 1969 in NY.
Donor(s): Stephen Leeman,‡ May Cavin Leeman.‡
Financial data (yr. ended 06/30/01): Grants paid, $152,150; assets, $3,090,770 (M); expenditures, $195,343; qualifying distributions, $171,748.
Limitations: Giving primarily in New York, NY.
Publications: Annual report.
Application information: New York/New Jersey Common Application Form as modified by the foundation. Application form required.
Officers and Directors:* Cavin P. Leeman, M.D.,* Pres. and Treas.; Diane L. Zimmerman,* V.P. and Secy.; Gina Trent.
EIN: 237057183
Codes: FD2

34816
Grace R. and Allan D. Marcus Foundation
7 W. 81st St., Apt. 5B
New York, NY 10024-6049

Established in 1990 in NY.
Donor(s): Grace R. Marcus.‡
Financial data (yr. ended 12/31/01): Grants paid, $151,950; assets, $3,100,877 (M); expenditures, $189,814; qualifying distributions, $152,491.
Limitations: Applications not accepted. Giving primarily in NY.
Application information: Contributes only to pre-selected organizations.
Trustees: Theodore P. Halperin, Daniel Soba.
EIN: 136928240
Codes: FD2

34817
Laura Steinberg Tisch Foundation, Inc.
778 Park Ave.
New York, NY 10021-3554

Established in 1995 in NY and DE.
Financial data (yr. ended 12/31/00): Grants paid, $151,890; assets, $2,744,030 (M); expenditures, $177,829; qualifying distributions, $151,890.
Limitations: Applications not accepted. Giving primarily in New York, NY.
Application information: Contributes only to pre-selected organizations.
Officer: Laura Steinberg Tisch, Pres.
EIN: 311641039
Codes: FD2

34818
Abraham Kamber Foundation
521 5th Ave., 22nd Fl.
New York, NY 10175 (212) 972-8844
FAX: (212) 972-0620; E-mail: steven@kamber.inc.com
Contact: Steven M. Levy, Tr.

Established in 1950 in NY.
Donor(s): Steven M. Levy, Peter B. Levy, Gloria K. Levy, Stanley H. Levy.
Financial data (yr. ended 12/31/99): Grants paid, $151,521; assets, $3,715,906 (M); gifts received,

34818—NEW YORK

$129,400; expenditures, $172,720; qualifying distributions, $157,185.
Limitations: Giving primarily in Westchester County and New York, NY.
Application information: Application form not required.
Trustees: Peter B. Levy, Steven M. Levy.
EIN: 136102029
Codes: FD2

34819
The David & Tricia Rogers Foundation
c/o Goldman Sachs & Co.
85 Broad St., Tax Dept.
New York, NY 10004

Established in 1994 in CT.
Donor(s): J. David Rogers.
Financial data (yr. ended 02/28/01): Grants paid, $151,493; assets, $7,467,708 (M); gifts received, $2,720,755; expenditures, $290,672; qualifying distributions, $151,611.
Limitations: Applications not accepted. Giving primarily in Darien, CT, and New York, NY.
Application information: Contributes only to pre-selected organizations.
Trustees: J. David Rogers, Tricia Rogers.
EIN: 133789004
Codes: FD2

34820
The Riklis Family Foundation, Inc.
c/o Fiduciary Trust Co. Intl.
600 5th Ave.
New York, NY 10020 (212) 861-1595
Application address: 1020 5th Ave., New York, NY 10028
Contact: Simona R. Ackerman, Pres.

Incorporated in 1960 in NY.
Financial data (yr. ended 06/30/01): Grants paid, $151,490; assets, $2,953,028 (M); expenditures, $160,225; qualifying distributions, $153,466.
Limitations: Giving on a national basis, with emphasis on New York, NY.
Application information: Application form not required.
Officers: Simona R. Ackerman, Pres.; Meeshulam Riklis, V.P.
EIN: 136163061
Codes: FD2

34821
Toufic Srour Foundation, Inc.
c/o Parigi Group Ltd.
112 W. 34th St., Ste. 836
New York, NY 10120-0800

Established in 1999 in NY.
Donor(s): Esther Jamal, Marco Srour, Morris Srour.
Financial data (yr. ended 11/30/01): Grants paid, $151,417; assets, $46,703 (M); gifts received, $194,553; expenditures, $151,986; qualifying distributions, $151,806.
Limitations: Applications not accepted. Giving primarily in NJ and NY.
Application information: Contributes only to pre-selected organizations.
Officers: Marco Srour, Pres.; Morris Srour, Secy.; Esther Jamal, Treas.
EIN: 134088570
Codes: FD2

34822
The Nachum & Feige Stein Foundation
1675 52nd St.
Brooklyn, NY 11204 (718) 851-1483
Contact: Nachum Stein, Pres.

Established in 1975 in NY.
Donor(s): Nachum Stein, Feige Stein.
Financial data (yr. ended 06/30/01): Grants paid, $151,380; assets, $0 (M); gifts received, $223,876; expenditures, $151,510; qualifying distributions, $151,380.
Limitations: Giving primarily in NY.
Application information: Application form not required.
Officers and Trustees:* Nachum Stein,* Pres.; Feige Stein,* Secy.; Alexander Hasenfeld.
EIN: 510142287
Codes: FD2

34823
The Dobbins Foundation
c/o Edward R. Finch
862 Park Ave.
New York, NY 10021

Established in 1999 in DE.
Donor(s): Hope J. Dobbins.
Financial data (yr. ended 12/31/00): Grants paid, $151,307; assets, $3,317,091 (M); gifts received, $3,410,625; expenditures, $171,175; qualifying distributions, $155,712.
Limitations: Applications not accepted. Giving primarily in MA.
Application information: Contributes only to pre-selected organizations.
Officers: Hope J. Dobbins, Chair.; Edward R. Finch, Pres.; Holly R. Dobbins, V.P. and Treas.; Heather Dobbins, V.P.; Michelle Dobbins Dodge, Secy.
EIN: 134078241
Codes: FD2

34824
The Margaret & Daniel Ranzman Foundation, Inc.
(Formerly Margaret Kuo Family Foundation, Inc.)
c/o Leonard S. Schwartz & Co.
1740 Broadway, 3rd Fl.
New York, NY 10019-4315

Established in 1984 in DE.
Donor(s): Margaret Kuo Ranzman.
Financial data (yr. ended 05/31/01): Grants paid, $151,000; assets, $1,861,292 (M); expenditures, $158,637; qualifying distributions, $152,985.
Limitations: Applications not accepted. Giving on a national basis.
Application information: Contributes only to pre-selected organizations.
Officers: Margaret Kuo Ranzman, Pres.; Sylvia Sotto, V.P.; Russell Knapp, Secy.
EIN: 226384497
Codes: FD2

34825
Kurtz Foundation
55 Rome St.
Farmingdale, NY 11735

Established in 1965 in NY.
Financial data (yr. ended 12/31/01): Grants paid, $150,835; assets, $749,242 (M); expenditures, $166,660; qualifying distributions, $150,780.
Limitations: Applications not accepted. Giving primarily in NY.
Application information: Contributes only to pre-selected organizations.
Officers and Directors:* Robert Kurtz,* Pres.; Ruth G. Kurtz,* C.F.O.; Alfred Kurtz.
EIN: 116046601
Codes: FD2

34826
The Giff-Som Back Foundation, Inc.
(Formerly The Amy Morgan Sommer Foundation)
810 7th Ave., Ste. 2900
New York, NY 10019

Established in 1985 in NY.
Donor(s): Amy Morgan Sommer.
Financial data (yr. ended 06/30/01): Grants paid, $150,828; assets, $2,296,655 (M); expenditures, $156,716; qualifying distributions, $150,353.
Limitations: Applications not accepted. Giving primarily in Los Angeles, CA, and Wellesley, MA.
Application information: Contributes only to pre-selected organizations.
Officers: Amy Morgan Sommer, Pres.; Beverly Sommer, V.P.
Director: Frank J. Stella.
EIN: 133319142
Codes: FD2

34827
Edward and Marjorie Goldberger Foundation
J.H. Cohn
1212 Ave. of Americas, 12th Fl.
New York, NY 10036

Established in 1957 in NY.
Donor(s): Marjorie Goldberger.
Financial data (yr. ended 12/31/01): Grants paid, $150,616; assets, $2,893,912 (M); expenditures, $183,439; qualifying distributions, $165,998.
Limitations: Applications not accepted. Giving primarily in NY.
Application information: Contributes only to pre-selected organizations.
Officers: Ann Jurdem, Chair. and V.P.; Susan Jacoby, Pres. and Secy.
EIN: 136084528
Codes: FD2

34828
The Painted Flower Foundation, Inc.
420 E. 51st St., Ste. 99
New York, NY 10022
Contact: Barbara Freedman, Dir.

Established in 1998 in NY.
Financial data (yr. ended 12/31/01): Grants paid, $150,613; assets, $1,528,319 (M); expenditures, $172,257; qualifying distributions, $150,613.
Limitations: Giving primarily in New York, NY, with some giving in CA and Washington, DC.
Directors: Barbara Freedman, Nancy Goldhill.
EIN: 133901528

34829
L. & I. Shamah Foundation, Inc.
c/o Catton Bros. Co.
112 W. 34th St.
New York, NY 10120
Contact: Irwin Shamah, Dir.

Established in 1987.
Donor(s): Irwin Shamah, Leon Shamah.
Financial data (yr. ended 12/31/01): Grants paid, $150,577; assets, $318 (M); gifts received, $45,000; expenditures, $152,689; qualifying distributions, $150,577.
Limitations: Giving primarily in Brooklyn, NY.
Application information: Application form not required.
Directors: Irwin Shamah, Leon Shamah.
EIN: 133440114

34830
John R. and Tawna B. Farmer Foundation
c/o BCRS Associates, LLC
67 Wall St., 8th Fl.
New York, NY 10005

Established in 1985 in CA.
Donor(s): John R. Farmer.
Financial data (yr. ended 03/31/01): Grants paid, $150,500; assets, $201,432 (M); expenditures, $152,350; qualifying distributions, $151,430.
Limitations: Applications not accepted. Giving on a national basis.
Application information: Contributes only to pre-selected organizations.
Trustees: John R. Farmer, Tawna B. Farmer.
EIN: 942988628
Codes: FD2

34831
Lockwood Family Foundation
c/o Hecht and Co., PC
111 W. 40th St.
New York, NY 10018

Established in 1999 in NY.
Donor(s): Christopher J. Lockwood.
Financial data (yr. ended 12/31/01): Grants paid, $150,500; assets, $347,576 (M); expenditures, $159,277; qualifying distributions, $152,846.
Limitations: Applications not accepted. Giving primarily in NY.
Application information: Contributes only to pre-selected organizations.
Officers: Susan E. Lockwood, Pres.; Kristen M. Lockwood, Secy.; Christopher J. Lockwood, Treas.
EIN: 134094392
Codes: FD2

34832
Sandpiper Fund, Inc.
c/o Hecht and Co., PC
111 W. 40th St.
New York, NY 10018

Established in 1990 in NY.
Donor(s): Daniel Scheuer, Shelley Leizman.
Financial data (yr. ended 12/31/01): Grants paid, $150,500; assets, $2,875,627 (M); gifts received, $100,000; expenditures, $176,861; qualifying distributions, $152,008.
Limitations: Applications not accepted. Giving primarily in New York, NY.
Application information: Contributes only to pre-selected organizations.
Officers: Daniel Scheuer, Pres.; Shelley Leizman, V.P.
EIN: 133557069
Codes: FD2

34833
The Thomas P. & Cynthia D. Sculco Foundation
132 E. 95th St.
New York, NY 10128
Contact: Thomas P. Sculco, M.D., Pres.

Established in 1997 in NY.
Donor(s): Thomas P. Sculco, M.D., Cynthia D. Sculco.
Financial data (yr. ended 02/28/01): Grants paid, $150,450; assets, $2,795,178 (M); gifts received, $550,063; expenditures, $154,024; qualifying distributions, $150,450.
Application information: Application form not required.
Officers: Thomas P. Sculco, M.D., Pres.; Cynthia D. Sculco, Secy.
EIN: 133952927
Codes: FD2

34834
Schulz Charitable Foundation, Inc.
c/o Winston & Winston
22 Greendald Rd.
Scarsdale, NY 10583 (914) 967-7000
FAX: (914) 967-7112
Contact: Allan B. Winston, Pres.

Established in 1999 in DE.
Donor(s): Adalbert Schulz.‡
Financial data (yr. ended 12/31/01): Grants paid, $150,380; assets, $3,344,758 (M); expenditures, $197,566; qualifying distributions, $171,627.
Limitations: Giving primarily in NY; some giving also in Asia.
Application information: Application form not required.
Officers and Directors:* Allan B. Winston,* Pres.; Diane Folkerts,* V.P.; Joseph A. Miller III,* V.P.; Diana B. Winston,* Secy.
EIN: 133977549
Codes: FD2

34835
The Box of Rain Foundation
c/o Amiel Peretz
78 White Birch Rd.
Pound Ridge, NY 10576

Established in 2001 in NY.
Donor(s): Amiel M. Peretz.
Financial data (yr. ended 11/30/01): Grants paid, $150,000; assets, $191,139 (M); gifts received, $178,282; expenditures, $156,431; qualifying distributions, $150,000.
Limitations: Applications not accepted. Giving primarily in NY.
Trustees: Amiel M. Peretz, Michelle Young Peretz.
EIN: 134157443
Codes: FD2

34836
The Dionne Foundation, Inc.
46 Summit Ave.
Bronxville, NY 10708
Application address: Joseph L. Dionne, Pres., 195 N. Wilton Rd., New Canaan, CT 06890
Contact: John L. Cady, Secy.-Treas.

Established in 1997 in NY.
Donor(s): Joseph L. Dionne.
Financial data (yr. ended 12/31/00): Grants paid, $150,000; assets, $2,615,706 (M); expenditures, $153,801; qualifying distributions, $150,000.
Limitations: Giving primarily in CT.
Officers: Joseph L. Dionne, Pres.; Joan Dionne, V.P.; John L. Cady, Secy.-Treas.
EIN: 133797466
Codes: FD2

34837
The Durst Family Foundation
1155 Ave. of The Americas
New York, NY 10036

Established in 2000 in NY.
Financial data (yr. ended 12/31/01): Grants paid, $150,000; assets, $5,163,792 (M); expenditures, $218,121; qualifying distributions, $150,000.
Limitations: Applications not accepted.
Application information: Contributes only to pre-selected organizations.
Officers and Directors: Wendy Durst Kreeger,* Pres.; Laurel Durst Strong,* V.P.; Nan Rothschild Cooper,* Secy.; Ira Marx, Treas.; Peter Askin, Joshua Durst, Leslie B. Durst, Peter D. Durst.
EIN: 522262647

34838
John B. Faile Foundation, Inc.
(also known as The Faile Foundation Advisory Account)
c/o The Bank of New York
1 Wall St., Tax Dept., 28th Fl.
New York, NY 10286

Established in 1994 in FL.
Financial data (yr. ended 12/31/01): Grants paid, $150,000; assets, $3,677,884 (M); expenditures, $174,300; qualifying distributions, $160,006.
Limitations: Applications not accepted.
Application information: Contributes only to pre-selected organizations.
Trustee: The Bank of New York.
EIN: 061379812
Codes: FD2

34839
The Sarah E. Grant Foundation
c/o Goldman Sachs & Co.
85 Broad St., Tax Dept.
New York, NY 10004

Established in 1997 in NY.
Donor(s): Geoffrey T. Grant.
Financial data (yr. ended 05/31/01): Grants paid, $150,000; assets, $1,257,492 (M); expenditures, $181,300; qualifying distributions, $150,250.
Limitations: Applications not accepted. Giving primarily in New York, NY; giving also in London, England.
Application information: Contributes only to pre-selected organizations.
Trustees: Peter C. Gerhard, Annette M. Grant, Geoffrey T. Grant.
EIN: 133931292
Codes: FD2

34840
Alton E. Peters Charitable Trust
c/o Marcum & Kliegman, LLP
655 3rd Ave., Ste. 1610
New York, NY 10017

Established in 1999 in NY.
Donor(s): Alton E. Peters.‡
Financial data (yr. ended 12/31/00): Grants paid, $150,000; assets, $821,204 (M); gifts received, $523; expenditures, $157,202; qualifying distributions, $150,000.
Limitations: Applications not accepted. Giving primarily in NH and NY.
Application information: Contributes only to pre-selected organizations.
Trustees: Emily A. Fletcher, Elizabeth I. Peters, Rachel C. Peters.
EIN: 137197068
Codes: FD2

34841
The Ralph A. Pfeiffer and Jane C. Pfeiffer Foundation, Inc.
1 Rockefeller Plz., Ste. 1210
New York, NY 10020

Established in 1997 in CT.
Donor(s): Jane C. Pfeiffer.
Financial data (yr. ended 12/31/01): Grants paid, $150,000; assets, $2,144,613 (M); gifts received, $21,650; expenditures, $191,052; qualifying distributions, $146,644.
Limitations: Applications not accepted.
Application information: Contributes only to pre-selected organizations.
Officers and Directors:* Jane C. Pfeiffer,* Pres.; Jonathan Smith, Secy.-Treas.; John J. Cahill, John T. Lewis.
EIN: 061480028
Codes: FD2

34842
The Alexander Schneider Foundation
201 W. 54th St., No. 1C
New York, NY 10019
Contact: Frank Salomon, Tr.

Established in 1982 in NY.
Donor(s): Alexander Schneider.
Financial data (yr. ended 12/31/01): Grants paid, $150,000; assets, $2,581,843 (M); expenditures, $208,549; qualifying distributions, $166,244.
Limitations: Applications not accepted. Giving primarily in New York, NY.
Application information: Contributes only to pre-selected organizations.
Trustees: Natascha Furst, Frank Salomon, Isaac Stern.
EIN: 133116302
Codes: FD2

34843
The Stebbins Fund, Inc.
c/o Anchin Block & Anchin, LLP
1375 Broadway, 18th Fl.
New York, NY 10018 (212) 840-3456
Contact: Gary S. Castle, Secy.

Incorporated in 1947 in NY.
Donor(s): Members of the Stebbins family.
Financial data (yr. ended 12/31/99): Grants paid, $150,000; assets, $5,132,496 (M); expenditures, $227,472; qualifying distributions, $161,178.
Limitations: Applications not accepted. Giving primarily in NY.
Application information: Contributes only to pre-selected organizations.
Officers and Directors:* Theodore E. Stebbins,* Pres.; Jane S. Sykes,* V.P. and Treas.; James F. Stebbins, V.P.; Gary S. Castle, Secy.; Victoria Stebbins Greenleaf, J. Wright Rumbough, Jr., Edwin E.F. Stebbins, Michael Morgan Stebbins.
EIN: 116021709
Codes: FD2

34844
The Sumner Scholarship Foundation, Inc.
(Formerly The Sarah Gardner Tiers Scholarship Foundation)
1211 Park Ave.
New York, NY 10128-1703 (212) 831-7987
E-mail: SRULONM270@AOL.com
Contact: Sumner Rulon-Miller

Established in 1996 in NY.
Donor(s): Elena Rulon-Miller.
Financial data (yr. ended 06/30/01): Grants paid, $150,000; assets, $194,411 (M); gifts received, $100; expenditures, $160,817; qualifying distributions, $150,000.
Limitations: Applications not accepted. Giving primarily in Tangier, Morocco; some giving in New York, NY.
Application information: Contributes only to pre-selected organizations.
Trustees: Henry G. Rulon-Miller, Patrick Rulon-Miller, Sumner Rulon-Miller III.
EIN: 133899466
Codes: FD2

34845
Lorber Charitable Fund
70 E. Sunrise Hwy.
Valley Stream, NY 11581 (516) 872-1000
Contact: Brian Lorber, Pres.

Established in 1997 in NY.
Donor(s): Howard Lorber.
Financial data (yr. ended 12/31/01): Grants paid, $149,605; assets, $598,405 (M); gifts received, $101,691; expenditures, $149,871; qualifying distributions, $149,364.
Limitations: Giving primarily in NY.
Officers: Brian Lorber, Pres.; Michael Lorber, Treas.
Director: Ira Stechell.
EIN: 113375574
Codes: FD2

34846
Margaret De Fleur Foundation, Inc.
c/o Joseph D. Stilwell
P.O. Box 1367
New York, NY 10011

Established in 1990 in NY.
Donor(s): Joseph D. Stilwell.
Financial data (yr. ended 11/30/01): Grants paid, $149,585; assets, $349,508 (M); gifts received, $53,165; expenditures, $153,635; qualifying distributions, $148,961.
Limitations: Applications not accepted. Giving on a national basis.
Application information: Contributes only to pre-selected organizations.
Officers and Directors:* Joseph D. Stilwell,* Pres. and Treas.; Howard Rich, Secy.; John Stilwell.
EIN: 133613195
Codes: FD2

34847
Lucius P. Wasserman Foundation, Inc.
c/o J. Soley
30 Griffen Ave.
Scarsdale, NY 10583

Incorporated in 1951 in NY.
Donor(s): L.P. Wasserman.‡
Financial data (yr. ended 12/31/01): Grants paid, $149,525; assets, $2,810,335 (M); expenditures, $159,980; qualifying distributions, $159,837.
Limitations: Applications not accepted. Giving primarily in NY.
Application information: Contributes only to pre-selected organizations. Unsolicited requests for funds not accepted.
Officers: Peter J. Wasserman, Pres.; Judy Soley, V.P.; Robert Soley, V.P.; Judi Wasserman, V.P.
EIN: 136098895
Codes: FD2

34848
The Craigmyle Foundation
c/o Kelly Drye & Warren, LLP
101 Park Ave., 30th Fl.
New York, NY 10178

Established in 1951 in NY.
Donor(s): Ronald M. Craigmyle.
Financial data (yr. ended 12/31/01): Grants paid, $149,500; assets, $2,621,283 (M); expenditures, $157,966; qualifying distributions, $148,986.
Limitations: Applications not accepted. Giving primarily in NY.
Application information: Contributes only to pre-selected organizations.
Trustees: William C. Blind, Rosemary Craigmyle, Terry Tetreault.
EIN: 136109205
Codes: FD2

34849
The Perennial Foundation
c/o BPB Associates, Ltd.
150 E. 52nd St., Ste. 1800
New York, NY 10022

Established in 1993 in NY.
Donor(s): Louis Ricciardelli, Harris Sufian.
Financial data (yr. ended 06/30/01): Grants paid, $149,500; assets, $222,967 (M); gifts received, $100,000; expenditures, $151,554; qualifying distributions, $151,178.
Limitations: Applications not accepted. Giving primarily in New York, NY.
Application information: Contributes only to pre-selected organizations.
Officer: Louis Ricciardelli, Pres.
Director: Karen Ricciardelli.
EIN: 133747131
Codes: FD2

34850
Thomas M. and Esther C. Flanagan Charitable Trust
c/o NBT Bank, N.A.
52 S. Broad St.
Norwich, NY 13815-1646
Contact: Sandra E. Colton, Trust Off.

Established in 1958 in NY.
Donor(s): Thomas M. Flanagan, Esther C. Flanagan.
Financial data (yr. ended 12/31/01): Grants paid, $149,463; assets, $2,344,843 (M); gifts received, $59,320; expenditures, $163,329; qualifying distributions, $157,589.
Limitations: Giving primarily in Norwich, NY.
Publications: Grants list.
Application information: Application form not required.
Trustees: W. Carroll Coyne, Thomas M. Flanagan, Mrs. Thomas M. Flanagan, NBT Bank, N.A.
EIN: 166043564
Codes: FD2

34851
Taub Family Foundation, Inc.
c/o David S. Taub
345 Underhill Blvd.
Syosset, NY 11791

Established in 2000 in FL.
Donor(s): Palm Bay Imports, Inc., Linda Taub, Richard Taub, David S. Taub.
Financial data (yr. ended 12/31/01): Grants paid, $149,333; assets, $43,660 (M); gifts received, $140,833; expenditures, $149,967; qualifying distributions, $149,967.
Limitations: Giving primarily in NY; some giving in FL.
Application information: Unsolicited request for funds not accepted.
Officers: David S. Taub, Pres. and Treas.; Richard Taub, V.P. and Secy.
Director: Linda Taub.
EIN: 651052540
Codes: CS

34852
Bertram Teich Foundation, Inc.
150 Central Park South, Apt. 2901
New York, NY 10019

Established around 1991.
Donor(s): Bertram Teich.
Financial data (yr. ended 12/31/00): Grants paid, $149,312; assets, $295,050 (M); expenditures, $150,677; qualifying distributions, $150,370.
Limitations: Giving primarily in NY.
Officers: Bertram Teich, Pres.; Harvey Martin, Secy.
EIN: 133628720
Codes: FD2

34853
The Doris & Stanley Tananbaum Foundation
c/o Charles Cangialosi, Ernst & Young, LLP
787 7th Ave.
New York, NY 10019

Established in 1998 in NY.
Donor(s): Doris Tananbaum, Stanley Tananbaum.

Financial data (yr. ended 12/31/99): Grants paid, $149,050; assets, $5,968,021 (M); gifts received, $3,056,051; expenditures, $158,670; qualifying distributions, $151,126.
Limitations: Applications not accepted. Giving primarily in NY.
Application information: Contributes only to pre-selected organizations.
Trustees: Ricki Conway, Doris Tananbaum, Stanley Tananbaum.
EIN: 137161531
Codes: FD2

34854
Harriet G. & Esteban Vicente Charitable Trust
c/o Executive Monetary Mgmt., Inc.
220 E. 42nd St., 32nd Fl.
New York, NY 10017

Established in 1986 in NY.
Donor(s): Harriet G. Vicente, Esteban Vicente.
Financial data (yr. ended 12/31/01): Grants paid, $148,900; assets, $601,123 (M); expenditures, $159,104; qualifying distributions, $148,541.
Limitations: Applications not accepted.
Application information: Contributes only to pre-selected organizations.
Trustees: Esteban Vicente, Harriet G. Vicente, Robert Washaw.
EIN: 133386415
Codes: FD2

34855
The Richard Hogan and Carron Sherry Foundation, Inc.
c/o Spear, Leeds & Kellogg
120 Broadway
New York, NY 10271
Contact: Richard Hogan, Pres.

Established in 1995 in NY.
Donor(s): Education for Youth Society, Richard Hogan.
Financial data (yr. ended 09/30/01): Grants paid, $148,889; assets, $2,736,324 (M); gifts received, $2,184,137; expenditures, $150,116; qualifying distributions, $149,084.
Limitations: Applications not accepted.
Application information: Contributes only to pre-selected organizations.
Officers: Richard Hogan, Pres. and Treas.; Carron Sherry, V.P. and Secy.; Douglas Endorf, V.P.
EIN: 133860420
Codes: FD2

34856
Seymour Eisenberg Memorial Foundation
c/o The Granite Capital International Group
126 E. 56th St., 25th Fl.
New York, NY 10022

Established in 1979 in NY.
Donor(s): Lewis M. Eisenberg.
Financial data (yr. ended 07/31/01): Grants paid, $148,823; assets, $280,567 (M); gifts received, $198,173; expenditures, $151,748; qualifying distributions, $148,823.
Limitations: Applications not accepted. Giving primarily in NJ and New York, NY.
Application information: Contributes only to pre-selected organizations.
Officer and Trustees:* Lewis M. Eisenberg,* Secy.; Judith Ann Eisenberg, Eugene Mercy, Jr.
EIN: 133001003
Codes: FD2

34857
The Huguenot Society of America
122 E. 58th St.
New York, NY 10022

Established in 1883 in NY.
Donor(s): Jacqueline Wells Charitable Unitrust.
Financial data (yr. ended 02/28/01): Grants paid, $148,650; assets, $4,217,115 (M); gifts received, $183,557; expenditures, $342,510; qualifying distributions, $232,145.
Limitations: Applications not accepted.
Officers: Courtney A. Haff, Pres.; Firta H. Fabend, V.P.; John Mark Hilliard, V.P.; Pamela S. Fulweiler, Secy.; Henri Eschauzier, Treas.
EIN: 136117102
Codes: FD2, GTI

34858
Fein Foundation
P.O. Box 482
Purchase, NY 10577

Established in 1954 in NY.
Donor(s): Bernard Fein.
Financial data (yr. ended 12/31/99): Grants paid, $148,565; assets, $2,640,353 (M); expenditures, $155,805; qualifying distributions, $149,411.
Limitations: Applications not accepted. Giving primarily in the metropolitan New York, NY, area.
Application information: Contributes only to pre-selected organizations.
Trustees: Adam Fein, Bernard Fein, Elaine Fein, Daniel Zawel.
EIN: 136161610
Codes: FD2

34859
The Belle O. & Carl A. Morse Foundation
(Formerly Carl A. Morse Foundation)
c/o Savrin & Berson
60 E. 42nd St., Ste. 533
New York, NY 10165 (212) 367-9644
Contact: Susan M. Berson, Pres.

Established about 1966 in NY.
Donor(s): Belle O. Morse,‡ Carl A. Morse, Morse-Diesel, Inc., Susan Berson.
Financial data (yr. ended 12/31/01): Grants paid, $148,500; assets, $934,106 (M); gifts received, $5,000; expenditures, $162,252; qualifying distributions, $162,252.
Limitations: Giving primarily in NY.
Application information: Application form required.
Officers: Susan M. Berson, Pres.; Leonard Berson, V.P.
EIN: 136208704
Codes: FD2

34860
The Augustine Foundation
151 W. 26th St., 4th Fl.
New York, NY 10001
Application address: 50 W. 10th St., New York, NY 10001
Contact: Rose L. Augustine, Pres.

Established in 1980 in NY.
Donor(s): Rose L. Augustine.
Financial data (yr. ended 06/30/01): Grants paid, $148,225; assets, $3,765,736 (M); gifts received, $100,000; expenditures, $149,214; qualifying distributions, $149,214.
Limitations: Giving primarily in New York, NY.
Application information: Application form not required.
Officers and Trustees:* Rose L. Augustine,* Pres. and Mgr.; Martha C. Silber,* Secy.; Harry J. Silber,* Treas.; David S. Silber.
EIN: 132997450

Codes: FD2

34861
Stephen Moss Foundation, Inc.
c/o BCRS Associates, LLC
100 Wall St., 11th Fl.
New York, NY 10005

Established in 1994 in NY.
Donor(s): Stephen Moss, Education for Youth Society.
Financial data (yr. ended 10/31/01): Grants paid, $148,221; assets, $324,799 (M); gifts received, $63,116; expenditures, $148,718; qualifying distributions, $148,255.
Limitations: Applications not accepted. Giving primarily in NY.
Application information: Contributes only to pre-selected organizations.
Officers: Stephen Moss, Pres. and Treas.; Robert Moss, Sr. V.P.; Linda Burns, V.P.; Nicole Moss, V.P.; Steven Moss, V.P.
EIN: 133799260
Codes: FD2

34862
The Joseph C. Nugent Charitable Trust
c/o Deutsche Trust Co. of NY
P.O. Box 1297, Church St. Sta.
New York, NY 10008

Established in 1992 in NY.
Donor(s): Joseph C. Nugent.‡
Financial data (yr. ended 12/31/01): Grants paid, $148,200; assets, $2,725,866 (M); expenditures, $198,761; qualifying distributions, $163,508.
Limitations: Applications not accepted. Giving primarily in New York, NY.
Application information: Contributes only to pre-selected organizations.
Trustee: Deutsche Bank.
EIN: 133692614
Codes: FD2

34863
The Layden Family Foundation
c/o US Trust Co.
114 W. 47th St.,TAXVAS
New York, NY 10036

Established in 2000 in PA.
Financial data (yr. ended 12/31/00): Grants paid, $148,000; assets, $9,653 (M); gifts received, $160,313; expenditures, $151,200; qualifying distributions, $148,000.
Limitations: Applications not accepted.
Application information: Unsolicited requests for funds not accepted.
Trustees: Barbara Layden, Donald W. Layden.
EIN: 233039715
Codes: FD2

34864
Robert Winthrop Charitable Trust
c/o Bonnie Mgmt. Co., Inc.
53 N. Park Ave., Ste. 53
Rockville Centre, NY 11570

Donor(s): Robert Winthrop,‡ Cornelia W. Bonnie.
Financial data (yr. ended 11/30/01): Grants paid, $148,000; assets, $970,471 (M); expenditures, $155,700; qualifying distributions, $148,000.
Limitations: Applications not accepted. Giving on a national basis.
Application information: Contributes only to pre-selected organizations.
Trustee: Cornelia W. Bonnie.
EIN: 237441147
Codes: FD2

34865
Kramer Foundation
c/o Wald & Wald
1 Penn Plz., Ste. 4307
New York, NY 10119-0001
Contact: Saul Kramer, Pres.

Established about 1951 in NY.
Donor(s): Saul Kramer.
Financial data (yr. ended 12/31/01): Grants paid, $147,856; assets, $2,198,733 (M); gifts received, $52,560; expenditures, $157,115; qualifying distributions, $146,944.
Limitations: Giving primarily in Palm Beach, FL, and NY.
Officers and Directors:* Saul Kramer,* Pres.; Lola Kramer,* V.P. and Secy.; Kathie Rudy,* V.P. and Secy.; Robert Kramer,* V.P. and Treas.; Laurence Wald, Secy.
EIN: 221713053
Codes: FD2

34866
Philip & Gussie Diamond Foundation, Inc.
c/o Cummings & Carroll, PC
175 Great Neck Rd., Ste. 405
Great Neck, NY 11021

Established around 1948 in NY.
Financial data (yr. ended 12/31/01): Grants paid, $147,745; assets, $3,474,553 (M); expenditures, $156,454; qualifying distributions, $147,745.
Limitations: Applications not accepted. Giving primarily in the greater New York, NY, area.
Application information: Contributes only to pre-selected organizations.
Officers: Marvin R. Neuwirth, Pres.; Felice Neuwirth, V.P.; Barbara Braun, Secy.
EIN: 136116411
Codes: FD2

34867
Marjorie and John Buyers Foundation
c/o Mason, Benz & Atkinson, LLP
3605 Eggert Rd.
Orchard Park, NY 14127-1992

Established in 1992 in NY.
Donor(s): John W. Buyers, Marjorie S. Buyers.
Financial data (yr. ended 12/31/01): Grants paid, $147,500; assets, $2,493,971 (M); expenditures, $147,785; qualifying distributions, $146,371.
Limitations: Giving limited to NY.
Directors: Bruce Buyers, John W. Buyers, Jr., Marjorie S. Buyers, Wendy Schintzius Griffin.
EIN: 161428487
Codes: FD2

34868
Gerson & Judith Leiber Foundation
7 Park Ave.
New York, NY 10016

Established in 1993.
Donor(s): Gerson Leiber, Judith Leiber.
Financial data (yr. ended 08/31/01): Grants paid, $147,500; assets, $30,275 (M); expenditures, $163,792; qualifying distributions, $147,255.
Limitations: Applications not accepted. Giving primarily in NY.
Application information: Contributes only to pre-selected organizations.
Directors: Gerson Leiber, Judith Leiber.
EIN: 133680342
Codes: FD2

34869
Herbert W. Nurnberg Trust
c/o Hays & Co.
477 Madison Ave.
New York, NY 10022-5892

Established in 1983.
Financial data (yr. ended 02/28/01): Grants paid, $147,500; assets, $864,044 (M); expenditures, $160,949; qualifying distributions, $146,144.
Limitations: Applications not accepted. Giving on a national basis.
Application information: Contributes only to pre-selected organizations.
Trustee: James P. Schreiber.
EIN: 136844536
Codes: FD2

34870
The Ezra Charitable Trust
515 Ave. I
Brooklyn, NY 11230
Contact: Ezra Birnbaum, Pres.

Donor(s): Ezra Birnbaum.
Financial data (yr. ended 12/31/99): Grants paid, $147,383; assets, $397,721 (M); gifts received, $272,307; expenditures, $149,267; qualifying distributions, $146,553.
Officer: Ezra Birnbaum, Pres.
EIN: 116487876
Codes: FD2

34871
The Mermelstein Foundation
33-00 Northern Blvd.
Long Island City, NY 11101-2215

Established in 1983 in NY.
Donor(s): Joseph Mermelstein, Bernard Mermelstein.
Financial data (yr. ended 11/30/00): Grants paid, $147,300; assets, $1,139,191 (M); expenditures, $148,299; qualifying distributions, $147,300.
Limitations: Applications not accepted. Giving primarily in NY.
Application information: Contributes only to pre-selected organizations.
Directors: Bernard Mermelstein, Helen Mermelstein, Joseph Mermelstein.
EIN: 112669722
Codes: FD2

34872
The Joseph and Bernice Tanenbaum Foundation
43-29 Bell Blvd.
Bayside, NY 11361 (718) 224-6300
Contact: Joseph Tanenbaum, Tr.

Established in 1995 in NY.
Donor(s): Joseph Tanenbaum, Bernice R. Tanenbaum.
Financial data (yr. ended 06/30/01): Grants paid, $147,270; assets, $658,038 (M); expenditures, $147,897; qualifying distributions, $145,311.
Limitations: Giving primarily in New York, NY.
Trustees: Bernice R. Tanenbaum, Joseph Tanenbaum, Richard E. Tanenbaum.
EIN: 113300825
Codes: FD2

34873
John R. & Dorothy D. Caples Fund
c/o Deutsche Trust Co. of NY
P.O. Box 1297, Church St. Sta.
New York, NY 10008

Established in 1994 in NY.
Financial data (yr. ended 12/31/01): Grants paid, $147,200; assets, $3,667,461 (M); expenditures, $192,037; qualifying distributions, $168,122.
Limitations: Applications not accepted.
Application information: Contributes only to pre-selected organizations.
Trustees: Charles V. O'Neill, Deutsche Bank.
EIN: 311441038
Codes: FD2

34874
Brach Family Foundation, Inc.
1600 63rd St.
Brooklyn, NY 11204-2713
Contact: Zigmond Brach, Pres.

Established in 1991 in NY.
Donor(s): Zigmond Brach, Sound Around, Corp.
Financial data (yr. ended 12/31/00): Grants paid, $147,150; assets, $1,880,244 (M); gifts received, $314,550; expenditures, $147,871; qualifying distributions, $146,212.
Limitations: Giving primarily in Brooklyn, NY.
Application information: Application form not required.
Officer: Zigmond Brach, Pres.
EIN: 113067698
Codes: FD2

34875
The Mendell Family Fund, Inc.
(Formerly The Ira L. & Margaret P. Mendell Fund, Inc.)
1 W. Purdy Ave.
Rye, NY 10580-2922

Established in 1954 in NY.
Donor(s): Ira L. Mendell.
Financial data (yr. ended 11/30/01): Grants paid, $147,030; assets, $3,930,580 (M); expenditures, $151,834; qualifying distributions, $147,688.
Limitations: Applications not accepted. Giving primarily in FL and NY.
Application information: Contributes only to pre-selected organizations.
Officer: Ira L. Mendell, Mgr.
EIN: 136159009
Codes: FD2

34876
Walter Kann Foundation, Inc.
c/o David Berdon & Co.
415 Madison Ave.
New York, NY 10017-1111

Established in 1986 in NY.
Donor(s): Walter Kann.
Financial data (yr. ended 09/30/01): Grants paid, $147,000; assets, $637,110 (M); gifts received, $5,760; expenditures, $152,760; qualifying distributions, $147,000.
Limitations: Applications not accepted. Giving primarily in NY.
Application information: Contributes only to pre-selected organizations.
Directors: Jacqueline Kann, Michael A. Kann, Walter Kann.
EIN: 133381799

34877
Haji Usman & Hazarbai Mundia Foundation, Inc.
159 Locust Ave.
Garden City, NY 11530
Contact: Abdul Mundia, M.D., Dir.

Established in 1994 in NY.
Donor(s): Abdul Mundia, M.D.
Financial data (yr. ended 12/31/01): Grants paid, $146,826; assets, $1 (M); gifts received, $124,079; expenditures, $146,826; qualifying distributions, $146,826.
Limitations: Giving primarily in India.

Directors: Michael Goldstein, Abdul Mundia, M.D., Roshanara Mundia.
EIN: 113236306
Codes: FD2

34878
The Austin and Kathryn Hearst Foundation
c/o Jaime Taicher
345 W. 58th St., Apt. 9C
New York, NY 10019

Donor(s): Austin Hearst.
Financial data (yr. ended 12/31/01): Grants paid, $146,701; assets, $737,495 (M); gifts received, $75,000; expenditures, $150,717; qualifying distributions, $146,267.
Limitations: Applications not accepted.
Application information: Contributes only pre-selected organizations.
Trustees: Austin Hearst, Kathryn Parlan Hearst, James Taicher.
EIN: 226748476
Codes: FD2

34879
The McEwen Family Foundation
c/o U.S. Trust
114 W. 47th St.
New York, NY 10036

Established in 1996 in PA.
Donor(s): Arthur I. McEwen.
Financial data (yr. ended 12/31/99): Grants paid, $146,650; assets, $145 (M); gifts received, $129,100; expenditures, $149,920; qualifying distributions, $147,270.
Limitations: Applications not accepted.
Application information: Contributes only to pre-selected organizations.
Trustees: Arthur I. McEwen, Jane E. McEwen.
EIN: 237852050
Codes: FD2

34880
The William P. Goldman and Brothers Foundation, Inc.
1270 Ave. of the Americas
New York, NY 10020   (212) 485-9700
Contact: Sidney Kraines, Pres.

Incorporated in 1951 in NY.
Donor(s): William P. Goldman,‡ William P. Goldman & Brothers, Inc., Byron Golman.
Financial data (yr. ended 12/31/01): Grants paid, $146,600; assets, $3,930,116 (M); gifts received, $1,000,000; expenditures, $149,920; qualifying distributions, $146,600.
Limitations: Giving primarily in NY.
Application information: Application form not required.
Officers: Sidney Kraines, Pres.; Jeffrey L. Kraines, V.P.; Merrill M. Kraines, Treas.
EIN: 136163100
Codes: FD2

34881
Walter & Franziska Petschek Family Trust
c/o United Continental Corp.
122 E. 42nd St., 34th Fl.
New York, NY 10168-0002

Donor(s): Alfred E. Petschek, Susan Petschek, Walter Petschek,‡ Stephen R. Petschek.
Financial data (yr. ended 06/30/01): Grants paid, $146,500; assets, $249,269 (M); gifts received, $127,294; expenditures, $147,170; qualifying distributions, $145,860.
Limitations: Applications not accepted. Giving primarily in MA and NY.
Application information: Contributes only to pre-selected organizations.
Trustees: Hugh McLoughlin, Hugh O'Donnell, Alfred E. Petschek, Charles I. Petschek.
EIN: 136085291

34882
The Roberts Charitable Foundation
c/o Bessemer Trust Co., N.A., Tax Dept.
630 5th Ave.
New York, NY 10111

Established in 1994 in NY.
Financial data (yr. ended 12/31/00): Grants paid, $146,495; assets, $286,249 (M); gifts received, $186,260; expenditures, $146,595; qualifying distributions, $145,213.
Limitations: Applications not accepted. Giving primarily in New York, NY.
Application information: Contributes only to pre-selected organizations.
Trustees: David Roberts, William B. Roberts.
EIN: 137047910
Codes: FD2

34883
Shaykin Family Foundation
c/o Shaykin & Co.
630 5th Ave., Ste. 3110
New York, NY 10111
Contact: Leonard Shaykin, Pres.

Established in 1986 in NY.
Donor(s): Leonard Shaykin.
Financial data (yr. ended 11/30/01): Grants paid, $146,439; assets, $2,349,896 (M); gifts received, $1,800; expenditures, $229,070; qualifying distributions, $223,713.
Limitations: Applications not accepted. Giving primarily in NY.
Application information: Contributes only to pre-selected organizations.
Officers: Leonard Shaykin, Pres.; Rabbi Simcha Weinberg, Exec. Dir.
Directors: Margy-Ruth Davis, Sandra Poole.
EIN: 363486772
Codes: FD2

34884
Robert F. Cummings, Jr. Foundation
c/o BCRS Assocs., LLC
100 Wall St., 11th Fl.
New York, NY 10005

Established in 1987 in NY.
Donor(s): Robert F. Cummings, Jr.
Financial data (yr. ended 08/31/01): Grants paid, $146,320; assets, $1,386,984 (M); expenditures, $148,109; qualifying distributions, $147,320.
Limitations: Applications not accepted. Giving primarily in New York, NY.
Application information: Contributes only to pre-selected organizations.
Trustees: Diane Benson Cummings, Robert F. Cummings, Jr., Alfred C. Eckert III.
EIN: 133437927
Codes: FD2

34885
Sykes Family Foundation
c/o Goldman Sachs & Co.
85 Broad St., Tax Dept.
New York, NY 10004

Established in 1993 in CA.
Donor(s): Gene T. Sykes.
Financial data (yr. ended 06/30/01): Grants paid, $145,900; assets, $5,421,204 (M); gifts received, $218,769; expenditures, $218,769; qualifying distributions, $145,947.
Limitations: Applications not accepted. Giving on a national basis.

Application information: Contributes only to pre-selected organizations.
Trustee: Gene T. Sykes.
EIN: 133748075
Codes: FD2

34886
B. C. & Phyllis Lifshitz Charitable Foundation
1159 E. 31st St.
Brooklyn, NY 11210

Established in 1997.
Donor(s): Benjamin C. Lifshitz.
Financial data (yr. ended 11/30/99): Grants paid, $145,800; assets, $1,005,720 (M); gifts received, $37,500; expenditures, $158,458; qualifying distributions, $156,046.
Limitations: Applications not accepted. Giving primarily in Brooklyn, NY.
Application information: Contributes only to pre-selected organizations.
Trustees: Benjamin C. Lifshitz, Daniel Lifshitz, Menachem E. Lifshitz, Phyllis Lifshitz.
EIN: 116481171
Codes: FD2

34887
Mary Tyler Moore and S. Robert Levine, M.D. Charitable Foundation
c/o Lance Valdez & Assoc., PC
375 Park Ave., Ste. 3707
New York, NY 10152

Established in 1994 in CA.
Donor(s): Mary Tyler Moore Levine.
Financial data (yr. ended 12/31/01): Grants paid, $145,741; assets, $15,951 (M); gifts received, $154,714; expenditures, $145,741; qualifying distributions, $145,741.
Limitations: Applications not accepted. Giving primarily in New York, NY.
Application information: Contributes only to pre-selected organizations.
Officer: Mary Tyler Moore Levine, Pres.
EIN: 954431020
Codes: FD2

34888
Sol Cohn Foundation
23 Sinclair Dr.
Kings Point, NY 11024   (516) 482-3907
Contact: Seymour Cohn, Secy.

Established in 1952 in NY.
Financial data (yr. ended 04/30/02): Grants paid, $145,550; assets, $2,216,030 (M); expenditures, $158,907; qualifying distributions, $144,477.
Limitations: Giving primarily in NY.
Application information: Application form not required.
Officers and Directors:* Bernard Cohn,* Pres.; Doris Cohn,* Secy.; Seymour Cohn,* Secy.
EIN: 116005703
Codes: FD2

34889
The Shirah Kober Zeller Foundation, Inc.
15 W. 72nd St., Apt. 28B
New York, NY 10023

Established in 1997 in NY.
Donor(s): Shirah Kober Zeller.
Financial data (yr. ended 12/31/00): Grants paid, $145,465; assets, $16,572 (M); gifts received, $76,703; expenditures, $150,971; qualifying distributions, $150,971.
Limitations: Applications not accepted. Giving primarily in New York, NY.
Application information: Contributes only to pre-selected organizations.

34889—NEW YORK

Officers and Director:* Mitchell K. Zeller, V.P.; Shirah Kober Zeller,* Secy.
EIN: 132757689
Codes: FD2

34890
The Beatrice & Roy Backus Foundation, Inc.
246B Heritage Hills
Somers, NY 10589 (914) 277-3024
Contact: Inge T. Stephens, Pres.

Established in 1988 in NY.
Donor(s): Beatrice Backus,‡ Roy Backus.‡
Financial data (yr. ended 12/31/01): Grants paid, $145,290; assets, $1,691,893 (M); expenditures, $205,699; qualifying distributions, $179,297.
Limitations: Giving on a national basis.
Publications: Annual report, application guidelines, financial statement, grants list.
Application information: Application form not required.
Officers and Directors:* Inge T. Stephens,* Pres.; Christopher H. Stephens,* V.P. and Secy.; Adolf Haasen.
EIN: 133442922
Codes: FD2

34891
Schwartz Foundation
c/o Goldman Sachs & Co.
85 Broad St., Tax Dept.
New York, NY 10004

Established in 1996 in NY.
Donor(s): Eric S. Schwartz.
Financial data (yr. ended 08/31/01): Grants paid, $145,032; assets, $6,011,239 (M); gifts received, $1,949,000; expenditures, $257,831; qualifying distributions, $148,032.
Limitations: Applications not accepted. Giving primarily in NY.
Application information: Contributes only to pre-selected organizations.
Trustee: Eric S. Schwartz.
EIN: 133957291
Codes: FD2

34892
Dr. Lillian Chutick and Dr. Rebecca Chutick Foundation
c/o Rose & Boxer
1065 Ave. of the Americas
New York, NY 10018

Established in 1992 in NY.
Financial data (yr. ended 08/31/01): Grants paid, $145,000; assets, $2,975,445 (M); expenditures, $146,435; qualifying distributions, $143,629.
Limitations: Applications not accepted. Giving primarily in New York, NY.
Application information: Contributes only to pre-selected organizations.
Trustees: Lillian Chutick, Herbert B. Rose.
EIN: 136991663
Codes: FD2

34893
The Ganlee Fund
c/o Pat Doudna, Ernst & Young
787 7th Ave.
New York, NY 10019

Established in 1966 in NY.
Financial data (yr. ended 12/31/00): Grants paid, $145,000; assets, $2,127,807 (M); expenditures, $151,755; qualifying distributions, $143,940.
Limitations: Applications not accepted. Giving primarily in NY.
Application information: Contributes only to pre-selected organizations.
Trustee: Sandra I. Van Heerden.
EIN: 136069298
Codes: FD2

34894
The RLG Foundation, Inc.
c/o Gotham Capital
520 Madison Ave., Ste. 32nd Fl.
New York, NY 10022

Established in 2000 in NY.
Donor(s): Robert Goldstein.
Financial data (yr. ended 10/31/01): Grants paid, $145,000; assets, $132,130 (M); gifts received, $56,775; expenditures, $145,048; qualifying distributions, $145,000.
Limitations: Giving primarily in NJ and NY.
Officers and Directors:* Robert Goldstein,* Pres. and Treas.; Alfred Goldstein,* Secy.; Hope Goldstein.
EIN: 134144882
Codes: FD2

34895
The Shimkin Foundation
257 Central Park West, Apt. 10A
New York, NY 10024
Additional address: 30 Mallard Lake Rd., Pound Ridge, NY 10576; E-mail: mshimkin@aol.com
Contact: Michael Shimkin, Secy.-Treas.

Established in 1985 in NY.
Donor(s): Leon Shimkin,‡ Michael Shimkin.
Financial data (yr. ended 12/31/01): Grants paid, $145,000; assets, $1,100,000 (M); expenditures, $150,000; qualifying distributions, $150,000.
Limitations: Applications not accepted. Giving on an international basis to El Salvador.
Application information: Contributes only to pre-selected organizations. Unsolicited requests for funds not considered.
Officers and Directors:* Emily S. Gindin,* V.P.; Michael Shimkin,* Secy.-Treas.
EIN: 136022234
Codes: FD2

34896
International Council of Shopping Centers Educational Foundation, Inc.
1221 Ave. of the Americas, 41st Fl.
New York, NY 10020-1099 (646) 728-3800
FAX: (212) 589-5555; E-mail: RCohen@icsc.org
Contact: Rochelle Cohen, Educational Fdn. Coord.

Established in 1989 in NY.
Donor(s): International Council of Shopping Centers, Inc.
Financial data (yr. ended 12/31/99): Grants paid, $144,835; assets, $1,270,345 (M); gifts received, $180,000; expenditures, $305,616; qualifying distributions, $297,431; giving activities include $153,263 for programs.
Limitations: Applications not accepted. Giving on a national basis.
Application information: Unsolicited requests for funds not accepted.
Officer and Trustees:* John Konarski, Exec. Dir.; Gary Brown, John L. Bucksbaum, Roy P. Drachman, Susan Kamei, Michael P. Kercheral, Bruce Ludwig, Bruce A. MacLeod, Michael P. McCarthy, Harry Newman, Jr., John T. Riordan, Molly Madsen Seuth, Ian F. Thomas, Cynthia Ray Walker.
EIN: 133525440
Codes: FD2

34897
Morris and Esther Ades Foundation
c/o Morris Ades, S & A Stores, Inc.
450 7th Ave., Ste. 701
New York, NY 10123

Established around 1993.
Donor(s): Morris Ades, Esther Ades.
Financial data (yr. ended 12/31/01): Grants paid, $144,810; assets, $170,373 (M); gifts received, $128,798; expenditures, $145,590; qualifying distributions, $144,810.
Limitations: Applications not accepted. Giving primarily in the metropolitan New York, NY, area.
Application information: Contributes only to pre-selected organizations.
Officers: Morris Ades, Pres.; Esther Ades, Secy.-Treas.
EIN: 223216484
Codes: FD2

34898
The Tamagni Foundation
c/o Lazard Freres & Co., LLC
30 Rockefeller Plz.
New York, NY 10020
Contact: John S. Tamagni, Pres.

Established in 1985 in NY.
Donor(s): Janet B. Tamagni, John S. Tamagni.
Financial data (yr. ended 09/30/01): Grants paid, $144,700; assets, $105,155 (M); gifts received, $185,240; expenditures, $145,830; qualifying distributions, $144,830.
Limitations: Giving primarily in NJ and NY.
Officers and Directors:* John S. Tamagni,* Pres.; Janet B. Tamagni,* V.P.; Howard Sontag,* Secy.-Treas.
EIN: 133318229
Codes: FD2

34899
Chaim and Rose Fraiman Foundation, Inc.
247 Seeley St.
Brooklyn, NY 11218-1207 (718) 965-1500
Contact: Chaim Fraiman, Pres.

Established in 1983.
Donor(s): Chaim Fraiman, Rose Fraiman.
Financial data (yr. ended 11/30/01): Grants paid, $144,690; assets, $419,507 (M); gifts received, $108,200; expenditures, $144,755; qualifying distributions, $144,690.
Limitations: Giving primarily in the greater New York, NY, area.
Officers: Chaim Fraiman, Pres.; Rose Fraiman, V.P.; Steve Adelsberg, Secy.; Theodore Weinberger, Treas.
EIN: 112689575
Codes: FD2

34900
General William Mayer Foundation, Inc.
c/o Graber & Co.
1100 Franklin Ave., No. 300
Garden City, NY 11530-1601
Application address: c/o Deborah O'Brien, 17 Nauyaug Point Rd., Mystic, CT 06355, tel.: (860) 536-1684

Established in 1968 in NY.
Financial data (yr. ended 12/31/01): Grants paid, $144,650; assets, $2,352,209 (M); expenditures, $184,481; qualifying distributions, $183,565.
Limitations: Giving primarily in the Northeast.
Officer: Gerald M. Mayer, Jr., Mgr.
EIN: 132625602
Codes: FD2

34901
Rochester Female Charitable Society
c/o JPMorgan Chase Bank
P.O. Box 31412
Rochester, NY 14603-1412 (716) 258-9796
Contact: Margaret Trevett

Established in 1822 in NY.
Financial data (yr. ended 03/31/01): Grants paid, $144,371; assets, $2,930,740 (M); gifts received, $1,000; expenditures, $168,389; qualifying distributions, $145,313.
Limitations: Giving limited to the greater Rochester, NY, area.
Publications: Grants list.
Application information: Individuals must be referred by greater Rochester area social workers. Application form not required.
Board Members: Margaret Trevett, and 23 additional board members.
Trustee: JPMorgan Chase Bank.
EIN: 237166180
Codes: FD2, GTI

34902
Hyman & Ann Arbesfeld Foundation, Inc.
150 E. 50th St.
New York, NY 10022
Contact: Hyman Arbesfeld, Dir.

Established in 1984 in NY.
Donor(s): Ann Arbesfeld, Hyman Arbesfeld.
Financial data (yr. ended 11/30/01): Grants paid, $144,190; assets, $3,793,885 (M); expenditures, $181,313; qualifying distributions, $144,190.
Limitations: Applications not accepted. Giving primarily in New York, NY.
Publications: Annual report.
Application information: Contributes only to pre-selected organizations.
Directors: Ann Arbesfeld, Benjamin Arbesfeld, Hyman Arbesfeld.
EIN: 133253358
Codes: FD2

34903
DeMuth Family Foundation
c/o Deutsche Trust Co. of NY
P.O. Box 829, Church St. Sta.
New York, NY 10008
Application address: c/o Christopher C. DeMuth, Tr., 1150 17th St. N.W., Washington, D.C. 20036

Established in 1992 in DC.
Donor(s): Harry C. DeMuth.‡
Financial data (yr. ended 12/31/01): Grants paid, $144,000; assets, $446,000 (M); expenditures, $149,087; qualifying distributions, $145,580.
Limitations: Giving primarily in IA.
Application information: Application form not required.
Trustees: Stephanie Alnot, Christopher DeMuth, Leilani DeMuth, Philip DeMuth, Deutsche Bank.
EIN: 367029894
Codes: FD2

34904
The Zelmanowicz Foundation, Inc.
3525 Baychester Ave.
Bronx, NY 10466 (718) 798-8900
Contact: Chaim M. Zelmanowicz, Pres.

Established in 1980 in NY.
Donor(s): Chaim M. Zelmanowicz.
Financial data (yr. ended 10/31/00): Grants paid, $143,860; assets, $11,333 (M); gifts received, $143,130; expenditures, $144,173; qualifying distributions, $143,860.
Limitations: Giving primarily in New York, NY.
Application information: Application form not required.
Officer: Chaim M. Zelmanowicz, Pres.
EIN: 133067430
Codes: FD2

34905
The Robert G. & Ellen S. Gutenstein Foundation, Inc.
c/o M.R. Weiser & Co., LLP
3000 Marcus
New Hyde Park, NY 11042-1066

Established in 1967 in DE and NY.
Donor(s): Robert G. Gutenstein, Ellen S. Gutenstein.
Financial data (yr. ended 10/31/01): Grants paid, $143,825; assets, $2,735,512 (M); gifts received, $750,000; expenditures, $160,528; qualifying distributions, $154,147.
Limitations: Applications not accepted.
Application information: Contributes only to pre-selected organizations.
Officers: Robert G. Gutenstein, Pres.; Ellen S. Gutenstein, V.P.; Charles Salomon, Secy.
EIN: 136227087
Codes: FD2

34906
N've Shalom Foundation, Inc.
411 5th Ave.
New York, NY 10016

Incorporated about 1938 in NY.
Donor(s): Joseph Attie.‡
Financial data (yr. ended 12/31/99): Grants paid, $143,783; assets, $2,668,616 (M); gifts received, $1,635; expenditures, $148,232; qualifying distributions, $144,103.
Limitations: Applications not accepted. Giving primarily in NY.
Application information: Contributes only to pre-selected organizations.
Officers: Joseph Shalom, Pres.; Henry Shalom, V.P. and Secy.; Stephen Shalom, Treas.
EIN: 136168301
Codes: FD2

34907
The Johnson Foundation
17 Christopher St.
New York, NY 10014

Established in 1992 in NY and DE.
Donor(s): Peter James Johnson.
Financial data (yr. ended 06/30/01): Grants paid, $143,750; assets, $2,232,088 (M); expenditures, $146,634; qualifying distributions, $142,132.
Limitations: Applications not accepted. Giving primarily in NY.
Application information: Contributes only to pre-selected organizations.
Officers and Directors:* Christopher Johnson,* Chair.; Peter James Johnson, Jr.,* V.P.; Veronica Johnson,* Treas.; Peter James Johnson.
EIN: 133696561
Codes: FD2

34908
Strausman Family Fund, Inc.
c/o Strausman Construction Co.
98 Cutter Mill Rd.
Great Neck, NY 11021-3152 (516) 482-6650
Contact: Edward Strausman, Pres.

Established in 1981 in NY.
Donor(s): Edward Strausman, George Strausman.
Financial data (yr. ended 11/30/99): Grants paid, $143,686; assets, $1,910,255 (M); gifts received, $75,000; expenditures, $146,755; qualifying distributions, $142,758.
Limitations: Giving primarily in NY.
Application information: Application form not required.
Officers: Edward Strausman, Pres.; George Strausman, V.P.; Samuel Strausman, V.P.; David Strausman, Secy.; Susan Rietti, Treas.
EIN: 112587343
Codes: FD2

34909
The Wm. Brian & Judith A. Little Charitable Trust
630 5th Ave., Ste. 2620
New York, NY 10111

Established in 1992 in NY.
Donor(s): Wm. Brian Little.‡
Financial data (yr. ended 12/31/00): Grants paid, $143,500; assets, $4,018,105 (M); expenditures, $249,730; qualifying distributions, $146,979.
Limitations: Applications not accepted. Giving primarily in New York, NY.
Application information: Contributes only to pre-selected organizations.
Trustees: Gregory Little, Jacqueline Little, Judith A. Little, Wm. Brian Little.
EIN: 136995435
Codes: FD2

34910
Victor & Monica Markowicz Charitable Trust
c/o Martin B. Jaffee
31 W. 56th St.
New York, NY 10019

Established in 1997 in FL.
Donor(s): Victor Markowicz.
Financial data (yr. ended 04/30/02): Grants paid, $143,500; assets, $810,905 (M); gifts received, $675; expenditures, $147,434; qualifying distributions, $143,500.
Limitations: Applications not accepted. Giving primarily in New York, NY.
Application information: Contributes only to pre-selected organizations.
Officer: Martin B. Jaffee, Admin.
Trustees: Clara Markowicz, Monica Markowicz, Victor Markowicz.
EIN: 137118108

34911
The Mattone Family Charitable Foundation
c/o David M. Brickman, C.P.A.
6 E. 43rd St., 19th Fl.
New York, NY 10017

Established in 1995 in NJ.
Donor(s): Vincent Mattone.
Financial data (yr. ended 12/31/00): Grants paid, $143,400; assets, $2,125,706 (M); expenditures, $144,288; qualifying distributions, $143,408.
Limitations: Applications not accepted. Giving on a national basis.
Application information: Contributes only to pre-selected organizations.
Trustee: Alan Mattone, Michelle Mattone.
EIN: 133800750
Codes: FD2

34912
Rifkind Family Foundation
c/o KLS
641 Lexington Ave.
New York, NY 10022

Established in 1997 in NY.
Financial data (yr. ended 12/31/00): Grants paid, $143,400; assets, $1,586,297 (M); gifts received, $282; expenditures, $151,899; qualifying distributions, $142,644.

34912—NEW YORK

Limitations: Applications not accepted. Giving primarily in MA and NY.
Application information: Contributes only to pre-selected organizations.
Officer: Richard A. Rifkind, Mgr.
Trustee: Carole Rifkind.
EIN: 133963803
Codes: FD2

34913
The Elbert Lenrow Fund, Inc.
420 Lexington Ave.
New York, NY 10170
Contact: William Holm, Mgr.

Established in 1979 in NY.
Donor(s): Elbert Lenrow.
Financial data (yr. ended 06/30/01): Grants paid, $143,000; assets, $2,411,083 (M); expenditures, $188,280; qualifying distributions, $143,000.
Limitations: Giving primarily in New York, NY.
Application information: Application by invitation only to graduates of the Fieldston School, via the College Counselor and Dean of Senior Students. Applicants must have received scholarship aid while at Fieldston. Application form required.
Officers: Emilie de Rohan-Chandor, Pres.; Deborah Hample, V.P.; Yvonne Korshak, Secy.; Linda Phillips Sigelow, Treas.; William Holm, Mgr.
Directors: Robert L. Bachner, Arnold Corrigan, Michael Mayers, Giuliana Robertson, Robert H. Siegel.
EIN: 132997431
Codes: FD2, GTI

34914
Beatrice R. & Joseph A. Coleman Foundation
130 E. 59th St.
New York, NY 10022 (212) 836-1358
Contact: Lauren Katzowitz, Exec. Dir.

Established in 1998 in NY.
Donor(s): Ida & William Rosenthal Foundation, Inc.
Financial data (yr. ended 12/31/01): Grants paid, $142,850; assets, $2,908,091 (M); expenditures, $217,492; qualifying distributions, $179,250.
Limitations: Applications not accepted. Giving primarily on the East Coast.
Application information: Contributes only to pre-selected organizations.
Officers: Elizabeth Coleman, Pres.; Robert Stroup, V.P.
Trustee: Kristin M. Houser.
EIN: 133981351
Codes: FD2

34915
The Bracebridge H. Young, Jr. Foundation
c/o BCRS Assoc., LLC
100 Wall St., 11th Fl.
New York, NY 10005

Established in 1989 in NY.
Donor(s): Bracebridge H. Young, Jr.
Financial data (yr. ended 05/31/01): Grants paid, $142,833; assets, $3,465,511 (M); expenditures, $172,439; qualifying distributions, $145,201.
Limitations: Applications not accepted. Giving primarily in Nantucket, MA.
Application information: Contributes only to pre-selected organizations.
Trustees: Bracebridge H. Young, Jr., Mary-Elizabeth Young, Yuriko Jane Young.
EIN: 133531986
Codes: FD2

34916
Emy & Emil Herzfeld Foundation, Inc.
420 Lexington Ave., Ste. 1745
New York, NY 10170
Contact: William P. Holm, Esq., Secy.

Established in 1952 in NY.
Financial data (yr. ended 12/31/01): Grants paid, $142,500; assets, $2,197,490 (M); expenditures, $186,643; qualifying distributions, $142,500.
Limitations: Giving primarily in the metropolitan New York, NY, area.
Officers: Countess Emilie de Rohan-Chandor, Pres.; William P. Holm, Secy.
Directors: Esther R. Dyer, Jane H. Rowen, Gary B. Schreiner, Alice E. Schwartz.
EIN: 136161598
Codes: FD2

34917
Robbins Foundation, Inc.
515 Madison Ave.
New York, NY 10022

Established in 1945 in NC and NY.
Financial data (yr. ended 02/28/02): Grants paid, $142,450; assets, $2,809,851 (M); expenditures, $218,591; qualifying distributions, $142,450.
Limitations: Applications not accepted. Giving primarily in NY.
Application information: Contributes only to pre-selected organizations.
Officers: Allan J. Robbins, Pres.; Carl B. Robbins, V.P.; Cera Robbins, V.P.; Stanley B. Rich, Treas.
EIN: 136116442
Codes: FD2

34918
The Norman E. Alexander Family Foundation
200 Park Ave.
New York, NY 10166
Contact: Norman E. Alexander, Pres.

Donor(s): Norman E. Alexander.
Financial data (yr. ended 03/31/01): Grants paid, $142,315; assets, $3,684,041 (M); gifts received, $1,258,347; expenditures, $142,950; qualifying distributions, $142,850.
Limitations: Giving primarily in NY.
Application information: Application form not required.
Officers: Norman E. Alexander, Pres.; Marjorie E. Alexander, V.P.; Stuart Z. Krinsly, Secy.
EIN: 136161205

34919
Alconda-Owsley Foundation
116 E. 68th St., Apt. 10C
New York, NY 10021-5905

Established in 1982 in NY.
Donor(s): Lucy Ball Owsley, David T. Owsley.
Financial data (yr. ended 12/31/01): Grants paid, $142,299; assets, $1,852,330 (M); expenditures, $162,986; qualifying distributions, $142,299.
Limitations: Applications not accepted. Giving limited to the U.S., with emphasis on IN, New York, NY and TX.
Application information: Contributes only to pre-selected organizations.
Trustee: David T. Owsley.
EIN: 133156527

34920
Hochman Family Foundation
1100 Park Ave.
New York, NY 10128
Application address: 505 Park Ave., Ste. 1700, New York, NY 10022
Contact: Richard H. Hockman, Secy.-Treas.

Established in 1998 in NY.
Donor(s): Richard Hochman, Carol Hochman.
Financial data (yr. ended 12/31/01): Grants paid, $142,212; assets, $0 (M); gifts received, $2,500; expenditures, $142,354; qualifying distributions, $142,193.
Limitations: Giving primarily in NY.
Officers: Carol J. Hochman, Pres.; Richard H. Hochman, Secy.-Treas.
Director: Matthew Sirovich.
EIN: 134010994
Codes: FD2

34921
The William & Sylvia Silberstein Foundation, Inc.
93 Rye Rd.
Rye, NY 10580-1045 (914) 698-6636
Contact: William Silberstein, Admin.

Established in 1969.
Donor(s): William Silberstein, Sylvia Silberstein.
Financial data (yr. ended 11/30/01): Grants paid, $142,142; assets, $4,874,955 (M); gifts received, $399,939; expenditures, $166,064; qualifying distributions, $142,142.
Limitations: Giving primarily in the New York, NY, area.
Officer: William Silberstein, Admin.
EIN: 237108375
Codes: FD2

34922
J. & L. Adler Foundation
12 Mountain Ave.
Monsey, NY 10952-2944
Contact: Lillian Adler, Pres.

Established in 1985 in NY.
Donor(s): Joseph Adler, Lillian Adler.
Financial data (yr. ended 12/31/01): Grants paid, $142,070; assets, $1,017,007 (M); gifts received, $25,000; expenditures, $151,721; qualifying distributions, $151,330.
Limitations: Giving primarily in Rockland County, NY.
Officer: Lillian Adler, Pres.
EIN: 132737530
Codes: FD2

34923
Sofaer Foundation, Inc.
c/o TAG Assocs., Ltd.
75 Rockefeller Plz., Ste. 900
New York, NY 10019

Established in 1985 in NY.
Donor(s): Marian B. Scheuer-Sofaer, Abraham D. Sofaer.
Financial data (yr. ended 11/30/01): Grants paid, $142,020; assets, $45,815 (M); gifts received, $121,635; expenditures, $145,933; qualifying distributions, $142,170.
Limitations: Applications not accepted. Giving primarily in Washington, DC, and the metropolitan New York, NY, areas.
Application information: Contributes only to pre-selected organizations.
Officers and Directors:* Marian B. Scheuer-Sofaer,* Pres. and Treas.; Abraham D. Sofaer,* V.P. and Secy.; Richard J. Scheuer.
EIN: 133336722
Codes: FD2

34924
The Ponagansett Foundation, Inc.
c/o Patterson, Belknap, Webb & Tyler
1133 Ave. of the Americas, Ste. 2200
New York, NY 10036-6710

Established in 1972 in NY.
Donor(s): Mary B. Shea.
Financial data (yr. ended 12/31/01): Grants paid, $141,848; assets, $3,378,168 (M); expenditures, $166,646; qualifying distributions, $160,397.
Limitations: Applications not accepted. Giving primarily in the greater metropolitan New York, NY, area, and NJ; giving also in the metropolitan Washington, DC, area, and New England, with emphasis on CT and RI.
Application information: Contributes only to pre-selected organizations.
Officers and Trustees:* Mary B. Shea,* Pres.; Antonia M. Grumbach,* V.P.; Kevin A. McCreadie,* V.P.; Robert B. Shea,* V.P.; Mary Ellen Leyden,* Secy.; Mimi J. Kaplansky,* Treas.; Stephen J. Schreiber.
EIN: 237179101
Codes: FD2

34925
Stephen C. Swid and Nan G. Swid Foundation
152 W. 57th St.
New York, NY 10019-3301

Established in 1985 in NY.
Donor(s): Stephen C. Swid, Charles Koppleman, Martin Bandier.
Financial data (yr. ended 09/30/01): Grants paid, $141,796; assets, $1,985,910 (M); expenditures, $153,104; qualifying distributions, $142,331.
Limitations: Applications not accepted. Giving primarily in New York, NY.
Application information: Contributes only to pre-selected organizations.
Officers: Stephen C. Swid, Pres.; Nan G. Swid, Secy.
EIN: 133369493
Codes: FD2

34926
The Chernin Family Foundation, Inc.
c/o Executive Monetary Mgt.
919 3rd Ave.
New York, NY 10022

Established in 2000 in DE.
Donor(s): Peter Chernin, Megan Chernin.
Financial data (yr. ended 12/31/01): Grants paid, $141,775; assets, $247,199 (M); gifts received, $252,466; expenditures, $167,399; qualifying distributions, $141,775.
Limitations: Applications not accepted.
Application information: Contributes only to pre-selected organizations.
Officers: Peter Chernin, Pres.; Megan Chernin, V.P. and Treas.; John D. Dadakis, Secy. and Dir.
EIN: 522281012

34927
Agway Foundation
P.O. Box 4933
Syracuse, NY 13221-4933 (315) 449-6474
Contact: Stephen H. Hoefer, Chair.

Established in 1967 in NY.
Donor(s): Agway, Inc.
Financial data (yr. ended 06/30/01): Grants paid, $141,650; assets, $2,565,786 (M); expenditures, $149,850; qualifying distributions, $141,650.
Limitations: Giving primarily in the northeastern states of CT, DE, MA, MD, ME, NH, NJ, NY, OH, PA, RI, and VT.
Publications: Application guidelines.

Application information: Application form not required.
Officer: Stephen H. Hoefer, Chair.
Trustees: Courtney B. Burdette, Daniel J. Edinger, Martin P. Frankenfield, Jeffrey C. McIntyre, Joel L. Wenger, William W. Young.
EIN: 166089932
Codes: CS, FD2, CD

34928
Sonya Staff Foundation, Inc.
467 W. 22nd St., Apt. F
New York, NY 10011
Additional address: P.O. Box 1211, New York, NY 10113; E-mail: mbanz@mindspring.com
Contact: Marion Banzhaf

Established in 1983.
Financial data (yr. ended 12/31/01): Grants paid, $141,500; assets, $1,312,331 (M); expenditures, $167,551; qualifying distributions, $141,408.
Limitations: Applications not accepted. Giving primarily in New York, NY.
Publications: Grants list, informational brochure.
Application information: Contributes only to pre-selected organizations.
Advisors: Amelia Augustus, Marion Banzhaf, Eve Staff Rosahn, Debra Schaffer.
EIN: 133230154
Codes: FD2

34929
David A. & Leah Ray Werblin Foundation, Inc.
c/o Harvey Ginsberg & Co.
675 3rd Ave., Ste. 2800
New York, NY 10017
Contact: Harvey Ginsberg, Secy.

Established about 1961 in NY.
Financial data (yr. ended 11/30/01): Grants paid, $141,500; assets, $1,528,961 (M); expenditures, $164,261; qualifying distributions, $142,143.
Limitations: Giving primarily in NJ and NY.
Officers and Directors:* Thomas D. Werblin,* Pres.; Harvey Ginsberg,* Secy.
EIN: 131958083
Codes: FD2

34930
The Judith Ammerman Foundation
3 Heath Pl.
Garden City, NY 11530-3003

Established in 1998 in NY.
Donor(s): Judith Ammerman.
Financial data (yr. ended 06/30/01): Grants paid, $141,000; assets, $273,466 (M); gifts received, $369,839; expenditures, $265,232; qualifying distributions, $141,000.
Limitations: Applications not accepted. Giving primarily in CT, IL, and NY.
Application information: Contributes only to pre-selected organizations.
Officers: Judith Ammerman, Pres.; Joan Gittleson, Secy.
EIN: 134026194
Codes: FD2

34931
The Merow Foundation
c/o Sullivan & Cromwell
125 Broad St.
New York, NY 10004
Contact: John E. Merow

Established in 1997 in NY.
Donor(s): John E. Merow.
Financial data (yr. ended 12/31/01): Grants paid, $140,960; assets, $2,277,168 (M); expenditures, $151,140; qualifying distributions, $139,656.
Limitations: Applications not accepted.

Application information: Contributes only to pre-selected organizations.
Trustees: John E. Merow, Mary Alyce Merow.
EIN: 133913625
Codes: FD2

34932
The Robert & Deann Halper Foundation
271 Central Park W., No. 9E
New York, NY 10024-3020
Contact: Robert Halper, Pres.

Established in 1991 in NY.
Donor(s): Deann Halper, Robert Halper.
Financial data (yr. ended 12/31/00): Grants paid, $140,625; assets, $1,396,945 (M); gifts received, $1,100,000; expenditures, $143,312; qualifying distributions, $140,725.
Officers: Robert Halper, Pres.; Deann Halper, V.P.; Murray Halper, Secy.-Treas.
EIN: 223121072
Codes: FD2

34933
Leslie C. Quick, Jr. & Regina A. Quick Charitable Trust Foundation
c/o AMCO
505 Park Ave., 20th Fl.
New York, NY 10022-9306

Established in 1988 in FL.
Donor(s): Leslie C. Quick, Jr.
Financial data (yr. ended 10/31/01): Grants paid, $140,573; assets, $10,024,668 (M); gifts received, $3,825,000; expenditures, $142,084; qualifying distributions, $141,724.
Limitations: Applications not accepted. Giving primarily in FL and NY.
Application information: Contributes only to pre-selected organizations.
Trustee: Regina A. Quick.
EIN: 650083436
Codes: FD2

34934
Earl C. Hull Charitable Trust
(Formerly Earl C. Hull Foundation, Inc.)
c/o HSBC Bank USA
1 HSBC Bank USA Plz.
Buffalo, NY 14240

Established in 1980 in NY.
Donor(s): Hilda C. Hull.
Financial data (yr. ended 12/31/00): Grants paid, $140,472; assets, $1,096,238 (M); gifts received, $1,300; expenditures, $153,566; qualifying distributions, $141,128.
Limitations: Applications not accepted. Giving primarily in Buffalo, NY.
Application information: Contributes only to pre-selected organizations.
Trustee: HSBC Bank USA.
EIN: 226689555
Codes: FD2

34935
The Lichtenstein Family Foundation
1531 54th St.
Brooklyn, NY 11219-4346

Established in 1997 in NY.
Donor(s): George Lichtenstein.
Financial data (yr. ended 12/31/01): Grants paid, $140,370; assets, $111,326 (M); expenditures, $142,875; qualifying distributions, $141,698.
Limitations: Applications not accepted.
Application information: Contributes only to pre-selected organizations.
Directors: Alan Lichtenstein, George Lichtenstein, David Singer.
EIN: 113377455

34936
Margaret S. & Henry Hart Rice Foundation, Inc.
c/o Marcum & Kliegman, LLP
655 3rd Ave., Ste. 1610
New York, NY 10017
Contact: Margaret S. Rice, Pres.

Established in 1954 in NY.
Donor(s): Margaret S. Rice, Henry Hart Rice.
Financial data (yr. ended 09/30/01): Grants paid, $140,365; assets, $949,342 (M); expenditures, $155,387; qualifying distributions, $148,224.
Limitations: Giving primarily in the greater New York, NY, area.
Officer: Margaret S. Rice, Pres. and Secy.
EIN: 136062838
Codes: FD2

34937
The Ironhill Foundation
c/o The Granite Capital Intl. Group
126 E. 56th St., 25th Fl.
New York, NY 10022

Established in 1994 in NY.
Donor(s): Lewis M. Eisenberg.
Financial data (yr. ended 12/31/01): Grants paid, $140,325; assets, $75,498 (M); gifts received, $74,669; expenditures, $145,355; qualifying distributions, $139,609.
Limitations: Applications not accepted. Giving on a national basis, with emphasis on the Northeast.
Application information: Contributes only to pre-selected organizations.
Trustee: Lewis M. Eisenberg.
EIN: 137012477
Codes: FD2

34938
The Ida and William Rosenthal Foundation, Inc.
67A E. 77th St.
New York, NY 10021-1813 (212) 737-1011
Contact: Catherine Coleman Brawer, Pres.

Incorporated in 1953 in NY.
Donor(s): Ida Rosenthal,‡ William Rosenthal.‡
Financial data (yr. ended 08/31/01): Grants paid, $140,301; assets, $3,584,527 (M); expenditures, $185,687; qualifying distributions, $151,425.
Limitations: Giving on a national basis.
Publications: Informational brochure (including application guidelines), grants list.
Application information: Application form not required.
Officers and Directors:* Catherine Coleman Brawer,* Pres.; Robert A. Brawer,* Secy.; Christopher P. Brawer,* Treas.; Meredith D. Brawer, Nicholas A. Brawer, Wendy H. Brawer, Ann Brownell Stone.
EIN: 136141274
Codes: FD2

34939
The Katherine and George Walker Foundation
c/o Goldman Sachs & Co.
85 Broad St., Tax Dept.
New York, NY 10004

Established in 2000 in NY.
Donor(s): George H. Walker IV.
Financial data (yr. ended 11/30/01): Grants paid, $140,250; assets, $728,906 (M); gifts received, $543,668; expenditures, $166,685; qualifying distributions, $140,250.
Limitations: Applications not accepted. Giving primarily in CT, NJ, NY, and PA.
Application information: Contributes only to pre-selected organizations.
Trustees: George H. Walker IV, Katherine Grant Walker.
EIN: 134092798

34940
Yad Kaila, Inc.
137-13 72nd Rd.
Flushing, NY 11367

Established in 1997.
Donor(s): Joseph Hoch.
Financial data (yr. ended 12/31/00): Grants paid, $140,224; assets, $48,681 (L); gifts received, $80,000; expenditures, $140,586; qualifying distributions, $140,224.
Limitations: Applications not accepted.
Application information: Contributes only to pre-selected organizations.
Director: Joseph Hoch.
EIN: 113353103
Codes: FD2

34941
The Covington-Gilmore Foundation
15 E. 26th St.
New York, NY 10010

Established in 1995 in NY.
Donor(s): Members of the Gilmore family.
Financial data (yr. ended 02/28/01): Grants paid, $140,000; assets, $127,316 (M); expenditures, $141,428; qualifying distributions, $140,175.
Limitations: Applications not accepted. Giving primarily in NY.
Application information: Contributes only to pre-selected organizations.
Directors: Abby Gilmore, David Gilmore, Karen Gilmore, Michael Gilmore.
EIN: 133832005
Codes: FD2

34942
DB Foundation
c/o Goldman Sachs & Co.
85 Broad St., Tax Dept.
New York, NY 10004

Established in 1999 in NY.
Donor(s): Richard Bronks.
Financial data (yr. ended 10/31/01): Grants paid, $140,000; assets, $1,264,214 (M); gifts received, $2,500; expenditures, $149,843; qualifying distributions, $142,408.
Limitations: Applications not accepted. Giving primarily in New York, NY.
Application information: Contributes only to pre-selected organizations.
Trustees: Richard Bronks, Christopher Carrera.
EIN: 134088704
Codes: FD2

34943
Peter R. Gimbel & Elga Andersen-Gimbel Memorial Trust
c/o Paneth, Haber & Zimmerman, LLP
622 3rd Ave.
New York, NY 10017

Established in 1996 in NY.
Financial data (yr. ended 12/31/01): Grants paid, $140,000; assets, $2,442,314 (M); expenditures, $193,556; qualifying distributions, $144,878.
Limitations: Applications not accepted. Giving primarily in New York, NY.
Application information: Contributes only to pre-selected organizations.
Trustees: Leslie Gimbel, Thomas S.T. Gimbel, Russell Kagen.
EIN: 137055292
Codes: FD2

34944
The Maurer Family Foundation
c/o U.S. Trust
114 W. 47th St.
New York, NY 10036
FAX: (212) 852-3377
Contact: Carolyn L. Larke, Asst. V.P. or Linda Franciscovich, Sr. V.P.

Established in 1996 in FL.
Donor(s): Gilbert C. Maurer, Ann E. Maurer.
Financial data (yr. ended 12/31/00): Grants paid, $140,000; assets, $1,914,277 (M); gifts received, $575,000; expenditures, $171,690; qualifying distributions, $165,610.
Limitations: Applications not accepted. Giving on a national basis, with emphasis on the East Coast.
Application information: Contributes only to pre-selected organizations.
Officers and Directors:* Gilbert C. Maurer,* Chair.; Ann E. Maurer,* Pres.; Meredith M. Hutchinson,* V.P.; Christopher C. Maurer,* V.P.; David W. Maurer,* V.P.; Jonathan G. Maurer,* V.P.; Peter J. Maurer,* V.P.
EIN: 311469474
Codes: FD2

34945
Richard Nelson Ryan Foundation
787 7th Ave.
New York, NY 10019-6099
Contact: Augusta L. Packer, Secy.

Established in 1950 in NY.
Financial data (yr. ended 12/31/01): Grants paid, $140,000; assets, $2,136,633 (M); expenditures, $144,421; qualifying distributions, $140,469.
Limitations: Giving primarily in Seattle, WA.
Application information: Application form not required.
Officers: Richard N. Ryan, Jr., Pres.; Hope R. Garrett, V.P. and Treas.; Hope Farnell, V.P.; Augusta L. Packer, Secy.
EIN: 136161617
Codes: FD2

34946
The Smachlo Foundation
100 Vischer Ferry Rd.
Rexford, NY 12148-1643 (518) 371-5344
Contact: Walter Smachlo, Tr.

Established in 1965 in NY.
Donor(s): Walter Smachlo, Madeleine Smachlo, Trembaly Investment Co.
Financial data (yr. ended 11/30/01): Grants paid, $140,000; assets, $2,598,904 (M); expenditures, $154,159; qualifying distributions, $137,617.
Limitations: Giving primarily in NY.
Trustees: Madeleine Smachlo, Mark Smachlo, Walter Smachlo.
EIN: 146030393
Codes: FD2

34947
Keren Eliyahu, Inc.
c/o Alexander Scharf
305 West End Ave.
New York, NY 10024

Donor(s): Senior Home Care, Inc.
Financial data (yr. ended 12/31/99): Grants paid, $139,900; assets, $1,240 (M); gifts received, $125,000; expenditures, $139,943; qualifying distributions, $139,900.
Limitations: Applications not accepted.
Application information: Contributes only to pre-selected organizations.
Officers: Alexander Scharf, Pres. and Treas.; Susan Diamond, Secy.
Director: David Scharf.

EIN: 133978200
Codes: FD2

34948
The Ralph and Elizabeth Friedus Foundation, Inc.
c/o Reitman & Reitman, LLP
369 Lexington Ave., 26th Fl.
New York, NY 10017

Established in 1991 in NY.
Donor(s): Elizabeth S. Friedus.‡
Financial data (yr. ended 05/31/00): Grants paid, $139,645; assets, $1,359,945 (M); expenditures, $141,929; qualifying distributions, $139,645.
Limitations: Giving primarily in NY.
Officers and Directors:* Joan R. Saltzman,* Pres. and Secy.; Eric F. Saltzman,* Treas.
EIN: 132620057
Codes: FD2

34949
James and Barbara Block Foundation, Inc.
575 Lexington Ave., 4th Fl.
New York, NY 10022
Contact: James A. Block, Pres.

Established in 1975 in NJ.
Financial data (yr. ended 06/30/00): Grants paid, $139,500; assets, $83,631 (M); gifts received, $100,000; expenditures, $139,783; qualifying distributions, $139,652.
Limitations: Giving primarily in NY.
Officers and Trustees:* James A. Block,* Pres.; Barbara Block,* Exec. V.P.; Peter M. Block, V.P.; Valerie M. Block, V.P.; William Bush,* Secy.-Treas.
EIN: 510138517
Codes: FD2

34950
Mercury Aircraft Foundation
c/o Mercury Aircraft, Inc.
17 Wheeler Ave.
Hammondsport, NY 14840

Established in 1952 in NY.
Donor(s): Mercury Aircraft, Inc., Mercury Minnesota, Inc.
Financial data (yr. ended 12/31/01): Grants paid, $139,500; assets, $2,374,021 (M); gifts received, $40,000; expenditures, $140,359; qualifying distributions, $138,206.
Limitations: Giving primarily in western NY.
Application information: Application form not required.
Officer and Trustees:* Gregory Hintz,* Mgr.; Marcia M. Coon, Joseph F. Meade, Jr., J.E. Meade III.
EIN: 166028162
Codes: CS, FD2, CD

34951
David & Yetta Cohen Foundation
c/o Jules Cohen
30 E. 60th St., Ste. 903
New York, NY 10022

Established about 1944 in NY.
Donor(s): Jules Cohen.
Financial data (yr. ended 12/31/00): Grants paid, $139,461; assets, $584,534 (M); expenditures, $141,979; qualifying distributions, $140,420.
Limitations: Applications not accepted. Giving primarily in NY.
Application information: Contributes only to pre-selected organizations.
Officer: Jules Cohen, Pres.
EIN: 136127102
Codes: FD2

34952
I. & B. Neuman Foundation, Inc.
122 E. 42nd St.
New York, NY 10017-5600

Established in 1956 in NY.
Donor(s): Irving Neuman,‡ Herbert Neuman, Sheldon Neuman.‡
Financial data (yr. ended 12/31/01): Grants paid, $139,383; assets, $1,015,554 (M); expenditures, $150,458; qualifying distributions, $139,121.
Limitations: Applications not accepted. Giving primarily in NY.
Application information: Contributes only to pre-selected organizations.
Officers: Irving Neuman, Pres. and Treas; Herbert Neuman, V.P.
EIN: 136161492
Codes: FD2

34953
The Gelfond Family Foundation
1120 5th Ave., Rm. 11A
New York, NY 10128

Established in 1996 in NY.
Donor(s): Linda Gelfond, Richard Gelfond.
Financial data (yr. ended 05/31/01): Grants paid, $139,378; assets, $224,436 (M); expenditures, $142,086; qualifying distributions, $139,574.
Limitations: Applications not accepted. Giving primarily in NY.
Application information: Contributes only to pre-selected organizations.
Trustees: Linda Gelfond, Richard Gelfond.
EIN: 137118118
Codes: FD2

34954
The Viniar Family Foundation
c/o Goldman Sachs & Co.
85 Broad St., Tax Dept.
New York, NY 10004

Established in 1992 in NJ.
Donor(s): David A. Viniar.
Financial data (yr. ended 06/30/01): Grants paid, $139,294; assets, $5,492,942 (M); gifts received, $2,140,875; expenditures, $194,319; qualifying distributions, $139,294.
Limitations: Applications not accepted. Giving primarily in the Northeast.
Application information: Contributes only to pre-selected organizations.
Trustees: David A. Viniar, Susan M. Viniar.
EIN: 133748089
Codes: FD2

34955
John S. and Florence G. Lawrence Foundation, Inc.
99 W. Hawthorne Ave., Ste. 300
Valley Stream, NY 11580 (516) 872-0477
Contact: John S. Lawrence, Pres.

Established in 1955 in NY.
Donor(s): John S. Lawrence.
Financial data (yr. ended 04/30/01): Grants paid, $139,226; assets, $5,211,984 (M); expenditures, $232,766; qualifying distributions, $207,681.
Limitations: Giving primarily in NY.
Application information: Application form not required.
Officers and Directors:* John S. Lawrence,* Pres. and Treas.; Florence G. Lawrence,* V.P. and Secy.; James G. Lawrence,* V.P.; Betsy P. Schiff,* V.P.; David M. Levitan.
EIN: 136099026
Codes: FD2

34956
Maier Foundation, Inc.
c/o Yoga Zone
40 Cuttermill Rd., No. 501
Great Neck, NY 11021-3213

Established in 1994 in NY.
Donor(s): Howard S. Maier.
Financial data (yr. ended 12/31/99): Grants paid, $139,200; assets, $2,418,774 (M); gifts received, $960; expenditures, $164,265; qualifying distributions, $139,112.
Limitations: Applications not accepted. Giving primarily in CA.
Application information: Contributes only to pre-selected organizations.
Officers and Directors:* Howard S. Maier,* Pres.; Margaret Cuomo Maier,* Secy.; Richard Leland, Allen Miller, Daniel P. Nolan, Jeffrey A. Zankel.
EIN: 133774001
Codes: FD2

34957
Stella Matutina Foundation, Inc.
c/o J. Garrett
Clinton Sq., P.O. Box 31051
Rochester, NY 14603

Established in 1992 in NY.
Donor(s): John H. Dessauer,‡ Margaret Lee Dessauer.
Financial data (yr. ended 09/30/01): Grants paid, $139,000; assets, $333,492 (M); gifts received, $123,696; expenditures, $151,081; qualifying distributions, $146,626.
Limitations: Applications not accepted. Giving primarily in Rochester, NY.
Application information: Contributes only to pre-selected organizations.
Officers: John H. Glavin, Pres.; Kathleen Whekhan, V.P. and Treas.; John L. Garrett, Secy.
Advisor: Margaret Lee Dessauer.
EIN: 161399369
Codes: FD2

34958
Judy & Warren Tenney Foundation
c/o Judy Tenney
845 Forest Ave.
Rye, NY 10580

Established in 1989 in NY.
Donor(s): Warren Tenney.‡
Financial data (yr. ended 12/31/01): Grants paid, $138,905; assets, $2,997,430 (M); gifts received, $14,750; expenditures, $204,373; qualifying distributions, $142,085.
Limitations: Applications not accepted. Giving primarily in New York, NY.
Application information: Contributes only to pre-selected organizations.
Officer: Judy E. Tenney, Pres.
EIN: 133482305
Codes: FD2

34959
The Alan N. Cohen Foundation, Inc.
(Formerly The Alan N. & Joan M. Cohen Foundation, Inc.)
c/o Alpine Resources, LLC
1700 Broadway, 17th Fl.
New York, NY 10019

Established in 1985 in NY.
Donor(s): Alan N. Cohen, Morton B. Ernstein.
Financial data (yr. ended 11/30/01): Grants paid, $138,800; assets, $95,729 (M); expenditures, $141,525; qualifying distributions, $138,971.
Limitations: Applications not accepted. Giving primarily in New York, NY.

Application information: Contributes only to pre-selected organizations.
Directors: Alan N. Cohen, Carol F. Cohen, Gordon Geoffrey Cohen, Laurie Cohen-Fenster.
EIN: 133296783
Codes: FD2

34960
Stanley R. & Elisabeth G. Jacobs Foundation
c/o Stroock & Stroock & Lavan
180 Maiden Ln.
New York, NY 10038

Established in 1954 in NY.
Donor(s): Helene B. Jacobs.‡
Financial data (yr. ended 05/31/01): Grants paid, $138,797; assets, $2,785,005 (M); expenditures, $177,656; qualifying distributions, $143,398.
Limitations: Applications not accepted. Giving primarily in New York, NY.
Application information: Contributes only to pre-selected organizations.
Trustees: Elisabeth G. Jacobs, Michael R. Linburn, Ronald J. Stein.
EIN: 136087036
Codes: FD2

34961
Jack & Janet Teich Foundation
20 Polly Park Dr.
Rye, NY 10580

Established in 1995 in NY.
Donor(s): Jack Teich.
Financial data (yr. ended 12/31/00): Grants paid, $138,751; assets, $385,072 (M); gifts received, $100,000; expenditures, $139,404; qualifying distributions, $138,413.
Limitations: Applications not accepted.
Application information: Contributes only to pre-selected organizations.
Officers: Jack Teich, Pres.; Janet Teich, V.P. and Secy.
EIN: 133839630
Codes: FD2

34962
The Ong Family Foundation
c/o Koo, Larrabee & Lau-Kee, LLP
410 Saw Mill River Rd., LL 110
Ardsley, NY 10502

Established in 1997 in NY.
Donor(s): Danny O. Yee.
Financial data (yr. ended 01/31/01): Grants paid, $138,450; assets, $4,918,890 (M); gifts received, $1,185,750; expenditures, $138,813; qualifying distributions, $101,454.
Limitations: Applications not accepted.
Application information: Contributes only to pre-selected organizations.
Trustees: Danny O. Yee, Donald Ong Yee, Larry Ong Yee, Stephanie L. Yee.
EIN: 133986239
Codes: FD2

34963
The Rhodes Foundation
(Formerly The Thom Rhodes Foundation)
c/o BCRS Assocs., LLC
100 Wall St., 11th Fl.
New York, NY 10005

Established in 1987 in CT.
Donor(s): Thomas L. Rhodes.
Financial data (yr. ended 07/31/01): Grants paid, $138,400; assets, $206,663 (M); gifts received, $172,768; expenditures, $143,829; qualifying distributions, $139,350.
Limitations: Applications not accepted. Giving on a national basis, primarily along the East Coast.

Application information: Contributes only to pre-selected organizations.
Trustees: Gleaves Rhodes, Thomas L. Rhodes.
EIN: 133437891
Codes: FD2

34964
The Heyday Foundation
(Formerly The Fred P. Hochberg Foundation)
c/o Nathan Berkman & Co.
29 Broadway, Rm. 2900
New York, NY 10006-3296

Established in 1990 in NY.
Donor(s): Fred P. Hochberg.
Financial data (yr. ended 09/30/01): Grants paid, $137,950; assets, $1,832,390 (M); expenditures, $177,496; qualifying distributions, $137,950.
Limitations: Applications not accepted. Giving primarily in New York, NY.
Application information: Contributes only to pre-selected organizations.
Trustee: Fred P. Hochberg.
EIN: 136956580

34965
Johny Melohn Foundation
c/o Altman & Dick
350 Broadway, Ste. 205
New York, NY 10013-3911

Established in 1986 in NY.
Donor(s): Johny Melohn.
Financial data (yr. ended 11/30/01): Grants paid, $137,682; assets, $383,212 (M); gifts received, $125,100; expenditures, $137,782; qualifying distributions, $137,682.
Limitations: Applications not accepted. Giving primarily in NY.
Application information: Contributes only to pre-selected organizations.
Officer: Johny Melohn, Pres.
EIN: 133395220
Codes: FD2

34966
Goldstone Fund, Inc.
c/o Tanton & Co., LLP
37 W. 57th St., 5th Fl.
New York, NY 10019-6708
Contact: Arthur H. Goldstone, Pres.

Established in 1959 in NY.
Donor(s): Herbert A. Goldstone.‡
Financial data (yr. ended 05/31/01): Grants paid, $137,500; assets, $7,555,556 (M); expenditures, $218,211; qualifying distributions, $140,750.
Limitations: Giving primarily in New York, NY.
Officers and Directors:* Arthur H. Goldstone,* Pres.; Jane G. Rittmaster,* V.P.; Janet L. Mulligan,* Secy.-Treas.
EIN: 136028782
Codes: FD2

34967
The Maks & Lea Rothstein Foundation, Inc.
535 W. 110th St.
New York, NY 10025

Established in 1992 in NY.
Donor(s): Maks Rothstein, Lea Rothstein.
Financial data (yr. ended 12/31/01): Grants paid, $137,500; assets, $1,424,965 (M); gifts received, $99,727; expenditures, $176,227; qualifying distributions, $137,449.
Limitations: Applications not accepted. Giving primarily in New York, NY.
Application information: Contributes only to pre-selected organizations.

Officers: Maks Rothstein, Pres.; Sergio Rothstein, V.P.
EIN: 133610040
Codes: FD2

34968
The John H. Hobbs Charitable Trust
466 Lexington Ave., 18th Fl.
New York, NY 10017-3149

Established in 1984 in NY.
Donor(s): John H. Hobbs.
Financial data (yr. ended 12/31/01): Grants paid, $137,301; assets, $554,840 (M); gifts received, $400,000; expenditures, $137,481; qualifying distributions, $137,481.
Limitations: Applications not accepted. Giving primarily in NY.
Application information: Contributes only to pre-selected organizations.
Trustee: John H. Hobbs.
EIN: 136847765
Codes: FD2

34969
Robert Mapplethorpe Foundation, Inc.
120 Wooster St.
New York, NY 10012 (212) 941-4760
FAX: (212) 941-4764
Contact: Launa Beuhler, Exec. Dir.

Established in 1988 in NY.
Donor(s): Robert Mapplethorpe.‡
Financial data (yr. ended 05/31/01): Grants paid, $137,194; assets, $399,407 (M); gifts received, $414,100; expenditures, $424,684; qualifying distributions, $407,808.
Limitations: Giving on a national basis.
Publications: Application guidelines, grants list.
Application information: Application form not required.
Officers: Michael Ward Stout, Pres.; Lynn Davis, V.P.; Dimitri Levas, V.P.; Burton Lipsky, Secy.-Treas.
Director: Stewart Shining.
EIN: 133480472
Codes: FD2

34970
The Hycliff Foundation, Inc.
c/o Siegel, Sacks & Co.
630 3rd Ave.
New York, NY 10017

Incorporated in 1977 in DE as partial successor to The Bernhard Foundation, Inc.
Donor(s): The Bernhard Foundation, Inc.
Financial data (yr. ended 02/28/02): Grants paid, $137,084; assets, $1,920,471 (M); expenditures, $157,586; qualifying distributions, $136,423.
Limitations: Applications not accepted. Giving primarily in New York, NY.
Application information: Contributes only to pre-selected organizations; funds are fully committed.
Officers: Robert A. Bernhard, Pres.; Joan M. Bernhard, V.P.; Adele B. Neufeld, Secy.; Michael Bernhard, Treas.
Trustees: Steven G. Bernhard, Susan Bernhard Collins.
EIN: 132893039
Codes: FD2

34971
The Prescott Fund for Children & Youth, Inc.
521 5th Ave., Rm. 1700
New York, NY 10175-1799

Established in 1947 in NY.
Financial data (yr. ended 12/31/01): Grants paid, $137,050; assets, $2,335,764 (M); expenditures, $206,450; qualifying distributions, $137,050.

Limitations: Giving limited to NY.
Officers: Robert Knakal, Pres.; Robert K. Boyer, V.P.; Rhonda Levy, Secy.
EIN: 131674446
Codes: FD2

34972
Hershman Family Foundation, Inc.
43 Willow Rd.
Woodmere, NY 11598 (516) 627-1155
Contact: Ronnie A. Hershman, Pres. and Hannah Hershman, V.P.

Established in 1993 in NY.
Donor(s): Ronnie A. Hershman, Hannah A. Hershman.
Financial data (yr. ended 08/31/00): Grants paid, $137,029; assets, $565,027 (M); gifts received, $25,000; expenditures, $140,814; qualifying distributions, $138,259.
Limitations: Giving primarily in NY.
Officers: Ronnie A. Hershman, Pres.; Hannah Hershman, V.P.
EIN: 113178650

34973
Barbara Bell Cumming Foundation
c/o Kelley Drye & Warren, LLP
101 Park Ave.
New York, NY 10178
Contact: Michael S. Insel, Tr.

Established in 1992 in NY.
Donor(s): Barbara Bell Cumming.‡
Financial data (yr. ended 09/30/01): Grants paid, $137,000; assets, $2,785,489 (M); expenditures, $202,850; qualifying distributions, $138,448.
Limitations: Giving primarily in New York, NY.
Application information: Application form not required.
Trustee: Michael S. Insel.
EIN: 136999946
Codes: FD2

34974
The Neil and Judith Auerbach Foundation, Inc.
15 Langeries Dr.
Monsey, NY 10952-1907

Established in 1999 in NY.
Donor(s): Neil Auerbach, Judith Auerbach.
Financial data (yr. ended 12/31/00): Grants paid, $136,850; assets, $66,444 (M); gifts received, $150,000; expenditures, $139,490; qualifying distributions, $136,839.
Limitations: Applications not accepted. Giving primarily in NY.
Application information: Contributes only to pre-selected organizations.
Directors: Judith Auerbach, Neil Auerbach, Michael Kutzin.
EIN: 134088697
Codes: FD2

34975
M. Zalles Wells College, et al. Trust
c/o JPMorgan Chase Bank
P.O. Box 31412
Rochester, NY 14603
Application address: 1 Chase Manhattan Plz., New York, NY 10081, tel.: (212) 552-0800
Contact: Donald Mills, V.P., JPMorgan Chase Bank

Established around 1979.
Financial data (yr. ended 11/30/01): Grants paid, $136,825; assets, $2,263,885 (M); expenditures, $169,868; qualifying distributions, $157,238.
Limitations: Giving primarily in the metropolitan New York, NY, area.

Application information: Contributes to some pre-selected organizations. Application form not required.
Trustees: David N. Bottoms, Jr., JPMorgan Chase Bank.
EIN: 136761281
Codes: FD2

34976
The Henry & Rose Moskowitz 1999 Family Foundation
50 W. 17th St.
New York, NY 10011

Established in 2000 in NY.
Donor(s): Henry Moskowitz.
Financial data (yr. ended 12/31/00): Grants paid, $136,677; assets, $437,284 (M); gifts received, $369,913; expenditures, $136,677; qualifying distributions, $136,677.
Limitations: Applications not accepted.
Application information: Contributes only to pre-selected organizations.
Officers: Henry Moskowitz, Pres.; Rose Moskowitz, V.P.; Mark Moskowitz, Secy.
EIN: 116537576
Codes: FD2

34977
The Gershwind Family Foundation
153 E. 53rd St., 45th Fl.
New York, NY 10022

Established in 1998 in NY.
Donor(s): Marjorie Gershwind.
Financial data (yr. ended 12/31/99): Grants paid, $136,489; assets, $1,342,976 (M); gifts received, $150,070; expenditures, $136,559; qualifying distributions, $136,559.
Limitations: Applications not accepted. Giving primarily in NY.
Application information: Contributes only to pre-selected organizations.
Officers and Directors:* Marjorie Gershwind,* Pres.; Mark Gershwind,* V.P.; Joseph Getraer,* Secy.
EIN: 113359917
Codes: FD2

34978
Mary A. & Thomas F. Grasselli Endowment Foundation
c/o Fiduciary Trust Co. International
600 Fifth Ave.
New York, NY 10020
Contact: Grace Grasselli Fowler, Pres.

Established in 1965 in DE.
Financial data (yr. ended 12/31/01): Grants paid, $136,200; assets, $2,172,141 (M); expenditures, $158,823; qualifying distributions, $142,037.
Limitations: Giving primarily in NJ and NY.
Officers and Trustees:* Grace Grasselli Fowler, Pres.; W. Timothy Cashman,* V.P.; Robert A. Fowler,* Secy.; David J. Garrett, Robert H. Phelps.
EIN: 516018870
Codes: FD2

34979
Robert and Patricia Colby Foundation
c/o M&T Bank
P.O. Box 22900
Rochester, NY 14692

Established in 1989 in NY.
Financial data (yr. ended 12/31/01): Grants paid, $136,000; assets, $1,136,183 (M); expenditures, $150,096; qualifying distributions, $135,999.
Limitations: Applications not accepted. Giving limited to Buffalo, NY.

Application information: Contributes only to pre-selected organizations.
Trustees: James M. Wadsworth, M & T Bank.
EIN: 161315877
Codes: FD2

34980
The Marcus Wallenberg Foundation
c/o Sullivan & Cromwell
125 Broad St.
New York, NY 10004-2498 (212) 558-4000
Contact: Charles Dowling

Established in 1983 in NY.
Donor(s): National Union Electric Corp., The Tappan Co.
Financial data (yr. ended 03/31/01): Grants paid, $136,000; assets, $2,674,701 (M); expenditures, $172,266; qualifying distributions, $136,250.
Limitations: Giving to Swedish nationals attending graduate business schools in the U.S.
Officers and Directors:* Peter Wallenberg,* Pres.; Henry Christensen III,* V.P.; Johan Stalhand, Secy.; P. Henry Mueller,* Treas.; Ulla Rasch Anderson, Thomas Gerrity.
EIN: 133176307
Codes: FD2, GTI

34981
The Nazem Family Foundation
c/o Marks Paneth
88 Froehlich Farm Blvd., 2nd Fl.
Woodbury, NY 11797

Established in 1994.
Donor(s): Fred Nazem, Phil Barak.
Financial data (yr. ended 11/30/00): Grants paid, $135,300; assets, $1,075,141 (M); expenditures, $140,614; qualifying distributions, $135,300.
Limitations: Applications not accepted. Giving primarily in NY.
Application information: Contributes only to pre-selected organizations.
Directors: Phil Barak, Susie Gharib, Fred Nazem.
EIN: 113241976
Codes: FD2

34982
McCrory Corporation Needy & Worthy Employees Trust
c/o JPMorgan Chase Bank
P.O. Box 31412
Rochester, NY 14603

Donor(s): McCrory Corporation.
Financial data (yr. ended 12/31/01): Grants paid, $135,217; assets, $1,235,525 (M); expenditures, $194,621; qualifying distributions, $48,601.
Limitations: Giving limted to headquarters city and major operating areas.
Application information: Unsolicited requests for funds not accepted.
Trustee: JPMorgan Chase Bank.
EIN: 136022694
Codes: CS, FD2, CD, GTI

34983
The Patricia and Clarke Bailey Foundation, Inc.
10 Oxford Rd.
Larchmont, NY 10538

Established in 1996 in NY.
Donor(s): Clarke Bailey, Patricia Bailey.
Financial data (yr. ended 11/30/00): Grants paid, $135,179; assets, $897,209 (M); expenditures, $138,649; qualifying distributions, $136,037.
Limitations: Applications not accepted.
Application information: Contributes only to pre-selected organizations.
Officers: Patricia Bailey, Pres.; Clarke Bailey, Secy.
EIN: 133921652

34983—NEW YORK

Codes: FD2

34984
The Ord Foundation
c/o U.S. Trust
114 W. 47th St.
New York, NY 10036

Established in 1994 in NY.
Donor(s): Thomas O. Treadwell.
Financial data (yr. ended 08/31/01): Grants paid, $135,021; assets, $1,532,472 (M); expenditures, $153,508; qualifying distributions, $144,786.
Limitations: Applications not accepted. Giving primarily in NY.
Application information: Contributes only to pre-selected organizations.
Trustees: John R. Treadwell, Penelope A. Treadwell, Thomas O. Treadwell.
EIN: 146172329
Codes: FD2

34985
The Cremona Fund, Inc.
120 W. 45th St., 7th Fl.
New York, NY 10036
Contact: Phillip P. Goodkin, Pres.

Established in 1960 in NY.
Financial data (yr. ended 06/30/01): Grants paid, $135,000; assets, $882,396 (M); expenditures, $147,144; qualifying distributions, $137,075.
Limitations: Applications not accepted. Giving primarily in New York, NY.
Application information: Contributes only to pre-selected organizations.
Officers and Directors:* Philip P. Goodkin,* Pres. and Treas.; Lawrence B. Rodman,* V.P.; Leroy E. Rodman,* Secy.; Theodore A. Landau.
EIN: 136028790
Codes: FD2

34986
Cross Ridge Foundation, Inc.
c/o Davidson, Dawson & Clark
330 Madison Ave., 35th Fl.
New York, NY 10017 (212) 557-7700
Contact: Berkeley D. Johnson, Jr., Secy.

Established around 1958.
Donor(s): Amy Klose.‡
Financial data (yr. ended 09/30/01): Grants paid, $135,000; assets, $2,142,289 (M); expenditures, $150,062; qualifying distributions, $134,544.
Limitations: Giving primarily in northern CA, Westchester County, NY, and VT.
Application information: Application form not required.
Officers: Tracy M. Brown, Pres.; Ferenc Dobronyi, V.P.; Joseph B. Dobronyi, V.P.; Berkeley D. Johnson, Jr., Secy.; Charles Smithers, Treas.
EIN: 136089083
Codes: FD2

34987
Betty Byrne De Zahara 1997 Charitable Trust
c/o The Bank of New York
1 Wall St., Tax Dept., 28th Fl.
New York, NY 10286

Established in 1997 in RI.
Financial data (yr. ended 11/30/01): Grants paid, $135,000; assets, $2,759,664 (M); expenditures, $210,410; qualifying distributions, $161,664.
Limitations: Applications not accepted. Giving primarily in Strasburg, PA.
Application information: Contributes only to pre-selected organizations.
Trustees: Richard Sayer, The Bank of New York.
EIN: 137155996
Codes: FD2

34988
Dixon-Comstock Art, 4th, 5th & 6th Trust
c/o The Bank of New York-Tax Dept.
1 Wall St., 28th Fl.
New York, NY 10286

Established in 2000 in NY.
Financial data (yr. ended 03/31/01): Grants paid, $135,000; assets, $2,366,620 (M); gifts received, $3,173,470; expenditures, $141,954; qualifying distributions, $136,172.
Limitations: Applications not accepted. Giving primarily in NY.
Application information: Contributes only to pre-selected organizations.
Trustee: The Bank of New York.
EIN: 137258003
Codes: FD2

34989
The Gantcher Foundation
c/o HPB Assocs.
65 E. 55th St., 30th Fl.
New York, NY 10022

Established in 1985 in NY.
Donor(s): Nathan Gantcher.
Financial data (yr. ended 06/30/01): Grants paid, $135,000; assets, $4,945,796 (M); gifts received, $677,249; expenditures, $175,505; qualifying distributions, $135,250.
Limitations: Applications not accepted. Giving primarily in New York, NY.
Application information: Contributes only to pre-selected organizations.
Trustees: Alice Gantcher, Joel Gantcher, Kimberly Gantcher, Michael Gantcher, Nathan Gantcher.
EIN: 133320425
Codes: FD2

34990
The Herbert and Lorraine Podell Foundation
605 3rd Ave.
New York, NY 10158-0180

Donor(s): Herbert Podell, Lorraine Podell.
Financial data (yr. ended 12/31/01): Grants paid, $134,992; assets, $553,788 (M); gifts received, $138,588; expenditures, $137,557; qualifying distributions, $134,346.
Limitations: Applications not accepted. Giving primarily in the Bronx, NY.
Application information: Contributes only to pre-selected organizations.
Trustees: Herbert Podell, Lorraine Podell.
EIN: 133798538
Codes: FD2

34991
Bridge Lane Foundation
c/o Rochelle Gutman
P.O. Box 040-331
Brooklyn, NY 11204 (718) 851-6259

Established in NY in 2000.
Donor(s): G & L Equities, LLC.
Financial data (yr. ended 11/30/01): Grants paid, $134,700; assets, $4,853 (M); gifts received, $139,650; expenditures, $134,797; qualifying distributions, $134,700.
Trustees: Rochelle Gutman, Teresa Lerner.
EIN: 113573668

34992
The Carl & Marsha Hewitt Foundation, Inc.
c/o BCRS Assoc., LLC
100 Wall St., 11th Fl.
New York, NY 10005

Established in 1994 in NY.

Donor(s): Education for Youth Society, Carl N. Newitt.
Financial data (yr. ended 10/31/01): Grants paid, $134,635; assets, $2,385,908 (M); gifts received, $1,471,664; expenditures, $141,700; qualifying distributions, $135,047.
Limitations: Applications not accepted. Giving primarily in the greater metropolitan New York, NY, area.
Application information: Contributes only to pre-selected organizations.
Officers: Carl H. Hewitt, Pres. and Treas.; Marsha A. Hewitt, V.P. and Secy.; Thomas J. McCabe, V.P.
EIN: 133798937
Codes: FD2

34993
Zaleski Family Foundation
c/o Michel Zaleski
300 Central Park West, Ste. 29D
New York, NY 10024

Established in 1996 in DE and NY.
Donor(s): Michel Zaleski.
Financial data (yr. ended 06/30/99): Grants paid, $134,500; assets, $2,351,654 (M); expenditures, $175,757; qualifying distributions, $134,500.
Limitations: Applications not accepted.
Officers: Michel Zaleski, Pres. and Secy.; Caroline Rob Zaleski, V.P. and Treas.
EIN: 133911432
Codes: FD2

34994
Charles S. Raizen Foundation, Inc.
31 Meadow Rd.
Scarsdale, NY 10583

Established in 1945 in NY.
Donor(s): Charles S. Raizen,‡ Patricia T. Raizen.‡
Financial data (yr. ended 12/31/01): Grants paid, $134,425; assets, $2,113,350 (M); expenditures, $146,195; qualifying distributions, $132,982.
Limitations: Applications not accepted. Giving on a national basis.
Application information: Contributes only to pre-selected organizations.
Officers: Roy Raizen, Pres.; David Raizen, V.P.; Nancy Raizen, V.P.; Susan R. Sperber, Secy.; Jill R. Serling, Treas.
EIN: 136122579
Codes: FD2

34995
The Tripp Foundation, Inc.
1 W. Church St.
Elmira, NY 14901

Established in 1972.
Financial data (yr. ended 04/30/01): Grants paid, $134,389; assets, $2,142,135 (M); expenditures, $153,839; qualifying distributions, $134,389.
Limitations: Giving primarily in the Cheming County and Dundee, NY, areas.
Application information: Application form required.
Officers and Trustees:* Frank T. Rose,* Pres.; Edward T. Marks,* V.P.; Susan M. Pawtak,* Secy.; Henry M. Kimball,* Treas.; Nancy F. Fulkerson, Ann M. Hazlitt, Howard H. Kimball, Polly M. Smith.
EIN: 160986346
Codes: FD2

34996
Zichron Avraham Abba Foundation
1360 E. 14th St., Ste. 101
Brooklyn, NY 11230

Established in 1998 in NY.
Donor(s): Leon Goldenberg, Chaim Goldenberg.

Financial data (yr. ended 12/31/00): Grants paid, $134,246; assets, $370,784 (M); gifts received, $235,120; expenditures, $136,151; qualifying distributions, $132,991.
Limitations: Applications not accepted.
Application information: Contributes only to pre-selected organizations.
Officers: Leon Goldenberg, Pres.; Agnes Goldenberg, V.P.
Trustee: Chaim Goldenberg.
EIN: 113412101
Codes: FD2

34997
The Lucy Foundation
10 Gracie Sq.
New York, NY 10028-8031
Contact: Diane Schafer, Tr.

Established in 1995 in DE and NY.
Donor(s): The Schafer Family Foundation, Diane H. Schafer.
Financial data (yr. ended 12/31/01): Grants paid, $134,239; assets, $534,661 (M); expenditures, $151,918; qualifying distributions, $136,367.
Limitations: Applications not accepted. Giving primarily in New York, NY.
Application information: Contributes only to pre-selected organizations.
Officer and Director:* Diane H. Schafer,* Pres.
EIN: 133860958
Codes: FD2

34998
JSO Foundation, Inc.
21 Richbell Rd.
Scarsdale, NY 10583
Contact: Berenice Oettinger, Pres.

Established about 1953 in NY.
Donor(s): Joseph Oettinger.
Financial data (yr. ended 12/31/01): Grants paid, $134,225; assets, $1,791,601 (M); expenditures, $146,138; qualifying distributions, $135,333.
Limitations: Giving primarily in NY.
Application information: Application form not required.
Officers: Berenice Oettinger, Pres.; Betty Hutman, V.P. and Secy.; Nancy Oettinger, V.P. and Secy.
EIN: 116038127
Codes: FD2

34999
Julius Seaman Family Foundation
500 N. Broadway, Ste. 238
Jericho, NY 11753

Established in 1987 in NY.
Donor(s): Morton Seaman.
Financial data (yr. ended 10/31/01): Grants paid, $134,200; assets, $4,055,979 (M); expenditures, $158,789; qualifying distributions, $152,536.
Limitations: Applications not accepted. Giving primarily in NY.
Application information: Contributes only to pre-selected organizations.
Officers: Morton Seaman, Pres.; Jeffrey Seaman, V.P.; Lois Seaman, V.P.; Jill Seaman Plancher, Secy.
EIN: 112951057
Codes: FD2

35000
Richard Hampton Jenrette Foundation, Inc.
c/o CSAM
466 Lexington Ave.
New York, NY 10017

Established in 1967 in NY.
Donor(s): Richard H. Jenrette.

Financial data (yr. ended 11/30/99): Grants paid, $133,930; assets, $677,403 (M); expenditures, $145,045; qualifying distributions, $135,096.
Limitations: Applications not accepted. Giving primarily in NC, NY, and SC.
Application information: Contributes only to pre-selected organizations.
Officers and Directors:* William L. Thompson,* Pres.; Joseph M. Jenrette III,* V.P.; Marjorie S. White, Secy.-Treas.; Scott Bessent, Michael A. Boyd, Charles H.P. Duell, Richard H. Jenrette, John W. Smith.
EIN: 136271770
Codes: FD2

35001
Richard S. and Karen Lefrak Charitable Foundation, Inc.
97-77 Queens Blvd.
Rego Park, NY 11374
Contact: Maxwell Goldpin

Established in 1989 in NY.
Donor(s): Richard S. Lefrak.
Financial data (yr. ended 11/20/00): Grants paid, $133,840; assets, $97,551 (M); gifts received, $150,937; expenditures, $135,660; qualifying distributions, $133,802.
Limitations: Applications not accepted. Giving primarily in New York, NY.
Application information: Contributes only to pre-selected organizations.
Officer: Richard S. Lefrak, Pres.
EIN: 112994678
Codes: FD2

35002
Herbert & Noemi Frank Family Foundation
814 Coney Island Ave.
Brooklyn, NY 11218
Contact: Herbert Frank, Tr.

Established in 1999 in NY.
Donor(s): Herbert Frank, Noemi Frank, Barry Frank.
Financial data (yr. ended 12/31/00): Grants paid, $133,637; assets, $193,487 (M); gifts received, $175,000; expenditures, $135,501; qualifying distributions, $133,637.
Limitations: Giving primarily in NY.
Trustees: Barry Frank, Herbert Frank, Noemi Frank.
EIN: 113522063
Codes: FD2

35003
The Lorne Michaels Foundation, Inc.
c/o Hecht & Co.
111 W. 40th St., 20th Fl.
New York, NY 10018

Established in 1990 in DE and NY.
Donor(s): Lorne Michaels, Broadway Video, Inc.
Financial data (yr. ended 12/31/01): Grants paid, $133,600; assets, $251,390 (M); expenditures, $137,493; qualifying distributions, $135,499.
Limitations: Applications not accepted. Giving primarily in NY.
Application information: Contributes only to pre-selected organizations.
Officer: Lorne Michaels, Pres.
EIN: 133584269
Codes: FD2

35004
Ziv Israel Association
c/o Kamerman
885 2nd Ave., 26th Fl.
New York, NY 10017

Established in 1989 in NY.

Donor(s): Emanuel Toporowitz.
Financial data (yr. ended 12/31/00): Grants paid, $133,560; assets, $90,745 (M); gifts received, $122,995; expenditures, $135,435; qualifying distributions, $135,435.
Limitations: Applications not accepted. Giving limited to Haifa, Israel.
Application information: Contributes only to pre-selected organizations.
Trustees: Arie Bodenstein, Emanuel Toporowitz.
EIN: 237321981
Codes: FD2

35005
Rose Family Foundation
c/o Brown Brothers Harriman Trust Co.
63 Wall St.
New York, NY 10005-2831

Established in 1998 in DE and NY.
Financial data (yr. ended 12/31/00): Grants paid, $133,537; assets, $6,272,556 (M); expenditures, $184,649; qualifying distributions, $142,825.
Limitations: Applications not accepted. Giving primarily in NY.
Application information: Contributes only to pre-selected organizations.
Officers: Marian H. Rose, Pres.; Ann R. Podlipny, V.P.; David H. Rose, Secy.; Simon M. Rose, Treas.
EIN: 134016964
Codes: FD2

35006
The Philip and Roberta Puschel Foundation
79 Madison Ave., 16th Fl.
New York, NY 10016-7878

Established in 1997 in NY.
Donor(s): Philip Puschel.
Financial data (yr. ended 12/31/01): Grants paid, $133,500; assets, $869,769 (M); gifts received, $457,214; expenditures, $133,914; qualifying distributions, $133,548.
Limitations: Applications not accepted. Giving primarily in NY.
Application information: Contributes only to pre-selected organizations.
Officer: Philip Puschel, Pres.
Directors: Gerald Puschel, Roberta Puschel.
EIN: 133949073
Codes: FD2

35007
The Schonfeld Family Foundation, Inc.
57 W. 57th St., Ste. 512
New York, NY 10019
Contact: Arnold Schonfeld, Tr.

Established around 1971.
Donor(s): Arnold Schonfeld, Sidney Schonfeld.
Financial data (yr. ended 12/31/00): Grants paid, $133,491; assets, $2,719,371 (M); gifts received, $200,000; expenditures, $139,314; qualifying distributions, $131,646.
Limitations: Giving primarily in NY.
Trustee: Arnold Schonfeld.
EIN: 237113225
Codes: FD2

35008
SDF Family Foundation
1442 51st St.
Brooklyn, NY 11219-3605

Established in 1997 in NY.
Donor(s): Samuel D. Friedman.
Financial data (yr. ended 12/31/00): Grants paid, $133,422; assets, $39,572 (L); gifts received, $441,586; expenditures, $440,082; qualifying distributions, $134,836.
Limitations: Applications not accepted.

Application information: Contributes only to pre-selected organizations.
Directors: Chaya V. Friedman, Samuel D. Friedman.
EIN: 113347643
Codes: FD2

35009
The Dilmaghani Foundation
540 Central Park Ave.
Scarsdale, NY 10583-1099

Donor(s): Dianne Aronian, Dennis Dilmaghani, Camp Hillard.
Financial data (yr. ended 07/31/01): Grants paid, $133,000; assets, $864,601 (M); gifts received, $22,000; expenditures, $135,391; qualifying distributions, $133,000.
Limitations: Applications not accepted. Giving primarily in CT and NY.
Application information: Contributes only to pre-selected organizations.
Officers and Trustees:* Dennis Dilmaghani,* Chair.; Margot Dilmaghani,* Secy.; Dianne Aronian,* Treas.
EIN: 136159975
Codes: FD2

35010
The Max Rosenfeld Foundation, Inc.
c/o David Berdon & Co.
415 Madison Ave.
New York, NY 10017

Established in 1945 in DE.
Financial data (yr. ended 11/30/01): Grants paid, $133,000; assets, $2,076,989 (M); expenditures, $140,184; qualifying distributions, $137,093.
Limitations: Applications not accepted. Giving primarily in New York, NY; some giving also in MA and Portland, ME.
Application information: Contributes only to pre-selected organizations.
Directors: Suzanne Lehmann, Michael Rosenfeld, Maxine Sclar.
EIN: 136137869
Codes: FD2

35011
Wellington Foundation, Inc.
14 Wall St., Ste. 1702
New York, NY 10005

Incorporated in 1955 in NY.
Donor(s): Herbert G. Wellington,‡ Herbert G. Wellington, Jr., Elizabeth D. Wellington.‡
Financial data (yr. ended 12/31/01): Grants paid, $133,000; assets, $1,835,772 (M); expenditures, $140,950; qualifying distributions, $133,436.
Limitations: Applications not accepted. Giving primarily in NY.
Application information: Contributes only to pre-selected organizations.
Officers: Charles H. Wellington, Pres. and Treas.; Patricia B. Wellington, V.P.; Thomas D. Wellington, Secy.
EIN: 136110175
Codes: FD2

35012
Michael F. & Edith H. Weinberg Charitable Foundation
3 Red Ground Rd.
Old Westbury, NY 11568

Established in 1997 in NY.
Donor(s): Michael F. Weinberg, Edith H. Weinberg, Robert Littman.
Financial data (yr. ended 12/31/01): Grants paid, $132,959; assets, $1,004,454 (M); expenditures, $138,203; qualifying distributions, $132,417.

Limitations: Applications not accepted. Giving primarily in NY.
Application information: Contributes only to pre-selected organizations.
Trustees: Robert Littman, Edith H. Weinberg, Michael F. Weinberg.
EIN: 113410989
Codes: FD2

35013
Goldberg Berbeco Foundation, Inc.
1250 Pittsford Victor Rd., Ste. 110
Pittsford, NY 14534
E-mail: gbf@goldberg-online.net; *URL:* http://goldberg-online.net/gbf
Contact: Paul Goldberg, Pres.

Established in 1960 in NY.
Donor(s): Emanuel Goldberg.‡
Financial data (yr. ended 09/30/01): Grants paid, $132,869; assets, $1,241,312 (M); expenditures, $205,092; qualifying distributions, $131,260.
Limitations: Giving primarily in Rochester, NY.
Publications: Application guidelines.
Officers: Paul S. Goldberg, Pres.; Nathalie Goldberg, V.P. and Secy.; Sandra J. Berbeco, V.P.; E. Barry Kaplan, Treas.
EIN: 166038171
Codes: FD2

35014
The Ainslie Foundation, Inc.
c/o W. Michael Reickert, The Ayco Co., LP
P.O. Box 8009, 855 Rte. 146, Ste. 120
Clifton Park, NY 12065-8009

Established in 1997 in DE.
Donor(s): Michael Ainslie, Suzanne Ainslie.
Financial data (yr. ended 12/31/01): Grants paid, $132,825; assets, $505,247 (M); gifts received, $267,796; expenditures, $142,270; qualifying distributions, $132,825.
Limitations: Applications not accepted.
Application information: Contributes only to pre-selected organizations.
Directors: Michael Ainslie, Suzanne Ainslie.
EIN: 522066094

35015
The Gullquist Family Charitable Trust
c/o Lazard Freres & Co., LLC
30 Rockefeller Plz.
New York, NY 10020
Contact: Herbert Gullquist, Tr.

Established in 1991 in NY.
Donor(s): Herbert W. Gullquist.
Financial data (yr. ended 12/31/01): Grants paid, $132,825; assets, $1,616,816 (M); expenditures, $138,155; qualifying distributions, $133,155.
Limitations: Giving primarily in CT.
Trustees: Anne K. Gullquist, Herbert W. Gullquist, Charles Stieglitz.
EIN: 136982699
Codes: FD2

35016
The Sara Chait Memorial Foundation, Inc.
c/o Marilyn Chait
860 5th Ave.
New York, NY 10021-5856

Incorporated in 1959 in NY.
Donor(s): Abraham Chait,‡ Murray Backer,‡ Burton D. Chait, Marilyn Chait, and others.
Financial data (yr. ended 12/31/01): Grants paid, $132,800; assets, $2,288,059 (M); expenditures, $134,290; qualifying distributions, $134,105.
Limitations: Applications not accepted. Giving primarily in NY.

Application information: Contributes only to pre-selected organizations.
Officers: Richard D. Kuhn, Pres.; Lawrence E. May, V.P.; Marilyn Chait, Treas.
Trustees: Sheldon Blackman, Alfred Gollomp, Donald Kent, Seymour Sobel.
EIN: 136121596
Codes: FD2

35017
The University Place Foundation, Inc.
(Formerly Ambase Foundation, Inc.)
99 University Pl., 7th Fl.
New York, NY 10003-4528 (212) 473-0028
Contact: Lester J. Mantell, V.P.

Incorporated in 1963 in MO.
Donor(s): AmBase Corp.
Financial data (yr. ended 12/31/01): Grants paid, $132,750; assets, $132,071 (M); expenditures, $133,129; qualifying distributions, $132,659.
Limitations: Giving primarily in NY.
Application information: Application form not required.
Officers and Directors:* David G. Ormsby,* Pres.; Lester J. Mantell,* V.P., Treas., and Cont.
EIN: 133246657
Codes: CS, FD2, CD

35018
Patrick J. Ward and Family Foundation
c/o Goldman Sachs & Co.
85 Broad St., Tax Dept.
New York, NY 10004

Established in 1991 in IL.
Donor(s): Patrick J. Ward.
Financial data (yr. ended 03/31/01): Grants paid, $132,647; assets, $1,005,386 (M); expenditures, $152,180; qualifying distributions, $132,216.
Limitations: Applications not accepted. Giving primarily in London, England.
Application information: Contributes only to pre-selected organizations.
Trustees: Robert K. Steel, Kathleen M. Ward, Patrick J. Ward.
EIN: 133639293
Codes: FD2

35019
The Berrilla Kerr Foundation, Inc.
c/o Hummel
220 Mineola Blvd.
Mineola, NY 11501

Established in 1985 in NY.
Donor(s): Berrilla Kerr.‡
Financial data (yr. ended 12/31/00): Grants paid, $132,500; assets, $350,818 (M); expenditures, $148,941; qualifying distributions, $132,203.
Limitations: Applications not accepted. Giving primarily in NY.
Application information: Unsolicited requests for funds not considered.
Officers and Directors:* Arlene Nadel,* Pres.; Janet N. Swords,* Secy.-Treas.; Austin Pendleton, Lanie Robertson, Sybil Rosen, Sloane Shelton.
EIN: 133304383
Codes: FD2, GTI

35020
The Pollock Foundation
c/o Ingalls & Snyder
61 Broadway
New York, NY 10006-2701

Established in 1983 in NY.
Donor(s): Oscar S. Pollock.
Financial data (yr. ended 11/30/01): Grants paid, $132,500; assets, $1,315,988 (M); gifts received,

$11,540; expenditures, $155,037; qualifying distributions, $143,903.
Limitations: Applications not accepted. Giving primarily in NY.
Application information: Contributes only to pre-selected organizations.
Officers: Oscar S. Pollock, Pres.; Mary Nan Pollock, V.P.
EIN: 133195928
Codes: FD2

35021
Milton Tenenbaum Charitable Foundation
c/o The Bank of New York, Tax Dept.
1 Wall St., 28th Fl.
New York, NY 10286
Application address: c/o The Bank of New York, 235 Main St., White Plains, NY 10601
Contact: Patricia Healy

Established in 1999 in NY.
Financial data (yr. ended 05/31/02): Grants paid, $132,500; assets, $1,484,377 (M); expenditures, $157,226; qualifying distributions, $132,500.
Trustee: The Bank of New York.
EIN: 137209332
Codes: FD2

35022
The Joyce Green Family Foundation
c/o Joyce Green
28 Harbour Rd.
Kings Point, NY 11024

Established in 1985 in NY.
Donor(s): Joyce Green.
Financial data (yr. ended 10/31/00): Grants paid, $132,450; assets, $2,290,160 (M); gifts received, $44,334; expenditures, $133,502; qualifying distributions, $132,415.
Limitations: Applications not accepted. Giving primarily in NY.
Application information: Contributes only to pre-selected organizations.
Officers and Directors:* Joyce Green,* Pres.; Brooke Green,* Secy.; Laurance Green, Secy.; Lee Green, Secy.
EIN: 112778328
Codes: FD2

35023
Long Mountain Road Foundation
c/o Baker & McKenzie
20 W. 64th St.
New York, NY 10023
Contact: Peter D. Lederer, Pres.

Established in 1989 in DE.
Donor(s): Peter D. Lederer.
Financial data (yr. ended 11/30/01): Grants paid, $132,400; assets, $141,058 (M); gifts received, $250,000; expenditures, $133,710; qualifying distributions, $132,400.
Limitations: Giving primarily in New York, NY.
Officer: Peter D. Lederer, Pres.
EIN: 521657562

35024
Federated Foundations, Inc.
c/o Theodore Present
40 Cuttermill Rd., Ste. 305
Great Neck, NY 11021

Incorporated in 1961 in NY.
Donor(s): Harry Keiser,‡ Edward Netter, Richard Netter.
Financial data (yr. ended 12/31/01): Grants paid, $132,340; assets, $765,420 (M); gifts received, $30,000; expenditures, $145,370; qualifying distributions, $133,771.

Limitations: Applications not accepted. Giving primarily in New York, NY.
Application information: Contributes only to pre-selected organizations.
Officer: Richard Netter, Pres.
EIN: 136143973
Codes: FD2

35025
Walter J. & Anna H. Burchan Charitable Trust
6 Ford Ave.
Oneonta, NY 13820-1818 (607) 432-6720
Contact: Ronald R. Haus, Tr.

Established in 1980 in NY.
Donor(s): Anna H. Burchan.
Financial data (yr. ended 12/31/01): Grants paid, $132,000; assets, $2,477,788 (M); expenditures, $144,971; qualifying distributions, $144,971.
Limitations: Giving primarily in Delaware and Otsego counties, NY.
Application information: Application form not required.
Officer and Trustees:* Ronald R. Haus,* Mgr.; Elsie I. Haus, Karen A. Haus.
EIN: 222294069
Codes: FD2

35026
Dr. Martin & Edith Horowitz Memorial Fund
1207 Delaware Ave., Ste. 208
Buffalo, NY 14209-1401

Financial data (yr. ended 12/31/00): Grants paid, $132,000; assets, $892,973 (M); expenditures, $31,084; qualifying distributions, $132,000.
Limitations: Applications not accepted. Giving on a national basis.
Application information: Contributes only to pre-selected organizations.
Trustee: Melisse H. Pinto.
EIN: 161416872
Codes: FD2

35027
The McInerney Foundation, Ltd.
c/o Cahill, Gordon & Reindel
80 Pine St.
New York, NY 10005-1702 (212) 701-3300

Established in 1991 in NY.
Donor(s): Denis McInerney.
Financial data (yr. ended 12/31/01): Grants paid, $132,000; assets, $1,082,657 (M); gifts received, $155; expenditures, $132,405; qualifying distributions, $131,761.
Limitations: Applications not accepted. Giving limited to the metropolitan New York, NY, area.
Application information: Contributes only to pre-selected organizations.
Officers and Directors:* Denis McInerney,* Pres.; Irene McInerney,* V.P.; Kathleen McInerney O'Hare,* Secy.-Treas.
EIN: 133633322
Codes: FD2

35028
The Nicholas G. Rutgers, Jr. Foundation, Inc.
c/o Morris & McVeigh, LLP
767 3rd Ave.
New York, NY 10017

Established in 1994 in NY.
Financial data (yr. ended 04/30/02): Grants paid, $132,000; assets, $1,349,270 (M); gifts received, $91,295; expenditures, $140,870; qualifying distributions, $132,000.
Limitations: Applications not accepted.
Application information: Contributes only to pre-selected organizations.

Officers: Nicholas G. Rutgers, Jr., Pres. and Treas.; Nancy H. Rutgers, V.P.; MacDonald Budd, Secy.
EIN: 133827542

35029
Jeffrey and Susan Goldenberg Foundation
c/o Goldman Sachs & Co., Tax Dept.
85 Broad St.
New York, NY 10004

Established in 1999 in NY.
Donor(s): Jeffrey Goldenberg.
Financial data (yr. ended 09/30/01): Grants paid, $131,960; assets, $1,751,734 (M); gifts received, $450,486; expenditures, $142,870; qualifying distributions, $131,960.
Limitations: Applications not accepted. Giving primarily in New York, NY.
Application information: Contributes only to pre-selected organizations.
Trustees: Jeffrey Goldenberg, Susan Goldenberg.
EIN: 134050662

35030
Summit Foundation
c/o Goldman Sachs & Co.
85 Broad St., Tax Dept.
New York, NY 10004

Established in 1994 in NY.
Donor(s): Cody J. Smith.
Financial data (yr. ended 09/30/01): Grants paid, $131,900; assets, $913,092 (M); gifts received, $1,500; expenditures, $142,800; qualifying distributions, $133,720.
Limitations: Applications not accepted. Giving primarily in Stanford, CA, Boston, MA, and New York, NY.
Application information: Contributes only to pre-selected organizations.
Trustee: Cody J. Smith.
EIN: 133805672
Codes: FD2

35031
The Baker Foundation
485 Washington Ave.
Pleasantville, NY 10570

Established in 1986 in NY.
Financial data (yr. ended 12/31/01): Grants paid, $131,780; assets, $2,276,233 (M); expenditures, $158,043; qualifying distributions, $131,092.
Limitations: Applications not accepted. Giving primarily in the metropolitan New York, NY, area.
Application information: Contributes only to pre-selected organizations. Unsolicited requests for funds not considered.
Officers: Mary Catherine Baker, Secy.; William A. Baker III, Treas.
EIN: 133405090
Codes: FD2

35032
Sol and Hilda Furst Foundation
380 N. Broadway, Ste. 310
Jericho, NY 11753-2109 (516) 745-0810

Incorporated in 1951 in NY.
Donor(s): Sol Furst.‡
Financial data (yr. ended 04/30/02): Grants paid, $131,708; assets, $2,423,749 (L); expenditures, $171,420; qualifying distributions, $154,048.
Limitations: Applications not accepted. Giving primarily in NY.
Application information: Contributes only to pre-selected organizations.
Officers and Directors:* Gerald Furst,* Pres.; Violet Furst,* V.P.; Ronald A. Furst,* Secy.
EIN: 136107416
Codes: FD2

35033
The Robyne Herbert L. Camp Charitable Foundation
c/o Cravath, Swaine & Moore
Worldwide Plz., 825 8th Ave., 45th Fl.
New York, NY 10019

Established in 1987 in NY.
Donor(s): Herbert L. Camp.
Financial data (yr. ended 12/31/00): Grants paid, $131,584; assets, $301,322 (M); expenditures, $131,864; qualifying distributions, $131,864.
Limitations: Applications not accepted. Giving primarily in MA and NY.
Application information: Contributes only to pre-selected organizations.
Trustee: Herbert L. Camp.
EIN: 133441312
Codes: FD2

35034
The Frederick H. Gillmore Fund
c/o Morris & McVeigh, LLP
767 3rd Ave.
New York, NY 10017-2023
Contact: Frederick H. Gillmore, Jr., Tr.

Established in 1979.
Donor(s): Frederick H. Gillmore.‡
Financial data (yr. ended 12/31/01): Grants paid, $131,500; assets, $1,002,020 (M); expenditures, $152,151; qualifying distributions, $137,462.
Limitations: Applications not accepted. Giving primarily in the greater New York, NY, area.
Application information: Contributes only to pre-selected organizations.
Trustees: Lyn G. Cook, Frederick H. Gillmore, Jr., Carol G. Tiffany.
EIN: 112516289
Codes: FD2

35035
The Joseph N. Mastrangelo and Ralph C. Arnold Foundation
(Formerly The Mastrangelo Charitable Trust)
P.O. Box 3937
Albany, NY 12203-0937 (518) 456-6544
FAX: (559) 851-8962; *E-mail:* Erik.Eddy@groupoe.com
Contact: Erik R. Eddy, Exec. Dir.

Established in 1987 in NY.
Donor(s): Angelo Mastrangelo, Kathleen Mastrangelo.
Financial data (yr. ended 12/31/01): Grants paid, $131,350; assets, $2,207,229 (M); expenditures, $188,288; qualifying distributions, $164,189.
Limitations: Giving primarily in upstate NY.
Publications: Annual report, program policy statement, occasional report, informational brochure (including application guidelines), financial statement.
Application information: Application form not required.
Officers and Directors:* Jack Beckett,* Pres.; John W. Clark,* Secy.-Treas.; Erik R. Eddy,* Exec. Dir.; Fr. Christopher Degiovine, Wesley Holloway, Jeanne Kobuszewski, John Kucij, Daniel P. Nolan.
EIN: 222861913
Codes: FD2

35036
Richard & Rebecca Evans Foundation
P.O. Box 753
Gloversville, NY 12078

Established in 1955 in NY.
Donor(s): Rebecca M. Evans,‡ Richard Evans II.‡
Financial data (yr. ended 03/31/01): Grants paid, $131,333; assets, $1,917,453 (M); expenditures, $154,343; qualifying distributions, $128,423.
Limitations: Applications not accepted. Giving primarily in CT, MA, and NY.
Application information: Contributes only to pre-selected organizations.
Officers and Directors:* Morris Evans,* Pres. and Treas.; Nancy Evans Hays,* V.P. and Secy.
EIN: 146016221
Codes: FD2

35037
The William & Mary Buckley Foundation
c/o BCRS Assocs., LLC
100 Wall St., 11th Fl.
New York, NY 10005

Established in 1993 in NY.
Donor(s): William J. Buckley.
Financial data (yr. ended 01/31/02): Grants paid, $131,286; assets, $1,707,252 (M); gifts received, $93,610; expenditures, $136,189; qualifying distributions, $132,768.
Limitations: Applications not accepted. Giving primarily in the Northeast.
Application information: Contributes only to pre-selected organizations.
Trustees: Mary K. Buckley, William J. Buckley.
EIN: 133748080
Codes: FD2

35038
The Gutman Family Foundation
c/o Goldman Sachs & Co.
85 Broad St., Tax Dept.
New York, NY 10004

Established in 1997 in IL.
Donor(s): Joseph D. Gutman.
Financial data (yr. ended 12/31/00): Grants paid, $131,250; assets, $3,315,936 (M); gifts received, $1,071,038; expenditures, $166,317; qualifying distributions, $131,317.
Limitations: Applications not accepted. Giving primarily in Chicago, IL and New York, NY.
Application information: Contributes only to pre-selected organizations.
Trustees: Joseph D. Gutman, Sheila H. Gutman.
EIN: 133936473
Codes: FD2

35039
Mathew & Edythe Gladstein Foundation, Inc.
85 Morris Ln.
Scarsdale, NY 10583-4440
Contact: Mathew Gladstein, V.P.

Established in 1964.
Donor(s): Edythe R. Gladstein, Mathew L. Gladstein, David Rosenthal.‡
Financial data (yr. ended 09/30/01): Grants paid, $131,084; assets, $1,771,357 (M); expenditures, $195,459; qualifying distributions, $131,334.
Limitations: Applications not accepted. Giving primarily in NY.
Application information: Contributes only to pre-selected organizations.
Officers and Directors:* Edythe R. Gladstein,* Pres.; Mathew L. Gladstein,* V.P.; Joshua Gladstein,* Secy.; Gina Gladstein,* Treas.
EIN: 136164867
Codes: FD2

35040
The George Zauderer Foundation
33 First Neck Ln.
Southampton, NY 11968

Established in 1959 in NY and DE.
Donor(s): Audrey Zauderer.
Financial data (yr. ended 12/31/00): Grants paid, $131,025; assets, $455,580 (M); gifts received, $8,460; expenditures, $131,970; qualifying distributions, $131,484.
Limitations: Applications not accepted. Giving primarily in NY.
Application information: Contributes only to pre-selected organizations.
Officer: Audrey Zauderer, Secy.
EIN: 136077837
Codes: FD2

35041
Merrill G. and Emita E. Hastings Foundation
c/o John T. Ablamsky
63 Reid Ave.
Port Washington, NY 11050

Trust established in 1966 in NY.
Donor(s): Emita E. Hastings.‡
Financial data (yr. ended 02/28/01): Grants paid, $130,935; assets, $4,102,480 (M); expenditures, $220,321; qualifying distributions, $185,587.
Limitations: Giving primarily in the New York, NY, area.
Application information: Application form not required.
Trustees: Janice Haggerty, Elizabeth H. Peterfreund, Joshua Peterfreund, Lisa Peterfreund.
EIN: 136203465
Codes: FD2

35042
Morris Horn Foundation
49 W. 44th St.
New York, NY 10036

Established in 1995 in NY.
Donor(s): Shimmie Horn.
Financial data (yr. ended 12/31/00): Grants paid, $130,680; assets, $126,851 (M); gifts received, $67,000; expenditures, $132,521; qualifying distributions, $130,680.
Officers: Shimmie Horn, Pres.; Esther Horn, Secy.
EIN: 113241230
Codes: FD2

35043
Doovin Trust
5223 15th Ave.
Brooklyn, NY 11219 (718) 871-4811
Contact: Chaim Landau, Tr.

Established in 1999 in NY.
Donor(s): Ephraim Landau, A & E Trust, Triangle Trust.
Financial data (yr. ended 11/30/01): Grants paid, $130,610; assets, $1,955,530 (M); expenditures, $141,844; qualifying distributions, $130,610.
Trustees: Chaim Landau, David Landau.
EIN: 116532369

35044
Donald L. Boudreau Foundation
10 Dudley Ln.
Larchmont, NY 10538

Established in 1997 in NY.
Financial data (yr. ended 12/31/99): Grants paid, $130,386; assets, $636,926 (M); expenditures, $130,556; qualifying distributions, $130,246.
Limitations: Applications not accepted. Giving primarily in NY.
Application information: Contributes only to pre-selected organizations.
Trustee: Susan G. Boudreau.
EIN: 137088657
Codes: FD2

35045
The Bert & Sandra Wasserman Foundation
126 E. 56th St., Ste. 12N
New York, NY 10022-3613

Established in 1997 in NY.
Donor(s): Bert W. wasserman.
Financial data (yr. ended 12/31/00): Grants paid, $130,105; assets, $5,772,511 (M); gifts received, $935,800; expenditures, $159,603; qualifying distributions, $130,105.
Limitations: Applications not accepted.
Application information: Contributes only to pre-selected organizations.
Officers and Directors:* Bert W. Wasserman,* Pres. and Treas.; Sandra Wasserman,* V.P.; Debra Wasserman-Amdursky,* Secy.
EIN: 133961422
Codes: FD2

35046
China Times Cultural Foundation
136-39 41st Ave., Ste. 1A
Flushing, NY 11355 (718) 460-4900
E-mail: ctcfmail@yahoo.com
Contact: Sophia Hsieh

Established in 1986 in CA.
Financial data (yr. ended 12/31/01): Grants paid, $130,000; assets, $2,599,155 (M); expenditures, $295,098; qualifying distributions, $234,703.
Limitations: Giving primarily in the U.S., China, and Canada.
Application information: Application form required.
Officers and Directors:* Chi-Chung Yu,* Pres.; Norman C.C. Fu,* V.P.; James Tu, Secy.; Louisa Y. Wong, Treas.; Ching-Chih Chuu, Tso-Yun Wang, Albert Yu, Alice Yu, Alice Tsai Yu, Franklin Yu.
EIN: 222711422
Codes: FD2, GTI

35047
The Leopold & Lydia Koss Foundation Trust
1185 Park Ave., Ste. 14K
New York, NY 10128

Established in 1999.
Donor(s): Leopold Koss, Lyndia Koss.
Financial data (yr. ended 12/31/01): Grants paid, $130,000; assets, $473,144 (M); gifts received, $50,623; expenditures, $130,737; qualifying distributions, $130,000.
Limitations: Giving primarily in NY.
Trustee: Leopold Koss.
EIN: 134087680

35048
Arthur & Barbara Crocker Charitable Trust
c/o The Bank of New York, Tax Dept.
1 Wall St., 28th Fl.
New York, NY 10286
Application address: 126 Mooring Park Dr., Naples, FL 33942
Contact: Arthur M. Crocker, Tr.

Established in 1967.
Donor(s): Arthur M. Crocker, Barbara S. Crocker.
Financial data (yr. ended 12/31/01): Grants paid, $129,977; assets, $285,647 (M); gifts received, $126,180; expenditures, $135,392; qualifying distributions, $129,915.
Trustees: Arthur M. Crocker, Barbara S. Crocker.
EIN: 116103376
Codes: FD2

35049
Neil V. Desena Foundation, Inc.
385 South End Ave., Ste. 2J
New York, NY 10280

Established in 1999 in NY.
Donor(s): Neil V. Desena.
Financial data (yr. ended 09/30/01): Grants paid, $129,950; assets, $340,802 (M); gifts received, $511,825; expenditures, $133,470; qualifying distributions, $129,950.
Limitations: Applications not accepted.
Application information: Contributes only to pre-selected organizations.
Officers: Neil V. Desena, Pres. and Treas.; Neil A. Desena, V.P. and Secy.; Marie S. Desena, V.P.
EIN: 134099412

35050
Ontario Children's Home
P.O. Box 82
Canandaigua, NY 14424
Application address: c/o Mrs. Richard Ogden, 210 W. Gibson St., Canandaigua, NY 14424

Established in 1863 in NY for civil war orphans.
Financial data (yr. ended 09/30/01): Grants paid, $129,900; assets, $2,936,146 (M); gifts received, $185; expenditures, $142,259; qualifying distributions, $129,900.
Limitations: Giving limited to children in Ontario County, NY.
Application information: Contact high school guidance counselors or school nurses in Ontario County, NY for application. Application form required.
Officers and Trustees:* Bruce Kennedy,* Pres.; Robert Blanck,* V.P.; Richard Hawks,* Secy.; Stephen Hamlin,* Treas.; and 3 additional trustees.
EIN: 166028318
Codes: FD2, GTI

35051
The Nan Tucker McEvoy Foundation, Inc.
c/o Cravath, Swaine & Moore
P.O. Box 825, Radio City Station, Ste. 4370C
New York, NY 10101-0825

Established in 1989 in NY.
Donor(s): Nan Tucker McEvoy.
Financial data (yr. ended 12/31/01): Grants paid, $129,850; assets, $18,560 (M); gifts received, $130,000; expenditures, $129,915; qualifying distributions, $129,850.
Limitations: Applications not accepted. Giving primarily in San Francisco, CA.
Application information: Contributes only to pre-selected organizations.
Officers and Director:* Nan Tucker McEvoy,* Pres.; Daniel L. Mosley, Secy.-Treas.
EIN: 133500024
Codes: FD2

35052
Barry & Teri Volpert Foundation
c/o Goldman Sachs & Co.
85 Broad St., Tax Dept.
New York, NY 10004

Established in 1995 in NY.
Donor(s): Barry S. Volpert.
Financial data (yr. ended 08/31/01): Grants paid, $129,769; assets, $4,096,941 (M); gifts received, $489,313; expenditures, $178,079; qualifying distributions, $133,079.
Limitations: Applications not accepted. Giving on a national basis.
Application information: Contributes only to pre-selected organizations.
Trustees: Joel Beckman, Barry S. Volpert, Teri C. Volpert.

EIN: 133802670
Codes: FD2

35053
The Lazar Stein Memorial Foundation
c/o RSM McGladrey, Inc.
380 Madison Ave., 15th Fl.
New York, NY 10017

Established in 1999 in NY.
Donor(s): Martin Stein.
Financial data (yr. ended 08/31/01): Grants paid, $129,607; assets, $209,352 (M); gifts received, $200,000; expenditures, $136,276; qualifying distributions, $135,048.
Limitations: Applications not accepted. Giving primarily in NJ and NY.
Application information: Contributes only to pre-selected organizations.
Officers: Martin Stein, Pres. and Treas.; Arlyne Stein, Secy.
Director: Steven Stein.
EIN: 134119091
Codes: FD2

35054
Ron Beller & Jennifer Moses Family Foundation, Inc.
85 Broad St., Tax Dept.
New York, NY 10004

Established in 1990 in NJ.
Donor(s): Ron Beller, Jennifer Moses.
Financial data (yr. ended 12/31/00): Grants paid, $129,587; assets, $5,499,934 (M); gifts received, $1,326,661; expenditures, $129,678; qualifying distributions, $129,587.
Limitations: Applications not accepted. Giving on an international basis.
Application information: Contributes only to pre-selected organizations.
Officers: Ron Beller, Pres.; Jennifer Moses, V.P.; Stephen J. Moses, Treas.
EIN: 223077176
Codes: FD2

35055
The William and Jane Overman Foundation, Inc.
605 3rd Ave., 42nd Fl.
New York, NY 10158
Contact: Jane Overman, Pres.

Established in 1986 in NY.
Donor(s): William Overman.
Financial data (yr. ended 11/30/01): Grants paid, $129,566; assets, $451,597 (M); expenditures, $136,317; qualifying distributions, $130,515.
Limitations: Applications not accepted. Giving primarily in NY.
Application information: Contributes only to pre-selected organizations.
Officer: Jane Overman, Pres.
EIN: 133386644
Codes: FD2

35056
The Leryna Foundation
111 8th Ave., Ste. 212
New York, NY 10011
Contact: Ely Levy, Tr.

Established in 1993 in NY.
Donor(s): Ely Levy, Joe Levy, Nissim Levy, Morris Nahmoud, Simcha Ryba, Thunderball Marketing, Inc.
Financial data (yr. ended 12/31/01): Grants paid, $129,550; assets, $1,512,939 (M); gifts received, $250,000; expenditures, $143,569; qualifying distributions, $129,550.

35056—NEW YORK

Trustees: Ely Levy, Joe Levy, Nissim Levy, Morris Nahmoud, Simcha Ryba.
EIN: 133693866
Codes: FD2

35057
The Kim and Deborah Fennebresque Family Foundation
c/o Sontag Advisory
261 Madison Ave.
New York, NY 10016

Established in 1997 in NY.
Donor(s): Edward McLaughlin.
Financial data (yr. ended 03/31/02): Grants paid, $129,482; assets, $719,761 (M); expenditures, $143,934; qualifying distributions, $129,482.
Limitations: Applications not accepted. Giving primarily in CT and NY.
Application information: Contributes only to pre-selected organizations.
Trustees: Deborah Fennebresque, Kim Fennebresque, Howard Sontag.
EIN: 137100772
Codes: FD2

35058
The Roby Foundation
c/o CSAM
466 Lexington Ave., 17th Fl.
New York, NY 10017-3140
Contact: Joe L. Roby

Established in 1996 in NY.
Donor(s): Joe L. Roby.
Financial data (yr. ended 12/31/01): Grants paid, $129,400; assets, $3,673,959 (M); gifts received, $1,861,500; expenditures, $145,909; qualifying distributions, $129,750.
Limitations: Giving primarily in New York, NY.
Application information: Application form not required.
Distribution Committee: Hilppa A. Roby, Joe L. Roby.
Trustee: Winthrop Trust Co.
EIN: 133932915
Codes: FD2

35059
Elliot K. Wolk Family Foundation, Inc.
11 Morris Ln.
Scarsdale, NY 10583

Established in 1983 in NY.
Donor(s): Elliot K. Wolk.
Financial data (yr. ended 11/30/00): Grants paid, $129,400; assets, $1,921,386 (M); expenditures, $133,491; qualifying distributions, $130,179.
Limitations: Applications not accepted. Giving primarily in New York and Westchester County, NY.
Application information: Contributes only to pre-selected organizations.
Officers: Elliot K. Wolk, Pres. and Treas.; Nancy Wolk, V.P. and Secy.
Director: Andrew Wolk.
EIN: 133221847
Codes: FD2

35060
Albert A. & Bertram N. Linder Foundation, Inc.
305 E. 40th St., PH-C
New York, NY 10016
Contact: Bertram N. Linder, Pres.

Incorporated in 1947 in NY.
Donor(s): Bertram N. Linder, Albert A. Linder.‡
Financial data (yr. ended 05/31/02): Grants paid, $129,315; assets, $2,193,050 (M); expenditures, $186,552; qualifying distributions, $135,155.

Limitations: Giving primarily in New York, NY, and Scranton, PA.
Application information: Telephone calls will not be considered. Application form not required.
Officers and Trustees:* Bertram N. Linder,* Pres. and Treas.; Mary Ellen Linder,* V.P. and Secy.; Denise Dunbar,* V.P.
EIN: 136100590
Codes: FD2

35061
Lori & Mark Fife Foundation, Inc.
13 E. 75th St.
New York, NY 10021

Established in 1996 in NY.
Donor(s): Lori Fife, Mark Fife.
Financial data (yr. ended 06/30/01): Grants paid, $129,254; assets, $377,382 (M); expenditures, $129,294; qualifying distributions, $128,783.
Limitations: Applications not accepted. Giving primarily in New York, NY and PA.
Application information: Contributes only to pre-selected organizations.
Officers: Lori Fife, Pres.; Howard Ruthan, V.P.; Mark Fife, Secy.-Treas.
EIN: 522026744
Codes: FD2

35062
The Elbrun and Peter Kimmelman Foundation, Inc.
800 3rd Ave., Ste. 3103
New York, NY 10022

Established in 1979.
Donor(s): Peter Kimmelman.
Financial data (yr. ended 11/30/01): Grants paid, $129,238; assets, $624 (M); gifts received, $129,544; expenditures, $129,338; qualifying distributions, $129,338.
Limitations: Applications not accepted. Giving primarily in New York, NY.
Application information: Contributes only to pre-selected organizations.
Officers: Peter Kimmelman, Pres.; Barbara Blassberg, Secy.; Elbrun Kimmelman, Treas.
EIN: 132967083
Codes: FD2

35063
The Eleanor and Roy Nester Family Foundation
1295 Northern Blvd., Ste. 16
Manhasset, NY 11030-3093 (516) 365-9205
FAX: (516) 365-9208
Contact: Linda L. Cronin, Secy.

Established in 1980 in NY.
Donor(s): Royalnest Corp., Eleanor D. Nester, Roy G. Nester.
Financial data (yr. ended 03/31/02): Grants paid, $129,136; assets, $326,420 (M); gifts received, $100,000; expenditures, $129,136; qualifying distributions, $140,346.
Limitations: Giving primarily in NY, with emphasis on Long Island.
Application information: Application form not required.
Officers and Directors:* Roy G. Nester,* Pres.; Denis F. Cronin,* V.P.; Peter J. DiConza, Jr.,* V.P.; Eleanor D. Nester,* V.P.; John W. Nester,* V.P.; Linda L. Cronin,* Secy.; Carol A. DiConza,* Treas.
EIN: 112537407
Codes: CS, FD2, CD

35064
SSB Foundation
c/o David F. Bellet
60 E. 42nd St., Ste. 3405
New York, NY 10165

Established in 1994.
Donor(s): David F. Bellet.
Financial data (yr. ended 12/31/01): Grants paid, $128,943; assets, $727,811 (M); gifts received, $268,217; expenditures, $138,103; qualifying distributions, $128,943.
Limitations: Applications not accepted. Giving on a national basis, with emphasis on New York, NY.
Application information: Contributes only to pre-selected organizations.
Officers: David F. Bellet, Pres.; Tina Bellet, Secy.-Treas.
EIN: 137053080
Codes: FD2

35065
E. Garrett & Patricia C. Cleary Foundation
c/o JPMorgan Chase Bank
P.O. Box 31412
Rochester, NY 14603-1412

Established in 1990 in NY.
Donor(s): Patricia C. Cleary.
Financial data (yr. ended 06/30/01): Grants paid, $128,800; assets, $775,110 (M); expenditures, $142,509; qualifying distributions, $128,893.
Limitations: Applications not accepted. Giving primarily in Rochester, NY.
Application information: Contributes only to pre-selected organizations.
Trustee: JPMorgan Chase Bank.
EIN: 166350479
Codes: FD2

35066
Richard & Catherine Herbst Foundation
c/o Dalessio, Millner & Leben
245 5th Ave., 16th Fl.
New York, NY 10016

Established in 1987 in NJ.
Donor(s): Richard W. Herbst.
Financial data (yr. ended 08/31/01): Grants paid, $128,800; assets, $396,736 (M); expenditures, $132,219; qualifying distributions, $132,005.
Limitations: Applications not accepted. Giving primarily in NJ and New York, NY.
Application information: Unsolicited requests for funds not accepted.
Trustees: Catherine F. Herbst, Richard W. Herbst, Thomas G. Mendell.
EIN: 133442299
Codes: FD2

35067
Richenthal Foundation
122 E. 42nd St., Ste. 4400
New York, NY 10168-0002 (212) 687-8360
Contact: Arthur Richenthal, Dir.

Established in 1964 in NY.
Financial data (yr. ended 12/31/01): Grants paid, $128,775; assets, $2,793,663 (M); expenditures, $132,847; qualifying distributions, $128,775.
Limitations: Giving primarily in NY.
Directors: Arthur Richenthal, Donald Richenthal.
EIN: 136113616
Codes: FD2

35068
Chaya Foundation
1631 50th St.
Brooklyn, NY 11204

Established in 1998 in NY.

Donor(s): Helen Sieger.
Financial data (yr. ended 08/31/01): Grants paid, $128,750; assets, $3,160,707 (M); gifts received, $600,000; expenditures, $130,500; qualifying distributions, $129,625.
Limitations: Applications not accepted. Giving limited to Brooklyn, NY.
Application information: Contributes only to pre-selected organizations.
Officer and Director:* Helen Sieger,* Pres.
EIN: 113415146
Codes: FD2

35069
Mary and James G. Wallach Foundation
3 Manhattanville Rd.
Purchase, NY 10577

Established in 1968.
Donor(s): James G. Wallach, Asgot Securities, Inc.
Financial data (yr. ended 10/31/01): Grants paid, $128,675; assets, $3,063,972 (M); expenditures, $172,737; qualifying distributions, $135,817.
Limitations: Applications not accepted. Giving primarily in NY.
Application information: Contributes only to pre-selected organizations.
Officers and Directors:* Mary Wallach, Pres.; Andrew Wallach, V.P.; Ira D. Wallach,* V.P.; Peter C. Siegfried,* Secy.-Treas.
EIN: 136278694
Codes: FD2

35070
Rita & Henry Kaplan Foundation
269 Grand Central Pkwy., Ste. 30A
Floral Park, NY 11005
Contact: Rita Kaplan, Tr. or Henry Kaplan, Tr.

Established in 1992 in NY.
Donor(s): Henry Kaplan, Rita Kaplan.
Financial data (yr. ended 12/31/01): Grants paid, $128,618; assets, $912,869 (M); gifts received, $65,000; expenditures, $133,080; qualifying distributions, $133,080.
Limitations: Giving primarily in NY.
Trustees: Henry Kaplan, Rita Kaplan.
EIN: 113134230
Codes: FD2

35071
The Henrietta & David Whitcomb Family Foundation
c/o Goodkind, Labiton, Rudoff, Suchrow, LLP
100 Park Ave., 12th Fl.
New York, NY 10017

Established in 2000 in NY.
Donor(s): David K. Whitcomb, Henrietta Whitcomb.
Financial data (yr. ended 12/31/01): Grants paid, $128,455; assets, $40,009 (M); expenditures, $140,100; qualifying distributions, $128,455.
Limitations: Applications not accepted.
Application information: Contributes only to pre-selected organizations.
Trustees: Steven Rodman, David K. Whitcomb, Henrietta Whitcomb.
EIN: 137267896

35072
The Gordon Family Foundation
c/o Goldman Sachs & Co.
85 Broad St., Tax Dept.
New York, NY 10004

Established in 1999 in CA.
Donor(s): Andrew M. Gordon.
Financial data (yr. ended 08/31/01): Grants paid, $128,432; assets, $1,368,380 (M); gifts received, $295,038; expenditures, $164,322; qualifying distributions, $127,161.
Limitations: Applications not accepted. Giving primarily in CA.
Application information: Contributes only to pre-selected organizations.
Trustees: Amy S. Gordon, Andrew M. Gordon.
EIN: 134048199
Codes: FD2

35073
Boorstein Family Fund
145 E. 48th St., Ste. 25C
New York, NY 10017

Established in 1963 in NY.
Donor(s): Allen L. Boorstein.
Financial data (yr. ended 12/31/01): Grants paid, $128,315; assets, $381,577 (M); expenditures, $132,999; qualifying distributions, $128,495.
Limitations: Applications not accepted. Giving primarily in New York, NY.
Application information: Contributes only to pre-selected organizations.
Officers: Allen L. Boorstein, Pres.; Jane K. Boorstein, Secy.
EIN: 116032894
Codes: FD2

35074
Nippon Express Foundation, Inc.
c/o Nippon Express U.S.A., Inc.
590 Madison Ave.
New York, NY 10022

Established in 1992 in NY.
Donor(s): Nippon Express U.S.A., Inc.
Financial data (yr. ended 12/31/01): Grants paid, $128,092; assets, $1,357,088 (M); expenditures, $131,910; qualifying distributions, $131,114.
Limitations: Applications not accepted.
Application information: Contributes only to pre-selected organizations.
Officers: Tadaaki Hashimoto, Pres.; Nobuyuki Miyajima, Secy.; Takashi Masuda, Treas.
EIN: 133693444
Codes: CS, CD

35075
Daniel I. & Elaine B. Sargent Charitable Trust
138 Keeler Ln.
North Salem, NY 10560

Established about 1971 in NY.
Donor(s): Daniel I. Sargent, Elaine B. Sargent.
Financial data (yr. ended 06/30/01): Grants paid, $127,850; assets, $98,597 (M); expenditures, $130,584; qualifying distributions, $130,284.
Limitations: Applications not accepted. Giving primarily in New York, NY.
Application information: Contributes only to pre-selected organizations.
Trustee: Elaine B. Sargent.
EIN: 237084097
Codes: FD2

35076
Valerie Beth Schwartz Foundation
P.O. Box 96
New York, NY 10028

Established in 2000 in NY.
Donor(s): Bernard Schwartz, Ida Schwartz.
Financial data (yr. ended 12/31/01): Grants paid, $127,700; assets, $893,393 (M); gifts received, $711,220; expenditures, $131,458; qualifying distributions, $127,700.
Officer: Bernard Schwartz, Pres.
EIN: 134117395

35077
Martha Beeman Foundation, Inc.
c/o KeyBank, N.A.
P.O. Box 408
Niagara Falls, NY 14303 (716) 282-3588
Contact: William Sdao, 1st V.P.

Established in 1995 in NY.
Financial data (yr. ended 12/31/01): Grants paid, $127,650; assets, $1,652,416 (M); expenditures, $205,147; qualifying distributions, $151,769.
Application information: Application form required.
Officers and Directors:* Frederick Dolittle, Chair. of Operations, Finance Committee; Therese Quarantillo, Chair., Grant/Audit Committee; E. Marie Davis, Co-Chair., Grant Evaluation Committee; Diana Palumbo, Co-Chair., Grant Evaluation Committee; Donald H. Smith,* Pres.; Michelle Skiba, Secy.; Earl W. Brydges, Jr., Carmen A. Granto, William Kellick, William Sdao, Nancy Smith.
EIN: 160346980
Codes: FD2

35078
W. & J. Larson Family Foundation
c/o Kavinoky & Cook
120 Delaware Ave., Ste. 600
Buffalo, NY 14202-2700

Established in 1985 in NY.
Donor(s): Joan J. Larson, Wilfred J. Larson.
Financial data (yr. ended 10/31/01): Grants paid, $127,650; assets, $2,655,268 (M); gifts received, $162,750; expenditures, $131,766; qualifying distributions, $128,724.
Limitations: Applications not accepted. Giving on a national basis.
Application information: Contributes only to pre-selected organizations.
Trustees: Brian D. Baird, Joan J. Larson, Wilfred J. Larson, Joseph D. Mitchell, Larry J. Nelson.
EIN: 166281709
Codes: FD2

35079
Hefta Foundation, Inc.
c/o Cromwell Leather Co.
147 Palmer Ave.
Mamaroneck, NY 10543
Contact: Harry Fleisch, Pres.

Established in 1994 in NY.
Donor(s): Harry Fleisch, Eleanor Fleisch.
Financial data (yr. ended 10/31/01): Grants paid, $127,330; assets, $2,016,869 (M); expenditures, $141,419; qualifying distributions, $128,211.
Limitations: Applications not accepted. Giving primarily in NY.
Application information: Contributes only to pre-selected organizations.
Officers: Harry M. Fleisch, Pres.; Andrew P. Fleisch, V.P.; Thomas Fleisch, Secy.; Eleanor C. Fleisch, Treas.
EIN: 133796996
Codes: FD2

35080
The DiMenna Foundation, Inc.
(Formerly The DiMenna Family Foundation, Inc.)
1049 5th Ave., P3
New York, NY 10028

Established in 1998 in CT and NY.
Donor(s): Joseph A. DiMenna.
Financial data (yr. ended 12/31/00): Grants paid, $127,000; assets, $3,271,931 (M); expenditures, $167,161; qualifying distributions, $123,508.
Limitations: Applications not accepted. Giving primarily in New York, NY.

35080—NEW YORK

Application information: Contributes only to pre-selected organizations.
Officers: Joseph A. DiMenna, Pres.; Maureen DiMenna, Secy.
Director: Kevin P. Cannon.
EIN: 061534269
Codes: FD2

35081
The Duke of Omnium Fund
c/o Sullivan & Cromwell
125 Broad St.
New York, NY 10004-2498

Established in 1993 in NY.
Donor(s): Albert H. Gordon.
Financial data (yr. ended 12/31/01): Grants paid, $127,000; assets, $368,837 (M); expenditures, $128,000; qualifying distributions, $126,512.
Limitations: Giving primarily in MA and NH.
Trustee: Peter Coolidge.
EIN: 133740798
Codes: FD2

35082
The Shaare Dina Charitable Trust
c/o Shazdeh Fashions, Inc.
1375 Broadway
New York, NY 10018

Established in 1999 in NY.
Donor(s): Mansour Zar, Khana Zar, Babak Zar.
Financial data (yr. ended 12/31/00): Grants paid, $126,930; assets, $188,007 (M); gifts received, $586,410; expenditures, $128,019; qualifying distributions, $127,805.
Limitations: Applications not accepted. Giving on a national basis.
Application information: Contributes only to pre-selected organizations.
Trustees: Khana Zar, Mansour Zar.
EIN: 134041347
Codes: FD2

35083
Isdell 86 Foundation
(Formerly Kevin C. Toner Foundation)
c/o Aristeia Capital, LLC
383 5th Ave.
New York, NY 10016 (212) 274-1460
Application address: 277 Park Ave., 27th Fl.,
New York, NY 10172
Contact: Kevin C. Toner, Pres.

Established in 1994 in NY.
Financial data (yr. ended 12/31/01): Grants paid, $126,500; assets, $76,856 (M); expenditures, $223,932; qualifying distributions, $215,979.
Officer: Kevin C. Toner, Pres.
Director: Robert De Verna.
EIN: 223341359
Codes: FD2

35084
Samuel & Bertha Schwartz Foundation
P.O. Box 693
Auburn, NY 13021 (315) 253-6205
Contact: Vincent M. Klein, Secy.

Established in 1951.
Donor(s): Herman H. Schwartz.‡
Financial data (yr. ended 12/31/01): Grants paid, $126,500; assets, $3,150,149 (M); expenditures, $168,055; qualifying distributions, $126,500.
Limitations: Giving primarily in Palm Beach and Miami, FL, Boston, MA, and Auburn, Rochester and New York, NY.
Officers and Trustees:* Margaret A. Schwartz,* Pres. and Treas.; Vincent M. Klein,* Secy.; Lois Ellenoff, Bradley W. Schwartz.
EIN: 156017667

Codes: FD2

35085
The Burdick Foundation Trust
P.O. Box 3288
Syracuse, NY 13220
Contact: Louis Bregou, Tr.

Established in 1987 in NY.
Donor(s): Roger Burdick Auto Sales, Inc., Roger's Buick, Inc.
Financial data (yr. ended 12/31/00): Grants paid, $126,398; assets, $462,140 (M); gifts received, $366,500; expenditures, $127,668; qualifying distributions, $127,668.
Limitations: Giving primarily in Syracuse, NY.
Application information: Application form not required.
Trustees: Louis Bregou, David Burdick, Ruth Burdick.
EIN: 166294086
Codes: FD2

35086
Jean L. & Raymond S. Troubh Fund
c/o Richard A. Eisner & Co., LLP
575 Madison Ave., 8th Fl.
New York, NY 10022-2597

Established in 1964.
Donor(s): Jean L. Troubh.
Financial data (yr. ended 05/31/01): Grants paid, $126,243; assets, $603,316 (M); expenditures, $130,518; qualifying distributions, $128,373.
Limitations: Applications not accepted. Giving primarily in New York, NY.
Application information: Contributes only to pre-selected organizations.
Officers: Jean L. Troubh, Pres.; Raymond S. Troubh, V.P. and Secy.
EIN: 136178229
Codes: FD2

35087
Adele and Leonard Block Foundation, Inc.
499 7th Ave., 21st Fl. S.
New York, NY 10018-6803
Contact: Leonard N. Block, Pres.

Established in 1945 in NJ.
Donor(s): Leonard N. Block.
Financial data (yr. ended 11/30/01): Grants paid, $126,200; assets, $142,308 (M); gifts received, $238,026; expenditures, $126,828; qualifying distributions, $126,224.
Limitations: Giving primarily in NJ and NY.
Officers and Directors:* Leonard N. Block,* Pres.; Adele G. Block,* V.P.; Thomas Block,* V.P.; Peggy Danziger,* V.P.; John E. Peters, Secy.; Gordon J. Girvin, Treas.
EIN: 226026000
Codes: FD2

35088
Bunny Fund, Inc.
c/o Barbara Buckland
75 Central Park W.
New York, NY 10023

Established in 1992 in NY and DE.
Donor(s): Barbara R. Buckland.
Financial data (yr. ended 12/31/01): Grants paid, $126,150; assets, $1,581,303 (M); expenditures, $139,321; qualifying distributions, $127,008.
Limitations: Applications not accepted. Giving primarily in New York, NY.
Application information: Contributes only to pre-selected organizations.
Officers: Barbara R. Buckland, Pres.; Leslie H. Buckland, V.P.; Jill S. Burnett, Secy.
EIN: 133645324

Codes: FD2

35089
Levenstein Family Foundation, Inc.
75 Central Park W., Ste. 2CD
New York, NY 10023 (212) 874-8025
Contact: Alan Levenstein, Pres.

Established in 1999 in NY.
Donor(s): Alan Levenstein.
Financial data (yr. ended 12/31/01): Grants paid, $126,150; assets, $1,173,408 (M); expenditures, $134,688; qualifying distributions, $126,150.
Application information: Application form not required.
Officers: Alan Levenstein, Pres.; Gail Levenstein, Secy.-Treas.
EIN: 134072249

35090
Easton Family Fund
(Formerly Henry Katz Foundation, Inc.)
181 E. 65th St., Ste. 8B
New York, NY 10021
Contact: Joan Easton, Pres.

Established in 1952.
Financial data (yr. ended 06/30/01): Grants paid, $126,145; assets, $2,161,315 (M); expenditures, $152,402; qualifying distributions, $126,145.
Limitations: Giving primarily in New York, NY.
Application information: Application form not required.
Officers: Joan K. Easton, Pres.; Elizabeth Easton, V.P.; Thomas Easton, V.P.
EIN: 136103454
Codes: FD2

35091
The Pesky Family Foundation, Inc.
437 Madison Ave.
New York, NY 10022 (212) 339-7745
Contact: Wendy Pesky, Pres., or Alan Pesky, Tr.

Established in 1989 in NY.
Donor(s): Wendy Pesky.
Financial data (yr. ended 10/31/00): Grants paid, $126,061; assets, $2,424,964 (M); gifts received, $122,878; expenditures, $216,832; qualifying distributions, $124,235.
Limitations: Applications not accepted. Giving primarily in CT, ID, and New York, NY.
Application information: Contributes only to pre-selected organizations.
Trustees: Alan Pesky, Gregory Pesky, Wendy Pesky, Heidi Worcester.
EIN: 223008373
Codes: FD2

35092
The PTM Charitable Foundation
c/o R. Bradford Evans
791 Park Ave., Ste. 7B
New York, NY 10021

Financial data (yr. ended 12/31/00): Grants paid, $126,000; assets, $2,430,853 (M); expenditures, $197,286; qualifying distributions, $132,465.
Limitations: Applications not accepted.
Application information: Contributes only to pre-selected organizations.
Officers and Directors*: R. Bradford Evans,* Pres. and Treas.; Barbara Reed Evans,* V.P. and Secy.; Robert H. Arnold.
EIN: 133800384
Codes: FD2

35093
Beaver Fund, Inc.
c/o Federated Linen
866 United Nations Plz., No. 545
New York, NY 10017-1822

Established in 1976 in NY.
Donor(s): William B. Troy, Joanne J. Troy.
Financial data (yr. ended 12/31/01): Grants paid, $125,950; assets, $158,918 (M); gifts received, $122,264; expenditures, $126,924; qualifying distributions, $125,333.
Limitations: Applications not accepted. Giving primarily in New York, NY.
Application information: Contributes only to pre-selected organizations.
Officers: William B. Troy, Pres.; Joanne J. Troy, Secy.
Director: Bernard Furman.
EIN: 132841229
Codes: FD2

35094
Monsignor Francis J. Williams Foundation
5 Glenwood Rd.
Rockville Centre, NY 11570-1506
(516) 935-1200
Contact: Daniel D. McCarthy, Tr.

Established in 1968.
Donor(s): Daniel D. McCarthy.
Financial data (yr. ended 12/31/01): Grants paid, $125,900; assets, $16,392 (M); gifts received, $125,994; expenditures, $126,025; qualifying distributions, $126,007.
Limitations: Giving primarily in NY.
Trustees: Daniel D. McCarthy, Robert Scholy.
EIN: 116102263
Codes: FD2

35095
The Burton Foundation
105 Wooster St.
New York, NY 10012 (212) 343-4158
Contact: Burton B. Staniar, Tr.

Established in 1997.
Financial data (yr. ended 12/31/99): Grants paid, $125,800; assets, $2,500,985 (M); gifts received, $806,250; expenditures, $163,144; qualifying distributions, $106,061.
Trustee: Burton B. Staniar.
EIN: 133975899

35096
M.E.E.T. Ophthalmology Foundation, Inc.
c/o Garfunkel, Wild & Travis
111 Great Neck Rd.
Great Neck, NY 11021

Financial data (yr. ended 06/30/01): Grants paid, $125,518; assets, $2,983,969 (M); expenditures, $184,248; qualifying distributions, $124,048.
Limitations: Applications not accepted. Giving limited to New York, NY.
Application information: Contributes only to pre-selected organizations.
Officers and Directors:* Robert Brown, M.D.,* Pres.; Anthony Piscano, M.D., V.P.; Paul Orloff, M.D.,* Secy.; Jack Dodick, M.D.,* Treas.; Yale Fisher, M.D., Ray Fong, M.D., Richard Gibralter, M.D., Vincent Giovianazzo, M.D., Gary Hirshfield, M.D., Albert Hornblass, M.D., Melvin J. Rothberger, M.D., Andrew W. Wendling, M.D.
EIN: 510243492
Codes: FD2

35097
Rudolph & Greta Koppel Foundation, Inc.
c/o Meyrowitz, Langenthal & Co.
1 Linden Pl.
Great Neck, NY 11021-2640
Contact: Greta Koppel, Secy.

Donor(s): Greta Koppel.
Financial data (yr. ended 12/31/01): Grants paid, $125,473; assets, $860,683 (M); gifts received, $3,538; expenditures, $127,889; qualifying distributions, $125,473.
Limitations: Giving primarily in FL.
Application information: Application form not required.
Officer: Greta Koppel, Secy. and Mgr.
EIN: 136275116
Codes: FD2

35098
The Masinter Family Foundation
1 Colonial Rd.
White Plains, NY 10605

Established in 1997 in NY.
Donor(s): Edgar M. Masinter.
Financial data (yr. ended 12/31/01): Grants paid, $125,438; assets, $898,401 (M); expenditures, $133,442; qualifying distributions, $125,688.
Limitations: Applications not accepted. Giving on a national basis, with emphasis on NY and NJ.
Application information: Contributes only to pre-selected organizations.
Trustees: Catherine M. Hildenbrand, Edgar M. Masinter, Margery F. Masinter, Robert A. Masinter.
EIN: 137133021
Codes: FD2

35099
Torah Response, Inc.
12 Wallenberg Cir.
Monsey, NY 10952-2800

Donor(s): Gloria Adler, Ida Bobrowsky, Travel Inn, Inc., Morris Tacansky.
Financial data (yr. ended 12/31/00): Grants paid, $125,415; assets, $158,013 (M); gifts received, $131,045; expenditures, $268,073; qualifying distributions, $268,073; giving activities include $110,044 for programs.
Limitations: Applications not accepted. Giving primarily in NY.
Application information: Contributes only to pre-selected organizations.
Officers: Gloria Adler, Pres.; Jonathan Hook, Secy.; Rabbi H.G. Schwartz, Treas.; Ira N. Adler, Admin.
EIN: 133318244

35100
Frances S. Viele Scholarship Trust
170 E. 78th St., Ste. 8B
New York, NY 10021 (212) 608-1080
Application address: c/o Morea Financial Svcs., 120 Broadway, Ste. 101, New York, NY 10271
Contact: William D. Brennan, Tr.

Established in 1977 in CA.
Financial data (yr. ended 05/31/01): Grants paid, $125,276; assets, $3,290,601 (M); expenditures, $190,204; qualifying distributions, $125,276.
Limitations: Applications not accepted. Giving on a national basis.
Application information: Unsolicited requests for funds not accepted.
Trustees: William D. Brennan, Donald L. Twiss.
EIN: 953285561
Codes: FD2, GTI

35101
American Friends of Binyan-Av Foundation, Inc.
c/o Victor Kameo
2179 Ocean Pkwy.
Brooklyn, NY 11223

Established in 1999 in NY.
Financial data (yr. ended 12/31/99): Grants paid, $125,000; assets, $188,828 (M); gifts received, $312,707; expenditures, $125,000; qualifying distributions, $125,000.
Limitations: Applications not accepted.
Application information: Contributes only to pre-selected organizations.
Officer and Directors:* Victor Kameo,* Pres.; Julie Levy, Eli Shalam.
EIN: 113472950
Codes: FD2

35102
The John V. Deitchman Family Foundation
c/o U.S. Trust
114 W. 47th St.
New York, NY 10036

Established in 1997 in DE.
Donor(s): John V. Deitchman.
Financial data (yr. ended 12/31/00): Grants paid, $125,000; assets, $2,873,042 (M); gifts received, $69,559; expenditures, $154,987; qualifying distributions, $128,083.
Limitations: Applications not accepted.
Application information: Contributes only to pre-selected organizations.
Trustees: Amy Elizabeth Deitchman, John V. Deitchman, Kathryn Lynn Deitchman, Linda A. Deitchman, Peter Charles Deitchman.
EIN: 133979660
Codes: FD2

35103
Emerald Foundation, Inc.
c/o Solomon Pearl Blum Heymann & Stich
40 Wall St., 35th Fl.
New York, NY 10001

Established in 1998 in NY.
Financial data (yr. ended 12/31/00): Grants paid, $125,000; assets, $650,534 (M); gifts received, $114,096; expenditures, $173,000; qualifying distributions, $171,375.
Limitations: Applications not accepted. Giving primarily in Boston, MA and New York, NY.
Application information: Contributes only to pre-selected organizations.
Officers and Directors:* Olivia Flatto, Pres.; Andrew W. Heymann,* V.P. and Treas.; Francine Meyer.
EIN: 133912580
Codes: FD2

35104
Huberfeld Family Foundation, Inc.
152 W. 57th St.
New York, NY 10019
Contact: Murray Huberfeld, Pres.

Established in 1999 in NY.
Financial data (yr. ended 12/31/00): Grants paid, $125,000; assets, $9,237,658 (M); gifts received, $3,000,000; expenditures, $129,369; qualifying distributions, $125,000.
Officers and Directors:* Murray Huberfeld,* Pres.; Laura Huberfeld,* Secy.-Treas.; Rae Huberfeld.
EIN: 134042543
Codes: FD2

35105
Joseph and May Winston Foundation
(Formerly The Winston Foundation)
P.O. Box 569
Rye, NY 10580 (914) 967-7000
Contact: Allan Winston, Dir.

Established in 1987 in DE.
Financial data (yr. ended 12/31/01): Grants paid, $125,000; assets, $4,325,355 (M); expenditures, $299,463; qualifying distributions, $154,451.
Application information: Application form not required.
Officers: Allan Winston, Pres.; David M. Winston, Exec. V.P.; Deborah Winston, Secy.; Diana Winston, Treas.
Directors: Joshua Winston, Julia Winston.
EIN: 061148600
Codes: FD2

35106
Molecular Biology Support Foundation, Inc.
c/o Herbert Paul, PC
370 Lexington Ave., Ste. 1001
New York, NY 10017

Established in 1997 in NY.
Donor(s): Lennart Philipson.
Financial data (yr. ended 12/31/01): Grants paid, $124,998; assets, $130,613 (M); expenditures, $127,742; qualifying distributions, $127,742.
Limitations: Applications not accepted. Giving primarily in NY.
Application information: Contributes only to pre-selected organizations.
Officers: Lennart Philipson, Pres.; Herbert Paul, Secy.; Malin Philipson, Treas.
EIN: 133950344
Codes: FD2

35107
Richard L. Hirsch Foundation
c/o Lawrence R. Gross
18 York Dr.
Great Neck, NY 11021
Contact: Richard L. Hirsch, Pres.

Incorporated in 1986 in NY.
Donor(s): Richard L. Hirsch.
Financial data (yr. ended 12/31/01): Grants paid, $124,987; assets, $2,142,864 (M); expenditures, $145,019; qualifying distributions, $123,681.
Limitations: Applications not accepted. Giving primarily in New York, NY.
Application information: Contributes only to pre-selected organizations.
Officers: Richard L. Hirsch, Pres.; David A. Hirsch, V.P. and Treas.; Joyce Hirsch, V.P.; Lawrence R. Gross, Secy.
EIN: 133343606
Codes: FD2

35108
Sternberg Charitable Trust
c/o Spear, Leeds & Kellogg
120 Broadway, 8th Fl.
New York, NY 10271

Established in 1994 in NY.
Donor(s): Stuart L. Sternberg.
Financial data (yr. ended 12/31/99): Grants paid, $124,965; assets, $2,102,620 (M); gifts received, $1,105,153; expenditures, $125,147; qualifying distributions, $124,742.
Limitations: Applications not accepted. Giving limited to NY.
Application information: Contributes only to pre-selected organizations.
Trustee: Stuart L. Sternberg.
EIN: 137046097
Codes: FD2

35109
Moses and Yetta Braunstein Charitable Foundation, Inc.
1836 Ocean Pkwy.
Brooklyn, NY 11223

Established in 1992 in NY.
Donor(s): Yetta Braunstein.
Financial data (yr. ended 12/31/01): Grants paid, $124,500; assets, $2,063,974 (M); gifts received, $165,000; expenditures, $126,305; qualifying distributions, $124,162.
Limitations: Applications not accepted.
Application information: Contributes only to pre-selected organizations.
Trustees: Rachel Blass, Barry Braunstein, Israel Braunstein, Yetta Braunstein.
EIN: 113132886
Codes: FD2

35110
Joseph R. Daly Foundation
c/o Joseph R. Daly
437 Madison Ave.
New York, NY 10022

Donor(s): Joseph R. Daly.
Financial data (yr. ended 12/31/01): Grants paid, $124,500; assets, $2,389,200 (M); expenditures, $127,125; qualifying distributions, $123,011.
Limitations: Applications not accepted. Giving primarily in NY.
Trustees: Elizabeth S. Daly, Joseph R. Daly.
EIN: 116080611
Codes: FD2

35111
The Dilascio Family Foundation, Inc.
3 Pen Mor Dr.
East Norwich, NY 11732-1695

Established in 1999 in NY.
Donor(s): Stephen Dilascio.
Financial data (yr. ended 09/30/01): Grants paid, $124,500; assets, $235,246 (M); gifts received, $339,632; expenditures, $125,572; qualifying distributions, $125,165.
Limitations: Applications not accepted. Giving primarily in NY.
Application information: Contributes only to pre-selected organizations.
Officers: Stephen Dilascio, Pres. and Treas.; Rosemary Dilascio, V.P. and Secy.; Annette Dilascio, V.P.
EIN: 113542565
Codes: FD2

35112
The Cushman Foundation
c/o Cambrian Corp.
1114 Ave. of the Americas
New York, NY 10036
Contact: David J. Vezeris, Tr.

Established in 1999 in NY.
Donor(s): Anthony Brenninkmeyer.
Financial data (yr. ended 12/31/01): Grants paid, $124,450; assets, $2,716,737 (M); expenditures, $148,237; qualifying distributions, $123,841.
Limitations: Applications not accepted. Giving primarily in NY.
Application information: Unsolicited requests for funds not accepted.
Trustees: Anthony Brenninkmeyer, Hans Jaspers, David J. Vezeris.
EIN: 134086187
Codes: FD2

35113
Joseph & Juanita Leff Charitable Trust
111 W. 40th St., 28th Fl.
New York, NY 10018-2506

Established in 1987 in NY.
Donor(s): Joseph Leff.
Financial data (yr. ended 12/31/01): Grants paid, $124,410; assets, $761,885 (M); gifts received, $205,665; expenditures, $126,200; qualifying distributions, $123,743.
Limitations: Applications not accepted. Giving primarily in the metropolitan New York, NY, area.
Application information: Contributes only to pre-selected organizations.
Trustees: Joseph Leff, Juanita Leff.
EIN: 133382241
Codes: FD2

35114
Isabelle W. Yeager Trust
c/o HSBC Bank USA
1 HSBC Ctr., 16th Fl.
Buffalo, NY 14203

Established in 1979 in NY.
Financial data (yr. ended 10/31/01): Grants paid, $124,354; assets, $2,442,816 (M); expenditures, $151,627; qualifying distributions, $127,212.
Limitations: Applications not accepted. Giving primarily in Erie County, NY.
Application information: Contributes only to pre-selected organizations.
Trustees: Hilary P. Bradford, HSBC Bank USA.
EIN: 166231762
Codes: FD2

35115
Dexter & Carol Earle Foundation
c/o Citrin Cooperman & Co., LLP
529 5th Ave., 10th Fl.
New York, NY 10017-4667

Established in 1989 in NY.
Donor(s): Dexter D. Earle.
Financial data (yr. ended 01/31/02): Grants paid, $124,296; assets, $1,678,188 (M); expenditures, $137,033; qualifying distributions, $124,546.
Limitations: Applications not accepted. Giving primarily in NJ.
Application information: Contributes only to pre-selected organizations.
Trustees: Carol A. Earle, Dexter D. Earle.
EIN: 133532028
Codes: FD2

35116
Quadrangle Group Foundation, Inc.
375 Park Ave.
New York, NY 10152

Established in 2001 in NY and DE.
Donor(s): Peter Ezersky, Steven Rattner, Joshua Steiner, David Tanner.
Financial data (yr. ended 12/31/01): Grants paid, $124,000; assets, $5 (M); gifts received, $124,000; expenditures, $124,000; qualifying distributions, $124,000.
Limitations: Applications not accepted.
Application information: Contributes only to pre-selected organizations.
Directors: Peter Ezersky, Steven Rattner, Joshua Steiner, David Tanner.
EIN: 134193512
Codes: FD2

35117
Review Foundation, Inc.
20 Corporate Woods Blvd., Ste. 600
Albany, NY 12211-2370 (518) 465-4747

Established in 1993 in NY.
Donor(s): Rhea P. Clark, KMP Charitable Trust VII.
Financial data (yr. ended 12/31/01): Grants paid, $124,000; assets, $3,781,473 (M); gifts received, $347,500; expenditures, $163,515; qualifying distributions, $124,000.
Limitations: Applications not accepted. Giving primarily in NY.
Application information: Contributes only to pre-selected organizations.
Officers: Rhea P. Clark, Pres.; James Clark, Jr., V.P.; Elizabeth Clark, Treas.; Kathleen Clark, Treas.
EIN: 223252633
Codes: FD2

35118
The Toni Lieberman Family Charitable Trust
c/o L.H. Frishkoff & Co.
529 5th Ave.
New York, NY 10017

Established in 1992 in NY.
Donor(s): Toni Lieberman.
Financial data (yr. ended 12/31/01): Grants paid, $123,983; assets, $2,169,577 (M); gifts received, $195,000; expenditures, $135,804; qualifying distributions, $123,752.
Limitations: Applications not accepted. Giving primarily in New York, NY.
Application information: Contributes only to pre-selected organizations.
Trustee: John V. Perna.
EIN: 137005205
Codes: FD2

35119
Rodney L. White Foundation, Inc.
c/o RSM McGladrey, Inc.
380 Madison Ave., 15th Fl.
New York, NY 10017

Established in 1965 in NY.
Donor(s): Shelby White, Tracy White.
Financial data (yr. ended 06/30/01): Grants paid, $123,935; assets, $1,761,145 (M); gifts received, $32,625; expenditures, $127,859; qualifying distributions, $123,935.
Limitations: Applications not accepted. Giving primarily in New York, NY.
Application information: Contributes only to pre-selected organizations.
Officers: Shelby White, Pres.; Jack Nash, V.P.; Tracy White, Secy.
EIN: 136182934
Codes: FD2

35120
The Avital Family Foundation
c/o Anchin, Block & Anchin, LLP
1375 Broadway, 18th Fl.
New York, NY 10018

Established in 2000 in NY.
Donor(s): Jackie Avital Corp., Jack Avital.
Financial data (yr. ended 10/31/01): Grants paid, $123,923; assets, $76,127 (M); gifts received, $200,200; expenditures, $124,073; qualifying distributions, $124,073.
Limitations: Applications not accepted. Giving primarily in New York, NY.
Application information: Contributes only to pre-selected organizations.
Directors: Jack Avital, Shimon Avital, Sol Mayer.
EIN: 113579198
Codes: FD2

35121
Graham Hunter Foundation, Inc.
c/o McCarthy, Fingar, Donovan
11 Martine Ave., 12th Fl.
White Plains, NY 10606-1934

Established in 1946 in NY.
Donor(s): Graham Hunter.‡
Financial data (yr. ended 12/31/00): Grants paid, $123,815; assets, $2,396,575 (M); expenditures, $170,055; qualifying distributions, $128,534.
Limitations: Applications not accepted. Giving on a national basis.
Application information: Contributes only to pre-selected organizations.
Officers: Carol Hunter Kelley, Pres.; William R. MacClarence, V.P. and Secy.
Trustee: Thomas R. MacClarence.
EIN: 136161726
Codes: FD2

35122
The Hoyt Fund
c/o Marshall M. Green
1345 6th Ave., 42nd Fl.
New York, NY 10105-6008

Established in 1998 in NY.
Financial data (yr. ended 12/31/01): Grants paid, $123,782; assets, $1,262,063 (M); expenditures, $143,519; qualifying distributions, $123,782.
Limitations: Applications not accepted. Giving primarily in NY.
Application information: Contributes only to pre-selected organizations.
Trustees: Suzanne H. Garcia, Marshall M. Green, Henry H. Hoyt, Jr.
EIN: 137125482
Codes: FD2

35123
Leon J. Gerstle Family Foundation
1290 Ave. of the Americas
New York, NY 10104

Established in 1989 in NY.
Financial data (yr. ended 04/30/01): Grants paid, $123,740; assets, $584,860 (M); gifts received, $13,500; expenditures, $123,934; qualifying distributions, $123,610.
Limitations: Applications not accepted. Giving primarily in New York, NY.
Application information: Contributes only to pre-selected organizations.
Officers: Barbara Gerstle, Admin.; Jacob Gerstle, Admin.; Leon J. Gerstle, Admin.
EIN: 133347275
Codes: FD2

35124
Makioka Foundation
c/o BCRS Assocs., LLC
67 Wall St., 8th Fl.
New York, NY 10005

Established in 1993 in NY.
Donor(s): Jun Makihara.
Financial data (yr. ended 02/28/02): Grants paid, $123,720; assets, $935,966 (M); gifts received, $170,148; expenditures, $127,719; qualifying distributions, $123,720.
Limitations: Applications not accepted. Giving primarily in MA and NY.
Application information: Contributes only to pre-selected organizations.
Trustees: Jun Makihara, Megumi Oka.
EIN: 133748081

35125
Murray Mizrachi Family Foundation
c/o Franshaw, Inc.
1411 Broadway
New York, NY 10018 (212) 564-2510
Contact: Murray Mizrachi, Tr.

Established around 1992 in NY.
Donor(s): Franshaw, Inc.
Financial data (yr. ended 12/31/01): Grants paid, $123,605; assets, $2,118 (M); gifts received, $124,000; expenditures, $123,642; qualifying distributions, $123,605.
Limitations: Giving primarily in NY.
Trustees: Abraham Mizrachi, Joseph Mizrachi, Murray Mizrachi.
EIN: 133613889
Codes: FD2

35126
The Rothfeld Family Foundation
791 Park Ave., Ste. 12B
New York, NY 10021-3551

Established in 1997 in NY.
Donor(s): Michael B. Rothfeld.
Financial data (yr. ended 12/31/01): Grants paid, $123,444; assets, $2,856,476 (M); gifts received, $548,420; expenditures, $125,306; qualifying distributions, $118,534.
Limitations: Applications not accepted. Giving primarily in NY and PA.
Application information: Contributes only to pre-selected organizations.
Director: Eric A. Rothfeld.
EIN: 133975327
Codes: FD2

35127
Syman Family Foundation
c/o BCRS Assocs., LLC
100 Wall St., 11th Fl.
New York, NY 10005

Established in 1993 in NY.
Donor(s): Gary A. Syman.
Financial data (yr. ended 06/30/01): Grants paid, $123,400; assets, $1,087,280 (M); gifts received, $2,900; expenditures, $139,811; qualifying distributions, $124,039.
Limitations: Applications not accepted. Giving primarily in CA.
Application information: Contributes only to pre-selected organizations.
Trustees: Azita Raji, J. David Rogers, Gary A. Syman.
EIN: 133748543
Codes: FD2

35128
Janice Michelle Foundation, Inc.
c/o Spear, Leeds & Kellogg
120 Broadway
New York, NY 10271

Established in 1998 in NY.
Donor(s): George Varsam.
Financial data (yr. ended 09/30/01): Grants paid, $123,250; assets, $1,676,125 (M); gifts received, $1,095,692; expenditures, $124,953; qualifying distributions, $97,430.
Limitations: Applications not accepted.
Application information: Contributes only pre-selected organizations.
Officers: George Varsam, Pres. and Treas.; Lori Varsam, V.P. and Secy.; Fotios Varsam, V.P.
EIN: 113458719
Codes: FD2

35129
Trio Foundation
c/o Goldman Sachs, Tax Dept.
85 Broad St.
New York, NY 10004-2456

Established in 1999 in NY.
Donor(s): Mary Ann Casati.
Financial data (yr. ended 11/30/01): Grants paid, $123,150; assets, $1,047,886 (M); gifts received, $3,000; expenditures, $138,551; qualifying distributions, $124,192.
Limitations: Applications not accepted. Giving primarily in New York, NY.
Application information: Contributes only to pre-selected organizations.
Trustees: Mary Ann Casati, Geoff Judge.
EIN: 134057282
Codes: FD2

35130
C. H. Stuart Foundation
c/o JPMorgan Chase Bank
P.O. Box 31412
Rochester, NY 14603-1412
Contact: Janis Mosher, V.P., JPMorgan Chase Bank

Trust established in 1951 in NY.
Donor(s): Emmons Jewelers, Inc., Sarah Coventry, Inc.
Financial data (yr. ended 12/31/01): Grants paid, $123,147; assets, $1,417,081 (M); expenditures, $127,720; qualifying distributions, $123,337.
Limitations: Applications not accepted. Giving primarily in Wayne County and Newark, NY.
Application information: Contributes only to pre-selected organizations.
Trustee: JPMorgan Chase Bank.
EIN: 166015254
Codes: FD2

35131
Aston Plastic Surgery Foundation
c/o Mahoney, Cohen & Co., CPA, PC
111 W. 40th St.
New York, NY 10018-2506

Established in 1982.
Donor(s): Sherrell J. Aston, M.D.
Financial data (yr. ended 06/30/01): Grants paid, $123,079; assets, $215,113 (M); expenditures, $965,483; qualifying distributions, $963,148; giving activities include $818,804 for programs.
Limitations: Applications not accepted. Giving primarily in NY and VA.
Application information: Contributes only to pre-selected organizations.
Officer: Sherrell J. Aston, M.D., Mgr.
EIN: 133081813
Codes: FD2

35132
The Bawd Foundation
c/o Elmrock Capital
150 E. 52nd St., Ste. 800
New York, NY 10022-6276

Established in 1996 in DE.
Donor(s): David D. Elliman, Robert Model.
Financial data (yr. ended 11/30/00): Grants paid, $123,063; assets, $1,849,336 (M); expenditures, $126,818; qualifying distributions, $125,001.
Limitations: Applications not accepted. Giving on a national basis.
Application information: Contributes only to pre-selected organizations.
Officers: David D. Elliman, Pres. and Treas.; Andrea D. Branch, V.P.; Kathleen N. Corrado, Secy.
EIN: 133922346

Codes: FD2

35133
Bodner Family Foundation, Inc.
152 W. 57th St.
New York, NY 10019
Contact: David Bodner, Pres.

Established in 1999 in NY.
Financial data (yr. ended 12/31/00): Grants paid, $123,000; assets, $9,084,640 (M); gifts received, $3,000,000; expenditures, $125,092; qualifying distributions, $123,000.
Officers and Directors:* David Bodner,* Pres.; Naomi Bodner,* Secy.-Treas.; Moishe Bodner.
EIN: 134042545
Codes: FD2

35134
Chernow Fund, Inc.
P.O. Box 197
Larchmont, NY 10538-0197 (914) 834-1900
Contact: Gordon S. Oppenheimer, Treas.

Established in 1954 in NY.
Financial data (yr. ended 10/31/01): Grants paid, $122,980; assets, $2,004,730 (M); expenditures, $186,107; qualifying distributions, $126,497.
Limitations: Giving primarily in the northeastern U.S., with emphasis on CT, Washington, DC, and NY.
Application information: Application form not required.
Officers: Lynn A. Streim, Pres.; Edward H. Streim, V.P.; Gordon S. Oppenheimer, Treas.
EIN: 136127968
Codes: FD2

35135
William F. Harnisch Foundation, Inc.
51 Jones Rd.
P.O. Box 366
East Quogue, NY 11942
New York, NY, tel.: (212) 407-9481
Contact: William F. Harnisch, Pres.

Established in 1997 in NY.
Donor(s): William F. Harnisch.
Financial data (yr. ended 12/31/01): Grants paid, $122,940; assets, $1,835,789 (M); expenditures, $156,244; qualifying distributions, $132,037.
Limitations: Giving primarily in NY and Nashville, TN.
Application information: Application form not required.
Officers: William F. Harnisch, Pres.; Michelle Teramo, Secy.
EIN: 113353576
Codes: FD2

35136
The Triangle Fund
80 E. Market St., Ste. 300
Corning, NY 14830

Established in 1997 in NY.
Donor(s): Gratia H. Lassalle.
Financial data (yr. ended 12/31/01): Grants paid, $122,814; assets, $350,603 (M); gifts received, $262,035; expenditures, $129,292; qualifying distributions, $122,814.
Limitations: Giving primarily in Chemung, Schoyler, and Steuben counties, NY.
Officer: Marianne W. Young, Secy.
Directors: John W. Hollister, Alanson B. Houghton, Andrew A. Houghton, James D. Houghton, Nina B. Houghton, Robert W. Houghton, Gratia H. Lassalle, Lauren E. Walsh.
EIN: 311591261
Codes: FD2

35137
The RME Foundation, Inc.
(Formerly Neuroscience Foundation of Western New York, Inc.)
49 Cleveland Ave.
Buffalo, NY 14222-3457

Established in 1989 in NY.
Donor(s): L. Nelson Hopkins III, M.D.
Financial data (yr. ended 09/30/01): Grants paid, $122,685; assets, $687,060 (M); expenditures, $123,455; qualifying distributions, $122,476.
Limitations: Applications not accepted. Giving limited to Buffalo, NY.
Application information: Contributes only to pre-selected organizations.
Officers: L. Nelson Hopkins III, M.D.,* Pres. and Treas.; Ann Adam Hopkins,* V.P. and Secy.
Director: Gerald Lippes.
EIN: 222989388
Codes: FD2

35138
The Around Foundation
c/o James Gleick
1 Long & Winding Rd.
Garrison, NY 10524

Established in 1997 in NY.
Donor(s): James Gleick.
Financial data (yr. ended 04/30/01): Grants paid, $122,600; assets, $4,303,755 (M); gifts received, $5,071; expenditures, $151,995; qualifying distributions, $122,600.
Limitations: Applications not accepted. Giving primarily in NY.
Application information: Contributes only to pre-selected organizations.
Trustees: Cynthia Crossen, James Gleick.
EIN: 113377271
Codes: FD2

35139
Lipschitz Family Charitable Trust
5116 17th Ave.
Brooklyn, NY 11204

Established in 1994 in NY.
Donor(s): Solomon Lipschitz.
Financial data (yr. ended 07/31/01): Grants paid, $122,472; assets, $1,842,758 (M); expenditures, $124,581; qualifying distributions, $121,247.
Limitations: Applications not accepted. Giving primarily in Brooklyn, NY.
Application information: Contributes only to pre-selected organizations.
Trustees: Olga Lipschitz, Solomon Lipschitz.
EIN: 116446481
Codes: FD2

35140
Mary W. MacKinnon Fund
c/o Wilber National Bank, Trust Dept.
245 Main St.
Oneonta, NY 13820-2502 (607) 432-1700

Established in 1968 in NY.
Donor(s): Mary W. MacKinnon.‡
Financial data (yr. ended 12/31/00): Grants paid, $122,352; assets, $2,425,645 (M); expenditures, $141,409; qualifying distributions, $125,920.
Limitations: Giving limited to Sidney, NY, residents.
Application information: Application must be submitted through doctor or hospital. Application form required.
Trustees: Diane Munson, Rev. Michael Shank, Terry Watkins, Theodore Wilklow.
EIN: 237234921
Codes: FD2, GTI

35141
Fibromyalgia Project, Inc.
c/o S. Levin
670 White Plains Rd., Ste. 222
Scarsdale, NY 10583

Established in 2000 in NY.
Donor(s): Stephen Ehrlich.
Financial data (yr. ended 12/31/00): Grants paid, $122,332; assets, $95,189 (M); gifts received, $209,589; expenditures, $124,004; qualifying distributions, $123,837.
Limitations: Applications not accepted. Giving primarily in NY.
Application information: Contributes only to pre-selected organizations.
Officer: Emanuel Pearlman, Secy.
Trustees: Mary Ann Ehrlich, Stephen Ehrlich, James Halper, M.D., Alan Manevitz, M.D., Steve Paget, M.D., Lisa Pearlman.
EIN: 061567773
Codes: FD2

35142
G. & H. Snyder Memorial Trust
c/o JPMorgan Chase Bank
P.O. Box 31412
Rochester, NY 14603

Donor(s): Gladys Snyder.‡
Financial data (yr. ended 12/31/01): Grants paid, $122,291; assets, $2,238,170 (M); expenditures, $145,047; qualifying distributions, $123,893.
Limitations: Applications not accepted.
Application information: Contributes only to pre-selected organizations.
Trustee: JPMorgan Chase Bank.
EIN: 311598840
Codes: FD2

35143
The Friderika Fischer Foundation, Inc.
c/o Jan Vilcek, M.D.
920 5th Ave., No. 2A
New York, NY 10021

Established in 2000 in NY.
Donor(s): Jan Vilcek.
Financial data (yr. ended 11/30/01): Grants paid, $122,055; assets, $5,000,784 (M); gifts received, $4,944,833; expenditures, $204,119; qualifying distributions, $161,319; giving activities include $154,819 for programs.
Limitations: Applications not accepted. Giving primarily in NM and NY.
Application information: Contributes only to pre-selected organizations. Unsolicited requests for funds not accepted.
Officers and Directors:* Jan Vilcek,* Pres. and Treas.; Marica Vilcek,* V.P. and Secy.; Bruce Cronstein, M.D.; Rick A. Kinsel, Jennifer Olshin.
EIN: 510404790
Codes: FD2

35144
Linville Family Foundation
c/o Brown Bros. Harriman Trust Co., LLC
63 Wall St.
New York, NY 10005

Established in 2001 in NY.
Donor(s): Clarence Linville, Susanne Gay Linville.
Financial data (yr. ended 12/31/01): Grants paid, $122,000; assets, $150,347 (M); gifts received, $1,928; expenditures, $128,000; qualifying distributions, $122,000.
Limitations: Applications not accepted. Giving primarily in CT, NY, SC, and VT.
Application information: Contributes only to pre-selected organizations.
Trustees: James Coker Linville, John Evans Linville, Susanne Gay Linville.
EIN: 137177348
Codes: FD2

35145
JB Charitable Foundation, Ltd.
c/o Roth & Co.
5612 18th Ave.
Brooklyn, NY 11204

Established in 1996 in NY.
Donor(s): Jacob Berkowitz.
Financial data (yr. ended 02/28/01): Grants paid, $121,878; assets, $87,540 (M); gifts received, $152,700; expenditures, $130,406; qualifying distributions, $124,275.
Limitations: Applications not accepted.
Application information: Contributes only to pre-selected organizations.
Officers: Jacob Berkowitz, Pres.; Frederika Berkowitz, Secy.; Martin Berkowitz, Treas.
EIN: 113316616
Codes: FD2

35146
William F. & Mildred Feinbloom Foundation, Inc.
c/o Davie, Kaplan & Braverman, PC
1000 First Federal Plz.
Rochester, NY 14614
Contact: Harris Rusitzky, Pres.

Donor(s): Mildred Feinbloom.
Financial data (yr. ended 12/31/01): Grants paid, $121,873; assets, $219,888 (M); expenditures, $124,335; qualifying distributions, $121,598.
Limitations: Giving primarily in NY.
Officers and Trustees:* Harris Rusitzky,* Pres.; Joan F. Rusitzky,* V.P.; Nathan J. Robfogel,* Secy.; Ann F. Bloom,* Treas.; E. Barry Kaplan, C. John Matteson.
EIN: 166045782
Codes: TN

35147
The Kenneth S. Davidson Family Foundation
500 Park Ave., Ste. 510
New York, NY 10022 (212) 750-5770
Contact: Kenneth S. Davidson, Tr.

Established in 1987 in NY.
Donor(s): Kenneth S. Davidson.
Financial data (yr. ended 12/31/01): Grants paid, $121,793; assets, $718,601 (M); expenditures, $124,987; qualifying distributions, $121,671.
Limitations: Giving primarily in the metropolitan New York, NY, area.
Trustee: Kenneth S. Davidson.
EIN: 133367889
Codes: FD2

35148
Brooklyn Benevolent Society
488 Atlantic Ave.
Brooklyn, NY 11217 (718) 875-2066
Contact: Cornelius A. Heaney, Secy.

Incorporated in 1845 in NY.
Donor(s): Cornelius Heaney.‡
Financial data (yr. ended 12/31/01): Grants paid, $121,735; assets, $5,167,240 (M); expenditures, $264,819; qualifying distributions, $164,020.
Limitations: Giving limited to New York, NY, with emphasis on the borough of Brooklyn.
Officers: Arnold Ring, Pres.; James J. Daly, V.P.; Cornelius A. Heaney, Secy.; Thomas E. Powers, Treas.
Trustees: Joseph P. Altman, David V. Farrell, Duncan A. Fraser, John G. Ingram, Fred W. McPhilliamy, Michael C. O'Brien.
EIN: 111661344
Codes: FD2

35149
Kobrand Foundation
c/o Kelley Drye & Warren, LLP
101 Park Ave., 30th Fl.
New York, NY 10178
Application address: 134 E. 40th St., New York, NY 10016, tel.: (212) 490-9300
Contact: Charles S. Mueller, Chair.

Established in 1972.
Donor(s): R.C. Kopf.‡
Financial data (yr. ended 12/31/00): Grants paid, $121,651; assets, $2,852,407 (M); expenditures, $173,208; qualifying distributions, $123,460.
Limitations: Giving on a national basis.
Application information: Application form not required.
Officers: Charles S. Mueller, Chair.; Robert A. Aldridge, Pres.; Richard Reitman, V.P. and Treas.; Michael S. Insel, Secy.
EIN: 237309965
Codes: FD2

35150
Shirley & William R. Fleischer Foundation, Inc.
120 Elm Dr.
Roslyn, NY 11576

Established around 1967 in NY.
Donor(s): Shirley Fleischer, William R. Fleischer.
Financial data (yr. ended 12/31/00): Grants paid, $121,592; assets, $2,669,426 (M); gifts received, $144,166; expenditures, $131,115; qualifying distributions, $121,905.
Limitations: Giving primarily in NY.
Application information: Application form not required.
Officers: Shirley Fleischer, Pres. and Secy.; William R. Fleischer, V.P.
EIN: 116048777
Codes: FD2

35151
Peck Stacpoole Foundation
17 W. 94th St., 1st Fl.
New York, NY 10025
FAX: (212) 932-0316
Contact: Robert W. Ashton, Secy.-Treas.

Established in 1997 in NY.
Donor(s): S. Allyn Peck.‡
Financial data (yr. ended 06/30/01): Grants paid, $121,550; assets, $3,666,093 (M); gifts received, $9,246; expenditures, $179,203; qualifying distributions, $121,113.
Limitations: Applications not accepted. Giving primarily in NY.
Application information: Unsolicited requests for funds not accepted.
Officers: Frederic W. Schaen, Pres.; Robert W. Ashton, Secy.-Treas.
Trustee: Lawrence L. Reger.
EIN: 133966373
Codes: FD2

35152
Cathedral Fund
c/o Perelson Weiner, LLP
1 Dag Hammarskjold Plz., 42nd Fl.
New York, NY 10017

Established in 1995 in MA.
Donor(s): Frances P. Caille, Harvey Picker, Branta Foundation.
Financial data (yr. ended 12/31/01): Grants paid, $121,500; assets, $1,213,465 (M); expenditures, $132,884; qualifying distributions, $122,835.

35152—NEW YORK

Limitations: Applications not accepted. Giving primarily in Boston, MA.
Application information: Contributes only to pre-selected organizations.
Trustee: Frances P. Caille.
EIN: 133843243
Codes: FD2

35153
Francis T. Hindelong Memorial Trust
c/o CSAM
466 Lexington Ave., 17th Fl.
New York, NY 10017-3140

Established in 1999 in NJ.
Financial data (yr. ended 12/31/01): Grants paid, $121,500; assets, $637,505 (M); gifts received, $445,700; expenditures, $125,855; qualifying distributions, $116,361.
Limitations: Applications not accepted. Giving on a national basis.
Application information: Contributes only to pre-selected organizations.
Distribution Committee: Aimee Hindelong, Donna Hindelong, John Hindelong, John Hindelong, Jr.
Trustee: Winthrop Trust Co.
EIN: 137224702
Codes: FD2

35154
The Wisch Family Foundation
c/o Goldman Sachs & Co.
85 Broad St., Tax Dept.
New York, NY 10004

Established in 1996 in NY.
Donor(s): Steven J. Wisch.
Financial data (yr. ended 04/30/02): Grants paid, $121,484; assets, $2,068,045 (M); expenditures, $122,343; qualifying distributions, $121,484.
Limitations: Applications not accepted. Giving primarily in Boston, MA and New York, NY.
Application information: Contributes only to pre-selected organizations.
Trustees: Debra Wisch, Steven J. Wisch.
EIN: 133938863
Codes: FD2

35155
The Coach Dairy Goat Farm Foundation
c/o The Coach Farm
105 Mill Hill Rd.
Pine Plains, NY 12567

Established in 1990 in NY.
Donor(s): Lillian Cahn, Miles Cahn.
Financial data (yr. ended 06/30/01): Grants paid, $121,450; assets, $174,704 (M); expenditures, $121,550; qualifying distributions, $121,414.
Limitations: Applications not accepted. Giving primarily in NY.
Application information: Contributes only to pre-selected organizations.
Trustees: Lillian Cahn, Miles Cahn.
EIN: 223075602
Codes: FD2

35156
Aaron M. Schreiber Family Foundation, Inc.
460 W. 34th St.
New York, NY 10001

Established in 1964 in NY.
Donor(s): Simeon Schreiber, Joel Schreiber, David Schreiber.
Financial data (yr. ended 12/31/99): Grants paid, $121,228; assets, $993,146 (M); gifts received, $17,556; expenditures, $123,745; qualifying distributions, $122,763.

Limitations: Applications not accepted. Giving primarily in NY.
Application information: Contributes only to pre-selected organizations.
Officers: Aaron Schreiber, Pres.; David Schreiber, V.P.; Simeon Schreiber, V.P; Joel Schreiber, Secy.
EIN: 136163551
Codes: FD2

35157
Mark E. Ross Charitable Trust
c/o Tag Assoc.
75 Rockefeller Plz., Ste. 900
New York, NY 10019

Established in 1997 in NY.
Donor(s): Mark E. Ross.
Financial data (yr. ended 04/30/01): Grants paid, $121,153; assets, $399,304 (M); gifts received, $100; expenditures, $124,529; qualifying distributions, $121,052.
Trustees: Cynthia C. Ross, Mark E. Ross.
EIN: 137117871
Codes: FD2

35158
Posner-Wallace Foundation
(Formerly Lillian & Stanley Posner Foundation)
300 W. 108th St., Apt. 15-C
New York, NY 10025
E-mail: posnerplus@aol.com
Contact: James R. Posner, Chair.

Established in 1957 in DC.
Donor(s): Irving Wallace, Stanley Posner,‡ Lillian Posner Wallace.‡
Financial data (yr. ended 12/31/00): Grants paid, $121,150; assets, $1,893,812 (M); gifts received, $79,150; expenditures, $133,710; qualifying distributions, $128,165.
Limitations: Giving primarily in the Washington, DC, area, Latin America, and Israel.
Application information: Contributes primarily to pre-selected organizations. Application form required.
Officers and Trustee:* James Posner, Chair.; Irving Wallace, Chair. Emeritus; Lawrence Posner, Secy.; Elisabeth Posner Schouten,* General Mgr.
EIN: 526037555
Codes: FD2

35159
Sollar Foundation, Inc.
805 3rd Ave., 11th Fl.
New York, NY 10022-7513

Established around 1969 in NY.
Donor(s): Arel Co., Arnold R. Sollar, Sienna Sollar, Elaine Eisen.
Financial data (yr. ended 12/31/00): Grants paid, $120,977; assets, $32,344 (M); gifts received, $130,463; expenditures, $121,094; qualifying distributions, $121,027.
Limitations: Applications not accepted. Giving primarily in New York, NY.
Application information: Contributes only to pre-selected organizations.
Officer: Arnold R. Sollar, Pres.
Director: Elaine Eisen.
EIN: 237024525
Codes: FD2

35160
Charles H. Douglas Charitable Trust
c/o Trustco Bank, N.A.
P.O. Box 380
Schenectady, NY 12301

Established in 1999 in NY.
Donor(s): Stephanie Bugden.

Financial data (yr. ended 12/31/01): Grants paid, $120,845; assets, $4,824,856 (M); expenditures, $156,484; qualifying distributions, $134,875.
Limitations: Applications not accepted. Giving primarily in Washington, DC, and NY.
Application information: Contributes only to pre-selected organizations.
Trustees: John Van Norden, Trustco Bank, N.A.
EIN: 141814550
Codes: FD2

35161
Benjamin and Elizabeth Abrams Foundation, Inc.
c/o S&E Azriliant
36 W. 44th St., Ste. 1100
New York, NY 10036

Incorporated in 1943 in NY.
Donor(s): Benjamin Abrams,‡ Elizabeth Abrams Kramer.‡
Financial data (yr. ended 12/31/01): Grants paid, $120,707; assets, $2,165,968 (M); expenditures, $150,716; qualifying distributions, $123,276.
Limitations: Applications not accepted. Giving primarily in Palm Beach County, FL, and NY.
Application information: Contributes only to pre-selected organizations.
Officers and Directors:* Cynthia Hochman,* Pres.; Geraldine A. Kory,* V.P. and Secy.; Marjorie A. Hyman,* Treas.
EIN: 136092960
Codes: FD2

35162
The Jack and Mimi Leviton Amsterdam Foundation
c/o Czarnowski & Beer
720 5th Ave.
New York, NY 10019

Established in 1977 in DE.
Donor(s): Jack Amsterdam.‡
Financial data (yr. ended 12/31/01): Grants paid, $120,696; assets, $3,074,972 (M); expenditures, $133,137; qualifying distributions, $123,137.
Limitations: Applications not accepted. Giving primarily in DE and NY.
Application information: Contributes only to pre-selected organizations.
Officers: Dasha Epstein, Pres.; Danielle Epstein, V.P.
EIN: 510220854
Codes: FD2

35163
Society for the Relief of Women & Children
c/o McLaughlin & Stern
260 Madison Ave., 18th Fl.
New York, NY 10116-2404
FAX: (212) 448-6260

Established in 1802 in NY.
Financial data (yr. ended 10/31/01): Grants paid, $120,692; assets, $2,802,132 (M); gifts received, $1,000; expenditures, $142,531; qualifying distributions, $137,141.
Limitations: Giving limited to New York, NY.
Application information: Grants to individuals are made only on recommendation of a church or social welfare agency. Unsolicited applications are discouraged. Application form not required.
Officers and Directors:* Mrs. John Parkinson III,* Pres.; Mrs. Charles S. Whitman, Jr.,* V.P.; Mrs. J. Michael Loening,* Secy.; Mrs. Frederick L. Liebolt,* Treas.; and 14 additional directors.
EIN: 136161272
Codes: FD2, GTI

35164
The Bernard H. Willig Foundation
15 Ashington Dr.
Ossining, NY 10562

Established in 2000.
Financial data (yr. ended 12/31/01): Grants paid, $120,660; assets, $104,752 (M); expenditures, $121,509; qualifying distributions, $120,263.
Limitations: Giving primarily in NY.
Trustees: Fay Stahl, Leonard Stahl.
EIN: 133947838
Codes: FD2

35165
The Richard Salomon Family Foundation, Inc.
(Formerly Richard & Edna Salomon Foundation, Inc.)
c/o Richard E. Salomon
610 5th Ave., 7th Fl.
New York, NY 10020

Established in 1964 in NY.
Donor(s): Richard B. Salomon,‡ Richard E. Salomon.
Financial data (yr. ended 12/31/99): Grants paid, $120,502; assets, $8,709,160 (M); gifts received, $117,238; expenditures, $216,616; qualifying distributions, $120,502.
Limitations: Applications not accepted. Giving primarily in New York, NY.
Application information: Contributes only to pre-selected organizations.
Officers and Directors:* Richard E. Salomon,* Pres.; Edna B. Salomon,* V.P.; Frederick Lubcher,* Secy.; Robyn S. Transport,* Treas.; Evanne S. Gargiulo, Laura A. Landro, Christina Salomon, David Salomon, Jennifer Salomon.
EIN: 136163521
Codes: FD2

35166
The Bender Family Foundation
111 Washington Ave.
Albany, NY 12210   (518) 446-9638
Application address: c/o The Community Foundation for the Capital Region, Exec. Park Dr., Albany, NY 12203
Contact: Jackie Mahoney, Dir. of Grantmaking and Donor Svcs.

Established in 1997 in NY.
Donor(s): Matthew Bender IV.
Financial data (yr. ended 12/31/01): Grants paid, $120,450; assets, $2,653,635 (M); expenditures, $159,054; qualifying distributions, $119,898.
Limitations: Giving primarily in Albany County, NY.
Publications: Application guidelines.
Application information: Contact Community Foundation for the Capital Region for application procedures. Application form required.
Officers: Matthew Bender IV, Pres.; Phoebe P. Bender, V.P.; M. Christian Bender, Secy.; Jeffrey P. Bender, Treas.
EIN: 161526228
Codes: FD2

35167
The Garber Fund
508 Hemlock Dr.
Cedarhurst, NY 11516

Established in 1987 in NY.
Donor(s): Harvey Brecher, Eli S. Garber, Harriette Garber.
Financial data (yr. ended 09/30/01): Grants paid, $120,193; assets, $704,883 (M); expenditures, $151,900; qualifying distributions, $270,293; giving activities include $350,000 for program-related investments.
Limitations: Applications not accepted. Giving primarily in NY.
Application information: Contributes only to pre-selected organizations.
Officers and Directors:* Eli S. Garber,* Pres.; Harriette Garber,* V.P.; Harvey Brecher.
EIN: 112910964
Codes: FD2

35168
Samuel Stark Foundation
1455 49th St., Ste. 5-D
Brooklyn, NY 11219-3255

Established in 1999 in NY.
Donor(s): Samuel Stark.
Financial data (yr. ended 12/31/00): Grants paid, $120,182; assets, $29,690 (M); gifts received, $130,626; expenditures, $120,497; qualifying distributions, $120,285.
Limitations: Applications not accepted. Giving primarily in Brooklyn, NY.
Application information: Contributes only to pre-selected organizations.
Director: Samuel Stark.
EIN: 316618100
Codes: FD2

35169
ANH Foundation
1060 Amsterdam Ave.
New York, NY 10025
Contact: Larry Thompson, Tr.

Established in 1996 in NY.
Financial data (yr. ended 12/31/00): Grants paid, $120,000; assets, $2,668,289 (M); expenditures, $129,415; qualifying distributions, $117,090.
Limitations: Giving limited to the upper West Side of Manhattan in New York City.
Trustees: H. Thomas Dyett, Joseph C. Hoopes, Jr., Lawrence B. Thompson, Dyer S. Wadsworth.
EIN: 137099598
Codes: FD2

35170
Asclepius Foundation, Inc.
Pantherkill Rd.
P.O. Box 70
Phoenicia, NY 12464-0070

Established in 1999 in NY.
Donor(s): Fiona Druckenmiller.
Financial data (yr. ended 10/31/00): Grants paid, $120,000; assets, $3,728,896 (M); gifts received, $1,667,640; expenditures, $481,005; qualifying distributions, $1,477,907.
Limitations: Applications not accepted. Giving primarily in NY.
Application information: Contributes only to pre-selected organizations.
Officers: Susan Kessler, Pres.; Rick Allen, Secy.; Andrew Kramer, Treas.
Directors: Barbara App, Carol Hornig, Frank Lipman, M.D.
EIN: 061530626
Codes: FD2

35171
Clark Family Foundation, Inc.
430 Park Ave., Ste. 1800
New York, NY 10022

Established in 1986 in NY.
Donor(s): John Sheldon Clark, Valer Clark Austin.
Financial data (yr. ended 12/31/99): Grants paid, $120,000; assets, $2,155,611 (M); expenditures, $169,743; qualifying distributions, $120,000.
Limitations: Applications not accepted. Giving primarily in AZ and Washington, DC.
Application information: Contributes only to pre-selected organizations.
Officers and Trustees:* John Sheldon Clark,* Pres.; Valer Clark Austin,* Treas.; Josia T. Austin.
EIN: 133322083
Codes: FD2

35172
The Gettinger Foundation
1407 Broadway, Ste. 3310
New York, NY 10018-5103   (212) 944-6090
Contact: Robert Gettinger, Pres.

Established in 1986 in NY.
Donor(s): Robert Gettinger.
Financial data (yr. ended 10/31/00): Grants paid, $120,000; assets, $3,215,748 (M); gifts received, $19,000; expenditures, $134,262; qualifying distributions, $121,109.
Limitations: Giving primarily in NY.
Application information: Application form not required.
Officers: Robert Gettinger, Pres.; Carol A. Edelson, Secy.
EIN: 133387105
Codes: FD2

35173
The Block Grausman Fund
c/o Stroock & Stroock & Lavan
180 Maiden Ln.
New York, NY 10038

Established around 1947.
Financial data (yr. ended 12/31/01): Grants paid, $120,000; assets, $1,798,274 (M); expenditures, $149,062; qualifying distributions, $122,837.
Limitations: Applications not accepted. Giving primarily in New York, NY.
Application information: Contributes only to pre-selected organizations.
Trustees: Philip Grausman, Richard Grausman, Jerome A. Manning.
EIN: 136086092
Codes: FD2

35174
The Hutchins Family Foundation, Inc.
400 Midtown Tower
Rochester, NY 14604

Established in 1997 in NY.
Donor(s): Frank M. Hutchins.
Financial data (yr. ended 12/31/01): Grants paid, $120,000; assets, $2,353,100 (M); expenditures, $133,731; qualifying distributions, $126,426.
Limitations: Applications not accepted. Giving primarily in NY.
Application information: Contributes only to pre-selected organizations.
Officers and Directors:* Jeanne B. Hutchins,* Pres. and Treas.; Frank M. Hutchins,* V.P. and Secy.; Constance H. Mills, Patricia H. Murphy, Virginia H. Valkenburgh, Katharine H. Welling.
EIN: 161520006
Codes: FD2

35175
The Latainer Family Foundation, Inc.
65 Lyon Ridge Rd.
Katonah, NY 10536-3715
Contact: Gary Latainer, Pres.

Established in 1999 in NY.
Donor(s): Gary Latainer.
Financial data (yr. ended 12/31/01): Grants paid, $120,000; assets, $230,919 (M); gifts received, $26,913; expenditures, $122,235; qualifying distributions, $121,960.
Limitations: Giving primarily in CO, MO, and NY.

35175—NEW YORK

Officers: Gary Latainer, Pres. and Treas.; Nydia Latainer, V.P. and Secy.
Director: Millie Chervin.
EIN: 134089614
Codes: FD2

35176
The Williams Family Philanthropic Foundation
77 Spruce St., Ste. 203
Cedarhurst, NY 11516

Established in 1985 in NY.
Donor(s): Jerry Williams, Esther Williams.
Financial data (yr. ended 11/30/01): Grants paid, $119,888; assets, $8,975 (M); gifts received, $123,000; expenditures, $121,065; qualifying distributions, $119,888.
Limitations: Applications not accepted. Giving primarily in the greater metropolitan New York, NY, area, including Long Island.
Application information: Contributes only to pre-selected organizations.
Officer: Jerry Williams, Pres.
Directors: Esther Williams, Judith Williams, Mortimer Williams.
EIN: 112849607
Codes: FD2

35177
D. & E. Steinmetz Foundation
202 Keap St.
Brooklyn, NY 11211
Contact: David Steinmetz, Tr.

Established in 1999 in NY.
Donor(s): Fort Management, Sherman Management, Town Management.
Financial data (yr. ended 06/30/01): Grants paid, $119,772; assets, $83,592 (M); gifts received, $53,400; expenditures, $120,254; qualifying distributions, $118,622.
Application information: Application form not required.
Trustees: David Steinmetz, Esther Steinmetz.
EIN: 113522236
Codes: FD2

35178
Gruder Family Foundation, Inc.
143-22 84th Ave.
Jamaica, NY 11435-2136
Contact: Selma Horowitz, Dir.

Established in 1993.
Donor(s): Selma Horowitz.
Financial data (yr. ended 08/31/01): Grants paid, $119,706; assets, $36,509 (M); gifts received, $60,000; expenditures, $121,506; qualifying distributions, $119,906.
Limitations: Giving on a national basis.
Application information: Application form not required.
Directors: Pearl Field, Selma Horowitz, Romina Field Weiss.
EIN: 133738851
Codes: FD2

35179
The Steven M. and Anita C. Heller Family Foundation
c/o Goldman Sachs & Co.
85 Broad St., Tax Dept.
New York, NY 10004

Established in 1993 in CT.
Donor(s): Steven M. Heller.
Financial data (yr. ended 05/31/01): Grants paid, $119,700; assets, $5,485,690 (M); gifts received, $1,100; expenditures, $183,329; qualifying distributions, $120,800.

Limitations: Applications not accepted. Giving primarily in NY.
Application information: Contributes only to pre-selected organizations.
Trustees: Anita C. Heller, Steven M. Heller.
EIN: 133792292

35180
Stanley Steyer Family Foundation, Inc.
c/o Harold Orlin
60 E. 42nd St., Ste. 458
New York, NY 10165

Established in 1983 in DE.
Donor(s): Helen Steyer, Thomas M. Steyer.
Financial data (yr. ended 05/31/01): Grants paid, $119,650; assets, $591,985 (M); gifts received, $65,178; expenditures, $124,690; qualifying distributions, $124,047.
Limitations: Applications not accepted. Giving primarily in NY.
Application information: Contributes only to pre-selected organizations.
Officers: Stanley Steyer, Pres.; Thomas M. Steyer, V.P.; Helen Steyer, Secy.
EIN: 133207413
Codes: FD2

35181
H. T. Edwards Charitable Trust Foundation
P.O. Box 2004
New York, NY 10108-1910
Application address: U.S. Trust of NY, 114 W. 47th St., New York, NY 10036
Contact: Harriet F. Leahy, Trust Off., U.S. Trust

Established in 1994 in NY.
Donor(s): U.S. Trust Co.
Financial data (yr. ended 12/31/01): Grants paid, $119,635; assets, $2,982,224 (M); expenditures, $140,512; qualifying distributions, $127,837.
Trustee: U.S. Trust.
EIN: 367071830
Codes: FD2

35182
Roger and Barbara Michaels Family Fund, Inc.
c/o David Tarlow & Co., PC
60 E. 42nd St., Ste. 2212
New York, NY 10165
Contact: Roger A. Michaels, Dir.

Established in 1980.
Financial data (yr. ended 12/31/00): Grants paid, $119,571; assets, $2,892,048 (M); expenditures, $166,343; qualifying distributions, $121,508.
Limitations: Giving primarily in NY.
Directors: Alice M. Ginandes, Barbara R. Michaels, Roger A. Michaels.
EIN: 133022845
Codes: FD2

35183
M. A. & L. J. Bennett Scholarship Fund
c/o JPMorgan Chase Bank
1211 6th Ave., 34th Fl.
New York, NY 10036
Application address: c/o Capt. Vincent Doherty, Emerald Society, 677 83rd St., Brooklyn, NY 11228, tel.: (718) 383-9232

Established in 1989 in NY.
Financial data (yr. ended 05/31/01): Grants paid, $119,500; assets, $2,932,058 (M); expenditures, $158,121; qualifying distributions, $136,510.
Limitations: Giving primarily in the metropolitan New York, NY, area.
Application information: Application form not required.
Trustee: JPMorgan Chase Bank.
EIN: 133544931

Codes: FD2, GTI

35184
The Mike Delaney Foundation
c/o BCRS Assocs., LLC
100 Wall St., 11th Fl.
New York, NY 10005

Established in 1987 in CT.
Donor(s): Michael C. Delaney.
Financial data (yr. ended 05/31/01): Grants paid, $119,500; assets, $587,424 (M); expenditures, $126,105; qualifying distributions, $119,837.
Limitations: Applications not accepted. Giving primarily in CT and New York, NY.
Application information: Contributes only to pre-selected organizations.
Trustees: Charlotte Delaney, Michael C. Delaney, Frederic B. Garonzik.
EIN: 133437923
Codes: FD2

35185
Charles A. & Marna Davis Foundation
c/o BCRS Assocs., LLC
67 Wall St., 8th Fl.
New York, NY 10005

Established in 1987 in NY.
Donor(s): Charles A. Davis, Charles A. Davis II.
Financial data (yr. ended 04/30/01): Grants paid, $119,455; assets, $1,416,792 (M); gifts received, $110; expenditures, $125,523; qualifying distributions, $120,064.
Limitations: Applications not accepted. Giving primarily in CT, NY and VT.
Application information: Contributes only to pre-selected organizations.
Trustees: Charles A. Davis, Marna Davis.
EIN: 133437924
Codes: FD2

35186
Russo Family Charitable Foundation
6553 Boston State Rd.
Hamburg, NY 14075

Established in 1988 in NY.
Donor(s): Celia Russo, John A. Russo, Joseph L. Russo.
Financial data (yr. ended 12/31/01): Grants paid, $119,350; assets, $5,812,821 (M); gifts received, $4,753,473; expenditures, $123,017; qualifying distributions, $119,350.
Limitations: Applications not accepted. Giving primarily in NY.
Application information: Contributes only to pre-selected organizations.
Officers: Joseph L. Russo, Pres.; Celia Russo, V.P.; John A. Russo, Secy.-Treas.
EIN: 161339086
Codes: FD2

35187
The Eileen & Peter Lehrer Family Foundation, Inc.
888 7th Ave.
New York, NY 10019 (212) 459-1818
Contact: Peter M. Lehrer, V.P.

Established in 1999 in MD and NY.
Donor(s): Eileen G. Lehrer, Peter M. Lehrer.
Financial data (yr. ended 12/31/01): Grants paid, $119,275; assets, $628,448 (M); gifts received, $375,000; expenditures, $120,750; qualifying distributions, $119,275.
Limitations: Giving limited to the U.S.
Officers and Directors:* Eileen G. Lehrer,* Pres.; Peter M. Lehrer,* V.P. and Secy.-Treas.
EIN: 522205396
Codes: FD2

35188
The Telcom Foundation Trust
c/o D. Landau
1225 39th St.
Brooklyn, NY 11218

Established in 1999 in NY.
Donor(s): Triangle Trust, Concord Trust, A & E Trust, David Landau.
Financial data (yr. ended 12/31/01): Grants paid, $119,265; assets, $1,014,584 (M); expenditures, $120,265; qualifying distributions, $119,265.
Limitations: Applications not accepted.
Application information: Contributes only to pre-selected organizations.
Director: David Landau.
EIN: 116532344

35189
Frances Schreiber Feder Foundation, Inc.
c/o Alro Plumbing, Inc.
414 Flushing Ave.
Brooklyn, NY 11205-1582
Contact: Ruth Shapiro, Pres.

Established in 1965.
Donor(s): Frances Feder.‡
Financial data (yr. ended 12/31/01): Grants paid, $119,058; assets, $526,210 (M); expenditures, $119,670; qualifying distributions, $119,058.
Limitations: Giving primarily in New York, NY.
Officers: Ruth Shapiro, Pres.; Matthew M. Zuckerman, V.P.; Samuel Shapiro, Secy.; Irwin Shapiro, Treas.
EIN: 136183142

35190
Peter and Devon Briger Foundation
c/o BCRS Assocs.
67 Wall St., 8th Fl.
New York, NY 10005

Established in 1997 in NY.
Donor(s): Peter L. Briger, Jr.
Financial data (yr. ended 12/31/00): Grants paid, $119,000; assets, $2,308,590 (M); expenditures, $163,273; qualifying distributions, $119,250.
Limitations: Applications not accepted. Giving primarily in MA, NJ, and NY.
Application information: Contributes only to pre-selected organizations.
Trustees: Peter L. Briger, Jr., Devon Elizabeth Fenton.
EIN: 133939006
Codes: FD2

35191
U.S. Friends of Loyola Foundation, Inc.
c/o Larry R. Carriere
3 Silver Thorne Dr.
Williamsville, NY 14221

Established in 1998 in NY.
Donor(s): Thomas R. Pirelli, Robert H. Beriault.
Financial data (yr. ended 12/31/01): Grants paid, $119,000; assets, $390,484 (M); gifts received, $224,725; expenditures, $126,301; qualifying distributions, $122,680.
Limitations: Applications not accepted.
Application information: Contributes only to pre-selected organizations.
Officers: Terrance A. Fairholm, Pres.; Larry R. Carriere, V.P. and Treas.; Jim Pearson, Secy.
Directors: Robert H. Beriault, David P. Bossy, Thomas R. Pirelli.
EIN: 161536779
Codes: FD2

35192
The Solan Family Foundation, Inc.
1 Dolma Rd.
Scarsdale, NY 10583-4505

Established in 1996 in NY.
Donor(s): Henry Solan.
Financial data (yr. ended 12/31/00): Grants paid, $118,867; assets, $1,741,135 (M); expenditures, $137,895; qualifying distributions, $128,614.
Limitations: Applications not accepted.
Application information: Contributes only to pre-selected organizations.
Officers: Henry Solan, Pres.; Miriam Solan, V.P.; Samara Verne Solan, Secy.; Alicia Ila Solan-Teglasi, Treas.
EIN: 133921332
Codes: FD2

35193
Lee Romney Foundation, Inc.
c/o M.A. Romney & Co.
200 Park Ave. S., Ste. 1018
New York, NY 10003 (212) 982-1405
FAX: (212) 982-2045
Contact: Mark A. Romney, Treas.

Established in 1988.
Donor(s): Mark A. Romney, Vera J. Tucker, Leonor Romney Charitable Lead Trust.
Financial data (yr. ended 11/30/01): Grants paid, $118,860; assets, $1,949,830 (M); gifts received, $107,936; expenditures, $139,903; qualifying distributions, $125,464.
Limitations: Applications not accepted. Giving primarily in NY.
Application information: Contributes only to pre-selected organizations.
Officers and Directors:* Sharon Rosenfeld Scott,* Pres.; Michael H. Romney,* V.P.; Mark A. Romney,* Treas.; Martin E. Greif.
EIN: 133187997
Codes: FD2

35194
Bentley Holden Fund
7784 S. Main St.
Pine Plains, NY 12567
FAX: (518) 398-1000
Contact: Carol Adams, Dir.

Established in 1966 in NY.
Financial data (yr. ended 12/31/01): Grants paid, $118,800; assets, $2,899,695 (M); expenditures, $165,650; qualifying distributions, $123,169.
Limitations: Applications not accepted. Giving limited to NY; communications grants limited to Dutchess County.
Application information: Contributes only to pre-selected organizations. Unsolicited applications not accepted or acknowledged.
Directors: Carol Adams, Jon H. Adams.
EIN: 146018221
Codes: FD2

35195
Herring-Finn Foundation, Inc.
10 E. 68th St.
New York, NY 10021-4326
Contact: John Herring, Pres., or Paul Herring, V.P.

Established in 1947 in NY and DE.
Donor(s): Gladys F. Herring,‡ John D. Herring, Paul L. Herring.
Financial data (yr. ended 12/31/01): Grants paid, $118,696; assets, $1,377,781 (M); gifts received, $20,000; expenditures, $124,063; qualifying distributions, $120,809.
Limitations: Applications not accepted. Giving primarily in NY.
Application information: Contributes only to pre-selected organizations.
Officers: John D. Herring, Pres.; Paul L. Herring, V.P.
EIN: 136137676
Codes: FD2

35196
The Jack S. & Shirley M. Silver Foundation
920 5th Ave.
New York, NY 10021

Established in 1985 in NY.
Donor(s): Jack S. Silver, Shirley M. Silver.
Financial data (yr. ended 05/31/01): Grants paid, $118,571; assets, $267,003 (M); expenditures, $120,878; qualifying distributions, $118,571.
Limitations: Applications not accepted. Giving primarily in New York, NY.
Application information: Contributes only to pre-selected organizations.
Trustees: Jack S. Silver, Shirley M. Silver.
EIN: 133343294
Codes: FD2

35197
The Severson Family Foundation
c/o BCRS Assoc., LLC
100 Wall St., 11th Fl.
New York, NY 10005

Established in 1993 in CA.
Donor(s): Ralph F. Severson.
Financial data (yr. ended 06/30/01): Grants paid, $118,550; assets, $867,104 (M); expenditures, $129,582; qualifying distributions, $119,875.
Limitations: Applications not accepted. Giving primarily in CA and UT.
Application information: Contributes only to pre-selected organizations.
Trustees: Joseph H. Clark, Ralph F. Severson, Sue Clark Severson.
EIN: 133748066
Codes: FD2

35198
Kathryn & Gilbert Miller Fund, Inc.
c/o Proskauer, Rose, LLP
1585 Broadway
New York, NY 10036
Contact: Charles Looker, Pres.

Incorporated in 1952 in NY.
Donor(s): Kathryn B. Miller.‡
Financial data (yr. ended 03/31/01): Grants paid, $118,400; assets, $201,793 (M); expenditures, $125,247; qualifying distributions, $124,310.
Limitations: Giving primarily in New York, NY.
Application information: Application form not required.
Officers and Directors:* Charles Looker,* Pres.; Lawrence J. Rothenberg,* V.P.; Jerold Zieselman,* Secy.
EIN: 136121254
Codes: FD2

35199
The Kennedy Smith Foundation, Inc.
500 Fifth Ave., Ste. 1710
New York, NY 10110-0002

Established in 1988 in NY.
Donor(s): Jean K. Smith.
Financial data (yr. ended 12/31/00): Grants paid, $118,250; assets, $500,054 (M); expenditures, $122,506; qualifying distributions, $118,250.
Limitations: Applications not accepted. Giving primarily in Washington, DC.
Application information: Contributes only to pre-selected organizations.

IN THIS SECTION, WITHIN EACH STATE, FOUNDATIONS ARE LISTED IN DESCENDING ORDER BY TOTAL GRANTS PAID

35199—NEW YORK

Officers: Jean K. Smith, Pres.; Charles J. O'Byrne, Secy.; Joseph E. Hakim, Treas.
EIN: 061238388
Codes: FD2

35200
The Ruth M. Knight Foundation, Inc.
c/o Parker, Duryee, Rosoff & Haft
529 5th Ave.
New York, NY 10017-4608

Established in 1957 in NY.
Donor(s): Ruth M. Knight Trust, George W. Naumburg, Jr., Elizabeth H. Naumburg, Michele Naumburg, Eric Naumburg, Judith Bluestone, Christopher London.
Financial data (yr. ended 12/31/00): Grants paid, $118,181; assets, $1,514,472 (M); gifts received, $102,994; expenditures, $128,908; qualifying distributions, $116,278.
Limitations: Applications not accepted. Giving primarily in NY.
Application information: Contributes only to pre-selected organizations.
Officers and Directors:* George W. Naumburg, Jr.,* Pres.; Michele Naumburg,* V.P.; Philip N. Naumburg,* V.P.; Arthur H. Brown, Jr.,* Secy; Leonard F. Howard,* Treas.; Elizabeth H. Naumburg, Eric Naumburg, Janet Naumburg, Judith Ellen Naumburg.
EIN: 136093663
Codes: FD2

35201
The BWF Foundation
c/o National Artists Management Co.
165 W. 46th St., Ste. 1202
New York, NY 10036 (888) 485-4720
Application address: 8621 Coral Gables Ln., Vienna, VA 22182; FAX: (703) 255-4756
Contact: Cindy Harney, Dir.

Established in 1999 in NY.
Donor(s): Barry Weissler, National Artists Mgmt. Co.
Financial data (yr. ended 11/30/01): Grants paid, $118,050; assets, $902,846 (M); gifts received, $21,600; expenditures, $273,533; qualifying distributions, $260,259.
Limitations: Giving on a national basis, with emphasis on New York, NY.
Publications: Application guidelines, grants list.
Application information: Application form required.
Officers: Barry Weissler, Pres.; Fran Weissler, V.P. and Secy.
Director: Cindy Rosenberg Harney.
EIN: 134036563
Codes: FD2

35202
The Hertz Charitable Foundation
95 Rockwell Pl.
Brooklyn, NY 11217

Financial data (yr. ended 01/31/00): Grants paid, $118,000; assets, $194 (M); expenditures, $118,000; qualifying distributions, $118,000.
Limitations: Applications not accepted. Giving limited in NY.
Application information: Contributes only to pre-selected organizations.
Trustee: Barry Hertz.
EIN: 133515234
Codes: FD2

35203
The Saperston Family Foundation
237 Main St., Ste. 1100
Buffalo, NY 14203-2718

Established in 1992 in NY.
Donor(s): Willard B. Saperston.
Financial data (yr. ended 12/31/01): Grants paid, $118,000; assets, $383,710 (M); gifts received, $3,797; expenditures, $119,954; qualifying distributions, $117,944.
Limitations: Applications not accepted. Giving primarily in Buffalo, NY.
Application information: Contributes only to pre-selected organizations.
Trustees: Willard B. Saperston, Bruce Warner.
EIN: 161428874
Codes: FD2

35204
William P. & Gertrude Schweitzer Foundation, Inc.
c/o Theodore R. Shiffman
317 Madison Ave., Ste. 1410
New York, NY 10017

Established in 1961 in NY.
Donor(s): Gertrude Schweitzer.‡
Financial data (yr. ended 12/31/01): Grants paid, $118,000; assets, $2,206,381 (M); expenditures, $127,782; qualifying distributions, $117,407.
Limitations: Applications not accepted. Giving primarily in New York, NY; some giving also in Washington, DC.
Application information: Contributes only to pre-selected organizations.
Officer: Peter W. Schweitzer, C.E.O. and Pres.
EIN: 136160772
Codes: FD2

35205
McGowan Gin Rosica Family Foundation, Inc.
115 Windemere Rd.
Rochester, NY 14610

Established in 1994 in DC.
Financial data (yr. ended 06/30/01): Grants paid, $117,928; assets, $1,675,122 (M); expenditures, $152,512; qualifying distributions, $117,098.
Limitations: Applications not accepted. Giving primarily in Aurora, IL.
Application information: Contributes only to pre-selected organizations.
Officers and Trustees:* Kathryn Rosica,* Pres.; A. Joseph Rosica,* Secy.; Mark Rosica,* Treas.
EIN: 521827834
Codes: FD2

35206
Seevers Family Foundation
c/o BCRS Assocs., LLC
100 Wall St., 11th Fl.
New York, NY 10005

Established in 1987 in NY.
Donor(s): Gary L. Seevers.
Financial data (yr. ended 07/31/01): Grants paid, $117,820; assets, $4,223,076 (M); gifts received, $247,500; expenditures, $171,041; qualifying distributions, $129,551.
Limitations: Applications not accepted. Giving on a national basis, primarily in New York, NY.
Application information: Contributes only to pre-selected organizations.
Trustees: Gary L. Seevers, Gary L. Seevers, Jr., Sharon Seevers.
EIN: 133437890
Codes: FD2

35207
Stanley F. Goldfein Foundation, Inc.
60 E. 42nd St., No. 2015
New York, NY 10165

Established in 1967.
Donor(s): Stanley F. Goldfein.
Financial data (yr. ended 05/31/01): Grants paid, $117,805; assets, $2,056,780 (M); expenditures, $118,220; qualifying distributions, $116,532.
Limitations: Applications not accepted.
Application information: Contributes only to pre-selected organizations.
Officer: Stanley F. Goldfein, Pres.
EIN: 237444440
Codes: FD2

35208
The Peter and Julie Borish Family Foundation
c/o Davis & Graber
150 E. 58th St., 22nd Fl.
New York, NY 10155

Established in 1999 in NY and DE.
Donor(s): Peter Borish.
Financial data (yr. ended 12/31/00): Grants paid, $117,500; assets, $559,246 (M); expenditures, $123,055; qualifying distributions, $117,951.
Limitations: Applications not accepted. Giving primarily in NY.
Application information: Contributes only to pre-selected organizations.
Officers: Peter Borish, Pres.; Julie Borish, V.P.; David Ginsberg, Secy.
EIN: 510381289
Codes: FD2

35209
The Evelyn Paige Foundation, Inc.
c/o Muchnick, Golieb & Golieb, PC
200 Park Ave., Ste. 1700
New York, NY 10003 (212) 315-5575
Contact: Margaret G. Axelrod, Pres.

Established in 1987 in NY.
Donor(s): Evelyn Paige.‡
Financial data (yr. ended 12/31/01): Grants paid, $117,500; assets, $3,488,155 (M); gifts received, $1,232,731; expenditures, $158,663; qualifying distributions, $139,982.
Limitations: Giving limited to New York, NY.
Application information: Application form not required.
Officers and Directors:* Margaret G. Axelrod,* Pres.; John A. Golieb,* Secy.-Treas.; Abner J. Golieb.
EIN: 133435542
Codes: FD2

35210
Esther & Morton Wohlgemuth Foundation, Inc.
c/o Irwin M. Thorpe
440 Park Ave. S., Ste. 5
New York, NY 10016

Incorporated in 1956 in NY.
Donor(s): Morton Wohlgemuth,‡ Esther Wohlgemuth, Alexander Wohlgemuth, Robert Wohlgemuth.
Financial data (yr. ended 12/31/01): Grants paid, $117,500; assets, $3,665,421 (M); expenditures, $132,720; qualifying distributions, $127,715.
Limitations: Applications not accepted. Giving primarily in NY.
Application information: Contributes only to pre-selected organizations.
Officers: Alexander Wohlgemuth, V.P.; Robert Wohlgemuth, V.P.; Irwin M. Thrope, Secy.
Trustee: Zeena S. Thrope.
EIN: 136086849
Codes: FD2

35211
Handy & Harman Foundation
555 Theodore Fremd Ave.
Rye, NY 10580 (914) 921-5200
Contact: P.E. Dixon, Secy.

Established in 1974 in NY.
Donor(s): Handy & Harman.
Financial data (yr. ended 12/31/01): Grants paid, $117,499; assets, $317,710 (M); gifts received, $137,500; expenditures, $118,433; qualifying distributions, $118,433.
Application information: Application form not required.
Officers and Directors:* R.D. Le Blanc,* Pres.; P.E. Dixon,* Secy.; D.C. Kelly,* Treas.
EIN: 237408431
Codes: CS, FD2, CD

35212
The Allendale Fund
c/o Bessemer Trust Co., N.A.
630 5th Ave.
New York, NY 10111-0333

Established in 1991 in NC.
Donor(s): Everette E. Mills III.
Financial data (yr. ended 12/31/01): Grants paid, $117,070; assets, $1,414,592 (M); expenditures, $127,700; qualifying distributions, $117,104.
Limitations: Applications not accepted. Giving limited to NC.
Application information: Contributes only to a pre-selected organization.
Officers: Everette E. Mills III, Pres.; Madeline J. Mills, Secy.
Director: William S. Jones.
EIN: 561757536
Codes: FD2

35213
The Fortunoff Foundation, Inc.
11 E. 36th St.
New York, NY 10016-3318

Established in 1952.
Donor(s): Everett M. Fortunoff, Robert Fortunoff.
Financial data (yr. ended 12/31/01): Grants paid, $117,065; assets, $25,800 (M); gifts received, $123,934; expenditures, $117,065; qualifying distributions, $117,065.
Limitations: Applications not accepted. Giving primarily in NY.
Application information: Contributes only to pre-selected organizations.
Trustees: Everett M. Fortunoff, Robert Fortunoff.
EIN: 136182916
Codes: FD2

35214
Fred & Annemarie Kambeitz Foundation, Inc.
23 Pleasant Ridge Rd.
Harrison, NY 10528

Established in 1997 in NY.
Donor(s): Fred Kambeitz.
Financial data (yr. ended 09/30/01): Grants paid, $116,975; assets, $1,609,185 (M); gifts received, $1,408,706; expenditures, $117,337; qualifying distributions, $117,337.
Limitations: Applications not accepted.
Application information: Contributes only to pre-selected organizations.
Officers: Fred Kambeitz, Pres. and Treas.; Annemarie Kambeitz, V.P. and Secy.; Lorraine Freed, V.P.
EIN: 133986882
Codes: FD2

35215
Fred & Gertrude Perlberg Foundation, Inc.
c/o Levine Sullivan & Menendez, LLP
5510 Merrick Rd.
Massapequa, NY 11758-6216 (516) 795-2500
Contact: William F. Sullivan, Dir.

Established in 1956 in NY.
Donor(s): Perlberg Holding Corp.
Financial data (yr. ended 07/31/01): Grants paid, $116,950; assets, $1,366,063 (M); expenditures, $117,289; qualifying distributions, $116,950.
Limitations: Applications not accepted. Giving primarily in NY.
Application information: Contributes only to pre-selected organizations.
Officers: Edward Perlberg, Pres. and C.E.O.; Ferderick A. B. Perlberg, Treas.
Director: William F. Sullivan.
EIN: 136100032

35216
The Phyllis and Leonard Rosen Family Foundation
c/o Wachtell, Lipton, Rosen & Katz
51 W. 52nd St.
New York, NY 10019

Established in 1986 in NY.
Donor(s): Leonard M. Rosen, Phyllis Rosen.
Financial data (yr. ended 04/30/01): Grants paid, $116,825; assets, $646,880 (M); gifts received, $164,898; expenditures, $116,925; qualifying distributions, $116,204.
Limitations: Applications not accepted. Giving primarily in NY.
Application information: Contributes only to pre-selected organizations.
Officers and Directors:* Leonard M. Rosen,* Pres. and Treas.; Phyllis Rosen,* V.P. and Secy.; David M. Einhorn.
EIN: 133389561
Codes: FD2

35217
The Helen Matchett DeMario Foundation, Inc.
61 Broadway, 18th Fl.
New York, NY 10006-2794 (212) 797-9100
Contact: Roy Sparber, Secy.; or David A. Brauner, Tr.

Established in 1984 in NJ.
Financial data (yr. ended 12/31/01): Grants paid, $116,750; assets, $2,978,895 (M); expenditures, $155,100; qualifying distributions, $123,530.
Limitations: Giving primarily in NY.
Application information: Application form not required.
Officers and Trustees:* Norman H. Sparber,* Pres.; David A. Brauner,* V.P.; Michael L. Goldstein,* V.P.; Roy M. Sparber,* Secy.; Elias Rosenzweig,* Treas.
EIN: 133213185
Codes: FD2

35218
The Francesco & Mary Giambelli Foundation, Inc.
(Formerly The Francesco Giambelli Foundation, Inc.)
46 E. 50th St.
New York, NY 10022

Established in 1990 in NY.
Donor(s): Francesco Giambelli.
Financial data (yr. ended 04/30/02): Grants paid, $116,600; assets, $507,739 (M); gifts received, $200,000; expenditures, $117,985; qualifying distributions, $116,600.
Limitations: Applications not accepted. Giving limited to NY.

Application information: Contributes only to pre-selected organizations.
Officers: Francesco Giambelli, Pres.; Angelo Vivolo, V.P.; Mary Giambelli, Secy.; Samuel B. Keller, Treas.
EIN: 133580886

35219
Donald Grant & Ann Martin Calder Foundation
c/o Alan S. Berlin
101 Park Ave., Ste. 3500
New York, NY 10178-1061

Established in 1996 in DE.
Donor(s): Ann Martin Calder.
Financial data (yr. ended 12/31/01): Grants paid, $116,500; assets, $1,205,467 (M); expenditures, $120,330; qualifying distributions, $116,500.
Limitations: Applications not accepted.
Application information: Contributes only to pre-selected organizations.
Directors: Ann Martin Calder, Cornelia Martin Calder, Donald Grant Calder, Donald Grant Calder, Jr., Isabella Swift Calder.
EIN: 133917776

35220
Moses & Miriam Vogel Foundation
1130 E. 22nd St.
Brooklyn, NY 11210

Established in 1992 in NY.
Donor(s): Moses Vogel, Miriam Vogel, Sara Gross.
Financial data (yr. ended 12/31/01): Grants paid, $116,428; assets, $1,393,741 (M); gifts received, $316,684; expenditures, $120,531; qualifying distributions, $116,428.
Limitations: Applications not accepted.
Application information: Contributes only to pre-selected organizations.
Trustees: Miriam Vogel, Moses Vogel.
EIN: 136991651

35221
Morrie & Susan Golick Family Foundation, Inc.
50 E. 79th St., Ste. 15E
New York, NY 10021-0231
Contact: Susan Golick, Secy.-Treas.

Established in 1997 in FL.
Donor(s): Morrie Golick.
Financial data (yr. ended 09/30/01): Grants paid, $116,270; assets, $1,821,438 (M); expenditures, $158,451; qualifying distributions, $149,704.
Limitations: Applications not accepted.
Application information: Contributes only to pre-selected organizations.
Officers: Morrie Golick, Pres.; Susan Golick, Secy.-Treas.
EIN: 650798174
Codes: FD2

35222
The Joan C. & David L. Henle Foundation
c/o Goldman Sachs & Co.
85 Broad St., Tax Dept.
New York, NY 10004-2456

Established in 1996 in NY.
Donor(s): David L. Henle.
Financial data (yr. ended 08/31/01): Grants paid, $116,210; assets, $2,571,510 (M); gifts received, $1,463,188; expenditures, $129,097; qualifying distributions, $120,097.
Limitations: Applications not accepted. Giving primarily in NY.
Application information: Contributes only to pre-selected organizations.
Trustees: David L. Henle, Joan C. Henle.
EIN: 137103244
Codes: FD2

35223—NEW YORK

35223
Ellen M. Violett and Mary P. R. Thomas Foundation
(Formerly Ellen M. Violett Foundation, Inc.)
230 E. 50th St.
New York, NY 10022

Established in 1994 in NY.
Donor(s): Ellen M. Violett.
Financial data (yr. ended 04/30/01): Grants paid, $116,200; assets, $8,082 (M); gifts received, $100,300; expenditures, $117,966; qualifying distributions, $117,062.
Limitations: Applications not accepted. Giving primarily in New York, NY.
Application information: Contributes only to pre-selected organizations.
Officers: Ellen M. Violett, Pres.; Mary P.R. Thomas, V.P.; Herbert Bard, Secy.
EIN: 133767145
Codes: FD2

35224
William and Radine Spier Foundation
444 Madison Ave., 38th Fl.
New York, NY 10022-6903
Contact: William Spier, Pres.

Established in 1993 in NY.
Donor(s): William Spier, Radine Spier.
Financial data (yr. ended 11/30/00): Grants paid, $116,005; assets, $18,008 (M); gifts received, $99,158; expenditures, $118,291; qualifying distributions, $117,096.
Limitations: Giving primarily in NY.
Officers: William Spier, Pres. and Treas.; Radine Spier, V.P. and Secy.
EIN: 133749134

35225
Lazare and Charlotte Kaplan Foundation, Inc.
c/o Rouis & Co., LLP
P.O. Box 209
Wurtsboro, NY 12790
Application address: c/o P.O. Box 456, Livingston Manor, NY 12758
Contact: Leon Siegel, Pres.

Established in 1965 in NY.
Donor(s): George Kaplan, Lazare Kaplan.‡
Financial data (yr. ended 12/31/01): Grants paid, $115,800; assets, $1,815,957 (M); expenditures, $141,437; qualifying distributions, $115,328.
Limitations: Giving primarily in Livingston Manor, NY school district and Town of Rockland.
Application information: Payments are made directly to colleges on behalf of individuals; contact high school guidance counselor for information. Application form required.
Officers: Leon Siegel, Pres.; Mary Fried, Secy.; Irving Avery, Treas.
Trustee: George Kaplan.
EIN: 136193153
Codes: FD2, GTI

35226
The Ring Foundation, Inc.
20 W. 47th St., PH
New York, NY 10036

Established in 1979 in NY.
Donor(s): Frank Ring, Leo Ring, Michael Ring, Freda Ring.
Financial data (yr. ended 05/31/01): Grants paid, $115,790; assets, $4,062,294 (M); gifts received, $13,600; expenditures, $121,140; qualifying distributions, $115,790.
Limitations: Applications not accepted. Giving primarily in NY.

Application information: Contributes only to pre-selected organizations. Unsolicited requests for funds not considered.
Officers: Frank Ring, Pres.; Michael Ring, Secy.
EIN: 133015418
Codes: FD2

35227
Eulalia Dempsey Charitable Trust
201 N. Union St.
P.O. Box 690
Olean, NY 14760

Financial data (yr. ended 12/31/00): Grants paid, $115,750; assets, $1,425,682 (M); expenditures, $138,952; qualifying distributions, $115,750.
Trustees: Patrick Geary, Mary Jean Lucco, Community Bank.
EIN: 237909658
Codes: FD2

35228
Barbash Family Fund, Inc.
265 W. Main St.
Babylon, NY 11702-3419

Established in 1993 in NY.
Donor(s): Maurice Barbash, Lillian Barbash.
Financial data (yr. ended 12/31/00): Grants paid, $115,730; assets, $615,180 (M); gifts received, $300,000; expenditures, $115,930; qualifying distributions, $115,930.
Limitations: Applications not accepted. Giving primarily in NY.
Application information: Contributes only to pre-selected organizations.
Officers: Maurice Barbash, Pres.; Lillian Barbash, V.P.; Susan Barbash, Secy.
EIN: 113184479
Codes: FD2

35229
The McGrath Family Charitable Foundation Trust
c/o Thomas J. McGrath
988 5th Ave.
New York, NY 10021

Established in 1998 in NY.
Donor(s): Thomas J. McGrath.
Financial data (yr. ended 12/31/00): Grants paid, $115,701; assets, $11,434 (M); gifts received, $80,074; expenditures, $116,886; qualifying distributions, $115,661.
Limitations: Applications not accepted. Giving primarily in NY.
Application information: Contributes only to pre-selected organizations.
Trustees: Diahn W. McGrath, Thomas J. McGrath.
EIN: 137144702
Codes: FD2

35230
The Offensend Family Foundation
19 Monroe Pl.
Brooklyn, NY 11201

Established in 1998 in NY.
Financial data (yr. ended 12/31/01): Grants paid, $115,661; assets, $427,142 (M); expenditures, $124,588; qualifying distributions, $118,091.
Limitations: Applications not accepted. Giving primarily in Brooklyn, NY.
Application information: Contributes only to pre-selected organizations.
Trustees: David G. Offensend, Janet Mawdsley Offensend.
EIN: 134011882
Codes: FD2

35231
Zichron Yehuda Foundation, Inc.
1127 53rd St.
Brooklyn, NY 11219

Established in 1996 in NY.
Donor(s): Ernest Paskes.
Financial data (yr. ended 12/31/99): Grants paid, $115,553; assets, $454,741 (M); gifts received, $16,006; expenditures, $120,364; qualifying distributions, $120,364.
Limitations: Applications not accepted.
Application information: Contributes only to pre-selected organizations.
Officers: Ernest Paskes, Pres.; Yeheida Gutwein, Treas.
EIN: 113137557
Codes: FD2

35232
Goldhirsch Foundation
200 E. 61st St., Ste. 40B
New York, NY 10021

Donor(s): Fred P. Goldhirsch.
Financial data (yr. ended 12/31/01): Grants paid, $115,526; assets, $134,048 (M); gifts received, $20,000; expenditures, $119,203; qualifying distributions, $116,564.
Limitations: Applications not accepted. Giving primarily in New York, NY.
Application information: Contributes only to pre-selected organizations.
Officer: Fred P. Goldhirsch, Pres.
EIN: 136143944
Codes: FD2

35233
The Morningstar Foundation
5 Shalvah Pl.
Monsey, NY 10952-2427   (845) 356-1114
Contact: George Morgenstern, Tr.

Established in 1995 in NY.
Donor(s): George Morgenstern.
Financial data (yr. ended 08/31/01): Grants paid, $115,293; assets, $407,780 (M); gifts received, $108,432; expenditures, $116,924; qualifying distributions, $116,821.
Trustee: George Morgenstern.
EIN: 137049647
Codes: FD2

35234
The Morris & Ida Newman Family Foundation, Inc.
c/o Melvin D. Newman
145 Central Park West
New York, NY 10023-2004

Established in 1955 in NY.
Donor(s): Melvin Newman, Carol Newman.
Financial data (yr. ended 12/31/00): Grants paid, $115,227; assets, $949,666 (M); expenditures, $117,477; qualifying distributions, $114,046.
Limitations: Applications not accepted. Giving primarily in NY.
Application information: Contributes only to pre-selected organizations.
Officers: Melvin D. Newman, Pres.; Carol Newman, V.P.
Director: Joshua Newman.
EIN: 136162759
Codes: FD2

35235
Marcel and Veronica Weissman Family Foundation
70-24 170th St.
Flushing, NY 11365

Established in 1998 in NY.
Donor(s): Marcel Weissman.
Financial data (yr. ended 06/30/01): Grants paid, $115,086; assets, $14,954 (M); gifts received, $115,000; expenditures, $115,086; qualifying distributions, $230,171.
Limitations: Giving primarily in NY.
Directors: Marcel Weissman, Veronika Weissman.
EIN: 137153243
Codes: FD2

35236
Cloud Mountain Foundation
c/o Louis Sternbach & Co.
1212 6th Ave.
New York, NY 10036

Established in 1999 in MA.
Donor(s): Benjamin Friedman.
Financial data (yr. ended 12/31/00): Grants paid, $115,000; assets, $5,855,760 (M); gifts received, $5,059,908; expenditures, $116,011; qualifying distributions, $115,000.
Limitations: Applications not accepted.
Application information: Contributes only to pre-selected organizations.
Officer: Benjamin Friedman, Pres.
EIN: 043493352
Codes: FD2

35237
The Kallinikeion Foundation
c/o Bessemer Trust Co., N.A.
630 5th Ave, Tax Dept.
New York, NY 10111
Contact: Helen Hadjiyannakis Bender, Secy.

Established in 1994 in DE.
Donor(s): Alexandra Kallin.
Financial data (yr. ended 12/31/01): Grants paid, $115,000; assets, $3,153,972 (M); expenditures, $169,170; qualifying distributions, $133,510.
Limitations: Applications not accepted.
Application information: Contributes only to pre-selected organizations.
Officers: Alexandra Kallin, Pres.; Bishop Philotheos of Meloa, V.P.; Helen Hadjiyannakis Bender, Secy.; Froso Beys, Treas.
Directors: Emanuel G. Demos, Simos C. Dimas, Iakim of Chaklcedon, Robert G. Stephanopoulos.
EIN: 133752109
Codes: FD2

35238
Kane Lodge Foundation, Inc.
c/o The Bank of New York, Tax Dept.
1 Wall St., 28th Fl.
New York, NY 10286
Application address: 641 Lexington Ave., 18th Fl., New York, NY 10022
Contact: John Stichter, Pres.

Established in 1960 in NY.
Financial data (yr. ended 09/30/01): Grants paid, $115,000; assets, $2,110,907 (M); gifts received, $50,000; expenditures, $140,742; qualifying distributions, $122,177.
Limitations: Giving primarily in NY.
Officers: John Stichter, Pres.; Herman E. Muller, Jr., V.P.; John R. Ahlgren, Secy.; Peter Sulick, Jr., Treas.
Directors: P. Michael Puleo, Victor G. Webb, Rodney I. Woods.
EIN: 136105390
Codes: FD2

35239
Lockhart Family Charitable Trust
c/o U.S. Trust
P.O. Box 2004
New York, NY 10109-1910

Established in 1998.
Donor(s): Eugene Lockhart, Harry Lockhart.
Financial data (yr. ended 12/31/01): Grants paid, $115,000; assets, $75,858 (M); expenditures, $117,424; qualifying distributions, $118,450.
Limitations: Applications not accepted.
Application information: Contributes only to pre-selected organizations.
Trustees: Andrew J. Lockhart, H. Eugene Lockhart, Julia C. Lockhart, Terry J. Lockhart, U.S. Trust.
EIN: 066470176
Codes: FD2

35240
The Manton Foundation
c/o Eisenberg & Blau
150 Broadway, Ste. 1102
New York, NY 10038

Established in 1991 in NY.
Donor(s): Edwin A.G. Manton, Florence V. Manton.
Financial data (yr. ended 12/31/01): Grants paid, $115,000; assets, $3,259,046 (M); expenditures, $121,265; qualifying distributions, $115,000.
Limitations: Applications not accepted. Giving primarily in NY.
Application information: Contributes only to pre-selected organizations.
Trustees: Edwin A.G. Manton, Florence V. Manton, Diana H. Morton.
EIN: 133636372

35241
A. B. & J. Noyes Foundation, Inc.
50 Broad St.
New York, NY 10004-2307

Established in 1957 in NY.
Financial data (yr. ended 12/31/00): Grants paid, $115,000; assets, $1,585,773 (M); expenditures, $140,789; qualifying distributions, $115,325.
Limitations: Applications not accepted.
Application information: Contributes only to pre-selected organizations.
Officers: Jansen Noyes III, Pres. and Treas.; Marie L. Cusic, Secy.
Directors: Alfred F. King III, Shirley N. Lathrop, Margaret T. Noyes.
EIN: 136161124
Codes: FD2

35242
The RHP Family Foundation, Inc.
c/o Heidi G.C. Rieger
800 Old Post Rd.
Bedford, NY 10506

Established in 2000 in NY.
Donor(s): Heidi G.C. Rieger, Richard O. Rieger.
Financial data (yr. ended 09/30/01): Grants paid, $115,000; assets, $911,235 (M); expenditures, $125,684; qualifying distributions, $115,000.
Limitations: Applications not accepted. Giving primarily in New York, NY.
Application information: Contributes only to pre-selected organizations.
Officers: Heidi G.C. Rieger, Pres.; Richard O. Rieger, V.P. and Secy.-Treas.
Director: Jerome L. Levins.
EIN: 134093927

35243
Bella & Israel Unterberg Foundation, Inc.
c/o Leipziger & Breskin, LLP
6 E. 43rd St., 22nd Fl.
New York, NY 10017-4609

Incorporated in 1948 in NY.
Donor(s): Members of the Unterberg family.
Financial data (yr. ended 12/31/01): Grants paid, $115,000; assets, $1,112,521 (M); expenditures, $136,950; qualifying distributions, $115,000.
Limitations: Applications not accepted. Giving primarily in NY, with emphasis on the greater metropolitan New York, area.
Application information: Contributes only to pre-selected organizations.
Officers: Thomas I. Unterberg, Pres.; Mary A. DeBare, V.P. and Secy.; Andrew Arno, Treas.
EIN: 136099080
Codes: FD2

35244
The Walters Family Foundation, Inc.
c/o U.S. Trust, Attn.: Linda Franciscovich
114 W. 47th St., Tax VS
New York, NY 10036
Application address: 742B Cieneguitas Rd., Santa Barbara, CA 93110; E-mail: waltersfamilyfoundation@yahoo.com
Contact: Sarah K. Walters, Pres.

Established in 1960 in NY.
Financial data (yr. ended 12/31/00): Grants paid, $115,000; assets, $3,276,910 (M); expenditures, $141,177; qualifying distributions, $117,750.
Limitations: Giving on a national basis.
Application information: Application form not required.
Officers and Directors:* Sarah Walters,* Pres. and Secy.; Kathryn S. Walters,* V.P.; Mary E. Rust,* Treas.
EIN: 136107423
Codes: FD2

35245
Henry & Louise Loeb Fund
c/o Richard A. Eisner & Co.
575 Madison Ave.
New York, NY 10022

Established in 1975 in NY.
Donor(s): Henry A. Loeb.‡
Financial data (yr. ended 11/30/01): Grants paid, $114,915; assets, $377,199 (M); expenditures, $123,006; qualifying distributions, $118,010.
Limitations: Applications not accepted. Giving primarily in New York, NY.
Application information: Contributes only to pre-selected organizations.
Officer: Louise S. Loeb, Pres. and Treas.
EIN: 136085597
Codes: FD2

35246
The Shafran Foundation
(Formerly Steven and Janet Shafron Foundation)
c/o Behan, Ling, & Ruta, CPA
358 5th Fl., 9th Fl.
New York, NY 10001

Established in 1996 in NY.
Donor(s): Steven M. Shafran.
Financial data (yr. ended 06/30/01): Grants paid, $114,750; assets, $1,256,474 (M); expenditures, $146,545; qualifying distributions, $113,991.
Limitations: Applications not accepted.
Application information: Contributes only to pre-selected organizations.
Trustees: Janet Shafran, Steven M. Shafran.
EIN: 133954349
Codes: FD2

35247
Sani Family Foundation, Inc.
c/o RSM McGladrey, Inc.
380 Madison Ave.
New York, NY 10017-2513

Established in 1965 in NY.
Donor(s): Lal C. Sani, Ashok Sani, CGS Industries, Inc.
Financial data (yr. ended 01/31/01): Grants paid, $114,731; assets, $1,223,190 (M); gifts received, $382,500; expenditures, $115,715; qualifying distributions, $115,181.
Limitations: Applications not accepted. Giving primarily in NY.
Application information: Contributes only to pre-selected organizations.
Officers and Directors:* Sham G. Sani, Pres.; Lal C. Sani,* V.P. and Secy.; Ashok Sani.
Trustees: Sunil Sani, Suresh Sani.
EIN: 136201183
Codes: FD2

35248
Helen & Robert Cahill Foundation, Inc.
c/o Glenn Zalk, CPA
60 E. 42nd St., Ste. 1313
New York, NY 10165

Established in 1955 in NY.
Donor(s): Helen F. Cahill, Robert Cahill, Robert L. Cahill, Jr., Dover Fund.
Financial data (yr. ended 11/30/00): Grants paid, $114,550; assets, $194,494 (M); gifts received, $180,660; expenditures, $117,210; qualifying distributions, $115,126.
Limitations: Applications not accepted. Giving primarily in New York, NY.
Application information: Contributes only to pre-selected organizations.
Officers: Robert L. Cahill, Jr., Pres.; Helen F. Cahill, V.P.; Terence S. Meehan, Secy.
EIN: 136061289
Codes: FD2

35249
The Colonna Chang Family Foundation, Inc.
2 Litchfield Rd.
Port Washington, NY 11050
Contact: Barbara Chang, Secy.

Established in 1997 in NY.
Donor(s): Jerome Colonna, Barbara Chang.
Financial data (yr. ended 12/31/01): Grants paid, $114,480; assets, $89,627 (M); expenditures, $116,905; qualifying distributions, $114,801.
Limitations: Giving primarily in NY.
Officers: Jerome D. Colonna, Pres.; Barbara T. Chang, Secy.; Richard Krainin, Treas.
EIN: 113411145
Codes: FD2

35250
The Robert J. and Michele K. O'Shea Foundation
c/o BCRS Associates
67 Wall St., 8th FL.
New York, NY 10005

Established in 1996 in NJ.
Donor(s): Robert J. O'Shea.
Financial data (yr. ended 10/31/01): Grants paid, $114,350; assets, $5,533,864 (M); gifts received, $2,120,829; expenditures, $197,369; qualifying distributions, $114,350.
Limitations: Applications not accepted. Giving primarily in NJ.
Application information: Contributes only to pre-selected organizations.
Trustees: Michele K. O'Shea, Robert J. O'Shea.
EIN: 133926380

35251
Wahrsager Foundation
c/o American Express, Tax & Bus Svcs., Inc.
1185 6th Ave.
New York, NY 10036-2602

Established in 1961 in NY.
Donor(s): Members of the Wahrsager family.
Financial data (yr. ended 09/30/01): Grants paid, $114,268; assets, $1,873,809 (M); expenditures, $144,748; qualifying distributions, $127,976.
Limitations: Applications not accepted. Giving primarily in New York, NY.
Application information: Contributes only to pre-selected organizations.
Officer and Directors:* Karel Wahrsager,* Pres. and Treas.; Eve W. Linn.
EIN: 136034241
Codes: FD2

35252
Joseph R. Takats Foundation
135 Delaware Ave., Penthouse
Buffalo, NY 14202-2410

Established in 1977 in NY.
Donor(s): Joseph R. Takats, Jr., Joseph R. Takats III, Vanguard Industries, Inc.
Financial data (yr. ended 12/31/01): Grants paid, $114,150; assets, $2,845,039 (M); expenditures, $137,330; qualifying distributions, $114,150.
Limitations: Applications not accepted. Giving primarily in Buffalo, NY.
Application information: Contributes only to pre-selected organizations.
Trustees: Maura Lynn Leavitt, Joseph R. Takats III, Lee A. Takats.
EIN: 161098026
Codes: FD2

35253
Benjamin Gittlin Foundation
21 Penn Plz., Ste. 1000
360 West St.
New York, NY 10001

Established in 1953 in NJ.
Donor(s): Benjamin Co.
Financial data (yr. ended 12/31/00): Grants paid, $114,063; assets, $258,991 (M); gifts received, $108,000; expenditures, $117,108; qualifying distributions, $114,063.
Limitations: Applications not accepted. Giving primarily in FL, NJ, and NY.
Application information: Contributes only to pre-selected organizations.
Officer and Trustees:* B. Morton Gittlin,* Pres.; Bruce Gittlin, Steven Robert Gittlin.
EIN: 237041492
Codes: FD2

35254
James L. Greenwald Foundation
510 Park Ave.
New York, NY 10022-1105

Donor(s): James L. Greenwald.
Financial data (yr. ended 12/31/00): Grants paid, $113,741; assets, $1,031,888 (M); expenditures, $126,604; qualifying distributions, $119,426.
Limitations: Applications not accepted. Giving primarily in CT and New York, NY.
Application information: Contributes only to pre-selected organizations.
Trustees: James L. Greenwald, Marilee Greenwald.
EIN: 133799397
Codes: FD2

35255
The Muccia Family Fund
c/o First Manhattan Co.
437 Madison Ave.
New York, NY 10022

Established in 1993 in NY.
Donor(s): Carrol A. Muccia, Jr., Margaret D. Muccia.
Financial data (yr. ended 12/31/01): Grants paid, $113,670; assets, $982,590 (M); expenditures, $117,479; qualifying distributions, $112,316.
Limitations: Applications not accepted.
Application information: Contributes only to pre-selected organizations.
Officer: Carrol A. Muccia, Jr., Chair.
Trustee: Margaret D. Muccia.
EIN: 137002560
Codes: FD2

35256
The Walsh Family Foundation
c/o Marcum & Kliegman
130 Crossways Park Dr.
Woodbury, NY 11797

Established in 1998 in NY.
Financial data (yr. ended 12/31/01): Grants paid, $113,566; assets, $134,549 (M); gifts received, $96,400; expenditures, $130,157; qualifying distributions, $113,566.
Limitations: Applications not accepted. Giving primarily in NY.
Application information: Contributes only to pre-selected organizations.
Officer: Brian E. Walsh, Pres.
EIN: 133950961
Codes: FD2

35257
The Ashkin Family Foundation, Inc.
c/o Darby Group Co.
865 Merrick Ave.
Westbury, NY 11590   (516) 812-5675
Contact: Rose Sommer

Established in 1997.
Donor(s): Michael Ashkin.
Financial data (yr. ended 12/31/99): Grants paid, $113,500; assets, $2,291,944 (M); expenditures, $118,980; qualifying distributions, $113,850.
Limitations: Giving primarily in NY.
Officers and Directors:* Michael Ashkin,* Pres.; Laura Kahn,* Secy.; Carl Ashkin,* Treas.; Carl Kaplan, David Oifer, Joel Salon.
EIN: 133948212
Codes: FD2

35258
The Diana Bonnor Lewis Foundation, Inc.
c/o John D.B. Lewis
99 Hudson St.
New York, NY 10013

Established in 1985 in NY.
Donor(s): Diana Bonnor Lewis,‡ John D.B. Lewis.
Financial data (yr. ended 10/31/01): Grants paid, $113,500; assets, $403,538 (M); expenditures, $120,500; qualifying distributions, $113,847.
Limitations: Applications not accepted. Giving primarily in MT.
Application information: Contributes only to pre-selected organizations.
Officers and Directors:* John D.B. Lewis,* Pres. and Treas.; James Kaufman,* V.P. and Secy.; Lewis M. Steel.
EIN: 133314838
Codes: FD2

35259
The Alan & Laraine Fischer Foundation
28 Pryer Ln.
Larchmont, NY 10538
Contact: Alan Fischer, Pres.

Established in 1984 in NY.
Donor(s): Alan A. Fischer, Laraine Fischer.
Financial data (yr. ended 05/31/01): Grants paid, $113,478; assets, $20,997 (M); gifts received, $134,500; expenditures, $115,004; qualifying distributions, $113,478.
Limitations: Applications not accepted. Giving primarily in the greater New York, NY, area.
Application information: Contributes only to pre-selected organizations.
Officers and Directors:* Alan A. Fischer,* Pres.; Laraine Fischer,* Secy.-Treas.; Bernard Mindich.
EIN: 133235209
Codes: FD2

35260
The Reichmann Family Foundation
15 Harbor Park Dr.
Port Washington, NY 11050

Established in 1986 in NY.
Donor(s): Andre Reichmann.
Financial data (yr. ended 12/31/01): Grants paid, $113,426; assets, $466,513 (M); gifts received, $216,298; expenditures, $118,387; qualifying distributions, $113,426.
Limitations: Applications not accepted. Giving primarily in Kings and Queens counties, NY.
Application information: Contributes only to pre-selected organizations.
Officers: Charles Reichmann, Pres.; Andre Reichmann, V.P.; Louis Reichmann, V.P.; Marianne Reichmann, V.P.
EIN: 112813890
Codes: FD2

35261
Pamela and Stuart Rothenberg Foundation
c/o Goldman Sachs & Co.
85 Broad St., Tax Dept.
New York, NY 10004

Established in 1996 in NY.
Donor(s): Stuart M. Rothenberg.
Financial data (yr. ended 07/31/01): Grants paid, $113,361; assets, $1,749,438 (M); gifts received, $3,000; expenditures, $158,205; qualifying distributions, $116,705.
Limitations: Applications not accepted. Giving primarily in New York, NY.
Application information: Contributes only to pre-selected organizations.
Trustees: Pamela Rothenberg, Stuart M. Rothenberg.
EIN: 137109412
Codes: FD2

35262
Murray I. & Florence Zarin Foundation, Inc.
10 Lighthouse Rd.
Great Neck, NY 11024-1138

Donor(s): Florence Zarin.
Financial data (yr. ended 04/30/00): Grants paid, $113,225; assets, $3,283,213 (M); expenditures, $165,985; qualifying distributions, $117,415.
Limitations: Applications not accepted. Giving limited to NY.
Application information: Contributes only to pre-selected organizations.
Officers: Florence Zarin, Pres.; Murray I. Zarin, Treas.
EIN: 237039737

35263
John Michael Evans Foundation
c/o Goldman Sachs & Co.
85 Broad St., Tax Dept.
New York, NY 10004

Donor(s): John Michael Evans.
Financial data (yr. ended 05/31/01): Grants paid, $113,000; assets, $3,664,313 (M); gifts received, $1,459,687; expenditures, $155,330; qualifying distributions, $113,330.
Limitations: Applications not accepted. Giving primarily in Princeton, NJ, and New York, NY.
Application information: Contributes only to pre-selected organizations.
Trustees: Heather Richards Evans, John Michael Evans.
EIN: 133933323
Codes: FD2

35264
The Fadem Family Foundation, Inc.
10 Melrose Dr.
New Rochelle, NY 10804-4610

Established in 1996 in NY.
Donor(s): Leroy Fadem, Edna Mae Fadem.
Financial data (yr. ended 12/31/01): Grants paid, $112,900; assets, $2,190,150 (M); gifts received, $75,995; expenditures, $128,137; qualifying distributions, $112,900.
Limitations: Applications not accepted.
Application information: Contributes only to pre-selected organizations.
Officers: Edna Mae Fadem, Pres.; Leroy Fadem, Exec. V.P.; Barbara Fadem, Secy.; Steven Fadem, Treas.
EIN: 133907052
Codes: FD2

35265
Charles and Richard Oestreich Foundation, Inc.
c/o David A. Oestreich
641 Lexington Ave., 15th Fl.
New York, NY 10022

Established in 1946 in NY.
Financial data (yr. ended 11/30/01): Grants paid, $112,891; assets, $1,821,624 (M); expenditures, $131,583; qualifying distributions, $109,094.
Limitations: Applications not accepted. Giving primarily in NY.
Application information: Contributes only to pre-selected organizations.
Officers: David A. Oestreich, Pres.; Joan E. Kend, V.P.; Jay D. Waxenberg, Secy.; Lawrence M. Schallop, Treas.
EIN: 136097539
Codes: FD2

35266
The Oliver R. Grace Charitable Foundation
c/o Waldman, Hirsch, & Co., LLP
855 Ave. of the Americas, Ste. 623
New York, NY 10001
Contact: Lorraine G. Grace, Dir.

Established in 1992 in NY.
Donor(s): Lorraine G. Grace.
Financial data (yr. ended 12/31/00): Grants paid, $112,845; assets, $685,316 (M); expenditures, $118,148; qualifying distributions, $112,845.
Limitations: Applications not accepted. Giving primarily in Washington, DC, and NY.
Application information: Contributes only to pre-selected organizations.
Director: Lorraine G. Grace.
EIN: 113105739
Codes: FD2

35267
Bethesda Foundation, Inc.
396 Cleveland Ave.
Hornell, NY 14843-0296 (607) 324-1616
Application address: P.O. Box 296, Hornell, NY 14843-0296
Contact: Duane T. Heineman, Exec. Dir.

Established in 1987 in NY.
Financial data (yr. ended 12/31/01): Grants paid, $112,842; assets, $2,182,202 (M); gifts received, $50; expenditures, $168,222; qualifying distributions, $125,813.
Limitations: Giving limited to the Hornell, NY, area.
Publications: Informational brochure, application guidelines.
Application information: Application form required.
Officers and Directors:* Joseph Latham,* Pres.; Robert Wright,* V.P.; Jane Jamison,* Secy.; James VanBrunt,* Treas.; Duane T. Heineman,* Exec. Dir.; and 20 additional directors.
EIN: 160350390
Codes: FD2

35268
Abettor Foundation
135 Central Park W.
New York, NY 10023-2465

Established in 1998 in NY.
Donor(s): Bernice Manocherian.
Financial data (yr. ended 12/31/01): Grants paid, $112,836; assets, $9,222,354 (M); gifts received, $154,413; expenditures, $124,694; qualifying distributions, $115,586.
Limitations: Applications not accepted. Giving primarily in NY.
Application information: Contributes only to pre-selected organizations.
Trustee: Bernice Manocherian.
EIN: 137151571
Codes: FD2

35269
John-Christophe Schlesinger Foundation
14 West Ln.
Pound Ridge, NY 10576

Established in 1997 in NY.
Donor(s): Richard Schlesinger.
Financial data (yr. ended 12/31/01): Grants paid, $112,801; assets, $1,760,321 (M); gifts received, $52,100; expenditures, $145,617; qualifying distributions, $112,801.
Limitations: Applications not accepted.
Application information: Contributes only to pre-selected organizations.
Directors: A. Lauren Schlesinger, Katherine Schlesinger, Richard Schlesinger, Sheila Schlesinger.
EIN: 133984550

35270
Noah and Sadie Wachtel Foundation, Inc.
158 Fox Meadow Rd.
Scarsdale, NY 10583
Contact: Bernice R. Clyman, Secy.

Established in 1965 in NY.
Donor(s): Bernice R. Clyman, Arthur A. Wachtel, Sadie K. Wachtel.‡
Financial data (yr. ended 12/31/01): Grants paid, $112,772; assets, $1,805,093 (M); expenditures, $113,128; qualifying distributions, $111,766.
Limitations: Applications not accepted. Giving primarily in NY.
Application information: Contributes only to pre-selected organizations.

Officers and Trustees:* Arthur A. Wachtel,* Pres.; Sidney Clyman,* V.P.; Bernice R. Clyman,* Secy.; Phyllis Wachtel,* Treas.
EIN: 136204681
Codes: FD2

35271
Lucille A. Herold Trust
c/o HSBC Bank USA
126 State St.
Albany, NY 12207
Application address: c/o Richard P. Wallace, Esq., Martin Shudt Law Firm, 279 River St., Troy, NY 12180

Established around 1976.
Donor(s): Lucille A. Herold.‡
Financial data (yr. ended 10/31/01): Grants paid, $112,700; assets, $2,177,575 (M); expenditures, $175,877; qualifying distributions, $116,860.
Limitations: Giving primarily in Troy and Albany, NY.
Trustees: Robert B. MacChesney, Richard Wallace, HSBC Bank USA.
EIN: 146100040
Codes: FD2

35272
Ahavas Chesed Foundation
c/o Kruger
1565 51st St.
Brooklyn, NY 11219

Established in 2000 in NY.
Financial data (yr. ended 12/31/00): Grants paid, $112,680; assets, $1,532,917 (M); gifts received, $290,000; expenditures, $332,016; qualifying distributions, $112,680.
Trustees: Marilyn Gips, Leah Lefkovitz, Toby Salczer.
EIN: 113534362
Codes: FD2

35273
Jacobowitz Chesed Fund
c/o Howard & Carol Jacobowitz
P.O. Box 667
Staten Island, NY 10314

Established in 1997 in NY.
Donor(s): Carol Jacobowitz, Howard Jacobowitz.
Financial data (yr. ended 12/31/01): Grants paid, $112,599; assets, $1,110,961 (M); gifts received, $1,000; expenditures, $116,079; qualifying distributions, $111,720.
Limitations: Applications not accepted.
Application information: Contributes only to pre-selected organizations.
Trustees: Carol Jacobowitz, Howard Jacobowitz.
EIN: 133932576
Codes: FD2

35274
The SES Foundation, Inc.
1650 63rd St.
Brooklyn, NY 11204-2713

Established in 2000 in NY.
Donor(s): Gericare Pharmaceuticals.
Financial data (yr. ended 11/30/01): Grants paid, $112,580; assets, $17,398 (M); gifts received, $130,000; expenditures, $112,732; qualifying distributions, $112,580.
Officer: Eli Shindler, Pres.
EIN: 113579451
Codes: FD2

35275
W. Bruce Cook and Mary Louise Cook Foundation
c/o U.S. Trust
114 W. 47th St., TaxVas
New York, NY 10036
Contact: Linda Franciscovich, Sr. VP and Trust Off., U.S. Trust

Established in 1998 in FL.
Donor(s): W. Bruce Cook.
Financial data (yr. ended 12/31/00): Grants paid, $112,500; assets, $2,287,045 (M); expenditures, $124,069; qualifying distributions, $114,911.
Limitations: Applications not accepted.
Application information: Contributes only to pre-selected organizations.
Trustee: W. Bruce Cook.
EIN: 656285872
Codes: FD2

35276
Timothy Dattels and Kristine Johnson Foundation
c/o Goldman Sachs & Co.
85 Broad St., Tax Dept.
New York, NY 10004-2456

Established in 1998 in NY.
Donor(s): Timothy Dattels.
Financial data (yr. ended 03/31/02): Grants paid, $112,500; assets, $864,822 (M); gifts received, $1,182; expenditures, $112,743; qualifying distributions, $112,743.
Limitations: Applications not accepted.
Application information: Contributes only to pre-selected organizations.
Trustees: Timothy D. Dattels, Kristine Johnson, Thomas S. Murphy, Jr.
EIN: 133931294
Codes: FD2

35277
The Peter Jennings Foundation, Inc.
c/o Squadron, Ellenoff, Plesent & Sheinfeld
551 5th Ave.
New York, NY 10176

Established in 1998 in DE and NY.
Donor(s): Peter Jennings.
Financial data (yr. ended 12/31/01): Grants paid, $112,500; assets, $1,595,306 (M); gifts received, $123,693; expenditures, $147,253; qualifying distributions, $112,500.
Limitations: Applications not accepted. Giving primarily in NY.
Application information: Contributes only to pre-selected organizations.
Officers: Peter Jennings, Pres.; Mark J. Weinstein, Treas.
EIN: 134033625
Codes: FD2

35278
Samourkas Foundation of New York
(Formerly Athena Cultural Foundation)
c/o Theodoros Samourkas
350 5th Ave., Ste. 3304
New York, NY 10118

Donor(s): Theodoros Samourkas.
Financial data (yr. ended 12/31/01): Grants paid, $112,500; assets, $58,576 (M); gifts received, $170,000; expenditures, $112,790; qualifying distributions, $112,500.
Limitations: Applications not accepted. Giving primarily in CT, MA, and New York, NY.
Application information: Contributes only to pre-selected organizations.
Officer: Theodoros Samourkas, Pres.
EIN: 521386946

Codes: FD2

35279
Shahmoon Family Foundation, Inc.
c/o Diana Blustain
P.O. Box 488
Remsenburg, NY 11960

Established in 1993 in DE.
Financial data (yr. ended 12/31/01): Grants paid, $112,500; assets, $1,812,350 (M); expenditures, $115,078; qualifying distributions, $114,032.
Limitations: Applications not accepted. Giving primarily in NY.
Application information: Contributes only to pre-selected organizations.
Officers: Rebecca Shahmoon, Pres.; Diana Blustain, V.P.; Sassoon Shahmoon, Secy.
EIN: 133668964
Codes: FD2

35280
Erdle Foundation, Inc.
1500 Jefferson Rd.
Rochester, NY 14623-3162
Contact: Jack A. Erdle, Pres.

Established around 1964 in NY.
Donor(s): Jack A. Erdle, Norma Erdle.
Financial data (yr. ended 12/31/01): Grants paid, $112,393; assets, $2,414,975 (M); gifts received, $300,000; expenditures, $114,079; qualifying distributions, $112,602.
Limitations: Applications not accepted. Giving primarily in FL and NY.
Application information: Contributes only to pre-selected organizations.
Officers: Jack A. Erdle, Pres.; Harvey B. Erdle, V.P.; Brenda Moss, V.P.; Norma Erdle, Secy.; Erin M. Kaplan.
EIN: 237002682
Codes: FD2

35281
Saranac Lake Voluntary Health Association, Inc.
70 Main St.
Saranac Lake, NY 12983-1706

Established in 1942 in NY.
Financial data (yr. ended 03/31/01): Grants paid, $112,368; assets, $2,931,383 (M); gifts received, $2,670; expenditures, $140,205; qualifying distributions, $126,787.
Limitations: Applications not accepted. Giving limited to Saranac Lake, NY.
Application information: Contributes only to pre-selected organizations.
Officers: Robert Allen, M.D., Pres.; Roger Neill, V.P.; Cathy Kraft, Secy.; Chester Beeman, Treas.
Directors: Leonard Bristol, M.D., Irving B. Hunt, Richard Kasulke, M.D., Alexander Mitchell, Charles Monts, Donald A. Richter, M.D., Lynn Saar, Jeannette Sheppard, William A. Sweeny, Alice Wareham, Robert E. White.
EIN: 150532253
Codes: FD2, GTI

35282
Schlein Foundation, Inc.
23 Sleepy Hollow Rd.
Rye Brook, NY 10573-1045

Established in 1948 in NY.
Donor(s): Jeffrey G. Schlein, Richard S. Schlein.
Financial data (yr. ended 12/31/00): Grants paid, $112,350; assets, $3,109,695 (M); gifts received, $2,500; expenditures, $121,617; qualifying distributions, $112,350.
Limitations: Applications not accepted. Giving primarily in NY.

Application information: Contributes only to pre-selected organizations.
Officers: Barbara S. Schlein, Pres.; Jennifer Schlein, V.P.; Robert Schlein, V.P.; Jeffrey G. Schlein, Secy.-Treas.
EIN: 237416728
Codes: FD2

35283
The Low Foundation, Inc.
c/o Grant Thornton, LLP
60 Broad St.
New York, NY 10004

Established in 1952.
Donor(s): Barbara L. Karatz.
Financial data (yr. ended 08/31/01): Grants paid, $112,305; assets, $1,212,184 (M); expenditures, $132,592; qualifying distributions, $115,829.
Limitations: Applications not accepted. Giving primarily in NY.
Application information: Contributes only to pre-selected organizations.
Officers and Directors:* William W. Karatz,* Pres.; Joshua L. Gutfreund, V.P.; Nicholas Gutfreund, V.P.; Owen D. Gutfreund, V.P.; Lawrence Buttenwieser,* Treas.
EIN: 136062712
Codes: FD2

35284
The Stanley J. Arkin Foundation, Inc.
c/o Rose Ridge Mgmt. Co.
575 Lexington Ave., 9th Fl.
New York, NY 10122-6102
Contact: Stanley J. Arkin, Pres.

Established in 1982 in NY.
Donor(s): Stanley J. Arkin.
Financial data (yr. ended 09/30/01): Grants paid, $112,300; assets, $555,679 (M); gifts received, $21,594; expenditures, $133,965; qualifying distributions, $119,953.
Limitations: Applications not accepted. Giving primarily in New York, NY.
Application information: Contributes only to pre-selected organizations.
Officers and Directors:* Stanley J. Arkin,* Pres.; Harold Cohen,* V.P.; Barbara D. Arkin,* Secy.-Treas.
EIN: 133105382
Codes: FD2

35285
Mele Foundation, Inc.
c/o Adolph Levin
53-04 192nd St.
Flushing, NY 11365

Established in 1954 in NY.
Donor(s): Edward V. Mele, Joseph E. Mele, Mele Manufacturing Co., Inc.
Financial data (yr. ended 12/31/01): Grants paid, $112,266; assets, $5,094,680 (M); gifts received, $43,737; expenditures, $139,320; qualifying distributions, $112,266.
Limitations: Giving primarily in KY and NY.
Officers: Edward V. Mele, Pres.; Joseph E. Mele, V.P.
EIN: 116005883
Codes: FD2

35286
The Austin Foundation, Inc.
480 Broadway, Ste. 250
Saratoga Springs, NY 12866

Established in 1994 in NY.
Donor(s): Jane G. Head.
Financial data (yr. ended 11/30/00): Grants paid, $112,200; assets, $3,902,708 (M); expenditures, $149,039; qualifying distributions, $112,200.
Limitations: Applications not accepted. Giving primarily in MD and WI.
Application information: Contributes only to pre-selected organizations.
Officers: Stephen R. Markovits, Pres.; Jane G. Head, Secy.-Treas.
Directors: Kim A. Head, Mark Head, Karen H. Schlegel.
EIN: 141777852
Codes: FD2

35287
Hymowitz Family Foundation Trust
c/o Speer & Fulvio, LLP
60 E. 62nd St., Ste. 1313
New York, NY 10165-0006

Established in 1999 in NY.
Donor(s): Gregg S. Hymowitz.
Financial data (yr. ended 06/30/00): Grants paid, $112,093; assets, $19,826 (M); gifts received, $153,072; expenditures, $112,108; qualifying distributions, $112,093.
Limitations: Applications not accepted. Giving primarily in New York, NY.
Application information: Contributes only to pre-selected organizations.
Trustees: Deborah Hymowitz, Gregg S. Hymowitz.
EIN: 134089721
Codes: FD2

35288
The Warwick Savings Foundation
591 Rte. 17M
P.O. Box 507
Monroe, NY 10950

Established in 1997 in NY.
Donor(s): Newburgh, Inc.
Financial data (yr. ended 12/31/00): Grants paid, $112,000; assets, $2,244,881 (M); expenditures, $122,129; qualifying distributions, $111,301.
Limitations: Applications not accepted.
Application information: Contributes only to pre-selected organizations.
Officers: Timothy A. Dempsey, Pres.; Ronald J. Gentile, Exec. V.P.; Arthur W. Budich, V.P. and Treas.; Nancy L. Sobotor-Littell, Secy.
Directors: Peter H. Alberghini, Frances M. Groish, Michael Hoffman, Thomas F. Lawrence, Jr., Sr. Ann Sakac, Robert H. Smith.
EIN: 061504632
Codes: FD2

35289
The Buccino Foundation
200 E. 69th St., Rm. 310-C
New York, NY 10021
Contact: Gerald P. Buccino, Pres.

Established in 1990 IL.
Donor(s): Gerald P. Buccino.
Financial data (yr. ended 12/31/00): Grants paid, $111,988; assets, $961,368 (M); gifts received, $49,864; expenditures, $114,091; qualifying distributions, $111,988.
Limitations: Giving on a national basis.
Application information: Application form required.
Officers and Directors:* Gerald P. Buccino,* Pres.; Lorraine M. Buccino, Secy.; Gerard J. Buccino,* Treas.
EIN: 363743267
Codes: FD2

35290
The Balsamo Family Foundation, Inc.
c/o BCRS Assoc(s). LLC
100 Wall St., 11th Fl.
New York, NY 10005

Established in 1999 in NY.
Donor(s): Stephen Balsamo.
Financial data (yr. ended 09/30/01): Grants paid, $111,756; assets, $1,095,748 (M); gifts received, $1,088,334; expenditures, $114,872; qualifying distributions, $112,319.
Limitations: Applications not accepted. Giving primarily in NY.
Application information: Contributes only to pre-selected organizations.
Officers: Stephen Balsamo, Pres. and Treas.; Susan Balsamo, V.P. and Secy.; Kathryn Balsamo, V.P.
EIN: 134101107
Codes: FD2

35291
The Angerman Foundation
16 Easthaven Ln.
White Plains, NY 10605

Established in 1999 in NY.
Financial data (yr. ended 09/30/01): Grants paid, $111,720; assets, $1,310,620 (M); expenditures, $122,556; qualifying distributions, $117,400.
Limitations: Applications not accepted.
Application information: Contributes only to pre-selected organizations.
Directors: Arnold Angerman, Dorothy Angerman, Irving Angerman.
EIN: 134090169
Codes: FD2

35292
Joan Stanton Irrevocable Charitable Trust
c/o Starr & Co.
350 Park Ave.
New York, NY 10022

Established in 1988 in NY.
Donor(s): Joan A. Stanton.
Financial data (yr. ended 12/31/01): Grants paid, $111,550; assets, $3,222 (M); gifts received, $110,000; expenditures, $111,576; qualifying distributions, $111,549.
Limitations: Applications not accepted. Giving primarily in NY.
Application information: Contributes only to pre-selected organizations.
Trustee: Joan A. Stanton.
EIN: 136892875
Codes: FD2

35293
The Furniss Foundation
c/o Smith Barney Pr. Tr. Co.
153 E. 53rd St., 23rd Fl.
New York, NY 10043
Application address: 320 Handy Rd., Newnan, GA 30263
Contact: Peter Furniss, Tr.

Established in 1996 in GA.
Donor(s): Gail S. Furniss, Peter Furniss.
Financial data (yr. ended 12/31/01): Grants paid, $111,500; assets, $1,582,468 (M); expenditures, $127,443; qualifying distributions, $110,672.
Limitations: Giving primarily in West Palm Beach, FL.
Application information: Application form required.
Trustee: Peter Furniss.
EIN: 582273968
Codes: FD2

35294
Gerson Family Foundation, Inc.
19 W. 95th St.
New York, NY 10025

Established in 1993 in NY.
Donor(s): James Gerson, Ruth Joffe, Barbara N. Gerson.
Financial data (yr. ended 09/30/01): Grants paid, $111,500; assets, $1,815,034 (M); expenditures, $114,915; qualifying distributions, $113,591.
Limitations: Applications not accepted. Giving primarily in CT, MA, and NY.
Application information: Contributes only to pre-selected organizations.
Officer: James Gerson, Pres.
Directors: Barbara N. Gerson, Richard A. Krantz.
EIN: 133750336
Codes: FD2

35295
Martin D. & Jean Shafiroff Foundation
c/o Barry M. Strauss Assoc., Ltd.
307 5th Ave., 8th Fl.
New York, NY 10016-6517

Established in 1986 in NY.
Donor(s): Martin D. Shafiroff.
Financial data (yr. ended 03/31/01): Grants paid, $111,437; assets, $644,013 (M); gifts received, $530,550; expenditures, $110,774; qualifying distributions, $111,437.
Limitations: Applications not accepted. Giving primarily in NY.
Application information: Contributes only to pre-selected organizations.
Trustees: John Lutri, Jean Shafiroff, Martin D. Shafiroff.
EIN: 136880147

35296
Aaron Laub Memorial Foundation, Inc.
17-20 Whitestone Expwy.
Whitestone, NY 11357

Established in 1988 in NY.
Donor(s): Norman A. Septimies, Perry Chemical Corp.
Financial data (yr. ended 11/30/01): Grants paid, $111,373; assets, $791,768 (M); gifts received, $263,400; expenditures, $113,096; qualifying distributions, $113,096.
Limitations: Applications not accepted. Giving primarily in NY, especially Brooklyn and Queens County, and NJ; giving also in Israel.
Application information: Contributes only to pre-selected organizations.
Officers: Eva Lamb Kunstler, Pres.; Irving Laub, V.P.; Jack Feigenbaum, Secy.
EIN: 113018695
Codes: FD2

35297
Herman & Lenore Rottenberg Foundation, Inc.
c/o Spitz & Greenstein, CPA
21 E. 40th St., No. 1006
New York, NY 10016-0501 (212) 889-7776
Application address: 115 Central Park West,
New York, NY 10023
Contact: Herman Rottenberg, Pres.

Donor(s): Herman Rottenberg.
Financial data (yr. ended 01/31/02): Grants paid, $111,290; assets, $1,855,202 (M); expenditures, $119,207; qualifying distributions, $111,290.
Limitations: Giving primarily in New York, NY.
Officer: Herman Rottenberg, Pres.
EIN: 136132611
Codes: FD2

35298
The Judith Riklis Foundation
c/o George V. Delson Assocs.
110 E. 59th St.
New York, NY 10022

Established in 1982 in NY.
Donor(s): Marcia Hirschfeld, Judith Riklis.
Financial data (yr. ended 08/31/01): Grants paid, $111,270; assets, $147,897 (M); gifts received, $101,390; expenditures, $112,809; qualifying distributions, $112,434.
Limitations: Applications not accepted. Giving primarily in NY.
Application information: Contributes only to pre-selected organizations.
Trustees: George V. Delson, Sylvia Garland, Judith Riklis.
EIN: 133139781
Codes: FD2

35299
The William Brown Foundation, Inc.
c/o Morrison, Cohen, Singer & Weinstein, LLP
750 Lexington Ave., 8th Fl.
New York, NY 10022 (212) 735-8600

Established in 1986 in NY.
Donor(s): William Brown.
Financial data (yr. ended 12/31/01): Grants paid, $111,000; assets, $2,224,529 (M); gifts received, $161,659; expenditures, $124,281; qualifying distributions, $109,880.
Limitations: Applications not accepted. Giving primarily in NY.
Application information: Contributes only to pre-selected organizations.
Directors: Geoffrey Bareket, Jerome Tarnoff, Mark Weingarten.
EIN: 133307838
Codes: FD2

35300
Alfred & Jane Ross Foundation, Inc.
c/o Yohalem Gillman & Co., LLP
477 Madison Ave.
New York, NY 10022
Contact: Elizabeth Morin, Acct.

Established in 1992 in DE.
Donor(s): Arthur Ross, Jane Ross.
Financial data (yr. ended 12/31/01): Grants paid, $110,992; assets, $4,772,144 (M); expenditures, $192,867; qualifying distributions, $120,350.
Limitations: Applications not accepted. Giving on a national basis.
Application information: Contributes only to pre-selected organizations.
Officers: Alfred F. Ross, Pres.; Jane Ross, V.P.; Stanley Gillman, Secy.-Treas.
EIN: 133680380
Codes: FD2

35301
Mirimac Fund, Inc.
301 Roaring Brook Rd.
Chappaqua, NY 10514

Established in 1958 in NY.
Donor(s): Maxwell W. Passerman,‡ Miriam R. Passerman.
Financial data (yr. ended 07/31/01): Grants paid, $110,875; assets, $1,810,130 (M); expenditures, $128,050; qualifying distributions, $115,716.
Limitations: Applications not accepted. Giving primarily in FL, ME, and NY.
Application information: Contributes only to pre-selected organizations.
Officers: Louise Rosenfeld, Pres.; Steven R. Passerman, V.P.; Gabriel I. Rosenfeld, Secy.; Harriet Passerman, Treas.
EIN: 136100575
Codes: FD2

35302
Susan & David Horowitz Foundation
(Formerly Abraham & Florence Horowitz Foundation)
1285 Ave. of the Americas, 21st Fl.
New York, NY 10019

Established in 1990 in NY.
Donor(s): Florence B. Horowitz, David H. Horowitz.
Financial data (yr. ended 06/30/01): Grants paid, $110,540; assets, $996,075 (M); expenditures, $119,443; qualifying distributions, $110,540.
Limitations: Applications not accepted. Giving limited to Washington, DC, Santa Fe, NM, and New York, NY.
Application information: Contributes only to pre-selected organizations.
Directors: David H. Horowitz, Susan W. Horowitz.
EIN: 133593961
Codes: FD2

35303
Meier Bernstein Foundation
10 Plaza St., Apt. 9G
Brooklyn, NY 11238-4932

Established in 1989.
Financial data (yr. ended 12/31/01): Grants paid, $110,500; assets, $2,088,388 (M); expenditures, $146,829; qualifying distributions, $135,019.
Limitations: Applications not accepted. Giving primarily in FL and Brooklyn, NY.
Application information: Contributes only to pre-selected organizations.
Officers and Directors:* Carol Leshner,* Pres.; Michael D'Antuono,* V.P.
EIN: 110017047
Codes: FD2

35304
Curtis & Katharine Welling Foundation
c/o Siegel Sacks & Co.
630 3rd Ave.
New York, NY 10017

Established in 1987 in NY.
Financial data (yr. ended 12/31/01): Grants paid, $110,495; assets, $105,632 (M); expenditures, $122,490; qualifying distributions, $110,405.
Limitations: Applications not accepted. Giving primarily in CT and NY.
Application information: Contributes only to pre-selected organizations.
Officers and Trustees:* Curtis Welling,* Pres.; Katharine Welling,* V.P.
EIN: 112848995
Codes: FD2

35305
The Joseph & Rachel Ades Foundation
(Formerly Ades Foundation, Inc.)
80 Cuttermill Rd., Ste. 205
Great Neck, NY 11021

Incorporated in 1945 in NY.
Donor(s): Joseph Ades,‡ Isaac Ades, Irving Baron, Barney Bernstein, Joseph Karp.
Financial data (yr. ended 12/31/01): Grants paid, $110,444; assets, $796,421 (M); expenditures, $113,674; qualifying distributions, $110,444.
Limitations: Applications not accepted. Giving primarily in New York, NY.
Application information: Contributes only to pre-selected organizations.
Officers: Albert Ades, Pres.; Robert Ades, V.P.; Joseph A. Ades, Secy.; Michael Ades, Treas.

EIN: 136077369
Codes: FD2

35306
Helen Thomas Howland Testamentary Trust Foundation
c/o M&T Bank, Tax Dept.
P.O. Box 22900
Rochester, NY 14692-2900
Application address: c/o M&T Bank, 2 Court St., Binghamton, NY 13901

Established in 1991 in NY.
Financial data (yr. ended 06/30/01): Grants paid, $110,356; assets, $2,060,611 (M); expenditures, $128,200; qualifying distributions, $110,553.
Limitations: Giving primarily in Broome and Tompkins counties, NY.
Trustee: M & T Bank.
EIN: 166353030
Codes: FD2

35307
Shai Charitable Trust
4 Misty Ln.
Suffern, NY 10901
Contact: Gilbert Backenroth, Tr.; or Ruth Backenroth, Tr.

Established in 1996 in NY.
Donor(s): Gilbert Backenroth, Ruth Backenroth.
Financial data (yr. ended 12/31/01): Grants paid, $110,176; assets, $45,565 (M); gifts received, $50,000; expenditures, $110,176; qualifying distributions, $110,176.
Limitations: Applications not accepted. Giving primarily in NY.
Application information: Contributes only to pre-selected organizations.
Trustees: Gilbert Backenroth, Ruth Backenroth.
EIN: 137083787
Codes: FD2

35308
Rose & Robert Edelman Foundation, Inc.
187-11 Aberdeen Rd.
Jamaica, NY 11432-5810 (718) 454-1978
Contact: Irving A. Olshever, Tr.

Established in 1983 in NY.
Donor(s): Robert Edelman.
Financial data (yr. ended 06/30/01): Grants paid, $110,098; assets, $2,077,120 (M); expenditures, $330,784; qualifying distributions, $110,098.
Limitations: Giving primarily in New York, NY.
Trustees: Samuel Edelman, Irving A. Olshever, Shirley E. Olshever.
EIN: 133209599
Codes: FD2

35309
The Jacob Marley Foundation, Inc.
c/o Diana Holden
49 Amherst Rd.
Port Washington, NY 11050

Established in 1993 in NY.
Donor(s): Christopher Quackenbush,‡ Traci Quackenbush.
Financial data (yr. ended 12/31/00): Grants paid, $110,044; assets, $3,517,998 (M); gifts received, $1,104,796; expenditures, $247,325; qualifying distributions, $132,233; giving activities include $67,867 for programs.
Limitations: Applications not accepted. Giving primarily in New York, NY.
Application information: Unsolicited requests for funds not accepted.
Officers and Directors:* Traci Quackenbush,* V.P. and Treas.; Carlton D. Brown,* V.P.; James J. Dunne III, Michael A. Quakenbush.

EIN: 113165445
Codes: FD2

35310
Leibowitz and Greenway Family Charitable Foundation
80 Pierrepoint St., Ste. 4
Brooklyn, NY 11201

Established in 2000 in FL and NY.
Donor(s): Lawrence Leibowitz.
Financial data (yr. ended 12/31/01): Grants paid, $110,000; assets, $885,198 (M); gifts received, $500,000; expenditures, $112,568; qualifying distributions, $110,000.
Limitations: Applications not accepted.
Application information: Contributes only to pre-selected organizations.
Trustees: Tara Greenway-Leibowitz, Lawrence Leibowitz.
EIN: 656358233

35311
James A. Moore Foundation for Otologic Research
c/o Neuberger & Berman
605 3rd Ave.
New York, NY 10158

Financial data (yr. ended 12/31/00): Grants paid, $110,000; assets, $649,020 (M); expenditures, $121,131; qualifying distributions, $110,000.
Limitations: Applications not accepted. Giving limited to MA, NC, and NY.
Application information: Contributes only to pre-selected organizations.
Officers: Eleanor M. Sterne, Pres. and Treas.; Douglas Moore, V.P. and Secy.
EIN: 136153634
Codes: FD2

35312
Peter S. Reed Foundation, Inc.
(Formerly The Concrete Foundation, Inc.)
c/o Holland & Knight, LLP
195 Broadway, 23rd Fl.
New York, NY 10007
Contact: Mary Ellen Sweeney, Legal Asst.

Established in 1979.
Donor(s): Peter S. Reed.‡
Financial data (yr. ended 06/30/02): Grants paid, $110,000; assets, $2,128,105 (M); expenditures, $153,929; qualifying distributions, $129,726.
Limitations: Applications not accepted. Giving primarily in the New York, NY, area.
Application information: Unsolicited requests for funds not accepted.
Officers and Directors:* Arne Svenson,* Pres.; Foster Reed,* V.P.; Frances Murdock,* Secy.; Mark McDonald,* Treas.; Rosalind Lichter, Dorothy Reed.
EIN: 133036536
Codes: FD2

35313
The Squirrel Foundation
c/o BCRS Associates, LLC
100 Wall St., 11th Fl.
New York, NY 10005

Established in 1995 in NJ.
Donor(s): Zachariah Cobrinik.
Financial data (yr. ended 08/31/01): Grants paid, $110,000; assets, $1,007,957 (M); gifts received, $1,088,383; expenditures, $112,800; qualifying distributions, $110,750.
Limitations: Applications not accepted. Giving primarily in New York, NY.
Application information: Contributes only to pre-selected organizations.

Trustees: Zachariah Cobrinik, Latifa Louah.
EIN: 133797377
Codes: FD2

35314
The Tiffany and Co. Foundation
727 5th Ave.
New York, NY 10022 (212) 230-6591
URL: http://www.tiffanyandcofoundation.org
Contact: Fernanda M. Kellogg, V.P.

Established in 1999 in NY.
Donor(s): Tiffany and Co.
Financial data (yr. ended 01/31/02): Grants paid, $110,000; assets, $6,003,268 (M); gifts received, $2,000,000; expenditures, $118,485; qualifying distributions, $118,485.
Limitations: Giving on a national basis.
Officers: Michael J. Kowalski, Pres.; James N. Fernandez, Exec. V.P.; Fernanda M. Kellogg, V.P.; Patrick B. Dorsey, Secy.; Michael W. Connolly, Treas.
EIN: 134096178
Codes: CS, FD2, CD

35315
Tsadra Foundation
P.O. Box 20192
New York, NY 10014

Established in 2000 in NY.
Donor(s): Eric Colombel.
Financial data (yr. ended 12/31/00): Grants paid, $110,000; assets, $26,579 (M); gifts received, $140,000; expenditures, $113,421; qualifying distributions, $73,421.
Limitations: Applications not accepted. Giving on a national and international basis.
Trustee: Eric Colombel.
EIN: 137224970
Codes: FD2

35316
Pierre J. Wertheimer Foundation, Inc.
9 W. 57th St.
New York, NY 10019

Established in 1960 in NY.
Financial data (yr. ended 10/31/01): Grants paid, $110,000; assets, $80,510 (M); gifts received, $110,000; expenditures, $110,144; qualifying distributions, $110,144.
Limitations: Giving primarily in New York, NY.
Officers: Alain Wertheimer, Pres.; Michael Rena, V.P.; Charles Heilbronn, Secy.
EIN: 136161226
Codes: FD2

35317
The Martin & Barbara Zweig Family Foundation, Inc.
900 3rd Ave.
New York, NY 10022

Established in 1998 in NY.
Donor(s): Martin Zweig.
Financial data (yr. ended 12/31/00): Grants paid, $110,000; assets, $4,524,707 (M); gifts received, $2,000,000; expenditures, $116,714; qualifying distributions, $110,000.
Limitations: Applications not accepted. Giving primarily in NY.
Application information: Contributes only to pre-selected organizations.
Officers: Martin Zweig, Pres.; Barbara Zweig, Secy.
EIN: 061534181
Codes: FD2

35318—NEW YORK

35318
Blumenkrantz Foundation
880 5th Ave.
New York, NY 10021

Established around 1949.
Financial data (yr. ended 10/31/01): Grants paid, $109,930; assets, $1,523,069 (M); expenditures, $112,097; qualifying distributions, $109,930.
Limitations: Applications not accepted. Giving primarily in NY.
Application information: Contributes only to pre-selected organizations.
Trustees: Neil Allen, Robert Allen, Selma B. Allen, Michelle Jacobs.
EIN: 136097509
Codes: FD2

35319
The Arell Foundation, Inc.
c/o Listowel, Inc.
2 Park Ave., Ste. 1525
New York, NY 10016-5790

Established in 1978 in NY.
Donor(s): Ralph Landau.
Financial data (yr. ended 12/31/01): Grants paid, $109,898; assets, $2,701,081 (M); expenditures, $116,888; qualifying distributions, $113,876.
Limitations: Applications not accepted. Giving primarily in Stanford, CA.
Application information: Contributes only to pre-selected organizations.
Officers: Lewis Gasorek, Pres.; Gisele M. Glynn, Secy.
Director: Edward Rover.
EIN: 132943420
Codes: FD2

35320
Marjorie B. Flickinger Family Foundation
P.O. Box 60
Buffalo, NY 14240
Contact: Charles E. Milch, Dir.

Established in 1996 in NY.
Donor(s): Marjorie B. Flickinger.
Financial data (yr. ended 05/31/00): Grants paid, $109,700; assets, $0 (M); expenditures, $111,246; qualifying distributions, $109,665.
Limitations: Applications not accepted. Giving primarily in Buffalo, NY.
Application information: Contributes only to pre-selected organizations.
Directors: Peter B. Flickinger, Charles E. Milch, Catherine F. Schweitzer.
EIN: 161509274
Codes: FD2

35321
The John C. & Katherine M. Morris Foundation, Inc.
c/o John C. Morris
15 E. 93rd St.
New York, NY 10021

Established in 1994 in MA.
Donor(s): John C. Morris.
Financial data (yr. ended 12/31/01): Grants paid, $109,668; assets, $601,676 (M); expenditures, $112,657; qualifying distributions, $110,035.
Limitations: Applications not accepted. Giving primarily in NY.
Application information: Contributes only to pre-selected organizations.
Officers: Katherine M. Morris, Pres.; John C. Morris, Treas.
Director: James E. Rouen.
EIN: 043241999
Codes: FD2

35322
Sander/Ray Epstein Charitable Foundation
c/o Buchbinder Tunick & Co., LLP
1 Penn Plz., No. 5335
New York, NY 10119
Contact: Seymour Epstein, Pres.

Established in 1962 in NY.
Financial data (yr. ended 12/31/01): Grants paid, $109,653; assets, $1,639,415 (M); expenditures, $119,560; qualifying distributions, $108,999.
Limitations: Applications not accepted. Giving primarily in New York, NY.
Application information: Contributes only to pre-selected organizations.
Officers: Seymour Epstein, Pres.; Wayne Epstein, V.P.; Peter Schneider, Secy.
Director: Richard Rothenberg.
EIN: 136218324
Codes: FD2

35323
The George M. Yeager Family Foundation
(Formerly The Yeager-Wood Foundation)
630 5th Ave., Ste. 2900
New York, NY 10111-0001

Established in 1985 in NY.
Donor(s): George M. Yeager.
Financial data (yr. ended 12/31/01): Grants paid, $109,650; assets, $2,090,335 (M); expenditures, $111,141; qualifying distributions, $108,988.
Limitations: Applications not accepted. Giving primarily in NY.
Application information: Contributes only to pre-selected organizations.
Officers and Directors:* George M. Yeager,* Pres.; Barbara G. Yeager,* V.P.; Gordon M. Marchand,* Secy.-Treas.; Kerry Yeager Stevens, Scott A. Yeager.
EIN: 133314441
Codes: FD2

35324
Musicians Foundation, Inc.
875 6th Ave., Ste. 2303
New York, NY 10001 (212) 239-9137
FAX: (212) 239-9138; *E-mail:* info@musiciansfoundation.org; *URL:* http://www.musiciansfoundation.org
Contact: B.C. Vermeersch, Exec. Dir.

Established in 1914 in NY.
Donor(s): Olin Downes,‡ Fritz Kreisler,‡ Isidor Philipp,‡ Theodore Steinway,‡ Arturo Toscanini,‡ Clyde Burrows,‡ Gottfried Galston,‡ Helen Huntington Hull,‡ Yolanda Mero-Irion,‡ Sam Morgenstern,‡ Noel Haskins Murphy,‡ Ernest Schelling,‡ Vladimir Horowitz,‡ Mary Burrows,‡ Wanda Horowitz,‡ Philip Lieson Miller,‡ Anne Bigelow Stern, Brent Williams.‡
Financial data (yr. ended 04/30/01): Grants paid, $109,039; assets, $2,616,542 (M); gifts received, $219,798; expenditures, $198,749; qualifying distributions, $172,989.
Limitations: Giving on a national basis.
Publications: Application guidelines.
Application information: Application form required.
Officers and Directors:* Ann Stern,* Pres.; Hans E. Tausig,* V.P.; Richard Flender,* Secy.; Joseph Hertzberg,* Treas.; B.C. Vermeersch, Exec. Dir.
EIN: 131790739
Codes: FD2, GTI

35325
The Eric and Edith Siday Charitable Foundation
c/o M. Ginsberg
747 3rd Ave., 3rd Fl.
New York, NY 10017

Established in 1997 in NY.
Financial data (yr. ended 12/31/00): Grants paid, $109,025; assets, $1,079,681 (M); expenditures, $136,600; qualifying distributions, $121,354.
Limitations: Applications not accepted. Giving primarily in New York, NY.
Application information: Contributes only to pre-selected organizations.
Officers: Nathaniel Lewis Gerber, Pres.; Deborah Gerber, Secy.
EIN: 133960545
Codes: FD2

35326
High Five Foundation
136 Harold Rd.
Woodmere, NY 11598
Contact: Gerald P. Kaminsky, Pres.

Established in 1996 in NY.
Donor(s): Gerald P. Kaminsky.
Financial data (yr. ended 10/31/01): Grants paid, $108,961; assets, $1,915,371 (M); gifts received, $31,100; expenditures, $120,138; qualifying distributions, $106,758.
Limitations: Applications not accepted.
Application information: Contributes only to pre-selected organizations.
Officers: Gerald P. Kaminsky, Pres.; Gary J. Kaminsky, V.P.; Jaclyn Kaminsky, Secy.; Michael J. Kaminsky, Treas.
EIN: 113358107
Codes: FD2

35327
The Dunwiddie Foundation
c/o JPMorgan Chase Bank
1211 6th Ave., 34th Fl.
New York, NY 10036-8890

Established in 1997 in NY.
Financial data (yr. ended 04/30/01): Grants paid, $108,906; assets, $1,438,243 (M); expenditures, $135,680; qualifying distributions, $109,918.
Limitations: Applications not accepted. Giving limited to NY and SC.
Application information: Contributes only to 2 pre-selected organizations.
Trustee: JPMorgan Chase Bank.
EIN: 526940078

35328
Bossak-Heilbron Charitable Foundation, Inc.
c/o Shulman, Jones, & Co.
200 E. Post Rd.
White Plains, NY 10601
Application address: 720 Milton Rd., Rye, NY 10580, tel.: (914) 967-5828
Contact: Jane Heilbron, Pres.

Established in 1995 in NY.
Donor(s): Jane Heilbron, Carolyn Bossak.
Financial data (yr. ended 10/31/01): Grants paid, $108,750; assets, $2,071,617 (M); gifts received, $65,406; expenditures, $112,582; qualifying distributions, $107,849.
Limitations: Giving primarily in Seattle, WA.
Application information: Application form required.
Officers and Directors:* Jane Heilbron,* Pres.; Gail Steinitz,* Secy.; Alan B. Heilbron,* Treas.
EIN: 133862827
Codes: FD2, GTI

35329
The Ravengate Foundation
c/o Bessemer Trust Co., N.A., Tax Dept.
630 5th Ave.
New York, NY 10111

Established in 1999 in CT.
Financial data (yr. ended 11/30/01): Grants paid, $108,725; assets, $113,606 (M); gifts received, $460; expenditures, $109,627; qualifying distributions, $109,172.
Limitations: Applications not accepted. Giving primarily in CT and NY.
Application information: Contributes only to pre-selected organizations.
Trustees: John D. Chadwick, Patricia Walsh Chadwick.
EIN: 066492514
Codes: FD2

35330
Edward & Susan Blumenfeld Foundation
6800 Jericho Tpke.
Syosset, NY 11791
Contact: Edward Blumenfeld, Pres.

Established in 1998 in NY.
Donor(s): Edward Blumenfeld.
Financial data (yr. ended 04/30/02): Grants paid, $108,715; assets, $1,845,599 (M); gifts received, $100,000; expenditures, $109,045; qualifying distributions, $107,118.
Application information: Application form not required.
Officers: Edward Blumenfeld, Pres.; Brad Blumenfeld, V.P.; David Blumenfeld, V.P.; Susan Blumenfeld, Secy.-Treas.
EIN: 113377549
Codes: FD2

35331
Jaffer Family Foundation
790 Summa Ave.
Westbury, NY 11590

Established in 2000 in NY.
Donor(s): Sadique Jaffer.
Financial data (yr. ended 12/31/00): Grants paid, $108,630; assets, $728 (M); gifts received, $111,500; expenditures, $110,772; qualifying distributions, $110,772.
Limitations: Giving primarily in NY.
Trustee: Sameer Hajee.
EIN: 113505408
Codes: FD2

35332
Robert & Mary Lou Morgado Charitable Trust
(Formerly The I'll Be There Foundation)
c/o Tag Assocs.
75 Rockefeller Plz., Ste. 900
New York, NY 10019

Established in 1995 in NY.
Donor(s): Mary Lou Morgado, Robert J. Morgado.
Financial data (yr. ended 11/30/01): Grants paid, $108,601; assets, $6,580,435 (M); expenditures, $145,439; qualifying distributions, $108,851.
Limitations: Applications not accepted. Giving on a national basis.
Application information: Contributes only to pre-selected organizations.
Trustees: Mary Lou Morgado, Robert J. Morgado.
EIN: 137072672
Codes: FD2

35333
Isaac & Toni Lieber Family Foundation
1050 Park Ave.
New York, NY 10028-1031
Contact: Edith Wolf Greenspan, Tr.

Established in 1985 in NY.
Financial data (yr. ended 09/30/01): Grants paid, $108,600; assets, $160,725 (M); gifts received, $10,800; expenditures, $109,042; qualifying distributions, $108,558.
Limitations: Applications not accepted. Giving primarily in New York, NY.
Application information: Contributes only to pre-selected organizations.
Trustees: Edith Wolf Greenspan, Arnold Lieber, Zalman Solowiedczyk.
EIN: 133054166
Codes: FD2

35334
Dorys McConnell Duberg Charitable Trust
c/o The Bank of New York, Tax Dept.
1 Wall St., 28th Fl.
New York, NY 10286
Application address: c/o Putnam Trust Co., Pequot Ave., Southport, CT 06490
Contact: Vincent Griffin, Jr.

Trust established in 1969 in CT.
Donor(s): Dorys McConnell Faile Duberg.‡
Financial data (yr. ended 01/31/02): Grants paid, $108,573; assets, $2,281,317 (M); expenditures, $126,441; qualifying distributions, $114,484.
Limitations: Giving primarily in Fairfield County, CT.
Application information: Application form not required.
Trustees: David Hall Faile, Jr., Robert B. Hutchinson, Toni F. Lyerly.
EIN: 237016974
Codes: FD2

35335
Michael J. Zamkow & Sue E. Berman Foundation
c/o Goldman Sachs & Co.
85 Broad St., Tax Dept.
New York, NY 10004

Established in 1995 in NY.
Donor(s): Michael J. Zamkow.
Financial data (yr. ended 02/28/01): Grants paid, $108,560; assets, $4,015,989 (M); gifts received, $128,453; expenditures, $109,810; qualifying distributions, $108,810.
Limitations: Applications not accepted. Giving primarily in New York, NY and London, England.
Application information: Contributes only to pre-selected organizations.
Trustees: Sue E. Berman, Michael J. Zamkow.
EIN: 133867834
Codes: FD2

35336
The David and Sheila Cornstein Foundation
c/o Blank Rome Tenzer Greenblatt
405 Lexington Ave.
New York, NY 10174-0208

Established in 1989 in NY.
Donor(s): David Cornstein, Sheila Cornstein.
Financial data (yr. ended 12/31/01): Grants paid, $108,330; assets, $754,970 (M); expenditures, $114,544; qualifying distributions, $109,027.
Limitations: Applications not accepted. Giving primarily in NY.
Application information: Contributes only to pre-selected organizations.
Trustees: David Cornstein, Sheila Cornstein.
EIN: 133519327

Codes: FD2

35337
Thomas Jefferson Rosenberg Foundation, Inc.
5 Hanover Sq., Ste. 200
New York, NY 10004-2614 (212) 869-1490
Contact: Henry Rosenberg, Pres.

Established around 1989 in NY.
Donor(s): Henry Rosenberg.
Financial data (yr. ended 12/31/00): Grants paid, $108,255; assets, $563,179 (M); gifts received, $77,000; expenditures, $123,392; qualifying distributions, $112,599.
Limitations: Giving primarily in NY.
Application information: Application form not required.
Officers: Henry Rosenberg, Pres. and Treas.; Gail Rosenberg, V.P.; Carol Rosner, V.P.; Eitan Eadan, Secy.
EIN: 133436858
Codes: FD2

35338
The Karp Foundation
(Formerly The Harvey L. Karp Foundation)
P.O. Box 30
East Hampton, NY 11937-0030

Established in 1968 in NY.
Financial data (yr. ended 06/30/01): Grants paid, $108,142; assets, $2,408,829 (M); expenditures, $112,273; qualifying distributions, $109,847.
Limitations: Applications not accepted. Giving primarily in New York, NY.
Application information: Contributes only to pre-selected organizations.
Officers: Harvey L. Karp, Pres. and Treas.; Robert B. Hodes, Secy.
Directors: David A. Karp, Karen Karp.
EIN: 132621240
Codes: FD2

35339
Zichron Avraham Charitable Foundation
506 Ave. I
Brooklyn, NY 11230 (718) 253-6799
Contact: Frieda Wadler, Tr.

Established in 2000 in NY.
Donor(s): Sobel Family Trust.
Financial data (yr. ended 12/31/00): Grants paid, $108,040; assets, $26,671 (M); gifts received, $132,677; expenditures, $108,240; qualifying distributions, $108,040.
Limitations: Giving primarily in NY.
Trustees: Rose Levine, Frieda Wadler.
EIN: 137173273
Codes: FD2

35340
Arthur F. and Arnold M. Frankel Foundation, Inc.
266 West End Ave.
New York, NY 10023
Contact: Jedd Wider, Tr.

Established in 1990 in NY.
Donor(s): Arthur F. Frankel,‡ Sidney Roffman, Joseph Lapatin, Jed Wider, Todd Wider.
Financial data (yr. ended 06/30/01): Grants paid, $108,000; assets, $2,861,555 (M); expenditures, $108,325; qualifying distributions, $108,065.
Limitations: Giving primarily in NY.
Application information: Application form not required.
Trustees: Jed Wider, Todd Wider.
EIN: 133615586
Codes: FD2

35341
Kaufmann Foundation, Inc.
c/o Yohalem Gillman & Co.
477 Madison Ave.
New York, NY 10022-5802

Established in 1990 in NY.
Donor(s): Peter Kaufmann, and other members of the Kaufmann family.
Financial data (yr. ended 12/31/00): Grants paid, $108,000; assets, $2,016,034 (M); gifts received, $75,000; expenditures, $115,753; qualifying distributions, $109,213.
Limitations: Applications not accepted. Giving primarily in CT and NY.
Application information: Contributes only to pre-selected organizations.
Officers and Directors:* Peter Kaufmann,* Chair.; Andrew Kaufmann,* Pres.; Ronald Kaufmann,* V.P.; Ruth Kaufmann,* V.P.; Jacqueline Tooter,* Secy.; Howard Tooter,* Treas.
EIN: 133603247
Codes: FD2

35342
The R. and D. Fund, Inc.
c/o Gray Seifert & Co.
380 Madison Ave., 22nd Fl.
New York, NY 10017-2513

Incorporated in 1952 in NY.
Donor(s): Donald B. Straus, Members of the Straus Family.
Financial data (yr. ended 12/31/99): Grants paid, $107,989; assets, $13,106 (M); gifts received, $39,300; expenditures, $110,253; qualifying distributions, $107,483.
Limitations: Applications not accepted.
Application information: Contributes only to pre-selected organizations.
Officer: Donald B. Straus, V.P.
EIN: 136118829
Codes: FD2

35343
Harold & Bette Wolfson Schapiro Foundation
c/o Rodney H. Ertischek
20 Fuller St.
Briarcliff Manor, NY 10510 (914) 762-5018

Established about 1957 in NY.
Donor(s): Gerald E. Schapiro, Joan Schapiro, Stuart Schapiro.
Financial data (yr. ended 02/28/02): Grants paid, $107,953; assets, $409,802 (M); gifts received, $88,000; expenditures, $158,900; qualifying distributions, $107,953.
Limitations: Applications not accepted.
Application information: Contributes only to pre-selected organizations.
Officers: Stuart Schapiro, Pres.; Gerald E. Schapiro, V.P. and Treas.; Joan Schapiro, V.P.
EIN: 136157602
Codes: FD2

35344
The Ann & Erlo Van Waveren Foundation, Inc.
210 E. 86th St., Ste. 204
New York, NY 10128 (212) 517-0060
FAX: (212) 876-0886; E-mail: obernier@aol.com
Contact: Olivier Bernier, Pres.

Incorporated in 1986 in NY.
Donor(s): Ann Van Waveren.‡
Financial data (yr. ended 12/31/99): Grants paid, $107,819; assets, $1,817,924 (M); expenditures, $212,851; qualifying distributions, $189,669; giving activities include $82,421 for programs.
Application information: Application form required.

Officers: Olivier Bernier, Pres.; Diana Swayer, Secy.; Theodore Young, Treas.
EIN: 133343738
Codes: FD2, GTI

35345
Keyser Family Foundation
c/o Bessemer Trust Co., N.A.
630 5th Ave.
New York, NY 10111

Established in 1997 in IL.
Donor(s): John P. Keyser, Elizabeth I. Keyser.
Financial data (yr. ended 12/31/01): Grants paid, $107,800; assets, $1,658,567 (M); expenditures, $112,230; qualifying distributions, $107,823.
Limitations: Applications not accepted. Giving primarily in San Francisco, CA; Washington, DC; Chicago, IL; Williamstown, MA; and New York, NY.
Application information: Contributes only to pre-selected organizations.
Officers and Directors:* John P. Keyser,* Pres. and Treas.; Elizabeth I. Keyser,* V.P. and Secy.; Kevin W. Keyser, Leigh M. Keyser.
EIN: 364180940
Codes: FD2

35346
The Frank L. Ciminelli Family Foundation
350 Essjay Rd., Ste. 101
Williamsville, NY 14221
Contact: Frank L. Ciminelli, Pres.

Established in 1998 in NY.
Donor(s): Frank L. Ciminelli.
Financial data (yr. ended 05/31/01): Grants paid, $107,532; assets, $537,444 (M); gifts received, $286,210; expenditures, $109,687; qualifying distributions, $107,463.
Limitations: Giving primarily in NY.
Officers: Frank L. Ciminelli, Pres.; Rosalie G. Ciminelli, V.P.; Angela Bontempo, Treas.
EIN: 161552205
Codes: FD2

35347
John and Dorothy Sprague Foundation
770 Park Ave., Apt. 7D
New York, NY 10021

Established in 1994 in NY.
Financial data (yr. ended 11/30/01): Grants paid, $107,516; assets, $1,006,155 (M); expenditures, $150,230; qualifying distributions, $111,166.
Limitations: Applications not accepted. Giving primarily in NY.
Application information: Contributes only to pre-selected organizations.
Trustees: John A. Sprague, Dorothy S. Whitmarsh.
EIN: 137053818
Codes: FD2

35348
The Fezzik Foundation, Inc.
c/o Shapiro & Lobel, LLP
111 W. 40th St., 8th Fl.
New York, NY 10018

Established 1986 in NY.
Donor(s): William Goldman.
Financial data (yr. ended 12/31/01): Grants paid, $107,500; assets, $813,260 (M); expenditures, $108,239; qualifying distributions, $106,153.
Limitations: Applications not accepted. Giving primarily in NY.
Application information: Contributes only to pre-selected organizations.
Officers: William Goldman, Pres.; Henry Charles Shays, Secy.-Treas.
Director: Aaron Shapiro.

EIN: 133382077
Codes: FD2

35349
The Franz W. Sichel Foundation
941 Park Ave.
New York, NY 10028
Contact: Peter M.F. Sichel, Pres.

Incorporated in 1961 in NY.
Donor(s): Employees of Fromm & Sichel, Inc.
Financial data (yr. ended 05/31/01): Grants paid, $107,497; assets, $1,357,140 (M); expenditures, $123,970; qualifying distributions, $113,254.
Limitations: Applications not accepted. Giving primarily in New York, NY.
Application information: Contributes only to pre-selected organizations.
Officers: Peter M.F. Sichel, Pres. and Treas.; Shepherd Raimi, Secy.
Directors: Richard Brown, Alexandra Sichel, Margaret Sichel.
EIN: 136115904
Codes: FD2

35350
Warner LeRoy Foundation, Inc.
c/o Starr & Co.
350 Park Ave.
New York, NY 10022

Established in 1981 in NY.
Donor(s): Warner LeRoy.
Financial data (yr. ended 12/31/99): Grants paid, $107,450; assets, $346,840 (M); expenditures, $109,351; qualifying distributions, $107,114.
Limitations: Applications not accepted. Giving primarily in NY.
Application information: Contributes only to pre-selected organizations.
Officers and Directors:* Warner LeRoy,* Pres.; Stanley Weiss,* Secy.; Kay LeRoy.
EIN: 133097097
Codes: FD2

35351
BBL Charitable Foundation, Inc.
P.O. Box 12789
Albany, NY 12203-2789

Established in 1999 in NY.
Donor(s): Donald Led Duke, BBL Construction Services, LLC.
Financial data (yr. ended 12/31/01): Grants paid, $107,400; assets, $65,992 (M); gifts received, $74,000; expenditures, $107,771; qualifying distributions, $107,467.
Limitations: Applications not accepted. Giving primarily in NY.
Application information: Contributes only to pre-selected organizations.
Directors: Michael Bette, Donald Led Duke, Stephen Obermayer.
EIN: 141810413
Codes: FD2

35352
The Lifton Family Foundation
3333 New Hyde Park Rd., Ste. 203
New Hyde Park, NY 11042

Established in 1998 in NY.
Donor(s): Martin Lifton.
Financial data (yr. ended 05/31/01): Grants paid, $107,376; assets, $1,763,258 (M); expenditures, $124,367; qualifying distributions, $107,376.
Limitations: Applications not accepted.
Application information: Contributes only to pre-selected organizations.
Trustees: Elinor Lifton, Judie B. Lifton, Martin Lifton, Steven J. Lifton.

EIN: 137154190
Codes: FD2

35353
Steven B. Schonfeld Foundation, Inc.
1 Jericho Plz.
Jericho, NY 11753

Established in 2001 in DE.
Donor(s): Steven B. Schonfeld.
Financial data (yr. ended 12/31/01): Grants paid, $107,375; assets, $1,168,581 (M); gifts received, $1,250,000; expenditures, $113,256; qualifying distributions, $113,239.
Limitations: Applications not accepted.
Application information: Contributes only to pre-selected organizations.
Officers: Steven B. Schonfeld, Pres.; Kathyrn Licursi, V.P. and Secy.; Herbert Schonfeld, V.P. and Treas.; Harriet Sue Schonfeld, V.P.
EIN: 134166757

35354
The Norman and Julia Bobrow Family Foundation
17 W. John St.
Hicksville, NY 11801-1001

Established in 1997.
Donor(s): Julia Bobrow, Norman Bobrow.
Financial data (yr. ended 12/31/01): Grants paid, $107,328; assets, $533,532 (M); gifts received, $150,000; expenditures, $110,578; qualifying distributions, $107,258.
Limitations: Applications not accepted. Giving primarily in New York, NY.
Application information: Contributes only to pre-selected organizations.
Trustees: Julia Bobrow, Norman Bobrow.
EIN: 137111547

35355
L'Maan Ameinu Foundation, Inc.
315 Westchester Ave., 2nd Fl.
Port Chester, NY 10573

Established in 2001 in NY.
Donor(s): Betty Cohen.
Financial data (yr. ended 12/31/01): Grants paid, $107,300; assets, $34,237 (M); gifts received, $142,941; expenditures, $107,448; qualifying distributions, $107,300.
Limitations: Applications not accepted.
Application information: Contributes only to pre-selected organizations.
Officers: Beity S. Cohen, Pres. and Treas.; Zev Cohen, V.P.; Esther Cohen Brooks, Secy.
EIN: 311775151
Codes: FD2

35356
Bernard M. Twersky Foundation
c/o Kaye, Scholer, Fierman, Hays & Handler
425 Park Ave.
New York, NY 10022
Contact: Julius Berman, Tr.

Established in 1980.
Donor(s): Bernard Twersky.‡
Financial data (yr. ended 10/31/01): Grants paid, $107,154; assets, $1,031,307 (M); expenditures, $119,496; qualifying distributions, $108,525.
Limitations: Applications not accepted. Giving primarily in NJ and NY.
Application information: Contributes only to pre-selected organizations.
Trustees: Julius Berman, Saul Roth, Abraham T. Twersky.
EIN: 133016544
Codes: FD2

35357
The G. Wallace and Frances T. Bates Charitable Trust
c/o Fiduciary Trust Co.
600 Fifth Ave.
New York, NY 10020
Contact: Anne Wilson Bates, Tr.

Established in 1987 in CT.
Donor(s): G. Wallace Bates.‡
Financial data (yr. ended 09/30/01): Grants paid, $107,000; assets, $649,851 (M); expenditures, $117,693; qualifying distributions, $108,038.
Limitations: Giving primarily in Boston, MA.
Trustees: Anne Wilson Bates, Fiduciary Trust Co.
EIN: 136868427
Codes: FD2

35358
The Winfield Foundation
c/o Hollyer, Brady
551 5th Ave., 27th Fl.
New York, NY 10176
Contact: Helen Hooke, Tr.

Incorporated in 1941 in NY.
Financial data (yr. ended 12/31/01): Grants paid, $107,000; assets, $2,144,056 (M); expenditures, $136,867; qualifying distributions, $111,032.
Limitations: Giving primarily in NY.
Application information: Application form not required.
Officers and Trustees:* Franklin W. McCann,* Pres. and Treas.; D. Chase Troxell,* V.P. and Secy.; Jonathan W. McCann,* V.P.; Margaret M. Fenhagen, Helen Hooke, Douglas Irwin.
EIN: 136158017
Codes: FD2

35359
Cornerstone Foundation
1358 47th St.
Brooklyn, NY 11219

Established in 1998 in NY.
Donor(s): Moses Eckstein.
Financial data (yr. ended 10/31/01): Grants paid, $106,965; assets, $3,078,123 (M); gifts received, $175,000; expenditures, $110,377; qualifying distributions, $105,408.
Limitations: Applications not accepted.
Application information: Contributes only to pre-selected organizations.
Director: Moses Eckstein.
EIN: 113462646
Codes: FD2

35360
Michael Chernow Trust 2
P.O. Box 197
Larchmont, NY 10538-0197 (914) 834-1900
Contact: Gordon S. Oppenheimer

Trust established in 1968 in NY.
Financial data (yr. ended 06/30/01): Grants paid, $106,800; assets, $2,644,657 (M); expenditures, $184,872; qualifying distributions, $140,760.
Limitations: Giving primarily in New York, NY.
Application information: Application form not required.
Trustees: Albert Krassner, Martin P. Krassner, Lynn Streim.
EIN: 136758228
Codes: FD2

35361
Abraham & Lillian Rosenberg Foundation, Inc.
80 White St.
New York, NY 10013

Established in 1964 in NY.

Financial data (yr. ended 04/30/01): Grants paid, $106,800; assets, $1,775,863 (M); expenditures, $133,494; qualifying distributions, $107,125.
Limitations: Applications not accepted. Giving primarily in New York, NY.
Application information: Contributes only to pre-selected organizations.
Officers: Martin Weinstein, Pres.; Gerald Weinstein, Secy.-Treas.
EIN: 136167434
Codes: FD2

35362
The Jim Henson Foundation
(Formerly The Henson Foundation)
584 Broadway, Ste. 1007
New York, NY 10012 (212) 680-1400
E-mail: info@hensonfoundation.org; **URL:** http://www.hensonfoundation.org
Contact: Meg Daniel, Fdn. Mgr.

Established in 1982 in NY.
Donor(s): James M. Henson,‡ members of the Henson Family.
Financial data (yr. ended 07/31/01): Grants paid, $106,762; assets, $3,308,746 (M); expenditures, $196,044; qualifying distributions, $105,284; giving activities include $52,908 for programs.
Limitations: Giving on a national basis.
Application information: Grants only available to American artists. Guidelines and application form are available on website, and by mail.
Officers: Cheryl Henson, Pres.; Jane Henson, V.P.; Allelu Kurten, Secy.; Louis Borodinsky, Treas.
EIN: 133133702

35363
R. B. Hazard Family Charitable Trust
4830 Cavalry Green
Manlius, NY 13104-1430 (315) 637-9097
Contact: Robert B. Hazard, Tr.

Established in 1989 in NY.
Donor(s): Robert B. Hazard.
Financial data (yr. ended 12/31/01): Grants paid, $106,600; assets, $364,705 (M); gifts received, $197,842; expenditures, $110,553; qualifying distributions, $106,600.
Limitations: Giving on a national basis.
Trustees: Janet H. Ambrose, Kimberly Gunderson, Martha G. Hazard, Robert B. Hazard, Robert B. Hazard, Jr., Valorie R. Stevens.
EIN: 166316219

35364
The Dall Foundation
c/o Grant Thornton, LLP
60 Broad St., 24th Fl.
New York, NY 10004-2501

Established in 1985.
Donor(s): Robert F. Dall.
Financial data (yr. ended 11/30/99): Grants paid, $106,472; assets, $2,916 (M); gifts received, $116,040; expenditures, $106,630; qualifying distributions, $106,630.
Limitations: Applications not accepted. Giving primarily in New York, NY.
Application information: Contributes only to pre-selected organizations.
Officers: Robert F. Dall, Pres. and Treas.; Rosalie A. Dall, V.P. and Secy.
EIN: 133319146
Codes: FD2

35365
The Lemoy Charitable Trust
c/o Rephael Lieberman
6201 16th Ave.
Brooklyn, NY 11204

Established in 1997 in NY.
Financial data (yr. ended 11/30/00): Grants paid, $106,465; assets, $775,157 (M); gifts received, $10,206; expenditures, $115,405; qualifying distributions, $113,567.
Officer: Rephael Lieberman, Mgr.
EIN: 116466175
Codes: FD2

35366
Leo Fink Foundation
c/o Julius Berman, Kaye, Scholer, LLP
425 Park Ave.
New York, NY 10022-3598

Established in 1986 in NY.
Financial data (yr. ended 05/31/01): Grants paid, $106,450; assets, $1,345,663 (M); gifts received, $30,000; expenditures, $107,281; qualifying distributions, $106,450.
Limitations: Applications not accepted.
Application information: Contributes only to pre-selected organizations.
Trustee: Julius Berman.
EIN: 133351504
Codes: FD2

35367
The DJR Trust
c/o Bessemer Trust Co., N.A.
630 5th Ave.
New York, NY 10111

Established in 1998 in NY.
Donor(s): Dan I. Rather, Jean G. Rather.
Financial data (yr. ended 12/31/00): Grants paid, $106,284; assets, $2,299,538 (M); expenditures, $135,806; qualifying distributions, $104,306.
Limitations: Applications not accepted. Giving primarily in New York, NY and TX.
Application information: Contributes only to pre-selected organizations.
Trustees: Dan I. Rather, Jean G. Rather, Bessemer Trust Co., N.A.
EIN: 137148229

35368
Louis P. Singer Fund, Inc.
c/o Christy & Viener
620 5th Ave.
New York, NY 10020

Established in 1961.
Donor(s): Berkshire Hathaway, Inc.
Financial data (yr. ended 08/31/01): Grants paid, $105,975; assets, $2,771,383 (M); expenditures, $137,694; qualifying distributions, $106,245.
Limitations: Giving primarily in NY.
Officers: Midge Korczak, Pres.; John D. Viener, Secy.-Treas.
EIN: 136077788
Codes: FD2

35369
Cygnus Management Foundation, Inc.
(Formerly Fay's Foundation)
100 E. Washington St., Ste. 206
Syracuse, NY 13202 (315) 478-8877
Contact: Warren D. Wolfson, Secy.-Treas.

Established in 1981 in NY.
Donor(s): Fay's, Inc.
Financial data (yr. ended 01/31/02): Grants paid, $105,925; assets, $1,051,109 (M); expenditures, $125,871; qualifying distributions, $105,925.
Limitations: Giving primarily in the Northeast, with emphasis on NY and PA.
Application information: Application form not required.
Officers and Directors:* James F. Poole, Jr.,* Pres.; David H. Panasci,* V.P.; Warren D. Wolfson,* Secy.-Treas.; Henry A. Panasci, Jr.
EIN: 222353455

35370
Barry Wish Family Foundation, Inc.
c/o Myer, Greene & Degge
P.O. Box 930
Pearl River, NY 10965

Established in 1996 in FL.
Donor(s): Barry N. Wish, Jonathan Adess Wish, Stacey Adess Silverstein.
Financial data (yr. ended 12/31/01): Grants paid, $105,900; assets, $1,191,941 (M); expenditures, $111,950; qualifying distributions, $105,423.
Limitations: Applications not accepted. Giving on a national basis.
Application information: Contributes only to pre-selected organizations.
Officers: Barry N. Wish, Pres.; Jonathan Adess Wish, Secy.; Stacey Adess Silverstein, Treas.
EIN: 650720792
Codes: FD2

35371
Abraham Ben Israel Memorial Fund, Inc.
c/o J. Kravitz
P.O. Box 701
Merrick, NY 11566

Established in 1961.
Donor(s): Abram I. Dusowitz, Dorothy Dusowitz.
Financial data (yr. ended 12/31/00): Grants paid, $105,837; assets, $337,241 (M); gifts received, $211,000; expenditures, $157,164; qualifying distributions, $110,437.
Limitations: Applications not accepted. Giving primarily in NY.
Application information: Contributes only to pre-selected organizations.
Directors: Abram Dusowitz, Chaya Dusowitz.
EIN: 136161126
Codes: FD2

35372
The Perlow Family Charitable Foundation Trust
1410 E. 5th St.
Brooklyn, NY 11230-5605

Established in 1993 in NY.
Donor(s): Ari Perlow.
Financial data (yr. ended 12/31/01): Grants paid, $105,802; assets, $2,215,590 (M); expenditures, $107,524; qualifying distributions, $107,202.
Limitations: Applications not accepted. Giving primarily in Brooklyn, NY.
Application information: Contributes only to pre-selected organizations.
Trustees: Ari Perlow, Doris May Perlow.
EIN: 116436661
Codes: FD2

35373
BSD Foundation
1761 E. 21st St.
Brooklyn, NY 11229

Established in 1999 in NY.
Financial data (yr. ended 10/31/00): Grants paid, $105,728; assets, $71,747 (M); gifts received, $185,000; expenditures, $117,628; qualifying distributions, $105,728.
Trustee: S. Slater.
EIN: 113518540
Codes: FD2

35374
Morris & Arlene Goldfarb Family Foundation, Inc.
21 Fairway Dr.
Mamaroneck, NY 10543

Established in 1996 in DE & NY.
Donor(s): Morris Goldfarb.
Financial data (yr. ended 08/31/01): Grants paid, $105,675; assets, $921,864 (M); gifts received, $762,500; expenditures, $107,896; qualifying distributions, $103,746.
Limitations: Applications not accepted. Giving primarily in NY.
Application information: Contributes only to pre-selected organizations.
Officers: Morris Goldfarb, Pres.; Arlene Goldfarb, Secy.
EIN: 133925695
Codes: FD2

35375
The Nancy Terner Behrman Foundation
885 Park Ave.
New York, NY 10021

Established in 1998 in NY.
Donor(s): Nancy T. Behrman.
Financial data (yr. ended 12/31/00): Grants paid, $105,664; assets, $1,302,847 (M); gifts received, $333,333; expenditures, $125,942; qualifying distributions, $105,618.
Limitations: Applications not accepted. Giving primarily in NY.
Application information: Contributes only to pre-selected organizations.
Officers and Directors:* Nancy Terner Behrman,* Pres.; Peter Grayson,* Secy.; Joshua S. Rubenstein,* Treas.
EIN: 133949093
Codes: FD2

35376
The Vogel Family Foundation
c/o Stephen Vogel
800 Park Ave.
New York, NY 10021

Established in 1998 in NY.
Donor(s): Sherman C. Vogel.
Financial data (yr. ended 12/31/01): Grants paid, $105,620; assets, $282,592 (M); gifts received, $130,595; expenditures, $107,150; qualifying distributions, $105,576.
Limitations: Applications not accepted.
Application information: Contributes only to pre-selected organizations.
Officers and Directors:* Stephen A. Vogel,* Pres.; Jeanette Vogel,* V.P.; Sherman C. Vogel,* Secy.; Laurie Vogel,* Treas.
EIN: 133981608
Codes: FD2

35377
James Keene Foundation
c/o M. Kirschenbaum
2130 Broadway
New York, NY 10023

Established in 1998.
Financial data (yr. ended 12/31/99): Grants paid, $105,545; assets, $281,117 (M); expenditures, $116,100; qualifying distributions, $105,545.
Limitations: Applications not accepted.
Application information: Contributes only to pre-selected organizations.
Directors: A. Kirschenbaum, M. Kirschenbaum.
EIN: 133377892
Codes: FD2

35378
The Geszel Family Foundation
c/o Bear Stearns Co.
245 Park Ave.
New York, NY 10167

Established in 2000 in NY.
Donor(s): Irving M. Geszel, Yetta Geszel.
Financial data (yr. ended 11/30/01): Grants paid, $105,527; assets, $6,227 (M); gifts received, $55,215; expenditures, $110,788; qualifying distributions, $105,527.
Limitations: Applications not accepted.
Application information: Contributes only to pre-selected organizations.
Trustees: Irving M. Geszel, Yetta Geszel.
EIN: 134142812

35379
The Mezzacappa Foundation
c/o Lazard Freres & Co., LLC
30 Rockefeller Plz.
New York, NY 10020-1902
Contact: Damon Mezzacappa, Pres.

Established in 1984 in NY.
Donor(s): Damon Mezzacappa.
Financial data (yr. ended 06/30/01): Grants paid, $105,500; assets, $851,681 (M); gifts received, $469,555; expenditures, $119,676; qualifying distributions, $105,600.
Limitations: Giving primarily in the greater New York, NY area.
Officers and Directors:* Damon Mezzacappa,* Pres.; Elizabeth Mezzacappa,* V.P.; Helen A. Bartholomew, Secy.; Francis J. Conroy,* Treas.
EIN: 133246104
Codes: FD2

35380
St. Vincent De Paul Foundation, Inc.
1045 Park St., Ste. C
Peekskill, NY 10566-3891
E-mail: stvinfdn@aol.com
Contact: Thomas R. Langan, V.P.

Established about 1980 in NY.
Financial data (yr. ended 12/31/00): Grants paid, $105,400; assets, $3,105,237 (M); gifts received, $2,283; expenditures, $160,264; qualifying distributions, $129,890.
Limitations: Giving on a national basis.
Application information: Application form not required.
Officers and Directors:* Thomas J. Langan, Jr.,* Chair. and Pres.; Thomas R. Langan,* V.P.; M. Eileen Dolphin,* Secy.; Robert V. Tiburzi, Sr.,* Treas.; John Duffy, Jr., Lucia Marett, Robert V. Tiburzi, Jr.
EIN: 135596824
Codes: FD2

35381
The Mindich Family Foundation
c/o Goldman Sachs & Co.
85 Broad St., Tax Dept.
New York, NY 10004

Established in 1996 in NY.
Donor(s): Eric M. Mindich.
Financial data (yr. ended 07/31/01): Grants paid, $105,350; assets, $5,345,299 (M); gifts received, $2,340,029; expenditures, $237,202; qualifying distributions, $109,430.
Limitations: Applications not accepted. Giving primarily in NY.
Application information: Contributes only to pre-selected organizations.
Trustees: Eric M. Mindich, Stacey B. Mindich.
EIN: 137085272
Codes: FD2

35382
The Tianaderrah Foundation
Butternut Rd.
P.O. Box 139
Unadilla, NY 13849 (607) 369-9401
Contact: Robert L. Gipson, Tr.

Established in 1996 in NY.
Donor(s): Robert L. Gipson.
Financial data (yr. ended 12/31/01): Grants paid, $105,350; assets, $2,679,582 (M); expenditures, $107,226; qualifying distributions, $105,350.
Limitations: Giving primarily in NY.
Trustees: Robert L. Gipson, Thomas L. Gipson, Sally Gipson Tully.
EIN: 166445118
Codes: FD2

35383
Hara Museum Fund
c/o Grant Thornton, LLP
60 Broad St.
New York, NY 10004

Established in 1984 in NY.
Donor(s): Keiko Hara, Umeko Hara, Sasakawa Peace Foundation, Chase Manhattan Foundation.
Financial data (yr. ended 06/30/01): Grants paid, $105,250; assets, $1,022,933 (M); gifts received, $1,000; expenditures, $138,041; qualifying distributions, $135,449.
Limitations: Applications not accepted.
Application information: Contributes only to pre-selected organizations.
Officers and Directors:* Toshio Hara,* Pres.; Ko-Yung Tung,* Secy.; Masajiro Shinkawa,* Treas.; Richard E. Greer, Sumiko Ito, John Powers.
EIN: 133236892
Codes: FD2

35384
The Robert and Karen Sobel Charitable Foundation
20 Westerleigh Rd.
Purchase, NY 10577

Established in 1999 in NY.
Donor(s): Robert J. Sobel.
Financial data (yr. ended 12/31/01): Grants paid, $105,250; assets, $12,265 (M); gifts received, $101,000; expenditures, $105,275; qualifying distributions, $105,250.
Officers: Robert J. Sobel, Pres.; Karen Sobel, V.P.
EIN: 137196988
Codes: FD2

35385
Lee Gottlieb Fund, Inc.
1 Liberty Plz.
New York, NY 10006

Established in 1955 in NY.
Donor(s): Leo Gottlieb.
Financial data (yr. ended 12/31/01): Grants paid, $105,174; assets, $1,792,443 (M); expenditures, $109,901; qualifying distributions, $106,345.
Limitations: Applications not accepted. Giving primarily in NY.
Application information: Contributes only to pre-selected organizations.
Officers: Elinor Gottlieb Mannucci, Pres. and Treas.; Mark Lee Mannucci, V.P. and Secy.; Anthony James Mannucci, V.P.
EIN: 136088831
Codes: FD2

35386
Alan H. Cummings Family Foundation
c/o Bessemer Trust Co., N.A., Tax Dept.
630 5th Ave.
New York, NY 10111
Application address: c/o Bessemer Trust Co. of FL, 222 Royal Palm Way, Palm Beach, FL 33480

Established in 1987 in FL.
Donor(s): Nathan Cummings.‡
Financial data (yr. ended 12/31/00): Grants paid, $105,150; assets, $1,247,992 (M); expenditures, $123,407; qualifying distributions, $105,150.
Limitations: Giving primarily in West Palm Beach, FL.
Officers and Directors:* Ruth Cummings Sorenson,* V.P. and Secy.; Helene C. Karp,* V.P. and Treas.
EIN: 592635536
Codes: FD2

35387
The J. C. & A. J. Bowling-Bowling Family Foundation
c/o U.S. Trust
P.O. Box 2004
New York, NY 10109-1910

Established in 1997.
Financial data (yr. ended 12/31/01): Grants paid, $105,000; assets, $2,253,062 (M); expenditures, $119,582; qualifying distributions, $105,000.
Limitations: Applications not accepted.
Application information: Contributes only to pre-selected organizations.
Trustees: Belinda B. Bewkes, Ann J. Bowling, Nancy B. Gramps, Stephanie B. Zeigler, U.S. Trust.
EIN: 311522458

35388
Chadbourne & Parke, LLP Foundation
30 Rockefeller Plz.
New York, NY 10112

Established in 2001 in DE.
Donor(s): Chadbourne & Parke LLP.
Financial data (yr. ended 12/13/01): Grants paid, $105,000; assets, $398,774 (M); gifts received, $503,770; expenditures, $105,000; qualifying distributions, $105,000.
Limitations: Applications not accepted. Giving primarily in New York, NY.
Application information: Contributes only to pre-selected organizations.
Officers: Charles K. O'Neill, Pres.; Lauren D. Kelly, V.P. and Secy.; Aniello Branco, V.P. and Treas.
EIN: 134197648
Codes: CS, FD2

35389
Jack & Bonnie Eizikovitz Charitable Fund, Inc.
(Formerly Mary & Bennett Grau Charitable Fund, Inc.)
c/o Zell & Ettinger
3001 Ave. M
Brooklyn, NY 11210

Established in 1988 in NY.
Donor(s): Jack Eizikovitz.
Financial data (yr. ended 12/31/99): Grants paid, $105,000; assets, $0 (M); gifts received, $196,000; expenditures, $118,385; qualifying distributions, $105,000.
Limitations: Applications not accepted.
Application information: Contributes only to pre-selected organizations.
Officers: Jack Eizikovitz, Pres.; Bonnie Eizikovitz, V.P.; Jeffrey Zell, Secy.
EIN: 133463056
Codes: FD2

35390
Samuel Field Family Foundation
c/o Adams & Co.
411 5th Ave.
New York, NY 10016-2203   (212) 579-5500
Contact: Claire Perlman, Tr.

Established about 1970 in NY.
Donor(s): Helen Field,‡ Claire Perlman, Jean F. Ruth.
Financial data (yr. ended 10/31/01): Grants paid, $105,000; assets, $2,167,812 (M); expenditures, $114,444; qualifying distributions, $105,000.
Limitations: Applications not accepted. Giving primarily in New York, NY.
Application information: Contributes only to pre-selected organizations.
Trustees: Claire Perlman, Jean F. Ruth, Toni Young.
EIN: 136111664
Codes: FD2

35391
The Dennis & Brooks Holt Foundation
c/o Lewis Braff & Co.
60 E. 42nd St., Ste. 850
New York, NY 10165

Established in 1997 in NY.
Donor(s): Brooks Holt, Dennis Holt.
Financial data (yr. ended 12/31/00): Grants paid, $105,000; assets, $48,078 (M); expenditures, $105,000; qualifying distributions, $104,983.
Limitations: Applications not accepted. Giving primarily in CA.
Application information: Contributes only to pre-selected organizations.
Officers and Directors:* Dennis Holt,* Pres.; Brooks Holt,* Secy.
EIN: 137097809
Codes: FD2

35392
The Philip J. and Anne M. Kemper Charitable Foundation
c/o Owl Wire & Cable
P.O. Box 187
Canastota, NY 13032

Established in 1999 in NY.
Donor(s): Philip J. Kemper, Anne M. Kemper.
Financial data (yr. ended 12/31/01): Grants paid, $105,000; assets, $2,156,063 (M); expenditures, $107,167; qualifying distributions, $103,928.
Limitations: Applications not accepted. Giving primarily in NY.
Application information: Contributes only to pre-selected organizations.
Trustees: Anne M. Kemper, Philip J. Kemper.
EIN: 161562659
Codes: FD2

35393
New York Institute for Vascular Studies, Inc.
330 Birdsall Dr.
Yorktown Heights, NY 10598
Contact: Steven Levine

Established in 1987 in NY.
Financial data (yr. ended 12/31/00): Grants paid, $105,000; assets, $971,133 (M); expenditures, $234,082; qualifying distributions, $224,609.
Limitations: Giving primarily in NY.
Officer: Carol Veith, Secy.
Director: Frank J. Veith.
EIN: 133376282
Codes: FD2

35394
The Peg Santvoord Foundation, Inc.
c/o Meyer Handelman Co.
P.O. Box 817
Purchase, NY 10577-0817
Application address: 200 Waverly Pl., New York, NY 10014, tel.: (212) 242-5249
Contact: Donn Russell, Dir.

Incorporated in 1966 in NY.
Financial data (yr. ended 06/30/01): Grants paid, $105,000; assets, $1,997,447 (M); expenditures, $122,608; qualifying distributions, $113,004.
Limitations: Giving limited to New York, NY.
Application information: Application form not required.
Officers and Directors:* William R. Handelman,* Pres. and Treas.; Russell J. Handelman,* V.P. and Secy.; Joseph W. Handelman, Donn Russell.
EIN: 136183822
Codes: FD2

35395
Hedwig van Ameringen Foundation
c/o Fulton, Rowe, Hart & Coon
1 Rockefeller Plz., Ste. 301
New York, NY 10020-2002   (212) 586-0700

Established in 1972 in NY.
Donor(s): Mrs. Arnold L. van Ameringen.
Financial data (yr. ended 12/31/01): Grants paid, $105,000; assets, $48,295 (M); expenditures, $105,880; qualifying distributions, $105,565.
Limitations: Applications not accepted. Giving primarily in NY.
Application information: Contributes only to pre-selected organizations.
Trustee: George Rowe, Jr.
EIN: 237181576
Codes: TN

35396
The Willkie 9/11 Victims Relief Fund, Inc.
c/o Willkie Farr & Gallagher
787 7th Ave.
New York, NY 10019

Established in 2001 in NY.
Donor(s): Willike Farr & Gallagher.
Financial data (yr. ended 12/31/01): Grants paid, $105,000; assets, $269,988 (M); gifts received, $375,260; expenditures, $105,272; qualifying distributions, $105,272.
Limitations: Applications not accepted. Giving primarily in New York, NY.
Application information: Contributes only to pre-selected organizations.
Officers and Directors:* Jack H. Nusbaum,* Pres.; Myron Trepper,* Secy.; Richard K. Descherer,* Treas.
EIN: 134188717
Codes: FD2

35397
Helene Foundation
c/o M. Rispler
18 Heyward St.
Brooklyn, NY 11211

Established in 1994.
Donor(s): Elsa Bistricer.
Financial data (yr. ended 11/30/00): Grants paid, $104,980; assets, $214,478 (M); expenditures, $105,119; qualifying distributions, $104,980.
Limitations: Applications not accepted.
Application information: Contributes only to pre-selected organizations.
Trustee: Elsa Bistricer.
EIN: 113220015
Codes: FD2

35398
The Braun Family Foundation
c/o Edith Braun
1775 Broadway, 26th Fl.
New York, NY 10019

Established in 1996 in NY.
Donor(s): Edith Braun.
Financial data (yr. ended 11/30/01): Grants paid, $104,977; assets, $656,872 (M); expenditures, $118,339; qualifying distributions, $107,705.
Limitations: Applications not accepted.
Application information: Contributes only to pre-selected organizations.
Officer: Edith Braun, Pres.
Director: Israel Braun.
EIN: 133932398
Codes: FD2

35399
Donald & Linda Gross Foundation, Inc.
c/o Dan's Supreme Supermarkets, Inc.
474 Fulton Ave.
Hempstead, NY 11550

Established in 1996 in NY.
Donor(s): Dan's Supreme Supermarkets, Inc.
Financial data (yr. ended 12/31/00): Grants paid, $104,955; assets, $1,466,101 (M); expenditures, $105,533; qualifying distributions, $103,995.
Directors: Donald Gross, Kenneth Gross, Linda Gross.
EIN: 113352790
Codes: CS, FD2, CD

35400
The Krauthammer Foundation, Inc.
c/o Fried, Frank & Harris
1 New York Plz.
New York, NY 10004

Established in 1988 in NY.
Financial data (yr. ended 09/30/01): Grants paid, $104,824; assets, $1,930,225 (M); expenditures, $133,401; qualifying distributions, $104,824.
Limitations: Applications not accepted. Giving primarily in Washington, DC, MD, and VA.
Application information: Contributes only to pre-selected organizations.
Directors: Charles Krauthammer, Marcel Krauthammer, Howard J. Stanislawski.
EIN: 222927289
Codes: FD2

35401
G. & S. Stern Gemilath Chesed Foundation
1407 48th St.
Brooklyn, NY 11219-3244

Established in 1998 in NY.
Donor(s): Alexander Stern.
Financial data (yr. ended 11/30/00): Grants paid, $104,569; assets, $705,190 (M); gifts received, $496,500; expenditures, $110,414; qualifying distributions, $104,569.
Limitations: Applications not accepted.
Application information: Contributes only to pre-selected organizations.
Trustee: Alexander Stern.
EIN: 113481301
Codes: FD2

35402
The Hartstein Foundation
1564 52nd St.
Brooklyn, NY 11219

Established in 1997 in NY.
Donor(s): Henry Hartstein.
Financial data (yr. ended 12/31/01): Grants paid, $104,500; assets, $298,960 (M); gifts received,

$198,000; expenditures, $104,500; qualifying distributions, $104,500.
Limitations: Applications not accepted.
Application information: Contributes only to pre-selected organizations.
Trustees: Henry Hartstein, Rachel Hartstein.
EIN: 113364149

35403
Henry C. and Karin J. Barkhorn Foundation
1095 Park Ave.
New York, NY 10128

Established in 1989 in NY.
Donor(s): Henry C. Barkhorn III.
Financial data (yr. ended 01/31/01): Grants paid, $104,250; assets, $1,919,200 (M); expenditures, $123,214; qualifying distributions, $104,863.
Limitations: Applications not accepted. Giving on a national basis, with some emphasis on NY.
Application information: Contributes only to pre-selected organizations.
Trustees: Henry C. Barkhorn III, Karin J. Barkhorn, Joan Barkhorn Hass.
EIN: 133531980
Codes: FD2

35404
The Preservation Fund
c/o Julius Paige, PC
45 W. 45th St., 12th Fl.
New York, NY 10036

Established in 1992 in NY.
Financial data (yr. ended 10/31/00): Grants paid, $104,200; assets, $2,270,934 (M); expenditures, $116,028; qualifying distributions, $112,474.
Limitations: Applications not accepted. Giving primarily in NY.
Application information: Contributes only to pre-selected organizations.
Officers: Ponchitto Pierce, Pres.; Jay Julien, V.P.; Rev. Andrew Young, Secy.; Julius Paige, Treas.
EIN: 133690790
Codes: FD2

35405
Jacqueline & Todd Goodwin Charitable Trust
600 Madison Ave.
New York, NY 10022-1615

Established in 1986 in NY.
Financial data (yr. ended 10/31/01): Grants paid, $104,095; assets, $1,673,791 (M); expenditures, $143,833; qualifying distributions, $143,833.
Limitations: Applications not accepted. Giving primarily in NY.
Application information: Contributes only to pre-selected organizations.
Trustees: Jacqueline Goodwin, Todd Goodwin.
EIN: 133389802
Codes: FD2

35406
The Beacon Light Foundation, Inc.
c/o Charles Bennett
34 Hammond Rd.
Glen Cove, NY 11542-3416 (516) 765-2981

Financial data (yr. ended 12/31/00): Grants paid, $104,025; assets, $2,076,376 (M); expenditures, $106,665; qualifying distributions, $103,653.
Limitations: Giving primarily in NY.
Officers: Alice Bennett, Pres.; Scott Bennett, Secy.; Charles T. Bennett, Treas.
EIN: 113333751
Codes: FD2

35407
The Niermeyer Foundation
c/o Michael Zukerman
450 Plaza Dr.
Vestal, NY 13850-3657

Established in 1991 in NY.
Donor(s): David Niermeyer.
Financial data (yr. ended 12/31/01): Grants paid, $103,830; assets, $145,451 (M); gifts received, $69,943; expenditures, $105,755; qualifying distributions, $105,583.
Limitations: Applications not accepted. Giving primarily in upstate NY.
Application information: Contributes only to pre-selected organizations.
Trustees: David Niermeyer, Eric Niermeyer, Florence Niermeyer, Robert J. Niermeyer.
EIN: 223136955
Codes: FD2

35408
Alfred & Harriet Feinman Foundation
134 Lincoln Ave.
Purchase, NY 10577-2303
Contact: Alfred Feinman, Pres.

Established in 1968 in NY.
Donor(s): Alfred Feinman.
Financial data (yr. ended 11/30/01): Grants paid, $103,780; assets, $1,118,245 (M); gifts received, $6,908; expenditures, $142,594; qualifying distributions, $120,675.
Limitations: Giving primarily in the greater New York, NY, area.
Application information: Application form not required.
Officers: Alfred Feinman, Pres.; Andrew Feinman, Secy.-Treas.
Directors: Martin Feinman, Robert Feinman.
EIN: 237007870
Codes: FD2

35409
D. W. Frankel Foundation, Inc.
160 E. 65th St.
New York, NY 10021-6654

Established in 1976 in NY.
Donor(s): David F. Frankel, Diane F. Sherman.
Financial data (yr. ended 12/31/99): Grants paid, $103,760; assets, $3,065,889 (M); gifts received, $118,150; expenditures, $119,744; qualifying distributions, $107,080.
Limitations: Applications not accepted. Giving on a national basis.
Application information: Contributes only to pre-selected organizations.
Officer: David F. Frankel, Pres.
Trustees: Linda Frankel, Diane F. Sherman.
EIN: 132874447
Codes: FD2

35410
Daniel & Flavia Gernatt Family Foundation
Richardson Rd.
Collins, NY 14034 (716) 337-0223

Established in 1988 in NY.
Financial data (yr. ended 12/31/01): Grants paid, $103,735; assets, $2,624,766 (M); gifts received, $149,859; expenditures, $106,142; qualifying distributions, $102,800.
Limitations: Giving primarily in the Collins and Gowanda, NY, areas.
Application information: Application form not required.
Trustees: Daniel Gernatt, Sr., Daniel Gernatt, Jr., Cynthia Peglowski, Patricia Regmann, Phyllis Ulmer.
EIN: 222914177

Codes: FD2

35411
Ferguson Foundation, Inc.
333 Ellicott St.
Buffalo, NY 14203-1678 (716) 852-2010
Contact: Whitworth Ferguson, Jr., Pres.

Established in 1954 in NY.
Donor(s): Ferguson Construction Co.
Financial data (yr. ended 12/31/01): Grants paid, $103,709; assets, $2,002,902 (M); gifts received, $73,000; expenditures, $107,643; qualifying distributions, $105,488.
Limitations: Giving limited to Buffalo, NY.
Application information: Application form not required.
Officers: Whitworth Ferguson, Jr., Pres. and Treas.; Donald R. Ferguson, Secy.
Trustee: Dorothy Ferguson.
EIN: 166043861
Codes: FD2

35412
The Guinzburg Fund
305 7th Ave., 15th Fl.
New York, NY 10001
Contact: Thomas H. Guinzburg, Pres.

Incorporated in 1955 in NY.
Donor(s): Harold K. Guinzburg.‡
Financial data (yr. ended 12/31/01): Grants paid, $103,405; assets, $116,897 (M); gifts received, $31,177; expenditures, $144,788; qualifying distributions, $102,574.
Limitations: Giving primarily in NY.
Application information: Application form not required.
Officer: Thomas H. Guinzburg, Pres.
EIN: 136108425
Codes: FD2

35413
Joan Rothenberg Family Foundation, Inc.
(Formerly Rothenberg Family Foundation, Inc.)
1111 Lac De Ville Blvd., Ste. 302
Rochester, NY 14618
E-mail: rothenberg@rothenbergfamilyfoundation.org;
URL: http://www.rothenbergfamilyfoundation.org
Contact: Sandra Rothenberg, Treas.

Established in 1998 in NY.
Donor(s): Martin Rothenberg.
Financial data (yr. ended 12/31/01): Grants paid, $103,360; assets, $1,478,547 (M); expenditures, $112,848; qualifying distributions, $103,360.
Limitations: Giving primarily in central and western NY.
Officers: Sandra Rothenberg, Pres. and Treas.; Marcia Rothenberg, Secy.
Directors: Larry Rothenberg, Martin Rothenberg.
EIN: 133940229
Codes: FD2

35414
James M. Large, Jr. Family Foundation
14 Underhill Rd.
Locust Valley, NY 11560

Established in 1997 in NY.
Donor(s): James M. Large, Jr.
Financial data (yr. ended 12/31/00): Grants paid, $103,341; assets, $564,058 (M); expenditures, $112,521; qualifying distributions, $102,976.
Limitations: Applications not accepted.
Application information: Contributes only to pre-selected organizations.
Officer: James M. Large, Jr., Pres.
EIN: 113382951
Codes: FD2

35415
The Paul F. Jacobson Foundation
c/o BCRS Associates, LLC
100 Wall St., 11th Fl.
New York, NY 10005-3101

Established in 1989 in NY.
Donor(s): Paul F. Jacobson.
Financial data (yr. ended 07/31/01): Grants paid, $103,281; assets, $6,638 (M); gifts received, $50; expenditures, $103,331; qualifying distributions, $103,329.
Limitations: Applications not accepted. Giving primarily in Washington, DC, and NY.
Application information: Contributes only to pre-selected organizations.
Trustees: Andrew M. Forbes, Paul F. Jacobson.
EIN: 223012500
Codes: FD2

35416
A. G. Burnham Charitable Fund, Inc.
P.O. Box 2449
Aquebogue, NY 11931 (631) 722-4703
FAX: (631) 722-0001; E-mail: RLWPHD@aol.com
Contact: R. Winslow, V.P.

Established in 1992 in NY.
Financial data (yr. ended 12/31/01): Grants paid, $103,200; assets, $2,450,032 (M); expenditures, $132,500; qualifying distributions, $128,387.
Limitations: Applications not accepted. Giving primarily in NY.
Application information: Contributes only to pre-selected organizations.
Officers: Alicia Winslow, Pres.; Richard Winslow, V.P. and Exec. Dir.
EIN: 133629337
Codes: FD2

35417
Confort Foundation Trust
660 White Plains Rd., Ste. 450
Tarrytown, NY 10591
Application address: c/o Scholarship Coordinator, 47-47 Austell Pl., Long Island City, NY 11101
Contact: Martin L. Riker, Tr.

Established in 1994 in NY.
Donor(s): John Confort.
Financial data (yr. ended 12/31/01): Grants paid, $103,182; assets, $603,811 (M); gifts received, $64,675; expenditures, $123,107; qualifying distributions, $120,000.
Limitations: Giving primarily to residents of Long Island City, NY.
Application information: Application form required.
Trustees: John Confort, Martin L. Riker.
EIN: 137053704
Codes: FD2, GTI

35418
The Paul & Ann Lego Charitable Foundation
c/o W. Michael Reickert, The Ayco Co., LP
P.O. Box 8019
Ballston Spa, NY 12020-8019

Established in 1993 in PA.
Donor(s): Paul E. Lego, Ann Lego.
Financial data (yr. ended 12/31/01): Grants paid, $103,175; assets, $295,579 (M); expenditures, $107,164; qualifying distributions, $103,175.
Limitations: Applications not accepted. Giving primarily in Pittsburgh, PA.
Application information: Contributes only to pre-selected organizations.
Officers: Paul E. Lego, Pres.; Ann Lego, Secy.-Treas.

Directors: Douglas E. Lego, Michael J. Lego, Paul G. Lego, Debra A. Lego-Wathen.
EIN: 251704275
Codes: FD2

35419
William B. and Anne S. Harrison Foundation
c/o JPMorgan Chase Bank
1211 Ave. of the Americas, 34th Fl.
New York, NY 10036

Established in 1998 in NY.
Financial data (yr. ended 12/31/01): Grants paid, $103,125; assets, $160,629 (M); expenditures, $106,007; qualifying distributions, $104,978.
Limitations: Applications not accepted.
Application information: Contributes only to pre-selected organizations.
Trustee: Anne S. Harrison, William B. Harrison, Jr., JPMorgan Chase Bank.
EIN: 526925583
Codes: FD2

35420
Otsar Kassin Foundation, Inc.
313 5th Ave.
New York, NY 10016 (212) 889-7602
Contact: Saul Kassin, Pres.

Established in 1974 in NY.
Donor(s): Saul Kassin, Members of the Kassin family, Transworld Textile.
Financial data (yr. ended 11/30/00): Grants paid, $103,090; assets, $10,313 (M); gifts received, $47,500; expenditures, $103,226; qualifying distributions, $103,226.
Limitations: Giving primarily in NY.
Officer: Saul Kassin, Pres.
EIN: 510168548
Codes: FD2

35421
The Pamela and Richard Rubinstein Foundation
131 Turkey Ln.
Cold Spring Harbor, NY 11724
Contact: Richard Rubinstein, Tr.

Donor(s): Pamela Rubinstein, Richard Rubinstein.
Financial data (yr. ended 12/31/01): Grants paid, $103,000; assets, $935,011 (M); gifts received, $250,000; expenditures, $104,548; qualifying distributions, $104,548.
Limitations: Giving primarily in NY.
Publications: Informational brochure.
Application information: Application form not required.
Trustees: Marissa Rubinstein, Pamela Rubinstein, Richard Rubinstein.
EIN: 137092964
Codes: FD2

35422
Gordon and Norma Smith Family Foundation
200 Madison Ave.
New York, NY 10016 (212) 696-0600
Contact: Gordon H. Smith, Dir.

Established in 1986 in NY.
Donor(s): Gordon H. Smith, Norma K. Smith.
Financial data (yr. ended 10/31/01): Grants paid, $103,000; assets, $284,731 (M); gifts received, $112,112; expenditures, $104,742; qualifying distributions, $103,000.
Limitations: Giving primarily in New York, NY.
Application information: Application form not required.
Directors: Randy Aberg, Gordon H. Smith, Norma K. Smith, Robin Smith.
EIN: 133379370
Codes: FD2

35423
The Arnow Family Fund, Inc.
1114 Ave. of the Americas, Ste. 3400
New York, NY 10036-7703

Established in 1984 in NY.
Donor(s): Robert H. Arnow, Joan W. Arnow.
Financial data (yr. ended 12/31/01): Grants paid, $102,900; assets, $2,086,121 (M); gifts received, $1,007,500; expenditures, $113,781; qualifying distributions, $104,235.
Limitations: Applications not accepted. Giving primarily in NY.
Application information: Contributes only to pre-selected organizations.
Officers and Directors:* Robert H. Arnow,* Pres.; David Arnow,* V.P.; Joshua Arnow, V.P.; Peter Arnow, V.P.; Ruth Arnow, V.P.; Joan W. Arnow, Secy.-Treas.
EIN: 133188773
Codes: FD2

35424
The Sunshine Fund
c/o Dalessio, Millner and Leben, LLP
245 5th Ave., 16th Fl.
New York, NY 10016

Established in 1987 in NY.
Donor(s): P. Henry James.
Financial data (yr. ended 04/30/01): Grants paid, $102,895; assets, $856,683 (M); expenditures, $106,403; qualifying distributions, $106,403.
Limitations: Applications not accepted. Giving primarily in Seattle, WA.
Application information: Contributes only to pre-selected organizations.
Trustees: Kathryn Anne James, Mary Ann James, Matthew Lee James, Michael Clay James, P. Henry James.
EIN: 133437889

35425
Muzio Family Foundation
c/o BCRS Assoc., LLC
67 Wall St., 8th Fl.
New York, NY 10005

Established in 1991 in NY.
Donor(s): Gaetano J. Muzio.
Financial data (yr. ended 03/31/01): Grants paid, $102,890; assets, $1,284,577 (M); expenditures, $112,666; qualifying distributions, $104,540.
Limitations: Applications not accepted. Giving on a national basis, with some emphasis on CA.
Application information: Contributes only to pre-selected organizations.
Trustees: Gaetano J. Muzio, Maria T. Muzio, James R. Rosencranz.
EIN: 133632761
Codes: FD2

35426
Goldsmith Family Charitable Foundation
620 5th Ave., 7th Fl.
New York, NY 10020

Established in 1996 in NY.
Donor(s): Jay S. Goldsmith.
Financial data (yr. ended 12/31/01): Grants paid, $102,845; assets, $299,158 (M); gifts received, $312,285; expenditures, $103,492; qualifying distributions, $103,492.
Limitations: Applications not accepted.
Application information: Contributes only to pre-selected organizations.
Officers: Jay S. Goldsmith, Pres.; Diane F. Goldsmith, V.P.; Lisa Goldsmith, Secy.; David Goldsmith, Treas.
EIN: 133891125
Codes: FD2

35427
Alex & Irene Eisenberg Foundation
900 5th Ave.
New York, NY 10021-4157 (212) 794-8567
Contact: Irene Eisenberg, Dir.

Donor(s): Alex Eisenberg.‡
Financial data (yr. ended 11/30/00): Grants paid, $102,840; assets, $733,246 (M); expenditures, $108,228; qualifying distributions, $105,057.
Limitations: Giving primarily in New York, NY.
Directors: Irene Eisenberg, Stanley Eisenberg, Walter Eisenberg.
EIN: 116026827
Codes: FD2

35428
William T. Foley Foundation, Inc.
46 Summit Ave.
Bronxville, NY 10708 (914) 779-1691
Contact: John L. Cady, Secy.-Treas.

Established in 1962 in NY.
Donor(s): Juliette Rupley, Louise Riley.‡
Financial data (yr. ended 06/30/00): Grants paid, $102,700; assets, $1,326,371 (M); expenditures, $118,352; qualifying distributions, $107,700.
Limitations: Giving primarily in New York, NY.
Application information: Rarely funds new applicants. Application form not required.
Officers: Robert Cady, Pres.; Margaret Cady, V.P.; John L. Cady, Secy.-Treas.
EIN: 136161354
Codes: FD2

35429
Fried Family Foundation
c/o Phoenix Realty
535 Madison Ave.
New York, NY 10022

Established in 1995 in NY.
Donor(s): J. Michael Fried.
Financial data (yr. ended 12/31/00): Grants paid, $102,700; assets, $70,957 (M); gifts received, $100,000; expenditures, $103,085; qualifying distributions, $102,674.
Limitations: Applications not accepted. Giving on a national basis, with emphasis on New York, NY.
Application information: Contributes only to pre-selected organizations.
Directors: J. Michael Fried, Janet C. Fried, Alan Hirmes.
EIN: 133807053
Codes: FD2

35430
Henry & Wendy Breck Foundation
550 Park Ave.
New York, NY 10021
Contact: Henry Breck, Pres.

Established in 1993 in NY.
Donor(s): Henry Breck.
Financial data (yr. ended 12/31/01): Grants paid, $102,562; assets, $939,846 (M); expenditures, $104,756; qualifying distributions, $102,562.
Limitations: Applications not accepted. Giving primarily in MA and New York, NY.
Application information: Contributes only to pre-selected organizations.
Officers: Henry Breck, Pres. and Treas.; Wendy Breck, V.P. and Secy.
Director: Christopher Breck.
EIN: 133669369
Codes: FD2

35431
The Nathan and Marilyn Silberman Foundation
c/o Nathan and Marilyn Silberman
1388 E. 24th St.
Brooklyn, NY 11210

Established in 2000 in NY.
Donor(s): Marilyn Silberman, Nathan Silberman.
Financial data (yr. ended 12/31/01): Grants paid, $102,524; assets, $11,676 (M); gifts received, $114,000; expenditures, $103,428; qualifying distributions, $103,427.
Limitations: Applications not accepted.
Application information: Contributes only to pre-selected organizations.
Trustees: Marilyn Silberman, Nathan Silberman.
EIN: 116534409
Codes: FD2

35432
The Spionkop Charitable Trust
c/o C. Pratt & Co.
355 Lexington Ave., 8th Fl.
New York, NY 10017-6603

Established in 1997 in NY.
Financial data (yr. ended 12/31/01): Grants paid, $102,500; assets, $2,389,048 (M); expenditures, $165,421; qualifying distributions, $112,193.
Limitations: Applications not accepted. Giving primarily in CT, MA and NY.
Application information: Contributes only to pre-selected organizations.
Trustees: Mary Offutt Pratt, Richardson Pratt, Jr.
EIN: 137087319
Codes: FD2

35433
Adina & Jeffrey Rubin Foundation
c/o M. Pinter & Co.
1406 57th St.
Brooklyn, NY 11219

Established in 1997 in NY.
Donor(s): Adina Rubin, Jeffrey Rubin.
Financial data (yr. ended 12/31/99): Grants paid, $102,369; assets, $52,840 (M); expenditures, $103,516; qualifying distributions, $102,285.
Limitations: Giving primarily in NY.
Trustees: Adina Rubin, Jeffrey Rubin.
EIN: 137124403
Codes: FD2

35434
Ayres/Baechle Foundation
c/o U.S. Trust
114 W. 47th St.
New York, NY 10036

Established in 1998.
Financial data (yr. ended 12/31/99): Grants paid, $102,350; assets, $2,629,085 (M); expenditures, $126,678; qualifying distributions, $101,877.
Limitations: Applications not accepted.
Application information: Contributes only to pre-selected organizations.
Officers: Christine Baechle, Chair.; Charles Ayres, Vice-Chair. and Pres.; James J. Baechle, V.P. and Secy.-Treas.
EIN: 522006012
Codes: FD2

35435
Eugene and Carol Atkinson Family Foundation
c/o BCRS Associates, LLC
67 Wall St., 8th Fl.
New York, NY 10005

Established in 1985 in NJ.
Donor(s): Eugene D. Atkinson.
Financial data (yr. ended 06/30/01): Grants paid, $102,294; assets, $1,655,532 (M); expenditures, $138,493; qualifying distributions, $102,294.
Limitations: Applications not accepted. Giving primarily in the tri-state CT, NJ, and NY, area.
Application information: Contributes only to pre-selected organizations.
Trustees: Carol A. Atkinson, Eugene D. Atkinson.
EIN: 133318157

35436
Weg Foundation, Inc.
8 Ruth Ct.
Monsey, NY 10952 (845) 357-4740
Contact: Noah Weg, M.D., Dir.

Established in 1987 in NY.
Donor(s): Noah Weg, M.D., Yetta Weg.
Financial data (yr. ended 11/30/99): Grants paid, $102,184; assets, $174,627 (M); gifts received, $100,313; expenditures, $102,394; qualifying distributions, $102,184.
Limitations: Giving primarily in Monsey and Brooklyn, NY.
Directors: Joseph N. Lieder, Noah Weg, M.D., Renee H. Weg.
EIN: 133439686
Codes: FD2

35437
Tilles Foundation
c/o BCRS Assocs., LLC
100 Wall St., 11th Fl.
New York, NY 10005

Established in 1989 in NY.
Donor(s): Gary S. Gensler.
Financial data (yr. ended 05/31/01): Grants paid, $102,180; assets, $1,184,921 (M); expenditures, $104,330; qualifying distributions, $103,028.
Limitations: Applications not accepted. Giving primarily in Washington, DC and MD.
Application information: Contributes only to pre-selected organizations.
Trustees: Francesca Danieli, Gary S. Gensler.
EIN: 133541870
Codes: FD2

35438
First Albany Foundation, Inc.
30 S. Pearl St.
Albany, NY 12207

Established in 1993 in NY.
Donor(s): First Albany Companies Inc., First Albany Corp.
Financial data (yr. ended 12/31/01): Grants paid, $102,050; assets, $185,708 (M); gifts received, $149,350; expenditures, $102,158; qualifying distributions, $102,067.
Limitations: Applications not accepted. Giving primarily in Albany, NY.
Application information: Contributes only to pre-selected organizations.
Officers and Directors:* George McNamee,* Pres.; Hugh Johnson,* V.P.; Alan P. Goldberg,* Treas.
EIN: 141749789
Codes: CS, FD2, CD

35439
Apple Lane Foundation
(Formerly De Sieyes Family Foundation)
c/o U.S. Trust
114 W. 47th St.
New York, NY 10036
FAX: (212) 852-3377
Contact: Andrew Lane, Asst. V.P.

Established in 1998 in CT.
Donor(s): Virginia De Sieyes.

35439—NEW YORK

Financial data (yr. ended 12/31/00): Grants paid, $102,011; assets, $3,300,656 (M); expenditures, $115,314; qualifying distributions, $102,011.
Limitations: Applications not accepted.
Application information: Contributes only to pre-selected organizations.
Officers and Directors:* Charles J. De Sieyes,* Pres.; David C. De Sieyes,* V.P.; Virginia Risley.
EIN: 061501640
Codes: FD2

35440
The Donnet Fund, Inc.
302 W. 12th St.
New York, NY 10014

Established in 1990 in NY.
Donor(s): Jacqueline Donnet.
Financial data (yr. ended 12/31/01): Grants paid, $102,000; assets, $11,357 (M); gifts received, $115,600; expenditures, $108,139; qualifying distributions, $102,000.
Limitations: Applications not accepted. Giving primarily in CA and New York, NY.
Application information: Contributes only to pre-selected organizations.
Officer: Jacqueline Donnet, Pres.
EIN: 133532583
Codes: FD2

35441
Judith and Frank Greenberg Foundation, Inc.
c/o Anchin, Block & Anchin, LLP
1375 Broadway, 18th Fl.
New York, NY 10018

Established in 1995 in NY.
Donor(s): Frank Greenberg.
Financial data (yr. ended 01/31/02): Grants paid, $101,925; assets, $682,159 (M); expenditures, $111,958; qualifying distributions, $104,890.
Limitations: Applications not accepted. Giving primarily in New York, NY.
Application information: Contributes only to pre-selected organizations.
Officers: Judith Greenberg, Pres.; Frank Greenberg, V.P. and Treas.; Richard Werman, Secy.
EIN: 113295586
Codes: FD2

35442
David & Minnie Berk Foundation, Inc.
1000 Woodbury Rd., Ste. 212A
Woodbury, NY 11797
Contact: Ronald Berk, Pres.

Established in 1961 in NY.
Donor(s): Members and friends of the Berk family.
Financial data (yr. ended 10/31/01): Grants paid, $101,750; assets, $2,360,457 (M); expenditures, $147,052; qualifying distributions, $101,187.
Limitations: Giving primarily in the tri-state NJ, NY, and PA, area.
Application information: Application form required.
Officers and Trustees:* Ronald Berk,* Pres.; Joy Levien,* 1st V.P.; Bruce Ostrow,* 2nd V.P.; Hope Reiner,* Secy.; Amy Berk Kuhn,* Treas.
EIN: 116038062
Codes: FD2

35443
Rosalind & Eugene J. Glaser Foundation
784 Park Ave., Ste. 15C
New York, NY 10021-3553

Established in 1999 in NY.
Donor(s): Rosalind Glaser, Eugene J. Glaser.
Financial data (yr. ended 12/31/01): Grants paid, $101,690; assets, $1,179,184 (M); expenditures, $109,432; qualifying distributions, $101,690.

Limitations: Applications not accepted. Giving primarily in NY.
Application information: Contributes only to pre-selected organizations.
Trustees: Alexis Glaser, Blair Glaser, Eugene J. Glaser, Rosalind Glaser.
EIN: 137193893
Codes: FD2

35444
Cowen Foundation
c/o Financial Square Partners
60 E. 42nd St., Ste. 1535
New York, NY 10165

Established in 1990 in NY.
Donor(s): Cowen & Co., SG Cowen Securities Corporation, Dover Fund, Arthur Cowen Charitable Lead Trust.
Financial data (yr. ended 12/31/01): Grants paid, $101,520; assets, $123,349 (M); gifts received, $21,202; expenditures, $104,175; qualifying distributions, $102,650.
Limitations: Applications not accepted. Giving primarily in NY.
Application information: Contributes only to pre-selected organizations.
Officers and Directors:* Joseph M. Cohen,* Pres.; Creighton H. Peet,* V.P.; Robert M. Greenberger,* Treas.; Stephen R. Weber.
EIN: 133550779
Codes: CS, TN

35445
The Robert M. Conway Foundation
(Formerly Robert M. & Lois Conway Foundation)
c/o BCRS Assocs., LLC
67 Wall St., 8th Fl.
New York, NY 10005

Established in 1982 in NY.
Donor(s): Robert M. Conway.
Financial data (yr. ended 09/30/01): Grants paid, $101,500; assets, $1,694,150 (M); expenditures, $105,975; qualifying distributions, $101,500.
Limitations: Applications not accepted. Giving in the U.S. and England.
Application information: Contributes only to pre-selected organizations.
Trustees: Robert M. Conway, Robert J. Hurst.
EIN: 133153721

35446
John & Joan D'Addario Foundation, Inc.
c/o Carney, Tiger, et al.
100 Crossways Park W., Ste. 112
Woodbury, NY 11797

Established in 1998 in NY.
Donor(s): John D'Addario, Jr., Joan D'Addario.
Financial data (yr. ended 05/31/01): Grants paid, $101,359; assets, $174,942 (M); expenditures, $103,938; qualifying distributions, $101,359.
Limitations: Applications not accepted. Giving primarily in NY.
Application information: Contributes only to pre-selected organizations.
Officers: John D'Addario, Jr., Pres.; Joan D'Addario, Secy.-Treas.
Directors: John D'Addario III, Laura D'Addario, Michael D'Addario, Suzanne D'Addario.
EIN: 113440873
Codes: FD2

35447
Elizabeth Goldberg Charitable Foundation, Inc.
(Formerly Bernard & Elizabeth Goldberg Charitable Foundation, Inc.)
8 E. 83rd St.
New York, NY 10028
Contact: Elizabeth Goldberg, Pres.

Established in 1990 in NY.
Donor(s): Bernard Goldberg, Elizabeth Goldberg.
Financial data (yr. ended 03/31/01): Grants paid, $101,310; assets, $886,173 (M); gifts received, $79,738; expenditures, $106,732; qualifying distributions, $101,473.
Limitations: Applications not accepted. Giving primarily in New York, NY.
Application information: Contributes only to pre-selected organizations.
Officers and Directors:* Elizabeth Goldberg,* Pres. and Treas.; Tamar Goldberg Olitsky,* V.P. and Secy.; Emanuel Gruss, Riane Gruss.
EIN: 133100096
Codes: FD2

35448
The Weisz Family Charitable Foundation
58 Joseph Ave.
Staten Island, NY 10314
Contact: Bentzie Weisz, Tr. or Estee Weisz, Tr.

Established in 1996 in NY.
Donor(s): Bentzie Weisz, Estie Weisz.
Financial data (yr. ended 12/31/01): Grants paid, $101,300; assets, $341,626 (M); gifts received, $95,000; expenditures, $109,435; qualifying distributions, $101,300.
Trustees: Bentzie Weisz, Estee Weisz.
EIN: 133922399

35449
Lila Gruber Research Foundation
301 Baltustrol Cir.
Roslyn, NY 11576
Contact: Murray P. Gruber, Tr.

Established in 1962.
Donor(s): Barry Gruber, Daryl Gruber Kulok, Murray P. Gruber, Helen Gruber.
Financial data (yr. ended 12/31/01): Grants paid, $101,150; assets, $2,636,508 (M); gifts received, $664,016; expenditures, $143,192; qualifying distributions, $101,150.
Limitations: Giving primarily in NY.
Application information: Application form not required.
Trustees: Helen Gruber, Murray P. Gruber, Daryl Gruber Kulok.
EIN: 116035223
Codes: FD2

35450
The Wolverine Foundation
350 Park Ave., 18th Fl.
New York, NY 10022

Established in 1999 in DE.
Donor(s): Alan W. Breed.
Financial data (yr. ended 12/31/00): Grants paid, $101,075; assets, $767,689 (M); expenditures, $111,559; qualifying distributions, $104,743.
Limitations: Applications not accepted. Giving primarily in CT.
Application information: Contributes only to pre-selected organizations.
Officers: Alan W. Breed, Pres. and Treas.; Ellen G. Breed, V.P.; Michael S. Breed, Secy.
EIN: 510394484
Codes: FD2

35451
Drasner Family Foundation
450 W. 33rd St.
New York, NY 10001-2603

Established in 1996 in NY.
Donor(s): Fred Drasner.
Financial data (yr. ended 12/31/00): Grants paid, $101,000; assets, $1,324,176 (M); gifts received, $1,480; expenditures, $102,880; qualifying distributions, $101,000.
Limitations: Applications not accepted. Giving primarily in NY.
Application information: Contributes only to pre-selected organizations.
Directors: Fred Drasner, Kenneth Drasner, Martin D. Krall.
EIN: 133924566
Codes: FD2

35452
Harry & Rose Jacobs Foundation, Inc.
c/o Yeshiva University
500 W. 185th St., 6th Fl.
New York, NY 10033
Contact: A. Gleicher

Donor(s): Harry Jacobs.
Financial data (yr. ended 12/31/01): Grants paid, $101,000; assets, $1,787,029 (M); expenditures, $102,430; qualifying distributions, $99,919.
Limitations: Applications not accepted. Giving limited to NY.
Application information: Contributes only to pre-selected organizations.
Officers: Norman Lamm, Pres.; Sheldon E. Socol, V.P.; Bernard Pittinsky, Secy.
EIN: 136161740
Codes: FD2

35453
Pells-Mayton Foundation, Inc.
c/o John Parker
18 Hemlock Rd.
Bronxville, NY 10708-3213

Established in 1983 in NY.
Financial data (yr. ended 12/31/00): Grants paid, $101,000; assets, $2,006,147 (M); expenditures, $158,034; qualifying distributions, $107,262.
Limitations: Applications not accepted. Giving primarily in NY.
Application information: Contributes only to pre-selected organizations.
Officers: Gladys M. Parker, Pres.; John J. Parker, Secy.-Treas.
EIN: 133187866
Codes: FD2

35454
Botwinick-Wolfensohn Foundation, Inc.
277 Park Ave., 49th Fl.
New York, NY 10172 (212) 207-5509
FAX: (212) 909-0831
Contact: Bridget Batson, Asst. Dir.

Established in 1952 in NY.
Donor(s): James D. Wolfensohn, Benjamin Botwinick, Edward Botwinick.
Financial data (yr. ended 12/31/00): Grants paid, $100,887; assets, $9,809,511 (M); gifts received, $4,804,065; expenditures, $104,261; qualifying distributions, $100,887.
Limitations: Applications not accepted. Giving primarily in New York, NY.
Application information: Contributes only to pre-selected organizations.
Officers: James D. Wolfensohn, Chair.; Edward Botwinick, Pres.; Adam Wolfensohn, V.P.; Elaine R. Wolfensohn, V.P.; Andrew Botwinick, Co-Secy.;
Sara R. Wolfensohn, Secy.; Naomi R. Wolfensohn, Treas.
EIN: 136111833
Codes: FD2

35455
The Zenna Family Foundation, Inc.
c/o SLK
120 Broadway, 8th Fl.
New York, NY 10271

Established in 1998 in NY.
Donor(s): Alphonse Zenna.
Financial data (yr. ended 09/30/01): Grants paid, $100,725; assets, $1,110,529 (M); gifts received, $678,015; expenditures, $101,450; qualifying distributions, $98,650.
Limitations: Applications not accepted. Giving primarily in NY.
Application information: Contributes only to pre-selected organizations.
Officers: Alphonse Zenna, Pres. and Treas.; Kathleen Zenna, V.P. and Secy.; Gregory Zenna, V.P.
EIN: 134039072
Codes: FD2

35456
Barbara and Donald Tober Foundation
c/o Jack Vivinetto, Sugar Foods Corp.
950 3rd Ave.
New York, NY 10022

Established in 1999 in NY.
Donor(s): Barbara Tober, Donald Tober.
Financial data (yr. ended 12/31/01): Grants paid, $100,615; assets, $115,977 (M); gifts received, $94,144; expenditures, $107,280; qualifying distributions, $101,930.
Limitations: Applications not accepted.
Application information: Contributes only to pre-selected organizations.
Trustees: Myron Stein, Barbara Tober, Donald G. Tober, Jack Vivinetto.
EIN: 137192894
Codes: FD2

35457
Janis and Alan Menken Foundation, Inc.
c/o Mason & Co., LLP
400 Park Ave., Ste. 1200
New York, NY 10022
Contact: Alan Menken, Pres.

Established in 1996 in NY.
Donor(s): Alan Menken.
Financial data (yr. ended 12/31/01): Grants paid, $100,582; assets, $90,788 (M); gifts received, $150,000; expenditures, $101,370; qualifying distributions, $101,359.
Limitations: Giving primarily in NY.
Officers and Directors:* Alan Menken,* Pres.; Janis Menken,* V.P.; Eric Kunis, Secy.; David Gotterer.
EIN: 133920424
Codes: FD2

35458
C. J. Huang Foundation
36 E. 74th St.
New York, NY 10021

Established around 1993.
Financial data (yr. ended 08/31/01): Grants paid, $100,550; assets, $1,937,451 (M); gifts received, $121,855; expenditures, $107,239; qualifying distributions, $106,264.
Limitations: Applications not accepted. Giving primarily in the northeastern U.S., with emphasis on CT, MA, NY, and RI.

Application information: Contributes only to pre-selected organizations.
Director: Paul Huang.
EIN: 133437209
Codes: FD2

35459
Welfare Trust Fund of the Twenty-Five Year Club
c/o The Bank of New York, Tax Dept.
1 Wall St., 28th Fl.
New York, NY 10286

Established in 1955 in NY.
Donor(s): The Twenty-Five Year Club.
Financial data (yr. ended 12/31/01): Grants paid, $100,500; assets, $228,117 (M); gifts received, $65,000; expenditures, $102,785; qualifying distributions, $100,295.
Limitations: Applications not accepted.
Application information: Contributes only to pre-selected organizations.
Trustee: The Bank of New York.
EIN: 136064124
Codes: FD2, GTI

35460
Woodshouse Foundation
(Formerly The Biggs Foundation)
c/o Josephine Glass
1221 Ave. of the Americas
New York, NY 10020
Application address: Les Chetifs Champs, St. Aubin Le Monial, France 03160
Contact: Wende Biggs Ratcliffe, Dir.

Established in 1992 in CT.
Financial data (yr. ended 12/31/01): Grants paid, $100,500; assets, $4,142,268 (M); expenditures, $155,748; qualifying distributions, $100,500.
Limitations: Giving primarily in the U.S. and France.
Trustees: Barton W. Biggs, Gretchen Biggs, Wende Biggs Ratcliffe.
EIN: 136983078
Codes: FD2

35461
The Sussman Family Charitable Foundation
c/o Ira Sussman
50 Parkville Ave.
Brooklyn, NY 11230

Established in 1993 in NY.
Donor(s): Ira Sussman, Judy Sussman.
Financial data (yr. ended 12/31/99): Grants paid, $100,485; assets, $1,480,646 (M); gifts received, $594,959; expenditures, $101,415; qualifying distributions, $101,321.
Limitations: Applications not accepted. Giving primarily in Brooklyn, NY.
Application information: Contributes only to pre-selected organizations.
Trustees: Ira Sussman, Judy Sussman.
EIN: 116436659
Codes: FD2

35462
Alice W. C. Koon Scholastic Fund
c/o HSBC Bank USA
1 HSBC Center, 17th Fl.
Buffalo, NY 14203

Established in 1967 in NY.
Financial data (yr. ended 12/31/01): Grants paid, $100,482; assets, $1,750,688 (M); expenditures, $129,273; qualifying distributions, $103,127.
Limitations: Applications not accepted. Giving limited to students residing in Cayuga County, NY.
Application information: Students may only apply through the superintendent of schools in the Southern Cayuga Central School District.

35462—NEW YORK

Trustee: HSBC Bank USA.
EIN: 166071002
Codes: FD2, GTI

35463
E. & M. Schreiber Family Foundation
180 Riverside Dr.
New York, NY 10024
Contact: Mary Schreiber, Pres.

Established in 1988 in NY.
Donor(s): Emanuel Schreiber, Mary Schreiber.
Financial data (yr. ended 06/30/01): Grants paid, $100,450; assets, $1,420,036 (M); gifts received, $134,106; expenditures, $102,404; qualifying distributions, $100,450.
Limitations: Giving primarily in NJ and NY.
Officers and Trustees:* Emanuel Schreiber,* Pres.; Mary Schreiber,* Pres.; Morris Schreiber,* Pres.
EIN: 133475648
Codes: FD2

35464
The Green River Foundation
c/o Goldman Sachs & Co.
85 Broad St., Tax Dept.
New York, NY 10004

Established in 1989 in NY.
Donor(s): John P. Curtin, Jr.
Financial data (yr. ended 02/28/01): Grants paid, $100,300; assets, $1,506,681 (M); gifts received, $3,000; expenditures, $104,230; qualifying distributions, $100,630.
Limitations: Applications not accepted. Giving primarily in New York, NY, and Newport, RI.
Application information: Contributes only to pre-selected organizations.
Trustees: Anne N. Curtin, John P. Curtin, Charles B. Mayer, Jr.
EIN: 133532021
Codes: FD2

35465
The Marilyn B. & Stanley L. Cohen Foundation, Inc.
c/o Tanton & Co., LLP
37 W. 57th St., 5th Fl.
New York, NY 10019

Established in 1977 in NY.
Donor(s): Stanley L. Cohen.
Financial data (yr. ended 06/30/01): Grants paid, $100,057; assets, $590,225 (M); expenditures, $103,348; qualifying distributions, $99,732.
Limitations: Applications not accepted. Giving primarily in New York, NY.
Application information: Contributes only to pre-selected organizations.
Officers: Stanley L. Cohen, Pres. and Treas.; Marilyn B. Cohen, V.P. and Secy.
Directors: Adam S. Cohen, Edward Small.
EIN: 132920362
Codes: FD2

35466
Heilbrunn Foundation
c/o Herbert Paul
370 Lexington Ave., Rm. 1001
New York, NY 10017-2416

Established in 1960.
Donor(s): Robert Heilbrunn,‡ Berkshire Hathaway, Inc.
Financial data (yr. ended 12/31/01): Grants paid, $100,036; assets, $165,465 (M); expenditures, $103,146; qualifying distributions, $103,146.
Limitations: Applications not accepted. Giving primarily in New York, NY.
Application information: Contributes only to pre-selected organizations.

Officer: Robert Heilbrunn, Pres.; Harriet Heilbrunn, Secy.-Treas.
EIN: 136138257
Codes: FD2

35467
Bertelsmann Foundation U.S., Inc.
1540 Broadway
New York, NY 10036-4094

Established in 1996 in NY.
Donor(s): Bertelsmann, Inc., Bertelsmann Stiftung, The Chase Manhattan Bank, N.A., BMG Music, Random House, Inc.
Financial data (yr. ended 06/30/00): Grants paid, $100,000; assets, $720,190 (M); gifts received, $812,250; expenditures, $991,523; qualifying distributions, $991,523; giving activities include $624,066 for programs.
Limitations: Applications not accepted. Giving primarily in New York, NY.
Application information: Contributes only to pre-selected organizations.
Officers and Directors:* Robert J. Sorrentino,* Pres.; Jacqueline Chasey,* V.P. and Secy.; Evelyn Alvarado, Treas.; Rafael Ortiz, Exec. Dir.; Wolfgang Keochstadt, Melanie Phillips.
EIN: 133777740
Codes: CS, FD2, CD

35468
The C.O.U.Q. Foundation, Inc.
c/o George V. Delson Assocs.
110 E. 59th St.
New York, NY 10022

Established in 1998 in NY.
Donor(s): Jeffrey E. Epstein.
Financial data (yr. ended 02/28/01): Grants paid, $100,000; assets, $47,821 (M); expenditures, $183,875; qualifying distributions, $183,255.
Limitations: Applications not accepted. Giving on an international basis.
Application information: Contributes only to pre-selected organizations.
Officers and Directors:* Jeffrey E. Epstein,* Pres.; Darren K. Indyke,* V.P.; Ghislaine Maxwell,* Treas.
EIN: 133996471
Codes: FD2

35469
Copperfield Fund
30 Rockefeller Plz., Rm. 5600
New York, NY 10112-0230

Established in 1965.
Donor(s): Neva R. Goodwin.
Financial data (yr. ended 11/30/01): Grants paid, $100,000; assets, $918 (M); gifts received, $101,000; expenditures, $100,599; qualifying distributions, $100,000.
Limitations: Applications not accepted. Giving on a national basis.
Application information: Contributes only to pre-selected organizations.
Trustees: Neva R. Goodwin, David W. Kaiser, Miranda M. Kaiser, Bruce Mazlish.
EIN: 136208454

35470
Frank J. Fee Foundation, Inc.
525 N. MacQuesten Pkwy.
Mount Vernon, NY 10552-2609
Contact: Frank J. Fee III, Pres.

Donor(s): The Reliable Automatic Sprinkler Co., Inc.
Financial data (yr. ended 08/31/01): Grants paid, $100,000; assets, $41,505 (M); gifts received, $125,000; expenditures, $100,038; qualifying distributions, $100,000.

Limitations: Giving primarily in MA.
Application information: Application form not required.
Officers: Frank J. Fee III, Pres.; Kevin T. Fee, Secy.; Eugene Carbine, Treas.
Trustees: Candida M. Fee, Michael R. Fee.
EIN: 136130510
Codes: FD2

35471
The Flagler Foundation, Inc.
c/o Sullivan & Cromwell
125 Broad St.
New York, NY 10004-2498

Established around 1985.
Donor(s): G.F. Robert Hanke.
Financial data (yr. ended 12/31/01): Grants paid, $100,000; assets, $1,187,071 (M); gifts received, $10,000; expenditures, $104,110; qualifying distributions, $100,302.
Limitations: Applications not accepted. Giving primarily in New York, NY, and Quantico, VA.
Application information: Contributes only to pre-selected organizations.
Officers: Frederick A. Terry, Jr., Pres.; G.F. Robert Hanke, Exec. V.P.; Lynn S. Washburn, V.P.; James I. Black III, Secy.-Treas.
EIN: 133236910
Codes: FD2

35472
Evelyn Fraites Foundation, Inc.
61 Broadway, 18th Fl.
New York, NY 10006-2794
Application address: c/o Prudential Securities, Inc., 1 Financial Sq., 32 Old Slip, 6th Fl., New York, NY 10292, tel.: (212) 804-7880
Contact: Joseph L. Fraites, Sr., Pres.

Established in 1984 in NJ.
Donor(s): Joseph Lawrence Fraites, Sr.
Financial data (yr. ended 11/30/99): Grants paid, $100,000; assets, $151,346 (M); gifts received, $101,698; expenditures, $103,537; qualifying distributions, $100,407.
Limitations: Applications not accepted. Giving limited to residents of Cranford, NJ.
Officers and Trustees:* Joseph Lawrence Fraites, Sr.,* Pres.; Christopher George Fraites,* V.P.; Ellen M. Fraites,* V.P.; Joseph Lawrence Fraites, Jr.,* V.P.; Lisa Fraites Dworkin,* Secy.
EIN: 133241845
Codes: FD2, GTI

35473
Gramercy Foundation, Inc.
2169 Grand Concourse
Bronx, NY 10453-2201
Contact: Kurt Struver, Dir.

Established in 1990 in NY.
Financial data (yr. ended 12/31/01): Grants paid, $100,000; assets, $841,255 (M); expenditures, $148,145; qualifying distributions, $107,445.
Limitations: Applications not accepted. Giving primarily in Blairstown, NJ.
Application information: Contributes only to pre-selected organizations.
Officers and Directors:* Lawrence Dix,* Treas.; Murray Struver,* Exec. Dir.; Kurt Struver.
EIN: 135625601
Codes: FD2

35474
Aaron & Marion Gural Foundation
c/o Newmark & Co. Real Estate Inc.
125 Park Ave., 11th Fl.
New York, NY 10017-5529
Contact: Aaron Gural, Pres.

Established in 1986 in NY.
Donor(s): Aaron Gural.
Financial data (yr. ended 12/31/99): Grants paid, $100,000; assets, $1,709,114 (M); expenditures, $106,316; qualifying distributions, $98,735.
Limitations: Applications not accepted. Giving primarily in New York, NY.
Application information: Contributes only to pre-selected organizations.
Officer: Aaron Gural, Pres.
Director: Jane Gural Senders.
EIN: 133377362
Codes: FD2

35475
The Henkind Foundation
2 Gannett Dr.
White Plains, NY 10604 (914) 694-1533
Contact: Lewis Henkind

Donor(s): Sol Henkind.
Financial data (yr. ended 12/31/00): Grants paid, $100,000; assets, $1,727,004 (M); expenditures, $100,758; qualifying distributions, $99,238.
Trustee: Sol Henkind.
EIN: 136165710
Codes: FD2

35476
Libby Holman Foundation, Inc.
121 E. 61st St.
New York, NY 10021-8146 (212) 751-6475
Contact: Jack Clareman, Pres.

Established in 1962 in NY.
Donor(s): Libby Holman Reynolds.‡
Financial data (yr. ended 02/28/01): Grants paid, $100,000; assets, $2,217,521 (M); expenditures, $119,933; qualifying distributions, $109,411.
Limitations: Giving primarily in New York, NY.
Application information: Application form not required.
Officers and Directors:* Jack Clareman,* Pres. and Secy.; Anthony Reynolds,* V.P.; Timothy H. Reynolds,* V.P.; Lloyd S. Clareman,* Treas.; Brooke Cheney, Mary Reynolds.
EIN: 116037769
Codes: FD2

35477
Keren Yisrole Efraim Fishel
10 W. 33rd St., No. 230
New York, NY 10001

Established in 1996 in NY.
Donor(s): Zolton Goldstein, Rosalia Goldstein.
Financial data (yr. ended 12/31/01): Grants paid, $100,000; assets, $1,660,625 (M); gifts received, $749,500; expenditures, $1,211,721; qualifying distributions, $99,864.
Trustees: Rosalia Goldstein, Zolton Goldstein.
EIN: 116167234

35478
Lawrence Family Foundation
c/o JPMorgan Chase Bank
P.O. Box 31412
Rochester, NY 14603

Established in 2000 in CA.
Donor(s): Mary K. Lawrence,‡ John K. Lawrence.
Financial data (yr. ended 12/31/01): Grants paid, $100,000; assets, $1,714,004 (M); gifts received, $1,101,177; expenditures, $176,070; qualifying distributions, $89,747.
Limitations: Applications not accepted. Giving primarily in CA and NY.
Application information: Contributes only to pre-selected organizations.
Officers: John K. Lawrence, Pres.; Barbara Kulik Lawrence, C.F.O.
Directors: Francis H. Lawrence, Helen Lawrence.
EIN: 954820107
Codes: FD2

35479
The Reuben and Jane Leibowitz Foundation, Inc.
911 Park Ave.
New York, NY 10021
Contact: Reuben S. Leibowitz, Tr.

Established in 1986 in NY.
Donor(s): Reuben S. Leibowitz.
Financial data (yr. ended 11/30/01): Grants paid, $100,000; assets, $2,322,598 (M); expenditures, $118,183; qualifying distributions, $104,176.
Limitations: Applications not accepted. Giving primarily in NY.
Application information: Contributes only to pre-selected organizations.
Trustees: Jane Leibowitz, Reuben S. Leibowitz, David Warmflash.
EIN: 133382812
Codes: FD2

35480
Lui and Wan Foundation
Murray Hill Sta.
P.O. Box 150
New York, NY 10156 (212) 689-4939
Contact: Francis C. Lui, Pres.

Established in 2001 in NY.
Donor(s): Francis C. Lui, Livia Wan Lui.
Financial data (yr. ended 02/28/02): Grants paid, $100,000; assets, $899,845 (M); gifts received, $1,002,500; expenditures, $4,155; qualifying distributions, $104,155.
Limitations: Giving primarily in VA.
Officers and Directors:* Francis C. Lui,* Pres.; Lawrence Lui,* V.P.; Yvonne Lui,* Secy.; Livia Wan Lui,* Treas.
EIN: 134161117

35481
Messinger Family Foundation, Inc.
140 Osborn Rd.
Harrison, NY 10528-1018

Established in 1998 in NY.
Donor(s): Martin Messinger.
Financial data (yr. ended 11/30/01): Grants paid, $100,000; assets, $1,915,633 (M); expenditures, $100,141; qualifying distributions, $99,700.
Limitations: Applications not accepted. Giving primarily in NY.
Application information: Contributes only to pre-selected organizations.
Directors: Daryl Messinger, Joan Messinger, Lisa Messinger, Martin Messinger, Sarah Messinger, Alice Messinger Rosenblatt.
EIN: 133979672
Codes: FD2

35482
Sidney & Jeanne Mishkin Foundation
c/o Hermine Mishkin
880 5th Ave., Apt. 14D
New York, NY 10021-4951

Established about 1945 in NY.
Financial data (yr. ended 12/31/00): Grants paid, $100,000; assets, $1,066,112 (M); gifts received, $54,980; expenditures, $102,756; qualifying distributions, $99,122.
Limitations: Applications not accepted. Giving primarily in the greater New York, NY, area.
Application information: Contributes only to pre-selected organizations.
Directors: Phyliss Meyers, Hermine Mishkin, Jeanne Mishkin, Joseph Mishkin.
EIN: 136142376
Codes: FD2

35483
Charles Schleussner Charitable Trust
c/o JPMorgan Chase Bank
1211 6th Ave., 34th Fl.
New York, NY 10036

Established in 1996 in NY.
Financial data (yr. ended 08/31/00): Grants paid, $100,000; assets, $4,524,898 (M); expenditures, $239,745; qualifying distributions, $126,951.
Limitations: Applications not accepted.
Application information: Contributes only to pre-selected organizations.
Trustees: Eugene E. Ressler, JPMorgan Chase Bank.
EIN: 136852499
Codes: FD2

35484
Ida Miriam Stern Memorial Fund, Inc.
1333 Broadway, Ste. 730
New York, NY 10018 (212) 760-0601
Contact: Richard M. Orin, Pres.

Established in 1991 in NY.
Financial data (yr. ended 10/31/01): Grants paid, $100,000; assets, $965,482 (M); expenditures, $110,884; qualifying distributions, $99,692.
Limitations: Giving primarily in New York, NY.
Officers: Richard M. Orin, Pres.; Dorothy Bergeron, Secy.; Eli Robins, Treas.
EIN: 133646296
Codes: FD2

35485
Raybin Q. Wong Foundation
c/o Martin Young
5 Roland Dr.
White Plains, NY 10605-5406

Established in 2000 in NY.
Financial data (yr. ended 12/31/01): Grants paid, $100,000; assets, $1,687,343 (M); gifts received, $6,671,895; expenditures, $100,024; qualifying distributions, $100,000.
Trustees: Peizhen Shao, Martin Young.
EIN: 113472626

35486
The Brennan Family Foundation
46 Hoaglands Ln.
Old Brookville, NY 11545
FAX: (516) 656-5953
Contact: Eileen B. Oakley, Dir.

Established in 1995 in DE and NY.
Donor(s): Patricia A. Brennan.
Financial data (yr. ended 12/31/01): Grants paid, $99,970; assets, $779,586 (M); gifts received, $7,030; expenditures, $115,813; qualifying distributions, $109,796.
Limitations: Giving primarily in New York, NY.
Officers: Donald P. Brennan, Pres.; Patricia A. Brennan, V.P.
Director: Eileen B. Oakley.
EIN: 133757539
Codes: FD2

35487
Nicholas & Christina Raho Foundation, Inc.
350 Theodore Fremd Ave.
Rye, NY 10580-1573

Established in 1980.
Donor(s): Nicholas Raho, Christina Raho, Peter Raho, Joseph Raho.
Financial data (yr. ended 06/30/01): Grants paid, $99,818; assets, $2,150,215 (M); gifts received, $326,063; expenditures, $103,656; qualifying distributions, $102,656.
Limitations: Applications not accepted. Giving on a national basis, with emphasis on NY.
Application information: Contributes only to pre-selected organizations.
Officers: Mary R. Julian, Pres.; Christina Raho, V.P.
Director: Nicholas Raho.
EIN: 133049641
Codes: FD2

35488
Scientific Research Foundation, Inc.
c/o Carl Loeb III
210 E. 65th St., Apt. 14A
New York, NY 10021

Established in 1963.
Donor(s): Carl M. Loeb III.
Financial data (yr. ended 11/30/00): Grants paid, $99,765; assets, $288,802 (M); gifts received, $65,600; expenditures, $101,840; qualifying distributions, $99,765.
Limitations: Applications not accepted. Giving primarily in New York, NY.
Application information: Contributes only to pre-selected organizations.
Officers: Carl M. Loeb III, Pres.; Alexandra M. Loeb, V.P.; Dahlia M. Loeb, V.P.; Hadassah M. Loeb, Treas.
EIN: 136085601

35489
The Marilyn S. and Robert F. Weinberg Foundation, Inc.
(Formerly Robert F. Weinberg Foundation)
100 Clearbrook Rd.
Elmsford, NY 10523

Financial data (yr. ended 04/30/02): Grants paid, $99,765; assets, $686,482 (M); expenditures, $100,735; qualifying distributions, $99,765.
Limitations: Applications not accepted.
Application information: Contributes only to pre-selected organizations.
Officer: Robert F. Weinberg, Mgr.
EIN: 133107638
Codes: FD2

35490
The Walter Rich Charitable Foundation
1 Railroad Ave.
Cooperstown, NY 13326

Established in 1996 in NY.
Financial data (yr. ended 06/30/01): Grants paid, $99,488; assets, $402,449 (M); gifts received, $76,374; expenditures, $124,255; qualifying distributions, $111,142; giving activities include $111,534 for programs.
Limitations: Applications not accepted. Giving primarily in NY.
Application information: Contributes only to pre-selected organizations.
Trustees: Sherwood Boehlert, Karine Rich, Walter Rich, Lester Sittler, Bruno Talevi.
EIN: 161515001
Codes: FD2

35491
Harry Chapin Foundation
196 E. Main St.
Huntington, NY 11743 (631) 423-7558
FAX: (631) 423-7596; *E-mail:* chapinpro@aol.com; *URL:* http://fdncenter.org/grantmaker/harrychapin
Contact: Leslie Ramme, Exec. Dir.

Established in 1981 in DC as a public charity; changed to a private foundation in 1999.
Financial data (yr. ended 12/31/00): Grants paid, $99,471; assets, $1,590,336 (M); gifts received, $294,665; expenditures, $144,690; qualifying distributions, $132,605.
Limitations: Giving on a national basis.
Publications: Application guidelines, grants list.
Application information: Application form required.
Officers and Directors:* Sandra Chapin,* Pres.; Anthony Curto,* Secy.; Jason Chapin,* Treas.; Jaime Chapin, Gerald Dempsey, Jason Dermer, Msgr. Thomas Hartman.
EIN: 521227851
Codes: FD2

35492
The Joseph Bruder Family Foundation
39 Taymil Rd.
New Rochelle, NY 10804-2816

Established in 1996 in NY.
Donor(s): Jack Bruder, Rhonda Bruder.
Financial data (yr. ended 10/31/01): Grants paid, $99,462; assets, $525 (M); gifts received, $91,000; expenditures, $99,512; qualifying distributions, $99,462.
Limitations: Applications not accepted.
Application information: Contributes only to pre-selected organizations.
Trustees: Jack Bruder, Rhonda Bruder.
EIN: 137098606
Codes: FD2

35493
Indonesian Cultural Foundation, Inc.
605 3rd Ave., Ste. 1501
New York, NY 10158
Contact: Carl J. Morelli, Secy.-Treas.

Established in 1970 in NY.
Financial data (yr. ended 12/31/01): Grants paid, $99,426; assets, $1,848,956 (M); expenditures, $157,233; qualifying distributions, $124,587.
Limitations: Giving primarily to Indonesian graduate students studying in the U.S.
Publications: Annual report.
Application information: Application form required.
Officers and Directors:* Padraic Fisher,* Pres.; Col. George C. Benson,* V.P.; Carl J. Morelli,* Secy.-Treas.; Wayne J. Forrest, Dorodjatun Kuntjoro-Jakti, Mappa Nasrun, Nguran Swetja, Makmur Widodo.
EIN: 237055841
Codes: FD2, GTI

35494
Howard Foundation, Inc.
200 Petersville Rd.
New Rochelle, NY 10801

Established in 1947.
Financial data (yr. ended 12/31/00): Grants paid, $99,150; assets, $1,036,232 (M); expenditures, $141,861; qualifying distributions, $118,394.
Limitations: Applications not accepted. Giving primarily in Westchester County, NY.
Application information: Contributes only to pre-selected organizations.
Officers: F.B. Powers, Jr., Pres.; J. Miressi, V.P.

EIN: 131840461
Codes: FD2

35495
The Barbara White Fishman Foundation
c/o Rochlin & Greenblah
225 W. 34th St., Ste. 1115
New York, NY 10024

Established in 1993 in NY.
Donor(s): Barbara Fishman.
Financial data (yr. ended 11/30/00): Grants paid, $99,000; assets, $31,796 (M); gifts received, $75,000; expenditures, $99,796; qualifying distributions, $98,915.
Limitations: Applications not accepted. Giving primarily in New York, NY.
Application information: Contributes only to pre-selected organizations.
Officer: Leslie Fishman, Pres.
EIN: 137024064
Codes: FD2

35496
Sloman Foundation, Inc.
c/o Peggy Stallman
21 Carol Dr.
Mount Kisco, NY 10549

Established around 1969 in NY.
Donor(s): Betty S. Price.
Financial data (yr. ended 12/31/00): Grants paid, $99,000; assets, $2,381,772 (M); expenditures, $105,497; qualifying distributions, $101,391.
Limitations: Applications not accepted. Giving primarily in NY.
Application information: Contributes only to pre-selected organizations.
Trustees: Betty S. Price, Peggy Stallman.
EIN: 237011941
Codes: FD2

35497
IRT Foundation
c/o Rachela Tauber
1145 45th St.
Brooklyn, NY 11219 (718) 435-1759

Established in 2001 in NY.
Donor(s): IRT Trust, Israel Tauber.
Financial data (yr. ended 02/28/02): Grants paid, $98,966; assets, $12,544 (M); gifts received, $111,614; expenditures, $99,666; qualifying distributions, $99,666.
Limitations: Giving primarily in NY.
Trustee: Rachela Tauber.
EIN: 133509921

35498
Kenneth C. Townson Fund
c/o JPMorgan Chase Bank
P.O. Box 31412
Rochester, NY 14603-1412 (716) 258-5169
Contact: Kate Noble, V.P., JPMorgan Chase Bank

Established in 1961 as Mr. & Mrs. Kenneth C. Townson Fund.
Financial data (yr. ended 12/31/01): Grants paid, $98,833; assets, $1,468,241 (M); expenditures, $115,415; qualifying distributions, $102,304.
Limitations: Giving primarily in Rochester, NY.
Trustee: JPMorgan Chase Bank.
EIN: 510244200
Codes: FD2

35499
Benzaquen Family Foundation
15 E. 69th St., Ste. 7A
New York, NY 10021-4997

Established in 1994 in NY.
Donor(s): Norman Benzaquen.

Financial data (yr. ended 09/30/01): Grants paid, $98,817; assets, $385,047 (M); expenditures, $111,235; qualifying distributions, $102,704.
Limitations: Applications not accepted. Giving primarily in New York, NY.
Application information: Contributes only to pre-selected organizations.
Officer: Norman Benzaquen, Pres.
Director: Stephanie Benzaquen.
EIN: 133796971
Codes: FD2

35500
The Ghatan Foundation
1226 Ocean Pkwy.
Brooklyn, NY 11230

Established in 1997 in NY.
Donor(s): Eliot Ghatan.
Financial data (yr. ended 11/30/01): Grants paid, $98,810; assets, $0 (M); gifts received, $50,000; expenditures, $98,810; qualifying distributions, $98,810.
Trustees: Aviva Ghatan, Eliot Ghatan.
EIN: 113350880
Codes: FD2

35501
Lindenbaum Family Charitable Trust
575 Madison Ave.
New York, NY 10022
FAX: (212) 940-8563
Contact: Samuel H. Lindenbaum, Tr.

Established in 1989 in NY.
Donor(s): Samuel H. Lindenbaum.
Financial data (yr. ended 09/30/01): Grants paid, $98,749; assets, $666,064 (M); gifts received, $200; expenditures, $109,021; qualifying distributions, $99,870.
Limitations: Applications not accepted. Giving primarily in New York, NY.
Application information: Contributes only to pre-selected organizations.
Trustees: Belle Lindenbaum, Samuel H. Lindenbaum.
EIN: 136929327
Codes: FD2

35502
Lotty Zucker Foundation
27 W. 44th St.
New York, NY 10036
Contact: Bernard Zucker, Tr.

Established in 1986 in NY.
Financial data (yr. ended 12/31/01): Grants paid, $98,710; assets, $416,399 (M); gifts received, $20,000; expenditures, $98,810; qualifying distributions, $98,171.
Limitations: Giving primarily in New York, NY.
Application information: Application form not required.
Trustees: Margot Minrish, Bernard Zucker.
EIN: 133340061
Codes: FD2

35503
Charlpeg Foundation, Inc.
c/o Meyer Handelman Co.
P.O. Box 817
Purchase, NY 10577

Incorporated in 1958 in NY.
Donor(s): Charles M. Grace.
Financial data (yr. ended 10/31/01): Grants paid, $98,700; assets, $242,501 (M); gifts received, $88,018; expenditures, $100,148; qualifying distributions, $98,732.
Limitations: Applications not accepted. Giving on a national basis.

Application information: Contributes only to pre-selected organizations.
Officers and Directors:* Charles M. Grace,* Pres.; Margaret V. Grace,* V.P.; John R. Young,* Secy.; Donald E. Handelman,* Treas.; William R. Handelman.
EIN: 136076805
Codes: FD2

35504
Gilbert & Snyder Foundation
c/o John J. Gilbert
29 E. 64th St., Apt. 11A
New York, NY 10021

Established in 1953.
Financial data (yr. ended 11/30/99): Grants paid, $98,685; assets, $1,139,201 (M); expenditures, $116,016; qualifying distributions, $105,056.
Limitations: Applications not accepted. Giving primarily in New York, NY.
Application information: Contributes only to pre-selected organizations.
Trustees: John Gilbert, Gilbert Snyder.
EIN: 136089999
Codes: FD2

35505
Maasim Tovim Foundation, Inc.
1342 E. 5th St.
Brooklyn, NY 11230-4626
Contact: Raphael Grossman, CPA

Established in 1998 in NY.
Financial data (yr. ended 12/31/01): Grants paid, $98,643; assets, $1,215,018 (M); gifts received, $34,318; expenditures, $103,343; qualifying distributions, $102,594.
Limitations: Giving primarily in NJ and NY.
Trustees: Abraham Berkowitz, Ernest Berkowitz, Hershy Berkowitz, Mindy Berkowitz, Sharon Silberstein.
EIN: 133978279
Codes: FD2

35506
Bull's Head Foundation, Inc.
c/o J. Maynard, Reboul, MacMurray, et al.
45 Rockefeller Plz.
New York, NY 10111

Established in 1950 in NY.
Donor(s): Walter Maynard.‡
Financial data (yr. ended 12/31/01): Grants paid, $98,500; assets, $1,645,595 (M); expenditures, $111,053; qualifying distributions, $100,718.
Limitations: Applications not accepted. Giving primarily in the northeastern states, including CT, Washington, DC, MA, and NY.
Application information: Unsolicited requests for funds not accepted.
Officers and Directors:* Walter Maynard, Jr.,* Pres.; John Maynard,* V.P. and Secy.; Augusta Maynard, Sheila M. Platt.
EIN: 136084014
Codes: FD2

35507
The Paneth Family Charitable Trust
3900 Shore Pkwy.
Brooklyn, NY 11235

Established in 1992 in NY.
Donor(s): Morton Paneth, Samuel Paneth, Leah Werner, Thomas Paneth.
Financial data (yr. ended 12/31/00): Grants paid, $98,500; assets, $3,590,641 (M); gifts received, $645,000; expenditures, $105,758; qualifying distributions, $98,820.
Limitations: Applications not accepted. Giving primarily in Brooklyn, NY.

Application information: Contributes only to pre-selected organizations.
Trustees: Morton Paneth, Samuel Paneth, Thomas Paneth, Leah Werner.
EIN: 116415770
Codes: FD2

35508
Benmen Fund
48 Concord Dr.
Monsey, NY 10952

Established in 1991 in NY.
Donor(s): Harvey Brecher, Miriam Brecher.
Financial data (yr. ended 11/30/01): Grants paid, $98,464; assets, $124,567 (M); gifts received, $195,140; expenditures, $100,787; qualifying distributions, $156,681; giving activities include $60,000 for loans.
Limitations: Applications not accepted. Giving primarily in Monsey, NY.
Application information: Contributes only to pre-selected organizations.
Officers and Directors:* Harvey Brecher,* Pres. and Treas.; Miriam Brecher,* V.P. and Secy.; Yossie Brecher,* V.P.; Malkie Kahn,* V.P.; Eli S. Garber.
EIN: 133620970
Codes: FD2

35509
Marcia and Phillip Rothblum Foundation, Inc.
(Formerly David Rothblum Foundation, Inc.)
c/o Philip Rothblum
545 Madison Ave., Ste. 700
New York, NY 10022-4219

Established in 1998 in NY.
Donor(s): Philip Rothblum, Marcia Rothblum.
Financial data (yr. ended 11/30/01): Grants paid, $98,350; assets, $96,157 (M); gifts received, $120,000; expenditures, $98,774; qualifying distributions, $98,563.
Limitations: Applications not accepted. Giving primarily in Mineola and New York, NY.
Application information: Contributes only to pre-selected organizations.
Officers: Philip Rothblum, Pres.; Marcia Rothblum, Secy.-Treas.
EIN: 112125721
Codes: FD2

35510
Stiefel Foundation for Dermatological Research, Inc.
P.O. Box 97
East Durham, NY 12423
Application address: 255 Alhambra Cir., No. 1000, Coral Gables, FL 33134, tel.: (305) 443-3800
Contact: Teresita L. Brunken, Secy.

Established around 1968.
Donor(s): Werner K. Stiefel, Stiefel Laboratories.
Financial data (yr. ended 12/31/01): Grants paid, $98,153; assets, $612,018 (M); gifts received, $87,771; expenditures, $98,393; qualifying distributions, $98,153.
Limitations: Giving on a national basis.
Application information: Application form not required.
Officers: Werner K. Stiefel, Pres.; Charles W. Stiefel, V.P.; Teresita L. Brunken, Secy.; Matt Pattullo, Treas.
EIN: 237002608

35511—NEW YORK

35511
The Shuman Family Foundation, Inc.
465 Main St., Ste. 600
Buffalo, NY 14203

Donor(s): Charles E. Shuman, Hyman B. Shuman, Philip Shuman & Sons, Inc.
Financial data (yr. ended 06/30/01): Grants paid, $98,000; assets, $907,897 (M); gifts received, $40,000; expenditures, $111,688; qualifying distributions, $97,854.
Limitations: Giving primarily in Buffalo, NY.
Officers: Charles E. Shuman, Pres.; Hyman B. Shuman, V.P.; Irving M. Shuman, Secy.
EIN: 237408428
Codes: FD2

35512
The Wikstrom Foundation
c/o Fleet National Bank
1 East Ave., NYRO M03A
Rochester, NY 14604
Contact: William A. McKee, V.P.

Established in 1960 in NY.
Donor(s): A.S. Wikstrom,‡ Wikstrom Liquidating Trust.
Financial data (yr. ended 12/31/01): Grants paid, $98,000; assets, $1,612,345 (M); expenditures, $106,038; qualifying distributions, $99,572.
Limitations: Giving primarily in NY, with emphasis on Onondaga.
Application information: Application form not required.
Trustee: Fleet National Bank.
EIN: 146014286
Codes: FD2

35513
Daniel J. and Edith A. Ehrlich Family Foundation
1070 Park Ave.
New York, NY 10128

Established in 1997 in NY.
Donor(s): Daniel J. Ehrlich.
Financial data (yr. ended 12/31/01): Grants paid, $97,900; assets, $998,126 (M); gifts received, $97,936; expenditures, $103,751; qualifying distributions, $99,303.
Limitations: Giving primarily in NY.
Trustee: Daniel J. Ehrlich.
EIN: 133977042
Codes: FD2

35514
The Goldstein Family Charitable Foundation, Inc.
35 Essex St.
New York, NY 10002

Established in 2000 in NY.
Donor(s): Emerich Goldstein.
Financial data (yr. ended 12/31/01): Grants paid, $97,869; assets, $245,043 (M); gifts received, $200,000; expenditures, $99,969; qualifying distributions, $97,869.
Trustee: Emerich Goldstein.
EIN: 522264339

35515
Saul & Marion Kleinkramer Foundation
c/o Bessemer Trust Co, N.A.
630 5th Ave.
New York, NY 10111

Established in 1997 in NY.
Donor(s): Saul Kleinkramer, Marion Kleinkramer.
Financial data (yr. ended 12/31/01): Grants paid, $97,750; assets, $847,454 (M); expenditures, $104,840; qualifying distributions, $99,881.
Limitations: Applications not accepted. Giving primarily in Montauk, NY.
Application information: Contributes only to pre-selected organizations.
Officers: Saul Kleinkramer, Pres.; Marion Kleinkramer, Secy.
Trustee: Sandra L. Bruschi.
EIN: 113336273
Codes: FD2

35516
Jotkowitz Family Charitable Foundation, Inc.
c/o Lonnie Wollin
350 5th Ave., Ste. 2822
New York, NY 10118

Established in 1994 in DE.
Donor(s): Seymour Jotkowitz, Annette Jotkowitz.
Financial data (yr. ended 09/30/01): Grants paid, $97,706; assets, $16,082 (M); gifts received, $30,675; expenditures, $99,710; qualifying distributions, $97,283.
Limitations: Applications not accepted. Giving primarily in NJ and NY.
Application information: Contributes only to pre-selected organizations.
Officers: Seymour Jotkowitz, Pres.; Annette Jotkowitz, V.P.; Lonnie Wollin, Secy.
EIN: 223270738
Codes: FD2

35517
S. & A. Agate Foundation, Inc.
c/o Yohalem Gillman & Co., LLP
477 Madison Ave.
New York, NY 10022-5802

Donor(s): Anita Agate.
Financial data (yr. ended 12/31/01): Grants paid, $97,657; assets, $3,229,026 (M); expenditures, $127,531; qualifying distributions, $97,657.
Limitations: Applications not accepted. Giving primarily in CA.
Application information: Contributes only to pre-selected organizations.
Officer: Constance A. Austin, Pres.
EIN: 136109670
Codes: FD2

35518
Rachem Bechasdecha Foundation
208 Hewes St.
Brooklyn, NY 11211 (718) 349-6166
Contact: Jacob Steinmetz, Tr.

Established in 2000 in NY.
Donor(s): Jacob Steinmetz, Esther Steinmetz.
Financial data (yr. ended 11/30/01): Grants paid, $97,493; assets, $234,227 (M); gifts received, $78,390; expenditures, $97,618; qualifying distributions, $96,322.
Application information: Application form not required.
Trustees: Jacob Steinmetz, Judith Steinmetz.
EIN: 113468795
Codes: FD2

35519
Biggs Family Charitable Foundation
240 E. 47th St., Ste. 23D
New York, NY 10017

Established in 2000 in NY.
Donor(s): John H. Biggs, Penelope P. Biggs.
Financial data (yr. ended 12/31/01): Grants paid, $97,450; assets, $1,083,234 (M); gifts received, $428,873; expenditures, $102,657; qualifying distributions, $97,450.
Limitations: Applications not accepted.
Application information: Contributes only to pre-selected organizations.
Directors: Henry P. Biggs, John H. Biggs, Penelope P. Biggs, Theresa McShane Biggs.
EIN: 364375110

35520
Henry L. O'Brien Foundation, Inc.
P.O. Box 1145
Westhampton Beach, NY 11978-1145

Established in 1954 in NY.
Financial data (yr. ended 12/31/01): Grants paid, $97,443; assets, $1,506,432 (M); expenditures, $99,517; qualifying distributions, $96,178.
Limitations: Applications not accepted. Giving primarily in NY.
Application information: Contributes only to pre-selected organizations.
Officers: Natalie O. Conklin, Pres.; Theodore B. Conklin, Jr., V.P.; Verity V. O'Brien, Secy.-Treas.
EIN: 136116284
Codes: FD2

35521
Zeitz Foundation, Inc.
c/o Becker, Ross, Stone, et al.
317 Madison Ave.
New York, NY 10017-5372 (212) 697-2310
Contact: Jesse Margolin, Dir.

Established in 1943 in FL.
Financial data (yr. ended 06/30/01): Grants paid, $97,429; assets, $2,427,698 (M); expenditures, $121,072; qualifying distributions, $108,182.
Limitations: Giving primarily in NY.
Officers and Directors:* Willard Zeitz,* Pres.; Wilbur Levin,* V.P. and Secy.; Robert Rosenthal,* V.P. and Treas.; Jesse Margolin.
EIN: 116037021
Codes: FD2

35522
Zichron Yitzchok Hacohen Foundation
2607 Nostrand Ave.
Brooklyn, NY 11210

Established in 1999 in NY.
Financial data (yr. ended 12/31/99): Grants paid, $97,411; assets, $0 (M); gifts received, $93,700; expenditures, $97,783; qualifying distributions, $97,411.
Director: Steve Wallerstein.
EIN: 113491317
Codes: FD2

35523
The Cooper Family Foundation, Inc.
c/o Jacqueline Vanoutryve
50 W. 34th St., No. 18-B-8
New York, NY 10001-3097

Established in 1992 in FL.
Donor(s): Donald Cooper.‡
Financial data (yr. ended 12/31/01): Grants paid, $97,300; assets, $547,206 (M); expenditures, $104,352; qualifying distributions, $97,300.
Limitations: Applications not accepted. Giving primarily in New York, NY.
Application information: Contributes only to pre-selected organizations.
Officer: Arlene Cooper, Mgr.
Trustee: Harry Wendroff.
Director: Richard Cooper.
EIN: 650354458
Codes: FD2

35524
Matin D. Gutmacher Family Foundation
c/o R. Gutmacher
781 5th Ave., Ste. 309
New York, NY 10022-1012

Established in 1998 in NY.

Donor(s): Gutmacher Enterprises.
Financial data (yr. ended 12/31/01): Grants paid, $97,300; assets, $111,189 (M); gifts received, $67,327; expenditures, $99,048; qualifying distributions, $97,300.
Limitations: Applications not accepted.
Application information: Contributes only to pre-selected organizations.
Directors: Barbara Girard, David Nadler, Seymour Zises.
EIN: 134036276
Codes: FD2

35525
The Flaherty Family Foundation
130 E. 95th St.
New York, NY 10128-1705

Established in 1996 in DE & NY.
Donor(s): Peter A. Flaherty.
Financial data (yr. ended 10/31/01): Grants paid, $97,185; assets, $668,107 (M); expenditures, $100,391; qualifying distributions, $97,185.
Limitations: Applications not accepted.
Application information: Contributes only to pre-selected organizations.
Officer: Peter A. Flaherty, Pres.
Trustee: Pamela P. Flaherty.
EIN: 133919502

35526
Morgan & Marjorie L. Miller Charitable Trust
11 Normandy Ln.
Scarsdale, NY 10583-7620

Established in 1987 in NY.
Donor(s): Marjorie Miller, Eleanor Leff.
Financial data (yr. ended 12/31/01): Grants paid, $97,025; assets, $1,244,277 (M); expenditures, $106,719; qualifying distributions, $97,025.
Limitations: Applications not accepted. Giving primarily in NY.
Application information: Contributes only to pre-selected organizations.
Trustees: Marjorie Miller, Morgan Miller.
EIN: 061187583
Codes: FD2

35527
The Lerer Family Charitable Foundation, Inc.
c/o Tag Associates, LLC
75 Rockefeller Plz., Ste. 900
New York, NY 10019

Established in 2000 in NY.
Donor(s): Kenneth B. Lerer.
Financial data (yr. ended 08/31/01): Grants paid, $97,000; assets, $97,039 (M); gifts received, $59,693; expenditures, $98,423; qualifying distributions, $98,423.
Limitations: Applications not accepted. Giving primarily in New York, NY.
Application information: Contributes only to pre-selected organizations.
Officers: Kenneth B. Lerer, Pres.; Katherine R. Sailer, V.P.
EIN: 311753295
Codes: FD2

35528
White Birch Foundation
c/o Marion Kaplan
450 West End Ave., Ste. 16B
New York, NY 10024

Established in 1997 in NY.
Donor(s): Irwin Kaplan, Marion Kaplan.
Financial data (yr. ended 12/31/01): Grants paid, $97,000; assets, $698,538 (M); expenditures, $110,866; qualifying distributions, $104,962.
Limitations: Applications not accepted. Giving on a national basis.
Application information: Unsolicited requests for funds not accepted.
Trustees: Irwin Kaplan, Marion Kaplan.
EIN: 137105149
Codes: FD2

35529
The Michael & Shirley Cayre Foundation
417 5th Ave., 9th Fl.
New York, NY 10016 (212) 726-0773
Contact: Michael Cayre, Pres.

Established in 2000 in DE.
Donor(s): Michael Cayre, Shirley Cayre.
Financial data (yr. ended 12/31/01): Grants paid, $96,983; assets, $371,391 (M); gifts received, $56,500; expenditures, $103,152; qualifying distributions, $96,821.
Officers: Michael Cayre, Pres.; Shirley Cayre, V.P.
EIN: 134109353
Codes: FD2

35530
The Schechter Foundation
P.O. Box 4822
New York, NY 10185-4822 (212) 698-1317
FAX: (212) 698-1321; *E-mail:* schechtertenrock@aol.com
Contact: Alfred Schechter, Pres.

Established in 1983 in NY.
Donor(s): Alfred Schechter.
Financial data (yr. ended 12/31/01): Grants paid, $96,945; assets, $1,501,138 (M); gifts received, $100,000; expenditures, $134,596; qualifying distributions, $108,700.
Limitations: Giving on a national basis, primarily in NY.
Application information: Application form available for scholarships. Application form required.
Officers and Directors:* Alfred Schechter,* Pres. and Treas.; Shirley Schechter,* V.P. and Secy.; Claudia Schechter, Robert Schechter.
EIN: 133157311
Codes: FD2, GTI

35531
Steinwachs Family Foundation
5600 Armor Duells Rd.
Orchard Park, NY 14127

Established in 1999 in NY.
Financial data (yr. ended 12/31/01): Grants paid, $96,830; assets, $2,602,908 (M); expenditures, $100,261; qualifying distributions, $95,547.
Limitations: Applications not accepted. Giving on a national basis, with emphasis on upstate NY.
Application information: Contributes only to pre-selected organizations.
Directors: Jeffrey P. Steinwachs, Paul C. Steinwachs, Sharon A. Steinwachs.
EIN: 161574554
Codes: FD2

35532
El Hefe Charitable Trust
1290 E. 21st St.
Brooklyn, NY 11210
Contact: Gladys Eisenstadt, Tr.

Established in 2000 in NY.
Financial data (yr. ended 12/31/01): Grants paid, $96,750; assets, $84,717 (M); expenditures, $98,250; qualifying distributions, $97,500.
Trustee: Gladys Eisenstadt.
EIN: 116533178
Codes: FD2

35533
American Friends of Halichot Am Israel, Inc.
1600 Broadway, Ste. 514C
New York, NY 10019

Established in 1993.
Donor(s): Ruth Silver.
Financial data (yr. ended 12/31/00): Grants paid, $96,500; assets, $920 (M); gifts received, $83,200; expenditures, $97,723; qualifying distributions, $97,140.
Limitations: Applications not accepted.
Application information: Contributes only to pre-selected organizations.
Directors: Ephraim Nagar, Jonathan Yaheb, Hadar Zabari.
EIN: 133583652
Codes: FD2

35534
Edelman Foundation
(Formerly Matz Foundation - Edelman Division)
14 Sutton Pl. S., Ste. 4B
New York, NY 10022
Contact: Richard M. Edelman, Tr.

Trust established in 1970 in NY as one of two successor trusts to the Matz Foundation.
Donor(s): Israel Matz,‡ Ethel & Irvin Edelman Foundation.
Financial data (yr. ended 06/30/01): Grants paid, $96,500; assets, $2,008,125 (M); expenditures, $103,157; qualifying distributions, $96,500.
Limitations: Applications not accepted. Giving primarily in NY.
Application information: Contributes only to pre-selected organizations.
Trustees: David A. Edelman, Jonathan S. Edelman, Richard M. Edelman, Anne C. Holbach.
EIN: 237082997
Codes: FD2

35535
Young Foundation
c/o John E. Young
380 Madison Ave., 7th Fl.
New York, NY 10017

Established in 2000 in NY.
Donor(s): John E. Young.
Financial data (yr. ended 12/31/01): Grants paid, $96,500; assets, $38,250 (M); gifts received, $100,101; expenditures, $100,100; qualifying distributions, $95,591.
Limitations: Applications not accepted. Giving primarily in New York, NY.
Application information: Contributes only to pre-selected organizations.
Trustee: John E. Young.
EIN: 134073167
Codes: FD2

35536
Max & Ida Strauss Foundation, Inc.
630 5th Ave., Rm. 2263
New York, NY 10111-0221

Established in 1958 in NY.
Donor(s): Fred S. Strauss.
Financial data (yr. ended 12/31/00): Grants paid, $96,491; assets, $2,291,702 (M); expenditures, $162,310; qualifying distributions, $99,937.
Limitations: Applications not accepted. Giving primarily in NY.
Application information: Contributes only to pre-selected organizations.
Officer: Fred S. Strauss, Pres. and Mgr.
Directors: Iris J. Strauss, Michael A. Strauss.
EIN: 136161575
Codes: FD2

35537
The Coulson Family Foundation
(Formerly Frank and Linda Coulson Family Foundation)
c/o Goldman Sachs & Co.
85 Broad St., Tax Dept.
New York, NY 10004

Established in 1991 in PA.
Donor(s): Frank L. Coulson, Jr.
Financial data (yr. ended 02/28/01): Grants paid, $96,465; assets, $78,105 (M); expenditures, $102,465; qualifying distributions, $96,394.
Limitations: Applications not accepted. Giving primarily in PA.
Application information: Contributes only to pre-selected organizations.
Trustees: Elizabeth H. Coulson, Frank L. Coulson, Jr., Frank L. Coulson III, Katheryn C. Coulson, Edward E. Crawford, Kimberly Lynn Macaione.
EIN: 133632762
Codes: FD2

35538
Solomon and Machla Tzedaka Fund Trust
1830 59th St.
Brooklyn, NY 11204

Established in 1998 in NY.
Donor(s): Solomon Abramczyk.
Financial data (yr. ended 11/30/01): Grants paid, $96,410; assets, $453,814 (M); gifts received, $506,646; expenditures, $97,178; qualifying distributions, $96,410.
Limitations: Applications not accepted.
Application information: Contributes only to pre-selected organizations.
Trustees: Machla Abramczyk, Solomon Abramczyk.
EIN: 116516261
Codes: FD2

35539
The Fred I. and Gilda Nobel Foundation, Inc.
c/o David Ehrlich & Co., LLP
515 Madison Ave.
New York, NY 10022-5403

Established in 1993 in NY.
Donor(s): Fred I. Nobel.
Financial data (yr. ended 11/30/01): Grants paid, $96,165; assets, $1,742,880 (M); expenditures, $100,560; qualifying distributions, $100,560.
Limitations: Applications not accepted. Giving primarily in Long Island and New York, NY.
Application information: Contributes only to pre-selected organizations.
Officers and Directors:* Fred I. Nobel,* Pres.; Laurie B. Everitt,* V.P.; Judy A. Jackups,* V.P.; Barry I. Nobel,* V.P.; Gilda Nobel,* V.P.
EIN: 113187562
Codes: FD2

35540
Sky Rink Winter Games Training Facilities, Inc.
Chelsea Piers - Pier 62, Ste. 300
New York, NY 10011-1015

Established in 1994 in DE and NY.
Financial data (yr. ended 08/31/01): Grants paid, $96,041; assets, $182,099 (M); gifts received, $115,321; expenditures, $152,824; qualifying distributions, $147,187.
Limitations: Applications not accepted.
Application information: Contributes only to pre-selected organizations.
Officers: David A. Tewksbury, Pres.; Kenneth Shelley, V.P.; Ashley Goodale, Secy.
Directors: Joel A. Elin, Ph.D., Robert Lowe, Ken Moir, Ron Talerico.
EIN: 133550784

Codes: FD2

35541
The Arde Bulova Memorial Fund, Inc.
c/o Joseph P. Catera
1081 Palmer Ave.
Larchmont, NY 10538

Established in 1962 in NY.
Donor(s): Louise B. Guilden.
Financial data (yr. ended 12/31/00): Grants paid, $96,000; assets, $2,331,047 (M); expenditures, $116,959; qualifying distributions, $105,860.
Limitations: Applications not accepted. Giving primarily in NY.
Application information: Contributes only to pre-selected organizations.
Officers and Directors:* Paul B. Guilden,* Pres.; Joseph P. Catera,* Secy.; Peter Gale,* Treas.; Lynn Gale.
EIN: 136117194
Codes: TN

35542
The VIYU Foundation
591 Main St., Ste. 200
East Aurora, NY 14052-1753
Contact: William Dann, Tr.

Established in 1989 in NY.
Donor(s): Members of the Dann family.
Financial data (yr. ended 07/31/01): Grants paid, $96,000; assets, $1,614,554 (M); expenditures, $97,029; qualifying distributions, $92,222.
Limitations: Giving primarily in Buffalo, NY.
Application information: Application form not required.
Trustees: Jesse C. Dann, Marion Dann, William Dann, William R. Dann, Jr., E.W. Dann Stevens.
EIN: 043064835
Codes: FD2

35543
The Roisen Family Foundation, Inc.
15 W. 47th St.
New York, NY 10036   (212) 819-0505
Contact: Jacques Roisen, Pres.

Established in 1997 in NY.
Donor(s): Jacques Roisen.
Financial data (yr. ended 12/31/01): Grants paid, $95,985; assets, $344,405 (M); gifts received, $149,800; expenditures, $96,790; qualifying distributions, $95,985.
Limitations: Giving primarily in NY.
Officers and Directors:* Jacques Roisen,* Pres.; Alina Roisen,* Secy.; Rita Kwiat, Sheldon Kwiat, Shelley Roisen.
EIN: 133944290

35544
Margaret Mayhall Moore Foundation
c/o U.S. Trust
114 W. 47th St.
New York, NY 10036

Established in 1997.
Financial data (yr. ended 12/31/01): Grants paid, $95,968; assets, $8,340,625 (M); expenditures, $101,419; qualifying distributions, $97,925.
Limitations: Applications not accepted.
Application information: Contributes only to pre-selected organizations.
Trustee: U.S. Trust.
EIN: 137119294
Codes: FD2

35545
The Scully-Peretsman Foundation
9 E. 79th St.
New York, NY 10021

Established in 1997 in NY.
Donor(s): Robert W. Scully, Nancy B. Peretsman.
Financial data (yr. ended 12/31/01): Grants paid, $95,923; assets, $1,877,146 (M); expenditures, $100,163; qualifying distributions, $97,023.
Limitations: Applications not accepted. Giving primarily in NY.
Application information: Contributes only to pre-selected organizations.
Trustees: Nancy B. Peretsman, Robert W. Scully.
EIN: 133982344
Codes: FD2

35546
Goldome Foundation
P.O. Box 22900
Rochester, NY 14692-2900

Established in 1969 in NY.
Donor(s): Goldome.
Financial data (yr. ended 12/31/01): Grants paid, $95,500; assets, $123,185 (M); expenditures, $102,722; qualifying distributions, $95,420.
Limitations: Applications not accepted. Giving limited to NY, with emphasis on western NY (Buffalo, Rochester and Syracuse); some support also in the metropolitan New York area.
Application information: Contributes only to pre-selected organizations.
Officer: Sharon D. Randaccio, Pres.
Directors: Thomas Crandall, Robert B. Rakoczy, Maureen A. Ronning.
EIN: 237029266
Codes: CS, FD2, CD

35547
The Kaltman Family Foundation
(Formerly The Martin Kaltman Foundation)
8 Coachmans Ct.
Old Westbury, NY 11568-1324
Contact: Eric Kaltman, Tr.

Established in 1985 in NY.
Donor(s): Martin Kaltman, Eric Kaltman.
Financial data (yr. ended 09/30/01): Grants paid, $95,445; assets, $1,018,379 (M); gifts received, $200,000; expenditures, $97,804; qualifying distributions, $95,875.
Officer and Trustees:* Martin Kaltman,* Mgr.; Eric Kaltman.
EIN: 112773179
Codes: FD2

35548
C. & M. Herzka Foundation
3177 Bedford Ave.
Brooklyn, NY 11210

Established in 1997 in NY.
Donor(s): Charles H. Herzka.
Financial data (yr. ended 06/30/01): Grants paid, $95,300; assets, $47,894 (M); gifts received, $102,800; expenditures, $95,373; qualifying distributions, $95,373.
Limitations: Applications not accepted.
Application information: Contributes only to pre-selected organizations.
Trustees: Charles H. Herzka, Miriam Herzka, Joseph Neumann.
EIN: 113407376
Codes: FD2

NEW YORK—35560

35549
The Lempert Family Foundation
35 Ohayo Mountain Rd.
Woodstock, NY 12498-1441
Contact: Norbert Lempert, Pres.

Donor(s): Norbert Lempert.
Financial data (yr. ended 12/31/00): Grants paid, $95,289; assets, $100,315 (M); gifts received, $100,003; expenditures, $95,439; qualifying distributions, $95,289.
Officer: Norbert Lempert, Pres.
Directors: Edith Lempert, Noreen Lempert.
EIN: 141802971
Codes: FD2

35550
The Lone Rock Foundation, Inc.
(Formerly Herring Creek Foundation, Inc.)
635 Madison Ave., 18th Fl.
New York, NY 10022

Established in 1994 in NY.
Donor(s): Susan Scheuer.
Financial data (yr. ended 12/31/00): Grants paid, $95,222; assets, $696,694 (M); gifts received, $75,250; expenditures, $98,697; qualifying distributions, $94,264.
Limitations: Applications not accepted. Giving primarily in MA and NY.
Application information: Contributes only to pre-selected organizations.
Officers: Susan Scheuer, Pres.; Jonathan Lipnick, Secy.
Director: Judith Scheuer.
EIN: 133783380
Codes: FD2

35551
Joseph Chehebar Family Foundation
1000 Pennsylvania Ave.
Brooklyn, NY 11207

Established in 1998 in NY.
Donor(s): Joseph Chehebar.
Financial data (yr. ended 12/31/01): Grants paid, $95,214; assets, $178,052 (M); gifts received, $121,000; expenditures, $95,401; qualifying distributions, $95,214.
Limitations: Applications not accepted.
Application information: Contributes only to pre-selected organizations.
Officer: Joseph Chehebar, Mgr.
EIN: 113388342
Codes: FD2

35552
The Jacquelyn & Gregory Zehner Foundation
c/o Goldman Sachs & Co.
85 Broad St., Tax Dept.
New York, NY 10004

Established in 1996 in NY.
Donor(s): Gregory Zehner.
Financial data (yr. ended 07/31/01): Grants paid, $95,170; assets, $2,895,205 (M); gifts received, $3,750; expenditures, $160,312; qualifying distributions, $99,312.
Limitations: Applications not accepted. Giving primarily in the New York, NY, area.
Application information: Contributes only to pre-selected organizations.
Trustees: Jacquelyn M. Hoffman-Zehner, Gregory Zehner.
EIN: 133971019
Codes: FD2

35553
The Sterling Foundation
12 Schoolhouse Ln.
Great Neck, NY 11020
Contact: Daniel S. Sterling, Tr.

Established in 1982.
Financial data (yr. ended 12/31/01): Grants paid, $95,092; assets, $1,458,115 (M); expenditures, $98,337; qualifying distributions, $97,072.
Limitations: Giving primarily in FL, NJ, and NY.
Trustees: Daniel S. Sterling, Helene Sterling.
EIN: 112590105
Codes: FD2

35554
Viola W. Bernard Foundation, Inc.
(Formerly Tappanz Foundation, Inc.)
c/o Neuberger, Berman, LLC
605 3rd Ave., 21st Fl.
New York, NY 10158
Application address: 19 E. 72nd St., Apt. 5A, New York, NY 10021
Contact: Cary A. Koplin, Dir.

Established in 1968.
Donor(s): Viola W. Bernard, M.D.‡
Financial data (yr. ended 12/31/00): Grants paid, $95,000; assets, $287,642 (M); gifts received, $57,162; expenditures, $97,504; qualifying distributions, $96,656.
Limitations: Giving primarily in New York, NY.
Officers: Perry Ottenberg, M.D., Pres.; Stephen Wise Tulin, Secy.-Treas.
Directors: Cary Koplin, Luba Lynch, Peter Neubauer, M.D., Jeanne Spurlock, M.D., Joan Wofford.
EIN: 132621140
Codes: FD2

35555
Castle Foundation
500 Mamaroneck Ave.
Harrison, NY 10528-1600

Established in 1989 in NY.
Financial data (yr. ended 12/31/01): Grants paid, $95,000; assets, $12,701 (M); gifts received, $95,000; expenditures, $95,056; qualifying distributions, $95,000.
Limitations: Applications not accepted. Giving primarily in NY.
Application information: Contributes only to pre-selected organizations.
Trustees: Camille Romita, Mauro C. Romita, Michael Romita.
EIN: 133490144

35556
The Jerome P. & Carol B. Kenney Trust
c/o Merrill Lynch
2 World Financial Ctr., 38 Fl.
New York, NY 10281-6100

Established in 1999 in NY.
Donor(s): Jerome P. Kenney, Carol B. Kenney.
Financial data (yr. ended 12/31/00): Grants paid, $95,000; assets, $609,719 (M); gifts received, $7,695; expenditures, $102,225; qualifying distributions, $95,000.
Limitations: Applications not accepted. Giving primarily in CT and NY.
Application information: Contributes only to pre-selected organizations.
Trustees: Carol B. Kenney, Jerome P. Kenney.
EIN: 137202044
Codes: FD2

35557
Bella Spewack Article 5 Trust
c/o The Bank of New York, Tax Dept.
1 Wall St., 28th Fl.
New York, NY 10286
Application address: 98 Riverside Dr., New York, NY 10024
Contact: Arthur Elias, Tr.

Established in 1991 in NY.
Donor(s): Bella Spewack.‡
Financial data (yr. ended 06/30/01): Grants paid, $95,000; assets, $1,744,522 (M); expenditures, $124,450; qualifying distributions, $99,112.
Limitations: Giving primarily in New York, NY.
Trustees: Arthur Elias, Lois Elias, The Bank of New York.
EIN: 133669246
Codes: FD2

35558
Dolly & Robert K. Raisler Foundation, Inc.
(Formerly The Robert K. Raisler Foundation)
c/o Eisner & Lubin LLP
444 Madison Ave.
New York, NY 10022

Incorporated in 1958 in NY.
Financial data (yr. ended 12/31/01): Grants paid, $94,965; assets, $2,087,664 (M); expenditures, $102,255; qualifying distributions, $99,785.
Limitations: Applications not accepted. Giving primarily in New York, NY.
Application information: Contributes only to pre-selected organizations.
Officers and Directors:* Robert K. Raisler,* Pres. and Treas.; Harold K. Raisler,* V.P. and Secy.
EIN: 136094433
Codes: FD2

35559
The Margolis Foundation, Inc.
147 E. 48th St.
New York, NY 10017
Contact: David I. Margolis, Pres.

Established in 1969.
Donor(s): David I. Margolis.
Financial data (yr. ended 12/31/01): Grants paid, $94,925; assets, $749,264 (M); expenditures, $95,586; qualifying distributions, $94,765.
Limitations: Giving primarily in New York, NY.
Officers and Directors:* David I. Margolis,* Pres.; Barbara A. Margolis,* V.P. and Secy.-Treas.; Brian Margolis,* V.P.; Nancy Margolis,* V.P.; Peter Margolis,* V.P.; Robert Margolis,* V.P.
EIN: 237009667
Codes: FD2

35560
Charles F. Wolf Scholarship Fund
c/o Pagones, Cross & VanTuyl
355 Main St.
Beacon, NY 12508-0550

Established in 1977 in NY.
Donor(s): Charles F. Wolf, M.D.‡
Financial data (yr. ended 05/31/01): Grants paid, $94,924; assets, $2,626,629 (M); expenditures, $141,979; qualifying distributions, $100,980.
Limitations: Giving limited to New York, NY.
Application information: Scholarships limited to students accepted by the NYU School of Medicine.
Trustee: Pagones, Cross & VanTuyl.
EIN: 141580597
Codes: FD2, GTI

35561
Wexler-Zimmerman Charitable Trust
83 Jane St.
New York, NY 10014-1731

Established in 1997 in NY.
Donor(s): Tanya Wexler.
Financial data (yr. ended 03/31/02): Grants paid, $94,920; assets, $243,336 (M); gifts received, $300; expenditures, $95,794; qualifying distributions, $94,920.
Limitations: Applications not accepted.
Application information: Contributes only to pre-selected organizations.
Trustees: Tanya Wexler, Amy Zimmerman.
EIN: 133981367
Codes: FD2

35562
Zichron Yona V'Sara Charitable Foundation
6 Lenore Ave.
Monsey, NY 10952

Established in 1998 in NY.
Donor(s): Herman Herzog, Aaron Herzog, Michael B. Herzog.
Financial data (yr. ended 12/31/01): Grants paid, $94,900; assets, $219,464 (M); gifts received, $100,000; expenditures, $94,979; qualifying distributions, $94,830.
Limitations: Applications not accepted.
Application information: Contributes only to pre-selected organizations.
Officers: Herman Herzog, Pres.; Michael B. Herzog, V.P.; Aaron Herzog, Secy.
EIN: 137171873
Codes: FD2

35563
Lassalle Fund, Inc.
c/o Norman Foundation
147 E. 48th St.
New York, NY 10017-1223
Contact: Nancy N. Lassalle, Pres.

Established in 1966 in NY.
Donor(s): Norman Foundation.
Financial data (yr. ended 12/31/00): Grants paid, $94,893; assets, $3,812,459 (M); gifts received, $1,443,169; expenditures, $129,619; qualifying distributions, $100,457.
Limitations: Giving primarily in New York, NY.
Officers: Nancy N. Lassalle, Pres.; Andrew E. Norman, V.P.
EIN: 136213551
Codes: FD2

35564
The Dilona Foundation, Inc.
c/o Daniel Okolica
9 Cloverdale Ln.
Monsey, NY 10952

Established in 1998 in NY.
Financial data (yr. ended 11/30/99): Grants paid, $94,843; assets, $6,693 (M); gifts received, $100,000; expenditures, $95,843; qualifying distributions, $95,843.
Directors: Daniel Okolica, Helen Okolica.
EIN: 134036569
Codes: FD2

35565
The Lubin Family Foundation
310 Old Country Rd., Ste. 201
Garden City, NY 11530 (516) 248-9300
Contact: Sara L. Schupf, Tr.

Established in 1993 in NY.
Donor(s): Tillie K. Lubin.
Financial data (yr. ended 12/31/01): Grants paid, $94,782; assets, $3,522,212 (M); gifts received, $203,050; expenditures, $115,460; qualifying distributions, $95,947.
Limitations: Applications not accepted. Giving on a national basis.
Application information: Contributes only to pre-selected organizations.
Trustee: Sara L. Schupf.
EIN: 136991626
Codes: FD2

35566
848 Charity Fund
848 E. 13th St.
Brooklyn, NY 11230

Established in 1989 in NY.
Donor(s): Bernard Newman.
Financial data (yr. ended 12/31/00): Grants paid, $94,650; assets, $1,711,228 (M); gifts received, $25,605; expenditures, $97,740; qualifying distributions, $93,458.
Limitations: Applications not accepted. Giving primarily in NY.
Application information: Contributes only to pre-selected organizations.
Officers: Bernard Newman, Pres.; Sarah Newman, V.P.; Leslie Honikman, Secy.-Treas.
EIN: 112994491
Codes: FD2

35567
The Stanley R. Miller Foundation
c/o BCRS Assocs., LLC
67 Wall St., 8th Fl.
New York, NY 10005

Established in 1961.
Donor(s): Catherine M. Miller.
Financial data (yr. ended 06/30/02): Grants paid, $94,625; assets, $1,238,228 (M); expenditures, $106,937; qualifying distributions, $94,625.
Limitations: Applications not accepted. Giving primarily in CT and NY.
Application information: Contributes only to pre-selected organizations.
Trustees: Pamela M. Gerard, Catherine M. Miller, Gail M. Stoddart.
EIN: 136028809

35568
Marie Lamfrom Charitable Foundation
c/o U.S. Trust
114 W. 47th St.
New York, NY 10036

Established in 1998 in OR.
Donor(s): Gertrude Boyle.
Financial data (yr. ended 12/31/00): Grants paid, $94,573; assets, $1,081,192 (M); expenditures, $102,407; qualifying distributions, $97,156.
Limitations: Applications not accepted. Giving primarily in OR.
Application information: Contributes only to pre-selected organizations.
Trustees: David C. Bany, Sarah A. Bany.
EIN: 931254171
Codes: FD2

35569
Solomon & Blanche De Jonge Foundation, Inc.
1585 Broadway, Rm. 24-114
New York, NY 10036-8200 (212) 446-4400
Contact: Lawrence J. Rothenberg, Pres.

Financial data (yr. ended 12/31/01): Grants paid, $94,500; assets, $1,215,230 (M); expenditures, $119,918; qualifying distributions, $101,577.
Officers: Lawrence J. Rothenberg, Pres. and Treas.; Adele Doyle, V.P.; Henry J. Leibowitz, Secy.
EIN: 136085831
Codes: FD2

35570
Leopold R. Gellert Family Trust
122 E. 42nd St., 34th Fl.
New York, NY 10168-0070

Established in 1962.
Donor(s): Robert J. Gellert, Max E. Gellert, Donald N. Gellert.
Financial data (yr. ended 05/31/01): Grants paid, $94,500; assets, $927,684 (M); expenditures, $102,751; qualifying distributions, $94,373.
Limitations: Applications not accepted. Giving primarily in NY.
Application information: Contributes only to pre-selected organizations.
Trustees: Donald N. Gellert, Max E. Gellert, Robert J. Gellert, Hugh McLoughlin, Jr., William R. Peters.
EIN: 136085289
Codes: FD2

35571
John P. and June D. Heffernan Foundation
420 Lexington Ave., Ste. 331
New York, NY 10170
Contact: John P. Heffernan, Tr.

Established in 1999 in NY.
Donor(s): John P. Heffernan.
Financial data (yr. ended 06/30/01): Grants paid, $94,500; assets, $1,385,318 (M); expenditures, $116,427; qualifying distributions, $93,331.
Trustees: John P. Heffernan, June D. Heffernan.
EIN: 137214979
Codes: FD2

35572
Gifford Rudin Foundation, Inc.
47-50 30th St.
Long Island City, NY 11101-3404
(718) 784-5900
Contact: Stephen Rudin, Pres.

Established in 1974.
Donor(s): Milton Paper Co., Inc.
Financial data (yr. ended 04/30/02): Grants paid, $94,445; assets, $790,149 (M); gifts received, $5,885; expenditures, $103,493; qualifying distributions, $93,762.
Limitations: Giving primarily in NY.
Officers: Stephen Rudin, Pres.; Stephen Verp, Secy.
EIN: 237375850
Codes: FD2

35573
Hennessy Foundation, Inc.
c/o Syska & Hennessy, Inc.
11 W. 42nd St.
New York, NY 10036-8002 (212) 921-2300
Contact: John F. Hennessy, III, Pres.

Established in 1953.
Donor(s): Hensey Properties, Inc.
Financial data (yr. ended 12/31/00): Grants paid, $94,300; assets, $1,998,180 (M); expenditures, $95,457; qualifying distributions, $95,457.
Limitations: Giving primarily in NY.
Officers: John F. Hennessy, Pres.; David B. Hennessy, V.P.; Kathleen Hennessy, V.P.
EIN: 136153737
Codes: FD2

35574
The JIA Charitable Foundation
2722 Ave. K
Brooklyn, NY 11210-3722

Established in 1999 in NY.
Donor(s): George Grossberger.

Financial data (yr. ended 12/31/01): Grants paid, $94,213; assets, $30,768 (M); gifts received, $74,015; expenditures, $94,378; qualifying distributions, $94,209.
Trustees: George Grossberger, Vickie Grossberger.
EIN: 113522310
Codes: FD2

35575
Jonathan and Susan Dolgen Family Foundation, Inc.
c/o Esanu, Katsky, Karins & Siger
605 3rd Ave., Ste. 16
New York, NY 10158

Established in 1997 in CA.
Donor(s): Jonathan Dolgen, Susan Dolgen.
Financial data (yr. ended 12/31/01): Grants paid, $94,185; assets, $782,217 (M); gifts received, $206,390; expenditures, $99,380; qualifying distributions, $94,185.
Limitations: Applications not accepted.
Application information: Contributes only to pre-selected organizations.
Officers: Susan Dolgen, Pres. and Treas.; Jonathan Dolgen, V.P. and Secy.
EIN: 133993946
Codes: FD2

35576
The Devlin Foundation
c/o Bessemer Trust
630 5th Ave.
New York, NY 10111
Contact: Katharine B. Devlin, Pres.

Established in 1998 in TX.
Donor(s): Robert M. Devlin, Katharine B. Devlin.
Financial data (yr. ended 12/31/01): Grants paid, $94,100; assets, $21,111,341 (M); gifts received, $20,144,198; expenditures, $94,663; qualifying distributions, $94,100.
Limitations: Giving on a national basis, with some emphasis on MA and NY.
Officers: Katharine B. Devlin, Pres.; Matthew B. Devlin, V.P.; Michael H. Devlin, V.P.; Robert M. Devlin, V.P.; Erin C. Devlin, Secy.
EIN: 760574063
Codes: FD2

35577
The Della Rosa Family Foundation
c/o Goldman Sachs & Co.
85 Broad St., Tax Dept.
New York, NY 10004

Established in 1994 in NJ.
Donor(s): Joseph Della Rosa.
Financial data (yr. ended 08/31/01): Grants paid, $94,000; assets, $5,433,954 (M); gifts received, $1,949,000; expenditures, $208,994; qualifying distributions, $96,994.
Limitations: Applications not accepted. Giving on a national basis, with emphasis on NY and NJ.
Application information: Contributes only to pre-selected organizations.
Trustees: Cheryl Della Rosa, Joseph Della Rosa.
EIN: 133797964
Codes: FD2

35578
Coleman Foundation
c/o BCRS Assocs., LLC
100 Wall St., 11th Fl.
New York, NY 10005-3101

Established in 1979.
Donor(s): Francis X. Coleman, Jr.
Financial data (yr. ended 07/31/01): Grants paid, $93,985; assets, $657,571 (M); gifts received, $138,700; expenditures, $112,289; qualifying distributions, $96,535.
Limitations: Applications not accepted. Giving primarily in NY.
Application information: Contributes only to pre-selected organizations.
Trustees: Agnes C. Coleman, Francis X. Coleman, Jr., Robert N. Downey.
EIN: 133001011
Codes: FD2

35579
The William R. Gruver Foundation
c/o Oscar Capital Management
900 3rd Ave., No. 200
New York, NY 10022
Contact: Anthony Scaramucci, Tr.

Established in 1989 in NJ.
Donor(s): William R. Gruver, Joan L. Gruver.
Financial data (yr. ended 02/28/02): Grants paid, $93,946; assets, $2,874,158 (M); expenditures, $114,543; qualifying distributions, $95,209.
Limitations: Applications not accepted. Giving on a national basis.
Application information: Contributes only to pre-selected organizations.
Trustees: Joan L. Gruver, William R. Gruver, Jill G. Puleo, Anthony Scaramucci.
EIN: 133531965
Codes: FD2

35580
Topol Foundation
825 Orienta Ave.
Mamaroneck, NY 10543-4314
Contact: Robert M. Topol, Pres.

Established in 1968.
Donor(s): Robert M. Topol, D'Vera Topol.
Financial data (yr. ended 12/31/00): Grants paid, $93,916; assets, $351,117 (M); gifts received, $99,104; expenditures, $95,147; qualifying distributions, $120,490.
Limitations: Giving primarily in the greater New York, NY, area.
Application information: Application form not required.
Officers and Directors:* Robert M. Topol,* Pres. and Treas.; D'Vera Topol,* V.P.; Martha Kirby,* Secy.; Clifford Topol, Gail Topol, Phyllis Topol.
EIN: 237002556
Codes: FD2

35581
Ralph R. Wilkins Foundation, Inc.
222 Groton Ave.
Cortland, NY 13045
Application address: P.O. Box 628, Cortland, NY 13045-0628, tel.: (607) 758-4953
Contact: John Kimmich, Pres.

Established in 1981 in NY.
Donor(s): Ralph Wilkins,‡ Carrie Wilkins.‡
Financial data (yr. ended 09/30/01): Grants paid, $93,900; assets, $1,730,307 (M); expenditures, $100,886; qualifying distributions, $99,050.
Limitations: Giving limited to Cortland County, NY.
Publications: Informational brochure (including application guidelines).
Application information: Application form required.
Officers and Directors:* John Kimmich,* Pres.; Patricia K. Porter,* V.P.; Harley M. Albro,* Secy.-Treas.; David Camp, Grant Van Sant.
EIN: 161188525
Codes: FD2

35582
The Peace Foundation
c/o Hartman & Craven
460 Park Ave.
New York, NY 10022

Established in 1997 in NY.
Donor(s): Peace Sullivan.
Financial data (yr. ended 12/31/01): Grants paid, $93,800; assets, $189,795 (M); gifts received, $152,902; expenditures, $95,369; qualifying distributions, $93,800.
Officer: Peace Sullivan, Pres.
EIN: 133949034
Codes: FD2

35583
The Marvin and Eleanor Winter Charitable Foundation
641 Lexington Ave.
New York, NY 10022
Contact: Eleanor L. Winter, Tr.

Established in 1989 in NY.
Donor(s): Marvin S. Winter, Eleanor Winter.
Financial data (yr. ended 12/31/01): Grants paid, $93,606; assets, $1,981,567 (M); gifts received, $96,580; expenditures, $95,072; qualifying distributions, $93,606.
Limitations: Giving primarily in New York, NY.
Application information: Application form not required.
Trustee: Eleanor Winter.
EIN: 136927039
Codes: FD2

35584
William & Vina B. Yerdon Foundation
c/o Triumpho Agency
P.O. Box 391
Fort Plain, NY 13339-0391

Established in 1975 in NY.
Donor(s): Lucile Yerdon.‡
Financial data (yr. ended 04/30/01): Grants paid, $93,600; assets, $2,041,941 (M); expenditures, $109,496; qualifying distributions, $101,391; giving activities include $12,632 for programs.
Limitations: Applications not accepted. Giving limited within a ten-mile radius of Fort Plain Village, NY.
Application information: Contributes only to pre-selected organizations.
Officer: David Briggs, Pres.
EIN: 237366678
Codes: FD2

35585
Gurney Foundation, Inc.
c/o Cummings & Carroll
175 Great Neck Rd.
Great Neck, NY 11021

Established in 1945 in NC.
Financial data (yr. ended 08/31/01): Grants paid, $93,565; assets, $1,942,029 (M); expenditures, $105,175; qualifying distributions, $89,660.
Limitations: Applications not accepted. Giving primarily in New York, NY.
Application information: Contributes only to pre-selected organizations.
Officers and Trustees:* Gloria Gurney,* Pres. and Treas.; Robert Wittes,* V.P. and Secy.; Jack Erlinger.
EIN: 566061042
Codes: FD2

35586
Alyad Foundation, Inc.
c/o Perlysky
9 Beechwood Dr.
Lawrence, NY 11559

Donor(s): Irwin Perlysky, Laya Perlysky.
Financial data (yr. ended 11/30/01): Grants paid, $93,497; assets, $825,334 (M); gifts received, $237,314; expenditures, $102,325; qualifying distributions, $93,497.
Officers and Directors:* Laya Perlysky,* Pres. and Treas.; Dov Perlysky,* V.P.; Esther Stahler,* Secy.
EIN: 113189339

35587
Gold Family Foundation
1 Carter Ln.
Monsey, NY 10952-1108

Established in 1998 in NY.
Donor(s): Mendel Gold.
Financial data (yr. ended 12/31/00): Grants paid, $93,420; assets, $120,223 (M); gifts received, $76,100; expenditures, $101,969; qualifying distributions, $93,420.
Limitations: Applications not accepted. Giving primarily in NY.
Application information: Contributes only to pre-selected organizations.
Officer: Mendel Gold, Pres.
EIN: 134001734
Codes: FD2

35588
Price Family Foundation
c/o Wiener, Frushtick & Straub
500 5th Ave., Ste. 2610
New York, NY 10110

Established in 1997 in NJ.
Donor(s): Michael Price.
Financial data (yr. ended 12/31/99): Grants paid, $93,350; assets, $508,501 (M); gifts received, $527,101; expenditures, $100,045; qualifying distributions, $93,350.
Limitations: Applications not accepted.
Application information: Contributes only to pre-selected organizations.
Trustees: Michael Price, Vikki Price, Howard Sontag.
EIN: 137137846

35589
Keith and Rose Reinhard Family Foundation
c/o Davis & Gilbert
1740 Broadway, 3rd Fl.
New York, NY 10019-4315

Established in 1999 in DE.
Donor(s): Keith Reinhard.
Financial data (yr. ended 08/31/02): Grants paid, $93,326; assets, $664,709 (M); gifts received, $521,217; expenditures, $95,576; qualifying distributions, $93,326.
Limitations: Applications not accepted.
Application information: Contributes only to pre-selected organizations.
Officers: Keith Reinhard, Pres.; Rose-Lee Reinhard, Secy.-Treas.
EIN: 134057552

35590
The Lynne & Richard Kaiser Family Foundation
c/o Hartman & Craven
460 Park Ave.
New York, NY 10022

Established in 1986 in NY.
Donor(s): Richard Kaiser.‡

Financial data (yr. ended 12/31/01): Grants paid, $93,320; assets, $3,151,420 (M); expenditures, $98,210; qualifying distributions, $94,320.
Limitations: Applications not accepted. Giving primarily in New York, NY.
Application information: Contributes only to pre-selected organizations.
Trustee: Lynne Kaiser.
EIN: 133385649
Codes: FD2

35591
The Treiber Family Foundation, Inc.
377 Oak St.
Garden City, NY 11530

Financial data (yr. ended 12/31/01): Grants paid, $93,300; assets, $2,248,711 (M); expenditures, $100,618; qualifying distributions, $92,759.
Limitations: Applications not accepted. Giving primarily in NY.
Application information: Contributes only to pre-selected organizations.
Officers: H. Craig Treiber, Pres.; John H. Treiber, V.P.; Peter S. Trieber, Secy.; Scott R. Triber, Treas.
EIN: 113440919
Codes: FD2

35592
The Waldorf Family Foundation, Inc.
17 Beach Dr.
Huntington, NY 11743 (631) 423-9500

Established in 1992 in NY.
Donor(s): Christopher V. Waldorf, Christopher V. Waldorf, Jr., Helyn Waldorf.
Financial data (yr. ended 12/31/01): Grants paid, $93,265; assets, $265,779 (M); gifts received, $100,000; expenditures, $95,315; qualifying distributions, $95,315.
Limitations: Applications not accepted. Giving primarily in NY.
Application information: Contributes only to pre-selected organizations.
Officers: Christopher V. Waldorf, Pres. and Treas.; Helyn Waldorf, V.P. and Secy.
Directors: Christopher V. Waldorf, Jr., Pamela Jeanne Waldorf.
EIN: 113136497
Codes: FD2

35593
Anthony C. Molinari Foundation, Inc.
7 Elyse Dr.
New City, NY 10956-3307
Application address: P.O. Box 515, New City, NY 10956, tel.: (914) 634-6506
Contact: Jane M. McNaught, Pres.

Established in 1959 in NY.
Financial data (yr. ended 12/31/00): Grants paid, $93,250; assets, $1,894,242 (M); expenditures, $98,325; qualifying distributions, $94,063.
Limitations: Giving primarily in central NY.
Officers: Jane M. McNaught, Pres.; Julianne M. Butch, V.P.; Richard P. McNaught, Secy.-Treas.
EIN: 166039202
Codes: FD2

35594
Harriet & Eli Cooper Foundation, Inc.
53-30 Concord St.
Little Neck, NY 11362

Established in 1997 in NY.
Donor(s): Eli Cooper, Harriet Cooper, Avrom Vann, Harry Koslow.
Financial data (yr. ended 12/31/00): Grants paid, $93,172; assets, $10,231,324 (M); gifts received, $9,297,896; expenditures, $101,676; qualifying distributions, $101,676.

Limitations: Applications not accepted.
Application information: Contributes only to pre-selected organizations.
Trustees: Harriet Cooper, Avrom Vann.
EIN: 113378441
Codes: FD2

35595
Blumenberg Family Foundation, Inc.
(also known as Blumfam Foundation, Inc.)
150 W. 26th St.
New York, NY 10001 (212) 691-1222
Contact: Efraim Blumenberg, Tr.

Established in 1996 in NY.
Donor(s): Efraim Blumenberg.
Financial data (yr. ended 12/31/00): Grants paid, $93,084; assets, $648,517 (M); gifts received, $16,000; expenditures, $142,719; qualifying distributions, $93,084.
Limitations: Giving primarily in NY.
Trustees: Efraim Blumenberg, Yehudith Blumenberg.
EIN: 113293808
Codes: FD2

35596
CTW Fund, Inc.
42 Division St.
Amsterdam, NY 12010
Contact: William E. Moore, Secy.

Established in 1997 in NY.
Financial data (yr. ended 12/31/00): Grants paid, $93,000; assets, $1,726,525 (M); expenditures, $106,229; qualifying distributions, $103,529.
Officers: Justin C. Brusgul, Pres.; Norberta Krupczak, V.P.; William E. Moore, Secy.; R. Elizabeth Long, Treas.
Board Member: William Martuscello.
EIN: 141787317
Codes: FD2

35597
JZL Foundation
87-09 Clio St.
Hollis, NY 11423-1229

Established in 1992 in NY.
Donor(s): Mickey Wohl.
Financial data (yr. ended 12/31/00): Grants paid, $92,911; assets, $315,258 (M); gifts received, $80,000; expenditures, $94,170; qualifying distributions, $92,911.
Limitations: Applications not accepted. Giving primarily in NY.
Application information: Contributes only to pre-selected organizations.
Director: Mickey Wohl.
EIN: 113137086
Codes: FD2

35598
Ethel & Alexander Nichoson Foundation
18 W. Carver St., Ste. 2
Huntington, NY 11743
Contact: Arthur Goldstein, Tr.

Established in 1970.
Financial data (yr. ended 05/31/01): Grants paid, $92,897; assets, $1,909,051 (M); expenditures, $115,285; qualifying distributions, $92,897.
Limitations: Giving primarily in NY.
Application information: Application form not required.
Trustee: Arthur Goldstein.
EIN: 116101005
Codes: FD2

35599
The James E. and Jacob A. Barkey Memorial Foundation
(Formerly J. Barkey Memorial Fund)
c/o Citibank, N.A., Tax Dept.
1 Court Sq., 22nd Fl.
Long Island City, NY 11120
Additional address: c/o Citi Trust Services, P.O. Box 6008, 701 E. 60th St., North Sioux Falls, SD 57117
Contact: Donna Konstanz, Trust Off., Citibank, N.A.

Established in 1970 in NY.
Donor(s): Jeanne E. Barkey.‡
Financial data (yr. ended 12/31/01): Grants paid, $92,816; assets, $1,784,972 (M); expenditures, $120,243; qualifying distributions, $91,977.
Limitations: Applications not accepted. Giving primarily in New York, NY.
Application information: Contributes only to pre-selected organizations.
Trustees: Robert M. Arias, Citibank, N.A.
EIN: 136327373
Codes: FD2

35600
Avanessians Family Foundation
c/o Goldman Sachs & Co.
85 Broad St., Tax Dept.
New York, NY 10004

Established in 1995 in NY.
Donor(s): Armen Avanessians.
Financial data (yr. ended 02/28/01): Grants paid, $92,800; assets, $2,252,977 (M); expenditures, $136,383; qualifying distributions, $93,383.
Limitations: Applications not accepted. Giving primarily in New York, NY.
Application information: Contributes only to pre-selected organizations.
Trustees: Armen Avanessians, Janette Avanessians.
EIN: 133862934
Codes: FD2

35601
Martin & Joan Rosen Foundation
1305 Club Dr.
Hewlett Harbor, NY 11557

Established in 1986 in NY.
Donor(s): Joan Rosen, Martin Rosen.
Financial data (yr. ended 12/31/00): Grants paid, $92,694; assets, $154,170 (M); gifts received, $50,000; expenditures, $94,285; qualifying distributions, $92,694.
Limitations: Applications not accepted. Giving primarily in NY.
Application information: Contributes only to pre-selected organizations.
Officers and Directors:* Martin Rosen,* Pres.; Joan Rosen,* Secy.-Treas.; Ilene Cohen, Nancy Stern.
EIN: 133378018
Codes: FD2

35602
The Roone Arledge Charitable Foundation
778 Park Ave., 15th Fl.
New York, NY 10021-3554

Established in 1997 in NY.
Donor(s): Roone Arledge.
Financial data (yr. ended 12/31/00): Grants paid, $92,690; assets, $1,996,369 (M); gifts received, $1,003,832; expenditures, $104,728; qualifying distributions, $83,561.
Limitations: Applications not accepted. Giving primarily in Southampton and New York, NY.
Application information: Contributes only to pre-selected organizations.
Trustees: Gigi Arledge, Roone Arledge, Ronald S. Konecky.
EIN: 133922166
Codes: FD2

35603
The Jay H. Perry Foundation, Inc.
c/o Grant Thornton
50 Broad St.
New York, NY 10004-2501

Financial data (yr. ended 06/30/00): Grants paid, $92,625; assets, $657,141 (M); expenditures, $99,815; qualifying distributions, $96,115.
Limitations: Applications not accepted. Giving primarily in New York, NY.
Application information: Contributes only to pre-selected organizations.
Officers: Nancy A. Crotty-Perry, Pres. and Treas.; Jeffrey R. Perry, V.P.
Directors: John Perry, Susan L. Perry.
EIN: 237101744
Codes: FD2

35604
Michael & Margaret Picotte Foundation, Inc.
20 Corporate Woods Blvd., Ste. 600
Albany, NY 12211

Established in 1990 in NY.
Donor(s): Kathleen M. Picotte.
Financial data (yr. ended 12/31/01): Grants paid, $92,603; assets, $2,672,061 (M); gifts received, $250,001; expenditures, $116,099; qualifying distributions, $92,603.
Limitations: Applications not accepted.
Application information: Contributes only to pre-selected organizations.
Officer: Michael B. Picotte, Pres.
Director: Margaret L. Picotte.
EIN: 061307349

35605
The SLA Foundation
778 Park Ave.
New York, NY 10021

Established in 1985 in DE.
Donor(s): Ralph E. Ablon.
Financial data (yr. ended 11/30/01): Grants paid, $92,563; assets, $1,847,081 (M); expenditures, $103,208; qualifying distributions, $93,075.
Limitations: Applications not accepted. Giving primarily in New York, NY.
Application information: Contributes only to pre-selected organizations.
Directors: Ralph E. Ablon, Sylvia L. Ablon, Robert E. Smith.
EIN: 133316015
Codes: FD2

35606
Max B. Cohn Family Foundation
c/o Milton Cohn
36 Sunset Rd.
Kings Point, NY 11024

Established in 1952 in NY.
Donor(s): Milton S. Cohn, Max B. Cohn.‡
Financial data (yr. ended 05/31/01): Grants paid, $92,485; assets, $1,273,096 (M); expenditures, $102,870; qualifying distributions, $92,485.
Limitations: Applications not accepted. Giving primarily in the greater New York, NY, area.
Application information: Contributes only to pre-selected organizations.
Officers and Board Members:* Milton S. Cohn,* Pres.; Melvin Roth,* V.P.; Maurice J. Cohn,* Secy.-Treas.
EIN: 116005709
Codes: FD2

35607
The Benjamin & Susan Winter Foundation
c/o The Winter Organization
641 Lexington Ave.
New York, NY 10022

Established in 1996 in NY.
Donor(s): Benjamin J. Winter, Susan Winter.
Financial data (yr. ended 10/31/01): Grants paid, $92,485; assets, $267,315 (M); gifts received, $65,000; expenditures, $94,665; qualifying distributions, $92,300.
Limitations: Applications not accepted.
Application information: Contributes only to pre-selected organizations.
Trustees: Benjamin J. Winter, Susan Winter.
EIN: 137107477
Codes: FD2

35608
Zichron Chaim Foundation
8 Elenar Ln.
Spring Valley, NY 10977-2521
(845) 356-7947
Contact: Yechiel Kleinman, Tr.

Financial data (yr. ended 12/31/00): Grants paid, $92,313; assets, $1,380 (M); gifts received, $94,374; expenditures, $92,759; qualifying distributions, $92,759.
Limitations: Giving primarily in New York, NY.
Trustees: Livia Deutsch, Zoltan Deutsch, Marge Kleinman, Yechiel Kleinman, Devora Kresch.
EIN: 311607517
Codes: FD2

35609
The Medin Foundation
c/o Joseph Furst
1244 49th St.
Brooklyn, NY 11219

Established in 1995 in NY.
Donor(s): Van Wald Holding Corp.
Financial data (yr. ended 12/31/00): Grants paid, $92,292; assets, $144,674 (M); gifts received, $31,000; expenditures, $93,325; qualifying distributions, $91,797.
Limitations: Applications not accepted.
Application information: Contributes only to pre-selected organizations.
Trustees: D. Gutfruend, M. Gutfruend.
EIN: 113271700
Codes: CS, FD2, CD

35610
The Ridings Foundation, Inc.
100 Clinton Sq., Ste. 101
Syracuse, NY 13202
Contact: David A.A. Ridings, Pres.

Established in 1998 in NY.
Donor(s): David A.A. Ridings.
Financial data (yr. ended 12/31/01): Grants paid, $92,203; assets, $763,413 (M); expenditures, $103,075; qualifying distributions, $95,052.
Limitations: Applications not accepted.
Officers: David A.A. Ridings, Pres. and Treas.; Sybil Oakes, Secy.
Director: Nancy R. Andrepoint.
EIN: 311589066
Codes: FD2

35611
Mitchell & Elaine Yanow Charitable Trust
c/o Carter, Ledyard & Milburn
2 Wall St.
New York, NY 10005

Established in 1997 in MO.
Donor(s): Mitchell Yanow.‡

Financial data (yr. ended 04/30/02): Grants paid, $92,200; assets, $1,637,819 (M); expenditures, $99,105; qualifying distributions, $92,200.
Limitations: Applications not accepted. Giving primarily in MO.
Application information: Contributes only to pre-selected organizations.
Trustees: Barbara Lichtenstein, Robert A. Ouimette, Caryl E. Yanow.
EIN: 137111098

35612
Margarita Victoria Delacorte Foundation
c/o U.S. Trust
114 W. 47th St.
New York, NY 10036-1532
Contact: Margarita V. Delacorte

Established in 1966 in NY.
Donor(s): Margarita V. Delacorte.
Financial data (yr. ended 12/31/01): Grants paid, $92,050; assets, $332,099 (M); expenditures, $98,343; qualifying distributions, $96,027.
Limitations: Giving primarily in New York, NY.
Trustee: U.S. Trust.
EIN: 136197777
Codes: FD2

35613
International Federation of Parkinson's Disease Foundations, Inc.
1200 5th Ave., Ste. 12D
New York, NY 10029-5214
Contact: Melvin D. Yahr, M.D., Pres.

Donor(s): Horace W. Goldsmith Foundation.
Financial data (yr. ended 12/31/01): Grants paid, $92,000; assets, $1,308,355 (M); gifts received, $70; expenditures, $111,205; qualifying distributions, $92,000.
Limitations: Giving primarily in New York, NY.
Officers and Directors:* Melvin D. Yahr, M.D.,* Pres.; Daniel Moros,* Secy.; Kenneth Aidekman, Sally Leung, Irwin Shapiro.
EIN: 133020604

35614
S. & W. Greenbaum Charitable Trust
1175 Park Ave., Ste. 9C
New York, NY 10128 (212) 737-6565
Contact: Shalom Greenbaum, Tr.

Established in 1990.
Donor(s): Shalom Greenbaum.
Financial data (yr. ended 12/31/00): Grants paid, $91,925; assets, $106,375 (M); gifts received, $77,536; expenditures, $96,668; qualifying distributions, $96,601.
Limitations: Giving primarily in New York, NY.
Trustees: Shalom Greenbaum, Wendy Greenbaum.
EIN: 136961553
Codes: FD2

35615
The Gusti Brandt Foundation
c/o Nathan Berkman & Co.
29 Broadway, Rm. 2900
New York, NY 10006-3296

Established in 1950.
Donor(s): Louis Brandt, Bernard Brandt.‡
Financial data (yr. ended 12/31/00): Grants paid, $91,911; assets, $1,286,341 (M); expenditures, $108,043; qualifying distributions, $91,911.
Limitations: Applications not accepted. Giving primarily in NY.
Application information: Contributes only to pre-selected organizations.
Directors: Gary Brandt, John Brandt, Robert Brandt, Ruth Brandt.
EIN: 136185337
Codes: FD2

35616
The David P. Nolan Foundation, Inc.
c/o Isaac Jarmark, Spear, Leeds, & Kellogg
120 Broadway
New York, NY 10271-0093

Established in 1985 in NY.
Donor(s): David P. Nolan.
Financial data (yr. ended 11/30/00): Grants paid, $91,865; assets, $210,955 (M); gifts received, $82,936; expenditures, $92,340; qualifying distributions, $91,144.
Limitations: Applications not accepted. Giving primarily in New York, NY.
Application information: Contributes only to pre-selected organizations.
Officers: David P. Nolan, Pres. and Treas.; James Nolan, V.P. and Secy.
EIN: 133343293
Codes: FD2

35617
Louella Cook Foundation
c/o U.S. Trust
114 W. 47th St.
New York, NY 10036
FAX: (212) 852-3377
Contact: Carolyn L. Larke, Asst. V.P.; or Linda Franciscovich, Sr. V.P., U.S. Trust Co. of New York

Established in 1976 in WA.
Financial data (yr. ended 07/31/01): Grants paid, $91,800; assets, $4,949,324 (M); expenditures, $149,539; qualifying distributions, $136,816.
Limitations: Giving primarily in WA, with emphasis on Seattle.
Publications: Application guidelines.
Application information: Application form not required.
Trustees: Caroline C. Jansing, Christopher C. Jansing, John Christopher Jansing, John Cook Jansing, U.S. Trust.
EIN: 911098016
Codes: FD2

35618
The Diandra De Morrell Douglas Foundation
c/o Starr & Co., LLC
350 Park Ave., 9th Fl.
New York, NY 10022
Contact: Diandra De Morrell Douglas, Pres.

Established in 2000 in CA.
Donor(s): Diandra De Morrell Douglas, Michael Douglas.
Financial data (yr. ended 12/31/00): Grants paid, $91,725; assets, $2,491,041 (M); gifts received, $2,525,610; expenditures, $94,100; qualifying distributions, $91,725.
Limitations: Giving primarily in CA and New York, NY.
Officers: Diandra De Morrell Douglas, Pres.; Luisa Del Valle Firouz, Secy.; Stuart Sundlund, C.F.O.
EIN: 954688616
Codes: FD2

35619
MMG Charitable Foundation
82-33 Beverly Rd.
Kew Gardens, NY 11415

Established in 1996 in NY.
Donor(s): Michael Gross.
Financial data (yr. ended 12/31/01): Grants paid, $91,655; assets, $372,797 (M); expenditures, $92,610; qualifying distributions, $92,081.
Limitations: Applications not accepted. Giving primarily in NY.
Application information: Contributes only to pre-selected organizations.
Trustees: Benjamin Gross, Bernard Gross, Mathilda Gross, Michael Gross.
EIN: 116480264
Codes: FD2

35620
The Hirschhorn/Baumann Family Foundation
c/o Perelson Weiner
1 Dag Hammarskjold Plz.
New York, NY 10017

Established in 1993 in NY.
Donor(s): Hannah H. Baumann.‡
Financial data (yr. ended 12/31/01): Grants paid, $91,605; assets, $2,229,618 (M); gifts received, $65,000; expenditures, $111,726; qualifying distributions, $95,175.
Limitations: Applications not accepted. Giving primarily in New York, NY.
Application information: Contributes only to pre-selected organizations.
Trustee: James S. Baumann.
EIN: 137020953
Codes: FD2

35621
Maureen & Mark Rossi Charitable Foundation, Inc.
13 Kirby Ln.
Rye, NY 10580

Established in 1997 in NY.
Donor(s): Maureen Rossi, Mark Rossi.
Financial data (yr. ended 03/31/01): Grants paid, $91,603; assets, $417,376 (M); expenditures, $96,978; qualifying distributions, $91,603.
Limitations: Applications not accepted.
Application information: Contributes only to pre-selected organizations.
Managers: Mark Rossi, Maureen Rossi.
EIN: 133945122
Codes: FD2

35622
The Timothy J. Rooney Foundation
c/o Timothy J. Rooney, Jr.
Yonkers Raceway Central Park Ave.
Yonkers, NY 10710

Established in 1994 in NY.
Donor(s): Timothy J. Rooney.
Financial data (yr. ended 12/31/01): Grants paid, $91,500; assets, $646,938 (M); gifts received, $313,600; expenditures, $91,600; qualifying distributions, $91,424.
Limitations: Applications not accepted.
Application information: Contributes only to pre-selected organizations.
Trustees: Margaret R. Galterio, Kathleen Mara, Bridget Rooney, Cara Rooney, Timothy J. Rooney, Timothy J. Rooney, Jr.
EIN: 133723406
Codes: FD2

35623
Byrne Foundation
240 Oneida St.
Syracuse, NY 13202-3373
Contact: James Coughlin

Established in 1960 in NY.
Donor(s): Byrne Dairy, Inc., Sonbyrne Sales, Inc., McMahon's of Central Square, Inc.
Financial data (yr. ended 04/30/01): Grants paid, $91,438; assets, $122,462 (M); gifts received, $86,000; expenditures, $92,585; qualifying distributions, $91,374.

Limitations: Applications not accepted. Giving primarily in Syracuse, NY.
Application information: Contributes only to pre-selected organizations.
Officer: William M. Byrne, Jr., Mgr.
EIN: 166052248
Codes: FD2

35624
IMS Foundation
506 Quentin Rd.
Brooklyn, NY 11223

Established in 1999 in NY.
Financial data (yr. ended 12/31/00): Grants paid, $91,401; assets, $213 (M); gifts received, $88,018; expenditures, $91,590; qualifying distributions, $91,590.
Officer: Raymond J. Salem, Pres.
EIN: 134026345
Codes: FD2

35625
Morningstar Foundation
6500 Main St., Ste. 5
Williamsville, NY 14221

Established in 1997 in NY.
Donor(s): Jamey L. Moran.
Financial data (yr. ended 12/31/01): Grants paid, $91,394; assets, $60,464 (M); gifts received, $12,867; expenditures, $91,601; qualifying distributions, $91,394.
Limitations: Applications not accepted.
Application information: Contributes only to pre-selected organizations.
Trustee: William C. Moran.
EIN: 161517613
Codes: FD2

35626
M. & H. Neiman Foundation, Inc.
c/o Marvin Neiman
39 Broadway, Ste. 2510
New York, NY 10006 (212) 269-1000

Established in 1972 in NY.
Donor(s): Marvin Neiman.
Financial data (yr. ended 10/31/01): Grants paid, $91,380; assets, $1,515 (M); gifts received, $100,075; expenditures, $91,380; qualifying distributions, $91,380.
Limitations: Applications not accepted. Giving primarily in Brooklyn, NY.
Application information: Contributes only to pre-selected organizations.
Officers: Marvin Neiman, Pres.; Louis Neiman, V.P.; Helen Neiman, Secy.
EIN: 237042788
Codes: FD2

35627
The Framarb Foundation
c/o George H. Beane
225 W. 80th St., Ste. 2B
New York, NY 10024-7003

Donor(s): Frank E. Bean, Mary H. Beane.
Financial data (yr. ended 03/31/01): Grants paid, $91,250; assets, $1,227,729 (M); gifts received, $230,907; expenditures, $99,481; qualifying distributions, $91,250.
Limitations: Applications not accepted. Giving primarily in the New York, NY, and Nashville, TN, areas.
Application information: Contributes only to pre-selected organizations.
Trustees: George H. Beane, Mary H. Beane.
EIN: 066105334
Codes: FD2

35628
William and Jane Brachfeld Foundation
4455 Douglas Ave.
Riverdale, NY 10471-3519

Established in 1971.
Financial data (yr. ended 06/30/01): Grants paid, $91,080; assets, $1,630,329 (M); expenditures, $96,870; qualifying distributions, $90,431.
Limitations: Giving primarily in New York, NY.
Officers: William Brachfeld, Pres.; Jane Brachfeld, Secy.
Directors: Jonathan Brachfeld, Kenneth Brachfeld.
EIN: 132688349
Codes: FD2

35629
The KCEG Foundation
14 Melnick Dr.
P.O. Box 765
Monsey, NY 10952

Established in 1997.
Donor(s): Ephraim Grossman.
Financial data (yr. ended 12/31/00): Grants paid, $91,058; assets, $128,708 (M); gifts received, $165,300; expenditures, $92,352; qualifying distributions, $92,081.
Limitations: Applications not accepted. Giving primarily in NY.
Application information: Contributes only to pre-selected organizations.
Trustees: Ephraim Grossman, Hendel Grossman.
EIN: 137103161
Codes: FD2

35630
The Krupman Family Foundation, Inc.
2 Ponds Ln.
Purchase, NY 10577

Established in 1997 in NY.
Donor(s): William A. Krupman.
Financial data (yr. ended 12/31/01): Grants paid, $91,057; assets, $55,149 (M); gifts received, $90,000; expenditures, $92,002; qualifying distributions, $91,873.
Officer: William A. Krupman, Chair.
EIN: 137098705
Codes: FD2

35631
The Strong-Cuevas Foundation, Inc.
211 Central Park West
New York, NY 10024 (212) 724-6358
Contact: Elizabeth Decuevas, Pres.

Established in 1995 in NY.
Donor(s): Elizabeth Decuevas.
Financial data (yr. ended 09/30/01): Grants paid, $91,025; assets, $368,410 (M); gifts received, $521,039; expenditures, $98,294; qualifying distributions, $91,025.
Limitations: Giving primarily in NY.
Officers: Elizabeth Decuevas, Pres.; Deborah Carmichael, V.P.; Melvin Seiden, Treas.
EIN: 133818287
Codes: FD2

35632
Nicklas Family Foundation
c/o Lexington Partners
660 Madison Ave.
New York, NY 10021
Contact: Brent Nicklas, Secy.-Treas.

Established in 1997 in NY.
Donor(s): Brent Nicklas, Sylvia Nicklas.
Financial data (yr. ended 12/31/01): Grants paid, $91,000; assets, $1,587,411 (M); expenditures, $101,357; qualifying distributions, $91,000.
Limitations: Giving primarily in NY.
Officers and Director:* Sylvia Nicklas,* Pres.; Brent Nicklas, Secy.-Treas.
EIN: 133942200
Codes: FD2

35633
The Freeman-Harrison Family Foundation
535 E. 86th St., Ste. 10-D
New York, NY 10028-7533
E-mail: bfnc1926@cs.com
Contact: Burton M. Freeman, Pres.

Established in 1998 in NY.
Donor(s): Burton M. Freeman.
Financial data (yr. ended 12/31/01): Grants paid, $90,950; assets, $999,590 (M); expenditures, $93,950; qualifying distributions, $92,157.
Limitations: Applications not accepted. Giving primarily in New York, NY.
Application information: Contributes only to pre-selected organizations.
Officer and Directors:* Burton M. Freeman,* Pres.; Kenneth D. Freeman, Sandra T. Freeman, Marjorie P. Harrison.
EIN: 134010197
Codes: FD2

35634
The Campbell Family Foundation
c/o William I. Campbell
375 Park Ave., Ste. 1501
New York, NY 10152

Established in 2000 in NY and DE.
Donor(s): William I. Campbell, Christine Wachter-Campbell.
Financial data (yr. ended 12/31/01): Grants paid, $90,842; assets, $1,994,693 (M); gifts received, $300,000; expenditures, $118,975; qualifying distributions, $90,842.
Limitations: Applications not accepted.
Application information: Contributes only to pre-selected organizations.
Officers: William I. Campbell, Pres.; Christine Wachter-Campbell, V.P.
EIN: 134149591

35635
Morse G. Dial Foundation
c/o M. Dial
12 E 37247
Clayton, NY 13624

Established in 1955.
Financial data (yr. ended 12/31/01): Grants paid, $90,826; assets, $623,307 (M); expenditures, $129,808; qualifying distributions, $124,359.
Limitations: Applications not accepted. Giving primarily in MA, NJ, and NY.
Application information: Contributes only to pre-selected organizations.
Trustees: Todd Atkinson, Mary T. Dial, Morse G. Dial, Jr.
EIN: 136106437
Codes: FD2

35636
The John W. Hill/Hill and Knowlton Foundation, Inc.
466 Lexington Ave.
New York, NY 10017-3140
Contact: Mark Thorne, Secy.

Established in 1957.
Donor(s): John Hill.‡
Financial data (yr. ended 12/31/01): Grants paid, $90,750; assets, $1,877,753 (M); expenditures, $105,802; qualifying distributions, $90,750.
Limitations: Giving on a national basis.

35636—NEW YORK

Application information: Application form required.
Officers and Directors:* Howard Paster,* Pres.; Mark Thorne,* Secy.-Treas.
EIN: 136161529
Codes: FD2

35637
The Scott and Linda Pinkus Foundation
c/o BCRS Associates, LLC
100 Wall St., 11th Fl.
New York, NY 10005

Established in 1999 in NJ.
Donor(s): Scott Pinkus.
Financial data (yr. ended 10/31/01): Grants paid, $90,740; assets, $1,597,673 (M); gifts received, $100; expenditures, $111,583; qualifying distributions, $91,117.
Limitations: Applications not accepted. Giving primarily in New York, NY.
Application information: Contributes only to pre-selected organizations.
Trustees: Linda Pinkus, Scott Pinkus.
EIN: 134051212
Codes: FD2

35638
Felberbaum Family Foundation
800 Park Ave.
New York, NY 10021

Established in 1986 in NY.
Donor(s): Barbara Felberbaum, Roger Felberbaum.
Financial data (yr. ended 09/30/01): Grants paid, $90,725; assets, $456,087 (M); gifts received, $74,782; expenditures, $95,379; qualifying distributions, $92,100.
Limitations: Applications not accepted. Giving primarily in the greater metropolitan New York, NY, area.
Application information: Contributes only to pre-selected organizations.
Trustees: Barbara Felberbaum, Roger Felberbaum.
EIN: 133385574
Codes: FD2

35639
The Allan Morrow Foundation, Inc.
825 3rd Ave., Ste. 3315
New York, NY 10022 (212) 593-4600

Established in 1989 in NY.
Donor(s): Allan Morrow.‡
Financial data (yr. ended 12/31/00): Grants paid, $90,611; assets, $1,613,814 (M); expenditures, $94,144; qualifying distributions, $92,720.
Limitations: Giving primarily in New York, NY.
Application information: Application form required.
Officers and Directors:* James Pepper,* Pres.; Vivian Shapiro, V.P.; Arline West,* Secy.; Mark R. Imowitz, Treas.; Norma Hillman, Bernice Manocherian, Lawrence Newman, Jeffrey Soref.
EIN: 133566764
Codes: FD2

35640
Charles E. Burchfield Foundation, Inc.
c/o Cohen & Swados
70 Niagara St.
Buffalo, NY 14202 (716) 856-4600
Contact: John P. Dee

Incorporated in 1966 in NY.
Donor(s): Charles E. Burchfield.‡
Financial data (yr. ended 12/31/01): Grants paid, $90,600; assets, $2,498,042 (M); expenditures, $167,308; qualifying distributions, $597,797.
Limitations: Giving on a national basis.

Publications: Annual report.
Application information: Application form not required.
Officers and Directors:* C. Arthur Burchfield,* Pres.; Sally R. Hill,* V.P.; Robert D. Mustain,* Secy.; Violet P. Burchfield, Phyllis S. Mustain.
EIN: 166073522
Codes: FD2

35641
Sharon and Lewis Korman Foundation
444 Madison Ave., Ste. 601
New York, NY 10019
Contact: Lewis J. Korman, Tr. or Sharon B. Korman, Tr.

Established in 1989 in NY.
Donor(s): Lewis J. Korman.
Financial data (yr. ended 12/31/01): Grants paid, $90,500; assets, $143,339 (M); gifts received, $100,000; expenditures, $91,130; qualifying distributions, $90,580.
Limitations: Giving primarily in New York, NY.
Trustees: Lewis J. Korman, Sharon B. Korman.
EIN: 133556710
Codes: FD2

35642
Jackson E. & Evelyn G. Spears Foundation, Inc.
c/o Daniel Levine, CPA
1 Huntington Quad., Ste. 3502
Melville, NY 11747
Application address: 18 Canaan Close, New Canaan, CT 06840, tel.: (203) 966-1677
Contact: Jackson E. Spears, Pres.

Financial data (yr. ended 12/31/01): Grants paid, $90,500; assets, $1,716,234 (M); expenditures, $105,858; qualifying distributions, $90,500.
Limitations: Giving on a national basis, with emphasis on CT and NY.
Application information: Application form not required.
Officers and Trustees:* Jackson E. Spears,* Pres.; Brian Spears, Secy.; William G. Spears, Treas.; Wendy Connors, Joan Spears.
EIN: 136085261
Codes: FD2

35643
Abraham Perlman Foundation, Inc.
1165 Park Ave.
New York, NY 10128
Contact: Nell Moskowitz, Mgr.

Established about 1959 in NY.
Donor(s): Abraham Perlman.‡
Financial data (yr. ended 05/31/01): Grants paid, $90,425; assets, $1,588,752 (M); expenditures, $98,353; qualifying distributions, $89,851.
Limitations: Giving primarily in the greater Boston, MA, area and New York, NY.
Officer: Nell Moskowitz, Mgr.
EIN: 116036673
Codes: FD2

35644
The Cohen Family Foundation, Inc.
c/o The Ayco Company, LLP
P.O. Box 8019
Ballston Spa, NY 12020-8019
Contact: W. Michael Reickert

Incorporated in 1986 in NY.
Donor(s): Florence Cohen, Peter A. Cohen, William L. Cohen, and other members of the Cohen family.
Financial data (yr. ended 12/31/00): Grants paid, $90,311; assets, $102,066 (M); gifts received, $82,925; expenditures, $94,605; qualifying distributions, $90,311.

Limitations: Applications not accepted. Giving primarily in New York, NY.
Application information: Contributes only to pre-selected organizations.
Officers: Peter A. Cohen, Pres. and Treas.; William Cohen, V.P. and Secy.
Director: Michelle Cohen.
EIN: 133183001
Codes: FD2

35645
F. Weiler Charity Fund
1114 Ave. of the Americas, Ste. 3400
New York, NY 10036

Trust established in 1946 in NY.
Donor(s): Robert H. Arnow, Alan G. Weiler, Weiler family and associates.
Financial data (yr. ended 12/31/01): Grants paid, $90,306; assets, $291,562 (M); gifts received, $100,000; expenditures, $92,911; qualifying distributions, $90,491.
Limitations: Applications not accepted. Giving primarily in NY.
Application information: Contributes only to pre-selected organizations.
Trustees: Robert H. Arnow, Alan G. Weiler.
EIN: 136161247
Codes: FD2

35646
Richard Rodney Dennett Trust
c/o JPMorgan Chase Bank
1211 Ave. of the Americas, 34th Fl.
New York, NY 10036

Established around 1981.
Financial data (yr. ended 12/31/01): Grants paid, $90,159; assets, $1,505,920 (M); expenditures, $111,285; qualifying distributions, $91,968.
Limitations: Applications not accepted.
Application information: Contributes only to pre-selected organizations.
Trustee: JPMorgan Chase Bank.
EIN: 136022784
Codes: FD2

35647
The Hope Tang Goodwin Foundation, Ltd.
231 Cleft Rd.
Mill Neck, NY 11765-1003

Established in 1997 in NY.
Donor(s): James Goodwin, James C. Kralik, Sykes Family Foundation.
Financial data (yr. ended 08/31/01): Grants paid, $90,059; assets, $696,631 (M); gifts received, $16,500; expenditures, $91,553; qualifying distributions, $90,459.
Limitations: Applications not accepted. Giving primarily in New York, NY.
Application information: Contributes only to pre-selected organizations.
Officers: James Goodwin, Pres. and Treas.; Cynthia Faustino, V.P. and Secy.
EIN: 113402983
Codes: FD2

35648
Y. A. Frenkel Family Foundation, Inc.
1487 E. 13th St.
Brooklyn, NY 11230-6603

Established in 1995 in NY.
Donor(s): Laszlo Frenkel.
Financial data (yr. ended 12/31/00): Grants paid, $90,018; assets, $396,992 (M); gifts received, $71,000; expenditures, $92,006; qualifying distributions, $89,803.
Limitations: Applications not accepted. Giving limited to Brooklyn, NY.

Application information: Contributes only to pre-selected organizations.
Officers: Laszlo Frenkel, Pres.; Marilyn Frenkel, V.P.
Director: Cheryl Frenkel.
EIN: 133857306
Codes: FD2

35649
Jacob & Eugenie Bucky Memorial Foundation, Inc.
c/o O'Neill, Whalen & Fitzgerald
P.O. Box 701
Sleepy Hollow, NY 10591-0701
(914) 631-4226
Contact: Robert C. Thomson, Jr., Pres.

Established in 1957.
Financial data (yr. ended 12/31/00): Grants paid, $90,000; assets, $1,943,755 (M); expenditures, $110,458; qualifying distributions, $95,273.
Limitations: Giving primarily in the Northeast, with emphasis on NJ, NY, and PA.
Application information: Application form required.
Officers and Directors:* Robert C. Thomson, Jr.,* Pres. and Treas.; Dennis M. Fitzgerald,* V.P. and Secy.; Michele C. Fitzgerald, Linda T. Murray, Eloise T. Schundler.
EIN: 136098493
Codes: FD2

35650
Clinton Seed Fund, Inc.
c/o Manhattan Plz.
400 W. 43rd St.
New York, NY 10036-6301

Established in 1992 in NY.
Financial data (yr. ended 05/31/01): Grants paid, $90,000; assets, $1,052,038 (M); expenditures, $103,799; qualifying distributions, $90,000.
Limitations: Giving limited to New York, NY, with emphasis on the Clinton District.
Officers: Mary D'Elia, Chair.; Susan Cole, Secy.; Mary Wing, Treas.
EIN: 133032253

35651
Thomas Dean Family Foundation
c/o Thompson Dean
550 Park Ave., Ste. 10E
New York, NY 10021

Established in 1998 in NY.
Donor(s): Thompson Dean III.
Financial data (yr. ended 12/31/99): Grants paid, $90,000; assets, $512,145 (M); expenditures, $92,208; qualifying distributions, $90,000.
Limitations: Giving primarily in MA and NY.
Officers and Director:* Thompson Dean III, Chair.; Caroline W. Dean,* Pres.; Hume R. Steyer, Secy.
EIN: 133942201
Codes: FD2

35652
Mae Cadwell Rovensky Trust
c/o U.S. Trust
P.O. Box 2004
New York, NY 10109-1910

Established in 1961 in NY.
Financial data (yr. ended 12/31/01): Grants paid, $90,000; assets, $1,662,388 (M); expenditures, $92,266; qualifying distributions, $91,279.
Limitations: Applications not accepted. Giving on a national basis.
Application information: Contributes only to pre-selected organizations.
Trustee: U.S. Trust.

EIN: 136071671
Codes: FD2

35653
Michele Snyder Foundation, Inc.
c/o U.S. Trust
114 W. 47th St., TAXVAS
New York, NY 10036

Established in 2000 in MD.
Donor(s): Michele Snyder.
Financial data (yr. ended 12/31/01): Grants paid, $90,000; assets, $1,799,090 (M); gifts received, $7,250; expenditures, $144,132; qualifying distributions, $90,000.
Limitations: Applications not accepted.
Application information: Unsolicited requests for funds not accepted.
Director: Michele Snyder.
EIN: 522272965

35654
The Whitehead Charitable Foundation
c/o Shulman, Jones & Co.
200 E. Post Rd.
White Plains, NY 10601
Application address: 140 Royal Palm Way, No. 201, Palm Beach, FL 33480, tel.: (561) 822-9906
Contact: Thomas Victory, Jr., Secy.

Established in 1976 in DE.
Donor(s): Edwin C. Whitehead.‡
Financial data (yr. ended 11/30/99): Grants paid, $90,000; assets, $4,003,629 (M); gifts received, $10,000; expenditures, $151,644; qualifying distributions, $90,000.
Limitations: Giving primarily in Alexandria, VA.
Officers and Directors:* John J. Whitehead,* Pres.; Peter J. Whitehead,* V.P.; Thomas Victory, Jr., Secy.; Susan Whitehead.
EIN: 060956618
Codes: FD2

35655
The Benjy & Adina Goldstein Charitable Foundation, Inc.
35 Essex St.
New York, NY 10002

Established in 2000 in NY.
Donor(s): Benjamin Goldstein.
Financial data (yr. ended 12/31/01): Grants paid, $89,968; assets, $226,269 (M); gifts received, $200,000; expenditures, $92,058; qualifying distributions, $89,968.
Trustee: Benjamin Goldstein.
EIN: 522264340

35656
Samuel J. & Ethel Lefrak Foundation, Inc.
97-77 Queens Blvd.
Rego Park, NY 11374-3317

Established in 1963.
Donor(s): Samuel J. Lefrak, L.S.S. Leasing Corp.
Financial data (yr. ended 12/31/00): Grants paid, $89,923; assets, $18,009 (M); expenditures, $90,715; qualifying distributions, $89,896.
Limitations: Applications not accepted. Giving primarily in New York, NY.
Application information: Contributes only to pre-selected organizations.
Officer: Samuel J. Lefrak, Pres.
EIN: 116043788
Codes: FD2

35657
Jehovah-Jireh, Inc.
3 Clinton Sq.
Albany, NY 12207 (518) 465-4717
Contact: Larry Deason, Dir.

Established in 1978 in NY.
Financial data (yr. ended 03/31/02): Grants paid, $89,866; assets, $1,374,150 (M); gifts received, $80,000; expenditures, $190,796; qualifying distributions, $176,032.
Director: Larry Deason.
EIN: 222239206
Codes: FD2

35658
The Bruns Foundation
c/o BCRS Assocs., LLC
100 Wall St., 11th Fl.
New York, NY 10005

Established in 1999 in IL.
Donor(s): John C. Ryan.
Financial data (yr. ended 09/30/01): Grants paid, $89,500; assets, $1,083,263 (M); gifts received, $780,500; expenditures, $126,031; qualifying distributions, $91,030.
Limitations: Applications not accepted. Giving primarily in Chicago, IL.
Application information: Contributes only to pre-selected organizations.
Trustees: Helen Bruns Ryan, John C. Ryan.
EIN: 137225243
Codes: FD2

35659
Butler Family Foundation
P.O. Box 137
Westhampton Beach, NY 11978

Established in 1999.
Donor(s): Abbey Butler, Ilene Butler.
Financial data (yr. ended 12/31/00): Grants paid, $89,500; assets, $23,925 (M); gifts received, $1,000; expenditures, $90,956; qualifying distributions, $89,500.
Limitations: Applications not accepted.
Application information: Contributes only to pre-selected organizations.
Officers: Abbey Butler, Pres.; Ilene Butler, V.P.
EIN: 113518798
Codes: FD2

35660
The Norman and Bettina Roberts Foundation, Inc.
11 5th Ave.
New York, NY 10003
Contact: Norman Roberts, Pres.

Established in 1992 in NY.
Donor(s): Norman Roberts, Bettina Roberts.‡
Financial data (yr. ended 09/30/01): Grants paid, $89,500; assets, $2,059,509 (M); gifts received, $1,059,017; expenditures, $108,554; qualifying distributions, $109,554.
Limitations: Giving primarily in New York, NY.
Officers: Norman Roberts, Pres. and Treas.; Joseph R. Canciglia, V.P. and Secy.
Directors: Lawrence Magid, David McIntee, Alice Perez.
EIN: 133702467
Codes: FD2

35661
The Old Mill Foundation, Inc.
c/o Martin & Selinger Co.
225 Broadway, Ste. 1501
New York, NY 10007

Established in 1982.

Donor(s): Annabelle G. Coleman, Denis P. Coleman, Jr.
Financial data (yr. ended 05/31/01): Grants paid, $89,480; assets, $517,163 (M); expenditures, $105,877; qualifying distributions, $89,480.
Limitations: Applications not accepted. Giving primarily in FL and NY.
Application information: Contributes only to pre-selected organizations.
Directors: Annabelle G. Coleman, Denis P. Coleman, Jr.
EIN: 133157302
Codes: FD2

35662
A. & L. Borg Private Foundation, Inc.
1636 50th St.
Brooklyn, NY 11204 (212) 865-9670
Contact: Abraham Borg or Lola Borg, Trustees

Established in 1989 in NY.
Donor(s): Abraham Borg, Lola Borg.
Financial data (yr. ended 12/31/01): Grants paid, $89,406; assets, $1,320,229 (M); gifts received, $252,500; expenditures, $90,431; qualifying distributions, $89,406.
Limitations: Giving primarily in NY.
Application information: Application form not required.
Trustees: Abraham Borg, Lola Borg.
EIN: 112944989
Codes: FD2

35663
Herbert T. Dyett Foundation, Inc.
218 N. Washington St.
Rome, NY 13440 (315) 336-1441
Scholarship application addresses: c/o Principal, Rome Free Academy, Rome, NY 13440, tel.: (315) 338-2222, or c/o Principal, Rome Catholic High School, Rome, NY 13440, tel.: (315) 336-6190
Contact: James P. Kehoe, Jr., Secy.

Established in 1957 in NY.
Financial data (yr. ended 12/31/01): Grants paid, $89,375; assets, $1,730,598 (M); expenditures, $97,070; qualifying distributions, $89,375.
Limitations: Giving limited to Rome, NY.
Application information: Recipients are selected on the basis of financial need, personality, character, leadership, citizenship, and health. Application form required.
Officers: John W. Grow, Pres.; Marion Bartell, V.P.; James P. Kehoe, Jr., Secy.; H. Thomas Dyett II, Treas.
Directors: Holly Amidon, Robert Blocher, William Blocher, Carole Fowler, David Guggi, Barbara Oliver, William Schenck.
EIN: 166041857
Codes: FD2, GTI

35664
Whalesback Foundation
3 World Financial Ctr., 16th Fl.
New York, NY 10285

Established in 1996 in PA.
Donor(s): Theodore Roosevelt III, Theodore Roosevelt IV.
Financial data (yr. ended 12/31/00): Grants paid, $89,359; assets, $1,608,288 (M); expenditures, $91,747; qualifying distributions, $89,220.
Limitations: Applications not accepted.
Application information: Contributes only to pre-selected organizations.
Officers and Trustees:* Theodore Roosevelt III,* Pres.; Theodore Roosevelt IV,* Secy.-Treas.; Constance Roosevelt.
EIN: 311478498

Codes: FD2

35665
The Leiman Fund
c/o Fulbright & Jaworski, LLP
666 Fifth Ave.
New York, NY 10103

Established in 1985 in NY.
Donor(s): Leonard M. Leiman, Joan M. Leiman.
Financial data (yr. ended 12/31/01): Grants paid, $89,200; assets, $482,783 (M); gifts received, $36,355; expenditures, $89,784; qualifying distributions, $89,200.
Limitations: Applications not accepted. Giving primarily in New York, NY.
Application information: Contributes only to pre-selected organizations.
Officers: Leonard M. Leiman, Pres.; Richard J. Cunningham, V.P. and Secy.; Joan M. Leiman, V.P. and Secy.; Wilbur A. Cowett, V.P.
EIN: 133317738

35666
The Schoenfeld Foundation
c/o Tanton and Co., LLP
37 W. 57th St., 5th Fl.
New York, NY 10019-6016

Established in 1987 in NY.
Donor(s): Peter M. Schoenfeld.
Financial data (yr. ended 12/31/01): Grants paid, $89,105; assets, $207,336 (M); gifts received, $57,373; expenditures, $89,584; qualifying distributions, $89,511.
Limitations: Giving primarily in NY.
Officers: Peter M. Schoenfeld, Pres. and Treas.; Charlotte Schoenfeld, V.P. and Secy.
Director: Michael Greenberg.
EIN: 133373006
Codes: FD2

35667
Belmont Foundation
330 Belmont Ave.
Brooklyn, NY 11207-4010

Established in 1950 in NY.
Donor(s): Belmont Metals, Inc., Members of the Henning family.
Financial data (yr. ended 12/31/01): Grants paid, $89,075; assets, $231,253 (M); gifts received, $20,349; expenditures, $90,873; qualifying distributions, $89,075.
Limitations: Applications not accepted. Giving primarily in NY.
Application information: Contributes only to pre-selected organizations.
Trustees: Richard G. Henning, Robert V. Henning, Robert V. Henning, Jr., Theodore W. Henning.
EIN: 116036932
Codes: CS, FD2, CD

35668
The Sassoon Family Foundation
c/o Goldman Sachs & Co.
85 Broad St., Tax Dept.
New York, NY 10004

Established in 1993 in NY.
Donor(s): Joseph Sassoon.
Financial data (yr. ended 05/31/02): Grants paid, $89,055; assets, $1,015,614 (M); expenditures, $91,885; qualifying distributions, $89,055.
Limitations: Applications not accepted.
Application information: Contributes only to pre-selected organizations.
Trustees: Joseph Sassoon, Patrick J. Ward.
EIN: 133748087

35669
S. Forest Company, Inc.
c/o Walter, Conston, Alexander & Green
90 Park Ave.
New York, NY 10016

Established in 1952.
Donor(s): Dean W. Mathey, Sidney Roffman, The Bank of New York.
Financial data (yr. ended 12/31/01): Grants paid, $89,000; assets, $6,287 (M); gifts received, $100,000; expenditures, $97,710; qualifying distributions, $89,000.
Limitations: Applications not accepted. Giving primarily in NJ and New York, NY.
Application information: Contributes only to pre-selected organizations.
Officers and Directors:* Paul M. Frank,* Pres.; Glenn G. Fox,* V.P.; Iwona Cegielski, Secy.-Treas.
EIN: 136069185
Codes: FD2

35670
Newcastle Foundation
c/o Brown Brothers Harriman Trust Co., LLC
63 Wall St.
New York, NY 10005

Established in 2000 in MA.
Financial data (yr. ended 12/31/01): Grants paid, $89,000; assets, $2,118,293 (M); expenditures, $109,569; qualifying distributions, $89,000.
Limitations: Applications not accepted.
Application information: Contributes only to pre-selected organizations.
Trustees: Timothy J. Barberich, Eileen P. Gebrian, Brown Brothers Harriman Trust Co., LLC.
EIN: 522283813

35671
The Webel Fund
85 Forest Ave.
Locust Valley, NY 11560

Established in 1966.
Donor(s): Geoffrey Kimball.
Financial data (yr. ended 10/31/01): Grants paid, $89,000; assets, $2,094,677 (M); gifts received, $7,000; expenditures, $214,064; qualifying distributions, $180,354.
Limitations: Applications not accepted. Giving on a national basis.
Application information: Contributes only to pre-selected organizations.
Trustees: Philip Rauch, Richard C. Webel.
EIN: 136207867
Codes: FD2

35672
Dadourian Foundation
168 Canal St., Ste. 600
New York, NY 10013 (212) 334-0990
Contact: Haig Dadourian, Pres.

Established in 1961 in NY.
Donor(s): Dadour Dadourian.
Financial data (yr. ended 04/30/01): Grants paid, $88,920; assets, $2,928,960 (M); expenditures, $155,246; qualifying distributions, $140,666.
Limitations: Giving primarily in the metropolitan New York, NY, area.
Application information: Application form not required.
Officers: Haig Dadourian, Pres.; Alexander A. Dadourian, V.P.; Peter Dadourian, Treas.
EIN: 136125022
Codes: FD2

35673
The Herbert & Kitty Glantz Charitable Foundation
16 Court St., 30th Fl.
Brooklyn, NY 11241 (718) 488-9400
Contact: Herbert Glantz, Tr.

Established in 1990 in NY.
Donor(s): Herbert T. Glantz, Kitty Glantz, N. Glantz & Son, Inc.
Financial data (yr. ended 12/31/00): Grants paid, $88,920; assets, $24,764 (M); gifts received, $75,000; expenditures, $92,188; qualifying distributions, $88,918.
Limitations: Giving primarily in Brooklyn, NY.
Trustees: Herbert T. Glantz, Kitty Glantz, Joseph C. Hartman.
EIN: 113032861
Codes: FD2

35674
Cheek Family Foundation
c/o JPMorgan Chase Bank
1211 6th Ave., 34th Fl.
New York, NY 10036
Contact: Ronald Lelen, V.P., JPMorgan Chase Bank

Established in 1989 in VA.
Donor(s): Leslie Cheek, Jr.
Financial data (yr. ended 02/28/01): Grants paid, $88,880; assets, $1,823,524 (M); expenditures, $115,050; qualifying distributions, $101,152.
Limitations: Giving primarily in MA and Richmond, VA.
Application information: Application form not required.
Trustee: JPMorgan Chase Bank.
EIN: 136930808
Codes: FD2

35675
The Schwebel Foundation
82-29 Abingdon Rd.
Kew Gardens, NY 11415
Contact: Philip Schwebel, Tr.

Established in 1958.
Financial data (yr. ended 10/31/99): Grants paid, $88,872; assets, $0 (M); expenditures, $93,093; qualifying distributions, $88,863.
Limitations: Giving primarily in the greater New York, NY, area.
Trustee: Philip Schwebel.
EIN: 116037220
Codes: FD2

35676
Meno Lissauer Foundation
c/o Peter Eliel
25 E. 86th St.
New York, NY 10021

Incorporated in 1951 in NY.
Donor(s): Associated Metals and Minerals Corp.
Financial data (yr. ended 12/31/01): Grants paid, $88,850; assets, $1,228,588 (M); expenditures, $113,954; qualifying distributions, $97,536.
Limitations: Applications not accepted. Giving primarily in NY.
Application information: Contributes only to pre-selected organizations.
Officer: Peter Eliel, Mgr.
EIN: 136161478
Codes: FD2

35677
The Sonia Alden Foundation, Inc.
146 Central Park W.
New York, NY 10023
Contact: Beth Friedman

Established in 1991 in NY.
Donor(s): Sonia Alden.‡
Financial data (yr. ended 12/31/01): Grants paid, $88,751; assets, $1,400,507 (M); expenditures, $99,958; qualifying distributions, $88,751.
Limitations: Giving on a national basis, with emphasis on New York, NY.
Officers and Directors:* Beth Holland,* Pres.; Cathy Feyer,* V.P. and Treas.; Ellen Silverman.
EIN: 113037134
Codes: FD2

35678
Lawrence S. Huntington Fund
46 E. 70th St., 4th Fl.
New York, NY 10021 (212) 717-8633
Contact: Lawrence S. Huntington, Dir.

Established in 1997 in NY.
Donor(s): Lawrence S. Huntington.
Financial data (yr. ended 12/31/00): Grants paid, $88,670; assets, $10,862 (M); gifts received, $114,255; expenditures, $107,711; qualifying distributions, $107,139.
Application information: Application form not required.
Director: Lawrence S. Huntington.
EIN: 133985928
Codes: FD2

35679
Kristina and Guy Wildenstein Foundation
c/o Wildenstein & Co., Inc.
19 E. 64th St.
New York, NY 10021

Established in 1999 in NY.
Donor(s): Guy Wildenstein.
Financial data (yr. ended 12/31/01): Grants paid, $88,500; assets, $6,241 (M); gifts received, $92,975; expenditures, $89,627; qualifying distributions, $88,500.
Limitations: Applications not accepted.
Application information: Contributes only to pre-selected organizations.
Officers: Guy Wildenstein, Pres.; Vanessa Wildenstein, V.P.; David Wildenstein, V.P.; Claudine Godts, Secy.; Kristina Wildenstein, Treas.
EIN: 134060977
Codes: FD2

35680
Beim Charitable Trust
c/o Barry M. Strauss Assocs., Ltd.
307 5th Ave., 8th Fl.
New York, NY 10016-6517

Established in 1984 in NY.
Donor(s): David O. Beim.
Financial data (yr. ended 12/31/01): Grants paid, $88,364; assets, $787,994 (M); expenditures, $98,392; qualifying distributions, $90,483.
Limitations: Applications not accepted. Giving primarily in NY.
Application information: Contributes only to pre-selected organizations.
Trustees: David O. Beim, Elizabeth A. Beim.
EIN: 136848409
Codes: FD2

35681
The Keith Haring Foundation, Inc.
676 Broadway, 5th Fl.
New York, NY 10012

Established in 1989 in NY.
Donor(s): Keith Haring,‡ ACT-UP.
Financial data (yr. ended 09/30/01): Grants paid, $88,250; assets, $2,649,424 (M); gifts received, $60; expenditures, $139,403; qualifying distributions, $101,509.
Limitations: Applications not accepted.
Application information: Contributes only to pre-selected organizations.
Officers: Kermit Oswald, Pres.; Gilbert Vazquez, V.P.; David Stark, Secy.; Allen Haring, Treas.; Julia Gruen, Exec. Dir.
Director: Kristen Haring.
EIN: 110249024
Codes: FD2

35682
The Hamilton Foundation
c/o DDK & Co., LLP
1500 Broadway, 12th Fl.
New York, NY 10036-4015
Contact: Charles H. Hamilton, Tr.

Established in 1993 in IL.
Financial data (yr. ended 12/31/01): Grants paid, $88,200; assets, $1,331,803 (M); expenditures, $98,701; qualifying distributions, $89,607.
Limitations: Applications not accepted. Giving primarily in CT, Washington, DC, and NY.
Application information: Contributes only to pre-selected organizations.
Trustees: Carol E. Hamilton, Charles H. Hamilton.
EIN: 367048494
Codes: FD2

35683
The Yaspan-Unterberg Foundation, Inc.
c/o Robert Yaspan
290 Hewlett Neck Rd.
Woodmere, NY 11598

Established in 1991 in NY.
Donor(s): Barbara Yaspan, Richard Yaspan, Robert Yaspan, David Yaspan, Janet Meltzer, Peggy Shapiro.
Financial data (yr. ended 12/31/01): Grants paid, $88,050; assets, $1,672,248 (M); gifts received, $162,195; expenditures, $112,195; qualifying distributions, $87,375.
Limitations: Applications not accepted. Giving primarily in New York, NY.
Application information: Contributes only to pre-selected organizations.
Officers and Directors:* Robert Yaspan,* Pres.; David Yaspan,* Secy.; Barbara Yaspan,* Treas.; Janet Meltzer, Peggy Shapiro, Richard Yaspan.
EIN: 133608916
Codes: FD2

35684
J. Robert and Barrie C. Blumenthal Foundation
5 Lynn Dr.
Muttontown, NY 11791

Established in 1997 in NY.
Donor(s): J. Robert Blumenthal, Barrie C. Blumenthal.
Financial data (yr. ended 12/31/01): Grants paid, $88,000; assets, $1,158,297 (M); expenditures, $109,906; qualifying distributions, $108,250.
Limitations: Giving primarily in NY.
Trustees: Barrie C. Blumenthal, J. Robert Blumenthal, Jill Blumenthal, Lisa Blumenthal.
EIN: 116487716
Codes: FD2

35685
The D-B Trust
1 M&T Plz., Ste. 2000
Buffalo, NY 14203-2391

Established in 1984 in NY.
Financial data (yr. ended 12/31/01): Grants paid, $88,000; assets, $1,620,318 (M); expenditures, $105,689; qualifying distributions, $87,876.
Limitations: Applications not accepted. Giving primarily in CT and NY, with emphasis on Buffalo.
Application information: Contributes only to pre-selected organizations.
Trustees: Elizabeth S. Mitchell, Anna H. Swift, Douglas G. Swift, Harlan J. Swift, Jr., Margaret G. Swift.
EIN: 222589701
Codes: FD2

35686
GBH Foundation Trust
c/o Brown Brothers Harriman Trust Co.
63 Wall St.
New York, NY 10005

Established in 1998 in PA.
Financial data (yr. ended 12/31/00): Grants paid, $88,000; assets, $1,576,780 (M); expenditures, $95,659; qualifying distributions, $87,466.
Limitations: Applications not accepted. Giving primarily in southeastern PA.
Application information: Contributes only to pre-selected organizations.
Trustees: Gordon B. Hattersley, Jr., Brown Brothers Harriman Trust Co.
EIN: 232966565
Codes: FD2

35687
Zichron Yisroel Vesther Foundation
5401 15th Ave.
Brooklyn, NY 11219-4322 (718) 894-2000
Contact: Albert Weinstock, Tr.

Established in 1999 in NY.
Financial data (yr. ended 09/30/01): Grants paid, $87,940; assets, $163,682 (M); gifts received, $272,124; expenditures, $91,065; qualifying distributions, $91,040.
Limitations: Giving primarily in NJ and Brooklyn, NY.
Trustees: Albert Weinstock, Mendel Weinstock.
EIN: 113519911
Codes: FD2

35688
Marc & Diane Spilker Foundation
c/o Goldman Sachs & Co.
85 Broad St., Tax Dept.
New York, NY 10004

Established in 1996 in NY.
Donor(s): Marc Spilker.
Financial data (yr. ended 04/30/01): Grants paid, $87,915; assets, $1,850,676 (M); gifts received, $2,750; expenditures, $164,922; qualifying distributions, $120,922.
Limitations: Applications not accepted. Giving primarily in Washington, DC, and New York, NY.
Application information: Contributes only to pre-selected organizations.
Trustees: Diane Spilker, Marc Spilker.
EIN: 133933345
Codes: FD2

35689
The Seeja Foundation
c/o Judith S. Peck
1 W. 72nd St., Apt. 57
New York, NY 10023

Established in 1981 in NY.
Donor(s): Judith S. Peck.
Financial data (yr. ended 09/30/01): Grants paid, $87,900; assets, $189,641 (M); gifts received, $75,000; expenditures, $90,493; qualifying distributions, $87,872.
Limitations: Applications not accepted. Giving primarily in NY.
Application information: Contributes only to pre-selected organizations.
Officers: Judith S. Peck, Pres.; Susan Green, V.P.; Charlotte Faulk, Secy.
EIN: 133064158
Codes: FD2

35690
The Sears Family Foundation of Rome, New York
c/o Marion A. Sears
1914 Black River Blvd.
Rome, NY 13440

Established in 1995 in NY.
Donor(s): Marion A. Sears.
Financial data (yr. ended 12/31/01): Grants paid, $87,870; assets, $2,362,182 (M); gifts received, $2,222,839; expenditures, $88,373; qualifying distributions, $87,870.
Limitations: Applications not accepted. Giving limited to Rome, NY.
Application information: Contributes only to pre-selected organizations.
Trustees: Barbara S. Dehiner, Howard P. Sears, Jr., Marion A. Sears, Thomas A. Sears.
EIN: 137039118

35691
The John S. & Amy S. Weinberg Foundation
c/o Goldman Sachs & Co.
85 Broad St., Tax Dept.
New York, NY 10004

Established in 1993 in NY.
Donor(s): John S. Weinberg.
Financial data (yr. ended 07/31/01): Grants paid, $87,714; assets, $6,897,142 (M); gifts received, $1,460,788; expenditures, $117,308; qualifying distributions, $89,064.
Limitations: Applications not accepted. Giving primarily in the metropolitan New York, NY, area.
Application information: Contributes only to pre-selected organizations.
Trustees: Amy S. Weinberg, John S. Weinberg.
EIN: 133749671
Codes: FD2

35692
The Anderman Foundation
108-18 Queens Blvd.
Forest Hills, NY 11375-4760

Donor(s): Arthur A. Anderman.
Financial data (yr. ended 12/31/01): Grants paid, $87,600; assets, $1,149,285 (M); gifts received, $10,600; expenditures, $98,330; qualifying distributions, $87,389.
Limitations: Applications not accepted. Giving primarily in NY.
Application information: Contributes only to pre-selected organizations.
Officers: Arthur A. Anderman, Pres.; Carole J. Anderman, Treas.
EIN: 112547291
Codes: FD2

35693
Helen and Philip Delman Foundation, Inc.
35 Sutton Pl.
New York, NY 10022
Contact: Neil Delman, Mgr.

Established in 1985 in NY.
Donor(s): Neil Delman.
Financial data (yr. ended 12/31/01): Grants paid, $87,600; assets, $2,182,328 (M); gifts received, $68,970; expenditures, $95,020; qualifying distributions, $88,700.
Limitations: Applications not accepted. Giving primarily in the U.S.; some giving also in Canada.
Application information: Unsolicited requests for funds not accepted.
Manager: Neil Delman.
Trustees: Aimee Delman, Steven Delman.
EIN: 133249486
Codes: FD2

35694
Gleason Fund, Inc. Life Benefit Plan
1000 University Ave.
P.O. Box 22970
Rochester, NY 14692

Established in 1948.
Donor(s): Gleason Memorial Fund, Inc.
Financial data (yr. ended 12/31/01): Grants paid, $87,594; assets, $12,288 (M); gifts received, $60,000; expenditures, $87,703; qualifying distributions, $87,703.
Limitations: Applications not accepted. Giving limited to NY.
Application information: Only grants previously approved prior to merger with Gleason Foundation are being paid. Funding is closed to new applicants. Unsolicited requests for funds are not accepted.
Trustee: JPMorgan Chase Bank.
EIN: 166024331
Codes: TN, GTI

35695
The David Hochberg Foundation
1 Theall Rd.
Rye, NY 10580

Established in 1994 in NY.
Donor(s): David Hochberg.
Financial data (yr. ended 11/30/00): Grants paid, $87,500; assets, $1,175,790 (M); gifts received, $5,000; expenditures, $89,450; qualifying distributions, $87,050.
Limitations: Applications not accepted. Giving primarily in Washington DC, New York, NY, and VA.
Application information: Contributes only to pre-selected organizations.
Trustee: David Hochberg.
EIN: 133800403
Codes: FD2

35696
Mortimer D. Sackler Foundation, Inc.
17 E. 62nd St.
New York, NY 10021-7204

Established in 1967 in NY.
Donor(s): Varns Investments, Ltd.
Financial data (yr. ended 12/31/00): Grants paid, $87,500; assets, $2,600,335 (M); expenditures, $92,048; qualifying distributions, $87,500.
Limitations: Applications not accepted.
Application information: Contributes only to pre-selected organizations.
Officers and Directors:* Mortimer D. Sackler,* Pres.; K.A. Sackler,* V.P. and Secy.; M.D.A. Sackler,* V.P. and Treas.; I. Lefcourt,* V.P.; S.S. Sackler,* V.P.; T.E. Sackler,* V.P.

EIN: 237022461
Codes: FD2

35697
Windhover Foundation
80 E. Market St., Ste. 300
Corning, NY 14830

Established in 1998 in NY.
Donor(s): James R. Houghton.
Financial data (yr. ended 12/31/00): Grants paid, $87,500; assets, $1,004,433 (M); expenditures, $94,940; qualifying distributions, $86,184.
Limitations: Giving primarily in NY.
Officers: James R. Houghton, Pres.; May K. Houghton, V.P.; Nina B. Houghton, Secy.; James D. Houghton, Treas.
Directors: Connie B. Coburn, Kent E. George, Jr.
EIN: 311630033
Codes: FD2

35698
Esther & Nathan Maidenbaum Foundation, Inc.
460 W. 34th St.
New York, NY 10001-2320

Donor(s): Esther Maidenbaum, David Schreiber.
Financial data (yr. ended 12/31/00): Grants paid, $87,487; assets, $84,451 (M); gifts received, $108,552; expenditures, $93,187; qualifying distributions, $88,834.
Limitations: Applications not accepted.
Application information: Contributes only to pre-selected organizations.
Officers: Esther Maidenbaum, Pres.; Shalom Maidenbaum, V.P.
EIN: 237055848

35699
The Marsal Family Foundation
c/o Alvarez & Marsal, Inc.
599 Lexington Ave., Ste. 2700
New York, NY 10022

Established in 1996 in CO.
Donor(s): Bryan Marsal, Kathleen Marsal.
Financial data (yr. ended 12/31/00): Grants paid, $87,467; assets, $889,130 (M); expenditures, $93,713; qualifying distributions, $87,481.
Limitations: Applications not accepted.
Application information: Contributes only to pre-selected organizations.
Officers: Bryan Marsal, Pres.; Kathleen Marsal, V.P.
EIN: 841367157
Codes: FD2

35700
Montague Family Charitable Foundation
P.O. Box 810
Amherst, NY 14226-0810
Contact: William P. Montague, Chair.

Established in 1989 in NY.
Donor(s): William P. Montague.
Financial data (yr. ended 12/31/01): Grants paid, $87,400; assets, $1,405,484 (M); expenditures, $116,314; qualifying distributions, $87,400.
Limitations: Giving primarily in NY.
Officers: William P. Montague, Chair.; Susan J. Montague, Pres.; William Peter Montague, V.P.; Susan Lynne Laine, Secy.
EIN: 223021981
Codes: FD2

35701
Catherine Stickney Steck Foundation
c/o Behan, Ling & Ruta
358 5th Ave.
New York, NY 10001

Established in 2000 in NY.

Donor(s): Catherine Stickney Steck, Frederic E. Steck.
Financial data (yr. ended 09/30/01): Grants paid, $87,335; assets, $613,820 (M); gifts received, $506,414; expenditures, $88,923; qualifying distributions, $87,335.
Limitations: Applications not accepted. Giving primarily in New York, NY.
Application information: Contributes only to pre-selected organizations.
Trustees: Alexander Peters, Catherine S. Steck, Elizabeth Strickler.
EIN: 134100192

35702
The Maurer Foundation, Inc.
c/o Jack E. Maurer
641 Lexington Ave., Ste. 1400
New York, NY 10022

Donor(s): Indicator Research Group, Inc., Jack E. Maurer.
Financial data (yr. ended 12/31/99): Grants paid, $87,200; assets, $152,458 (M); expenditures, $87,786; qualifying distributions, $86,720.
Limitations: Applications not accepted. Giving primarily in the metropolitan New York, NY, area.
Application information: Contributes only to pre-selected organizations.
Officers: Jack E. Maurer, Pres.; Rona Maurer, V.P.
EIN: 237048522
Codes: FD2

35703
The Deborah Rose Foundation
200 Madison Ave., 5th Fl.
New York, NY 10016

Established in 1999 in DE.
Financial data (yr. ended 12/31/00): Grants paid, $87,120; assets, $367,996 (M); gifts received, $250,000; expenditures, $87,395; qualifying distributions, $87,120.
Limitations: Applications not accepted.
Application information: Contributes only to pre-selected organizations.
Director: Deborah Rose.
EIN: 134088811
Codes: FD2

35704
Frank E. Perrella Charitable Trust
c/o City National Bank & Trust Co.
14 N. Main St.
Gloversville, NY 12078-3004 (518) 773-7911
Contact: William N. Smith, Pres.

Established in 1995 in NY.
Donor(s): Frank E. Perrella.
Financial data (yr. ended 12/31/01): Grants paid, $87,060; assets, $1,831,253 (M); expenditures, $94,754; qualifying distributions, $86,265.
Limitations: Giving primarily in Gloversville, NY, and surrounding areas.
Officer: William N. Smith, Pres.
Trustees: George A. Morgan, City National Bank & Trust Co.
EIN: 146173371
Codes: FD2

35705
The Gallagher Charitable Fund
(Formerly The Christopher F. Gallagher Charitable Fund)
c/o James D. Miller & Co., LLP
350 5th Ave., Ste. 5019
New York, NY 10118-0080

Established in 1990 in NY.
Donor(s): Christopher F. Gallagher.

Financial data (yr. ended 12/31/99): Grants paid, $87,050; assets, $1,674,061 (M); expenditures, $103,311; qualifying distributions, $91,890.
Limitations: Applications not accepted. Giving primarily in NY.
Application information: Contributes only to pre-selected organizations.
Trustees: Christopher F. Gallagher, Regina A. Gallagher.
EIN: 226488953
Codes: FD2

35706
F. Irving Hutchins Charitable Trust
c/o JPMorgan Chase Bank
P.O. Box 31412
Rochester, NY 14603-1412

Financial data (yr. ended 12/31/01): Grants paid, $87,020; assets, $1,744,978 (M); expenditures, $105,729; qualifying distributions, $86,607.
Limitations: Applications not accepted. Giving primarily in Rochester, NY.
Application information: Contributes only to pre-selected organizations.
Trustee: JPMorgan Chase Bank.
EIN: 166015204
Codes: FD2

35707
Carlos A. Cordeiro Foundation
c/o Goldman Sachs & Co.
85 Broad St., Tax Dept.
New York, NY 10004

Donor(s): Carlos A. Cordeiro.
Financial data (yr. ended 08/31/01): Grants paid, $87,000; assets, $3,860,602 (M); gifts received, $2,750; expenditures, $155,708; qualifying distributions, $90,309.
Limitations: Applications not accepted. Giving primarily in MA, with emphasis on Cambridge.
Application information: Contributes only to pre-selected organizations.
Trustee: Carlos A. Cordeiro.
EIN: 133926136
Codes: FD2

35708
The Jatoma Charitable Foundation
c/o E-J Electric Installation Co.
46-41 Vernon Blvd.
Long Island City, NY 11101

Established in 2000 in NY.
Donor(s): Carol Mann.
Financial data (yr. ended 11/30/01): Grants paid, $87,000; assets, $1,384,790 (M); expenditures, $125,515; qualifying distributions, $87,000.
Limitations: Applications not accepted. Giving primarily in New York, NY.
Application information: Contributes only to pre-selected organizations.
Trustees: Margaret Berenblum, J. Robert Mann, Jr., Anthony E. Mann, Jack R. Mann III.
EIN: 137198355

35709
The Jeffrey David Walerstein Foundation
3 Main St., No. 604
Nyack, NY 10960 (914) 353-2111
Contact: Ronald M. Walerstein, Tr.

Established in 1989 in NY.
Donor(s): Ronald M. Walerstein.
Financial data (yr. ended 12/31/00): Grants paid, $87,000; assets, $963,719 (M); gifts received, $122,448; expenditures, $87,575; qualifying distributions, $86,417.
Limitations: Giving primarily in NY.

35709—NEW YORK

Trustees: Gail Walerstein, Mark J. Walerstein, Ronald M. Walerstein.
EIN: 133541932
Codes: FD2

35710
The Joseph & Idii Lieber Foundation
1167 E. 26th St.
Brooklyn, NY 11210

Established in 1996 in NY.
Donor(s): Joseph Lieber.
Financial data (yr. ended 12/31/01): Grants paid, $86,966; assets, $588,337 (M); gifts received, $265,000; expenditures, $87,809; qualifying distributions, $86,966.
Limitations: Applications not accepted.
Application information: Contributes only to pre-selected organizations.
Trustees: Idii Lieber, Joseph Lieber.
EIN: 113352010
Codes: FD2

35711
Costanza Family Charitable Trust
c/o Citibank, N.A., Tax Dept.
1 Court Sq., 22nd Fl.
Long Island City, NY 11120
Application address: c/o Betty Ott, 153 E. 53rd. St., New York, NY 10043

Established in 1993 in NY.
Donor(s): Gesualdo A. Costanzo.
Financial data (yr. ended 12/31/00): Grants paid, $86,952; assets, $2,113,614 (M); expenditures, $89,932; qualifying distributions, $86,552.
Limitations: Giving primarily in NC.
Trustee: Citibank, N.A.
EIN: 116432843
Codes: FD2

35712
The Stuart Family Foundation, Inc.
c/o Kohlberg, Kravis, Roberts & Co.
9 W. 57th St.
New York, NY 10019-2600

Established in 1995 in NY.
Donor(s): Scott M. Stuart.
Financial data (yr. ended 11/30/01): Grants paid, $86,900; assets, $1,883,936 (M); gifts received, $573,438; expenditures, $107,969; qualifying distributions, $92,627.
Limitations: Applications not accepted. Giving primarily in CT and NY.
Application information: Contributes only to pre-selected organizations.
Officers: Scott M. Stuart, Pres.; Lisa G. Stuart, V.P.; James M. Goldrick, Secy.-Treas.
EIN: 133861861
Codes: FD2

35713
Historical Research Foundation, Inc.
c/o Sanford Becker & Co.
1430 Broadway, 6th Fl.
New York, NY 10018 (212) 921-9000
Application address: c/o National Review, 215 Lexington Ave., New York, NY 10016
Contact: Frances Bronson, Secy.

Established in 1958 in NY.
Donor(s): Lawrence Fertig,‡ Walten Judd Foundation.
Financial data (yr. ended 12/31/01): Grants paid, $86,865; assets, $197,084 (M); expenditures, $97,567; qualifying distributions, $97,567.
Limitations: Giving on a national basis.
Officers: Thomas L. Rhodes, Pres.; Frances Bronson, Secy.; Evan Gailbraith, Treas.
Director: William Buckley.

Trustee: Jeffrey Hart.
EIN: 136059836
Codes: FD2, GTI

35714
John W. and Laura S. Stewart Foundation, Inc.
270 Madison Ave.
New York, NY 10016-0601
Contact: Daniel Gersen, Pres.

Financial data (yr. ended 04/30/02): Grants paid, $86,850; assets, $729,139 (M); expenditures, $92,472; qualifying distributions, $86,850.
Limitations: Giving primarily in the New York, NY, area.
Officers and Directors:* Daniel Gersen,* Pres.; Judy Blum, V.P.; Richard Blakeman,* Secy.-Treas.
EIN: 136108690

35715
The Laurel Fund, Inc.
c/o Yohalem Gillman & Co., LLP
477 Madison Ave.
New York, NY 10022-5802

Established in 1964 in NY.
Donor(s): Walter N. Rothschild, Jr.
Financial data (yr. ended 12/31/01): Grants paid, $86,770; assets, $110,683 (M); gifts received, $99,985; expenditures, $88,661; qualifying distributions, $86,452.
Limitations: Applications not accepted. Giving primarily in MA and NY.
Application information: Contributes only to pre-selected organizations.
Officers: Walter N. Rothschild, Jr., Pres. and Treas.; Virginia T. Rothschild, V.P.; Jerome H. Manning, Secy.
Director: Walter N. Rothschild III.
EIN: 116037811
Codes: FD2

35716
Benjamin & Hedwig Sulzle Foundation, Inc.
26 E. 73rd St.
New York, NY 10021
Contact: Wendy R. Flanagan, Mgr.

Established in 1966 in NY.
Donor(s): H.G. Sulzle.‡
Financial data (yr. ended 09/30/01): Grants paid, $86,750; assets, $1,161,178 (M); gifts received, $400; expenditures, $91,400; qualifying distributions, $85,840.
Limitations: Applications not accepted. Giving primarily in MA and NY.
Application information: Unsolicited requests for funds not accepted.
Officer and Trustees:* Wendy R. Flanagan,* Mgr.; L.H. Flanagan.
EIN: 166075456
Codes: FD2

35717
Charles Thorwelle Foundation
c/o Rouis and Co., LLP
P.O. Box 209
Wurtsboro, NY 12790
Application address: c/o Fleet National Bank, Curtis Bldg., Callicoon, NY 12723, tel.: (845) 887-4400
Contact: Robert C. Curtis, Tr.

Financial data (yr. ended 12/31/01): Grants paid, $86,750; assets, $1,650,274 (M); expenditures, $126,899; qualifying distributions, $85,945.
Limitations: Giving limited to the Delaware Valley, NY, area.
Application information: Application form required for scholarships only. Application form required.

Trustees: Ruth R. Brustman, Robert C. Curtis, Maurice Roche.
EIN: 146047928
Codes: FD2, GTI

35718
Bauer Family Foundation
60 Waterfront Cir.
Buffalo, NY 14202
Contact: Paul D. Bauer, Tr.

Established in 1991 in NY.
Donor(s): Paul D. Bauer.
Financial data (yr. ended 12/31/01): Grants paid, $86,650; assets, $1,092,458 (M); expenditures, $87,607; qualifying distributions, $86,650.
Limitations: Giving primarily in NY.
Trustees: David P. Bauer, Lisa M. Bauer, Mary Grace Bauer, Paul D. Bauer.
EIN: 161390793
Codes: FD2

35719
The Alan & Peggy Tishman Foundation, Inc.
55 E. 59th St.
New York, NY 10022 (212) 326-4884
Contact: Alan V. Tishman, Pres.

Incorporated in 1956 in NY; name changed in 1988.
Donor(s): Alan V. Tishman, Margaret Tishman.
Financial data (yr. ended 11/30/01): Grants paid, $86,573; assets, $1,004,986 (M); expenditures, $87,815; qualifying distributions, $86,417.
Limitations: Applications not accepted. Giving primarily in New York, NY.
Application information: Contributes only to pre-selected organizations.
Officers: Alan V. Tishman, Pres.; Peggy Tishman, V.P.
EIN: 136099395
Codes: FD2

35720
The Kahan Family Foundation
1531 54th St.
Brooklyn, NY 11219-4346

Established in 1999 in NY.
Donor(s): Leslie Kahan, Chana Kahan, Jacob Kasirer, Barry Braunstein.
Financial data (yr. ended 12/31/01): Grants paid, $86,536; assets, $664,968 (M); gifts received, $410,641; expenditures, $94,467; qualifying distributions, $89,544.
Limitations: Applications not accepted. Giving primarily in NY.
Application information: Contributes only to pre-selected organizations.
Trustees: Chana Kahan, Leslie Kahan.
EIN: 113493767
Codes: FD2

35721
The Hurlbut Foundation
740 East Ave.
Rochester, NY 14607
Contact: Robert H. Hurlbut, Pres.

Established in 1993 in NY.
Donor(s): Robert H. Hurlbut.
Financial data (yr. ended 06/30/01): Grants paid, $86,500; assets, $611,452 (M); expenditures, $89,000; qualifying distributions, $85,887.
Application information: Application form not required.
Officers: Robert H. Hurlbut, Pres.; Christine A. Bean, V.P.; Robert W. Hurlbut, V.P.; C. Richard Cole, Secy.; Jerald J. Rotenberg, Treas.
EIN: 161445751
Codes: FD2

35722
Lotte Kaliski Foundation for Gifted Children, Inc.
225 W. 34th St.
New York, NY 10122
Contact: Dennis Stamm Kaliski

Established in 1989 in NY.
Financial data (yr. ended 12/31/99): Grants paid, $86,400; assets, $1,074,557 (M); expenditures, $150,700; qualifying distributions, $85,756.
Limitations: Giving primarily in NY.
Application information: Grants are restricted to no more than $4,000 per school year per recipient. Application form required.
Directors: Arthur Block, Siegbert Weinberger.
EIN: 133453837
Codes: FD2, GTI

35723
Carolyn D. & Rush Taggart Foundation
c/o U.S. Trust
114 W. 47th St.
New York, NY 10036

Financial data (yr. ended 06/30/01): Grants paid, $86,400; assets, $1,233,276 (M); expenditures, $91,156; qualifying distributions, $86,400.
Limitations: Applications not accepted. Giving primarily in NY.
Application information: Contributes only to pre-selected organizations.
Trustee: U.S. Trust.
EIN: 136185668
Codes: FD2

35724
The Lionel Gilels Family Foundation
2921 Erie Blvd. E.
Syracuse, NY 13224-1430

Established in 1985 in NY.
Donor(s): Lionel Gilels, Empire Vision Center, Inc.
Financial data (yr. ended 12/31/01): Grants paid, $86,300; assets, $173,350 (M); gifts received, $48,396; expenditures, $89,359; qualifying distributions, $86,183.
Limitations: Applications not accepted. Giving primarily in Syracuse, NY.
Application information: Contributes only to pre-selected organizations.
Trustees: Jacquelyn Gilels, Lionel Gilels.
EIN: 222672857
Codes: FD2

35725
The Karen & David Eisner Foundation
c/o David Eisner
165 West End Ave.
New York, NY 10023

Established in 1997 in NY.
Donor(s): David Eisner, Karen Eisner.
Financial data (yr. ended 06/30/01): Grants paid, $86,282; assets, $1,211,583 (M); gifts received, $1,158; expenditures, $89,392; qualifying distributions, $76,393.
Limitations: Applications not accepted.
Application information: Contributes only to pre-selected organizations.
Officers and Directors:* David Eisner,* Pres.; Karen Eisner,* V.P. and Secy.; Milton J. Kain.
EIN: 133979797
Codes: FD2

35726
Friedlander Family Foundation, Inc.
c/o Roger B. Friedlander
181 Clover Hills Dr.
Rochester, NY 14618

Established in 1994 in NY.
Donor(s): Roger B. Friedlander.
Financial data (yr. ended 03/31/01): Grants paid, $86,206; assets, $349,883 (M); expenditures, $91,699; qualifying distributions, $85,689.
Limitations: Applications not accepted. Giving primarily in NY.
Application information: Contributes only to pre-selected organizations.
Trustees: Carolyn T. Friedlander, David Friedlander, Jonathan Friedlander, Roger B. Friedlander, Deborah F. Haen, Robert Oppenheimer, Jerald J. Rotenberg.
EIN: 161459698
Codes: FD2

35727
The Nomi P. Ghez Foundation
c/o Goldman Sachs & Co.
85 Broad St., Tax Dept.
New York, NY 10004

Established in 1994 in NY.
Donor(s): Nomi P. Ghez.
Financial data (yr. ended 09/30/01): Grants paid, $86,173; assets, $1,036,771 (M); gifts received, $1,099,563; expenditures, $91,313; qualifying distributions, $89,173.
Limitations: Applications not accepted. Giving limited to New York, NY.
Application information: Contributes only to pre-selected organizations.
Trustee: Nomi P. Ghez.
EIN: 133801608
Codes: FD2

35728
Nancy & Robert S. Blank Foundation
c/o Plymouth Rock Assocs.
110 W. 51st St., Rm. 4310
New York, NY 10020-1203

Established in 1993 in PA.
Donor(s): Robert S. Blank, Nancy L. Blank.
Financial data (yr. ended 08/31/01): Grants paid, $86,041; assets, $695,538 (M); gifts received, $9,494; expenditures, $97,550; qualifying distributions, $86,171.
Limitations: Applications not accepted. Giving primarily in NY and PA.
Application information: Contributes only to pre-selected organizations.
Officers: Robert S. Blank, Pres.; Nancy L. Blank, V.P.
EIN: 232738179
Codes: FD2

35729
Fred Hazan Foundation, Inc.
189 Priscilla Rd.
Woodmere, NY 11598
Contact: Lawrence Hazan, Tr.

Established in 1955 in NY.
Donor(s): Isaac M. Hazan, Victor Hazan, Aaron Hazan, Lawrence Hazan, Lloyd Sportswear, Inc.
Financial data (yr. ended 01/31/01): Grants paid, $86,037; assets, $1,484,163 (M); expenditures, $88,001; qualifying distributions, $86,037.
Limitations: Giving primarily in NY.
Trustees: Aaron Hazan, Isaac Hazan, Lawrence Hazan, Victor Hazan.
EIN: 136159194
Codes: FD2

35730
A. R. Landsman Foundation, Inc.
(Formerly Landsman & Katz Foundation, Inc.)
c/o Hilva Landsman
800 5th Ave., Ste. 21B
New York, NY 10021-8970

Established in 1953 in NY.
Financial data (yr. ended 12/31/00): Grants paid, $86,000; assets, $504,914 (M); expenditures, $92,957; qualifying distributions, $88,462.
Limitations: Applications not accepted. Giving primarily in the greater New York, NY, area.
Application information: Contributes only to pre-selected organizations.
Officers: Hilva Landsman, Pres.; Lisa Ann Landsman, V.P.; Jerome Pustilnik, Secy.
EIN: 136128661
Codes: FD2

35731
Allen F. Pierce Foundation
33 Gates Cir., Apt. A
Buffalo, NY 14209
Contact: Jean M. Elfvin, Pres.

Financial data (yr. ended 12/31/01): Grants paid, $86,000; assets, $1,662 (M); expenditures, $88,818; qualifying distributions, $85,193.
Limitations: Giving limited to Bradford County, PA.
Application information: Application form not required.
Officer and Directors:* Jean Margaret Elfvin,* Pres.; Ann D. DiLauro, Carole DiLauro, Hon. John T. Elfvin, Janet A. Knapp.
Agent: First Union National Bank.
EIN: 232044356
Codes: FD2

35732
The Ping Y. Tai Foundation, Inc.
18 E. 67th St.
New York, NY 10021

Established in 1997 in NY.
Donor(s): Ping Y. Tai,‡ J.T. Tai & Co., Inc.
Financial data (yr. ended 11/30/01): Grants paid, $86,000; assets, $2,350,728 (M); gifts received, $150,254; expenditures, $113,523; qualifying distributions, $107,373.
Limitations: Applications not accepted. Giving primarily in NY.
Application information: Contributes only to pre-selected organizations.
Officers: Michael Duffalo, Pres.; Yueh Chuen Chen, Secy.-Treas.
EIN: 133980789
Codes: FD2

35733
The Ripple Foundation
c/o Wien & Malkin, LLP
60 E. 42nd St.
New York, NY 10165
Contact: Richard Shapiro

Established in 1999 in DE.
Donor(s): Anthony E. Malkin, Rachelle B. Malkin.
Financial data (yr. ended 12/31/00): Grants paid, $85,996; assets, $1,380,656 (M); gifts received, $390,687; expenditures, $87,753; qualifying distributions, $85,996.
Officers and Directors:* Anthony E. Malkin,* Pres. and Treas.; Rachelle B. Malkin,* Secy.
EIN: 134081347
Codes: FD2

35734
Blum-Merians Foundation, Inc.
10 Bonnie Briar Ln.
Larchmont, NY 10538
Contact: Melvin Merians, Tr.

Established in 1992 in NY.
Financial data (yr. ended 12/31/01): Grants paid, $85,905; assets, $16,019 (M); gifts received, $71,888; expenditures, $46,385; qualifying distributions, $86,385.
Limitations: Giving on a national basis.
Trustees: Diane Burrows, Edward Merians, Linda Merians, Melvin Merians.
EIN: 133689669
Codes: FD2

35735
American Chai Trust
c/o Perlman & Perlman, Attn.: Grant application
220 5th Ave., 7th Fl.
New York, NY 10001
Contact: Clifford Perlman, Tr.

Established in 1968 in NY.
Financial data (yr. ended 02/28/01): Grants paid, $85,750; assets, $1,651,944 (M); expenditures, $98,434; qualifying distributions, $97,046.
Limitations: Giving primarily in the metropolitan New York, NY, area.
Publications: Application guidelines.
Application information: Application form required.
Trustees: Lis Brewer, Pauline Doynow, Kaye Hirsch, Clifford Perlman, Walter Stern.
EIN: 136130992
Codes: FD2

35736
The Rieger Charitable Foundation Trust
c/o Noam Mgmt.
1646 49th St.
Brooklyn, NY 11204 (718) 436-2326
Contact: Abraham Rieger, Dir.

Established in 1998 in NY.
Donor(s): Abraham Jacob Rieger.
Financial data (yr. ended 12/31/00): Grants paid, $85,580; assets, $2,905,304 (M); gifts received, $640,000; expenditures, $86,931; qualifying distributions, $85,580.
Limitations: Giving primarily in Brooklyn, NY.
Application information: Application form not required.
Directors: Abraham Rieger, Rachel Rieger.
EIN: 116508164
Codes: FD2

35737
Perle Charitable Foundation
250 W. 57th St., Rm. 1018
New York, NY 10107-0001
Contact: Bendet Perle, Tr.

Established in 1989.
Financial data (yr. ended 12/31/00): Grants paid, $85,552; assets, $1 (M); gifts received, $74,799; expenditures, $85,552; qualifying distributions, $85,552.
Limitations: Applications not accepted.
Application information: Contributes only to pre-selected organizations.
Trustees: Bendet Perle, Isaac Perle, Lawrence Perle.
EIN: 136938518
Codes: FD2

35738
Leib and Hermann Merkin Foundation, Inc.
415 Madison Ave., 3rd Fl.
New York, NY 10017-1111

Incorporated in 1950 in NY.
Donor(s): Leib Merkin,‡ Hermann Merkin,‡ Ursula Merkin.
Financial data (yr. ended 06/30/99): Grants paid, $85,511; assets, $246,724 (M); gifts received, $181,179; expenditures, $94,119; qualifying distributions, $85,724.
Limitations: Applications not accepted. Giving primarily in New York, NY.
Application information: Contributes only to pre-selected organizations.
Officer: Ursula Merkin, Pres. and Secy.
EIN: 136093666
Codes: FD2

35739
Mel & Pamela Shaftel Foundation, Inc.
211 Central Park W., Apt. 15-G
New York, NY 10024-6020

Established in 1994 in NJ.
Donor(s): Mel Shaftel, Pamela Shaftel.
Financial data (yr. ended 07/31/00): Grants paid, $85,500; assets, $551,862 (M); expenditures, $89,565; qualifying distributions, $83,696.
Limitations: Applications not accepted. Giving primarily in New Haven, CT.
Application information: Contributes only to pre-selected organizations.
Officers: Mel Shaftel, Mgr.; Pamela Shaftel, Mgr.
EIN: 223342427

35740
Silberstein-Boesky Family Foundation, Inc.
Northview, Sarles St.
Mount Kisco, NY 10549

Established in 1997 in NY.
Financial data (yr. ended 12/31/99): Grants paid, $85,500; assets, $2,447,566 (M); gifts received, $1,009,030; expenditures, $89,378; qualifying distributions, $84,273.
Limitations: Applications not accepted. Giving primarily in NY.
Application information: Contributes only to pre-selected organizations.
Officers and Directors:* Seema S. Boesky,* Pres.; William T. Ward,* Secy.; Georgina J. Slade.
EIN: 061498058
Codes: FD2

35741
The O'Toole Family Foundation
c/o Goldman Sachs & Co.
85 Broad St., Tax Dept.
New York, NY 10004

Established in 1993 in NJ.
Donor(s): Terence M. O'Toole.
Financial data (yr. ended 03/31/01): Grants paid, $85,380; assets, $6,234,224 (M); gifts received, $1,459,688; expenditures, $153,380; qualifying distributions, $85,380.
Limitations: Applications not accepted. Giving primarily in CA, NJ, NY, and PA.
Application information: Contributes only to pre-selected organizations.
Trustees: Paula M. O'Toole, Terence M. O'Toole.
EIN: 133748068

35742
The Patricia Chernoff Charitable Trust
c/o U.S. Trust
114 W. 47th St.
New York, NY 10036
Contact: Karen Francois

Established in 1991 in NY.
Financial data (yr. ended 12/31/00): Grants paid, $85,000; assets, $1,980,417 (M); expenditures, $97,808; qualifying distributions, $92,000.
Limitations: Applications not accepted. Giving primarily in ME; some giving also in Washington, DC.
Trustees: Karen Heath, Richard L. Ottinger.
EIN: 136971188
Codes: FD2

35743
Melvin & Mildred Eggers Family Charitable Foundation
c/o J. Witmeyer
P.O. Box 31051
Rochester, NY 14603

Established in 1995 in NY.
Donor(s): Mildred Eggers.‡
Financial data (yr. ended 05/31/01): Grants paid, $85,000; assets, $1,917,039 (M); expenditures, $94,341; qualifying distributions, $86,370.
Limitations: Applications not accepted. Giving primarily in NY.
Application information: Contributes only to pre-selected organizations.
Trustees: Richard M. Eggers, William D. Eggers.
EIN: 161490519
Codes: FD2

35744
Fred L. Lavanburg Foundation
950 3rd Ave., 30th Fl.
New York, NY 10022 (212) 371-5060
FAX: (212) 755-4439
Contact: Oscar S. Straus II, Pres.

Incorporated in 1927 in NY.
Donor(s): Fred L. Lavanburg.‡
Financial data (yr. ended 12/31/01): Grants paid, $85,000; assets, $2,376,047 (M); expenditures, $158,020; qualifying distributions, $128,581.
Limitations: Giving primarily in NY.
Publications: Multi-year report.
Application information: Application form not required.
Officers and Trustees:* Oscar S. Straus II,* Chair. and Pres.; Anne Lindgren,* V.P.; Joan M. Straus,* V.P.; Charles T. Locke III,* Secy.; Percy Preston, Jr.,* Treas.; Amanda Brainard, Alan Hockstader, Peter D. Salins, Oscar S. Schafer, Jr.
EIN: 131850830
Codes: FD2

35745
Leviant Foundation
c/o Richard A. Eisner & Co., LLP
575 Madison Ave., 7th Fl.
New York, NY 10022-2597

Established in 1992 in NY.
Financial data (yr. ended 09/30/01): Grants paid, $85,000; assets, $630,101 (M); expenditures, $85,753; qualifying distributions, $84,962.
Limitations: Applications not accepted. Giving limited to New York, NY.
Application information: Contributes only to pre-selected organizations.
Trustee: Jacques Leviant.
EIN: 137000812
Codes: FD2

35746
Clara A. March Scholarship Fund
15 Knoerl Ave.
Buffalo, NY 14210-2329
Application address: c/o Dean of the Medical School, 40 Biomedical Bldg., SUNY, Buffalo, NY 14214
Contact: Dennis A. Nadler, Assoc. Dean

Established in 1971 in NY.
Donor(s): Clara A. March.‡
Financial data (yr. ended 12/31/01): Grants paid, $85,000; assets, $1,701,664 (M); expenditures, $101,440; qualifying distributions, $84,295.
Limitations: Giving limited to Buffalo, NY.
Application information: Contributes only to students enrolled at SUNY Buffalo Medical School. Application form required.
Trustees: M. Jane Dickman, Brian E. Keating, Timothy A. McCarthy.
EIN: 166119078
Codes: FD2, GTI

35747
Paul J. Roth Family Foundation
c/o Howard W. Roth
1 Columbia Cir.
Albany, NY 12203

Established in 1998 in NY.
Financial data (yr. ended 12/31/01): Grants paid, $85,000; assets, $1,553,024 (M); expenditures, $106,979; qualifying distributions, $84,861.
Limitations: Giving primarily in Albany, NY.
Trustees: Arthur J. Roth, Howard W. Roth.
EIN: 141805156
Codes: FD2

35748
Oaklands Fund, Inc.
c/o Anthony M. O'Connor
1158 5th Ave.
New York, NY 10029-6917

Financial data (yr. ended 12/31/01): Grants paid, $84,900; assets, $1,195,066 (M); expenditures, $87,282; qualifying distributions, $86,092.
Limitations: Applications not accepted. Giving primarily in NY.
Application information: Contributes only to pre-selected organizations.
Officers: Mary Wistar O'Connor, Pres.; Suzzane P. O'Connor, Secy.; Anthony M. O'Connor, Treas.
Trustees: Anthony M. O'Connor, Jr., Robert B. O'Connor, Jr.
EIN: 136161671
Codes: FD2

35749
The Grubstake Foundation
c/o F. Ginsberg
155 Highland Rd.
Rye, NY 10580-1707

Financial data (yr. ended 12/31/00): Grants paid, $84,860; assets, $31,502 (M); gifts received, $62,280; expenditures, $85,067; qualifying distributions, $84,860.
Limitations: Applications not accepted. Giving primarily in NY.
Application information: Contributes only to pre-selected organizations.
Trustees: Carolyn B. Ginsberg Durcan, Frances Ginsberg.
EIN: 132829303
Codes: FD2

35750
The DiPaolo Foundation
c/o Lorraine and Gordon DiPaolo
47 Plaza St. W.
Brooklyn, NY 11217

Established in 1996 in NY.
Donor(s): Gordon DiPaolo, Lorraine DiPaolo.
Financial data (yr. ended 11/30/01): Grants paid, $84,819; assets, $355,456 (M); gifts received, $37,987; expenditures, $88,282; qualifying distributions, $86,757.
Limitations: Applications not accepted. Giving primarily in Brooklyn, NY.
Application information: Contributes only to pre-selected organizations.
Trustees: Gordon DiPaolo, Lorraine DiPaolo.
EIN: 133923411
Codes: FD2

35751
Appel Family Foundation
c/o Robert J. Appel
700 Park Ave.
New York, NY 10021

Established in 1997 in NY.
Donor(s): Robert Appel, Helen Appel, Susan C. Slavin, Debra L. Weinberg.
Financial data (yr. ended 06/30/01): Grants paid, $84,800; assets, $1,332,763 (M); gifts received, $442,571; expenditures, $119,453; qualifying distributions, $79,855.
Limitations: Applications not accepted.
Application information: Contributes only to pre-selected organizations.
Directors: Helen Appel, Robert Appel, Susan C. Slavin, Debra L. Weinberg.
EIN: 113433017
Codes: FD2

35752
Alan & Carol Schechter Charity Fund, Inc.
76-02 174 St.
Flushing, NY 11366

Established in 1996.
Financial data (yr. ended 11/30/01): Grants paid, $84,659; assets, $86,713 (M); gifts received, $126,050; expenditures, $84,659; qualifying distributions, $84,659.
Limitations: Applications not accepted.
Application information: Contributes only to pre-selected organizations.
Officers and Directors:* Alan Schechter,* Pres.; Carol Schechter,* V.P.; Brian Schechter.
EIN: 133353393
Codes: FD2

35753
Abraham D. & Annette Cohen Foundation
c/o The Garnet Group, Inc.
825 3rd Ave., 40th Fl.
New York, NY 10022   (212) 775-7577
Contact: Sharon Grasser

Established in 1984.
Donor(s): Annette Cohen, David A. Cohen, Joseph A. Cohen.
Financial data (yr. ended 10/31/01): Grants paid, $84,634; assets, $231,292 (M); expenditures, $85,019; qualifying distributions, $84,734.
Limitations: Applications not accepted. Giving primarily in New York, NY.
Application information: Contributes only to pre-selected organizations.
Officers and Directors:* Joseph A. Cohen,* Pres.; David A. Cohen,* Secy.-Treas.
EIN: 112715279
Codes: FD2

35754
Waterhill Foundation
P.O. Box 549
East Aurora, NY 14052-0549

Established in 1990 in NY.
Donor(s): Richard W. Bowen II.
Financial data (yr. ended 12/31/00): Grants paid, $84,614; assets, $22,472 (M); gifts received, $84,614; expenditures, $87,629; qualifying distributions, $84,586.
Limitations: Applications not accepted. Giving primarily in CA and MI.
Application information: Contributes only to pre-selected organizations.
Trustees: Richard W. Bowen II, Thomas R. Emmerling.
EIN: 166348320
Codes: FD2

35755
The Ruth and David Sutton Family Foundation
1937 E. 3rd St.
Brooklyn, NY 11223

Established in 1993 in NY.
Donor(s): David Sutton, Paul Sutton, Cudlie Accessories, LLC.
Financial data (yr. ended 05/31/01): Grants paid, $84,596; assets, $0 (M); gifts received, $60,000; expenditures, $84,696; qualifying distributions, $84,696.
Limitations: Applications not accepted.
Application information: Contributes only to pre-selected organizations.
Trustees: David Sutton, Paul Sutton, Steven Sutton.
EIN: 137014537
Codes: FD2

35756
Rapaport Family Charitable Trust
c/o Rita Barrison, C.P.A.
1000 Park Blvd., Ste. 212
Massapequa Park, NY 11762

Established in 1993 in NY.
Donor(s): Peter M. Rapaport, Jessica F. Shapiro.
Financial data (yr. ended 12/31/01): Grants paid, $84,452; assets, $2,126,784 (M); gifts received, $326,435; expenditures, $135,528; qualifying distributions, $84,452.
Limitations: Applications not accepted. Giving primarily in New York, NY.
Application information: Contributes only to pre-selected organizations.
Trustee: Peter Rapaport.
EIN: 137029273
Codes: FD2

35757
The Margules Foundation, Inc.
21 Manor Ln.
Lawrence, NY 11559
Contact: Sheldon Margules, Tr.

Established in 1992 in NY.
Donor(s): Sheldon Margules.
Financial data (yr. ended 06/30/01): Grants paid, $84,422; assets, $104,767 (M); expenditures, $88,595; qualifying distributions, $84,422.
Limitations: Applications not accepted. Giving primarily in NY.
Application information: Contributes only to pre-selected organizations.
Trustee: Sheldon Margules.
EIN: 113129095
Codes: FD2

35758
The Bowman Family Foundation
c/o Merrill Lynch & Co.
250 Vesey St.
New York, NY 10281-1327
Contact: Matthias B. Bowman, Pres.

Established in 1994 in DE.
Donor(s): Matthias B. Bowman, Penny M. Bowman.
Financial data (yr. ended 12/31/99): Grants paid, $84,400; assets, $3,161,228 (M); gifts received, $183,114; expenditures, $124,166; qualifying distributions, $84,400.
Limitations: Applications not accepted. Giving primarily in NY.
Application information: Contributes only to pre-selected organizations.
Officers: Matthias B. Bowman, Pres.; Penny M. Bowman, V.P.
EIN: 133801244
Codes: FD2

35759
Alfred T. Stanley Foundation
c/o Daniel Jacobs
P.O. Box 1320
Bronx, NY 10471-0620

Established in 1983 in NY.
Financial data (yr. ended 12/31/01): Grants paid, $84,400; assets, $1,554,985 (M); expenditures, $87,185; qualifying distributions, $84,400.
Limitations: Applications not accepted. Giving primarily in New York, NY.
Application information: Contributes only to pre-selected organizations. Unsolicited requests for funding not considered.
Officers: John Crane, Pres.; Theodore Storey, V.P.; Louise Pitkin, Secy.; Alfred T. Stanley, Treas.
EIN: 136133796
Codes: FD2

35760
Paul and Susan Efron Foundation
c/o Goldman Sachs & Co.
85 Broad St., Tax Dept.
New York, NY 10004

Established in 1999 in NY.
Donor(s): Paul S. Efron.
Financial data (yr. ended 09/30/01): Grants paid, $84,350; assets, $781,901 (M); gifts received, $559,044; expenditures, $98,090; qualifying distributions, $88,090.
Limitations: Applications not accepted. Giving primarily in New York, NY.
Application information: Contributes only to pre-selected organizations.
Trustees: Paul S. Efron, Susan G. Efron.
EIN: 134082155
Codes: FD2

35761
The Kestenbaum Foundation
135 Rockaway Tpke.
Lawrence, NY 11559
Application address: 200 Wildacre Ave., Lawrence, NY 11559
Contact: Leonard A. Kestenbaum, Tr.

Established in 1995 in NY.
Donor(s): Leonard A. Kestenbaum.
Financial data (yr. ended 12/31/01): Grants paid, $84,185; assets, $6,021 (M); gifts received, $60,000; expenditures, $84,749; qualifying distributions, $84,185.
Limitations: Giving primarily in New York, NY.
Trustees: Aliza Kestenbaum, Leonard A. Kestenbaum.
EIN: 136986909

Codes: FD2

35762
Alfred J. Lippman Foundation
c/o Silverman & Mordfin
150 Great Neck Rd.
Great Neck, NY 11021
Contact: Harold Silverman, Dir.

Established in 1999 in NY.
Financial data (yr. ended 06/30/01): Grants paid, $84,100; assets, $1,060,170 (M); expenditures, $85,896; qualifying distributions, $83,655.
Directors: Gerald Y. Mordfin, Stuart Mordfin, Harold H. Silverman.
EIN: 113500406
Codes: FD2

35763
The Seymour & Dorothy Weinstein Foundation
339 Albany Post Rd.
Croton-on-Hudson, NY 10520-1521

Established in 1988 in NY.
Donor(s): Seymour Weinstein.
Financial data (yr. ended 12/31/00): Grants paid, $84,050; assets, $14,272 (M); gifts received, $81,964; expenditures, $84,128; qualifying distributions, $84,124.
Limitations: Applications not accepted. Giving primarily in NY.
Application information: Contributes only to pre-selected organizations.
Officer: Seymour Weinstein, Pres.
EIN: 133477889
Codes: FD2

35764
The Welfare to Work Foundation
(Formerly Theodore V. Buerger Foundation)
394 Bedford Rd.
Pleasantville, NY 10570

Financial data (yr. ended 03/31/02): Grants paid, $83,999; assets, $12,376 (M); gifts received, $84,825; expenditures, $85,772; qualifying distributions, $83,999.
Limitations: Applications not accepted. Giving limited to Briarcliff, NY.
Application information: Contributes only to a pre-selected organization.
Trustees: Theodore V. Buerger, Joann Frey.
EIN: 137079094
Codes: TN

35765
Steven & Bede Levinson Foundation, Inc.
c/o Wollin Assoc.
350 5th Ave., Ste. 2822
New York, NY 10118

Donor(s): Steven Levinson, Bede Levinson.
Financial data (yr. ended 06/30/00): Grants paid, $83,995; assets, $1,695,886 (M); expenditures, $90,438; qualifying distributions, $84,365.
Limitations: Applications not accepted. Giving primarily in NY.
Application information: Contributes only to pre-selected organizations.
Officers: Steven Levinson, Pres.; Beatrice Levinson, V.P.; Lonnie E. Wollin, Secy.
EIN: 133251182
Codes: FD2

35766
Burton & Suzanne Rubin Foundation
c/o Rubin Baum, LLP
30 Rockefeller Plz., 29th Fl.
New York, NY 10112-2999
Contact: Burton Rubin, Pres.

Established in 1999 in NY.

Donor(s): Burton Rubin, Suzanne Rubin.
Financial data (yr. ended 06/30/00): Grants paid, $83,850; assets, $33,289 (M); gifts received, $117,158; expenditures, $83,870; qualifying distributions, $83,850.
Application information: Application form not required.
Officers: Burton Rubin, Pres.; Suzanne Rubin, V.P. and Secy.; Frederic Rubin, V.P. and Treas.; Margot Rubin, V.P.
EIN: 134081339

35767
Feldstein Family Charitable Foundation, Inc.
745 5th Ave., Rm. 709
New York, NY 10151-0105

Established in 1987 in NY.
Financial data (yr. ended 12/31/01): Grants paid, $83,708; assets, $460,153 (M); expenditures, $84,138; qualifying distributions, $83,708.
Limitations: Applications not accepted. Giving primarily in New York, NY.
Application information: Contributes only to pre-selected organizations.
Officers: Richard Feldstein, Pres. and Treas.; Judith Feldstein, V.P. and Secy.
EIN: 133412554
Codes: FD2

35768
Griff Family Foundation
c/o Stuart Perl
1523 E. 22nd St.
Brooklyn, NY 11210-5124

Established in 1999 in NY.
Financial data (yr. ended 12/31/01): Grants paid, $83,706; assets, $6,463 (M); gifts received, $45,000; expenditures, $83,706; qualifying distributions, $83,706.
Limitations: Applications not accepted. Giving primarily in NY.
Application information: Contributes only to pre-selected organizations.
Trustee: Iris D. Perl.
EIN: 113507399

35769
The Ahavas Tzedakah Foundation Trust
370 Rugby Rd.
Cedarhurst, NY 11516
Contact: Aaron Salomon, Tr.

Established in 1999.
Financial data (yr. ended 12/31/01): Grants paid, $83,700; assets, $1,638,035 (M); gifts received, $100,000; expenditures, $91,715; qualifying distributions, $83,700.
Trustees: Aaron Salomon, Chaya Rachel Salomon.
EIN: 116527334
Codes: FD2

35770
Randolph Lewisohn Fund
c/o JPMorgan Chase Bank
1211 6th Ave., 34th Fl.
New York, NY 10036
Application address: c/o Presbytery of NYC, 7 W. 11th St., New York, NY 10011, tel.: (212) 691-9650

Established in 1996 in NY.
Financial data (yr. ended 12/31/01): Grants paid, $83,693; assets, $1,612,420 (M); expenditures, $105,078; qualifying distributions, $85,043.
Trustee: JPMorgan Chase Bank.
EIN: 133408705
Codes: FD2

35771
Rachel & Ezra Shamah Foundation
c/o Franshaw, Inc.
1411 Broadway, 18th Fl.
New York, NY 10018
Contact: Ezra Shamah, Tr.

Established in 1991 in NY.
Donor(s): Franshaw, Inc.
Financial data (yr. ended 12/31/01): Grants paid, $83,543; assets, $315 (M); gifts received, $84,000; expenditures, $83,826; qualifying distributions, $83,543.
Limitations: Giving primarily in Brooklyn, NY.
Application information: Application form not required.
Trustees: Ezra Shamah, Rachel Shamah.
EIN: 133613890
Codes: FD2

35772
LLS Foundation, Inc.
c/o Family Management, LLC
477 Madison Ave.
New York, NY 10022

Established in 1985 in NY.
Donor(s): Laura Lee Scheuer.
Financial data (yr. ended 11/30/01): Grants paid, $83,500; assets, $1,250,139 (M); expenditures, $125,842; qualifying distributions, $83,361.
Limitations: Applications not accepted. Giving primarily in Washington, DC, and New York, NY.
Application information: Contributes only to pre-selected organizations.
Officers and Directors:* Laura Lee Scheuer,* Pres. and Treas.; Emily Malino Scheuer,* V.P.; Elizabeth Scheuer,* Secy.
EIN: 133282712
Codes: FD2

35773
The Belsky Foundation, Inc.
111 Arrandale Rd.
Rockville Centre, NY 11570-1599
Contact: Burton Belsky, Secy.

Established in 1959.
Donor(s): The Belsky Co.
Financial data (yr. ended 11/30/01): Grants paid, $83,456; assets, $966,128 (M); gifts received, $35,000; expenditures, $85,312; qualifying distributions, $82,937.
Limitations: Applications not accepted. Giving primarily in NY.
Application information: Contributes only to pre-selected organizations.
Officers: Murray Belsky, Pres.; Bruce Belsky, V.P.; Burton Belsky, Secy.
EIN: 136145483
Codes: FD2

35774
The Kris and Kathy Heinzelman Foundation
c/o Cravath, Swaine & Moore
825 8th Ave.
New York, NY 10019-7475

Established in 1999 in NY.
Donor(s): Kathy Heinzelman, Kris F. Heinzelman.
Financial data (yr. ended 12/31/01): Grants paid, $83,455; assets, $223,744 (M); expenditures, $92,070; qualifying distributions, $83,398.
Limitations: Applications not accepted. Giving primarily in CT, MA, NJ, NY, and RI.
Application information: Contributes only to pre-selected organizations.
Trustees: Kathy Heinzelman, Kris F. Heinzelman.
EIN: 134081145
Codes: FD2

35775
Kim and Ralph Rosenberg Family Foundation
c/o Goldman Sachs & Co.
85 Broad St., Tax Dept.
New York, NY 10004

Established in 1999 in NY.
Donor(s): Ralph Rosenberg.
Financial data (yr. ended 10/31/01): Grants paid, $83,422; assets, $889,986 (M); gifts received, $3,500; expenditures, $88,991; qualifying distributions, $87,041.
Limitations: Applications not accepted. Giving primarily in NY.
Application information: Contributes only to pre-selected organizations.
Trustees: Kim Rosenberg, Ralph Rosenberg, Stuart Rothenberg.
EIN: 134052243
Codes: FD2

35776
Nathan Tannenbaum Foundation, Inc.
350 5th Ave., 10th Fl.
New York, NY 10118-0199

Established in 1951 in NY.
Donor(s): Nathan Tannenbaum.
Financial data (yr. ended 12/31/01): Grants paid, $83,421; assets, $1,495,023 (M); expenditures, $115,495; qualifying distributions, $83,064.
Limitations: Applications not accepted. Giving primarily in NY.
Application information: Contributes only to pre-selected organizations.
Officers: Morton Tannenbaum, Pres. and Treas.; Rhea Tannenbaum, V.P.; Robert Tannenbaum, V.P.; Sydelle Tannenbaum, Secy.
EIN: 136116415
Codes: FD2

35777
The Nola Foundation
200 Madison Ave., 5th Fl.
New York, NY 10016

Established in 1998 in DE.
Donor(s): Susan & Elihu Rose Foundation, Inc.
Financial data (yr. ended 12/31/00): Grants paid, $83,308; assets, $7,953 (M); gifts received, $90,000; expenditures, $83,583; qualifying distributions, $83,308.
Limitations: Applications not accepted. Giving primarily in New York, NY.
Application information: Contributes only to pre-selected organizations.
Officers and Directors:* Amy Rose Silverman,* Pres.; Jeffrey Silverman,* V.P.
EIN: 134014432
Codes: FD2

35778
The Roni & Bruce Sokoloff Foundation
c/o Reliance Group Holdings, Inc.
55 E. 52nd St.
New York, NY 10055

Established in 1996 in DE and NY.
Donor(s): Bruce Sokoloff, Roni Sokoloff.
Financial data (yr. ended 11/30/99): Grants paid, $83,250; assets, $597,849 (M); gifts received, $5,523; expenditures, $86,026; qualifying distributions, $83,250.
Officers: Bruce Sokoloff, Pres. and Treas.; Roni Sokoloff, V.P. and Secy.
EIN: 522006410
Codes: FD2

35779
The Hillsberg Foundation
265 E. 66th St., Rm. 20-B
New York, NY 10021

Donor(s): Herbert Hillsberg, Sanford J. Hillsberg, Allen Filstein, Vicki Filstein.
Financial data (yr. ended 07/31/01): Grants paid, $83,245; assets, $166,894 (M); gifts received, $85,403; expenditures, $87,737; qualifying distributions, $83,245.
Limitations: Applications not accepted.
Application information: Contributes only to pre-selected organizations.
Officers: Herbert Hillsberg, Pres.; Vicki Filstein, V.P.; Madeline Hillsberg, V.P.; Mindy Hillsberg, V.P.; Sanford J. Hillsberg, Treas.
EIN: 521417579
Codes: FD2

35780
Marshall Family Foundation
5800 Lake Bluff Rd.
North Rose, NY 14516

Established in 1995 in NY.
Donor(s): W. Gilman Marshall, Ina Marshall.
Financial data (yr. ended 10/31/00): Grants paid, $83,000; assets, $2,171,429 (M); gifts received, $220,000; expenditures, $111,598; qualifying distributions, $85,449.
Limitations: Giving limited to Rose, NY.
Trustees: Gary Marshall, Gilman Marshall, Ina Marshall, Kent Marshall, Kris T. Marshall.
EIN: 166430502
Codes: FD2

35781
The Mark Twain Foundation
c/o JPMorgan Chase Bank
1211 Ave. of the Americas, 38th Fl.
New York, NY 10036
E-mail: jones_ed_l@JPMorgan.com
Contact: Edward L. Jones, V.P.

Established in 1978.
Financial data (yr. ended 10/31/01): Grants paid, $83,000; assets, $1,569,617 (M); expenditures, $135,708; qualifying distributions, $85,743.
Limitations: Applications not accepted. Giving on a national basis, with emphasis on Hartford, CT, and Elmira, NY.
Application information: Unsolicited requests for funds not accepted.
Trustee: JPMorgan Chase Bank.
EIN: 133058782
Codes: FD2

35782
The Bandier Family Foundation, Inc.
P.O. Box 2190, Gin Ln.
Southampton, NY 11969
Contact: Martin Bandier, Pres.

Established in 1994 in NY.
Donor(s): Martin Bandier.
Financial data (yr. ended 11/30/01): Grants paid, $82,956; assets, $57,909 (M); gifts received, $95,000; expenditures, $84,047; qualifying distributions, $83,983.
Limitations: Giving primarily in New York, NY.
Officers and Directors:* Martin Bandier,* Pres.; Dorothy Bandier,* Secy.-Treas.; Janice Brock.
EIN: 133803092
Codes: FD2

35783
The Elias Foundation
c/o U.S. Trust Co. of NY
114 W. 47th St., TAXVAS
New York, NY 10036

Established in 1999 in DE.
Donor(s): Jacqueline Mann, James E. Mann.
Financial data (yr. ended 12/31/00): Grants paid, $82,950; assets, $1,323,575 (M); gifts received, $995,784; expenditures, $123,957; qualifying distributions, $90,809.
Limitations: Applications not accepted.
Officers: Jacqueline Mann, Pres.; Alison Mann, V.P.; Anastasia Mann, V.P.; James E. Mann, Secy.; Eldar Shafir, Treas.
EIN: 134092287
Codes: FD2

35784
Arts and Letters Foundation, Inc.
c/o J. Gerton
230 E. 50th St., Ste. 3B
New York, NY 10022-7702 (212) 688-6488

Established in 1997 in DE and NY.
Donor(s): Janice Gerton.
Financial data (yr. ended 12/31/00): Grants paid, $82,873; assets, $1,226,566 (M); gifts received, $106,500; expenditures, $90,251; qualifying distributions, $85,735.
Limitations: Applications not accepted.
Application information: Contributes only to pre-selected organizations.
Officers and Directors:* Janice Gerton,* Pres.; Henry Bear,* V.P. and Secy.-Treas.
EIN: 522069719
Codes: FD2

35785
Kuperman Family Foundation, Inc.
43 W. 33rd St.
New York, NY 10001

Established in 1998 in NY.
Donor(s): Joseph Kuperman, Leo Kuperman, Sarah Tarnofsky.
Financial data (yr. ended 12/31/00): Grants paid, $82,781; assets, $380,878 (M); expenditures, $82,845; qualifying distributions, $82,725.
Limitations: Applications not accepted.
Application information: Contributes only to pre-selected organizations.
Directors: Joseph Kuperman, Leo Kuperman, Sarah Tarnofsky.
EIN: 113467834
Codes: FD2

35786
Conway Foundation
101 Park Ave., 30th Fl.
New York, NY 10178
Application address: c/o I. Stanley Kriegel, 2 Penn Plz., Ste. 1914, New York, NY 10121

Established in 1986 in NY.
Donor(s): E. Virgil Conway.
Financial data (yr. ended 12/31/00): Grants paid, $82,755; assets, $1,364,735 (M); expenditures, $93,801; qualifying distributions, $91,730.
Limitations: Giving primarily in NY.
Officer: E. Virgil Conway, Pres.
EIN: 133392387
Codes: FD2

35787
The Friedman Family Charitable Foundation
c/o EOS Partners, LP
320 Park Ave., 22nd Fl.
New York, NY 10022-6838

Established in 1991 in NY.
Donor(s): Steven M. Friedman.
Financial data (yr. ended 06/30/01): Grants paid, $82,750; assets, $394,902 (M); gifts received, $3,350; expenditures, $86,200; qualifying distributions, $83,201.
Limitations: Giving primarily in NY; some funding also in Philadelphia, PA, and Chicago, IL.
Trustee: Steven M. Friedman.
EIN: 136976452

35788
The Murray and Renee Nadel Family Foundation
433 Beechmont Dr.
New Rochelle, NY 10804-4617

Established in 1997 in NY.
Donor(s): Murray Nadel, Renee Nadel.
Financial data (yr. ended 12/31/01): Grants paid, $82,750; assets, $146,768 (M); expenditures, $84,217; qualifying distributions, $82,749.
Limitations: Applications not accepted.
Application information: Contributes only to pre-selected organizations.
Officers: Murray Nadel, Pres.; Renee Nadel, V.P.
EIN: 133975463
Codes: FD2

35789
Leo W. & Lilyan E. Cole Fund
c/o JPMorgan Private Bank
1211 Ave. of the Americas, 38th Fl.
New York, NY 10036 (212) 789-5679
FAX: (212) 596-3712; E-mail: elias_jacqueline@jpmorgan.com
Contact: Jacqueline Elias, V.P., JPMorgan Chase Bank

Established in 1974 in NY.
Financial data (yr. ended 05/31/02): Grants paid, $82,700; assets, $1,145,480 (M); expenditures, $102,217; qualifying distributions, $82,700.
Limitations: Applications not accepted. Giving primarily in New York, NY.
Application information: Proposals will be solicited by the fund. Unsolicited proposals will not be accepted.
Trustee: JPMorgan Chase Bank.
EIN: 136686039
Codes: FD2

35790
The Wechsler Foundation, Inc.
c/o Seymour M. Ettinger, CPA
1935 Allison Dr.
Bellmore, NY 11710

Donor(s): Robert Wechsler.
Financial data (yr. ended 12/31/99): Grants paid, $82,633; assets, $85,931 (M); expenditures, $96,318; qualifying distributions, $96,270.
Limitations: Applications not accepted. Giving primarily in New York, NY.
Application information: Contributes only to pre-selected organizations.
Officers and Directors:* Robert Wechsler,* Pres. and Treas.; Evelene Wechsler,* Secy.; Seymour M. Ettinger.
EIN: 112779306
Codes: FD2

35791
Louis D. Mauro, Sr. Charitable Trust
c/o NBT Bank, N.A.
52 S. Broad St.
Norwich, NY 13815
Application address: c/o NBT Bank, 199 2nd Ave. Ext., Gloversville, NY 12078

Financial data (yr. ended 06/30/01): Grants paid, $82,595; assets, $1,057,659 (M); expenditures, $93,102; qualifying distributions, $82,691.
Limitations: Giving limited to residents of Gloversville and Fulton County, NY.
Application information: Application form required.
Trustees: David Seward, NBT Bank, N.A.
EIN: 146153728
Codes: FD2

35792
Vijaydev Mistry Foundation, Inc.
579 Broadway, Apt. 2F
New York, NY 10012 (212) 226-7537
Contact: Harishchandra V. Mistry, Dir.

Established in 1987 in NY.
Donor(s): Bhika Ratanjee, Harishchandra V. Mistry, Harshadrai V. Mistry.
Financial data (yr. ended 10/31/01): Grants paid, $82,571; assets, $440,804 (M); gifts received, $50,000; expenditures, $96,193; qualifying distributions, $96,193.
Application information: Application form not required.
Directors: Harishchandra V. Mistry, Harshadrai V. Mistry, Bhika Ratanjee.
EIN: 133440329
Codes: FD2

35793
Benjamin & Sophie Scher Charitable Foundation
48 W. 38th St., 11th Fl.
New York, NY 10018

Established in 1997 in NY.
Financial data (yr. ended 08/31/01): Grants paid, $82,500; assets, $3,517,410 (M); expenditures, $287,129; qualifying distributions, $248,525.
Limitations: Applications not accepted.
Application information: Contributes only to pre-selected organizations.
Trustees: Sandra O'Neill, David Scher, Robert Scher.
EIN: 133965996
Codes: FD2

35794
Societe des Professeurs Francais et Franophones d'Amerique
(Formerly Societe des Professeurs Francais en Amerique)
c/o Yorkville Financial Sta.
P.O. Box 6641
New York, NY 10128
FAX: (212) 996-2367
Contact: Gerard Roubichou, Pres.

Established in 1904 in NY.
Donor(s): Louise Dufrenoy,‡ Jeanne Marandon.‡
Financial data (yr. ended 12/31/99): Grants paid, $82,500; assets, $3,339,778 (M); gifts received, $21,599; expenditures, $165,621; qualifying distributions, $129,119.
Limitations: Giving exclusively to U.S. citizens.
Publications: Grants list, informational brochure.
Application information: Application form required.
Officers and Directors:* Gerard Roubichou, Pres.; Simone Ackerman, 1st V.P.; Marie Naudin,* Secy.; Clement M'Bom, Treas.; Jean-Francois Briere, Carmen Coll, Charles Hill, Frantz-Antoine

Leconte, Brigitte Mahuzier, Francoise Mead, Anne Mullen-Hohl, Diane Paravazian, Renaud Redien-Collot, Claude Roquin, Peter Schulman, Hughes St. Fort.
EIN: 133150248
Codes: FD2, GTI

35795
The Ullendorff Memorial Foundation
(Formerly Emma Ullendorff Memorial Foundation)
c/o American Express, TBS, Inc.
1185 Ave. of the Americas
New York, NY 10036-2602

Established in 1986 in NY.
Donor(s): Henry Ullendorff, Regina Ullendorff, Danielle Ullendorff.
Financial data (yr. ended 12/31/00): Grants paid, $82,500; assets, $2,826,993 (M); gifts received, $63,000; expenditures, $296,519; qualifying distributions, $142,282.
Limitations: Applications not accepted. Giving on a national basis, with emphasis on New York, NY.
Application information: Contributes only to pre-selected organizations.
Trustees: Jacqueline Ahrens, Danielle Ullendorff, David Ullendorff, Doris Ullendorff, Henry Ullendorff, Regina Ullendorff.
EIN: 135674318
Codes: FD2

35796
Ernie Wolk Charitable Trust
c/o HSBC Bank USA
1 Marine Midland Ctr., 16th Fl.
Buffalo, NY 14240

Established in 1963 in NY.
Financial data (yr. ended 12/31/01): Grants paid, $82,500; assets, $1,347,205 (M); expenditures, $97,865; qualifying distributions, $83,986.
Limitations: Applications not accepted. Giving primarily in Rochester, NY.
Application information: Contributes only to pre-selected organizations.
Trustee: HSBC Bank USA.
EIN: 166050723
Codes: FD2

35797
The Handal Foundation, Inc.
c/o Donald Handal
10 E. 34th St., 3rd Fl.
New York, NY 10016-4327

Donor(s): Wright's Knitwear Corp.
Financial data (yr. ended 11/30/01): Grants paid, $82,400; assets, $143,691 (M); expenditures, $88,872; qualifying distributions, $87,362.
Limitations: Applications not accepted. Giving primarily in NY.
Application information: Contributes only to pre-selected organizations.
Officers: Joseph Handal, Pres.; Donald Handal, V.P.; Eileen Silverman, Secy.; Richard Handal, Treas.
EIN: 133162054
Codes: FD2

35798
APAS Foundation
c/o Andrew Steffan
160 E. 72nd St., Ste. 6E
New York, NY 10021

Established in 1997 in NY.
Donor(s): Andrew Steffan, Patricia Steffan.
Financial data (yr. ended 12/31/01): Grants paid, $82,108; assets, $946,981 (M); expenditures, $86,660; qualifying distributions, $82,108.

Limitations: Applications not accepted. Giving primarily in NY.
Application information: Contributes only to pre-selected organizations.
Officers: Andrew Steffan, Pres. and Treas.; Patricia Steffan, V.P.; Alexander Steffan, Secy.
EIN: 133981269
Codes: FD2

35799
The Hilson Fund, Inc.
c/o Epiphany Nursery School
510 E. 74th St.
New York, NY 10021
Contact: Wendy F. Levey, Pres.

Established in 1947 in NY.
Donor(s): John S. Hilson,‡ Mildred S. Hilson.‡
Financial data (yr. ended 11/30/99): Grants paid, $82,000; assets, $1,546,602 (M); expenditures, $96,463; qualifying distributions, $80,411.
Limitations: Applications not accepted. Giving primarily in NY.
Application information: Contributes only to pre-selected organizations.
Officers: Wendy F. Levey, Pres.; Steven F. Flink, Secy.-Treas.
EIN: 136028783
Codes: FD2

35800
Zarin/Rosenfeld Family Foundation
110 Riverside Dr., Ste. 13AC
New York, NY 10024

Established in 2000 in NY.
Donor(s): Gerald Rosenfeld, Judith Zarin.
Financial data (yr. ended 12/31/00): Grants paid, $82,000; assets, $369,789 (M); gifts received, $449,061; expenditures, $82,500; qualifying distributions, $82,000.
Limitations: Applications not accepted.
Application information: Contributes only to pre-selected organizations.
Trustees: Gerald Rosenfeld, Judith Zarin.
EIN: 134116103
Codes: FD2

35801
Harry & Helen Ostreicher Family Foundation
c/o Zell & Ettinger
3001 Ave. M
Brooklyn, NY 11210

Established in 1996.
Donor(s): Harry Ostreicher.
Financial data (yr. ended 07/31/01): Grants paid, $81,940; assets, $0 (M); gifts received, $1,292,125; expenditures, $82,038; qualifying distributions, $80,391.
Officer: Harry Ostreicher, Pres. and V.P.
EIN: 113241598
Codes: FD2

35802
The Seidenfeld Family Foundation
5807 12th Ave.
Brooklyn, NY 11219

Established in 1996 in NY.
Donor(s): Norman Seidenfeld.
Financial data (yr. ended 12/31/00): Grants paid, $81,875; assets, $0 (M); gifts received, $81,799; expenditures, $82,335; qualifying distributions, $82,335.
Limitations: Applications not accepted. Giving primarily in NY.
Application information: Contributes only to pre-selected organizations.
Director: Norman Seidenfeld.
EIN: 116465379

Codes: FD2

35803
Robert A. & Leslie N. Cenci Foundation
c/o BCRS Assocs., LLC
100 Wall St., 11th Fl.
New York, NY 10005

Established in 1987 in CT.
Donor(s): Robert A. Cenci.
Financial data (yr. ended 03/31/01): Grants paid, $81,765; assets, $912,277 (M); expenditures, $108,851; qualifying distributions, $83,656.
Limitations: Applications not accepted. Giving primarily in CT, NY, and VT.
Application information: Contributes only to pre-selected organizations.
Trustees: Leslie N. Cenci, Robert A. Cenci.
EIN: 133437928
Codes: FD2

35804
Sternklar Family Foundation, Inc.
(Formerly Bezalel Art Foundation)
156 William St., Ste. 802
New York, NY 10038

Donor(s): Jack Sternklar, Lila Sternklar.
Financial data (yr. ended 06/30/01): Grants paid, $81,663; assets, $684,477 (M); expenditures, $81,742; qualifying distributions, $80,279.
Limitations: Applications not accepted. Giving primarily in the metropolitan New York, NY, area.
Application information: Contributes only to pre-selected organizations.
Officers: Jack Sternklar, Pres.; Lila Sternklar, V.P.
EIN: 133041079
Codes: FD2

35805
JJR Foundation
c/o RHO Capital Partners, Inc.
152 W. 57th St.
New York, NY 10019

Established in 1993 in NY.
Donor(s): Joshua Ruch, Human Genome Sciences (NY) Inc., Millenium Pharmaceuticals, Shire Pharmaceuticals, Habib Kairouz.
Financial data (yr. ended 09/30/01): Grants paid, $81,640; assets, $4,764,640 (M); gifts received, $815,782; expenditures, $121,097; qualifying distributions, $85,515.
Limitations: Applications not accepted. Giving primarily in New York, NY.
Application information: Contributes only to pre-selected organizations.
Trustees: Joshua Ruch, Julia M. Ruch.
EIN: 133740793
Codes: FD2

35806
The Nina & Ivan Selin Family Foundation, Inc
c/o Neuberger Berman Trust Co.
605 3rd Ave.
New York, NY 10158-3698

Established in 1994 in MD.
Donor(s): Nina E. Selin, Ivan Selin.
Financial data (yr. ended 12/31/00): Grants paid, $81,500; assets, $1,555,638 (M); expenditures, $104,871; qualifying distributions, $81,474.
Limitations: Applications not accepted. Giving primarily in Washington, DC.
Application information: Contributes only to pre-selected organizations.
Officers: Nina E. Selin, Pres.; Ivan Selin, V.P.; Jessica B. Selin, Secy.; Douglas S. Selin, Treas.
EIN: 521891582
Codes: FD2

35807—NEW YORK

35807
The William and Jacqueline Shaw Family Foundation, Inc.
237 Ferndale Rd.
Scarsdale, NY 10583

Established in NY in 1997.
Donor(s): William Shaw.
Financial data (yr. ended 12/31/00): Grants paid, $81,470; assets, $2,604,560 (M); expenditures, $101,720; qualifying distributions, $101,532.
Limitations: Applications not accepted. Giving primarily in CA, MA, and NY.
Application information: Contributes only to pre-selected organizations.
Officers: William Shaw, Pres.; Linda Shaw Goodman, V.P. and Secy.; Deborah Shaw Sevy, V.P. and Treas.
EIN: 133948877
Codes: FD2

35808
Kyodai Foundation
c/o B. Rosenblatt
14 E. 60th St., No. 702
New York, NY 10022-7125

Established in 1988 in DE.
Financial data (yr. ended 12/31/01): Grants paid, $81,400; assets, $1,207,782 (M); expenditures, $88,829; qualifying distributions, $82,935.
Limitations: Applications not accepted. Giving primarily in CA and New York, NY.
Application information: Contributes only to pre-selected organizations.
Officers: Stephanie P. Levi, Pres.; Melissa Posen, Secy.; Daniel L. Posen, Treas.
EIN: 133446242
Codes: FD2

35809
Jacob & Anita Flaks Foundation
3825 Oceanview Ave.
Brooklyn, NY 11224

Established in 1986 in NY.
Donor(s): Anita Flaks, Jacob Flaks.
Financial data (yr. ended 06/30/01): Grants paid, $81,201; assets, $260,373 (M); gifts received, $8,000; expenditures, $83,702; qualifying distributions, $82,867.
Limitations: Applications not accepted. Giving primarily in NY.
Application information: Contributes only to pre-selected organizations.
Trustees: Anita Flaks, Jacob Flaks.
EIN: 112812614
Codes: FD2

35810
The Dorsky Foundation, Inc.
(Formerly Samuel Dorsky Foundation, Inc.)
379 W. Broadway
New York, NY 10012
Contact: Karen A. Dorsky, Dir.

Donor(s): Samuel Dorsky.
Financial data (yr. ended 10/31/00): Grants paid, $81,000; assets, $1,206,664 (M); gifts received, $400; expenditures, $90,303; qualifying distributions, $87,197.
Limitations: Giving primarily in New York, NY.
Directors: David A. Dorsky, Karen A. Dorsky, Noah P. Dorsky.
EIN: 136121016
Codes: FD2

35811
The Virginia & Warren Schwerin Family Foundation, Inc.
c/o Related Properties
2 Manhattanville Rd.
Purchase, NY 10577

Established in 1997 in DE.
Donor(s): Warren Schwerin.
Financial data (yr. ended 12/31/01): Grants paid, $81,000; assets, $491,592 (M); gifts received, $32,934; expenditures, $87,774; qualifying distributions, $82,282.
Limitations: Applications not accepted. Giving primarily in NY.
Application information: Contributes only to pre-selected organizations.
Officers: Warren Schwerin, Pres.; Virginia Schwerin, V.P.; Sherri D. Wilson, Treas.
EIN: 133620145
Codes: FD2

35812
Von Seebeck Charitable Trust
c/o The Bank of New York, Tax Dept.
1 Wall St., 28th Fl.
New York, NY 10286
Contact: Willis Pruitt

Established in 1991 in NY.
Financial data (yr. ended 09/30/01): Grants paid, $81,000; assets, $926,219 (M); expenditures, $94,822; qualifying distributions, $83,399.
Limitations: Applications not accepted. Giving primarily in New York, NY.
Trustee: The Bank of New York.
EIN: 137001906
Codes: FD2

35813
Ludwig Vogelstein Foundation, Inc.
P.O. Box 510
Shelter Island, NY 11964-0510
Contact: Willi Kirkham, Exec. Dir.

Incorporated in 1947 in NY.
Donor(s): Julie Braun-Vogelstein.‡
Financial data (yr. ended 12/31/01): Grants paid, $80,900; assets, $1,001,792 (M); expenditures, $141,620; qualifying distributions, $127,408.
Limitations: Giving primarily in the U.S.; some giving internationally.
Publications: Application guidelines.
Application information: Application guidelines available anytime; grants are strictly for individuals. Telephone calls not accepted. Application form not required.
Officers: Robert S. Braunschweig, Pres.; Ellen Peckham, V.P.; Virginia Gorodnitzki, Secy.; Willi Kirkham, Exec. Dir.
Directors: Catherine Brooks, Marjorie Chadbourne, Mary Cox, Robert Harris.
EIN: 136185761
Codes: FD2, GTI

35814
Bengualid Foundation, Inc.
400 E. 111th St.
New York, NY 10029

Established in 1988 in NY.
Donor(s): Henri Bengualid, Mark Bengualid, Victoria Bengualid.
Financial data (yr. ended 12/31/01): Grants paid, $80,850; assets, $2,530,076 (M); gifts received, $104,008; expenditures, $81,184; qualifying distributions, $80,190.
Limitations: Applications not accepted. Giving primarily in NY.
Application information: Contributes only to pre-selected organizations.
Trustee: Henri Bengualid.
EIN: 133458300
Codes: FD2

35815
Jean L. and Robert A. Stern Foundation, Inc.
(Formerly PRR Foundation, Inc.)
4 Cradle Rock Rd.
Pound Ridge, NY 10576-2208 (914) 764-0451
Contact: Jean L. Stern, Pres.

Established in 1992 in NY.
Donor(s): Jean L. Stern, Robert A. Stern.
Financial data (yr. ended 09/30/01): Grants paid, $80,770; assets, $4,889,099 (M); gifts received, $4,442,444; expenditures, $83,106; qualifying distributions, $81,299.
Limitations: Giving primarily in the metropolitan New York, NY, area.
Application information: Application form required.
Officers: Jean L. Stern, Pres.; Robert A. Stern, V.P. and Secy.-Treas.
Director: Robert J. Stern.
EIN: 133682636
Codes: FD2

35816
Raible Foundation, Inc.
47 Middle Rd.
Port Washington, NY 11050 (516) 767-0760

Financial data (yr. ended 12/31/01): Grants paid, $80,700; assets, $714,461 (M); expenditures, $83,273; qualifying distributions, $80,891.
Limitations: Applications not accepted. Giving primarily in CT and NY.
Application information: Contributes only to pre-selected organizations.
Officer: Charlotte Kappenberg, Chair.
EIN: 116078700
Codes: FD2

35817
Barnard School Foundation
1636 3rd Ave., No. 416
New York, NY 10128-3655 (212) 426-3204
Contact: Lofton S. Moore, Secy.

Established in 1993 in NY.
Financial data (yr. ended 06/30/01): Grants paid, $80,500; assets, $1,369,269 (M); expenditures, $116,069; qualifying distributions, $79,339.
Limitations: Giving limited to New York, NY.
Application information: Application form not required.
Officers and Trustees:* Kit Wallace,* Pres.; Miriam Westheimer,* V.P.; Lofton S. Moore, Secy.; Gail Weinstein,* Treas.; Virginia Conner, Diane Davis, Howard Johnson, Annette Lintz, Verne Oliver, Jon Sinonian, Michele Sola, Thomas Tinker, John Varjabedian.
EIN: 130468890
Codes: FD2

35818
Arnold & Dorothy Neustadter Foundation
c/o Esanu, Katsky, Korins & Siger
605 3rd Ave.
New York, NY 10158 (212) 953-6000

Donor(s): Arnold Neustadter,‡ Dorothy Neustadter, Richard M. Neustadter.
Financial data (yr. ended 12/31/01): Grants paid, $80,480; assets, $1,206,837 (M); gifts received, $3,500; expenditures, $95,920; qualifying distributions, $80,480.
Limitations: Applications not accepted. Giving primarily in New York, NY.
Application information: Contributes only to pre-selected organizations.

Trustees: Martha Mendelsohn, Dorothy Neustadter, Richard M. Neustadter, Jane Revasch.
EIN: 136202507

35819
The McGroddy Family Foundation, Inc.
796 Long Hill Rd. W.
Briarcliff Manor, NY 10510-2123

Established in 1998 in NY.
Financial data (yr. ended 12/31/00): Grants paid, $80,440; assets, $1,215,331 (M); expenditures, $82,599; qualifying distributions, $79,945.
Limitations: Applications not accepted. Giving primarily in NY.
Application information: Contributes only to pre-selected organizations.
Officers: James C. McGroddy, Pres.; Sheree Wen, V.P.; Kathleen McGroddy, Secy.
EIN: 133982834
Codes: FD2

35820
Allade, Inc.
c/o Arthur D. Emil
919 3rd Ave.
New York, NY 10022

Established in 1956 in NY.
Donor(s): Allan D. Emil, Arthur D. Emil, Kate S. Emil.
Financial data (yr. ended 12/31/00): Grants paid, $80,394; assets, $2,223,983 (M); expenditures, $105,837; qualifying distributions, $80,394.
Limitations: Applications not accepted. Giving primarily in NY.
Application information: Contributes only to pre-selected organizations.
Trustee: Arthur D. Emil.
Directors: Arthur Aeder, Lydia Depolo, David Emil.
EIN: 136097697
Codes: FD2

35821
The Jerrold & Sally Fine Foundation, Inc.
c/o Richard A. Eisner & Co., LLP
750 3rd Ave.
New York, NY 10017

Established in 1986 in DE.
Donor(s): Jerrold Fine.
Financial data (yr. ended 12/31/01): Grants paid, $80,350; assets, $1,689,314 (M); expenditures, $82,145; qualifying distributions, $80,645.
Limitations: Applications not accepted. Giving primarily in CT and PA.
Application information: Contributes only to pre-selected organizations.
Directors: Jerrold Fine, Sally Fine, Paul Roth.
EIN: 222774146
Codes: FD2

35822
Snyder Family Foundation
82 Meadow Rd.
Buffalo, NY 14216

Established in 1999 in NY.
Donor(s): Barry Snyder.
Financial data (yr. ended 12/31/01): Grants paid, $80,325; assets, $2,312,129 (M); gifts received, $50,948; expenditures, $93,747; qualifying distributions, $80,325.
Limitations: Applications not accepted.
Application information: Contributes only to pre-selected organizations.
Trustees: Barry Snyder, Louise Snyder.
EIN: 161575410

35823
The New Kalman Sunshine Fund, Inc.
c/o Loveman Kornreich
711 Westchester Ave.
White Plains, NY 10604-3504
Contact: Lee A. Furman, Pres.

Established in 1984.
Donor(s): Philip Amin.‡
Financial data (yr. ended 12/31/01): Grants paid, $80,292; assets, $937,269 (M); expenditures, $94,907; qualifying distributions, $9,459.
Limitations: Giving primarily in NY.
Officers and Directors:* Lee A. Furman,* Pres.; Robert Furman,* V.P.; Warren Weiss,* Secy.; Andrew Furman, David Furman, Ronald Furman.
EIN: 133228316
Codes: FD2

35824
Harry S. Fredenburgh Scholarship Fund
c/o JPMorgan Chase Bank
P.O. Box 1412
Rochester, NY 14603-1412
Application address: c/o JPMorgan Chase Bank, 31 Main St., Canandaigua, NY 14424, tel.: (716) 394-7675
Contact: Janis Mosher, V.P., JPMorgan Chase Bank

Established in 1979.
Financial data (yr. ended 12/31/01): Grants paid, $80,250; assets, $1,543,225 (M); expenditures, $94,383; qualifying distributions, $80,236.
Limitations: Giving limited to Seneca Falls, NY.
Application information: Application form required.
Trustee: JPMorgan Chase Bank.
EIN: 166229781
Codes: FD2, GTI

35825
Jesse and Dorothy Hartman Foundation
c/o Proskauer, Rose, LLP
1585 Broadway
New York, NY 10036-8200

Established in 1954 in NY.
Donor(s): Jesse Hartman.‡
Financial data (yr. ended 12/31/00): Grants paid, $80,225; assets, $1,237,092 (M); expenditures, $90,646; qualifying distributions, $80,475.
Limitations: Applications not accepted. Giving primarily in CT, FL, NY and VT.
Application information: Contributes only to pre-selected organizations.
Officers: Margot Hartman Tenney, Pres.; Kenneth S. Hilton, V.P.; Milton Mann, Secy.-Treas.
Director: Delbert Tenney.
EIN: 066044501
Codes: FD2

35826
Harry Levine Memorial Foundation
c/o Beldock Levine & Hoffman, LLP
99 Park Ave., Ste. 1600
New York, NY 10016

Established in 1966 in NY.
Donor(s): Lawrence S. Levine, Alan H. Levine, Nancy L. Rosen.
Financial data (yr. ended 12/31/99): Grants paid, $80,150; assets, $449,383 (M); gifts received, $11,349; expenditures, $82,177; qualifying distributions, $80,689.
Limitations: Applications not accepted. Giving primarily in NY.
Application information: Contributes only to pre-selected organizations.
Trustees: Alan H. Levine, Lawrence S. Levine, Nancy L. Rosen.

EIN: 136209282
Codes: FD2

35827
The Milton & Jena Berlinski Foundation
c/o Goldman Sachs & Co.
85 Broad St., Tax Dept.
New York, NY 10004

Established in 1997 in NY.
Donor(s): Milton Berlinski.
Financial data (yr. ended 05/31/02): Grants paid, $80,147; assets, $1,204,233 (M); gifts received, $397,825; expenditures, $93,600; qualifying distributions, $80,147.
Limitations: Applications not accepted.
Application information: Contributes only to pre-selected organizations.
Trustees: Jena Berliniski, Milton Berlinski, John McNulty.
EIN: 133992649

35828
The Peter and Carmen Lucia Buck Foundation
14 E. 90th St., Apt. 9A
New York, NY 10128-0711
Contact: Christopher Buck, Pres.

Established in 1999 in CT.
Financial data (yr. ended 06/30/01): Grants paid, $80,140; assets, $589,181 (M); expenditures, $112,840; qualifying distributions, $84,326.
Limitations: Applications not accepted. Giving primarily in CT and NY.
Application information: Unsolicited requests for funds not accepted.
Officers: Carmen Lucia Buck, Chair.; Christopher Buck, Pres. and Treas.; Michael Buck, Secy.
EIN: 061547852
Codes: FD2

35829
Robert & Patricia O'Hara III Foundation
c/o BCRS Assocs.
67 Wall St., 8th Fl.
New York, NY 10005

Established in 1989 in NJ.
Donor(s): Robert E. O'Hara III.
Financial data (yr. ended 03/31/01): Grants paid, $80,055; assets, $219,777 (M); expenditures, $82,416; qualifying distributions, $81,276.
Limitations: Applications not accepted. Giving primarily in CT, NJ and NY.
Application information: Contributes only to pre-selected organizations.
Trustees: Patricia F. O'Hara, Robert E. O'Hara III.
EIN: 133532023
Codes: FD2

35830
Yablon Foundation
c/o Scott Yablon
2 Fargo Ln.
Irvington, NY 10533-1202

Established in 1992 in NY.
Donor(s): Leonard H. Yablon.
Financial data (yr. ended 12/31/01): Grants paid, $80,050; assets, $1,929,383 (M); expenditures, $83,453; qualifying distributions, $80,194.
Limitations: Applications not accepted. Giving primarily in NY.
Application information: Contributes only to pre-selected organizations.
Directors: Bonnie M. Yablon, Leonard H. Yablon, Pamela F. Yablon, Patricia L. Yablon, Scott R. Yablon.
EIN: 133674038
Codes: FD2

35831
Charles P. Berolzheimer Foundation, Inc.
61 Broadway, 18th Fl.
New York, NY 10006-2794 (212) 797-9100
FAX: (212) 797-9161

Donor(s): California Cedar Products Co.
Financial data (yr. ended 06/30/01): Grants paid, $80,000; assets, $1,075,209 (M); expenditures, $93,999; qualifying distributions, $79,689.
Limitations: Applications not accepted. Giving on a national basis.
Application information: Contributes only to pre-selected organizations.
Officers: Philip C. Berolzheimer, V.P.; Michael L. Goldstein, V.P.; David R. Kay, Secy.-Treas.
EIN: 136066046
Codes: FD2

35832
The Coby Foundation, Ltd.
977 Ave. of the Americas, Ste. 810
New York, NY 10018 (212) 563-2282
FAX: (212) 563-5584
Contact: Rosemarie Garipoli, Exec. Dir.

Established in 1994.
Donor(s): Irene Zambelli Silverman.
Financial data (yr. ended 12/31/01): Grants paid, $80,000; assets, $8,000,000 (M); expenditures, $151,147; qualifying distributions, $80,000.
Limitations: Giving primarily in the Mid-Atlantic and northeastern U.S.
Application information: Applicants must use NY/NJ Area Common Application Form. Application form required.
Officers and Directors:* Leslie Shanken,* Chair.; Rosemarie Garipoli,* Exec. Dir.; Martha C. Howell, Lucille A. Roussin, James Shenton.
EIN: 133781874

35833
Friends of Or Baruch, Inc.
c/o Mitzi
1 E. 33rd St.
New York, NY 10016

Established in 1986 in NY.
Donor(s): The Benard Foundation, Jacob Hidery Foundation.
Financial data (yr. ended 12/31/99): Grants paid, $80,000; assets, $23,521 (L); gifts received, $35,700; expenditures, $80,145; qualifying distributions, $80,000.
Limitations: Applications not accepted. Giving primarily in Jerusalem, Israel.
Application information: Contributes only to pre-selected organizations.
Directors: Sol Betesh, Charles S. Maddard, Albert Shammam.
EIN: 133137300
Codes: FD2

35834
The Harry P. Kamen Family Foundation
c/o Morgan, Lewis & Bockius, LLP
101 Park Ave.
New York, NY 10178

Established in 1999 in NY.
Donor(s): Harry P. Kamen.
Financial data (yr. ended 12/31/01): Grants paid, $80,000; assets, $963,415 (M); gifts received, $30,000; expenditures, $101,118; qualifying distributions, $80,000.
Limitations: Applications not accepted.
Application information: Contributes only to pre-selected organizations.
Trustees: Barbara Kamen, Harry P. Kamen.
EIN: 137218993

35835
Dana and Jesse Lehman Foundation
c/o The Georgian Press, Inc.
175 Varick St.
New York, NY 10014

Established in 1999 in NY.
Financial data (yr. ended 02/28/01): Grants paid, $80,000; assets, $900,627 (M); expenditures, $81,364; qualifying distributions, $80,000.
Limitations: Applications not accepted.
Application information: Contributes only to pre-selected organizations.
Trustees: Dana Lehman, Jesse Lehman.
EIN: 137186931
Codes: FD2

35836
The Dunlevy Milbank Foundation, Inc.
c/o Sullivan & Cromwell
125 Broad St.
New York, NY 10004
Contact: Charles T. Dowling

Incorporated in 1941 in NY.
Donor(s): Dunlevy Milbank.‡
Financial data (yr. ended 12/31/01): Grants paid, $80,000; assets, $990,099 (M); gifts received, $17,843; expenditures, $90,579; qualifying distributions, $84,422.
Limitations: Giving primarily in New York, NY.
Application information: Application form not required.
Officers and Directors:* Barbara Foshay-Miller,* Pres.; Henry Christensen III,* V.P.; Donald R. Osborn,* Secy.-Treas.
EIN: 136096738
Codes: FD2

35837
The Irma Reich Foundation
650 Park Ave., Apt. 4C
New York, NY 10021-6115
Contact: Michael Reich, Tr.

Established in 1998 in NY.
Donor(s): Michael Reich.
Financial data (yr. ended 12/31/00): Grants paid, $80,000; assets, $42,852 (M); gifts received, $30,000; expenditures, $80,008; qualifying distributions, $79,984.
Limitations: Giving primarily in NY.
Trustees: Daniel Reich, David Reich, Elliot Reich, Michael Reich.
EIN: 134036669
Codes: FD2

35838
Nathanson-Abrams Family Foundation
860 United Nations Plz.
New York, NY 10017
E-mail: rna860@aol.com
Contact: Roberta Abrams, Pres.

Established in 1980 in NY.
Financial data (yr. ended 02/28/01): Grants paid, $79,983; assets, $1,151,801 (M); expenditures, $99,292; qualifying distributions, $80,558.
Limitations: Applications not accepted. Giving primarily in NY; some giving also in Israel.
Application information: Contributes only to pre-selected organizations.
Officers and Directors:* Roberta Abrams,* Pres; Noel Nathanson,* V.P. and Secy.; Susan Nathanson,* Treas.
EIN: 133030314
Codes: FD2

35839
The Aaron and Esther Fogel Foundation, Inc.
18 Lord Ave.
Lawrence, NY 11559

Established in 1998 in NY.
Donor(s): Aaron Fogel, Max Karfiol.
Financial data (yr. ended 07/31/00): Grants paid, $79,930; assets, $1,253,194 (M); gifts received, $500,391; expenditures, $93,224; qualifying distributions, $79,930.
Limitations: Giving primarily in Brooklyn, NY.
Directors: Aaron Fogel, Esther Fogel, Rebecca Fogel, Frady Kalter, Moshe Kalter.
EIN: 113459020
Codes: FD2

35840
The Christopher K. and E. Carter Norton Foundation
c/o Goldman Sachs & Co.
85 Broad St., Tax Dept.
New York, NY 10004

Established in 1996 in CT.
Donor(s): Christopher K. Norton.
Financial data (yr. ended 03/31/02): Grants paid, $79,838; assets, $79,012 (M); gifts received, $2,500; expenditures, $82,338; qualifying distributions, $79,838.
Limitations: Applications not accepted. Giving primarily in CT.
Application information: Contributes only to pre-selected organizations.
Trustees: Christopher K. Norton, E. Carter Norton.
EIN: 133918282
Codes: FD2

35841
The RMF Foundation, Inc.
c/o Richard Friedberg
452 Riverside Dr.
New York, NY 10027-6837

Established in 1994 in NY.
Donor(s): Richard M. Friedberg.
Financial data (yr. ended 06/30/01): Grants paid, $79,671; assets, $109,600 (M); gifts received, $100,000; expenditures, $96,587; qualifying distributions, $96,587.
Limitations: Applications not accepted. Giving on a national basis.
Application information: Contributes only to pre-selected organizations.
Directors: Barbara Friedberg, Richard M. Friedberg, Carol Walter.
EIN: 133797799

35842
Gregory & Raissa Shlomm Foundation
c/o Amicale Industries, Inc.
1375 Broadway
New York, NY 10018-7001

Established in 1959.
Financial data (yr. ended 04/30/00): Grants paid, $79,668; assets, $194,925 (M); gifts received, $1,000; expenditures, $80,208; qualifying distributions, $79,530.
Limitations: Applications not accepted. Giving primarily in New York, NY.
Application information: Contributes only to pre-selected organizations.
Officers: Boris Shlomm, Pres.; Alexander Shlomm, V.P.; Laura Shlomm, V.P.; Daniel Shlomm, Treas.
EIN: 136120939
Codes: FD2

35843
Ezra Jack Keats Foundation, Inc.
1005 E. 4th St.
Brooklyn, NY 11230
Application address for mini-grants: 450 14th St., Brooklyn, NY 11215
Contact: Deborah Pope, V.P.

Established in 1964.
Financial data (yr. ended 12/31/01): Grants paid, $79,662; assets, $1 (M); expenditures, $131,198; qualifying distributions, $79,662.
Limitations: Giving on a national basis.
Application information: Application form required.
Officers and Directors:* Martin Pope,* Pres.; Deborah Pope, V.P. and Exec. Dir.; Lillie Pope,* Secy.; Reynold Ruffins,* Treas.
EIN: 237072750
Codes: FD2

35844
Neena Rao Charitable Corporation
369 Guy Park Ave.
Amsterdam, NY 12010 (518) 843-4414
Contact: C.K.G. Rao, Pres.

Established in 1999 in NY.
Donor(s): C.K.G. Rao, Jyoti Rao.
Financial data (yr. ended 12/31/01): Grants paid, $79,614; assets, $640,753 (M); gifts received, $2,778; expenditures, $80,451; qualifying distributions, $79,614.
Limitations: Giving primarily in Montgomery, NY.
Officers: C.K.G. Rao, Pres.; Jyoti Rao, V.P.
EIN: 141816910
Codes: FD2

35845
Rosedorf Foundation
1139 57th St.
Brooklyn, NY 11219
Contact: David Weisz, Pres.

Established in 1999 in NY.
Donor(s): David Weisz.
Financial data (yr. ended 12/31/01): Grants paid, $79,610; assets, $474,033 (M); gifts received, $546,487; expenditures, $79,659; qualifying distributions, $79,610.
Officer: David Weisz, Pres.
EIN: 113523188
Codes: FD2

35846
B & L Foundation
c/o Goodkind
100 Park Ave., 12th Fl.
New York, NY 10017

Established in 1998 in NJ and NY.
Donor(s): David Cushing, Bonnie Cushing.
Financial data (yr. ended 12/31/01): Grants paid, $79,585; assets, $1,891,999 (M); expenditures, $90,877; qualifying distributions, $90,110.
Limitations: Giving primarily in NJ and NY.
Trustees: Bonnie Cushing, David Cushing.
EIN: 137172629
Codes: FD2

35847
Har Hazetim Foundation
c/o Again Trading Corp.
1239 Broadway, 12th Fl.
New York, NY 10001
Contact: Bonyammine Zeitouni, Tr.

Established in 1994 in NY.
Donor(s): Bonyammine Zeitouni.
Financial data (yr. ended 12/31/01): Grants paid, $79,400; assets, $134,405 (M); gifts received, $22,000; expenditures, $79,524; qualifying distributions, $79,400.
Limitations: Giving primarily in Brooklyn, NY.
Trustees: Bonyammine Zeitouni, David Zeitouni, Moussa Zeitouni.
EIN: 133800971

35848
The David Kozicki Memorial Foundation
c/o Gross
691 Dahill Rd.
Brooklyn, NY 11218

Established in 1995 in NY.
Donor(s): Zvi Kozicki.
Financial data (yr. ended 12/31/00): Grants paid, $79,357; assets, $923,984 (M); gifts received, $64,407; expenditures, $100,030; qualifying distributions, $84,831.
Limitations: Applications not accepted.
Application information: Contributes only to pre-selected organizations.
Directors: Judy Kuzicki, Zvi Kuzicki, Sarah Rosen.
EIN: 113208317
Codes: FD2

35849
Tradition Foundation
c/o Martin Vegh
121 Joseph Ave.
Staten Island, NY 10314

Financial data (yr. ended 12/31/01): Grants paid, $79,317; assets, $4,088,962 (M); gifts received, $1,503,572; expenditures, $79,317; qualifying distributions, $79,317.
Limitations: Applications not accepted.
Application information: Contributes only to pre-selected organizations.
Trustees: Martin Vegh, Susan Vegh.
EIN: 137112949
Codes: FD2

35850
The Friedman Family Foundation
500 7th Ave., 7th Fl.
New York, NY 10018 (212) 354-8550
Contact: Isidore Friedman, Pres.

Established in 1983 in NY.
Financial data (yr. ended 12/31/00): Grants paid, $79,300; assets, $1,317,923 (M); expenditures, $80,041; qualifying distributions, $79,300.
Limitations: Giving primarily in the greater metropolitan New York, NY, area, including Nassau County.
Application information: Application form not required.
Officers: Isidore Friedman, Pres.; Marilyn Friedman, V.P.; Mark L. Friedman, V.P.
Directors: Gary H. Friedman, Paul A. Friedman, Robin Friedman Klatt.
EIN: 133181247
Codes: FD2

35851
Pincus & Regina Peterseil Foundation, Inc.
335 Central Ave.
Lawrence, NY 11559
Application address: 711 Mulberry Pl., N. Woodmere, NY 11581, tel.: (516) 374-0356
Contact: Pincus Peterseil

Established in 1998.
Donor(s): Pincus Peterseil.
Financial data (yr. ended 07/31/01): Grants paid, $79,300; assets, $10,035 (M); gifts received, $47,000; expenditures, $79,854; qualifying distributions, $79,292.
Limitations: Giving primarily in NY.

Application information: Application form not required.
Trustees: Helene Berkowitz, Susan Nerenberg, Pincus Peterseil, Regina Peterseil.
EIN: 113411610
Codes: FD2

35852
N. & D. Rausman Foundation
20 Herschel Terr.
Monsey, NY 10952

Established in 1999 in NY.
Donor(s): Norman Rausman.
Financial data (yr. ended 11/30/00): Grants paid, $79,300; assets, $261,965 (M); gifts received, $78,750; expenditures, $95,423; qualifying distributions, $79,294.
Application information: Application form not required.
Trustee: Norman Rausman.
EIN: 134036959
Codes: FD2

35853
The Linton Foundation, Inc.
c/o Leslie/Linton Entertainment
1370 Ave. of the Americas
New York, NY 10019

Donor(s): Robert E. Linton, Margot T. Linton.
Financial data (yr. ended 12/31/01): Grants paid, $79,227; assets, $1,290,465 (M); gifts received, $207,831; expenditures, $89,506; qualifying distributions, $80,117.
Limitations: Applications not accepted. Giving primarily in NY.
Application information: Contributes only to pre-selected organizations.
Officers: Robert E. Linton, Pres.; Margot T. Linton, Treas.
EIN: 136077023
Codes: FD2

35854
The Brimstone Fund
c/o Brown Brothers Harriman Trust Co.
63 Wall St.
New York, NY 10005
Contact: Cristy West, Tr.

Established in 1995 in NY.
Donor(s): Barbara West,‡ Cristy West.
Financial data (yr. ended 12/31/01): Grants paid, $79,000; assets, $1,545,780 (M); gifts received, $4,735; expenditures, $92,409; qualifying distributions, $84,131.
Limitations: Applications not accepted. Giving primarily in Washington, DC, and ME; some support for national organizations.
Application information: Contributes only to pre-selected organizations. Unsolicited requests for funds not considered or acknowledged.
Trustees: Margaret P. Hanson, Cristy West.
EIN: 237811366
Codes: FD2

35855
Helfen Foundation, Inc.
100 Corporate Pkwy., Ste. 410
Amherst, NY 14226
Contact: Ellen E. Koessler, Pres.

Established in 2000 in NY.
Donor(s): Ellen E. Koessler.
Financial data (yr. ended 12/31/01): Grants paid, $79,000; assets, $232,717 (M); expenditures, $79,195; qualifying distributions, $79,000.
Limitations: Giving primarily in Buffalo, NY.
Officers and Directors:* Ellen E. Koessler,* Pres.; Joanne P. Lana,* Secy.; Paul C. Hilbert,* Treas.

35855—NEW YORK

EIN: 311708687

35856
Hooper Foundation
3243 S. Creek Rd.
Hamburg, NY 14075-6167
Contact: W. Stanley Hooper, Tr.

Donor(s): Lois A. Hooper, W. Stanley Hooper.
Financial data (yr. ended 09/30/01): Grants paid, $79,000; assets, $1,353,688 (M); expenditures, $80,017; qualifying distributions, $79,455.
Limitations: Giving primarily in MN and Buffalo, NY.
Trustees: Keith Hooper, Lois A. Hooper, W. Stanley Hooper, Linda Hooper Ward.
EIN: 237045144
Codes: FD2

35857
James & Chantal Sheridan Foundation
c/o Goldman Sachs & Co.
85 Broad St., Tax Dept.
New York, NY 10004

Established in 1996 in CT.
Donor(s): James M. Sheridan.
Financial data (yr. ended 02/28/01): Grants paid, $79,000; assets, $3,197,162 (M); gifts received, $1,103,329; expenditures, $113,025; qualifying distributions, $79,525.
Limitations: Applications not accepted. Giving primarily in New England and NY.
Application information: Contributes only to pre-selected organizations.
Trustees: Chantal Sheridan, James M. Sheridan, Robert E. Sheridan.
EIN: 133933347
Codes: FD2

35858
Max & Pearl Ann Marco Family Foundation, Inc.
c/o Mahoney Cohen & Co.
111 W. 40th St.
New York, NY 10018

Established in 1996 in FL.
Donor(s): Max Marco.
Financial data (yr. ended 12/31/00): Grants paid, $78,960; assets, $284,161 (M); expenditures, $79,517; qualifying distributions, $78,888.
Limitations: Applications not accepted.
Application information: Contributes only to pre-selected organizations.
Directors: David Marco, Max Marco, Pearl Ann Marco.
EIN: 650713646
Codes: FD2

35859
The Eshe Fund
P.O. Box 65, Madison Sq. Sta.
New York, NY 10159-0065
Contact: Henry H. Steiner, Secy.

Established in 1984 in NY.
Donor(s): Etta K. Steiner.
Financial data (yr. ended 12/31/01): Grants paid, $78,836; assets, $1,677,803 (M); gifts received, $52,100; expenditures, $82,893; qualifying distributions, $80,337.
Limitations: Giving primarily in New Haven, CT, Boston, MA and MO.
Officers and Directors:* Etta K. Steiner,* Pres.; Sarah K. Steiner,* V.P.; Henry H. Steiner,* Secy.; Elizabeth K. Steiner,* Treas.
EIN: 133247309
Codes: FD2, GTI

35860
Helen and Carlton M. Fishel Foundation, Inc.
c/o Penelope F. McDermott
76 Island Dr.
Rye, NY 10580-4306

Established in 1997 in NY.
Financial data (yr. ended 12/31/01): Grants paid, $78,800; assets, $307,714 (M); gifts received, $164,000; expenditures, $83,659; qualifying distributions, $78,800.
Limitations: Applications not accepted.
Application information: Contributes only to pre-selected organizations.
Directors: Kathleen F. McCullough, Kristen D. McCullough, Penelope F. McDermott, Douglas J. McDermott.
EIN: 133975322
Codes: FD2

35861
The Drummond C. & Ruth A. Bell Foundation
c/o The Bank of New York
1 Wall St., Tax Dept., 28th Fl.
New York, NY 10286

Established in 1996 in CT.
Donor(s): Drummond C. Bell III, Ruth A. Bell.
Financial data (yr. ended 11/30/01): Grants paid, $78,700; assets, $1,210,786 (M); gifts received, $164,188; expenditures, $82,916; qualifying distributions, $79,325.
Limitations: Applications not accepted. Giving primarily in CT.
Application information: Contributes only to pre-selected organizations.
Trustees: Drummond C. Bell III, Ruth A. Bell.
EIN: 061458477
Codes: FD2

35862
Sussman Family Foundation
c/o American Express Tax & Business Service
1185 Ave. of the Americas, 6th Fl.
New York, NY 10036
Application address: 7 Thomas Jefferson Dr., Warren, NJ 07059
Contact: Bernard M. Sussman, Tr.

Established in 1991 in NJ.
Donor(s): Bernard M. Sussman.
Financial data (yr. ended 05/31/01): Grants paid, $78,650; assets, $138,596 (M); gifts received, $47,194; expenditures, $90,091; qualifying distributions, $78,650.
Limitations: Giving primarily in New York, NY.
Trustees: Bernard M. Sussman, Phyllis Sussman.
EIN: 133634386

35863
Jay and Joyce Weitzman Foundation, Inc.
816 Ave. I
Brooklyn, NY 11230 (718) 963-2200
Contact: Jay Weitzman, Pres. or Joyce Weitzman, V.P.

Established in 1998 in NY.
Donor(s): Jay Weitzman.
Financial data (yr. ended 11/30/99): Grants paid, $78,649; assets, $1,007 (M); gifts received, $75,000; expenditures, $80,843; qualifying distributions, $78,640.
Officers: Jay Weitzman, Pres.; Joyce Weitzman, V.P.
EIN: 113411787
Codes: FD2

35864
Olin Family Foundation, Inc.
105 Firestone Cir., North Hills
Roslyn, NY 11576

Established in 1998 in NY.
Financial data (yr. ended 12/31/01): Grants paid, $78,570; assets, $1,697,165 (M); expenditures, $81,530; qualifying distributions, $77,950.
Officers and Directors:* Susanne C. Olin,* Pres.; Gerald D. Olin,* Secy.; Laura Odell, Daniel R. Olin.
EIN: 113332090
Codes: FD2

35865
Cortland Savings Foundation
1 N. Main St.
P.O. Box 5628
Cortland, NY 13045 (607) 756-5643

Established in 1998 in NY.
Financial data (yr. ended 12/31/01): Grants paid, $78,500; assets, $1,759,486 (M); expenditures, $92,023; qualifying distributions, $77,933.
Limitations: Giving primarily in Cortland, NY.
Officers: Wesley D. Stisser, Pres.; Thomas E. Gallagher, V.P.; Sandy Samson, Secy.; F. Michael Stapleton, Treas.
Director: Harvey Kaufman.
EIN: 161561037
Codes: FD2

35866
Sam Pomeranz Trust
c/o Sheldon G. Kall
3522 James St., Ste. 101
Syracuse, NY 13206
Application address: c/o Abraham Shankman, 551 Salt Springs Rd., Syracuse, NY 13224

Established in 2001.
Financial data (yr. ended 12/31/01): Grants paid, $78,500; assets, $7,281,181 (M); expenditures, $78,500; qualifying distributions, $78,500.
Limitations: Giving primarily in NY.
Trustees: Sheldon G. Kall, Abraham Shankman.
EIN: 166514459

35867
Catton Brothers Foundation, Inc.
112 W. 34th St.
New York, NY 10120 (212) 695-6343
Contact: Sam Catton, Pres.

Established in 1969 in NY.
Donor(s): Edward Catton,‡ Harry Catton, Catton Bros. Corp., Frieda Catton.
Financial data (yr. ended 12/31/00): Grants paid, $78,486; assets, $37,711 (M); gifts received, $69,400; expenditures, $80,357; qualifying distributions, $79,535.
Limitations: Giving primarily in the metropolitan New York, NY, area.
Officers: Sam Catton, Pres.; Rae Catton, V.P.; Edward Catton, Secy.; Harry Catton, Treas.
EIN: 237112579
Codes: FD2

35868
Leiden University Fund (U.S.A.), Inc.
c/o Deforest & Duer
90 Broad St., 18th Fl.
New York, NY 10004

Established in 1998 in NY.
Financial data (yr. ended 12/31/00): Grants paid, $78,431; assets, $2,818 (M); gifts received, $26,509; expenditures, $79,822; qualifying distributions, $78,427.

Officers and Directors:* Hendrik Laverge,* Pres. and Treas.; Isaac E. Druker,* V.P.; A.M. Irvin-Helb.
EIN: 133974605
Codes: FD2

35869
Buffalo Sabres Alumni Association
724 Ransom Rd.
Grand Island, NY 14072
Contact: Larry Playfair, Pres.

Established in 1989 in NY.
Financial data (yr. ended 12/31/01): Grants paid, $78,400; assets, $113,104 (M); expenditures, $154,746; qualifying distributions, $78,365.
Limitations: Giving limited to western NY.
Officers and Directors:* Fred Stanfield,* Chair.; Larry Playfair,* Pres.; Danny Gare,* V.P.; Derek Smith,* V.P.; Gregory T. Ivancic,* Secy.; Bob Engel.
EIN: 161356116
Codes: FD2

35870
Steven A. Klar Foundation
2580 Hempstead Tpke.
East Meadow, NY 11554
Contact: Steven A. Klar, Pres.

Established in 1994 in NY.
Donor(s): Steven A. Klar.
Financial data (yr. ended 06/30/01): Grants paid, $78,379; assets, $120,643 (M); gifts received, $135,000; expenditures, $79,429; qualifying distributions, $78,379.
Limitations: Giving primarily in NY.
Officers: Steven A. Klar, Pres.; Marvin F. Milich, Secy.
EIN: 113241722
Codes: FD2

35871
The Miriam & Harold Steinberg Foundation, Inc.
c/o Steinberg Priest Capital MgmtL.
12 E. 49th St., Ste. 1202
New York, NY 10017-1028

Established in 1960 in NY.
Financial data (yr. ended 06/30/01): Grants paid, $78,350; assets, $1,957,843 (M); expenditures, $101,684; qualifying distributions, $79,980.
Limitations: Applications not accepted. Giving primarily in the San Francisco Bay Area, CA, and New York, NY.
Application information: Contributes only to pre-selected organizations.
Officers: Michael A. Steinberg, Pres.; Carole A. Krumland, V.P. and Secy.; James D. Steinberg, V.P. and Treas.
EIN: 136126000
Codes: FD2

35872
William B. & Jane E. Bram Foundation
970 Park Ave.
New York, NY 10028-0324

Donor(s): Jane E. Bram, William B. Bram.
Financial data (yr. ended 12/31/00): Grants paid, $78,284; assets, $307,124 (M); gifts received, $105,257; expenditures, $80,509; qualifying distributions, $78,317.
Limitations: Applications not accepted. Giving primarily in New York, NY.
Application information: Contributes only to pre-selected organizations.
Officers and Trustees:* William B. Bram,* Pres.; Jane E. Bram,* V.P.
EIN: 136077391
Codes: FD2

35873
Gerald K. & Virginia Hornung Family Foundation, Inc.
c/o Lipsky, Goodkin & Co.
120 W. 45th St., 7th Fl.
New York, NY 10036

Established in 1969 in NY.
Donor(s): Gerald K. Hornung II, Virginia Ann Hornung.
Financial data (yr. ended 11/30/01): Grants paid, $78,270; assets, $1,889,152 (M); expenditures, $107,002; qualifying distributions, $80,100.
Limitations: Applications not accepted. Giving primarily in VT.
Application information: Contributes only to pre-selected organizations.
Officers and Directors:* Gerald K. Hornung II,* Pres.; Virginia Ann Hornung,* V.P. and Treas.; Milton Hosack, Secy.; Dana Elizabeth Hornung, Gerald Kenneth Hornung III, Kimberly Hornung Marcy, Theodore Wendel Marcy, Leslie Hornung Wallstrom, Timothy Clarke Wallstrom.
EIN: 237057216
Codes: FD2

35874
Daughters of the Cincinnati
c/o Goldstein & Morris
36 W. 44th St., Ste. 1010
New York, NY 10036
Application address: 122 E. 58th St., New York, NY 10022, tel.: (212) 319-6915; URL: http://fdncenter.org/grantmaker/cincinnati
Contact: Scholarship Admin.

Established in 1894.
Financial data (yr. ended 12/31/01): Grants paid, $78,200; assets, $2,383,242 (M); gifts received, $44,343; expenditures, $198,947; qualifying distributions, $109,878.
Limitations: Giving on a national basis.
Publications: Annual report.
Application information: Application form required.
Officers: Lynn S. Manager, Pres.; Mrs. John G. Walthausen, V.P.; Gabrielle Bielnstein, Secy.; Mrs. Robert G. Shaw, Treas.
EIN: 136096069
Codes: GTI

35875
Idalia Whitcomb Charitable Trust
c/o JPMorgan Private Bank, Global Foundations Group
1211 Ave. of the Americas, 38th Fl.
New York, NY 10036 (212) 789-5715
Contact: Lisa Philp, V.P.

Established in 1989 in NY.
Financial data (yr. ended 06/30/01): Grants paid, $78,155; assets, $2,171,323 (M); expenditures, $128,919; qualifying distributions, $98,386.
Limitations: Applications not accepted. Giving primarily in Warren, RI.
Application information: Contributes only to pre-selected organizations.
Trustees: Thomas E. Wright, JPMorgan Chase Bank.
EIN: 136912627
Codes: FD2

35876
Hinerfeld Trust
c/o Norman Hinerfeld
11 Oak Ln.
Larchmont, NY 10538-3917

Donor(s): Norman Hinerfeld.
Financial data (yr. ended 12/31/01): Grants paid, $78,090; assets, $442,757 (M); gifts received, $4,038; expenditures, $95,737; qualifying distributions, $77,344.
Limitations: Applications not accepted. Giving primarily in New York, NY.
Application information: Contributes only to pre-selected organizations.
Trustees: Norman Hinerfeld, Ruth Hinerfeld.
EIN: 136286972
Codes: FD2

35877
Sol and Lillian Ash Foundation, Inc.
420 Lexington Ave., Ste. 2150
New York, NY 10170 (212) 687-6776
Contact: Robert Siegel, Pres.

Established in 1959.
Financial data (yr. ended 12/31/01): Grants paid, $78,000; assets, $1,490,362 (M); expenditures, $96,790; qualifying distributions, $77,781.
Limitations: Giving primarily in the greater New York, NY, area.
Officers: Robert Siegel, Pres.; Edward Yelon, Treas.
EIN: 136159050
Codes: FD2

35878
The Beau Bogan Foundation
c/o U.S. Trust
P.O. Box 2004
New York, NY 10109-1910

Established in 1989 in FL.
Donor(s): Harney S. Bogan, Jr.
Financial data (yr. ended 12/31/01): Grants paid, $78,000; assets, $185,337 (M); gifts received, $1,575; expenditures, $83,810; qualifying distributions, $79,917.
Limitations: Applications not accepted. Giving primarily in the Palm Beach, FL, area, and New York, NY.
Application information: Contributes only to pre-selected organizations.
Trustee: U.S. Trust.
EIN: 650126326
Codes: FD2

35879
The Marshall Fund
c/o U.S. Trust
114 W. 47th St.
New York, NY 10036
Application address: P.O. Box 881, Kingston, NH 03848-0881

Established in 1993 in NH.
Donor(s): Robert L.V. French, Shirley S. French.
Financial data (yr. ended 12/31/99): Grants paid, $78,000; assets, $2,087,334 (M); expenditures, $95,197; qualifying distributions, $79,120.
Limitations: Giving primarily in the New England area.
Application information: Application form required.
Trustees: Pamela F. Evarts, Jameson S. French, Robert L.V. French, Shirley S. French, Steven B. French.
EIN: 020467589
Codes: FD2

35880
The Bill Bernbach Foundation
c/o Reminick Aarons & Co., LLP
685 3rd Ave.
New York, NY 10017

Established in 1969.
Donor(s): Evelyn Bernbach.‡
Financial data (yr. ended 12/31/00): Grants paid, $77,986; assets, $1,453,646 (M); expenditures, $86,357; qualifying distributions, $77,986.

Limitations: Applications not accepted. Giving primarily in NY.
Application information: Contributes only to pre-selected organizations.
Officer: Paul Bernbach, Pres.
Director: John Bernbach.
EIN: 237060333
Codes: FD2

35881
The John and Jayne Summers Foundation, Inc.
195 St. Paul St.
Rochester, NY 14604

Established in 2000 in NY.
Donor(s): John M. Summers, Jayne C. Summers.
Financial data (yr. ended 12/31/01): Grants paid, $77,875; assets, $277,253 (M); gifts received, $176,000; expenditures, $82,478; qualifying distributions, $81,425.
Limitations: Applications not accepted. Giving primarily in Rochester, NY.
Application information: Contributes only to pre-selected organizations.
Officers: Douglas J. Summers, Pres.; Kenneth A. Marvald, V.P. and Secy.; John M. Summers, Treas.
Directors: Susan Schmid, Jayne C. Summers.
EIN: 161596923
Codes: FD2

35882
Physicians Relief Fund
c/o Virginia Kanick, M.D.
560 Riverside Dr., 17B
New York, NY 10027
Application address: 3330 N. Leisure World Blvd., No. 1025, Silver Spring, MD 20906, tel.: (301) 598-9488
Contact: Ruth G. Altman, Exec. Dir.

Established in 1929 in NY; incorporated in 1974.
Financial data (yr. ended 12/31/00): Grants paid, $77,850; assets, $1,920,096 (M); gifts received, $4,850; expenditures, $125,052; qualifying distributions, $96,227.
Limitations: Giving primarily in New York, NY.
Application information: Application form required.
Officers and Directors:* Virginia Kanick, M.D.,* Pres.; Leslie Baer, Treas.; Ruth G. Altman, Exec. Dir.
EIN: 237426275
Codes: FD2, GTI

35883
Inisfad Foundation, Inc.
c/o U.S. Trust
114 W. 47th St.
New York, NY 10036
Application address: 12 Hunt St., Rowayton, CT 06853
Contact: Lawrence D. Cavanaugh, Jr., Dir.

Established in 1925 in NY.
Financial data (yr. ended 12/31/00): Grants paid, $77,825; assets, $1,415,849 (M); expenditures, $102,499; qualifying distributions, $88,812.
Limitations: Giving primarily in CT and NY.
Directors: Jan Cavanaugh, Lawrence D. Cavanaugh, Jr., Eleanor Reimer.
EIN: 136157475
Codes: FD2

35884
Helen Frankenthaler Foundation, Inc.
c/o Hecht & Co., PC
111 W. 40th St., 20th Fl.
New York, NY 10018-2588

Donor(s): Helen Frankenthaler.
Financial data (yr. ended 12/31/01): Grants paid, $77,700; assets, $1,208,684 (M); gifts received, $181,440; expenditures, $87,361; qualifying distributions, $77,700.
Limitations: Applications not accepted. Giving primarily in New York, NY.
Application information: Contributes only to pre-selected organizations.
Officers and Director:* Helen Frankenthaler,* Pres.; Maureen St. Onge, V.P. and Secy.; Michael Hecht, Treas.
EIN: 133244308
Codes: FD2

35885
Tarky Lombardi Foundation, Inc.
555 E. Genesee St.
Syracuse, NY 13210 (315) 442-0100
Contact: Tarky Lombardi, Jr., Pres.

Donor(s): Tarky Lombardi, Jr.
Financial data (yr. ended 12/31/01): Grants paid, $77,586; assets, $1,277,547 (M); gifts received, $5,000; expenditures, $79,528; qualifying distributions, $77,586.
Limitations: Giving primarily in Syracuse, NY.
Officers and Directors:* Tarky Lombardi, Jr.,* Pres.; Francis T. Lombardi,* V.P. and Treas.
EIN: 160966705

35886
The Alex & Ruth Fruchthandler Foundation, Inc.
111 Broadway, 20th Fl.
New York, NY 10006

Established in 1945.
Donor(s): Olympia & York Financial Co., Fruchthandler Bros. Enterprises.
Financial data (yr. ended 12/31/00): Grants paid, $77,554; assets, $7,311,542 (M); gifts received, $2,868,000; expenditures, $78,045; qualifying distributions, $77,554.
Limitations: Applications not accepted. Giving on a national basis.
Application information: Contributes only to pre-selected organizations.
Officers: Abraham Fruchthandler, Pres.; Zachary Fruchthandler, Secy.-Treas.
EIN: 136156031
Codes: FD2

35887
The Cheryl and Edward S. Gordon Foundation
c/o Cheryl Gordon
1301 Ave. of the Americas
New York, NY 10019-6022

Established in 1999 in NY.
Donor(s): Cheryl Gordon.
Financial data (yr. ended 09/30/01): Grants paid, $77,550; assets, $1,853,918 (M); gifts received, $1,388,010; expenditures, $94,129; qualifying distributions, $85,682.
Limitations: Applications not accepted. Giving primarily in NY.
Application information: Contributes only to pre-selected organizations.
Trustees: Cheryl Gordon, Anthony M. Saytanides.
EIN: 134082835
Codes: FD2

35888
The Carol & Arnold Wolowitz Foundation, Inc.
888 Veterans Memorial Hwy., Ste. 520
Hauppauge, NY 11788

Established in 1998 in NY.
Donor(s): William Hirschfeld, Arnold Wolowitz.
Financial data (yr. ended 12/31/01): Grants paid, $77,540; assets, $1,131,084 (M); gifts received, $40,000; expenditures, $109,523; qualifying distributions, $77,540.
Limitations: Applications not accepted. Giving primarily in NY.
Application information: Contributes only to pre-selected organizations.
Officers: Arnold Wolowitz, Pres.; Carol Wolowitz, V.P.; Kathleen Meade, Secy.
EIN: 237201382
Codes: FD2

35889
Columbian Foundation, Inc.
110 Genesee St., Ste. 300
Auburn, NY 13021-3655 (315) 253-0326
FAX: (315) 253-4968; *E-mail:* jpmclane@boylefirm.com
Contact: John P. McLane, Pres.

Established in 1957 in NY.
Financial data (yr. ended 12/31/01): Grants paid, $77,507; assets, $1,567,900 (M); gifts received, $4,260; expenditures, $86,503; qualifying distributions, $81,504.
Limitations: Giving limited to Cayuga and Onondaga counties, NY.
Application information: Application form required.
Officers and Directors:* Peter Flint Metcalf,* Pres.; Charles R. Adams,* V.P.; Charles W. Loomis,* V.P.; Karen E. Spinelli,* Secy.; John P. McLane,* Treas.
EIN: 156017838
Codes: FD2

35890
The Ames Family Fund, Inc.
c/o Lazard Freres & Co.
30 Rockefeller Plz.
New York, NY 10020-1902
Contact: George J. Ames, Pres.

Established in 1981 in NY.
Donor(s): George J. Ames.
Financial data (yr. ended 09/30/01): Grants paid, $77,500; assets, $26,957 (M); gifts received, $75,000; expenditures, $78,642; qualifying distributions, $77,605.
Limitations: Giving primarily in NY; some giving also in CO, CT, and MA.
Officers and Directors:* George J. Ames,* Pres.; Ruth A. Solie,* V.P.; Joan A. Berkowitz,* Secy.; Margery E. Ames,* Treas.; Bess R. Ames, Dorothy A. Cummings, John A. Solie.
EIN: 133064660
Codes: FD2

35891
Judith S. Randal Foundation
c/o Deutsche Trust Co. of NY
P.O. Box 1297, Church St. Sta.
New York, NY 10008
Application address: c/o Judith S. Randal, 1080 5th Ave., New York, NY 10128

Established in 1986 in NY.
Donor(s): Judith S. Randal.
Financial data (yr. ended 11/30/01): Grants paid, $77,500; assets, $1,522,806 (M); expenditures, $101,801; qualifying distributions, $87,206.
Limitations: Giving primarily in New York, NY.
Application information: Application form not required.
Trustee: Deutsche Bank.
EIN: 136881560
Codes: FD2

NEW YORK—35903

35892
The Frankel Family Foundation, Inc.
c/o Stuart Frankel & Co., Inc.
55 Water St.
New York, NY 10041

Established in 1998 in NY.
Donor(s): Stuart Frankel.
Financial data (yr. ended 09/30/01): Grants paid, $77,400; assets, $10,030 (M); gifts received, $86,000; expenditures, $77,625; qualifying distributions, $77,400.
Limitations: Applications not accepted. Giving primarily in New York, NY.
Application information: Contributes only to pre-selected organizations.
Officers and Directors:* Stuart Frankel,* Pres. and Treas.; Andrew Frankel,* V.P.; Jeffrey Frankel,* Secy.
EIN: 134026241
Codes: FD2

35893
The Rose Shield Fund
666 3rd Ave., 29th Fl.
New York, NY 10017-4011

Established in 1982 in NY.
Donor(s): Alice R. Sigelman.
Financial data (yr. ended 04/30/01): Grants paid, $77,250; assets, $1,706,996 (M); expenditures, $98,733; qualifying distributions, $77,415.
Limitations: Applications not accepted. Giving primarily in New York, NY.
Application information: Contributes only to pre-selected organizations.
Officers: Alice R. Sigelman, Chair.; Jesse L. Sigelman, Pres.; David P. Steinmann, Secy.-Treas.
EIN: 133174406
Codes: FD2

35894
Slocum-Dickson Foundation, Inc.
1729 Burrstone Rd.
New Hartford, NY 13413

Established in 1955 in NY.
Financial data (yr. ended 12/31/01): Grants paid, $77,237; assets, $1,474,977 (M); gifts received, $745; expenditures, $95,381; qualifying distributions, $77,237.
Limitations: Giving primarily in Utica, NY.
Officers: Frank Dubeck, Pres.; Joan W. Compson, V.P.; Pi Gentile, Secy.; David Armstrong, Treas.
Directors: John H. Story, and 10 additional directors.
EIN: 156018016

35895
Harweb Foundation
c/o Henry U. Harris, Jr., Smith Barney & Co.
388 Greenwich St.
New York, NY 10013 (212) 808-7843

Donor(s): Henry U. Harris,‡ Mary W. Harris.‡
Financial data (yr. ended 12/31/00): Grants paid, $77,200; assets, $976,112 (M); expenditures, $81,827; qualifying distributions, $77,650.
Limitations: Applications not accepted. Giving primarily in NY.
Application information: Contributes only to pre-selected organizations.
Officer: Loretta Cronin, Treas.
Trustees: David W. Harris, Henry U. Harris, Jr., Joan H. Hawkey.
EIN: 136161742
Codes: FD2

35896
Bedik/Muran Foundation, Inc.
(Formerly Van & Lilyan Muran Foundation, Inc.)
200 Armstrong Rd.
Garden City Park, NY 11040
Contact: Lilyan Muran, V.P.

Established in 1994 in NY.
Donor(s): Mary Bedik, Van Muran.
Financial data (yr. ended 09/30/01): Grants paid, $77,150; assets, $1,473,740 (M); gifts received, $200,000; expenditures, $120,499; qualifying distributions, $102,236.
Limitations: Giving primarily in NY.
Officers: Van Muran, Pres.; Lilyan Muran, V.P. and Treas.; William Muran, Secy.
EIN: 113241924
Codes: FD2

35897
Clive J. Davis Foundation
c/o Executive Monetary Mgmt.
919 3rd Ave., 11th Fl.
New York, NY 10022

Established in 1995 in NY.
Donor(s): Clive J. Davis.
Financial data (yr. ended 12/31/99): Grants paid, $77,150; assets, $2,226,945 (M); gifts received, $1,150; expenditures, $106,877; qualifying distributions, $77,150.
Limitations: Applications not accepted. Giving primarily in IL.
Application information: Contributes only to pre-selected organizations.
Trustee: Clive J. Davis.
EIN: 137079336
Codes: FD2

35898
Victoria Loconsolo Foundation, Inc.
c/o Pauline Rosenberg
2660 Coney Island Ave.
Brooklyn, NY 11223

Established in 1981 in NY.
Financial data (yr. ended 12/31/01): Grants paid, $77,080; assets, $1,798,527 (M); gifts received, $77,270; expenditures, $88,772; qualifying distributions, $76,568.
Limitations: Applications not accepted. Giving primarily in New York, NY.
Officers: John A. Loconsolo, Chair.; Regina Dedick, Pres.
Directors: Maria Caccese, Antoinette Chiaro, Janet D'Aurio, Elizabeth Loconsolo, Jacqueline Loconsolo, Rose Marie Rizzo.
EIN: 112577394

35899
Kanter-Plaut Foundation, Inc.
c/o Herbert C. Kantor
51 E. 42nd St.
New York, NY 10017 (212) 682-8383

Established in 1956 in NY.
Donor(s): Harry Kanter.‡
Financial data (yr. ended 12/31/01): Grants paid, $77,050; assets, $1,543,887 (M); expenditures, $108,486; qualifying distributions, $97,739.
Limitations: Applications not accepted. Giving primarily in New York, NY.
Application information: Contributes only to pre-selected organizations.
Directors: Peter Bullough, Lillian Guide, Gerry Kallman, John Kallman, Michael Kanter, Herbert Kantor, Marshall Kreisler, Regina Maes, John Mazzarella, David Noakes, Debbie Pollack, Laura Stewart.
EIN: 136206770
Codes: FD2

35900
Jean & Albert Nerken Foundation
c/o Yohalem Gillman & Co., LLP
477 Madison Ave.
New York, NY 10022-5802
Contact: Jean Nerken, Tr.

Established in 1988 in NY.
Donor(s): Albert Nerken,‡ Jean Nerken.
Financial data (yr. ended 10/31/01): Grants paid, $77,025; assets, $3,685,545 (M); expenditures, $109,553; qualifying distributions, $94,155.
Limitations: Applications not accepted. Giving primarily in New York, NY.
Application information: Contributes only to pre-selected organizations.
Trustees: Etta Brandman, Jean Nerken, Ruth Nerken.
EIN: 133499349
Codes: FD2

35901
American Friends of Maccabee Institute Foundation
61 Broadway, 18th Fl.
New York, NY 10006-2794

Established in 1992 in DE and NY.
Donor(s): Charles Cohen, Fred Leibowitz, Martha Leibowitz, Tony Montalbano, Heather Montalbano, Barry Septimus, Ronald Stern, Beth Stern, Beit Midrash Jerusalem Foundation, Grand Street Boys Foundation, Herman Goldman Foundation.
Financial data (yr. ended 12/31/00): Grants paid, $77,000; assets, $34,859 (M); gifts received, $98,616; expenditures, $79,668; qualifying distributions, $79,668.
Limitations: Applications not accepted. Giving primarily in Jerusalem, Israel.
Application information: Contributes only to pre-selected organizations.
Officers: Maye L. Feld, Pres.; David Feld, V.P.; Abraham Peter, M.D., V.P.; Nina Dagan, Treas.
Directors: Rabbi Avraham Cantor, Larry Dominich.
EIN: 133673810

35902
The Brown Brothers Harriman & Company Undergraduate Fund
c/o Brown Brothers Harriman & Co., Human Resources Dept.
59 Wall St.
New York, NY 10005-2818
FAX: (212) 493-7287

Established in 1964.
Donor(s): Brown Brothers Harriman & Co.
Financial data (yr. ended 07/31/01): Grants paid, $77,000; assets, $1,060,823 (M); expenditures, $88,218; qualifying distributions, $86,191.
Limitations: Applications not accepted. Giving limited to areas of company operations.
Application information: Applicants must be children of employees. Unsolicited requests for funds not accepted.
Officers and Trustees:* Landon Hilliard III,* Chair.; Susan C. Livingston, Michael W. McConnell, Jeffrey A. Schoenfeld, W. Carter Sullivan III.
EIN: 136169140
Codes: CS, FD2, CD, GTI

35903
DBL Foundation, Inc.
P.O. Box 944
Glens Falls, NY 12801-0944

Established in 1993 in NY.
Donor(s): Joan B. Lapham.

35903—NEW YORK

Financial data (yr. ended 12/31/01): Grants paid, $77,000; assets, $2,792,774 (M); gifts received, $2,035,632; expenditures, $77,447; qualifying distributions, $77,000.
Limitations: Applications not accepted. Giving primarily in NY.
Application information: Contributes only to pre-selected organizations.
Officers: John D. Lapham, Pres.; Michael R. Lapham, V.P.; Thomas Lapham, Secy.; Joan B. Lapham, Treas.
EIN: 141756361

35904
Robert & Margaret Gartland Family Foundation
c/o U.S. Trust Co. of NY
114 W. 47th St.
New York, NY 10036

Established in 1999 in NY.
Donor(s): Robert F. Gartland.
Financial data (yr. ended 12/31/01): Grants paid, $77,000; assets, $1,476,904 (M); gifts received, $250; expenditures, $102,463; qualifying distributions, $75,936.
Limitations: Applications not accepted. Giving primarily in NY.
Application information: Contributes only to pre-selected organizations.
Officers: Robert F. Gartland, Pres.; Monica Gartland, V.P.; Margaret Gartland, Secy.-Treas.
EIN: 134092491
Codes: FD2

35905
The Kenneth Kolker Foundation, Inc.
c/o KRT Business Mgmt., Inc.
500 5th Ave.
New York, NY 10110

Established in 1999 in NY.
Donor(s): Kenneth Kolker.
Financial data (yr. ended 12/31/01): Grants paid, $77,000; assets, $1,344,345 (M); expenditures, $97,066; qualifying distributions, $77,000.
Officers: Kenneth Kolker, Pres.; Donna Seeherman, V.P.; Barry Klarberg, Treas.
EIN: 134071790

35906
The Anna D. Mahan Foundation
800 Mony Tower I
Syracuse, NY 13202-2721 (315) 474-6448
Application address: 499 S. Warren St., 8th Fl., Syracuse, NY 13202
Contact: John J. Costello, Secy.

Established in 1984 in NY.
Financial data (yr. ended 06/30/01): Grants paid, $77,000; assets, $1,329,601 (M); expenditures, $88,191; qualifying distributions, $76,295.
Limitations: Giving limited to central NY.
Publications: Informational brochure (including application guidelines).
Application information: Application form not required.
Officers: Charlotte G. Holstein, Chair.; John J. Costello, Secy.
Director: Msgr. Charles J. Fahey.
EIN: 222695315
Codes: FD2

35907
The O'Neal Foundation, Inc.
c/o Merrill Lynch Fog
2 World Financial Ctr., 38th Fl.
New York, NY 10281

Established in 2000 in NY.
Donor(s): Nancy A. Garvey, E. Stanley O'Neal.

Financial data (yr. ended 09/30/01): Grants paid, $77,000; assets, $945,341 (M); expenditures, $95,447; qualifying distributions, $77,000.
Limitations: Applications not accepted.
Application information: Contributes only to pre-selected organizations.
Officers: E. Stanley O'Neal, Pres.; John D. Dadakis, Secy.; Nancy A. Garvey, Treas.
EIN: 134122557

35908
K. & M. Demay Charitable Foundation
c/o Karl Demay & Mildred Demay
114 Linden Ave.
Newark, NY 14513-1931 (716) 238-3300

Established in 1998 in NY.
Donor(s): Karl Demay, Mildred Demay.
Financial data (yr. ended 12/31/00): Grants paid, $76,827; assets, $595,544 (M); gifts received, $11,077; expenditures, $80,584; qualifying distributions, $76,827.
Limitations: Giving primarily in NY.
Officer and Trustees:* Karl Demay,* Chair.; Mildred Demay.
EIN: 161560448
Codes: FD2

35909
Heshy & Chaya Gross Special Account Foundation
c/o Harry and Harriette Gross
6 Bartlett Rd.
Monsey, NY 10952

Established in 1994 in NY.
Donor(s): Harriette Gross, Harry Gross.
Financial data (yr. ended 12/31/00): Grants paid, $76,780; assets, $56,979 (M); gifts received, $91,600; expenditures, $76,961; qualifying distributions, $76,780.
Limitations: Applications not accepted. Giving primarily in Brooklyn, NY.
Application information: Contributes only to pre-selected organizations.
Trustees: Harriette Gross, Harry Gross.
EIN: 137039705
Codes: FD2

35910
Swede Anderson Foundation Trust
c/o Leonard A. Anderson and Peter R. Travers, Jr.
905 Harlem Rd.
West Seneca, NY 14224-1066

Established in 1972 in NY.
Financial data (yr. ended 12/31/99): Grants paid, $76,691; assets, $2,254,326 (M); expenditures, $97,864; qualifying distributions, $86,902.
Limitations: Applications not accepted. Giving primarily in NY, with some emphasis on Buffalo.
Application information: Contributes only to pre-selected organizations.
Trustees: Elise E. Travers, Jeffrey P. Travers, Judith E. Travers, Mark J. Travers, Peter R. Travers, Jr.
EIN: 166208191
Codes: FD2

35911
The Jedra Charitable Foundation, Inc.
110-11 Queens Blvd., Apt. 20B
Forest Hills, NY 11375 (718) 263-4956
Contact: David Shechet, Pres.

Established in 1964 in NY.
Donor(s): David Shechet.
Financial data (yr. ended 06/30/01): Grants paid, $76,638; assets, $8,592,606 (M); expenditures, $77,553; qualifying distributions, $77,458.
Limitations: Giving primarily in FL and New York, NY.

Application information: Application form not required.
Officers: David Shechet, Pres.; Arthur Shechet, V.P.; Arlene Shechet, V.P.; Jean Shechet, Secy.
EIN: 136163612
Codes: FD2

35912
The Michael M. Wiseman and Helen A. Garten Charitable Foundation
c/o Sullivan & Cromwell
125 Broad St.
New York, NY 10004

Established in 2000 in CT.
Donor(s): Michael M. Wiseman.
Financial data (yr. ended 12/31/01): Grants paid, $76,617; assets, $176,207 (M); gifts received, $75,000; expenditures, $78,073; qualifying distributions, $76,617.
Limitations: Applications not accepted.
Application information: Contributes only to pre-selected organizations.
Trustees: Helen A. Garten, Michael M. Wiseman.
EIN: 134149893

35913
David Yurman Humanitarian Foundation, Inc.
c/o Yohalem Gillman & Co., LLP
477 Madison Ave.
New York, NY 10022-5802

Established in 2000 in NY.
Donor(s): David Yurman, Sybil Yurman.
Financial data (yr. ended 12/31/01): Grants paid, $76,601; assets, $456,556 (M); gifts received, $272,964; expenditures, $84,273; qualifying distributions, $76,601.
Limitations: Applications not accepted.
Application information: Contributes only to pre-selected organizations.
Officers and Directors:* David Yurman,* Pres.; Sybil Yurman,* V.P.; Ralph Galasso,* Secy.
EIN: 582586156

35914
Martone Foundation
166 Sea Cliff Ave.
Glen Cove, NY 11542-4150

Established in 1972 in NY.
Donor(s): Members of the Martone family.
Financial data (yr. ended 07/31/01): Grants paid, $76,600; assets, $768,344 (M); expenditures, $79,496; qualifying distributions, $76,440.
Limitations: Applications not accepted. Giving primarily on Long Island, NY.
Application information: Contributes only to pre-selected organizations.
Officers: Lawrence J. Martone, Pres.; Lorenzo A. Martone, V.P.; Louise A. Peluso, Secy.-Treas.
Directors: Andrew A. Martone, Catherine M. Martone, John J. Martone.
EIN: 237283011
Codes: FD2

35915
Blanche T. Enders Charitable Trust
c/o JPMorgan Private Bank
1211 Ave. of the Americas, 38th Fl.
New York, NY 10036 (212) 789-5679
FAX: (212) 596-3712; E-mail: elias_jacqueline@jpmorgan.com
Contact: Jacqueline Elias, V.P., JPMorgan Chase Bank

Financial data (yr. ended 12/31/00): Grants paid, $76,500; assets, $1,457,683 (M); expenditures, $94,264; qualifying distributions, $75,113.
Limitations: Giving primarily in New York, NY.
Trustee: J.P. Morgan Private Bank.

EIN: 136140674

35916
The Harry & Susan Newton Charitable Foundation
c/o Harry Newton
205 W. 19th St., Ste. 9
New York, NY 10011

Established in 1998 in NY.
Donor(s): Harry Newton, Susan Newton.
Financial data (yr. ended 12/31/99): Grants paid, $76,500; assets, $78,588 (M); gifts received, $5,000; expenditures, $73,588; qualifying distributions, $73,588.
Directors: Muriel Fullam, Harry Newton, Susan Newton.
EIN: 134023608

35917
The Kayden Foundation
550 Mamaroneck Ave., Ste. 404
Harrison, NY 10528-1612
Application address: 10312 Shireoaks Ln., Boca Raton, FL 33498
Contact: Bernard H. Kayden, Pres.

Established in 1962 in NY.
Financial data (yr. ended 12/31/00): Grants paid, $76,450; assets, $2,121,060 (M); expenditures, $88,770; qualifying distributions, $70,824.
Limitations: Giving primarily in the greater New York, NY, area.
Officers: Bernard H. Kayden, Pres.; Mildred Kayden, Secy.-Treas.
EIN: 136137280
Codes: FD2

35918
The Fried Foundation, Inc.
40 Exchange Pl.
New York, NY 10005

Established in 1966 in DE and NY.
Donor(s): Albert Fried, Jr.
Financial data (yr. ended 01/31/02): Grants paid, $76,400; assets, $1,353,839 (M); gifts received, $531,375; expenditures, $78,435; qualifying distributions, $77,874.
Limitations: Applications not accepted. Giving primarily in NJ and NY.
Application information: Contributes only to pre-selected organizations.
Officers: Albert Fried, Jr., Pres.; Christina E. Fried, V.P.; John P. Vazzana, Secy.-Treas.
EIN: 136197403
Codes: FD2

35919
Hoffman Article 3 Charitable Trust
c/o JPMorgan Chase Bank
1211 6th Ave., 34th Fl.
New York, NY 10036

Established in 1996 in FL.
Financial data (yr. ended 09/30/01): Grants paid, $76,400; assets, $3,211,541 (M); expenditures, $151,189; qualifying distributions, $134,044.
Limitations: Applications not accepted. Giving limited to CA.
Application information: Contributes only to pre-selected organizations.
Trustees: Robert S. Warshaw, JPMorgan Chase Bank.
EIN: 137102174
Codes: FD2

35920
Tripifoods Foundation
c/o Hodgson, Russ, Andrews, Woods & Good
1800 One M&T Plz., Ste. 2000
Buffalo, NY 14203

Established in 1986 in NY.
Donor(s): Tripifoods, Inc.
Financial data (yr. ended 06/30/01): Grants paid, $76,300; assets, $129,892 (M); gifts received, $52,000; expenditures, $76,623; qualifying distributions, $76,300.
Limitations: Applications not accepted. Giving primarily in western NY, with some giving also in NJ and CT; minor support also in France and Africa.
Application information: Contributes only to pre-selected organizations.
Officer: Anthony Dutton, Secy.
Trustees: Leonard Schrutt, Gregory G. Tripi.
EIN: 133399842
Codes: CS, FD2, CD

35921
Ratner Family Foundation
400 Garden City Plz., Ste. 210
Garden City, NY 11530 (516) 294-8550
Contact: Dennis Ratner, Tr.

Established in 1997 in NY.
Donor(s): Arthur Ratner, Dennis Ratner.
Financial data (yr. ended 12/31/01): Grants paid, $76,290; assets, $347,341 (M); expenditures, $82,459; qualifying distributions, $76,290.
Trustees: Dennis Ratner, Felice Bassin Seeman.
EIN: 116496216

35922
Martha Lovenheim Siegel Charitable Trust
134 E. 93rd St., Ste. 8B
New York, NY 10128
Contact: John E. Lovenheim, Tr.

Established in 1993 in NY.
Donor(s): Clifford N. Lovenheim.‡
Financial data (yr. ended 12/31/01): Grants paid, $76,230; assets, $1,074,777 (M); expenditures, $101,819; qualifying distributions, $76,230.
Limitations: Applications not accepted.
Application information: Contributes only to pre-selected organizations.
Trustees: John E. Lovenheim, Martha Lovenheim Siegel.
EIN: 166383848
Codes: FD2

35923
The Kirby Family Foundation
c/o W. Michael Reickert, The Ayco Corp.
P.O. Box 8019
Ballston Spa, NY 12020-8019

Established in 1985 in PA.
Donor(s): Robert E. Kirby.‡
Financial data (yr. ended 12/31/00): Grants paid, $76,200; assets, $3,210,548 (M); expenditures, $77,188; qualifying distributions, $76,200.
Limitations: Applications not accepted. Giving primarily in FL, MA, and PA.
Application information: Contributes only to pre-selected organizations.
Officer: Linda K. Mewshaw, Pres.
EIN: 251513507
Codes: FD2

35924
The Thomas R. Pura and Sara Weinheimer Foundation
(Formerly The Thomas R. Pura Foundation)
BCRS Associates LLC
100 Wall St., FL. 11
New York, NY 10005-3701

Established in 1993 in NY.
Donor(s): Thomas R. Pura.
Financial data (yr. ended 04/30/00): Grants paid, $76,200; assets, $274,860 (M); expenditures, $80,542; qualifying distributions, $77,424.
Limitations: Applications not accepted. Giving primarily in New York, NY.
Application information: Contributes only to pre-selected organizations.
Trustees: Thomas R. Pura, Sara J. Weinheimer.
EIN: 133748053

35925
Thomas E. Dewey Fund
230 Park Ave., Ste. 1450
New York, NY 10169-1452 (212) 867-4949
Contact: Thomas E. Dewey, Jr., Tr.

Established in 1958 in NY.
Donor(s): Thomas E. Dewey.‡
Financial data (yr. ended 12/31/01): Grants paid, $76,160; assets, $1,451,924 (M); expenditures, $80,409; qualifying distributions, $78,110.
Limitations: Giving primarily in New York, NY.
Trustees: Ann R.L. Dewey, Thomas E. Dewey, Jr.
EIN: 136111376
Codes: FD2

35926
The Julia & Seymour Gross Foundation, Inc.
1000 Park Ave.
New York, NY 10028
Contact: Inez K. Gross, Chair.

Donor(s): Inez Gross.
Financial data (yr. ended 06/30/01): Grants paid, $76,150; assets, $351,701 (M); gifts received, $40,000; expenditures, $77,263; qualifying distributions, $76,958.
Limitations: Applications not accepted. Giving primarily in NY.
Application information: Contributes only to pre-selected organizations.
Officers: Inez K. Gross, Chair.; Menard M. Gertler, M.D., Pres.
EIN: 136122092
Codes: FD2

35927
B O Fund
1499 E. 29th St.
Brooklyn, NY 11229

Established in 1999 in NY.
Financial data (yr. ended 12/31/01): Grants paid, $76,146; assets, $232,972 (M); gifts received, $85,000; expenditures, $85,595; qualifying distributions, $76,146.
Limitations: Applications not accepted.
Application information: Contributes only to pre-selected organizations.
Trustees: Abraham Oksenberg, Zvi Oksenberg.
EIN: 113519105
Codes: FD2

35928
The Jarx Foundation, Inc.
c/o Janet Moses
P.O. Box 407
Harrison, NY 10528

Established in 1997.
Donor(s): Ellen M. Capra, James R. Capra.

35928—NEW YORK

Financial data (yr. ended 12/31/01): Grants paid, $76,123; assets, $484,147 (M); gifts received, $7,000; expenditures, $82,789; qualifying distributions, $76,289.
Limitations: Applications not accepted. Giving primarily in New York, NY. Some giving also in the West Indies.
Application information: Contributes only to pre-selected organizations.
Officers and Directors:* James R. Capra,* Pres.; Ellen M. Capra,* V.P.; Janet Moses,* Secy.
EIN: 133946523
Codes: FD2

35929
Judith and Paul Hochhauser Foundation, Inc.
1 Bay Blvd.
Lawrence, NY 11559 (516) 239-3600

Established in 1989 in NY.
Donor(s): Paul Hochhauser.
Financial data (yr. ended 12/31/01): Grants paid, $76,081; assets, $501,343 (M); expenditures, $76,604; qualifying distributions, $76,081.
Limitations: Applications not accepted.
Application information: Contributes only to pre-selected organizations.
Officers: Paul Hochhauser, Pres.; Judith Hochhauser, V.P. and Secy.; Robert Schulman, Treas.
EIN: 113014573

35930
The Elizabeth Foundation
P.O. Box 801
Millbrook, NY 12545

Established in 1999 in CA.
Donor(s): Karen E. Lemons Charitable Lead Unitrust.
Financial data (yr. ended 12/31/01): Grants paid, $76,000; assets, $2,112,229 (M); gifts received, $642,000; expenditures, $87,559; qualifying distributions, $74,343.
Limitations: Applications not accepted. Giving primarily in CA and PA.
Application information: Contributes only to pre-selected organizations.
Trustee: Karen Lemons Hollins.
EIN: 770497261
Codes: FD2

35931
The Lenox Foundation
20 Corporate Woods Blvd.
Albany, NY 12211

Established in 1997.
Financial data (yr. ended 12/31/01): Grants paid, $76,000; assets, $2,603,849 (M); gifts received, $347,500; expenditures, $99,325; qualifying distributions, $76,000.
Limitations: Applications not accepted.
Application information: Contributes only to pre-selected organizations.
Officer: Marcia P. Floyd, Pres. and Treas.
Trustee: Rhea P. Clark.
EIN: 311532337

35932
Shaarei Hatzlacha Foundation
1353 47th St.
Brooklyn, NY 11219
Contact: Josef Janklowicz, Dir.

Donor(s): Jack Janklowicz, Josef Janklowicz.
Financial data (yr. ended 10/31/01): Grants paid, $76,000; assets, $664,924 (M); gifts received, $120,898; expenditures, $76,000; qualifying distributions, $76,000.

Officer and Directors:* Josef Janklowicz,* Pres.; Jack Janklowicz, Leonard Janklowicz.
EIN: 113405704
Codes: FD2

35933
Steele Family Foundation
c/o Bessemer Trust Co., N.A.
630 5th Ave.
New York, NY 10111 (212) 708-9216
Application address: c/o Michael C. Steele, Bessemer Trust Co., N.A., 100 Woodbridge Ctr. Dr., Woodbridge, NJ 07095

Established in 1996 in NJ.
Donor(s): Edward C. Steele, Joan M. Steele.
Financial data (yr. ended 12/31/01): Grants paid, $76,000; assets, $820,534 (M); gifts received, $320,158; expenditures, $78,000; qualifying distributions, $76,000.
Limitations: Giving on a national basis, with some emphasis on NY.
Trustees: Edward C. Steele, Joan M. Steele, Michael C. Steele.
EIN: 223431692

35934
Peco Foundation
c/o DDK & Co.
1500 Broadway
New York, NY 10036
Contact: Jeffrey S. Feinman, C.P.A.

Established in 1969.
Donor(s): Catherine G. Curran.
Financial data (yr. ended 12/31/01): Grants paid, $75,994; assets, $7,683,680 (M); gifts received, $10,650; expenditures, $88,678; qualifying distributions, $82,631.
Limitations: Applications not accepted. Giving primarily in New York, NY.
Application information: Contributes only to pre-selected organizations.
Trustee: Catherine G. Curran.
EIN: 237031675
Codes: FD2

35935
Golden Family Charitable Fund, Inc.
229 W. 43rd St., Rm. 1031
New York, NY 10036-3959

Established in 1987 in NY.
Donor(s): Arthur S. Golden, Michael Golden, Stephen A.O. Golden, Lynn G. Dolnick.
Financial data (yr. ended 12/31/00): Grants paid, $75,950; assets, $179,430 (M); expenditures, $79,150; qualifying distributions, $76,050.
Limitations: Applications not accepted. Giving primarily in the Boston, MA, area, and New York, NY.
Application information: Contributes only to pre-selected organizations.
Officers and Directors:* Arthur S. Golden,* Pres.; Stephen A.O. Golden,* V.P.; Lynn G. Dolnick,* Secy.; Michael Golden,* Treas.
EIN: 133470016
Codes: FD2

35936
The Edgar A. & Ida M. Alekna Foundation
c/o Piakar & Lyons, PC
P.O. Box 247
Vestal, NY 13851-0247

Established in 1988 in NY.
Donor(s): Edgar A. Alekna.
Financial data (yr. ended 12/31/01): Grants paid, $75,855; assets, $80,039 (M); expenditures, $76,512; qualifying distributions, $76,294.

Limitations: Applications not accepted. Giving primarily in NY and PA.
Application information: Contributes only to pre-selected organizations.
Trustees: Edgar A. Alekna, Ida M. Alekna, James J. Lewis, Michael H. Zuckerman.
EIN: 222933659
Codes: FD2

35937
The David Wasserman Foundation, Inc.
Adirondack Ctr., 4722 State Hwy. 30
Amsterdam, NY 12010 (518) 843-2800
Contact: Norbert J. Sherbunt, Pres.

Incorporated in 1953 in NY.
Donor(s): David Wasserman.‡
Financial data (yr. ended 02/28/01): Grants paid, $75,853; assets, $1,556,594 (M); expenditures, $147,697; qualifying distributions, $104,067.
Limitations: Giving limited to Montgomery County, NY.
Publications: Financial statement.
Application information: Application form not required.
Officers and Directors:* Norbert J. Sherbunt,* Pres. and Treas.; Judith M. Sherbunt,* V.P. and Secy.
EIN: 237183522
Codes: FD2

35938
Lowenstein Family Foundation
1060 Seven Oaks Ln.
Mamaroneck, NY 10543

Established in 1993 in DE.
Financial data (yr. ended 04/30/01): Grants paid, $75,778; assets, $632,031 (M); expenditures, $77,685; qualifying distributions, $75,778.
Limitations: Applications not accepted. Giving primarily in NY.
Application information: Contributes only to pre-selected organizations.
Officers: Richard Lowenstein, Pres.; Michael Lowenstein, V.P.; Rita Lowenstein, Secy.; Wendy Sandler, Treas.
EIN: 133745065
Codes: FD2

35939
Mario and Annunziatina Sbarro Family Foundation, Inc.
(Formerly Sbarro Family Foundation, Inc.)
405 Lexington Ave., 8th Fl.
New York, NY 10174
Contact: Carol F. Burger

Established in 1993 in DE.
Donor(s): Mario Sbarro.
Financial data (yr. ended 10/31/01): Grants paid, $75,700; assets, $891 (M); gifts received, $12,800; expenditures, $75,855; qualifying distributions, $75,700.
Limitations: Applications not accepted. Giving primarily in NY and PA.
Application information: Contributes only to pre-selected organizations.
Officers: Mario Sbarro, Pres.; Annunziatina Sbarro, V.P.; Bernard Zimmerman, Secy.-Treas.
EIN: 133188018
Codes: FD2

35940
Daniels Family Foundation
c/o CAI Advisors & Co.
767 5th Ave.
New York, NY 10153

Established in 1994 in NY.
Donor(s): Leslie B. Daniels.

Financial data (yr. ended 12/31/01): Grants paid, $75,606; assets, $708,834 (M); expenditures, $78,180; qualifying distributions, $75,606.
Limitations: Applications not accepted. Giving primarily in NY.
Application information: Contributes only to pre-selected organizations.
Trustees: Elizabeth Daniels, Leslie B. Daniels.
EIN: 133799459

35941
The Gustave A. and Geraldine S. Werner Foundation
c/o Gayle Fish
7084 Kinne Rd.
Lockport, NY 14094

Established in 1995 in NY.
Donor(s): Geraldine S. Werner.
Financial data (yr. ended 12/31/01): Grants paid, $75,600; assets, $2,239,635 (M); gifts received, $278,482; expenditures, $82,141; qualifying distributions, $80,521.
Limitations: Applications not accepted. Giving limited to NY.
Application information: Contributes only to pre-selected organizations.
Trustees: Gayle Fish, Myrl Gelb, Marcel Mundry, Geraldine S. Werner.
EIN: 161491845
Codes: FD2

35942
The Walter H. & Mary Beth Buck Foundation, Inc.
c/o Maxwell Shmerler & Co.
1 N. Lexington Ave.
White Plains, NY 10601

Established in 1994 in NY.
Donor(s): Walter H. Buck.
Financial data (yr. ended 10/31/01): Grants paid, $75,500; assets, $1,165,121 (M); gifts received, $310,954; expenditures, $79,112; qualifying distributions, $76,389.
Limitations: Applications not accepted. Giving primarily in NY.
Application information: Contributes only to pre-selected organizations.
Officers: Walter H. Buck, Pres.; Mary Beth Buck, Secy.-Treas.
EIN: 133797578
Codes: FD2

35943
The Caiola Family Foundation, Inc.
c/o Bettina Equities Co.
230 E. 83rd St.
New York, NY 10028
Contact: Rosemarie Caiola-Musacchia, Secy.-Treas.

Established in 2000 in NY.
Donor(s): Sal Caiola.
Financial data (yr. ended 12/31/01): Grants paid, $75,500; assets, $326,514 (M); gifts received, $200,000; expenditures, $77,643; qualifying distributions, $75,500.
Officers: Maria Sciortino, Pres.; Bettina Caiola, V.P.; Rosemarie Caiola-Musacchia, Secy.-Treas.
EIN: 134132591

35944
D. S. and R. H. Gottesman Foundation
3 Manhattanville Rd.
Purchase, NY 10577

Incorporated in 1941 in NY.
Financial data (yr. ended 10/31/01): Grants paid, $75,500; assets, $1,609,178 (M); expenditures, $80,685; qualifying distributions, $76,203.

Limitations: Applications not accepted. Giving primarily in New York, NY; giving also in Israel.
Application information: Contributes only to pre-selected organizations.
Officers and Directors:* Ira D. Wallach,* Pres.; Armand P. Bartos,* V.P.; Edgar Wachenheim III, V.P.; Kenneth L. Wallach, V.P.; Peter C. Siegfried, Secy.-Treas.; Celeste G. Bartos, Miriam G. Wallach.
EIN: 136101701
Codes: FD2

35945
Robert L. Stott Foundation, Inc.
c/o American Express Tax & Business Svcs.
1185 Ave. of the Americas
New York, NY 10036-2602

Incorporated in 1957 in NY.
Donor(s): Robert L. Stott,‡ Robert L. Stott, Jr., Donald B. Stott.
Financial data (yr. ended 12/31/01): Grants paid, $75,500; assets, $2,919,999 (M); expenditures, $90,334; qualifying distributions, $79,335.
Limitations: Applications not accepted. Giving primarily in FL and NY.
Application information: Contributes only to pre-selected organizations.
Officers: Robert L. Stott, Jr., Pres.; Heidi Stott, Secy.; Donald B. Stott, Treas.
EIN: 136061943
Codes: FD2

35946
The Bonnie Johnson Sacerdote Foundation
c/o BCRS Assoc., LLC
100 Wall St., 11th Fl.
New York, NY 10005

Established in 1994 in NY.
Donor(s): Bonnie Johnson Sacerdote, Peter M. Sacerdote.
Financial data (yr. ended 07/31/01): Grants paid, $75,450; assets, $510,496 (M); gifts received, $204,531; expenditures, $78,139; qualifying distributions, $75,030.
Limitations: Applications not accepted. Giving primarily in New York, NY.
Application information: Contributes only to pre-selected organizations.
Trustee: Bonnie Johnson Sacerdote.
EIN: 133796736
Codes: FD2

35947
J. F. Schoellkopf Silver Wedding Fund
P.O. Box 22900
Rochester, NY 14692 (716) 827-4500
Application Address: c/o Paul D. Gilmour, Buffalo Color Corp., 100 Lee St., P.O. Box 7027, Buffalo, NY 14240

Established in 1909.
Financial data (yr. ended 12/31/01): Grants paid, $75,450; assets, $1,530,638 (M); expenditures, $98,571; qualifying distributions, $75,079.
Limitations: Giving primarily in Buffalo, NY.
Application information: Application forms are available from the Mutual Aid Society. Application form required.
Trustee: M & T Bank.
EIN: 166030147
Codes: FD2, GTI

35948
The John Cavanagh Trust
c/o JPMorgan Chase Bank, Tax Dept.
1211 6th Ave., 34th Fl.
New York, NY 10036 (212) 270-9100
Contact: Ervin G. Jones, V.P.

Financial data (yr. ended 12/31/01): Grants paid, $75,357; assets, $1,082,679 (M); expenditures, $107,799; qualifying distributions, $77,241.
Limitations: Giving primarily in AZ.
Trustees: Ogden Phipps, JPMorgan Chase Bank.
EIN: 136045253
Codes: FD2

35949
The Pierce Family Charitable Foundation
c/o Frederick G. Pierce, II
70 W. Chippewa St., Ste. 500
Buffalo, NY 14202 (716) 566-2950

Established in 1996 in NY.
Donor(s): Frederick G. Pierce II, Lisa N. Pierce II.
Financial data (yr. ended 12/31/01): Grants paid, $75,200; assets, $1,637,988 (M); gifts received, $72,235; expenditures, $96,986; qualifying distributions, $73,362.
Officers: Frederick G. Pierce II, Pres. and Treas.; Lisa N. Pierce II, V.P. and Secy.
Directors: Alan Gordon, Seymour H. Knox IV.
EIN: 133914726
Codes: FD2

35950
Richard Ravitch Foundation, Inc.
c/o Richard Ravitch
31 E. 79th St., Apt. 9E
New York, NY 10021

Established in 1949 in NY.
Donor(s): Richard Ravitch.
Financial data (yr. ended 11/30/01): Grants paid, $75,155; assets, $1,835,495 (M); gifts received, $291,260; expenditures, $86,471; qualifying distributions, $75,155.
Limitations: Applications not accepted. Giving primarily in NY.
Application information: Contributes only to pre-selected organizations.
Officers and Directors:* Richard Ravitch,* Pres. and Principal Mgr.; Judah Gribetz,* V.P.; Joseph Ravitch,* V.P.; Donald Rice,* Secy.; Michael Ravitch,* Treas.
EIN: 136093139
Codes: FD2

35951
Salo W. and Jeannette M. Baron Foundation, Inc.
c/o Davis & Gilbert
1740 Broadway, 3rd Fl.
New York, NY 10019 (212) 468-4902
Contact: Russell S. Knapp, Pres.

Established in 1987 in DE.
Donor(s): Salo W. Baron.‡
Financial data (yr. ended 12/31/01): Grants paid, $75,000; assets, $1,223,105 (M); expenditures, $77,165; qualifying distributions, $75,000.
Limitations: Giving primarily in New York, NY.
Officers: Russell S. Knapp, Pres.; Shoshana Tancer, V.P.; Tobey Gitelle, Secy.-Treas.
EIN: 133416976

35952
Clarkson Family Foundation
45 Sutton Pl. S.
New York, NY 10022

Established in 1996 in NY.
Donor(s): Bayard D. Clarkson.

35952—NEW YORK

Financial data (yr. ended 12/31/01): Grants paid, $75,000; assets, $1,069,423 (M); expenditures, $87,330; qualifying distributions, $75,134.
Limitations: Applications not accepted.
Application information: Contributes only to pre-selected organizations.
Trustees: Bayard D. Clarkson, Virginia C. Clarkson.
EIN: 137088453

35953
Eleanor & Anthony Defrancis Scholarship Fund
c/o JPMorgan Chase Bank
1211 6th Ave., 34th Fl.
New York, NY 10036

Established in 2000 in NY.
Donor(s): Nicholas Defancis.
Financial data (yr. ended 02/28/01): Grants paid, $75,000; assets, $1,277,034 (M); gifts received, $1,739,341; expenditures, $75,000; qualifying distributions, $75,000.
Limitations: Giving primarily in AR, CA, and MA.
Trustee: JPMorgan Chase Bank.
EIN: 527153399

35954
1101 Foundation
c/o Hodgson, Russ, Andrews, Woods & Goodyear
1 M&T Plz., Ste. 200
Buffalo, NY 14203

Established in 1995 in NY.
Donor(s): Donald L. Meyer.
Financial data (yr. ended 12/31/00): Grants paid, $75,000; assets, $9,791,570 (M); gifts received, $9,827,401; expenditures, $152,018; qualifying distributions, $75,000.
Limitations: Applications not accepted.
Application information: Contributes only to pre-selected organizations.
Trustees: Donald L. Meyer, Doris C. Meyer.
EIN: 161478622

35955
Steve Brian Kerr Charitable Foundation, Inc.
c/o Joseph A. Broderick
P.O. Box 309
East Northport, NY 11731

Established in 1997 in NY.
Donor(s): Marcia Kerr.
Financial data (yr. ended 12/31/01): Grants paid, $75,000; assets, $561,036 (M); expenditures, $89,384; qualifying distributions, $75,000.
Limitations: Applications not accepted. Giving primarily in NY.
Application information: Contributes only to pre-selected organizations.
Officers: Marcia Kerr, Pres.; Lisa Parlo, Secy.; Eric Kerr, Treas.
EIN: 133967303

35956
Anne Boyd Lichtenstein Foundation
c/o Bessemer Trust Co., N.A.
630 5th Ave., 37th Fl.
New York, NY 10111

Established in 1959.
Financial data (yr. ended 12/31/01): Grants paid, $75,000; assets, $1,670,294 (M); expenditures, $90,514; qualifying distributions, $78,387.
Limitations: Applications not accepted. Giving primarily in New York, NY.
Application information: Contributes only to pre-selected organizations.
Officer: John D. Dale, Jr., Pres.
Trustees: Edward W.T. Gray III, Ethel Harper, Gordon A. Millspaugh, Jr.
EIN: 136067980

35957
Robert J. Nolan Foundation, Inc.
P.O. Box 765
Glens Falls, NY 12801 (518) 793-6611
Contact: John C. Mannix, Pres.

Established in 1986 in NY.
Donor(s): Robert J. Nolan.
Financial data (yr. ended 09/30/01): Grants paid, $75,000; assets, $871,465 (M); expenditures, $86,358; qualifying distributions, $79,884.
Limitations: Giving limited to residents of the greater Glens Falls, NY, area.
Application information: Application form required.
Officers: John C. Mannix, Pres.; Paul Krihak, V.P.; Daniel Robertson, Secy.; Judy Dee, Treas.
Directors: Michael Massiano, Richard O'Connor, Judy Sicard.
EIN: 222826285
Codes: GTI

35958
The Rice Family Foundation
c/o Clayton, Dubilier & Rice, Inc.
375 Park Ave.
New York, NY 10152
Contact: J. Rice

Established in 1998 in NY.
Donor(s): Joseph L. Rice III.
Financial data (yr. ended 12/31/01): Grants paid, $75,000; assets, $1,227,452 (M); expenditures, $85,728; qualifying distributions, $75,000.
Limitations: Applications not accepted. Giving primarily in NY.
Application information: Contributes only to pre-selected organizations.
Trustees: Franci J. Blassberg, Joseph L. Rice.
EIN: 137152866

35959
The Hope Sheridan Foundation
c/o Schulte Roth & Zabel LLP
919 3rd Ave.
New York, NY 10022

Established in 2001 in NY.
Financial data (yr. ended 12/31/01): Grants paid, $75,000; assets, $471,450 (M); gifts received, $567,472; expenditures, $75,000; qualifying distributions, $75,000.
Limitations: Applications not accepted. Giving primarily in New York, NY.
Application information: Contributes only to pre-selected organizations.
Trustees: Linda Dawson, Howard F. Scharfstein.
EIN: 137257964

35960
R. L. Stine & J. W. Stine Foundation, Inc.
300 West End Ave.
New York, NY 10023-8156

Established in 1996 in NY.
Donor(s): Robert L. Stine.
Financial data (yr. ended 12/31/00): Grants paid, $75,000; assets, $544,015 (M); gifts received, $100,000; expenditures, $75,000; qualifying distributions, $75,000.
Limitations: Applications not accepted. Giving on a national basis, with emphasis on New York, NY.
Application information: Contributes only to pre-selected organizations.
Officers: Robert L. Stine, Pres.; Jane Stine, Secy.
EIN: 133919173

35961
Henry Y. Sugimoto Charitable Foundation
c/o Young & Moriwaki
777 3rd Ave., 19th Fl.
New York, NY 10017

Established in 1999 in NY.
Donor(s): Madeleine Sugimoto.
Financial data (yr. ended 12/31/01): Grants paid, $75,000; assets, $117,650 (M); gifts received, $10,000; expenditures, $85,259; qualifying distributions, $75,000.
Trustees: Gary S. Moriwaki, Craig Sugimoto, Madeleine Sugimoto.
EIN: 137170113

35962
Voelker-Orth Museum
149-19 38th Ave.
Flushing, NY 11354
Contact: Catherine Abrams, Dir.

Established in 1999 in NY.
Donor(s): Elisabeth Catherine Orth.
Financial data (yr. ended 07/31/00): Grants paid, $75,000; assets, $7,138,740 (M); gifts received, $2,781,175; expenditures, $98,768; qualifying distributions, $75,000.
Limitations: Giving primarily in New York, NY.
Directors: Lee Cogan, Stanley Cogan, Anthony DiBrita, Catherine Fitts, Paul Kerson, Joan S. Kingsley, Barbara Levin, Chun Soo Pyn, Rolan G. Wade.
EIN: 113498583
Codes: FD2

35963
J. Lawrence Werther Research Foundation
c/o J. Lawrence Werther
1060 5th Ave.
New York, NY 10028

Established in 1990 in NY.
Donor(s): Alfredo Lehman, Ethel Moses, Kenneth Berg, John Pomerantz, Leon Black, Abraham Goldstein, The Benjamin Jacobson & Sons Foundation.
Financial data (yr. ended 12/31/01): Grants paid, $75,000; assets, $1,416,003 (M); gifts received, $101,560; expenditures, $90,184; qualifying distributions, $84,420; giving activities include $3,176 for programs.
Limitations: Applications not accepted. Giving primarily in NY.
Application information: Contributes only to pre-selected organizations.
Officer: J. Lawrence Werther, Pres.
Trustees: John Pomerantz, Laura Pomerantz.
EIN: 133553537

35964
Wolf Family Foundation
1505 Coney Island Ave.
Brooklyn, NY 11230-4713
Contact: Hirsch Wolf, Pres.

Established in 1999.
Donor(s): Hirsch Wolf.
Financial data (yr. ended 06/30/01): Grants paid, $75,000; assets, $35,431 (M); gifts received, $100,000; expenditures, $75,375; qualifying distributions, $75,000.
Limitations: Giving primarily in NY.
Officers: Hirsch Wolf, Pres.; Gershon Ginsburg, V.P.; Raquel Wolf, Secy.
EIN: 112988920

35965
The Wright Foundation, Inc.
c/o Yohalem Gillman & Co.
477 Madison Ave.
New York, NY 10022

Established in 2000 in CT.
Donor(s): Peter A. Wright.
Financial data (yr. ended 12/31/01): Grants paid, $75,000; assets, $2,090,864 (M); gifts received, $1,000,000; expenditures, $102,781; qualifying distributions, $80,968.
Limitations: Applications not accepted.
Application information: Contributes only to pre-selected organizations.
Officers and Directors:* Peter A. Wright,* Pres.; Jonathan K. Golden,* V.P.; Wendy Wright,* Secy.-Treas.
EIN: 134141287
Codes: FD2

35966
The Birnbaum Foundation, Inc.
620 Guard Hill Rd.
Bedford, NY 10506

Established about 1956.
Financial data (yr. ended 12/31/01): Grants paid, $74,865; assets, $768,911 (M); expenditures, $90,933; qualifying distributions, $74,865.
Limitations: Applications not accepted. Giving primarily in Westchester County and New York, NY.
Application information: Contributes only to pre-selected organizations.
Officer: Ira Birnbaum, Pres.
EIN: 136098221

35967
Eddie & Shawna Azar Charitable Foundation
1060 E. 8th St.
Brooklyn, NY 11230-4102
Contact: Eddie Azar, Tr.

Established in 1998.
Financial data (yr. ended 05/31/00): Grants paid, $74,755; assets, $3,945 (L); gifts received, $110,000; expenditures, $75,355; qualifying distributions, $74,755.
Limitations: Giving primarily in Brooklyn, NY.
Trustees: Eddie Azar, Shawna Azar.
EIN: 116493594

35968
Gershowitz-Gardyn Family Foundation, Ltd.
85 E. Hoffman Ave.
Lindenhurst, NY 11757

Established in 1988 in NY.
Donor(s): Paul W. Gardyn.
Financial data (yr. ended 12/31/00): Grants paid, $74,753; assets, $821,618 (M); expenditures, $103,626; qualifying distributions, $72,837.
Limitations: Applications not accepted. Giving primarily in Boca Raton, FL.
Application information: Contributes only to pre-selected organizations.
Officers: Paul W. Gardyn, Pres.; Debra Gershowitz, Secy.
Director: Steven Landau.
EIN: 112888340

35969
The Mazel Charitable Trust
1621 50th St.
Brooklyn, NY 11204

Financial data (yr. ended 12/31/01): Grants paid, $74,694; assets, $468 (M); gifts received, $35,000; expenditures, $74,694; qualifying distributions, $74,694.
Limitations: Applications not accepted.
Application information: Contributes only to pre-selected organizations.
Trustees: Jupah Blan, Marilyn Blan.
EIN: 116466161

35970
Donald N. Tweedy Charitable Trust
c/o JPMorgan Chase Bank
P.O. Box 31412
Rochester, NY 14603
Application address: c/o Sheela Amembal, Trust Off., JPMorgan Chase Bank, 999 Broad St., Bridgeport, CT 06604, tel.: (203)382-6548

Established in 1948.
Financial data (yr. ended 09/30/01): Grants paid, $74,682; assets, $1,036,739 (M); expenditures, $92,449; qualifying distributions, $76,207.
Limitations: Giving limited to Danbury, CT.
Application information: Application form not required.
Trustee: JPMorgan Chase Bank.
EIN: 066022779

35971
Orin Lehman Foundation, Inc.
c/o Margolin, Lowenstein & Co., LLP
60 Cutter Mill Rd., No. 512
Great Neck, NY 11021
Contact: Orin Lehman, Pres.

Incorporated in 1953 in NY.
Donor(s): Orin Lehman.
Financial data (yr. ended 12/31/00): Grants paid, $74,640; assets, $74,434 (M); gifts received, $51,155; expenditures, $74,877; qualifying distributions, $74,640.
Limitations: Applications not accepted. Giving primarily in New York, NY.
Application information: Contributes only to pre-selected organizations.
Officer: Orin Lehman, Pres.
EIN: 136094016

35972
Viram Foundation, Inc.
61 Jane St., Ste. 12B
New York, NY 10014

Established in 2000 in NY.
Donor(s): Viren Mehta, Amita Rodman Mehta.
Financial data (yr. ended 12/31/01): Grants paid, $74,608; assets, $2,742,229 (M); expenditures, $112,108; qualifying distributions, $74,608.
Limitations: Applications not accepted.
Application information: Contributes only to pre-selected organizations.
Officers and Directors:* Viren Mehta,* Pres.; Kevin Rodman Conare,* V.P.; Amita Rodman Mehta,* Secy.-Treas.; Kamal Mehta.
EIN: 134140025

35973
The Kraus Family Foundation
c/o Goldman Sachs & Co.
85 Broad St., Tax Dept.
New York, NY 10004
Application address: c/o Marcum & Kleigman, LLP, 130 Crossways Park Dr., Woodbury, NY 11797
Contact: Peter S. Kraus, Tr.

Established in 1996 in NY.
Donor(s): Peter S. Kraus.
Financial data (yr. ended 08/31/00): Grants paid, $74,584; assets, $4,192,769 (M); gifts received, $3,752,894; expenditures, $80,577; qualifying distributions, $78,699.
Limitations: Giving primarily in New York, NY and Salisbury, VT.
Trustees: Jill G. Kraus, Peter S. Kraus.
EIN: 133921376

35974
Mark and Hilda Posner Family Foundation Trust
1950 52nd St.
Brooklyn, NY 11204
Application address: 581 McDonald Ave., Brooklyn, NY 11218
Contact: Mark Posner, Dir.

Established in 1998 in NY.
Donor(s): Mark Posner.
Financial data (yr. ended 12/31/01): Grants paid, $74,572; assets, $109,963 (M); gifts received, $90,000; expenditures, $75,122; qualifying distributions, $74,572.
Directors: Hilda Posner, Mark Posner.
EIN: 116508144

35975
The George Backer Family Foundation, Inc.
c/o Brown Rudnick et al.
120 W. 45th St.
New York, NY 10036

Established in 1989 in NY.
Donor(s): George Backer.‡
Financial data (yr. ended 12/31/01): Grants paid, $74,500; assets, $2,016,544 (M); expenditures, $95,888; qualifying distributions, $85,193.
Limitations: Applications not accepted. Giving primarily in New York, NY.
Application information: Contributes only to pre-selected organizations.
Officers: Phyllis Morrelli, Pres.; Joan Meer, V.P.; John D. Morelli, Treas.
EIN: 133537126

35976
The Giordano Family Foundation
c/o BCRS Assocs., LLC
67 Wall St.
New York, NY 10005

Established in 1991 in NY.
Donor(s): Robert M. Giordano.
Financial data (yr. ended 03/31/01): Grants paid, $74,500; assets, $592,506 (M); expenditures, $89,888; qualifying distributions, $75,465.
Limitations: Applications not accepted. Giving primarily in New York, NY.
Application information: Contributes only to pre-selected organizations.
Trustees: Jane W. Giordano, Robert M. Giordano, Robert E. Shauffer.
EIN: 133632759

35977
Richard Nye Foundation
c/o Baker Nye Investments
477 Madison Ave., Ste. 1600
New York, NY 10022
Contact: Richard B. Nye, Pres.

Established in 1986 in NY.
Donor(s): Richard B. Nye, Hethea Nye, Griffis Foundation.
Financial data (yr. ended 12/31/01): Grants paid, $74,500; assets, $386,467 (M); gifts received, $25,000; expenditures, $75,848; qualifying distributions, $74,929.
Limitations: Giving primarily in NY.
Application information: Application form not required.
Officer: Richard B. Nye, Pres.
EIN: 133368971

35978
The Storehouse Trust
333 International Dr., Ste. B-3
Williamsville, NY 14221
Contact: Anne V. McCune, Tr.; or Leroy V. McCune, Tr.

Established in 1989 in NY.
Financial data (yr. ended 12/31/01): Grants paid, $74,500; assets, $885,779 (M); expenditures, $84,171; qualifying distributions, $74,361.
Limitations: Giving primarily in MA and NY.
Trustees: Anne V. McCune, Leroy V. McCune.
EIN: 166331396

35979
The Robert & Linda Friedman Foundation
c/o BCRS Assoc., LLC
67 Wall St., 8th Fl.
New York, NY 10005

Established in 1981 in NY.
Donor(s): Robert A. Friedman.
Financial data (yr. ended 01/31/01): Grants paid, $74,338; assets, $2,267,494 (M); expenditures, $102,052; qualifying distributions, $84,838.
Limitations: Applications not accepted. Giving primarily in NY; funding also in Boston, MA.
Application information: Contributes only to pre-selected organizations.
Trustees: David M. Friedman, Linda S. Friedman, Robert A. Friedman, Stephen R. Goldenberg.
EIN: 133102976

35980
Joseph L. Briggs Trust
c/o JPMorgan Chase Bank
P.O. Box 31412
Rochester, NY 14603-1412
Application address: c/o Edward Cavelier, East Jr.-Sr. High School, 1801 E. Main St., Rochester, NY 14609, tel.: (716) 288-3130

Established in 1967.
Financial data (yr. ended 08/31/01): Grants paid, $74,316; assets, $1,369,971 (M); expenditures, $88,958; qualifying distributions, $75,481.
Limitations: Giving primarily in NY.
Application information: Funding awarded in excess of those paid for scholarships are limited to pre-selected organizations. Application form not required.
Trustee: JPMorgan Chase Bank.
EIN: 166108736

35981
Fima Fidelman Charitable Trust
c/o The Bank of New York, Tax Dept.
1 Wall St., 28th Fl.
New York, NY 10286

Established in 1997 in NY.
Financial data (yr. ended 12/31/01): Grants paid, $74,148; assets, $2,182,968 (M); expenditures, $95,205; qualifying distributions, $78,372.
Limitations: Applications not accepted. Giving primarily in NY.
Application information: Contributes only to pre-selected organizations.
Trustee: The Bank of New York.
EIN: 137146273

35982
The JW Foundation
520 Woodmere Blvd.
Woodmere, NY 11598

Established in 1997 in NY.
Donor(s): Jeffrey Weinberg, Sharona Weinberg.
Financial data (yr. ended 11/30/99): Grants paid, $74,130; assets, $2,445 (M); gifts received, $75,000; expenditures, $74,189; qualifying distributions, $74,150.
Trustees: Jeffrey Weinberg, Sharona Weinberg.
EIN: 113412512

35983
McDermott Family Foundation, Inc.
571 Boughton Hill Rd.
Honeoye Falls, NY 14472

Established in 1997 in NY.
Donor(s): Thomas C. McDermott.
Financial data (yr. ended 12/31/01): Grants paid, $74,037; assets, $398,616 (M); expenditures, $81,400; qualifying distributions, $75,893.
Limitations: Applications not accepted. Giving primarily in NY.
Application information: Contributes only to pre-selected organizations.
Officers and Directors:* Gloria P. McDermott,* Pres.; Thomas C. McDermott,* Secy.-Treas.; Andrew C. McDermott, James C. McDermott, Mark C. McDermott, Thomas C. McDermott III.
EIN: 161526083

35984
Jack & Phyllis Wertenteil Foundation
c/o Arye Ringel
1750 44th St.
Brooklyn, NY 11204-1050

Established in 1988 in NY.
Donor(s): Jack Wertenteil.
Financial data (yr. ended 06/30/01): Grants paid, $74,032; assets, $11,610 (M); gifts received, $76,438; expenditures, $74,449; qualifying distributions, $74,132.
Limitations: Applications not accepted. Giving primarily in the greater metropolitan New York, NY, area.
Application information: Contributes only to pre-selected organizations.
Trustees: Jack Wertenteil, Phyllis Wertenteil.
EIN: 116352918

35985
Rohit & Katharine Desai Foundation
540 Madison Ave.
New York, NY 10022

Established in 1984 in NY.
Donor(s): Rohit Desai, Katharine Desai.
Financial data (yr. ended 12/31/01): Grants paid, $74,000; assets, $1,270,446 (M); expenditures, $77,692; qualifying distributions, $75,777.
Limitations: Applications not accepted. Giving primarily in Brooklyn, NY.
Application information: Contributes only to pre-selected organizations.
Trustees: Katharine Desai, Rohit Desai.
EIN: 133260252

35986
Carl Forstmann Memorial Foundation
c/o Forstmann, Little & Co.
767 5th Ave., 44th Fl.
New York, NY 10153

Established in 1922.
Financial data (yr. ended 12/31/99): Grants paid, $74,000; assets, $1,753,375 (M); expenditures, $98,392; qualifying distributions, $75,490.
Limitations: Applications not accepted. Giving primarily in MD and NY.
Application information: Contributes only to pre-selected organizations.
Officers: Dorothy M. Sammis, Pres.; Cecily Lyle, Secy.; Nicholas C. Forstmann, Treas.
Trustees: Sarah Cambier, Christina Giammalva, Susie Kealy, Elissa L. Moran, John G. Scott, Charles Severs, Steven K. Wilson.
EIN: 226042706

35987
Ada G. & Stanley I. Halbreich Foundation, Inc.
1 Gracie Terr., Ste. 14F
New York, NY 10028 (212) 988-3692
Contact: Ada G. Halbreich, Dir.

Established in 1998.
Donor(s): Ada G. Halbreich.
Financial data (yr. ended 12/31/00): Grants paid, $74,000; assets, $159,814 (M); gifts received, $133,242; expenditures, $75,518; qualifying distributions, $74,979.
Director: Ada G. Halbreich.
EIN: 137100026

35988
Stringer Foundation
174 N. Brookside Ave.
Freeport, NY 11520-1904 (516) 623-6400
Contact: Irving M. Wall, Secy.

Established in 1995 in NY.
Donor(s): Tipton S. Conrad.
Financial data (yr. ended 06/30/02): Grants paid, $74,000; assets, $2,003,565 (M); expenditures, $241,843; qualifying distributions, $74,000.
Limitations: Giving on a national basis.
Application information: Application form not required.
Officers and Directors:* Tipton S. Conrad,* Pres.; Irving M. Wall, Secy. and Treas.; Donald R. Wall.
EIN: 113288229

35989
Arnold & Jeanne Bernstein Fund
420 Lexington Ave., Ste. 2150
New York, NY 10170
Contact: Arnold Bernstein, Pres.

Established about 1958 in NY.
Financial data (yr. ended 12/31/01): Grants paid, $73,995; assets, $1,195,661 (M); expenditures, $84,948; qualifying distributions, $73,995.
Limitations: Giving primarily in NY.
Officers and Trustee:* Arnold J. Bernstein,* Pres.; Jeanne P. Bernstein, Treas.
EIN: 136095410

35990
The Schoor Family Foundation
c/o C. Burger, Jenkens & Gilchrist
405 Lexington Ave.
New York, NY 10174

Established in 2000 in NY.
Donor(s): Kalman Schoor, Jordana Schoor, Acqua Wellington Foundation.
Financial data (yr. ended 12/31/01): Grants paid, $73,800; assets, $74,101 (M); gifts received, $90,000; expenditures, $73,984; qualifying distributions, $73,800.
Limitations: Applications not accepted. Giving primarily in New York, NY.
Application information: Contributes only to pre-selected organizations.
Directors: Martin Kofman, Jordana Schoor, Kalman Schoor.
EIN: 134126814

35991
Martin Tananbaum Foundation, Inc.
c/o Gary M. Orkin, CPA
125 Jericho Tpke., Ste. 300
Jericho, NY 11753 (516) 279-5432

Incorporated in 1958 in NY.
Donor(s): Martin Tananbaum.‡
Financial data (yr. ended 12/31/00): Grants paid, $73,745; assets, $787,471 (M); expenditures, $106,441; qualifying distributions, $91,309.

Limitations: Applications not accepted. Giving primarily in NY, with emphasis on the greater metropolitan New York, NY area.
Application information: Contributes only to pre-selected organizations.
Officers: Barbara Tananbaum DeGeorge, Secy.; Elbert Brodsky, Treas.
Directors: Amy Coplon, Janet Weiner DeWinter, Florence Levine, Minnie Lee Tananbaum.
EIN: 136162900

35992
PCS Foundation, Inc.
6 Timber Trail
Rye, NY 10580

Financial data (yr. ended 12/31/01): Grants paid, $73,725; assets, $1,049,155 (M); gifts received, $611,678; expenditures, $77,260; qualifying distributions, $73,725.
Limitations: Applications not accepted.
Application information: Contributes only to pre-selected organizations.
Officers: Parag Saxena, Pres.; Radha Saxena, V.P.; Usha Saxena, Secy.-Treas.
EIN: 133836874

35993
Machiz Family Foundation
39 Evergreen Cir.
Manhasset, NY 11030

Established in 1997 in NY.
Donor(s): Leon Machiz.
Financial data (yr. ended 12/31/01): Grants paid, $73,711; assets, $175,419 (M); expenditures, $78,011; qualifying distributions, $147,422.
Limitations: Applications not accepted. Giving primarily in FL and NY.
Application information: Contributes only to pre-selected organizations.
Trustees: Leon Machiz, Lorraine Machiz.
EIN: 061485970

35994
The Rosenfeld Foundation
c/o Cleary, Gottlieb, Steen & Hamilton
1 Liberty Plz.
New York, NY 10006

Established in 1991 in NY.
Donor(s): Eric R. Rosenfeld, Faith Rosenfeld.
Financial data (yr. ended 12/31/01): Grants paid, $73,700; assets, $57,781 (M); gifts received, $70,000; expenditures, $76,200; qualifying distributions, $76,008.
Limitations: Applications not accepted. Giving on a national basis, with some emphasis on MA and NY.
Application information: Contributes only to pre-selected organizations.
Trustees: Eric R. Rosenfeld, Fran W. Rosenfeld.
EIN: 133640005

35995
The Bridgewater Fund, Inc.
c/o Paul Kaplan
40 5th Ave.
New York, NY 10011

Established in 1971 in NY and DE.
Donor(s): Ursula Lerse, Reginald Fullerton, Charles A. Rivkin, Paul J. Sperry, Paul D. Kaplan.
Financial data (yr. ended 11/30/01): Grants paid, $73,663; assets, $369,204 (M); gifts received, $47,938; expenditures, $76,314; qualifying distributions, $73,540.
Limitations: Applications not accepted. Giving in the East, with emphasis on NY and RI.
Application information: Contributes only to pre-selected organizations.

Officers and Directors:* Paul D. Kaplan,* Pres.; Robert Tofel, Secy.; Patricia Kaplan.
EIN: 237442465

35996
The Robert and Gail Edelstein Foundation, Inc.
10 Old Jackson Ave.
Hastings-on-Hudson, NY 10706
(914) 478-3108
Contact: Robert Edelstein, Pres.

Established in 1997 in DE.
Donor(s): Robert Edelstein.
Financial data (yr. ended 04/30/01): Grants paid, $73,634; assets, $1,321,757 (M); expenditures, $105,335; qualifying distributions, $73,634.
Limitations: Giving primarily in FL and NY.
Application information: Application form not required.
Officers: Robert Edelstein, Pres.; Gail Edelstein, Secy.
EIN: 133948948

35997
Northcote Parkinson Fund
67A E. 77th St.
New York, NY 10021
Contact: John Train, Chair.

Established in 1987 in NY.
Donor(s): Smith Richardson Foundation, Inc., H. Smith Richardson Charitable Trust, Nelson Peltz, Olin Foundation, Frederick W. Richmond Foundation, The J.M. Kaplan Fund, Randolph Foundation.
Financial data (yr. ended 12/31/00): Grants paid, $73,600; assets, $218,006 (M); gifts received, $144,660; expenditures, $217,258; qualifying distributions, $214,264.
Limitations: Applications not accepted. Giving on a national basis.
Application information: Contributes only to pre-selected organizations.
Officers and Board Members:* John Train,* Chair. and Treas.; Virginia Armat Hurt,* Secy.
Director: Ed Tuck.
EIN: 133391238

35998
Grace Franco and Sons Foundation
350 5th Ave., Ste. 5001
New York, NY 10118-5099

Established in 1994.
Donor(s): Grace Franco, Fine Sheer Industries, Inc.
Financial data (yr. ended 12/31/01): Grants paid, $73,584; assets, $2,442 (M); gifts received, $74,100; expenditures, $73,690; qualifying distributions, $73,690.
Limitations: Applications not accepted. Giving primarily in NY.
Application information: Contributes only to pre-selected organizations.
Officer: Grace Franco, Pres.
EIN: 133755626

35999
Max Mainzer Memorial Foundation, Inc.
180 West End Ave., Ste. 27R
New York, NY 10023
Contact: Carlos Dornberg, V.P.

Donor(s): Helga Welles,‡ Fred L. Marx.‡
Financial data (yr. ended 03/31/01): Grants paid, $73,550; assets, $124,431 (M); gifts received, $26,500; expenditures, $76,525; qualifying distributions, $76,301.
Limitations: Giving primarily in NY.
Application information: Application form not required.

Officers: Hans Kaiser, Pres.; Carlos Dornberg, V.P. and Treas.
EIN: 116008008
Codes: GTI

36000
Janssen Meyers Foundation for Excellence
c/o Janssen Meyers Assocs., LLP
1345 Old Northern Blvd.
Roslyn, NY 11576

Established in 1993 in NY.
Donor(s): Peter Janssen, Bruce Meyers, Todd Nejaime.
Financial data (yr. ended 12/31/00): Grants paid, $73,530; assets, $279,441 (M); gifts received, $153,375; expenditures, $73,874; qualifying distributions, $73,874.
Limitations: Giving on a national basis, with emphasis on CA and NY.
Officers: Peter Janssen, Pres.; Julia Venturino, Secy.
EIN: 133688985

36001
Case Family Foundation
44 W. 77th St., Ste. 7E
New York, NY 10024

Established in 1997 in NY.
Donor(s): Robert A. Case.
Financial data (yr. ended 12/31/00): Grants paid, $73,500; assets, $2,695,438 (M); gifts received, $109,465; expenditures, $86,002; qualifying distributions, $72,684.
Limitations: Applications not accepted.
Application information: Contributes only to pre-selected organizations.
Trustees: Mary-Suzanne P. Case, Robert A. Case.
EIN: 137105895

36002
Wurtele Foundation, Inc.
1 W. Church St.
Elmira, NY 14901

Established in 1981 in NY.
Donor(s): Joanna Wurtele.
Financial data (yr. ended 04/30/01): Grants paid, $73,364; assets, $1,494,451 (M); gifts received, $446,992; expenditures, $96,454; qualifying distributions, $73,364.
Limitations: Applications not accepted. Giving primarily in Corning, NY.
Application information: Contributes only to pre-selected organizations.
Officers and Trustees:* Joanna Wurtele,* Pres.; Clover M. Drinkwater, Secy.-Treas.; Elizabeth McCullough.
EIN: 133098760

36003
The Batim Foundation
1225 39th St.
Brooklyn, NY 11218

Established in 1994 in NY.
Donor(s): Park Estates, The Landau Family Trust.
Financial data (yr. ended 11/30/01): Grants paid, $73,282; assets, $1,993,300 (M); gifts received, $72,040; expenditures, $74,182; qualifying distributions, $73,282.
Limitations: Applications not accepted. Giving primarily in NY.
Application information: Contributes only to pre-selected organizations.
Trustees: M. Eckstein, D. Landau.
EIN: 113237411

36004
The Judith and Elliot Horowitz Foundation
2095 E. 3rd St.
Brooklyn, NY 11223

Established in 1998 in NY.
Donor(s): Elliot Horowitz.
Financial data (yr. ended 12/31/01): Grants paid, $73,270; assets, $151,136 (M); gifts received, $100,000; expenditures, $74,319; qualifying distributions, $73,238.
Limitations: Applications not accepted. Giving primarily in NY.
Application information: Contributes only to pre-selected organizations.
Officers and Trustee:* Elliot Horowitz,* Chair.; Judith Horowitz, Mgr.
EIN: 113464810

36005
The Eddie R. Betesh Foundation, Inc.
913 First Ct.
Brooklyn, NY 11223

Established in 1999 in NY.
Donor(s): Eddie Betesh.
Financial data (yr. ended 12/31/00): Grants paid, $73,267; assets, $40 (M); gifts received, $30,276; expenditures, $75,907; qualifying distributions, $75,907.
Limitations: Applications not accepted.
Application information: Contributes only to pre-selected organizations.
Officers: Eddie Betesh, Pres.; Albert Betesh, V.P.; Shelly Betesh, Secy.-Treas.
EIN: 113528015

36006
The David G. Lambert Foundation
c/o Goldman Sachs & Co.
85 Broad St., Tax Dept.
New York, NY 10004

Established in 1996 in NY.
Financial data (yr. ended 05/31/01): Grants paid, $73,225; assets, $847,489 (M); gifts received, $3,500; expenditures, $97,825; qualifying distributions, $75,075.
Limitations: Applications not accepted. Giving primarily in MA and NY.
Application information: Contributes only to pre-selected organizations.
Trustee: David G. Lambert.
EIN: 133933625

36007
The Alberto Foundation
c/o Craig N. Aroons
55 Old Turnpike Rd., Ste. 212
Nanuet, NY 10954

Established in 1996 in DE.
Financial data (yr. ended 12/31/01): Grants paid, $73,200; assets, $1,498 (M); expenditures, $74,176; qualifying distributions, $73,200.
Limitations: Applications not accepted. Giving primarily in NJ.
Application information: Contributes only to pre-selected organizations.
Officers and Directors:* Charles M. Alberto, Jr.,* Pres.; Joan Alberto,* V.P.; Steve Alberto,* V.P.; Lenard H. Mandel,* Secy.-Treas.
EIN: 133919996

36008
The Granoff Family Foundation
2 Fir Dr.
Great Neck, NY 11024-1529
Contact: Gary C. Granoff, V.P.

Established in 1978 in NY.
Financial data (yr. ended 10/31/00): Grants paid, $73,139; assets, $1,014,797 (M); expenditures, $75,347; qualifying distributions, $73,139.
Limitations: Applications not accepted. Giving on a national basis.
Application information: Contributes only to pre-selected organizations.
Officers: N. Henry Granoff, Pres.; Gary C. Granoff, V.P. and Secy.; Dan Granoff, M.D., V.P.; Jeanette Granoff, V.P.
EIN: 132981867

36009
Asch Foundation, Inc.
380 Madison Ave.
New York, NY 10017

Donor(s): George Asch, Phyllis E. Asch, Palais Royal of Houston, The Madeline and Lawrence Greenwald Foundation, Moselle Pollack.
Financial data (yr. ended 06/30/01): Grants paid, $73,075; assets, $554,597 (M); expenditures, $81,739; qualifying distributions, $76,775.
Limitations: Applications not accepted. Giving primarily in NY.
Application information: Contributes only to pre-selected organizations.
Officers and Director:* George Asch,* Pres.; Phyllis E. Asch, Secy.-Treas.
EIN: 133060664

36010
The David A. Dechman Foundation
c/o Goldman Sachs & Co.
85 Broad St., Tax Dept.
New York, NY 10004

Established in 1999 in NY.
Donor(s): David A. Dechman.
Financial data (yr. ended 03/31/01): Grants paid, $73,000; assets, $2,067,852 (M); gifts received, $659,487; expenditures, $100,752; qualifying distributions, $66,573.
Limitations: Applications not accepted. Giving primarily in MA and NY.
Application information: Contributes only to pre-selected organizations.
Trustee: David A. Dechman.
EIN: 134087830

36011
Daniel & Mary Reeves Foundation
c/o Louis Sternbach & Co.
1333 Broadway
New York, NY 10018

Established in 1955.
Financial data (yr. ended 12/31/01): Grants paid, $73,000; assets, $1,142,457 (M); expenditures, $92,867; qualifying distributions, $74,200.
Limitations: Applications not accepted. Giving on a national basis.
Application information: Contributes only to pre-selected organizations.
Officers: Susan Reeves, Pres.; Sheila O'Donnell, V.P.; Daniel F. Reeves, Jr., V.P.; Donald I. Altman, Secy.-Treas.
EIN: 136065955

36012
Griffith-McLouth Foundation
c/o Fleet National Bank
1 East Ave., 3rd Fl.
Rochester, NY 14638
Contact: Janet H. Schumacher, Trust Off., Fleet National Bank

Established in 1981 in NY.
Donor(s): Charles McLouth III, Agnes McLouth Griffith.
Financial data (yr. ended 07/31/01): Grants paid, $72,991; assets, $1,558,015 (M); expenditures, $84,262; qualifying distributions, $78,125.
Limitations: Giving limited to the Palmyra, NY, area.
Application information: Application form required.
Trustee: Fleet National Bank.
EIN: 222420223

36013
Kenwood Benevolent Society
131 Sherrill Rd.
Sherrill, NY 13461-1099 (315) 363-6580
Contact: Paul V. Noyes, Admin.

Established in 1902 in NY.
Financial data (yr. ended 12/31/00): Grants paid, $72,975; assets, $1,177,301 (M); gifts received, $300; expenditures, $77,364; qualifying distributions, $74,512.
Limitations: Giving primarily in Madison and Oneida counties, NY.
Application information: Application form not required.
Officers and Directors:* Jeanne N. Garner,* Pres.; Cornelia N. Hatcher, Secy.; Paul V. Noyes, Admin.; Wilbur D. Allen, Susan Campanie, Meredith Leonard, Kelly N. Rose, Rhoda R. Vanderwall, Paul Wayland-Smith.
EIN: 156018962

36014
The Richard F. and Lynne Barnes Leahy Foundation
c/o Cleary Gottlieb
1 Liberty Plz.
New York, NY 10006

Established in 1993 in NY.
Donor(s): Richard F. Leahy, Lynne Barnes Leahy.
Financial data (yr. ended 12/31/01): Grants paid, $72,900; assets, $9,237 (M); expenditures, $75,455; qualifying distributions, $75,279.
Limitations: Applications not accepted. Giving primarily in NY.
Application information: Contributes only to pre-selected organizations.
Trustees: Lynne Barnes Leahy, Richard F. Leahy.
EIN: 137010878

36015
Alice L. Kulick Foundation, Inc.
P.O. Box 621
Harrison, NY 10528

Established in 1998 in NY.
Donor(s): Alice L. Kulick.
Financial data (yr. ended 12/31/00): Grants paid, $72,789; assets, $90,298 (M); gifts received, $83,100; expenditures, $74,052; qualifying distributions, $72,789.
Limitations: Applications not accepted. Giving primarily in NY.
Application information: Contributes only to pre-selected organizations.
Officers and Directors:* Alice L. Kulick, Pres. and Treas.; Rene Kulick,* Secy.; Eugene Wallach.
EIN: 134036648

36016
The Gutfruend Zedaka Fund
c/o J. Furst
1244 49th St.
Brooklyn, NY 11219

Established in 1995 in NY.
Financial data (yr. ended 12/31/00): Grants paid, $72,761; assets, $229,012 (M); expenditures, $74,084; qualifying distributions, $72,072.

Limitations: Applications not accepted. Giving primarily in Brooklyn, NY.
Application information: Contributes only to pre-selected organizations.
Trustees: D. Gutfruend, M. Gutfruend.
EIN: 113271701

36017
Salvatore & Anna Beltrone Family Foundation
(Formerly Beltrone Family Foundation)
16 Hemlock St.
Latham, NY 12110-2217 (518) 785-6611

Established in 1995 in NY.
Donor(s): Salvatore Beltrone, Anna Beltrone.
Financial data (yr. ended 06/30/01): Grants paid, $72,708; assets, $3,202,829 (M); gifts received, $494,069; expenditures, $99,865; qualifying distributions, $72,708.
Limitations: Applications not accepted. Giving primarily in NY.
Application information: Contributes only to pre-selected organizations.
Trustees: Antonia Beltrone, Kara Conway Love, Brian Nobis.
EIN: 141790563

36018
Isabelle Russek Leeds Foundation
c/o Private Financial Svcs.
570 Lexington Ave., 42nd Fl.
New York, NY 10022

Established in 1986 in NY.
Donor(s): Isabelle R. Leeds.
Financial data (yr. ended 10/31/00): Grants paid, $72,600; assets, $1,396,302 (M); expenditures, $94,529; qualifying distributions, $72,600.
Limitations: Applications not accepted. Giving limited to New York, NY.
Application information: Contributes only to pre-selected organization.
Officers and Trustees:* Isabelle R. Leeds,* Pres.; Amy Beth Leeds, V.P. and Secy.; David R. Leeds,* V.P.
EIN: 133384086

36019
The Levien Foundation, Inc.
745 5th Ave., Ste. 812
New York, NY 10151-0016

Established in 1960 in NY.
Financial data (yr. ended 12/31/01): Grants paid, $72,570; assets, $1,327,350 (M); expenditures, $94,905; qualifying distributions, $83,405.
Limitations: Applications not accepted. Giving primarily in NY; some giving in the West Palm Beach, FL, area.
Application information: Contributes only to pre-selected organizations.
Director: Janice Levien.
EIN: 136077798

36020
Zwick Family Charitable Foundation
930 E. 24th St.
Brooklyn, NY 11210 (718) 258-8871
Contact: Martin Zwick, Pres.

Established in 2000 in NY.
Donor(s): Abraham N. Klein, Martin Zwick, Irene David.‡
Financial data (yr. ended 12/31/01): Grants paid, $72,568; assets, $284,725 (M); gifts received, $74,300; expenditures, $73,102; qualifying distributions, $72,568.
Officers: Martin Zwick, Pres.; Gail Zwick, V.P.
EIN: 316637541

36021
Morris & Rose Danzig Charitable Trust
c/o JPMorgan Chase Private Bank
1211 Ave. of the Americas, 38th Fl.
New York, NY 10036 (212) 789-5715
E-mail: philip_lisa@JPMorgan.com
Contact: Lisa Philp

Financial data (yr. ended 12/31/01): Grants paid, $72,500; assets, $1,268,956 (M); expenditures, $92,534; qualifying distributions, $74,579.
Limitations: Applications not accepted. Giving primarily in the New York, NY metropolitan area.
Application information: Unsolicited requests for funds not accepted.
Trustees: Arthur A. Anderman, JPMorgan Chase Bank.
EIN: 136609939

36022
The Sarah D. Klingenstein Foundation
787 Seventh Ave., 6th Fl.
New York, NY 10019
Contact: Sarah Klingenstein, Pres.

Established in 1999 in DE.
Donor(s): Sarah D. Klingenstein.
Financial data (yr. ended 12/31/01): Grants paid, $72,500; assets, $252,205 (M); gifts received, $10,396; expenditures, $78,418; qualifying distributions, $69,931.
Limitations: Applications not accepted.
Application information: Contributes only to pre-selected organizations.
Officers and Trustee:* Sarah D. Klingenstein,* Pres.; Arthur Sederbaum, Secy.; Andrew Klingenstein, Treas.
EIN: 134078024

36023
Bettina Baruch Foundation, Inc.
c/o Marks Paneth & Shron LLP
622 3rd Ave.
New York, NY 10017

Established in 2001 in NY.
Donor(s): Betty Baruch Y, Bette Baruch Char. Remainder Trust.
Financial data (yr. ended 12/31/01): Grants paid, $72,487; assets, $3,107,023 (M); gifts received, $3,605,504; expenditures, $84,025; qualifying distributions, $72,487.
Limitations: Applications not accepted. Giving primarily in NY.
Application information: Contributes only to pre-selected organizations.
Officers: Patricia Joseph, Pres.; Robert Edmonds, V.P. and Secy.; Robert Lewis, Treas.
EIN: 134066646

36024
Stewart Family Foundation, Inc.
c/o Seymour Stewart
5 Meadow Ln.
Manhasset, NY 11030

Established in 1998 in NY.
Donor(s): Seymour Stewart.
Financial data (yr. ended 12/31/00): Grants paid, $72,430; assets, $284,691 (M); expenditures, $75,466; qualifying distributions, $72,685.
Limitations: Applications not accepted. Giving primarily in NY.
Application information: Contributes only to pre-selected organizations.
Directors: Beth Cotler, Michele Elson, Lisa S. Jacobs, Gloria Stewart, Seymour Stewart.
EIN: 113442511

36025
The Ruth, Victor, & Paul Levy Foundation, Inc.
200 Central Park S., Ste. 28A
New York, NY 10019-1448
Contact: Ruth Levy, Tr.

Established in 1998 in NY.
Donor(s): Ruth Levy, Victor Levy.
Financial data (yr. ended 09/30/01): Grants paid, $72,400; assets, $31,278 (M); expenditures, $74,658; qualifying distributions, $72,400.
Limitations: Applications not accepted. Giving primarily in New York, NY.
Application information: Contributes only to pre-selected organizations.
Trustees: Ruth Levy, Victor Levy.
EIN: 134031036

36026
The Aaron & Kreindel Twerski Foundation
1772 49th St.
Brooklyn, NY 11204

Established in 1989 in NY.
Donor(s): Aaron Twerski.
Financial data (yr. ended 11/30/01): Grants paid, $72,400; assets, $253,293 (M); gifts received, $26,433; expenditures, $77,773; qualifying distributions, $72,400.
Limitations: Applications not accepted. Giving primarily in Brooklyn, NY.
Application information: Contributes only to pre-selected organizations.
Trustee: Aaron Twerski.
EIN: 112999938

36027
The Finkelstein Foundation
c/o J. Furst
1244 49th St.
Brooklyn, NY 11219-3011

Established in 1995 in NY.
Financial data (yr. ended 12/31/00): Grants paid, $72,260; assets, $181,983 (M); expenditures, $73,557; qualifying distributions, $71,661.
Limitations: Applications not accepted.
Application information: Contributes only to pre-selected organizations.
Trustees: Samuel Finkelstein, Shaindel Finkelstein.
EIN: 113271690

36028
The Beirne Foundation, Inc.
c/o Paul R. Beirne
25 Central Park W., Ste. 31-0
New York, NY 10023

Established in 1991 in DE.
Donor(s): Paul R. Beirne.
Financial data (yr. ended 12/31/99): Grants paid, $72,180; assets, $309,220 (M); gifts received, $50,000; expenditures, $76,313; qualifying distributions, $74,300.
Limitations: Giving limited to New York, NY.
Officer: Paul R. Beirne, Pres.
Directors: Beverly Beirne, Greg Beirne.
EIN: 133583634

36029
Elisabeth Dye Curtis Trust
1 HSBC Ctr., 16th Fl.
Buffalo, NY 14203-2885

Established in 1985 in NY.
Financial data (yr. ended 12/31/01): Grants paid, $72,145; assets, $1,173,523 (M); expenditures, $86,443; qualifying distributions, $73,214.
Limitations: Applications not accepted. Giving primarily in NY.

36029—NEW YORK

Application information: Contributes only to pre-selected organizations.
Trustee: HSBC Bank USA.
EIN: 166021304

36030
Rothschild Family Foundation
805 E. Genesee St.
Syracuse, NY 13210

Established in 1998.
Donor(s): Alan W. Rothschild.
Financial data (yr. ended 12/31/01): Grants paid, $72,080; assets, $1 (M); expenditures, $72,080; qualifying distributions, $72,080.
Limitations: Applications not accepted.
Application information: Contributes only to pre-selected organizations.
Trustee: Alan W. Rothschild.
EIN: 222992381

36031
The Gutman Family Foundation, Inc.
700 Park Ave.
New York, NY 10021-4930

Established in 1994 in NY.
Donor(s): Edward S. Gutman.
Financial data (yr. ended 10/31/99): Grants paid, $72,070; assets, $748,236 (M); gifts received, $61,131; expenditures, $72,870; qualifying distributions, $70,654.
Limitations: Giving primarily in NY.
Application information: Application form not required.
Officers: Edward S. Gutman, Pres. and Treas.; Patricia Gutman, V.P.; Robert Gutman, V.P.; Heidi Gutman, Secy.
EIN: 133798838

36032
The Martin A. Posner Hand Foundation
2 E. 88th St.
New York, NY 10020

Established in 1987 in NY.
Donor(s): Natasha Gelman.
Financial data (yr. ended 12/31/00): Grants paid, $72,063; assets, $1,278,722 (M); gifts received, $1,600; expenditures, $88,045; qualifying distributions, $83,913.
Limitations: Applications not accepted. Giving primarily in New York, NY.
Application information: Contributes only to pre-selected organizations.
Directors: Steven Green, M.D., Martin A. Posner, M.D., Jerome Sloane.
EIN: 133375430

36033
The George E. & Kathleen E. Austin Foundation
29 Boulder Trail
Bronxville, NY 10708-5903
Contact: George E. Austin, Pres.

Established in 1997 in NY.
Donor(s): George E. Austin, Kathleen E. Austin.
Financial data (yr. ended 12/31/01): Grants paid, $72,000; assets, $1,553,982 (M); gifts received, $100,000; expenditures, $89,208; qualifying distributions, $74,385.
Limitations: Applications not accepted.
Application information: Contributes only to pre-selected organizations.
Directors: Carter W. Austin, Elizabeth E. Austin, George E. Austin, Kathleen E. Austin, Peter L. Austin.
EIN: 133948814

36034
Bruce Wesson Charitable Foundation
c/o Galen Assoc.
610 5th Ave.
New York, NY 10020

Donor(s): Bruce F. Wesson.
Financial data (yr. ended 12/31/00): Grants paid, $71,962; assets, $1,194,822 (M); gifts received, $732,000; expenditures, $83,481; qualifying distributions, $71,936.
Limitations: Giving primarily in NJ and NY.
Application information: Application form not required.
Trustee: Bruce F. Wesson.
EIN: 133980742

36035
The Jacob and Jean Stein Foundation, Inc.
20 Jerusalem Ave.
Hicksville, NY 11801

Established in 1999 in NY.
Donor(s): Jacob Stein, Jean Stein.
Financial data (yr. ended 06/30/01): Grants paid, $71,915; assets, $23,556 (M); gifts received, $84,905; expenditures, $73,612; qualifying distributions, $73,034.
Limitations: Giving primarily in NY.
Officers: Jacob Stein, Pres.; Jean Stein, Secy.
Directors: Richard A. Stein, M.D., Stuart J. Stein, Linda G. Whalen.
EIN: 113506883

36036
Cynthia and Ronald Beck Foundation
c/o Ronald N. Beck
830 Park Ave., Ste. 200
New York, NY 10021-2757

Established in 1999 in NY.
Donor(s): Cynthia Lewis Beck, Ronald N. Beck.
Financial data (yr. ended 12/31/01): Grants paid, $71,900; assets, $330,292 (M); expenditures, $71,900; qualifying distributions, $71,789.
Limitations: Applications not accepted. Giving primarily in Los Angeles, CA and New York, NY.
Application information: Contributes only to pre-selected organizations.
Directors: Cynthia Lewis Beck, Ronald N. Beck.
EIN: 134045208

36037
The Hunter Foundation, Inc.
c/o Hertz, Herson & Co., LLP
2 Park Ave., Ste. 1500
New York, NY 10016-5675

Donor(s): Allan B. Hunter.
Financial data (yr. ended 12/31/01): Grants paid, $71,851; assets, $956,278 (M); expenditures, $75,034; qualifying distributions, $72,357.
Limitations: Applications not accepted. Giving primarily in NY.
Application information: Contributes only to pre-selected organizations.
Trustees: Andre Hunter, Renate Hunter, Peter Strauss.
EIN: 136094021

36038
The Marah Moshe Foundation
5014 16th Ave., Ste. 155
Brooklyn, NY 11204-1404

Established in 1995 in NY.
Donor(s): Shmuel B. Loffler.
Financial data (yr. ended 11/30/00): Grants paid, $71,848; assets, $608,256 (M); gifts received, $103,543; expenditures, $77,571; qualifying distributions, $71,848.

Limitations: Applications not accepted.
Application information: Contributes only to pre-selected organizations.
Officers: Shmuel B. Loffler, Pres.; Liba U. Loffler, V.P.; Josef Loffler, Secy.
Trustee: Iby Loffler.
EIN: 113305583

36039
Samuel J. & Ethel Lefrak Charitable Foundation, Inc.
97-77 Queens Blvd.
Rego Park, NY 11374-3317

Established in 1989 in DE.
Donor(s): Samuel J. Lefrak.
Financial data (yr. ended 11/30/99): Grants paid, $71,825; assets, $1,000,394 (M); gifts received, $13,000; expenditures, $88,560; qualifying distributions, $71,825.
Limitations: Applications not accepted. Giving primarily in NY.
Application information: Contributes only to pre-selected organizations.
Officer: Samuel J. Lefrak, Pres.
EIN: 112994768

36040
The Mayer Family Foundation
c/o BCRS Assocs., LLC
67 Wall St., 8th Fl.
New York, NY 10005

Established in 1989 in CT.
Donor(s): Charles B. Mayer, Jr.
Financial data (yr. ended 03/31/02): Grants paid, $71,750; assets, $1,089,572 (M); expenditures, $73,500; qualifying distributions, $71,750.
Limitations: Applications not accepted. Giving primarily in New York, NY.
Application information: Contributes only to pre-selected organizations.
Trustees: Charles B. Mayer, Charles B. Mayer, Jr.
EIN: 133531984

36041
The Alexander S. Onassis Public Benefit Foundation (U.S.A.), Inc.
645 5th Ave., 3rd Fl.
New York, NY 10022-5910

Established in 1999 in NY.
Financial data (yr. ended 06/30/01): Grants paid, $71,650; assets, $292,334 (M); gifts received, $1,400,412; expenditures, $1,537,318; qualifying distributions, $71,650.
Limitations: Applications not accepted.
Application information: Contributes only to pre-selected organizations.
Officers and Board Members:* Stelio A. Papadimitriou,* Pres. and Treas.; Michael Sotirhos,* V.P.; Paul Ioannides,* Secy.; Georgios Babiniotis, John Brademas, Michael Jaharis, Jr., Amb. Vassilios Vitsaxis.
EIN: 134037172

36042
The Horowitch Family Foundation
(Formerly Maurice & Sheldon Horowitch Foundation)
6709 Brooklawn Pkwy.
Syracuse, NY 13211 (800) 234-9955
Contact: Sheldon J. Horowitch, Tr.

Established in 1969.
Donor(s): Sheldon J. Horowitch.
Financial data (yr. ended 12/31/99): Grants paid, $71,625; assets, $2,024,725 (M); gifts received, $38,012; expenditures, $74,776; qualifying distributions, $73,300.
Limitations: Giving primarily in central NY.

Trustees: Jill B. Greiss, Sheldon J. Horowitch, M.D., Samuel K. Levene.
EIN: 237046081

36043
The Murray & Isabella Rayburn Foundation, Inc.
c/o Speer & Fulvio, LLP
60 E. 42 St., Ste. 1313
New York, NY 10165-0006

Established in 1980 as Murray & Marjorie Rayburn Foundation.
Donor(s): Murray B. Rayburn Charitable Lead Trust.
Financial data (yr. ended 06/30/01): Grants paid, $71,550; assets, $107,044 (M); gifts received, $161,416; expenditures, $76,766; qualifying distributions, $74,933.
Limitations: Applications not accepted. Giving primarily in New York, NY.
Application information: Contributes only to pre-selected organizations.
Officers and Directors:* Isabella Rayburn,* Pres.; Raymond W. Merritt,* Secy.; Martin Helpern,* Treas.; James H. Carey.
EIN: 133077508

36044
Arabel Foundation, Inc.
c/o Arthur Rebell
160 W. 66th St., Ste. 5500
New York, NY 10023-6555

Incorporated in 1955 in NY.
Donor(s): Harry Rebell, Arthur Rebell, Michael A. Rebell.
Financial data (yr. ended 12/31/00): Grants paid, $71,532; assets, $161,356 (M); expenditures, $79,511; qualifying distributions, $79,503.
Limitations: Applications not accepted. Giving primarily in NY.
Application information: Contributes only to pre-selected organizations.
Officers: Arthur Rebell, Pres. and Treas.; Michael A. Rebell, V.P.; Phyllis Rebell, Secy.
EIN: 136089983

36045
Shirley Borak Foundation, Inc.
454 Succabone Rd.
Bedford Corners, NY 10549 (914) 234-7091
Contact: Allison Sachs, Treas.

Donor(s): Allison Sachs.
Financial data (yr. ended 12/31/00): Grants paid, $71,500; assets, $92,590 (M); gifts received, $33,150; expenditures, $85,585; qualifying distributions, $70,729.
Officers: Patricia Hockler, Pres.; Allison Sachs, Treas.
Trustees: Scott Hockler, Barbara Reiff.
EIN: 237009728

36046
Helen & Herman Gimbel Charity Fund, Inc.
24 Suncrest Dr.
Dix Hills, NY 11746
Contact: Stephanie Prince, Dir.

Established in 1969.
Financial data (yr. ended 03/31/01): Grants paid, $71,454; assets, $1,713,134 (M); expenditures, $77,376; qualifying distributions, $77,376.
Limitations: Giving primarily in FL and NY.
Directors: Herman Gimbel, Joseph Gimbel, David Prince, Stephanie Prince.
EIN: 237010047

36047
Jill & Jayne Franklin Charitable Trust
c/o The Bank of New York-Tax Dept.
1 Wall St., 28th Fl.
New York, NY 10286

Established in 1999 in NY.
Financial data (yr. ended 01/31/02): Grants paid, $71,411; assets, $1,948,116 (M); expenditures, $97,078; qualifying distributions, $71,411.
Limitations: Applications not accepted.
Application information: Contributes only to pre-selected organizations.
Trustee: The Bank of New York.
EIN: 137206444

36048
Elsmere Foundation, Inc.
c/o Angelo, Gordon & Co.
245 Park Ave.
New York, NY 10167

Incorporated in 1955 in NY.
Donor(s): Kate S. Heming, Henry L. Heming, Henry A. Cohn, Abraham S. Platt, Richard H. Baer, Walter W. Hess, Jr., Herbert H. Weitsman,‡ Chester Viale, Stephen Kovacs, Alexander Bing III.
Financial data (yr. ended 12/31/01): Grants paid, $71,400; assets, $318,085 (M); gifts received, $48,118; expenditures, $79,617; qualifying distributions, $74,485.
Limitations: Applications not accepted. Giving primarily in NY.
Application information: Contributes only to pre-selected organizations.
Officers: Walter W. Hess, Jr., Pres.; Alexander Bing III, 2nd V.P.; Robert Schoenthal, Treas.
EIN: 136061343

36049
Putnam Hospital Center Charitable Trust
c/o The Bank of New York, Tax Dept.
1 Wall St., 28th Fl.
New York, NY 10286

Established in 1998 in NY.
Financial data (yr. ended 07/31/01): Grants paid, $71,352; assets, $1,123,763 (M); expenditures, $83,903; qualifying distributions, $73,499.
Limitations: Applications not accepted.
Application information: Contributes only to pre-selected organizations.
Trustee: The Bank of New York.
EIN: 137161850

36050
Propp Foundation, Inc.
405 Park Ave., Ste. 1103
New York, NY 10022-4405

Established in 1930.
Donor(s): E. Propp, M.J. Propp.
Financial data (yr. ended 12/31/01): Grants paid, $71,310; assets, $1,251,992 (M); expenditures, $75,392; qualifying distributions, $71,310.
Limitations: Applications not accepted.
Application information: Contributes only to pre-selected organizations.
Officers: M.J. Propp, Pres.; E. Propp, Exec. V.P. and Treas.; Florence Klein, V.P.
EIN: 136098342

36051
The Philippe and Deborah Dauman Foundation
c/o DND Capital Partners
9 W. 57th St., Ste. 4615
New York, NY 10019
Contact: Philippe P. Dauman, Pres.

Established in 2000 in NY.
Donor(s): Philippe P. Dauman, Deborah Ross Dauman.
Financial data (yr. ended 12/31/01): Grants paid, $71,250; assets, $1,313,748 (M); gifts received, $500,487; expenditures, $94,468; qualifying distributions, $71,380.
Limitations: Giving primarily in NY.
Application information: Application form not required.
Officers: Philippe P. Dauman, Pres. and Treas.; Deborah Ross Dauman, V.P. and Secy.
EIN: 134097014

36052
The Emanuel and Anna Weinstein Foundation
c/o M. Bedney, Graf, Repetti, & Co.
1114 Ave. of the Americas, 17th Fl.
New York, NY 10036
Application address: 50 E. 89th St., New York, NY 10128, tel.: (212) 534-1504
Contact: Harvey J. Weinstein, Tr.

Established in 1985 in NY.
Donor(s): Harvey J. Weinstein.
Financial data (yr. ended 12/31/00): Grants paid, $71,100; assets, $1,123,099 (M); gifts received, $15,383; expenditures, $73,292; qualifying distributions, $71,100.
Limitations: Giving primarily in NY.
Trustees: Harvey J. Weinstein, George Youngerman.
EIN: 133313447

36053
Bweta Family Foundation
c/o Jamil Ezra
514 E. 84th St.
New York, NY 10028

Established in 1998 in NY.
Donor(s): Jamil Ezra.
Financial data (yr. ended 12/31/00): Grants paid, $71,089; assets, $667,063 (M); gifts received, $240,400; expenditures, $77,981; qualifying distributions, $71,089.
Limitations: Applications not accepted. Giving primarily in NY.
Application information: Contributes only to pre-selected organizations.
Trustees: Jamil Ezra, Ruth Ezra.
EIN: 134020892

36054
Kurz-Kneiger Foundation, Inc.
168 Doughty Blvd.
Inwood, NY 11096

Established in 1984 in NY.
Donor(s): Milton Kurz.
Financial data (yr. ended 12/31/01): Grants paid, $71,078; assets, $1,138,248 (M); gifts received, $50,000; expenditures, $93,260; qualifying distributions, $71,078.
Limitations: Applications not accepted. Giving primarily in the tri-state CT, NJ, and NY, area.
Application information: Contributes only to pre-selected organizations.
Officers: Milton Kurz, Pres.; Edward Schlussel, V.P.; Jonathan Kurz, Secy.; David Kurz, Treas.
EIN: 112680139

36055
Lippes Family Charitable Foundation
700 Guaranty Bldg.
28 Church St.
Buffalo, NY 14202 (716) 853-5100
Contact: Gerald S. Lippes, Chair.

Established in 1989 in NY.
Donor(s): Gerald S. Lippes.

Financial data (yr. ended 12/31/01): Grants paid, $71,017; assets, $2,327,036 (M); expenditures, $87,941; qualifying distributions, $71,017.
Limitations: Giving primarily in Buffalo, NY.
Officers: Gerald S. Lippes, Chair.; Sandra F. Lippes, Pres.; Adam S. Lippes, V.P.; David F. Lippes, V.P.; Tracy G. Lippes, V.P.
EIN: 223019880

36056
The Brooklyn Home for Aged Men
c/o Nancy K. Munson
9701 Shore Rd.
Brooklyn, NY 11209 (718) 745-1638

Established in 1878 in NY.
Financial data (yr. ended 12/31/01): Grants paid, $71,000; assets, $998,298 (M); gifts received, $12,596; expenditures, $119,593; qualifying distributions, $105,408.
Limitations: Applications not accepted. Giving primarily in Brooklyn, NY.
Publications: Informational brochure.
Application information: Contributes only to pre-selected organizations.
Officers and Directors:* Nancy K. Munson,* Pres.; Dorothy C. Beckmann,* V.P.; George C. Schaefer,* Secy.-Treas.; Gary A. Henningsen, Eleanor M. Kaufmann, Annette E. Schaefer, Jean C. Weber.
EIN: 111630754

36057
Vivian and Paul Olum Charitable Foundation
c/o Levene, Gouldin & Thompson, LLP
450 Plaza Dr.
Vestal, NY 13850 (607) 763-9200

Established in 1984 in NY.
Financial data (yr. ended 12/31/01): Grants paid, $70,950; assets, $1,031,488 (M); gifts received, $589,868; expenditures, $74,414; qualifying distributions, $70,950.
Limitations: Applications not accepted. Giving primarily in NY.
Application information: Contributes only to pre-selected organizations.
Trustees: Paul Olum, Michael H. Zuckerman.
EIN: 222559174

36058
Joan & Arthur Sarnoff Foundation
151 Central Park W.
New York, NY 10023-1514 (212) 362-2628
Contact: Arthur Sarnoff, Pres.

Established in 1966 in NY.
Donor(s): Arthur Sarnoff, Joan Sarnoff.
Financial data (yr. ended 12/31/01): Grants paid, $70,950; assets, $202,004 (M); gifts received, $50,722; expenditures, $75,349; qualifying distributions, $70,401.
Limitations: Giving primarily in New York, NY.
Officers: Arthur Sarnoff, Pres.; Joan Sarnoff, V.P.
Directors: Susan Sarnoff Bram, Elizabeth Sarnoff Cohen.
EIN: 136211155

36059
Grant Family Foundation
(Formerly The Max L. Grant Charitable Foundation)
c/o Theodore Ranzal, C.P.A.
108 Corporate Park Dr., Ste. 105
White Plains, NY 10604

Established in 1985 in RI.
Financial data (yr. ended 12/31/00): Grants paid, $70,900; assets, $651,094 (M); expenditures, $72,528; qualifying distributions, $70,941.

Limitations: Applications not accepted. Giving primarily in CT and VT.
Application information: Contributes only to pre-selected organizations.
Officers: Gardner L. Grant, Pres.; Ellen P. Grant, V.P.; Laura R. Zimmerman, Secy.; Gardner Grant, Jr., Treas.
EIN: 133264113

36060
The Haugland Family Foundation, Inc.
8 Meadow Creek Ct.
East Islip, NY 11730

Established in 1998 in NY.
Donor(s): William J. Haugland, Hogwild Associates, Inc.
Financial data (yr. ended 12/31/00): Grants paid, $70,900; assets, $166,789 (M); gifts received, $12,938; expenditures, $71,408; qualifying distributions, $70,900.
Limitations: Applications not accepted.
Application information: Contributes only to pre-selected organizations.
Officers: William J. Haugland, Pres.; Linda Haugland, V.P.; Myron S. Bloom, Secy.-Treas.
EIN: 113440392

36061
Nosson Charitable Trust
2500 Ave. I
Brooklyn, NY 11210-2830
Application address: 1342 E. 5th St., Brooklyn, NY 11230
Contact: Raphael Grossman

Established in 2000 in NY.
Financial data (yr. ended 12/31/00): Grants paid, $70,888; assets, $15,603 (M); gifts received, $86,500; expenditures, $71,388; qualifying distributions, $71,388.
Trustees: Chana Gelbfish, Joseph Gelbfish.
EIN: 117448965

36062
The Phelan Foundation
7 Split Rock Ct.
Melville, NY 11747

Established in 2000 in NY.
Donor(s): Frank Phelan.
Financial data (yr. ended 12/31/00): Grants paid, $70,852; assets, $37,871 (M); gifts received, $110,000; expenditures, $75,529; qualifying distributions, $70,940.
Officers and Directors:* Frank Phelan,* Pres.; Mary Phelan,* V.P. and Secy.; Charles Feuerstein.
EIN: 113531781

36063
Louis & Lillian Detkin Foundation, Inc.
269-23H Grand Central Pkwy.
Floral Park, NY 11005 (718) 631-3543
Contact: Paul G. Detkin, Mgr.

Financial data (yr. ended 11/30/01): Grants paid, $70,835; assets, $1,142,841 (M); expenditures, $75,370; qualifying distributions, $69,482.
Limitations: Giving primarily in NY.
Officer: Paul G. Detkin, Mgr.
EIN: 136109925

36064
The Rita & Irwin Hochberg Family Foundation
c/o Bloom, Hochberg & Co.
450 7th Ave.
New York, NY 10123

Donor(s): Hochberg Assocs., LP.
Financial data (yr. ended 12/31/01): Grants paid, $70,800; assets, $499,596 (M); gifts received, $26,287; expenditures, $73,647; qualifying distributions, $70,558.
Limitations: Applications not accepted.
Application information: Contributes only to pre-selected organizations.
Officers: Irwin Hochberg, Pres.; Rita Hochberg, V.P.; Jonathan Hochberg, Secy.; Mitchell Hochberg, Treas.
EIN: 137100740

36065
Constance Saltonstall Foundation for the Arts, Inc.
P.O. Box 6607
Ithaca, NY 14851-6607 (607) 277-4933
FAX: (607) 277-4933; E-mail: artsfound@clarityconnect.com; URL: http://www.saltonstall.org
Contact: Lee-Ellen Marvin, Exec. Dir.

Established in 1996.
Donor(s): Constance Saltonstall.‡
Financial data (yr. ended 12/31/01): Grants paid, $70,760; assets, $4,688,652 (M); gifts received, $251,942; qualifying distributions, $202,745.
Limitations: Giving limited to residents of central and western counties of NY.
Publications: Application guidelines.
Application information: Unsolicited requests for funds not accepted. Application form required.
Officers: Alison Lurie, Pres.; Victoria Romanoff, V.P.; Dede Hatch, Secy.; Kathy Durland Dewart, Treas.; Lee-Ellen Marvin, Exec. Dir.
Directors: Kenneth McClane, James McConkey, Marilyn Rivchin.
EIN: 161481219
Codes: GTI

36066
The Trena Koval Danels Memorial Foundation, Inc.
c/o Melvin Koval
370 Old Country Rd.
Garden City, NY 11530

Established in 1985 in NY.
Donor(s): Melvin Koval, Selma Koval, Irwin Danels.
Financial data (yr. ended 02/28/01): Grants paid, $70,657; assets, $141,557 (M); expenditures, $88,432; qualifying distributions, $70,563.
Limitations: Applications not accepted.
Application information: Contributes only to pre-selected organizations. Unsolicited requests for funds not considered.
Trustees: Irwin Danels, Melvin Koval.
EIN: 112729201

36067
Samuel & Rose Mitchell Foundation
c/o Estral Assoc.
3 E. 69th St., No. M1
New York, NY 10021

Established in 1954 in DE.
Donor(s): Estelle M. Konheim.
Financial data (yr. ended 12/31/01): Grants paid, $70,571; assets, $691,365 (M); expenditures, $80,030; qualifying distributions, $70,571.
Limitations: Applications not accepted. Giving primarily in the greater New York, NY, area.
Application information: Contributes only to pre-selected organizations.
Officer: Estelle M. Konheim, Pres.
EIN: 136128527

36068
Doris G. Quinn Foundation
P.O. Box 591
Bedford, NY 10506
Contact: David A. Barnebl, C.E.O.

Established in 1986 in NY.
Donor(s): Doris G. Quinn.
Financial data (yr. ended 12/31/00): Grants paid, $70,500; assets, $4,610,887 (M); gifts received, $16,397; expenditures, $125,551; qualifying distributions, $72,227.
Limitations: Applications not accepted. Giving primarily in NC, NJ and NY.
Application information: Contributes only to pre-selected organizations.
Trustees: David A. Barnebl, Eugene J. Callahan, Linda G. Grandey, Richard P. Terbrusch.
EIN: 133406777

36069
Grace, George & Judith Silverburgh Foundation, Inc.
c/o Leipziger & Breskin
6 E. 43rd St., 22nd Fl.
New York, NY 10017-4696

Established in 1990 in NY.
Donor(s): George Silverburgh.‡
Financial data (yr. ended 08/31/01): Grants paid, $70,500; assets, $3,207,192 (M); expenditures, $103,654; qualifying distributions, $100,517.
Limitations: Applications not accepted. Giving primarily in Bridgeport and Mystic, CT.
Application information: Contributes only to pre-selected organizations.
Officers: Roger C. Wollen, Pres.; Dori Wollen, V.P.; Leonard Weintraub, Treas.
EIN: 133585189

36070
Lowenthal Family Foundation, Inc.
1123 Broadway, Ste. 907
New York, NY 10010
Contact: Walter Lowenthal, Pres.

Established in 1993 in NY.
Donor(s): Walter Lowenthal, Randie Lowenthal.
Financial data (yr. ended 03/31/01): Grants paid, $70,449; assets, $69,659 (L); gifts received, $37,039; expenditures, $71,752; qualifying distributions, $71,752.
Limitations: Giving primarily in NY.
Officers: Walter Lowenthal, Pres.; Randie Lowenthal, V.P.; Paul Lowenthal, Secy.; Edward Lowenthal, Treas.
EIN: 133714728

36071
The Philene Foundation
24 North Dr.
Great Neck, NY 11021
Contact: Philip R. Herzig, Tr.

Established in 1999 in NY.
Donor(s): Philip Herzig, Helene Herzig.
Financial data (yr. ended 12/31/00): Grants paid, $70,432; assets, $1,671,255 (M); gifts received, $1,500,000; expenditures, $78,024; qualifying distributions, $70,432.
Trustees: Helene Herzig, Philip R. Herzig.
EIN: 113520681

36072
Noiles Family Foundation
c/o The Bank of New York
1 Wall St., Tax Dept., 28th Fl.
New York, NY 10286
Application address: c/o Douglas G. Noiles, 114 Elm Pl., New Canaan, CT 06840

Established in 1998 in CT.
Financial data (yr. ended 04/30/01): Grants paid, $70,400; assets, $1,818,962 (M); expenditures, $88,272; qualifying distributions, $75,707.
Trustees: Douglas G. Noiles, Edna T. Noiles.
EIN: 043384454

36073
Charles Hertzig Foundation
FDR Sta.
P.O. Box 1030
New York, NY 10150

Established in 1958.
Donor(s): Saul Hertzig, Rita Hertzig.
Financial data (yr. ended 10/31/01): Grants paid, $70,345; assets, $1,016,440 (M); expenditures, $96,021; qualifying distributions, $69,869.
Limitations: Applications not accepted. Giving primarily in the Northeast and Southeast.
Publications: Annual report.
Application information: Contributes only to pre-selected organizations.
Officers: Saul Hertzig, Pres.; Rita Hertzig, Secy.; Melvin Hertzig, Treas.
EIN: 136098084

36074
Rivendell Foundation
c/o The Philanthropic Group
630 5th Ave., 20th Fl.
New York, NY 10111-0254 (212) 501-7785
Contact: Barbara R. Greenberg, Consultant

Established in 1987 in NJ.
Donor(s): Kenneth J. Goldman.
Financial data (yr. ended 12/31/01): Grants paid, $70,337; assets, $113,781 (M); gifts received, $193,652; expenditures, $94,846; qualifying distributions, $70,337.
Limitations: Applications not accepted. Giving primarily in NJ for Newark teachers and public school children.
Application information: Applications by invitation only.
Trustee: Kenneth J. Goldman.
Staff Consultant: Barbara R. Greenberg.
EIN: 222876727

36075
Samuel & Anna Jacobs Foundation, Inc.
350 5th Ave., Ste. 3505
New York, NY 10118

Established in 1964.
Donor(s): Samuel Jacobs.‡
Financial data (yr. ended 12/31/00): Grants paid, $70,300; assets, $1,257,425 (M); gifts received, $152,244; expenditures, $76,337; qualifying distributions, $73,043.
Limitations: Applications not accepted. Giving primarily in New York, NY.
Application information: Contributes only to pre-selected organizations.
Officers: Ernest Rubenstein, V.P.; William S. Rubenstein, Secy.
EIN: 116039709

36076
Nathan & Helen Kohler Foundation
c/o Berg, Kaminsky & Klein, LLP
350 Jericho Tpke.
Jericho, NY 11753-1351
Contact: Marilyn Ellman Buel, Pres.

Established in 1962.
Donor(s): Helen Kohler.‡
Financial data (yr. ended 10/31/01): Grants paid, $70,300; assets, $1,283,050 (M); expenditures, $78,229; qualifying distributions, $70,300.
Limitations: Giving primarily in NY.
Application information: Application form not required.
Officer and Directors:* Marilyn Ellman Buel,* Pres.; Eugene Baumstein, Dolores Kreisman.
EIN: 136161880

36077
Busfield Foundation
c/o Steven F. Feehan
175 Garrett Rd.
Windsor, NY 13865

Established in 1995 in NY.
Financial data (yr. ended 12/31/00): Grants paid, $70,200; assets, $1,542,203 (M); expenditures, $94,218; qualifying distributions, $92,293.
Limitations: Applications not accepted. Giving primarily in NY.
Application information: Contributes only to pre-selected organizations.
Trustees: Stephen Feehan, Suzanne Feehan, June Nolan, Joan Rees.
EIN: 161468338

36078
The Salvatore & Alice Federico Foundation, Inc.
335 W. 38th St., 12th Fl.
New York, NY 10018

Established in 1992 in NY.
Financial data (yr. ended 12/31/00): Grants paid, $70,200; assets, $1,339,240 (M); expenditures, $80,226; qualifying distributions, $71,922.
Limitations: Applications not accepted. Giving primarily in NY.
Application information: Contributes only to pre-selected organizations.
Officers: Salvatore Federico, Pres.; Alice L. Federico, V.P.; David Feeney, V.P.
EIN: 133700940

36079
City Lights Charity Foundation
c/o Abraham Fishoff
1000 Stanley Ave.
Brooklyn, NY 11208

Established in 2000 in NY.
Donor(s): Abraham Fishoff.
Financial data (yr. ended 12/31/01): Grants paid, $70,178; assets, $169,246 (M); gifts received, $187,275; expenditures, $71,712; qualifying distributions, $70,178.
Director: Abraham Fishoff.
EIN: 113578664

36080
The Michele and Martin Cohen Family Foundation
75 E. End Ave.
New York, NY 10028-7909

Established in 1995 in NY.
Donor(s): Martin Cohen, Michele Cohen.
Financial data (yr. ended 12/31/00): Grants paid, $70,026; assets, $542,947 (M); gifts received, $270,000; expenditures, $71,618; qualifying distributions, $71,518.

36080—NEW YORK

Limitations: Applications not accepted. Giving primarily in CA, Washington, DC, IL, and NY.
Application information: Contributes only to pre-selected organizations.
Trustees: Martin Cohen, Michele Cohen.
EIN: 133863473

36081
The Frances Alexander Foundation
(Formerly The Ann F. Kaplan & Robert Fippinger Foundation)
c/o Goldman Sachs & Co.
85 Broad St., Tax Dept.
New York, NY 10004

Established in 1991 in NY.
Donor(s): Ann F. Kaplan.
Financial data (yr. ended 04/30/02): Grants paid, $70,000; assets, $6,822,287 (M); gifts received, $1,661,276; expenditures, $134,993; qualifying distributions, $70,000.
Limitations: Applications not accepted. Giving primarily in MA.
Application information: Contributes only to pre-selected organizations.
Trustees: Robert A. Fippinger, Ann F. Kaplan.
EIN: 133638507

36082
Nathan Z. Armour Foundation, Inc.
c/o Stroock & Stroock & Lavan
180 Maiden Ln.
New York, NY 10038-4925

Financial data (yr. ended 12/31/01): Grants paid, $70,000; assets, $1,264,776 (M); expenditures, $73,633; qualifying distributions, $69,289.
Limitations: Applications not accepted. Giving primarily in New York, NY.
Application information: Contributes only to pre-selected organizations.
Officers: Jerome A. Manning, Pres. and Treas.; Ronald J. Stein, V.P. and Secy.
EIN: 136090314

36083
Casdin Family Foundation
230 Park Ave., 20th Fl.
New York, NY 10169

Established in 2000 in NY.
Donor(s): Jeffrey W. Casdin.
Financial data (yr. ended 12/31/01): Grants paid, $70,000; assets, $691,002 (M); expenditures, $76,437; qualifying distributions, $70,000.
Trustees: Jeffrey W. Casdin, Sharon Casdin.
EIN: 137257954

36084
Angelo Donghia Foundation, Inc.
c/o Levy Sonet & Siegel, LLP
630 3rd Ave., 23rd Fl.
New York, NY 10017

Established in 2001 in NY.
Donor(s): Angelo Donghia.‡
Financial data (yr. ended 12/31/01): Grants paid, $70,000; assets, $22,133,820 (M); gifts received, $24,096,913; expenditures, $112,083; qualifying distributions, $83,149.
Limitations: Giving primarily in New York, NY.
Officers and Trustees:* Jerrold M. Sonet,* Pres.; Alan M. Siegel,* Secy.; Steven G. Sonet,* Treas.
EIN: 133523056

36085
The Pauline V. and William F. Garvey Foundation, Inc.
c/o Joseph Trenk
19 W. 44th St., Rm. 1415
New York, NY 10036-5903

Established in 1990 in NY.
Donor(s): Pauline V. Garvey.‡
Financial data (yr. ended 05/31/01): Grants paid, $70,000; assets, $1,091,260 (M); expenditures, $89,968; qualifying distributions, $70,000.
Limitations: Applications not accepted. Giving primarily in White Plains, NY.
Application information: Contributes only to pre-selected organizations.
Officers and Directors:* James A. Garvey,* Pres.; Bernard Colletti,* Secy.; John Wyles,* Treas.
EIN: 133575677

36086
Grubman Graham Foundation, Inc.
270 Madison Ave., 9th Fl.
New York, NY 10016
Contact: C. Baller, Secy.

Established in 1998 in NY.
Donor(s): Wallace K. Graham.
Financial data (yr. ended 12/31/01): Grants paid, $70,000; assets, $149,790 (M); gifts received, $31,950; expenditures, $93,918; qualifying distributions, $70,000.
Limitations: Applications not accepted. Giving primarily in MD and NY.
Application information: Contributes only to pre-selected organizations.
Officers and Directors:* Wallace K. Graham,* Pres.; Ruth Graham,* V.P.; Steven L. Graham,* V.P.; Charles H. Baller, Secy.; Eric P. Grubman,* Treas.
EIN: 134011395

36087
Margaret Q. Landenberger Research Foundation
c/o Brown Brothers Harriman Trust Co.
63 Wall St.
New York, NY 10005

Established around 1992.
Financial data (yr. ended 12/31/01): Grants paid, $70,000; assets, $1,337,968 (M); expenditures, $81,287; qualifying distributions, $71,980.
Limitations: Applications not accepted. Giving primarily in PA.
Application information: Contributes only to pre-selected organizations.
Trustees: Margaret Q. Landenberger, Brown Brothers Harriman Trust Co.
EIN: 650350358

36088
Irene Lewisohn Trust
c/o Citibank, N.A.
1 Court Sq., 22nd Fl.
Long Island City, NY 11120

Financial data (yr. ended 12/31/00): Grants paid, $70,000; assets, $1,379,705 (M); expenditures, $88,850; qualifying distributions, $68,616.
Limitations: Applications not accepted. Giving primarily in NY.
Application information: Contributes only to pre-selected organizations.
Trustee: Citibank, N.A.
EIN: 136054133

36089
The Securitas Foundation
55 E. 52nd St.
New York, NY 10055

Established in 1998 in NY.
Donor(s): Securitas Partners.
Financial data (yr. ended 12/31/99): Grants paid, $70,000; assets, $12,111 (M); gifts received, $23,200; expenditures, $83,089; qualifying distributions, $71,089.
Limitations: Applications not accepted. Giving on a national and international basis.
Application information: Contributes only to pre-selected organizations.
Officers: John J. Hendrickson, Chair.; Michael J. Cuddy, Pres.; Elaine Mizer Paulsen, V.P. and Secy.; Cathryn C. Crites, Treas.
EIN: 223624166

36090
Shoshana Foundation, Inc.
870 United Nations Plz., Ste. 14A
New York, NY 10017

Established in 1986 in NY.
Donor(s): Richard F. Gold.‡
Financial data (yr. ended 12/31/00): Grants paid, $70,000; assets, $879,398 (M); expenditures, $78,303; qualifying distributions, $72,281; giving activities include $72,886 for programs.
Limitations: Applications not accepted. Giving primarily in CO, Washington, DC, FL, IA, MA, NY, PA, and VA.
Application information: Students are nominated for scholarships by one of 14 opera educational institutions.
Officers: William Odenkirk, Pres.; Denes Striny, V.P.; Flavia M. Gale, Secy.; Melanie L. Amhorwitz, Treas.
Directors: Melissa Ann Coyne, Barden Gale, Rita Gold.
EIN: 133317859
Codes: GTI

36091
Edith P. Taylor Charitable Trust
c/o JPMorgan Chase Bank
1211 6th Ave., 34th Fl.
New York, NY 10036
Application address: John Andrus, c/o JPMorgan Chase Bank, 225 South St., Morristown, NJ 07960

Established in 1997 in NJ.
Donor(s): Edith P. Taylor.‡
Financial data (yr. ended 09/30/01): Grants paid, $70,000; assets, $1,265,931 (M); gifts received, $63,719; expenditures, $85,080; qualifying distributions, $75,151.
Limitations: Giving primarily in NJ.
Application information: Application form not required.
Trustee: JPMorgan Chase Bank.
EIN: 137133247

36092
Kahle Family Foundation
2255 Bailey Ave.
Buffalo, NY 14211

Established in 1987 in NY.
Financial data (yr. ended 12/31/99): Grants paid, $69,925; assets, $1,708,983 (M); expenditures, $77,265; qualifying distributions, $72,148.
Limitations: Applications not accepted. Giving primarily in NY.
Application information: Contributes only to pre-selected organizations.
Trustees: Marilyn Kahle, Mark Kahle, William C. Moran.

EIN: 166305763

36093
The Tulchin Family Foundation, Inc.
c/o Mahoney Cohen and Co.
1065 Ave. of the Americas
New York, NY 10018

Established in 1996 in NY.
Financial data (yr. ended 12/31/01): Grants paid, $69,925; assets, $1,595,515 (M); expenditures, $78,573; qualifying distributions, $69,925.
Limitations: Applications not accepted.
Application information: Contributes only to pre-selected organizations.
Officers: Stanley Tulchin, Pres.; Jeffrey Tulchin, V.P.; Steven Tulchin, V.P.; Susan P. Tulchin, Secy.; Jill Tulchin, Treas.
EIN: 113352595

36094
The Carter Fund
c/o Citibank, N.A.
PBG Tax Dept., Sort 4850
New York, NY 10043

Trust established in 1958 in NY.
Donor(s): James W. Carter, Margaret W. Carter.‡
Financial data (yr. ended 12/31/01): Grants paid, $69,857; assets, $1,465,798 (M); expenditures, $90,378; qualifying distributions, $69,857.
Limitations: Applications not accepted. Giving primarily in the metropolitan New York, NY, area.
Application information: Contributes only to pre-selected organizations.
Trustee: Citibank, N.A.
EIN: 136057027

36095
Davidson-Hooker Fund
c/o U.S. Trust
P.O. Box 2004
New York, NY 10109-1910
Application address: 114 W. 47th St., New York, NY 10036
Contact: Edith Ross Parker, Tr.

Financial data (yr. ended 12/31/01): Grants paid, $69,800; assets, $724,975 (M); expenditures, $83,918; qualifying distributions, $69,800.
Trustees: Mary B. Davidson, Edith Ross Parker, U.S. Trust.
EIN: 136070070

36096
Morris Glickman Foundation, Inc.
105 Creedkside Rd.
Mount Kisco, NY 10549
Application address: 13 Churchill Ln., Rancho Mirage, CA 92270-3038
Contact: Marvin S. Glickman, Pres.

Donor(s): Marvin S. Glickman.
Financial data (yr. ended 06/30/00): Grants paid, $69,770; assets, $651,831 (M); expenditures, $71,912; qualifying distributions, $69,458.
Limitations: Giving primarily in CA, and New York, NY.
Officers: Marvin S. Glickman, Pres. and Treas.; Linda Levine, V.P.; Nancy Lipton, V.P.; Joanne Singer, V.P.; Alma Glickman, Secy.
EIN: 116015697

36097
The Vern Cormie Foundation
c/o KRT Business Mgmt.
500 5th Ave., Ste. 3000
New York, NY 10110

Established in 1997 in CA.
Donor(s): Marian Cormie.
Financial data (yr. ended 12/31/01): Grants paid, $69,750; assets, $42,037 (M); expenditures, $71,229; qualifying distributions, $69,750.
Trustees: James M. Cormie, John D. Cormie, Marian M. Cormie.
EIN: 237880446

36098
David and Andrea Baum Foundation
c/o Goldman Sachs & Co.
85 Broad St., Tax Dept.
New York, NY 10004-2456

Established in 2000 in NJ.
Donor(s): David M. Baum.
Financial data (yr. ended 11/30/01): Grants paid, $69,552; assets, $1,440,575 (M); gifts received, $630,944; expenditures, $92,086; qualifying distributions, $72,086.
Limitations: Applications not accepted. Giving on a national basis.
Application information: Contributes only to pre-selected organizations.
Trustees: Andrea Terzi Baum, David M. Baum.
EIN: 137178822

36099
Lederman Family Foundation
c/o Carol Lederman
6 Hasley Farm Dr.
Southampton, NY 11968

Established in 1999 in NY.
Financial data (yr. ended 12/31/00): Grants paid, $69,505; assets, $1,120,636 (M); gifts received, $337,253; expenditures, $84,440; qualifying distributions, $69,314.
Limitations: Applications not accepted.
Application information: Contributes only to pre-selected organizations.
Directors: Carol Lederman, Mark Lederman.
EIN: 137202850

36100
Jasper & Isabella Richards Scholarship Trust
10 Erie Rd.
Canajoharie, NY 13317 (518) 673-3321
Contact: Richard G. Rose, Tr.

Financial data (yr. ended 12/31/01): Grants paid, $69,500; assets, $425,153 (M); expenditures, $73,629; qualifying distributions, $69,500.
Limitations: Giving limited to Canajoharie, NY.
Application information: Application form required.
Trustee: Richard G. Rose.
EIN: 166379853

36101
Hecht Foundation
1378 E. 5th St.
Brooklyn, NY 11230 (718) 283-8544
Contact: Nancy Moses

Established in 2000 in NY.
Financial data (yr. ended 12/31/00): Grants paid, $69,470; assets, $2,189 (M); gifts received, $61,300; expenditures, $70,321; qualifying distributions, $70,321; giving activities include $850 for programs.
Trustee: Abraham Hecht.
EIN: 137177312

36102
Samuel & Mollie Jemal Foundation
1 Penn Plaza, Ste. 1514
New York, NY 10119 (212) 265-5570
Contact: Jack Jemal, Pres.

Established in 1990 in NY.
Donor(s): Jack Jemal, Isaac Jemal, Joseph Jemal.
Financial data (yr. ended 04/30/01): Grants paid, $69,387; assets, $31,556 (M); gifts received, $89,900; expenditures, $71,412; qualifying distributions, $71,291.
Limitations: Giving primarily in the greater New York, NY, area.
Application information: Application form not required.
Officers: Jack Jemal, Pres.; Joseph Jemal, Secy.; Abraham Jemal, Treas.
Director: Isaac Jemal.
EIN: 237315121

36103
Allan G. and M. J. Gohr McTaggart Foundation
282 North St.
Buffalo, NY 14201-1307

Established in 1986.
Donor(s): Allan G. McTaggart,‡ Marilyn J. Gohr McTaggart.
Financial data (yr. ended 06/30/01): Grants paid, $69,375; assets, $801,362 (M); expenditures, $71,027; qualifying distributions, $69,375; giving activities include $1,652 for programs.
Limitations: Giving primarily in Buffalo, NY.
Application information: Application form not required.
Officers: Marilyn J. Gohr McTaggart, Pres. and Treas.; Thomas J. Filipski, Secy.
Director: Robert J. Plache.
EIN: 161257513

36104
Mark Stuart, Jr. Foundation
c/o Stuart, Scotto & Cella
20 Broad St.
New York, NY 10005-2601

Donor(s): Mark J. Stuart, Jr.
Financial data (yr. ended 02/28/02): Grants paid, $69,201; assets, $261,071 (M); gifts received, $50,000; expenditures, $70,201; qualifying distributions, $69,201.
Limitations: Applications not accepted. Giving primarily in NY.
Application information: Contributes only to pre-selected organizations.
Trustee: Mark J. Stuart, Jr.
EIN: 237008867

36105
The Goldie & David Blanksteen Foundation
c/o Hoberman, Miller, Goldstein & Lesser
226 W. 26th St., 8th Fl.
New York, NY 10001
Application address: 45 Underwood Rd., Forest Hills, NY 11385
Contact: David Blanksteen, Tr.

Established in 1995 in NY.
Donor(s): David Blanksteen, Goldie Blanksteen.
Financial data (yr. ended 06/30/02): Grants paid, $69,158; assets, $1,061,115 (M); gifts received, $169,547; expenditures, $87,190; qualifying distributions, $69,158.
Limitations: Giving primarily in NY.
Trustees: David Blanksteen, Goldie Blanksteen.
EIN: 137072675

36106
E. Evan Foundation, Inc.
P.O. Box 185
Slingerlands, NY 12159-0185

Established in 1985 in NY.
Donor(s): Pittsfield News Co., Inc., Eitan Evan, Malka Evan.
Financial data (yr. ended 08/31/01): Grants paid, $69,100; assets, $1,203,773 (M); gifts received,

36106—NEW YORK

$75,752; expenditures, $76,936; qualifying distributions, $69,100.
Limitations: Applications not accepted. Giving primarily in Albany, NY.
Application information: Contributes only to pre-selected organizations.
Officers: Eitan Evan, Pres.; Malka Evan, Secy.
Directors: Amir Evan, Lior Evan, Shye Evan.
EIN: 141675495

36107
Rimerman Family Foundation
c/o Ira S. Rimerman, et al.
63 Sands Point Rd.
Sands Point, NY 11050

Established in 1997 in NY.
Donor(s): Ira S. Rimerman.
Financial data (yr. ended 12/31/01): Grants paid, $69,045; assets, $1,377,068 (M); expenditures, $71,730; qualifying distributions, $70,541.
Limitations: Applications not accepted. Giving primarily in NY.
Application information: Contributes only to pre-selected organizations.
Trustees: Ira S. Rimerman, Iris J. Rimerman.
EIN: 116484281

36108
Mr. and Mrs. Robert C. Baker Family Foundation
c/o National Realty and Development Corp.
3 Manhattanville Rd.
Purchase, NY 10577-2116   (914) 694-4444
Contact: Robert C. Baker, Pres.

Established in 1995 in NY.
Donor(s): Robert C. Baker.
Financial data (yr. ended 12/31/01): Grants paid, $69,007; assets, $4,925 (M); expenditures, $76,161; qualifying distributions, $68,989.
Officer: Robert C. Baker, Pres.
EIN: 133798665

36109
Jack I. & Lillian L. Poses Foundation
c/o Barbara Kafka
23 E. 92nd St.
New York, NY 10128

Financial data (yr. ended 12/31/01): Grants paid, $69,000; assets, $846,574 (M); expenditures, $78,708; qualifying distributions, $71,383.
Limitations: Applications not accepted. Giving primarily in NY.
Application information: Contributes only to pre-selected organizations.
Trustee: Barbara Kafka.
EIN: 136068601

36110
Jessie Ridley Foundation, Inc.
250 W. 57th St.
New York, NY 10019

Incorporated in 1973 in NY.
Financial data (yr. ended 12/31/01): Grants paid, $69,000; assets, $1,961,751 (M); expenditures, $94,679; qualifying distributions, $69,000.
Limitations: Applications not accepted. Giving on a national basis, with some emphasis on NY.
Application information: Contributes only to pre-selected organizations.
Officers: Murray Kalik, Pres.; P. Douglas Martin, V.P.; Mark Kalik, Secy.; Hon. Edward Ridley Finch, Jr., Treas.
Trustees: Elizabeth Lathrop Finch, Lawrence Kalik, Mildred Kalik, Richard W. Martin, Mary M. Walker.
EIN: 237379436

36111
The Bernheim Foundation, Inc.
c/o Charles A. Bernheim
33 E. 70th St., Apt. 5E
New York, NY 10021-4956

Established in 1955 in NY.
Donor(s): Charles A. Bernheim, Elinor K. Bernheim,‡ Leonard H. Bernheim, Jr.,‡ Stephanie Bernheim, Rachel Bernheim.
Financial data (yr. ended 12/31/01): Grants paid, $68,883; assets, $777,079 (M); gifts received, $158,932; expenditures, $76,121; qualifying distributions, $71,447.
Limitations: Applications not accepted. Giving primarily in New York, NY.
Application information: Contributes only to pre-selected organizations.
Officers: Charles A. Bernheim, Pres.; Joshua Rubenstein, V.P. and Secy.; Stephanie Bernheim, V.P.
EIN: 136084144

36112
Joseph Safdya & Sons Foundation
1960 E. 4th St.
Brooklyn, NY 11223
Contact: Joseph Saff, Tr.

Established in 1991 in NY.
Donor(s): Joseph Saff, Franshaw, Inc.
Financial data (yr. ended 12/31/01): Grants paid, $68,872; assets, $1,238 (M); gifts received, $69,555; expenditures, $68,872; qualifying distributions, $68,872.
Limitations: Giving primarily in NY.
Application information: Application form not required.
Trustees: Celia Saff, Eddie Saff, Isaac Saff, Joseph Saff.
EIN: 133613886

36113
Renfield-Miller Foundation, Inc.
888 Park Ave.
New York, NY 10021

Donor(s): Jean Renfield-Miller, Michael Reid-Schwartz.
Financial data (yr. ended 11/30/01): Grants paid, $68,795; assets, $377,808 (M); expenditures, $70,456; qualifying distributions, $68,795.
Limitations: Applications not accepted. Giving primarily in NY.
Application information: Contributes only to pre-selected organizations.
Officers: Jean Renfield-Miller, Pres.; Douglas C. Renfield-Miller, V.P.
Director: Michael Reid-Schwartz.
EIN: 133052250

36114
The Harold K. Raisler Foundation, Inc.
c/o Eisner & Lubin, LLP
444 Madison Ave.
New York, NY 10022

Incorporated in 1957 in NY.
Financial data (yr. ended 12/31/01): Grants paid, $68,780; assets, $1,977,058 (M); expenditures, $76,078; qualifying distributions, $72,880.
Limitations: Applications not accepted. Giving primarily in New York, NY.
Application information: Contributes only to pre-selected organizations.
Directors: Aline Raisler, Jeanne Raisler.
EIN: 136094406

36115
The Irving Siegel Charitable Foundation
c/o Staks Mgmt. Co.
326 Broadway
Bethpage, NY 11714-3021   (516) 433-6450
Contact: Irving Siegel, Tr.

Established in 1995.
Donor(s): Irving Siegel.
Financial data (yr. ended 12/31/01): Grants paid, $68,740; assets, $642,272 (M); expenditures, $72,289; qualifying distributions, $68,740.
Limitations: Giving on a national basis.
Trustees: Diane Siegel, Irving Siegel, Joel Zychick.
EIN: 116465350

36116
American Friends of Toras Chaim
1880 54th St.
Brooklyn, NY 11204   (718) 283-8544
Contact: Raphael Z. Grossman, Tr.

Financial data (yr. ended 12/31/00): Grants paid, $68,731; assets, $5,515 (M); gifts received, $69,211; expenditures, $70,201; qualifying distributions, $70,201.
Limitations: Giving on an international basis, primarily in Ramat Jerusalem, Israel.
Trustee: Raphael Z. Grossman.
EIN: 113411887

36117
Lawrence Schacht Foundation, Inc.
c/o Rivkin, Radler & Kremer
EAB Plz.
Uniondale, NY 11556
Contact: Bernard Feigen, Dir.

Established in 1951 in NY.
Donor(s): Lawrence Schacht.‡
Financial data (yr. ended 12/31/00): Grants paid, $68,696; assets, $3,338,073 (M); expenditures, $137,453; qualifying distributions, $68,696.
Limitations: Giving primarily in NJ and NY.
Application information: Application form not required.
Director: Barbara Schacht Wasserberg.
EIN: 136106088

36118
John L. McHugh Foundation, Inc.
60 E. 42nd St., Rm. 428
New York, NY 10165-0006   (212) 490-0190
Contact: Stanley B. Rich, Mgr.

Established in 1958.
Donor(s): John L. McHugh.‡
Financial data (yr. ended 09/30/01): Grants paid, $68,650; assets, $1,167,717 (M); expenditures, $124,301; qualifying distributions, $68,650.
Limitations: Giving primarily in MA and NY.
Officers and Trustees:* Trumbull Barton,* Pres.; Sally R. Harwood,* V.P.; Chas. Hollerith,* V.P.; Stanley B. Rich,* Treas. and Mgr.
EIN: 136141528

36119
Jonas Ehrlich Charitable Foundation II, Inc.
1341 47th St.
Brooklyn, NY 11219

Established in 2001.
Donor(s): Jonas Ehrlich.‡
Financial data (yr. ended 12/31/01): Grants paid, $68,600; assets, $3,475,580 (M); gifts received, $3,500,000; expenditures, $222,924; qualifying distributions, $71,100.
Limitations: Giving primarily in Brooklyn, NY.
EIN: 113621521

36120
Edward R. Hughes and Irene E. Hughes Foundation
7219 3rd Ave.
Brooklyn, NY 11209-2198 (718) 238-3360
Contact: Harry G. English, Chair.

Established in 1993 in NY.
Financial data (yr. ended 06/30/01): Grants paid, $68,600; assets, $1,556,227 (M); expenditures, $124,109; qualifying distributions, $88,921.
Limitations: Giving primarily in NY.
Officers: Harry G. English, Chair.; Muriel T. Dorff, Secy.; Eileen E. English, Treas.
EIN: 116420370

36121
Louis & Rose Russek Foundation
c/o Private Financial Svcs.
570 Lexington Ave., 42nd Fl.
New York, NY 10022

Established in 1967.
Financial data (yr. ended 10/31/01): Grants paid, $68,570; assets, $900,239 (M); expenditures, $93,666; qualifying distributions, $68,570.
Limitations: Applications not accepted. Giving primarily in Palm Beach, FL and Wellesley, MA.
Application information: Contributes only to pre-selected organizations.
Officers and Trustees:* Isabelle R. Leeds,* Pres.; Norma Grabler,* V.P.; Judith Fields, Amy Beth Leeds.
EIN: 136227389

36122
The W. J. Barney Foundation, Inc.
c/o John W. Pegg & Co.
P.O. Box 702
Hartsdale, NY 10530-0702

Donor(s): W.J. Barney Corp., William Joshua Barney, Jr.‡
Financial data (yr. ended 12/31/00): Grants paid, $68,560; assets, $3,420,145 (M); expenditures, $69,586; qualifying distributions, $68,500.
Limitations: Applications not accepted. Giving primarily in NY.
Application information: Contributes only to pre-selected organizations.
Officer: John W. Pegg, Secy.-Treas.
EIN: 136108758

36123
Mollie Zweig Foundation
625 Park Ave.
New York, NY 10021

Established in 1999 in NY.
Financial data (yr. ended 12/31/00): Grants paid, $68,550; assets, $2,007,491 (M); expenditures, $73,458; qualifying distributions, $71,255.
Limitations: Applications not accepted.
Application information: Contributes only to pre-selected organizations.
Officer: Mollie Zweig, Pres.
EIN: 134091662

36124
Harold E. Hirsch Foundation, Inc.
P.O. Box 610
Millwood, NY 10546
Contact: Michael Kirsch, Tr.

Established in 1961.
Financial data (yr. ended 10/31/01): Grants paid, $68,536; assets, $1,891,624 (M); expenditures, $90,893; qualifying distributions, $82,481.
Limitations: Giving primarily in New York, NY, and Philadelphia, PA.

Trustees: Elmer Kirsch, Martin Kirsch, Michael Kirsch.
EIN: 136160989

36125
Effron Family Foundation
1 Clifton Ln.
White Plains, NY 10605-4707

Established in 1998 in NY.
Financial data (yr. ended 12/31/01): Grants paid, $68,405; assets, $285,281 (M); expenditures, $77,292; qualifying distributions, $76,931.
Limitations: Giving primarily in NY.
Officers: Barry J. Effron, Pres.; Michelle S. Effron, V.P.; Leslie A. Effron, Secy.
Trustee: Tova A. Effron.
EIN: 061531012

36126
Grano Family Foundation
c/o UBS- Paineweber
1285 Ave. of Americas, 14th Fl.
New York, NY 10019
Contact: Joseph J. Grano, Tr.

Established in 2000 in NJ.
Donor(s): Joseph J. Grano, Jr.
Financial data (yr. ended 12/31/01): Grants paid, $68,333; assets, $750,170 (M); expenditures, $79,057; qualifying distributions, $70,108.
Limitations: Giving primarily in NJ and NY.
Trustees: Andrea J. Grano, Angela L. Grano, Joseph C. Grano, Joseph J. Grano, Jr., Kathleen J. Grano.
EIN: 134150690

36127
Ronny and Sheila Apfel Charitable Trust
c/o Donald G. Koch
26 Broadway, Ste. 2100
New York, NY 10004
Application address: 1664 Hanover St., Teaneck, NJ 07666-2222, tel.: (917) 855-7632
Contact: Ronny Apfel, Tr.

Established in 1994 in NY.
Donor(s): Ronny Apfel, Sheila Apfel.
Financial data (yr. ended 12/31/01): Grants paid, $68,298; assets, $169,264 (M); expenditures, $75,816; qualifying distributions, $75,816.
Limitations: Giving on a national basis.
Application information: Application form required.
Trustees: Ronny Apfel, Sheila Apfel.
EIN: 137053192

36128
The Mitchell and Roslyn Barash Foundation, Inc.
(Formerly The Mitchell Barash Foundation)
95 Hickory Dr.
Roslyn, NY 11576

Established in 1964 in NY.
Donor(s): Mitchell Barash.
Financial data (yr. ended 12/31/01): Grants paid, $68,276; assets, $1,036,930 (M); expenditures, $78,159; qualifying distributions, $76,210.
Limitations: Applications not accepted.
Application information: Contributes only to pre-selected organizations.
Officers: Mitchell Barash, Pres.; Roslyn Barash, Secy.
EIN: 112062341

36129
Grove W. & Agnes M. Hinman Charitable Foundation
P.O. Box 209
Hamilton, NY 13346-0209
Contact: Susan Schapiro, Tr.

Established in 1970 in NY.
Financial data (yr. ended 04/30/01): Grants paid, $68,220; assets, $916,936 (M); expenditures, $82,413; qualifying distributions, $69,180.
Limitations: Giving primarily in the Hamilton, Madison, and Morrisville-Eaton, NY, school districts.
Application information: Application form required.
Trustees: Robert Kallet, Raymond P. Ryan, Susan Schapiro, Frank O. White.
EIN: 237194828
Codes: GTI

36130
Se Foundation
c/o Shimon Eidlisz
1449 59th St.
Brooklyn, NY 11219

Established in 1999.
Donor(s): Shimon Eidlisz.
Financial data (yr. ended 12/31/00): Grants paid, $68,150; assets, $131,220 (M); gifts received, $100,000; expenditures, $68,780; qualifying distributions, $68,150.
Officer: Shimon Eidlisz, Pres.
Directors: Ann Eidlisz, Osher A. Itzkowitz.
EIN: 113523882

36131
The Penny Charitable Trust
c/o Bryan Cave
245 Park Ave.
New York, NY 10176-0034

Donor(s): Ilse R. Sternberg.
Financial data (yr. ended 11/30/01): Grants paid, $68,100; assets, $10,873 (M); gifts received, $94,847; expenditures, $70,470; qualifying distributions, $68,791.
Limitations: Applications not accepted. Giving on an international basis.
Application information: Contributes only to pre-selected organizations.
Trustees: Dyke M. Davies, Judith S. Neaman, Ilse R. Sternberg.
EIN: 137070450

36132
Robert G. Wehle Charitable Trust
c/o JPMorgan Chase Bank
P.O. Box 31412
Rochester, NY 14603-1412
Contact: Patricia S. Burns, V.P., JPMorgan Chase Bank

Established in 1965 in NY.
Donor(s): Elizabeth Wehle Charitable Trust.
Financial data (yr. ended 12/31/01): Grants paid, $68,037; assets, $799,158 (M); gifts received, $15,200; expenditures, $77,492; qualifying distributions, $68,999.
Limitations: Applications not accepted.
Application information: Contributes only to pre-selected organizations.
Trustee: JPMorgan Chase Bank.
EIN: 166065271

36133
Chesed Avrhom Hacohn Foundation
c/o Staten Island Bank & Trust
1591 Richmond Rd.
Staten Island, NY 10304
Application addresses: 5312 17th Ave.,
Brooklyn, NY 11204
Contact: A. Romi Cohn, Chair.

Established in 1985 in NY.
Donor(s): A. Romi Cohn.
Financial data (yr. ended 12/31/01): Grants paid, $68,000; assets, $686,711 (M); expenditures, $95,537; qualifying distributions, $88,535.
Limitations: Giving primarily in Jerusalem, Israel.
Application information: Applicants must be pursuing Jewish studies. Application form required.
Officer: A. Romi Cohn, Chair.
Trustees: Aryeh Lieb Geldzahler, Joseph Geldzahler, Solomon Kohn, Joseph Ullman, Staten Island Bank & Trust.
EIN: 116313080
Codes: GTI

36134
Congel-Pyramid Trust
4 Clinton Sq., Ste. 106
Syracuse, NY 13202-1075 (315) 476-0532
Contact: Robert V. Hunter, Tr.

Established in 1986 in NY.
Donor(s): Robert J. Congel, Pyramid Co., and subsidiaries.
Financial data (yr. ended 09/30/01): Grants paid, $68,000; assets, $744,091 (M); expenditures, $71,359; qualifying distributions, $68,000.
Limitations: Giving primarily in Syracuse, NY.
Trustees: Robert J. Congel, Suzanne M. Congel, Robert V. Hunter, Bruce A. Kenan, George J. Schunck.
EIN: 166291475

36135
The Herman E. & Estelle Goodman Foundation, Inc.
c/o S. Loeb-Cleary Gottleib, et al.
1 Liberty Plz.
New York, NY 10006-1470

Established in 1957.
Financial data (yr. ended 11/30/01): Grants paid, $68,000; assets, $478,449 (M); expenditures, $74,133; qualifying distributions, $68,100.
Limitations: Applications not accepted. Giving primarily in New York, NY.
Application information: Contributes only to pre-selected organizations.
Officers: Adam J. Goodman, Pres. and Treas.; Steven M. Loeb, V.P. and Secy.
Director: Michelle Leibson.
EIN: 136106697

36136
The Topor Family Foundation
c/o Hoberman, Miller, Goldstein & Lesser
226 W. 26th St.
New York, NY 10001

Established in 1986 in NY.
Donor(s): Shimon Topor.
Financial data (yr. ended 08/31/01): Grants paid, $67,996; assets, $2,614,183 (M); expenditures, $91,375; qualifying distributions, $67,996.
Limitations: Applications not accepted. Giving primarily in the metropolitan New York, NY, area.
Application information: Contributes only to pre-selected organizations.
Trustees: Hava Topor, Shimon Topor.
EIN: 136880413

36137
The Heller Family Charitable Foundation
1717 45th St.
Brooklyn, NY 11204

Established in 1998 in NY.
Donor(s): Oscar Heller, Adelaide Heller.
Financial data (yr. ended 12/31/01): Grants paid, $67,863; assets, $469,091 (M); gifts received, $18,000; expenditures, $68,859; qualifying distributions, $67,863.
Limitations: Applications not accepted.
Application information: Contributes only to pre-selected organizations.
Trustees: Adelaide Heller, Oscar Heller.
EIN: 137120572

36138
Dana and Anne Low Foundation
c/o JPMorgan Chase Bank
1211 Ave. of the Americas, 34th Fl.
New York, NY 10036

Established in 1998.
Financial data (yr. ended 12/31/01): Grants paid, $67,798; assets, $393,090 (M); expenditures, $75,012; qualifying distributions, $69,240.
Limitations: Applications not accepted. Giving primarily in Greenwich, CT.
Application information: Contributes only to pre-selected organizations.
Trustees: Anne E. Low, Dana E. Low, JPMorgan Chase Bank.
EIN: 526940074

36139
The Ostgrodd Foundation, Inc.
1035 5th Ave.
New York, NY 10028
Contact: Barbara Grodd, Pres.

Established in 1995 in NY.
Donor(s): Barbara Grodd, Clifford Grodd.
Financial data (yr. ended 12/31/01): Grants paid, $67,750; assets, $2,023,835 (M); gifts received, $50,830; expenditures, $82,736; qualifying distributions, $68,080.
Limitations: Giving primarily in New York, NY.
Application information: Application form not required.
Officers: Barbara Grodd, Pres. and Treas.; Patricia Grodd Stone, Secy.
Directors: Clifford Grodd, James Grodd.
EIN: 133826884

36140
The Bado Foundation, Inc.
c/o Siegel, Sacks & Co.
630 3rd Ave., 22nd Fl.
New York, NY 10017-6779

Established in 1961 in NY.
Financial data (yr. ended 12/31/01): Grants paid, $67,742; assets, $393,144 (M); expenditures, $80,641; qualifying distributions, $67,742.
Limitations: Applications not accepted. Giving primarily in NY.
Application information: Contributes only to pre-selected organizations.
Officers: Doris C. Brown, Chair.; David Banker, Pres. and Treas.; Douglas H. Banker, V.P.; Vincent C. Banker, V.P.; Jean B. Angell, Secy.
EIN: 136166867

36141
Keren Ish Foundation
31B Lynch St.
Brooklyn, NY 11206

Established in NY in 1998.
Donor(s): Arnold Kohn.
Financial data (yr. ended 12/31/01): Grants paid, $67,730; assets, $870,530 (M); gifts received, $323,900; expenditures, $68,405; qualifying distributions, $67,730.
Limitations: Applications not accepted.
Application information: Contributes only to pre-selected organizations.
Trustees: Arnold Kohn, Sara Kohn.
EIN: 137171843

36142
The Harburg Foundation, Inc.
225 Lafayette St., Rm. 813
New York, NY 10012 (212) 343-9668
FAX: (212) 343-9453; *E-mail:* ernie@harburgfoundation.org
Contact: Nick Markovich, Exec. Admin.

Established in 1981 in NY.
Donor(s): E.Y. Harburg.‡
Financial data (yr. ended 06/30/01): Grants paid, $67,688; assets, $455,945 (M); expenditures, $391,783; qualifying distributions, $390,233; giving activities include $36,572 for programs.
Limitations: Giving primarily on a national basis.
Publications: Informational brochure (including application guidelines).
Application information: Application form required.
Officers: Ernest Harburg, Pres.; Marjorie Harburg, V.P.; Arnold Corrigan, Secy.-Treas.; Nick Markovich, Exec. Admin.; Deena Rosenberg, Artistic Dir.
EIN: 133101075
Codes: GTI

36143
The Benaid Foundation
c/o A. Stanley Gluck
1251 Ave. of the Americas
New York, NY 10020

Established in 1972.
Financial data (yr. ended 12/31/01): Grants paid, $67,675; assets, $1,607,454 (M); gifts received, $14,000; expenditures, $92,355; qualifying distributions, $67,675.
Limitations: Applications not accepted. Giving primarily in New York, NY.
Application information: Contributes only to pre-selected organizations.
Officers: A. Stanley Gluck, Pres. and Treas.; Ann Begley, V.P.; Robert Dujarric, V.P.; Isaac Stern, V.P.; Robert de Rothschild, Secy.
EIN: 237169525

36144
American Agriculturist Foundation, Inc.
c/o Cornell Univ.
418 Warren Hall
Ithaca, NY 14850 (607) 225-1599
Contact: Wayne Knoblauch, Secy.

Established in 1935 in NY.
Financial data (yr. ended 12/31/01): Grants paid, $67,641; assets, $1,321,216 (M); expenditures, $81,797; qualifying distributions, $67,641.
Limitations: Giving limited to the Northeast.
Officers and Directors:* Judith Riehlman,* Chair.; Craig Buckout,* Vice-Chair.; Wayne Knoblauch, Secy.; Thomas Todd, Treas.; Gordon Conklin, Clifford Crouch, Robert Everingham, Willis Hayes, Bernard Potter, Robert Smith, Bernard Stanton, Paul Steiger.
EIN: 166050706

36145
Sunlit Uplands Foundation
(Formerly Ramussen Family Foundation)
P.O. Box 1
Walton, NY 13856
Application address: Dunk Hill Rd., Walton, NY 13856
Contact: Arthur E. Rasmussen, Tr. and Joann Spain Rasmussen, Tr.

Established in 1997 in NY.
Donor(s): Arthur E. Rasmussen, Joann Spain Rasmussen.
Financial data (yr. ended 12/31/01): Grants paid, $67,600; assets, $1,420,139 (M); gifts received, $111,000; expenditures, $70,751; qualifying distributions, $67,600.
Application information: Application form not required.
Trustees: Arthur E. Rasmussen, Joann Spain Rasmussen.
EIN: 166461442

36146
The Carlilian Foundation
1532 Dorwaldt Blvd.
Schenectady, NY 12309-5111 (518) 374-5464
E-mail: cyfx63a@mindspring.com
Contact: C.W. Carl, Jr., Tr.

Established in 1968.
Donor(s): C.W. Carl, Jr.
Financial data (yr. ended 12/31/01): Grants paid, $67,446; assets, $1,209,339 (M); gifts received, $134,538; expenditures, $73,356; qualifying distributions, $67,446.
Limitations: Giving limited to Albany, Montgomery, Rensselaer, Saratoga, and Schenectady counties, NY.
Publications: Annual report.
Application information: Application form not required.
Trustees: Patricia Whalen Bennett, C.W. Carl, Jr., W.H. Milton III, K.T. Schmidt.
EIN: 146049444

36147
Schoenheimer Foundation
c/o Radix Corp.
230 Park Ave., Rm. 630
New York, NY 10169-0076
Contact: Pierre Schoenheimer, Dir.

Established in 1980.
Financial data (yr. ended 11/30/01): Grants paid, $67,345; assets, $888,767 (M); gifts received, $106,093; expenditures, $69,420; qualifying distributions, $67,345.
Directors: Robert C. Lapin, Linda McCurdy, Joyce A. Schoenheimer, Pierre L. Schoenheimer.
EIN: 133055927

36148
Semlitz/Glaser Foundation
1 Gracie Sq., Apt. 11
New York, NY 10028

Established in 1991 in NY.
Donor(s): Stephen M. Semlitz, Cathy Glaser.
Financial data (yr. ended 04/30/02): Grants paid, $67,310; assets, $515,870 (M); gifts received, $34,648; expenditures, $69,785; qualifying distributions, $67,310.
Limitations: Applications not accepted. Giving primarily in New York, NY.
Application information: Contributes only to pre-selected organizations.
Trustees: Cathy Glaser, Stephen M. Semlitz.
EIN: 133632754

36149
Gill Charitable Foundation Inc.
c/o C. Sackett
P.O. Box 31051
Rochester, NY 14603

Established in 1997 in NY.
Donor(s): Daniel E. Gill.
Financial data (yr. ended 12/31/01): Grants paid, $67,300; assets, $619,097 (M); expenditures, $78,891; qualifying distributions, $69,532.
Limitations: Applications not accepted. Giving primarily in IL, NY, and PA.
Application information: Contributes only to pre-selected organizations.
Officers and Directors:* Dorothy A. Gill,* Pres.; Diane G. Denning,* Secy.; Daniel E. Gill,* Treas.; and 7 additional directors.
EIN: 161520831

36150
The Ferman Family Foundation, Inc.
579 Fifth Ave., 5th Fl.
New York, NY 10017-1917
Contact: Symon Ferman, Pres.

Established in 1997 in NY.
Donor(s): Symon Ferman.
Financial data (yr. ended 12/31/01): Grants paid, $67,125; assets, $238,598 (M); gifts received, $20,544; expenditures, $67,430; qualifying distributions, $67,125.
Limitations: Giving primarily in New York, NY.
Officers and Directors:* Symon Ferman,* Pres.; Eda Ferman,* Secy.; Gary Ferman, Gary Lehrer.
EIN: 133944287

36151
The GGM Trust
70 E. 10 St., Ste. 6U
New York, NY 10003

Established in 1997.
Donor(s): Gertrude G. Michelson.
Financial data (yr. ended 12/31/01): Grants paid, $67,000; assets, $292,798 (M); expenditures, $70,974; qualifying distributions, $67,000.
Limitations: Applications not accepted. Giving primarily in NY.
Application information: Contributes only to pre-selected organizations.
Trustees: Gertrude G. Michelson, Horace Michelson.
EIN: 137097804

36152
Barking Foundation, Inc.
c/o Arthur B. Greene & Co.
101 Park Ave.
New York, NY 10178 (212) 661-8200

Established in 1997 in ME.
Donor(s): Stephen E. King, Tabitha King.
Financial data (yr. ended 12/31/00): Grants paid, $66,944; assets, $2,105,689 (M); gifts received, $1,000,000; expenditures, $74,738; qualifying distributions, $71,363.
Limitations: Giving on a national basis.
Application information: Scholarship awards are paid directly to the educational institution on behalf of the individual recipient.
Officers: Stephen E. King, Pres.; Tabitha King, V.P.; Arthur B. Greene, Secy.
EIN: 010511020

36153
Linda Pinsky Memorial Foundation, Inc.
c/o Richard Mezan, Esq.
460 Park Ave.
New York, NY 10022
Contact: Gerald Pinsky, Pres.

Established in 1986 in NY.
Donor(s): Gerald Pinsky, Sandra Pinsky.‡
Financial data (yr. ended 12/31/01): Grants paid, $66,940; assets, $510,943 (M); expenditures, $74,899; qualifying distributions, $66,940.
Limitations: Applications not accepted.
Application information: Contributes only to pre-selected organizations.
Officer and Trustees:* Gerald Pinsky,* Pres.; Barbara Levkovich, Morris Pinsky.
EIN: 133316623

36154
Mary D. Comerford Charitable Trust
c/o M&T Bank
1 M&T Plz., 8th Fl.
Buffalo, NY 14203
Application address: c/o M&T Bank, 1 S. Centre St., Pottsville, PA 17901, tel.: (570) 628-9309
Contact: Lynn Veach

Established in 1982.
Donor(s): Mary Comerford.‡
Financial data (yr. ended 09/30/01): Grants paid, $66,785; assets, $872,729 (M); expenditures, $77,107; qualifying distributions, $65,843.
Limitations: Giving primarily in Pottsville, PA.
Trustees: Robert N. Bohorad, Lois Griffiths, M & T Bank.
EIN: 232193785

36155
Harold & Nancy L. Oelbaum Foundation
220 White Plains Rd.
Tarrytown, NY 10591

Established in 1993 in NY.
Donor(s): Harold Oelbaum, Nancy L. Oelbaum.
Financial data (yr. ended 12/31/01): Grants paid, $66,720; assets, $5,794 (M); expenditures, $67,595; qualifying distributions, $66,711.
Limitations: Applications not accepted. Giving primarily in NY.
Application information: Contributes only to pre-selected organizations.
Trustees: Harold Oelbaum, Nancy L. Oelbaum.
EIN: 133741076

36156
The Heffer Family Foundation, Inc.
c/o Lenat Co.
315 Westchester Ave.
Port Chester, NY 10573 (914) 937-0100

Established in 1997 in NY.
Donor(s): John Heffer.
Financial data (yr. ended 12/31/01): Grants paid, $66,671; assets, $728,658 (M); gifts received, $98,080; expenditures, $71,454; qualifying distributions, $66,070.
Limitations: Applications not accepted.
Application information: Contributes only to pre-selected organizations.
Trustees: Alison Heffer, Barbara Heffer, Douglas Heffer, John Heffer.
EIN: 133989464

36157
The Patricia M. & H. William Smith, Jr. Foundation
975 County Rd., Ste. 10A
Norwich, NY 13815
Contact: H. William Smith, Jr., Secy.-Treas.

Established in 1999 in NY.
Donor(s): H. William Smith, Jr., Patricia M. Smith.
Financial data (yr. ended 12/31/01): Grants paid, $66,625; assets, $261,846 (M); gifts received, $11,995; expenditures, $67,953; qualifying distributions, $66,625.
Limitations: Giving primarily in CO, MA, and NY.
Officers: Patricia M. Smith, Pres.; H. William Smith, Jr., Secy.-Treas.
Directors: Tracy L. Fauver, H. William Smith III.
EIN: 161552523

36158
Diana & Eli Zborowski Foundation, Inc.
c/o Eli Zborowski
500 5th Ave., Ste. 1600
New York, NY 10110

Established in 1997 in NY.
Donor(s): Diana Zborowski, Eli Zborowski.
Financial data (yr. ended 06/30/02): Grants paid, $66,600; assets, $332,931 (M); gifts received, $43,932; expenditures, $67,501; qualifying distributions, $66,600.
Officers: Diana Zborowski, Pres.; Lillian Naveh, V.P.; Morris Zborowski, V.P.; Eli Zborowski, Secy.-Treas.
Director: Ori Gutman.
EIN: 133981045

36159
The Rosenberg Zelniker Foundation, Inc.
c/o Econoco Corp.
300 Karin Ln.
Hicksville, NY 11801
Contact: Barry A. Rosenberg, Co-Chair.

Established in 1945.
Donor(s): Econoco Corp.
Financial data (yr. ended 12/31/01): Grants paid, $66,502; assets, $789,976 (M); gifts received, $10,000; expenditures, $81,993; qualifying distributions, $66,502.
Limitations: Applications not accepted. Giving primarily in Nassau County and New York, NY.
Application information: Contributes only to pre-selected organizations.
Officers: Barry Rosenberg, Co-Chair.; Mark Zelniker, Co-Chair.
Directors: Joseph Klinow, Laurie Klinow, Marjorie Rosenberg, Jan Scherr, Jeffrey Scherr, Elaine Zelniker.
EIN: 136160042

36160
The Berenson Family Fund
888 Park Ave., Ste. 12A
New York, NY 10021-0235

Established in 1999 in NY.
Donor(s): Jeffrey Berenson.
Financial data (yr. ended 10/31/01): Grants paid, $66,500; assets, $119,226 (M); expenditures, $82,050; qualifying distributions, $73,999.
Officer: Jeffrey Berenson, Pres.
EIN: 134090152

36161
Finsen Family Foundation
c/o U.S. Trust
P.O. Box 2004
New York, NY 10109-1910

Established in 1997.
Financial data (yr. ended 12/31/01): Grants paid, $66,500; assets, $1,299,055 (M); expenditures, $86,158; qualifying distributions, $66,500.
Limitations: Applications not accepted.
Application information: Contributes only to pre-selected organizations.
Agent: U.S. Trust.
EIN: 223520273

36162
Litzenberger Family Foundation
c/o Goldman Sachs & Co.
85 Broad St., Tax Dept.
New York, NY 10004

Established in 1998 in CT.
Donor(s): Robert H. Litzenberger.
Financial data (yr. ended 08/31/01): Grants paid, $66,500; assets, $1,892,260 (M); gifts received, $415,427; expenditures, $78,500; qualifying distributions, $66,500.
Limitations: Applications not accepted.
Application information: Contributes only to pre-selected organizations.
Trustee: Robert H. Litzenberger.
EIN: 134038156

36163
Stephen J. Potter Memorial Foundation, Inc.
47 Sunnyside E.
Queensbury, NY 12804
Contact: John Austin, Jr., Secy.-Treas.

Established in 1955 in NY.
Donor(s): Stephen J. Potter.‡
Financial data (yr. ended 09/30/01): Grants paid, $66,500; assets, $712,923 (M); expenditures, $74,245; qualifying distributions, $69,731.
Limitations: Giving primarily in Ticonderoga, NY.
Application information: Application form not required.
Officers and Directors:* Jane M. Lape,* Pres.; John McDonald,* V.P.; John Austin, Jr.,* Secy.-Treas.; Gerald Abbott, William B. Wetherbee.
EIN: 146016858
Codes: GTI

36164
Richard and Ann Solomon Family Foundation, Inc.
(Formerly Sidney L. Solomon Foundation, Inc.)
c/o Yohalem Gillman & Co.
477 Madison Ave.
New York, NY 10022-5802

Established in 1950 in NY.
Donor(s): Peter J. Solomon.
Financial data (yr. ended 01/31/02): Grants paid, $66,500; assets, $794,500 (M); expenditures, $72,540; qualifying distributions, $66,500.
Limitations: Applications not accepted. Giving primarily in the New England area and NY.
Application information: Contributes only to pre-selected organizations.
Officers: Jeanette R. Solomon, Pres. and Treas.; Richard H. Solomon, V.P. and Secy.
EIN: 136154884

36165
The Lappin Foundation
c/o Nathan Berkman & Co.
29 Broadway, Ste. 2900
New York, NY 10006-3103

Established in 1981 in CT.
Financial data (yr. ended 08/31/01): Grants paid, $66,482; assets, $1,176,419 (M); expenditures, $71,357; qualifying distributions, $66,482.
Limitations: Applications not accepted. Giving primarily in West Palm Beach, FL.
Application information: Contributes only to pre-selected organizations.
Trustee: W. Robert Lappin.
EIN: 133087999

36166
The Mann Family Foundation, Inc.
c/o Mann & Bros.
48 W. 37th St.
New York, NY 10018-7408 (212) 868-3535
Contact: Nathan Mann, Pres.

Established in 1996 in NY.
Donor(s): Jack Mann.
Financial data (yr. ended 12/31/00): Grants paid, $66,474; assets, $59,581 (M); gifts received, $52,000; expenditures, $66,534; qualifying distributions, $66,534.
Limitations: Giving primarily in New York, NY.
Application information: Application form not required.
Officers: Nathan Mann, Pres.; Jack Mann, Treas.
EIN: 133861360

36167
Tilia Foundation
c/o Leigh Miller
1170 5th Ave., Ste. 8B
New York, NY 10029

Established in 1997 in NY.
Donor(s): Mrs. Alexander B. Hawes.
Financial data (yr. ended 01/31/01): Grants paid, $66,400; assets, $321,005 (M); gifts received, $116,960; expenditures, $67,268; qualifying distributions, $66,400.
Trustees: Rosilla H. Hawes, A. Gifford Miller, Leigh M. Miller, Lynden B. Miller, Marshall L. Miller.
EIN: 133931536

36168
The Monaghan Foundation, Inc.
c/o Monaghan
165 Perry St., Ste. PH6
New York, NY 10014

Established in 2000 in NJ.
Donor(s): William I. Monaghan, William S. Monaghan.
Financial data (yr. ended 12/31/01): Grants paid, $66,389; assets, $779,285 (M); expenditures, $88,733; qualifying distributions, $66,389.
Limitations: Applications not accepted.
Application information: Contributes only to pre-selected organizations.
Directors: William I. Monaghan, William S. Monaghan.
EIN: 134096155

36169
C. Steven Duncker Foundation
c/o Goldman Sachs & Co.
85 Broad St., Tax Dept.
New York, NY 10004

Established in 1998 in NY.
Donor(s): C. Steven Duncker.
Financial data (yr. ended 07/31/01): Grants paid, $66,300; assets, $1,586,970 (M); expenditures, $102,343; qualifying distributions, $66,300.
Limitations: Applications not accepted. Giving primarily in NY.
Application information: Contributes only to pre-selected organizations.
Trustees: Christy Helen Blumenhorst, C. Steven Duncker.
EIN: 133932635

36170
The Saxe Family Foundation
P.O. Box 4185
Albany, NY 12204

Donor(s): Eliot Saxe, Walter A. Saxe, Chaylie L. Saxe.
Financial data (yr. ended 05/31/02): Grants paid, $66,294; assets, $278,474 (M); expenditures, $68,280; qualifying distributions, $66,294.
Limitations: Applications not accepted. Giving primarily in Albany, NY.
Application information: Contributes only to pre-selected organizations.
Officers: Joshua A. Saxe, Pres.; Walter A. Saxe, V.P.
EIN: 141504967

36171
The Munschauer Family Foundation
c/o Frederick E. Munschauer Jr.
303 Ruskin Rd.
Eggertsville, NY 14226-4238

Established in 1992 in NY.
Donor(s): Frederick E. Munschauer, Jr.
Financial data (yr. ended 01/31/02): Grants paid, $66,280; assets, $1,425,929 (M); expenditures, $67,564; qualifying distributions, $66,280.
Limitations: Applications not accepted. Giving primarily in NY.
Application information: Contributes only to pre-selected organizations.
Trustees: Carol Ann Munschauer, Frederick E. Munschauer, Jr., Frederick E. Munschauer III.
EIN: 161428095

36172
Lovinger Family Foundation
1 W. 72nd St.
New York, NY 10023

Established in 1993 in NY.
Financial data (yr. ended 04/30/01): Grants paid, $66,200; assets, $863,877 (M); expenditures, $67,163; qualifying distributions, $66,058.
Limitations: Applications not accepted. Giving primarily in NY.
Application information: Contributes only to pre-selected organizations.
Officers and Trustees:* Jeffrey Lovinger,* Pres.; Pamela Lovinger,* Secy.; Caitlin Lovinger.
EIN: 133722501

36173
I. Jack & Elsie L. Bernstein Foundation, Inc.
445 5th Ave., Rm. 21H
New York, NY 10016 (917) 770-1111
Contact: Paul Bernstein, Pres.

Established about 1961 in NY.
Donor(s): Paul Bernstein, Bernstein and Sons Shirt Corp.
Financial data (yr. ended 08/31/01): Grants paid, $66,155; assets, $613,981 (M); gifts received, $5,400; expenditures, $81,563; qualifying distributions, $66,155.
Limitations: Giving primarily in New York, NY.
Officer: Paul E. Bernstein, Pres.
EIN: 136164853

36174
Carl E. Touhey Foundation
c/o Pine West Plaza Bldg.
2 Washington Ave.
Albany, NY 12205 (518) 452-3191

Established in 1989.
Donor(s): Carl E. Touhey.
Financial data (yr. ended 12/31/00): Grants paid, $66,105; assets, $615,281 (M); gifts received, $408,609; expenditures, $68,847; qualifying distributions, $65,589.
Limitations: Applications not accepted.
Application information: Contributes only to pre-selected organizations.
Directors: Carl E. Touhey, Charles L. Touhey, Lila M. Touhey, Virgina E. Touhey.
EIN: 223016226

36175
Morris Levine Key Food Stores Foundation, Inc.
(Formerly Key Food Stores Foundation, Inc.)
8925 Ave. D
Brooklyn, NY 11236-1679

Established in 1962 in NY.
Donor(s): Key Food Stores Cooperative, Inc., Allen Newman, Man-Dell Food Stores, Inc., Pick Quickfoods, Inc., Dan's Supreme Supermarkets, Inc.
Financial data (yr. ended 08/31/01): Grants paid, $66,100; assets, $164,199 (M); gifts received, $171,995; expenditures, $168,094; qualifying distributions, $168,952.
Limitations: Applications not accepted. Giving primarily in NY.
Application information: Contributes only to pre-selected organizations.
Directors: Sheldon Geller, Jules Levine, Lawrence Mandel, Richard Pallitto.
EIN: 116035538
Codes: CS, CD

36176
The Mark Zurack & Kathy Ferguson Foundation
c/o BCRS Assocs., LLC
100 Wall St., 11th Fl.
New York, NY 10005

Established in 1996 in NY.
Donor(s): Mark Zurack.
Financial data (yr. ended 10/31/01): Grants paid, $66,100; assets, $2,100,478 (M); expenditures, $113,420; qualifying distributions, $66,420.
Limitations: Applications not accepted. Giving limited to New York, NY.
Application information: Contributes only to pre-selected organizations.
Trustees: Kathy Ferguson, Mark Zurack.
EIN: 133926309

36177
Yashresh Yaakov, Inc.
1931 Homecrest Ave.
Brooklyn, NY 11229 (718) 376-4041
Contact: Raphael Attie, Secy.

Established in 1993 in NY.
Donor(s): Raphael Attie.
Financial data (yr. ended 12/31/01): Grants paid, $66,099; assets, $33,068 (M); expenditures, $67,199; qualifying distributions, $66,649.
Limitations: Giving on a national basis.
Application information: Application form not required.
Officers and Directors:* Rabbi Jacob Attie,* Pres.; Raphael Attie,* Secy.; Leah Attie,* Treas.; Jack Attie, Rabbi Shlomo Attie.
EIN: 113179027

36178
James D'Addario Family Foundation, Inc.
5 Woodland Rd.
Old Westbury, NY 11568

Established in 1998 in NY.
Donor(s): James D'Addario, Janet D'Addario.
Financial data (yr. ended 05/31/01): Grants paid, $66,050; assets, $343,785 (M); gifts received, $299,965; expenditures, $69,176; qualifying distributions, $66,050.
Limitations: Applications not accepted. Giving on a national basis.
Application information: Contributes only to pre-selected organizations.
Officers: James D'Addario, Pres.; Janet D'Addario, Secy.-Treas.
Directors: Amy D'Addario, Robert D'Addario, Julie Zerbo.
EIN: 113440871

36179
Gadfly Foundation
c/o Czarnowski & Beer
720 5th Ave., 10th Fl.
New York, NY 10019 (212) 832-3317
Contact: Charles L. Grimes, Mgr.

Established in 1968.
Donor(s): Charles L. Grimes.
Financial data (yr. ended 12/31/01): Grants paid, $66,000; assets, $600,001 (M); expenditures, $69,900; qualifying distributions, $66,100.
Limitations: Applications not accepted. Giving primarily in the northeastern U.S.
Application information: Contributes only to pre-selected organizations.
Manager: Charles L. Grimes.
EIN: 237066597

36180
Charles H. Goren Foundation, Inc.
122 E. 42nd St., Ste. 616
New York, NY 10168
Application address: 124 Stoneridge Dr., Chapel Hill, NC 27514, tel.: (919) 962-8504
Contact: Thomas L. Hazen, Pres. or Lisa Hazen, V.P.

Established in 1992.
Financial data (yr. ended 09/30/01): Grants paid, $66,000; assets, $1,224,119 (M); expenditures, $72,695; qualifying distributions, $66,000.
Limitations: Giving primarily in NC.
Application information: Application form not required.
Officers and Directors:* Thomas L. Hazen,* Pres.; Lisa Hazen,* V.P.
EIN: 133687588

36181
The Robert and Elaine LeBuhn Foundation, Inc.
77 Water St., 17th Fl.
New York, NY 10005 (212) 344-1866

Established in 1997 in NY.
Donor(s): Robert LeBuhn.
Financial data (yr. ended 12/31/01): Grants paid, $66,000; assets, $38,805 (M); gifts received, $99,600; expenditures, $71,555; qualifying distributions, $68,255.
Limitations: Applications not accepted. Giving on a national basis.
Application information: Contributes only to pre-selected organizations.
Officers and Directors:* Robert LeBuhn,* Pres. and Treas.; Elaine Lindley LeBuhn,* Secy.; Alfred Wheeler.
EIN: 133981546

36182
The Jonathan Otto Foundation, Inc.
c/o Jonathan Otto
305 Northern Blvd., Ste. 204
Great Neck, NY 11021

Established in 1999 in DE.
Donor(s): Jonathan Otto.
Financial data (yr. ended 12/31/01): Grants paid, $66,000; assets, $1,407 (M); gifts received, $30,000; expenditures, $68,156; qualifying distributions, $66,000.

Limitations: Applications not accepted.
Application information: Contributes only to pre-selected organizations.
Officers: Jonathan Otto, Pres. and Treas.; Jay Walker, Secy.
EIN: 113478921

36183
The Nash Aussenberg Memorial Foundation
c/o Alvin Rapp
1650 Broadway, Ste. 1007
New York, NY 10019-6833

Established in 1991.
Donor(s): Alvin Rapp, Nathan Kahn, Sandy Kahn, Alan Goldberg, Gross Life Monumente Funds, Inc., Empire Resources Corp.
Financial data (yr. ended 06/30/02): Grants paid, $65,955; assets, $9,906 (M); gifts received, $36,196; expenditures, $66,098; qualifying distributions, $65,955.
Limitations: Applications not accepted. Giving primarily in New York, NY.
Application information: Contributes only to pre-selected organizations.
Officers: Jacob J. Schacter, Pres.; Edith Aussenberg, V.P.; Moses Nussbaum, Secy.; Alvin Rapp, Treas.
EIN: 133650734

36184
Sidney E. and Amy O. Goodfriend Foundation
c/o US Trust Co. of New York
114 W. 47th St., TAXVAS
New York, NY 10004

Established in 1999 in NY.
Donor(s): Amy O. Goodfriend.
Financial data (yr. ended 12/31/00): Grants paid, $65,925; assets, $1,288,663 (M); expenditures, $71,675; qualifying distributions, $66,606.
Limitations: Applications not accepted. Giving primarily in NY.
Application information: Unsolicited requests for funds are not accepted.
Trustees: Amy O. Goodfriend, Sidney E. Goodfriend.
EIN: 134082157

36185
Robert and Sylvia Scher Charitable Foundation
51 Sycamore Rd.
Scarsdale, NY 10583
Contact: Ellen Gelboim, Tr.

Established in 1997 in NY.
Financial data (yr. ended 09/30/01): Grants paid, $65,910; assets, $1,556,031 (M); expenditures, $123,141; qualifying distributions, $100,404.
Limitations: Applications not accepted. Giving on a national basis.
Application information: Contributes only to pre-selected organizations.
Trustees: Avi Gelboim, Ellen Gelboim, Ricki Gelboim.
EIN: 133972066

36186
J. Walter Thompson Company Fund, Inc.
466 Lexington Ave.
New York, NY 10017 (212) 210-7000
Contact: Donald Gammon, Secy.

Incorporated in 1953 in NY.
Donor(s): J. Walter Thompson Co.
Financial data (yr. ended 11/30/00): Grants paid, $65,853; assets, $717,568 (M); expenditures, $69,071; qualifying distributions, $65,853.
Limitations: Giving primarily in New York, NY.
Publications: Annual report.

Application information: Employee-related scholarships are administered by the National Merit Scholarship Corporation. Application form not required.
Officers and Directors:* Lewis J. Trencher,* Chair.; Susan Mirsky,* V.P.; Donald Gammon,* Secy.; Donna Matteo, Treas.; Christopher Jones.
EIN: 136020644
Codes: CS, CD

36187
The Alden Foundation
30 Lincoln Plz.
New York, NY 10023-7103
Contact: Denise DeShane, Pres.

Established in 1990 in DE.
Donor(s): Denise DeShane, Alan Gelband.
Financial data (yr. ended 12/31/01): Grants paid, $65,747; assets, $776,948 (M); gifts received, $45,600; expenditures, $77,756; qualifying distributions, $65,747.
Limitations: Giving primarily in New York, NY.
Officers and Directors:* Denise DeShane,* Pres.; Alan Gelband,* V.P.; Rosslyn Shamash.
EIN: 133594676

36188
Schlam Family Foundation, Inc.
4 Beechwood Dr.
Lawrence, NY 11559

Established in 1999 in NY.
Financial data (yr. ended 06/30/01): Grants paid, $65,706; assets, $203,344 (M); gifts received, $4,300; expenditures, $66,396; qualifying distributions, $65,896.
Limitations: Applications not accepted.
Application information: Contributes only to pre-selected organizations.
Directors: Elisheva Schlam, Steven Schlam, Michelle Weiss.
EIN: 113522527

36189
Victor W. & Maxine Eimicke Foundation, Inc.
35 E. Grassy Sprain Rd., Ste. 403
Yonkers, NY 10710-4501

Established in 1984 in NY.
Donor(s): Victor W. Eimicke,‡ Laura E. Klimley, Alicia E. Barbieri.
Financial data (yr. ended 12/31/01): Grants paid, $65,683; assets, $397,045 (M); expenditures, $67,323; qualifying distributions, $65,683.
Limitations: Applications not accepted. Giving primarily in NY.
Application information: Contributes only to pre-selected organizations.
Officers: Alicia E. Barbieri, Pres.; Laura E. Klimley, V.P.; Maxine Eimicke, Secy.; John Palmero, Treas.
EIN: 133248497

36190
The Indira Foundation
c/o Goldman Sachs & Co.
85 Broad St., Tax Dept.
New York, NY 10004

Established in 1999 in CT.
Donor(s): Avi Nash.
Financial data (yr. ended 08/31/01): Grants paid, $65,670; assets, $849,977 (M); gifts received, $947,630; expenditures, $75,436; qualifying distributions, $65,670.
Limitations: Applications not accepted. Giving primarily in NY.
Application information: Contributes only to pre-selected organizations.
Trustees: Avi Nash, Sandra Nash.
EIN: 134051213

36191
The Thomas J. Edelman Charitable Foundation, Inc.
380 Madison Ave., 11th Fl.
New York, NY 10017

Established in 1993 in NY.
Donor(s): Thomas J. Edelman.
Financial data (yr. ended 12/31/01): Grants paid, $65,600; assets, $1,239,634 (M); expenditures, $77,801; qualifying distributions, $65,600.
Limitations: Applications not accepted. Giving primarily in New York, NY, CT, and NJ.
Application information: Contributes only to pre-selected organizations.
Officer: Thomas J. Edelman, Pres.
Directors: Albert I. Edelman, Cornelia S. Edelman.
EIN: 133762804

36192
Susan W. Rose Fund for Music, Inc.
200 Madison Ave., 5th Fl.
New York, NY 10016

Established in 1997 in DE.
Financial data (yr. ended 12/31/99): Grants paid, $65,510; assets, $2,403 (M); gifts received, $65,000; expenditures, $66,074; qualifying distributions, $65,510.
Limitations: Giving on a national basis.
Application information: Unsolicited requests for funds not accepted. Grant candidates are proposed by professionals and selected by foundation committee. Application form required.
Officers and Directors*: Susan W. Rose,* Pres.; Elihu Rose,* V.P.; Isabel Rose, Secy.; Michael D. Sullivan, Treas.
EIN: 133808182

36193
Schwartz Brothers Foundation
1070 E. 26th St.
Brooklyn, NY 11210

Established in 1994 in NY.
Donor(s): Joseph Schwartz, Software Solutions, Schwartz Investments.
Financial data (yr. ended 12/31/99): Grants paid, $65,500; assets, $2,125,536 (M); gifts received, $63,000; expenditures, $85,232; qualifying distributions, $65,750.
Limitations: Giving primarily in NY.
Directors: Charles Schwartz, Joseph Schwartz, Marcel Schwartz, Nathan Schwartz.
EIN: 113229922

36194
The David J. Mastrocola Foundation
c/o Goldman Sachs & Co.
85 Broad St., Tax Dept.
New York, NY 10004

Established in 1998 in NY.
Donor(s): David J. Mastrocola.
Financial data (yr. ended 12/31/01): Grants paid, $65,462; assets, $2,152 (M); expenditures, $65,512; qualifying distributions, $65,462.
Limitations: Applications not accepted.
Application information: Contributes only to pre-selected organizations.
Trustees: David J. Mastrocola, Steven C. Mero.
EIN: 134036266

36195
Herman & Gertrude Gross Foundation, Inc.
12 Jordan Dr.
Great Neck, NY 11021-2814

Established in 1968.
Donor(s): Herman Gross.

Financial data (yr. ended 09/30/01): Grants paid, $65,421; assets, $1,499,007 (M); expenditures, $65,887; qualifying distributions, $63,832.
Limitations: Giving on a national basis.
Officers: Herman Gross, Pres.; Gertrude Gross, Secy.; Elliot Gross, Treas.
EIN: 132623894

36196
Spetner Family Foundation
Roth and Co., LLP
Brooklyn, NY 11204

Established in 2000 in NY.
Donor(s): Abraham Spetner.
Financial data (yr. ended 12/31/00): Grants paid, $65,400; assets, $155,538 (M); gifts received, $221,000; expenditures, $65,462; qualifying distributions, $65,462.
Limitations: Applications not accepted. Giving primarily in NY.
Application information: Unsolicited requests for funds not accepted.
Officers: Abraham Spetner, Pres.; Rita Spetner, Secy.; Kenneth Spetner, Treas.
EIN: 113540386

36197
Raphael D. & Francine Friedlander Foundation
185 Great Neck Rd.
Great Neck, NY 11021-3312

Established in 1981.
Donor(s): Raphael D. Friedlander, Francine Friedlander.
Financial data (yr. ended 06/30/01): Grants paid, $65,325; assets, $1,006,853 (M); gifts received, $563,180; expenditures, $89,865; qualifying distributions, $65,325.
Limitations: Applications not accepted. Giving primarily in the greater New York, NY, area.
Application information: Contributes only to pre-selected organizations.
Officer: Francine Friedlander, Secy.
Director: Raphael D. Friedlander.
EIN: 112573096

36198
Williams Family Foundation, Inc.
c/o Fleet Investment Mgmt., Inc.
1 East Ave., NYROM03A
Rochester, NY 14604 (716) 546-9822
Contact: Janet H. Schumacher, Trust Off.

Established in 1998 in NY.
Financial data (yr. ended 12/31/01): Grants paid, $65,317; assets, $1,156,584 (M); expenditures, $218,813; qualifying distributions, $69,022.
Limitations: Giving limited to Ontario County in Geneva, NY.
Application information: Do not send videotapes. Incomplete proposals will not be considered. Application form required.
Officers: Nozomi Williams, Pres.; Peter Oddleifson, Secy.; Gary J. Lindsay, Treas.
EIN: 161549566

36199
The Mehra Family Foundation
c/o Goldman Sachs & Co.
85 Broad St., Tax Dept.
New York, NY 10004

Established in 1999 in CT.
Donor(s): Sanjeev Mehra.
Financial data (yr. ended 10/31/01): Grants paid, $65,290; assets, $1,098,362 (M); gifts received, $5,000; expenditures, $100,605; qualifying distributions, $65,290.
Limitations: Applications not accepted. Giving primarily in CT, MA, and NY.

Application information: Contributes only to pre-selected organizations.
Trustees: Karen Petersen Mehra, Sanjeev Mehra.
EIN: 134091997

36200
Landowne & Bloom Foundation, Inc.
888 7th Ave., 8th Fl.
New York, NY 10106 (212) 757-4760
Contact: Morton Landowne, Mgr.

Established in 1962 in NY.
Donor(s): Harry Bloom,‡ Morton Landowne, Rose Landowne, Sara Landowne, Ann Landowne, Elliott Landowne, Kate Landowne Gilbert.
Financial data (yr. ended 12/31/01): Grants paid, $65,279; assets, $404,029 (M); gifts received, $25,500; expenditures, $78,220; qualifying distributions, $65,279.
Limitations: Applications not accepted. Giving primarily in NY.
Officer: Morton Landowne, Mgr.
EIN: 136154524

36201
B. and R. Knapp Foundation, Inc.
(Formerly Silver Marshall Foundation, Inc.)
c/o David & Gilbert
1740 Broadway, 3rd Fl.
New York, NY 10019 (212) 468-4902
Contact: Russell S. Knapp, Pres.

Established in 1979 in DE.
Donor(s): Russell S. Knapp.
Financial data (yr. ended 12/31/01): Grants paid, $65,206; assets, $974,867 (M); expenditures, $67,160; qualifying distributions, $65,206.
Limitations: Giving primarily in New York, NY.
Officers and Directors:* Russell S. Knapp, Pres.; Bettina L. Knapp, Secy.-Treas.; Albert B. Knapp, Charles E. Knapp.
EIN: 132979552

36202
Nassimi Family Foundation, Inc.
c/o Nassimi Corp.
370 7th Ave., No. 1700
New York, NY 10001
Contact: Aghajan Nassimi, Mgr.

Established in 1994 in NY.
Donor(s): Aghajan Nassimi, Edward Nassimi, Medhi M. Nassimi, Sanfour Investment Group.
Financial data (yr. ended 02/28/02): Grants paid, $65,178; assets, $1,207 (M); gifts received, $58,000; expenditures, $65,758; qualifying distributions, $65,178.
Officers: Aghajan Nassimi, Mgr.; Edward Nassimi, Mgr.; Medhi M. Nassimi, Mgr.
EIN: 133781329

36203
The Arthur Foundation, Inc.
20 King St.
New York, NY 10014-4960 (646) 230-8389
Contact: Helen-Jean Arthur Dunn, Mgr.

Established in 1962 in NY.
Donor(s): Walter R. Arthur,‡ Hazel G. Arthur,‡ Peter Jay Sharp,‡ Alice Tully,‡ Helen-Jean Arthur Dunn, Evelyn Sharp.‡
Financial data (yr. ended 06/30/01): Grants paid, $65,100; assets, $931,257 (M); expenditures, $65,510; qualifying distributions, $64,751.
Limitations: Giving primarily in the tri-state CT, NJ, and NY, area.
Application information: Requests for funds from the video documentary department not accepted. Application form required.

Officers: Elisa Dunn, Mgr.; Helen-Jean Arthur Dunn, Mgr.; Kathleen Dunn, Mgr.; Michael Dunn, Mgr.
EIN: 136163541

36204
The Menche Foundation
39 Whitman Dr.
Brooklyn, NY 11234-6738

Established in 2000 in NY.
Donor(s): Aaron Menche, Aliza Menche.
Financial data (yr. ended 12/31/01): Grants paid, $65,071; assets, $7,240 (M); gifts received, $26,237; expenditures, $65,338; qualifying distributions, $65,071.
Limitations: Applications not accepted.
Application information: Contributes only to pre-selected organizations.
Directors: Aaron Menche, Aliza Menche, Helen Sultanik.
EIN: 113546426

36205
The Lipsay Family Charitable Foundation
c/o Seth Lipsay
46 Merrivale Rd.
Great Neck, NY 11020

Established in 1998 in NY.
Donor(s): Seth Lipsay, Deanne Lipsay.
Financial data (yr. ended 03/31/01): Grants paid, $65,022; assets, $93,346 (M); gifts received, $50,000; expenditures, $65,817; qualifying distributions, $65,357.
Limitations: Applications not accepted. Giving on a national basis, with emphasis on the greater metropolitan New York, NY, area.
Application information: Contributes only to pre-selected organizations.
Trustees: Deanne Lipsay, Seth Lipsay.
EIN: 137134842

36206
The Kristen Ann Carr Fund
648 Amsterdam Ave.
New York, NY 10025-7456 (212) 501-0748
FAX: (212) 724-0849; *URL:* http://www.sarcoma.com
Contact: Barbara Carr, Tr.; or David Marsh, Tr.

Established in 1994 in NY.
Donor(s): T.J. Martell Foundation.
Financial data (yr. ended 12/31/01): Grants paid, $65,000; assets, $1,869,632 (M); gifts received, $58,065; expenditures, $137,534; qualifying distributions, $65,000.
Limitations: Giving primarily in New York, NY.
Trustees: Barbara Carr, Sasha Carr, David Marsh.
EIN: 133800442

36207
Mike and Sylvia Chase Family Foundation
c/o Grant Thornton, LLP
60 Broad St.
New York, NY 10004

Established in 2000 in NY.
Donor(s): Sylvia Chase.
Financial data (yr. ended 09/30/01): Grants paid, $65,000; assets, $771,326 (M); expenditures, $74,136; qualifying distributions, $65,000.
Limitations: Applications not accepted.
Application information: Contributes only to pre-selected organizations.
Officers: Stephen H. Chase, Pres. and Treas.; Carol Oppenheimer Simon, V.P. and Secy.
EIN: 311693023

36208
The Robert J. and Martha B. Fierle Foundation
c/o James E. Kelly
5820 Main St., Ste. 600
Williamsville, NY 14221

Established in 1986 in NY.
Donor(s): Robert J. Fierle.
Financial data (yr. ended 12/31/01): Grants paid, $65,000; assets, $3,556,271 (M); expenditures, $129,117; qualifying distributions, $65,000.
Limitations: Applications not accepted. Giving primarily in Buffalo, NY.
Application information: Contributes only to pre-selected organizations.
Officer: James E. Kelly, Mgr.
Trustees: Gretchen Fierle Collins, Donna L. Fierle, Julia L. Fierle, Laura E. Fierle, Peter J. Fierle, Rachel A. Fierle, Robert J. Fierle, Jr., William C. Fierle, Karen F. Paulk.
EIN: 222779812

36209
Saul Fromkes Foundation, Inc.
122 E. 42nd St., Rm. 4400
New York, NY 10168-4999 (212) 447-8360
Contact: Otto Fromkes, Dir., and Arthur Richenthal, Dir.

Established in 1993 in NY.
Financial data (yr. ended 12/31/01): Grants paid, $65,000; assets, $1,310,335 (M); expenditures, $67,095; qualifying distributions, $65,000.
Limitations: Giving primarily in NJ and NY.
Directors: Otto Fromkes, Arthur Richenthal.
EIN: 133682406

36210
George and Alice Kevorkian Foundation, Inc.
19 Durham Dr.
Dix Hills, NY 11746-5310

Established in 2000 in NY.
Donor(s): George Kevorkian.
Financial data (yr. ended 12/31/01): Grants paid, $65,000; assets, $862,739 (M); expenditures, $70,085; qualifying distributions, $65,000.
Limitations: Applications not accepted.
Application information: Contributes only to pre-selected organizations.
Directors: George Kevorkian, John Michael Kevorkian, Steven Victor Kevorkian.
EIN: 113536312

36211
Tony Randall Theatrical Fund, Inc.
c/o A. Goldfine
225 W. 34th St., Ste. 1200
New York, NY 10122-0001
Contact: Anthony L. Randall, Pres.

Established in 1981 in NY.
Donor(s): Anthony L. Randall.
Financial data (yr. ended 06/30/02): Grants paid, $65,000; assets, $16,226 (M); expenditures, $65,130; qualifying distributions, $65,000.
Limitations: Giving primarily in New York, NY.
Officer: Anthony L. Randall, Pres.
EIN: 133082489

36212
The D. M. Solomon Family Foundation
c/o Goldman Sachs & Co.
85 Broad St., Tax Dept.
New York, NY 10004

Established in 2001 in NY.
Donor(s): David M. Solomon.
Financial data (yr. ended 12/31/01): Grants paid, $65,000; assets, $77,265 (M); gifts received, $142,343; expenditures, $71,431; qualifying distributions, $70,638.
Limitations: Applications not accepted. Giving primarily in New York, NY.
Application information: Contributes only to pre-selected organizations.
Officers: David M. Solomon, Chair. and Pres.; Mary C. Solomon, V.P. and Secy.; Andrew Solomon, Treas.
EIN: 134144079

36213
The Sunrise Klein Foundation, Inc.
c/o A. Klein
8 Sunrise Dr.
Monsey, NY 10952-3305

Established in 2000.
Donor(s): Julius Klein, Inc., Abraham Klein.
Financial data (yr. ended 01/31/01): Grants paid, $65,000; assets, $386,324 (M); gifts received, $452,298; expenditures, $69,608; qualifying distributions, $65,000.
Limitations: Applications not accepted.
Application information: Contributes only to pre-selected organizations.
Trustee: Abraham Klein.
EIN: 134097745

36214
The Louis E. & Frances B. Beatty Charitable Foundation
c/o NBT Bank, N.A.
52 S. Broad St.
Norwich, NY 13815
Contact: Sandra E. Colton, Asst. V.P. and Trust Off.

Established in 1993 in NY.
Donor(s): Louis E. Beatty.
Financial data (yr. ended 08/31/02): Grants paid, $64,900; assets, $1,144,070 (M); expenditures, $69,225; qualifying distributions, $60,862.
Limitations: Applications not accepted. Giving primarily in New Berlin, NY.
Application information: Contributes only to pre-selected organizations.
Trustees: Paul Marquit, Robert Wadsworth, John A. Wheeler, NBT Bank, N.A.
EIN: 161447310

36215
Arnold S. Penner Foundation, Inc.
246 E. 71st St.
New York, NY 10021
Contact: Arnold S. Penner, Dir.

Donor(s): Arnold S. Penner.
Financial data (yr. ended 02/28/02): Grants paid, $64,810; assets, $546,867 (M); expenditures, $66,002; qualifying distributions, $64,810.
Director: Arnold S. Penner.
EIN: 133935352

36216
The Martha Kamerman Memorial Foundation
(Formerly Micra Foundation)
885 2nd Ave., 26th Fl.
New York, NY 10017

Established in 1989 in NY; funded in 1990.
Financial data (yr. ended 12/31/01): Grants paid, $64,800; assets, $125,246 (M); gifts received, $500; expenditures, $65,935; qualifying distributions, $64,800.
Limitations: Applications not accepted. Giving limited to NY.
Application information: Contributes only to pre-selected organizations.
Trustees: Jerome Kamerman, Hilton Soniker.
EIN: 136935251

36217
Laurents Foundation
c/o Markowitz, Fenelon & Bank, LLP
608 Northville Tpke.
Riverhead, NY 11901 (631) 727-3626
Contact: Thomas Hatcher, Mgr.

Established in 1965.
Financial data (yr. ended 12/31/01): Grants paid, $64,750; assets, $1,674,253 (M); gifts received, $35,000; expenditures, $81,992; qualifying distributions, $64,750.
Limitations: Giving primarily in NY.
Officers and Trustees:* David Hatcher,* Mgr.; Thomas Hatcher,* Mgr.; Marcia Hefter, Arthur Laurents.
EIN: 136114331

36218
Kadrovach/Duckworth Family Foundation
c/o BCRS Assocs., LLC
67 Wall St., 8th Fl.
New York, NY 10005

Established in 1991 in IL.
Donor(s): Connie K. Duckworth.
Financial data (yr. ended 02/28/01): Grants paid, $64,735; assets, $5,979,882 (M); gifts received, $1,717,079; expenditures, $64,735; qualifying distributions, $64,735.
Limitations: Applications not accepted. Giving primarily in IL.
Application information: Contributes only to pre-selected organizations.
Trustees: Connie K. Duckworth, Thomas J. Duckworth, David B. Ford.
EIN: 133634387

36219
The Foundation for Light and Love, Inc.
c/o Burton Cohen, PC
950 3rd Ave.
New York, NY 10022
Application address: 10 Park Ave., New York, NY 10016, tel.: (212) 889-4986
Contact: Michele Risa, Dir.

Donor(s): Joel Goldberg.
Financial data (yr. ended 12/31/00): Grants paid, $64,595; assets, $289,209 (M); gifts received, $20,477; expenditures, $66,236; qualifying distributions, $64,595.
Directors: Joel Goldberg, Michele Risa.
EIN: 133922214

36220
Charles F. Brush Foundation
360 E. 72nd St., Ste. B211
New York, NY 10021

Donor(s): Charles F. Brush III.
Financial data (yr. ended 10/31/01): Grants paid, $64,500; assets, $29,826 (M); gifts received, $42,570; expenditures, $66,886; qualifying distributions, $65,006.
Limitations: Applications not accepted.
Application information: Contributes only to pre-selected organizations.
Officers: Charles F. Brush III, Pres.; Jean Taylor, Secy.
EIN: 136155648

36221
The Chang Foundation
5 Micole Ct.
Dix Hills, NY 11746

Established in 1997 in NY.
Donor(s): Dominic Chang, Irene Chang.

Financial data (yr. ended 04/30/01): Grants paid, $64,500; assets, $1,660,830 (M); expenditures, $78,546; qualifying distributions, $64,500.
Limitations: Applications not accepted. Giving primarily in NJ and NY.
Application information: Contributes only to pre-selected organizations.
Trustees: Irene Chang, Steven Chang.
EIN: 113393786

36222
The Christina Foundation
c/o Peter Robinson
1114 Ave. of the Americas, 28th Fl.
New York, NY 10036 (212) 704-2304

Established in 1968.
Donor(s): American Retail Group, Inc., American Retail Properties, Inc., Kevin Brenninkmeyer, Argidius Foundation.
Financial data (yr. ended 12/31/01): Grants paid, $64,500; assets, $17,279 (M); gifts received, $65,900; expenditures, $64,635; qualifying distributions, $64,500.
Application information: Application form not required.
Officers and Trustees:* Peter S. Robinson,* Pres.; David J. Vezeris, V.P. and Secy.; Kenneth R. Allex,* V.P. and Treas.; Howard Jackson, Treas.; Roland Hugo Brenninkmeyer, Roland M. Brenninkmeyer.
EIN: 136277184
Codes: CS

36223
The Tompkins County Trust Co. Charitable Fund
c/o The Commons
P.O. Box 460
Ithaca, NY 14851-0460

Established in 1994 in NY.
Financial data (yr. ended 12/31/01): Grants paid, $64,500; assets, $1,300,164 (M); expenditures, $78,714; qualifying distributions, $63,636.
Limitations: Applications not accepted. Giving primarily in Ithaca, NY.
Application information: Contributes only to pre-selected organizations.
Officers: James J. Byrnes, Chair.; Janet L. Hewitt, Secy.
Trustee: The Tompkins Trust Co.
Members: Francis M. Fetsko, Donald S. Stewart.
EIN: 223309880

36224
Dr. Edwin A. Ulrich Charitable Trust
c/o Pangia & Co.
55 Market St.
Poughkeepsie, NY 12601

Established in 1996 in NY.
Donor(s): Edwin A. Ulrich.
Financial data (yr. ended 12/31/01): Grants paid, $64,500; assets, $1,338,568 (M); expenditures, $93,520; qualifying distributions, $64,500.
Limitations: Applications not accepted. Giving primarily in NY.
Application information: Contributes only to pre-selected organizations.
Trustees: Jeffrey P. Armstrong, John R. Conklin, John Regan, Dieter H. Rennhack, Marco Smythe.
EIN: 146161493

36225
Kittay Foundation, Inc.
c/o Betty Zeidman
22 W. 38th St., Rm. 1003
New York, NY 10018-6299

Established in 1946 in NY.
Donor(s): Frieda Kittay Goldsmith.
Financial data (yr. ended 12/31/00): Grants paid, $64,475; assets, $488,073 (M); expenditures, $65,371; qualifying distributions, $64,475.
Limitations: Applications not accepted. Giving primarily in New York, NY.
Application information: Contributes only to pre-selected organizations; unsolicited requests for funds not considered.
Officers and Directors:* Frieda Kittay Goldsmith,* V.P.; Arlyn Imberman,* Secy.; Jeffrey Kittay,* Treas.
EIN: 136161657

36226
The Frances & David Pernick Family Foundation
c/o David Pernick
42 Hemlock Dr.
Kings Point, NY 11024

Established in 1998 in NY.
Donor(s): David Pernick.
Financial data (yr. ended 12/31/01): Grants paid, $64,458; assets, $415,535 (M); expenditures, $64,568; qualifying distributions, $64,458.
Officers: David Pernick, Pres.; Frances Pernick, Secy.
Directors: Jill Friedman, Bruce Pernick.
EIN: 113435389

36227
Asher Reuven Charity Fund
c/o Rabbi Chaim Pomerantz
1647 55th St.
Brooklyn, NY 11204

Established in 1989 in NY.
Donor(s): Ira Pomerantz, Herbert Lobel, Ronald Lowinger.
Financial data (yr. ended 09/30/01): Grants paid, $64,423; assets, $45,288 (M); gifts received, $67,985; expenditures, $64,956; qualifying distributions, $64,423.
Limitations: Applications not accepted. Giving primarily in NY.
Application information: Contributes only to pre-selected organizations.
Trustees: Rabbi Chaim Pomerantz, Mendy Pomerantz, Roslyn Pomerantz.
EIN: 112832051

36228
Petschek Foundation
c/o Grant Thornton, LLP
60 Broad St.
New York, NY 10004-2501

Established in 1955 in NY.
Donor(s): Thea P. Jervolino, Elaine Petschek, Charles Petschek.
Financial data (yr. ended 12/31/01): Grants paid, $64,287; assets, $156,636 (M); gifts received, $106,410; expenditures, $66,240; qualifying distributions, $64,287.
Limitations: Applications not accepted. Giving primarily in New York, NY.
Application information: Contributes only to pre-selected organizations.
Officers: Charles Petschek, Pres. and Treas.; Carol Petschek, V.P.; Elaine Petschek, V.P.; Jay Petschek, V.P.; Jill Petschek, V.P.; Nancy Petschek-Kohn, V.P.
EIN: 136065032

36229
The Richard and Natalie Jacoff Foundation, Inc.
c/o Berlack, Israels & Liberman
120 W. 45th St.
New York, NY 10036 (212) 704-0100

Established in 1985 in NY.
Donor(s): Richard Jacoff, Natalie Jacoff.
Financial data (yr. ended 12/31/01): Grants paid, $64,250; assets, $1,462,739 (M); expenditures, $86,056; qualifying distributions, $64,250.
Limitations: Applications not accepted. Giving primarily in NY.
Application information: Contributes only to pre-selected organizations.
Officers and Directors:* Rachel Mildred Jacoff,* Pres.; Kenneth R. Asher,* V.P. and Secy.; Richard Jacoff,* V.P. and Treas.
EIN: 133316233

36230
Rosenbaum Family Foundation, Inc.
c/o Bloom Hochberg & Co.
450 7th Ave.
New York, NY 10123

Established in 1986 in NY.
Donor(s): Irving Rosenbaum.
Financial data (yr. ended 12/31/01): Grants paid, $64,065; assets, $13,280 (M); gifts received, $144,644; expenditures, $149,872; qualifying distributions, $64,065.
Limitations: Applications not accepted. Giving primarily in NY.
Application information: Contributes only to pre-selected organizations.
Officers: Irving Rosenbaum, Pres.; Irwin Hochberg, Secy.-Treas.
EIN: 133354149

36231
MCM Charitable Foundation
3384 Bedford Ave.
Brooklyn, NY 11210
Application address: 116 39th St., Brooklyn, NY 11232
Contact: Sol Strimber

Established in 1999 in NY.
Donor(s): Murray Mandel.
Financial data (yr. ended 12/31/01): Grants paid, $64,051; assets, $138,271 (M); gifts received, $65,000; expenditures, $64,151; qualifying distributions, $64,051.
Trustees: Chanie Mandel, Murray Mandel.
EIN: 113522283

36232
JenJo Foundation
641 Lexington Ave., Ste. 1400
New York, NY 10022

Established in 1990 in NY.
Financial data (yr. ended 12/31/01): Grants paid, $64,010; assets, $1,845,453 (M); expenditures, $78,248; qualifying distributions, $78,248.
Limitations: Applications not accepted. Giving primarily in the greater Boston, MA area, and on Long Island, NY.
Application information: Unsolicited requests for funds not accepted.
Trustees: Elizabeth O'Heaney, William O'Heaney.
EIN: 136944768

36233
The Katherine Dalglish Foundation
c/o Capital Administration, Inc.
49 W. 24th St., 8th Fl.
New York, NY 10010
Contact: Pierre Tonachel, Tr.

Established in 1979 in NY.
Donor(s): Helen G. Swerling.‡
Financial data (yr. ended 06/30/01): Grants paid, $64,000; assets, $1,196,443 (M); expenditures, $79,618; qualifying distributions, $66,157.
Limitations: Giving primarily in lower Manhattan in New York, NY.
Publications: Application guidelines.

Application information: Application form not required.
Trustees: David Hapgood, Pierre Tonachel.
EIN: 132907888

36234
The Glad Foundation
132 W. 31st St., 18th Fl.
New York, NY 10001-3406

Established in 1971.
Donor(s): 132 W. 31st St. Realty Corp., Edna F. Lemle.
Financial data (yr. ended 04/30/02): Grants paid, $64,000; assets, $1,204,044 (M); expenditures, $68,601; qualifying distributions, $64,000.
Limitations: Applications not accepted. Giving primarily in New York, NY.
Application information: Contributes only to pre-selected organizations.
Officers: Edna F. Lemle, Pres.; Florence J. Lemle, V.P. and Secy.
EIN: 237123061

36235
The Grosevnor Foundation
22 W. 15th St., Ste. 9A
New York, NY 10011
Contact: David Handler, Tr.

Established in 2000 in NY.
Donor(s): David Handler.
Financial data (yr. ended 12/31/01): Grants paid, $63,783; assets, $208,327 (M); gifts received, $97,000; expenditures, $70,653; qualifying distributions, $63,783.
Trustee: David Handler.
EIN: 134104304

36236
The Lerner Family Foundation, Inc.
1020 Ocean Pkwy.
Brooklyn, NY 11230
Contact: Pinchos Lerner, Pres.

Established in 1996 in NY.
Donor(s): Chanie Lerner.
Financial data (yr. ended 12/31/00): Grants paid, $63,750; assets, $351,567 (M); gifts received, $100,000; expenditures, $64,960; qualifying distributions, $64,902; giving activities include $1,210 for programs.
Limitations: Applications not accepted.
Application information: Contributes only to pre-selected organizations.
Officers: Pinchos Lerner, Pres.; Chanie Lerner, V.P. and Secy.
EIN: 113333895

36237
David G. Salten Foundation
41 Park Ave.
New York, NY 10016 (212) 685-7009

Established in 1989 in NY.
Donor(s): David G. Salten.
Financial data (yr. ended 12/31/01): Grants paid, $63,735; assets, $380,451 (M); expenditures, $65,756; qualifying distributions, $63,735.
Limitations: Applications not accepted. Giving primarily in NY.
Application information: Contributes only to pre-selected organizations.
Trustee: David G. Salten.
EIN: 133552152

36238
The Frank and Domna Stanton Foundation, Inc.
c/o Domna Stanton
112 E. 74th St.
New York, NY 10021

Established in 1987 in NY.
Donor(s): World-Wide Holdings Corp.
Financial data (yr. ended 12/31/00): Grants paid, $63,621; assets, $777,173 (M); gifts received, $89,480; expenditures, $72,754; qualifying distributions, $62,673.
Limitations: Applications not accepted. Giving primarily in NY.
Application information: Contributes only to pre-selected organizations.
Officers: Domna Stanton, V.P.; James Stanton, Secy.; Michael Stanton, Treas.
EIN: 133416233
Codes: CS, CD

36239
Philip M. Waterman Foundation, Inc.
875 Park Ave.
New York, NY 10021-0341

Donor(s): Elise D. Waterman, Philip M. Waterman, Jr.
Financial data (yr. ended 04/30/02): Grants paid, $63,617; assets, $274,331 (M); gifts received, $46,690; expenditures, $63,919; qualifying distributions, $63,617.
Limitations: Applications not accepted. Giving primarily in NY.
Application information: Contributes only to pre-selected organizations.
Officers: Elise D. Waterman, Pres. and Treas.; Philip M. Waterman, Jr., V.P. and Secy.
EIN: 136059475

36240
The Alexander & Ilse Melamid Charitable Foundation
c/o American Express
1185 Ave. of the Americas
New York, NY 10036

Established in 1984 in NY.
Donor(s): Alexander Melamid,‡ Ilse Melamid.
Financial data (yr. ended 05/31/01): Grants paid, $63,600; assets, $119,461 (M); gifts received, $103,455; expenditures, $68,367; qualifying distributions, $65,256.
Limitations: Giving primarily in NY.
Application information: Application form not required.
Trustee: Ilse Melamid.
EIN: 133213720

36241
The Vanden Brul Foundation, Inc.
35 Briar Patch Rd.
Rochester, NY 14618-3804 (716) 381-2308

Established in 1981 in NY.
Donor(s): Herbert W. Vanden Brul.
Financial data (yr. ended 09/30/01): Grants paid, $63,515; assets, $85,028 (M); expenditures, $66,680; qualifying distributions, $63,472.
Limitations: Applications not accepted. Giving primarily in the greater Rochester, NY, area.
Application information: Contributes only to pre-selected organizations.
Officer: Herbert W. Vanden Brul, Pres.
Directors: Patricia Nunnari, Donald Vanden Brul, Kristin A. Vanden Brul-McDonald, William Vanden Brul.
EIN: 133098970

36242
William J. Burns Foundation, Inc.
60 E. 42nd St., Ste. 1760
New York, NY 10165

Established in 1987 in NY.
Financial data (yr. ended 12/31/01): Grants paid, $63,500; assets, $1,491,220 (M); expenditures, $83,063; qualifying distributions, $72,062.
Limitations: Applications not accepted. Giving primarily in NY.
Application information: Contributes only to pre-selected organizations.
Officers: Jeremiah E. Brown, Pres.; James J. Cronin, V.P.; William B. Benack, Secy.-Treas.
EIN: 133374325

36243
Natapow Family Foundation, Inc.
120 Corporate Woods, Ste. 100
Rochester, NY 14623

Established in 1986 in NY.
Donor(s): Ruben Natapow, Natapow Realty Corp., RAM, LP, Robert Natapow, Stephen Natapow.
Financial data (yr. ended 06/30/01): Grants paid, $63,500; assets, $244,288 (M); gifts received, $59,144; expenditures, $64,832; qualifying distributions, $63,500.
Limitations: Applications not accepted. Giving primarily in Rochester, NY.
Application information: Contributes only to pre-selected organizations.
Officers: Ruben Natapow, Pres.; Robert Natapow, Secy.; Stephen Natapow, Treas.
Trustees: Susan DeBlase, E. Barry Kaplan.
EIN: 222757393

36244
Jack P. Schleifer Foundation
60 E. 42nd St.
New York, NY 10017

Donor(s): Jack P. Schleifer, Natalie Schlass.
Financial data (yr. ended 12/31/01): Grants paid, $63,494; assets, $339,330 (M); gifts received, $280,850; expenditures, $63,622; qualifying distributions, $63,622.
Officers: Jack P. Schleifer, Pres.; Natalie Schlass, Secy.
Director: Daniel Schleifer.
EIN: 134146027

36245
Judith M. & Michael D. Sullivan Foundation
11 Elkof Ct.
Croton-on-Hudson, NY 10520-3426

Established in 1997 in DE.
Donor(s): Judith M. Sullivan, Michael D. Sullivan.
Financial data (yr. ended 09/30/01): Grants paid, $63,350; assets, $13,914 (M); gifts received, $30,000; expenditures, $63,826; qualifying distributions, $63,350.
Limitations: Applications not accepted.
Application information: Contributes only to pre-selected organizations.
Officers: Judith M. Sullivan, Pres. and Treas.; Michael D. Sullivan, V.P. and Secy.
EIN: 133972751

36246
John W. Danforth Company Foundation, Inc.
1940 Fillmore Ave.
Buffalo, NY 14214-2992 (716) 832-1940
Contact: Wayne R. Reilly, Dir.

Donor(s): John W. Danforth Company.
Financial data (yr. ended 12/31/01): Grants paid, $63,295; assets, $337,008 (M); gifts received,

$75,000; expenditures, $63,543; qualifying distributions, $63,295.
Limitations: Giving primarily in the western NY area.
Application information: Application form not required.
Director: Wayne R. Reilly.
EIN: 166027290
Codes: CS, CD

36247
Tioga County Senior Citizens Foundation
c/o Chemung Canal Trust Co.
P.O. Box 1522
Elmira, NY 14902 (607) 687-0229
Application address: P.O. Box 117, Owego, NY 13827-0117; E-mail: cjwright@stny.rr.com
Contact: Carolyn Wright, Secy.

Established in 1951 as a private foundation. Renamed in 1982 to current name.
Financial data (yr. ended 09/30/02): Grants paid, $63,294; assets, $1,224,000 (M); expenditures, $80,649; qualifying distributions, $66,912.
Limitations: Giving limited to Tioga County, NY.
Publications: Annual report, informational brochure.
Application information: Request application form. Application form required.
Officers and Directors:* J. Dickson Edson,* Pres.; Gary Williams,* V.P.; Carolyn Wright,* Secy.; Ralph Kelsey,* Treas.
EIN: 150543615

36248
Barbara Saltzman Charitable Foundation
30 E. 65th St., Apt. 5C
New York, NY 10021

Established in 1997 in NY.
Donor(s): Barbara Saltzman.
Financial data (yr. ended 12/31/01): Grants paid, $63,226; assets, $1,132,543 (M); expenditures, $69,422; qualifying distributions, $65,185.
Limitations: Giving primarily in New York, NY.
Officers: Barbara Saltzman, Pres.; Lawrence Saltzman, V.P.; Matthew Saltzman, V.P.; Neil Saltzman, V.P.; William Saltzman, Secy.
EIN: 133946884

36249
Bank of Utica Foundation, Inc.
c/o M & H
P.O. Box 477
Utica, NY 13503 (315) 797-2700
Application address: 222 Genesee St., Utica, NY 13502
Contact: Tom E. Sinnott, Chair.

Established in 1992 in NY.
Donor(s): Bank of Utica.
Financial data (yr. ended 12/31/01): Grants paid, $63,200; assets, $277,500 (M); expenditures, $63,598; qualifying distributions, $63,200.
Limitations: Giving limited to Utica, NY.
Officers: Tom E. Sinnott, Chair.; Roger J. Sinnott, Pres.; Joan M. Sinnott, V.P.
EIN: 161423958
Codes: CS, CD

36250
Kohanim Wallerstein Foundation, Inc.
1373 E. 13th St.
Brooklyn, NY 11230 (718) 627-4467
Contact: Shmuel Wallerstein, Dir.

Donor(s): Lou Wallerstein, Charlotte Wallerstein, Shmuel Wallerstein.
Financial data (yr. ended 09/30/00): Grants paid, $63,152; assets, $44,519 (M); gifts received, $58,601; expenditures, $63,446; qualifying distributions, $63,446.
Directors: Shmuel Wallerstein, Pres.; Chanig Wallerstein, Raphael Wallerstein.
EIN: 132895298

36251
Charles Spear Charitable Trust
115 E. 23rd St., 8th Fl.
New York, NY 10010-4560

Established in 1992 in NY.
Donor(s): Charles Spielberger.
Financial data (yr. ended 12/31/00): Grants paid, $63,100; assets, $1,874,820 (M); gifts received, $100,000; expenditures, $87,756; qualifying distributions, $63,100.
Limitations: Applications not accepted. Giving primarily in NY.
Application information: Contributes only to pre-selected organizations.
Trustee: Caroline Barrett.
EIN: 132113021

36252
The Engelberg Family Foundation
1014 E. 21st St.
Brooklyn, NY 11210

Established in 1993 in DE and NY.
Donor(s): Mindy Engelberg.
Financial data (yr. ended 11/30/01): Grants paid, $63,097; assets, $107,796 (M); gifts received, $36,428; expenditures, $68,700; qualifying distributions, $65,185.
Limitations: Applications not accepted. Giving primarily in Brooklyn, NY.
Application information: Contributes only to pre-selected organizations.
Officers: Mindy Engelberg, Pres.; Michael Engelberg, Secy.
EIN: 113162917

36253
William D. Witter Foundation, Inc.
1040 5th Ave.
New York, NY 10028

Established in 1998 in NY.
Donor(s): Susan Witter.
Financial data (yr. ended 09/30/01): Grants paid, $63,085; assets, $95,298 (M); gifts received, $65,432; expenditures, $71,518; qualifying distributions, $63,085.
Limitations: Applications not accepted.
Application information: Contributes only to pre-selected organizations.
Officers: Susan R. Witter, Pres. and Treas.; William P. Witter, V.P. and Secy.; Sidney W. Witter, V.P.; Virginia Witter Woods, V.P.; Elizabeth Tacy Witter, V.P.
EIN: 134065752

36254
The Handler Foundation
c/o Jerry S. Handler
151 W. 40th St.
New York, NY 10018-1903

Established about 1952.
Donor(s): Handro Properties.
Financial data (yr. ended 11/30/01): Grants paid, $63,075; assets, $565,325 (M); gifts received, $13,000; expenditures, $75,574; qualifying distributions, $63,075.
Limitations: Applications not accepted. Giving primarily in NY.
Application information: Contributes only to pre-selected organizations.
Trustee: Jerry S. Handler.
EIN: 136147244

36255
Charles and Els Bendheim Foundation, Inc.
c/o Wald & Wald
1 Penn Plz., Ste. 4307
New York, NY 10119
Application address: 1 Parker Plz., 14th Fl., Fort Lee, NJ 07024, tel.: (201) 944-6020
Contact: Els Bendheim, Pres.

Incorporated in 1947 in NY.
Donor(s): Nannette Bendheim,‡ Charles H. Bendheim,‡ Philip E. Bendheim.
Financial data (yr. ended 01/31/01): Grants paid, $63,050; assets, $21,131 (M); gifts received, $23,271; expenditures, $63,050; qualifying distributions, $63,037.
Limitations: Giving primarily in NY.
Officer: Els Bendheim, Pres.
EIN: 136103769

36256
James C. Hemphill Foundation
c/o BCRS Assocs., LLC
67 Wall St., 8th Fl.
New York, NY 10005

Established in 1958 in IL.
Financial data (yr. ended 06/30/01): Grants paid, $63,000; assets, $1,008,544 (M); expenditures, $65,135; qualifying distributions, $63,000.
Limitations: Applications not accepted. Giving primarily in Chicago, IL.
Application information: Contributes only to pre-selected organizations.
Officer and Directors:* Robert I. Lund,* Pres.; Wade Fetzer III, John F. Gilmore, Jr., James P. Gorter, Bruce Heyman, Pamela L. Kolzow, Susan Willetts.
EIN: 136028808

36257
Zichron Yosef Chesed Foundation
1320 E. 26th St.
Brooklyn, NY 11210
Application address: 1342 E. 5th St., Brooklyn, NY 11230, tel.: (718) 283-8544
Contact: Raphael Grossman

Established in 1998 in NY.
Financial data (yr. ended 11/30/01): Grants paid, $62,814; assets, $159,161 (M); gifts received, $75,000; expenditures, $63,264; qualifying distributions, $63,242.
Limitations: Giving primarily in New York, NY; some giving also in Israel.
Trustee: Zev Pollak.
EIN: 113483759

36258
The Kaye Family Foundation
c/o E. M. Warburg Pincus
466 Lexington Ave., 11th Fl.
New York, NY 10017

Established in 1999 in NY.
Donor(s): Charles R. Kaye.
Financial data (yr. ended 11/30/01): Grants paid, $62,800; assets, $418,354 (M); gifts received, $2,680; expenditures, $72,041; qualifying distributions, $62,800.
Limitations: Applications not accepted. Giving primarily in New York, NY.
Application information: Contributes only to pre-selected organizations.
Trustees: Charles R. Kaye, Sheryl Kaye.
EIN: 134092284

36259
Walter A. and Mary Catherine Scott Foundation
c/o U.S. Trust
114 W. 47th St., TaxVas
New York, NY 10036

Established in 2000 in DE.
Donor(s): Mary C. Scott, Walter A. Scott.
Financial data (yr. ended 12/31/01): Grants paid, $62,800; assets, $984,482 (M); expenditures, $90,148; qualifying distributions, $62,800.
Limitations: Applications not accepted.
Application information: Unsolicited requests for funds not accepted.
Officers: Walter A. Scott, Pres.; Mary C. Scott, V.P.; C. Reed Scott, Secy.; Alisa A. Scott, Treas.
EIN: 134171575

36260
Andrew & Julie Klingenstein Family Fund, Inc.
c/o Tanton and Co., LLP
37 W. 57th St., 5th Fl.
New York, NY 10019

Established in 2000 in MD.
Donor(s): Andrew Klingenstein, Andrew Klingenstein Charitable Lead Trust.
Financial data (yr. ended 12/31/01): Grants paid, $62,750; assets, $1,240,713 (M); gifts received, $138,993; expenditures, $68,695; qualifying distributions, $62,750.
Officers and Directors:* Julie Klingenstein,* Pres.; Thomas D. Klingenstein,* V.P.; Andrew Klingenstein,* Secy.-Treas.
EIN: 522126870

36261
Evan Philip Scheuer Foundation, Inc.
23 E. 4th St., 8th Fl.
New York, NY 10003-7023

Established in 1996.
Financial data (yr. ended 12/31/00): Grants paid, $62,750; assets, $1,260,038 (M); expenditures, $73,582; qualifying distributions, $62,750.
Limitations: Applications not accepted.
Application information: Contributes only to pre-selected organizations.
Officer: Evan Philip Scheuer, Pres.
EIN: 133882430

36262
The William and May D. Norris Foundation
c/o Ingber & Ingber
P.O. Box 977
Monticello, NY 12701-1723

Established in 1995 in NY.
Financial data (yr. ended 12/31/01): Grants paid, $62,714; assets, $1,173,122 (M); expenditures, $101,802; qualifying distributions, $62,714.
Limitations: Applications not accepted. Giving primarily in NY.
Application information: Contributes only to pre-selected organizations.
Trustees: Ann Culligan, James Culligan, Jack S. Ingber, Keith Ingber.
EIN: 141777064

36263
Sargol Charitable Trust
412 Ave. C
Brooklyn, NY 11218-4518 (212) 603-6141
Contact: Yitzchok Goodman, Tr.

Financial data (yr. ended 12/31/01): Grants paid, $62,621; assets, $1,616,855 (M); gifts received, $360,420; expenditures, $63,721; qualifying distributions, $62,721.
Limitations: Giving primarily in Brooklyn, NY.

Trustees: Rachel Goodman, Yitzchok Goodman, Raphael Grossman.
EIN: 116478559

36264
The Braewold Fund
153 Wood Rd.
Mount Kisco, NY 10549

Financial data (yr. ended 12/31/01): Grants paid, $62,505; assets, $660,476 (M); expenditures, $70,652; qualifying distributions, $62,497.
Limitations: Applications not accepted. Giving primarily in NY.
Application information: Contributes only to pre-selected organizations.
Trustees: Frances Wood, James Wood.
EIN: 137196658

36265
The Ogilvy Foundation
c/o WPP Group (PX Gratt)
125 Park Ave., 4th Fl.
New York, NY 10017
Application address: 309 W. 49th St., New York, NY 10019
Contact: Nancy Nolan

Established in 1984 in NY.
Donor(s): Ogilvy & Mather Worldwide, Inc.
Financial data (yr. ended 06/30/00): Grants paid, $62,500; assets, $1,290,545 (M); expenditures, $77,383; qualifying distributions, $76,976.
Limitations: Giving on a national and international basis.
Officers and Directors:* Rochelle Lazarus,* Pres.; John Elliott, Jr.,* V.P.; William E. Phillips,* V.P.; Richard DeMilt, Treas.
EIN: 133230406
Codes: CS, CD

36266
The Aaron & Shirley Feder Family Foundation, Inc.
812 5th Ave., Apt. 3A
New York, NY 10021-7253

Established in 1990 in NY.
Donor(s): Aaron Feder, Shirley Feder, Marc Feder, Daniel Feder, Gabriel Feder.
Financial data (yr. ended 12/31/01): Grants paid, $62,465; assets, $162,579 (M); gifts received, $26,000; expenditures, $66,297; qualifying distributions, $62,465.
Limitations: Applications not accepted.
Application information: Contributes only to pre-selected organizations.
Trustees: Aaron Feder, Marc Feder, Shirley Feder.
EIN: 113040576

36267
The Hyde Family Charitable Fund
1800 1 M&T Plz.
Buffalo, NY 14203

Established in 1996 in NY.
Donor(s): Charles F. Hyde, Jr.
Financial data (yr. ended 12/31/01): Grants paid, $62,383; assets, $1,523,976 (M); gifts received, $975; expenditures, $71,800; qualifying distributions, $62,383.
Limitations: Applications not accepted. Giving primarily in Buffalo, NY.
Application information: Contributes only to pre-selected organizations.
Trustees: Charles F. Hyde, Jr., Douglas W. Hyde, Joyce W. Hyde, Thomas R. Hyde, Margaret H. Wachtel.
EIN: 161502229

36268
The Wonderful Foundation
277 West End Ave.
New York, NY 10023
Contact: Loraine F. Gardner, Pres.

Established in 1990 in NY.
Donor(s): Stephen Gardner.
Financial data (yr. ended 12/31/01): Grants paid, $62,374; assets, $1,173,015 (M); expenditures, $72,286; qualifying distributions, $63,508.
Limitations: Giving on a national basis.
Officers: Loraine F. Gardner, Pres. and Treas.; Barbara Dolgin, V.P.; Daniel Dolgin, V.P.
EIN: 363693741

36269
The Spiro Family Foundation, Inc.
c/o Arthur M. Spiro
19 Harbour Rd.
Great Neck, NY 11024-1203

Established in 1965.
Donor(s): Arthur M. Spiro.
Financial data (yr. ended 06/30/02): Grants paid, $62,348; assets, $235,971 (M); gifts received, $180,000; expenditures, $101,023; qualifying distributions, $62,348.
Limitations: Applications not accepted. Giving on a national basis.
Application information: Contributes only to pre-selected organizations.
Officers: Arthur M. Spiro, Pres.; Joan Spiro, Secy.
EIN: 116049401

36270
The Lawrence Foundation
112 W. 34th St.
New York, NY 10120-0101 (212) 947-8900
Contact: Leonard S. Bernstein, Tr.

Donor(s): Candlesticks, Inc., Lancaster Industries, Inc.
Financial data (yr. ended 09/30/01): Grants paid, $62,300; assets, $1,284,378 (M); gifts received, $5,000; expenditures, $62,654; qualifying distributions, $61,921.
Limitations: Giving for scholarships limited to Mount Joy, PA.
Application information: Application form required.
Trustees: Jay S. Bernstein, Lawrence Bernstein, Leonard S. Bernstein.
EIN: 132880731
Codes: CS, CD

36271
Otis A. Thompson Foundation, Inc.
c/o NBT Bank, N.A.
52 S. Broad St.
Norwich, NY 13815-1646 (607) 337-6193
Contact: Sandra E. Colton

Established in 1962.
Donor(s): Raymond O. Thompson,‡ NBT Bank, N.A.
Financial data (yr. ended 12/31/01): Grants paid, $62,300; assets, $1,634,244 (M); expenditures, $68,036; qualifying distributions, $62,300.
Limitations: Giving primarily in Chenango, Delaware, and Otsego counties, NY.
Application information: Application form required.
Officers: Everett A. Gilmour, Chair.; Daryl Forsythe, Pres.; William Sluiter, V.P.; Jacob K. Weinman, V.P.; Charles D. Lord, Secy.-Treas.
Agent: NBT Bank, N.A.
EIN: 166046540

36272
The Herman & Ruth Albert Foundation, Inc.
The Crossing at Blind Brook
Purchase, NY 10577

Established in 1993 in DE and NY.
Donor(s): Herman Albert,‡ Ruth Albert.
Financial data (yr. ended 11/30/01): Grants paid, $62,225; assets, $14,897 (M); expenditures, $62,455; qualifying distributions, $62,203.
Limitations: Applications not accepted. Giving primarily in West Palm Beach, FL.
Application information: Contributes only to pre-selected organizations.
Officer: Ruth Albert, Secy.
EIN: 133744236

36273
Daniels Family Foundation, Inc.
1095 Park Ave.
New York, NY 10128

Established in 1997 in NY.
Donor(s): Aaron Daniels.
Financial data (yr. ended 12/31/01): Grants paid, $62,180; assets, $475,693 (M); gifts received, $201; expenditures, $74,447; qualifying distributions, $62,180.
Limitations: Applications not accepted. Giving primarily in New York, NY.
Application information: Contributes only to pre-selected organizations.
Directors: Aaron Daniels, Judy Daniels.
EIN: 133948882

36274
The Brownwood Family Foundation
c/o Cravath, Swaine & Moore
825 8th Ave., 46th Fl.
New York, NY 10019-7475
Contact: David O. Brownwood, Tr.

Established in 1993 in CT.
Donor(s): David O. Brownwood.
Financial data (yr. ended 12/31/01): Grants paid, $62,130; assets, $16,297 (M); expenditures, $62,440; qualifying distributions, $62,004.
Limitations: Applications not accepted.
Application information: Contributes only to pre-selected organizations.
Trustee: David O. Brownwood.
EIN: 061367934

36275
Keren Yad Sarah, Inc.
c/o Solomon B. Elias
1441 45th St.
Brooklyn, NY 11219

Established in 1999 in NY.
Donor(s): Solomon B. Elias.
Financial data (yr. ended 06/30/01): Grants paid, $62,050; assets, $22,380 (M); gifts received, $56,673; expenditures, $65,192; qualifying distributions, $65,192.
Limitations: Giving primarily in Brooklyn, NY.
Officer: Solomon B. Elias, Mgr.
EIN: 311676073

36276
Bisgeier Family Foundation
400 West End Ave.
New York, NY 10024-5778
Contact: Howard Bisgeier, Pres. and Treas.

Established in 2001 in NY.
Donor(s): David Bisgeier, Susan Bisgeier.
Financial data (yr. ended 12/31/02): Grants paid, $62,000; assets, $1,101,015 (M); gifts received, $113,777; expenditures, $68,324; qualifying distributions, $62,000.
Limitations: Giving primarily in NY.
Officers and Directors:* Howard Bisgeier, Pres. and Treas.; Shirley Bisgeier,* V.P.; Bonnie Bisgeier, Craig Bisgeier.
EIN: 134111135

36277
The Four T's Foundation
c/o U.S. Trust
114 W. 47th St., TAXVAS
New York, NY 10036

Established in 2000 in NY.
Donor(s): John S. Reed.
Financial data (yr. ended 12/31/01): Grants paid, $62,000; assets, $2,215,902 (M); expenditures, $67,018; qualifying distributions, $62,000.
Limitations: Applications not accepted.
Application information: Unsolicited requests for funds not accepted.
Trustees: Cynthia Reed, John S. Reed.
EIN: 137219393

36278
The Abraham Gottlieb Foundation, Inc.
c/o Progressive Planning, Inc.
500 N. Broadway, Ste. 245
Jericho, NY 11753

Financial data (yr. ended 12/31/01): Grants paid, $62,000; assets, $877,529 (M); expenditures, $75,777; qualifying distributions, $75,777.
Limitations: Applications not accepted. Giving primarily in NY.
Application information: Contributes only to pre-selected organizations.
Officer: Lynn Gilbert, Mgr.
EIN: 136139188

36279
W. F. Reilly Foundation, Inc.
375 Park Ave., Ste. 1507
New York, NY 10152
Contact: William F. Reilly, Dir.

Established in 2000 in NY.
Donor(s): William F. Reilly, William F. Reilly.
Financial data (yr. ended 12/31/00): Grants paid, $62,000; assets, $1,716,541 (M); gifts received, $3,069,500; expenditures, $119,496; qualifying distributions, $83,242.
Limitations: Giving primarily in NY.
Directors: Anthony C. Reilly, Jane W. Reilly, William F. Reilly.
EIN: 134104179

36280
Wagner-Braunsberg Family Foundation, Inc.
c/o Frank Lionel
1800 Northern Blvd., Ste. 212
Roslyn, NY 11576-1124

Established in 1997 in DE.
Donor(s): K. Peter Wagner, Yvonne R. Wagner.
Financial data (yr. ended 12/31/01): Grants paid, $62,000; assets, $1,347,363 (M); gifts received, $363,611; expenditures, $65,882; qualifying distributions, $62,000.
Limitations: Applications not accepted.
Application information: Contributes only to pre-selected organizations.
Officers and Directors:* K. Peter Wagner,* Pres.; Elizabeth S. Lieberman,* V.P.; Charles H.S. Wagner,* V.P.; Wayne L.B. Wagner,* V.P.; Yvonne R. Wagner,* V.P.; Frank Lionel,* Treas.
EIN: 113373671

36281
Edwin S. Lowe Foundation
31 W. 27th St.
New York, NY 10001

Established in 1961.
Financial data (yr. ended 10/31/01): Grants paid, $61,913; assets, $278,719 (M); expenditures, $68,889; qualifying distributions, $61,913.
Limitations: Applications not accepted. Giving primarily in CA and NY.
Application information: Contributes only to pre-selected organizations.
Officer: Barbara Lowe Fodor, Pres.
EIN: 136160967

36282
Edward Sulzberger Foundation, Inc.
250 W. 57th St., Ste. 2507
New York, NY 10107
Contact: Myron Sulzberger Rolfe, Pres.

Established in 1986 in DE and NY.
Donor(s): Edward Sulzberger.‡
Financial data (yr. ended 12/31/01): Grants paid, $61,850; assets, $1,522,967 (M); expenditures, $93,445; qualifying distributions, $61,850.
Limitations: Applications not accepted. Giving primarily in New York, NY.
Application information: Contributes only to pre-selected organizations.
Officers and Directors:* Myron Sulzberger Rolfe,* Pres. and Mgr.; Susan S. Rolfe,* Secy.-Treas.; Maye Sulzberger.
EIN: 133385799

36283
The Diana Foundation, Inc.
29-28 41st Ave., 12th Fl.
Long Island City, NY 11101-3303

Established in 1991 in NY.
Donor(s): Merle Hoffman.
Financial data (yr. ended 12/31/99): Grants paid, $61,780; assets, $154,694 (M); gifts received, $187; expenditures, $64,691; qualifying distributions, $61,679.
Limitations: Applications not accepted. Giving primarily in the greater metropolitan New York, NY, area.
Application information: Contributes only to pre-selected organizations.
Officer and Trustees:* Merle Hoffman,* Pres.; Ruth Hoffman.
EIN: 223208840

36284
Milton B. Rosenbluth Foundation, Inc.
955 Lexington Ave.
New York, NY 10021
Contact: Michael J. Samek, Treas.

Established in 1988 in NY.
Financial data (yr. ended 12/31/00): Grants paid, $61,750; assets, $712,515 (M); gifts received, $88,800; expenditures, $70,634; qualifying distributions, $66,508.
Limitations: Giving primarily in NY.
Officers and Directors:* Helen S. Tucker,* Chair.; Michael A. Rosenbluth, M.D.,* Pres.; Werner H. Kramarsky,* Secy.; Michael J. Samek,* Treas.; Anne H. Bass, Catherine R. Rosenbluth, and 5 additional directors.
EIN: 133460707
Codes: GTI

36285
Still Point Fund
c/o Eisenberg and Blau, C.P.A.
150 Broadway, Ste. 1102
New York, NY 10038

Established in 1997 in VT.
Donor(s): Brenda Ross Winter.
Financial data (yr. ended 12/31/01): Grants paid, $61,700; assets, $949,937 (M); expenditures, $64,398; qualifying distributions, $61,700.
Limitations: Applications not accepted. Giving primarily in PA and VA.
Application information: Contributes only to pre-selected organizations.
Trustee: Brenda Ross Winter.
EIN: 043370051

36286
The Beckman Family Foundation
8 Hathaway Rd.
Scarsdale, NY 10583

Established in 1993 in NY.
Donor(s): Joel S. Beckman.
Financial data (yr. ended 10/31/01): Grants paid, $61,680; assets, $63,845 (M); expenditures, $61,680; qualifying distributions, $61,680.
Limitations: Applications not accepted. Giving primarily in NY.
Application information: Contributes only to pre-selected organizations. Unsolicited requests for funds not accepted.
Trustees: Joel S. Beckman, Shari L. Beckman.
EIN: 137034350

36287
The Barry and Alison Goodman Foundation
c/o The Millburn Corporation
1270 Ave. of the Americas
New York, NY 10020 (212) 332-7300

Established in 1995 in NY.
Donor(s): Barry Goodman.
Financial data (yr. ended 12/31/01): Grants paid, $61,650; assets, $460,358 (M); expenditures, $64,960; qualifying distributions, $61,650.
Limitations: Applications not accepted. Giving primarily in NY.
Application information: Contributes only to pre-selected organizations.
Officers: Barry Goodman, Pres.; Alison Goodman, Secy.
Director: Harvey Beker.
EIN: 133861629

36288
The Mid-York Foundation
160 Broad St.
P.O. Box 505
Hamilton, NY 13346-0629 (315) 825-3111
Contact: Ann P. Cochran, Pres.

Incorporated in 1990 in NY.
Donor(s): Mid-York Family Health Center Assn., Inc.
Financial data (yr. ended 12/31/01): Grants paid, $61,500; assets, $8,177 (M); gifts received, $69,924; expenditures, $62,787; qualifying distributions, $61,500.
Limitations: Giving limited to Chenango and Madison counties, NY.
Officers and Directors:* Ann P. Cochran,* Pres.; Donald DuBois,* V.P.; Alice Lahue,* Secy.; Lawrence Baker,* Treas.; Jennifer Caloia, Terrence Murphy, Paul Noyes, James Plesniarski, Eleanor Ross.
EIN: 161378925

36289
Robin and Charles B. Moss, Jr. Family Charitable Trust
(Formerly Charles B. Moss, Jr. Family Charitable Trust)
c/o Anchin, Block & Anchin, LLP
1375 Broadway, 18th Fl.
New York, NY 10018

Donor(s): Charles B. Moss, Jr.
Financial data (yr. ended 09/30/01): Grants paid, $61,400; assets, $716,410 (M); expenditures, $63,927; qualifying distributions, $61,400.
Limitations: Applications not accepted. Giving primarily in CO and NY.
Application information: Contributes only to pre-selected organizations.
Trustees: Charles B. Moss, Jr., Robin H. Moss.
EIN: 112846796

36290
The Rato Dratsang Foundation
107 E. 31st St., 5th Fl.
New York, NY 10016 (212) 779-1841

Financial data (yr. ended 12/31/00): Grants paid, $61,300; assets, $35,806 (M); gifts received, $15,786; expenditures, $62,115; qualifying distributions, $61,300.
Limitations: Applications not accepted. Giving on an international basis, with emphasis on India.
Application information: Contributes only to pre-selected organizations.
Officers: Khyongla Rato, Pres.; Anthony Spina, V.P. and Secy.
EIN: 133355619

36291
Allan Shedlin Foundation, Inc.
945 5th Ave.
New York, NY 10021-2655

Established in 1958 in NY.
Donor(s): Allan Shedlin, Ann Shedlin Trust, Lilly Shedlin.
Financial data (yr. ended 12/31/01): Grants paid, $61,255; assets, $1,155,875 (M); expenditures, $72,466; qualifying distributions, $61,255.
Limitations: Applications not accepted. Giving primarily in New York, NY.
Application information: Contributes only to pre-selected organizations.
Officer: Allan Shedlin, Pres.
EIN: 136106763

36292
Lewis M. & Mabel C. Fowler Memorial Foundation, Inc.
(also known as Lewis Fowler Scholarship)
c/o Central National Bank
24 Church St.
Canajoharie, NY 13317-1101

Established in 1954 in NY.
Financial data (yr. ended 12/31/01): Grants paid, $61,250; assets, $1,081,026 (M); expenditures, $75,039; qualifying distributions, $61,250.
Limitations: Giving primarily in the St. Johnsville, NY, area.
Trustees: Peter Corso, Robert Moyer, Edward F. Skoda.
EIN: 146030197

36293
The Johnson Family Foundation, Inc.
149 E. 73rd St.
New York, NY 10021

Established in 1997 in NY.
Donor(s): Thomas S. Johnson.
Financial data (yr. ended 12/31/01): Grants paid, $61,250; assets, $3,397,820 (M); gifts received, $742,200; expenditures, $85,408; qualifying distributions, $61,250.
Limitations: Applications not accepted. Giving primarily in CT, IL, MA, NJ, and the metropolitan New York, NY, area.
Application information: Contributes only to pre-selected organizations.
Officers and Directors:* Margaret Ann Johnson,* Chair.; Thomas S. Johnson, Treas.; Scott M. Johnson, Thomas P. Johnson.
EIN: 137118242

36294
Theodore & Elizabeth Weicker Foundation
2 E. 70th St.
New York, NY 10021-4913 (212) 988-0646

Established in 1958.
Donor(s): Elizabeth W. Fondaras.
Financial data (yr. ended 12/31/01): Grants paid, $61,250; assets, $721,199 (M); gifts received, $28,857; expenditures, $117,798; qualifying distributions, $61,250.
Limitations: Giving primarily in NY.
Officers: Elizabeth W. Fondaras, Pres.; Charles F. Gibbs, Secy.; Theodore Weicker, Jr., Treas.
EIN: 131959247

36295
The Bistritzky Family Foundation, Inc.
4815-15th Ave.
Brooklyn, NY 11219
Contact: Issacher Bristritzky, Tr.

Donor(s): Alexander Bistritzky, Rebecka Rhein.
Financial data (yr. ended 09/30/01): Grants paid, $61,110; assets, $93,978 (M); gifts received, $3,500; expenditures, $61,995; qualifying distributions, $61,110.
Trustees: Issacher Bistritzky, Rebecka Rhein.
EIN: 136082492

36296
Robert & Ellen Bach Foundation, Inc.
c/o The Bank of New York, Tax Dept.
1 Wall St., 28th Fl.
New York, NY 10286
Application address: 35 E. 75th St., New York, NY 10021
Contact: Ellen Bach, Tr.

Established in 1961.
Donor(s): Robert Bach, Ellen Bach.
Financial data (yr. ended 07/31/01): Grants paid, $61,010; assets, $1,213,311 (M); expenditures, $95,419; qualifying distributions, $61,010.
Limitations: Giving primarily in New York, NY.
Trustees: Ellen Bach, The Bank of New York.
EIN: 136083790

36297
Abelow Family Foundation
c/o Goldman Sachs & Co.
85 Broad Street-Tax Dept.
New York, NY 10004

Established in 1999 in NY.
Donor(s): Bradley I. Abelow.
Financial data (yr. ended 09/30/01): Grants paid, $61,000; assets, $1,091,341 (M); gifts received, $197,375; expenditures, $69,450; qualifying distributions, $61,000.
Limitations: Applications not accepted.
Application information: Contributes only to pre-selected organizations.
Directors: Bradley I. Abelow, Carolyn J. Murray.
EIN: 134053987

36298
Kantor Foundation, Inc.
420 Lexington Ave.
New York, NY 10170
Contact: Steven I. Levin, Pres.

Established in 1965 in NY.
Donor(s): Mabelle Kantor,‡ Russell P. Kantor.‡
Financial data (yr. ended 06/30/02): Grants paid, $61,000; assets, $1,087,925 (M); expenditures, $68,436; qualifying distributions, $61,000.
Application information: Application form not required.
Officers: Steven I. Levin, Pres. and Treas.; Ida Jane Stiner, V.P. and Secy.
Directors: Kenneth Halajian, Hillary Siegel, Alan Stiner.
EIN: 136188244

36299
The Newcomb-Hargraves Foundation
c/o Newcomb & Hargraves
7 W. 81st St., Ste. 11B
New York, NY 10024

Established in 2000 in NY.
Donor(s): John A. Hargraves, Nancy S. Newcomb.
Financial data (yr. ended 12/31/01): Grants paid, $61,000; assets, $1,902,480 (M); gifts received, $900,840; expenditures, $74,432; qualifying distributions, $61,000.
Limitations: Applications not accepted.
Application information: Contributes only to pre-selected organizations.
Trustees: John A. Hargraves, Nancy S. Newcomb.
EIN: 316650840

36300
The Drogen Foundation
R.R. No. 2, Box 3101
Oneonta, NY 13820

Established in 1997 in NY.
Donor(s): Mildred P. Drogen.
Financial data (yr. ended 12/31/01): Grants paid, $60,870; assets, $1 (M); gifts received, $44,200; expenditures, $61,037; qualifying distributions, $60,870.
Limitations: Applications not accepted. Giving limited to Oneonta, NY.
Application information: Contributes only to pre-selected organizations.
Trustees: Arnold Drogen, Mildred P. Drogen.
EIN: 166443320

36301
Savio & Patty Tung Foundation, Inc.
c/o Urbach Kahn & Werlin Advisors, Inc.
250 Park Ave. S., Ste. 600
New York, NY 10003-1494

Established in 1999 in NY.
Donor(s): Savio Tung, Patty Tung.
Financial data (yr. ended 11/30/01): Grants paid, $60,795; assets, $409,879 (M); expenditures, $63,895; qualifying distributions, $60,795.
Limitations: Applications not accepted. Giving primarily in New York, NY.
Application information: Contributes only to pre-selected organizations.
Trustees: Patty Tung, Savio Tung.
EIN: 134036105

36302
C.D. Foundation for Retarded Children
c/o Chill, Graubard, Mollen, & Miller
600 3rd Ave.
New York, NY 10016

Established in 1992 in NY.
Donor(s): Alice Lawrence Foundation, Inc., Julius Brody, C. Daniel Chill.
Financial data (yr. ended 12/31/01): Grants paid, $60,750; assets, $1,370,552 (M); expenditures, $105,827; qualifying distributions, $60,750.
Limitations: Applications not accepted.
Application information: Contributes only to pre-selected organizations.
Officers and Directors:* C. Daniel Chill,* Pres.; Vivian Chill,* Secy.; Adam Chill,* Treas.
EIN: 133653352

36303
The Zorn Foundation, Inc.
1120 Park Ave.
New York, NY 10128-1242 (212) 722-3598
Contact: Richard L. Zorn, Pres.

Established about 1968 in NY.
Donor(s): Lillian R. Zorn.
Financial data (yr. ended 07/31/01): Grants paid, $60,741; assets, $601,614 (M); gifts received, $376,587; expenditures, $65,901; qualifying distributions, $59,837.
Limitations: Giving primarily in NY.
Officers and Director:* Richard L. Zorn, Pres. and Treas.; Lillian R. Zorn,* V.P.; George P. Felleman, Secy.
EIN: 132620481

36304
The Alexander Family Foundation
c/o Margo Alexander
138 E. 92nd St.
New York, NY 10128

Established in 2000 in NY.
Donor(s): Margo N. Alexander.
Financial data (yr. ended 12/31/01): Grants paid, $60,700; assets, $3,270,081 (M); gifts received, $443; expenditures, $143,333; qualifying distributions, $60,700.
Limitations: Applications not accepted.
Application information: Contributes only to pre-selected organizations.
Officer and Trustees:* Margo N. Alexander,* Pres.; James R. Alexander, Nichol C. Alexander, Robert C. Alexander.
EIN: 134140292

36305
Ronald & Adele Tauber Foundation
c/o Sage Capital Mgmt.
120 Bloomingdale Rd.
White Plains, NY 10605

Established in 1983.
Donor(s): Ronald S. Tauber.
Financial data (yr. ended 12/31/01): Grants paid, $60,700; assets, $326,627 (M); gifts received, $31,610; expenditures, $64,702; qualifying distributions, $60,700.
Limitations: Giving primarily in the Northeast.
Trustees: Ronald J. Stein, Adele S. Tauber, Ronald S. Tauber.
EIN: 133199597

36306
Shmerler Foundation
(Formerly Gutner Foundation)
1 N. Lexington Ave.
White Plains, NY 10601

Established in 1947 in NY.
Financial data (yr. ended 12/31/01): Grants paid, $60,696; assets, $2,240,555 (M); expenditures, $62,392; qualifying distributions, $108,925.
Limitations: Applications not accepted. Giving primarily in NY.
Application information: Contributes only to pre-selected organizations.
Officers: Edwin Shmerler, Pres.; William Shmerler, Secy.
EIN: 136067203

36307
The Manuel S. Betanzos Foundation, Inc.
125 Queen St.
Staten Island, NY 10314
Contact: Odon Betanzos, Pres.

Established in 1994 in NY.
Donor(s): Amalia V. Betanzos, Odon Betanzos.
Financial data (yr. ended 12/31/01): Grants paid, $60,567; assets, $34,252 (M); gifts received, $46,368; expenditures, $61,333; qualifying distributions, $60,567.
Limitations: Giving primarily in NY.
Officers and Directors:* Odon Betanzos,* Pres.; Amalia V. Betanzos,* V.P. and Secy.-Treas.; Antonio Ramirez Almanzo, Theodore Beardsley, Tonio Burgos, Eulalio Ferrer, Joaquin Segura, Rev. Jose Maria Padilla Vallencia.
EIN: 133772247

36308
Marvin J. Herskowitz Foundation, Inc.
342 Madison Ave., Ste. 1008
New York, NY 10173

Established around 1966.
Donor(s): Marvin J. Herskowitz.
Financial data (yr. ended 12/31/01): Grants paid, $60,531; assets, $106,223 (M); gifts received, $80,950; expenditures, $60,678; qualifying distributions, $60,531.
Limitations: Applications not accepted. Giving primarily in the greater metropolitan New York, NY, area.
Application information: Contributes only to pre-selected organizations.
Officer: Marvin J. Herskowitz, Pres.
EIN: 136197776

36309
The Weinig Foundation, Inc.
25 Sutton Pl. N.
New York, NY 10022-2453 (212) 223-0231
Contact: Dr. S. Weinig

Established in 1995 in NY.
Donor(s): Sheldon Weinig.
Financial data (yr. ended 12/31/01): Grants paid, $60,500; assets, $770,326 (M); gifts received, $72,866; expenditures, $75,613; qualifying distributions, $60,500.
Limitations: Giving primarily in Chicago, IL, and NY.
Application information: Application form required.
Directors: James Lyon, Marike Weinig, Mary Joe Weinig, Sheldon Weinig.
EIN: 133854362

36310
Isaac & Doris Russo Foundation, Inc.
184-10 Jamaica Ave.
Hollis, NY 11423

Donor(s): Isaac J. Russo.
Financial data (yr. ended 04/30/01): Grants paid, $60,477; assets, $544,182 (M); gifts received, $195,268; expenditures, $60,903; qualifying distributions, $59,674.
Limitations: Giving primarily in New York, NY.
Officer: Isaac J. Russo, Mgr.
EIN: 136265203

36311
Marsicano Foundation
50 Bank St.
New York, NY 10014 (212) 243-7757
Contact: Laurance W. Nagin, Pres.

Established around 1971.
Donor(s): Philomena Marsicano.‡
Financial data (yr. ended 12/31/01): Grants paid, $60,250; assets, $808,275 (M); expenditures, $80,681; qualifying distributions, $60,250.
Limitations: Applications not accepted. Giving limited to NY.
Application information: Contributes only to pre-selected organizations.
Officer: Laurance W. Nagin, Pres.
EIN: 131823716

36312
Paul Moos Foundation
c/o Cleary, Gottlieb, et al.
1 Liberty Plz.
New York, NY 10006-1470
Application address: 880 5th Ave., New York, NY 10021
Contact: Pearl Lamberg, Tr.

Established in 1964.
Financial data (yr. ended 01/31/02): Grants paid, $60,246; assets, $1,066,293 (M); expenditures, $63,296; qualifying distributions, $60,246.
Limitations: Giving primarily in New York, NY.
Trustees: Carol Lamberg, Pearl Lamberg, Anne L. Zeff.
EIN: 237275464

36313
Claire Wagner Estate Heinbach-Wagner Trust
c/o Deutsche Trust Co. of NY
P.O. Box 829, Church St. Sta.
New York, NY 10008
Application address: c/o David Wolkenbrod, Deutsche Trust Co. of NY, 280 Park Ave., New York, NY 10017

Established in 1962.
Financial data (yr. ended 12/31/01): Grants paid, $60,234; assets, $1,238,984 (M); expenditures, $79,005; qualifying distributions, $68,418.
Limitations: Giving primarily in NJ and NY.
Trustee: Deutsche Bank.
EIN: 136182244
Codes: GTI

36314
WRG Foundation
c/o Galen Assocs.
610 5th Ave., 5th Fl.
New York, NY 10020

Established in 1986 in NY.
Donor(s): William R. Grant.
Financial data (yr. ended 12/31/00): Grants paid, $60,200; assets, $10,183,510 (M); gifts received, $4,104,000; expenditures, $81,180; qualifying distributions, $60,200.
Limitations: Applications not accepted. Giving primarily in NJ, NY, and RI.
Application information: Contributes only to pre-selected organizations.
Trustees: Byron A. Grant, William R. Grant.
EIN: 133407905

36315
City National Bank Foundation
c/o City National Bank & Trust Co.
14 N. Main St.
Gloversville, NY 12078 (518) 773-7911
Contact: William N. Smith, Pres.

Established in 1987 in NY.
Donor(s): City National Bank & Trust Company.
Financial data (yr. ended 12/31/01): Grants paid, $60,173; assets, $76,311 (M); gifts received, $50,000; expenditures, $60,577; qualifying distributions, $60,173.
Limitations: Giving primarily in Gloversville, NY.
Application information: Application form not required.
Officer and Trustees:* William N. Smith,* Pres.; George A. Morgan, City National Bank & Trust Co.
EIN: 222816974
Codes: CS, CD

36316
Newman-Tanner Foundation
c/o Harold Tanner
650 Madison Ave., 23rd Fl.
New York, NY 10022-1004

Established in 1990 in NY.
Donor(s): Estelle Tanner, Harold Tanner.
Financial data (yr. ended 12/31/01): Grants paid, $60,170; assets, $860,181 (M); expenditures, $86,714; qualifying distributions, $59,283.
Limitations: Applications not accepted.
Application information: Contributes only to pre-selected organizations.
Trustees: Karen Tanner Allen, David Tanner, Estelle Newman Tanner, Harold Tanner, James Tanner.
EIN: 136942897

36317
The Brooks Family Foundation, Inc.
14 Lawson Ln.
Great Neck, NY 11023-1041 (516) 433-7676
Contact: Louis E. Brooks, Dir.

Established in 1998 in NY.
Donor(s): Louis E. Brooks.
Financial data (yr. ended 05/31/01): Grants paid, $60,135; assets, $1,110,644 (M); expenditures, $63,603; qualifying distributions, $60,135.
Limitations: Giving primarily in NY.
Directors: Francine Brooks, Jeanette Brooks, Louis E. Brooks, Mark Brooks.
EIN: 134009547

36318
The Peter & Caroline Striano Foundation, Inc.
65-45 Fresh Meadow Ln.
Flushing, NY 11365

Established in 1991 in NY.
Donor(s): Peter Striano, Unity Electric Co., Inc.
Financial data (yr. ended 12/31/01): Grants paid, $60,100; assets, $417,050 (M); gifts received, $350,000; expenditures, $61,240; qualifying distributions, $60,200.
Limitations: Applications not accepted. Giving primarily in NJ and NY.
Application information: Contributes only to pre-selected organizations.
Officers: Peter Striano, Pres.; Caroline Striano, V.P.; Christine Striano, Secy.; Marisa Siegel, Treas.
EIN: 113078596

36319
Ethel and Philip Adelman Charitable Foundation
c/o N. Berkowitz
114 W. 47th St.
New York, NY 10036-8401

Established in 1996.
Donor(s): Philip Adelman.‡
Financial data (yr. ended 12/31/01): Grants paid, $60,000; assets, $1,248,768 (M); gifts received, $1,346; expenditures, $60,000; qualifying distributions, $60,000.
Limitations: Giving primarily in NY.
Trustee: Philip Adelman.
EIN: 133917004

36320
Robert B. and Emilie W. Betts Foundation
c/o RBB Asset Mgmt.
85 Tripp St.
Bedford Corners, NY 10549

Established in 1993 in NY.
Donor(s): Emilie W. Betts.
Financial data (yr. ended 12/31/01): Grants paid, $60,000; assets, $1,116,297 (M); gifts received, $150,000; expenditures, $87,651; qualifying distributions, $67,901.
Limitations: Applications not accepted. Giving primarily in WY.
Application information: Contributes only to pre-selected organizations.
Officers: Emilie W. Betts, Pres.; Robert B. Betts, Jr., V.P. and Secy.; Brooks Betts MacDuff, V.P. and Treas.
EIN: 830305462

36321
Boardman Family Foundation
c/o The Bank of New York, Tax Dept., 28th Fl.
1290 6th Ave., 5th Fl.
New York, NY 10286-0001
Contact: Stella Lau, V.P., The Bank of New York

Established in 1998 in NJ.
Donor(s): Jean R. Boardman.
Financial data (yr. ended 05/31/02): Grants paid, $60,000; assets, $977,486 (M); expenditures, $70,242; qualifying distributions, $60,000.
Trustee: The Bank of New York.
EIN: 137166339

36322
Buffalo Eye Bank Foundation, Inc.
68 Thistle Ave.
Tonawanda, NY 14150 (716) 847-7272
Contact: Gerald A. Lee, Treas.

Financial data (yr. ended 12/31/01): Grants paid, $60,000; assets, $1,156,721 (M); expenditures, $73,877; qualifying distributions, $61,166.
Limitations: Giving primarily in NY.
Officers: Roger Haase, Pres.; Thomas Reinagel, V.P.; Helen Kossuth, Secy.; Gerald A. Lee, Treas.
Trustees: Joseph Mach, Matthew X. Wagner, Jr., Donald J. Young.
EIN: 166027186

36323
The Gardner Cowles III Charitable Foundation
P.O. Box 1704
Sag Harbor, NY 11963
Contact: Pat Cowles

Established in 1987 in NY.
Donor(s): Gardner Cowles III.
Financial data (yr. ended 12/31/01): Grants paid, $60,000; assets, $1,051,942 (M); expenditures, $63,974; qualifying distributions, $60,000.
Limitations: Giving primarily in CT, MA, and NY.
Trustee: Gardner Cowles III.
EIN: 133444590

36324
Betti S. & Loomis J. Grossman Foundation, Inc.
c/o Maier, Markey & Menashi
1890 Palmer Ave.
Larchmont, NY 10538

Donor(s): Betti S. Grossman, Loomis J. Grossman.‡
Financial data (yr. ended 12/31/01): Grants paid, $60,000; assets, $186,508 (M); expenditures, $65,730; qualifying distributions, $60,000.

Limitations: Applications not accepted. Giving primarily in Westchester County and New York, NY.
Application information: Contributes only to pre-selected organizations.
Officer and Director:* Betti S. Grossman,* V.P. and Secy.
EIN: 136160880

36325
Noel and Harriette Levine Foundation, Inc.
c/o Noel Levine
885 Third Ave., Ste. 1780
New York, NY 10022

Established in 1999 in NY.
Donor(s): Noel Levine, Harriette Levine.
Financial data (yr. ended 12/31/01): Grants paid, $60,000; assets, $731,396 (M); gifts received, $4,000; expenditures, $78,005; qualifying distributions, $60,000.
Limitations: Applications not accepted.
Application information: Contributes only to pre-selected organizations.
Officers: Noel Levine, Pres.; Harriette Levine, Secy.-Treas.
EIN: 134074336

36326
The Second Foundation
c/o Brand, Sonnenschine & Co.
377 Broadway, 9th Fl.
New York, NY 10013-3907

Established in 1993 in NJ.
Financial data (yr. ended 12/31/01): Grants paid, $60,000; assets, $452,219 (M); gifts received, $361,721; expenditures, $61,050; qualifying distributions, $60,000.
Limitations: Applications not accepted. Giving limited to Little Ferry, NJ.
Application information: Contributes only to pre-selected organizations.
Trustee: Richard Factor.
EIN: 133727668

36327
John T. Underwood Foundation
c/o U.S. Trust
P.O. Box 2004
New York, NY 10109-1910 (212) 852-3294
FAX: (212) 852-3377; E-mail: alane@ustrust.com
Contact: Andrew Lane, Asst. V.P., U.S. Trust

Financial data (yr. ended 12/31/01): Grants paid, $60,000; assets, $1,095,476 (M); expenditures, $82,422; qualifying distributions, $60,000.
Limitations: Applications not accepted. Giving primarily in Brooklyn, NY.
Application information: Contributes only to pre-selected organizations.
Trustee: U.S. Trust.
EIN: 136072078

36328
Warren J. & Florence Sinsheimer Foundation, Inc.
22 Murray Hill Rd.
Scarsdale, NY 10583

Established in 1968.
Donor(s): Warren J. Sinsheimer.
Financial data (yr. ended 12/31/01): Grants paid, $59,997; assets, $261,110 (M); expenditures, $62,468; qualifying distributions, $59,997.
Limitations: Applications not accepted. Giving primarily in Westchester County and New York, NY.
Application information: Contributes only to pre-selected organizations.

Officers: Warren J. Sinsheimer, Pres.; Florence Sinsheimer, V.P.
EIN: 132625039

36329
Donald F. and Edna G. Bishop Scholarship Foundation
(also known as Bishop Scholarship Foundation)
c/o BSB Bank & Trust
58-68 Exchange St.
Binghamton, NY 13901-3483

Established in 1989 in NY.
Donor(s): Donald Bishop, Edna G. Bishop.
Financial data (yr. ended 09/30/01): Grants paid, $59,989; assets, $507,777 (M); gifts received, $75,280; expenditures, $66,322; qualifying distributions, $60,406.
Limitations: Applications not accepted. Giving primarily in NY.
Trustee: BSB Bank & Trust.
EIN: 166332120

36330
Lederer Foundation, Inc.
c/o Theodore Ranzal
108 Corporate Park Dr., Ste. 105
White Plains, NY 10604-3503

Established in 1950 in NY.
Donor(s): Ann L. Beaver, M. Fehsenfeld,‡ Carol Lederer,‡ Richard M. Lederer, Jr.
Financial data (yr. ended 12/31/01): Grants paid, $59,877; assets, $969,403 (M); gifts received, $3,500; expenditures, $67,808; qualifying distributions, $59,877.
Limitations: Applications not accepted. Giving primarily in New York and Westchester County, NY.
Application information: Contributes only to pre-selected organizations.
Officers and Directors:* Ann L. Beaver,* Pres.; Theodore Ranzal,* Treas.; Elaine Granata.
EIN: 136108527

36331
Brumberger Foundation, Inc.
74 Putnam Blvd.
Atlantic Beach, NY 11509

Financial data (yr. ended 02/28/01): Grants paid, $59,785; assets, $935,042 (M); expenditures, $61,413; qualifying distributions, $61,413.
Limitations: Applications not accepted. Giving primarily in CA, FL and NY.
Application information: Contributes only to pre-selected organizations.
Officers: Richard Brumberger, Pres. and Secy.; Adrienne Gruber, V.P. and Treas.
EIN: 166035604

36332
Lyndonville Area Foundation, Inc.
P.O. Box 545
Lyndonville, NY 14098-0545

Established in 1967 in NY.
Financial data (yr. ended 12/31/01): Grants paid, $59,755; assets, $1,430,014 (M); gifts received, $13,560; expenditures, $1,497,373.
Limitations: Giving limited to Lyndonville, NY.
Application information: Students must meet academic standards and financial needs; must also have completed one semester of college.
Officers and Directors:* Rev. Stephen P. Devine,* Pres.; Herbert Walck,* V.P.; Patricia Harris,* Secy.; Douglas W. Hedges,* Treas.; Stanley R. Barry, William Gerling, Orville Harris, Russell Martino, Marc Scarr, Marion E. Smith.
EIN: 166073941
Codes: CM

36333
The Morris & Eva Guttman Family Charitable Trust
2 Cloverdale Ln.
Monsey, NY 10952

Established in 1998 in NY.
Donor(s): Morris Guttman, Eva Guttman.
Financial data (yr. ended 12/31/01): Grants paid, $59,665; assets, $1,141,823 (M); expenditures, $62,680; qualifying distributions, $59,665.
Limitations: Applications not accepted.
Application information: Contributes only to pre-selected organizations.
Trustee: Shirley Bersson, Charles Guttman, David Guttman, Eva Guttman, Morris Guttman, Freida Harris.
EIN: 116502055

36334
Goldberg-Rhapsody Foundation, Inc.
c/o Larkspur America, Inc.
550 White Plains Rd., Ste. 230
Tarrytown, NY 10591-5102
Contact: Murray Goldberg, Pres.

Established in 1980 in NY.
Financial data (yr. ended 09/30/01): Grants paid, $59,650; assets, $1,753,875 (M); expenditures, $63,089; qualifying distributions, $63,089.
Limitations: Applications not accepted. Giving primarily in NY.
Application information: Contributes only to pre-selected organizations.
Officers: Murray Goldberg, Pres.; Charlotte Goldberg, V.P.
EIN: 133013026

36335
Schonfeld Tzodoko Fund
1565 55th St.
Brooklyn, NY 11219

Established in 1995 in NY.
Donor(s): Frank Schonfeld.
Financial data (yr. ended 12/31/01): Grants paid, $59,531; assets, $40,929 (M); gifts received, $100,000; expenditures, $60,207; qualifying distributions, $59,531.
Limitations: Applications not accepted.
Application information: Contributes only to pre-selected organizations.
Officers: Frank Schonfeld, Pres.; Freeda Karmel, V.P.; David Schonfeld, Treas.
EIN: 113290862

36336
The Weiser Family Foundation
(Formerly Kenmar Foundation)
c/o M.R. Weiser & Co.
135 W. 50th St.
New York, NY 10020-1299

Donor(s): Kenneth D. Weiser, Carol Weiser.
Financial data (yr. ended 12/31/01): Grants paid, $59,455; assets, $147,066 (M); gifts received, $72,243; expenditures, $60,816; qualifying distributions, $59,505.
Limitations: Applications not accepted. Giving primarily in NY.
Application information: Contributes only to pre-selected organizations.
Officers: Kenneth D. Weiser, Pres. and Treas.; Carol Weiser, Secy.
EIN: 136164693

36337
ALSTOM Signaling Foundation, Inc.
(Formerly General Railway Signal Foundation, Inc.)
150 Sawgrass Dr.
Rochester, NY 14620-4609   (716) 783-2000
Contact: Ann Kerwick, Pres.

Established in 1952 in NY.
Donor(s): General Railway Signal Corp.
Financial data (yr. ended 09/28/01): Grants paid, $59,406; assets, $1,102,853 (M); gifts received, $3,121; expenditures, $83,146; qualifying distributions, $68,343.
Limitations: Giving primarily in Rochester, NY.
Application information: Application form not required.
Officers and Directors:* James Balliet, Chair. and V.P.; Ann Kerwick,* Pres.; Janis Navarra, Secy.; Jeff Cash, Treas.
EIN: 237447593
Codes: CS, CD

36338
Ushkow Charitable Fund, Inc.
c/o Jerome Serchuck
Tower 56, 126 E. 56th St.
New York, NY 10022

Established in 1989 in NY.
Financial data (yr. ended 12/31/01): Grants paid, $59,344; assets, $2,497,394 (M); expenditures, $65,291; qualifying distributions, $59,344.
Limitations: Applications not accepted. Giving primarily in NY.
Application information: Contributes only to pre-selected organizations.
Officers: Joan Serchuck, Pres.; Jerome Serchuck, V.P.
EIN: 112954310

36339
Young Agency Foundation
500 Plum St., Bridgewater Pl.
Syracuse, NY 13204-1480   (315) 474-3374
Contact: Robert D. Young, Tr.

Established in 1987 in NY.
Donor(s): The Young Agency, Inc.
Financial data (yr. ended 12/31/01): Grants paid, $59,335; assets, $83,285 (M); gifts received, $131,400; expenditures, $59,335; qualifying distributions, $59,335.
Limitations: Giving primarily in Syracuse, NY.
Trustees: Roy S. Moore III, George J. Schunck, Robert D. Young.
EIN: 161298185
Codes: CS, CD

36340
Turula Family Fund, Inc.
140 Allens Creek Rd.
Rochester, NY 14618-3307
Contact: B. Andrew Dutcher

Established in 2000 in NY.
Donor(s): Eugene Turula.‡
Financial data (yr. ended 12/31/00): Grants paid, $59,280; assets, $2,553,984 (M); gifts received, $2,603,957; expenditures, $99,191; qualifying distributions, $59,280.
Limitations: Applications not accepted.
Application information: Contributes only to pre-selected organizations.
Directors: Gabriel Turula, Stephen Turula.
EIN: 311655968

36341
David M. Martin Trust Fund
3522 James St.
Syracuse, NY 13206   (315) 437-3321

Established in 1993 in NY.
Financial data (yr. ended 09/30/01): Grants paid, $59,269; assets, $386,730 (M); expenditures, $73,595; qualifying distributions, $59,269.
Limitations: Giving limited to residents of central New York.
Trustees: Mateele S. Kall, Sheldon G. Kall.
EIN: 166385390

36342
The Chalsty Family Foundation
c/o CSAM
466 Lexington Ave., 17th Fl.
New York, NY 10017
Contact: John S. Chalsty

Established in 1997 in NJ.
Donor(s): John S. Chalsty.
Financial data (yr. ended 12/31/01): Grants paid, $59,200; assets, $1,351,673 (M); expenditures, $77,988; qualifying distributions, $59,200.
Limitations: Giving primarily in CA and NJ.
Application information: Application form not required.
Distribution Committee: Deborah A. Chalsty, Jennifer A. Chalsty, John S. Chalsty, Susan C. Neely.
Trustee: Winthrop Trust Co.
EIN: 133932914

36343
Judy and Fred Wilpon Family Foundation, Inc.
111 Great Neck Rd., Ste. 408
Great Neck, NY 11021-5476
Contact: Fred Wilpon, Pres.

Established in 1982.
Donor(s): Fred Wilpon.
Financial data (yr. ended 12/31/00): Grants paid, $59,198; assets, $2,246,050 (M); gifts received, $1,058,500; expenditures, $63,239; qualifying distributions, $59,198.
Limitations: Giving primarily in the greater metropolitan New York, NY, area, including Long Island.
Application information: Application form not required.
Officer and Directors:* Fred Wilpon,* Pres.; Robin Wilpon Wachtler, Jeffrey Wilpon, Judith Wilpon.
EIN: 112626618

36344
Philip & Lena Berger Foundation
c/o Albert Berger
141-22 68th Dr.
Flushing, NY 11367

Established in 1986 in NY.
Donor(s): Albert Berger.
Financial data (yr. ended 09/30/01): Grants paid, $59,074; assets, $88,124 (M); gifts received, $55,516; expenditures, $59,396; qualifying distributions, $59,074.
Limitations: Applications not accepted. Giving primarily in NY.
Application information: Contributes only to pre-selected organizations.
Officer and Director:* Albert Berger,* Pres.
EIN: 136880016

36345
The Gary W. Parr Family Foundation, Inc.
174 E. Lake Rd.
Tuxedo Park, NY 10987-4243
Contact: Gary W. Parr, Chair.

Established in 1996 in NC.
Donor(s): Gary W. Parr.
Financial data (yr. ended 12/31/00): Grants paid, $59,017; assets, $1,161,916 (M); gifts received, $467,091; expenditures, $61,108; qualifying distributions, $60,455.
Officers: Gary W. Parr, Chair.; Cheri S. Parr, V.P.
EIN: 562003520

36346
Arthur D. Dana Foundation, Inc.
230 Park Ave., Ste. 1521
New York, NY 10169-1599

Established in 1961 in NY.
Donor(s): Arthur D. Dana, Jr.
Financial data (yr. ended 11/30/01): Grants paid, $59,000; assets, $360,269 (M); gifts received, $25,000; expenditures, $59,478; qualifying distributions, $59,000.
Limitations: Applications not accepted. Giving primarily in NY and VT.
Application information: Contributes only to pre-selected organizations.
Officers and Directors:* William D. Dana, Jr.,* V.P.; James D. Dana,* Secy.; Olga H. Dana, Alice D. Spencer.
EIN: 136160860

36347
The Price Foundation
c/o Goldman Sachs & Co.
85 Broad St., Tax Dept.
New York, NY 10004

Established in 1999 in NY.
Donor(s): Michael A. Price.
Financial data (yr. ended 10/31/01): Grants paid, $59,000; assets, $1,343,604 (M); gifts received, $2,500; expenditures, $86,665; qualifying distributions, $59,000.
Limitations: Applications not accepted. Giving primarily in NY.
Application information: Contributes only to pre-selected organizations.
Trustees: Jodi L. Price, Michael A. Price.
EIN: 134089164

36348
Schulman Family Foundation
c/o Robert E. Schulman
18 Pine Tree Dr.
Great Neck, NY 11024-1108

Established in 1994 in NY.
Donor(s): Robert E. Schulman, Carol Schulman.
Financial data (yr. ended 12/31/01): Grants paid, $59,000; assets, $1,137,875 (M); expenditures, $94,124; qualifying distributions, $94,123.
Limitations: Applications not accepted. Giving primarily in NY.
Application information: Contributes only to pre-selected organizations.
Officers: Robert E. Schulman, Pres.; Marjorie Schulman, V.P.; Richard Schulman, V.P.; Nancy Solefer, V.P.; Carol Schulman, Secy.
EIN: 113242213

36349
The Edwin Schlossberg Foundation
641 Ave. of Americas
New York, NY 10011   (212) 989-3393
Contact: Edwin A. Schlossberg, Tr.

Donor(s): Edwin Schlossberg, Inc.

Financial data (yr. ended 12/31/01): Grants paid, $58,984; assets, $4,009 (M); gifts received, $53,334; expenditures, $59,168; qualifying distributions, $58,981.
Limitations: Giving primarily in the New York, NY, area.
Application information: Application form not required.
Trustees: Caroline B. Kennedy, Edwin A. Schlossberg.
EIN: 042748882

36350
Nussen Family Foundation
1460 59th St.
Brooklyn, NY 11219

Donor(s): William Nussen.
Financial data (yr. ended 12/31/00): Grants paid, $58,936; assets, $662,259 (M); gifts received, $100,000; expenditures, $61,309; qualifying distributions, $58,936.
Limitations: Applications not accepted. Giving primarily in NY.
Application information: Contributes only to pre-selected organizations.
Trustees: Malka Nussen, William Nussen.
EIN: 113370425

36351
The Arkin Foundation, Inc.
4 E. 70th St.
New York, NY 10021

Established in 1998 in NY.
Donor(s): Andrew Arkin.
Financial data (yr. ended 12/31/01): Grants paid, $58,925; assets, $725,155 (M); expenditures, $83,024; qualifying distributions, $58,925.
Limitations: Applications not accepted. Giving primarily in New York, NY.
Application information: Contributes only to pre-selected organizations.
Officers and Directors:* Andrew Arkin,* Pres.; Jason Arkin,* V.P. and Secy.-Treas.; Amy Arkin.
EIN: 133986430

36352
Bernard J. & Valerie Daenzer Foundation, Inc.
c/o F. Palazzolo, Marine Midland Bank
386 Park Ave. S., Ste. 414
New York, NY 10016

Established in 1997 in FL.
Donor(s): Bernard Daenzer, Valerie Daenzer.
Financial data (yr. ended 12/31/01): Grants paid, $58,860; assets, $208,383 (M); expenditures, $64,626; qualifying distributions, $58,860.
Limitations: Applications not accepted.
Application information: Contributes only to pre-selected organizations.
Officers: Bernard Daenzer, Pres.; Jean V. Aiken, V.P.; Valerie Daenzer, V.P.; John C. Daenzer, Secy.-Treas.
EIN: 650757200

36353
The Phyllida and Glenn Earle Foundation
c/o Goldman Sachs & Co.
85 Broad St., Tax Dept.
New York, NY 10004

Established in 1997 in NY.
Donor(s): Glenn P. Earle.
Financial data (yr. ended 04/30/02): Grants paid, $58,826; assets, $32,836 (M); gifts received, $3,500; expenditures, $62,508; qualifying distributions, $58,826.
Limitations: Applications not accepted. Giving on an international basis, primarily London, England.

Application information: Contributes only to pre-selected organizations.
Trustees: Glenn P. Earle, Phyllida Earle, Jide J. Zmitlin.
EIN: 133963597

36354
Peter and Lynn Tishman Fund, Inc.
(Formerly Peter Tishman Fund, Inc.)
645 Madison Ave.
New York, NY 10022-1010

Donor(s): Peter V. Tishman.
Financial data (yr. ended 11/30/01): Grants paid, $58,799; assets, $429,748 (M); expenditures, $71,336; qualifying distributions, $58,799.
Limitations: Applications not accepted. Giving primarily in NY.
Application information: Contributes only to pre-selected organizations.
Officers: Peter V. Tishman, Pres.; Rita Tishman, V.P. and Secy.
EIN: 136099396

36355
The Marcelle Foundation
P.O. Box 14043
Albany, NY 12212-4043
Contact: Ruth Ann Marcelle, Pres.

Established in 1983.
Donor(s): Ann W. Marcelle, Ruth Ann Marcelle, Rev. Edward Marcelle, Mrs. Edward Marcelle.
Financial data (yr. ended 12/31/01): Grants paid, $58,730; assets, $439,423 (M); gifts received, $12,000; expenditures, $68,547; qualifying distributions, $58,730.
Limitations: Applications not accepted. Giving primarily in Albany, NY.
Application information: Contributes only to pre-selected organizations.
Officers and Directors:* Ann W. Marcelle,* Chair.; Ruth Ann Marcelle, Pres.; Michael Sonnenreich, Secy.
EIN: 112647245

36356
The Himmel Foundation, Inc.
711 Westchester Ave., 2nd Fl.
White Plains, NY 10604

Donor(s): Arthur B. Himmel.
Financial data (yr. ended 11/30/01): Grants paid, $58,711; assets, $540,866 (M); expenditures, $59,178; qualifying distributions, $58,711.
Limitations: Applications not accepted. Giving primarily in NY.
Application information: Contributes only to pre-selected organizations.
Officers and Directors:* Arthur B. Himmel,* Pres.; Betty H. Himmel,* V.P.; Jeffrey A. Himmel,* Treas.
EIN: 133294776

36357
Yonasan & Aharon Memorial Foundation
1362 46th St.
Brooklyn, NY 11219

Established in 1998 in NY.
Donor(s): Elisabeth Bleier.
Financial data (yr. ended 12/31/01): Grants paid, $58,710; assets, $39,109 (M); gifts received, $75,000; expenditures, $58,710; qualifying distributions, $58,710.
Limitations: Applications not accepted.
Application information: Contributes only to pre-selected organizations.
Trustees: Alex Bleier, Elisabeth Bleier, Erwin Bleier, Robert Bleier.
EIN: 113438224

36358
Milton Carpenter Foundation, Inc.
P.O. Box 226
Jefferson Valley, NY 10535-0226
(845) 621-2819
FAX: (845) 621-2819; E-mail: mcfarlane@rcn.com
Contact: Arlene Stoffel, Secy.

Established in 1984.
Donor(s): Milton Carpenter.‡
Financial data (yr. ended 12/31/01): Grants paid, $58,690; assets, $1,232,113 (M); expenditures, $71,995; qualifying distributions, $70,584.
Limitations: Giving limited to residents of Putnam and northern Westchester counties, NY.
Publications: Informational brochure (including application guidelines).
Application information: Contact high school guidance counselor; personal interview required. Application form required.
Officers: Marcelle Caccioppoli, V.P.; Arlene Stoffel, Secy. and Admin.
Directors: Henrietta Lodge, Ralph Pasacrita, Carol Schweitzer.
EIN: 061102502
Codes: GTI

36359
Dyckman's Foundation, Inc.
73 W. 47th St.
New York, NY 10036
Contact: Dina Dyckman, Pres.

Established in 1958 in NY.
Donor(s): Dina Dyckman, Moses Dyckman.
Financial data (yr. ended 08/31/01): Grants paid, $58,626; assets, $2,254 (M); gifts received, $63,450; expenditures, $58,731; qualifying distributions, $58,731.
Limitations: Giving primarily in Brooklyn and New York, NY.
Application information: Application form not required.
Officers: Dina Dyckman, Pres.; Jacob Dyckman, Secy.-Treas.
EIN: 136163219

36360
The Morris Foundation, Inc.
165 Perry St., Rm. PH 6
New York, NY 10014

Established in 1999 in NY.
Financial data (yr. ended 12/31/01): Grants paid, $58,610; assets, $1,072,879 (M); expenditures, $66,400; qualifying distributions, $66,400.
Limitations: Applications not accepted.
Application information: Contributes only to pre-selected organizations.
Directors: Gail Marcus, William Monaghan.
EIN: 134047659

36361
The Silbert Family Foundation
(Formerly Theodore H. Silbert Foundation, Inc.)
444 Madison Ave., 8th Fl.
New York, NY 10022 (212) 829-9924
Contact: Jeffrey Greener

Established in 1945 in NY.
Donor(s): Theodore H. Silbert.
Financial data (yr. ended 12/31/01): Grants paid, $58,550; assets, $1,412,929 (M); expenditures, $162,854; qualifying distributions, $58,550.
Limitations: Applications not accepted. Giving primarily in New York, NY.
Publications: Financial statement.
Application information: Contributes only to pre-selected organizations.

36361—NEW YORK

Officers and Director:* Michael L. Silbert,* Pres.; Scott J. Silbert, V.P. and Treas.; Benjamin O. Silbert, V.P.; Elyssa B. Silbert, V.P.; Theodore H. Silbert, V.P.
EIN: 136085153

36362
Leo & Marjorie P. Stern Foundation
c/o Capital Research Co.
630 5th Ave.
New York, NY 10111
Contact: Walter P. Stern, Tr.

Established in 1958.
Financial data (yr. ended 12/31/00): Grants paid, $58,534; assets, $483,478 (M); expenditures, $60,090; qualifying distributions, $58,803.
Limitations: Applications not accepted. Giving on a national basis.
Application information: Contributes only to pre-selected organizations.
Trustees: Richard D. Stern, Walter P. Stern.
EIN: 136084394

36363
The Mary Hilem Taylor Foundation
c/o A. Kozak and Co., LLP
192 Lexington Ave., Ste. 1100
New York, NY 10016

Established in 1995 in FL.
Donor(s): Mary Schott.
Financial data (yr. ended 12/31/01): Grants paid, $58,525; assets, $53,760 (M); gifts received, $33,750; expenditures, $58,725; qualifying distributions, $58,525.
Limitations: Applications not accepted.
Application information: Contributes only to pre-selected organizations.
Trustee: Felicia Taylor.
EIN: 656191958

36364
The Farbman Family Foundation
1286 Hardscrabble Rd.
Chappaqua, NY 10514

Established in 1998 in NY.
Donor(s): Steven Farbman, Eileen Farbman.
Financial data (yr. ended 12/31/01): Grants paid, $58,500; assets, $774,699 (M); expenditures, $63,836; qualifying distributions, $58,500.
Limitations: Applications not accepted. Giving primarily in NY.
Application information: Contributes only to pre-selected organizations.
Officers: Eileen Farbman, Mgr.; Steven Farbman, Mgr.
EIN: 134008937

36365
The Widder Foundation, Inc.
570 7th Ave.
New York, NY 10018-1603
Application address: 210 E. 68th St., New York, NY 10018, tel.: (212) 921-5230
Contact: Ruth Widder, V.P.

Donor(s): Ruth Widder, Herman Widder,‡ Ruwid Fabrics Corp.
Financial data (yr. ended 12/31/01): Grants paid, $58,499; assets, $1,172,571 (M); gifts received, $594; expenditures, $58,940; qualifying distributions, $58,499.
Limitations: Giving primarily in New York, NY.
Officers: Ruth Widder, V.P.; Albert Widder, Secy.
Directors: Norman Elliott, Laurette Widder, Lynnette Widder.
EIN: 136115433

36366
Harry R. & Rita White Foundation, Inc.
c/o Schooler, Weinstein, Minsky & Lester
325 Merrick Ave.
East Meadow, NY 11554

Established in 1976.
Financial data (yr. ended 11/30/99): Grants paid, $58,480; assets, $1,693,195 (M); expenditures, $119,908; qualifying distributions, $58,480.
Limitations: Applications not accepted. Giving primarily in NY.
Application information: Contributes only to pre-selected organizations.
Officers and Directors:* Harry R. White II,* Pres.; Rita Afzelius,* V.P.; Lonnie Wollin, Treas.; Harry R. White, Rita White.
EIN: 132874801

36367
The Harvey & Ruth Gelfenbein Charitable Foundation, Inc.
c/o Cornick, Garber & Sandler, LLP
630 3rd Ave., 10th Fl.
New York, NY 10017

Established in 1980.
Donor(s): Harvey Gelfenbein, Ruth Gelfenbein.
Financial data (yr. ended 11/30/01): Grants paid, $58,400; assets, $1,018,547 (M); expenditures, $59,600; qualifying distributions, $58,400.
Limitations: Applications not accepted. Giving primarily in NY.
Application information: Contributes only to pre-selected organizations.
Officers: Harvey Gelfenbein, Pres. and Treas.; Ruth Gelfenbein, Secy.
Director: Emanuel Gruss.
EIN: 133056514

36368
Louise Hauss Miller Foundation
c/o Winthrop, Stimson, Putnam & Roberts
1 Battery Park Pl., Ste. 32
New York, NY 10004-1490
Contact: H. Williamson Ghriskey, Secy.-Treas.

Established in 1982 in DE.
Financial data (yr. ended 01/31/02): Grants paid, $58,400; assets, $1,273,421 (M); expenditures, $82,148; qualifying distributions, $58,400.
Limitations: Applications not accepted.
Application information: Contributes only to pre-selected organizations.
Officers: Allen Carlow Phillips, Pres.; Susan Phillips Decker, V.P.; H. Williamson Ghriskey, Secy.-Treas.
Trustee: Bonnie Barnes.
EIN: 133109190

36369
Gitterman Intra-Family Trust Gift
c/o Norman Malter, Raich Ende Malter & Co.
90 Merrick Ave.
East Meadow, NY 11554-1571

Established in 1997 in CT.
Donor(s): Joseph L. Gitterman III.
Financial data (yr. ended 12/31/01): Grants paid, $58,397; assets, $596,687 (M); expenditures, $63,389; qualifying distributions, $58,261.
Limitations: Applications not accepted.
Application information: Contributes only to pre-selected organizations.
Trustees: Joanna C.H. Gitterman, Joseph L. Gitterman III, Paul D. Gitterman, Thomas H. Gitterman, Victoria K. Gitterman.
EIN: 066445597

36370
The Frank Pace, Jr. Foundation
565 Rt. 25A
Miller Place, NY 11764-2600 (631) 821-8037
Contact: William F. Quinn, Treas.

Established around 1960 in NY.
Financial data (yr. ended 11/30/01): Grants paid, $58,300; assets, $1,553,727 (M); expenditures, $68,947; qualifying distributions, $60,852.
Limitations: Giving primarily in the Northeast.
Officers: Ward B. Chamberlin, Jr., Pres.; Priscilla Janney-Pace, V.P.; Paula Pace, V.P.; William F. Quinn, Treas.
EIN: 136117487

36371
The Simpson Foundation, Inc.
4949 Pineledge Dr.
Clarence, NY 14031
Contact: Nancy H. Simpson, Pres.

Established in 1983.
Donor(s): James W. Simpson.
Financial data (yr. ended 12/31/01): Grants paid, $58,300; assets, $684,468 (M); expenditures, $62,232; qualifying distributions, $58,300.
Limitations: Giving primarily in Buffalo, NY.
Application information: Application form not required.
Officers: Nancy H. Simpson, Pres.; Susan Simpson, Secy.; James W. Simpson, Treas.
EIN: 222592275

36372
The Olive R. Ringo Charitable Trust
618 Brisbane Bldg.
Buffalo, NY 14203 (716) 856-4091
Contact: Gordon Gannon, Jr., Tr.

Established in 1989 in NY.
Financial data (yr. ended 12/31/01): Grants paid, $58,235; assets, $1,140,630 (M); expenditures, $80,920; qualifying distributions, $58,235.
Limitations: Giving primarily in the Sarasota, FL, and Buffalo, NY, areas.
Trustees: Kenneth Fradin, Gordon Gannon, Jr.
EIN: 222957363

36373
Frank R. & Emilie E. Stamer Foundation, Inc.
55 Central Park W.
New York, NY 10023-6003 (212) 866-5274
Contact: Joan M. Lewis, Pres.

Established in 1963.
Financial data (yr. ended 12/31/01): Grants paid, $58,230; assets, $1,229,144 (M); expenditures, $61,230; qualifying distributions, $58,230.
Limitations: Giving primarily in New York, NY.
Application information: Application form not required.
Officers: Joan M. Lewis, Pres.; Joanna L. Cole, V.P.; George Lewis, Secy.
Directors: Jonathan R. Cole, Sheila B. Kamerman.
EIN: 116041806

36374
Barbara Davies Troisi Foundation
230 Park Ave., Ste. 1000
New York, NY 10169 (212) 808-3035
Contact: Frank X. Troisi, Tr.

Established in 1989 in NY.
Donor(s): Frank X. Troisi.
Financial data (yr. ended 12/31/00): Grants paid, $58,216; assets, $560,679 (M); gifts received, $66,738; expenditures, $67,800; qualifying distributions, $58,216.
Limitations: Giving primarily in NJ and NY.

Trustees: Costa L. Papson, James F. Sassano, Frank X. Troisi.
EIN: 133534989

36375
The Willman-Crowley Foundation
c/o Goldman Sachs & Co.
85 Broad St., Tax Dept.
New York, NY 10004

Established in 1999 in NY.
Donor(s): Kenneth W. Willman, Rosemary C. Willman.
Financial data (yr. ended 12/31/01): Grants paid, $58,200; assets, $201,989 (M); expenditures, $58,351; qualifying distributions, $58,200.
Limitations: Applications not accepted.
Application information: Contributes only to pre-selected organizations.
Trustees: Kenneth W. Willman, Rosemary C. Willman.
EIN: 316629933

36376
Yemen Education Fund
c/o J.A. Smith
1130 Park Ave., Ste. 4-1
New York, NY 10128-1255
Application addresses: c/o Abdulaziz Saqqaf, Chair., Faculty of Economics and Commerce, Sana's University, Sana's Republic of Yemen, c/o M.M. Er Selcuk, 318 W. 102nd St., New York, NY 10025

Established around 1984.
Donor(s): M.M. Er Selcuk.
Financial data (yr. ended 12/31/99): Grants paid, $58,102; assets, $43,912 (M); gifts received, $37,420; expenditures, $59,100; qualifying distributions, $101,905.
Limitations: Giving primarily in the Republic of Yemen.
Officers: M.M. Er Selcuk, Pres.; J.A. Smith, Secy.
EIN: 133316326

36377
The Bagby Foundation for the Musical Arts, Inc.
501 5th Ave., Ste. 1401
New York, NY 10017-6107
Contact: J. Andrew Lark, Exec. Dir.

Established in 1925 in NY.
Donor(s): Eugene M. Grant, John H. Steinway.‡
Financial data (yr. ended 12/31/01): Grants paid, $58,081; assets, $2,264,042 (M); gifts received, $14,675; expenditures, $140,185; qualifying distributions, $115,548.
Limitations: Giving primarily in the metropolitan New York, NY, area.
Officers and Trustees:* Rose Bampton Pelletier,* Co-Chair.; Jarmila Packard,* Co-Chair.; F. Malcolm Graff, Jr.,* Pres.; Winthrop Rutherford, Jr.,* Secy.; Blanche Lark Christerson,* Treas.; J. Andrew Lark, Exec. Dir.; and 13 additional trustees.
EIN: 131873289
Codes: GTI

36378
Norger Foundation
64 Lincoln Rd.
Scarsdale, NY 10583

Established in 1996 in NY.
Donor(s): Geraldine F. Merksamer, Norman J. Merksamer.
Financial data (yr. ended 09/30/01): Grants paid, $58,050; assets, $584,128 (M); gifts received, $77,630; expenditures, $61,809; qualifying distributions, $58,050.
Limitations: Applications not accepted. Giving primarily in NY.
Application information: Contributes only to pre-selected organizations.
Officers: Norman J. Merksamer, Chair. and Treas.; Geraldine F. Merksamer, Pres.; Gregg D. Merksamer, V.P.; Hume R. Steyer, Secy.
EIN: 133916069

36379
Donmarel Foundation
c/o HSBC Bank USA
P.O. Box 4203
Buffalo, NY 14240

Established in 1966 in NY.
Financial data (yr. ended 12/31/01): Grants paid, $58,000; assets, $760,735 (M); expenditures, $68,940; qualifying distributions, $58,000.
Limitations: Applications not accepted. Giving on a national basis.
Application information: Contributes only to pre-selected organizations.
Trustee: HSBC Bank USA.
EIN: 166069804

36380
The Mary Ellen and Michael G. Ferrel Foundation, Inc.
c/o Cornick Garber & Sandler, LLP
630 3rd Ave.
New York, NY 10017

Established in 2000 in DE.
Donor(s): Michael G. Ferrel.
Financial data (yr. ended 12/31/01): Grants paid, $58,000; assets, $157,259 (M); expenditures, $64,001; qualifying distributions, $58,000.
Limitations: Applications not accepted.
Application information: Contributes only to pre-selected organizations.
Officers: Michael G. Ferrel, Pres. and Treas.; Mary Ellen Ferrel, V.P. and Secy.
EIN: 043531549

36381
Arthur and Louise Wasserman Foundation
1920 Liberty Bldg.
Buffalo, NY 14202-8232 (716) 856-2112
Contact: Arthur Wasserman, Tr.

Established in 1987 in NY.
Donor(s): Arthur Wasserman, Louise Wasserman.
Financial data (yr. ended 12/31/00): Grants paid, $58,000; assets, $671,377 (M); expenditures, $77,886; qualifying distributions, $58,000.
Limitations: Giving primarily in Buffalo, NY.
Trustees: David Heymann, James E. Kelly, Arlene Wasserman.
Directors: Keith Bookbinder, Daniel A. McCaffrey, Virginia Parsons, Gerald Price.
EIN: 222866780

36382
Pitterman Family Foundation, Inc.
515 E. 79th St., Apt. 25A
New York, NY 10021
Contact: Lawrence Pitterman, Dir.

Established in 1997 in KY.
Donor(s): Lawrence Pitterman.
Financial data (yr. ended 12/31/01): Grants paid, $57,959; assets, $483,280 (M); expenditures, $66,456; qualifying distributions, $57,513.
Limitations: Giving primarily in NY.
Application information: Application form not required.
Directors: Cara Pitterman, Hallee Pitterman, Lawrence Pitterman, Marjorie Pitterman.
EIN: 611315347

36383
Leo V. Berger Fund
c/o Harvey Schwartz
845 3rd Ave.
New York, NY 10022-6601

Donor(s): Leo V. Berger.‡
Financial data (yr. ended 12/31/00): Grants paid, $57,930; assets, $1,996,624 (M); gifts received, $2,008,237; expenditures, $57,957; qualifying distributions, $56,611.
Limitations: Applications not accepted. Giving primarily in FL, MD, and NY.
Application information: Contributes only to pre-selected organizations.
Officer: Milton S. Shapiro, Pres.
Directors: Sigmund Kassap, Harvey Schwartz.
EIN: 510196887

36384
Thayer Family Scholarship Trust
c/o Key Bank, N.A.
P.O. Box 1965
Albany, NY 12201-1965

Financial data (yr. ended 07/31/01): Grants paid, $57,882; assets, $2,752,790 (M); gifts received, $1,726,658; expenditures, $70,526; qualifying distributions, $57,392.
Limitations: Applications not accepted. Giving primarily in Cooperstown, NY.
Trustee: KeyBank, N.A.
EIN: 146134451
Codes: GTI

36385
The Willard and Roberta Block Family Foundation
c/o Krass & Lund, PC
54 Cornwall Ln.
Sands Point, NY 11050-1345

Established in 1994 in DE.
Donor(s): Willard Block, Roberta Block.
Financial data (yr. ended 12/31/01): Grants paid, $57,825; assets, $483,231 (M); expenditures, $57,845; qualifying distributions, $57,825.
Limitations: Applications not accepted. Giving primarily in NY.
Application information: Contributes only to pre-selected organizations.
Officers and Directors:* Willard Block,* Chair.; Roberta Block,* Secy.
EIN: 133793675

36386
Eliscu and Sisenwein Fund, Inc.
c/o Buck Sturmer & Co.
521 5th Ave.
New York, NY 10175

Financial data (yr. ended 12/31/00): Grants paid, $57,810; assets, $1,794,787 (M); gifts received, $298,407; expenditures, $58,409; qualifying distributions, $57,810.
Limitations: Applications not accepted. Giving primarily in NY.
Application information: Contributes only to pre-selected organizations.
Officers: Irving Sisenwein, Pres.; Branna Sisenwein, Treas.
EIN: 136141483

36387
I. Kingdon and Didi Hirsch Foundation
c/o Nathan Berkman & Co.
29 Broadway, Ste. 2900
New York, NY 10006

Donor(s): Nancy Rubin.

36387—NEW YORK

Financial data (yr. ended 09/30/01): Grants paid, $57,760; assets, $223,876 (M); expenditures, $58,166; qualifying distributions, $57,355.
Limitations: Applications not accepted.
Application information: Contributes only to pre-selected organizations.
Trustee: Nancy Rubin.
EIN: 133987111

36388
Richard F. Walsh/Alfred W. Ditolla Foundation
(Formerly Richard F. Walsh Foundation)
c/o I.A.T.S.E.
1515 Broadway, Ste. 600
New York, NY 10036

Financial data (yr. ended 09/30/01): Grants paid, $57,750; assets, $313,797 (M); gifts received, $42,387; expenditures, $58,228; qualifying distributions, $57,750.
Limitations: Applications not accepted.
Application information: Contributes only to pre-selected organizations.
Officer: Thomas C. Short, Chair.
Trustees: Edward C. Powell, Harold P. Spivak.
EIN: 136208834

36389
The J. & H. Weldon Foundation, Inc.
382 Further Ln.
P.O. Box 422
Amagansett, NY 11930

Donor(s): Henry H. Weldon.
Financial data (yr. ended 11/30/01): Grants paid, $57,550; assets, $1,112,299 (M); expenditures, $73,890; qualifying distributions, $57,550.
Limitations: Applications not accepted. Giving primarily in New York, NY.
Application information: Contributes only to pre-selected organizations.
Officers: June de H. Weldon, Pres.; Henry H. Weldon, V.P. and Treas.; James R. Weldon, Secy.
EIN: 133151515

36390
Fleur Harlan Foundation
817 5th Ave.
New York, NY 10021

Established in 1999 in NY.
Donor(s): Fleur Harlan.
Financial data (yr. ended 11/30/01): Grants paid, $57,500; assets, $130,686 (M); expenditures, $58,607; qualifying distributions, $116,023.
Limitations: Applications not accepted. Giving primarily in New York, NY.
Application information: Contributes only to pre-selected organizations.
Trustee: Fleur Harlan.
EIN: 137176145

36391
The Margarita & John Hennessy Family Foundation
435 E. 52nd St., Apt. 7C
New York, NY 10022

Established in 1997 in NY.
Donor(s): John Hennessy.
Financial data (yr. ended 12/31/00): Grants paid, $57,500; assets, $1,168,245 (M); gifts received, $2,000; expenditures, $70,742; qualifying distributions, $57,500.
Officers: Margarita C.T. Hennessy, Pres.; James H. Lowell, V.P.; John Novograd, Secy.; John M. Hennessy, Treas.
Directors: Alexandra Hennessy, Grace Hennessy, Miguel Hennessy.
EIN: 133978602

36392
Sidney & Judith Kranes Charitable Trust
420 Lexington Ave., Ste. 626
New York, NY 10170 (212) 218-7575
Application address: 30 Rockefeller Plz., Ste. 4340, New York, NY 10112
Contact: Thomas J. Sweeney, and Thomas J. Hubbard, Trustees

Established in 1992 in NY.
Donor(s): Judith E. Kranes.‡
Financial data (yr. ended 12/31/01): Grants paid, $57,500; assets, $2,667,212 (M); expenditures, $77,244; qualifying distributions, $69,333.
Limitations: Giving primarily in New York, NY.
Trustees: Thomas J. Hubbard, Thomas J. Sweeney.
EIN: 136981197

36393
Peter Simon Veeder Scholarship Fund
c/o JPMorgan Chase Bank
P.O. Box 31412
Rochester, NY 14603
Application address: c/o Southeast Fountain High School, 744 E. U.S. 136, Veedersburg, IN 47987
Contact: Robert Baker

Established in 1997 in CT.
Financial data (yr. ended 12/31/01): Grants paid, $57,500; assets, $799,688 (M); expenditures, $71,103; qualifying distributions, $58,475.
Trustee: JPMorgan Chase Bank.
EIN: 066115230

36394
Thalheim Family Foundation, Inc.
264 Sparrow Dr.
Manhasset, NY 11030

Established in 1999 in NY.
Donor(s): Jay Thalheim.
Financial data (yr. ended 12/31/01): Grants paid, $57,350; assets, $336,870 (M); gifts received, $201,909; expenditures, $57,676; qualifying distributions, $57,350.
Limitations: Applications not accepted.
Application information: Contributes only to pre-selected organizations.
Directors: Amy Handwerker, David Thalheim, Jay Thalheim, Neil Thalheim.
EIN: 113476785

36395
The Howard D. & Sandra Taylor Family Foundation, Inc.
c/o Schroder & Co., Inc.
1633 Broadway Tax Dept., 9th Fl.
New York, NY 10019 (212) 237-0403
Application address: 787 7th Ave., NY, NY 10019
Contact: Janet Mulligan, Pres.

Donor(s): Howard D. Taylor.
Financial data (yr. ended 11/30/01): Grants paid, $57,265; assets, $533,072 (M); expenditures, $66,806; qualifying distributions, $57,265.
Limitations: Giving primarily in FL and NY.
Application information: Application form not required.
Officers and Directors:* Janet Mulligan,* Pres.; Sandra Taylor,* V.P.; Leon R. Blain,* Treas.; Jill Conner, Jeff Taylor, Roger Yaseen.
EIN: 237075720

36396
The Chancellor Foundation, Inc.
c/o Sigmund Balaban & Co.
40 Broad St.
New York, NY 10004

Established in 1999 in NV.
Donor(s): Steven Dinetz.
Financial data (yr. ended 11/30/01): Grants paid, $57,100; assets, $77,715 (M); expenditures, $65,689; qualifying distributions, $57,100.
Limitations: Applications not accepted.
Application information: Contributes only to pre-selected organizations.
Trustees: Lawrence Dinetz, Marvin Dinetz, Steven Dinetz, Arnold E. Reiter.
EIN: 311675414

36397
Hoselton Foundation
6 Stoney Clover Ln.
Pittsford, NY 14534-4601
Application address: 909 Fairport Rd., East Rochester, NY 14445, tel.: (716) 586-7373
Contact: David C. Hoselton, Pres.

Established in 1973 in NY.
Donor(s): David C. Hoselton.
Financial data (yr. ended 11/30/01): Grants paid, $57,100; assets, $533,689 (M); gifts received, $104,268; expenditures, $58,341; qualifying distributions, $57,100.
Limitations: Giving primarily in Rochester, NY.
Application information: Application form not required.
Officers: David C. Hoselton, Pres.; Corale B. Hoselton, V.P.; Thomas Burns, Secy.-Treas.
Directors: William J. Crothers, Eugene F. Miller, Robert Whitmore.
EIN: 237356701

36398
The Nupik Foundation, Inc.
7 Stonehenge Rd.
Great Neck, NY 11023-1007

Established in 2000 in NY.
Donor(s): Nina Miner.
Financial data (yr. ended 12/31/00): Grants paid, $57,074; assets, $104,959 (M); gifts received, $13,956; expenditures, $57,113; qualifying distributions, $57,113.
Limitations: Giving primarily in NY.
Officers: George Miner, Pres.; Leslie Kule, V.P. and Secy.; Michael Leventhal, V.P. and Treas.
EIN: 113488418

36399
The Corita Charitable Trust
44 E. 64th St.
New York, NY 10021 (212) 486-2409
Contact: Clarence F. Michalis, Chair.

Established in 1986 in NY.
Donor(s): Clarence F. Michalis.
Financial data (yr. ended 11/30/01): Grants paid, $57,010; assets, $652,718 (M); gifts received, $43,220; expenditures, $60,063; qualifying distributions, $57,010.
Limitations: Giving primarily in NY.
Application information: Application form not required.
Officer: Clarence F. Michalis, Chair.
Trustee: Cora B. Michalis.
EIN: 136895007

36400
Saul Z. & Amy S. Cohen Family Foundation, Inc.
c/o 61 Assocs.
350 5th Ave., Ste. 1413
New York, NY 10118

Established in 1979 in NY.
Donor(s): Amy Scheuer Cohen.
Financial data (yr. ended 11/30/01): Grants paid, $57,000; assets, $2,643 (M); gifts received, $45,000; expenditures, $57,105; qualifying distributions, $57,105.
Limitations: Applications not accepted. Giving primarily in NY.
Application information: Contributes only to pre-selected organizations.
Officers: Amy Scheuer Cohen, Pres.; David Zahner, Secy.-Treas.
EIN: 133032459

36401
Endowment for the Neurosciences
2824 Sawmill Rd.
North Bellmore, NY 11710 (516) 781-9311
Contact: Melvin Greenberg, Treas.

Established in 1986 in NC.
Financial data (yr. ended 12/31/01): Grants paid, $57,000; assets, $8,455 (M); gifts received, $57,000; expenditures, $57,210; qualifying distributions, $57,052.
Limitations: Giving primarily in Buffalo, NY.
Application information: Application submitted by a M.D. or Ph.D. on behalf of an institution engaged in full time basic or clinical study under the auspices of a medical center teaching hospital or an institution which has established a record of bona fide scientific research in neurological and related fields. Application form required.
Officers: Steven Greenberg, Pres.; Melvin Greenberg, Treas.
EIN: 581679620

36402
The Quinn Family Foundation, Inc.
c/o Geller & Co., LLC
800 3rd Ave., 19th FL.
New York, NY 10022
Contact: Simon Levin

Established in 1997 in NJ.
Donor(s): Michael L. Quinn.
Financial data (yr. ended 12/31/01): Grants paid, $57,000; assets, $1,193,656 (M); expenditures, $70,303; qualifying distributions, $55,948.
Limitations: Applications not accepted.
Application information: Contributes only to pre-selected organizations.
Officer and Trustees:* Michael L. Quinn,* Pres.; Colleen Quinn, Conor Quinn, Janice L. Quinn, Ryan Quinn.
EIN: 223512077

36403
Frank G. & Frances Revoir Foundation
c/o KeyBank, N.A.
201 S. Warren St.
Syracuse, NY 13202
Application address: c/o Frederick S. Marty, V.P., Hiscock & Barclay, LP, P.O. Box 4878, Syracuse, NY 13221
Contact: William C. Francher, Tr.

Established in 1989 in NY.
Financial data (yr. ended 12/31/00): Grants paid, $57,000; assets, $990,968 (M); expenditures, $72,257; qualifying distributions, $57,000.
Limitations: Giving primarily in Syracuse and central NY.
Publications: Informational brochure, application guidelines.
Application information: Application form not required.
Trustees: William C. Francher, Horace J. Landry, Frederick S. Marty.
EIN: 166098220

36404
Helen & Anthony J. Scala Foundation
26 Archer Rd.
Harrison, NY 10528

Established in 1986 in NY.
Donor(s): Anthony J. Scala.
Financial data (yr. ended 12/31/00): Grants paid, $57,000; assets, $889,035 (M); gifts received, $50,000; expenditures, $56,670; qualifying distributions, $57,000.
Limitations: Giving on a national basis.
Application information: Application form not required.
Officer: Anthony J. Scala, Pres.
EIN: 133399838

36405
Charles and Susan Edelstein Charity Foundation
1159 E. 28th St.
Brooklyn, NY 11210

Established in 1997 in NY.
Donor(s): Charles Edelstein.
Financial data (yr. ended 12/31/99): Grants paid, $56,945; assets, $2,887 (M); gifts received, $61,500; expenditures, $58,649; qualifying distributions, $56,945.
Limitations: Applications not accepted.
Application information: Contributes only to pre-selected organizations.
Trustees: Charles Edelstein, Susan Edelstein.
EIN: 137112950

36406
The Isidore Grossman Foundation, Inc.
125 Mineola Ave., Ste. 107
Roslyn Heights, NY 11577-2041
Contact: Irwin Grossman, Secy.-Treas.

Established in 1943.
Financial data (yr. ended 12/31/01): Grants paid, $56,800; assets, $1,145,750 (M); expenditures, $64,295; qualifying distributions, $56,800.
Limitations: Applications not accepted. Giving primarily in NY.
Application information: Contributes only to pre-selected organizations.
Officers: William J. Grossman, Pres.; Irwin Grossman, Secy.-Treas.
EIN: 136091872

36407
Fritzi and Herbert Owens Family Foundation
50 E. 79th St.
New York, NY 10021-0232

Established in 1994 in NY.
Donor(s): Fritzi Owens, Herbert Owens.
Financial data (yr. ended 12/31/01): Grants paid, $56,775; assets, $0 (M); gifts received, $50,000; expenditures, $57,407; qualifying distributions, $56,775.
Limitations: Applications not accepted. Giving primarily in New York, NY.
Application information: Contributes only to pre-selected organizations.
Directors: Fritzi Owens, Herbert Owens, Mark Owens, Robert O. Owens, Ruth Owens.
EIN: 133774411

36408
The Fried Family Charitable Foundation
215 Lagoon Dr., E.
Lido Beach, NY 11561

Established in 2000.
Financial data (yr. ended 12/31/01): Grants paid, $56,760; assets, $16,630 (M); expenditures, $57,365; qualifying distributions, $56,760.
Limitations: Applications not accepted.
Application information: Contributes only to pre-selected organizations.
Trustees: Bert Fried, Sara Fried.
EIN: 116533149

36409
The Richard Meier Foundation
475 10th Ave., 6th Fl.
New York, NY 10018-2259 (212) 967-6060
Contact: Richard Meier, Tr.

Established in 1997 in NY.
Donor(s): Richard Meier.
Financial data (yr. ended 12/31/01): Grants paid, $56,625; assets, $1,292,540 (M); expenditures, $59,355; qualifying distributions, $56,625.
Limitations: Giving primarily in NY.
Application information: Application form not required.
Trustees: Jordan Davis, Richard Meier.
EIN: 133978415

36410
Whitworth and Dorothy Ferguson Foundation
48 Huntington Ct.
Williamsville, NY 14221

Established in 2000 in NY.
Donor(s): Whitworth Ferguson, Jr.
Financial data (yr. ended 12/31/01): Grants paid, $56,519; assets, $156,294 (M); gifts received, $100,000; expenditures, $58,060; qualifying distributions, $56,519.
Limitations: Applications not accepted.
Application information: Contributes only to pre-selected organizations.
Trustees: Dorothymae Taylor Ferguson, Whitworth Ferguson, Jr.
EIN: 161597103

36411
Herbert and Jeanine Coyne Foundation
c/o Loeb & Loeb
345 Park Ave.
New York, NY 10154-0037

Established in 1983 in NY.
Donor(s): Herbert J. Coyne, Jeanine Coyne.
Financial data (yr. ended 12/31/01): Grants paid, $56,500; assets, $26,648 (M); gifts received, $60,000; expenditures, $57,589; qualifying distributions, $56,500.
Limitations: Applications not accepted. Giving primarily in FL, MA, and New York, NY.
Application information: Contributes only to pre-selected organizations.
Officers: Herbert J. Coyne, Pres. and Treas.; Jeanine Coyne, V.P. and Secy.
Director: Robert Pelz.
EIN: 133206423

36412
Arthur Zimtbaum Foundation, Inc.
c/o Elihu M. Modlin
777 3rd Ave., 30th Fl.
New York, NY 10017 (212) 832-1600
Contact: Rose LeVantine, Pres.

Incorporated in 1955 in NY.
Donor(s): Arthur Zimtbaum,‡ Rose B. LeVantine.

36412—NEW YORK

Financial data (yr. ended 12/31/01): Grants paid, $56,500; assets, $2,137,534 (M); expenditures, $111,476; qualifying distributions, $83,323.
Limitations: Giving on a national basis, primarily in MA and NY.
Application information: Application form not required.
Officers: Rose B. LeVantine, Pres.; Elihu H. Modlin, V.P. and Secy.; Herbert Merin, Treas.
Directors: William J. Burke, Paulette L. LeVantine, Andrew Merin, Charles Modlin.
EIN: 116016391

36413
Meyer Handelman Fund
P.O. Box 817
Purchase, NY 10577-2515

Donor(s): Donald E. Handelman, Joseph W. Handelman, William R. Handelman.
Financial data (yr. ended 12/31/01): Grants paid, $56,450; assets, $1,133,295 (M); gifts received, $62,024; expenditures, $57,854; qualifying distributions, $56,450.
Limitations: Applications not accepted. Giving primarily in New York, NY.
Application information: Contributes only to pre-selected organizations.
Officers: Donald E. Handelman, Pres.; William R. Handelman, V.P. and Secy.; Joseph W. Handelman, V.P. and Treas.
EIN: 136110502

36414
Grotheer Memorial Fund
c/o JPMorgan Chase Bank
P.O. Box 1412
Rochester, NY 14603

Donor(s): Dwight Blackstone.‡
Financial data (yr. ended 12/31/01): Grants paid, $56,432; assets, $422,979 (M); expenditures, $68,328; qualifying distributions, $56,432.
Limitations: Applications not accepted. Giving primarily in NY.
Application information: Contributes only to pre-selected organizations.
Trustee: JPMorgan Chase Bank.
EIN: 136754169

36415
Paul A. Cohen Foundation
c/o Kranz & Co.
145 E. 57th St.
New York, NY 10022

Financial data (yr. ended 12/31/01): Grants paid, $56,416; assets, $779,888 (M); expenditures, $74,705; qualifying distributions, $56,416.
Limitations: Applications not accepted. Giving primarily in New York, NY.
Application information: Contributes only to pre-selected organizations.
Officer and Trustees:* Carol R. Cohen,* Pres.; Paul Thomas Cohen.
EIN: 136162767

36416
Alex Gabay Foundation
111 W. 67th St.
New York, NY 10023

Donor(s): Alex Gabay.
Financial data (yr. ended 12/31/00): Grants paid, $56,400; assets, $140,037 (M); gifts received, $72,538; expenditures, $57,449; qualifying distributions, $56,400.
Limitations: Applications not accepted. Giving primarily in NY.
Application information: Contributes only to pre-selected organizations.

Officers: Alex Gabay, Pres.; Patricia Gabay, Secy.
EIN: 133333930

36417
Costanza Family Foundation
14 Franklin St., Ste. 800
Rochester, NY 14604

Established in 2000 in NY.
Donor(s): James Costanza, Angelo Costanza, Linda Shepard.
Financial data (yr. ended 12/31/01): Grants paid, $56,390; assets, $24,249 (M); gifts received, $73,225; expenditures, $56,405; qualifying distributions, $56,390.
Limitations: Applications not accepted. Giving primarily in NY.
Application information: Contributes only to pre-selected organizations.
Trustees: Andrew Costanza, Angelo Costanza, James Costanza, Maria M. Costanza, Nicholas Costanza, Linda Shepard.
EIN: 161580788

36418
Naueltschi Foundation
(Formerly The Nancy J. Gavin Foundation)
c/o RSM McGladrey, Inc.
555 Fifth Ave.
New York, NY 10017-2416

Established in 1998 in DE.
Donor(s): Albert L. Ueltschi.
Financial data (yr. ended 12/31/01): Grants paid, $56,355; assets, $1,962,684 (M); gifts received, $40,500; expenditures, $57,557; qualifying distributions, $57,557.
Limitations: Applications not accepted. Giving primarily in WA.
Application information: Contributes only to pre-selected organizations.
Officer: Nancy J. Gavin, Pres.
EIN: 061519389

36419
Bnei Brocho Foundation
2075 75th St.
Brooklyn, NY 11204
Contact: Yitzchok Kaplan, Mgr.

Established in 1997 in NY.
Financial data (yr. ended 09/30/01): Grants paid, $56,300; assets, $300,235 (M); expenditures, $57,072; qualifying distributions, $56,300.
Officer: Yitzchok Kaplan, Mgr.
EIN: 137053362

36420
The Kiev Foundation
(Formerly Social Psychiatry Research Institute, Inc.)
150 E. 69th St.
New York, NY 10021-5766 (212) 249-6829
Contact: Ari Kiev, M.D., Pres.

Established in 1974 in NY.
Financial data (yr. ended 12/31/01): Grants paid, $56,286; assets, $1,454,886 (M); gifts received, $948,056; expenditures, $90,224; qualifying distributions, $56,286.
Limitations: Giving primarily in NJ and NY.
Officer and Trustee:* Ari Kiev, M.D.,* Pres.
EIN: 237070393

36421
Gary Williams Foundation
c/o Goldman Sachs & Co.
85 Broad St., Tax Dept.
New York, NY 10004

Established in 1998 in VA.
Donor(s): The Buffett Foundation, Gary Williams.

Financial data (yr. ended 01/31/01): Grants paid, $56,198; assets, $2,717,876 (M); expenditures, $104,520; qualifying distributions, $56,448.
Limitations: Applications not accepted. Giving primarily in NY; some giving also in CT and France.
Application information: Contributes only to pre-selected organizations.
Trustees: Wiet H. Pot, Gary W. Williams.
EIN: 133989532

36422
Rosenthal Family Foundation, Inc.
117 E. 29th St.
New York, NY 10016-8090

Established in 1984 in NY.
Donor(s): Jack Rosenthal.
Financial data (yr. ended 11/30/01): Grants paid, $56,079; assets, $864,131 (M); gifts received, $60,580; expenditures, $56,262; qualifying distributions, $56,079.
Limitations: Applications not accepted. Giving primarily in New York, NY.
Application information: Contributes only to pre-selected organizations.
Officers: Jack Rosenthal, Pres.; Elizabeth Rosenthal, V.P.; Stewart Rosenthal, Secy.-Treas.
EIN: 133263916

36423
The Durst Foundation, Inc.
1155 Ave. of the Americas
New York, NY 10036

Established in 1944 in NY.
Donor(s): Durst Partners, Durst Building Corp., David Durst, 46-47 Assocs., LLC, Durst Organization, LP, St. Rud Construction, 205 Assocs.
Financial data (yr. ended 12/31/01): Grants paid, $56,000; assets, $19,157 (M); expenditures, $56,228; qualifying distributions, $56,203.
Limitations: Applications not accepted. Giving primarily in NY.
Application information: Contributes only to pre-selected organizations.
Officers and Directors:* Douglas Durst,* Pres.; David Durst,* V.P.; Peter Durst, V.P.
EIN: 131656537

36424
The Seymour V. & Zena Lipkowitz Foundation, Inc.
c/o Cummings & Carroll
175 Great Neck Rd.
Great Neck, NY 11021-3313

Established in 1992 in NJ.
Donor(s): Seymour V. Lipkowitz.
Financial data (yr. ended 12/31/01): Grants paid, $56,000; assets, $882,525 (M); gifts received, $2,822; expenditures, $74,875; qualifying distributions, $56,000.
Limitations: Applications not accepted. Giving primarily in New York, NY.
Application information: Contributes only to pre-selected organizations.
Officers and Trustees:* Elliot Lipkowitz,* Chair.; Sharon Henderson,* Secy.; Ivan Linden.
EIN: 521775837

36425
Fishel Family Charitable Foundation, Inc.
627 Broadway
New York, NY 10012

Incorporated in DE in 1996.
Financial data (yr. ended 12/31/01): Grants paid, $55,955; assets, $711,348 (M); expenditures, $59,467; qualifying distributions, $55,955.

Limitations: Applications not accepted.
Application information: Contributes only to pre-selected organizations.
Officers and Directors:* Kenneth Fishel,* Pres.; Robert Fishel,* Secy.
EIN: 133879107

36426
O.C.F. Foundation, Inc.
1067 5th Ave.
New York, NY 10128
Contact: Gregor Leinsdorf, Pres.

Incorporated in 1940 in NY.
Donor(s): International Minerals and Metals Corp.
Financial data (yr. ended 12/31/01): Grants paid, $55,950; assets, $1,954,659 (M); expenditures, $71,184; qualifying distributions, $65,540.
Limitations: Applications not accepted. Giving primarily in NY.
Application information: Contributes only to pre-selected organizations.
Officers: Gregor Leinsdorf, Pres.; Mary Leinsdorf, V.P.
Director: Jack Elam.
EIN: 136007727

36427
Thomas A. Famigletti Foundation
3A Bowden Ln.
Glen Head, NY 11545
Contact: Judith A. Famigletti, Mgr.

Established in 1989 in NY.
Donor(s): Thomas A. Famigletti.
Financial data (yr. ended 12/31/01): Grants paid, $55,870; assets, $995,858 (M); gifts received, $10,000; expenditures, $72,081; qualifying distributions, $55,870.
Officers and Trustees:* Douglas Famigletti,* Mgr.; Judith A. Famigletti,* Mgr.; Brian Famigletti.
EIN: 112997256

36428
Ralph G. Cator Trust
One HSBC Center, 17th Fl.
Buffalo, NY 14240-2801

Established in 1997 in NY.
Financial data (yr. ended 02/28/02): Grants paid, $55,758; assets, $419,197 (M); expenditures, $71,526; qualifying distributions, $55,758.
Limitations: Applications not accepted.
Application information: Contributes only to pre-selected organizations.
Trustees: Lee Hunter, HSBC Bank USA.
EIN: 166448557

36429
The Tsvi-Ora foundation
16 Dover St.
Brooklyn, NY 11235

Established in 1997.
Donor(s): Mitchell Vilinsky, Ruvane Vilinsky, Edward Vilinsky.
Financial data (yr. ended 12/31/01): Grants paid, $55,756; assets, $9,262 (L); gifts received, $65,500; expenditures, $57,576; qualifying distributions, $55,756.
Officers: Mitchell Vilinsky, Pres.; Ruvane Vilinsky, V.P.; Edward Vilinsky, Secy.-Treas.
EIN: 113433976

36430
Ruthanne Koffman Charitable Foundation
c/o Piaker & Lyons
P.O. Box 247
Vestal, NY 13851

Established in 1985 in NY.
Donor(s): Ruthanne Koffman.

Financial data (yr. ended 12/31/01): Grants paid, $55,600; assets, $1,220,885 (M); gifts received, $5; expenditures, $57,000; qualifying distributions, $55,905.
Limitations: Applications not accepted. Giving primarily in NY.
Application information: Contributes only to pre-selected organizations.
Trustees: David Koffman, Elizabeth Koffman, Ruthanne Koffman.
EIN: 222624220

36431
The Grossman-Southern Container Foundation
P.O. Box 1060
Smithtown, NY 11787

Established in 1985 in NY.
Donor(s): Southern Container Corp.
Financial data (yr. ended 11/30/01): Grants paid, $55,566; assets, $1,288,336 (M); gifts received, $500,000; expenditures, $56,386; qualifying distributions, $55,566.
Limitations: Applications not accepted. Giving primarily in NY.
Application information: Contributes only to pre-selected organizations.
Officers and Directors:* Steven Grossman,* Pres.; Steven Hill, V.P. and Secy.; Robert Grossman.
EIN: 112778329
Codes: CS, CD

36432
The Martin and Irene Taub Memorial Fund
c/o JPMorgan Chase Bank
345 Park Ave., 8th Fl.
New York, NY 10154-1002

Established in 1996 in NY.
Financial data (yr. ended 12/31/01): Grants paid, $55,498; assets, $916,429 (M); expenditures, $71,059; qualifying distributions, $57,087.
Limitations: Applications not accepted.
Application information: Contributes only to pre-selected organizations.
Trustee: JPMorgan Chase Bank.
EIN: 137075767

36433
The Goodman Charitable Trust
c/o Peter E. Buell, C.P.A., Marks Paneth & Shron
622 3rd Ave., 7th Fl.
New York, NY 10017

Established in 1996 in NY.
Donor(s): James Goodman.
Financial data (yr. ended 12/31/01): Grants paid, $55,468; assets, $313,103 (M); gifts received, $132,445; expenditures, $57,225; qualifying distributions, $57,082.
Limitations: Applications not accepted.
Application information: Contributes only to pre-selected organizations.
Trustees: Stephen M. Breitstone, Andrew Goodman, Bruce Goodman, Barry B. Seidel.
EIN: 116479000

36434
The David and Lauren Gorter Foundation
c/o BCRS Assocs., LLC
67 Wall St., 8th Fl.
New York, NY 10005

Established in 1992 in IL; funded in 1993.
Donor(s): David F. Gorter, Lauren A. Gorter.
Financial data (yr. ended 12/31/01): Grants paid, $55,436; assets, $214,836 (M); expenditures, $55,505; qualifying distributions, $55,436.
Limitations: Applications not accepted.
Application information: Contributes only to pre-selected organizations.

Directors: Grace Arnold, David F. Gorter, Lauren A. Gorter.
EIN: 363872803

36435
The Horn Foundation, Inc.
c/o L & S Realty Co.
434 Hempstead Tpke.
West Hempstead, NY 11552

Established in 1992 in NY.
Financial data (yr. ended 08/31/01): Grants paid, $55,400; assets, $658,550 (M); expenditures, $65,641; qualifying distributions, $55,400.
Limitations: Applications not accepted. Giving primarily on Long Island, NY.
Application information: Contributes only to pre-selected organizations.
Directors: Larry Horn, Rita Horn, Phillip Trost.
EIN: 113140354

36436
Abraham & Lillian Hecht Foundation
2110 Ocean Pkwy.
Brooklyn, NY 11223 (718) 283-8544
Contact: Abraham Hecht, Tr.

Financial data (yr. ended 12/31/99): Grants paid, $55,390; assets, $11,210 (M); gifts received, $56,636; expenditures, $55,709; qualifying distributions, $55,390.
Trustee: Abraham Hecht.
EIN: 113456882

36437
Wellspring Charity Fund
315 Westchester Ave., 2nd Fl.
Port Chester, NY 10573

Established in 1998 in NY.
Donor(s): Gloria S. Deitsch.
Financial data (yr. ended 12/31/01): Grants paid, $55,363; assets, $224,832 (M); gifts received, $82,346; expenditures, $55,787; qualifying distributions, $55,211.
Limitations: Applications not accepted.
Application information: Contributes only to pre-selected organizations.
Officers and Directors:* Gloria S. Deitsch,* Pres.; Deborah D. Feh,* V.P.; Rebecca D. Sklar,* Secy.; Irving Kaplan,* Treas.
EIN: 133994337

36438
Henry M. Butzel Family Foundation, Inc.
3 Clinton Sq.
Albany, NY 12207 (518) 465-4717
Contact: Daniel A. Lombardi, Dir.

Donor(s): Miriam Butzel.
Financial data (yr. ended 10/31/00): Grants paid, $55,350; assets, $2,163,718 (M); gifts received, $561,769; expenditures, $91,995; qualifying distributions, $55,350.
Limitations: Giving primarily in NY.
Directors: Daniel A. Lombardi, Joanne Stillman, Philip Stillman.
EIN: 141789042

36439
Frankel Brothers Foundation
32 Court St., Rm. 505
Brooklyn, NY 11201 (718) 855-0741

Donor(s): Jacob Frankel, Naftali Frankel, Rosa Frankel.
Financial data (yr. ended 12/31/01): Grants paid, $55,315; assets, $527,037 (M); gifts received, $78,000; expenditures, $55,366; qualifying distributions, $55,315.
Limitations: Giving primarily in NY.

36439—NEW YORK

Application information: Application form not required.
Trustees: Naftali Frankel, Rosa Frankel.
EIN: 112643090

36440
The Henry & Shirlee Benach Foundation
22 Longview Ln.
Chappaqua, NY 10514

Established in 1966 in NY.
Donor(s): Henry Benach,‡ Shirlee Benach.
Financial data (yr. ended 12/31/01): Grants paid, $55,312; assets, $316,210 (M); gifts received, $483; expenditures, $56,145; qualifying distributions, $55,312.
Limitations: Applications not accepted. Giving primarily in the greater New York, NY, area.
Application information: Contributes only to pre-selected organizations.
Trustee: Shirlee Benach.
EIN: 136206005

36441
SKCK Foundation
1259 East 27th St.
Brooklyn, NY 11210-4622 (718) 283-8544
Contact: Steven Klein, Tr.

Established in 2001 in NY.
Donor(s): SKCK Trust.
Financial data (yr. ended 01/31/02): Grants paid, $55,300; assets, $418,684 (M); gifts received, $482,050; expenditures, $63,366; qualifying distributions, $63,366.
Limitations: Giving primarily in NY.
Trustees: Israel Braun, Chana Klein, Herman Klein, Steven Klein.
EIN: 113620904

36442
Robert and Caroline Schwartz Foundation
c/o Robert G. Schwartz, Metropolitan Life Insurance Co.
200 Park Ave., Ste. 5700
New York, NY 10166-0114

Established in 1986 in DE.
Donor(s): Robert G. Schwartz.
Financial data (yr. ended 12/31/01): Grants paid, $55,272; assets, $1,118,529 (M); expenditures, $60,695; qualifying distributions, $55,272.
Limitations: Applications not accepted. Giving primarily in NJ and NY.
Application information: Contributes only to pre-selected organizations.
Officers: Robert G. Schwartz, Pres. and Treas.; Caroline Schwartz, V.P. and Secy.
Directors: Joanne Schwartz Carter, Tracy Schwartz Parks, Robert G. Schwartz, Jr.
EIN: 133386282

36443
Anti-Defamation League Foundation Common Fund, Inc.
823 United Nations Plz.
New York, NY 10017-3518

Established in 1982.
Financial data (yr. ended 06/30/01): Grants paid, $55,267; assets, $234,055 (M); gifts received, $8,400; expenditures, $56,935; qualifying distributions, $55,267.
Limitations: Applications not accepted.
Application information: Contributes only to pre-selected organizations.
Directors: Howard P. Berkowitz, Maxwell E. Greenberg, Burton M. Joseph, David Strassler.
EIN: 133095748

36444
The Linda and Isaac Stern Charitable Foundation
c/o Joshua A. Rednor
1979 Marcus Ave.
New Hyde Park, NY 11042

Established in 1997 in NY.
Financial data (yr. ended 12/31/00): Grants paid, $55,250; assets, $87,943 (M); expenditures, $55,417; qualifying distributions, $55,250.
Limitations: Applications not accepted. Giving primarily in NY.
Application information: Contributes only to pre-selected organizations.
Officers and Directors:* Isaac Stern,* Pres. and Treas.; Linda Stern,* Secy.; Catherine Gevers.
EIN: 522112066

36445
George Duffy Foundation
c/o Richard J. Cordovano, C.P.A.
One Clair Pass
Saratoga Springs, NY 12866-7505
Application address: P.O. Box 230, Fort Plain, NY 13339

Financial data (yr. ended 12/31/00): Grants paid, $55,200; assets, $2,836,038 (M); expenditures, $91,135; qualifying distributions, $55,200.
Limitations: Giving limited to Canajoharie, Fort Plain, and St. Johnsville, NY.
Publications: Informational brochure.
Application information: Application form required.
Officers: Frederick J. Kirkpatrick, Pres.; Robert H. Diefendorf, 1st V.P.; Myron H. Walton, 2nd V.P.; Shirley E. Diefendorf, Secy.-Treas.
EIN: 146016445
Codes: GTI

36446
The Pomegranate Foundation
c/o Kathleen Peratis
110 E. 59th St.
New York, NY 10022-7604

Financial data (yr. ended 12/31/01): Grants paid, $55,200; assets, $770,325 (M); gifts received, $2,121; expenditures, $55,975; qualifying distributions, $55,200.
Limitations: Applications not accepted. Giving primarily in New York, NY.
Application information: Contributes only to pre-selected organizations.
Trustee: Kathleen Peratis.
EIN: 133798585

36447
Grunebaum Foundation, Inc.
30 Vesey St.
New York, NY 10007-2914 (212) 267-6420
Contact: Ernest F. Grunebaum, Secy.

Established in 1950 in NY.
Donor(s): Ernest F. Grunebaum, Ruth G. Sondheimer.
Financial data (yr. ended 12/31/01): Grants paid, $55,183; assets, $925,715 (M); expenditures, $59,214; qualifying distributions, $55,313.
Officers: Ruth G. Sondheimer, Pres.; Ernest F. Grunebaum, Secy.
EIN: 136089084

36448
Krutz Foundation, Inc.
c/o Robinson Brog
1345 Ave. of the Americas
New York, NY 10105-0302

Established in 2000 in NY.
Donor(s): Eve Krutz.
Financial data (yr. ended 09/30/01): Grants paid, $55,100; assets, $1,532,966 (M); expenditures, $131,808; qualifying distributions, $55,100.
Limitations: Applications not accepted. Giving primarily in Rockland County, NY.
Application information: Contributes only to pre-selected organizations.
Officers and Directors:* Adele Horton,* Pres. and Treas.; Ronald Lemberger,* V.P.; Marshall J. Gluck,* Secy.
EIN: 134075906

36449
The Ballard Family Foundation
c/o Goldman Sachs & Co.
85 Broad St., Tax Dept.
New York, NY 10004

Established in 1982 in NJ.
Donor(s): Claude M. Ballard.
Financial data (yr. ended 05/31/01): Grants paid, $55,086; assets, $1,402,422 (M); expenditures, $56,961; qualifying distributions, $56,121.
Limitations: Applications not accepted. Giving primarily in NY, PA and TX.
Application information: Contributes only to pre-selected organizations.
Trustees: Claude M. Ballard, Mary B. Ballard, Mary Melinda Ballard, Karen Ballard Hart, Robyn B. Ziperski.
EIN: 133153733

36450
The Namm Foundation, Inc.
1202 Lexington Ave., Ste. 234
New York, NY 10028-1425
Contact: Andrew I. Namm, Pres.

Financial data (yr. ended 12/31/01): Grants paid, $55,070; assets, $1,268,091 (M); expenditures, $71,548; qualifying distributions, $55,070.
Limitations: Giving primarily in NY and VT.
Application information: Application form not required.
Officers and Trustees:* Andrew Namm,* Pres.; Anne Namm,* V.P. and Secy.; James Doran,* V.P. and Treas.; Georgia Mackay,* Treas. and Exec. Dir.; Benjamin Cohen.
EIN: 136069191

36451
Acquavella Family Foundation
c/o William R. Acquavella
18 E. 79th St.
New York, NY 10021

Established in 1997 in NY.
Donor(s): William Acquavella, H. Anthony Ittleson.
Financial data (yr. ended 12/31/01): Grants paid, $55,000; assets, $328,708 (M); gifts received, $20,000; expenditures, $59,197; qualifying distributions, $55,718.
Limitations: Applications not accepted. Giving primarily in NY.
Application information: Contributes only to pre-selected organizations.
Trustees: Donna Jo Acquavella, William R. Acquavella.
EIN: 137140356

36452
Dorothy Carnegie Foundation
c/o AJG Tax Consulting Corp.
350 5th Ave., Ste. 609
New York, NY 10118-0685 (212) 594-9861
Contact: Arnold J. Gitomer, Treas.

Donor(s): Dorothy Carnegie.‡

Financial data (yr. ended 12/31/00): Grants paid, $55,000; assets, $746,292 (M); gifts received, $100; expenditures, $66,541; qualifying distributions, $55,000.
Limitations: Giving on a national basis.
Application information: Application form not required.
Officers and Trustees:* Donna Dale Carnegie,* Pres.; J. Oliver Crom,* V.P.; Michael Crom,* Secy.; Arnold J. Gitomer,* Treas.; David Rivkin, Troy C. White.
EIN: 136219844

36453
Robert & Pamela Delaney Family Foundation
(Formerly Delaney Family Foundation)
c/o Goldman Sachs & Co.
85 Broad St., Tax Dept.
New York, NY 10004

Established in 1997 in NJ.
Donor(s): Robert V. Delaney.
Financial data (yr. ended 06/30/01): Grants paid, $55,000; assets, $634,495 (M); gifts received, $101,063; expenditures, $61,850; qualifying distributions, $55,000.
Limitations: Applications not accepted. Giving limited to Clinton, NY.
Application information: Contributes only to pre-selected organizations.
Trustees: Pamela J. Craig, Charles J. Delaney, Robert V. Delaney.
EIN: 133984315

36454
Charles L. Grannon Foundation
c/o BCRS Assoc., LLC
67 Wall St., 8th Fl.
New York, NY 10005

Established in 1977 in NY.
Donor(s): Charles L. Grannon.
Financial data (yr. ended 02/28/02): Grants paid, $55,000; assets, $138,800 (M); gifts received, $2,400; expenditures, $57,597; qualifying distributions, $55,000.
Limitations: Applications not accepted. Giving primarily in Boca Raton, FL.
Application information: Contributes only to pre-selected organizations.
Trustees: Charles L. Grannon, Craig C. Grannon, Mark W. Grannon, Michael L. Grannon.
EIN: 132921501

36455
Gullabi Gulbenkian Foundation, Inc.
168 Canal St., Rm. 600
New York, NY 10013-4503 (212) 334-0990
Contact: Alex Dadourian, Treas.

Financial data (yr. ended 12/31/01): Grants paid, $55,000; assets, $1,076,553 (M); expenditures, $62,711; qualifying distributions, $55,000.
Limitations: Giving limited to New York, NY.
Officers: Edward H. Gulbenkian, Jr., Pres.; Stephen Dadourian, Secy.; Alex Dadourian, Treas.
EIN: 136104842

36456
The Melvin & Doris Sirow Foundation, Inc.
777 3rd Ave., 26th Fl.
New York, NY 10017

Established in 1957.
Donor(s): Real Estate Industrials, Inc., Realty Enterprises of New Jersey.
Financial data (yr. ended 11/30/01): Grants paid, $54,976; assets, $73,560 (M); gifts received, $46,820; expenditures, $56,702; qualifying distributions, $54,976.

Limitations: Applications not accepted. Giving primarily in the greater New York, NY, area.
Application information: Contributes only to pre-selected organizations.
Officers: Melvin Sirow, Pres.; Doris Sirow, V.P.
EIN: 116036948

36457
The Ellman Foundation, Inc.
c/o Silverman & Mardfin
150 Great Neck Rd.
Great Neck, NY 11021-3309
Application address: 4356 Kasso Cir, Boca Raton, FL 33431
Contact: Esther Ellman, Pres.

Donor(s): Lee E. Ellman, Esther Ellman.
Financial data (yr. ended 11/30/01): Grants paid, $54,950; assets, $944,309 (M); gifts received, $100,000; expenditures, $58,405; qualifying distributions, $54,302.
Limitations: Giving primarily in the southeastern and northeastern regions of the U.S.
Officers: Esther Ellman, Pres.; Jan Ellman, Treas.
EIN: 136160971

36458
Shanok Foundation, Inc.
P.O. Box D, Wykagyl Sta.
New Rochelle, NY 10804-0123

Financial data (yr. ended 09/30/01): Grants paid, $54,882; assets, $763,641 (M); expenditures, $80,104; qualifying distributions, $63,032.
Limitations: Applications not accepted.
Application information: Contributes only to pre-selected organizations.
Officers: Dorothy Shanok, Pres. and Mgr.; Charles Shanok, V.P. and Secy.
EIN: 136081795

36459
The Heckmann Family Foundation
c/o U.S. Trust Co. of New York
114 W. 47 St.
New York, NY 10036

Established in 1997 in CA.
Donor(s): Richard J. Heckmann.
Financial data (yr. ended 12/31/01): Grants paid, $54,846; assets, $1,348,357 (M); gifts received, $645,335; expenditures, $128,242; qualifying distributions, $54,846.
Limitations: Applications not accepted.
Application information: Contributes only to pre-selected organizations.
Officers: Richard J. Heckmann, Pres. and Treas.; Mary M. Heckmann, Secy.
Directors: Brock P. Heckmann, Scott M. Heckmann, Thomas R. Heckmann.
EIN: 330758328

36460
John E. Lovenheim & Barbara P. Lovenheim Charitable Trust
24 Grove St.
Rochester, NY 14605-2813
Contact: John E. Lovenheim, Tr.

Established in 1993 in NY.
Donor(s): Clifford N. Lovenheim.‡
Financial data (yr. ended 12/31/01): Grants paid, $54,843; assets, $1,080,306 (M); expenditures, $68,161; qualifying distributions, $54,639.
Limitations: Applications not accepted. Giving primarily in Rochester, NY.
Application information: Contributes only to pre-selected organizations.
Trustees: Barbara P. Lovenheim, John E. Lovenheim.
EIN: 166383847

36461
Bentley Fund
7784 S. Main St.
Pine Plains, NY 12567
Contact: Carol Adams, Dir.

Established in 1960.
Financial data (yr. ended 12/31/01): Grants paid, $54,809; assets, $1,116,160 (M); expenditures, $82,016; qualifying distributions, $58,598.
Limitations: Applications not accepted. Giving primarily in Pine Plains, NY.
Application information: Contributes only to pre-selected organizations.
Directors: Carol Adams, Jon H. Adams.
EIN: 146018200

36462
Carol Colman Timmis Foundation, Ltd.
c/o American Express Tax & Business Svcs., Inc.
1185 Ave. of the Americas
New York, NY 10036

Established in 1997 in NY.
Donor(s): Carol Colman.
Financial data (yr. ended 09/30/01): Grants paid, $54,785; assets, $872,164 (M); gifts received, $32,520; expenditures, $89,939; qualifying distributions, $54,785.
Limitations: Applications not accepted. Giving primarily in NY.
Application information: Contributes only to pre-selected organizations.
Officers: Carol Colman Timmis, Pres.; Thomas W. Colman, V.P.; John H. Timmis, Secy.
EIN: 133917290

36463
Pat Covelli Foundation, Inc.
c/o Paddy Lee Fashions, Inc.
48-49 35th St.
Long Island City, NY 11101-2314

Established in 1999 in NY.
Donor(s): Paddy Lee Fashions, Inc., Daniel Levy, Paula Levy, Ralph Covelli, Sr.
Financial data (yr. ended 12/31/01): Grants paid, $54,770; assets, $91,341 (M); gifts received, $126,935; expenditures, $110,744; qualifying distributions, $109,421.
Limitations: Applications not accepted. Giving primarily in Greenvale and New York, NY.
Application information: Contributes only to pre-selected organizations.
Directors: John Covelli, Ralph Covelli, Sr., Ralph Covelli, Jr.
EIN: 113475576
Codes: CS, CD

36464
The Rothschild Inc. Foundation
1251 Ave. of the Americas
New York, NY 10020

Established around 1969.
Donor(s): Rothschild, Inc.
Financial data (yr. ended 12/31/01): Grants paid, $54,757; assets, $46 (M); gifts received, $54,757; expenditures, $54,837; qualifying distributions, $54,837.
Limitations: Applications not accepted. Giving primarily in New York, NY.
Application information: Contributes only to pre-selected organizations.
Officer: Charles Levine, Chair.
EIN: 132618415
Codes: CS, CD

36465
TYF Foundation
c/o Brand Sonnenschine & Co.
377 Broadway, 9th Fl.
New York, NY 10013

Established in 1994 in NY.
Donor(s): Raphael Yenowitz, Hyde Park Nursing Home, Inc.
Financial data (yr. ended 12/31/01): Grants paid, $54,675; assets, $1,280,920 (M); gifts received, $80,000; expenditures, $57,143; qualifying distributions, $54,675.
Limitations: Applications not accepted. Giving primarily in Spring Valley, NY.
Application information: Contributes only to pre-selected organizations.
Trustees: Raphael Yenowitz, Yaakov Simcha Yenowitz.
EIN: 133798939

36466
Jack and Jane Rivkin Foundation
P.O. Box 2249
Amagansett, NY 11930
Contact: Jane Rivkin

Established in 1999 in NY.
Donor(s): Jack Rivkin, Jane Rivkin.
Financial data (yr. ended 12/31/00): Grants paid, $54,649; assets, $1,278,312 (M); gifts received, $163,798; expenditures, $127,006; qualifying distributions, $54,649.
Application information: Application form not required.
Trustees: Dawn Bushell, Arnold Gitomer, Michael Rink, Jack Rivkin, Jane Rivkin, Susan Rivkin.
EIN: 113518069

36467
E. Brink Scholarship Trust Fund
c/o HSBC Bank, USA
1 HSBC Ctr., 16th Fl.
Buffalo, NY 14203-2885

Financial data (yr. ended 12/31/01): Grants paid, $54,600; assets, $984,441 (M); expenditures, $69,167; qualifying distributions, $55,855.
Limitations: Applications not accepted. Giving limited to students in the Union-Endicott Central School District, NY.
Application information: Unsolicited requests for funds not accepted.
Trustee: HSBC Bank USA.
EIN: 166076060
Codes: GTI

36468
Rudolph and Hilda U. Forchheimer Foundation, Inc.
1 Oakstwain Rd.
Scarsdale, NY 10583-2019

Donor(s): Rudolph Forchheimer.
Financial data (yr. ended 12/31/01): Grants paid, $54,571; assets, $712,283 (M); expenditures, $56,875; qualifying distributions, $54,841.
Limitations: Applications not accepted.
Application information: Contributes only to pre-selected organizations.
Officers and Directors:* Rudolph Forchheimer,* Pres. and Treas.; Hilda U. Forchheimer,* V.P. and Secy.; Constance F. Heller, Audrey F. Stever.
EIN: 136222282

36469
Helen R. Brady Memorial Fund
(Formerly Charles F. Brady Memorial Fund)
c/o HSBC Bank USA
1 HSBC Ctr., 16th Fl.
Buffalo, NY 14203-2885

Established in 1988 in NY.
Financial data (yr. ended 12/31/01): Grants paid, $54,500; assets, $706,678 (M); expenditures, $65,444; qualifying distributions, $55,327.
Limitations: Applications not accepted. Giving limited to Onondaga County, NY.
Application information: Contributes only to pre-selected organizations.
Trustee: HSBC Bank USA.
EIN: 156022438

36470
E.D. Foundation
P.O. Box 628
Woodmere, NY 11598
Application address: 414 Devon St., Kearney, NJ 07032
Contact: Carol Puchyr

Established in 1968 in NY.
Donor(s): Enrico Donati.
Financial data (yr. ended 12/31/01): Grants paid, $54,500; assets, $1,332,725 (M); expenditures, $69,645; qualifying distributions, $54,500.
Limitations: Giving on a national basis.
Application information: Application form required.
Trustees: Adele Donati, Enrico Donati, David Oxman.
EIN: 136319615
Codes: GTI

36471
Foulke Foundation Trust
10 Linden Ave.
Larchmont, NY 10538 (914) 834-0905
Contact: Mrs. Roy A. Foulke, Jr., Tr.

Established in 1994 in NY.
Donor(s): Roy A. Foulke, Jr.‡
Financial data (yr. ended 12/31/01): Grants paid, $54,500; assets, $1,420,280 (M); expenditures, $73,527; qualifying distributions, $54,500.
Limitations: Giving on a national basis.
Trustee: Maureen Foulke.
EIN: 137033827

36472
Chansoo & Elisabeth Bittner Joung Foundation
c/o Goldman Sachs & Co.
85 Broad St.
New York, NY 10004

Established in 1999 in CT.
Financial data (yr. ended 12/31/01): Grants paid, $54,500; assets, $394,977 (M); gifts received, $1,500; expenditures, $69,875; qualifying distributions, $56,540.
Limitations: Applications not accepted. Giving primarily in CT.
Application information: Contributes only to pre-selected organizations.
Trustees: Chansoo Joung, Elisabeth Bittner Joung.
EIN: 134091397

36473
Sol W. and Hermina Cantor Foundation
465 Park Ave.
New York, NY 10022-1902

Established in 1962.
Donor(s): Sol W. Cantor.
Financial data (yr. ended 12/31/00): Grants paid, $54,490; assets, $305,596 (M); gifts received, $50,250; expenditures, $55,760; qualifying distributions, $54,490.
Limitations: Applications not accepted. Giving primarily in FL and New York, NY.
Application information: Contributes only to pre-selected organizations.
Officers: Sol W. Cantor, Pres.; Ellen Cantor, V.P.
EIN: 136104263

36474
The Cogitare Foundation
(Formerly The Leonard & Charlotte Cooper Foundation)
304 W. 78th St., Apt. 2
New York, NY 10024
E-mail: ES93@yahoo.com
Contact: Elaine Scialo, Pres.

Established in 1998 in DE.
Donor(s): Peter D. Cooper.
Financial data (yr. ended 03/31/01): Grants paid, $54,447; assets, $1,233,871 (M); gifts received, $40; expenditures, $59,060; qualifying distributions, $54,447.
Limitations: Giving primarily in NY.
Officers and Directors:* Elaine Scialo,* Pres.; Peter D. Cooper,* V.P. and Secy.; Randall Cooper, Sloan Cooper.
EIN: 133998983

36475
The Watt Family Foundation
c/o Lazard Freres & Co., LLC
30 Rockefeller Plz.
New York, NY 10020
Contact: William D. Watt, Pres.

Established in 1986 in NY.
Donor(s): William D. Watt.
Financial data (yr. ended 09/30/01): Grants paid, $54,425; assets, $158,283 (M); gifts received, $14,261; expenditures, $55,105; qualifying distributions, $54,489.
Limitations: Giving primarily in CT and New York, NY.
Officers and Directors:* William D. Watt,* Pres.; Andrew B. Watt,* V.P.; Karen B. Watt,* V.P.; Howard Sontag,* Secy.-Treas.
EIN: 133373456

36476
Olga Havel Foundation, Inc.
c/o Constantin Associates
575 Madison Ave., 25th Fl.
New York, NY 10022

Established in 1995 in NY.
Financial data (yr. ended 06/30/01): Grants paid, $54,405; assets, $1,303,750 (M); expenditures, $216,514; qualifying distributions, $54,405.
Limitations: Giving primarily in Prague, Czech Republic.
Officer: Alain Coblence, Pres.
Director: Diana Phipps.
EIN: 133584362

36477
The Pollio Family Foundation, Inc.
c/o John H. Lavelle
450 New Karner Rd., Ste. 200
Albany, NY 12205

Established in 1992 in NY.
Donor(s): Joseph L. Pollio, Sr.
Financial data (yr. ended 12/31/01): Grants paid, $54,400; assets, $1,194,616 (M); gifts received, $2,600; expenditures, $57,699; qualifying distributions, $54,400.
Limitations: Applications not accepted. Giving primarily in New York, NY, and Grafton, VT.

Application information: Contributes only to pre-selected organizations.
Officer: Joseph L. Pollio, Sr., Chair.
Directors: Joseph L. Pollio, Jr., Ruth Pollio.
EIN: 030334275

36478
Schonberger Family Foundation
166 Hillair Cir.
White Plains, NY 10605

Established around 1987 in NY.
Donor(s): Elias Schonberger.
Financial data (yr. ended 10/31/01): Grants paid, $54,352; assets, $1,312,632 (M); gifts received, $190,601; expenditures, $68,601; qualifying distributions, $54,602.
Limitations: Applications not accepted. Giving primarily in NY.
Application information: Contributes only to pre-selected organizations.
Officers: Elias Schonberger, Pres. and Treas.; David Schonberger, V.P.; Mark Schonberger, V.P.
EIN: 133314123

36479
The Silberstein Family Foundation, Inc.
784 Park Ave., Ste. 19C
New York, NY 10021

Established in 1995 in NY.
Financial data (yr. ended 04/30/02): Grants paid, $54,231; assets, $1,118,819 (M); expenditures, $80,755; qualifying distributions, $54,231.
Limitations: Applications not accepted. Giving limited to NY.
Application information: Contributes only to pre-selected organizations.
Directors: Corey Shdaimah, Alan M. Silberstein, Andrew Silberstein, Susan K. Silberstein.
EIN: 133836426

36480
The Philip J. Hahn Foundation
200 E. 62nd St.
New York, NY 10021-8209
Contact: Philip J. Hahn, Mgr.

Established in 1997 in NY.
Donor(s): Philip J. Hahn.
Financial data (yr. ended 12/31/01): Grants paid, $54,150; assets, $318,454 (M); gifts received, $30,000; expenditures, $54,643; qualifying distributions, $54,150.
Officer: Philip J. Hahn, Mgr.
EIN: 133945802

36481
The Feuerring Foundation
c/o Denise Weiner
138 Havilands Ln.
White Plains, NY 10605

Donor(s): Gertrude Feuerring.‡
Financial data (yr. ended 12/31/01): Grants paid, $54,102; assets, $1,231,928 (M); gifts received, $510,000; expenditures, $68,844; qualifying distributions, $54,102.
Limitations: Applications not accepted. Giving primarily in New York, NY.
Application information: Contributes only to pre-selected organizations.
Directors: Ralph Feuerring, Eric Sondheimer, Denise Weiner.
EIN: 136221072

36482
The Sidney and Betty Shames Foundation, Inc.
c/o Sidney Shames
57 Holly Pl.
Briarcliff Manor, NY 10510

Established in 1993 in NJ.
Donor(s): Sidney J. Shames.
Financial data (yr. ended 12/31/00): Grants paid, $54,050; assets, $765,002 (M); expenditures, $63,238; qualifying distributions, $54,050.
Limitations: Applications not accepted. Giving primarily in New York, NY.
Application information: Contributes only to pre-selected organizations.
Officers and Trustees:* Sidney J. Shames,* Pres. and Treas.; Beatrice Shames,* Secy.; Leila S. Shames.
EIN: 223255723

36483
The Morris & Beatrice Eigen Foundation
(Formerly The Judith Ann Foundation)
c/o Nathan Berkman & Co.
29 Broadway, Rm. 2900
New York, NY 10006

Established in 1990 in NY.
Donor(s): Judith Eigen, Morris Eigen.‡
Financial data (yr. ended 09/30/01): Grants paid, $54,015; assets, $84,710 (M); expenditures, $60,391; qualifying distributions, $54,015.
Limitations: Applications not accepted. Giving primarily in New York, NY.
Application information: Contributes only to pre-selected organizations.
Trustees: Judith Eigen, Morris Eigen, Morris Sarna, Shirley Sarna.
EIN: 133587600

36484
Grove Foundation, Inc.
125 Jericho Turnpike, Ste. 200
Jericho, NY 11753

Established in 1959.
Financial data (yr. ended 10/31/01): Grants paid, $54,000; assets, $756,985 (M); gifts received, $250; expenditures, $54,925; qualifying distributions, $54,000.
Limitations: Applications not accepted. Giving primarily in CT.
Application information: Contributes only to pre-selected organizations.
Officers: Jack Sanford Davis, Pres.; Vivian Davis, V.P.; Helen Davis, Treas.
EIN: 136160952

36485
Hoyt Foundation
c/o Marshall M. Green
1345 6th Ave., 42nd Fl.
New York, NY 10105

Established in 1998 in NY.
Financial data (yr. ended 12/31/01): Grants paid, $54,000; assets, $815,489 (M); expenditures, $54,854; qualifying distributions, $54,000.
Limitations: Applications not accepted. Giving primarily in NY.
Application information: Contributes only to pre-selected organizations.
Trustees: Marshall M. Green, Henry H. Hoyt, Jr.
EIN: 137125483

36486
Rose & Louis Klosk Fund
c/o JPMorgan Chase Bank
P.O. Box 31412
Rochester, NY 14603-1412
Contact: M. Peterson

Donor(s): Rose Klosk.‡
Financial data (yr. ended 12/31/01): Grants paid, $54,000; assets, $1,161,194 (M); expenditures, $71,260; qualifying distributions, $54,961.
Limitations: Applications not accepted.
Application information: Contributes only to pre-selected organizations. Unsolicited requests for funds not accepted.
Trustees: Michael Klosk, JPMorgan Chase Bank.
EIN: 136334348

36487
Holtz Family Foundation
855 Merrick Ave.
Westbury, NY 11590-6604 (516) 222-0335

Established in 1990 in NY.
Donor(s): Irving Holtz.
Financial data (yr. ended 12/31/01): Grants paid, $53,950; assets, $493,258 (M); expenditures, $59,575; qualifying distributions, $53,950.
Limitations: Applications not accepted. Giving limited to NY.
Application information: Contributes only to pre-selected organizations.
Officers and Directors:* Irving Holtz,* Pres.; Jonathan Holtz,* V.P.; Charles Carnival,* Secy.; Manuel Holtz.
EIN: 133617083

36488
David Aronow Foundation, Inc.
12 Wildwood Dr.
Great Neck, NY 11024-1124
Contact: Shirley A. Samis, Pres.

Established about 1948.
Donor(s): David Aronow.‡
Financial data (yr. ended 12/31/01): Grants paid, $53,893; assets, $1,040,552 (M); expenditures, $60,547; qualifying distributions, $53,893.
Limitations: Applications not accepted. Giving primarily in NY.
Application information: Contributes only to pre-selected organizations.
Officers: Shirley A. Samis, Pres.; Peter S. Samis, V.P.; Robert A. Samis, V.P.; Jill A. Woller, Secy.-Treas.
EIN: 136161452

36489
Edwin J. Wadas Foundation, Inc.
c/o Feldman, Domagal and Kupiec
246 Genesse St.
Utica, NY 13502-4385
Application address: 22 Greenman Ave., New York Mills, NY 13417
Contact: Edwin J. Wadas, Pres.

Established in 1990 in NY.
Donor(s): Edwin J. Wadas, A.W. Lawrence & Co., Inc.
Financial data (yr. ended 12/31/00): Grants paid, $53,822; assets, $978,553 (M); expenditures, $59,268; qualifying distributions, $59,268.
Limitations: Giving limited to Clinton, New York Mills, Whitesboro, and Whitestown, NY.
Application information: Application form required.
Officers: Edwin J. Wadas, Pres.; John E. Short, Secy.; Alfred J. Kupiec, Jr., Treas.
EIN: 161361881

36490
David J. Simon Family Charitable Foundation
c/o David J. Simon
230 Park Ave., Ste. 7th Fl.
New York, NY 10169-0935

Established in 2001 in NY.
Donor(s): David Simon.
Financial data (yr. ended 12/31/01): Grants paid, $53,800; assets, $84,816 (M); gifts received, $133,175; expenditures, $58,754; qualifying distributions, $53,800.
Officer: David Simon, Chair.
EIN: 134189190

36491
Lois Lenski Covey Foundation, Inc.
c/o Moses & Singer
1301 Ave. of the Americas
New York, NY 10019-6076 (212) 554-7826
Contact: Arthur F. Abelman, Tr.

Established in NY.
Donor(s): Lois Lenski Covey.‡
Financial data (yr. ended 12/31/01): Grants paid, $53,785; assets, $1,235,079 (M); expenditures, $77,128; qualifying distributions, $53,785.
Application information: Application form required.
Trustees: Arthur F. Abelman, Michael C. Covey, Paul A. Covey, Stephen Covey, Gloria Koltmeyer, Paula Quint.
EIN: 136223036

36492
Zichron Chaya Tzedaka Foundation, Inc.
c/o Beryl Jachimowitz
1725 59th St.
Brooklyn, NY 11204

Established in 1995 in NY.
Donor(s): Fred Mehl,‡ Beryl Jachimowitz, A. Schwartz.
Financial data (yr. ended 12/31/01): Grants paid, $53,706; assets, $36,131 (M); gifts received, $39,369; expenditures, $54,370; qualifying distributions, $53,706.
Limitations: Applications not accepted.
Application information: Contributes only to pre-selected organizations.
Officers: Beryl Jachimowitz, Pres.; Yisroel Chaim Jachimowitz, V.P.; Tzvi Jachimowitz, Secy.
EIN: 116459124

36493
Goldfein Family Foundation, Inc.
(Formerly Phillip & Pauline Goldfein Foundation, Inc.)
60 E. 42nd St., Ste. 2015
New York, NY 10165

Donor(s): Phillip Goldfein, Robert J. Goldfein.
Financial data (yr. ended 12/31/01): Grants paid, $53,694; assets, $812,653 (M); gifts received, $321; expenditures, $53,827; qualifying distributions, $53,694.
Limitations: Applications not accepted.
Application information: Contributes only to pre-selected organizations.
Officers: Phillip Goldfein, Pres.; Doris Cohen, V.P.; Robert J. Goldfein, Secy.
EIN: 237021255

36494
The Oneida Savings Bank Charitable Foundation
182 N. Main St.
P.O. Box 240
Oneida, NY 13421-1676 (315) 363-2000
Contact: Eric Stickels, Secy.-Treas.

Established in 1998.
Donor(s): Oneida Financial Corp.
Financial data (yr. ended 12/31/01): Grants paid, $53,635; assets, $1,583,190 (M); expenditures, $54,687; qualifying distributions, $53,759.
Limitations: Giving in NY, in areas of company operations.
Officers: Michael R. Kallet, Pres.; Eric Stickles, Secy.-Treas.
Directors: Thomas H. Dixon, William Matthews, Ann K. Pierz.
EIN: 161561680
Codes: CS, CD

36495
Zedek Foundation
P.O. Box 2344
New York, NY 10185-2344

Established in 1986.
Financial data (yr. ended 09/30/01): Grants paid, $53,600; assets, $1,156,519 (M); expenditures, $54,618; qualifying distributions, $53,600.
Limitations: Applications not accepted. Giving primarily in New York, NY.
Application information: Contributes only to pre-selected organizations.
Officers: Falel Ostrow, Pres.; Harry Ostrow, Secy.
EIN: 112785199

36496
Barry & Jill Lafer Foundation
1060 5th Ave.
New York, NY 10128

Established in 1986 in NY.
Donor(s): Barry S. Lafer.
Financial data (yr. ended 12/31/01): Grants paid, $53,595; assets, $75,118 (M); gifts received, $121,030; expenditures, $54,975; qualifying distributions, $53,731.
Limitations: Applications not accepted. Giving primarily in New York, NY.
Application information: Contributes only to pre-selected organizations.
Trustee: Barry S. Lafer.
EIN: 133386384

36497
The JED Fund
c/o McGrath, Doyle & Phair
150 Broadway
New York, NY 10038 (212) 571-2300

Established in 1996 in NY.
Donor(s): Edith S.N. Muma.
Financial data (yr. ended 12/31/00): Grants paid, $53,589; assets, $216,514 (M); expenditures, $54,301; qualifying distributions, $53,589.
Limitations: Applications not accepted.
Application information: Contributes only to pre-selected organizations.
Trustees: Nicholas Jacangelo, Dorothy E. Muma, Edith S.N. Muma, Edwin F. Tuccio.
EIN: 133831989

36498
Elliot Family Charitable Trust Fund
760 Forest Ave.
Rye, NY 10580-3220

Financial data (yr. ended 12/31/01): Grants paid, $53,564; assets, $214,132 (M); expenditures, $55,031; qualifying distributions, $53,564.
Director: Paul Elliot.
EIN: 137104670

36499
The Krauss Charitable Foundation
c/o Joseph B. Sprung
545 Madison Ave., Ste. 801
New York, NY 10022-9239
Application address: 43 Loscharros Ln., Portola Valley, CA 94028
Contact: Melvyn Krauss, Pres.

Established in 1994.
Donor(s): Melvyn Krauss.
Financial data (yr. ended 12/31/01): Grants paid, $53,520; assets, $1,467,827 (M); gifts received, $50,000; expenditures, $53,520; qualifying distributions, $53,520.
Limitations: Giving primarily in NY.
Officer: Melvyn Krauss, Pres.
EIN: 113183212

36500
David Alan and Susan Berkman Rahm Foundation
c/o Stroock, Stroock & Lavan
180 Maiden Ln.
New York, NY 10038-4982 (212) 806-5470
Contact: David A. Rahm, Secy.-Treas.

Established in 1997 in NY.
Donor(s): David A. Rahm, Susan B. Rahm.
Financial data (yr. ended 11/30/01): Grants paid, $53,505; assets, $518,747 (M); gifts received, $60,305; expenditures, $58,329; qualifying distributions, $54,460.
Limitations: Giving primarily in NY.
Application information: Application form not required.
Officers: Susan B. Rahm, Pres.; David A. Rahm, Secy.-Treas.
EIN: 133979557

36501
Boquet Foundation, Inc.
c/o Kaplan, Choate & Co.
880 3rd Ave., 3rd Fl.
New York, NY 10022-1902 (212) 319-2700
Contact: Peter S. Paine, Jr., Pres.

Established around 1962.
Donor(s): Peter S. Paine, Peter S. Paine, Jr., Ellen Lea Paine.
Financial data (yr. ended 12/31/00): Grants paid, $53,500; assets, $1,416,076 (M); expenditures, $66,126; qualifying distributions, $53,500.
Limitations: Applications not accepted. Giving primarily in Essex County, NY and the greater New York, NY, area.
Application information: Grants are limited to organizations known to the managers.
Officers and Directors:* Peter S. Paine, Jr.,* Pres.; Lea Paine Highet,* V.P.; Richard E. Carlson, Secy.-Treas.; Peter S. Paine III.
EIN: 136114419

36502
Tannenhauser Family Foundation
c/o Robert Tannenhauser
210 E. 68th St.
New York, NY 10021-6047

Established in 1995 in NY.
Donor(s): Mae Tannenhauser.
Financial data (yr. ended 04/30/02): Grants paid, $53,500; assets, $30,733 (M); gifts received, $35,000; expenditures, $54,654; qualifying distributions, $53,500.
Limitations: Applications not accepted.
Application information: Contributes only to pre-selected organizations.
Officers: Robert Tannenhauser, Pres.; Michael Tannenhauser, Secy.
EIN: 133837480

36503
Unterman Family Foundation
GEM Capital Mgmt., Inc.
70 E. 55th St.
New York, NY 10022

Established in 1998 in NY.
Donor(s): Gerald Unterman, Elaine Unterman.
Financial data (yr. ended 12/31/01): Grants paid, $53,475; assets, $745,444 (M); expenditures, $57,073; qualifying distributions, $53,473.
Limitations: Applications not accepted. Giving primarily in NY.
Application information: Contributes only to pre-selected organizations.
Trustees: Elaine Unterman, Gerald B. Unterman.
EIN: 134009057

36504
The Stoll Family Charitable Trust
185 S. Country Rd.
East Patchogue, NY 11772-5413
Contact: Harry H. Stoll, Tr.

Established in 1998.
Donor(s): Harry H. Stoll.
Financial data (yr. ended 12/31/01): Grants paid, $53,471; assets, $148,477 (M); expenditures, $57,856; qualifying distributions, $53,471.
Trustees: Harry H. Stoll, Helga Stoll, Sanford Stoll.
EIN: 116514196

36505
Diane & Howard Wohl Family Foundation, Inc.
141 Heather Ln.
Mill Neck, NY 11765

Established in 1999 in NY.
Donor(s): Howard Wohl.
Financial data (yr. ended 12/31/01): Grants paid, $53,450; assets, $1,182,258 (M); gifts received, $280,000; expenditures, $63,590; qualifying distributions, $53,450.
Limitations: Applications not accepted.
Application information: Contributes only to pre-selected organizations.
Officers and Directors: Howard Wohl,* Pres.; Diane Wohl,* Secy.-Treas.; Alexander D. Wohl, Allison K. Wohl, Hillary J. Wohl, Pamela B. Wohl.
EIN: 113493603

36506
The Adams-Baldock Foundation
c/o B. Strauss Assoc., Ltd.
307 5th Ave., 8th Fl.
New York, NY 10016-6517

Established in 1998 in CT.
Donor(s): Michael Baldock.
Financial data (yr. ended 10/31/00): Grants paid, $53,350; assets, $63,449 (M); gifts received, $24,813; expenditures, $53,519; qualifying distributions, $53,183.
Limitations: Applications not accepted.
Application information: Contributes only to pre-selected organizations.
Trustee: Michael Baldock.
EIN: 061533126

36507
The Tondowski Family Foundation
1415 47th St.
Brooklyn, NY 11219

Established in 2000 in NY.
Donor(s): Samuel Tondowski.
Financial data (yr. ended 12/31/01): Grants paid, $53,286; assets, $102,632 (M); gifts received, $128,913; expenditures, $53,286; qualifying distributions, $53,286.
Limitations: Applications not accepted.
Application information: Contributes only to pre-selected organizations.
Trustees: Rifka Tondowski, Samuel Tondowski.
EIN: 113575473

36508
PBP Foundation of New York, Inc.
c/o BNY Capital Markets, Inc.
445 Park Ave., 12th Fl.
New York, NY 10022
Contact: Arthur D. Kowaloff, Pres.

Incorporated in 1978 in NY.
Donor(s): Fiona Field Kay.
Financial data (yr. ended 12/31/01): Grants paid, $53,270; assets, $149,920 (M); gifts received, $50,667; expenditures, $76,918; qualifying distributions, $69,697.
Limitations: Giving primarily in New York, NY.
Officers and Directors: Arthur D. Kowaloff,* Pres. and Treas.; Marina Rust,* V.P. and Secy.
EIN: 132939192

36509
Thuna Family Foundation, Inc.
c/o Paul Miller
12-06 149th St.
Whitestone, NY 11357

Established in 2000 in NY.
Financial data (yr. ended 12/31/00): Grants paid, $53,211; assets, $6,018 (M); gifts received, $59,229; expenditures, $53,211; qualifying distributions, $0.
Limitations: Applications not accepted.
Application information: Contributes only to pre-selected organizations.
Officers: Marty Thuna, Pres.; Marcus Thuna, V.P.; Sonia Thuna, V.P.
EIN: 113541209

36510
Joseph G. & Hortense L. Mintzer Trust
c/o Urbach, Kahn & Werlin
250 Park Ave. S.
New York, NY 10003
Application address: 53 Loudonwood E., Loundonville, NY 12211
Contact: Hortense L. Mintzer, Tr.

Established in 1964 in NY.
Financial data (yr. ended 11/30/01): Grants paid, $53,101; assets, $554,679 (M); expenditures, $57,872; qualifying distributions, $53,101.
Limitations: Applications not accepted.
Application information: Contributes only to pre-selected organizations.
Trustees: Hortense L. Mintzer, Joanne Mintzer, Dale M. Raisig, Alice Sandler.
EIN: 146034010

36511
The Palette Foundation
c/o George V. Delson Assoc.
110 E. 59th St.
New York, NY 10022

Established in 1998 in NY.
Donor(s): Rand Skolnick.
Financial data (yr. ended 05/31/02): Grants paid, $53,100; assets, $2,353 (M); expenditures, $53,259; qualifying distributions, $53,100.
Limitations: Applications not accepted. Giving primarily in New York, NY.
Application information: Contributes only to pre-selected organizations.
Trustees: Michael Daboin, Rand Skolnick.
EIN: 137147307

36512
The Viola Foundation
c/o Bernath & Rosenberg, P.C.
1140 6th Ave., Ste. 16
New York, NY 10036

Established in 1997 in NY.
Donor(s): James H. Bernath.
Financial data (yr. ended 12/31/01): Grants paid, $53,072; assets, $21,344 (M); gifts received, $53,500; expenditures, $53,551; qualifying distributions, $53,072.
Limitations: Applications not accepted. Giving on a national basis.
Application information: Contributes only to pre-selected organizations.
Trustees: James H. Bernath, Susi Bernath.
EIN: 133915359

36513
Rodgers & Hammerstein Foundation
1065 Ave. of the Americas, Ste. 2400
New York, NY 10018

Established about 1953 in NY.
Donor(s): Dorothy F. Rodgers,‡ Hammerstein Music & Theater, Inc.
Financial data (yr. ended 12/31/01): Grants paid, $53,000; assets, $11,135 (M); expenditures, $55,446; qualifying distributions, $53,000.
Limitations: Applications not accepted. Giving primarily in New York, NY.
Application information: Contributes only to pre-selected organizations.
Officer: William Hammerstein, Secy.
EIN: 136084412

36514
The Dorothy Strelsin Foundation, Inc.
c/o The Bank of New York, Tax Dept.
1 Wall St., 28th Fl.
New York, NY 10286

Established in 1990 in NY.
Donor(s): Dorothy Strelsin.‡
Financial data (yr. ended 07/31/01): Grants paid, $53,000; assets, $1,201,581 (M); gifts received, $41,118; expenditures, $57,296; qualifying distributions, $53,825.
Limitations: Applications not accepted. Giving primarily in NY.
Application information: Contributes only to pre-selected organizations.
Trustee: Enid Nemy.
EIN: 133561352

36515
Foundation of Westchester Clubmen, Inc.
35 Old Tarrytown Rd.
White Plains, NY 10603 (914) 761-0834
Contact: Oscar M. Graves, Treas.

Financial data (yr. ended 12/31/01): Grants paid, $52,970; assets, $304,683 (M); gifts received, $54,250; expenditures, $64,946; qualifying distributions, $52,970.
Limitations: Giving limited to Westchester County, NY.
Officers: John Mitchel, Pres.; Lou Hyacinthe, Secy.; Oscar M. Graves, Treas.
EIN: 237003466

36516
The Jack Cayre Foundation, Inc.
16 E. 40th St., 12th Fl.
New York, NY 10016
Contact: Jack J. Cayre, Pres.

Established in 1995 in DE.
Donor(s): Jack J. Cayre, The Michael & Shirley Cayre Foundation.

36516—NEW YORK

Financial data (yr. ended 12/31/01): Grants paid, $52,966; assets, $651,793 (M); gifts received, $55,000; expenditures, $53,196; qualifying distributions, $52,966.
Limitations: Giving primarily in NY.
Application information: Application form not required.
Officer: Jack J. Cayre, Pres.
EIN: 133869478

36517
The Renee and Carl Landegger Family Charitable Trust
c/o Yohalem Gillman & Co., LLP
477 Madison Ave., 9th Fl.
New York, NY 10022-5802

Established in 1997 in NY.
Donor(s): Carl C. Landegger, The Black Clawson Co.
Financial data (yr. ended 12/31/01): Grants paid, $52,875; assets, $1,037,854 (M); expenditures, $59,394; qualifying distributions, $52,809.
Limitations: Applications not accepted.
Application information: Contributes only to pre-selected organizations.
Trustees: Carl C. Landegger, Renee Landegger.
EIN: 137126904

36518
Harold and Isabel Feld Foundation
1016 5th Ave., Ste. 10C
New York, NY 10028-0132 (212) 744-7285
Contact: Harold Feld, Tr.

Established in 1985 in NY.
Donor(s): Harold Feld.
Financial data (yr. ended 12/31/01): Grants paid, $52,820; assets, $747,498 (M); expenditures, $54,417; qualifying distributions, $52,820.
Limitations: Giving primarily in New York, NY.
Application information: Application form not required.
Trustee: Harold Feld.
EIN: 133286304

36519
Howard Memorial Fund
120 Wall St., 8th Fl.
New York, NY 10005 (212) 558-5420
Contact: DeLoris V. Greene, Chair.

Established in 1948 in NY.
Financial data (yr. ended 06/30/01): Grants paid, $52,800; assets, $1,055,974 (M); gifts received, $200; expenditures, $55,534; qualifying distributions, $55,037.
Limitations: Giving limited to residents of the five boroughs of New York City, and Nassau and Suffolk counties, NY.
Application information: Application form required.
Officers: W. Gerald Davenport, Pres.; James Wood, V.P.; Elizabeth LeC. Stubbs, Secy.-Treas.
Scholarship Committee: DeLoris W. Greene, Chair.; Selma Clark, John M. Friedman, Jr., Anne James, Arnold P. Keith, Jr., Donna Long, Mildred L. Love, Elizabeth Schouenborg, Charles J. Tanenbaum.
Members: Milton L. Little, Jr., Gayle F. Robinson, Janyce Q. Vaugh.
EIN: 136161770
Codes: GTI

36520
Hoskins Foundation
(Formerly Hoskins Family Foundation)
1 M&T Plz., Ste. 2000
Buffalo, NY 14203-2391 (716) 848-1406
E-mail: dbennett@hodgsonruss.com

Established in 1995 in NY.
Donor(s): John Hoskins, Susan Hoskins, Curtis Screw Co., Inc.
Financial data (yr. ended 12/31/01): Grants paid, $52,761; assets, $257,560 (M); expenditures, $55,344; qualifying distributions, $52,761.
Limitations: Applications not accepted. Giving primarily in Buffalo, NY.
Application information: Contributes only to pre-selected organizations.
Trustees: Dianne Bennett, Barbara Billings, Bruce J. Glor, Beth Lynne Hoskins, John T. Hoskins, John T. Hoskins, Jr., Susan Hoskins.
EIN: 161490629

36521
The Jerrold R. & Shirley Golding Foundation, Inc.
60 Cuttermill Rd., Ste. 212
Great Neck, NY 11021 (516) 487-0440

Established in 1969 in NY.
Donor(s): Montvale Imperial, Inc.
Financial data (yr. ended 12/31/99): Grants paid, $52,704; assets, $503,697 (M); expenditures, $53,279; qualifying distributions, $53,105.
Limitations: Applications not accepted. Giving primarily in FL.
Application information: Contributes only to pre-selected organizations.
Officers: Harriet Golding, Pres. and Treas.; Rachael Martin, V.P.; Sheryl Klein, Secy.
EIN: 237046427

36522
Moskowitz Foundation
c/o Lou Moskowitz
10 Fox Meadow Ct.
Woodbury, NY 11797-1505

Financial data (yr. ended 12/31/01): Grants paid, $52,585; assets, $721,665 (M); expenditures, $62,234; qualifying distributions, $52,585.
Limitations: Applications not accepted. Giving primarily in NJ and NY.
Application information: Contributes only to pre-selected organizations.
Officers: Lou Moskowitz, Pres. and Treas.; Al Rowitz, Secy.
EIN: 116013731

36523
Valani Foundation, Inc.
18 E. 48th St., Ste. 801
New York, NY 10017

Donor(s): Rajnikant Shah, Kumar Pal Shah.
Financial data (yr. ended 12/31/01): Grants paid, $52,576; assets, $6,024 (M); gifts received, $51,000; expenditures, $52,576; qualifying distributions, $52,576.
Limitations: Applications not accepted. Giving primarily in Elmhurst, NY.
Application information: Contributes only to pre-selected organizations.
Officers: Rajnikant Shah, Pres.; Kumar Pal Shah, V.P.; Shekhar Shah, Secy.; Niranjana Shah, Treas.
Director: Mridula Shah.
EIN: 134071416

36524
Andrew B. Kim/Wan Kyun Rha Kim Family Foundation, Inc.
22 E. 94th St.
New York, NY 10028

Established in 1993 in NY.
Donor(s): Andrew B. Kim.
Financial data (yr. ended 12/31/01): Grants paid, $52,565; assets, $223,558 (M); gifts received, $112,590; expenditures, $54,456; qualifying distributions, $52,565.
Limitations: Applications not accepted.
Application information: Contributes only to pre-selected organizations.
Officers: Andrew B. Kim, Chair. and Treas.; Wan Kyun R. Kim, Pres. and Secy.; Gene Y. Kim, V.P.; Ty Y. Kim, V.P.
EIN: 133732636

36525
John & Barbara Samuelson Foundation, Inc.
c/o Prager & Fenton
675 3rd Ave.
New York, NY 10017

Established in 1999 in NY.
Donor(s): John Samuelson, Barbara Samuelson.
Financial data (yr. ended 12/31/01): Grants paid, $52,550; assets, $224,377 (M); gifts received, $11,686; expenditures, $56,348; qualifying distributions, $52,550.
Limitations: Applications not accepted.
Application information: Contributes only to pre-selected organizations.
Officers and Directors:* Barbara Samuelson,* Pres.; John Samuelson,* V.P.; Charles A. Samuelson,* Secy.; Richard A. Samuelson,* Treas.
EIN: 134045935

36526
The Marsha and David Veit Charitable Foundation, Inc.
43 Cowdin Ln.
Chappaqua, NY 10514

Established in 1998 in NY.
Donor(s): David M. Veit.
Financial data (yr. ended 12/31/01): Grants paid, $52,545; assets, $310,567 (M); expenditures, $55,610; qualifying distributions, $52,545.
Limitations: Applications not accepted.
Application information: Contributes only to pre-selected organizations.
Officers and Directors:* David M. Veit,* Pres.; Marsha Veit,* Secy.-Treas.
EIN: 134007110

36527
The Adikes Family Foundation
c/o Brosnan & Hegler, LLP
1415 Kellum Pl., No. 203
Garden City, NY 11530
Application address: 7 Horse Hill Rd., Brookville, NY 11417
Contact: Park T. Adikes, Tr.

Established in 2001 in NY.
Donor(s): Park T. Adikes, Maryedith Adikes.
Financial data (yr. ended 12/31/01): Grants paid, $52,500; assets, $2,043,211 (M); gifts received, $2,053,337; expenditures, $62,533; qualifying distributions, $56,877.
Limitations: Giving primarily in NY.
Officer: Patricia Adikes-Hill, Exec. Dir.
Trustees: Maryedith Adikes, Park T. Adikes.
EIN: 116560827

36528
Goldenberg Foundation
c/o Harold Goldenberg
2600 Nostrand Ave.
Brooklyn, NY 11210-4642

Established in 1993 in NY.
Donor(s): Harold Goldenberg.
Financial data (yr. ended 09/30/01): Grants paid, $52,500; assets, $442,830 (M); expenditures, $54,960; qualifying distributions, $52,500.
Limitations: Applications not accepted. Giving primarily in Brooklyn, NY.
Application information: Contributes only to pre-selected organizations.
Directors: Esther Baker, Harold Goldenberg, Macky Goldenberg, Samuel Raab.
EIN: 113182539

36529
The Eisenreich Family Foundation
c/o Mr. Avery Eisenreich
3269 Bedford Ave.
Brooklyn, NY 11210

Established in 1997 in NY.
Donor(s): Commercial Security Mortgage Credit, Inc., Avery Eisenreich.
Financial data (yr. ended 12/31/00): Grants paid, $52,483; assets, $497,531 (M); gifts received, $50,000; expenditures, $196,727; qualifying distributions, $52,483.
Limitations: Applications not accepted.
Application information: Contributes only to pre-selected organizations.
Trustees: Avery Eisenreich, Toby Eisenreich.
EIN: 137118478

36530
Gottlieb Family Charitable Foundation
44 Arrowhead Ln.
Lawrence, NY 11559

Established in 1999 in NY.
Financial data (yr. ended 02/28/01): Grants paid, $52,480; assets, $633,988 (M); gifts received, $658,046; expenditures, $52,600; qualifying distributions, $52,480.
Officers and Trustees:* Eli Gottlieb,* Pres.; Linda Gottlieb,* Treas.
EIN: 134035645

36531
Temper of the Times Charitable Foundation, Inc.
555 Theodore Fremd Ave., Ste. B-103
Rye, NY 10580-1456
Application address: 20710 S.W. 87th Ave., Vashon, WA 98070; Rye, NY tel.: (914) 925-0022, ext. 210; Vashon, WA tel.: (206) 463-7855; FAX: (206) 463-7856
Contact: Vita Nelson, Pres.

Established in 1997 in NY.
Financial data (yr. ended 12/31/00): Grants paid, $52,400; assets, $958,956 (M); gifts received, $18,180; expenditures, $70,690; qualifying distributions, $60,265.
Application information: Application form required.
Officers and Directors:* Vita Nelson,* Pres.; Lester Nelson,* Secy.; Cora Nelson, Exec. Dir.; Lucy Banker, Lee R. Nelson.
EIN: 133900955

36532
Marion Rose Foundation, Inc.
c/o Landau & Co., C.P.A.
85 E. Hoffman Ave.
Lindenhurst, NY 11757

Established in 1961 in NY.
Donor(s): Ethel R. Wells.
Financial data (yr. ended 04/30/02): Grants paid, $52,346; assets, $717,270 (M); expenditures, $52,585; qualifying distributions, $52,346.
Limitations: Applications not accepted.
Application information: Contributes only to pre-selected organizations.
Trustee: Ethel R. Wells.
EIN: 116037046

36533
Eissa A. Bateh & Brothers Foundation, Inc.
255 47th St.
Brooklyn, NY 11220
Contact: Albert J. Bateh, Pres.

Financial data (yr. ended 12/31/01): Grants paid, $52,300; assets, $961,460 (M); expenditures, $53,246; qualifying distributions, $52,300.
Limitations: Giving primarily in NY.
Officers: Albert J. Bateh, Pres.; Janan J. Bateh, V.P.; James A. Bateh, Secy.; Essa M. Bateh, Treas.
EIN: 136081893

36534
Seymour and Barbara J. Leslie Foundation
810 Channel Rd.
Woodmere, NY 11598-1828

Established in 1969.
Donor(s): Seymour Leslie.
Financial data (yr. ended 12/31/01): Grants paid, $52,298; assets, $750,901 (M); expenditures, $53,428; qualifying distributions, $52,018.
Limitations: Giving primarily in NY.
Officers: Barbara Leslie, Mgr.; Seymour Leslie, Mgr.
EIN: 237010481

36535
K.E.D.S. Foundation, Inc.
c/o U.S. Trust
114 W. 47th St.
New York, NY 10036

Donor(s): David S. Van Pelt.
Financial data (yr. ended 12/31/01): Grants paid, $52,250; assets, $924,329 (M); expenditures, $64,120; qualifying distributions, $52,250.
Publications: Application guidelines.
Application information: Unsolicited requests for funds not accepted at this time.
Directors: David S. Van Pelt, Elizabeth A. Van Pelt, Kathryn S. Van Pelt, Spencer Van Pelt.
EIN: 134011246

36536
The Kazickas Family Foundation, Inc.
120 E. 38th St.
New York, NY 10016

Established in 1998 in NY.
Donor(s): Victor Gruodis, John Kazickas, Joseph M. Kazickas, Joseph P. Kazickas, Michael Kazickas.
Financial data (yr. ended 12/31/00): Grants paid, $52,250; assets, $2,079,884 (M); gifts received, $550,190; expenditures, $57,487; qualifying distributions, $55,552.
Limitations: Applications not accepted. Giving primarily in New York, NY.
Application information: Contributes only to pre-selected organizations.
Officers and Directors:* Jurate Kazickas,* Pres.; John Kazickas,* Secy.-Treas.; Alexandra Kazickas, Joseph Kazickas, Lucy Muhlfeld.
EIN: 134011883

36537
Monomoy Fund, Inc.
c/o A.B. Greene & Co.
101 Park Ave.
New York, NY 10178

Established in 1994 in MI.
Donor(s): Dorette L. Fleishmann.
Financial data (yr. ended 12/31/00): Grants paid, $52,250; assets, $842,554 (M); expenditures, $62,875; qualifying distributions, $52,250.
Limitations: Applications not accepted.
Application information: Contributes only to pre-selected organizations.
Officers: Dorette L. Fleischmann, Pres.; Robert B. Deans, Jr., Treas.
EIN: 383190289

36538
The Lawrence & Anne Frisman Foundation
c/o Spear, Leeds & Kellogg
120 Broadway
New York, NY 10271
Contact: Isaac Jarmark

Established in 1985 in NY.
Donor(s): Lawrence Frisman.
Financial data (yr. ended 11/30/99): Grants paid, $52,215; assets, $1,600,272 (M); expenditures, $98,911; qualifying distributions, $70,755.
Limitations: Applications not accepted.
Application information: Contributes only to pre-selected organizations.
Officers: Lawrence Frisman, Pres. and Treas.; Carl Hewitt, Secy.
EIN: 133339955

36539
Joseph Gluck Foundation
60 E. 42nd St., Ste. 2232
New York, NY 10165 (212) 949-1830
FAX: (212) 986-7408
Contact: Sanford O. Gluck, Tr.

Established in 1945 in NY.
Financial data (yr. ended 12/31/01): Grants paid, $52,149; assets, $1,244,773 (M); gifts received, $10,000; expenditures, $54,681; qualifying distributions, $52,149.
Limitations: Applications not accepted. Giving primarily in New York, NY.
Publications: Annual report.
Application information: Contributes only to pre-selected organizations.
Trustee: Sanford O. Gluck.
EIN: 136154141

36540
The Baptist Women of Metro NY, Inc.
1A Glenwood Ave.
Lynbrook, NY 11563

Established in 1999 in NY.
Financial data (yr. ended 01/31/01): Grants paid, $52,111; assets, $1,101,689 (M); expenditures, $72,234; qualifying distributions, $53,890.
Limitations: Applications not accepted.
Application information: Contributes only to pre-selected organizations.
Officers: Joy A. Zregler, Pres.; Kathleen Van Essendelft, V.P.; Ruth Pleines, Secy.; Barbara E. Fiegas, Treas.
Directors: Ruth Arnao, Menlyn Blake, Cynthia Lord, Jacky Moraglu, Dona Pastore, Rose Wolk, Lorraine Wright.
EIN: 131656650

36541
The Morris & Jules Levine Family Foundation
c/o Mark Peltz, Miller, Ellin & Co., LLP
750 Lexington Ave.
New York, NY 10022

Established in 1999 in NY.
Donor(s): Jules B. Levine.
Financial data (yr. ended 11/30/01): Grants paid, $52,100; assets, $886,750 (M); gifts received, $200,000; expenditures, $55,440; qualifying distributions, $52,100.
Limitations: Applications not accepted. Giving primarily in NY.
Application information: Contributes only to pre-selected organizations.
Officer: Jules B. Levine, Mgr.
Trustees: Krishan L. Malik, Stanley Schlesinger.
EIN: 134089821

36542
Louis Weinberg Foundation, Inc.
c/o HSBC Bank USA
P.O. Box 4203, 17th Fl.
Buffalo, NY 14240

Established in 1964 in NY.
Financial data (yr. ended 12/31/01): Grants paid, $52,100; assets, $1,022,572 (M); gifts received, $11,370; expenditures, $64,717; qualifying distributions, $52,100.
Limitations: Applications not accepted. Giving primarily in NY.
Application information: Contributes only to pre-selected organizations.
Officer and Trustees:* Rita B. Cohen,* Pres.; Lambert L. Ginsberg,* Secy.-Treas.; Hymen Cohen, Harry Dolgin, Michael E. Ginsberg, Myril Green, John J. Quinlan, HSBC Bank USA.
EIN: 146030952

36543
The Millie Chessin Memorial Foundation for Torah Education, Inc.
16 Howard Dr.
Spring Valley, NY 10977
Contact: Mayer Schiller, Dir.

Established in 1999 in NY.
Donor(s): Kenneth Greif, Zachary Prensky.
Financial data (yr. ended 12/31/01): Grants paid, $52,083; assets, $966,459 (M); gifts received, $1,000; expenditures, $75,501; qualifying distributions, $52,083.
Directors: Riva Prensky, Zachary Prensky, Mayer Schiller.
EIN: 134111588

36544
CDL Foundation, Inc.
7 Rolling Hill Ln.
Lawrence, NY 11559

Established in 1997 in NY.
Donor(s): Steven Krausman, Lisa Krausman.
Financial data (yr. ended 12/31/00): Grants paid, $52,011; assets, $192,060 (M); gifts received, $32,551; expenditures, $62,274; qualifying distributions, $52,011.
Limitations: Applications not accepted. Giving primarily in NY.
Application information: Contributes only to pre-selected organizations.
Directors: Lisa Krausman, Steven Krausman, Jonathan Scheiner.
EIN: 061492452

36545
Elias A. Cohen Foundation, Inc.
c/o Richard Lawrence
39 Broadway, Ste. 1701
New York, NY 10006 (212) 483-1200
Contact: Richard Lawrence, Treas.

Incorporated in 1951 in NY.
Donor(s): Elias A. Cohen,‡ David Schlang, Joseph Schlang, Maurice H. Schlang, Cohen Family Fund, Mildred Cohn.‡
Financial data (yr. ended 12/31/00): Grants paid, $52,000; assets, $1,637,060 (M); expenditures, $54,645; qualifying distributions, $51,245.
Limitations: Giving primarily in NY.
Application information: Application form not required.
Officers: Marc Cohen, Pres.; Seymour Cohen, V.P.; Robin Diamont, V.P.; Maurice Schlang, V.P.; Craig Snow, Recording Secy.; Richard Lawrence, Treas.
EIN: 136113003

36546
Foundation for Fairer Capitalism
c/o Ted L. Greenberg
225 W. 80th St., Apt. 10D
New York, NY 10024

Established in 1989 in DE and NY.
Donor(s): Ted L. Greenberg.
Financial data (yr. ended 06/30/02): Grants paid, $52,000; assets, $760,711 (M); expenditures, $55,502; qualifying distributions, $52,000.
Limitations: Applications not accepted. Giving primarily in New York, NY.
Application information: Contributes only to pre-selected organizations.
Officers: Ted L. Greenberg, Pres.; Jed Alpert, Secy.
EIN: 133544872

36547
The Loughlin Foundation, Inc.
c/o Bessemer Trust Co., N.A.
630 5th Ave.
New York, NY 10111

Established in 1998 in NJ.
Financial data (yr. ended 12/31/01): Grants paid, $52,000; assets, $209,679 (M); gifts received, $140,700; expenditures, $55,491; qualifying distributions, $53,011.
Limitations: Applications not accepted. Giving on a national basis.
Application information: Contributes only to pre-selected organizations.
Officers: William D. Loughlin, Pres.; Mark T. Loughlin, Secy.; John P. Loughlin, Treas.
Trustees: James M. Loughlin, Thomas G. Loughlin.
EIN: 223547366

36548
U & E Foundation
471 Bedford Ave.
Brooklyn, NY 11211
Contact: Usher Steinmetz, Tr.

Established in 1998 in NY.
Donor(s): Usher Steinmetz.
Financial data (yr. ended 11/30/01): Grants paid, $52,000; assets, $191,445 (M); gifts received, $101,281; expenditures, $52,211; qualifying distributions, $52,000.
Trustees: Esther Steinmetz, Usher Steinmetz.
EIN: 113465275

36549
Y. E. Beyda Trust
1133 Broadway, Rm. 210
New York, NY 10010

Established in 1993 in NY.
Donor(s): Kinetic Mktg., Inc.
Financial data (yr. ended 12/31/00): Grants paid, $51,873; assets, $98,449 (M); gifts received, $10,000; expenditures, $52,998; qualifying distributions, $51,873.
Limitations: Applications not accepted.
Application information: Contributes only to pre-selected organizations.
Trustees: Charles Beyda, Yachova E. Beyda.
EIN: 137031366

36550
Friedrich H. Oettel Foundation
200 Theater Pl.
Buffalo, NY 14202

Donor(s): Friedrich H. Oettel.
Financial data (yr. ended 12/31/01): Grants paid, $51,800; assets, $60,841 (M); gifts received, $52,000; expenditures, $51,857; qualifying distributions, $51,800.
Limitations: Applications not accepted. Giving primarily in Buffalo, NY.
Application information: Contributes only to pre-selected organizations.
Trustees: Thomas R. Beecher, Eugene D. Mahaney.
EIN: 222492066

36551
John V. Romeo Foundation, Inc.
c/o Fiberwave Technologies, Inc.
125 2nd St.
Brooklyn, NY 11231

Established in 1998 in NY.
Donor(s): John Romeo.
Financial data (yr. ended 12/31/01): Grants paid, $51,800; assets, $109,136 (M); expenditures, $55,728; qualifying distributions, $51,722.
Limitations: Applications not accepted.
Application information: Contributes only to pre-selected organizations.
Officer and Director:* John Romeo,* Pres.
EIN: 134036633

36552
Sydney & Helen Jacoff Foundation, Inc.
c/o Berlack, Israels & Liberman
120 W. 45th St.
New York, NY 10036

Established in 1990 in NY.
Donor(s): Sydney Jacoff, Helen Jacoff.
Financial data (yr. ended 12/31/01): Grants paid, $51,744; assets, $1,312,376 (M); gifts received, $48,113; expenditures, $56,508; qualifying distributions, $51,744.
Limitations: Applications not accepted. Giving primarily in NY.
Application information: Contributes only to pre-selected organizations.
Officers: Sydney Jacoff, Pres.; Daniel Jacoff, V.P. and Secy.; Michael Jacoff, V.P. and Treas.
EIN: 133570162

36553
The Hess-Levy Family Foundation
c/o Sullivan & Cromwell
125 Broad St.
New York, NY 10004-2498

Established in 1993 in NY.
Donor(s): Betty L. Hess.
Financial data (yr. ended 11/30/01): Grants paid, $51,648; assets, $1,085,010 (M); gifts received,

$47,777; expenditures, $52,978; qualifying distributions, $51,648.
Limitations: Applications not accepted. Giving primarily in NY.
Application information: Contributes only to pre-selected organizations.
Directors: Betty L. Hess, Rodger Hess, Nadine Levy, Peter A. Levy.
EIN: 133763129

36554
Lawrence H. Schur Foundation, Inc.
2432 Grand Concourse
Bronx, NY 10458 (718) 733-6300
Contact: Lawrence H. Schur, Pres.

Established in 1969.
Donor(s): Lawrence H. Schur.
Financial data (yr. ended 12/31/01): Grants paid, $51,557; assets, $14,532 (M); gifts received, $18,240; expenditures, $51,747; qualifying distributions, $51,557.
Limitations: Applications not accepted.
Application information: Contributes only to pre-selected organizations.
Officer: Lawrence H. Schur, Pres.
EIN: 237062626

36555
Thomas E. & Paula J. Christman Foundation
c/o U.S. Trust
114 W. 47th St., TaxVS
New York, NY 10036
Contact: Thomas E. Christman, Dir.

Established in 1981 in NY.
Donor(s): Paula J. Christman, Thomas E. Christman.
Financial data (yr. ended 12/31/01): Grants paid, $51,500; assets, $635,065 (M); expenditures, $58,073; qualifying distributions, $51,500.
Limitations: Giving primarily in NY.
Directors: Paula J. Christman, Thomas E. Christman, James J. Mc Entee.
EIN: 112585913

36556
Simple Gifts Fund
241 Main St., Ste. 100
Buffalo, NY 14203-2703 (716) 852-2200
Contact: Phyllis Wendt Pierce, Tr.

Established in 1996 in NY.
Donor(s): Phyllis Wendt Pierce.
Financial data (yr. ended 11/30/01): Grants paid, $51,500; assets, $863,415 (M); gifts received, $72,235; expenditures, $59,796; qualifying distributions, $52,534.
Limitations: Giving primarily in NY.
Trustee: Phyllis Wendt Pierce.
EIN: 161512132

36557
Lee and Marvin Traub Charitable Fund
c/o Lee & Marvin Traub
524 E. 72nd St.
New York, NY 10023

Established in 2000 in NY.
Donor(s): Lee Traub, Marvin S. Traub.
Financial data (yr. ended 11/30/01): Grants paid, $51,439; assets, $60,480 (M); gifts received, $129,000; expenditures, $52,610; qualifying distributions, $51,955.
Limitations: Applications not accepted.
Application information: Contributes only to pre-selected organizations.
Trustees: Lee Traub, Marvin S. Traub.
EIN: 137267366

36558
Bela & Catherine Schick Foundation, Inc.
c/o Robert Markewich
175 Riverside Dr.
New York, NY 10024

Financial data (yr. ended 12/31/01): Grants paid, $51,437; assets, $813,422 (M); expenditures, $62,825; qualifying distributions, $51,437.
Limitations: Applications not accepted. Giving primarily in New York, NY.
Application information: Contributes only to pre-selected organizations.
Officers: Murray Kalik, Pres.; Mark Kalik, V.P.; Eva Rachel Markewich, Secy.; Robert Markewich, Treas.
EIN: 132976336

36559
Robert & Anne Pietrafesa Family Foundation
c/o B.G. Sulzle
7573 Hunt Ln.
Fayetteville, NY 13066-2560
Contact: Robert D. Pietrafesa, Sr., Tr.

Established in 1985 in NY.
Donor(s): Robert D. Pietrafesa, Sr.
Financial data (yr. ended 12/31/01): Grants paid, $51,375; assets, $194,012 (M); gifts received, $63,130; expenditures, $53,116; qualifying distributions, $51,375.
Limitations: Giving limited to central NY.
Application information: Application form not required.
Trustees: Anne H. Pietrafesa, Robert D. Pietrafesa, Sr., Robert E. Pietrafesa II.
EIN: 222600674

36560
Gallant Family Foundation, Inc.
(Formerly Flatbush-Midwood Community Art Foundation, Inc.)
156 William St., Ste. 802
New York, NY 10038

Established in 1993 in DE and NY.
Donor(s): Stanley Gallant, Susan Gallant.
Financial data (yr. ended 06/30/01): Grants paid, $51,350; assets, $838,471 (M); expenditures, $56,710; qualifying distributions, $49,996.
Limitations: Applications not accepted. Giving primarily in New Milford, CT, and Brooklyn, NY.
Application information: Contributes only to pre-selected organizations.
Officers: Stanley Gallant, Pres.; Susan Gallant, V.P.
EIN: 133039604

36561
The Arthur and Phyllis Milton Foundation, Inc.
425 E. 58th St., Ste. 43A
New York, NY 10022-2300 (212) 355-7770
Contact: Arthur Milton, Pres.

Established in 1996 in NY.
Donor(s): Arthur Milton.
Financial data (yr. ended 12/31/01): Grants paid, $51,330; assets, $646,349 (M); expenditures, $53,359; qualifying distributions, $53,260.
Limitations: Applications not accepted. Giving primarily in NY.
Application information: Unsolicited requests for funds not accepted.
Officers and Directors:* Arthur Milton,* Pres.; Phyllis Milton,* Secy.-Treas.; David Gotterer.
EIN: 133922759

36562
Emily L. and Robert E. Smith Foundation
165 E. 72nd St., Ste. 5L
New York, NY 10021

Established in 1997 in NY.
Donor(s): Robert E. Smith, Emily L. Smith.
Financial data (yr. ended 12/31/01): Grants paid, $51,250; assets, $453,606 (M); expenditures, $59,526; qualifying distributions, $51,250.
Limitations: Applications not accepted.
Application information: Contributes only to pre-selected organizations.
Officers and Directors:* Emily L. Smith,* Pres.; Amy Lynn Smith,* V.P.; Karen Gail Smith,* V.P.; Victoria Ann Smith,* V.P.; Robert E. Smith,* Secy.-Treas.
EIN: 133980754

36563
Newcombe Foundation
c/o Davidson, Dawson & Clark
330 Madison Ave.
New York, NY 10017

Donor(s): Amos R. Newcombe.
Financial data (yr. ended 12/31/00): Grants paid, $51,120; assets, $1,057,939 (M); expenditures, $57,392; qualifying distributions, $51,120.
Limitations: Applications not accepted. Giving primarily in Kingston, NY.
Application information: Contributes only to pre-selected organizations.
Trustees: Amos R. Newcombe, Helen Newcombe, Lydia Newcombe.
EIN: 146039070

36564
The Milton Weinstock Charitable Foundation
c/o Brand Sonnenschine
377 Broadway
New York, NY 10013

Established in 1998 in NY.
Donor(s): Milton Weinstock.
Financial data (yr. ended 12/31/01): Grants paid, $51,114; assets, $357,774 (M); gifts received, $60,700; expenditures, $52,389; qualifying distributions, $51,114.
Limitations: Applications not accepted.
Application information: Contributes only to pre-selected organizations.
Trustee: Esther Weinstock.
EIN: 134011013

36565
The Dake Education Foundation
P.O. Box 435
Saratoga Springs, NY 12866

Established in 1999.
Financial data (yr. ended 12/31/00): Grants paid, $51,100; assets, $948,023 (M); gifts received, $998,914; expenditures, $51,228; qualifying distributions, $51,094.
Limitations: Giving primarily in NY.
Application information: Application form required.
Officer: Bradford G. Dake, Pres.
EIN: 141794001

36566
Rhonie & George F. Berlinger Foundation, Inc.
1120 Park Ave.
New York, NY 10128
Contact: Rhonie H. Berlinger, Pres.

Incorporated in 1958 in NY.
Donor(s): George F. Berlinger,‡ Rhonie H. Berlinger.

Financial data (yr. ended 05/31/01): Grants paid, $51,069; assets, $250,930 (M); gifts received, $117,138; expenditures, $53,544; qualifying distributions, $52,044.
Limitations: Giving primarily in New York, NY.
Application information: Application form not required.
Officers: Rhonie H. Berlinger, Pres.; Nancy K. Stone, Secy.-Treas.
Director: Mary Ellen Klee.
EIN: 136084411

36567
Jih Foundation, Inc.
c/o Sussman
1247 55th St.
Brooklyn, NY 11219-4119

Established in 2000 in NY.
Donor(s): Harold Sussman, Ira Sussman, Joel Sussman.
Financial data (yr. ended 11/30/01): Grants paid, $51,036; assets, $7,977 (M); gifts received, $52,500; expenditures, $51,039; qualifying distributions, $51,036.
Limitations: Applications not accepted.
Application information: Contributes only to pre-selected organizations.
Directors: Harold Sussman, Ira Sussman, Joel Sussman.
EIN: 113521826

36568
St. John Fisher Fund for Religious, Educational and Charitable Activities
c/o Rev. Msgr. Daniel S. Hamilton
210 S. Wellwood Ave.
Lindenhurst, NY 11757-4927

Established in 2000 in NY.
Donor(s): Rev. Msgr. Daniel S. Hamilton.
Financial data (yr. ended 12/31/01): Grants paid, $51,000; assets, $916,884 (M); gifts received, $281,900; expenditures, $52,772; qualifying distributions, $51,000.
Limitations: Applications not accepted. Giving on a national basis, with emphasis on Chicago, IL, and the greater metropolitan New York, NY, area.
Application information: Contributes only to pre-selected organizations.
Officer: Rev. Msgr. Daniel S. Hamilton, Exec. Dir.
Trustees: Rev. Msgr. James M. McDonald, Rev. Edward J. Walsh.
EIN: 311675287

36569
Frontier Corporation-Educational Fund
(Formerly Rochester Telephone Corporation-Educational Fund)
c/o HSBC Bank USA
One HSBC Center, 16th Fl.
Buffalo, NY 14203-2801

Established in 1971.
Donor(s): Frontier Corp.
Financial data (yr. ended 08/31/01): Grants paid, $51,000; assets, $476,483 (M); expenditures, $51,445; qualifying distributions, $50,760.
Limitations: Applications not accepted. Giving on a national basis in areas of company operation.
Trustee: HSBC Bank USA.
EIN: 237167280
Codes: CS, CD, GTI

36570
The Schwarz Family Foundation
70 Cowdin Ln.
Chappaqua, NY 10514

Established in 1967.

Financial data (yr. ended 12/31/01): Grants paid, $50,928; assets, $970,185 (M); expenditures, $64,633; qualifying distributions, $51,212.
Limitations: Applications not accepted. Giving primarily in NJ.
Application information: Contributes only to pre-selected organizations.
Officers: Inge Schwarz Westreich, Pres.; Jeffrey Schwarz, V.P.; Karen Schlansky, Secy.-Treas.
EIN: 226100120

36571
The Caroline P. Hirsch Foundation
c/o Caroline P. Hirsch
860 United Nations Plz.
New York, NY 10017

Established in 1990 in NY.
Donor(s): Caroline P. Hirsch.
Financial data (yr. ended 12/31/99): Grants paid, $50,870; assets, $469,669 (M); expenditures, $59,226; qualifying distributions, $50,870.
Limitations: Applications not accepted. Giving primarily in New York, NY.
Application information: Contributes only to pre-selected organizations.
Trustee: Caroline P. Hirsch.
EIN: 136951414

36572
Jonathan Larson Performing Arts Foundation, Inc.
c/o Nancy Kassak Diekmann
P.O. Box 672, Prince St. Station
New York, NY 10012 (212) 529-0814
FAX: (212) 253-7604; E-mail: JLPAF@jlpaf.org;
URL: http://www.jlpaf.org

Established in 1996 in NY.
Donor(s): Allan S. Larson, Allan Gordon, Kevin McCollum, Jeffrey Seller, William Carver, Jay Harris, Victoria Leacock.
Financial data (yr. ended 12/31/01): Grants paid, $50,700; assets, $1,082,418 (M); gifts received, $507,435; expenditures, $268,204; qualifying distributions, $239,966.
Limitations: Giving on a national basis.
Application information: Download application form from foundation's Web site. Support for individuals is focused on those in early to mid-career who have not yet received a significant level of acclaim in their field. Application form required.
Trustees and Board Members:* Jonathan Burkhart, William Craver, Allan S. Gordon,* Jay S. Harris,* Allan S. Larson,* Julie Larson,* Victoria Leacock, Jesse L. Martin, Kevin McCollum, Peter Parcher, Todd Robinson.
EIN: 133902358

36573
Scher Family Foundation, Inc.
48 W. 38th St.
New York, NY 10016 (212) 382-2266
Contact: Robert Scher, V.P.

Established in 1958 in NY.
Donor(s): Members of the Scher family.
Financial data (yr. ended 12/31/01): Grants paid, $50,700; assets, $147,568 (M); expenditures, $51,092; qualifying distributions, $50,700.
Limitations: Giving primarily in the greater New York, NY, area.
Application information: Application form not required.
Officers: Benjamin Scher, Pres.; Robert Scher, V.P.
EIN: 136110427

36574
Kenneth and Agnes Zitter Family Foundation
9 Dogwood Ln.
Lawrence, NY 11559-1820 (516) 239-9050

Financial data (yr. ended 12/31/00): Grants paid, $50,680; assets, $186,879 (M); gifts received, $80,000; expenditures, $50,935; qualifying distributions, $50,680.
Limitations: Giving primarily in NY.
Board Members: Agnes Zitter, Kenneth Zitter.
EIN: 113465807

36575
Gordon Salmon and Marjorie R. Present Charitable Foundation
3940 East Ave.
Rochester, NY 14618 (716) 586-4165
Contact: James R. Present, Tr.

Established in 1987 in NY.
Financial data (yr. ended 12/31/01): Grants paid, $50,623; assets, $480,849 (M); expenditures, $53,407; qualifying distributions, $50,623.
Limitations: Giving primarily in FL, MA, and NY.
Trustees: Barbara Present, Gordon S. Present, James R. Present, Marjorie R. Present, Nancy Van Broekhoven, Paul Van Broekhoven.
EIN: 222861959

36576
The Lawrence Charitable Foundation
388 Kenridge Rd.
Lawrence, NY 11559 (516) 295-5350
Contact: Gary Gettenberg, Tr.

Established in 2000 in NY.
Financial data (yr. ended 12/31/00): Grants paid, $50,608; assets, $187,927 (M); gifts received, $422,096; expenditures, $58,858; qualifying distributions, $58,858.
Trustees: Gary Gettenberg, Lynn Gettenberg.
EIN: 311709120

36577
The Elizabeth J. Abrahams Charity Foundation
75 E. End Ave., Apt. 14B
New York, NY 10028-7918
Contact: Harvey W. Abrahams, Pres.

Established in 1994 in NY.
Donor(s): Harvey W. Abrahams.
Financial data (yr. ended 09/30/01): Grants paid, $50,564; assets, $3,500 (M); gifts received, $41,500; expenditures, $50,731; qualifying distributions, $50,564.
Limitations: Giving primarily in NY.
Officers: Harvey W. Abrahams, Pres.; Jacqueline Abrahams, V.P.; Jesse T. Abrahams, V.P.; William T. Abrahams, V.P.
EIN: 113230416

36578
The Yisroel David Charitable Foundation
c/o Paradise
116 39th St.
Brooklyn, NY 11232
Contact: S. Strimber

Established in 1999 in NY.
Donor(s): Paul Friedman.
Financial data (yr. ended 12/31/01): Grants paid, $50,560; assets, $30,928 (M); gifts received, $30,000; expenditures, $50,560; qualifying distributions, $50,560.
Trustees: Jack Friedman, Paul Friedman.
EIN: 113522289

36579
The Jeffrey Paley Family Foundation
812 Park Ave.
New York, NY 10021

Established in 1999 in NY.
Donor(s): Dorothy Hirshon.‡
Financial data (yr. ended 12/31/01): Grants paid, $50,540; assets, $39,798 (M); expenditures, $50,673; qualifying distributions, $50,479.
Limitations: Applications not accepted. Giving primarily in CT, MA, and NY.
Application information: Contributes only to pre-selected organizations.
Officer and Trustee:* Jeffrey Paley,* Pres.
EIN: 134077416

36580
Phi Delta Theta Educational Foundation of Meadville, Pennsylvania
P.O. Box 830
Jamestown, NY 14702-0830 (716) 664-2966
Contact: Gregory J. Edwards, V.P.

Financial data (yr. ended 06/30/02): Grants paid, $50,536; assets, $248,183 (M); gifts received, $2,930; expenditures, $57,291; qualifying distributions, $50,536.
Limitations: Giving limited to Meadville, PA.
Officers: Stephen R. Kaufman, Pres.; Gregory J. Edwards, V.P.; Jerry A. Goodrick, Secy.; John B. Lloyd, Treas.
EIN: 256065091

36581
LMP Foundation, Inc.
203 Whistle Stop Rd.
Pittsford, NY 14534

Established in 2000 in NY.
Financial data (yr. ended 12/31/01): Grants paid, $50,500; assets, $938,723 (M); expenditures, $61,964; qualifying distributions, $50,500.
Limitations: Applications not accepted. Giving primarily in Rochester, NY.
Application information: Contributes only to pre-selected organizations.
Officer: Lynette P. Blake, Pres.
Directors: David E. Anderson, James E. Blake, Gloria G. Harrington, Frances H. Snhenck.
EIN: 161578637

36582
The Novogratz-Caceres Family Foundation
(Formerly The Novogratz Family Foundation)
c/o BCRS Assocs., LLC
67 Wall St., 8th Fl.
New York, NY 10005

Established in 1999 in NY.
Donor(s): Michael Novogratz.
Financial data (yr. ended 12/31/01): Grants paid, $50,500; assets, $857,955 (M); gifts received, $100; expenditures, $50,817; qualifying distributions, $50,500.
Limitations: Applications not accepted.
Application information: Contributes only to pre-selected organizations.
Trustees: Dora Caceres, Jacqueline Novogratz, Michael Novogratz.
EIN: 134083989

36583
William C. & Joyce C. O'Neill Charitable Trust
c/o JPMorgan Chase Bank
1211 Ave. of the Americas, 34th Fl.
New York, NY 10036
Application address: c/o JPMorgan Chase Bank, 205 Royal Palm Way, Palm Beach, FL 33480
Contact: Betsy E. May, V.P., JPMorgan Chase Bank

Established in 1993.
Donor(s): Joyce C. O'Neil.
Financial data (yr. ended 12/31/01): Grants paid, $50,500; assets, $635,142 (M); expenditures, $81,628; qualifying distributions, $74,860.
Application information: Application form not required.
Trustees: Lois Conway Crabhill, Hollis Russell, JPMorgan Chase Bank.
EIN: 656110806

36584
Lothar von Ziegesar Foundation, Inc.
c/o Buchbinder Tunick & Co.
1 Penn Plz., Rm. 5335
New York, NY 10119 (212) 695-5003
Contact: David Sands

Established in 1991 in NY.
Donor(s): Franz von Ziegesar.
Financial data (yr. ended 12/31/00): Grants paid, $50,500; assets, $718,542 (M); gifts received, $26,563; expenditures, $85,258; qualifying distributions, $50,500.
Limitations: Giving primarily in CT and NY.
Officers and Directors:* Elizabeth von Ziegesar,* Pres.; Franz von Ziegesar,* Pres.; F. Peter von Ziegesar,* Secy.; George Haibloom,* Treas.
EIN: 133615178

36585
The Schell Family Foundation
336 Central Park W., Ste. 4A
New York, NY 10025

Established in 2000 in DE and NY.
Donor(s): J. Michael Schell, Kathleen Schell.
Financial data (yr. ended 12/31/01): Grants paid, $50,450; assets, $294,380 (M); gifts received, $151,926; expenditures, $55,954; qualifying distributions, $50,450.
Limitations: Applications not accepted.
Application information: Contributes only to pre-selected organizations.
Officers and Directors:* J. Michael Schell,* Pres. and Secy.-Treas.; Kathleen O. Schell, V.P.; Jennifer Schell, John Michael Schell, Jr.
EIN: 134141369

36586
Hanna Foundation
c/o M&T Bank
1 M&T Plz., 8th Fl.
Buffalo, NY 14203

Donor(s): Paul J. Hanna, Lee E. Hanna.
Financial data (yr. ended 11/30/01): Grants paid, $50,412; assets, $600,072 (M); gifts received, $90; expenditures, $56,006; qualifying distributions, $50,412.
Limitations: Applications not accepted. Giving primarily in FL.
Application information: Contributes only to pre-selected organizations.
Officers and Directors:* Paul J. Hanna,* Chair.; Lee E. Hanna,* Pres.; Melinda M. Hanna,* Secy.; Paul J. Hanna II,* C.F.O. and Treas.; Deborah G. Hanna.
Trustee: M & T Bank.
EIN: 236868675

36587
Robert & Florence Kaufman Foundation, Inc.
777 3rd Ave.
New York, NY 10017

Established in 1987 in NY.
Donor(s): Florence Kaufman, Robert Kaufman, William and Ester Kaufman Foundation.
Financial data (yr. ended 12/31/01): Grants paid, $50,220; assets, $741,319 (M); expenditures, $63,326; qualifying distributions, $50,220.
Limitations: Applications not accepted. Giving primarily in NY.
Application information: Contributes only to pre-selected organizations.
Officers: Robert Kaufman, Pres.; Ronna Dipersia, V.P.; Cathy Iger, V.P.; Julie McAlpine, V.P.; Florence Kaufman, Secy.-Treas.
EIN: 112848313

36588
The Feldman Frater Family Foundation, Inc.
876 Park Ave., Ste. 9S
New York, NY 10021

Established in 2000 in NY.
Donor(s): Hugh R. Frater.
Financial data (yr. ended 12/31/01): Grants paid, $50,158; assets, $448,254 (M); expenditures, $50,217; qualifying distributions, $50,158.
Limitations: Applications not accepted.
Application information: Contributes only to pre-selected organizations.
Directors: Kristen J. Feldman, Hugh R. Frater.
EIN: 134150058

36589
Ernst Foundation, Inc.
c/o Alvin Schulman, Moses & Singer, LLP
1301 Ave. of the Americas
New York, NY 10019

Donor(s): Beatrice Ernst Doffner, Howard Ernst.
Financial data (yr. ended 12/31/01): Grants paid, $50,101; assets, $914,249 (M); expenditures, $120,301; qualifying distributions, $50,101.
Limitations: Applications not accepted. Giving primarily in New York, NY.
Application information: Contributes only to pre-selected organizations.
Officers: Beatrice Ernst Daffner, Pres.; Naomi Paley, Secy.; Stuart Paley, Secy.
Directors: Howard Ernst, Victor Linn.
EIN: 116004939

36590
David N. Judelson Family Charitable Trust
375 Park Ave., Ste. 2507
New York, NY 10152

Established in 1967.
Financial data (yr. ended 12/31/01): Grants paid, $50,030; assets, $1,249,838 (M); gifts received, $50,000; expenditures, $57,351; qualifying distributions, $50,030.
Limitations: Applications not accepted. Giving primarily in New York, NY.
Application information: Contributes only to pre-selected organizations.
Trustees: David N. Judelson, Maria O. Judelson.
EIN: 136264357

36591
Ahearn Foundation
c/o M&T Bank
P.O. Box 22900
Rochester, NY 14692
Application address: P.O. Box 259, Vestal, NY 13851-0259; FAX: (607) 724-3180; E-mail: ahearnfoundation@usa.net
Contact: Anne M. Ahearn, Exec. Secy.

Financial data (yr. ended 12/31/01): Grants paid, $50,000; assets, $2,283,044 (M); gifts received, $1,250,000; expenditures, $81,974; qualifying distributions, $65,108.
Limitations: Giving primarily in Broome County, NY.
Application information: Application form not required.
Officers and Advisory Committee:* Donald Ahearn,* Chair.; Robert J. Ahearn,* Vice-Chair.; Anne M. Ahearn,* Exec. Secy.; Wilbur Bud Dahlgren,* Secy.; William C. Ahearn, David J. Cahill.
Trustee Bank: M&T Bank.
EIN: 222266031

36592
The John D. & Eleanore Carifa Foundation
c/o Alliance Capital Mgmt.
1345 Ave. of the Americas
New York, NY 10105-0302

Established in 2000 in NY.
Donor(s): Eleanore Carifa, John D. Carifa.
Financial data (yr. ended 11/30/01): Grants paid, $50,000; assets, $758,762 (M); gifts received, $999,528; expenditures, $58,000; qualifying distributions, $54,250.
Limitations: Applications not accepted.
Application information: Contributes only to pre-selected organizations.
Directors: Eleanore Carifa, John D. Carifa, John D. Carifa, Jr., William Carifa.
EIN: 943382710

36593
Kwen Chen International Law Foundation, Inc.
250 Park Ave. S., 6th Fl.
New York, NY 10003-1494   (212) 867-1818
Contact: P.G. Chen

Donor(s): Kwen Chen.
Financial data (yr. ended 04/30/00): Grants paid, $50,000; assets, $115,900 (M); gifts received, $50,000; expenditures, $51,000; qualifying distributions, $50,000.
Officer: Kwen Chen, Pres.
Directors: Peter G. Chen, Kai Ling Wong.
EIN: 133944801

36594
The Michele Klipstein Cohen Foundation, Inc.
67-38 108th St., Apt. 027
Forest Hills, NY 11375

Established in 1999 in NY.
Financial data (yr. ended 05/31/02): Grants paid, $50,000; assets, $337,464 (M); expenditures, $102,523; qualifying distributions, $50,000.
Directors: Robyn Cassel, Berthe Klipstein, Lucette Sevi.
EIN: 582475384

36595
Coplex Foundation
315 E. 62nd St., 6th Fl.
New York, NY 10021-7767

Donor(s): Benson A. Selzer.
Financial data (yr. ended 12/31/01): Grants paid, $50,000; assets, $410,798 (M); expenditures, $95,795; qualifying distributions, $50,000.
Limitations: Applications not accepted. Giving primarily in the New York, NY, area.
Application information: Contributes only to pre-selected organizations.
Trustees: Joel Handel, John A. Selzer.
EIN: 236448671

36596
C. J. Devine Charitable Residuary Trust
c/o The Bank of New York, Tax Dept.
1 Wall St., 28th Fl.
New York, NY 10286
Contact: Joan Buchanan, Trust Off., The Bank of New York

Financial data (yr. ended 12/31/00): Grants paid, $50,000; assets, $1,180,212 (M); expenditures, $53,969; qualifying distributions, $48,989.
Limitations: Giving limited to NJ and NY.
Trustee: The Bank of New York.
EIN: 136265759

36597
John Dewey Foundation
c/o S.D. Daniels and Co., PC
342 Madison Ave., No. 1620
New York, NY 10173
Contact: Steven Cahn, Pres.

Established in 1964 in DE.
Donor(s): Mrs. John Dewey.‡
Financial data (yr. ended 12/31/01): Grants paid, $50,000; assets, $417,794 (M); expenditures, $59,007; qualifying distributions, $50,000.
Limitations: Giving primarily in IL.
Officers: Steven M. Cahn, Pres.; Israel Scheffler, Secy.-Treas.
Directors: Karen Hanson, Richard Rorty, Robert Westbrook.
EIN: 136172348

36598
Edelweiss Foundation
c/o Griffin, Coogan, & Veneruso, PC
51 Pondfield Rd.
Bronxville, NY 10708

Established in 1999 in NY.
Donor(s): Robert Abplanalp.
Financial data (yr. ended 12/31/00): Grants paid, $50,000; assets, $2,078,771 (M); gifts received, $450,000; expenditures, $50,000; qualifying distributions, $50,000.
Limitations: Applications not accepted.
Application information: Contributes only to pre-selected organizations.
Directors: John Abplanalp, Josephine Abplanalp, Robert H. Abplanalp, Marie Holcombe.
EIN: 134090193

36599
Enable Hope Foundation
c/o Trust Co.
114 W. 47th St., TaxVAS
New York, NY 10036

Established in 1997 in MA.
Donor(s): Benjamin B. Baker.
Financial data (yr. ended 12/31/01): Grants paid, $50,000; assets, $1,369,114 (M); gifts received, $505,767; expenditures, $53,849; qualifying distributions, $50,000.
Limitations: Applications not accepted. Giving primarily in MA.
Application information: Contributes only to pre-selected organizations.
Trustees: Benjamin B. Baker, Deborah A. Baker.
EIN: 043372484

36600
Anne & Isidore Falk Charitable Foundation
188 E. 70th St., Ste. 29A
New York, NY 10021

Established in 1994 in NY.
Donor(s): Isidore Falk.
Financial data (yr. ended 12/31/01): Grants paid, $50,000; assets, $2,370,732 (M); gifts received, $500,000; expenditures, $53,000; qualifying distributions, $53,000.
Limitations: Applications not accepted.
Application information: Contributes only to pre-selected organizations.
Officer: Isidore Falk, Mgr.
EIN: 116444209

36601
Cary L. Guy Foundation
c/o Christine A Kehoe, Admin. Dir., Piper Rudnick LLP
1251 Ave. of the Americas, 29th Fl.
New York, NY 10020
FAX: (212) 835-6001

Established in 1986 in NY.
Donor(s): Cary L. Guy, M.D.‡
Financial data (yr. ended 12/31/01): Grants paid, $50,000; assets, $1,267,549 (M); expenditures, $79,354; qualifying distributions, $60,945.
Limitations: Giving primarily in NY.
Officer and Director:* Richard D. Roberts, M.D.,* Pres.
EIN: 133399029

36602
W. Averell and Pamela C. Harriman Foundation
c/o Brown Brothers Harriman Trust Co.
63 Wall St., 8th Fl.
New York, NY 10005-3099

Established in 1969 in NY.
Donor(s): W. Averell Harriman.‡
Financial data (yr. ended 12/31/00): Grants paid, $50,000; assets, $5,302,013 (M); gifts received, $579,048; expenditures, $130,726; qualifying distributions, $64,031.
Limitations: Applications not accepted. Giving primarily in Washington, DC.
Application information: Contributes only to pre-selected organizations.
Officers and Directors:* Kathleen L. Ames,* Pres.; Robert C. Fisk,* V.P.; Kathleen L. Mortimer,* Secy.; Averill H. Mortimer,* Treas.
EIN: 510193921

36603
KH Foundation
c/o Perelson Weiner, LLP
1 Dag Hammarskjold Plz., 42nd Fl.
New York, NY 10017

Established in 1988 in NY.
Donor(s): Ruth M. Guffee.
Financial data (yr. ended 12/31/01): Grants paid, $50,000; assets, $10,162 (M); gifts received, $50,000; expenditures, $50,605; qualifying distributions, $50,605.
Limitations: Applications not accepted. Giving primarily in NY.
Application information: Contributes only to pre-selected organizations.
Trustee: Ruth M. Guffee.
EIN: 061236515

36604
The Mathilde and Arthur B. Krim Foundation, Inc.
870 United Nations Plz., Apt. 27E
New York, NY 10017

Established in 1967.
Donor(s): Arthur B. Krim,‡ Mathilde Krim.
Financial data (yr. ended 12/31/01): Grants paid, $50,000; assets, $1,166 (M); gifts received, $50,000; expenditures, $50,000; qualifying distributions, $50,000.
Limitations: Applications not accepted. Giving primarily in NY.
Application information: Contributes only to pre-selected organizations.
Officers and Director:* Mathilde Krim,* Pres.; Daphna Krim, Secy.-Treas.
EIN: 136219851

36605
The Liu Foundation
c/o Arthur Liu
449 Broadway
New York, NY 10013
Contact: Yvonne Liu, Pres.

Established in 1997 in NY.
Donor(s): Arthur Liu.
Financial data (yr. ended 12/31/01): Grants paid, $50,000; assets, $2,002,212 (M); gifts received, $2,000,000; expenditures, $60,056; qualifying distributions, $50,000.
Officer: Yvonne Liu, Pres.
Directors: Arthur Liu, Laura Parsons, Fred Teng, Whiting Wu.
EIN: 133945839

36606
The Helen & Rita Lurie Foundation, Inc.
1111 Park Ave.
New York, NY 10128

Donor(s): Philip Morris Co.
Financial data (yr. ended 10/31/01): Grants paid, $50,000; assets, $4,706,464 (M); gifts received, $3,969,573; expenditures, $55,239; qualifying distributions, $50,000.
Limitations: Applications not accepted. Giving primarily in New York, NY.
Application information: Contributes only to pre-selected organizations.
Officers: Henrie Lurie, Pres.; Joseph R. Stern, Secy.; Hans J. Frank, Treas.
EIN: 133316656

36607
Michaels Philanthropic Foundation
1028 Channel Dr.
Hewlett, NY 11557 (516) 295-0255
Contact: James Michaels, Pres.

Financial data (yr. ended 04/30/02): Grants paid, $50,000; assets, $947,794 (M); expenditures, $54,320; qualifying distributions, $50,000.
Limitations: Giving primarily in New York, NY.
Officers: James Michaels, Pres.; Phyllis Michaels, V.P.; Sherri Michaels, Secy.
EIN: 116047540

36608
The Norumbega Fund
c/o The Bank of New York, Tax Dept.
1 Wall St., 28th Fl.
New York, NY 10286 (212) 635-1520

Established in 1957.
Financial data (yr. ended 12/31/01): Grants paid, $50,000; assets, $169,265 (M); expenditures, $50,960; qualifying distributions, $50,000.
Limitations: Applications not accepted. Giving primarily in CT.
Application information: Contributes only to pre-selected organizations.
Trustee: The Bank of New York.
EIN: 136078791

36609
C. B. Ramsay Foundation, Inc.
c/o Davidson, Dawson & Clark, LLP
330 Madison Ave.
New York, NY 10017

Financial data (yr. ended 12/31/01): Grants paid, $50,000; assets, $780,662 (M); expenditures, $55,711; qualifying distributions, $50,000.
Limitations: Applications not accepted. Giving primarily in Washington, DC.
Application information: Contributes only to pre-selected organizations.
Officers and Directors:* Jean Ramsay Bower,* Pres.; William C. Ramsay,* V.P.; Jennifer Just,* Secy.
EIN: 116037054

36610
Mitchell and Deborah Rechler Foundation
225 Broadhollow Rd., Ste. CS 5341
Melville, NY 11747

Established in 1999 in NY.
Donor(s): Mitchell Rechler, Deborah Rechler.
Financial data (yr. ended 12/31/01): Grants paid, $50,000; assets, $68,264 (M); expenditures, $50,150; qualifying distributions, $50,000.
Directors: Deborah Rechler, Donald Rechler, Mitchell Rechler.
EIN: 113522138

36611
The Roche Family Foundation, Inc.
c/o Clarfeld Financial Advisors
560 White Plains Rd., 5th Fl.
Tarrytown, NY 10591

Established in 1999 in NY.
Donor(s): John J. Roche.
Financial data (yr. ended 09/30/01): Grants paid, $50,000; assets, $1,607,504 (M); expenditures, $113,610; qualifying distributions, $50,000.
Directors: Janet E. Roche, John J. Roche, Keith S. Roche, Patricia K. Roche.
EIN: 134092374

36612
The Ann Schermerhorn Foundation
c/o Raymond & Feldman
110 E. 59th St.
New York, NY 10022

Established in 1986 in NY.
Financial data (yr. ended 10/31/01): Grants paid, $50,000; assets, $423,851 (M); expenditures, $53,628; qualifying distributions, $50,000.
Limitations: Applications not accepted. Giving primarily in NY.
Application information: Contributes only to pre-selected organizations.
Officers: Peter Allen, Pres.; Diane Allen, V.P.; Steven P. Raymond, Secy.-Treas.
EIN: 133402217

36613
The Robert F. & Anna Marie Shapiro Family Foundation, Inc.
c/o Tanton & Co. LLP
37 W. 57th St., 5th Fl.
New York, NY 10019-3411
Contact: Janet L. Mulligan

Donor(s): Robert F. Shapiro, Anna Marie Shapiro.
Financial data (yr. ended 11/30/01): Grants paid, $50,000; assets, $315,637 (M); gifts received, $1,000; expenditures, $55,392; qualifying distributions, $51,250.
Limitations: Applications not accepted. Giving primarily in New York, NY.
Application information: Contributes only to pre-selected organizations.
Officers and Trustees:* Robert F. Shapiro,* Chair. and V.P.; Anna Marie Shapiro,* Pres.; Peter J. Repetti, Secy.; Edwin E. Jedeikin, Treas.
EIN: 133140202

36614
Shendell Foundation
c/o Gordon Oppenheimer
P.O. Box 197
Larchmont, NY 10538-0197

Established in 1962 in NY.
Donor(s): Isaac Shendell.
Financial data (yr. ended 10/31/01): Grants paid, $50,000; assets, $1,247,533 (M); expenditures, $60,009; qualifying distributions, $51,423.
Limitations: Applications not accepted. Giving primarily in the metropolitan New York, NY, area.
Application information: Contributes only to pre-selected organizations.
Trustees: Gordon S. Oppenheimer, Robert Segal.
EIN: 136097659

36615
The Sullivan & Cromwell Foundation
125 Broad St., Ste. 2533
New York, NY 10004-2498

Established in 2001 in NY.
Donor(s): Sullivan & Cromwell.
Financial data (yr. ended 12/31/01): Grants paid, $50,000; assets, $1,851,943 (M); gifts received, $1,901,742; expenditures, $50,000; qualifying distributions, $50,000.
Limitations: Applications not accepted. Giving primarily in NY.
Application information: Contributes only to pre-selected organizations.
Officers and Directors:* H. Rodgin Cohen,* Chair. and Pres.; Ricardo A. Mestres, Jr.,* Secy.; John E. Merow,* Treas.
EIN: 311809780
Codes: CS

36616
The Father Peter G. Young, Jr. Foundation, Inc.
P.O. Box 1338
Albany, NY 12201
Contact: Jackie Gentile, Comp.

Established in 1996 in NY.
Donor(s): Carolyn Bardos, Cohoes Savings.
Financial data (yr. ended 03/31/02): Grants paid, $50,000; assets, $203,183 (M); gifts received, $45,729; expenditures, $65,418; qualifying distributions, $50,000.
Limitations: Giving primarily in Albany, NY.
Officers: Rev. Peter G. Young, C.E.O.; William Hennessey, Chair.; Maureen Dumas, Secy.; Jackie Gentile, Comp.
EIN: 223207792

36617
The Zukerman Charitable Trust
450 Park Ave., 6th Fl.
New York, NY 10022

Established in 1999.
Financial data (yr. ended 12/31/00): Grants paid, $50,000; assets, $1,120,306 (M); expenditures, $68,473; qualifying distributions, $7,380.
Limitations: Applications not accepted. Giving primarily in MA.

Application information: Contributes only to pre-selected organizations.
Trustees: Karen D. Zukerman, Laura B. Zukerman, Morris E. Zukerman.
EIN: 137213846

36618
The Irene Levoy Foundation, Inc.
26 Martin Ct.
Kings Point, NY 11024

Established in 1988 in NY.
Financial data (yr. ended 11/30/01): Grants paid, $49,975; assets, $1,094,201 (M); gifts received, $2,924; expenditures, $58,687; qualifying distributions, $49,975.
Limitations: Applications not accepted. Giving primarily in NY.
Application information: Contributes only to pre-selected organizations.
Officers and Directors:* Irene Levoy,* Pres.; Leon Oxman,* Secy.; Calvin Good,* Treas.
EIN: 112946575

36619
Samuel & Hannah Holzman Trust
254-21 Walden Ave.
Great Neck, NY 11020-1017 (516) 487-7893
Contact: Herbert Baum, Tr.

Established in 1974 in NY.
Financial data (yr. ended 05/31/02): Grants paid, $49,950; assets, $859,567 (M); expenditures, $58,101; qualifying distributions, $49,950.
Limitations: Giving primarily in NY.
Trustees: Herbert Baum, Herbert Stein.
EIN: 136601520

36620
Paul & Georgina Roth Charitable Foundation
(Formerly Philip & Samuel Roth Charitable Foundation)
4983 Tall Oaks Dr.
Fayetteville, NY 13066-9776

Established in 1953 in NY.
Donor(s): Paul B. Roth.
Financial data (yr. ended 12/31/01): Grants paid, $49,886; assets, $532,384 (M); expenditures, $56,534; qualifying distributions, $49,886.
Limitations: Applications not accepted. Giving primarily in Onondaga County, NY, with emphasis on Syracuse.
Application information: Contributes only to pre-selected organizations.
Trustees: Georgina H. Roth, Paul B. Roth.
EIN: 156020475

36621
Erwin and Ruth Zafir Foundation, Inc.
1551 53rd St.
Brooklyn, NY 11219

Established in 1992 in NY.
Donor(s): Erwin Zafir, Ruth Zafir.
Financial data (yr. ended 12/31/01): Grants paid, $49,883; assets, $378,529 (M); gifts received, $3,186,000; expenditures, $50,221; qualifying distributions, $49,883.
Limitations: Applications not accepted. Giving primarily in New York, NY.
Application information: Contributes only to pre-selected organizations.
Directors: Erwin Zafir, Ruth Zafir.
EIN: 113135109

36622
Rodeph Chesed Foundation
841 63rd St.
Brooklyn, NY 11220

Established in 1990 in NY.

Donor(s): Scents International.
Financial data (yr. ended 12/31/01): Grants paid, $49,867; assets, $138,541 (M); gifts received, $75,555; expenditures, $51,641; qualifying distributions, $49,867.
Limitations: Applications not accepted. Giving primarily in NY.
Application information: Contributes only to pre-selected organizations.
Trustees: Edward Berger, Ruth Berger.
EIN: 113093692

36623
Morna R. Schwartz Foundation, Inc.
c/o Michael Reid-Schwartz
1185 Park Ave.
New York, NY 10128-1313

Donor(s): Morna Reid-Schwartz.
Financial data (yr. ended 12/31/01): Grants paid, $49,859; assets, $996,382 (M); expenditures, $56,689; qualifying distributions, $49,859.
Limitations: Applications not accepted. Giving primarily in NY.
Application information: Contributes only to pre-selected organizations.
Officers: Morna Reid-Schwartz, Pres.; Joseph W. Renfield, V.P.; Michael Reid-Schwartz, Secy.-Treas.
EIN: 136192221

36624
The Grant and Donna Berry Foundation
18 Wampus Close
Armonk, NY 10504-1941

Established in 1997 in NY.
Donor(s): Grant Berry, Donna Berry.
Financial data (yr. ended 11/30/01): Grants paid, $49,839; assets, $307,794 (M); expenditures, $51,863; qualifying distributions, $49,839.
Limitations: Applications not accepted. Giving primarily in NY.
Application information: Contributes only to pre-selected organizations.
Officer: Grant Berry, Pres.
EIN: 113410448

36625
The Zeidman Family Charitable Foundation
115 E. 87th St., Ste. 33A
New York, NY 10128

Established in 2000 in NY.
Donor(s): Morton I. Zeidman.
Financial data (yr. ended 12/31/01): Grants paid, $49,745; assets, $1 (M); gifts received, $60,190; expenditures, $51,745; qualifying distributions, $49,745.
Limitations: Giving primarily in NY.
Trustees: Daniel J. Zeidman, Morton I. Zeidman.
EIN: 134089229

36626
Ralph F. Peo Foundation, Inc.
1100 Rand Bldg.
Buffalo, NY 14203

Financial data (yr. ended 12/31/01): Grants paid, $49,700; assets, $1,089,542 (M); expenditures, $60,006; qualifying distributions, $49,700.
Limitations: Giving primarily in Buffalo, NY.
Application information: Application form not required.
Directors: Samuel C. Armstrong, James L. Magavern, William J. Magavern II, Isabel K. Smith.
EIN: 166052065

36627
Henry Unger Family Foundation, Inc.
c/o Oberfest
287 King St.
Chappaqua, NY 10514

Established in 1995 in CT.
Financial data (yr. ended 06/30/00): Grants paid, $49,700; assets, $1,789,209 (M); gifts received, $350; expenditures, $51,582; qualifying distributions, $49,423.
Limitations: Applications not accepted. Giving limited to Westport, CT.
Application information: Contributes only to pre-selected organizations.
Officers and Trustees:* Barbara Unger Wales,* Pres.; Teresa Foster,* V.P.; Dane Unger,* V.P.; Jan Unger,* V.P.; Mark Unger,* V.P.; Bruce D. Oberfest,* Secy.-Treas.
EIN: 061457223

36628
Kenneth Rosenberg Foundation
c/o Aaron Halper & Co.
270 Madison Ave., 7th Fl.
New York, NY 10016-0601

Financial data (yr. ended 12/31/99): Grants paid, $49,650; assets, $1,274,203 (M); expenditures, $52,815; qualifying distributions, $49,650.
Limitations: Applications not accepted. Giving primarily in NY.
Application information: Contributes only to pre-selected organizations.
Officer: Kenneth Rosenberg, Pres.
EIN: 136593765

36629
GB Charitable Foundation, Ltd.
c/o Roth & Co.
5612 18th Ave.
Brooklyn, NY 11204

Established in 1996 in NY.
Donor(s): George Berkowitz.
Financial data (yr. ended 02/28/01): Grants paid, $49,644; assets, $20,937 (M); gifts received, $52,000; expenditures, $51,354; qualifying distributions, $51,289.
Limitations: Applications not accepted.
Application information: Contributes only to pre-selected organizations.
Officers: George Berkowitz, Pres.; Frederika Berkowitz, Secy.; Martin Berkowitz, Treas.
EIN: 113316617

36630
The Hannah & Ryan Barry Memorial Foundation
1220 Park Ave.
New York, NY 10128 (212) 508-9400
Contact: Thomas C. Barry, Tr.

Established in 1985 in NY.
Donor(s): Thomas C. Barry, Patricia R. Barry, Kathleen M. Doyle.
Financial data (yr. ended 12/31/01): Grants paid, $49,500; assets, $744,162 (M); expenditures, $64,026; qualifying distributions, $63,020.
Limitations: Giving primarily in New York, NY.
Application information: Application form not required.
Trustees: Michael C. Barry, Patricia R. Barry, Thomas C. Barry, Kathleen M. Doyle, Lynn Rauch.
EIN: 521374362

36631
Robert & Ann Newburger Foundation, Inc.
c/o Robert Newburger
P.O. Box 1625
Westhampton Beach, NY 11978-7625
Contact: Ann L. Newburger, V.P.

Donor(s): Robert L. Newburger.
Financial data (yr. ended 09/30/01): Grants paid, $49,450; assets, $878,308 (M); expenditures, $53,488; qualifying distributions, $49,450.
Limitations: Giving primarily in NY.
Officers and Director:* Robert L. Newburger,* Pres.; Ann L. Newburger, V.P. and Treas.
EIN: 136084395

36632
The Merrilyn Foundation
111 Piping Rock Rd.
Locust Valley, NY 11560

Established in 1998 in NY.
Donor(s): Vernon L. Merrill.‡
Financial data (yr. ended 12/31/01): Grants paid, $49,374; assets, $322,884 (M); expenditures, $53,017; qualifying distributions, $49,374.
Limitations: Applications not accepted. Giving primarily in NY.
Application information: Contributes only to pre-selected organizations.
Trustee: Lynn Gray.
EIN: 137144968

36633
The Fredericka V. Slingerland Family Foundation
4 Edgewood Cir.
Albany, NY 12204

Established in 1997 in NY.
Donor(s): Slingerland Foundation, Fredericka V. Slingerland.
Financial data (yr. ended 12/31/01): Grants paid, $49,300; assets, $981,352 (M); gifts received, $250; expenditures, $66,120; qualifying distributions, $49,300.
Limitations: Applications not accepted.
Application information: Contributes only to pre-selected organizations.
Trustees: Alan R. Ekstein, Frank H. Slingerland, Fredericka V. Slingerland.
EIN: 166459896

36634
The Weiss Foundation, Inc.
c/o Lipsky, Goodkin & Co.
120 W. 45th St.
New York, NY 10036

Established in 1954 in NY.
Donor(s): Margaret A. Weiss.
Financial data (yr. ended 09/30/01): Grants paid, $49,295; assets, $12,490 (M); expenditures, $49,533; qualifying distributions, $49,345.
Limitations: Applications not accepted. Giving primarily in New York, NY.
Application information: Contributes only to pre-selected organizations.
Officers and Directors:* John F. Weiss,* Pres.; Georgia W. Morris,* V.P.; Philip P. Goodkin,* Secy.-Treas.
EIN: 136067984

36635
Powell Family Foundation
c/o B. Strauss Assoc., Ltd.
307 5th Ave., 8th Fl.
New York, NY 10016-6517

Established in 2000 in CT.
Donor(s): William B. Powell.
Financial data (yr. ended 04/30/02): Grants paid, $49,260; assets, $86,082 (M); gifts received, $688; expenditures, $50,073; qualifying distributions, $49,260.
Limitations: Applications not accepted.
Application information: Contributes only to pre-selected organizations.
Trustees: Linda B. Powell, William P. Powell.
EIN: 061602798

36636
The Kornblau Family Foundation
47 E. 88th St.
New York, NY 10128

Established in 1993 in NY.
Financial data (yr. ended 11/30/01): Grants paid, $49,250; assets, $569,806 (M); gifts received, $40,462; expenditures, $50,727; qualifying distributions, $49,250.
Limitations: Applications not accepted. Giving limited to New York, NY.
Application information: Contributes only to pre-selected organizations.
Officers: Helen W. Kornblau, Pres.; Katherine J. Kornblau, Secy.; David L. Kornblau, Treas.
EIN: 133745043

36637
Pro Deo Guild, Inc.
P.O. Box 304
Hartsdale, NY 10530-0304

Financial data (yr. ended 02/28/02): Grants paid, $49,238; assets, $524,512 (M); expenditures, $55,601; qualifying distributions, $55,361.
Limitations: Applications not accepted. Giving on a worldwide basis.
Application information: Unsolicited requests for funds not considered or acknowledged.
Officers: Regina Brown, Pres.; John Brown, V.P.; Helen O'Donnell, Secy.; Doris Salley, Treas.
Directors: Georgena Cummings, Jane Murphy.
EIN: 133311305
Codes: GTI

36638
The Zichron Sarah Foundation
1409 E. 24th St.
Brooklyn, NY 11210-5144
Contact: Philip Huberfeld, Tr.

Established in 1997.
Donor(s): Philip Huberfeld, Rae Huberfeld.
Financial data (yr. ended 12/31/01): Grants paid, $49,168; assets, $849,096 (M); expenditures, $54,134; qualifying distributions, $49,168.
Trustees: Murray A. Huberfeld, Philip Huberfeld, Rae Huberfeld.
EIN: 116497906

36639
Zichron Devorah Foundation
70-56 136th St.
Flushing, NY 11367

Donor(s): Joseph Biderman.
Financial data (yr. ended 12/31/01): Grants paid, $49,162; assets, $46,020 (M); gifts received, $310; expenditures, $49,762; qualifying distributions, $49,162.
Limitations: Applications not accepted. Giving primarily in New York, NY.
Application information: Contributes only to pre-selected organizations.
Trustees: David J. Biderman, Esther Biderman, Joseph Biderman.
EIN: 113189455

36640
Robert B. & Addie P. Thomson Trust
c/o The Delaware National Bank of Delhi
124-126 Main St.
Delhi, NY 13753

Established in 1976 in NY.
Financial data (yr. ended 12/31/01): Grants paid, $49,160; assets, $1,198,213 (M); expenditures, $56,770; qualifying distributions, $49,160.
Limitations: Giving limited to Delaware County, NY, including the Hobart and Stamford area.
Trustees: Evelyn Goodspeed, Fred Joedicke, The Delaware National Bank of Delhi.
EIN: 166043464

36641
Lawrence and Elizabeth Krulik Foundation
400 Wireless Blvd.
Hauppauge, NY 11788

Established in 1995 in NY.
Donor(s): Elizabeth Krulik.
Financial data (yr. ended 12/31/01): Grants paid, $49,125; assets, $173,327 (M); gifts received, $100,000; expenditures, $49,239; qualifying distributions, $49,182.
Officers: Elizabeth Krulik, Pres.; Richard Krulik, Secy.; Sheryl Weisberg, Treas.
EIN: 133731987

36642
Otto and Fran Walter Foundation, Inc.
(Formerly Walter & Lorenz Foundation, Inc.)
866 United Nations Plz., Rm. 471
New York, NY 10017-1822
Contact: Otto L. Walter, Pres.

Established in 1954 in NY.
Donor(s): Anton Lorenz.‡
Financial data (yr. ended 12/31/01): Grants paid, $49,084; assets, $153,466 (M); expenditures, $103,540; qualifying distributions, $49,084.
Limitations: Applications not accepted. Giving primarily in NY.
Publications: Annual report.
Application information: Contributes only to pre-selected organizations.
Officers and Directors:* Otto L. Walter,* Pres. and Treas.; Frank G. Helman,* Secy.
EIN: 131625529

36643
The Holmes Family Foundation, Inc.
(Formerly The Jay T. & Karen E. Holmes Foundation, Inc.)
c/o Patrick D. Martin
P.O. Box 1051
Rochester, NY 14603-1051

Established in 1991 in NY.
Donor(s): Jay T. Holmes.
Financial data (yr. ended 12/31/01): Grants paid, $49,026; assets, $408,571 (M); gifts received, $14,949; expenditures, $55,029; qualifying distributions, $49,026.
Limitations: Applications not accepted. Giving on a national basis.
Application information: Contributes only to pre-selected organizations.
Officers and Directors:* Jay T. Holmes,* Pres.; Karen T. Holmes,* Secy.-Treas.; Susan C. Delligatti, Daniel J. Holmes, Jayne H. Wilson.
EIN: 161398330

36644
Cintas Foundation, Inc.
c/o William B. Warren
1301 Ave. of the Americas, Ste. 2537
New York, NY 10019-6092
Application address: c/o Institute of International Education, 809 United Nations Plz., New York, NY 10017, tel.: (212) 984-5370

Incorporated in 1957 in NY as Cuban Art Foundation, Inc.
Donor(s): Oscar B. Cintas.‡
Financial data (yr. ended 08/31/01): Grants paid, $49,000; assets, $2,175,878 (M); expenditures, $114,153; qualifying distributions, $78,479.
Limitations: Giving primarily to organizations benefiting Cuba.
Publications: Application guidelines.
Application information: Application form required.
Officers and Directors:* William B. Warren,* Pres.; Hortensia Sampedro,* Treas.; Dan Cameron, Margarita Cano, Leonor Lovo DeGonzalez, Manuel Gonzales, Cathy Leff, Roger D. Stone.
EIN: 131980389
Codes: GTI

36645
The Bertha Koempel Foundation, Inc.
c/o Gasser & Hayes
150 Purchase St.
Rye, NY 10580
Contact: James J. Beha, II, Pres.

Established in 1954 in NY.
Financial data (yr. ended 12/31/00): Grants paid, $49,000; assets, $26,842 (M); expenditures, $54,201; qualifying distributions, $49,000.
Limitations: Giving primarily in New York, NY.
Officers and Trustees:* James J. Beha II,* Pres.; William P.D. Bailey,* V.P.; Ida Brown,* Secy.; Robert Sarosy,* Treas.
EIN: 136086899
Codes: TN

36646
Morris Kirschner Perpetual Charitable Trust
c/o Deutsche Trust Co. of NY
P.O. Box 1297, Church St. Sta.
New York, NY 10008

Established in 1998 in NY.
Financial data (yr. ended 12/31/01): Grants paid, $48,938; assets, $1,064,293 (M); gifts received, $20; expenditures, $72,334; qualifying distributions, $59,804.
Limitations: Applications not accepted.
Application information: Contributes only to pre-selected organizations.
Trustee: Deutsche Bank.
EIN: 137122586

36647
The Dweck and Rahmey Family Foundation
c/o Jacmel Jewelry
30-00 47th Ave.
Long Island City, NY 11101

Donor(s): Jack Rahmey, Morris Dweck.
Financial data (yr. ended 12/31/99): Grants paid, $48,850; assets, $0 (M); gifts received, $37,940; expenditures, $49,022; qualifying distributions, $48,850.
Limitations: Applications not accepted. Giving primarily in NY.
Application information: Contributes only to pre-selected organizations.
Officer: Morris Dweck, Secy.
Directors: Thomas Milillo, Jack Rahmey.
EIN: 113391169

36648
Lewis Foundation
c/o Leona T. Lewis
40 Autumn Dr.
Slingerlands, NY 12159

Established in 1969.
Financial data (yr. ended 12/31/99): Grants paid, $48,836; assets, $2,255,034 (M); expenditures, $61,812; qualifying distributions, $54,439.
Limitations: Applications not accepted. Giving primarily in central NY.
Application information: Contributes only to pre-selected organizations.
Trustees: Susan L. Coyne, Leona T. Lewis.
EIN: 146049219

36649
Simon and Marie Jaglom Foundation, Inc.
115 E. 82nd St., Ste. 1B
New York, NY 10028-0828
Contact: Michael E. Jaglom, Pres.

Established in 1962 in NY.
Donor(s): Marie Jaglom,‡ Simon Jaglom.‡
Financial data (yr. ended 11/30/01): Grants paid, $48,793; assets, $12,368,231 (M); expenditures, $50,390; qualifying distributions, $48,793.
Limitations: Applications not accepted. Giving primarily in New York, NY.
Application information: Unsolicited requests for funds not accepted.
Officers and Directors:* Michael E. Jaglom,* Pres.; Henry D. Jaglom,* Secy.
EIN: 136105676

36650
Laura and Matthew Berdon Foundation
c/o Ferro Berdon & Co.
250 Park Ave. S., 6th Fl.
New York, NY 10003-1402

Donor(s): Matthew A. Berdon.
Financial data (yr. ended 02/28/02): Grants paid, $48,778; assets, $2,964 (M); gifts received, $46,500; expenditures, $48,883; qualifying distributions, $48,778.
Limitations: Applications not accepted. Giving primarily in CA and New York, NY.
Application information: Contributes only to pre-selected organizations.
Officers and Trustees:* Laura M. Berdon,* Mgr.; Matthew A. Berdon,* Mgr.
EIN: 136121240

36651
The Anne & John J. Walsh Foundation
c/o Lord Abbett & Co
767 5th Ave.
New York, NY 10153-0101

Established in 1987 in NY.
Donor(s): John J. Walsh, Anne Walsh.
Financial data (yr. ended 11/30/01): Grants paid, $48,750; assets, $792,010 (M); gifts received, $200,708; expenditures, $51,108; qualifying distributions, $48,750.
Limitations: Applications not accepted. Giving primarily in Queens County, NY.
Application information: Contributes only to pre-selected organizations.
Trustees: Anne Walsh, John J. Walsh.
EIN: 136880921

36652
The Rabinowitz Charitable Foundation
c/o Martin Rabinowitz, Odyssey Partners
1500 Broadway, No. 1020
New York, NY 10036-4015

Established in 1991 in NY.
Donor(s): Martin J. Rabinowitz.
Financial data (yr. ended 06/30/01): Grants paid, $48,743; assets, $773,022 (M); gifts received, $5,000; expenditures, $49,770; qualifying distributions, $48,743.
Limitations: Applications not accepted. Giving primarily in NY.
Application information: Contributes only to pre-selected organizations.
Trustees: Ann Rabinowitz, Martin J. Rabinowitz, Nancy J. Rabinowitz, Steven M. Rabinowitz, Susan A. Rabinowitz.
EIN: 133704156

36653
The Grunebaum Family Fund
282 Katonah Ave., Ste. 250
Katonah, NY 10536

Financial data (yr. ended 10/31/01): Grants paid, $48,637; assets, $1,153,099 (M); expenditures, $113,969; qualifying distributions, $52,745.
Limitations: Applications not accepted. Giving primarily in NY.
Application information: Contributes only to pre-selected organizations.
Directors: Ernest Grunebaum, George Grunebaum, Lauren Grunebaum, Peter Grunebaum.
EIN: 136112767

36654
Saul and Janice Linzer Foundation
c/o Max Wasser
132 Nassau St., Ste. 300
New York, NY 10038

Established in 1988 in NY.
Donor(s): Saul Linzer, Janice Linzer.
Financial data (yr. ended 11/30/01): Grants paid, $48,636; assets, $512,759 (M); expenditures, $51,422; qualifying distributions, $48,636.
Limitations: Applications not accepted.
Application information: Contributes only to pre-selected organizations.
Trustees: Janice Linzer, Saul Linzer.
EIN: 136917099

36655
The Green Foundation
941 Park Ave.
New York, NY 10028-0318

Established in 1953 in MA.
Donor(s): Greenal, Inc., Peggy Gee Fashions, Peter Green.
Financial data (yr. ended 12/31/01): Grants paid, $48,557; assets, $819,296 (M); expenditures, $51,338; qualifying distributions, $49,481.
Limitations: Applications not accepted.
Application information: Contributes only to pre-selected organizations.
Officer: Peter Green, Pres. and Treas.
EIN: 136114110

36656
Huguenot Historical Association of New Rochelle Foundation
c/o Norman Herzberg
46 Longue Vue Ave.
New Rochelle, NY 10804-4119

Financial data (yr. ended 12/31/01): Grants paid, $48,500; assets, $672,395 (M); expenditures, $50,828; qualifying distributions, $48,500.
Limitations: Applications not accepted. Giving limited to New Rochelle, NY.
Application information: Contributes only to pre-selected organizations.
Trustees: Norman J. Herzberg, Gregory Varian.
EIN: 136213135

36657
The Echo Foundation
(Formerly Edgar & Theresa Hyman Foundation)
10 E. 40th St.
New York, NY 10016-0203

Donor(s): Lynn T. Roberts, Steven D. Roberts, Dorothy H. Roberts.
Financial data (yr. ended 05/31/02): Grants paid, $48,495; assets, $49,757 (M); gifts received, $50,151; expenditures, $48,688; qualifying distributions, $48,495.
Limitations: Applications not accepted. Giving primarily in New York, NY.
Application information: Contributes only to pre-selected organizations.
Officers: Dorothy H. Roberts, Pres.; Steven D. Roberts, V.P.; Lynn T. Roberts, Secy.-Treas.
EIN: 237123039

36658
David Lowy Family Foundation, Inc.
c/o Dalow Industries, Inc.
31-00 47th Ave.
Long Island City, NY 11101

Established in 1992 in NY.
Donor(s): David Lowy.
Financial data (yr. ended 12/31/01): Grants paid, $48,480; assets, $6,188 (M); gifts received, $46,000; expenditures, $48,480; qualifying distributions, $48,480.
Limitations: Applications not accepted. Giving primarily in the metropolitan New York, NY, area.
Application information: Contributes only to pre-selected organizations.
Officer: David Lowy, Pres.
EIN: 133669134

36659
George & Jane Pfaff Family Foundation
23 Springwood Manor Dr.
Loudonville, NY 12211

Established in 1997 in NY.
Donor(s): George O. Pfaff.
Financial data (yr. ended 12/31/01): Grants paid, $48,450; assets, $53,922 (M); expenditures, $49,507; qualifying distributions, $49,457.
Limitations: Applications not accepted. Giving primarily in NY.
Application information: Contributes only to pre-selected organizations.
Officers: George O. Pfaff, Pres. and Treas.; Jane Pfaff, V.P. and Secy.
EIN: 161516413

36660
The Martin Family Foundation
c/o P. Kosmach, Bessemer Trust Co.
630 5th Ave.
New York, NY 10111

Established in 2000 in NJ.
Donor(s): William F. Martin.
Financial data (yr. ended 12/31/01): Grants paid, $48,400; assets, $423,749 (M); expenditures, $49,497; qualifying distributions, $48,400.
Limitations: Applications not accepted.
Application information: Contributes only to pre-selected organizations.
Trustees: Brian P. Martin, Janet E. Martin, Suzanne Martin, William F. Martin, Bessemer Trust Co. of NJ.
EIN: 527142691

36661
M. J. Love Foundation
760 Carlton Rd.
Clifton Park, NY 12065-1015
Contact: John R. Mackenzie, Tr.

Financial data (yr. ended 05/31/02): Grants paid, $48,339; assets, $3,850 (M); gifts received, $48,867; expenditures, $49,290; qualifying distributions, $48,339.
Limitations: Giving on a national and international basis.
Application information: Application form required.
Trustees: John R. Mackenzie, Mary E. Mackenzie.
EIN: 141800229

36662
Connie S. & Betty L. Maniatty Foundation, Inc.
c/o Speer & Fulvio, LLP
60 E. 42nd St., Ste. 1313
New York, NY 10165
Contact: Connie S. Maniatty, Pres.

Established in 1975 in NY.
Financial data (yr. ended 06/30/01): Grants paid, $48,263; assets, $690,524 (M); expenditures, $52,667; qualifying distributions, $51,613.
Limitations: Applications not accepted. Giving primarily in CT and New York, NY.
Application information: Contributes only to pre-selected organizations.
Officers and Directors:* Connie S. Maniatty, Pres. and Treas.; Betty L. Maniatty,* V.P. and Secy.; Vincent B. Murphy, Jr., Richard J. Schmeelk.
EIN: 510180480

36663
The Gresco Foundation
c/o Scott Rechler
225 Broadhollow Rd., CS 5341
Melville, NY 11747

Established in 1998 in NY.
Financial data (yr. ended 12/31/01): Grants paid, $48,215; assets, $52,221 (M); expenditures, $51,927; qualifying distributions, $50,031.
Limitations: Applications not accepted. Giving primarily in NY.
Application information: Contributes only to pre-selected organizations.
Directors: Gregg Rechler, Roger Rechler, Scott Rechler.
EIN: 113464963

36664
Kenneth S. Michael Foundation, Inc.
800 West End Ave.
New York, NY 10025
Application address: 292 Cherry Ln., Teaneck, NJ 07666, tel.: (201) 836-7014
Contact: Jenny Michael, Pres.

Established in 1967 in NY.
Donor(s): Kenneth S. Michael.‡
Financial data (yr. ended 08/31/01): Grants paid, $48,175; assets, $1,115,145 (M); expenditures, $54,725; qualifying distributions, $48,175.
Officer: Jenny Michael, Pres.
EIN: 136257692

36665
Mr. & Mrs. Richard A. Baker Family Foundation
c/o National Realty & Development Corp.
3 Manhattanville Rd.
Purchase, NY 10577 (914) 694-4444
Contact: Richard A. Baker, Tr.

Established in 1997 in NY.
Donor(s): Richard A. Baker.
Financial data (yr. ended 12/31/01): Grants paid, $48,139; assets, $31,977 (M); expenditures, $50,288; qualifying distributions, $48,181.
Limitations: Giving primarily in CT and NY.
Trustee: Richard A. Baker.
EIN: 133944372

36666
Norman D. Cohen Family Foundation
P.O. Box 20487, D.H.C.C.
New York, NY 10017

Donor(s): Norman D. Cohen.
Financial data (yr. ended 12/31/01): Grants paid, $48,065; assets, $422,767 (M); expenditures, $50,063; qualifying distributions, $48,065.
Limitations: Applications not accepted. Giving primarily in Palm Beach, FL and New York, NY.
Application information: Contributes only to pre-selected organizations.
Trustee: Norman D. Cohen.
EIN: 042770997

36667
The Stainman Family Foundation, Inc.
c/o Arthur J. Stainman
320 E. 72nd St.
New York, NY 10021-4769

Donor(s): Arthur J. Stainman, Lois Stainman.
Financial data (yr. ended 12/31/00): Grants paid, $48,003; assets, $953,726 (M); gifts received, $29,563; expenditures, $53,578; qualifying distributions, $47,829.
Officers: Arthur J. Stainman, Pres.; Lois Stainman, V.P.; Evan Stainman, Secy.
EIN: 133980213

36668
Nathaniel Saltonstall Arts Fund
c/o Behan, Ling & Ruta
358 5th Ave., 9th Fl.
New York, NY 10001
Application address: c/o Palmer Dodge, 1 Beacon St., Boston, MA 02134
Contact: Nathaniel S. Gardiner, Tr.

Established in 1959 in MA.
Donor(s): Nathaniel Saltonstall.
Financial data (yr. ended 12/31/01): Grants paid, $48,002; assets, $852,743 (M); expenditures, $67,930; qualifying distributions, $48,002.
Limitations: Giving limited to the New England area.
Trustees: Michael Baldwin, Nathaniel S. Gardiner, Eloise W. Hodge.
EIN: 046124122

36669
The Robert W. and Virginia Hassler Family Foundation
97 Gianelli Ave.
Merrick, NY 11566 (516) 379-4701
Contact: Virginia Hassler, Dir.

Established in 1998 in NY.
Financial data (yr. ended 09/30/01): Grants paid, $48,000; assets, $57,985 (M); gifts received, $106,129; expenditures, $51,008; qualifying distributions, $48,000.
Limitations: Giving primarily in NY.
Application information: Application form not required.
Directors: Barbara Fromm, Virginia Hassler, Anthony C. Sgueglia, Vincent Tenety, Christine Tonry.
EIN: 113459359

36670
John R. and Joyce McC. Hupper Charitable Trust
c/o Cravath, Swaine & Moore
825 8th Ave., Worldwide Plz.
New York, NY 10019

Established in 1985 in NY.
Donor(s): John R. Hupper, Joyce McC. Hupper.
Financial data (yr. ended 12/31/01): Grants paid, $48,000; assets, $1,298,418 (M); gifts received, $189,370; expenditures, $50,895; qualifying distributions, $47,872.
Limitations: Applications not accepted. Giving primarily in MA and NY.
Application information: Contributes only to pre-selected organizations.
Trustees: John R. Hupper, Joyce McC. Hupper.
EIN: 133359911

36671
James IV Association of Surgeons, Inc.
500 E. 85th St., PH 1
New York, NY 10028 (212) 249-3700
FAX: (212) 249-4433; E-mail: jamesIVassoc.surg@aol.com
Contact: Veronica Johannesson

Established in 1957 in NY.
Financial data (yr. ended 12/31/99): Grants paid, $48,000; assets, $1,418,408 (M); expenditures, $93,275; qualifying distributions, $82,059.
Limitations: Giving on a national basis, with some giving in Australia, Hong Kong, and Mexico.
Application information: Applications accepted from active members of the James IV Associations of Surgeons and from chairpersons of national academic departments of surgery. Application form required.
Officers: Richard J. Finley, M.D., Pres.; C. James Carrico, M.D., V.P.; Stewart M. Hamilton, M.D., V.P.; Prof. Robin C.N. Williamson, V.P.; Stephen F. Lowry, M.D., Secy.; Murray F. Brennan, M.D., Treas.
Directors: Arnold G. Diethelm, M.D., Victor Fazio, M.D., R. Scott Jones, M.D., Ernest Manders, M.D., Layton F. Rikkers, M.D., Courtney Townsend, M.D., and 9 additional directors.
EIN: 136138272

36672
George Libert Foundation
c/o Citibank, N.A.
1 Court Sq., 22nd Fl.
Long Island City, NY 11120

Financial data (yr. ended 12/31/00): Grants paid, $48,000; assets, $866,676 (M); expenditures, $61,429; qualifying distributions, $47,085.
Limitations: Applications not accepted. Giving primarily in NY.
Application information: Contributes only to pre-selected organizations.
Trustee: Citibank, N.A.
EIN: 136056417

36673
Norr Fund, Inc.
8 Tory Ln.
Scarsdale, NY 10583-2315

Established in 1968.
Donor(s): David Norr.
Financial data (yr. ended 12/31/01): Grants paid, $48,000; assets, $842,257 (M); gifts received, $47,168; expenditures, $48,325; qualifying distributions, $48,000.
Limitations: Applications not accepted. Giving limited to New York, NY.
Application information: Contributes only to pre-selected organizations.

Officers: David Norr, Pres.; Carol B. Norr, V.P.; Philip M. Susswein, Secy.
EIN: 136256450

36674
The Robert N. DeBenedictis Foundation
227 E. 56th St., Ste. 400
New York, NY 10022 (212) 753-2357
Application address: 1400 N.E. 14th St., Fort Lauderdale, FL 33304, FAX: (212) 888-6828, FAX: (954) 766-2655; E-mail: robert.debenedictis@verizon.net; URL: http://fdncenter.org/grantmaker/rnd

Incorporated in 1997 in NY.
Donor(s): Robert N. DeBenedictis.
Financial data (yr. ended 12/31/01): Grants paid, $47,940; assets, $5,510 (M); gifts received, $82,021; expenditures, $76,803; qualifying distributions, $47,940.
Limitations: Applications not accepted. Giving primarily in PA.
Application information: Contributes only to pre-selected organizations.
Officers: Robert N. DeBenedictis, Chair. and Pres.; George S. Trisciuzzi, Vice-Chair. and V.P.; Paul Galluccio, Secy.; Julie Martino, Treas.; Ariana Testamarck, Exec. Dir.
EIN: 133989370

36675
Leni & Peter May Family Foundation, Inc.
280 Park Ave., 41st Fl.
New York, NY 10017

Established in 1989.
Donor(s): Peter W. May, Leni F. May.
Financial data (yr. ended 12/31/01): Grants paid, $47,850; assets, $203 (M); gifts received, $6,500; expenditures, $47,850; qualifying distributions, $47,850.
Limitations: Applications not accepted. Giving on a national basis.
Application information: Contributes only to pre-selected organizations.
Directors: Jonathan May, Leni F. May, Leslie May, Peter W. May.
EIN: 133557827

36676
Harry Herskowitz Foundation, Inc.
975 Park Ave., Apt. 7B
New York, NY 10028 (212) 737-9170
Contact: Dr. Ruth Skydell, Pres.

Established in 1958 in NY.
Financial data (yr. ended 11/30/01): Grants paid, $47,841; assets, $495,955 (M); gifts received, $800; expenditures, $85,927; qualifying distributions, $47,841.
Limitations: Giving primarily in the metropolitan New York, NY, area.
Application information: Application form not required.
Officers and Directors:* Ruth H. Skydell,* Pres.; Harry Skydell,* V.P.; Laurie S. Goldberg,* Secy.
EIN: 136115242

36677
Bessie Rattner Foundation, Inc.
180 E. End Ave.
New York, NY 10028
Contact: Milton S. Rattner, Tr.

Donor(s): Hansel 'N' Gretel Brand, Inc., Milton S. Rattner.
Financial data (yr. ended 12/31/01): Grants paid, $47,840; assets, $2,285,650 (M); gifts received, $800; expenditures, $48,184; qualifying distributions, $47,840.
Limitations: Giving primarily in New York, NY.

Trustee: Milton S. Rattner.
EIN: 136169194

36678
Nancy & Craig Gibson Charitable Trust
c/o AMCO
505 Park Ave., 20th Fl.
New York, NY 10022-1106

Established in 1997 in NY.
Donor(s): Nancy Quick Gibson.
Financial data (yr. ended 12/31/01): Grants paid, $47,800; assets, $288,073 (M); gifts received, $3,274; expenditures, $52,209; qualifying distributions, $47,800.
Limitations: Applications not accepted. Giving primarily in MA.
Application information: Contributes only to pre-selected organizations.
Trustees: Craig B. Gibson, Nancy Quick Gibson.
EIN: 043410276

36679
World Gratitude Day, Inc.
132 W. 31st St.
New York, NY 10001-3406

Established in 1975 in NY.
Financial data (yr. ended 08/31/01): Grants paid, $47,751; assets, $1,005,753 (M); gifts received, $56,305; qualifying distributions, $47,751.
Limitations: Applications not accepted. Giving primarily in NY.
Application information: Contributes only to pre-selected organizations.
Officers: Edna F. Lemle, Pres.; Florence J. Lemle, V.P.
EIN: 237365629

36680
Peter Dion Family Foundation
1100 Franklin Ave., Ste. 205
Garden City, NY 11530-1601
Contact: Peter Dion, Pres.

Established in 1997.
Donor(s): Peter Dion, Diana Dion, Stephen Kutulos, Harriet Kutulos, Bessie Dion.
Financial data (yr. ended 06/30/01): Grants paid, $47,750; assets, $57,127 (M); gifts received, $20,000; expenditures, $47,905; qualifying distributions, $47,873.
Officers: Peter Dion, Pres.; Bessie Dion, V.P.; Harriet Kutulos, V.P.; Stephen Kutulos, Secy.
EIN: 133973378

36681
The Cannon Fund
c/o Bessemer Trust Co., N.A., Trust Dept.
630 5th Ave.
New York, NY 10111
Application address: 30 E. Huron St., Apt. 2908, Chicago, IL 60611
Contact: Carolyn Cannon, Tr.

Donor(s): George W. Cannon, Jr.
Financial data (yr. ended 08/31/01): Grants paid, $47,550; assets, $938,702 (M); expenditures, $61,609; qualifying distributions, $49,128.
Limitations: Giving on a national basis.
Trustees: Carolyn Cannon, George W. Cannon, Jr., Betty Medema.
EIN: 386055654

36682
Roney-Fitzpatrick Foundation
c/o The Bank of New York, Tax Dept.
1 Wall St., 28th Fl.
New York, NY 10286
Application address: 43 Swan Rd., Winchester, MA 01890
Contact: Edwin J. Fitzpatrick, Jr., Tr.

Financial data (yr. ended 12/31/01): Grants paid, $47,541; assets, $793,425 (M); expenditures, $53,098; qualifying distributions, $47,541.
Limitations: Giving limited to central NJ.
Trustees: Anne R. Fitzpatrick, Edwin J. Fitzpatrick, Jr., Ward H. Nessen.
EIN: 596147880

36683
The Weiner Foundation
c/o Arthur C. Weiner
305 Aerie Ct.
Manhasset, NY 11030-4053

Established in 1997 in NY.
Donor(s): Arthur C. Wiener.
Financial data (yr. ended 12/31/01): Grants paid, $47,525; assets, $10,118 (M); gifts received, $47,500; expenditures, $47,630; qualifying distributions, $47,525.
Limitations: Applications not accepted. Giving primarily in New York, NY.
Application information: Contributes only to pre-selected organizations.
Officers: Arthur C. Wiener, Pres.; Gale Wiener, V.P.; Glenn Wiener, V.P.
EIN: 113371282

36684
Abbot A. & Selma C. Harman Foundation
c/o Richard S. Harman & Co.
146 Central Park West
New York, NY 10023 (212) 218-1062
Contact: Richard S. Harman, Mgr.

Established in 1985 in NY.
Financial data (yr. ended 12/31/00): Grants paid, $47,515; assets, $66,957 (M); expenditures, $53,711; qualifying distributions, $47,515.
Limitations: Giving primarily in the New York, NY, area.
Application information: Application form not required.
Officer: Richard S. Harman, Mgr.
EIN: 133338031

36685
The Flanagan Family Foundation
c/o Louis Sternbach & Co.
1333 Broadway, Ste. 516
New York, NY 10018

Financial data (yr. ended 12/31/01): Grants paid, $47,500; assets, $826,871 (M); expenditures, $52,340; qualifying distributions, $47,500.
Limitations: Applications not accepted.
Application information: Contributes only to pre-selected organizations.
Officer: Robert M. Flanagan, Chair.
EIN: 134037250

36686
Gulati Family Foundation, Inc.
c/o Ravi Gulati
29 Bobs Ln.
Setauket, NY 11733

Established in 1997 in NY.
Donor(s): Ravi Gulati.
Financial data (yr. ended 12/31/01): Grants paid, $47,500; assets, $358,555 (M); expenditures, $51,930; qualifying distributions, $47,500.
Limitations: Applications not accepted.
Application information: Contributes only to pre-selected organizations.
Officers and Directors:* Ravi Gulati,* Pres. and Treas.; Janet Gulati,* V.P. and Secy.; Nicole L. Gulati, Sheila M. Gulati.
EIN: 113361970

36687
Erland & Rose Marie Karlsson Foundation
c/o Goldman Sachs & Co.
85 Broad St., Tax Dept.
New York, NY 10004

Established in 1996 in NY.
Donor(s): Erland S. Karlsson.
Financial data (yr. ended 03/31/02): Grants paid, $47,500; assets, $1,091,857 (M); gifts received, $2,500; expenditures, $50,330; qualifying distributions, $47,500.
Limitations: Applications not accepted.
Application information: Contributes only to pre-selected organizations.
Trustees: Erland S. Karlsson, Rose Marie Karlsson, Eric Mindich.
EIN: 133933311

36688
The Tonamora Foundation
c/o The Cox Office
419 Park Ave. S., 13th Fl.
New York, NY 10016-8410

Established in 1998 in NY.
Donor(s): Ambrose M. O'Donnell.
Financial data (yr. ended 05/31/02): Grants paid, $47,500; assets, $1,334,400 (M); expenditures, $57,621; qualifying distributions, $47,500.
Limitations: Applications not accepted. Giving limited to New York, NY.
Application information: Contributes only to pre-selected organizations.
Officers: Ambrose M. O'Donnell, Pres.; Thomas A. Cox, V.P.; David E. Stutzman, Secy.
EIN: 134014643

36689
Thomas J. & Marie C. Murrin Foundation
c/o W. Michael Reickert, The Ayco Corp., LP
P.O. Box 8019
Ballston Spa, NY 12020-8019

Established in 1989 in PA.
Donor(s): Marie C. Murrin, Thomas J. Murrin.
Financial data (yr. ended 12/31/01): Grants paid, $47,498; assets, $3,209 (M); expenditures, $47,548; qualifying distributions, $47,498.
Limitations: Applications not accepted. Giving primarily in Pittsburgh, PA.
Application information: Contributes only to pre-selected organizations.
Officers: Thomas J. Murrin, Pres.; Marie C. Murrin, Secy.-Treas.
EIN: 251602947

36690
Cornyn Foundation, Inc.
48 Tobey Ct.
Pittsford, NY 14534
Contact: Virginia R. Cornyn, Pres.

Established in 1997 in NY.
Donor(s): Virginia R. Cornyn.
Financial data (yr. ended 12/31/01): Grants paid, $47,325; assets, $760,890 (M); expenditures, $53,251; qualifying distributions, $47,325.
Limitations: Giving primarily in MA and NY.
Officers and Directors:* Virginia R. Cornyn,* Pres.; Kelly Zusman,* V.P.; Carolyn G. Clemons,* Secy.; Kathleen R. Arnold, James E. Clemons, Nora Clemons, John E. Cornyn, Michelle M. Watts.
EIN: 161517828

36691
Evans Devereux Memorial Fund
(also known as Virginia Evans Devereux Memorial Fund)
120 Delaware Ave.
Buffalo, NY 14202 (716) 845-6000
Contact: Sue S. Gardner, Tr.

Financial data (yr. ended 12/31/00): Grants paid, $47,300; assets, $1,143,788 (M); gifts received, $80,622; expenditures, $71,829; qualifying distributions, $47,300.
Limitations: Giving primarily in Buffalo, NY.
Trustees: Carol J. Alaimo, Grace Marie Ange, Sue S. Gardner.
EIN: 223115623

36692
The Planethood Foundation
63 Ralph Ave.
White Plains, NY 10606 (914) 948-8839
Contact: Donald Ferencz, Secy.-Treas.

Established in 1996 in NY.
Donor(s): Benjamin Ferencz.
Financial data (yr. ended 12/31/01): Grants paid, $47,138; assets, $1,900,048 (M); expenditures, $87,796; qualifying distributions, $47,138.
Officers: Benjamin Ferencz, Chair.; Gertrude Ferencz, Vice-Chair.; Donald Ferencz, Secy.-Treas.
EIN: 311830855

36693
The Amy and Steve Unfried Foundation
76 Park Ave.
Bronxville, NY 10708-1703

Established in 1991 in NY.
Donor(s): Stephen M. Unfried.
Financial data (yr. ended 12/31/00): Grants paid, $47,122; assets, $1,103,127 (M); gifts received, $157,743; expenditures, $48,628; qualifying distributions, $47,059.
Limitations: Applications not accepted. Giving primarily in CT.
Application information: Contributes only to pre-selected organizations.
Trustees: Amy B. Unfried, Stephen M. Unfried.
EIN: 133614341

36694
Literary Society Foundation, Inc.
Gracie Mansion Sta.
P.O. Box 155
New York, NY 10028-0002

Financial data (yr. ended 12/31/00): Grants paid, $47,115; assets, $1,959,768 (M); expenditures, $74,622; qualifying distributions, $47,115.
Limitations: Giving primarily in the northeastern U.S., with emphasis on CT, NJ, NY, and PA.
Officers: Johann Giel, Pres.; Helga Kelly, Secy.; Hans Schumacher, Treas.
EIN: 136115059

36695
The Wallace Family Foundation
c/o The Broadstone Group
888 7th Ave., Ste. 3400
New York, NY 10106

Established in 1992 in NY.
Donor(s): Paul F. Wallace, Avocet, Sombra Corporation.
Financial data (yr. ended 12/31/01): Grants paid, $47,089; assets, $5,957 (M); gifts received, $53,500; expenditures, $48,083; qualifying distributions, $48,083.

Limitations: Applications not accepted.
Application information: Contributes only to pre-selected organizations.
Officers: Paul F. Wallace, Pres.; Deirdre Wallace, V.P.; Stephanie Wallace, V.P.; Paul F. Wallace, Jr., Secy.-Treas.
EIN: 133663224

36696
Sam & Louise Campe Foundation, Inc.
c/o U.S. Trust Co. of New York
114 W. 47th St.
New York, NY 10036-1510
Application address: c/o Frankenthaler, Kohn, Schneider & Katz, 26 Broadway, New York, NY 10004
Contact: Henry Kohn

Financial data (yr. ended 12/31/01): Grants paid, $47,033; assets, $698,935 (M); expenditures, $64,207; qualifying distributions, $47,033.
Limitations: Giving primarily in NY.
EIN: 136123925

36697
The Caliban Foundation
c/o Goldman Sachs & Co.
85 Broad St., Tax Dept.
New York, NY 10004

Established in 1998 in NY.
Donor(s): Michael S. Rubinoff, Michael S. Rubinoff.
Financial data (yr. ended 04/30/01): Grants paid, $47,027; assets, $1,851,846 (M); gifts received, $671,871; expenditures, $90,119; qualifying distributions, $47,027.
Limitations: Applications not accepted. Giving primarily in MA and NY; some giving also in India.
Application information: Contributes only to pre-selected organizations.
Trustees: Lecia Rosenthal, Michael S. Rubinoff.
EIN: 137178636

36698
The Brout Foundation, Inc.
c/o Alan Brout
82 Brook Hills Cir.
White Plains, NY 10605

Established in 1961 in NY.
Donor(s): Alan Brout.
Financial data (yr. ended 08/31/01): Grants paid, $47,000; assets, $489,642 (M); expenditures, $47,603; qualifying distributions, $47,000.
Limitations: Applications not accepted. Giving primarily in NY.
Application information: Contributes only to pre-selected organizations.
Officers: Alan Brout, Pres.; Joan Brout, V.P.; Amy B. McHugh, Secy.; Ellen L. Brout, Treas.
EIN: 136160889

36699
The Correspondents Fund
c/o Rosenman & Colin
575 Madison Ave.
New York, NY 10022
Application address: c/o The New York Times, 229 W. 43rd St., New York, NY 10036-3913
Contact: James L. Greenfield, Pres.

Financial data (yr. ended 04/30/01): Grants paid, $47,000; assets, $961,099 (M); expenditures, $68,567; qualifying distributions, $52,515.
Limitations: Giving on a national basis.
Application information: Application form not required.
Officers: James L. Greenfield, Pres.; R. Edward Jackson, V.P.; Bonnie Angelo, V.P.; Ralph R. Schulz, Treas.

Directors: Ann Cooper, Barbara Crossette, Osborne Elliott, Elmer Lower, Herbert Mitgang, William Orme, Morley Safer, William Sheehan, Richard Wald, Ben Wright.
EIN: 136100568
Codes: GTI

36700
Arthur Dubow Foundation
c/o Glenn Allan Zalk, C.P.A.
60 E. 42nd St., Ste. 1313
New York, NY 10165

Established in 1986 in NY.
Donor(s): Arthur M. Dubow.
Financial data (yr. ended 06/30/01): Grants paid, $47,000; assets, $876,222 (M); expenditures, $50,442; qualifying distributions, $47,422.
Limitations: Applications not accepted. Giving primarily in the Northeast.
Application information: Contributes only to pre-selected organizations.
Trustees: Arthur M. Dubow, Charles Dubow, Barbara Shattuck.
EIN: 116327839

36701
The Robert H. Kemper, Jr. and Norma E. Kemper Charitable Foundation
P.O. Box 308
Canastota, NY 13032

Established in 2000 in NY.
Donor(s): Norma E. Kemper, Robert H. Kemper, Jr.
Financial data (yr. ended 12/31/01): Grants paid, $47,000; assets, $1,063,183 (M); expenditures, $48,130; qualifying distributions, $47,000.
Limitations: Applications not accepted.
Application information: Contributes only to pre-selected organizations.
Trustees: Norma E. Kemper, Robert H. Kemper, Jr.
EIN: 161562673

36702
Urstadt Conservation Foundation
c/o Urstadt Property Company, Inc.
2 Park Pl., Off. 3
Bronxville, NY 10708

Established in 1998 in NY.
Donor(s): Charles Urstadt, Elinor Urstadt.
Financial data (yr. ended 12/31/01): Grants paid, $47,000; assets, $1,080,521 (M); expenditures, $49,410; qualifying distributions, $47,000.
Directors: Charles Urstadt, Elinor Urstadt.
EIN: 137154898

36703
Neil & Virginia Weiss Foundation in Memory of Steven Weiss
c/o Knitastiks, Inc.
1411 Broadway
New York, NY 10018-3403

Established in 1997 in NY.
Donor(s): Neil Weiss, Virginia Weiss.
Financial data (yr. ended 01/31/02): Grants paid, $47,000; assets, $907,652 (M); gifts received, $48,709; expenditures, $47,318; qualifying distributions, $47,000.
Limitations: Applications not accepted. Giving primarily in NY.
Application information: Contributes only to pre-selected organizations.
Officers: Neil Weiss, Pres.; Douglas Dimonda, V.P.; Elizabeth Dimonda, V.P.; Virginia Weiss, Secy.; Kenneth Weiss, Treas.
EIN: 133940173

36704
NBC Family Charitable Foundation
300 Gleed Ave.
East Aurora, NY 14052

Established in 1997 in NY.
Financial data (yr. ended 12/31/01): Grants paid, $46,853; assets, $958,205 (M); expenditures, $58,983; qualifying distributions, $46,853.
Limitations: Applications not accepted.
Application information: Contributes only to pre-selected organizations.
Officer: Neil M. Chur, Pres.
EIN: 161520430

36705
Frieda & George Zinberg Foundation, Inc.
c/o Arthur D. Zinberg
66 Ave. A
New York, NY 10009-7202

Financial data (yr. ended 04/30/02): Grants paid, $46,850; assets, $836,810 (M); expenditures, $50,072; qualifying distributions, $46,850.
Limitations: Applications not accepted. Giving primarily in New York, NY.
Application information: Contributes only to pre-selected organizations.
Officers: Eugene Zinberg, Pres.; Joel M. Zinberg, V.P.; Arthur D. Zinberg, Secy.-Treas.
EIN: 133626368

36706
Zichron Lea Schonfeld Foundation
1540 56th St.
Brooklyn, NY 11219 (718) 853-6427
Contact: Susan Feldman, Tr.

Established in 2000 in NY.
Financial data (yr. ended 10/30/01): Grants paid, $46,809; assets, $14,151 (M); gifts received, $62,500; expenditures, $48,349; qualifying distributions, $48,349; giving activities include $1,540 for programs.
Limitations: Giving primarily in NY.
Trustees: Shlomo Feldman, Steven Feldman, Eli Silberstein.
EIN: 116553082

36707
Whiting Foundation Trust
c/o HSBC Bank USA
1 HSBC Ctr., 17th Fl.
Buffalo, NY 14203

Financial data (yr. ended 02/28/02): Grants paid, $46,800; assets, $641,576 (M); expenditures, $57,565; qualifying distributions, $46,800.
Limitations: Applications not accepted. Giving primarily in upstate NY.
Application information: Contributes only to pre-selected organizations.
Trustee: HSBC Bank USA.
EIN: 166148416

36708
Betty Parsons Foundation
61 Broadway, 18th Fl.
New York, NY 10006-2794 (212) 797-9100
Contact: Christopher C. Schwabacher, V.P.

Established in 1983 in NY.
Donor(s): Betty Parsons.‡
Financial data (yr. ended 08/31/00): Grants paid, $46,750; assets, $946,284 (M); expenditures, $77,073; qualifying distributions, $65,975; giving activities include $19,377 for programs.
Limitations: Giving primarily in NY.
Publications: Annual report.
Application information: Application form not required.

Officers: William P. Rayner, Pres.; Christopher C. Schwabacher, V.P.
EIN: 133193737

36709
Bountiful Resources Foundation
14 Chesham Way
Fairport, NY 14450

Established in 2001 in NY.
Donor(s): Kevin Clawson.
Financial data (yr. ended 12/31/01): Grants paid, $46,723; assets, $27,600 (M); gifts received, $27,600; expenditures, $46,723; qualifying distributions, $0.
Limitations: Applications not accepted.
Application information: Contributes only to pre-selected organizations.
Officers: Kevin Clawson, Pres.; Genevieve Pelissie, V.P.; Toi Clawson, Secy.-Treas.
EIN: 010563957

36710
J. R. Morris Charitable Foundation, Inc.
154 N. Glenora Rd.
Dundee, NY 14837 (607) 243-7771
Contact: Jeffrey R. Morris, Pres.

Established in 1995 in NY.
Donor(s): Jeffrey R. Morris.
Financial data (yr. ended 10/31/01): Grants paid, $46,700; assets, $846,908 (M); expenditures, $50,786; qualifying distributions, $46,700.
Limitations: Giving limited to residents of Allegany, Steuben and Yates counties, NY.
Officers and Directors:* Jeffrey R. Morris,* Pres.; Laurie Richer,* Secy.; Betty D. Morris.
EIN: 161490773

36711
Heyman Family Fund, Inc.
c/o John Butler
119-25 180th St.
Jamaica, NY 11434
Application address: P.O. Box 1202 Old Chelsea Sta., New York, NY 10011, tel.: (212) 627-4897
Contact: William D. Heyman, Pres.

Established in 1985 in NY.
Donor(s): D. John Heyman.
Financial data (yr. ended 12/31/00): Grants paid, $46,600; assets, $1,148,618 (M); expenditures, $74,686; qualifying distributions, $57,177.
Application information: Application form not required.
Officers: William D. Heyman, Pres.; Lynn Sedranak, Treas.
Trustee: Stephen Hayman.
EIN: 136087901

36712
The Alan & Tonia Gould Family Foundation, Inc.
c/o Pegg & Pegg
370 Lexington Ave., Ste. 1007
New York, NY 10017
Application address: 9 Village Ln., Santa Fe, NM 87505, tel.: (505) 988-1150
Contact: Alan Gould, Treas.

Established in 1997 in NM.
Donor(s): Gould Family Foundation, Inc.
Financial data (yr. ended 12/31/01): Grants paid, $46,580; assets, $1,038,990 (M); gifts received, $25,000; expenditures, $67,542; qualifying distributions, $56,479.
Limitations: Giving on a national basis, with some emphasis on Santa Fe, NM.
Application information: Application form not required.

Officers and Directors:* Tonia Gould,* Pres.; Michelle Daniels,* V.P.; Abigail Gould,* Secy.; Alan M. Gould,* Treas.; Melissa Gould, Robyn Tsapis.
EIN: 742844699

36713
The Julia Regina Smith Foundation, Inc.
75 East End Ave.
New York, NY 10028 (212) 988-1113
Contact: E. Ward Smith, Pres.

Financial data (yr. ended 12/31/01): Grants paid, $46,579; assets, $105,574 (M); expenditures, $48,850; qualifying distributions, $46,579.
Application information: Application form not required.
Officers: E. Ward Smith, Pres.; Carolyn L. Smith, V.P.
EIN: 476046922

36714
The Rome Sisters Foundation, Inc.
1 Mohegan Pl.
New Rochelle, NY 10804 (914) 633-7766
Contact: Robert Bases, M.D., Dir.

Established in 1987 in NY.
Donor(s): Lillian Rome,‡ Robert Bases, M.D., Judith Bases.
Financial data (yr. ended 09/30/01): Grants paid, $46,569; assets, $95,605 (M); gifts received, $126,000; expenditures, $70,023; qualifying distributions, $46,569.
Limitations: Applications not accepted. Giving limited to NY.
Application information: Contributes only to pre-selected organizations.
Directors: Judith Bases, Leonard Bases, M.D., Robert Bases, M.D.
EIN: 133441297

36715
The Rubin-Henry Family Foundation
c/o Howard Rubin
120 E. End Ave., Apt. 2
New York, NY 10028-7552

Established in 2000 in NY.
Donor(s): Mary Henry, Howard Rubin.
Financial data (yr. ended 08/31/01): Grants paid, $46,555; assets, $0 (M); gifts received, $600,000; expenditures, $46,555; qualifying distributions, $46,555.
Limitations: Applications not accepted.
Application information: Contributes only to pre-selected organizations.
Trustees: Mary Henry, Howard Rubin.
EIN: 137255537

36716
The Fagin Family Foundation
110-46 68th Rd.
Forest Hills, NY 11375-2959

Established in 1999 in NY.
Donor(s): Allen I. Fagin.
Financial data (yr. ended 12/31/01): Grants paid, $46,525; assets, $106,686 (M); gifts received, $130,000; expenditures, $48,010; qualifying distributions, $46,525.
Limitations: Applications not accepted.
Application information: Contributes only to pre-selected organizations.
Officers and Directors:* Allen I. Fagin,* Pres. and Treas.; Judith H. Fagin,* V.P. and Secy.; Charles G. Fagin, Miriam Fagin, Robert B. Fagin.
EIN: 113493014

36717
American Friends of the Claude Pompidou Foundation
c/o Abbe G. Shapiro
30 Rockefeller Plz.
New York, NY 10112

Established in 1998 in NY.
Financial data (yr. ended 12/31/00): Grants paid, $46,500; assets, $10,605 (M); gifts received, $5,000; expenditures, $75,827; qualifying distributions, $75,827.
Limitations: Applications not accepted. Giving on an international basis, primarily Paris, France.
Application information: Contributes only to pre-selected organizations.
Officers and Trustees:* Allan M. Chapin,* Pres.; Claude Roland,* Secy.; Thomas Pompidou,* Treas.; Hon. Evan G. Galbraith, George M. Gudefin, Daniel Moquay, Ieoh Ming Pei.
EIN: 133567614

36718
Downeast Conservation Foundation, Inc.
81 Skunks Misery Rd.
Locust Valley, NY 11560
Contact: F. Thomas Powers, Dir.

Donor(s): Elaine E. & Frank T. Powers, Jr. Foundation.
Financial data (yr. ended 12/31/01): Grants paid, $46,500; assets, $765,389 (M); expenditures, $53,042; qualifying distributions, $46,500.
Limitations: Giving primarily in Locust Valley, NY.
Directors: David A. Lewis, F. Thomas Powers, Sarah E. Powers.
EIN: 113346666

36719
Marine Society of the City of New York
17 Battery Pl.
New York, NY 10004 (212) 425-0448

Established in 1770 in NY.
Financial data (yr. ended 12/31/99): Grants paid, $46,467; assets, $3,235,406 (M); gifts received, $1,940; expenditures, $166,411; qualifying distributions, $125,876.
Limitations: Giving primarily on the East Coast, with emphasis on NY.
Publications: Newsletter.
Application information: Application form not required.
Officers: Frank Shellenbarger, Pres.; Leo Kraszeski, 1st V.P.; A. Smith, Secy.; Henry Engelbrecht, Treas.
EIN: 135643623
Codes: GTI

36720
The Diamond Family Charitable Foundation, Inc.
401 Pea Pond Rd.
P.O. Box 477
Bedford, NY 10506

Established in 1997 in NY.
Donor(s): Robert L. Diamond.
Financial data (yr. ended 12/31/01): Grants paid, $46,450; assets, $135,552 (M); expenditures, $49,790; qualifying distributions, $46,450.
Limitations: Applications not accepted.
Application information: Contributes only to pre-selected organizations.
Officers: Robert L. Diamond, Pres.; William Diamond, V.P.; Janice Diamond, Secy.; James Diamond, Treas.
EIN: 133938127

36721
The Mandell Family Foundation, Inc.
c/o Richard Mandell
666 Greenwich St., Ste. 434
New York, NY 10014

Established in 1999 in FL.
Donor(s): Leonore Schenker.
Financial data (yr. ended 06/30/01): Grants paid, $46,426; assets, $355,692 (M); expenditures, $59,970; qualifying distributions, $46,426.
Limitations: Applications not accepted.
Application information: Contributes only to pre-selected organizations.
Officer and Directors:* Leonore Schenker,* Pres.; James Mandell, Richard Mandell, Margery Sugarman.
EIN: 650937789

36722
Carl Tripi Foundation
c/o Rev. Msgr. Dino Lorenzetti
69 O'Hara Rd.
Tonawanda, NY 14150

Established in 2000 in NY.
Donor(s): Tripifoods Foundation.
Financial data (yr. ended 12/31/01): Grants paid, $46,401; assets, $383,940 (M); expenditures, $48,661; qualifying distributions, $46,401.
Limitations: Applications not accepted. Giving primarily in Buffalo, NY.
Application information: Contributes only to pre-selected organizations.
Directors: Rev. David Lipuma, Rev. Msgr. Dino Lorenzetti, Nanette L. Luczak, Joseph C. Tripi II.
EIN: 161577823

36723
Persian Heritage Foundation
c/o Committee on Awards
450 Riverside Dr., No. 4
New York, NY 10027-6821   (212) 851-5723
FAX: (212) 749-9524

Established in 1985 in DE.
Donor(s): Ehsan Yarshater.
Financial data (yr. ended 06/30/00): Grants paid, $46,400; assets, $3,450,139 (M); gifts received, $453,927; expenditures, $108,464; qualifying distributions, $107,920.
Limitations: Giving on an international basis.
Application information: Manuscript should be accompanied by 2 letters from scholars in the field stating that the work merits publication. Application form not required.
Officers: Ehsan Yarshater, Pres.; Dina Amin, V.P.; Raymond J. McRory, V.P.
EIN: 133201819

36724
The Hornet Foundation
c/o Morris & McVeigh, LLP
767 3rd Ave.
New York, NY 10017

Donor(s): Thomas Barbour.
Financial data (yr. ended 12/31/01): Grants paid, $46,300; assets, $269,114 (M); expenditures, $46,630; qualifying distributions, $46,300.
Limitations: Applications not accepted.
Application information: Contributes only to pre-selected organizations.
Officers: Thomas Barbour, Pres. and Treas.; MacDonald Budd, Secy.
Directors: Philip Brockman, Alison B. Fox.
EIN: 133143515

36725
The Scoroposki Foundation
(Formerly Jim and Lynn Scoroposki Foundation)
189 South St.
Oyster Bay, NY 11771   (516) 922-2266

Financial data (yr. ended 12/31/00): Grants paid, $46,273; assets, $1,014,822 (M); gifts received, $5,603; expenditures, $46,890; qualifying distributions, $46,273.
Limitations: Giving primarily in NY.
Trustees: James R. Scoroposki, Lidwina Scoroposki.
EIN: 113379285

36726
The Katcher Family Foundation
c/o Wachtell, Lipton, Rosen & Katz
51 W. 52nd St.
New York, NY 10019

Established in 1998 in NY.
Donor(s): Richard D. Katcher.
Financial data (yr. ended 12/31/01): Grants paid, $46,250; assets, $122,143 (M); expenditures, $46,303; qualifying distributions, $46,250.
Limitations: Applications not accepted.
Application information: Contributes only to pre-selected organizations.
Officers and Directors:* Richard D. Katcher,* Pres. and Treas.; Susan Katcher,* V.P. and Secy.; Andrew Katcher, Daniel Katcher.
EIN: 134036332

36727
Dublin Fund, Inc.
c/o Yohalem Gillman & Co., LLP
477 Madison Ave.
New York, NY 10022-5802

Donor(s): John McCurdy Eaton, Justine E. Auchincloss, Edward H. Auchincloss, Frederick M. Eaton.
Financial data (yr. ended 12/31/01): Grants paid, $46,150; assets, $615,689 (M); expenditures, $53,063; qualifying distributions, $47,857.
Limitations: Applications not accepted. Giving primarily in NY.
Application information: Contributes only to pre-selected organizations.
Officers and Directors:* Justine A. Eaton,* Pres.; Justine E. Auchincloss,* V.P. and Secy.; Frederick A. Eaton,* V.P. and Treas.; Edward H. Auchincloss,* V.P.; John McCurdy Eaton,* V.P.
EIN: 136076804

36728
The Yaseen Family Foundation, Inc.
(Formerly Leonard and Helen Yassen Foundation, Inc.)
c/o Becker & Co., PC
551 Madison Ave.
New York, NY 10022

Donor(s): Leonard C. Yaseen,‡ Helen F. Yaseen,‡ Roger Yaseen.
Financial data (yr. ended 07/31/01): Grants paid, $46,055; assets, $713,292 (M); expenditures, $52,632; qualifying distributions, $46,055.
Limitations: Applications not accepted. Giving primarily in NY.
Application information: Contributes only to pre-selected organizations.
Officers: Roger Yaseen, Pres.; Nicole Yaseen, V.P.; Marc Yaseen, Secy.-Treas.
EIN: 132964529

36729
Aaron and Debbie Cywiak Foundation, Inc.
1418 E. 24th St.
Brooklyn, NY 11210

Established in 1999 in NY.
Donor(s): Aaron Cywiak, Michael Cywiak.
Financial data (yr. ended 09/30/01): Grants paid, $46,020; assets, $4,817 (M); expenditures, $47,137; qualifying distributions, $46,944.
Limitations: Applications not accepted.
Application information: Contributes only to pre-selected organizations.
Officers: Aaron Cywiak, Pres.; Debbie Cywiak, V.P.; Michael Cywiak, Secy.-Treas.
EIN: 113520083

36730
E. A. Barvoets Fund
136 Railroad Ave. Ext
Albany, NY 12205

Established in 1953 in NY.
Donor(s): Williams Press, Inc.
Financial data (yr. ended 12/31/01): Grants paid, $46,000; assets, $863,644 (M); expenditures, $69,347; qualifying distributions, $46,000.
Limitations: Applications not accepted. Giving primarily in NY.
Application information: Contributes only to pre-selected organizations.
Trustees: Barbara Barvoets, Brooks R. Barvoets, Ernest Barvoets, Suzanne Barvoets, David F. Kunz.
EIN: 146020337

36731
The Brooke-McCarragher Foundation
21 E. 90th St., Apt. 14A
New York, NY 10128-6501

Established in 2000 in NY.
Donor(s): Paul A. Brooke, Kathleen McCarragher.
Financial data (yr. ended 12/31/01): Grants paid, $46,000; assets, $669,232 (M); expenditures, $51,275; qualifying distributions, $46,000.
Limitations: Giving on a national basis.
Officers and Directors:* Paul A. Brooke,* Pres.; Kathleen McCarragher,* V.P.
EIN: 626369585

36732
Sam and Jennie Rovit Memorial Foundation
c/o Richard Rovit
42 Brite Ave.
Scarsdale, NY 10583

Financial data (yr. ended 12/31/01): Grants paid, $46,000; assets, $760,845 (M); gifts received, $327,502; expenditures, $54,409; qualifying distributions, $46,000.
Limitations: Applications not accepted.
Application information: Contributes only to pre-selected organizations.
Trustees: Lawrence Rothenberg, Barbara Rovit, Earl Rovit, Richard Rovit.
EIN: 133935633

36733
The Stony Creek Fund
c/o AKO, MMcGuire
1251 6th Ave.
New York, NY 10020-1182

Financial data (yr. ended 12/31/01): Grants paid, $46,000; assets, $482,900 (M); expenditures, $50,100; qualifying distributions, $45,476.
Limitations: Applications not accepted. Giving primarily in MA and New York, NY.
Application information: Contributes only to pre-selected organizations.

Officers: Jonathan M. Weld, Pres.; Jane P. Weld, V.P. and Treas.; Jack D. Gunther, Jr., Secy.
EIN: 133800567

36734
The Rosalind & Alfred Berger Foundation
30 E. 62nd St.
New York, NY 10021
Contact: Alfred Berger, Dir.

Established in 1989 in NY.
Donor(s): Alfred Berger.
Financial data (yr. ended 12/31/01): Grants paid, $45,956; assets, $1,306,676 (M); gifts received, $91,768; expenditures, $56,268; qualifying distributions, $56,268.
Limitations: Giving primarily in NY.
Director: Alfred Berger.
EIN: 133537910

36735
The Ferris Foundation, Inc.
(Formerly Susan Henshaw Jones Foundation, Inc.)
c/o Mahoney Cohen & Co.
111 W. 40th St.
New York, NY 10018

Established in 1998 in DC.
Donor(s): Susan Henshaw Jones.
Financial data (yr. ended 12/31/01): Grants paid, $45,827; assets, $971,810 (M); expenditures, $59,436; qualifying distributions, $45,827.
Limitations: Applications not accepted. Giving primarily in Washington, DC.
Application information: Contributes only to pre-selected organizations.
Officers: Susan Henshaw Jones, Pres.; Richard Eaton, Secy.
EIN: 134013680

36736
Victor C. & Clara C. Battin Foundation
c/o Clara C. Battin
956 5th Ave.
New York, NY 10021-1737   (212) 879-7433
Contact: Miriam Cahn, Tr.

Financial data (yr. ended 08/31/01): Grants paid, $45,780; assets, $1,043,872 (M); expenditures, $66,014; qualifying distributions, $49,818.
Limitations: Giving primarily in New York, NY.
Trustees: Clara C. Battin, Miriam Cahn.
EIN: 136124399

36737
Ansonia Foundation, Inc.
c/o The Bank of New York
1 Wall St., 28th Fl., Tax Dept.
New York, NY 10286
Application address: c/o Putnam Trust Co., P.O. Box 2610, Greenwich, CT 06836
Contact: Peter Roberge

Financial data (yr. ended 09/30/01): Grants paid, $45,750; assets, $678,448 (M); expenditures, $54,605; qualifying distributions, $45,750.
Limitations: Giving primarily in the Northeast.
Officer: Jeffrey C. Sturgess, Pres.
Trustee: Putnam Trust Co.
EIN: 066033969

36738
S. Spencer Scott Fund, Inc.
c/o O'Connor, Davies & Co., LLP
60 E. 42nd St., Ste. 3600
New York, NY 10165
Application address: Lord Hill, Old Lyme, CT 06371
Contact: S. Spencer Scott, Jr., Pres.

Established in 1949 in NY.

Financial data (yr. ended 12/31/00): Grants paid, $45,750; assets, $919,298 (M); expenditures, $55,496; qualifying distributions, $45,750.
Limitations: Giving on a national basis.
Officers: S. Spencer Scott, Jr., Pres.; Deborah Flagg Scott, V.P.
EIN: 136113359

36739
George and Joyce Wein Foundation
c/o Berlin & Kolin
1790 Broadway, Rm. 705
New York, NY 10019-1412

Established in 1991 in DE.
Donor(s): George T. Wein, Joyce Wein.
Financial data (yr. ended 12/31/01): Grants paid, $45,700; assets, $578,861 (M); gifts received, $372,364; expenditures, $46,453; qualifying distributions, $45,700.
Limitations: Applications not accepted. Giving primarily in New York, NY.
Application information: Contributes only to pre-selected organizations.
Officers and Directors:* George T. Wein,* Pres.; Joyce Wein,* V.P.; Lester Dembitzer,* Secy.-Treas.
EIN: 133599335

36740
Nori Foundation, Inc.
2 Highpoint Terr.
Scarsdale, NY 10583

Donor(s): Dattatreyudu Nori.
Financial data (yr. ended 12/31/00): Grants paid, $45,676; assets, $114,900 (M); gifts received, $61,000; expenditures, $60,335; qualifying distributions, $0.
Officers: Dattatreyudu Nori, Pres.; Priya Nori, V.P.; Satish Nori, V.P.; Subhadra Nori, V.P.
EIN: 134006662

36741
Ficalora Foundation
173 Aldershot Ln.
Manhasset, NY 11030

Established in 1998 in NY.
Donor(s): Joseph R. Ficalora, Alice B. Ficalora.
Financial data (yr. ended 12/31/00): Grants paid, $45,665; assets, $1,513,959 (M); gifts received, $137,850; expenditures, $46,982; qualifying distributions, $45,321.
Limitations: Applications not accepted.
Application information: Contributes only to pre-selected organizations.
Officers: Alice B. Ficalora, Pres.; Joseph R. Ficalora, V.P.; John J. Ficalora, Treas.
EIN: 113441781

36742
Braver Foundation, Inc.
1185 Ave. of the Americas
New York, NY 10036-2602
Contact: David A. Braver, Pres.

Established in 1968 in NY.
Donor(s): David A. Braver.
Financial data (yr. ended 12/31/01): Grants paid, $45,611; assets, $257,905 (M); expenditures, $46,395; qualifying distributions, $45,611.
Limitations: Applications not accepted. Giving primarily in New York, NY.
Application information: Contributes only to pre-selected organizations.
Officer: David A. Braver, Pres.
EIN: 136277869

36743
Ben & Estelle Sommers Foundation, Inc.
c/o Gayle Miller
61 W. 62nd St.
New York, NY 10023

Established in 1994 in NY.
Donor(s): Estelle Sommers.‡
Financial data (yr. ended 12/31/01): Grants paid, $45,554; assets, $191,407 (M); expenditures, $54,299; qualifying distributions, $45,554.
Limitations: Giving primarily in New York, NY.
Application information: Application form not required.
Director: Gayle Miller.
EIN: 133733418

36744
The Troy Savings Bank Charitable Foundation, Inc.
32 2nd St.
Troy, NY 12180
Application address: Hedley Park Pl., 433 River St., Troy, NY 12180, tel.: (518) 270-4932
Contact: Daniel J. Hogarty, Jr., Pres.

Established in 1998 in NY.
Donor(s): The Troy Savings Bank.
Financial data (yr. ended 12/31/01): Grants paid, $45,545; assets, $4,937,121 (M); expenditures, $121,509; qualifying distributions, $120,134.
Limitations: Giving primarily in NY.
Officers and Directors:* Daniel J. Hogarty, Jr.,* Pres.; Kevin M. O'Bryan,* Secy.; David DeLuca,* Treas.; The Troy Savings Bank.
EIN: 141813865
Codes: CS, CD

36745
AMP Foundation, Inc.
Tardinotocci & Goldstein, LLP
122 E. 42nd St., Ste. 1518
New York, NY 10168

Established in 1990 in NY.
Donor(s): Christopher Fallon.
Financial data (yr. ended 11/30/00): Grants paid, $45,500; assets, $1,127 (L); expenditures, $53,071; qualifying distributions, $45,445.
Limitations: Applications not accepted. Giving primarily in NY.
Application information: Contributes only to pre-selected organizations.
Officers: Christopher Fallon, Pres.; John Fallon, Secy.; Elaine Ryan, Treas.
EIN: 133557167

36746
James Foundation, Inc.
c/o American Express Tax and Business Svcs.
1185 Ave. of the Americas
New York, NY 10036-2602

Established in 1984 in NJ.
Donor(s): James Chromiak, Virginia Gilder.
Financial data (yr. ended 11/30/01): Grants paid, $45,500; assets, $1,513,530 (M); expenditures, $59,739; qualifying distributions, $45,500.
Limitations: Applications not accepted. Giving limited to NJ and PA.
Application information: Contributes only to pre-selected organizations.
Officers and Directors:* James Chromiak, Pres. and Treas.; Virginia Gilder,* V.P.; Susan Chromiak,* Secy.
EIN: 133319281

36747
David M. Milton Charitable Trust
c/o George D. O'Neill
30 Rockefeller Plz., Rm. 5432
New York, NY 10012-0245

Financial data (yr. ended 05/31/02): Grants paid, $45,500; assets, $883,469 (M); expenditures, $53,813; qualifying distributions, $45,500.
Limitations: Applications not accepted. Giving primarily in New York, NY.
Application information: Contributes only to pre-selected organizations.
Trustees: Jacob Isbrandsten, George D. O'Neill, J. Davidge Warfield.
EIN: 136876120

36748
Barbara Forst Charitable Trust
Migdal, Pollack, Rosenkrantz & Migdal LLP
41 E. 57th St., 15th Fl.
New York, NY 10022
Contact: Lester C. Migdal, Tr.

Established in 1999.
Financial data (yr. ended 12/31/01): Grants paid, $45,432; assets, $1,419,132 (M); gifts received, $500,000; expenditures, $54,124; qualifying distributions, $45,432.
Trustees: Jesse Forst, Matthew Forst, Lester C. Migdal, Fernande Sommers.
EIN: 311627706

36749
Allen Foundation, Inc.
255 E. 2nd St.
Mineola, NY 11501

Established in 1959.
Financial data (yr. ended 12/31/01): Grants paid, $45,321; assets, $506,467 (M); expenditures, $45,919; qualifying distributions, $45,321.
Limitations: Giving primarily in the greater New York, NY, area.
Director: Alton K. Allen.
EIN: 116036302

36750
The Tarasoff Foundation
c/o Schroeder & Co., Inc.
1633 Broadway, 9th Fl. Tax Dept.
New York, NY 10019-6708
Contact: Michael A. Casciato

Established in 1997 in DE.
Donor(s): Barry Tarasoff.
Financial data (yr. ended 02/28/02): Grants paid, $45,300; assets, $199,576 (M); gifts received, $53,927; expenditures, $45,613; qualifying distributions, $45,300.
Officers and Directors:* Barry J. Tarasoff,* Pres. and Treas.; Sylvia Tarasoff,* Secy.; Joshua Tarasoff.
EIN: 061476857

36751
DBS Foundation, Inc.
c/o Nathan Berkman & Co.
29 Broadway, Rm. 2900
New York, NY 10006

Financial data (yr. ended 08/31/01): Grants paid, $45,295; assets, $457,544 (M); gifts received, $100,000; expenditures, $48,549; qualifying distributions, $45,295.
Limitations: Applications not accepted. Giving primarily in NY.
Application information: Contributes only to pre-selected organizations.
Trustees: David B. Strauss, Jr., Susan Strauss.
EIN: 132575461

36752
Sarah Hamlet Charitable Foundation
36 Causeway
Lawrence, NY 11559-1514 (516) 371-5854
Contact: Sarah Hamlet, Tr.

Established in 1998 in NY.
Financial data (yr. ended 11/30/01): Grants paid, $45,275; assets, $2,951 (M); gifts received, $49,000; expenditures, $46,275; qualifying distributions, $46,275.
Limitations: Giving primarily in NY.
Trustees: Rochelle Hamlet, Sarah Hamlet, Frank Schwartz.
EIN: 116506163

36753
Wood Kalb Foundation
c/o F.D.R. Station
P.O. Box 5315
New York, NY 10150-5315

Established in 1953 in NY.
Donor(s): Julia A. Murphy, Social Research Foundation, Inc.
Financial data (yr. ended 12/31/01): Grants paid, $45,275; assets, $436,730 (M); expenditures, $61,074; qualifying distributions, $45,275.
Limitations: Applications not accepted. Giving on a national basis, with emphasis on New York, NY, and Washington, DC.
Application information: Contributes only to pre-selected organizations.
Trustee: Julia A. Murphy.
EIN: 136105376

36754
Lawrence and Marilyn Kaplan Foundation
c/o Kabro Associates
113 Crossways Park Dr.
Woodbury, NY 11797

Established in 2000 in NY.
Donor(s): Lawrence Kaplan, Marilyn Kaplan.
Financial data (yr. ended 12/31/01): Grants paid, $45,175; assets, $257,444 (M); gifts received, $199,998; expenditures, $45,325; qualifying distributions, $45,175.
Limitations: Applications not accepted.
Application information: Contributes only to pre-selected organizations.
Directors: Lori Decostanzo, Bonnie Farello, Lawrence Kaplan, Marilyn Kaplan, Steven Kaplan, Sherry Stolzeberg.
EIN: 113545707

36755
Meryl & Christopher Lewis Foundation
60 Mystic Dr.
Ossining, NY 10562-1967
Contact: Christopher A.H. Lewis, Chair.

Established in 1986 in NY.
Donor(s): Christopher A.H. Lewis, Meryl B. Lewis.
Financial data (yr. ended 06/30/01): Grants paid, $45,155; assets, $883,001 (M); gifts received, $25; expenditures, $46,250; qualifying distributions, $44,639.
Limitations: Giving limited to Cape Ann, MA, and Westchester County, NY.
Application information: Application form required.
Officer: Christopher A.H. Lewis, Chair.; Meryl Lewis, Secy.
Trustee: Ellen Blank.
EIN: 133369933

36756
Madjack Foundation, Inc.
665 Titicus Rd.
North Salem, NY 10560

Established in 2000 in NY.
Donor(s): Peter Kamenstyin.
Financial data (yr. ended 12/31/00): Grants paid, $45,150; assets, $47,508 (M); gifts received, $92,012; expenditures, $45,450; qualifying distributions, $45,450.
Officers and Directors:* Peter Kamenstyin,* Pres. and Treas.; Jacalyn Kamenstyin,* Secy.
EIN: 134104916

36757
The Edward L. Anderson, Jr. Foundation, Inc.
c/o Pustorino, Puglisi & Co., LLP
515 Madison Ave., 22nd Fl.
New York, NY 10022

Established in 1980.
Donor(s): Edward L. Anderson.
Financial data (yr. ended 12/31/01): Grants paid, $45,117; assets, $209,790 (M); gifts received, $102,005; expenditures, $47,044; qualifying distributions, $45,785.
Limitations: Applications not accepted. Giving on a national basis.
Application information: Contributes only to pre-selected organizations.
Officers: Edward L. Anderson, Jr., Pres.; David W. Anderson, V.P.; Steven B. Anderson, Secy.
EIN: 222302121

36758
The Baker Foundation
71 N. Country Club Dr.
Rochester, NY 14618

Established in 1995 in NY.
Donor(s): Robert W. Baker, Sr.
Financial data (yr. ended 12/31/01): Grants paid, $45,100; assets, $684,520 (M); gifts received, $36,144; expenditures, $50,037; qualifying distributions, $45,100.
Limitations: Applications not accepted. Giving primarily in NY.
Application information: Contributes only to pre-selected organizations.
Officer: Robert W. Baker, Sr., Mgr.
Trustees: Nancy Baker, Natalie P. Baker, Robert Baker, Jr., Susan Sheridan.
EIN: 161462951

36759
The Greylock Foundation
c/o Bruce H. Sobel, C.P.A.
6 E. 43rd St., 19th Fl.
New York, NY 10017-4609

Established in 1994 in NY.
Financial data (yr. ended 11/30/01): Grants paid, $45,100; assets, $867,923 (M); gifts received, $100,000; expenditures, $48,826; qualifying distributions, $45,100.
Limitations: Applications not accepted. Giving primarily in CA and MA.
Application information: Contributes only to pre-selected organizations.
Trustee: Thomas E. Gallagher.
EIN: 956982534

36760
NAMSB Foundation, Inc.
309 5th Ave., Ste. 303
New York, NY 10016 (212) 685-4550
E-mail: info@nsi-show.com; *URL:* http://www.nsi-shows.com
Contact: Jack Herschlag, Chair.

Established in 1968 in NY.
Financial data (yr. ended 01/31/02): Grants paid, $45,100; assets, $1,042,385 (M); expenditures, $48,900; qualifying distributions, $45,100.
Limitations: Applications not accepted.
Application information: Contributes only to pre-selected organizations.
Officers and Trustees:* Myron Sperber,* Pres.; Charles Alberts,* V.P.; Arthur H. Taylor, Jr.,* V.P.; Perry Brenner,* Secy.; Marvin A. Blumenfeld,* Treas.; William Hefner, Joseph S. Klein, Charles Linz, George Newman.
EIN: 132642749

36761
Colet Foundation, Ltd.
c/o Robert Engel, Gleacher & Co.
660 Madison Ave., 19th Fl.
New York, NY 10021
Contact: Directors

Donor(s): John Weitz, Eyal Ofer.
Financial data (yr. ended 10/31/00): Grants paid, $45,079; assets, $27,508 (M); gifts received, $26,000; expenditures, $50,096; qualifying distributions, $45,048.
Officers: John Weitz, Chair.; Simon Strauss, Secy.; Robert Engel, Treas.
Director: Stephen Baldock.
EIN: 133593839

36762
Heinz and Suze Rehfuss Memorial Fund
c/o Mark L. Stulmaker
42 Delaware Ave., Ste. 300
Buffalo, NY 14202-3901
Application address: c/o Melisse H. Pinto, 156 David Rd., Rutland, VT, 05701

Established in 1991 in NY.
Donor(s): Heinz Rehfuss.‡
Financial data (yr. ended 12/31/00): Grants paid, $45,052; assets, $386,104 (M); expenditures, $53,375; qualifying distributions, $46,638.
Limitations: Giving limited to Buffalo, NY.
Application information: Application form required.
Trustee: Melisse H. Pinto.
EIN: 166356877
Codes: GTI

36763
Arcadia Foundation
(Formerly John B. Ryan Foundation, Inc.)
c/o Marcum & Kliegman
130 Crossways Park Dr.
Woodbury, NY 11797-2027

Donor(s): John B. Ryan.
Financial data (yr. ended 12/31/00): Grants paid, $45,000; assets, $594,993 (M); gifts received, $68,956; expenditures, $49,424; qualifying distributions, $45,000.
Limitations: Applications not accepted. Giving primarily in New York, NY.
Officer and Directors:* John B. Ryan,* Pres.; Thomas Ryan.
EIN: 133398050

36764
Romare Howard Bearden Foundation, Inc.
305 7th Ave.
New York, NY 10001-6008

Established in 1988 in NY.
Donor(s): Romare Howard Bearden.‡
Financial data (yr. ended 09/30/01): Grants paid, $45,000; assets, $3,642,161 (M); expenditures, $241,320; qualifying distributions, $45,000.
Limitations: Applications not accepted. Giving primarily in NC.
Application information: Contributes only to pre-selected organizations.
Officers: Marie L. Rohan, Chair.; Tallal Elboushi, Vice-Chair.; Diedre Harris-Kelley, Secy.; Dorothe Rohan Dow, Treas.
EIN: 136902775

36765
Eva H. Brown Foundation, Inc.
P.O. Box 359
New Hyde Park, NY 11040
Application address: 2000 Plaza Ave., P.O. Box 148, Hew Hyde Park, NY 11040, tel.: (516) 328-1400
Contact: Ann M. Henken, Secy.

Donor(s): Milton V. Brown.
Financial data (yr. ended 05/31/00): Grants paid, $45,000; assets, $1,065,292 (M); expenditures, $47,950; qualifying distributions, $47,450.
Limitations: Giving limited to Long Island, NY.
Application information: Application form required.
Officers: Kalman I. Nulman, Pres.; Bruce D. Brown, V.P.; Ann M. Henken, Secy.; Allan G. Brown, Treas.
EIN: 510203745

36766
Bulrush Foundation
(Formerly The Siegfried Family Foundation)
c/o J. Witmeyer
P.O. Box 31051
Rochester, NY 14603

Established in 1995 in NY.
Donor(s): Carolyn W. Siegfried.
Financial data (yr. ended 09/30/01): Grants paid, $45,000; assets, $1,189,282 (M); gifts received, $337,930; expenditures, $45,222; qualifying distributions, $54,057.
Limitations: Applications not accepted. Giving primarily in Baltimore, MD; giving also in Columbia and Ontario, Canada.
Application information: Contributes only to pre-selected organizations.
Officers and Directors:* Carolyn Gale Siegfried,* Pres.; Elizabeth Hathaway Siegfried,* V.P.; James H. Ridgely, Secy.; James H. McBride, Treas.
EIN: 161491119

36767
The Frances & Townsend Burden Foundation
c/o Ambrose O'Connell
600 5th Ave.
New York, NY 10020

Financial data (yr. ended 12/31/01): Grants paid, $45,000; assets, $903,094 (M); expenditures, $48,941; qualifying distributions, $45,000.
Limitations: Applications not accepted. Giving on a national basis.
Application information: Contributes only to pre-selected organizations.
Officers: Childs Burden, Pres.; Frances Burden, V.P.; Dixon Burden, Secy.; Henry Burden, Treas.
EIN: 136085379

36768
Carver Scholarship Fund, Inc.
75 W. 125th St.
New York, NY 10027 (212) 876-4747
Contact: Richard T. Greene, Chair.

Donor(s): Carver Federal Savings Bank.
Financial data (yr. ended 12/31/00): Grants paid, $45,000; assets, $825,395 (M); expenditures, $49,306; qualifying distributions, $45,000.
Limitations: Giving primarily in New York, NY.
Publications: Informational brochure.
Application information: The foundation has discontinued making scholarship awards directly to individuals. Application form required.
Officer: Richard T. Greene, Chair.
Trustees: Earl Andrews, David Dinkins, David Jones, Marcella Maxwell, Deborah Wright.
EIN: 133277661
Codes: CS, CD

36769
Camilla Davis Foundation
c/o Starr & Co.
350 Park Ave.
New York, NY 10022

Donor(s): Daniel B. Hrdy.
Financial data (yr. ended 06/30/01): Grants paid, $45,000; assets, $94,864 (M); gifts received, $683; expenditures, $45,050; qualifying distributions, $45,000.
Limitations: Applications not accepted. Giving primarily in CA.
Application information: Contributes only to pre-selected organizations.
Officer: Daniel B. Hrdy, Pres.
EIN: 746310617

36770
David F. and Frances A. Eberhart Foundation
305 E. 87th St.
New York, NY 10128-4801

Established in 1998 in NY.
Donor(s): David Eberhart, Frances Eberhart.
Financial data (yr. ended 12/31/01): Grants paid, $45,000; assets, $1,253,400 (M); gifts received, $450,030; expenditures, $56,795; qualifying distributions, $45,000.
Officer: David F. Eberhart, Pres.
EIN: 133958121

36771
The Enable Foundation
c/o Torys
237 Park Ave.
New York, NY 10017

Financial data (yr. ended 12/31/02): Grants paid, $45,000; assets, $3,903 (M); gifts received, $45,000; expenditures, $46,004; qualifying distributions, $45,000.
Limitations: Applications not accepted.
Application information: Contributes only to pre-selected organizations.
Trustees: Gregory E. Mulroy, Susan B. Robinson, Mark B. Waldstein.
EIN: 522133009

36772
Floors Foundation
1329 E. 24th St.
Brooklyn, NY 11210 (718) 951-6596
Contact: Jacob Feldman, Tr.

Established in 1997.
Donor(s): Leah Feldman.
Financial data (yr. ended 12/31/01): Grants paid, $45,000; assets, $296,352 (M); gifts received,

36772—NEW YORK

$76,923; expenditures, $46,159; qualifying distributions, $45,000.
Limitations: Giving primarily in NY.
Trustees: Jacob Feldman, Leah Feldman.
EIN: 116473852

36773
Brian P. Friedman Family Foundation
520 Madison Ave., 8th Fl.
New York, NY 10022

Established in 1992 in NY.
Donor(s): Brian P. Friedman.
Financial data (yr. ended 11/30/01): Grants paid, $45,000; assets, $118,967 (M); expenditures, $45,268; qualifying distributions, $45,102.
Limitations: Applications not accepted.
Application information: Contributes only to pre-selected organizations.
Officer and Directors:* Brian P. Friedman,* Pres.; Etta Brandman, Barbara J. Shulman.
EIN: 133705915

36774
Clara & Kurt Hellmuth Foundation
c/o JPMorgan Chase Bank
1211 6th Ave., 34th Fl.
New York, NY 10036
Application address: 9 Market Ln., Great Neck, NY 11020
Contact: Michael F. Berger, Pres.

Established around 1986.
Financial data (yr. ended 12/31/01): Grants paid, $45,000; assets, $928,473 (M); expenditures, $70,798; qualifying distributions, $57,743.
Officer and Directors:* Michael F. Berger,* Pres. and Secy.; Tobas N. Berger.
EIN: 510202860

36775
The Hurlburt Foundation, Inc.
c/o SP Cooper and Collp
1 Exec. Blvd., 4th Fl.
Yonkers, NY 10701 (914) 709-1100
Contact: Herbert G. Kanarick, Treas.

Established in 1998 in FL.
Donor(s): Wilbur F. Hurlburt, Jr.
Financial data (yr. ended 12/31/01): Grants paid, $45,000; assets, $4,911,722 (M); gifts received, $723,934; expenditures, $167,146; qualifying distributions, $45,000.
Limitations: Giving primarily in FL.
Application information: Application form required.
Officers and Directors:* Jean L. Hurlburt,* Pres.; Nancy Hurlburt,* V.P.; Wilbur F. Hurlburt III,* V.P.; Michael H. Kline, Sr.,* Secy.; Herbert G. Kanarick,* Treas.; John S. Bohatch.
EIN: 650795533

36776
The Rona Jaffe Foundation
201 E. 62nd St., No. 14D
New York, NY 10021-7627

Donor(s): Rona F. Jaffe.
Financial data (yr. ended 09/30/01): Grants paid, $45,000; assets, $378,144 (M); gifts received, $125,000; expenditures, $146,496; qualifying distributions, $45,000.
Limitations: Applications not accepted. Giving primarily in NY.
Application information: Unsolicited requests for funds not accepted.
Officers and Directors:* Rona F. Jaffe,* Pres.; Alan Rothfeld,* Secy.; Philip F. Strassler,* Treas.
EIN: 133383860

36777
Herman H. & Ruth S. Kahn Foundation, Inc.
c/o B. Strauss Assoc., Ltd.
307 5th Ave., 8th Fl.
New York, NY 10016-6517

Established in 1954 in NY.
Donor(s): Herman H. Kahn, Ruth S. Kahn.
Financial data (yr. ended 06/30/01): Grants paid, $45,000; assets, $672,789 (M); gifts received, $100; expenditures, $42,378; qualifying distributions, $45,100.
Limitations: Applications not accepted. Giving in the U.S., with emphasis on NY.
Application information: Contributes only to pre-selected organizations.
Officers: Geraldine K. Karetsky, V.P.; Ann Finkelson, Secy.; Barry M. Strauss, Treas.
EIN: 136094014

36778
Louis Levin Foundation
c/o A. Zell
392 Central Park W., Apt. 12M
New York, NY 10025-5040
Contact: Joan Rose, Pres.

Established in 1967.
Financial data (yr. ended 12/31/99): Grants paid, $45,000; assets, $1,147,555 (M); expenditures, $127,990; qualifying distributions, $101,500.
Limitations: Giving primarily in NY.
Application information: Application form not required.
Officers: Joan Rose, Pres.; David Rose, V.P.; Saul Rose, Secy.
EIN: 226076671

36779
The Francis & Gloria McAlpin Charitable Foundation, Inc.
617 Old Woods Rd.
Webster, NY 14580
Application address: 255 Hollenbeck St., Rochester, NY 14621, tel.: (716) 266-3060
Contact: Michael J. McAlpin, Secy.

Established in 2000 in NY.
Donor(s): McAlpin Industries, Inc.
Financial data (yr. ended 12/31/01): Grants paid, $45,000; assets, $1,095 (M); expenditures, $50,356; qualifying distributions, $45,000.
Application information: Application form not required.
Officers and Directors:* Francis K. McAlpin,* Pres.; Gloria G. McAlpin,* V.P.; Michael J. McAlpin,* Secy.; Kenneth M. McAlpin,* Treas.
EIN: 161597707

36780
The Andrew J. and Katalin S. Novak Foundation
c/o The Cox Office
419 Park Ave. S., 13th Fl.
New York, NY 10016-8410

Established in 1999 in NY.
Financial data (yr. ended 10/31/01): Grants paid, $45,000; assets, $787,247 (M); expenditures, $69,214; qualifying distributions, $69,214.
Limitations: Giving primarily in TX.
Officers: Andrew J. Novak, Pres.; Katalin S. Novak, V.P.; David E. Stutzman, Secy.; Thomas A. Cox, Treas.
EIN: 134091512

36781
The Burton and Judith Resnick Foundation
110 E. 59th St., 37th Fl.
New York, NY 10022

Established in 1989.

Donor(s): Burton P. Resnick.
Financial data (yr. ended 03/31/01): Grants paid, $45,000; assets, $2,086,652 (M); gifts received, $1,901,000; expenditures, $46,067; qualifying distributions, $45,000.
Limitations: Giving primarily in NY.
Officers and Directors:* Burton P. Resnick,* Pres. and Treas.; Judith B. Resnick,* V.P. and Secy.; Steven J. Rotter.
EIN: 133524116

36782
Waldo Foundation, Inc.
c/o Paul R. Mendelsohn
175 E. 74th St., Rm. 9A
New York, NY 10021-3218

Donor(s): Walter Mendelsohn.
Financial data (yr. ended 09/30/01): Grants paid, $45,000; assets, $1,009,824 (M); gifts received, $90,472; expenditures, $52,035; qualifying distributions, $45,000.
Limitations: Applications not accepted. Giving limited to NY.
Application information: Contributes only to pre-selected organizations.
Officers: Sue M. Mellins, Chair.; Paul R. Mendelsohn, Pres.; Robert B. Mellins, V.P.; Lore H. Mendelsohn, Secy.-Treas.
EIN: 136082687

36783
Carol and Stuart Schlesinger Foundation
c/o Goldman Sachs & Co.
85 Broad St., Tax Dept.
New York, NY 10004

Established in 1989 in NY.
Donor(s): Stuart J. Schlesinger, Carol Schlesinger.
Financial data (yr. ended 04/30/02): Grants paid, $44,950; assets, $297,188 (M); expenditures, $45,148; qualifying distributions, $44,950.
Limitations: Applications not accepted. Giving primarily in New York, NY.
Application information: Contributes only to pre-selected organizations.
Trustees: Carol Schlesinger, David A. Schlesinger, Rachel L. Schlesinger, Stuart J. Schlesinger.
EIN: 133532017

36784
The Debra and Jeffrey Geller Family Foundation
71 Carolyn Pl.
Chappaqua, NY 10514 (914) 238-6712
Contact: Jeffrey Geller, Tr.

Established in 2000 in NY.
Donor(s): Jeffrey Geller, Debra Geller.
Financial data (yr. ended 12/31/01): Grants paid, $44,813; assets, $0 (M); gifts received, $600,000; expenditures, $47,604; qualifying distributions, $44,431.
Limitations: Giving primarily in NY.
Trustees: Debra Geller, Jeffrey Geller.
EIN: 134138500

36785
John and Anne Oros Foundation
c/o BCRS Associates, LLC
67 Wall St., 8th Fl.
New York, NY 10005

Established in 1988 in NJ.
Donor(s): John J. Oros, Anne Oros.
Financial data (yr. ended 06/30/01): Grants paid, $44,810; assets, $965,469 (M); gifts received, $148,922; expenditures, $50,187; qualifying distributions, $44,810.
Limitations: Applications not accepted. Giving limited to Madison, NJ, New York, NY, and Madison, WI.

Application information: Contributes only to pre-selected organizations.
Trustees: Anne W. Oros, John J. Oros, John L. Oros.
EIN: 133502405

36786
BLL Foundation
c/o Sullivan and Cromwell
125 Broad St.
New York, NY 10004-2498

Established in 1999 in NY.
Financial data (yr. ended 12/31/01): Grants paid, $44,707; assets, $764,231 (M); expenditures, $45,068; qualifying distributions, $44,401.
Limitations: Applications not accepted.
Application information: Contributes only to pre-selected organizations.
Trustees: Barbara G. Landau, W. Loeber Landau.
EIN: 134038296

36787
The Baker Foundation, Inc.
c/o Robert Taisey
156 W. 56th St.
New York, NY 10019-3800
Contact: Robert D. Taisey, Secy.-Treas.

Established in 1988 in NY.
Donor(s): John De Cuevas, Margaret De Cuevas, Sue Lonoff De Cuevas.
Financial data (yr. ended 12/31/99): Grants paid, $44,700; assets, $12,440 (M); gifts received, $45,000; expenditures, $45,595; qualifying distributions, $44,700.
Limitations: Giving primarily in MA and NY.
Application information: Application form not required.
Officers and Trustees:* John De Cuevas,* Pres.; Margaret De Cuevas,* V.P.; Robert D. Taisey,* Secy.-Treas.; Sue Lonoff De Cuevas, Vincent McGee.
EIN: 133490498

36788
Led Charitable Foundation
371 Crown St.
Brooklyn, NY 11225
Contact: Louis Dubov, Tr.

Established in 2001 in NY.
Financial data (yr. ended 12/31/01): Grants paid, $44,692; assets, $1,726 (L); gifts received, $46,991; expenditures, $45,265; qualifying distributions, $45,265.
Trustees: Evelyn Dubov, Louis Dubov, Reize Margulis.
EIN: 113556325

36789
Theresa Alessandra Russo Foundation, Inc.
c/o Russo & Atlas
1600 Stewart Ave., Ste. 300
Westbury, NY 11590

Established in 1992 in NY.
Financial data (yr. ended 12/31/01): Grants paid, $44,688; assets, $63,700 (M); gifts received, $80,710; expenditures, $86,023; qualifying distributions, $44,688.
Limitations: Applications not accepted.
Application information: Contributes only to pre-selected organizations.
Officers: Susan Russo, Pres.; Fr. James Maltese, V.P.; Judy Murdaugh Jackson, Secy.; Vincent J. Russo, Treas.
EIN: 113126316

36790
The Kopp Family Foundation, Inc.
c/o Philip Kopp, III
181-63 Tudor Rd.
Jamaica, NY 11432-1446

Established in 2000 in NY.
Donor(s): Philip Kopp III.
Financial data (yr. ended 09/30/01): Grants paid, $44,664; assets, $139,487 (M); gifts received, $168,197; expenditures, $45,475; qualifying distributions, $44,664.
Limitations: Applications not accepted.
Application information: Contributes only to pre-selected organizations.
Officers: Philip Kopp III, Pres. and Treas.; Elaine Kopp, V.P. and Secy.; Gloria M. Kopp, V.P.
EIN: 113542564

36791
Straus Family Foundation, Inc.
c/o Wald & Wald
1 Penn Plz., Ste. 4307
New York, NY 10119-4307
Contact: Walter Straus, Pres.

Established in 1986 in NY.
Donor(s): Walter Straus.
Financial data (yr. ended 11/30/01): Grants paid, $44,638; assets, $243,779 (M); expenditures, $44,988; qualifying distributions, $44,638.
Limitations: Giving primarily in New York, NY.
Officer: Walter Straus, Pres.
EIN: 133381673

36792
Botnick Family Foundation
197 Riverside Dr.
Binghamton, NY 13905
Application address: 159-163 Front St., P.O. Box 765, Binghamton, NY 13902

Established in 1986 in NY.
Donor(s): Richard W. Botnick, Matthew Botnick, Judith Carmody, Mrs. Richard W. Botnick.
Financial data (yr. ended 12/31/99): Grants paid, $44,500; assets, $940,868 (M); gifts received, $250,150; expenditures, $51,926; qualifying distributions, $44,930.
Limitations: Giving primarily in Binghamton, NY.
Application information: Application form not required.
Trustees: Matthew G. Botnick, Richard W. Botnick, Mrs. Richard W. Botnick, Judith Carmody, Addison Keeler.
EIN: 222818488

36793
The Semper Foundation
230 Sarles St.
Bedford Corners, NY 10549

Established in 2000 in NY.
Donor(s): Faith Rosenfeld.
Financial data (yr. ended 12/31/01): Grants paid, $44,500; assets, $13,574 (M); expenditures, $46,877; qualifying distributions, $44,500.
Limitations: Applications not accepted. Giving primarily in NY.
Application information: Contributes only to pre-selected organizations.
EIN: 134141897

36794
Peggy and Adam Young Charitable Foundation
c/o Prager & Fenton
675 3rd Ave.
New York, NY 10017

Established in 1999 in FL.
Donor(s): Adam Young.
Financial data (yr. ended 09/30/01): Grants paid, $44,447; assets, $395,237 (M); expenditures, $58,275; qualifying distributions, $44,447.
Limitations: Applications not accepted. Giving primarily in NY.
Application information: Contributes only to pre-selected organizations.
Trustees: Adam Young, Margaret Young.
EIN: 650958638

36795
The Menno & Helen Ratzker Charitable Trust
c/o Oram, Yelon & Bernstein, PC
420 Lexington Ave., Ste. 2150
New York, NY 10170

Established in 1985 in NY.
Donor(s): Menno Ratzker.
Financial data (yr. ended 06/30/02): Grants paid, $44,441; assets, $44,097 (M); gifts received, $22,499; expenditures, $44,605; qualifying distributions, $44,441.
Limitations: Applications not accepted. Giving primarily in NY.
Application information: Contributes only to pre-selected organizations.
Directors: Helen Ratzker, Menno Ratzker.
EIN: 133318143

36796
Broughton Charitable Foundation
600 5th Ave.
New York, NY 10020
Contact: Pascal Wirz

Established in 1992 in MA.
Financial data (yr. ended 11/30/01): Grants paid, $44,260; assets, $349,657 (M); expenditures, $61,371; qualifying distributions, $44,260.
Officer: Watson Reid, Pres. and Treas.
EIN: 223186876

36797
Pape Family Foundation
114 W. 47th St., TAXVAS
New York, NY 10036

Established in 1997 in OR.
Donor(s): Shirley N. Pape.
Financial data (yr. ended 12/31/01): Grants paid, $44,100; assets, $1,170,588 (M); expenditures, $57,092; qualifying distributions, $44,100.
Limitations: Applications not accepted.
Application information: Contributes only to pre-selected organizations.
Trustees: Alyson Charles Pape, Gary D. Pape, Michael Frederick Pape, Randall C. Pape, Rebekah Anne Pape, Ryan Charles Pape, Shirley N. Pape, Terrance E. Pape, Dian Pape Tooke.
EIN: 931231080

36798
The David A. & Robin E. Jaye Foundation Charitable Trust
c/o M. Blumenreich & Co.
342 Madison Ave., Ste. 826
New York, NY 10173
Contact: David A. Jaye, Tr.

Established in 1992 in MA.
Donor(s): David A. Jaye.
Financial data (yr. ended 12/31/01): Grants paid, $44,030; assets, $756,075 (M); expenditures, $47,169; qualifying distributions, $44,030.
Trustee: David A. Jaye.
EIN: 046718903

36799
The Heslin Institute for Eye Research
185 Madison Ave.
New York, NY 10016 (212) 689-7676

Financial data (yr. ended 07/31/01): Grants paid, $44,000; assets, $835,878 (M); gifts received, $86,746; expenditures, $60,122; qualifying distributions, $46,525.
Limitations: Applications not accepted.
Application information: Contributes only to pre-selected organizations.
Officer: K. Budl Heslin, M.D., Pres.
EIN: 133133150

36800
The Mangurian Foundation, Inc.
c/o Joseph A. Platania
1 S. Washington St., Ste. 240
Rochester, NY 14614

Established in 1999 in NY.
Donor(s): Harry T. Mangurian, Jr.
Financial data (yr. ended 12/31/01): Grants paid, $44,000; assets, $7,298,950 (M); gifts received, $2,500,000; expenditures, $76,329; qualifying distributions, $44,000.
Limitations: Applications not accepted. Giving primarily in Rochester, NY.
Application information: Contributes only to pre-selected organizations.
Officers and Directors:* Harry T. Mangurian, Jr.,* Pres.; Gordon W. Latz,* V.P.; Dorothy J. Mangurian,* V.P.; Terry M. Skuse,* V.P.; Tracy L. Aherron,* Secy.; Stephen G. Mehallis,* Treas.; Beth L. Panesh, Cont.; J. Ernest Brophy.
EIN: 161578255

36801
Daniel & Susan Pollack Foundation, Inc.
131 E. 66th St.
New York, NY 10021

Donor(s): Daniel A. Pollack.
Financial data (yr. ended 11/30/01): Grants paid, $44,000; assets, $283,530 (M); expenditures, $45,070; qualifying distributions, $44,000.
Limitations: Applications not accepted. Giving primarily in Cambridge, MA, New York, NY, and Haverford, PA.
Application information: Contributes only to pre-selected organizations.
Trustees: Daniel A. Pollack, Susan Pollack.
EIN: 133381723

36802
Harry & Andrew H. Rosenthal Foundation, Inc.
c/o Maxwell Shmerler & Co.
1 N. Lexington Ave., 5th Fl.
White Plains, NY 10601

Donor(s): Andrew H. Rosenthal.
Financial data (yr. ended 02/28/02): Grants paid, $44,000; assets, $886,522 (M); gifts received, $65,000; expenditures, $44,891; qualifying distributions, $44,000.
Limitations: Applications not accepted. Giving primarily in NY.
Application information: Contributes only to pre-selected organizations.
Officers: Andrew H. Rosenthal, Pres.; Edwin Shmerler, Secy.
EIN: 132631210

36803
The Scholarships Foundation, Inc.
P.O. Box 6020
New York, NY 10128
URL: http://fdncenter.org/grantmaker/scholarships

Established in 1921.

Financial data (yr. ended 06/30/01): Grants paid, $44,000; assets, $774,145 (M); expenditures, $76,924; qualifying distributions, $63,064.
Limitations: Giving primarily in NY.
Application information: Application form required.
Officers and Directors:* Mrs. Charles L. Fleming,* Pres.; Mrs. Warren Gunderson,* V.P.; Mrs. Rodman Benedict,* Corresponding Secy.; Mrs. Gerald R. Philips,* Recording Secy.; Phoebe R. Stanton,* Treas.; Mrs. Philip D. Wiedel.
EIN: 066043809
Codes: GTI

36804
Wu Zhong-Yi Scholarship Foundation, Inc.
15 Claremont Ave., Apt. 73
New York, NY 10027-6814
Contact: Luke C.L. Yuan, Pres.

Established around 1987.
Donor(s): Chien-Shiung Wu.
Financial data (yr. ended 10/31/00): Grants paid, $44,000; assets, $1,081,481 (M); gifts received, $1,600; expenditures, $58,133; qualifying distributions, $46,582.
Limitations: Giving primarily in China.
Officers and Trustees:* Luke C.L. Yuan, Pres.; Xu Wu,* Treas.; Qiao Guoyu, Su Wu.
EIN: 133387111

36805
Eugene M. Sullivan, M.D. Foundation
c/o M.J. Kelley
15 Stepping Stone Ln.
Orchard Park, NY 14127-2238

Financial data (yr. ended 12/31/01): Grants paid, $43,900; assets, $589,937 (M); expenditures, $50,909; qualifying distributions, $43,900.
Limitations: Applications not accepted. Giving primarily in NY.
Application information: Contributes only to pre-selected organizations.
Trustees: Patricia S. Hunt, Mary Jane Kelley, E. Michael Sullivan, Jr., M.D., John J. Sullivan.
EIN: 222234066

36806
The Lenore Linsky Hecht Foundation, Inc.
(Formerly Jack and Belle Linsky Foundation, Inc.)
c/o Paneth, Haber & Zimmerman
600 3rd Ave.
New York, NY 10016
Application address: 325 West End Ave., New York, NY 10023
Contact: Lenore Linsky Hecht, Pres.

Established in 1979.
Donor(s): Belle Linsky.‡
Financial data (yr. ended 12/31/01): Grants paid, $43,890; assets, $673,955 (M); expenditures, $47,589; qualifying distributions, $43,890.
Limitations: Giving primarily in Washington, DC and NY.
Officer: Lenore Linsky Hecht, Pres.
EIN: 133006623

36807
Robert G. Boehmler Community Foundation, Inc.
c/o Davie Reid
100 Linden Oaks, Ste. 202
Rochester, NY 14625-2831

Financial data (yr. ended 12/31/01): Grants paid, $43,809; assets, $1,241,965 (M); gifts received, $35,000; expenditures, $73,831; qualifying distributions, $43,809.
Director: Robert G. Boehmler.
Trustee: David C. Reid.

EIN: 161510757

36808
Give Thanks Fund
c/o Walter J. Handelman
1 N. Broadway, Rm. 1001
White Plains, NY 10601

Financial data (yr. ended 12/31/01): Grants paid, $43,800; assets, $1,408,534 (M); expenditures, $54,533; qualifying distributions, $43,800.
Limitations: Applications not accepted. Giving primarily in NY.
Application information: Contributes only to pre-selected organizations.
Officers and Directors:* Charles C. Lee,* Pres. and Treas.; Walter J. Handelman,* V.P. and Secy.; Ogden White, Jr.
EIN: 136075266

36809
Frank & Janina Petschek Foundation, Inc.
300 Central Park W.
New York, NY 10024

Established in 1958.
Financial data (yr. ended 08/31/01): Grants paid, $43,800; assets, $341,614 (M); expenditures, $46,953; qualifying distributions, $43,800.
Limitations: Applications not accepted. Giving primarily in New York, NY.
Application information: Contributes only to pre-selected organizations.
Officers: Elisabeth De Picciotto, Pres.; Maria P. Smith, V.P.; Maurice De Picciotto, Treas.
EIN: 136062709

36810
James G. Dinan Foundation, Inc.
c/o James G. Dinan
350 Park Ave., 4th Fl.
New York, NY 10022

Established in 1997 in NY.
Donor(s): James G. Dinan.
Financial data (yr. ended 06/30/99): Grants paid, $43,750; assets, $1,812,655 (M); expenditures, $89,327; qualifying distributions, $40,181.
Limitations: Applications not accepted. Giving primarily in New York, NY.
Application information: Contributes only to pre-selected organizations.
Officers: James G. Dinan, Pres. and Treas.; Elizabeth Miller, Secy.
Director: William A. Dinan.
EIN: 133976827

36811
Paul J. Sperry Charitable Fund
c/o M.Z. Ottenstein & Co.
516 5th Ave., Ste. 1006
New York, NY 10036

Established in 1965 in NY.
Financial data (yr. ended 12/31/01): Grants paid, $43,745; assets, $211,999 (M); gifts received, $2,903; expenditures, $47,205; qualifying distributions, $43,745.
Limitations: Applications not accepted. Giving primarily in New York, NY.
Application information: Contributes only to pre-selected organizations.
Trustee: Paul J. Sperry.
EIN: 136178892

36812
Living Archives, Inc.
262 W. 91st St.
New York, NY 10024
Contact: Diane Brown, Dir.

Established in 1987 in NY.

Financial data (yr. ended 10/31/00): Grants paid, $43,675; assets, $7,254 (M); gifts received, $33,127; expenditures, $46,925; qualifying distributions, $43,675.
Limitations: Applications not accepted. Giving primarily in New York, NY.
Officer: D.A. Pennebaker, Pres.
Directors: Steve Benedict, Diane Brown, Richard Leacock.
EIN: 132896424

36813
Norman and Elinor Belfer Foundation
80 Cuttermill Rd., Ste. 200
Great Neck, NY 11021-3152

Established in 1987 in DE.
Donor(s): Elinor Belfer, Norman Belfer.
Financial data (yr. ended 12/31/01): Grants paid, $43,592; assets, $781,093 (M); gifts received, $3,000; expenditures, $62,108; qualifying distributions, $43,592.
Limitations: Applications not accepted. Giving primarily in FL and NY.
Application information: Contributes only to pre-selected organizations.
Officer: Norman Belfer, Pres.
EIN: 133387391

36814
Irwin & Sylvia Schnurmacher Foundation, Inc.
175 Great Neck Rd., Ste. 407
Great Neck, NY 11021
Contact: Stephen Schnurmacher, Pres.

Donor(s): Irwin Schnurmacher,‡ Sylvia Schnurmacher.‡
Financial data (yr. ended 08/31/01): Grants paid, $43,567; assets, $827,202 (M); expenditures, $50,975; qualifying distributions, $43,567.
Limitations: Giving primarily in NY.
Application information: Application form required.
Officers: Stephen Schnurmacher, Pres.; Laurie Tomchin, V.P.; Leonard Schnurmacher, Secy.-Treas.
EIN: 132938933

36815
RJL Charitable Foundation
c/o Michael Kessler
42-09 235th St.
Douglaston, NY 11363

Established in 1999 in NY.
Donor(s): Jeffrey Levine, Randi Levine.
Financial data (yr. ended 12/31/00): Grants paid, $43,565; assets, $2,479 (M); gifts received, $44,800; expenditures, $45,140; qualifying distributions, $43,565.
Limitations: Applications not accepted.
Application information: Contributes only to pre-selected organizations.
Directors: Michael Kessler, Jeffrey Levine, Randi Levine.
EIN: 113508299

36816
The Robert & Elizabeth Muller Foundation, Inc.
c/o Dayton & D'Amato
42-40 Bell Blvd.
Bayside, NY 11361-2861
Contact: Lawrence L. D'Amato, V.P.

Donor(s): Robert Muller.‡
Financial data (yr. ended 12/31/00): Grants paid, $43,500; assets, $978,430 (M); expenditures, $53,933; qualifying distributions, $48,497.
Limitations: Giving primarily in New York, NY.
Publications: Financial statement.
Officers: June D'Amato, Pres.; Lawrence L. D'Amato, V.P.

EIN: 112587773

36817
The Lowell and Fern Kwiat Family Foundation, Inc.
12 Howard Dr.
Syosset, NY 11791

Established in 1998 in NY.
Donor(s): Lowell Kwiat, Fern Kwiat.
Financial data (yr. ended 12/31/01): Grants paid, $43,480; assets, $157,755 (M); expenditures, $43,844; qualifying distributions, $43,480.
Limitations: Applications not accepted.
Application information: Contributes only to pre-selected organizations.
Directors: Fern Kwiat, Greg Kwiat, Lowell Kwiat.
EIN: 311607301

36818
The Order of Colonial Lords of Manors in America, Inc.
c/o James D. Miller & Co.
350 5th Ave., Ste. 5019
New York, NY 10118-0080 (212) 483-2323

Financial data (yr. ended 12/31/01): Grants paid, $43,450; assets, $898,041 (M); expenditures, $57,370; qualifying distributions, $48,173.
Limitations: Applications not accepted. Giving primarily in NY.
Application information: Contributes only to pre-selected organizations.
Officers: Timothy F. Beard, Pres.; Joseph Pistell, Secy.; William W. Reese, Treas.
EIN: 136104057

36819
EBA Foundation
c/o Eric Kaplan
335 Madison Ave., Ste. 1500
New York, NY 10017

Established in 2000 in NY.
Donor(s): Seymour Milstein.
Financial data (yr. ended 12/31/01): Grants paid, $43,265; assets, $749,204 (M); gifts received, $250,000; expenditures, $43,685; qualifying distributions, $43,265.
Limitations: Applications not accepted. Giving primarily in NY.
Application information: Contributes only to pre-selected organizations.
Trustees: Abigail Black Elbaum, Seymour Milstein, Vivian Milstein.
EIN: 134098940

36820
The Scott & Suling Mead Foundation
c/o Goldman Sachs & Co.
85 Broad St., Tax Dept.
New York, NY 10004

Established in 1996 in DC.
Donor(s): E. Scott Mead.
Financial data (yr. ended 04/30/01): Grants paid, $43,261; assets, $2,868,791 (M); gifts received, $1,851,703; expenditures, $81,761; qualifying distributions, $43,261.
Limitations: Applications not accepted. Giving on an international basis, with emphasis on London, England.
Application information: Contributes only to pre-selected organizations.
Trustees: E. Scott Mead, James M. Mead, Suling C. Mead.
EIN: 133921104

36821
Mark & Helene Eisner Foundation, Inc.
c/o Speer & Fulvio
750 Lexington Ave.
New York, NY 10165-1301

Established in 1987 in NY.
Donor(s): Helene Rittenberg.‡
Financial data (yr. ended 08/31/01): Grants paid, $43,168; assets, $622,185 (M); expenditures, $44,810; qualifying distributions, $43,168.
Limitations: Applications not accepted. Giving primarily in New York, NY.
Application information: Contributes only to pre-selected organizations.
Officers: Barbara Lans, Pres.; Deborah Lans, V.P. and Secy.; Alan Lans, V.P.; Stephen Lans, V.P.
EIN: 133357583

36822
Robert Gladstone Family Foundation, Inc.
c/o Peyser & Alexander
500 5th Ave., Ste. 2700
New York, NY 10110
Contact: Shawn Gladstone, Dir.

Established in 1997 in NY.
Financial data (yr. ended 12/31/01): Grants paid, $43,114; assets, $100,367 (M); expenditures, $43,446; qualifying distributions, $43,114.
Application information: Application form not required.
Directors: Shawn Gladstone, Dana Miller, Tony Peyser.
EIN: 133942022

36823
Loewy Family Foundation
c/o Malakoff, Wasserman, & Pecker, C.P.A.
1 Old Country Rd., Ste. 340
Carle Place, NY 11514

Donor(s): Jeffrey M. Loewy, Nancy Jane Loewy.
Financial data (yr. ended 12/31/01): Grants paid, $43,112; assets, $176,126 (M); expenditures, $45,452; qualifying distributions, $43,112.
Trustees: Jeffrey M. Loewy, Nancy Jane Loewy.
EIN: 137088887

36824
Goldenberg-Malina Foundation
c/o A. Carl Goldenberg
170 Valley Rd.
New Rochelle, NY 10804

Established in 1985 in NY.
Donor(s): A. Carl Goldenberg, Robert S. Malina.
Financial data (yr. ended 11/30/01): Grants paid, $43,100; assets, $152,345 (M); gifts received, $18,963; expenditures, $44,292; qualifying distributions, $43,100.
Limitations: Applications not accepted. Giving primarily in NY.
Application information: Contributes only to pre-selected organizations.
Officers and Directors:* A. Carl Goldenberg,* Pres.; Robert S. Malina,* Treas.; Sondra Goldenberg, Fran Malina.
EIN: 133249397

36825
Abraham & Gizella Berger Foundation for Cancer Research
c/o George Lipkin, M.D.
77 Park Ave., Ste. 3A
New York, NY 10016-2556

Donor(s): George Lipkin, Sari Lipkin.
Financial data (yr. ended 09/30/01): Grants paid, $43,096; assets, $23,439 (M); gifts received,

$39,030; expenditures, $43,000; qualifying distributions, $43,093.
Limitations: Applications not accepted. Giving primarily in New York, NY.
Application information: Contributes only to pre-selected organizations.
Officers: George Lipkin, M.D., Pres.; Sari Lipkin, Treas.
Trustee: Stanley I. Schachter.
EIN: 132970313

36826
The Buchalter Foundation
c/o Goldman Sachs & Co.
85 Broad St., Tax Dept.
New York, NY 10004

Established in 1996 in NJ.
Donor(s): Lawrence R. Buchalter.
Financial data (yr. ended 08/31/01): Grants paid, $43,067; assets, $777,835 (M); gifts received, $583,875; expenditures, $55,067; qualifying distributions, $43,067.
Limitations: Applications not accepted.
Application information: Contributes only to pre-selected organizations.
Trustees: Lawrence R. Buchalter, Robin Buchalter.
EIN: 137109408

36827
Syzfra Miriam Foundation
c/o Mrs. Spira
42 Calvert Dr.
Monsey, NY 10952

Established around 1981.
Donor(s): Mortin Spira, Congregation Ahavas Tzedoka, Zeu Edelman, Aron Spira.
Financial data (yr. ended 12/31/00): Grants paid, $43,036; assets, $1,102,930 (M); gifts received, $60,000; expenditures, $50,372; qualifying distributions, $43,036.
Limitations: Applications not accepted. Giving primarily in NY.
Application information: Contributes only to pre-selected organizations.
Officer: Esther Spira, Pres.
EIN: 237115027

36828
Gary J. and Susan O. Ferrentino Foundation
170 Circle Rd.
Syosset, NY 11791

Established in 1996 in NY.
Donor(s): Gary J. Ferrentino, Susan O. Ferrentino.
Financial data (yr. ended 09/30/01): Grants paid, $43,000; assets, $660,869 (M); gifts received, $163,219; expenditures, $49,174; qualifying distributions, $43,000.
Limitations: Applications not accepted. Giving on a national basis.
Application information: Contributes only to pre-selected organizations.
Trustees: Gary J. Ferrentino, Susan O. Ferrentino.
EIN: 137099576

36829
Gerard Family Foundation
239 Central Park West
New York, NY 10024-6038

Established in 1998 in NY.
Donor(s): Egon Gerard, Karen Gerard.
Financial data (yr. ended 12/31/01): Grants paid, $43,000; assets, $668,932 (M); expenditures, $45,409; qualifying distributions, $43,000.
Limitations: Applications not accepted. Giving primarily in CT, MA, and NY.
Application information: Contributes only to pre-selected organizations.
Trustees: Egon Gerard, Karen Gerard.
EIN: 134007575

36830
John C. & Susan K. Hubbard Foundation
c/o John C. Hubbard, Jr.
36 Pinewood Dr.
Glenville, NY 12302-4734

Donor(s): Susan K. Hubbard.‡
Financial data (yr. ended 12/31/00): Grants paid, $43,000; assets, $906,324 (M); expenditures, $43,645; qualifying distributions, $43,000.
Limitations: Applications not accepted. Giving primarily in NJ.
Application information: Contributes only to pre-selected organizations.
Director: John C. Hubbard, Jr.
EIN: 226108097

36831
The Plato Malozemoff Foundation
c/o Ann A. Dessylas
59 E. 54th. St., Ste. 94
New York, NY 10022 (212) 207-9082

Incorporated in 1986 in DE.
Donor(s): Plato Malozemoff.‡
Financial data (yr. ended 12/31/01): Grants paid, $43,000; assets, $743,629 (M); expenditures, $49,557; qualifying distributions, $43,000.
Application information: Application form not required.
Officer: Alexandra Malozemoff, Pres.
Trustees: Alexis P. Malozemoff, Irene Weigle.
EIN: 133382155

36832
William G. & Rhoda B. Partridge Memorial Scholarship Fund
c/o NBT Bank, N.A.
52 S. Broad St.
Norwich, NY 13815 (607) 337-6193
Contact: Sandra E. Colton, Trust Off., NBT Bank, N.A.

Financial data (yr. ended 06/30/01): Grants paid, $43,000; assets, $958,949 (M); expenditures, $46,794; qualifying distributions, $45,065.
Limitations: Giving limited to residents of Edinburg and Northville, NY.
Publications: Application guidelines.
Application information: Application form required.
Trustee: NBT Bank, N.A.
EIN: 141597911
Codes: GTI

36833
The Sirota Foundation, Inc.
575 Park Ave.
New York, NY 10021 (212) 688-3235
Contact: Norman L. Sirota, Pres.

Donor(s): Norman L. Sirota.
Financial data (yr. ended 06/30/99): Grants paid, $43,000; assets, $883,896 (M); gifts received, $2,000; expenditures, $56,958; qualifying distributions, $43,000.
Limitations: Giving primarily in FL.
Officers: Norman L. Sirota, Pres.; Niki Sirota, V.P.; Stephanie A. Sirota, Secy.
EIN: 136112056

36834
Henry and Gertrude Rothschild Foundation, Inc.
c/o Edward I. Speer, C.P.A.
550 Mamaroneck Ave., Ste. 504
Harrison, NY 10528

Established in 1986 in NY.
Donor(s): Henry Rothschild, Gertrude Rothschild.
Financial data (yr. ended 08/31/01): Grants paid, $42,850; assets, $252,070 (M); expenditures, $43,881; qualifying distributions, $42,850.
Limitations: Applications not accepted.
Application information: Contributes only to pre-selected organizations.
Officers and Directors:* Gertrude Rothschild,* Pres. and Treas.; Henry Rothschild,* V.P. and Secy.
EIN: 133370395

36835
Alexander Charitable Foundation
c/o J. Alexander
301 W. 57th St., Ste. 34AB
New York, NY 10019

Established in 2000 in NY.
Donor(s): J. Kobi Alexander.
Financial data (yr. ended 12/31/01): Grants paid, $42,700; assets, $3,134,675 (M); expenditures, $42,709; qualifying distributions, $42,700.
Limitations: Applications not accepted.
Application information: Contributes only to pre-selected organizations.
Trustees: J. Kobi Alexander, Hana Basal Alexander.
EIN: 137263003

36836
John J. Creedon Foundation
c/o John J. Creedon
200 Park Ave., Ste. 5700
New York, NY 10166

Established in 1987 in DE.
Donor(s): John J. Creedon.
Financial data (yr. ended 12/31/01): Grants paid, $42,700; assets, $723,746 (M); expenditures, $44,706; qualifying distributions, $42,700.
Limitations: Applications not accepted. Giving primarily in New York, NY.
Application information: Contributes only to pre-selected organizations.
Officers: John J. Creedon, Pres. and Treas.; Diane A. Creedon, V.P. and Secy.
Director: Juliette H. Kvernland.
EIN: 133387874

36837
Washington County Home for Aged Women, Inc.
c/o Glens Falls National Bank
P.O. Box 307, 250 Glen St.
Glens Falls, NY 12801-9989
Application address: Alvin E. Dunnem, 1 Washington St., Cambridge, NY 12816, tel.: (518) 677-3130

Donor(s): J. Sheldon Trust.
Financial data (yr. ended 09/30/01): Grants paid, $42,662; assets, $860,181 (M); gifts received, $4,364; expenditures, $55,685; qualifying distributions, $42,662.
Limitations: Giving limited to Washington County, NY.
Application information: Application form required.
Officer and Directors:* Charles R. Clark,* Pres.; James A. Catalfimo, Clyde Cook, Lawrence E. Corbett, Jr., Robert I. Rozell, Seta Smith.
EIN: 141372655

36838
Forst Family Foundation
c/o Goldman Sachs & Co., Tax Dept.
85 Broad St.
New York, NY 10004

Established in 1999 in NY.
Donor(s): Edward C. Forst.

Financial data (yr. ended 05/31/02): Grants paid, $42,654; assets, $282,845 (M); gifts received, $300,490; expenditures, $46,418; qualifying distributions, $42,654.
Limitations: Applications not accepted. Giving primarily in Cambridge, MA and NY.
Application information: Contributes only to pre-selected organizations.
Trustees: Edward C. Forst, Susan R. Forst.
EIN: 134046414

36839
Herbert Rogowsky Foundation, Inc.
125 N. Main St., Ste. 203
Port Chester, NY 10573-4221
Contact: Martin Rogowsky, Pres.

Donor(s): Stephen Rogowsky, Martin Rogowsky.
Financial data (yr. ended 02/28/02): Grants paid, $42,603; assets, $750,682 (M); expenditures, $46,974; qualifying distributions, $42,603.
Officers and Directors:* Martin Rogowsky,* Pres.; Stephen Rogowsky,* Treas.
EIN: 237011944

36840
The Fowler Family Foundation
c/o John M. Fowler
2 Northwest Way
Bronxville, NY 10708-4306

Established in 1998 in NY.
Donor(s): John M. Fowler.
Financial data (yr. ended 12/31/01): Grants paid, $42,500; assets, $844,220 (M); gifts received, $50,000; expenditures, $44,897; qualifying distributions, $42,500.
Limitations: Applications not accepted.
Application information: Contributes only to pre-selected organizations.
Trustees: Evan A. Fowler, John M. Fowler, William E. Fowler III.
EIN: 522106855

36841
Alice & Murray Giddings Foundation
c/o Dr. Joseph Lalka
P.O. Box 182
Chatham, NY 12037

Established in 1995 in NY.
Financial data (yr. ended 12/31/01): Grants paid, $42,500; assets, $957,994 (M); expenditures, $55,426; qualifying distributions, $42,500.
Limitations: Giving primarily in NY.
Officers: Joseph Lalka, Pres.; Seth Rapport, V.P.; Merle Gold, Secy.; Winnie Behrens, Treas.
EIN: 141781248

36842
The Hodson Family Foundation, Inc.
48 Litchfield Rd.
Port Washington, NY 11050

Established in 1986 in FL.
Donor(s): Robert G. Hodson, Patricia A. Hodson.
Financial data (yr. ended 10/31/01): Grants paid, $42,500; assets, $235,321 (M); expenditures, $42,650; qualifying distributions, $42,346.
Limitations: Giving primarily in FL and VT.
Trustee: Robert P. Hodson.
EIN: 222774070

36843
The Richard C. Welden Foundation
420 Lexington Ave.
New York, NY 10170
URL: http://www.welden.org
Contact: Ivan V. Ivanoff, Exec. Dir.

Established in 1999 in NY.

Financial data (yr. ended 12/31/01): Grants paid, $42,500; assets, $68,376 (M); expenditures, $75,093; qualifying distributions, $42,500.
Limitations: Giving primarily in CA and MA.
Officers: Thorn T. Welden, Pres.; Ivan V. Ivanoff, Exec. Dir.
EIN: 311636932

36844
Laurence D. Belfer Family Foundation
c/o Belfer Mgmt., LLC
767 5th Ave., 46th Fl.
New York, NY 10153

Established in 1999 in NY.
Donor(s): Laurence D. Belfer.
Financial data (yr. ended 12/31/00): Grants paid, $42,457; assets, $1,084,955 (M); gifts received, $469,562; expenditures, $65,844; qualifying distributions, $38,141.
Limitations: Giving primarily in New York, NY.
Trustee: Laurence D. Belfer.
EIN: 137208162

36845
The Anthony and Claire Pace Foundation, Inc.
276 Southdown Rd.
Lloyd Harbor, NY 11743

Established in 1995 in NY.
Donor(s): Anthony J. Pace, Claire Pace.
Financial data (yr. ended 12/31/01): Grants paid, $42,425; assets, $50,325 (M); gifts received, $26,000; expenditures, $42,979; qualifying distributions, $42,425.
Limitations: Applications not accepted.
Application information: Contributes only to pre-selected organizations.
Officers: Anthony J. Pace, Pres.; Claire Pace, V.P.; Anthony J. Cincotta, Secy.
EIN: 113300843

36846
J. & S. Heidenberg Foundation, Inc.
c/o Tabb, Conigliaro & McGann
200 Madison Ave., Ste. 2200
New York, NY 10016-3903

Established in 1942 in NY.
Donor(s): Sylvia Heidenberg, Robert Heidenberg.
Financial data (yr. ended 12/31/00): Grants paid, $42,418; assets, $552,277 (M); gifts received, $167,761; expenditures, $43,186; qualifying distributions, $42,418.
Officer: Susan Laden, Pres. and Secy.
EIN: 136138798

36847
The Gary N. Siegler Foundation
c/o Perelson Weiner
1 Dag Hammarskjold Plz., 42nd Fl.
New York, NY 10017-2286
Contact: Gary N. Siegler, Pres.

Established in 1990 in NY.
Donor(s): Gary N. Siegler.
Financial data (yr. ended 12/31/01): Grants paid, $42,404; assets, $1,427,346 (M); expenditures, $49,712; qualifying distributions, $42,404.
Limitations: Applications not accepted. Giving primarily in New York, NY.
Application information: Contributes only to pre-selected organizations.
Officer: Gary N. Siegler, Pres.
EIN: 133548642

36848
Dubofsky Family Foundation
5 Harbor Way
Kings Point, NY 11024-2116
Contact: Robert L. Dubofsky, Tr.

Financial data (yr. ended 11/30/01): Grants paid, $42,400; assets, $43,382 (M); gifts received, $76,894; expenditures, $42,528; qualifying distributions, $42,400.
Limitations: Giving primarily in NY.
Trustee: Robert L. Dubofsky.
EIN: 116291278

36849
Werwaiss Family Charitable Trust
230 Park Ave., Ste. 945
New York, NY 10169-0095
Contact: John A. Werwaiss, Tr.

Established in 1986 in NY.
Donor(s): John A. Werwaiss.
Financial data (yr. ended 08/31/01): Grants paid, $42,374; assets, $7,466 (M); expenditures, $42,545; qualifying distributions, $42,374.
Limitations: Giving primarily in NY.
Trustee: John A. Werwaiss.
EIN: 133386924

36850
Nawab Bibi Charitable Trust
180 Progress Rd.
Gloversville, NY 12078
Contact: Rahman Bashir, Tr.

Established in 1997.
Financial data (yr. ended 06/30/02): Grants paid, $42,333; assets, $663,550 (M); gifts received, $2,703; expenditures, $72,209; qualifying distributions, $42,333.
Limitations: Giving primarily in MD.
Trustees: Bashir Rahman, Hamid Aziz Rehman, Rashida A. Rahman.
EIN: 141797883

36851
The Peter & Ellen Jakobson Foundation, Inc.
c/o Peter Jakobson
1025 5th Ave.
New York, NY 10028

Established in 1999 in NY.
Donor(s): Peter Jakobson, Ellen Jakobson.
Financial data (yr. ended 12/31/00): Grants paid, $42,310; assets, $48,375 (M); gifts received, $42,125; expenditures, $42,358; qualifying distributions, $42,310.
Limitations: Applications not accepted. Giving primarily in New York, NY.
Application information: Contributes only to pre-selected organizations.
Officers and Directors:* Peter Jakobson, Sr.,* Pres.; Ellen Jakobson,* Secy.; Patricia Marshall.
EIN: 134058721

36852
Barnett and Anne Berch Foundation, Inc.
c/o Dabar Mgmt. Co., Inc.
120 E. Prospect Ave.
Mount Vernon, NY 10550

Donor(s): Anne Berch.
Financial data (yr. ended 11/30/01): Grants paid, $42,250; assets, $704,043 (M); expenditures, $45,490; qualifying distributions, $42,250.
Limitations: Applications not accepted. Giving primarily in NY.
Application information: Contributes only to pre-selected organizations.
Officer: Anne Berch, Mgr.
EIN: 136135111

36853
The Anna E. Gallagher Charitable Trust
58-26 Roosevelt Ave.
Woodside, NY 11377
Contact: Frederic P. Szostek, Tr.

Established in 1986 in NY.
Financial data (yr. ended 12/31/00): Grants paid, $42,210; assets, $787,933 (M); expenditures, $48,181; qualifying distributions, $42,210.
Limitations: Giving primarily in NY.
Trustees: Carolyn I. Szostek, Frederic P. Szostek.
EIN: 112818822

36854
Freya & Richard Block Family Foundation
c/o Richard Block
336 Central Park West, Ste. 14A
New York, NY 10025

Established in 1999 in NY.
Donor(s): Richard H. Block, Freya Block.
Financial data (yr. ended 07/31/01): Grants paid, $42,200; assets, $443,227 (M); gifts received, $338,896; expenditures, $48,270; qualifying distributions, $42,200.
Limitations: Applications not accepted. Giving primarily in NY.
Application information: Contributes only to pre-selected organizations.
Directors: Freya Block, Richard H. Block.
EIN: 134092442

36855
The Visiting Nurse Association of Rye, Inc.
c/o Bryon Hawkins
131 Old Post Rd.
Rye, NY 10580-1401
Application address: 7 Pine Island Rd., Rye, NY 10580, tel.: (914) 967-5718
Contact: Frances T. Wiener, Pres.

Established in 1967 in NY.
Donor(s): Agatha A. Durland Trust.‡
Financial data (yr. ended 12/31/01): Grants paid, $42,200; assets, $240,664 (M); gifts received, $46,024; expenditures, $44,503; qualifying distributions, $42,741.
Limitations: Giving limited to Rye, NY.
Application information: Application form required.
Officers and Directors:* Frances T. Wiener, Pres.; Nancy Steed, V.P.; Ann Sexton,* Secy.; Marie Meena, Treas.; Anne Bschorr,* Chair., Scholarship Comm.; Ruth Diefenbach, Emory Freeman, Robert Freeman, Bryon Hawkins, Sandy Jacoby, Janice Pierce.
EIN: 131825945
Codes: GTI

36856
The Alan C. Greenberg Foundation, Inc.
c/o Bear Stearns Companies, Inc.
383 Madison Ave.
New York, NY 10179 (212) 272-2000

Established in 1964.
Donor(s): Alan C. Greenberg.
Financial data (yr. ended 12/31/01): Grants paid, $42,176; assets, $33,545 (M); gifts received, $33,662; expenditures, $45,966; qualifying distributions, $44,076.
Limitations: Applications not accepted. Giving primarily in NY.
Application information: Contributes only to pre-selected organizations.
Officers: Alan C. Greenberg, Pres. and Treas.; Maynard Greenberg, V.P.
EIN: 136271740

36857
Brian R. Zipp Charitable Foundation
c/o B. Strauss Assoc., Ltd.
307 5th Ave., 8th Fl.
New York, NY 10016-6517

Established in 1994 in NY.
Donor(s): Brian R. Zipp.
Financial data (yr. ended 03/31/02): Grants paid, $42,165; assets, $788,042 (M); gifts received, $575,742; expenditures, $46,009; qualifying distributions, $42,165.
Limitations: Applications not accepted.
Application information: Contributes only to pre-selected organizations.
Trustees: Msgr. Robert Charlebois, Brian R. Zipp, Thomas M. Zipp.
EIN: 133800329

36858
The First Lake Foundation, Inc.
c/o Philip Evans
41 Notre Dame Ln.
Utica, NY 13502-4817

Established in 1994 in NY.
Financial data (yr. ended 06/30/01): Grants paid, $42,100; assets, $413,832 (M); expenditures, $49,396; qualifying distributions, $41,988.
Limitations: Applications not accepted. Giving primarily in Utica, NY.
Application information: Contributes only to pre-selected organizations.
Officers: James S. Ely, Jr., Pres.-Treas.; Phil Evans, V.P.; Nell E. Wendler, V.P.
EIN: 161471873

36859
Sarkisian Brothers Foundation
11 Charlotte St.
Binghamton, NY 13905-2683
Contact: Renee S. Reilly, Tr.

Established in 1987 in NY.
Financial data (yr. ended 12/31/99): Grants paid, $42,050; assets, $836,343 (M); expenditures, $44,960; qualifying distributions, $42,050.
Limitations: Giving primarily in Binghamton, NY.
Trustees: Renee S. Reilly, George K. Sarkisian, Gregg A. Sarkisian.
EIN: 161313362

36860
The Abraham and Pearl Reinfeld Charitable Foundation
c/o Pearl Reinfeld
325 West End Ave.
New York, NY 10023

Established in 1998 in NY.
Financial data (yr. ended 12/31/01): Grants paid, $42,047; assets, $4,666 (M); gifts received, $51; expenditures, $43,067; qualifying distributions, $42,047.
Trustees: Ira Nordlight, David Reinfeld, Pearl Reinfeld, Carol Soltz.
EIN: 134039884

36861
Donald Hicks Dew Foundation
125 Rasbach St.
Canastota, NY 13032-1430
Contact: Donald H. Dew, Tr.

Donor(s): Diemolding Corp., Lois Brooks.
Financial data (yr. ended 12/31/01): Grants paid, $42,000; assets, $8,566 (M); gifts received, $44,200; expenditures, $42,059; qualifying distributions, $42,059.
Limitations: Giving primarily in NY.
Application information: Application form not required.
Trustees: B. Jarvis Dew, Donald F. Dew, Donald H. Dew.
EIN: 166062084
Codes: CS

36862
The Dorothy G. Griffin Charitable Foundation
c/o Dorothy G. Griffin, Varflex Corporation
512 W. Court St.
Rome, NY 13440 (315) 336-4400

Established in 1997 in NY.
Donor(s): Dorothy G. Griffin, William L. Griffin.
Financial data (yr. ended 12/31/01): Grants paid, $42,000; assets, $1,047,141 (M); expenditures, $47,638; qualifying distributions, $42,000.
Limitations: Giving restricted to Rome, NY, and neighboring communities.
Application information: Application form not required.
Trustees: Edwin L. Cates, Dorothy G. Griffin, William L. Griffin, Charles J. Schoff.
EIN: 161541273

36863
Kennedy-Hanly Foundation, Inc.
c/o Gasser & Hayes
150 Purchase St.
Rye, NY 10580-0215

Established in 1987 in NY.
Donor(s): Joan K. Hanly.
Financial data (yr. ended 03/31/01): Grants paid, $42,000; assets, $666,171 (M); expenditures, $43,399; qualifying distributions, $42,000.
Limitations: Applications not accepted. Giving primarily in the Northeast.
Application information: Contributes only to pre-selected organizations.
Officers: Joan K. Hanly, Pres.; Kenneth Hanly, V.P. and Treas.; James A. Beha II, V.P.
EIN: 133433075

36864
Harold E. Klue Trust
c/o The Bank of New York
1 Wall St., Tax Dept., 28th Fl.
New York, NY 10286
Application address: c/o Patricia A. Healy, V.P., The Bank of New York, White Plains, NY 10602

Established in 1994 in NY.
Financial data (yr. ended 12/31/01): Grants paid, $42,000; assets, $843,881 (M); expenditures, $49,685; qualifying distributions, $42,000.
Application information: Application form required.
Trustee: The Bank of New York.
EIN: 136963401

36865
Jacques and Yulla Lipchitz Foundation, Inc.
369 Lexington Ave.
New York, NY 10017
Contact: Hanno D. Mott, V.P.

Established in 1962.
Donor(s): Yulla Lipchitz.
Financial data (yr. ended 02/28/02): Grants paid, $42,000; assets, $1,809,771 (M); expenditures, $42,330; qualifying distributions, $330.
Limitations: Applications not accepted.
Application information: Contributes only to pre-selected organizations.
Officers and Directors:* Yulla Lipchitz,* Pres.; Lolya Lipchitz, V.P.; Hanno D. Mott,* V.P.
EIN: 136151503

36866
N & M Foundation
356 Marcy Ave.
Brooklyn, NY 11206 (718) 599-7177
Contact: Naftali Steinmetz, Tr.

Established in 2000 in NY.
Financial data (yr. ended 06/30/01): Grants paid, $42,000; assets, $125,326 (M); gifts received, $76; expenditures, $42,000; qualifying distributions, $42,000.
Application information: Application form not required.
Trustees: Miriam Steinmetz, Naftali Steinmetz.
EIN: 113588879

36867
Egon & Telsi Birnbaum Foundation
1721 50th St.
Brooklyn, NY 11204-1259

Donor(s): Egon Birnbaum, Telsi Birnbaum.
Financial data (yr. ended 09/30/01): Grants paid, $41,980; assets, $1 (M); gifts received, $38,025; expenditures, $42,069; qualifying distributions, $41,980.
Limitations: Applications not accepted.
Application information: Contributes only to pre-selected organizations.
Officers: Egon Birnbaum, Mgr.; Telsi Birnbaum, Mgr.
EIN: 112678412

36868
Chasdei Zahavi Foundation
1574 Carroll St.
Brooklyn, NY 11213-5330
Contact: Tzirl Goldman, Tr.

Established in 2000 in NY.
Financial data (yr. ended 08/31/01): Grants paid, $41,937; assets, $3,152 (M); gifts received, $46,031; expenditures, $42,937; qualifying distributions, $42,937; giving activities include $500 for programs.
Limitations: Giving primarily in Brooklyn, NY.
Trustee: Tzirl Goldman.
EIN: 113527951

36869
Bob and Sheila Friedland Foundation, Inc.
656 Central Park Ave.
Yonkers, NY 10704

Established in 1986 in DE and NY.
Donor(s): Friedland Realty, Inc., Robert Friedland, Sheila Freidland.
Financial data (yr. ended 11/30/01): Grants paid, $41,925; assets, $31,270 (M); gifts received, $50,000; expenditures, $43,241; qualifying distributions, $41,925.
Limitations: Applications not accepted. Giving primarily in Westchester County and New York, NY.
Application information: Contributes only to pre-selected organizations.
Officers and Directors:* Robert Friedland,* Pres. and Treas.; Sheila G. Friedland,* Secy.
EIN: 133442016
Codes: CS, CD

36870
E. Florence Richards Fund, Inc.
c/o Donald E. Snyder
14 Hidden Springs Dr.
Pittsford, NY 14534-2897

Established in 1973 in NY.
Donor(s): Donald E. Snyder, E. Florence Richards.‡

Financial data (yr. ended 08/31/01): Grants paid, $41,875; assets, $368,357 (M); expenditures, $45,808; qualifying distributions, $41,875.
Limitations: Applications not accepted. Giving primarily in NY.
Application information: Contributes only to pre-selected organizations.
Officers and Directors:* Donald E. Snyder,* Pres. and Treas.; Dorothy E. Snyder,* V.P.; Beverly L. Shank,* Secy.
EIN: 237424750

36871
The Helen & Nathaniel Wisch Foundation, Inc.
733 Park Ave.
New York, NY 10021

Established in 1986 in NY.
Financial data (yr. ended 11/30/01): Grants paid, $41,850; assets, $12,628 (M); expenditures, $42,068; qualifying distributions, $41,850.
Limitations: Applications not accepted. Giving primarily in Los Angeles, CA.
Application information: Contributes only to pre-selected organizations.
Officers: Nathaniel Wisch, Pres.; Helen Wisch, Treas.
EIN: 133394212

36872
The Benjamin & Lorelei Hammerman Foundation, Ltd.
605 Park Ave.
New York, NY 10021 (212) 677-3355

Donor(s): Benjamin Hammerman, Lorelei Hammerman, Judith M. Weiss, Hillel S. Hammerman, Deborah E. Born.
Financial data (yr. ended 12/31/01): Grants paid, $41,786; assets, $996,752 (M); gifts received, $30,000; expenditures, $43,267; qualifying distributions, $41,786.
Limitations: Applications not accepted.
Application information: Contributes only to pre-selected organizations.
Officers and Directors:* Lorelei Hammerman,* Pres.; Benjamin Hammerman,* Secy.-Treas.; Deborah E. Born, Hillel S. Hammerman, Judith M. Weiss.
EIN: 133593279

36873
The Feigenbaum Foundation, Inc.
150 Thompson St., Ste. 2D
New York, NY 10021

Established in 1996 in NY.
Donor(s): Marvin Feigenbaum.
Financial data (yr. ended 08/31/01): Grants paid, $41,771; assets, $69,414 (M); gifts received, $24,000; expenditures, $42,665; qualifying distributions, $41,771.
Limitations: Applications not accepted. Giving primarily in NY; some giving also in Israel.
Application information: Contributes only to pre-selected organizations.
Officer: Marvin Feigenbaum, Pres.
EIN: 133912764

36874
Hudson Valley Foundation for Youth Health, Inc.
120 Lawrenceville St., Ste. 113
Kingston, NY 12401-0903
Contact: George Sisco, Chair.

Established in 1994 in NY.
Financial data (yr. ended 12/31/01): Grants paid, $41,769; assets, $2,253,346 (M); expenditures, $70,183; qualifying distributions, $47,134.
Limitations: Giving primarily in NY.

Application information: Application form not required.
Officers: George A. Sisco, Chair.; Audrey Frost, Vice-Chair.; Harold Shorr, Treas.
Trustees: Mary Ann Brown, Lehanne Sisco, Jennifer Weil.
EIN: 222484912

36875
Robins Family Foundation, Inc.
370 E. 76th St., Ste. B1901
New York, NY 10021

Donor(s): Fred Robins, Matilda Robins,‡ Mervin I. Robins.‡
Financial data (yr. ended 12/31/01): Grants paid, $41,720; assets, $815,763 (M); expenditures, $54,471; qualifying distributions, $41,720.
Limitations: Applications not accepted. Giving primarily in NY.
Application information: Contributes only to pre-selected organizations.
Officers: Fred Robins, Pres.; David Robins, V.P.; Karen Robins, Secy.; Eric Robins, Treas.
EIN: 116039896

36876
The Reddy Foundation
c/o Goldman Sachs & Co.
85 Broad St., Tax Dept.
New York, NY 10004

Established in 1996 in NY.
Donor(s): Girish Reddy.
Financial data (yr. ended 02/28/01): Grants paid, $41,700; assets, $1,451,821 (M); gifts received, $340,594; expenditures, $65,538; qualifying distributions, $41,700.
Limitations: Applications not accepted.
Application information: Contributes only to pre-selected organizations.
Trustee: Girish Reddy.
EIN: 133943919

36877
Scott-Jenkins Fund
c/o Wilber National Bank
245 Main St.
Oneonta, NY 13820
Application address: Financial Aid Office, Netzer Administration Building, SUCO Oneonta, NY 13820, tel.: (607) 436-2532

Donor(s): Ann E. Scott.‡
Financial data (yr. ended 12/31/01): Grants paid, $41,678; assets, $817,510 (M); expenditures, $45,571; qualifying distributions, $41,162.
Limitations: Giving limited to Oneonta, NY.
Officer: Alan Donovan, Chair.
Trustee: Wilber National Bank.
EIN: 166199427
Codes: GTI

36878
Biegelsen Foundation, Inc.
90 State St., Ste. 1436
Albany, NY 12207-1713
Application address: P.O. Box 210, Hollywood, FL 33022, tel.: (954) 463-6581
Contact: Jeffrey Biegelsen, V.P.

Financial data (yr. ended 09/30/01): Grants paid, $41,650; assets, $883,492 (M); expenditures, $44,602; qualifying distributions, $42,287.
Limitations: Giving primarily in Broward County, FL.
Application information: Application form not required.
Officers: Joseph Z. Biegelsen, Pres.; Jeffrey P. Biegelsen, V.P. and Secy.-Treas.
EIN: 136103887

36879
Hans E. Schapira, M.D. Foundation, Inc.
3333 Henry Hudson Pkwy., Apt. 17S
Riverdale, NY 10463 (718) 796-3633
Contact: Ruth Schapira, Pres.

Financial data (yr. ended 02/28/02): Grants paid, $41,600; assets, $605,334 (M); expenditures, $56,981; qualifying distributions, $46,389.
Limitations: Giving primarily in New York, NY.
Officers and Directors:* Ruth Schapira,* Pres.; Ralph Schapira, V.P.; Paul Schapira,* Secy.; Leonard Steel.
EIN: 133338059
Codes: GTI

36880
The Woodward Charitable Foundation
c/o Condon O'Meara, McGinty & Donnelly, LLP
3 New York Plz.
New York, NY 10004-2442

Established in 1953 in NY.
Financial data (yr. ended 04/30/01): Grants paid, $41,600; assets, $1,890,253 (M); expenditures, $112,214; qualifying distributions, $52,919.
Limitations: Applications not accepted. Giving primarily in New York, NY.
Application information: Contributes only to pre-selected organizations.
Trustee: Lisa Woodward.
EIN: 136117375

36881
Berkowitz-Blau Foundation, Inc.
1226 E. 22nd. St.
Brooklyn, NY 11210

Established in 1998 in NY.
Donor(s): Calvin Berkowitz, Zvi Baruch Berkowitz, Peretz Berkowitz.
Financial data (yr. ended 12/31/01): Grants paid, $41,590; assets, $466,140 (M); gifts received, $159,425; expenditures, $43,051; qualifying distributions, $41,590.
Limitations: Applications not accepted. Giving primarily in NY.
Application information: Contributes only to pre-selected organizations.
Directors: Bertha Berkowitz, Calvin Berkowitz, Peretz Berkowitz, Zvi Baruch Berkowitz.
EIN: 113426810

36882
Nfada Charitable Foundation
1144 Wherle Dr.
P.O. Box 9019
Williamsville, NY 14231

Established in 1999 in NY.
Financial data (yr. ended 12/31/01): Grants paid, $41,520; assets, $61,562 (M); gifts received, $18,287; expenditures, $121,887; qualifying distributions, $41,520.
Limitations: Applications not accepted. Giving primarily in NY.
Application information: Contributes only to pre-selected organizations.
Trustees: Kevin J. Campbell, James M. Culligan, James J. Doyle II, Russell F. Marong, Lawrence Schreiber, Paul Stasiak.
EIN: 166486097

36883
Daisy S. Bacon Scholarship Fund
14 Vanderventer Ave.
Port Washington, NY 11050-3737
Contact: Harry J. Mulry, Jr., Tr.

Established in 1992.

Financial data (yr. ended 12/31/01): Grants paid, $41,500; assets, $643,776 (M); expenditures, $54,170; qualifying distributions, $54,170.
Limitations: Giving limited to residents of Port Washington, NY.
Publications: Annual report, grants list, application guidelines.
Application information: Application form required.
Trustee: Harry J. Mulry, Jr.
EIN: 116386052
Codes: GTI

36884
The Helmar Foundation
c/o Yohalem Gillman & Co., LLP
477 Madison Ave.
New York, NY 10022-5802

Established in 1997 in NY.
Financial data (yr. ended 04/30/02): Grants paid, $41,500; assets, $927,070 (M); expenditures, $49,294; qualifying distributions, $41,500.
Limitations: Applications not accepted. Giving primarily in NY.
Application information: Contributes only to pre-selected organizations.
Trustees: Marilyn Haykin, Helene Stein.
EIN: 137097803

36885
Donald W. Layden, Jr. and Mary Jo Layden Family Foundation, Inc.
c/o U.S. Trust Co. of NY
114 W. 47th St., TAXRGR
New York, NY 10036

Established in 1999 in WI.
Donor(s): Donald W. Layden, Jr., Mary Jo Layden.
Financial data (yr. ended 11/30/01): Grants paid, $41,500; assets, $269,875 (M); expenditures, $41,975; qualifying distributions, $41,449.
Limitations: Applications not accepted. Giving primarily in NY.
Application information: Contributes only to pre-selected organizations.
Officers and Directors:* Donald W. Layden, Jr.,* Pres.; Mary Jo Layden,* V.P.; Donald W. Layden, Sr.
EIN: 391980153

36886
The Bishop Robert L. Paddock Trust
c/o Ball Baker Leake
122 E. 42nd St., Ste. 810
New York, NY 10168
Application address: c/o Mid-Hudson Regional Offices Diocese of NY, 30 Pine Grove Ave., Kingston, NY 12401

Donor(s): Bishop Robert L. Paddock.‡
Financial data (yr. ended 12/31/01): Grants paid, $41,500; assets, $521,401 (M); expenditures, $74,040; qualifying distributions, $41,500.
Trustees: Very Rev. James C. Fenhagen, Rev. Janice M. Robinson, Rt. Rev. Mark S. Sisk.
EIN: 526049591

36887
Katherine A. & Clinton R. Black, Jr. Foundation
c/o Warshaw Burstein, et al., LLP
555 5th Ave.
New York, NY 10017-2416

Established in 1955 in NY and DE.
Financial data (yr. ended 12/31/01): Grants paid, $41,400; assets, $100,216 (M); expenditures, $45,620; qualifying distributions, $42,011.
Limitations: Applications not accepted. Giving primarily in New York, NY.

Application information: Contributes only to pre-selected organizations.
Officers: Crawford A. Black, Pres.; Clinton R. Black, Jr., V.P.; Joan E. Black, Secy.-Treas.
EIN: 136092706

36888
Susan Porter & James Clark Giving Fund
(Formerly James Mott Clark Foundation)
350 Park Ave., 9th Fl.
New York, NY 10022

Established in 1988 in NY and DE.
Donor(s): James Mott Clark, Jr.
Financial data (yr. ended 06/30/01): Grants paid, $41,333; assets, $147,509 (M); gifts received, $2,142; expenditures, $43,020; qualifying distributions, $42,125.
Limitations: Applications not accepted. Giving primarily in New York, NY.
Application information: Contributes only to pre-selected organizations.
Officers: James Mott Clark, Jr., Pres. and Secy.; Susanna L. Porter, V.P.; Kenneth R. Wasiak, Treas.
EIN: 133489504

36889
The Slade Family Foundation, Inc.
P.O. Box 1530
Port Washington, NY 11050
Contact: Edward Slade, Pres.

Established in 1993 in NY.
Financial data (yr. ended 12/31/01): Grants paid, $41,251; assets, $1,004,625 (M); gifts received, $54,000; expenditures, $44,609; qualifying distributions, $43,011.
Limitations: Giving primarily in NY.
Application information: Unsolicited requests for funds not accepted.
Officers and Directors:* Edward Slade,* Pres.; Andrea Slade Weitzner,* V.P.; Dorothy Slade,* Secy.; Carol Tarshis,* Treas.; Lawrence Slade, Stefanie Slade, Michael Weitzner.
EIN: 113134746

36890
Loomis J. Grossman, Jr. Foundation, Inc.
150 White Plains Rd.
Tarrytown, NY 10591-5521

Established in NY.
Donor(s): Loomis J. Grossman, Jr.
Financial data (yr. ended 12/31/01): Grants paid, $41,250; assets, $192,919 (M); expenditures, $46,508; qualifying distributions, $40,855.
Limitations: Applications not accepted. Giving primarily in New York, NY and UT.
Application information: Contributes only to pre-selected organizations.
Officers and Trustees:* Loomis J. Grossman, Jr.,* Pres.; Robert C. Baker,* Secy.; Thomas J. Dee.
EIN: 237077822

36891
Harden Foundation, Inc.
8550 Mill Pond Way
McConnellsville, NY 13401 (315) 245-1000
Contact: David Harden, Dir.

Established in 1944 in NY.
Financial data (yr. ended 12/31/01): Grants paid, $41,250; assets, $875,610 (M); expenditures, $50,986; qualifying distributions, $41,250.
Limitations: Giving primarily in NY.
Directors: Anne Babcock, David Harden, Neil Harden.
EIN: 156017586
Codes: GTI

36892
The Peters Family Foundation
c/o U.S. Trust
114 W. 47th St.
New York, NY 10036

Established in 2000 in WA.
Donor(s): Janice C. Peters, Michael P. Peters.
Financial data (yr. ended 12/31/01): Grants paid, $41,250; assets, $2,826,541 (M); expenditures, $58,050; qualifying distributions, $41,250.
Limitations: Applications not accepted. Giving primarily in IA and WA.
Application information: Contributes only to pre-selected organizations.
Trustees: Janice C. Peters, Michael P. Peters.
EIN: 916505643

36893
Craigielea Educational Fund, Inc.
c/o Fleet National Bank
159 E. Main St.
Rochester, NY 14638
Application address: 50 Trevor Court, Rd., Rochester, NY 14610
Contact: Eric Hope, Pres.

Financial data (yr. ended 04/30/00): Grants paid, $41,205; assets, $1,042,585 (M); expenditures, $48,422; qualifying distributions, $45,488.
Limitations: Giving primarily in Ithaca, NY.
Officers: Eric Hope, Pres.; David Collum, Secy.; Wayne D. Wetzel, Jr., Treas.
Trustee: Fleet National Bank.
EIN: 166048156

36894
The Walter F. Blaine Foundation
c/o BCRS Associates
67 Wall St., 8th Fl
New York, NY 10005

Donor(s): Walter F. Blaine,‡ Phyllis M. Blaine.
Financial data (yr. ended 11/30/00): Grants paid, $41,171; assets, $609,419 (M); gifts received, $34,063; expenditures, $41,718; qualifying distributions, $41,259.
Limitations: Applications not accepted. Giving primarily in NJ, and New York, NY.
Application information: Contributes only to pre-selected organizations.
Trustees: Phyllis M. Blaine, Claire Robert, Margaret Wenzel.
EIN: 136028805

36895
JMF Charitable Foundation
1470 59TH St.
Brooklyn, NY 11219

Established in 2001 in NY.
Financial data (yr. ended 05/31/02): Grants paid, $41,170; assets, $59,398 (M); gifts received, $101,618; expenditures, $42,220; qualifying distributions, $41,170.
Trustee: Jacob Friedman.
EIN: 113602012

36896
Ashley Family Foundation, Inc.
600 Power Bldg.
16 W. Main St.
Rochester, NY 14614 (716) 454-4840
Contact: Janice Ashley, Pres.

Established in 1996 in NY.
Donor(s): Janice Ashley, Stephen Ashley.
Financial data (yr. ended 12/31/01): Grants paid, $41,142; assets, $642,106 (M); gifts received, $74,514; expenditures, $49,083; qualifying distributions, $41,038.

Officers and Directors:* Janice G. Ashley,* Pres.; Stephen B. Ashley,* V.P.; Jillian Martin, Secy.; Joan Markham, Treas.; Jonathan M. Ashley, Leeson K. Ashley.
EIN: 161515899

36897
The Acqua Wellington Foundation
c/o Oracle Svcs., Inc.
1010 Northern Blvd., Ste. 208
Great Neck, NY 11021

Financial data (yr. ended 12/31/01): Grants paid, $41,100; assets, $41,993 (M); expenditures, $42,375; qualifying distributions, $41,100.
Limitations: Applications not accepted. Giving primarily in CA and NY; some giving also in Canada.
Application information: Contributes only to pre-selected organizations.
Officers and Director:* Isser Elishis,* Pres.; Claude Robillard, V.P. and Secy.; Kalman Schoor, V.P. and Treas.; Wayne Coleson, V.P.; Barry Foster, V.P.; Cassandra Luhur, V.P.; Beth Rosenberg, V.P.
EIN: 134115482

36898
Lin and Susie Chen Foundation, Inc.
210 Canal St., Ste. 611
New York, NY 10013-4510 (212) 964-2480
Contact: Rose Chao, Secy.

Established in 1993 in NY.
Donor(s): Susie Chen.
Financial data (yr. ended 12/31/01): Grants paid, $41,055; assets, $1,431,959 (M); gifts received, $591,702; expenditures, $49,609; qualifying distributions, $41,055.
Limitations: Giving primarily in New York, NY, and NJ; some giving also in Fuzhou, China.
Officers and Directors:* Whiting Wu,* Pres.; Alan Winton,* V.P.; Rose Chao,* Secy.-Treas.
EIN: 133742616

36899
Paul W. Zuccaire Foundation
44 Merrivale Rd.
Great Neck, NY 11020

Established in 1999 in NY.
Donor(s): Estelle Zuccaire.
Financial data (yr. ended 12/31/01): Grants paid, $41,050; assets, $2,992,032 (M); gifts received, $400,100; expenditures, $127,804; qualifying distributions, $41,050.
Limitations: Applications not accepted.
Application information: Contributes only to pre-selected organizations.
Officers: Alice Jean Zuccaire, Pres.; Arnold Y. Claman, V.P. and Secy.; Robert Connell, V.P.
EIN: 113523633

36900
Shabse Rubin Tzedaka Foundation, Inc.
84 Franklin St.
New York, NY 10013
Contact: Sarah Roz, Tr.

Donor(s): Sam Rubin, Herschel Roz, Sarah Roz.
Financial data (yr. ended 12/31/01): Grants paid, $41,018; assets, $0 (M); gifts received, $35,000; expenditures, $41,728; qualifying distributions, $41,728.
Limitations: Giving primarily in the New York, NY, area.
Trustee: Sarah Roz.
EIN: 116084162

36901
Braxton Fund, Inc.
c/o Theron H. Worth
10 Terrace Heights
Katonah, NY 10536

Donor(s): Frances C. Braxton.
Financial data (yr. ended 10/31/01): Grants paid, $41,000; assets, $664,719 (M); expenditures, $44,602; qualifying distributions, $40,846.
Limitations: Applications not accepted. Giving primarily in NY.
Application information: Contributes only to pre-selected organizations.
Officers and Directors:* Theron H. Worth,* Pres. and Treas.; Jaqueline M.B. Wren,* V.P. and Secy.; Christopher S. Wren.
EIN: 136162097

36902
The Fremarch Foundation
c/o Frederick M.R. Smith
784 Park Ave., Ste. 18B
New York, NY 10021

Established in 1997 in NY.
Donor(s): Frederick M.R. Smith.
Financial data (yr. ended 12/31/01): Grants paid, $41,000; assets, $320,429 (M); expenditures, $49,271; qualifying distributions, $41,000.
Limitations: Applications not accepted.
Application information: Contributes only to pre-selected organizations.
Trustee: Frederick M.R. Smith.
EIN: 137118610

36903
Mr. & Mrs. Roman Martinez, IV Foundation
c/o Mahoney, Cohen, & Co.
111 W. 40th St.
New York, NY 10018-2506

Established in 1994 in NY.
Donor(s): Roman Martinez.
Financial data (yr. ended 11/30/01): Grants paid, $41,000; assets, $40,792 (M); gifts received, $33,286; expenditures, $41,275; qualifying distributions, $41,000.
Limitations: Applications not accepted. Giving on the East Coast, primarily in CT, MA, and NY.
Application information: Contributes only to pre-selected organizations.
Trustees: Helena Martinez, Roman Martinez IV.
EIN: 137044724

36904
The Stevenson Family Foundation
c/o Michael Kauffman
459 Pulaski St.
Syracuse, NY 13202

Established in 1984.
Donor(s): Milton Stevenson, Ann Stevenson.
Financial data (yr. ended 02/28/02): Grants paid, $41,000; assets, $78,284 (M); expenditures, $41,000; qualifying distributions, $41,000.
Limitations: Applications not accepted. Giving primarily in Syracuse, NY.
Application information: Contributes only to pre-selected organizations.
Trustees: Ann Stevenson, Milton Stevenson.
EIN: 222586535

36905
The C. & J. Unanue Foundation, Inc.
c/o Bessemer Trust Co., N.A.
630 5th Ave.
New York, NY 10111

Established in 1995 in NJ.
Donor(s): Joseph A. Unanue, Carmen Unanue.

Financial data (yr. ended 06/30/01): Grants paid, $41,000; assets, $6,064,592 (M); gifts received, $1,100,100; expenditures, $73,737; qualifying distributions, $43,270.
Limitations: Applications not accepted. Giving on a national basis.
Application information: Contributes only to pre-selected organizations.
Officers and Trustees:* Carmen Unanue,* Pres.; Andrew Unanue,* V.P.; Joseph A. Unanue,* Secy.-Treas.
EIN: 223382542

36906
The Lew Wasserman Scholarship Foundation
P.O. Box 5023
New York, NY 10150

Donor(s): Universal Studios, Inc.
Financial data (yr. ended 06/30/01): Grants paid, $41,000; assets, $717,958 (M); gifts received, $25,627; expenditures, $66,627; qualifying distributions, $40,783.
Limitations: Applications not accepted.
Application information: Contributes only to pre-selected organizations.
Officers and Directors:* Ron Meyer,* Pres.; Karen Randall,* Exec. V.P., Secy.; Hellene S. Runtagh, Exec. V.P.; Deborah S. Rosen,* Sr. V.P.; William A. Sutman, Sr. V.P.; Kevin Conway, V.P.; H. Stephen Gorden, V.P.; Marc Palotay, V.P.; John R. Preston, V.P.; Pamela F. Cherney, Treas.
EIN: 954479463
Codes: CS

36907
The Marc Wolinsky & Barry C. Skovgaard Foundation, Inc.
c/o Wachtell, Lipton, Rosen & Katz
51 W. 52nd St.
New York, NY 10019

Established in 1987 in NY.
Donor(s): Marc Wolinsky, Barry C. Skovgaard.
Financial data (yr. ended 04/30/02): Grants paid, $41,000; assets, $48,306 (M); gifts received, $1,000; expenditures, $41,007; qualifying distributions, $41,000.
Limitations: Giving primarily in NY.
Officers and Directors:* Marc Wolinsky,* Pres.; Barry C. Skovgaard,* V.P.; Michael Himmel.
EIN: 133442970

36908
The Frieman Foundation, Inc.
c/o Rivka Frieman
1175 Park Ave., Apt. 10C
New York, NY 10128

Established in 1989 in NY.
Donor(s): Rivka Frieman.
Financial data (yr. ended 11/30/01): Grants paid, $40,930; assets, $9,460 (M); gifts received, $40,225; expenditures, $42,896; qualifying distributions, $40,930.
Limitations: Applications not accepted.
Application information: Contributes only to pre-selected organizations.
Officers: Rivka Frieman, Pres.; Morris Platt, Treas.
EIN: 133549076

36909
Barbara Irene Lovenheim Charitable Trust
190 Council Rock
Rochester, NY 14610-3335

Established in 1993 in NY.
Financial data (yr. ended 12/31/01): Grants paid, $40,919; assets, $1,092,333 (M); expenditures, $104,286; qualifying distributions, $40,919.
Limitations: Applications not accepted.

Directors: Barbara I. Lovenheim, John E. Lovenheim.
EIN: 166383849

36910
The Dreifus Family Foundation
c/o Lazard, Freres & Co., LLC
30 Rockefeller Plz.
New York, NY 10020
Contact: Charles Dreifus, Pres.

Established in 1986 in NY.
Donor(s): Charles Dreifus.
Financial data (yr. ended 06/30/01): Grants paid, $40,900; assets, $55,095 (M); expenditures, $40,965; qualifying distributions, $40,900.
Limitations: Giving primarily in NJ and New York, NY.
Officers and Directors:* Charles Dreifus,* Pres.; Erika Dreifus,* V.P.; Joanna Dreifus,* V.P.; Madeline Dreifus,* V.P.; Paul Cohen,* Secy.-Treas.
EIN: 222726738

36911
Pickman Foundation, Inc.
118-21 Queens Blvd.
Forest Hills, NY 11375 (718) 575-0045
Contact: Theresa Schwartz, Secy.

Established around 1959 in NY.
Donor(s): Morton Pickman.
Financial data (yr. ended 05/31/99): Grants paid, $40,890; assets, $2,418,250 (M); expenditures, $42,456; qualifying distributions, $83,290.
Limitations: Giving primarily in the greater New York, NY, area.
Officers: Morton Pickman, Pres.; Theresa Schwartz, Secy.
EIN: 116036666

36912
Mashitz Family Charitable Foundation
17 S. Parker Dr.
Monsey, NY 10952

Established in 1997 in NY.
Financial data (yr. ended 12/31/99): Grants paid, $40,790; assets, $26,788 (M); expenditures, $40,790; qualifying distributions, $40,790.
Limitations: Applications not accepted.
Application information: Contributes only to pre-selected organizations.
Trustees: Isaac Mashitz, Rivka Mashitz.
EIN: 133939863

36913
Saltzman Foundation, Inc.
350 5th Ave., Ste. 8008
New York, NY 10118-0001
Contact: Arnold A. Saltzman, Pres.

Established in 1950 in NY.
Financial data (yr. ended 03/31/00): Grants paid, $40,785; assets, $2,862,379 (M); gifts received, $73,816; expenditures, $54,780; qualifying distributions, $40,785.
Limitations: Giving on a national basis.
Application information: Application form not required.
Officers and Directors:* Arnold A. Saltzman,* Pres. and Treas.; Joan Saltzman,* Secy.; Roger Haber, Marian Saltzman.
EIN: 136142471

36914
Cylia G. Siedenburg and William G. Siedenburg Foundation
400 E. 56th St., 36th Fl.
New York, NY 10022

Established in 1996.
Donor(s): William G. Siedenburg.

Financial data (yr. ended 12/31/01): Grants paid, $40,744; assets, $236,949 (M); expenditures, $47,669; qualifying distributions, $40,744.
Limitations: Applications not accepted. Giving on a national basis.
Application information: Contributes only to pre-selected organizations.
Trustees: Marvin Lauterbach, Cylia G. Siedenburg, William G. Siedenburg, Richard C. Weidenbaum.
EIN: 137096555

36915
Marcus Foundation, Inc.
980 Ave. of the Americas
New York, NY 10018-5443

Established in 1930 in NY.
Donor(s): Marcus Brothers Textiles, Inc.
Financial data (yr. ended 07/31/01): Grants paid, $40,689; assets, $153,875 (M); gifts received, $20,000; expenditures, $43,438; qualifying distributions, $40,261.
Limitations: Applications not accepted. Giving primarily in the greater New York, NY, area.
Application information: Contributes only to pre-selected organizations.
Officers: Arthur Marcus, Pres.; Jay H. Marcus, V.P.; Martin S. Marcus, V.P.
EIN: 136116660
Codes: CS, CD

36916
The Family of Samuel H. Schwartz Foundation
P.O. Box 790
Babylon, NY 11702-0790

Established in 1987 in New York.
Donor(s): Lillian S. Kraut.
Financial data (yr. ended 09/30/01): Grants paid, $40,659; assets, $1,083,680 (M); expenditures, $68,713; qualifying distributions, $40,659.
Limitations: Applications not accepted. Giving primarily in NY.
Application information: Contributes only to pre-selected organizations.
Officers: Lillian S. Kraut, Pres.; Paul Ades, Secy.; Doris Brody, Treas.
EIN: 133438198

36917
The Stainrook Foundation
c/o Judith Swann Stainrook
150 Columbus Ave., No. 4A
New York, NY 10023

Established in 1997 in NY.
Donor(s): Harry R. Stainrook, Judith Swann Stainrook.
Financial data (yr. ended 12/31/01): Grants paid, $40,600; assets, $814,137 (M); expenditures, $46,266; qualifying distributions, $40,600.
Limitations: Applications not accepted. Giving primarily in Philadelphia, PA; some giving in Washington, DC, MD, and NY.
Application information: Contributes only to pre-selected organizations.
Directors: Harry R. Stainrook, Judith S. Stainrook.
EIN: 161535406

36918
Edward Handelman Fund
c/o Walter J. Handelman
1 N. Broadway, No. 1001
White Plains, NY 10601

Donor(s): Blanche B. Handelman.
Financial data (yr. ended 12/31/01): Grants paid, $40,596; assets, $733,677 (M); expenditures, $49,402; qualifying distributions, $40,596.
Limitations: Applications not accepted. Giving primarily in Westchester County, NY.

Application information: Contributes only to pre-selected organizations.
Officers and Directors:* Alice H. Model,* Pres.; Judith A. Handelman,* V.P.; Walter J. Handelman,* Secy.; Alan L. Model,* Treas.
EIN: 136273229

36919
The Hancock Foundation
c/o Barry F. Schwartz
35 E. 62nd St.
New York, NY 10021 (212) 572-5170

Established in 1997 in CT.
Donor(s): Barry F. Schwartz.
Financial data (yr. ended 12/31/01): Grants paid, $40,501; assets, $154,705 (M); gifts received, $25,000; expenditures, $40,615; qualifying distributions, $40,501.
Limitations: Giving primarily in Greenwich, CT.
Application information: Application form not required.
Trustee: Barry F. Schwartz.
EIN: 133941584

36920
Bonnell Cove Foundation
c/o James D. Phyfe, Davis, Polk & Wardwell
450 Lexington Ave.
New York, NY 10017-3911

Established in 1989 in NY.
Donor(s): The Cruising Club of America, Inc.
Financial data (yr. ended 12/31/99): Grants paid, $40,500; assets, $634,707 (M); gifts received, $16,800; expenditures, $43,873; qualifying distributions, $40,500.
Limitations: Applications not accepted.
Application information: Contributes only to pre-selected organizations.
Officers and Directors:* Robert E. Drew,* Pres.; James C. Pitney,* V.P.; Gordon Abbott, Jr.,* Secy.; George M. Isdale, Jr.,* Treas.; Vincent Monte-Sano, Thomas O. Otto, Ross E. Sherbrooke, Kaighn Smith, M.D., Charles P. Schutt, Jr., Ronald Trossbach.
EIN: 133556721

36921
The Devery Foundation
49 Broadway
P.O. Box 586
Lake Luzerne, NY 12846

Financial data (yr. ended 06/30/02): Grants paid, $40,500; assets, $246,939 (M); expenditures, $47,503; qualifying distributions, $40,500.
Limitations: Applications not accepted. Giving primarily in Schenectady, NY.
Application information: Contributes only to pre-selected organizations.
Officer: Judith A. Lynch, Chair.
Trustees: M. Mary Thomas, Edward VanHeusen.
EIN: 222134697

36922
The Glastenbury Foundation, Inc.
33 E. 70th St., Ste. 6D
New York, NY 10021
Contact: Robert G. Scott, Pres.

Established in 1999 NY and DE.
Donor(s): Robert G. Scott.
Financial data (yr. ended 12/31/01): Grants paid, $40,500; assets, $739,624 (M); gifts received, $3,240; expenditures, $47,037; qualifying distributions, $40,500.
Limitations: Giving primarily in NY.
Officers: Robert G. Scott, Pres.; Karen M. Scott, Secy.; Matthew R. Scott, Treas.
Directors: Jessica A. Scott, Megan E. Scott.

EIN: 134092164

36923
Endowment Fund of the Fifth Masonic District of Manhattan
71 W. 23rd St.
New York, NY 10010-4102
Contact: William Evers, Secy.

Financial data (yr. ended 12/31/00): Grants paid, $40,480; assets, $1,016,929 (M); expenditures, $53,917; qualifying distributions, $56,917; giving activities include $3,000 for loans to individuals.
Limitations: Giving primarily in New York, NY.
Application information: Application form required.
Officers: Andrew Marshall, Pres.; Alan Berk, V.P.; William Evers, Secy.; Richard Meshejian, Treas.
Trustee: Frank Messemer.
EIN: 136097064

36924
Gantz Family Foundation
c/o B. Strauss Assoc., Ltd.
307 5th Ave., 8th Fl.
New York, NY 10016-6517

Established in 1999 in NY.
Donor(s): Emanuel Gantz.
Financial data (yr. ended 11/30/01): Grants paid, $40,386; assets, $30,141 (M); expenditures, $41,681; qualifying distributions, $40,386.
Limitations: Applications not accepted.
Application information: Contributes only to pre-selected organizations.
Trustees: Emanuel Gantz, Patricia Gantz.
EIN: 134108684

36925
The Abraham & Sarah Charitable Foundation
1554 49th St.
Brooklyn, NY 11219

Established in 1999 in NY.
Donor(s): Leib Mandelbaum, Bertha Mandelbaum.
Financial data (yr. ended 12/31/00): Grants paid, $40,310; assets, $257,434 (M); gifts received, $256,368; expenditures, $41,299; qualifying distributions, $40,310.
Limitations: Applications not accepted.
Application information: Contributes only to pre-selected organizations.
Trustees: Bertha Mandelbaum, Chaim Mandelbaum, Leib Mandelbaum, Mordechai Mandelbaum.
EIN: 113493969

36926
Harold and Ruth Allen Foundation
30 Pheasant Run
Kings Point, NY 11024-1523
Application address: 901 E. Camino Real, Boca Raton, FL 33432
Contact: Harold Allen, Tr.

Donor(s): Harold Allen, Ruth Allen.
Financial data (yr. ended 09/30/02): Grants paid, $40,300; assets, $195,726 (M); gifts received, $20,000; expenditures, $40,810; qualifying distributions, $40,300.
Limitations: Giving primarily in NY.
Trustees: Harold Allen, Ruth Allen, Janet Lynn Dippell.
EIN: 116007325

36927
The Kotler Family Foundation, Inc.
c/o Schroder & Co., Inc.
1633 Broadway, Tax Dept., 9th Fl.
New York, NY 10019-6708

Established in 1991 in DE.
Donor(s): Steven Kotler.
Financial data (yr. ended 02/28/02): Grants paid, $40,300; assets, $826,523 (M); expenditures, $44,322; qualifying distributions, $40,300.
Limitations: Applications not accepted.
Application information: Contributes only to pre-selected organizations.
Officers: Steven Kotler, Pres. and Secy.; Carolyn Kotler, V.P. and Treas.
EIN: 133617743

36928
The William and Sara Mittler Foundation
c/o Frendel, Brown & Weissman
655 3rd Ave., Ste. 1400
New York, NY 10017

Established in 1997 in NY.
Financial data (yr. ended 11/30/01): Grants paid, $40,300; assets, $469,577 (M); expenditures, $59,349; qualifying distributions, $40,300.
Limitations: Applications not accepted. Giving primarily in New York, NY.
Application information: Contributes only to pre-selected organizations.
Trustees: Joel S. Weissman, Paul Weissman.
EIN: 133964632

36929
William & Marion Zeckendorf Foundation, Inc.
770 Lexington Ave., 3rd Fl.
New York, NY 10021

Established in 1961 in NY.
Donor(s): William Zeckendorf, Nancy Zeckendorf.
Financial data (yr. ended 07/31/01): Grants paid, $40,250; assets, $74,632 (M); expenditures, $45,757; qualifying distributions, $42,808.
Limitations: Applications not accepted. Giving primarily in NM and NY.
Application information: Contributes only to pre-selected organizations.
Officers and Directors:* Nancy Zeckendorf,* V.P.; William Zeckendorf,* V.P.; Margaret Fletcher, Mgr.
EIN: 136095627

36930
The Michael Tenenbaum Educational Trust
1637 50th St.
Brooklyn, NY 11204

Established in 2000 in NY.
Donor(s): Michael Tenenbaum.
Financial data (yr. ended 12/31/01): Grants paid, $40,180; assets, $558,008 (M); gifts received, $100,000; expenditures, $41,992; qualifying distributions, $40,180.
Limitations: Applications not accepted.
Application information: Contributes only to pre-selected organizations.
EIN: 116552379

36931
Jacob & Belle Rosenbaum Foundation
22 Hilltop Pl.
Monsey, NY 10952

Established in 1982 in NY.
Financial data (yr. ended 12/31/00): Grants paid, $40,136; assets, $722,544 (M); gifts received, $5,000; expenditures, $43,582; qualifying distributions, $40,144.
Limitations: Applications not accepted. Giving on a national basis.

Directors: Belle Rosenbaum, Jacob Rosenbaum.
EIN: 133100072

36932
The Marks Foundation
c/o Goldman Sachs & Co.
85 Broad St., Tax Dept.
New York, NY 10004

Donor(s): Ronald G. Marks.
Financial data (yr. ended 04/30/02): Grants paid, $40,105; assets, $895,588 (M); expenditures, $42,220; qualifying distributions, $40,105.
Limitations: Applications not accepted.
Application information: Contributes only to pre-selected organizations.
Trustees: Lynne Marks, Ronald G. Marks.
EIN: 133933322

36933
Marc Galler Research Foundation, Inc.
111 E. Hawthorne Ave.
Valley Stream, NY 11580 (516) 561-8225

Established in 1969.
Donor(s): William Galler, Beatrice Galler, Heterochemical Corp., Lynn Galler.
Financial data (yr. ended 10/31/01): Grants paid, $40,055; assets, $373,875 (M); gifts received, $79,063; expenditures, $40,455; qualifying distributions, $40,155.
Limitations: Giving primarily in NY.
Application information: Application form not required.
Officers: Lynn Galler, Pres.; Beatrice Galler, V.P.; Raymond Berutti, Secy.-Treas.
EIN: 217013433

36934
The Scott & Susan Davidson Foundation, Inc.
885 3rd Ave.
New York, NY 10022

Established in 1999 in NY.
Donor(s): Marvin H. Davidson Foundation, Scott Davidson, Susan Davidson.
Financial data (yr. ended 12/31/01): Grants paid, $40,045; assets, $1,124,459 (M); gifts received, $71,647; expenditures, $57,564; qualifying distributions, $40,045.
Limitations: Applications not accepted.
Application information: Contributes only to pre-selected organizations.
Officers and Directors:* Scott E. Davidson,* Pres.; Susan Davidson,* Secy.; Stephen Dowicz,* Secy.
EIN: 134088730

36935
The Aleph Foundation for Humanities
c/o Euristates
667 Madison Ave., 11th Fl.
New York, NY 10021

Established in 1999 in DE and NY.
Financial data (yr. ended 12/31/01): Grants paid, $40,000; assets, $1,716,921 (M); gifts received, $40,000; expenditures, $48,135; qualifying distributions, $48,027.
Limitations: Applications not accepted. Giving primarily in New York, NY.
Application information: Contributes only to pre-selected organizations.
Officers and Directors:* Jean-Charles Naouri,* Pres.; Benjamin Lichaa,* Treas.; Maurice Friedrich, Joel Ornstein.
EIN: 061532031

36936
Blue Earth Foundation, Inc.
c/o U.S. Trust
114 W. 47th St., TaxVas
New York, NY 10036

Established in 2000 in DE.
Donor(s): Daniel F. Akerson, Karin A. Akerson.
Financial data (yr. ended 12/31/00): Grants paid, $40,000; assets, $1,450,106 (M); gifts received, $2,723,858; expenditures, $61,036; qualifying distributions, $55,825.
Application information: Unsolicited request for funds not accepted.
Officers and Directors:* Daniel F. Akerson, Chair.; Karin A. Akerson,* Pres.; Keith D. Akerson,* Secy.; Elizabeth C. Akerson,* Treas.
EIN: 541991343

36937
The Haskell and Gay Duncan Foundation, Inc.
c/o Myer, Greene & Degge
P.O. Box 930
Pearl River, NY 10965

Established in 1999 in NC.
Donor(s): Haskell A. Duncan.
Financial data (yr. ended 12/31/01): Grants paid, $40,000; assets, $287,057 (M); expenditures, $45,683; qualifying distributions, $40,000.
Limitations: Applications not accepted.
Application information: Contributes only to pre-selected organizations.
Officers: Haskell A. Duncan, Pres.; Wayne E. Jordan, V.P.; Mark D. Vaughn, Secy.-Treas.
EIN: 562163266

36938
The Edward & Carol Goldberg Family Foundation, Inc.
c/o Merrill Lynch
2 World Financial Ctr., 38th Fl.
New York, NY 10281-6100

Established in 1998 in NY.
Donor(s): Edward L. Goldberg, Carol Goldberg.
Financial data (yr. ended 05/31/01): Grants paid, $40,000; assets, $1,417,350 (M); gifts received, $75,599; expenditures, $50,309; qualifying distributions, $32,864.
Limitations: Applications not accepted.
Application information: Contributes only to pre-selected organizations.
Officers: Carol Goldberg, Pres.; Edward L. Goldberg, V.P.
Director: Erica D. Goldberg.
EIN: 223591660

36939
William H. Hazen Foundation
c/o William H. Hazen
55 Remsen St.
Brooklyn, NY 11201

Established in 1997 in NY.
Donor(s): William H. Hazen.
Financial data (yr. ended 12/31/00): Grants paid, $40,000; assets, $883,500 (M); gifts received, $100,250; expenditures, $43,200; qualifying distributions, $42,566.
Limitations: Giving primarily in ME and NY.
Application information: Unsolicited requests for funds not accepted.
Trustees: Judith E. Hazen, William H. Hazen.
EIN: 116487867

36940
The Johnson-Stillman Family Foundation
c/o Frances D. Spier
135 E. 71st St., Ste. 11A
New York, NY 10021-4258

Established in 1996 in NY.
Donor(s): Frances D. Spier.
Financial data (yr. ended 12/31/01): Grants paid, $40,000; assets, $905,204 (M); expenditures, $40,574; qualifying distributions, $40,000.
Limitations: Applications not accepted. Giving primarily in Washington, DC, and New York, NY.
Application information: Contributes only to pre-selected organizations.
Officer: Frances D. Spier, Pres.
EIN: 137097866

36941
Lainoff Family Foundation, Inc.
c/o Hertz, Herson, & Co., LLP
2 Park Ave., Ste. 1500
New York, NY 10016

Established in 1997 in NY.
Donor(s): Irwin Lainoff.
Financial data (yr. ended 12/31/01): Grants paid, $40,000; assets, $1,109,861 (M); gifts received, $309,616; expenditures, $44,269; qualifying distributions, $40,000.
Limitations: Applications not accepted. Giving primarily in Washington, DC.
Application information: Contributes only to pre-selected organizations.
Officers and Directors:* Irwin Lainoff,* Pres.; Carole Lainoff,* V.P.; Michael Lainoff,* Treas.; Steven Lainoff,* Treas.
EIN: 133949510

36942
Lichtenstein Foundation, Inc.
c/o Garan, Inc.
350 5th Ave.
New York, NY 10118-0001 (212) 563-2000
Contact: Seymour Lichtenstein, Pres.

Donor(s): Seymour Lichtenstein.
Financial data (yr. ended 11/30/01): Grants paid, $40,000; assets, $810,532 (M); expenditures, $40,180; qualifying distributions, $40,000.
Limitations: Giving primarily in New York, NY.
Officers and Directors:* Seymour Lichtenstein,* Pres.; Marvin Robinson,* Secy.
EIN: 136121017

36943
The Meg Foundation
5316 15th Ave.
Brooklyn, NY 11219

Established in 2000.
Financial data (yr. ended 12/31/01): Grants paid, $40,000; assets, $34,664 (M); gifts received, $16,397; expenditures, $46,827; qualifying distributions, $40,000.
Directors: Anne Gottlieb, Miklos Gottlieb, July Lichtschein, Laurie Netzer.
EIN: 113510392

36944
The Raydan Foundation
c/o Kirkland Investment Corp.
527 Madison Ave., 17th. Fl.
New York, NY 10022-4212

Established in 1985 in NY.
Donor(s): Joel Kirschbaum.
Financial data (yr. ended 06/30/01): Grants paid, $40,000; assets, $6,506 (M); expenditures, $40,050; qualifying distributions, $40,000.

Limitations: Applications not accepted. Giving primarily in NY.
Application information: Contributes only to pre-selected organizations.
Trustees: Joel Kirschbaum, Michelle Kirschbaum.
EIN: 133318164

36945
C. Frank Reavis Foundation, Inc.
c/o Fulbright & Jaworski, LLP
666 5th Ave.
New York, NY 10103

Financial data (yr. ended 10/31/01): Grants paid, $40,000; assets, $613,578 (M); expenditures, $44,046; qualifying distributions, $40,000.
Limitations: Applications not accepted. Giving primarily in NY.
Application information: Contributes only to pre-selected organizations.
Officers: Berry Eitel Walter, Pres.; Peter J. Repetti, Secy.; Walter T. Eitel, Treas.
EIN: 136272713

36946
W. Eugene Smith Memorial Fund, Inc.
1133 Ave. of the Americas
New York, NY 10036 (212) 857-6038
Additional tel.: (212) 857-9751, ext. 138; URL: http://www.smithfund.org
Contact: Helen Marcus, Pres.

Established in 1980 in NY.
Donor(s): Nikon, Inc.
Financial data (yr. ended 02/28/02): Grants paid, $40,000; assets, $6,975 (M); gifts received, $50,350; expenditures, $56,007; qualifying distributions, $39,997.
Limitations: Giving on a national and international basis.
Application information: Application form available on foundation website. Application form required.
Officers and Trustees:* Helen Marcus,* Pres.; Kathy Ryan,* Secy.; Jeanette Chapnick, Treas.; and 12 additional trustees.
EIN: 133060631
Codes: CS, CD, GTI

36947
Arline J. Smith Trust
c/o JPMorgan Chase Bank
P.O. Box 31412
Rochester, NY 14603-1412
Application address: c/o Dir. of Financial Aid, Juilliard School of Music, 60 Lincoln Ctr. Plz., Rm. 235, New York, NY 10023-6591, tel.: (212) 799-5000, Ext. 211

Donor(s): Arline J. Smith.‡
Financial data (yr. ended 08/31/01): Grants paid, $40,000; assets, $820,037 (M); expenditures, $69,417; qualifying distributions, $41,160.
Limitations: Giving limited to residents of CT.
Application information: Application form required.
Trustee: JPMorgan Chase Bank.
EIN: 066246639
Codes: GTI

36948
Tambil Foundation Trust
c/o Deutsche Trust Co. of NY
P.O. Box 1297, Church St. Sta.
New York, NY 10008
Application address: S. Tattersall, Trust Off, Deutsche Trust Co. of NY, 280 Park Ave., New York, NY 10017
Contact: S. Tattersall, Trust Off., Deutsche Trust Co. of NY

Financial data (yr. ended 12/31/01): Grants paid, $40,000; assets, $385,851 (M); expenditures, $45,087; qualifying distributions, $42,067.
Limitations: Giving primarily in FL.
Trustee: Deutsche Bank.
EIN: 136043082

36949
William & Jerry Ungar Foundation, Inc.
c/o Rosen, Seymour, Shapss, Martin & Co.
757 3rd Ave.
New York, NY 10017-2049

Established in 1974.
Financial data (yr. ended 11/30/01): Grants paid, $40,000; assets, $627,365 (M); gifts received, $40,000; expenditures, $41,917; qualifying distributions, $40,000.
Limitations: Applications not accepted. Giving primarily in NY.
Application information: Contributes only to pre-selected organizations.
Officers: Jerry Ungar, Mgr.; William Ungar, Mgr.
EIN: 237420557

36950
The Ville Medieval De Cardona Foundation Charitable Trust
c/o Fuster
14 E. 75th St., Ste. 11D
New York, NY 10021

Established in 1997 in NY.
Financial data (yr. ended 12/31/99): Grants paid, $40,000; assets, $846 (M); gifts received, $40,000; expenditures, $43,232; qualifying distributions, $43,232; giving activities include $4,091 for programs.
Limitations: Applications not accepted.
Application information: Contributes only to pre-selected organizations.
Trustees: Maria Fuster, Valentin Fuster.
EIN: 133937112

36951
Reid Williams Foundation
13 Vandam St.
New York, NY 10013
Contact: Reid Williams, Pres.

Established in 2000 in NY.
Donor(s): Reid Williams.
Financial data (yr. ended 12/31/01): Grants paid, $40,000; assets, $696,510 (M); gifts received, $165,640; expenditures, $48,458; qualifying distributions, $40,000.
Officer and Director:* Reid Williams,* Pres.
EIN: 316653377

36952
The Willinphila Foundation
c/o Linda S. Musser
167 E. 82nd St.
New York, NY 10028-1856

Financial data (yr. ended 11/30/01): Grants paid, $40,000; assets, $418,917 (M); expenditures, $43,017; qualifying distributions, $40,000.
Limitations: Applications not accepted.

Application information: Contributes only to pre-selected organizations.
Trustees: William L. Musser, Jr., Lila Ruth Musser, Linda S. Musser, Philip Adrian Musser.
EIN: 133933663

36953
Jon & Kathy Savitz Foundation
c/o Goldman Sachs & Co.
85 Broad St., Tax Dept.
New York, NY 10004

Established in 1999 in NY.
Donor(s): Jonathan Savitz.
Financial data (yr. ended 10/31/01): Grants paid, $39,850; assets, $2,330,784 (M); gifts received, $975,875; expenditures, $65,061; qualifying distributions, $39,850.
Limitations: Applications not accepted.
Application information: Contributes only to pre-selected organizations.
Trustees: Jonathan Savitz, Katalin Savitz, Peter Savitz.
EIN: 134052242

36954
The Amphion Foundation
c/o The Bank of New York, Tax Dept.
1 Wall St., 28th Fl.
New York, NY 10286-0001
Application address: P.O. Box 38, Church St. Sta., New York, NY 10008-0030
Contact: Elliott C. Carter, Jr., Pres.

Established in 1988 in NY.
Donor(s): Elliott C. Carter.
Financial data (yr. ended 12/31/01): Grants paid, $39,800; assets, $1,699,890 (M); gifts received, $500,000; expenditures, $53,118; qualifying distributions, $39,800.
Officers and Directors:* Elliott C. Carter, Jr.,* Pres. and Treas.; Helen J. Carter,* V.P. and Secy.; Allen F. Edwards,* Admin.; Jean Bowen, James M. Kendrick.
EIN: 133438528

36955
The Joan Danforth Foundation
c/o BCRS Associates, LLC
67 Wall Street, 8th Fl.
New York, NY 10005

Established in 1997 in CA.
Donor(s): Joan Danforth.
Financial data (yr. ended 11/30/01): Grants paid, $39,750; assets, $603,397 (M); expenditures, $41,598; qualifying distributions, $39,750.
Limitations: Applications not accepted.
Application information: Contributes only to pre-selected organizations.
Trustees: Joan Danforth, Carole Levine, Toni Rembe.
EIN: 133976343

36956
The Frank and Brynde Berkowitz Family Foundation, Inc.
100 Jericho Quad, Ste. 226
Jericho, NY 11753
Application address: 240 Broadway, Lawrence, NY 11559
Contact: Frank Berkowitz, Pres.

Established in 1995 in NY.
Donor(s): Brynde Berkowitz, Frank Berkowitz, Total Medical Svcs. and Supplies, Inc.
Financial data (yr. ended 12/31/00): Grants paid, $39,721; assets, $378,827 (M); gifts received, $200,000; expenditures, $64,130; qualifying distributions, $39,721.
Limitations: Giving primarily in Brooklyn, NY.

Officers: Frank Berkowitz, Pres.; Stephen Seltzer, Secy.; Brynde Berkowitz, Treas.
EIN: 113294061

36957
Donald and Judy Gruhn Foundation
c/o U.S. Trust
114 W. 47th St., Tax VAS
New York, NY 10036

Established in 1997 in NY.
Donor(s): Donald Gruhn, Judy Gruhn.
Financial data (yr. ended 12/31/00): Grants paid, $39,615; assets, $606,582 (M); gifts received, $49,469; expenditures, $49,567; qualifying distributions, $39,800.
Limitations: Applications not accepted. Giving limited to NY.
Application information: Unsolicited requests for funds are not accepted.
Officers: Donald Gruhn, Chair.; Judy Gruhn, V.P. and Treas.; Richard Hewitt, Secy.
EIN: 137110193

36958
The Courtside Charitable Foundation
c/o Goldstein
1700 Broadway, 17th Fl.
New York, NY 10019

Established in 1993 in NJ.
Financial data (yr. ended 11/30/01): Grants paid, $39,600; assets, $357,722 (M); expenditures, $44,166; qualifying distributions, $39,600.
Limitations: Applications not accepted. Giving primarily in New York, NY.
Application information: Contributes only to pre-selected organizations.
Trustee: Candice Goldstein.
EIN: 133746646

36959
Belovsky Family Foundation
202 Pleasant Valley Rd.
Alfred Station, NY 14803-9601
(607) 587-8173

Donor(s): Mildred Belovsky.‡
Financial data (yr. ended 12/31/01): Grants paid, $39,475; assets, $755,390 (M); expenditures, $41,380; qualifying distributions, $39,475.
Limitations: Giving primarily in Alfred, NY.
Trustee: Keith E. Patrick.
EIN: 166281726

36960
Larry & Judy Cohen Foundation, Inc.
c/o Spear, Leeds and Kellogg
120 Broadway, 8th Fl., Tax Dept.
New York, NY 10271

Established in 1998 in NJ.
Donor(s): Larry Cohen.
Financial data (yr. ended 09/30/99): Grants paid, $39,475; assets, $10,183 (M); gifts received, $49,727; expenditures, $40,333; qualifying distributions, $40,333.
Limitations: Applications not accepted. Giving primarily in NY.
Application information: Contributes only to pre-selected organizations.
Officers: Larry Cohen, Pres. and Treas.; Judy Cohen, V.P. and Secy; Jerome Cohen, V.P.
EIN: 223627225

36961
Marsellus Family Fund
P.O. Box 4968
Syracuse, NY 13221 (315) 422-2306
Contact: John D. Marsellus, V.P.

Donor(s): Marsellus Casket Co., Inc., John F. Marsellus.
Financial data (yr. ended 04/30/02): Grants paid, $39,470; assets, $526,839 (M); expenditures, $42,564; qualifying distributions, $39,470.
Limitations: Giving primarily in central NY.
Officers: John F. Marsellus, Pres.; John D. Marsellus, V.P.; Brian B. Greenhouse, Secy.-Treas.
EIN: 156017922

36962
The Townes Foundation
c/o Arye Ringel
1750 44th St.
Brooklyn, NY 11204-1050

Established in 1984.
Financial data (yr. ended 12/31/01): Grants paid, $39,439; assets, $802,763 (M); gifts received, $1,821; expenditures, $66,731; qualifying distributions, $39,439.
Limitations: Applications not accepted. Giving primarily in NY.
Application information: Contributes only to pre-selected organizations.
Trustees: David K. Townes, Priscilla A. Townes.
EIN: 133159105

36963
Access Capital Foundation
c/o Miles M. Stuchin
405 Park Ave.
New York, NY 10022

Established in 1997 in NY.
Donor(s): Miles Stuchin.
Financial data (yr. ended 06/30/01): Grants paid, $39,435; assets, $1,644,547 (M); expenditures, $59,109; qualifying distributions, $39,435.
Limitations: Applications not accepted. Giving primarily in New York, NY.
Application information: Contributes only to pre-selected organizations.
Trustees: Marcie Stuchin, Miles M. Stuchin.
EIN: 367190561

36964
Joseph and Martha Melohn Charitable Foundation
1995 Broadway, 14th Fl.
New York, NY 10023-5882 (212) 787-2500
Contact: Leon Melohn, Tr.

Established in 1986 in NY.
Donor(s): Leon Melohn.
Financial data (yr. ended 11/30/01): Grants paid, $39,302; assets, $175,085 (M); expenditures, $40,685; qualifying distributions, $39,302.
Limitations: Giving primarily in the metropolitan New York, NY, area.
Trustee: Leon Melohn.
EIN: 133395216

36965
Michael and Zora Marton Foundation
3720 Independence Ave.
Riverdale, NY 10463-1429

Donor(s): Michael Marton.
Financial data (yr. ended 12/31/00): Grants paid, $39,295; assets, $636,306 (M); gifts received, $47,000; expenditures, $40,450; qualifying distributions, $39,295.
Limitations: Applications not accepted. Giving primarily in NY.

Application information: Contributes only to pre-selected organizations.
Officer and Trustee:* Michael Marton,* Mgr.
EIN: 133325263

36966
The Norman S. Levy Family Foundation, Inc.
c/o Global Imports
140 58th St., Bldg. B, Unit 5F
Brooklyn, NY 11220

Established in 1994.
Donor(s): Norman S. Levy.
Financial data (yr. ended 12/31/01): Grants paid, $39,285; assets, $6,075 (M); gifts received, $10,000; expenditures, $39,361; qualifying distributions, $39,285.
Limitations: Applications not accepted.
Application information: Contributes only to pre-selected organizations.
Officers: Norman S. Levy, Pres.; Jeffrey Sitt, V.P.; Morris Sitt, Secy.
EIN: 133773989

36967
The Poppiti Foundation
(Formerly The Edward and Marie Poppiti Foundation)
c/o BCRS Assocs., LLC
100 Wall St., 11th Fl.
New York, NY 10005

Established in 1989 in NJ.
Donor(s): Edward A. Poppiti, Jr.
Financial data (yr. ended 04/30/02): Grants paid, $39,240; assets, $139,670 (M); expenditures, $41,690; qualifying distributions, $40,465.
Limitations: Applications not accepted. Giving primarily in NJ and NY.
Application information: Contributes only to pre-selected organizations.
Trustees: Edward A. Poppiti, Gerald Rudnet.
EIN: 133536550

36968
Mary Muldoon Fund
159 Wolf Rd.
Albany, NY 12212-5003

Established in 1927.
Financial data (yr. ended 08/31/01): Grants paid, $39,200; assets, $1,366,949 (M); expenditures, $63,310; qualifying distributions, $48,812.
Limitations: Giving limited to NY.
Application information: Application form not required.
Trustees: Antonia Cortese, Jeannette DiLorenzo, Dennis Tracey.
EIN: 146030191

36969
Irving & Estelle Levy Foundation
c/o Jerome R. Klein
465 Park Ave., No.10A
New York, NY 10022 (212) 832-9690

Financial data (yr. ended 12/31/01): Grants paid, $39,175; assets, $520,308 (M); gifts received, $32,000; expenditures, $47,465; qualifying distributions, $39,175.
Limitations: Applications not accepted. Giving primarily in CA, NY, and TX.
Application information: Contributes only to pre-selected organizations.
Officer and Trustees:* Jerome C. Klein,* Mgr.; Jerome R. Klein, Ann Wittenberg.
EIN: 136133195

36970
Rabbi Isaac Kellman Foundation, Inc.
c/o Ira Kellman
840 West End Ave.
New York, NY 10025-8440

Donor(s): Ira Kellman.
Financial data (yr. ended 12/31/00): Grants paid, $39,145; assets, $109,881 (M); gifts received, $17,345; expenditures, $64,251; qualifying distributions, $39,145.
Limitations: Applications not accepted. Giving primarily in New York, NY.
Application information: Contributes only to pre-selected organizations.
Officer: Ira Kellman, Pres.
EIN: 136204698

36971
Azriel Yehudah & Leah Respler - Yitzchak Aron & Sarah Kramer Foundation
c/o Jeffrey Respler
37-11 47th Ave.
Long Island City, NY 11101

Established in 1996 in NY.
Donor(s): Jeffrey Respler, Jerome Respler, Dorothy Respler.
Financial data (yr. ended 06/30/01): Grants paid, $39,098; assets, $29,802 (M); expenditures, $39,463; qualifying distributions, $39,098.
Application information: Unsolicited requests for funds not accepted.
Directors: Dorothy Respler, Jeffrey Respler, Jerome Respler.
EIN: 113340077

36972
Ezrat Limud Fund, Inc.
1502 46th St.
Brooklyn, NY 11219
Additional address: 111 Broadway, New York, NY 10006
Contact: Henry Hirsch, Dir.

Established in 1996 in NY.
Donor(s): Henry Hirsch.
Financial data (yr. ended 12/31/01): Grants paid, $39,097; assets, $81,262 (M); gifts received, $61,114; expenditures, $39,216; qualifying distributions, $101,001.
Limitations: Applications not accepted.
Application information: Contributes only to pre-selected organizations.
Directors: Lee Hanover, Henry Hirsch, Mitchel Lisker.
EIN: 113347443

36973
Sire Foundation
c/o Judson P. Reis
630 5th Ave., Ste. 3101
New York, NY 10111

Established in 1998 in NY.
Donor(s): Judson P. Reis.
Financial data (yr. ended 12/31/01): Grants paid, $39,080; assets, $649,206 (M); expenditures, $40,000; qualifying distributions, $39,080.
Limitations: Applications not accepted. Giving primarily in CT, NJ, and NY tri-state area.
Application information: Contributes only to pre-selected organizations.
Officer: Judson P. Reis, Pres.
EIN: 134012985

36974
Melville House, Inc.
330 Willis Ave.
Roslyn Heights, NY 11577 (516) 621-1500
Contact: Alexander Casella, Chair.

Established in 1994 in NY.
Financial data (yr. ended 06/30/01): Grants paid, $39,061; assets, $0 (M); expenditures, $51,927; qualifying distributions, $51,927.
Application information: Application form required.
Officer and Directors:* Alexander Casella,* Chair.; Ann Arkin, Archie Arrington, Vincent Caruso, Ronald Carver, C.J. Rubino, Frank W. Sluter.
EIN: 112289338

36975
The Bump Family Charitable Foundation, Inc.
29 Indian Summer Blvd.
Windsor, NY 13865

Established in 2001 in NY.
Financial data (yr. ended 12/31/01): Grants paid, $39,050; assets, $35,018 (M); gifts received, $75,000; expenditures, $41,470; qualifying distributions, $0.
Directors: Jeffrey Bump, Susan Bump, Rick Heichemer, James Orband, Robert Sedor.
EIN: 161595755

36976
Daniel S. Loeb - Third Point Foundation
7 MacDougal Alley
New York, NY 10011
Contact: Daniel S. Loeb, Pres.

Established in 2000 in NY.
Donor(s): Daniel S. Loeb.
Financial data (yr. ended 12/31/01): Grants paid, $39,050; assets, $641,998 (M); expenditures, $41,506; qualifying distributions, $39,050.
Officers and Directors:* Daniel S. Loeb,* Pres. and Treas.; John Josephson, Secy.; Ronald Loeb, Carter Pottash.
EIN: 522251371

36977
The Padela Family Foundation
185 Hill Cir.
Calverton, NY 11933

Established in 2000.
Financial data (yr. ended 12/31/01): Grants paid, $39,008; assets, $965 (L); gifts received, $39,430; expenditures, $39,008; qualifying distributions, $39,008.
Limitations: Giving primarily in NY.
Trustees: Asif Padela, Muhammad Ilyas Padela, Parveen I. Padela.
EIN: 113536767
Codes: TN

36978
Ack Family Foundation
c/o Bessemer Trust Co.
630 5th Ave.
New York, NY 10111

Established in 2000 in DE.
Donor(s): Arie L. Kopelman.
Financial data (yr. ended 01/31/02): Grants paid, $39,000; assets, $351,433 (M); expenditures, $41,297; qualifying distributions, $39,000.
Limitations: Applications not accepted.
Application information: Contributes only to pre-selected organizations.
Directors: Arie L. Kopelman, Corinne F. Kopelman, Jill A. Kopelman, William F. Kopelman.
EIN: 134152569

36979
James Hubert Blake Scholarship Fund
(also known as Eubie Blake Scholarship Fund)
c/o Beldock, Levine & Hoffman
99 Park Ave., Ste. 1600
New York, NY 10016-1503 (212) 490-0400
Contact: Elliot L. Hoffman, Tr.

Established about 1984 in NY.
Donor(s): James Hubert Blake a.k.a. Eubie Blake,‡ Marion Blake.‡
Financial data (yr. ended 03/31/02): Grants paid, $39,000; assets, $433,502 (M); expenditures, $48,494; qualifying distributions, $39,000.
Limitations: Giving on a national and international basis.
Application information: Application form required.
Trustees: Elliot L. Hoffman, Elizabeth L. Jordan.
EIN: 136836085
Codes: GTI

36980
Boatwright Foundation, Inc.
c/o James D. Miller & Co.
350 5th Ave., Ste. 5019
New York, NY 10118-0080 (212) 268-9888

Financial data (yr. ended 12/31/01): Grants paid, $39,000; assets, $631,618 (M); expenditures, $54,534; qualifying distributions, $40,206.
Limitations: Applications not accepted.
Application information: Contributes only to pre-selected organizations.
Officers: Eugene W. Stetson III, Pres.; Jane Watson Stetson, V.P.; Erik A. Hanson, Secy.-Treas.
Director: James S. Sligar.
EIN: 133048884

36981
The Brown Family Foundation
1053 E. 19th St.
Brooklyn, NY 11230-4501
Contact: Sidney Browne, Tr.

Established in 1999 in NY.
Donor(s): Sidney Browne, Esther Browne.
Financial data (yr. ended 12/31/00): Grants paid, $39,000; assets, $268,161 (M); gifts received, $170,000; expenditures, $43,856; qualifying distributions, $39,000.
Trustees: Esther Browne, Sidney Browne.
EIN: 113521827

36982
Richard A. Grossman Foundation, Inc.
150 White Plains Rd.
Tarrytown, NY 10591-5521

Established in 1969 in NY.
Donor(s): Richard A. Grossman.
Financial data (yr. ended 12/31/01): Grants paid, $39,000; assets, $172,819 (M); expenditures, $43,275; qualifying distributions, $38,629.
Limitations: Applications not accepted. Giving primarily in Easton, PA.
Application information: Contributes only to pre-selected organizations.
Officer: Richard A. Grossman, Pres.
Trustees: Robert C. Baker, Thomas J. Dee.
EIN: 237093493

36983
Simon & Stella Sheib Foundation
40 County Rte. 51
Campbell Hall, NY 10916
Contact: David Sheib, Dir.

Financial data (yr. ended 12/31/01): Grants paid, $39,000; assets, $597,169 (M); expenditures, $51,494; qualifying distributions, $39,000.

36983—NEW YORK

Limitations: Giving primarily in Westchester County, NY.
Director: David Sheib.
EIN: 136216916

36984
Sound Federal Savings and Loan Association Charitable Foundation
c/o Sound Federal Savings and Loan Assoc.
300 Mamaroneck Ave.
Mamaroneck, NY 10543-2647

Established in 1998 in DE.
Donor(s): Sound Federal Bancorp.
Financial data (yr. ended 12/31/00): Grants paid, $39,000; assets, $898,102 (M); expenditures, $39,976; qualifying distributions, $39,000.
Limitations: Giving limited to headquarters city and major operating areas.
Application information: Application form required.
Directors: Bruno J. Giafre, Richard P. McStravick, Allan Salzman.
EIN: 134046178
Codes: CS, CD

36985
The Strelsin Foundation, Inc.
20 Beekman Pl., Apt. 6F
New York, NY 10022-8032 (212) 838-6333
Contact: David Fromkin, Pres.

Donor(s): David Fromkin.
Financial data (yr. ended 12/31/01): Grants paid, $39,000; assets, $714,470 (M); gifts received, $32; expenditures, $54,001; qualifying distributions, $39,000.
Limitations: Giving primarily in NY.
Officer: David Fromkin, Pres.
EIN: 136097736

36986
The Zausner Foundation, Inc.
c/o Martin Zausner
923 5th Ave.
New York, NY 10021-2649

Financial data (yr. ended 12/31/01): Grants paid, $38,935; assets, $652,560 (M); expenditures, $43,655; qualifying distributions, $38,935.
Limitations: Applications not accepted. Giving primarily in New York, NY.
Application information: Contributes only to pre-selected organizations.
Officers and Directors:* Martin Zausner,* Pres. and Treas.; Adrienne B. Zausner,* V.P. and Secy.; Joan M. Harper.
EIN: 136089201

36987
The Carole & Alvin Schragis Foundation, Inc.
10 Birch Ln.
Scarsdale, NY 10583

Established in 1988 in NY.
Donor(s): Alvin Schragis, Carole Schragis.
Financial data (yr. ended 12/31/01): Grants paid, $38,917; assets, $16,904 (M); gifts received, $32,126; expenditures, $38,995; qualifying distributions, $38,995.
Limitations: Applications not accepted. Giving primarily in NY.
Application information: Contributes only to pre-selected organizations.
Officers and Directors:* Carole Schragis, Pres.; Alvin Schragis,* V.P.; Steven Schragis,* Secy.; Cathy Heller, Gary Schragis.
EIN: 133505306

36988
The Olive Tree Foundation
c/o U.S. Trust
114 W. 47th St., TaxVAS
New York, NY 10036

Established in SC in 1997.
Donor(s): Katherine Green, Dennis O. Green.
Financial data (yr. ended 12/31/00): Grants paid, $38,835; assets, $1,138,133 (M); expenditures, $51,834; qualifying distributions, $43,548.
Application information: Unsolicited request for funds not accepted at this time.
Officers and Directors:* Katherine Green,* Pres.; Dennis O. Green,* 1st V.P.; Earlonzo O. Houge,* 2nd V.P.; Cassandra F. Green,* Secy.; Leslie D. Green,* Treas.; Damon S. Green,* Mgr.
EIN: 582359736

36989
Maon Noam, Inc.
c/o Ritter
25 Smith St.
Nanuet, NY 10954

Established in 1999.
Financial data (yr. ended 12/31/01): Grants paid, $38,769; assets, $19,490 (M); gifts received, $19,388; expenditures, $46,743; qualifying distributions, $38,769.
Officers: Alexander Poltorak, Chair.; Valeria Poltorak, Secy.
EIN: 311689936

36990
Rodd D. Brickell Foundation, Inc.
c/o Richard Brickell, Joseph P. Day Realty
9 E. 40th St.
New York, NY 10016-0402

Financial data (yr. ended 11/30/01): Grants paid, $38,691; assets, $234,413 (M); gifts received, $100,500; expenditures, $40,722; qualifying distributions, $38,691.
Limitations: Giving primarily in New York, NY.
Director: Richard Brickell.
EIN: 133320286

36991
McInerney Family Foundation
320 Park Ave., Ste. 2500
New York, NY 10022
FAX: (914) 761-9074; *E-mail:* info@mcinerneyfoundation.org
Contact: Lori McInerney, Dir.

Established in 1997 in NY.
Financial data (yr. ended 04/30/02): Grants paid, $38,690; assets, $1,385,022 (M); expenditures, $54,692; qualifying distributions, $38,690.
Limitations: Giving primarily in CT, NJ, and NY.
Application information: Application form not required.
Trustees: Paula McInerney, Thomas E. McInerney.
Director: Lori McInerney.
EIN: 133949885

36992
The Lewart Family Charitable Trust
c/o Eleanor Lewart
201 E. 77th St.
New York, NY 10021

Established in 1993 in NY.
Donor(s): Jerry Lewart, Eleanor Lewart.
Financial data (yr. ended 11/30/01): Grants paid, $38,620; assets, $827,086 (M); gifts received, $251,357; expenditures, $49,401; qualifying distributions, $38,620.
Limitations: Applications not accepted. Giving primarily in New York, NY.

Application information: Contributes only to pre-selected organizations.
Trustees: Eleanor Lewart, Jerry Lewart.
EIN: 137030069

36993
The Nussbaum Family Foundation, Inc.
c/o Peyser & Alexander
500 5th Ave., Ste. 2700
New York, NY 10110
Application address: 83 Village Rd., Roslyn, NY 11577
Contact: Sandi Nussbaum, Dir.

Financial data (yr. ended 12/31/01): Grants paid, $38,596; assets, $90,433 (M); expenditures, $38,749; qualifying distributions, $38,596.
Application information: Application form not required.
Directors: David Miller, Sandi Nussbaum, Tony Peyser.
EIN: 223326246

36994
The Kahle Foundation, Inc.
c/o John L. Cady
46 Summit Ave.
Bronxville, NY 10708
Application address: c/o Loren Kahle, Jr., 1801 Lavoca, Austin, TX 78701

Donor(s): Loren F. Kahle.
Financial data (yr. ended 11/30/00): Grants paid, $38,509; assets, $311,208 (M); expenditures, $38,659; qualifying distributions, $38,509.
Limitations: Giving primarily in ID and TX.
Officers: Loren F. Kahle, Pres.; Elizabeth Kahle, V.P.; John L. Cady, Secy.-Treas.
EIN: 742804791

36995
Gloria & Harvey Levine Charitable Foundation
228 Cedar Ave.
Hewlett Bay Park, NY 11557

Established in 2000 in NY.
Donor(s): Harvey L. Levine.
Financial data (yr. ended 12/31/01): Grants paid, $38,500; assets, $812,820 (M); gifts received, $339,676; expenditures, $43,125; qualifying distributions, $37,660.
Limitations: Applications not accepted.
Application information: Contributes only to pre-selected organizations.
Officers and Directors:* Harvey L. Levine,* Pres.; Gloria Levine,* V.P. and Treas.; Richard Rubel,* Secy.
EIN: 113562809

36996
N.C. & B.C. Foundation, Inc.
c/o R. Terris
200 Garden City Plz., Ste. 224
Garden City, NY 11530 (516) 877-2770
Contact: Noel L. Cohen, Dir.

Established in 1996 in NY.
Donor(s): Noel L. Cohen, Baujke P. Cohen.
Financial data (yr. ended 12/31/01): Grants paid, $38,500; assets, $1,273,816 (M); expenditures, $38,993; qualifying distributions, $38,500.
Limitations: Giving primarily in NY.
Directors: Baujke P. Cohen, Mark Cohen, Noel L. Cohen, Erwin L. Corwin, Richard Terris.
EIN: 113349321

36997
Sea Island Foundation Trust
c/o U.S. Trust
114 W. 47th St., TaxVS
New York, NY 10036-1510

Established in 1994 in NY.
Donor(s): Paul Haklisch, Carmela Haklisch.
Financial data (yr. ended 12/31/01): Grants paid, $38,500; assets, $703,685 (M); expenditures, $52,309; qualifying distributions, $38,500.
Limitations: Applications not accepted. Giving primarily in NY.
Application information: Contributes only to pre-selected organizations.
Trustee: U.S. Trust.
EIN: 137053448

36998
U & R Foundation
471 Bedford Ave.
Brooklyn, NY 11211 (718) 384-4160
Contact: Usher Wagshall, Dir.

Established in 2000 in NY.
Financial data (yr. ended 06/30/01): Grants paid, $38,500; assets, $61,780 (M); gifts received, $100,000; expenditures, $38,500; qualifying distributions, $38,500.
Limitations: Giving primarily in NY.
Application information: Application form not required.
Directors: Rita Wagshall, Usher Wagshall.
EIN: 522283939

36999
George K. and Cynthia R. Cooney Charitable Foundation
9 Eastway
Bronxville, NY 10708

Established in 1998 in NY.
Donor(s): George K. Cooney.
Financial data (yr. ended 05/31/01): Grants paid, $38,400; assets, $726,646 (M); gifts received, $25,000; expenditures, $38,732; qualifying distributions, $38,400.
Limitations: Applications not accepted.
Application information: Contributes only to pre-selected organizations.
Trustees: Cynthia R. Cooney, George K. Cooney.
EIN: 137159912

37000
The George A. & Frances R. Katz Family Foundation
c/o Wachtell, Lipton, Rosen & Katz
51 W. 52nd St.
New York, NY 10019

Established in 1986.
Financial data (yr. ended 04/30/01): Grants paid, $38,380; assets, $649,690 (M); expenditures, $46,649; qualifying distributions, $38,380.
Limitations: Applications not accepted. Giving primarily in New York, NY.
Application information: Contributes only to pre-selected organizations.
Officers and Directors:* Frances R. Katz,* Chair.; Deborah S. Katz,* Pres.; Jodi M. Katz,* 1st V.P.; Amy B. Katz,* 2nd V.P.; Margaret M. Lowry, 3rd V.P.
EIN: 133363230

37001
Nathan J. & Helen Goldrich Foundation, Inc.
600 Mamaroneck Ave., 4th Fl.
Harrison, NY 10528-1632 (914) 381-7300
Contact: David L. Goldrich, Secy.

Donor(s): Helen Goldrich.
Financial data (yr. ended 12/31/01): Grants paid, $38,375; assets, $616,779 (M); expenditures, $38,652; qualifying distributions, $38,047.
Limitations: Giving primarily in CT and NY.
Officers: Helen Goldrich, Pres.; Robert F. Goldrich, V.P.; David L. Goldrich, Secy.; Michael J. Goldrich, Treas.
Director: Laura N. Goldrich.
EIN: 136193029

37002
Bartenura Foundation
c/o Evelyn & Samuel Shechter
55 Central Park W. Ste. 5F
New York, NY 10023-6003

Established in 2000 in NY.
Donor(s): Samuel D. Shechter, Evelyn Musher Shechter.
Financial data (yr. ended 12/31/01): Grants paid, $38,330; assets, $16,360 (M); gifts received, $2,800; expenditures, $38,957; qualifying distributions, $38,330.
Limitations: Applications not accepted.
Application information: Contributes only to pre-selected organizations.
Directors: Evelyn Musher Shechter, Joshua Musher, Samuel D. Shechter.
EIN: 134134990

37003
Rosa C. & Henry A. Sauter Scholarship Fund
c/o The Bank of New York
1 Wall St., 28th Fl.
New York, NY 10286

Established in 1999 in NY.
Donor(s): Rosa C. Sauter.‡
Financial data (yr. ended 12/31/01): Grants paid, $38,320; assets, $1,531,131 (M); expenditures, $68,734; qualifying distributions, $38,320.
Trustees: Shirley L. Sauter, The Bank of New York.
EIN: 137221515

37004
The Davidowitz Family Foundation
1858 East 26th Street
Brooklyn, NY 11229

Established in 1999 in NY.
Financial data (yr. ended 06/30/01): Grants paid, $38,250; assets, $441,803 (M); gifts received, $250,000; expenditures, $41,097; qualifying distributions, $38,250.
Limitations: Applications not accepted. Giving primarily in Brooklyn, NY.
Application information: Contributes only to pre-selected organizations.
Officers: Jacob Davidowitz, Pres.; Leah Davidowitz, V.P.; Tova Rubin, Secy.
EIN: 113517517

37005
J. and L. Smith Foundation
10 Rockefeller Plz., Ste. 916
New York, NY 10020

Established in 2000 in NY.
Donor(s): James S. Smith.
Financial data (yr. ended 12/31/01): Grants paid, $38,250; assets, $624,859 (M); expenditures, $44,119; qualifying distributions, $38,250.
Trustees: James S. Smith, Laura B. Smith.
EIN: 134136600

37006
Gellin Foundation, Inc.
c/o Regina Cane
30 Marjory Ln.
Scarsdale, NY 10583-6906

Donor(s): William Gellin,‡ Jeannette S. Gellin,‡ Alex Birnbaum.
Financial data (yr. ended 10/31/01): Grants paid, $38,225; assets, $893,753 (M); gifts received, $1,350; expenditures, $45,588; qualifying distributions, $38,225.
Limitations: Applications not accepted. Giving primarily in NY.
Application information: Contributes only to pre-selected organizations.
Officers: Gilda Zalaznick, Pres. and Treas.; Regina Cane, V.P. and Secy.
EIN: 136125385

37007
Hazan Family Foundation
1407 Broadway, No. 707
New York, NY 10018-5107
Contact: Ira Hazan, Tr.

Established in 1993 in NY.
Financial data (yr. ended 07/31/01): Grants paid, $38,202; assets, $55,636 (M); expenditures, $38,470; qualifying distributions, $37,959.
Limitations: Giving primarily in NY.
Trustees: Ira Hazan, Marilyn Hazan, Bruce Pomerantz.
EIN: 226607830

37008
W. & M. Kaye Foundation, Inc.
c/o Julius Page, C.P.A.
545 Madison Ave., Ste. 801
New York, NY 10022

Established in 1985 in NY.
Financial data (yr. ended 12/31/99): Grants paid, $38,200; assets, $679,482 (M); expenditures, $48,865; qualifying distributions, $47,925.
Limitations: Applications not accepted. Giving primarily in NY.
Application information: Contributes only to pre-selected organizations.
Officers: Marjorie Kaye, Pres.; Warren Kaye, Secy.-Treas.
EIN: 112688528

37009
Daniella Maria Arturi Foundation, Inc.
c/o Frendel, Brown & Weissman
655 3rd Ave., Ste. 1400
New York, NY 10017

Established in 1996 in NY.
Donor(s): Emanuel Arturi.
Financial data (yr. ended 06/30/01): Grants paid, $38,175; assets, $258,836 (M); gifts received, $224,595; expenditures, $176,258; qualifying distributions, $174,487; giving activities include $115,419 for programs.
Limitations: Applications not accepted. Giving primarily in NY.
Application information: Contributes only to pre-selected organizations.
Directors: Emanuel Arturi, Marie Clarke Arturi, John P. Cifichiello, Margaret Zoeller.
EIN: 133915004

37010
The Solomon Wilson Family Foundation, Inc.
225 W. 22nd St.
New York, NY 10011-2702
Contact: Frederick R. Wilson, Pres.

Established in 2000 in NY.

37010—NEW YORK

Donor(s): Frederick R. Wilson.
Financial data (yr. ended 12/31/01): Grants paid, $38,175; assets, $1,465 (M); expenditures, $40,019; qualifying distributions, $38,175.
Limitations: Giving primarily in NY.
Officers and Directors:* Frederick R. Wilson, Pres. and Treas.; Joanne S. Wilson,* V.P. and Secy.; Susan G. Soloman.
EIN: 134092426

37011
Howard & Sue Simon Family Foundation, Inc.
c/o Weston Equities, Inc.
370 Lexington Ave.
New York, NY 10017

Established in 2000 in NY.
Donor(s): Sue Simon.
Financial data (yr. ended 12/31/00): Grants paid, $38,116; assets, $9,872 (M); gifts received, $47,149; expenditures, $38,202; qualifying distributions, $38,116.
Limitations: Applications not accepted. Giving primarily in NY.
Application information: Contributes only to pre-selected organizations.
Officers: Howard I. Simon, Pres.; Sue Simon, V.P.; Jonathan Simon, Secy.; Jill Simon, Treas.
EIN: 134102149

37012
The Dominie Foundation Trust
11 Bruce St.
Scotia, NY 12302 (518) 374-1883
Contact: Wallace M. Campbell, Tr.

Established in 1990 in NY.
Donor(s): Wallace M. Campbell.
Financial data (yr. ended 12/31/01): Grants paid, $38,113; assets, $183,682 (M); gifts received, $250; expenditures, $40,342; qualifying distributions, $38,113.
Limitations: Giving primarily in upstate NY.
Trustee: Wallace M. Campbell.
EIN: 146144692

37013
The Seymour & Shirley Rubin Charitable Trust
30 Randolph Dr.
Dix Hills, NY 11746-8331

Donor(s): Seymour Rubin, Shirley Rubin.
Financial data (yr. ended 12/31/01): Grants paid, $38,103; assets, $120,431 (M); gifts received, $5,500; expenditures, $38,765; qualifying distributions, $38,103.
Officers: Seymour Rubin, Pres.; Shirley Rubin, V.P.
EIN: 116450742

37014
Steven Lloyd Weinrib Charitable Foundation
c/o ABC Carpet Co., Inc.
888 Broadway
New York, NY 10003

Established in 1998 in NY.
Financial data (yr. ended 12/31/00): Grants paid, $38,075; assets, $141,357 (M); expenditures, $38,435; qualifying distributions, $38,384.
Limitations: Applications not accepted. Giving primarily in New York, NY.
Application information: Contributes only to pre-selected organizations.
Officers: Jerome Weinrib, Pres.; Norma Weinrib, V.P.; Paulette Cole, Secy.; Madeline Weinrib, Treas.
EIN: 134034582

37015
The Albert G. Lowenthal Foundation
(Formerly A. G. & C. F. Lowenthal Foundation)
188 Mamaroneck Rd.
Scarsdale, NY 10583-4526

Established in 1992 in NY.
Donor(s): Albert G. Lowenthal, Carol F. Lowenthal.
Financial data (yr. ended 12/31/00): Grants paid, $38,046; assets, $723,440 (M); gifts received, $125,010; expenditures, $38,146; qualifying distributions, $38,046.
Limitations: Applications not accepted.
Application information: Contributes only to pre-selected organizations.
Trustees: Albert G. Lowenthal, Carol F. Lowenthal.
EIN: 133697893

37016
Decams Foundation
c/o The Bank of New York, Tax Dept.
One Wall St., 28th Fl.
New York, NY 10286
Application address: 481 Ravine Dr., Aurora, OH 44202
Contact: Michael Degennaro, Pres.

Established in 1999 in OH.
Donor(s): Michael Degennaro.
Financial data (yr. ended 12/31/01): Grants paid, $38,000; assets, $986,067 (M); gifts received, $100,196; expenditures, $50,382; qualifying distributions, $38,000.
Limitations: Giving primarily in OH.
Officers: Michael Degennaro, Pres. and Treas.; Sherry L. Degennaro, V.P. and Secy.
Trustees: Christine Branem, Amy Degennaro.
EIN: 341908593

37017
The Eierman Foundation, Inc.
(Formerly The Irvin Greif Foundation, Inc.)
2 Deshon Ave.
Bronxville, NY 10708-2119 (914) 779-9648
Contact: Kimberly S. Eierman, Pres.

Financial data (yr. ended 11/30/01): Grants paid, $38,000; assets, $697,211 (M); expenditures, $39,895; qualifying distributions, $38,000.
Officers and Directors:* Kimberly S. Eierman,* Pres.; Jane B. Eierman,* V.P. and Secy.; S. Gregory Eierman,* V.P. and Treas.; Kathy B. Eierman,* V.P.; George Fantaousakis.
EIN: 520745714

37018
Koller Family Foundation, Inc.
300 E. 42nd St., 15th Fl.
New York, NY 10017

Donor(s): Howard Sloan Koller Group Inc.
Financial data (yr. ended 12/31/01): Grants paid, $38,000; assets, $20,209 (M); gifts received, $40,000; expenditures, $38,519; qualifying distributions, $37,988.
Limitations: Applications not accepted.
Application information: Contributes only to pre-selected organizations.
Directors: Michael J. Deutsch, Edward R. Koller, Jr., Edward R. Koller III, Ross Koller.
EIN: 134091674
Codes: CS

37019
Rolf and Elizabeth Rosenthal Family Foundation
31 The Glen
Locust Valley, NY 11560-2211

Established in 1993 in NY.
Donor(s): Rolf W. Rosenthal, Elizabeth Rosenthal.
Financial data (yr. ended 12/31/01): Grants paid, $38,000; assets, $750,092 (M); gifts received, $380; expenditures, $45,833; qualifying distributions, $38,000.
Limitations: Applications not accepted. Giving primarily in Washington, DC, MA, and NY.
Application information: Contributes only to pre-selected organizations.
Officer and Trustee:* Rolf W. Rosenthal,* Pres.
EIN: 116429817

37020
Eugen Friedlaender Foundation, Inc.
180 Maiden Ln.
New York, NY 10038-4982 (212) 806-6018
Contact: Ronald J. Stein, Dir.

Established in 1953 in NY.
Donor(s): Helmut N. Friedlaender, Edith S.E. Bondi.
Financial data (yr. ended 12/31/01): Grants paid, $37,990; assets, $894,945 (M); gifts received, $500; expenditures, $54,961; qualifying distributions, $40,555.
Limitations: Giving primarily in New York, NY.
Application information: Application form not required.
Officers and Directors:* Helmut N. Friedlaender,* Pres.; Thomas M. Franck,* V.P.; Judith G. Friedlaender,* Secy.; Jean Titlow,* Treas.; John R. Menke, Ronald J. Stein.
EIN: 136077311

37021
Olga & Joseph H. Hirshhorn Foundation, Inc.
(Formerly Joseph H. Hirshhorn Foundation, Inc.)
c/o David Tarlow & Co.
60 E. 42nd St., Rm. 2212
New York, NY 10165

Incorporated in 1955 in NY.
Donor(s): Joseph H. Hirshhorn.
Financial data (yr. ended 12/31/01): Grants paid, $37,973; assets, $19,911 (M); expenditures, $38,436; qualifying distributions, $37,973.
Limitations: Applications not accepted. Giving primarily in Washington, DC and Naples, FL.
Application information: Contributes only to pre-selected organizations.
Officers: Olga Hirshhorn, Pres.; John P. Cunningham, V.P.; John McDermott, V.P.; David Schaengold, V.P.
EIN: 131984847

37022
The Joel B. Leff Foundation, Inc.
25 Sutton Pl.
New York, NY 10022-2453

Donor(s): Joel B. Leff.
Financial data (yr. ended 11/30/01): Grants paid, $37,953; assets, $366,987 (M); expenditures, $38,644; qualifying distributions, $38,453.
Limitations: Applications not accepted. Giving primarily in the greater New York, NY, area.
Application information: Contributes only to pre-selected organizations.
Officer: Joel B. Leff, Pres.
EIN: 133192850

37023
Jeanne S. Friedman Foundation
825 3rd Ave., 25th Fl.
New York, NY 10022-7519

Established in 1984 in NY.
Donor(s): Jeanne S. Friedman.
Financial data (yr. ended 12/31/01): Grants paid, $37,872; assets, $173,124 (M); gifts received, $5,780; expenditures, $42,102; qualifying distributions, $37,872.

Limitations: Applications not accepted. Giving primarily in Los Angeles, CA.
Application information: Contributes only to pre-selected organizations.
Trustees: Eugene J. Callahan, Douglas E. Friedman, Jeanne S. Friedman, Gwen S. McGuire.
EIN: 133230661

37024
J. G. R. and J. E. Rovensky Charitable Trust
c/o U.S. Trust
114 W. 47th St., TaxVAS
New York, NY 10036

Established in 1988 in NY.
Financial data (yr. ended 12/31/01): Grants paid, $37,865; assets, $914,542 (M); expenditures, $39,365; qualifying distributions, $37,865.
Limitations: Applications not accepted. Giving on a national basis.
Application information: Contributes only to pre-selected organizations.
Trustee: U.S. Trust.
EIN: 136903101

37025
Max Blechner Charitable Fund, Inc.
c/o Norbert Blechner
7 W. 81st St.
New York, NY 10024

Established in 1953.
Donor(s): Norbert Blechner, Hannah Blechner.
Financial data (yr. ended 12/31/01): Grants paid, $37,858; assets, $981,103 (M); expenditures, $40,945; qualifying distributions, $37,858.
Limitations: Applications not accepted. Giving primarily in the greater New York, NY, area.
Application information: Contributes only to pre-selected organizations.
Officers and Trustees:* Norbert Blechner, Pres.; Hannah Blechner, Secy.
EIN: 136183059

37026
Lisa Wendel Memorial Foundation
c/o Brian Wendel
342 Madison Ave., Ste. 826
New York, NY 10173

Established in 1990 in FL.
Donor(s): Gerald Wendel, Joshua Wendel.
Financial data (yr. ended 12/31/99): Grants paid, $37,857; assets, $1,348,767 (M); gifts received, $288,527; expenditures, $41,862; qualifying distributions, $37,857.
Limitations: Applications not accepted. Giving primarily in Aspen, CO and Miami, FL.
Application information: Contributes only to pre-selected organizations.
Officers: Gerald Wendel, Pres.; Thomas Ergman, V.P.; David Dorfman, Secy.; Michael Wendel, Treas.
EIN: 133217479

37027
Elyon Foundation
c/o A. Katzberg
1328 41st St.
Brooklyn, NY 11218-3506

Established in 2000 in NY.
Donor(s): Abraham Katzberg.
Financial data (yr. ended 11/30/01): Grants paid, $37,855; assets, $47,145 (M); gifts received, $85,000; expenditures, $37,855; qualifying distributions, $37,855.
Trustees: Abraham Katzberg, Carol Katzberg.
EIN: 113564336

37028
The Umin Fund
c/o The National Review
215 Lexington Ave., 4th Fl.
New York, NY 10016

Established in 1986 in NY.
Donor(s): William F. Buckley, Jr.
Financial data (yr. ended 06/30/01): Grants paid, $37,855; assets, $19,281 (M); expenditures, $41,173; qualifying distributions, $39,012.
Limitations: Applications not accepted. Giving on a national basis.
Application information: Contributes only to pre-selected organizations.
Trustees: Priscilla L. Buckley, William F. Buckley, Jr., Steven M. Umin.
EIN: 133379960

37029
Felsen Family Foundation
2064 Ridge Rd.
Muttontown, NY 11791

Established in 2000 in NY.
Donor(s): Esther Felsen, Harvey Felsen.
Financial data (yr. ended 12/31/01): Grants paid, $37,812; assets, $347,959 (M); gifts received, $60,210; expenditures, $48,395; qualifying distributions, $37,812.
Limitations: Applications not accepted.
Application information: Contributes only to pre-selected organizations.
Directors: Barry Arnold, Esther Felsen, Harvey Felsen.
EIN: 113576191

37030
Sellin Charitable Trust
2030 Erie Blvd. E.
Syracuse, NY 13224

Established in 1992 in NY.
Financial data (yr. ended 12/31/01): Grants paid, $37,800; assets, $117,825 (M); expenditures, $40,333; qualifying distributions, $37,800.
Limitations: Applications not accepted. Giving primarily in Syracuse, NY.
Application information: Contributes only to pre-selected organizations.
Trustee: Arnold J. Hodes.
EIN: 166367092

37031
Pot Family Foundation
c/o Goldman Sachs & Co.
85 Broad St., Tax Dept.
New York, NY 10005

Established in 1996 in NY.
Donor(s): Wiet H.M. Pot.
Financial data (yr. ended 03/31/01): Grants paid, $37,749; assets, $1,304,288 (M); expenditures, $56,642; qualifying distributions, $37,749.
Limitations: Applications not accepted. Giving primarily in the United Kingdom, Belgium, France, and Holland.
Application information: Contributes only to pre-selected organizations.
Trustees: Carien C.C. Pot Mees, Wiet H.M. Pot, Robert K. Steel.
EIN: 133936466

37032
Levy Hermanos Foundation, Inc.
c/o Anna Theresa Petrak
1075 Park Ave.
New York, NY 10128   (718) 932-0979

Donor(s): Selma Levy Hermanos,‡ Susan S. Hermanos.
Financial data (yr. ended 10/31/01): Grants paid, $37,720; assets, $118,450 (M); gifts received, $26,047; expenditures, $39,089; qualifying distributions, $37,720.
Limitations: Giving primarily in New York, NY.
Application information: Application form not required.
Officers: Robert Hermanos, Pres.; Miriam H. Knapp, V.P.; Robert C. Knapp, Secy.; Susan S. Hermanos, Treas.
EIN: 136099351

37033
Lippman Rose Schnurmacher Fund, Inc.
175 Great Neck Rd., No. 407
Great Neck, NY 11021
Contact: Stephen Schnurmacher, Pres.

Incorporated in 1945 in NY.
Donor(s): Rose Schnurmacher.‡
Financial data (yr. ended 08/31/01): Grants paid, $37,700; assets, $664,209 (M); expenditures, $44,772; qualifying distributions, $37,700.
Limitations: Giving primarily in NY.
Application information: Application form required.
Officers: Stephen Schnurmacher, Pres.; Laurie Tomchin, V.P.; Leonard Schnurmacher, Secy.-Treas.
EIN: 136126002

37034
Rubin-Wollman Foundation, Inc.
c/o Mac Corkindale
137 Broadway, Ste. H
Amityville, NY 11701

Donor(s): Warren Rubin, Rabbit Hill, Inc.
Financial data (yr. ended 09/30/01): Grants paid, $37,700; assets, $789,726 (M); gifts received, $35,508; expenditures, $55,222; qualifying distributions, $37,700.
Limitations: Applications not accepted. Giving primarily in CT and NY.
Application information: Contributes only to pre-selected organizations.
Officers: Warren Rubin, Pres.; Bruce Mac Corkindale, Secy.; Bernice Wollman, Treas.
EIN: 061529668

37035
K. & M. Weisburgh Charitable Fund, Inc.
103 Hickory Grove Dr.
Larchmont, NY 10538

Donor(s): Karin Weisburgh, Mitchell Weisburgh.
Financial data (yr. ended 12/31/01): Grants paid, $37,612; assets, $675,707 (M); expenditures, $37,612; qualifying distributions, $37,612.
Limitations: Giving primarily in NY.
Trustees: Martha Nierenberg, Karin Weisburgh, Mitchell Weisburgh.
EIN: 134065871

37036
Herbert H. & Mariea L. Brown Charitable Trust Foundation
c/o NBT Bank, N.A.
52 S. Broad St.
Norwich, NY 13815-0000

Established in 1984 in NY.
Donor(s): Herbert H. Brown,‡ Mariea L. Brown.
Financial data (yr. ended 09/30/01): Grants paid, $37,600; assets, $816,510 (M); expenditures, $40,049; qualifying distributions, $39,102.
Limitations: Giving limited to Chenango County and the greater Sherburne, NY, area.
Trustees: Martha M. Adams, William D. Craine, W. Howard Sullivan, NBT Bank, N.A.
EIN: 166271541

37037
M. H. Yager Foundation, Inc.
96 Clovercrest Dr.
Rochester, NY 14618-2529

Financial data (yr. ended 12/31/01): Grants paid, $37,600; assets, $307,634 (M); expenditures, $59,105; qualifying distributions, $37,600.
Limitations: Applications not accepted. Giving primarily in central NY.
Application information: Contributes only to pre-selected organizations.
Officers and Directors:* Penelope S. Martin,* Pres.; Robert W. Martin,* V.P.; Gertrude M. Yager,* Secy.; Patrick D. Martin,* Treas.
EIN: 146018102

37038
Josiah H. Danforth Memorial Fund
8 Fremont St.
Gloversville, NY 12078 (518) 725-0653

Financial data (yr. ended 12/31/01): Grants paid, $37,589; assets, $685,503 (M); expenditures, $45,137; qualifying distributions, $37,139.
Limitations: Giving limited to residents of Fulton County, NY.
Application information: Application form required.
Officers and Directors:* David Clough,* Pres.; Carol J. Edwards,* Secy.; Jeanette Tinney,* Treas.; James W. Holtzworth, Wayne G. Jones.
EIN: 146023489
Codes: GTI

37039
Lisa Bilotti Foundation, Inc.
c/o Kelley, Drye & Warren, LLP
101 Park Ave., 30th Fl.
New York, NY 10178

Established in 1990 in NJ.
Donor(s): Lisa Bilotti.‡
Financial data (yr. ended 09/30/00): Grants paid, $37,500; assets, $859,228 (M); expenditures, $40,750; qualifying distributions, $38,000.
Limitations: Applications not accepted. Giving primarily in New York, NY.
Application information: Contributes only to pre-selected organizations.
Officers and Directors:* Margaret S. Bilotti,* Pres. and Treas.; Carlo F. Bilotti,* V.P.; Talbott Miller,* Secy.
EIN: 133578733

37040
Herbert R. and Blanche L. Brinberg Foundation
c/o Herbert Brinberg
145 E. 48th St.
New York, NY 10017

Established in 2000 in NY.
Donor(s): Herbert R. Brinberg.
Financial data (yr. ended 12/31/01): Grants paid, $37,500; assets, $58,801 (M); gifts received, $500; expenditures, $42,520; qualifying distributions, $37,500.
Limitations: Applications not accepted.
Application information: Contributes only to pre-selected organizations.
Trustees: Blanche L. Brinberg, Herbert R. Brinberg, Todd M. Brinberg.
EIN: 134148814

37041
Carrier & Bryant Distributors' Educational Foundation
(Formerly William A. Blees Educational Foundation)
c/o R. Jarmac
P.O. Box 4808, Carrier Pkwy.
Syracuse, NY 13221 (315) 433-4512
FAX: (315) 433-4213
Application address: c/o Maclin Richardson, Dir. of Scholarship Svcs., P.O. Box 770728, Lakewood, OH 44107, tel.: (440) 333-4381

Donor(s): Marco Sales, Inc.
Financial data (yr. ended 07/31/01): Grants paid, $37,500; assets, $546,448 (M); expenditures, $44,464; qualifying distributions, $42,993.
Limitations: Giving limited to areas of company operations.
Application information: Application form required.
Officers and Directors:* Joseph Kaelin,* Pres. and Treas.; Richard Jarmac,* Secy.; Warren Farr, Jr., Anthony Jokerst, Robert Kesterton, Frank Rau, Jr., George Sanders, Jr., and 5 additional directors.
EIN: 161153992
Codes: GTI

37042
Sylvia & Howard Minsky Fund
c/o JPMorgan Chase Bank
1211 6th Ave., 34th Fl.
New York, NY 10036
Application address: Susanne Capodanno, Trust Off., c/o JPMorgan Chase Bank, 205 Royal Palm Way, Palm Beach, FL 33480

Established in 1998 in FL.
Donor(s): Howard G. Minsky, Sylvia Minsky.
Financial data (yr. ended 12/31/00): Grants paid, $37,500; assets, $57,406 (M); expenditures, $38,418; qualifying distributions, $37,609.
Limitations: Applications not accepted. Giving primarily in FL.
Application information: Contributes only to pre-selected organizations.
Trustee: JPMorgan Chase Bank.
EIN: 061528345

37043
Rosesther Charity Fund
975 E. 8th St.
Brooklyn, NY 11230

Established in 1989 in NY.
Donor(s): Leslie Honikman.
Financial data (yr. ended 12/31/99): Grants paid, $37,500; assets, $314,962 (L); gifts received, $60,000; expenditures, $37,625; qualifying distributions, $37,413.
Limitations: Applications not accepted. Giving primarily in Brooklyn, NY.
Application information: Contributes only to pre-selected organizations.
Officers: Leslie Honikman, Pres.; Lia Honikman, V.P.; Bertha Deutch, Secy.-Treas.
EIN: 116378655

37044
D. & N. Sayaset Foundation
627 Ave. O
Brooklyn, NY 11230

Established in 1999.
Donor(s): Eliyahu M. Levin.
Financial data (yr. ended 12/31/01): Grants paid, $37,500; assets, $897,414 (M); gifts received, $83,154; expenditures, $51,874; qualifying distributions, $37,500.
Limitations: Applications not accepted. Giving primarily in Boston, MA.

Application information: Contributes only to pre-selected organizations.
Trustees: Daniel Stilerman, Nacham Stilerman.
EIN: 137153241

37045
The C. F. Roe Slade Foundation
c/o U.S. Trust Co. of NY
114 W. 47th St.
New York, NY 10016

Established in 1969 in NY.
Donor(s): Marie-Antoinette Slade.‡
Financial data (yr. ended 06/30/01): Grants paid, $37,500; assets, $2,779,938 (M); gifts received, $1,982,141; expenditures, $65,612; qualifying distributions, $63,445.
Limitations: Applications not accepted. Giving primarily in NY.
Application information: Contributes only to pre-selected organizations.
Trustees: John H. Bell, Jr., Kathleen McLaughlin Jeffords.
EIN: 136205873

37046
Veillette-Nifosi Foundation, Inc.
86 Elliot Rd.
East Chatham, NY 12060

Established in 1998 in NY and DE.
Donor(s): Fran Veillette, Paul Veillette.
Financial data (yr. ended 12/31/01): Grants paid, $37,500; assets, $883,998 (M); expenditures, $49,405; qualifying distributions, $38,011.
Limitations: Applications not accepted. Giving primarily in NY.
Application information: Contributes only to pre-selected organizations.
Directors: Fran Veillette, Paul Veillette.
EIN: 141800600

37047
Cill Dara Foundation
c/o Brown Brothers Harriman Trust Co.
63 Wall St.
New York, NY 10005

Established in 1998 in MN.
Financial data (yr. ended 12/31/01): Grants paid, $37,490; assets, $398,289 (M); expenditures, $41,456; qualifying distributions, $39,858.
Limitations: Applications not accepted. Giving primarily in IA and MN.
Application information: Contributes only to pre-selected organizations.
Trustees: Ann Hank Monahan, Daniel J. Monahan.
EIN: 364225328

37048
Jane Chu Foundation
7 Chatham Sq., Ste. 403
New York, NY 10038

Established in 2000 in NY.
Financial data (yr. ended 11/30/00): Grants paid, $37,460; assets, $1,905,380 (M); expenditures, $131,769; qualifying distributions, $1,811,762; giving activities include $1,811,762 for programs.
Limitations: Applications not accepted.
Application information: Contributes only to pre-selected organizations.
Trustees: Stephen Chang, Merrill Lynch.
EIN: 114091402

37049
Cogar Foundation, Inc.
1001 Broad St.
Utica, NY 13501

Financial data (yr. ended 12/31/99): Grants paid, $37,450; assets, $831,022 (M); expenditures,

$42,774; qualifying distributions, $40,796; giving activities include $9,809 for programs.
Limitations: Giving limited to Herkimer County, NY.
Application information: Application form required.
Officers: Robert McLaughlin, Pres.; Albert Mazloom, V.P. and Secy.; James Anderson, Treas.
EIN: 237035415
Codes: GTI

37050
Israel Matz Foundation
14 E. 4th St., Ste. 403
New York, NY 10012 (212) 673-8142
Contact: Milton Arfa, Chair.

Trust established in 1925 in NY.
Donor(s): Israel Matz.‡
Financial data (yr. ended 12/31/01): Grants paid, $37,425; assets, $1,380,396 (M); expenditures, $134,474; qualifying distributions, $62,709.
Limitations: Giving primarily in New York, NY; giving also in Israel.
Officer: Milton Arfa, Chair.
Trustees: Hiam Arfa, Rachel Arfa, Shlomo Sharan.
EIN: 136121533
Codes: GTI

37051
Lisben Charitable Foundation, Inc.
c/o Beno Sternlicht
123 Partridge Run
Schenectady, NY 12309

Established in 1998 in NY.
Donor(s): Beno Sternlicht, Lisa Sternlicht.
Financial data (yr. ended 05/31/01): Grants paid, $37,361; assets, $193,504 (M); expenditures, $37,471; qualifying distributions, $37,361.
Application information: Application form not required.
Directors: Hugh Janow, Beno Sternlicht, Lisa Sternlicht.
EIN: 582395697

37052
Fraydun Foundation, Inc.
c/o Pan Am Equities Inc.
3 New York Plz.
New York, NY 10004 (212) 837-4800
Contact: Fraydun Manocherian, Dir.

Established in 1981 in NY.
Donor(s): Fraydun Manocherian.
Financial data (yr. ended 12/31/00): Grants paid, $37,350; assets, $2,517,566 (M); expenditures, $48,055; qualifying distributions, $37,350.
Limitations: Giving primarily in NY.
Application information: Application form not required.
Directors: Fraydun Manocherian, Jennifer Manocherian, Kimberly Strelov.
EIN: 133185696

37053
Susan Jaffe Tane Foundation
12 Sands Light Rd.
Sands Point, NY 11050

Established in 1996 in DE.
Donor(s): Susan Jaffe Tane.
Financial data (yr. ended 12/31/99): Grants paid, $37,338; assets, $295,378 (M); expenditures, $41,608; qualifying distributions, $41,608.
Limitations: Applications not accepted.
Application information: Contributes only to pre-selected organizations.
Officer: Susan Jaffe Tane, Mgr.
Director: Irwin R. Tane.
EIN: 113352629

37054
Ravenswood Foundation
c/o U.S. Trust
114 W. 47th St., TaxVAS
New York, NY 10036

Established in 1995 in NY.
Donor(s): Kevin E. Crowe, Lynn Crowe.
Financial data (yr. ended 11/30/01): Grants paid, $37,312; assets, $419,454 (M); expenditures, $40,962; qualifying distributions, $37,312.
Limitations: Applications not accepted. Giving primarily in WV.
Application information: Contributes only to pre-selected organizations.
Trustees: Kevin E. Crowe, Lynn Crowe.
EIN: 137079320

37055
Jerome and Phyllis Charney Foundation
P.O. Box 6545
Syracuse, NY 13217

Established in 1993 in NY.
Donor(s): Phyllis L. Charney, Melvyn Charney, Karen Kruth.
Financial data (yr. ended 12/31/01): Grants paid, $37,300; assets, $385,758 (M); expenditures, $39,300; qualifying distributions, $37,300.
Limitations: Applications not accepted. Giving primarily in NY.
Application information: Contributes only to pre-selected organizations.
Trustees: Melvyn Charney, Phyllis L. Charney, Karen Kruth.
EIN: 161449220

37056
Foundation for the Advancement of Arts & Sciences from India, Inc.
150-56 Melbourne Ave.
Flushing, NY 11367-1439 (718) 268-5977
Contact: Ravi Kulkarni, V.P.

Established in 1993 in NY.
Financial data (yr. ended 12/31/01): Grants paid, $37,300; assets, $283,632 (M); gifts received, $11,050; expenditures, $41,102; qualifying distributions, $28.
Limitations: Giving limited to India.
Officers: Raju Kulkarni, Pres.; Ravi Kulkarni, V.P.; Hemant Joglekar, Secy.
Trustee: Rajkumar Singh.
EIN: 113174234

37057
Rose and Alvin Gindel Foundation
36 Wenwood Dr.
Glen Head, NY 11545

Established in 1986 in NY.
Donor(s): Alvin Gindel.
Financial data (yr. ended 12/31/01): Grants paid, $37,289; assets, $61,112 (M); gifts received, $2,000; expenditures, $43,510; qualifying distributions, $37,289.
Limitations: Applications not accepted. Giving primarily in NY.
Application information: Contributes only to pre-selected organizations.
Officers and Directors:* Alvin Gindel,* Pres.; Rose Gindel,* Secy.-Treas.; Michael Gindel.
EIN: 112837189

37058
James P. & Ruth C. Gillroy Foundation, Inc.
125 Park Ave., 3rd Fl.
New York, NY 10017 (212) 697-2710
Contact: Edmund C. Grainger, Jr., Pres.

Established in 1970 in NY.
Donor(s): Ruth C. Gilroy.‡
Financial data (yr. ended 05/31/02): Grants paid, $37,250; assets, $1,132,931 (M); expenditures, $52,765; qualifying distributions, $46,150.
Limitations: Giving limited to New York, NY.
Publications: Application guidelines.
Application information: Requests by undergraduates, as well as educational institutions for grants for needy students, are considered.
Officers and Trustees:* Edmund C. Grainger, Jr.,* Pres.; Joseph J. Reilly,* V.P.; Kathryn G. Hobbins,* Secy.
EIN: 237129473
Codes: GTI

37059
Hyman and Marjorie Weinberg Foundation
c/o BCRS Assocs.
100 Wall St., 11th Fl.
New York, NY 10005

Established in 1979.
Donor(s): Hyman Weinberg Charitable Lead Trust, Hyman Weinberg.
Financial data (yr. ended 07/31/01): Grants paid, $37,250; assets, $489,910 (M); expenditures, $44,431; qualifying distributions, $40,816.
Limitations: Applications not accepted. Giving limited to NY.
Application information: Contributes only to pre-selected organizations.
Trustees: Robert A. Friedman, Bruce S. Weinberg, Joyce Weinberg, Marjorie P. Weinberg-Berman.
EIN: 133025977

37060
N. M. Leff Foundation, Inc.
2 Sutton Pl. S.
New York, NY 10022-3070

Donor(s): Norman M. Leff.
Financial data (yr. ended 12/31/99): Grants paid, $37,228; assets, $59,491 (M); gifts received, $70,702; expenditures, $41,964; qualifying distributions, $37,228.
Limitations: Applications not accepted. Giving primarily in New York, NY.
Application information: Contributes only to pre-selected organizations.
Officer: Norman M. Leff, Pres.
EIN: 136271784

37061
The Green Family Foundation
c/o BCRS Associates LLC
67 Wall St., 8th Fl.
New York, NY 10005
Contact: J. Markham Green, Tr.

Established in 1985 in NY.
Donor(s): J. Markham Green.
Financial data (yr. ended 04/30/02): Grants paid, $37,000; assets, $492,292 (M); gifts received, $139; expenditures, $39,932; qualifying distributions, $37,000.
Limitations: Applications not accepted. Giving primarily in New York, NY.
Application information: Contributes only to pre-selected organizations.
Trustee: J. Markham Green.
EIN: 133318152

37062
Carl & Anne Hirsch Family Charitable Foundation
c/o U.S. Trust
114 W. 47th St
New York, NY 10036

Established in 1998 in SC.

37062—NEW YORK

Financial data (yr. ended 12/31/01): Grants paid, $37,000; assets, $461,903 (M); expenditures, $42,272; qualifying distributions, $37,000.
Trustees: Anne D. Hirsch, Carl H. Hirsch, U.S. Trust.
EIN: 137141065

37063
Theodore & Lucille Kaufman Foundation
150 E. 69th St., Ste. 8-Q
New York, NY 10021
Contact: Lucille Kaufman, Dir.

Established in 1999 in NY.
Donor(s): Theodore Kaufman, Lucille Kaufman.
Financial data (yr. ended 12/31/01): Grants paid, $37,000; assets, $297,094 (M); gifts received, $48,364; expenditures, $37,351; qualifying distributions, $37,000.
Directors: Lucille Kaufman, Stephen Kaufman, Theodore Kaufman.
EIN: 134047209

37064
Leeds Family Foundation
c/o Lipsky, Goodkin & Co.
120 W. 45th St., 7th Fl.
New York, NY 10036

Established in 1999 in NY.
Donor(s): Laurence C. Leeds, Jr.
Financial data (yr. ended 12/31/01): Grants paid, $37,000; assets, $797,371 (M); gifts received, $170,924; expenditures, $40,359; qualifying distributions, $37,000.
Limitations: Applications not accepted.
Application information: Contributes only to pre-selected organizations.
Trustees: Dalia Leeds, Laurence C. Leeds, Jr.
EIN: 137219856

37065
The Scone Foundation
c/o Ross D. Perry, C.P.A.
10 E. 40th St., Ste. 710
New York, NY 10016

Established in 1998 in NY.
Donor(s): Stanley Cohen.
Financial data (yr. ended 12/31/01): Grants paid, $37,000; assets, $913,776 (M); expenditures, $60,101; qualifying distributions, $35,403.
Limitations: Applications not accepted.
Application information: Contributes only to pre-selected organizations.
Trustees: Laura Cohen, Stanley Cohen, Stuart Schneiderman.
EIN: 113427118

37066
David & Sylvia Teitelbaum Fund, Inc.
c/o Donovan, Leisure, Newton & Irvine
250 Cold Brook Rd.
Bearsville, NY 12409

Financial data (yr. ended 12/31/00): Grants paid, $37,000; assets, $1,175,698 (M); gifts received, $33,921; expenditures, $53,173; qualifying distributions, $37,000.
Limitations: Giving primarily in FL, and New York, NY.
Officers and Directors:* David Teitelbaum,* Pres. and Treas.; Richard Teitelbaum,* V.P. and Secy.; Tim Teitelbaum,* V.P.; Bernard Teitelbaum.
EIN: 136130525

37067
The Wyler Family Foundation, Inc.
(Formerly Alfred & Marguerite Wyler Family Foundation, Inc.)
7 Sage Ct.
White Plains, NY 10605-4408
Contact: Victor A. Wyler, Pres.

Donor(s): Victor A. Wyler.
Financial data (yr. ended 12/31/01): Grants paid, $36,961; assets, $380,396 (M); gifts received, $14,065; expenditures, $37,932; qualifying distributions, $36,961.
Limitations: Giving primarily in New York, NY.
Officers: Victor A. Wyler, Pres. and Treas.; Petronella Wyler, V.P.; Frederick Lubcher, Secy.
EIN: 136162973

37068
Kahal Foundation, Inc.
c/o Paul Josephson, C.P.A.
91 Broad Hollow Rd.
Melville, NY 11747
Application address: 225 W. 86th St., New York, NY 10024
Contact: Hugo Kahn, Mgr.

Donor(s): Hugo Kahn.
Financial data (yr. ended 12/31/01): Grants paid, $36,924; assets, $870,312 (M); expenditures, $44,528; qualifying distributions, $36,924.
Limitations: Giving primarily in NY.
Officer and Trustee:* Hugo Kahn,* Mgr.
EIN: 136262272

37069
The Wieder Family Foundation, Inc.
1450 E. 27th St.
Brooklyn, NY 11210 (718) 692-1025
Contact: Moshe H. Wieder, Tr.

Established in 1994 in NY.
Donor(s): Moshe H. Wieder.
Financial data (yr. ended 12/31/01): Grants paid, $36,862; assets, $135,360 (M); gifts received, $70,000; expenditures, $37,032; qualifying distributions, $36,862.
Limitations: Giving primarily in Brooklyn, NY.
Trustees: Beth I. Wieder, Moshe H. Wieder.
EIN: 113200948

37070
The William & Anita Newman Foundation
1120 Ave. of the Americas
New York, NY 10036

Established in 1985 in NY.
Donor(s): William Newman, Anita Newman.
Financial data (yr. ended 09/30/01): Grants paid, $36,792; assets, $3,616,731 (M); gifts received, $825,000; expenditures, $45,027; qualifying distributions, $36,792.
Limitations: Applications not accepted. Giving primarily in NY.
Application information: Contributes only to pre-selected organizations.
Officer and Directors:* William Newman,* Pres.; Anita Newman.
EIN: 133352983

37071
Mary Denny Wray Foundation
c/o Shustek & Assocs.
1710 1st Ave., Ste. 180
New York, NY 10128-4902

Established in 1998 in NY.
Donor(s): Mary Denny Wray.
Financial data (yr. ended 05/31/00): Grants paid, $36,788; assets, $212,610 (M); expenditures, $48,725; qualifying distributions, $36,788.

Limitations: Applications not accepted. Giving on a national basis, with emphasis on VA.
Application information: Contributes only to pre-selected organizations.
Officers and Directors:* Mary Denny Wray,* Pres.; Marshall Bagley Reid,* Secy.; Buford Scott Reid, James Garnett Reid.
EIN: 223592054

37072
The NASFT Scholarship & Research Fund, Inc.
c/o NASFT
120 Wall St., 27th Fl.
New York, NY 10005-4001 (212) 482-6440
Contact: John Roberts

Donor(s): National Assn. for the Specialty Food Trade, Inc.
Financial data (yr. ended 01/31/02): Grants paid, $36,601; assets, $87,699 (M); expenditures, $39,416; qualifying distributions, $36,601.
Limitations: Giving primarily in NY.
Application information: Application form required.
Officers: Joan Rubschlager, Pres.; Richard Watson, V.P.; Richard Long, Treas.
Trustees: Tim Ashman, Bob Budd.
EIN: 133168002

37073
David Sauber Foundation
c/o Abe Friedman
1555 54th St., No.3
Brooklyn, NY 11219
Application address: 609 Ave. K, Brooklyn, NY 11230, tel.: (718) 338-2996
Contact: Debby Rebenwurzel

Established in 1995 in NY.
Donor(s): David Sauber, The David Sauber Charitable Lead Annuity Trust.
Financial data (yr. ended 12/31/01): Grants paid, $36,600; assets, $40,062 (M); gifts received, $42,120; expenditures, $36,680; qualifying distributions, $36,600.
Limitations: Giving primarily in NY; some giving also in Israel.
Trustees: Leslie Feldman, Debby Rebenwurzel.
EIN: 113266044

37074
The Banon Family Foundation, Inc.
(Formerly The Sidney and Louise Banon Foundation, Inc.)
c/o Sid Banon
150 E. 69th St.
New York, NY 10021

Established in NY 1998.
Financial data (yr. ended 11/30/01): Grants paid, $36,582; assets, $168,329 (M); gifts received, $42,500; expenditures, $37,833; qualifying distributions, $36,582.
Limitations: Applications not accepted.
Application information: Contributes only to pre-selected organizations.
Officer: Sidney Banon, Pres.
EIN: 134035808

37075
Katz Family Foundation, Inc.
700 Park Ave.
New York, NY 10021

Established in 1997 in NY.
Donor(s): Stanley Katz.
Financial data (yr. ended 11/30/01): Grants paid, $36,560; assets, $1,403,710 (M); expenditures, $93,513; qualifying distributions, $36,965.
Limitations: Applications not accepted.

Application information: Contributes only to pre-selected organizations.
Officers: Stanley Katz, Pres.; Andrew Katz, V.P.; Cheryl Katz, V.P.; Judith Katz, Secy.-Treas.
EIN: 133980692

37076
Martin & Roberta Goldstein Family Foundation
501 Chestnut Ridge Rd.
Chestnut Ridge, NY 10977-5629
Contact: Martin L. Goldstein, Tr.

Established in 1996 in NY.
Donor(s): Martin Goldstein, Roberta Goldstein.
Financial data (yr. ended 12/31/01): Grants paid, $36,537; assets, $121,972 (M); gifts received, $36,244; expenditures, $36,627; qualifying distributions, $36,496.
Trustees: Michelle Eisler, Martin L. Goldstein, Roberta Goldstein, Alison Isenstein.
EIN: 137104328

37077
Gerald Abell Foundation, Inc.
260 W. Broadway, Apt. 2B
New York, NY 10002-2260

Established in 1998 in NY.
Donor(s): Keith Wayne Abell.
Financial data (yr. ended 12/31/00): Grants paid, $36,500; assets, $317,080 (M); expenditures, $38,677; qualifying distributions, $36,218.
Limitations: Applications not accepted.
Application information: Contributes only to pre-selected organizations.
Officers and Directors:* Keith Wayne Abell,* Pres.; Cathleen Ruth Ann Fedoruk,* Secy.; Ellen Abell, Lisa Frisone.
EIN: 134011765

37078
Mary and Frank Skillern Foundation
127 E. 62nd St.
New York, NY 10021
Contact: Frank Skillern, Pres.

Established in 1997 in UT.
Donor(s): Frank Skillern, Mary Skillern.
Financial data (yr. ended 12/31/01): Grants paid, $36,500; assets, $519,658 (M); expenditures, $38,298; qualifying distributions, $36,500.
Officers: Frank Skillern, Pres.; Mary Skillern, Treas.
Director: Christopher Skillern.
EIN: 870572197

37079
Dr. Morris Smoller Social Service Fund
99 Madison Ave., 6th Fl.
New York, NY 10016

Financial data (yr. ended 06/30/02): Grants paid, $36,500; assets, $680,091 (M); gifts received, $6,500; expenditures, $38,553; qualifying distributions, $36,500.
Officers: David Negrin, Pres.; Murray Lipton, V.P.; Alan Krell, Treas.
EIN: 136225308

37080
The Edgard and Geraldine Feder Foundation
c/o Allan D. Goodridge
140 Broadway, Ste. 3100
New York, NY 10005-9998

Established in 1991 in NY.
Donor(s): Geraldine Feder.
Financial data (yr. ended 12/31/01): Grants paid, $36,494; assets, $1,012 (M); gifts received, $36,000; expenditures, $36,494; qualifying distributions, $36,494.
Limitations: Applications not accepted. Giving primarily in CT.

Application information: Contributes only to pre-selected organizations.
Trustees: Edward Ehrenberg, Geraldine Feder, Yves Feder, Allan D. Goodridge.
EIN: 133618530

37081
George Sayour Family Foundation, Inc.
59 88th St.
Brooklyn, NY 11209-5523
Contact: Joseph G. Sayour, Pres.

Financial data (yr. ended 07/31/01): Grants paid, $36,455; assets, $367,991 (M); expenditures, $56,141; qualifying distributions, $36,455.
Officers: Joseph G. Sayour, Pres.; Victor Sayour, Secy.; Richard Sayour, Treas.
EIN: 237345988

37082
The Sewell Foundation
c/o Albert Kalter
225 Broadway
New York, NY 10007

Established in 1992 in NY.
Financial data (yr. ended 12/31/01): Grants paid, $36,447; assets, $1,247,794 (M); expenditures, $83,882; qualifying distributions, $36,447.
Limitations: Applications not accepted.
Application information: Contributes only to pre-selected organizations.
Officers: Lawrence Newman, Pres.; Brenda Kalter, V.P.; Helaine Newman, V.P.; Albert Kalter, Secy.-Treas.
EIN: 133679462

37083
McLain Foundation
49 Colony Ct.
Amherst, NY 14226-3526
Contact: David M. Wright, Tr.

Financial data (yr. ended 12/31/01): Grants paid, $36,417; assets, $857,587 (M); expenditures, $40,241; qualifying distributions, $36,417.
Limitations: Giving primarily in western NY.
Trustees: David M. Wright, Douglas F. Wright, James N. Wright, Jonathan Wright, Laurence C. Wright.
EIN: 166032078

37084
The Chilmark Foundation
c/o FG Asset Mgmt.
635 Madison Ave., Ste. 1700
New York, NY 10022 (212) 832-3112
Contact: Julius Rosenwald II, Chair.

Established in 1964 in PA.
Donor(s): Julia K. Rosenwald, Julius Rosenwald II, Julius Rosenwald III.
Financial data (yr. ended 12/31/01): Grants paid, $36,400; assets, $547,039 (M); gifts received, $100,585; expenditures, $44,655; qualifying distributions, $36,400.
Limitations: Giving primarily in Philadelphia, PA.
Application information: Application form not required.
Officers and Trustees:* Julius Rosenwald II,* Chair.; Julia K. Rosenwald,* Vice-Chair.; Julius Rosenwald III, Secy.; Fred Grossman,* Treas.
EIN: 236291605

37085
Stanley and Catherine Maas Foundation
(Formerly Stanley E. Maas Foundation)
38 Mallard Rd.
Manhasset, NY 11030-1220

Established in 1984 in NY.
Donor(s): Catherine T. Maas.

Financial data (yr. ended 04/30/02): Grants paid, $36,400; assets, $1,264,122 (M); expenditures, $41,741; qualifying distributions, $36,400.
Limitations: Applications not accepted. Giving primarily in NY.
Application information: Contributes only to pre-selected organizations.
Officers: Catherine T. Maas, Pres.; Evelyn Lev, Secy.
EIN: 112690167

37086
Untitled Foundation
c/o David Deutsch
226-228 E. 49th St.
New York, NY 10017

Established in 2000 in NY.
Donor(s): David Deutsch.
Financial data (yr. ended 12/31/01): Grants paid, $36,300; assets, $11,390 (M); expenditures, $38,084; qualifying distributions, $36,300.
Officers: David Deutsch, Chair. and Pres.; Shawn Gannon, V.P.; Vicki Sambunaris, Secy.
EIN: 134090868

37087
Jacob Herzka Charitable Trust Foundation
1446 59th St.
Brooklyn, NY 11219

Established in 1999 in NY.
Donor(s): Jacob Herzka.
Financial data (yr. ended 12/31/00): Grants paid, $36,110; assets, $653,230 (M); gifts received, $425,000; expenditures, $36,610; qualifying distributions, $36,110.
Limitations: Applications not accepted.
Application information: Contributes only to pre-selected organizations.
Trustee: Jacob Herzka.
EIN: 912057543

37088
Dengrove Family Foundation, Inc.
1133 Broadway, Ste. 502
New York, NY 10010-7901

Donor(s): Sylvia M. Dengrove.
Financial data (yr. ended 09/30/01): Grants paid, $36,070; assets, $744,438 (M); expenditures, $39,991; qualifying distributions, $36,070.
Limitations: Applications not accepted. Giving primarily in New York, NY.
Application information: Contributes only to pre-selected organizations.
Officers and Directors:* Jay L. Dengrove,* Pres. and Treas.; Sylvia M. Dengrove,* V.P. and Secy.; Abraham Goldstein.
EIN: 136125285

37089
George D. Benjamin Foundation
c/o Fiduciary Trust Intl.
600 5th Ave.
New York, NY 10020

Established in 1997 in NJ.
Donor(s): George D. Benjamin.
Financial data (yr. ended 12/31/00): Grants paid, $36,050; assets, $797,881 (M); expenditures, $43,977; qualifying distributions, $38,122.
Limitations: Applications not accepted. Giving primarily in New York, NY.
Application information: Contributes only to pre-selected organizations.
Trustees: Evelyn J. Benjamin, George D. Benjamin, Nell D. Benjamin.
EIN: 223515588

37090
Anrol Foundation
Tag Associates, LTD.
75 Rockefeller Plz., Ste. 900
New York, NY 10019

Established in 1998 in NY.
Donor(s): Edwin Goodman Charitable Lead Trust.
Financial data (yr. ended 12/31/01): Grants paid, $36,000; assets, $267,518 (M); gifts received, $55,029; expenditures, $45,283; qualifying distributions, $36,000.
Limitations: Applications not accepted.
Application information: Contributes only to pre-selected organizations.
Officers: Edwin Goodman, Chair. and Treas.; Lorna Goodman, Pres.; Hume Steyer, Secy.
EIN: 133951510

37091
Sheila & Getzel Cohen Family Foundation
c/o Alexander Cohen
255 W. 88th St., Ste. 7A
New York, NY 10024

Established in 2000 in NY.
Donor(s): Alexander Z. Cohen.
Financial data (yr. ended 12/31/01): Grants paid, $36,000; assets, $96,607 (M); gifts received, $1,250; expenditures, $37,050; qualifying distributions, $36,000.
Limitations: Applications not accepted.
Application information: Contributes only to pre-selected organizations.
Trustees: Alexander Z. Cohen, C. Sheila Cohen, Getzel M. Cohen.
EIN: 066504220

37092
The Goodman-Klein-Pinckney Family Foundation, Inc.
950 Reynolds Arcade Bldg.
Rochester, NY 14614
Contact: Donald Bilgore, Secy.

Established in 2001 in NY.
Donor(s): The Charles & Minnie Goodman Charitable Remainder Trust.
Financial data (yr. ended 12/31/01): Grants paid, $36,000; assets, $798,918 (M); gifts received, $864,540; expenditures, $51,182; qualifying distributions, $45,869.
Limitations: Giving primarily in Rochester, NY.
Application information: Application form not required.
Officers and Directors:* Melvin Klein,* Pres.; Donald L. Bilgore,* Secy.; Morton Goodman, Anita G. Pinckney, Norman J. Reich.
EIN: 311707904

37093
The M & M Foundation
1303 53rd St., Ste 260
Brooklyn, NY 11219

Established in 1999 in NY.
Donor(s): Mordechai Mayer, Mordechai Ainhorn.
Financial data (yr. ended 12/31/01): Grants paid, $36,000; assets, $2,035 (M); expenditures, $36,062; qualifying distributions, $36,000.
Limitations: Applications not accepted.
Application information: Contributes only to pre-selected organizations.
Trustees: Mordechai Ainhorn, Mordechai Mayer.
EIN: 113521343

37094
The Pearl Family Foundation
c/o Edelstein
P.O. Box 1534
Pearl River, NY 10965

Established in 1994.
Donor(s): Richard Pearl.
Financial data (yr. ended 12/31/01): Grants paid, $36,000; assets, $698,282 (M); expenditures, $43,814; qualifying distributions, $36,000.
Limitations: Applications not accepted. Giving primarily in NH, NY, and VT.
Application information: Contributes only to pre-selected organizations.
Officers and Directors:* Richard Pearl,* Pres.; Jane Pearl,* V.P.; Jennifer Pearl,* Secy.; Meddie Pearl,* Treas.
EIN: 133772783

37095
Van de Vrande Charitable Foundation
100 Park Ave., Fl. 23
New York, NY 10017   (917) 747-8666

Established in 1998 in IL.
Donor(s): Karen van de Vrande.
Financial data (yr. ended 12/31/00): Grants paid, $36,000; assets, $91,609 (M); expenditures, $37,496; qualifying distributions, $35,800.
Limitations: Giving primarily in IL.
Trustee: Karen van de Vrande.
EIN: 367210192

37096
Carl & Madeline Glick Foundation, Inc.
211 E. 70th St., Ste. 8B
New York, NY 10021

Donor(s): Carl Glick, Madeline Glick.
Financial data (yr. ended 09/30/01): Grants paid, $35,968; assets, $7,886 (M); expenditures, $38,868; qualifying distributions, $35,968.
Limitations: Applications not accepted. Giving primarily in New York, NY.
Application information: Contributes only to pre-selected organizations.
Officers and Directors:* Carl Glick,* Co-Pres.; Madeline Glick,* Co-Pres.; Marianne Rohrlich.
EIN: 132989779

37097
Silverberg Family Foundation, Inc.
40 Bluebird Hill Ct.
Manhasset, NY 11030   (516) 625-3750

Donor(s): Irwin W. Silverburg.
Financial data (yr. ended 12/31/01): Grants paid, $35,950; assets, $1,030,207 (M); expenditures, $48,783; qualifying distributions, $35,950.
Limitations: Applications not accepted. Giving primarily in NJ and NY.
Application information: Contributes only to pre-selected organizations.
Officers and Directors:* Irwin Silverberg,* Pres.; Ronnie L. Silverberg,* V.P. and Secy.; Suzanne Silverberg,* Treas.
EIN: 113228373

37098
Shapiro E. Familia Foundation, Inc.
c/o Mordecai J. Elazary
1084 E. 17th St.
Brooklyn, NY 11230

Established in 1991 in NY.
Donor(s): Soloman Shapiro.
Financial data (yr. ended 08/31/01): Grants paid, $35,882; assets, $17,725 (M); gifts received, $25,000; expenditures, $36,466; qualifying distributions, $35,868.
Limitations: Applications not accepted. Giving primarily in New York, NY.
Application information: Contributes only to pre-selected organizations.
Officers: Joseph N. Shapiro, Pres.; Mordecai J. Elazary, V.P.; Miriam B. Elazary, Secy.
EIN: 113094778

37099
Abraham Wassner & Sons Foundation, Inc.
c/o Berlack, Israels & Liberman, LLP
120 W. 45th St.
New York, NY 10036-4041

Established in 1981 in NY.
Donor(s): Abraham Wassner.
Financial data (yr. ended 12/31/01): Grants paid, $35,878; assets, $740,596 (M); expenditures, $39,861; qualifying distributions, $35,878.
Limitations: Applications not accepted. Giving primarily in New York, NY.
Application information: Contributes only to pre-selected organizations.
Officer and Directors:* Diane Wassner,* Pres.; Judah Wassner, Leonard Wassner.
EIN: 136219360

37100
A. & J. Saks Foundation, Inc.
350 E. 81st St.
New York, NY 10028-3931
Contact: Arnold Saks, Pres.

Established in 1998 in NY.
Donor(s): U.S. Bancorp, Household International, Inc.
Financial data (yr. ended 12/31/01): Grants paid, $35,870; assets, $212,374 (M); expenditures, $38,847; qualifying distributions, $35,870.
Limitations: Giving primarily in New York, NY.
Officer: Arnold Saks, Pres.
EIN: 133933281

37101
Joseph L. & Ray L. Freund Foundation
102 Franklin St.
New York, NY 10013-2946
Contact: David J. Freund, Pres.

Financial data (yr. ended 12/31/01): Grants paid, $35,850; assets, $556,106 (M); expenditures, $40,345; qualifying distributions, $35,850.
Application information: Application form not required.
Officer: David J. Freund, Pres.
EIN: 136163058

37102
Trafton M. & Maude W. Crandall Foundation A
c/o JPMorgan Chase Bank
P.O. Box 31412
Rochester, NY 14603-1412

Financial data (yr. ended 12/31/01): Grants paid, $35,750; assets, $646,671 (M); expenditures, $43,317; qualifying distributions, $36,299.
Limitations: Applications not accepted. Giving primarily in Washington, DC, and NY.
Application information: Contributes only to pre-selected organizations.
Trustee: JPMorgan Chase Bank.
EIN: 166069495

37103
The Thall Family Foundation, Inc.
165 Feeks Ln.
Lattingtown, NY 11560

Established in 2000 in DE.
Donor(s): Richard S. Thall.
Financial data (yr. ended 12/31/01): Grants paid, $35,750; assets, $48,884 (M); gifts received,

$501; expenditures, $43,753; qualifying distributions, $35,750.
Limitations: Applications not accepted.
Application information: Contributes only to pre-selected organizations.
Directors: Diana Levin, Alice Thall, Carolyn R. Thall, Richard S. Thall.
EIN: 113577946

37104
John N. Matthews Family Foundation, Inc.
c/o Gilbert, Segall & Young, LLP
430 Park Ave.
New York, NY 10022-3505

Donor(s): Donald J. Matthews, R.F. Matthews.
Financial data (yr. ended 09/30/01): Grants paid, $35,700; assets, $217,405 (M); expenditures, $38,382; qualifying distributions, $35,700.
Limitations: Applications not accepted. Giving primarily in NY.
Application information: Contributes only to pre-selected organizations.
Officers: Donald J. Matthews, Pres.; R.F. Matthews, V.P.; D.K. Kinsey, Treas.
EIN: 136066034

37105
Lund Family Foundation
c/o BCRS Assoc., LLC
67 Wall St., 8th Fl.
New York, NY 10005

Established in 1989 in IL.
Donor(s): Robert I. Lund.
Financial data (yr. ended 03/31/02): Grants paid, $35,686; assets, $238,389 (M); expenditures, $38,906; qualifying distributions, $35,686.
Limitations: Applications not accepted. Giving primarily in Chicago, IL.
Application information: Contributes only to pre-selected organizations.
Trustees: Richard S. Atlas, Robert I. Lund, Sandra Lund.
EIN: 133532034

37106
Granovsky Family Foundation
c/o Robert J. Granovsky
420 E. 54th St., Ste. 12A
New York, NY 10022

Established in 1997 in NJ.
Donor(s): Barbara M. Granovsky, Robert J. Granovsky.
Financial data (yr. ended 12/31/01): Grants paid, $35,653; assets, $155,697 (M); expenditures, $35,653; qualifying distributions, $35,653.
Trustees: Barbara M. Granovsky, Robert J. Granovsky.
EIN: 311526136

37107
The Elaine Terner Cooper Foundation
980 5th Ave.
New York, NY 10021

Established in 1998 in NY.
Donor(s): Elaine Terner Cooper, The Terner Foundation.
Financial data (yr. ended 12/31/99): Grants paid, $35,600; assets, $1,056,526 (M); gifts received, $991,450; expenditures, $38,761; qualifying distributions, $36,935.
Limitations: Applications not accepted.
Application information: Contributes only to pre-selected organizations.
Trustee: Elaine Terner Cooper.
EIN: 132073897

37108
Ruth & Peter Fleck Foundation, Inc.
c/o Polakoff & Michaelson, C.P.A.
90 West St., Ste. 1605
New York, NY 10006

Established in 1955.
Donor(s): G. Peter Fleck,‡ Ruth Fleck.
Financial data (yr. ended 12/31/01): Grants paid, $35,600; assets, $679,390 (M); expenditures, $41,449; qualifying distributions, $35,600.
Limitations: Applications not accepted. Giving primarily in MA and NY.
Application information: Contributes only to pre-selected organizations.
Officer and Directors:* Ruth Fleck,* Pres.; Andrea Fleck Clardy, Ann Fleck Henderson, Marjorie Fleck Withers.
EIN: 136075581

37109
Arthur H. Connor Charitable Trust
c/o The Bank of New York, Tax Dept.
1 Wall St., 28th Fl.
New York, NY 10286-0001 (212) 635-1520

Financial data (yr. ended 12/31/01): Grants paid, $35,592; assets, $794,450 (M); expenditures, $41,417; qualifying distributions, $35,592.
Limitations: Applications not accepted.
Application information: Contributes only to pre-selected organizations.
Trustee: The Bank of New York.
EIN: 133728333

37110
Levin Foundation
c/o Louis Sternbach & Co.
1212 Ave. of the Americas, 6th Fl.
New York, NY 10036-1602

Donor(s): I. Victor Levin.
Financial data (yr. ended 12/31/01): Grants paid, $35,550; assets, $317,661 (M); gifts received, $20,000; expenditures, $36,006; qualifying distributions, $35,550.
Limitations: Applications not accepted. Giving primarily in NY.
Application information: Contributes only to pre-selected organizations.
Director: I. Victor Levin.
EIN: 136271765

37111
The Carol and Alan Brumberger Foundation
1016 5th Ave.
New York, NY 10028

Established in 2000 in NY.
Donor(s): Carol Brumberger, Alan E. Brumberger.
Financial data (yr. ended 07/31/01): Grants paid, $35,500; assets, $149,827 (M); gifts received, $3,127; expenditures, $36,748; qualifying distributions, $35,500.
Limitations: Applications not accepted. Giving primarily in New York, NY.
Application information: Contributes only to pre-selected organizations.
Trustees: Alan E. Brumberger, Carol Brumberger.
EIN: 137253670

37112
The John Doar Foundation, Inc.
c/o Doar, Rieck & Mack
233 Broadway, Rm. 1001
New York, NY 10279-0173

Donor(s): John Doar.
Financial data (yr. ended 12/31/01): Grants paid, $35,500; assets, $825,718 (M); gifts received, $25,000; expenditures, $36,025; qualifying distributions, $35,600.
Limitations: Applications not accepted. Giving on a national basis, with emphasis on WI.
Application information: Contributes only to pre-selected organizations.
Officers and Directors:* John Doar,* Pres.; Robert Doar, V.P.; Karla MacKesson, Secy.-Treas.; Gael Doar, Michael Doar.
EIN: 133318264

37113
Gouverneur Foundation, Inc.
133 E. Barney St.
Gouverneur, NY 13642-1193 (315) 287-4836
Contact: Gale Ferguson, Pres.

Donor(s): Max Levinson.
Financial data (yr. ended 06/30/01): Grants paid, $35,500; assets, $421,933 (M); gifts received, $66,823; expenditures, $35,855; qualifying distributions, $35,500.
Limitations: Giving limited to Gouverneur, NY.
Application information: Application form required.
Officers and Directors:* Gale Ferguson,* Pres.; Norton Taylor,* Secy.; William Bodah,* Treas.; Charles Graves, Max Levinson.
EIN: 146048653

37114
The Perlmutter Family Foundation
(Formerly The Barbara and Louis Perlmutter Foundation)
c/o Lazard Freres & Co., LLC
30 Rockefeller Plz.
New York, NY 10020
Contact: Louis Perlmutter, Pres.

Established in 1986 in NY.
Donor(s): Louis Perlmutter.
Financial data (yr. ended 06/30/01): Grants paid, $35,500; assets, $653,075 (M); gifts received, $7,000; expenditures, $35,904; qualifying distributions, $35,381.
Limitations: Giving primarily in NY.
Officers and Directors:* Louis Perlmutter,* Pres.; Eric Perlmutter,* V.P.; Kermit Perlmutter,* V.P.; Barbara Perlmutter,* Secy.-Treas.
EIN: 133423720

37115
The Rum Fund
200 Madison Ave., 5th Fl.
New York, NY 10016

Established in 1998 in DE.
Donor(s): Susan and Elihu Rose Foundation, Inc.
Financial data (yr. ended 12/31/00): Grants paid, $35,466; assets, $7,316 (M); gifts received, $40,000; expenditures, $35,741; qualifying distributions, $35,466.
Limitations: Applications not accepted.
Application information: Contributes only to pre-selected organizations.
Officers: Abigail Rose, Pres.; Michael Blum, V.P.
EIN: 134022921

37116
Richard G. McDermott, Jr. Family Foundation, Inc.
c/o Louis Sternbach and Co.
1333 Broadway, Ste. 516
New York, NY 10018

Established in 1992 in CT.
Donor(s): Richard G. McDermott, Jr.
Financial data (yr. ended 12/31/01): Grants paid, $35,457; assets, $652,440 (M); gifts received, $315; expenditures, $42,783; qualifying distributions, $35,457.

Limitations: Applications not accepted. Giving limited to Babson Park, MA.
Application information: Contributes only to pre-selected organizations.
Officer: Richard G. McDermott, Jr., Pres.
EIN: 061332539

37117
Owenoke Foundation
c/o Perelson Weiner, LLP
1 Dag Hammarskjold Plz., 42nd Fl.
New York, NY 10017-2286

Established in 1996 in NY.
Donor(s): Nancy Schwartz.
Financial data (yr. ended 12/31/01): Grants paid, $35,400; assets, $534,423 (M); expenditures, $35,400; qualifying distributions, $35,400.
Limitations: Applications not accepted.
Application information: Contributes only to pre-selected organizations.
Trustee: Nancy Schwartz.
EIN: 137102683

37118
The Hartman Charitable Trust
1639 52nd St.
Brooklyn, NY 11204

Financial data (yr. ended 12/31/00): Grants paid, $35,360; assets, $738,366 (M); expenditures, $36,646; qualifying distributions, $34,873.
Limitations: Applications not accepted.
Application information: Contributes only to pre-selected organizations.
Trustees: Alexander Hartman, Sima Hartman.
EIN: 137023749

37119
Ralph J. Valentino Family Foundation, Inc.
8 Bonnie Ct.
Merrick, NY 11566

Established in 1996 in NY.
Donor(s): Ralph J. Valentino.
Financial data (yr. ended 09/30/01): Grants paid, $35,350; assets, $111,342 (M); gifts received, $5,000; expenditures, $35,540; qualifying distributions, $35,350.
Limitations: Applications not accepted.
Application information: Contributes only to pre-selected organizations.
Officers: Ralph J. Valentino, Pres. and Treas.; Antoinette Valentino, V.P. and Secy.; Ralph L. Valentino, V.P.
EIN: 113353743

37120
The Silber Family Foundation, Inc.
1259 56th St.
Brooklyn, NY 11219

Established in 1997 in NY.
Donor(s): Zalman Silber.
Financial data (yr. ended 12/31/99): Grants paid, $35,334; assets, $0 (M); gifts received, $34,700; expenditures, $36,363; qualifying distributions, $36,363; giving activities include $1,029 for programs.
Officers: Zalman Silber, Pres.; Sharon Silber, Secy.-Treas.
EIN: 113296320

37121
The Rita & Sheldon Kwiat Family Foundation, Inc.
15 Cypress Ave.
Great Neck, NY 11024

Established in 1997 in NY.
Donor(s): Rita Kwiat, Sheldon Kwiat.

Financial data (yr. ended 12/31/01): Grants paid, $35,324; assets, $73,797 (M); expenditures, $35,500; qualifying distributions, $35,324.
Limitations: Applications not accepted.
Application information: Contributes only to pre-selected organizations.
Officers: Sheldon Kwiat, Chair.; Rita Kwiat, Pres.; Michelle Kwiat, V.P. and Secy.
EIN: 133944749

37122
The Olian Foundation, Inc.
(Formerly Cyrus & Jacob Olian Foundation, Inc.)
c/o Howard Olian
Shepherds Ln.
Sands Point, NY 11050

Established in 1952.
Donor(s): Westwood, Inc., Howard Olian.
Financial data (yr. ended 11/30/02): Grants paid, $35,259; assets, $1,081,737 (M); expenditures, $80,266; qualifying distributions, $35,259.
Limitations: Applications not accepted. Giving primarily in NY.
Application information: Contributes only to pre-selected organizations.
Officers: Joanne Olian, Pres.; Howard Olian, Secy.-Treas.
EIN: 136160914

37123
Rome Savings Bank Foundation
100 W. Dominick St.
Rome, NY 13440

Established in 1999 in DE and NY.
Donor(s): Rome Bancorp, Inc.
Financial data (yr. ended 12/31/01): Grants paid, $35,250; assets, $1,257,858 (M); expenditures, $35,835; qualifying distributions, $35,013.
Limitations: Giving limited to Rome, NY.
Application information: Unsolicited request for funds not accepted.
Officers and Directors:* Charles M. Sprock,* C.E.O. and Pres.; Marion C. Scoville,* Secy.; David C. Nolan, C.F.O. and Treas.; Bruce R. Englebert, David C. Grow, Kirk B. Hinman, T. Richard Leidig, Richard H. McMahon, Michael J. Valentine.
EIN: 161581034
Codes: CS, CD

37124
The Slone Family Foundation
c/o Richard Slone
P.O. Box 308
New Hyde Park, NY 11040-0251

Established in 1997 in NY.
Donor(s): Richard Slone, Urethane Products Co., Inc.
Financial data (yr. ended 12/31/01): Grants paid, $35,190; assets, $634,389 (M); expenditures, $35,710; qualifying distributions, $35,190.
Officer: Richard Slone, Pres.
EIN: 113368339

37125
Haro Foundation
324 Savage Farm Rd.
Ithaca, NY 14850-2260
Contact: Rose S. Bethe, Tr.

Donor(s): Hans A. Bethe, Rose S. Bethe.
Financial data (yr. ended 12/31/01): Grants paid, $35,175; assets, $492,035 (M); expenditures, $37,358; qualifying distributions, $35,175.
Limitations: Giving primarily in NY.
Officers and Trustees:* Hans A. Bethe,* Pres.; Laura H. Holmberg,* Secy.; Henry G. Bethe, Rose S. Bethe.

EIN: 166093007

37126
Mitchell B. Modell Foundation
498 17th Ave., 20th Fl.
New York, NY 10018 (212) 822-1000
Contact: Mitchell Modell, Tr.

Established in NY in 1998.
Financial data (yr. ended 12/31/01): Grants paid, $35,140; assets, $40,173 (M); gifts received, $20,000; expenditures, $35,290; qualifying distributions, $35,140.
Trustee: Mitchell Modell.
EIN: 311577879

37127
Koplik Foundation
c/o Perry H. Koplik & Sons, Inc.
505 Park Ave.
New York, NY 10022-1106 (212) 339-1700
Contact: Perry H. Koplik, Pres.

Established in 1962.
Donor(s): Perry H. Koplik.
Financial data (yr. ended 12/31/01): Grants paid, $35,100; assets, $716,169 (M); gifts received, $50,000; expenditures, $35,380; qualifying distributions, $35,100.
Limitations: Giving primarily in New York, NY.
Officer: Perry H. Koplik, Pres.
EIN: 136161653

37128
Waldbaum Foundation
c/o Waldbaum, Inc.
Hemlock St. and Boulevard Ave.
Central Islip, NY 11722

Financial data (yr. ended 12/31/01): Grants paid, $35,100; assets, $0 (M); gifts received, $11,438; expenditures, $35,100; qualifying distributions, $35,100.
Officers: David Smithies,* Pres.; Anthony Gasparo,* V.P.; Kevin McDonnell,* V.P.; Kenneth Uhl, Treas.; Neil Falcone, Joan Lizzi, Denis McCrary, Robert Ulrich.
EIN: 113514151

37129
Sperandio Family Foundation
18 Twin Ponds Dr.
Spencerport, NY 14559
Contact: Jacqueline Sperandio, V.P.

Established in 1995 in NY.
Donor(s): Robert V. Sperandio, Jacqueline Sperandio.
Financial data (yr. ended 12/31/01): Grants paid, $35,050; assets, $1,987,231 (M); expenditures, $52,537; qualifying distributions, $35,050.
Officers: Robert V. Sperandio, Pres. and Secy.; Jacqueline Sperandio, V.P.
Trustees: Elizabeth S. Rickert, Mark C. Sperandio.
EIN: 161490918

37130
David & Ilse Appel Family Foundation
c/o S. Mintz
305 Broadway, Ste. 1002
New York, NY 10007-1109

Donor(s): David Appel.
Financial data (yr. ended 12/31/01): Grants paid, $35,032; assets, $40,528 (M); gifts received, $61,600; expenditures, $35,064; qualifying distributions, $35,032.
Limitations: Applications not accepted.
Application information: Contributes only to pre-selected organizations.
Trustee: David Appel.
EIN: 116437191

37131
Chencinski Brothers Charitable Foundation, Inc.
c/o Issac Gottesman
1879 48th St.
Brooklyn, NY 11204-1239

Established in 1994.
Donor(s): Isaac Chencinski, Moses Chencinski.
Financial data (yr. ended 12/31/01): Grants paid, $35,025; assets, $158,669 (M); expenditures, $37,816; qualifying distributions, $35,025.
Limitations: Applications not accepted. Giving primarily in Brooklyn, NY.
Application information: Contributes only to pre-selected organizations.
Officers: Moses Chencinski, Pres.; Isaac Chencinski, Secy.-Treas.
EIN: 521892265

37132
Gottesman Family Foundation
825 West End Ave.
New York, NY 10025
Contact: Alexander Gottesman, Pres.

Established in 1994 in NY.
Donor(s): Alexander Gottesman.
Financial data (yr. ended 07/31/01): Grants paid, $35,020; assets, $683,583 (M); gifts received, $71,727; expenditures, $36,627; qualifying distributions, $35,020.
Application information: Application form not required.
Officers: Alexander Gottesman, Pres.; Ronald Gottesman, V.P.; Steven Garrin, Secy.
EIN: 137042162

37133
The Bayberry Foundation, Inc.
33 Bayberry Rd.
Lawrence, NY 11559-2724

Established in 1996 in DE & NY.
Donor(s): Joseph S. Reiss, M.D.
Financial data (yr. ended 12/31/01): Grants paid, $35,004; assets, $141,674 (M); expenditures, $40,269; qualifying distributions, $35,004.
Limitations: Applications not accepted. Giving primarily in NY.
Application information: Contributes only to pre-selected organizations.
Officers and Directors:* Joseph S. Reiss, M.D.,* Pres.; Brenda H. Reiss,* Secy.-Treas.
EIN: 113378915

37134
Antoinette E. "Mimi" & Herman Boehm Foundation, Inc.
c/o Ronald M. Appel
295 Madison Ave.
New York, NY 10017-6304

Established in 1994 in NY.
Donor(s): Herman Boehm.
Financial data (yr. ended 12/31/01): Grants paid, $35,000; assets, $593,857 (M); gifts received, $34,390; expenditures, $37,595; qualifying distributions, $36,081.
Limitations: Applications not accepted. Giving primarily in NY.
Application information: Contributes only to pre-selected organizations.
Officers and Directors:* Herman Boehm,* Pres.; Ronald M. Appel, V.P.; Andrew Weiss, Secy.; Adeline Sherr, Treas.; Eric Weinberger.
EIN: 133763458

37135
Theodore and Maria Bollt Family Foundation
c/o Bessemer Trust Co., N.A.
630 5th Ave., 34th Fl.
New York, NY 10111
Application address: c/o Bessemer Trust Co. of FL, 801 Brickell Ave., Miami, FL 33131

Established in 1993 in FL.
Donor(s): Theodore Bollt, Maria Bollt.
Financial data (yr. ended 04/30/02): Grants paid, $35,000; assets, $622,403 (M); expenditures, $43,767; qualifying distributions, $34,865.
Limitations: Giving primarily in FL.
Advisory Committee Members: Maria Bollt, Theodore Bollt.
Trustee: Bessemer Trust Co., N.A.
EIN: 656113538

37136
Children's Immunology Research Fund, Inc.
c/o Gluckman & Gevirman
597 5th Ave.
New York, NY 10017

Established in 1999 in NY.
Financial data (yr. ended 06/30/01): Grants paid, $35,000; assets, $214,467 (M); gifts received, $30,800; expenditures, $38,560; qualifying distributions, $34,928.
Limitations: Applications not accepted. Giving primarily in New York, NY.
Application information: Contributes only to pre-selected organizations.
Officers: Arye Rubinstein, Pres.; Herbert Gevirman, Secy.-Treas.
Directors: Joyce H. Lowinson, Anita Septimus.
EIN: 133106729

37137
The Conable Family Foundation, Inc.
10532 Alexander Rd., Box 218
Alexander, NY 14005

Established in 1999 in NY.
Donor(s): Barber Conable, Jr., Charlotte Conable.
Financial data (yr. ended 12/31/01): Grants paid, $35,000; assets, $774,702 (M); gifts received, $24,078; expenditures, $36,728; qualifying distributions, $35,000.
Limitations: Applications not accepted. Giving primarily in NY.
Application information: Contributes only to pre-selected organizations.
Officers: Barber B. Conable, Jr., Chair.; Charlotte W. Conable, V. Chair.; Jane C. Schmieder, Secy.-Treas.
Trustees: Emily C. Conable, Samuel W. Conable.
EIN: 161565050

37138
The Chaim J. and Fay R. Fortgang Family Foundation
c/o Wachtell, Lipton, Rosen & Katz
51 W. 52nd St.
New York, NY 10019

Established in 1986 in NY.
Donor(s): Ron LaBow, Chaim J. Fortgang, Fay R. Fortgang.
Financial data (yr. ended 04/30/02): Grants paid, $35,000; assets, $283,576 (M); expenditures, $35,100; qualifying distributions, $35,000.
Limitations: Applications not accepted. Giving primarily in New York, NY.
Application information: Contributes only to pre-selected organizations.
Directors: Chaim J. Fortgang, Fay R. Fortgang, Pinkas Fortgang.
EIN: 133387892

37139
Larry and Anne Glenn Foundation, Inc.
50 Town Cocks Ln.
Locust Valley, NY 11560

Established in 1997 in NY.
Donor(s): Larry Glenn, Anne Glenn.
Financial data (yr. ended 12/31/01): Grants paid, $35,000; assets, $219,791 (M); gifts received, $15,000; expenditures, $41,702; qualifying distributions, $35,000.
Officers and Directors:* Lawrence R. Glenn,* Chair.; Anne D. Glenn,* Pres.; Lawrence R. Glenn, Jr.,* Secy.; Darcy A. Glenn,* Treas.
EIN: 113380037

37140
Klein Family Foundation
c/o Brand Sonnenschine, LLP
377 Broadway
New York, NY 10013

Established in 1999 in NY.
Donor(s): Abraham Klein, Sarah Dinah Klein.
Financial data (yr. ended 12/31/00): Grants paid, $35,000; assets, $4,067,783 (M); gifts received, $4,044,393; expenditures, $35,500; qualifying distributions, $35,000.
Limitations: Applications not accepted.
Application information: Contributes only to pre-selected organizations.
Trustees: Abraham Klein, Sarah Dinah Klein.
EIN: 134092608

37141
Lazar Charitable Trust
6250 Quintard Rd.
P.O. Box 514
Jamesville, NY 13078-9725
Contact: Michael J. Lazar, Tr.

Established in 1990 in NY.
Donor(s): Michael J. Lazar.
Financial data (yr. ended 12/31/01): Grants paid, $35,000; assets, $732,544 (M); expenditures, $36,118; qualifying distributions, $35,000.
Limitations: Giving primarily in Syracuse, NY.
Trustees: Judith Abby Lazar, Michael J. Lazar, Michelle L. Lazar.
EIN: 161384317

37142
The Kero Mantzouras Foundation
100 Cedar St., Ste. A42
Dobbs Ferry, NY 10522-1019

Established in 1992.
Financial data (yr. ended 12/31/01): Grants paid, $35,000; assets, $578,223 (M); expenditures, $42,106; qualifying distributions, $35,000.
Limitations: Applications not accepted. Giving primarily in MA.
Application information: Contributes only to pre-selected organizations.
Trustee: Demetrios Sophides.
EIN: 133666144

37143
1959 Foundation, Inc.
c/o American Express, Tax & Business Svcs.
1185 Ave. of the Americas
New York, NY 10036

Established in 2000.
Donor(s): William W. Powell.
Financial data (yr. ended 12/31/01): Grants paid, $35,000; assets, $277,659 (M); gifts received, $6,243; expenditures, $41,243; qualifying distributions, $35,000.
Limitations: Applications not accepted.

37143—NEW YORK

Application information: Contributes only to pre-selected organizations.
Officers: William W. Powell, Pres.; Joanne Paladino, Secy.; Moshe Metzger, Treas.
EIN: 134140002

37144
Piper Foundation
c/o B. Strauss Assoc., Ltd.
307 5th Ave., 8th Fl.
New York, NY 10016-6517

Established in 1996 in CT.
Donor(s): Thomas L. Piper III.
Financial data (yr. ended 10/31/01): Grants paid, $35,000; assets, $144,298 (M); expenditures, $38,013; qualifying distributions, $35,000.
Limitations: Applications not accepted.
Application information: Contributes only to pre-selected organizations.
Trustees: Andrew K. Piper, Ann R. Piper, Thomas L. Piper III, Thomas L. Piper IV.
EIN: 133949039

37145
Sankey Logan Foundation
c/o Yvonne L. Logan-Sankey
40 E. 89th St., Ste. 15E
New York, NY 10128

Established in 1998 in NY.
Donor(s): Yvonne L. Logan-Sankey, Martin A. Sankey.
Financial data (yr. ended 12/31/01): Grants paid, $35,000; assets, $283,371 (M); expenditures, $35,656; qualifying distributions, $35,000.
Limitations: Applications not accepted.
Application information: Contributes only to pre-selected organizations.
Trustees: Elizabeth Doyle Asgairis, Yvonne L. Logan-Sankey, Martin A. Sankey.
EIN: 133979483

37146
The Barbara Tober Foundation
c/o Sugar Foods Corp.
950 3rd Ave.
New York, NY 10022-2705

Established in 1994 in NY.
Donor(s): Barbara Tober.
Financial data (yr. ended 11/30/01): Grants paid, $35,000; assets, $344,680 (M); expenditures, $40,110; qualifying distributions, $35,000.
Limitations: Applications not accepted. Giving primarily in New York, NY.
Application information: Contributes only to pre-selected organizations.
Officer: Barbara Tober, Mgr.
EIN: 133883171

37147
The Gurdon W. Wattles Fund
c/o Simpson Thatcher & Bartlett
425 Lexington Ave.
New York, NY 10017-3909

Financial data (yr. ended 12/31/01): Grants paid, $35,000; assets, $854,897 (M); expenditures, $42,174; qualifying distributions, $35,000.
Limitations: Applications not accepted. Giving primarily in CT and NY.
Application information: Contributes only to pre-selected organizations.
Trustees: Alexander B. Wattles, Gurdon B. Wattles, Gurdon S. Wattles, Elizabeth W. Wilkes.
EIN: 237027979

37148
Irving N. Tolkin Foundation, Inc.
270 Pepperidge Rd.
Hewlett, NY 11557-2749

Donor(s): Jennifer Dale, Inc., Marvin Tolkin.
Financial data (yr. ended 12/31/01): Grants paid, $34,962; assets, $148,707 (M); gifts received, $375; expenditures, $42,410; qualifying distributions, $34,962.
Limitations: Applications not accepted.
Application information: Contributes only to pre-selected organizations.
Officer: Marvin Tolkin, Pres. and Treas.
EIN: 116021069

37149
Norton's Foundation
c/o David Seaman
51 E. 42nd St.
New York, NY 10017

Established in 1997 in NY.
Donor(s): Elaine E. & Frank T. Poers, Jr. Foundation.
Financial data (yr. ended 05/31/02): Grants paid, $34,933; assets, $183,163 (M); expenditures, $38,985; qualifying distributions, $34,933.
Limitations: Applications not accepted.
Application information: Contributes only to pre-selected organizations.
Officers: Marjorie P. Ade, Pres.; William B. Ade, V.P.; Oliver M. Ade, Secy.; Dylan P. Ade, Treas.
EIN: 113358375

37150
Blue Hill Road Foundation, Inc.
c/o Leshkowitz & Co.
270 Madison Ave.
New York, NY 10016
Application address: 8 E. 96th St., New York, NY 10028, tel.: (212) 532-5550
Contact: Fred Lee Barber, Pres.

Established in 1994 in NY.
Donor(s): Fred Lee Barber Co., Inc.
Financial data (yr. ended 12/31/01): Grants paid, $34,925; assets, $1,887,449 (M); gifts received, $150,000; expenditures, $35,584; qualifying distributions, $34,925.
Limitations: Giving primarily in NY.
Officers: Fred Lee Barber, Pres.; David Barber, Secy.; Daniel Barber, Treas.
EIN: 133799422

37151
The Linda and Richard Horowitz Foundation, Inc.
5 Fir Dr.
Kings Point, NY 11024

Established in 1998 in NY.
Donor(s): Richard Horowitz.
Financial data (yr. ended 12/31/01): Grants paid, $34,892; assets, $84,958 (M); gifts received, $30,000; expenditures, $34,892; qualifying distributions, $34,892.
Officer: Richard Horowitz, Mgr.
EIN: 113431167

37152
House of Gross Foundation, Inc.
c/o Jack M. Gross
307 7th Ave., Ste. 2306
New York, NY 10001-5010

Donor(s): Jess E. Gross Co.
Financial data (yr. ended 06/30/01): Grants paid, $34,891; assets, $6,718 (M); gifts received, $20,500; expenditures, $35,005; qualifying distributions, $34,889.

Limitations: Applications not accepted. Giving limited to NY.
Application information: Contributes only to pre-selected organizations.
Officer: Jack M. Gross, Pres.
EIN: 136066596
Codes: CS, CD

37153
Benedict Family Charitable Foundation, Inc.
82 Wall St.
New York, NY 10005-3668

Donor(s): Alfred Benedict.
Financial data (yr. ended 12/31/01): Grants paid, $34,854; assets, $432,646 (L); expenditures, $41,478; qualifying distributions, $34,560.
Limitations: Applications not accepted. Giving primarily in NY.
Application information: Contributes only to pre-selected organizations.
Officers: Dolly Benedict, Pres. and Secy.; Kathy Benedict, V.P. and Treas.
EIN: 132945086

37154
Lilly and Philip Schwebel Foundation Trust
82-29 Abingdon Rd.
Kew Gardens, NY 11415

Established in 1998 in NY.
Financial data (yr. ended 12/31/01): Grants paid, $34,780; assets, $561,805 (M); gifts received, $7,270; expenditures, $41,465; qualifying distributions, $34,780.
Trustee: Lilly Schwebel.
EIN: 137144663

37155
Braus Family Foundation
c/o Todd Joseph, Hodgson
1800 1 M&T Plz.
Buffalo, NY 14203-2391
Application address: 1300 Federal Hwy., No. 202, Boca Raton, FL 33432-2848, tel.: (561) 391-6444
Contact: Jay R. Braus, Tr.

Established in 1995 in NY.
Donor(s): Jay R. Braus.
Financial data (yr. ended 12/31/00): Grants paid, $34,779; assets, $786,049 (M); expenditures, $34,779; qualifying distributions, $34,779.
Application information: Application form not required.
Trustees: Jane Braus, Jay R. Braus, Patricia Braus, Paul Braus.
EIN: 161490867

37156
Barry & Adrienne Gray Foundation, Inc.
707 Westchester Ave., Ste. 405
White Plains, NY 10604-3102 (914) 681-4404

Established in 1994 in NY.
Donor(s): Barry W. Gray.
Financial data (yr. ended 12/31/01): Grants paid, $34,750; assets, $5,982 (M); gifts received, $10,250; expenditures, $35,905; qualifying distributions, $34,732.
Limitations: Applications not accepted.
Application information: Contributes only to pre-selected organizations.
Officers: Barry W. Gray, Pres.; Adrienne Gray, Secy.
EIN: 133792900

37157
Ferer Foundation
1107 5th Ave., Ste. 3S
New York, NY 10128-0145

Established in 1998 in NY.
Donor(s): Christy Ferer.
Financial data (yr. ended 12/31/00): Grants paid, $34,700; assets, $36,467 (M); gifts received, $25,000; expenditures, $38,535; qualifying distributions, $34,680.
Trustees: Christy Ferer, Michael Fuchs, Neal Levin, Howard Milstein.
EIN: 134028435

37158
Mark & Amy Tercek Foundation
85 Broad St., Tax Dept.
New York, NY 10004

Established in 1996 in NY.
Donor(s): Mark R. Tercek.
Financial data (yr. ended 05/31/01): Grants paid, $34,700; assets, $970,818 (M); gifts received, $343,344; expenditures, $53,640; qualifying distributions, $34,700.
Limitations: Applications not accepted.
Application information: Contributes only to pre-selected organizations.
Trustees: Amy Tercek, Mark R. Tercek.
EIN: 133931295

37159
M. & L. Gross Foundation
c/o Max Wasser
132 Nassau St., Ste. 300
New York, NY 10038

Established in 1994 in NY.
Financial data (yr. ended 05/31/01): Grants paid, $34,649; assets, $196,885 (M); gifts received, $20,000; expenditures, $34,759; qualifying distributions, $34,649.
Limitations: Applications not accepted.
Application information: Contributes only to pre-selected organizations.
Trustee: Ronald Gross.
EIN: 137042169

37160
John Winter Family Fund
c/o Richard G. Parker
587 Main St., Ste. 101
New York Mills, NY 13417
Contact: Richard G. Parker, Tr.

Established in 2000 in NY.
Financial data (yr. ended 12/31/01): Grants paid, $34,601; assets, $1,095,772 (M); gifts received, $2,220; expenditures, $46,219; qualifying distributions, $34,601.
Limitations: Giving limited to NY.
Application information: Application form required.
Trustees: Richard G. Parker, Katharine S. Winter.
EIN: 166494705

37161
The Emil and Ann Schachter Foundation
915 E. 24th St.
Brooklyn, NY 11210

Established in 1996 in NJ.
Donor(s): Emil Schachter, Ann Schachter.
Financial data (yr. ended 12/31/01): Grants paid, $34,600; assets, $64,137 (M); gifts received, $27,517; expenditures, $34,696; qualifying distributions, $34,600.
Limitations: Applications not accepted. Giving primarily in Brooklyn, NY.
Application information: Contributes only to pre-selected organizations.
Officers: Emil Schachter, Pres.; Ann Schachter, V.P.
EIN: 113353135

37162
The Kislev Benevolent Foundation
520 W. Nyack Rd.
Monsey, NY 10952

Established in 1997 in NY.
Donor(s): Chaim Breuer, Jack Werzberger.
Financial data (yr. ended 11/30/01): Grants paid, $34,577; assets, $1,129 (M); gifts received, $35,000; expenditures, $35,602; qualifying distributions, $34,577.
Limitations: Applications not accepted.
Application information: Contributes only to pre-selected organizations.
Trustees: Chaim Breuer, Jack Werzberger.
EIN: 137103152

37163
The Harry & Sally Sacks Foundation
c/o Seltzer, Sussman & Habermann
100 Jericho Quadrangle, Ste. 226
Jericho, NY 11753 (631) 435-3600
Contact: Martin S. Sussman, Tr.

Established in 1990 in NY.
Donor(s): Sally Sacks.‡
Financial data (yr. ended 12/31/01): Grants paid, $34,550; assets, $176,533 (M); expenditures, $38,147; qualifying distributions, $34,550.
Trustee: Martin S. Sussman.
EIN: 226498009

37164
Roberts Family Foundation
1112 Park Ave.
New York, NY 10128

Established in 1993 in NY.
Donor(s): Anthony W. Roberts.
Financial data (yr. ended 10/31/01): Grants paid, $34,542; assets, $314,923 (M); expenditures, $39,694; qualifying distributions, $34,542.
Limitations: Applications not accepted.
Application information: Contributes only to pre-selected organizations.
Officers: Anthony W. Roberts, Pres.; Susan M. Roberts, Secy.-Treas.
Director: Jeffrey W. Roberts.
EIN: 133741295

37165
Herbert Lee Grayson Foundation, Inc.
93 Mercer St.
New York, NY 10012-4424 (212) 226-3480
Contact: Neil Grayson, Mgr.

Established in 1996 in NY.
Financial data (yr. ended 12/31/01): Grants paid, $34,520; assets, $351,091 (M); expenditures, $35,795; qualifying distributions, $34,520.
Limitations: Giving primarily in New York, NY.
Officer: Neil Grayson, Mgr.
EIN: 133871882

37166
Stanley M. & Marjorie S. Verby Foundation, Inc.
P.O. Box 363
Holtsville, NY 11742

Donor(s): H. Verby Co., H. Verby Equipment Co., H. Verby Holding Co., Thermo Samlite Industries, Inc.
Financial data (yr. ended 10/31/01): Grants paid, $34,505; assets, $91,711 (M); gifts received, $10,000; expenditures, $34,854; qualifying distributions, $34,505.
Limitations: Applications not accepted. Giving primarily in NY.
Application information: Contributes only to pre-selected organizations.
Officers: Stanley M. Verby, Pres.; Marjorie S. Verby, V.P.
EIN: 116010298

37167
The Michael & Dudley Del Balso Charitable Trust
466 Lexington Ave.
New York, NY 10017

Established in 1986 in NY.
Donor(s): Jennison Assocs. Capital Corp., Michael Del Balso.
Financial data (yr. ended 12/31/01): Grants paid, $34,500; assets, $893,518 (M); gifts received, $10,527; expenditures, $45,027; qualifying distributions, $34,500.
Limitations: Applications not accepted. Giving primarily in CT, NJ, and NY.
Application information: Contributes only to pre-selected organizations.
Trustees: Dudley Del Balso, Michael Del Balso.
EIN: 136878848

37168
Harris J. & Geraldine S. Nelson Foundation
c/o Julius P. Fouts
300 E. 40th St.
New York, NY 10016

Donor(s): Geraldine S. Nelson Trust.
Financial data (yr. ended 12/31/02): Grants paid, $34,500; assets, $718,006 (M); expenditures, $54,286; qualifying distributions, $39,863.
Limitations: Applications not accepted. Giving primarily in MA.
Application information: Contributes only to pre-selected organizations.
Trustees: Richard C. Doyle, Julius P. Fouts.
EIN: 046029911

37169
Richard F. Odenbach Family Charitable Trust
1 E. Main St.
Rochester, NY 14614

Established in 2001 in NY.
Donor(s): Janice S. Odenbach.
Financial data (yr. ended 12/31/01): Grants paid, $34,500; assets, $25,146 (M); gifts received, $60,250; expenditures, $35,104; qualifying distributions, $35,104.
Limitations: Applications not accepted. Giving primarily in NY.
Application information: Contributes only to pre-selected organizations.
Trustees: Virginia Embrey, James S. Grossman, Joseph M. Odenbach, Richard J. Odenbach.
EIN: 166526029

37170
Bais Yisrael Foundation
c/o Y. Israel
1680 59th St.
Brooklyn, NY 11204

Established in 1992 in NY.
Donor(s): Yonoson Israel.
Financial data (yr. ended 12/31/01): Grants paid, $34,477; assets, $57,258 (M); expenditures, $35,125; qualifying distributions, $34,477.
Limitations: Applications not accepted. Giving primarily in NY.
Application information: Contributes only to pre-selected organizations.
Officers: Moshe Ekstein, Pres.; Chava Israel, V.P.; Yonoson Israel, Secy.-Treas.

37170—NEW YORK

EIN: 113137727

37171
The Dress Barn Fund
c/o The Dress Barn, Inc.
30 Dunnigan Dr.
Suffern, NY 10901 (845) 369-4624

Established in 1985 in CT.
Donor(s): The Dress Barn, Inc.
Financial data (yr. ended 12/31/00): Grants paid, $34,468; assets, $3,486 (M); gifts received, $35,000; expenditures, $34,468; qualifying distributions, $34,468.
Limitations: Applications not accepted. Giving primarily in areas of company operations in CT and NY.
Application information: Unsolicited requests for funds not accepted.
Trustees: Elliot S. Jaffe, Roslyn Jaffe.
EIN: 222731305
Codes: CS, CD

37172
The Zern Family Foundation
11 Glen Eagles Dr.
Larchmont, NY 10538
Contact: Allen W. Zern, Tr.

Established in 1997 in NY.
Financial data (yr. ended 12/31/01): Grants paid, $34,450; assets, $476,132 (M); expenditures, $39,005; qualifying distributions, $34,450.
Trustees: Allen W. Zern, Judith H. Zern.
EIN: 137107908

37173
The Adar Foundation
c/o Harry Bram
111 Broadway, Ste. 7
New York, NY 10006

Donor(s): Harry Bram, Sidney Gable.
Financial data (yr. ended 12/31/01): Grants paid, $34,435; assets, $7,092 (M); gifts received, $3,380; expenditures, $34,442; qualifying distributions, $34,435.
Limitations: Applications not accepted. Giving primarily in the metropolitan New York, NY, area.
Application information: Contributes only to pre-selected organizations.
Trustees: Harry Bram, Sidney Gable.
EIN: 136940521

37174
The Sloan Foundation, Inc.
(Formerly Sloan Institute of Applied Technology, Inc.)
c/o Irving Sloan
535 E. 86th St., Apt. 18D
New York, NY 10028

Established in 1990 in NY.
Donor(s): Irving Sloan.
Financial data (yr. ended 06/30/02): Grants paid, $34,369; assets, $269,397 (M); expenditures, $35,286; qualifying distributions, $34,369.
Limitations: Applications not accepted. Giving primarily in New York, NY.
Application information: Contributes only to pre-selected organizations.
Officers: Irving Sloan, Pres.; Hilda Sloan, V.P. and Secy.
EIN: 061308676

37175
Reiss Foundation, Inc.
60 E. 42nd St., Rm. 2201
New York, NY 10165

Financial data (yr. ended 11/30/01): Grants paid, $34,351; assets, $799,254 (M); gifts received, $15,000; expenditures, $35,744; qualifying distributions, $34,351.
Limitations: Applications not accepted. Giving primarily in New York, NY.
Application information: Contributes only to pre-selected organizations.
Officers: Arthur Reiss, Pres.; Linda Heffner, V.P.; Arline Reiss, V.P.; Roberta Miller, Secy.-Treas.
EIN: 136130783

37176
The Parker Family Foundation, Inc.
230 Park Ave., Ste. 1150
New York, NY 10169

Established in 1998 in NY.
Donor(s): Jeffrey Parker, Shelley Lieff.
Financial data (yr. ended 12/31/01): Grants paid, $34,325; assets, $77,400 (M); expenditures, $34,425; qualifying distributions, $34,325.
Limitations: Giving primarily in NY.
Officers: Jeffrey M. Parker, Pres.; Shelley Lieff, V.P.
EIN: 134035373

37177
The Gehring Foundation
c/o Gehring Tricot Corp.
64 Ransom St.
Dolgeville, NY 13329-1333
Application address: 1 W. 34th St., New York, NY 10001, tel.: (212) 279-9700
Contact: Gregory G. Gehring, Tr.

Established in 1964 in NY.
Donor(s): George G. Gehring, Gehring Textiles, Inc., Gehring Tricot Corp., Militex, Inc.
Financial data (yr. ended 12/31/00): Grants paid, $34,316; assets, $327,942 (M); gifts received, $24,500; expenditures, $34,329; qualifying distributions, $34,344.
Limitations: Giving primarily in NY.
Trustees: George G. Gehring, Patricia C. Gehring.
EIN: 136169670

37178
Schonkopf Family Foundation
c/o Albert Schonkopf
580 5th Ave., Ste. 712
New York, NY 10036

Established in 1997 in NY.
Donor(s): Albert Schonkopf.
Financial data (yr. ended 12/31/01): Grants paid, $34,308; assets, $192 (M); gifts received, $34,500; expenditures, $34,944; qualifying distributions, $34,308.
Limitations: Applications not accepted.
Application information: Contributes only to pre-selected organizations.
Trustees: Albert Schonkopf, Tova Schonkopf.
EIN: 133935025

37179
Temple Foundation
c/o Hy Allen
399 Knollwood Rd., Ste. 107
White Plains, NY 10603

Financial data (yr. ended 12/31/00): Grants paid, $34,280; assets, $1 (M); gifts received, $12,144; expenditures, $126,973; qualifying distributions, $34,280.
Limitations: Giving primarily in San Miquel, Mexico.
Director: Roberta Aiken.
EIN: 133920664

37180
Bolshoi Ballet & Opera Foundation, Inc.
c/o T. Bassing Mantenfel, CPA
303 E. 81st St.
New York, NY 10028

Established in 1995 in NY.
Donor(s): Trust for Mutual Understanding, Jeane Welcu, Ginger Minges, Stanislov Maximov, T. Bassing Mantenfel.
Financial data (yr. ended 12/31/01): Grants paid, $34,260; assets, $77,568 (M); expenditures, $72,289; qualifying distributions, $31,092.
Limitations: Applications not accepted. Giving primarily in New York, NY.
Application information: Contributes only to pre-selected organizations.
Officers: Mrs. Paul Lepercq, Chair.; Vladimir Vasiliev, Vice-Chair.; Val Golovitser, Treas.
EIN: 133848110

37181
Rocking Chair Foundation
c/o BMC&F
67 N. Main St.
New City, NY 10956-8070

Established in 1991 in NY and DE.
Donor(s): Jeffrey I. Sussman, Susan H. Sussman.
Financial data (yr. ended 06/30/01): Grants paid, $34,200; assets, $106,433 (M); expenditures, $35,766; qualifying distributions, $34,200.
Limitations: Applications not accepted.
Application information: Contributes only to pre-selected organizations.
Officers and Directors:* Jeffrey I. Sussman,* Pres.; Susan H. Sussman,* Secy.
EIN: 133639647

37182
Arthur I. & Susan Maier Fund, Inc.
320 Glendale Rd.
Scarsdale, NY 10583
Contact: Arthur I. Maier, Pres.

Established in 1985 in NY.
Donor(s): Arthur I. Maier, Susan Maier.
Financial data (yr. ended 11/30/01): Grants paid, $34,170; assets, $767,807 (M); gifts received, $468,592; expenditures, $38,835; qualifying distributions, $34,170.
Limitations: Giving primarily in NY.
Officers: Arthur I. Maier, Pres.; Susan Maier, V.P. and Treas.; Nancy Maier, Secy.
EIN: 133322380

37183
The Harry & Phyllis Manko Family Foundation
40 W. Creek Farms Rd.
Sands Point, NY 11050

Established in 1999 in NY.
Donor(s): Harry Manko.
Financial data (yr. ended 12/31/01): Grants paid, $34,165; assets, $349,256 (M); expenditures, $35,165; qualifying distributions, $34,165.
Limitations: Applications not accepted.
Application information: Contributes only to pre-selected organizations.
Officers: Harry Manko, Pres. and Treas.; Phyllis S. Manko, V.P. and Secy.
Directors: Clifford M. Manko, Elizabeth Manko.
EIN: 113463208

37184
The Schwimmers Foundation
266 Keap St.
Brooklyn, NY 11211
Contact: Leiser Schwimmer

Established in 1998 in NY.

Donor(s): Leiser Schwimmer.
Financial data (yr. ended 12/31/01): Grants paid, $34,103; assets, $8,186 (M); gifts received, $31,700; expenditures, $35,433; qualifying distributions, $34,103.
Trustee: Leiser Schwimmer.
EIN: 116480133

37185
Oswego County Charitable Foundation
44 E. Bridge St.
Oswego, NY 13126

Established in 1999 in DE and NY.
Donor(s): Oswego County Bancorp, Inc.
Financial data (yr. ended 12/31/01): Grants paid, $34,075; assets, $278,737 (M); gifts received, $33,330; expenditures, $34,075; qualifying distributions, $34,075.
Directors: Sara S. Barclay, Gregory J. Kreis, Bruce Phelps, Ruth Sayer, Carl K. Walrath.
EIN: 161570671

37186
The Crunch Foundation, Inc.
800 S. State St.
Syracuse, NY 13202-3015

Established in 1996 in NY.
Financial data (yr. ended 12/31/01): Grants paid, $34,059; assets, $5,281 (M); gifts received, $39,565; expenditures, $36,525; qualifying distributions, $34,059.
Limitations: Giving primarily in Syracuse, NY.
Directors: Howard Dolgon, Alexander S. Pasquale, Todd Smith, Paul Solomon.
Trustee: Vance Lederman.
EIN: 161499992

37187
Josten Fund, Inc.
880 5th Ave., PH F
New York, NY 10021-4951
Contact: Peter Josten, Pres.

Donor(s): Peter Josten.
Financial data (yr. ended 06/30/01): Grants paid, $34,050; assets, $81,777 (M); gifts received, $44,063; expenditures, $35,847; qualifying distributions, $34,910.
Limitations: Giving primarily in New York, NY.
Officer: Peter Josten, Pres. and Treas.
Trustee: Robert Morganthau.
EIN: 136115871

37188
Sam & Anna Lopin Foundation, Inc.
c/o M. Finkelstein
2012 Victory Blvd.
Staten Island, NY 10314-3524
Application address: 320 E. 52nd St., New York, NY 10021, tel.: (212) 758-5045
Contact: Ellen L. Blair, Pres.

Established in 1968.
Donor(s): Sam Lopin,‡ Anna Lopin.‡
Financial data (yr. ended 06/30/00): Grants paid, $34,050; assets, $963,254 (M); expenditures, $40,003; qualifying distributions, $36,688.
Limitations: Giving primarily in NY.
Officers and Director:* Ellen L. Blair,* Pres.; Michael B. Yudin, V.P. and Treas.; William G. Blair, Secy.
EIN: 136275108

37189
New England Society in the City of Brooklyn
c/o David Goodrich
155 Congress St.
Brooklyn, NY 11201-6103
Application address: c/o Harrison Davis, 215 Adams St., Apt. 2-J, Brooklyn, NY 11201, tel.: (718) 625-1291

Established in 1883 in NY.
Financial data (yr. ended 12/31/01): Grants paid, $34,040; assets, $624,770 (M); gifts received, $6,175; expenditures, $40,088; qualifying distributions, $34,524.
Limitations: Giving limited to Brooklyn and Long Island, NY.
Publications: Program policy statement, application guidelines.
Application information: Application form required.
Officers: Franklin Ciaccio, Pres.; Suzanne Lover, V.P.; John Gillespie, Secy.; David Goodrich, Treas.
EIN: 116036708
Codes: GTI

37190
Marina Kellen French Foundation
c/o Joel E. Sammet & Co.
20 Exchange Pl.
New York, NY 10005

Established in 2001 in NY.
Donor(s): Michael Kellen, A.M. & S.M. Kellen Foundation.
Financial data (yr. ended 12/31/01): Grants paid, $34,036; assets, $261,929 (M); gifts received, $295,000; expenditures, $37,032; qualifying distributions, $36,653.
Limitations: Applications not accepted. Giving primarily in NY.
Application information: Contributes only to pre-selected organizations.
Trustee: Marina Kellen French.
EIN: 137270721

37191
Lawrence P. Castellani Family Foundation
403 Main St., Ste 430
Buffalo, NY 14203

Established in 1993 in NY.
Donor(s): Lawrence P. Castellani, Joan J. Castellani.
Financial data (yr. ended 12/31/01): Grants paid, $34,000; assets, $70,012 (M); expenditures, $36,982; qualifying distributions, $35,175.
Limitations: Applications not accepted. Giving primarily in NY.
Application information: Contributes only to pre-selected organizations.
Trustees: Joan J. Castellani, Lawrence P. Castellani.
EIN: 166399132

37192
FII Foundation
c/o Bessemer Trust Co., N.A., Tax Dept.
630 5th Ave.
New York, NY 10111-0100 (212) 708-9216

Established in 1991 in DE.
Donor(s): Allan R. Dragone.
Financial data (yr. ended 12/31/01): Grants paid, $34,000; assets, $225,955 (M); expenditures, $40,586; qualifying distributions, $34,000.
Limitations: Applications not accepted.
Application information: Contributes only to pre-selected organizations.
Officers and Directors:* Allan R. Dragone,* Chair.; Jennifer D. Ouellette,* Pres. and Treas.; Jane B. Dragone, V.P. and Secy.
EIN: 133608974

37193
Julius Kass Family Foundation, Inc.
c/o Stephen Kass-Carter, Ledyard & Milburn
2 Wall St.
New York, NY 10005

Established in 1990 in NY.
Donor(s): Eleanor L. Kass.
Financial data (yr. ended 12/31/01): Grants paid, $34,000; assets, $326,659 (M); expenditures, $39,771; qualifying distributions, $34,000.
Limitations: Applications not accepted. Giving primarily in Dade County, FL, Boston, MA, and the New York, NY area.
Application information: Contributes only to pre-selected organizations.
Directors: Andrew R. Kass, Eleanor L. Kass, James M. Kass, Jeffrey S. Kass, Joan S. Kass, Stephen L. Kass, Emme K. Pedinielli, F. Daniele Pedinielli, Jean-Pierre R. Pedinielli.
EIN: 133598268

37194
Louis & Ida Katz Foundation, Inc.
530 Park Ave.
New York, NY 10021-8015

Established in 1944.
Financial data (yr. ended 12/31/01): Grants paid, $34,000; assets, $942,964 (M); expenditures, $56,157; qualifying distributions, $34,000.
Limitations: Applications not accepted.
Application information: Contributes only to pre-selected organizations.
Trustees: Barbara Goldblatt, Ruth Haberman, Stephen G. Katz.
EIN: 136165617

37195
Nordemann Foundation, Inc.
c/o Reisner & Co.
137 S. Babylon Tpke.
Merrick, NY 11566-4206
Application address: P.O. Box 740, Huntington, NY 11743, tel.: (631) 549-0505
Contact: Hans B.H. Nordemann, Dir.

Established in 1983 in NY.
Donor(s): Bernhard Nordemann.
Financial data (yr. ended 12/31/00): Grants paid, $34,000; assets, $598,263 (M); expenditures, $34,000; qualifying distributions, $34,000.
Limitations: Giving primarily in Huntington, NY.
Application information: Application form not required.
Directors: Bernhard Nordemann, Deborah J. Nordemann, Hans B.H. Nordemann, Helene Nordemann.
EIN: 112667115

37196
Orisha Foundation, Inc.
305 Broadway
New York, NY 10007 (212) 822-1460
Contact: William Waterman, Jr., Pres.

Donor(s): William Waterman, Jr.
Financial data (yr. ended 12/31/01): Grants paid, $34,000; assets, $592,409 (M); expenditures, $35,690; qualifying distributions, $34,000.
Limitations: Giving primarily in New York, NY.
Application information: Application form not required.
Officers and Directors:* William Waterman, Jr.,* Pres. and Treas.; Gertrude B. Pajaron,* V.P. and Secy.; Maria Luisa Nunes,* V.P.
EIN: 237036173

37197
William R. Salomon Scholarship Fund
c/o Salomon Smith Barney Holdings Inc.
666 5th Ave., 3rd Fl., Zone 13
New York, NY 10103

Donor(s): Salomon Brothers Inc.
Financial data (yr. ended 06/30/00): Grants paid, $34,000; assets, $1,856,128 (M); expenditures, $38,275; qualifying distributions, $35,250.
Limitations: Applications not accepted. Giving primarily in areas of company operations.
Officers and Director:* Deryck C. Maughan,* Pres.; Gary P. Hediger, V.P.; Andrew W. Alter, Secy.; Gedale B. Horowitz, Treas.
EIN: 132986194
Codes: CS, CD, GTI

37198
A. E. Ventures Foundation, Inc.
P.O. Box 20069
New York, NY 10011

Donor(s): Anson Peckham, Ellen Peckham.
Financial data (yr. ended 12/31/99): Grants paid, $34,000; assets, $581,543 (M); expenditures, $47,536; qualifying distributions, $33,499.
Limitations: Giving primarily in NY.
Officer: Anson W. Peckham, Pres.
Trustees: Ellen Peckham, Frank Spring, Betty Winkler.
EIN: 133999711

37199
The Fried Foundation
(Formerly Moses Fried Foundation)
20 Sutton Pl. S.
New York, NY 10022-4165
Contact: Patricia Fried, Tr.

Financial data (yr. ended 12/31/01): Grants paid, $33,990; assets, $639,589 (M); expenditures, $53,704; qualifying distributions, $33,990.
Limitations: Giving primarily in New York, NY.
Application information: Application form not required.
Trustee: Patricia S. Fried.
EIN: 136183077

37200
Abraham I. & Jean Sherr Foundation, Inc.
700 Park Ave., Apt. 5B
New York, NY 10021-4930

Financial data (yr. ended 12/31/01): Grants paid, $33,970; assets, $812,617 (M); expenditures, $39,803; qualifying distributions, $33,970.
Limitations: Applications not accepted. Giving primarily in New York, NY.
Application information: Contributes only to pre-selected organizations.
Officer: Rita M. Sherr, Treas.
EIN: 136100738

37201
Robert E. Martin Trust Foundation
c/o HSBC Bank USA
P.O. Box 4203
Buffalo, NY 14240-4203

Established in 1996 in NY.
Financial data (yr. ended 12/31/01): Grants paid, $33,959; assets, $490,539 (M); expenditures, $67,235; qualifying distributions, $33,959.
Limitations: Applications not accepted. Giving primarily in NY.
Application information: Contributes only to pre-selected organizations.
Trustee: HSBC Bank USA.
EIN: 166369746

37202
The Misasi Foundation
12 Mercurio Way
Hampton, NY 12837

Established in 1998 in NY.
Donor(s): Steven Misasi, Frank Misasi.
Financial data (yr. ended 12/31/01): Grants paid, $33,945; assets, $247,910 (M); expenditures, $36,474; qualifying distributions, $33,945.
Limitations: Applications not accepted.
Application information: Contributes only to pre-selected organizations.
Officers: Steven Misasi, Pres. and Treas.; Louise Misasi, V.P. and Secy.; Frank Misasi, V.P.
EIN: 141805957

37203
The Zucker Family Foundation
c/o Samuel Zucker
1132 E. 26th St.
Brooklyn, NY 11210

Established in 1997.
Donor(s): Samuel Zucker, The Zucker Family Trust.
Financial data (yr. ended 12/31/00): Grants paid, $33,942; assets, $280,585 (M); expenditures, $38,263; qualifying distributions, $33,909.
Trustee: Samuel Zucker.
EIN: 113410634

37204
Maurice I. Parisier Foundation, Inc.
c/o Joel Isaacson & Co., Inc.
516 5th Ave., 11th Fl.
New York, NY 10036-7501

Donor(s): Jeanine Plottel, Roland Plottel.
Financial data (yr. ended 12/31/01): Grants paid, $33,900; assets, $665,028 (M); gifts received, $12,574; expenditures, $38,349; qualifying distributions, $33,900.
Limitations: Applications not accepted. Giving primarily in New York, NY.
Application information: Contributes only to pre-selected organizations.
Officers: Jeanine Plottel, Pres.; Roland Plottel, Secy.
EIN: 136220483

37205
Children's Home Association of Genesee County, Inc.
P.O. Box 1730
Batavia, NY 14021-1730 (585) 343-2376

Financial data (yr. ended 12/31/01): Grants paid, $33,874; assets, $539,618 (M); expenditures, $48,132; qualifying distributions, $35,463.
Limitations: Giving limited to Genesee County, NY.
Officers: Martha Spinnegan, Pres.; Rosalie Maguire, V.P.; Leta Sackett, Secy.; Tina Thornton, Treas.
Directors: Mary Ellen Ames, Maryanne Bowman, Susan Dambra, Selby Davis, Chris Fix, Bill McMullen, Sheila Molaro, Jane Scott, Diane Torcello.
EIN: 160743955

37206
The Nassau Foundation
21 Fir Dr.
Great Neck, NY 11024-1528
Contact: Joel Pashcow, Tr.

Established in 1987 in NY.
Financial data (yr. ended 12/31/01): Grants paid, $33,750; assets, $420,565 (M); gifts received, $15,000; expenditures, $34,551; qualifying distributions, $33,750.
Trustee: Joel Pashcow.
EIN: 112837194

37207
Harlyn Foundation, Inc.
24 Central Park S.
New York, NY 10019
Contact: Evelyn B. Silver, Pres.

Established in 1961 in NY.
Financial data (yr. ended 03/31/02): Grants paid, $33,703; assets, $698,829 (M); expenditures, $52,264; qualifying distributions, $33,703.
Limitations: Giving primarily in CA and MA.
Application information: Application form not required.
Officer and Directors:* Evelyn B. Silver,* Pres.; Eduardo Acaso, Andrew J. Silver, Patricia M. Silver.
EIN: 136136916

37208
Friedner Family Foundation
11 Arleigh Rd.
Great Neck, NY 11021 (212) 350-7222
Contact: Ralph Friedner, Tr.

Established in 2000 in NY.
Donor(s): Ralph Friedner.
Financial data (yr. ended 12/31/01): Grants paid, $33,700; assets, $68,908 (M); expenditures, $36,099; qualifying distributions, $33,700.
Limitations: Giving primarily in MA and NY.
Trustees: Audrey Friedner, Ralph Friedner.
EIN: 113523658

37209
Daiwa Securities America Foundation
c/o Brad Brenner
32 Old Slip
New York, NY 10005-3504

Established in 1993 in NY.
Donor(s): Daiwa Securities America Inc.
Financial data (yr. ended 02/28/02): Grants paid, $33,685; assets, $669,713 (M); expenditures, $33,685; qualifying distributions, $33,685.
Limitations: Giving primarily in areas of company operations and its affiliates.
Application information: Unsolicited request for funds not accepted.
Officer and Directors:* Masayasu Ohi,* Chair.; Richard Beggs, Brad Brenner, Hideaki Matsuura.
EIN: 133637516
Codes: CS, CD, GTI

37210
The Gregory & Vera Kiernan Foundation
300 Millwood Rd.
Chappaqua, NY 10514-1424

Established in 1996 in NY.
Donor(s): Gregory Kiernan.
Financial data (yr. ended 12/31/01): Grants paid, $33,675; assets, $10,869 (M); expenditures, $34,742; qualifying distributions, $33,675.
Limitations: Applications not accepted.
Application information: Contributes only to pre-selected organizations.
Trustees: Gregory Kiernan, Vera Kiernan.
EIN: 137095660

37211
The Rabinowitz Foundation, Inc.
911 Park Ave.
New York, NY 10021 (212) 535-7945
Contact: Allan C. Rabinowitz, Secy.

Financial data (yr. ended 06/30/01): Grants paid, $33,662; assets, $772,576 (M); expenditures, $41,044; qualifying distributions, $34,824.

Limitations: Giving primarily in the Northeast.
Application information: Individuals must include financial statements. Organizations must include proof of exempt status.
Officers and Directors:* Wilbur M. Rabinowitz,* Pres.; Allan C. Rabinowitz,* Secy.
EIN: 116015583

37212
The Belvedere Foundation
c/o U.S. Trust
114 W. 47th St., TaxVS
New York, NY 10036

Established in 1992 in NY.
Donor(s): Inisfad Foundation.
Financial data (yr. ended 12/31/01): Grants paid, $33,650; assets, $1,165,914 (M); expenditures, $54,427; qualifying distributions, $33,650.
Limitations: Applications not accepted. Giving primarily on the East Coast.
Application information: Contributes only to pre-selected organizations.
Trustees: Carroll J. Cavanagh, Deirdre B. Cavanagh, Mona Cavanagh, Monica Cavanagh.
EIN: 136992357

37213
The Cousins Charitable Foundation
c/o BDO Seidman, Attn: J. Seidman
330 Madison Ave., 3rd Fl.
New York, NY 10017-5001

Established in 1997 in NY.
Donor(s): Caroline Urvater, Diego L. Hidalgo, Marc V. Schnur.
Financial data (yr. ended 12/31/01): Grants paid, $33,650; assets, $483,135 (M); gifts received, $257,450; expenditures, $35,091; qualifying distributions, $33,650.
Limitations: Applications not accepted.
Application information: Contributes only to pre-selected organizations.
Trustees: Diego L. Hidalgo, Caroline Urvater.
EIN: 133946691

37214
Sohn Foundation
c/o Dalessio, Millner, and Leben, LLP
245 5th Ave., 16th Fl.
New York, NY 10016

Established in 1993.
Donor(s): Robert C. Sohn, Tina Sohn.
Financial data (yr. ended 12/31/01): Grants paid, $33,650; assets, $758,964 (M); gifts received, $3,964; expenditures, $36,678; qualifying distributions, $33,650.
Officers: Tina Sohn, Pres.; Barry Shapiro, V.P. and Secy.; Norman Leben, V.P. and Treas.
EIN: 990306576

37215
Ditchek Family Foundation
1834 E. 28th St.
Brooklyn, NY 11229

Established in 1996 in NY.
Donor(s): Stuart H. Ditchek.
Financial data (yr. ended 12/31/00): Grants paid, $33,600; assets, $2,727 (M); gifts received, $28,400; expenditures, $33,698; qualifying distributions, $33,600.
Limitations: Applications not accepted.
Application information: Contributes only to pre-selected organizations.
Trustees: Frances Ditchek, Stuart H. Ditchek.
EIN: 113353760

37216
The Zurich Foundation, Inc.
c/o Zurich Capital Markets
1 Chase Manhattan Plz., 4th Fl.
New York, NY 10005

Established in 2000 in NY.
Donor(s): Zurich Capital Markets Inc.
Financial data (yr. ended 12/31/01): Grants paid, $33,600; assets, $2,030,645 (M); expenditures, $52,153; qualifying distributions, $50,559.
Limitations: Applications not accepted.
Application information: Contributes only to pre-selected organizations.
Officers: Randall K.C. Kau, Pres. and Exec. Dir.; Stephen J. Lerner, V.P.; Jonathan Lewis, Secy.; Rhoda Chen, Treas.
EIN: 134147153
Codes: CS

37217
Ellen Stark Charitable Trust
c/o HSBC Bank USA
One HSBC Center
Buffalo, NY 14203-2885

Established in 1992 in NY.
Financial data (yr. ended 04/30/02): Grants paid, $33,574; assets, $604,099 (M); expenditures, $41,937; qualifying distributions, $33,574.
Limitations: Applications not accepted. Giving limited to NY.
Application information: Contributes only to pre-selected organizations.
Trustee: HSBC Bank USA.
EIN: 166377339

37218
New York Health & Racquet Club Foundation, Inc.
c/o Fraydun Manocherian
3 New York Plz.
New York, NY 10004

Established around 1985 in NY.
Donor(s): New York Health and Racquet Club, Pamela Equities Inc.
Financial data (yr. ended 04/30/01): Grants paid, $33,536; assets, $1,053,051 (M); gifts received, $20,996; expenditures, $55,565; qualifying distributions, $38,184.
Limitations: Giving limited to New York, NY.
Application information: Unsolicited request for funds not accepted.
Directors: Fraydun Manocherian, John Manocherian, Kimberly Strelov.
EIN: 133165187
Codes: CS, CD

37219
DeRose Family Foundation
c/o Michael J. DeRose
891 Delaware Ave.
Buffalo, NY 14209-2097

Donor(s): Michael J. DeRose, Rita DeRose.
Financial data (yr. ended 12/31/01): Grants paid, $33,500; assets, $541,052 (M); expenditures, $33,684; qualifying distributions, $33,500.
Limitations: Applications not accepted. Giving primarily in Buffalo, NY.
Application information: Contributes only to pre-selected organizations.
Trustee: Michael J. DeRose.
EIN: 161189989

37220
Infant Jesus of Prague, Inc.
P.O. Box 1260
Tupper Lake, NY 12986

Financial data (yr. ended 12/31/01): Grants paid, $33,495; assets, $2,102 (M); gifts received, $32,000; expenditures, $33,520; qualifying distributions, $33,495.
Directors: Jeremiah M. Hayes, Rev. Donald Kramberg, Rev. Robert Shurtleff.
EIN: 161536247

37221
Thorn Family Foundation
400 Bradford Pkwy.
Syracuse, NY 13224-1802

Established in 1999 in NY.
Donor(s): Thomas L. Thorn, Joan Thorn.
Financial data (yr. ended 12/31/01): Grants paid, $33,491; assets, $455,226 (M); gifts received, $50,200; expenditures, $34,813; qualifying distributions, $33,491.
Limitations: Applications not accepted.
Application information: Contributes only to pre-selected organizations.
Trustees: Joan Thorn, Thomas L. Thorn.
EIN: 161575913

37222
Steven A. and Marianne M. Mills Charitable Foundation
16 Prescott Ave.
Bronxville, NY 10708

Established in 2001 in NY.
Donor(s): Steven A. Mills.
Financial data (yr. ended 12/31/01): Grants paid, $33,370; assets, $169,954 (M); gifts received, $205,879; expenditures, $35,668; qualifying distributions, $33,370.
Limitations: Applications not accepted. Giving primarily in NY.
Application information: Contributes only to pre-selected organizations.
Officers: Steven A. Mills, Pres.; Marianne M. Mills, V.P. and Treas.; John Charles Mills, Secy.
EIN: 311764912

37223
Tzdaka Vechesed, Inc.
400 E. 56th St., Ste. 345
New York, NY 10022
Contact: Fred Keshner, Dir.

Established in 1995 in NY.
Donor(s): A.R. Acquisition Corp.
Financial data (yr. ended 12/31/01): Grants paid, $33,350; assets, $484 (M); gifts received, $30,200; expenditures, $37,575; qualifying distributions, $33,350.
Limitations: Giving primarily in Brooklyn, NY.
Application information: Application form not required.
Directors: Yoram Ginach, Fred Keshner, Tova Schapira.
EIN: 133782839

37224
Upstate New York Cancer Research & Education Foundation
211 White Spruce Blvd.
Rochester, NY 14623

Established in 1996 in NY.
Financial data (yr. ended 12/31/00): Grants paid, $33,333; assets, $495,756 (M); gifts received, $211,821; expenditures, $597,434; qualifying distributions, $266,912; giving activities include $266,912 for programs.

37224—NEW YORK

Limitations: Applications not accepted.
Application information: Contributes only to pre-selected organizations.
Officers and Directors:* Laszlo Boros,* V.P.; Jonathan Rubins,* V.P.; Robert F. Asbury,* Secy.; James Fetten,* Treas.
EIN: 161501967

37225
The Neil Family Foundation, Inc.
321 Depew Ave.
Buffalo, NY 14214

Established in 2001 in NY.
Donor(s): Richard A. Neil, Christopher Neil.
Financial data (yr. ended 12/31/01): Grants paid, $33,325; assets, $168,489 (M); gifts received, $200,100; expenditures, $33,342; qualifying distributions, $33,334.
Limitations: Applications not accepted. Giving primarily in Buffalo, NY.
Application information: Contributes only to pre-selected organizations.
Directors: Marilyn E. Neil, Matthew R. Neil, Richard A. Neil.
EIN: 161598200

37226
Dajoy Family Foundation, Inc.
(Formerly Wolowitz Family Foundation, Inc.)
2614 Frances St.
Bellmore, NY 11710

Established in 1986 as the Wolowitz Family Foundation, Inc.; reorganized in 1993 under current name.
Donor(s): David Michael.
Financial data (yr. ended 12/31/01): Grants paid, $33,300; assets, $90,714 (M); gifts received, $47,400; expenditures, $33,300; qualifying distributions, $33,300.
Limitations: Applications not accepted.
Application information: Contributes only to pre-selected organizations.
Officers: David Michael, Pres. and Treas.; Joyce Michael, V.P.; Max Michael, Secy.
EIN: 133384435

37227
Wyman Foundation, Inc.
709 Westchester Ave., Ste. 206
White Plains, NY 10604

Established in 1999 in NY.
Donor(s): William B. Owen.
Financial data (yr. ended 12/31/01): Grants paid, $33,296; assets, $72,931 (M); gifts received, $130; expenditures, $33,426; qualifying distributions, $33,296.
Limitations: Applications not accepted. Giving primarily in White Plains, NY.
Application information: Contributes only to pre-selected organizations.
Officers: William B. Owen, Pres.; Ann L. Owen, V.P.; Phillip L. Owen, Treas.
EIN: 134064024

37228
Joseph & Arkadi Gerney Foundation
860 United Nations Plaza, Ste. 29C
New York, NY 10017-1817

Financial data (yr. ended 12/31/01): Grants paid, $33,275; assets, $673,663 (M); expenditures, $34,099; qualifying distributions, $33,275.
Limitations: Applications not accepted. Giving primarily in MA, MD, and NY.
Application information: Contributes only to pre-selected organizations.
Trustees: Brigitte Gerney, Michael Gerney, Robert S. Puder.

EIN: 237000460

37229
Harold and Beatrice Renfield Foundation, Inc.
10 Gracie Sq.
New York, NY 10028
Contact: Beatrice Renfield, Pres.

Established in 1974 in NY.
Donor(s): Beatrice Renfield.
Financial data (yr. ended 12/31/99): Grants paid, $33,269; assets, $25,686 (M); gifts received, $2,820; expenditures, $35,481; qualifying distributions, $33,889.
Limitations: Giving primarily in New York, NY.
Officers: Beatrice Renfield, Pres.; Martin J. Milston, Secy.-Treas.
Director: Thomas A. Milfe.
EIN: 510156925

37230
The Marx Foundation, Inc.
c/o H.D. Silver and Co.
11 Riverside Dr., Ste. 13HW
New York, NY 10023

Established in 1948 in NY.
Financial data (yr. ended 03/31/02): Grants paid, $33,250; assets, $1,504,180 (M); expenditures, $40,100; qualifying distributions, $33,250.
Limitations: Giving primarily in the greater New York, NY, area.
Officers: Lawrence Marx, Jr., Pres. and Treas.; Lawrence Marx III, V.P.; Paul J. Rachbach, Secy.
EIN: 136087683

37231
Neuhaus Family Charitable Foundation
c/o Armin Neuhaus
12 Cedar Ln.
Monsey, NY 10952

Established in 1998 in NY.
Donor(s): Armin Neuhaus, Magda Neuhaus.
Financial data (yr. ended 12/31/01): Grants paid, $33,250; assets, $228,005 (M); expenditures, $33,250; qualifying distributions, $33,250.
Limitations: Applications not accepted.
Application information: Contributes only to pre-selected organizations.
Trustee: Armin Neuhaus.
EIN: 116498168

37232
P.D.P. Foundation
c/o Polakoff & Michaelson, C.P.A.
90 West St., Ste. 1605
New York, NY 10006

Established in 1967 in CA.
Donor(s): Jacqueline Piatigorsky.
Financial data (yr. ended 07/31/01): Grants paid, $33,248; assets, $700,780 (M); gifts received, $2,187; expenditures, $44,604; qualifying distributions, $33,248.
Limitations: Applications not accepted. Giving primarily in FL.
Application information: Contributes only to pre-selected organizations.
Officers and Trustees:* Jacqueline Piatigorsky,* Pres.; Jephta Drachman,* V.P.; Joram Piatigorsky,* V.P.; Michael A. Varet,* Secy.
EIN: 132617132

37233
The Blumenfeld Family Foundation
73 Carlton Rd.
Monsey, NY 10952-2435
Contact: Alvin Blumenfeld, Pres.

Established in 1988 in NY.
Donor(s): Alvin Blumenfeld, Lois Blumenfeld.

Financial data (yr. ended 10/31/01): Grants paid, $33,243; assets, $35,612 (M); gifts received, $57,350; expenditures, $33,768; qualifying distributions, $33,225.
Limitations: Giving primarily in NY.
Officers: Alvin Blumenfeld, Pres.; Lois Blumenfeld, V.P.; Howard Blumenfeld, Secy.
EIN: 133263128

37234
Aronson Family Charitable Foundation
c/o Joel Aronson
12 Jeffrey Pl.
Monsey, NY 10952

Established in 1999 in NY.
Financial data (yr. ended 10/31/01): Grants paid, $33,240; assets, $1,928,001 (M); gifts received, $1,851,201; expenditures, $37,845; qualifying distributions, $33,240.
Limitations: Applications not accepted. Giving primarily in NY.
Application information: Contributes only to pre-selected organizations.
Officers: Joel Aronson, Pres.; Abraham Igel, V.P.; Seymour Saslow, Secy.; Joseph Levine, Treas.
Director: Simon Bineth.
EIN: 134092176

37235
Irving & Barbara Rousso Foundation
860 United Nations Plz.
New York, NY 10017
Contact: Irving L. Rousso, Pres.

Established in 1993 in NY.
Donor(s): Irving L. Rousso.
Financial data (yr. ended 12/31/01): Grants paid, $33,193; assets, $251,066 (M); gifts received, $10,000; expenditures, $35,295; qualifying distributions, $33,193.
Limitations: Giving primarily in NY.
Application information: Application form not required.
Officer: Irving L. Rousso, Pres.
EIN: 113142291

37236
Jack & Esther Hirth Foundation
210 W. 70th St.
New York, NY 10023

Established in 1997 in NY.
Donor(s): Sam Yellin, Akiva Hirth.
Financial data (yr. ended 12/31/01): Grants paid, $33,175; assets, $35,305 (M); gifts received, $6,200; expenditures, $33,675; qualifying distributions, $33,175.
Limitations: Applications not accepted.
Application information: Contributes only to pre-selected organizations.
Directors: Akiva Hirth, Heshie Hirth, Mordechai Hirth.
EIN: 133952181

37237
The Ginsberg 1995 Charitable Trust
c/o Marvin M. Brown
666 3rd. Ave., Ste. 2700
New York, NY 10017

Established in 1996 in NY.
Donor(s): Schering-Plough Corp.
Financial data (yr. ended 12/31/01): Grants paid, $33,160; assets, $156,057 (M); expenditures, $35,025; qualifying distributions, $32,944.
Limitations: Applications not accepted. Giving primarily in NY.
Application information: Contributes only to pre-selected organizations.
Trustees: Marvin M. Brown, Richard I. Ginsberg.

EIN: 137078691

37238
Abraham Ben Jacob Sutton Foundation, Inc.
310 Franklin Blvd.
Long Beach, NY 11561-3742 (516) 432-8885
Contact: Adele Sutton, Pres.

Donor(s): Adele Sutton.
Financial data (yr. ended 12/31/01): Grants paid, $33,149; assets, $27,172 (M); gifts received, $27,500; expenditures, $33,721; qualifying distributions, $33,149.
Limitations: Giving primarily in NY.
Officer: Adele Sutton, Pres.
EIN: 116036975

37239
Candle in the Darkness Foundation, Inc.
15 Bardolier Ln.
Bay Shore, NY 11706

Established in 1998 in NY.
Financial data (yr. ended 12/31/99): Grants paid, $33,000; assets, $3,551 (M); gifts received, $41,110; expenditures, $37,977; qualifying distributions, $37,977.
Limitations: Applications not accepted.
Application information: Contributes only to pre-selected organizations.
Officers: Stephen Costello, Pres.; Gregg Richard, V.P.; Stanley Skorupski, V.P.
EIN: 113456237

37240
Humanist Trust
c/o Fiduciary Trust
600 5th Ave.
New York, NY 10020 (212) 466-4100
Contact: Jeffery Wolfert

Financial data (yr. ended 12/31/01): Grants paid, $33,000; assets, $663,299 (M); expenditures, $36,913; qualifying distributions, $33,591.
Limitations: Giving primarily in New York, NY.
Trustees: Peter S. Alsop, Alexander G. Houston Bowden, John D. Gordan III.
EIN: 116006530

37241
Lovenheim Foundation, Inc.
c/o Davie, Kaplan & Braverman, PC
1000 1st Federal Plz.
Rochester, NY 14614-1916

Donor(s): Andrew Lovenheim, Clifford Lovenheim.
Financial data (yr. ended 11/30/01): Grants paid, $33,000; assets, $137,328 (M); gifts received, $9,165; expenditures, $40,725; qualifying distributions, $33,000.
Limitations: Applications not accepted. Giving limited to Rochester, NY.
Application information: Contributes only to pre-selected organizations.
Officer: Andrew Lovenheim, Secy.-Treas.
Trustees: Earl Lovenheim, Peter Lovenheim.
EIN: 166032159

37242
Raffiani Family Foundation, Inc.
24 Claudet Way
Eastchester, NY 10709 (914) 829-7121
E-mail: phil@raffiani.com
Contact: Philip Raffiani, Pres.

Established in 1999 in CT and NY.
Donor(s): Philip Raffiani, Laura Raffiani.
Financial data (yr. ended 12/31/01): Grants paid, $33,000; assets, $3,977,053 (M); gifts received, $2,000,000; expenditures, $53,170; qualifying distributions, $33,000.

Limitations: Giving on a national basis.
Officers and Board Members:* Philip Raffiani,* Pres.; Laura Raffiani,* V.P.
EIN: 061566990

37243
The Sumac Foundation
c/o JPMorgan Chase Bank
1121 Ave. of the Americas, Fl. 34
New York, NY 10036-8890

Financial data (yr. ended 03/31/02): Grants paid, $33,000; assets, $683,361 (M); gifts received, $20,000; expenditures, $39,261; qualifying distributions, $33,000.
Limitations: Applications not accepted.
Application information: Contributes only to pre-selected organizations.
Trustees: Donald K. Freebairn, Elizabeth A. Freebairn, Kenneth T. Freebairn, Lucrecia B. Freebairn, William A. Freebairn.
EIN: 137115395

37244
The K. K. & T. Y. Tse Foundation
11 E. 86th St., Apt. 20A
New York, NY 10028-0501

Established in 2000 in NY.
Financial data (yr. ended 12/31/01): Grants paid, $33,000; assets, $709,528 (M); expenditures, $46,437; qualifying distributions, $33,000.
Limitations: Giving primarily in New York, NY.
Trustees: Erik Wei Yi Cheng, Virginia Yung-Chung Tse.
EIN: 316646640

37245
Osborne Memorial Association
34 Grover St.
Auburn, NY 13021
Contact: Frederik R.L. Osborne, Dir.

Financial data (yr. ended 11/30/01): Grants paid, $32,850; assets, $643,856 (M); expenditures, $35,000; qualifying distributions, $32,850.
Limitations: Giving limited to Cayuga County, NY.
Application information: Application form not required.
Directors: Robert R. Gallo, Samuel V. Kennedy, Donna C. Osborne, Frederik R.L. Osborne, Minturn S. Osborn.
EIN: 237230444

37246
George Sakier Foundation, Inc.
c/o Sam J. Nole, C.P.A.
60 E. 42nd St., Ste. 1201
New York, NY 10169

Established in 1984 in DE.
Financial data (yr. ended 12/31/99): Grants paid, $32,850; assets, $373,081 (M); expenditures, $44,299; qualifying distributions, $41,399.
Limitations: Applications not accepted. Giving primarily in New York, NY.
Application information: Contributes only to pre-selected organizations.
Officers: Jacob Israel, Pres.; Mrs. Jacob Israel, Pres.; Robert Coe, Secy.; Philip J. Frank, Treas.
Director: Donald Underwood.
EIN: 133228888

37247
Stanley Penksa Foundation, Inc.
c/o Getman & Getman
P.O. Box 613
Oneonta, NY 13820
Contact: Frank W. Getman, Pres.

Established in 1988 in NY.

Financial data (yr. ended 12/31/01): Grants paid, $32,830; assets, $928,566 (M); expenditures, $35,410; qualifying distributions, $32,830.
Limitations: Giving primarily in Worcester, NY.
Officers: Frank W. Getman, Pres.; Melinda Frost, Secy.-Treas.
Trustee: Henry Cooley.
EIN: 133444662

37248
Bert Mitchell Family Foundation
c/o Mitchell/Titus & Co.
1 Battery Park Plz., 27th Fl.
New York, NY 10004-1405
Contact: Bert N. Mitchell, Chair.

Established in 1992 in NY.
Donor(s): Bert Mitchell, Carole B. Mitchell.
Financial data (yr. ended 12/31/00): Grants paid, $32,797; assets, $245,391 (M); gifts received, $61,200; expenditures, $33,267; qualifying distributions, $32,797.
Limitations: Giving primarily in New York, NY.
Officers and Directors:* Bert N. Mitchell,* Chair. and Pres.; Tracey Mitchell,* Secy.; Carole Mitchell,* Treas.; Robbin Mitchell, Ronald Mitchell.
EIN: 133617553

37249
The Shlomo Boruch & Brina Charitable Trust
65-46 167th St.
Flushing, NY 11365-1938

Financial data (yr. ended 12/31/00): Grants paid, $32,796; assets, $91,996 (M); expenditures, $24,485; qualifying distributions, $32,299.
Limitations: Applications not accepted. Giving primarily in the greater metropolitan New York, NY, area.
Application information: Contributes only to pre-selected organizations.
Trustees: Barbara Perkal, Martin Samson.
EIN: 116446279

37250
ZDS Foundation
1761 E. 21st St.
Brooklyn, NY 11229

Established in 2000 in NY.
Financial data (yr. ended 10/31/00): Grants paid, $32,790; assets, $1,949 (M); gifts received, $37,500; expenditures, $35,896; qualifying distributions, $32,790.
Limitations: Giving primarily in NY.
Trustee: Susan Slater.
EIN: 113518543

37251
Blumberg Foundation, Inc.
111 N. Central Ave.
Hartsdale, NY 10530

Donor(s): William T. Blumberg, Robert Blumberg, Hazel Blumberg.
Financial data (yr. ended 03/31/02): Grants paid, $32,775; assets, $492,593 (M); expenditures, $34,797; qualifying distributions, $32,775.
Limitations: Applications not accepted. Giving primarily in NY.
Application information: Contributes only to pre-selected organizations.
Officers and Directors:* Hazel Blumberg,* Pres.; Robert Blumberg,* V.P.; Louise Albin,* Secy.-Treas.
EIN: 136109155

37252
Richard Dollinger Trust
c/o HSBC Bank, USA
P.O. Box 4203, 17th Fl.
Buffalo, NY 14240

Established in 1998 in NY.
Financial data (yr. ended 12/31/99): Grants paid, $32,755; assets, $623,923 (M); expenditures, $45,005; qualifying distributions, $33,609.
Limitations: Applications not accepted.
Application information: Contributes only to pre-selected organizations.
Trustee: HSBC Bank USA.
EIN: 161548435

37253
Kane Family Foundation
c/o U.S. Trust
114 W. 47th St., TaxVAS
New York, NY 10036

Established in 1987 in NJ.
Financial data (yr. ended 12/31/00): Grants paid, $32,720; assets, $657,744 (M); gifts received, $82,192; expenditures, $43,046; qualifying distributions, $34,720.
Limitations: Applications not accepted. Giving on a national basis.
Application information: Contributes only to pre-selected organizations.
Trustees: Laura L. Kane, Scott C. Kane, Shirley T. Kane, Ward T. Kane.
EIN: 222783771

37254
Stuart & Mildred Reiner Foundation
31 Haights Cross Rd.
Chappaqua, NY 10514

Established in 1985 in NY.
Donor(s): Mildred Reiner.
Financial data (yr. ended 12/31/01): Grants paid, $32,698; assets, $137,624 (M); gifts received, $1,000; expenditures, $33,366; qualifying distributions, $32,698.
Limitations: Applications not accepted. Giving primarily in NY.
Application information: Contributes only to pre-selected organizations.
Officers: Mildred Reiner, Pres.; Daniel Reiner, V.P.; Peter Reiner, Secy.; Andrew Reiner, Treas.
EIN: 133317252

37255
Marlissa & John E. Westerfield Foundation
26 Locust Ln.
Bronxville, NY 10708
Contact: John Westerfield, Tr.

Established in 2000 in NY.
Donor(s): John E. Westerfield, Marlissa Westerfield.
Financial data (yr. ended 12/31/01): Grants paid, $32,541; assets, $108,221 (M); gifts received, $42,020; expenditures, $37,530; qualifying distributions, $32,541.
Limitations: Giving primarily in NY.
Trustees: John E. Westerfield, Marlissa Westerfield, Evan B. Westerfield.
EIN: 134149868

37256
Life Saving Benevolent Association of New York
c/o Helen Delaney
140 Broadway
New York, NY 10005-1101

Established in 1849 in NY.
Financial data (yr. ended 12/31/01): Grants paid, $32,535; assets, $759,390 (M); expenditures, $40,500; qualifying distributions, $39,897.
Limitations: Giving primarily in NY.
Application information: Application form required.
Officers and Directors:* Klaus G. Dorfi,* Co-Chair. and C.E.O.; Niels W. Johnsen,* Co-Chair.; Richard A. Cook,* Co-Pres.; Walter Kramer,* Co-Pres.; Capt. James McNamara,* Co-Pres.; Kermit C. Smith,* Co-Pres.; Gordon Stewart,* Co-Pres.; Daniel H. Olmsted,* V.P.; Richard DeSimone,* Sr. V.P., Marine; Joseph P. Decaminada,* Secy.-Treas.; Cornelius E. Golding,* C.F.O.; Rev. Peter Larom, Exec. Dir.; J. Carter Bacot, Percy Chubb III, Emil Kratovil, John J. Mackowski, George M. Marshall, and 8 additional directors.
EIN: 136104148
Codes: GTI

37257
The Anna M. Day Foundation
c/o Brown Brothers Harriman Trust Co.
63 Wall St.
New York, NY 10005

Established in 2000 in VA.
Donor(s): Anna M. Day.
Financial data (yr. ended 12/31/01): Grants paid, $32,500; assets, $553,229 (M); gifts received, $128,206; expenditures, $37,190; qualifying distributions, $32,500.
Limitations: Applications not accepted.
Application information: Contributes only to pre-selected organizations.
Officer: Anna M. Day.
Directors: Edward G. Dinwiddie, Elizabeth Day Dinwiddie.
EIN: 542000049

37258
The Ruder Family Foundation, Inc.
(Formerly William & Helen Ruder Family Foundation, Inc.)
301 E. 57th St., 3rd Fl.
New York, NY 10022-1304

Established in 1952 in NY.
Donor(s): William Ruder, Helen Ruder.
Financial data (yr. ended 11/30/01): Grants paid, $32,500; assets, $57,102 (M); expenditures, $33,438; qualifying distributions, $32,500.
Limitations: Applications not accepted. Giving primarily in NY.
Application information: Contributes only to pre-selected organizations.
Officer: William Ruder, Pres. and Treas.
EIN: 136179259

37259
The Salzman Family Foundation
Goldman Sachs & Co.
85 Broad St., Tax Dept.
New York, NY 10004

Established in 1994.
Donor(s): Jack L. Salzman.
Financial data (yr. ended 08/31/01): Grants paid, $32,500; assets, $115,811 (M); expenditures, $33,579; qualifying distributions, $32,500.
Limitations: Applications not accepted.
Application information: Contributes only to pre-selected organizations.
Trustees: Jack L. Salzman, Rene Salzman.
EIN: 133801225

37260
The Charles and Samuel Meltzer Foundation, Inc.
250 E. Hartsdale Ave., Ste. 44
Hartsdale, NY 10530

Financial data (yr. ended 12/31/01): Grants paid, $32,485; assets, $154,364 (M); expenditures, $33,672; qualifying distributions, $32,485.
Limitations: Applications not accepted. Giving primarily in New York, NY.
Application information: Contributes only to pre-selected organizations.
Officers: Steven Meltzer, Secy.; Harvey Silverman, Treas.
EIN: 132917938

37261
M Y B Foundation
1327H 46th St.
Brooklyn, NY 11219

Established in 2000 in NY.
Financial data (yr. ended 12/31/01): Grants paid, $32,469; assets, $10,091 (M); gifts received, $36,000; expenditures, $32,497; qualifying distributions, $32,469.
Limitations: Applications not accepted.
Application information: Contributes only to pre-selected organizations.
Trustee: Ann Kahn.
EIN: 116472759

37262
Nathaniel L. & Etta M. Goldstein Foundation
c/o Morris & McVeigh, LLP
767 3rd Ave.
New York, NY 10017-2023

Established in 1963.
Financial data (yr. ended 10/31/01): Grants paid, $32,415; assets, $29,670 (M); gifts received, $18,000; expenditures, $32,440; qualifying distributions, $32,411.
Limitations: Applications not accepted. Giving primarily in New York, NY.
Application information: Contributes only to pre-selected organizations.
Trustees: Steven Goldstein, Lois E. Lowenstein.
EIN: 136144078

37263
The Rebecca Amitai & Morty Schaja Foundation, Inc.
c/o Spear, Leeds & Kellogg
120 Broadway, Ste. 840
New York, NY 10271

Established in 1997 in NY.
Donor(s): Rebecca Amitai, Morty Schaja.
Financial data (yr. ended 09/30/01): Grants paid, $32,398; assets, $496,390 (M); gifts received, $210,995; expenditures, $33,476; qualifying distributions, $31,078.
Limitations: Applications not accepted.
Application information: Contributes only to pre-selected organizations.
Officers: Rebecca Amitai, Pres. and Treas.; Morty Schaja, V.P. and Secy.; Regine Schaja, V.P.
EIN: 133986720

37264
Alan & Elisabeth H. Doft Foundation, Inc.
c/o Doft & Co., Inc.
645 Madison Ave., 16th Fl.
New York, NY 10022-1010

Established in 1995 in NY.
Financial data (yr. ended 12/31/01): Grants paid, $32,283; assets, $619,711 (M); expenditures, $33,368; qualifying distributions, $32,283.

Limitations: Applications not accepted. Giving primarily in New York, NY.
Application information: Contributes only to pre-selected organizations.
Officers: Alan Doft, Pres.; Elisabeth Doft, Secy.
Directors: Jonathan Doft, Michael Doft, Rachel Doft.
EIN: 133748894

37265
Gutnik Family Foundation
2677 National Dr.
Brooklyn, NY 11234

Established in 1999 in NY.
Donor(s): Oleg Gutnik.
Financial data (yr. ended 12/31/01): Grants paid, $32,270; assets, $27,954 (M); expenditures, $33,427; qualifying distributions, $32,270.
Limitations: Applications not accepted. Giving primarily in NY.
Application information: Contributes only to pre-selected organizations.
Trustee: Oleg Gutnik.
EIN: 113508581

37266
Peter A. Ridings Memorial Foundation
8 Audubon Dr.
Cazenovia, NY 13035 (315) 655-2917
Contact: D. John Ridings, Mgr.

Donor(s): Jane B. Ridings, D. John Ridings.
Financial data (yr. ended 12/31/01): Grants paid, $32,260; assets, $626,709 (M); expenditures, $34,419; qualifying distributions, $32,260.
Limitations: Giving primarily in NY.
Application information: Application form not required.
Officer and Trustees:* D. John Ridings,* Mgr.; Jane B. Ridings, Peter B. Ridings.
EIN: 156021539

37267
Joseph & Lilly Aboudi Foundation
c/o Elan Eliau
1410 Broadway, Ste. 901
New York, NY 10018

Established in 1997 in NY.
Donor(s): XES-NY, Ltd.
Financial data (yr. ended 12/31/01): Grants paid, $32,201; assets, $2,206 (M); gifts received, $30,000; expenditures, $34,618; qualifying distributions, $34,618.
Limitations: Applications not accepted. Giving primarily in NY.
Application information: Contributes only to pre-selected organizations.
Trustee: Elan Eliau.
EIN: 134036636

37268
Richard A. & James F. Corroon Foundation, Inc.
c/o Willis Corroon Corp. of NY
7 Hanover Sq., 11th Fl.
New York, NY 10004 (212) 344-8888

Established in 1968.
Donor(s): John A. Corroon, Robert F. Corroon,‡ Claire C. Shields, Mari C. Stearns.
Financial data (yr. ended 12/31/99): Grants paid, $32,200; assets, $762,618 (M); expenditures, $34,340; qualifying distributions, $32,200.
Limitations: Applications not accepted. Giving on a national basis.
Application information: Contributes only to pre-selected organizations.
Officers and Trustees:* Richard F. Corroon, Pres.; John A. Corroon, V.P.; James M. Corroon,* Secy.-Treas.; Christopher L. Corroon.
EIN: 237000812

37269
The Safir Foundation, Inc.
317 Cantitoe St.
Bedford Hills, NY 10507

Donor(s): Alan P. Safir, Marc A. Safir.
Financial data (yr. ended 11/30/01): Grants paid, $32,190; assets, $62,792 (M); gifts received, $17,203; expenditures, $35,196; qualifying distributions, $32,919.
Limitations: Applications not accepted. Giving primarily in New York, NY.
Application information: Contributes only to pre-selected organizations.
Officers: Alan P. Safir, Pres.; Joan A. Safir, V.P.
EIN: 222327444

37270
Eugenie S. Wright Foundation, Inc.
c/o Meighan & Necarsulmer
P.O. Box 370
Mamaroneck, NY 10543
Contact: Jefferson D. Meighan, Pres.

Established in 1948 in NY.
Donor(s): Eugenie S. Wright.‡
Financial data (yr. ended 12/31/01): Grants paid, $32,180; assets, $970,012 (M); expenditures, $65,810; qualifying distributions, $32,180.
Limitations: Giving primarily in Larchmont, Mamaroneck, and Westchester County, NY.
Officers: Jefferson D. Meighan, Pres. and Treas.; Elisa Colleluori, Secy.
EIN: 136130913

37271
Miller-Morse Family Foundation
c/o David Morse
6 Chestnut Ave.
Bronxville, NY 10708

Established in 1999 in NY.
Donor(s): Kimberly Morse, David Morse.
Financial data (yr. ended 12/31/01): Grants paid, $32,150; assets, $100,587 (M); gifts received, $55,000; expenditures, $34,712; qualifying distributions, $32,150.
Limitations: Applications not accepted.
Application information: Contributes only to pre-selected organizations.
Trustees: David Morse, Kimberly Morse.
EIN: 137210208

37272
The Rodolitz Foundation
849 Smith Ln.
Woodmere, NY 11598 (718) 649-1750
Contact: Allan J. Rodolitz, Pres.

Financial data (yr. ended 04/30/02): Grants paid, $32,150; assets, $198,219 (M); gifts received, $19,900; expenditures, $34,719; qualifying distributions, $32,150.
Officers: Allan Rodolitz, Pres.; Anita Rodolitz, Secy.
EIN: 112827598

37273
W & C Corp., Inc.
24 Estate Dr.
Jericho, NY 11753

Established in 1994 in NY.
Donor(s): Walter Cosel.
Financial data (yr. ended 12/31/01): Grants paid, $32,141; assets, $648,641 (M); expenditures, $45,290; qualifying distributions, $32,141.
Limitations: Giving primarily in upstate NY.
Trustee: Elinore Cullen.
EIN: 113225006

37274
The Jeffrey P. Reich Family Foundation
c/o David M. Brickman, C.P.A.
6 E. 43rd St., 19th Fl.
New York, NY 10017

Established in 1996 in NY.
Donor(s): Jeffrey P. Reich.
Financial data (yr. ended 12/31/00): Grants paid, $32,100; assets, $714 (M); gifts received, $33,375; expenditures, $32,100; qualifying distributions, $31,942.
Limitations: Applications not accepted. Giving primarily in Washington, DC.
Application information: Contributes only to pre-selected organizations.
Trustees: Jeffrey P. Reich, Stacy Patterson Reich.
EIN: 133911296

37275
Stupell Foundation, Inc.
79 Penn Rd.
Scarsdale, NY 10583 (914) 472-6357
Contact: Audrey Dorsen, Dir.

Established in 1980 in NY.
Donor(s): Leo K. Stupell.‡
Financial data (yr. ended 05/31/01): Grants paid, $32,100; assets, $742,577 (M); expenditures, $34,854; qualifying distributions, $34,382.
Limitations: Giving primarily in NY.
Application information: Application form not required.
Directors: Rosalie Antin, Audrey Dorsen.
EIN: 136106669

37276
M & S Foundation, Inc.
405 Lexington Ave., Ste. 2634
New York, NY 10174-2699

Established in 1986 in NJ.
Financial data (yr. ended 12/31/01): Grants paid, $32,090; assets, $773,115 (M); expenditures, $39,736; qualifying distributions, $32,090.
Limitations: Applications not accepted. Giving primarily in New York, NY.
Application information: Contributes only to pre-selected organizations.
Trustees: Michael C. Palitz, Suzanne L. Palitz.
EIN: 222787681

37277
Gage Fund, Inc.
c/o Alan Kroll, Davis & Gilbert
1740 Broadway
New York, NY 10016
Application address: 310 Stonehill Rd., Pound Ridge, NY 10576; tel.: (914) 764-5256
Contact: Michele L. Gage, V.P.

Donor(s): Robert T. Gage.
Financial data (yr. ended 11/30/99): Grants paid, $32,040; assets, $1,238,182 (M); gifts received, $21,000; expenditures, $32,890; qualifying distributions, $32,340.
Limitations: Giving limited to Pound Ridge, NY.
Application information: Application form not required.
Officers: Robert T. Gage, Pres.; Michele L. Gage, V.P.; Thomas Gage, V.P.
EIN: 136197404

37278
The Biddle Family Foundation
970 Bullis Rd.
P.O. Box 420
Elma, NY 14059-0420

Established in 2001 in NY.
Donor(s): James E. Biddle, Sr., James E. Biddle, Jr.

37278—NEW YORK

Financial data (yr. ended 12/31/01): Grants paid, $32,000; assets, $13,857 (M); gifts received, $45,864; expenditures, $32,016; qualifying distributions, $32,000.
Limitations: Applications not accepted.
Application information: Contributes only to pre-selected organizations.
Officers: James E. Biddle, Pres.; Kevin G. Biddle, V.P.; James E. Biddle, Jr., Secy.-Treas.
EIN: 311799154

37279
Fannie C. Hyde Testamentary Trust
c/o Chemung Canal Trust Co.
P.O. Box 1522
Elmira, NY 14902 (800) 836-3711
Contact: Doug Bissonette

Established in 1963 in NY.
Donor(s): Fannie C. Hyde.‡
Financial data (yr. ended 04/30/02): Grants paid, $32,000; assets, $1,538,349 (M); expenditures, $57,976; qualifying distributions, $32,000.
Limitations: Giving limited to the village of Owego, NY.
Publications: Annual report.
Application information: Application form not required.
Trustee: Chemung Canal Trust Co.
EIN: 156020596

37280
Loeb Rhoades Employee Welfare Fund, Inc.
61 Broadway
New York, NY 10006 (212) 483-7047

Donor(s): Loeb Partners Corporation.
Financial data (yr. ended 12/31/01): Grants paid, $32,000; assets, $77,991 (M); expenditures, $32,227; qualifying distributions, $32,000.
Limitations: Applications not accepted. Giving limited to headquarters city and major operating areas.
Application information: Contributes only to pre-selected organizations.
Trustees: Thomas L. Kempner, Andrew J. McLaughlin, Jr.
EIN: 132618946
Codes: CS, CD

37281
The Statue Foundation, Inc.
c/o B. Eisold
353 Central Park West
New York, NY 10025

Established in 1997 in NY.
Donor(s): Barbara K. Eisold.
Financial data (yr. ended 12/31/01): Grants paid, $32,000; assets, $404,778 (M); gifts received, $21,033; expenditures, $63,592; qualifying distributions, $32,000.
Limitations: Applications not accepted. Giving primarily in New York, NY.
Application information: Contributes only to pre-selected organizations.
Officer: Barbara K. Eisold, Pres.
Directors: Elizabeth Eisold Blaylock, Kenneth Eisold, Katherine Eisold Miller.
EIN: 133947134

37282
The Todd A. Stuart Foundation, Inc.
c/o Spear, Leeds & Kellogg
120 Broadway
New York, NY 10271

Established in 1999 in NY.
Donor(s): Todd A. Stuart.
Financial data (yr. ended 06/30/01): Grants paid, $32,000; assets, $1,033,712 (M); gifts received, $1,010,712; expenditures, $44,656; qualifying distributions, $32,100.
Limitations: Applications not accepted.
Application information: Contributes only to pre-selected organizations.
Officers: Todd A. Stuart, Pres. and Treas.; Gregg L. Stuart, V.P.; Lisa B. Stuart, Secy.
EIN: 134023827

37283
Harry & Rose Zaifert Foundation
c/o Robert A. Kadison, C.P.A., PC
420 Lexington Ave., Ste. 2020
New York, NY 10170

Financial data (yr. ended 12/31/01): Grants paid, $32,000; assets, $552,169 (M); expenditures, $38,117; qualifying distributions, $32,000.
Limitations: Applications not accepted. Giving primarily in NY.
Application information: Contributes only to pre-selected organizations.
Officers: Ina Haas, Pres. and Treas.; Jerome Haas, V.P. and Secy.
Director: Bernard Newman.
EIN: 226046906

37284
Carl & Rene Cohen Foundation, Inc.
c/o Goldstein, Golub, Kessler & Co., PC
1185 Ave. of the Americas
New York, NY 10036

Financial data (yr. ended 12/31/01): Grants paid, $31,887; assets, $1,028,265 (M); expenditures, $43,527; qualifying distributions, $31,887.
Limitations: Applications not accepted. Giving primarily in Santa Fe, NM, and New York, NY.
Application information: Contributes only to pre-selected organizations.
Officer: James Cohen, Pres.
Director: Robert M. Cohen.
EIN: 136096255

37285
Max Solomon Foundation, Inc.
c/o Lester Tomback
88 Lake Shore Dr.
Eastchester, NY 10709

Established in 1955 in NY.
Financial data (yr. ended 04/30/02): Grants paid, $31,850; assets, $392,458 (M); expenditures, $35,969; qualifying distributions, $33,909.
Limitations: Applications not accepted. Giving primarily in NY.
Application information: Contributes only to pre-selected organizations.
Officers and Directors:* Lester E. Tomback,* Pres. and Treas.; Elinor T. Fine,* V.P. and Secy.; Edward Gaines, David M. Levitan.
EIN: 136059184

37286
Walter and Sylvia Brownstone Foundation
c/o CBIZ Business Solutions, Inc.
225 W. 34th St., Rm. 400
New York, NY 10122 (212) 244-1100
Contact: Clyde R. Brownstone, Pres.

Established in 1956 in NY.
Donor(s): Members of the Brownstone family.
Financial data (yr. ended 03/31/02): Grants paid, $31,840; assets, $562,931 (M); expenditures, $38,422; qualifying distributions, $31,366.
Limitations: Giving primarily in the metropolitan New York, NY, area.
Officer: Clyde R. Brownstone, Pres. and Secy.-Treas.
EIN: 136096687

37287
The Copen Foundation
c/o Robert S. Lusthaus
497 S. Oyster Bay Rd.
Plainview, NY 11803-3316
Application address: 70 Woodmere Blvd., Woodmere, NY 11598, tel.: (516) 569-5391
Contact: Ileen Gusoff, Pres.

Financial data (yr. ended 12/31/01): Grants paid, $31,838; assets, $190,458 (M); expenditures, $36,199; qualifying distributions, $31,838.
Limitations: Giving primarily in NY.
Officers: Ileen Gusoff, Pres. and Treas.; Pamela Cott, V.P. and Secy.
EIN: 116018654

37288
The TLK Foundation
(Formerly TLK Foundation, Inc.)
c/o Tanton & Co.
37 W. 57th St.
New York, NY 10019

Established in 1997 in NJ.
Donor(s): Ilan Kaufthal.
Financial data (yr. ended 12/31/01): Grants paid, $31,800; assets, $437,929 (M); expenditures, $34,705; qualifying distributions, $31,800.
Officers: Joshua Kaufthal, Pres.; Linda Kaufthal, Secy.; David Kaufthal, Treas.
EIN: 133936569

37289
Audio Engineering Society Educational Foundation, Inc.
60 E. 42nd St.
New York, NY 10165
Contact: Emil Torick, Pres.

Established in 1983 in NY.
Financial data (yr. ended 12/31/01): Grants paid, $31,750; assets, $299,811 (M); gifts received, $23,500; expenditures, $33,404; qualifying distributions, $33,314.
Limitations: Giving on a national basis.
Application information: Application form required.
Officers and Directors:* Emil Torick,* Pres.; Donald J. Plunkett,* Secy.; Roger K. Furness, Treas.; John J. Bubbers, Julius P. Fouts.
EIN: 112664807
Codes: GTI

37290
The Khatib Foundation, Inc.
86-74 Palermo St.
Hollis, NY 11423

Established in 1999 in NY.
Donor(s): Reza Khatib, M.D., Georgianna Khatib.
Financial data (yr. ended 12/31/01): Grants paid, $31,750; assets, $1 (M); gifts received, $130,000; expenditures, $40,770; qualifying distributions, $31,750.
Directors: David P. Callahan, Georgianna Khatib, Reza Khatib, M.D.
EIN: 113522346

37291
The Rosenberger Foundation, Inc.
c/o Robert Todd Lang
767 5th Ave.
New York, NY 10022 (212) 310-8200

Financial data (yr. ended 11/30/01): Grants paid, $31,750; assets, $358,661 (M); expenditures, $35,597; qualifying distributions, $31,750.
Limitations: Giving primarily in FL, MA, and NY.

Officers: Mrs. Leo Rosenberger, Chair.; Robert Todd Lang, Pres. and Treas.; Gerrie Soman, V.P.; Roger Soman, V.P.; Joann Lang, Secy.
EIN: 136129057

37292
The Frank G. Raichle Foundation
800 Fleet Bank Bldg.
Buffalo, NY 14202-2292 (716) 843-3846
E-mail: rhalpern@jaeckle.com
Contact: Ralph L. Halpern, Tr.

Established in 1983 in NY.
Donor(s): Joelle G. Raichle, Frank G. Raichle.‡
Financial data (yr. ended 12/31/01): Grants paid, $31,715; assets, $868,955 (M); gifts received, $26,228; expenditures, $33,775; qualifying distributions, $33,775.
Limitations: Applications not accepted. Giving primarily in western NY state.
Application information: Contributes only to pre-selected organizations.
Trustees: Ralph L. Halpern, Joelle G. Raichle.
EIN: 112654942

37293
James P. Gordon Foundation
c/o JPMorgan Chase Bank
130 S. Main St.
Canandaigua, NY 14424
Application address: Janice Mosher, c/o JPMorgan Chase Bank, 5 Seneca St., Geneva, NY 14456, tel.: (716) 394-7675; E-mail: janis.l.mosher@chase.com
Contact: Janis Mosher, V.P., JPMorgan Chase Bank

Financial data (yr. ended 12/31/01): Grants paid, $31,714; assets, $924,118 (M); expenditures, $43,049; qualifying distributions, $32,758.
Limitations: Giving primarily in Penn Yan and Yates County, NY.
Trustee: JPMorgan Chase Bank.
EIN: 166226344

37294
The Ellen and Andrew G. Celli Foundation, Inc.
c/o Eli Greenberg
270 Madison Ave.
New York, NY 10016
Application address: 10 E. 50th St., New York, NY 10022

Established in 1999 in DE.
Donor(s): Ellen Unterberg Celli, Andrew G. Celli, Jr., Emily Satloff.
Financial data (yr. ended 03/31/02): Grants paid, $31,705; assets, $2,549 (M); gifts received, $24,159; expenditures, $32,776; qualifying distributions, $31,705.
Limitations: Giving primarily in NY.
Directors: Andrew G. Celli, Jr., Ellen Unterberg Celli, Emily Satloff.
EIN: 134087933

37295
Foundation "Q"
c/o Arye Ringel
1750 44th St.
Brooklyn, NY 11204-1050

Established in 1990 in NY.
Donor(s): Stuart V. Rubinfeld.
Financial data (yr. ended 05/31/02): Grants paid, $31,699; assets, $31,443 (M); gifts received, $45,000; expenditures, $31,779; qualifying distributions, $31,699.
Limitations: Applications not accepted. Giving primarily in the New York, NY, area.
Application information: Contributes only to pre-selected organizations.

Trustees: Stuart V. Rubinfeld, Teena C. Rubinfeld.
EIN: 113014673

37296
Dreizel Glueck Bikur Cholim Foundation
1333 Broadway, Ste. 516
New York, NY 10081
Application Address: 200 Riverside Blvd., Apt. 6N, New York, NY 10069
Contact: Jacob Glueck, Tr.

Financial data (yr. ended 12/31/01): Grants paid, $31,695; assets, $457,517 (M); gifts received, $75,000; expenditures, $33,509; qualifying distributions, $31,695.
Limitations: Giving primarily in NY.
Trustee: Jacob Glueck.
EIN: 133718076

37297
The Ernest and Joan Liu Foundation
c/o BCRS Assocs.
67 Wall St., 8th Fl.
New York, NY 10005

Established in 1989 in NJ.
Donor(s): Ernest S. Liu.
Financial data (yr. ended 03/31/02): Grants paid, $31,665; assets, $565,724 (M); gifts received, $120; expenditures, $33,415; qualifying distributions, $31,665.
Limitations: Applications not accepted. Giving primarily in New York, NY.
Application information: Contributes only to pre-selected organizations.
Trustees: Erica Sze-Hua Liu, Ernest S. Liu, Joan S. Liu.
EIN: 133531987

37298
Bernard J. & Helen Sheftman Foundation, Inc.
c/o Jack Scharf
630 3rd Ave., 18th Fl.
New York, NY 10017

Financial data (yr. ended 12/31/01): Grants paid, $31,655; assets, $736,997 (M); expenditures, $38,902; qualifying distributions, $31,655.
Limitations: Applications not accepted.
Application information: Contributes only to pre-selected organizations.
Officers: Jack Scharf, Pres.; Sherman S. Lawrence, Secy.
EIN: 237399857

37299
Panchiaki Korais Society, Inc.
c/o Psyllos & Psyllos
213-35 40th Ave.
Bayside, NY 11361

Financial data (yr. ended 06/30/01): Grants paid, $31,650; assets, $582,037 (M); gifts received, $4,145; expenditures, $174,063; qualifying distributions, $31,650.
Limitations: Applications not accepted. Giving primarily in Queens County, NY.
Application information: Contributes only to pre-selected organizations.
Officers and Directors:* Stelios Eerazounis,* Pres.; James Psaltakis,* V.P.; Emmanuel Moraitis,* Treas.
EIN: 237024590

37300
Ungar Family Foundation
c/o Jane Ungar
15 W. 81st St., Ste. 5B
New York, NY 10024-6022
Contact: Jane Ungar, Tr.

Established in 2001 in NY.

Donor(s): Jane Ungar, Elizabeth Ungar.
Financial data (yr. ended 12/31/01): Grants paid, $31,648; assets, $22,019 (M); gifts received, $58,238; expenditures, $33,727; qualifying distributions, $33,727.
Limitations: Giving primarily in New York, NY.
Application information: Application form not required.
Trustees: Elizabeth Ungar, Jane Ungar.
EIN: 134152714

37301
Peggy and Peter Pressman Family Foundation
125 E. 72nd St.
New York, NY 10021

Established in 1999 in NY.
Donor(s): Peggy Pressman, Peter Pressman.
Financial data (yr. ended 11/30/01): Grants paid, $31,600; assets, $682,503 (M); expenditures, $36,740; qualifying distributions, $31,600.
Limitations: Applications not accepted.
Application information: Contributes only to pre-selected organizations.
Officers: Peggy Pressman, Pres.; Peter Pressman, V.P.; Stanley Fishkin, Secy.; Stephen Edelstein, Treas.
EIN: 134088192

37302
Cole Family Foundation
c/o Tag Associates, R. Transport
75 Rockefeller Plz., Ste. 900
New York, NY 10019

Established in 1999 in NY.
Donor(s): Kenneth Cole.
Financial data (yr. ended 04/30/01): Grants paid, $31,500; assets, $553,830 (M); gifts received, $31,500; expenditures, $31,675; qualifying distributions, $31,500.
Limitations: Applications not accepted.
Application information: Contributes only to pre-selected organizations.
Trustees: Kenneth Cole, Maria Cuomo Cole.
EIN: 137176155

37303
The Gerta Charitable Trust
525 E. 72 St., Ste. 320
New York, NY 10021

Established in 1994 in NY.
Donor(s): Gertrude Conner.
Financial data (yr. ended 12/31/01): Grants paid, $31,500; assets, $201,652 (M); expenditures, $34,329; qualifying distributions, $31,500.
Limitations: Applications not accepted. Giving primarily in NY.
Application information: Contributes only to pre-selected organizations.
Trustees: Gertrude Conner, Paul Windels.
EIN: 137038773

37304
Gunnar & Lillian Nicholson Foundation
c/o JPMorgan Chase Bank
P.O. Box 31412
Rochester, NY 14603-1412
Application address: c/o JPMorgan Chase Bank, P.O. Box 92920, Rochester, NY 14692, tel.: (800) 850-7222

Financial data (yr. ended 12/31/01): Grants paid, $31,478; assets, $163,970 (M); expenditures, $35,135; qualifying distributions, $31,763.
Limitations: Giving primarily in New York, NY.
Trustee: JPMorgan Chase Bank.
EIN: 136023698

37305
RWS Foundation, Inc.
c/o Marks, Paneth, and Shron, LLP
622 3rd Ave.
New York, NY 10017

Donor(s): Robert W. Sarnoff.‡
Financial data (yr. ended 09/30/01): Grants paid, $31,411; assets, $355,752 (M); gifts received, $129; expenditures, $36,006; qualifying distributions, $31,411.
Limitations: Applications not accepted. Giving primarily in New York, NY.
Application information: Contributes only to pre-selected organizations.
Officer: Anna Moffo Sarnoff, Pres.
EIN: 136084874

37306
Wabash Magnetics Scholarship Foundation
c/o DKM Corp.
565 5th Ave., 4th Fl.
New York, NY 10017

Donor(s): Wabash Magnetics.
Financial data (yr. ended 12/31/01): Grants paid, $31,375; assets, $65,256 (M); gifts received, $28,000; expenditures, $31,375; qualifying distributions, $31,403.
Application information: Unsolicited request for funds not accepted.
Directors: Casimer V. Kroll,* Pres.; Robert L. Stouder,* Secy.; Christopher N. Carmien,* Treas.; Mary Bach, Gail Whitenack.
Trustees: Pamela K. Bedwell, Debra A. Bonner, Mildred J. Clay, Kathy Friermood, Joseph R. Haupert, Robert H. Paupenfuss, Linda Ridgeway, Suzie D. Stephens.
EIN: 356205883
Codes: CS, CD, GTI

37307
Jack G. Lubelle Foundation, Inc.
19 W. Main St., Ste. 821
Rochester, NY 14614
Contact: Richard S. Levin, Secy.-Treas.

Financial data (yr. ended 12/31/01): Grants paid, $31,300; assets, $811,672 (M); expenditures, $83,038; qualifying distributions, $31,300.
Limitations: Giving primarily in Rochester, NY.
Officers and Trustees:* Eileen Serling,* Pres.; Dorothy Cummings,* V.P.; Albert G. Krenitsky,* V.P.; A. Clark Pieper,* V.P.; Richard S. Levin,* Secy.-Treas.; D. Rosenberg, M. Rosenberg.
EIN: 166092145

37308
The Joseph K. Miller Tzedaka Fund, Inc.
(Formerly The Joseph K. Miller Memorial Fund, Inc.)
381 Westwood Rd.
Woodmere, NY 11598

Donor(s): Sharon Miller.
Financial data (yr. ended 12/31/99): Grants paid, $31,298; assets, $146,906 (M); gifts received, $107,500; expenditures, $31,462; qualifying distributions, $31,348.
Limitations: Applications not accepted.
Officers: Rhoda Miller, Pres.; Alan Miller, V.P. and Treas.
EIN: 112965427

37309
Savino and Virginia Nanula Foundation
8940 Main St.
Clarence, NY 14031
Contact: Savino P. Nanula, Tr.

Established in 1997 in NY.
Donor(s): Savino P. Nanula.
Financial data (yr. ended 12/31/01): Grants paid, $31,260; assets, $56,545 (M); expenditures, $31,260; qualifying distributions, $31,242.
Limitations: Giving primarily in NY.
Trustee: Savino P. Nanula.
EIN: 137112396

37310
The Ruskin, Moscou, Evans & Faltischek Foundation, Inc.
170 Old Country Rd.
Mineola, NY 11501-4366

Established in 1998 in NY.
Donor(s): Douglas J. Good, Raymond S. Evans, Michael L. Faltischek, Gregory J. Naclerio, Benjamin Weinstock, Douglas A. Cooper, Dennis Alan Eagle, Neil Goldman.
Financial data (yr. ended 04/30/01): Grants paid, $31,200; assets, $4,526 (M); gifts received, $19,746; expenditures, $31,285; qualifying distributions, $31,200.
Limitations: Giving primarily in NY.
Officers and Directors:* Raymond S. Evans,* Pres.; Gregory J. Naclerio,* Secy.; Michael L. Faltischek,* Treas.; Irvin Brum, Michael K. Feigenbaum, Douglas J. Good, Melvyn B. Ruskin, Benjamin Weinstock, Jeffrey A. Wurst.
EIN: 113436897

37311
Kopczynski Family Foundation
1671 Sweeney St.
North Tonawanda, NY 14120

Established in 1995 in NY.
Donor(s): John Kopczynski, Sr., John Kopczynski, Jr., Michael R. Kopczynsk, St. Mary Manufacturing Corp.
Financial data (yr. ended 01/31/02): Grants paid, $31,169; assets, $213,594 (M); gifts received, $35,000; expenditures, $32,197; qualifying distributions, $31,169.
Limitations: Applications not accepted. Giving primarily in North Tonawanda, NY.
Application information: Contributes only to pre-selected organizations.
Trustees: Michael R. Kopczynski, Arnold Weiss.
EIN: 161483359

37312
Hegeman Memorial Trust Fund
c/o Met. Life
1 Madison Ave., Area 3H
New York, NY 10010-3690 (212) 578-6953
Contact: Ben LoCasto, Dir., Employee Assistance Dept.

Established in 1952 in NY.
Donor(s): Metropolitan Life Insurance Co.
Financial data (yr. ended 12/31/01): Grants paid, $31,153; assets, $1,052,472 (M); gifts received, $20,700; expenditures, $31,153; qualifying distributions, $31,153.
Limitations: Giving limited to MetLife employees in the U.S.
Application information: Application form required.
Officers and Trustee:* Catherine A. Rein,* Pres.; Louis J. Ragusa, Sr. V.P.; Judy E. Weiss, Exec. V.P.; John V. Fleming, V.P.
EIN: 133043763
Codes: CS, CD, GTI

37313
Schoen Family Foundation
c/o U.S. Trust
114 W. 47th St., TaxVas
New York, NY 10036

Established in 1998.
Donor(s): Paul Schoen.
Financial data (yr. ended 12/31/01): Grants paid, $31,153; assets, $136,844 (M); expenditures, $33,269; qualifying distributions, $31,153.
Limitations: Giving limited to NJ.
Trustee: U.S. Trust.
EIN: 137151365

37314
The Guthart Family Foundation
3 Expressway Plz.
Roslyn Heights, NY 11577

Established in 2000 in NY.
Donor(s): Leo A. Guthart.
Financial data (yr. ended 12/31/01): Grants paid, $31,145; assets, $397,262 (M); expenditures, $33,156; qualifying distributions, $31,145.
Limitations: Applications not accepted. Giving primarily in Washington, DC and New York, NY.
Application information: Contributes only to pre-selected organizations.
Trustees: Laura Guthart, Leo A. Guthart, Rebecca Guthart, Margaret G. Strauss.
EIN: 256688535

37315
The Martin Revson Foundation, Inc.
445 Park Ave.
New York, NY 10022-2606 (212) 753-3683

Donor(s): Martin Revson.
Financial data (yr. ended 12/31/00): Grants paid, $31,140; assets, $17,974 (M); expenditures, $31,165; qualifying distributions, $31,140.
Limitations: Applications not accepted. Giving primarily in New York, NY.
Application information: Contributes only to pre-selected organizations.
Trustee: Martin Revson.
EIN: 136161565

37316
Gouray Fund, Inc.
45 E. 85th St.
New York, NY 10028-0957
Contact: Paul Gouray, Pres.

Donor(s): Paul Gouray.
Financial data (yr. ended 09/30/01): Grants paid, $31,105; assets, $367,295 (M); expenditures, $32,015; qualifying distributions, $32,015.
Limitations: Giving primarily in New York, NY.
Officers: Paul Gouray, Pres. and Secy.; John P. Gouray, V.P.; Marianne C. Gouray, Treas.
EIN: 136095276

37317
Michael Berman Family Foundation
240 E. 39th St., Ste. 49H
New York, NY 10016

Established in 1997 in NY.
Donor(s): Michael Berman.
Financial data (yr. ended 12/31/00): Grants paid, $31,100; assets, $1,503,292 (M); gifts received, $25,009; expenditures, $57,841; qualifying distributions, $31,350.
Limitations: Applications not accepted.
Application information: Contributes only to pre-selected organizations.
Directors: Barbara Berman, Louise Berman, Michael Berman.
EIN: 133947917

37318
Robin Smith Charitable Trust
154 Little Neck Rd.
Centerport, NY 11721-1142

Established in 1986 in NY.
Donor(s): Robin Smith.
Financial data (yr. ended 12/31/01): Grants paid, $31,100; assets, $1,446,754 (M); gifts received, $523,480; expenditures, $32,829; qualifying distributions, $32,645.
Limitations: Applications not accepted. Giving primarily in NY.
Application information: Contributes only to pre-selected organizations.
Trustees: Heather Smith, Robin Smith.
EIN: 116330786

37319
AOH Foundation
c/o Marshall Green
1345 6th Ave., 42nd Fl.
New York, NY 10105

Established in 1994 in NY.
Donor(s): Anna O. Hoyt.
Financial data (yr. ended 11/30/00): Grants paid, $31,000; assets, $1,515,223 (M); gifts received, $4,500; expenditures, $47,457; qualifying distributions, $31,000.
Limitations: Applications not accepted. Giving on a national basis.
Application information: Contributes only to pre-selected organizations.
Trustee: Suzanne H. Garcia.
EIN: 137044726

37320
Ariowitsch Family Foundation, Inc.
512 7th Ave., Ste. 2900
New York, NY 10018-4729
Application address: 3593 Silver Plume Ct., Bouldor, CO 80305
Contact: Tim Ariowitsch, Tr.

Established in 1968.
Financial data (yr. ended 12/31/01): Grants paid, $31,000; assets, $662,246 (M); expenditures, $33,163; qualifying distributions, $31,000.
Limitations: Giving primarily in New York, NY.
Trustee: Tim Ariowitsch.
EIN: 136279580

37321
The Doris Duke Foundation, Inc.
650 5th Ave., 19th Fl.
New York, NY 10019
Contact: Grants Mgr.

Incorporated in 1934 in DE.
Donor(s): Doris Duke.‡
Financial data (yr. ended 12/31/01): Grants paid, $31,000; assets, $6,229,446 (M); expenditures, $101,112; qualifying distributions, $74,029.
Limitations: Applications not accepted. Giving primarily in NJ and NY.
Officers and Directors:* James F. Gill,* Chair.; Marion Oates Charles,* Vice-Chair.; Joan E. Spero, Pres.; Alan Altschuler, C.F.O.; Harry Demopoulos, J. Carter Browl, Anthony S. Fauci, Nannerl O. Keohane, John J. Mack.
EIN: 131655241

37322
The M. N. Emmerman and P. A. Stockhausen Foundation
300 E. 40th St., No. 27K
New York, NY 10016

Established in 1996 in NY.
Financial data (yr. ended 12/31/01): Grants paid, $31,000; assets, $210,408 (M); expenditures, $32,023; qualifying distributions, $31,000.
Limitations: Applications not accepted.
Application information: Contributes only to pre-selected organizations.
Officer: Michael Emmerman, Mgr.
Trustee: Patricia A. Stockhausen.
EIN: 133913381

37323
Foundation for Mood Disorders
c/o O'Conner, Davies & Co.
60 E. 42nd St., Ste. 3600
New York, NY 10165-3698
Application address: c/o D. Nelson Adams, Davis, Polk & Wardwell, 450 Lexington Ave., New York, NY 10017, tel.: (212) 772-3400

Established in 1994 in NY.
Donor(s): Foundation for Depression and Manic Depression, Inc.
Financial data (yr. ended 06/30/00): Grants paid, $31,000; assets, $3,224,113 (M); expenditures, $247,139; qualifying distributions, $216,770; giving activities include $216,720 for programs.
Limitations: Giving primarily in NY.
Officers: D. Nelson Adams, Pres.; Ronald R. Fieve, M.D., V.P.; Katia Fieve, Secy.
EIN: 133735967

37324
The Kikis Family Foundation
c/o Deltec Asset Mgmt.
720 5th Ave., 9th Fl.
New York, NY 10019
Contact: James E. Hughes, Jr., Tr.

Established in 1993 in NY.
Financial data (yr. ended 09/30/01): Grants paid, $31,000; assets, $212,116 (M); expenditures, $44,273; qualifying distributions, $31,000.
Limitations: Giving primarily in New York, NY.
Trustees: James E. Hughes, Jr., Helen Kikis, Peter T. Kikis, Thomas Kikis.
EIN: 133744409

37325
Klein Family Health Sciences Foundation
c/o Fairchild Properties, Ltd.
20 E. 46th St.
New York, NY 10017

Established in 1994 in NY.
Financial data (yr. ended 12/31/99): Grants paid, $31,000; assets, $72,525 (M); gifts received, $103,500; expenditures, $31,185; qualifying distributions, $31,000.
Limitations: Applications not accepted. Giving primarily in CT and NY.
Application information: Unsolicited requests for funds not accepted.
Trustees: Leslie Klein, Sam Klein.
EIN: 137043233

37326
Charlotte A. Koch Foundation
300 E. 42nd St.
New York, NY 10017-5947

Established in 1986 in NY.
Donor(s): Charlotte A. Koch.‡
Financial data (yr. ended 12/31/01): Grants paid, $31,000; assets, $365,897 (M); expenditures, $33,818; qualifying distributions, $30,855.
Limitations: Applications not accepted. Giving primarily in NY.
Application information: Contributes only to pre-selected organizations.
Directors: Carol H. Baldi, David W. Baum, Joseph M. Cassin, Henry W. Grady.
EIN: 133276467

37327
The Messer Foundation
200 Theater Pl.
Buffalo, NY 14202 (716) 853-8671
Contact: Thomas R. Beecher, Jr., Tr.

Donor(s): Thomas R. Beecher, Jr.
Financial data (yr. ended 12/31/01): Grants paid, $31,000; assets, $521,541 (M); expenditures, $35,590; qualifying distributions, $31,000.
Limitations: Giving primarily in Buffalo, NY.
Trustees: Kathleen S. Beecher, Thomas R. Beecher, Jr., Thomas R. Beecher III.
EIN: 166025317

37328
Michelle Pitcher Foundation, Inc.
c/o L. Wollin
350 5th Ave., Ste. 2822
New York, NY 10118

Established in 2000 in DE.
Financial data (yr. ended 09/30/01): Grants paid, $31,000; assets, $137,428 (M); gifts received, $200,000; expenditures, $35,054; qualifying distributions, $30,990.
Limitations: Applications not accepted.
Application information: Contributes only to pre-selected organizations.
Officers: Michelle Pitcher Duffy, Pres.; James Duffy, V.P.; Lonnie Wollin, Secy.
EIN: 223769248

37329
Maxwell Lide Stanback Foundation, Inc.
2 Springdale Rd.
Larchmont, NY 10538-1520 (914) 834-7194

Financial data (yr. ended 12/31/01): Grants paid, $31,000; assets, $770,703 (M); expenditures, $38,250; qualifying distributions, $31,000.
Limitations: Applications not accepted. Giving limited to NY.
Application information: Contributes only to pre-selected organizations.
Officer: T.M. Stanback, Jr., Pres. and Mgr.
EIN: 237188213

37330
Royal Heritage Foundation, Inc.
836 Hempstead Ave.
West Hempstead, NY 11552-3433
Tel.: (516) 485-9600 ext. 13
Contact: Shelby Goldgrab, Dir.

Donor(s): Shelby Goldgrab, Robin Goldgrab.
Financial data (yr. ended 09/30/01): Grants paid, $30,967; assets, $56,961 (M); gifts received, $12,312; expenditures, $31,649; qualifying distributions, $30,834.
Limitations: Giving primarily in NY.
Directors: Barry Goldgrab, Jeffrey Goldgrab, Robin Goldgrab, Shelby Goldgrab.
EIN: 112883957

37331
The Marlene & Edward Landau Foundation, Inc.
c/o Edward J. Landau
250 Park Ave., Ste. 1000
New York, NY 10177

Established in 1991 in NY.
Donor(s): Fred and Anne Landau Foundation, Edward J. Landau, Marlene Landau.
Financial data (yr. ended 12/31/01): Grants paid, $30,925; assets, $296,726 (M); expenditures, $31,957; qualifying distributions, $30,925.
Limitations: Applications not accepted.
Application information: Contributes only to pre-selected organizations.

37331—NEW YORK

Officers: Edward J. Landau, Pres.; Marlene Landau, V.P.
Director: Patrick J. Costello.
EIN: 133561924

37332
Victor and Phyllis Grann Family Foundation, Inc.
812 5th Ave., Apt. 4A
New York, NY 10021-7253

Established in 1991 in CT.
Donor(s): Victor Grann, Phyllis Grann.
Financial data (yr. ended 12/31/01): Grants paid, $30,900; assets, $881,177 (M); gifts received, $54,076; expenditures, $46,706; qualifying distributions, $30,900.
Limitations: Applications not accepted. Giving primarily in CA and New York, NY.
Application information: Contributes only to pre-selected organizations.
Officer: Victor Grann, Pres.
EIN: 223106701

37333
Joseph Camhi Foundation, Inc.
20 Muriel Ave.
Lawrence, NY 11559
Contact: Joseph Camhi, Pres.

Donor(s): Joseph Camhi, Dorothy Undergarment Co.
Financial data (yr. ended 11/30/01): Grants paid, $30,878; assets, $616,530 (M); expenditures, $34,045; qualifying distributions, $30,878.
Officers: Joseph Camhi, Pres.; Stanley Camhi, V.P.; Regina Camhi, Secy.; Sydell Chernoff, Treas.
EIN: 136109420

37334
Goodman-Lipman Family Foundation, Inc.
1013 Cove Rd.
Mamaroneck, NY 10543

Established in 1999 in NY.
Donor(s): Robert P. Goodman, Jane Sarah Lipman.
Financial data (yr. ended 12/31/01): Grants paid, $30,850; assets, $38,129 (M); gifts received, $17,708; expenditures, $39,254; qualifying distributions, $30,850.
Limitations: Applications not accepted.
Application information: Contributes only to pre-selected organizations.
Directors: James S. Goodman, Robert P. Goodman, Jane Sarah Lipman.
EIN: 134052449

37335
The Bender/Fishbein Foundation, Inc.
c/o T. Richard Fishbein
200 Park Ave.
New York, NY 10166

Established in 1998 in NY.
Donor(s): T. Richard Fishbein.
Financial data (yr. ended 12/31/01): Grants paid, $30,820; assets, $553,192 (M); expenditures, $40,043; qualifying distributions, $30,820.
Limitations: Applications not accepted. Giving primarily in New York, NY.
Application information: Contributes only to pre-selected organizations.
Officers: T. Richard Fishbein, Pres.; Estelle Bender, V.P.
EIN: 134010009

37336
Rita & Herbert Z. Gold Charitable Trust
P.O. Box 319
Rockville Centre, NY 11570

Established in 1996 in NY.
Donor(s): Herbert Z. Gold.
Financial data (yr. ended 12/31/01): Grants paid, $30,817; assets, $306,807 (M); expenditures, $33,063; qualifying distributions, $31,226; giving activities include $109 for programs.
Limitations: Applications not accepted. Giving limited to residents of Rockville Centre, NY.
Trustees: Herbert Z. Gold, Rita Gold.
EIN: 116465852
Codes: GTI

37337
Society of Daughters of Holland Dames
c/o B.A. Brinkley
200 Central Park South, Ste. 20G
New York, NY 10019

Financial data (yr. ended 12/31/01): Grants paid, $30,710; assets, $303,087 (L); gifts received, $2,550; expenditures, $61,074; qualifying distributions, $50,701.
Limitations: Applications not accepted. Giving primarily in NY.
Application information: Contributes only to pre-selected organizations.
Officers: Martha V. Glass, Treas.; Barbara A. Brinkley, Exec. Dir.
EIN: 136163969
Codes: GTI

37338
Magavern Pool, Inc.
1100 Rand Bldg.
Buffalo, NY 14203 (716) 856-3500

Established in 1985 in NY.
Financial data (yr. ended 12/31/01): Grants paid, $30,700; assets, $681,352 (M); expenditures, $33,496; qualifying distributions, $30,700.
Limitations: Applications not accepted. Giving primarily in Buffalo, NY.
Application information: Contributes only to pre-selected organizations.
Officers and Directors:* William J. Magavern II,* Pres.; James L. Magavern,* Secy.; Donald J. Egan.
EIN: 222583121

37339
Tarandi Foundation
2992 St., Rt. 48
Oswego, NY 13126-5734 (315) 592-7375
Contact: Ravindra F. Shah, M.D., Tr.

Established in 1988 in NY.
Donor(s): Ravindra F. Shah, M.D., Manjula R. Shah, M.D.
Financial data (yr. ended 12/31/01): Grants paid, $30,660; assets, $687,387 (M); gifts received, $73,680; expenditures, $31,843; qualifying distributions, $30,660.
Limitations: Giving primarily in India; some giving also in Providence, RI.
Application information: Application form not required.
Trustees: Manjula R. Shah, M.D., Ravindra F. Shah, M.D.
EIN: 161314643

37340
The Ambler Family Foundation, Inc.
c/o Michael Ambler
655 Park Ave.
New York, NY 10021

Established in 1997 in DE.
Financial data (yr. ended 12/31/01): Grants paid, $30,640; assets, $661,303 (M); expenditures, $31,522; qualifying distributions, $30,640.
Limitations: Applications not accepted.
Application information: Contributes only to pre-selected organizations.
Officers: Michael N. Ambler, Pres. and Treas.; Marsha D. Ambler, V.P. and Secy.
Directors: Christian D. Ambler, Michael N. Ambler, Jr.
EIN: 133940885

37341
Robert K. Scripps Family Foundation
c/o U.S. Trust
114 W. 47th St., TaxVas
New York, NY 10036

Established in 1998 in FL.
Donor(s): Robert K. Scripps.
Financial data (yr. ended 12/31/01): Grants paid, $30,600; assets, $786,833 (M); expenditures, $37,234; qualifying distributions, $30,600.
Application information: Unsolicited requests for funds not accepted.
Officers and Directors:* Robert K. Scripps, Pres.; Elizabeth Scripps, Secy.; Suzanne Scripps LaFlamme, Christina Scripps.
EIN: 650824010

37342
Bruno Walter Memorial Foundation
c/o Yohalem Gillman & Co., LLP
477 Madison Ave.
New York, NY 10022-5802

Established in 1965 in NY.
Donor(s): Bruno Walter.
Financial data (yr. ended 04/30/02): Grants paid, $30,580; assets, $649,196 (M); expenditures, $40,981; qualifying distributions, $30,580.
Limitations: Applications not accepted. Giving primarily in New York, NY.
Application information: Contributes only to pre-selected organizations.
Officers: Stanley Gillman, Pres.; Todd M. Brinberg, Secy.
Trustees: Hannie Gillman, Christoph Scholz, Craig Shumate, Margaret Sichel.
EIN: 136174444

37343
The Harriet and Charles Ballon Foundation, Inc.
800 5th Ave., No. 6B
New York, NY 10021-7216

Established in 1963 in NY.
Donor(s): Charles Ballon,‡ Harriet Ballon.
Financial data (yr. ended 12/31/01): Grants paid, $30,575; assets, $107,264 (M); gifts received, $10,000; expenditures, $31,095; qualifying distributions, $30,575.
Limitations: Applications not accepted. Giving primarily in New York, NY.
Application information: Contributes only to pre-selected organizations.
Officers and Directors:* Harriet Ballon Lucks,* Pres.; Hilary Ballon Kramer,* Secy.; Howard Ballon,* Treas.; Carla Gorell.
EIN: 136144787

37344
The Raquel and Jack Benun Charitable Foundation, Inc.
818 Ave. R
Brooklyn, NY 11223

Established in 1999 in NY.
Donor(s): Jack Benun.
Financial data (yr. ended 12/31/01): Grants paid, $30,543; assets, $80,166 (M); gifts received, $44,057; expenditures, $30,543; qualifying distributions, $30,543.
Limitations: Applications not accepted.
Application information: Contributes only to pre-selected organizations.
Director: Jack Benun.

EIN: 113499470

37345
The David W. Bermant Foundation: Color, Light, Motion, Inc.
c/o Prager & Fenton
675 3rd Ave., 9th Fl.
New York, NY 10017
Application address: 1104 La Vista Rd., Santa Barbara, CA 93110, tel.: (805) 687-5239

Established in 1986 in NY.
Donor(s): David W. Bermant.
Financial data (yr. ended 01/31/00): Grants paid, $30,500; assets, $805,572 (M); gifts received, $56,300; expenditures, $47,282; qualifying distributions, $46,062; giving activities include $15,168 for programs.
Limitations: Giving limited to NY.
Application information: Application form not required.
Officers and Directors:* Andrew Bermant, David W. Bermant, Jeffrey Bermant, Susan Hopmans Bermant, Robert Margolies, Sandra Powers, Victoria Vesna.
EIN: 133376746

37346
Hanson Family Foundation, Inc.
c/o Fredric Hanson
380 W. 12th St., Apt. 6E
New York, NY 10014 (212) 627-7320

Established in 1997 in NY.
Donor(s): Margery W. Hanson.
Financial data (yr. ended 12/31/01): Grants paid, $30,500; assets, $290,831 (M); expenditures, $33,380; qualifying distributions, $30,500.
Limitations: Applications not accepted.
Application information: Contributes only to pre-selected organizations.
Officers and Directors:* Margery W. Hanson,* Pres.; Fredric Hanson,* V.P., and Secy.-Treas.; Diana Kash Hanson, Sarah Elizabeth Hanson.
EIN: 133780362

37347
The James G. McMurtry III Foundation
330 W. 42nd St., 18th Fl.
New York, NY 10036-6902 (212) 967-9080
Contact: Elliot Blumenthal, Dir.

Established in 1994.
Donor(s): James G. McMurtry III.
Financial data (yr. ended 12/31/01): Grants paid, $30,500; assets, $5,082 (M); gifts received, $34,900; expenditures, $30,896; qualifying distributions, $30,500.
Limitations: Giving limited to New York, NY.
Directors: Elliot Blumenthal, Hugh Ferguson, James G. McMurtry III.
EIN: 133796627

37348
Thomas and Lois Mills Scholarship Trust
c/o HSBC Bank USA
P.O. Box 4203, 17th Fl.
Buffalo, NY 14240

Financial data (yr. ended 06/30/99): Grants paid, $30,482; assets, $700,415 (M); gifts received, $1,000; expenditures, $39,573; qualifying distributions, $31,320.
Limitations: Giving limited to NY.
Trustee: HSBC Bank USA.
EIN: 166136606

37349
Lawrence & Alice Valenstein Fund, Inc.
c/o Fleischman & Company
307 5th Ave.
New York, NY 10016-6517

Donor(s): Alice Valenstein.
Financial data (yr. ended 12/31/01): Grants paid, $30,404; assets, $668,604 (M); gifts received, $98,013; expenditures, $40,305; qualifying distributions, $30,404.
Limitations: Applications not accepted. Giving primarily in CA, CT, and NY.
Application information: Contributes only to pre-selected organizations.
Officers: John Valenstein, Pres.; Linda Elkind, V.P.; Alice Valenstein, Secy.-Treas.
EIN: 136183947

37350
Abraham Woursell Foundation
c/o Citibank, N.A., Tax Dept.
1 Court Sq., 22nd Fl.
Long Island City, NY 11120

Financial data (yr. ended 12/31/99): Grants paid, $30,399; assets, $2,358,239 (M); expenditures, $58,291; qualifying distributions, $30,719.
Limitations: Applications not accepted. Giving to individuals on an international basis.
Trustee: Citibank, N.A.
EIN: 136140514

37351
Joseph Jaspan Foundation, Inc.
300 Garden City Plz.
Garden City, NY 11530
Contact: Arthur W. Jaspan, Dir.

Donor(s): Joseph Jaspan.
Financial data (yr. ended 12/31/01): Grants paid, $30,317; assets, $57,819 (M); gifts received, $68,451; expenditures, $30,335; qualifying distributions, $30,317.
Limitations: Giving primarily in NY.
Application information: Application form not required.
Directors: Arthur W. Jaspan, Rosalyn Jaspan.
EIN: 116044710

37352
Jonathan Rinehart Family Foundation
c/o Jonathan Rinehart
150 E. 73rd St., Ste. 7D
New York, NY 10021-4362

Established in 1996 in NY.
Donor(s): Jonathan Rinehart.
Financial data (yr. ended 12/31/01): Grants paid, $30,302; assets, $503,676 (M); expenditures, $34,423; qualifying distributions, $30,302.
Limitations: Applications not accepted.
Application information: Contributes only to pre-selected organizations.
Trustees: David L. Duffy, Jonathan Rinehart.
EIN: 137103967

37353
The Griffin-Cole Fund
c/o Goldman Sachs & Co.
85 Broad St., Tax Dept.
New York, NY 10004

Established in 1996 in NJ.
Donor(s): Christopher A. Cole.
Financial data (yr. ended 07/31/01): Grants paid, $30,300; assets, $4,935,837 (M); gifts received, $1,462,438; expenditures, $100,050; qualifying distributions, $33,050.
Limitations: Applications not accepted. Giving primarily in Princeton, NJ.
Application information: Contributes only to pre-selected organizations.
Trustees: Christopher A. Cole, Barbara Griffin-Cole.
EIN: 137109406

37354
Elenore and Maurice Rosenthal Foundation
25 Sutton Pl. S.
New York, NY 10022

Established in 1999 in NY.
Financial data (yr. ended 12/31/01): Grants paid, $30,275; assets, $56,259 (M); expenditures, $30,646; qualifying distributions, $30,275.
Directors: Elenore Rosenthal, Maurice Rosenthal.
EIN: 137128237

37355
Joseph B. Corpina, Jr. Memorial Foundation, Inc.
46 Candlewood Rd.
Scarsdale, NY 10583
Contact: Joseph B. Corpina, Dir.

Donor(s): Joseph B. Corpina, Nancy B. Corpina.
Financial data (yr. ended 12/31/00): Grants paid, $30,200; assets, $198,597 (M); gifts received, $37,305; expenditures, $38,015; qualifying distributions, $38,015; giving activities include $6,739 for programs.
Limitations: Giving primarily in Scarsdale, NY.
Director: Joseph B. Corpina.
EIN: 133188830

37356
Clifford A. Howell Foundation
420 E. 72nd St.
New York, NY 10021
Contact: Jerrold T. Doros, Dir.

Established in 1990 in DE.
Donor(s): Clifford Howell.‡
Financial data (yr. ended 12/31/01): Grants paid, $30,200; assets, $503,337 (M); gifts received, $3,510; expenditures, $52,184; qualifying distributions, $30,200.
Limitations: Giving primarily in New York, NY.
Application information: Application form not required.
Director: Jerrold T. Doros.
EIN: 133602787

37357
Segal Charitable Foundation
c/o Esther Friedman
104 Ross St., Apt. 4K
Brooklyn, NY 11211-7677

Established in 1998 in NY.
Donor(s): Arthur Goldberger, Arthur Friedman, Isidore Friedman.
Financial data (yr. ended 12/31/01): Grants paid, $30,200; assets, $118,581 (M); gifts received, $42,981; expenditures, $31,100; qualifying distributions, $30,200.
Limitations: Applications not accepted.
Application information: Contributes only to pre-selected organizations.
Trustees: Arthur Friedman, Esther Friedman.
EIN: 113412302

37358
Else and Max Schuster Foundation
1212 Ave. of the Americas
New York, NY 10036

Established in 1983 in NY.
Financial data (yr. ended 12/31/01): Grants paid, $30,183; assets, $929 (M); gifts received, $30,000; expenditures, $30,440; qualifying distributions, $30,183.

37358—NEW YORK

Directors: Else Schuster, Max Schuster.
EIN: 133185313

37359
The John C. Hover Foundation, Inc.
c/o U.S. Trust
114 W. 47th St., TaxVAS
New York, NY 10036
Application address: c/o John C. Hover, II, P.O. Box 676, 3039 Durham Rd., Buckingham, PA 18912

Financial data (yr. ended 12/31/01): Grants paid, $30,131; assets, $209,022 (M); expenditures, $31,961; qualifying distributions, $30,131.
Limitations: Giving primarily in MA, NJ, and NY.
Officers and Directors:* John C. Hover II,* Pres. and Treas.; Judith H. Harper,* V.P. and Secy.; Margaretta H. Lundell,* V.P.; Jacqueline W. Hover, Margaret B. Hover, Eric R. Lundell.
EIN: 136213663

37360
Paul and Else Blum Private Foundation
c/o Bernard Blum
437 Franklin St.
Buffalo, NY 14202

Established in 1993 in NY.
Financial data (yr. ended 12/31/00): Grants paid, $30,130; assets, $1,020,963 (M); gifts received, $90,000; expenditures, $33,247; qualifying distributions, $30,130.
Limitations: Applications not accepted.
Application information: Contributes only to pre-selected organizations.
Trustee: Bernard Blum.
EIN: 166394946

37361
Benjamin Kurz Foundation
c/o Irene Reaback
217 Juniper Cir. N.
Lawrence, NY 11559-1915

Financial data (yr. ended 12/31/00): Grants paid, $30,105; assets, $1 (M); expenditures, $31,519; qualifying distributions, $30,105.
Limitations: Applications not accepted. Giving primarily in NY.
Application information: Contributes only to pre-selected organizations.
Officer: Irene Reaback, Mgr.
EIN: 116036890

37362
The Hampton Foundation of Manhattan
c/o Vohalem Gillman & Co., LLP
477 Madison Ave., 9th Fl.
New York, NY 10022

Established in 1990 in DE.
Donor(s): Robert Stern.
Financial data (yr. ended 12/31/01): Grants paid, $30,102; assets, $846,103 (M); expenditures, $55,954; qualifying distributions, $39,277.
Limitations: Applications not accepted. Giving primarily in New York, NY.
Application information: Contributes only to pre-selected organizations.
Officers: Robert Stern, Pres.; Susan Hays Stern, Secy.-Treas.
EIN: 521654921

37363
The Emily Unterberg Satloff and James Eliot Satloff Foundation, Inc.
c/o Eli Greenberg
270 Madison Ave.
New York, NY 10016
Application address: 10 E. 50th St., New York, NY 10022-6831

Established in 1999 in DE.
Donor(s): Emily Satloff.
Financial data (yr. ended 03/31/02): Grants paid, $30,100; assets, $8,123 (M); gifts received, $26,734; expenditures, $31,180; qualifying distributions, $30,100.
Directors: Ellen Unterberg Celli, Emily Satloff, James Satloff.
EIN: 134085329

37364
Stanley & Gene Lasdon Charitable Trust
280 N. Bedford Rd.
Mount Kisco, NY 10549
Application address: 980 5th Ave., Apt. 12B, New York, NY 10021-0126
Contact: Gene S. Lasdon, Tr.

Established in 1992 in NY.
Donor(s): Stanley S. Lasdon, Gene S. Lasdon.
Financial data (yr. ended 12/31/00): Grants paid, $30,050; assets, $919,058 (M); expenditures, $33,856; qualifying distributions, $30,050.
Limitations: Giving primarily in New York, NY.
Application information: Application form not required.
Trustees: Gene S. Lasdon, Jeffrey S. Lasdon.
EIN: 136999395

37365
The Sheila and Henry Marcus Foundation, Inc.
76 Fraser St.
Staten Island, NY 10314
Contact: Henry Marcus, Pres.

Established in 1995.
Donor(s): Henry Marcus.
Financial data (yr. ended 12/31/00): Grants paid, $30,049; assets, $323,847 (M); expenditures, $30,347; qualifying distributions, $30,049.
Limitations: Giving primarily in NY.
Officer: Henry Marcus, Pres.
EIN: 133862964

37366
Sussman Charitable Trust
50 Doxsee Dr.
Freeport, NY 11520

Established in 1980 in NY.
Donor(s): Lori Sussman, Marc Sussman, Morris Sussman, Elaine Sussman, Port Plastics.
Financial data (yr. ended 11/30/01): Grants paid, $30,040; assets, $264,801 (M); gifts received, $73,665; expenditures, $31,559; qualifying distributions, $30,040.
Limitations: Applications not accepted. Giving primarily in NY.
Application information: Contributes only to pre-selected organizations.
Trustees: Elaine Sussman, Lori Sussman, Marc Sussman, Morris Sussman.
EIN: 133030269

37367
Martin & Betty Schwab Foundation, Inc.
71 Sheldrake Rd.
Scarsdale, NY 10583

Established in 1961 in NY.
Donor(s): The Charitable Lead Trust.

Financial data (yr. ended 12/31/01): Grants paid, $30,024; assets, $105,871 (M); expenditures, $32,061; qualifying distributions, $30,024.
Limitations: Applications not accepted. Giving primarily in the greater New York, NY, area.
Application information: Contributes only to pre-selected organizations.
Officers: Betty B. Schwab, Pres.; Jerome A. Manning, Secy.; Martin Schwab, Treas.
EIN: 136077133

37368
James T. and Linda M. Flynn Family Foundation
340 E. 72nd St.
New York, NY 10021-4768

Established in 1997 in NY.
Donor(s): James T. Flynn, Linda M. Flynn.
Financial data (yr. ended 12/31/01): Grants paid, $30,000; assets, $24,280 (M); gifts received, $18,000; expenditures, $31,325; qualifying distributions, $30,000.
Limitations: Applications not accepted. Giving primarily in NY.
Application information: Contributes to pre-selected organizations.
Trustees: James T. Flynn, Linda M. Flynn.
EIN: 137106287

37369
Foundation for Research of the New York Academy of Osteopathy, Inc.
P.O. Box 170
Old Westbury, NY 11568-0170
Contact: Stanley Schiowitz, Pres.

Financial data (yr. ended 08/31/99): Grants paid, $30,000; assets, $384,451 (M); expenditures, $31,468; qualifying distributions, $30,000.
Limitations: Giving limited to NY.
Officers and Directors:* Stanley Schiowitz,* Pres.; Michael Sutula, V.P.; Rita Sears, Secy.; Brian Waldron,* Treas.; Michael Burruano, Eileen DiGiovanna, Dennis Dowling, and 10 additional directors.
EIN: 136159697

37370
The Michael Gardner Foundation
c/o Baytree Capital
40 Wall St., 58th Fl.
New York, NY 10005-2301 (212) 504-1200
FAX: (212) 363-4231
Contact: Michael Gardner, Pres.

Established in 1999.
Financial data (yr. ended 12/31/00): Grants paid, $30,000; assets, $295,640 (M); gifts received, $53,780; expenditures, $743,214; qualifying distributions, $29,892.
Limitations: Giving on a national basis, with emphasis on New York, NY and Boston, MA.
Application information: Application form not required.
Officer: Michael Gardner, Pres.
EIN: 134086681

37371
The Lionel Goldfrank III Foundation
667 Madison Ave., 20th Fl.
New York, NY 10021-8029

Established in 1999 in NY.
Donor(s): Lionel Goldfrank III.
Financial data (yr. ended 04/30/00): Grants paid, $30,000; assets, $96,874 (M); gifts received, $118,963; expenditures, $34,729; qualifying distributions, $30,000.
Limitations: Applications not accepted.
Application information: Contributes only to pre-selected organizations.

Officer: Lionel Goldfrank III, Pres.
EIN: 316623852

37372
Graham Family Charitable Foundation
200 Park Ave., Ste. 3900
New York, NY 10166 (212) 808-7430
Contact: Janet Howard, Tr.

Established in 1999 in NY.
Financial data (yr. ended 12/31/99): Grants paid, $30,000; assets, $1,373,507 (M); gifts received, $1,150,000; expenditures, $40,002; qualifying distributions, $40,002; giving activities include $10,002 for programs.
Limitations: Giving primarily in New York, NY.
Trustees: Kevin Graham, Monica Graham, Janet Howard.
EIN: 134021970

37373
Susan Klingenstein Fund
c/o Tanton & Co.
37 W. 57th St., 5th Fl.
New York, NY 10019

Established in 2000 in IL.
Donor(s): Susan Klingenstein.
Financial data (yr. ended 12/31/01): Grants paid, $30,000; assets, $113,318 (M); gifts received, $282; expenditures, $32,097; qualifying distributions, $30,000.
Limitations: Applications not accepted.
Application information: Contributes only to pre-selected organizations.
Trustee: Susan Klingenstein.
EIN: 364392412

37374
Charles Looney Memorial Fund
c/o Grand Lodge F. & A.M.
71 W. 23rd St.
New York, NY 10010-4102 (212) 741-4512
Contact: Frank S. Grado, Tr.

Financial data (yr. ended 12/31/01): Grants paid, $30,000; assets, $645,436 (M); expenditures, $33,905; qualifying distributions, $33,332.
Limitations: Giving primarily in New York, NY.
Trustees: Robert E. Bearse, Frank S. Grado, Edward M. Weigert.
EIN: 132937671

37375
Anna L. Mabey Foundation
c/o NBT Bank, N.A.
52 S. Broad St.
Norwich, NY 13815-1646 (607) 337-6193
Contact: Barbara North, Tr.

Established in 1978 in NY.
Financial data (yr. ended 08/31/01): Grants paid, $30,000; assets, $489,085 (M); expenditures, $33,705; qualifying distributions, $30,000.
Limitations: Giving limited to Chenango, Delaware, and Otsego counties, NY.
Trustees: Charlotte Barnes, Barbara North, Richard North, NBT Bank, N.A.
EIN: 166073588

37376
Pancretan Endowment Fund
220 Delhi Rd.
Scarsdale, NY 10583-1520
E-mail: Evelivasakis@LZAtechnology.com
Contact: Emmanuel E. Velivasakis, Pres.

Established in 1995 in IL.
Financial data (yr. ended 12/31/01): Grants paid, $30,000; assets, $585,096 (M); gifts received, $30,811; expenditures, $34,995; qualifying distributions, $30,000.

Limitations: Applications not accepted. Giving limited to the Island of Crete.
Publications: Biennial report.
Application information: Contributes only to pre-selected organizations.
Officers: Emmanuel Velivasakis, Pres.; George Charatis, Secy.-Treas.
Trustees: Anthony Saris, Carol Travayakis, Emmanuel Tsikoudakis, Steve Zeimbekakis, Terry Zervos.
EIN: 363685805

37377
The Perrin Foundation
72 Reade St.
New York, NY 10027
Application address: 926 Coolidge St., Westfield, NJ 07090, tel.: (732) 449-8890
Contact: John G. Jeffers, Pres.

Established in 1928 in NY.
Donor(s): Mary Ricks.
Financial data (yr. ended 12/31/01): Grants paid, $30,000; assets, $368,859 (M); expenditures, $31,666; qualifying distributions, $30,000.
Limitations: Giving primarily in NJ.
Application information: Application form not required.
Officers: John G. Jeffers, Pres.; Robert Q. Bennett, V.P.; David C. Wohlgemuth, Secy.
Directors: Robert Dadd, George MacKenzie, Mary Ricks.
EIN: 226049335

37378
River Charitable Trust
69 5th Ave., Ste. 12J
New York, NY 10003

Established in 2001 in NY.
Donor(s): Gene Bierhorst.
Financial data (yr. ended 12/31/01): Grants paid, $30,000; assets, $79 (M); gifts received, $30,000; expenditures, $30,000; qualifying distributions, $30,000.
Limitations: Applications not accepted. Giving primarily in New York, NY.
Directors: Gene Bierhorst, Susan Bierhorst.
EIN: 134153587

37379
The Barrie and Emmanuel Roman Foundation
c/o Goldman Sachs & Co.
85 Broad St., Tax Dept.
New York, NY 10004

Established in 1999 in NY.
Donor(s): Emmanuel Roman.
Financial data (yr. ended 10/31/01): Grants paid, $30,000; assets, $342,455 (M); gifts received, $2,500; expenditures, $34,180; qualifying distributions, $33,180.
Limitations: Applications not accepted. Giving primarily in Stanford, CA, and Chicago, IL.
Application information: Contributes only to pre-selected organizations.
Trustees: Barrie Roman, Emmanuel Roman.
EIN: 134088971

37380
The Sapp Family Foundation
c/o Goldman Sachs & Co.
85 Broad St., Tax Dept.
New York, NY 10004

Established in 1991 in NY.
Donor(s): Richard A. Sapp.
Financial data (yr. ended 04/30/01): Grants paid, $30,000; assets, $8,014,118 (M); gifts received, $2,435,563; expenditures, $200,214; qualifying distributions, $31,839.

Limitations: Applications not accepted. Giving on a national basis.
Application information: Contributes only to pre-selected organizations.
Trustees: Richard A. Sapp, Shari M. Sapp.
EIN: 133632757

37381
Selgreen Foundation, Inc.
c/o Kurz & Kurz
122 E. 42nd St.
New York, NY 10168

Financial data (yr. ended 12/31/00): Grants paid, $30,000; assets, $578,926 (M); expenditures, $32,555; qualifying distributions, $30,000.
Limitations: Giving on an international basis.
Application information: Application form not required.
Officer: Leon A. Weil, Pres.
EIN: 136162783

37382
Sandra & Lawrence Simon Family Foundation, Inc.
c/o Lawrence & Sandra Simon
58 Tammy's Ln.
Syosset, NY 11791

Established in 1999 in NY.
Donor(s): Lawrence Simon, Sandra Simon.
Financial data (yr. ended 12/31/01): Grants paid, $30,000; assets, $667,867 (M); gifts received, $150,000; expenditures, $40,450; qualifying distributions, $30,000.
Limitations: Applications not accepted.
Application information: Contributes only to pre-selected organizations.
Officers: Lawrence Simon, Pres.; Sandra Simon, Secy.-Treas.
EIN: 113511169

37383
Singh Family Foundation
c/o Goldman Sachs & Co.
85 Broad St.
New York, NY 10004

Established in 1999 in NY.
Donor(s): Dinakar Singh.
Financial data (yr. ended 10/31/01): Grants paid, $30,000; assets, $613,107 (M); gifts received, $2,500; expenditures, $34,330; qualifying distributions, $33,330.
Limitations: Applications not accepted. Giving primarily in Libertyville, IL.
Application information: Contributes only to pre-selected organizations.
Trustees: Dinakar Singh, Florence Ann Singh, Ravi Mo Singh.
EIN: 134115900

37384
Shin Yang Foundation
225 E. 70th St., Ste. 2G
New York, NY 10021
Contact: Luguang Yang, Tr.

Established in 2001 in NY.
Donor(s): Luguang Yang.
Financial data (yr. ended 01/30/02): Grants paid, $30,000; assets, $60,402 (M); gifts received, $70,000; expenditures, $32,000; qualifying distributions, $32,000.
Limitations: Giving primarily in Hunan Province, China.
Trustee: Luguang Yang.
EIN: 134138338

37385
Penn Schoellkopf Fund, Inc.
c/o Paul A. Schoellkopf
P.O. Box 1210, Ellicott Station
Buffalo, NY 14205-1210

Donor(s): Paul A. Schoellkopf.
Financial data (yr. ended 12/31/01): Grants paid, $29,950; assets, $335,513 (M); gifts received, $24,510; expenditures, $34,229; qualifying distributions, $29,950.
Limitations: Applications not accepted. Giving primarily in Buffalo, NY.
Application information: Contributes only to pre-selected organizations.
Officers and Directors:* Paul A. Schoellkopf,* Pres.; Ann S. Jewett,* V.P.; Donna Y. Yungbluth, Secy.-Treas.; Jane S. Banta, Susan Schoellkopf.
EIN: 166071354

37386
JMA Foundation, Inc.
888 Park Ave., Ste. 9C
New York, NY 10021-0235

Donor(s): Jane Saltoun, Munir Saltoun.
Financial data (yr. ended 11/30/01): Grants paid, $29,908; assets, $1,199,220 (M); expenditures, $30,509; qualifying distributions, $29,908.
Limitations: Applications not accepted.
Application information: Contributes only to pre-selected organizations.
Officers: Jane Saltoun,* Mgr.; Munir Saltoun,* Mgr.
EIN: 133743913

37387
Toras Chachom Charitable Foundation
1419 47th St.
Brooklyn, NY 11219

Contact: Yitzchok Kalish, Tr.

Established in 1999 in NY.
Financial data (yr. ended 12/31/01): Grants paid, $29,894; assets, $82,577 (M); gifts received, $23,675; expenditures, $31,787; qualifying distributions, $29,894.
Application information: Applicants are nominated by community leaders.
Trustees: Yitzchok Kalish, Samuel Leifer.
EIN: 113438015

37388
Nicholas Patterson Perpetual Fund
P.O. Box 887
Buffalo, NY 14205
Contact: Frederick B. Cohen, Tr.

Established in 1987 in NY.
Financial data (yr. ended 12/31/00): Grants paid, $29,890; assets, $517,584 (M); expenditures, $37,725; qualifying distributions, $7,885.
Limitations: Giving primarily in NY.
Trustee: Frederick B. Cohen.
EIN: 222806714
Codes: GTI

37389
The Yale Fishman Family Foundation
445 Central Ave., Ste. 201
Cedarhurst, NY 11516

Established in 2001 in NY.
Donor(s): Yale Fishman.
Financial data (yr. ended 12/31/01): Grants paid, $29,850; assets, $220,218 (M); gifts received, $300,000; expenditures, $30,469; qualifying distributions, $30,350.
Limitations: Applications not accepted.
Application information: Contributes only to pre-selected organizations.
Directors: Joseph Fishman, Yale Fishman, Rebecca Silverstein.
EIN: 113579520

37390
The Klee Fund, Inc.
c/o Marcum & Kliegman, LLP
655 3rd Ave., Ste. 1610
New York, NY 10017

Donor(s): Mary Ellen Klee, Nancy K. Stone, Robert Stone.
Financial data (yr. ended 12/31/01): Grants paid, $29,840; assets, $526,955 (M); gifts received, $30,122; expenditures, $37,392; qualifying distributions, $29,840.
Limitations: Applications not accepted. Giving primarily in NY.
Application information: Contributes only to pre-selected organizations.
Officers: Nancy K. Stone, Pres.; Mary Ellen Klee, V.P.; John Furth, Treas.
EIN: 136086141

37391
Louis Auer Foundation
38 Oneck Rd.
Westhampton Beach, NY 11978-2206
(631) 288-2137
Contact: Louis Auer, Tr.

Donor(s): Louis Auer.
Financial data (yr. ended 12/31/01): Grants paid, $29,800; assets, $687,392 (M); gifts received, $28,284; expenditures, $32,902; qualifying distributions, $29,800.
Trustee: Louis Auer.
EIN: 136173083

37392
Whitehall Foundation, Inc.
c/o C. Sackett
P.O. Box 31051
Rochester, NY 14603

Established in 2000 in NY.
Donor(s): Lucius R. Gordon, Marie A. Gordon.
Financial data (yr. ended 12/31/01): Grants paid, $29,800; assets, $636,272 (M); gifts received, $593,731; expenditures, $36,339; qualifying distributions, $24,345.
Limitations: Applications not accepted. Giving primarily in GA and MA.
Application information: Contributes only to pre-selected organizations.
Officers and Directors:* Lucia G. Gumaer,* Pres.; Elliott W. Gumaer, Jr.,* Secy.-Treas.; Lucius R. Gordon.
EIN: 912090135

37393
Gerald Tsai Foundation
200 Park Ave., Ste. 4522
New York, NY 10166

Established in 1988 in NY.
Donor(s): Gerald Tsai, Jr.
Financial data (yr. ended 12/31/00): Grants paid, $29,773; assets, $663,349 (M); expenditures, $78,846; qualifying distributions, $29,773.
Limitations: Applications not accepted. Giving primarily in New York, NY.
Application information: Contributes only to pre-selected organizations.
Officers: Gerald Tsai, Pres.; Maryalice Tait, V.P. and Secy.; Patricia Fitzgerald, V.P.
EIN: 133513057

37394
Suzanne H. Lee Trust
c/o JPMorgan Chase Bank
P.O. Box 31412
Rochester, NY 14603-1412

Financial data (yr. ended 08/31/01): Grants paid, $29,750; assets, $558,163 (M); expenditures, $30,872; qualifying distributions, $29,713.
Limitations: Giving primarily in NY, with some emphasis on Rochester and Brockport.
Application information: Application form not required.
Trustee: JPMorgan Chase Bank.
EIN: 166016523

37395
Grace Norton Dudley Fund
c/o JPMorgan Chase Bank
P.O. Box 31412
Rochester, NY 14603-1412
Application addresses: c/o Guidance Office for the Bridgeport, CT high schools; c/o JPMorgan Chase Bank, 999 Broad St., Bridgeport, CT 06606, tel.: (203) 382-6548

Established in 2000 in VT.
Financial data (yr. ended 12/31/01): Grants paid, $29,734; assets, $1,710,575 (M); expenditures, $52,203; qualifying distributions, $31,987.
Limitations: Giving limited to residents of Bridgeport, CT.
Trustee: JPMorgan Chase Bank.
EIN: 066079557

37396
Oppenheimer Foundation
137-79 70th Rd.
Flushing, NY 11367 (718) 283-8544
Contact: Stuart Vestandig, Tr.

Established in 1999 in NY.
Financial data (yr. ended 12/31/01): Grants paid, $29,700; assets, $26,006 (M); gifts received, $21,656; expenditures, $30,200; qualifying distributions, $29,700.
Trustee: Stuart Verstandig.
EIN: 113489146

37397
Deborah Salem Foundation
2011 E. 4th St.
Brooklyn, NY 11223

Established in 1996.
Financial data (yr. ended 09/30/01): Grants paid, $29,700; assets, $271,619 (M); gifts received, $5,933; expenditures, $30,535; qualifying distributions, $30,410.
Limitations: Applications not accepted.
Application information: Contributes only to pre-selected organizations.
Directors: Jeff A. Cohen, Joseph Mizrachi, Jess J. Salem, Sam Salem, Carey Sutton.
EIN: 112947586

37398
Richard & Eslyn Bassuk Foundation, Inc.
45 Mamaroneck Rd.
Scarsdale, NY 10583

Donor(s): Richard Bassuk, Eslyn Bassuk.
Financial data (yr. ended 12/31/01): Grants paid, $29,692; assets, $72,436 (M); gifts received, $50,000; expenditures, $29,932; qualifying distributions, $29,932.
Limitations: Applications not accepted. Giving primarily in Westchester County and New York, NY.
Application information: Contributes only to pre-selected organizations.

Officers: Richard Bassuk, Pres.; Eslyn Bassuk, V.P. and Secy.; Jack H. Nusbaum, Treas.
EIN: 133372836

37399
Garman Family Foundation
578 Mill Rd.
East Aurora, NY 14052-2831

Established in 2000 in NY.
Donor(s): Richard E. Garman.
Financial data (yr. ended 12/31/01): Grants paid, $29,666; assets, $4,439,615 (M); expenditures, $75,170; qualifying distributions, $29,666.
Limitations: Applications not accepted.
Application information: Contributes only to pre-selected organizations.
Officers: Richard E. Garman, Pres.; Patricia H. Garman, V.P.; Melissa G. Baumgart, Secy.-Treas.
EIN: 161592064

37400
Obrtlik School Fund
c/o M&T Bank
1 M&T Plz., 8th Fl.
Buffalo, NY 14203

Established in 2000 in NY.
Financial data (yr. ended 12/31/00): Grants paid, $29,644; assets, $473,476 (M); gifts received, $480,484; expenditures, $35,159; qualifying distributions, $29,644.
Limitations: Giving primarily in Binghamton, NY.
Trustee: M & T Bank.
EIN: 912129566

37401
The Harris Trust
37 Brookville Rd.
Glen Head, NY 11545

Established in 1960 in NY.
Donor(s): Henry U. Harris, Jr., Mary Jeanne Harris.‡
Financial data (yr. ended 12/31/01): Grants paid, $29,625; assets, $316,687 (M); expenditures, $33,046; qualifying distributions, $30,123.
Limitations: Applications not accepted. Giving primarily in NY.
Application information: Contributes only to pre-selected organizations.
Trustee: Henry U. Harris, Jr.
EIN: 116033492

37402
The Judith & Benjamin Marks Family Foundation, Inc.
c/o Spear, Leeds & Kellogg
120 Broadway, 8th Fl., Tax Dept.
New York, NY 10271

Established in 1996 in NY.
Donor(s): Benjamin Marks, The Marks Family, L.P.
Financial data (yr. ended 09/30/01): Grants paid, $29,585; assets, $157,171 (M); expenditures, $30,551; qualifying distributions, $29,585.
Limitations: Applications not accepted.
Application information: Contributes only to pre-selected organizations.
Officers: Benjamin Marks, Pres.; Judith Marks, V.P.; Nancy Phillips, Secy.-Treas.
EIN: 133919882

37403
The Helen R. & Harold C. Mayer Foundation, Inc.
c/o Mariner Mgmt.
516 5th Ave., Ste. 701
New York, NY 10036

Financial data (yr. ended 09/30/01): Grants paid, $29,507; assets, $527,716 (M); expenditures, $31,329; qualifying distributions, $29,507.
Limitations: Applications not accepted. Giving primarily in NY.
Application information: Contributes only to pre-selected organizations.
Officers and Directors:* Harold C. Mayer, Jr.,* Pres.; Sue Ellen Rittmaster,* V.P.; Joan Mayer, Treas.
EIN: 136062833

37404
Laurie Kayden Foundation
c/o Robert Horan, Phillips, Nizer, Benjamin, Krim & Ballon
666 5th Ave.
New York, NY 10103

Established in 1990 in NY.
Donor(s): Suzanne Kayden.
Financial data (yr. ended 12/31/01): Grants paid, $29,500; assets, $108,207 (M); gifts received, $16,500; expenditures, $30,831; qualifying distributions, $29,500.
Limitations: Applications not accepted. Giving limited to New York, NY.
Application information: Contributes only to pre-selected organizations.
Trustees: Robert Horan, Suzanne Kayden.
EIN: 133557216

37405
The Ruth McDayton Foundation
c/o Chamberlain, Willi, et al.
15 Maiden Ln., Ste. 705
New York, NY 10038

Financial data (yr. ended 05/31/02): Grants paid, $29,500; assets, $76,107 (M); expenditures, $29,703; qualifying distributions, $29,500.
Trustees: Robert D. Oucherloney, Richard A. Watson.
EIN: 133788809

37406
The Palmer-Walker Foundation
c/o Nancy Bick
173 Morris Ave.
Rockville Centre, NY 11570

Established in 1989 in NY.
Donor(s): Robert E. Palmer.
Financial data (yr. ended 12/31/01): Grants paid, $29,500; assets, $727,775 (M); expenditures, $31,320; qualifying distributions, $29,500.
Limitations: Applications not accepted.
Application information: Contributes only to pre-selected organizations.
Directors: Jane Bennett, Nancy Bick, R. Bruce Palmer.
EIN: 112988666

37407
The Storper Family Foundation Trust
c/o Ellen Rosen
45 E. Broadway, Ste. 9
Long Beach, NY 11561-4106

Established in 1998 in NY.
Financial data (yr. ended 12/31/01): Grants paid, $29,500; assets, $487,156 (M); expenditures, $45,698; qualifying distributions, $29,500.
Trustees: Sarah Field, Ellen Rosen, Barbara Storper, Dan Storper.
EIN: 116502064

37408
The Love Foundation, Inc.
(Formerly Joseph Love Foundation, Inc.)
215 Hilton Ave.
Hempstead, NY 11551-1200
Application address: P.O. Box 1200, Hempstead, NY 11551-1200, tel.: (516) 538-2400
Contact: Gerald N. Daffner, Tr.

Established in 1945 in DE.
Donor(s): Stanley J. Love.
Financial data (yr. ended 05/31/02): Grants paid, $29,458; assets, $389,581 (M); expenditures, $31,613; qualifying distributions, $29,458.
Limitations: Giving primarily in NY.
Officers: William K. Love, Pres. and Treas.; Victoria Love, V.P. and Secy.; Diane Love, V.P.
Trustee: Gerald N. Daffner.
EIN: 136110440

37409
Eva Shapiro Foundation, Inc.
1 Commander Sq.
Oyster Bay, NY 11771

Financial data (yr. ended 12/31/01): Grants paid, $29,425; assets, $784,472 (M); expenditures, $33,876; qualifying distributions, $29,425.
Limitations: Applications not accepted.
Application information: Contributes only to pre-selected organizations.
Directors: Harold Shapiro, Leonard Shapiro, Mark Shapiro, Steven Shapiro.
EIN: 112463637

37410
The Mandel Foundation
129-09 Jamaica Ave.
Richmond Hill, NY 11418

Established in 1987 in NY.
Donor(s): Robert Mandel.
Financial data (yr. ended 12/31/01): Grants paid, $29,400; assets, $78,914 (M); expenditures, $29,626; qualifying distributions, $29,400.
Limitations: Applications not accepted.
Application information: Contributes only to pre-selected organizations.
Trustees: Donald R. Deitrich, Daniel Mandel, Robert Mandel, Alfred J. Mernone.
EIN: 116330126

37411
Shipps Foundation
c/o Richard Davis
1185 Park Ave., Ste. 5G
New York, NY 10128

Established in 1999 in NY.
Donor(s): Richard R. Davis.
Financial data (yr. ended 12/31/00): Grants paid, $29,400; assets, $444,124 (M); gifts received, $185,872; expenditures, $49,202; qualifying distributions, $33,438.
Limitations: Applications not accepted.
Application information: Contributes only to pre-selected organizations.
Officer and Director:* Richard R. Davis,* Pres.
EIN: 134090870

37412
Packin Family Trust
110 Varick Ave.
Brooklyn, NY 11237 (718) 386-6119
Contact: David B. Packin, Mgr.

Donor(s): David B. Packin.
Financial data (yr. ended 12/31/99): Grants paid, $29,365; assets, $266,766 (M); gifts received,

37412—NEW YORK

$45,000; expenditures, $29,521; qualifying distributions, $29,521.
Application information: Application form not required.
Officer: David B. Packin, Mgr.
EIN: 133160359

37413
The Siegle Foundation, Inc.
75 S. Main St.
Homer, NY 13077
Application address: 30 Hunter Ln., Rochester, NY 14618
Contact: Joanne A. Siegle, V.P.

Established in 1988 in NY.
Donor(s): Victor G. Siegle, Ann H. Siegle.
Financial data (yr. ended 12/31/01): Grants paid, $29,356; assets, $515,160 (M); expenditures, $67,107; qualifying distributions, $29,356.
Limitations: Giving primarily in the central NY area.
Officers: Victor G. Siegle, Pres.; Joanne A. Siegle, V.P.; Ann H. Siegle, Exec. Dir.
Directors: Paul Handman, Amy Lagambino, Ronald Siegle.
EIN: 161341056

37414
The McCormick Family Foundation
4 Orama Dr.
Sands Point, NY 11050-1251

Established in 2000 in NY.
Donor(s): Michael McCormick, Genine McCormick.
Financial data (yr. ended 11/30/01): Grants paid, $29,350; assets, $188,564 (M); gifts received, $192,042; expenditures, $36,582; qualifying distributions, $29,350.
Limitations: Applications not accepted. Giving primarily in NY.
Application information: Contributes only to pre-selected organizations.
Officer: Genine McCormick, Secy.
Director: Michael McCormick.
EIN: 113532010

37415
The Eig Family Foundation, Inc.
c/o Lazard Freres & Co., LLC
30 Rockefeller Plz.
New York, NY 10020
Contact: Norman Eig, Pres.

Established in 1986 in NY.
Donor(s): Norman Eig.
Financial data (yr. ended 09/30/01): Grants paid, $29,325; assets, $604,055 (M); expenditures, $30,130; qualifying distributions, $29,325.
Limitations: Giving primarily in NJ and NY.
Officers and Directors:* Norman Eig,* Pres.; Barbara Eig,* V.P.; Charles W. Steiglitz,* Secy.-Treas.
EIN: 133384957

37416
The Lewis Foundation
c/o Maria L. Phillips
196 E. 7th St.
New York, NY 10021

Financial data (yr. ended 12/31/01): Grants paid, $29,300; assets, $535,922 (M); expenditures, $31,970; qualifying distributions, $29,300.

Limitations: Applications not accepted. Giving primarily in CT, New York, NY, and VA.
Application information: Contributes only to pre-selected organizations.
Trustees: Maria B. Lewis, Chair.; Charles W. Lewis, Jr., Maria L. Phillips.
EIN: 136059553

37417
Christiane L. and Richard J. Hiegel Charitable Foundation
Worldwide Plz.
825 8th Ave., Ste. 4550
New York, NY 10019

Established in 1987 in NY.
Donor(s): Christiane L. Hiegel, Richard J. Hiegel.
Financial data (yr. ended 12/31/01): Grants paid, $29,265; assets, $62,889 (M); expenditures, $29,660; qualifying distributions, $29,660.
Limitations: Applications not accepted. Giving primarily in NY.
Application information: Contributes only to pre-selected organizations.
Trustees: Christiane L. Hiegel, Richard J. Hiegel.
EIN: 136879590

37418
The Fernandez Family Foundation, Inc.
c/o Perelson Weiner, LLP
1 Dag Hammarskjold Plz., 42nd Fl.
New York, NY 10017

Established in 1994 in CT.
Donor(s): Manuel Fernandez.
Financial data (yr. ended 11/30/01): Grants paid, $29,250; assets, $941,780 (M); gifts received, $82,654; expenditures, $41,587; qualifying distributions, $37,250.
Limitations: Applications not accepted. Giving on a national basis.
Application information: Contributes only to pre-selected organizations.
Officers and Directors:* Joanne Fernandez,* Pres.; Manuel Fernandez,* Treas.; Christina Fernandez, Kimberly Ann Fernandez.
EIN: 061414462

37419
Zichron Yehoshua Beirach Foundation
1274 49th St., Ste. 66
Brooklyn, NY 11219-3011
Contact: Alan Wohlberg, Tr.

Established in 1999.
Financial data (yr. ended 08/31/00): Grants paid, $29,240; assets, $2,297 (M); gifts received, $32,500; expenditures, $30,712; qualifying distributions, $30,712; giving activities include $1,472 for programs.
Limitations: Giving primarily in NY.
Trustee: Alan Wohlberg.
EIN: 113499566

37420
The Ilex Foundation
c/o Rockefeller & Co., Inc.
30 Rockefeller Plz., Ste. 5600
New York, NY 10112

Established in 1999 in OH.
Donor(s): Olga Davidson Nagy.
Financial data (yr. ended 01/31/02): Grants paid, $29,180; assets, $188,877 (M); gifts received,

$487,900; expenditures, $459,099; qualifying distributions, $29,180.
Limitations: Applications not accepted. Giving primarily in MA and NJ.
Application information: Contributes only to pre-selected organizations.
Officer: Olga Davidson Nagy, Chair.
Trustees: Mohammed J. Mahallati, Hossein Modaressi, Roy P. Mottahedeh, Gregory Nagy, T. Michael Searson, Richard T. Watson.
EIN: 347089903

37421
Richard Blumenthal & Linda Morgan Foundation
488 Madison Ave., 8th Fl.
New York, NY 10022-5702

Established in 1996 in NY.
Donor(s): Richard Blumenthal.
Financial data (yr. ended 12/31/01): Grants paid, $29,160; assets, $367,206 (M); gifts received, $27,621; expenditures, $30,143; qualifying distributions, $29,767.
Limitations: Applications not accepted.
Application information: Contributes only to pre-selected organizations.
Trustees: Richard Blumenthal, Linda Morgan.
EIN: 137097699

37422
Edward Sykes Foundation
(Formerly Edward Sykes Endowment Trust)
c/o JPMorgan Chase Bank
P.O. Box 31412
Rochester, NY 14603-1412
Application address: 1 Chase Manhattan Plz., 4th Fl., New York, NY 10081, tel.: (212) 552-2869
Contact: Anthony Sorge, Trust Off., JPMorgan Chase Bank

Financial data (yr. ended 12/31/01): Grants paid, $29,135; assets, $393,307 (M); expenditures, $34,622; qualifying distributions, $29,718.
Limitations: Giving limited to New York, NY.
Trustee: JPMorgan Chase Bank.
EIN: 136023438

37423
Antoinette & Lawrence Iannotti Foundation
c/o Cassin, Cassin & Joseph
300 E. 42nd St.
New York, NY 10017-5947

Established in 2000 in NY.
Donor(s): Antoinette Iannottie Trust, New Whitehouse Food Market, Inc., Francesca Iannotti.
Financial data (yr. ended 12/31/00): Grants paid, $29,100; assets, $591,839 (M); gifts received, $578,339; expenditures, $30,045; qualifying distributions, $13,501.
Limitations: Applications not accepted. Giving primarily in NY.
Application information: Contributes only to pre-selected organizations.
Directors: Joseph M. Cassin, Lawrence P. Iannotti, Jr., Nina Maguire.
EIN: 132518466

NEW YORK—37437

37424
The Drs. Maxwell and Maria Mintz Family Foundation
54 Westwood Dr.
Glens Falls, NY 12804
Application address: c/o Dugan, Colthart & Zoch, P.A., P.O. Box 576, Closter, NJ 07624
Contact: Kenneth Parlin, Secy.

Established in 1999 in DE.
Donor(s): Mildred Fitzgerald.
Financial data (yr. ended 12/31/01): Grants paid, $29,100; assets, $89,538 (M); gifts received, $20,795; expenditures, $32,895; qualifying distributions, $29,100.
Limitations: Giving primarily in NY.
Officers: Dr. Maxwell Mintz, Chair.; Kenneth B. Parlin, Secy.; Andrew S. Parlin, Treas.
EIN: 141812970

37425
Alan & Elaine Lichtenberg Foundation
c/o Barbara Mironov
10 Pond Park Rd.
Great Neck, NY 11023-2012

Established in 1999 in NY.
Donor(s): Alan Lichtenberg.
Financial data (yr. ended 09/30/00): Grants paid, $29,087; assets, $233,490 (M); gifts received, $226,567; expenditures, $31,456; qualifying distributions, $31,406.
Limitations: Applications not accepted. Giving primarily in NY.
Application information: Contributes only to pre-selected organizations.
Officers: Barbara Mironov, Pres.; Susan Karelitz, V.P.; Richard Lichtenberg, Secy.; Diane Lichtenberg-Scanlan, Treas.
EIN: 116530618

37426
Louis & Lena Minkoff Foundation, Inc.
(Formerly Louis & Lena Minkoff Memorial Foundation)
28 Wildwood Dr.
Kings Point, NY 11024-1246

Established in 1967 in NY.
Donor(s): Harry Minkoff, Gift Pax, Inc.
Financial data (yr. ended 12/31/01): Grants paid, $29,060; assets, $1,580,842 (M); expenditures, $50,655; qualifying distributions, $29,060.
Limitations: Giving primarily in NY.
Officers: Lawrence A. Minkoff, Pres.; George Minkoff, V.P.; Ruth Minkoff, Secy.; Harry Minkoff, Treas.
EIN: 116078778

37427
Athas Zaharis Agoriani Trust
58-29 213th St.
Oakland Gardens, NY 11364
Contact: John Zaharis, Tr.

Financial data (yr. ended 12/31/00): Grants paid, $29,054; assets, $408,582 (M); expenditures, $32,567; qualifying distributions, $31,467.
Limitations: Giving limited to the town of Agoriani in Sparta, Greece.
Trustees: Theodore Dimon, John Zaharis.
EIN: 112801980
Codes: GTI

37428
Atkins Family Foundation
350 E. 57th St., Ste. 8A
New York, NY 10022

Established in 1999 in PA.
Donor(s): Patrick Atkins.
Financial data (yr. ended 12/30/01): Grants paid, $29,000; assets, $805,752 (M); gifts received, $89,091; expenditures, $32,910; qualifying distributions, $29,976.
Limitations: Applications not accepted. Giving primarily in NC, NY, and PA.
Application information: Contributes only to pre-selected organizations.
Officers: Patrick Atkins, Pres.; John Michael Atkins, V.P.; Lee Anne Mangone, Secy.; Michele R. Atkins, Treas.
EIN: 251844415

37429
Feder Family Foundation
733 Cornaga Ct.
Far Rockaway, NY 11691
Application address: 277 Broadway, New York, NY 10007, tel.: (212) 962-5999
Contact: Abraham Feder, Dir.

Established in 1994 in NY.
Donor(s): Abraham Feder.
Financial data (yr. ended 12/31/01): Grants paid, $29,000; assets, $8,221 (M); gifts received, $24,930; expenditures, $29,065; qualifying distributions, $29,000.
Limitations: Giving primarily in NY.
Directors: Abraham Feder, Estelle Feder.
EIN: 113221108

37430
Annesta R. Gardner Trust
c/o JPMorgan Chase Bank
P.O. Box 31412
Rochester, NY 14603
Contact: Dick Hamilton, Trust Off., JPMorgan Chase Bank

Donor(s): Annesta R. Gardner.‡
Financial data (yr. ended 11/30/01): Grants paid, $29,000; assets, $324,097 (M); expenditures, $37,635; qualifying distributions, $30,435.
Limitations: Giving primarily in New York, NY.
Application information: Application form not required.
Trustees: Howard N. Golden, JPMorgan Chase Bank.
EIN: 136715780

37431
The Toldos Yaakov Foundation
c/o Max Wassor
132 Nassau St.
New York, NY 10036

Financial data (yr. ended 09/30/99): Grants paid, $29,000; assets, $2,300 (M); gifts received, $28,831; expenditures, $29,236; qualifying distributions, $29,000.
Limitations: Applications not accepted. Giving primarily in New York, NY.
Application information: Contributes only to pre-selected organizations.
Trustees: Rabbi Shaya Klor, Yossie Rieder.
EIN: 118061085

37432
Wildermuth Memorial Foundation, Inc.
560 Delaware Rd.
Kenmore, NY 14223 (716) 877-2251
Contact: Nancy Gesicki, Pres.

Established in 1990 in NY.
Financial data (yr. ended 12/31/01): Grants paid, $29,000; assets, $1,461,890 (M); expenditures, $56,167; qualifying distributions, $29,000.
Limitations: Giving primarily in NY.
Officers and Directors:* Nancy Gesicki,* Pres. and Treas.; Robert J. Gesicki,* V.P.; Lorraine Schuster,* Secy.; Jean Donoghue,* Research Prog. Dir.
EIN: 161378283

37433
Amos Foundation, Inc.
120 E. Washington St., Ste. 600
Syracuse, NY 13202 (315) 428-9446
Contact: William P. Christy, Jr., Tr.

Established in 1957.
Donor(s): John Amos,‡ George Dowley, C.L. Amos Co., Inc.
Financial data (yr. ended 12/31/01): Grants paid, $28,950; assets, $903,626 (M); expenditures, $41,446; qualifying distributions, $28,950.
Limitations: Giving primarily in Syracuse, NY.
Officer: Charmaine S. Hanreck, Secy.-Treas.
Trustee: William P. Christy, Jr.
EIN: 156017561

37434
The Seligson Foundation
Valley Rd.
Locust Valley, NY 11560 (516) 997-4212
Contact: Alan Seligson, Pres.

Established in 1982 in NY.
Donor(s): Alan Seligson.
Financial data (yr. ended 11/30/01): Grants paid, $28,929; assets, $668,229 (M); expenditures, $30,979; qualifying distributions, $28,929.
Limitations: Giving primarily in NY.
Officers: Alan Seligson, Pres.; Kate Seligson, V.P.; Nancy Seligson, V.P.; Edith Seligson, Secy.
EIN: 112625463

37435
The Gilbert Brownstone Foundation, Inc.
166 E. 61st St.
New York, NY 10021
Contact: Michael L. Sher

Established in 1999 in NY.
Donor(s): Gilbert Brownstone.
Financial data (yr. ended 06/30/01): Grants paid, $28,915; assets, $301,044 (M); expenditures, $58,907; qualifying distributions, $28,915.
Officers: Gilbert Brownstone, Pres. and Treas.; Catherine Brownstone, V.P. and Secy.
EIN: 134103052

37436
Sydney & Marjory Krause Foundation, Inc.
c/o Jean Krause Bauman
18 Ridgetop Dr.
Tomkins Cove, NY 10986-1647
Application address: 3208 44th St. N.W., Washington, DC 20016
Contact: Ralph Krause, Pres.

Financial data (yr. ended 12/31/00): Grants paid, $28,900; assets, $464,272 (M); expenditures, $30,735; qualifying distributions, $28,900.
Limitations: Giving primarily in NY.
Application information: Application form not required.
Officers: Ralph Krause, Pres.; Jean Krause Bauman, V.P. and Secy.; Ellen Krause Citron, Treas.
EIN: 237028886

37437
Security Trust
c/o Steven Hill
18 Jill Ln.
Monsey, NY 10952

Established in 1997 in NY.
Donor(s): Steven Hill.
Financial data (yr. ended 11/30/00): Grants paid, $28,894; assets, $46,336 (M); gifts received,

37437—NEW YORK

$19,450; expenditures, $29,423; qualifying distributions, $28,882.
Limitations: Applications not accepted. Giving primarily in NY.
Application information: Contributes only to pre-selected organizations.
Trustees: Rachel Hill, Steven Hill.
EIN: 137129971

37438
The Babajide Foundation
c/o Goldman Sachs & Co.
85 Broad St., Tax Dept.
New York, NY 10004

Established in 1997 in NY.
Donor(s): Jide J. Zeitlin.
Financial data (yr. ended 12/31/00): Grants paid, $28,850; assets, $19,549 (M); gifts received, $15,350; expenditures, $28,900; qualifying distributions, $28,824.
Limitations: Applications not accepted. Giving primarily in MA and NY.
Application information: Contributes only to pre-selected organizations.
Trustee: Jide J. Zeitlin.
EIN: 133931289

37439
Margaret B. Monahan and Alberta W. Laighton Memorial Fund
P.O. Box 788
Pawling, NY 12564-0788

Financial data (yr. ended 12/31/01): Grants paid, $28,850; assets, $515,174 (M); expenditures, $30,052; qualifying distributions, $28,488.
Limitations: Applications not accepted. Giving limited to Pawling, NY.
Trustees: John Daniels, M.D., Anna Loper, Charlotte Whaley, C. Ross Daniels, Jr.
EIN: 146022154
Codes: GTI

37440
The Perillo Tours Foundation
c/o Tornatore & Co.
6075 E. Molloy Rd., Bldg. 5
Syracuse, NY 13211

Established in 1995 in NJ.
Donor(s): Mario P. Perillo.
Financial data (yr. ended 12/31/01): Grants paid, $28,850; assets, $569,651 (M); expenditures, $28,877; qualifying distributions, $28,850.
Limitations: Applications not accepted. Giving primarily in New York, NY.
Application information: Contributes only to pre-selected organizations.
Trustees: Mario P. Perillo, Stephen Perillo, Samuel T. Tornatore.
EIN: 226665506

37441
The Lawrence & Carol Saper Foundation
c/o Swidler, Berlin, Shereff & Friedman
405 Lexington Ave., 11th Fl.
New York, NY 10174-1100

Established in 1996 in NY.
Donor(s): Lawrence Saper.
Financial data (yr. ended 12/31/01): Grants paid, $28,840; assets, $2,788,709 (M); gifts received, $1,000,000; expenditures, $31,170; qualifying distributions, $28,840.
Limitations: Applications not accepted. Giving primarily in NY.
Application information: Contributes only to pre-selected organizations.
Officers: Lawrence Saper, Chair.; Carol Saper, V.P. and Treas.; Martin Nussbaum, Secy.
EIN: 133946616

37442
Solomon & Clara Rabinowitz Foundation, Inc.
18 Hummingbird Rd.
Roslyn, NY 11576 (516) 621-1040
Application address: 4 Joy Dr., New Hyde Park, NY 11040
Contact: Stanley Rabinowitz, Tr. or Milton Rabinowitz, Tr.

Established in 1987 in NY.
Donor(s): Clara Rabinowitz, Solomon Rabinowitz.
Financial data (yr. ended 04/30/01): Grants paid, $28,823; assets, $429,946 (M); expenditures, $33,796; qualifying distributions, $28,823.
Limitations: Giving primarily in the metropolitan New York, NY, area.
Trustees: Milton Rabinowitz, Stanley Rabinowitz.
EIN: 112556174

37443
Davidsohn Family Foundation, Inc.
1471 55th St.
Brooklyn, NY 11219

Established in 1994 in NY.
Donor(s): George Davidsohn.
Financial data (yr. ended 11/30/01): Grants paid, $28,782; assets, $23,432 (M); gifts received, $50,000; expenditures, $29,594; qualifying distributions, $28,780.
Limitations: Applications not accepted.
Application information: Contributes only to pre-selected organizations.
Officer: George Davidsohn, Pres.
Trustee: Denise Davidsohn.
EIN: 133799767

37444
Alan & Janis Goldberg Foundation, Inc.
10 Kenneth Ct.
Great Neck, NY 11024
Contact: Alan Goldberg, Pres.

Established in 1984.
Donor(s): Alan Goldberg, Murray Goldberg, Charlotte Goldberg.
Financial data (yr. ended 05/31/02): Grants paid, $28,760; assets, $274,645 (M); expenditures, $28,940; qualifying distributions, $28,760.
Limitations: Giving primarily in NY.
Officers: Alan Goldberg, Pres.; Janis Goldberg, Secy.
EIN: 133234427

37445
Seymour Schuman Foundation, Inc.
36-04 Skillman Ave.
Long Island City, NY 11101

Donor(s): Propper Manufacturing Co., Beatrice Schuman.
Financial data (yr. ended 06/30/01): Grants paid, $28,755; assets, $53,256 (M); gifts received, $62,000; expenditures, $28,786; qualifying distributions, $28,775.
Limitations: Applications not accepted. Giving primarily in New York, NY.
Application information: Contributes only to pre-selected organizations.
Officers: Seymour Schuman, Pres.; Beatrice Schuman, V.P.
EIN: 136224245
Codes: CS

37446
The Westlake Foundation, Inc.
c/o Konigsberg, Wolf & Co.
440 Park Ave. S.
New York, NY 10016
Contact: Paul Konigsberg, Pres.

Established in 1986 in NY.
Donor(s): Robert Konigsberg, PLR Assocs.
Financial data (yr. ended 12/31/01): Grants paid, $28,750; assets, $288,595 (M); gifts received, $10,800; expenditures, $29,455; qualifying distributions, $28,750.
Limitations: Applications not accepted. Giving primarily in New York, NY.
Officers: Paul J. Konigsberg, Pres.; Robert Konigsberg, Secy.
EIN: 133393042

37447
Austen-Stokes Ancient Americas Foundation, Inc.
507 N. Midland Ave.
Upper Nyack, NY 10960

Established in 1999 in NY.
Donor(s): John A. Stokes, Jr.
Financial data (yr. ended 12/31/01): Grants paid, $28,749; assets, $525,167 (M); gifts received, $24,071; expenditures, $52,324; qualifying distributions, $48,098.
Limitations: Applications not accepted.
Application information: Contributes only to pre-selected organizations.
Officers: John A. Stokes, Jr., Pres. and Treas.; Marisol Hernandez De Stokes, Secy.
Director: Elena Austen Stokes.
EIN: 134052244

37448
Butler Foundation, Inc.
550 Park Ave., Ste. 10W
New York, NY 10021-7369

Established in 1988 in FL.
Donor(s): William J. Butler, Patricia Butler.
Financial data (yr. ended 12/31/01): Grants paid, $28,700; assets, $26,125 (M); expenditures, $28,922; qualifying distributions, $28,700.
Limitations: Applications not accepted. Giving primarily in NY.
Application information: Contributes only to pre-selected organizations.
Officers: William Jack Butler, Pres.; Patricia Fleming Butler, V.P.
Director: Peter Butler.
EIN: 592898825

37449
David and Lucille Gildin Foundation
6 Xavier Dr., Ste. 311A
Yonkers, NY 10704-1361

Donor(s): David Gildin, Lucille Gildin.‡
Financial data (yr. ended 12/31/99): Grants paid, $28,677; assets, $342,585 (M); gifts received, $20,395; expenditures, $31,993; qualifying distributions, $29,644.
Limitations: Applications not accepted. Giving primarily in NY.
Application information: Contributes only to pre-selected organizations.
Officers: David Gildin, Pres.; Marsha Gildin, Secy.-Treas.
EIN: 133178179

37450
Birsh Foundation, Inc.
c/o Arthur T. Birsh
52 Vanderbilt Ave.
New York, NY 10017

Established in 1948 in NY.
Donor(s): Playbill, Inc.
Financial data (yr. ended 06/30/02): Grants paid, $28,600; assets, $12,809 (M); gifts received, $20,000; expenditures, $29,455; qualifying distributions, $28,600.
Limitations: Applications not accepted. Giving primarily in New York, NY.
Application information: Contributes only to pre-selected organizations.
Officer: Arthur T. Birsh, Mgr.
EIN: 136160082

37451
The Gladys & Murray Goldstein Foundation, Inc.
10 Iroquois Trail
Harrison, NY 10528

Donor(s): Gladys Goldstein, Murray Goldstein, Sanford M. Goldstein, Richard Goldstein.
Financial data (yr. ended 11/30/99): Grants paid, $28,585; assets, $128,810 (M); gifts received, $21,100; expenditures, $29,372; qualifying distributions, $28,585.
Limitations: Applications not accepted. Giving primarily in New Rochelle and the greater New York, NY, area.
Application information: Contributes only to pre-selected organizations.
Officers: Gladys Goldstein, Pres.; Murray Goldstein, Secy.; Richard Goldstein, Mgr.
EIN: 113083067

37452
Mandeville Foundation, Inc.
60 E. 42nd St., Rm. 843
New York, NY 10165-0843 (212) 697-4785
Contact: Hubert T. Mandeville, Pres.

Incorporated in 1963 in CT.
Donor(s): Ernest W. Mandeville.
Financial data (yr. ended 12/31/01): Grants paid, $28,536; assets, $673,059 (M); expenditures, $305,358; qualifying distributions, $143,678.
Limitations: Giving primarily in CT and NY.
Application information: Application form not required.
Officers and Directors:* Hubert T. Mandeville,* Pres. and Treas.; P. Kempton Mandeville,* V.P.; Maurice C. Greenbaum,* Secy.; Meredith H. Hollis, Matthew T. Mandeville.
EIN: 066043343

37453
Leora E. Belknap Trust
2224 Burdett Ave.
Troy, NY 12180

Financial data (yr. ended 12/31/01): Grants paid, $28,500; assets, $378,207 (M); expenditures, $30,550; qualifying distributions, $30,300.
Limitations: Applications not accepted.
Application information: Contributes only to pre-selected organizations.
Trustee: David Tomlinson.
EIN: 146155391

37454
Emanuel & Zelda Bruckenstein Family Trust
1877 E. 9th St.
Brooklyn, NY 11233
Contact: Yehudah Leib Puretz, Tr.

Established in 1994.
Donor(s): Emanuel Bruckenstein.‡
Financial data (yr. ended 07/31/01): Grants paid, $28,500; assets, $312,317 (M); gifts received, $8,036; expenditures, $34,792; qualifying distributions, $34,566.
Trustees: Israel Grossman, Yehudah Leib Puretz.
EIN: 116441005

37455
The David and Esther Goldstein Charitable Trust
5413 17th Ave.
Brooklyn, NY 11204

Established in 1999 in NY.
Donor(s): Esther Goldstein.
Financial data (yr. ended 12/31/01): Grants paid, $28,500; assets, $672,609 (M); gifts received, $213,500; expenditures, $28,729; qualifying distributions, $28,500.
Limitations: Applications not accepted.
Application information: Contributes only to pre-selected organizations.
Trustees: David Goldstein, Armin Kaufman.
EIN: 116519669

37456
The Hatrick Foundation
c/o Cleary Gottlieb
One Liberty Plz.
New York, NY 10006

Established in 2001 in NY.
Donor(s): Karin Lopp.
Financial data (yr. ended 12/31/01): Grants paid, $28,500; assets, $263,485 (M); gifts received, $290,956; expenditures, $28,500; qualifying distributions, $28,500.
Limitations: Applications not accepted. Giving primarily in White Plains, NY.
Application information: Contributes only to pre-selected organizations.
Trustees: Steve M. Loeb, Karin Lopp.
EIN: 134146008

37457
The JTK Foundation
c/o Rosen Seymour Shapss Martin & Co., LLP
757 3rd Ave.
New York, NY 10017

Established in 1996 in NY.
Financial data (yr. ended 12/31/01): Grants paid, $28,500; assets, $1,465,768 (M); gifts received, $99,498; expenditures, $42,038; qualifying distributions, $28,500.
Limitations: Giving primarily in NY.
Trustees: Jayne T. Keith, Walter C. Teagle III.
EIN: 133923848

37458
George C. Karlson Foundation
c/o Magdalen Gaynor
10 Bank St., Ste. 650
White Plains, NY 10601

Financial data (yr. ended 12/31/01): Grants paid, $28,500; assets, $371,148 (M); expenditures, $30,275; qualifying distributions, $28,500.
Limitations: Applications not accepted. Giving primarily in NY.
Application information: Contributes only to pre-selected organizations.
Trustee: Roger A. Karlson.
EIN: 116043764

37459
Morris Levy Foundation for Children
(Formerly Strawberries Trust for Children)
c/o Sunnyview Farm
140 Arch Bridge Rd.
Ghent, NY 12075
Contact: Adam R. Levy, Tr.

Donor(s): Morris Levy.
Financial data (yr. ended 12/31/01): Grants paid, $28,500; assets, $359,167 (M); expenditures, $31,224; qualifying distributions, $28,500.
Limitations: Giving primarily in NY.
Trustees: Adam R. Levy, Jules Weinstein.
EIN: 222827058

37460
Edith W. MacGuire Charitable Trust
c/o Leon D. Alpern & Co.
200 Garden City Plz., Ste. 224
Garden City, NY 11530
Contact: Edith W. MacGuire, Tr.

Established in 1998 in NY.
Donor(s): Edith MacGuire.
Financial data (yr. ended 12/31/01): Grants paid, $28,500; assets, $762,649 (M); gifts received, $250,000; expenditures, $39,988; qualifying distributions, $28,680.
Trustee: Edith W. MacGuire.
EIN: 311627048

37461
Dr. Joseph B. & Lillian Stiefel Foundation, Inc.
269 Kneeland Ave.
Yonkers, NY 10705

Established in 1999.
Financial data (yr. ended 12/31/01): Grants paid, $28,500; assets, $527,428 (M); expenditures, $31,223; qualifying distributions, $28,500.
Limitations: Applications not accepted.
Application information: Contributes only to pre-selected organizations.
Officers: Noah Weinshell, Pres.; Marcia Weinshell, Secy.
EIN: 223639034

37462
Aram Soba Foundation
(Formerly Maaser, Inc.)
c/o Kramer Levin, et al.
919 3rd Ave., 41st Fl.
New York, NY 10022-3902
Application address: 1780 E. 9th St., Brooklyn, NY 11223
Contact: Jimmy Sitt, Pres.

Established in 1990.
Financial data (yr. ended 12/31/99): Grants paid, $28,484; assets, $637 (M); gifts received, $26,516; expenditures, $28,554; qualifying distributions, $28,554.
Officers: Jimmy Sitt, Pres.; Jack Kuessous, V.P.; Saul E. Burian, Secy.
EIN: 133517185
Codes: GTI

37463
Sonnenblick Foundation, Inc.
712 5th Ave.
New York, NY 10019 (212) 841-9200
Contact: Arthur I. Sonnenblick, Pres.

Established in 1954 in NY.
Donor(s): Arthur I. Sonnenblick, Jack E. Sonnenblick.
Financial data (yr. ended 03/31/01): Grants paid, $28,480; assets, $1 (M); gifts received, $11,000; expenditures, $29,608; qualifying distributions, $28,480.

37463

Limitations: Giving primarily in NY.
Officers and Directors:* Arthur I. Sonnenblick,* Pres.; Sybil Sonnenblick,* Secy.; Steven Sonnenblick,* Treas.
EIN: 136122775

37464
Philip Scaturro Foundation
c/o Allen & Co.
711 5th Ave., 9th Fl.
New York, NY 10022
Contact: Philip Scaturro, Pres.

Established in 1988 in NY.
Donor(s): Philip Scaturro.
Financial data (yr. ended 11/30/00): Grants paid, $28,434; assets, $766,810 (M); expenditures, $32,820; qualifying distributions, $32,767.
Limitations: Giving primarily in NY.
Officer: Philip Scaturro, Pres.
EIN: 133541859

37465
Fertig Family Foundation
105 Joseph Ave.
Staten Island, NY 10314-5054

Established in 1998 in NY.
Donor(s): Seymour Fertig.
Financial data (yr. ended 12/31/01): Grants paid, $28,414; assets, $185,176 (M); gifts received, $28,055; expenditures, $29,373; qualifying distributions, $28,414.
Limitations: Applications not accepted.
Application information: Contributes only to pre-selected organizations.
Director: Seymour Fertig.
EIN: 137159763

37466
AJM Foundation
2003 Ave. J, Ste. 1C
Brooklyn, NY 11210

Established in 1996 in NY.
Donor(s): Lieberman Family.
Financial data (yr. ended 12/31/01): Grants paid, $28,383; assets, $9,793 (M); expenditures, $28,388; qualifying distributions, $28,383.
Limitations: Applications not accepted. Giving primarily in NJ and NY.
Application information: Contributes only to pre-selected organizations.
Trustee: Lillian Lieberman.
EIN: 113326328

37467
Sylvan Schefler Trust Foundation
540 Madison Ave., 15th Fl.
New York, NY 10022-3213
Contact: Sylvan Schefler, Mgr.

Established in 1985 in NY.
Donor(s): Sylvan Schefler.
Financial data (yr. ended 12/31/01): Grants paid, $28,355; assets, $1,778 (M); gifts received, $21,825; expenditures, $28,433; qualifying distributions, $28,355.
Limitations: Giving primarily in NY.
Officer: Sylvan Schefler, Mgr.
EIN: 136270065

37468
Takako and Paul Richards Foundation, Inc.
1 Lincoln Ctr.
20 W. 64th St., Apt. 29E
New York, NY 10023

Donor(s): Paul D. Richards.
Financial data (yr. ended 12/31/01): Grants paid, $28,350; assets, $339,373 (M); expenditures, $29,100; qualifying distributions, $28,350.

Limitations: Applications not accepted. Giving primarily in New York, NY.
Application information: Contributes only to pre-selected organizations.
Officer: Paul D. Richards, Pres.; Takako Richards, Secy.-Treas.
EIN: 133967587

37469
J. Perlbinder Foundation
429 E. 52nd St.
New York, NY 10022-6478

Donor(s): J. Perlbinder.
Financial data (yr. ended 12/31/01): Grants paid, $28,305; assets, $34,823 (M); gifts received, $25,000; expenditures, $29,295; qualifying distributions, $28,305.
Limitations: Applications not accepted.
Application information: Contributes only to pre-selected organizations.
Officers: Julius Perlbinder, Pres.; Martin Berger, V.P.; Stephen Perlbinder, V.P.; Lillian West, V.P.; Bernard West, Secy.; Augusta Berger, Treas.
EIN: 136217042

37470
The Donald F. & Barbara L. Newman Family Foundation
2440 Sheriadan Dr.
Tonawanda, NY 14150

Established in 1998 in NY.
Donor(s): Donald F. Newman.
Financial data (yr. ended 12/31/01): Grants paid, $28,300; assets, $719,195 (M); gifts received, $19,258; expenditures, $43,675; qualifying distributions, $28,300.
Limitations: Giving primarily in FL and MI.
Officers: Donald F. Newman, Pres. and Treas.; Barbara L. Newman, V.P.; James D. Newman, V.P.; Michael F. Newman, V.P.; Robert L. Newman, V.P.; Thomas B. Newman, V.P.; Paul A. Battaglia, Secy.
EIN: 311593672

37471
James M. Slattery Foundation, Inc.
1 Hollow Ln., Ste. 311
New Hyde Park, NY 11042

Donor(s): James M. Slattery,‡ Slattery Investors Corp.
Financial data (yr. ended 03/31/01): Grants paid, $28,295; assets, $497,487 (M); expenditures, $38,418; qualifying distributions, $28,295.
Limitations: Applications not accepted. Giving primarily in Palm Beach, FL, and New York, NY.
Application information: Contributes only to pre-selected organizations.
Directors: Gloria T. Confort, Bernard Richards.
EIN: 116011688

37472
Grosser Family Foundation Trust
c/o Shane Yurman
127 Rte. 59
Monsey, NY 10952

Established in 1996 in NY.
Donor(s): Robert Grosser.
Financial data (yr. ended 11/30/01): Grants paid, $28,254; assets, $0 (M); gifts received, $109,594; expenditures, $28,254; qualifying distributions, $28,254.
Trustees: Steven Heller, Patricia Kantor.
EIN: 133936219

37473
The A. J. Perella Foundation
c/o Joseph R. Perella
998 5th Ave.
New York, NY 10028

Established in 2001 in NY.
Donor(s): Mrs. Joseph Perella, Joseph Perella.
Financial data (yr. ended 12/31/01): Grants paid, $28,250; assets, $126,009 (M); gifts received, $154,201; expenditures, $28,250; qualifying distributions, $28,250.
Limitations: Applications not accepted.
Application information: Contributes only to pre-selected organizations.
Trustees: Amy M. Perella, Joseph R. Perella.
EIN: 134200954

37474
Joseph & Laura Wortman Foundation
c/o Citibank, N.A., Tax Dept.
1 Court Sq., 22nd Fl.
Long Island City, NY 11120

Established in 1989 in NY.
Financial data (yr. ended 12/31/00): Grants paid, $28,249; assets, $521,932 (M); expenditures, $39,682; qualifying distributions, $27,879.
Limitations: Applications not accepted.
Application information: Contributes only to pre-selected organizations.
Trustees: Barry M. Berkeley, Citibank, N.A.
EIN: 136919339

37475
The Dorothy and Marshall M. Reisman Foundation
4555 E. Lake Rd.
Cazenovia, NY 13035 (315) 652-3771
Contact: Marshall M. Reisman, Tr.

Established in 1991 in NY.
Donor(s): Dorothy Reisman, Marshall M. Reisman, Andan Services, Inc.
Financial data (yr. ended 01/31/00): Grants paid, $28,245; assets, $541,698 (M); expenditures, $35,913; qualifying distributions, $29,661.
Limitations: Giving limited to NY.
Trustee: Marshall M. Reisman.
EIN: 166353565

37476
McCabe Family Foundation
c/o Barry Strauss Assocs., Ltd.
307 5th Ave., 8th Fl.
New York, NY 10016-6517

Established in 1994 in NY.
Donor(s): Robert A. McCabe.
Financial data (yr. ended 06/30/01): Grants paid, $28,224; assets, $139,728 (M); gifts received, $1,281; expenditures, $30,495; qualifying distributions, $28,999.
Limitations: Applications not accepted. Giving primarily in Cambridge, MA.
Application information: Contributes only to pre-selected organizations.
Trustees: Anne E. McCabe, Constantina McCabe, George F. McCabe, Robert A. McCabe.
EIN: 133786334

37477
Rosenbaum-Zell Family Foundation, Inc.
c/o Joseph Graf & Co., LLP
6 E. 43rd St.
New York, NY 10017

Established around 1966.
Donor(s): Ilse Rosenbaum,‡ Werner Rosenbaum.
Financial data (yr. ended 02/28/02): Grants paid, $28,187; assets, $23,104 (M); gifts received,

$30,155; expenditures, $28,485; qualifying distributions, $28,187.
Limitations: Applications not accepted. Giving primarily in the greater New York, NY, area.
Application information: Contributes only to pre-selected organizations.
Officers: Walter Hecht, Pres.; Werner Rosenbaum, V.P.
EIN: 136204700

37478
The Polsky Foundation
667 Madison Ave.
New York, NY 10021

Donor(s): Alexander Polsky, Cynthia Polsky.
Financial data (yr. ended 12/31/00): Grants paid, $28,125; assets, $1,636,773 (M); gifts received, $102,346; expenditures, $41,956; qualifying distributions, $28,125.
Limitations: Applications not accepted. Giving primarily in NY.
Application information: Contributes only to pre-selected organizations.
Officers: Cynthia H. Polsky, Chair.; Leon Polsky, Pres.; Alexander Polsky, V.P. and Treas.; Nicholas Polsky, Secy.
EIN: 510245812

37479
The Brear Foundation
c/o BBH Trust Co.
63 Wall St.
New York, NY 10005

Established in 2000 in MA.
Donor(s): Robert S. Ross, Betsy Glaser.
Financial data (yr. ended 12/31/01): Grants paid, $28,100; assets, $359,668 (M); expenditures, $47,045; qualifying distributions, $28,100.
Limitations: Applications not accepted. Giving primarily in Cambridge, MA and Flushing, NY.
Application information: Contributes only to pre-selected organizations.
Trustees: Betsy Glaser, Robert S. Ross, Brown Bros. Harriman Trust Co. of PA.
EIN: 043541794

37480
The Mirabito Foundation
6 James St.
Sidney, NY 13838-1406 (607) 563-9333
Contact: John Mirabito, Tr.

Established in 1995 in NY.
Donor(s): John Mirabito, Thomas Mirabito, Sr.
Financial data (yr. ended 12/31/01): Grants paid, $28,100; assets, $116,659 (M); gifts received, $15,755; expenditures, $28,283; qualifying distributions, $28,100.
Limitations: Applications not accepted. Giving primarily in Sidney, NY.
Application information: Contributes only to pre-selected organizations.
Trustees: John Dowd, Cheryl Mirabito, Concetta Mirabito, John Mirabito, Thomas Mirabito, Sr.
EIN: 166427316

37481
The Jay and Mary Goldberg Charitable Trust
c/o Jay Goldberg
1 W. 72nd St., Apt. 44
New York, NY 10023

Established in 1998 in NY.
Donor(s): Jay Goldberg, Mary Cirillo-Goldberg.
Financial data (yr. ended 12/31/01): Grants paid, $28,098; assets, $907,319 (M); expenditures, $39,413; qualifying distributions, $28,098.
Limitations: Applications not accepted. Giving primarily in New York, NY.

Application information: Contributes only to pre-selected organizations.
Trustees: Mary Cirillo-Goldberg, Jay Goldberg.
EIN: 137163815

37482
Ruth & David A. Goodkind Foundation, Inc.
c/o Port, Rella & Co.
21 E. 40th St., Ste. 1006
New York, NY 10016

Financial data (yr. ended 12/31/00): Grants paid, $28,095; assets, $1,018,909 (M); expenditures, $65,213; qualifying distributions, $41,166.
Limitations: Applications not accepted. Giving primarily in New York, NY.
Application information: Contributes only to pre-selected organizations.
Officers: Robert Goodkind, Pres.; Irene Goodkind, V.P.
EIN: 136085606

37483
The D. Nelson Adams Charitable Trust
c/o Davis Polk-Wardwell
450 Lexington Ave.
New York, NY 10017-3911

Established in 1993 in NY.
Donor(s): D. Nelson Adams.
Financial data (yr. ended 12/31/01): Grants paid, $28,072; assets, $27,955 (M); gifts received, $1,924; expenditures, $29,556; qualifying distributions, $28,072.
Limitations: Applications not accepted.
Application information: Contributes only to pre-selected organizations.
Trustee: D. Nelson Adams.
EIN: 137022115

37484
The George F., Jr., & Myra Shaskan Foundation, Inc.
c/o Lipsky, Goodkin & Co.
120 W. 45th St., 7th Fl.
New York, NY 10036
Contact: George F. Shaskan, Jr., Pres.

Established in 1969 in NY.
Donor(s): George F. Shaskan, Jr., Myra Shaskan, H. Luria.
Financial data (yr. ended 12/31/01): Grants paid, $28,060; assets, $540,410 (M); gifts received, $6,211; expenditures, $30,789; qualifying distributions, $29,389.
Limitations: Applications not accepted. Giving primarily in the Washington, DC, area, and New York, NY.
Application information: Contributes only to pre-selected organizations.
Officers and Directors:* George F. Shaskan, Jr.,* Pres.; Myra Shaskan,* V.P.; Phillip P. Goodkin, Secy.-Treas.
EIN: 237070134

37485
Cleveland Foundation
c/o Mortimer C. Low
25 Park Pl.
Bronxville, NY 10708-3978

Financial data (yr. ended 12/31/01): Grants paid, $28,048; assets, $895,593 (M); expenditures, $34,043; qualifying distributions, $28,048.
Limitations: Applications not accepted. Giving primarily in MN, the greater New York, NY, area, and WY.
Application information: Contributes only to pre-selected organizations.
Trustees: Charles A. Cleveland, Sr., John L. Cleveland, Elizabeth C. Lackey.

EIN: 136037214

37486
Evelyn & Morton Barrow Foundation, Inc.
c/o Martin R. Egre, CPA
585 Stewart Ave., Ste. 326
Garden City, NY 11530 (516) 222-1890
Contact: Morton Barrow, Pres.

Donor(s): Morton Barrow, Evelyn Barrow.
Financial data (yr. ended 11/30/01): Grants paid, $28,025; assets, $68,665 (M); expenditures, $29,543; qualifying distributions, $28,025.
Limitations: Giving primarily in NY.
Officers: Morton Barrow, Pres.; Evelyn Barrow, V.P.; Peter Barrow, Secy.
EIN: 112723683

37487
Angelus Foundation, Inc.
c/o Helen A. Brandes
480 Park Ave.
New York, NY 10022-1613

Financial data (yr. ended 12/31/01): Grants paid, $28,013; assets, $505,121 (M); expenditures, $30,423; qualifying distributions, $28,013.
Limitations: Giving primarily in New York, NY.
Application information: Application form not required.
Officers: Helen A. Brandes, V.P. and Secy.; Anita S. Rosenbloom, V.P.
EIN: 136092849

37488
Claire Phillips Barnet Foundation, Inc.
220 E. 42nd St., Ste. 3000
New York, NY 10017-5806

Established in 1985 in NY.
Financial data (yr. ended 12/31/01): Grants paid, $28,000; assets, $172,304 (M); expenditures, $29,486; qualifying distributions, $28,000.
Limitations: Applications not accepted. Giving primarily in New York, NY.
Application information: Contributes only to pre-selected organizations.
Officers and Directors:* Richard E. Burns,* Pres.; Martha F. Burns, V.P.; Catherine Atwood,* Secy.-Treas.
EIN: 133267127

37489
Theresa Costa Scholarship Fund
c/o HSBC Bank USA
One HSBC Plz., 16th Fl.
Buffalo, NY 14203-2885

Financial data (yr. ended 02/28/02): Grants paid, $28,000; assets, $323,338 (M); expenditures, $33,049; qualifying distributions, $28,620.
Limitations: Applications not accepted. Giving primarily in NY.
Trustee: HSBC Bank USA.
EIN: 166417356
Codes: GTI

37490
Fellowship Foundation, Inc.
c/o W. Kolbert
9 Summerwind Dr.
Glen Head, NY 11545

Established in 1996 in NY.
Donor(s): Elly Jansen, Notz, Stucki & Cie.
Financial data (yr. ended 12/31/00): Grants paid, $28,000; assets, $0 (L); gifts received, $71,413; expenditures, $266,415; qualifying distributions, $266,415; giving activities include $256,192 for programs.
Limitations: Giving limited to St. George, Barbados.

37490—NEW YORK

Application information: Application form not required.
Officers: Elly Jansen, Chair.; George Whitehouse, Treas.
Directors: David Klein, Greta Soggot.
Trustees: Cef Suarez, Anna Maria Whitehouse, Natasha Whitehouse.
EIN: 132968071

37491
Gladys Tozier Memorial Scholarship Trust
c/o M&T Bank
1 M&T Plz., 8th Fl.
Buffalo, NY 14203
Application address: 1400 Woodmont Ave., Williamsport, PA 17701
Contact: Evan Rosser, Jr., Tr.

Established in 1991 in PA.
Donor(s): Gladys Tozier.‡
Financial data (yr. ended 12/31/01): Grants paid, $28,000; assets, $522,016 (M); expenditures, $38,124; qualifying distributions, $28,000.
Limitations: Giving limited to residents of Clearfield, Elk, and Lycoming counties, PA.
Application information: Application form required.
Trustees: Evan Rosser, Jr., M & T Bank.
EIN: 232650705
Codes: GTI

37492
Dominick & Rose Ciampa Foundation, Inc.
100 Hilton Ave.
Garden City, NY 11530

Established in 1999 in NY.
Financial data (yr. ended 12/31/01): Grants paid, $27,850; assets, $1,603,295 (M); gifts received, $91,150; expenditures, $30,378; qualifying distributions, $27,850.
Limitations: Applications not accepted.
Application information: Contributes only to pre-selected organizations.
Officers: Dominick Ciampa, Chair. and Pres.; Rose Ciampa, V.P.; Benjamin Ciampa, Secy.-Treas.; Christine Ciampa, Mgr.
EIN: 113466090

37493
The Demille Family Foundation
734 Franklin Ave., Ste. 351
Garden City, NY 11530

Established in 2000 in NY.
Donor(s): Nelson Demille.
Financial data (yr. ended 12/31/01): Grants paid, $27,850; assets, $61,159 (M); gifts received, $16,456; expenditures, $34,863; qualifying distributions, $27,850.
Directors: Daniel Barbiero, Thomas Eschmann, Leonard M. Ridini, Jr., David Westermann, Jr.
EIN: 113544948

37494
The Prince Foundation
c/o Alfred N. Prince
349 Stone Hill Rd.
Pound Ridge, NY 10576

Established in 1996 in NY.
Donor(s): Alfred N. Prince.
Financial data (yr. ended 12/31/01): Grants paid, $27,850; assets, $57,340 (M); gifts received, $50,000; expenditures, $28,864; qualifying distributions, $27,850.
Trustees: Alfred N. Prince, Noriko Y. Prince.
EIN: 133841670

37495
Conde Family Foundation
33 E. 70th St., Ste. 6F
New York, NY 10021-4941
Contact: Cristobal Conde, Pres.

Established in 1999 in NY.
Donor(s): Cristobal Conde, Susan Conde.
Financial data (yr. ended 10/31/00): Grants paid, $27,826; assets, $305,896 (M); gifts received, $381,200; expenditures, $27,916; qualifying distributions, $27,916.
Limitations: Giving primarily in NY.
Officer and Directors:* Cristobal Conde,* Pres.; Susan Conde.
EIN: 134089589

37496
The Joshua Foundation, Inc.
c/o Joseph F. Girzone
1071 Joshua Ln.
Altamont, NY 12009

Established in 1990.
Financial data (yr. ended 03/31/01): Grants paid, $27,825; assets, $394,020 (M); gifts received, $473,236; expenditures, $149,739; qualifying distributions, $140,132; giving activities include $112,307 for programs.
Limitations: Applications not accepted. Giving limited to the Altamont, NY, area.
Application information: Unsolicited requests for funds not accepted.
Trustees: Joseph F. Girzone, Russell L. McGrath, Richard G. Della Ratta.
EIN: 223072537
Codes: GTI

37497
The Victor and Milia Shacalo Foundation, Inc.
302 5th Ave., 7th Fl.
New York, NY 10001
Application address: 2446 Ocean Pkwy., Brooklyn, NY 11235, tel.: (212) 564-2655
Contact: Victor Shacalo, Pres.

Established in 1997 in NY.
Donor(s): Victor Shacalo, Milia Shacalo.
Financial data (yr. ended 12/31/00): Grants paid, $27,796; assets, $22,396 (M); gifts received, $10,000; expenditures, $27,871; qualifying distributions, $27,796.
Limitations: Giving primarily in NY.
Officers: Victor Shacalo, Pres.; Toby Shacalo, V.P.; Milia Shacalo, Secy.
EIN: 133975597

37498
Hanna Andersson Children's Foundation
c/o US Trust Company of NY
114 W. 47th St., TAXRGR
New York, NY 10036

Established in 2001 in OR.
Financial data (yr. ended 12/31/01): Grants paid, $27,765; assets, $418,130 (M); gifts received, $450,661; expenditures, $33,425; qualifying distributions, $33,425.
Limitations: Applications not accepted.
Application information: Contributes only to pre-selected organizations.
Directors: Gun K.E. Denhart, Jeffrey S. Mills, Gretchen A. Peterson, Courtney L. Russell.
EIN: 931325900

37499
Catherine Scripps Rodriguez Family Foundation, Inc.
c/o U.S. Trust
114 W. 47th St., TaxVas
New York, NY 10036

Established in 1999 in NY.
Donor(s): Catherine Scripps Rodriguez.
Financial data (yr. ended 12/31/01): Grants paid, $27,727; assets, $769,725 (M); expenditures, $34,674; qualifying distributions, $27,727.
Limitations: Giving on a national basis.
Application information: Unsolicited requests for funds not accepted.
Directors: Samantha Loud, Shawn Loud, Catherine Scripps Rodriguez, Ismael Rodriguez.
EIN: 650831285

37500
The Worby Charitable Foundation
11 Martine Ave., Ste. PH
White Plains, NY 10606
Contact: David E. Worby, Tr.

Established in 1993 in NY.
Donor(s): David E. Worby.
Financial data (yr. ended 12/31/01): Grants paid, $27,700; assets, $247,869 (M); gifts received, $40,537; expenditures, $41,616; qualifying distributions, $27,700.
Application information: Application form not required.
Trustee: David E. Worby.
EIN: 137031450

37501
Zukowski Diamond Foundation
c/o Yohalem Gillman & Co.
477 Madison Ave., 9th Fl.
New York, NY 10022-5802

Established in 1999 in NY.
Donor(s): David M. Diamond.
Financial data (yr. ended 09/30/01): Grants paid, $27,685; assets, $68,290 (M); gifts received, $31,007; expenditures, $29,775; qualifying distributions, $27,902.
Limitations: Applications not accepted. Giving primarily in New York, NY.
Application information: Contributes only to pre-selected organizations.
Officers: David M. Diamond, Pres. and Secy.; Karen Zukowski, V.P.
EIN: 223690492

37502
The Cottonwood Foundation
c/o Brown Brothers Harriman Trust Co.
63 Wall St.
New York, NY 10005

Established in 1997 in MN.
Donor(s): Carol Hoffmann.
Financial data (yr. ended 12/31/01): Grants paid, $27,659; assets, $614,148 (M); gifts received, $25,874; expenditures, $31,059; qualifying distributions, $27,659.
Limitations: Applications not accepted.
Application information: Contributes only to a pre-selected organization.
Trustees: Carol Hoffmann, William Hoffmann.
EIN: 364156747

37503
Murphy Foundation, Inc.
P.O. Box 369
Stamford, NY 12167 (607) 652-7581
Contact: William J. Murphy, Pres.

Established in 1960 in NY.

Financial data (yr. ended 12/31/01): Grants paid, $27,636; assets, $903,774 (M); expenditures, $33,446; qualifying distributions, $27,636.
Limitations: Giving primarily in NY.
Officers and Directors:* William J. Murphy,* Pres.; Edward J. McCabe, Jr.,* V.P.; Douglas Murphy, Secy.-Treas.; William F. Murphy.
EIN: 150621420

37504
Martin Romerovski Foundation, Inc.
812 5th Ave.
New York, NY 10021 (212) 758-1638

Established in 1965.
Donor(s): Martin Romerovski,‡ Romerovski Bros., Inc.
Financial data (yr. ended 12/31/00): Grants paid, $27,607; assets, $76,345 (M); expenditures, $27,754; qualifying distributions, $27,607.
Limitations: Applications not accepted. Giving primarily in New York, NY.
Application information: Contributes only to pre-selected organizations.
Officer: Rose Romerovski, Secy.
EIN: 136172511

37505
The Benno Bordiga Foundation, Inc.
737 Park Ave., Ste. 2B
New York, NY 10021-4256

Established in 1990 in NY.
Donor(s): Allomatic Industries, Inc., Benno Bordiga.
Financial data (yr. ended 11/30/01): Grants paid, $27,600; assets, $210,913 (M); expenditures, $35,757; qualifying distributions, $27,600.
Limitations: Applications not accepted. Giving primarily in New York, NY.
Application information: Contributes only to pre-selected organizations.
Officer: Benno Bordiga, Pres.
EIN: 133594551

37506
Ironwood Foundation, Inc.
c/o Jack Stadler
1030 Constable Dr.
Mamaroneck, NY 10543

Donor(s): Jack Stadler.
Financial data (yr. ended 01/31/02): Grants paid, $27,585; assets, $862,123 (M); expenditures, $33,070; qualifying distributions, $32,765.
Limitations: Applications not accepted. Giving primarily in NY.
Application information: Contributes only to pre-selected organizations.
Officers: Jack Stadler, Pres. and Treas.; Anne Stadler Klass, V.P. and Secy.; John Stadler, V.P.
EIN: 133033569

37507
William & Jane Rosenau Foundation, Inc.
23 Crossing at Blind Brk.
Purchase, NY 10577

Established in 1967.
Donor(s): William W. Rosenau, John R. Redmond, Jane S. Rosenau.
Financial data (yr. ended 11/30/01): Grants paid, $27,550; assets, $601,533 (M); gifts received, $28,355; expenditures, $39,561; qualifying distributions, $27,550.
Limitations: Applications not accepted. Giving primarily in NY.
Application information: Contributes only to pre-selected organizations.
Officers: Jane S. Rosenau, Pres. and Treas.; Robert Todd Lang, Secy.

EIN: 237011889

37508
Zizmor Foundation
c/o Jonathan Zizmor
5021 Iselin Ave.
Riverdale, NY 10471-2914

Established in 1990 in DE.
Donor(s): Jonathan Zizmor.
Financial data (yr. ended 11/30/01): Grants paid, $27,520; assets, $156,960 (M); expenditures, $29,698; qualifying distributions, $27,520.
Limitations: Applications not accepted. Giving limited to New York, NY.
Application information: Contributes only to pre-selected organizations.
Officers and Directors:* Jonathan Zizmor,* Pres.; Wendy Zizmor,* Secy.
EIN: 133594045

37509
Money for Women/Barbara Deming Memorial Fund, Inc.
P.O. Box 630125
Bronx, NY 10463-0805
Contact: Susan Pliner, Exec. Dir.

Established by 1975 in NY.
Donor(s): Mary Meigs, Barbara Deming.
Financial data (yr. ended 07/31/01): Grants paid, $27,515; assets, $65,846 (M); gifts received, $38,219; expenditures, $48,397; qualifying distributions, $47,807.
Limitations: Giving on a national basis; some giving also in Canada.
Application information: Applicants must submit a $5 processing fee with each application; applications sent by express mail or registered mail are not accepted. Application form required.
Officers: Nancy Fried, Pres.; Cheryl Grau, Secy.-Treas.; Susan Pliner, Exec. Dir.
Directors: Maureen Brady, Lise Weil.
EIN: 510176956
Codes: GTI

37510
Samuel Feder Family Foundation, Inc.
c/o Aaron Feder, Carolace
1350 Broadway, Ste. 210
New York, NY 10018

Donor(s): Samuel Feder, Aaron E. Feder.
Financial data (yr. ended 10/31/01): Grants paid, $27,500; assets, $273,705 (M); expenditures, $37,792; qualifying distributions, $27,331.
Limitations: Applications not accepted. Giving primarily in NY.
Application information: Contributes only to pre-selected organizations.
Officer: Aaron Feder, Pres.
Directors: Walter Feder, Doris Getzler.
EIN: 136161404

37511
William and Diane Hein Foundation
(Formerly William S. Hein Foundation)
c/o William C. Moran
6500 Main St., Ste. 5
Buffalo, NY 14221

Established in 1995 in NY.
Donor(s): William S. Hein, William S. Hein, Jr.
Financial data (yr. ended 12/31/01): Grants paid, $27,500; assets, $1,846,981 (M); gifts received, $200,000; expenditures, $43,537; qualifying distributions, $30,849.
Limitations: Applications not accepted. Giving primarily in NY.
Application information: Contributes only to pre-selected organizations.

Officers and Directors:* William S. Hein, Jr.,* Pres.; Diane S. Hein,* Secy.; William C. Moran.
EIN: 161484562

37512
Laskin Charitable Foundation, Inc.
545 Madison Ave., 4th Fl.
New York, NY 10022 (212) 751-5822
Contact: Sallie Felzen, Pres.

Established in 1994 in FL.
Donor(s): Louise Laskin.
Financial data (yr. ended 12/31/00): Grants paid, $27,500; assets, $143,782 (M); expenditures, $29,462; qualifying distributions, $27,500.
Application information: Application form not required.
Officers and Directors:* Sallie Felzen,* Pres.; Paul Felzen,* Secy.
EIN: 133245633

37513
Helenka and Guido Pantaleoni Foundation, Inc.
c/o Fulbright & Jaworski
666 5th Ave.
New York, NY 10103-0001

Established in 1988 in NY.
Financial data (yr. ended 12/31/01): Grants paid, $27,500; assets, $466,266 (M); expenditures, $33,959; qualifying distributions, $27,500.
Limitations: Applications not accepted. Giving primarily in NY.
Application information: Contributes only to pre-selected organizations.
Officers: Guido Pantaleoni, Pres.; Nina Hillgarth, V.P.; Michael Pantaleoni, V.P.; Anthony Pantaleoni, Secy.
EIN: 133506104

37514
Waterman Family Fund
P.O. Box 8009
Clifton Park, NY 12065-8009

Established in 1996 in FL.
Donor(s): Richard M. Waterman.
Financial data (yr. ended 12/31/01): Grants paid, $27,500; assets, $64,280 (M); expenditures, $27,585; qualifying distributions, $27,500.
Limitations: Applications not accepted. Giving primarily in NY.
Application information: Contributes only to pre-selected organizations.
Trustee: Richard M. Waterman.
EIN: 237858682

37515
The Burrows Foundation, Inc.
777 3rd Ave., 26th Fl.
New York, NY 10017-1401

Established in 1954 in NY.
Donor(s): Selig S. Burrows,‡ Real Estate Industrials, Inc., Sam Spatt Foundation, Inc.
Financial data (yr. ended 05/31/02): Grants paid, $27,410; assets, $36,272 (M); gifts received, $30,200; expenditures, $27,515; qualifying distributions, $27,410.
Limitations: Applications not accepted. Giving primarily in FL and NY.
Application information: Contributes only to pre-selected organizations.
Officers: Kenneth D. Burrows, Pres.; Jonathan L. Burrows, V.P.; Patricia Burrows, Secy.-Treas.
EIN: 132709563

IN THIS SECTION, WITHIN EACH STATE, FOUNDATIONS ARE LISTED IN DESCENDING ORDER BY TOTAL GRANTS PAID.

37516
The Ada Lieb Goldstein Foundation
c/o Equity Group, Inc.
800 3rd Ave., 36th Fl.
New York, NY 10022

Established in 1991 in NY and DE.
Donor(s): Robert D. Goldstein.
Financial data (yr. ended 12/31/01): Grants paid, $27,400; assets, $154,601 (M); expenditures, $30,225; qualifying distributions, $27,339.
Limitations: Applications not accepted.
Application information: Contributes only to pre-selected organizations.
Officers: Robert D. Goldstein, Pres.; Judy A. Goldstein, Secy.-Treas.
EIN: 133640275

37517
The Venetos Foundation, Inc.
P.O. Box 847
New Rochelle, NY 10801-6360

Financial data (yr. ended 12/31/01): Grants paid, $27,400; assets, $621,755 (M); expenditures, $34,696; qualifying distributions, $27,400.
Limitations: Applications not accepted. Giving primarily in NY.
Application information: Contributes only to pre-selected organizations.
Officers: Melvyn H. Bergman, Pres.; Eugene Bergman, V.P.; Keith Bergman, V.P.; Maxine Bergman, Secy.-Treas.
EIN: 136224081

37518
The Rutkowski Family Foundation, Inc.
282 Harrison Ave.
Harrison, NY 10528

Established in 1997 in New York.
Donor(s): Paul C. Rutkowski.
Financial data (yr. ended 09/30/01): Grants paid, $27,375; assets, $489,281 (M); expenditures, $31,184; qualifying distributions, $27,375.
Officers: Paul C. Rutkowski, Pres.; Monika M. Rutkowski, V.P.; Nicole K. Rutkowski, Secy.
EIN: 133970954

37519
Bershad Foundation, Inc.
c/o Carol A. Abrams
42 Lawridge Dr.
Rye Brook, NY 10573-1021

Established in 1965 in NY.
Financial data (yr. ended 12/31/01): Grants paid, $27,350; assets, $415,536 (M); expenditures, $28,984; qualifying distributions, $27,350.
Limitations: Applications not accepted. Giving primarily in CT, NY, and PA.
Application information: Contributes only to pre-selected organizations.
Officers: Ronnie B. Backman, Pres.; Carol A. Abrams, Secy.
EIN: 136181437

37520
Irving and Muriel Fischer Foundation, Inc.
P.O. Box 367
Bedford Hills, NY 10507

Established in 1986 in NY.
Donor(s): Irving R. Fischer.
Financial data (yr. ended 11/30/01): Grants paid, $27,300; assets, $177,438 (M); gifts received, $9,138; expenditures, $27,950; qualifying distributions, $27,300.
Limitations: Applications not accepted. Giving primarily in New York, NY.

Application information: Contributes only to pre-selected organizations.
Officers and Directors:* Irving R. Fischer,* Pres.; Michael Fischer,* V.P.; Muriel Fischer,* Secy.-Treas.
EIN: 133387376

37521
Koegel Foundation, Inc.
7 Chesterfield Rd.
Scarsdale, NY 10583

Financial data (yr. ended 12/31/01): Grants paid, $27,300; assets, $305,872 (M); expenditures, $28,075; qualifying distributions, $27,300.
Limitations: Applications not accepted. Giving primarily in NY.
Application information: Contributes only to pre-selected organizations.
Officers: William F. Koegel, Pres. and Treas.; Ruth K. Macreery, V.P.; James E. Koegel, Secy.
EIN: 136099147

37522
The Brecher Fund
48 Concord Dr.
Monsey, NY 10952

Established in 1985 in NY.
Donor(s): Harvey Brecher, Miriam Brecher.
Financial data (yr. ended 05/31/01): Grants paid, $27,293; assets, $135,528 (M); gifts received, $180,095; expenditures, $27,368; qualifying distributions, $27,188.
Limitations: Applications not accepted. Giving primarily in NY.
Application information: Contributes only to pre-selected organizations.
Officers and Directors:* Harvey Brecher,* Pres. and Treas.; Miriam Brecher,* V.P. and Secy.; Eli S. Garber.
EIN: 133288971

37523
Joseph & Faye Liberman Foundation
5121 17th Ave.
Brooklyn, NY 11204

Established in 1996 in NY.
Donor(s): Joseph Liberman, Faye Liberman.
Financial data (yr. ended 05/31/02): Grants paid, $27,293; assets, $9,668 (M); gifts received, $25,000; expenditures, $27,818; qualifying distributions, $27,293.
Limitations: Applications not accepted. Giving primarily in NY.
Application information: Contributes only to pre-selected organizations.
Directors: Faye Liberman, Joseph Liberman.
EIN: 137061682

37524
The Lamport Foundation, Inc.
c/o Bessemer Trust Co., N.A.
630 5th Ave.
New York, NY 10111-0002
Application address: 380 Lexington Ave., 54th Fl., New York, NY 10168
Contact: Cynthia H. Lamport, V.P.

Established in 1960.
Donor(s): Anthony M. Lamport.
Financial data (yr. ended 10/31/01): Grants paid, $27,292; assets, $318,798 (M); expenditures, $30,317; qualifying distributions, $27,292.
Limitations: Giving primarily in New York, NY.
Officers: Anthony M. Lamport, Pres. and Treas.; Aaron M. Lamport, V.P.; Cynthia H. Lamport, V.P.; Sarah W. Laurence, V.P.; Kim Hall, Secy.
EIN: 060775428

37525
The J & E Charitable Foundation Trust
1440 59th St.
Brooklyn, NY 11219

Established in 1999 in NY.
Donor(s): Joseph Parnes, Estelle Parnes.
Financial data (yr. ended 12/31/00): Grants paid, $27,260; assets, $179,709 (M); gifts received, $70,050; expenditures, $30,041; qualifying distributions, $30,041.
Limitations: Applications not accepted.
Application information: Contributes only to pre-selected organizations.
Trustees: Estelle Parnes, Joseph Parnes.
EIN: 116532363

37526
Eli & Marilyn Hertz Foundation
24 Greenway St.
Forest Hills, NY 11375-5943

Established in 1996 in NY.
Donor(s): Eli Hertz, Marilyn Hertz.
Financial data (yr. ended 09/30/01): Grants paid, $27,250; assets, $133,380 (M); gifts received, $70,240; expenditures, $27,416; qualifying distributions, $27,250.
Trustees: Eli Hertz, Marilyn Hertz.
EIN: 116481726

37527
Mordechai and Mirrel Eissenberg Foundation, Inc.
1460 57th St.
Brooklyn, NY 11219 (718) 633-7700

Donor(s): Mordechai Eissenberg.
Financial data (yr. ended 12/31/01): Grants paid, $27,247; assets, $26,978 (M); gifts received, $27,000; expenditures, $27,893; qualifying distributions, $27,893.
Limitations: Applications not accepted. Giving primarily in NY.
Application information: Contributes only to pre-selected organizations.
Trustees: Mirrel Eissenberg, Mordechai Eissenberg.
EIN: 112996900

37528
Arthur and Joan Boyd Family Foundation, Inc.
605 Oakhurst Rd.
Mamaroneck, NY 10543

Established in 1985 in NY.
Donor(s): Arthur Boyd, Joan Boyd.
Financial data (yr. ended 11/30/01): Grants paid, $27,220; assets, $244,684 (M); expenditures, $27,582; qualifying distributions, $27,220.
Limitations: Applications not accepted. Giving primarily in New York, NY.
Application information: Contributes only to pre-selected organizations.
Directors: Arthur Boyd, Joan Boyd.
EIN: 133317569

37529
The Geri Bauer Foundation, Inc.
99 Madison Ave.
New York, NY 10016

Established in 1999 in NY.
Financial data (yr. ended 11/30/01): Grants paid, $27,200; assets, $156,867 (M); gifts received, $31,531; expenditures, $34,224; qualifying distributions, $27,200.
Limitations: Applications not accepted. Giving primarily in NY.
Application information: Contributes only to pre-selected organizations.

Officers and Directors:* Geri Bauer,* Pres.; Rachel Dimayuga,* Secy.; Kurt Kiess.
EIN: 134091905

37530
The Anne Claire Lester Foundation, Inc.
c/o Muriel S. Kessler
60 E. 42nd St., Rm. 1136
New York, NY 10165-0156 (212) 986-0960

Established in 1990 in NY.
Donor(s): Anne Claire Lester.
Financial data (yr. ended 12/31/01): Grants paid, $27,200; assets, $490,375 (M); expenditures, $39,715; qualifying distributions, $27,200.
Limitations: Applications not accepted. Giving primarily in New York, NY.
Application information: Contributes only to pre-selected organizations.
Officers: Anne Claire Lester, Pres.; Muriel S. Kessler, Secy.; Jack Scharf, Treas.
EIN: 133579342

37531
The Sunrise Foundation
637 Yonkers Ave.
Yonkers, NY 10704

Established in 1996 in NY.
Donor(s): A.G. Khakee.
Financial data (yr. ended 12/31/00): Grants paid, $27,200; assets, $511,110 (M); gifts received, $99,378; expenditures, $31,150; qualifying distributions, $27,200.
Limitations: Applications not accepted.
Application information: Contributes only to pre-selected organizations.
Officer and Director:* A.G. Khakee,* Pres.
EIN: 133924702

37532
SRG Foundation
c/o Rita Gottlieb
1417 56th St.
Brooklyn, NY 11219-4618
Contact: Rita Gottlieb, Tr.

Established in 1999 in NY.
Donor(s): Rita Gottlieb.
Financial data (yr. ended 12/31/01): Grants paid, $27,178; assets, $79,158 (M); gifts received, $65,000; expenditures, $27,303; qualifying distributions, $27,178.
Application information: Application form not required.
Trustee: Rita Gottlieb.
EIN: 113306281

37533
Clarisse B. Kampel Foundation, Inc.
c/o Bruce MacCorkindale
3960 Merrick Rd.
Seaford, NY 11783
Application address: 135 E. 83rd St., New York, NY 10028
Contact: Carl Battaglia, Exec. Dir.

Established in 1986 in NY.
Donor(s): Daniel S. Kampel, Clarisse B. Kampel,‡ Billy Rose Foundation, Annie Laurie Aiken Foundation.
Financial data (yr. ended 06/30/01): Grants paid, $27,125; assets, $405,655 (M); gifts received, $50,250; expenditures, $64,954; qualifying distributions, $61,954.
Limitations: Giving primarily in NY.
Application information: Informal oral review required.
Officers: Daniel S. Kampel, V.P.; John B. Ritter, Secy.; Bruce MacCorkindale, Treas.; Carl Battaglia, Exec. Dir.

EIN: 133347805
Codes: GTI

37534
Max Brooks Foundation, Inc.
3120 Palisade Ave.
Bronx, NY 10463-1014

Donor(s): Max Brooks.
Financial data (yr. ended 12/31/01): Grants paid, $27,050; assets, $423,407 (M); gifts received, $25,000; expenditures, $27,631; qualifying distributions, $27,050.
Limitations: Applications not accepted.
Officers: Max Brooks, Pres.; Sydell Brooks, Secy.
Trustees: Jeffrey S. Brooks, Toby G. Feder, Bernice Hornblass.
EIN: 136125549

37535
MIG Charitable Foundation, Ltd.
c/o Roth & Co.
5612 18th Ave.
Brooklyn, NY 11204

Established in 1998 in NY.
Donor(s): Michael Gross.
Financial data (yr. ended 02/28/02): Grants paid, $27,046; assets, $1,691 (M); gifts received, $24,500; expenditures, $29,046; qualifying distributions, $27,046.
Limitations: Applications not accepted.
Application information: Contributes only to pre-selected organizations.
Officers: Michael Gross, Pres.; Regina Gross, Secy.; Solomon Gross, Treas.
EIN: 113316618

37536
Joan and Joseph Birman Foundation
100 Wellington Ave.
New Rochelle, NY 10804

Established in 1996 in NY.
Donor(s): Helen Kimmel, Joan S. Birman, Joseph L. Birman.
Financial data (yr. ended 11/30/01): Grants paid, $27,000; assets, $425,210 (M); expenditures, $37,124; qualifying distributions, $28,066.
Limitations: Applications not accepted. Giving primarily in New York, NY.
Application information: Contributes only to pre-selected organizations.
Trustees: Joan S. Birman, Joseph L. Birman, Kenneth P. Birman.
EIN: 137102288

37537
The Carper Foundation
1 W. 72nd St., Ste. 55
New York, NY 10023-3486 (212) 848-1811
Contact: Daniel E. Carper, Tr.

Established in 1986 in NY.
Donor(s): Daniel E. Carper, Margaret A. Carper.
Financial data (yr. ended 11/30/01): Grants paid, $27,000; assets, $745,917 (M); gifts received, $59,000; expenditures, $28,899; qualifying distributions, $28,524.
Limitations: Giving primarily in New York, NY.
Trustees: Daniel E. Carper, Margaret A. Carper.
EIN: 133381129

37538
The Frank DiMino Family Trust
(Formerly The Raymond DiMino Memorial Foundation)
4400 9 Mile Point Rd.
Fairport, NY 14450

Established in 1988 in NY.
Donor(s): Frank DiMino.

Financial data (yr. ended 06/30/01): Grants paid, $27,000; assets, $2,823,003 (M); expenditures, $64,109; qualifying distributions, $27,575.
Limitations: Applications not accepted. Giving limited to Rochester, NY.
Application information: Contributes only to pre-selected organizations.
Trustees: Jack M. Battaglia, Michael Bree, Rebecca Bree, Cortland L. Brovitz, Kimberly D'Amico, Frank DiMino, Frank DiMino, Jr., Helen DiMino, Ronald DiMino, Donna Karabinakis, Peter Thummler.
EIN: 222985922

37539
Falconer Foundation, Inc.
c/o Gilbert, Segall & Young
430 Park Ave.
New York, NY 10022-3592
Application address: 3350 Loma Alta Ln., Santa Cruz, CA 95065, tel.: (831) 464-1261
Contact: Robert Falconer, Pres.

Financial data (yr. ended 12/31/01): Grants paid, $27,000; assets, $574,742 (M); expenditures, $65,316; qualifying distributions, $27,000.
Limitations: Giving primarily in CA.
Officers: Robert Falconer, Pres.; James A. Kenney, V.P.; Donald Davies, M.D., Secy.-Treas.
Directors: Fremont DeArmond, Alan Richards, Ph.D.
EIN: 136267404

37540
Josephs Family Foundation, Inc.
100 Rt. 306
Monsey, NY 10952

Established in 1999 in NY.
Donor(s): Rubin Josephs, Judy Josephs.
Financial data (yr. ended 08/31/01): Grants paid, $27,000; assets, $327,614 (M); gifts received, $100,000; expenditures, $27,016; qualifying distributions, $27,000.
Limitations: Applications not accepted. Giving primarily in Spring Valley, NY.
Application information: Contributes only to pre-selected organizations.
Directors: Judy Josephs, Rubin Josephs, Ruth Josephs.
EIN: 133968855

37541
Levine Family Foundation, Inc.
c/o Bernard Segal
53 Trenor Dr.
New Rochelle, NY 10804-3718

Established in 1988 in NY.
Donor(s): Linda Rothman Levine.
Financial data (yr. ended 12/31/01): Grants paid, $27,000; assets, $2,309,157 (M); gifts received, $34,643; expenditures, $59,674; qualifying distributions, $59,674.
Limitations: Applications not accepted. Giving primarily in NY.
Application information: Contributes only to pre-selected organizations.
Officers: Linda Rothman Levine, Pres.; Marvin Levine, V.P.; Bernard Segal, Secy.
EIN: 133476578

37542
The Else Sackler Foundation
c/o Else Sackler
461 E. 57th St.
New York, NY 10022

Established in 1991 in NY.
Donor(s): Else Sackler.

Financial data (yr. ended 12/31/00): Grants paid, $27,000; assets, $1,889,469 (M); gifts received, $32,000; expenditures, $54,850; qualifying distributions, $30,945.
Limitations: Applications not accepted. Giving primarily in Washington, DC.
Application information: Contributes only to pre-selected organizations.
Officers: Carol Master, Pres.; Sherry L. Mayrent, V.P. and Secy.; Elizabeth Sackler, Secy.-Treas.
EIN: 133549168

37543
The Siegel Family Foundation, Inc.
(Formerly William Siegel Foundation, Inc.)
c/o Retail Apparel Svc. Corp.
71 Clinton Rd., Lower Level
Garden City, NY 11530-4728

Established in 1985 in NY.
Donor(s): William Siegel.
Financial data (yr. ended 12/31/01): Grants paid, $27,000; assets, $491,709 (M); expenditures, $27,150; qualifying distributions, $27,000.
Limitations: Applications not accepted.
Application information: Contributes only to pre-selected organizations.
Officer: William Siegel, Mgr.
EIN: 133315499

37544
Danielle Whalen Memorial Foundation
296 Blake Ave.
Bohemia, NY 11716

Established in 1999 in NY.
Donor(s): James W. Whalen III, Jeanne L. Whalen.
Financial data (yr. ended 11/30/01): Grants paid, $27,000; assets, $438,014 (M); expenditures, $34,533; qualifying distributions, $27,000.
Limitations: Applications not accepted.
Application information: Contributes only to pre-selected organizations.
Officers: James W. Whalen III, Pres.; Jeanne L. Whalen, V.P.; James W. Whalen IV, Secy.-Treas.
EIN: 113465851

37545
Irving Fabrikant Foundation
1016 5th Ave., Apt. 9C
New York, NY 10028
Contact: Geraldine Fabrikant, Mgr.

Financial data (yr. ended 02/28/01): Grants paid, $26,970; assets, $410,597 (M); expenditures, $27,616; qualifying distributions, $26,970.
Limitations: Giving primarily in New York, NY.
Officer: Geraldine Fabrikant, Mgr.
EIN: 136160022

37546
Herbert & Yvonne Missry Foundation
1872 E. 2nd St.
Brooklyn, NY 11223

Established in 2000.
Financial data (yr. ended 12/31/00): Grants paid, $26,968; assets, $20,157 (M); gifts received, $47,000; expenditures, $27,008; qualifying distributions, $26,968.
Officer: Morris Missry, Chair.
EIN: 113522784

37547
Gellert Family Charitable Trust
122 E. 42nd St., 34th Fl.
New York, NY 10168

Donor(s): Members of the Gellert family, Catherine G. Ross.
Financial data (yr. ended 11/30/01): Grants paid, $26,950; assets, $42,033 (M); expenditures, $27,192; qualifying distributions, $26,950.
Limitations: Applications not accepted.
Application information: Contributes only to pre-selected organizations.
Trustees: Hubert J. Gellert, Martin F. Gellert, Peter J. Gellert, Robert J. Gellert, Catherine G. Ross.
EIN: 136307135

37548
Joan & Leonard Baron Foundation, Inc.
c/o Schwartz & Co.
2580 Sunrise Hwy.
Bellmore, NY 11710 (516) 409-5000
Application address: 2100 S. Ocean Blvd., Palm Beach, FL 33480
Contact: Leonard Baron, Pres.

Established in 1993.
Donor(s): Leonard Baron.
Financial data (yr. ended 12/31/00): Grants paid, $26,920; assets, $265,859 (M); expenditures, $28,333; qualifying distributions, $26,920.
Officers and Directors:* Leonard Baron,* Pres.; Joan Baron,* V.P. and Treas.; Manley H. Thaler, Secy.
EIN: 650375771

37549
The Robert A. Jaye Charitable Trust
c/o M. Blumenreich & Co.
342 Madison Ave., Ste. 826
New York, NY 10173-0002
Contact: Robert A. Jaye, Tr.

Established in 1992 in NY.
Donor(s): Robert A. Jaye, Sylvia Jaye.
Financial data (yr. ended 12/31/01): Grants paid, $26,915; assets, $1,036,087 (M); expenditures, $30,239; qualifying distributions, $26,915.
Limitations: Giving primarily in NY.
Application information: Application form not required.
Trustee: Robert A. Jaye.
EIN: 046718853

37550
The Peter Nager Charitable Trust
121 Beaver Dam Rd.
Katonah, NY 10536-3716

Established in 1999 in NY.
Donor(s): Peter Nager.
Financial data (yr. ended 06/30/01): Grants paid, $26,850; assets, $686,572 (M); expenditures, $32,884; qualifying distributions, $26,850.
Limitations: Applications not accepted. Giving primarily in New York, NY.
Application information: Contributes only to pre-selected organizations.
Trustee: Peter Nager.
EIN: 137196662

37551
Thomas J. Walsh & Ann L. Walsh Charitable Trust
c/o JPMorgan Chase Bank
P.O. Box 31412
Rochester, NY 14603-1412
Application address: c/o JPMorgan Chase Bank, Personal Asset Mgmt. Svcs., P.O. Box 92920, Rochester, NY 14692-9020, tel.: (800) 850-7222

Financial data (yr. ended 12/31/01): Grants paid, $26,850; assets, $469,855 (M); expenditures, $33,544; qualifying distributions, $27,507.
Limitations: Giving primarily in CT.
Trustees: Kevin A. Walsh, JPMorgan Chase Bank.
EIN: 136211050

37552
Ethan & Tamar Benovitz Foundation, Inc.
c/o L. Wollin
350 5th Ave., Ste. 2822
New York, NY 10118

Established in 2000 in DE.
Donor(s): Ethan Benovitz, Tamar Benovitz.
Financial data (yr. ended 09/30/01): Grants paid, $26,845; assets, $204,622 (M); gifts received, $225,000; expenditures, $31,069; qualifying distributions, $26,738.
Limitations: Applications not accepted. Giving primarily in NY.
Application information: Contributes only to pre-selected organizations.
Officers: Ethan Benovitz, Pres.; Tamar Benovitz, V.P.; Lonnie Wilson, Secy.
EIN: 223770259

37553
Margaret Bartlett Scholarship Foundation
c/o Glasser & Haims, C.P.A.
99 W. Hawthorne Ave., Ste. 418
Valley Stream, NY 11580-6101

Financial data (yr. ended 12/31/01): Grants paid, $26,800; assets, $233,290 (M); gifts received, $43,254; expenditures, $27,367; qualifying distributions, $26,990.
Limitations: Applications not accepted. Giving primarily in VT.
Application information: Contributes only to pre-selected organizations.
Trustee: Roger Berkley.
EIN: 222570746

37554
The Victor & Pearl Tumpeer Foundation
c/o Ruth Tumpeer
24 Central Park S., Ste 9W
New York, NY 10019

Established in 1958 in NY.
Donor(s): Joseph J. Tumpeer, Ruth Tumpeer.
Financial data (yr. ended 12/31/01): Grants paid, $26,796; assets, $400,853 (M); expenditures, $30,165; qualifying distributions, $26,796.
Limitations: Applications not accepted. Giving primarily in New York, NY.
Application information: Contributes only to pre-selected organizations.
Trustees: Marc F. Sroge, Ruth Tumpeer.
EIN: 366102201

37555
Sanford M. & Nancy E. Epstein Foundation
8 Ridge Rd.
Red Spring Colony
Glen Cove, NY 11542-1720
Contact: Sanford M. Epstein, Pres.

Donor(s): Sanford M. Epstein.
Financial data (yr. ended 02/28/02): Grants paid, $26,785; assets, $590,160 (M); expenditures, $30,611; qualifying distributions, $26,785.
Application information: Application form not required.
Officers and Directors:* Sanford M. Epstein,* Pres. and V.P.; Nancy E. Epstein,* Secy.-Treas.; Scott K. Epstein, Steven K. Epstein.
EIN: 237425359

37556
Stuart A. Shikiar Family Foundation
30 E. 85th St., Apt. 24B
New York, NY 10028 (212) 888-6565
Contact: Stuart A. Shikiar, Tr.

Established in 1994 in NY.
Donor(s): Stuart A. Shikiar.

Financial data (yr. ended 11/30/01): Grants paid, $26,775; assets, $1,148,258 (M); gifts received, $252,250; expenditures, $58,470; qualifying distributions, $26,775.
Limitations: Giving primarily in NY.
Application information: Contact foundation for application information and deadlines.
Trustee: Stuart A. Shikiar.
EIN: 137052572

37557
Oceana Charitable Foundation, Inc.
21 Princeton Pl.
Orchard Park, NY 14127

Established in 1996 in NY.
Donor(s): Oceana Matrix, Ltd.
Financial data (yr. ended 10/31/01): Grants paid, $26,750; assets, $11,287 (M); gifts received, $14,200; expenditures, $26,750; qualifying distributions, $26,750.
Limitations: Applications not accepted. Giving primarily in NY and PA.
Application information: Contributes only to pre-selected organizations.
Directors: Mark Alan Rand, Michael Rand, Richard F. Rand.
EIN: 161539913
Codes: CS, CD

37558
Rabbi Leib Geliebter Memorial Foundation, Inc.
25 Herrick Dr.
Lawrence, NY 11559

Established in 1991 in NY.
Donor(s): Florence Geliebter, Joseph Geliebter.
Financial data (yr. ended 12/31/01): Grants paid, $26,706; assets, $467,455 (M); expenditures, $31,222; qualifying distributions, $26,706.
Limitations: Applications not accepted.
Application information: Contributes only to pre-selected organizations.
Directors: Florence Geliebter, Joseph Geliebter, Mark Geliebter.
EIN: 113045604

37559
Rosalthea M. Judd Trust
c/o The Bank of New York
1 Wall St., 28th Fl.
New York, NY 10286

Established in 1990 in NY.
Financial data (yr. ended 10/31/01): Grants paid, $26,659; assets, $282,116 (M); expenditures, $28,573; qualifying distributions, $26,659.
Limitations: Applications not accepted. Giving primarily in Port Chester, NY.
Application information: Contributes only to pre-selected organizations.
Trustee: The Bank of New York.
EIN: 136062252

37560
The Schallamach Family Foundation, Inc.
7 Locust Dr.
Great Neck, NY 11021-1724

Established in 1986 in NY.
Donor(s): Arno Schallamach.
Financial data (yr. ended 06/30/01): Grants paid, $26,649; assets, $55,847 (M); gifts received, $10,000; expenditures, $28,779; qualifying distributions, $26,649.
Limitations: Applications not accepted. Giving primarily in NY.
Application information: Contributes only to pre-selected organizations.
Officers: Arno Schallamach, Pres. and Treas.; Paula Schallamach, V.P. and Secy.

EIN: 133381803

37561
Jacob Bluestein Foundation
c/o Marion Galison
115 Central Park West, Ste. 11A
New York, NY 10023

Established in 1958 in NY.
Donor(s): Allan I. Bluestein,‡ Milton J. Bluestein.‡
Financial data (yr. ended 04/30/02): Grants paid, $26,600; assets, $753,311 (M); expenditures, $44,682; qualifying distributions, $26,600.
Limitations: Applications not accepted. Giving primarily in FL and NY.
Application information: Contributes only to pre-selected organizations.
Officers and Directors:* Marion Galison,* Pres.; Peter Galison,* V.P.; Gerald Galison,* Secy.-Treas.
EIN: 136116536

37562
Justice Foundation, Inc.
1 New York Plz., 30th Fl.
New York, NY 10004 (212) 908-9504
Contact: Nelson Schaenen, Jr., Pres.

Financial data (yr. ended 06/30/01): Grants paid, $26,600; assets, $704,272 (M); expenditures, $34,697; qualifying distributions, $28,670.
Limitations: Giving primarily in Ithaca, NY.
Application information: Scholarships limited to members of Delta Upsilon Chapter at Cornell University.
Officers: Nelson Schaenen, Jr., Pres.; Robert J. Verna, Secy.-Treas.
EIN: 221713051

37563
The Kevin Kelly Foundation
c/o BCRS Assocs.
85 Broad St.-Tax Dept.
New York, NY 10005

Established in 1996 in NY.
Donor(s): Kevin Kelly.
Financial data (yr. ended 10/31/01): Grants paid, $26,600; assets, $82,462 (M); expenditures, $28,125; qualifying distributions, $26,600.
Limitations: Applications not accepted. Giving primarily in Garden City, NY.
Application information: Contributes only to pre-selected organizations.
Trustees: Kevin Kelly, Patricia Kelly.
EIN: 133919770

37564
S. & H. Korn Foundation, Inc.
1658 52nd St.
Brooklyn, NY 11219
Contact: Solomon Korn, Pres.

Established in 1994.
Donor(s): Helen Korn, Solomon Korn.
Financial data (yr. ended 12/31/00): Grants paid, $26,600; assets, $668,375 (M); gifts received, $151,670; expenditures, $26,651; qualifying distributions, $26,298.
Limitations: Giving limited to Brooklyn, NY.
Officer: Solomon Korn, Pres.
Directors: Helen Korn, Hindy G. Korn, Hyman Korn.
EIN: 113215884

37565
Handel Foundation
(Formerly The Handel Charitable Foundation)
75 Washington St.
Poughkeepsie, NY 12603-2303

Established in 1997 in NY.
Donor(s): Bernard Handel.

Financial data (yr. ended 06/30/01): Grants paid, $26,585; assets, $141,138 (M); gifts received, $49,941; expenditures, $26,690; qualifying distributions, $26,690.
Limitations: Giving primarily in Dutchess County, NY.
Trustees: Bernard Handel, Shirley M. Handel.
EIN: 141800699

37566
Marietta & Andrew Romay Foundation, Inc.
c/o Robert S. Braunschweig
420 Lexington Ave., Ste. 336
New York, NY 10170

Established in 1991 in NY.
Donor(s): Andrew Romay, Marietta Romay.
Financial data (yr. ended 12/31/01): Grants paid, $26,584; assets, $669,658 (M); gifts received, $22,313; expenditures, $30,958; qualifying distributions, $26,584.
Limitations: Applications not accepted.
Application information: Contributes only to pre-selected organizations.
Directors: Robert S. Braunschweig, Andrew Romay, Marietta Romay.
EIN: 133596234

37567
Joseph L. Aurichio Foundation, Inc.
44 Midvale Rd.
Hartsdale, NY 10530-3607
Application address: 2 Jeffreys Rd., Hopewell Jct., NY 12533
Contact: John F. Tierney Jr., Treas.

Established in 1997.
Donor(s): Joseph L. Aurichio.
Financial data (yr. ended 12/31/01): Grants paid, $26,570; assets, $462,788 (M); expenditures, $39,447; qualifying distributions, $26,570.
Officers: Joseph L. Aurichio, Pres.; Carol Actis, Secy.; John F. Tierney, Treas.
EIN: 133940934

37568
The Berley Family Foundation, Inc.
216 Greenway N.
Forest Hills, NY 11375

Established in 1998 in DE and NY.
Donor(s): Noah M. Berley, Rhoda Berley, Berley Industries, Inc.
Financial data (yr. ended 12/31/01): Grants paid, $26,570; assets, $534,816 (M); expenditures, $27,848; qualifying distributions, $26,570.
Limitations: Applications not accepted.
Application information: Contributes only to pre-selected organizations.
Officers and Directors:* Noah M. Berley,* Pres.; Saul A. Berley,* V.P.; Eve Brooks,* V.P.; Rhoda Berley,* Treas.
EIN: 113445775

37569
Kevin D. Gorter Memorial Foundation
C/O BCRS Assocs,, LLC
67 Wall St., 8th Fl.
New York, NY 10005

Established in 1989 in IL.
Donor(s): James P. Gorter.
Financial data (yr. ended 12/31/01): Grants paid, $26,550; assets, $392,092 (M); expenditures, $31,675; qualifying distributions, $26,550.
Limitations: Applications not accepted. Giving primarily in MA.
Application information: Contributes only to pre-selected organizations.
Officers: Jennifer G. Daly, Pres.; Audrey F. Gorter, V.P.; James P. Gorter, Treas.

37569—NEW YORK

Director: Mary Gorter Krey.
EIN: 363683638

37570
Fisher-Raviv Family Foundation
c/o Adi Raviv
512 7th Ave., 17th Fl.
New York, NY 10018

Established in 1999 in NY.
Donor(s): Adi Raviv.
Financial data (yr. ended 12/31/00): Grants paid, $26,533; assets, $125,467 (M); expenditures, $26,533; qualifying distributions, $26,533.
Limitations: Applications not accepted.
Application information: Contributes only to pre-selected organizations.
Trustees: Laura Fisher, Adi Raviv.
EIN: 137224548

37571
The David Johnson Foundation
1419 E. 27th St.
Brooklyn, NY 11223

Financial data (yr. ended 10/31/01): Grants paid, $26,510; assets, $197,666 (M); gifts received, $150,000; expenditures, $28,156; qualifying distributions, $26,510.
EIN: 061565092

37572
The Te Leng Wu Charitable Trust
35 Nantucket Pl.
Scarsdale, NY 10583-4719

Donor(s): Te Leng Wu.
Financial data (yr. ended 12/31/01): Grants paid, $26,510; assets, $34,565 (M); gifts received, $82,000; expenditures, $26,510; qualifying distributions, $26,510.
Limitations: Giving in an international basis primarily China.
Trustees: Te Leng Wu, Mrs. Bao Cheng Lee Wu.
EIN: 137157094

37573
The Philip Devon Family Foundation, Inc.
c/o Edward J. Landau
250 Park Ave., Ste. 1000
New York, NY 10177-0076

Established in 1989 in NY.
Financial data (yr. ended 12/31/01): Grants paid, $26,500; assets, $423,459 (M); expenditures, $26,775; qualifying distributions, $26,500.
Limitations: Applications not accepted.
Application information: Contributes only to pre-selected organizations.
Directors: Dana Devon, Dwight Devon, Edward J. Landau.
EIN: 133498743

37574
Olive B. & A. Lindsay O'Connor Educational Fund
c/o U.S. Trust
P.O. Box 2004
New York, NY 10109-1910

Established in 1997 in NY.
Financial data (yr. ended 12/31/01): Grants paid, $26,500; assets, $503,772 (M); expenditures, $33,929; qualifying distributions, $26,500.
Limitations: Applications not accepted. Giving primarily in NY.
Application information: Contributes only to pre-selected organizations.
Trustee: U.S. Trust.
EIN: 133951708

37575
The Peter Daniel Seligman Foundation
c/o Robert Konigsberg
440 Park Ave. S., 10th Fl.
New York, NY 10016

Established in 2000 in NY.
Donor(s): Robert Konigsberg.
Financial data (yr. ended 09/30/01): Grants paid, $26,500; assets, $24,018 (M); gifts received, $51,097; expenditures, $27,079; qualifying distributions, $26,500.
Limitations: Applications not accepted. Giving primarily in WI.
Application information: Contributes only to pre-selected organizations.
Officers and Directors:* Robert Konigsberg,* Pres.; Stephanie Balint,* V.P.; Suzanne Reimer,* V.P.; Bonnie Konigsberg,* Secy.-Treas.
EIN: 134136972

37576
The Sharp-Curtis Foundation
c/o Peter Sharp & Co., Inc.
545 Madison Ave.
New York, NY 10022

Established in 1996 in NY.
Donor(s): James T. Curtis, Caroline M. Sharp.
Financial data (yr. ended 12/31/00): Grants paid, $26,500; assets, $590,321 (M); gifts received, $7,000; expenditures, $31,920; qualifying distributions, $26,500.
Limitations: Applications not accepted. Giving primarily in New York, NY.
Application information: Contributes only to pre-selected organizations.
Officers and Directors:* Caroline M. Sharp,* Pres.; James T. Curtis,* V.P.; Barry Tobias, Secy.-Treas.; Caroline Cronson.
EIN: 133864243

37577
Neil R. Austrian Foundation, Inc.
c/o Barry M. Strauss Assocs., Ltd.
307 5th Ave., 8th Fl.
New York, NY 10016-6517

Established in 1985 in CT.
Donor(s): Neil R. Austrian.
Financial data (yr. ended 11/30/01): Grants paid, $26,400; assets, $154,835 (M); gifts received, $685; expenditures, $27,095; qualifying distributions, $26,400.
Limitations: Applications not accepted.
Application information: Contributes only to pre-selected organizations.
Officers: Neil R. Austrian, Pres.; Nancy Austrian, Secy.
Director: Neil R. Austrian, Jr.
EIN: 133322785

37578
St. Andrew's Society of the City of Albany
150 Washington Ave.
Albany, NY 12210

Financial data (yr. ended 10/31/01): Grants paid, $26,400; assets, $577,435 (M); expenditures, $54,600; qualifying distributions, $26,400.
Limitations: Applications not accepted. Giving primarily in the Albany, NY, area.
Application information: Contributes only to pre-selected organizations.
Trustees: Roger Creighton, Edward R. McEwan.
EIN: 146050437

37579
William F. Treacy Scholarship Fund
115-06 Myrtle Ave.
Richmond Hill, NY 11418 (718) 847-8484
Contact: John T. Ahern, Tr. or Ed Ford, Tr.

Financial data (yr. ended 12/31/01): Grants paid, $26,400; assets, $31,522 (M); expenditures, $50,690; qualifying distributions, $33,335.
Limitations: Giving limited to residents of NY.
Application information: Scholarship awards not to exceed $1000 per year, up to 4 years, at any accredited undergraduate college or university. Application form required.
Trustees: John T. Ahern, Ed Ford.
EIN: 237442878
Codes: GTI

37580
The Trainor Family Foundation, Inc.
8 Captain Honeywells Rd.
Ardsley-on-Hudson, NY 10503-1504

Established in 1999 in NY.
Donor(s): Lawrence Trainor.
Financial data (yr. ended 09/30/01): Grants paid, $26,313; assets, $412,379 (M); gifts received, $515,685; expenditures, $29,892; qualifying distributions, $26,313.
Limitations: Applications not accepted.
Application information: Contributes only to pre-selected organizations.
Officers: Lawrence Trainor, Pres. and Treas.; Elena Trainor, V.P. and Secy.; Francis Trainor, V.P.
EIN: 134090695

37581
A. Haigh Cundey Foundation Inc.
c/o Marvin Ringer
673 Colfax Pl.
Valley Stream, NY 11581

Donor(s): A. Haigh Cundey.
Financial data (yr. ended 12/31/01): Grants paid, $26,300; assets, $203,525 (M); expenditures, $30,054; qualifying distributions, $26,300.
Limitations: Applications not accepted.
Application information: Contributes only to pre-selected organizations.
Officer: A. Haigh Cundey, Pres.
EIN: 132619233

37582
The Grove Creek Fund
c/o Estabrook Capital Management
1633 Broadway, 30th Fl.
New York, NY 10019

Established in 1999 in NY.
Donor(s): Charles T. Foley.
Financial data (yr. ended 12/31/01): Grants paid, $26,300; assets, $1,014,705 (M); gifts received, $229,175; expenditures, $47,474; qualifying distributions, $25,125.
Limitations: Applications not accepted.
Application information: Contributes only to pre-selected organizations.
Trustees: Charles T. Foley, Charles T. Foley II, David P. Foley, Kathleen M. Foley.
EIN: 134094405

37583
Just So Foundation
c/o JPMorgan Chase Bank
1211 6th Ave., 34th Fl.
New York, NY 10036
Application address: 2832 Vista Butte Dr., Las Vegas, NV 89134
Contact: Curtis Cushman, Tr.

Established in 1998.

Financial data (yr. ended 12/31/01): Grants paid, $26,300; assets, $496,886 (M); expenditures, $27,212; qualifying distributions, $26,175.
Limitations: Giving primarily in NV.
Application information: Application form not required.
Trustees: Curtis Cushman, Dorothy Barta Cushman, JPMorgan Chase Bank.
EIN: 656270560

37584
Elwer Foundation, Inc.
c/o Rothenberg, Peters & Co.
1 Linden Pl., Ste. 211
Great Neck, NY 11021-2697

Established in 1986 in NY.
Donor(s): Eleanor Werner.
Financial data (yr. ended 11/30/01): Grants paid, $26,273; assets, $615,971 (M); gifts received, $29,010; expenditures, $29,452; qualifying distributions, $26,443.
Limitations: Applications not accepted. Giving primarily in Hartford, CT.
Application information: Contributes only to pre-selected organizations.
Officers: Frederic Werner, Pres. and Treas.; Kenneth Werner, V.P.; Robert Werner, V.P.; Jacqueline Werner, Secy.
EIN: 136145851

37585
Berk Krauss Foundation, Inc.
c/o KBL Healthcare, Inc.
645 Madison Ave., 14th Fl.
New York, NY 10022

Established in 1996 in NY.
Financial data (yr. ended 12/31/01): Grants paid, $26,200; assets, $169,687 (M); expenditures, $27,578; qualifying distributions, $26,200.
Limitations: Applications not accepted.
Application information: Contributes only to pre-selected organizations.
Trustees: Zachery C. Berk, Marlene R. Krauss.
EIN: 133925354

37586
Sunrise Support, Inc.
126 E. 56 St., Ste. 2300
New York, NY 10022

Established in 1998 in NY.
Donor(s): Jacqueline Aron.
Financial data (yr. ended 12/31/01): Grants paid, $26,171; assets, $45,842 (M); gifts received, $115,000; expenditures, $100,999; qualifying distributions, $99,507.
Limitations: Giving primarily in NY and PA.
Officer: Jacqueline Aron, Pres., V.P., and Secy.-Treas.
EIN: 133948309

37587
Jerome Taishoff Foundation, Inc.
c/o Frendel, Brown & Weissman
655 3rd Ave.
New York, NY 10017-9117 (212) 867-9630

Established in 1954 in NY.
Financial data (yr. ended 12/31/01): Grants paid, $26,153; assets, $213,643 (M); expenditures, $41,255; qualifying distributions, $26,153.
Limitations: Applications not accepted. Giving primarily in CA.
Application information: Contributes only to pre-selected organizations.
Trustees: Vally T. Chamberlain, Paul Weissman.
EIN: 136161521

37588
V'Natan Lecha Rahamin Foundation
c/o Raymond Beyda
408 Ave. O
Brooklyn, NY 11230

Established in 1999 in NY.
Donor(s): Raymond Joseph Beyda.
Financial data (yr. ended 12/31/00): Grants paid, $26,140; assets, $8,063 (M); gifts received, $35,248; expenditures, $27,650; qualifying distributions, $26,140.
Limitations: Applications not accepted.
Application information: Contributes only to pre-selected organizations.
Directors: Raymond Joseph Beyda, Jamie Lynn Beyda, Joseph Raymond Beyda.
EIN: 113503465

37589
John & Laree Caughey Foundation
c/o Rachel May
655 Allen St.
Syracuse, NY 13210

Financial data (yr. ended 12/31/01): Grants paid, $26,100; assets, $459,237 (M); expenditures, $37,993; qualifying distributions, $26,100.
Limitations: Applications not accepted. Giving on a national basis, with emphasis on CA.
Application information: Contributes only to pre-selected organizations.
Officers and Directors:* Edwin Bingham,* Pres.; Pia Welch,* V.P.; Rachel May,* Treas. and Mgr.; Stephen Dow Beckham, Robert Hine, Norris Hundley, Jo Beth van Gelderen.
EIN: 952505709

37590
F. Gerard McGrath Foundation
c/o Windels Marx, et al.
156 W. 56th St.
New York, NY 10019

Established in 1986 in DE.
Donor(s): F. Gerard McGrath.
Financial data (yr. ended 12/31/01): Grants paid, $26,100; assets, $666,456 (M); gifts received, $91,000; expenditures, $29,231; qualifying distributions, $26,100.
Limitations: Applications not accepted. Giving primarily in CT, and Notre Dame, IN.
Application information: Contributes only to pre-selected organizations.
Officers and Directors:* F. Gerard McGrath,* Pres.; Carolyn M. McGrath,* Secy.-Treas.; Charles Seidler, Jr.
EIN: 061188137

37591
United States Science Education Foundation
c/o Hameeda Shaikh
49 Applegate Dr.
Central Islip, NY 11722-1901

Financial data (yr. ended 12/31/01): Grants paid, $26,050; assets, $13,715 (M); gifts received, $26,524; expenditures, $27,972; qualifying distributions, $0.
Trustees: Roshan Shaikh, Muhammad Paryal Soomro.
EIN: 116489027

37592
Black Cat Foundation
c/o Henry Berinstein
320 E. 72nd St., Ste. 6A
New York, NY 10021

Established in 1997.
Donor(s): Rodney A. Berinstein.
Financial data (yr. ended 12/31/01): Grants paid, $26,000; assets, $407,680 (M); gifts received, $100,000; expenditures, $27,325; qualifying distributions, $26,563.
Trustees: Henry W. Berinstein, Rodney A. Berinstein, Dennis B. Poster.
EIN: 133959068

37593
The Brout Family Foundation, Inc.
4 Trails End
Rye, NY 10580

Established in 2000 in NY.
Donor(s): Edward Brout.
Financial data (yr. ended 09/30/01): Grants paid, $26,000; assets, $84,173 (M); gifts received, $60,347; expenditures, $26,575; qualifying distributions, $26,000.
Limitations: Applications not accepted.
Application information: Contributes only to pre-selected organizations.
Officers: Edward Brout, Pres. and Treas.; Jennifer Brout, V.P. and Secy.; David Brout, V.P.
EIN: 134090677

37594
Richard T. Button Foundation, Inc.
250 W. 57th St., Ste. 1818
New York, NY 10107

Established in 2000 in NY.
Donor(s): Richard T. Button.
Financial data (yr. ended 10/31/01): Grants paid, $26,000; assets, $384,266 (M); gifts received, $190; expenditures, $47,889; qualifying distributions, $26,000.
Limitations: Applications not accepted. Giving primarily in NY.
Application information: Contributes only to pre-selected organizations.
Officers: Richard T. Button, Pres.; Edward Button, V.P.; Emily Button, Secy.-Treas.
EIN: 134089796

37595
Family Associates Foundation, Inc.
28 Whitestone Ln.
Rochester, NY 14618

Established in 1997 in NY.
Donor(s): William M. Balderston III.
Financial data (yr. ended 12/31/01): Grants paid, $26,000; assets, $506,275 (M); expenditures, $29,752; qualifying distributions, $26,000.
Limitations: Applications not accepted.
Application information: Contributes only to pre-selected organizations.
Officers and Directors:* William M. Balderston III,* Pres. and Treas.; David M. Balderston,* V.P.; Peter R. Balderston,* V.P.; William Balderston IV,* V.P.; Mary B. Somerby,* V.P.; Ruth M. Balderston,* Secy.
EIN: 161522170

37596
The Alexander & Charlotte Herman Foundation
c/o Abe I. Friedman
1555 54th St., Ste. 3
Brooklyn, NY 11219

Established in 1995 in NY.
Donor(s): Charlotte Herman.
Financial data (yr. ended 12/31/01): Grants paid, $26,000; assets, $95,677 (M); gifts received, $100,000; expenditures, $26,081; qualifying distributions, $26,081.
Limitations: Applications not accepted. Giving primarily in New York, NY; giving also in Israel.
Application information: Contributes only to pre-selected organizations.

37596—NEW YORK

Trustees: Charlotte Herman, Debby Rebenwurzel, Miriam Widawsky, Naomi Wiener.
EIN: 113230339

37597
Kenmore Rotary Foundation, Inc.
3200 Elmwood Ave.
Kenmore, NY 14217-1232

Financial data (yr. ended 12/31/01): Grants paid, $26,000; assets, $439,215 (M); gifts received, $27,550; expenditures, $30,729; qualifying distributions, $26,000.
Limitations: Applications not accepted. Giving primarily in NY.
Application information: Contributes only to pre-selected organizations.
Officers: William Brucker, Pres.; James McLaine, V.P. and Treas.; Lawrence Ward, Secy.
EIN: 222141650

37598
The Mai Family Foundation
c/o Mahoney Cohen & Co.
111 W. 40th St., 12th Fl.
New York, NY 10018

Established in 1996 in NY.
Donor(s): Vincent A. Mai.
Financial data (yr. ended 12/31/01): Grants paid, $26,000; assets, $3,135,338 (M); expenditures, $69,105; qualifying distributions, $26,000.
Limitations: Applications not accepted. Giving primarily in NY.
Application information: Contributes only to pre-selected organizations.
Officers and Directors:* Vincent A. Mai,* Pres. and Treas.; Anne Mai,* V.P.; Lisa Moore, Secy.; Sanford Krieger.
EIN: 133915987

37599
Masonic Toys for Tots Foundation
c/o Harry D. Diven Jr.
315 W. 70th St., Apt. 101
New York, NY 10023-3514

Established in 2001 in NY.
Financial data (yr. ended 12/31/01): Grants paid, $26,000; assets, $7,739 (M); gifts received, $43,869; expenditures, $36,130; qualifying distributions, $26,000.
Limitations: Applications not accepted.
Application information: Contributes only to pre-selected organizations.
Officers: Ivan Obolensky, Pres.; Todd Myers, Exec. V.P.; Harry J. Diven, Jr., Secy.-Treas.
EIN: 134123681

37600
The Kipp Nelson Foundation
c/o Goldman Sachs & Co.
85 Broad St., Tax Dept.
New York, NY 10004

Established in 1998 in NY.
Donor(s): Kipp N. Nelson.
Financial data (yr. ended 07/31/00): Grants paid, $26,000; assets, $1,674,540 (M); gifts received, $1,608,348; expenditures, $26,129; qualifying distributions, $26,000.
Limitations: Applications not accepted.
Application information: Contributes only to pre-selected organizations.
Trustees: Carlos A. Cordiero, Kipp N. Nelson.
EIN: 133936467

37601
The P. C. Richard Foundation
c/o P.C. Richard & Son
150 Price Pkwy.
Farmingdale, NY 11735-1315 (516) 843-4300

Established in 1994 in NY.
Donor(s): P.C. Richard & Son.
Financial data (yr. ended 12/31/00): Grants paid, $26,000; assets, $39,377 (M); expenditures, $99,272; qualifying distributions, $99,272.
Limitations: Applications not accepted. Giving primarily in NY.
Application information: Contributes only to pre-selected organizations.
Officers: Gary Richard, C.E.O. and Pres.; Thomas Ponmer, V.P. and C.F.O.; Kevin Hughey, Treas.
EIN: 113213607
Codes: CS, CD

37602
Jane Schenck Estate Trust
(Formerly Jane Schenck Estate)
c/o NBT Bank, N.A.
52 S. Broad St.
Norwich, NY 13815-1646
Application addresses: c/o Superintendent, Greene Central School, Greene, NY 13778; c/o Superintendent, Afton Central School, Afton, NY 13730

Financial data (yr. ended 06/30/01): Grants paid, $26,000; assets, $212,981 (M); expenditures, $28,447; qualifying distributions, $28,351; giving activities include $26,000 for loans to individuals.
Limitations: Giving limited to Greene and Afton, NY.
Application information: Application form required.
Trustees: Vernice N. Church, Robert Fiester, Margery Secrest, Frederick Taroli, NBT Bank, N.A.
EIN: 166052404

37603
The Howard and Debbie Schiller Foundation
c/o Golman Sachs & Co.
85 Broad St., Tax Dept.
New York, NY 10004

Established in 1996 in NY.
Donor(s): Howard B. Schiller.
Financial data (yr. ended 06/30/01): Grants paid, $26,000; assets, $2,360,344 (M); gifts received, $247,281; expenditures, $78,174; qualifying distributions, $26,000.
Limitations: Applications not accepted. Giving primarily in New York, NY.
Application information: Contributes only to pre-selected organizations.
Trustees: Debbie Schiller, Howard B. Schiller.
EIN: 133933626

37604
Rudolph and Rose Wollner Charitable Trust
1 E. Main St., Ste. 510
Rochester, NY 14614 (716) 325-6700
Contact: Robert G. Lamb, Jr., Tr.

Established in 2000 in NY.
Donor(s): Rose Wollner.‡
Financial data (yr. ended 12/31/01): Grants paid, $26,000; assets, $1,183,907 (M); gifts received, $625,007; expenditures, $53,549; qualifying distributions, $26,000.
Trustees: Anne B. Francis, Maureen P. Lamb, Robert G. Lamb, Jr.
EIN: 166508097

37605
S. & G. Kaplan Fund, Inc.
1144 Sage St.
Far Rockaway, NY 11691
Contact: Simon Kaplan, Pres., or Gertrude Kaplan, Secy.

Donor(s): Simon Kaplan, Gertrude Kaplan.
Financial data (yr. ended 12/31/01): Grants paid, $25,781; assets, $236,064 (M); gifts received, $2,000; expenditures, $26,885; qualifying distributions, $25,781.
Limitations: Giving primarily in NY.
Officers: Simon Kaplan, Pres.; Gertrude Kaplan, Secy.; Joseph Kaplan, Treas.
EIN: 112835155

37606
Charles R. Brewer Charitable Trust
c/o Wilber National Bank
245 Main St.
Oneonta, NY 13820

Established in 1999 in NY.
Donor(s): Charles R. Brewer.‡
Financial data (yr. ended 12/31/01): Grants paid, $25,776; assets, $616,402 (M); expenditures, $33,674; qualifying distributions, $25,776.
Limitations: Applications not accepted.
Application information: Contributes only to pre-selected organizations.
Trustee: Wilber National Bank.
EIN: 166202755

37607
Reuben and Ethel Frieman Foundation, Inc.
c/o Carol Finkel
401 E. 89th St., Apt. 15-A
New York, NY 10128-6724

Financial data (yr. ended 12/31/01): Grants paid, $25,750; assets, $116,782 (M); expenditures, $27,130; qualifying distributions, $25,750.
Limitations: Applications not accepted. Giving limited to NY.
Application information: Contributes only to pre-selected organizations.
Officers: Carol Finkel, Pres.; Arnold Kivelson, Secy.
EIN: 136169165

37608
The Dr. Nicholas D. and Patricia B. Trbovich Foundation
28 Tanglewood Dr. W.
Orchard Park, NY 14127

Established in 1984 in NY.
Donor(s): Nicholas D. Trbovich.
Financial data (yr. ended 11/30/01): Grants paid, $25,740; assets, $210,044 (M); gifts received, $15,900; expenditures, $29,524; qualifying distributions, $25,740.
Limitations: Applications not accepted. Giving primarily in Saratoga Springs, NY.
Application information: Contributes only to pre-selected organizations.
Officer: Kathleen A. Trbovich, Exec. Dir.
Trustees: Michael D. Trbovich, Nicholas D. Trbovich.
EIN: 222581401

37609
The Anikstein Family Foundation, Inc.
213 Roslyn Rd.
Roslyn Heights, NY 11577-1338

Established in 1985 in NY.
Donor(s): Members of the Anikstein family.
Financial data (yr. ended 11/30/01): Grants paid, $25,652; assets, $84,443 (M); gifts received,

$10,000; expenditures, $25,812; qualifying distributions, $25,652.
Limitations: Applications not accepted. Giving primarily on the East Coast; some giving in CA.
Application information: Contributes only to pre-selected organizations.
Directors: Albert Anikstein, Harvey Anikstein.
EIN: 112737109

37610
Mule Family Foundation
c/o Goldman Sachs & Co.
85 Broad St., Tax Dept.
New York, NY 10004-2456

Established in 1994 in NY.
Donor(s): Edward A. Mule.
Financial data (yr. ended 08/31/01): Grants paid, $25,620; assets, $1,147,607 (M); gifts received, $392,000; expenditures, $54,664; qualifying distributions, $25,620.
Limitations: Applications not accepted. Giving primarily in New York, NY.
Application information: Contributes only to pre-selected organizations.
Trustee: Edward A. Mule.
EIN: 133801234

37611
The Oberoi Family Foundation
c/o Goldman Sachs & Co.
85 Broad St., Tax Dept.
New York, NY 10004

Established in 1997 in NY.
Donor(s): Alok Oberoi.
Financial data (yr. ended 05/31/01): Grants paid, $25,535; assets, $1,972,722 (M); gifts received, $2,750; expenditures, $72,744; qualifying distributions, $25,535.
Limitations: Applications not accepted.
Application information: Contributes only to pre-selected organizations.
Trustees: Alok Oberoi, Majini Oberoi.
EIN: 133932623

37612
Livingston Foundation, Inc.
445 E. 80th St.
New York, NY 10021
Contact: Tamara Weintraub, Pres.

Established in 1945 in NY.
Financial data (yr. ended 09/30/01): Grants paid, $25,509; assets, $1,125,940 (M); expenditures, $28,810; qualifying distributions, $27,116.
Limitations: Applications not accepted. Giving primarily in New York, NY.
Application information: Contributes only to pre-selected organizations.
Officers: Tamara Weintraub, Pres.; Louis B. Livingston, V.P. and Treas.
EIN: 136171684

37613
The Joy J. & John M. Nevin Foundation
c/o Joseph Abraham
655 3rd Ave., Ste. 1400
New York, NY 10017

Established in 1997 in NY.
Donor(s): John M. Nevin.
Financial data (yr. ended 12/31/01): Grants paid, $25,500; assets, $190,727 (M); expenditures, $28,402; qualifying distributions, $25,500.
Limitations: Applications not accepted.
Application information: Contributes only to pre-selected organizations.
Directors: John Nevin, Jr., John M. Nevin, Joy J. Nevin.
EIN: 133979362

37614
Philip J. Spincola Memorial Children's Fund, Inc.
88 Luquer Rd.
Manhasset, NY 11030

Established in 2000 in NY.
Donor(s): Joyce Spincola, Laura Spincola, Dana Spincola.
Financial data (yr. ended 12/31/01): Grants paid, $25,500; assets, $61,966 (M); gifts received, $15,000; expenditures, $25,537; qualifying distributions, $25,500.
Limitations: Applications not accepted. Giving primarily in NY.
Application information: Contributes only to pre-selected organizations.
Officers and Directors:* Dana Spincola,* Pres.; Laura Spincola,* V.P. and Treas.; Joyce Spincola,* Secy.
EIN: 113548511

37615
Tziterman Memorial Trust
195 Wildacre Ave.
Lawrence, NY 11559

Established in 2000 in NY.
Donor(s): IDT Corp.
Financial data (yr. ended 06/30/01): Grants paid, $25,473; assets, $384,011 (M); gifts received, $250,000; expenditures, $25,473; qualifying distributions, $25,473.
Limitations: Applications not accepted.
Application information: Contributes only to pre-selected organizations.
Trustee: Devora May Smith.
EIN: 137257263
Codes: CS

37616
Edwin M. Johnston, Jr. Family Foundation
1350 1 M&T Plaza
Buffalo, NY 14203-2395

Established in 1999 in NY.
Donor(s): Edwin M. Johnston, Jr.
Financial data (yr. ended 12/31/01): Grants paid, $25,423; assets, $1,029,431 (M); gifts received, $161,564; expenditures, $29,798; qualifying distributions, $25,423.
Limitations: Applications not accepted. Giving primarily in St. Louis, MO, and Buffalo, NY.
Application information: Contributes only to pre-selected organizations.
Trustees: Jennifer J. Demuth, Edwin M. Johnston, Jr., Edwin M. Johnston III, Susan S. Johnston, Sarah J. Mitchell.
EIN: 161578180

37617
The Hammerman Charitable Trust
c/o David L. Hammerman
14 Manor Ln.
Lawrence, NY 11559

Established in 1992 in NY.
Donor(s): David Hammerman.
Financial data (yr. ended 12/31/01): Grants paid, $25,395; assets, $645,883 (M); gifts received, $337,775; expenditures, $25,689; qualifying distributions, $25,395.
Limitations: Applications not accepted.
Application information: Contributes only to pre-selected organizations.
Trustees: David L. Hammerman, Marc Z. Hammerman.
EIN: 116417695

37618
Dr. Robert R. Eckert Memorial Fund
c/o The National Bank of Delaware County
P.O. Box 389
Walton, NY 13856 (607) 865-4126

Established in 1985 in NY.
Financial data (yr. ended 12/31/00): Grants paid, $25,382; assets, $823,479 (M); expenditures, $28,223; qualifying distributions, $27,287.
Limitations: Giving limited to residents of the Downsville School District and Roscoe Central School District, NY.
Trustee: The National Bank of Delaware County.
EIN: 166280587
Codes: GTI

37619
Murel Foundation, Inc.
125 E. 72nd St.
New York, NY 10021 (212) 249-1838
Contact: Ellin Kalmus, Pres.

Established in 1981 in TX.
Financial data (yr. ended 12/31/01): Grants paid, $25,380; assets, $81,244 (M); expenditures, $26,878; qualifying distributions, $25,380.
Limitations: Giving primarily in NY.
Officers: Ellin Kalmus, Pres.; Lester C. Migdal, Secy.
EIN: 136155520

37620
The Simon Savitt Charitable Foundation, Inc.
260 Madison Ave., 22nd Fl.
New York, NY 10016-2401

Established in 1994 in NY.
Financial data (yr. ended 12/31/01): Grants paid, $25,380; assets, $52,654 (M); gifts received, $2,787; expenditures, $28,826; qualifying distributions, $25,510.
Limitations: Applications not accepted. Giving primarily in NY.
Application information: Contributes only to pre-selected organizations.
Officers: Ephraim Savitt, Pres.; Fern Savitt, V.P.; Sylvia Savitt, Secy.; Leah Savitt, Treas.
EIN: 133790071

37621
Esther & Louis Wertenteil Foundation
(Formerly Werber Foundation)
c/o Arye Ringel
1750 44th St.
Brooklyn, NY 11204-1050

Donor(s): Louis Wertenteil, Esther Wertenteil.
Financial data (yr. ended 06/30/02): Grants paid, $25,342; assets, $17,377 (M); gifts received, $29,260; expenditures, $25,685; qualifying distributions, $25,342.
Limitations: Applications not accepted. Giving primarily in NY.
Application information: Contributes only to pre-selected organizations.
Trustees: Teena C. Rubinfeld, Aron Wertenteil, Esther Wertenteil.
EIN: 112690412

37622
Reiss Family Foundation
7 Beverly Rd.
Great Neck, NY 11021

Established in 1997 in NY.
Donor(s): Barbara Reiss, Marc Reiss.
Financial data (yr. ended 12/31/01): Grants paid, $25,335; assets, $16,808 (M); gifts received, $16,525; expenditures, $25,928; qualifying distributions, $25,335.

37622—NEW YORK

Limitations: Applications not accepted. Giving primarily in New York, NY.
Application information: Contributes only to pre-selected organizations.
Trustees: Barbara Reiss, Marc Reiss.
EIN: 116485298

37623
Sugar Family Charitible Foundation
Lefferts St. Station
P.O. Box 220
Brooklyn, NY 11233-0220
Application address: 462 Malbone St., Brooklyn, NY 11225
Contact: Yissachor Sugar, Tr.

Established in 1999 in NY.
Financial data (yr. ended 12/31/01): Grants paid, $25,318; assets, $211,241 (M); gifts received, $28,000; expenditures, $27,068; qualifying distributions, $25,318.
Limitations: Giving primarily in Brooklyn, NY.
Trustees: Jaime Sugar, Yissachor Dov Sugar.
EIN: 113436854

37624
Dishy Family Foundation
(Formerly Dishy-Easton Foundation, Inc.)
50 Riverside Dr.
New York, NY 10024

Donor(s): Bernard Dishy.
Financial data (yr. ended 03/31/01): Grants paid, $25,285; assets, $120,043 (M); expenditures, $27,639; qualifying distributions, $25,285.
Limitations: Applications not accepted. Giving primarily in New York, NY.
Application information: Contributes only to pre-selected organizations.
Officers: Bernard Dishy, Pres.; David Dishy, V.P.; Linda Dishy, Secy.; Andrea Dishy, Treas.
EIN: 136223436

37625
Gottheil Family Fund
1433 55th St.
Brooklyn, NY 11219

Established in 1992.
Donor(s): Zelman Gottheil, Fannie Gottheil.
Financial data (yr. ended 11/30/00): Grants paid, $25,250; assets, $111,101 (M); gifts received, $34,000; expenditures, $25,250; qualifying distributions, $25,250.
Limitations: Applications not accepted.
Application information: Contributes only to pre-selected organizations.
Officers: Zelman Gottheil, Pres.; Fannie Gottheil, V.P.
EIN: 133040342

37626
Media Association of Social Scientists and Artists, Inc.
9 Riverview Ave.
Ardsley, NY 10502 (914) 674-4003
Contact: Randi M. Hoffmann, Pres.

Established in 1999 in NY.
Donor(s): Randi M. Hoffmann.
Financial data (yr. ended 06/30/00): Grants paid, $25,250; assets, $3,919 (M); gifts received, $15,000; expenditures, $39,385; qualifying distributions, $25,245.
Limitations: Giving on a national and international basis.
Application information: Application form required.
Officers and Directors:* Randi M. Hoffmann,* Pres.; Flavia Goldson,* Secy.; Noa Ain,* Treas.;

Ellen Baxter, Lee Blumer, Lisa Kalomeris, Arthur Salvadore, Bill Stanton.
EIN: 133354834

37627
Joseph Family Charitable Trust
15 W. 72nd St., Apt. 29C
New York, NY 10023-3472
Contact: Patricia S. Joseph, Tr.

Financial data (yr. ended 07/31/01): Grants paid, $25,240; assets, $595,976 (M); expenditures, $26,934; qualifying distributions, $26,934.
Limitations: Giving primarily in NY.
Application information: Application form not required.
Trustees: Claire W. Joseph, Patricia S. Joseph, Jean U. Kumar, Mohan U. Kumar.
EIN: 226233373

37628
The Geisser Family Foundation
c/o Andrea Geisser-Fenway Partners
152 W. 57th St.
New York, NY 10019

Established in 1998 in NY.
Financial data (yr. ended 12/31/01): Grants paid, $25,200; assets, $419,831 (M); gifts received, $55,150; expenditures, $29,594; qualifying distributions, $25,200.
Limitations: Applications not accepted.
Application information: Contributes only to pre-selected organizations.
Trustees: Andrea Geisser, Mary Ellen Geisser.
EIN: 061507919

37629
A. H. & N. Leeseberg Trust
c/o Staten Island Savings Bank
1591 Richmond Rd.
Staten Island, NY 10304

Established in 1999 in NY.
Financial data (yr. ended 12/31/01): Grants paid, $25,200; assets, $475,361 (M); gifts received, $495; expenditures, $34,093; qualifying distributions, $25,200.
Limitations: Applications not accepted.
Application information: Contributes only to pre-selected organizations.
Trustee: Staten Island Savings Bank.
EIN: 137244618

37630
The Joyce & Gary Wenglowski Foundation
c/o BCRS Assocs., LLC
67 Wall St.
New York, NY 10005

Established in 1986 in NY.
Donor(s): Gary M. Wenglowski, Joyce Wenglowski.
Financial data (yr. ended 04/30/02): Grants paid, $25,200; assets, $297,631 (M); expenditures, $27,280; qualifying distributions, $25,200.
Limitations: Applications not accepted. Giving primarily in ME and NY.
Application information: Contributes only to pre-selected organizations.
Trustees: Gary M. Wenglowski, Joyce Wenglowski.
EIN: 133376368

37631
Mark & Marilyn Talve Foundation
c/o Mark Talve
85 Harbor Rd.
Port Washington, NY 11050

Established in 1998 in NY.

Financial data (yr. ended 12/31/01): Grants paid, $25,191; assets, $43,211 (M); expenditures, $25,427; qualifying distributions, $25,191.
Limitations: Applications not accepted.
Application information: Contributes only to pre-selected organizations.
Officers: Mark Talve, Pres.; Marilyn Talve, Secy.
EIN: 113381725

37632
The Michelle O'Neill Foundation, Inc.
26 Oregon St.
Long Beach, NY 11561
Contact: Carol O'Neill, Pres.

Established in 1999 in NY.
Financial data (yr. ended 12/31/01): Grants paid, $25,185; assets, $54,227 (M); gifts received, $49,335; expenditures, $39,793; qualifying distributions, $25,185.
Officers: Carol O'Neill, Pres.; Carol-Ann O'Neill, V.P. and Secy.; Jacquelin O'Neill, Treas.
EIN: 134044538

37633
George A. Tucker Charitable Trust
6500 Bogusville Hill Rd.
Deansboro, NY 13328

Financial data (yr. ended 06/30/01): Grants paid, $25,105; assets, $278,860 (M); expenditures, $2,628; qualifying distributions, $2,628.
Limitations: Applications not accepted.
Application information: Contributes only to pre-selected organizations.
Trustees: Phillip Morse, Sharon Zombek.
EIN: 161525296

37634
Kahn Family Foundation, Inc.
c/o Nathan Kahn
4663 Waldo Ave.
Riverdale, NY 10471-3061

Established in 1996 in NY.
Financial data (yr. ended 12/31/99): Grants paid, $25,100; assets, $2,114 (M); gifts received, $15,000; expenditures, $27,896; qualifying distributions, $25,100.
Limitations: Applications not accepted.
Application information: Contributes only to pre-selected organizations.
Directors: Nathan Kahn, Sandra Kahn.
EIN: 133863402

37635
The Raymond R. Konopka, Jr. Foundation, Inc.
c/o Klarberg, Raiola & Assoc.
500 5th Ave., Ste. 3000
New York, NY 10110

Established in 1998 in NY.
Donor(s): Louise Konopka.
Financial data (yr. ended 12/31/01): Grants paid, $25,090; assets, $15,930 (M); gifts received, $38,500; expenditures, $25,126; qualifying distributions, $25,090.
Limitations: Applications not accepted.
Application information: Contributes only to pre-selected organizations.
Directors: Lee Konopka, Louise Konopka, Steven Konopka, Susan Konopka.
EIN: 133989453

37636
The Cornell Delta Phi Educational Fund
c/o Snow Becker Krauss
605 Third Ave.
New York, NY 10158
Contact: P. Michael Puleo, Tr.

Established in 1955 in NY.

Financial data (yr. ended 03/31/01): Grants paid, $25,050; assets, $470,163 (M); expenditures, $36,129; qualifying distributions, $33,441.
Limitations: Giving limited to residents of Ithaca, NY.
Application information: Applicant must include most recent transcript from Cornell University. Application form required.
Trustees: Fred D. Barre, Craig W. Fanning, P. Michael Puleo, H. Stewart Wheller.
EIN: 136123284
Codes: GTI

37637
Yisachar Zevulun Scholarship Fund, Inc.
7 Andover Ln.
Lawrence, NY 11559
Contact: Jeff Mansbach, Pres.

Established in 1996 in NY.
Donor(s): Murray Friedman, Mrs. Murray Friedman.
Financial data (yr. ended 12/31/99): Grants paid, $25,050; assets, $2,606 (M); gifts received, $26,515; expenditures, $25,200; qualifying distributions, $25,050.
Limitations: Giving primarily in NY.
Officers: Jeff Mansbach, Pres. and Treas.; Sol Hartman, V.P.; Jonathan Herman, V.P.
EIN: 113327971

37638
The Beuth Foundation
464 Lake Shore Dr.
Putnam Valley, NY 10579
Contact: Philip R. Beuth, Pres.

Established in 1997 in NY.
Donor(s): Philip R. Beuth.
Financial data (yr. ended 12/31/00): Grants paid, $25,000; assets, $408,605 (M); expenditures, $27,757; qualifying distributions, $25,000.
Application information: Application form not required.
Officers: Philip R. Beuth, Pres.; Jane M. Beuth, V.P.; Mary G. Beuth, Secy.-Treas.
Directors: Philip S. Beuth, Robert A. Beuth.
EIN: 061479737

37639
The Bloomberg Sisters Foundation
c/o Geller & Co.
800 3rd Ave., 19th Fl.
New York, NY 10022

Established in 1998 in NY.
Donor(s): Michael R. Bloomberg.
Financial data (yr. ended 12/31/01): Grants paid, $25,000; assets, $503,760 (M); expenditures, $25,391; qualifying distributions, $24,844.
Limitations: Applications not accepted.
Application information: Contributes only to pre-selected organizations.
Trustees: Emma Bloomberg, Susan E.B. Bloomberg, Patti Harris.
EIN: 137151342

37640
Jack Teigh Blume Foundation, Inc.
150 W. 56th St., No. 5204
New York, NY 10019-3839 (212) 265-4904

Established in 1961.
Financial data (yr. ended 12/31/99): Grants paid, $25,000; assets, $71,284 (M); expenditures, $26,998; qualifying distributions, $25,000.
Limitations: Applications not accepted. Giving primarily in New York, NY.
Application information: Contributes only to pre-selected organizations.
Officer and Director:* Abby Brown,* Pres.

EIN: 136226232

37641
Sylvan E. Bowles Scholarship Fund
c/o Lenard Marlow
666 Old Country Rd., Ste. 705
Garden City, NY 11530-2018

Established in 1963.
Donor(s): Sylvan E. Bowles.‡
Financial data (yr. ended 12/31/00): Grants paid, $25,000; assets, $488,706 (M); expenditures, $27,351; qualifying distributions, $25,000.
Limitations: Giving primarily in the West Indies.
Trustees: Lenard Marlow, Richard Marlow.
EIN: 116100871

37642
The Captiva Foundation
200 Theater Pl.
Buffalo, NY 14202 (716) 853-8671
Contact: Thomas R. Beecher, Jr., Tr.

Established in 1997 in NY.
Donor(s): Max W. Jacobs, Matthew C. Jacobs, Thomas R. Beecher, Jr.
Financial data (yr. ended 12/31/01): Grants paid, $25,000; assets, $493,658 (M); gifts received, $98,721; expenditures, $26,267; qualifying distributions, $25,000.
Application information: Application form not required.
Trustees: Thomas R. Beecher, Jr., Matthew C. Jacobs.
EIN: 161537263

37643
The Ernest & Jeanette Dicker Charitable Foundation
c/o Davidoff & Malto
605 3rd Ave., Ste. 34
New York, NY 10158

Donor(s): Ernest Dicker, Jeanette Dicker.
Financial data (yr. ended 12/31/01): Grants paid, $25,000; assets, $47,657 (M); gifts received, $16,922; expenditures, $25,816; qualifying distributions, $25,000.
Limitations: Applications not accepted. Giving primarily in NY.
Application information: Contributes only to a pre-selected organization.
Directors: Ernest Dicker, Jeanette Dicker.
EIN: 133887585

37644
The Dorothy and Jack Entratter Foundation
969 3rd Ave.
New York, NY 10022

Established in 1998 in NY.
Donor(s): The Dorothy and Jack Entratter Children's Homes Association.
Financial data (yr. ended 12/31/01): Grants paid, $25,000; assets, $440,805 (M); expenditures, $29,222; qualifying distributions, $25,000.
Limitations: Applications not accepted.
Application information: Contributes only to pre-selected organizations.
Officers: Caryl Palin, Pres.; Michelle Wolkoff, V.P.; Gerald Wolkoff, Secy.; Michael Palin, Treas.
EIN: 134022704

37645
Federman Scholarship Fund
c/o M&T Bank
P.O. Box 22900
Rochester, NY 14692 (716) 258-8445
Application address: c/o Trust & Investment Svcs., 1 M&T Plz., Buffalo, NY 14203-2301, tel.: (716) 842-5527

Financial data (yr. ended 12/31/01): Grants paid, $25,000; assets, $301,037 (M); expenditures, $30,294; qualifying distributions, $26,205.
Limitations: Giving primarily in Erie County, NY.
Application information: Application form not required.
Trustee: M & T Bank.
EIN: 166223968
Codes: GTI

37646
Mortimer J. Harrison Article 11(F) Trust
c/o Torys
237 Park Ave.
New York, NY 10017
Application address: c/o Arthur E. Lashinsky, 810 S. Springfield Ave., NJ 07081

Established in 1996 in NY.
Donor(s): Mortimer J. Harrison.‡
Financial data (yr. ended 12/31/00): Grants paid, $25,000; assets, $40,770 (M); gifts received, $50,000; expenditures, $32,549; qualifying distributions, $24,973.
Limitations: Giving primarily in New York, NY.
Trustee: Arthur E. Lashinsky.
EIN: 137075865

37647
Katherine Hassett Foundation for Charitable Purposes
7219 3rd Ave.
Brooklyn, NY 11209-2198 (718) 238-3360
Contact: Harry G. English, Mgr.

Established in 1995 in GA.
Financial data (yr. ended 12/31/01): Grants paid, $25,000; assets, $663,090 (M); expenditures, $47,276; qualifying distributions, $25,000.
Limitations: Giving primarily in NY.
Officers and Trustees:* Erica R. Brand de Mena, Secy.; Eileen E. English,* Treas.; Harry G. English,* Mgr.
EIN: 112811217

37648
Heller Family Foundation
c/o RSM McGladrey, Inc.
555 5th Ave., 5th Fl.
New York, NY 10017-2416

Established in 1999 in NY.
Donor(s): Anne Heller.
Financial data (yr. ended 12/31/01): Grants paid, $25,000; assets, $485,575 (M); expenditures, $29,613; qualifying distributions, $25,000.
Limitations: Applications not accepted. Giving primarily in NY.
Application information: Contributes only to pre-selected organizations.
Trustees: Anne Heller, James A. Heller, Susan K. Heller.
EIN: 137204248

37649
Learning Disability Funding Organization, Inc.
7 Cobblestone Ct.
Centerport, NY 11721
Application address: 400 E. 66th St., New York, NY 10021, tel.: (646) 314-9826
Contact: Josh Swartz, Pres.

Donor(s): Josh Swartz, Jerome Swartz.
Financial data (yr. ended 12/31/99): Grants paid, $25,000; assets, $824 (M); gifts received, $20,000; expenditures, $29,275; qualifying distributions, $25,000.
Limitations: Giving limited to Suffolk County, NY.
Application information: Application form not required.
Officer and Director:* Josh Swartz,* Pres. and Treas.
EIN: 113390095

37650
The LG-MEP Family Foundation
(Formerly Beryl Plaut Family Foundation)
c/o Darren Berger
1350 Ave. of the Americas, Ste. 1207
New York, NY 10019-4896

Established in 2000 in DE.
Donor(s): Beryl Plaut.
Financial data (yr. ended 12/31/01): Grants paid, $25,000; assets, $451,347 (M); gifts received, $400,000; expenditures, $25,029; qualifying distributions, $25,000.
Limitations: Applications not accepted.
Application information: Contributes only to pre-selected organizations.
Officer: Beryl Plaut, Pres.
EIN: 134148983

37651
A. Marchionne Foundation for Scientific Study
c/o Richard H. Nevers
11 Tulip Tree Ln.
Niskayuna, NY 12309

Established in 2000 in NY.
Donor(s): Anthony Marchionne.
Financial data (yr. ended 12/31/01): Grants paid, $25,000; assets, $2,000,157 (M); gifts received, $752,074; expenditures, $36,804; qualifying distributions, $25,000.
Limitations: Applications not accepted.
Application information: Contributes only to pre-selected organizations.
Officers and Directors:* Richard H. Nevers,* Pres.; Hon. C. Ross Lander,* Treas.; Bruce Lord.
EIN: 141826951

37652
The Jules Mayer Foundation
91 Central Park W.
New York, NY 10023

Established in 1998 in NY.
Donor(s): Helen W. Mayer.
Financial data (yr. ended 12/31/01): Grants paid, $25,000; assets, $68,009 (M); expenditures, $25,100; qualifying distributions, $25,000.
Limitations: Applications not accepted. Giving primarily in New York, NY.
Application information: Contributes only to pre-selected organizations.
Trustees: Helen W. Mayer, Max D. Mayer.
EIN: 137150795

37653
Carl and Hilda Morris Foundation
c/o Berman and Sosman, LLC
2492 Merrick Rd.
Bellmore, NY 11710

Established in 1997 in OR.
Financial data (yr. ended 12/31/01): Grants paid, $25,000; assets, $2,504,064 (M); expenditures, $66,322; qualifying distributions, $25,000.
Limitations: Giving primarily in Tacoma, WA.
Director: David C. Moreu.
EIN: 936285843

37654
James M. Nederlander Foundation, Inc.
1450 Broadway, 6th Fl.
New York, NY 10018 (800) 223-6715
Contact: James M. Nederlander, Dir.

Donor(s): James M. Nederlander.
Financial data (yr. ended 09/30/01): Grants paid, $25,000; assets, $7,837 (M); gifts received, $25,000; expenditures, $25,790; qualifying distributions, $25,000.
Officers and Directors:* James L. Nederlander,* Pres.; David Malkin,* Secy.; Nicholas Scandalios,* Treas.; Charlene S. Nederlander, James M. Nederlander.
EIN: 133980285

37655
The Norinchukin Foundation, Inc.
c/o The Norinchukin Bank-NY Branch
245 Park Ave., 29th Fl.
New York, NY 10167-0104
FAX: (212) 697-5754
Contact: Toshiyuki Futaoka, Pres.

Established in 1994 in NY.
Donor(s): The Norinchukin Bank.
Financial data (yr. ended 12/31/01): Grants paid, $25,000; assets, $513,362 (M); expenditures, $26,529; qualifying distributions, $25,000.
Limitations: Giving primarily in NY.
Application information: Application form not required.
Officers and Directors:* Yoshiro Niiro,* Chair.; Toshiyuki Futaoka,* Pres.; Ken Niyomura,* Secy.; Fumiko Kato, Treas.; Robert G. Thomas.
Trustee: The Norinchukin Bank.
EIN: 133738532

37656
Plaut Family Foundation
28 Lord Ave.
Lawrence, NY 11559

Established in 2001.
Donor(s): Murray Plaut.
Financial data (yr. ended 12/31/01): Grants paid, $25,000; assets, $125,160 (M); gifts received, $150,010; expenditures, $25,000; qualifying distributions, $25,000.
Officer: Murray Plaut, Pres.
EIN: 113630176

37657
Walter Reade Foundation, Inc.
c/o Simpson Thacher & Bartlett
425 Lexington Ave.
New York, NY 10017

Established in 1951.
Donor(s): Walter Reade Organization, Inc.
Financial data (yr. ended 12/31/00): Grants paid, $25,000; assets, $1,071,768 (M); expenditures, $45,719; qualifying distributions, $25,000.
Limitations: Applications not accepted. Giving primarily in NY.
Application information: Contributes only to pre-selected organizations.
Officers: Ronnie Reade, Pres.; Wendy Reade, Secy.-Treas.
EIN: 216014506

37658
The Rothfeld Family Foundation
c/o Marks, Paneth and Shron, LLP
622 3rd Ave., 7th Fl.
New York, NY 10017-6701

Established in 1997 in NY.
Financial data (yr. ended 12/31/01): Grants paid, $25,000; assets, $59,768 (M); expenditures, $28,250; qualifying distributions, $27,950.
Limitations: Applications not accepted. Giving on a national basis.
Application information: Contributes only to pre-selected organizations.
Trustees: Henry Christensen III, Ella Foshay, Michael B. Rothfeld.
EIN: 311588462

37659
Maurice S. Sage Foundation, Inc.
200 Central Park S.
New York, NY 10023
Application address: 45 Christopher St., New York, NY 10014
Contact: Martin Sage, Pres.

Established in 1994.
Donor(s): Lillian Sage, Malcolm Sage, Howard Miller, Lynn Florio.
Financial data (yr. ended 12/31/01): Grants paid, $25,000; assets, $626,334 (M); gifts received, $22,500; expenditures, $27,250; qualifying distributions, $25,000.
Application information: Application form required.
Officers: Martin Sage, Pres.; Malcolm Sage, Secy.-Treas.
EIN: 133799408

37660
Schneider Kaufman Foundation, Inc.
350 East 82nd St., Ste. 11B
New York, NY 10028

Established in 2000 in NY.
Donor(s): Edward Kaufman, Nathan Schneider.
Financial data (yr. ended 06/30/02): Grants paid, $25,000; assets, $28,209 (M); expenditures, $26,940; qualifying distributions, $25,000.
Limitations: Applications not accepted. Giving primarily in NY.
Application information: Contributes only to pre-selected organizations.
Officers: Nathan Schneider, Pres.; Edward Kaufman, V.P.
Director: Julie Kaufman.
EIN: 311732649

37661
Strulovic Family Foundation
543 Bedford Ave., Box 205
Brooklyn, NY 11211
Contact: Zalmen Strulovic, Secy.-Treas.

Established in 2000 in NY.
Donor(s): Miriam Strulovic.
Financial data (yr. ended 05/31/01): Grants paid, $25,000; assets, $0 (M); gifts received, $25,000; expenditures, $25,000; qualifying distributions, $25,000.
Limitations: Giving primarily in Monroe, NY.
Officer: Zalmen Strulovic, Secy.-Treas.
EIN: 061588375

37662
John G. Ullman and Associates Foundation, Inc.
P.O. Box 1424
Corning, NY 14830

Established in 1994 in NY.
Donor(s): John G. Ullman, Barbara Ullman.
Financial data (yr. ended 12/31/01): Grants paid, $25,000; assets, $475,141 (M); gifts received, $126,814; expenditures, $26,393; qualifying distributions, $25,000.
Limitations: Applications not accepted. Giving limited to Corning, NY.
Application information: Contributes only to pre-selected organizations.
Trustees: Robert Cole, M.D., Barbara Ullman, John G. Ullman.
EIN: 223275145

37663
The Vizcarrondo Family Foundation
c/o Wachtell, Lipton, Rosen & Katz
51 W. 52nd St.
New York, NY 10019

Established in 1999 in NY.
Donor(s): Paul Vizcarrondo, Jr.
Financial data (yr. ended 12/31/01): Grants paid, $25,000; assets, $180,567 (M); gifts received, $95,304; expenditures, $25,059; qualifying distributions, $25,000.
Limitations: Applications not accepted.
Application information: Contributes only to pre-selected organizations.
Officers and Directors:* Paul Vizcarrondo, Jr.,* Pres. and Treas.; Andrea L. Vizcarrondo,* V.P. and Secy.; Michael F. Baumeister.
EIN: 134059776

37664
William L. Waytena Foundation
9230 Valley Stream Rd.
Clarence, NY 14031-1522

Established in 1983.
Donor(s): William L. Waytena.
Financial data (yr. ended 08/31/02): Grants paid, $25,000; assets, $106,087 (M); expenditures, $26,599; qualifying distributions, $25,000.
Limitations: Applications not accepted. Giving on a national basis, with some emphasis on AZ and NY.
Application information: Contributes only to pre-selected organizations.
Trustees: Louise M. Waytena, William L. Waytena.
EIN: 161206316

37665
Dwight W. Winkelman Foundation, Inc.
P.O. Box 708
Skaneateles, NY 13152-0708

Donor(s): Dwight W. Winkelman,‡ Marguerite P. Winkelman.‡
Financial data (yr. ended 12/31/01): Grants paid, $25,000; assets, $184,803 (M); expenditures, $25,967; qualifying distributions, $24,965.
Limitations: Giving primarily in central NY.
Officers: Scott C. Winkelman, Pres.; Raymond T. Ryan, V.P.; Carolyn Winkelman, Secy.-Treas.
Director: D. William Winkelman.
EIN: 166052941

37666
The Limpe Foundation
c/o Petro-Chem Development Co., Inc.
122 E. 42nd St., Ste. 2308
New York, NY 10017-5600

Established in 1991 in NY.
Donor(s): Emily Limpe, Anthony Limpe.
Financial data (yr. ended 12/31/01): Grants paid, $24,975; assets, $606,357 (M); expenditures, $26,287; qualifying distributions, $24,975.
Limitations: Applications not accepted. Giving primarily in CT and NY.
Application information: Contributes only to pre-selected organizations.
Trustees: Anthony Limpe, Emily Limpe.
EIN: 133639369

37667
Joe and Pasena Maroun Family Foundation Trust
c/o The Bank of New York, Tax Dept.
1 Wall St., 28th Fl.
New York, NY 10286

Established in 2000 in NY.
Financial data (yr. ended 12/31/01): Grants paid, $24,975; assets, $709,816 (M); gifts received, $212,420; expenditures, $31,338; qualifying distributions, $24,975.
Limitations: Applications not accepted.
Application information: Contributes only to pre-selected organizations.
Trustee: The Bank of New York.
EIN: 311702817

37668
The Robert L. & Ellen D. Stern Foundation, Inc.
c/o Marcum & Kliegman, LLP
655 3rd Ave., Ste. 1610
New York, NY 10017-5617
Application address: 720 Milton Rd, Apt. L7, Rye, NY 10580-3248
Contact: Robert L. Stern, Pres.

Donor(s): Robert L. Stern.
Financial data (yr. ended 12/31/01): Grants paid, $24,974; assets, $453,229 (M); expenditures, $26,646; qualifying distributions, $24,974.
Limitations: Giving primarily in NY.
Officers: Robert L. Stern, Pres.; Ellen D. Stern, V.P.; Robert L. Stern, Jr., Secy.
EIN: 136084393

37669
Niagara Educational Foundation, Inc.
c/o M. Roth
346 Riverview Dr.
Youngstown, NY 14174
Contact: Grant Comm.

Financial data (yr. ended 08/31/01): Grants paid, $24,905; assets, $374,879 (M); expenditures, $25,919; qualifying distributions, $24,710.
Limitations: Giving limited to Niagara County, NY.
Officers and Directors:* Peter Wendel,* Chair.; William Ross,* Vice-Chair.; Nancy Post Lange,* Secy.; Merrill Roth,* Treas.; Thea Brandt, and 18 additional directors.
EIN: 166060150

37670
Belgravia Foundation
c/o S. Thaler
20 Crossways Park N., Ste. 412
Woodbury, NY 11797

Donor(s): Ralph A. Fields.
Financial data (yr. ended 09/30/01): Grants paid, $24,870; assets, $480,376 (M); gifts received, $575; expenditures, $34,422; qualifying distributions, $24,870.
Limitations: Applications not accepted. Giving primarily in New York, NY.
Application information: Contributes only to pre-selected organizations.
Officers and Directors:* Ralph A. Fields,* Pres.; Linda Kilby,* Secy.; Martin Felcher, Treas.
EIN: 133109042

37671
Allyn's Creek Foundation, Inc.
c/o Marie G. Whitbeck
24 Woodbury Pl.
Rochester, NY 14618

Established in 2001 in NY.
Donor(s): Lucius R. Gordon, Marie A. Gordon.
Financial data (yr. ended 12/31/01): Grants paid, $24,835; assets, $560,580 (M); gifts received, $579,753; expenditures, $28,507; qualifying distributions, $25,230.
Limitations: Applications not accepted.
Application information: Contributes only to pre-selected organizations.
Officers and Directors:* Marie G. Whitbeck,* Pres.; Ernest C. Whitbeck III,* Secy.-Treas.; Lucius R. Gordon.
EIN: 912092057

37672
The Dorothy L. Lappin Foundation
c/o Nathan Berkman & Co.
29 Broadway, Ste. 2900
New York, NY 10006

Donor(s): Dorothy L. Lappin.
Financial data (yr. ended 07/31/01): Grants paid, $24,825; assets, $210,148 (M); gifts received, $18,105; expenditures, $27,251; qualifying distributions, $24,825.
Trustee: Dorothy L. Lappin.
EIN: 133963447

37673
Bellucci DePaoli Family Foundation, Inc.
162 E. 71st St.
New York, NY 10021

Established in 1997 in NY.
Donor(s): Richard Bellucci, Richard G. Hamermesh.
Financial data (yr. ended 12/31/01): Grants paid, $24,805; assets, $130,747 (M); gifts received, $77,100; expenditures, $29,086; qualifying distributions, $4,281.
Limitations: Applications not accepted. Giving primarily in NY.
Application information: Contributes only to pre-selected organizations.
Trustees: Lori Hamermesh, Richard G. Hamermesh.
EIN: 133944033

37674
BSW Foundation, Inc.
c/o U.S. Trust of New York
114 W. 47th St., TAXVS
New York, NY 10036
Application address: Sandra Wright, Tr., c/o B.S.W., Inc., 1815 16th St., Washington, DC 20009

Established in 1994 in MI.
Donor(s): Sandra Wright.
Financial data (yr. ended 12/31/00): Grants paid, $24,800; assets, $506,980 (M); expenditures, $55,736; qualifying distributions, $44,039.
Trustees: Michael D. Gibson, J. Hayes Kavanaugh, Winifred E. Ohrstrom, Sandra Wright.
EIN: 383122375

37675
M. & H. Sommer Foundation
P.O. Box 238
Rye, NY 10580
Contact: Helene Wright, Pres.

Financial data (yr. ended 12/31/01): Grants paid, $24,800; assets, $412,595 (M); expenditures, $31,857; qualifying distributions, $24,800.

37675—NEW YORK

Limitations: Giving limited to the Northeast.
Officers and Trustees:* Helen Wright,* Pres.; George H. Meehan,* V.P.; Stanley Wright,* Secy.-Treas.
EIN: 136209298

37676
Gelbstein Family Foundation
144 Hewes St.
Brooklyn, NY 11211 (718) 782-7590
Contact: Joseph Gelbstein, Mgr.

Established in 1998.
Donor(s): Joseph Gelbstein, Robert Gelbstein.
Financial data (yr. ended 12/31/01): Grants paid, $24,715; assets, $38,503 (M); gifts received, $3,500; expenditures, $25,005; qualifying distributions, $24,715.
Officer: Joseph Gelbstein, Mgr.
EIN: 113446734

37677
The Arthur & Joyce Fein Family Foundation
26 Briarcliff Dr.
Monsey, NY 10952

Established in 1996 in NY.
Financial data (yr. ended 12/31/00): Grants paid, $24,713; assets, $252,666 (M); gifts received, $120,000; expenditures, $26,054; qualifying distributions, $24,629.
Limitations: Applications not accepted.
Application information: Contributes only to pre-selected organizations.
Officers: Arthur Fein, Pres.; Joyce Fein, V.P.; Alan Fein, Secy.
EIN: 061403178

37678
William Russell Fawcett Fund
c/o Deutsche Trust Co. of NY
P.O. Box 829, Church St. Sta.
New York, NY 10008

Donor(s): Priscilla Damon Fawcett.
Financial data (yr. ended 12/31/01): Grants paid, $24,711; assets, $631,029 (M); expenditures, $33,362; qualifying distributions, $28,820.
Limitations: Applications not accepted.
Application information: Contributes only to pre-selected organizations.
Trustee: Deutsche Bank.
EIN: 136223755

37679
Rye Rotary Foundation, Inc.
c/o Frank J. LaRusso, C.P.A.
P.O. Box 736
Harrison, NY 10528
Application address: P.O. Box 404, Rye, NY 10580
Contact: Geoffrey M. Beringer, Pres.

Established in 1967 in NY.
Financial data (yr. ended 09/30/01): Grants paid, $24,640; assets, $74,000 (M); gifts received, $157; expenditures, $24,852; qualifying distributions, $24,591.
Limitations: Giving limited to residents of Rye, NY.
Application information: Application form required.
Officers: Geoffrey M. Beringer, Pres.; Steven Johnson, Treas.
Trustees: Peter Crozier, Irving C. Herman.
EIN: 133041401
Codes: GTI

37680
The Jane Baldwin Holbritter Charitable Trust
720 Walden Pond Rd.
Albany, NY 12203
Contact: Margaret F. Holbritter, Tr.

Established in 1999 in DE.
Donor(s): Jane B. Holbritter.
Financial data (yr. ended 12/31/00): Grants paid, $24,627; assets, $481,171 (M); expenditures, $28,458; qualifying distributions, $24,627.
Trustees: Margaret F. Holbritter, Eleanor H. Nasner.
EIN: 146197876

37681
The Shuch Family Foundation
c/o BCRS Assoc., LLC
67 Wall St.
New York, NY 10005

Established in 1986.
Donor(s): Alan A. Shuch.
Financial data (yr. ended 08/31/01): Grants paid, $24,545; assets, $471,344 (M); gifts received, $99,969; expenditures, $30,070; qualifying distributions, $24,545.
Limitations: Applications not accepted. Giving primarily in NJ.
Application information: Contributes only to pre-selected organizations.
Trustees: David B. Ford, Alan A. Shuch, Ann Frances Shuch.
EIN: 133385066

37682
Enrico Fermi Educational Fund of Yonkers, Inc.
c/o Anthony Maddalena
13 Ann Marie Pl.
Yonkers, NY 10703
Application address: c/o Rosalind Mariani, Scholarship Comm., 67 Garfield St., Yonkers, NY 10701

Financial data (yr. ended 06/30/01): Grants paid, $24,500; assets, $239,082 (M); gifts received, $22,785; expenditures, $36,244; qualifying distributions, $33,113.
Limitations: Giving limited to residents of Yonkers, NY.
Officers: Lucia Trovato, Pres.; Lorraine Beta Cummaro, V.P.; James C. Grosso, Secy.; Anthony Maddalena, Treas.
EIN: 136159001
Codes: GTI

37683
The Prince Family Foundation
20 Griffin Ave.
Scarsdale, NY 10583

Established in 2000 in DE.
Donor(s): Steven J. Prince.
Financial data (yr. ended 12/31/01): Grants paid, $24,500; assets, $112,900 (M); gifts received, $2,950; expenditures, $30,688; qualifying distributions, $24,500.
Application information: Application form not required.
Officers: Steven J. Prince, Pres.; Debra L. Prince, V.P.
EIN: 364368404

37684
Peter and Gail Salvatore Foundation, Inc.
c/o William G. Peskoff, Spear, Leeds, & Kellogg
120 Broadway
New York, NY 10271

Established in 1993 in NY.
Donor(s): Peter J. Salvatore.
Financial data (yr. ended 10/31/01): Grants paid, $24,500; assets, $456,535 (M); gifts received, $45,426; expenditures, $24,974; qualifying distributions, $24,500.
Limitations: Applications not accepted.
Application information: Contributes only to pre-selected organizations.
Officers: Peter J. Salvatore, Pres.; Gail Salvatore, V.P.; Maryann Jecewiz, Secy.-Treas.
EIN: 133748370

37685
Ros-Herb Foundation, Inc.
c/o Joseph Stern & Co.
733 Yonkers Ave., Ste. 301
Yonkers, NY 10704
Contact: Herbert R. Silverman, Pres.

Donor(s): Herbert R. Silverman.
Financial data (yr. ended 05/31/00): Grants paid, $24,494; assets, $35,695 (M); gifts received, $15,000; expenditures, $24,589; qualifying distributions, $24,494.
Limitations: Giving primarily in NY.
Officer: Herbert R. Silverman, Pres.
EIN: 136083244

37686
Samuel I. & Regina Gross Foundation, Inc.
30 Bay St.
Staten Island, NY 10301
Contact: Avery J. Gross, Pres.

Established in 1951.
Donor(s): Avery Gross.
Financial data (yr. ended 11/30/01): Grants paid, $24,457; assets, $422,214 (M); expenditures, $27,827; qualifying distributions, $24,457.
Limitations: Giving primarily in the greater New York, NY, area.
Application information: Application form not required.
Officer: Avery Gross, Pres.
EIN: 136161406

37687
Carl & Lucile Oestreicher Foundation, Inc.
630 Park Ave.
New York, NY 10021-7246 (212) 249-4171
Contact: Irma Oestreicher, Pres.

Donor(s): Gerard Oestreicher.‡
Financial data (yr. ended 11/30/01): Grants paid, $24,450; assets, $84,746 (M); expenditures, $26,378; qualifying distributions, $24,450.
Limitations: Applications not accepted. Giving primarily in NY.
Application information: Contributes only to pre-selected organizations.
Officers: Irma Oestreicher, Pres.; Lynn Jeffrey, Secy.
EIN: 136089871

37688
Faith, Hope and Charity Foundation, Inc.
1716 Central Ave.
Albany, NY 12205

Donor(s): Frank A. Tate, Jr.
Financial data (yr. ended 10/31/01): Grants paid, $24,426; assets, $5,788 (M); gifts received, $26,100; expenditures, $24,426; qualifying distributions, $24,426.
Limitations: Applications not accepted. Giving primarily in NY.
Application information: Contributes only to pre-selected organizations.
Officers and Directors:* Frank A. Tate, Jr.,* Pres.; Michael E. Tate,* V.P.; Lisa Field,* Secy.; Robyn Magee,* Treas.
EIN: 237154630

37689
The Albert A. Arditti Foundation, Inc.
c/o Birkenfeld Horwitz & Chu
137 Broadway, Ste. B
Amityville, NY 11701
Application address: c/o Directors, P.O. Box 4506, Warren, NJ 07060

Established in 1966 in NY.
Financial data (yr. ended 12/31/01): Grants paid, $24,400; assets, $649,398 (M); expenditures, $27,101; qualifying distributions, $24,400.
Limitations: Giving primarily in NJ and NY.
Officers: Arthur A. Arditti, Pres.; Andrew Arditti, V.P.; Alice Simoni, Secy.; Shirley Arditti, Treas.
EIN: 136208776

37690
Helen & Aron Bistricer Torah Foundation
1458 47th St.
Brooklyn, NY 11219-2634

Donor(s): Aron Bistricer, Frances Bistricer, Bracha Retter.
Financial data (yr. ended 12/31/01): Grants paid, $24,374; assets, $675,887 (M); gifts received, $25,000; expenditures, $25,728; qualifying distributions, $24,374.
Limitations: Applications not accepted.
Application information: Contributes only to pre-selected organizations.
Trustees: Aron Bistricer, Frances Klein, Bracha Retter.
EIN: 112707376

37691
The Paturick Foundation, Inc.
c/o Sara Paturick
188 E. 64th St., Ste. 1706
New York, NY 10021

Donor(s): Arthur Paturick, Charles Paturick.
Financial data (yr. ended 06/30/02): Grants paid, $24,350; assets, $73,787 (M); gifts received, $40,000; expenditures, $25,705; qualifying distributions, $24,350.
Limitations: Applications not accepted. Giving primarily in New York, NY.
Application information: Contributes only to pre-selected organizations.
Officers: Charles Paturick, Pres. and Treas.; Roberta Paturick, V.P.; Sarah Paturick, V.P.
EIN: 136270038

37692
Charles D. & Mary A. Bauer Foundation
102 Brookedge Dr.
Williamsville, NY 14221

Established in 1996 in NY.
Donor(s): Charles D. Bauer.
Financial data (yr. ended 08/31/02): Grants paid, $24,300; assets, $460,453 (M); gifts received, $21,900; expenditures, $25,764; qualifying distributions, $24,300.
Limitations: Applications not accepted. Giving primarily in NY.
Application information: Contributes only to pre-selected organizations.
Trustee: Charles D. Bauer.
EIN: 161525643

37693
The Gutnick Foundation, Inc.
827 Montgomery St.
Brooklyn, NY 11213-5280 (718) 771-0001
Contact: Meir Gutnick, Pres.

Established in 2000 in NY.
Donor(s): Meir Gutnick.
Financial data (yr. ended 12/31/00): Grants paid, $24,251; assets, $12,835 (M); gifts received, $39,100; expenditures, $26,265; qualifying distributions, $26,265.
Application information: Application form not required.
Officer: Meir Gutnick, Pres.
EIN: 113539242

37694
Adler Family Charitable Foundation
c/o Allen Adler Enterprises
220 E. 42nd St., 32nd Fl.
New York, NY 10017

Established in 1994 in NY.
Donor(s): Allen Adler.
Financial data (yr. ended 12/31/01): Grants paid, $24,200; assets, $467,021 (M); gifts received, $1,077; expenditures, $26,077; qualifying distributions, $25,000.
Limitations: Applications not accepted. Giving primarily in NY.
Application information: Contributes only to pre-selected organizations.
Trustees: Allen Adler, Frances Beatty Adler.
EIN: 137053894

37695
Frederick J. Haug Family Foundation, Inc.
506 E. 74th St.
New York, NY 10021

Established in 1997 in NY.
Donor(s): Frederick J. Haug.
Financial data (yr. ended 12/31/01): Grants paid, $24,175; assets, $313,041 (M); expenditures, $44,331; qualifying distributions, $24,175.
Limitations: Applications not accepted.
Application information: Contributes only to pre-selected organizations.
Officer: Frederick J. Haug, Pres.
EIN: 133946783

37696
North Star Foundation, Inc.
216 Redwood Rd.
Sag Harbor, NY 11963 (631) 794-2323
Contact: Peter E. Heller, Pres.

Financial data (yr. ended 12/31/01): Grants paid, $24,168; assets, $270,491 (M); expenditures, $27,108; qualifying distributions, $24,168.
Limitations: Giving primarily in the greater New York, NY, area.
Application information: Application form not required.
Officers: Peter E. Heller, Pres. and Treas.; Anita De La Garza, Secy.
EIN: 136158559

37697
The Seligman Foundation
900 5th Ave.
New York, NY 10021
Contact: Benjamin Seligman, Tr.

Donor(s): Benjamin Seligman, Florence Seligman.
Financial data (yr. ended 11/30/01): Grants paid, $24,166; assets, $415,077 (M); expenditures, $26,566; qualifying distributions, $24,166.
Limitations: Giving primarily in New York, NY.
Trustees: Benjamin Seligman, Florence Seligman.
EIN: 136092864

37698
Howard R. Alper Foundation, Inc.
c/o Arthur Friedman, C.P.A.
280 Madison Ave., No. 1007
New York, NY 10016

Established in 1991 in NY.
Donor(s): Howard R. Alper.
Financial data (yr. ended 11/30/01): Grants paid, $24,150; assets, $32,639 (M); expenditures, $24,168; qualifying distributions, $24,150.
Limitations: Applications not accepted. Giving primarily in New York, NY.
Application information: Contributes only to pre-selected organizations.
Officer: Marilyn Alper, Pres.
EIN: 133405512

37699
Joan Berg Victor Family Charitable Foundation
c/o Joan Berg Victor
863 Park Ave., Ste. 11E
New York, NY 10021

Established in 1998 in NY.
Donor(s): Joan Berg Victor.
Financial data (yr. ended 12/31/01): Grants paid, $24,102; assets, $43,195 (M); gifts received, $12,705; expenditures, $25,652; qualifying distributions, $24,102.
Director: Joan Berg Victor.
EIN: 137157525

37700
Allegany County Area Foundation, Inc.
P.O. Box 494
Wellsville, NY 14895

Established in 1983 in NY.
Financial data (yr. ended 04/30/01): Grants paid, $24,096; assets, $3,103,797 (M); gifts received, $2,683,143; expenditures, $27,574.
Limitations: Giving limited to Allegany County, NY.
Application information: Scholarship applications available through the guidance offices of school districts serving Allegany County. Application form required.
Officers and Directors:* Kenneth Nielsen,* Pres.; Thomas Brown,* V.P.; John Carter,* Secy.-Treas.; Leslie Haggstrom, Woodie Lange, Carolyn Miller, Marcia Moore, Robert Mountain, Joan Sinclair.
EIN: 222506596
Codes: CM

37701
American Friends of Torah Umesorah of Latino America
16 Cameo Ridge Rd.
Monsey, NY 10952-2513 (845) 356-9243
Contact: David Ehrman, Pres.

Financial data (yr. ended 08/31/01): Grants paid, $24,031; assets, $562 (M); gifts received, $21,073; expenditures, $24,171; qualifying distributions, $24,031.
Officers: David Ehrman, Pres.; Ruth Ehrman, V.P.; Daniel Kugielsky, Treas.
EIN: 133752354

37702
Peter & Mary Stone Foundation
c/o Starr & Co.
350 Park Ave.
New York, NY 10022

Donor(s): Peter H. Stone.
Financial data (yr. ended 12/31/00): Grants paid, $24,030; assets, $0 (M); gifts received, $23,000; expenditures, $25,279; qualifying distributions, $25,279.
Limitations: Applications not accepted.
Application information: Contributes only to pre-selected organizations.
Officers: Peter H. Stone, Pres.; Mary O. Stone, Treas.
EIN: 237130116

37703
Eisen Foundation, Inc.
609 5th Ave., 6th Fl.
New York, NY 10017 (212) 832-4000

Donor(s): Edward R. Eisen.
Financial data (yr. ended 12/31/01): Grants paid, $24,025; assets, $16,290 (M); gifts received, $13,598; expenditures, $24,130; qualifying distributions, $24,025.
Limitations: Applications not accepted. Giving primarily in NY.
Application information: Contributes only to pre-selected organizations.
Officer: Edwin R. Eisen, Pres.
EIN: 133503659

37704
Sacco Family Foundation
121 Concourse W.
Brightwaters, NY 11718

Established in 1998 in NY.
Donor(s): Donald J. Sacco.
Financial data (yr. ended 12/31/01): Grants paid, $24,013; assets, $184,612 (M); gifts received, $38,440; expenditures, $25,389; qualifying distributions, $24,013.
Limitations: Applications not accepted. Giving primarily in NY and RI.
Application information: Contributes only to pre-selected organizations.
Trustees: Donald J. Sacco, Geraldine B. Sacco, Lori Sacco Spellman.
EIN: 113442011

37705
Anne & Jacob Starr Foundation
830 12th Ave.
New York, NY 10018
Application address: 8484 Northstar Ct., Boynton Beach, FL 33436
Contact: Jean M. Starr, Pres.

Incorporated in 1964 in NY.
Donor(s): Jacob Starr.
Financial data (yr. ended 11/30/01): Grants paid, $24,013; assets, $612,730 (M); gifts received, $100; expenditures, $27,322; qualifying distributions, $24,013.
Officers: Jean M. Starr, Pres.; Tama Starr, V.P.
EIN: 136193022

37706
The Bonoff Foundation, Inc.
12 Split Tree Rd.
Scarsdale, NY 10583-7900

Established in 1998 in NY.
Financial data (yr. ended 12/31/00): Grants paid, $24,000; assets, $299,589 (M); expenditures, $24,000; qualifying distributions, $23,948.
Limitations: Applications not accepted.
Application information: Contributes only to pre-selected organizations.
Officers: Peter F. Bonoff, Pres. and Treas.; Amy L. Bonoff, V.P. and Secy.; Daniel R. Bonoff, V.P.; Jennifer Bonoff Koppel, V.P.
EIN: 133946925

37707
Frances L. Carpenter Foundation
c/o William W. Cantwell
P.O. Box 508
Saranac Lake, NY 12983-0508

Donor(s): Frances L. Carpenter.‡
Financial data (yr. ended 12/31/01): Grants paid, $24,000; assets, $459,131 (M); expenditures, $26,875; qualifying distributions, $24,000.
Limitations: Applications not accepted. Giving primarily in Saranac Lake, NY.
Application information: Contributes only to pre-selected organizations.
Officers: William W. Cantwell, Pres.; Irving B. Hunt, V.P.; Frances C. Shepard, Secy.
Trustees: Kenneth Hunt, Henry Jakobe.
EIN: 141579255

37708
Children's Foundation of Columbia County, Inc.
c/o Pattison, Koskey & Rath, PC
502 Union St.
Hudson, NY 12534
Application address: 17 Reuter Ln., Claverack, NY 12513
Contact: Joseph McCrudden, Treas.

Established in 1843 in NY.
Financial data (yr. ended 04/30/02): Grants paid, $24,000; assets, $662,404 (M); expenditures, $26,518; qualifying distributions, $24,000.
Limitations: Giving limited to Columbia County, NY.
Publications: Annual report, financial statement.
Officers: Richard Koskey, Pres.; Thomas Kline, V.P.; Catherine Van Denburg, Secy.; Joseph McCrudden, Treas.
Directors: Sandra Florio, Richard Koweek, Beverly Schopp, Kathy Whitbeck.
EIN: 140763850

37709
Doshi Family Foundation, Inc.
6 Bridle Path Ct.
Glen Head, NY 11545
Contact: Nitin V. Doshi, Dir.

Established in 1991 in NY.
Donor(s): Leena N. Doshi, Nitin V. Doshi.
Financial data (yr. ended 12/31/01): Grants paid, $24,000; assets, $14,801 (M); expenditures, $24,000; qualifying distributions, $24,000.
Application information: Application form not required.
Directors: Leena N. Doshi, Nitin V. Doshi, Narendra V. Lakhani.
EIN: 113088579

37710
The Dounoucos Family Foundation
c/o Fleet National Bank
169 E. Main St.
Rochester, NY 14638

Established in 1997 in NY.
Financial data (yr. ended 12/31/00): Grants paid, $24,000; assets, $126,195 (M); expenditures, $25,177; qualifying distributions, $24,639.
Limitations: Applications not accepted.
Application information: Contributes only to pre-selected organizations.
Trustee: Fleet National Bank.
EIN: 161527196

37711
Charles and Anna Elenberg Foundation, Inc.
c/o Jack Scharf
630 3rd Ave., 18th Fl.
New York, NY 10017

Donor(s): Anna Elenberg.
Financial data (yr. ended 06/30/01): Grants paid, $24,000; assets, $777,866 (M); expenditures, $43,005; qualifying distributions, $39,727.
Limitations: Applications not accepted.
Application information: Application forms are distributed to pre-selected educational institutions on a rotating basis.
Officers: Rabbi David B. Hollander, Pres.; Fay Hollander, Secy.; Abraham Gross, Treas.
EIN: 116042334
Codes: GTI

37712
Arthur J. Gavrin Foundation, Inc.
1865 Palmer Ave., Ste. 108
Larchmont, NY 10538-3037
Application address: c/o Guidance Dept., New Rochelle High School, New Rochelle, NY 10802, tel.: (914) 576-4542

Donor(s): David M. Gavrin, Tena P. Gavrin.
Financial data (yr. ended 12/31/01): Grants paid, $24,000; assets, $270,765 (M); expenditures, $24,416; qualifying distributions, $24,067.
Limitations: Giving limited to residents of New Rochelle, NY.
Application information: Applicant must include transcript.
Officers: David M. Gavrin, Pres.; Ira C. Gavrin, V.P.; Robert J. Gavrin, V.P.; Tena P. Gavrin, Treas.
EIN: 136265245
Codes: GTI

37713
Mycenaean Foundation, Inc.
c/o The Millburn Corporation
1270 Ave. of the Americas
New York, NY 10020
Application address: c/o Philip Betancourt, Institute for Aegean Prehistory, 3550 Market St., Ste. 100, Philadelphia, PA 19104

Established in 1985 in MO.
Financial data (yr. ended 12/31/01): Grants paid, $24,000; assets, $575,360 (M); expenditures, $39,019; qualifying distributions, $32,771.
Limitations: Giving limited to Greece.
Officer: Philip P. Betancourt, Pres. and Secy.-Treas.
Directors: Gerald Cohn, Henry P. Davis, Patricia G. Hecker, James Muhly, Carolyn S. Wiener, Malcolm H. Wiener.
EIN: 436070522
Codes: GTI

37714
Augustus J. Pleuthner Religious Foundation
43 State St., No. 4D
Skaneateles, NY 13152 (315) 685-5536
Contact: Anne P. McCall, Secy.

Financial data (yr. ended 12/31/01): Grants paid, $24,000; assets, $381,327 (M); expenditures, $25,448; qualifying distributions, $24,000.
Limitations: Giving primarily in CT and NY.
Application information: Application form not required.
Officers: Andrew G. Green, Pres.; Lynne P. Greene, V.P.; Anne P. McCall, Secy.; Kathleen Walters, Treas.
EIN: 136108435

37715
Barbara and William Rosenthal Family Foundation
c/o Citibank, N.A., Tax Dept.
PBG Tax Sort 4850
New York, NY 10043

Established in 1998 in NY.
Financial data (yr. ended 06/30/01): Grants paid, $24,000; assets, $1,323,860 (M); gifts received, $192,863; expenditures, $63,022; qualifying distributions, $24,000.
Limitations: Applications not accepted. Giving primarily in New York, NY.
Application information: Contributes only to pre-selected organizations.
Trustee: Citibank, N.A.
EIN: 226753977

37716
Myers-Ball Foundation, Inc.
c/o Barbara Myers
349 E. 84th St.
New York, NY 10028

Established in 1991 in IL.
Donor(s): Barbara Q. Myers.
Financial data (yr. ended 12/31/01): Grants paid, $23,871; assets, $608,078 (M); expenditures, $26,519; qualifying distributions, $25,487.
Limitations: Applications not accepted. Giving primarily in New York, NY.
Application information: Contributes only to pre-selected organizations.
Officers: Barbara Q. Myers, Pres. and Treas.; Barbara Klett, Secy.
EIN: 363763373

37717
The Charles & Kaaren Hale Family Foundation
c/o CSAM
466 Lexington Ave., 17th Fl.
New York, NY 10017

Established in 1997 in DE.
Financial data (yr. ended 12/31/01): Grants paid, $23,860; assets, $354,828 (M); expenditures, $26,325; qualifying distributions, $23,860.
Limitations: Applications not accepted.
Application information: Contributes only to pre-selected organizations.
Officers: Charles Hale, Pres.; Kaaren A. Hale, Secy.
EIN: 133940900

37718
The Mazur Family Foundation
c/o Wachtell, Lipton, Rosen & Katz
51 W. 52nd St.
New York, NY 10019

Established in 1999 in NY.
Donor(s): Robert B. Mazur, Marilyn Mazur.
Financial data (yr. ended 12/31/01): Grants paid, $23,850; assets, $468,844 (M); gifts received, $72,898; expenditures, $24,507; qualifying distributions, $23,850.
Limitations: Applications not accepted. Giving primarily in NY.
Application information: Contributes only to pre-selected organizations.
Officers and Directors:* Robert B. Mazur,* Pres. and Treas.; Marilyn Mazur,* V.P. and Secy.; Matthew L. Mazur, Zachery E. Mazur.
EIN: 134075471

37719
The Tsang Family Foundation
c/o Goldman Sachs & Co.
85 Broad St., Tax Dept.
New York, NY 10004

Established in 1989 in NY.
Donor(s): Moses K. Tsang.
Financial data (yr. ended 05/31/01): Grants paid, $23,802; assets, $5,226,114 (M); expenditures, $23,902; qualifying distributions, $23,802.
Limitations: Applications not accepted. Giving primarily in NH.
Application information: Contributes only to pre-selected organizations.
Trustees: Angela O. Cheung, Moses K. Tsang.
EIN: 133536524

37720
Myles F. Wittenstein Charitable Foundation, Inc.
135 Lawn Ln.
Oyster Bay, NY 11771
Contact: Myles F. Wittenstein, Pres.

Established in 1999 in NY.
Donor(s): Myles F. Wittenstein.
Financial data (yr. ended 12/31/01): Grants paid, $23,796; assets, $209,415 (M); expenditures, $26,115; qualifying distributions, $23,796.
Officer: Myles F. Wittenstein, Pres.
EIN: 116507428

37721
The Gips Foundation, Inc.
1442 47th St.
Brooklyn, NY 11219

Established in 2000 in NY.
Donor(s): Bernard Gips, Enercon Mechanical.
Financial data (yr. ended 12/31/01): Grants paid, $23,771; assets, $1,509 (M); gifts received, $23,800; expenditures, $24,915; qualifying distributions, $23,771.
Limitations: Applications not accepted.
Application information: Contributes only to pre-selected organizations.
Officers: Bernard Gips, Pres.; Malkie Gips, V.P.; Shlome Zalman Gips, Secy.; Yechiel Zev Gips, Treas.
EIN: 113539608

37722
Saldanha Family Foundation
110 Meadow Rd.
Buffalo, NY 14216-3614

Donor(s): Robert A. Saldanha, Anne L. Saldanha.
Financial data (yr. ended 12/31/01): Grants paid, $23,770; assets, $63,053 (M); gifts received, $20,055; expenditures, $24,714; qualifying distributions, $23,770.
Limitations: Applications not accepted. Giving primarily in Buffalo, NY.
Application information: Contributes only to pre-selected organizations.
Trustee: Anne L. Saldanha.
EIN: 161289451

37723
James Marston Fitch Charitable Foundation
c/o The Neighborhood Preservation Center
232 E. 11th St.
New York, NY 10003   (212) 252-6809
FAX: (212) 471-9987; *E-mail:* FitchFoundation@aol.com; *URL:* http://www.fitchfoundation.org
Contact: Margaret Evans

Established in 1998 in NY.
Donor(s): James Marston Fitch.
Financial data (yr. ended 12/31/00): Grants paid, $23,750; assets, $411,087 (M); gifts received, $32,043; expenditures, $32,378; qualifying distributions, $31,515.
Limitations: Giving on a national basis.
Officers and Trustees:* Richard Blinder,* Chair.; Eric DeLony,* Vice-Chair.; Page Ayres Cowley,* Secy.; Theodore Prudon,* Treas.; Laurie Beckelman, Mary Diericlx, William J. Higgins, and 5 additional directors.
EIN: 133993856

37724
Arnold Family Foundation
4 Glenn Pl.
Hastings-on-Hudson, NY 10706-3107

Established in 1986 in NY.
Donor(s): Justin B. Arnold.
Financial data (yr. ended 09/30/01): Grants paid, $23,731; assets, $414,744 (M); expenditures, $25,671; qualifying distributions, $23,731.
Limitations: Applications not accepted. Giving primarily in NY.
Application information: Contributes only to pre-selected organizations.
Officers: Justin B. Arnold, Pres.; Bernice G. Arnold, Treas.
EIN: 133382157

37725
Srybnik Foundation, Inc.
140 53rd St.
Brooklyn, NY 11232

Financial data (yr. ended 12/31/01): Grants paid, $23,723; assets, $5,624 (M); gifts received, $25,000; expenditures, $23,809; qualifying distributions, $23,723.
Limitations: Applications not accepted. Giving primarily in New York, NY.
Application information: Contributes only to pre-selected organizations.
Officers: Simon Srybnik, Pres.; Louis D. Srybnik, V.P.
EIN: 116036965

37726
Suskram Family Foundation
c/o U.S. Trust
114 W. 47th St., TaxVAS
New York, NY 10036

Established in 1997 in DE.
Donor(s): Bernard Kramarsky.
Financial data (yr. ended 12/31/00): Grants paid, $23,700; assets, $179,846 (M); expenditures, $27,405; qualifying distributions, $25,323.
Limitations: Applications not accepted.
Application information: Contributes only to pre-selected organizations.
Trustees: Bernard Kramarsky, Helga Kramarsky.
EIN: 133941827

37727
The Cynthia & Philip Kaplan Foundation
14 Augusta Ln.
Manhasset, NY 11030

Donor(s): Philip Kaplan.
Financial data (yr. ended 12/31/01): Grants paid, $23,660; assets, $146,223 (M); expenditures, $24,998; qualifying distributions, $23,660.
Limitations: Applications not accepted.
Application information: Contributes only to pre-selected organizations.
Directors: Andrew Kaplan, Cynthia Kaplan, Philip Kaplan.
EIN: 113409764

37728
The John Christopher Smith Foundation, Inc.
P.O. Box 367
Walden, NY 12586
Application address: P.O. Box 668, Pine Bush, NY 12566, tel.: (914) 744-2095
Contact: Richard J. Smith, Dir.

Established in 1987 in NY.
Donor(s): Richard J. Smith.
Financial data (yr. ended 10/31/01): Grants paid, $23,654; assets, $13,640 (M); expenditures, $26,958; qualifying distributions, $23,654.
Limitations: Giving primarily in NY.
Directors: Elizabeth Smith, Richard J. Smith.
EIN: 141701015

37729
Clark R. Green Charitable Foundation
c/o Clark R. Green
145 Hicks St., Apt. B51
Brooklyn, NY 11201-2300

Established in 1996 NY.
Donor(s): Clark R. Green.
Financial data (yr. ended 11/30/01): Grants paid, $23,650; assets, $731,620 (M); gifts received, $33,705; expenditures, $25,550; qualifying distributions, $23,650.
Limitations: Applications not accepted. Giving primarily in New York, NY.
Application information: Contributes only to pre-selected organizations.
Officer: Clark R. Green, Pres.
Trustees: Gloria G. Brown, Richard D. Green.
EIN: 113296925

37730
The Joseph Torgueman Foundation, Inc.
302 5th Ave., 7th Fl.
New York, NY 10001
Application address: 2214 Ave. T, Brooklyn, NY 11229, tel.: (212)564-2655
Contact: Joseph Torgueman, Pres.

Established in NY in 1997.
Financial data (yr. ended 12/31/00): Grants paid, $23,618; assets, $235 (M); gifts received, $3,452; expenditures, $23,693; qualifying distributions, $23,618.
Limitations: Giving primarily in NY.
Officers: Joseph Torgueman, Pres.; Victor Shacalo, V.P.; Rozie Torgueman, Secy.
EIN: 133975595

37731
Bohensky Charitable Foundation
920 E. 17th St., Ste. 504
Brooklyn, NY 11230-3723

Established in 1999.
Donor(s): Fred Bohensky.
Financial data (yr. ended 09/30/01): Grants paid, $23,557; assets, $2,060 (M); gifts received, $21,121; expenditures, $23,557; qualifying distributions, $23,557.
Limitations: Applications not accepted.
Application information: Contributes only to pre-selected organizations.
Officers and Director:* Fred Bohensky,* Pres.; Esther Bohensky, V.P.; Chana R. Jacobs, Secy.
EIN: 061559044

37732
Gilbert & Virginia McCurdy Charitable Trust
c/o JPMorgan Chase Bank
P.O. Box 31412
Rochester, NY 14603-1412

Financial data (yr. ended 12/31/01): Grants paid, $23,551; assets, $357,197 (M); expenditures, $22,972; qualifying distributions, $23,677.
Limitations: Applications not accepted. Giving primarily in Rochester, NY.
Application information: Contributes only to pre-selected organizations.
Trustee: JPMorgan Chase Bank.
EIN: 166015246

37733
Budd Levinson Foundation, Inc.
c/o Markowitz, Fenelon & Bank
30 Park Pl.
East Hampton, NY 11937
Application address: P.O. Box 1976, East Hampton, NY 11937, tel.: (631) 324-3998
Contact: Budd Levinson, Chair.

Donor(s): Irvin A. Levinson.
Financial data (yr. ended 10/31/01): Grants paid, $23,525; assets, $629,343 (M); gifts received, $5,000; expenditures, $26,370; qualifying distributions, $97,630.
Limitations: Giving primarily in FL and NY.
Officers and Directors:* Budd Levinson,* Chair.; Kevin W. Crowley,* Pres.; Curtis D. Becker,* Secy.-Treas.
EIN: 136098912

37734
Samuel Gutner Foundation, Inc.
c/o Kaplan & Kaplan
330 7th Ave., 18th Fl.
New York, NY 10001

Established in 1993 in NY.
Donor(s): Elizabeth Gutner.
Financial data (yr. ended 11/30/99): Grants paid, $23,511; assets, $23,717 (M); gifts received, $43,844; expenditures, $25,126; qualifying distributions, $23,511.
Limitations: Applications not accepted.
Application information: Contributes only to pre-selected organizations.
Officer and Trustee:* Elizabeth Gutner,* Pres.
EIN: 133745301

37735
Abe L. Blinder Foundation, Inc.
c/o Mark Weinstein, Squadron, Ellenoff, et al.
551 5th Ave.
New York, NY 10176

Established in 1993 in NY.
Donor(s): Abe L. Blinder.
Financial data (yr. ended 12/31/00): Grants paid, $23,500; assets, $1,491 (M); gifts received, $25,000; expenditures, $25,477; qualifying distributions, $23,500.
Limitations: Applications not accepted. Giving primarily in New York, NY.
Application information: Contributes only to pre-selected organizations.
Directors: Abe L. Blinder, Henry David Blinder, Jonathon Blinder, Mark J. Weinstein.
EIN: 133743974

37736
Joseph & Josephine Ciricleo Trust
22 Claudet Way
Eastchester, NY 10709-1539

Established in 1986 in NY.
Financial data (yr. ended 11/30/01): Grants paid, $23,500; assets, $92,661 (M); expenditures, $24,880; qualifying distributions, $23,500.
Limitations: Applications not accepted. Giving primarily in NY.
Application information: Contributes only to pre-selected organizations.
Trustees: Joseph Ciricleo, Josephine Ciricleo.
EIN: 133393026

37737
May Foundation Trust
2080 Town Harbor Ln.
Southold, NY 11971 (631) 765-1739

Donor(s): John M. May, Elinor M. May, Marilyn May.
Financial data (yr. ended 12/31/01): Grants paid, $23,500; assets, $403,238 (M); gifts received, $26,000; expenditures, $29,729; qualifying distributions, $23,500.
Limitations: Applications not accepted. Giving limited to Southold, NY.
Application information: Contributes only to pre-selected organizations.
Trustees: Elinor M. May, Joan E. May, Marilyn May, Robert D. May.
EIN: 112978693

37738
Noteworthy Foundation, Inc.
100 Church St.
Amsterdam, NY 12010 (518) 842-2734
Contact: John Colangelo, Treas.

Donor(s): Thomas B. Constantino.‡
Financial data (yr. ended 04/30/02): Grants paid, $23,500; assets, $41,475 (M); gifts received, $31,040; expenditures, $23,500; qualifying distributions, $23,500.
Limitations: Giving primarily in Amsterdam, NY.
Officers and Directors:* Carol L. Constantino,* Pres.; Thomas J. Cummings,* V.P.; Diane Santos, Secy.; John Colangelo, Treas.; Hon. Gene Catena, Msgr. Paul Lenz, Stanley J. Wawrejko.
EIN: 223058335

37739
R. A. Rendich Foundation Educational Fund
c/o U.S. Trust
114 W. 47th St.
New York, NY 10036
Contact: Carolyn Larke, Asst. V.P. and Trust Off., U.S. Trust

Established in 1993 in NY.
Financial data (yr. ended 12/31/99): Grants paid, $23,500; assets, $955,641 (M); expenditures, $33,778; qualifying distributions, $30,409.
Limitations: Giving primarily in NY.
Trustee: U.S. Trust.
EIN: 136074171

37740
Kenneth M. Schmidt Family Foundation, Inc.
c/o Barry Strauss Assoc., Ltd.
307 5th Ave., 8th Fl.
New York, NY 10016-6517

Established in 1997 in NY.
Donor(s): Kenneth M. Schmidt.
Financial data (yr. ended 02/28/02): Grants paid, $23,500; assets, $99,263 (M); gifts received, $24,360; expenditures, $24,072; qualifying distributions, $23,500.
Limitations: Applications not accepted.
Application information: Contributes only to pre-selected organizations.
Officers: Kenneth M. Schmidt, Pres.; Tracy S. Trafficanda, V.P.; Terry E. Schmidt, Treas.
EIN: 133949094

37741
The Carolyn S. Schwartz Charitable Trust
15 W. 72nd St.
New York, NY 10023-3402

Established in 1995 in NY.
Donor(s): Renee Schwartz, Alfred Schwartz.
Financial data (yr. ended 12/31/00): Grants paid, $23,500; assets, $22,012 (M); gifts received, $18; expenditures, $23,543; qualifying distributions, $23,500.
Limitations: Applications not accepted. Giving primarily in New York, NY.
Application information: Contributes only to pre-selected organizations.

Trustees: Alfred Schwartz, Carolyn Schwartz, Renee Schwartz.
EIN: 137079061

37742
The Tekakwitha Foundation, Inc.
1 Cobble Hill Rd.
Loudonville, NY 12211 (518) 462-1321
Contact: Thomas D. O'Connor, Pres.

Established in 1957 in NY.
Financial data (yr. ended 12/31/01): Grants paid, $23,500; assets, $75,602 (M); expenditures, $26,425; qualifying distributions, $23,500.
Limitations: Giving primarily in CT, NH, and central NY.
Officers: Thomas D. O'Connor, Pres. and Treas.; Nancy B. O'Connor, Secy.
EIN: 146017389

37743
The Volcker Family Foundation, Inc.
c/o Kirlin, Campbell & Keating
5 Hanover Sq., 14th Fl.
New York, NY 10004

Established in 1996 in DE.
Donor(s): Paul A. Volcker.
Financial data (yr. ended 12/31/00): Grants paid, $23,500; assets, $2,313,955 (M); gifts received, $500,000; expenditures, $43,317; qualifying distributions, $23,500.
Limitations: Giving primarily in Washington, DC, and New York, NY.
Officers and Directors:* Paul A. Volcker,* Pres.; Ernesto V. Luzzatto, Secy.-Treas.; Robert Kavesh, Marshall P. Keating, James P. Volcker, Janis Volcker Zima.
EIN: 133917327

37744
Rudolph & Lentilhon G. Von Fluegge Foundation, Inc.
c/o Pegg & Pegg
370 Lexington Ave., Rm. 1007
New York, NY 10017-6598 (212) 532-4287
Contact: Robert R. Pegg, Secy.-Treas.

Financial data (yr. ended 12/31/01): Grants paid, $23,500; assets, $511,214 (M); expenditures, $28,760; qualifying distributions, $23,500.
Limitations: Giving primarily in New York, NY.
Application information: Application form not required.
Officers and Directors:* Hans Henning Von Fluegge,* Pres.; Isabel Lentilhon Von Fluegge,* V.P.; Robert R. Pegg,* Secy.-Treas.
EIN: 133086697

37745
Kluger Obstfeld Family Foundation
1134 E. 22nd St.
Brooklyn, NY 11210

Established in 1999 in NY.
Donor(s): Jack Kluger, Anna Obstfeld.
Financial data (yr. ended 09/30/01): Grants paid, $23,470; assets, $313 (M); gifts received, $2,590; expenditures, $25,081; qualifying distributions, $23,470.
Limitations: Giving primarily in NY.
Directors: Ari Kluger, Jack Kluger, Rachel Kluger.
EIN: 113524360

37746
The F. Jackson Fund, Inc.
c/o Albert Kalter, PC
225 Broadway
New York, NY 10007

Established in 1998 in NY.

Financial data (yr. ended 12/31/01): Grants paid, $23,460; assets, $722,477 (M); expenditures, $53,511; qualifying distributions, $43,056.
Limitations: Applications not accepted. Giving primarily in NY.
Application information: Contributes only to pre-selected organizations.
Officers and Directors:* Lawrence Newman,* Pres.; Helaine Newman,* V.P.; Brenda Kalter,* V.P.; Albert Kalter,* Treas.
EIN: 133997827

37747
The Jesse Bayer Foundation
c/o Robert Bayer
1350 Ave. of the Americas
New York, NY 10019

Established in 1986 in NY.
Financial data (yr. ended 12/31/01): Grants paid, $23,450; assets, $454,311 (M); expenditures, $31,693; qualifying distributions, $23,450.
Limitations: Applications not accepted. Giving primarily in FL and New England.
Application information: Contributes only to pre-selected organizations.
Trustees: Mary Ellen Bayer, Robert I. Bayer, Irwin Grossman.
EIN: 133369906

37748
Chaim Leib & Chaya Sara Kahan Memorial
c/o Brand Sonnenschine, LLP
377 Broadway, 9th Fl.
New York, NY 10013-3972

Established in 1999 in NY.
Donor(s): Michael Silberberg.
Financial data (yr. ended 12/31/00): Grants paid, $23,445; assets, $5,288 (M); gifts received, $32,500; expenditures, $27,386; qualifying distributions, $27,045.
Officers: Simon Perlmutter, Pres.; Michael Silberberg, V.P. and Treas.; Joseph Zelmanowitz, Secy.
EIN: 134057201

37749
Edward & Lee Lawrence Foundation
20 Round Hill Ln.
Port Washington, NY 11050
Contact: Edward A. Lawrence, Dir.

Established in 1967 in NY.
Donor(s): Edward A. Lawrence.
Financial data (yr. ended 12/31/01): Grants paid, $23,430; assets, $151,696 (M); gifts received, $1,816; expenditures, $27,379; qualifying distributions, $23,430.
Limitations: Giving primarily in NY.
Application information: Application form not required.
Director: Edward A. Lawrence.
EIN: 116084773

37750
Garland E. Wood Foundation
67 Wall St., 8th Fl.
New York, NY 10005

Established in 1987 in NY.
Donor(s): Garland E. Wood.
Financial data (yr. ended 08/31/01): Grants paid, $23,400; assets, $169,637 (M); gifts received, $10,000; expenditures, $23,500; qualifying distributions, $23,400.
Limitations: Applications not accepted. Giving primarily in New York, NY.
Application information: Contributes only to pre-selected organizations.
Trustees: Curtis A. Wood, Jr., Garland E. Wood.

EIN: 133437869

37751
William H. Herrman Foundation, Inc.
1120 Park Ave.
New York, NY 10128-1242

Donor(s): Morton M. Watnik,‡ William H. Herrman.
Financial data (yr. ended 04/30/02): Grants paid, $23,350; assets, $397,618 (M); expenditures, $29,511; qualifying distributions, $23,350.
Limitations: Applications not accepted. Giving on a national basis, with emphasis on New York, NY.
Application information: Contributes only to pre-selected organizations.
Officers and Directors:* William H. Herrman,* Pres. and Treas.; Judith H. Herrman,* V.P. and Secy.; William Herrman II.
EIN: 136201333

37752
The Dossie Schattman Foundation
c/o Albert Kalter, PC
225 Broadway, 32nd Fl.
New York, NY 10007

Established in 1991 in NY.
Donor(s): The Dossie K. Schattman Charitable Trust.
Financial data (yr. ended 12/31/01): Grants paid, $23,350; assets, $800,456 (M); expenditures, $58,572; qualifying distributions, $23,350.
Limitations: Applications not accepted. Giving primarily in NY.
Application information: Contributes only to pre-selected organizations.
Officers and Directors:* Lawrence Newman,* Pres.; Brenda Kalter,* V.P.; Helaine Newman,* V.P.; Albert Kalter,* Secy.-Treas.
EIN: 133570163

37753
Dayle H. and Michael Katz Foundation, Inc.
c/o Sterling Equities, Inc.
111 Great Neck Rd., Ste. 408
Great Neck, NY 11021

Financial data (yr. ended 12/31/00): Grants paid, $23,315; assets, $373,254 (M); gifts received, $161,450; expenditures, $26,074; qualifying distributions, $23,315.
Officers and Directors:* Michael Katz,* Pres.; Gregory Katz, V.P.; Howard Katz, V.P.; Dayle H. Katz,* Secy.-Treas.
EIN: 113464795

37754
The Edith and William Landau Foundation, Inc.
(Formerly Fred & Anna Landau Foundation)
43 Murray Hill Rd.
Scarsdale, NY 10583 (914) 725-3314

Established in 1974 in NY.
Donor(s): Fred Landau,‡ Mann, Judd, Landau, William Landau, M.D.,‡ Landau Foundation, Edith L. Landau.
Financial data (yr. ended 12/31/01): Grants paid, $23,300; assets, $694,911 (M); expenditures, $24,394; qualifying distributions, $23,300.
Limitations: Applications not accepted. Giving primarily in NY.
Application information: Contributes only to pre-selected organizations.
Officers: Edith L. Landau, Pres.; Deborah J. Landau, Secy.; Margaret E. Landau, Treas.
EIN: 237325237

37755
Marilyn and Saul Spilke Foundation
111 W. 40th St., Ste. 1702
New York, NY 10018

Established in 1998 in NY.
Donor(s): Marilyn Spilke.
Financial data (yr. ended 12/31/01): Grants paid, $23,300; assets, $707,271 (M); gifts received, $51,816; expenditures, $30,307; qualifying distributions, $23,300.
Limitations: Applications not accepted. Giving primarily in NY.
Application information: Contributes only to pre-selected organizations.
Officers and Directors:* Marilyn Spilke-Hudson,* Pres.; Joseph Bartfield,* Secy.; Harry Rabinowitz,* Treas.
EIN: 133988541

37756
Keren Binyamin Foundation, Inc.
c/o Robert Kolman
35 Rodney St.
Brooklyn, NY 11211 (718) 875-4000

Established in 1999 in NY.
Donor(s): Robert Kolman.
Financial data (yr. ended 12/31/01): Grants paid, $23,259; assets, $110,599 (M); gifts received, $24,556; expenditures, $25,911; qualifying distributions, $23,259.
Officers: Robert Kolman, Pres.; Susan Kolman, V.P.; Herman Neuschloss, Secy.
EIN: 113514936

37757
Butler Family Foundation
c/o J.E. Butler
522 Cayuga Heights Rd.
Ithaca, NY 14850

Established in 1998 in NY.
Financial data (yr. ended 12/31/01): Grants paid, $23,250; assets, $392,877 (M); expenditures, $25,000; qualifying distributions, $23,612.
Limitations: Applications not accepted. Giving primarily in AZ and UT.
Application information: Contributes only to pre-selected organizations.
Trustees: Don H. Butler, John E. Butler, Karl D. Butler, Jr., Linda S. Butler, Robert T. Butler.
EIN: 161526176

37758
M & R Charitable Trust
10 Lenore Ave.
Monsey, NY 10952

Financial data (yr. ended 12/31/01): Grants paid, $23,178; assets, $3,108 (L); gifts received, $13,200; expenditures, $23,575; qualifying distributions, $23,575.
Trustee: Meyer Steg.
EIN: 116545610

37759
Elyachar Welfare Corporation
8 E. 48th St., No. 6E
New York, NY 10017

Established about 1951 in NY.
Donor(s): Ralph Elyachar, Daniel Elyachar, Gerel Corp., Timston Corp., Ruradan Corp.
Financial data (yr. ended 12/31/00): Grants paid, $23,143; assets, $1,230,726 (M); gifts received, $22,000; expenditures, $23,328; qualifying distributions, $23,143.
Limitations: Applications not accepted. Giving primarily in New York, NY.

Application information: Contributes only to pre-selected organizations.
Officers: Ralph Elyachar, Pres.; Daniel Elyachar, V.P.
EIN: 136161372

37760
David Wasserman Scholarship Fund, Inc.
Adirondack Ctr.
4722 State Hwy. 30
Amsterdam, NY 12010 (518) 843-2800
Contact: Norbert Sherbunt

Financial data (yr. ended 04/30/01): Grants paid, $23,100; assets, $930 (M); gifts received, $43,500; expenditures, $59,169; qualifying distributions, $48,345.
Limitations: Giving limited to residents of Montgomery County, NY.
Application information: Application form required.
Officers: Norbert J. Sherbunt, Pres. and Treas.; Judith M. Sherbunt, V.P. and Secy.
EIN: 146030181
Codes: GTI

37761
Paul de Lima Foundation
c/o Paul de Lima Co., Inc.
P.O. Box 4813
Syracuse, NY 13221

Established in 1986 in NY.
Donor(s): Paul de Lima Company, Inc., Paul de Lima, Jr., Peter H. Miller.
Financial data (yr. ended 12/31/01): Grants paid, $23,050; assets, $37,200 (M); gifts received, $23,050; expenditures, $23,050; qualifying distributions, $23,050.
Limitations: Applications not accepted. Giving primarily in the Syracuse, NY, area.
Application information: Contributes only to pre-selected organizations.
Trustees: Paul de Lima, Jr., Peter H. Miller.
EIN: 222789206
Codes: CS, CD

37762
AVR Foundation, Inc.
c/o Daniel Rous
194 Riverside Dr.
New York, NY 10025-7259 (212) 877-9717

Donor(s): Vivian Rous.
Financial data (yr. ended 12/31/01): Grants paid, $23,000; assets, $267,896 (M); expenditures, $25,555; qualifying distributions, $23,000.
Limitations: Applications not accepted.
Application information: Contributes only to pre-selected organizations.
Officers: Vivian Rous, Pres. and Treas.; Daniel Rous, Secy.
EIN: 237025598

37763
Bernard F. Conners Foundation
(Formerly Bernard F. Conners Trust)
c/o Francis W. Coughlin
4 British American Blvd.
Latham, NY 12110-1419

Financial data (yr. ended 11/30/01): Grants paid, $23,000; assets, $428,574 (M); expenditures, $27,206; qualifying distributions, $23,000.
Limitations: Applications not accepted. Giving primarily in NY.
Application information: Contributes only to pre-selected organizations.
Trustees: Bernard F. Conners, Catherine C. Conners, Francis W. Coughlin.
EIN: 146102668

37764
Taraknath Das Foundation
c/o Southern Asian Institute, Columbia Univ.
420 W. 118th St., Ste. 1131
New York, NY 10027-7296
Contact: Leonard A. Gordon, V.P.

Established in 1930; incorporated in 1935.
Donor(s): Mary Keatinge Das, Taraknath Das, Ph.D., Ranen Das.
Financial data (yr. ended 12/31/99): Grants paid, $23,000; assets, $694,598 (M); gifts received, $200; expenditures, $37,711; qualifying distributions, $35,861.
Limitations: Giving limited to organizations and citizens of India.
Application information: Applicant must include transcript and letters of recommendation. Application form required.
Officers: Felix Gross, Pres.; Leonard A. Gordon, V.P.
EIN: 136161284
Codes: GTI

37765
The Fenton Family Foundation
c/o U.S. Trust
114 W. 47th St., TaxVas
New York, NY 10036

Established in 2000 in CA.
Donor(s): Noel Fenton, Sarah Fenton.
Financial data (yr. ended 12/31/00): Grants paid, $23,000; assets, $3,715,603 (M); gifts received, $5,892,661; expenditures, $25,018; qualifying distributions, $25,018.
Limitations: Applications not accepted. Giving primarily in CA.
Application information: Contributes only to pre-selected organizations.
Officers: Noel Fenton, Pres.; Wendy Fenton, Secy.; Sarah Fenton, C.F.O.
Directors: Devon Fenton, Lance Fenton, Peter Fenton.
EIN: 943380876

37766
Ruth & Sheldon Goldstein Foundation
c/o LGT
P.O. Box F-1706
Binghamton, NY 13902-0106

Established in 1995 in NY.
Donor(s): Sheldon Goldstein, Ruth Goldstein.
Financial data (yr. ended 12/31/01): Grants paid, $23,000; assets, $278,329 (M); gifts received, $110,000; expenditures, $23,955; qualifying distributions, $23,000.
Limitations: Applications not accepted. Giving primarily in NY.
Application information: Contributes only to pre-selected organizations.
Trustees: Ruth Goldstein, Sheldon Goldstein, Michael H. Zuckerman.
EIN: 161478693

37767
Grandma Brown Foundation, Inc.
Scenic and Watson Aves.
P.O. Box 230
Mexico, NY 13114-0230 (315) 963-7221
Contact: Sandra L. Brown, Tr.

Established in 1961 in NY.
Donor(s): Grandma Brown's Beans, Inc.
Financial data (yr. ended 03/31/01): Grants paid, $23,000; assets, $22,882 (M); expenditures, $23,048; qualifying distributions, $23,009.
Limitations: Giving primarily in the town of Mexico and the counties of Oswego and Onondoga, NY.

Application information: Application form not required.
Trustee: Sandra L. Brown.
EIN: 166052275
Codes: CS, CD

37768
The John P. Picone Charitable Foundation, Inc.
31 Garden Ln.
P.O. Box 336
Lawrence, NY 11559

Established in 2000 in NY.
Donor(s): John P. Picone Inc.
Financial data (yr. ended 12/31/01): Grants paid, $23,000; assets, $102,706 (M); expenditures, $23,601; qualifying distributions, $22,992.
Limitations: Applications not accepted. Giving primarily in NY.
Application information: Contributes only to pre-selected organizations.
Directors: John P. Picone, Patrice Picone, Gerald E. Rossettie.
EIN: 113524076
Codes: CS

37769
Theodore T. & Hilda Rose Foundation, Inc.
630 Park Ave.
New York, NY 10021-6544
Contact: Linda C. Rose, Pres.

Financial data (yr. ended 04/30/02): Grants paid, $23,000; assets, $348,955 (M); expenditures, $24,818; qualifying distributions, $23,000.
Limitations: Giving primarily in New York, NY.
Application information: Application form not required.
Officers: Linda C. Rose, Pres.; Judith Gingold, Secy.-Treas.
EIN: 136122491

37770
The Robert Hampton Tapp Foundation
c/o Union League Club
38 E. 37th St.
New York, NY 10016-3095

Established in 1993 in NY.
Donor(s): Hallie Jane Tapp.
Financial data (yr. ended 12/31/01): Grants paid, $23,000; assets, $417,608 (M); gifts received, $175,135; expenditures, $25,445; qualifying distributions, $23,000.
Limitations: Applications not accepted. Giving primarily in NY.
Application information: Contributes only to pre-selected organizations.
Officers and Directors:* E. Nicholson Stewart,* Pres.; John P. Casey,* Treas.; John Paul Reiner,* Secy.; Robert F. Fairchild, Stuart E. Prall, Hallie Jane Tapp.
EIN: 133737788

37771
Jophed/Thomas Foundation
(Formerly Fannie & Victor Tomshinsky Foundation, Inc.)
c/o Arthur Friedman, C.P.A.
280 Madison Ave., Ste. 1007
New York, NY 10016-0801

Donor(s): George M. Thomas,‡ Bernice Thomas, Joan E. Thomas, Philip S. Thomas.
Financial data (yr. ended 12/31/01): Grants paid, $22,997; assets, $460,240 (M); expenditures, $27,149; qualifying distributions, $23,066.
Limitations: Applications not accepted. Giving primarily in New York, NY.
Application information: Contributes only to pre-selected organizations.

Officers: Bernice Thomas, Pres.; Philip S. Thomas, V.P.; Joan E. Thomas, Secy.
EIN: 136147801

37772
The Gifting Alternatives Foundation
(Formerly Heritage of Values Foundation, Inc.)
21 Gordon Ave.
Briarcliff Manor, NY 10510 (914) 762-8824
Contact: Frederick C. Veit, Exec. Dir.

Established in 1995.
Donor(s): Eljer Industries, Frederick C. Veit.
Financial data (yr. ended 12/31/00): Grants paid, $22,924; assets, $21,253 (M); gifts received, $26,645; expenditures, $54,031; qualifying distributions, $22,924.
Limitations: Giving primarily in NY.
Officer and Directors:* Frederick C. Veit,* Exec. Dir.; James Jensen, Frederick D. Veit, Lois E. Veit.
EIN: 133718069
Codes: TN

37773
Edwin & Terese Trent Foundation, Inc.
781 5th Ave.
New York, NY 10022

Established in 1960 in NY.
Donor(s): Terese Trent.
Financial data (yr. ended 12/31/00): Grants paid, $22,922; assets, $111,408 (M); expenditures, $24,240; qualifying distributions, $22,922.
Limitations: Applications not accepted. Giving primarily in the New York, NY, area.
Application information: Contributes only to pre-selected organizations.
Officers: Terese Trent, Pres. and Treas.; Walter Trent, V.P. and Secy.
EIN: 136084853

37774
Emet Foundation, Inc.
c/o Roshwalb
1155 Ave. of the Americas
New York, NY 10036

Established in 1990 in NY.
Donor(s): Stavisky Family Foundation, Inc.
Financial data (yr. ended 12/31/01): Grants paid, $22,900; assets, $1,012,293 (M); expenditures, $33,989; qualifying distributions, $22,900.
Limitations: Giving primarily in the metropolitan New York, NY, area.
Officer: Aron Stavisky, Pres.
EIN: 133580782

37775
Robert and Nettie Benenson Foundation, Inc.
445 Park Ave., Ste. 1902
New York, NY 10022-2667
Contact: Edward H. Benenson, Pres.

Established about 1957 in NY.
Financial data (yr. ended 12/31/01): Grants paid, $22,893; assets, $1,422,428 (M); expenditures, $34,380; qualifying distributions, $22,893.
Limitations: Giving primarily in NY.
Officers: Edward H. Benenson, Pres.; Albert Fleischman, V.P.; Lisa Quattrocchi, Secy.
EIN: 510173119

37776
Deblinger Family Foundation, Inc.
219 Wardell Rd.
Rush, NY 14543

Established in 1997 in NY.
Donor(s): Joseph Deblinger.
Financial data (yr. ended 06/30/01): Grants paid, $22,779; assets, $524,306 (M); gifts received, $39,778; expenditures, $31,505; qualifying distributions, $22,779.
Limitations: Applications not accepted. Giving primarily in Washington, DC.
Application information: Contributes only to pre-selected organizations.
Directors: Albert Altesman, H. Cecile Deblinger, Joann Deblinger.
EIN: 161550624

37777
The Gallagher Family Foundation
15 White Hill Rd.
Cold Spring Harbor, NY 11724

Established in 1986 in DE.
Donor(s): James G. Gallagher.
Financial data (yr. ended 12/31/01): Grants paid, $22,750; assets, $58,355 (M); expenditures, $25,113; qualifying distributions, $23,930.
Limitations: Applications not accepted. Giving primarily in Cold Spring Harbor, NY.
Application information: Contributes only to pre-selected organizations.
Officer and Director:* James G. Gallagher,* Pres.
EIN: 112834532

37778
The Saidel Family Foundation, Inc.
(Formerly The Saul Saidel Charitable Foundation)
350 5th Ave., Ste. 3112A
New York, NY 10118-0110 (212) 279-1117
Contact: Samuel Saidel, Dir.

Donor(s): Samuel Saidel.
Financial data (yr. ended 11/30/01): Grants paid, $22,750; assets, $56,219 (M); gifts received, $12,500; expenditures, $78,683; qualifying distributions, $22,750.
Limitations: Giving primarily in NJ and PA.
Directors: Robert Feldstein, Wallace Musoff, Daniel Saidel, Lawrence Saidel, Samuel Saidel, Scott Saidel.
EIN: 133524943

37779
The Mack Foundation
150 E. 85th St.
New York, NY 10028
Contact: Jeremy Mack, Pres.

Donor(s): David Mack, Jeremy Mack.
Financial data (yr. ended 12/31/01): Grants paid, $22,745; assets, $294,094 (M); expenditures, $28,217; qualifying distributions, $22,547.
Limitations: Giving primarily in NY.
Officers: Jeremy Mack, Pres.; David Mack, V.P.
EIN: 221710927

37780
The Manning and Napier Foundation, Inc.
1100 Chase Sq.
Rochester, NY 14604-1905 (716) 325-6880

Financial data (yr. ended 12/31/01): Grants paid, $22,742; assets, $13,265 (M); gifts received, $4,275; expenditures, $23,985; qualifying distributions, $22,742.
Limitations: Giving primarily in Rochester, NY.
Officers: Francis J. Ward, Pres.; Edward George, V.P.; Richard Barrington, Secy.-Treas.
EIN: 161481662

37781
Samuel H. Christenfeld Foundation, Inc.
c/o Cohen & Friedman, C.P.A.
119 N. Park Ave., Ste. 310
Rockville Centre, NY 11570 (516) 766-6266
Contact: Stanley Christenfeld, Pres.

Financial data (yr. ended 12/31/01): Grants paid, $22,721; assets, $389,395 (M); expenditures, $24,272; qualifying distributions, $22,721.
Limitations: Giving primarily in NY.
Officers: Stanley Christenfeld, Pres.; Adele Golby, V.P.; Emily Christenfeld, Secy.-Treas.
EIN: 136157666

37782
John T. and Eileen M. White Charitable Foundation
1A Century Rd.
Palisades, NY 10964

Established in 1999 in NY.
Donor(s): Eileen M. White, John T. White.
Financial data (yr. ended 12/31/01): Grants paid, $22,714; assets, $164,022 (M); gifts received, $100,000; expenditures, $22,714; qualifying distributions, $22,714.
Limitations: Applications not accepted. Giving primarily in NY.
Application information: Contributes only to pre-selected organizations.
Trustees: Eileen M. White, John T. White.
EIN: 311660684

37783
Hazel L. Wilbur Charitable Trust
c/o NBT Bank, N.A.
52 S. Broad St.
Norwich, NY 13815

Established in 1995 in NY.
Financial data (yr. ended 11/30/01): Grants paid, $22,711; assets, $571,912 (M); expenditures, $25,262; qualifying distributions, $22,711.
Limitations: Applications not accepted.
Application information: Contributes only to pre-selected organizations.
Trustee: NBT Bank, N.A.
EIN: 166429714

37784
Patrick J. Broderick Memorial Foundation
c/o Cusack & Stiles, LLP
61 Broadway, Ste. 2100
New York, NY 10006

Established in 1961 in NY.
Donor(s): Most Rev. Edwin B. Broderick.
Financial data (yr. ended 12/31/01): Grants paid, $22,700; assets, $394,053 (M); gifts received, $8,674; expenditures, $27,485; qualifying distributions, $22,700.
Limitations: Applications not accepted. Giving primarily in NY.
Application information: Contributes only to pre-selected organizations.
Officers and Directors:* Most Rev. Edwin B. Broderick,* Pres. and Treas.; Patricia Broderick,* V.P. and Secy.; Douglas Broderick, Edwin T. Broderick, Robert D. Broderick.
EIN: 136143792

37785
The Leonard A. Feiner Foundation, Inc.
178 Wildacre Ave.
Lawrence, NY 11559-1413

Donor(s): Leonard A. Feiner.
Financial data (yr. ended 12/31/01): Grants paid, $22,665; assets, $71,342 (M); gifts received, $59,375; expenditures, $22,665; qualifying distributions, $22,665.
Limitations: Applications not accepted. Giving primarily in New York, NY.
Application information: Contributes only to pre-selected organizations.
Officer: Leonard A. Feiner, Pres.
EIN: 112794650

37786
Edgar & Eva Galson Charitable Trust
236 Lockwood Rd.
Syracuse, NY 13214-2035

Established in 1998 in NY.
Donor(s): Edgar Galson, Eva Galson.
Financial data (yr. ended 12/31/01): Grants paid, $22,665; assets, $57,785 (M); expenditures, $24,605; qualifying distributions, $23,140.
Limitations: Applications not accepted.
Application information: Contributes only to pre-selected organizations.
Trustees: Edgar Galson, Eva Galson.
EIN: 166483155

37787
Armellino Family Foundation
c/o BCRS Assocs., LLC
67 Wall St., 8th Fl.
New York, NY 10005

Established in 1987 in NJ.
Donor(s): Michael R. Armellino.
Financial data (yr. ended 01/31/02): Grants paid, $22,650; assets, $1,553,288 (M); expenditures, $36,485; qualifying distributions, $22,650.
Limitations: Applications not accepted. Giving primarily in NJ and New York, NY.
Application information: Contributes only to pre-selected organizations.
Trustees: Michael R. Armellino, Steven G. Einhorn, William J. Kealy.
EIN: 133437932

37788
Freed Foundation, Inc.
72 Exeter St.
Brooklyn, NY 11235 (718) 648-7959

Financial data (yr. ended 12/31/01): Grants paid, $22,643; assets, $307,195 (M); expenditures, $24,254; qualifying distributions, $22,643.
Limitations: Applications not accepted.
Application information: Contributes only to pre-selected organizations.
Officers: Lawrence Freed, Pres.; Sherie Freed, Secy.; Ronald Freed, Treas.
EIN: 116034865

37789
Matalon Family Foundation, Inc.
1075 E. 7th St.
Brooklyn, NY 11230-3501

Established in 1974.
Donor(s): Robert Matalon, Barbara Matalon, Miriam Sinitsky.
Financial data (yr. ended 12/31/01): Grants paid, $22,600; assets, $164,444 (M); gifts received, $20,000; expenditures, $28,884; qualifying distributions, $22,600.
Limitations: Applications not accepted. Giving primarily in New York, NY.
Application information: Contributes only to pre-selected organizations.
Officers: Robert Matalon, Pres.; Barbara Matalon, Secy.; Morris Matalon, Treas.
EIN: 237419408

37790
Frances Cohen Foundation
4505 Beach 45th St.
Brooklyn, NY 11224-1001 (718) 946-0068
Contact: Samuel W. Cohen, Tr.

Financial data (yr. ended 12/31/01): Grants paid, $22,530; assets, $1 (M); gifts received, $21,390; expenditures, $23,121; qualifying distributions, $22,530.
Trustee: Samuel W. Cohen.
EIN: 113496034

37791
Douglas C. James Charitable Trust
P.O. Box 32
Woodstock, NY 12498

Established in 1993 in NY.
Donor(s): Douglas C. James.
Financial data (yr. ended 12/31/01): Grants paid, $22,525; assets, $384,100 (M); gifts received, $1,000; expenditures, $25,859; qualifying distributions, $25,558.
Limitations: Applications not accepted. Giving primarily in Woodstock, NY.
Application information: Contributes only to pre-selected organizations.
Trustees: David F. James, Douglas C. James.
EIN: 141764010

37792
Feder Family Charitable Trust
c/o Arthur A. Feder
25 W 81st St.
New York, NY 10024

Donor(s): Arthur A. Feder.
Financial data (yr. ended 03/31/02): Grants paid, $22,520; assets, $4,596 (M); gifts received, $14,724; expenditures, $23,347; qualifying distributions, $22,520.
Limitations: Applications not accepted.
Application information: Contributes only to pre-selected organizations.
Trustee: Arthur A. Feder.
EIN: 136271757

37793
Robert M. Brown III Foundation, Inc.
(Formerly The Yvonne P. and Robert M. Brown III Foundation)
c/o Barry Strauss Assoc., Ltd.
307 5th Ave., 8th Fl.
New York, NY 10016-6517

Established in 1986 in CT.
Donor(s): Robert M. Brown III.
Financial data (yr. ended 10/31/01): Grants paid, $22,500; assets, $229,368 (M); gifts received, $94,000; expenditures, $22,797; qualifying distributions, $22,775.
Limitations: Applications not accepted. Giving primarily in Darien, CT.
Application information: Contributes only to pre-selected organizations.
Directors: Jessica L. Brown, Robert M. Brown III, Robert M. Brown IV.
EIN: 133451201

37794
Frederic R. Coudert Foundation
c/o Coudert Bros.
1114 Ave. of the Americas
New York, NY 10036
Contact: Kenneth R. Page

Established in 1999 in NY.
Donor(s): Frederic R. Coudert III.
Financial data (yr. ended 12/31/01): Grants paid, $22,500; assets, $798,407 (M); gifts received,

$24,616; expenditures, $61,700; qualifying distributions, $22,500.
Trustee: Frederic R. Coudert III.
EIN: 137180778

37795
The Dann Foundation, Inc.
c/o Geoffrey Dann: Lingold Associates
500 Fifth Ave., 50th Fl.
New York, NY 10110

Donor(s): Elliot W. Dann.
Financial data (yr. ended 12/31/01): Grants paid, $22,500; assets, $210,894 (M); expenditures, $24,393; qualifying distributions, $22,500.
Limitations: Applications not accepted. Giving primarily in NY.
Application information: Contributes only to pre-selected organizations.
Officers and Directors:* Deborah Dann,* Pres.; Jennifer A. Dann,* V.P.; Geoffrey Dann,* Secy.
EIN: 133266717

37796
Leonard Tingle Foundation
c/o Ide, Haigney & Rado
176 E. 71 St.
New York, NY 10021-5159

Donor(s): Jeanette Hobart.
Financial data (yr. ended 09/30/01): Grants paid, $22,500; assets, $488,504 (M); expenditures, $27,051; qualifying distributions, $26,223.
Limitations: Applications not accepted. Giving primarily in AZ, with emphasis on Phoenix and Carefree; giving also in New London, CT.
Application information: Contributes only to pre-selected organizations.
Officers: Lenore T. Howard, Pres.; John E. Haigney, Secy.; Harry S. Howard, Treas.
EIN: 136158846

37797
The Dana Wigutoff Memorial Foundation, Inc.
c/o Edwin Wigutoff
267 Glen Ave.
Sea Cliff, NY 11579-1543

Established in 1985 in NY.
Donor(s): Edwin D. Wigutoff, Gilbert Levy, Frances Wigutoff, Sharon S. Wigutoff.
Financial data (yr. ended 06/30/00): Grants paid, $22,490; assets, $71,319 (M); expenditures, $22,677; qualifying distributions, $22,664.
Limitations: Applications not accepted. Giving primarily in NY, and Bryan, OH.
Application information: Contributes only to pre-selected organizations.
Officers: Edwin D. Wigutoff, Pres.; Sharon S. Wigutoff, V.P.
EIN: 112720503

37798
Foundation of the Alumnae Association of Mount Sinai Hospital School of Nursing, Inc.
c/o Anne Taberna
1 Gustave L. Levy Pl.
New York, NY 10029 (212) 289-5566

Financial data (yr. ended 09/30/01): Grants paid, $22,471; assets, $195,372 (M); gifts received, $23,178; expenditures, $36,724; qualifying distributions, $22,471.
Officers: Judith Jones Scher, Pres.; Sylvia M. Barker, V.P.; Sheila Kurtzman Boubli, Secy.-Treas.
Directors: Carole Daly Garabedian, Phyliss Shanley Hansell, Charlotte Nussbaum Isler, Edith Lustbader Jaffe, Marjorie Seelinger Labarbera, Marjorie Gulla Lewis, Marjorie Finkelstein Mendelsohn, Catherine O'Donnell, Karen Attanasio Zygmunt.

EIN: 136096777
Codes: GTI

37799
Zichron Arye, Inc.
345 Kent Ave.
Brooklyn, NY 11211
Contact: Eugene Buchinger, Pres.

Donor(s): Eugene Buchinger.
Financial data (yr. ended 12/31/01): Grants paid, $22,467; assets, $165,915 (M); gifts received, $40,000; expenditures, $23,432; qualifying distributions, $22,467.
Officer: Eugene Buchinger, Pres.
EIN: 113273749

37800
Francesca Kress Foundation
c/o Francesca M. Kress
1020 5th Ave.
New York, NY 10028

Established in 1994.
Donor(s): Francesca M. Kress.
Financial data (yr. ended 12/31/00): Grants paid, $22,447; assets, $201,980 (M); gifts received, $20,000; expenditures, $31,969; qualifying distributions, $22,447.
Limitations: Applications not accepted. Giving primarily in New York, NY, and Charleston, SC.
Application information: Contributes only to pre-selected organizations.
Officers: Francesca M. Kress, Pres.; Jessica Kress Mayberry, V.P.; John N. Mayberry, Secy.-Treas.
EIN: 133773333

37801
Susseles Family Philanthropies, Inc.
c/o Siders
180 E. End Ave.
New York, NY 10128

Donor(s): Patricia Siders.
Financial data (yr. ended 12/31/01): Grants paid, $22,426; assets, $72,758 (M); gifts received, $20,000; expenditures, $23,156; qualifying distributions, $22,426.
Limitations: Giving primarily in NY.
Officer: Patricia Siders, Pres.
EIN: 136144669

37802
The Banks Family Foundation, Inc.
14 E. 75th St., Ste. 9A
New York, NY 10021
Contact: Russell Banks, Pres.

Established in 1994.
Financial data (yr. ended 12/31/01): Grants paid, $22,420; assets, $187,410 (M); expenditures, $22,892; qualifying distributions, $22,420.
Limitations: Giving primarily in New York, NY.
Officers: Russell Banks, Pres.; Gordon Banks, V.P.; Janice Banks, Secy.-Treas.
EIN: 133799347

37803
The Sinai Foundation, Inc.
c/o Annette Gross
1054 59th St.
Brooklyn, NY 11219

Established in 1993 in NY.
Donor(s): Annette Gross.
Financial data (yr. ended 11/30/01): Grants paid, $22,416; assets, $80,216 (M); gifts received, $15,180; expenditures, $23,909; qualifying distributions, $22,416.
Limitations: Applications not accepted. Giving limited to NY.

Application information: Contributes only to pre-selected organizations.
Officers: Annette Gross, Pres.; Sara Gross, V.P.; Barbara Nussbaum, Secy.-Treas.
EIN: 113188874

37804
Kevin Scott Dalrymple Foundation
21 Brundige Dr.
Goldens Bridge, NY 10526
Contact: Richard W. Dalrymple, Tr.

Established in 1994 in NY.
Donor(s): Richard W. Dalrymple, Kathleen M. Dalrymple.
Financial data (yr. ended 12/31/01): Grants paid, $22,410; assets, $541,179 (M); gifts received, $1,705; expenditures, $26,747; qualifying distributions, $23,596.
Limitations: Giving primarily in Katonah, NY.
Trustees: Kathleen M. Dalrymple, Richard W. Dalrymple.
EIN: 133746904

37805
Jonathan & Isabel Ezrow Foundation
200 Madison Ave.
New York, NY 10016

Donor(s): Susan & Elihu Rose Foundation.
Financial data (yr. ended 12/31/00): Grants paid, $22,410; assets, $11,982 (M); gifts received, $30,000; expenditures, $23,185; qualifying distributions, $22,410.
Limitations: Applications not accepted.
Application information: Contributes only to pre-selected organizations.
Officers and Directors:* Isabel Rose,* Pres.; Jonathan Ezrow,* V.P.
EIN: 134066366

37806
Joseph Letson Charitable Trust
52 S. Broad St.
Norwich, NY 13815

Established in 2000 in NY.
Financial data (yr. ended 12/31/01): Grants paid, $22,356; assets, $543,844 (M); expenditures, $26,097; qualifying distributions, $25,008.
Limitations: Applications not accepted.
Application information: Contributes only to pre-selected organizations.
Trustee: NBT Bank, N.A.
EIN: 166305073

37807
The Arta Foundation
185 W. End Ave.
New York, NY 10023

Established in 1999 in NY.
Donor(s): Bina Presser.
Financial data (yr. ended 12/31/01): Grants paid, $22,300; assets, $387,152 (M); gifts received, $76,010; expenditures, $26,705; qualifying distributions, $22,300.
Limitations: Applications not accepted. Giving primarily in NY.
Application information: Contributes only to pre-selected organizations.
Trustee: Bina Presser.
EIN: 134057328

37808
Alpert Zusman Family, Inc.
271 Madison Ave.
New York, NY 10016-1001 (212) 532-4416

Financial data (yr. ended 12/31/01): Grants paid, $22,300; assets, $148,919 (M); gifts received,

37808—NEW YORK

$10,000; expenditures, $22,571; qualifying distributions, $22,300.
Limitations: Applications not accepted. Giving primarily in NY.
Application information: Contributes only to pre-selected organizations.
Officers: Jack Alpert, Pres.; Charles Alpert, Secy.; Joseph Alpert, Treas.
EIN: 111876776

37809
Seymour D. & Sonia Schneiderman Foundation
c/o Sonnenschein Nath
1221 Ave. of the Americas, 26th Fl.
New York, NY 10020

Established in 1999 in DE and NY.
Donor(s): Seymour D. Schneiderman.
Financial data (yr. ended 08/31/01): Grants paid, $22,295; assets, $257,745 (M); expenditures, $22,445; qualifying distributions, $22,295.
Limitations: Applications not accepted.
Application information: Contributes only to pre-selected organizations.
Directors: Gerald Barandes, Seymour D. Schneiderman, Sonia Schneiderman.
EIN: 134092157

37810
Arthur A. & Carla Rand Foundation
c/o Arthur A. Rand
110-26 68th Dr.
Forest Hills, NY 11375-2953

Established in 1997 in NY.
Donor(s): Arthur A. Rand, Carla Rand.
Financial data (yr. ended 10/31/01): Grants paid, $22,294; assets, $206,219 (M); gifts received, $47,512; expenditures, $22,773; qualifying distributions, $22,294.
Limitations: Applications not accepted. Giving primarily in New York, NY.
Application information: Contributes only to pre-selected organizations.
Officers: Arthur A. Rand, Pres.; Carla Rand, V.P.
EIN: 113350839

37811
The J. Posner Family Trust
1545 45th St.
Brooklyn, NY 11219

Established in 1998 in NY.
Donor(s): Jason Posner.
Financial data (yr. ended 12/31/01): Grants paid, $22,259; assets, $204,825 (M); gifts received, $90,000; expenditures, $22,809; qualifying distributions, $22,259.
Director: Jacob Posner.
EIN: 116508143

37812
Jacob & Rose Olum Foundation
c/o Levene, Gouldin & Thompson, LLP
P.O. Box F 1706
Binghamton, NY 13902-0106 (607) 763-9200

Donor(s): Charitable Remainder Annuity Trust.
Financial data (yr. ended 12/31/01): Grants paid, $22,250; assets, $506,080 (M); expenditures, $27,070; qualifying distributions, $22,250.
Limitations: Applications not accepted. Giving limited to Binghamton, NY.
Application information: Contributes only to pre-selected organizations.
Trustee: Michael H. Zuckerman.
EIN: 237034984

37813
Imago Foundation, Ltd.
425 Riverside Dr., Ste. 12J
New York, NY 10025

Established in 1999 in NY.
Financial data (yr. ended 04/30/00): Grants paid, $22,200; assets, $200 (M); gifts received, $25,000; expenditures, $24,800; qualifying distributions, $22,800.
Directors: Karen Gaskin, Michael Hsu, Roy P. Kinsey, Jr.
EIN: 134061069

37814
Efraim and Judith Schwartz Charitable Foundation
1051 E. 22nd St.
Brooklyn, NY 11210

Established in 2000 in NY.
Donor(s): Efraim Schwartz, Judith Schwartz.
Financial data (yr. ended 12/31/00): Grants paid, $22,190; assets, $26,196 (M); gifts received, $48,188; expenditures, $22,261; qualifying distributions, $22,190.
Trustee: Joseph Schwartz.
EIN: 116635559

37815
Dr. Nancy A. K. Perkins Charitable Foundation
16 N. Main St.
Pittsford, NY 14534 (716) 383-1111

Donor(s): Nancy A.K. Perkins, M.D.
Financial data (yr. ended 12/31/01): Grants paid, $22,158; assets, $619,020 (M); expenditures, $26,298; qualifying distributions, $22,158.
Limitations: Applications not accepted.
Application information: Contributes only to pre-selected organizations.
Trustees: Nancy A.K. Perkins, M.D., Klaus E.T. Siebert.
EIN: 166439639

37816
Marcell and Maria Roth Fund, Inc.
c/o Hanna L. Tennen
90 Riverside Dr., Apt. 15E
New York, NY 10024

Financial data (yr. ended 05/31/01): Grants paid, $22,140; assets, $236,278 (M); expenditures, $23,160; qualifying distributions, $22,140.
Limitations: Applications not accepted. Giving primarily in New York, NY.
Application information: Contributes only to pre-selected organizations.
Officers: Irene E. Pipes, Pres.; Hanna L. Tennen, Secy.-Treas.
EIN: 237176256

37817
Kwitman Family Foundation, Inc.
c/o H. Kwitman
261 5th Ave., Ste. 1504
New York, NY 10016-7701

Established in 1996 in NY.
Donor(s): Benjamin Kwitman.
Financial data (yr. ended 12/31/01): Grants paid, $22,138; assets, $750,614 (M); gifts received, $71,297; expenditures, $26,675; qualifying distributions, $22,138.
Limitations: Applications not accepted. Giving primarily in NY.
Application information: Contributes only to pre-selected organizations.
Directors: Ann Kwitman, Harold L. Kwitman, William H. Kwitman, Lois S. Michaels.
EIN: 133885787

37818
The Markowitz Family Foundation
c/o Eugene Markowitz
4 Crestview Terr.
Monsey, NY 10952

Established in 1999 in NY.
Donor(s): Eugene Markowitz.
Financial data (yr. ended 06/30/00): Grants paid, $22,114; assets, $26,644 (M); gifts received, $41,310; expenditures, $22,114; qualifying distributions, $22,114.
Trustees: Eugene Markowitz, Renee Markowitz.
EIN: 134035030

37819
Segulas Israel Charitable Foundation
34 Wallenberg Cir.
Monsey, NY 10952 (845) 772-4312
Contact: Mark Lipschitz, Tr.

Established in 1999 in NY.
Financial data (yr. ended 12/31/99): Grants paid, $22,038; assets, $31 (M); gifts received, $22,519; expenditures, $22,488; qualifying distributions, $22,488.
Trustees: Malkie Lipschitz, Mark Lipschitz.
EIN: 134018250

37820
Carolyn Jenkins Trust f/b/o Scott-Jenkins Fund
c/o Wilber National Bank
245 Main St.
Oneonta, NY 13820-2502 (607) 432-1700
Application address: c/o Donald Moore, State University College, Education Bldg., Rm. 123, Oneonta, NY 13820-2502, tel.: (607) 432-2532

Established in 1976 in NY.
Donor(s): Carolyn Jenkins.‡
Financial data (yr. ended 12/31/02): Grants paid, $22,017; assets, $429,157 (M); expenditures, $23,981; qualifying distributions, $21,861.
Limitations: Giving primarily in Oneonta, NY.
Application information: Application form required.
Scholarship Committee Member: Alan Donovan, Chair.
Trustee: Wilber National Bank.
EIN: 166183805
Codes: GTI

37821
Ellen Harvey Foundation, Inc.
(Formerly Monroe Coblens Foundation, Inc.)
c/o Sugarman & Thorpe, PC
1501 Broadway, Ste. 1503
New York, NY 10036

Established in 1984 in NY.
Financial data (yr. ended 10/31/01): Grants paid, $22,016; assets, $419,461 (M); expenditures, $24,685; qualifying distributions, $22,016.
Limitations: Applications not accepted. Giving primarily in FL and NY.
Application information: Contributes only to pre-selected organizations.
Officers: Ellen Harvey, Pres.; Roger Harvey, V.P.; Irwin M. Thorpe, Secy.
EIN: 136082368

37822
Anne F. Bourne Memorial Fund, Inc.
c/o Nugent & Haeussler, PC
101 Bracken Rd.
Montgomery, NY 12549

Established in 1947 in NY.
Donor(s): Anne F. Bourne.‡

Financial data (yr. ended 12/31/01): Grants paid, $22,000; assets, $694,000 (M); expenditures, $24,483; qualifying distributions, $22,000.
Limitations: Applications not accepted.
Application information: Contributes only to pre-selected organizations.
Officers: Walter Grannum, Pres.; Kenneth DeWitt, Secy.; John Smith, Treas.
Trustee: Richard Goodrich.
EIN: 146013841

37823
The Mitch Miller Foundation, Inc.
345 W. 58th St., Apt. 11J
New York, NY 10019-1115
Contact: Mitchell W. Miller, Tr.

Financial data (yr. ended 12/31/01): Grants paid, $22,000; assets, $480,003 (M); gifts received, $2,000; expenditures, $22,323; qualifying distributions, $22,100.
Limitations: Applications not accepted. Giving primarily in NY and PA.
Application information: Contributes only to pre-selected organizations.
Officers and Trustees:* Mitchell W. Miller,* Chair.; Mitchell A. Miller,* Vice-Chair.; Andrea Miller,* Secy.; Margaret Reuther,* Treas.
EIN: 136161712

37824
The Reese Foundation
c/o Lazard Freres & Co.
30 Rockefeller Plz.
New York, NY 10020
Contact: Frances R. Olivieri, Pres.

Established in 1986 in NY.
Donor(s): Willis L.M. Reese,‡ Frances R. Olivieri.
Financial data (yr. ended 06/30/01): Grants paid, $22,000; assets, $335 (M); expenditures, $22,049; qualifying distributions, $22,000.
Limitations: Giving primarily in the greater New York, NY, area.
Application information: Application form not required.
Officers: Frances R. Olivieri, Pres.; John R. Reese, V.P.; William W. Reese, Secy.-Treas.
EIN: 133373455

37825
John H. Watts Charitable Foundation
c/o Charter Atlantic
200 Park Ave., 46th Fl.
New York, NY 10166   (212) 681-3018
Contact: John H. Watts, Tr.

Donor(s): John H. Watts.
Financial data (yr. ended 11/30/99): Grants paid, $22,000; assets, $448,430 (M); expenditures, $22,274; qualifying distributions, $22,000.
Limitations: Giving primarily in New York, NY.
Trustee: John H. Watts.
EIN: 136881097

37826
Berru Charitable Foundation
c/o Joseph Tel & Co.
200 Park Ave., Fl. 24
New York, NY 10166-0005
Contact: Bernard Weinflash, Tr.

Donor(s): Bernard Weinflash.
Financial data (yr. ended 09/30/01): Grants paid, $21,950; assets, $314,956 (M); expenditures, $30,736; qualifying distributions, $21,950.
Trustees: Bernard Weinflash, Ruth Weinflash.
EIN: 237003289

37827
Oliner Foundation
195 Central Ave.
Lawrence, NY 11559
Contact: Martin Oliner, Dir.

Established in 1990 in NY.
Donor(s): Martin Oliner.
Financial data (yr. ended 12/31/01): Grants paid, $21,913; assets, $353,863 (M); expenditures, $21,913; qualifying distributions, $21,913.
Limitations: Giving limited to Lawrence, NY.
Director: Martin Oliner.
EIN: 113062528

37828
American Cancer Foundation, Inc.
707 Westchester Ave.
White Plains, NY 10604
Application address: 10 Berol Close, Chappaqua, NY, tel.: (914) 328-9696
Contact: Marc Straus, Chair.

Financial data (yr. ended 12/31/00): Grants paid, $21,880; assets, $0 (M); expenditures, $21,880; qualifying distributions, $21,880.
Officer: Marc Straus, Chair.
Trustees: Jeffrey Ambinder, Eliot Friedman.
EIN: 133556723

37829
Milton & Mildred Rosen Foundation, Inc.
9520 Seaview Ave.
Brooklyn, NY 11236-5432
Contact: Milton Rosen, Pres.

Donor(s): M. Gurvitch.
Financial data (yr. ended 12/31/01): Grants paid, $21,848; assets, $698,793 (M); gifts received, $24,823; expenditures, $24,671; qualifying distributions, $21,848.
Application information: Application form not required.
Officers: Milton Rosen, Pres.; Janet Gurvitch, Secy.
EIN: 237068822

37830
The Bartlett Foundation
7 Bartlett Rd.
Monsey, NY 10952
Contact: Samuel Dobner, Tr.

Established in 1999 in NY.
Donor(s): Samuel Dobner.
Financial data (yr. ended 09/30/01): Grants paid, $21,756; assets, $7,890 (M); gifts received, $10,000; expenditures, $22,725; qualifying distributions, $21,756.
Limitations: Giving primarily in NY.
Trustee: Samuel Dobner.
EIN: 137223793

37831
Dorothy Setzler Fund
3921 Lincoln St.
Seaford, NY 11783   (516) 785-8948
Contact: William E. Setzler, Pres.

Established in 1991 in DE.
Donor(s): William E. Setzler.
Financial data (yr. ended 12/31/01): Grants paid, $21,700; assets, $288,751 (M); gifts received, $516; expenditures, $22,445; qualifying distributions, $21,700.
Limitations: Giving on a national basis, with emphasis on the metropolitan New York, NY, area.
Application information: Maximum grant not likely to exceed $10,000.
Officers and Directors:* William E. Setzler,* Pres. and Treas.; Lenore M. Kelly,* V.P. and Secy.
EIN: 113087798

37832
The Eduardo & Antonella Salvati Foundation, Inc.
25 Sutton Pl. S., Ste. 20K
New York, NY 10022
Contact: Antonella Salvati

Established n 1997 in NY.
Financial data (yr. ended 06/30/01): Grants paid, $21,650; assets, $767,273 (M); expenditures, $21,965; qualifying distributions, $21,650.
Directors: Antonella Salvati, Eduardo Salvati.
EIN: 133983391

37833
Garth Family Foundation
c/o Barbara Thomas, Squadron, Ellenoff, et al.
551 5th Ave.
New York, NY 10176-0001

Established in 1992 in CO.
Donor(s): Hugh C. Garth, Donna Garth.
Financial data (yr. ended 12/31/01): Grants paid, $21,632; assets, $285,858 (M); expenditures, $27,536; qualifying distributions, $21,632.
Limitations: Applications not accepted. Giving primarily in Steamboat Springs, CO.
Application information: Contributes only to pre-selected organizations.
Officers: Hugh C. Garth, Pres. and Treas.; Donna Garth, V.P. and Secy.
EIN: 841199676

37834
Lawrence S. Mayers Fund, Inc.
c/o Moses and Schreiber
3000 Marcus Ave.
New Hyde Park, NY 11042
Application address: 32 Robin Hood Rd., Pound Ridge, NY 10576
Contact: Lawrence S. Mayers, Tr.

Financial data (yr. ended 04/30/02): Grants paid, $21,618; assets, $248,662 (M); expenditures, $24,554; qualifying distributions, $21,618.
Limitations: Giving primarily in New York, NY.
Trustee: Lawrence S. Mayers.
EIN: 136089967

37835
John Alexander Memorial Scholarship Fund
c/o Trustco Bank, N.A.
P.O. Box 380
Schenectady, NY 12305
Application address: c/o C. Koury, 525 State St., Schenectady, NY 12305, tel.: (518) 374-1200

Financial data (yr. ended 06/30/01): Grants paid, $21,600; assets, $618,815 (M); expenditures, $29,328; qualifying distributions, $22,284.
Limitations: Giving limited to residents of Schenectady County, NY.
Application information: Application form required.
Trustee: Trustco Bank, N.A.
EIN: 146111436
Codes: GTI

37836
The Liebowitz Foundation
5 Vanderbilt Dr.
Sands Point, NY 11050

Established in 1994.
Donor(s): Leo Liebowitz.
Financial data (yr. ended 12/31/01): Grants paid, $21,575; assets, $906,753 (M); expenditures, $24,180; qualifying distributions, $21,575.
Limitations: Applications not accepted. Giving primarily in New York, NY.

37836—NEW YORK

Application information: Contributes only to pre-selected organizations.
Trustees: Leo Liebowitz, Rose Liebowitz.
EIN: 113240737

37837
The Feldman Family Foundation Trust
Hust Rd., Calicoon Township
Jeffersonville, NY 12748

Established in 2000.
Donor(s): Larry Feldman, Jaffa Feldman.
Financial data (yr. ended 12/31/01): Grants paid, $21,560; assets, $48 (M); gifts received, $21,153; expenditures, $21,645; qualifying distributions, $21,560.
Trustees: Jaffa Feldman, Larry Feldman.
EIN: 316649842

37838
Saul and Edna Glotzer Foundation, Inc.
c/o Glen Ross
2 Stone Hollow Way
Armonk, NY 10504

Established in 1998 in NY.
Donor(s): Glen Ross.
Financial data (yr. ended 12/31/00): Grants paid, $21,525; assets, $408,885 (M); expenditures, $21,525; qualifying distributions, $21,282.
Limitations: Applications not accepted.
Application information: Contributes only to pre-selected organizations.
Trustees: Edna Glotzer, Glen Ross, Rhoda Ross.
EIN: 134033339

37839
Max Sussman & Rosalind Sussman Foundation, Inc.
99-41 64th Ave., Ste. C-17
Rego Park, NY 11374-2653

Donor(s): Max Sussman, Rosalind Sussman.
Financial data (yr. ended 12/31/01): Grants paid, $21,512; assets, $31,185 (M); gifts received, $26,000; expenditures, $21,644; qualifying distributions, $21,512.
Limitations: Applications not accepted.
Application information: Contributes only to pre-selected organizations.
Officer: Max Sussman, Pres.
EIN: 237244163

37840
The Abraham & Rebecca Crystal Foundation, Inc.
160-08 Booth Memorial Ave.
Flushing, NY 11365
Application address: c/o Graubard, Mollen, & Miller, 600 3rd Ave., New York, NY 10016-2097, tel.: (212) 818-8800
Contact: Allen Greenberg

Established in 1995.
Donor(s): Abraham Crystal, Rebecca Crystal.
Financial data (yr. ended 12/31/01): Grants paid, $21,500; assets, $610,902 (M); gifts received, $50,000; expenditures, $22,714; qualifying distributions, $21,500.
Limitations: Giving primarily in NY.
Officers: Abraham J. Crystal, Pres.; Rebecca Crystal, Secy.-Treas.
Directors: Milton S. Shapiro, Philip Shapiro.
EIN: 113272593

37841
Mary L. Kenzie Family Foundation
c/o Mary Roche
700 Guaranty Bldg., 28 Church St.
Buffalo, NY 14202

Established in 2000 in NY.
Donor(s): Mary L. Kenzie.
Financial data (yr. ended 12/31/01): Grants paid, $21,500; assets, $641,835 (M); gifts received, $48,810; expenditures, $23,709; qualifying distributions, $21,500.
Limitations: Applications not accepted.
Application information: Contributes only to pre-selected organizations.
Officers: Mary L. Kenzie, Pres.; Rachel K. King, V.P.; Langley H. Kenzie, Secy.; Ross B. Kenzie, Treas.
EIN: 161589308

37842
The Paul Miller Family Foundation, Inc.
2969 Clover St.
Pittsford, NY 14534-1725

Established in 1994 in NY.
Donor(s): Louise J. Miller.
Financial data (yr. ended 12/31/01): Grants paid, $21,500; assets, $569,015 (M); expenditures, $38,833; qualifying distributions, $21,500.
Limitations: Applications not accepted.
Application information: Contributes only to pre-selected organizations.
Officers and Directors:* Louise J. Miller,* Pres.; Elizabeth K. Miller, Secy.; Kenper W. Miller,* Treas.; Jean M. Gordon, Paul T. Miller, Ranne J. Miller.
EIN: 161469652

37843
Trombly Foundation
c/o Cowen & Co.
80 State St.
Albany, NY 12207-2544 (518) 463-5244
Contact: Kenneth Nirenberg, Tr.

Established in 1986 in NY.
Donor(s): Francis H. Trombly.
Financial data (yr. ended 11/30/01): Grants paid, $21,500; assets, $10,992 (M); gifts received, $16,621; expenditures, $22,025; qualifying distributions, $21,500.
Limitations: Giving primarily in the Albany, NY, area.
Trustees: Kenneth Nirenberg, Edward J. Trombly, Francis H. Trombly.
EIN: 146131632

37844
The Barbara Bagden Roberts Foundation, Inc.
299 W. 12th St.
New York, NY 10014

Established in 1998 in DE.
Donor(s): Barbara Roberts.
Financial data (yr. ended 11/30/01): Grants paid, $21,480; assets, $284 (M); expenditures, $24,027; qualifying distributions, $21,480.
Limitations: Applications not accepted.
Application information: Contributes only to pre-selected organizations.
Officer: Barbara B. Roberts, Pres.
EIN: 133981550

37845
Ella Gayle Hamlin Foundation, Inc.
(Formerly Ella Hamlin Johnson Foundation)
c/o Robert Lewis
319 N. Salem Rd.
North Salem, NY 10560

Established in 1982.
Donor(s): Ella Gayle Hamlin.‡
Financial data (yr. ended 12/31/01): Grants paid, $21,467; assets, $777,774 (M); expenditures, $40,251; qualifying distributions, $21,467.
Limitations: Giving primarily in CA, and New York, NY.

Officers and Directors:* Meri M. Hammon,* Pres.; Julia Bailey,* V.P.; Robert Lewis,* Secy.-Treas.; Walter Hammon, Annabel Santana.
EIN: 133106723

37846
The Reade Family Foundation
c/o JPMorgan Chase Bank
1211 6th Ave., 38th Fl.
New York, NY 10036 (212) 789-5263
Contact: Kenneth Gheno, V.P., JPMorgan Chase Bank

Established in 1997 in NY.
Financial data (yr. ended 06/30/01): Grants paid, $21,450; assets, $520,884 (M); expenditures, $33,222; qualifying distributions, $22,621.
Trustees: Pamela L. Bimson, K. Deane Reade, JPMorgan Chase Bank.
EIN: 066455460

37847
The Sipos Foundation, Inc.
50-02 Queens Blvd.
Woodside, NY 11377-4491 (718) 457-7400
Contact: Howard Taub, Pres.

Financial data (yr. ended 12/31/00): Grants paid, $21,450; assets, $365,720 (M); expenditures, $21,978; qualifying distributions, $21,450.
Limitations: Giving primarily in NY.
Officer and Trustee:* Howard Taub,* Pres.
EIN: 237316423

37848
Fred C. and Carl Colvin Memorial Trust
c/o M&T Bank
One M&T Plaza, 8th FL.
Buffalo, NY 14203-2309

Established in 1998 in PA.
Financial data (yr. ended 09/30/01): Grants paid, $21,415; assets, $598,119 (M); expenditures, $30,081; qualifying distributions, $21,415.
Limitations: Applications not accepted.
Application information: Contributes only to pre-selected organizations.
Trustee: M & T Bank.
EIN: 256579869

37849
Sterling Fund & Fellowship Foundation
c/o JPMorgan Chase Bank
P.O. Box 31412
Rochester, NY 14603-1412
Application address: 999 Broad St., Bridgeport, CT 06604, tel.: (203) 382-6548
Contact: Sheela Amembal, Trust Off., JPMorgan Chase Bank

Financial data (yr. ended 11/30/01): Grants paid, $21,375; assets, $397,201 (M); expenditures, $28,439; qualifying distributions, $21,915.
Limitations: Giving on a national basis.
Trustee: JPMorgan Chase Bank.
EIN: 066057010

37850
Walter H. Weil Family Foundation
146 Central Park West
New York, NY 10023 (212) 496-1382
Contact: Walter H. Weil, Tr.

Established in 1990 in NY.
Donor(s): Walter H. Weil.
Financial data (yr. ended 12/31/01): Grants paid, $21,360; assets, $352,937 (M); expenditures, $23,009; qualifying distributions, $21,360.
Limitations: Giving primarily in NY.
Trustees: Emily Weil, Jennifer Weil, Walter H. Weil.
EIN: 133569423

37851
Timber Lake Foundation
85 Crescent Beach Rd.
Glen Cove, NY 11542
Contact: Jay Jacobs, Dir.

Established in 1988 in NY.
Donor(s): Jay S. Jacobs.
Financial data (yr. ended 05/31/01): Grants paid, $21,350; assets, $0 (M); gifts received, $26,500; expenditures, $28,255; qualifying distributions, $21,350.
Limitations: Giving primarily in NY.
Directors: John Donnelly, Jay S. Jacobs, Sandy Lavitt, David O'Brien, Jennifer Quinn, Andy Siegel.
EIN: 112940875

37852
Jerome & Laura Dorfman Charitable Foundation
35 Sutton Pl., Ste. 15B
New York, NY 10022
Contact: Ilene Giaquinta, Vice-Chair.

Established in 2000 in NY.
Financial data (yr. ended 12/31/01): Grants paid, $21,340; assets, $63 (M); gifts received, $22,100; expenditures, $22,340; qualifying distributions, $21,340.
Limitations: Giving primarily in New York, NY.
Application information: Application form not required.
Officers: Laura Dorfman, Chair.; Ilene Giaquinta, Vice-Chair.
EIN: 134087928

37853
Philip & Dorothy Hirth Foundation
210 W. 70th St.
New York, NY 10023

Financial data (yr. ended 12/31/01): Grants paid, $21,290; assets, $9,751 (M); gifts received, $23,950; expenditures, $22,890; qualifying distributions, $21,290.
Limitations: Applications not accepted.
Application information: Contributes only to pre-selected organizations.
Director: Mitchell Hirth, Sydney Hirth, Sheila Melkman.
EIN: 133942774

37854
Leon Finley Trust B Charitable
(Formerly Leon Finley Trust f/b/o St. John's University, et al. Trust B)
c/o JPMorgan Chase Bank
1211 6th Ave., 34th Fl.
New York, NY 10036

Established in 1989 in NY; Amended in 1998.
Financial data (yr. ended 12/31/00): Grants paid, $21,250; assets, $418,702 (M); expenditures, $27,056; qualifying distributions, $21,937.
Limitations: Applications not accepted. Giving primarily in NY.
Application information: Contributes only to pre-selected organizations.
Trustee: JPMorgan Chase Bank.
EIN: 526955768

37855
The Joslin Family Foundation, Inc.
c/o Braun
6 E. 45th St., Ste. 1401
New York, NY 10017

Established in 1998 in NY.
Financial data (yr. ended 12/31/01): Grants paid, $21,250; assets, $883,260 (M); expenditures, $30,174; qualifying distributions, $21,250.
Limitations: Applications not accepted.

Application information: Contributes only to pre-selected organizations.
Officers and Directors:* Raymond E. Joslin, Pres.; Jennifer Joslin Clendening,* V.P.; David Joslin,* V.P.; Jeffrey Joslin,* V.P.
EIN: 133947603

37856
The Klimley Foundation
125 Parkway Rd., Ste. 1316
Bronxville, NY 10708 (914) 793-3804
Contact: Brooks J. Klimley, Pres.

Established in 1998 in DE and NY.
Donor(s): Brooks J. Klimley.
Financial data (yr. ended 12/31/01): Grants paid, $21,250; assets, $387,592 (M); gifts received, $63,438; expenditures, $24,051; qualifying distributions, $21,250.
Officers: Brooks J. Klimley, Pres. and Treas.; Laura E. Klimley, Secy.
EIN: 133993555

37857
The Morris and Luba Perlman Foundation
1664 51st St.
Brooklyn, NY 11204-1416
Application address: P.O. Box 311, Parkville Sta., Brooklyn, NY 11204, tel.: (718) 851-7433
Contact: Morris Perlman, Pres., or Luba Perlman, Secy.-Treas.

Donor(s): Luba Perlman, Morris Perlman.
Financial data (yr. ended 08/31/01): Grants paid, $21,243; assets, $262,725 (M); gifts received, $15,000; expenditures, $22,093; qualifying distributions, $21,243.
Limitations: Giving primarily in NY.
Application information: Application form not required.
Officers: Morris Perlman, Pres.; Manya P. Fisher, V.P.; Luba Perlman, Secy.-Treas.
EIN: 112165219

37858
Bella and Seymour Goldberg Foundation, Inc.
c/o Woods Mgmt. Co.
98 Cutter Mill Rd.
Great Neck, NY 11021

Established in 1989 in NY.
Donor(s): Goldberg Charitable Lead Trust.
Financial data (yr. ended 06/30/01): Grants paid, $21,229; assets, $19,098 (M); gifts received, $20,000; expenditures, $21,256; qualifying distributions, $21,229.
Limitations: Applications not accepted. Giving primarily in NY.
Application information: Contributes only to pre-selected organizations.
Officer and Directors:* Seymour Goldberg,* Pres.; Ruth Gerver, Michael G. Tannenbaum.
EIN: 136938293

37859
The Dorothy D. & John C. Fitterer Foundation, Inc.
c/o Lipsky Goodkin & Co.
120 W. 45th St., 7th Fl.
New York, NY 10036

Donor(s): Dorothy D. Fitterer, John C. Fitterer.
Financial data (yr. ended 06/30/02): Grants paid, $21,200; assets, $326,739 (M); expenditures, $23,576; qualifying distributions, $21,200.
Limitations: Applications not accepted. Giving primarily in NJ and NY.
Application information: Contributes only to pre-selected organizations.

Officers and Directors:* John C. Fitterer, Jr.,* Pres.; Lorraine F. Kaplan,* V.P.; Philip P. Goodkin, Secy.-Treas.
EIN: 136211439

37860
Murray Goodgold Foundation, Inc.
1020 Park Ave.
New York, NY 10028
Contact: Sally Goodgold, Tr.

Established in 1996 in NY.
Donor(s): Jay Goodgold.
Financial data (yr. ended 03/31/01): Grants paid, $21,200; assets, $196,273 (M); gifts received, $50,050; expenditures, $23,307; qualifying distributions, $21,200.
Trustee: Sally Goodgold.
EIN: 133891430

37861
Hedbring Foundation
c/o Teal, Becker, & Chiaramonte
3 Washington Sq.
Albany, NY 12205

Established in 1992 in NY.
Donor(s): Olle E.S. Hedbring, The Fort Miller Group.
Financial data (yr. ended 12/31/01): Grants paid, $21,200; assets, $84,521 (M); expenditures, $22,184; qualifying distributions, $21,200.
Limitations: Applications not accepted. Giving primarily in MA and NY.
Application information: Contributes only to pre-selected organization.
Officers: John T. Hedbring, Pres.; Olle E.S. Hedbring, Secy.; Claudine Hedbring, Treas.
EIN: 223121049

37862
A. J. Ostriker Foundation, Inc.
2 Pondview E.
Purchase, NY 10577-1608

Financial data (yr. ended 05/31/02): Grants paid, $21,200; assets, $199,017 (M); expenditures, $22,112; qualifying distributions, $21,200.
Limitations: Applications not accepted. Giving primarily in the metropolitan New York, NY, area.
Application information: Contributes only to pre-selected organizations.
Officers: Joy Helman, Pres.; Gilbert Helman, Secy.; Denice Rein, Treas.
EIN: 136067326

37863
Mukhtyar Family Scholarship & Charitable Foundation, Inc.
85 Hamilton Oval
New Rochelle, NY 10805-2901
Contact: Dilip Mukhtyar, Pres.

Established in 1995 in NY.
Donor(s): Dilip Mukhtyar.
Financial data (yr. ended 12/31/01): Grants paid, $21,177; assets, $208,762 (M); gifts received, $27,722; expenditures, $21,927; qualifying distributions, $21,177.
Limitations: Giving primarily in India.
Officers: Dilip Mukhtyar, Pres.; Usha Mukhtyar, V.P.; Shailja Mukhtyar, Secy.
EIN: 133865576

37864
Irma & Arthur Miller Family Foundation, Inc.
995 5th Ave.
New York, NY 10028

Established in 1997 in NY.
Donor(s): Irma A. Miller.

37864—NEW YORK

Financial data (yr. ended 08/31/01): Grants paid, $21,150; assets, $281,687 (M); expenditures, $22,268; qualifying distributions, $21,150.
Limitations: Applications not accepted.
Application information: Contributes only to pre-selected organizations.
Directors: Judith Ann Abrams, Irma A. Miller, Jon Stevens.
EIN: 133980940

37865
Jay & Sandra Harris Foundation, Inc.
c/o Goldsmith & Harris
80 Pine St.
New York, NY 10005-1702

Established in 1986 in NY.
Donor(s): Jay R. Harris.
Financial data (yr. ended 12/31/01): Grants paid, $21,145; assets, $529,973 (M); gifts received, $180; expenditures, $22,660; qualifying distributions, $21,145.
Limitations: Applications not accepted. Giving primarily in New York, NY.
Application information: Contributes only to pre-selected organizations.
Officers: Jay R. Harris, Pres.; Lisa Eng, V.P.; Arthur Friedman, Secy.
EIN: 133389570

37866
The Muchnick Family Foundation
(Formerly Max Muchnick Foundation)
P.O. Box 10
Blue Point, NY 11715-0010

Financial data (yr. ended 09/30/01): Grants paid, $21,145; assets, $93,961 (M); gifts received, $3,111; expenditures, $21,910; qualifying distributions, $21,145.
Limitations: Applications not accepted.
Application information: Contributes only to pre-selected organizations.
Trustee: Saul Muchnick.
EIN: 112587660

37867
Community Foundation of Unadilla, New York, Inc.
P.O. Box 608
Unadilla, NY 13849-0608

Financial data (yr. ended 05/31/00): Grants paid, $21,138; assets, $468,052 (M); gifts received, $5,434; expenditures, $21,484.
Limitations: Giving limited to Unadilla, NY.
Officers: Charles Fisk, Pres.; William Bauer, V.P.; Ruth Lord, Secy.; Jon Fisher, Treas.
EIN: 237066561
Codes: CM

37868
The Robert D. Flickinger Foundation
161 Hidden Ridge Common
Williamsville, NY 14221 (716) 633-6278

Established in 1985 in NY.
Donor(s): Robert D. Flickinger.
Financial data (yr. ended 12/31/01): Grants paid, $21,135; assets, $473,728 (M); expenditures, $22,321; qualifying distributions, $20,805.
Limitations: Applications not accepted. Giving primarily in NY.
Application information: Contributes only to pre-selected organizations.
Trustees: Greta L. Flickinger, Louise A. Flickinger, Robert D. Flickinger.
EIN: 161265415

37869
The O. & M. Abraham Foundation
955 E. 12th St.
Brooklyn, NY 11230

Established in 1993 in NY.
Donor(s): Oscar Abraham.
Financial data (yr. ended 12/31/01): Grants paid, $21,121; assets, $283,825 (M); expenditures, $21,319; qualifying distributions, $21,164.
Limitations: Applications not accepted. Giving primarily in Brooklyn, NY.
Application information: Contributes only to pre-selected organizations.
Trustees: Marilyn Abraham, Oscar Abraham.
EIN: 113181204

37870
Robert & Nancy Ellin Family Foundation
c/o Miller, Ellin & Co., LLP
750 Lexington Ave.
New York, NY 10022-1200

Established in 1999 in NY.
Donor(s): Robert Ellin.
Financial data (yr. ended 11/30/01): Grants paid, $21,116; assets, $58,193 (M); expenditures, $21,570; qualifying distributions, $21,116.
Limitations: Applications not accepted. Giving primarily in Riverdale, NY.
Application information: Contributes only to pre-selected organizations.
Trustee: S. Wakeham.
EIN: 134092847

37871
Jack & Hilda Schulder Foundation, Inc.
350 5th Ave.
New York, NY 10118 (212) 244-1200
Contact: Jacob J. Schulder, Pres.

Donor(s): Jacob J. Schulder, Hilda Schulder.
Financial data (yr. ended 06/30/02): Grants paid, $21,050; assets, $158,364 (M); expenditures, $24,315; qualifying distributions, $21,050.
Limitations: Giving primarily in the greater New York, NY, area.
Application information: Application form not required.
Officer and Directors:* Jacob J. Schulder,* Pres. and Treas.; Diane Schulder Abrams, Sylvia Schulder Fisher.
EIN: 136203666

37872
Medwick Foundation, Inc.
22 Greene Ln.
White Plains, NY 10605 (914) 428-9437
Contact: Shirley Medwick, Pres.

Donor(s): Maury P. Medwick.‡
Financial data (yr. ended 12/31/01): Grants paid, $21,038; assets, $200,363 (M); expenditures, $21,187; qualifying distributions, $21,013.
Limitations: Giving primarily in Larchmont and New York, NY.
Officers: Shirley Medwick, Pres.; Cathleen Silberman, Treas.
EIN: 136154188

37873
Meade Foundation, Inc.
425 E. Lake Rd.
Hammondsport, NY 14840
Contact: J.F. Meade, Jr., Tr.

Established in 1989 in NY.
Donor(s): J.F. Meade, Jr.
Financial data (yr. ended 12/31/01): Grants paid, $21,033; assets, $2,320,000 (M); gifts received, $587; expenditures, $173,186; qualifying distributions, $21,033.
Limitations: Giving primarily in Hammondsport, NY.
Application information: Application form not required.
Trustees: Helen B. Meade, J.F. Meade, Jr., J.F. Meade III.
EIN: 161339424

37874
Basser Arts Foundation
c/o Harold Bobroff
795 Hampton Rd.
Woodmere, NY 11598
Application address: 225 Central Park W., New York, NY 10024
Contact: Wendy Orange, Mgr.

Donor(s): Wendy Orange.
Financial data (yr. ended 12/31/99): Grants paid, $21,000; assets, $92,560 (M); gifts received, $32,500; expenditures, $22,136; qualifying distributions, $21,823.
Limitations: Giving primarily in Washington, DC, and NY; some giving also in Israel.
Application information: Application form not required.
Managers: Harold Bobroff, Wendy Orange.
EIN: 133193560

37875
Chinese Christian Fellowship, Inc.
549 W. 123rd St.
New York, NY 10027

Financial data (yr. ended 09/30/99): Grants paid, $21,000; assets, $157,902 (M); gifts received, $48,393; expenditures, $55,985; qualifying distributions, $0.
Limitations: Applications not accepted.
Officers: Xuan-He Sha, Pres.; Alice Wong, Treas.
Directors: Timothy Chang, Yen Fung.
EIN: 136169142

37876
Joseph L. Fisher Foundation, Inc.
45 E. Broadway
Long Beach, NY 11561-4106 (516) 431-5765
Contact: Ellen M. Rosen, Secy.

Financial data (yr. ended 11/30/01): Grants paid, $21,000; assets, $434,635 (M); expenditures, $28,222; qualifying distributions, $24,986.
Limitations: Giving primarily in New York, NY.
Application information: Application form not required.
Officers: Dan Storper, Pres.; Ellen M. Rosen, Secy.
EIN: 136124971

37877
JMB Hope Foundation
c/o Cleary, Gottlieb, Steen & Hamilton
1 Liberty Plz.
New York, NY 10006-1470

Established in 1998 in NY.
Donor(s): Thomas W. Brock, Julie M. Brock.
Financial data (yr. ended 05/31/01): Grants paid, $21,000; assets, $1,284,714 (M); expenditures, $28,500; qualifying distributions, $21,000.
Limitations: Applications not accepted. Giving primarily in NY.
Application information: Contributes only to pre-selected organizations.
Trustee: Julie M. Brock.
EIN: 134014003

37878
John Allen Jones Family Charitable Foundation
55 Pineapple St., Ste. 1D
Brooklyn, NY 11201

Established in 2000.
Financial data (yr. ended 12/31/01): Grants paid, $21,000; assets, $446,476 (M); expenditures, $21,897; qualifying distributions, $21,000.
Trustee: Bonnie S. Jones.
EIN: 116540455

37879
Schilthuis Foundation, Inc.
315 E. 72nd St.
New York, NY 10021 (212) 734-1169
Contact: Carel Schilthuis, Treas.

Financial data (yr. ended 12/31/01): Grants paid, $21,000; assets, $284,818 (M); gifts received, $300; expenditures, $23,043; qualifying distributions, $21,000.
Limitations: Giving primarily in CT.
Officers: Sally Johnson, Pres.; Pamela Rossback, V.P.; Joel Karp, Secy.; Carel Schilthuis, Treas.
EIN: 066036024

37880
The Wendy Foundation
c/o Starr & Co.
350 Park Ave.
New York, NY 10022

Established in 1995.
Donor(s): Gus Van Sant, Jr.
Financial data (yr. ended 12/31/01): Grants paid, $21,000; assets, $144,413 (M); gifts received, $52,479; expenditures, $21,676; qualifying distributions, $21,000.
Limitations: Applications not accepted. Giving primarily in Portland, OR.
Application information: Contributes only to pre-selected organizations.
Directors: D.J. Haanraadts, Gus Van Sant, Sr., Gus Van Sant, Jr.
EIN: 931191915

37881
Siegmund and Irma Rosenthal Foundation
c/o David A. Weiner
35 Doctor Frank Rd.
Spring Valley, NY 10977-2518
(845) 425-1305
Contact: Jonathan Herlands, Secy.

Established in 1995 in NY.
Donor(s): Irma Rosenthal.‡
Financial data (yr. ended 12/31/01): Grants paid, $20,990; assets, $395,245 (M); expenditures, $25,297; qualifying distributions, $20,990.
Officers: David Wiener, Pres. and Treas.; Harry Eisenstein, V.P.; Jonathan Herlands, Secy.
EIN: 133764063

37882
Arthur L. Horniker Trust
5 Lattingtown Wood Ct.
Lattingtown, NY 11560-1319

Established in 1999 in NY.
Donor(s): Arthur L. Horniker.‡
Financial data (yr. ended 12/31/00): Grants paid, $20,935; assets, $486,900 (M); expenditures, $42,058; qualifying distributions, $20,935.
Limitations: Applications not accepted. Giving primarily in New York, NY.
Application information: Contributes only to pre-selected organizations.
Trustees: Alexander Edelman, Neal Merbaum.
EIN: 137140153

37883
David Gotterer Charitable Trust
400 Park Ave., Ste. 1200
New York, NY 10022-4406 (212) 826-6000
Contact: David Gotterer, Tr.

Established in 1986 in NY.
Donor(s): David Gotterer.
Financial data (yr. ended 11/30/01): Grants paid, $20,928; assets, $308,217 (M); expenditures, $21,301; qualifying distributions, $20,928.
Limitations: Giving primarily in NY.
Application information: Application form not required.
Trustees: David Gotterer, Marilyn Gotterer.
EIN: 133389544

37884
R & R Family Foundation
c/o M. Rausman
270 Grandview Ave.
Monsey, NY 10952-2947

Established in 1985 in NY.
Donor(s): Joe Newmann, Emil Rausman, Martin Rausman, Maseld Realty, R & R Assocs., Rauscher Assocs.
Financial data (yr. ended 06/30/01): Grants paid, $20,913; assets, $494,005 (M); gifts received, $437,579; expenditures, $25,339; qualifying distributions, $20,913.
Limitations: Applications not accepted. Giving primarily in NY.
Application information: Contributes only to pre-selected organizations.
Officers: Martin Rausman, Pres.; Herbert Rausman, Secy.
EIN: 227112485

37885
Albert N. & Esther B. Cory Foundation, Inc.
109 Montgomery Ave.
Scarsdale, NY 10583-5531

Financial data (yr. ended 12/31/00): Grants paid, $20,910; assets, $907,643 (M); expenditures, $24,004; qualifying distributions, $20,910.
Limitations: Applications not accepted. Giving primarily in New York, NY.
Application information: Contributes only to pre-selected organizations.
Trustees: David Cory, Ellen C. Epstein.
EIN: 136161966

37886
Frank Cassata Family Foundation
200 W. Main St., Ste. 102
Babylon, NY 11702

Established in 1995 in NY.
Donor(s): Frank Cassata.
Financial data (yr. ended 12/31/01): Grants paid, $20,900; assets, $824,270 (M); gifts received, $200,000; expenditures, $68,181; qualifying distributions, $34,110.
Limitations: Giving primarily in Long Island, NY.
Trustees: Frank Cassata, Rosaron C. Cassata, Rosario S. Cassata, Vincent Cassata.
EIN: 113270612

37887
David & Rae Wiener Foundation, Inc.
c/o Lipsky, Goodkin & Co.
120 W. 45th St., Ste. 11A
New York, NY 10036

Financial data (yr. ended 04/30/02): Grants paid, $20,874; assets, $475,207 (M); expenditures, $23,643; qualifying distributions, $20,874.
Limitations: Applications not accepted.
Application information: Contributes only to pre-selected organizations.
Officers: Norma Van Riper, Pres.; Harrison Wiener, V.P.; Louis Wiener, Secy.
EIN: 136151883

37888
Gerald and Nedra Bloch Family Foundation
c/o Gerald Bloch
21 E. 87st St.
New York, NY 10128

Established in 1994.
Donor(s): Gerald Bloch.
Financial data (yr. ended 12/31/00): Grants paid, $20,861; assets, $359,215 (M); expenditures, $21,357; qualifying distributions, $20,861.
Limitations: Applications not accepted. Giving primarily in New York, NY.
Application information: Contributes only to pre-selected organizations.
Officers: Gerald Bloch, Pres.; Nedra Bloch, Secy.
EIN: 133711606

37889
The Theodore N. Mirvis Foundation
c/o Wachtell, Lipton, Rosen & Katz
51 W. 52nd St.
New York, NY 10019

Donor(s): Theodore N. Mirvis.
Financial data (yr. ended 04/30/01): Grants paid, $20,833; assets, $140,698 (M); gifts received, $54,710; expenditures, $22,183; qualifying distributions, $20,833.
Limitations: Applications not accepted.
Application information: Contributes only to pre-selected organizations.
Officers and Directors:* Theodore N. Mirvis,* Pres.; Ruth Lynn Mirvis,* V.P.; Michael G. Jesselson.
EIN: 133386656

37890
Benjamin & Rivka Gelbtuch Charitable Trust
4900 Blackstone Ave.
Riverdale, NY 10471

Established in 1997 in NY.
Donor(s): Benjamin Gelbtuch, Rivka Gelbtuch.
Financial data (yr. ended 12/31/01): Grants paid, $20,800; assets, $106,078 (M); gifts received, $30,000; expenditures, $22,357; qualifying distributions, $22,357.
Limitations: Applications not accepted.
Application information: Contributes only to pre-selected organizations.
Officers: Benjamin Gelbtuch, Pres.; Rivka Gelbtuch, V.P.
EIN: 226726579

37891
Weisbuch Aid Fund
c/o Paul Berman
455 W. 34th St., Apt. 5-F
New York, NY 10001

Donor(s): Manuel Weisbuch.‡
Financial data (yr. ended 12/31/01): Grants paid, $20,775; assets, $319,984 (M); expenditures, $21,430; qualifying distributions, $20,595.
Limitations: Giving primarily in MA and NY.
Trustee: Paul Berman.
EIN: 116037951

37892
The Tashlik Family Charitable Foundation
9 Overlook Cir.
Manhasset, NY 11030-3933

Established in 1996 in NY.
Donor(s): Susan Tashlik.

Financial data (yr. ended 12/31/01): Grants paid, $20,710; assets, $316,258 (M); gifts received, $400; expenditures, $22,987; qualifying distributions, $20,710.
Limitations: Applications not accepted.
Application information: Contributes only to pre-selected organizations.
Trustees: Ivy N. Tashlik, Jill D. Tashlik, Scott J. Tashlik, Susan A. Tashlik, Theodore William Tashlik.
EIN: 113350060

37893
The Nossen Foundation, Inc.
c/o Israel A. Press
1280 Ocean Pkwy.
Brooklyn, NY 11230

Established in 1990 in NY.
Donor(s): A. Grosz, Robert Frankel.
Financial data (yr. ended 11/30/01): Grants paid, $20,700; assets, $366,318 (M); gifts received, $50,000; expenditures, $21,172; qualifying distributions, $20,700.
Limitations: Applications not accepted. Giving primarily in Passaic, NJ, and Brooklyn, NY.
Application information: Contributes only to pre-selected organizations.
Officers: Israel A. Press, Pres. and Secy.; Robert Frankel, V.P. and Treas.
EIN: 113038143

37894
University Associates Philanthropic Foundation, Inc.
c/o The Rockefeller University
1230 York Ave.
New York, NY 10021-6399

Established in 1981.
Financial data (yr. ended 06/30/01): Grants paid, $20,683; assets, $511,410 (M); gifts received, $215,871; expenditures, $28,086; qualifying distributions, $20,683.
Limitations: Applications not accepted. Giving primarily in NY.
Application information: Unsolicited requests for funds not accepted.
Officers and Directors:* Richard M. Furlaud,* Pres.; Maren E. Imhoff, Secy.; John J. Harrigan, Cont.; Alexander Forger.
EIN: 061051736

37895
Kleinow Family Foundation, Inc.
c/o Charles D. Kleinow
P.O. Box 598
Scarsdale, NY 10583

Established in 1997 in NY.
Donor(s): Lisa Kleinow, Charles D. Kleinow.
Financial data (yr. ended 12/31/01): Grants paid, $20,660; assets, $197,684 (M); gifts received, $10,400; expenditures, $23,194; qualifying distributions, $20,641.
Limitations: Applications not accepted. Giving primarily in NY.
Application information: Contributes only to pre-selected organizations.
Directors: Charles D. Kleinow, Lisa Kleinow, Russell Vergess.
EIN: 133940659

37896
Lucy & Hyman Grotsky Foundation, Inc.
c/o Muchnick, Golieb & Golieb, PC
200 Park Ave. S., Ste. 1700
New York, NY 10003 (212) 315-5575
Contact: Stephen Grotsky, Mgr.

Established in 1975.
Donor(s): Hyman Grotsky,‡ Lucy Grotsky.‡
Financial data (yr. ended 09/30/02): Grants paid, $20,600; assets, $1,896 (M); expenditures, $22,050; qualifying distributions, $20,600.
Limitations: Giving on a national basis.
Officer and Trustees:* Stephen Grotsky,* Mgr.; Barton Sadowsky, Connie Sadowsky.
EIN: 510164587

37897
LGT Foundation
c/o Lenore Tawney
32 W. 20th St., No. 5
New York, NY 10011

Established in 1995 in NY.
Donor(s): Lenore Tawney.
Financial data (yr. ended 07/31/01): Grants paid, $20,600; assets, $479,746 (M); expenditures, $22,388; qualifying distributions, $20,600.
Limitations: Applications not accepted.
Application information: Contributes only to pre-selected organizations.
Officers: Lenore Tawney, Pres.; Kathleen Mangan, Secy.; Ellyn A. Sosin, Treas.
Directors: Rebecca Rawson, Paul J. Smith, Toshiko Takaezu.
EIN: 061281494

37898
Florence & Ben Barrack Foundation, Inc.
25 Sutton Pl., S.
New York, NY 10022-2441 (212) 755-7525
Contact: Florence Barrack, Dir.

Donor(s): Ben Barrack,‡ Florence Barrack.
Financial data (yr. ended 09/30/01): Grants paid, $20,560; assets, $454,930 (M); expenditures, $23,116; qualifying distributions, $20,560.
Limitations: Giving primarily in NY.
Directors: Florence Barrack, Martin Feldman, Sinclair Korman.
EIN: 136188601

37899
The Marans Family Foundation Trust
564 Redwood Dr.
Cedarhurst, NY 11516

Established in 2000 in NY.
Donor(s): Arnold Marans, Zipporah Marans.
Financial data (yr. ended 12/31/01): Grants paid, $20,556; assets, $45,480 (M); expenditures, $23,552; qualifying distributions, $20,556.
Limitations: Applications not accepted. Giving primarily in the greater metropolitan New York, NY, area.
Application information: Contributes only to pre-selected organizations.
Trustees: Arnold Marans, Zipporah Marans.
EIN: 113556962

37900
S.J. Rosica Family Foundation
100 Corporate Pkwy., Ste.136
Amherst, NY 14226-1200

Established in 1997 in NY.
Donor(s): Msgr. Andrew J. McGowan, Sebastian J. Rosica.
Financial data (yr. ended 12/31/01): Grants paid, $20,540; assets, $464,118 (M); gifts received, $1,000; expenditures, $29,403; qualifying distributions, $20,540.
Limitations: Applications not accepted. Giving primarily in NY.
Application information: Contributes only to pre-selected organizations.
Officers and Directors:* Sebastian J. Rosica,* Pres.; Mark J. Rosica,* V.P. and Treas.; Lenore M. Rosica,* Secy.; A. Joseph Rosica, Daniel J. Rosica, Francis X. Rosica, Kathryn A. Rosica, Marianne Rosica-Brand.
EIN: 161526591

37901
Edward E. & Mildred E. Finch Foundation, Inc.
1400 Old Country Rd.
Westbury, NY 11590

Donor(s): Edward E. Finch.
Financial data (yr. ended 06/30/02): Grants paid, $20,520; assets, $330,667 (M); expenditures, $22,329; qualifying distributions, $20,520.
Limitations: Applications not accepted.
Application information: Contributes only to pre-selected organizations.
Directors: Edward E. Finch, Mildred E. Finch, Raymond E. Finch.
EIN: 113410806

37902
Chenango County Medical Society & Otsego County Medical Society, Trustees for the Van Wagner Scholarship
c/o NBT Bank, N.A.
52 S. Broad St.
Norwich, NY 13815-1646
Application address: c/o Kathleen E. Dyman, 4311 Middle Settlement Rd., New Hartford, NY 13413

Established in 1970 in NY.
Financial data (yr. ended 04/30/02): Grants paid, $20,500; assets, $308,128 (M); gifts received, $2,000; expenditures, $25,395; qualifying distributions, $24,389.
Limitations: Giving limited to residents of Chenango and Otsego counties, NY.
Application information: Application form required.
Officer and Trustees: John R. Brereton, M.D., Cynthia Briglin, M.D., Robert V. Davidson, M.D., Grace D. Holmes, M.D., Joseph Hughes, M.D., John Lusins, M.D., Paul Orioli, M.D., Donald Raddatz, M.D.
EIN: 237325443
Codes: GTI

37903
Graywood Foundation, Inc.
c/o Kenton Wood
779 CR 403
Greenville, NY 12083

Donor(s): Kenton Wood.
Financial data (yr. ended 11/30/01): Grants paid, $20,500; assets, $443,995 (M); expenditures, $21,850; qualifying distributions, $20,500.
Limitations: Giving primarily in NY.
Officers and Directors:* Kenton Wood,* Pres. and Treas.; Katrina Wood,* V.P. and Secy.; Jennifer Wood.
EIN: 133800478

37904
Irenaeus Foundation
800 Fleet Bank Bldg.
Buffalo, NY 14202-2292
Application address: 37 Larsen Ln., West Seneca, NY 14224, tel.: (716) 843-3850
Contact: Peter M. Heffernan, Tr.

Established in 1992 in NY.
Donor(s): John J. Heffernan Trust.
Financial data (yr. ended 12/31/99): Grants paid, $20,500; assets, $2,902 (M); gifts received, $22,000; expenditures, $20,780; qualifying distributions, $20,780.
Limitations: Giving primarily in NY.
Application information: Application form not required.

Trustees: J.J. Cordes, M.O. Heffernan, N.C. Heffernan, Peter M. Heffernan.
EIN: 161428687

37905
M. Jeanne Place Charitable Foundation
2859 River Rd.
Niskayuna, NY 12309-1132

Established in 1998 in NY.
Donor(s): M. Jeanne Place.
Financial data (yr. ended 12/31/01): Grants paid, $20,500; assets, $80,008 (M); gifts received, $11,805; expenditures, $21,319; qualifying distributions, $20,500.
Officer: M. Jeanne Place, Pres.
Director: A.H. Lowe, Jr.
EIN: 141805031

37906
Seven Lamps Foundation, Inc.
40 Oxford Rd.
New Rochelle, NY 10804

Donor(s): Madeleine F. Stebbins.
Financial data (yr. ended 12/31/01): Grants paid, $20,500; assets, $220,273 (M); expenditures, $22,497; qualifying distributions, $20,500.
Limitations: Applications not accepted. Giving primarily in NY.
Application information: Contributes only to pre-selected organizations.
Officers: Madeleine F. Stebbins, Pres.; Henrietta Schwartz, V.P.; Gerald E. Murray, Secy.
EIN: 131988881

37907
The Shoe Charitable Foundation
c/o Theodore C.C. Chu
127 E. 30th St., Ste. 5B
New York, NY 10016-7373

Established in 1999 in NY.
Donor(s): Theodore C.C. Chu.
Financial data (yr. ended 12/31/01): Grants paid, $20,500; assets, $763 (M); expenditures, $20,500; qualifying distributions, $20,500.
Limitations: Applications not accepted. Giving primarily in New York, NY.
Application information: Contributes only to pre-selected organizations.
Officers: Theodore C.C. Chu, Pres. and Treas.; Yvonee C. Meinwald, V.P.; Chia-Kun Chu, Secy.
EIN: 134090052

37908
Wolinetz Family Foundation
14 Cloverdale Ln.
Monsey, NY 10952

Established in 1999 in NY.
Financial data (yr. ended 12/31/01): Grants paid, $20,500; assets, $13,179 (M); gifts received, $25,784; expenditures, $20,539; qualifying distributions, $20,499.
Limitations: Applications not accepted.
Application information: Contributes only to pre-selected organizations.
Officers: Harvey Wolinetz, Pres.; Naomi Wolinetz, V.P.; Rena Katz, Treas.
EIN: 137186953

37909
The Brinckerhoff Foundation
68 Main St.
P.O. Box 424
Fishkill, NY 12524

Established in 1998 in DE.
Donor(s): Brinckerhoff & Neuville, Inc.
Financial data (yr. ended 10/31/01): Grants paid, $20,487; assets, $61,894 (M); gifts received, $23,280; expenditures, $22,209; qualifying distributions, $21,789.
Limitations: Applications not accepted. Giving primarily in NY.
Application information: Contributes only to pre-selected organizations.
Officers: Barbara B. Tead, Pres.; Beverly Brinckerhoff, V.P.; Mary E. Brinckerhoff, Secy.; Margaret Brinckerhoff Gentsch, Treas.
EIN: 141805812
Codes: CS, CD

37910
Badger State Civic Fund, Inc.
1331 Broad St.
Syracuse, NY 13224-1919 (315) 446-4433
Contact: Dr. Hans Hartenstein, Pres.; or Mary Louise Hartenstein, Secy.

Donor(s): Hans Hartenstein, Mrs. Hans Hartenstein.
Financial data (yr. ended 12/31/01): Grants paid, $20,450; assets, $259,135 (M); gifts received, $11,000; expenditures, $21,815; qualifying distributions, $20,450.
Limitations: Giving primarily in Syracuse, NY.
Officers: Hans Hartenstein, Pres.; Ann Hartenstein, V.P.; Julie Hartenstein, V.P.; Mary Louise Hartenstein, Secy.
EIN: 396074988

37911
Delaware National Bank of Delhi Corporate Charitable Trust
c/o Delaware Nat'l Bank
124-126 Main St.
Delhi, NY 13753

Established in 1996 in NY.
Donor(s): Delaware National Bank.
Financial data (yr. ended 12/31/01): Grants paid, $20,400; assets, $108,252 (M); expenditures, $20,817; qualifying distributions, $20,383.
Limitations: Applications not accepted. Giving primarily in DE.
Application information: Contributes only to pre-selected organizations.
Trustee: The Delaware National Bank of Delhi.
EIN: 166447080
Codes: CS

37912
Goldner Family Charitable Foundation
1251 46th St.
Brooklyn, NY 11219

Established in 1998.
Financial data (yr. ended 12/31/01): Grants paid, $20,400; assets, $60,253 (M); expenditures, $20,450; qualifying distributions, $20,400.
Trustee: Sandor Goldner.
EIN: 113419243

37913
Norman P. Rappaport Foundation, Inc.
650 Park Ave.
New York, NY 10021-6115
Contact: Norman P. Rappaport, Pres.

Donor(s): Norman P. Rappaport.
Financial data (yr. ended 11/30/01): Grants paid, $20,385; assets, $49,049 (M); gifts received, $17,560; expenditures, $20,559; qualifying distributions, $20,385.
Limitations: Giving primarily in NY.
Officer: Norman P. Rappaport, Pres.
EIN: 132881142

37914
The Shore Family Foundation, Inc.
Lighthouse Rd.
Sands Point, NY 11050

Established in 1997 in NY.
Financial data (yr. ended 12/31/01): Grants paid, $20,347; assets, $1,167,189 (M); expenditures, $24,282; qualifying distributions, $20,347.
Limitations: Applications not accepted.
Application information: Unsolicited requests for funds not accepted.
Officers and Directors:* Jerry Shore, Chair., Pres. and Treas.; Cecile Shore,* V.P. and Secy.; Brian Shore,* V.P.; Peter Shore,* V.P.; Robin Shore,* V.P.
EIN: 133920312

37915
Margaret T. Biddle Paragraph Twelfth Trust
c/o Cusack & Stiles, LLP
61 Broadway, Ste. 2100
New York, NY 10006-2894

Donor(s): Margaret T. Biddle.‡
Financial data (yr. ended 12/31/01): Grants paid, $20,300; assets, $392,104 (M); expenditures, $20,480; qualifying distributions, $19,927.
Application information: Unsolicited requests for funds not accepted.
Trustees: Christian Hohenlohe, Peter Boyce Schulze, Richard A. Smith.
EIN: 136066488
Codes: GTI

37916
Haskell Family Foundation
c/o B. Strauss Assoc., Ltd.
245 5th Ave., No. 1102
New York, NY 10016-8775

Established in 1994 in NY.
Donor(s): John H.F. Haskell, Jr.
Financial data (yr. ended 02/28/02): Grants paid, $20,300; assets, $1,307,340 (M); gifts received, $1,000,300; expenditures, $22,474; qualifying distributions, $20,300.
Limitations: Applications not accepted.
Application information: Contributes only to pre-selected organizations.
Trustees: Diana F.T. Haskell, Francine L.R. Haskell, John H.F. Haskell, Jr.
EIN: 133757928

37917
The Draizin Foundation, Inc.
287 Bowman Ave.
Purchase, NY 10577
Contact: Stephen S. Draizin, Pres.

Established in 1985 in NY.
Donor(s): RAD Oil Co., Inc.
Financial data (yr. ended 12/31/01): Grants paid, $20,270; assets, $512,046 (M); expenditures, $21,639; qualifying distributions, $20,270.
Limitations: Giving primarily in CT and NY.
Officers: Stephen S. Draizin, Pres.; Donald J. Draizin, V. P.; Jennifer Fuchs, Secy.-Treas.; Adam Draizin, Treas.
EIN: 133275008

37918
Gordon Foundation, Inc.
c/o Mrs. W.L. Landau
510 Park Ave.
New York, NY 10022-1160

Financial data (yr. ended 12/31/01): Grants paid, $20,260; assets, $701,789 (M); expenditures, $24,664; qualifying distributions, $23,110.
Limitations: Applications not accepted. Giving on a national basis, with emphasis on NY.

37918—NEW YORK

Application information: Contributes to pre-selected organizations.
Officers: Barbara G. Landau, Pres.; W. Loeber Landau, V.P.; Elaine G. Yaffe, V.P.; Donna Landau Hardiman, Secy.
EIN: 136161724

37919
H & E Foundation
1661 E. 24th St.
Brooklyn, NY 11229

Established in 1998 in NY.
Donor(s): Harry Fuhrer, Evelyn Fuhrer.
Financial data (yr. ended 06/30/01): Grants paid, $20,255; assets, $283,658 (M); expenditures, $20,868; qualifying distributions, $20,255.
Director: Evelyn Fuhrer.
EIN: 113465167

37920
CD 101.9 Smooth Jazz Foundation
395 Hudson St., 7th Fl.
New York, NY 10014
Application address: 30 Derby Ct., Oyster Bay, NY 11771
Contact: Frank Iemmitti

Established in 1999 in NY.
Financial data (yr. ended 12/31/01): Grants paid, $20,250; assets, $14,226 (M); expenditures, $20,779; qualifying distributions, $20,250.
Application information: Application form required.
Officers: Connie Francis Avila, Pres.; Judith Ellis, Secy.; Robert Finley, Treas.
EIN: 134018495

37921
The Andrew M. Carter Charitable Trust
c/o Hyperion Capital Mgmt., Inc.
165 Broadway, 36th Fl.
New York, NY 10006-1404

Established in 1984 in NY.
Donor(s): Andrew M. Carter.
Financial data (yr. ended 12/31/00): Grants paid, $20,225; assets, $798,335 (M); expenditures, $21,900; qualifying distributions, $20,225.
Limitations: Applications not accepted. Giving primarily in Boston, MA.
Application information: Contributes only to pre-selected organizations.
Trustees: Nancy M. Bozhardt, Andrew M. Carter, Joseph P. Lombard.
EIN: 046519030

37922
The Druskin Family Foundation, Inc.
c/o W. Michael Reickert
855 Rte. 146, Ste. 120, P.O. Box 8009
Clifton Park, NY 12065-8009

Established in 1997 in NJ.
Donor(s): Robert Druskin, Harriet Druskin.
Financial data (yr. ended 12/31/99): Grants paid, $20,220; assets, $286,540 (M); expenditures, $22,485; qualifying distributions, $20,220.
Limitations: Applications not accepted.
Application information: Contributes only to pre-selected organizations.
Officer: Robert A. Druskin, Pres.
Trustee: Ben Druskin.
EIN: 223512395

37923
E. Magnus Oppenheim Foundation, Inc.
551 5th Ave.
New York, NY 10176-0516

Donor(s): E. Magnus Oppenheim.
Financial data (yr. ended 12/31/01): Grants paid, $20,206; assets, $1,798 (M); gifts received, $17,503; expenditures, $20,220; qualifying distributions, $20,206.
Limitations: Giving primarily in New York, NY.
Officers: E. Magnus Oppenheim, Pres.; Rachel Oppenheim, V.P.
EIN: 133050265

37924
The Little Star Foundation
c/o BCRS Assocs., LLC
67 Wall St., 8th Fl.
New York, NY 10005

Donor(s): Thomas J. Macirowski.
Financial data (yr. ended 09/30/01): Grants paid, $20,200; assets, $189,320 (M); expenditures, $21,997; qualifying distributions, $20,200.
Limitations: Applications not accepted. Giving primarily in St. Louis, MO.
Application information: Contributes only to pre-selected organizations.
Trustees: Thomas J. Macirowski, Christina Torbinski-MacRae.
EIN: 133801276

37925
The Dorf Foundation, Inc.
c/o James Dorf
425 E. 79th St.
New York, NY 10021

Donor(s): Dorf International, Inc. of Texas.
Financial data (yr. ended 12/31/01): Grants paid, $20,175; assets, $557,668 (M); expenditures, $21,500; qualifying distributions, $20,650.
Limitations: Applications not accepted. Giving primarily in NY.
Application information: Unsolicited request for funds not accepted.
Officers: Charles B. Dorf, Pres.; James A. Dorf, Treas.
EIN: 136119402
Codes: CS, CD

37926
Brown Family Foundation, Inc.
27 E. 65th St., Ste. 5B
New York, NY 10021

Established in 1993 in NY.
Donor(s): Julius Brown, Gertrude Brown.
Financial data (yr. ended 09/30/02): Grants paid, $20,160; assets, $12,354 (M); gifts received, $25,038; expenditures, $20,240; qualifying distributions, $20,160.
Limitations: Applications not accepted. Giving primarily in NY.
Application information: Contributes only to pre-selected organizations.
Officers: Julius Brown, Pres.; Gertrude Brown, V.P. and Treas.; Catherine Brown, V.P.; Susan Brown, V.P.
EIN: 113177394

37927
Linda B. Gross and Daniel J. Gross Family Foundation, Inc.
c/o Daniel J. Gross
50 Central Park W.
New York, NY 10023

Donor(s): Daniel Gros.
Financial data (yr. ended 12/31/99): Grants paid, $20,150; assets, $127,891 (M); expenditures, $20,433; qualifying distributions, $20,150.
Limitations: Applications not accepted.
Application information: Contributes only to pre-selected organizations.

Officers and Directors:* Linda Gross,* Pres.; Daniel Gross,* Secy.-Treas.; Suzanne Rost.
EIN: 133952035

37928
The Herman Karpel Memorial Foundation, Inc.
c/o Israeloff, Trattner & Co., C.P.A.
11 Sunrise Plz.
Valley Stream, NY 11580
Application address: 1255 N. Ave., New Rochelle, NY 10804
Contact: Phoebe Karpel, Pres.

Donor(s): Victoria Fisher, Phoebe Karpel.‡
Financial data (yr. ended 12/31/01): Grants paid, $20,120; assets, $43,552 (M); gifts received, $10,000; expenditures, $20,342; qualifying distributions, $20,120.
Limitations: Giving primarily in NY.
Application information: Application form not required.
Officers: Phoebe Karpel, Pres.; Victoria Fisher, V.P.; Susan Levine, V.P.; Roberta Silman, V.P.
EIN: 133137962

37929
The Bank of Greene County Charitable Foundation
425 Main St.
Catskill, NY 12414-1300

Established in 1999 in DE and NY.
Donor(s): The Bank of Greene County.
Financial data (yr. ended 06/30/01): Grants paid, $20,100; assets, $516,217 (M); expenditures, $21,651; qualifying distributions, $19,969.
Limitations: Giving primarily in areas of company operations in NY.
Officers and Directors:* J. Bruce Whittaker,* Pres.; Bruce P. Egger, Secy.; Michelle M. Plummer, C.F.O.; Edmund L. Smith, Treas.; Walter H. Ingalls, David H. Jenkins, Raphael Klein, Dennis R. O'Grady, Paul Slutzky, Martin C. Smith.
EIN: 141810419
Codes: CS

37930
The Levi Family Foundation
c/o James H. Levi
85 Larchmont Ave.
Larchmont, NY 10538

Established in 1996 in NY.
Donor(s): James H. Levi.
Financial data (yr. ended 12/31/01): Grants paid, $20,080; assets, $54,070 (M); expenditures, $20,905; qualifying distributions, $20,080.
Limitations: Applications not accepted.
Application information: Contributes only to pre-selected organizations.
Trustees: Constance A. Levi, James H. Levi.
EIN: 137105498

37931
Joseph Suchman Memorial Foundation
c/o Jerry Suchman
46 Hwy.
Chappaqua, NY 10514

Financial data (yr. ended 12/31/01): Grants paid, $20,071; assets, $235,465 (M); expenditures, $22,073; qualifying distributions, $20,071.
Limitations: Applications not accepted.
Application information: Contributes only to pre-selected organizations.
Officers: Ruth Suchman, Pres.; Carol Rosenblum, V.P.; Jerry Suchman, Secy.-Treas.
EIN: 136113177

37932
Yvar Mikhashoff Trust for New Music
P.O. Box 8
Forestville, NY 14062-0008 (716) 965-2128

Established in 1994 in NY.
Financial data (yr. ended 12/31/01): Grants paid, $20,069; assets, $309,175 (M); gifts received, $760; expenditures, $28,569; qualifying distributions, $20,069.
Trustee: Jan Williams.
EIN: 161466808

37933
Carnegie Fund for Authors
1 Old Country Rd.
Carle Place, NY 11514

Financial data (yr. ended 12/31/01): Grants paid, $20,050; assets, $857,702 (M); expenditures, $34,436; qualifying distributions, $26,896.
Limitations: Giving primarily in NY.
Application information: Application form required.
Trustees: Scott Albarella, Barbara Magalnick, William L. Rothenberg.
EIN: 136084244
Codes: GTI

37934
Social Services League of Ithaca, Inc.
200 E. Buffalo St.
Ithaca, NY 14850-4232
Application address: c/o Human Services Coalition, 313 N. Aurora St., Ithaca, NY 14850, tel.: (607) 273-8686
Contact: Nancy Burston

Established in 1989 in NY.
Financial data (yr. ended 12/31/01): Grants paid, $20,050; assets, $357,191 (M); expenditures, $21,506; qualifying distributions, $20,050.
Limitations: Giving limited to Tompkins County, NY.
Officers and Directors:* Annie Wall,* Pres.; Glen Gordon,* V.P.; Frank Smith,* Secy.; Brent Stephans,* Treas.; Judy Jackson, and 5 additional directors.
EIN: 150539122

37935
The John S. and Ann Kaufman Foundation
14 Chedworth Rd.
Scarsdale, NY 10583-3310

Donor(s): Helene M. Kaufman Charitable Lead Annuity Trust B, Central Carolina Warehouses.
Financial data (yr. ended 12/31/01): Grants paid, $20,014; assets, $59,201 (M); gifts received, $15,400; expenditures, $20,097; qualifying distributions, $20,014.
Limitations: Applications not accepted. Giving primarily in the New York, NY, area.
Application information: Contributes only to pre-selected organizations.
Trustee: John S. Kaufman.
EIN: 133140165

37936
Richard Henry Arnold, M.D. and Lazar Joseph Halpern, M.D. Memorial Fund
2785 W. 5th St., Ste. 2A
Brooklyn, NY 11224

Donor(s): Nathalie Halpern Arnold, Gloria Halpern, Harold Halpern.
Financial data (yr. ended 12/31/00): Grants paid, $20,000; assets, $351,536 (M); expenditures, $26,119; qualifying distributions, $22,710.
Limitations: Applications not accepted.
Application information: Contributes only to pre-selected organizations.
Trustees: Gloria Halpern, Harold Halpern.
EIN: 113200916
Codes: GTI

37937
Chappel Foundation, Inc.
727 New Loudon Rd.
Latham, NY 12110 (518) 783-1951
Contact: Louis Pelligrino

Established in 1996 in NY.
Financial data (yr. ended 12/31/00): Grants paid, $20,000; assets, $162,692 (M); expenditures, $20,291; qualifying distributions, $20,000.
Directors: Gregory Finin, Conrad Kupillas, Kevin G. Langan.
EIN: 223143582

37938
The Atsuko Chiba Foundation, Inc.
c/o Berlin Koiln
1790 Broadway, Rm. 705
New York, NY 10019

Established in 1989 in NY.
Donor(s): Atsuko Chiba.
Financial data (yr. ended 01/31/02): Grants paid, $20,000; assets, $954,791 (M); gifts received, $1,000; expenditures, $23,508; qualifying distributions, $20,000.
Limitations: Applications not accepted. Giving primarily in MA.
Application information: Contributes only to pre-selected organizations.
Officer and Directors:* Norman Pearlstine,* Pres.; Dolores Langone, V.P.; Lester Dembitzer, Secy.-Treas.
EIN: 133467232

37939
The Sally Stowe Clemence Family Foundation
c/o U.S. Trust
114 W. 47th St., TaxVas
New York, NY 10036

Established in 1990 in FL.
Donor(s): Sally Stowe Clemence.
Financial data (yr. ended 12/31/01): Grants paid, $20,000; assets, $270,427 (M); expenditures, $23,105; qualifying distributions, $22,741.
Limitations: Applications not accepted. Giving primarily in CT and FL.
Application information: Contributes only to pre-selected organizations.
Officers: Sally Stowe Clemence, Pres. and Treas.; Joan R. Stowe, V.P. and Secy.; John C. Jacques, V.P.; William F. Jacques II, V.P.
EIN: 650147695

37940
Joseph D. and Chaya Cohen Torah Fund
257 W. 86th St., Apt. 2B
New York, NY 10024

Established in 1994.
Donor(s): Joseph Cohen, Chaya Cohen.
Financial data (yr. ended 12/31/01): Grants paid, $20,000; assets, $43,848 (M); gifts received, $25,000; expenditures, $21,229; qualifying distributions, $20,000.
Limitations: Applications not accepted. Giving primarily in the greater metropolitan New York, NY, area.
Application information: Contributes only to pre-selected organizations.
Trustees: Chaya Cohen, Joseph Cohen.
EIN: 137054601

37941
J. Stanley Coyne Foundation, Inc.
P.O. Box 303, 130 Albany St.
Cazenovia, NY 13035 (315) 655-2481
Contact: Raymond T. Ryan, Treas.

Established in 1959.
Donor(s): Coyne International Enterprises, Inc.
Financial data (yr. ended 07/31/01): Grants paid, $20,000; assets, $11,017 (M); gifts received, $20,000; expenditures, $20,025; qualifying distributions, $20,025.
Limitations: Giving primarily in central NY.
Officers and Trustees:* Thomas M. Coyne,* Pres.; Alexander Pobedinsky,* Secy.; Raymond T. Ryan,* Treas.
EIN: 156022086

37942
John Steuart Curry Foundation, Inc.
c/o J. Witmeyer
1300 Clinton Sq.
Rochester, NY 14603

Established in 1997 in NY.
Donor(s): Daniel B. Schuster.‡
Financial data (yr. ended 12/31/00): Grants paid, $20,000; assets, $466,527 (M); expenditures, $22,249; qualifying distributions, $21,935.
Limitations: Applications not accepted.
Application information: Contributes only to pre-selected organizations.
Officers and Directors:* Sarah G. Schuster,* Pres. and Treas.; Lucy Mathiak,* V.P.; Allen C. Smith,* Secy.
EIN: 223127112

37943
Mary Lecomte du Nouy Trust for LDN Foundation
(Formerly Mary Lecomte du Nouy Trust for the Pierre Lecomte du Nouy France Foundation)
c/o U.S. Trust
114 W. 47th St., TaxVas
New York, NY 10036

Financial data (yr. ended 12/31/01): Grants paid, $20,000; assets, $486,515 (M); expenditures, $30,163; qualifying distributions, $20,000.
Limitations: Giving primarily in New York, NY.
Trustee: U.S. Trust.
EIN: 136786343

37944
Ecolint-American Foundation
c/o Salibello & Broder
633 Third Ave., 13th Fl.
New York, NY 10017-6708 (212) 315-5000

Financial data (yr. ended 12/31/01): Grants paid, $20,000; assets, $38,548 (M); gifts received, $38,923; expenditures, $21,798; qualifying distributions, $20,000.
Limitations: Applications not accepted.
Application information: Contributes only to pre-selected organizations.
Officers and Trustees:* Theodore J. Killheffer,* Pres.; Zachary Greenhill,* Secy.; Marcia Crabtree, Jonathan Greenhill, Elaine McClure, Asha Singh-Williams.
EIN: 237056392

37945
The Eisner Charitable Foundation, Inc.
1716 47th St.
Brooklyn, NY 11204

Established in 1998 in NY.
Donor(s): Abe Eisner.

37945—NEW YORK

Financial data (yr. ended 11/30/01): Grants paid, $20,000; assets, $95,785 (M); expenditures, $20,234; qualifying distributions, $20,000.
Limitations: Applications not accepted.
Application information: Contributes only to pre-selected organizations.
Officers: Abe Eisner, Pres.; Nellie Eisner, V.P.; Miriam Eder, Treas.
EIN: 134030709

37946
Galewitz Family Foundation
c/o JPMorgan Chase Bank
P.O. Box 31412
Rochester, NY 14603
Application address: 1 Chase Manhattan Plz., 5th Fl., New York, NY 10081-1000, tel.: (212) 552-2576
Contact: Andrew Noll, Trust Off., JPMorgan Chase Bank

Financial data (yr. ended 12/31/01): Grants paid, $20,000; assets, $267,239 (M); expenditures, $23,453; qualifying distributions, $20,151.
Limitations: Giving primarily in NY.
Application information: Application form not required.
Trustee: JPMorgan Chase Bank.
EIN: 136030936

37947
The Grey Blanket Foundation
200 Theater Pl.
Buffalo, NY 14202 (716) 853-8671
Contact: Thomas R. Beecher, Jr., Tr.

Established in 1997 in NY.
Donor(s): Michele Jacobs.
Financial data (yr. ended 12/31/01): Grants paid, $20,000; assets, $438,624 (M); gifts received, $93,245; expenditures, $23,986; qualifying distributions, $20,000.
Limitations: Giving primarily in CA.
Trustees: Thomas R. Beecher, Jr., Luke T. Jacobs, Michele Jacobs.
EIN: 166454226

37948
E. T. Harmax Foundation
54 Riverside Dr., Apt. 16A
New York, NY 10024-6553 (212) 580-7660
Contact: Mark Levine, Pres.

Established in 1986 in NY.
Donor(s): Mark Levine.
Financial data (yr. ended 11/30/01): Grants paid, $20,000; assets, $43,043 (M); expenditures, $20,013; qualifying distributions, $20,000.
Limitations: Giving primarily in New York, NY.
Officer: Mark Levine, Pres.
Trustee: Elizabeth Levine.
EIN: 133416101

37949
Heffner Rosenwald Howard Foundation, Inc.
101 S. Bedford Rd., Ste. 203A
Mount Kisco, NY 10549

Established in 1989 in NY.
Donor(s): Barnaby J. Howard.
Financial data (yr. ended 09/30/01): Grants paid, $20,000; assets, $203,535 (M); gifts received, $50; expenditures, $22,141; qualifying distributions, $20,000.
Limitations: Applications not accepted.
Application information: Contributes only to pre-selected organizations.
Officer and Directors:* Barnaby J. Howard,* Pres.; Michael Heffner.
EIN: 133562092

37950
Salem and Annabel Jacoff Family Foundation, Inc.
c/o Berlack, Israels & Liberman
120 W. 45th St.
New York, NY 10036

Established in 1991 in NY.
Donor(s): Salem Jacoff,‡ Annabel Jacoff.‡
Financial data (yr. ended 12/31/01): Grants paid, $20,000; assets, $378,011 (M); expenditures, $24,773; qualifying distributions, $20,000.
Limitations: Applications not accepted. Giving primarily in NY.
Application information: Contributes only to pre-selected organizations.
Officers: Robert Jacoff, Pres. and Treas.; Mark Jacoff, V.P. and Secy.
EIN: 133637754

37951
The Jennifer Foundation, Inc.
c/o J. Huntley
89 Mill River Rd.
Oyster Bay, NY 11771

Established in 1997 in NY.
Donor(s): Jennifer S. Huntley.
Financial data (yr. ended 12/31/01): Grants paid, $20,000; assets, $545,229 (M); gifts received, $3,361; expenditures, $23,361; qualifying distributions, $20,000.
Limitations: Applications not accepted. Giving primarily in NY.
Application information: Contributes only to pre-selected organizations.
Officers: Jennifer S. Huntley, Pres.; Helen Brosseau, V.P.; Cynthia Smith DaCosta, V.P.
EIN: 113295380

37952
Jewish Renaissance Foundation, Inc.
767 Fifth Ave., Ste. 4600
New York, NY 10153

Established in 1996 in NY.
Donor(s): Ronald S. Lauder.
Financial data (yr. ended 12/31/99): Grants paid, $20,000; assets, $19,315,507 (M); expenditures, $971,491; qualifying distributions, $2,082,064; giving activities include $802,576 for programs.
Limitations: Applications not accepted.
Application information: Contributes only to pre-selected organizations.
Officers and Directors:* Ronald S. Lauder,* Pres.; Menachem Z. Rosensaft, Exec. V.P. and Secy.; Jacob Z. Schuster, Treas.; Louis Begley, Rabbi Chaskel O. Besser.
EIN: 133906533

37953
Linda & Alan Kahn Foundation, Inc.
49 Overhill Rd.
Forest Hills, NY 11375-6021

Established in 1999 in NY.
Donor(s): Irving Kahn.
Financial data (yr. ended 03/31/01): Grants paid, $20,000; assets, $198,943 (M); expenditures, $20,156; qualifying distributions, $20,000.
Limitations: Applications not accepted.
Application information: Contributes only to pre-selected organizations.
Officers: Alan Kahn, Pres.; Irving Kahn, V.P.; Linda Kahn, Secy.
EIN: 113483455

37954
The Seymour L. Kaplan Scholarship Foundation
c/o Natalie J. Roberts
315 Glendale Rd.
Scarsdale, NY 10583

Established in 1992 in NY.
Donor(s): Dorothy Kaplan.
Financial data (yr. ended 12/31/01): Grants paid, $20,000; assets, $396,178 (M); expenditures, $21,951; qualifying distributions, $20,000.
Limitations: Applications not accepted.
Officers: Dorothy Kaplan, Chair.; Natalie J. Roberts, Vice-Chair.
EIN: 137004964
Codes: GTI

37955
Max & Rose Katz Foundation, Inc.
c/o Sara Seiden
101-20 Ascan Ave.
Forest Hills, NY 11375-5951

Financial data (yr. ended 10/31/01): Grants paid, $20,000; assets, $203,599 (M); expenditures, $21,880; qualifying distributions, $20,000.
Limitations: Applications not accepted. Giving on a national basis, with emphasis on the East.
Application information: Contributes only to pre-selected organizations.
Officers and Directors:* Jeanne Katz,* Pres.; Sara Seiden, Secy.-Treas.; Laura Baron, Helen W. Samuels.
EIN: 136138846

37956
Peter Krueger-Christie's Foundation
c/o Barry Strauss Assocs., Ltd.
307 5th Ave., 8th Fl.
New York, NY 10016-6517

Established in 1988 in NY.
Financial data (yr. ended 02/28/02): Grants paid, $20,000; assets, $307,822 (M); expenditures, $25,122; qualifying distributions, $20,000.
Limitations: Applications not accepted.
Application information: Contributes only to pre-selected organizations.
Officers: Catherine Cahill, Pres.; Constance Krueger, Secy.; Jay Cantor, Treas.
EIN: 133504108

37957
Long Island Commercial Bank Foundation
1 Suffolk Sq.
Islandia, NY 11749

Established in 1999 in NY.
Donor(s): Long Island Commercial Bank.
Financial data (yr. ended 12/31/01): Grants paid, $20,000; assets, $10,348 (M); gifts received, $28,843; expenditures, $20,004; qualifying distributions, $23,996.
Limitations: Applications not accepted.
Application information: Contributes only to pre-selected organizations.
Officers: Perry B. Duryea, Jr., Chair.; Douglas C. Manditch, Pres.; Thomas Buonaiuto, Treas.
Director: Roy M. Kern, Sr.
EIN: 113391428
Codes: CS, CD

37958
Donald and Bonnie Maharam Charitable Foundation
45 Rasons Ct.
Hauppauge, NY 11788

Established in 2001 in NY.
Financial data (yr. ended 12/31/01): Grants paid, $20,000; assets, $230,752 (M); gifts received,

$250,000; expenditures, $20,000; qualifying distributions, $20,000.
Trustees: Harvey S. Feuerstein, Hillary Maharam, Michael Maharam, Patricia Maharam, Stephen Maharam.
EIN: 912151218

37959
Newton Family Fund
c/o U.S. Trust
114 W. 47th St., TaxVas
New York, NY 10036

Established in 1998 in CO.
Donor(s): Quigg Newton, Virginia S. Newton.
Financial data (yr. ended 12/31/01): Grants paid, $20,000; assets, $618,958 (M); gifts received, $12,942; expenditures, $29,564; qualifying distributions, $20,000.
Limitations: Applications not accepted.
Application information: Contributes only to pre-selected organizations.
Officers: Quigg Newton, Pres.; Virginia S. Newton, 1st V.P. and Secy.-Treas.; Virginia M. Newton, 2nd V.P.
EIN: 841462523

37960
The Ohr Foundation, Inc.
c/o Abraham Roth
5612 18th Ave.
Brooklyn, NY 11204

Established in 1999 in NY.
Donor(s): Meir Akerman, Eugene Loevinger.
Financial data (yr. ended 12/31/01): Grants paid, $20,000; assets, $815,265 (M); gifts received, $620,000; expenditures, $20,257; qualifying distributions, $20,000.
Officers: Eugene Loevinger, Pres.; Meir Akerman, V.P.; Margaret Loevinger, Secy.; Ruth Akerman, Treas.
EIN: 113503916

37961
The Palm Tree Foundation
c/o Bessemer Trust Co., N.A.
630 5th Ave., Tax Dept.
New York, NY 10111

Established in 2001 in CA.
Donor(s): Lev J. Leytes, Galina I. Leytes.
Financial data (yr. ended 12/31/01): Grants paid, $20,000; assets, $3,492,833 (M); gifts received, $3,442,163; expenditures, $42,330; qualifying distributions, $26,903.
Limitations: Applications not accepted. Giving primarily in CA.
Application information: Contributes only to pre-selected organizations.
Officers: Lev J. Leytes, Pres.; Galina I. Leytes, Secy. and C.F.O.
EIN: 943387977

37962
Panosian Family Foundation, Inc.
111 N. Main St.
Elmira, NY 14901

Established in 1995 in NY.
Donor(s): Panosian Enterprises.
Financial data (yr. ended 12/31/01): Grants paid, $20,000; assets, $313,146 (M); gifts received, $29,963; expenditures, $20,468; qualifying distributions, $20,000.
Limitations: Applications not accepted. Giving primarily in NY, with emphasis on Elmira; giving also in Colorado Springs, CO.
Application information: Contributes only to pre-selected organizations.
Officers: Lucille A. Panosian, Pres.; Manual N. Panosian, V.P.; Daniel P. Panosian, Secy.-Treas.
Directors: Susan P. Frisbie, David M. Panosian, Ronald N. Panosian, Sandra L. White.
EIN: 161487436

37963
The Helen Polonsky Educational Fund, Inc.
160 W. 66th St., Ste. 55A
New York, NY 10023-6569
Contact: Jay B. Polonsky, Pres.

Established in 1991 in MD and NY.
Donor(s): Jay B. Polonsky.
Financial data (yr. ended 12/31/01): Grants paid, $20,000; assets, $42,782 (M); expenditures, $20,078; qualifying distributions, $20,078.
Limitations: Giving primarily in the New York, NY, area.
Application information: Application form not required.
Officers and Directors:* Jay B. Polonsky,* Pres.; Leonard Polonsky,* V.P.; Ivan Polonsky,* Treas.
EIN: 061334621

37964
Luetz Riedel Charitable Trust
233 Broadway, Ste. 4701
New York, NY 10279

Established in 1998.
Donor(s): Fred P. Riedel.
Financial data (yr. ended 12/31/01): Grants paid, $20,000; assets, $478,034 (M); expenditures, $21,503; qualifying distributions, $20,000.
Trustees: Norbert Dengler, Theobald Dengler.
EIN: 137156955

37965
Arthur W. & Nellie W. Schmidt Charitable Foundation, Inc.
100 Highview Ave.
Nanuet, NY 10954-3315

Financial data (yr. ended 12/31/01): Grants paid, $20,000; assets, $5,742 (M); expenditures, $20,978; qualifying distributions, $20,000.
Limitations: Applications not accepted. Giving primarily in Rockland County, NY.
Application information: Contributes only to pre-selected organizations.
Officers: Arthur W. Schmidt, Jr., Pres.; A.D. Schmidt, Secy.-Treas.
EIN: 136208780

37966
Saint Elizabeth Ann Bayley Seton Foundation, Inc.
c/o Richard Dioguardi, C.P.A.
5 Old Rd.
Elmsford, NY 10523-3306

Established in 1999 in NY.
Donor(s): Seton Shanley.
Financial data (yr. ended 12/31/99): Grants paid, $20,000; assets, $24,933 (M); gifts received, $44,749; expenditures, $20,000; qualifying distributions, $20,000.
Limitations: Applications not accepted. Giving primarily in NY.
Application information: Contributes only to pre-selected organizations.
Officer: Seton Shanley, Pres.
EIN: 133506766

37967
Sontag Foundation, Inc.
c/o Bessemer Trust Co., N.A.
630 5th Ave., Tax Dept.
New York, NY 10111

Established in 2000 in FL.
Donor(s): Frederick B. Sontag.
Financial data (yr. ended 12/31/00): Grants paid, $20,000; assets, $4,822,600 (M); gifts received, $5,005,136; expenditures, $49,569; qualifying distributions, $29,840.
Limitations: Applications not accepted. Giving primarily in Tampa, FL and Chicago, IL.
Application information: Contributes only to pre-selected organizations.
Officers: Frederick B. Sontag, Pres.; Susan T. Sontag, V.P.; Cindy L. Sontag, Secy.; Frederick T. Sontag, Treas.
EIN: 593634325

37968
Sung Family Foundation
c/o John J. Sung
9765 Rocky Pt.
Clarence, NY 14031-1589

Established in 2001 in NY.
Donor(s): John J. Sung, Janet H. Sung.
Financial data (yr. ended 12/31/01): Grants paid, $20,000; assets, $995 (M); gifts received, $26,000; expenditures, $25,005; qualifying distributions, $25,005.
Limitations: Applications not accepted. Giving primarily in Seoul, Korea.
Application information: Contributes only to pre-selected organizations.
Trustees: Janet H. Sung, John J. Sung.
EIN: 166522877

37969
The Kenneth J. Tedaldi Foundation, Inc.
38 Oak St.
Patchogue, NY 11772-2883
Contact: Kenneth J. Tedaldi, Pres.

Established in 1993 in NY.
Donor(s): Kenneth J. Tedaldi.
Financial data (yr. ended 12/31/01): Grants paid, $20,000; assets, $339,784 (M); gifts received, $237,195; expenditures, $20,370; qualifying distributions, $20,000.
Limitations: Giving primarily in NY.
Application information: Application form not required.
Officers: Kenneth J. Tedaldi, Pres.; Neil B. Esposito, Secy.
EIN: 113190508

37970
The Warner Foundation
c/o P. Gartner
114 W. 47th St., 22nd Fl.
New York, NY 10036-1510

Established in 2001 in NY.
Financial data (yr. ended 12/31/01): Grants paid, $20,000; assets, $929,140 (M); gifts received, $902,505; expenditures, $42,135; qualifying distributions, $20,400.
Limitations: Applications not accepted.
Application information: Contributes only to pre-selected organizations.
Officers: Ann Warner, Pres.; Susan Reed, V.P. and Treas.; Paul Gartner, Secy.
EIN: 010620097

37971
David A. Weir, Jr. Family Foundation Trust
c/o C.L. King & Assoc., Inc.
9 Elk St.
Albany, NY 12207-1002
Contact: Candace K. Weir, Dir.

Donor(s): Candace K. Weir, David A. Weir.
Financial data (yr. ended 12/31/01): Grants paid, $20,000; assets, $231,777 (M); expenditures, $22,050; qualifying distributions, $22,017.

Limitations: Giving primarily in Washington, DC.
Trustees: Meredith Prime, Amelia F. Weir, Candace K. Weir, David A. Weir.
EIN: 141687589

37972
The Zichron Aryeh Leib Foundation
c/o J. Meller
3084 Bedford Ave.
Brooklyn, NY 11210

Established in 1997 in NY.
Donor(s): Stuart M. Fischman.
Financial data (yr. ended 12/31/01): Grants paid, $20,000; assets, $7,422 (M); gifts received, $25,500; expenditures, $20,000; qualifying distributions, $20,000.
Limitations: Applications not accepted.
Application information: Contributes only to pre-selected organizations.
Trustees: Stuart M. Fischman, Rita Francis.
EIN: 137101874

37973
Ida Braunova Memorial Fund
121 E. 60th St.
New York, NY 10022 (212) 759-0884
Contact: Helen Braun, Tr.

Financial data (yr. ended 12/31/01): Grants paid, $19,995; assets, $221,768 (M); gifts received, $30,000; expenditures, $20,720; qualifying distributions, $19,995.
Limitations: Giving primarily in NJ and NY.
Trustees: Ernest Block, Nina Block, Helen Braun, Juraj Braun.
EIN: 223572181

37974
Moshe Lehmann Foundation, Inc.
90 Pinehurst Ave.
New York, NY 10033-1701

Donor(s): Felix F. Lehmann.
Financial data (yr. ended 12/31/01): Grants paid, $19,949; assets, $4,135 (M); gifts received, $17,525; expenditures, $20,314; qualifying distributions, $19,949.
Limitations: Applications not accepted. Giving primarily in the greater New York, NY, area.
Application information: Contributes only to pre-selected organizations.
Officer: Felix F. Lehmann, Pres.
EIN: 132748860

37975
Victoria Lea Smith Foundation
1160 Park Ave.
New York, NY 10128

Established in 1999 in NY.
Donor(s): Victoria Lea Smith.
Financial data (yr. ended 12/31/00): Grants paid, $19,925; assets, $1,422,112 (M); gifts received, $105,356; expenditures, $57,619; qualifying distributions, $18,780.
Limitations: Applications not accepted.
Application information: Contributes only to pre-selected organizations.
Officer: Victoria Lea Smith, Pres.
EIN: 137212742

37976
Dr. Clarence A. Tyler Scholarship Fund
120 Delaware Ave., Ste. 100
Buffalo, NY 14202
Application address: c/o Alden High School, Alden, NY 14004
Contact: Timothy Shannon, Principal

Financial data (yr. ended 12/31/00): Grants paid, $19,920; assets, $335,058 (M); expenditures, $22,847; qualifying distributions, $19,690.
Limitations: Giving primarily in NY.
Application information: Application form not required.
Trustee: Melissa P. Sullivan De Castro.
EIN: 166037864

37977
Walter & Marion David Foundation, Inc.
15 W. 47th St.
New York, NY 10036 (212) 719-2220
Contact: Walter David, Tr.

Donor(s): Walter David.
Financial data (yr. ended 12/31/01): Grants paid, $19,907; assets, $4,788 (M); gifts received, $17,025; expenditures, $20,077; qualifying distributions, $19,907.
Limitations: Giving primarily in NY.
Trustees: Marion David, Sheldon David, Walter David.
EIN: 133130696

37978
Spitzer Family Foundation
355 7th Ave.
New York, NY 10001

Financial data (yr. ended 12/31/01): Grants paid, $19,900; assets, $334,616 (M); gifts received, $21,000; expenditures, $21,300; qualifying distributions, $19,900.
Limitations: Applications not accepted. Giving primarily in New York, NY.
Application information: Contributes only to pre-selected organizations.
Officers: Linda Spitzer, Pres.; Richard Spitzer, Secy.; Gilbert Spitzer, Treas.
EIN: 133478597

37979
Brunick Family Foundation
c/o U.S. Trust
114 W. 47th St., TaxVas
New York, NY 10036

Established in 1999 in CO.
Donor(s): David R. Brunick, Mary S. Brunick.
Financial data (yr. ended 12/31/00): Grants paid, $19,870; assets, $234,687 (M); gifts received, $60,000; expenditures, $24,059; qualifying distributions, $21,994.
Application information: Unsolicited requests for funds not accepted.
Directors: David R. Brunick, Mary S. Brunick.
EIN: 841524927

37980
Kahn Foundation, Inc.
c/o Kahn-Lucas-Lancaster, Inc.
100 W. 33rd St., Ste. 921
New York, NY 10001
Contact: Andrew Kahn, Dir.

Established in 1987 in NY.
Donor(s): Kahn-Lucas-Lancaster, Inc.
Financial data (yr. ended 12/31/01): Grants paid, $19,850; assets, $31,996 (M); gifts received, $12,115; expenditures, $20,140; qualifying distributions, $19,875.
Limitations: Giving primarily in NY and PA.

Directors: Andrew Kahn, Peggy Anne Kahn.
EIN: 236343794
Codes: CS, CD

37981
Masal Foundation
c/o Meyer Lamet
1431 46th St.
Brooklyn, NY 11219-2633

Donor(s): Meyer Lamet.
Financial data (yr. ended 11/30/01): Grants paid, $19,800; assets, $126,518 (M); expenditures, $21,390; qualifying distributions, $19,800.
Limitations: Applications not accepted. Giving primarily in Brooklyn, NY.
Application information: Contributes only to pre-selected organizations.
Trustee: Meyer Lamet.
EIN: 237076785

37982
Albert and Cleovia Starling Foundation, Inc.
45 Thomas Jefferson Ln.
Snyder, NY 14226-3806 (716) 824-5353
Application address: 2025 Clinton St., Buffalo, NY 14206

Established in 1994 in NY.
Financial data (yr. ended 07/31/01): Grants paid, $19,800; assets, $197,248 (M); expenditures, $23,229; qualifying distributions, $19,800.
Application information: Application form required.
Officers: Chester Bochenek, Pres.; Robert Busch, V.P.; Michael J. Stachowski, Secy.-Treas.
EIN: 161464878

37983
ABC Charitable Foundation
845 W. End Ave., Ste. 4D
New York, NY 10025 (212) 864-6501
Contact: Chava Bistritzky, Pres.

Established in 1999 in NY.
Donor(s): Chava Bistritzky.
Financial data (yr. ended 11/30/01): Grants paid, $19,773; assets, $199,242 (M); gifts received, $120,000; expenditures, $20,264; qualifying distributions, $19,773.
Officers: Chava Bistritzky, Pres.; Issacher Bistritzky, V.P.; Isaac Bistritzky, Secy.
EIN: 134092579

37984
Cornelius T. & Elizabeth Lynch Scholarship Fund
(Formerly Cornelius T. & Elizabeth Lynch Scholarship Trust)
c/o M&T Bank
P.O. Box 22900
Rochester, NY 14692-2900
Application address: c/o M&T Bank, Trust Dept., 225 East Ave., Rochester, NY 14604-2625

Financial data (yr. ended 03/31/02): Grants paid, $19,768; assets, $250,759 (M); expenditures, $24,046; qualifying distributions, $19,898.
Limitations: Giving limited to the Geneva, NY, area.
Application information: Application form not required.
Trustee: M & T Bank.
EIN: 166014594
Codes: GTI

37985
Jerilee Family Foundation
108 Old Mountain Rd.
Upper Nyack, NY 10960 (845) 358-2221
Contact: Jerome Johnson, Pres.

Established in 1998 in DE.

Financial data (yr. ended 05/31/02): Grants paid, $19,750; assets, $962,697 (M); expenditures, $20,387; qualifying distributions, $19,750.
Limitations: Giving primarily in NY.
Officers: Jerome Johnson, Pres.; Lee Johnson, Treas.
Directors: Jill S. Tanz, Ronald E. Tanz.
EIN: 134011030

37986
The Wise Family Charitable Foundation
P.O. Box 572
Chester, NY 10918

Established in 1995 in NY.
Financial data (yr. ended 10/31/01): Grants paid, $19,750; assets, $286,963 (M); gifts received, $111,737; expenditures, $19,920; qualifying distributions, $19,750.
Limitations: Applications not accepted.
Application information: Contributes only to pre-selected organizations.
Officer and Trustees:* Barrie Edwards,* Pres.; John Castaldo, Robert Wise.
EIN: 133861747

37987
Salzman/Holstein Foundation, Inc.
(Formerly Holstein Foundation)
115 Central Park W.
New York, NY 10023

Established in 1948.
Financial data (yr. ended 12/31/01): Grants paid, $19,726; assets, $75,596 (M); expenditures, $24,644; qualifying distributions, $19,726.
Limitations: Applications not accepted. Giving primarily in NY.
Application information: Contributes only to pre-selected organizations.
Officers: Susan C. Saltzman, Pres.; Lee Saltzman, Secy.
EIN: 156020258

37988
Nathaniel A. Mesnikoff Foundation, Inc.
35 Scenic Dr.
Hastings-on-Hudson, NY 10706-1211

Donor(s): Lucille Savin.
Financial data (yr. ended 12/31/01): Grants paid, $19,700; assets, $367,461 (M); expenditures, $23,734; qualifying distributions, $19,700.
Limitations: Applications not accepted. Giving primarily in NY.
Application information: Contributes only to pre-selected organizations.
Officer and Directors:* Alvin Mesnikoff,* Pres.; Norman Mesnikoff, Lillian Savin.
EIN: 237450437

37989
Gertrude & Morris Bienenfeld Charitable Foundation
c/o Richard Mezan
460 Park Ave.
New York, NY 10022

Established about 1956.
Donor(s): Bestform Foundations, Inc.
Financial data (yr. ended 07/31/01): Grants paid, $19,698; assets, $1,146,297 (M); gifts received, $135,000; expenditures, $22,311; qualifying distributions, $19,698.
Limitations: Applications not accepted. Giving primarily in NY.
Application information: Contributes only to pre-selected organizations.
Trustees: Hadassah Bienenfeld, Marvin Bienenfeld, Morris Bienenfeld.
EIN: 116013176

37990
The Cunningham-Gardiner Foundation
c/o Joan S. Brown
4 Beechwood Way
Scarborough, NY 10510

Established in 1998 in NY.
Donor(s): Joan S. Brown.
Financial data (yr. ended 12/31/01): Grants paid, $19,695; assets, $522,894 (M); gifts received, $22,517; expenditures, $24,786; qualifying distributions, $19,695.
Trustees: Joan S. Brown, Martha G. Dale, Sarah S. Rivers, John C. Simons, Thomas S. Simons.
EIN: 137152819

37991
Arthur J. Bellinzoni Foundation
P.O. Box 5
Aurora, NY 13026-0005 (315) 364-3296
Contact: Arthur J. Bellinzoni, Tr.

Established in 1956 in NY.
Donor(s): Arthur J. Bellinzoni.
Financial data (yr. ended 10/31/01): Grants paid, $19,690; assets, $171,190 (M); expenditures, $21,062; qualifying distributions, $19,690.
Limitations: Giving primarily in NY.
Trustees: Arthur J. Bellinzoni, Attilio R'Ezzonico.
EIN: 136075443

37992
Frederick M. Peyser, Jr. Foundation
c/o Seth E. Frank
125 W. 55th St.
New York, NY 10019
Application address: 1255 Winding Oak Cir., Vero Beach, FL 32963
Contact: Frederick M. Peyser, Jr., Pres.

Established in 1989 in NY.
Financial data (yr. ended 12/31/01): Grants paid, $19,670; assets, $417,434 (M); expenditures, $22,020; qualifying distributions, $19,670.
Limitations: Giving on a national basis, with emphasis on the Northeast.
Officers: Frederick M. Peyser, Jr., Pres. and Treas.; Seth E. Frank, V.P.; Selina Peyser Lamb, V.P.
EIN: 133484411

37993
The Edward and Karen Levene Charitable Foundation Trust
9 Vincent Ct.
Binghamton, NY 13905-4427
Contact: Edward R. Levene, Tr.

Established in 1985 in NY.
Financial data (yr. ended 12/31/01): Grants paid, $19,642; assets, $227,744 (M); expenditures, $21,517; qualifying distributions, $19,642.
Limitations: Giving primarily in Binghamton, NY.
Trustees: Edward R. Levene, Karen Levene, David Stearns.
EIN: 166283714

37994
The Murray Alon Charitable Foundation
163-06 71st Ave., 1st Fl.
Flushing, NY 11365-4207
Application address: 64-40 Ellwell Cir., Rego Park, NY 11374
Contact: Murray Alon, Pres.

Established in 1986 in NY.
Donor(s): Murray Alon, Metropole, LLC.
Financial data (yr. ended 11/30/01): Grants paid, $19,627; assets, $558 (M); gifts received, $20,100; expenditures, $20,022; qualifying distributions, $20,022.
Limitations: Giving primarily in the metropolitan New York, NY, area, including Long Island.
Officers: Murray Alon, Pres.; Bruce Osterhoudt, V.P.; Grace Osterhoudt, Secy.-Treas.
EIN: 133446203

37995
Ira and Priscilla Kleinberg Foundation
4 Kennilworth Terr.
Great Neck, NY 11024-1206

Established in 1995 in NY.
Donor(s): Ira Kleinberg, Priscilla Kleinberg.
Financial data (yr. ended 01/31/02): Grants paid, $19,601; assets, $102,889 (M); gifts received, $20,000; expenditures, $19,601; qualifying distributions, $19,601.
Limitations: Applications not accepted.
Application information: Contributes only to pre-selected organizations.
Officers: Ira Kleinberg, Pres.; Susan Bushell, V.P.; Addy Fritzhand, V.P.; Steven Kleinberg, V.P.; Priscilla Kleinberg, Secy.-Treas.
EIN: 113249972

37996
Erna & Isaac Stern Foundation, Inc.
15 Purchase Hills Dr.
Purchase, NY 10577
Contact: Constance Flaum, Pres.

Financial data (yr. ended 01/31/02): Grants paid, $19,600; assets, $437,808 (M); expenditures, $24,522; qualifying distributions, $19,600.
Limitations: Giving primarily in New York and Westchester County, NY.
Officers: Constance Flaum, Pres.; Mitchel Flaum, V.P.; Stephen Flaum, Treas.
EIN: 136116794

37997
The Asher & Deborah Fensterheim Foundation
565 Taxter Rd.
Elmsford, NY 10523
Contact: Ricky Rothstein, Pres.

Established in 1997 in NY.
Donor(s): Asher Fensterheim.
Financial data (yr. ended 11/30/01): Grants paid, $19,562; assets, $98,306 (M); expenditures, $24,070; qualifying distributions, $19,562.
Limitations: Giving primarily in FL and NY.
Officers: Ricky Rothstein, Pres.; Lisa Eisenberger, V.P. and Secy.; David Fensterheim, V.P. and Treas.
EIN: 133922985

37998
The John J. & Margaret R. Gilbert Foundation, Inc.
c/o John J. Gilbert
29 E. 64th St., Ste. 11A
New York, NY 10021

Financial data (yr. ended 11/30/01): Grants paid, $19,502; assets, $904,139 (M); expenditures, $33,664; qualifying distributions, $26,583.
Limitations: Applications not accepted. Giving primarily in CO and NY.
Application information: Contributes only to pre-selected organizations.
Trustees: John Gilbert, Margot Gilbert.
EIN: 134044703

37999
Ruth and Ralph Friedman Foundation, Inc.
B. Strauss Assoc., Ltd.
307 5th Ave., 8th Fl.
New York, NY 10016-6517

Financial data (yr. ended 12/31/01): Grants paid, $19,500; assets, $59,746 (M); expenditures, $19,819; qualifying distributions, $19,500.

Limitations: Applications not accepted.
Application information: Contributes only to pre-selected organizations.
Officer: Robert Friedman, Pres.
EIN: 136107390

38000
Sears Family Foundation
250 W. 90th St.
New York, NY 10024
Contact: Austin N. Sears, Tr.

Donor(s): Austin N. Sears, Margarita Sears.
Financial data (yr. ended 12/31/99): Grants paid, $19,500; assets, $1,055,156 (M); gifts received, $126,400; expenditures, $120,393; qualifying distributions, $95,220; giving activities include $95,220 for programs.
Limitations: Giving primarily in NY.
Trustees: Austin N. Sears, Margarita Sears.
EIN: 117040015

38001
The Woodcock No. 4 Foundation
30 Rockefeller Plz., Rm. 5600
New York, NY 10112
Application address: c/o Stuart Davidson, 400 Seaport Ct., Ste. 250, Redwood City, CA 94063

Established in 1992 in NY.
Financial data (yr. ended 11/30/01): Grants paid, $19,500; assets, $371,243 (M); gifts received, $76,915; expenditures, $25,970; qualifying distributions, $19,500.
Trustees: John H.J. Guth, Richard T. Watson.
EIN: 133717633

38002
The Norman & Carol Stahl Family Foundation, Inc.
(Formerly The Stahl Family Foundation, Inc.)
401 E. 60th St., Ste. 28A
New York, NY 10001-1596

Established in 1993 in NY.
Financial data (yr. ended 03/31/01): Grants paid, $19,479; assets, $2,299 (M); expenditures, $21,142; qualifying distributions, $19,385.
Limitations: Applications not accepted. Giving primarily in NY.
Application information: Contributes only to pre-selected organizations.
Officer: Carol Stahl, V.P. and Secy.
EIN: 113137943

38003
Hoffman Family Foundation, Inc.
20 Old Mamaroneck Rd.
White Plains, NY 10605-2026
Application address: c/o Michael Masters & Co., 175 Memorial Hwy., New Rochelle, NY 10801
Contact: Burton P. Hoffman, Dir.

Donor(s): Burton P. Hoffman.
Financial data (yr. ended 11/30/00): Grants paid, $19,475; assets, $3,074 (M); expenditures, $19,585; qualifying distributions, $19,475.
Limitations: Giving primarily in NY.
Directors: Burton P. Hoffman, Jeffrey Hoffman.
EIN: 133355615

38004
The GH Foundation
(Formerly The Deborah and Richard Cole Foundation)
800 Fleet Bank Bldg.
Buffalo, NY 14202-2292

Established in 1962 in NY.
Financial data (yr. ended 09/30/01): Grants paid, $19,364; assets, $14,115 (M); gifts received, $11,844; expenditures, $19,396; qualifying distributions, $19,353.
Limitations: Applications not accepted. Giving primarily in NY.
Application information: Contributes only to pre-selected organizations.
Trustees: Deborah M. Greenberg, Ralph L. Halpern.
EIN: 136161389

38005
Abel E. Peck Memorial Fund
c/o The National Bank of Delaware County
P.O. Box 389
Walton, NY 13856
Application address: c/o Guidance Dept., Walton Central High School, Walton, NY 13856, tel.: (607) 865-4116

Financial data (yr. ended 11/30/01): Grants paid, $19,356; assets, $788,898 (M); expenditures, $22,738; qualifying distributions, $20,756.
Limitations: Giving limited to Walton, NY.
Application information: Application form required.
Trustee: The National Bank of Delaware County.
EIN: 166254479
Codes: GTI

38006
Fay & Charles Greenbaum Foundation, Inc.
c/o Edward Selter
14 Steven Ln.
Kings Point, NY 11024

Donor(s): Fay Greenbaum, Charles Greenbaum.
Financial data (yr. ended 11/30/01): Grants paid, $19,350; assets, $307,591 (M); expenditures, $23,815; qualifying distributions, $19,350.
Limitations: Applications not accepted. Giving primarily in New York, NY.
Application information: Contributes only to pre-selected organizations.
Officers: Ruth Selter, Pres. and Treas.; Jocelyn Sass, Secy.
EIN: 133089902

38007
Maldeb Foundation, Inc.
c/o M. Joel Mandelbaum
39-49 46th St.
Sunnyside, NY 11104

Established in 1988 in NY.
Financial data (yr. ended 04/30/02): Grants paid, $19,350; assets, $284,870 (M); expenditures, $21,277; qualifying distributions, $19,350.
Limitations: Applications not accepted. Giving limited to New York, NY.
Application information: Contributes only to pre-selected organizations.
Officers: M. Joel Mandelbaum, Pres.; Ellen Mandelbaum, V.P.
Director: Burton Malkiel.
EIN: 133444156

38008
The Rogers Family Foundation
P.O. Box 44
Armonk, NY 10504

Established in 1998 in NY.
Financial data (yr. ended 12/31/01): Grants paid, $19,350; assets, $358,082 (M); expenditures, $19,700; qualifying distributions, $19,350.
Limitations: Applications not accepted. Giving primarily in NY.
Application information: Contributes only to pre-selected organizations.
Directors: Donald J. Rogers, Kenneth G. Rogers, Stephen Rogers, Sylvia Rogers.
EIN: 134031082

38009
Maggiotto Family Charitable Trust
930 Park Ave., Ste. 4S
New York, NY 10028

Established in 1998 in NY.
Donor(s): Rocco Magiotto, Kathleen Fisher.
Financial data (yr. ended 12/31/00): Grants paid, $19,325; assets, $22,186 (M); gifts received, $18,000; expenditures, $22,450; qualifying distributions, $19,325.
Limitations: Applications not accepted.
Application information: Contributes only to pre-selected organizations.
Trustee: Rocco J. Maggiotto.
EIN: 137171419

38010
The Nadler Family Foundation
260 Madison Ave., 3rd Fl.
New York, NY 10016 (212) 309-9898
Contact: Donna Nadler

Established in 2001 in NY and DE.
Donor(s): David Nadler.
Financial data (yr. ended 12/31/01): Grants paid, $19,300; assets, $2,801 (M); gifts received, $32,724; expenditures, $29,925; qualifying distributions, $29,925.
Limitations: Giving primarily in New York, NY.
Officers and Directors:* David Nadler,* Pres.; Francesca Nadler,* V.P.; Amy Nadler,* Secy.; Cara Nadler,* Treas.
EIN: 134168889

38011
The Justin & Deborah Scheer Family Foundation, Inc.
75 Washington St.
Poughkeepsie, NY 12601 (845) 452-1383
Contact: Eugene H. Fleishman

Established in 1992 in NY.
Donor(s): Justin Scheer, M.D., Deborah S. Scheer.
Financial data (yr. ended 12/31/01): Grants paid, $19,295; assets, $475,186 (M); expenditures, $25,191; qualifying distributions, $19,295.
Limitations: Giving primarily in NY.
Application information: Application form not required.
Officers: Deborah S. Scheer, Pres. and Treas.; Justin Scheer, M.D., V.P. and Secy.
Directors: Peter E. Scheer, Stephen A. Scheer, William R. Scheer.
EIN: 141756646

38012
Mai Vilms Charitable Foundation, Inc.
c/o Inverness Council, Inc.
545 Madison Ave.
New York, NY 10022

Established in 1997 in MI and NY.
Donor(s): Mai V. Hallingby.
Financial data (yr. ended 12/31/01): Grants paid, $19,190; assets, $394,807 (M); expenditures, $27,569; qualifying distributions, $19,190.
Limitations: Applications not accepted.
Application information: Contributes only to pre-selected organizations.
Officers and Directors:* Mai V. Hallingby,* Pres.; Stephanie A. Ercklentz,* V.P.; Cornelia M. Ercklentz,* Secy.; Philip S. Lawrence,* Treas.
EIN: 383353877

38013
Alfred A. and Hanina Z. Shasha Foundation
15 Cotswold Way
Scarsdale, NY 10583

Established in 1985 in NY.
Donor(s): Alfred A. Shasha.
Financial data (yr. ended 05/31/01): Grants paid, $19,186; assets, $1,026,513 (M); expenditures, $29,859; qualifying distributions, $19,186.
Limitations: Applications not accepted.
Application information: Contributes only to pre-selected organizations.
Officer: Alfred A. Shasha, Pres.
EIN: 133229188

38014
Afghan Jewish Foundation, Inc.
c/o Amerind, Inc.
580 5th Ave., Rm. 2407
New York, NY 10036-4714

Financial data (yr. ended 12/31/01): Grants paid, $19,172; assets, $369,209 (M); gifts received, $23,465; expenditures, $20,758; qualifying distributions, $19,172.
Limitations: Applications not accepted.
Officer: Solomon Gad, Pres.
EIN: 136216150

38015
Carpat Foundation, Inc.
10 E. 70th St., Apt. 14C
New York, NY 10021   (212) 988-2981
Contact: Patricia M. Erpf, Pres.

Donor(s): Patricia M. Erpf.
Financial data (yr. ended 04/30/02): Grants paid, $19,160; assets, $19,362 (M); expenditures, $21,375; qualifying distributions, $19,160.
Limitations: Giving primarily in New York, NY.
Officer and Directors:* Patricia M. Erpf,* Pres. and V.P.; Douglas Erpf, John Heimerdinger, Ellen Erpf Miller.
EIN: 136193278

38016
Manes Family Foundation, Inc.
P.O. Box 330
North Salem, NY 10560-0330
Contact: John P. Manes, Pres.

Established in 1986 in NY.
Financial data (yr. ended 04/30/02): Grants paid, $19,150; assets, $322,265 (M); gifts received, $10,000; expenditures, $24,562; qualifying distributions, $19,150.
Limitations: Giving primarily in NY.
Officers: John P. Manes, Pres.; Seymour Berkman, Secy.-Treas.
EIN: 133429516

38017
Acker Family Foundation, Inc.
P.O. Box 429
Shoreham, NY 11786-0429

Established in 1997 in FL.
Donor(s): Bruce Acker.
Financial data (yr. ended 12/31/01): Grants paid, $19,101; assets, $316,302 (M); expenditures, $19,166; qualifying distributions, $19,101.
Limitations: Applications not accepted. Giving primarily in MA and NY.
Application information: Contributes only to pre-selected organizations.
Officers and Directors:* Bruce Acker,* Pres.; Holly Acker,* V.P.; Heather Acker,* V.P.; Anna Andrews,* Secy.-Treas.
EIN: 650754941

38018
The Maletta Foundation
30 West Ave.
Livonia, NY 14487   (716) 346-2136
Contact: Anthony G. Maletta, Tr.

Established in 1995 NY.
Donor(s): Anthony G. Maletta, Adriana P. Maletta.
Financial data (yr. ended 12/31/01): Grants paid, $19,040; assets, $248,459 (M); gifts received, $1,297; expenditures, $20,095; qualifying distributions, $19,040.
Trustees: Adriana P. Maletta, Anthony G. Maletta, Dana P. Woolever.
EIN: 161484555

38019
Allan and Sherry Martin Family Foundation
c/o Wachtell, Lipton, Rosen & Katz
51 W. 52nd St.
New York, NY 10019

Established in 1999 in NY.
Donor(s): Allan A. Martin, Sheryl A. Martin.
Financial data (yr. ended 12/31/01): Grants paid, $19,021; assets, $142,069 (M); expenditures, $21,021; qualifying distributions, $19,021.
Limitations: Applications not accepted.
Application information: Contributes only to pre-selected organizations.
Officers and Directors:* Allan A. Martin,* Pres. and Treas.; Sheryl A. Martin,* V.P. and Secy.; Gregory C. Martin, Kevin B. Martin, Rachel L. Martin.
EIN: 134091735

38020
Agnes K. Haverly Foundation, Inc.
c/o Alan Zheutlin
275 W. 96th St., Ste. 10Q
New York, NY 10025-6261

Established around 1977.
Donor(s): John G. Haverly.
Financial data (yr. ended 12/31/01): Grants paid, $19,000; assets, $228,639 (M); expenditures, $21,393; qualifying distributions, $20,530.
Limitations: Applications not accepted. Giving primarily in New York, NY.
Application information: Contributes only to pre-selected organizations.
Directors: Arthur Chu, Delia Haverly, John G. Haverly, Mary Ann McKenna, Max Needleman.
EIN: 132890781

38021
The James N. & Marcia L. Kannry Charitable Trust
466 Lexington Ave., 18th Fl.
New York, NY 10017

Established in 1999 in NY.
Donor(s): James N. Kannry.
Financial data (yr. ended 12/31/00): Grants paid, $19,000; assets, $80,254 (M); expenditures, $19,046; qualifying distributions, $19,046.
Limitations: Applications not accepted.
Application information: Contributes only to pre-selected organizations.
Trustees: James N. Kannry, Marcia L. Kannry.
EIN: 137229066

38022
Kaster-Sherman Foundation, Inc.
(Formerly Benjamin & Bessie Sherman Foundation, Inc.)
c/o Lewis R. Kaster
1290 Ave. of the Americas
New York, NY 10104

Donor(s): Lewis R. Kaster.
Financial data (yr. ended 11/30/01): Grants paid, $19,000; assets, $24,247 (M); gifts received, $41,013; expenditures, $19,622; qualifying distributions, $19,000.
Limitations: Applications not accepted. Giving primarily in FL.
Application information: Contributes only to pre-selected organizations.
Officers and Directors:* Lewis Sherman,* V.P.; Lewis R. Kaster,* Secy.-Treas.
EIN: 136160874

38023
The Lillis Foundation
c/o U.S. Trust
114 W. 47th St.
New York, NY 10036

Established in 2000 in WA.
Donor(s): Charles M. Lillis, Gwendolyn H. Lillis.
Financial data (yr. ended 12/31/01): Grants paid, $19,000; assets, $4,071,325 (M); expenditures, $137,416; qualifying distributions, $19,000.
Limitations: Applications not accepted.
Trustees: Jessica L. Barker, Charles M. Lillis, Gwendolyn H. Lillis, Michael B. Lillis, Timothy S. Lillis.
EIN: 916520620

38024
The Little-Kittinger Foundation, Inc.
c/o Neil R. Farmelo
1500 Statler Towers
Buffalo, NY 14202

Established in 1994 in NY.
Donor(s): Josephine L. Kittinger.
Financial data (yr. ended 12/31/01): Grants paid, $19,000; assets, $2,315,827 (M); expenditures, $77,398; qualifying distributions, $24,085.
Limitations: Applications not accepted. Giving primarily in CA.
Application information: Contributes only to pre-selected organizations.
Directors: Dale B. Demyanick, Neil R. Farmelo, Barry K. Hutten, Edward Hutten, Jeffrey K. Hutten, Lois K. Hutten.
EIN: 161468031

38025
Oser-Braun Foundation for the Visually Impaired, Inc.
c/o Seltzer, Sussman & Haberman
100 Jericho Quadrangle, Ste. 226
Jericho, NY 11753
Application address: 440 E. 62nd St., New York, NY 10021
Contact: Gustav Oser, Pres.

Established in 1986 in NY.
Donor(s): Gustav Oser, Eva Oser.‡
Financial data (yr. ended 12/31/01): Grants paid, $19,000; assets, $146,263 (M); gifts received, $18,300; expenditures, $21,105; qualifying distributions, $19,000.
Limitations: Giving primarily in NJ and NY.
Officers and Directors:* Gustav Oser,* Pres.; Stephen Seltzer,* Secy.
EIN: 133330428

38026
The David J. Supino Foundation
c/o Lazard Freres & Co., LLC
30 Rockefeller Plz.
New York, NY 10020
Contact: David J. Supino, Pres.

Established in 1986 in NY.
Donor(s): David J. Supino.
Financial data (yr. ended 09/30/01): Grants paid, $19,000; assets, $9,713 (M); gifts received,

$20,000; expenditures, $19,105; qualifying distributions, $19,000.
Limitations: Giving primarily in NY.
Officers and Directors:* David J. Supino,* Pres.; Charles M. Stieglitz,* V.P.; Howard Sontag,* Secy.-Treas.
EIN: 133371585

38027
White Stone Fund, Inc.
1140 5th Ave.
New York, NY 10128

Established in 1999 in MO.
Donor(s): Alfred C. Sikes.
Financial data (yr. ended 12/31/00): Grants paid, $19,000; assets, $500,379 (M); gifts received, $499,813; expenditures, $21,749; qualifying distributions, $19,000.
Directors: Marcia Sikes Cole, Christine Sikes McNary, Alfred C. Sikes, Deborah Sikes, Martha H. Sikes.
EIN: 364324010

38028
The James & Dena Hammerstein Foundation, Inc.
c/o A. Kozak and Co., LLP
192 Lexington Ave., Ste. 1100
New York, NY 10016

Established in 1997 in DE.
Donor(s): James Hammerstein, Dena Hammerstein.
Financial data (yr. ended 12/31/00): Grants paid, $18,853; assets, $220,922 (M); gifts received, $9,027; expenditures, $94,530; qualifying distributions, $89,495; giving activities include $70,057 for programs.
Limitations: Applications not accepted. Giving primarily in NY.
Application information: Contributes only to pre-selected organizations.
Officers: Dena Hammerstein, Pres.; Jennifer Hammerstein, Secy.; Suzanne Davis, Treas.
EIN: 133981053

38029
George & Alice Javian Foundation
34 Harbor Park Dr.
Port Washington, NY 11050 (516) 484-5470
Contact: George Javian, Pres.

Financial data (yr. ended 11/30/01): Grants paid, $18,827; assets, $172,660 (M); expenditures, $22,171; qualifying distributions, $20,730.
Limitations: Giving primarily in NY.
Application information: Application form not required.
Officers: George Javian, Pres. and Treas.; Ronald Javian, V.P.; Alice Javian, Secy.
EIN: 112563387

38030
The Schachter Family Charitable Trust
901 E. 23rd St.
Brooklyn, NY 11210-3621

Established in 1993 in NJ.
Donor(s): Benzion Schachter.
Financial data (yr. ended 12/31/00): Grants paid, $18,816; assets, $598,423 (M); gifts received, $2,600; expenditures, $19,736; qualifying distributions, $18,816.
Limitations: Applications not accepted. Giving primarily in NY.
Application information: Contributes only to pre-selected organizations.
Trustees: Benzion Schachter, Judith Schachter.
EIN: 116436542

38031
King's Daughters Home for Children, Inc.
c/o Betty Hudson
6 Wheeler Ave.
Cortland, NY 13045-1123
Application address: Sears Rd., Cortland, NY 13045
Contact: Mrs. Fritz Downes

Financial data (yr. ended 12/31/01): Grants paid, $18,809; assets, $457,220 (M); gifts received, $200; expenditures, $27,168; qualifying distributions, $18,809.
Limitations: Giving limited to Cortland County, NY.
Officers: Mrs. Fritz Downes, Pres. and Project Chair; Barbara Latimer, Secy.; Betty Hudson, Treas.
EIN: 166054829

38032
The Llewellyn Miller Fund of the American Society of Journalists and Authors Charitable Trust
(Formerly The American Society of Journalists and Authors Charitable Trust)
1501 Broadway, Ste. 302
New York, NY 10036
Contact: Katharine O. Fishman, Chair.

Established in 1972 in NY; became operational in 1982.
Donor(s): New York Times Foundation, Reader's Digest Foundation, Newhouse Foundation.
Financial data (yr. ended 08/31/01): Grants paid, $18,750; assets, $173,409 (M); gifts received, $26,926; expenditures, $22,131; qualifying distributions, $18,750.
Officer and Trustees:* Katharine O. Fishman,* Chair.; Murray T. Bloom, Patricia Carbine, John M. Carter, Patricia S. Estees, Ray Robinson, Al Silverman, Grace W. Weinstein.
EIN: 136625578
Codes: GTI

38033
Morton & Joyce Certilman Foundation, Inc.
c/o Certilman, Balin, Adler & Hyman
90 Merrick Ave.
East Meadow, NY 11554

Donor(s): Morton Certilman, Joyce Certilman.
Financial data (yr. ended 12/31/01): Grants paid, $18,735; assets, $3,309 (M); gifts received, $400; expenditures, $18,760; qualifying distributions, $18,735.
Limitations: Applications not accepted. Giving primarily in NY.
Application information: Contributes only to pre-selected organizations.
Directors: Bernard Certilman, Joyce Certilman, Morton Certilman.
EIN: 237052320

38034
AMS Foundation
1295 President St.
Brooklyn, NY 11213

Established in 2000 in NY.
Donor(s): Ari Sperlin, Malka Sperlin.
Financial data (yr. ended 06/30/02): Grants paid, $18,725; assets, $15,526 (M); gifts received, $12,482; expenditures, $52,732; qualifying distributions, $18,725.
Limitations: Applications not accepted. Giving primarily in NY.
Application information: Contributes only to pre-selected organizations.
Trustees: Ari Sperlin, Malka Sperlin.
EIN: 113569319

38035
Ernest A. Fort Charitable Trust
39 Seminary Hill Rd.
Carmel, NY 10512

Established in 1999 in NY.
Donor(s): Ernest A. Fort.
Financial data (yr. ended 12/31/00): Grants paid, $18,710; assets, $291,658 (M); expenditures, $19,210; qualifying distributions, $18,710.
Limitations: Applications not accepted. Giving primarily in FL and GA.
Application information: Contributes only to pre-selected organizations.
EIN: 066422706

38036
The Eleanor and Alexander Holtzman Foundation
190 E. 72nd St., Ste. 31C
New York, NY 10021
Contact: Alexander Holtzman, Pres.

Established in 1998 in NY.
Donor(s): Alexander Holtzman.
Financial data (yr. ended 12/31/00): Grants paid, $18,704; assets, $310,447 (M); expenditures, $22,705; qualifying distributions, $18,704.
Officer: Alexander Holtzman, Pres.
EIN: 134035862

38037
The David Eisenberger Foundation
22 Washington Ave.
Spring Valley, NY 10977 (914) 354-6258
Contact: Inrich Katz, Pres.

Established in 1998 in NY.
Financial data (yr. ended 12/31/01): Grants paid, $18,700; assets, $152,312 (M); expenditures, $18,804; qualifying distributions, $18,617.
Limitations: Giving primarily in Spring Valley, NY.
Officers: Inrich Katz, Pres. and Treas.; David Soifer, Secy.
EIN: 137076152

38038
Rothkopf/Greenberg Family Foundation
9 Sparrow Ln.
Woodbury, NY 11797

Established in 1989 in NY.
Donor(s): George Rothkopf.
Financial data (yr. ended 05/31/02): Grants paid, $18,700; assets, $527,006 (M); gifts received, $3,000; expenditures, $19,192; qualifying distributions, $18,700.
Limitations: Applications not accepted.
Application information: Contributes only to pre-selected organizations.
Trustee: George Rothkopf.
EIN: 112975013

38039
The Beatrice & Samuel Robins Educational Scholarship Foundation
70 Marcus Dr.
Melville, NY 11747-4210

Established in 1995.
Financial data (yr. ended 06/30/00): Grants paid, $18,674; assets, $784 (M); gifts received, $19,300; expenditures, $18,836; qualifying distributions, $18,674.
Limitations: Applications not accepted. Giving primarily in NY.
Trustee: Marilyn Jurick.
EIN: 113268877

38040
Solomon J. & Edith K. Freedman Charitable Foundation, Inc.
342 Madison Ave., Ste. 1220
New York, NY 10173-1220

Financial data (yr. ended 12/31/00): Grants paid, $18,650; assets, $163,932 (M); gifts received, $9,057; expenditures, $23,305; qualifying distributions, $18,650.
Limitations: Applications not accepted.
Application information: Contributes only to pre-selected organizations.
Officers and Directors*: Solomon J. Freedman,* Pres.; Edith K. Freedman,* V.P.; Bruce A. Rosen,* Treas.
EIN: 133977223

38041
Dundalk Foundation
c/o Geometry Group
110 E. 59th St.
New York, NY 10022
Contact: William D. Birch, Tr.

Established in 1998 in NY.
Donor(s): William D. Birch.
Financial data (yr. ended 12/31/01): Grants paid, $18,645; assets, $315,303 (M); expenditures, $20,860; qualifying distributions, $18,645.
Trustee: William D. Birch.
EIN: 137158386

38042
Kunstler Charitable Foundation, Inc.
c/o Samuel Kunstler
108-18 Queens Blvd.
Forest Hills, NY 11375

Established in 1997.
Donor(s): Samuel Kunstler.
Financial data (yr. ended 12/31/01): Grants paid, $18,564; assets, $89,929 (M); expenditures, $18,564; qualifying distributions, $18,564.
Officer: Samuel Kunstler, Mgr.
EIN: 113364013

38043
Arnold and Susan Scharf Foundation, Inc.
40 Tuthill Rd.
East Moriches, NY 11940

Established in 1997 in DE and NY.
Donor(s): Arnold Scharf.
Financial data (yr. ended 12/31/00): Grants paid, $18,550; assets, $480,471 (M); expenditures, $18,556; qualifying distributions, $18,550.
Limitations: Applications not accepted. Giving primarily in New York, NY.
Application information: Contributes only to pre-selected organizations.
Officers: Arnold Scharf, Pres. and Treas.; Susan Scharf, V.P. and Secy.
Director: Judy Goldstein.
EIN: 113375888

38044
Guido and Ellen Palma Foundation, Inc.
1348 Shoecraft Rd.
Webster, NY 14580

Established in 1998 in NY.
Donor(s): Kimberly L. Palma, Roger P. Palma, Richard Magere.
Financial data (yr. ended 09/30/01): Grants paid, $18,540; assets, $425,212 (M); gifts received, $51,266; expenditures, $26,349; qualifying distributions, $18,540.
Limitations: Applications not accepted. Giving primarily in NY.
Application information: Contributes only to pre-selected organizations.
Officers and Directors:* Roger P. Palma,* Pres. and Treas.; Kimberly L. Palma,* V.P. and Secy.; Richard Magere.
EIN: 161559984

38045
Shirley & Donald Bronsky Foundation, Inc.
28 Kenilworth Rd.
Binghamton, NY 13903

Established in 2000.
Donor(s): Donald Bronsky, Shirley Bronsky.
Financial data (yr. ended 12/31/01): Grants paid, $18,521; assets, $0 (M); expenditures, $18,521; qualifying distributions, $18,521.
Directors: Donald A. Bronsky, Mark Bronsky, Peter Bronsky, Shari Bronsky, Shirley Bronsky.
EIN: 161586942

38046
The Anglican Foundation, Inc.
c/o Peters & Welsh, C.P.A.
580 Mineola Ave.
Carle Place, NY 11514
Contact: Stuart Newby, V.P.

Financial data (yr. ended 10/31/01): Grants paid, $18,500; assets, $579,947 (M); gifts received, $650; expenditures, $27,893; qualifying distributions, $18,500.
Limitations: Giving on a national basis, with emphasis on NY.
Officers: Rev. Canon George Monroe, Pres.; Stuart Newby, V.P.; Katherine Klein, Secy.; Paula F. MacLean, Treas.
Trustees: C. Casey, Rev. W. Stokes.
EIN: 116035577

38047
Baumgarten Foundation
c/o Frederic H. Baumgarten
989 Ave. of the Americas
New York, NY 10018-5410

Established in 1963 in NY.
Donor(s): H.W. Baumgarten,‡ Frederic H. Baumgarten.
Financial data (yr. ended 09/30/00): Grants paid, $18,500; assets, $196,061 (M); expenditures, $18,742; qualifying distributions, $18,500.
Limitations: Applications not accepted. Giving primarily in New York, NY.
Application information: Contributes only to pre-selected organizations.
Trustees: Frederic H. Baumgarten, George A. Baumgarten.
EIN: 136170020

38048
The J. S. and Martin B. Bloch Foundation, Inc.
42 Greenway Terr.
Forest Hills, NY 11375

Established in 2000 in MI and NY.
Donor(s): Martin B. Bloch.
Financial data (yr. ended 12/31/01): Grants paid, $18,500; assets, $265,099 (M); gifts received, $2,077; expenditures, $26,924; qualifying distributions, $18,500.
Limitations: Applications not accepted.
Application information: Contributes only to pre-selected organizations.
Officers: Jerry Bloch, Pres. and Treas.; Helen L. Bloch, Secy.
Director: Sam E. Bloch.
EIN: 311726454

38049
Harvey & Lois Dann Foundation, Inc.
c/o Tyler Dann
P.O. Box 226
Chappaqua, NY 10514-0226

Established in 1997 in NY.
Donor(s): Lois Dann.‡
Financial data (yr. ended 12/31/00): Grants paid, $18,500; assets, $314,969 (M); expenditures, $19,268; qualifying distributions, $18,500.
Limitations: Applications not accepted. Giving primarily in NY.
Application information: Contributes only to pre-selected organizations.
Officers: Tyler Dann, V.P.; Harvey Dann IV, Secy.; Sarah B. Dann, Treas.
EIN: 133941600

38050
Eagleton War Memorial Scholarship Fund, Inc.
Box 980
Bridgehampton, NY 11932-0980
Application address: c/o Superintendent of Schools, Bridgehampton High School, Bridgehampton, NY 11932

Financial data (yr. ended 12/31/01): Grants paid, $18,500; assets, $252,316 (M); expenditures, $19,460; qualifying distributions, $37,638.
Limitations: Giving limited to Bridgehampton, NY.
Application information: Application form not required.
Officers: Al Kalina, Pres.; Craig Gibson, Secy.-Treas.
Directors: Harold King, John Nealon, Helen Smith.
EIN: 237149864
Codes: GTI

38051
James & Janice Stanton Foundation, Inc.
c/o World Wide Holdings Corp.
150 E. 58th St.
New York, NY 10155-0002

Established in 1995 in NY.
Donor(s): Frank & Domna Stanton Foundation.
Financial data (yr. ended 12/31/00): Grants paid, $18,461; assets, $211,667 (M); expenditures, $20,053; qualifying distributions, $10,291.
Limitations: Applications not accepted. Giving primarily in New York, NY.
Application information: Contributes only to pre-selected organizations.
Officers: James Stanton, Pres.; Janice Stanton, V.P.
EIN: 133831451

38052
Janet Yaseen Foundation, Inc.
(Formerly Roger & Janet Yaseen Foundation, Inc.)
c/o BDO Seidman, LLP
812 5th Ave.
New York, NY 10021

Donor(s): Roger Yaseen, Janet Yaseen.
Financial data (yr. ended 12/31/01): Grants paid, $18,450; assets, $356,264 (M); expenditures, $20,280; qualifying distributions, $18,450.
Limitations: Applications not accepted. Giving primarily in New York, NY.
Application information: Contributes only to pre-selected organizations.
Officers: Janet Yaseen, Pres. and V.P.; Marc Yaseen, Secy.
EIN: 136266495

38053
Wm. B. Thompson Fund
c/o Cusack & Stiles, LLP
61 Broadway, Ste. 2100
New York, NY 10006

Established in 1927.
Financial data (yr. ended 11/30/00): Grants paid, $18,400; assets, $487,213 (M); expenditures, $20,543; qualifying distributions, $19,216.
Limitations: Applications not accepted.
Trustees: Christian C. Hohenlohe, Peter B. Schulze, Richard A. Smith.
EIN: 136089682

38054
The Elizabeth S. & Irving G. Kaufmann Foundation, Inc.
c/o Rifkin & Lubcher
477 Madison Ave., 10th Fl.
New York, NY 10022

Donor(s): Elizabeth S. Kaufmann, Irving G. Kaufmann.‡
Financial data (yr. ended 02/28/01): Grants paid, $18,384; assets, $5,807 (M); gifts received, $2,785; expenditures, $21,454; qualifying distributions, $18,384.
Limitations: Applications not accepted. Giving primarily in NY.
Application information: Contributes only to pre-selected organizations.
Trustee: Elizabeth S. Kaufmann.
EIN: 136061303

38055
The Langdon Family Foundation, Inc.
c/o Karen P. Langdon
157 E. 32nd St., Ste. 22c
New York, NY 10016

Established in 1999 in NY.
Donor(s): Karen P. Langdon.
Financial data (yr. ended 10/31/01): Grants paid, $18,380; assets, $19,106 (M); gifts received, $30,480; expenditures, $21,240; qualifying distributions, $18,380.
Limitations: Applications not accepted.
Application information: Contributes only to pre-selected organizations.
Officers: Karen P. Langdon, Pres.; William S. Langdon III, V.P.; Thomas Legotte, Secy.
EIN: 134114123

38056
Alan Weinstein Charitable Trust
c/o Israeloff, Trattner & Co.
350 5th Ave., Ste. 1000
New York, NY 10118

Established in 1997 in NY.
Donor(s): Alan Weinstein.
Financial data (yr. ended 12/31/01): Grants paid, $18,375; assets, $11,182 (M); gifts received, $838; expenditures, $21,029; qualifying distributions, $18,375.
Limitations: Applications not accepted.
Application information: Contributes to pre-selected organizations.
Officer: Alan Weinstein, Pres. and Treas.
EIN: 133959223

38057
Kesher Trust Fund
30 Concord Dr.
Monsey, NY 10952 (845) 425-0253
Contact: Uri Nussbaum, Tr.

Established in 1995.
Donor(s): Uri Nussbaum.
Financial data (yr. ended 12/31/00): Grants paid, $18,360; assets, $57,925 (M); gifts received, $5,000; expenditures, $18,862; qualifying distributions, $18,360.
Limitations: Giving primarily in Rockland County, NY.
Application information: Application form required.
Trustees: Annie Nussbaum, Chany Nussbaum, Uri Nussbaum.
EIN: 136911481

38058
Able Trust
c/o Melvin L. Bedrick
825 8th Ave., Rm. 4570B
New York, NY 10019-7415
URL: http://www.abletrust.org

Established in 1987 in NY.
Donor(s): Melvin L. Bedrick.
Financial data (yr. ended 12/31/01): Grants paid, $18,350; assets, $252,483 (M); expenditures, $18,655; qualifying distributions, $18,890.
Limitations: Applications not accepted. Giving primarily in CT and New York, NY.
Application information: Contributes only to pre-selected organizations.
Trustee: Melvin L. Bedrick.
EIN: 133388412

38059
Institute for Ethical Behavior
c/o James T. Michaelson
22 Gouverner St.
Canton, NY 13617
Application address: 7 Annette St., Heuvelton, NY 13654
Contact: Wesley L. Stitt, Tr.

Financial data (yr. ended 12/31/01): Grants paid, $18,300; assets, $140,889 (M); expenditures, $24,835; qualifying distributions, $18,300.
Limitations: Giving limited to St. Lawrence, Franklin, and Jefferson counties, NY.
Officers: James T. Michaelson, Pres.; Floyd Morter, Jr., V.P.; Ruth F. Garner, Secy.; Carolyn Badger, Treas.
Trustee: Wesley L. Stitt.
EIN: 161277306

38060
The Gay and Marie Milbrandt Charitable Trust
40 South Rd.
Tivoli, NY 12583

Established in 1986 in NY.
Donor(s): Gay Milbrandt.
Financial data (yr. ended 12/31/01): Grants paid, $18,290; assets, $272,538 (M); expenditures, $20,245; qualifying distributions, $18,290.
Limitations: Applications not accepted. Giving primarily in NY.
Application information: Contributes only to pre-selected organizations.
Trustees: Nadja C. McKay, Marie L. Milbrandt.
EIN: 226424440

38061
Zichron Avroham Moshe Foundation
9 Underwood Rd.
Monsey, NY 10952-1815 (845) 425-7702
Contact: Jeffry Hollander, Tr.

Established in 1996 in NY.
Financial data (yr. ended 12/31/01): Grants paid, $18,275; assets, $35,369 (M); gifts received, $29,610; expenditures, $18,300; qualifying distributions, $18,275.
Limitations: Giving primarily in Brooklyn, NY.
Trustee: Jeffry Hollander.
EIN: 133918253

38062
The Lipton Family Foundation
c/o Yohalem Gillman & Co., LLP
477 Madison Ave.
New York, NY 10022-5802

Established in 1993 in NY.
Donor(s): Roger Lipton.
Financial data (yr. ended 12/31/01): Grants paid, $18,270; assets, $158,207 (M); expenditures, $20,033; qualifying distributions, $18,270.
Limitations: Applications not accepted.
Application information: Contributes only to pre-selected organizations.
Officers: Roger Lipton, Pres.; Mary Lipton, V.P.
Director: Solomon Lipton.
EIN: 133716472

38063
Usha Foundation
226 Idlewood Rd.
Rochester, NY 14618 (716) 244-3632
Contact: Brijen Gupta, Exec. Dir.

Established in 1998 in IA.
Financial data (yr. ended 12/31/01): Grants paid, $18,252; assets, $38,522 (M); gifts received, $18,000; expenditures, $26,642; qualifying distributions, $18,252.
Limitations: Giving in the U.S. and India.
Officers: Nalini Mullapudi, Pres.; George Nachos, Treas.; Brijen Gupta, Exec. Dir.
EIN: 391900020

38064
The John and Katherine Naudin Foundation, Inc.
c/o Washburn, et al.
P.O. Box 1219
Gloversville, NY 12078-0354

Financial data (yr. ended 10/31/01): Grants paid, $18,250; assets, $451,609 (M); expenditures, $19,826; qualifying distributions, $18,250.
Limitations: Applications not accepted. Giving primarily in FL.
Application information: Contributes only to pre-selected organizations.
Officers: Elizabeth N. Snedeker, Pres.; Sedgwick Snedeker, Secy.; Nancy H. Seagren, Treas.
EIN: 146016106

38065
Donald & Gladys Heath Scholarship Memorial Fund
c/o Fleet National Bank
159 E. Main St.
Rochester, NY 14638

Financial data (yr. ended 02/28/00): Grants paid, $18,222; assets, $538,436 (M); expenditures, $24,822; qualifying distributions, $22,692.
Limitations: Giving limited to Mount Morris, Livonia, and Retsof, NY.
Application information: Recipient recommended by high schools. Application form not required.
Trustee: Fleet National Bank.
EIN: 166355023
Codes: GTI

38066
The Arthur S. and Marilyn Penn Charitable Trust
c/o Elmrock
150 E. 52nd St., 8th Fl.
New York, NY 10022

Established in 1987 in NY.
Donor(s): Arthur S. Penn, Marilyn Penn.

Financial data (yr. ended 12/31/01): Grants paid, $18,210; assets, $310,860 (M); expenditures, $23,233; qualifying distributions, $19,890.
Limitations: Applications not accepted. Giving primarily in NY.
Application information: Contributes only to pre-selected organizations.
Trustees: Arthur S. Penn, Marilyn Penn.
EIN: 133386164

38067
Bigajer Family Foundation
1235 E. 24th St.
Brooklyn, NY 11210

Financial data (yr. ended 12/31/01): Grants paid, $18,197; assets, $24,089 (M); gifts received, $10,750; expenditures, $18,932; qualifying distributions, $18,197.
Limitations: Applications not accepted.
Application information: Contributes only to pre-selected organizations.
Trustee: Charles Bigajer.
EIN: 113404280

38068
The Kate and Isaac Brody Foundation, Inc.
1450 Coolidge Ave.
Baldwin, NY 11510
Contact: Samuel A. Brody, M.D., V.P.

Financial data (yr. ended 05/31/01): Grants paid, $18,188; assets, $412,579 (M); expenditures, $20,259; qualifying distributions, $18,188.
Officers: Ethel Brody, M.D., Pres.; Samuel Brody, M.D., V.P. and Secy.; Paul Brody, M.D., V.P.; Jane Brody, M.D., Treas.
EIN: 112161565

38069
The Beverly Karp Foundation, Inc.
146 Central Park W., Apt. 4-E
New York, NY 10023

Established in 1988 in NY.
Donor(s): Beverly Karp.
Financial data (yr. ended 12/31/01): Grants paid, $18,150; assets, $479,756 (M); expenditures, $22,898; qualifying distributions, $18,150.
Limitations: Applications not accepted. Giving primarily in New York, NY.
Application information: Contributes only to pre-selected organizations.
Officers: Beverly Karp, Pres.; Nicholas Karp, Secy.; David Karp, Treas.
EIN: 133452802

38070
Aloha Foundation
c/o Kall & Kall, C.P.A.
3522 James St.
Syracuse, NY 13206

Established in 1989 in NY.
Donor(s): Earle Buck, Minna R. Buck.
Financial data (yr. ended 12/31/01): Grants paid, $18,123; assets, $608,067 (M); gifts received, $19,248; expenditures, $37,321; qualifying distributions, $20,965.
Limitations: Applications not accepted. Giving primarily in NY.
Application information: Contributes only to pre-selected organizations.
Trustees: Earle Buck, Minna R. Buck.
EIN: 161365260

38071
Marjorie Gilbert Foundation, Inc.
3 Purchase Hill Dr.
Purchase, NY 10577

Donor(s): Marjorie Gilbert.

Financial data (yr. ended 05/31/01): Grants paid, $18,100; assets, $143,670 (M); gifts received, $149,808; expenditures, $20,389; qualifying distributions, $20,389.
Limitations: Applications not accepted. Giving primarily in NY.
Application information: Contributes only to pre-selected organizations.
Officer: Marjorie Gilbert, Mgr.
EIN: 134100158

38072
The Nora and Roger Gimbel Family Foundation, Inc.
10 E. 70th St., 15 Fl.
New York, NY 10021
Contact: Roger Gimbel, Pres.

Established in 1997 in NY.
Donor(s): Roger Gimbel.
Financial data (yr. ended 06/30/01): Grants paid, $18,100; assets, $136,049 (M); expenditures, $23,123; qualifying distributions, $18,100.
Officers: Roger Gimbel, Pres.; Nora Gimbel, V.P.; Geoffry Gimbel, Secy.
EIN: 133973929

38073
The Renee and Chaim Gross Foundation, Inc.
526 LaGuardia Pl.
New York, NY 10012
Contact: April Paul, Collection Curator

Established in 1974 in NY.
Donor(s): Howard Dunitz,‡ Chaim Gross,‡ Chaim Gross Foundation.
Financial data (yr. ended 12/31/00): Grants paid, $18,100; assets, $5,619,351 (M); gifts received, $7,984; expenditures, $88,291; qualifying distributions, $18,100.
Limitations: Giving primarily in NY.
Application information: Contributes primarily to pre-selected organizations. Application form not required.
Officers and Directors:* Irwin Hersey,* Pres.; Miriam Gross,* V.P. and Secy.; Renee Gross,* Treas.
EIN: 133490010

38074
The Polen Foundation
c/o Marks Paneth & Shron, LLP
622 3rd Ave.
New York, NY 10017

Established in 1995 in NY.
Financial data (yr. ended 12/31/01): Grants paid, $18,100; assets, $298,258 (M); expenditures, $20,533; qualifying distributions, $18,100.
Limitations: Applications not accepted. Giving primarily in Boca Raton, FL.
Application information: Contributes only to pre-selected organizations.
Directors: Signe Adam, Edward Polen, Russell Polen, Shirley Polen, Tara Polen.
EIN: 133860198

38075
Dymash Foundation Trust
1244 49th St.
Brooklyn, NY 11219 (718) 436-3335
Contact: Samuel Halberstam, Dir.

Established in 1998 in NY.
Donor(s): Samuel Halberstam.
Financial data (yr. ended 12/31/01): Grants paid, $18,055; assets, $53,037 (M); gifts received, $25,000; expenditures, $18,523; qualifying distributions, $18,055.
Limitations: Giving primarily in NY.

Directors: Malkie Halberstam, Samuel Halberstam.
EIN: 113466273

38076
MCY Foundation
c/o Sam Eisenberg
P.O. Box 1079
Monroe, NY 10950

Established in 2000 in NY.
Financial data (yr. ended 12/31/01): Grants paid, $18,033; assets, $153,704 (M); gifts received, $150,000; expenditures, $19,292; qualifying distributions, $18,033.
Limitations: Applications not accepted.
Application information: Contributes only to pre-selected organizations.
Trustees: Meilech Eisenberg, Sam Eisenberg, Sarah Eisenberg.
EIN: 134148123

38077
The Sukenik Foundation
118-75 Metropolitan Ave., Ste. 1B
Kew Gardens, NY 11415
Contact: Daniel B. Sukenik, Pres.

Donor(s): William Sukenik,‡ Malka Sukenik, Rachel L. Sukenik.
Financial data (yr. ended 11/30/01): Grants paid, $18,020; assets, $41,259 (M); gifts received, $11,000; expenditures, $18,144; qualifying distributions, $18,020.
Limitations: Giving primarily in NY.
Officer: Daniel B. Sukenik, Pres.
EIN: 136059787

38078
Richard L. and Marian P. Cook Foundation
c/o NBT Bank, N.A.
52 S. Broad St.
Norwich, NY 13815

Established in NY in 1998.
Donor(s): Richard L. Cook, Marian P. Cook.
Financial data (yr. ended 10/31/01): Grants paid, $18,000; assets, $370,246 (M); expenditures, $21,411; qualifying distributions, $20,035.
Limitations: Giving primarily in Norwich, NY.
Trustees: Richard L. Cook, Timothy J. Handy, John D. Roberts, Peter V. Smith, NBT Bank, N.A.
EIN: 166482985

38079
Dolores and Theodore Ehrenreich Foundation
c/o Mariner Mgmt.
516 5th Ave., Ste. 701
New York, NY 10036

Established in 1997.
Financial data (yr. ended 06/30/99): Grants paid, $18,000; assets, $483 (M); gifts received, $20,000; expenditures, $31,024; qualifying distributions, $24,254.
Officers: Dolores Ehrenreich, Chair.; Arthur Aeder, Pres.; Mitchel Aeder, Treas.
Directors: Ruth Manor, Ruth Wolman.
EIN: 133960677

38080
Katherine & George Fan Foundation
Cedar Ln.
Ossining, NY 10562
Contact: George Fan, Tr.

Established in 1994 in DE.
Donor(s): George Fan, Katherine Fan.
Financial data (yr. ended 08/31/99): Grants paid, $18,000; assets, $1,569 (M); gifts received, $3,783; expenditures, $21,200; qualifying distributions, $18,000.

38080—NEW YORK

Application information: Application form not required.
Officer: George Fan.
EIN: 133784702

38081
Friends of La Nueva Esperanza, Inc.
477 Old Best Rd.
West Sand Lake, NY 12196

Established in 1994 in NY.
Donor(s): George A. Saxton, Anne K. Saxton.
Financial data (yr. ended 06/30/01): Grants paid, $18,000; assets, $2,534 (M); gifts received, $15,000; expenditures, $19,950; qualifying distributions, $18,000.
Limitations: Applications not accepted. Giving primarily in the Dominican Republic.
Application information: Contributes only to pre-selected organizations.
Officers: George A. Saxton, Pres.; Anne K. Saxton, Secy.-Treas.
Directors: Peter Barus, Natalie Perez, Victor Perez.
EIN: 223133452

38082
Marie Josephine Hartford Foundation
c/o Chamberlain & Steward
400 Park Ave., 6th Fl.
New York, NY 10022

Financial data (yr. ended 05/31/01): Grants paid, $18,000; assets, $222,841 (M); expenditures, $24,295; qualifying distributions, $18,000.
Limitations: Applications not accepted. Giving primarily in New York, NY.
Application information: Contributes only to pre-selected organizations.
Officers and Trustees:* Norman H. Volk,* Pres. and Treas.; Nuala O'Donnell Pell,* V.P.; Lawrence Bukzin,* Secy.
EIN: 136168640

38083
The Paul & Klara Porzelt Foundation
c/o Carter, Ledyard & Milburn
2 Wall St.
New York, NY 10005-2001
Contact: Theodore R. Wagner, Tr.

Established in 1986 in NY.
Financial data (yr. ended 12/31/01): Grants paid, $18,000; assets, $433,738 (M); expenditures, $20,611; qualifying distributions, $18,000.
Limitations: Giving primarily in New York, NY.
Trustees: Paul Porzelt, Henry Hope Reed, Theodore R. Wagner.
EIN: 133267108

38084
RBM Foundation
c/o Darwin R. Wales
P.O. Box 5250, 700 Security Mutual Bldg.
Binghamton, NY 13901
Application address: 3525 NY Rte. 79, Harpursville, NY 13787
Contact: Barbara Mathews, Chair.

Established in 1992 in NY.
Donor(s): Barbara Mathews.
Financial data (yr. ended 09/30/01): Grants paid, $18,000; assets, $372,675 (M); expenditures, $21,556; qualifying distributions, $18,000.
Limitations: Giving limited to Broome, Chenango, Tioga, Delaware, and Otsego counties, NY.
Application information: Application form not required.
Officer and Trustees:* Barbara Mathews,* Chair.; Eugene Gilliand, Lawrence R. Jones, Richard B. Long, Margery Secrest.
EIN: 166379904

38085
Morris & Dvora Scharf Foundation, Inc.
1659 58th St.
Brooklyn, NY 11204

Established in 2000 in NY.
Donor(s): Morris Scharf, Dvora Scharf.
Financial data (yr. ended 12/31/01): Grants paid, $18,000; assets, $365,683 (M); gifts received, $18,000; expenditures, $19,100; qualifying distributions, $18,000.
Limitations: Applications not accepted.
Application information: Contributes only to pre-selected organizations.
Directors: Dvora Scharf, Lipa Scharf, Morris Scharf.
EIN: 134115138

38086
Schuster Charitable Trust
1212 Ave. of the Americas
New York, NY 10036-1602

Established around 1966.
Financial data (yr. ended 12/31/01): Grants paid, $18,000; assets, $19,551 (M); gifts received, $31,649; expenditures, $18,000; qualifying distributions, $18,000.
Limitations: Applications not accepted.
Application information: Contributes only to pre-selected organizations.
Trustee: H. Schuster.
EIN: 136197720

38087
The Sheffield Foundation, Inc.
451 Sheffield Rd.
Ithaca, NY 14850-9246

Established in 2000 in NY.
Donor(s): Jan Suwinski, Susan Suwinski.
Financial data (yr. ended 12/31/01): Grants paid, $18,000; assets, $528,172 (M); gifts received, $196,735; expenditures, $21,293; qualifying distributions, $18,000.
Limitations: Applications not accepted. Giving on a national basis.
Application information: Contributes only to pre-selected organizations.
Officer and Directors:* Jan Suwinski,* Mgr.; Karen Suwinski, Susan Suwinski.
EIN: 161587911

38088
The Wayen Charitable Foundation
c/o Oded Aboodi
1285 Ave. of the Americas, 21st Fl.
New York, NY 10019

Established in 1988 in NJ.
Financial data (yr. ended 10/31/01): Grants paid, $18,000; assets, $206,840 (M); expenditures, $18,304; qualifying distributions, $18,000.
Limitations: Applications not accepted. Giving primarily in NJ and NY.
Application information: Contributes only to pre-selected organizations.
Trustee: Oded Aboodi.
EIN: 133466312

38089
Tannen Family Foundation
c/o Michael Tannen
90 Riverside Dr., Ste. 5B
New York, NY 10024

Established in 1993 in NY.
Donor(s): Michael Tannen.
Financial data (yr. ended 12/31/00): Grants paid, $17,995; assets, $320,394 (M); expenditures, $22,108; qualifying distributions, $21,886.
Limitations: Applications not accepted. Giving primarily in New York, NY.
Application information: Contributes only to pre-selected organizations.
Officers: Michael Tannen, Pres.; Catherine Tannen, V.P.; Mary Tannen, V.P.; Noah Tannen, V.P.
EIN: 133742562

38090
Patsy and Joyce DiMarzo Family Foundation
c/o M&T Bank
P.O. Box 22900
Rochester, NY 14692-2900

Established in 1986 in NY.
Financial data (yr. ended 06/30/02): Grants paid, $17,950; assets, $56,339 (M); expenditures, $19,005; qualifying distributions, $17,950.
Limitations: Applications not accepted. Giving primarily in Rochester, NY.
Application information: Contributes only to pre-selected organizations.
Trustees: Joyce DiMarzo, M & T Bank.
EIN: 222782413

38091
Rudolph Joseph Foundation
261 Prince Ave.
Freeport, NY 11520-1021

Donor(s): Rudolph Joseph, Mildred Joseph.
Financial data (yr. ended 12/31/01): Grants paid, $17,945; assets, $1,496,851 (M); expenditures, $33,358; qualifying distributions, $17,945.
Limitations: Giving primarily in FL and NY.
Trustees: Mildred Joseph, Rudolph Joseph.
EIN: 116110951

38092
Nathan & Jacqueline Goldman Foundation, Inc.
(Formerly Nathan Goldman Foundation, Inc.)
712 5th Ave.
New York, NY 10019   (212) 841-9246
Contact: Nathan Goldman, Pres.

Established in 1960 in NY.
Donor(s): Nathan Goldman, Jacqueline Goldman.
Financial data (yr. ended 06/30/99): Grants paid, $17,918; assets, $250 (M); expenditures, $21,720; qualifying distributions, $17,918.
Limitations: Giving primarily in FL and New York, NY; some giving in Israel.
Officers: Nathan Goldman, Pres.; Jacqueline Goldman, Secy.; Robert Goldman, Treas.
EIN: 136122780

38093
NSMF Charitable Foundation
c/o Louis M. Friedman
1006 E. 28th St.
Brooklyn, NY 11210-3742

Established in 1998.
Donor(s): L. Friedman, H. Friedman.
Financial data (yr. ended 12/31/01): Grants paid, $17,907; assets, $94,833 (M); expenditures, $18,877; qualifying distributions, $17,907.
Limitations: Applications not accepted.
Application information: Contributes only to pre-selected organizations.
Trustees: Hennie Friedman, Louis M. Friedman.
EIN: 113466146

38094
The Jeffrey A. Altman Foundation, Inc.
c/o Jeffrey A. Altman
205 E. 22nd St.
New York, NY 10016

Established in 1997 in NY.
Donor(s): Jeffrey A. Altman.

Financial data (yr. ended 11/30/00): Grants paid, $17,800; assets, $124,828 (M); gifts received, $59,500; expenditures, $17,865; qualifying distributions, $17,800.
Limitations: Applications not accepted.
Application information: Contributes only to pre-selected organizations.
Directors: Georgia Altman, Jeffrey A. Altman, Lawrence Altman.
EIN: 133979282

38095
The New York Classical Club, Inc.
c/o Mary C. English
324 Weaver St.
Larchmont, NY 10538

Established in 1998 in NY.
Donor(s): The New York Classical Club's Greek and Latin Scholars Fund.
Financial data (yr. ended 03/31/02): Grants paid, $17,775; assets, $328,615 (M); gifts received, $3,414; expenditures, $28,539; qualifying distributions, $23,704.
Limitations: Giving primarily in New York, NY.
Officers: Donna Wilson, Pres.; Susan Brockman, V.P.; Mary English, Secy.; David J. Murphy, Treas.
EIN: 133970766

38096
Morris Shaver Scholarship Fund
P.O. Box 4203
Buffalo, NY 14240-4203

Established in 1998 in NY.
Financial data (yr. ended 05/31/02): Grants paid, $17,773; assets, $280,621 (M); expenditures, $21,854; qualifying distributions, $17,773.
Limitations: Applications not accepted.
Application information: Contributes only to pre-selected organizations.
Trustee: HSBC Bank USA.
EIN: 316617961

38097
Connors Foundation, Inc.
c/o Smith, Ranschi, et al.
235 Main St.
White Plains, NY 10601

Established in 2000 in NY.
Donor(s): Mark Connors, Kelly Connors.
Financial data (yr. ended 12/31/00): Grants paid, $17,760; assets, $112,107 (M); gifts received, $101,000; expenditures, $17,760; qualifying distributions, $17,760.
Officers: Mark Connors, Pres.; Kelly Connors, V.P. and Treas.; Paul Connors, Secy.
EIN: 134099359

38098
Samuel Schneider Foundation, Inc.
c/o Schneider Trading, Inc.
462 7th Ave., 23rd Fl.
New York, NY 10018
Contact: Albert Schneider, Tr.

Established in 1951 in NJ.
Donor(s): Schneider Mills, Inc., Schneider Trading, Inc.
Financial data (yr. ended 02/28/02): Grants paid, $17,750; assets, $107,954 (M); gifts received, $50,000; expenditures, $18,099; qualifying distributions, $17,750.
Limitations: Giving primarily in New York, NY.
Application information: Application form not required.
Trustees: Albert Schneider, Martha Stein, Morris Stein.
EIN: 136101811

38099
The Charles and Mary Crossed Foundation
109 Pickwick Dr.
Rochester, NY 14618

Established in 1993 in NY.
Donor(s): Carol N. Crossed, Richard Crossed.
Financial data (yr. ended 12/31/01): Grants paid, $17,749; assets, $141,863 (M); gifts received, $5,600; expenditures, $30,242; qualifying distributions, $22,447.
Limitations: Applications not accepted.
Application information: Contributes only to pre-selected organizations.
Officers: Carol N. Crossed, Pres.; Jessica Crossed, Secy.; David Crossed, Treas.
Directors: Andrew I. Crossed, Amy Crossed-Rieck.
EIN: 161440339

38100
Zichron Chaya Leah Foundation
1274 49th St., Ste. 66
Brooklyn, NY 11219-3011 (718) 283-8544
Contact: S. Wohlberg, Tr.

Established in 1999.
Financial data (yr. ended 08/31/01): Grants paid, $17,730; assets, $276 (M); expenditures, $18,250; qualifying distributions, $17,730.
Trustee: S. Wohlberg.
EIN: 113497829

38101
The Gogel Family Foundation
c/o Donald J. Gogel
31 Masterton Rd.
Bronxville, NY 10708

Established in 1997 in NY.
Donor(s): Jeffrey Bagatin, Donald J. Gogel.
Financial data (yr. ended 12/31/01): Grants paid, $17,715; assets, $322,200 (M); gifts received, $15,080; expenditures, $18,145; qualifying distributions, $17,715.
Limitations: Applications not accepted. Giving primarily in NY.
Application information: Contributes only to pre-selected organizations.
Trustees: Donald J. Gogel, Leah Gogel, Rebecca Gogel, Georgia Wall.
EIN: 137119435

38102
The Tartell Family Foundation, Inc.
690 Hawthorne St.
West Hempstead, NY 11552
Contact: Robert M. Tartell, Pres.

Established in 1992 in NY.
Donor(s): Robert M. Tartell, Lottie Tartell.
Financial data (yr. ended 07/31/01): Grants paid, $17,695; assets, $313,716 (M); gifts received, $45,000; expenditures, $21,367; qualifying distributions, $17,695.
Limitations: Giving primarily in New York, NY.
Officers: Robert M. Tartell, Pres. and Treas.; Lottie Tartell, V.P. and Secy.
EIN: 113149830

38103
Richard & Barbara Roaman Foundation, Inc.
7 The Tulips
Roslyn, NY 11576

Established in 1966.
Financial data (yr. ended 12/31/01): Grants paid, $17,692; assets, $59,860 (M); expenditures, $18,833; qualifying distributions, $17,692.
Limitations: Applications not accepted. Giving primarily in NY.
Application information: Contributes only to pre-selected organizations.
Officers: Richard A. Roaman, Pres.; Barbara Roaman, Secy.
EIN: 132573869

38104
The Mulholland Family Foundation, Inc.
c/o Brown Bros. Harriman Trust Co.
63 Wall St.
New York, NY 10005

Established in 1998 in FL.
Donor(s): James S. Mulholland III.
Financial data (yr. ended 12/31/01): Grants paid, $17,650; assets, $515,503 (M); gifts received, $17,313; expenditures, $18,757; qualifying distributions, $17,650.
Limitations: Applications not accepted.
Application information: Contributes only to pre-selected organizations.
Directors: Geraldine M. Kempton, James S. Mulholland III, Susan K. Mulholland.
EIN: 650881822

38105
The Shirley W. and William L. Griffin Foundation
c/o Edwin L. Cates
512 W. Court St.
Rome, NY 13440-4010

Established in 1994.
Financial data (yr. ended 12/31/01): Grants paid, $17,623; assets, $322,670 (M); expenditures, $20,912; qualifying distributions, $17,623.
Limitations: Applications not accepted. Giving primarily in Rome, NY.
Application information: Contributes only to pre-selected organizations.
Trustees: Edwin L. Cates, Dorothy G. Griffin, R. James Williams, Warren E. Williams.
EIN: 161471540

38106
Henry & Rosa Segal Foundation, Inc.
927 5th Ave., 5th Fl.
New York, NY 10021 (212) 861-1952
Contact: Claire Edersheim, Pres.

Donor(s): Rosa Segal Vernikov.
Financial data (yr. ended 12/31/01): Grants paid, $17,620; assets, $745,603 (M); expenditures, $22,269; qualifying distributions, $17,620.
Limitations: Giving primarily in the greater New York, NY, area.
Application information: Individual applicants should submit brief academic resume, including outline of proposed investigation and budget.
Officer: Claire Edersheim, Pres.
EIN: 136163177

38107
The Schnell Family Foundation
10 E. 70th St.
New York, NY 10021

Established in 1998 in NY.
Donor(s): Seymour Schnell.
Financial data (yr. ended 12/31/01): Grants paid, $17,600; assets, $502,429 (M); gifts received, $3,631; expenditures, $17,600; qualifying distributions, $17,600.
Limitations: Applications not accepted. Giving primarily in NY.
Application information: Contributes only to pre-selected organizations.
Officers: Seymour Schnell, Pres.; Paul T. Schnell, V.P. and Secy.; Marianne Schnell, V.P. and Treas.; Joanne Schnell, V.P.
EIN: 134012194

38108
Saw Mill Fund, Inc.
c/o Yohalem, Gillman & Co.
477 Madison Ave.
New York, NY 10022-5802

Donor(s): Phyllis Farley.
Financial data (yr. ended 06/30/01): Grants paid, $17,576; assets, $99,924 (M); expenditures, $18,622; qualifying distributions, $17,576.
Limitations: Applications not accepted. Giving primarily in the metropolitan New York, NY, area.
Application information: Contributes only to pre-selected organizations.
Officers: Philip Farley, Pres. and Treas.; Phyllis Farley, V.P. and Secy.
EIN: 237075737

38109
Charles M. De Forest Foundation
c/o Fiduciary Trust Co.
600 5th Ave.
New York, NY 10020 (212) 466-4100
Contact: Ellen Cosgrove

Established in 1968.
Financial data (yr. ended 12/31/01): Grants paid, $17,573; assets, $205,638 (M); expenditures, $22,883; qualifying distributions, $17,573.
Limitations: Giving primarily in HI.
Trustees: Katherine Bailey, Elizabeth Solstad, Kenneth Solstad, Fiduciary Trust Co.
EIN: 237003463

38110
Susan Daniels Family Charitable Foundation
c/o Becker & Co.
551 Madison Ave.
New York, NY 10022

Established in 1998.
Financial data (yr. ended 06/30/01): Grants paid, $17,571; assets, $157,647 (M); expenditures, $17,828; qualifying distributions, $17,571.
Limitations: Applications not accepted. Giving primarily in NY.
Application information: Contributes only to pre-selected organizations.
Trustees: Gregory Daniels, Kenneth Daniels, Marc Daniels, Susan Daniels.
EIN: 043338422

38111
The Bertram Steinman Family Foundation, Inc.
c/o B. Steinman
103 Crows Nest Ct.
Manhasset, NY 11030

Established in 2000 in NY.
Financial data (yr. ended 12/31/01): Grants paid, $17,565; assets, $82,047 (M); expenditures, $20,622; qualifying distributions, $17,565.
Limitations: Applications not accepted.
Application information: Contributes only to pre-selected organizations.
Officers: Bertram Steinman, Pres.; Jeffrey Q. Steinman, V.P.; Stuart L. Steinman, V.P.; Dorothy Steinman, Secy.-Treas.
EIN: 113570704

38112
Henry & Betty Necarsulmer Foundation
c/o Barry M. Straus Assocs., Ltd.
307 5th Ave., 8th Fl.
New York, NY 10016-6517

Donor(s): Henry Necarsulmer, Elizabeth Necarsulmer.
Financial data (yr. ended 12/31/01): Grants paid, $17,507; assets, $88,654 (M); expenditures, $18,333; qualifying distributions, $17,507.
Limitations: Applications not accepted. Giving primarily in NY.
Application information: Contributes only to pre-selected organizations.
Officers: Henry Necarsulmer, Pres.; Elizabeth Necarsulmer, V.P.; Barry M. Strauss, Secy.
EIN: 136088223

38113
David Gill Memorial Foundation, Inc.
c/o W. Michael Reickert, The Ayco Co.
P.O. Box 8019
Ballston Spa, NY 12020-8019

Established in 1983.
Donor(s): American Express Foundation, Yvonne Gill, Edwin Gill, Peter A. Cohen.
Financial data (yr. ended 09/30/01): Grants paid, $17,501; assets, $127,999 (M); expenditures, $19,816; qualifying distributions, $17,501.
Limitations: Applications not accepted. Giving primarily in Providence, RI.
Application information: Contributes only to pre-selected organizations.
Officers: Edwin Gill, Pres.; Yvonne Gill, V.P.; Peter A. Cohen, Secy.-Treas.
EIN: 133181479

38114
The Abraham Foundation
c/o Kathleen Seltzer
22 The Circle
East Hampton, NY 11937

Established in 1998 in NY.
Donor(s): Gloria Seltzer.
Financial data (yr. ended 12/31/01): Grants paid, $17,500; assets, $270,174 (M); expenditures, $19,161; qualifying distributions, $17,500.
Limitations: Applications not accepted.
Application information: Contributes only to pre-selected organizations.
Trustee: Kathleen Seltzer.
EIN: 311586077

38115
Beavertides Foundation
c/o Cravath, Swaine & Moore
825 8th Ave., Ste. 2282
New York, NY 10019

Established in 1997 in NY.
Donor(s): Katherine L. Schrenk, William J. Schrenk, Jr.
Financial data (yr. ended 12/31/01): Grants paid, $17,500; assets, $283,907 (M); gifts received, $100; expenditures, $17,662; qualifying distributions, $17,345.
Limitations: Applications not accepted. Giving on a national basis, with emphasis on NY.
Application information: Contributes only to pre-selected organizations.
Trustees: Katherine L. Schrenk, William J. Schrenk, Jr.
EIN: 133860124

38116
The Andrea and Charles Bronfman Foundation, Inc.
375 Park Ave., 4th Fl.
New York, NY 10152-0192

Established in 1998 in DE and NY.
Donor(s): Charles R. Bronfman, Stepworth Holdings, Inc.
Financial data (yr. ended 12/31/01): Grants paid, $17,500; assets, $2,070,138 (M); expenditures, $25,786; qualifying distributions, $17,500.
Limitations: Applications not accepted. Giving on a national basis.
Application information: Contributes only to pre-selected organizations.
Officers and Directors:* Charles R. Bronfman,* Chair. and V.P.; Andrea M. Bronfman,* Vice-Chair. and V.P.; Jeffrey Solomon,* Pres.; Geri Craig, Secy.; Andrew Parsons, Treas.
EIN: 133999708

38117
CF Foundation, Inc.
83 Woodcrest Blvd.
Kenmore, NY 14223

Established in 1987 in NY.
Donor(s): James E. Campbell, June K. Campbell.
Financial data (yr. ended 12/31/01): Grants paid, $17,500; assets, $271,396 (M); gifts received, $74; expenditures, $19,998; qualifying distributions, $18,370.
Limitations: Applications not accepted. Giving primarily in Buffalo, NY.
Application information: Contributes only to pre-selected organizations.
Directors: Mary Kate Balkin, James E. Campbell, Jay B. Campbell, June K. Campbell.
EIN: 161310858

38118
Eve Dorfzaun Foundation, Inc.
c/o Lynn Igel
250 W. 90th St.
New York, NY 10024

Established in 1997 in NY.
Donor(s): Eve Dorfzaun.
Financial data (yr. ended 12/31/01): Grants paid, $17,500; assets, $245,081 (M); expenditures, $18,311; qualifying distributions, $17,500.
Limitations: Applications not accepted.
Application information: Contributes only to pre-selected organizations.
Trustee: Eve Dorfzaun, Dir.
EIN: 133945115

38119
Benjamin & Sara Greenspan Fund, Inc.
420 Lexington Ave., Ste. 2150
New York, NY 10170 (212) 953-0500
Contact: Edward Yelon, Treas.

Financial data (yr. ended 12/31/01): Grants paid, $17,500; assets, $570,261 (M); expenditures, $26,300; qualifying distributions, $17,500.
Limitations: Giving primarily in New Haven, CT, and New York, NY.
Officers: Richard Greenspan, Pres.; Edward Yelon, Treas.
EIN: 136092196

38120
The Hecht Foundation, Inc.
c/o Diamant, Katz, Kahn
6 E. 43rd St., 24th Fl.
New York, NY 10017

Incorporated in 1944 in NY.
Donor(s): George J. Hecht,‡ Parents' Magazine Enterprises, Inc., and others.
Financial data (yr. ended 12/31/01): Grants paid, $17,500; assets, $488,834 (M); expenditures, $21,774; qualifying distributions, $17,500.
Limitations: Applications not accepted.
Application information: Contributes only to pre-selected organizations.
Officer: Susan H. Toefel, Pres.
EIN: 136110380

38121
Orion Foundation, Inc.
c/o Shanholt, Glassman, Klein, & Kramer
488 Madison Ave., 10th Fl.
New York, NY 10022-5702

Established in 1989 in NY.
Donor(s): Miles Morgan.
Financial data (yr. ended 12/31/00): Grants paid, $17,500; assets, $3,058 (M); gifts received, $10,055; expenditures, $18,613; qualifying distributions, $18,613.
Limitations: Applications not accepted.
Application information: Contributes only to pre-selected organizations.
Officers: Miles Morgan, Pres.; Robert Ackart, Secy.; Christie Barter, Treas.
EIN: 133535900

38122
Joan Whitney and Charles Shipman Payson Charitable Foundation
c/o CSAM
466 Lexington Ave., 17th Fl.
New York, NY 10017-3140   (212) 201-9188

Established in 1987 in ME.
Donor(s): John W. Payson.
Financial data (yr. ended 10/31/01): Grants paid, $17,500; assets, $375,834 (M); expenditures, $18,870; qualifying distributions, $17,950.
Limitations: Applications not accepted. Giving primarily in ME.
Application information: Contributes only to pre-selected organizations.
Trustee: John W. Payson.
EIN: 010430129

38123
The Yen Family Charitable Foundation
c/o Oded Aboodi
1285 Ave. of the Americas, 21st Fl.
New York, NY 10019

Established in 1988 in NJ.
Financial data (yr. ended 10/31/01): Grants paid, $17,500; assets, $208,410 (M); expenditures, $17,808; qualifying distributions, $17,500.
Limitations: Applications not accepted. Giving primarily in NY.
Application information: Contributes only to pre-selected organizations.
Trustee: Oded Aboodi.
EIN: 133466314

38124
Gertrude Wachtler Cohen Memorial Foundation
76 S. Central Ave.
Valley Stream, NY 11580-5405

Donor(s): Edward S. Orzac, M.D.
Financial data (yr. ended 12/31/01): Grants paid, $17,477; assets, $241,749 (M); gifts received, $3,000; expenditures, $19,409; qualifying distributions, $17,606.
Limitations: Applications not accepted.
Application information: Contributes only to pre-selected organizations.
Officers: Sidney Orzac, Pres.; Edward S. Orzac, M.D., Secy.-Treas.
EIN: 237173642

38125
The Desperito Foundation, Inc.
46 Summit Ave.
Bronxville, NY 10708
Contact: John L. Cady, Secy.-Treas.

Established in 1997 in NY.
Donor(s): Ernest Desperito, Paula Desperito.
Financial data (yr. ended 12/31/00): Grants paid, $17,465; assets, $320,013 (M); gifts received, $70,393; expenditures, $29,645; qualifying distributions, $17,465.
Limitations: Giving primarily in Bedford, NY.
Officers: Ernest Desperito, Pres.; John L. Cady, Secy.-Treas.
EIN: 133967406

38126
L. William Eagan Family Foundation
104 Cottage Grove Dr.
Minoa, NY 13116
Contact: Robert J. Alexander, Jr., Mgr.

Established in 1986 in NY.
Financial data (yr. ended 06/30/99): Grants paid, $17,460; assets, $92,840 (M); expenditures, $20,389; qualifying distributions, $20,259.
Limitations: Giving primarily in central NY.
Application information: Application form not required.
Officer and Trustees:* Robert J. Alexander, Jr.,* Mgr.; Edward W. Eagan, Mary K. Eagan, Timothy A. Eagan, David A. Firley.
EIN: 222765887

38127
High Hopes Foundation, Inc.
c/o Michael Kennedy
425 Park Ave., 26th Fl.
New York, NY 10022

Established in 1989 in NY.
Donor(s): Trans-High Corp.
Financial data (yr. ended 05/31/02): Grants paid, $17,450; assets, $1,018 (M); gifts received, $16,950; expenditures, $17,450; qualifying distributions, $17,450.
Limitations: Applications not accepted. Giving primarily in New York, NY.
Application information: Contributes only to pre-selected organizations.
Officers and Directors:* Eleanore Kennedy,* Pres.; Michael Kennedy,* Secy.; Judith Baker,* Treas.; Laurabelle Goodson.
EIN: 133527256
Codes: CS, CD

38128
Jack A. Lesnow Family Foundation, Inc.
1111 Park Ave., No. 11D
New York, NY 10128-1234
Contact: Kalman Noselson, Pres.

Donor(s): Bertha Lesnow.‡
Financial data (yr. ended 12/31/01): Grants paid, $17,447; assets, $140,295 (M); expenditures, $21,374; qualifying distributions, $17,447.
Limitations: Applications not accepted. Giving primarily in NY.
Application information: Contributes only to pre-selected organizations.
Officers: Kalman Noselson, Pres.; Betsy Hockstein, V.P.; Susie Koltun, Secy.; Judith Noselson, Treas.
EIN: 116047859

38129
Vincent A. Greco Memorial Foundation
c/o Claire Friedlander
30 W. 70th St., Ste. 4A
New York, NY 10023

Established in 2000 in NY.
Donor(s): Claire Friedlander.
Financial data (yr. ended 04/30/02): Grants paid, $17,440; assets, $393,886 (M); gifts received, $53; expenditures, $18,178; qualifying distributions, $17,440.
Limitations: Giving primarily in Philadelphia, PA.
Trustee: Claire Friedlander.
EIN: 134133935

38130
Hugh & Betsy Lamle Foundation
c/o Hugh Lamle
555 Dune Rd.
Westhampton Beach, NY 11978

Established in 1994 in NY.
Financial data (yr. ended 09/30/01): Grants paid, $17,435; assets, $163,943 (M); expenditures, $19,628; qualifying distributions, $17,435.
Limitations: Applications not accepted.
Application information: Contributes only to pre-selected organizations.
Officers: Hugh Lamle, Pres. and Treas.; Betsy Lamle, V.P. and Secy.
EIN: 113241586

38131
Yetta & Abraham Lester Family Foundation, Inc.
750 Kappock St.
Riverdale, NY 10463
Contact: Yetta Lester, V.P.

Established in 1991 in NY.
Donor(s): Abraham Lester,‡ Yetta Lester.
Financial data (yr. ended 09/30/01): Grants paid, $17,400; assets, $286,290 (M); gifts received, $2,681; expenditures, $20,080; qualifying distributions, $17,400.
Limitations: Giving primarily in NY.
Officers: Yetta Lester, V.P.; Anne Lester Stone, Secy.
EIN: 133632497

38132
Ateres Shimon Dovid Memorial Foundation
c/o Eliyahu Zukierman
386 E. 8th St.
Brooklyn, NY 11218-4204

Donor(s): Nora Zukierman.
Financial data (yr. ended 12/31/01): Grants paid, $17,272; assets, $206,458 (M); expenditures, $18,341; qualifying distributions, $17,272.
Limitations: Applications not accepted. Giving primarily in the metropolitan New York, NY, area.
Application information: Contributes only to pre-selected organizations.
Trustees: Ida Feman, Eliyahu Zukierman, Miriam Zukierman, Nora Zukierman.
EIN: 116416907

38133
The Chapel of the Good Shepherd Foundation
50 Fountain Plz., Ste. 301
Buffalo, NY 14202

Established in 1999 in NY.
Financial data (yr. ended 02/28/02): Grants paid, $17,213; assets, $23,383 (M); gifts received, $31,220; expenditures, $18,173; qualifying distributions, $17,213.
Limitations: Applications not accepted. Giving primarily in NY.
Application information: Contributes only to pre-selected organizations.
Officer: Ronald Hermance, Jr., Chair.
Trustees: Robert Allison, Alan Anderson, Rev. Gordon De La Vars, James S. Fanning, James Groninger, Kris Hermance, Gerald F. Lahey, Jane Y. Lahey, Anne McIntosh, Walter McIntosh, Rev. Ross McKenzie, Mark Raynor.
EIN: 061540224

38134
Zichron Lea Foundation
112 Rutledge St.
Brooklyn, NY 11211

Established in 2000 in NY.

38134
Donor(s): Goldberger Family Trust.
Financial data (yr. ended 12/31/00): Grants paid, $17,210; assets, $71,646 (L); gifts received, $88,864; expenditures, $17,294; qualifying distributions, $17,210.
Director: Marc Goldberger.
EIN: 113537369

38135
The Conza Foundation, Inc.
c/o Becker & Co., LLC
551 Madison Ave.
New York, NY 10022

Financial data (yr. ended 06/30/02): Grants paid, $17,200; assets, $594,901 (M); gifts received, $556,000; expenditures, $30,707; qualifying distributions, $17,200.
Limitations: Applications not accepted.
Application information: Contributes only to pre-selected organizations.
Trustees: Stuart Becker, Anthony P. Conza, Scott Ehrenpreis.
EIN: 133921217

38136
The Butterfly Foundation, Inc.
43 Burton Ave.
Woodmere, NY 11598-1747

Established in 1997.
Donor(s): Stanley Sheidlower, Edith Sheidlower.
Financial data (yr. ended 12/31/00): Grants paid, $17,190; assets, $283,367 (M); expenditures, $22,936; qualifying distributions, $17,190.
Limitations: Applications not accepted.
Application information: Contributes only to pre-selected organizations.
Officers: Edith Sheidlower, Pres.; Stanley Sheidlower, V.P.
Directors: Amy Sheidlower Flynn, Jesse T. Sheidlower, Norman Sheidlower.
EIN: 113379746

38137
Helene & Harvey Benovitz Foundation, Inc.
c/o L. Wollin
350 5th Ave., Ste. 2822
New York, NY 10118

Established in 1999 in DE.
Financial data (yr. ended 06/30/01): Grants paid, $17,188; assets, $10,703 (M); gifts received, $10,000; expenditures, $18,873; qualifying distributions, $17,188.
Limitations: Applications not accepted. Giving primarily in NY.
Application information: Contributes only to pre-selected organizations.
Officers: Helene Benovitz, Pres.; Harvey Benovitz, V.P.; Lonnie Wollin, Secy.
EIN: 223623902

38138
Abraham Haas, et al. Trust - David Haas Memorial
c/o Deutsche Trust Co.
P.O. Box 1297, Church St. Sta.
New York, NY 10008-0829

Financial data (yr. ended 12/31/01): Grants paid, $17,157; assets, $239,006 (M); expenditures, $21,692; qualifying distributions, $18,730.
Limitations: Applications not accepted.
Application information: Contributes only to a pre-selected organization.
Trustee: Deutsche Bank.
EIN: 136042010

38139
Herbert and Irene Wheeler Foundation
(Formerly The Wheeler Foundation, Inc.)
P.O. Box 300507
Brooklyn, NY 11230-0507
Contact: Irene Wheeler, Treas.

Donor(s): Irene Wheeler.
Financial data (yr. ended 05/31/00): Grants paid, $17,153; assets, $90,066 (M); gifts received, $50,338; expenditures, $24,997; qualifying distributions, $21,036.
Limitations: Giving primarily in the New York City tri-state area.
Officer: Irene Wheeler, Treas.
EIN: 133673063
Codes: GTI

38140
Jay I. Firman Foundation, Inc.
465 Park Ave.
New York, NY 10022-1902
Contact: Liuba Firman, Pres.

Donor(s): Liuba Firman.
Financial data (yr. ended 11/30/01): Grants paid, $17,125; assets, $30,428 (M); gifts received, $17,000; expenditures, $17,780; qualifying distributions, $17,780.
Limitations: Giving primarily in NY.
Application information: Application form not required.
Officer: Liuba Firman, Pres.
EIN: 116035636

38141
Friends of Hama'ayan Institution, Inc.
c/o Paul Schwartz, C.P.A.
222 W. 83rd St., Ste. 4C
New York, NY 10024
Application address: c/o Jacob Paskesz, 1353 56th St., Brooklyn, NY 11219
Contact: Mordechai Krashinsky, Pres.

Financial data (yr. ended 12/31/00): Grants paid, $17,100; assets, $101,911 (M); gifts received, $36,287; expenditures, $22,442; qualifying distributions, $22,442.
Limitations: Giving limited to residents of Jerusalem, Israel.
Officers: Mordechai Krashinsky, Pres.; Henry Wolf, V.P. and Treas.; Jacob Paskesz, Secy.
EIN: 112686188
Codes: GTI

38142
The Robert and Barbara Sablowsky Foundation
c/o Nathan Berkman & Co.
29 Broadway, Ste. 2900
New York, NY 10006

Established in 2000 in NY.
Donor(s): Robert Sablowsky, Barbara Sablowsky.
Financial data (yr. ended 08/31/01): Grants paid, $17,100; assets, $33,772 (M); gifts received, $61,215; expenditures, $17,100; qualifying distributions, $17,100.
Limitations: Applications not accepted. Giving primarily in NY.
Application information: Contributes only to pre-selected organizations.
Trustees: Barbara Sablowsky, Robert Sablowsky.
EIN: 134137519

38143
Judith & Richard Wolf Foundation, Inc.
P.O. Box 356
Hewlett, NY 11557-0356

Established in 1990 in NY.
Donor(s): Richard Wolf, Judith Wolf.

Financial data (yr. ended 12/31/01): Grants paid, $17,090; assets, $8,764 (M); expenditures, $17,180; qualifying distributions, $17,176.
Limitations: Applications not accepted.
Application information: Unsolicited requests for funds not accepted.
Directors: Cynthia Atlas, Judith Wolf, Richard Wolf.
EIN: 112971364

38144
Dr. Elvira M. Carota Foundation
c/o Fein & Fein
31 Tompkins Rd.
Scarsdale, NY 10583

Established in 1998 in NY.
Donor(s): Elvira M. Carota.
Financial data (yr. ended 12/31/01): Grants paid, $17,000; assets, $25,352 (M); expenditures, $17,430; qualifying distributions, $17,425.
Limitations: Applications not accepted.
Application information: Contributes only to pre-selected organizations.
Officer: Elvira M. Carota, Pres.
Trustees: Marian Edvardsen, Howard Fein.
EIN: 134024566

38145
The Endowment for Vietnamese Education, Inc.
(Formerly The Stewart Family Foundation)
c/o Michele Stewart
527 Madison Ave., Ste. 24
New York, NY 10022-4304

Established in 1991 in DE.
Donor(s): William P. Stewart, Barbara Stewart, Michele Stewart.
Financial data (yr. ended 12/31/01): Grants paid, $17,000; assets, $24,405 (M); gifts received, $549,000; expenditures, $5,577,175; qualifying distributions, $557,312; giving activities include $540,717 for programs.
Limitations: Applications not accepted. Giving limited to the benefit of Vietnam.
Application information: Contributes only to pre-selected organizations.
Officer and Director:* Michele Stewart,* V.P.
EIN: 133292282

38146
The Escher Foundation, Inc.
1197 Post Rd.
Scarsdale, NY 10583-2023

Financial data (yr. ended 12/31/01): Grants paid, $17,000; assets, $304,300 (M); expenditures, $18,925; qualifying distributions, $17,000.
Limitations: Giving primarily in NY.
Application information: Application form not required.
Officers: Doris J.W. Escher, M.D., Pres.; Jeffrey Escher, M.D., V.P.; Daralynn Gordon, Secy.-Treas.
EIN: 237003465

38147
The Phyllis A. and Daryl R. Forsythe Foundation
21 Ridgeland Rd.
Norwich, NY 13815

Established in 1998 in NY.
Donor(s): Daryl R. Forsythe.
Financial data (yr. ended 03/31/02): Grants paid, $17,000; assets, $235,494 (M); gifts received, $14,000; expenditures, $18,548; qualifying distributions, $17,000.
Officer and Director:* Caryl R. Forsythe,* Pres.
EIN: 161550690

38148
The Jacques & Margot W. Kohn Foundation, Inc.
45 E. 89th St., Ste. 29E
New York, NY 10128

Established in 2000 in NY.
Donor(s): Jacques Kohn, Margot W. Kohn.
Financial data (yr. ended 12/31/01): Grants paid, $17,000; assets, $258,611 (M); gifts received, $100,149; expenditures, $18,304; qualifying distributions, $17,000.
Limitations: Applications not accepted.
Application information: Contributes only to pre-selected organizations.
Officers: Jacques Kohn, Pres.; Bernard J. Wald, Secy.; Margot W. Kohn, Treas.
EIN: 134088271

38149
The McMahon Family Foundation
(Formerly T. Gordon & Karen McMahon Family Foundation)
c/o Richard A. Eisner & Co., LLP
575 Madison Ave.
New York, NY 10022

Established in 1985 in NY.
Donor(s): T. Gordon McMahon.
Financial data (yr. ended 12/31/01): Grants paid, $17,000; assets, $513,602 (M); gifts received, $180; expenditures, $19,780; qualifying distributions, $17,000.
Limitations: Applications not accepted. Giving primarily in New York, NY.
Application information: Contributes only to pre-selected organizations.
Trustee: T. Gordon McMahon.
EIN: 133318163

38150
Tabor Foundation
c/o Myron Rindsberg
191 Sharon Rd.
Millerton, NY 12546
Application address: P.O. Box AZ, Millerton, NY 12546, tel.: (518) 789-4442
Contact: Ed Downey, Chair.

Donor(s): Josephine Demarest.
Financial data (yr. ended 12/31/00): Grants paid, $17,000; assets, $335,882 (M); gifts received, $1,200; expenditures, $19,273; qualifying distributions, $16,794.
Limitations: Giving primarily in CT and Millerton, NY.
Officers: Ed Downey, Chair.; Walter Davis, Secy.; Myron Rindsberg, Treas.
Director: Gertrude Schley.
EIN: 146616107

38151
The Henry Sears Foundation, Inc.
c/o Bessemer Trust Co., N.A.
630 5th Ave., 34th Fl.
New York, NY 10111-0333

Established in 1995 in MD.
Financial data (yr. ended 12/31/00): Grants paid, $16,988; assets, $823,768 (M); expenditures, $51,546; qualifying distributions, $40,581.
Limitations: Applications not accepted. Giving on the East Coast.
Application information: Contributes only to pre-selected organizations.
Officers: Henry F. Sears, Pres.; Christopher Sears, V.P.; Philip W. Hoon, Secy.-Treas.
Director: Sharon Bushnell.
EIN: 521933579

38152
Allen & Nirelle Galson Charitable Trust
5717 Thompson Rd.
Syracuse, NY 13214

Established in 1998 in NY.
Donor(s): Allen E. Galson, Nirelle J. Galson.
Financial data (yr. ended 12/31/01): Grants paid, $16,956; assets, $117,175 (M); expenditures, $24,681; qualifying distributions, $16,956.
Limitations: Applications not accepted.
Application information: Contributes only to pre-selected organizations.
Trustees: Allen E. Galson, Nirelle J. Galson.
EIN: 166483632

38153
The Kennedy Family Foundation
c/o Mark J. Bonner
3600 Marine Midland Ctr.
Buffalo, NY 14203

Established in 1998 in NY.
Donor(s): Bernard J. Kennedy.
Financial data (yr. ended 12/31/01): Grants paid, $16,950; assets, $205,503 (M); expenditures, $17,216; qualifying distributions, $16,950.
Officer and Director:* Bernard J. Kennedy,* Pres.
EIN: 311599316

38154
Schlinkert Family Foundation
c/o Cleary, Gottlieb, Steen & Hamilton
1 Liberty Plz.
New York, NY 10006-1470

Established in 1999 in CT.
Donor(s): Leo Schlinkert.
Financial data (yr. ended 12/31/01): Grants paid, $16,950; assets, $37,513 (M); expenditures, $18,069; qualifying distributions, $16,950.
Limitations: Applications not accepted.
Application information: Contributes only to pre-selected organizations.
Trustees: Diane Dickey, Leo Schlinkert.
EIN: 134094420

38155
The Reinsberg Family Foundation
c/o Lazard Freres & Co.
30 Rockefeller Plz.
New York, NY 10020
Contact: John R. Reinsberg, Tr.

Established in 1998 in NY.
Donor(s): Susie Reinsberg, Kurt Reinsberg, John R. Reinsberg.
Financial data (yr. ended 12/31/01): Grants paid, $16,933; assets, $325,350 (M); expenditures, $17,738; qualifying distributions, $16,933.
Limitations: Giving primarily in New York, NY.
Trustees: Nicole R. Kubin, John R. Reinsberg, Kurt E. Reinsberg, Susie R. Reinsberg.
EIN: 134023614

38156
Louis J. & Dorothy Gribetz Foundation, Inc.
c/o Grace Glasser
180 Riverside Dr., Apt. 12C
New York, NY 10024

Donor(s): David Glasser, Leo Glasser, Grace Glasser, Sharon Jaffe.
Financial data (yr. ended 12/31/01): Grants paid, $16,900; assets, $256,278 (M); gifts received, $15,034; expenditures, $18,514; qualifying distributions, $16,900.
Limitations: Giving primarily in NY.
Officers: Grace Glasser, Pres.; David G. Glasser, V.P.; Dorothy Weiss, Secy.
EIN: 116013983

38157
Brockway Foundation for the Needy of the Village and Township of Homer, New York
c/o KeyBank, N.A.
25 S. Main St.
Homer, NY 13077-1314
Contact: Kevin Crosley

Financial data (yr. ended 12/31/01): Grants paid, $16,875; assets, $538,177 (M); expenditures, $24,104; qualifying distributions, $17,725.
Limitations: Giving limited to the Homer, NY, area.
Officers: Jean Alexander, Pres.; Genevive Stafford, Secy.; Virginia Swartwout, Treas.
Board Members: Kevin Crosley, John Englebrecht.
EIN: 156021436
Codes: GTI

38158
Joseph Feldschuh Foundation, Inc.
50 5th Ave., Ste. 7120
New York, NY 10118

Established in 1997 in NY.
Donor(s): Joseph Feldschuh.
Financial data (yr. ended 12/31/99): Grants paid, $16,817; assets, $341,200 (M); gifts received, $29,000; expenditures, $17,072; qualifying distributions, $16,817.
Limitations: Applications not accepted.
Application information: Contributes only to pre-selected organizations.
Directors: Joseph Feldschuh, Shirley Harrison.
EIN: 311574943

38159
The Muller Fund, Inc.
P.O. Box 102
Diamond Point, NY 12824-0102

Financial data (yr. ended 08/31/01): Grants paid, $16,810; assets, $454,074 (M); expenditures, $18,250; qualifying distributions, $16,810.
Limitations: Applications not accepted. Giving primarily in NY.
Application information: Contributes only to pre-selected organizations.
Trustees: Phillip McIntyre, Evelyn Muller, Herman E. Muller, Jr.
EIN: 136122627

38160
Jam Foundation, Inc.
c/o Arnold Spellun
529 5th Ave., 8th Fl.
New York, NY 10017-4608

Established in 1998 in NY.
Financial data (yr. ended 12/31/99): Grants paid, $16,800; assets, $133,543 (M); expenditures, $17,519; qualifying distributions, $16,800.
Limitations: Applications not accepted.
Application information: Contributes only to pre-selected organizations.
Officer: Arnold Spellun, Pres.
EIN: 134037390

38161
The Mendel & Zlata Hoffman Foundation
6 Sunrise Dr.
Monsey, NY 10952

Established in 1995.
Donor(s): Mendel Hoffman.
Financial data (yr. ended 12/31/00): Grants paid, $16,793; assets, $29,809 (M); gifts received, $18,028; expenditures, $20,040; qualifying distributions, $16,793.
Limitations: Applications not accepted. Giving primarily in NY; some giving to Israel.

38161—NEW YORK

Application information: Unsolicited requests for funds not accepted.
Trustees: Leah Hoffman, Mendel Hoffman, Zlata Hoffman.
EIN: 137067552

38162
Karp Foundation, Inc.
c/o Three Arrows Co.
600 Mamaroneck Ave., Ste. 302
Harrison, NY 10528

Established about 1965 in NY.
Donor(s): Three Arrows Co.
Financial data (yr. ended 12/31/00): Grants paid, $16,763; assets, $24,851 (M); gifts received, $10,600; expenditures, $17,005; qualifying distributions, $16,763.
Limitations: Applications not accepted. Giving primarily in NY.
Application information: Contributes only to pre-selected organizations.
Officers: Eileen Karp, Pres.; David Karp, V.P.; Howard Karp, V.P.; Morris Karp, Treas.
EIN: 136173515

38163
Irving and Shari Weinberger Foundation
56-15 175th St.
Flushing, NY 11365-1621

Established in 1997 in NY.
Donor(s): Irving Weinberger.
Financial data (yr. ended 12/31/01): Grants paid, $16,763; assets, $358,407 (M); expenditures, $17,169; qualifying distributions, $16,763.
Limitations: Applications not accepted. Giving primarily in New York, NY.
Application information: Contributes only to pre-selected organizations.
Trustees: Irving Weinberger, Shari Weinberger.
EIN: 113352180

38164
John J. Conefry, Jr. Foundation
5 Butler Pl.
Garden City, NY 11530-4602

Established in 1997 in NY.
Donor(s): John J. Conefry, Jr.
Financial data (yr. ended 12/31/00): Grants paid, $16,750; assets, $568,919 (M); gifts received, $403,344; expenditures, $19,429; qualifying distributions, $16,750.
Limitations: Applications not accepted. Giving primarily in the New York, NY, area.
Application information: Contributes only to pre-selected organizations.
Trustees: Christopher J. Conefry, John J. Conefry, Mary Ellen Conefry, Sarah Conefry.
EIN: 113378781

38165
M S Foundation
c/o D. Soifer, C.P.A.
24 Jackson Ave.
Spring Valley, NY 10977
Contact: Nathan Steinmetz, Dir.

Established in 1999.
Financial data (yr. ended 06/30/01): Grants paid, $16,750; assets, $250,038 (M); gifts received, $46,920; expenditures, $22,242; qualifying distributions, $16,750.
Director: Nathan Steinmetz.
EIN: 113477941

38166
The Dorothy & Dennis Sheahan Charitable Family Foundation
84 Hayground Cove Rd.
P.O. Box 1194
Water Mill, NY 11976

Established in 2000 in NY.
Donor(s): Dennis P. Sheahan.
Financial data (yr. ended 12/31/00): Grants paid, $16,750; assets, $223,752 (M); gifts received, $234,653; expenditures, $20,165; qualifying distributions, $16,750.
Limitations: Applications not accepted. Giving primarily in NY.
Application information: Contributes only to pre-selected organizations.
Trustees: Dennis P. Sheahan, Dorothy Sheahan.
EIN: 522229353

38167
The Jungreis Foundation
50 Broadway, 5th Fl.
New York, NY 10004

Established in 1999 in NY.
Donor(s): Aron Jungreis.
Financial data (yr. ended 11/30/00): Grants paid, $16,740; assets, $208,368 (M); gifts received, $207,810; expenditures, $19,100; qualifying distributions, $19,100.
Officers: Aron Jungreis, Pres.; Ruth Jungreis, V.P.
EIN: 113466420

38168
Kathleen & Edward Scheider Foundation, Inc.
c/o Hartmeyer & Duncan
P.O. Box 69
Fleischmanns, NY 12430-0069
(845) 254-4553

Donor(s): Edward J. Scheider, Kathleen Scheider.‡
Financial data (yr. ended 12/31/01): Grants paid, $16,715; assets, $144,272 (M); expenditures, $18,637; qualifying distributions, $16,715.
Limitations: Giving primarily in New York, NY.
Officers: Edward J. Scheider, V.P.; Harry Bower, Secy.-Treas.
EIN: 133155234

38169
Tyler Foundation, Inc.
5021 Theall Rd.
Rye, NY 10580-1445 (914) 925-9331
Contact: Parker R. Tyler, Jr., Pres.

Donor(s): Parker R. Tyler, Jr., Jo Tyler, Xanthos Valan, GCS Service, Inc., Gloria B. Tyler.
Financial data (yr. ended 12/31/01): Grants paid, $16,704; assets, $83,788 (M); gifts received, $6,358; expenditures, $19,293; qualifying distributions, $16,704.
Limitations: Giving on a national basis, with emphasis on the Northeast.
Officers and Directors:* Parker R. Tyler, Jr.,* Pres.; Gloria B. Tyler,* Secy.-Treas.; Hilary Tyler, Wesley B. Tyler.
EIN: 132838499

38170
Herman & Ruth Rosenthal Foundation, Inc.
c/o Judith Eydenberg
115 Andover Rd.
Roslyn Heights, NY 11577

Established in 1947.
Financial data (yr. ended 12/31/01): Grants paid, $16,630; assets, $22,291 (M); expenditures, $16,746; qualifying distributions, $16,630.
Limitations: Giving primarily in NY.
Officer: Judith Eydenberg, Pres.

EIN: 136130054

38171
S. C. Benjamin Foundation
(Formerly Sidney Cannold Charitable Foundation)
c/o Sheryl C. Benjamin
10 Indian Trail
Harrison, NY 10528-1829

Established in 1914 in NY; classified as a private operating foundation in 2001.
Financial data (yr. ended 04/30/02): Grants paid, $16,616; assets, $747,213 (M); gifts received, $7,000; expenditures, $21,870; qualifying distributions, $16,616.
Limitations: Applications not accepted. Giving primarily in NY.
Application information: Contributes only to pre-selected organizations.
Officer: Sheryl C. Benjamin, Pres.
EIN: 136120578

38172
Barrie & Mark Handelman Family Foundation
1555 Lexington Pkwy.
Schenectady, NY 12309

Established in 1986 in NY.
Financial data (yr. ended 10/31/01): Grants paid, $16,591; assets, $200,278 (M); expenditures, $18,623; qualifying distributions, $16,591.
Limitations: Applications not accepted. Giving primarily in Schenectady, NY.
Application information: Contributes only to pre-selected organizations.
Trustee: Mark Handelman.
EIN: 222782416

38173
J. M. Hodges Educational Fund Trust
c/o Community Bank, N.A.
P.O. Box 690, 201 N. Union St.
Olean, NY 14760-2738

Financial data (yr. ended 12/31/99): Grants paid, $16,500; assets, $266,044 (M); gifts received, $1,500; expenditures, $20,197; qualifying distributions, $33,687; giving activities include $16,500 for loans to individuals.
Limitations: Giving limited within a ten-mile radius of Olean, NY.
Trustee: Community Bank.
EIN: 166136464

38174
Lipke Foundation
(Formerly Gibraltar Foundation)
3556 Lake Shore Rd.
P.O. Box 2028
Buffalo, NY 14219-0228

Donor(s): Gibraltar Steel.
Financial data (yr. ended 12/31/01): Grants paid, $16,500; assets, $347,596 (M); expenditures, $24,648; qualifying distributions, $22,422.
Limitations: Applications not accepted. Giving primarily in NY.
Application information: Contributes only to pre-selected organizations.
Trustees: Brian J. Lipke, Meredith A. Lipke.
EIN: 510176074

38175
The McAloon-Wettlaufer Foundation, Inc.
72 Cleveland Dr.
Buffalo, NY 14222-1610 (716) 829-2890
Additional tel.: (716) 881-0458
Contact: Margaret McAloon, Pres.

Established in 1991 in NY.

Donor(s): C. Penn Wettlaufer,‡ Mrs. C. Penn Wettlaufer, Margaret McAloon.
Financial data (yr. ended 06/30/01): Grants paid, $16,500; assets, $102,300 (M); gifts received, $41,000; expenditures, $18,722; qualifying distributions, $16,500.
Limitations: Giving limited to western NY.
Officers: Margaret McAloon, Pres.; Anne R. Berthoff, V.P.; Elizabeth Wettlaufer, Secy.; Jeffrey Vinz, Treas.
Trustees: Mary Jo Giambelluca, Karen Klimczak, David Mahoney, Ron Smith.
EIN: 223090446

38176
The O'Hara Family Foundation
410 Bryant Ave.
Roslyn, NY 11576

Established in 1998 in NY.
Donor(s): Richard L. O'Hara, Dolores O'Hara.
Financial data (yr. ended 12/31/01): Grants paid, $16,500; assets, $298,388 (M); gifts received, $22,300; expenditures, $43,726; qualifying distributions, $16,500.
Limitations: Giving limited to NY.
Officers and Directors:* Richard L. O'Hara,* Pres.; Dolores O'Hara,* V.P.; Ann Maria Kinney,* Secy.-Treas.
EIN: 113411369

38177
The Armstrong-Nickoll Family Foundation
c/o Benjamin E. Nickoll
34 Gramercy Park E. Ste. 2A
New York, NY 10003

Established in 1998 in NY.
Donor(s): Benjamin E. Nickoll.
Financial data (yr. ended 12/31/00): Grants paid, $16,445; assets, $503,285 (M); gifts received, $450,249; expenditures, $16,545; qualifying distributions, $16,445.
Trustees: Christine M. Armstrong, Benjamin E. Nickoll.
EIN: 134007198

38178
The Robert and Marcia Horowitz Foundation
1 Valerie Dr.
Glen Head, NY 11545-2913

Established in 1997.
Financial data (yr. ended 12/31/01): Grants paid, $16,445; assets, $365,533 (M); expenditures, $28,074; qualifying distributions, $16,445.
Limitations: Applications not accepted.
Application information: Contributes only to pre-selected organizations.
Trustee: Robert Horowitz.
EIN: 113375157

38179
Luigi Fatato Foundation, Inc.
318 2nd St.
Brooklyn, NY 11215-2401

Donor(s): Theresa Striano.
Financial data (yr. ended 05/31/01): Grants paid, $16,435; assets, $213,316 (M); expenditures, $17,932; qualifying distributions, $16,435.
Limitations: Applications not accepted.
Application information: Contributes only to pre-selected organizations.
Officers: Ronald J. Fatato, Pres. and Secy.; Francis Fatato, V.P.; Louis M. Fatato, V.P.; Thomas R. Fatato, V.P.
EIN: 116039857

38180
Barbara J. & Lawrence J. Goldstein Do Good Foundation, Inc.
1865 Palmer Ave.
Larchmont, NY 10538

Established in 1996 in NY.
Donor(s): Lawrence J. Goldstein.
Financial data (yr. ended 12/31/01): Grants paid, $16,430; assets, $347,315 (M); gifts received, $66,675; expenditures, $20,411; qualifying distributions, $16,430.
Limitations: Applications not accepted.
Application information: Contributes only to pre-selected organizations.
Officers: Lawrence J. Goldstein, Chair.; Barbara J. Goldstein, Pres.; David Michael, Secy.
EIN: 133915414

38181
David H. Gold Foundation, Inc.
c/o Frendel, Brown & Weissman
655 3rd Ave., Ste. 1400
New York, NY 10017-5617

Financial data (yr. ended 12/31/01): Grants paid, $16,380; assets, $145,648 (M); expenditures, $19,214; qualifying distributions, $16,380.
Limitations: Applications not accepted. Giving primarily in NY.
Application information: Contributes only to pre-selected organizations.
Officers: Adrienne Gossett, Pres.; Harvey Gossett, V.P.
EIN: 116034212

38182
The Barry & Renee Brandeis Foundation
15 Cooper Dr.
Great Neck, NY 11023

Established in 1999 in NY.
Donor(s): Barry Brandeis, Renee Brandeis.
Financial data (yr. ended 12/31/01): Grants paid, $16,375; assets, $299,310 (M); gifts received, $50,000; expenditures, $17,331; qualifying distributions, $16,375.
Limitations: Applications not accepted.
Application information: Contributes only to pre-selected organizations.
Directors: Barry Brandeis, Renee Brandeis, David Kessler.
EIN: 113527406

38183
Arlene L. & Jerome R. Gerber Family Foundation
c/o Arthur Liberman
P.O. Box 6545
Syracuse, NY 13217

Financial data (yr. ended 12/31/01): Grants paid, $16,350; assets, $119,097 (M); expenditures, $18,038; qualifying distributions, $16,350.
Limitations: Applications not accepted.
Application information: Contributes only to pre-selected organizations.
Officers and Directors:* Arthur Liberman,* Pres.; Robert Gerber,* V.P.; Sheldon B. Kruth,* Secy. and Treas.
EIN: 161538711

38184
Mayer Family Foundation
c/o Wassermann
235 E. 22nd St., No. 11-J
New York, NY 10010-4616
Contact: Hannah D. Wassermann, Pres.

Donor(s): Hannah D. Wassermann, Felix E. Wassermann.
Financial data (yr. ended 12/31/01): Grants paid, $16,350; assets, $51,780 (M); gifts received, $16,825; expenditures, $16,605; qualifying distributions, $16,350.
Officers: Hannah D. Wassermann, Pres.; Felix E. Wassermann, Secy.
EIN: 136161693

38185
KMC Foundation
12 Ocean Blvd.
Point Lookout, NY 11569
Application address: c/o Padell, 156 W. 56th St., New York, NY 10019
Contact: Kevin Cahill, Pres.

Established in 1999 in NY.
Financial data (yr. ended 12/31/01): Grants paid, $16,348; assets, $475,507 (M); gifts received, $200,000; expenditures, $16,612; qualifying distributions, $16,348.
Officers and Directors:* Kevin Cahill,* Pres.; Kathryn Cahill,* Secy.-Treas.; Brendan Cahill, Chris Cahill, Denis Cahill, Kevin Cahill, Jr., Sean Cahill.
EIN: 113487471

38186
The Thousand Cranes Foundation
101 Central Park W., Ste. PH-C
New York, NY 10023-4204
Contact: Barbara Ann Klein, Pres.

Financial data (yr. ended 12/31/00): Grants paid, $16,341; assets, $32,881 (M); expenditures, $16,596; qualifying distributions, $16,341.
Limitations: Giving primarily in NY.
Officers and Directors:* Barbara Ann Klein,* Pres.; Edward G. Schwartz,* Secy.; Lauren-Marie Taylor.
EIN: 133850642

38187
Loomis Foundation
c/o Alfred L. Loomis, III
237 Park Ave., Ste. 900
New York, NY 10017

Established in 1957 in NY.
Donor(s): Alfred L. Loomis, Jr.‡
Financial data (yr. ended 12/31/01): Grants paid, $16,308; assets, $419,388 (M); expenditures, $18,528; qualifying distributions, $16,308.
Limitations: Applications not accepted. Giving primarily in Jacksonville, FL.
Application information: Contributes only to pre-selected organizations.
Officers: Alfred L. Loomis III, Pres.; Virginia D. Loomis, V.P.; Virginia Peterson, Secy.-Treas.
EIN: 136077032

38188
Dill Foundation
1 Vink Dr.
Carmel, NY 10512 (845) 225-0050
Contact: Fred L. Dill, Sr., Tr.

Established in 1981 in NY.
Donor(s): Fred L. Dill, Sr.
Financial data (yr. ended 02/28/02): Grants paid, $16,300; assets, $385,009 (M); gifts received, $50,000; expenditures, $17,195; qualifying distributions, $16,300.
Limitations: Giving primarily in Westchester and Putnam counties, NY.
Trustees: Fred L. Dill, Sr., Stephen Dill, Marvin I. Gruss.
EIN: 061043550

38189
Selma & Alvin Silverman Foundation, Inc.
c/o Wien & Malkin, LLP
60 E. 42nd St.
New York, NY 10165-0001

Donor(s): Alvin Silverman.
Financial data (yr. ended 10/31/01): Grants paid, $16,270; assets, $183,477 (M); expenditures, $18,677; qualifying distributions, $16,270.
Limitations: Applications not accepted. Giving primarily in NY.
Application information: Contributes only to pre-selected organizations.
Officers: Selma Silverman, Pres. and Treas.; Alvin Silverman, V.P. and Secy.
EIN: 136142185

38190
The Duhl Foundation, Inc.
311 E. 50th St.
New York, NY 10022

Established in 1961.
Donor(s): Roger N. Duhl, Benjamin Duhl.
Financial data (yr. ended 12/31/01): Grants paid, $16,250; assets, $1,641,786 (M); gifts received, $1,500,000; expenditures, $20,082; qualifying distributions, $16,250.
Limitations: Applications not accepted. Giving primarily in NY.
Application information: Contributes only to pre-selected organizations.
Officers: Benjamin Duhl, Pres.; Andrew P. Segal, V.P.; Roger N. Duhl, Secy.-Treas.
EIN: 136161491

38191
Robert J. Rohr, III and Mary C. Rohr Charitable Trust
(Formerly Robert and Mary C. Rohr Charitable Trust)
c/o U.S. Trust
114 W. 47th St., TaxVas
New York, NY 10036

Established in 1988 in NY.
Financial data (yr. ended 09/30/01): Grants paid, $16,200; assets, $140,688 (M); expenditures, $17,933; qualifying distributions, $16,200.
Limitations: Applications not accepted.
Application information: Contributes only to pre-selected organizations.
Trustee: U.S. Trust.
EIN: 136923367

38192
John V. Cioffi Family Foundation
c/o Yohalem, Gillman & Co., LLP
477 Madison Ave.
New York, NY 10022-5802

Donor(s): John V. Cioffi.
Financial data (yr. ended 12/31/00): Grants paid, $16,185; assets, $434,068 (M); gifts received, $42,938; expenditures, $24,897; qualifying distributions, $16,185.
Limitations: Applications not accepted. Giving primarily in New York, NY.
Application information: Contributes only to pre-selected organizations.
Trustee: John V. Cioffi.
EIN: 237650708

38193
Muller Foundation
247 W. 87th St., Ste. 7J
New York, NY 10024-2848
Contact: Efrat Muller-Lefkowitz, Pres.

Established in 1993 in IL.
Donor(s): Efrat Muller-Lefkowitz.
Financial data (yr. ended 12/31/00): Grants paid, $16,125; assets, $279,868 (M); expenditures, $18,596; qualifying distributions, $16,125.
Limitations: Giving primarily in the New York, NY area.
Officer: Efrat Muller-Lefkowitz, Pres.
Director: Jacob Laufer.
EIN: 133736440

38194
Malina Foundation, Inc.
c/o Victor Levinson
565 Park Ave., Ste. 7E
New York, NY 10021

Donor(s): Arthur Malina.
Financial data (yr. ended 12/31/00): Grants paid, $16,098; assets, $232,111 (M); expenditures, $18,031; qualifying distributions, $16,098.
Limitations: Applications not accepted. Giving primarily in NY.
Application information: Contributes only to pre-selected organizations.
Officers: Edythe Charnas, Pres.; Evelyn Malina, V.P.; Jane Levinson, Secy.-Treas.
EIN: 136092407

38195
Adelphic Cornell Educational Fund, Inc.
c/o Stewart Howe Alumni Svcs.
P.O. Box 876
Ithaca, NY 14851-0876
Application address: P.O. Box 5000, Berkely, CA 94705-0050, tel.: (415)-921-2382
Contact: J. Thomas Chirurg, Pres.

Donor(s): Robert E. Reed, Thomas S. Foulkes.
Financial data (yr. ended 04/30/02): Grants paid, $16,074; assets, $426,721 (M); gifts received, $9,909; expenditures, $19,851; qualifying distributions, $16,074.
Limitations: Giving limited to Ithaca, NY.
Application information: Application form not required.
Officers: J. Thomas Chirurg, Pres.; Ron E. Schaefer, Secy.-Treas.
EIN: 166023220

38196
American Friends for Advocacy Training, Inc.
400 E. 56th St.
New York, NY 10022 (212) 832-2598
Contact: Florence Galkin, Pres.

Financial data (yr. ended 12/31/00): Grants paid, $16,051; assets, $11,319 (M); gifts received, $72,131; expenditures, $89,478; qualifying distributions, $63,021; giving activities include $46,970 for programs.
Limitations: Giving on an international basis, primarily in Israel.
Officers: Florence Galkin, Pres.; Martin Hochbaum, Secy.
Trustees: Doron Abraham, Yuly Ben-Levi, Sharon Binyamin, J. Brener, Sharon Burde, Meryl Greenfield, Mark Pelavin, Alison Pepper, Gail Pressberg, Rabbi David Rabson, Judith Recanaty, Bar-Yoset Rivka, Phillip Superia, Amin Hage Yehia.
EIN: 133807458

38197
Fund for Astrophysical Research, Inc.
(also known as F.A.R.)
919 3rd Ave., 2nd Fl.
New York, NY 10022-3904 (212) 909-6595
FAX: (212) 909-6836; *E-mail:* wbdunham@debevoise.com; *URL:* http://fdncenter.org/grantmaker/fundastro
Contact: Wolcott B. Dunham, Jr., Pres.

Established in 1936.
Donor(s): Charles G. Thompson, Alice Bemis Thompson.
Financial data (yr. ended 12/31/01): Grants paid, $16,039; assets, $235,856 (M); gifts received, $13,667; expenditures, $16,379; qualifying distributions, $16,150.
Limitations: Giving in Australia, New Zealand, and the U.S.
Application information: See fund's Web site for full application requirements and conditions.
Officers and Trustees:* Wolcott B. Dunham, Jr.,* Pres. and Treas.; Arthur R. Upgren,* V.P.; Mary Dunham Thompson, Secy.; George N. Apell, Kenneth A. Janes, Richard G. Kron, A.G. Davis Philip, Harry L. Shipman.
Advisor: James G. Baker.
EIN: 136161246

38198
Blarney Fund Education Trust
c/o Bell & Co.
15 E. 26th St., Ste. 1605
New York, NY 10010-1599
Application address: P.O. Box 214, Swanton, VT 05488, tel.: (802) 868-2755
Contact: Michael Emmet Walsh, Tr.

Established in 1990 in VT.
Donor(s): Michael Emmet Walsh.
Financial data (yr. ended 05/31/01): Grants paid, $16,000; assets, $305,888 (M); gifts received, $21,744; expenditures, $16,094; qualifying distributions, $16,094.
Limitations: Giving limited to Franklin County, VT.
Application information: Recipients selected by the Guidance Dept. and Scholarship Comm. of participating high schools.
Trustee: Michael Emmet Walsh.
EIN: 036051035
Codes: GTI

38199
Adele and Hyman S. Frank Fund
1134 Beach 9th St.
Far Rockaway, NY 11691

Established in 1990 in NY.
Financial data (yr. ended 12/31/01): Grants paid, $16,000; assets, $0 (M); expenditures, $17,224; qualifying distributions, $15,958.
Limitations: Applications not accepted. Giving primarily in NY.
Application information: Contributes only to pre-selected organizations.
Trustees: Anita Bashkowitz, Gloria Simon-Hoch.
EIN: 136940685

38200
Kleinbaum Fund, Inc.
c/o Lipsky, Goodkin & Co.
120 W. 45th St., 7th Fl.
New York, NY 10036

Financial data (yr. ended 05/31/02): Grants paid, $16,000; assets, $374,428 (M); expenditures, $18,211; qualifying distributions, $16,000.
Limitations: Applications not accepted.
Application information: Contributes only to pre-selected organizations.

Officer and Directors:* Harriette A. Gifford,* Pres.; Philip P. Goodkin.
EIN: 136028781

38201
Martocci Memorial Foundation, Inc.
c/o Ronald J. McDowan
169 Mountain Rd.
Cornwall-on-Hudson, NY 12520
(845) 534-7918

Established in 1998 in NY.
Financial data (yr. ended 12/31/99): Grants paid, $16,000; assets, $39,140 (M); expenditures, $17,050; qualifying distributions, $17,050.
Limitations: Giving primarily in NY.
Officer: Ronald J. McGowan, Pres.
EIN: 141801944

38202
Ruth & Morris Natelson Foundation
c/o Barry Strauss Assocs., Ltd.
307 5th Ave., 8th Fl.
New York, NY 10016-6517

Financial data (yr. ended 09/30/01): Grants paid, $16,000; assets, $292,307 (M); expenditures, $18,760; qualifying distributions, $16,000.
Limitations: Applications not accepted. Giving primarily in NY.
Application information: Contributes only to pre-selected organizations.
Trustees: Arthur W. Fried, Pamela N. Irving, Barry M. Strauss.
EIN: 237002929

38203
PGJM Foundation
39 The Oaks
Roslyn, NY 11576

Financial data (yr. ended 12/31/00): Grants paid, $16,000; assets, $650,313 (M); expenditures, $22,489; qualifying distributions, $16,000.
Limitations: Applications not accepted.
Application information: Contributes only to pre-selected organizations.
Officers: Gene M. Bernstein, Pres.; Pamela A. Bernstein, V.P.
Directors: Jennifer A. Bernstein, Melinda J. Bernstein.
EIN: 113440511

38204
Planning & Community Relations Corporation of Southern Brooklyn, Inc.
4520 18th Ave.
Brooklyn, NY 11204

Established in 1997 in NY.
Financial data (yr. ended 07/31/01): Grants paid, $16,000; assets, $299,847 (M); expenditures, $25,515; qualifying distributions, $16,000.
Limitations: Applications not accepted.
Application information: Contributes only to pre-selected organizations.
Officers: Menachem Shayovich, Chair. and Secy.; David Singer, Pres.; Max Berg, V.P.
EIN: 112693623

38205
Aaron Siskind Foundation
c/o The School of Visual Arts, MFA Photography
214 E. 21st St.
New York, NY 10010-7460

Donor(s): Aaron Siskind.‡
Financial data (yr. ended 12/31/00): Grants paid, $16,000; assets, $41,512 (M); expenditures, $49,525; qualifying distributions, $16,000.
Limitations: Giving primarily in Providence, RI.
Application information: Application form required.
Officer and Directors:* Anne Coleman Torrey,* Exec. Dir.; Judith Jacobs, Ira Lowe, Victor Schrager, Charles Traub.
EIN: 521359961

38206
Annie Sonnenblick Scholarship Fund, Inc.
c/o Republic National Bank of New York
452 5th Ave., 27th Fl.
New York, NY 10018-2706
Contact: Evelyn Hanson, Chair.

Financial data (yr. ended 11/30/99): Grants paid, $16,000; assets, $500 (M); gifts received, $25,559; expenditures, $25,559; qualifying distributions, $25,559.
Limitations: Giving on a national basis, with emphasis on the Northeast.
Application information: Application form required.
Officers: Evelyn Hanson, Chair. and V.P.; Robert Stadelman, V.P.; Patricia Howard, Secy.
EIN: 133010491
Codes: GTI

38207
The Robert & Gail Spiegel Foundation, Inc.
c/o M.R. Weiser & Co., LLP
135 W. 50th St.
New York, NY 10020-1299

Donor(s): Robert Spiegel.
Financial data (yr. ended 08/31/01): Grants paid, $16,000; assets, $475,628 (M); expenditures, $21,023; qualifying distributions, $16,000.
Limitations: Applications not accepted. Giving primarily in NJ and NY.
Application information: Contributes only to pre-selected organizations.
Officers: Gail Spiegel, Co-Pres.; Robert Spiegel, Co-Pres.
EIN: 237048454

38208
The Star Foundation
c/o David Landau
1358 47th St.
Brooklyn, NY 11219

Established in 1995 in NY.
Financial data (yr. ended 12/31/01): Grants paid, $16,000; assets, $365,432 (M); expenditures, $18,075; qualifying distributions, $16,000.
Limitations: Applications not accepted.
Application information: Contributes only to pre-selected organizations.
Trustee: M. Eckstein, David Landau.
EIN: 113272301

38209
Telfeyan Evangelical Fund, Inc.
24 Windsor Rd.
Great Neck, NY 11021-3910

Financial data (yr. ended 09/30/01): Grants paid, $16,000; assets, $268,803 (M); gifts received, $385; expenditures, $18,992; qualifying distributions, $16,000.
Limitations: Applications not accepted. Giving primarily in NJ, and New York, NY.
Application information: Contributes only to pre-selected organizations.
Officers: Sarkis Telfeyan, Pres.; Elida N. Telfeyan, V.P.
EIN: 116034149

38210
The Von Damm Family Evergreen Foundation
46-17 28th Ave.
Astoria, NY 11103
Contact: Henry Von Damm, Tr.

Established in 2000 in NY.
Donor(s): Henry Von Damm, Jr.
Financial data (yr. ended 04/30/01): Grants paid, $16,000; assets, $148,212 (M); gifts received, $164,270; expenditures, $16,058; qualifying distributions, $16,000.
Trustees: Henry Von Damm, Louise Von Damm.
EIN: 137252003

38211
Katherine Benton Dollinger Walsh Charitable Trust
c/o James G. Vazzana
5 S. Fitzhugh St., Ste. 230
Rochester, NY 14614-1413 (716) 454-5850
Contact: James G. Vazzana, Tr.

Established in 1999 in NY.
Financial data (yr. ended 12/31/01): Grants paid, $16,000; assets, $305,666 (M); expenditures, $29,578; qualifying distributions, $16,000.
Trustees: Thomas McElligott, Elizabeth Jo Walsh Parrish, James G. Vazzana.
EIN: 166497200

38212
The Axelrod Family Foundation, Inc.
c/o Muchnick, Golieb & Golieb
200 Park Ave., Ste. 1700
New York, NY 10003-1503
Application address: 45 W. 139th St., New York, NY 10037, tel.: (212) 368-8110
Contact: Mrs. Mott

Established in 1994 in NY.
Donor(s): Bernard M. Axelrod, Carlin S. Axelrod.
Financial data (yr. ended 12/31/01): Grants paid, $15,975; assets, $1,867 (M); gifts received, $17,500; expenditures, $18,140; qualifying distributions, $17,262.
Limitations: Giving primarily in Delano Village, NY.
Application information: Application form required.
Officers and Directors:* Bernard M. Axelrod,* Pres.; Jay G. Axelrod,* Secy.; Carlin S. Axelrod.
EIN: 133775791
Codes: GTI

38213
Robert L. Pelz Foundation, Inc.
345 Park Ave., 18th Fl.
New York, NY 10154-0004

Donor(s): Mary Jane Pelz, Robert L. Pelz.
Financial data (yr. ended 03/31/01): Grants paid, $15,975; assets, $47,530 (M); gifts received, $33,188; expenditures, $16,107; qualifying distributions, $15,975.
Limitations: Applications not accepted. Giving primarily in New York, NY.
Application information: Contributes only to pre-selected organizations.
Officers: Robert L. Pelz, Pres.; Mary Jane Pelz, V.P. and Treas.; Katie Pelz-Davis, Secy.; Robert L. Pelz, Jr., Treas.
EIN: 136105206

38214
Lucy & Richard K. Manoff Foundation
c/o Nathan Berkman & Co.
29 Broadway, Rm. 2900
New York, NY 10006-3102

Donor(s): Richard K. Manoff.

Financial data (yr. ended 12/31/01): Grants paid, $15,930; assets, $53,276 (M); expenditures, $18,219; qualifying distributions, $15,930.
Limitations: Applications not accepted. Giving primarily in NY.
Application information: Contributes only to pre-selected organizations.
Trustees: Gregory P. Manoff, Richard K. Manoff, Robert K. Manoff.
EIN: 136115271

38215
Second District Dental Society of the State of New York Relief Fund
c/o Callaghan
500 Merrick Rd.
Rockville Centre, NY 11570

Financial data (yr. ended 12/31/01): Grants paid, $15,850; assets, $30,988 (M); gifts received, $300; expenditures, $17,580; qualifying distributions, $15,850.
Limitations: Giving limited to NY.
Officer: Bernard W. Haekett, Exec. Dir.
EIN: 116102934

38216
Tikvah Charitable Trust
c/o Mr. Berel Fink
1909 59th St.
Brooklyn, NY 11204-2341

Established in 1992 in NY.
Donor(s): Berel Fink.
Financial data (yr. ended 12/31/01): Grants paid, $15,825; assets, $310,725 (M); expenditures, $20,450; qualifying distributions, $15,825.
Limitations: Applications not accepted. Giving primarily in Brooklyn, NY.
Application information: Contributes only to pre-selected organizations.
Trustees: Allan C. Bell, Berel Fink, Esther Fink, Nellie Fink.
EIN: 223196452

38217
JJJ Family Foundation
(Formerly The Janie and Tino Galluzzo Foundation)
c/o Lenat Co.
315 Westchester Ave.
Port Chester, NY 10573

Established in 1985 in CT.
Donor(s): Agostino Galluzzo, Jane H. Galluzzo.
Financial data (yr. ended 12/31/01): Grants paid, $15,762; assets, $21,308 (M); gifts received, $34,926; expenditures, $15,777; qualifying distributions, $19,660.
Limitations: Applications not accepted. Giving primarily in Greenwich, CT.
Application information: Contributes only to pre-selected organizations.
Trustees: Agostino Galluzzo, Jane H. Galluzzo, Jay A. Galluzzo, John Heffer.
EIN: 136881122

38218
Irene and Nathaniel M. Aycock Foundation
7 Cobblestone Ct.
Centerport, NY 11721

Established in 1998 in NY.
Donor(s): Irene R. Aycock.‡
Financial data (yr. ended 12/31/00): Grants paid, $15,700; assets, $369,601 (M); expenditures, $20,384; qualifying distributions, $15,700.
Limitations: Applications not accepted.
Application information: Contributes only to pre-selected organizations.

Officers and Directors:* Bruce A. Rosen,* Pres.; Sally Tate,* V.P.; Alan Fell,* Treas.
EIN: 113357089

38219
Select Equity Group Foundation
380 Lafayette St., Ste. 6
New York, NY 10003-6933

Established in 2000 in NY.
Donor(s): Select Equity Group, Inc.
Financial data (yr. ended 12/31/01): Grants paid, $15,700; assets, $163,213 (M); gifts received, $104,754; expenditures, $18,797; qualifying distributions, $15,700.
Limitations: Applications not accepted.
Application information: Contributes only to pre-selected organizations.
Trustees: Christopher Arndt, John Britton, George S. Loening, Darren Seirer, Amor Towles.
EIN: 134148796
Codes: CS

38220
Watkins Foundation
c/o Jacqueline Slifka
799 Park Ave.
New York, NY 10021

Donor(s): Jacqueline Slifka.
Financial data (yr. ended 11/30/01): Grants paid, $15,696; assets, $224,181 (M); expenditures, $18,038; qualifying distributions, $16,501.
Limitations: Applications not accepted. Giving primarily in New York, NY.
Application information: Contributes only to pre-selected organizations.
Officer: Jacqueline Slifka, Pres.
EIN: 133109460

38221
The George W. Gorham Family Foundation
200 E. 66th St., Ste. E1107
New York, NY 10021

Established in 2001 in DE.
Donor(s): George W. Gorham.
Financial data (yr. ended 12/31/01): Grants paid, $15,650; assets, $87,758 (M); gifts received, $102,375; expenditures, $15,725; qualifying distributions, $15,650.
Limitations: Applications not accepted. Giving primarily in NY.
Application information: Contributes only to pre-selected organizations.
Directors: Ann Gorham, George W. Gorham, John Gorham, Sarah C. Gorham.
EIN: 134169993

38222
John and Dolores Clarke Charitable Foundation
4 Holly Ln.
Rye, NY 10580

Established in 1997 in NY.
Donor(s): Dolores M. Clarke, John M. Clarke.
Financial data (yr. ended 12/31/01): Grants paid, $15,610; assets, $217,298 (M); expenditures, $15,755; qualifying distributions, $15,610.
Limitations: Applications not accepted. Giving primarily in NY.
Application information: Contributes only to pre-selected organizations.
Trustees: Christa J. Clarke, Dolores M. Clarke, John M. Clarke, John M. Clarke, Jr.
EIN: 137118308

38223
Laurence & Bernice Kaperst Foundation
c/o B. Strauss Assoc., Ltd.
307 5th Ave., 8th Fl.
New York, NY 10016-6517

Established in 2000 in FL.
Donor(s): Bernice Kaperst, Stuart Kaperst.
Financial data (yr. ended 04/30/02): Grants paid, $15,608; assets, $126,236 (M); gifts received, $65,000; expenditures, $16,258; qualifying distributions, $15,608.
Trustees: Bernice Kaperst, Robin Kaperst, Stuart Kaperst.
EIN: 582589401

38224
The Darivoff Family Foundation
c/o Goldman Sachs & Co.
85 Broad St., Tax Dept.
New York, NY 10004

Established in 1999 in NJ.
Donor(s): Philip M. Darivoff.
Financial data (yr. ended 11/30/01): Grants paid, $15,605; assets, $989,944 (M); gifts received, $563,989; expenditures, $32,529; qualifying distributions, $18,355.
Limitations: Applications not accepted. Giving primarily in NJ and PA.
Application information: Contributes only to pre-selected organizations.
Trustees: Betsy S. Darivoff, Philip M. Darivoff.
EIN: 134039056

38225
The Yaacov and Ronit Gross Foundation
53 Cedarhurst Ave.
Lawrence, NY 11559

Established in 1996 in NY.
Donor(s): Yaacov M. Gross.
Financial data (yr. ended 12/31/00): Grants paid, $15,600; assets, $328,655 (M); gifts received, $51,187; expenditures, $17,212; qualifying distributions, $15,600.
Limitations: Applications not accepted.
Application information: Contributes only to pre-selected organizations.
Officer: Yaacov M. Gross, Pres.
EIN: 113353298

38226
Bradley Spencer Parlo Foundation, Inc.
c/o Joseph A. Broderick
P.O. Box 309
East Northport, NY 11731

Established in 1997 in NY.
Donor(s): Marcia Kerr.
Financial data (yr. ended 12/31/00): Grants paid, $15,600; assets, $679,349 (M); expenditures, $24,209; qualifying distributions, $15,600.
Limitations: Applications not accepted.
Application information: Contributes only to pre-selected organizations.
Officers: Marcia Kerr, Pres.; Lisa Parlo, Secy.; Eric Kerr, Treas.
EIN: 133967577

38227
R.H.M. Foundation, Inc.
c/o Golenbuck, Eiseman, Assor, & Bell
437 Madison Ave., 35th Fl.
New York, NY 10022
Contact: Donald Hamburg, Secy.

Donor(s): Marianne D. Meyer.
Financial data (yr. ended 02/28/02): Grants paid, $15,575; assets, $478,743 (M); gifts received,

$16,746; expenditures, $29,594; qualifying distributions, $15,575.
Limitations: Applications not accepted. Giving primarily in New York, NY.
Application information: Contributes only to pre-selected organizations.
Officers and Directors:* Marianne D. Meyer,* Pres. and Treas.; Ruth Ellen Bruce,* V.P.; Donald Hamburg,* Secy.
EIN: 136090865

38228
Barney N. Salen Foundation
4114 9th Ave.
Brooklyn, NY 11232-4005 (718) 648-0107
Contact: Milton E. Salen, Pres.

Financial data (yr. ended 11/30/01): Grants paid, $15,511; assets, $371 (M); gifts received, $15,000; expenditures, $18,811; qualifying distributions, $15,511.
Limitations: Giving limited to the metropolitan New York, NY, area.
Application information: Generally contributes only to pre-selected organizations. Application form not required.
Officer: Milton E. Salen, Pres.
EIN: 112516155

38229
San Kiang Charitable Association, Inc.
25 Division St.
New York, NY 10002

Established in 1996 in NY.
Financial data (yr. ended 12/31/01): Grants paid, $15,511; assets, $681,514 (M); gifts received, $12,790; expenditures, $114,256; qualifying distributions, $15,511.
Limitations: Applications not accepted.
Application information: Contributes only to pre-selected organizations.
Officers: Yong Y. Hur, Secy.; Chau H. Hai, Treas.; Tom Wong, Exec. Dir.
EIN: 135513175

38230
Howard R. & Grayce B. Bendixen Memorial Trust
c/o M&T Bank
Box 4983, 101 S. Salina St., 3rd Fl.
Syracuse, NY 13202

Established in 1987 in NY.
Financial data (yr. ended 06/30/01): Grants paid, $15,500; assets, $530,707 (M); expenditures, $24,837; qualifying distributions, $15,500.
Limitations: Giving primarily in Syracuse, NY.
Trustee: M & T Bank.
EIN: 166315029

38231
The John Brademas Foundation
53 Washington Sq. S., 3rd Fl.
New York, NY 10012-1098

Established in 1993 in NY.
Financial data (yr. ended 12/31/99): Grants paid, $15,500; assets, $125,256 (M); gifts received, $782; expenditures, $15,657; qualifying distributions, $15,500.
Limitations: Applications not accepted.
Application information: Contributes only to pre-selected organizations.
Trustees: David A. Berenson, John Brademas.
EIN: 133708587

38232
The Guenther Scholarship Fund
c/o Steuben Trust Co.
1 Steuben Sq.
Hornell, NY 14843-1699

Financial data (yr. ended 12/31/00): Grants paid, $15,500; assets, $472,813 (M); gifts received, $70,350; expenditures, $17,020; qualifying distributions, $15,500.
Limitations: Applications not accepted. Giving limited to Hornell, NY.
Trustee: Steuben Trust Co.
EIN: 222314303
Codes: GTI

38233
IJM Charitable Foundation
c/o Inder J. Mahendru
Half Moon Ln.
Sands Point, NY 11050

Established in 2000 in NY.
Donor(s): Inder J. Mahendru.
Financial data (yr. ended 12/31/00): Grants paid, $15,500; assets, $3,468 (M); gifts received, $19,000; expenditures, $15,532; qualifying distributions, $15,532.
Limitations: Giving primarily in India.
Director: Inder J. Mahendru.
EIN: 061583696

38234
The James H. and Margaret Tabeling Foundation, Inc.
c/o Jared J. Scharf
1025 Westchester, A305
White Plains, NY 10604-3536
Application address: P.O. Box 602, Hartsdale, NY 10530

Established in 1989 in NY.
Financial data (yr. ended 12/31/01): Grants paid, $15,475; assets, $996,341 (M); gifts received, $1,118,168; expenditures, $16,818; qualifying distributions, $15,475.
Application information: Application form not required.
Officers: S.L. Scharf, Pres.; Eve Scharf, Secy.
Trustee: Jared J. Scharf.
EIN: 133540286

38235
Marilyn & Erwin Ezzes Foundation
875 5th Ave.
New York, NY 10021

Established in 2000 in NY.
Donor(s): Marilyn Ezzes.
Financial data (yr. ended 12/31/01): Grants paid, $15,465; assets, $21,036 (M); gifts received, $33,134; expenditures, $19,204; qualifying distributions, $15,465.
Limitations: Applications not accepted. Giving primarily in NY.
Application information: Contributes only to pre-selected organizations.
Directors: Erwin H. Ezzes, Marilyn H. Ezzes, Beryl Kreisel.
EIN: 134148794

38236
Irving Bravman and Rose B. Bravman Family Foundation, Inc.
75-23 171st St.
Flushing, NY 11366

Donor(s): Irving Bravman, Rose Bravman.
Financial data (yr. ended 12/31/99): Grants paid, $15,434; assets, $81,056 (M); gifts received, $11,900; expenditures, $15,604; qualifying distributions, $15,422.
Limitations: Applications not accepted.
Application information: Contributes only to pre-selected organizations.
Officers: Irving Bravman, Pres.; Rose Bravman, Secy.
EIN: 113349625

38237
Lawrence L. Ashinoff Foundation, Inc.
c/o Hecht & Co., PC
111 W. 40th St.
New York, NY 10018

Donor(s): Lawrence L. Ashinoff.
Financial data (yr. ended 02/28/02): Grants paid, $15,391; assets, $262,532 (M); gifts received, $20,000; expenditures, $15,903; qualifying distributions, $15,391.
Limitations: Applications not accepted. Giving primarily in VA.
Application information: Contributes only to pre-selected organizations.
Directors: Carole Ashinoff, Lawrence L. Ashinoff, Donald Hecht.
EIN: 133010478

38238
Alfred F. and Kathryne M. Krause Foundation
3189-A E. Lake Rd.
Skaneateles, NY 13152-9002 (315) 685-6762
Contact: Alfred F. Krause, Tr.

Established in 1986 in NY.
Donor(s): Alfred F. Krause, Kathryn M. Krause.
Financial data (yr. ended 12/31/01): Grants paid, $15,366; assets, $112,775 (M); gifts received, $496; expenditures, $17,055; qualifying distributions, $15,366.
Limitations: Giving primarily in Troy, NY.
Trustees: Alfred F. Krause, Kathryn M. Krause.
EIN: 222779806

38239
The John Franco Charitable Foundation, Inc.
c/o Lonstein Law Office, PC
1 Terrace Hill, Box 351
Ellenville, NY 12428
Contact: Wayne Lonstein

Established in 1997 in NY.
Donor(s): John Franco.
Financial data (yr. ended 12/31/00): Grants paid, $15,325; assets, $460,093 (M); gifts received, $10,250; expenditures, $16,554; qualifying distributions, $15,325.
Directors: James R. Franco, Rose Franco, Dennis J. Gilbert.
EIN: 141798180

38240
Joe W. Gerrity, Jr. Foundation
P.O. Box 46
Newtonville, NY 12128

Financial data (yr. ended 12/31/00): Grants paid, $15,312; assets, $239,386 (M); gifts received, $66,267; expenditures, $31,041; qualifying distributions, $15,243.
Limitations: Applications not accepted. Giving primarily in Albany, NY, and surrounding counties.
Application information: Contributes only to pre-selected organizations.
Officer: Joe W. Gerrity, Jr., Pres.
EIN: 237042416

38241
The AVOT Charitable Trust
75 Roanoke St.
Staten Island, NY 10314

Established in 1994 in NY.
Donor(s): Israel Goldstein, Sharon Goldstein.
Financial data (yr. ended 12/31/01): Grants paid, $15,300; assets, $16,766 (M); gifts received, $5,000; expenditures, $17,039; qualifying distributions, $15,300.
Limitations: Applications not accepted. Giving primarily in the New York, NY, area.
Application information: Contributes only to pre-selected organizations.
Trustees: Israel Goldstein, Sharon Goldstein.
EIN: 116450573

38242
The Efrein Foundation, Inc.
(Formerly Harry & Margaret A. Bookshin Foundation, Inc.)
c/o Robert E. Driscoll
60 E. 42nd St., Ste. 1061
New York, NY 10165

Financial data (yr. ended 05/31/02): Grants paid, $15,265; assets, $269,969 (M); expenditures, $18,177; qualifying distributions, $15,265.
Limitations: Applications not accepted. Giving primarily in HI.
Officers: Nan Seley Efrein, Pres. and Treas.; Robert E. Driscoll, Secy.
EIN: 116017909

38243
The Steven and Suzanne Feldman Family Foundation
1085 Park Ave., Ste. 148
New York, NY 10028 (212) 922-5633
Contact: Steven & Suzanne Feldman

Established in 1998 in NY.
Donor(s): Steven Feldman.
Financial data (yr. ended 12/31/01): Grants paid, $15,257; assets, $192,248 (M); gifts received, $25,000; expenditures, $15,823; qualifying distributions, $15,257.
Directors: Steven Feldman, Suzanna Studier Feldman, Anthony Scaramucci.
EIN: 133991132

38244
Wylie Wallace Fults Family Foundation
c/o Janvey, Gordon, Herlands, et al.
355 Lexington Ave.
New York, NY 10017

Established in 2000 in NY.
Donor(s): Holly B. Wallace.
Financial data (yr. ended 12/31/01): Grants paid, $15,250; assets, $259,802 (M); gifts received, $37,289; expenditures, $20,523; qualifying distributions, $15,250.
Limitations: Applications not accepted.
Application information: Contributes only to pre-selected organizations.
Officers: Holly B. Wallace, Pres.; Edwin M. Baum, V.P. and Secy.; Rosana F. Meloy, V.P.
EIN: 134147868

38245
Sherry and Joel Mallin Family Foundation
110 E. 59th St., Ste. 3202
New York, NY 10022
Contact: Sherry Mallin, Pres.

Established in 2000 in NY.
Donor(s): Klondike Resources, Inc.
Financial data (yr. ended 05/31/01): Grants paid, $15,250; assets, $750 (M); gifts received, $16,000; expenditures, $15,250; qualifying distributions, $0.
Limitations: Giving primarily in Chicago, IL and New York, NY.
Officers and Directors:* Sherry Mallin,* Pres.; Kenneth Greenberg,* V.P.; Noah Mallin,* Secy.-Treas.
EIN: 522279277
Codes: CS

38246
Alpha Lodge Sunshine Foundation, Inc.
(also known as Alpha Sunshine Foundation, Inc.)
c/o Gary M. Waters
4403 Bedford Ave.
Brooklyn, NY 11229-4928

Financial data (yr. ended 12/31/01): Grants paid, $15,242; assets, $124,518 (M); gifts received, $55,366; expenditures, $31,498; qualifying distributions, $15,242.
Limitations: Applications not accepted. Giving primarily in NY.
Application information: Contributes only to pre-selected organizations.
Officers: Allan Greenberg, Pres.; William D. Rubin, V.P.; Gary M. Walters, Fin. Secy.; Sid Wieder, Recording Secy.; Lowell Goldberg, Treas.
EIN: 116035562

38247
Mark Brent Dolinsky Memorial Foundation, Inc.
205 Soundview Ave.
White Plains, NY 10606-3825

Established in 1982 in NY.
Donor(s): Muriel Dolinsky.
Financial data (yr. ended 01/31/02): Grants paid, $15,239; assets, $129,727 (M); gifts received, $16,998; expenditures, $21,164; qualifying distributions, $15,239.
Limitations: Giving primarily in Westchester County, NY.
Application information: Application form not required.
Officer and Directors:* Muriel Dolinsky,* Pres.; Edward M. Berman, Diane J. Dolinsky, Sara L. Dolinsky.
EIN: 133105431

38248
The Adela and Lawrence Elow Foundation
P.O. Box 277
Bedford, NY 10506-0277

Established in 1986 in NY.
Financial data (yr. ended 08/31/02): Grants paid, $15,180; assets, $28,020 (M); expenditures, $16,984; qualifying distributions, $15,180.
Limitations: Applications not accepted. Giving primarily in NY.
Application information: Contributes only to pre-selected organizations.
Officers: Lawrence Elow, Pres.; Adela Elow, V.P.
EIN: 133365078

38249
Beth and Dale G. Frost Foundation, Inc.
155 Noye Ln.
Woodmere, NY 11598-1836

Established in 1987 in NY.
Donor(s): Beth Frost, Dale G. Frost.
Financial data (yr. ended 12/31/01): Grants paid, $15,175; assets, $248 (M); gifts received, $14,575; expenditures, $15,250; qualifying distributions, $15,175.
Limitations: Applications not accepted. Giving primarily in Long Island, NY.
Application information: Contributes only to pre-selected organizations.
Officer: Dale G. Frost, Mgr.
EIN: 133369859

38250
The Jacob K. Javits Foundation, Inc.
c/o Marion B. Javits
322 E. 57th St., 12th Fl.
New York, NY 10022

Established in 2000 in NY.
Financial data (yr. ended 12/31/00): Grants paid, $15,133; assets, $3,822,777 (M); gifts received, $10,500; expenditures, $81,921; qualifying distributions, $172,415.
Limitations: Giving primarily in New York, NY.
Officers and Directors:* Marian B. Javits,* Chair. and Pres.; Carla I. Javits,* Vice-Chair.; Mark Kaufman,* Treas.; Richard Aurelio, W. Don Cornwell, Sen. Roy M. Goodman, Hon. Joshua M. Javits, Jeffrey C. Kell, Donald S. Kellerman, Dr. John Marburger, Hon. Charles McC. Mathias, Jr., Senator Daniel Patrick Moynihan, Patricia K. Perlman, Lewis Rudin, Senator Alan K. Simpson, John Trubio, Hon. William J. Vanden Heuvel.
EIN: 133226735

38251
The Joseph Katz and Shirley Katz Charitable Trust
c/o Meltzer, Lippe & Goldstein
190 Willis Ave.
Mineola, NY 11501

Established in 1994 in NY.
Donor(s): Joseph Katz.
Financial data (yr. ended 12/31/01): Grants paid, $15,126; assets, $242,807 (M); gifts received, $10,000; expenditures, $16,526; qualifying distributions, $15,126.
Limitations: Applications not accepted. Giving primarily in NY.
Application information: Contributes only to pre-selected organizations.
Trustees: Joseph Katz, Shirley Katz.
EIN: 113242441

38252
The Fisher Landau Foundation
c/o Fisher Bros.
299 Park Ave.
New York, NY 10017

Established in 1983 in NY.
Donor(s): Emily Landau, Cleaning Service Co.
Financial data (yr. ended 06/30/01): Grants paid, $15,100; assets, $481,965 (M); gifts received, $21,616; expenditures, $22,658; qualifying distributions, $22,007.
Limitations: Applications not accepted. Giving primarily in New York, NY.
Application information: Contributes only to pre-selected organizations.
Trustees: Joseph Curry, M. Anthony Fisher, Caryl Frankenberger, Emily Landau.
EIN: 133267201

38253
Lerner-Gray Foundation, Inc.
c/o Joel Popkin & Co., Inc.
1430 Broadway, Ste. 1805
New York, NY 10018

Financial data (yr. ended 12/31/00): Grants paid, $15,100; assets, $217,261 (M); gifts received, $25,000; expenditures, $18,758; qualifying distributions, $15,100.
Officer: Arthur Gray, Jr., Pres. and Treas.
EIN: 136113576

38254
Raymond C. & Dorothy I. Schlotterer Trust
c/o John Lyttle, Windels, Marx, et. al
156 W. 56th St.
New York, NY 10019

Established in 1992 in NY.
Donor(s): Dorothy I. Schlotterer.‡
Financial data (yr. ended 12/31/01): Grants paid, $15,073; assets, $468,524 (M); expenditures, $18,190; qualifying distributions, $15,118; giving activities include $15,073 for loans to individuals.
Limitations: Giving limited to NY.
Application information: Application form required.
Trustee: Edward Pennfield.
EIN: 136966814
Codes: GTI

38255
The Redel Foundation, Inc.
c/o Irving Redel
911 Park Ave.
New York, NY 10021

Established in 1980.
Donor(s): Irving Redel.
Financial data (yr. ended 10/31/01): Grants paid, $15,025; assets, $494,631 (M); gifts received, $6,250; expenditures, $17,866; qualifying distributions, $15,025.
Limitations: Applications not accepted. Giving primarily in NY.
Application information: Contributes only to pre-selected organizations.
Officers and Directors:* Irving Redel,* Pres.; Jessica Redel Greenes,* V.P.; Victoria Redel.
EIN: 133082842

38256
The Jeff Bernstein & Lisa Marrocchino Family Foundation, Inc.
1 W. 72nd St., Ste. 67
New York, NY 10023

Donor(s): Jeff Bernstein.
Financial data (yr. ended 12/31/99): Grants paid, $15,000; assets, $88,740 (M); expenditures, $15,000; qualifying distributions, $15,000.
Limitations: Applications not accepted.
Application information: Contributes only to pre-selected organizations.
Directors: Jeff Bernstein, Lisa Marrocchino.
EIN: 134049638

38257
Chu & Chan Foundation
c/o D. Chan
401 Broadway, Ste. 1100
New York, NY 10013
Contact: Tony Chu, Pres.

Established in 1998 in NY.
Donor(s): Lam Chu.‡
Financial data (yr. ended 04/30/00): Grants paid, $15,000; assets, $1,124 (M); gifts received, $1,000; expenditures, $16,150; qualifying distributions, $15,146.
Officers: Tony Chu, Pres.; Jeff Sobel, V.P.; Thomas Sobel, Secy.
Director: Emily Chu.
EIN: 113440906

38258
John A. & Margaret H. Cook Fund, Inc.
c/o L.H. Firshkoff & Co.
529 5th Ave., Ste. 907
New York, NY 10017
Application address: 1040 5th Ave., New York, NY 10128
Contact: Margaret H. Cook, Pres.

Established in 1996 in NY.
Donor(s): John A. Cook.‡
Financial data (yr. ended 09/30/01): Grants paid, $15,000; assets, $364,352 (M); expenditures, $22,503; qualifying distributions, $15,000.
Limitations: Giving primarily in New York, NY.
Application information: Application form not required.
Officers: Margaret H. Cook, Pres. and Treas.; Mariana Cook, V.P.; Ralph Lerner, Secy.
EIN: 136141526

38259
Charles B. Decker Memorial Fund
HCR2, 24 Coreys Rd.
Tupper Lake, NY 12986-9613 (518) 359-3119
Contact: Janet P. Decker, Tr.

Established in 1991 in NY.
Donor(s): Alfred M. Decker, Janet P. Decker.
Financial data (yr. ended 06/30/01): Grants paid, $15,000; assets, $188,625 (M); gifts received, $3,000; expenditures, $15,050; qualifying distributions, $15,050.
Limitations: Giving primarily to residents of the Adirondack region, NY.
Application information: Application form required.
Trustees: Alfred M. Decker, Janet P. Decker, John W. Decker, Ann E. Merkel.
EIN: 223130400
Codes: GTI

38260
Elsie del Fierro Trust
c/o Kelley, Drye & Warren, LLP
101 Park Ave., Ste. 3030
New York, NY 10178-0002

Established in 1979 in NY.
Financial data (yr. ended 12/31/00): Grants paid, $15,000; assets, $4,879 (M); expenditures, $15,138; qualifying distributions, $15,087.
Limitations: Applications not accepted. Giving primarily in New York, NY.
Application information: Contributes only to pre-selected organizations.
Trustees: Michael S. Insel, Hilde Siegel.
EIN: 136348894

38261
The Elias Family Foundation, Inc.
c/o Barbara Elias
31 Halston Pkwy.
East Amherst, NY 14051-1843
Contact: Barbara Elias, Pres.

Established in 2000 in NY.
Donor(s): Barbara Elias.
Financial data (yr. ended 12/31/01): Grants paid, $15,000; assets, $249,785 (M); gifts received, $2,428; expenditures, $18,763; qualifying distributions, $15,000.
Application information: Application form not required.
Officer and Directors:* Barbara Elias,* Pres.; Kristin Linthwaite, Kelly Ostrowski.
EIN: 161591822

38262
Fogel Family Foundation
c/o Samuel Fogel
1160 E. 9th St.
Brooklyn, NY 11230

Established in 1997.
Donor(s): Samuel Fogel.
Financial data (yr. ended 12/31/01): Grants paid, $15,000; assets, $72,253 (M); expenditures, $15,197; qualifying distributions, $15,000.
Limitations: Applications not accepted. Giving primarily in NY.
Application information: Contributes only to pre-selected organizations.
Officers: Samuel Fogel, Pres.; Tamar Fogel, Secy.-Treas.
Director: Hersh Fogel.
EIN: 113408112

38263
The Fridno Trust
142 Sutton Pl. S.
Lawrence, NY 11559

Established in 1998.
Donor(s): Norman Rabenstein.
Financial data (yr. ended 12/31/01): Grants paid, $15,000; assets, $173,395 (M); gifts received, $60,000; expenditures, $16,301; qualifying distributions, $15,000.
Trustees: Frida Rabenstein, Norman Rabenstein.
EIN: 116508114

38264
The Goodrich Foundation, Inc.
c/o John L. Cady
46 Summit Ave.
Bronxville, NY 10708

Established in 1998 in NY.
Donor(s): John K. Goodrich.
Financial data (yr. ended 12/31/00): Grants paid, $15,000; assets, $288,416 (M); expenditures, $25,125; qualifying distributions, $15,000.
Limitations: Applications not accepted.
Application information: Contributes only to pre-selected organizations.
Officer: John K. Goodrich, Pres.
EIN: 134036967

38265
The Grogan Foundation
25 Lester Pl.
New Rochelle, NY 10804

Established in 1985 in DE.
Donor(s): John J. Grogan.
Financial data (yr. ended 10/31/01): Grants paid, $15,000; assets, $55,892 (M); expenditures, $16,171; qualifying distributions, $14,989.
Limitations: Applications not accepted. Giving limited to NY.
Application information: Contributes only to pre-selected organizations.
Officers and Directors:* John J. Grogan,* Pres. and Treas.; Margaret P. Grogan,* V.P. and Secy.; Timothy C. Grogan.
EIN: 133325341

38266
The Hampshire Foundation
c/o Bessemer Trust Co., N.A.
630 5th Ave., Tax Dept.
New York, NY 10111

Established in 2000 in CT.
Donor(s): The Hadley Trust.
Financial data (yr. ended 12/31/01): Grants paid, $15,000; assets, $2,267,011 (M); expenditures, $26,478; qualifying distributions, $15,000.

38266—NEW YORK

Limitations: Applications not accepted.
Application information: Contributes only to pre-selected organizations.
Trustees: Nicholas N. Cournoyer, Sabina E. Cournoyer, Sabina G. Cournoyer.
EIN: 061584535

38267
The Arthur & Patricia Hill Foundation
c/o U.S. Trust
P.O. Box 2004
New York, NY 10109-1910
Application address: U.S. Trust, 114 W. 47th St., New York, NY 10036, tel.: (212) 852-1000

Established in 2000 in NY.
Donor(s): Arthur B. Hill.
Financial data (yr. ended 12/31/01): Grants paid, $15,000; assets, $76,172 (M); expenditures, $23,247; qualifying distributions, $15,000.
Trustee: U.S. Trust.
EIN: 256717749

38268
J.L.M. Benevolent Fund
c/o Kelley, Drye & Warren, LLP
101 Park Ave., 30th Fl.
New York, NY 10178-0002 (212) 808-7933
Contact: Michael S. Insel, Tr.

Established around 1947 in NY.
Donor(s): Francois Monohan.‡
Financial data (yr. ended 10/31/01): Grants paid, $15,000; assets, $47,734 (M); gifts received, $24,948; expenditures, $16,322; qualifying distributions, $15,000.
Limitations: Giving primarily in NH and NY; some giving also in France.
Trustees: John J. Costello, Michael S. Insel, Winthrop Munyan.
EIN: 136272298

38269
The Jewish Documentation Center, Inc.
757 Third Ave.
New York, NY 10017

Established in 1994.
Donor(s): Alfred Goldstein.‡
Financial data (yr. ended 12/31/01): Grants paid, $15,000; assets, $235,257 (M); gifts received, $67,514; expenditures, $15,201; qualifying distributions, $15,000.
Limitations: Applications not accepted.
Application information: Contributes only to pre-selected organizations.
Officers: Martin Rosen, Pres.; Ralph Engel, V.P.; Jack Sevita, Treas.
EIN: 136163581

38270
Peter S. Kalikow Foundation, Inc.
c/o H.J. Kalikow & Co., LLC
101 Park Ave., 25th Fl.
New York, NY 10178
Contact: Peter S. Kalikow, Pres.

Established in 1983 in NY.
Donor(s): Peter S. Kalikow.
Financial data (yr. ended 06/30/02): Grants paid, $15,000; assets, $186,190 (M); gifts received, $25,000; expenditures, $15,322; qualifying distributions, $15,000.
Limitations: Giving primarily in NY.
Application information: Application form not required.
Officers: Peter S. Kalikow, Pres.; Gerald Schrager, V.P.; Daniel F. Cremins, Treas.
EIN: 133182633

38271
Kass Family Foundation
250 E. Hartsdale Ave., Ste. 30
Hartsdale, NY 10530-3507

Established in 2000 in NY.
Donor(s): Aileen Kass.
Financial data (yr. ended 12/31/01): Grants paid, $15,000; assets, $140,000 (M); gifts received, $50,000; expenditures, $19,635; qualifying distributions, $15,000.
Directors: Aileen Kass, Arthur Kroll.
EIN: 134133946

38272
D'Elbert & Selma Keenan Family Foundation, Inc.
c/o Moses & Schreiber, LLP
3000 Marcus Ave., Ste. 1W5
New Hyde Park, NY 11042 (516) 352-7700
Contact: David L. Moses, Treas.

Donor(s): Selma Keenan.
Financial data (yr. ended 08/31/01): Grants paid, $15,000; assets, $209,909 (M); gifts received, $30,092; expenditures, $16,048; qualifying distributions, $15,000.
Officers: Selma Keenan, Pres.; David L. Moses, Treas.
EIN: 136192089

38273
Harold L. Korda Foundation, Inc.
110 E. 59th St., 29th Fl.
New York, NY 10022-1304 (212) 317-0777
Contact: Fay Holloschitz, Dir.

Financial data (yr. ended 06/30/02): Grants paid, $15,000; assets, $253,693 (M); expenditures, $22,089; qualifying distributions, $15,000.
Limitations: Giving primarily in NY.
Directors: Fay Holloschitz, Henry L. Karet, Harry Schall.
EIN: 237133390

38274
The Korobkin Foundation, Inc.
c/o Jerry Rosenband, C.P.A.
370 Lexington Ave., Ste. 905
New York, NY 10017

Established in 1998 in NY.
Financial data (yr. ended 12/31/01): Grants paid, $15,000; assets, $230,879 (M); expenditures, $15,873; qualifying distributions, $15,000.
Limitations: Applications not accepted. Giving primarily in New York, NY.
Application information: Contributes only to pre-selected organizations.
Officers: Barry J. Korobkin, Pres.; Nancy Korobkin, V.P.; David B. Korobkin, Secy.-Treas.
EIN: 133985413

38275
The Barbara & Mark Kronman Foundation
316 W. 79th St., Ste. 10E
New York, NY 10024

Established in 1996 in NY.
Donor(s): Barbara Kronman, Mark Kronman.
Financial data (yr. ended 11/30/01): Grants paid, $15,000; assets, $161,941 (M); expenditures, $16,343; qualifying distributions, $15,000.
Limitations: Applications not accepted.
Application information: Contributes only to pre-selected organizations.
Officers: Mark J. Kronman, Pres.; Stanley I. Cullen, V.P.; Barbara Kronman, Secy.
EIN: 133922801

38276
The Mandy Foundation
c/o U.S. Trust
114 W. 47th St.
New York, NY 10036

Established in 2000 in NY.
Donor(s): Jeffrey S. Maurer.
Financial data (yr. ended 12/31/01): Grants paid, $15,000; assets, $536,798 (M); expenditures, $17,214; qualifying distributions, $15,000.
Limitations: Applications not accepted.
Application information: Contributes only to pre-selected organizations.
Officers and Directors:* Jeffrey S. Maurer,* Pres.; Wendy S. Maurer,* V.P.; Brooke Maurer,* Secy.; Craig Maurer,* Treas.
EIN: 113557574

38277
Marantha Foundation
30 Edison Dr.
Schenectady, NY 12309

Established in 2000 in NY.
Donor(s): Douglas Stoner, Barbara Stoner.
Financial data (yr. ended 11/30/01): Grants paid, $15,000; assets, $257,640 (M); gifts received, $282,012; expenditures, $15,000; qualifying distributions, $15,000.
Trustees: Barbara Stoner, Douglas Stoner.
EIN: 141829273

38278
New York Foundation for Architecture, Inc.
200 Lexington Ave., Rm. 602
New York, NY 10016-6255 (212) 683-0023
URL: http://www.aiany.org

Established in 1966 in NY.
Financial data (yr. ended 12/31/00): Grants paid, $15,000; assets, $1,070,732 (M); gifts received, $221,035; expenditures, $294,132; qualifying distributions, $223,561.
Limitations: Applications not accepted. Giving primarily to residents of New York, NY.
Officers: Paul Segal, Pres.-Elect; Bartholomew Voorsanger, Pres.; Ronnette Railey, Secy.-Treas.
Trustees: Frederick Bland, Cora Cahan, Robert Geddes, Walter Hunt, Jr., Peter Marino, Rolf H. Ohlhausen, Rebecca Robertson, Robert Silman, Kenneth Walker, Margot Wellington.
EIN: 223047700
Codes: TN, GTI

38279
New Yorkers Need to Know Foundation
c/o Dave H. & Reba W. Williams
1345 Ave. of the Americas
New York, NY 10105

Established in 1999 in NY.
Donor(s): Dave H. Williams, Reba W. Williams.
Financial data (yr. ended 12/31/01): Grants paid, $15,000; assets, $36,790 (M); gifts received, $50,000; expenditures, $88,877; qualifying distributions, $88,617.
Limitations: Applications not accepted. Giving primarily in NY.
Application information: Contributes only to pre-selected organizations.
Directors: Dave H. Williams, Reba W. Williams.
EIN: 134039633

38280
The Kathleen Norman Trust f/b/o Visually Impaired Students
29 John St., Ste. 1004
New York, NY 10038
Contact: Jack D. Matza, Tr.

Established in 2000 in NY.
Financial data (yr. ended 12/31/00): Grants paid, $15,000; assets, $111,334 (M); gifts received, $125,331; expenditures, $18,027; qualifying distributions, $18,027.
Trustee: Jack D. Matza.
EIN: 137221435

38281
Ohr Torah Foundation
1615 52nd St.
Brooklyn, NY 11204

Established in 1997 in NY.
Donor(s): Israel Lefkowitz.
Financial data (yr. ended 12/31/99): Grants paid, $15,000; assets, $215,622 (M); gifts received, $84,000; expenditures, $16,657; qualifying distributions, $15,000.
Limitations: Applications not accepted.
Application information: Contributes only to pre-selected organizations.
Directors: Esther Lefkowitz, Solomon Lefkowitz, Miriam Nevenasky.
EIN: 113401521

38282
Otten-Robbins Foundation, Inc.
c/o Louis O. Robbins
40 E. 88th St., Ste. 3A
New York, NY 10128

Financial data (yr. ended 04/30/02): Grants paid, $15,000; assets, $275,467 (M); expenditures, $17,061; qualifying distributions, $15,000.
Limitations: Applications not accepted. Giving primarily in NY.
Application information: Contributes only to pre-selected organizations.
Officers and Directors:* Lois O. Robbins,* Pres.; Michael Otten,* V.P.; Louis Otten,* Secy.-Treas.; Evelyn B. Otten, Michael D. Robbins.
EIN: 136091616

38283
Henry & Sally Pearce Foundation
c/o Sarah Pearce
1050 5th Ave.
New York, NY 10028-0109

Donor(s): Henry Pearce,‡ Sarah E. Pearce.
Financial data (yr. ended 09/30/01): Grants paid, $15,000; assets, $218,158 (M); expenditures, $15,000; qualifying distributions, $15,000.
Limitations: Applications not accepted. Giving primarily in NY.
Application information: Contributes only to pre-selected organizations.
Director: Sarah E. Pearce.
EIN: 237339646

38284
Max & Helen Philipson Foundation
c/o Tanklow, Hollender & Co.
450 7th Ave., Ste. 1802
New York, NY 10123-1899

Financial data (yr. ended 12/31/01): Grants paid, $15,000; assets, $286,792 (M); expenditures, $19,272; qualifying distributions, $15,000.
Limitations: Applications not accepted. Giving primarily in Charleston, SC.
Application information: Contributes only to pre-selected organizations.

Officer and Trustee:* Hilary Philipson,* Pres.
EIN: 237070142

38285
The Pointer Foundation
c/o CRM Mgmt., Inc.
P.O. Box 778
New York, NY 10013
Contact: Yana Konstani

Established in 1990 in CA.
Donor(s): Amy Irving.
Financial data (yr. ended 12/31/01): Grants paid, $15,000; assets, $202,830 (M); expenditures, $26,676; qualifying distributions, $15,000.
Limitations: Applications not accepted. Giving limited to Los Angeles, CA.
Application information: Contributes only to pre-selected organizations.
Officers: Michael Rutman, Pres., Secy., and C.F.O.; Amy Irving, V.P.
EIN: 954269110

38286
Project Pericles
535 5th Ave., Ste. 906
New York, NY 10017
Contact: Eugene M. Lang, Chair.

Established in 2000 in NY.
Donor(s): Eugene M. Lang Foundation.
Financial data (yr. ended 12/31/01): Grants paid, $15,000; assets, $9,773 (M); gifts received, $10,000; expenditures, $20,760; qualifying distributions, $20,759.
Officers and Directors:* Eugene M. Lang,* Chair. and Treas.; Alfred H. Bloom, David A. Caputo, Arthur Levine, and 5 other directors.
EIN: 134097541

38287
The Schenk Family Foundation
3 Brookside Rd.
Binghamton, NY 13903

Established in 2000 in NY.
Donor(s): Laurence Schenk.
Financial data (yr. ended 12/31/01): Grants paid, $15,000; assets, $62,475 (M); expenditures, $15,060; qualifying distributions, $15,000.
Limitations: Applications not accepted. Giving on a national basis.
Application information: Contributes only to pre-selected organizations.
Officers: Maura Santagelo, Pres.; Laurence Schenk, Secy.-Treas.
EIN: 166498914

38288
Turan Family Foundation
c/o M. Turan
183 Harbor Rd.
Cold Spring Harbor, NY 11724

Financial data (yr. ended 12/31/01): Grants paid, $15,000; assets, $221,434 (M); gifts received, $235,000; expenditures, $15,000; qualifying distributions, $15,000.
Officers: Nina J. Turan, Pres.; Madeline A. Turan, Secy.
Directors: Danielle Turan, Donna Turan, Mark E. Turan, Sari M. Turan.
EIN: 113515284

38289
Loraine Vichey Memorial Trust
c/o Julius Mendalis
160 Broadway
New York, NY 10038-4205

Financial data (yr. ended 10/31/01): Grants paid, $15,000; assets, $404,771 (M); expenditures, $17,551; qualifying distributions, $17,551.
Limitations: Applications not accepted. Giving primarily in New York, NY.
Application information: Contributes only to pre-selected organizations.
Trustee: Vincent W. Quinn.
EIN: 136734079

38290
Sherali Fazal Visram Memorial Foundation, Inc.
c/o Holiday Inn
2-8 Hawley St.
Binghamton, NY 13901

Established in 2000 in MA.
Donor(s): Vista Property Management, LLC.
Financial data (yr. ended 12/31/00): Grants paid, $15,000; assets, $5 (M); gifts received, $15,000; expenditures, $15,000; qualifying distributions, $15,000.
Limitations: Applications not accepted. Giving on an international basis, primarily in India.
Application information: Contributes only to pre-selected organizations.
Officer: Amin Sherali Visram, Pres.
Director: Azim Visram.
EIN: 043279667
Codes: CS

38291
Jerry Vogel Foundation, Inc.
100 E. 42nd St.
New York, NY 10017

Financial data (yr. ended 09/30/01): Grants paid, $15,000; assets, $627,358 (M); expenditures, $33,610; qualifying distributions, $15,000.
Limitations: Applications not accepted. Giving primarily in Rye, NY.
Directors: John Drew, Edmund C. Grainger, Jr., Edmund C. Grainger III.
EIN: 136120914

38292
Webster Foundation
c/o Bessemer Trust Co., N.A.
630 5th Ave., Tax Dept.
New York, NY 10111

Financial data (yr. ended 12/31/01): Grants paid, $15,000; assets, $274,123 (M); expenditures, $18,928; qualifying distributions, $15,000.
Limitations: Applications not accepted. Giving primarily in Nashville, TN.
Application information: Contributes only to pre-selected organizations.
Trustee: Bessemer Trust Co., N.A.
EIN: 626033117

38293
Robert H. Wentorf Foundation, Inc.
c/o Alan Wrigley
27 W. Main St.
Cambridge, NY 12816

Donor(s): Robert H. Wentorf, Jr.‡
Financial data (yr. ended 12/31/01): Grants paid, $15,000; assets, $270,615 (M); expenditures, $15,741; qualifying distributions, $15,000.
Limitations: Applications not accepted.
Application information: Contributes only to pre-selected organizations.

38293—NEW YORK

Officers: Rolf C. Wentorf, Pres. and Secy.; Debra Wentorf, Secy.; Alan Wrigley, Treas.
Trustee: Mike Greason.
EIN: 141775761

38294
Ronald A. Wilford Foundation for Conductors, Inc.
c/o U.S. Trust
114 W. 47th St., TaxVas
New York, NY 10036-1510

Donor(s): Nelly Walter, Sarah Wilford.
Financial data (yr. ended 12/31/01): Grants paid, $15,000; assets, $351,394 (M); expenditures, $17,882; qualifying distributions, $15,000.
Limitations: Applications not accepted. Giving primarily in Boston, MA.
Application information: Contributes only to pre-selected organizations.
Officers: Ronald A. Wilford, Pres.; Jonathan Brill, Secy.; Peter Gelb, Treas.
EIN: 133486646

38295
The Kathryn Aguirre Worth Memorial Foundation, Inc.
c/o White & Case LLP
1155 Avenue of the Americas Ste. 3748
New York, NY 10036-2787
Application address: c/o Selection Committee Faculty of Law, National University of Singapore, 38 Law Link, Singapore, 117589

Established in 1998 in NY.
Donor(s): White & Case LLP, Standard Chartered Bank.
Financial data (yr. ended 12/31/01): Grants paid, $15,000; assets, $271,964 (M); expenditures, $15,000; qualifying distributions, $15,000.
Limitations: Giving limited to Singapore.
Officers: James B. Hurlock, Pres.; Winthrop Rutherfurd, Jr., V.P.; Elizather P. Munson, Secy.; James J. Latchford, Treas.
Directors: J. Haywood Blakemore, Kenneth C. Ellis, David A. Worth.
EIN: 133983778

38296
William F. Zentler, Jr. Charitable Foundation
c/o U.S. Trust
P.O. Box 2004
New York, NY 10109-1910
Application address: c/o U.S. Trust, 114 W. 47th St., TaxVas, New York, NY 10036

Established in 1998.
Donor(s): William F. Zentler, Jr.
Financial data (yr. ended 12/31/01): Grants paid, $15,000; assets, $232,125 (M); expenditures, $23,999; qualifying distributions, $15,000.
Trustee: U.S. Trust.
EIN: 526952259

38297
Turpin Foundation, Inc.
P.O. Box 492
Rhinebeck, NY 12572

Established in 1999.
Donor(s): J. Louis Turpin.
Financial data (yr. ended 12/31/01): Grants paid, $14,988; assets, $619,744 (M); gifts received, $100,000; expenditures, $44,616; qualifying distributions, $14,988.
Officer and Directors:* Julie Ivers Turpin,* Pres.; Kris Ivers Hayes, J. Louis Turpin.
EIN: 141818722

38298
Arthur & Hadassah Marcus Foundation, Inc.
207 W. 86th St.
New York, NY 10024-3340
Contact: Arthur Marcus, V.P.

Donor(s): Arthur Marcus.
Financial data (yr. ended 04/30/02): Grants paid, $14,950; assets, $22,813 (M); gifts received, $14,300; expenditures, $14,950; qualifying distributions, $14,950.
Officers: Hadassah K. Marcus, Pres.; Arthur Marcus, V.P. and Secy.-Treas.; Jay H. Marcus, V.P.
EIN: 237111006

38299
Warshawsky Foundation, Inc.
35 Melville Park Rd.
Melville, NY 11747

Financial data (yr. ended 10/31/01): Grants paid, $14,937; assets, $70,382 (M); gifts received, $14,700; expenditures, $15,165; qualifying distributions, $15,140.
Limitations: Applications not accepted. Giving primarily in Long Island, NY.
Application information: Contributes only to pre-selected organizations.
Trustees: Allan Warshawsky, Jerome Warshawsky.
EIN: 237378932

38300
Hess Family Foundation, Inc.
c/o Yohalem Gillman & Co., LLP
477 Madison Ave.
New York, NY 10022-5802

Donor(s): Marion N. Hess, Mortimer H. Hess, Jr.
Financial data (yr. ended 03/31/01): Grants paid, $14,880; assets, $156 (M); expenditures, $16,705; qualifying distributions, $14,880.
Limitations: Applications not accepted. Giving primarily in NY.
Application information: Contributes only to pre-selected organizations.
Officers: Mortimer H. Hess, Jr., Pres.; Margaret M. Hess, V.P.; Robert L. Pelz, Secy.-Treas.
EIN: 136216279

38301
Evergreen Foundation, Inc.
c/o Myer, Greene & Degge
P.O. Box 930
Pearl River, NY 10965

Established in 1997 in CT.
Donor(s): Mead M. Brownell, K. Hyde Brownell, Thomas H. Brownell.
Financial data (yr. ended 12/31/01): Grants paid, $14,810; assets, $475,846 (M); gifts received, $100,231; expenditures, $15,360; qualifying distributions, $14,614.
Limitations: Applications not accepted.
Application information: Contributes only to pre-selected organizations.
Officers: Mead M. Brownell, Pres.; K. Hyde Brownell, Secy.; Gerald G. Walters, Treas.
Directors: George S. Brownell, Kenneth C. Brownell.
EIN: 061482180

38302
Ju Tang Chu & Wu Ping Chu Foundation
c/o R. Lawrence/Cadwalader
100 Maiden Ln.
New York, NY 10038

Established in 1999 in NY.
Donor(s): Chia-Kun Chu, Theodore C.C. Chu.

Financial data (yr. ended 12/31/01): Grants paid, $14,800; assets, $23,387 (M); expenditures, $21,180; qualifying distributions, $14,800.
Limitations: Applications not accepted. Giving primarily in New York, NY, and Paris, France.
Application information: Contributes only to pre-selected organizations.
Officers and Directors:* Chia-Kun Chu,* Pres. and Treas.; Robert C. Lawrence III,* V.P. and Secy.; Theodore C.C. Chu.
EIN: 134069047

38303
The Hallett Family Charitable Foundation
c/o Marvin M. Brown
666 3rd Ave., Ste. 2700
New York, NY 10017-5683

Established in 1997.
Donor(s): Fred R. Hallett.
Financial data (yr. ended 12/31/01): Grants paid, $14,800; assets, $246,847 (M); expenditures, $18,309; qualifying distributions, $14,800.
Limitations: Applications not accepted.
Application information: Contributes only to pre-selected organizations.
Trustees: Fred R. Hallett, Joan Hallett, John D. Hallett, Maryl P. Hallett.
EIN: 166455854

38304
Life Enrichment Foundation
c/o Aaron Rosenberg
597 Woodmere Rd.
Woodmere, NY 11598

Donor(s): Aaron Rosenberg.
Financial data (yr. ended 12/31/00): Grants paid, $14,800; assets, $256,464 (M); gifts received, $86,000; expenditures, $28,845; qualifying distributions, $14,800.
Limitations: Applications not accepted.
Application information: Contributes only to pre-selected organizations.
Trustee: Aaron Rosenberg.
EIN: 113411821

38305
The Kroo-Grunfeld Family Foundation, Inc.
15 W. 81st St., Ste. 15F
New York, NY 10024-6022 (212) 580-9153
Contact: Katherina Grunfeld, Pres.

Established in 2000 in NY.
Donor(s): Paul Grunfeld, Katherina Grunfeld.
Financial data (yr. ended 11/30/01): Grants paid, $14,795; assets, $158,961 (M); gifts received, $60,030; expenditures, $16,693; qualifying distributions, $14,795.
Officers: Katherina Grunfeld, Pres.; Paul Grunfeld, V.P.; Nicole Grunfeld, Secy.
EIN: 134093705

38306
Max & Helen Abrams Foundation, Inc.
c/o Fred Abrams
270-29A Grand Central Pkwy.
Floral Park, NY 11005-1119

Established in 1943.
Financial data (yr. ended 12/31/01): Grants paid, $14,782; assets, $197,031 (M); expenditures, $16,408; qualifying distributions, $14,782.
Limitations: Applications not accepted. Giving primarily in New York, NY, area.
Application information: Contributes only to pre-selected organizations.
Officers and Directors:* Marilyn Katz,* V.P.; Fred Abrams,* Secy.-Treas.; Roberta Bologna, Steven Katz.
EIN: 136090811

38307
Abboud Abadi Charitable Foundation, Inc.
1236 Avenue S
Brooklyn, NY 11229-2732

Established in 2000 in NY.
Donor(s): Abboud Abadi.
Financial data (yr. ended 12/31/01): Grants paid, $14,765; assets, $85,703 (M); gifts received, $30,000; expenditures, $16,665; qualifying distributions, $14,765.
Limitations: Applications not accepted.
Application information: Contributes only to pre-selected organizations.
Officer: Abboud Abadi, Pres.
EIN: 113565508

38308
The Wayne Family Foundation
c/o BMC&F
67 N. Main St.
New City, NY 10956

Established in 1996 in DE.
Donor(s): Jane Z. Wayne, James G. Wayne.
Financial data (yr. ended 06/30/01): Grants paid, $14,740; assets, $177,968 (M); gifts received, $24,297; expenditures, $16,162; qualifying distributions, $14,740.
Limitations: Applications not accepted.
Application information: Contributes only to pre-selected organizations.
Officers: Jane Z. Wayne, Pres.; James G. Wayne, V.P.
Director: Thomas A. Condon.
EIN: 061468568

38309
Stanley B. Tunick Foundation
21 Meadow Rd.
Scarsdale, NY 10583-7642

Donor(s): Mildred S. Tunick, Erica B. Tunick, Robert N. Tunick, Richard D. Tunick, Stanley B. Tunick Trust.
Financial data (yr. ended 12/31/01): Grants paid, $14,700; assets, $359,591 (M); expenditures, $14,888; qualifying distributions, $14,700.
Limitations: Applications not accepted. Giving primarily in NY.
Application information: Contributes only to pre-selected organizations.
Trustees: Andrew J. Tunick, Mildred S. Tunick, Richard D. Tunick.
EIN: 116007076

38310
Barbara & Howard Wise Endowment for the Arts, Inc.
110 W. 13th St.
New York, NY 10011-7802

Established in 1990 in NY.
Financial data (yr. ended 12/31/01): Grants paid, $14,700; assets, $186,670 (M); expenditures, $16,829; qualifying distributions, $14,700.
Limitations: Applications not accepted. Giving limited to NY.
Application information: Contributes only to pre-selected organizations.
Officers: Barbara S. Wise, Pres.; Juliet Wise Reubens, V.P. and Secy.; Daniel Wise, V.P. and Treas.
EIN: 133593706
Codes: GTI

38311
The Platt Family Foundation, Inc.
47 Stanton Cir.
New Rochelle, NY 10804
Contact: Harold Platt, Pres.; or Ann Platt, Secy.-Treas.

Established in 1986 in DE and NY.
Donor(s): Ann Platt, Harold Platt.
Financial data (yr. ended 12/31/01): Grants paid, $14,660; assets, $17,811 (M); expenditures, $14,845; qualifying distributions, $14,660.
Limitations: Giving primarily in NY.
Officers: Harold Platt, Pres.; Ann Platt, Secy.-Treas.
EIN: 061192164

38312
Brian A. Dellomo Scholarship Trust
c/o Anthony Dellomo
55 Lakeland Rd.
Staten Island, NY 10314-2505

Established in 2000.
Financial data (yr. ended 12/31/01): Grants paid, $14,659; assets, $67,081 (M); gifts received, $2,165; expenditures, $15,105; qualifying distributions, $15,056.
Limitations: Applications not accepted.
Application information: Contributes only to pre-selected organizations.
Officers and Directors:* Anthony E. Dellomo,* Pres.; Patricia K. Dellomo,* Secy.
EIN: 134076626

38313
Stanley J. and Doris Fenvessy Foundation
167 E. 61st St.
New York, NY 10021

Established in 1986 in NY.
Donor(s): Stanley J. Fenvessy, Doris Fenvessy.
Financial data (yr. ended 10/31/01): Grants paid, $14,656; assets, $16,363 (M); gifts received, $5,000; expenditures, $16,215; qualifying distributions, $14,655.
Limitations: Applications not accepted. Giving primarily in New York, NY.
Application information: Contributes only to pre-selected organizations.
Officer: Doris Fenvessy, Pres. and Secy.
EIN: 133387065

38314
The James M. Coogan Family Foundation
51 Pondfield Rd.
Bronxville, NY 10708

Established in 1999 in NY.
Donor(s): James M. Coogan.
Financial data (yr. ended 12/31/01): Grants paid, $14,625; assets, $332,333 (M); expenditures, $14,809; qualifying distributions, $14,625.
Officers: James M. Coogan, Pres.; Robin Coogan, Secy.
EIN: 134090179

38315
Charles L. & Elizabeth P. Gerli Foundation, Inc.
502 Union St.
Hudson, NY 12534

Financial data (yr. ended 12/31/01): Grants paid, $14,608; assets, $243,635 (M); expenditures, $21,185; qualifying distributions, $14,608.
Limitations: Applications not accepted. Giving primarily in NY.
Officer: Charles Gerli, Jr., Mgr.
EIN: 136133907

38316
Lewis and Colleen Golub Foundation
c/o Lewis Golub
501 Duanesburg Rd.
Schenectady, NY 12306

Established in 1998 in DE.
Donor(s): Lewis Golub.
Financial data (yr. ended 12/31/01): Grants paid, $14,600; assets, $137,300 (M); expenditures, $14,987; qualifying distributions, $14,942.
Limitations: Applications not accepted.
Application information: Contributes only to pre-selected organizations.
Officers and Trustees:* Lewis Golub,* Pres.; Colleen Golub,* V.P.; Jerel Golub,* Secy.
EIN: 141807047

38317
Morton A. & Phyllis B. Simon Foundation
c/o Morton A. Simon
3 Chestnut Dr.
Pomona, NY 10970

Established in 1989 in NY.
Donor(s): Morton A. Simon, Phyllis B. Simon.
Financial data (yr. ended 10/31/01): Grants paid, $14,594; assets, $55,521 (M); expenditures, $17,038; qualifying distributions, $14,594.
Limitations: Applications not accepted.
Application information: Contributes only to pre-selected organizations.
Officers: Morton A. Simon, Pres.; Phyllis B. Simon, V.P. and Secy.
EIN: 223010423

38318
Tridan Foundation, Inc.
c/o Yohalem, Gillman & Co., LLP
477 Madison Ave., 9th Fl.
New York, NY 10022-5802

Donor(s): Peter Goodman, Barbara S. Goodman.
Financial data (yr. ended 12/31/01): Grants paid, $14,550; assets, $332,192 (M); gifts received, $20,000; expenditures, $15,082; qualifying distributions, $14,550.
Limitations: Applications not accepted.
Application information: Contributes only to pre-selected organizations.
Officers: Peter Goodman, Pres. and Treas.; Barbara S. Goodman, V.P. and Secy.; Elizabeth Smith Goodman, V.P.; Geoffrey Adams Goodman, V.P.; Mark H. Goodman, V.P.
EIN: 136161296

38319
F.G. Foundation
c/o Frada Nager
150 E. 69th St.
New York, NY 10021

Established in 1997 in NY.
Donor(s): Frada Nager.
Financial data (yr. ended 06/30/01): Grants paid, $14,535; assets, $110,278 (M); gifts received, $20,125; expenditures, $15,714; qualifying distributions, $15,281.
Trustees: Mimi Graham, Michael Krengel, Frada Nager.
EIN: 223577769

38320
Irving J. Aibel Foundation, Inc.
c/o Jack Kane & Co., PC
70 W. 40th St., 4th Fl.
New York, NY 10018

Established about 1944 in NY.
Donor(s): Benjamin Aibel.

38320—NEW YORK

Financial data (yr. ended 12/31/01): Grants paid, $14,500; assets, $366,975 (M); gifts received, $15,282; expenditures, $17,928; qualifying distributions, $17,928.
Limitations: Applications not accepted. Giving primarily in NY.
Application information: Contributes only to pre-selected organizations.
Officers: Benjamin Aibel, Pres.; Bertha G. Aibel, Treas.
Directors: James H. Aibel, Judy Brickman, Robert Todd Lane.
EIN: 136090013

38321
Jasmine L. Cantor Foundation, Inc.
307 Chase Lincoln First Bank Bldg.
Jamestown, NY 14702-1279

Financial data (yr. ended 12/31/01): Grants paid, $14,500; assets, $335,132 (M); expenditures, $18,977; qualifying distributions, $18,977.
Limitations: Applications not accepted. Giving limited to residents of Jamestown, NY.
Application information: Unsolicited requests for funds not accepted.
Trustees: Sherwood S. Caldwell, Eddy Cantor, Joseph Yelich.
EIN: 161287432
Codes: GTI

38322
The Farash Fund for Manufacturing Education
919 Winton Rd. S.
Rochester, NY 14618-1633

Established in 1995 in NY.
Donor(s): Max M. Farash.
Financial data (yr. ended 12/31/01): Grants paid, $14,500; assets, $286,339 (M); expenditures, $15,485; qualifying distributions, $14,500.
Limitations: Applications not accepted.
Application information: Contributes only to pre-selected organizations.
Trustees: Arthur E. Aspengren, Max M. Farash, Eric R. Fox.
EIN: 166396808

38323
The Howard A. Glickstein Fund
3 St. Jode Ct.
Northport, NY 11768 (631) 754-4526
Contact: Howard A. Glickstein, Tr.

Financial data (yr. ended 08/31/01): Grants paid, $14,500; assets, $1 (M); expenditures, $15,210; qualifying distributions, $14,500.
Limitations: Giving primarily in Huntington, NY.
Trustees: Howard A. Glickstein, Lawrence Newman.
EIN: 226403573

38324
The Piluso Foundation
c/o Long Island Telephone Co.
875 Merrick Ave.
Westbury, NY 11590

Established in 1999 in NY.
Donor(s): Charles Piluso.
Financial data (yr. ended 12/31/01): Grants paid, $14,500; assets, $177,866 (M); expenditures, $16,585; qualifying distributions, $14,500.
Trustees: Joanne Panzarella-Piluso, Charles Piluso.
EIN: 061477860

38325
Preferred Mutual Insurance Company Foundation
c/o Preferred Mutual Insurance Co.
1 Preferred Way
New Berlin, NY 13411
E-mail: info@pminsco.com; URL: http://www.pminsco.com
Contact: John G. Frisch, Advisory Comm. Member

Established in 1985 in NY.
Donor(s): Preferred Mutual Insurance Co.
Financial data (yr. ended 12/31/01): Grants paid, $14,500; assets, $392,616 (M); gifts received, $50,250; expenditures, $15,033; qualifying distributions, $14,500.
Limitations: Giving limited to Chenango, Delaware, and Otsego counties, NY.
Application information: Application form required for scholarships available Feb. of each year. Application form required.
Officers and Trustees:* Robert A. Wadsworth,* C.E.O. and Pres.; Gary G. Strong,* Secy.; John G. Frisch, Alan Pole, NBT Bank, N.A.
EIN: 226423721
Codes: CS, CD, GTI

38326
The Philippe Weissberg Charitable Trust
c/o Winthrop Trust Co.
466 Lexington Ave., 17th Fl.
New York, NY 10017-3140

Established in 2000 in NY.
Donor(s): Philippe Weissberg.
Financial data (yr. ended 12/31/01): Grants paid, $14,500; assets, $875,973 (M); expenditures, $40,079; qualifying distributions, $14,500.
Limitations: Applications not accepted.
Application information: Contributes only to pre-selected organizations.
Distrib. Comm. Member: Philippe Weissberg.
Trustee: Winthrop Trust Co.
EIN: 527142501

38327
Wild Woods Foundation
c/o Myer, Greene & Degge
P.O. Box 930
Pearl River, NY 10965

Established in 1996 in DE.
Donor(s): Janet U. McAlpin.
Financial data (yr. ended 11/30/01): Grants paid, $14,500; assets, $849,915 (M); gifts received, $116,276; expenditures, $33,743; qualifying distributions, $14,500.
Limitations: Applications not accepted. Giving primarily in AK, CA, and OR.
Application information: Contributes only to pre-selected organizations.
Officers: Janet U. McAlpin, Pres.; Ann R. McAlpin, Secy.
Director: David E. Godsey.
EIN: 133929814

38328
Anna, Karin J. & David B. Dillard Foundation
c/o Lazard Freres & Co.
30 Rockefeller Plz.
New York, NY 10020
Contact: David B. Dillard, V.P.

Established in 1985 in NY.
Donor(s): David B. Dillard.
Financial data (yr. ended 12/31/00): Grants paid, $14,472; assets, $2,121,528 (M); gifts received, $64,200; expenditures, $23,520; qualifying distributions, $13,177.
Limitations: Giving on a national basis.

Officers and Directors:* Christopher Dillard,* Pres.; Anna Karin J. Dillard,* V.P.; David B. Dillard,* V.P.; James Dillard, Secy.; Patrick Dillard, Treas.
EIN: 133318826

38329
Waka Foundation, Inc.
c/o Strauss, Comas, & Modansky, LLP
462 7th Ave., 22nd Fl.
New York, NY 10018

Established in 1998 in NY.
Financial data (yr. ended 08/31/01): Grants paid, $14,453; assets, $573,419 (M); expenditures, $171,264; qualifying distributions, $14,453; giving activities include $7,564 for programs.
Limitations: Applications not accepted.
Application information: Contributes only to pre-selected organizations.
Officers and Directors:* Hans Li,* Pres.; Connie S. P. Chen,* Secy.-Treas.; Carina Courtright.
EIN: 133973868

38330
Bruce M. Epstein Family Charitable Trust
c/o Jennison Assocs.
466 Lexington Ave., 18th Fl.
New York, NY 10017-3140

Established in 1984 in NY.
Donor(s): Bruce M. Epstein, Jennison Assocs. Capital Corp.
Financial data (yr. ended 12/31/01): Grants paid, $14,440; assets, $309,186 (M); gifts received, $2,000; expenditures, $17,100; qualifying distributions, $14,440.
Limitations: Applications not accepted.
Application information: Contributes only to pre-selected organizations.
Trustee: Barbara Epstein.
EIN: 226389588

38331
Varflex Educational Foundation
512 W. Court St.
Rome, NY 13440
Contact: Dorothy G. Griffin, Tr.

Established in 1994.
Financial data (yr. ended 12/31/01): Grants paid, $14,400; assets, $255,827 (M); expenditures, $18,392; qualifying distributions, $14,374.
Application information: Application form required.
Trustees: Edwin L. Cates, Dorothy G. Griffin, William L. Griffin.
EIN: 161471541
Codes: GTI

38332
Robert & Renee Kelly Foundation
c/o Fiduciary Trust Co. International
600 5th Ave.
New York, NY 10020-2326
Application address: 3855 Via Nona Maria, No. 103A, Carmel, CA 93923
Contact: Robert Kelly, Pres.

Established in 2000 in CA.
Donor(s): Robert Kelly, Renee Kelly.
Financial data (yr. ended 12/31/01): Grants paid, $14,390; assets, $583,422 (M); expenditures, $30,126; qualifying distributions, $14,390.
Officers: Robert Kelly, Pres. and C.F.O.; Renee Kelly, V.P. and Secy.
EIN: 770547275

IN THIS SECTION, WITHIN EACH STATE, FOUNDATIONS ARE LISTED IN DESCENDING ORDER BY TOTAL GRANTS PAID

38333
Nabi Foundation
83 Beach Rd.
Great Neck, NY 11023
Contact: Stanley A. Nabi, Tr.

Financial data (yr. ended 12/31/01): Grants paid, $14,350; assets, $180,712 (M); expenditures, $14,500; qualifying distributions, $14,350.
Limitations: Giving primarily in NY.
Trustees: Bette E. Nabi, Stanley A. Nabi.
EIN: 136168274

38334
Valerie and Jeffrey S. Wilpon Foundation
111 Great Neck Rd., Ste. 408
Great Neck, NY 11021
Contact: Jeffrey S. Wilpon, Pres.

Established in 2000 in NY.
Donor(s): Jeffrey S. Wilpon, Valerie Wilpon.
Financial data (yr. ended 12/31/00): Grants paid, $14,350; assets, $168,448 (M); gifts received, $178,996; expenditures, $14,350; qualifying distributions, $14,350.
Officers and Directors:* Jeffrey S. Wilpon,* Pres.; Valerie Wilpon,* V.P.
EIN: 113555767

38335
The Samuel & Natalie Lipsett Foundation
c/o Bessemer Trust Co.
630 5th Ave.
New York, NY 10111

Established in 1999 in FL.
Donor(s): Natalie Kahn Lipsett, Samuel N. Lipsett.
Financial data (yr. ended 12/31/01): Grants paid, $14,342; assets, $424,011 (M); expenditures, $19,482; qualifying distributions, $14,342.
Limitations: Applications not accepted.
Application information: Contributes only to pre-selected organizations.
Trustees: Natalie Kahn Lipsett, Samuel N. Lipsett.
EIN: 656319168

38336
The Ames Family Foundation
c/o U.S. Trust
114 W. 47th St., TaxVas
New York, NY 10036

Established in 2000 in WA.
Donor(s): A. Gary Ames.
Financial data (yr. ended 12/31/00): Grants paid, $14,313; assets, $3,882,820 (M); gifts received, $5,032,152; expenditures, $23,285; qualifying distributions, $14,313.
Application information: Unsolicited request for funds not accepted.
Trustees: A. Gary Ames, Barbara J. Ames, Eric C. Ames, Megan E. Barjesteh.
EIN: 912042889

38337
Folger Family Foundation
c/o Oscar Folger
521 5th Ave., 24th Fl.
New York, NY 10175

Established in 2000 in NY.
Donor(s): Rita Folger.
Financial data (yr. ended 12/31/01): Grants paid, $14,310; assets, $30,564 (M); expenditures, $14,353; qualifying distributions, $14,310.
Limitations: Applications not accepted. Giving primarily in NJ and Brooklyn, NY.
Application information: Contributes only to pre-selected organizations.
Trustees: Oscar D. Folger, Rita Folger.
EIN: 134092976

38338
Alvin F. and Ruth K. Thiem Charitable Foundation, Inc.
c/o Richard F. O'Connor
311 Alexander St., Ste. 319
Rochester, NY 14604-2613

Established in 1992 in NY.
Donor(s): Alvin F. Thiem.
Financial data (yr. ended 12/31/01): Grants paid, $14,300; assets, $144,334 (M); expenditures, $15,795; qualifying distributions, $14,300.
Limitations: Applications not accepted.
Application information: Contributes only to pre-selected organizations.
Officers: Alvin F. Thiem, Pres.; Richard O'Connor, V.P. and Secy.; Mark Klafen, Treas.
EIN: 161419723

38339
Siraben Trust
c/o Ciaschi, Dietershagen, et al.
11 Spruce Ln.
Ithaca, NY 14850-1766

Established in 1964 in NY.
Donor(s): Rachel Siegel, Benjamin M. Siegel.‡
Financial data (yr. ended 12/31/01): Grants paid, $14,299; assets, $87,662 (M); gifts received, $10,364; expenditures, $15,212; qualifying distributions, $14,299.
Limitations: Applications not accepted. Giving primarily in Tompkins County, NY; some giving also in Israel.
Application information: Contributes only to pre-selected organizations.
Officer: Rachel J. Siegel, Mgr.
EIN: 166058687

38340
Peter J. Weiller Foundation
c/o Leonard L. Stark
60 E. 42nd St., Ste. 1115
New York, NY 10165-0095

Established in 1986 in NY.
Financial data (yr. ended 12/31/01): Grants paid, $14,275; assets, $94,432 (M); expenditures, $14,472; qualifying distributions, $14,126.
Limitations: Applications not accepted. Giving primarily in Westchester County, NY.
Application information: Contributes only to pre-selected organizations.
Trustee: Douglas R. Weiller.
EIN: 133381120

38341
Walters Charitable Trust
P.O. Box 128
New York, NY 10150

Established in 1999 in NY.
Financial data (yr. ended 12/31/01): Grants paid, $14,252; assets, $325,185 (M); expenditures, $14,252; qualifying distributions, $14,252.
Officer: Milt Walters, Pres.
EIN: 066478368

38342
The Bell-Hoving Family Foundation
c/o Nancy Hoving
150 E. 73rd St.
New York, NY 10021-4362

Established in 1992 in NY.
Donor(s): Amelia Lange Bell.
Financial data (yr. ended 12/31/01): Grants paid, $14,250; assets, $371,063 (M); expenditures, $16,405; qualifying distributions, $14,250.
Limitations: Applications not accepted. Giving primarily in New York, NY.
Application information: Contributes only to pre-selected organizations.
Officers and Directors:* Nancy B. Hoving,* Pres.; Petrea B. Hoving,* Secy.; Thomas P.F. Hoving,* Treas.
EIN: 133679550

38343
The Stern Family Foundation
861 E. 24th St.
Brooklyn, NY 11210-2821
Contact: Samuel Stern, Pres.

Donor(s): Samuel Stern.
Financial data (yr. ended 03/31/01): Grants paid, $14,250; assets, $1,334,987 (M); gifts received, $1,114,997; expenditures, $32,321; qualifying distributions, $14,250.
Officers: Samuel Stern, Pres.; Martin Orstein, Secy.-Treas.
EIN: 133956806

38344
Obernier Family Foundation
c/o BDO Seidman, LLP
330 Madison Ave.
New York, NY 10017-5001

Established in 1998 in CT.
Donor(s): Robert Obernier.
Financial data (yr. ended 12/31/01): Grants paid, $14,200; assets, $112,819 (M); gifts received, $48,489; expenditures, $14,527; qualifying distributions, $14,200.
Limitations: Applications not accepted.
Application information: Contributes only to pre-selected organizations.
Trustees: Robert Obernier, Rosemarie Obernier.
EIN: 066462350

38345
The Slater Foundation
159 W. 13th St., Ste. 4
New York, NY 10011-7867

Established in 1998 in NY.
Financial data (yr. ended 05/31/02): Grants paid, $14,200; assets, $411,877 (M); expenditures, $16,736; qualifying distributions, $14,200.
Trustee: Jacqueline R. Slater.
EIN: 367237697

38346
Benjamin M. Stein Foundation, Inc.
60 Louden Ave.
Amityville, NY 11701 (631) 842-1515

Donor(s): Benjamin M. Stein, M.D., Brunswick Hospital Ctr.
Financial data (yr. ended 12/31/01): Grants paid, $14,150; assets, $9,339 (M); gifts received, $15,000; expenditures, $14,660; qualifying distributions, $14,150.
Limitations: Applications not accepted. Giving primarily in Palm Beach, FL, and Great Neck and New York, NY.
Application information: Contributes only to pre-selected organizations.
Officers: Benjamin M. Stein, M.D., Pres. and Mgr.; Douglas N. Stein, V.P.; Claire W. Stein, Secy.-Treas.
EIN: 116037936

38347
Virginia Moshang and Herbert Lau Kee Foundation
c/o Herbert Lau Kee
345 Broome St., Apt. 6D
New York, NY 10013

Established in 1992 in NY.

38347—NEW YORK

Financial data (yr. ended 08/31/01): Grants paid, $14,109; assets, $1 (M); expenditures, $15,074; qualifying distributions, $14,109.
Limitations: Applications not accepted. Giving primarily in New York, NY.
Application information: Contributes only to pre-selected organizations.
Officers: Virginia Moshang Kee, Pres.; Herbert Lau Kee, Secy.-Treas.
Director: Glenn Lau Kee.
EIN: 133632294

38348
The Glendale Foundation, Inc.
126 E. 56th St., 10th Fl.
New York, NY 10022

Financial data (yr. ended 12/31/01): Grants paid, $14,100; assets, $650,755 (M); expenditures, $24,885; qualifying distributions, $20,432.
Limitations: Applications not accepted. Giving primarily in NY.
Application information: Contributes only to pre-selected organizations.
Officers and Directors:* Stephen L. Schwartz,* Pres.; Mary Ann Van Clief,* V.P.; Jeanette Pereira,* Secy.-Treas.; Karen Hart.
EIN: 133288476

38349
Stein-Grandt Fund
702 Euclid Ave.
Elmira, NY 14905-1919 (607) 734-0718
Contact: Edward J. Grandt, Pres.

Donor(s): Edward J. Grandt.
Financial data (yr. ended 04/30/02): Grants paid, $14,100; assets, $86,008 (M); expenditures, $15,226; qualifying distributions, $14,100.
Limitations: Giving limited to NY.
Officers and Trustees:* Edward J. Grandt,* Pres. and Treas.; Irene Stein Grandt,* V.P. and Secy.; John S. Grandt.
EIN: 161367574

38350
The Holmes Charitable Foundation
c/o Weber Moses & Co.
225 Broadway, Ste. 2620
New York, NY 10007

Established in 1999 in IL.
Donor(s): H. Robert Holmes.
Financial data (yr. ended 12/31/01): Grants paid, $14,085; assets, $162,150 (M); expenditures, $22,720; qualifying distributions, $14,085.
Limitations: Applications not accepted.
Application information: Contributes only to pre-selected organizations.
Trustees: Debra J. Holmes, H. Robert Holmes, Kelly Elizabeth Holmes.
EIN: 364296450

38351
S. G. Rosenbaum Foundation, Inc.
c/o Louis Sternbach & Co.
1333 Broadway, No. 516
New York, NY 10018

Donor(s): Francis Rosenbaum, Jr.
Financial data (yr. ended 12/31/01): Grants paid, $14,075; assets, $245,876 (M); gifts received, $116; expenditures, $16,905; qualifying distributions, $14,075.
Limitations: Applications not accepted. Giving limited to New York, NY.
Application information: Contributes only to pre-selected organizations.
Officers: Francis F. Rosenbaum, Jr., Pres.; Joyce K. Rosenbaum, V.P.

Directors: Michael F. Rosenbaum, Jr., Steve L. Rosenbaum.
EIN: 136059702

38352
Judith and Arthur Mintz Foundation, Inc.
1346 Boxwood Dr. E.
Hewlett, NY 11557-2205

Established in 1986 in NY.
Donor(s): Arthur Mintz, Judith Mintz.
Financial data (yr. ended 12/31/01): Grants paid, $14,073; assets, $26,101 (M); gifts received, $40,100; expenditures, $14,153; qualifying distributions, $14,073.
Limitations: Applications not accepted. Giving primarily in NY.
Application information: Contributes only to pre-selected organizations.
Officer: Arthur Mintz, Pres.
EIN: 133369793

38353
The Joan & Fred Hirschhorn, Jr. Foundation, Inc.
c/o Fiduciary Trust Co. International
600 Fifth Ave.
New York, NY 10020

Financial data (yr. ended 12/31/01): Grants paid, $14,055; assets, $118,433 (M); expenditures, $14,944; qualifying distributions, $14,055.
Limitations: Applications not accepted. Giving primarily in NY.
Application information: Contributes only to pre-selected organizations.
Officers: Fred Hirschhorn, Jr., Pres.; Joan H. Bright, V.P.; Elinor H. Hirschhorn, V.P.; Elizabeth S. Hirschhorn, V.P.; Joan M. Hirschhorn, V.P.
EIN: 136129653

38354
The Carol and George Henry Family Foundation
P.O. Box 621
Armonk, NY 10504-0621

Established in 1986 in NY.
Donor(s): Carol Henry, George Henry.
Financial data (yr. ended 12/31/01): Grants paid, $14,050; assets, $278,913 (M); expenditures, $14,558; qualifying distributions, $14,050.
Limitations: Applications not accepted.
Application information: Contributes only to pre-selected organizations.
Trustees: Carol Henry, Dena Lynn Henry, George Henry, Robin Ann Henry.
EIN: 133389028

38355
Lalchandani Family Foundation
6135 98th St., Apt. 16E
Rego Park, NY 11374-1425

Established in 1998.
Donor(s): Nathir Lalchandani.
Financial data (yr. ended 12/31/01): Grants paid, $14,006; assets, $61,967 (L); gifts received, $8,776; expenditures, $14,729; qualifying distributions, $14,006.
Limitations: Applications not accepted.
Application information: Contributes only to pre-selected organizations.
Officers: Nathir Lalchandani, Pres.; Kaushalya Lalchandani, V.P.; Ram Lalchandani, Secy.; Sita Lalchandani, Treas.
EIN: 113462799

38356
The Corso Family Foundation, Inc.
c/o Joseph Corso, Jr.
167 Zock Rd.
New York, NY 10271-0093

Established in 1994 in NY.
Donor(s): Joseph Corso, Sr., Joseph Corso, Jr., Education for Youth Society Foundation.
Financial data (yr. ended 10/31/01): Grants paid, $14,000; assets, $457,857 (M); expenditures, $15,189; qualifying distributions, $14,000.
Limitations: Applications not accepted. Giving primarily in NY.
Application information: Contributes only to pre-selected organizations.
Officers: Joseph Corso, Jr., Pres. and Treas.; Joseph Corso, Sr., V.P. and Secy.; Christina Corso, V.P.
EIN: 133799201

38357
Alfred Erk Charitable Education Trust
c/o JPMorgan Chase Bank
P.O. Box 31412
Rochester, NY 14603
Application address: c/o Cheryl Kleiman, JPMorgan Chase Bank, 20 S. Clinton Ave., Ste. S-4, Rochester, NY 14606, tel.: (800) 850-7222

Established in 1985 in CT.
Financial data (yr. ended 09/30/01): Grants paid, $14,000; assets, $191,569 (M); expenditures, $20,636; qualifying distributions, $15,388.
Limitations: Giving limited to residents of Middlebury, CT.
Application information: Application form required.
Trustee: JPMorgan Chase Bank.
EIN: 066287322

38358
Stuart M. Johnson Foundation
8 Haven Ave., Ste. 203
Port Washington, NY 11050

Established in 2000 in NY.
Donor(s): Stuart M. Johnson.
Financial data (yr. ended 12/31/01): Grants paid, $14,000; assets, $653,304 (M); gifts received, $2,000; expenditures, $21,890; qualifying distributions, $14,000.
Limitations: Applications not accepted.
Application information: Contributes only to pre-selected organizations.
Officers and Directors:* Stuart M. Johnson,* Pres.; Craig M. Johnson,* V.P. and Treas.; Stanley Fishkin, Irwin S. Meyer, Jay A. Odintz.
EIN: 113558145

38359
The Kaplan Family Private Foundation
19 Rivers Edge
Newburgh, NY 12550

Established in 1998 in NY.
Donor(s): William Kaplan, Elaine Kaplan.
Financial data (yr. ended 12/31/00): Grants paid, $14,000; assets, $571,933 (M); gifts received, $1,378; expenditures, $14,600; qualifying distributions, $14,600.
Limitations: Applications not accepted. Giving primarily in NY.
Application information: Contributes only to pre-selected organizations.
Officers: William Kaplan, Pres.; Elaine Kaplan, V.P.; Richard Drake, Secy.; Fred Jadrosich, Treas.
Directors: Richard Bauer, Joan Kaplan, Sheila Rubin.
EIN: 141803630

38360
Paul Family Foundation, Inc.
c/o Lonnie E. Wollin
350 5th Ave., Ste. 2822
New York, NY 10118

Established around 1984.
Donor(s): Boris Paul.
Financial data (yr. ended 09/30/01): Grants paid, $14,000; assets, $86,570 (M); expenditures, $14,710; qualifying distributions, $14,234.
Limitations: Applications not accepted.
Application information: Contributes only to pre-selected organizations.
Officers: Boris Paul, Pres.; Lonnie E. Wollin, Secy.
EIN: 133245058

38361
The Paul Family Foundation
20 Woodside Ln.
Pittsford, NY 14534
Contact: John W. Paul, Tr.

Established in 1997 in NY.
Donor(s): Lillian E. Paul.
Financial data (yr. ended 12/31/01): Grants paid, $14,000; assets, $278,425 (M); expenditures, $14,728; qualifying distributions, $14,000.
Limitations: Giving limited to Broome County, NY.
Trustees: David M. Paul, John W. Paul, Lillian E. Paul.
EIN: 166466665

38362
The Spiegel-Pollock Family Foundation
(Formerly The Arthur & Pollock Spiegel Foundation)
28 Fox Ln.
Mount Kisco, NY 10549 (914) 234-0085
Contact: L. Pollock Spiegal, Dir.

Established in 1997 in NY.
Donor(s): Arthur Spiegel, Pollock Spiegel.
Financial data (yr. ended 01/31/02): Grants paid, $14,000; assets, $252,777 (M); gifts received, $3,000; expenditures, $14,176; qualifying distributions, $14,000.
Limitations: Giving primarily in NY.
Directors: Arthur H. Spiegal III, L. Pollock Spiegel.
EIN: 133933188

38363
Susan S. and Kenneth L. Wallach Foundation
c/o Irwin Markow
3 Manhattan Rd.
Purchase, NY 10577

Financial data (yr. ended 12/31/01): Grants paid, $14,000; assets, $770,936 (M); gifts received, $100,869; expenditures, $20,650; qualifying distributions, $14,000.
Trustees: Kenneth L. Wallach, Susan S. Wallach.
EIN: 137147899

38364
The Wang Family Charitable Foundation
c/o Manny Ruchelsman
1285 6th Ave., 21st Fl.
New York, NY 10019-6028

Financial data (yr. ended 10/31/01): Grants paid, $14,000; assets, $95,498 (M); expenditures, $14,305; qualifying distributions, $14,000.
Limitations: Applications not accepted. Giving primarily in New York, NY.
Application information: Contributes only to pre-selected organizations.
Trustee: Robert J. Morgado.
EIN: 133192845

38365
The Floyd & Barbara Warkol Charitable Foundation
Meadow Ln.
Purchase, NY 10577-2511

Established in 1990 in NY.
Donor(s): Floyd Warkol, Barbara Warkol.
Financial data (yr. ended 12/31/01): Grants paid, $14,000; assets, $466,126 (M); expenditures, $14,348; qualifying distributions, $14,000.
Limitations: Applications not accepted.
Application information: Contributes only to pre-selected organizations.
Trustees: Barbara Warkol, Floyd Warkol.
EIN: 226485772

38366
Woodward Foundation, Inc.
10 Tuthill Dr.
Shelter Island Heights, NY 11965

Established in 1998 in NY.
Financial data (yr. ended 12/31/00): Grants paid, $14,000; assets, $290,142 (M); expenditures, $16,209; qualifying distributions, $16,044.
Limitations: Applications not accepted. Giving primarily in NY and VA.
Application information: Contributes only to pre-selected organizations.
Officers: John E. Woodward III, Pres. and Treas.; James E. Ballowe, Jr., Secy.
EIN: 133542606

38367
Amy & Eugene Lynn Foundation, Inc.
c/o Tanton & Co., LLP
37 W. 57th St., 5th Fl.
New York, NY 10019
Contact: Robin Lynn, Pres.

Donor(s): Eugene Lynn, Amy Lynn, Robin Lynn.
Financial data (yr. ended 05/31/00): Grants paid, $13,975; assets, $22,261 (M); gifts received, $2,030; expenditures, $14,305; qualifying distributions, $14,062.
Officers and Directors:* Robin Lynn,* Pres. and Treas.; Bruce C. Lynn,* V.P. and Secy.; Daniel G. Ross.
EIN: 136085827

38368
Harold and Helen Derfner Foundation
c/o Derfner Mgmt., Inc.
245 E. 80th St.
New York, NY 10021

Established in 1992 in NY and FL.
Donor(s): Michael Braunstein, Barbara Braunstein.
Financial data (yr. ended 12/31/01): Grants paid, $13,950; assets, $265,062 (M); gifts received, $250,000; expenditures, $264,018; qualifying distributions, $14,044.
Limitations: Applications not accepted. Giving primarily in Palm Beach, FL.
Application information: Contributes only to pre-selected organizations.
Trustees: Harold Derfner, Helen Derfner, Jay Lieberman.
EIN: 133661341

38369
Julius and Evelyn Melnick Foundation, Inc.
225 Willow Ave.
Bronx, NY 10454 (718) 292-6400
Contact: Evelyn Melnick, Pres. or Michael Melnick, Secy.-Treas.

Financial data (yr. ended 04/30/02): Grants paid, $13,943; assets, $403,914 (M); gifts received, $10,000; expenditures, $14,302; qualifying distributions, $13,943.
Limitations: Giving primarily in NY.
Officers: Evelyn Melnick, Pres.; Michael Melnick, Secy.-Treas.
EIN: 136277918

38370
John R. & Hope Reese Foundation
c/o Lazard Freres & Co., LLC
30 Rockefeller Plz.
New York, NY 10020
Contact: John R. Reese, Pres.

Established in 1986 in NY.
Donor(s): John R. Reese.
Financial data (yr. ended 06/30/01): Grants paid, $13,900; assets, $78,602 (M); expenditures, $15,765; qualifying distributions, $13,900.
Limitations: Giving primarily in NY.
Officers: John R. Reese, Pres. and Secy.-Treas.; Hope Reese, V.P.
EIN: 133371584

38371
The Waterman Foundation, Inc.
c/o Reminick, Aarons & Co., LLP
685 3rd Ave., 19th Fl.
New York, NY 10017

Established in 1991 in TX.
Financial data (yr. ended 04/30/01): Grants paid, $13,900; assets, $229,090 (M); expenditures, $18,189; qualifying distributions, $13,900.
Limitations: Applications not accepted. Giving primarily in Santa Fe, NM.
Application information: Contributes only to pre-selected organizations.
Officer: Neil S. Waterman, Jr., Pres.
EIN: 752267289

38372
The Hyman Family Foundation
16 E. 73rd St., Ste. 2F
New York, NY 10021

Established in 1998 in NY.
Financial data (yr. ended 12/31/00): Grants paid, $13,897; assets, $309,311 (M); expenditures, $13,997; qualifying distributions, $13,897.
Directors: Carol Hyman, Gerald Hyman.
EIN: 113431731

38373
Myra Lee and Albert Fleischman Foundation, Inc.
1823 Gerritsen Ave.
Brooklyn, NY 11229

Established in 1996.
Donor(s): Albert Fleischman, Myra Lee Fleischman, RNB Foundation, Inc.
Financial data (yr. ended 12/31/01): Grants paid, $13,860; assets, $226,469 (M); expenditures, $14,458; qualifying distributions, $13,860.
Limitations: Applications not accepted.
Application information: Contributes only to pre-selected organizations.
Officers: Albert Fleischman, Pres. and Treas.; Myra Lee Fleischman, V.P. and Secy.; Rabbi Vicki Nan Lieberman, V.P.
EIN: 113299443

38374
MRM Charitable Foundation, Inc.
342 Madison Ave., Ste. 1923
New York, NY 10173-1999
Contact: Steve Vago, Pres.

Established in 1995 in NY.

38374—NEW YORK

Financial data (yr. ended 12/31/00): Grants paid, $13,855; assets, $70,477 (M); expenditures, $18,648; qualifying distributions, $18,573.
Officers: Steve Vago, Pres.; Hannah Vago, V.P.; Reynold Polk, Secy.
EIN: 133864872

38375
Vincenza and Joseph Vasile Foundation
39 State St., Ste. 700
Rochester, NY 14614

Established in 1996 in NY.
Financial data (yr. ended 09/30/01): Grants paid, $13,850; assets, $195,267 (M); expenditures, $17,101; qualifying distributions, $13,850.
Limitations: Applications not accepted. Giving primarily in Rochester, NY.
Application information: Contributes only to pre-selected organizations.
Directors: Gerald J. Vasile, Joseph Vasile.
EIN: 161516424

38376
Gottsegen Family Foundation
c/o CAI Advisors
767 5th Ave.
New York, NY 10153

Established in 1999.
Donor(s): Peter M. Gottsegen.
Financial data (yr. ended 12/31/01): Grants paid, $13,800; assets, $197,733 (M); expenditures, $16,475; qualifying distributions, $13,800.
Limitations: Applications not accepted.
Application information: Contributes only to pre-selected organizations.
Trustee: Peter M. Gottsegen.
EIN: 134067123

38377
A. M. Kleeman, Jr. Scholarship Fund
c/o Orange County Trust Co.
75 North St.
Middletown, NY 10940
Application address: c/o Warwick Valley Central School District, Warwick, NY 10990
Contact: Joseph Natale, Superintendent

Established around 1986 in NY.
Financial data (yr. ended 05/31/02): Grants paid, $13,800; assets, $217,406 (M); expenditures, $17,124; qualifying distributions, $13,707.
Limitations: Giving limited to Central School District No. 1 in Warwick and Chester in Orange County, NY.
Application information: Application form required.
Trustee: Orange County Trust Co.
EIN: 133586537
Codes: GTI

38378
Seymour Wiener Family Foundation
902 Broadway, 7th Fl.
New York, NY 10010-6002

Donor(s): Louis Frey Co., Inc.
Financial data (yr. ended 12/31/00): Grants paid, $13,800; assets, $12,408 (M); gifts received, $13,500; expenditures, $13,875; qualifying distributions, $13,800.
Limitations: Applications not accepted. Giving primarily in New York, NY.
Application information: Contributes only to pre-selected organizations.
Officer: Seymour Wiener, Mgr.
EIN: 136201184

38379
Sarah and Sasson Shalam Foundation
10 W. 33rd St., No. 702
New York, NY 10001 (212) 967-6868
Contact: Sasson Shalam, Pres.

Established in 1993.
Donor(s): Sonny Shalam.
Financial data (yr. ended 12/31/00): Grants paid, $13,798; assets, $1,108,996 (M); expenditures, $15,475; qualifying distributions, $13,798.
Limitations: Applications not accepted. Giving primarily in NY.
Application information: Contributes only to pre-selected organizations.
Officers: Sasson Shalam, Pres.; Abraham Shalam, Treas.
EIN: 133731350

38380
Page & William Black Foundation
1 Premium Point
New Rochelle, NY 10801

Donor(s): Page M. Black.
Financial data (yr. ended 11/30/01): Grants paid, $13,795; assets, $184,703 (M); gifts received, $50; expenditures, $24,506; qualifying distributions, $13,795.
Limitations: Applications not accepted. Giving primarily in New York, NY.
Application information: Contributes only to pre-selected organizations.
Trustees: Page M. Black, Allen Kezsbom.
EIN: 136113854

38381
The Gratch Foundation
c/o Ariel Gratch
40 E. 88th St., Ste. 15E
New York, NY 10128

Established in 1998 in NY.
Donor(s): Ariel Gratch.
Financial data (yr. ended 12/31/00): Grants paid, $13,785; assets, $166,961 (M); expenditures, $14,115; qualifying distributions, $13,785.
Limitations: Applications not accepted.
Application information: Contributes only to pre-selected organizations.
Officers: Ariel Gratch, Pres. and Treas.; Orit Gratch, V.P. and Secy.
EIN: 133993558

38382
The Jeffrey and Rita Wilder Foundation, Inc.
c/o Popper, Seger & Popper, LLP
192 Lexington Ave.
New York, NY 10016

Established in 1985 in NY.
Donor(s): Jeffrey Wilder.
Financial data (yr. ended 12/31/00): Grants paid, $13,778; assets, $488,876 (M); expenditures, $14,586; qualifying distributions, $13,778.
Limitations: Applications not accepted. Giving primarily in NY.
Application information: Contributes only to pre-selected organizations.
Officers: Jeffrey Wilder, Pres.; Rita Wilder, Secy.
Director: Lawrence Drath.
EIN: 133389241

38383
Smidinger Trust
P.O. Box 343
Scarborough, NY 10510

Donor(s): Arthur Smidinger, Marion Smidinger.

Financial data (yr. ended 12/31/99): Grants paid, $13,777; assets, $554,454 (M); expenditures, $15,852; qualifying distributions, $15,852.
Limitations: Applications not accepted. Giving primarily in New York, NY.
Application information: Contributes only to pre-selected organizations.
Trustees: Marion Smidinger, Peter Smidinger, Susan Smidinger.
EIN: 133096937

38384
W.I.L.D. Foundation
c/o Myer, Greene & Degge
P.O. Box 930
Pearl River, NY 10965

Financial data (yr. ended 11/30/01): Grants paid, $13,750; assets, $981,867 (M); gifts received, $106,248; expenditures, $22,956; qualifying distributions, $13,750.
Limitations: Applications not accepted.
Application information: Contributes only to pre-selected organizations.
Officers: David M. McAlpin, Pres.; Nanci H. McAlpin, Secy.
EIN: 133930285

38385
The Brackenridge Foundation, Inc.
9 Elm Ln.
Bronxville, NY 10708-1941

Established in 1994 in NY.
Donor(s): A. Bruce Brackenridge, Barbara Brackenridge.
Financial data (yr. ended 12/31/01): Grants paid, $13,749; assets, $273,008 (M); expenditures, $15,166; qualifying distributions, $13,749.
Limitations: Applications not accepted. Giving primarily in NY.
Application information: Contributes only to pre-selected organizations.
Officers: A. Bruce Brackenridge, Pres.; Barbara Brackenridge, Secy.
Directors: Alexander Brackenridge, Catherine Brackenridge, Martha B. Sayre.
EIN: 133751202

38386
Raymond and Nicole Bigar Foundation, Inc.
c/o Raymond Bigar
1107 5th Ave.
New York, NY 10128

Donor(s): Raymond Bigar, Nicole Bigar.
Financial data (yr. ended 12/31/01): Grants paid, $13,748; assets, $84,088 (M); gifts received, $5,000; expenditures, $14,235; qualifying distributions, $13,748.
Limitations: Applications not accepted. Giving primarily in NY.
Application information: Contributes only to pre-selected organizations.
Officer: Raymond Bigar, Pres.
EIN: 136172512

38387
Kamlani Foundation, Inc.
c/o Sham Kamlani
1407 Broadway, Ste. 1708
New York, NY 10018

Established in 1998 in NY.
Financial data (yr. ended 12/31/01): Grants paid, $13,720; assets, $189,414 (M); expenditures, $16,560; qualifying distributions, $13,720.
Limitations: Applications not accepted.
Application information: Contributes only to pre-selected organizations.
Trustee: Kavita Kamlani.

EIN: 134022323

38388
Y. H. Mirzoeff & Sons Foundation, Inc.
71 W. 47th St., Ste. 1402
New York, NY 10036 (212) 869-5888
Contact: Janice Ewenstein, Dir.

Established in 1986 in NY.
Donor(s): Israel Mirzoeff.
Financial data (yr. ended 12/31/01): Grants paid, $13,700; assets, $317,659 (M); expenditures, $18,114; qualifying distributions, $13,700.
Director: Janice Ewenstein.
EIN: 133355469

38389
The Robert Model Charitable Foundation
c/o Elmrock Capital
18 E. 74th St.
New York, NY 10021

Established in 1997 in WY.
Donor(s): Robert Model.
Financial data (yr. ended 12/31/01): Grants paid, $13,700; assets, $282,375 (M); expenditures, $15,429; qualifying distributions, $13,700.
Limitations: Applications not accepted.
Application information: Contributes only to pre-selected organizations.
Trustees: Robert Carlson, Robert Model, Arthur Penn.
EIN: 841400882

38390
Ridgefield Foundation Trust
c/o JPMorgan Chase Bank
1211 Ave. of the Americas, 34th Fl.
New York, NY 10036

Established in 2000.
Financial data (yr. ended 12/31/01): Grants paid, $13,656; assets, $68,818 (M); expenditures, $21,167; qualifying distributions, $14,356.
Limitations: Applications not accepted. Giving primarily in Ridgefield, CT.
Application information: Contributes only to pre-selected organizations.
Trustees: Rebecca Mucchetti, Stephen Mucchetti, JPMorgan Chase Bank.
EIN: 137260377

38391
Sam & Rose Fox Foundation
c/o Sam Fox
1938 Grand Ave.
Baldwin, NY 11510

Established in 1990 in NY.
Donor(s): Sam Fox.
Financial data (yr. ended 12/31/01): Grants paid, $13,655; assets, $81,082 (M); gifts received, $20,000; expenditures, $13,657; qualifying distributions, $13,657.
Limitations: Applications not accepted. Giving primarily in NY.
Application information: Contributes only to pre-selected organizations.
Trustees: Fred Fox, Rose Fox, Sam Fox.
EIN: 113040709

38392
The Sam and Gerry Ward Foundation, Inc.
P.O. Box 310
East Amherst, NY 14051-0310

Established in 1997 in NY.
Donor(s): Samuel F. Ward.
Financial data (yr. ended 12/31/01): Grants paid, $13,650; assets, $242,565 (M); expenditures, $15,369; qualifying distributions, $13,650.
Limitations: Applications not accepted.
Application information: Contributes only to pre-selected organizations.
Officers and Directors:* Samuel F. Ward,* Pres. and Treas.; Geraldine W. Ward,* V.P.; Daniel W. Judge,* Secy.
EIN: 222892136

38393
Weisser Foundation
c/o Lehman, Newman, & Flynn
225 W. 34th St., Ste. 2220
New York, NY 10122

Established in 1998 in NY.
Donor(s): Philip Weisser, Marcia Weisser.
Financial data (yr. ended 12/31/01): Grants paid, $13,628; assets, $62,896 (M); expenditures, $14,189; qualifying distributions, $13,628.
Limitations: Giving primarily in NY.
Trustees: Marcia Weisser, Philip Weiser.
EIN: 137174317

38394
JDSM Family Foundation, Inc.
c/o Jack Cohen
3703 Bernard Dr.
Wantagh, NY 11793

Established in 1999.
Donor(s): Jack Cohen, Mrs. Jack Cohen.
Financial data (yr. ended 06/30/01): Grants paid, $13,600; assets, $93,174 (M); gifts received, $20,000; expenditures, $30,709; qualifying distributions, $13,600.
Limitations: Applications not accepted. Giving primarily in Long Island, NY.
Application information: Contributes only to pre-selected organizations.
Officers and Directors:* Jack Cohen,* Pres.; Solomon Cohen,* V.P.; Dale Cohen,* Secy.-Treas.
EIN: 113523343

38395
Edward & Alice McLaughlin Scholarship Fund
c/o M&T Bank
One M&T Plz., 8th Fl.
Buffalo, NY 14203

Donor(s): The Edward A. McLaughlin Trust.
Financial data (yr. ended 09/30/01): Grants paid, $13,595; assets, $155,481 (M); expenditures, $17,445; qualifying distributions, $13,610.
Limitations: Applications not accepted. Giving primarily in PA.
Application information: Contributes only to pre-selected organizations.
Trustee: M&T Bank.
EIN: 237851151

38396
Peter & Maria DuBois Foundation, Inc.
c/o Lipsky, Goodkin & Co.
120 W. 45th St., 7th Fl.
New York, NY 10036

Financial data (yr. ended 11/30/01): Grants paid, $13,575; assets, $356,264 (M); expenditures, $13,956; qualifying distributions, $13,575.
Limitations: Applications not accepted.
Application information: Contributes only to pre-selected organizations.
Officers and Directors:* Joan D. Hunziker,* Pres.; Margaret McCann DuBois, V.P.; Robert Hunziker,* V.P.; Susan D. Shyne,* V.P.; Philip P. Goodkin, Secy.-Treas.
EIN: 136028784

38397
Zelig & Sarah Grossman Foundation
c/o Zell & Ettinger, C.P.A.
3001 Ave. M
Brooklyn, NY 11210

Established in 1994 in NY.
Donor(s): Zelig Grossman.
Financial data (yr. ended 12/31/01): Grants paid, $13,560; assets, $1 (M); gifts received, $13,000; expenditures, $13,855; qualifying distributions, $13,560.
Officers: Zelig Grossman, Pres.; Sarah Grossman, V.P.; Jeffrey Zell, Secy.
EIN: 113215110

38398
James J. Bloomer Charitable Trust
c/o Chemung Canal Trust Co.
P.O. Box 1522
Elmira, NY 14902
Application address: Saint Patrick's Roman Catholic Church Society, Elmira, NY 14901, tel.: (607) 733-6661

Established in 1954 in NY.
Donor(s): James L. Bloomer.‡
Financial data (yr. ended 12/31/00): Grants paid, $13,500; assets, $272,996 (M); expenditures, $15,446; qualifying distributions, $13,804.
Limitations: Giving limited to residents of Elmira, NY.
Application information: Application form not required.
Trustee: Chemung Canal Trust Co.
EIN: 166022129
Codes: GTI

38399
The Grace & Bert Lytell & Helen Menken Foundation, Inc.
c/o Donald Klein
7-11 S. Broadway, Ste. 208
White Plains, NY 10601

Financial data (yr. ended 12/31/01): Grants paid, $13,500; assets, $362,657 (M); expenditures, $16,318; qualifying distributions, $13,500.
Limitations: Applications not accepted. Giving primarily in New York, NY.
Application information: Contributes only to pre-selected organizations.
Officers: Donald Klein, Pres. and V.P.; Barbara Klein, V.P.; Zoe Klein, Secy.; Jason Klein, Treas.
EIN: 133051739

38400
The Birny Mason, Jr. Foundation, Inc.
6 Island Dr.
Rye, NY 10580-4306

Financial data (yr. ended 12/31/01): Grants paid, $13,500; assets, $424,052 (M); expenditures, $17,322; qualifying distributions, $13,500.
Limitations: Applications not accepted. Giving primarily in NY.
Application information: Contributes only to pre-selected organizations.
Trustees: Betty Smith Mason, Jerome A. Mason, Louise K. Mason, Candy L. Wood.
EIN: 136102737

38401
The Helena Segy Foundation
c/o Allan D. Goodridge
330 Madison Ave.
New York, NY 10017

Established in 1991 in NY.
Donor(s): Helena Segy.

38401
Financial data (yr. ended 12/31/01): Grants paid, $13,500; assets, $250,777 (M); gifts received, $17,180; expenditures, $30,146; qualifying distributions, $13,500.
Limitations: Applications not accepted. Giving primarily in New York, NY.
Application information: Contributes only to pre-selected organizations.
Trustees: Allan D. Goodridge, Helena Segy.
EIN: 136978310

38402
Sutton Area Community Fund Corporation
405 Lexington Ave.
New York, NY 10174-0002

Established in 1989 in NY.
Financial data (yr. ended 12/31/01): Grants paid, $13,500; assets, $41,979 (M); expenditures, $14,856; qualifying distributions, $13,500.
Limitations: Applications not accepted. Giving primarily in New York, NY.
Application information: Contributes only to pre-selected organizations.
Officers and Directors:* Richard Eyen,* Pres.; Elise Shapiro, V.P.; Patricia McHugh,* Secy.; Connie Klager,* Treas.; Sheldon Gordon, Nancy Katzoff, Ted Lynn, Jess Velona.
EIN: 133169753

38403
Beane Foundation
c/o Lionel & Belonsky, LLP
1800 Northern Blvd., Rm. 212
Roslyn, NY 11576

Donor(s): Alpheus C. Beane,‡ Alpheus C. Beane, Jr.
Financial data (yr. ended 12/31/01): Grants paid, $13,485; assets, $149,636 (M); expenditures, $16,240; qualifying distributions, $13,485.
Limitations: Applications not accepted.
Application information: Contributes only to pre-selected organizations.
Trustees: Alexander S. Beane, Alpheus C. Beane, Jr., Alpheus C. Beane III, Linda M. Beane.
EIN: 136096278

38404
The Harley & Marie-Christine Lippman Charitable Foundation, Inc.
1021 Park Ave.
New York, NY 10028

Established in 1996 in NY.
Donor(s): Harley Lippman.
Financial data (yr. ended 11/30/01): Grants paid, $13,485; assets, $119,271 (M); gifts received, $50; expenditures, $14,115; qualifying distributions, $13,485.
Limitations: Applications not accepted.
Application information: Contributes only to pre-selected organizations.
Officer: Harley Lippman, Pres.
Directors: John S. Erwin, Stuart Kessler.
EIN: 133949052

38405
Keren Bertha Chernofsky, Inc.
P.O. Box 197
Larchmont, NY 10538-0197

Financial data (yr. ended 12/31/01): Grants paid, $13,482; assets, $250,303 (M); expenditures, $17,771; qualifying distributions, $13,482.
Limitations: Applications not accepted. Giving primarily in NY.
Application information: Contributes only to pre-selected organizations.
Officer: Philip Chernofsky, Pres.
EIN: 237067955

38406
Rebekah & George Wisoff Foundation, Inc.
c/o Siegel
6 Carol Ln.
New Rochelle, NY 10804-1713

Established in 1986 in NY.
Donor(s): George Wisoff, Rebekah Wisoff.
Financial data (yr. ended 11/30/01): Grants paid, $13,481; assets, $60,173 (M); expenditures, $15,206; qualifying distributions, $13,481.
Limitations: Applications not accepted. Giving primarily in NY.
Application information: Contributes only to pre-selected organizations.
Directors: George Wisoff, Jill Wisoff, Rebekah Wisoff.
EIN: 133456896

38407
E.R.G. Foundation
c/o Century 21, Attn: Raymond Gindi
22 Cortlandt St.
New York, NY 10007

Established in 2001 in NY.
Donor(s): Raymond Gindi, Elizabeth Gindi.
Financial data (yr. ended 12/31/01): Grants paid, $13,456; assets, $244,298 (M); gifts received, $260,000; expenditures, $16,175; qualifying distributions, $13,583.
Limitations: Applications not accepted. Giving primarily in New York City.
Application information: Contributes only to pre-selected organizations.
Directors: Elizabeth Gindi, Raymond Gindi, Ezra Sutton.
EIN: 134171703

38408
Herbert & Hilda Daitch Foundation, Inc.
c/o O'Conner, Davies & Co.
925 Westchester Ave., Ste. 309
White Plains, NY 10604

Donor(s): Herbert C. Daitch.
Financial data (yr. ended 12/31/01): Grants paid, $13,435; assets, $47,336 (M); expenditures, $14,532; qualifying distributions, $13,435.
Limitations: Applications not accepted.
Application information: Contributes only to pre-selected organizations.
Officers: Herbert C. Daitch, Pres.; Hilda Daitch, V.P.; Sandra Flanagan Vegan, Secy.-Treas.
EIN: 136176870

38409
The Bardon-Cole Foundation, Inc.
2 5th Ave.
New York, NY 10011 (212) 995-6027
Contact: Donald R. Cole, Pres.

Established in 1965.
Donor(s): Donald R. Cole.
Financial data (yr. ended 12/31/01): Grants paid, $13,429; assets, $500,511 (M); expenditures, $55,854; qualifying distributions, $13,429.
Limitations: Giving on a national basis, with some emphasis on CT and NY.
Officers and Trustees:* Donald R. Cole,* Pres.; Carol A. Cole,* V.P. and Secy.-Treas.; Phyllis Bradford.
EIN: 136173920

38410
Getzler Foundation, Inc.
12 W. 96th St.
New York, NY 10025
Contact: Abraham E. Getzler, Pres.

Donor(s): Abraham E. Getzler, Eva Getzler.
Financial data (yr. ended 12/31/01): Grants paid, $13,424; assets, $263,078 (M); gifts received, $20,000; expenditures, $14,241; qualifying distributions, $13,424.
Limitations: Giving primarily in NY.
Officers: Abraham E. Getzler, Pres.; Joel Getzler, V.P.
EIN: 136091641

38411
Len, Michael & Deyva Schreier Family Foundation
c/o Sterling Equities, Inc.
111 Great Neck Rd., Ste. 408
Great Neck, NY 11021

Financial data (yr. ended 12/31/00): Grants paid, $13,375; assets, $419,428 (M); gifts received, $248,625; expenditures, $13,932; qualifying distributions, $13,375.
Officers and Directors:* Leonard J. Schreier, Pres.; Deyva Schreier, V.P.; Michael Schreier, Secy.
EIN: 113464797

38412
The Boris & Renee Joffe Foundation, Inc.
c/o William Schapiro
800 Fleet Bank Bldg., 12 Fountain Plz.
Buffalo, NY 14202 (716) 832-4248
Application address: 367 Starin Ave., Buffalo, NY 14216
Contact: Boris B. Joffe, Pres.

Financial data (yr. ended 12/31/01): Grants paid, $13,339; assets, $184,647 (M); expenditures, $15,611; qualifying distributions, $15,532.
Limitations: Giving primarily in Buffalo, NY.
Officers: Boris B. Joffe, Pres. and Treas.; Renee Joffe, V.P.; William Schapiro, Secy.
EIN: 166071848

38413
Claire Williams O'Neil Foundation
c/o Ann O'Neil
830 Holley Rd.
Elmira, NY 14905

Established in 2000 in PA and NY.
Donor(s): Roger O'Neil.
Financial data (yr. ended 12/31/01): Grants paid, $13,332; assets, $421,584 (M); gifts received, $200; expenditures, $16,005; qualifying distributions, $13,332.
Limitations: Applications not accepted.
Application information: Contributes only to pre-selected organizations.
Officers: Roger O'Neil, Pres.; Joan Mathewson O'Neil, V.P.; Carolyn Flanagan, Secy.; Ann O'Neil, Treas.
EIN: 233058554

38414
The A. & I. Shapiro Foundation, Inc.
414 Flushing Ave.
Brooklyn, NY 11205-1511
Contact: Irwin Shapiro, Pres.

Established around 1963.
Donor(s): Irwin Shapiro.
Financial data (yr. ended 12/31/01): Grants paid, $13,326; assets, $292,034 (M); expenditures, $15,253; qualifying distributions, $13,326.
Limitations: Giving primarily in NY.
Application information: Application form not required.
Officer: Irwin Shapiro, Pres.
EIN: 116037026

38415
Irving L. & Phyllis Bernstein Foundation, Inc.
28 Doral Dr.
Manhasset, NY 11030

Established in 1984 in NY.
Donor(s): Irving L. Bernstein, Phyllis Bernstein.
Financial data (yr. ended 12/31/01): Grants paid, $13,321; assets, $290,012 (M); gifts received, $8,844; expenditures, $15,667; qualifying distributions, $13,321.
Limitations: Applications not accepted. Giving primarily in NJ.
Application information: Contributes only to pre-selected organizations.
Officers: Irving L. Bernstein, Pres.; Steven Bernstein, V.P.; Phyllis Bernstein, Secy.-Treas.
EIN: 112713264

38416
Mary Anne Hunting Foundation
186 Riverside Dr., Ste. 16C
New York, NY 10024

Established in 1998 in NY.
Donor(s): Mary Anne Hunting.
Financial data (yr. ended 12/31/01): Grants paid, $13,300; assets, $325,852 (M); gifts received, $60,000; expenditures, $14,733; qualifying distributions, $13,300.
Limitations: Applications not accepted.
Application information: Contributes only to pre-selected organizations.
Officers and Directors:* Mary Anne Hunting,* Pres. and Treas.; Thomas H. Remien,* Secy.
EIN: 134008762

38417
The Ann M. and David E. Harden Foundation, Inc.
8550 Mill Pond Way
McConnellsville, NY 13401-1800
Contact: David E. Harden

Established in 1997 in NY.
Donor(s): David E. Harden.
Financial data (yr. ended 12/31/01): Grants paid, $13,265; assets, $252,089 (M); expenditures, $13,422; qualifying distributions, $13,265.
Directors: Gregory Harden, Tracey Harden, Daniel Trataglia.
EIN: 161527441

38418
Milton & Moselle B. Pollack Foundation, Inc.
(Formerly Milton & Lillian Pollack Foundation, Inc.)
480 Park Ave.
New York, NY 10022-1613
Contact: Milton Pollack, Pres.

Established in 1957.
Donor(s): Milton Pollack.
Financial data (yr. ended 07/31/01): Grants paid, $13,261; assets, $993,595 (M); expenditures, $15,938; qualifying distributions, $13,396.
Limitations: Giving primarily in New York, NY.
Application information: Application form not required.
Officer: Milton Pollack, Pres.
EIN: 136161330

38419
The Dorothy & Harry Gometz Fund, Inc.
225 Central Park West
New York, NY 10024-6026 (212) 877-7065
Contact: Dorothy W. Gometz, Pres.

Financial data (yr. ended 06/30/02): Grants paid, $13,250; assets, $61,235 (M); gifts received, $13,350; expenditures, $14,259; qualifying distributions, $13,250.
Limitations: Giving primarily in New York, NY.
Officers: Dorothy W. Gometz, Pres.; Susan Sokol, Secy.
Directors: Janice Levien, Leone J. Peters, Edward H. Streim, Lyn Streim.
EIN: 132962679

38420
Chasdei Efraim Foundation
29 South Parker Dr.
Monsey, NY 10952

Established in 1998 in NY.
Donor(s): Saul Katz.
Financial data (yr. ended 12/31/01): Grants paid, $13,230; assets, $1,072 (M); gifts received, $14,350; expenditures, $13,230; qualifying distributions, $13,230.
Limitations: Applications not accepted.
Application information: Contributes only to pre-selected organizations.
Trustees: Esther Katz, Saul Katz.
EIN: 113420583

38421
The Martin B. Greenberg Foundation, Inc.
1 N. End Ave., Ste. 1117
New York, NY 10282

Established in 1993 in DE and NY.
Donor(s): Martin Greenberg.
Financial data (yr. ended 12/31/00): Grants paid, $13,219; assets, $408,894 (M); expenditures, $20,508; qualifying distributions, $13,219.
Limitations: Applications not accepted. Giving primarily in the New York, NY, area.
Application information: Contributes only to pre-selected organizations.
Officers: Martin Greenberg, Pres.; Howard Malzberg, Secy.; Paul Reichenberg, Treas.
EIN: 510352079

38422
The Pierre Simon Foundation
988 5th Ave.
New York, NY 10021

Established in 1992 in NY.
Donor(s): Pierre Simon.
Financial data (yr. ended 12/31/01): Grants paid, $13,185; assets, $233,479 (M); expenditures, $14,349; qualifying distributions, $13,185.
Limitations: Applications not accepted.
Application information: Contributes only to pre-selected organizations.
Directors: Jacqueline Simon, Pierre Simon.
EIN: 133687546

38423
The Taub Family Charitable Trust
c/o Louis M. Friedman, C.P.A.
1006 E. 28th St.
Brooklyn, NY 11210-3742

Donor(s): Jeffrey Taub, Perl Taub.
Financial data (yr. ended 12/31/01): Grants paid, $13,181; assets, $59,983 (M); gifts received, $10,000; expenditures, $13,260; qualifying distributions, $13,181.
Limitations: Applications not accepted.
Application information: Contributes only to pre-selected organizations.
Trustees: Jeffrey Taub, Perl Taub.
EIN: 116532364

38424
Cabot Scholarship Fund
c/o JPMorgan Chase Bank
P.O. Box 31412
Rochester, NY 14603-1412
Application address: c/o Anthony Teravainen, Washington Citizens' Scholarship Fdn., Shepaug Valley Regional High School, South St., Washington, CT 06793

Financial data (yr. ended 02/28/02): Grants paid, $13,168; assets, $246,469 (M); expenditures, $16,913; qualifying distributions, $13,489.
Limitations: Giving limited to residents of Washington, CT.
Application information: Application form available from Shepaug Valley Regional High School guidance office. Application form required.
Trustee: JPMorgan Chase Bank.
EIN: 066113079
Codes: GTI

38425
The Certe Foundation, Inc.
c/o Richard W. Cohen
1125 Park Ave., Apt. 6C
New York, NY 10128

Donor(s): Constance P. Cohen, Richard W. Cohen.
Financial data (yr. ended 08/31/01): Grants paid, $13,166; assets, $208,425 (M); gifts received, $11,750; expenditures, $13,933; qualifying distributions, $13,166.
Limitations: Applications not accepted. Giving primarily in New York, NY.
Officers and Directors:* Richard W. Cohen,* Pres.; Constance P. Cohen,* V.P. and Secy.; Albert A. Blinder.
EIN: 132624114

38426
Gleason Works Foundation, Inc.
P.O. Box 22970
Rochester, NY 14692-2970 (716) 256-8760
Contact: Edward J. Pelta, Secy.-Treas.

Donor(s): Gleason Corp., Gleason Foundation.
Financial data (yr. ended 12/31/01): Grants paid, $13,160; assets, $199,272 (M); expenditures, $15,293; qualifying distributions, $13,160.
Limitations: Giving primarily in NY.
Officers and Directors:* David J. Burns,* Pres.; Gary J. Kimmet,* V.P.; Edward J. Pelta, Secy.-Treas.
EIN: 166023236
Codes: CS, CD

38427
Pajwell Foundation
c/o Ernst & Young, P. Doudna
787 7th Ave., Ste. 2008
New York, NY 10019

Established in 1999 in CO.
Donor(s): Pamela Joseph.
Financial data (yr. ended 12/31/00): Grants paid, $13,150; assets, $2,425,573 (M); gifts received, $1,917,342; expenditures, $13,195; qualifying distributions, $13,150.
Director: Pamela Joseph.
EIN: 522192469

38428
Robert & Elaine Weiss Charitable Foundation
c/o Shufro, Rose & Co., LLC
745 5th Ave., 26th Fl.
New York, NY 10151

Established in 2000 in NY.
Financial data (yr. ended 12/31/01): Grants paid, $13,125; assets, $91,648 (M); expenditures, $16,735; qualifying distributions, $13,125.

38428—NEW YORK

Limitations: Applications not accepted. Giving primarily in NY.
Application information: Contributes only to pre-selected organizations.
Trustees: Elaine Weiss, Robert Weiss.
EIN: 134136349

38429
Charles Schwartz Foundation for Music, Inc.
269 Sycamore St.
West Hempstead, NY 11552
Contact: Ellen Anzovino, Pres.

Financial data (yr. ended 06/30/01): Grants paid, $13,120; assets, $95,516 (M); gifts received, $124,814; expenditures, $35,686; qualifying distributions, $25,630.
Officers: Ellen Anzovino, Pres.; Louis Anzovino, V.P.; Alice Schwartz, Secy.-Treas.; Donald Schwartz, Exec. Dir.
EIN: 133617098

38430
Marc A. Somberg Memorial Foundation
7 Wimbledon Ct.
Jericho, NY 11753-2822

Established in 1995 in NY.
Donor(s): Milton Somberg, Marilyn Somberg.
Financial data (yr. ended 12/31/01): Grants paid, $13,100; assets, $82,893 (M); gifts received, $40,000; expenditures, $13,748; qualifying distributions, $13,100.
Limitations: Giving primarily in NY.
Trustees: Marilyn Somberg, Milton A. Somberg.
EIN: 113295557

38431
Maurice Villency Foundation, Inc.
c/o American Express Tax & Business Services, Inc.
1185 Ave. of the Americas
New York, NY 10036-2602
Application address: 200 Madison Ave., New York, NY 10016
Contact: Robert Villency, Dir.

Established in 1988 in NY.
Donor(s): Maurice Villency, Inc., Robert Villency, The David Everett Foundation, The Kids Fund.
Financial data (yr. ended 05/31/01): Grants paid, $13,092; assets, $3,883 (M); expenditures, $13,392; qualifying distributions, $13,392.
Limitations: Giving primarily in the metropolitan New York, NY, area.
Application information: Application form required.
Directors: Stuart Kessler, Robert Villency.
EIN: 133487733
Codes: CS, CD, GTI

38432
Jill E. Solomon Charitable Foundation
10 Willows Ln.
White Plains, NY 10605-4212

Established in 1999 in NY.
Donor(s): Leonard Solomon, Carole Solomon.
Financial data (yr. ended 12/31/01): Grants paid, $13,069; assets, $221,256 (M); gifts received, $23,277; expenditures, $13,734; qualifying distributions, $13,069.
Limitations: Applications not accepted. Giving primarily in NY.
Application information: Contributes only to pre-selected organizations.
Trustees: Betsy Hallerman, William Shmerler, Carole Solomon, Leonard Solomon, Steven Solomon, Bethanie Tomkiewicz.
EIN: 137176441

38433
P. V. and A. S. Brown Foundation
c/o US Trust Co. of NY
P.O. Box 2004
New York, NY 10109

Established in 2001.
Financial data (yr. ended 12/31/01): Grants paid, $13,050; assets, $420,427 (M); expenditures, $38,499; qualifying distributions, $17,529.
Limitations: Applications not accepted. Giving primarily in Bronx, NY.
Application information: Contributes only to pre-selected organizations.
Trustee: US Trust Co. of NY.
EIN: 136614122

38434
Buddy & Dorothy Martin Foundation, Inc.
60 The Intervale
Roslyn, NY 11576-1909

Established in 1986 in NY.
Donor(s): Buddy Martin, Dorothy Martin.
Financial data (yr. ended 12/31/99): Grants paid, $13,050; assets, $155,713 (M); expenditures, $13,388; qualifying distributions, $13,050.
Limitations: Applications not accepted.
Application information: Contributes only to pre-selected organizations.
Officers and Directors:* Buddy Martin,* Pres.; Dorothy Martin,* Secy.; David Martin.
EIN: 133378019

38435
Niels W. Johnsen Foundation, Inc.
61 Broadway, 18th Fl.
New York, NY 10006-2794

Established in 1994 in DE and NJ.
Donor(s): Niels W. Johnsen.
Financial data (yr. ended 11/30/01): Grants paid, $13,018; assets, $100,924 (M); gifts received, $11,500; expenditures, $15,284; qualifying distributions, $13,018.
Limitations: Applications not accepted. Giving primarily in NY.
Application information: Contributes only to pre-selected organizations.
Officers and Directors:* Niels W. Johnsen,* Pres.; Millicent M. Johnsen,* V.P. and Treas.; Stanley M. Klein,* Secy.; Niels M. Johnsen.
EIN: 133505841

38436
The Amadeus Fund, Inc.
c/o Weiler & Arnow
1114 Ave. of the Americas, Ste. 3400
New York, NY 10036

Established in 1989 in NY.
Donor(s): Robert H. Arnow, The Arnow Family Fund, Inc.
Financial data (yr. ended 08/31/01): Grants paid, $13,000; assets, $1,648 (M); gifts received, $13,000; expenditures, $13,502; qualifying distributions, $12,999.
Limitations: Applications not accepted. Giving primarily in New York, NY.
Officers and Directors:* Joan Arnow,* Pres.; Robert H. Arnow,* Secy.; David Arnow, Joan B. Caplan, Marilyn Gaylin, Bridgett Paolucci.
EIN: 133545537
Codes: GTI

38437
Simon Cohen Foundation
c/o Robert J. Reed
22 Elaine Dr.
Oceanside, NY 11572

Established in 1964 in NY.
Financial data (yr. ended 11/30/01): Grants paid, $13,000; assets, $350,144 (M); expenditures, $14,913; qualifying distributions, $14,805.
Limitations: Giving primarily in NY.
Officers and Directors:* Robert J. Reed,* Pres.; Robert Cohen,* V.P.; Judah Feinerman,* Secy.; Steven Cohen,* Treas.; Barry Cohen, Irene Cohen, Richard B. Davis.
EIN: 116037743

38438
The Dulude Family Foundation, Inc.
c/o Patrick D. Martin
P.O. Box 1051
Rochester, NY 14603-1051

Established in 1997 in NY.
Donor(s): Richard Dulude.
Financial data (yr. ended 12/31/01): Grants paid, $13,000; assets, $271,371 (M); expenditures, $20,508; qualifying distributions, $13,000.
Limitations: Applications not accepted.
Application information: Contributes only to pre-selected organizations.
Officers and Directors:* Richard Dulude,* Pres.; Joel L. Dulude,* V.P.; Jonathan M. Dulude,* Secy.; Jean M. Dulude,* Treas.; Lezli A. Dulude.
EIN: 161521663

38439
William L. Edwards & Mary A. Edwards Foundation
c/o W. Edwards
194 Kensington Rd.
Garden City, NY 11530

Established in 1999 in NY.
Donor(s): William L. Edwards, Michael H. Edwards, Christopher W. Edwards.
Financial data (yr. ended 12/31/01): Grants paid, $13,000; assets, $279,535 (M); gifts received, $5,265; expenditures, $15,475; qualifying distributions, $13,000.
Limitations: Applications not accepted. Giving primarily in New York, NY.
Application information: Contributes to pre-selected organizations.
Directors: Christopher W. Edwards, Mary Ann Edwards, Michael H. Edwards, William L. Edwards.
EIN: 113499752

38440
Justus Heijmans Foundation
641 Lexington Ave., 29th Fl.
New York, NY 10022-4599
Application address: 387 Park Ave. S., New York, NY 10016, tel.: (212) 661-8700
Contact: Edgar M. Cullman, Sr., Tr.

Established in 1968.
Financial data (yr. ended 08/31/01): Grants paid, $13,000; assets, $401,321 (M); expenditures, $15,900; qualifying distributions, $13,000.
Limitations: Giving primarily in CT and NY.
Trustees: Edgar M. Cullman, Sr., Edgar M. Cullman, Jr.
EIN: 136272082

38441
David Herzog Foundation
1618 51st St.
Brooklyn, NY 11204

Established in 1995 in NY.
Donor(s): David Herzog.
Financial data (yr. ended 12/31/00): Grants paid, $13,000; assets, $329,690 (M); gifts received, $110,000; expenditures, $13,118; qualifying distributions, $12,979.
Limitations: Applications not accepted.
Application information: Contributes only to pre-selected organizations.
Officers: David Herzog, Pres.; Raquel Herzog, V.P.; Philip Herzog, Secy.
EIN: 113281610

38442
Larchmont Chamber Music Circle, Inc.
c/o American Express TBS
1185 Ave. of the Americas
New York, NY 10036-2602

Financial data (yr. ended 12/31/01): Grants paid, $13,000; assets, $10,956 (M); gifts received, $14,700; expenditures, $13,339; qualifying distributions, $13,335.
Application information: Application form not required.
Officers: Hannah I. Noether, Pres.; Joan Lear Sher, Secy.
EIN: 136157956
Codes: GTI

38443
Joseph B. & Christina A. Mathewson Foundation
c/o Tompkins County Trust Co.
P.O. Box 460
Ithaca, NY 14851-0460 (607) 272-3210

Donor(s): Joseph B. Mathewson,‡ Christina A. Mathewson.
Financial data (yr. ended 12/31/01): Grants paid, $13,000; assets, $264,145 (M); expenditures, $17,738; qualifying distributions, $13,000.
Limitations: Giving primarily in CT and NY.
Trustees: William Paleen, Christina M. Salerno, Reynolds M. Salerno, Donald S. Stewart.
EIN: 166051577

38444
The Old Boys Foundation
c/o White & Case LLP
1155 Ave. of the Americas, Ste. 3436
New York, NY 10036-2787

Donor(s): Maurice E. Pinto.
Financial data (yr. ended 12/31/01): Grants paid, $13,000; assets, $172,254 (M); expenditures, $15,094; qualifying distributions, $13,000.
Limitations: Applications not accepted.
Application information: Contributes only to pre-selected organizations.
Officers and Directors:* Maurice E. Pinto,* Pres.; Andrew Auchincloss,* Secy.-Treas.
EIN: 522060504

38445
The Reinhardt Family Scholarship Trust
1207 Delaware Ave., Ste. 208
Buffalo, NY 14209-1401
Application address: c/o Selection Comm., Holland Central High School, 103 Canada, Holland, NY 14080, tel.: (716) 537-2231

Established in 1996 in NY.
Donor(s): Frederick F. Reinhardt.
Financial data (yr. ended 12/31/01): Grants paid, $13,000; assets, $129,538 (M); expenditures, $14,209; qualifying distributions, $13,000.
Limitations: Giving limited to residents of Holland, NY.
Application information: Application form required.
Trustees: Frederick F. Reinhardt, Rosaland E. Reinhardt.
EIN: 161512484

38446
B. F. S. Schaefer Foundation, Inc.
West Creek Farms Rd.
Sands Point, NY 11050
Contact: Franklyn Schaefer, Mgr.

Established in 1961 in NY.
Financial data (yr. ended 03/31/02): Grants paid, $13,000; assets, $266,509 (M); expenditures, $16,348; qualifying distributions, $13,000.
Limitations: Giving primarily in NY.
Officer: Franklyn Schaefer, Mgr.
EIN: 510205694

38447
Schmell Family Foundation, Inc.
937 Rogers Ave.
Brooklyn, NY 11226
Application address: 10 E. 40th St., New York, NY 10016, tel.: (212) 532-7580
Contact: Israel Schmell, Tr.

Donor(s): Israel Schmell.
Financial data (yr. ended 12/31/01): Grants paid, $13,000; assets, $125,931 (M); gifts received, $17,000; expenditures, $13,050; qualifying distributions, $13,000.
Limitations: Giving primarily in NY.
Trustees: Israel Schmell, Martin Schmell.
EIN: 237022476

•38448
The Dhuanne S. and Douglas T. Tansill Foundation, Inc.
c/o Davidson, Dawson and Clark
330 Madison Ave.
New York, NY 10017

Established in 1986 in NY.
Donor(s): Douglas T. Tansill.
Financial data (yr. ended 12/31/01): Grants paid, $13,000; assets, $197,349 (M); expenditures, $15,715; qualifying distributions, $13,000.
Limitations: Applications not accepted. Giving primarily in CT and NY.
Application information: Contributes only to pre-selected organizations.
Officers and Directors:* Douglas T. Tansill,* Pres. and Treas.; Douglas F. Tansill, V.P.; Peyton E. Tansill,* V.P.; Dhuanne S. Tansill,* Secy.; William H. Miller, Jr.
EIN: 133402031

38449
Samuel D. & Rosalie K. Bierman Foundation
108 E. 82nd St.
New York, NY 10028
Contact: Stephen K. Bierman, Tr.

Established around 1965.
Financial data (yr. ended 12/31/01): Grants paid, $12,985; assets, $31,496 (M); gifts received, $900; expenditures, $13,978; qualifying distributions, $12,985.
Limitations: Giving primarily in New York, NY.
Application information: Application form not required.
Trustee: Stephen K. Bierman.
EIN: 136169154

38450
William J. Tully Foundation
678 Colonial Ave.
Pelham, NY 10803-2542

Financial data (yr. ended 12/31/00): Grants paid, $12,963; assets, $286,801 (M); gifts received, $24,000; expenditures, $14,043; qualifying distributions, $12,963.
Limitations: Giving primarily in NY.
Application information: Application form not required.
Trustees: Kathryn M. Tully, William J. Tully.
EIN: 136192373

38451
Munshi Bishan Singh Kochhar Foundation, Inc.
52 E. 7th St.
New York, NY 10003

Established in 2000 in NY.
Donor(s): Pritpal S. Kochhar.
Financial data (yr. ended 12/31/01): Grants paid, $12,959; assets, $346,963 (M); gifts received, $301; expenditures, $14,559; qualifying distributions, $12,959.
Limitations: Applications not accepted.
Application information: Contributes only to pre-selected organizations.
Officers: Amrik S. Kochhar, Pres.; Evert Marechal, V.P.; Pritpal S. Kochhar, Secy.-Treas.
EIN: 134147472

38452
The David M. Mahood Memorial Fund
c/o Citibank, N.A., Tax Dept.
1 Court Sq., 22nd Fl.
Long Island City, NY 11120
Application address: c/o PBG Trust, 153 E. 53rd St., New York, NY 10043

Financial data (yr. ended 12/31/00): Grants paid, $12,944; assets, $329,563 (M); expenditures, $14,230; qualifying distributions, $12,944.
Trustee: Citibank, N.A.
EIN: 136053998

38453
The Ruth and Louis Gerstle Foundation, Inc.
15 Gould St.
Great Neck, NY 11023
Contact: Ruth Gerstle, Pres.

Established in 1988 in NY.
Donor(s): Ruth Gerstle, Louis Gerstle.
Financial data (yr. ended 12/31/00): Grants paid, $12,928; assets, $101,389 (M); gifts received, $11,781; expenditures, $13,201; qualifying distributions, $12,780.
Limitations: Giving primarily in NY.
Application information: Application form not required.
Officers and Directors:* Ruth Gerstle,* Pres.; Louis Gerstle,* V.P.; Judith Farbman, Leonard Gerstle.
EIN: 112942782

38454
Pauline Yuells Markel Charitable Trust
c/o Lucille Greenblatt
430 E. 56th St., Ste. 8B
New York, NY 10022

Established in 1958.
Financial data (yr. ended 11/30/01): Grants paid, $12,900; assets, $553,842 (M); expenditures, $13,905; qualifying distributions, $12,900.
Limitations: Giving primarily in NY.
Application information: Application form not required.
Trustee: Lucille Greenblatt.

38454—NEW YORK

EIN: 136110485

38455
Jean & Henry Pollak Foundation
1410 Broadway, 7th Fl.
New York, NY 10018-5007

Donor(s): Jean deBeer Pollak, Henry Pollak II.
Financial data (yr. ended 10/31/01): Grants paid, $12,900; assets, $269,181 (M); expenditures, $13,704; qualifying distributions, $12,900.
Limitations: Applications not accepted. Giving primarily in NY.
Application information: Contributes only to pre-selected organizations.
Officers: Henry Pollak II, Pres.; Jean deBeer Pollak, Secy.
EIN: 237042008

38456
Esther Esh Sternberg Foundation
c/o Joel Weissman
655 3rd Ave., Ste. 1400
New York, NY 10017

Established in 1997 in NY.
Donor(s): Esther Sternberg.
Financial data (yr. ended 12/31/01): Grants paid, $12,890; assets, $320,006 (M); expenditures, $15,403; qualifying distributions, $12,890.
Limitations: Applications not accepted. Giving primarily in New York, NY.
Application information: Contributes only to pre-selected organizations.
Trustees: Esther Esh Sternberg, Lewis Sternberg.
EIN: 133944955

38457
C. Gerald Goldsmith Foundation, Inc.
c/o Chamberlain & Steward Assocs., Ltd.
400 Park Ave., 6th Fl.
New York, NY 10022 (212) 371-4980
Contact: C. Gerald Goldsmith, Pres.

Donor(s): C. Gerald Goldsmith.
Financial data (yr. ended 12/31/00): Grants paid, $12,880; assets, $129,232 (M); gifts received, $750; expenditures, $14,430; qualifying distributions, $12,930.
Limitations: Giving primarily in FL.
Officers and Directors:* C. Gerald Goldsmith,* Pres. and Treas.; Andrew Goldsmith,* V.P. and Secy.; Alice Elgart,* V.P.
EIN: 136077571

38458
The Elizabeth and Stanley D. Scott Foundation, Inc.
1 Sutton Pl. S.
New York, NY 10022

Established in 2000 in NY.
Donor(s): Elizabeth Scott, Stanley D. Scott.
Financial data (yr. ended 06/30/01): Grants paid, $12,878; assets, $1,319,133 (M); gifts received, $1,315,133; expenditures, $13,977; qualifying distributions, $13,774.
Limitations: Applications not accepted.
Application information: Contributes only to pre-selected organizations.
Directors: Peter Kimmelman, Elizabeth Scott, Stanley D. Scott.
EIN: 134144166

38459
The Nico Fund
c/o Nancy H. Biddle
784 Park Ave.
New York, NY 10021

Established in 1989 in NY.
Donor(s): Nancy H. Biddle.
Financial data (yr. ended 12/31/01): Grants paid, $12,877; assets, $109,847 (M); gifts received, $9,305; expenditures, $12,877; qualifying distributions, $12,877.
Limitations: Applications not accepted.
Application information: Contributes only to pre-selected organizations.
Trustees: Nancy H. Biddle, Pandora Biddle Hentic, Lucile Herbert.
EIN: 136934664

38460
Rand Foundation, Inc.
c/o Spielman, Koenigsberg & Parker
888 7th Ave., 35th Fl.
New York, NY 10106

Financial data (yr. ended 12/31/01): Grants paid, $12,850; assets, $67,235 (M); expenditures, $14,215; qualifying distributions, $12,850.
Limitations: Applications not accepted.
Application information: Contributes only to pre-selected organizations.
Officers: Judith Shongut, Pres.; George Miller, V.P. and Secy.; Nancy Miller, Treas.
EIN: 116022011

38461
John O. Middlebrook Trust
c/o E.J. Lehman, Winston & Strawn
200 Park Ave., 42nd Fl.
New York, NY 10166 (212) 808-7843

Financial data (yr. ended 12/31/01): Grants paid, $12,836; assets, $305,489 (M); expenditures, $22,906; qualifying distributions, $12,836.
Limitations: Applications not accepted.
Application information: Contributes only to pre-selected organizations.
Trustees: Grace A. DeVoto, Gladys T. Middlebrook.
EIN: 136117753

38462
The Alexander Fischbein Foundation
c/o Andrew Goldstein
909 3rd Ave., 17th Fl.
New York, NY 10022-4731 (212) 826-2000

Established in 1990 in NY.
Donor(s): Sarah Korein, L. Pollack Spiegel.
Financial data (yr. ended 12/31/01): Grants paid, $12,800; assets, $314,305 (M); gifts received, $13,830; expenditures, $13,050; qualifying distributions, $12,800.
Limitations: Giving primarily in NY.
Officers: Mimi Fischbein, Pres.; Alan Lotterman, V.P.; Bruce Bronster, Treas.
EIN: 133578576

38463
Andrew J. and Anita G. Frankel Family Foundation, Inc.
(Formerly Andrew J. and Anita G. Frankel Foundation, Inc.)
c/o Mary Lou Holcombe
630 5th Ave., Ste. 2401
New York, NY 10111-0100

Established in 1964 in NY.
Financial data (yr. ended 12/31/01): Grants paid, $12,800; assets, $346,493 (M); gifts received, $42,510; expenditures, $15,212; qualifying distributions, $12,800.
Limitations: Applications not accepted. Giving primarily in New York, NY.
Application information: Contributes only to pre-selected organizations.
Officers: Andrew J. Frankel, Pres.; Anita G. Frankel, V.P.; Mary Lou Holcombe, Secy.-Treas.
EIN: 136167961

38464
A.J.Y.W. Foundation
543 Bedford Ave., Ste. 201
Brooklyn, NY 11211
Application address: 151 Ross St., Brooklyn, NY 11211, tel.: (718) 486-5448
Contact: Abraham Weiss, Tr.

Established in 1999.
Financial data (yr. ended 10/31/01): Grants paid, $12,790; assets, $58,496 (M); gifts received, $9,500; expenditures, $13,690; qualifying distributions, $12,790.
Limitations: Giving limited to Brooklyn, NY.
Trustees: Abraham Weiss, Yitta Weiss.
EIN: 137171842

38465
Wilfred J. & Norma Halpern Foundation, Inc.
220 Steven Pl.
Woodmere, NY 11598

Established in 1989 in NY.
Donor(s): Wilfred J. Halpern.
Financial data (yr. ended 10/31/01): Grants paid, $12,750; assets, $60,144 (M); gifts received, $30; expenditures, $12,973; qualifying distributions, $12,750.
Limitations: Applications not accepted. Giving primarily in New York, NY.
Application information: Contributes only to pre-selected organizations.
Officers and Directors:* Wilfred J. Halpern,* Pres. and Treas.; Norma Halpern,* V.P. and Secy.; John A. Halpern.
EIN: 112937667

38466
The Susan & Edward Kopelowitz Charitable Trust
147 Midgely Dr.
Hewlett, NY 11557

Donor(s): Edward Kopelowitz, Susan Kopelowitz.
Financial data (yr. ended 10/31/00): Grants paid, $12,740; assets, $757 (M); expenditures, $13,685; qualifying distributions, $12,740.
Limitations: Applications not accepted.
Application information: Contributes only to pre-selected organizations.
Trustees: Edward Kopelowitz, Susan Kopelowitz, Gerschwin Kurlander.
EIN: 237424749

38467
S.M.B. Foundation
c/o J. Lorch
147-29 72nd Dr.
Flushing, NY 11367

Donor(s): Samson R. Breuer.‡
Financial data (yr. ended 12/31/01): Grants paid, $12,729; assets, $4,107 (M); gifts received, $11,573; expenditures, $12,808; qualifying distributions, $12,729.
Limitations: Applications not accepted.
Application information: Contributes only to pre-selected organizations.
Officers: Janie Rosenfeld, Pres.; Howard B. Lorch, Mgr.
EIN: 132710489

38468
The Donohue Family Foundation
6 Northern Ave.
Bronxville, NY 10708-2221

Established in 2000 in NY.
Donor(s): Barbara Donohue.

Financial data (yr. ended 12/31/01): Grants paid, $12,728; assets, $904,624 (M); expenditures, $17,946; qualifying distributions, $12,728.
Limitations: Giving primarily in NY.
Trustees: Barbara Donohue, Benjamin S. Donohue, Claire B. Donohue, Michael S. Donohue.
EIN: 137228785

38469
The Milbourne Christopher Foundation, Inc.
c/o Eaton & Van Winkle
3 Park Ave.
New York, NY 10016

Established in 1991 in NY.
Donor(s): Maurine Christopher.
Financial data (yr. ended 12/31/01): Grants paid, $12,721; assets, $213,704 (M); gifts received, $30,200; expenditures, $14,818; qualifying distributions, $12,721.
Officer and Trustees:* Maurine Christopher,* Chair.; John Bohannon, John D. Brooks, Jr.
EIN: 133660593

38470
Soloman & Celia F. Heiferman Family Foundation
58-58 Grand Ave.
Maspeth, NY 11378-3295

Donor(s): Celia F. Heiferman.
Financial data (yr. ended 11/30/01): Grants paid, $12,700; assets, $45,111 (M); gifts received, $20,000; expenditures, $12,727; qualifying distributions, $12,700.
Limitations: Applications not accepted. Giving primarily in NY.
Application information: Contributes only to pre-selected organizations.
Officer: Celia F. Heiferman, Pres.
EIN: 116017349

38471
Robert E. Nederlander Foundation
1450 Broadway
New York, NY 10018

Established in 1998 in NY.
Donor(s): Robert E. Nederlander.
Financial data (yr. ended 12/31/01): Grants paid, $12,700; assets, $86,214 (M); expenditures, $12,768; qualifying distributions, $12,700.
Limitations: Applications not accepted. Giving primarily in NY.
Application information: Contributes only to pre-selected organizations.
Officer: Robert E. Nederlander, Pres.
Directors: Gladys Nederlander, Leonard Toboroff.
EIN: 133934374

38472
The Jonathan George Ellis Leukemia Foundation
c/o Nathan Berkman & Co.
29 Broadway, Ste. 2900
New York, NY 10006-3296

Donor(s): Neil Ellis, Elizabeth Ellis.
Financial data (yr. ended 05/31/01): Grants paid, $12,650; assets, $2,164 (M); gifts received, $12,800; expenditures, $12,664; qualifying distributions, $12,650.
Limitations: Applications not accepted.
Application information: Contributes only to pre-selected organizations.
Trustees: Elizabeth Ellis, Neil Ellis.
EIN: 066068895

38473
Sam & Julia Selkowitz Foundation
c/o Levene, Gouldin & Thompson
P.O. Box F-1706
Binghamton, NY 13902

Financial data (yr. ended 12/31/01): Grants paid, $12,650; assets, $313,927 (M); expenditures, $17,975; qualifying distributions, $12,650.
Limitations: Applications not accepted. Giving primarily in NY.
Application information: Contributes only to pre-selected organizations.
Trustees: Donald Green, Michael H. Zuckerman.
EIN: 237032221

38474
Spencer Raphael Jaffe Charitable Foundation
43 Lawrence Ave.
Lawrence, NY 11559-1446

Established in 1993 in NY.
Donor(s): Solange Jaffe.
Financial data (yr. ended 12/31/00): Grants paid, $12,600; assets, $443,651 (M); gifts received, $2,577; expenditures, $20,561; qualifying distributions, $12,600.
Limitations: Applications not accepted. Giving primarily in Stamford, CT.
Application information: Contributes only to pre-selected organizations.
Officer and Trustees:* Solange Jaffe,* Pres.; Jonathan M. Jaffe, Meryl Jo Jaffe.
EIN: 113144593

38475
Kaufman Family Foundation, Inc.
450 7th Ave.
New York, NY 10123-0001

Financial data (yr. ended 04/30/99): Grants paid, $12,600; assets, $176,273 (M); expenditures, $13,415; qualifying distributions, $12,794.
Limitations: Applications not accepted. Giving primarily in NY.
Application information: Contributes only to pre-selected organizations.
Trustees: George S. Kaufman, Steven J. Kaufman.
EIN: 136181041

38476
The Jacob Perlman Memorial Foundation
c/o Joseph C. Pearlman
902 Ocean Pkwy., Apt. 6B
Brooklyn, NY 11230

Financial data (yr. ended 06/30/02): Grants paid, $12,600; assets, $228 (M); gifts received, $13,000; expenditures, $12,800; qualifying distributions, $12,600.
Officers: Joseph E. Perlman, Pres.; Solomon Perlman, Pres.
EIN: 113366446

38477
Craine Family Foundation
1 N. Main St.
Sherburne, NY 13460
Application address: 53 Chenango Ave., Sherburne, NY 13460, tel.: (607) 674-7400
Contact: William C. Craine, Tr.

Established in 1996.
Donor(s): William C. Craine, William D. Craine.
Financial data (yr. ended 12/31/01): Grants paid, $12,575; assets, $67,223 (M); gifts received, $48,280; expenditures, $13,229; qualifying distributions, $12,575.
Limitations: Giving primarily in NY.
Trustees: L. David Craine, William C. Craine, William D. Craine.

EIN: 161495551

38478
Lake Mahopac Rotary Foundation, Inc.
c/o Nussbaum
504 Woodland Ct.
Mahopac, NY 10541

Financial data (yr. ended 12/31/01): Grants paid, $12,550; assets, $154,682 (M); gifts received, $1,000; expenditures, $13,167; qualifying distributions, $12,550.
Officer: Catherine Cavanaugh, Pres.
EIN: 141746381

38479
The Rosenfeld Family Foundation
1630 47th St.
Brooklyn, NY 11204

Established in 1997 in NY.
Donor(s): Berl Rosenfeld, Leah Rosenfeld.
Financial data (yr. ended 12/31/01): Grants paid, $12,528; assets, $249,090 (M); gifts received, $16,613; expenditures, $12,549; qualifying distributions, $12,528.
Limitations: Applications not accepted.
Application information: Contributes only to pre-selected organizations.
Trustees: Berl Rosenfeld, Leah Rosenfeld.
EIN: 113410721

38480
David & Ester Bistricer Foundation
4611 12th Ave.
Brooklyn, NY 11219-2539

Established in 1988 in NY.
Donor(s): David Bistricer, Ester Bistricer.
Financial data (yr. ended 12/31/01): Grants paid, $12,525; assets, $613,707 (M); expenditures, $12,575; qualifying distributions, $12,525.
Limitations: Applications not accepted. Giving primarily in NY.
Application information: Contributes only to pre-selected organizations.
Trustees: David Bistricer, Ester Bistricer.
EIN: 112910261

38481
Bernard Aronson Foundation, Inc.
c/o Berinstein
320 E. 72nd St., Apt. 6A
New York, NY 10021-4769

Financial data (yr. ended 08/31/00): Grants paid, $12,500; assets, $96,746 (M); expenditures, $13,972; qualifying distributions, $12,500.
Limitations: Applications not accepted. Giving primarily in NY.
Application information: Contributes only to pre-selected organizations.
Officer: Audrey Aronson, Pres.
EIN: 136115743

38482
The Philip Birnbaum Foundation, Inc.
c/o Janet Jaffin
230 Park Ave., Ste. 430
New York, NY 10169

Established in 1988 in NY.
Donor(s): Philip Birnbaum.‡
Financial data (yr. ended 09/30/02): Grants paid, $12,500; assets, $464,209 (M); expenditures, $15,493; qualifying distributions, $12,500.
Limitations: Applications not accepted. Giving primarily in New York, NY.
Application information: Contributes only to pre-selected organizations.
Officers and Directors:* Janet Jaffin,* Pres.; Doris Greenburg,* Secy.; Lois Levine,* Treas.

38482—NEW YORK

EIN: 133526188

38483
J. H. & E. R. Carson Foundation, Inc.
c/o E.I. Speer
550 Maharoueck, Ste. 504
Harrison, NY 10528

Financial data (yr. ended 12/31/01): Grants paid, $12,500; assets, $396,520 (M); expenditures, $22,383; qualifying distributions, $12,500.
Limitations: Applications not accepted. Giving primarily in NY.
Application information: Contributes only to pre-selected organizations.
Officers and Directors:* Elizabeth R. Carson,* Pres.; Hartley C. Etheridge,* V.P.; George DeSipio,* Secy.-Treas.; Randal Etheridge.
EIN: 136088819

38484
The Gristmill Foundation
c/o Candida S. Cucharo
P.O. Box 1203
Manhasset, NY 11030

Established in 1998 in NY.
Donor(s): Candida S. Cucharo.
Financial data (yr. ended 12/31/01): Grants paid, $12,500; assets, $216,246 (M); gifts received, $800; expenditures, $14,413; qualifying distributions, $12,500.
Limitations: Applications not accepted.
Application information: Contributes only to pre-selected organizations.
Trustees: Emmet J. Agoglia, Candida S. Cucharo, Mary Giordano, John McKegney, Robert Spano.
EIN: 113433997

38485
Odin/Berkana Foundation
P.O. Box 246
Clarence, NY 14031 (716) 759-8160
Contact: Mary L. Whitcomb, Pres.

Established in 1995 in NY.
Donor(s): Mary L. Whitcomb.
Financial data (yr. ended 12/31/01): Grants paid, $12,500; assets, $312,606 (M); gifts received, $59,718; expenditures, $21,890; qualifying distributions, $12,500.
Limitations: Giving on a national basis, with emphasis on Clarence, NY.
Officers and Directors:* Mary L. Whitcomb,* Pres. and Treas.; Ericka Greatbatch,* V.P.; Virginia Telfer,* Secy.
EIN: 161474895

38486
The Gerald and Louise Puschel Family Foundation
79 Madison Ave., 16th Fl.
New York, NY 10016-7878

Established in 1997 in NY.
Donor(s): Walter E. Puschel.
Financial data (yr. ended 12/31/01): Grants paid, $12,500; assets, $244,789 (M); gifts received, $140,000; expenditures, $12,637; qualifying distributions, $12,500.
Limitations: Applications not accepted. Giving primarily in CT.
Application information: Contributes only to pre-selected organizations.
Officer: Gerald W. Puschel, Pres.
Directors: Louise C. Puschel, Philip P. Puschel.
EIN: 133957261

38487
Giles & Florence P. St. Clair Foundation
c/o JPMorgan Chase Bank
1211 Ave. of the Americas, 34th Fl.
New York, NY 10036
Application address: 225 South St., Morristown, NJ 07960
Contact: Gregory Kirk, V.P., JPMorgan Chase Bank

Financial data (yr. ended 08/31/01): Grants paid, $12,500; assets, $233,649 (M); expenditures, $14,622; qualifying distributions, $12,686.
Trustee: JPMorgan Chase Bank.
EIN: 226083505

38488
Stevenson Foundation Trust
c/o JPMorgan Chase Bank
P.O. Box 31412
Rochester, NY 14603-1412
Application address: c/o JPMorgan Chase Bank, Trust Division, 1 Lincoln Sq., Rochester, NY 14643, tel.: (716) 258-5254

Financial data (yr. ended 12/31/01): Grants paid, $12,500; assets, $151,170 (M); expenditures, $14,435; qualifying distributions, $12,715.
Limitations: Giving limited to residents of Canandaigua, NY.
Trustee: JPMorgan Chase Bank.
EIN: 166102231
Codes: GTI

38489
The Tenafly Citizenship Scholarship Award, Inc.
c/o Ira Tokayer
1114 6th Ave., 26th Fl.
New York, NY 10036
Application address: c/o Tenafly High School, Guidance Office, 19 Columbus Dr., Tenafly, NJ 07670, tel.: (201) 816-6640

Established in 1996 in NY.
Donor(s): Ira Tokayer.
Financial data (yr. ended 06/30/00): Grants paid, $12,500; assets, $5,239 (M); expenditures, $13,109; qualifying distributions, $13,109.
Limitations: Giving limited to residents of Tenafly, NJ.
Application information: Application form required.
Officer: Ira Tokayer, Pres.
EIN: 133920785

38490
M & J Family Foundation
577 Madison Ave.
West Hempstead, NY 11552 (516) 481-2957
Contact: Mardelle Cagen, Pres.

Established in 1991 in NY.
Donor(s): The Kleinman Foundation.
Financial data (yr. ended 10/31/01): Grants paid, $12,494; assets, $396,593 (M); gifts received, $300; expenditures, $14,013; qualifying distributions, $12,494.
Limitations: Giving primarily in New York, NY.
Officer and Director:* Mardelle Cagen,* Pres.
EIN: 113044190

38491
Scollard Family Foundation, Inc.
1461 Franklin Ave.
Garden City, NY 11530
Contact: Patrick J. Scollard, Chair.

Established in 1999 in NY.
Donor(s): Patrick J. Scollard.
Financial data (yr. ended 12/31/01): Grants paid, $12,425; assets, $163,345 (M); expenditures, $17,704; qualifying distributions, $12,425.
Officers: Patrick J. Scollard, Chair.; Gloria A. Scollard, Pres.; Maureen A. Bauer, Secy.
Board Members: Brian C. Scollard, Daniel J. Scollard, Kevin P. Scollard, Thomas M. Scollard.
EIN: 113517260

38492
Elizabeth Wolf Scholarship Fund
c/o Pagones, Cross & VanTuyl, PC
355 Main St.
Beacon, NY 12508
Application address: c/o Nick Coto, Principal, Beacon High School, Beacon, NY 12508, tel.: (914) 838-6950

Established in 1977 in NY.
Donor(s): Charles F. Wolf, M.D.‡
Financial data (yr. ended 05/31/01): Grants paid, $12,420; assets, $0 (M); expenditures, $15,443; qualifying distributions, $14,406.
Limitations: Giving limited to residents of Beacon, NY.
Application information: Application form required.
Trustees: Francois Cross, Anthony L. Pagones.
EIN: 141580472
Codes: GTI

38493
Elizabeth Roosa Buisch Memorial Scholarship Fund
c/o Steuban Trust Co.
1 Steuban Sq.
Hornell, NY 14843-1699

Established in 1996 in NY.
Donor(s): Louis G. Buisch, Sr.
Financial data (yr. ended 12/31/01): Grants paid, $12,400; assets, $293,045 (M); expenditures, $17,017; qualifying distributions, $12,400.
Limitations: Applications not accepted. Giving primarily in Hornell, NY.
Application information: Unsolicited requests for funds not accepted.
Trustee: Steuben Trust Co.
EIN: 161501166

38494
Elmo M. Royce Youth Fund
c/o HSBC Bank USA
P.O. Box 4203
Buffalo, NY 14240-4203

Established in 1987 in NY.
Financial data (yr. ended 12/31/00): Grants paid, $12,377; assets, $229,517 (M); expenditures, $15,577; qualifying distributions, $12,456.
Limitations: Applications not accepted.
Application information: Contributes only to pre-selected organizations.
Trustee: HSBC Bank USA.
EIN: 237004745

38495
Jadot-Rops Foundation, Inc.
41-41 24th St., 2nd Fl.
Long Island City, NY 11101

Financial data (yr. ended 09/30/01): Grants paid, $12,375; assets, $234,308 (M); gifts received, $75,000; expenditures, $76,685; qualifying distributions, $67,022.
Limitations: Applications not accepted.
Application information: Contributes only to pre-selected organizations.
Officer: Roberto Mitrotti, Pres.
EIN: 133858379

38496
The Bonfire Foundation
c/o The Rockaway Partners, Ltd.
45 Theodore Fremd Ave.
Rye, NY 10580-2932

Established in 1998 in NY.
Donor(s): Tod Parrott.
Financial data (yr. ended 12/31/99): Grants paid, $12,351; assets, $693,149 (M); expenditures, $16,285; qualifying distributions, $13,775.
Limitations: Applications not accepted. Giving primarily in Rye, NY.
Application information: Contributes only to pre-selected organizations.
Directors: Robert De Concini, Kristen Parrott, Tod Parrott.
EIN: 134039331

38497
Gottlieb Family Foundation
519 Chauncey Ln.
Lawrence, NY 11559

Established in 1992 in NY.
Donor(s): Feivel Gottlieb.
Financial data (yr. ended 06/30/01): Grants paid, $12,305; assets, $183,123 (M); expenditures, $17,585; qualifying distributions, $12,305.
Limitations: Applications not accepted.
Application information: Contributes only to pre-selected organizations.
Officer: Feivel Gottlieb, Secy.
EIN: 137001089

38498
Edmac Foundation, Inc.
c/o Edtech, Inc.
349 W. Commercial St., Ste. 2990
East Rochester, NY 14445

Established in 2000 in DE.
Donor(s): Edward D. McDonald.
Financial data (yr. ended 06/30/02): Grants paid, $12,300; assets, $191,533 (M); gifts received, $18,000; expenditures, $15,646; qualifying distributions, $12,300.
Limitations: Applications not accepted. Giving primarily in Rochester, NY.
Application information: Contributes only to pre-selected organizations.
Officers: Edward D. McDonald, Pres.; Edward B. McDonald, V.P.; Carol Ross, Secy.; David K. McDonald, Treas.
EIN: 161595406

38499
William F. Ray Foundation
c/o Brown Brothers Harriman & Co.
59 Wall St.
New York, NY 10005

Donor(s): William F. Ray.
Financial data (yr. ended 12/31/01): Grants paid, $12,300; assets, $394,961 (M); expenditures, $12,738; qualifying distributions, $12,300.
Limitations: Applications not accepted. Giving primarily in Wellesley, MA, and the New York, NY, area.
Application information: Contributes only to pre-selected organizations.
Trustee: William F. Ray III.
EIN: 136271610

38500
Pechman Foundation
27116E Grand Central Pkwy.
Floral Park, NY 11005-1209

Donor(s): Stanley Pechman.
Financial data (yr. ended 12/31/01): Grants paid, $12,294; assets, $178,496 (M); expenditures, $16,080; qualifying distributions, $12,294.
Limitations: Giving primarily in NY.
Trustee: Stanley Pechman.
EIN: 136113703

38501
Isaac S. Franco Family Foundation
350 5th Ave., Ste. 5001
New York, NY 10118

Donor(s): Isaac S. Franco.
Financial data (yr. ended 12/31/01): Grants paid, $12,290; assets, $58 (M); gifts received, $12,250; expenditures, $12,308; qualifying distributions, $12,290.
Limitations: Applications not accepted. Giving primarily in NY.
Application information: Contributes only to pre-selected organizations.
Officer: Isaac S. Franco, Pres.
EIN: 133759142

38502
The Laufer Family Foundation
1541 46th St.
Brooklyn, NY 11219-2726

Established in 1995 in NY.
Donor(s): Moshe Laufer.
Financial data (yr. ended 11/30/00): Grants paid, $12,290; assets, $1,060 (M); gifts received, $12,745; expenditures, $12,440; qualifying distributions, $12,440.
Limitations: Applications not accepted. Giving primarily in NY.
Trustee: Moshe Laufer.
EIN: 113275150

38503
Singh Foundation, Inc.
c/o Rajasekhar Ramakrishnan
50 W. 97th St., Apt. 15T
New York, NY 10025-0681 (212) 866-1616

Established in 1993 in NY.
Financial data (yr. ended 12/31/01): Grants paid, $12,254; assets, $181,529 (M); gifts received, $17,255; expenditures, $25,492; qualifying distributions, $12,254.
Limitations: Giving limited to India.
Officers: Deepak Kapur, Pres.; B. Mathew, V.P.; Mriganka Sur, V.P.; Rajasekhar Ramakrishnan, Secy.-Treas.
EIN: 133719319

38504
G.R.M. Foundation, Inc.
c/o Pan Am Equities, Inc.
3 New York Plz.
New York, NY 10004

Donor(s): Greg Manocherian, Jed Manocherian.
Financial data (yr. ended 12/31/00): Grants paid, $12,250; assets, $113,803 (M); gifts received, $25,000; expenditures, $65,558; qualifying distributions, $52,869.
Limitations: Applications not accepted.
Application information: Contributes only to pre-selected organizations.
Officers and Directors:* Greg Manocherian,* Pres.; John Manocherian, V.P.; Jed Manocherian,* Secy.; Jerome H. Katz, Treas.; Fred Manocherian.
EIN: 133840700

38505
Soul Support Foundation, Inc.
240 W. 101st St.
New York, NY 10025 (212) 666-0046
Contact: Sharon Strassfeld, Pres.

Established in 1984 in NY.
Donor(s): Michael Strassfeld, Sharon Strassfeld.
Financial data (yr. ended 12/31/01): Grants paid, $12,250; assets, $127,969 (M); gifts received, $10,000; expenditures, $12,625; qualifying distributions, $11,674.
Limitations: Giving primarily in New York, NY.
Application information: Application form not required.
Officers: Sharon Strassfeld, Pres.; Michael Strassfeld, V.P.
Trustee: Matthew Schuster.
EIN: 133373753

38506
The Christy Turlington Charitable Foundation
c/o Gelfand, Rennert & Feldman, LLC
360 Hamilton Ave., Ste. 100
White Plains, NY 10601

Established in 1998 in NY.
Donor(s): Christy Turlington.
Financial data (yr. ended 12/31/00): Grants paid, $12,250; assets, $199,786 (M); expenditures, $13,631; qualifying distributions, $13,151.
Limitations: Applications not accepted.
Application information: Contributes only to pre-selected organizations.
Trustees: Kelly Maria Carter, Christy Turlington, Maria Elizabeth Turlington, Erin Elizabeth Whitaker.
EIN: 134007581

38507
Coleman and Grace Brandt Foundation
330 W. 72nd St., Ste. 10-A
New York, NY 10023-2649

Established in 1998 in NY.
Donor(s): Coleman Brandt.
Financial data (yr. ended 05/31/01): Grants paid, $12,225; assets, $1,031,111 (M); expenditures, $16,552; qualifying distributions, $12,225.
Limitations: Applications not accepted.
Application information: Contributes only to pre-selected organizations.
Trustees: Coleman Brandt, Grace Brandt.
EIN: 134010168

38508
Demakos Foundation, Inc.
4568 Bailey Ave.
Amherst, NY 14226-2138 (716) 837-4422
Contact: Peter G. Demakos, Pres.

Established in 1987 in NY.
Donor(s): Gregory Demakos.
Financial data (yr. ended 06/30/01): Grants paid, $12,162; assets, $240,074 (M); expenditures, $13,747; qualifying distributions, $13,362.
Limitations: Giving primarily in NY.
Application information: Application form required.
Officers: Peter G. Demakos, Pres. and Treas.; Rebecca G. Demakos, V.P.; Dean C. Stathacos, Secy.
EIN: 222847414

38509
The Carol and Philip Mehler Charitable Foundation, Inc.
54 Birchall Dr.
Scarsdale, NY 10583

Established in 1997 in NY.

38509—NEW YORK

Financial data (yr. ended 10/31/01): Grants paid, $12,129; assets, $64,428 (M); expenditures, $13,738; qualifying distributions, $12,129.
Limitations: Applications not accepted. Giving primarily in New York, NY.
Application information: Contributes only to pre-selected organizations.
Officers: Philip R. Mehler, Pres. and Secy.; Philip R.M. Mehler, V.P.; Carol K. Mehler, Treas.
EIN: 133980160

38510
Michele & Thomas Kahn Foundation, Inc.
25 Central Park W., Ste. 16J
New York, NY 10023-7209

Established in 1999 in NY.
Donor(s): Irving Kahn.
Financial data (yr. ended 03/31/01): Grants paid, $12,125; assets, $259,265 (M); expenditures, $12,339; qualifying distributions, $12,125.
Limitations: Applications not accepted.
Application information: Contributes only to pre-selected organizations.
Officers: Thomas Kahn, Pres.; Irving Kahn, V.P.; Michelle Kahn, Secy.
EIN: 134049922

38511
S. Arthur & Dorothy R. Neufeld Foundation
100 W. 57th St., Apt. 5N
New York, NY 10019-3327

Established in 1997 in NY.
Donor(s): Dorothy R. Neufeld, S. Arthur Neufeld.
Financial data (yr. ended 12/31/01): Grants paid, $12,125; assets, $266,314 (M); gifts received, $59,146; expenditures, $17,245; qualifying distributions, $12,125.
Limitations: Applications not accepted.
Application information: Contributes only to pre-selected organizations.
Officers and Directors:* S. Arthur Neufeld,* Pres.; Dorothy R. Neufeld,* V.P. and Secy.; Peter A. Wright,* V.P.
EIN: 133947020

38512
Anna D. & William Baker Memorial Fund
c/o Chemung Canal Trust Co.
P.O. Box 1522
Elmira, NY 14902-1522 (607) 737-3896
Contact: Alan Nathenson, Tr.

Established in 1968 in NY.
Donor(s): Anita D. Baker,‡ William Baker.‡
Financial data (yr. ended 12/31/01): Grants paid, $12,100; assets, $253,002 (M); expenditures, $14,295; qualifying distributions, $12,100.
Limitations: Giving limited to Elmira, NY.
Trustees: Alan Nathenson, David B. Slohm, Chemung Canal Trust Co.
EIN: 166096575

38513
The Mary G. Krey & Bradley R. Krey Charitable Foundation
c/o BCRS Associates
67 Wall St., 6th Fl.
New York, NY 10005 (212) 440-0800

Established in 1997 in IL.
Donor(s): Bradley R. Krey, Mary G. Krey.
Financial data (yr. ended 12/31/01): Grants paid, $12,100; assets, $112,082 (M); expenditures, $12,462; qualifying distributions, $12,100.
Limitations: Applications not accepted. Giving primarily in IL.
Application information: Contributes only to pre-selected organizations.

Officers and Directors:* Mary G. Krey,* Pres. and Treas.; Bradley R. Krey,* V.P. and Secy.; David F. Gorter.
EIN: 364120661

38514
Donald L. Davis Foundation
2277 Niagara Falls Blvd.
Amherst, NY 14228

Donor(s): Donald L. Davis.
Financial data (yr. ended 12/31/01): Grants paid, $12,088; assets, $56,504 (M); expenditures, $13,844; qualifying distributions, $12,088.
Limitations: Applications not accepted. Giving primarily in NY.
Application information: Contributes only to pre-selected organizations.
Trustees: Donald Davis, John Davis.
EIN: 166065355

38515
Jobarr Foundation, Inc.
c/o Joseph Rubin
71-55 171st St.
Flushing, NY 11365-3337

Established in 1987 in NY.
Donor(s): Joseph Rubin.
Financial data (yr. ended 12/31/01): Grants paid, $12,082; assets, $479,050 (M); gifts received, $230,685; expenditures, $12,097; qualifying distributions, $12,082.
Application information: Application form not required.
Officers: Joseph Rubin, Pres.; R. Rubin, V.P. and Secy.
EIN: 237015552

38516
Second Star Foundation
P.O. Box 1091
Jamesport, NY 11947-1091
Application address: 33 W. 2nd St., Riverhead, NY 11901, tel.: (631) 727-2180
Contact: Jay P. Quartararo

Established in 2000 in NY.
Donor(s): Ellen Berger, Steve Berger, Bethany Clare Berger.
Financial data (yr. ended 12/31/01): Grants paid, $12,062; assets, $168,613 (M); gifts received, $20,229; expenditures, $32,718; qualifying distributions, $12,062.
Application information: Application form not required.
Directors: Bethany Clare Berger, Ellen Berger, Steve Berger, Richard Wines.
EIN: 113528701

38517
Dickstein Family Foundation
5 Dorchester Dr.
Glen Head, NY 11545

Established in 1997 in NY.
Donor(s): Richard Dickstein.
Financial data (yr. ended 12/31/01): Grants paid, $12,025; assets, $32,270 (M); expenditures, $12,110; qualifying distributions, $12,025.
Limitations: Applications not accepted. Giving primarily in NY.
Application information: Contributes only to pre-selected organizations.
Trustees: Marilyn Dickstein, Richard Dickstein.
EIN: 116483288

38518
Joan and Peter Andrews Family Foundation
Pitt Petri Bldg.
374 Delaware Ave., Rm. 203
Buffalo, NY 14202

Established in 1996 in VA.
Donor(s): Peter C. Andrews.
Financial data (yr. ended 09/30/02): Grants paid, $12,000; assets, $158,806 (M); expenditures, $14,180; qualifying distributions, $12,000.
Limitations: Applications not accepted.
Application information: Contributes only to pre-selected organizations.
Trustees: Joan K. Andrews, Peter C. Andrews.
EIN: 166443273

38519
The Borgia Family Foundation
43 Woodland Dr.
Oyster Bay Cove, NY 11771

Established in 2000 in NY.
Donor(s): Michael Borgia, Tere Borgia.
Financial data (yr. ended 12/31/01): Grants paid, $12,000; assets, $250,093 (M); gifts received, $29,419; expenditures, $13,823; qualifying distributions, $12,000.
Limitations: Applications not accepted.
Application information: Contributes only to pre-selected organizations.
Trustees: Michael Borgia, Tere Borgia.
EIN: 134153115

38520
Irving T. Bush Foundation, Inc.
c/o Paul Silberberg
112 Madison Ave., 3rd Fl.
New York, NY 10016

Financial data (yr. ended 07/31/01): Grants paid, $12,000; assets, $240,995 (M); expenditures, $14,731; qualifying distributions, $12,000.
Limitations: Applications not accepted. Giving primarily in NY.
Application information: Contributes only to pre-selected organizations.
Officers and Trustees:* Paul Silberberg,* Pres.; Edward J. Walsh, Jr.,* V.P. amd Secy.; Ralph Holt.
EIN: 136043483

38521
Cantor-Lynn-Wasserman Foundation, Inc.
(Formerly H. B. Cantor Foundation, Inc.)
c/o Teitler & Teitler
1114 Ave. of the Americas, 45th Fl.
New York, NY 10036

Donor(s): Gertrude L. Cantor.‡
Financial data (yr. ended 12/31/01): Grants paid, $12,000; assets, $251,482 (M); expenditures, $13,429; qualifying distributions, $12,000.
Limitations: Applications not accepted.
Application information: Contributes only to pre-selected organizations.
Officers and Directors:* David A. Cantor,* Pres.; Marcia Wasserman,* V.P.; Nancy Lynn,* Secy.
EIN: 136120607

38522
Carr Family Foundation
c/o Goldman Sachs & Co.
85 Broad St.
New York, NY 10004

Donor(s): Michael J. Carr.
Financial data (yr. ended 11/30/01): Grants paid, $12,000; assets, $641,090 (M); gifts received, $2,500; expenditures, $22,324; qualifying distributions, $14,818.

Limitations: Applications not accepted. Giving primarily in New York, NY.
Application information: Contributes only to pre-selected organizations.
Trustees: Michael J. Carr, Shelley L. Sporleder.
EIN: 134089115

38523
Dr. Joy To The World, Inc.
c/o KRT Business Mgmt.
500 5th Ave., Ste. 3000
New York, NY 10110

Established in 1998 in NY.
Donor(s): Joy Browne.
Financial data (yr. ended 12/31/00): Grants paid, $12,000; assets, $299,421 (M); gifts received, $105,000; expenditures, $12,000; qualifying distributions, $12,000.
Limitations: Applications not accepted. Giving primarily in NY.
Application information: Contributes only to pre-selected organizations.
Directors: Joy Browne, Patience Brown, Alannah Sinclaire.
EIN: 134036600

38524
Sidney A. & Libby Fine Foundation, Inc.
317 Madison Ave., Ste. 2310
New York, NY 10017-5301
Contact: Burton M. Fine, Mgr.

Established in 1958.
Donor(s): Burton M. Fine, Alex Birnbaum.
Financial data (yr. ended 08/31/01): Grants paid, $12,000; assets, $115,449 (M); gifts received, $10,000; expenditures, $12,774; qualifying distributions, $12,000.
Limitations: Giving primarily in NY.
Officer: Burton M. Fine, Mgr.
EIN: 136127142

38525
Olga Forrai Foundation, Inc.
c/o Oram, Yelon & Bernstein
420 Lexington Ave., Ste. 2150
New York, NY 10170
Application address: 205 E. 82nd St., New York, NY 10028
Contact: Erika Urbach, Treas.

Financial data (yr. ended 12/31/01): Grants paid, $12,000; assets, $663,980 (M); expenditures, $32,712; qualifying distributions, $28,703.
Limitations: Giving limited to residents of New York, NY.
Officers: Robert M. Walsh, Pres.; Erna Gwillim, Secy.; Erika Urbach, Treas.
EIN: 133182161
Codes: GTI

38526
The GK Foundation
P.O. Box 748120
Rego Park, NY 11374-8120 (718) 897-6500
Contact: David Kuppermann, Tr.

Established in 1987 in NY.
Donor(s): David Kuppermann, Pola Kuppermann.
Financial data (yr. ended 11/30/01): Grants paid, $12,000; assets, $455,217 (M); gifts received, $103,730; expenditures, $14,494; qualifying distributions, $12,000.
Limitations: Giving primarily in New York, NY.
Trustees: Jacob Dyckman, Jay Fenster, David Kuppermann, Pola Kuppermann, Simeon Zoimen.
EIN: 136892493

38527
Imatra Foundation
c/o Saasto
26 Court St., Ste. 1304
Brooklyn, NY 11242

Financial data (yr. ended 12/31/01): Grants paid, $12,000; assets, $100,523 (M); expenditures, $13,760; qualifying distributions, $12,000.
Officer: Robert A. Saasto, Pres.
EIN: 113324668

38528
Institute for Continuing Education in Law and Librarianship
75 Main St.
Dobbs Ferry, NY 10522
Contact: David R. Cohen, Pres.

Established in 1983.
Donor(s): Glanville Publications, Inc.
Financial data (yr. ended 01/31/02): Grants paid, $12,000; assets, $1 (M); expenditures, $13,038; qualifying distributions, $12,000.
Limitations: Giving primarily in St. Louis, MO and NY.
Officers: David R. Cohen, Pres.; Julius J. Marke, V.P.; Fay Cohen, Secy.-Treas.
EIN: 133170913

38529
George & Janet Jaffin Foundation, Inc.
230 Park Ave., Ste. 510
New York, NY 10169-0005

Donor(s): George M. Jaffin, Janet Jaffin, James Cohen, Milton Cohen.
Financial data (yr. ended 11/30/01): Grants paid, $12,000; assets, $248,712 (M); expenditures, $13,765; qualifying distributions, $13,356.
Limitations: Giving primarily in New York, NY.
Officers and Director:* George M. Jaffin,* Pres.; Janet Jaffin, V.P.
EIN: 136101281

38530
The E. R. H. Lee Foundation
530 5th Ave., 2nd Fl.
New York, NY 10036

Established in 1997 in NY.
Donor(s): Dwight Lee.
Financial data (yr. ended 12/31/01): Grants paid, $12,000; assets, $245,258 (M); expenditures, $17,943; qualifying distributions, $12,000.
Limitations: Applications not accepted.
Application information: Contributes only to pre-selected organizations.
Trustee: Dwight E. Lee.
EIN: 137124812

38531
Joseph F. Meade Memorial Science Fund
c/o JPMorgan Chase Bank
P.O. Box 31412
Rochester, NY 14603-1412

Financial data (yr. ended 12/31/01): Grants paid, $12,000; assets, $242,307 (M); gifts received, $10,000; expenditures, $14,243; qualifying distributions, $12,222.
Limitations: Applications not accepted. Giving limited to residents of Hammondsport, NY.
Application information: Students chosen by a selection committee consisting of administrators and residents of Hammondsport Central School District, NY.
Trustee: JPMorgan Chase Bank.
EIN: 166015269
Codes: GTI

38532
MEH Foundation, Inc.
Fairgrounds Dr.
P.O. Box 527
Manlius, NY 13104

Financial data (yr. ended 09/30/01): Grants paid, $12,000; assets, $177,539 (M); gifts received, $51,684; expenditures, $12,350; qualifying distributions, $12,000.
Limitations: Applications not accepted. Giving primarily in Syracuse, NY.
Application information: Contributes only to pre-selected organizations.
Officers: Ahmad El-Hindi, Pres.; Elizabeth El-Hindi, V.P.; Maryam Wasmund, Treas.
EIN: 161199638

38533
The Charles B. & Winifred R. Weber Foundation
c/o Winthrop, Stimson, Putnam & Roberts
1 Battery Park Plz.
New York, NY 10004-1490

Established in 1999 in NY.
Donor(s): Mrs. Charles R. Weber.
Financial data (yr. ended 12/31/01): Grants paid, $12,000; assets, $156,853 (M); expenditures, $13,394; qualifying distributions, $12,145.
Limitations: Applications not accepted. Giving primarily in NY.
Application information: Contributes only to pre-selected organizations.
Officers: Daniel J. McSwiggan, V.P. and Secy.; Robert Anthoine, V.P.; Fred P. Eckhardt, V.P.; Robert Frankel, Secy.-Treas.
EIN: 136167132

38534
Allan Silverstein Family Foundation, Inc.
c/o L. Wollin
350 5th Ave.
New York, NY 10118

Donor(s): Allan Silverstein.
Financial data (yr. ended 09/30/01): Grants paid, $11,989; assets, $205,323 (M); gifts received, $20,000; expenditures, $13,116; qualifying distributions, $11,989.
Limitations: Applications not accepted.
Application information: Contributes only to pre-selected organizations.
Officer: Allan Silverstein.
EIN: 133862104

38535
The Hudson Charitable Foundation, Inc.
c/o William Berger
1407 46th St.
Brooklyn, NY 11219

Established in 1983 in NY.
Donor(s): Hudson Neckwear Co., Irving Berger, William Berger, Leo Lieber.
Financial data (yr. ended 06/30/01): Grants paid, $11,969; assets, $130,903 (M); gifts received, $66,000; expenditures, $12,260; qualifying distributions, $11,969.
Limitations: Applications not accepted.
Application information: Contributes only to pre-selected organizations.
Officer: William Berger, Treas.
EIN: 133202380
Codes: CS, CD

38536
Eleanor G. & John S. Karger Foundation, Inc.
116 E. 66th St.
New York, NY 10021
Contact: John S. Karger, Pres.

Donor(s): John S. Karger.
Financial data (yr. ended 12/31/01): Grants paid, $11,956; assets, $46,890 (M); expenditures, $13,408; qualifying distributions, $11,956.
Limitations: Giving primarily in NY.
Officers: John S. Karger, Pres.; Thomas S. Karger, V.P. and Secy.; Ann Price Karger, V.P. and Treas.
EIN: 136180308

38537
The Michael P. Canno Scholarship Foundation
P.O. Box 925
Rye, NY 10580

Established in 2000 in NY.
Donor(s): Lauren Canno-Tabachnick.
Financial data (yr. ended 09/30/01): Grants paid, $11,933; assets, $12,227 (M); gifts received, $22,500; expenditures, $19,458; qualifying distributions, $11,933.
Limitations: Giving primarily in NY.
Application information: Application forms available through Rye Neck High School NY guidance department. Application form required.
Trustees: Lauren Canno-Tabachnick, Mark P. Canno, Melinda Canno-Velez.
EIN: 137219336

38538
The Michael Miller Foundation, Inc.
(Formerly The Michael & Carol Miller Foundation, Inc.)
R. Terris
200 Garden City Plz., Rm. 224
Garden City, NY 11530 (516) 877-2770
Contact: Michael Miller, Pres.

Donor(s): Michael Miller, Carol Miller.
Financial data (yr. ended 06/30/01): Grants paid, $11,904; assets, $216,654 (M); expenditures, $12,055; qualifying distributions, $12,041.
Limitations: Giving primarily in NY.
Officers: Michael Miller, Pres.; Richard Terris, Secy.
EIN: 133054113

38539
Lewis Wilmot Fund Charitable Trust
24 Main St.
Middleport, NY 14105 (716) 434-9904
Application address: 6 Alfred St., Middleport, NY 14105
Contact: Bernard J. Dujenski, Chair.

Financial data (yr. ended 12/31/01): Grants paid, $11,900; assets, $154,569 (M); gifts received, $5,000; expenditures, $13,331; qualifying distributions, $11,900.
Limitations: Giving limited to Royalton, Hartland, and Middleport, NY.
Officer: Bernard J. Dujenski, Chair.
Trustees: Ann Bates, Charles Perry, Pauline Willcapp.
EIN: 166170483

38540
Alzheimer's Research Association, Inc.
(Formerly J. Murray Tyson Foundation, Inc.)
c/o Lonnie E. Wollin
350 5th Ave., Ste. 2822
New York, NY 10118-2896

Financial data (yr. ended 10/31/01): Grants paid, $11,896; assets, $144,406 (M); gifts received, $11,312; expenditures, $28,882; qualifying distributions, $11,896.
Limitations: Applications not accepted. Giving primarily in CA and NY.
Application information: Contributes only to pre-selected organizations.
Officers and Directors:* Gary Wollin,* Pres.; Lonnie E. Wollin,* Secy.-Treas.
EIN: 237438025

38541
Abraham Ellis Foundation, Inc.
c/o Cambridge Essex Stamp Co.
393 5th Ave., 4th Fl.
New York, NY 10016

Financial data (yr. ended 12/31/00): Grants paid, $11,890; assets, $142,681 (M); expenditures, $13,519; qualifying distributions, $13,243.
Limitations: Applications not accepted.
Application information: Contributes only to pre-selected organizations.
Director: Richard Ellis.
EIN: 136154731

38542
Adolph H. Schreiber Family Foundation, Inc.
460 W. 34th St.
New York, NY 10001-2320

Donor(s): Irving Eisenman.
Financial data (yr. ended 12/31/01): Grants paid, $11,886; assets, $363,873 (M); gifts received, $218; expenditures, $13,394; qualifying distributions, $11,886.
Limitations: Applications not accepted.
Application information: Contributes only to pre-selected organizations.
Officers: Elliot Schreiber, Pres.; Irving Eisenman, Secy.
EIN: 136163552

38543
Keren Yechiel Charitable Foundation
1711 44th St.
Brooklyn, NY 11204
Application address: 760 Montgomery St., Brooklyn, NY 11213
Contact: Elliot Seide, Tr.

Established in 1998 in NY.
Financial data (yr. ended 09/30/01): Grants paid, $11,881; assets, $26,751 (M); gifts received, $20,000; expenditures, $13,131; qualifying distributions, $11,881.
Limitations: Giving primarily in Brooklyn, NY.
Trustees: Elliot Seide, Yosef Seide.
EIN: 311612765

38544
EESCO Foundation, Inc.
10 Roosevelt Ave.
Port Jefferson Station, NY 11776-3337
Contact: George T. Foundotos, Pres.

Financial data (yr. ended 12/31/01): Grants paid, $11,850; assets, $117,299 (M); expenditures, $11,916; qualifying distributions, $11,916.
Limitations: Giving primarily to residents of Greenport, NY.
Application information: Application form required.
Officers: George T. Foundotos, Pres.; George A. Burrell, Secy.; Walter H. Burden III, Treas.
EIN: 112547290

38545
Irving Rothlein Foundation
1740 Rte. 32
Saugerties, NY 12477
Contact: Travis C. Rothlein, Tr.

Donor(s): Travis C. Rothlein.
Financial data (yr. ended 12/31/01): Grants paid, $11,830; assets, $491,178 (M); expenditures, $15,337; qualifying distributions, $11,830.
Limitations: Giving primarily in New York, NY.
Application information: Application form not required.
Trustees: Nancy C. Rothlein, Travis C. Rothlein.
EIN: 136098364

38546
The Herman Liebmann Foundation
c/o Marks Paneth & Shron, LLP
622 3rd Ave.
New York, NY 10017

Financial data (yr. ended 10/31/01): Grants paid, $11,825; assets, $276,034 (M); expenditures, $12,748; qualifying distributions, $12,748.
Limitations: Giving primarily in New York, NY.
Trustee: Herman Liebmann.
EIN: 136190605

38547
The Debrah Lee Charatan Foundation
515 Madison Ave., 12th Fl.
New York, NY 10022

Established in 2000 in NY.
Donor(s): Debrah Lee Charatan, Robert Durst.
Financial data (yr. ended 03/31/01): Grants paid, $11,800; assets, $59,725 (M); gifts received, $75,000; expenditures, $15,275; qualifying distributions, $15,275.
Officer: Debrah Lee Charatan, Pres.
EIN: 134126715

38548
Morris & Ruth B. Cowan Foundation, Inc.
320 Central Park W., Ste. 8G
New York, NY 10025

Established in 1999 in NY.
Donor(s): Ruth B. Cowan.
Financial data (yr. ended 12/31/01): Grants paid, $11,800; assets, $10,279 (M); gifts received, $11,811; expenditures, $13,199; qualifying distributions, $11,800.
Limitations: Applications not accepted. Giving primarily in New York, NY.
Application information: Contributes only to pre-selected organizations.
Officers: Ruth B. Cowan, Pres.; Sharon Ann Miller, Secy.
EIN: 134067362

38549
Sheldon & Marilyn David Foundation
15 W. 47th St.
New York, NY 10036
Contact: Sheldon David, Tr.

Donor(s): Sheldon David.
Financial data (yr. ended 12/31/01): Grants paid, $11,782; assets, $398 (M); gifts received, $11,400; expenditures, $11,782; qualifying distributions, $11,782.
Limitations: Giving primarily in NY.
Trustees: Marilyn David, Sheldon David, Jack Walker.
EIN: 133133925

38550
Milton and Shirley Glaser Foundation, Inc.
207 E. 32nd St.
New York, NY 10016 (212) 889-3161
Contact: Milton Glaser, Pres. or Shirley Glaser, V.P.

Established in 1994 in NY.
Donor(s): Milton Glaser.
Financial data (yr. ended 12/31/01): Grants paid, $11,750; assets, $25,782 (M); gifts received, $20,000; expenditures, $13,805; qualifying distributions, $11,750.
Limitations: Giving primarily in New York, NY.
Officers: Milton Glaser, Pres.; Shirley Glaser, V.P.
Trustee: James McMullan.
EIN: 133754244

38551
Regina Goldwasser Foundation
56 W. 45th St., No. 1600
New York, NY 10036 (212) 869-5015
Contact: Henry Goldwasser, Mgr.

Financial data (yr. ended 12/31/01): Grants paid, $11,707; assets, $91,086 (M); expenditures, $11,900; qualifying distributions, $11,707.
Limitations: Giving primarily in NY.
Officer and Trustee:* Henry Goldwasser,* Mgr.
EIN: 132926389

38552
Michael Stanton Foundation
c/o Michael Stanton
150 E. 58th St.
New York, NY 10155

Established in 1995 in NY.
Financial data (yr. ended 12/31/00): Grants paid, $11,700; assets, $232,144 (M); expenditures, $16,290; qualifying distributions, $11,700.
Limitations: Applications not accepted.
Application information: Contributes only to pre-selected organizations.
Officer: Michael Stanton.
EIN: 133837975

38553
Rita and Leo Greenland Family Foundation
1056 5th Ave., Ste. 10A
New York, NY 10028

Established in 1999 in NY.
Donor(s): Leo Greenland.
Financial data (yr. ended 12/31/01): Grants paid, $11,691; assets, $149,534 (M); expenditures, $18,374; qualifying distributions, $11,691.
Limitations: Applications not accepted.
Application information: Contributes only to pre-selected organizations.
Trustee: Leo Greenland.
EIN: 137196982

38554
David T. Nash Charitable Foundation
c/o Bessemer Trust Co., N.A.
630 5th Ave.
New York, NY 10111

Established in 1996 in NY.
Donor(s): David T. Nash, Ellen C. Nash.
Financial data (yr. ended 12/31/99): Grants paid, $11,650; assets, $100,472 (M); expenditures, $13,385; qualifying distributions, $11,761.
Limitations: Applications not accepted.
Application information: Contributes only to pre-selected organizations.
Trustees: David T. Nash, Ellen C. Nash, Robert M. Nash, Stephen D. Nash.
EIN: 911846057

38555
William & Alice Rossi Foundation, Inc.
26 Gaynor Ave.
Nesconset, NY 11767

Established in 1997 in NY.
Donor(s): William Rossi.
Financial data (yr. ended 09/30/01): Grants paid, $11,650; assets, $291,075 (M); expenditures, $12,241; qualifying distributions, $11,650.
Limitations: Applications not accepted. Giving primarily in NY.
Application information: Contributes only to pre-selected organizations.
Officers: William Rossi, Pres. and Treas.; Alice Rossi, V.P. and Secy.; William Gardner, V.P.
EIN: 113416821

38556
DeSpirt Foundation, Inc.
1085 E. Delavan Ave.
Buffalo, NY 14215

Established prior to 1969 in NY.
Financial data (yr. ended 11/30/01): Grants paid, $11,600; assets, $154,241 (M); expenditures, $12,973; qualifying distributions, $11,600.
Limitations: Applications not accepted. Giving primarily in Buffalo, NY.
Application information: Contributes only to pre-selected organizations.
Officers and Directors:* Rita D. Heffernan,* Pres.; Michelle O. Heffernan, Secy.; William Busgaglia, Michael DeSpirt, Peter M. Heffernan.
EIN: 166034186

38557
The Sydney Foundation, Inc.
c/o Marcum & Kliegman, LLP
655 3rd Ave., 16th Fl.
New York, NY 10017
Application address: 770 Park Ave., New York, NY 10021
Contact: Juliet Frank, Pres.

Established in 1947.
Financial data (yr. ended 06/30/01): Grants paid, $11,600; assets, $176,629 (M); expenditures, $15,862; qualifying distributions, $11,600.
Limitations: Giving primarily in NY.
Application information: Application form not required.
Officers: Juliet Frank, Pres.; Diane M. Coffey, Secy.
EIN: 136120736

38558
The Goldberg Family Foundation
7 Hastings Rd.
Old Westbury, NY 11568-1146

Established in 1997 in NY.
Donor(s): Allen Goldberg.
Financial data (yr. ended 12/31/01): Grants paid, $11,550; assets, $30,484 (M); expenditures, $12,098; qualifying distributions, $11,550.
Limitations: Applications not accepted. Giving primarily in New York, NY.
Application information: Contributes only to pre-selected organizations.
Trustees: Allen Goldberg, Patricia Goldberg.
EIN: 116484637

38559
Elizabeth & Joseph Travaglini Educational Fund
19 Chenango St., Ste. 802
Binghamton, NY 13902 (607) 722-5511
Contact: James M. Barber, Tr.

Financial data (yr. ended 11/30/00): Grants paid, $11,529; assets, $177,672 (M); expenditures, $14,314; qualifying distributions, $12,492.
Limitations: Giving limited to Cavaglietto and Barengo, Italy.
Trustee: James M. Barber.
EIN: 161132981
Codes: GTI

38560
The Edelman Foundation
717 5th Ave., 4th Fl.
New York, NY 10022-8111

Established in 1989 in NY.
Donor(s): Asher Edelman.
Financial data (yr. ended 12/31/01): Grants paid, $11,500; assets, $401 (M); gifts received, $12,180; expenditures, $12,080; qualifying distributions, $11,500.
Limitations: Applications not accepted. Giving primarily in New York, NY.
Application information: Contributes only to pre-selected organizations.
Trustees: Asher B. Edelman, Irving Garfinkel.
EIN: 136936290

38561
Clark Gillies Foundation
2095 Express Dr. N.
Hauppauge, NY 11788 (631) 851-1700

Established in 1998.
Financial data (yr. ended 12/31/99): Grants paid, $11,500; assets, $96,229 (M); gifts received, $46,600; expenditures, $14,283; qualifying distributions, $11,500.
Limitations: Giving primarily in NY.
Application information: Application form required.
Directors: John Danzi, Joe Duerr, George Wafer.
EIN: 113386742

38562
Hyman and Ruth Muss Foundation, Inc.
118-35 Queens Blvd.
Forest Hills, NY 11375

Established in 1989 in NY.
Donor(s): Hyman Moss.
Financial data (yr. ended 12/31/01): Grants paid, $11,500; assets, $1,543,132 (M); gifts received, $339,862; expenditures, $15,123; qualifying distributions, $11,500.
Limitations: Applications not accepted. Giving primarily in NY.
Application information: Contributes only to pre-selected organizations.
Officers: Ruth Muss, Pres.; Stanley H. Muss, V.P. and Treas.
EIN: 112987980

38563
The Jack & Mae Rosenberg Charitable Trust
c/o Curtis Mallet
101 Park Ave., Ste. 3500
New York, NY 10178-0061

Established in 1995 in NY.
Donor(s): Herbert Stoller.
Financial data (yr. ended 12/31/01): Grants paid, $11,500; assets, $4,236,083 (M); gifts received, $247,770; expenditures, $50,333; qualifying distributions, $28,225.
Limitations: Applications not accepted. Giving primarily in Baltimore, MD.
Application information: Contributes only to pre-selected organizations.
Trustee: Herbert Stoller.
EIN: 137050361

38564
Nat Sherman Foundation, Inc.
629 W. 54th St.
New York, NY 10019-3581
Contact: Myrna Sherman, Treas.

Financial data (yr. ended 12/31/01): Grants paid, $11,500; assets, $20,615 (M); expenditures, $11,516; qualifying distributions, $11,500.
Officers: Ethel Person, Pres.; Annette Sherman, Secy.; Myrna Sherman, Treas.
EIN: 133250137

38565
Stein Family Foundation, Inc.
5 Willow Ln.
Scarsdale, NY 10583

Established in 1986 in NY.
Donor(s): Malcolm L. Stein.
Financial data (yr. ended 11/30/01): Grants paid, $11,500; assets, $2,448 (M); gifts received, $10,000; expenditures, $11,740; qualifying distributions, $11,500.
Limitations: Applications not accepted. Giving primarily in NY.
Application information: Contributes only to pre-selected organizations.
Officers and Directors:* Malcolm L. Stein,* Pres.; Harriet W. Stein,* V.P.
EIN: 133439998

38566
Alexander Wasserman and Evelyn Wasserman Foundation, Inc.
1603 McDonald Ave.
Brooklyn, NY 11230

Established in 1997 in NY.
Donor(s): Alexander Wasserman, Evelyn Wasserman.
Financial data (yr. ended 12/31/01): Grants paid, $11,500; assets, $248,940 (M); expenditures, $11,614; qualifying distributions, $11,614.
Limitations: Applications not accepted. Giving primarily in Brooklyn and Long Beach, NY.
Application information: Contributes only to pre-selected organizations.
Officers: Alexander Wasserman, Pres.; Susan Wasserman, V.P.; Evelyn Wasserman, Secy.-Treas.
EIN: 113379626

38567
Brooks Bar-B-Que Charitable Foundation
9401 State Hwy. 23
Oneonta, NY 13820
Contact: Jean Brooks, Tr. or John W. Brooks, Tr.

Established in 2000 in NY.
Donor(s): John W. Brooks, Joan E. Brooks, Brooks Bar-B-Que, Inc.
Financial data (yr. ended 12/31/01): Grants paid, $11,450; assets, $89,856 (M); gifts received, $31,000; expenditures, $12,374; qualifying distributions, $11,450.
Limitations: Giving primarily in Oneonta, NY.
Trustees: Joan E. Brooks, John W. Brooks, Ryan A. Brooks.
EIN: 166503425

38568
The Guthrie Foundation
c/o D.W. Hiscock, Patterson, Delknap
1133 Ave. of the Americas, 20th Fl.
New York, NY 10036
Application address: 14 E. 75th St., New York, NY 10021

Donor(s): Randolph H. Guthrie, Mabel W. Guthrie, Randolph H. Guthrie, Sr.‡
Financial data (yr. ended 11/30/01): Grants paid, $11,450; assets, $248,636 (M); expenditures, $17,202; qualifying distributions, $11,450.
Limitations: Giving primarily in NY.
Application information: Application form not required.
Trustees: George G. Guthrie, Jo Carol Guthrie.
EIN: 132881832

38569
Samuel K. Ohlstein Foundation, Inc.
120 W. 45th St., 7th Fl.
New York, NY 10036

Established in 1993 in NY.
Donor(s): Samuel K. Ohlstein.‡
Financial data (yr. ended 12/31/01): Grants paid, $11,450; assets, $310,423 (M); expenditures, $19,278; qualifying distributions, $11,450.
Limitations: Applications not accepted. Giving primarily in NY.
Application information: Contributes only to pre-selected organizations.
Officers: Robert W. Ohlstein, Pres. and Treas.; Kenneth Berger, V.P. and Secy.
EIN: 133702716

38570
David & Sarah Jane Fuchs Charitable Trust
15 W. 34th St.
New York, NY 10001

Established in 1998 in NY.
Donor(s): David Fuchs, Sarah Jane Fuchs.
Financial data (yr. ended 12/31/01): Grants paid, $11,440; assets, $31,162 (M); gifts received, $6,000; expenditures, $12,025; qualifying distributions, $11,440.
Trustees: Sondra Eichel, Cynthia Fuchs, Steven Fuchs.
EIN: 137083793

38571
The Cecelia B. and Kenneth B. Cutler Foundation
10 Westway
Bronxville, NY 10708

Established in 1986 in NY.
Donor(s): Cecelia B. Cutler, Kenneth B. Cutler.
Financial data (yr. ended 11/30/01): Grants paid, $11,425; assets, $256,922 (M); expenditures, $12,609; qualifying distributions, $11,922.
Limitations: Applications not accepted. Giving primarily in MI, NY, and PA.
Application information: Contributes only to pre-selected organizations.
Trustees: Cecelia B. Cutler, Kenneth B. Cutler.
EIN: 133316060

38572
The Cicely Tyson Foundation, Inc.
c/o PFM
152 W. 57th St., 19 Fl.
New York, NY 10019-3301

Established in 1998 in NY.
Financial data (yr. ended 12/31/01): Grants paid, $11,425; assets, $25,342 (M); gifts received, $11,000; expenditures, $11,681; qualifying distributions, $11,425.
Limitations: Applications not accepted.
Application information: Contributes only to pre-selected organizations.
Officer: Cicely Tyson, Pres.
EIN: 133997217

38573
Raymond & Madalin Beaton Charitable Trust
c/o Evergreen Bank, N.A.
237 Glen St.
Glens Falls, NY 12801

Established in 1987 in NY.
Financial data (yr. ended 06/30/99): Grants paid, $11,416; assets, $357,104 (M); expenditures, $13,154; qualifying distributions, $12,106.
Limitations: Applications not accepted.
Application information: Contributes only to pre-selected organizations.
Trustee: Evergreen Bank, N.A.
EIN: 146134428

38574
The Gluckman Foundation
c/o Fownes Bros. & Co.
411 5th Ave.
New York, NY 10016

Financial data (yr. ended 05/31/02): Grants paid, $11,411; assets, $187,426 (M); expenditures, $13,241; qualifying distributions, $11,411.
Limitations: Applications not accepted. Giving primarily in New York, NY.
Application information: Contributes only to pre-selected organizations.
Officers: Roby Gluckman, Treas.; Thomas Gluckman, Mgr.
EIN: 136175029

38575
Martin and Irene Kofman Foundation, Inc.
226 Franklin St.
Brooklyn, NY 11222-1333

Donor(s): Martin I. Kofman.
Financial data (yr. ended 11/30/01): Grants paid, $11,380; assets, $11,320 (M); gifts received, $20,000; expenditures, $11,380; qualifying distributions, $11,380.
Limitations: Applications not accepted. Giving primarily in Brooklyn, NY.
Application information: Contributes only to pre-selected organizations.
Trustees: Irene Kofman, Martin I. Kofman.
EIN: 112730617

38576
Edith & Robert Korn Foundation
210 E. 68th St.
New York, NY 10021

Established in 1997 in NY.
Financial data (yr. ended 12/31/00): Grants paid, $11,350; assets, $216,001 (M); expenditures, $11,619; qualifying distributions, $11,350.
Limitations: Applications not accepted.
Application information: Contributes only to pre-selected organizations.
Officer: Edward Korn, V.P.
EIN: 133981480

38577
The Noon Foundation, Inc.
c/o Angelo Natoli, C.P.A.
316 E. 53rd St.
New York, NY 10022 (212) 935-4720

Established in 1964 in NY.
Donor(s): Samuel Neaman, Cecilia Neaman.
Financial data (yr. ended 12/31/01): Grants paid, $11,310; assets, $96,852 (M); gifts received, $20,230; expenditures, $11,785; qualifying distributions, $11,248.
Limitations: Applications not accepted.
Application information: Contributes only to pre-selected organizations.

Officers and Directors:* Samuel Neaman,* Pres.; Angelo Natoli, Secy.; Thomas Hardy, Zehev Tadmor.
EIN: 133284401

38578
Finerman Foundation, Inc.
c/o Ralph Finerman
65 Central Park W., Rm. 8G
New York, NY 10023

Donor(s): Ralph Finerman.
Financial data (yr. ended 06/30/01): Grants paid, $11,300; assets, $181,867 (M); gifts received, $17,580; expenditures, $12,396; qualifying distributions, $11,333.
Limitations: Applications not accepted. Giving primarily in New York, NY.
Application information: Contributes only to pre-selected organizations.
Officers: Ralph Finerman, Pres.; Adam Finerman, V.P.; Alissa Finerman, V.P.
EIN: 237024610

38579
Will & Stella Gratz Foundation, Inc.
15 Bishop Pl.
Larchmont, NY 10538-3801

Financial data (yr. ended 12/31/00): Grants paid, $11,300; assets, $179,459 (M); expenditures, $12,724; qualifying distributions, $11,300.
Limitations: Applications not accepted. Giving primarily in NY.
Application information: Contributes only to pre-selected organizations.
Officers: Donald S. Gratz, Pres. and Chair.; William F. Gratz, V.P. and Treas.; Roberta Brandes Gratz, Secy.
EIN: 136152139

38580
Murray Hazan Family Foundation
Todd Dr.
Sands Point, NY 11050
Contact: Murray Hazan, Mgr.

Established in 1994 in NY.
Donor(s): Murray Hazan.
Financial data (yr. ended 11/30/01): Grants paid, $11,276; assets, $210,546 (M); expenditures, $11,607; qualifying distributions, $11,276.
Officer and Trustees:* Murray Hazan,* Mgr.; Barbara Hazan, Steven Hazan.
EIN: 226642389

38581
The Leonard Milton Foundation, Inc.
124 Windsor Gate
Great Neck, NY 11020-1632
Contact: Hilda Milton, Pres.

Financial data (yr. ended 10/31/01): Grants paid, $11,260; assets, $204,392 (M); expenditures, $12,685; qualifying distributions, $11,260.
Limitations: Giving primarily in NY.
Officers: Hilda Milton, Pres. and Treas.; Rand Paul Milton, V.P. and Secy.
EIN: 116036417

38582
Lessing Foundation
c/o Helen Lessing
25 E. 86th St., Apt. 11C
New York, NY 10028-0553

Established in 1981 in NY.
Donor(s): F.W. Lessing, Joan Lessing.
Financial data (yr. ended 11/30/01): Grants paid, $11,250; assets, $204,678 (M); gifts received, $1,500; expenditures, $13,729; qualifying distributions, $11,250.

Limitations: Applications not accepted. Giving primarily in New York, NY.
Application information: Contributes only to pre-selected organizations.
Officers: Helen D. Lessing, Pres.; Joan Lessing, V.P.
EIN: 133092013

38583
The Schuur Foundation
163 E. 82nd St.
New York, NY 10028-1856

Established in 1994 in NY.
Donor(s): Robert G. Schuur, Susan E. Schuur.
Financial data (yr. ended 06/30/02): Grants paid, $11,250; assets, $156,692 (M); gifts received, $18,200; expenditures, $11,512; qualifying distributions, $11,250.
Limitations: Applications not accepted.
Application information: Contributes only to pre-selected organizations.
Trustees: Robert G. Schuur, Susan E. Schuur.
EIN: 137050902

38584
Doris and Daniel Solomon Charitable Foundation
c/o Daniel Solomon
795 Wilson St.
Valley Stream, NY 11581-3527

Established in 1999 in NY.
Donor(s): Daniel Solomon, Doris Solomon.
Financial data (yr. ended 11/30/01): Grants paid, $11,246; assets, $75,252 (M); gifts received, $34,720; expenditures, $13,220; qualifying distributions, $11,246.
Directors: Susan Hartman, Daniel Solomon, Doris Solomon, Gary Solomon.
EIN: 113521129

38585
Delta Phi Epsilon/Tillie Oderbolz Trust
c/o JPMorgan Chase Bank
1211 6th Ave., 34th Fl.
New York, NY 10036

Established in 1994 in TX.
Financial data (yr. ended 12/31/01): Grants paid, $11,187; assets, $284,768 (M); expenditures, $17,865; qualifying distributions, $11,187.
Limitations: Applications not accepted. Giving primarily in Austin, TX.
Application information: Contributes only to pre-selected organizations.
Trustee: JPMorgan Chase Bank.
EIN: 746193411

38586
Naphtaly Levy Memorial Foundation
c/o Miriam Levy
461 Ft. Washington Ave.
New York, NY 10033

Donor(s): Miriam Levy.
Financial data (yr. ended 12/31/01): Grants paid, $11,183; assets, $114,072 (M); expenditures, $12,847; qualifying distributions, $11,183.
Limitations: Applications not accepted.
Application information: Contributes only to pre-selected organizations.
Trustees: Monica Deitz, Isaiah Levy, Miriam Levy, Rae Zachal.
EIN: 137102431

38587
Eugene & Janet Dimet Foundation
481 Mountainview Dr.
Lewiston, NY 14092-1938

Donor(s): Eugene Dimet, Janet Dimet.

Financial data (yr. ended 12/31/01): Grants paid, $11,182; assets, $2,229 (M); gifts received, $11,000; expenditures, $11,340; qualifying distributions, $11,182.
Limitations: Applications not accepted. Giving limited to the Buffalo, NY, area.
Application information: Contributes only to pre-selected organizations.
Trustees: Eugene Dimet, Janet Dimet, Jason Dimet, Lauren Dimet.
EIN: 223021283

38588
Rachel & Isaac Bukstein Foundation, Inc.
c/o Lissner & Lissner, LLP
250 W. 57th St., Ste. 615
New York, NY 10107-0699

Established in 1999 in NY.
Donor(s): Gregory Bukstein.
Financial data (yr. ended 12/31/01): Grants paid, $11,178; assets, $5,034 (M); gifts received, $12,500; expenditures, $19,928; qualifying distributions, $11,178.
Limitations: Applications not accepted.
Application information: Contributes only to pre-selected organizations.
Officers: Gregory Z. Bukstein, Pres.; Michael D. Lissner, V.P.; Alexander Kagan, Secy.; Leo Elkin, Treas.
EIN: 137177001

38589
The Gort Foundation, Inc.
c/o Sydney & Ganim
122 E. 42nd St., Ste. 2800
New York, NY 10168

Donor(s): Seymour Gort, Douglas Gort, Dorchester Inc.
Financial data (yr. ended 08/31/02): Grants paid, $11,175; assets, $279,999 (M); expenditures, $16,635; qualifying distributions, $11,175.
Limitations: Applications not accepted. Giving primarily in New York, NY.
Application information: Contributes only to pre-selected organizations.
Officers: Seymour Gort, Pres.; Douglas Gort, V.P.; Cliff Gort, Secy.
Director: Herbert P. Sydney.
EIN: 133317197

38590
The MARMA Foundation
(also known as Mason & Margot Adams Foundation)
c/o Newson & Haberman
225 W. 34th St., Ste. 2007
New York, NY 10122-2090

Established in 1998 in NY.
Donor(s): Mason Adams.
Financial data (yr. ended 12/31/01): Grants paid, $11,150; assets, $226,946 (M); expenditures, $11,280; qualifying distributions, $11,150.
Officer: Mason Adams, Mgr.
EIN: 061519128

38591
LLENROC Foundation
22 Locust Rd.
Brookhaven, NY 11719
Application address: 329 W. 19th St., New York, NY 10011-3901, tel.: (212) 691-4796
Contact: Keith Johnson, Chair.

Established in 1993.
Financial data (yr. ended 12/31/00): Grants paid, $11,140; assets, $298,680 (M); gifts received, $103,560; expenditures, $23,572; qualifying distributions, $11,140.

38591—NEW YORK

Limitations: Giving limited to Tompkins County, NY.
Officer: Keith Johnson, Chair.
Trustees: Michael W. Barry, Ezra Cornell, Craig Fanning, Larry Phillips.
EIN: 133680647

38592
The Stephen Robert Foundation
c/o Robert Capital Mgmt., LLC
610 5th Ave.
New York, NY 10020

Established in 1986 in NY.
Donor(s): Stephen Robert.
Financial data (yr. ended 06/30/01): Grants paid, $11,132; assets, $720,722 (M); gifts received, $463,366; expenditures, $11,182; qualifying distributions, $6,336.
Limitations: Applications not accepted. Giving primarily in NY and RI.
Application information: Contributes only to pre-selected organizations.
Trustee: Stephen Robert.
EIN: 133385607

38593
Lewis and Seymour Roth Foundation
800 Hiawatha Blvd. W.
P.O. Box 1354
Syracuse, NY 13201 (315) 475-8431
Contact: Lewis Roth, Tr.

Financial data (yr. ended 12/31/01): Grants paid, $11,125; assets, $4,788 (M); expenditures, $11,698; qualifying distributions, $11,694.
Limitations: Applications not accepted. Giving primarily in NY.
Application information: Contributes only to pre-selected organizations.
Trustees: Lewis Roth, Seymour Roth.
EIN: 237439362

38594
Elizabeth & Richard S. Fuld Foundation
Clinton Ln.
Harrison, NY 10528

Donor(s): Elizabeth S. Fuld, Richard S. Fuld, Jr.
Financial data (yr. ended 09/30/01): Grants paid, $11,105; assets, $41,144 (M); gifts received, $12,500; expenditures, $12,927; qualifying distributions, $12,927.
Limitations: Applications not accepted. Giving primarily in NY.
Application information: Contributes only to pre-selected organizations.
Officers: Richard S. Fuld, Pres. and Treas.; Richard S. Fuld, Jr., V.P. and Secy.
EIN: 133139002

38595
The Irving Family Foundation
237 Main St., Ste. 1100
Buffalo, NY 14203-2718

Established in 1992 in NY.
Donor(s): John W. Irving.
Financial data (yr. ended 12/31/01): Grants paid, $11,104; assets, $341,469 (M); gifts received, $152,625; expenditures, $14,461; qualifying distributions, $11,104.
Limitations: Giving primarily in Manchester, VT.
Trustees: John W. Irving, Willard B. Saperston, Bruce Warner.
EIN: 161428873

38596
Nakash Family Foundation
c/o Jordache Enterprises, Inc.
1400 Broadway, 14th Fl.
New York, NY 10018
Contact: Joseph Nakash, Pres., Avi Nakash, V.P. or Ralph Nakash, Secy.-Treas.

Established in 1984 in NY.
Donor(s): Jordache Ltd., Jordache Enterprises, Inc.
Financial data (yr. ended 12/31/01): Grants paid, $11,100; assets, $2,123,216 (M); gifts received, $69,765; expenditures, $86,382; qualifying distributions, $60,634; giving activities include $20,300 for programs.
Officers: Joseph Nakash, Pres.; Avi Nakash, V.P.; Ralph Nakash, Secy.-Treas.
EIN: 133030267
Codes: CS

38597
Furman Foundation
c/o Robert M. Furman
1070 Park Ave., Ste. 15C
New York, NY 10128

Established in 1965 in NY.
Donor(s): Robert M. Furman, Ellen P. Furman, Carol Miller Furman.
Financial data (yr. ended 10/31/01): Grants paid, $11,046; assets, $8,143 (M); gifts received, $10,000; expenditures, $11,182; qualifying distributions, $11,046.
Limitations: Applications not accepted. Giving primarily in NY.
Application information: Contributes only to pre-selected organizations.
Trustees: Carol Miller Furman, Matthew S. Furman, Robert M. Furman.
EIN: 136167663

38598
Wolfson Jacobson Raisler Foundation, Inc.
910 5th Ave.
New York, NY 10021-4155
Contact: Steven Jacobson, V.P.

Donor(s): Steven Jacobson, Diane Sokolowski, Dolly Raisler.‡
Financial data (yr. ended 10/31/01): Grants paid, $11,025; assets, $209,080 (M); expenditures, $15,603; qualifying distributions, $11,025.
Limitations: Giving primarily in NY.
Officers: Gordon Jacobson, Pres.; Steven Jacobson, V.P.
EIN: 136183255

38599
Jade Foundation
14 Cabriolet Ln.
Melville, NY 11747 (631) 367-7446
Contact: David Wasserman, Pres.

Established in 1994 in NY.
Donor(s): David Wasserman, Ellen Wasserman, Lawrence Siegel.
Financial data (yr. ended 12/31/00): Grants paid, $11,004; assets, $158,720 (M); gifts received, $8,813; expenditures, $18,069; qualifying distributions, $11,004.
Limitations: Giving primarily in Washington, DC, NY, and PA.
Application information: Application form not required.
Officers and Directors:* David Wasserman,* Pres.; Ellen Wasserman,* Secy.-Treas.; Lawrence Siegel.
EIN: 113237282

38600
Disc Graphics Foundation, Inc.
10 Gilpin Ave.
Hauppauge, NY 11788
Contact: Dr. Ruth Schwartz Cowan

Established in 1999 in NY.
Donor(s): Disc Graphics, Inc.
Financial data (yr. ended 12/31/00): Grants paid, $11,000; assets, $1,041 (M); gifts received, $11,000; expenditures, $11,000; qualifying distributions, $11,000.
Limitations: Giving primarily in NY.
Application information: Application form required.
Officers: Don Sinkin, Pres.; Stephen Frey, V.P. and Secy.; Margaret Krumholz, V.P. and Treas.; Frank A. Bress, V.P.; John Rebecchi, V.P.
EIN: 113509720
Codes: CS

38601
Furth Family Foundation
25 Sutton Pl. S., Apt. 3G
New York, NY 10022-2467

Established in 1986 in NY.
Financial data (yr. ended 11/30/00): Grants paid, $11,000; assets, $1,235 (M); expenditures, $11,129; qualifying distributions, $11,000.
Limitations: Applications not accepted. Giving primarily in New York, NY.
Application information: Contributes only to pre-selected organizations.
Officers: Frank Furth, Admin.; Valerie Furth, Admin.
EIN: 133355695

38602
Dr. Joseph J. Lawrence Trust
c/o JPMorgan Chase Bank
P.O. Box 31412
Rochester, NY 14603-1412

Financial data (yr. ended 12/31/01): Grants paid, $11,000; assets, $281,510 (M); expenditures, $12,398; qualifying distributions, $11,000.
Limitations: Applications not accepted. Giving primarily in Greenwich, CT.
Application information: Contributes only to pre-selected organizations.
Trustee: JPMorgan Chase Bank.
EIN: 956093764

38603
Max J. and Winnie Rosenshein Foundation, Inc.
(Formerly Ruth P. Sachs Memorial Foundation)
450 Park Ave., Ste. 1000
New York, NY 10022 (212) 755-4321
Contact: Robert D. Costello, V.P.

Donor(s): Winnie S. Rosenshein.
Financial data (yr. ended 12/31/01): Grants paid, $11,000; assets, $615,853 (M); gifts received, $550,000; expenditures, $51,922; qualifying distributions, $11,000.
Officers: Winnie S. Rosenshein, Pres.; Robert D. Costello, V.P. and Secy.; Bruce I. Gould, V.P.
EIN: 136260339

38604
Sugahara Foundation
c/o Kamerman
509 Madison Ave., Ste. 1114
New York, NY 10022-5501

Established in 1997 in NY.
Donor(s): Yone Sugahara.
Financial data (yr. ended 12/31/01): Grants paid, $11,000; assets, $182,974 (M); expenditures, $14,314; qualifying distributions, $11,000.

Trustees: Kathryn M. Clough, Abigail L.H. Sugahara, Alexandra N.F. Sugahara, Christopher K.B. Sugahara, Lisabeth A. Sugahara.
EIN: 133966227

38605
Olia & Michael Zetkin Memorial Scholarship
481 Carol Pl.
Pelham, NY 10803-2111   (914) 738-4998
Contact: Arthur Rabin, Pres.

Financial data (yr. ended 05/31/00): Grants paid, $11,000; assets, $217,944 (M); expenditures, $11,324; qualifying distributions, $11,429.
Limitations: Giving limited to residents of NY.
Officers: Arthur Rabin, Pres.; Rita Rabin, Treas.
EIN: 133010508
Codes: GTI

38606
Zichron Shimon Charity Foundation
1865 52nd. St., Ste. 1G
Brooklyn, NY 11204
Contact: Norman Goldner, Pres.

Established in 1998.
Financial data (yr. ended 12/31/01): Grants paid, $11,000; assets, $60,059 (M); gifts received, $36,000; expenditures, $11,025; qualifying distributions, $11,000.
Officer: Norman Goldner, Pres.
EIN: 113419245

38607
The Eastboro Foundation Charitable Trust
c/o Jacob Rosenberg
1140 Ave. of the Americas, 16th Fl.
New York, NY 10036-5803

Donor(s): Jacob Rosenberg, Esther Rosenberg.
Financial data (yr. ended 12/31/00): Grants paid, $10,990; assets, $142,711 (M); gifts received, $55,000; expenditures, $11,136; qualifying distributions, $11,040.
Limitations: Applications not accepted. Giving primarily in NY.
Application information: Contributes only to pre-selected organizations.
Trustees: Esther Rosenberg, Jacob I. Rosenberg.
EIN: 133915453

38608
Starr Hacker Memorial Scholarship Fund
350 Daniel St.
Lindenhurst, NY 11757-3547
Application address: 300 Charles St., Lindenhurst, NY 11757, tel.: (631) 226-7567
Contact: Lee Paseltiner, Tr.

Financial data (yr. ended 11/30/01): Grants paid, $10,990; assets, $256,314 (M); expenditures, $13,208; qualifying distributions, $10,990.
Limitations: Giving limited to Lindenhurst, NY.
Application information: Application form required.
Trustees: Niel Lederer, Lee Paseltiner.
EIN: 112487557
Codes: GTI

38609
Youth Educational Council, Inc.
c/o L. Goldberg & Co.
97-45 Queens Blvd.
Rego Park, NY 11374-2101

Financial data (yr. ended 12/31/00): Grants paid, $10,986; assets, $95,755 (M); expenditures, $11,113; qualifying distributions, $10,986.
Limitations: Applications not accepted.
Application information: Contributes only to pre-selected organizations.

Officers: Leonard Lampert, Pres.; David Rosen, Secy.
EIN: 116046796

38610
The Burton and Sarina Gwirtzman Foundation
P.O. Box 257
Southfields, NY 10975-0257

Established in 1998 in NY.
Donor(s): Burton Gwirtzman.
Financial data (yr. ended 12/31/01): Grants paid, $10,980; assets, $241,909 (M); gifts received, $23,729; expenditures, $12,880; qualifying distributions, $10,980.
Limitations: Applications not accepted.
Application information: Contributes only to pre-selected organizations.
Directors: Burton Gwirtzman, Sarina Gwirtzman.
EIN: 137193628

38611
The WKLW Foundation
c/o Max Wasser
132 Nassau St., Ste. 300
New York, NY 10038

Established in 1986 in NY.
Donor(s): Max Wasser.
Financial data (yr. ended 09/30/01): Grants paid, $10,946; assets, $652 (M); gifts received, $10,800; expenditures, $11,094; qualifying distributions, $10,946.
Limitations: Applications not accepted. Giving primarily in NY.
Application information: Contributes only to pre-selected organizations.
Trustees: Michael Lipstein, Max Wasser.
EIN: 133374593

38612
Blatte Family Foundation
c/o Lawrence A. Blatte
198 Harbor View N.
Lawrence, NY 11559

Donor(s): Lawrence A. Blatte.
Financial data (yr. ended 12/31/00): Grants paid, $10,943; assets, $15,228 (M); expenditures, $11,008; qualifying distributions, $10,943.
Limitations: Applications not accepted.
Application information: Contributes only to pre-selected organizations.
Officers: Lawrence A. Blatte, Pres.; Barbara Blatte, V.P.; Amy Blatte Braunstein, Secy.; David C. Blatte, Treas.
EIN: 113435540

38613
Richard Allan Shankman Memorial Fund, Inc.
3580 Rte. 44
Millbrook, NY 12545
Contact: Leonard Shankman, Pres.

Donor(s): Leonard Shankman.
Financial data (yr. ended 11/30/01): Grants paid, $10,925; assets, $96,570 (M); expenditures, $18,560; qualifying distributions, $10,925.
Limitations: Giving primarily in NY.
Officers: Leonard Shankman, Pres.; Richard Shankman, V.P.; Roseann Shankman, Treas.
EIN: 136093371

38614
Joseph W. Houth Charitable Trust
c/o Deutsche Bank
P.O. Box 1297, Church St. Sta.
New York, NY 10008

Established in 1999 in FL.
Donor(s): Joseph W. Houth.‡

Financial data (yr. ended 07/31/01): Grants paid, $10,911; assets, $642,111 (M); expenditures, $58,063; qualifying distributions, $24,340.
Limitations: Applications not accepted.
Application information: Contributes only to pre-selected organizations.
Trustee: Deutsche Bank.
EIN: 656299087

38615
Nagelberg Family Foundation
139 Harborview S.
Lawrence, NY 11559

Established in 2000 in NY.
Donor(s): Bernard Nagelberg, Janet Nagelberg.
Financial data (yr. ended 02/28/02): Grants paid, $10,841; assets, $99 (M); gifts received, $11,204; expenditures, $11,161; qualifying distributions, $10,841.
Trustee: Janet Nagelberg.
EIN: 061574558

38616
Hyman J. & Florence Hammerman Family Foundation
43 Mill Hill Rd.
P.O. Box 1123
Woodstock, NY 12498
Contact: Stuart A. Hammerman, Tr.

Established in 1993 in NY.
Donor(s): Stuart A. Hammerman.
Financial data (yr. ended 12/31/01): Grants paid, $10,825; assets, $168,595 (M); gifts received, $5,000; expenditures, $13,548; qualifying distributions, $10,825.
Limitations: Giving primarily in NY.
Application information: Application form not required.
Trustees: Elizabeth R. Hammerman, Stuart A. Hammerman.
EIN: 141766382

38617
Frederick B. Kilmer Foundation
46 Woodbury Way
Fairport, NY 14450-2475   (716) 223-7142
Contact: Martha J. Jack, Tr.

Established in 2000 in NY.
Donor(s): John L. Jack, Martha J. Jack.
Financial data (yr. ended 12/31/01): Grants paid, $10,817; assets, $347,604 (M); gifts received, $1,200; expenditures, $15,063; qualifying distributions, $10,817.
Trustees: Jennifer Dund, John L. Jack, Martha J. Jack, Kathleen E. Weintraub.
EIN: 161589634

38618
The Kurzman Fund
c/o The Bank of New York, Tax Dept.
1 Wall St., 28th Fl.
New York, NY 10286
Contact: William Wiseman, V.P., The Bank of New York

Established in 1985 in NY.
Financial data (yr. ended 12/31/00): Grants paid, $10,808; assets, $306,320 (M); expenditures, $12,451; qualifying distributions, $11,059.
Limitations: Giving primarily in NY.
Trustee: The Bank of New York.
EIN: 136078699

38619
Lawton W. Fitt and James I. McLaren Foundation
c/o Goldman Sachs & Co.
85 Broad St., Tax Dept.
New York, NY 10004

Established in 1996 in NY.
Donor(s): Lawton W. Fitt.
Financial data (yr. ended 09/30/01): Grants paid, $10,800; assets, $2,969,935 (M); gifts received, $2,750; expenditures, $66,226; qualifying distributions, $13,965.
Limitations: Applications not accepted. Giving primarily in NY.
Application information: Contributes only to pre-selected organizations.
Trustees: Lawton W. Fitt, James I. McLaren.
EIN: 133919763

38620
The Fletcher Foundation
22 E. 67th St.
New York, NY 10021

Established in 1999 in NY.
Donor(s): Alphonse Fletcher, Jr.
Financial data (yr. ended 12/31/01): Grants paid, $10,800; assets, $352,829 (M); expenditures, $11,200; qualifying distributions, $10,800.
Limitations: Applications not accepted. Giving primarily in CT, MA, and NY.
Application information: Contributes only to pre-selected organizations.
Officer: Alphonse Fletcher, Jr., Pres.
Directors: Bettye Fletcher, Geoffrey S. Fletcher, Todd J. Fletcher.
EIN: 133775587

38621
New York Alpha Tau Omega Students Aid Fund, Inc.
2 Houston Way
Averill Park, NY 12018-2622 (518) 674-5457
Contact: Norman Case, Treas.

Financial data (yr. ended 08/31/01): Grants paid, $10,800; assets, $188,731 (M); expenditures, $11,238; qualifying distributions, $10,800.
Limitations: Giving limited to residents of Syracuse, NY.
Application information: Recipients are nominated by Chapter Scholarship Chair.
Officers: Alan Coates, Pres.; Robert Young, V.P.; Roger Wooster, Secy.; Norman Case, Treas.
EIN: 156018434
Codes: GTI

38622
Clarence Rotary Foundation
P.O. Box 157
Clarence, NY 14031-0157
Contact: Thomas Coseo, Pres.

Financial data (yr. ended 12/31/01): Grants paid, $10,799; assets, $88,728 (M); gifts received, $5,561; expenditures, $11,482; qualifying distributions, $10,799.
Limitations: Giving limited to Clarence, NY.
Application information: Request application form. Application form required.
Officers and Directors:* Thomas Coseo,* Pres.; David Thielman,* Secy.; Stephen D. Carlson,* Treas.; Patrick Casilio, Jr., Robert Friedman, Robert Geiger, Paul Justinger, Frank Lombardo.
EIN: 222974207

38623
Hornblow Foundation
c/o Alvin Goldfine
225 W. 34th St., Ste. 2007
New York, NY 10122-0008
Application address: 875 5th Ave., New York, NY 10022
Contact: Leonora Hornblow, Tr.

Donor(s): Leonora Hornblow.
Financial data (yr. ended 12/31/01): Grants paid, $10,796; assets, $133,650 (M); expenditures, $12,701; qualifying distributions, $10,796.
Limitations: Giving primarily in New York, NY.
Trustees: Alvin Goldfine, Leonora Hornblow, Michael Hornblow.
EIN: 136021426

38624
Benyumen Shekhter Foundation for the Advancement of Standard Yiddish
926 Sunrise Hwy.
West Babylon, NY 11704
Application address: 3328 Bainbridge Ave., Bronx, NY 10467
Contact: Mordkhe Schaechter, Pres.

Financial data (yr. ended 12/31/00): Grants paid, $10,763; assets, $195,823 (M); expenditures, $12,073; qualifying distributions, $10,763.
Limitations: Giving primarily in New York, NY.
Officers: Mordkhe Schaechter, Pres.; Leoyl Kahn, Secy.
EIN: 237060332

38625
The Lee and Yum Foundation
24 Madison Ave.
Endicott, NY 13760

Established in 2000 in NY.
Donor(s): Bai O. Lee, Jung H. Yum.
Financial data (yr. ended 12/31/01): Grants paid, $10,750; assets, $335,448 (M); gifts received, $181,310; expenditures, $13,778; qualifying distributions, $10,750.
Trustees: Bai O. Lee, Jung H. Yum.
EIN: 166503671

38626
Barbara and Ray Ranta Charitable Foundation
150 W. 79th St.
New York, NY 10024

Established in 1996 in NY.
Donor(s): Barbara Ranta, Ray Ranta.
Financial data (yr. ended 12/31/01): Grants paid, $10,700; assets, $59,802 (M); gifts received, $39; expenditures, $11,289; qualifying distributions, $10,700.
Limitations: Applications not accepted. Giving primarily in New York, NY.
Application information: Contributes only to pre-selected organizations.
Directors: Martin Lieberman, Barbara Ranta, Ray Ranta.
EIN: 133923086

38627
Woo's Foundation
79-02 Ankener Ave.
Elmhurst, NY 11373

Established in 1997 in NY.
Donor(s): Cheng-Kee Woo.‡
Financial data (yr. ended 12/31/99): Grants paid, $10,700; assets, $296,835 (M); gifts received, $296,635; expenditures, $12,037; qualifying distributions, $12,037.
Limitations: Applications not accepted. Giving primarily in NY.
Application information: Unsolicited requests for funds not accepted.
Officers: Shian Bian Woo, C.F.O.; Ching Hung Woo, Exec. Dir.
Directors: Xiang Lin Luo, Mee Wah See.
EIN: 111217247

38628
Herman Koenigsberg Memorial Foundation, Inc.
130 William St.
New York, NY 10038

Financial data (yr. ended 03/31/01): Grants paid, $10,685; assets, $98,657 (M); expenditures, $10,974; qualifying distributions, $10,685.
Limitations: Applications not accepted.
Application information: Contributes only to pre-selected organizations.
Officers: Herman M. Koenigsberg, Pres.; Shirley G. Koenigsberg, V.P.; Goldie Badek, Secy.
EIN: 132735119

38629
Harold Schwartz Memorial Child Welfare Fund
c/o Saul Rasnick
133 Brooklawn Dr.
Rochester, NY 14618

Established in 1990 in NY.
Financial data (yr. ended 06/30/02): Grants paid, $10,650; assets, $166,618 (M); gifts received, $155; expenditures, $12,948; qualifying distributions, $10,650.
Limitations: Applications not accepted. Giving primarily in Rochester, NY.
Application information: Contributes only to pre-selected organizations.
Officers: Arthur Cassidy, Pres.; Lloyd Krieger, V.P.; Mort Stein, Secy.; Abe Rudnick, Treas.
EIN: 510243188

38630
Morris B. Rettner Foundation, Inc.
481 Main St.
New Rochelle, NY 10801-6398
(914) 636-7000
Contact: Ronald Rettner, Secy.

Donor(s): Ronald Rettner.
Financial data (yr. ended 12/31/01): Grants paid, $10,600; assets, $131,309 (M); expenditures, $12,056; qualifying distributions, $10,600.
Limitations: Giving primarily in NY.
Application information: Application form not required.
Officers: Marcella Mandelbaum, Pres.; Ronald Rettner, Secy.
EIN: 132843494

38631
Harry & Roberta Salter Foundation, Inc.
322 Central Park W., Ste. 9A
New York, NY 10025-7629

Financial data (yr. ended 12/31/01): Grants paid, $10,585; assets, $312,933 (M); expenditures, $13,600; qualifying distributions, $13,600.
Limitations: Applications not accepted. Giving primarily in NY.
Application information: Contributes only to pre-selected organizations.
Officers: Roberta Salter, Pres.; Victoria Salter, Treas.
EIN: 237441858

38632
Dorothy Dickinson Trust
c/o NBT Bank, N.A.
52 S. Broad St.
Norwich, NY 13815-1646

Donor(s): Dorothy Dickinson.‡

Financial data (yr. ended 10/31/01): Grants paid, $10,584; assets, $203,951 (M); expenditures, $11,937; qualifying distributions, $10,584.
Limitations: Applications not accepted. Giving limited to Bainbridge, NY.
Trustee: NBT Bank, N.A.
EIN: 166130872

38633
Cantor Family Foundation
(Formerly Helaine & Paul Cantor Charitable Foundation)
c/o Cantor Weiss Friedner
880 3rd Ave.
New York, NY 10022 (212) 350-7200

Established in 1996 in NY.
Donor(s): Helaine Cantor, Paul Cantor.
Financial data (yr. ended 12/31/01): Grants paid, $10,580; assets, $18,243 (M); expenditures, $10,580; qualifying distributions, $10,580.
Limitations: Applications not accepted.
Application information: Contributes only to pre-selected organizations.
Trustees: Helaine Cantor, Paul Cantor.
EIN: 133865204

38634
Deo Gratias Foundation
c/o Lisa Horn
P.O. Box 794
Locust Valley, NY 11560

Donor(s): Thomas J. Salvatore.
Financial data (yr. ended 12/31/01): Grants paid, $10,580; assets, $331,129 (M); gifts received, $64,000; expenditures, $10,895; qualifying distributions, $10,895.
Limitations: Applications not accepted.
Application information: Contributes only to pre-selected organizations.
Directors: Lisa Horn, Jeanne Salvatore, Paul Salvatore.
EIN: 113434234

38635
Buffalo Police Foundation, Inc.
74 Franklin St., Ste. 216
Buffalo, NY 14202

Established in 1995 in NY.
Donor(s): Alfiero Family Foundation, KeyBank, N.A., Lippes, Silverstein, Mathis & Wexler.
Financial data (yr. ended 06/30/01): Grants paid, $10,578; assets, $74,699 (M); gifts received, $42,345; expenditures, $13,974; qualifying distributions, $10,578.
Limitations: Applications not accepted.
Application information: Contributes only to pre-selected organizations.
Officers and Director:* Mark Hamister,* Chair.; Patrick Fagan, Vice-Chair.; Michael E. Ferdman, Secy.; Mark Koziel, Treas.
EIN: 161494420

38636
Phyllis & Bennett Cerf Foundation, Inc.
132 E. 62nd St.
New York, NY 10021-8104

Donor(s): Bennett Cerf,‡ Phyllis Cerf Wagner.
Financial data (yr. ended 11/30/01): Grants paid, $10,550; assets, $386,164 (M); expenditures, $12,272; qualifying distributions, $11,505.
Limitations: Applications not accepted. Giving primarily in New York, NY.
Application information: Contributes only to pre-selected organizations.
Officers: Phyllis Cerf Wagner, Pres.; Christopher B. Cerf, V.P.; Jonathan Cerf, V.P.
EIN: 136142796

38637
Danzi Family Foundation, Inc.
45A King Arthurs Ct.
St. James, NY 11780

Established in 1998 in NY.
Donor(s): John A. Danzi.
Financial data (yr. ended 12/31/01): Grants paid, $10,550; assets, $251,985 (M); gifts received, $160,257; expenditures, $10,680; qualifying distributions, $10,680.
Limitations: Applications not accepted.
Application information: Contributes only to pre-selected organizations.
Officer and Director:* John A. Danzi,* Pres.
EIN: 113428923

38638
The David & Shirley Seiler Foundation, Inc.
c/o Munir Saltoun
888 Park Ave., Ste. 9
New York, NY 10021

Donor(s): David Seiler, Shirley Seiler.
Financial data (yr. ended 12/31/01): Grants paid, $10,544; assets, $340,266 (M); expenditures, $11,099; qualifying distributions, $10,544.
Limitations: Applications not accepted. Giving primarily in NY and Providence, RI.
Application information: Contributes only to pre-selected organizations.
Officer: Munir Saltoun, Mgr.
EIN: 581473538

38639
Franklyn Ellenbogen, Jr. Memorial Foundation
c/o Marjorie Ellenbogen
45 Sutton Pl. S., Ste. 14C
New York, NY 10022-3058

Donor(s): Marjorie Ellenbogen.
Financial data (yr. ended 01/31/02): Grants paid, $10,518; assets, $200,516 (M); gifts received, $11,032; expenditures, $10,913; qualifying distributions, $10,518.
Limitations: Applications not accepted. Giving primarily in NY.
Application information: Contributes only to pre-selected organizations.
Officers: Marjorie Ellenbogen, Pres.; Nancy K. Nachman, V.P.; Ralph M. Engel, Secy.
EIN: 136110723

38640
Meisel Foundation, Inc.
7 Cowpath
Glen Head, NY 11545-3113

Established in 1988 in NY.
Donor(s): Ben Meisel.
Financial data (yr. ended 05/31/02): Grants paid, $10,501; assets, $79,115 (M); gifts received, $2,000; expenditures, $11,714; qualifying distributions, $10,501.
Limitations: Applications not accepted. Giving primarily in the New York, NY, area.
Application information: Contributes only to pre-selected organizations.
Officers and Directors:* Sybil R. Meisel,* Pres.; Andrew H. Meisel,* V.P.; Robin H. Meisel,* V.P.; Sheri M. Meisel,* V.P.; Edward L. Meisel,* Treas.
EIN: 112918946

38641
Andretta Foundation
9 Twin Ponds Dr.
Kingston, NY 12402
Contact: Vincent J. Andretta, Jr., Tr.

Financial data (yr. ended 12/31/01): Grants paid, $10,500; assets, $249,490 (M); expenditures, $11,813; qualifying distributions, $10,500.
Limitations: Giving limited to Kingston, NY.
Application information: Application form not required.
Trustee: Vincent J. Andretta, Jr.
EIN: 146048022

38642
The Attai Foundation
55 Field Terrace
Irvington, NY 10533

Established in 1999 in DE.
Donor(s): Lari Attai.
Financial data (yr. ended 12/31/01): Grants paid, $10,500; assets, $214,648 (M); expenditures, $11,785; qualifying distributions, $10,500.
Limitations: Applications not accepted. Giving primarily in NY.
Application information: Contributes only to pre-selected organizations.
Officers: Lari Attai, Pres.; Sheila Attai, V.P.
EIN: 134034791

38643
Camp Cool J Foundation
c/o Virtu Management Group, Ltd.
405 Park Ave.
New York, NY 10022-4405

Established in 1996 in DE and NY.
Donor(s): Polygram Inc.
Financial data (yr. ended 06/30/01): Grants paid, $10,500; assets, $1,753 (M); expenditures, $14,078; qualifying distributions, $13,320.
Limitations: Applications not accepted.
Application information: Contributes only to pre-selected organizations.
Officers: James Todd Smith, Chair.; Cynthia Cooper, Exec. Dir.
EIN: 113365540

38644
Carton Foundation, Inc.
1508 Genesee St., Ste. 1220
Utica, NY 13502
Contact: Bartle Gorman, Tr.

Donor(s): Matthew A. Carton.
Financial data (yr. ended 12/31/01): Grants paid, $10,500; assets, $228,294 (M); expenditures, $11,153; qualifying distributions, $10,500.
Limitations: Giving primarily in Utica, NY.
Trustees: Vincent Corrou, Bartle Gorman.
EIN: 156025480

38645
Margaret A. Jamison Memorial, Inc.
21 Jenkinstown Rd.
New Paltz, NY 12561
Application address: c/o Richard W. Lent, P.O. Box 368, New Paltz, NY 12561, tel.: (845) 255-0900

Financial data (yr. ended 12/31/01): Grants paid, $10,500; assets, $160,493 (M); expenditures, $21,895; qualifying distributions, $10,500.
Limitations: Giving limited to New Paltz and Ulster County, NY.
Officers: Dirk R. DeWitt, Pres. and Treas.; Sally Rhoades, V.P.
Directors: Drew Lent, Howard Major, Mary Jane Ordway.

38645—NEW YORK

EIN: 146024095

38646
Ledes Foundation
16 E. 40th St., Apt. 3F
New York, NY 10016

Established in 1995 in NY.
Donor(s): Sally C. Ledes.
Financial data (yr. ended 12/31/01): Grants paid, $10,500; assets, $634,612 (M); expenditures, $14,641; qualifying distributions, $10,500.
Limitations: Applications not accepted. Giving primarily in NY.
Application information: Contributes only to pre-selected organizations.
Directors: Joseph H. Graces, John C. Ledes, Sally C. Ledes.
EIN: 133800534

38647
The Millennium Foundation Trust
c/o Meltzeer & Lewis
190 Willis Ave.
Mineola, NY 11501-2693

Established in 1995.
Donor(s): Lewis Meltzer.
Financial data (yr. ended 12/31/01): Grants paid, $10,500; assets, $2,739 (M); gifts received, $12,545; expenditures, $10,791; qualifying distributions, $10,500.
Limitations: Applications not accepted. Giving primarily in NY.
Application information: Contributes only to pre-selected organizations.
Trustee: Lewis S. Meltzer.
EIN: 116451183

38648
The Mitchell Family Charitable Trust
211 E. 70th St., Ste. 23G
New York, NY 10021

Established in 1998 in NY.
Donor(s): Michael W. Mitchell.
Financial data (yr. ended 12/31/01): Grants paid, $10,500; assets, $31,315 (M); gifts received, $1,292; expenditures, $11,141; qualifying distributions, $10,500.
Limitations: Applications not accepted.
Application information: Contributes only to pre-selected organizations.
Trustees: Caroline S. Mitchell, Michael W. Mitchell.
EIN: 134031578

38649
J. Malcolm Mossman Charitable Trust
c/o JPMorgan Chase Bank
P.O. Box 31412
Rochester, NY 14603-1412
Application address: c/o JPMorgan Chase Bank, 1 Chase Manhattan Plz., 4th Fl., New York, NY 10081, tel.: (212) 552-2576
Contact: Andrew Noll, Trust Off.

Established in 1971.
Financial data (yr. ended 12/31/01): Grants paid, $10,500; assets, $120,082 (M); expenditures, $12,350; qualifying distributions, $10,767.
Limitations: Giving primarily in the greater metropolitan New York, NY, area.
Application information: Application form not required.
Trustee: JPMorgan Chase Bank.
EIN: 136354042

38650
Margaret & Frank Stinchfield Foundation
c/o Frendel, Brown & Weissman
655 3rd Ave., Rm. 1400
New York, NY 10017

Established in 1960 in NY.
Financial data (yr. ended 12/31/01): Grants paid, $10,500; assets, $862,991 (M); expenditures, $18,567; qualifying distributions, $11,919.
Limitations: Applications not accepted. Giving primarily in New York, NY.
Application information: Contributes only to pre-selected organizations.
Trustees: Jay Goodman, Lee Stinchfield, Joel Weissman.
EIN: 136082200

38651
TAT Foundation
c/o Hirsch Oelbaum Bram
111 Broadway
New York, NY 10006

Established in 1982 in NY.
Financial data (yr. ended 06/30/01): Grants paid, $10,500; assets, $9,242 (M); gifts received, $24,217; expenditures, $10,717; qualifying distributions, $10,500.
Limitations: Giving primarily in NY.
Application information: Unsolicited request for funds not accepted.
Trustees: Josef Jofman, Eliezer Kuperman.
EIN: 133033450

38652
John & Maude Matouk Charitable Foundation
37 W. 26th St.
New York, NY 10010-1006

Financial data (yr. ended 11/30/01): Grants paid, $10,490; assets, $200,130 (M); gifts received, $24,125; expenditures, $10,639; qualifying distributions, $10,490.
Limitations: Applications not accepted.
Application information: Contributes only to a pre-selected organization.
Trustees: George Matouk, Selma Matouk.
EIN: 136170716

38653
The David & Beatrice S. Kugel Foundation, Inc.
c/o Abbott L. Lambert
1025 5th Ave.
New York, NY 10028

Financial data (yr. ended 09/30/01): Grants paid, $10,440; assets, $95,983 (M); expenditures, $11,022; qualifying distributions, $10,440.
Limitations: Applications not accepted. Giving primarily in Westport, CT.
Application information: Contributes only to pre-selected organizations.
Officers: Abbott L. Lambert, Pres.; Barbara K. Herne, Secy.-Treas.
Director: Mary Herne.
EIN: 136167917

38654
Keren Tifereth Yisroel Foundation
45 White St.
New York, NY 10013 (212) 219-3944
Contact: Yehuda Lieb Braun, Tr.

Established in 1999 in NY.
Donor(s): Jeffrey Braun.
Financial data (yr. ended 06/30/00): Grants paid, $10,418; assets, $486 (M); gifts received, $11,000; expenditures, $10,542; qualifying distributions, $10,418.

Trustees: Yehuda Leib Braun, Norman Dick, Rabbi Mendel Silverberg.
EIN: 134073684

38655
Medica Foundation, Inc.
570 Park Ave., Ste. 8-C
New York, NY 10021-7370 (212) 888-7840
Contact: Daniel Macken, Pres.

Established in 1990 in NY.
Donor(s): John Peace, Henry Blackstone, Arnold Jacobs, James E. Robinson Foundation.
Financial data (yr. ended 12/31/99): Grants paid, $10,404; assets, $328,724 (M); gifts received, $25,450; expenditures, $29,952; qualifying distributions, $10,404.
Limitations: Giving primarily in New York, NY.
Officers: Daniel Macken, Pres.; Maritza Macken, Treas.
EIN: 237250067

38656
The Davidson Family Foundation, Inc.
(Formerly A. & D. Davidson Foundation, Inc.)
P.O. Box 696
Oyster Bay, NY 11771
Contact: Deborah Davidson, Pres.

Financial data (yr. ended 12/31/01): Grants paid, $10,400; assets, $150,590 (M); expenditures, $11,891; qualifying distributions, $10,400.
Officers and Directors:* Deborah Davidson,* Pres.; Carol Davidson,* V.P.; Jonathan Davidson,* Secy.; Paul Landsman, Treas.
EIN: 133097034

38657
Danielle Antar Foundation, Inc.
c/o Zell & Ettinger, C.P.A.
3001 Ave. M
Brooklyn, NY 11210

Established in 1996 in NY.
Financial data (yr. ended 12/31/01): Grants paid, $10,300; assets, $1 (M); gifts received, $53,405; expenditures, $54,904; qualifying distributions, $10,300.
Limitations: Giving primarily in NY.
Directors: James Lore, Michael Marino, Mark Styczen.
EIN: 113279421

38658
The Fried Foundation, Inc.
c/o Marks, Paneth & Shron LLP
622 3rd Ave.
New York, NY 10017

Financial data (yr. ended 05/31/01): Grants paid, $10,300; assets, $189,406 (M); expenditures, $12,964; qualifying distributions, $10,300.
Limitations: Applications not accepted. Giving primarily in NY.
Application information: Contributes only to pre-selected organizations.
Officers: Ann Fried, Pres.; Sarah Scott, V.P.; Lovelia Albright, Mgr.
EIN: 136120029

38659
Jack and Inez Lippes Family Foundation
31 Hampton Hill Dr.
Williamsville, NY 14221

Established in 1996.
Donor(s): Jack Lippes, Inez Lippes.
Financial data (yr. ended 12/31/01): Grants paid, $10,295; assets, $154,069 (M); expenditures, $12,470; qualifying distributions, $10,188.
Limitations: Applications not accepted. Giving limited to Buffalo, NY.

Application information: Contributes only to pre-selected organizations.
Trustees: Inez Lippes, Jack Lippes.
EIN: 161532286

38660
Cool Schools Corporation of New York City
88th St. & E. End Ave.
New York, NY 10128
Contact: Karen Kolster, V.P.

Donor(s): Authentic Fitness Corporation, Samuel and Mary Rudin Foundation, Invemed Associates.
Financial data (yr. ended 06/30/01): Grants paid, $10,280; assets, $95,701 (M); expenditures, $14,719; qualifying distributions, $14,575.
Limitations: Giving limited to NY.
Officers: Donna Hanover Giuliani, Pres.; Karen Kolster, V.P.
Directors: M. Silverman, Truda Yewett.
EIN: 133763089

38661
Pearlman Foundation
112 W. 56th St.
New York, NY 10019-3841

Established in 1997 in DE and NY.
Financial data (yr. ended 12/31/01): Grants paid, $10,271; assets, $52,619 (M); expenditures, $12,069; qualifying distributions, $10,271.
Limitations: Applications not accepted.
Application information: Contributes only to pre-selected organizations.
Officers: Leonard D. Pearlman, Pres. and Treas.; Emanuel Pearlman, Secy.
EIN: 133948508

38662
Joseph and Sheila Thal Foundation
c/o Jean-Pierre Delbecq
110 E. 55th St., 11th Fl.
New York, NY 10022
Application address: 1020 Park Ave., Ste. 12D, New York, NY 10028
Contact: Joseph Thal, Tr.

Established in 1999 in NY.
Donor(s): Joseph H. Thal.
Financial data (yr. ended 12/31/01): Grants paid, $10,260; assets, $304,274 (M); gifts received, $137,574; expenditures, $10,310; qualifying distributions, $10,260.
Application information: Application form not required.
Trustees: Jean-Pierre Delbecq, Joseph H. Thal, Sheila Thal.
EIN: 134096667

38663
Avon Community Foundation, Inc.
72 W. Main St.
Avon, NY 14414

Established in 1999 in NY.
Financial data (yr. ended 12/31/01): Grants paid, $10,250; assets, $188,548 (M); gifts received, $6,000; expenditures, $12,456; qualifying distributions, $10,250.
Application information: Application form required.
Officer: William S. Nevin, Pres.
EIN: 161576758

38664
The Goodkind Family Foundation, Inc.
100 Park Ave., 12th Fl.
New York, NY 10017

Financial data (yr. ended 12/31/00): Grants paid, $10,250; assets, $24,596 (M); expenditures, $10,250; qualifying distributions, $10,250.

Officers: Peter L. Goodkind, Pres.; John D. Goodkind, Secy.
Director: Elisa Ann Mandelbaum.
EIN: 133922446

38665
Marilyn & Joseph H. Dukoff Foundation
224 Everit Ave.
Hewlett, NY 11557-2225 (516) 374-4305
Contact: Joseph H. Dukoff, Pres.

Donor(s): Joseph H. Dukoff, Marilyn Dukoff.
Financial data (yr. ended 12/31/01): Grants paid, $10,241; assets, $76,699 (M); gifts received, $9,000; expenditures, $10,605; qualifying distributions, $10,241.
Limitations: Giving primarily in NY.
Officer: Joseph H. Dukoff, Pres. and V.P.
EIN: 237115979

38666
Catskill Revitalization Corporation, Inc. Endowment Fund
c/o National Bank of Stamford
1 Churchill Ave.
Stamford, NY 12167

Established in 1996 in NY.
Financial data (yr. ended 12/31/01): Grants paid, $10,220; assets, $185,042 (M); expenditures, $10,220; qualifying distributions, $10,220.
Limitations: Applications not accepted. Giving primarily in NY.
Application information: Contributes only to pre-selected organizations.
Officers: Robin Turner, Chair.; Victor Mace, Vice-Chair.; Stephen Walker, Secy.
Trustee: National Bank of Stamford.
EIN: 166428524

38667
Albert Nordheimer Trust Fund
350 5th Ave.
New York, NY 10118-0110
Contact: Hubert J. Brandt, Tr.

Financial data (yr. ended 12/31/01): Grants paid, $10,200; assets, $164,781 (M); expenditures, $10,439; qualifying distributions, $10,200.
Limitations: Giving primarily in NY.
Trustee: Hubert J. Brandt.
EIN: 136758013

38668
The Anthony A. Sirna Foundation, Inc.
20 E. 74th St.
New York, NY 10021 (212) 988-9145
Contact: Barbara M. Sirna, Pres.

Established in 1985 in NY.
Financial data (yr. ended 12/31/01): Grants paid, $10,200; assets, $263,652 (M); expenditures, $11,126; qualifying distributions, $10,200.
Officers: Barbara M. Sirna, Pres. and Treas.; Alexander G. Anagnos, V.P.; Anthony A. Sirna IV, Secy.
EIN: 133265429

38669
Morris & Gertrude Furman Foundation
810 7th Ave., 28th Fl.
New York, NY 10019 (212) 265-6600
Contact: Robert Murray, Mgr.

Established in 1992.
Donor(s): Jay Furman.
Financial data (yr. ended 06/30/02): Grants paid, $10,115; assets, $177,073 (M); expenditures, $11,495; qualifying distributions, $10,115.
Limitations: Giving primarily in New York, NY.
Officer: Robert Murray, Mgr.
EIN: 136178557

38670
Janet Traeger Salz Charitable Foundation
700 Park Ave., Apt. 12C
New York, NY 10021
Contact: Janet Salz, Pres.

Donor(s): Janet Salz.
Financial data (yr. ended 06/30/01): Grants paid, $10,108; assets, $270,638 (M); expenditures, $10,368; qualifying distributions, $10,233.
Limitations: Applications not accepted. Giving primarily in New York, NY.
Application information: Contributes only to pre-selected organizations.
Officer: Janet Salz, Pres.
EIN: 136920344

38671
Alan and Patricia B. Davidson Family Foundation
c/o Berlack, et al
120 W. 45th St.
New York, NY 10036

Established in 1999.
Financial data (yr. ended 12/31/01): Grants paid, $10,100; assets, $15,046 (M); gifts received, $16; expenditures, $11,800; qualifying distributions, $10,100.
Limitations: Giving primarily in NY.
Officers: Alan Davidson, Pres. and Treas.; Patricia B. Davidson, V.P. and Secy.
EIN: 134066594

38672
McCann Charitable Foundation, Inc.
c/o James McCann
1600 Stewart Ave.
Westbury, NY 11590

Established in 1997 in NY.
Donor(s): James McCann.
Financial data (yr. ended 12/31/01): Grants paid, $10,100; assets, $451,838 (M); gifts received, $317,500; expenditures, $10,253; qualifying distributions, $10,100.
Limitations: Applications not accepted.
Application information: Contributes only to pre-selected organizations.
Officers and Directors:* John J. Gartland, Jr.,* Pres; Richard V. Corbally,* Secy.; Dennis J. Murray, Michael G. Gartland.
EIN: 113328892

38673
M. Stoklos Educational Foundation
c/0 MBP Associates, Inc.
110 E. 55th St., 11th Fl.
New York, NY 10022-4540

Established in 1998 in NY.
Donor(s): Mary Stoklos.
Financial data (yr. ended 04/30/02): Grants paid, $10,053; assets, $124,442 (M); gifts received, $5,000; expenditures, $10,889; qualifying distributions, $10,053.
Limitations: Applications not accepted. Giving primarily in AZ.
Application information: Contributes only to pre-selected organizations.
Trustees: Jean Pierre Delbecq, Mary Stoklos, Michael R. Stoklos.
EIN: 134010071

38674
John & Mark Boyar Foundation, Inc.
18 Terrace Ct.
Old Westbury, NY 11568

Established in 1997 in NY.
Donor(s): Joan Boyar, Mark Boyar.

38674—NEW YORK

Financial data (yr. ended 11/30/01): Grants paid, $10,050; assets, $147,526 (M); gifts received, $8,364; expenditures, $10,188; qualifying distributions, $10,050.
Limitations: Applications not accepted.
Application information: Contributes only to pre-selected organizations.
Officers and Directors:* Mark A. Boyer,* Pres.; Jonathan Boyar,* V.P.; Lee B. Boyar,* V.P.; Joan L. Boyar,* Secy.-Treas.
EIN: 113410278

38675
Morse & Sadie Gould Foundation
7 Little John Pl.
White Plains, NY 10605-3502

Financial data (yr. ended 12/31/00): Grants paid, $10,040; assets, $176,800 (M); expenditures, $10,082; qualifying distributions, $10,040.
Limitations: Applications not accepted. Giving limited to New York, NY.
Application information: Contributes only to pre-selected organizations.
Trustees: Alan Gould, Kenneth J. Gould, Gary Greenbaum.
EIN: 136128159

38676
H. & R. Langner Foundation
c/o M. Neiman
39 Broadway, Ste. 2510
New York, NY 10006

Financial data (yr. ended 02/28/02): Grants paid, $10,026; assets, $8,213 (M); gifts received, $13,809; expenditures, $10,046; qualifying distributions, $10,026.
Officer: Hershel Langner, Pres.
EIN: 133996646

38677
The Alvarez Educational Foundation, Inc.
c/o Alvarez & Marsal, Inc.
599 Lexington Ave., Ste. 2700
New York, NY 10022-4834
Application address: 626 Floyd St., Englewood Cliffs, NJ 07632, tel.:(212) 759-4433
Contact: Monica Alvarez-Mitchell, Secy.-Treas.

Established in 1996 in NJ.
Donor(s): Abigail C. Alvarez, Antonio C. Alvarez.
Financial data (yr. ended 12/31/01): Grants paid, $10,000; assets, $166,418 (M); expenditures, $10,427; qualifying distributions, $10,000.
Limitations: Giving primarily in the Philippines.
Officers: Antonio C. Alvarez, Pres.; Abigail C. Alvarez, V.P.; Monica Alvarez-Mitchell, Secy.-Treas.
EIN: 223479932

38678
Article 5 DeCoizart Perpetual Charitable Trust
c/o JPMorgan Chase Bank
1211 6th Ave., 34th Fl.
New York, NY 10036
Contact: Philip Dimaulo, V.P., JPMorgan Chase Bank

Established in 1996.
Financial data (yr. ended 11/30/01): Grants paid, $10,000; assets, $454,606 (M); expenditures, $18,448; qualifying distributions, $14,316.
Limitations: Giving primarily in NY.
Application information: Application form not required.
Trustees: Carl S. Forsythe III, JPMorgan Chase Bank.
EIN: 137049947

38679
Atlantis Foods Foundations, Inc.
c/o Fiberwave Technologies, Inc.
125 2nd St.
Brooklyn, NY 11231

Established in 2000 in NY.
Donor(s): John V. Romeo Foundation, Inc.
Financial data (yr. ended 12/31/00): Grants paid, $10,000; assets, $4,888 (M); gifts received, $21,000; expenditures, $16,112; qualifying distributions, $10,000.
Limitations: Applications not accepted. Giving primarily in Millwood, NY.
Application information: Contributes only to pre-selected organizations.
Officer and Director:* John Romeo,* Pres.
EIN: 134124917

38680
Barry Family Foundation
1220 Park Ave.
New York, NY 10128

Established in 1999 in NY.
Donor(s): Thomas C. Barry, Patricia R. Barry.
Financial data (yr. ended 12/31/01): Grants paid, $10,000; assets, $263,424 (M); expenditures, $15,356; qualifying distributions, $10,000.
Limitations: Applications not accepted.
Application information: Contributes only to pre-selected organizations.
Trustees: Patricia R. Barry, Thomas C. Barry.
EIN: 137184282

38681
James A. Beha Foundation, Inc.
c/o Gasser & Hayes
106-19 Metropolitan Ave.
Forest Hills, NY 11375

Donor(s): James J. Beha.
Financial data (yr. ended 12/31/01): Grants paid, $10,000; assets, $112,236 (M); gifts received, $24,148; expenditures, $10,744; qualifying distributions, $10,000.
Limitations: Applications not accepted. Giving primarily in NY.
Application information: Contributes only to pre-selected organizations.
Officers: James J. Beha, Pres.; Macy Ann Beha, V.P.; Ida Brown, Secy.; Robert A. Sarosy, Treas.
EIN: 136059716

38682
George and Patricia Bellesis Foundation
28 Campbell Dr.
Dix Hills, NY 11746

Donor(s): George Bellesis, Patricia Bellesis, Port Plastics.
Financial data (yr. ended 11/30/01): Grants paid, $10,000; assets, $87,492 (M); expenditures, $10,637; qualifying distributions, $9,905.
Limitations: Applications not accepted.
Application information: Contributes only to pre-selected organizations.
Officers: George Bellesis, Pres. and Treas.; Patricia Bellesis, V.P.; Suzanne Kompogiorgas, Secy.
EIN: 112577723

38683
Borrego Foundation, Inc.
2 Beach Ave.
Larchmont, NY 10538-4005

Established in 1997 in DE and NY.
Donor(s): Susan A. Lieber.
Financial data (yr. ended 12/31/00): Grants paid, $10,000; assets, $405,642 (M); gifts received, $175; expenditures, $13,299; qualifying distributions, $8,745.
Limitations: Applications not accepted.
Application information: Contributes only to pre-selected organizations.
Officers: Mary E. Rubin, Pres.; Samuel A. Lieber, V.P. and Secy.-Treas.
EIN: 133980920

38684
Burke Family Foundation
20 Island Dr.
Rye, NY 10580-4306

Established in 1997 in NY.
Donor(s): Daniel Burke.
Financial data (yr. ended 12/31/01): Grants paid, $10,000; assets, $1,165,953 (M); gifts received, $3,883; expenditures, $14,943; qualifying distributions, $10,000.
Limitations: Applications not accepted. Giving primarily in, but not limited to, Portland, ME, New York, NY, and VT.
Application information: Contributes only to pre-selected organizations.
Trustees: Daniel Burke, Harriet Burke.
EIN: 137119979

38685
Belle C. Burnett Foundation
P.O. Box 573
Salem, NY 12865-0573
Application address: c/o Guidance Office, Salem Central School, E. Broadway, Salem, NY 12865, tel.: (518) 854-7855

Financial data (yr. ended 12/31/01): Grants paid, $10,000; assets, $125,226 (M); expenditures, $10,585; qualifying distributions, $10,417.
Limitations: Giving primarily in NY.
Application information: Application form required.
Officer: Katharine L. Tomasi, Secy.-Treas.
Directors: Polly Craig, Jane Hanks, Althea Lewis, Barbara Norman, Nancy Rogers, Nancy White.
EIN: 146018940
Codes: GTI

38686
John Mack & Sharlyn Carter Family Foundation
c/o Braun Business Mgmt.
6 E. 45th St., Ste. 1401
New York, NY 10017-2414

Donor(s): John Mack Carter.
Financial data (yr. ended 12/31/00): Grants paid, $10,000; assets, $191,154 (M); expenditures, $10,050; qualifying distributions, $10,000.
Limitations: Applications not accepted.
Application information: Contributes only to pre-selected organizations.
Officers: John Mack Carter, Pres.; Sharlyn R. Carter, Secy.
Directors: John M. Carter II, Jonna Carter Low.
EIN: 133672416

38687
Castroviejo-Schneider Eye Surgery Foundation, Inc.
1034 5th Ave.
New York, NY 10028 (212) 628-2300
Contact: Howard J. Schneider, M.D., Mgr.

Established in 1990 in NY.
Donor(s): Bernard Marden.
Financial data (yr. ended 12/31/01): Grants paid, $10,000; assets, $20,559 (M); gifts received, $850; expenditures, $13,880; qualifying distributions, $10,000.
Limitations: Giving primarily in New York, NY.

Application information: Application form not required.
Officer and Directors:* Howard J. Schneider, M.D.,* Mgr.; Leona L. Chen, M.D.
EIN: 133541586

38688
The Shirley C. Chu Memorial Fund
12 Laura Ln.
Ithaca, NY 14850-9784

Financial data (yr. ended 12/31/01): Grants paid, $10,000; assets, $790,623 (M); expenditures, $12,864; qualifying distributions, $10,000.
Limitations: Applications not accepted. Giving primarily in Taiwan.
Application information: Contributes only to pre-selected organizations.
Officers: C.C. Chu, Pres. and Treas.; Yuh-Hsu Pan, V.P.
Trustee: Robert Chen.
EIN: 161266518

38689
Bernard and Judy Cornwell Foundation, Inc.
c/o Squadron, Ellenoff, et al.
551 Fifth Ave.
New York, NY 10176

Established in 1999 in MA.
Financial data (yr. ended 12/31/01): Grants paid, $10,000; assets, $33,312 (M); gifts received, $20,000; expenditures, $10,000; qualifying distributions, $10,000.
Limitations: Applications not accepted.
Application information: Contributes only to pre-selected organizations.
Officers: Bernard Wiggins, Pres.; Mark Weinstein, Secy.; Jill Cashdollar, Treas.
EIN: 134033628

38690
William Henry Cosby, Jr. and Camille Olivia Cosby Foundation, Inc.
c/o John R. Schmitt
1133 Ave. of the Americas, Ste. 2200
New York, NY 10036-6710

Established in 1987 in NY.
Donor(s): Camille Olivia Cosby, William Henry Cosby, Jr.
Financial data (yr. ended 06/30/01): Grants paid, $10,000; assets, $6,112 (M); gifts received, $12,310; expenditures, $15,225; qualifying distributions, $15,220.
Limitations: Giving primarily in NY and PA.
Application information: Unsolicited request for funds not accepted.
Officers and Directors:* Camille Olivia Cosby,* Pres. and Treas.; William Henry Cosby, Jr.,* V.P.; John P. Schmitt, Secy.
EIN: 133408842
Codes: GTI

38691
The DeCaro Family Foundation
c/o BCRS Associates, LLC
67 Wall St., 8th Fl.
New York, NY 10004

Established in 1988 in NY.
Donor(s): Angelo DeCaro.
Financial data (yr. ended 03/31/02): Grants paid, $10,000; assets, $311,241 (M); expenditures, $12,250; qualifying distributions, $10,000.
Limitations: Applications not accepted. Giving primarily in CT and NY.
Application information: Contributes only to pre-selected organizations.
Trustees: Angelo DeCaro, Brian DeCaro, Keith DeCaro, Donna Falci.

EIN: 133501180

38692
Ernest Erickson Foundation, Inc.
c/o Jerome Levine
345 Park Ave.
New York, NY 10154-0037 (212) 407-4820

Financial data (yr. ended 12/31/01): Grants paid, $10,000; assets, $389,555 (M); expenditures, $14,937; qualifying distributions, $10,000.
Limitations: Applications not accepted. Giving primarily in New York, NY.
Application information: Contributes only to pre-selected organizations.
Officers: Abraham Guterman, Pres.; Lauries Ruckel, V.P.; Jerome L. Levine, Secy.-Treas.
EIN: 136161599

38693
The Espoir Foundation
P.O. Box 616, Ansonia Sta.
New York, NY 10023-0616 (212) 595-1075

Established in 1983 in NY.
Donor(s): Douglas R. Boyan.‡
Financial data (yr. ended 07/31/00): Grants paid, $10,000; assets, $197,132 (M); expenditures, $10,310; qualifying distributions, $10,000.
Limitations: Giving primarily in New York, NY.
Officers: Michael Sheafe, Pres.; Joe M. Pumphrey, V.P. and Treas.; Herman Phillips, Secy.
EIN: 133213139

38694
Thomas F. & Helen A. Fagan Foundation
c/o John A. Dowd
63 Cherry Ln.
Syosset, NY 11791-1822 (516) 921-1144

Financial data (yr. ended 11/30/01): Grants paid, $10,000; assets, $8,878 (M); gifts received, $10,000; expenditures, $10,010; qualifying distributions, $10,000.
Limitations: Applications not accepted. Giving primarily in NY.
Application information: Contributes only to pre-selected organizations.
Trustees: John T. Fagan, Robert E. Fagan.
EIN: 136212066

38695
The Gloria and Hilliard Farber Foundation
45 Broadway
New York, NY 10006

Established in 2000 in NY.
Donor(s): Gloria Farber, Hilliard Farber.
Financial data (yr. ended 05/31/01): Grants paid, $10,000; assets, $168,332 (M); gifts received, $175,700; expenditures, $10,714; qualifying distributions, $10,700.
Limitations: Applications not accepted. Giving primarily in New York, NY.
Application information: Contributes only to pre-selected organizations.
Directors: Gloria Farber, Hilliard Farber, Jennifer Farber, Melissa Farber.
EIN: 134132864

38696
Fran-Man Foundation, Inc.
156 E. 79th St., Apt. 12A
New York, NY 10021
Application address: 156 E. 69th St., New York, NY 10021, tel.: (212) 570-9836
Contact: Susan L. West, Pres.

Financial data (yr. ended 12/31/01): Grants paid, $10,000; assets, $158,174 (M); expenditures, $12,722; qualifying distributions, $10,000.

Application information: Application form not required.
Officers: Susan L. West, Pres.; Richard A. Lewis, V.P.; Amanda Lewis Morrow, Secy.; Deborah West Madoff, Treas.
EIN: 136149942

38697
Genesis Foundation, Inc.
800 3rd Ave., 33rd Fl.
New York, NY 10022 (212) 872-1647
Contact: Carolina Esquenazi, Pres.

Established in 2000 in FL.
Donor(s): Genesis Offshore, Khronos Capital Research, David Mayer, Gally Mayer.
Financial data (yr. ended 12/31/01): Grants paid, $10,000; assets, $121,693 (M); gifts received, $137,000; expenditures, $15,319; qualifying distributions, $10,000.
Limitations: Giving primarily in the U.S. and Latin America.
Officers: Carolina Esquenazi, Pres.; Herbert Seltzer, Secy.-Treas.
Directors: Becky Mayer, Gally Mayer, Vivian Mayer.
EIN: 912120744

38698
Herman B. Giddings Foundation, Inc.
c/o Lonnie Wollin
350 5th Ave., Ste. 2822
New York, NY 10118

Established in 1995 in DE.
Donor(s): Herman B. Giddings.
Financial data (yr. ended 06/30/01): Grants paid, $10,000; assets, $113,732 (M); gifts received, $5,888; expenditures, $10,915; qualifying distributions, $9,693.
Limitations: Applications not accepted. Giving primarily in Los Angeles, CA, and Nashville, TN.
Application information: Contributes only to pre-selected organizations.
Officers: Herman B. Giddings, Pres.; Lonnie Wollin, Secy.
EIN: 133844650

38699
Conrad H. and Anna Belle Gillen Scholarship Fund
(Formerly Conrad H. and Anna Belle Gillen Trust Fund)
c/o NBT Bank, N.A.
52 S. Broad St.
Norwich, NY 13815

Financial data (yr. ended 12/31/01): Grants paid, $10,000; assets, $309,416 (M); expenditures, $11,914; qualifying distributions, $11,030.
Limitations: Giving limited to residents of Fulton County, NY.
Application information: Application available from the guidance directors at the participating schools: Gloversville High School, Northville Central, Johnstown High School, Mayfield Central, Broadalbin-Perth, and Perth Christian Bible. Application form required.
Trustee: NBT Bank, N.A.
EIN: 146016128
Codes: GTI

38700
The Everett and Pearl Gilmour Foundation, Inc.
c/o NBT Bank, N.A.
52 S. Broad St.
Norwich, NY 13815

Donor(s): Everett A. Gilmour.
Financial data (yr. ended 12/31/01): Grants paid, $10,000; assets, $189,087 (M); gifts received,

$25,000; expenditures, $11,429; qualifying distributions, $10,000.
Limitations: Giving primarily in WY.
Application information: Application form required.
Directors: Everett A. Gilmour, Pearl J. Gilmour, Edward J. Lee.
EIN: 223270902

38701
Samuel H. Golding Foundation, Inc.
c/o Irwin M. Thrope
440 Park Ave. S.
New York, NY 10016

Donor(s): Rachel Golding.
Financial data (yr. ended 12/31/01): Grants paid, $10,000; assets, $215,095 (M); expenditures, $11,438; qualifying distributions, $10,542.
Limitations: Applications not accepted.
Application information: Contributes only to pre-selected organizations.
Officers and Directors:* Bernard H. Greene,* Pres.; Irwin M. Thrope,* V.P.; Bernard Finkelstein,* Secy.; Zeena S. Thrope,* Treas.
EIN: 136067670

38702
Mark & Marcelle Halpern Foundation, Inc.
c/o Moses & Schreiber
3000 Marcus Ave., Ste. 1W5
Lake Success, NY 11042

Financial data (yr. ended 05/31/02): Grants paid, $10,000; assets, $748 (M); gifts received, $8,000; expenditures, $10,770; qualifying distributions, $10,000.
Limitations: Applications not accepted. Giving primarily in New York, NY.
Application information: Contributes only to pre-selected organizations.
Officers: Marcelle P. Halpern, Pres.; Mark Halpern, V.P.; David L. Moses, Secy.
EIN: 237067926

38703
The Nancy and John Hoffmann Foundation
1192 Park Ave.
New York, NY 10128

Established in 1997 in NY.
Donor(s): John Hoffmann.
Financial data (yr. ended 12/31/01): Grants paid, $10,000; assets, $101,621 (M); expenditures, $11,704; qualifying distributions, $10,000.
Limitations: Applications not accepted.
Application information: Contributes only to pre-selected organizations.
Trustees: Catherine Hoffmann, John Hoffmann, Nancy Hoffmann.
EIN: 133947796

38704
The Israeli American Public Education Fund
c/o W.J. Schriber
1585 Broadway, 25th Fl.
New York, NY 10036-8299

Financial data (yr. ended 12/31/01): Grants paid, $10,000; assets, $438,452 (M); expenditures, $13,809; qualifying distributions, $10,000.
Limitations: Applications not accepted. Giving primarily in Jerusalem, Israel.
Application information: Contributes only to pre-selected organizations.
Officer and Directors:* Jay Zises,* Chair.; Selig Zises.
EIN: 133863705

38705
Amelia G. Jachym Scholarship Fund
600 Hotel Jamestown Office Bldg.
Jamestown, NY 14702-3236

Established in 1982 in NY.
Donor(s): John J. Jachym.
Financial data (yr. ended 08/31/01): Grants paid, $10,000; assets, $304,469 (M); gifts received, $15,270; expenditures, $16,231; qualifying distributions, $63,141.
Limitations: Giving limited to residents of NY.
Application information: Contact Pine Valley Central School for application information.
Trustees: Richard L. Earle, Richard L. Girst, Charles T. Hall, Debbie Ormsby, Kathy Stoltenberg, Vincent J. Vecchiarella.
EIN: 112599257
Codes: GTI

38706
Jolika Foundation
c/o John A. Friede
1 Shore Rd.
Rye, NY 10580

Established in 2000 in NY.
Donor(s): John A. Friede.
Financial data (yr. ended 12/31/00): Grants paid, $10,000; assets, $26,541 (M); gifts received, $40,000; expenditures, $13,459; qualifying distributions, $10,000.
Limitations: Giving primarily in New York, NY.
Trustees: John A. Friede, Marcia Friede, Henry Welt.
EIN: 134096979

38707
The William F. Kerby and Robert S. Potter Fund
c/o Peter G. Skinner, Dow Jones & Co.
200 Liberty St.
New York, NY 10281

Established in 1990.
Donor(s): James H. Ottaway, Jr.
Financial data (yr. ended 12/31/01): Grants paid, $10,000; assets, $213,808 (M); expenditures, $12,548; qualifying distributions, $12,382.
Limitations: Giving primarily in Reston, VA.
Application information: Application form not required.
Officers and Directors:* Peter G. Skinner,* Pres. and Treas.; Stuart Karle,* V.P.; Anne K. Hilker,* Secy.; James H. Ottaway, Jr., Isabel R. Potter, Robert D. Sack.
EIN: 223021227
Codes: GTI

38708
Morris & Jeanette Kessel Fund
200 E. 57th St.
New York, NY 10022

Established in 1955.
Financial data (yr. ended 12/31/01): Grants paid, $10,000; assets, $736,948 (M); gifts received, $2,275; expenditures, $13,875; qualifying distributions, $10,000.
Limitations: Applications not accepted. Giving primarily in NY.
Application information: Contributes only to pre-selected organizations.
Officers: Morris C. Kessel, Pres.; Paul Kessel, V.P.
EIN: 136161715

38709
Kiwi Foundation
6 Heather Ridge Rd.
Averill Park, NY 12018

Established in 2000 in NY.

Financial data (yr. ended 12/31/00): Grants paid, $10,000; assets, $1,178,339 (M); expenditures, $10,769; qualifying distributions, $10,000.
Limitations: Giving primarily in Poestenkill, NY.
Directors: Chester Opalka, Karen Opalka.
EIN: 141823331

38710
The Koren Foundation
c/o Bierdman, Greenwald, Kresch, & Gerbasi
888 7th Ave.
New York, NY 10106-0001

Established in 1998 in CT.
Donor(s): John Y. Koren.
Financial data (yr. ended 12/31/01): Grants paid, $10,000; assets, $100,439 (M); expenditures, $11,310; qualifying distributions, $10,000.
Limitations: Applications not accepted.
Application information: Contributes only to pre-selected organizations.
Officers and Directors:* John Y. Koren,* Pres. and Treas.; Kate M. Koren,* V.P.
EIN: 061534165

38711
Paul C. Kovi Foundation
c/o Reminick, Aarons & Co., LLP
685 3rd Ave., 19th Fl.
New York, NY 10017-4037

Donor(s): Paul C. Kovi, Tom Margittai.
Financial data (yr. ended 12/31/00): Grants paid, $10,000; assets, $60,137 (M); expenditures, $10,071; qualifying distributions, $10,000.
Limitations: Applications not accepted. Giving primarily in NY.
Application information: Contributes only to pre-selected organizations.
Officers: Paul C. Kovi, Pres.; Alex Von Bidder, V.P.; Michael Tannenbaum, Secy.
EIN: 133395955

38712
The Lanie and Ethel Foundation
10 E. 40th St., Ste. 3806
New York, NY 10016-0301

Established in 2001 in NY.
Donor(s): James T. Smithgall.
Financial data (yr. ended 12/31/01): Grants paid, $10,000; assets, $41,184 (M); gifts received, $64,824; expenditures, $23,465; qualifying distributions, $16,982.
Limitations: Applications not accepted. Giving primarily in New York, NY.
Application information: Contributes only to pre-selected organizations.
Trustees: Katherine Gill, Alf Hubay, John Roberts, James T. Smithgall, Daniel Tucker.
EIN: 134133103

38713
Mako Foundation, Inc.
c/o Howard Nusbaum
60 Park Terr. W., Ste. 84
New York, NY 10034

Established in 1997 in NJ.
Donor(s): Arthur Nusbaum.
Financial data (yr. ended 12/31/01): Grants paid, $10,000; assets, $222,183 (M); expenditures, $11,202; qualifying distributions, $10,000.
Limitations: Applications not accepted.
Application information: Contributes only to pre-selected organizations.
Officer and Trustees:* Arthur Nusbaum,* Pres.; Howard Nusbaum, Robert Nusbaum, Barbara Selick.
EIN: 223551789

38714
Manowitz and Drillings Family Foundation, Inc.
(Formerly Manowitz Family Foundation, Inc.)
93-19 68th Ave., Apt. 1
Forest Hills, NY 11375

Donor(s): J. William Manowitz, Mrs. J. William Manowitz.
Financial data (yr. ended 12/31/01): Grants paid, $10,000; assets, $585,611 (M); gifts received, $297,478; expenditures, $13,561; qualifying distributions, $10,000.
Limitations: Applications not accepted. Giving primarily in FL and NY.
Application information: Contributes only to pre-selected organizations.
Officers: J. William Manowitz, Pres.; Joanne G. Manowitz, V.P.; Jane W. Manowitz, Secy.; Jane A. Lazarus, Treas.
EIN: 113227265

38715
Margate Foundation
c/o Paneth, Haber & Zimmerman, LLP
600 3rd Ave.
New York, NY 10016

Established in 1981 in DE and NY.
Donor(s): Joy G. Ungerleider-Mayerson,‡ Peter Ungerleider,‡ Steven Ungerleider, Andrew Ungerleider, Jeane Ungerleider-Springer.
Financial data (yr. ended 10/31/00): Grants paid, $10,000; assets, $3,050 (M); expenditures, $14,406; qualifying distributions, $12,303.
Limitations: Applications not accepted. Giving on a national basis.
Application information: Contributes only to pre-selected organizations.
Officers and Directors:* Steven Ungerleider,* Pres.; Andrew Ungerleider,* V.P.; Peter Ungerleider,* V.P.; Jeane Ungerleider-Springer,* V.P.
EIN: 133115331

38716
David Merin Foundation
64-57 Woodhaven Blvd.
Rego Park, NY 11374

Established in 2000 in NY.
Donor(s): David Merin Associates.
Financial data (yr. ended 12/31/00): Grants paid, $10,000; assets, $100,514 (M); gifts received, $134,672; expenditures, $10,100; qualifying distributions, $10,000.
Limitations: Applications not accepted. Giving primarily in New York, NY.
Application information: Contributes only to pre-selected organizations.
Officers: David Merin, Pres.; Ian Fan, V.P.; Alan Rosenberg, Secy.; Jay Waxenberg, Treas.
EIN: 134134807
Codes: CS

38717
The Netanya Foundation, Inc.
c/o Jerome Kowalsky
883 3rd Ave., Ste. 2800
New York, NY 10022

Established in 1990 in NY.
Donor(s): Theodore H. Cutler Family Charitable Trust, Irwin Chafetz Family Charitable Trust, Helen R. Cyker, Monte Goldman, Rita Goldman, Farla H. Krentzman, Viacom International, Inc., Northeast Theater Corp., Foundation for Global Community.
Financial data (yr. ended 12/31/01): Grants paid, $10,000; assets, $62,573 (M); gifts received, $10,080; expenditures, $12,244; qualifying distributions, $10,000.
Limitations: Applications not accepted. Giving primarily in Israel.
Application information: Contributes only to pre-selected organizations.
Officers: Zvi Poley, Chair.; Shalom Kraus, Pres.; Jerome Kowalsky, Secy.
Director: Rabbi Henry D. Michaelman.
EIN: 521594262

38718
The Herbert and Marsha Newman Family Foundation
1 Dag Hammarskjold Plz., 42nd Fl.
New York, NY 10017-2286

Established in 1986 in NY.
Donor(s): Herbert Newman,‡ Marsha L. Newman.
Financial data (yr. ended 12/31/01): Grants paid, $10,000; assets, $46,037 (M); expenditures, $10,130; qualifying distributions, $10,000.
Limitations: Applications not accepted. Giving primarily in Westchester County, NY.
Application information: Contributes only to pre-selected organizations.
Trustee: Marsha L. Newman.
EIN: 136879726

38719
Maria E. Orr Foundation for Charitable Purposes, Inc.
7219 3rd Ave.
Brooklyn, NY 11209 (718) 238-3360
Contact: Harry G. English, Chair.

Established in 2000 in GA.
Financial data (yr. ended 12/31/01): Grants paid, $10,000; assets, $118,643 (M); expenditures, $12,978; qualifying distributions, $10,000.
Officers and Trustees:* Harry G. English,* Chair.; Erica R. Brand,* Secy.; Eileen E. English,* Treas.
EIN: 582459022

38720
Overlook Foundation
c/o Goldman Sachs & Co.
85 Broad St., Tax Dept.
New York, NY 10004

Established in 1995 in NY.
Donor(s): Walter H. Haydock.
Financial data (yr. ended 08/31/01): Grants paid, $10,000; assets, $176,561 (M); gifts received, $2,750; expenditures, $13,146; qualifying distributions, $10,000.
Limitations: Applications not accepted.
Application information: Contributes only to pre-selected organizations.
Trustees: Walter H. Haydock, Alicia H. Mummell, Julia H. Walsh.
EIN: 133801607

38721
The Park Ridge Organization Scholarship Fund, Inc.
5018 Express Dr. S., Ste. 200
Ronkonkoma, NY 11779
Application address: c/o David Woods, Park Ridge Scholarship Fund Comm., P.O. Box 53, Stony Brook, NY 11790, tel.: (631) 751-6460

Established in 1993 in NY.
Financial data (yr. ended 12/31/01): Grants paid, $10,000; assets, $55,072 (M); expenditures, $10,000; qualifying distributions, $9,952.
Limitations: Giving limited to residents of NY.
Application information: Application form required.
Officers and Directors:* Charles B. Mancini,* Pres.; Julius Vizzi,* V.P.; Octavius Vizzi,* V.P.; Stanley Mishkin,* Secy.-Treas.
EIN: 113161541
Codes: GTI

38722
Samuel P. Pejo, M.D. Private Foundation
P.O. Box 247
Vestal, NY 13850

Financial data (yr. ended 12/31/00): Grants paid, $10,000; assets, $0 (M); expenditures, $10,060; qualifying distributions, $10,000.
Director: Thomas J. Murphy.
EIN: 166496867

38723
The Marion D. and Jane E. Piper Charitable Foundation
c/o M&T Bank
P.O. Box 22900
Rochester, NY 14692

Financial data (yr. ended 06/30/02): Grants paid, $10,000; assets, $194,035 (M); expenditures, $12,924; qualifying distributions, $10,000.
Limitations: Applications not accepted. Giving primarily in Rochester, NY, and Memphis, TN.
Application information: Contributes only to pre-selected organizations.
Trustee: M & T Bank.
EIN: 222641092

38724
Louis Posner Family Foundation
19 Brookfield Rd.
New Hyde Park, NY 11040 (516) 437-0383
Contact: Marcia Posner, Dir.

Established in 1998 in NY.
Donor(s): Marcia Posner.
Financial data (yr. ended 12/31/01): Grants paid, $10,000; assets, $12,484 (M); gifts received, $1,206; expenditures, $10,000; qualifying distributions, $10,000.
Limitations: Giving primarily in NY.
Director: Marcia Posner.
EIN: 113411218

38725
The Ranger Family Charitable Trust
c/o CSAM
466 Lexington Ave., 17th Fl.
New York, NY 10017

Established in 1999 in NJ.
Financial data (yr. ended 12/31/01): Grants paid, $10,000; assets, $980,283 (M); gifts received, $391,987; expenditures, $13,521; qualifying distributions, $10,000.
Limitations: Applications not accepted.
Application information: Contributes only to pre-selected organizations.
Distribution Committee Members: Michael W. Ranger, Virginia Ray Ranger.
Trustee: Winthrop Trust Co.
EIN: 137213551

38726
The Roger Rechler Foundation, Inc.
c/o Roger Rechler
225 Broadhollow Rd., CS 5341
Melville, NY 11747

Established in 1998 in NY.
Donor(s): Roger Rechler.
Financial data (yr. ended 12/31/01): Grants paid, $10,000; assets, $156,830 (M); gifts received, $19,059; expenditures, $16,460; qualifying distributions, $10,000.
Directors: Gregg Rechler, Roger Rechler, Scott Rechler, Todd Rechler.
EIN: 113442610

38727
The William Ellis Robinson Foundation
255 W. 88th St., Ste. 13A
New York, NY 10024

Established in 1998 in NY.
Donor(s): Mrs. Stancie Robinson.
Financial data (yr. ended 12/31/01): Grants paid, $10,000; assets, $35,831 (M); gifts received, $10,512; expenditures, $12,580; qualifying distributions, $10,000.
Limitations: Applications not accepted.
Application information: Contributes only to pre-selected organizations.
Officers and Directors:* M. David Sherrill,* Pres. and Treas.; Stancie Robinson,* Secy.; Lucien S.Y. Guthrie.
EIN: 311607491

38728
The Rita G. Rudel Foundation
81 Cross Ridge Rd.
Chappaqua, NY 10514 (914) 238-6428
Application address: International Neuropsychological Society, 700 Ackerman Rd., Ste. 550, Columbus, OH 43202

Established in 1985 in NY.
Donor(s): Julius Rudel.
Financial data (yr. ended 12/31/99): Grants paid, $10,000; assets, $1,852 (M); gifts received, $1,500; expenditures, $11,771; qualifying distributions, $10,000.
Publications: Application guidelines.
Application information: Applicants must hold a Ph.D. or M.D. degree and should be in post-doctoral or at mid-career at the time of application. Awards not granted to persons holding tenure.
Trustees: Martha Bridge Denckla, M.D., Darryl DeVivo, M.D., Rita Haggerty, Bettyann Kevles, Ph.D., Lewis P. Rowland, M.D., Rose Lynn Sherr, Ph.D., Paula Tallal, Ph.D., Ralph Wharton, M.D.
EIN: 133262903

38729
Albert & Hanna Rosa Schweid Foundation, Inc.
1440 55th St.
Brooklyn, NY 11219
Contact: Chaim Schweid, Pres.

Financial data (yr. ended 12/31/01): Grants paid, $10,000; assets, $85,025 (M); gifts received, $50,000; expenditures, $10,050; qualifying distributions, $10,000.
Officers and Trustee:* Chaim Schweid,* Pres.; Mache Dov Schweid, Treas.
Directors: Joseph Z. Schweid, Meir I. Schweid.
EIN: 113448055

38730
Louis Schweitzer Charitable Trust
c/o Hecht & Co., PC
111 W. 40th St.
New York, NY 10018

Trust established in 1972 in NY.
Donor(s): Louis Schweitzer.‡
Financial data (yr. ended 04/30/02): Grants paid, $10,000; assets, $701,290 (M); expenditures, $15,136; qualifying distributions, $10,000.
Limitations: Applications not accepted. Giving primarily in New York, NY.
Application information: Contributes only to pre-selected organizations.
Trustees: James J. Ross, M. Peter Schweitzer.
EIN: 136517711

38731
Joseph & Rena Sellin Charitable Trust
c/o Arnold J. Hodes
2030 Eric Blvd. E.
Syracuse, NY 13224

Established in 2001 in NY.
Financial data (yr. ended 12/31/01): Grants paid, $10,000; assets, $90,824 (M); gifts received, $100,000; expenditures, $10,500; qualifying distributions, $9,988.
Limitations: Applications not accepted.
Application information: Contributes only to pre-selected organizations.
Trustee: Arnold J. Hodes.
EIN: 166514682

38732
The Serio Foundation
c/o Dominic Serio
54-22 65th Pl.
Maspeth, NY 11378

Established in 2000 in NY.
Donor(s): Dominic Serio.
Financial data (yr. ended 12/31/01): Grants paid, $10,000; assets, $173,639 (M); expenditures, $13,171; qualifying distributions, $10,000.
Limitations: Applications not accepted.
Application information: Contributes only to pre-selected organizations.
Trustees: Dominic Serio, Lorraine Serio.
EIN: 137252339

38733
Shapiro-Silverberg Foundation
c/o Yohalem, Gillman & Co.
477 Madison Ave.
New York, NY 10022

Established in 2000 in NY.
Donor(s): John M. Shapiro.
Financial data (yr. ended 12/31/01): Grants paid, $10,000; assets, $3,748,771 (M); gifts received, $806,511; expenditures, $67,753; qualifying distributions, $3,966.
Limitations: Applications not accepted.
Application information: Contributes only to pre-selected organizations.
Officers: John M. Shapiro, Pres.; Shonni J. Silverberg, V.P.
EIN: 134151366

38734
Anatol Shulkin Memorial Scholarship
c/o Arthur Rabin
481 Carol Pl.
Pelham, NY 10803-2111 (914) 738-4998

Financial data (yr. ended 05/31/02): Grants paid, $10,000; assets, $229,931 (M); expenditures, $10,286; qualifying distributions, $10,186.
Limitations: Giving primarily in New York, NY.
Officers: Arthur Rabin, Pres.; Rita Rabin, Treas.
EIN: 133010477

38735
The Estelle Silverstone Foundation for Jewish Spiritual Revival, Inc.
2 Century Trail
Harrison, NY 10528-1702

Financial data (yr. ended 12/31/01): Grants paid, $10,000; assets, $166,409 (M); gifts received, $674; expenditures, $20,836; qualifying distributions, $10,000.
Limitations: Applications not accepted. Giving primarily in NY.
Application information: Contributes only to pre-selected organizations.
Officers and Directors:* Alfredo F. Borodowski,* Pres.; Isaac Jeret,* Secy.; Shira Leibowitz,* Treas.
EIN: 134134982

38736
The Sokol Family Foundation
60 Oak Dr.
Syosset, NY 11791

Established in 1994 in NY.
Donor(s): Aaron Sokol.
Financial data (yr. ended 06/30/01): Grants paid, $10,000; assets, $91,493 (M); expenditures, $35,947; qualifying distributions, $9,943.
Limitations: Applications not accepted.
Application information: Contributes only to pre-selected organizations.
Directors: Michelle Bratsafolis, Sharon Feldstein.
EIN: 113182086

38737
Mike & Stella B. Spanakos Scholarship Fund, Ltd.
7207 Ft. Hamilton Pkwy.
Brooklyn, NY 11228
Application address: 50 Livingston St., Brooklyn, NY 11201
Contact: George M. Spanakos, Pres.

Established in 1990 in NY.
Donor(s): William M. Spanakos.
Financial data (yr. ended 11/30/00): Grants paid, $10,000; assets, $29,307 (M); gifts received, $25,000; expenditures, $11,510; qualifying distributions, $11,504.
Application information: Application form required.
Officers: George M. Spanakos, Pres.; Stella L. Spanakos, V.P.; William M. Spanakos, Secy.-Treas.
EIN: 113027031

38738
Bernard & Marion Stein Foundation, Inc.
c/o Freedman & Co.
61 Broadway, Ste. 1405
New York, NY 10006

Established in 1959.
Donor(s): Bernard Stein, Marion Stein.
Financial data (yr. ended 09/30/01): Grants paid, $10,000; assets, $205,255 (M); gifts received, $125; expenditures, $11,950; qualifying distributions, $10,000.
Limitations: Applications not accepted. Giving primarily in NY.
Application information: Contributes only to pre-selected organizations.
Officers: Bernard Stein, Pres.; Marion Stein, V.P.
Directors: Ellen Lazarus, Robert Stein.
EIN: 136062837

38739
William & Dorothea Titus Foundation, Inc.
c/o Lipsky, Goodkin & Co.
120 W. 45th St., 7th Fl.
New York, NY 10036

Financial data (yr. ended 05/31/01): Grants paid, $10,000; assets, $322,724 (M); expenditures, $11,425; qualifying distributions, $10,000.
Limitations: Applications not accepted. Giving primarily in NY.
Application information: Contributes only to pre-selected organizations.
Officers: Susan T. Goldstone, Pres.; Arthur H. Goldstone, V.P. and Secy.; Philip P. Goodkin, Treas.
EIN: 136028780

38740
George W. Tower Foundation
130 E. Main St.
Waterville, NY 13480-1108
Application address: P.O. Box 26, Waterville, NY 13480, tel.: (315) 841-8021
Contact: Richard S. Woodman, Treas.

Financial data (yr. ended 12/31/01): Grants paid, $10,000; assets, $212,200 (M); expenditures, $10,548; qualifying distributions, $10,000.
Limitations: Giving limited to the Waterville, NY, area.
Officers: Gail H. Gale, Pres.; Richard S. Woodman, Treas.
EIN: 150543664

38741
Anthony Tudor Trust
P.O. Box 783
Ocean Beach, NY 11770-0783

Financial data (yr. ended 12/31/01): Grants paid, $10,000; assets, $57,480 (M); expenditures, $39,383; qualifying distributions, $10,000.
Limitations: Applications not accepted. Giving primarily in NY.
Application information: Contributes only to pre-selected organizations.
Trustee: Sally Brayley Bliss.
EIN: 136905798

38742
Jacob M. Wallerstein Foundation, Inc.
720 Gramatan Ave.
Mount Vernon, NY 10550

Established in 1950 in NY.
Financial data (yr. ended 12/31/01): Grants paid, $10,000; assets, $179,316 (M); expenditures, $10,788; qualifying distributions, $10,000.
Limitations: Applications not accepted. Giving primarily in NY.
Application information: Contributes only to pre-selected organizations.
Trustees: Jordan Sedler, Sally Sedler, Gussie Wallerstein.
EIN: 136059795

38743
The Welwart Family Charitable Foundation
377 Broadway, 9th Fl.
New York, NY 10013

Established in 1999 in NY.
Donor(s): William Welwart, Judy Welwart.
Financial data (yr. ended 12/31/99): Grants paid, $10,000; assets, $49 (M); gifts received, $10,000; expenditures, $10,000; qualifying distributions, $10,000.
Limitations: Applications not accepted. Giving primarily in Brooklyn, NY.
Application information: Contributes only to pre-selected organizations.
Trustees: Judy Welwart, William Welwart.
EIN: 137205902

38744
The Wisnefski Foundation, Inc.
594 Jewett Ave.
Staten Island, NY 10314

Established in 1999 in NY.
Financial data (yr. ended 12/31/01): Grants paid, $10,000; assets, $145,699 (M); gifts received, $51,712; expenditures, $10,940; qualifying distributions, $10,000.
Limitations: Applications not accepted. Giving primarily in NY.
Application information: Contributes only to pre-selected organizations.

Officers and Directors:* Patricia Cirbus,* Pres. and Treas.; Joanne W. Durkin,* V.P. and Secy.
EIN: 134040944

38745
The Wolstencroft Family Foundation
c/o Goldman Sachs & Co.
85 Broad St., Tax Dept.
New York, NY 10004

Established in 1997 in IL.
Donor(s): Tracy Wolstencroft.
Financial data (yr. ended 10/31/01): Grants paid, $10,000; assets, $251,294 (M); gifts received, $3,500; expenditures, $16,585; qualifying distributions, $10,000.
Limitations: Applications not accepted.
Application information: Contributes only to pre-selected organizations.
Trustees: Catherine Wolstencroft, Tracy Wolstencroft.
EIN: 133976344

38746
The Edward and Karen Wydra Charitable Foundation Trust
c/o Edward Wydra
82 Arleigh Rd.
Great Neck, NY 11021

Established in 2001.
Donor(s): Edward Wydra, Karen Wydra.
Financial data (yr. ended 12/31/01): Grants paid, $10,000; assets, $90,000 (M); gifts received, $100,000; expenditures, $10,000; qualifying distributions, $10,000.
Limitations: Giving primarily in Brooklyn, NY.
Application information: Unsolicited request for funds not accepted.
Trustees: Edward Wydra, Karen Wydra.
EIN: 116565553

38747
The Martin and Zipporah Wydra Charitable Foundatuib Trust
c/o Martin Wydra
8313 Bay Pkwy., LL
Brooklyn, NY 11214

Established in 2001 in NY.
Donor(s): Martin Wydra.
Financial data (yr. ended 12/31/01): Grants paid, $10,000; assets, $90,000 (M); gifts received, $100,000; expenditures, $10,000; qualifying distributions, $10,000.
Limitations: Giving primarily in Brooklyn, NY.
Application information: Unsolicited request for funds not accepted.
Trustees: Martin Wydra, Zipporah Wydra.
EIN: 116565552

38748
The Ellen Yerman Charitable Foundation, Inc.
1015 Cherokee Rd.
Scotia, NY 12302 (518) 399-7521
Contact: Alexander J. Yerman, Pres.

Established in 1997 in NY.
Donor(s): Alexander J. Yerman.
Financial data (yr. ended 03/31/02): Grants paid, $10,000; assets, $150,192 (M); gifts received, $2,000; expenditures, $10,640; qualifying distributions, $10,000.
Officers: Alexander J. Yerman, Pres. and Treas.; Teresa Yerman, Secy.
Directors: E. Francis Cullen, Sharlayna Yerman.
EIN: 161527697

38749
Z.B.F. Foundation, Inc.
4600 14th Ave., Ste. 3E
Brooklyn, NY 11219-2605

Established in 1999 in NY.
Donor(s): Zev Fishman.
Financial data (yr. ended 06/30/01): Grants paid, $10,000; assets, $27,448 (M); gifts received, $22,700; expenditures, $13,007; qualifying distributions, $10,000.
Limitations: Giving primarily in Brooklyn, NY.
Officer: Zev Fishman, Mgr.
EIN: 311676062

38750
Isaac Ziering Foundation, Inc.
c/o Herman Ziering
103 Wilmot Rd.
New Rochelle, NY 10804

Established in 1988 in NY.
Donor(s): Herman Ziering, Mark Ziering, Miriam Ziering.
Financial data (yr. ended 12/31/01): Grants paid, $10,000; assets, $652,520 (M); gifts received, $550,950; expenditures, $32,746; qualifying distributions, $10,000.
Limitations: Applications not accepted. Giving primarily in New York, NY.
Application information: Contributes only to pre-selected organizations.
Officer: Herman Ziering, Mgr.
EIN: 133429634

38751
Eisenberg Family Foundation, Inc.
1483 60th St.
Brooklyn, NY 11219

Established in 2000 in NY.
Donor(s): Solomon Eisenberg, Joseph H. & Miriam F. Wells Foundation, Inc.
Financial data (yr. ended 12/31/00): Grants paid, $9,960; assets, $382,617 (M); gifts received, $477,502; expenditures, $9,960; qualifying distributions, $9,960.
Limitations: Applications not accepted.
Application information: Contributes only to pre-selected organizations.
Directors: Edward H. Birnbaum, Miriam Eisenberg, Solomon Eisenberg.
EIN: 113543069

38752
Farber Family Foundation
144-39 70th Ave.
Flushing, NY 11367
Contact: Nathan G. Farber, Tr.

Established in 1996 in NY.
Donor(s): Nathan G. Farber.
Financial data (yr. ended 06/30/01): Grants paid, $9,960; assets, $17,363 (M); gifts received, $11,416; expenditures, $10,110; qualifying distributions, $10,019.
Trustees: Nathan G. Farber, Sharon A. Seligman.
EIN: 113353198

38753
The Saint Anargyrios Foundation, Inc.
21-63 37th St.
Astoria, NY 11105

Established in 2000 in NY.
Financial data (yr. ended 12/31/00): Grants paid, $9,950; assets, $25,811 (M); gifts received, $39,368; expenditures, $10,950; qualifying distributions, $0.
Limitations: Giving primarily for the benefit of Greece.

38753—NEW YORK

Officers: Demetrios S. Katos, Pres.; E.B. Karydas, V.P.; Kalliope Koutsoubis, Secy.; Despina Mantikas, Treas.
EIN: 113554156

38754
Minkowitz Charitable Foundation
c/o Lionel Lewis
1075 Central Park Ave.
Scarsdale, NY 10583

Financial data (yr. ended 12/31/01): Grants paid, $9,944; assets, $58,129 (M); gifts received, $15,000; expenditures, $15,974; qualifying distributions, $9,944.
Officer: Martin Minkowitz, Pres.
EIN: 223325869

38755
Leo Billet Family Foundation, Inc.
10 E. 40th St.
New York, NY 10016-0200 (212) 532-7580
Contact: Leo Billet, Tr.

Donor(s): Leo Billet.
Financial data (yr. ended 12/31/00): Grants paid, $9,940; assets, $16,942 (M); gifts received, $5,000; expenditures, $10,040; qualifying distributions, $9,940.
Limitations: Giving primarily in NY.
Trustee: Leo Billet.
EIN: 237010244

38756
Benjamin Lehr Foundation, Inc.
c/o Robert M. Lehr
500 5th Ave., Ste. 3120
New York, NY 10010

Donor(s): Werner J. Kaplan, Robert M. Lehr.
Financial data (yr. ended 12/31/01): Grants paid, $9,930; assets, $25,707 (M); gifts received, $15,000; expenditures, $10,489; qualifying distributions, $9,930.
Limitations: Applications not accepted. Giving primarily in NY.
Application information: Contributes only to pre-selected organizations.
Officers: Robert M. Lehr, Pres.; Werner J. Kaplan, Treas.
Director: Gilda Kaplan.
EIN: 136151178

38757
The ENS Foundation, Inc.
c/o Sandy Levine
338 Travis Ave.
Staten Island, NY 10314-6129

Established in 1985 in NY.
Financial data (yr. ended 06/30/01): Grants paid, $9,908; assets, $10,650 (M); gifts received, $10,979; expenditures, $16,325; qualifying distributions, $9,908.
Limitations: Applications not accepted.
Application information: Contributes only to pre-selected organizations.
Officers: Sandy Levine, Pres.; Ken Henry, V.P.; Jerry Chosak, Corresponding Secy.; Milton Hymowitz, Recording Secy.; Jay Unger, Treas.
Directors: Bruce Balsam, Mike Chosak, Bill Danenberg, Al Nadler, Richie Shenton, Charles Wantman.
EIN: 112818706

38758
The McGinley Family Charitable Trust
c/o McGrath, Doyle & Phair
150 Broadway, Ste. 1703
New York, NY 10038

Established in 1997 in NJ.

Donor(s): Gerald H. McGinley.
Financial data (yr. ended 04/30/02): Grants paid, $9,905; assets, $57,607 (M); expenditures, $9,964; qualifying distributions, $9,905.
Limitations: Applications not accepted.
Application information: Contributes only to pre-selected organizations.
Trustees: Gerald H. McGinley, Mary P. McGinley.
EIN: 137111084

38759
Doris and Abraham Getzler Family Foundation, Inc.
12 W. 96th St.
New York, NY 10025 (212) 697-2400
Contact: Abraham E. Getzler, Pres.

Established in 1997 in NY.
Financial data (yr. ended 12/31/01): Grants paid, $9,820; assets, $228,037 (M); gifts received, $110,500; expenditures, $10,258; qualifying distributions, $9,820.
Limitations: Giving primarily in the New York, NY, area.
Officers: Abraham E. Getzler, Pres.; Joel Getzler, V.P.; Marion Kramer, V.P.; Renee Septimus, V.P.; Doris Getzler, Secy.
EIN: 133861344

38760
Gertrude Hale Memorial Scholarship Fund
c/o NBT Bank, N.A.
52 S. Broad St.
Norwich, NY 13815 (607) 337-6193

Established in 1988 in NY.
Financial data (yr. ended 12/31/01): Grants paid, $9,810; assets, $199,723 (M); expenditures, $11,051; qualifying distributions, $9,810.
Limitations: Giving limited to the Gloversville, NY, area.
Application information: Application form required.
Trustee: NBT Bank, N.A.
EIN: 146138824

38761
Anabelle Stack Brown Charitable Trust
178 Delaware Ave.
Freeport, NY 11520 (516) 623-3302
Contact: Leonard A. Goldman, Tr.

Established in 1998 in NY.
Financial data (yr. ended 12/31/01): Grants paid, $9,800; assets, $81,806 (M); expenditures, $10,944; qualifying distributions, $9,800.
Limitations: Giving primarily in CA and IA.
Trustee: Leonard A. Goldman.
EIN: 116499463

38762
The Mark B. Isaacs Foundation, Inc.
c/o David Isaacs
25 Chapel Pl., Ste. 2-C
Great Neck, NY 11021

Financial data (yr. ended 04/30/02): Grants paid, $9,797; assets, $130,798 (M); expenditures, $23,127; qualifying distributions, $9,797.
Limitations: Applications not accepted. Giving primarily in NY.
Application information: Contributes only to pre-selected organizations.
Officer: David Isaacs, Exec. Dir.
Directors: Marion Barber, Renee Schutzer.
EIN: 136159809

38763
The Adam Paul Spizz Memorial Foundation
c/o Alex and Marika Spizz
2558 Glenn Dr.
Bellmore, NY 11710

Established in 2000 in NY.
Donor(s): Alex Spizz, Marika Spizz.
Financial data (yr. ended 12/31/01): Grants paid, $9,760; assets, $65,624 (M); gifts received, $225; expenditures, $10,115; qualifying distributions, $9,760.
Limitations: Applications not accepted. Giving primarily in NY.
Application information: Contributes only to pre-selected organizations.
Trustees: Alex Spizz, Marika Spizz.
EIN: 113540986

38764
Weinman Family Foundation, Inc.
c/o NBT Bank, N.A.
52 S. Broad St.
Norwich, NY 13815-1646
Additional application address: 183 N. Broad St., Norwich, NY 13815
Contact: Jacob K. Weinman, Pres.

Donor(s): Jacob K. Weinman.
Financial data (yr. ended 12/31/01): Grants paid, $9,750; assets, $169,773 (M); expenditures, $10,870; qualifying distributions, $9,750.
Limitations: Giving primarily in Norwich, NY.
Officer: Jacob K. Weinman, Pres.
Trustee: Paul Karan.
EIN: 136183070

38765
Peter N. Whitcher Trust
c/o Richard S. Scolaro
90 Presidential Plz.
Syracuse, NY 13202
Application address: P.O. Box 259, Skaneateles, NY
Contact: Daniel C. Labelle, Exec. Dir.

Donor(s): Peter N. Whitcher.‡
Financial data (yr. ended 05/31/01): Grants paid, $9,750; assets, $276,976 (M); expenditures, $33,360; qualifying distributions, $29,923.
Limitations: Giving limited to western NY and vicinity.
Application information: Application form required.
Trustee: Richard S. Scolaro.
EIN: 112552891
Codes: GTI

38766
New World Gospel Mission, Inc.
355 Stafford Ave.
Staten Island, NY 10312

Financial data (yr. ended 12/31/99): Grants paid, $9,703; assets, $891,063 (M); expenditures, $30,224; qualifying distributions, $0.
Officers: Abraham Kim, Pres.; Jae Eun Noe, V.P.; Byung W. Suh, Secy.; Kap Chon Chai, Treas.
EIN: 113325506

38767
The James E. and Elizabeth B. Hughes Family Foundation
126 E. 56th St., 17th Fl.
New York, NY 10022
Contact: Douglas R. Drucker, Jr., Secy.

Established in 1999 in DE.
Financial data (yr. ended 12/31/01): Grants paid, $9,700; assets, $136,621 (M); gifts received,

$30,000; expenditures, $10,012; qualifying distributions, $9,700.
Limitations: Giving primarily in NY.
Officers: James E. Hughes, Jr., Pres.; Douglas R. Drucker, Jr., Secy.; Robert H. Gibson, Treas.
Directors: Barbara Gibson, Elizabeth B. Hughes, James E. Hughes, Sr., Peter B. Hughes, Elisabeth D. Templeton.
EIN: 134046240

38768
Bocko Mayo and Anna Mayo Foundation, Inc.
31 Emm Ln.
Roslyn, NY 11576-2005

Financial data (yr. ended 12/31/01): Grants paid, $9,700; assets, $131,391 (M); expenditures, $11,694; qualifying distributions, $9,700.
Limitations: Applications not accepted. Giving primarily in NY.
Application information: Contributes only to pre-selected organizations.
Officer: Hyman M. Matza, Pres.
EIN: 136077586

38769
Richard & Sarah Munschauer Foundation
755 Renaissance Dr.
Williamsville, NY 14221-8045

Established in 1992 in NY.
Donor(s): Richard W. Munschauer, Sarah J. Munschauer.
Financial data (yr. ended 07/31/01): Grants paid, $9,700; assets, $37,411 (M); expenditures, $10,313; qualifying distributions, $9,700.
Limitations: Applications not accepted. Giving limited to Buffalo, NY.
Application information: Contributes only to pre-selected organizations.
Trustees: David A. Munschauer, John J. Munschauer, Richard W. Munschauer, Sarah J. Munschauer, Thomas L. Munschauer.
EIN: 223194998

38770
The Lynn E. and Mattie G. McConnell Foundation and Scholarship Fund
c/o Bath National Bank
44 Liberty St.
Bath, NY 14810
Contact: B. Graham, Trust Off., Bath National Bank

Donor(s): Mattie G. McConnell.‡
Financial data (yr. ended 12/31/01): Grants paid, $9,660; assets, $274,767 (M); expenditures, $13,554; qualifying distributions, $9,660.
Limitations: Giving primarily to residents of the Bath, NY, area.
Application information: Application form required.
Trustee: Bath National Bank.
EIN: 166237917
Codes: GTI

38771
The Lance & Janiece Gad Foundation, Inc.
6 Peter Cooper Rd., Apt. 8F
New York, NY 10010

Established in 1987 in NY.
Donor(s): Lance S. Gad.
Financial data (yr. ended 04/30/02): Grants paid, $9,658; assets, $256,084 (M); expenditures, $10,196; qualifying distributions, $9,658.
Limitations: Applications not accepted. Giving primarily in CT and NY.
Application information: Contributes only to pre-selected organizations.

Officers: Lance S. Gad, Pres. and Treas.; Janiece F. Gad, V.P. and Secy.
Director: Claire Gad.
EIN: 133452161

38772
Byrne Family Foundation
89 Halston Pkwy.
East Amherst, NY 14051-1843

Established in 2000 in NY.
Donor(s): John J. Byrne.
Financial data (yr. ended 12/31/01): Grants paid, $9,650; assets, $79,091 (M); expenditures, $9,961; qualifying distributions, $9,650.
Limitations: Applications not accepted. Giving primarily in Buffalo, NY.
Application information: Contributes only to pre-selected organizations.
Officers: John J. Byrne, Pres.; Marguerite R. Byrne, V.P.
Directors: Carolyn R. Byrne, Heathe M. Byrne.
EIN: 161590273

38773
Vonder Linden Charitable Trust
c/o Leonard Rachmilowitz, C.P.A.
P.O. Box 334
Rhinebeck, NY 12572-0334
Application address: c/o Fund Admin., P.O. Box 452, Rhinebeck, NY 12572

Financial data (yr. ended 06/30/01): Grants paid, $9,640; assets, $510,294 (L); expenditures, $27,080; qualifying distributions, $27,080.
Limitations: Giving limited to Dutchess and Ulster counties, NY.
Trustees: Stephen Kelly, Michael Mazzarella, Howard C. St. John.
EIN: 146102155
Codes: GTI

38774
Kane Paper Scholarship Fund, Inc.
12 Marjorie Dr.
Suffern, NY 10901
Application address: 2365 Milburn Ave., Baldwin, NY 11510-3384, tel.: (516) 223-8120
Contact: James G. Kane, Treas.

Donor(s): Kane Paper Corp., B & M Container Corp.
Financial data (yr. ended 12/31/01): Grants paid, $9,622; assets, $8,554 (M); expenditures, $10,693; qualifying distributions, $9,622.
Limitations: Giving limited to NY.
Application information: Application form required.
Officer: James G. Kane, Treas. and Mgr.
EIN: 116082733
Codes: CS, CD, GTI

38775
National Self Government Committee, Inc.
c/o L.I. University Hospital Prog.
475 Seaview Ave., 102AC
Brooklyn, NY 11201
Contact: Diana Voelker

Financial data (yr. ended 12/31/01): Grants paid, $9,620; assets, $223,926 (M); expenditures, $11,677; qualifying distributions, $10,787.
Limitations: Giving limited to New York, NY.
Officers: Rick Richardson, Chair.; Linda Lafrado, Vice-Chair.; Fred Feus, Treas.
EIN: 136118197

38776
The Foundation of the Binghamton Breakfast Rotary Club
P.O. Box 2302
Binghamton, NY 13902-2302
Contact: Charitable Comm.

Established in 1999 in NY.
Financial data (yr. ended 06/30/01): Grants paid, $9,589; assets, $1 (M); gifts received, $4,000; expenditures, $9,694; qualifying distributions, $9,589.
Limitations: Giving primarily in Binghamton, NY.
Officer: Robert Tornblom, Treas.
Trustees: Mary Lou Bush, James Hayes, Ronald Smeltzer.
EIN: 161484013

38777
Yakov Zvi Friedman Trust
92 Wilson St.
Brooklyn, NY 11211

Financial data (yr. ended 09/30/01): Grants paid, $9,563; assets, $3,681 (M); gifts received, $10,025; expenditures, $10,309; qualifying distributions, $9,563.
Trustees: Jacob Friedman, Leah Friedman.
EIN: 112589174

38778
Fair Return League, Inc.
c/o Eric M. Javits
1345 Ave. of the Americas, 31st Fl.
New York, NY 10105 (212) 586-4050

Established in 1942.
Donor(s): Eric M. Javits, Earle Mack.
Financial data (yr. ended 12/31/01): Grants paid, $9,560; assets, $274,428 (M); gifts received, $10,000; expenditures, $11,045; qualifying distributions, $9,560.
Limitations: Applications not accepted. Giving primarily in New York, NY.
Application information: Contributes only to pre-selected organizations.
Officer: Eric M. Javits, Pres.
EIN: 136125334

38779
The Bess and Israel Workman Foundation
(Formerly Israel Workman Foundation)
60 Gramercy Park
New York, NY 10010 (212) 254-5900
Contact: Peter Workman, Tr.

Donor(s): Bernard Workman.
Financial data (yr. ended 12/31/01): Grants paid, $9,550; assets, $209,782 (M); expenditures, $11,966; qualifying distributions, $11,776.
Trustee: Peter Workman.
EIN: 136208824

38780
Animal Farm Foundation, Inc.
318 E. 51st St.
New York, NY 10022

Established in 1985 in NY.
Donor(s): Jane R. Berkey.
Financial data (yr. ended 06/30/01): Grants paid, $9,545; assets, $47,845 (M); gifts received, $69,025; expenditures, $80,981; qualifying distributions, $56,378.
Limitations: Applications not accepted.
Application information: Contributes only to pre-selected organizations.
Officers: Jane R. Berkey, Pres.; Donald Cleary, Secy.-Treas.
EIN: 222386955

38781
Cambyland Foundation
c/o Phil Goldstein
300 Rector Pl., 7A
New York, NY 10280-1420

Established in 1998 in CT.
Donor(s): Marcus Camby.
Financial data (yr. ended 12/31/99): Grants paid, $9,515; assets, $33,049 (M); gifts received, $109,393; expenditures, $78,070; qualifying distributions, $42,887.
Limitations: Giving primarily in CT.
Officer: Kelvin Moore, Exec. Dir.
Trustees: Janice Camby, Marcus Camby, Alex Johnson.
Directors: Olivia Almagro, Rodney Baker, Chuck Cummings, and 8 additional directors.
EIN: 611319058

38782
The Mildred Arcadipane Foundation, Inc.
c/o Mildred Arcadipane
222 Crestwood Ave.
Tuckahoe, NY 10707

Established in 1999 in NY.
Donor(s): Mildred Arcadipane.
Financial data (yr. ended 12/31/01): Grants paid, $9,500; assets, $199,077 (M); expenditures, $13,510; qualifying distributions, $9,500.
Officers: Mildred Arcadipane, Pres.; Joseph Cassin, V.P.; Nancy Chinchar, Treas.
Directors: Charles Arcadipane, Ben Wetchler.
EIN: 134047164

38783
Vito Battista Atelier Foundation, Inc.
141 Willoughby St.
Brooklyn, NY 11201-5317

Established around 1991.
Financial data (yr. ended 04/30/02): Grants paid, $9,500; assets, $380,039 (M); expenditures, $12,300; qualifying distributions, $9,500.
Officers: Vincent Battista, Pres.; Paul DiNatale, Secy.; John Anselmo, Treas.
EIN: 223089545

38784
The S. H. Bourne Foundation, Inc.
5 W. 37th St.
New York, NY 10018

Donor(s): Bourne Co.
Financial data (yr. ended 11/30/01): Grants paid, $9,500; assets, $10,988 (M); expenditures, $9,500; qualifying distributions, $9,499.
Limitations: Applications not accepted. Giving primarily in New York, NY.
Application information: Contributes only to pre-selected organizations.
Trustee: Beebe Bourne.
EIN: 136128213
Codes: CS, CD

38785
Anthony M. and Carol E. DiMarzo Family Foundation
11 Pine Acres Dr.
Rochester, NY 14618

Established in 1986 in NY.
Donor(s): Anthony DiMarzo, Carol DiMarzo.
Financial data (yr. ended 06/30/02): Grants paid, $9,500; assets, $139,967 (M); expenditures, $12,616; qualifying distributions, $9,500.
Limitations: Applications not accepted. Giving primarily in NY.
Application information: Contributes only to pre-selected organizations.
Trustees: Anthony DiMarzo, Carol DiMarzo, M & T Bank.
EIN: 222781180

38786
The Gottlieb-Schwartz Family Foundation
724 Collfield Ave.
Staten Island, NY 10314

Established in 1994 in NY.
Donor(s): Martin Gottlieb, Michael Schwartz, Steven Schwartz.
Financial data (yr. ended 12/31/01): Grants paid, $9,500; assets, $553 (M); gifts received, $6,000; expenditures, $9,500; qualifying distributions, $9,500.
Limitations: Applications not accepted. Giving primarily in NY.
Application information: Contributes only to pre-selected organizations.
Officers: Michael Gottlieb, Pres.; Steven Schwartz, Treas.
EIN: 133794021

38787
The Iwazumi Foundation, Inc.
125 Bramble Brook Rd.
Ardsley, NY 10502-2206

Established in 1993 in NY.
Donor(s): Tatsuo Iwazumi.
Financial data (yr. ended 12/31/01): Grants paid, $9,500; assets, $164,809 (M); expenditures, $18,375; qualifying distributions, $9,500.
Limitations: Applications not accepted. Giving primarily in CA.
Application information: Contributes only to pre-selected organizations.
Officers and Directors:* Tatsuo Iwazumi,* Pres.; Mikiko Iwazumi,* Secy.; Ray Iwazumi, Hiroyuki Kitago.
EIN: 133717388

38788
The Charles T. and Ardith Mederrick Family Foundation
c/o Wachtell, Lipton, Rosen and Katz
51 W. 52nd St.
New York, NY 10019

Established in 1986 in NY.
Donor(s): Ardith L. Mederrick.
Financial data (yr. ended 04/30/01): Grants paid, $9,500; assets, $77,832 (M); expenditures, $9,624; qualifying distributions, $9,500.
Limitations: Applications not accepted. Giving primarily in NY.
Application information: Contributes only to pre-selected organizations.
Officers and Directors:* Charles T. Mederrick,* Pres.; Ardith L. Mederrick,* V.P.; Jodi J. Schwartz.
EIN: 133389557

38789
Nathan Rudy & Sons Foundation, Inc.
711 Ave. R
Brooklyn, NY 11223-2211

Established in 1989 in NY.
Donor(s): Edward M. Rudy, Isaac Rudy.
Financial data (yr. ended 12/31/00): Grants paid, $9,500; assets, $579,677 (M); gifts received, $400,000; expenditures, $9,675; qualifying distributions, $9,500.
Limitations: Applications not accepted. Giving primarily in Brooklyn, NY.
Application information: Contributes only to pre-selected organizations.
Trustees: Edward M. Rudy, Isaac Rudy.
EIN: 112943196

38790
Stephen & Mary Dowicz Foundation
c/o M.H. Davidson & Co.
885 3rd Ave., Ste. 3300
New York, NY 10022

Established in 2000 in NJ.
Donor(s): Stephen Dowicz, Mary Dowicz.
Financial data (yr. ended 12/31/01): Grants paid, $9,495; assets, $439,250 (M); gifts received, $61,829; expenditures, $23,570; qualifying distributions, $9,495.
Limitations: Applications not accepted.
Application information: Contributes only to pre-selected organizations.
Trustees: Mary Dowicz, Stephen Dowicz.
EIN: 223734687

38791
The Dr. Joseph F. Karpinski, Sr. Foundation
2 South St., Ste. 407
Auburn, NY 13021-3833

Established in 1998 in NY.
Donor(s): Joseph F. Karpinski.
Financial data (yr. ended 12/31/01): Grants paid, $9,480; assets, $615,004 (M); gifts received, $477,925; expenditures, $11,054; qualifying distributions, $9,480.
Limitations: Applications not accepted.
Application information: Contributes only to pre-selected organizations.
Trustees: John Bielejaski, Jr., Gary E. Duckett, Peter Emerson, Leonard A. Erdman, Joseph F. Karpinski, Sr.
EIN: 161538623

38792
Benjamin & Lilian Hertzberg Foundation, Inc.
c/o Joel E. Sammet & Co.
19 Rector St., Ste. 2400
New York, NY 10006-2303

Established around 1969 in NY.
Donor(s): Benjamin Hertzberg.
Financial data (yr. ended 01/31/02): Grants paid, $9,450; assets, $261,981 (M); expenditures, $9,950; qualifying distributions, $9,450.
Limitations: Applications not accepted. Giving primarily in NY.
Application information: Contributes only to pre-selected organizations.
Officers and Directors:* Benjamin Hertzberg,* Pres.; Lillian Hertzberg,* Secy.; Richard Rothberg.
EIN: 237011945

38793
The Gindi Foundation
c/o Moussa Gindi
2147 Ocean Pkwy.
Brooklyn, NY 11223

Established in 1999 in NY.
Donor(s): Moussa Gindi.
Financial data (yr. ended 12/31/01): Grants paid, $9,447; assets, $74,440 (M); gifts received, $30,000; expenditures, $9,447; qualifying distributions, $9,447.
Limitations: Applications not accepted.
Application information: Contributes only to pre-selected organizations.
Trustees: Moussa Gindi, Shella Gindi.
EIN: 113521545

38794
Bock Family Foundation
18 Stonewall Ln.
Mamaroneck, NY 10543
Application address: 1 Parker Plz., Fort Lee, NJ 07024
Contact: Morris Bock, Secy.-Treas.

Established in 1998.
Donor(s): Caroline B. Bock, Morris Bock.
Financial data (yr. ended 12/31/01): Grants paid, $9,430; assets, $193,986 (M); expenditures, $9,852; qualifying distributions, $9,430.
Officers and Directors:* Caroline B. Bock,* Pres.; Morris Bock,* Secy.-Treas.; Jay L. Bock.
EIN: 134012424

38795
Joseph J. Peltz Foundation, Inc.
c/o Michael Peltz
35 Fishermans Dr.
Port Washington, NY 11050

Established in 1991 in NY.
Financial data (yr. ended 12/31/01): Grants paid, $9,375; assets, $172,366 (M); expenditures, $12,597; qualifying distributions, $9,375.
Limitations: Giving primarily in NY.
Officers: David Peltz, Pres.; Michael Peltz, Secy.
EIN: 066071618

38796
Ben Kronish Memorial Foundation
1114 Ave. of the Americas, 46th Fl.
New York, NY 10036-7703

Financial data (yr. ended 12/31/01): Grants paid, $9,372; assets, $1,153 (M); gifts received, $2,500; expenditures, $10,126; qualifying distributions, $9,372.
Limitations: Applications not accepted. Giving primarily in New York, NY.
Application information: Contributes only to pre-selected organizations.
Officers: Herbert Kronish, Pres.; Paul Kronish, V.P.
EIN: 237029101

38797
Curran Music Scholarship Fund
(also known as Gertrude D. Curran Trust f/b/o Curran Music School)
1 HSBC Ctr., 17th Fl.
Buffalo, NY 14203-2885

Financial data (yr. ended 12/31/01): Grants paid, $9,350; assets, $188,102 (M); expenditures, $11,432; qualifying distributions, $9,506.
Limitations: Applications not accepted. Giving limited to Utica, NY.
Trustees: David K. Peet, HSBC Bank USA.
EIN: 156015514
Codes: GTI

38798
Leonard D. Hubbard Onodaga Nation School Trust
c/o Fleet National Bank
159 E. Main St.
Rochester, NY 14638
Application address: c/o Principal, Lafayette Central School, Lafayette, NY 12401

Established in 1990 in NY.
Financial data (yr. ended 05/30/00): Grants paid, $9,350; assets, $277,463 (M); expenditures, $13,008; qualifying distributions, $11,632.
Limitations: Giving limited to residents of Lafayette, NY.
Application information: Application form required.
Trustee: Fleet National Bank.
EIN: 226500878

38799
June & Jay Reich Foundation, Inc.
150 E. 69th St., Apt. 25M
New York, NY 10021-5704   (212) 772-3996

Donor(s): Jay Reich.
Financial data (yr. ended 12/31/01): Grants paid, $9,326; assets, $102,933 (M); gifts received, $5,000; expenditures, $9,353; qualifying distributions, $9,326.
Limitations: Applications not accepted.
Application information: Contributes only to pre-selected organizations.
Officer: Jay Reich, Pres.
EIN: 237003078

38800
Anna & David Zimmerman Foundation, Inc.
320 Central Park West, Apt. 15C
New York, NY 10025-7659   (212) 873-4874
Contact: Ely Zimmerman, Secy.-Treas.

Donor(s): Bernard Zimmerman, Ely Zimmerman.
Financial data (yr. ended 11/30/01): Grants paid, $9,306; assets, $263,510 (M); expenditures, $10,788; qualifying distributions, $9,306.
Limitations: Giving primarily in NY.
Officers and Directors:* Bernard Zimmerman,* Pres.; Robert Zimmerman, V.P.; Ely Zimmerman,* Secy.-Treas.
EIN: 136099447

38801
Lynn Favrot Nolan Family Fund
1037 Clove Rd.
Lagrangeville, NY 12540-6504
(845) 621-2819
Contact: Lynn Favrot Nolan, Chair.

Established in 1995 in NY and LA.
Donor(s): Aimee F. Bell, Thomas B. Favrot, Jr.
Financial data (yr. ended 12/31/01): Grants paid, $9,300; assets, $126,058 (M); expenditures, $11,647; qualifying distributions, $9,300.
Limitations: Giving primarily in LA and NY.
Application information: Application form not required.
Officers: Lynn Favrot Nolan, Chair. and Pres.; Aimee F. Bell, V.P.; Thomas B. Favrot, Jr., V.P.; William T. Nolan, Secy.-Treas.
EIN: 141790059

38802
Emile C. Riendeau Foundation, Inc.
22 Oakwood Rd.
Huntington, NY 11743   (631) 423-6634
Contact: Clifford E. Starkins, Dir.

Established in 1998 in CT.
Donor(s): Emile C. Riendeau.
Financial data (yr. ended 12/31/01): Grants paid, $9,300; assets, $61,915 (M); expenditures, $16,496; qualifying distributions, $9,300.
Directors: H.R. Nicholson, Emile C. Riendeau, Clifford E. Starkins.
EIN: 113365701

38803
Nassau Family Foundation, Inc.
c/o Buchbinder
1 Penn Plz., Ste. 5335
New York, NY 10119

Established in 1990 in NY.
Donor(s): Paul Nassau, Chloe Nassau.
Financial data (yr. ended 06/30/02): Grants paid, $9,250; assets, $19,652 (M); expenditures, $9,450; qualifying distributions, $9,250.
Limitations: Applications not accepted. Giving primarily in MA, and New York, NY.
Application information: Contributes only to pre-selected organizations.
Officers: Paul Nassau, Pres.; Chloe Nassau, Secy.; Barry Sprung, Treas.
EIN: 133599580

38804
David & Laura Finn Family Foundation, Inc.
90 Wellington Ave.
New Rochelle, NY 10804

Donor(s): David Finn.
Financial data (yr. ended 03/31/02): Grants paid, $9,246; assets, $270,202 (M); expenditures, $9,481; qualifying distributions, $9,246.
Limitations: Applications not accepted. Giving primarily in New York, NY.
Application information: Contributes only to pre-selected organizations.
Officers: David Finn, Pres. and Treas.; Laura Finn, V.P.
EIN: 136179414

38805
The Itzkowitz Family Foundation
1434 49th St.
Brooklyn, NY 11219
Contact: Joseph and Sarah Itzkowitz

Established in 1997.
Financial data (yr. ended 12/31/01): Grants paid, $9,239; assets, $107,661 (M); gifts received, $14,036; expenditures, $10,151; qualifying distributions, $9,221.
Trustees: Joseph Itzkowitz, Sarah Itzkowitz.
EIN: 113410920

38806
William J. Cox Memorial Fund
9600 Main St., Ste. 3
Clarence, NY 14031-2093

Established in 1999 in NY.
Donor(s): Forest Industries Trust.
Financial data (yr. ended 12/31/99): Grants paid, $9,200; assets, $204,575 (M); gifts received, $50,000; expenditures, $10,432; qualifying distributions, $9,200.
Officers: James M. Norton, Pres.; Jeanne M. Schmidt, Secy.-Treas.
Directors: Douglas L. Cotton, William J. Cox, Edward G. Wright.
EIN: 161494319

38807
Max & Fanny Kessel Charitable Trust
c/o Leshaw
306 W. 38th St., Ste. 1503
New York, NY 10018
Application address: 2 Yorkshire Dr., Monroe Township, NJ 08831
Contact: Fanny Kessel, Pres.

Financial data (yr. ended 12/31/00): Grants paid, $9,200; assets, $118,512 (M); expenditures, $10,372; qualifying distributions, $9,200.
Officer: Fanny Kessel, Pres. and Treas.
EIN: 226425453

38808
Joyce and Sanford Bookstein Foundation
4 Avis Dr.
Latham, NY 12110   (518) 783-6531
Contact: Joyce H. Bookstein, Pres.

Established in 1994 in NY.
Financial data (yr. ended 12/31/01): Grants paid, $9,190; assets, $168,333 (M); expenditures, $9,319; qualifying distributions, $9,190.
Officers and Directors:* Joyce H. Bookstein,* Pres.; Donald Bookstein,* V.P.; Paul Bookstein,* V.P.; Sanford Bookstein,* Secy.-Treas.

38808—NEW YORK

EIN: 141776759

38809
Sidney & Grace Horowitz Foundation, Inc.
300 Smith St.
Farmingdale, NY 11735

Donor(s): Sidney Horowitz, Grace Horowitz.
Financial data (yr. ended 12/31/01): Grants paid, $9,189; assets, $0 (M); gifts received, $10,500; expenditures, $9,450; qualifying distributions, $9,189.
Limitations: Applications not accepted. Giving primarily in Greenwich, CT.
Application information: Contributes only to pre-selected organizations.
Trustee: Sidney Horowitz, Mgr.
EIN: 237008189

38810
Hotchkiss-Stow Foundation
c/o Neslon Holdings, LTD
71 Frederick St.
Binghamton, NY 13901   (607) 723-6411
Contact: Mark Hotchkiss, Tr.

Established in 1983 in NY.
Financial data (yr. ended 12/31/01): Grants paid, $9,150; assets, $109,751 (M); expenditures, $10,281; qualifying distributions, $9,150.
Limitations: Giving primarily in NY.
Trustees: Clarence F. Hotchkiss, Jr., Edna Hotchkiss, Mark Hotchkiss, Walter Plevyak.
EIN: 222505557

38811
Keren Kinyan Torah Foundation
1225 50th St.
Brooklyn, NY 11219-3541   (718) 853-8154
Contact: Eugene Gubner, Pres.

Financial data (yr. ended 12/31/01): Grants paid, $9,137; assets, $14,102 (M); gifts received, $500; expenditures, $10,137; qualifying distributions, $10,137.
Limitations: Giving primarily in Brooklyn, NY; some giving also in Israel.
Officer: Eugene Gubner, Pres.
EIN: 113416696

38812
Edith M. Schweckendieck Trust
c/o Citibank, N.A.
1 Court Sq., 22nd Fl.
Long Island City, NY 11120
Application address: 153 E. 53rd. St., New York, NY 10022
Contact: Michael Festa, Trust Off., Citibank, N.A.

Established around 1971.
Financial data (yr. ended 12/31/00): Grants paid, $9,125; assets, $392,461 (M); expenditures, $14,140; qualifying distributions, $9,300.
Trustee: Citibank, N.A.
EIN: 136055136

38813
The Elise and Andrew Brownstein Charitable Trust
c/o Wachtell, Lipton, Rosen & Katz
51 W. 52nd St.
New York, NY 10019-6119

Established in 1988 in NY.
Donor(s): Andrew R. Brownstein.
Financial data (yr. ended 12/31/01): Grants paid, $9,100; assets, $213,281 (M); expenditures, $9,447; qualifying distributions, $9,100.
Limitations: Applications not accepted. Giving primarily in New York, NY.
Application information: Contributes only to pre-selected organizations.

Trustees: Andrew R. Brownstein, Elise Jaffe Brownstein.
EIN: 136900303

38814
Marsha H. & Murray M. Jaros Family Foundation
2118 Rosendale Rd.
Schenectady, NY 12309

Established in 1991 in NY.
Donor(s): Marsha H. Jaros, Murray M. Jaros.
Financial data (yr. ended 12/31/01): Grants paid, $9,100; assets, $171,507 (M); gifts received, $9,975; expenditures, $10,244; qualifying distributions, $9,100.
Limitations: Applications not accepted. Giving limited to Schenectady, NY.
Application information: Contributes only to pre-selected organizations.
Trustees: Marsha H. Jaros, Murray M. Jaros.
EIN: 226545554

38815
The Jack Shammah Foundation
720 Ave. I
Brooklyn, NY 11230

Established in 1999 in NY.
Donor(s): Jack Shammah.
Financial data (yr. ended 12/31/01): Grants paid, $9,100; assets, $38,163 (M); gifts received, $30,000; expenditures, $9,100; qualifying distributions, $9,100.
Limitations: Applications not accepted.
Application information: Contributes only to pre-selected organizations.
Trustees: Jack Shammah, Margrette Shammah.
EIN: 113523634

38816
The Federbush Family Foundation
1020 5th Ave.
New York, NY 10028-0133   (212) 675-5700
Contact: Alexander Federbush, Dir.

Established in 1997 in NY.
Donor(s): Alexander P. Federbush, Marjorie Federbush.
Financial data (yr. ended 12/31/00): Grants paid, $9,094; assets, $109,779 (M); gifts received, $5,429; expenditures, $10,496; qualifying distributions, $9,023.
Directors: Alexander P. Federbush, Marjorie Federbush.
EIN: 133945188

38817
Ramsleg Foundation
c/o AMCO
667 Madison Ave., 20th Fl.
New York, NY 10021

Donor(s): Rudolph J. Schaefer III.
Financial data (yr. ended 12/31/01): Grants paid, $9,066; assets, $188,845 (M); gifts received, $2,750; expenditures, $9,617; qualifying distributions, $9,066.
Limitations: Applications not accepted. Giving primarily in Rye, NY and Providence, RI.
Application information: Contributes only to pre-selected organizations.
Officers and Directors:* Martha H. Schaefer,* Pres.; Jane I. Schaefer,* V.P.; Greta J. Schaefer,* Secy.; Rudolph J. Schaefer III,* Treas.; Lauriston Castleman, Jr., Lucia S. Chase, Randolph J. Schaefer IV, Edmee S. Zahringer.
EIN: 133153643

38818
The Bear Foundation
c/o Goldman Sachs & Co.
85 Broad St., Tax Dept.
New York, NY 10004-2456

Established in 1993 in NY.
Donor(s): Robert B. Morris III.
Financial data (yr. ended 03/31/02): Grants paid, $9,050; assets, $1,257,957 (M); gifts received, $1,215,331; expenditures, $10,680; qualifying distributions, $9,050.
Limitations: Applications not accepted. Giving on an international basis, with emphasis on London, England.
Application information: Contributes only to pre-selected organizations.
Trustees: Thomas Blueher, Cristina Ortega Morris, Robert B. Morris III.
EIN: 133749040

38819
Neil Sedaka Foundation, Inc.
c/o AJG Tax Consulting Corp.
350 5th Ave., Ste. 602
New York, NY 10118-0685   (212) 594-9861
Contact: Esther Strassberg

Donor(s): Neil Sedaka.
Financial data (yr. ended 12/31/00): Grants paid, $9,050; assets, $59,999 (M); gifts received, $10,000; expenditures, $23,080; qualifying distributions, $23,773.
Limitations: Giving primarily in NY.
Application information: Application form not required.
Officers: Leba Sedaka, Pres.; Neil Sedaka, V.P.; Arnold Gitomer, Secy.
EIN: 132881758

38820
Shikiar Charitable Foundation
(Formerly The Adam Shikiar Charitable Foundation)
30 E. 85th St., Ste. 9D
New York, NY 10028   (212) 888-6565
Contact: Stuart A. Shikiar, Tr.

Established in 1989 in NY.
Donor(s): Stuart Shikiar, Diana Shikiar.
Financial data (yr. ended 12/31/01): Grants paid, $9,022; assets, $266,898 (M); gifts received, $278; expenditures, $12,075; qualifying distributions, $9,022.
Limitations: Giving primarily in NY.
Trustees: Diana Shikiar, Stuart Shikiar.
EIN: 136922675

38821
The Bluthenthal-Toff Family Foundation
c/o Ruth B. Toff
277 Beverly Rd.
Scarsdale, NY 10583-5070

Established in 1998 in NY.
Donor(s): Ruth B. Toff.
Financial data (yr. ended 04/30/02): Grants paid, $9,000; assets, $226,686 (M); gifts received, $5,068; expenditures, $11,517; qualifying distributions, $9,000.
Limitations: Applications not accepted.
Application information: Contributes only to pre-selected organizations.
Trustees: Nancy E. Toff, Ruth B. Toff.
EIN: 134004905

38822
Evelyn A. Gardner Family Foundation
c/o Thomas A. Gardner
480 Broadway, Ste. 250
Saratoga Springs, NY 12866

Established in 2000 in NY.
Donor(s): Evelyn A. Gardner.
Financial data (yr. ended 12/31/01): Grants paid, $9,000; assets, $144,322 (M); expenditures, $9,205; qualifying distributions, $9,000.
Limitations: Applications not accepted.
Application information: Contributes only to pre-selected organizations.
Trustees: Evelyn A. Gardner, Thomas A. Gardner.
EIN: 141823038

38823
The Gifts of Time Charitable Foundation, Inc.
2452 Hilltop Rd.
Niskayuna, NY 12309 (518) 372-3200
Contact: Kathryn Kuhmerker Appel, Pres.

Established in 1998 in NY.
Donor(s): Lisa Kuhmerker Living Trust.
Financial data (yr. ended 12/31/01): Grants paid, $9,000; assets, $333,095 (M); expenditures, $12,945; qualifying distributions, $9,000.
Officers and Directors:* Kathryn Kuhmerker Appel, Pres. and Treas.; Joseph Gerstein,* V.P.; Gloria Levitas, Secy.; Muriel Bebeau.
EIN: 141800468

38824
Elaine and John Godina Foundation
c/o Joseph Lapatin
977 6th Ave., Ste. 810
New York, NY 10018

Established in 1995 in DE.
Donor(s): John M. Godina.
Financial data (yr. ended 06/30/01): Grants paid, $9,000; assets, $34,275 (M); expenditures, $9,000; qualifying distributions, $8,991.
Limitations: Applications not accepted.
Application information: Contributes only to pre-selected organizations.
Officers and Directors:* John M. Godina,* Pres. and Treas.; Elaine L. Godina,* V.P.; Joseph Lapatin,* Secy.
EIN: 061442623

38825
Sam and Adele Golden Foundation for the Arts
c/o Mark Golden
188 Bell Rd.
New Berlin, NY 13411 (607) 847-8158
FAX: (607) 847-8158; *E-mail:* info@goldenfoundation.org; *URL:* http://www.goldenfoundation.org
Contact: Lucy Tower Funke

Established in 1997 in NY.
Donor(s): GOLDEN Artist Colors, Inc.
Financial data (yr. ended 12/31/01): Grants paid, $9,000; assets, $375,459 (L); gifts received, $107,579; expenditures, $38,991; qualifying distributions, $21,964.
Limitations: Giving on a national basis to cultural organizations and on a national and international basis to professional artists who are working in paint.
Publications: Application guidelines.
Application information: Artists must submit 8 color slides of high quality. Application form required.
Officers: Mark Golden, Pres.; Tom Golden, V.P.; Barbara Golden, Secy.-Treas.
Directors: Tania Golden Bowling, Jean Marc Golden.
EIN: 161523983

Codes: CS, CD

38826
The Lily Harmon Charitable Trust
c/o Kronish Lieb Weiner & Hellman, LLP
1114 Ave. of the Americas
New York, NY 10036

Established in 2000 in NY.
Donor(s): Lily Harmon.‡
Financial data (yr. ended 12/31/01): Grants paid, $9,000; assets, $146,639 (M); expenditures, $20,369; qualifying distributions, $9,000.
Limitations: Applications not accepted.
Application information: Contributes only to pre-selected organizations.
Trustee: Jo Ann Hirshhorn.
EIN: 137245228

38827
Keren Chana V'Yitzchok Koch, Inc.
c/o Martin Moshel
65 Rte. 59
Monsey, NY 10952-3739

Established in 1989 in NY.
Donor(s): Chana Koch.
Financial data (yr. ended 01/31/01): Grants paid, $9,000; assets, $97,611 (M); gifts received, $2,200; expenditures, $9,410; qualifying distributions, $8,913.
Limitations: Applications not accepted.
Application information: Contributes only to pre-selected organizations.
Officers: Chana Koch, Pres.; Abraham Garfinkel, V.P.; Martin Moshel, Treas.
Trustee: Sushe Hecht.
EIN: 112955847

38828
Elsie P. and Lucius B. McCowan Private Foundation
8056 Tonawanda Creek Rd.
East Amherst, NY 14051

Established in 1997 in NY.
Donor(s): Elsie P. McCowan.
Financial data (yr. ended 12/31/01): Grants paid, $9,000; assets, $228,246 (M); expenditures, $9,759; qualifying distributions, $9,000.
Trustees: M. William Boller, Elsie P. McCowan.
EIN: 161527078

38829
Mereville Foundation
c/o Siegel, Sacks
630 3rd Ave.
New York, NY 10017

Established in 1996 in DE.
Financial data (yr. ended 06/30/02): Grants paid, $9,000; assets, $871,581 (M); expenditures, $18,277; qualifying distributions, $9,000.
Limitations: Applications not accepted. Giving primarily in NY.
Application information: Contributes only to pre-selected organizations.
Officers: Russell C. Wilkinson, Pres.; Eileen G. Wilkinson, Secy.
EIN: 133915954

38830
Arthur Miller Foundation
c/o J.L. Rosenhouse
250 W. 57th St., Ste. 2203
New York, NY 10019-3741 (212) 582-2438
Contact: Arthur Miller, Tr.

Established in 1999 in CT.
Donor(s): Arthur Miller.

Financial data (yr. ended 12/31/00): Grants paid, $9,000; assets, $90,817 (M); expenditures, $9,183; qualifying distributions, $9,183.
Trustees: Arthur Miller, Ingeborg M. Miller.
EIN: 223661214

38831
The Joel & Zehava Rosenfeld Foundation Trust
1175 58th St.
Brooklyn, NY 11219

Established in 1999.
Financial data (yr. ended 12/31/01): Grants paid, $9,000; assets, $138,737 (M); expenditures, $9,550; qualifying distributions, $9,000.
Limitations: Applications not accepted.
Application information: Contributes only to pre-selected organizations.
Trustees: Joel Rosenfeld, Zehava Rosenfeld.
EIN: 116527331

38832
Women's Medical Association of New York Financial Assistance Fund
33 E. 70th St., Ste. 9E
New York, NY 10021-4946 (212) 744-3473
Contact: Anne C. Carter, M.D., Tr.

Financial data (yr. ended 06/30/00): Grants paid, $9,000; assets, $106,876 (M); gifts received, $5,750; expenditures, $10,927; qualifying distributions, $10,898; giving activities include $1,927 for loans to individuals.
Limitations: Giving primarily in the metropolitan New York, NY, area.
Application information: Application form required.
Officer and Trustees:* Anne C. Carter, M.D.,* Chair. and Pres.; Barbara Bartlik, Clarita Herrera, Lois A. Katz, Rosalinda Rubenstein.
Committee Members: Jennifer Bell, M.D., Mary Ruth Buchness, M.D., Pamela Charney, Michelle Copeland, Grace Hughes, M.D., Bonnie Reichman, Carolyn Weber, M.D.
EIN: 133175056
Codes: GTI

38833
Deak Family Foundation
c/o Hoff, Metkiff & Romano LLP
575 Lexington Ave.
New York, NY 10022
Application address: c/o Westchester Country Club, Apt. 420, Rye, NY 10580, tel.: (914) 725-3256
Contact: Lisolette M. Deak, Tr.

Established in 1987 in NY.
Financial data (yr. ended 12/31/01): Grants paid, $8,995; assets, $207,326 (M); gifts received, $85,130; expenditures, $9,265; qualifying distributions, $8,995.
Limitations: Giving primarily in the New York, NY, area.
Trustees: Lisolette M. Deak, R. Leslie Deak.
EIN: 133440314

38834
Claire & Menahem Mansoor Foundation
212 W. 85th St., Ste. 3E
New York, NY 10024

Established in 1999 in NY.
Donor(s): Menaham Mansoor, Claire Mansoor, Daniel J. Mansoor.
Financial data (yr. ended 12/31/00): Grants paid, $8,987; assets, $115,795 (M); gifts received, $1,000; expenditures, $11,040; qualifying distributions, $11,100.
Limitations: Applications not accepted. Giving on a national basis.

38834—NEW YORK

Application information: Contributes only to pre-selected organizations.
Officers: Menaham Mansoor, Chair.; Claire Mansoor, Vice-Chair.; Daniel J. Mansoor, Pres.; Yardena Mansoor, Secy.
EIN: 134087749

38835
Harold J. Coleman Foundation
c/o JPMorgan Chase Bank
P.O. Box 31412
Rochester, NY 14603-1412

Financial data (yr. ended 12/31/01): Grants paid, $8,950; assets, $105,115 (M); expenditures, $10,369; qualifying distributions, $8,950.
Limitations: Applications not accepted. Giving primarily in NY.
Application information: Contributes only to pre-selected organizations.
Trustee: JPMorgan Chase Bank.
EIN: 166015175

38836
Honey & Norman Mann Foundation, Inc.
9 Cherrywood Ln.
Manhasset, NY 11030-3926

Donor(s): Norman Mann.
Financial data (yr. ended 12/31/01): Grants paid, $8,920; assets, $27,312 (M); gifts received, $80; expenditures, $8,950; qualifying distributions, $8,920.
Limitations: Applications not accepted. Giving limited to NY.
Application information: Contributes only to pre-selected organizations.
Officer: Norman Mann, Pres.
EIN: 237003111

38837
The Sid Barry Foundation, Inc.
c/o Arthur J. McGee
390 Plandome Rd., No. 204
Manhasset, NY 11030

Financial data (yr. ended 12/31/00): Grants paid, $8,916; assets, $126,320 (M); expenditures, $9,203; qualifying distributions, $9,132.
Limitations: Applications not accepted. Giving primarily in NY.
Application information: Contributes only to pre-selected organizations.
Officer: Bradford W. Barry, Pres.
EIN: 116035222

38838
Shareef Abdur Rahim Future Foundation, Inc.
c/o KRT Business Mgmt.
500 5th Ave., Ste. 3000
New York, NY 10110

Established in 1999 in WA.
Financial data (yr. ended 12/31/99): Grants paid, $8,902; assets, $19,171 (M); gifts received, $38,228; expenditures, $19,057; qualifying distributions, $8,902.
Officers: Eric Goodwin, Pres.; Rodney Sampson, V.P.; Keven Davis, Secy.; Shareef Adbur Rahim, Treas.
EIN: 911885812

38839
Mouse King Foundation
P.O. Box 1617
Sag Harbor, NY 11963-0058

Donor(s): Helen J. Batcheller.
Financial data (yr. ended 12/31/01): Grants paid, $8,900; assets, $137,312 (M); expenditures, $10,658; qualifying distributions, $8,900.
Limitations: Applications not accepted. Giving primarily in NY.
Application information: Contributes only to pre-selected organizations.
Trustees: Edward R. Batcheller, Helen J. Batcheller, Helen S. Tuony, John L. Walsh.
EIN: 112527924

38840
The Joseph E. Peter Foundation
6201 Turnwood Dr.
Jamesville, NY 13078

Established in 1998 in NY.
Donor(s): A.L. George Co.
Financial data (yr. ended 12/31/01): Grants paid, $8,900; assets, $26,699 (M); gifts received, $6,150; expenditures, $9,197; qualifying distributions, $8,900.
Limitations: Applications not accepted. Giving primarily in MI and NY.
Application information: Contributes only to pre-selected organizations.
Trustees: Robert Fagliarone, Joseph E. Peter.
EIN: 161545713

38841
May and Morris Newburger Foundation
c/o Marcum & Kliegman, LLP
655 3rd Ave., Ste. 1610
New York, NY 10017

Established in 1957 in NY.
Financial data (yr. ended 12/31/01): Grants paid, $8,893; assets, $232,235 (M); gifts received, $24,636; expenditures, $9,923; qualifying distributions, $9,485.
Limitations: Applications not accepted. Giving primarily in New York, NY.
Application information: Contributes only to pre-selected organizations.
Trustee: Maury Newburger.
EIN: 237418106

38842
Jacob Brenner Memorial Foundation
1790 Broadway, Ste. 705
New York, NY 10019

Financial data (yr. ended 10/31/01): Grants paid, $8,880; assets, $127,188 (M); expenditures, $10,290; qualifying distributions, $8,757.
Limitations: Applications not accepted. Giving primarily in NY.
Application information: Contributes only to pre-selected organizations.
Officers: Brunice Breiner, V.P.; Miriam B. Singer, V.P.; Pearl Wasserman, Secy.
EIN: 136102930

38843
Frank Soifer Foundation, Inc.
1 Parkwood Pl.
Rye Brook, NY 10573-1022
Contact: Janet Paul, Pres.

Financial data (yr. ended 01/31/02): Grants paid, $8,861; assets, $170,145 (M); gifts received, $3,000; expenditures, $9,825; qualifying distributions, $8,861.
Limitations: Giving primarily in FL.
Officers and Trustees:* Janet Paul,* Pres.; Robert Soifer,* Secy.
EIN: 510179118

38844
The World Partnership in Hope Fund
128 W. 37th St.
New York, NY 10018 (212) 868-2381
Contact: Msgr. Donald Sakano, Chair.

Established in 1997 in NY.
Donor(s): Frank J. Hahn.
Financial data (yr. ended 12/31/01): Grants paid, $8,858; assets, $43,507 (M); gifts received, $17,603; expenditures, $43,985; qualifying distributions, $8,858.
Limitations: Applications not accepted. Giving primarily in NY.
Application information: Contributes only to pre-selected organizations.
Officers: Msgr. Donald Sakano, Chair.; Frank J. Hahn, Secy.-Treas.
EIN: 133959229

38845
The Iris and Andrew Morse Foundation, Inc.
c/o Grant Thornton, LLP
7 Hanover Sq.
New York, NY 10004-2616

Established in 1986 in NY.
Donor(s): Andrew Morse, Iris Morse.
Financial data (yr. ended 09/30/01): Grants paid, $8,845; assets, $94,430 (M); expenditures, $11,895; qualifying distributions, $8,845.
Limitations: Applications not accepted. Giving primarily in NY.
Application information: Contributes only to pre-selected organizations.
Officers: Iris Morse, Pres. and Treas.; Andrew Morse, V.P. and Secy.
EIN: 133382133

38846
N. D. Glekel Foundation, Inc.
465 Park Ave., Ste. 7B
New York, NY 10022
Contact: Newton Glekel, Pres.

Donor(s): Newton Glekel.
Financial data (yr. ended 09/30/99): Grants paid, $8,766; assets, $143,394 (M); expenditures, $9,652; qualifying distributions, $8,766.
Limitations: Giving primarily in New York, NY.
Officers: Newton Glekel, Pres.; Trudy Glekel, Secy.
EIN: 136165582

38847
The Calamus Foundation
c/o Myer, Greene & Degge
P.O. Box 930
Pearl River, NY 10965

Established in 1996 in DE & NY.
Donor(s): Loring McAlpin.
Financial data (yr. ended 11/30/01): Grants paid, $8,750; assets, $1,377,521 (M); gifts received, $157,685; expenditures, $17,475; qualifying distributions, $8,750.
Limitations: Applications not accepted.
Application information: Contributes only to pre-selected organizations.
Officers: Loring McAlpin, Pres.; Daniel Wolfe, Secy.
Director: Gary Schwartz.
EIN: 133922034

38848
Arthur Gabler Scholarship Fund
(Formerly Arthur Gabler Scholarship Trust)
c/o JPMorgan Chase Bank
P.O. Box 31412
Rochester, NY 14603-1412
Application address: c/o Guidance Dept., Trumbull High School, Trumbull, CT 06611

Donor(s): Arthur Gabler.‡
Financial data (yr. ended 06/30/01): Grants paid, $8,750; assets, $606,489 (M); expenditures, $19,908; qualifying distributions, $9,442.
Limitations: Giving limited to residents of Trumbull, CT.

Application information: Include financial aid and tax information. Application form required.
Trustees: John J. Hunt, JPMorgan Chase Bank.
EIN: 066244605
Codes: GTI

38849
The Morning Foundation
333 E. 45th St.
New York, NY 10017

Established in 1999 in NY.
Financial data (yr. ended 12/31/01): Grants paid, $8,750; assets, $166,590 (M); expenditures, $11,028; qualifying distributions, $8,750.
Limitations: Applications not accepted. Giving primarily in New York, NY.
Application information: Contributes only to pre-selected organizations.
Officer: John Morning, Pres.
EIN: 137200463

38850
Honeybee Community Fund
c/o U.S. Trust
114 W. 47th St., TaxVAS
New York, NY 10036

Established in 1996 in NY.
Donor(s): Elizabeth K. Treadwell.
Financial data (yr. ended 12/31/01): Grants paid, $8,720; assets, $104,334 (M); gifts received, $2,580; expenditures, $9,887; qualifying distributions, $8,720.
Limitations: Applications not accepted.
Application information: Contributes only to pre-selected organizations.
Officers: Elizabeth K. Treadwell, Pres.; Susan Perley, Treas.
EIN: 141783794

38851
The McCue Memorial Foundation
21 Mountain Rise
Fairport, NY 14450
Contact: Gerald McCue, Tr.

Established in 1998 in NY.
Donor(s): Gerald McCue.
Financial data (yr. ended 12/31/01): Grants paid, $8,700; assets, $2,131 (M); gifts received, $10,000; expenditures, $8,765; qualifying distributions, $8,700.
Limitations: Giving primarily in NY.
Application information: Application form required.
Trustee: Gerald McCue.
EIN: 161556283

38852
Emil & Stelle Rogers Foundation, Inc.
c/o Emil Rogers
260 Madison Ave., 18 Fl.
New York, NY 10016-2401   (212) 448-1100
Contact: William D. Rogers, Pres.

Donor(s): William D. Rogers, Ellen R. Saxl.
Financial data (yr. ended 03/31/02): Grants paid, $8,665; assets, $186,797 (M); expenditures, $8,715; qualifying distributions, $8,665.
Officers: William D. Rogers, Pres.; Ellen R. Saxl, Treas.
EIN: 136124591

38853
Melanol Foundation, Inc.
c/o Eric S. Sondheimer
118 W. 79th St., Apt. 6B
New York, NY 10024-6445

Donor(s): Hannah I. Noether, Eric S. Sondheimer.
Financial data (yr. ended 10/31/01): Grants paid, $8,652; assets, $74,222 (M); gifts received, $16,000; expenditures, $9,126; qualifying distributions, $8,652.
Limitations: Applications not accepted. Giving primarily in New York, NY.
Application information: Contributes only to pre-selected organizations.
Officers: Hannah I. Noether, Pres.; Eric S. Sondheimer, V.P.; Philippe Blumenthal, Secy.; Ephraim Hochberg, Treas.
EIN: 136066278

38854
The Associated Charitable Foundation
c/o Schertz Realty
92 Washington Ave.
Cedarhurst, NY 11516

Established in 1998 in NY.
Financial data (yr. ended 01/31/02): Grants paid, $8,611; assets, $4,792 (M); gifts received, $11,000; expenditures, $11,119; qualifying distributions, $8,611.
Limitations: Applications not accepted.
Application information: Contributes only to pre-selected organizations.
Officers: Jacob Bronner, Pres. and Treas.; Israel Bronner, V.P.; Aryeh Victor, V.P.; Zwi Levy, Secy.
EIN: 133989618

38855
Charles M. Cappellino Foundation, Inc.
65 Soundview Ave.
Mattituck, NY 11952   (631) 298-4522
Contact: Charles M. Cappellino, M.D., Pres.

Donor(s): Charles M. Cappellino, M.D.
Financial data (yr. ended 12/31/01): Grants paid, $8,611; assets, $193,693 (M); expenditures, $17,109; qualifying distributions, $8,611.
Limitations: Giving primarily in New York, NY.
Application information: Application form not required.
Officers: Charles M. Cappellino, M.D., Pres. and Treas.; Louise Cappellino, Secy.
EIN: 237060338

38856
Louis & Florence Carp Memorial Foundation
c/o Del Mastro
475 Park Ave. S., Ste. 33
New York, NY 10016

Donor(s): Robert Carp.
Financial data (yr. ended 12/31/99): Grants paid, $8,600; assets, $309,395 (M); expenditures, $8,833; qualifying distributions, $8,600.
Limitations: Applications not accepted. Giving primarily in New York, NY.
Application information: Contributes only to pre-selected organizations.
Officer: Robert Carp, Pres.
EIN: 136191714

38857
Hirsch Family Foundation
c/o Leo Hirsch
1130 E. 23rd St.
Brooklyn, NY 11210

Established in 1993 in NY.
Donor(s): Leo Hirsch.
Financial data (yr. ended 09/30/01): Grants paid, $8,600; assets, $305,426 (M); gifts received, $48,240; expenditures, $9,263; qualifying distributions, $8,600.
Limitations: Applications not accepted. Giving primarily in Brooklyn, NY.
Application information: Contributes only to pre-selected organizations.
Trustees: Joseph Hirsch, Leo Hirsch, Libe Hirsch, Sara Simcha.
EIN: 113185637

38858
Sheldon H. Lischin Foundation, Inc.
189 Johnny Cake Hollow Rd.
Pine Plains, NY 12567
Contact: Michael Lischin, Treas.

Established in 1997.
Donor(s): Sheldon Lischin.
Financial data (yr. ended 12/31/00): Grants paid, $8,600; assets, $203,344 (M); expenditures, $12,933; qualifying distributions, $8,600.
Officers and Directors:* Malissa B. Lischin,* Secy.; Michael Lischin,* Treas.; Gary Lischin,* Mgr.
EIN: 311530694

38859
McDermott Family Charitable Trust
2229 Salt Point Tpke.
Clinton Corners, NY 12514

Established in 2000 in NY.
Donor(s): William P. McDermott.
Financial data (yr. ended 12/31/01): Grants paid, $8,575; assets, $189,963 (M); expenditures, $13,445; qualifying distributions, $8,575.
Limitations: Applications not accepted.
Application information: Contributes only to pre-selected organizations.
Officers: Willam McDermott, Pres.; Kerry W. McDermott, V.P.; Eileen M. Laramie, Secy.-Treas.
EIN: 146198226

38860
The Hunt Charitable Foundation, Inc.
5570 Main St., Ste. 201
Williamsville, NY 14221

Established in 2001 in NY.
Donor(s): Hunt Real Estate Corp.
Financial data (yr. ended 12/31/01): Grants paid, $8,542; assets, $35,020 (M); gifts received, $7,182; expenditures, $9,032; qualifying distributions, $8,173.
Limitations: Applications not accepted.
Application information: Contributes only to pre-selected organizations.
Officers and Directors:* Peter F. Hunt,* Pres.; Horace A. Gioia,* Secy.; Gary M. Kanaley.
EIN: 161584859
Codes: CS

38861
Martin & Sarah R. Honig Foundation
110-20 71st Rd.
Forest Hills, NY 11375-4901

Financial data (yr. ended 08/31/01): Grants paid, $8,534; assets, $101,630 (M); gifts received, $3,984; expenditures, $9,388; qualifying distributions, $8,471.
Limitations: Applications not accepted. Giving primarily in NY.
Application information: Contributes only to pre-selected organizations.
Officers: Sarah R. Honig, Pres.; Judith F. Rosenfeld, V.P.; David Rosenfeld, Secy.
Directors: Alisa Horn, Amy Rosenfeld.
EIN: 116079122

38862
The Jerome and Marlene Brody Foundation, Inc.
Leggett Rd.
Ghent, NY 12075

Established in 1990 in NY.
Donor(s): Jerome Brody,‡ Marlene Brody.
Financial data (yr. ended 12/31/01): Grants paid, $8,525; assets, $244,034 (M); gifts received,

38862—NEW YORK

$63,765; expenditures, $12,082; qualifying distributions, $8,525.
Limitations: Applications not accepted.
Application information: Contributes only to pre-selected organizations.
Officers: Marlene Brody, V.P. and Secy.
EIN: 141736554

38863
Bernard J. & Sylvia Aaron Foundation, Inc.
c/o FT Kleiger & Co.
80 Cuttermill Rd., Ste. 302
Great Neck, NY 11021-3108

Donor(s): Sylvia Aaron.
Financial data (yr. ended 12/31/01): Grants paid, $8,518; assets, $72,511 (M); expenditures, $8,667; qualifying distributions, $8,518.
Limitations: Applications not accepted. Giving primarily in NY.
Application information: Contributes only to pre-selected organizations.
Officer: Jeffrey Aaron, Pres.
EIN: 136165605

38864
Charles & Jennie Modica Foundation, Inc.
2166 Gerritsen Ave.
Brooklyn, NY 11229

Donor(s): Pauline Modica.
Financial data (yr. ended 05/31/02): Grants paid, $8,510; assets, $5,237 (M); gifts received, $7,130; expenditures, $9,084; qualifying distributions, $8,510.
Limitations: Applications not accepted. Giving primarily in NY.
Application information: Contributes only to pre-selected organizations.
Director: Pauline Modica.
EIN: 112722123

38865
The Elsa Becker Foundation
c/o Economy Novelty
407 Park Ave. S., Ste. 26A
New York, NY 10001-1215
Contact: Robert Becker, Pres.

Established in 1992 in NY.
Financial data (yr. ended 10/31/01): Grants paid, $8,500; assets, $123,989 (M); expenditures, $11,810; qualifying distributions, $0.
Application information: Application form not required.
Officers: Robert Becker, Pres.; Harold Truchman, Jr., V.P.; Warren Becker, Secy.
EIN: 133641188

38866
Myers Vitkin Foundation, Inc.
(also known as John Myers Foundation, Inc.)
c/o Fleischman & Co.
307 5th Ave.
New York, NY 10016-6517

Financial data (yr. ended 03/31/02): Grants paid, $8,500; assets, $308,183 (M); gifts received, $1,000; expenditures, $12,061; qualifying distributions, $8,500.
Limitations: Applications not accepted. Giving primarily in CA and NY.
Application information: Contributes only to pre-selected organizations.
Officers: L. Robert Vitkin, Pres.; Pamela Y. Tulman, V.P.; Angela V. Glosser, Secy.
EIN: 131777780

38867
Bernard and Eva Resnick Foundation, Inc.
51 E. 42nd St., Ste. 1700
New York, NY 10017 (212) 682-8383
Contact: Richard S. Davidoff, Mgr.

Financial data (yr. ended 12/31/01): Grants paid, $8,500; assets, $425,004 (M); expenditures, $13,638; qualifying distributions, $8,500.
Limitations: Giving primarily in NY.
Application information: Application form not required.
Officer and Director:* Richard S. Davidoff,* Mgr.
EIN: 132688094

38868
Roy & Pearl Rogers Foundation
c/o Steuben Trust Co.
P.O. Box 647
Hornell, NY 14843-0647

Financial data (yr. ended 12/31/01): Grants paid, $8,500; assets, $165,154 (M); expenditures, $10,992; qualifying distributions, $8,500.
Limitations: Applications not accepted.
Application information: Contributes only to pre-selected organizations.
Trustee: Steuben Trust Co.
EIN: 166022590

38869
The Kyle S. Rosen Foundation
4 E. 89th St., Apt. 7E
New York, NY 10128

Established in 1997 in NY.
Donor(s): Walter Rosen, Mrs. Walter Rosen, Paul Wattenberg, Mrs. Paul Wattenberg.
Financial data (yr. ended 12/31/01): Grants paid, $8,500; assets, $225,065 (M); gifts received, $61,600; expenditures, $9,751; qualifying distributions, $8,500.
Officers: Brett Rosen, Pres.; Debbie Wattenberg-Rosen, Secy.; Craig Effron, Treas.
EIN: 133981240

38870
Evelyn E. Stempfle Fund Trust
c/o NBT Bank, N.A.
52 S. Broad St.
Norwich, NY 13815-1699
Application address: c/o Guidance Dir., Gloversville High School, Gloversville, NY 12078, tel.: (518) 725-0674

Financial data (yr. ended 12/31/01): Grants paid, $8,500; assets, $175,993 (M); expenditures, $9,726; qualifying distributions, $8,500.
Limitations: Giving primarily in Gloversville, NY.
Application information: Application form required.
Trustee: NBT Bank, N.A.
EIN: 146036979

38871
Seth I. Weissman Foundation, Inc.
4 Rolling Hills Ln.
Harrison, NY 10528-1706

Donor(s): Kings Electronics.
Financial data (yr. ended 10/31/01): Grants paid, $8,500; assets, $2,024 (M); expenditures, $8,580; qualifying distributions, $8,500.
Limitations: Applications not accepted. Giving primarily in the greater New York, NY, area.
Application information: Contributes only to pre-selected organizations.
Officers: Estelle Fassler, Pres.; Leon Fassler, V.P.; Ronald H. Weissman, M.D., Treas.
EIN: 132931574

38872
Silvera Foundation
205 E. 63rd St.
New York, NY 10021

Established in 1997 in NY.
Donor(s): David Silvera.
Financial data (yr. ended 12/31/01): Grants paid, $8,468; assets, $90,279 (M); gifts received, $40,000; expenditures, $9,670; qualifying distributions, $8,468.
Limitations: Applications not accepted. Giving primarily in New York, NY.
Application information: Contributes only to pre-selected organizations.
Officers: Mayer Silvera, Pres.; David Silvera, Secy.; Batia Silvera, Treas.
EIN: 133969270

38873
The David and Dassie Schreiber Family Foundation, Inc.
460 W. 34th St.
New York, NY 10001

Established in 2001 in NY.
Donor(s): Aaron M. Schreiber Family Foundation, Inc.
Financial data (yr. ended 12/31/01): Grants paid, $8,442; assets, $194,381 (M); gifts received, $210,367; expenditures, $8,663; qualifying distributions, $8,656.
Limitations: Applications not accepted.
Application information: Contributes only to pre-selected organizations.
Director: David Schreiber.
EIN: 113589018

38874
The Clairmont Foundation
950 Third Ave., 9th Fl.
New York, NY 10022-2705
Contact: George B. Clairmont, Tr.

Established in 1978 in NY.
Donor(s): George B. Clairmont.
Financial data (yr. ended 07/31/01): Grants paid, $8,440; assets, $82,356 (M); expenditures, $8,580; qualifying distributions, $8,490.
Limitations: Giving primarily in New York, NY.
Application information: Application form not required.
Trustee: George B. Clairmont.
EIN: 132948477

38875
ADITI: Foundation for the Arts
c/o Kalpana Raina
252 Seventh Ave., Rm PH-H
New York, NY 10001-7352

Established in 1998 in NY.
Donor(s): Kalpana Raina.
Financial data (yr. ended 12/31/01): Grants paid, $8,400; assets, $217,365 (M); gifts received, $250; expenditures, $11,366; qualifying distributions, $8,400.
Limitations: Applications not accepted.
Application information: Contributes only to pre-selected organizations.
Director: Sabyasachi Bhattacharya, Kalpana Raina.
EIN: 134027439

38876
The McNamee Charitable Trust
c/o Cathy Mcbride, First Albany Corp.
30 S. Pearl St.
Albany, NY 12207

Donor(s): George C. McNamee.

Financial data (yr. ended 12/31/01): Grants paid, $8,400; assets, $169,272 (M); expenditures, $8,916; qualifying distributions, $8,400.
Limitations: Giving primarily in Albany, NY.
Trustee: Carl P. Carlucci.
EIN: 222779693

38877
Fink Family Foundation, Inc.
391 Broadway
New York, NY 10013
Contact: Donald Fink, Pres.

Established in 1996 in NY.
Donor(s): Donald Fink.
Financial data (yr. ended 12/31/01): Grants paid, $8,380; assets, $86,374 (M); gifts received, $1,000; expenditures, $9,908; qualifying distributions, $8,380.
Limitations: Giving primarily in NY.
Officer: Donald Fink, Pres.
EIN: 133872846

38878
The Schulman Foundation
100 Cleveland Ave.
Freeport, NY 11520-4053

Established in 1987 in NY.
Financial data (yr. ended 09/30/01): Grants paid, $8,380; assets, $1 (M); gifts received, $4,500; expenditures, $8,571; qualifying distributions, $8,380.
Limitations: Giving primarily in NY.
Directors: Fred Schulman, Howard Schulman, Molly Schulman.
EIN: 133381216

38879
David Finkelstein Foundation, Inc.
175 E. 62nd St., No. 12B
New York, NY 10021-7626 (212) 753-9004
Contact: Shep Forest, Pres.

Financial data (yr. ended 12/31/01): Grants paid, $8,340; assets, $100,805 (M); expenditures, $9,969; qualifying distributions, $8,340.
Officers: Shep Forest, Pres.
EIN: 136219843

38880
The Afghan Jewish Sisterhood Foundation, Inc.
c/o D. Elias
167-14 71st Ave.
Fresh Meadows, NY 11365

Financial data (yr. ended 12/31/01): Grants paid, $8,322; assets, $5,000 (M); expenditures, $8,354; qualifying distributions, $8,322.
Limitations: Applications not accepted.
Application information: Contributes only to pre-selected organizations.
Officer: Solomon Gad, Pres.
EIN: 112954347

38881
Heidecorn Family Foundation, Inc.
4 Gifford Lake Dr.
Armonk, NY 10504-2701

Established in 2000 in NY.
Donor(s): David Heidecorn, Deborah Heidecorn, Jeffrey Kapelman.
Financial data (yr. ended 12/31/01): Grants paid, $8,280; assets, $103,949 (M); gifts received, $9,500; expenditures, $13,327; qualifying distributions, $8,280.
Limitations: Applications not accepted. Giving primarily in NY and PA.
Application information: Contributes only to pre-selected organizations.

Officers and Directors:* David Heidecorn,* Pres. and Treas.; Deborah Heidecorn,* Secy.; Jeffrey Kapelman.
EIN: 061600573

38882
The Lenore & Howard Klein Foundation, Inc.
70-20 108th St., Apt. 12-H
Forest Hills, NY 11375 (718) 263-4777

Established in 1992 in NY.
Donor(s): Howard L. Klein,‡ Lenore Klein.
Financial data (yr. ended 12/31/00): Grants paid, $8,250; assets, $209,898 (M); gifts received, $5,000; expenditures, $11,883; qualifying distributions, $8,250.
Limitations: Applications not accepted. Giving primarily in New York, NY.
Application information: Contributes only to pre-selected organizations.
Officers: Lenore Klein, Pres.; Jane Laffend, V.P. and Treas.; Jennifer D. Port, Secy.
EIN: 133673818

38883
Harry and Jean Bunderoff Fund, Inc.
c/o Louis Weissman
100 Cedarhurst Ave., Ste. 200
Cedarhurst, NY 11516

Financial data (yr. ended 11/30/01): Grants paid, $8,235; assets, $184,199 (M); expenditures, $9,150; qualifying distributions, $8,235.
Limitations: Applications not accepted. Giving primarily in Palm Beach County, FL.
Application information: Contributes only to pre-selected organizations.
Directors: Charles B. Kamp, Muriel B. Kamp.
EIN: 136145558

38884
Riveredge Foundation
261 Broadway
Lawrence, NY 11559

Established in 2000 in NY.
Donor(s): Abraham Elias.
Financial data (yr. ended 12/31/00): Grants paid, $8,230; assets, $30,331 (M); gifts received, $64,200; expenditures, $8,330; qualifying distributions, $8,330.
Limitations: Applications not accepted.
Application information: Contributes only to pre-selected organizations.
Officers: Abraham Elias, Pres.; Edda Elias, Secy.-Treas.
EIN: 134110634

38885
Reynolds Charitable Foundation Trust
4 Pine Ridge Rd.
Larchmont, NY 10538-2616

Established in 1999 in NY.
Donor(s): William T. Reynolds, Emily Grady Reynolds.
Financial data (yr. ended 12/31/01): Grants paid, $8,225; assets, $33,613 (M); gifts received, $7,500; expenditures, $8,225; qualifying distributions, $8,225.
Limitations: Applications not accepted.
Application information: Contributes only to pre-selected organizations.
Trustees: Emily Grady Reynolds, William T. Reynolds.
EIN: 137172590

38886
Laura M. & Albert B. Gross Foundation, Inc.
c/o Freeman & Davis, LLP
225 W. 34th St., No. 320
New York, NY 10122 (212) 594-8155

Donor(s): Lillian G. Bauer, Irene G. Berton, Alice G. Fish.
Financial data (yr. ended 12/31/01): Grants paid, $8,200; assets, $21,659 (M); gifts received, $8,200; expenditures, $8,210; qualifying distributions, $8,200.
Limitations: Applications not accepted.
Application information: Contributes only to pre-selected organizations.
Officers: Lillian G. Bauer, Pres.; Alice G. Fish, Secy.; Irene G. Berzon, Treas.
EIN: 136116441

38887
William & Bernice Rose Foundation, Inc.
c/o Yohalem, Gillman & Co.
477 Madison Ave.
New York, NY 10022

Financial data (yr. ended 11/30/01): Grants paid, $8,200; assets, $160,868 (M); expenditures, $10,898; qualifying distributions, $8,200.
Limitations: Applications not accepted. Giving primarily in NY.
Application information: Contributes only to pre-selected organizations.
Officers: William S. Rose, Jr., Pres.; Victoria G. Rose, V.P.
EIN: 136143156

38888
Elmo M. Royce Benefit Fund
c/o HSBC Bank USA
P.O. Box 4203
Buffalo, NY 14240-4203

Established in 1987 in NY.
Financial data (yr. ended 12/31/01): Grants paid, $8,193; assets, $100,300 (M); expenditures, $10,034; qualifying distributions, $8,193.
Limitations: Applications not accepted. Giving primarily in NY.
Application information: Contributes only to pre-selected organizations.
Trustee: HSBC Bank USA.
EIN: 237004842

38889
689 Foundation
c/o Catherine Girardi
40 Central Park S., Ste. PH-B
New York, NY 10019

Established in 1999 in NY.
Donor(s): Catherine Girardi.
Financial data (yr. ended 10/31/01): Grants paid, $8,150; assets, $61,256 (M); gifts received, $12,931; expenditures, $10,847; qualifying distributions, $8,150.
Limitations: Applications not accepted.
Application information: Contributes only to pre-selected organizations.
Officers: Catherine Girardi, Pres.; Cecelia Girardi, Secy.; Teresa Liberto, Treas.
EIN: 134088234

38890
The Robert B. and Barbara C. Singer Family Foundation
135 Osborne Rd.
Northville, NY 12134

Established in 1998 in NY.
Donor(s): Robert Singer, Barbara Singer.

Financial data (yr. ended 12/31/01): Grants paid, $8,100; assets, $94,973 (M); expenditures, $9,122; qualifying distributions, $8,100.
Limitations: Applications not accepted.
Application information: Contributes only to pre-selected organizations.
Trustees: Suzanne Singer Boger, Elaine S. Eisenbraun, Karen S. Miller, Barbara C. Singer, Robert B. Singer, Steven A. Singer.
EIN: 146190343

38891
The Rosemarie & John A. Tokar Scholarship Foundation, Ltd.
c/o MMN & R
160 Middle Neck Rd.
Great Neck, NY 11021-1204

Established in 1995 in NY.
Donor(s): John A. Tokar, Rosemarie Tokar.
Financial data (yr. ended 12/31/01): Grants paid, $8,097; assets, $161,582 (M); gifts received, $63,986; expenditures, $9,175; qualifying distributions, $8,097.
Limitations: Applications not accepted.
Application information: Unsolicited requests for funds not accepted.
Officers and Directors:* John A. Tokar,* Pres. and Treas.; William J. Nielsen,* Exec. V.P.; Rosemarie Tokar,* V.P.; Rev. Kenneth J. Boller.
EIN: 113242960

38892
Emanuel & Evelyn Klimpl Foundation
c/o Elaine Katz, Parker, Chapin, Flattau & Klimpl, LLP
1211 Ave. of the Americas
New York, NY 10036-8701

Financial data (yr. ended 12/31/01): Grants paid, $8,078; assets, $49,932 (M); expenditures, $8,078; qualifying distributions, $8,078.
Limitations: Applications not accepted. Giving primarily in NY.
Application information: Contributes only to pre-selected organizations.
Officer: Evelyn Klimpl, Pres.
EIN: 136112802

38893
Lovestrand, Inc.
100 Grand Blvd.
Deer Park, NY 11729-3947

Established in 1994 in NY.
Donor(s): Doris Radford.
Financial data (yr. ended 12/31/01): Grants paid, $8,074; assets, $183,066 (M); gifts received, $17,192; expenditures, $16,838; qualifying distributions, $8,074.
Limitations: Applications not accepted.
Application information: Contributes only to pre-selected organizations.
Officers: Doris Radford, Pres.; Rudolph Migliore, V.P.; Ronald R. Radford, Secy.-Treas.
EIN: 112990677

38894
The Kess Foundation, Inc.
c/o Dayton & D'Amato
42-40 Bell Blvd.
Bayside, NY 11361
Application address: 4240 N. Bayview Rd., Southold, NY 11971, tel.: (631) 765-5041
Contact: Marie L. Schlegel, Pres.

Established in 1990 in NY.
Donor(s): Marie L. Schlegel.
Financial data (yr. ended 12/31/01): Grants paid, $8,050; assets, $171,836 (M); gifts received, $5,000; expenditures, $10,562; qualifying distributions, $8,050.
Limitations: Giving primarily in NY.
Officers: Marie L. Schlegel, Pres.; Lawrence L. D'Amato, Secy.
Trustees: Alexander J. Janlewicz, Jr., Cheryl E. Janlewicz.
EIN: 112998128

38895
The Simner Foundation
c/o Marvin E. Simner
785 Park Ave.
New York, NY 10021

Established in 1997 in NY.
Donor(s): Marvin E. Simner, Bertina Simner.
Financial data (yr. ended 12/31/01): Grants paid, $8,050; assets, $136,172 (M); gifts received, $25,000; expenditures, $8,050; qualifying distributions, $8,050.
Limitations: Applications not accepted.
Application information: Contributes only to pre-selected organizations.
Officers and Directors:* Marvin E. Simner,* Pres. and Treas.; Bertina Simner,* V.P. and Secy.; Herrick A. Simner.
EIN: 133932163

38896
The Milton and Ella Upsher Foundation
c/o Robert M. Tanenbaum
767 5th Ave., 43rd Fl.
New York, NY 10153-0097

Established in 1996 in NY.
Donor(s): Daniel C. Lubin.
Financial data (yr. ended 12/31/01): Grants paid, $8,050; assets, $22,209 (M); gifts received, $200; expenditures, $8,417; qualifying distributions, $8,050.
Limitations: Applications not accepted.
Application information: Contributes only to pre-selected organizations.
Trustees: Daniel C. Lubin, Flaminia Lubin, Robert M. Tanenbaum.
EIN: 137102549

38897
Max & Rosa Gold Foundation, Inc.
c/o Sydney Luria
521 5th Ave.
New York, NY 10017-4608 (212) 986-3131
Contact: Muriel Stevens, Pres., or Sydney A. Luria, Secy.

Financial data (yr. ended 12/31/00): Grants paid, $8,010; assets, $463,638 (M); expenditures, $9,757; qualifying distributions, $8,010.
Limitations: Giving primarily in NY.
Officers: Muriel Stevens, Pres.; Sydney A. Luria, Secy.; Rabbi Emanuel Rackman, Treas.
Trustees: Harvey Gold, Hillard Gold, Michael Gold, Norman Stevens.
EIN: 136114441

38898
Dr. Victor A. Bacile Scholarship Fund
c/o John W. Mazzetti
227 Mill St.
Poughkeepsie, NY 12601

Financial data (yr. ended 12/31/01): Grants paid, $8,000; assets, $99,719 (M); gifts received, $6,669; expenditures, $8,715; qualifying distributions, $7,951.
Limitations: Applications not accepted. Giving primarily in NY.
Application information: Unsolicited requests for funds not accepted.
Trustees: Peter Barone, John D. Bertolozzi, Jr., Gregory Chiaramonte, Anthony F. Comunale, Charles H. Fells, Patrick Ferrante, John Fiore, John W. Mazzetti, Gabriel F. Ponte, Joseph Scivolette.
EIN: 141730868

38899
Susan Devine Camilli Foundation
c/o U.S. Trust
114 W. 47th St., Ste. C-1
New York, NY 10036-1594

Established in 1991 in NY.
Donor(s): Bonaventura E. Devine.‡
Financial data (yr. ended 12/31/01): Grants paid, $8,000; assets, $7,407,055 (M); expenditures, $109,832; qualifying distributions, $185,579.
Limitations: Applications not accepted.
Application information: Contributes only to pre-selected organizations.
Directors: Andre Christopher Camilli, Susan Devine Camilli, Tura Christine Camilli, Anne Moore.
EIN: 133617665

38900
Herbert F. Darling Family Foundation
(also known as Herbert F. & Bertha W. Darling Trust)
c/o HSBC Bank USA
P.O. Box 4203, 17th Fl.
Buffalo, NY 14240

Established in 1984 in NY.
Financial data (yr. ended 09/30/01): Grants paid, $8,000; assets, $280,914 (M); expenditures, $12,349; qualifying distributions, $8,675.
Limitations: Applications not accepted. Giving primarily in NY.
Application information: Contributes only to pre-selected organizations.
Trustee: HSBC Bank USA.
EIN: 166021940

38901
Elliot Howard Folz Foundation
3401 Lawson Blvd.
Oceanside, NY 11572
Contact: Roger C. Folz, Pres.

Established in 1986 in NY.
Donor(s): Roger C. Folz.
Financial data (yr. ended 12/31/01): Grants paid, $8,000; assets, $49,345 (M); gifts received, $2,200; expenditures, $8,273; qualifying distributions, $8,000.
Limitations: Giving primarily in Oceanside, NY.
Application information: Application form not required.
Officers: Roger C. Folz, Pres. and Treas.; Adele Folz, V.P. and Secy.
EIN: 112839937

38902
Damon & Sara Gadd Family Foundation
c/o Ross D. Perry
10 E. 40th St., Ste. 710
New York, NY 10016 (212) 696-4235

Donor(s): Sara Gadd.
Financial data (yr. ended 12/31/01): Grants paid, $8,000; assets, $295,791 (M); expenditures, $11,560; qualifying distributions, $8,000.
Limitations: Applications not accepted.
Application information: Contributes only to pre-selected organizations.
Director: Sara Gadd.
Trustee: Samuel W. Meek, Jr.
EIN: 656172650

38903
The Hatzlacha Foundation
1301 47th St.
Brooklyn, NY 11219-2637

Established in 1998 in NY.
Donor(s): Jacque Werdyger.
Financial data (yr. ended 12/31/00): Grants paid, $8,000; assets, $177,054 (M); gifts received, $68,914; expenditures, $8,130; qualifying distributions, $8,000.
Trustees: Jacque Werdyger, Rivka Werdyger.
EIN: 113415194

38904
M. & G. Henderson Scholarship Fund
c/o The Bank of New York, Tax Dept.
48 Wall St., 28th Fl.
New York, NY 10286
Application address: 1 Wall St., New York, NY 10286
Contact: Annette Ferro, Trust Off., The Bank of New York

Financial data (yr. ended 12/31/00): Grants paid, $8,000; assets, $180,358 (M); expenditures, $8,485; qualifying distributions, $8,003.
Limitations: Giving limited to residents of Rye, NY.
Trustee: The Bank of New York.
EIN: 136062187

38905
Hunter Charitable Trust
94 Southlawn Ave.
Dobbs Ferry, NY 10522

Established in NY in 1997.
Donor(s): Harriette E. Hunter.
Financial data (yr. ended 12/31/01): Grants paid, $8,000; assets, $190,464 (M); expenditures, $8,625; qualifying distributions, $8,625.
Limitations: Applications not accepted. Giving primarily in Wilmington, DE, Boston, MA, Silver Spring, MD, Ann Arbor, Birmingham and Olivet, MI, and Dobbs Ferry, Poughkeepsie, and Yonkers, NY.
Application information: Contributes only to pre-selected organizations.
Trustees: David H. Hunter, Stephen K. Hunter.
EIN: 383326883

38906
National Junior Wheelchair Athletes' Fund
c/o Jay L. Mortimer
455 E. 57th St., Ste. 5A
New York, NY 10022

Established in 1995 in NY.
Financial data (yr. ended 12/31/99): Grants paid, $8,000; assets, $38,033 (M); expenditures, $9,404; qualifying distributions, $8,000.
Limitations: Applications not accepted.
Application information: Contributes only to pre-selected organizations.
Officer: Jay L. Mortimer, Pres.
EIN: 131852814

38907
The Nieuwendyk Foundation
c/o KRT Business Mgmt.
500 5th Ave.
New York, NY 10110

Established in 1998 in NY.
Donor(s): Joe Nieuwendyk, Cooksey/McGill Communications.
Financial data (yr. ended 12/31/00): Grants paid, $8,000; assets, $13,974 (M); expenditures, $8,000; qualifying distributions, $7,996.
Limitations: Applications not accepted. Giving primarily in Ithaca, NY.

Officers: Joe Nieuwendyk, Pres.; Barry Klarberg, V.P.; Robert Raiola, Treas.
EIN: 134012716

38908
The Satenik and Odom Ourian Educational Foundation
c/o Haig Nalbantian
395 Riverside Dr., Ste. 7C
New York, NY 10025-1844

Donor(s): Satenik Ourian.
Financial data (yr. ended 12/31/00): Grants paid, $8,000; assets, $196,241 (M); expenditures, $9,306; qualifying distributions, $8,000.
Limitations: Applications not accepted. Giving primarily in New York, NY.
Application information: Contributes only to pre-selected organizations.
Trustees: Haig Nalbantian, David Reynolds, Suzanne Reynolds.
EIN: 136896689

38909
Rabbi Leib and Minnie Potashnik Memorial Fund
P.O. Box 480
Lawrence, NY 11559

Established in 2001.
Donor(s): Prism Consultants, Shimon Feuer.
Financial data (yr. ended 12/31/01): Grants paid, $8,000; assets, $771 (M); gifts received, $11,000; expenditures, $10,229; qualifying distributions, $8,000.
Limitations: Applications not accepted.
Application information: Contributes only to pre-selected organizations.
Officers: Shimon Feuer, Pres.; Ettie Schoor, V.P. and Secy.; Chavi Feuer, Treas.
EIN: 113593631

38910
Francesca Primus Foundation, Inc.
c/o Bass and Lemer, LLP
836 Hempstead Ave.
West Hempstead, NY 11552
Application address: 200 Central Park S., New York, NY 10019, tel.: (212) 582-2338
Contact: Natalie Fewsmith, Dir.

Established in 1992 in NY.
Donor(s): Francesca Primus,‡ George Primus.‡
Financial data (yr. ended 02/28/02): Grants paid, $8,000; assets, $291,071 (M); expenditures, $9,332; qualifying distributions, $8,000.
Limitations: Giving primarily in NY.
Directors: Natalie Fewsmith, Barry Primus.
EIN: 133675567

38911
R. Rubin Family Foundation, Inc.
c/o Barry M. Strauss Assocs., Ltd.
307 5th Ave., 8th Fl.
New York, NY 10016-8775

Established in 1985 in NY.
Donor(s): Robert S. Rubin.
Financial data (yr. ended 03/31/02): Grants paid, $8,000; assets, $217,742 (M); expenditures, $9,578; qualifying distributions, $8,000.
Limitations: Applications not accepted.
Application information: Contributes only to pre-selected organizations.
Officers: Robert S. Rubin, Pres.; Martha Adams Rubin, V.P.; Barry M. Strauss, Secy.-Treas.
Directors: David Adams Rubin, James Samuel Rubin, Nathaniel Solomon Rubin, Rebecca J. Rubin.
EIN: 133275556

38912
S.A.A.M. Charitable Trust
c/o Andrew Heine
114 W. 47th St.
New York, NY 10036

Established in 1983 in NY.
Financial data (yr. ended 04/30/00): Grants paid, $8,000; assets, $91,566 (M); expenditures, $9,049; qualifying distributions, $8,754.
Limitations: Applications not accepted. Giving primarily in New York, NY.
Application information: Contributes only to pre-selected organizations.
Advisory Committee Members: Cynthia Colin, Spencer Partrich.
Trustee: Andrew Heine.
EIN: 136823322

38913
Harry and Mae Schetzen Foundation
c/o Frank Palazzolo, C.P.A.
386 Park Ave. S., Ste. 414
New York, NY 10016
Application address: 41 Centre St., Brookline, MA 02146
Contact: Martin Schetzen, Tr.

Donor(s): Harry Schetzen,‡ Mae Schetzen.
Financial data (yr. ended 04/30/02): Grants paid, $8,000; assets, $138,485 (M); expenditures, $14,746; qualifying distributions, $8,000.
Trustees: Ozzie Gaines, Mae Schetzen, Martin Schetzen.
EIN: 136204676

38914
Ralph M. Schwartz Foundation, Inc.
25 Sutton Pl., Ste. 3M
New York, NY 10022

Established in 1999 in NY.
Donor(s): Ralph Schwartz.
Financial data (yr. ended 12/31/01): Grants paid, $8,000; assets, $129,910 (M); gifts received, $19,500; expenditures, $10,522; qualifying distributions, $8,000.
Limitations: Applications not accepted. Giving primarily in CA.
Application information: Contributes only to pre-selected organizations.
Directors: Elsa A. Schwartz, Leo S. Schwartz, Ralph Schwartz, Richard M. Schwartz, Stephen R. Schwartz.
EIN: 134016984

38915
The Robert and Sara Smith Foundation, Inc.
291 Genesee St.
Utica, NY 13501

Established in 1993 in NY.
Financial data (yr. ended 12/31/01): Grants paid, $8,000; assets, $354,088 (M); gifts received, $48,942; expenditures, $9,507; qualifying distributions, $8,000.
Limitations: Applications not accepted.
Application information: Contributes only to pre-selected organizations.
Officers: Michael Silverman, Pres.; Charles Silverman, V.P.; Lois Silverman, Secy.-Treas.
EIN: 161448678

38916
Gerald Sutliff Trust f/b/o Hofstra University
c/o The Bank of New York, Tax Dept.
1 Wall St., 28th Fl.
New York, NY 10286
Application address: c/o Alfred E. Urban, Jr., William Bradford Turner Post, No. 265, P.O. Box 8, Garden City, NY 11530

Established in 1987 in NY.
Financial data (yr. ended 09/30/01): Grants paid, $8,000; assets, $265,507 (M); expenditures, $9,893; qualifying distributions, $8,364.
Limitations: Giving limited to Garden City, NY.
Application information: Application form required.
Trustee: The Bank of New York.
EIN: 133543303
Codes: GTI

38917
Vista Youth Foundation
2556 Arthur Kill Rd.
Staten Island, NY 10309

Established in 1999 in NY.
Financial data (yr. ended 10/31/01): Grants paid, $8,000; assets, $1 (M); expenditures, $8,550; qualifying distributions, $8,000.
Trustee: Marie Gambino.
EIN: 134089155

38918
Stanley Wohlgemuth Memorial
c/o J. David Bleich
400 E. 77th St., Ste. 3C
New York, NY 10021-2303

Financial data (yr. ended 12/31/01): Grants paid, $8,000; assets, $331,398 (M); expenditures, $8,352; qualifying distributions, $8,000.
Officer: J. David Bleich, Pres.
EIN: 134028218

38919
Ronald Ezring Charitable Foundation
72 Longview Rd.
Port Washington, NY 11050

Established in 1996 in NY.
Donor(s): Ronald Ezring.
Financial data (yr. ended 06/30/02): Grants paid, $7,981; assets, $157,168 (M); expenditures, $9,992; qualifying distributions, $7,981.
Limitations: Applications not accepted. Giving primarily in NY.
Application information: Contributes only to pre-selected organizations.
Trustees: Diana Ezring, Ronald Ezring, Leonard C. Green.
EIN: 113270489

38920
The Lattimer Family Fund, Inc.
161 Ft. Washington Ave., Ste. 1156
New York, NY 10032-3795 (212) 305-8902
Contact: John K. Lattimer, Pres.

Donor(s): John K. Lattimer.
Financial data (yr. ended 12/31/01): Grants paid, $7,960; assets, $116,416 (M); expenditures, $10,163; qualifying distributions, $7,960.
Limitations: Giving primarily in New York, NY.
Application information: Application form not required.
Officers and Trustees:* John K. Lattimer,* Pres.; Jamie Lattimer,* V.P.
EIN: 136197775

38921
Ber Mandel Family Foundation, Inc.
c/o L. Sanders
1718 Quentin Rd., Apt. 2D
Brooklyn, NY 11229-1235
Application address: 263 West End Ave., Apt. 11B, New York, NY 10023, tel.: (212) 875-0339
Contact: Yetta Mandel, Pres.

Donor(s): Ber Mandel, Harvey Mandel, Yetta Mandel.
Financial data (yr. ended 12/31/01): Grants paid, $7,946; assets, $14,685 (M); expenditures, $7,996; qualifying distributions, $7,946.
Application information: Application form not required.
Officers: Yetta Mandel, Pres.; Harvey Mandel, V.P.; Rene Schreber, Secy.; Avram Schreber, Treas.
EIN: 116047854

38922
Eric & Ruth Katzenstein Foundation, Inc.
1277 Ocean Pkwy.
Brooklyn, NY 11230 (718) 951-1234
Contact: Eric S. Katzenstein, Pres.

Established in 1960 in NY.
Donor(s): Leon L. Eisenman, Eric S. Katzenstein, K'Hal Adath Jeshurun, Inc.
Financial data (yr. ended 12/31/01): Grants paid, $7,910; assets, $10,979 (M); gifts received, $15,750; expenditures, $10,197; qualifying distributions, $7,910.
Limitations: Giving primarily in New York, NY.
Officers and Directors:* Eric S. Katzenstein,* Pres. and Treas.; Ruth B. Katzenstein,* V.P. and Secy.; Theodore D. Katzenstein, Morris M. Klugman.
EIN: 136089435

38923
The Reiner J. & Edith Auman Foundation
c/o Reiner J. Auman
80-30 169th St.
Jamaica, NY 11432

Established in 1996 in NY.
Donor(s): Reiner J. Auman.
Financial data (yr. ended 10/31/01): Grants paid, $7,900; assets, $40,012 (M); expenditures, $10,159; qualifying distributions, $7,900.
Limitations: Applications not accepted. Giving primarily in New York, NY.
Application information: Contributes only to pre-selected organizations.
Officers: Reiner J. Auman, Pres.; Richard F. Auman, V.P.; Edith Auman, Secy.; Adrian Auman, Treas.
EIN: 113350836

38924
Herman and Rhoda Bercow Foundation, Inc.
99 Park Ave., 17th Fl.
New York, NY 10016

Financial data (yr. ended 12/31/01): Grants paid, $7,900; assets, $107,163 (M); expenditures, $8,245; qualifying distributions, $7,900.
Limitations: Applications not accepted. Giving primarily in New York, NY.
Application information: Contributes only to pre-selected organizations.
Officer: Alan Bercow.
EIN: 136081904

38925
Heineman & Company Foundation, Inc.
c/o Heineman & Co.
151 W. 40th St.
New York, NY 10018 (212) 840-1400

Donor(s): Laurence Borgebohr, William Heineman, Heineman & Co.
Financial data (yr. ended 05/31/02): Grants paid, $7,900; assets, $157,383 (M); gifts received, $2,000; expenditures, $8,789; qualifying distributions, $7,900.
Limitations: Giving primarily in Williamstown, MA.
Officers and Directors:* William M. Heineman,* Pres.; Melvin Greenfield,* V.P. and Secy.; Howard Danzig, Stuart Heit.
EIN: 136131678
Codes: CS, CD

38926
Nannell Foundation, Inc.
66 W. Barclay St.
Hicksville, NY 11801

Donor(s): Johanna M. Utrecht, Elliott Utrecht.
Financial data (yr. ended 12/31/01): Grants paid, $7,900; assets, $146,994 (M); gifts received, $18,473; expenditures, $10,128; qualifying distributions, $7,900.
Limitations: Applications not accepted. Giving primarily in NY.
Application information: Contributes only to pre-selected organizations.
Officers and Trustees:* Johanna M. Utrecht,* Pres.; Elliott Utrecht,* V.P.; Gary Myerson.
EIN: 113190832

38927
G. P. Rooney Foundation, Inc.
15 The Hollows
East Norwich, NY 11732

Established in 1985 in NY.
Donor(s): Gerald P. Rooney.
Financial data (yr. ended 11/30/01): Grants paid, $7,900; assets, $199,117 (M); gifts received, $7,500; expenditures, $8,269; qualifying distributions, $7,900.
Limitations: Applications not accepted. Giving primarily in the New York, NY area.
Application information: Contributes only to pre-selected organizations.
Officers: Gerald P. Rooney, Pres. and Treas.; Claire S. Rooney, V.P.; John G. Rooney, V.P.; Michele R. Condello, Secy.
EIN: 112768745

38928
The Dr. John A. Burns Scholarship Fund
c/o HSBC Bank USA
P.O. Box 4203
Buffalo, NY 14240

Established in 1988 in NY.
Financial data (yr. ended 01/31/01): Grants paid, $7,899; assets, $91,300 (M); expenditures, $9,299; qualifying distributions, $8,068.
Limitations: Applications not accepted. Giving primarily in Buffalo, NY.
Trustee: HSBC Bank USA.
EIN: 166226548

38929
Chesed Foundation
3920 Cypress Ave.
Brooklyn, NY 11224

Established in 1997.
Donor(s): Michael Weiss.

Financial data (yr. ended 12/31/01): Grants paid, $7,898; assets, $225,099 (M); gifts received, $79,015; expenditures, $8,185; qualifying distributions, $7,898.
Limitations: Applications not accepted. Giving primarily in Brooklyn, NY.
Application information: Contributes only to pre-selected organizations.
Trustee: Michael Weiss.
EIN: 113364001

38930
Scalp and Blade Scholarship Trust
c/o M&T Bank
P.O. Box 22900
Rochester, NY 14692

Financial data (yr. ended 12/31/01): Grants paid, $7,875; assets, $95,428 (M); gifts received, $1,600; expenditures, $8,508; qualifying distributions, $7,897.
Limitations: Giving limited to Erie County, NY.
Application information: Request application through Erie County high schools, guidance counselor or principal. Application form required.
Trustee: M & T Bank.
EIN: 166020842
Codes: GTI

38931
Carl M. Siroty Foundation, Inc.
45 Doral Dr.
Manhasset, NY 11030-3907
Contact: Stanley Winikoff, Pres.

Financial data (yr. ended 12/31/01): Grants paid, $7,875; assets, $75,255 (M); expenditures, $11,805; qualifying distributions, $7,875.
Limitations: Giving primarily in FL and NY.
Officer: Stanley Winikoff, Pres.
EIN: 136193966

38932
The Gardner Family Foundation, Inc.
4 Darley Rd.
Great Neck, NY 11021

Established in 1997 in NY.
Donor(s): Herbert M. Gardner.
Financial data (yr. ended 11/30/01): Grants paid, $7,850; assets, $94,195 (M); expenditures, $9,400; qualifying distributions, $7,850.
Limitations: Applications not accepted. Giving primarily in NY.
Application information: Contributes only to pre-selected organizations.
Officers: Herbert M. Gardner, Pres. and Treas.; Mark K. Gardner, V.P. and Secy.
Directors: David S. Gardner, Elizabeth R. Gardner, Peter H. Gardner.
EIN: 113413198

38933
The Haupt Foundation, Inc.
198 Broadway, Ste. 506
New York, NY 10038

Donor(s): Ira Haupt II.
Financial data (yr. ended 12/31/01): Grants paid, $7,850; assets, $57,760 (M); gifts received, $14,550; expenditures, $9,045; qualifying distributions, $7,850.
Limitations: Applications not accepted. Giving primarily in NY.
Application information: Contributes only to pre-selected organizations.
Officer: Ira Haupt II, Pres.
EIN: 237049709

38934
The Hampshire Charitable Trust
925 Westchester Ave., Ste. 308
White Plains, NY 10604 (914) 993-0777
Application address: 39 Main St., North Hampton, MA 01060
Contact: William C. Newman, Tr.

Established in 1993 in NY.
Donor(s): Howard A. Newman.
Financial data (yr. ended 12/31/01): Grants paid, $7,810; assets, $139,037 (M); expenditures, $9,138; qualifying distributions, $7,810.
Limitations: Giving primarily in MA.
Trustees: Howard A. Newman, William C. Newman.
EIN: 223233353

38935
The Harmon Foundation
c/o BCRS Assocs. LLC
67 Wall St., 8th Fl.
New York, NY 10005

Established in 1981 in NJ.
Donor(s): Charles M. Harmon, Jr.,‡ Germaine F. Harmon.
Financial data (yr. ended 01/31/02): Grants paid, $7,800; assets, $186,243 (M); expenditures, $12,113; qualifying distributions, $7,800.
Limitations: Applications not accepted. Giving primarily in CO and FL.
Application information: Contributes only to pre-selected organizations.
Trustees: Germaine F. Harmon, Timothy B. Harmon.
EIN: 133102892

38936
Farrow Family Foundation, Inc.
c/o Joan Farrow
34 Benton Ave.
Monticello, NY 12701

Established in 1993 in NY.
Donor(s): Jesse M. Farrow, Joan R. Farrow.
Financial data (yr. ended 12/31/01): Grants paid, $7,795; assets, $78,604 (M); expenditures, $11,762; qualifying distributions, $7,795.
Limitations: Applications not accepted.
Application information: Contributes only to pre-selected organizations.
Directors: Jason A. Farrow, Joan R. Farrow, Jonathan M. Farrow, Jill F. Marrero.
EIN: 133741950

38937
BMW Foundation
2621 Palisades Ave.
Riverdale, NY 10463

Financial data (yr. ended 04/30/02): Grants paid, $7,791; assets, $18,228 (M); gifts received, $4,726; expenditures, $7,827; qualifying distributions, $7,791.
Trustee: Myron Weiss.
EIN: 137098618

38938
Nakoda Bherunath Scholarship Foundation, Inc.
c/o K.K. Mehta
42 Bristol Dr.
Manhasset, NY 11030-3944

Financial data (yr. ended 12/31/01): Grants paid, $7,750; assets, $149,363 (L); expenditures, $7,837; qualifying distributions, $7,697.
Limitations: Giving primarily in Jodhpur, India.
Officers: Rakesh Lunia, Pres.; Sanjay Bhandari, Secy.; Prabha Golia, Treas.
EIN: 113031192

38939
Melly & Rochelle Lifshitz Charitable Trust
22 Auerbach Ln.
Lawrence, NY 11559

Established in 1996 in NY.
Donor(s): Menachem E. Lifshitz.
Financial data (yr. ended 10/31/01): Grants paid, $7,750; assets, $3,772 (M); gifts received, $9,000; expenditures, $8,342; qualifying distributions, $9,000.
Limitations: Applications not accepted. Giving primarily in NY.
Application information: Contributes only to pre-selected organizations.
Directors: Daniel Lifshitz, Menachem E. Lifshitz.
EIN: 116478782

38940
Milchman Foundation
c/o Ben Milchman
147-26 70th Ave.
Flushing, NY 11367

Donor(s): Ben Milchman.
Financial data (yr. ended 11/30/01): Grants paid, $7,750; assets, $0 (M); gifts received, $10,152; expenditures, $7,929; qualifying distributions, $15,486.
Trustees: Allan Milchman, Ben Milchman, Evelyn Milchman.
EIN: 113297024

38941
A. J. O'Dell Foundation
4 Madison Ave.
Arcade, NY 14009-1320

Financial data (yr. ended 12/31/01): Grants paid, $7,750; assets, $545,242 (M); expenditures, $15,669; qualifying distributions, $15,667.
Limitations: Applications not accepted. Giving primarily in NY.
Application information: Contributes only to pre-selected organizations.
Trustees: Charles R. Newman, Chair.; Ernestine Howel, Frank Vadway, Lee S. Wishing, Anthony Zenter.
EIN: 160848946

38942
Anna L. Weissberger Foundation, Ltd.
c/o Jay Harris, Hall, Dickler, et al.
110 E. 59th St., 29th Fl.
New York, NY 10022

Established in 1992 in NY.
Donor(s): L. Arnold Weissberger.‡
Financial data (yr. ended 12/31/00): Grants paid, $7,750; assets, $2,343,233 (M); gifts received, $734,615; expenditures, $565,785; qualifying distributions, $152,949; giving activities include $166,004 for programs.
Limitations: Applications not accepted. Giving primarily in New York, NY.
Application information: Contributes only to pre-selected organizations.
Trustees: Fredda L. Harris, Jay S. Harris, Peter D. Raymond.
EIN: 132864367

38943
Hirschell E. and Deanna E. Levine Foundation
74 Lake End Rd.
Merrick, NY 11566-4612

Established in 1986 in NY.
Donor(s): Hirschell E. Levine, Deanna E. Levine.
Financial data (yr. ended 09/30/01): Grants paid, $7,740; assets, $117,281 (M); gifts received,

$15,987; expenditures, $7,923; qualifying distributions, $7,740.
Limitations: Applications not accepted. Giving primarily in NY.
Application information: Contributes only to pre-selected organizations.
Trustees: Deanna E. Levine, Hirschell E. Levine.
EIN: 222767247

38944
Fred Friedman Family Foundation, Inc.
80-46 Grenfell St.
Kew Gardens, NY 11415

Established in 2000 in NY.
Financial data (yr. ended 12/31/00): Grants paid, $7,730; assets, $12,467 (M); gifts received, $20,254; expenditures, $7,730; qualifying distributions, $7,730.
Limitations: Applications not accepted. Giving primarily in NY.
Application information: Contributes only to pre-selected organizations.
Directors: Leonard Elstein, Fred Friedman, Ruth Friedman.
EIN: 113554368

38945
Compass Foundation, Inc.
c/o Allan Rabinowitz
911 Park Ave.
New York, NY 10021

Financial data (yr. ended 12/31/01): Grants paid, $7,691; assets, $103,467 (M); gifts received, $1,039; expenditures, $8,615; qualifying distributions, $7,691.
Limitations: Applications not accepted. Giving on a national basis.
Application information: Contributes only to pre-selected organizations.
Officers: David Schaffer, Pres.; Marvin Broome, Secy.; Allan Rabinowitz, Treas.
EIN: 116018258

38946
H. & Z. Bistricer Charitable Foundation
1480 57th St.
Brooklyn, NY 11219 (718) 851-4623

Donor(s): Henry Bistricer, Jeannie Bistricer, Zahava Bistricer.
Financial data (yr. ended 12/31/01): Grants paid, $7,662; assets, $170,877 (M); expenditures, $8,370; qualifying distributions, $7,662.
Limitations: Applications not accepted. Giving primarily in NY.
Application information: Contributes only to pre-selected organizations.
Trustees: Jeannie Bistricer, Zahava Bistricer.
EIN: 112738322

38947
Sehorn's Corner Foundation, Inc.
c/o KRT Business Management, Inc.
500 5th Ave., Ste. 3000
New York, NY 10110-0002

Established in 1999 in FL.
Donor(s): Jason Sehorn.
Financial data (yr. ended 12/31/00): Grants paid, $7,660; assets, $70,734 (M); gifts received, $125,255; expenditures, $87,910; qualifying distributions, $7,660.
Officers: Jason Sehorn, Pres.; Barry Klarberg, Treas.
Directors: Nancy Benoit, Adam Bree, Richard Cohen, Marc Cooper, Mark Degorter, Jon Miller, Tracy Perlman, MET-RX.
EIN: 134068698

38948
Harold A. Schwartz Foundation, Inc.
855 Ave. of the Americas, No. 609
New York, NY 10001

Established in 1989 in NY.
Donor(s): Harold A. Schwartz.
Financial data (yr. ended 11/30/01): Grants paid, $7,656; assets, $184,145 (M); gifts received, $104,755; expenditures, $12,156; qualifying distributions, $7,656.
Limitations: Applications not accepted. Giving primarily in New York, NY.
Application information: Contributes only to pre-selected organizations.
Officers: Harold A. Schwartz, Pres.; Marilyn Schwartz, V.P. and Treas.; Barbara Schwartz, Secy.
EIN: 133548961

38949
Glatzer Family Foundation
c/o J. Glatzer
2392 Nostrand Ave.
Brooklyn, NY 11210 (718) 258-8700
Contact: Jay Glatzer, Pres.

Established in 2000 in NY.
Donor(s): Jay Glatzer.
Financial data (yr. ended 12/31/01): Grants paid, $7,650; assets, $22,983 (M); gifts received, $13,000; expenditures, $12,493; qualifying distributions, $7,650.
Limitations: Giving primarily in Brooklyn, NY.
Officer and Trustee:* Jay Glatzer,* Pres.
EIN: 113526564

38950
Juliette S. & George J. Lewin Foundation, Inc.
c/o Jacobs, Evall & Blumenfeld, LLP
420 Lexington Ave.
New York, NY 10170-2859

Financial data (yr. ended 11/30/01): Grants paid, $7,650; assets, $114,640 (M); expenditures, $9,299; qualifying distributions, $7,650.
Limitations: Applications not accepted. Giving primarily in FL, and New York, NY.
Application information: Contributes only to pre-selected organizations.
Officers and Directors:* Marjorie L. Ross,* Pres.; Peggy L. Walden,* V.P.; Mervin Ross,* Secy.; Joan L. Lynton,* Treas.; Julian Lynton.
EIN: 136150640

38951
Robert H. Johnson Foundation
50 Center St.
P.O. Box 503
Geneseo, NY 14454 (716) 245-5776
Colorado tel.: (303) 986-0107
Contact: Mary J. Hart, Tr.

Financial data (yr. ended 12/31/99): Grants paid, $7,645; assets, $107,829 (M); gifts received, $1,000; expenditures, $16,143; qualifying distributions, $7,645.
Limitations: Giving primarily in MN.
Trustee: Mary J. Hart.
EIN: 136169798

38952
Odyssey Foundation, Inc.
358 Townline Rd.
Ithaca, NY 14850

Established in 1991 in NY.
Financial data (yr. ended 12/31/00): Grants paid, $7,600; assets, $56,227 (M); expenditures, $8,247; qualifying distributions, $7,600.
Limitations: Applications not accepted. Giving primarily in Ithaca, NY.
Application information: Contributes only to pre-selected organizations.
Officers: Richard Platek, Pres. and Treas.; Evelyn Platek, Secy.
Director: Barbara Platek.
EIN: 223162714

38953
Stella & Abraham Friedhoff Fund, Inc.
1382 Lexington Ave.
New York, NY 10128-1611
Contact: Nancy Friedhoff

Established in 1980 in NY.
Donor(s): Arnold Friedhoff.
Financial data (yr. ended 12/31/00): Grants paid, $7,594; assets, $266,884 (M); expenditures, $8,946; qualifying distributions, $7,594.
Limitations: Giving primarily in San Francisco, CA, and New York, NY.
Application information: Application form not required.
Officers: Hulda Edelstein, Pres.; Robert Edelstein, V.P.; Arnold J. Friedhoff, Secy.; Frances Friedhoff, Treas.
EIN: 133098399

38954
Lawrence J. Israel Foundation
c/o Malakoff, Wasserman & Pecker, C.P.A.
1 Old Country Rd., No. 340
Carle Place, NY 11514-1807

Donor(s): Lawrence Israel.
Financial data (yr. ended 12/31/01): Grants paid, $7,587; assets, $19,367 (M); expenditures, $10,829; qualifying distributions, $7,587.
Trustee: Lawrence J. Israel.
EIN: 136350968

38955
Isabel & David Mahalick Foundation, Inc.
c/o L. Wollin
350 5th Ave., Ste. 2822
New York, NY 10118

Financial data (yr. ended 06/30/01): Grants paid, $7,565; assets, $98,122 (M); gifts received, $51,600; expenditures, $9,128; qualifying distributions, $7,565.
Officers: Isabel Mahalick, Pres.; David Mahalick, V.P.; Lonnie Wollin, Secy.
EIN: 223622986

38956
Helen & Daniel Kudler Foundation
c/o Gettry, Marcus, Stern & Lehrer
220 5th Ave., 4th Fl.
New York, NY 10001

Financial data (yr. ended 08/31/02): Grants paid, $7,560; assets, $12,415 (M); gifts received, $5,000; expenditures, $7,625; qualifying distributions, $7,560.
Limitations: Applications not accepted. Giving primarily in New York, NY.
Application information: Contributes only to pre-selected organizations.
Trustee: Helen Kudler.
EIN: 116112902

38957
The Herman & Regina Auslander Foundation, Inc.
c/o Gross
691 Dahill Rd.
Brooklyn, NY 11218

Established in 1999 in NY.
Donor(s): Regina Auslander.
Financial data (yr. ended 12/31/00): Grants paid, $7,554; assets, $249,272 (M); gifts received,

$100; expenditures, $8,029; qualifying distributions, $7,491.
Limitations: Applications not accepted.
Application information: Contributes only to pre-selected organizations.
Directors: Marcel Gross, Benjamin Kien, Sidney Kien.
EIN: 113453484

38958
The Fowler-Milburn Foundation, Inc.
c/o Gasser & Hayes
116-19 Metropolitan Ave.
Forest Hills, NY 11375

Donor(s): Dorothy Milburn Jessup.
Financial data (yr. ended 03/31/01): Grants paid, $7,550; assets, $160,221 (M); expenditures, $8,285; qualifying distributions, $8,220.
Limitations: Applications not accepted. Giving limited to NY.
Application information: Contributes only to pre-selected organizations.
Officers: J. Milburn Jessep, Pres.; Kathleen Jessep, V.P.; Horace J. Caulkens IV, Treas.
EIN: 133000349

38959
The Andrew & Sally Quale Foundation
11 Northern Ave.
Bronxville, NY 10708

Established in 1986 in NY.
Donor(s): Andrew C. Quale, Jr., Sally Quale.
Financial data (yr. ended 12/31/01): Grants paid, $7,550; assets, $179,879 (M); expenditures, $7,978; qualifying distributions, $7,550.
Limitations: Giving primarily in NY.
Officers and Directors:* Andrew C. Quale, Jr.,* Pres. and Treas.; Sally Quale,* V.P. and Secy.
EIN: 133390699

38960
Dorothy & Naomi Schimel Charitable Foundation, Inc.
39 Gramercy Park N.
New York, NY 10010

Established in 2000 in NY.
Donor(s): Dorothy L. Schimel.
Financial data (yr. ended 12/31/01): Grants paid, $7,541; assets, $158,059 (M); expenditures, $7,639; qualifying distributions, $7,541.
Officers: Dorothy L. Schimel, Pres.; Naomi Schimel, V.P. and Secy.; William M. Parente, Treas.
EIN: 134145637

38961
The Seymour Adler Charitable Foundation Trust
c/o ASI Solutions, Inc.
780 3rd Ave., 6th Fl.
New York, NY 10017-2024

Established in 1999 in NY.
Financial data (yr. ended 12/31/01): Grants paid, $7,525; assets, $137,708 (M); expenditures, $8,660; qualifying distributions, $7,525.
Limitations: Applications not accepted. Giving primarily in NJ and NY.
Application information: Contributes only to pre-selected organizations.
Trustee: Seymour Adler.
EIN: 137158290

38962
The Herman Foundation, Inc.
991 Benton St.
Woodmere, NY 11598-1706
Contact: Irwin Goldberger, V.P.

Financial data (yr. ended 05/31/02): Grants paid, $7,525; assets, $143,680 (M); expenditures, $8,314; qualifying distributions, $7,525.
Limitations: Giving primarily in NY.
Officers and Directors:* Muriel Goldberger,* Pres.; Linda Land,* V.P. and Secy.; Arlene Berrol,* V.P. and Treas.; Irwin Goldberger,* V.P.; Mollie Kaufman.
EIN: 136107985

38963
Baker Charitable Foundation, Inc.
(Formerly The LTT Foundation, Inc.)
c/o Stuart D. Baker
30 Rockefeller Plz., Ste. 3248
New York, NY 10112 (212) 408-5435

Established in 1994 in DE.
Donor(s): Stuart D. Baker.
Financial data (yr. ended 12/31/01): Grants paid, $7,500; assets, $227,791 (M); gifts received, $60,000; expenditures, $10,039; qualifying distributions, $7,500.
Limitations: Applications not accepted. Giving limited to NY.
Application information: Contributes only to pre-selected organizations.
Officers and Director:* Alixandra Baker, Chair. and Treas.; Stuart D. Baker,* Pres.; Antoinette M. Juliano, Secy.
EIN: 133760427

38964
The Blair A. & Elizabeth J. Boyer Charitable Trust
466 Lexington Ave., 18th Fl.
New York, NY 10017-3140

Established in 1993 in NY.
Donor(s): Jennison Assocs. Capital Corp.
Financial data (yr. ended 12/31/01): Grants paid, $7,500; assets, $124,544 (M); expenditures, $7,717; qualifying distributions, $7,500.
Limitations: Applications not accepted. Giving primarily in Chatham, NJ.
Application information: Contributes only to pre-selected organizations.
Trustees: Blair A. Boyer, Elizabeth J. Boyer.
EIN: 137030269

38965
Food for Thought Endowment Fund, Inc.
c/o Food Industry Alliance of NYS, Inc.
130 Washington Ave.
Albany, NY 12210 (518) 434-1900

Established in 1992 in NY.
Donor(s): NYS Food Merchant Assn., Inc.
Financial data (yr. ended 12/31/99): Grants paid, $7,500; assets, $28,172 (M); gifts received, $10,000; expenditures, $13,190; qualifying distributions, $7,495.
Application information: Scholarship applications should include the applicant's vision of the future of the food industry.
Officers and Trustee:* Lawrence T. McLoughlin,* Pres.; Michael Casey, V.P.; Peter Deeb, Treas.
EIN: 223293055

38966
L. K. Foote Family Memorial Fund Trust
c/o Community Bank, N.A.
P.O. Box 690, 201 N. Union St.
Olean, NY 14760-2738

Financial data (yr. ended 12/31/99): Grants paid, $7,500; assets, $181,412 (M); gifts received, $2,525; expenditures, $9,816; qualifying distributions, $15,494; giving activities include $7,500 for loans to individuals.
Limitations: Giving limited to residents of the Olean, NY, area.
Trustee: Community Bank.
EIN: 166031968

38967
Kroll Family Foundation
25 Rectory St.
Scarsdale, NY 10583 (914) 722-6341
Contact: Arthur Kroll, Pres.

Established in 2001 in NY.
Financial data (yr. ended 12/31/01): Grants paid, $7,500; assets, $92,500 (M); gifts received, $50,000; expenditures, $8,250; qualifying distributions, $0.
Limitations: Giving on a national basis.
Officer: Arthur Kroll, Pres.
EIN: 134154059

38968
Stuart T. Low Foundation, Inc.
c/o Seaman and Ashley
51 E. 42nd St., Ste. 1601
New York, NY 10017
Application address: 68 Queens Head St., London NI 8NG, England
Contact: Virginia S. Low, Pres.

Established in 1998 in NY.
Donor(s): Virginia S. Low.
Financial data (yr. ended 12/31/01): Grants paid, $7,500; assets, $108,159 (M); gifts received, $1,000; expenditures, $10,395; qualifying distributions, $7,500.
Officers and Trustees:* Virginia S. Low,* Pres.; Philip Boyle,* V.P.; David P. Seaman, Secy.; Ciannait Low.
EIN: 133978577

38969
The PBH Charitable Trust
466 Lexington Ave., 18th Fl.
New York, NY 10017

Established in 1987 in NY.
Donor(s): John H. Hobbs.
Financial data (yr. ended 12/31/01): Grants paid, $7,500; assets, $98,727 (M); gifts received, $5,000; expenditures, $10,835; qualifying distributions, $8,086.
Limitations: Applications not accepted.
Application information: Contributes only to pre-selected organizations.
Officer: John H. Hobbs, Mgr.
Trustee: Margaret M. Hobbs.
EIN: 136896043

38970
Shanken Family Foundation
387 Park Ave. S.
New York, NY 10016
Contact: Marvin Shanken, Pres.

Established in 1999 in NY.
Donor(s): M. Shanken Communications, Inc.
Financial data (yr. ended 12/31/00): Grants paid, $7,500; assets, $347,196 (M); gifts received, $200,000; expenditures, $7,525; qualifying distributions, $7,500.

38970—NEW YORK

Limitations: Applications not accepted.
Application information: Contributes only to pre-selected organizations.
Officer: Marvin Shanken, Pres.
EIN: 134027049
Codes: CS

38971
Marjorie R. Stermer Charitable Trust
c/o Chemung Canal Trust Co.
P.O. Box 1522
Elmira, NY 14902-1522 (607) 737-3896

Established in 1999.
Donor(s): Marjorie R. Stermer.
Financial data (yr. ended 09/30/01): Grants paid, $7,500; assets, $202,518 (M); expenditures, $14,947; qualifying distributions, $8,225.
Limitations: Giving primarily in NY.
Trustee: Chemung Canal Trust Co.
EIN: 166498259

38972
The Woodcock No. 2 Foundation
30 Rockefeller Plz., Ste. 5600
New York, NY 10112
Application address: 84 Revere St., Boston, MA 02114
Contact: Olga Davidson Nagy, Tr.

Established in 1991 in NY.
Donor(s): P.W. Guth Charitable Lead Unitrust No. 1, P.W. Guth Charitable Lead Unitrust No. 2, Polly W. Guth.
Financial data (yr. ended 11/30/01): Grants paid, $7,500; assets, $855,282 (M); gifts received, $193,141; expenditures, $14,369; qualifying distributions, $7,500.
Limitations: Giving primarily in Boston, MA.
Trustees: Olga Davidson Nagy, Richard T. Watson.
EIN: 133651418

38973
The Victoria S. and Peter T. Michaelis Foundation, Inc.
c/o Peter Michaelis
129 Maple Ave.
Katonah, NY 10536

Established in 2000 in NY.
Donor(s): Peter Michaelis, Victoria Michaelis.
Financial data (yr. ended 12/31/01): Grants paid, $7,490; assets, $299,754 (M); expenditures, $14,818; qualifying distributions, $7,490.
Limitations: Applications not accepted.
Application information: Contributes only to pre-selected organizations.
Officers and Trustees:* Peter Michaelis,* Pres.; Victoria Michaelis,* Secy.-Treas.; Frank E. Sisson III.
EIN: 134150538

38974
The Holliday Foundation
3 Murray Hill Rd.
Scarsdale, NY 10583

Established in 2000 in NY.
Donor(s): Marc Holliday.
Financial data (yr. ended 12/31/01): Grants paid, $7,464; assets, $67,753 (M); gifts received, $50,000; expenditures, $14,393; qualifying distributions, $7,464.
Officers: Marc Holliday, Pres.; Morton Holliday, V.P.; Sheree Holliday, Secy.-Treas.
EIN: 134152690

38975
Lewis M. & Maude L. Stevenson Foundation
110 Westwood Cir.
Roslyn Heights, NY 11577-1836

Financial data (yr. ended 12/31/01): Grants paid, $7,425; assets, $199,837 (M); expenditures, $11,874; qualifying distributions, $7,425.
Limitations: Applications not accepted. Giving primarily in NY.
Application information: Contributes only to pre-selected organizations.
Directors: George Bedor, Daniel L. Gaba.
EIN: 112567223

38976
Virgil and Jane Peck Ehle Scholarship Trust Fund
c/o City National Bank & Trust Co., Trust Off.
14 N. Main St.
Gloversville, NY 12078-3004 (518) 773-7911

Financial data (yr. ended 10/31/01): Grants paid, $7,400; assets, $222,483 (M); expenditures, $8,711; qualifying distributions, $7,400.
Limitations: Giving limited to residents of Gloversville, NY.
Application information: Application form required.
Trustee: City National Bank & Trust Co.
EIN: 146128271

38977
Bernard & Joyce Sillins Foundation
224 W. 49th St., Ste. 411
New York, NY 10019 (212) 262-6622
Additional tel.: (212) 221-1890
Contact: Bernard Sillins, Pres.

Donor(s): Bernard Sillins.
Financial data (yr. ended 12/31/01): Grants paid, $7,400; assets, $29,588 (M); expenditures, $9,090; qualifying distributions, $7,400.
Limitations: Giving primarily in NY.
Officers: Bernard Sillins, Pres.; Joyce Sillins, V.P.
EIN: 222336710

38978
The Troy Savings Bank Charitable Trust
c/o The Troy Savings Bank
32 2nd St.
Troy, NY 12180 (518) 270-3311
Contact: John W. Myer, Trust Off., The Troy Savings Bank

Established in 1997.
Donor(s): The Troy Savings Bank.
Financial data (yr. ended 09/30/01): Grants paid, $7,400; assets, $200,026 (M); expenditures, $11,541; qualifying distributions, $11,541.
Limitations: Giving limited to NY.
Application information: Application form required.
Trustee: The Troy Savings Bank.
EIN: 146189204
Codes: CS, CD

38979
Heartland Foundation
c/o Jon Bloostein
35 Union Square West
New York, NY 10003

Established in 1996 in NY.
Donor(s): Jon Bloostein.
Financial data (yr. ended 06/30/01): Grants paid, $7,390; assets, $118,519 (M); gifts received, $100,001; expenditures, $9,890; qualifying distributions, $8,602.
Limitations: Applications not accepted. Giving primarily in New York, NY.

Application information: Contributes only to pre-selected organizations.
Officer: Jon Bloostein.
EIN: 133864637

38980
David M. Weinberg Family Foundation
80-12 214th St.
Jamaica, NY 11427-1096

Donor(s): David M. Weinberg.
Financial data (yr. ended 04/30/00): Grants paid, $7,375; assets, $75,569 (M); expenditures, $7,532; qualifying distributions, $7,375.
Limitations: Applications not accepted. Giving on a national basis.
Application information: Contributes only to pre-selected organizations.
Trustees: Allen Weinberg, David M. Weinberg, Leonard Weinberg.
EIN: 237015348

38981
Abby and Michael Modell Family Foundation
c/o Michael Modell
498 Seventh Ave., 20th Fl.
New York, NY 10018 (212) 822-1000

Financial data (yr. ended 12/31/00): Grants paid, $7,350; assets, $55,455 (M); gifts received, $20,000; expenditures, $7,507; qualifying distributions, $7,350.
Officers and Directors:* Abby Modell,* Mgr.; Michael Modell,* Mgr.
EIN: 311577154

38982
The Joseph Kell Foundation
c/o Kelley, Drye, & Warren, LLP
101 Park Ave., Ste. 3065
New York, NY 10178

Donor(s): Joseph Kell.
Financial data (yr. ended 12/31/01): Grants paid, $7,321; assets, $102,601 (M); expenditures, $15,978; qualifying distributions, $11,674.
Limitations: Applications not accepted. Giving primarily in NY.
Application information: Contributes only to pre-selected organizations.
Trustees: Ethel Davis, Meyer Davis, Joseph Kell.
EIN: 133076738

38983
Altschul Fund
c/o Marylin B. Altschul
1040 Park Ave., Ste. 10E
New York, NY 10028-1032

Donor(s): Selig Altschul,‡ Marylin B. Altschul.
Financial data (yr. ended 12/31/01): Grants paid, $7,299; assets, $129,499 (M); expenditures, $8,348; qualifying distributions, $7,299.
Limitations: Applications not accepted. Giving primarily in New York, NY.
Application information: Contributes only to pre-selected organizations.
Trustees: Alfred S. Altschul, James S. Altschul, Marylin B. Altschul.
EIN: 136183010

38984
Helene & Richard Rubin Foundation, Inc.
36 The Crossings
Purchase, NY 10577

Donor(s): Helene Rubin, Richard Rubin.
Financial data (yr. ended 10/31/01): Grants paid, $7,284; assets, $10,281 (M); gifts received, $10,000; expenditures, $8,218; qualifying distributions, $7,284.

Limitations: Giving on a national basis, with emphasis on the New York, NY, area.
Application information: Application form not required.
Officers: Richard Rubin, Pres. and Treas.; Helene Rubin, Secy.
EIN: 136177968

38985
Jeanette Odasz Trust
c/o Trustco Bank, N.A.
P.O. Box 380
Schenectady, NY 12301-0380

Financial data (yr. ended 12/31/01): Grants paid, $7,278; assets, $115,154 (M); expenditures, $7,900; qualifying distributions, $7,278.
Limitations: Applications not accepted. Giving primarily in Schenectady, NY.
Application information: Selection by nominations.
Trustee: Trustco Bank, N.A.
EIN: 146105337

38986
Rudolph & Josephine DiPalma Foundation
9 Meadow Hill Pl.
Armonk, NY 10504-1103

Financial data (yr. ended 11/30/01): Grants paid, $7,267; assets, $73,640 (M); expenditures, $8,437; qualifying distributions, $7,267.
Limitations: Applications not accepted. Giving primarily in NY.
Application information: Contributes only to pre-selected organizations.
Officer: Rudolph DiPalma, Pres.
Director: Josephine DiPalma.
EIN: 133101367

38987
Jess Ward Foundation
1430 Broadway
New York, NY 10018-9208
Contact: Raymond Ward, Tr.

Financial data (yr. ended 11/30/01): Grants paid, $7,266; assets, $186,828 (M); expenditures, $7,298; qualifying distributions, $7,266.
Limitations: Giving primarily in NY.
Trustees: Raymond Ward, Sanford Ward.
EIN: 136141282

38988
Peter M. Olympia, Sr. and Edith P. Olympia Charitable Trust
18 Walnut Hill Rd.
Poughkeepsie, NY 12603

Financial data (yr. ended 12/31/99): Grants paid, $7,250; assets, $275,106 (M); expenditures, $9,815; qualifying distributions, $9,815.
Limitations: Applications not accepted.
Application information: Contributes only to pre-selected organizations.
Trustee: Peter M. Olympia, Jr.
EIN: 141789320

38989
Flora and William Surnamer Foundation, Inc.
15 E. 69th St.
New York, NY 10021

Donor(s): Joel M. Surnamer, Herbert Weissman.
Financial data (yr. ended 02/28/02): Grants paid, $7,250; assets, $126,306 (M); gifts received, $3,000; expenditures, $11,284; qualifying distributions, $7,250.
Limitations: Applications not accepted. Giving primarily in NY.
Application information: Contributes only to pre-selected organizations.

Officers: Joel M. Surnamer, Pres.; Glen Surnamer, Secy.
Director: Eric Surnamer.
EIN: 133207049

38990
Laura Schriber Gallik Memorial Scholarship Fund
c/o The National Bank of Delaware County
P.O. Box 389
Walton, NY 13856 (607) 865-4126

Donor(s): Dimitri M. Gallick.
Financial data (yr. ended 12/31/00): Grants paid, $7,232; assets, $192,331 (M); expenditures, $8,301; qualifying distributions, $7,890.
Limitations: Giving limited to Walton, NY.
Application information: Application form required.
Trustee: The National Bank of Delaware County.
EIN: 161406866
Codes: GTI

38991
Chaim Brachah Foundation
198 Hewes St.
Brooklyn, NY 11211
Contact: Joseph Rosner and Phillip Rosner

Established in 1998 in NY.
Financial data (yr. ended 12/31/00): Grants paid, $7,200; assets, $188,647 (M); gifts received, $110,180; expenditures, $9,217; qualifying distributions, $7,200.
Limitations: Giving primarily in Brooklyn, NY.
Trustees: Zisel Fisher, Josef Rosner, Phillip Rosner.
EIN: 137171868

38992
McAfee Foundation, Inc.
c/o Davidson, Dawson & Clark, LLP
330 Madison Ave., 35th Fl.
New York, NY 10017

Financial data (yr. ended 12/31/01): Grants paid, $7,200; assets, $197,212 (M); expenditures, $14,079; qualifying distributions, $7,200.
Limitations: Applications not accepted. Giving primarily in NY.
Application information: Contributes only to pre-selected organizations.
Officers and Directors:* Jean P. Tilt,* Pres.; Priscilla T. Pochna,* Secy.; Jean T. Sammis,* Treas.
EIN: 136051793

38993
Beck & Wiesenthal Charitable Foundation
c/o M. Wiesenthal
444 Madison Ave., Ste. 2802
New York, NY 10022-6903

Financial data (yr. ended 12/31/01): Grants paid, $7,175; assets, $25,673 (M); gifts received, $6,500; expenditures, $7,208; qualifying distributions, $7,175.
Limitations: Applications not accepted. Giving primarily in New York, NY.
Application information: Contributes only to pre-selected organizations.
Officers: Margery Wiesenthal, Pres.; Melvin L. Wiesenthal, Secy.
EIN: 366124662

38994
The Lubin Foundation, Inc.
(Formerly Louis & Anna P. Lubin Foundation, Inc.)
19 Hughes Ct.
Queensbury, NY 12804 (518) 761-0262
Contact: Stephen R. Lubin, Pres.

Financial data (yr. ended 05/31/02): Grants paid, $7,175; assets, $94,571 (M); expenditures, $12,948; qualifying distributions, $7,175.
Limitations: Giving primarily in NY.
Officers: Stephen R. Lubin, Pres.; Karen L. Vincent, V.P.; Denise L. Kohler, Secy.
EIN: 136117975

38995
St. Luke's Nurses' Benefit Fund
P.O. Box 250892, Columbia Station
New York, NY 10025
Application address: 3 Leewald Ln., City Island, NY 10464
Contact: Barbara Edwards Dennis, Tr.

Financial data (yr. ended 06/30/01): Grants paid, $7,170; assets, $445,841 (M); expenditures, $9,820; qualifying distributions, $7,170.
Limitations: Giving primarily in New York, NY.
Application information: Application form required.
Trustees: Barbara Edwards Dennis, Judith Gantly.
EIN: 136164433

38996
Marvin & Joy Moser Foundation, Inc.
13 Murray Hill Rd.
Scarsdale, NY 10583-2829

Established in 1984 in NY.
Donor(s): Marvin Moser.
Financial data (yr. ended 08/31/01): Grants paid, $7,155; assets, $13,068 (M); gifts received, $5,000; expenditures, $7,605; qualifying distributions, $7,155.
Limitations: Applications not accepted. Giving primarily in NY.
Application information: Contributes only to pre-selected organizations.
Officers: Marvin Moser, Pres.; Warren J. Sinsheimer, Secy.; Joy Moser, Treas.
EIN: 132617131

38997
Norman and Susan Ember Foundation
945 5th Ave.
New York, NY 10021-2655

Established in 1994 in NY.
Financial data (yr. ended 12/31/01): Grants paid, $7,145; assets, $114,437 (M); expenditures, $7,975; qualifying distributions, $7,145.
Limitations: Applications not accepted. Giving on a national basis, with emphasis on New York, NY.
Application information: Contributes only to pre-selected organizations.
Trustee: Norman Ember.
EIN: 133799925

38998
Star Welfare Foundation, Inc.
c/o Marks, Paneth & Shron, LLP
622 3rd Ave.
New York, NY 10017
Application address: 425 Underhill Blvd., Syosset, NY 11791
Contact: Martin Silver, Pres.

Established in 1944 in NY.
Donor(s): Star Industries, Inc., Star Liquor Imports, Inc.

38998—NEW YORK

Financial data (yr. ended 12/31/00): Grants paid, $7,125; assets, $115,380 (M); expenditures, $7,225; qualifying distributions, $7,064.
Limitations: Giving primarily in MA and NY.
Officer: Martin Silver, Pres. and Treas.
EIN: 136110450
Codes: CS, CD

38999
Jack & Belle Alpern Foundation, Inc.
140 8th Ave.
Brooklyn, NY 11215

Financial data (yr. ended 10/31/01): Grants paid, $7,110; assets, $176,381 (M); expenditures, $14,408; qualifying distributions, $7,110.
Limitations: Applications not accepted.
Application information: Contributes only to pre-selected organizations.
Officers: Robert A. Alpern, Pres. and Treas.; Sherry Alpern, V.P. and Secy.
EIN: 136198283

39000
The Paslaqua Charitable Foundation
510 Mt. Vernon Rd.
Snyder, NY 14226

Established in 2000 in NY.
Donor(s): Kenneth R. Paslaqua.
Financial data (yr. ended 12/31/01): Grants paid, $7,070; assets, $4,924 (M); expenditures, $8,350; qualifying distributions, $7,070.
Limitations: Applications not accepted.
Application information: Contributes only to pre-selected organizations.
Officers and Directors:* Kenneth R. Paslaqua,* Pres.; Nancy J. Trotter,* V.P.; Nancy J. L. Paslaqua,* Secy.
EIN: 161586282

39001
Luke & Anthony Santiago Foundation
c/o James C. Muffoletto, C.P.A.
228 Linwood Ave.
Buffalo, NY 14209

Established in 1996 in NY.
Donor(s): Luke Santiago Testamentary Trust.
Financial data (yr. ended 12/31/01): Grants paid, $7,030; assets, $162,180 (M); expenditures, $10,554; qualifying distributions, $7,030.
Limitations: Applications not accepted. Giving primarily in NY.
Application information: Contributes only to pre-selected organizations.
Officers: Vincent F. Pierino, Pres.; James C. Muffoletto, Secy.
Directors: Anna Maria Santiago Petrishin, Al Patrick Santiago, Anthony H. Santiago, Anthony John Santiago, Carmen Andrew Santiago.
EIN: 161502901

39002
William H. St. Thomas Family Foundation, Inc.
P.O. Box 913
Gloversville, NY 12078-0913

Financial data (yr. ended 12/31/01): Grants paid, $7,010; assets, $408,541 (M); expenditures, $7,773; qualifying distributions, $7,010.
Limitations: Applications not accepted.
Application information: Contributes only to pre-selected organizations.
Officers: James W. St. Thomas, Pres.; Ruth Van Huesen, Secy.-Treas.
EIN: 237175615

39003
Berent-Lott Charitable Trust
242 Pleasant Vale Rd.
Tivoli, NY 12583-5205   (845) 756-2577
Contact: Eberhard F. Berent, Tr. and Paul Lott, Tr.

Donor(s): Eberhard F. Berent, Paul Lott.
Financial data (yr. ended 12/31/01): Grants paid, $7,000; assets, $139,827 (M); gifts received, $300; expenditures, $7,495; qualifying distributions, $7,995.
Trustees: Eberhard F. Berent, Paul Lott.
EIN: 141787907

39004
BGM Foundation
P.O. Box 490
Johnson City, NY 13790-0490

Financial data (yr. ended 02/28/02): Grants paid, $7,000; assets, $174,279 (M); expenditures, $8,861; qualifying distributions, $8,861.
Limitations: Applications not accepted. Giving primarily in Binghamton, NY.
Application information: Contributes only to pre-selected organizations.
Trustees: Ferris Akel, George Akel, Ronald Akel.
EIN: 161255123

39005
The Aaron, Ida & Abraham Davidson Memorial Foundation
(Formerly The Aaron & Ida Davidson Foundation)
c/o Rabbi Gershon Rothstein
1529 E. 18th St.
Brooklyn, NY 11230

Established in 1952 in ME.
Donor(s): Rabbi David Rothstein.
Financial data (yr. ended 12/31/01): Grants paid, $7,000; assets, $143,349 (M); gifts received, $5,200; expenditures, $7,658; qualifying distributions, $7,000.
Limitations: Applications not accepted.
Application information: Contributes only to pre-selected organizations.
Officers and Directors:* Rabbi Eser Davidson,* Pres. and Treas.; Rabbi David Rothstein,* Secy.; Rabbi Gershon Rothstein,* Mgr.; Aaron Yitzchak Davidson, Sarah R. Honig, Rabbi J.H. Marcus, Lillian Marcus, Judith Rosenfeld, Lewis H. Rothstein, Bernard Slosberg, Irene Slosberg.
EIN: 016023919

39006
The Dillon-Presti Foundation
50 Broad St., No. 808
New York, NY 10004-2307

Established in 1993 in PA.
Donor(s): E. Lee Hennessee.
Financial data (yr. ended 12/31/01): Grants paid, $7,000; assets, $114,217 (M); gifts received, $1,000; expenditures, $7,844; qualifying distributions, $7,000.
Limitations: Giving primarily in NY and TN.
Trustees: Charles J. Gradante, E. Lee Hennessee.
EIN: 237743384

39007
Ralph Dean & Evelyn Peake Harby Scholarship Fund
c/o The National Bank of Delaware County
P.O. Box 389
Walton, NY 13856   (607) 865-4126

Financial data (yr. ended 12/31/00): Grants paid, $7,000; assets, $236,019 (M); expenditures, $8,168; qualifying distributions, $7,627.
Limitations: Giving limited to Walton, NY.

Application information: Unsolicited requests for funds not considered or acknowledged. Application form required.
Trustee: The National Bank of Delaware County.
EIN: 166210926
Codes: GTI

39008
Horwood C. and Alene S. Jones Foundation
c/o Nicholas Petrosillo
1416 Riverbend Rd.
Baldwinsville, NY 13027

Established in 1990 in NY.
Financial data (yr. ended 12/31/00): Grants paid, $7,000; assets, $183,023 (M); expenditures, $15,033; qualifying distributions, $10,564.
Application information: Application form required.
Trustees: Nicholas Petrosillo, Sylvia Petrosillo, Camilla Rivard, Mark Rivard.
EIN: 223032132

39009
Lespamtry Foundation
146 Central Park W.
New York, NY 10023-2005   (212) 724-9240
Contact: Harold B. Ehrlich, Tr.

Financial data (yr. ended 10/31/01): Grants paid, $7,000; assets, $62,389 (M); gifts received, $7,500; expenditures, $7,104; qualifying distributions, $7,000.
Limitations: Giving primarily in New York, NY.
Trustee: Harold B. Ehrlich.
EIN: 136212534

39010
Norma Murray Private Foundation
c/o Donald L. Murray
4802 Cavalry Green Dr.
Manlius, NY 13104

Established in 2001 in NY.
Financial data (yr. ended 12/31/01): Grants paid, $7,000; assets, $150,709 (M); gifts received, $149,644; expenditures, $7,925; qualifying distributions, $6,927.
Limitations: Applications not accepted.
Application information: Contributes only to pre-selected organizations.
Trustee: Donald L. Murray.
EIN: 161588986

39011
The Stoll-Kaufman Foundation
60 E. 42nd St., Ste. 3700
New York, NY 10165-0150   (212) 682-3488
Application address: c/o Barry E. Kaufman, 333 Clay St., Ste. 2700, Houston, TX 77002, tel.: (832) 476-3613
Contact: Martin A. Stroll, Tr.

Financial data (yr. ended 12/31/01): Grants paid, $7,000; assets, $92,530 (M); expenditures, $7,286; qualifying distributions, $7,000.
Limitations: Giving primarily in New York, NY, and Houston, TX.
Application information: Generally contributes to pre-selected organizations. Application form not required.
Trustees: Barry E. Kaufman, Martin A. Stoll.
EIN: 136129520

39012
Teitler Foundation, Inc.
c/o Teitler & Teitler
1114 Ave. of Americas, 45th Fl.
New York, NY 10036

Donor(s): Teitler & Teitler.

Financial data (yr. ended 12/31/01): Grants paid, $7,000; assets, $52,192 (M); expenditures, $7,170; qualifying distributions, $7,152.
Limitations: Applications not accepted.
Application information: Contributes only to pre-selected organizations.
Director: Michael F. Teitler.
EIN: 237123347
Codes: CS

39013
Philip Zwickler Charitable & Memorial Foundation
c/o Allen Zwickler
437 Madison Ave.
New York, NY 10022

Established in 1992 in NY.
Donor(s): Seymour Zwickler, Allen Zwickler.
Financial data (yr. ended 12/31/01): Grants paid, $6,995; assets, $81,125 (M); gifts received, $16,761; expenditures, $9,508; qualifying distributions, $6,995.
Limitations: Applications not accepted.
Application information: Contributes only to pre-selected organizations.
Trustees: Caren Levine, Allen Zwickler, Seymour Zwickler.
EIN: 116413445

39014
The Heckman-Takahara Family Foundation
(Formerly The Stanley D. Heckman Educational Trust)
1251 Ave. of Americas, 35th Fl.
New York, NY 10020

Established in 1986 in NY.
Donor(s): Stanley D. Heckman.
Financial data (yr. ended 12/31/01): Grants paid, $6,950; assets, $79,992 (M); expenditures, $7,173; qualifying distributions, $6,950.
Limitations: Applications not accepted. Giving primarily in New York, NY.
Application information: Contributes only to pre-selected organizations.
Trustee: Stanley D. Heckman.
EIN: 236796049

39015
The Melvin Stecher and Norman Horowitz Foundation, Inc.
(Formerly The Stecher and Horowitz Foundation, Inc.)
721 5th Ave., Apt. 40A
New York, NY 10022-2523

Established in 1987 in NY.
Financial data (yr. ended 12/31/01): Grants paid, $6,940; assets, $828 (M); gifts received, $5,648; expenditures, $7,248; qualifying distributions, $6,940.
Trustees: Norman Horowitz, Melvin Stecher.
EIN: 112842809

39016
The Richard & Hazel Rubin Foundation
c/o Eagle & Fein
342 Madison Ave., Ste. 1712
New York, NY 10173

Established in 1997 in NY.
Donor(s): Hazel Rubini.
Financial data (yr. ended 12/31/01): Grants paid, $6,925; assets, $45,728 (M); expenditures, $10,539; qualifying distributions, $6,925.
Limitations: Applications not accepted.
Application information: Contributes only to pre-selected organizations.
Officer: Hazel Rubin, Pres.
EIN: 133743289

39017
The Ebrahim Eshaghian Foundation, Inc.
215 Lexington Ave., Ste. 1103
New York, NY 10016

Established in 2000 in NY.
Donor(s): Ebrahim Eshaghian.‡
Financial data (yr. ended 12/31/01): Grants paid, $6,900; assets, $147,023 (M); expenditures, $6,990; qualifying distributions, $6,900.
Limitations: Applications not accepted.
Application information: Contributes only to pre-selected organizations.
Trustees: David Eshaghian, Esagh Eshaghian, Joseph Eshaghian, Massoud Eshaghian.
EIN: 134015292

39018
Hazel B. Truesdell Scholarship Fund
2486 Youngstown-Lockport Rd.
Ransomville, NY 14131-9644 (716) 791-3364
Contact: Susan E. Schafer, Tr.

Donor(s): Hazel B. Tresdell.‡
Financial data (yr. ended 12/31/99): Grants paid, $6,900; assets, $179,233 (M); expenditures, $7,363; qualifying distributions, $6,958.
Limitations: Giving limited to the Youngstown and Ransomville, NY, areas.
Application information: Applicant must provide transcript, SAT and ACT scores and letters of recommendation. Application form required.
Trustees: Dorothy Breckon, Mary Jo Hannah, Sue Holmes, Martin Miller, Susan E. Schafer, Christine S. "Munch" Zewin.
EIN: 223077990
Codes: GTI

39019
Gomel Chesed Foundation
c/o G. Hirsch
1252 46th St.
Brooklyn, NY 11219

Established in 1999 in NY.
Financial data (yr. ended 12/31/00): Grants paid, $6,886; assets, $16,339 (M); gifts received, $18,500; expenditures, $6,911; qualifying distributions, $6,886.
Limitations: Applications not accepted.
Application information: Contributes only to pre-selected organizations.
Trustees: Eleanor Hirsch, Gerald Hirsch.
EIN: 113521346

39020
Edward and Elaine L. Lee Foundation
50 E. Hartsdale Ave.
Hartsdale, NY 10530

Donor(s): Edward Lee, Elaine L. Lee.
Financial data (yr. ended 07/31/99): Grants paid, $6,886; assets, $78,881 (M); expenditures, $7,180; qualifying distributions, $6,842.
Limitations: Applications not accepted. Giving primarily in NY.
Application information: Contributes only to pre-selected organizations.
Officers: Elaine L. Lee, Pres. and Treas.; Donald B. Lee, V.P.; David S. Lee, Secy.
EIN: 136076021

39021
Moore-Church Scholarship Trust
c/o M&T Bank
1 M&T Plz., 8th Fl.
Buffalo, NY 14240
Application address: c/o Potomac State College, Keyser, WV 26726
Contact: Robert Eagle

Established in 1997 in WV.
Financial data (yr. ended 10/31/01): Grants paid, $6,885; assets, $221,189 (M); expenditures, $9,205; qualifying distributions, $6,885.
Limitations: Giving limited to residents of WV.
Trustee: M&T Bank.
EIN: 550755281

39022
Jacob and Paulette Levy Scholarship Fund
c/o David M. Brickman
6 E. 43rd St.
New York, NY 10017

Established in 1993 in NY.
Financial data (yr. ended 10/31/99): Grants paid, $6,865; assets, $113,806 (M); gifts received, $300; expenditures, $13,230; qualifying distributions, $11,883.
Limitations: Applications not accepted.
Application information: Contributes only to pre-selected organizations.
Trustees: Harry Bardin, Nissim Levy, Harry Minskoff, Sarah Newitter, Rabbi Arthur Schneier.
EIN: 136775325

39023
McLaughlin Family Fund, Inc.
(Formerly Edward B. McLaughlin Foundation, Inc.)
c/o Thomas B. Albertson
P.O. Box 211, 271 N. Ave.
New Rochelle, NY 10802

Established in 1967 in NY.
Donor(s): Edward B. McLaughlin, Marene G. McLaughlin.
Financial data (yr. ended 10/31/01): Grants paid, $6,850; assets, $200,139 (M); gifts received, $100; expenditures, $8,207; qualifying distributions, $6,850.
Limitations: Applications not accepted. Giving primarily in CT and FL.
Application information: Contributes only to pre-selected organizations.
Officers and Trustees:* Alexander M. Amos,* Chair.; Meredith Johnson, Pres.; Marene G. McLaughlin, V.P. and Secy.; Alexander M. Amos, Jonathan McLaughlin.
EIN: 136256925

39024
Tully & Michelle Plesser Foundation, Inc.
(Formerly Plesser Foundation, Inc.)
c/o T. Plesser
459 Butter Ln.
Bridgehampton, NY 11932

Donor(s): Tully Plesser, Zachary Plesser.
Financial data (yr. ended 12/31/01): Grants paid, $6,850; assets, $10,724 (M); gifts received, $5,000; expenditures, $7,036; qualifying distributions, $7,036.
Limitations: Giving primarily in NY.
Officer: Tully Plesser, Pres.
EIN: 136154226

39025
Hanna M. Earl Crematory Trust
c/o HSBC Bank USA
P.O. Box 4203, 16th Fl.
Buffalo, NY 14240

Established in 1987 in NY.
Financial data (yr. ended 07/31/01): Grants paid, $6,841; assets, $132,052 (M); expenditures, $8,869; qualifying distributions, $7,063.
Limitations: Applications not accepted.
Application information: Contributes only to pre-selected organizations.
Trustee: HSBC Bank USA.
EIN: 146018655

39026
Israel & Fenie Feit Family Foundation, Inc.
300 Central Ave.
Lawrence, NY 11559-1619

Donor(s): Dudley Feit.‡
Financial data (yr. ended 12/31/01): Grants paid, $6,831; assets, $79,084 (M); expenditures, $7,060; qualifying distributions, $6,831.
Limitations: Giving primarily in NY.
Trustee: Joseph Feit.
EIN: 136201462

39027
Mollie and Jack Epstein Foundation
c/o M. Camhi
9 Brooksite Dr.
Smithtown, NY 11787-3400
Application address: 106 Stone Oaks Dr., Hartsdale, NY 10530
Contact: Morris Epstein, Mgr.

Financial data (yr. ended 12/31/01): Grants paid, $6,818; assets, $38,372 (M); expenditures, $7,519; qualifying distributions, $6,818.
Limitations: Giving primarily in NY.
Application information: Application form not required.
Officer: Morris Epstein, Mgr.
EIN: 116016846

39028
Otsego 2000, Inc.
P.O. Box 173
Cooperstown, NY 13326-0173

Established in 1984 in NY.
Financial data (yr. ended 12/31/00): Grants paid, $6,812; assets, $252,852 (M); gifts received, $171,311; expenditures, $162,044; qualifying distributions, $153,347; giving activities include $141,893 for programs.
Limitations: Applications not accepted. Giving primarily in upstate NY.
Application information: Contributes only to pre-selected organizations.
Officers: Henry S.F. Cooper, Pres.; Kent Barwick, V.P.; Kurt Ofer, V.P.; Robert Poulson, V.P.; Polly Renckens, Secy.; Edward Wesnofske, Treas.
Directors: Martha McGowan, Michael Moffat, and 16 additional directors.
EIN: 112654945

39029
Edward Ariowitsch Foundation
c/o Nina Ariowitsch
305 E. 72nd St.
New York, NY 10022

Established in 1996.
Donor(s): Ariowitsch Family Foundation, Inc.
Financial data (yr. ended 12/31/01): Grants paid, $6,800; assets, $388,571 (M); expenditures, $9,729; qualifying distributions, $6,800.
Limitations: Applications not accepted. Giving primarily in New York, NY.
Application information: Contributes only to pre-selected organizations.
Officer: Tim Ariowitsch, Pres.
Trustees: Nina Ariowitsch, Audrey Wallrock.
EIN: 137096262

39030
The Nicholas J. & Katherine M. Campbell Foundation, Inc.
c/o Gasser & Hayes
106-19 Metropolitan Ave.
Forest Hills, NY 11375

Donor(s): Katherine M. Campbell.
Financial data (yr. ended 04/30/02): Grants paid, $6,800; assets, $40,667 (M); expenditures, $7,522; qualifying distributions, $6,800.
Limitations: Applications not accepted. Giving primarily in PA.
Application information: Contributes only to pre-selected organization.
Officers: Mary C. Caldwell, Pres.; Patrick Caldwell, V.P. and Treas.; John C. Campbell, Secy.
EIN: 133270981

39031
Simon and Eve Colin Foundation II
c/o Stephen Colin
350 E. 79th St., Ste. 14H
New York, NY 10021

Established in 2000 in DE.
Donor(s): Stephen Colin.
Financial data (yr. ended 12/31/01): Grants paid, $6,800; assets, $9,000 (M); gifts received, $8,275; expenditures, $7,497; qualifying distributions, $6,800.
Limitations: Applications not accepted.
Application information: Contributes only to pre-selected organizations.
Director: Stephen Colin.
EIN: 134075261

39032
Meringoff Foundation, Inc.
P.O. Box 175
Old Westbury, NY 11568-0175

Established in 1985 in NY and DE.
Donor(s): Paul Meringoff.
Financial data (yr. ended 06/30/01): Grants paid, $6,785; assets, $70,045 (M); expenditures, $10,472; qualifying distributions, $6,785.
Limitations: Applications not accepted. Giving primarily in NY.
Application information: Contributes only to pre-selected organizations.
Officer: Paul Meringoff, Pres. and Treas.
EIN: 112785580

39033
Morrie R. Yohai Foundation
18 Sinclair Dr.
Kings Point, NY 11024-1622

Donor(s): Morrie R. Yohai.
Financial data (yr. ended 11/30/01): Grants paid, $6,785; assets, $262,363 (M); expenditures, $7,117; qualifying distributions, $6,785.
Limitations: Applications not accepted. Giving primarily in New York, NY.
Application information: Contributes only to pre-selected organizations.
Officers: Morrie R. Yohai, Pres.; Phyllis Yohai, Secy.
EIN: 136195837

39034
The Couvert-Falcone Charitable Foundation
c/o Alfred & Francoise Falcone
5177 Pointe E. Dr.
Jamesville, NY 13078

Established in 1990 in NY.
Donor(s): Alfred E. Falcone, Francoise Falcone.
Financial data (yr. ended 11/30/01): Grants paid, $6,750; assets, $86,662 (M); gifts received, $21; expenditures, $9,267; qualifying distributions, $6,750.
Limitations: Applications not accepted. Giving primarily in Syracuse, NY.
Application information: Contributes only to pre-selected organizations.
Trustees: Alfred E. Falcone, Francoise Falcone.
EIN: 166352339

39035
Foundation for Science and Theology, Inc.
(Formerly The Globus Foundation, Inc.)
P.O. Box 18050
Hauppauge, NY 11788

Established in 1988 in NY.
Financial data (yr. ended 12/31/01): Grants paid, $6,750; assets, $243,226 (M); expenditures, $35,807; qualifying distributions, $6,750.
Limitations: Applications not accepted.
Application information: Contributes only to pre-selected organizations.
Officers: Alfred Globus, Pres.; Kenneth Globus, Secy.-Treas.
Director: Robert Rubinger.
EIN: 112728858

39036
Gerald B. H. Solomon Freedom Foundation, Inc.
P.O. Box 1246
South Glens Falls, NY 12803

Established in 1992 in NY.
Donor(s): Gerald B.H. Solomon.
Financial data (yr. ended 09/30/01): Grants paid, $6,750; assets, $115,880 (M); gifts received, $2,000; expenditures, $6,905; qualifying distributions, $6,865.
Limitations: Applications not accepted. Giving primarily in the Albany, NY, area.
Directors: Robert Avon, Preston L. Jenkins, Jr., Herb Koster, Dante Orsini, Freda Solomon, Gerald B.H. Solomon, J. Ronald Williams.
EIN: 223246773
Codes: GTI

39037
The Victor B. Cook Foundation
c/o George I. Raskin
23 Fox Hunt Ln.
Great Neck, NY 11020

Donor(s): George I. Raskin.
Financial data (yr. ended 10/31/99): Grants paid, $6,739; assets, $9,154 (M); gifts received, $8,000; expenditures, $6,999; qualifying distributions, $6,739.
Limitations: Applications not accepted. Giving primarily in New York, NY.
Application information: Contributes only to pre-selected organizations.
Trustee: George I. Raskin.
EIN: 136162323

39038
M. Bonnie Axthelm Charitable Foundation
c/o U.S. Trust
114 W. 47th St., TaxVas
New York, NY 10036

Established in 1997 in CT.

Donor(s): M. Bonnie Axthelm.‡
Financial data (yr. ended 12/31/00): Grants paid, $6,725; assets, $386,763 (M); expenditures, $10,425; qualifying distributions, $8,425.
Limitations: Applications not accepted.
Application information: Contributes only to pre-selected organizations.
Trustees: Nancy Axthelm, Stephen Axthelm, Megan A. Brown.
EIN: 066444196

39039
Perry & Teresa Pearson Foundation, Inc.
c/o Wollin Assocs.
350 5th Ave., Ste. 2822
New York, NY 10118

Established in 1991 in DE.
Donor(s): Gerald L. Pearson.
Financial data (yr. ended 09/30/01): Grants paid, $6,720; assets, $103,220 (M); expenditures, $8,671; qualifying distributions, $6,720.
Limitations: Applications not accepted. Giving limited to Winterset, IA.
Application information: Contributes only to pre-selected organizations.
Officers: Perry Pearson, Pres.; Teresa Pearson, V.P.; Lonnie Wollin, Secy.
EIN: 133636275

39040
Mimi Abrons Foundation, Inc.
28 Rigene Rd.
Harrison, NY 10528

Donor(s): Mimi Abrams.
Financial data (yr. ended 12/31/01): Grants paid, $6,715; assets, $84,075 (M); expenditures, $8,954; qualifying distributions, $6,715.
Limitations: Applications not accepted.
Application information: Contributes only to pre-selected organizations.
Officer: Mimi Abrons, Pres.
EIN: 133769282

39041
Robert and Arnold Hoffman Foundation, Inc.
c/o Cadwalader, Wickerson & Taft
100 Maiden Ln., Ste. 2106
New York, NY 10038
Application address: 5340 N. Campbell Ave., Tucson, AZ 85718
Contact: M. Richard Evarts, Pres.

Financial data (yr. ended 10/31/01): Grants paid, $6,695; assets, $90,803 (M); expenditures, $8,138; qualifying distributions, $7,628.
Limitations: Giving primarily in the eastern U.S.
Officers: M. Richard Evarts, Pres.; Carol Evarts, Secy.
EIN: 136161391

39042
Arnold & Mary Lehman Foundation, Inc.
c/o James R. Zuckerman
3000 Marcus Ave., No. 1E5
New Hyde Park, NY 11042

Financial data (yr. ended 06/30/02): Grants paid, $6,665; assets, $150,369 (M); expenditures, $9,263; qualifying distributions, $6,665.
Limitations: Applications not accepted. Giving primarily in NY.
Application information: Contributes only to pre-selected organizations.
Officers and Directors:* Victor Zelman,* Pres.; Dale L. Schlafer,* V.P.; James R. Zuckerman,* Secy.-Treas.
EIN: 136167633

39043
Nathan & Augusta Simpson Foundation
c/o M. Kanner, C.P.A.
7448 Amboy Rd.
Staten Island, NY 10307-1421

Financial data (yr. ended 09/30/01): Grants paid, $6,649; assets, $484,258 (M); expenditures, $34,179; qualifying distributions, $6,649.
Limitations: Applications not accepted. Giving primarily in New York, NY.
Application information: Contributes only to pre-selected organizations.
Trustees: Brach Simpson, Henry Simpson, Scott Simpson.
EIN: 136121503

39044
Frances & Solomon Petchers Foundation, Inc.
90 Union St.
New Rochelle, NY 10805 (914) 633-6759
Contact: Benjamin Petchers, Pres., or Esther Petchers, Tr.

Financial data (yr. ended 09/30/01): Grants paid, $6,635; assets, $251,663 (M); expenditures, $11,513; qualifying distributions, $6,635.
Limitations: Giving primarily in NY.
Officers and Trustees:* Benjamin Petchers,* Pres.; Marcia K. Petchers, Treas.; Esther Petchers.
EIN: 136159090

39045
Francesca Gennaro Testamentary Trust
c/o Michael Kertis
350 5th Ave., Ste. 330
New York, NY 10118-0399 (212) 629-8899

Established around 1993.
Financial data (yr. ended 12/31/99): Grants paid, $6,630; assets, $164,078 (M); expenditures, $9,840; qualifying distributions, $0.
Limitations: Giving primarily in Whitestone, NY.
Application information: Application form not required.
Officer and Trustees:* Michael F. Burke,* Mgr.; Michael Kertis.
EIN: 137006126

39046
Santo Gennaro Testamentary Trust
c/o Burke, Burke & Burke
350 5th Ave., Ste. 330
New York, NY 10118 (212) 629-8899
Contact: Michael F. Burke, Mgr.

Established around 1993.
Financial data (yr. ended 12/31/99): Grants paid, $6,628; assets, $164,078 (M); expenditures, $9,840; qualifying distributions, $9,840.
Limitations: Giving primarily to residents of Rye, NY.
Application information: Application form not required.
Officer and Trustees:* Michael F. Burke, Mgr.; Michael Kertis.
EIN: 137006127

39047
Shonan Foundation
c/o S. Skaist
685 Stewart Ave.
Staten Island, NY 10314-4218

Established in 1999 in NY.
Financial data (yr. ended 07/31/01): Grants paid, $6,620; assets, $250 (M); gifts received, $4,200; expenditures, $7,020; qualifying distributions, $6,620.
Limitations: Applications not accepted. Giving primarily in NJ.
Application information: Contributes only to pre-selected organizations.
Trustees: Nancy S. Skaist, Sholom Y. Skaist.
EIN: 134071855

39048
Irving L. Braverman Foundation, Inc.
c/o Louis Weissman
100 Cedarhurst Ave.
Cedarhurst, NY 11516-2129

Donor(s): Irving L. Braverman.
Financial data (yr. ended 05/31/02): Grants paid, $6,616; assets, $1,359 (M); expenditures, $6,649; qualifying distributions, $6,616.
Limitations: Applications not accepted. Giving primarily in New York, NY.
Application information: Contributes only to pre-selected organizations.
Officers: Irving L. Braverman, Pres.; Judith Braverman, Secy.
EIN: 136158917

39049
Richard & Martha Coopersmith Foundation
c/o R.D. Coopersmith
96 Spring St.
New York, NY 10012

Established in 1997.
Donor(s): Richard D. Coopersmith.
Financial data (yr. ended 12/31/01): Grants paid, $6,613; assets, $34,913 (M); gifts received, $10,000; expenditures, $6,718; qualifying distributions, $6,613.
Limitations: Applications not accepted.
Application information: Contributes only to pre-selected organizations.
Officers and Directors:* Richard D. Coopersmith,* Pres.; Martha Coopersmith,* Secy.; Ralph Elefant.
EIN: 133978468

39050
The Crawford-Doyle Charitable Foundation
c/o John K. Doyle
21 E. 90th St., Ste. 12-C
New York, NY 10128-0654

Established in 1999 in NY.
Donor(s): John Doyle, Judith Crawford.
Financial data (yr. ended 12/31/01): Grants paid, $6,600; assets, $527,282 (M); gifts received, $103,721; expenditures, $12,907; qualifying distributions, $8,188.
Limitations: Applications not accepted.
Application information: Contributes only to pre-selected organizations.
Trustees: Judith Crawford, John K. Doyle.
EIN: 137190672

39051
Gilrod Foundation
180 East End Ave.
New York, NY 10128-7763 (212) 737-1951
Contact: Stella D. Gilrod, Tr.

Donor(s): Stella D. Gilrod.
Financial data (yr. ended 12/31/01): Grants paid, $6,600; assets, $64,514 (M); expenditures, $7,253; qualifying distributions, $6,600.
Application information: Application form not required.
Trustee: Stella D. Gilrod.
EIN: 237027978

39052
The Morris & Bertha Hyman Foundation
Box 122, Roosevelt Terr.
Northville, NY 12134-0122
Application address: Rd. 1, Box 2265,
Northville, NY 12134
Contact: Bertha B. Hyman, Tr.

Established in 1991 in NY.
Donor(s): Members of the Hyman family.
Financial data (yr. ended 12/31/01): Grants paid, $6,600; assets, $117,553 (M); expenditures, $10,714; qualifying distributions, $6,600.
Limitations: Giving primarily in NY.
Trustees: Bertha B. Hyman, Morris A. Hyman.
EIN: 222175178

39053
The David G. Ormsby Charitable Foundation
c/o Cravath Swaine & Moore
825 8th Ave., Ste. 4200
New York, NY 10019-7475

Donor(s): David G. Ormsby.
Financial data (yr. ended 12/31/01): Grants paid, $6,600; assets, $2,662 (M); expenditures, $6,600; qualifying distributions, $6,600.
Limitations: Applications not accepted. Giving on a national basis.
Application information: Contributes only to pre-selected organizations.
Trustee: David G. Ormsby.
EIN: 133382151

39054
Raymond Crile Quick Scholarship Foundation
118 Horseshoe Rd.
Mill Neck, NY 11765
Application address: c/o The Old Westbury School of the Holy Child, 25 Storehill Rd., Old Westbury, NY 11568

Established in 1999 in NY.
Donor(s): Peter C. Quick, Crisler B. Quick.
Financial data (yr. ended 02/28/00): Grants paid, $6,600; assets, $488,396 (M); gifts received, $483,889; expenditures, $6,600; qualifying distributions, $6,600.
Limitations: Giving limited to Old Westbury, NY.
Application information: Contact The Old Westbury School of the Holy Child for application guidelines.
Trustees: Loretta Gallo, Mary E. O'Hern, Crisler B. Quick, Peter C. Quick, Raymond Vogel.
EIN: 134048403

39055
The Louis J. Schreiber Family Foundation, Inc.
121 Rand Pl.
Lawrence, NY 11559

Financial data (yr. ended 12/31/01): Grants paid, $6,600; assets, $23,868 (M); gifts received, $20,000; expenditures, $6,923; qualifying distributions, $6,600.
Trustee: Avram Schreiber.
EIN: 136163589

39056
Michael and Gila Rollhaus Foundation
147-24 75th Ave.
Flushing, NY 11367

Established in 1998 in NY.
Donor(s): Michael Rollhaus.
Financial data (yr. ended 12/31/00): Grants paid, $6,593; assets, $60,796 (M); expenditures, $6,593; qualifying distributions, $6,593.
Officers: Michael Rollhaus, Pres. and Treas.; Gila Rollhaus, V.P. and Secy.
EIN: 113414048

39057
Robert M. Ginsberg Foundation
275 W. 96th St.
New York, NY 10025

Donor(s): Robert M. Ginsberg.
Financial data (yr. ended 09/30/01): Grants paid, $6,585; assets, $129,807 (M); expenditures, $6,785; qualifying distributions, $6,585.
Limitations: Applications not accepted.
Application information: Contributes only to pre-selected organizations.
Officer: Robert M. Ginsberg, Pres.
EIN: 133437049

39058
The Elsa and Irving Nusblatt Foundation, Inc.
(Formerly Irving Nusblatt Foundation)
960 Smith Ln.
Woodmere, NY 11598

Financial data (yr. ended 10/31/01): Grants paid, $6,570; assets, $648 (M); gifts received, $7,250; expenditures, $6,570; qualifying distributions, $6,570.
Limitations: Applications not accepted. Giving primarily in CT and NY.
Application information: Contributes only to pre-selected organizations.
Officers: Edward Nusblatt, Pres.; Robert Jablow, V.P.; Jerome Schulman, V.P.
EIN: 510244268

39059
Samaritan Hospital School of Nursing Alumni Association Charitable Foundation
c/o Alumni Office
2215 Burdett Ave.
Troy, NY 12180 (518) 767-9332
Contact: Mary Beth Rutkowski, Dir.

Financial data (yr. ended 12/31/01): Grants paid, $6,525; assets, $128,169 (M); expenditures, $8,336; qualifying distributions, $6,525.
Limitations: Giving primarily in Troy, NY.
Application information: Application form required.
Officers and Directors:* Joan Gemmill,* Pres.; Robin Campbell,* V.P.; Tamara Auclaire,* Secy.; Mary E. Finkel,* Treas.; Mary Grace Cahill, Diane Clark, Denise D'Avella, Martha Dean, Helen Hendry, Dawn Baldwin Hurst, Tracy Lewis, Ellen Nicpon, Mary Beth Rutkowski, Florence Strang, Doris Yetto.
EIN: 141684557

39060
The Nicola L. Caruso Foundation
P.O. Box 575
Tully, NY 13159

Financial data (yr. ended 09/30/01): Grants paid, $6,510; assets, $143,196 (M); gifts received, $4,500; expenditures, $7,095; qualifying distributions, $6,510.
Limitations: Applications not accepted.
Application information: Contributes only to pre-selected organizations.
Trustee: Nicola L. Caruso.
EIN: 166883419

39061
Elayne & Donald Flamm Foundation
c/o Deutsche Trust Co. of NY
P.O. Box 1297, Church St. Sta.
New York, NY 10008
Application address: c/o Bankers Trust Forida Co., 350 Royal Palm Way, Palm Beach, FL 33480

Established in 1998 in FL.
Donor(s): Elayne Flamm.
Financial data (yr. ended 12/31/01): Grants paid, $6,500; assets, $45,370 (M); expenditures, $7,155; qualifying distributions, $6,812.
Trustees: Elayne Flamm, James Knee, Robert Knee, Robert Simses, Deutsche Bank.
EIN: 066463263

39062
Foundation for Clinical Research in Inflammatory Bowel Disease
12 E. 86th St.
New York, NY 10028 (212) 861-2000
Contact: Daniel H. Present, M.D., Pres.

Established in 1993 in NY.
Donor(s): Ira Trachtman.
Financial data (yr. ended 12/31/99): Grants paid, $6,500; assets, $473,917 (M); gifts received, $153,893; expenditures, $23,305; qualifying distributions, $22,280.
Application information: Application form not required.
Officers: Daniel H. Present, M.D., Pres.; Douglas A. Present, Secy.-Treas.
Directors: Robert Flug, Ira Trachtman, Nathaniel Wisch, M.D.
EIN: 133717235

39063
J. E. Howe Educational Fund Trust
c/o Community Bank, N.A., Trust Dept.
P.O. Box 690
Olean, NY 14760-2738

Established in 1987 in NY.
Financial data (yr. ended 12/31/99): Grants paid, $6,500; assets, $236,215 (M); gifts received, $6,525; expenditures, $9,734; qualifying distributions, $13,735; giving activities include $6,500 for loans to individuals.
Limitations: Giving limited to the greater Cattaraugus and Olean, NY, areas.
Trustee: Community Bank.
EIN: 166031953

39064
John Hung Foundation
170 Park Row, Ste. 16C
New York, NY 10038

Established in 2000.
Donor(s): John Hung.
Financial data (yr. ended 12/31/01): Grants paid, $6,500; assets, $139,954 (M); gifts received, $2,000; expenditures, $11,193; qualifying distributions, $6,500.
Officer and Trustee:* John Hung,* Mgr.
EIN: 134107942

39065
The Koenen Foundation
c/o Sharon L. Sputh, C.P.A., PC
1667 Sheepshead Bay Rd., 2nd Fl.
Brooklyn, NY 11235

Established in 1986 in NJ.
Donor(s): Austin V. Koenen.
Financial data (yr. ended 03/31/02): Grants paid, $6,500; assets, $118,307 (M); expenditures, $6,500; qualifying distributions, $6,500.
Limitations: Applications not accepted. Giving primarily in Montclair, NJ.
Application information: Contributes only to pre-selected organizations.
Trustees: Austin V. Koenen, Karestan Koenen, Kathleen Koenen.
EIN: 222777167

39066
Moscahlaidis Foundation
c/o Krinos Foods, Inc.
4700 Northern Blvd.
Long Island City, NY 11101-1028
Contact: Eric Moscahlaidis, V.P.

Established in 1983.
Donor(s): Eric Moscahlaidis, Quality Braid Corp., Standard Importing Co., Inc., Krinos Realty Corp., Busy Flea Market, Athens Foods, Athens Pastries.
Financial data (yr. ended 12/31/01): Grants paid, $6,500; assets, $624,166 (M); expenditures, $11,647; qualifying distributions, $6,500.
Limitations: Giving primarily in New York, NY.
Officers: John Moscahlaidis, Pres.; Eric Moscahlaidis, V.P.
EIN: 133127990

39067
The Michael Stewart Foundation
(Formerly Stuart M. Robinson Foundation)
49 Barlow Dr. N.
Brooklyn, NY 11234-6719
Application address: 853 7th Ave., New York, NY 10019, tel.: (212) 247-6133
Contact: Francine Pascal, Tr.

Financial data (yr. ended 12/31/01): Grants paid, $6,500; assets, $114,557 (M); expenditures, $7,710; qualifying distributions, $6,500.
Limitations: Giving primarily in NY.
Trustees: Francine Pascal, Burt N. Rubin.
EIN: 136179721

39068
Goldbereis Foundation
c/o Bernat Reisman
1426 56th St.
Brooklyn, NY 11219

Established in 1993 in NY.
Donor(s): Bernat Reisman.
Financial data (yr. ended 11/30/01): Grants paid, $6,474; assets, $176,788 (M); gifts received, $46,092; expenditures, $7,176; qualifying distributions, $6,474.
Limitations: Applications not accepted. Giving primarily in NY.
Application information: Contributes only to pre-selected organizations.
Trustee: Bernat Reisman.
EIN: 113191497

39069
Pollack Family Foundation, Inc.
c/o L. Wollin
350 5th Ave. Ste. 2822
New York, NY 10118

Established in 1997 in DE.
Donor(s): Alexander Pollack.
Financial data (yr. ended 09/30/01): Grants paid, $6,453; assets, $48,480 (M); gifts received, $478; expenditures, $8,479; qualifying distributions, $6,453.
Limitations: Applications not accepted.
Application information: Contributes only to pre-selected organizations.
Officers: Alexander Pollack, Pres.; Lonnie Wollin, Secy.
EIN: 223551936

39070
Needham September 11th Scholarship Fund
c/o Needham & Co., Inc.
445 Park Ave.
New York, NY 10022
URL: http://www.needhamco.com/About_Us/WTC_Scholarship_Fund/wtc_scholarship_fund.html

Established in 2001 in NY.
Donor(s): Needham & Co., Inc., John Michaelson, Warren Foss.
Financial data (yr. ended 12/31/01): Grants paid, $6,400; assets, $1,519,935 (M); gifts received, $1,545,915; expenditures, $26,795; qualifying distributions, $6,400.
Limitations: Giving primarily in NY.
Application information: Application for scholarships available through foundation website. Application form required.
Directors: Glen W. Albanese, John J. Prior, Jr., Joseph J. Turano.
EIN: 134196881
Codes: CS

39071
The Asriel and Marie Rackow Charitable Foundation
936 5th Ave., Ste. 8B
New York, NY 10021

Established in 2000 in DE.
Donor(s): Asriel Rackow.
Financial data (yr. ended 04/30/02): Grants paid, $6,400; assets, $14,475 (M); expenditures, $6,400; qualifying distributions, $6,400.
Limitations: Applications not accepted. Giving primarily in New York, NY.
Application information: Contributes only to pre-selected organizations.
Director: Asriel Rackow.
EIN: 311681288

39072
H. N. Raisler Fund, Inc.
4 Purchase Hills Dr.
Purchase, NY 10577-1611

Donor(s): Herbert Raisler.
Financial data (yr. ended 11/30/01): Grants paid, $6,390; assets, $221,027 (M); expenditures, $8,595; qualifying distributions, $6,390.
Limitations: Applications not accepted. Giving primarily in FL and NY.
Application information: Contributes only to pre-selected organizations.
Officers: Norma Raisler, Pres.; Kenneth Raisler, Secy.
EIN: 136094407

39073
The Alson Foundation
c/o Ernest S. Alson
150 E. 58th St.
New York, NY 10155-0002

Donor(s): Ernest Alson, Members of the Alson family.
Financial data (yr. ended 12/31/00): Grants paid, $6,375; assets, $40,831 (M); expenditures, $6,530; qualifying distributions, $6,375.
Limitations: Applications not accepted. Giving primarily in CT, NY, and Dorado, PR.
Application information: Contributes only to pre-selected organizations.
Trustees: Andrew Alson, Elaine Alson, Ernest S. Alson, Lynn Alson.
EIN: 136189381

39074
Ruth and Ezra Chesky Foundation
c/o Barry M. Strauss Assocs., Ltd.
307 5th Ave., 8th Fl.
New York, NY 10016-6517

Donor(s): Ezra M. Chesky.‡
Financial data (yr. ended 06/30/01): Grants paid, $6,375; assets, $100,950 (M); expenditures, $7,285; qualifying distributions, $7,084.
Limitations: Applications not accepted. Giving primarily in New York, NY.
Application information: Contributes only to pre-selected organizations.
Trustees: Joan Brandy, Ruth Chesky.
EIN: 237003092

39075
The Gertrude and Edward Wiener Charitable Foundation, Inc.
310 E. 46th St., Ste. 8E
New York, NY 10017
Contact: Arline E. Vogel, Dir.

Established in 1998 in NY.
Donor(s): Arline E. Vogel.
Financial data (yr. ended 12/31/00): Grants paid, $6,321; assets, $63,271 (M); gifts received, $15,000; expenditures, $7,116; qualifying distributions, $6,321.
Directors: Joseph P. Bornstein, Harry Precourt, Arline E. Vogel.
EIN: 526945787

39076
Gloria M. Barron Foundation
927 Ripley Ln.
Oyster Bay, NY 11771

Financial data (yr. ended 12/31/99): Grants paid, $6,300; assets, $148,329 (L); gifts received, $6,202; expenditures, $9,435; qualifying distributions, $9,435.
Limitations: Applications not accepted. Giving primarily in the New York, NY, area.
Application information: Contributes only to pre-selected organizations.
Trustee: Manuel H. Barron.
EIN: 237098551

39077
The Frederick Batrus Foundation
c/o Lazard Freres & Co., LLC
30 Rockefeller Plz.
New York, NY 10020
Contact: Frederick Harlan Batrus, Pres.

Established in 1986 in NY.
Donor(s): Frederick Harlan Batrus.
Financial data (yr. ended 09/30/01): Grants paid, $6,300; assets, $68,088 (M); expenditures, $6,430; qualifying distributions, $6,430.
Limitations: Giving primarily in New York, NY.
Officers and Directors:* Frederick Harlan Batrus,* Pres.; Eleanor Batrus Dugle,* V.P.; Howard Sontag,* Treas.
EIN: 133437447

39078
Free Loan Society, Inc.
118-75 Metropolitan Ave., Ste. 1B
Kew Gardens, NY 11415 (718) 846-7150
Contact: Daniel B. Sukenik, Pres.

Donor(s): Daniel B. Sukenik, Sukenik Foundation, Marvin Weistein.
Financial data (yr. ended 10/31/01): Grants paid, $6,300; assets, $2,570 (M); gifts received, $6,358; expenditures, $6,930; qualifying distributions, $6,300.
Officer: Daniel B. Sukenik, Pres.

39078—NEW YORK

EIN: 136265048

39079
The Douglas M. Lawson and Barbara A. Taylor Foundation, Inc.
303 E. 57th St.
New York, NY 10022 (212) 752-8138
Contact: Douglas M. Lawson, Dir.

Donor(s): Douglas M. Lawson, Barbara A. Taylor-Lawson.
Financial data (yr. ended 12/31/01): Grants paid, $6,300; assets, $156,153 (M); gifts received, $10,000; expenditures, $11,728; qualifying distributions, $6,300.
Directors: Douglas M. Lawson, Barbara A. Taylor-Lawson.
EIN: 133095633

39080
The Lister Foundation
c/o Howe & Addington
450 Lexington Ave.
New York, NY 10017

Established in 2001 in NY.
Financial data (yr. ended 12/31/01): Grants paid, $6,300; assets, $367,124 (M); gifts received, $379,093; expenditures, $10,400; qualifying distributions, $10,400.
Limitations: Applications not accepted.
Application information: Contributes only to pre-selected organizations.
Trustees: Madeleine Lister, Stephen A. Lister.
EIN: 137308114

39081
Prestia Family Foundation, Inc.
490 1st St.
Brooklyn, NY 11215
Contact: Angela R. Prestia, Dir.

Financial data (yr. ended 12/31/01): Grants paid, $6,300; assets, $159,487 (M); expenditures, $12,222; qualifying distributions, $6,300.
Application information: Application form required.
Directors: Angela Marie Prestia, Angela R. Prestia, Philip Prestia.
EIN: 113353670

39082
Joel M. Schreiber Family Foundation, Inc.
460 W. 34th St.
New York, NY 10001

Established in 2001 in NY.
Donor(s): Aaron Schreiber Family Foundation, Inc., Joel Schreiber.
Financial data (yr. ended 12/31/01): Grants paid, $6,300; assets, $210,484 (M); gifts received, $225,444; expenditures, $6,338; qualifying distributions, $6,329.
Limitations: Applications not accepted.
Application information: Contributes only to pre-selected organizations.
Officer: Joel Schreiber, Pres.
EIN: 134159859

39083
Adele & William Feder Private Foundation, Inc.
79 Oakdale Rd.
Roslyn Heights, NY 11577

Financial data (yr. ended 10/31/01): Grants paid, $6,294; assets, $141,841 (M); expenditures, $8,047; qualifying distributions, $6,294.
Limitations: Applications not accepted.
Application information: At present, selection criteria are based on schools attended by members of donor's family.

Officers and Directors:* Adele Feder,* V.P.; Stephen Feder,* Secy.; Jeanne Feder,* Treas.
EIN: 112614184

39084
Arya Family Foundation
2 Debra Ct.
Old Westbury, NY 11568
Contact: Yashpal Arya, Dir.

Established in 1995 in NY.
Donor(s): Yashpal Arya.
Financial data (yr. ended 12/31/00): Grants paid, $6,278; assets, $498,491 (M); expenditures, $7,146; qualifying distributions, $6,278.
Directors: Urmilesh Arya, Vijaypal Arya, Yashpal Arya.
EIN: 113296769

39085
Kellner-Kurtz Family Foundation
17 Brickston Dr.
Pittsford, NY 14534

Established in 1999 in NY.
Donor(s): Janet Kellner, James Kurtz.
Financial data (yr. ended 12/31/01): Grants paid, $6,275; assets, $10,875 (M); gifts received, $6,537; expenditures, $6,993; qualifying distributions, $6,275.
Limitations: Applications not accepted.
Application information: Contributes only to pre-selected organizations.
Directors: Stephen Jacobstein, Janet Kellner, James Kurtz.
EIN: 161576714

39086
The David and Shirley Fromer Foundation
c/o Ganer Grossbach
1995 Broadway, 16th Fl.
New York, NY 10023
Contact: David Fromer, Pres.

Established in 1988 in NY.
Donor(s): David Fromer.
Financial data (yr. ended 12/31/01): Grants paid, $6,270; assets, $57,984 (M); expenditures, $6,270; qualifying distributions, $6,270.
Limitations: Giving primarily in NY.
Officers and Trustees:* David Fromer,* Pres.; Shirley Fromer,* Secy.
EIN: 136901027

39087
The Lynda and Joseph Jurist Foundation
c/o Jurist Company, Inc.
175 Varick St.
New York, NY 10014

Established in 1995 in NY.
Donor(s): Lynda Jurist, Joseph Jurist.
Financial data (yr. ended 10/31/01): Grants paid, $6,268; assets, $15,550 (M); expenditures, $6,523; qualifying distributions, $6,348.
Limitations: Applications not accepted. Giving primarily in NY.
Application information: Contributes only to pre-selected organizations.
Officers and Directors:* Lynda Jurist,* Pres.; Joseph Jurist,* Secy.; David Shushansky.
EIN: 133864272

39088
The Frances C. Knight Charitable Foundation
90 Presidential Plz., 5th Fl.
Syracuse, NY 13202-2232

Established in 1989 in NY.
Donor(s): Frances C. Knight.

Financial data (yr. ended 12/31/01): Grants paid, $6,263; assets, $342,628 (M); expenditures, $14,047; qualifying distributions, $6,263.
Limitations: Applications not accepted. Giving primarily in West Palm Beach, FL.
Application information: Contributes only to pre-selected organizations.
Trustees: Frances C. Knight, Richard S. Scolaro.
EIN: 223010384

39089
Dinah Levine Moche Foundation
P.O. Box 98
Rye, NY 10580

Established in 1996 in NY.
Donor(s): Dinah Levine Moche.
Financial data (yr. ended 12/31/01): Grants paid, $6,259; assets, $148,533 (M); expenditures, $9,672; qualifying distributions, $6,259.
Limitations: Applications not accepted. Giving on a national basis.
Application information: Contributes only to pre-selected organizations.
Trustee: Dinah Levine Moche.
EIN: 133922804

39090
Elizabeth Hull-Kate Warriner Award
(also known as Hull-Warriner Award)
c/o The Bank of New York, Tax Dept.
1 Wall St., 28th Fl.
New York, NY 10286
Application address: c/o Dramatists Guild, 234 W. 44th St., New York, NY 10036

Financial data (yr. ended 12/31/99): Grants paid, $6,251; assets, $101,909 (M); expenditures, $6,918; qualifying distributions, $6,366.
Limitations: Giving limited to New York, NY.
Application information: Award to a playwright who has a play in progress.
Trustee: The Bank of New York.
EIN: 136263395

39091
The Samuel Garfinkel Family Foundation
c/o Lipsky, Goodkin & Co.
120 W. 45th St., 7th Fl.
New York, NY 10036

Donor(s): Rubin Garfinkel.
Financial data (yr. ended 07/31/01): Grants paid, $6,250; assets, $1,248 (M); gifts received, $7,000; expenditures, $6,617; qualifying distributions, $6,250.
Limitations: Applications not accepted. Giving primarily in NY.
Application information: Contributes only to pre-selected organizations.
Officer: Rubin Garfinkel, Pres.
EIN: 116013481

39092
Joyce & Elliot Liskin Foundation, Inc.
P.O. Box 497
Bronx, NY 10471-0497

Donor(s): Elliot Liskin.‡
Financial data (yr. ended 12/31/01): Grants paid, $6,250; assets, $146,952 (M); gifts received, $4,000; expenditures, $11,140; qualifying distributions, $6,250.
Limitations: Applications not accepted.
Application information: Contributes only to pre-selected organizations.
Officers: Joyce Liskin, Pres. and Treas.; Steven P. Liskin, V.P. and Secy.
Director: Ernest Feldman.
EIN: 133096929

39093
The Michael Hausman-Filmhaus Foundation, Inc.
736 Broadway, 8th Fl.
New York, NY 10003-9519 (212) 245-9060
Contact: Michael Hausman, Pres.

Established in 1993 in NY.
Donor(s): Michael Hausman.
Financial data (yr. ended 12/31/01): Grants paid, $6,200; assets, $192,618 (M); expenditures, $7,392; qualifying distributions, $6,200.
Limitations: Giving primarily in NY.
Officers: Michael Hausman, Pres.; Pamela Hausman, V.P. and Secy.; Richard Brick, V.P. and Treas.
EIN: 133721844

39094
I Dream a World Foundation, Inc.
c/o Suzanne Lehmann
101 Central Park West, Apt. 18F
New York, NY 10023

Established in 1997 in NY.
Donor(s): Suzanne Lehmann.
Financial data (yr. ended 12/31/99): Grants paid, $6,200; assets, $419,138 (M); gifts received, $89,600; expenditures, $7,800; qualifying distributions, $5,989.
Limitations: Applications not accepted.
Application information: Contributes only to pre-selected organizations.
Officers and Directors:* Suzanne Lehmann, Pres. and Treas.; Daniel Lehmann,* V.P. and Secy.; Fred Gluck, Jr.,* V.P.; Lisa Gluck,* V.P.; Susan Gluck,* V.P.
EIN: 133942097

39095
The LDK & RDK Charitable Foundation
c/o Satterlee, Stephens, Burke & Burke
230 Park Ave., Ste. 1130
New York, NY 10169

Donor(s): Loic De Kertanguy, Rebecca De Kertanguy.
Financial data (yr. ended 11/30/01): Grants paid, $6,200; assets, $31,485 (M); gifts received, $891; expenditures, $6,554; qualifying distributions, $6,200.
Limitations: Applications not accepted. Giving limited to New York, NY.
Application information: Contributes only to pre-selected organizations.
Trustees: Loic De Kertanguy, Rebecca De Kertanguy.
EIN: 133451003

39096
Wallrich Foundation
1 M & T Plaza, Ste. 2000
Buffalo, NY 14203-2301

Established in 1999 in NY.
Financial data (yr. ended 03/31/02): Grants paid, $6,200; assets, $6,904 (M); gifts received, $5,000; expenditures, $7,828; qualifying distributions, $6,200.
Limitations: Applications not accepted.
Application information: Contributes only to pre-selected organizations.
Trustees: Sara Wallrich Ryan, George M. Wallrich, Sr., George M. Wallrich, Jr., Virginia R. Wallrich.
EIN: 161570940

39097
The Avni Foundation, Inc.
c/o Ravit Avni-Singer
132 Todd Hill Rd.
LaGrangeville, NY 12540

Established in 1999 in NY.
Donor(s): Moshe Avni.
Financial data (yr. ended 12/31/00): Grants paid, $6,150; assets, $72,438 (M); gifts received, $350; expenditures, $6,150; qualifying distributions, $6,118.
Officers: Ravit Avni-Singer, Pres.; Michal Avni, V.P. and Secy.
EIN: 134093708

39098
Living Arts Foundation, Inc.
1200 5th Ave.
New York, NY 10029 (212) 348-8894
Contact: Wendy Levine, Pres.

Financial data (yr. ended 10/31/01): Grants paid, $6,150; assets, $24,192 (M); expenditures, $8,232; qualifying distributions, $6,150.
Limitations: Giving primarily in MA.
Officer: Wendy Levine, Pres.
EIN: 136161047

39099
Spartan Masonic Educational Foundation, Inc.
c/o Baldwin Masonic Temple
754 Prospect St.
Baldwin, NY 11510 (516) 223-3809
Application address: 576 Ashland Ave., Baldwin, NY 11510
Contact: Edward Callaghan, Treas.

Donor(s): John Walther.
Financial data (yr. ended 12/31/99): Grants paid, $6,150; assets, $126,308 (M); gifts received, $11,002; expenditures, $12,037; qualifying distributions, $12,019.
Application information: Application form required.
Officer: Edward Callaghan, Treas.
EIN: 237118957

39100
The Alper Foundation, Inc.
15 Crescent St.
Sag Harbor, NY 11963-2532
Contact: Bertram Alper, Pres.

Financial data (yr. ended 12/31/00): Grants paid, $6,142; assets, $190,422 (M); gifts received, $1,163; expenditures, $8,351; qualifying distributions, $6,142.
Limitations: Giving primarily in NY.
Officer: Bertram Alper, Pres. and Mgr.
EIN: 136182921

39101
The Terry and David Gary Foundation
c/o Terry Gary
5 Oak Valley Ln.
Purchase, NY 10577

Established in 1999 in NY.
Donor(s): Terry Weiss Gary, David Gary.
Financial data (yr. ended 12/31/01): Grants paid, $6,130; assets, $28,425 (M); expenditures, $6,130; qualifying distributions, $6,130.
Limitations: Applications not accepted. Giving primarily in NJ, NY, and PA.
Application information: Contributes only to pre-selected organizations.
Trustees: David Gary, Terry Weiss Gary, Mindy Hoffman.
EIN: 137222573

39102
The Mitchell David Solomon Foundation, Inc.
1148 5th Ave., Ste. 14C
New York, NY 10128

Donor(s): Irwin Solomon, Rebecca Solomon.
Financial data (yr. ended 10/31/01): Grants paid, $6,124; assets, $52,253 (M); gifts received, $10,000; expenditures, $6,504; qualifying distributions, $6,124.
Limitations: Applications not accepted. Giving primarily in NY.
Application information: Contributes only to pre-selected organizations.
Trustees: Gina Solomon, Irwin Solomon, Rebecca Solomon, Yale Solomon.
EIN: 136161090

39103
Marcus & Gertrude Adler Charitable Trust
32 W. 39th St.
New York, NY 10018-3810

Financial data (yr. ended 12/31/01): Grants paid, $6,113; assets, $65,975 (M); gifts received, $5,000; expenditures, $6,244; qualifying distributions, $6,113.
Limitations: Applications not accepted. Giving primarily in New York, NY.
Application information: Contributes only to pre-selected organizations.
Trustee: Gertrude Adler.
EIN: 237058139

39104
Jafis Foundation
275 Madison Ave., 30th Fl.
New York, NY 10016
Contact: Jack Forgash, Tr.

Established in 1997 in NY.
Financial data (yr. ended 12/31/00): Grants paid, $6,100; assets, $3,708 (M); gifts received, $208; expenditures, $6,100; qualifying distributions, $6,100.
Trustee: Jack Forgash.
EIN: 137113206

39105
Nathan Fluegelman Memorial Fund, Inc.
6 Old Lyme Rd.
Scarsdale, NY 10583

Financial data (yr. ended 12/31/01): Grants paid, $6,086; assets, $99,802 (M); gifts received, $7,000; expenditures, $7,378; qualifying distributions, $6,591.
Limitations: Applications not accepted. Giving primarily in New York, NY.
Application information: Contributes only to pre-selected organizations.
Officers: Helen Fluegelman, Pres. and Secy.; Joan Wexler, Treas.
Director: Bertram Josephson.
EIN: 136066168

39106
Tewani Charitable Foundation
9 Trapping Way
Pleasantville, NY 10570
Contact: Prakash Tewani, Dir.

Established in 1999 in NY.
Donor(s): Prakash Tewani, Raj Kumar Tewani, Jagdish Tewani.
Financial data (yr. ended 11/30/01): Grants paid, $6,077; assets, $4,147 (M); gifts received, $7,500; expenditures, $6,562; qualifying distributions, $6,077.
Directors: Jagdish Tewani, Prakash Tewani, Raj Kumar Tewani.

39106—NEW YORK

EIN: 134094714

39107
Mary Warren Free Institute of the City of Troy
132-136 8th St.
Troy, NY 12180

Financial data (yr. ended 10/31/01): Grants paid, $6,050; assets, $875,959 (M); expenditures, $40,556; qualifying distributions, $6,050.
Limitations: Applications not accepted. Giving limited to Troy, NY.
Application information: Contributes only to pre-selected organizations.
Officers: William E. Boyce, Pres.; William P. McGovern III, V.P.; Phyllis Morgan, Secy.; Robert J. Lutringer, Treas.
EIN: 141454088

39108
Henry Greenspan Foundation
c/o Bruce H. Sobel
6 E. 43rd St.
New York, NY 10017

Donor(s): Albert L. Greenspan.‡
Financial data (yr. ended 12/31/01): Grants paid, $6,045; assets, $250,638 (M); expenditures, $7,492; qualifying distributions, $6,045.
Limitations: Applications not accepted.
Application information: Contributes only to pre-selected organizations.
Officer: Henry Greenspan, Pres.
EIN: 237416723

39109
Churchwomen's League for Patriotic Service, Inc.
c/o House of the Redeemer
7 E. 95th St.
New York, NY 10128

Financial data (yr. ended 12/31/99): Grants paid, $6,040; assets, $558,672 (M); expenditures, $7,167; qualifying distributions, $7,167.
Limitations: Giving primarily in New York, NY.
Application information: Grants are made at the discretion of the Governing Board.
Officer: Mrs. Chalmers Dale, Pres.
EIN: 136174480

39110
Harvey and Ruth Spear Foundation
100 Maiden Ln., Rm. 1206
New York, NY 10038 (212) 504-6282
Contact: Harvey M. Spear, Pres.

Donor(s): Harvey M. Spear.
Financial data (yr. ended 11/30/01): Grants paid, $6,040; assets, $6,381 (M); expenditures, $6,120; qualifying distributions, $6,040.
Limitations: Giving primarily in NY.
Officer: Harvey M. Spear, Pres.
EIN: 136160997

39111
Lawrence A. Fauci Foundation
401 Edinboro Rd.
Staten Island, NY 10306

Donor(s): Lawrence A. Fauci.
Financial data (yr. ended 12/31/01): Grants paid, $6,027; assets, $104,478 (M); expenditures, $6,735; qualifying distributions, $6,027.
Limitations: Giving primarily in New York, NY.
Trustees: Florence Fauci, Lawrence A. Fauci.
EIN: 133501788

39112
Jim and Linda Ellis Foundation, Inc.
c/o James H. Ellis
36 Butler Rd.
Scarsdale, NY 10583

Established in 1998 in NY.
Donor(s): James H. Ellis.
Financial data (yr. ended 12/31/01): Grants paid, $6,025; assets, $223,640 (M); expenditures, $7,519; qualifying distributions, $6,025.
Limitations: Applications not accepted.
Application information: Contributes only to pre-selected organizations.
Officers: James H. Ellis, Chair.; Arthur U. Ellis, V.P.; Nancie J. Ellis, V.P.; James A. Ellis, Secy.-Treas.
EIN: 133995609

39113
The Benenson Foundation, Inc.
136 E. 76th St.
New York, NY 10021
Contact: Richard Benenson, Tr.

Financial data (yr. ended 12/31/99): Grants paid, $6,004; assets, $10,538 (M); expenditures, $6,500; qualifying distributions, $6,004.
Limitations: Giving primarily in New York, NY.
Trustees: Karen Allinson, Richard Benenson.
EIN: 510172991

39114
Amsterdam News Educational Foundation, Inc.
2340 Frederick Douglas Blvd.
New York, NY 10027
Application address: c/o Elinor Tatum, 41 2nd Ave., New York, NY 10003, tel.: (212) 529-9902

Donor(s): Amnews Corp.
Financial data (yr. ended 12/31/00): Grants paid, $6,000; assets, $34,708 (M); gifts received, $250; expenditures, $9,525; qualifying distributions, $6,025.
Officers: Wilbert Tatum, Pres.; Frank Graziadei, V.P.; Susan Tatum, V.P.; Ira A. McCown, Jr., Secy.
EIN: 133634817
Codes: CS

39115
Ronald J. Anania Family Foundation
74 Snell Rd.
Geneva, NY 14456
Contact: Ronald J. Anania, Tr.

Established in 1986 in NY.
Financial data (yr. ended 03/31/02): Grants paid, $6,000; assets, $30,224 (M); gifts received, $20,000; expenditures, $6,000; qualifying distributions, $6,000.
Limitations: Giving primarily in Geneva, NY.
Trustees: Ronald J. Anania, John A. Micek.
EIN: 222781771

39116
Josef & Yaye Breitenbach Charitable Foundation
c/o Peter C. Jones
125 E. 84th St.
New York, NY 10023

Established in 1998 in NY.
Donor(s): Yaye Togashi Breitenbach.
Financial data (yr. ended 12/31/00): Grants paid, $6,000; assets, $21,049 (M); gifts received, $23,000; expenditures, $6,000; qualifying distributions, $6,000.
Limitations: Giving primarily in AZ.
Trustees: Denise B. Bethel, Peter C. Jones.
EIN: 137007022

39117
Brueckner Family Charitable Foundation
c/o CSAM
466 Lexington Ave., 17th Fl.
New York, NY 10017

Established in 1999 in NJ.
Financial data (yr. ended 12/31/01): Grants paid, $6,000; assets, $458,853 (M); gifts received, $150,000; expenditures, $7,441; qualifying distributions, $6,000.
Limitations: Applications not accepted.
Application information: Contributes only to pre-selected organizations.
Advisory Committee: Richard P. Brueckner, Laurie C. Brueckner.
Trustee: Winthrop Trust Co.
EIN: 134092823

39118
Tom & Harriet Burnett Family Foundation
50 Broad St., Ste. 808
New York, NY 10004

Established in 2001 in DE.
Donor(s): Thomas Burnett.
Financial data (yr. ended 12/31/01): Grants paid, $6,000; assets, $467,235 (M); gifts received, $400,000; expenditures, $6,080; qualifying distributions, $6,000.
Limitations: Applications not accepted.
Application information: Contributes only to pre-selected organizations.
Directors: Harriet Burnett, Thomas Burnett.
EIN: 134183289

39119
Burns Memorial Trust Foundation
Graymoor, Rte. 9
Garrison, NY 10524
Contact: J.F. O'Reilly, Tr.

Established in 1995 in NY.
Donor(s): J. Burns.
Financial data (yr. ended 12/31/01): Grants paid, $6,000; assets, $116,231 (M); expenditures, $6,514; qualifying distributions, $6,000.
Trustees: J.F. Reilly, R. O'Rourke, R. Warren.
EIN: 066416177

39120
Hyman B. and Estelle Carroll Foundation, Inc.
c/o Cummings & Carroll
175 Great Neck Rd., Ste. 405
Great Neck, NY 11021-3366

Established in 1998 in NY.
Donor(s): Hyman B. Carroll.
Financial data (yr. ended 04/30/02): Grants paid, $6,000; assets, $59,727 (M); gifts received, $10,807; expenditures, $6,474; qualifying distributions, $6,000.
Limitations: Applications not accepted.
Application information: Contributes only to pre-selected organizations.
Officers: Hyman B. Carroll, Pres.; John S. Carroll, V.P.; Estelle Carroll, Secy.
EIN: 113444834

39121
Alexander W. Casdin Foundation
c/o L.H. Frishkoff & Co.
529 5th Ave.
New York, NY 10017

Established in 2001 in NY.
Financial data (yr. ended 12/31/01): Grants paid, $6,000; assets, $64,069 (M); gifts received, $66,826; expenditures, $6,104; qualifying distributions, $6,000.
Limitations: Applications not accepted.

Application information: Contributes only to pre-selected organizations.
Trustee: Alexander W. Casdin.
EIN: 137270729

39122
The CHH Charitable Trust
466 Lexington Ave., 18th Fl.
New York, NY 10017-3151

Established in 1987 in NY.
Financial data (yr. ended 12/31/01): Grants paid, $6,000; assets, $101,595 (M); gifts received, $5,000; expenditures, $8,917; qualifying distributions, $6,000.
Limitations: Applications not accepted.
Application information: Contributes only to pre-selected organizations.
Trustees: Catherine H. Hobbs, John H. Hobbs.
EIN: 136899018

39123
Cooperstown Community Foundation
9 Westridge Rd.
P.O. Box 4983
Cooperstown, NY 13326-1020

Financial data (yr. ended 11/30/01): Grants paid, $6,000; assets, $47,266 (M); expenditures, $6,179; qualifying distributions, $6,000.
Limitations: Applications not accepted. Giving primarily in the Cooperstown, NY, area.
Application information: Unsolicited requests for funds not accepted.
Officers: Linnea Nelson, Pres.; Elinor Pollock, V.P.; Barbara LaCava, Secy.; Henry J. Phillips, Treas.
EIN: 166090548

39124
Epsilon Association Charitable Trust
c/o Sciarabba, Walker & Co.
200 E. Buffalo St.
Ithaca, NY 14850

Established in 1954 in NY.
Donor(s): Lena Gilbert.‡
Financial data (yr. ended 05/31/01): Grants paid, $6,000; assets, $111,339 (M); expenditures, $7,245; qualifying distributions, $6,000.
Limitations: Giving limited to Ithaca, NY.
Application information: Application form required.
Trustees: Frederick D. Bloom, Charles R. Holcomb, Bruce E. Young.
EIN: 166076130

39125
Mercy and Patrick C. Ewing Charitable Foundation
c/o U.S. Trust
114 W. 47th St., TaxVas
New York, NY 10036

Established in 1999 in IL.
Donor(s): Jessie Ewing.
Financial data (yr. ended 12/31/00): Grants paid, $6,000; assets, $110,789 (M); gifts received, $4,000; expenditures, $9,342; qualifying distributions, $6,769.
Limitations: Applications not accepted. Giving primarily in Chicago, IL.
Application information: Contributes only to pre-selected organizations.
Trustee: Jessie V. Ewing.
EIN: 367257312

39126
Rita & Daniel Fraad Foundation
17 Oxford Rd.
Scarsdale, NY 10583

Donor(s): Daniel Fraad,‡ Rita Fraad.
Financial data (yr. ended 06/30/00): Grants paid, $6,000; assets, $374,725 (M); expenditures, $11,195; qualifying distributions, $6,000.
Limitations: Applications not accepted. Giving primarily in Washington, DC, and New York, NY.
Application information: Contributes only to pre-selected organizations.
Officer: Rita Fraad, Pres.
EIN: 136161390

39127
Friends of Toras Simcha
444 Madison Ave.
New York, NY 10022

Established in 1996 in NY.
Financial data (yr. ended 08/31/01): Grants paid, $6,000; assets, $36,324 (M); gifts received, $7,680; expenditures, $6,016; qualifying distributions, $6,016.
Limitations: Applications not accepted.
Application information: Contributes only to pre-selected organizations.
Directors: Hirschell E. Levine, Menachem Pinck, Rabbi Nate Siegel.
EIN: 133913533

39128
Jeannie L. Grant Recreation Camp Association, Inc.
356 Fulton St.
Brooklyn, NY 11201-5104
Application address: 1052 64th St., Brooklyn, NY 11219, tel.: (718) 504-6694
Contact: Robert Porta

Financial data (yr. ended 10/31/01): Grants paid, $6,000; assets, $122,782 (M); expenditures, $7,260; qualifying distributions, $7,260.
Limitations: Giving limited to the Brooklyn, NY, area.
Officers: Elaine Quinones, Pres.; Cassandra Jenkins, V.P.; Alfred Smith, Secy.-Treas.
EIN: 116000717

39129
The Handler/Michaels Foundation, Inc.
c/o Eileen Michaels
469 Old Court House Rd.
New Hyde Park, NY 11040

Financial data (yr. ended 12/31/99): Grants paid, $6,000; assets, $93,260 (M); expenditures, $8,634; qualifying distributions, $5,982; giving activities include $6,000 for programs.
Limitations: Applications not accepted.
Application information: Contributes only to pre-selected organizations.
Officers and Directors:* Eileen Michaels,* Pres.; Kenneth I. Handler,* Secy.; Philip J. Michaels.
EIN: 113437791

39130
Keren Torah Vchesed Foundation
c/o Abba Soloff
165 Ross St.
Brooklyn, NY 11211-7704

Established in 1997 in NY.
Donor(s): Abba Soloff, Abraham Soloff.
Financial data (yr. ended 10/31/01): Grants paid, $6,000; assets, $232,087 (M); gifts received, $50,000; expenditures, $20,859; qualifying distributions, $6,000.
Limitations: Applications not accepted.

Application information: Contributes only to pre-selected organizations.
Trustees: Abba Soloff, Abraham Soloff, Elsie Soloff.
EIN: 137123397

39131
Landmarks Foundation Protecting Sacred Sites Globally, Inc.
155 E. 75th St.
New York, NY 10021

Donor(s): Beards Fund, Samuel Adams Green, Kazuco, Carol and Joseph Lebworth Foundation, Caroline Newhouse Foundation, Schoenberg Foundation.
Financial data (yr. ended 12/31/01): Grants paid, $6,000; assets, $6,634 (M); gifts received, $38,990; expenditures, $36,271; qualifying distributions, $36,271; giving activities include $22,740 for programs.
Limitations: Applications not accepted.
Application information: Contributes only to pre-selected organizations.
Officer: Cristine M. Biddle, Secy.
Director: Samuel A. Green.
EIN: 133967980

39132
The Alvin Lehman Foundation, Inc.
c/o John A. Lehman
17 River St.
Warwick, NY 10990

Donor(s): Hanna L. Albert.
Financial data (yr. ended 06/30/01): Grants paid, $6,000; assets, $161,372 (M); expenditures, $6,966; qualifying distributions, $6,475.
Limitations: Applications not accepted.
Application information: Contributes only to pre-selected organizations.
Officers: John Lehman, Pres.; Alan Lehman, Secy.
Director: Ari Lehman.
EIN: 237304122

39133
Lillian S. Lusskin Orthopaedic Foundation, Inc.
47 E. 88th St.
New York, NY 10128-1152

Financial data (yr. ended 12/31/01): Grants paid, $6,000; assets, $190,517 (M); expenditures, $6,892; qualifying distributions, $6,817.
Limitations: Applications not accepted. Giving primarily in New York, NY.
Application information: Contributes only to pre-selected organizations.
Officer: Ralph Lusskin, Pres.
EIN: 136279591

39134
Thomas L. Manuel Charitable Foundation
c/o U.S. Trust
114 W. 47th St.
New York, NY 10036

Established in 1997 in NY.
Financial data (yr. ended 12/31/01): Grants paid, $6,000; assets, $206,553 (M); expenditures, $8,648; qualifying distributions, $6,000.
Limitations: Giving primarily in MN.
Trustee: U.S. Trust.
EIN: 137108052

39135
Meyer Family Foundation
5645 Harris Hill Rd.
Williamsville, NY 14221 (716) 741-0051
Contact: Paul N. Meyer, Tr.

Donor(s): Paul N. Meyer.

39135—NEW YORK

Financial data (yr. ended 12/31/01): Grants paid, $6,000; assets, $91,450 (M); expenditures, $6,650; qualifying distributions, $6,000.
Trustees: Jeffrey N. Meyer, Jennifer M. Meyer, Katherine A. Meyer, Lola J. Meyer, Michelle L. Meyer, Paul N. Meyer, Susan L. Meyer.
EIN: 161429865

39136
Moraes Sarmento Foundation, Inc.
c/o Anna Maria Sarmento
115 W. 11th St.
New York, NY 10011

Established in 2000 in NY.
Donor(s): Anna Maria Sarmento.
Financial data (yr. ended 12/31/01): Grants paid, $6,000; assets, $937,611 (M); gifts received, $1,000,000; expenditures, $17,677; qualifying distributions, $6,000.
Limitations: Giving primarily in Brazil.
Officers: Gretchen Anne Kuhn De Moraes Sarmento, Pres.; Ana Lucia Vaz De Carvalho, V.P.; Anna Maria Sarmento, V.P.; Guilherme Correa De Moraes Sarmento, Secy.; Carlos Correa De Oliveira, Secy.
EIN: 134147314

39137
Pemachrina Foundation, Inc.
c/o Inverness Counsel, Inc.
545 Madison Ave.
New York, NY 10022

Established in 2000 in MI.
Donor(s): Eriberto Scocimara, Marguerite S. Scocimara.
Financial data (yr. ended 12/31/01): Grants paid, $6,000; assets, $129,119 (M); gifts received, $5,400; expenditures, $12,572; qualifying distributions, $6,000.
Limitations: Applications not accepted.
Application information: Contributes only to pre-selected organizations.
Officers and Directors:* Christina I. Surtees,* Pres.; Julia Scocimara,* Secy.; Marguerite S. Scocimara,* Treas.
EIN: 383570952

39138
Irene Ritter Foundation
45 E. 89th St., Ste. 34F
New York, NY 10128-1232

Established in 1999 in NY.
Donor(s): David Ritter.
Financial data (yr. ended 11/30/01): Grants paid, $6,000; assets, $106,363 (M); gifts received, $8,000; expenditures, $6,816; qualifying distributions, $6,000.
Limitations: Applications not accepted.
Application information: Contributes only to pre-selected organizations.
Officers and Directors:* David Ritter,* Pres. and Treas.; Marie C. Ritter,* V.P. and Secy.; Jennifer Ritter, Michael Ritter.
EIN: 134090839

39139
Diana Roberts Memorial Scholarship Fund, Inc.
c/o Bernard L. Roberts
150 E. 69th St., Ste. 6G
New York, NY 10021

Established in 1994 in NY.
Donor(s): Bobby Jacobs, Trina Jacobs.
Financial data (yr. ended 12/31/00): Grants paid, $6,000; assets, $87,029 (M); gifts received, $2,650; expenditures, $6,306; qualifying distributions, $5,937.
Trustee: Bernard Roberts.

EIN: 133674048

39140
David M. & Hope G. Solinger Foundation, Inc.
c/o Betty Ann Solinger
33 E. 70th St., Apt. 3D
New York, NY 10021-4941 (212) 744-2227

Donor(s): David M. Solinger,‡ Hope G. Solinger.
Financial data (yr. ended 12/31/01): Grants paid, $6,000; assets, $391,017 (M); expenditures, $13,671; qualifying distributions, $6,000.
Limitations: Applications not accepted. Giving primarily in New York, NY.
Application information: Contributes only to pre-selected organizations.
Officers: Hope G. Solinger, Pres.; Betty Ann Solinger, V.P.; Lynn Stern, Secy.-Treas.
EIN: 136098429

39141
Stone Family Fund, Inc.
c/o Schulte Roth & Zabel, LLP
530 E. 86th St.
New York, NY 10028
Contact: Carol Pomerantz, or Toni Shore, Mgrs.

Established in 1986 in NY.
Donor(s): Janet Jacques Stone.
Financial data (yr. ended 12/31/01): Grants paid, $6,000; assets, $105,402 (M); expenditures, $7,531; qualifying distributions, $6,755.
Officers: Carol Pomerantz, Mgr.; Toni Shore, Mgr.
EIN: 133319677

39142
WWJD Foundation
P.O. Box 247
Vestal, NY 13850

Established in 1998.
Donor(s): Jeff Coghlan.
Financial data (yr. ended 12/31/00): Grants paid, $6,000; assets, $64,410 (L); gifts received, $25,380; expenditures, $6,530; qualifying distributions, $6,000.
Limitations: Giving primarily in NY.
Trustees: Jeff Coghlan, Thomas J. Murphy.
EIN: 166472548

39143
S.C.G. Foundation, Inc.
(also known as Service City-GEBA Foundation, Inc.)
74-61 220th St.
Oakland Gardens, NY 11364-1862
(718) 224-8947
Contact: Larry Schlesinger, Treas.

Financial data (yr. ended 12/31/01): Grants paid, $5,980; assets, $44,160 (M); expenditures, $6,669; qualifying distributions, $5,980.
Limitations: Giving primarily in Queens County, NY.
Officers: Lawrence Hammez, Jr., Pres.; Phillip Schwartzman, V.P.; Jamshed Ghadiali, Secy.; Larry Schlesinger, Treas.
EIN: 136272087

39144
Battenkill Foundation
c/o Brown Brothers Harriman Trust Co.
63 Wall St.
New York, NY 10005

Established in 1999 in MN.
Financial data (yr. ended 12/31/01): Grants paid, $5,975; assets, $104,061 (M); gifts received, $3,673; expenditures, $7,896; qualifying distributions, $5,975.
Limitations: Applications not accepted.

Application information: Contributes only to pre-selected organizations.
Trustees: Edward L. Requet, Margaret H. Requet.
EIN: 364297877

39145
The Joseph Marks Foundation, Inc.
c/o Theodore Marks
1 Mahopac Plz.
Mahopac, NY 10541

Financial data (yr. ended 05/31/01): Grants paid, $5,973; assets, $213,325 (M); gifts received, $109,144; expenditures, $6,675; qualifying distributions, $5,973.
Limitations: Applications not accepted. Giving primarily in NY.
Application information: Contributes only to pre-selected organizations.
Officer: Theodore Marks, Pres.
EIN: 237029103

39146
M. & L. Kandel Foundation, Inc.
c/o S.R. Buschel, B.D.O. Seidman
330 Madison Ave.
New York, NY 10017
Application address: 2774 Ocean Blvd., Palm Beach, FL 33480
Contact: Lottie Kandel, V.P.

Established in 1986 in NY.
Donor(s): Robert Kandel.
Financial data (yr. ended 11/30/99): Grants paid, $5,956; assets, $13,118 (M); expenditures, $6,721; qualifying distributions, $5,956.
Application information: Application form not required.
Officers: Morton Kandel, Pres.; Lottie Kandel, V.P.; Robert Kandel, Treas.
EIN: 133380646

39147
Chaman Gupta Foundation
9 Princeton Dr.
Plainview, NY 11803

Established in 2000 in NY.
Financial data (yr. ended 12/31/00): Grants paid, $5,953; assets, $10,312 (M); gifts received, $16,265; expenditures, $5,953; qualifying distributions, $0.
Limitations: Applications not accepted. Giving primarily in NY; some giving also in India.
Application information: Contributes only to pre-selected organizations.
Trustees: John Gupta, Mike Gupta.
EIN: 912130669

39148
Glick Family Foundation
5 Horsemans Ln.
Syosset, NY 11791-4402

Donor(s): Joel Glick.
Financial data (yr. ended 12/31/01): Grants paid, $5,930; assets, $81,081 (M); gifts received, $14,483; expenditures, $6,080; qualifying distributions, $5,903.
Limitations: Applications not accepted.
Application information: Contributes only to pre-selected organizations.
Directors: Carol Glick, Joel Glick, Marcie Glick.
EIN: 113549579

39149
Hakoras Hatov Charitable Foundation, Inc.
c/o Ira Zicherman
1540 E. 17th St.
Brooklyn, NY 11230

Established in 1991 in NY.

Donor(s): Ira Zicherman.
Financial data (yr. ended 08/31/01): Grants paid, $5,930; assets, $397,749 (M); gifts received, $35,000; expenditures, $6,555; qualifying distributions, $5,930.
Limitations: Applications not accepted. Giving primarily in Brooklyn, NY.
Application information: Contributes only to pre-selected organizations.
Officers and Directors:* Ira Zicherman,* Pres.; Brenda Zicherman,* Secy.-Treas.; Bernard Zicherman.
EIN: 113074851

39150
The Joseph Cohen Foundation, Inc.
302 5th Ave., 7th Fl.
New York, NY 10001
Application address: 1117 Avenue V, Brooklyn, NY 11223, tel.: (212) 564-2655
Contact: Joseph Cohen, Pres.

Established in 1997 in NY.
Donor(s): Joseph Cohen.
Financial data (yr. ended 12/31/00): Grants paid, $5,915; assets, $6,720 (M); expenditures, $5,990; qualifying distributions, $5,915.
Officers: Joseph Cohen, Pres.; Yechova Cohen, V.P.; David Shalam, Secy.
EIN: 133975599

39151
Dorothy M. Beskind Foundation
c/o Rogoff & Co.
275 Madison Ave., Ste. 1400
New York, NY 10016-1101
Contact: Dorothy M. Beskind, Pres.

Donor(s): Dorothy M. Beskind.
Financial data (yr. ended 12/31/00): Grants paid, $5,907; assets, $228,075 (M); expenditures, $6,555; qualifying distributions, $5,907.
Officer: Dorothy M. Beskind, Pres.
EIN: 136147945

39152
Newman Chesed Foundation
60 McLean Ave.
Yonkers, NY 10705-2356

Donor(s): Sidney Newman, Alice Newman.‡
Financial data (yr. ended 12/31/01): Grants paid, $5,900; assets, $41,933 (M); expenditures, $6,255; qualifying distributions, $5,900.
Limitations: Applications not accepted. Giving primarily in NY.
Application information: Contributes only to pre-selected organizations.
Trustees: Norman Fried, Robert Lewis, Sidney Newman.
EIN: 133403193

39153
The Bernard Rothfeld Children's Foundation, Inc.
c/o Eric Rothfield
111 W. 40th St.
New York, NY 10018-2506

Established in 1989 in FL.
Financial data (yr. ended 12/31/00): Grants paid, $5,900; assets, $106,633 (M); gifts received, $3,267; expenditures, $6,790; qualifying distributions, $5,900.
Limitations: Applications not accepted. Giving primarily in FL.
Application information: Contributes only to pre-selected organizations.
Directors: Hazel Goldman, Eric A. Rothfeld, Ruth Rothfeld.
EIN: 650143398

39154
The Dorren Foundation
27 Fairvale Dr.
Penfield, NY 14526
Application address: 6130 W. Flamingo Rd., Las Vegas, NV 89103
Contact: Harvey B. Dorren, Pres.

Donor(s): Harvey B. Dorren, Nobuko K. Dorren.
Financial data (yr. ended 12/31/01): Grants paid, $5,895; assets, $2,268 (M); gifts received, $7,000; expenditures, $6,644; qualifying distributions, $5,895.
Limitations: Giving primarily in CA.
Officers: Harvey B. Dorren, Pres.; Nobuko K. Dorren, V.P.; Martin R. Dorren, Secy.
EIN: 222579401

39155
The Mariom Foundation, Inc.
c/o Lita S. Greenwald
785 Park Ave., No. 8A
New York, NY 10021-3552

Donor(s): Lita S. Greenwald, Stephen Greenwald.
Financial data (yr. ended 12/31/01): Grants paid, $5,880; assets, $11,364 (M); gifts received, $8,153; expenditures, $5,963; qualifying distributions, $5,880.
Limitations: Applications not accepted. Giving primarily in NY.
Application information: Contributes only to pre-selected organizations.
Officers: Lita S. Greenwald, Pres.; Stephen Greenwald, Secy.-Treas.
EIN: 133574270

39156
The Scholl Family Foundation, Inc.
c/o U.S. Trust
114 W. 47th St., TaxVas
New York, NY 10036

Established in 1997 in NY.
Donor(s): Harold Scholl, Hannah Scholl.
Financial data (yr. ended 12/31/00): Grants paid, $5,880; assets, $100,518 (M); expenditures, $5,961; qualifying distributions, $5,940.
Limitations: Applications not accepted.
Application information: Contributes only to pre-selected organizations.
Directors: Eric Scholl, Hannah Scholl, Harold Scholl, Roger Scholl.
EIN: 223545911

39157
Zichron Simche Shlomo Foundation
1558 49th St.
Brooklyn, NY 11219 (718) 283-8544
Contact: Leo Lieber, Tr.

Established in 2000 in NY.
Financial data (yr. ended 12/31/01): Grants paid, $5,873; assets, $164,447 (M); gifts received, $9,088; expenditures, $6,923; qualifying distributions, $5,873.
Limitations: Giving primarily in Brooklyn, NY.
Trustees: Leo Lieber, Sarah Lieber.
EIN: 113514060

39158
Fund for Neediest Russian Emigrants, Inc.
111 5th Ave.
New York, NY 10003 (212) 387-0299
Contact: Lawrence Weinberg

Financial data (yr. ended 10/31/01): Grants paid, $5,800; assets, $0 (M); gifts received, $157,274; expenditures, $6,633; qualifying distributions, $0.
Officer: Lawrence Weinberg, Pres.
EIN: 132960150

39159
Slivka Family Foundation, Inc.
25 Trinity Pass
Pound Ridge, NY 10576

Established in 1998 in NY.
Donor(s): Abraham Slivka.
Financial data (yr. ended 12/31/00): Grants paid, $5,750; assets, $103,268 (M); expenditures, $5,970; qualifying distributions, $5,750.
Limitations: Applications not accepted. Giving primarily in NY.
Application information: Contributes only to pre-selected organizations.
Director: Abraham Slivka.
EIN: 134038747

39160
Stanley Jay Lagin Foundation
c/o Gettry Marcus
20 Crossways Park N., Ste. 304
Woodbury, NY 11797

Financial data (yr. ended 12/31/01): Grants paid, $5,737; assets, $16,469 (M); expenditures, $6,239; qualifying distributions, $5,737.
Limitations: Applications not accepted. Giving primarily in NY.
Application information: Contributes only to pre-selected organizations.
Officer: Ellen Ross, Mgr.
EIN: 116037584

39161
Fins Foundation
141 Tara Dr.
Roslyn, NY 11576-2727 (516) 625-1317
Contact: Donna Fins Miller, Tr.

Financial data (yr. ended 12/31/01): Grants paid, $5,728; assets, $36,690 (M); expenditures, $6,333; qualifying distributions, $5,728.
Application information: Application form not required.
Trustee: Donna Fins Miller.
EIN: 116076878

39162
The Hirschtritt Family Foundation
1185 Park Ave.
New York, NY 10128

Established in 1989 in NY.
Donor(s): David P. Steinmann, Joel S. Hirschtritt.
Financial data (yr. ended 12/31/01): Grants paid, $5,725; assets, $43,652 (M); expenditures, $6,023; qualifying distributions, $5,725.
Limitations: Applications not accepted.
Application information: Contributes only to pre-selected organizations.
Officer and Directors:* Joel S. Hirschtritt,* Pres.; Nancy Hirschtritt, David P. Steinmann.
EIN: 133525298

39163
Weissman Foundation, Inc.
c/o Paul Weissman
325 West End Ave.
New York, NY 10023

Financial data (yr. ended 11/30/01): Grants paid, $5,724; assets, $54,394 (M); expenditures, $5,764; qualifying distributions, $5,724.
Limitations: Applications not accepted.
Application information: Contributes only to pre-selected organizations.
Officer: Paul Weissman, Pres.
EIN: 136144182

IN THIS SECTION, WITHIN EACH STATE, FOUNDATIONS ARE LISTED IN DESCENDING ORDER BY TOTAL GRANTS PAID

39164
The Stedawill Art Foundation, Inc.
c/o L. Wollin
350 5th Ave., Ste. 2822
New York, NY 10118

Financial data (yr. ended 06/30/01): Grants paid, $5,720; assets, $39,176 (M); expenditures, $7,119; qualifying distributions, $5,992.
Limitations: Applications not accepted. Giving limited to New York, NY.
Application information: Contributes only to pre-selected organizations.
Officers: Gerald Hirschhorn, Pres.; Patricia Hirschhorn, V.P.; Lonnie Wollin, Secy.
EIN: 133002233

39165
Alice T. Miner Masonic Memorial Trust
c/o Fleet National Bank
159 E. Main St.
Rochester, NY 14638

Financial data (yr. ended 12/31/99): Grants paid, $5,704; assets, $102,411 (M); expenditures, $7,018; qualifying distributions, $6,346.
Limitations: Applications not accepted. Giving primarily in Plattsburgh, NY.
Application information: Contributes only to pre-selected organizations.
Trustee: Fleet National Bank.
EIN: 146014245

39166
Laura Pels International Foundation
200 W. 57th St., Ste. 803
New York, NY 10019

Established in 1997 in NY.
Donor(s): Laura Pels.
Financial data (yr. ended 12/31/01): Grants paid, $5,682; assets, $977,686 (M); expenditures, $11,203; qualifying distributions, $11,100.
Limitations: Applications not accepted.
Application information: Contributes only to pre-selected organizations. Unsolicited requests for funds not accepted. Grants are by invitation only.
Officers: Laura J. Pels, Pres.; Jeffrey S. Feinman, Treas.
Directors: Michael Colgan, Wilma Jordan, Juliette Meeus, Francis X. Morrissey.
EIN: 133926887

39167
The Gds Foundation
24 Jackson Ave.
Spring Valley, NY 10977 (845) 354-7293
Contact: David Soifer, Dir.

Established in 2000 in NY.
Donor(s): David Soifer, Miriam Soifer.
Financial data (yr. ended 06/30/01): Grants paid, $5,664; assets, $52,715 (M); gifts received, $57,665; expenditures, $7,130; qualifying distributions, $5,664.
Directors: Imrich Katz, David Soifer, Miriam Soifer.
EIN: 134147796

39168
Second Chance Foundation, Inc.
c/o Gelfand Rennert & Feldman
1301 Ave. of the Americas
New York, NY 10019-1847
Application address: P.O. Box 727, Vineyard Haven, MA 02568

Established in 1990 in NY.
Donor(s): Victor Pisano, Judith Belushi Pisano, The John Belushi Memorial Foundation.
Financial data (yr. ended 12/31/00): Grants paid, $5,660; assets, $182,550 (M); gifts received, $11,000; expenditures, $9,843; qualifying distributions, $5,695.
Limitations: Giving primarily in Martha's Vineyard, MA.
Officers: Judith Belushi Pisano, Co-Pres.; Victor Pisano, Co-Pres.
EIN: 223066512

39169
Aaron & Sonia Fishman Foundation for Yiddish Culture, Inc.
3616 Henry Hudson Pkwy., No. 7BN
Bronx, NY 10463
Contact: Joshua A. Fishman, Pres.

Financial data (yr. ended 12/31/01): Grants paid, $5,650; assets, $82,958 (M); expenditures, $5,700; qualifying distributions, $5,650.
Limitations: Giving primarily in CA.
Officers and Directors:* Joshua A. Fishman,* Pres.; Martin Horowitz,* V.P.; David Roskies,* V.P.; David E. Fishman,* Secy.; Gella S. Fishman,* Treas.
EIN: 133039721

39170
Kellogg Free Library
P.O. Box 150
Cincinnatus, NY 13040
Contact: Franklin W. Ufford, Pres.

Established in 1930 in NY.
Financial data (yr. ended 12/31/01): Grants paid, $5,650; assets, $4,071,690 (M); gifts received, $2,515; expenditures, $140,319; qualifying distributions, $5,650.
Limitations: Giving limited to Cortland County, NY, for libraries and the Cincinnatus, NY, School District for community development.
Application information: Application form not required.
Officers and Directors:* Franklin W. Ufford,* Pres.; George Pryor,* V.P.; Carol Harrington,* Secy.-Treas.
EIN: 150594533

39171
The Abner Rosen Foundation, Inc.
40 E. 69th St.
New York, NY 10021 (212) 249-1550
Contact: Jonathan P. Rosen, Pres.

Donor(s): Miriam N. Rosen.
Financial data (yr. ended 06/30/00): Grants paid, $5,650; assets, $8,547 (M); gifts received, $10,000; expenditures, $7,304; qualifying distributions, $5,650.
Officers and Directors:* Jonathan P. Rosen,* Pres.; Miriam N. Rosen,* V.P.; Irving S. Bobrow,* Secy.; Jeanette D. Rosen,* Treas.
EIN: 133841307

39172
The Simeon Schreiber Family Foundation, Inc.
460 W. 34th St.
New York, NY 10001

Established in 2001 in NY.
Donor(s): Aaron Schreiber Family Foundation, Inc., David and Dassie Schreiber Family Foundation, Inc.
Financial data (yr. ended 12/31/01): Grants paid, $5,650; assets, $216,981 (M); gifts received, $230,750; expenditures, $5,689; qualifying distributions, $5,680.
Limitations: Applications not accepted.
Application information: Contributes only to pre-selected organizations.
Officer: Simeon Schreiber, Pres.
EIN: 134157131

39173
The Wright Family Foundation
c/o Philip H. Wright
62 Whippoorwill Rd.
Armonk, NY 10504

Established in 1998 in DE.
Donor(s): Philip H. Wright.
Financial data (yr. ended 12/31/99): Grants paid, $5,628; assets, $70,141 (M); gifts received, $47,850; expenditures, $8,222; qualifying distributions, $5,628.
Officer: Philip H. Wright, Pres. and Treas.
EIN: 134011969

39174
The Selma Schechter Foundation, Inc.
2600 Nostrand Ave.
Brooklyn, NY 11210

Established in 1962.
Donor(s): Shelly Schechter, Sheila Brecher, Richard Schechter, Sam Schechter, Harold Schechter, Saul Schechter, Dov Schechter, Benjamin Brecher, Jeffrey Schechter, Jerry Schechter.
Financial data (yr. ended 06/30/01): Grants paid, $5,619; assets, $66,766 (M); gifts received, $3,000; expenditures, $8,869; qualifying distributions, $7,244.
Limitations: Applications not accepted. Giving primarily in Miami Beach, FL, New York, NY, and Cincinnati, OH.
Application information: Contributes only to pre-selected organizations.
Officers: Saul Schechter, Pres.; Dov Schechter, V.P.; Richard Schechter, V.P.; Jerry Schechter, Secy.-Treas.
EIN: 116044719

39175
The Morris & Natalie Forgash Foundation
c/o Rivkin Radler
EAB Plaza
Uniondale, NY 11556
Application address: 51 The Serpentine, Roslyn Estates, NY 11576
Contact: Doris Rosen, Tr.

Financial data (yr. ended 12/31/01): Grants paid, $5,600; assets, $121,253 (M); expenditures, $6,930; qualifying distributions, $5,600.
Limitations: Giving primarily in NY.
Application information: Application form not required.
Trustee: Doris Rosen.
EIN: 136220363

39176
David & Rebecca Goodman Foundation, Inc.
c/o Paul Goodman
2280 E. 28th St.
Brooklyn, NY 11229-5058

Financial data (yr. ended 11/30/99): Grants paid, $5,600; assets, $11,230 (M); gifts received, $8,100; expenditures, $5,615; qualifying distributions, $5,615.
Limitations: Applications not accepted.
Application information: Contributes only to pre-selected organizations.
Officers: Paul Goodman, Pres.; Lester Goodman, Treas.
EIN: 237082541

39177
The N Foundation, Inc.
c/o Eisman, Zucker, et al., LLP
120 Bloomingdale Rd. Ste 402
White Plains, NY 10605

Donor(s): Linda Nisselson, Peter Nisselson.
Financial data (yr. ended 08/31/01): Grants paid, $5,600; assets, $0 (M); gifts received, $5,680; expenditures, $5,680; qualifying distributions, $5,680.
Limitations: Applications not accepted. Giving limited to residents of Larchmont, NY.
Directors: Arthur E. Eisman, Linda Nisselson, Peter Nisselson.
EIN: 133361672
Codes: GTI

39178
The Frida Tredup Trust - Saratoga Springs Nurses Foundation
c/o Adirondack Trust Co., Trust Dept.
473 Broadway
Saratoga Springs, NY 12866-2262
Application address: 186 West Ave., Saratoga Springs, NY 12866
Contact: Duane T. Brown

Financial data (yr. ended 12/31/00): Grants paid, $5,600; assets, $53,690 (M); expenditures, $6,126; qualifying distributions, $5,742.
Trustee: Adirondack Trust Co.
EIN: 146149423

39179
Norbert and Paula Gits Foundation
c/o Bessemer Trust Co., N.A.
630 5th Ave., 37th Fl.
New York, NY 10111
Application address: c/o Philip C. Kalafatis, Bessemer Trust Co. of Florida, 222 Royal Palm Way, Palm Beach, FL 33480

Established in 2000 in FL.
Donor(s): Norbert Gits, Paula Gits.
Financial data (yr. ended 06/30/02): Grants paid, $5,599; assets, $531,074 (M); gifts received, $30,000; expenditures, $12,882; qualifying distributions, $5,599.
Limitations: Giving primarily in Lake Leelanau, MI; some giving also in FL.
Advisory Committee Members: Norbert Gits, Paula Gits.
Trustee: Bessemer Trust Co. of Florida.
EIN: 527109505

39180
Clifford Family Foundation, Inc.
201 Orchard Ridge Rd.
Chappaqua, NY 10514-2732
Contact: Katherine C. Cates, Secy.-Treas.

Established in 1997 in NY.
Donor(s): Mary L. Clifford.
Financial data (yr. ended 12/31/01): Grants paid, $5,587; assets, $106,861 (M); expenditures, $7,167; qualifying distributions, $5,587.
Officers and Directors:* Lawrence M. Clifford,* Pres.; James D. Clifford,* V.P.; Elizabeth C. Coan,* V.P.; Mary C. Wood,* V.P.; Katherine C. Cates,* Secy.-Treas.; Donald K. Clifford, Jr., Mary L. Clifford.
EIN: 133895333

39181
Chaim Veshulem, Inc.
14 Sunrise Dr.
Monsey, NY 10952

Established in 1998 in NY.
Donor(s): Aron Herman, Rachel Herman.
Financial data (yr. ended 11/30/00): Grants paid, $5,545; assets, $7,270 (M); gifts received, $22,000; expenditures, $6,653; qualifying distributions, $5,545.
Limitations: Applications not accepted.
Application information: Contributes only to pre-selected organizations.
Officers: Aron Herman, Pres. and Treas.; Solomon Rosenberg, V.P.; Rachel Herman, Secy.
EIN: 134041479

39182
The Kleiger Foundation, Inc.
c/o F.T. Kleiger & Co.
80 Cuttermill Rd., No. 302
Great Neck, NY 11021

Donor(s): Fannie R. Kleiger.‡
Financial data (yr. ended 12/31/01): Grants paid, $5,505; assets, $158,697 (M); gifts received, $5,000; expenditures, $7,061; qualifying distributions, $5,505.
Limitations: Applications not accepted.
Application information: Contributes only to pre-selected organizations.
Officer: Connie Goldstein, Pres.
EIN: 132532501

39183
Marilyn M. Barman Charitable Trust
20 Central Dr.
Port Washington, NY 11050
Application address: 146-01 45th Ave., Ste. 406, Flushing, NY 11355
Contact: A. Addison Barman, Tr.

Donor(s): A. Addison Barman.
Financial data (yr. ended 12/31/00): Grants paid, $5,500; assets, $133,993 (M); gifts received, $6,385; expenditures, $9,745; qualifying distributions, $5,500.
Trustees: A. Addison Barman, Melanie Barman, Russel Barman.
EIN: 116431196

39184
Brotherhood Research Institute, Inc.
c/o Rabbi Gerald Kaplan
P.O. Box 245005
Brooklyn, NY 11224-7005

Financial data (yr. ended 04/30/01): Grants paid, $5,500; assets, $48,000 (M); gifts received, $4,900; expenditures, $8,900; qualifying distributions, $5,500.
Limitations: Applications not accepted. Giving primarily in NY.
Application information: Unsolicited requests for funds not accepted.
Officers: Rabbi Gerald Kaplan, Pres.; Roslyn Lubrano, V.P.; Rabbi Charles Margolis, Treas.
Director: Rabbi Abraham Garmaize.
EIN: 112558007

39185
Joan & Palmer Dixon Fund
c/o Marks, Paneth, & Shron, LLP
622 3rd Ave.
New York, NY 10017
Application address: 79 E. 79th St., New York, NY 10021
Contact: Peter T. Dixon, V.P.

Financial data (yr. ended 04/30/01): Grants paid, $5,500; assets, $96,787 (M); expenditures, $5,560; qualifying distributions, $5,560.
Limitations: Giving primarily in NY.
Application information: Application form not required.
Officers: Peter T. Dixon, V.P. and Treas.; Palmer Dixon, Secy.

EIN: 136130931

39186
Harry & Anita Mayer Foundation
c/o Richard Kandel & Co.
100 Crossways Pk. W., Ste. 210
Woodbury, NY 11797

Established in 1994 in NY.
Financial data (yr. ended 12/31/01): Grants paid, $5,500; assets, $1,520,064 (M); gifts received, $1,497,882; expenditures, $7,175; qualifying distributions, $5,500.
Limitations: Applications not accepted. Giving primarily in New York, NY.
Application information: Contributes only to pre-selected organizations.
Officers: Richard Kandel, Pres.; David Kessler, Secy.
EIN: 113223907

39187
Elvera Svenningsen Memorial Foundation
1 N. Broadway, Ste. 1004
White Plains, NY 10601-2310

Established in 1994 in NY.
Donor(s): Christine Svenningsen.
Financial data (yr. ended 11/30/01): Grants paid, $5,500; assets, $48,976 (M); gifts received, $10,000; expenditures, $7,433; qualifying distributions, $7,433.
Limitations: Applications not accepted. Giving primarily in Stamford, CT, and NY.
Officers: Christine Svenningsen, Pres. and Treas.; Fanny Warren, V.P. and Secy.; Margo Warren Patterson, V.P.
EIN: 113325358

39188
Marshall and Marilyn R. Wolf Foundation, Inc.
Church St. Sta.
P.O. Box 566
New York, NY 10008-0566   (212) 321-2403

Established in 1987 in NY.
Donor(s): Marshall Wolf, Marilyn Wolf.
Financial data (yr. ended 12/31/01): Grants paid, $5,500; assets, $4,511 (M); gifts received, $6,085; expenditures, $5,585; qualifying distributions, $5,500.
Limitations: Giving primarily in New York, NY.
Officers: Marshall Wolf, Pres.; Marilyn R. Wolf, Secy.-Treas.
Director: Barbara Madej.
EIN: 133422706

39189
Matthew & Lee Love Foundation, Inc.
c/o Birkenfeld Horwitz & Chu, LLP
137 Broadway, Ste. P
Amityville, NY 11701

Financial data (yr. ended 04/30/00): Grants paid, $5,490; assets, $69,344 (M); expenditures, $5,597; qualifying distributions, $5,490.
Limitations: Applications not accepted. Giving primarily in NY.
Trustee: Matthew Love.
EIN: 237449869

39190
D. & S. Rubin Trust
1600 Hillside Ave., Ste. 203
New Hyde Park, NY 11040

Donor(s): David Rubin.
Financial data (yr. ended 12/31/01): Grants paid, $5,490; assets, $99,215 (M); gifts received, $50; expenditures, $5,600; qualifying distributions, $5,490.
Limitations: Applications not accepted.

39190—NEW YORK

Application information: Contributes only to pre-selected organizations.
Trustee: David Rubin.
EIN: 116391113

39191
The Herbert E. Stern Family Foundation, Inc.
c/o Walter H. Stern
755 Bryant Ave.
Roslyn, NY 11576-5000

Established around 1970 in NY.
Donor(s): Herbert E. Stern, Erna E. Stern,‡ Walter H. Stern.
Financial data (yr. ended 06/30/02): Grants paid, $5,477; assets, $34,168 (M); gifts received, $5,000; expenditures, $5,627; qualifying distributions, $5,477.
Limitations: Applications not accepted. Giving primarily in the Boca Raton, FL and New York, NY areas.
Application information: Contributes only to pre-selected organizations.
Officer: Walter H. Stern, Pres.
EIN: 136139105

39192
The Daidola Foundation
c/o John C. Daidola
P.O. Box 826
Huntington, NY 11743-8826

Established in 1993 in NY.
Donor(s): John C. Daidola.
Financial data (yr. ended 12/31/01): Grants paid, $5,467; assets, $127,931 (M); gifts received, $40,800; expenditures, $8,937; qualifying distributions, $5,467.
Limitations: Applications not accepted. Giving primarily in NY.
Application information: Contributes only to pre-selected organizations.
Directors: Paulette V. Butler, John C. Daidola, Nancy Daidola.
EIN: 113211929

39193
Shimshon M. & Chaya Adler Foundation, Inc.
3907 Seagate Ave.
Brooklyn, NY 11224

Established in 1996 in NY.
Donor(s): Robert Adler.
Financial data (yr. ended 12/31/00): Grants paid, $5,450; assets, $4,791 (M); gifts received, $8,195; expenditures, $6,075; qualifying distributions, $6,075.
Limitations: Applications not accepted. Giving primarily in Brooklyn, NY.
Application information: Contributes only to pre-selected organizations.
Directors: Devorah Adler, Robert Adler, Abraham Lewanoni.
EIN: 113300619

39194
The Eda & Leonard Geringer Family Foundation, Inc.
1150 Hardscrabble Rd.
Chappaqua, NY 10514-1902

Established in 1999 in NY.
Donor(s): Eda Geringer, Leonard Geringer.
Financial data (yr. ended 11/30/01): Grants paid, $5,450; assets, $85,159 (M); expenditures, $8,080; qualifying distributions, $5,450.
Limitations: Applications not accepted.
Application information: Contributes only to pre-selected organizations.
Officers: Leonard Geringer, Pres.; Eda Geringer, V.P.

EIN: 113464131

39195
The H. Carnie Lawson II Charitable Trust
14 Frogrock Rd.
Armonk, NY 10504-1012 (914) 273-8535

Established in 1985 in NY.
Donor(s): H. Carnie Lawson II.
Financial data (yr. ended 12/31/01): Grants paid, $5,450; assets, $115,611 (M); gifts received, $264; expenditures, $5,714; qualifying distributions, $5,450.
Limitations: Applications not accepted.
Application information: Contributes only to pre-selected organizations.
Trustees: Henry Carnie Lawson, Pamela Jane Lawson, Suzanne Lawson.
EIN: 136860709

39196
The Horbach Fund
c/o The Bank of New York
1 Wall St., 28th Fl.
New York, NY 10286 (212) 635-1520
Application address: c/o The Bank of New York, National Community Div., P.O. Box 1040, Little Falls, NJ 07424

Donor(s): Cynthia Lee Morgan.
Financial data (yr. ended 12/31/01): Grants paid, $5,440; assets, $100,201 (M); expenditures, $5,792; qualifying distributions, $5,440.
Limitations: Giving limited to NJ, NY, and southern New England.
Application information: Application form required.
Trustee: The Bank of New York.
EIN: 237171692

39197
Joshua S. Koenigsberg Memorial Foundation, Inc.
15 Maiden Ln.
New York, NY 10038
Contact: Herman Koenigsberg, Tr.

Donor(s): Herman Koenigsberg.
Financial data (yr. ended 06/30/00): Grants paid, $5,415; assets, $116,108 (M); expenditures, $5,467; qualifying distributions, $5,415.
Limitations: Applications not accepted. Giving primarily in the New York, NY, area.
Application information: Contributes only to pre-selected organizations.
Officers and Trustees:* Herman Koenigsberg,* Pres.; Bernard Koenigsberg,* V.P.; Shirley Koenigsberg,* Secy.
EIN: 132624874

39198
The Frederick M. & Susan Friedman Foundation, Inc.
911 Park Ave., Apt. 14B
New York, NY 10021

Established in 1986 in NY.
Donor(s): Frederick M. Friedman, Susan Friedman.
Financial data (yr. ended 12/31/00): Grants paid, $5,400; assets, $83,862 (M); gifts received, $6,000; expenditures, $5,486; qualifying distributions, $5,400.
Limitations: Applications not accepted. Giving primarily in NY.
Application information: Contributes only to pre-selected organizations.
Directors: Andrea Friedman, Frederick M. Friedman, Stephanie Friedman, Susan Friedman.
EIN: 132285060

39199
Norman H. Halper Foundation, Inc.
313 Madison Ave., 8th Fl.
New York, NY 10017

Financial data (yr. ended 04/30/02): Grants paid, $5,400; assets, $39,653 (M); expenditures, $5,425; qualifying distributions, $5,400.
Limitations: Applications not accepted. Giving limited to New York, NY.
Application information: Contributes only to pre-selected organizations.
Officer: Norman H. Halper, Pres.
EIN: 136271926

39200
S. & Y. Goltche Trust
137-35 75th Rd.
Flushing, NY 11367

Established in 1999 in NY.
Donor(s): Sion Goltche, Yaffa Goltche.
Financial data (yr. ended 12/31/00): Grants paid, $5,398; assets, $46,401 (M); expenditures, $6,023; qualifying distributions, $5,398.
Limitations: Applications not accepted.
Application information: Contributes only to pre-selected organizations.
Trustees: Sion Goltche, Yaffa Goltche.
EIN: 137224915

39201
Wollin Family Foundation
c/o Lonnie E. Wollin
350 5th Ave., Ste. 2822
New York, NY 10118

Established in 1985 in DE.
Donor(s): Lonnie E. Wollin.
Financial data (yr. ended 02/28/00): Grants paid, $5,395; assets, $5,000 (M); expenditures, $7,332; qualifying distributions, $5,390.
Limitations: Applications not accepted. Giving primarily in NY.
Application information: Contributes only to pre-selected organizations.
Officers: Gary Wollin, Pres.; Lonnie Wollin, Secy.
EIN: 222615242

39202
Gesoff Family Foundation
39 Cohawney Rd.
Scarsdale, NY 10583-2222

Donor(s): Richard S. Gesoff.
Financial data (yr. ended 06/30/99): Grants paid, $5,387; assets, $15,766 (M); expenditures, $5,696; qualifying distributions, $5,387.
Limitations: Applications not accepted. Giving primarily in Scarsdale and New York, NY.
Application information: Contributes only to pre-selected organizations.
Trustees: Linda Gesoff, Richard S. Gesoff.
EIN: 133383307

39203
The Peter D. Bregman Foundation
55 5th Ave, 14th Fl.
New York, NY 10003

Established in 1998.
Donor(s): Peter Bregman.
Financial data (yr. ended 11/30/01): Grants paid, $5,369; assets, $113,027 (M); gifts received, $13,465; expenditures, $6,390; qualifying distributions, $5,369.
Limitations: Applications not accepted. Giving primarily in NY.
Application information: Contributes only to pre-selected organizations.
Officer: Peter Bregman, Pres.

Directors: Anthony Bregman, Bertie Bregman.
EIN: 522135940

39204
Rousso Sportswear Foundation, Inc.
111 Cedar Ave.
Hewlett, NY 11557-2413
Contact: David E. Rousso, Pres.

Donor(s): David E. Rousso.
Financial data (yr. ended 12/31/00): Grants paid, $5,362; assets, $59,270 (M); expenditures, $5,773; qualifying distributions, $5,362.
Limitations: Giving primarily in NY.
Officers: David E. Rousso, Pres.; Eli D. Rousso, V.P.; Sandra Izhakoff, Secy.; Harilyn Rousso, Treas.
EIN: 136154248

39205
Leonardo Da Vinci Foundation, Inc.
c/o Ann C. Pizzorusso
30 5th Ave., PH-C
New York, NY 10011

Established in 1997.
Donor(s): Ann Pizzorusso.
Financial data (yr. ended 12/31/01): Grants paid, $5,350; assets, $124,314 (M); expenditures, $8,853; qualifying distributions, $5,350.
Limitations: Applications not accepted. Giving primarily in NY.
Application information: Contributes only to pre-selected organizations.
Officer: Ann C. Pizzorusso, Pres.
Directors: Charles Amore, David Nathan.
EIN: 133978242

39206
Gerald & Rhoda Blumberg Foundation, Inc.
(Formerly Gerald Blumberg Foundation)
521 5th Ave., 24th Fl.
New York, NY 10175

Donor(s): Gerald Blumberg, Rhoda Blumberg.
Financial data (yr. ended 11/30/01): Grants paid, $5,345; assets, $71,951 (M); expenditures, $7,263; qualifying distributions, $5,345.
Limitations: Applications not accepted. Giving primarily in NY.
Application information: Contributes only to pre-selected organizations.
Officers: Gerald Blumberg, Pres.; Rhoda Blumberg, V.P. and Secy.; Lawrence S. Blumberg, Treas.
EIN: 136199591

39207
The John Paul II Charitable Trust
(Formerly John and Marsha Bisgrove Charitable Trust)
5457 Martin Rd.
Auburn, NY 13021
Application address: R.D. No. 2, Auburn, New York, 13021, tel.: (315) 252-6322; FAX: (315) 252-8189
Contact: John Bisgrove, Jr., Tr.

Established in 1987 in NY.
Donor(s): John Bisgrove, Jr., Marsha Bisgrove.
Financial data (yr. ended 12/31/01): Grants paid, $5,322; assets, $18,844 (M); expenditures, $5,322; qualifying distributions, $5,322.
Limitations: Giving primarily in Auburn, NY.
Trustees: John Bisgrove, Jr., Marsha Bisgrove, John P. Doyle, Jr.
EIN: 222794788

39208
The Kurtis and Mary Reed Foundation
860 United Nations Plz.
New York, NY 10017

Established in 1997 in NY.
Donor(s): Kurtis Reed.‡
Financial data (yr. ended 12/31/00): Grants paid, $5,300; assets, $63,358 (M); expenditures, $5,440; qualifying distributions, $5,300.
Limitations: Applications not accepted.
Application information: Contributes only to pre-selected organizations.
Trustee: CitiBank, N.A.
EIN: 133953195

39209
Stacy and Miro Weinberger Foundation, Inc.
509 W. 122nd St., Ste. 11
New York, NY 10027

Established in 2000 in NY.
Donor(s): Miro Weinberger.
Financial data (yr. ended 12/31/01): Grants paid, $5,300; assets, $27,645 (M); gifts received, $5,000; expenditures, $7,053; qualifying distributions, $5,300.
Limitations: Applications not accepted. Giving primarily in Washington, DC, MA, NY, and VT.
Application information: Contributes only to pre-selected organizations.
Officers: Miro Weinberger, Pres.; Sarah Weinberger, Secy.; Stacy Weinberger, Treas.
EIN: 134092540

39210
The Golub Family Foundation, Inc.
7 Trail's End
Chappaqua, NY 10514

Established in 1997 in NY.
Donor(s): Gerald L. Golub.
Financial data (yr. ended 11/30/01): Grants paid, $5,286; assets, $69,377 (M); gifts received, $2,000; expenditures, $5,433; qualifying distributions, $5,292.
Limitations: Applications not accepted.
Application information: Contributes only to pre-selected organizations.
Officers: Gerald L. Golub, Pres.; Bonnie Golub, Secy.
Director: Laurie F. Golub.
EIN: 133936964

39211
Retep Fund, Inc.
P.O. Box 124
Irvington, NY 10533

Established in 2000 in NY.
Donor(s): Helen Loughlin Herlitz.
Financial data (yr. ended 06/30/01): Grants paid, $5,275; assets, $166,611 (M); gifts received, $7,670; expenditures, $6,049; qualifying distributions, $6,049.
Officers: Helen Loughlin Herlitz, Pres.; Suzanne H. Herlitz, V.P.; Frederick W. Herlitz, V.P.; Fred W. Herlitz, Secy.-Treas.
EIN: 134150948

39212
J & J Foundation, Inc.
50 E. 42nd St., Ste. 1809
New York, NY 10017

Donor(s): Jane Levy, Julius Levy.
Financial data (yr. ended 12/31/01): Grants paid, $5,260; assets, $13,899 (M); gifts received, $3,281; expenditures, $5,823; qualifying distributions, $5,260.

Limitations: Applications not accepted. Giving primarily in New York, NY.
Application information: Contributes only to pre-selected organizations.
Directors: Jane Levy, Julius Levy.
EIN: 237129023

39213
Martin & Rhoda Barr Foundation, Inc.
c/o Martin Barr
29 Harvard Ln.
Hastings-on-Hudson, NY 10706-3309

Established in 1968 in NY.
Donor(s): Martin Barr, Rhoda Barr.
Financial data (yr. ended 12/31/01): Grants paid, $5,250; assets, $102,828 (M); expenditures, $5,359; qualifying distributions, $5,250.
Limitations: Applications not accepted. Giving primarily in New York, NY.
Application information: Contributes only to pre-selected organizations.
Trustees: Martin Barr, Rhoda Barr.
EIN: 136277920

39214
Melvin H. Fillin Foundation, Inc.
c/o Morton E. Swetlitz
350 5th Ave., Ste. 6101
New York, NY 10118-0132

Donor(s): Melvin H. Fillin.
Financial data (yr. ended 12/31/00): Grants paid, $5,250; assets, $34,098 (M); gifts received, $5,816; expenditures, $6,683; qualifying distributions, $5,250.
Limitations: Applications not accepted. Giving primarily in NM.
Application information: Contributes only to pre-selected organizations.
Officers: Melvin H. Fillin, Pres.; Mary Stewart, Secy.
EIN: 237123612

39215
Parks Family Foundation
c/o Burruano, Dolan, Glaser & Traynor, LLP
1 Byram Brook Pl.
Armonk, NY 10504

Established in 1989 in NY.
Donor(s): R. Ralph Parks, Jr.
Financial data (yr. ended 04/30/01): Grants paid, $5,250; assets, $612,276 (M); gifts received, $3,256; expenditures, $10,454; qualifying distributions, $5,250.
Limitations: Applications not accepted.
Application information: Contributes only to pre-selected organizations.
Trustees: Robert J. Hurst, Gwendoline Parks, R. Ralph Parks, Jr.
EIN: 133531982

39216
David & Marguerite Reisfeld Foundation, Inc.
c/o Jerome Richard
20 Sutton Pl. S., Ste. 4A
New York, NY 10022-4165

Financial data (yr. ended 12/31/01): Grants paid, $5,250; assets, $76,173 (M); gifts received, $7,762; expenditures, $5,862; qualifying distributions, $5,862.
Limitations: Applications not accepted. Giving primarily in New York, NY.
Application information: Contributes only to pre-selected organizations.
Officer: Jerome H. Richard, Pres.
EIN: 222192164

39217
Kusum Family Foundation, Inc.
419 Park Ave. S., Ste. 1104
New York, NY 10016

Established in 2000 in NY.
Donor(s): Devendra Shah.
Financial data (yr. ended 12/31/01): Grants paid, $5,225; assets, $275,954 (M); gifts received, $100,000; expenditures, $8,729; qualifying distributions, $5,225.
Limitations: Applications not accepted. Giving primarily in NY.
Application information: Contributes only to pre-selected organizations.
Officers and Directors:* Devendra Shah,* Pres.; Yogesh Shah,* V.P.; Ashwin Shah, Secy.-Treas.
EIN: 134139226

39218
Raphael & Esther de Rothschild Foundation
(Formerly Nili and Nathaniel de Rothschild Foundation)
767 5th Ave., 46th Fl.
New York, NY 10153-0023

Established in 1994 in NY.
Financial data (yr. ended 12/31/01): Grants paid, $5,204; assets, $379,602 (M); gifts received, $57,465; expenditures, $34,802; qualifying distributions, $34,309.
Limitations: Applications not accepted. Giving primarily in NY.
Application information: Contributes only to pre-selected organizations.
Trustees: Nathaniel de Rothschild, Nili de Rothschild.
EIN: 137052577

39219
Joley Foundation, Inc.
301 E. 79th St., Apt. 7P
New York, NY 10021-0951 (212) 570-0443
Contact: Ethel S. Hirsch, Pres.

Financial data (yr. ended 10/31/01): Grants paid, $5,200; assets, $80,631 (M); expenditures, $5,795; qualifying distributions, $5,795.
Officers: Ethel S. Hirsch, Pres. and Treas.; Nathaniel Levy, V.P.; Robert G. Klein, Secy.
EIN: 116009019

39220
The Theresa E. and Frederick W. Krebs Foundation
c/o Harvey Ginsberg & Co.
675 3rd Ave., Ste. 2800
New York, NY 10017
Contact: Harvey Ginsberg, Pres.

Financial data (yr. ended 12/31/00): Grants paid, $5,177; assets, $1 (M); expenditures, $5,252; qualifying distributions, $5,177.
Limitations: Giving primarily in NY.
Officers: Harvey Ginsberg, Pres.; Anita Ginsberg, Secy.; Samuel Z. Ginsberg, Treas.
EIN: 132691010

39221
Yang Foundation
141 Paris Rd.
New Hartford, NY 13413-2455
(315) 724-5101
Contact: Chul Jo Yang, Tr.

Established in 1987 in NY.
Financial data (yr. ended 12/31/01): Grants paid, $5,175; assets, $98,564 (M); expenditures, $5,237; qualifying distributions, $5,175.
Limitations: Giving primarily in NY.
Directors: Jae Sook Yang, Michelle K. Yang.

Trustee: Chul Jo Yang.
EIN: 161318142

39222
Alissa Beth Bander Memorial Foundation, Inc.
2 Hemlock Hills
Chappaqua, NY 10514
Contact: Neil H. Bander, M.D., Chair.

Established in 1988 in NY.
Financial data (yr. ended 12/31/01): Grants paid, $5,150; assets, $391,471 (M); gifts received, $170,000; expenditures, $15,831; qualifying distributions, $5,150.
Limitations: Giving primarily in NY.
Application information: Application form not required.
Officers: Neil H. Bander, M.D., Chair. and Secy.-Treas.; Karen Bander, Ph.D., Pres.; Albert Weiss, V.P.
EIN: 133235052

39223
The Annie Audrey Ragin Foundation
c/o Luther M. Ragin, Jr.
160 Cabrini Blvd. Ste. 11
New York, NY 10033 (212) 740-0897

Donor(s): Luther M. Ragin, Jr., Deborah Fish Ragin.
Financial data (yr. ended 12/31/01): Grants paid, $5,150; assets, $14,112 (M); expenditures, $5,192; qualifying distributions, $5,150.
Limitations: Applications not accepted. Giving primarily in New York, NY.
Application information: Contributes only to pre-selected organizations.
Trustees: Deborah Fish Ragin, Luther M. Ragin, Jr.
EIN: 133639771

39224
Susan & Michael Shapiro Memorial Foundation
555 Green Pl.
Woodmere, NY 11598-1908

Established in 1987 in NY.
Donor(s): Adele Shapiro,‡ David Shapiro.
Financial data (yr. ended 12/31/01): Grants paid, $5,145; assets, $115,468 (M); gifts received, $26,394; expenditures, $5,481; qualifying distributions, $5,145.
Limitations: Applications not accepted. Giving primarily in NY.
Application information: Contributes only to pre-selected organizations.
Trustees: Adele Shapiro, David Shapiro, Deborah Shapiro.
EIN: 112852971

39225
Lawrence Evan Sloate Foundation, Inc.
c/o Hertz, Herson & Co., LLP
2 Park Ave., Rm. 1500
New York, NY 10016-5701

Donor(s): Morton Sloate.
Financial data (yr. ended 12/31/01): Grants paid, $5,128; assets, $17,921 (M); expenditures, $6,423; qualifying distributions, $5,128.
Limitations: Applications not accepted.
Application information: Contributes only to pre-selected organizations.
Officers: Morton Sloate, Pres.; Patricia Sloate, Secy.
EIN: 132672981

39226
Ruth Keeler Charitable Trust
c/o Robert Scheff
630 Park Ave., Ste. 10C
New York, NY 10021

Established in 1988 in NY.
Donor(s): Ruth Keeler.
Financial data (yr. ended 12/31/01): Grants paid, $5,123; assets, $3,771 (M); gifts received, $5,575; expenditures, $5,123; qualifying distributions, $5,123.
Limitations: Applications not accepted. Giving primarily in Westchester County, NY.
Application information: Contributes only to pre-selected organizations.
Trustees: Ruth Keeler, Robert Scheff.
EIN: 136918074

39227
Catskill Community Swimming Pool, Inc.
226 Rte. 385
Catskill, NY 12414

Established in 1997 in NY.
Financial data (yr. ended 12/31/01): Grants paid, $5,100; assets, $99,939 (M); gifts received, $100; expenditures, $5,705; qualifying distributions, $5,046.
Limitations: Giving primarily in Catskill, NY.
Officers: Nancy Ursprung, Pres.; Jack Guterman, V.P.; Patricia A. Delanoy, Secy.-Treas.
Directors: Nancy Cuddihy Guterman, Sara Wolven.
EIN: 237231520

39228
Abraham & Celia Linzer Foundation
c/o Joseph F. Linzer
73 Euclid Ave.
Hastings-on-Hudson, NY 10706-1109

Donor(s): Joseph F. Linzer.
Financial data (yr. ended 11/30/01): Grants paid, $5,100; assets, $41,398 (M); expenditures, $5,100; qualifying distributions, $5,100.
Limitations: Applications not accepted. Giving primarily in NY.
Application information: Contributes only to pre-selected organizations.
Officer: Joseph F. Linzer, Pres.
EIN: 136069437

39229
N.C. Charitable Trust
11 Peter Dr.
Wappingers Falls, NY 12590

Established in 1993.
Financial data (yr. ended 12/31/99): Grants paid, $5,100; assets, $251,037 (M); gifts received, $55,000; expenditures, $5,128; qualifying distributions, $5,128.
Officers: Bharet Magdalia, Pres.; Ramesh Jindal, V.P.; Vinod Jindal, Secy.; Pawan Jindal, Treas.
EIN: 141763869

39230
Katherine M. Stoner Trust
c/o M&T Trust Co.
1 M&T Plz., 8th Fl.
Buffalo, NY 14203
Application address: c/o John Schall, M&T Trust Co., 14 N. Main St., Chambersburg, PA 17201, tel.: (717) 267-7625

Financial data (yr. ended 12/31/01): Grants paid, $5,100; assets, $89,557 (M); expenditures, $6,556; qualifying distributions, $5,100.
Limitations: Giving limited to residents of PA.

Application information: Application form required.
Trustee: M & T Bank.
EIN: 256266025

39231
Weinshel/Goldfarb Foundation, Inc.
c/o L. Connie Wollin
350 5th Ave., No. 2822
New York, NY 10118

Established in 1997 in DE.
Donor(s): Joel Goldfarb, Elizabeth Weinshel.
Financial data (yr. ended 06/30/01): Grants paid, $5,100; assets, $204,868 (M); gifts received, $21,875; expenditures, $7,591; qualifying distributions, $5,944.
Limitations: Applications not accepted. Giving on a national basis.
Application information: Contributes only to pre-selected organizations.
Officers: Elizabeth Weinshel, Pres.; Joel Goldfarb, V.P.; Lonnie Wollin, Secy.
EIN: 223553567

39232
Walter J. Steffan Foundation
2660 N. Forest Rd., Apt. 118
Getzville, NY 14068-1529 (716) 688-7722
Contact: Norma Steffan, Tr.

Donor(s): Norma Steffan.
Financial data (yr. ended 12/31/01): Grants paid, $5,097; assets, $100,529 (M); expenditures, $6,497; qualifying distributions, $5,097.
Limitations: Giving primarily in NY.
Application information: Application form not required.
Trustees: Norma Steffan, W. John Steffan.
EIN: 166058429

39233
The Sottovoce Foundation
1586 Laurel Hollow Rd.
Syosset, NY 11791

Established in 1997.
Donor(s): F. Sedgwick Browne.
Financial data (yr. ended 02/28/02): Grants paid, $5,095; assets, $60,636 (M); expenditures, $6,989; qualifying distributions, $5,095.
Limitations: Applications not accepted. Giving on a national basis.
Application information: Contributes only to pre-selected organizations.
Trustees: F. Sedgwick Browne, Gloria Browne.
EIN: 113370114

39234
The West Mountain Mission
c/o Roger Smith, Pawling Corp.
157 Charles Colman Blvd.
Pawling, NY 12564

Established in 1992 in NY.
Financial data (yr. ended 12/31/01): Grants paid, $5,080; assets, $2,110 (M); gifts received, $402; expenditures, $8,304; qualifying distributions, $5,080.
Limitations: Giving primarily in Pawling, NY.
Trustees: Elizabeth Allen, Judith Collette, G. Theodore Nace, Beatrice D. Parent, Howard W. Smith, Roger W. Smith, Ronald L. Wozniak.
EIN: 146036732

39235
Babtkis Foundation
1347 40th St.
Brooklyn, NY 11218-3503
Contact: Lillian Babtkis, Mgr.

Established around 1969.
Financial data (yr. ended 07/31/02): Grants paid, $5,075; assets, $285,409 (M); expenditures, $11,172; qualifying distributions, $5,075.
Limitations: Giving primarily in the metropolitan New York, NY, area.
Officer: Lillian Babtkis, Mgr.
EIN: 237029237

39236
Jack Shelly Foundation
1010 Seawane Dr.
Hewlett, NY 11557 (516) 791-2500

Established in 1999 in NY.
Financial data (yr. ended 11/30/01): Grants paid, $5,075; assets, $102,418 (M); gifts received, $1,000; expenditures, $5,368; qualifying distributions, $5,075.
Officers: Leonard Schlussel, Pres.; Irving Schlussel, V.P.; Lee Schlussel, Treas.
EIN: 134106308

39237
Morris and Ester Sadock Foundation, Inc.
c/o Lady Ester Lingerie Corp.
16 E. 34th St.
New York, NY 10016

Established in 1981 in NY.
Donor(s): Lady Ester Lingerie Corp.
Financial data (yr. ended 01/31/01): Grants paid, $5,057; assets, $29,829 (M); expenditures, $5,095; qualifying distributions, $5,082.
Limitations: Applications not accepted. Giving primarily in the greater New York, NY, area.
Application information: Contributes only to pre-selected organizations.
Trustees: Karen Sadock, M. William Sadock, Robert T. Sadock.
EIN: 133084706

39238
The John J. Rydzewski Charitable Fund, Inc.
1 W. 72nd St., Ste. 30
New York, NY 10023

Financial data (yr. ended 12/31/01): Grants paid, $5,055; assets, $74,304 (M); gifts received, $34,250; expenditures, $11,475; qualifying distributions, $5,055.
Limitations: Applications not accepted. Giving primarily in Walnut Creek, CA.
Application information: Contributes only to pre-selected organizations.
Officers: John J. Rydzewski, Chair. and Pres.; Harold J. Philipps, Secy.; Bert E. Picot, Jr., Treas.
EIN: 522070195

39239
Doris & Mortimer Grossman Fund, Inc.
53 Cedarhurst Ave.
Lawrence, NY 11559

Financial data (yr. ended 12/31/01): Grants paid, $5,050; assets, $89,612 (M); expenditures, $5,556; qualifying distributions, $5,050.
Limitations: Applications not accepted. Giving primarily in NY.
Application information: Contributes only to pre-selected organizations.
Officer: Yaacov Gross, Pres.
EIN: 116005067

39240
The Posner Foundation, Inc.
110 E. 42nd St., Ste. 1406
New York, NY 10017-5611

Donor(s): Alan H. Posner, Lillian Posner.
Financial data (yr. ended 12/31/01): Grants paid, $5,050; assets, $8,459 (M); gifts received, $2,000; expenditures, $5,135; qualifying distributions, $5,050.
Limitations: Applications not accepted. Giving primarily in New York, NY.
Application information: Contributes only to pre-selected organizations.
Officers: Alan H. Posner, Pres.; Lillian Posner, V.P.
EIN: 136163961

39241
Burton I. Koffman Foundation, Inc.
c/o Piaker & Lyons, PC
P.O. Box 247
Vestal, NY 13851-0247

Donor(s): Burton I. Koffman.
Financial data (yr. ended 12/31/01): Grants paid, $5,048; assets, $3,710 (M); gifts received, $7,035; expenditures, $5,179; qualifying distributions, $5,048.
Limitations: Applications not accepted. Giving primarily in Binghamton, NY.
Application information: Contributes only to pre-selected organizations.
Trustees: Burton I. Koffman, Richard E. Koffman.
EIN: 237005613

39242
Rabinovitch Family Foundation
543 Bedford Rd.
Mount Kisco, NY 10549

Established in 1994 in NY.
Donor(s): Donald Rabinovitch.
Financial data (yr. ended 11/30/01): Grants paid, $5,029; assets, $27,536 (M); gifts received, $5,892; expenditures, $5,233; qualifying distributions, $5,029.
Limitations: Applications not accepted.
Application information: Contributes only to pre-selected organizations.
Officer: Donald Rabinovitch, Pres.
EIN: 133798061

39243
The Aeneas Capital Management Foundation
100 S. Bedford Rd., Ste. 240
Mount Kisco, NY 10549

Established in 2000 in NY.
Donor(s): Thomas Grossman.
Financial data (yr. ended 12/31/01): Grants paid, $5,000; assets, $17,427 (M); gifts received, $907; expenditures, $7,026; qualifying distributions, $5,000.
Trustee: Thomas Grossman.
EIN: 137232145

39244
Sidney and Beatrice Albert Foundation
c/o Marvin I. Honig
20 Corporate Woods, 5th Fl.
Albany, NY 12211

Established in 1994 in NY.
Financial data (yr. ended 05/31/02): Grants paid, $5,000; assets, $59,601 (M); expenditures, $5,000; qualifying distributions, $5,000.
Limitations: Giving primarily in NY.
Officers: Beatrice Albert, Pres. and Treas.; Marvin Honig, Secy.
EIN: 223267816

39245
The Barnard Family Foundation, Inc.
c/o David Barnard
1215 5th Ave., Apt. 2B
New York, NY 10029-5211

Established in 1986 in NY.
Donor(s): David Barnard.

39245—NEW YORK

Financial data (yr. ended 03/31/02): Grants paid, $5,000; assets, $17,491 (M); expenditures, $5,000; qualifying distributions, $5,000.
Limitations: Applications not accepted. Giving limited to New York, NY.
Application information: Contributes only to pre-selected organizations.
Officers: David Barnard, Pres. and Treas.; Janice Barnard, Secy.
EIN: 133348613

39246
The Jack & Deborah Becker Charitable Foundation
c/o Snow Becker Krauss, PC
605 3rd Ave.
New York, NY 10158-0125

Established in 1997 in NY.
Donor(s): Jack Becker.
Financial data (yr. ended 12/31/01): Grants paid, $5,000; assets, $72,274 (M); gifts received, $5,000; expenditures, $5,125; qualifying distributions, $5,000.
Limitations: Applications not accepted.
Application information: Contributes only to pre-selected organizations.
Directors: Barbara Lynn Becker, Deborah S. Becker, Jack Becker, Marjorie Anne Becker.
EIN: 133937865

39247
The Marc and Ruti Bell Foundation
157 E. 32nd St., Ste. 23A
New York, NY 10016-6036

Established in 2000 in DE and NY.
Donor(s): Marc Bell.
Financial data (yr. ended 11/30/01): Grants paid, $5,000; assets, $2,182,199 (M); gifts received, $2,891,636; expenditures, $5,000; qualifying distributions, $5,000.
Limitations: Applications not accepted.
Application information: Contributes only to pre-selected organizations.
Officers: Marc Bell, Pres.; Ruti Bell, V.P.
EIN: 134145737

39248
The Blickman Foundation
(Formerly The Blickman-Friman Foundation)
10 Rockefeller Plz., Ste. 700
New York, NY 10020

Established in 1984 in NY.
Donor(s): Jerry Blickman, Inc., Friman & Stein, Inc.
Financial data (yr. ended 01/31/02): Grants paid, $5,000; assets, $663 (M); gifts received, $5,500; expenditures, $5,263; qualifying distributions, $5,000.
Limitations: Applications not accepted. Giving primarily in NY.
Application information: Contributes only to pre-selected organizations.
Officers and Directors:* Michele Blickman,* Pres.; Mace Blickman,* Secy.; Nicole Miller, Treas.; Robert Hoberman.
EIN: 133204389

39249
Marvin A. & Lillian K. Block Foundation, Inc.
c/o Gross, Shuman, et al.
465 Main St.
Buffalo, NY 14203

Financial data (yr. ended 12/31/01): Grants paid, $5,000; assets, $146,068 (M); expenditures, $6,667; qualifying distributions, $5,000.
Limitations: Applications not accepted. Giving primarily in NY.

Application information: Contributes only to pre-selected organizations.
Officers: David Alexander, Pres.; James Burke, Secy.
EIN: 166028770

39250
Marlin E. Blosser Trust
c/o M&T Bank
1 M&T Plz., 8th Fl.
Buffalo, NY 14203
Application address: Carlisle High School, Counseling Center, 623 W. Penn St., Carlisle, PA 17013

Established in 1999 in PA.
Financial data (yr. ended 12/31/00): Grants paid, $5,000; assets, $293,638 (M); expenditures, $9,268; qualifying distributions, $4,870.
Limitations: Giving primarily to residents of Carlisle, PA.
Trustee: M & T Bank.
EIN: 256579913

39251
Adam J. Cirillo Scholarship Foundation
c/o Patricia Cuzzocrea
5 Morse Ave.
Staten Island, NY 10314

Established in 1996 in NY.
Financial data (yr. ended 12/31/01): Grants paid, $5,000; assets, $365,556 (M); expenditures, $8,021; qualifying distributions, $5,000.
Limitations: Giving limited to residents of Brooklyn, NY.
Application information: Application form required.
Director: Patricia Cuzzocrea.
EIN: 133844881

39252
The Charles & Ellen Cogut Family Foundation, Inc.
c/o Charles I. Cogut
36 Garden Pl.
Brooklyn, NY 11201

Established in 1995.
Donor(s): Ellen F. Cogut.
Financial data (yr. ended 11/30/01): Grants paid, $5,000; assets, $232,209 (M); gifts received, $10,000; expenditures, $6,400; qualifying distributions, $5,000.
Limitations: Applications not accepted. Giving primarily in NY.
Application information: Contributes only to pre-selected organizations.
Officers: Charles I. Cogut, Pres. and Treas.; Ellen F. Cogut, Exec. V.P. and Secy.; Pamela Cogut, V.P.
EIN: 113294488

39253
The Lester I. Conrad Research Foundation, Inc.
c/o Reisner and Co.
137 S. Babylon Tpke.
Merrick, NY 11566-4206

Established in 1983 in NY.
Donor(s): Muriel Conrad Reisner.
Financial data (yr. ended 11/30/99): Grants paid, $5,000; assets, $12,571 (M); expenditures, $5,080; qualifying distributions, $5,080.
Limitations: Applications not accepted.
Application information: Contributes only to pre-selected organizations.
Directors: Andrew Perlman, Alan Reisner, Muriel Conrad Reisner.
EIN: 133195596

39254
The Countess Moira Charitable Foundation
c/o Analytic Asset Mgmt., Inc.
600 3rd Ave., 17th Fl.
New York, NY 10016

Established in 2000 in NY.
Donor(s): Moira Rossi, Edward W.T. Gray III, Moira Forbes.
Financial data (yr. ended 06/30/01): Grants paid, $5,000; assets, $971,980 (M); gifts received, $1,090,622; expenditures, $9,468; qualifying distributions, $5,000.
Limitations: Applications not accepted. Giving primarily in Great Neck, NY.
Application information: Contributes only to pre-selected organizations.
Officers: Edward W.T. Gray III, Chair.; Michele J. Le Moal-Gray, Vice-Chair.; Carolyn B. Gray, Pres.; Peter G. Gray, V.P. and Secy.; Taylor T. Gray, V.P. and Treas.
Trustees: Moira Forbes, Moira Rossi.
EIN: 113551993

39255
Athena E. Coutsodontis Memorial Foundation
9 Northway
Bronxville, NY 10708

Financial data (yr. ended 12/31/01): Grants paid, $5,000; assets, $5,974 (M); gifts received, $5,200; expenditures, $6,638; qualifying distributions, $5,000.
Director: Francesca E. Coutsodontis.
EIN: 134101352

39256
The Cream Hill Foundation
c/o Yohalem, Gillman & Co.
477 Madison Ave.
New York, NY 10022-5802

Established in 2000 in NY.
Donor(s): George Labalme, Jr.
Financial data (yr. ended 12/31/01): Grants paid, $5,000; assets, $1,225,236 (M); gifts received, $991,701; expenditures, $28,000; qualifying distributions, $5,000.
Limitations: Applications not accepted.
Application information: Contributes only to pre-selected organizations.
Trustees: George Labalme, Jr., Henry G. Labalme, Jennifer R. Labalme, Patricia Hochschild Labalme, Victoria A. Labalme, Lisa L. Osterland.
EIN: 134148381

39257
The Cremer Foundation
c/o Willkie, Farr & Gallagher
787 7th Ave.
New York, NY 10019-6099 (212) 821-8008
Contact: Robert B. Hodes, Tr.

Financial data (yr. ended 12/31/01): Grants paid, $5,000; assets, $193,946 (M); expenditures, $6,008; qualifying distributions, $5,000.
Limitations: Giving primarily in NY.
Application information: Application form not required.
Trustee: Robert B. Hodes.
EIN: 136107846

39258
Dautch Family Foundation
c/o M&T Bldg.
1 M&T Plz., Rm. 1800
Buffalo, NY 14203-2310

Donor(s): Lawrence H. Dautch.

Financial data (yr. ended 12/31/01): Grants paid, $5,000; assets, $9,034 (M); expenditures, $5,159; qualifying distributions, $5,000.
Limitations: Applications not accepted. Giving on a national basis, with some emphasis on NY.
Application information: Contributes only to pre-selected organizations.
Trustees: Lawrence H. Dautch, Patricia E. Dautch.
EIN: 166342785

39259
The Deerfield Foundation, Inc.
645 Madison Ave., Ste. 500
New York, NY 10022-1010

Established in 1961.
Donor(s): Louis Marx, Jr.
Financial data (yr. ended 06/30/01): Grants paid, $5,000; assets, $767,350 (M); expenditures, $5,366; qualifying distributions, $5,366.
Limitations: Applications not accepted. Giving primarily in Long Island City, NY.
Application information: Contributes only to pre-selected organizations.
Officers: Louis Marx, Jr., Pres.; Seymour L. Wane, V.P.; Robert W. Lenthe, Secy.
EIN: 136613664

39260
The Winifred Crawford Dibert Foundation, Inc.
525 Fairmount Ave.
Jamestown, NY 14702-1198 (716) 483-1122
Contact: Edward P. Wright, Dir.

Established in 2000 in NY.
Donor(s): Winifred S. Dibert.
Financial data (yr. ended 12/31/01): Grants paid, $5,000; assets, $987,294 (M); expenditures, $7,204; qualifying distributions, $5,000.
Directors: Winifred S. Dibert, Jon A. Saff, Edward P. Wright.
EIN: 161589819

39261
Ester Eisenberg Charitable Trust
c/o Leon Eisenberg
160 E. Beech St.
Long Beach, NY 11561

Established in 1995 in NY.
Donor(s): Ester Eisenberg.‡
Financial data (yr. ended 12/31/01): Grants paid, $5,000; assets, $165,297 (M); expenditures, $6,258; qualifying distributions, $5,000.
Limitations: Applications not accepted. Giving primarily in NY.
Application information: Contributes only to pre-selected organizations.
Trustee: Leon Eisenberg.
EIN: 116460945

39262
Eng Family Charitable Trust
308 E. 38th St.
New York, NY 10016

Established in 2000 in NY.
Donor(s): Kenneth Eng, June Eng.
Financial data (yr. ended 12/31/01): Grants paid, $5,000; assets, $76,368 (M); expenditures, $7,444; qualifying distributions, $5,000.
Limitations: Applications not accepted. Giving primarily in NY.
Application information: Contributes only to pre-selected organizations.
Trustees: June Eng, Kenneth Eng.
EIN: 137237799

39263
Paul H. Epstein Foundation, Inc.
c/o Rose Proskauer, LLP
1585 Broadway
New York, NY 10036-8299

Donor(s): Paul H. Epstein.
Financial data (yr. ended 12/31/01): Grants paid, $5,000; assets, $82,866 (M); gifts received, $5,000; expenditures, $7,147; qualifying distributions, $5,000.
Limitations: Applications not accepted. Giving limited to New York, NY.
Application information: Contributes only to pre-selected organizations.
Officer: Paul H. Epstein, Pres.
EIN: 237024264

39264
The ETZ Chaim Charitable Trust
1520 50th St.
Brooklyn, NY 11219

Donor(s): Saul Wolf, Chaim Wolf, Chaim Meisels.
Financial data (yr. ended 12/31/01): Grants paid, $5,000; assets, $440,414 (M); gifts received, $160,294; expenditures, $5,289; qualifying distributions, $5,000.
Limitations: Applications not accepted. Giving primarily in Brooklyn, NY.
Trustees: Deborah Wolf, Saul Wolf.
EIN: 137138977

39265
Spencer & Linda Falk Family Foundation, Inc.
1 Cedar Island
Larchmont, NY 10538

Established in 2000.
Donor(s): Spencer Falk, Linda Falk.
Financial data (yr. ended 12/31/01): Grants paid, $5,000; assets, $3,018 (M); expenditures, $5,000; qualifying distributions, $5,000.
Limitations: Applications not accepted. Giving primarily in NY.
Application information: Contributes only to pre-selected organizations.
Officers and Trustees:* Spencer Falk, Pres. and Treas.; Linda Falk,* Secy.; Adrien Bergen.
EIN: 134117492

39266
Leo Feist Charities, Inc.
50 Tisdale Rd.
Scarsdale, NY 10583 (914) 725-3988
Contact: Richard Feist, Pres.

Established in 1940 in NY.
Donor(s): Leo Feist.‡
Financial data (yr. ended 12/31/99): Grants paid, $5,000; assets, $113,483 (M); expenditures, $6,608; qualifying distributions, $5,000.
Limitations: Giving primarily in NY.
Application information: Application form not required.
Officers: Richard Feist, Pres.; Marilyn Reiner, V.P.; Betsy Feist, Secy.-Treas.
EIN: 136163059

39267
The Fialkov Family Foundation
c/o Richard Kopeland
65 Colgate Rd.
Great Neck, NY 11023

Financial data (yr. ended 12/31/01): Grants paid, $5,000; assets, $93,351 (M); expenditures, $7,906; qualifying distributions, $2,906.
Limitations: Applications not accepted.
Application information: Contributes only to pre-selected organizations.
Directors: Carol Fialkov, Clare Fialkov, Jay Fialkov, Richard Kopeland.
EIN: 116478221

39268
Jerry Finkelstein Foundation, Inc.
c/o Tarlow & Tarlow, LLP
1505 Kellum Pl.
Mineola, NY 11501 (516) 873-0372
Contact: Jerry Finkelstein, Pres.

Established in 1986 in NY.
Donor(s): Jerry Finkelstein.
Financial data (yr. ended 03/31/01): Grants paid, $5,000; assets, $93,070 (M); gifts received, $301,250; expenditures, $5,000; qualifying distributions, $5,000.
Limitations: Giving primarily in MA and NY.
Officer: Jerry Finkelstein, Pres. and Treas.
EIN: 136167959

39269
Louise & Sidney Frank Foundation
11 Hillandale Dr.
New Rochelle, NY 10804-1921

Financial data (yr. ended 01/31/02): Grants paid, $5,000; assets, $13,118 (M); gifts received, $25; expenditures, $7,325; qualifying distributions, $5,000.
Limitations: Applications not accepted.
Application information: Contributes only to pre-selected organizations.
Officer: Sidney Frank, Pres.
EIN: 136076858

39270
Lawrence Friedland Foundation, Inc.
22 E. 65th St., 5th Fl.
New York, NY 10021

Established in 1986 in NY.
Donor(s): Lawrence Friedland.
Financial data (yr. ended 09/30/01): Grants paid, $5,000; assets, $195,994 (M); expenditures, $6,062; qualifying distributions, $5,000.
Limitations: Applications not accepted. Giving primarily in New York, NY.
Application information: Contributes only to pre-selected organizations.
Officers: Lawrence Friedland, Pres.; Marilyn Friedland, Secy.
Directors: Elizabeth Friedland, Pamela Friedland, William Friedland.
EIN: 133435718

39271
Samuel Friedman Foundation, Inc.
c/o Saperston & Day, P.C.
1100 M & T Ctr., 3 Fountain Plz.
Buffalo, NY 14203-1486
Contact: Richard J. Day, Dir.

Established in 1968.
Donor(s): Samuel Friedman.‡
Financial data (yr. ended 05/31/01): Grants paid, $5,000; assets, $94,258 (M); expenditures, $7,428; qualifying distributions, $5,000.
Limitations: Giving primarily in Buffalo, NY.
Application information: Application form not required.
Directors: Ann Cohn, Donald S. Day, Richard J. Day, Esther Kirtz, Miriam Sukernek.
EIN: 160955139

39272
Richard H. Goldman Memorial Foundation
150 E. 69th St., Apt. 7G
New York, NY 10021

Donor(s): Robert S. Goldman.

39272—NEW YORK

Financial data (yr. ended 12/31/01): Grants paid, $5,000; assets, $4,514 (M); expenditures, $5,106; qualifying distributions, $5,000.
Limitations: Applications not accepted. Giving primarily in Washington, DC, and New York, NY.
Application information: Contributes only to pre-selected organizations.
Trustees: Clifford Goldman, Robert S. Goldman.
EIN: 112538932

39273
Green Hills Charitable Foundation
c/o Brand Sonnenschine, LLP
377 Broadway, 9th Fl.
New York, NY 10013

Established in 1999 in NY.
Donor(s): Manuel Sanchez.
Financial data (yr. ended 12/31/01): Grants paid, $5,000; assets, $73,392 (M); gifts received, $10,000; expenditures, $5,000; qualifying distributions, $5,000.
Limitations: Applications not accepted.
Application information: Contributes only to pre-selected organizations.
Trustees: Anita Sanchez, Manuel Sanchez.
EIN: 134092628

39274
The Frank A. Gunther Foundation, Inc.
323 Port Richmond Ave.
Staten Island, NY 10302

Established in 2000 in NY.
Donor(s): Robert C. Gunther, Jayne C. Gunther.
Financial data (yr. ended 12/31/00): Grants paid, $5,000; assets, $50,085 (M); gifts received, $55,100; expenditures, $5,015; qualifying distributions, $5,000.
Limitations: Applications not accepted. Giving primarily in NJ.
Application information: Contributes only to pre-selected organizations.
Officers: Robert C. Gunther, Chair.; Jayne C. Gunther, Vice-Chair.; Roy K. Danischewski, Secy.
EIN: 061562793

39275
Carol Friedricks Gutman and Steven L. Gutman Foundation
200 E. 62nd St., Ste. 28-A
New York, NY 10021

Established in 2000.
Donor(s): Carol Gutman.
Financial data (yr. ended 12/31/01): Grants paid, $5,000; assets, $3,858 (M); expenditures, $5,000; qualifying distributions, $5,000.
Limitations: Applications not accepted.
Application information: Contributes only to pre-selected organizations.
Trustees: Carol Gutman, Robert Gutman, Steven Gutman.
EIN: 134014530

39276
Joseph G. Hayes Medical Education Foundation
c/o Stahl Real Estate
277 Park Ave., 4th Fl.
New York, NY 10172-0003

Established in 1991 in NY; funded in 1992.
Donor(s): Herbert Siegal, Stanley Stahl.
Financial data (yr. ended 12/31/01): Grants paid, $5,000; assets, $115,061 (M); gifts received, $20,000; expenditures, $8,090; qualifying distributions, $5,271.
Limitations: Applications not accepted. Giving primarily in New York, NY.
Application information: Contributes only to pre-selected organizations.

Officers: Joseph G. Hayes, Pres.; Herbert Siegal, V.P.; Richard Czaja, Secy.-Treas.
EIN: 133619283

39277
Florence M. Hetzler Memorial Art Fund Trust
P.O. Box 568
Orchard Park, NY 14127 (716) 648-0839
Application address: 4256 Tisbury Ln., Hamburg, NY 14075
Contact: Mary C. Rahill, Tr.

Donor(s): Mary C. Rahill.
Financial data (yr. ended 12/31/00): Grants paid, $5,000; assets, $41,645 (M); expenditures, $5,288; qualifying distributions, $5,000.
Limitations: Giving primarily in NY.
Trustees: Florence M. Hetzler, Mary C. Rahill.
EIN: 161450455

39278
Jewell Trust
85 Forest Ave.
Locust Valley, NY 11560-0506

Financial data (yr. ended 06/30/02): Grants paid, $5,000; assets, $8,091 (M); expenditures, $5,007; qualifying distributions, $4,997.
Limitations: Applications not accepted.
Application information: Contributes only to pre-selected organizations.
Officer and Trustees:* Geoffrey D. Kimball,* Mgr.; Pauline D. Webel.
EIN: 133230477

39279
Fannie Kantrowitz Trust
2802 Ave. K
Brooklyn, NY 11210
Contact: Kalman Finkel, Tr.

Financial data (yr. ended 12/31/00): Grants paid, $5,000; assets, $0 (M); expenditures, $5,033; qualifying distributions, $5,033.
Limitations: Giving primarily in NJ and New York, NY.
Trustee: Kalman Finkel.
EIN: 116314290

39280
The Bernard and Michele Kaplan Foundation, Inc.
c/o Arthur Lehman
52 Vanderbilt Ave.
New York, NY 10017

Established in 1998 in NY.
Donor(s): Bernard Kaplan, Michele Kaplan.
Financial data (yr. ended 12/31/01): Grants paid, $5,000; assets, $57,186 (M); expenditures, $5,000; qualifying distributions, $5,000.
Limitations: Applications not accepted.
Application information: Contributes only to pre-selected organizations.
Officers: Bernard Kaplan, Pres.; Michele Kaplan, V.P.; Ian Kaplan, Secy.
EIN: 134018418

39281
Elmont Duncan Kennedy Memorial Fund, Inc.
191 Freeman Ave.
Elmont, NY 11003-4906 (516) 285-7921
Contact: Joseph Greenblatt, Pres.

Established in 1998.
Donor(s): Joseph Greenblatt.
Financial data (yr. ended 12/31/99): Grants paid, $5,000; assets, $63,849 (M); gifts received, $1,000; expenditures, $6,941; qualifying distributions, $6,823.
Limitations: Giving limited to residents of Elmont, NY.

Application information: Application must be submitted by high school. Application form not required.
Officers: Joseph Greenblatt, Pres.; Nicholas Girardi, Secy.; Martin Koch, Treas.
EIN: 113311748

39282
Garabed and Aghavni Kouzoujian Benevolent Foundation, Inc.
51 Valentine Ave.
Huntington, NY 11743-4960

Established in 1996 in NY.
Donor(s): Aghavni Kouzoujian.
Financial data (yr. ended 06/30/02): Grants paid, $5,000; assets, $157,440 (M); expenditures, $6,489; qualifying distributions, $5,000.
Limitations: Giving primarily in NY; also some international giving.
Application information: Application form not required.
Directors: Mary Garabedian, Aghavni Kouzoujian, Jack Kouzoujian.
EIN: 113347450

39283
The Linda Krimsley Memorial Charitable Foundation Trust
1080 5th Ave., Apt. 3C
New York, NY 10128

Established in 1999 in NY.
Financial data (yr. ended 12/31/00): Grants paid, $5,000; assets, $54,079 (M); expenditures, $5,070; qualifying distributions, $4,988.
Limitations: Applications not accepted.
Application information: Contributes only to pre-selected organizations.
Trustees: Maxine Greene, Carole Saltz.
EIN: 116532356

39284
Michael J. & Barbara Kugler Foundation, Inc.
(Formerly Michael J. Kugler Foundation, Inc.)
c/o Goldstein, Golub, Kessler & Co., PC
1185 Ave. of the Americas
New York, NY 10036-2602

Established in 1986 in NY.
Donor(s): Michael J. Kugler.
Financial data (yr. ended 09/30/00): Grants paid, $5,000; assets, $0 (M); gifts received, $5,000; expenditures, $5,000; qualifying distributions, $5,000.
Limitations: Applications not accepted. Giving primarily in the greater metropolitan New York, NY, area.
Application information: Contributes only to pre-selected organizations.
Officers and Directors:* Michael J. Kugler,* Pres. and Treas.; David Warmflash,* V.P. and Secy.; Allan S. Sexter.
EIN: 133423317

39285
The George A. Long Foundation
c/o George A. Long
200 E. 65th St., Ste. 45-F
New York, NY 10021

Established in 2001 in NY.
Financial data (yr. ended 12/31/01): Grants paid, $5,000; assets, $895,219 (M); gifts received, $876,878; expenditures, $5,100; qualifying distributions, $5,000.
Limitations: Applications not accepted. Giving primarily in Chester, PA.
Application information: Contributes only to pre-selected organizations.

Officers and Directors:* George A. Long,* Pres.; David Warmflash,* Secy.; Shimon Wolf,* Treas.
EIN: 134187533

39286
B. William Mahoney Trust
c/o HSBC Bank USA
1 HSBC Ctr., 17th Fl., Tax Dept.
Buffalo, NY 14203

Established in 1997 in NY.
Donor(s): B. William Mahoney.
Financial data (yr. ended 09/30/00): Grants paid, $5,000; assets, $290,825 (M); gifts received, $52,716; expenditures, $8,086; qualifying distributions, $5,312.
Limitations: Applications not accepted. Giving primarily in CT, NY, and PA.
Application information: Unsolicited request for funds not accepted.
Trustee: HSBC Bank USA.
EIN: 146186780

39287
Rosalie J. & C. Daniel Maldari Family Charitable Foundation
c/o Russo & Burke
600 3rd Ave.
New York, NY 10016

Established in 1999 in NY.
Donor(s): C. Daniel Maldari.
Financial data (yr. ended 11/30/01): Grants paid, $5,000; assets, $93,997 (M); gifts received, $35,000; expenditures, $11,981; qualifying distributions, $5,000.
Limitations: Applications not accepted.
Application information: Contributes only to pre-selected organizations.
Directors: Joseph Cosenza, C. Daniel Maldari, Christopher A. Maldari, Rev. Donald Maldari.
EIN: 113521349

39288
Alan R. Miller Foundation
c/o David B. Miller
57 Duck Pond Rd.
Glen Cove, NY 11542

Established in 2001 in NY.
Donor(s): David B. Miller.
Financial data (yr. ended 12/31/01): Grants paid, $5,000; assets, $495,825 (M); gifts received, $500,000; expenditures, $5,000; qualifying distributions, $5,000.
Limitations: Applications not accepted.
Application information: Contributes only to pre-selected organizations.
Directors: David B. Miller, Marlys Miller, Rosemary Miller.
EIN: 113635469

39289
The Irving Mintz Foundation, Inc.
c/o Lisa M. Messinger
47 E. 87th St.
New York, NY 10128

Donor(s): Lisa Mintz Messinger, Elizabeth Mintz.
Financial data (yr. ended 06/30/01): Grants paid, $5,000; assets, $842 (M); expenditures, $5,320; qualifying distributions, $5,000.
Limitations: Applications not accepted.
Application information: Contributes only to pre-selected organizations.
Officers: Lisa Mintz Messinger, Pres.; Elizabeth R. Mintz, Treas.
EIN: 133171202

39290
Neighborhood Development Foundation
1731 Victory Blvd.
Staten Island, NY 10314

Financial data (yr. ended 12/31/01): Grants paid, $5,000; assets, $93,037 (M); expenditures, $5,218; qualifying distributions, $5,000.
Limitations: Giving primarily in Staten Island, NY.
Officers and Directors:* Paul E. Proske,* Pres.; Albert J. Regen,* Secy.-Treas.; John Alexander, David Ceci.
EIN: 133793566

39291
Joseph J. Nicholson - Robert D. McCarter Foundation
666 3rd Ave., 28th Fl.
New York, NY 10017

Established in 1993 in NY.
Donor(s): Joseph J. Nicholson.
Financial data (yr. ended 12/31/00): Grants paid, $5,000; assets, $90,863 (M); gifts received, $59,000; expenditures, $5,130; qualifying distributions, $5,000.
Trustees: Anthony Grillo, Joel S. Hirschtritt, Robert Michaels, Joseph J. Nicholson, David P. Steinmann.
EIN: 133676917

39292
The O'Grady and Fletcher Family Foundation, Inc.
(Formerly The John and Leeda O'Grady Family Foundation)
387 Croton Lake Rd.
Mount Kisco, NY 10549-4225
Application address: c/o Willkie, Farr & Gallagher, 787 7th Ave., New York, NY 10019, tel.: (212) 728-8000
Contact: Harvey L. Sperry, Dir.

Established in 1989 in NY.
Donor(s): Leeda J. O'Grady Fletcher.
Financial data (yr. ended 12/31/01): Grants paid, $5,000; assets, $115,208 (M); expenditures, $5,680; qualifying distributions, $5,000.
Limitations: Giving primarily in New York, NY.
Application information: Application form not required.
Officers and Directors:* Ralph Fletcher,* Pres.; Leeda J. O'Grady Fletcher,* Secy.-Treas.; Christine S. O'Grady, Michael O'Grady, Harvey L. Sperry.
EIN: 133526045

39293
George L. Ohrstrom, Jr. Foundation
c/o Curtis, Mallet-Prevost, Colt & Mosle
101 Park Ave., Ste. 3500
New York, NY 10178-0061

Donor(s): George L. Ohrstrom, Jr.
Financial data (yr. ended 12/31/01): Grants paid, $5,000; assets, $78,982 (M); gifts received, $280; expenditures, $5,198; qualifying distributions, $5,000.
Limitations: Applications not accepted. Giving primarily in VA.
Application information: Contributes only to pre-selected organizations.
Officers: George L. Ohrstrom, Jr., Pres.; Alan S. Berlin, V.P.; Dorothy A. Barry, Secy.
Directors: Peter A. Kalat, David W. Laughlin.
EIN: 133415874

39294
The Alexander Radoff Poulos Foundation, Inc.
9 Pebble Hill Rd. N.
Dewitt, NY 13214

Established in 2000 in NY.
Financial data (yr. ended 12/31/01): Grants paid, $5,000; assets, $15,616 (M); expenditures, $5,668; qualifying distributions, $5,000.
Officers: Nicholas P. Poulos, Pres.; Nancy H. Radoff, V.P.
Directors: Peter Chronis, Beth Poulos.
EIN: 161597582

39295
The Redsky Foundation for Immunizations
P.O. Box 208
Essex, NY 12936

Established in 1999 in NY.
Financial data (yr. ended 12/31/01): Grants paid, $5,000; assets, $111,910 (M); gifts received, $61,062; expenditures, $6,973; qualifying distributions, $5,000.
Limitations: Applications not accepted.
Application information: Contributes only to pre-selected organizations.
Officer: Laura Sells Doyle, Chair.
Trustees: John Doyle, Martin S. Fin.
EIN: 146197084

39296
Mike Richter Private Foundation
c/o Klarberg, Raiola & Assocs.
500 5th Ave., Ste. 2000
New York, NY 10110

Established in 1995 in NY.
Financial data (yr. ended 12/31/00): Grants paid, $5,000; assets, $53,501 (M); gifts received, $10,000; expenditures, $5,196; qualifying distributions, $5,000.
Directors: Barry Klarberg, Stephen Reed, Michael T. Richter, Brandon Steiner.
EIN: 133848982

39297
The Royster Family Foundation
1025 Northern Blvd.
Roslyn, NY 11576-1587

Established in 1998 in FL.
Donor(s): Caroline M.H. Royster.
Financial data (yr. ended 12/31/01): Grants paid, $5,000; assets, $105,896 (M); expenditures, $7,268; qualifying distributions, $5,000.
Limitations: Applications not accepted.
Application information: Contributes only to pre-selected organizations.
Trustees: Caroline M.H. Royster, Thomas S. Royster.
EIN: 311577057

39298
Harry & Harriet Ruchman Foundation, Inc.
80 Park Ave.
New York, NY 10016

Established in 1998 in NY.
Donor(s): Harry Ruchman, McNamara Sports, Inc.
Financial data (yr. ended 12/31/01): Grants paid, $5,000; assets, $289,099 (M); gifts received, $38,917; expenditures, $6,425; qualifying distributions, $5,000.
Limitations: Applications not accepted.
Application information: Contributes only to pre-selected organizations.
Directors: Irving Gotlieb, Harriet Ruchman, Harry Ruchman.
EIN: 134009941

39299
Salimbaceous Trust
124 W. 79th St., Ste. 15-C
New York, NY 10024

Established in 1996 in CA.
Donor(s): Gina K. Wilcox.‡
Financial data (yr. ended 12/31/01): Grants paid, $5,000; assets, $368,243 (M); expenditures, $6,998; qualifying distributions, $5,000.
Limitations: Applications not accepted. Giving primarily in Vancouver, WA.
Application information: Contributes only to pre-selected organizations.
Trustees: Nicholas Cass Hassol, Julie Tow Suess-Pierce, Liza Cass White.
EIN: 137062361

39300
San Jose Foundation, Inc.
c/o Valenzuela Capital Partners, LLC
1270 Ave. of the Americas, Ste. 508
New York, NY 10020-1804

Established in 1998 in NY.
Donor(s): Thomas N. Valenzuela.
Financial data (yr. ended 12/31/01): Grants paid, $5,000; assets, $96,038 (M); expenditures, $5,281; qualifying distributions, $5,090.
Limitations: Applications not accepted.
Application information: Contributes only to pre-selected organizations.
Officer: Thomas N. Valenzuela, Pres.
Director: Angelina M. Valenzuela.
EIN: 134036645

39301
Salem D. Shuchman & Barbara L. Klock Foundation
c/o Bessemer Trust Co.
630 5th Ave.
New York, NY 10111

Established in 2000 in PA.
Donor(s): Salem D. Shuchman.
Financial data (yr. ended 12/31/00): Grants paid, $5,000; assets, $220,788 (M); gifts received, $436,911; expenditures, $5,557; qualifying distributions, $5,000.
Limitations: Applications not accepted. Giving primarily in PA.
Application information: Contributes only to pre-selected organizations.
Trustees: Barbara L. Klock, Salem D. Shuchman.
EIN: 256747770

39302
The Sine Nomine Foundation
125 E. 74th St.
New York, NY 10021
Contact: William C. Stubing, Chair.

Established in 2001 in NY.
Donor(s): William C. Stubing.
Financial data (yr. ended 12/31/01): Grants paid, $5,000; assets, $101,261 (M); gifts received, $105,500; expenditures, $5,000; qualifying distributions, $5,000.
Limitations: Giving primarily in NY.
Application information: Application form not required.
Officers and Directors:* William C. Stubing,* Chair. and Treas.; Ronald L. Thomas,* Pres.; Karen Fisher Gutheil, V.P. and Secy.
EIN: 311713667

39303
Slobodkina Foundation
32 William St.
Glen Head, NY 11545

Established in 2000 in NY.
Donor(s): Esphyr Urqhuart Slobodkina.
Financial data (yr. ended 04/30/01): Grants paid, $5,000; assets, $87,279 (M); gifts received, $118,810; expenditures, $33,535; qualifying distributions, $26,431.
Officer: Esphyr Urqhuart Slobodkina, Pres.
Director: Ann Marie Mulhearn.
EIN: 113549979

39304
Starr Foundation
c/o U.S. Trust, Tax Dept.
114 W. 47th St.
New York, NY 10036

Established in 1993 in VA.
Donor(s): Alice M. Starr.
Financial data (yr. ended 12/31/00): Grants paid, $5,000; assets, $194,473 (M); expenditures, $8,132; qualifying distributions, $5,500.
Limitations: Applications not accepted.
Application information: Contributes only to pre-selected organizations.
Trustees: Alice M. Starr, Kenneth W. Starr.
EIN: 541690003

39305
The Mulchand & Parpati Thadhani Foundation, Inc.
70 Barker St., Ste. 603
Mount Kisco, NY 10549 (914) 241-2361
Contact: Sajni M. Thadani, Pres.

Established in 2000 in NY.
Donor(s): Sajni M. Thadani.
Financial data (yr. ended 05/31/01): Grants paid, $5,000; assets, $171,693 (M); gifts received, $200,000; expenditures, $14,903; qualifying distributions, $5,000.
Officer: Sajni M. Thadani, Pres.
EIN: 134126170

39306
The Jerry Weston Foundation, Inc.
1441 3rd. Ave., Ste. 22B
New York, NY 10028
Contact: Roseanne Weston, Pres.

Established in 1991 in NY.
Donor(s): Roseanne Weston.
Financial data (yr. ended 09/30/01): Grants paid, $5,000; assets, $55,440 (M); gifts received, $2,833; expenditures, $5,878; qualifying distributions, $5,000.
Limitations: Giving primarily in New York, NY.
Application information: Application form required.
Officer: Roseanne Weston, Pres.
Directors: Mara Cohen, Harvey Morgan, Gregory Weston.
EIN: 113064777

39307
Margaret W. Whitaker Charitable Foundation
100 Crossways Pk., Ste. 205
Woodbury, NY 11797
Contact: Joseph P. Scanlon, Tr.

Established in 1997 in NY.
Donor(s): Margaret W. Whitaker.
Financial data (yr. ended 12/31/99): Grants paid, $5,000; assets, $108,890 (M); gifts received, $25,000; expenditures, $5,374; qualifying distributions, $4,970.
Application information: Application form required.
Trustees: Edwin F. Black, Kevin Kennedy, Joseph P. Scanlon.
EIN: 116490479

39308
The White Plains Bridge of Friendship Foundation, Inc.
c/o Cuddy & Feder & Worby
90 Maple Ave.
White Plains, NY 10601

Financial data (yr. ended 12/31/01): Grants paid, $5,000; assets, $24,892 (M); expenditures, $5,000; qualifying distributions, $5,000.
Limitations: Giving primarily in White Plains, NY.
Directors: George Gretas, William Null, Saul Yanofsky.
EIN: 137040815

39309
Wilcox Family Foundation
c/o IBJ Whitehall Financial Bank
32 Park Ave.
New York, NY 10022

Established in 1989 in CT.
Donor(s): George G. Wilcox, Christina H. Wilcox.
Financial data (yr. ended 11/30/01): Grants paid, $5,000; assets, $87,575 (M); expenditures, $9,422; qualifying distributions, $5,000.
Limitations: Giving primarily in Newport, RI.
Officer and Trustees:* Christina W. McIntyre,* Mgr.; Gail W. Holmes, Christina H. Wilcox, G. Geer Wilcox, Peter B. Wilcox, IBJ Whitehall Financial Bank.
EIN: 226474493

39310
Nikita Zukov Foundation, Inc.
400 E. 57th St., Apt. 173
New York, NY 10022-3019 (212) 627-5000
Contact: Nikita Zukov, Pres.

Established in 1986 in NY.
Donor(s): Nikita Zukov.
Financial data (yr. ended 12/31/01): Grants paid, $5,000; assets, $41,923 (M); gifts received, $1,000; expenditures, $12,418; qualifying distributions, $11,580.
Limitations: Giving primarily in Croatia.
Application information: Application form not required.
Officers: Nikita Zukov, Pres.; Paula Zukov, Secy.
EIN: 133367432
Codes: GTI

39311
The Eisner Charitable Fund, Inc.
1107 5th Ave.
New York, NY 10128

Established in 1994 in NY.
Donor(s): Douglas Eisner, Joseph A. Eisner, Susan E. Eley, Michael Eisner, Hallie Eisner.
Financial data (yr. ended 09/30/01): Grants paid, $4,995; assets, $135,819 (M); expenditures, $5,244; qualifying distributions, $4,995.
Limitations: Applications not accepted. Giving primarily in New York, NY.
Application information: Contributes only to pre-selected organizations.
Officers: Douglas Eisner, Pres.; Joseph A. Eisner, V.P.; Susan E. Eley, V.P.; Hallie Eisner, Secy.; Michael Eisner, Co-Treas.; Richard Eisner, Co-Treas.
EIN: 133806069

39312
The Augusta Hugaboom Trust Scholarships Fund
c/o HSBC Bank USA
1 HSBC Ctr., 17th Fl.
Buffalo, NY 14240

Financial data (yr. ended 12/31/01): Grants paid, $4,988; assets, $73,910 (M); expenditures, $6,188; qualifying distributions, $5,137.
Limitations: Applications not accepted. Giving primarily in Hunter, Jewett, and Lexington, NY.
Application information: Unsolicited requests for funds not accepted.
Trustee: HSBC Bank USA.
EIN: 146073039

39313
Karl & Bertha Eisner Foundation
c/o Reminick, Aarons & Co., LLP
685 3rd Ave.
New York, NY 10017-4037

Financial data (yr. ended 12/31/01): Grants paid, $4,970; assets, $26,000 (M); expenditures, $6,710; qualifying distributions, $4,970.
Limitations: Applications not accepted. Giving on a national basis, with emphasis on the eastern U.S.
Application information: Contributes only to pre-selected organizations.
Trustees: Joseph Eisner, Nathan Eisner, Betty Siegel.
EIN: 116037740

39314
Masonic Charities of Carmel Corp.
11 Church St.
Carmel, NY 10512
Application address: 10 Chestnut Hill Rd., Sherman, CT 06784, tel.: (860) 354-3050
Contact: Richard Wolken, Pres.

Financial data (yr. ended 12/31/00): Grants paid, $4,970; assets, $301,837 (M); gifts received, $1,320; expenditures, $18,657; qualifying distributions, $18,657.
Officer: Richard Wolken, Pres. and Treas.
EIN: 061401324

39315
Ben & Ruth Smith Foundation, Inc.
202 Mamaroneck Ave.
White Plains, NY 10601

Donor(s): Donald Smith, B. Smith and Sons Furs, Inc.
Financial data (yr. ended 08/31/02): Grants paid, $4,964; assets, $704 (M); gifts received, $5,000; expenditures, $5,049; qualifying distributions, $4,964.
Limitations: Applications not accepted. Giving primarily in New York, NY.
Application information: Contributes only to pre-selected organizations.
Officer: Donald Smith, Mgr.
EIN: 136279923

39316
Ruth Abrams Foundation, Inc.
c/o Upen Saraiya, AB&A
1375 Broadway, 18th Fl.
New York, NY 10018-7086

Financial data (yr. ended 12/31/01): Grants paid, $4,928; assets, $211,802 (M); expenditures, $28,264; qualifying distributions, $4,928.
Limitations: Applications not accepted. Giving primarily in New York, NY.
Application information: Contributes only to pre-selected organizations.
Directors: Charles Haar, Susan E. Haar, Joseph Winston.
EIN: 133157934

39317
The Fligman Family Charitable Foundation
1545-A 56th St.
Brooklyn, NY 11219

Established in 1999.
Financial data (yr. ended 12/31/01): Grants paid, $4,905; assets, $65,572 (M); gifts received, $31,430; expenditures, $5,942; qualifying distributions, $4,905.
Trustee: Harry Fligman.
EIN: 113502207

39318
Ira & Marylou Alpert Foundation
630 Birdsall Dr.
Yorktown Heights, NY 10598

Established in 1986 in NY.
Donor(s): Ira Alpert.
Financial data (yr. ended 11/30/01): Grants paid, $4,900; assets, $76,910 (M); gifts received, $1,856; expenditures, $6,757; qualifying distributions, $6,217.
Limitations: Applications not accepted.
Application information: Contributes only to pre-selected organizations.
Trustees: Ira Alpert, Marylou Alpert.
EIN: 133406434

39319
The Bretton Foundation
Planetarium Station
P.O. Box 977
New York, NY 10024-0541

Donor(s): William C. McIntyre.
Financial data (yr. ended 12/31/01): Grants paid, $4,900; assets, $478 (M); gifts received, $4,200; expenditures, $5,010; qualifying distributions, $4,900.
Limitations: Applications not accepted.
Application information: Contributes only to pre-selected organizations.
Trustee: William C. McIntyre.
EIN: 137074268

39320
Litts Scholarship Fund
(also known as Litts Foundation)
469 Clark Rd.
Pulaski, NY 13142-2285
Contact: Debbie Love, Dir.

Established in 1997 in NY.
Donor(s): Clarence F. Litts, Robert E. Litts.
Financial data (yr. ended 12/31/01): Grants paid, $4,900; assets, $83,671 (M); gifts received, $20,025; expenditures, $4,986; qualifying distributions, $0.
Application information: Applications provided upon request. Application form required.
Directors: Korovena Levis, Clarence F. Litts, Robert E. Litts, Debbie Love.
EIN: 161530654

39321
Mancher Family Foundation
90 Highland Rd.
Scarsdale, NY 10583-1808
Contact: Leona R. Mancher, Pres.

Established in 1997 in NY.
Donor(s): Harry R. Mancher.
Financial data (yr. ended 12/31/00): Grants paid, $4,894; assets, $1 (M); expenditures, $4,996; qualifying distributions, $4,894.
Limitations: Giving primarily in New York, NY.
Officer: Leona R. Mancher, Pres.
Director: Harold M. Kase.
EIN: 237061249

39322
Wilks Family Foundation
c/o Shulman, Jones & Co.
200 E. Post Rd.
White Plains, NY 10601
Contact: Donald L. Wilks, Tr.

Established in 1999 in FL.
Donor(s): Patricia Wilks.
Financial data (yr. ended 06/30/01): Grants paid, $4,875; assets, $694,285 (M); gifts received, $233,145; expenditures, $11,103; qualifying distributions, $4,403.
Limitations: Giving primarily in MA.
Application information: Application form not required.
Trustees: Donald L. Wilks, Patricia Wilks.
EIN: 134092040

39323
Gregg Solomon Foundation, Inc.
230 W. 38th St.
New York, NY 10018-5800

Established in 1991 in NY.
Donor(s): Gregg Solomon.
Financial data (yr. ended 12/31/01): Grants paid, $4,850; assets, $7,485 (M); expenditures, $6,555; qualifying distributions, $4,850.
Limitations: Applications not accepted.
Application information: Contributes only to pre-selected organizations.
Directors: William Kass, Gerald Solomon, Gregg Solomon.
EIN: 133500470

39324
Day Is Done Foundation
c/o C.H. Specht
50 Montrose Rd.
Yonkers, NY 10710

Financial data (yr. ended 12/31/01): Grants paid, $4,825; assets, $1,763 (M); gifts received, $6,161; expenditures, $4,905; qualifying distributions, $4,825.
Limitations: Applications not accepted. Giving primarily in MA.
Application information: Contributes only to pre-selected organizations.
Officer: Peter Yarrow, Mgr.
EIN: 237042449

39325
Nathan & Minnie Goldstein Foundation
87 Grace Ave.
Great Neck, NY 11021 (516) 487-8675
Contact: Louis Goldstein, Mgr.

Donor(s): Louis Goldstein.
Financial data (yr. ended 08/31/99): Grants paid, $4,818; assets, $176,850 (M); gifts received, $550; expenditures, $5,059; qualifying distributions, $4,818.
Limitations: Giving primarily in NY.
Officer: Louis Goldstein, Mgr.
EIN: 116095970

39326
T. Stewart Foster Family Foundation
c/o HSBC Bank USA
P.O. Box 4203, 17th Fl.
Buffalo, NY 14240

Financial data (yr. ended 12/31/01): Grants paid, $4,800; assets, $129,490 (M); expenditures, $8,537; qualifying distributions, $4,800.
Limitations: Applications not accepted. Giving on a national basis.
Application information: Contributes only to pre-selected organizations.

39326—NEW YORK

Trustees: Theodore Foster II, Cynthia Ann Troiano, HSBC Bank USA.
EIN: 156015549

39327
Chana Leah & Herman J. Liberman Free Loan Fund
1054 E. 13th St., Ste. 2
Brooklyn, NY 11230 (718) 951-0492
Contact: Ira Liberman, Dir.

Financial data (yr. ended 12/31/00): Grants paid, $4,794; assets, $17,250 (M); gifts received, $500; expenditures, $6,364; qualifying distributions, $4,794.
Limitations: Giving limited to Brooklyn, NY.
Application information: Application form required.
Director: Ira Liberman.
EIN: 222626028

39328
Arnsten Foundation, Inc.
c/o Lawrence Arnsten
13 W. 74th St.
New York, NY 10023

Established in 1998 in NY.
Donor(s): Lawrence Arnsten, Dorothy Arnsten.
Financial data (yr. ended 12/31/01): Grants paid, $4,777; assets, $10,276 (M); gifts received, $14,000; expenditures, $5,477; qualifying distributions, $4,777.
Officers: Lawrence Arnsten, Pres.; Paul Arnsten, V.P.; Dorothy Arnsten, Secy.
EIN: 133975888

39329
The Daniel Foundation
c/o Roth & Co., LLP
5612 18th Ave.
Brooklyn, NY 11204

Established in 1983.
Financial data (yr. ended 09/30/01): Grants paid, $4,751; assets, $87,241 (M); gifts received, $4,967; expenditures, $5,159; qualifying distributions, $5,159.
Limitations: Applications not accepted. Giving primarily in Brooklyn, NY; also some international giving.
Trustees: G. Alexander Namdar, Israel Namdar, Samuel J. Namdar.
EIN: 133735718

39330
The Schneiderman Family Foundation, Inc.
151 N. Main St., Ste. 300
New City, NY 10956

Established in 1997 in NY.
Donor(s): Sanford Schneiderman, Rhona Schneiderman.
Financial data (yr. ended 06/30/01): Grants paid, $4,750; assets, $68,036 (M); expenditures, $5,050; qualifying distributions, $4,750.
Limitations: Applications not accepted.
Application information: Contributes only to pre-selected organizations.
Directors: Rhona Schneiderman, Sanford Schneiderman, Michael Steckler.
EIN: 133980193

39331
Gertrude Linzer Foundation
c/o Max Wasser
132 Nassau St., Ste. 300
New York, NY 10038-2403

Established in 1986 in NY.
Donor(s): Gertrude Linzer.

Financial data (yr. ended 09/30/01): Grants paid, $4,732; assets, $5,620 (M); gifts received, $4,000; expenditures, $4,732; qualifying distributions, $4,732.
Limitations: Applications not accepted.
Application information: Contributes only to pre-selected organizations.
Trustee: Gertrude Linzer.
EIN: 136885095

39332
Virgil and Judith Stark Foundation, Inc.
c/o Silverman Linden Higgins
330 W. 42nd St.
New York, NY 10036-0455
Contact: Frank Stark, Pres.

Incorporated in 1961 in NY.
Donor(s): Virgil Stark,‡ Judith Stark.‡
Financial data (yr. ended 12/31/01): Grants paid, $4,725; assets, $18,726 (M); expenditures, $4,953; qualifying distributions, $4,725.
Officer: Frank Stark, Pres.
EIN: 136107555

39333
The Digiacinto Family Foundation, Inc.
c/o Joseph W. Digiacinto
235 Main St., Penthouse
White Plains, NY 10601

Donor(s): Mary Digiacinto.
Financial data (yr. ended 12/31/01): Grants paid, $4,700; assets, $5,206 (M); gifts received, $10,000; expenditures, $5,590; qualifying distributions, $4,700.
Limitations: Applications not accepted. Giving primarily in Armonk, NY.
Application information: Contributes only to pre-selected organizations.
Officers and Directors:* Joseph W. Digiacinto,* Pres.; John D. Digiacinto,* V.P. and Treas.; James J. Digiacinto,* Secy.
EIN: 137091544

39334
The Raymond and Maria Floyd Family Foundation
c/o Bessemer Trust Co., N.A.
630 5th Ave.
New York, NY 10111

Established in 1999 in FL.
Donor(s): Raymond L. Floyd, Maria K. Floyd.
Financial data (yr. ended 12/31/00): Grants paid, $4,700; assets, $100,836 (M); gifts received, $107,229; expenditures, $7,425; qualifying distributions, $3,937.
Limitations: Applications not accepted.
Application information: Contributes only to pre-selected organizations.
Trustees: Maria K. Floyd, Raymond L. Floyd.
EIN: 522194504

39335
Spindler Family Foundation
c/o John Witmeyer
P.O. Box 31051
Rochester, NY 14603

Established in 1998.
Donor(s): Howard A. Spindler.
Financial data (yr. ended 12/31/01): Grants paid, $4,700; assets, $171,668 (M); expenditures, $8,409; qualifying distributions, $4,700.
Limitations: Applications not accepted.
Application information: Contributes only to pre-selected organizations.
Officers and Directors: Howard A. Spindler, Pres. and Treas; Jacqueline A. Spindler, V.P.; Kathryn R. Spindler-Virgin, V.P.; Howard R. Spindler, Secy.

EIN: 161550374

39336
Steven J. Yohay Family Foundation, Inc.
555 W. 57th St.
New York, NY 10019

Established in 1997 in NY.
Donor(s): Steven J. Yohay.
Financial data (yr. ended 12/31/01): Grants paid, $4,700; assets, $19,219 (M); gifts received, $18,000; expenditures, $6,905; qualifying distributions, $6,896.
Limitations: Applications not accepted.
Application information: Contributes only to pre-selected organizations.
Directors: Howard Field, Gary Schatsky, Joel Yohay, Steven J. Yohay.
EIN: 113410892

39337
Zichron Moshe Charitable Foundation
1120 53rd St.
Brooklyn, NY 11219-3439
Contact: Martin Guttman, Tr.

Established in 1998 in NY.
Financial data (yr. ended 10/31/01): Grants paid, $4,699; assets, $84,437 (M); gifts received, $5,190; expenditures, $6,009; qualifying distributions, $4,699.
Limitations: Giving primarily in Brooklyn, NY.
Trustees: Esther Guttman, Martin Guttman.
EIN: 113456885

39338
Eli & Arlene Wachtel Charitable Foundation
7 Shaw Rd.
Scarsdale, NY 10583-4427

Established in 1986 in NY.
Donor(s): Eli Wachtel.
Financial data (yr. ended 06/30/99): Grants paid, $4,660; assets, $3,065 (M); expenditures, $5,418; qualifying distributions, $5,418.
Limitations: Applications not accepted.
Application information: Contributes only to pre-selected organizations.
Officers: Arlene Wachtel, Pres.; Eli Wachtel, V.P.
EIN: 133401506

39339
Nordlys Foundation
110 Spring St.
Saratoga Springs, NY 12866

Established in 2000 in NY.
Donor(s): Barbara Glaser.
Financial data (yr. ended 06/30/01): Grants paid, $4,650; assets, $977,874 (M); gifts received, $971,991; expenditures, $8,163; qualifying distributions, $4,650.
Limitations: Applications not accepted. Giving primarily in NY.
Application information: Contributes only to pre-selected organizations.
Directors: Susan Bokan, Barbara Glaser, Kimara Glaser-Kirschenbaum.
EIN: 146205088

39340
The Rauscher Charitable Trust
70 Bennington Ave.
Freeport, NY 11520

Established in 1996 in NY.
Donor(s): Walter Rauscher, Kerry Rauscher.
Financial data (yr. ended 12/31/00): Grants paid, $4,650; assets, $1 (M); gifts received, $3,800; expenditures, $5,032; qualifying distributions, $4,650.
Trustee: Kerry Rauscher.

EIN: 113348511

39341
The Zacks Family Foundation, Inc.
7 Park Ave., Ste. 16D
New York, NY 10016

Financial data (yr. ended 12/31/01): Grants paid, $4,650; assets, $187,030 (M); gifts received, $131,851; expenditures, $4,780; qualifying distributions, $4,650.
Officers: Andrew Zacks, Pres.; Jeff Zacks, V.P.; Linda Zacks, V.P.
EIN: 134025048

39342
Sigel Charitable Trust
c/o Corporate Research Group, Inc.
524 North Ave.
New Rochelle, NY 10804

Established in 1992 in NY.
Donor(s): Efrem Sigel.
Financial data (yr. ended 12/31/01): Grants paid, $4,645; assets, $104,543 (M); gifts received, $9,000; expenditures, $4,836; qualifying distributions, $4,645.
Limitations: Applications not accepted. Giving primarily in NY.
Application information: Contributes only to pre-selected organizations.
Trustees: Efrem Sigel, Frederica Sigel.
EIN: 137003899

39343
M. B. Elizabeth Harriman Trust
(Formerly M. B. Elizabeth Harriman Trust f/b/o Oliver Bishop Harriman Foreign Service Scholarship)
c/o JPMorgan Chase Bank
P.O. Box 31412
Rochester, NY 14603
Application address: P.O. Box 92920, Rochester, NY 14692-9020, tel.: (800) 850-7222

Financial data (yr. ended 12/31/00): Grants paid, $4,625; assets, $93,904 (M); expenditures, $5,969; qualifying distributions, $4,507.
Limitations: Giving on a national basis.
Trustee: JPMorgan Chase Bank.
EIN: 136049845

39344
The Yale & Betty Citrin Foundation
54 Bradford Rd.
Scarsdale, NY 10583-7650

Financial data (yr. ended 11/30/01): Grants paid, $4,600; assets, $102,646 (M); expenditures, $4,611; qualifying distributions, $4,600.
Limitations: Applications not accepted. Giving primarily in New York, NY.
Application information: Contributes only to pre-selected organizations.
Officers: Yale Citrin, Pres.; Betty Citrin, V.P.
EIN: 133155933

39345
Mark and Elyssa Dickstein Foundation
660 Madison Ave., 16th Fl.
New York, NY 10021

Established in 1998 in NY.
Donor(s): Mark Dickstein.
Financial data (yr. ended 12/31/01): Grants paid, $4,600; assets, $106,796 (M); expenditures, $4,650; qualifying distributions, $4,600.
Trustees: Elyssa Dickstein, Mark Dickstein.
EIN: 226743850

39346
Pearle H. Evans Scholarship Fund
c/o M&T Bank
1 M&T Plz., 8th Fl. Tax Dept.
Buffalo, NY 14203
Contact: Ken Schmidt, V.P. and Trust Off, M&T Bank

Established in 1995.
Financial data (yr. ended 12/31/01): Grants paid, $4,550; assets, $128,738 (M); expenditures, $6,134; qualifying distributions, $4,479.
Limitations: Giving primarily in PA.
Trustee: M & T Bank.
EIN: 251766405

39347
Charles & Rita Baten Foundation, Inc.
c/o Frank J. Stella, Jr.
305 Northern Blvd., Ste. 302
Great Neck, NY 11021

Donor(s): Charles Baten.
Financial data (yr. ended 03/31/01): Grants paid, $4,549; assets, $12,019 (M); expenditures, $4,665; qualifying distributions, $4,549.
Limitations: Applications not accepted. Giving primarily in NY.
Application information: Contributes only to pre-selected organizations.
Officer and Directors:* Marvin Baten,* Mgr.; Charles Baten.
EIN: 136123893

39348
Eddie Barnes Memorial Music Scholarship Foundation
212-75 Whitehall Terr.
Queens Village, NY 11427-1892
Contact: Norli Bollag, Pres.

Donor(s): Norli Bollag.
Financial data (yr. ended 05/31/99): Grants paid, $4,500; assets, $8,234 (M); gifts received, $5,000; expenditures, $4,980; qualifying distributions, $4,981.
Limitations: Giving primarily in the metropolitan New York, NY, area.
Officer: Norli Bollag, Pres.
EIN: 112545501

39349
Marion Tyler Blake Trust
c/o Beldock, Levine & Hoffman
99 Park Ave., Ste. 1600
New York, NY 10016-1503   (212) 490-0400
Contact: Elliot L. Hoffman, Tr.

Donor(s): Marion Tyler Blake.‡
Financial data (yr. ended 03/31/02): Grants paid, $4,500; assets, $186,124 (M); expenditures, $7,061; qualifying distributions, $4,500.
Limitations: Giving primarily in the metropolitan New York, NY, area.
Application information: Applications are handled through the Eubie Blake Scholarship Fund. Preference given to students recommended by teachers known to the foundation. Application form required.
Trustees: Naomi Alleyne, Delma Marchand Goulbourne, Elliot L. Hoffman.
EIN: 136836084
Codes: GTI

39350
Satoko and Franz M. Joseph Foundation, Inc.
(Formerly American European Foundation, Inc.)
60 E. 42nd St., Ste. 1115
New York, NY 10165-0095

Donor(s): Franz M. Joseph.‡

Financial data (yr. ended 11/30/99): Grants paid, $4,500; assets, $164,129 (M); expenditures, $6,736; qualifying distributions, $4,500.
Limitations: Applications not accepted. Giving primarily in NY.
Application information: Contributes only to pre-selected organizations.
Officers and Directors:* Richard U. Koppel,* Pres. and Treas.; Barry Kessler,* V.P. and Secy.; Hannelore Koppel.
EIN: 136109358

39351
George Jay Kotick Memorial Trust
501 E. 79th St.
New York, NY 10021

Financial data (yr. ended 12/31/01): Grants paid, $4,500; assets, $71,153 (M); expenditures, $4,500; qualifying distributions, $4,500.
Limitations: Giving primarily in NY and WA.
Trustees: Dale Kotick, Joel M. Kotick, Bruce Schindler.
EIN: 133528597

39352
The Laszlo Family Foundation
Crossroads Bldg.
2 State St., Ste. 700
Rochester, NY 14614-1329

Established in 2000 in NY.
Financial data (yr. ended 12/31/01): Grants paid, $4,500; assets, $629,576 (M); expenditures, $4,630; qualifying distributions, $4,500.
Officers: Paul R. Messina, Chair.; Michael H. Messina, Pres.
EIN: 166514654

39353
Henry W. Meers Fund
c/o Walter J. Handelman
1 N. Broadway, Ste. 1001
White Plains, NY 10601   (914) 428-9305

Established in 1964 in NY.
Donor(s): Henry W. Meers.
Financial data (yr. ended 12/31/01): Grants paid, $4,500; assets, $57,155 (M); expenditures, $7,915; qualifying distributions, $4,500.
Limitations: Applications not accepted. Giving on a national basis, with emphasis on Chicago, IL.
Application information: Contributes only to pre-selected organizations.
Officers and Directors:* Evelyn H. Meers,* Pres.; Albert H. Meers, V.P.; Henry W. Meers, Jr., V.P.; Walter J. Handelman,* Secy.-Treas.
EIN: 136159559

39354
Syracuse Jewish Children's Foundation
120 E. Washington St.
Syracuse, NY 13202-4000

Financial data (yr. ended 12/31/01): Grants paid, $4,500; assets, $93,397 (M); expenditures, $5,222; qualifying distributions, $4,500.
Limitations: Applications not accepted. Giving primarily in Syracuse, NY.
Application information: Contributes only to pre-selected organizations.
Officers: Michael Moss, Pres.; Robert Rothman, Secy.-Treas.
Trustees: Richard Engel, Babbett Ferguson, Richard Gerber, Rosalind Gingold.
EIN: 166046143

39355
Verbeek Family Foundation, Inc.
c/o KRT Business Management, Inc.
500 5th Ave., Ste. 3000
New York, NY 10110

Established in 1999 in TX.
Donor(s): Pat Verbeek.
Financial data (yr. ended 12/31/01): Grants paid, $4,500; assets, $1 (M); gifts received, $1,157; expenditures, $4,500; qualifying distributions, $4,500.
Officers: Pat Verbeek, Pres.; Diane Verbeek, V.P.; Barry Klarberg, Treas.
EIN: 311630822

39356
Theresa Fatato Foundation, Inc.
115 School St.
Nyack, NY 10960-1510
Contact: Vincent T. Fatato, Secy.

Financial data (yr. ended 09/30/01): Grants paid, $4,495; assets, $165,782 (M); expenditures, $6,895; qualifying distributions, $4,495.
Limitations: Giving primarily in NY.
Officers: Louis T. Fatato, Pres.; Anthony Fatato, V.P.; Thomas P. Fatato, V.P.; Vincent T. Fatato, Secy.; Philip A. Fatato, Treas.
EIN: 133003679

39357
Zygfryd and Helene Wolloch Foundation
13 Overlook Rd.
Scarsdale, NY 10583

Financial data (yr. ended 12/31/00): Grants paid, $4,490; assets, $101,878 (M); expenditures, $5,340; qualifying distributions, $4,490.
Limitations: Applications not accepted. Giving primarily in NY.
Application information: Contributes only to pre-selected organizations.
Officers and Directors:* Zygfryd B. Wolloch,* Pres. and Treas.; Helene Wolloch,* V.P.; Richard D. Wolloch,* Secy.; Daniel J. Wolloch, Michael N. Wolloch, Norbert S. Wolloch.
EIN: 133380846

39358
Solzberg Foundation, Inc.
85 Greenwood Ln.
White Plains, NY 10607-1019

Financial data (yr. ended 12/31/01): Grants paid, $4,483; assets, $101,631 (M); expenditures, $5,396; qualifying distributions, $4,483.
Limitations: Applications not accepted. Giving primarily in FL.
Application information: Contributes only to pre-selected organizations.
Officer: Martin Solzberg, Pres.
EIN: 116034864

39359
Silverstein Brothers Foundation, Inc.
140 Riverside Dr.
New York, NY 10024

Established in 1947.
Donor(s): Samuel Silverstein,‡ Israel Silverstein.
Financial data (yr. ended 04/30/02): Grants paid, $4,471; assets, $111,304 (M); expenditures, $5,436; qualifying distributions, $4,471.
Limitations: Giving primarily in NY.
Trustee: Sadie Silverstein.
EIN: 136118638

39360
Paltrowitz Family Foundation, Inc.
c/o Lonnie Wollin
350 Fifth Ave., Ste. 2822
New York, NY 10118

Established in 1998.
Donor(s): Irving Paltrowitz.
Financial data (yr. ended 06/30/01): Grants paid, $4,470; assets, $90,850 (M); expenditures, $8,735; qualifying distributions, $4,470.
Limitations: Applications not accepted.
Application information: Contributes only to pre-selected organizations.
Officers: Irving Paltrowitz, Pres.; Danielle Paltrowitz, V.P.; Joanne Paltrowitz, V.P.; Justin Paltrowitz, V.P.; Laurence Paltrowitz, V.P.; Lonnie Wollin, Secy.
EIN: 223554915

39361
Esther Koven Foundation, Inc.
c/o Kranz & Co.
145 E. 57th St.
New York, NY 10022

Established in 2000 in NY.
Donor(s): Esther Koven Charitable Lead Annuity Trust.
Financial data (yr. ended 12/31/01): Grants paid, $4,468; assets, $130,435 (M); gifts received, $68,822; expenditures, $4,518; qualifying distributions, $4,468.
Limitations: Giving primarily in New York, NY.
Directors: Cory L. Koven, Jay B. Koven.
EIN: 137193520

39362
Fritz & Emily Darmstadter Foundation, Inc.
c/o Alan J. Garfunkel
63 Lincoln Rd.
Scarsdale, NY 10583-7533

Financial data (yr. ended 12/31/01): Grants paid, $4,450; assets, $106,646 (M); expenditures, $5,365; qualifying distributions, $4,450.
Limitations: Applications not accepted.
Application information: Contributes only to pre-selected organizations.
Officers and Directors:* Judith Darmstadter,* Pres.; Hannah Blechner,* V.P.; Margaret Kahn,* Secy.; Alan J. Garfunkel,* Treas.
EIN: 136274544

39363
David F. Schneeweiss & H. F. Schneeweiss Charitable Trust
85 Galileo Dr.
Williamsville, NY 14221-4517

Established in 2000 in NY.
Donor(s): David F. Schneeweiss, Hallie F. Schneeweiss.
Financial data (yr. ended 12/31/01): Grants paid, $4,450; assets, $61,566 (M); expenditures, $4,943; qualifying distributions, $4,450.
Limitations: Applications not accepted. Giving primarily in NY.
Application information: Contributes only to pre-selected organizations.
Trustees: David P. Schneeweiss, Hallie F. Schneeweiss.
EIN: 166500223

39364
Andrew Weissman Family Foundation
c/o Schwartz & Co.
2580 Sunrise Hwy.
Bellmore, NY 11710
Contact: Andrew Weissman, Pres.

Established in 2000 in NY.
Donor(s): Andrew Weissman.
Financial data (yr. ended 12/31/01): Grants paid, $4,450; assets, $18,504 (M); expenditures, $4,500; qualifying distributions, $4,450.
Application information: Application form not required.
Officers: Andrew Weissman, Pres. and Treas.; Susan Schachter, V.P. and Secy.
Director: Michael J. Schwartz.
EIN: 113572759

39365
The Cavior Foundation
c/o The Cavior Organization, Inc.
60 E. 42nd St.
New York, NY 10165

Donor(s): Jay M. Cavior, Shirley M. Cavior.
Financial data (yr. ended 12/31/01): Grants paid, $4,445; assets, $79,329 (M); expenditures, $6,998; qualifying distributions, $4,445.
Limitations: Applications not accepted. Giving primarily in New York, NY.
Application information: Contributes only to pre-selected organizations.
Trustees: Jay M. Cavior, Stephen R. Cavior, Warren J. Cavior, George I. Harris.
EIN: 237119917

39366
Companions in Courage Foundation
(Formerly The LaFontaine Foundation)
c/o Gibson, McAskill & Crosby
69 Delaware Ave., Rm 900
Buffalo, NY 14202-3809

Established in 1999 in NY.
Donor(s): Patrick LaFontaine.
Financial data (yr. ended 12/31/00): Grants paid, $4,422; assets, $32,531 (M); expenditures, $4,426; qualifying distributions, $4,422.
Limitations: Applications not accepted. Giving primarily in Buffalo, NY.
Application information: Contributes only to pre-selected organizations.
Directors: Marybeth LaFontaine, Patrick LaFontaine, Donald Meehan.
EIN: 161493691

39367
The Maurice A. Recanati Foundation, Inc.
P.O. Box 722
Bearsville, NY 12409-0722

Established in 1995 in NY.
Donor(s): Dimitri Recanati.
Financial data (yr. ended 06/30/02): Grants paid, $4,400; assets, $83,828 (M); gifts received, $2,000; expenditures, $6,625; qualifying distributions, $4,400.
Limitations: Applications not accepted. Giving primarily in NY.
Officers and Directors:* Maurice-Andre Recanati,* Chair. and Pres.; Roy F. Hutton,* V.P. and Secy.; Joyce Recanati,* V.P. and Treas.; Harvey C. Snyder,* V.P.; Dimitri Argyriades.
EIN: 141786386

IN THIS SECTION, WITHIN EACH STATE, FOUNDATIONS ARE LISTED IN DESCENDING ORDER BY TOTAL GRANTS PAID

39368
The Barbara Alden Taylor Foundation, Inc.
303 E. 57th St., Ste. 36F
New York, NY 10022 (212) 752-8138
Contact: Barbara Alden Taylor, Dir.

Established in 2000 in NY.
Financial data (yr. ended 12/31/01): Grants paid, $4,392; assets, $159,384 (M); gifts received, $9,964; expenditures, $7,341; qualifying distributions, $4,392.
Director: Barbara Alden Taylor.
EIN: 134123316

39369
The Lisa Ann Sharf Foundation
c/o Lisa Green
1070 Park Ave., Apt. 10-C
New York, NY 10128-1000

Established in 1989 in NY.
Donor(s): Evelyn P. Strouse.‡
Financial data (yr. ended 12/31/01): Grants paid, $4,390; assets, $526,245 (M); expenditures, $12,387; qualifying distributions, $4,390.
Limitations: Applications not accepted.
Application information: Contributes only to pre-selected organizations.
Directors: Lisa S. Green, Matthew H. Kamens.
EIN: 232575534

39370
Harrison Earl & Frances Smith Scholarship Fund
c/o Chemung Canal Trust Co.
P.O. Box 1522
Elmira, NY 14902
Application address: c/o Board of Education, Elmira Heights Central School District, Elmira Heights, NY 14903, tel.: (607) 734-7114

Established in 1963 in NY.
Donor(s): Harrison Earl,‡ Frances Smith.‡
Financial data (yr. ended 12/31/00): Grants paid, $4,386; assets, $90,012 (M); expenditures, $4,724; qualifying distributions, $4,408.
Limitations: Giving limited to residents of Elmira Heights, NY.
Application information: Application form not required.
Trustee: Chemung Canal Trust Co.
EIN: 166038545
Codes: GTI

39371
Joseph & Lillian Eaton Foundation
c/o Carol London
137 E. 66 St.
New York, NY 10021-6150

Donor(s): Jerome Eaton.
Financial data (yr. ended 02/28/02): Grants paid, $4,357; assets, $123,801 (M); expenditures, $7,547; qualifying distributions, $4,357.
Limitations: Applications not accepted. Giving primarily in NY.
Application information: Contributes only to pre-selected organizations.
Officers: Jerome Eaton, Pres.; Carol Eaton London, V.P.; Thomas Eaton, Secy.-Treas.
EIN: 136141239

39372
Stephen H. Shulman Family Foundation Trust
924 Upland Dr.
Elmira, NY 14905-1421

Established in 1984 in NY.
Donor(s): Stephen H. Shulman.
Financial data (yr. ended 12/31/01): Grants paid, $4,325; assets, $14,742 (M); expenditures, $4,435; qualifying distributions, $4,338.
Limitations: Applications not accepted. Giving primarily in Elmira, NY.
Application information: Contributes only to pre-selected organizations.
Trustees: Sherry K. Shulman, Stephen H. Shulman.
EIN: 166272861

39373
The Inez Benjamin Foundation
c/o Stephen M. Rosenberg, Jenkens & Gilchrist
405 Lexington Ave.
New York, NY 10174

Established in 2000 in NY.
Donor(s): The Inez Benjamin Trust.
Financial data (yr. ended 12/31/01): Grants paid, $4,300; assets, $251,596 (M); gifts received, $9,000; expenditures, $7,142; qualifying distributions, $4,300.
Limitations: Applications not accepted.
Application information: Contributes only to pre-selected organizations.
Trustee: Stephen M. Rosenberg.
EIN: 137119977

39374
Seltzer Foundation, Inc.
100 Jericho Quadrangle, Ste. 226
Jericho, NY 11753 (516) 935-3600
Contact: Stephen Seltzer, Pres.

Established in 1997 in NY.
Donor(s): Sandy Seltzer, Stephen Seltzer.
Financial data (yr. ended 12/31/01): Grants paid, $4,300; assets, $74,195 (M); gifts received, $5,007; expenditures, $4,467; qualifying distributions, $4,300.
Officers: Stephen Seltzer, Pres.; Sandra Seltzer, Secy.; Clifford Seltzer, Treas.
EIN: 113406238

39375
Felix Flateau - Alexander Rosenbaum Fund, Inc.
c/o Al Sussman
135 Elmira Loop
Brooklyn, NY 11239
Application address: 227 Duck Pond Dr., South Wantagh, NY 11793, tel.: (631) 826-8752
Contact: Lawrence Sussman, Pres.

Financial data (yr. ended 03/31/02): Grants paid, $4,260; assets, $67,899 (M); expenditures, $7,822; qualifying distributions, $4,260.
Limitations: Giving primarily in NY.
Officers: Lawrence Sussman, Pres.; Abraham Sussman, V.P.; William Nelson, Secy.
EIN: 136089982

39376
Rose L. Abrams Gemilath Chesed Association, Inc.
42 Stevens Pl.
Lawrence, NY 11559-1329 (516) 374-0800
Contact: Eliezer Horowitz, Pres.

Donor(s): Eliezer Horowitz, Joseph Horowitz, Sheldon Kahn.
Financial data (yr. ended 12/31/01): Grants paid, $4,250; assets, $35,427 (M); gifts received, $2,850; expenditures, $4,912; qualifying distributions, $4,250.
Limitations: Giving limited to NY.
Application information: Application form required.
Officers and Directors:* Eliezer Horowitz,* Pres. and Mgr.; Richard Glickman,* V.P.; Ruth Veit, V.P.; Naomi Nadata,* Secy.; Deborah Horowitz,* Treas.; Carole Boxer, Lawrence Cohen, Joseph Horowitz, Sheila Weisler.
EIN: 116020795

39377
Dworman Foundation, Inc.
c/o American Express Tax & Bus. Svcs., Inc.
1185 Avenue of the Americas, 6th Fl.
New York, NY 10036

Donor(s): Alvin Dworman.
Financial data (yr. ended 09/30/01): Grants paid, $4,250; assets, $24,394 (M); gifts received, $23,250; expenditures, $4,250; qualifying distributions, $4,250.
Limitations: Applications not accepted. Giving limited to New York, NY.
Application information: Contributes only to pre-selected organizations.
Officer: Alvin Dworman, Pres.
EIN: 116035630

39378
Charles G. & Elizabeth A. Mortimer Foundation
c/o Kenneth M. Katz
26-20 Bell Blvd.
Bayside, NY 11360-2539

Financial data (yr. ended 12/31/00): Grants paid, $4,250; assets, $161,958 (M); expenditures, $6,075; qualifying distributions, $4,250.
Directors: Kenneth M. Katz, Charles G. Mortimer, Jr., Charles G. Mortimer III, Nancy M. Wilson.
EIN: 136078073

39379
Sidney and Charlotte Feuerstein Charitable Foundation
630 Park Ave.
New York, NY 10021-6544

Financial data (yr. ended 06/30/01): Grants paid, $4,231; assets, $35,987 (M); gifts received, $20,000; expenditures, $4,618; qualifying distributions, $4,231.
Limitations: Applications not accepted. Giving primarily in NY.
Application information: Contributes only to pre-selected organizations.
Officers: Charlotte Feuerstein, Mgr.; Sidney S. Feuerstein, Mgr.; Ronnie Heyman, Mgr.
EIN: 132678789

39380
The Sheila Hoffman Bialek Foundation, Inc.
c/o Sheila Bialek
56 Fairfield Pond, P.O. Box 184
Sagaponack, NY 11962

Established in 1999 in NY.
Donor(s): Sheila Hoffman Bialek.
Financial data (yr. ended 12/31/01): Grants paid, $4,200; assets, $85,119 (M); expenditures, $6,362; qualifying distributions, $4,200.
Limitations: Giving primarily in NY.
Directors: Albert Bialek, Sheila Hoffman Bialek.
EIN: 134056685

39381
The Bertram M. Goldsmith Foundation
c/o Grant Thornton
60 Broad St.
New York, NY 10004

Financial data (yr. ended 05/31/01): Grants paid, $4,200; assets, $13,574 (M); expenditures, $4,526; qualifying distributions, $4,237.
Limitations: Applications not accepted. Giving on a national basis.
Application information: Contributes only to pre-selected organizations.
Trustee: Fannie Goldsmith.
EIN: 226064506

39382
David Goldstein Foundation, Inc.
33 Winfield Ave.
Harrison, NY 10528
Contact: Lawrence Goldstein, Pres.

Financial data (yr. ended 12/31/01): Grants paid, $4,200; assets, $74,705 (M); expenditures, $4,712; qualifying distributions, $4,250.
Limitations: Giving primarily in NY.
Officers: Lawrence Goldstein, Pres.; Lynn Goldstein, Secy.-Treas.
EIN: 136091593

39383
George & Ann Rosenberg Foundation, Inc.
c/o Dorothy R. Bloom
85 Club Pointe Dr.
White Plains, NY 10605

Established in 1944 in NY.
Donor(s): George Rosenberg,‡ Ann Rosenberg.‡
Financial data (yr. ended 12/31/01): Grants paid, $4,200; assets, $159,850 (M); expenditures, $5,009; qualifying distributions, $4,200.
Limitations: Applications not accepted. Giving primarily in NY.
Application information: Contributes only to pre-selected organizations.
Officer: Dorothy Rosenberg Bloom, Pres. and Treas.
EIN: 136110184

39384
The Lawrence C. Stewart Charitable Foundation
9 Signal Hill Rd.
Fayetteville, NY 13066-9674

Established in 1992 in NY.
Donor(s): Lawrence C. Stewart.
Financial data (yr. ended 12/31/01): Grants paid, $4,200; assets, $3,887 (M); expenditures, $4,231; qualifying distributions, $4,200.
Limitations: Applications not accepted. Giving limited to NY.
Application information: Contributes only to pre-selected organizations.
Trustees: Lawrence C. Stewart, Pamela Sunshine.
EIN: 161413000

39385
The Widoff Foundation
228 Mead Mountain Rd.
Woodstock, NY 12498-1016

Donor(s): Gerald J. Widoff.
Financial data (yr. ended 10/31/01): Grants paid, $4,190; assets, $23,107 (M); expenditures, $4,295; qualifying distributions, $4,190.
Limitations: Applications not accepted. Giving primarily in NY.
Application information: Contributes only to pre-selected organizations.
Officer: Gerald J. Widoff, Mgr.
Trustees: Adam Widoff, Antony J. Widoff.
EIN: 237035402

39386
Joseph A. D'Aiello, Jr. Memorial Fund
c/o Joseph A. D'Aiello
2574 Tiemann Ave.
Bronx, NY 10469

Established in 1995.
Donor(s): Joseph A. D'Aiello, Sr.
Financial data (yr. ended 09/30/01): Grants paid, $4,179; assets, $1,106 (M); gifts received, $3,250; expenditures, $4,240; qualifying distributions, $4,179.
Officers: Joseph A. D'Aiello, Pres.; Marie-Eleana D'Aiello, V.P. and Secy.

EIN: 133848797

39387
The Podhoretz Sarna Goldfeier Foundation
c/o Nathan Berkman & Co.
29 Broadway, Ste. 2900
New York, NY 10006-3296

Established in 1993 in NY.
Donor(s): Emanuel Podhoretz.
Financial data (yr. ended 06/30/01): Grants paid, $4,177; assets, $1 (M); expenditures, $4,527; qualifying distributions, $4,177.
Limitations: Applications not accepted.
Application information: Contributes only to pre-selected organizations.
Trustee: Emanuel Podhoretz.
EIN: 133722625

39388
Allegro Foundation
c/o Starr & Co.
350 Park Ave.
New York, NY 10022
Contact: Misha Dichter, Dir.

Established in 1999 in NY.
Donor(s): Lucy Dichter.
Financial data (yr. ended 12/31/00): Grants paid, $4,175; assets, $78,373 (M); expenditures, $11,435; qualifying distributions, $11,371.
Directors: Alexander Dichter, Cipa Dichter, Gabriel Dichter, Misha Dichter.
EIN: 134075001

39389
Fenton Foundation
Jackson St.
New Suffolk, NY 11956-9999

Donor(s): Joseph Fenton.
Financial data (yr. ended 09/30/01): Grants paid, $4,170; assets, $59,695 (M); expenditures, $4,345; qualifying distributions, $4,170.
Limitations: Applications not accepted. Giving primarily in NY and PA.
Application information: Contributes only to pre-selected organizations.
Trustees: Adelaide Fenton, Joseph Fenton.
EIN: 116080397

39390
Charlyn Foundation, Inc.
c/o Charles H. Hoffman
803 Weaver St.
Larchmont, NY 10538-1031

Financial data (yr. ended 12/31/01): Grants paid, $4,103; assets, $39,064 (M); expenditures, $4,198; qualifying distributions, $4,103.
Limitations: Applications not accepted.
Application information: Contributes only to pre-selected organizations.
Officers: Charles H. Hoffman, Pres.; Rowena Hoffman, V.P.
EIN: 136143927

39391
William Heiser Foundation for the Cure of Spinal Cord Injuries, Inc.
c/o William Heiser
3434 Hawthorne Dr. N.
Wantagh, NY 11793

Established in 1993 in NY.
Financial data (yr. ended 12/31/01): Grants paid, $4,100; assets, $13,187 (L); gifts received, $18,310; expenditures, $11,350; qualifying distributions, $11,350.
Limitations: Applications not accepted. Giving primarily in NY.

Application information: Contributes only to pre-selected organizations.
Officers: Joseph Sherman, Pres.; Christopher Hooker, V.P.; Karen Bennett, Secy.; Joseph Ruis, Treas.
EIN: 113174615
Codes: GTI

39392
Mayburn Foundation, Inc.
15 Honey Hollow Rd.
Pound Ridge, NY 10576

Established in 1997 in NY.
Donor(s): Christian Georges Mayaud, M.D.
Financial data (yr. ended 12/31/00): Grants paid, $4,100; assets, $206,663 (M); gifts received, $100; expenditures, $5,047; qualifying distributions, $4,100.
Officers and Directors:* Christian Georges Mayaud, M.D.,* Pres.; Hillary Burnett Mayaud,* V.P. and Treas.; Steven Hochberg,* Secy.
EIN: 133949457

39393
World Journal Culture Foundation, Inc.
c/o World Journal Newspaper
141-07 20th Ave., 6th Fl.
Flushing, NY 11357-6093
Contact: Howard Lee, Dir.

Donor(s): Chinese Daily News, Inc.
Financial data (yr. ended 06/30/01): Grants paid, $4,100; assets, $180,925 (M); expenditures, $132,038; qualifying distributions, $34,631; giving activities include $26,980 for programs.
Limitations: Giving on a national basis.
Application information: Application form required.
Directors: T.S. Chang, Howard Lee, Jacob Ma, P.L. Wang.
EIN: 112948645
Codes: CS, CD

39394
Klarberg Family Foundation, Inc.
1 Pheasant Run Rd.
Pleasantville, NY 10570

Established in 2000 in NY.
Donor(s): Barry Klarberg.
Financial data (yr. ended 12/31/00): Grants paid, $4,095; assets, $1 (M); gifts received, $4,611; expenditures, $4,610; qualifying distributions, $4,095.
Officer: Barry Klarberg, Pres.
EIN: 134101634

39395
Mellijor Charitable Foundation, Inc.
c/o William Borden
220 Estates Terr., S.
Manhasset, NY 11030

Financial data (yr. ended 12/31/01): Grants paid, $4,085; assets, $77,615 (M); expenditures, $4,085; qualifying distributions, $4,085.
Limitations: Applications not accepted.
Application information: Contributes only to pre-selected organizations.
Officers: Alfonso V. Mellijor, Pres.; Linda Mellijor, V.P.
EIN: 133936809

39396
Harry M. & Sylvia Wagner Foundation, Inc.
5 Tudor City Pl., Apt. 301
New York, NY 10017

Financial data (yr. ended 10/31/01): Grants paid, $4,055; assets, $17,165 (M); expenditures, $4,896; qualifying distributions, $4,055.

Limitations: Applications not accepted. Giving primarily in New York, NY.
Application information: Contributes only to pre-selected organizations.
Officer: Patricia Wagner, Pres. and Secy.
EIN: 136160994

39397
Whittaker Family Foundation
1 Bradford Heights Rd.
Syracuse, NY 13224

Donor(s): Gaylord D. Whittaker.
Financial data (yr. ended 06/30/02): Grants paid, $4,050; assets, $152,612 (M); expenditures, $8,642; qualifying distributions, $4,050.
Limitations: Applications not accepted. Giving on a national basis, with some emphasis on NY.
Application information: Contributes only to pre-selected organizations.
Trustees: Carolyn K. Whittaker Bray, Deborah J. Whittaker Villanueva, Gaylord D. Whittaker, Gaylord Daniel Whittaker, Jr., Ida Mae Whittaker, John David Whittaker, William Douglas Whittaker.
EIN: 161255224

39398
The Louviers Foundation
57 Lookout Rd.
Tuxedo Park, NY 10987-4033

Donor(s): David B. duPont, Barbara L. duPont.
Financial data (yr. ended 01/31/02): Grants paid, $4,030; assets, $94,980 (M); expenditures, $5,225; qualifying distributions, $4,030.
Limitations: Applications not accepted. Giving primarily in NY.
Application information: Contributes only to pre-selected organizations.
Trustees: Barbara L. duPont, David B. duPont.
EIN: 066286610

39399
Mabel M. Heid Scholarship Fund
c/o JPMorgan Chase Bank
P.O. Box 31412
Rochester, NY 14603-1412

Established in 1991 in NY.
Donor(s): Eugene A. Heid.‡
Financial data (yr. ended 09/30/01): Grants paid, $4,026; assets, $99,136 (M); expenditures, $5,419; qualifying distributions, $4,805.
Limitations: Giving limited to residents of Irondequoit, NY.
Application information: Application form required.
Trustee: JPMorgan Chase Bank.
EIN: 166357668

39400
Chai Foundation
4 Uxbridge St.
Staten Island, NY 10314

Established in 1998 in NY.
Donor(s): Chaya R. Ginsberg, Moshe L. Ginsberg.
Financial data (yr. ended 12/31/01): Grants paid, $4,025; assets, $257,473 (M); gifts received, $30,450; expenditures, $11,767; qualifying distributions, $4,025.
Limitations: Applications not accepted. Giving primarily in NY.
Application information: Contributes only to pre-selected organizations.
Trustees: Chaya R. Ginsberg, Moshe L. Ginsberg.
EIN: 134015543

39401
The Irving Chutick Foundation, Inc.
c/o F.T. Kleiger & Co.
80 Cuttermill Rd., Ste. 302
Great Neck, NY 11021-3108

Financial data (yr. ended 12/31/01): Grants paid, $4,025; assets, $98,396 (M); expenditures, $6,067; qualifying distributions, $4,025.
Limitations: Applications not accepted. Giving primarily in New York, NY.
Application information: Contributes only to pre-selected organizations.
Officers: Louise Terry, Pres.; Jack Terry, V.P.
EIN: 116014456

39402
The Frank J. Becker Educational Foundation
173 Earle Ave.
Lynbrook, NY 11563   (516) 599-1023
Contact: Robert G. Becker, Treas.

Financial data (yr. ended 12/31/99): Grants paid, $4,000; assets, $40,083 (M); expenditures, $4,451; qualifying distributions, $4,238.
Limitations: Giving limited to residents of Lynbrook, NY.
Application information: Application form required.
Officers and Directors:* William G. Fanuzzi,* Pres.; Luis E. Bejarano,* V.P.; Salvatore Gullo,* Secy.; Robert G. Becker,* Treas.; Hon. Francis X. Becker, Michael DeMarco.
EIN: 116103238

39403
Morton and Ruth Berger Foundation
c/o Max Wasser
132 Nassau St., Ste. 300
New York, NY 10038

Established in 1997 in NY.
Donor(s): Ruth Berger.‡
Financial data (yr. ended 12/31/00): Grants paid, $4,000; assets, $70,125 (M); gifts received, $72,920; expenditures, $4,043; qualifying distributions, $4,043.
Limitations: Applications not accepted.
Application information: Contributes only to pre-selected organizations.
Trustee: Stephen Berger.
EIN: 137098611

39404
Herbert Berger Scholarship Foundation
25 Bloomingdale Rd.
Staten Island, NY 10309
Application address: c/o Principal, Tottenville High School, Staten Island, NY 10312

Established in 1990 in NY.
Financial data (yr. ended 12/31/00): Grants paid, $4,000; assets, $56,628 (M); expenditures, $4,053; qualifying distributions, $4,000.
Limitations: Giving limited to residents of Staten Island, NY.
Application information: Application form not required.
Trustee: Shelby Berger Jakoby.
EIN: 136939674

39405
Cantor, Fitzgerald Foundation
c/o J. Ficarro
101 Park Ave., 34th Fl.
New York, NY 10172

Established in 1982 in NY.
Donor(s): Cantor, Fitzgerald Securities Corp.
Financial data (yr. ended 12/31/00): Grants paid, $4,000; assets, $18,904 (L); expenditures, $4,000; qualifying distributions, $4,000.
Limitations: Applications not accepted. Giving primarily in NY.
Application information: Contributes only to pre-selected organizations.
Officers and Directors:* Howard W. Lutnick,* Chair and Pres.; Douglas B. Gardner, V.P. and Treas.; Stuart Fraser,* V.P.; Philip Ginsberg,* V.P.; Stephen M. Merkel, Secy.; Iris Cantor.
EIN: 133117872
Codes: CS, CD

39406
David's Animal Foundation, Inc.
780-1 Broadway Ave.
Holbrook, NY 11741

Established in 1999 in NY.
Donor(s): Marion Brody.
Financial data (yr. ended 12/31/01): Grants paid, $4,000; assets, $124,109 (M); gifts received, $101,416; expenditures, $13,363; qualifying distributions, $4,000.
Limitations: Applications not accepted. Giving primarily in NY.
Application information: Contributes only to pre-selected organizations.
Officers: Philip S. Brody, Pres.; Debra Lynn Feliziani, V.P.
Directors: Marion Brody, Dawn E. Manzi, Kristin M. Siarkowicz.
EIN: 113477451

39407
Pesach and Pearl Feldman Foundation
1625 52nd St.
Brooklyn, NY 11204

Established in 1996 in NY.
Donor(s): Pearl Feldman, Pesach Feldman.
Financial data (yr. ended 08/31/01): Grants paid, $4,000; assets, $103,964 (M); gifts received, $50,000; expenditures, $5,184; qualifying distributions, $4,000.
Limitations: Applications not accepted.
Application information: Contributes only to pre-selected organizations.
Trustees: Paul Feldman, Pearl Feldman.
EIN: 137093164

39408
Genco Foundation for Health Sciences, Inc.
65 Livingston Pkwy.
Snyder, NY 14226

Established in 1997 in NY.
Financial data (yr. ended 12/31/01): Grants paid, $4,000; assets, $6,170 (M); expenditures, $5,541; qualifying distributions, $4,000.
Limitations: Applications not accepted.
Application information: Contributes only to pre-selected organizations.
Directors: Robert J. Genco, Sandra C. Genco, Deborah A. Powell.
EIN: 161541513

39409
Gentile Family Foundation
145 Briarhill Rd.
Williamsville, NY 14221

Established in 2000 in NY.
Financial data (yr. ended 12/31/01): Grants paid, $4,000; assets, $26 (M); expenditures, $4,210; qualifying distributions, $4,000.
Limitations: Giving primarily in South Bend, IN.
Trustees: Nancy Gentile, Nicholas Gentile, Donna M. Renelt.
EIN: 316650308

39410
Walter & Patricia Gladstone - Andes Scholarship Trust Fund
c/o The National Bank of Delaware County
P.O. Box 389
Walton, NY 13856
Application address: c/o Andes Central School Dist., Andes, NY 13731

Established in 1997 in NY.
Donor(s): Walter Gladstone, Patricia Gladstone.
Financial data (yr. ended 11/30/01): Grants paid, $4,000; assets, $113,867 (M); expenditures, $4,807; qualifying distributions, $4,000.
Limitations: Giving limited to Andes, NY.
Application information: Recipients chosen by school administration. Application form required.
Trustee: The National Bank of Delaware County.
EIN: 161541848

39411
Goldfinger Foundation for the Visual Arts, Inc.
220 Mead St.
Waccabuc, NY 10597
Contact: Myron Goldfinger, Pres.

Established in 1998 in NY.
Donor(s): Myron Goldfinger.
Financial data (yr. ended 12/31/00): Grants paid, $4,000; assets, $48,888 (M); expenditures, $4,000; qualifying distributions, $3,970.
Officers: Myron Goldfinger, Pres.; Djerba Goldfinger, V.P.; Thira Goldfinger, V.P.; June Goldfinger, Treas.
EIN: 134009859

39412
The Heroy Family Foundation
c/o IBJ Whitehall
320 Park Ave.
New York, NY 10022

Established in 1994 in AL.
Financial data (yr. ended 11/30/01): Grants paid, $4,000; assets, $58,578 (M); expenditures, $4,781; qualifying distributions, $4,000.
Limitations: Applications not accepted. Giving primarily in Baltimore, MD.
Application information: Contributes only to pre-selected organizations.
Officers and Directors:* Rosalie Braverman,* Pres.; Joseph Braverman,* V.P.; Myles Braverman,* Treas.
EIN: 137040712

39413
Krivit Foundation, Inc.
c/o Helen Krivit Fried
12 Carriage Way
White Plains, NY 10605
Application address: 18 Blue Ribbon Dr., Westport, CT 06880, tel.: (203) 227-9267
Contact: Marilyn K. Steiner, Pres.

Financial data (yr. ended 12/31/01): Grants paid, $4,000; assets, $70,005 (M); expenditures, $4,860; qualifying distributions, $4,000.
Limitations: Giving primarily in CT and NY.
Application information: Application form not required.
Officers: Marilyn K. Steiner, Pres. and Treas.; Monroe J. Steiner, V.P.
EIN: 136059758

39414
The Henry Lindenbaum Memorial Foundation, Inc.
480 Park Ave., Ste. 16C
New York, NY 10022

Established in 1992 in NY.
Donor(s): Ruth Lindenbaum.
Financial data (yr. ended 12/31/01): Grants paid, $4,000; assets, $31,555 (M); expenditures, $4,025; qualifying distributions, $4,000.
Limitations: Applications not accepted. Giving primarily in New York, NY.
Application information: Contributes only to pre-selected organizations.
Trustees: Belda Lindenbaum, Jean Lindenbaum, Ruth Lindenbaum.
EIN: 133469416

39415
Elkhanan Livian Endowment Foundation, Inc.
100 Greenway Terr.
Forest Hills, NY 11375
Application address: c/o The Higher Education Board of the United Mesehedi Jewish Community of America, 54 Steamboat Rd., Great Neck, NY 11024
Contact: Chamuel Livian, Dir.

Established in 1991 in NY.
Donor(s): Chamuel Livian.
Financial data (yr. ended 12/31/00): Grants paid, $4,000; assets, $0 (M); expenditures, $4,214; qualifying distributions, $4,000.
Limitations: Giving primarily in NY.
Application information: Application form required.
Directors: Avraham Dalmanian, Chamuel Livian, Gabriel Livian.
EIN: 113049419

39416
Louise H. & Arthur Malsin Foundation, Inc.
c/o Joseph Beberman
45 N. Village Ave., Ste. 10
Rockville Centre, NY 11570
Application address: 160 Converse Rd., Marion, MA 02738
Contact: Mary M. Merrow, Pres.

Financial data (yr. ended 10/31/01): Grants paid, $4,000; assets, $81,263 (M); expenditures, $5,406; qualifying distributions, $4,000.
Officers: Mary M. Merrow, Pres.; Lane M. Dunn, V.P. and Secy.; Louise M. Rothchild, V.P. and Secy.; Arthur Malsin, Jr., V.P.
EIN: 133465599

39417
The Mathewson Foundation
4302 S. Salina St.
Syracuse, NY 13205

Established in 1988 in NY.
Donor(s): Ann M. Mathewson, George A. Mathewson.
Financial data (yr. ended 09/30/01): Grants paid, $4,000; assets, $137,074 (M); expenditures, $4,748; qualifying distributions, $4,000.
Limitations: Applications not accepted. Giving primarily in Syracuse, NY.
Application information: Contributes only to pre-selected organizations.
Trustees: Ann M. Mathewson, George A. Mathewson.
EIN: 161340643

39418
The McCaddin-McQuirk Foundation, Inc.
P.O. Box 5001
New York, NY 10185
Contact: John J. Caffrey, Pres.

Incorporated in 1902 in NY.
Donor(s): Rt. Rev. John McQuirk,‡ Ann Eliza McCaddin Walsh.‡
Financial data (yr. ended 12/31/01): Grants paid, $4,000; assets, $4,387,045 (M); expenditures, $9,000; qualifying distributions, $6,891.
Limitations: Giving primarily in the U.S., Canada, South America, Africa, and Asia.
Application information: Applications must be made through a bishop, rector, or head of a seminary. Application form not required.
Officers: John J. Caffrey, Pres.; Frank Hardart III, Secy.; Robert G. Ix, Treas.
Trustees: Thomas F. Blaney, John J. Eager, Frederic J. Fuller, Francis M. Hartman, Henry J. Humphreys, Msgr. Thomas A. Modugno, Carrol A. Muccia, Jr., Martin W. Ronan, Jr., John G. Scott, Thomas A. Turley, William A. White.
EIN: 136134444

39419
Pauline McCarthy Charitable Trust
c/o HSBC Bank USA
P.O. Box 4203
Buffalo, NY 14240-4203

Financial data (yr. ended 12/31/01): Grants paid, $4,000; assets, $51,978 (M); expenditures, $4,829; qualifying distributions, $4,000.
Limitations: Applications not accepted. Giving primarily in NY.
Application information: Contributes only to pre-selected organizations.
Trustee: HSBC Bank USA.
EIN: 237297016

39420
The Old Timers-Jack Thompson Memorial Scholarship Fund
c/o JPMorgan Chase Bank
P.O. Box 31412
Rochester, NY 14603-1412

Financial data (yr. ended 08/31/01): Grants paid, $4,000; assets, $82,800 (M); expenditures, $5,621; qualifying distributions, $4,192.
Limitations: Giving limited to residents of CT.
Application information: Contact high school guidance counselor for application information.
Trustee: JPMorgan Chase Bank.
EIN: 066268930

39421
Oppenheim Students' Fund, Inc.
c/o Board of Education
607 Walnut Ave.
Niagara Falls, NY 14301-1729
Contact: Barbara Joyce

Financial data (yr. ended 12/31/01): Grants paid, $4,000; assets, $31,252 (M); expenditures, $5,047; qualifying distributions, $4,253.
Limitations: Giving limited to Niagara County, NY.
Officers and Directors:* Fred Barone,* Pres.; William L. Sdao, Secy.; Frank Orfano,* Treas.; James De Rusha, John Essler, Bruce Fraser.
EIN: 166040269
Codes: GTI

39422
Horace A. and Helen A. Pantano Family
c/o Horace A. Pantano
378 Chestnut St., No. 303
Fredonia, NY 14063-1632

Established in NY in 1998.
Donor(s): Horace A. Pantano.
Financial data (yr. ended 09/30/01): Grants paid, $4,000; assets, $79,420 (M); expenditures, $5,948; qualifying distributions, $4,000.
Limitations: Applications not accepted.
Application information: Contributes only to pre-selected organizations.

Directors: Helen A. Panatano, Horace A. Pantano, Steven R. Pantano.
EIN: 161558053

39423
Selby Parker Fund
5892 Main St.
Williamsville, NY 14221 (716) 632-6800
Contact: Jack A. Keenan, Tr.

Financial data (yr. ended 11/30/01): Grants paid, $4,000; assets, $92,098 (M); expenditures, $4,105; qualifying distributions, $4,000.
Limitations: Giving on a national basis.
Application information: Application form not required.
Trustee: Jack A. Keenan.
EIN: 166023149

39424
Elizabeth Pike Scholarship Fund
c/o JPMorgan Chase Bank
P.O. Box 31412
Rochester, NY 14603-1412

Financial data (yr. ended 12/31/01): Grants paid, $4,000; assets, $59,980 (M); expenditures, $5,490; qualifying distributions, $4,076.
Limitations: Applications not accepted. Giving limited to residents of Fairfield, CT.
Application information: Unsolicited requests for funds not accepted.
Trustee: JPMorgan Chase Bank.
EIN: 066022611

39425
Rancho Feedwell Foundation
125 Prince St.
New York, NY 10012-3153

Donor(s): Harold Milgrom, Ben Solomon.
Financial data (yr. ended 11/30/01): Grants paid, $4,000; assets, $81,518 (M); expenditures, $4,950; qualifying distributions, $4,000.
Application information: Application form not required.
Officer and Director:* Harold Milgrom,* Pres.
EIN: 521370162

39426
Henry Salzman Foundation, Inc.
c/o Paul Alexander
608 Dover Rd.
Oceanside, NY 11572

Established in 1991 in NJ.
Donor(s): Henry Salzman.‡
Financial data (yr. ended 09/30/01): Grants paid, $4,000; assets, $50,298 (M); expenditures, $4,140; qualifying distributions, $39,921.
Limitations: Applications not accepted. Giving limited to NJ and NY.
Application information: Contributes only to pre-selected organizations.
Officers: Paul Alexander, Pres.; Ellen Alexander, Secy.
EIN: 113031683

39427
The Shulsky Foundation
200 Central Park S., Ste. 20E
New York, NY 10019-1415

Established in 1996 in NY.
Donor(s): Rubin Shulsky,‡ 1220 Broadway, LLC.
Financial data (yr. ended 11/30/01): Grants paid, $4,000; assets, $14,080 (M); expenditures, $5,465; qualifying distributions, $4,029.
Limitations: Applications not accepted. Giving primarily in New York, NY.
Application information: Contributes only to pre-selected organizations.

Trustee: Rena Shulsky.
EIN: 137079079

39428
Thunen Family Foundation, Inc.
c/o Garret Thunen
7 Nichols Pl.
Briarcliff Manor, NY 10510

Established in 1999 in NY.
Donor(s): Garret Thunen.
Financial data (yr. ended 12/31/00): Grants paid, $4,000; assets, $124,870 (M); gifts received, $2,209; expenditures, $6,362; qualifying distributions, $4,050.
Limitations: Applications not accepted.
Application information: Contributes only to pre-selected organizations.
Officer: Garret Thunen, Pres.
EIN: 134046890

39429
The Tulip Fund
c/o Deborah Landau
64 E. 86th St.
New York, NY 10028

Established in 1985 in NY.
Donor(s): Deborah J. Landau, William Landau, M.D.
Financial data (yr. ended 10/31/01): Grants paid, $4,000; assets, $63,128 (M); gifts received, $583; expenditures, $4,583; qualifying distributions, $4,000.
Limitations: Applications not accepted. Giving primarily in NY.
Application information: Contributes only to pre-selected organizations.
Officers: Deborah J. Landau, Pres. and Treas.; Edith L. Landau, Secy.
EIN: 133320298

39430
John J. & Hester Van Buiten Charitable Fund
c/o MBP Assoc., Inc.
110 E. 55th St.
New York, NY 10022

Donor(s): John J. Van Buiten, Hester Van Buiten.
Financial data (yr. ended 12/31/01): Grants paid, $4,000; assets, $117,173 (M); expenditures, $8,339; qualifying distributions, $4,000.
Limitations: Applications not accepted. Giving primarily in NJ.
Application information: Contributes only to pre-selected organizations.
Trustees: Jean-Pierre Delbecq, A. Crew Schielke, Jr., Hester Van Buiten, John J. Van Buiten.
EIN: 133354759

39431
Heinemann & Rosa Vogelstein Foundation, Inc.
466 Lexington Ave., 10th Fl.
New York, NY 10017
Contact: John L. Vogelstein, Pres.

Financial data (yr. ended 12/31/01): Grants paid, $4,000; assets, $6,182 (M); expenditures, $5,200; qualifying distributions, $4,000.
Officers: John L. Vogelstein, Pres.; Andrew W. Vogelstein, V.P.; Hans A. Vogelstein, V.P.; Susan Larusso, Secy.
EIN: 136117270

39432
Sheldon J. Streisand Foundation
111 Great Neck Rd., Ste 412
Great Neck, NY 11021

Established in 1998.
Donor(s): Judith B. Streisand.

Financial data (yr. ended 12/31/01): Grants paid, $3,989; assets, $19,371 (M); expenditures, $6,019; qualifying distributions, $3,989.
Limitations: Applications not accepted.
Application information: Contributes only to pre-selected organizations.
Trustees: Erica S. Needle, Steven Needle, Judith B. Streisand, Sheldon J. Streisand.
EIN: 113440418

39433
Henry P. Kovarik Foundation for Poetry, Inc.
c/o Cedar, Strauss, & Holt
P.O. Box 2100
Selden, NY 11784-0614 (631) 732-6600
Contact: Lawrence J. Holt, Dir.

Financial data (yr. ended 04/30/99): Grants paid, $3,975; assets, $161,640 (M); expenditures, $5,125; qualifying distributions, $5,125.
Limitations: Giving limited to Middle Island, NY.
Application information: Application form required.
Directors: Eugene Dooley, Lawrence J. Holt, Karen Mouzakas.
EIN: 112781923

39434
The Woodcock No. 5 Foundation
c/o Rockefeller & Co.
30 Rockefeller Plz., Ste. 5600
New York, NY 10112
Application address: 400 Seaport Ct., Ste. 250, Redwood City, CA
Contact: Stuart Davidson, Tr.

Financial data (yr. ended 11/30/01): Grants paid, $3,972; assets, $70,014 (M); gifts received, $21,643; expenditures, $6,433; qualifying distributions, $3,972.
Limitations: Giving primarily in NY and OH.
Application information: Application form not required.
Trustees: Stuart P. Davidson, Richard T. Watson.
EIN: 133932862

39435
The Shalom Foundation, Inc.
P.O. Box 442
Tallman, NY 10982

Established in 1999.
Financial data (yr. ended 08/31/01): Grants paid, $3,968; assets, $1 (M); gifts received, $3,966; expenditures, $4,116; qualifying distributions, $3,968.
Officers: Aharon Friedman, Pres.; Max Uhr, Secy.; Margaret Friedman, Treas.
EIN: 134025619

39436
Marilyn Newmark and Leonard J. Meiselman Charitable Foundation, Inc.
22 Woodhollow Rd.
Roslyn Heights, NY 11577-2217
Contact: Marilyn Meiselman, Pres.

Established in 1996 in NY.
Donor(s): Marilyn Meiselman.
Financial data (yr. ended 12/31/01): Grants paid, $3,950; assets, $135,234 (M); expenditures, $5,853; qualifying distributions, $3,950.
Limitations: Giving primarily in NY.
Officers: Marilyn Meiselman, Pres.; Mindy Meiselman, V.P. and Secy.; John J. Reilly, Treas.
EIN: 113328754

39437
Smith-Weil Foundation, Inc.
1160 Park Ave.
New York, NY 10128

Established in 1993 in NY.
Donor(s): A. Lorne Weil.
Financial data (yr. ended 12/31/00): Grants paid, $3,950; assets, $0 (M); expenditures, $46,082; qualifying distributions, $3,950.
Limitations: Applications not accepted. Giving primarily in New York, NY.
Application information: Contributes only to pre-selected organizations.
Officers: Victoria Lea Smith, Pres. and Treas.; A. Lorne Weil, V.P.; John C. Novogrod, Secy.
EIN: 133751138
Codes: TN

39438
Debbie and Richard A. Wilpon Foundation
111 Great Neck Rd., Ste. 408
Great Neck, NY 11021
Contact: Richard A. Wilpon, Pres.

Established in 2000 in NY.
Donor(s): Richard A. Wilpon.
Financial data (yr. ended 12/31/00): Grants paid, $3,916; assets, $148,443 (M); gifts received, $149,175; expenditures, $3,916; qualifying distributions, $3,916.
Officers and Directors:* Richard A. Wilpon,* Pres.; Debbie Wilpon,* V.P.
EIN: 137257956

39439
The Michael and Estelle Sotirhos Family Foundation
3000 Marcus Ave., No. 3W10
New Hyde Park, NY 11042

Established in 1989 in DC.
Donor(s): Michael G. Sotirhos, Estelle Sotirhos.
Financial data (yr. ended 12/31/01): Grants paid, $3,910; assets, $12,557 (M); gifts received, $8,000; expenditures, $4,798; qualifying distributions, $3,910.
Limitations: Applications not accepted.
Application information: Contributes only to pre-selected organizations.
Officer and Trustees:* Michael G. Sotirhos,* Chair.; Estelle Sotirhos, Michael S. Sotirhos, Jr.
EIN: 133516219

39440
Gilbert L. and Linda A. Snyder Charitable Foundation, Inc.
45 E. 89th St., Ste. 7E
New York, NY 10128

Established in 1993 in DE.
Financial data (yr. ended 11/30/99): Grants paid, $3,905; assets, $903,953 (M); expenditures, $3,955; qualifying distributions, $3,930.
Limitations: Applications not accepted.
Application information: Contributes only to pre-selected organizations.
Officers: Gilbert L. Snyder, Pres. and Treas.; Linda A. Snyder, V.P. and Secy.
EIN: 133961524

39441
Joseph P. & Betty Jacobson Foundation, Inc.
c/o Wagner, Stott, Mercator
14 Wall St., 21st Fl.
New York, NY 10005

Financial data (yr. ended 10/31/01): Grants paid, $3,878; assets, $54,894 (M); expenditures, $5,110; qualifying distributions, $3,878.
Limitations: Applications not accepted. Giving primarily in New York, NY.
Application information: Contributes only to pre-selected organizations.
Officers and Directors:* Perry P. Jacobson,* V.P.; Thomas A. Jacobson,* V.P.; Sharon Jacobson,* Secy.; Sylvia G. Jacobson,* Treas.
EIN: 136062876

39442
The Royce W. Clark Memorial Trust
c/o The National Bank of Delaware County
P.O. Box 389
Walton, NY 13856-0389   (607) 865-4126

Established in 1989 in NY.
Donor(s): Gordon Watson.
Financial data (yr. ended 12/31/00): Grants paid, $3,875; assets, $148,504 (M); gifts received, $5,000; expenditures, $4,616; qualifying distributions, $4,304.
Limitations: Giving limited to Walton, NY.
Application information: Application form required.
Trustee: The National Bank of Delaware County.
EIN: 166333418

39443
Walter W. Oakley Trust
c/o JPMorgan Chase Bank
P.O. Box 31412
Rochester, NY 14603-1412

Financial data (yr. ended 12/31/01): Grants paid, $3,860; assets, $33,163 (M); expenditures, $4,591; qualifying distributions, $3,860.
Limitations: Applications not accepted.
Application information: Contributes only to pre-selected organizations.
Trustee: JPMorgan Chase Bank.
EIN: 166015436

39444
Aronauer Family Foundation, Inc.
265 Sparrow Dr.
Manhasset, NY 11030-4007
Contact: Irwin L. Aronauer, Pres.

Financial data (yr. ended 12/31/01): Grants paid, $3,857; assets, $27,793 (M); gifts received, $1,000; expenditures, $4,298; qualifying distributions, $3,857.
Limitations: Giving primarily in NY.
Officer: Irwin L. Aronauer, Pres.
EIN: 237043112

39445
Abe and Chaya Foundation
179 Grandview Ave.
Monsey, NY 10952
Contact: Abraham Jeremias, Tr.

Established in 1999 in NY.
Donor(s): Abaline Paper Products.
Financial data (yr. ended 12/31/00): Grants paid, $3,850; assets, $36,355 (M); gifts received, $44,200; expenditures, $3,868; qualifying distributions, $3,850.
Trustees: Abraham Jeremias, Chaya Jeremias.
EIN: 311682404

39446
Dave Luckman Memorial Foundation
240 Mineola Blvd.
Mineola, NY 11501
Contact: William Houslanger, Tr.

Financial data (yr. ended 04/30/99): Grants paid, $3,850; assets, $44,529 (M); expenditures, $3,988; qualifying distributions, $3,850.
Limitations: Giving primarily in New York, NY.
Trustees: Peter M. Luckman, Todd E. Houslanger, William Houslanger.
EIN: 116008972

39447
SGL Foundation
55 Dale Rd. E.
Rochester, NY 14625-2007

Financial data (yr. ended 11/30/01): Grants paid, $3,850; assets, $10,617 (M); expenditures, $3,986; qualifying distributions, $3,850.
Limitations: Applications not accepted. Giving primarily in Rochester, NY and PA.
Application information: Contributes only to pre-selected organizations.
Trustees: Alan Laties, David Laties, Victor Laties.
EIN: 046064800

39448
Zichron Beis Hillel Foundation
1356 55th St.
Brooklyn, NY 11219   (718) 851-6417
Contact: Pinchus Weinberger, Tr.

Established in 1999 in NY.
Financial data (yr. ended 12/31/01): Grants paid, $3,813; assets, $67,932 (M); gifts received, $6,000; expenditures, $4,363; qualifying distributions, $3,813.
Limitations: Giving primarily in Brooklyn, NY.
Trustees: Elena Weinberger, Pinches Weinberger.
EIN: 113487728

39449
Baldwinsville Marching Band Support Group, Inc.
P.O. Box 357
Baldwinsville, NY 13027

Financial data (yr. ended 03/31/02): Grants paid, $3,809; assets, $19,604 (M); gifts received, $3,270; expenditures, $77,166; qualifying distributions, $62,475.
Limitations: Giving limited to Baldwinsville, NY.
Application information: Unsolicited request for funds not accepted.
Officers: Robert Dupra, Pres.; Mary House, V.P.; Ozzie Calabrese, Secy.; John Mrawka, Treas.
EIN: 222542537

39450
America Share U.S.A., Inc.
c/o Taicoa Corp.
15 W. 26th St.
New York, NY 10010-1002

Established in 1991 in NY.
Financial data (yr. ended 12/31/00): Grants paid, $3,800; assets, $31,059 (M); gifts received, $4,698; expenditures, $3,830; qualifying distributions, $3,800.
Limitations: Applications not accepted.
Application information: Contributes only to pre-selected organizations.
Directors: Anna Pinto, Dennis Pinto, Fiona Pinto.
EIN: 133599586

39451
Jennie Grossinger Foundation, Inc.
271 Madison Ave., 22nd Fl.
New York, NY 10016

Established in 1970 in NY.
Donor(s): Charles Alpert, Joseph Alpert, Sheldon Small.
Financial data (yr. ended 06/30/00): Grants paid, $3,800; assets, $5,360 (M); gifts received, $5,000; expenditures, $3,895; qualifying distributions, $3,800.
Limitations: Applications not accepted. Giving primarily in NY.

Application information: Contributes only to pre-selected organizations.
Officers: Joseph Alpert, Secy.; Charles Alpert, Treas.
EIN: 132726085

39452
Isaac & Dinah Guzy Foundation, Inc.
230 Park Ave., Ste. 510
New York, NY 10169

Donor(s): Deborah Frankel.
Financial data (yr. ended 08/31/02): Grants paid, $3,800; assets, $111,770 (M); expenditures, $5,299; qualifying distributions, $3,800.
Limitations: Applications not accepted. Giving primarily in NY and PA.
Application information: Contributes only to pre-selected organizations.
Officers and Directors:* Janet Jaffin,* Pres.; Doris Greenberg,* Secy.; Lois Levine.
EIN: 136101287

39453
Bruce & Beverly Marmor Foundation
c/o S. Kruth
401 N. Salina St., No. 400
Syracuse, NY 13203

Donor(s): Bruce Marmor, Beverly Marmor.
Financial data (yr. ended 12/31/01): Grants paid, $3,800; assets, $54,653 (M); expenditures, $4,452; qualifying distributions, $3,800.
Limitations: Applications not accepted. Giving primarily in NY.
Application information: Contributes only to pre-selected organizations.
Trustees: Beverly Marmor, Bruce Marmor.
EIN: 166279140

39454
The Eunice Foundation
c/o Ronald Berman
150 W. 56th St., Ste. 6703
New York, NY 10019

Established in 2000 in DE.
Financial data (yr. ended 12/31/01): Grants paid, $3,783; assets, $349,921 (M); gifts received, $170,081; expenditures, $5,170; qualifying distributions, $3,783.
Limitations: Applications not accepted.
Application information: Contributes only to pre-selected organizations.
Officer: Ronald Berman, Pres.
EIN: 134108529

39455
Charles R. Vaughn Educational Trust
c/o Jeremiah F. Manning
27 Brookman Ave.
Delmar, NY 12054

Established in 1999 in NY.
Financial data (yr. ended 12/31/01): Grants paid, $3,782; assets, $374,367 (M); expenditures, $10,148; qualifying distributions, $3,782.
Trustee: Jeremiah F. Manning.
EIN: 141785189

39456
The Julian Autrey Song Foundation
98 Riverside Dr., Ste. 2A
New York, NY 10024

Established in 1999 in NY.
Donor(s): Jon Rupp, Patricia Wheeler.
Financial data (yr. ended 11/30/01): Grants paid, $3,780; assets, $297,660 (M); gifts received, $107,471; expenditures, $76,479; qualifying distributions, $3,780.

Officers: Jon Rupp, Pres.; Patricia Wheeler, V.P. and Secy.; John Piccinnini, Treas.
EIN: 137211068

39457
The Arthur M. Moren, Jr. Charitable Foundation
c/o William Janetschek
172 Willow St.
Garden City, NY 11530

Donor(s): Arthur M. Moren, Jr., Jennison Assocs. Capital Corp.
Financial data (yr. ended 12/31/01): Grants paid, $3,775; assets, $67,454 (M); expenditures, $7,209; qualifying distributions, $7,155.
Limitations: Applications not accepted.
Application information: Contributes only to pre-selected organizations.
Trustees: Arthur M. Moren, Jr., Deanna F. Moren.
EIN: 226389745

39458
The Louis R. Aidala Foundation, Inc
597 Fifth Ave., 9th Fl.
New York, NY 10017

Established in 2001 in NY.
Donor(s): Louis R. Aidala.
Financial data (yr. ended 12/31/01): Grants paid, $3,750; assets, $36,276 (M); gifts received, $40,000; expenditures, $3,750; qualifying distributions, $3,750.
Limitations: Giving primarily in New York, NY.
Officers: Louis R. Aidala, Chair.; Mary Ann Aidala, V.P.; Lori Bambina, Secy.
EIN: 134167428

39459
Paul & Patricia Gioia Foundation
38 Loudon Pkwy.
Loudonville, NY 12211

Established in 2000 in NY.
Donor(s): Paul Gioia, Patricia Gioia.
Financial data (yr. ended 12/31/01): Grants paid, $3,750; assets, $363,745 (M); gifts received, $160,000; expenditures, $7,065; qualifying distributions, $3,750.
Limitations: Applications not accepted.
Application information: Contributes only to pre-selected organizations.
Trustees: Patricia Gioia, Paul Gioia.
EIN: 141828523

39460
Elizabeth T. McNamee Memorial Fund, Inc.
19 Skipper Dr.
West Islip, NY 11795

Established in 1999 in NY.
Financial data (yr. ended 09/30/00): Grants paid, $3,750; assets, $200,933 (M); gifts received, $79,665; expenditures, $18,912; qualifying distributions, $3,750.
Limitations: Applications not accepted. Giving primarily in NJ and NY.
Officers: William E. McNamee, Pres.; Francis H. McNamee, V.P.; Maria McNamee, Secy.
EIN: 113457122

39461
Blake and Dorothy Washington Scholarship Fund, Inc.
10 Hamilton Ave.
P.O. Box 1444
Monticello, NY 12701 (845) 794-5110
Contact: Edward M. Cooke, Dir.

Established in 1988 in NY.
Financial data (yr. ended 04/30/99): Grants paid, $3,750; assets, $52,813 (M); expenditures, $4,165; qualifying distributions, $4,165.

Limitations: Giving limited to Monticello, NY.
Directors: Kay Kelly Bogdan, Edward M. Cooke, William Stickney.
EIN: 222957830

39462
The Kitchawan Institute
199 Pinesbridge Rd.
Ossining, NY 10562

Established in 1999.
Financial data (yr. ended 12/31/00): Grants paid, $3,715; assets, $31,333 (M); gifts received, $45,010; expenditures, $112,760; qualifying distributions, $3,715.
Limitations: Applications not accepted.
Application information: Contributes only to pre-selected organizations.
Officer: Sue Morrow Flanagan, Pres.
Directors: Gerald Geist, Emma Weston.
EIN: 134055160

39463
Peter & Lorinda Ezersky Family Foundation
c/o Quadrangle Group, LLC
375 Park Ave.
New York, NY 10152

Established in 2000 in NY.
Donor(s): Peter Ezersky.
Financial data (yr. ended 12/31/00): Grants paid, $3,700; assets, $17,102 (M); gifts received, $22,813; expenditures, $3,700; qualifying distributions, $3,487.
Limitations: Applications not accepted. Giving primarily in NY.
Application information: Contributes only to pre-selected organizations.
Officers: Peter Ezersky, Pres.; Lorinda Ezersky, V.P.; Howard Sontag, Treas.
EIN: 134135136

39464
Foundation for the Prevention and Treatment of Eye Diseases, Inc.
c/o David M. Brickman, C.P.A.
6 E. 43rd St., 19th Fl.
New York, NY 10017

Donor(s): Jack M. Dodick.
Financial data (yr. ended 04/30/02): Grants paid, $3,700; assets, $115,776 (M); gifts received, $43,671; expenditures, $11,821; qualifying distributions, $3,700.
Limitations: Applications not accepted. Giving primarily in the New York, NY, area.
Application information: Contributes only to pre-selected organizations.
Officers: Jack M. Dodick, M.D., Pres.; Lynne Dodick, V.P.
EIN: 133374516

39465
G.S.S. Foundation, Inc.
325 W. 86th St., Ste. H3B
New York, NY 10024-3114
Contact: Simone Schenker, Secy.

Financial data (yr. ended 12/31/01): Grants paid, $3,689; assets, $17,212 (M); gifts received, $600; expenditures, $3,734; qualifying distributions, $3,689.
Application information: Application form not required.
Officer: Simone Schenker, Secy.
EIN: 237028896

39466
Berel Segal Family Foundation, Inc.
53 Trenor Dr.
New Rochelle, NY 10804

Established in 1986 in NY.
Donor(s): Edward Chernoff.
Financial data (yr. ended 12/31/01): Grants paid, $3,677; assets, $8,488 (M); expenditures, $3,684; qualifying distributions, $3,677.
Limitations: Applications not accepted. Giving primarily in NY.
Application information: Contributes only to pre-selected organizations.
Officers: Bernard Segal, Pres.; Eleanor Segal, Secy.
EIN: 133384434

39467
The Acorn Foundation
620 Park Ave.
New York, NY 10021 (212) 249-4949
Contact: Anna Glen B. Vietor, Pres.

Established in 1955 in NY.
Donor(s): Anna Glen Butler Vietor.
Financial data (yr. ended 12/31/99): Grants paid, $3,676; assets, $65,820 (L); gifts received, $222,004; expenditures, $339,294; qualifying distributions, $296,565.
Limitations: Giving primarily in NY.
Application information: Application form not required.
Officers and Directors:* Anna Glen Butler Vietor,* Pres.; David B. Vietor,* Exec. Dir.
EIN: 136098172
Codes: TN

39468
The Capek Family Foundation, Inc.
106 81st Ave.
Kew Gardens, NY 11415-1108
Contact: Zdenek A. Capek, Pres.

Donor(s): Zdenek A. Capek.
Financial data (yr. ended 12/31/01): Grants paid, $3,660; assets, $83,292 (M); gifts received, $10,000; expenditures, $3,764; qualifying distributions, $3,660.
Limitations: Giving primarily in New York, NY.
Officer: Zdenek A. Capek, Pres.
EIN: 113052481

39469
Bruce Pollak Foundation, Inc.
c/o Martin M. Pollak
16 Springwood Path
Syosset, NY 11791

Financial data (yr. ended 12/31/01): Grants paid, $3,650; assets, $33,313 (M); expenditures, $3,922; qualifying distributions, $3,650.
Limitations: Applications not accepted. Giving primarily in NY.
Application information: Contributes only to pre-selected organizations.
Officers: Martin M. Pollak, Pres.; Ellen Pollak, V.P.; Jerome I. Feldman, Secy.-Treas.
EIN: 136222529

39470
Goldin and Rivin Foundation
21 S. End Ave., Ste. 425
New York, NY 10280 (212) 571-7111
Contact: Alexander Goldin, Tr.

Established in 1999 in NY.
Financial data (yr. ended 12/31/99): Grants paid, $3,620; assets, $50,529 (M); gifts received, $50,000; expenditures, $8,988; qualifying distributions, $8,888.
Limitations: Giving primarily in New York, NY.
Trustees: Alexander Goldin, Julia Rivin.
EIN: 113497040

39471
Abraham and Florence Mendel Foundation, Inc.
(Formerly Borg-Mendel Foundation, Inc.)
17 W. 17th St., 8th Fl.
New York, NY 10011-5510

Donor(s): Mendel Group, Inc., Judah Wolf & Co., Erlanger & Co., Abraham Mendel, Florence Mendel.
Financial data (yr. ended 06/30/01): Grants paid, $3,600; assets, $4,849 (M); gifts received, $7,840; expenditures, $3,620; qualifying distributions, $3,600.
Limitations: Applications not accepted.
Application information: Contributes only to pre-selected organizations.
Officers: Florence Mendel, Pres.; Abraham Mendel, V.P.
EIN: 133394958

39472
Montgomery Fund, Inc.
(Formerly Bolton Fund, Inc.)
c/o Waldman, Hirsch & Co.
855 Ave. of the Americas, Ste. 623
New York, NY 10001

Established in 1986 in NY.
Financial data (yr. ended 11/30/01): Grants paid, $3,585; assets, $6,357 (M); gifts received, $3,019; expenditures, $3,585; qualifying distributions, $3,585.
Limitations: Applications not accepted. Giving primarily in PA.
Application information: Contributes only to pre-selected organizations.
Officer: William B. Bolton, Pres. and Treas.
EIN: 133081440

39473
The Olga and Herman Wachtenheim Foundation
10 Sealy Dr.
Lawrence, NY 11559-2420

Established in 1993 in NY.
Donor(s): Olga Wachtenheim, Herman Wachtenheim.
Financial data (yr. ended 12/31/01): Grants paid, $3,577; assets, $222,809 (M); gifts received, $37,820; expenditures, $3,681; qualifying distributions, $3,577.
Limitations: Giving primarily in NY.
Officers: Olga Wachtenheim, Pres.; Herman Wachtenheim, V.P.
EIN: 113186796

39474
The Herman & Kate Caro Foundation
583 Cedar Hill Rd.
Far Rockaway, NY 11691

Donor(s): Herman Caro, Kate Caro.
Financial data (yr. ended 12/31/01): Grants paid, $3,550; assets, $32,716 (M); gifts received, $5,000; expenditures, $3,831; qualifying distributions, $3,550.
Limitations: Applications not accepted. Giving primarily in New York, NY.
Application information: Contributes only to pre-selected organizations.
Trustee: Kate Caro.
EIN: 116077126

39475
Foundation Mireille and James Levy (USA)
c/o Steven Kamerman
509 Madison Ave., Ste. 1114
New York, NY 10022-5501
Contact: James Levy, Tr.

Established in 1993 in NY.
Donor(s): James Levy, Mireille Levy.
Financial data (yr. ended 12/31/01): Grants paid, $3,550; assets, $20,757 (M); gifts received, $5,000; expenditures, $4,231; qualifying distributions, $3,550.
Limitations: Giving primarily in Rochester, MN.
Application information: Application form not required.
Trustees: James Levy, Mireille Levy.
EIN: 133703640

39476
IMM-MIN-ED Foundation
212-75 Whitehall Terr.
Queens Village, NY 11427
Contact: Eleanor Bollag, V.P.

Donor(s): George Bollag.
Financial data (yr. ended 05/31/99): Grants paid, $3,550; assets, $4,867 (M); gifts received, $5,000; expenditures, $3,925; qualifying distributions, $3,915.
Limitations: Giving primarily in NY.
Officers: George Bollag, Pres.; Eleanor Bollag, V.P.
EIN: 112556291

39477
David G. Osterer Foundation
c/o U.E. Systems, Inc.
14 Hayes St.
Elmsford, NY 10523

Financial data (yr. ended 12/31/01): Grants paid, $3,550; assets, $62,782 (M); expenditures, $4,745; qualifying distributions, $3,550.
Limitations: Applications not accepted.
Application information: Contributes only to pre-selected organizations.
Officers: Richard Osterer, Pres.; Michael Osterer, V.P.
EIN: 136143837

39478
The George T. Whalen, Jr. Foundation, Inc.
P.O. Box AC
Millbrook, NY 12545

Established in 2000 in NY.
Financial data (yr. ended 12/31/01): Grants paid, $3,550; assets, $102,632 (M); expenditures, $5,327; qualifying distributions, $3,550.
Limitations: Giving primarily in NY.
Application information: Application form not required.
Officers: George T. Whalen, Jr., Pres.; Ann D. Whalen, V.P.; Catherine R. Shanks, Secy.; George T. Whalen III, Treas.
EIN: 141820581

39479
Joseph M. Asselta Charitable Trust
c/o Louis Leogrande
16 Gary Ave.
New Hartford, NY 13413

Financial data (yr. ended 09/30/01): Grants paid, $3,537; assets, $174,984 (M); expenditures, $10,397; qualifying distributions, $3,537.
Limitations: Applications not accepted. Giving primarily in Utica, NY.
Application information: Contributes only to pre-selected organizations.

Trustees: J.R. Buckley, Garry Kopel, Louis Leogrande.
EIN: 166251762

39480
Lena B. McClain Trust
c/o M&T Bank
1 M&T Plz., 8th Fl.
Buffalo, NY 14203
Application address: Harrisonville, PA 17728
Contact: Clifford Berkstreser

Financial data (yr. ended 12/31/01): Grants paid, $3,530; assets, $72,183 (M); expenditures, $5,017; qualifying distributions, $3,530.
Limitations: Giving limited to Fulton County, PA.
Application information: Application form required.
Trustee: M & T Bank.
EIN: 236487847

39481
Elmo M. Royce Benevolent Fund
c/o HSBC Bank USA
P.O. Box 4203
Buffalo, NY 14240-4203

Established in 1987 in NY.
Financial data (yr. ended 12/31/01): Grants paid, $3,523; assets, $94,158 (M); expenditures, $4,966; qualifying distributions, $3,523.
Limitations: Applications not accepted. Giving primarily in NY.
Application information: Contributes only to pre-selected organizations.
Trustee: HSBC Bank USA.
EIN: 237004843

39482
Irving Wexler Foundation, Inc.
c/o Lila Greene
20 Chapel Pl., Ste. 2H
Great Neck, NY 11021

Financial data (yr. ended 11/30/01): Grants paid, $3,510; assets, $75,453 (M); expenditures, $4,744; qualifying distributions, $3,510.
Limitations: Applications not accepted. Giving primarily in NY.
Application information: Contributes only to pre-selected organizations.
Officers: Allan B. Greene, Pres.; Lila Greene, Secy.-Treas.
EIN: 116011322

39483
Mary Curtin Scholarship Trust
467 Foster Rd.
Vestal, NY 13850 (607) 754-7216
Contact: Michael J. Fidler, Tr.

Established in 1998 in NY.
Financial data (yr. ended 12/31/99): Grants paid, $3,500; assets, $15,781 (M); gifts received, $8,387; expenditures, $4,387; qualifying distributions, $3,500.
Limitations: Giving primarily in NY.
Trustees: Martin Curtin, Kathleen M Dwyer, Jeri Fidler, Meaghan Fidler, Michael J. Fidler.
EIN: 166467199

39484
Marion & Ben Duffy Foundation
c/o James A. Kelly, Jr.
15 Beekman St., Ste. 1000
New York, NY 10038-1509 (212) 267-5556

Financial data (yr. ended 12/31/01): Grants paid, $3,500; assets, $19,469 (M); expenditures, $3,651; qualifying distributions, $3,500.
Limitations: Applications not accepted.
Application information: Contributes only to pre-selected organizations.
Trustees: James A. Kelly, Jr., Regina M. Kelly.
EIN: 136212653

39485
Gelfand Generations, Inc.
99 DuBois Ave.
Sea Cliff, NY 11579

Financial data (yr. ended 09/30/01): Grants paid, $3,500; assets, $61,957 (M); gifts received, $3,083; expenditures, $3,580; qualifying distributions, $3,500.
Limitations: Applications not accepted. Giving primarily in NY.
Application information: Contributes only to pre-selected organizations.
Officers and Directors:* Joe Brodie,* Pres.; Jeffrey Lavender,* Secy.-Treas.; Gerald Aldrich, Jackie Ferkin, Howard Forbes, Gail Glick, Jacob Gordon, Miriam Klein, Isidore Schwartz.
EIN: 133407449

39486
The Gittleson Foundation
c/o Tarlow & Tarlow
1505 Kellum Pl.
Mineola, NY 11501

Established in 1994 in NY.
Donor(s): Allan Gittleson.
Financial data (yr. ended 12/31/00): Grants paid, $3,500; assets, $51,134 (M); gifts received, $3,000; expenditures, $4,436; qualifying distributions, $3,500.
Limitations: Applications not accepted.
Application information: Contributes only to pre-selected organizations.
Officers: Allan Gittleson, Pres.; June Gittleson, Mgr.
EIN: 116037665

39487
Michael Howard Educational Trust
c/o JPMorgan Chase Bank
P.O. Box 31412
Rochester, NY 14603-1412

Financial data (yr. ended 01/31/01): Grants paid, $3,500; assets, $123,181 (M); expenditures, $5,226; qualifying distributions, $3,726.
Limitations: Applications not accepted. Giving primarily to residents of NY.
Trustee: JPMorgan Chase Bank.
EIN: 166073270

39488
The Allan I. Kanter Charitable Foundation
4936 Tanglewood Ln.
Manlius, NY 13104

Established in 1992 in NY.
Donor(s): Allan I. Kanter.
Financial data (yr. ended 12/31/01): Grants paid, $3,500; assets, $18,805 (M); expenditures, $3,643; qualifying distributions, $3,500.
Limitations: Applications not accepted. Giving primarily in Syracuse, NY.
Application information: Contributes only to pre-selected organizations.
Trustees: Allan I. Kanter, Rita Kanter.
EIN: 166371916

39489
The Marlene A. Kaplan Foundation, Inc.
c/o Gary Kaplan
15 Sherwood Ln.
Cedarhurst, NY 11516

Financial data (yr. ended 12/31/00): Grants paid, $3,500; assets, $53,301 (M); gifts received, $1,000; expenditures, $3,617; qualifying distributions, $3,500.
Limitations: Applications not accepted. Giving primarily in Hewlett, Lawrence and New Hyde Park, NY.
Application information: Contributes only to pre-selected organizations.
Officer: Gary Kaplan, Mgr.
EIN: 113373504

39490
Philip Lehman Foundation, Inc.
c/o Hertz, Herson and Co., LLP
2 Park Ave., Ste. 1500
New York, NY 10016

Financial data (yr. ended 12/31/01): Grants paid, $3,500; assets, $140,758 (M); expenditures, $4,396; qualifying distributions, $3,500.
Limitations: Applications not accepted. Giving primarily in Sun Valley, ID, and New York, NY.
Application information: Contributes only to pre-selected organizations.
Officers: Philip H. Isles, Pres.; Paul E. Manheim, V.P.; Paul C. Guth, Secy.-Treas.
EIN: 136094017

39491
James E. Nunn Memorial Foundation, Inc.
c/o John Dillonm
286 Genesee St.
Utica, NY 13502-4639
Contact: John Dillon, Treas.

Financial data (yr. ended 11/30/01): Grants paid, $3,500; assets, $58,167 (M); gifts received, $990; expenditures, $3,689; qualifying distributions, $3,461.
Limitations: Giving primarily in NY.
Officers: Norma Schug, Pres.; Justin Kelly, Secy.; John Dillon, Treas.
EIN: 161129057

39492
Patriotic National Non-Profit Protestant Researchers, Inc.
P.O. Box 463
Baldwin Place, NY 10505

Donor(s): William Godsen,‡ Lucille Godsen.‡
Financial data (yr. ended 03/31/99): Grants paid, $3,500; assets, $96,380 (M); expenditures, $5,712; qualifying distributions, $5,551.
Limitations: Applications not accepted. Giving primarily in NY.
Officers: Nancy Godsen, Pres.; Constance Godsen, V.P.; Anthony Haruch, Secy.-Treas.
EIN: 237379939

39493
The Righteous Babe Foundation, Inc.
P.O. Box 95, Ellicot Sta.
Buffalo, NY 14205-0095

Established in 1998 in NY.
Donor(s): Righteous Babe Records, Inc.
Financial data (yr. ended 06/30/02): Grants paid, $3,500; assets, $31,009 (M); gifts received, $200; expenditures, $5,412; qualifying distributions, $3,500.
Limitations: Applications not accepted. Giving primarily in NY.
Application information: Contributes only to pre-selected organizations.
Officers: Ani DiFranco, Pres.; Scot Fisher, V.P.; Rocco Lucente II, Secy.
EIN: 161546071
Codes: CS, CD

39494
U.S.-China Educational Fund, Inc.
(Formerly The C. T. Loo Chinese Educational Fund, Inc.)
c/o C.T. Wu
320 Albany Post Rd.
Croton-on-Hudson, NY 10520
Contact: C.T. Wu, Pres.

Financial data (yr. ended 02/28/02): Grants paid, $3,500; assets, $112,688 (M); expenditures, $10,848; qualifying distributions, $3,500.
Limitations: Giving limited to NY.
Application information: Application form not required.
Officers: C.T. Wu, Pres.; Lionel Tsao, Secy.; Lydia Chang, Treas.
EIN: 136096706

39495
Michael H. Lerner Foundation
c/o Squadron, Ellenoff, et al.
551 5th Ave.
New York, NY 10176

Established in 1994.
Donor(s): Michael H. Lerner.
Financial data (yr. ended 12/31/01): Grants paid, $3,450; assets, $6,702 (M); expenditures, $5,172; qualifying distributions, $3,450.
Limitations: Applications not accepted. Giving primarily in New York, NY.
Application information: Contributes only to pre-selected organizations.
Officer and Directors:* Michael H. Lerner,* Pres.; Brett Mayer.
EIN: 510363067

39496
Joe's World Foundation
c/o Joe Patane
P.O. Box 8465
New York, NY 10116-8465

Financial data (yr. ended 12/31/01): Grants paid, $3,440; assets, $112 (M); gifts received, $47,379; expenditures, $38,042; qualifying distributions, $3,440.
Officers and Directors:* Mary Anna Patane,* Secy.; Joe Patane, Exec. Dir.; Philip Patane, Sr.
EIN: 134077232

39497
The Roschen Foundation, Inc.
60 E. 42nd St., No. 1760
New York, NY 10165

Financial data (yr. ended 10/31/01): Grants paid, $3,410; assets, $111,364 (M); expenditures, $5,252; qualifying distributions, $3,410.
Limitations: Applications not accepted. Giving primarily in NY.
Application information: Contributes only to pre-selected organizations.
Officers and Directors:* Otto T. Roschen,* Pres.; William E. Roschen, Jr.,* Secy.-Treas.; Delphine A. Roschen.
EIN: 136134641

39498
Tosei Foundation
271 Central Park W.
New York, NY 10024 (212) 595-2623
Contact: Gordon Cotler, Tr.

Financial data (yr. ended 07/31/02): Grants paid, $3,405; assets, $45,048 (M); gifts received, $2,700; expenditures, $4,372; qualifying distributions, $3,405.
Limitations: Giving primarily in New York, NY.
Trustee: Gordon Cotler.

EIN: 136158850

39499
Presidential Life Insurance Company Foundation, Inc.
c/o Presidential Life Corp.
69 Lydecker St.
Nyack, NY 10960

Established in 1989 in NY.
Donor(s): Presidential Life Insurance Co.
Financial data (yr. ended 12/31/01): Grants paid, $3,400; assets, $2,629 (M); expenditures, $3,425; qualifying distributions, $2,999.
Limitations: Applications not accepted. Giving primarily in NY.
Application information: Contributes only to pre-selected organizations.
Officers and Directors:* Herbert Kurz,* Pres.; Stanley Rubin, V.P.; Morton Silberman.
EIN: 133512544
Codes: CS, CD

39500
Murray Kramer Foundation, Inc.
200 Garden City Plz., Ste. 202
Garden City, NY 11530

Financial data (yr. ended 03/31/02): Grants paid, $3,395; assets, $2,983 (M); gifts received, $6,000; expenditures, $3,873; qualifying distributions, $3,395.
Limitations: Giving limited to NY.
Officer: Herbert G. Kramer, Pres.
EIN: 116033747

39501
Isabelle and Jerome E. Hyman Foundation
c/o Cleary, Gottlieb, Steen & Hamilton
1 Liberty Plz.
New York, NY 10006-1470

Established in 1986 in NY.
Donor(s): Jerome E. Hyman.
Financial data (yr. ended 11/30/01): Grants paid, $3,355; assets, $126,956 (M); expenditures, $4,162; qualifying distributions, $3,405.
Limitations: Applications not accepted. Giving primarily in New York, NY.
Application information: Contributes only to pre-selected organizations.
Trustees: Isabelle M. Hyman, Jerome E. Hyman.
EIN: 133386437

39502
Viener Foundation, Inc.
c/o Christy & Viener
620 5th Ave.
New York, NY 10020-2402

Donor(s): John D. Viener.
Financial data (yr. ended 12/31/01): Grants paid, $3,350; assets, $44,086 (M); expenditures, $4,211; qualifying distributions, $3,350.
Limitations: Applications not accepted.
Application information: Contributes only to pre-selected organizations.
Officer: John D. Viener, Pres.
EIN: 133669547

39503
Simcha Foundation, Inc.
430 E. 86th St., Apt. 7C
New York, NY 10028-6401

Financial data (yr. ended 09/30/01): Grants paid, $3,320; assets, $3,893 (M); gifts received, $3,378; expenditures, $3,645; qualifying distributions, $3,320.
Limitations: Applications not accepted. Giving primarily in New York, NY.

Application information: Contributes only to pre-selected organizations.
Officers: Seymour Kramer, Pres. and Treas.; Gail A. Kramer, Secy.
EIN: 133118381

39504
Andrew J. Baum Memorial Foundation, Inc.
150 E. 69th St.
New York, NY 10021 (212) 239-0080
Contact: Myron Baum, Pres.

Donor(s): Andrew Textile Corp.
Financial data (yr. ended 11/30/01): Grants paid, $3,316; assets, $16,115 (M); gifts received, $3,565; expenditures, $3,389; qualifying distributions, $3,307.
Limitations: Giving primarily in New York, NY.
Officers and Directors:* Myron Baum,* Pres.; Barbara Baum,* Secy.-Treas.; Charles Baum.
EIN: 112442926

39505
Cora A. Goodell and Menzo W. Goodell Scholarship Endowment Trust
c/o Wilber National Bank
245 Main St.
Oneonta, NY 13820-2502
Contact: Joan Van Valkenberg or Lawrence Bobnick

Established in 1987 in NY.
Financial data (yr. ended 12/31/01): Grants paid, $3,316; assets, $131,619 (M); expenditures, $5,839; qualifying distributions, $4,196.
Limitations: Applications not accepted. Giving limited to Worcester, NY.
Application information: Unsolicited requests for funds not accepted.
Trustee: Wilber National Bank.
EIN: 166272694

39506
The Nina Carroll Foundation
c/o John L. Carroll
515 Madison Ave., 32nd Fl.
New York, NY 10022

Financial data (yr. ended 12/31/01): Grants paid, $3,305; assets, $37,687 (M); expenditures, $4,784; qualifying distributions, $3,305.
Directors: Cornelia Carroll, John Lee Carroll, John Lee Carroll, Jr.
EIN: 133831481

39507
Kenneth M. Axtell, Jr. Foundation
c/o NBT Bank, N.A.
52 S. Broad St.
Norwich, NY 13815
Application address: c/o Branch Mgr., NBT Bank, N.A., 105 Front St., Deposit, NY 13754

Established in 1992 in NY.
Donor(s): Kenneth M. Axtell, Jr.
Financial data (yr. ended 06/30/02): Grants paid, $3,300; assets, $65,969 (M); expenditures, $3,816; qualifying distributions, $3,300.
Limitations: Giving limited to Delaware County and Deposit, NY.
Application information: Application form required.
Trustee: NBT Bank, N.A.
EIN: 166376529

39508
The Cobble Creek Foundation
c/o Nathan Berkman & Co.
29 Broadway, Ste. 2900
New York, NY 10006

Established in 1999 in CT.

Donor(s): Todd Rubin, Jon M. Rubin.
Financial data (yr. ended 05/31/01): Grants paid, $3,295; assets, $88,580 (M); expenditures, $14,667; qualifying distributions, $3,295.
Limitations: Applications not accepted.
Application information: Contributes only to pre-selected organizations.
Trustees: Jon M. Rubin, Todd Rubin.
EIN: 134060087

39509
Wang Family Foundation
1064 E. 64th St.
Brooklyn, NY 11210
Application address: 1064 E. 27th St., Brooklyn, NY 11210
Contact: Leonard Wang, Dir.

Established in 1999 in NY.
Financial data (yr. ended 12/31/01): Grants paid, $3,261; assets, $50,557 (M); expenditures, $3,936; qualifying distributions, $3,261.
Directors: Leonard Wang, Sabine Wang.
EIN: 134026361

39510
Figliolia Foundation Trust
1 Wall Street Ct.
New York, NY 10005
Donor(s): George Figliolia.
Financial data (yr. ended 12/31/99): Grants paid, $3,260; assets, $249,421 (M); gifts received, $52,000; expenditures, $6,291; qualifying distributions, $4,665.
Application information: Application form required.
Trustees: George Figliolia, Martin Riker.
EIN: 133922569

39511
Adamson Foundation, Inc.
c/o U.S. Trust
114 W. 47th St., TaxVas
New York, NY 10036-1594

Established in 1997 in MD.
Donor(s): Dorothea K. Lyas.
Financial data (yr. ended 12/31/01): Grants paid, $3,250; assets, $109,686 (M); expenditures, $4,622; qualifying distributions, $3,250.
Limitations: Applications not accepted.
Application information: Contributes only to pre-selected organizations.
Directors: Chester W. Gould, Dorothea K. Lyas, Karla N. Lyas.
EIN: 522069920

39512
Klein Foundation, Inc.
c/o L. Wollin
350 5th Ave., Ste. 2822
New York, NY 10118

Donor(s): Larry Klein.
Financial data (yr. ended 03/31/00): Grants paid, $3,250; assets, $79,390 (M); gifts received, $13,000; expenditures, $3,586; qualifying distributions, $3,247.
Limitations: Applications not accepted.
Application information: Contributes only to pre-selected organizations.
Officers: Larry Klein, Pres.; Lonnie Wollin, Secy.
EIN: 133864130

39513
Helen Mayer Charitable Trust
c/o Fleet National Bank
1 East Ave., NYRO3072
Rochester, NY 14638

Established in 1959 in NY.
Donor(s): Helen Shumway Mayer.
Financial data (yr. ended 11/30/01): Grants paid, $3,250; assets, $29,763 (M); expenditures, $3,346; qualifying distributions, $3,312.
Limitations: Applications not accepted. Giving primarily in New England.
Application information: Unsolicited requests for funds not considered or acknowledged.
Trustee: Fleet National Bank.
EIN: 166022958

39514
Mukhopadhyay Foundation, Inc.
210 Kingsland Ave.
Brooklyn, NY 11223

Established in 2001 in NY.
Donor(s): Rama Mukhopadhyay.
Financial data (yr. ended 12/31/01): Grants paid, $3,250; assets, $3,632 (M); gifts received, $7,100; expenditures, $3,468; qualifying distributions, $3,250.
Directors: Manjula Mukhopadhyay, Rama Mukhopadhyay, Sonaal Mukhopadhyay.
EIN: 582634086

39515
Richard H. & Cynthia A. Thompson Foundation
19 Onondaga St.
Rye, NY 10580-1719

Established in 1999 in TX.
Donor(s): Richard H. Thompson, Cynthia A. Thompson.
Financial data (yr. ended 12/31/00): Grants paid, $3,250; assets, $76,456 (M); gifts received, $12,000; expenditures, $5,375; qualifying distributions, $3,077.
Limitations: Applications not accepted.
Application information: Contributes only to pre-selected organizations.
Officers and Directors:* Cynthia A. Thompson,* Pres.; Richard H. Thompson,* V.P. and Secy.; Robert E. Thompson, Sr.
EIN: 752833621

39516
The Tietz Family Foundation
95 Reid Ave.
Port Washington, NY 11050

Established in 2000 in NY.
Donor(s): Larry Tietz.
Financial data (yr. ended 12/31/01): Grants paid, $3,250; assets, $25,548 (M); expenditures, $4,511; qualifying distributions, $3,250.
Limitations: Applications not accepted. Giving primarily in Port Washington, NY.
Application information: Contributes only to pre-selected organizations.
Director: Larry Tietz.
EIN: 137227588

39517
Lynn E. & Mattie G. McConnell Scholarship
c/o Bath National Bank
44 Liberty St.
Bath, NY 14810
Contact: B. Graham

Established in 1999 in NY.
Financial data (yr. ended 12/31/99): Grants paid, $3,243; assets, $285,392 (M); expenditures, $3,594; qualifying distributions, $3,243.
Application information: Application form required.
Trustee: Bath National Bank.
EIN: 166237717

39518
Metals Foundation, Inc.
c/o Theodore L. Diamond
30 Rockefeller Plz.
New York, NY 10112

Financial data (yr. ended 12/31/01): Grants paid, $3,240; assets, $98,435 (M); expenditures, $3,320; qualifying distributions, $3,299.
Limitations: Applications not accepted. Giving primarily in NY.
Application information: Contributes only to pre-selected organizations.
Officer: Theodore L. Diamond, Pres.
EIN: 136199751

39519
The D.T. Foundation, Inc.
120 East End Ave.
New York, NY 10028

Established in 1985 in NY.
Donor(s): David Tendler.
Financial data (yr. ended 06/30/02): Grants paid, $3,230; assets, $231 (M); gifts received, $32,642; expenditures, $34,444; qualifying distributions, $3,230.
Limitations: Applications not accepted. Giving primarily in New York, NY.
Application information: Contributes only to pre-selected organizations.
Trustees: Beatrice Tendler, David Tendler, Karen Tendler, Pearl Tendler.
EIN: 133315585

39520
Nutritional Research and Educational Foundation, Inc.
36 E. 36th St., Ste. 204
New York, NY 10016   (212) 213-3360
Contact: Linda Isaacs, Treas.

Financial data (yr. ended 04/30/01): Grants paid, $3,229; assets, $3,308 (M); gifts received, $5,525; expenditures, $5,137; qualifying distributions, $3,229.
Officers: Nicholas J. Gonzalez, M.D., Pres.; Linda Isaacs, Treas.
EIN: 133768831

39521
Tibbets Scholarship Trust
c/o JPMorgan Chase Bank
P.O. Box 31412
Rochester, NY 14603-1412
Application address: c/o Patricia Cyganovich, Principal, North Salem Central School District, Rte. 124, N. Salem, NY 10560

Financial data (yr. ended 12/31/00): Grants paid, $3,226; assets, $88,856 (M); expenditures, $4,539; qualifying distributions, $3,398.
Limitations: Giving limited to the North Salem Central School District, NY.
Application information: Application form required.
Trustee: JPMorgan Chase Bank.
EIN: 136283227

39522
The J. Marberger Stuart Foundation, Inc.
c/o Richard J. Stuart
369 Carpenter Ave.
Sea Cliff, NY 11579

Established in 1993 in NY.
Donor(s): Marjorie L. Stuart, Jane R. Stuart.
Financial data (yr. ended 12/31/99): Grants paid, $3,218; assets, $6,485 (M); gifts received, $9,000; expenditures, $3,345; qualifying distributions, $3,218.

39522—NEW YORK

Limitations: Applications not accepted.
Officers and Directors:* Jane Ruth Stuart,* Pres. and Treas.; Richard J. Stuart, Sr. V.P.; Alice M. Stuart,* V.P. and Secy.
EIN: 113151120

39523
Godfrey J. Jacobsen Memorial Scholarship Fund
c/o George T. Wolf
150 Perinton Hills Off. Pk.
Fairport, NY 14450-9107
Application address: c/o James E. Sperry High School, 1799 Lehigh Sta. Rd., Henrietta, NY 14467
Contact: Frank Giannone, Guidance Off.

Donor(s): Godfrey J. Jacobsen.‡
Financial data (yr. ended 05/31/00): Grants paid, $3,200; assets, $134,351 (M); expenditures, $4,407; qualifying distributions, $4,407.
Limitations: Giving limited to Henrietta, NY.
Application information: Application form required.
Officers and Directors:* Ruth S. Stork,* Pres.; Lowell T. Twitchell,* V.P.; George T. Wolf,* Secy.-Treas.
EIN: 161206307

39524
The Lutton Foundation
11 Donbrook Rd.
Pound Ridge, NY 10576

Established in 1989 in NY.
Donor(s): James H. Lynch, Jr., James E. Lutton.
Financial data (yr. ended 11/30/01): Grants paid, $3,200; assets, $4,133 (M); gifts received, $6,312; expenditures, $3,395; qualifying distributions, $3,200.
Limitations: Applications not accepted. Giving primarily in the tri-state CT, NJ, and NY, area.
Application information: Contributes only to pre-selected organizations.
Officers: James E. Lutton, Pres.; Carl H. Hewitt, Secy.-Treas.
EIN: 133539167

39525
Lillian S. Alexander Foundation, Inc.
52 Windmill Ct.
Huntington Station, NY 11746

Established in 1998 in NY.
Donor(s): Lillian S. Alexander.
Financial data (yr. ended 07/31/02): Grants paid, $3,181; assets, $8,880 (M); gifts received, $2,865; expenditures, $3,761; qualifying distributions, $3,181.
Limitations: Applications not accepted. Giving limited to Bronx, NY.
Application information: Contributes only to pre-selected organizations.
Officers: Lillian S. Alexander, Pres.; Norman J. Slawsky, V.P.; Donna Slawsky-Leon, Secy.; Renee Slawsky-Scalise, Treas.
EIN: 134022435

39526
Pan Karabournian Society of Minas, Inc.
28-07 Hobart St.
Woodside, NY 11377-7818
Contact: Nicholas Tassa, Pres.

Financial data (yr. ended 12/31/01): Grants paid, $3,180; assets, $57,276 (M); expenditures, $4,277; qualifying distributions, $3,180.
Limitations: Giving primarily in Jamaica, NY.
Officers: Nicholas Tassa, Pres.; Sophia Sideris, Treas.
EIN: 112676996

39527
Perl Rosenbach Hendel Foundation
7922 21st Ave.
Brooklyn, NY 11214 (718) 259-9398
Contact: Perl Hendel, Pres.

Established in 1989 in NY as a successor to the Joseph Rosenbach Foundation which was established in 1962.
Financial data (yr. ended 11/30/01): Grants paid, $3,173; assets, $61,211 (M); gifts received, $2,150; expenditures, $3,495; qualifying distributions, $3,229.
Officers: Perl Hendel, Pres.; Bonnie Besdim, V.P.; Abraham Hendel, Secy.; Amy Basson, Treas.
EIN: 112996143

39528
Jewish Charities Fund, Inc.
521 5th Ave., 24th Fl.
New York, NY 10175-0083

Donor(s): Rhoda Blumberg.
Financial data (yr. ended 11/30/01): Grants paid, $3,172; assets, $120,312 (M); expenditures, $4,997; qualifying distributions, $3,172.
Limitations: Applications not accepted.
Application information: Contributes only to pre-selected organizations.
Officers: Gerald Blumberg, Pres.; Rhoda Blumberg, V.P. and Secy.; Lawrence S. Blumberg, Treas.
EIN: 136115432

39529
Burton & Paula Geyer Foundation
P.O. Box 404
Pound Ridge, NY 10576 (914) 764-0250
Contact: Burton or Paula Geyer

Established in 1986 in NY.
Donor(s): Burton Geyer, Paula Geyer.
Financial data (yr. ended 11/30/01): Grants paid, $3,170; assets, $11,834 (M); gifts received, $10,000; expenditures, $3,170; qualifying distributions, $3,170.
Limitations: Giving on a national basis.
Trustees: Burton Geyer, Paula Geyer.
EIN: 112850558

39530
Jack Haim Charitable Trust
52 Riverside Ave.
New York, NY 10024

Established in 1985 in NY.
Donor(s): Jack D. Haim.
Financial data (yr. ended 11/30/01): Grants paid, $3,150; assets, $26,258 (M); expenditures, $3,423; qualifying distributions, $3,423.
Limitations: Applications not accepted. Giving primarily in NY.
Application information: Contributes only to pre-selected organizations.
Trustee: Jack D. Haim.
EIN: 136864168

39531
Marvin L. and Joyce A. Hartstein Foundation, Inc.
c/o Robert S. Braunschweig
420 Lexington Ave., No. 336
New York, NY 10170-0399

Established in 1986 in NY.
Donor(s): Marvin L. Hartstein, Joyce A. Hartstein.
Financial data (yr. ended 11/30/01): Grants paid, $3,150; assets, $5,354 (M); gifts received, $96; expenditures, $3,396; qualifying distributions, $3,150.
Limitations: Applications not accepted. Giving primarily in New York, NY.
Application information: Contributes only to pre-selected organizations.
Directors: Robert S. Braunschweig, Joyce A. Hartstein, Marvin L. Hartstein.
EIN: 133382030

39532
Eva & Harvey Kivelson Foundation, Inc.
35 E. 75th St.
New York, NY 10021-2761
Contact: Arnold Kivelson, Secy.-Treas.

Financial data (yr. ended 12/31/01): Grants paid, $3,150; assets, $176,500 (M); expenditures, $6,319; qualifying distributions, $3,150.
Limitations: Applications not accepted. Giving primarily in New York, NY.
Application information: Contributes only to pre-selected organizations.
Officer and Director:* Arnold Kivelson,* Secy.-Treas.
EIN: 136095762

39533
MIY Foundation
c/o Uri Langer
1823 49th St.
Brooklyn, NY 11204

Established in 2000 in NY.
Financial data (yr. ended 12/31/01): Grants paid, $3,150; assets, $55,411 (M); gifts received, $40,000; expenditures, $5,559; qualifying distributions, $3,150.
Limitations: Applications not accepted.
Application information: Contributes only to pre-selected organizations.
Trustees: Marsha Langner, Uri Langner.
EIN: 113579303

39534
Peterson Family Charitable Trust
c/o GWC
P.O. Box 7
Fly Creek, NY 13337

Established in 1994 in NY.
Donor(s): Earle Peterson, Cynthia Peterson, James Peterson.
Financial data (yr. ended 12/31/99): Grants paid, $3,150; assets, $798,759 (M); gifts received, $159,250; expenditures, $56,804; qualifying distributions, $146,642; giving activities include $128,314 for loans to individuals and $12,254 for programs.
Limitations: Applications not accepted. Giving limited to NY.
Application information: Contributes only to pre-selected organizations.
Trustees: Cynthia Peterson, Earle Peterson, James Peterson, Susan Peterson.
EIN: 161450463

39535
Margaret B. Tilt Scholarship Trust
c/o Orange County Trust Co.
75 North St.
Middletown, NY 10940-5022
Application address: c/o Allan Newton, Supervising Principal, Warwick Valley Central School District, Warwick, NY 10990, tel.: (914) 986-1181

Financial data (yr. ended 12/31/01): Grants paid, $3,130; assets, $16,808 (M); gifts received, $300; expenditures, $5,249; qualifying distributions, $3,130.
Limitations: Giving limited to residents of Warwick, NY.

Application information: Application form required.
Trustee: Orange County Trust Co.
EIN: 146086361
Codes: GTI

39536
Gollin Foundation
535 E. 86th St., Apt. 1C
New York, NY 10028-7533

Established in 1952 in NY.
Donor(s): Joshua G. Gollin.‡
Financial data (yr. ended 12/31/01): Grants paid, $3,125; assets, $53,963 (M); expenditures, $3,296; qualifying distributions, $3,125.
Limitations: Applications not accepted.
Application information: Contributes only to pre-selected organizations.
Officers: James Gollin, Pres. and Treas.; John Geoffrey Gollin, V.P. and Secy.
Director: Jane F. Gollin.
EIN: 136161257

39537
William F. Riecker Foundation, Inc.
350 5th Ave.
New York, NY 10118-0110
Application address: 690 Union Blvd., Totowa, NJ 07512-2208
Contact: Alfred J. Riecker, Treas.

Donor(s): William H. Riecker.
Financial data (yr. ended 12/31/99): Grants paid, $3,125; assets, $122,325 (M); expenditures, $3,446; qualifying distributions, $3,446.
Limitations: Giving primarily in NJ and NY.
Application information: Application form not required.
Officer and Trustees:* Alfred J. Riecker,* Treas.; Mildred H. Caradine.
EIN: 277060618

39538
The Mordecai & Elinor Gabriel Foundation, Inc.
(Formerly The David & Emily Rosenstein Foundation, Inc.)
c/o Mordecai L. Gabriel
120 Old Mill Rd.
Great Neck, NY 11023-1936

Donor(s): Mordecai L. Gabriel.
Financial data (yr. ended 12/31/01): Grants paid, $3,105; assets, $52,049 (M); expenditures, $3,205; qualifying distributions, $3,205.
Limitations: Applications not accepted. Giving primarily in NY.
Application information: Contributes only to pre-selected organizations.
Officers: Mordecai L. Gabriel, Pres.; Elinor Gabriel, Secy.
EIN: 136161374

39539
The John Mauro Memorial Scholarship Fund
c/o NBT Bank, N.A.
52 S. Broad St.
Norwich, NY 13815

Established in 1988 in NY.
Financial data (yr. ended 12/31/01): Grants paid, $3,100; assets, $64,411 (M); expenditures, $3,651; qualifying distributions, $3,100.
Limitations: Giving limited to Gloversville, NY.
Application information: Application form required.
Trustee: NBT Bank, N.A.
EIN: 146138823

39540
The Seris Foundation
4720 Delafield Ave.
Riverdale, NY 10471-3312

Established in 1997 in NY.
Donor(s): Israel Lefkowitz.
Financial data (yr. ended 12/31/01): Grants paid, $3,100; assets, $244,720 (M); gifts received, $22,000; expenditures, $7,611; qualifying distributions, $3,100.
Limitations: Applications not accepted.
Application information: Contributes only to pre-selected organizations.
Directors: Daniel A. Klapper, David A. Klapper, Erika P. Klapper, Raphael M. Klapper.
EIN: 133969875

39541
Zedek, Inc.
1725 52nd St.
Brooklyn, NY 11204-1516

Donor(s): Hillel Meyers.
Financial data (yr. ended 07/31/02): Grants paid, $3,064; assets, $563 (M); gifts received, $3,500; expenditures, $3,064; qualifying distributions, $3,064.
Limitations: Applications not accepted. Giving primarily in the metropolitan New York, NY, area.
Application information: Contributes only to pre-selected organizations.
Officer: Hillel Meyers, Pres.
EIN: 237146574

39542
Key to Health Foundation, Inc.
c/o L. Wollin
350 5th Ave., Ste. 2822
New York, NY 10118

Established in 1996.
Donor(s): Ann Louise Gittleman.
Financial data (yr. ended 06/30/01): Grants paid, $3,038; assets, $33,384 (M); gifts received, $50; expenditures, $7,737; qualifying distributions, $3,098.
Limitations: Applications not accepted. Giving primarily in New York, NY.
Application information: Contributes only to pre-selected organizations.
Officers: Ann Louise Gittleman, Pres.; Stuart Gittleman, V.P.; Lonnie Wollin, Secy.
EIN: 223482455

39543
Ruth M. Thomas Trust
c/o JPMorgan Chase Bank
P.O. Box 31412
Rochester, NY 14603-1412

Financial data (yr. ended 12/31/01): Grants paid, $3,032; assets, $116,082 (M); expenditures, $4,779; qualifying distributions, $3,179.
Limitations: Applications not accepted. Giving primarily in NY.
Application information: Contributes only to pre-selected organizations.
Trustee: JPMorgan Chase Bank.
EIN: 166253027

39544
Harold C. Burns Scholarship Fund
(also known as C. Burns Scholarship Fund)
c/o HSBC Bank USA
1 HSBC Ctr., 16th Fl.
Buffalo, NY 14203

Financial data (yr. ended 08/31/01): Grants paid, $3,000; assets, $85,235 (M); expenditures, $4,347; qualifying distributions, $3,159.

Limitations: Applications not accepted. Giving primarily in NY.
Trustee: HSBC Bank USA.
EIN: 166245166

39545
Camillus Optimist College Scholarship Fund
c/o A. Adorante
P.O. Box 600
Camillus, NY 13031 (315) 487-0210
Application address: c/o Community Service Awards, P.O. Box 33, Camillas, NY 13031

Financial data (yr. ended 08/31/01): Grants paid, $3,000; assets, $51,704 (M); gifts received, $79; expenditures, $3,079; qualifying distributions, $3,000.
Limitations: Giving limited to residents in Camillas, NY.
Application information: Application form required.
Officers: David Kenna, Pres.; Cheryl Crocket, Secy.; Anthony P. Adorante, Treas.
Directors: Lucille Adorante, Jay David Dickinson, Marlene Dickinson, Lorraine Gordon, William R. Gordon, Marie Kenna.
EIN: 161499188

39546
Deakins Family Charitable Foundation
3 Woodpath Dr.
Northport, NY 11768-3519
Application address: P.O. Box 1034, West Diver, VT 05356, tel.: (212) 422-1626
Contact: William Deakins, Tr.

Established in 2000 in NY.
Financial data (yr. ended 10/31/01): Grants paid, $3,000; assets, $58,476 (M); gifts received, $60,000; expenditures, $3,000; qualifying distributions, $2,985.
Limitations: Giving primarily in New York, NY.
Trustee: William Deakins.
EIN: 223771987

39547
Horst and Ruth Denk Foundation, Inc.
563 Park Ave.
New York, NY 10021-7314
Contact: Ruth E. Denk, Pres.

Donor(s): Ruth E. Denk.
Financial data (yr. ended 12/31/01): Grants paid, $3,000; assets, $3,221 (M); expenditures, $3,450; qualifying distributions, $3,000.
Limitations: Giving primarily in New York, NY.
Application information: Application form not required.
Officer: Ruth E. Denk, Pres.
EIN: 133142251

39548
East Williston Teachers' Association Scholarship Foundation
c/o The Wheatley School
11 Bacon Rd.
Old Westbury, NY 11568-1599

Established in 1996 in NY.
Financial data (yr. ended 12/31/99): Grants paid, $3,000; assets, $12,592 (M); gifts received, $18,525; expenditures, $11,826; qualifying distributions, $11,826.
Limitations: Giving limited to NY.
Trustees: David K. Israel, Chair.; Robert J. Bernstein, Majorie Mayerson, Roslyn Thurm.
EIN: 113321870

39549
B. Jeffrey Ebbels Memorial Scholarship Trust
283 Thompson Blvd.
Watertown, NY 13601-3622

Financial data (yr. ended 12/31/01): Grants paid, $3,000; assets, $8,809 (M); gifts received, $3,100; expenditures, $3,000; qualifying distributions, $3,000.
Trustee: Leo Archer.
EIN: 161074649

39550
Awdry G. Flickinger Family Foundation
c/o Charles E. Milch
P.O. Box 60
Buffalo, NY 14240

Established in 1996 in NY.
Financial data (yr. ended 05/31/01): Grants paid, $3,000; assets, $31,766 (M); expenditures, $3,128; qualifying distributions, $3,000.
Limitations: Applications not accepted. Giving limited to Buffalo, NY.
Application information: Contributes only to pre-selected organizations.
Directors: Thomas R. Flickinger, Thomas Raymond Flickinger, William S. Flickinger, Charles E. Milch.
EIN: 161512239

39551
The Foundation for the Jan Mitchell Prize, Inc.
595 Madison Ave.
New York, NY 10022 (212) 755-9760
Contact: Jan Mitchell, Pres.

Donor(s): Jan Mitchell.
Financial data (yr. ended 03/31/02): Grants paid, $3,000; assets, $2,221 (M); gifts received, $8,000; expenditures, $6,290; qualifying distributions, $6,290; giving activities include $6,290 for programs.
Limitations: Giving on a national and international basis.
Officers: George Weidenfeld, Chair.; Jan Mitchell, Pres.
EIN: 132898803
Codes: GTI

39552
Global Charitable Fund
c/o Sherman Taub
1214 Heyson Rd.
Far Rockaway, NY 11691

Established in 1997 in NY.
Donor(s): Sherman Taub.
Financial data (yr. ended 12/31/99): Grants paid, $3,000; assets, $74 (M); gifts received, $4,163; expenditures, $4,139; qualifying distributions, $4,139.
Limitations: Applications not accepted.
Application information: Contributes only to pre-selected organizations.
Trustees: Samuel Sonnenschine, Sherman Taub.
EIN: 116485332

39553
Jeffrey A. Goldstein Foundation, Inc.
c/o Forum Personnel, Inc.
342 Madison Ave., Ste. 509
New York, NY 10017

Established in 1999 in NY.
Financial data (yr. ended 06/30/00): Grants paid, $3,000; assets, $78,249 (M); gifts received, $6,293; expenditures, $3,014; qualifying distributions, $3,000.
Limitations: Applications not accepted.

Directors: Frank Fusaro, Joel Gazes, Matthew Goldstein, Steven Goldstein.
EIN: 113444302

39554
Jeff Hunter Charitable Trust
c/o Martin B. Jaffe
7 Holly Lane
Rye Brook, NY 10573

Donor(s): Jeff Hunter.
Financial data (yr. ended 11/30/01): Grants paid, $3,000; assets, $620,044 (M); expenditures, $5,879; qualifying distributions, $3,000.
Limitations: Applications not accepted. Giving primarily in NY.
Application information: Contributes only to pre-selected organizations.
Trustees: Jeff Hunter, Martin B. Jaffe.
EIN: 137141718

39555
Raymond H. Jackman Foundation Trust
c/o Ronald Martin
54 Sunset Ave.
Tupper Lake, NY 12986-2117

Financial data (yr. ended 02/28/02): Grants paid, $3,000; assets, $167,790 (M); expenditures, $5,966; qualifying distributions, $3,000.
Trustees: Fred Johnson, Ronald A. Martin, Mary Wood.
EIN: 146114061

39556
The Michael A. Kalman Foundation
823 Park Ave., Apt. 5C
New York, NY 10021

Established in 1988 in NY.
Donor(s): Michael A. Kalman.
Financial data (yr. ended 09/30/01): Grants paid, $3,000; assets, $72,121 (M); expenditures, $3,813; qualifying distributions, $3,000.
Limitations: Applications not accepted. Giving primarily in the metropolitan New York, NY, area.
Application information: Contributes only to pre-selected organizations.
Trustees: Michael A. Kalman, Jonathan Winer.
EIN: 133497063

39557
The Ann Marie Kempczinski Foundation
12 Evergreen Ave.
Rye, NY 10580

Established in 1998.
Financial data (yr. ended 08/31/01): Grants paid, $3,000; assets, $467 (M); gifts received, $2,300; expenditures, $3,844; qualifying distributions, $3,000.
Limitations: Giving primarily in MA.
Officers: Richard Kempczinski, Pres.; Chris Kempczinski, Secy.; Cathy Major, Secy.; Heather Kempczinski, Treas.
EIN: 311622117

39558
The Klein-Kaufman Family Foundation
134 W. Hills Rd.
Huntington Station, NY 11746

Established in 1993 in NY.
Donor(s): Klein Kaufman Corp.
Financial data (yr. ended 02/28/01): Grants paid, $3,000; assets, $5,447 (M); gifts received, $3,000; expenditures, $3,000; qualifying distributions, $3,000.
Limitations: Applications not accepted. Giving primarily in Huntington, NY.
Officer: Jonah Kaufman, Pres.

Directors: Melinda Kaufman, Irving Klein, Mina Klein.
EIN: 113185247
Codes: GTI

39559
Kluger Family Foundation, Inc.
28 Bayview Ave.
Great Neck, NY 11021-2904

Established in 1997 in NY.
Donor(s): Michael Kluger.
Financial data (yr. ended 06/30/02): Grants paid, $3,000; assets, $52,855 (M); expenditures, $10,633; qualifying distributions, $3,000.
Limitations: Applications not accepted. Giving primarily in NY.
Application information: Contributes only to pre-selected organizations.
Directors: Alan Kluger, Lawrence Kluger.
EIN: 113294590

39560
Robert Kohn Memorial Education Foundation
c/o Eric Sklar
2881 Mandalay Beach Rd.
Wantagh, NY 11793

Established in 1994 in NY.
Financial data (yr. ended 12/31/99): Grants paid, $3,000; assets, $27,602 (M); gifts received, $225; expenditures, $3,666; qualifying distributions, $3,685.
Limitations: Applications not accepted. Giving limited to residents of Commack, NY.
Officers: Barbara Kohn, Pres.; Eric Sklar, Treas.
EIN: 113205484

39561
Lois Korey Scholarship Fund
c/o Cindy Harwin, Korey Kay & Partners
130 5th Ave.
New York, NY 10011-4395

Established in 1991 in NY.
Financial data (yr. ended 12/31/01): Grants paid, $3,000; assets, $27,130 (M); expenditures, $3,080; qualifying distributions, $3,069.
Limitations: Giving primarily in New York, NY.
Application information: Application form required.
Officer: Kenneth Damsky, Admin.
Trustee: Allen Kay.
EIN: 133593420

39562
The Levitas Foundation
230 Park Ave., Ste. 1549
New York, NY 10169

Established in 1998 in NY.
Donor(s): James R. Levitas.
Financial data (yr. ended 12/31/00): Grants paid, $3,000; assets, $38,974 (M); gifts received, $1,000; expenditures, $3,106; qualifying distributions, $3,025.
Limitations: Applications not accepted. Giving primarily in New York, NY.
Application information: Contributes only to pre-selected organizations.
Trustees: Julie E. Greenhouse, Dana M. Levitas, Donna Levitas, James R. Levitas.
EIN: 134010965

39563
Albert & Blanca Levy Charitable Foundation
c/o Blanca Levy
1521 51st St.
Brooklyn, NY 11219-3756

Established around 1991.
Donor(s): Blanca Levy.

Financial data (yr. ended 12/31/00): Grants paid, $3,000; assets, $26,520 (M); gifts received, $3,030; expenditures, $3,025; qualifying distributions, $3,000.
Officers: Alejandro Levy, Pres.; Hilda Snyder, Secy.-Treas.
EIN: 113043092

39564
Arthur & Lillie Mayer Foundation, Inc.
9 Inverness Rd.
Scarsdale, NY 10583
Contact: Michael F. Mayer, Pres.

Financial data (yr. ended 12/31/01): Grants paid, $3,000; assets, $61,323 (M); expenditures, $3,780; qualifying distributions, $3,000.
Limitations: Giving primarily in NY.
Officer: Michael F. Mayer, Pres.
EIN: 136221493

39565
Toni Mendez Foundation, Inc.
400 Park Ave., Ste. 1200
New York, NY 10022
Contact: Toni Mendez, Pres.

Established in 1989 in NY.
Donor(s): Toni Mendez.
Financial data (yr. ended 12/31/00): Grants paid, $3,000; assets, $59,714 (M); gifts received, $675; expenditures, $6,014; qualifying distributions, $3,000.
Limitations: Giving primarily in New York, NY.
Officers and Director:* Toni Mendez,* Pres.; David Gotterer, V.P.; Robert J. Gotterer, V.P.; Cynthia Weil Mann, V.P.
EIN: 133528580

39566
Mieczslaw Munz Scholarship Fund, Inc.
c/o Walter Hautzig
505 West End Ave., Rm. 8D
New York, NY 10024-4305

Financial data (yr. ended 05/31/01): Grants paid, $3,000; assets, $19,456 (M); gifts received, $6,000; expenditures, $7,932; qualifying distributions, $3,000.
Limitations: Applications not accepted.
Application information: Contributes only to pre-selected organizations.
Officers: Walter Hautzig, Pres.; Ann Schein, V.P. and Treas.; Susan Wadswortin, Secy.
EIN: 133000494

39567
Nichol Family Foundation
5990 Belle Island Rd., No. 7
Syracuse, NY 13209
Contact: Pamela Woollis, Tr.

Established in 1997 in NY.
Financial data (yr. ended 12/31/01): Grants paid, $3,000; assets, $63,088 (M); expenditures, $4,792; qualifying distributions, $3,000.
Trustees: Mary Ann Nichol, Pamela Woollis.
EIN: 161509638

39568
The Liliane Piel Foundation
c/o A. Goodridge
330 Madison Ave., 14th Fl.
New York, NY 10017 (212) 973-8024

Established in 1998 in NY.
Donor(s): Liliane Piel.
Financial data (yr. ended 12/31/01): Grants paid, $3,000; assets, $58,796 (M); expenditures, $6,704; qualifying distributions, $3,000.
Limitations: Giving primarily in New York, NY.
Trustee: Liliane Piel.
EIN: 134008614

39569
The Reid Family Foundation, Inc.
P.O. Box 987
Lockport, NY 14095

Established in 1995 in NY.
Financial data (yr. ended 12/31/01): Grants paid, $3,000; assets, $207 (M); gifts received, $3,000; expenditures, $3,000; qualifying distributions, $3,000.
Officers: Paul D. Reid, Pres. and Treas.; Robert W. Reid, V.P. and Secy.
Directors: Arnold C. Keller, Robert A. Lipp, Matthew Murphy, Joseph A. Platania, J. Ward Reid, Regis Stevenson, John G. White.
EIN: 161465512

39570
W. L. Robinson Trust under paragraph 6A
1 HSBC Ctr., 16th Fl.
P.O. Box 4203, 17th Fl.
Buffalo, NY 14240

Donor(s): L. Robinson.‡
Financial data (yr. ended 12/31/01): Grants paid, $3,000; assets, $190,422 (M); expenditures, $6,233; qualifying distributions, $3,348.
Limitations: Applications not accepted. Giving primarily in Plattsburgh, NY.
Trustee: James E. Keable, HSBC Bank USA.
EIN: 146065385

39571
The Milton A. Schiff Foundation, Inc.
40 E. 21st St., No. 5
New York, NY 10010 (212) 674-4420
Contact: Patricia Schiff-Estess, Pres.

Financial data (yr. ended 05/31/00): Grants paid, $3,000; assets, $64,679 (M); expenditures, $4,320; qualifying distributions, $3,660; giving activities include $660 for programs.
Limitations: Giving on a national basis.
Application information: Application form required.
Officers: Patricia Schiff-Estess, Pres.; Abby Achs, V.P.
EIN: 133351960

39572
Seymour Schneidman Foundation
c/o Anchin, Block & Anchin, LLP
1375 Broadway
New York, NY 10018

Established in 1987 in NY.
Donor(s): Lorraine Schneidman.
Financial data (yr. ended 11/30/01): Grants paid, $3,000; assets, $6,591 (M); expenditures, $4,070; qualifying distributions, $3,000.
Limitations: Applications not accepted. Giving primarily in NY.
Application information: Contributes only to pre-selected organizations.
Officers and Directors:* Richard Schneidman,* Pres.; Lorraine Schneidman,* V.P.; Geraldine Sacks,* Secy.-Treas.
EIN: 133445651

39573
Shoppers Village/Maureen Nolan Memorial Fund
877 N. Corona Ave.
Valley Stream, NY 11580
Application address: 138 Woodfield Rd., West Hempstead, NY 11552, tel.: (516) 538-0800
Contact: Robert W. O'Brien, Secy.

Financial data (yr. ended 07/31/00): Grants paid, $3,000; assets, $29,102 (M); expenditures, $3,000; qualifying distributions, $3,000.
Limitations: Giving limited to residents of West Hempstead, NY.
Application information: Application form required.
Officers: Matthew G. Nizza, Pres.; Peter Morello, V.P.; Robert W. O'Brien, Secy.
EIN: 112617929
Codes: GTI

39574
Carl Slater Memorial Fund
16 Watkins Pl.
New Rochelle, NY 10801
Contact: Ruth Slater, Pres.

Established in 1986 in NY.
Donor(s): Matthew D. Slater, Julius Slater, Ruth Slater.
Financial data (yr. ended 04/30/99): Grants paid, $3,000; assets, $1,998 (M); gifts received, $100; expenditures, $5,806; qualifying distributions, $3,000.
Limitations: Giving primarily in New York, NY.
Officer: Ruth Slater, Pres.
EIN: 133412475

39575
The Tighe Hidalgo Foundation, Inc.
1320 York Ave., Apt. 36B
New York, NY 10021

Established in 1998 in NY.
Donor(s): David A. Hidalgo, M.D.
Financial data (yr. ended 12/31/01): Grants paid, $3,000; assets, $62,651 (M); gifts received, $6,000; expenditures, $3,000; qualifying distributions, $3,000.
Limitations: Applications not accepted.
Application information: Contributes only to pre-selected organizations.
Officers: Mary Ann Tighe, Pres.; Kim Tighe, V.P.; David A. Hidalgo, M.D., Secy.; Aaron Tighe, Treas.
EIN: 134014406

39576
Webster Foundation, Inc.
118 Wagstaff Ln.
West Islip, NY 11795

Financial data (yr. ended 12/31/01): Grants paid, $3,000; assets, $37,843 (M); expenditures, $3,410; qualifying distributions, $2,991.
Limitations: Applications not accepted. Giving primarily in Babylon, NY.
Application information: Contributes only to pre-selected organizations.
Officers: Arvon Webster, Pres.; Donald P. Webster, Secy.-Treas.
EIN: 116019409

39577
Wisniewski Foundation
c/o Krystyna Wisniewski
141 Nixon Ave.
Staten Island, NY 10304

Established in 1999.
Donor(s): Krystyna Wisniewski.

39577—NEW YORK

Financial data (yr. ended 12/31/00): Grants paid, $3,000; assets, $35,704 (M); expenditures, $3,130; qualifying distributions, $3,111.
Limitations: Applications not accepted. Giving on a national basis.
Application information: Contributes only to pre-selected organizations.
Director: Krystyna Wisniewski.
EIN: 134019998

39578
Mabel M. Witmer Trust
c/o M & T Bank
1 M&T Plz., 8th Fl.
Buffalo, NY 14203
Application address: c/o M & T Bank, 14 N. Main St., Chambersburg, PA 17201, tel.: (717) 267-7625
Contact: John Schall, V.P. and Trust Off., M & T Bank

Financial data (yr. ended 12/31/01): Grants paid, $3,000; assets, $84,658 (M); expenditures, $4,558; qualifying distributions, $3,000.
Limitations: Giving limited to residents of Franklin and Cumberland counties, PA.
Application information: Application form required.
Trustee: M & T Bank.
EIN: 256183584
Codes: GTI

39579
Robinson-Costas Charitable Foundation
c/o United Financial Svcs.
4773 Buckley Rd.
Liverpool, NY 13088

Financial data (yr. ended 12/31/99): Grants paid, $2,992; assets, $0 (M); gifts received, $3,040; expenditures, $3,027; qualifying distributions, $2,992.
Officer: Andres Costas, Pres.
EIN: 880306406

39580
The Christian Foundation, Inc.
c/o Joseph W. DeCrescenzo
30 Fleetwood Ave., Ste. 3J
Mount Vernon, NY 10552

Established around 1993.
Donor(s): Joseph W. DeCrescenzo.
Financial data (yr. ended 12/31/01): Grants paid, $2,966; assets, $46,975 (M); expenditures, $3,479; qualifying distributions, $2,966.
Limitations: Applications not accepted. Giving on a national basis, with emphasis on NY.
Application information: Contributes only to pre-selected organizations.
Officers: Joseph W. DeCrescenzo, Pres.; Michael Ferrigno, V.P.; Margaret DeCrescenzo, Secy.
EIN: 133694334

39581
The Heiser Family Foundation
c/o Nathan Berkman & Co.
29 Broadway, Rm. 2906
New York, NY 10006-3296

Established in 1990 in NY.
Donor(s): Freddy Heiser, Rozalia Heiser.
Financial data (yr. ended 07/31/00): Grants paid, $2,965; assets, $34,328 (M); gifts received, $2,000; expenditures, $3,011; qualifying distributions, $2,965.
Limitations: Applications not accepted. Giving primarily in New York, NY.
Application information: Contributes only to pre-selected organizations.

Trustees: David Heiser, Freddy Heiser, Rozalia Heiser.
EIN: 133585022

39582
C & R Fund, Inc.
45 E. End Ave.
New York, NY 10028

Donor(s): Charles Censor, Jacques Censor.
Financial data (yr. ended 12/31/01): Grants paid, $2,942; assets, $57,829 (M); expenditures, $3,700; qualifying distributions, $3,700.
Limitations: Applications not accepted.
Application information: Contributes only to pre-selected organizations.
Officer: Charles Censor, Pres.
EIN: 136121169

39583
Wiener Family Foundation
211 Broadway
Lynbrook, NY 11563
Application address: 1095 Cornwall Ave., Boca Raton, FL 33434
Contact: Louis Wiener, Mgr.

Established in 1986 in NY.
Donor(s): Louis Wiener.
Financial data (yr. ended 11/30/00): Grants paid, $2,928; assets, $150,883 (M); gifts received, $15,000; expenditures, $3,428; qualifying distributions, $2,928.
Limitations: Giving primarily in CA, Chicago, IL, and the New York, NY area.
Officer: Louis Wiener, Mgr.
EIN: 112852909

39584
The David Heckler Foundation
10-29 44th Rd.
Long Island City, NY 11101

Donor(s): David Heckler,‡ Charles Heckler.
Financial data (yr. ended 06/30/01): Grants paid, $2,917; assets, $12,130 (M); gifts received, $5,000; expenditures, $2,947; qualifying distributions, $2,942.
Limitations: Applications not accepted. Giving primarily in New York, NY.
Application information: Contributes only to pre-selected organizations.
Officers: Charles Heckler, V.P.; Marion Heckler, Treas.
EIN: 116035648

39585
Elsie L. & Peter H. Brandt Foundation
44 W. 77th St.
New York, NY 10024
Contact: Carol Ferranti, Tr.

Established in 1960 in NY.
Donor(s): Peter H. Brandt.
Financial data (yr. ended 12/31/00): Grants paid, $2,888; assets, $1 (M); expenditures, $3,263; qualifying distributions, $2,888.
Limitations: Giving primarily in NY.
Trustees: Carol Ferranti, Neil Ferranti.
EIN: 136159531

39586
William J. Butler Foundation, Inc.
c/o Butler & Jablow
280 Madison Ave., Ste. 805
New York, NY 10016

Donor(s): William J. Butler.
Financial data (yr. ended 12/31/01): Grants paid, $2,880; assets, $7,445 (M); expenditures, $3,030; qualifying distributions, $2,880.

Limitations: Applications not accepted. Giving primarily in NY.
Application information: Contributes only to pre-selected organizations.
Officer: William J. Butler, Pres.
EIN: 136199607

39587
Long Island Bassmasters, Inc.
P.O. Box 2547
Ronkonkoma, NY 11779-0410

Established around 1986.
Donor(s): Edward Goodwin, Jr. Bassmasters, Garman's Tackle, Charlie Kick, Jim Blair.
Financial data (yr. ended 11/30/01): Grants paid, $2,880; assets, $8,632 (M); gifts received, $1,809; expenditures, $9,506; qualifying distributions, $6,628.
Limitations: Giving primarily in NY.
Officers: Pat McNamara, Pres.; Brendan Cucinello, V.P.; Troy Duran, Secy.; T. Guiffrida, Treas.
EIN: 112772915

39588
Ruder & Finn Fund, Inc.
c/o Ruder Finn, Inc.
301 E. 57th St.
New York, NY 10022

Established in 1964 in NY.
Donor(s): Ruder Finn, Inc.
Financial data (yr. ended 08/31/02): Grants paid, $2,875; assets, $42,130 (M); gifts received, $3,000; expenditures, $2,900; qualifying distributions, $2,875.
Limitations: Applications not accepted. Giving primarily in areas of company operations.
Application information: Contributes only to pre-selected organizations.
Trustee: David Finn.
EIN: 136162874
Codes: CS, CD

39589
The Keith W. Fengler Memorial Foundation
202 Ruth Rd.
North Syracuse, NY 13212 (315) 458-3369
Contact: Henry J. Fengler, Tr.

Financial data (yr. ended 12/31/00): Grants paid, $2,871; assets, $103,798 (M); gifts received, $73,139; expenditures, $2,921; qualifying distributions, $2,871.
Limitations: Giving primarily in Syracuse, NY.
Application information: Application form required.
Trustee: Henry J. Fengler.
EIN: 166491840

39590
Zichron Mordchai Mayer & Frymet Charitable Foundation
226 Crafton Ave.
Staten Island, NY 10314 (718) 494-7199
Contact: Martin Friedman, Pres.

Established in 2000.
Donor(s): Josef Friedman.
Financial data (yr. ended 12/31/01): Grants paid, $2,861; assets, $19,753 (M); gifts received, $20,842; expenditures, $3,051; qualifying distributions, $2,861.
Officers and Trustees:* Martin Friedman,* Pres.; Devorah Goldner,* Secy.-Treas.; Joseph Friedman.
EIN: 134127969

39591
Anesthesia Group Charitable Foundation
301 Prospect St.
Syracuse, NY 13203
Contact: Anthony A. Ascioti, Dir.

Established in 1991 in NY.
Financial data (yr. ended 12/31/01): Grants paid, $2,850; assets, $7,924 (M); expenditures, $3,281; qualifying distributions, $2,850.
Directors: John D'Addario, Anthony A. Ascioti, Arturo Castro, Brian Chanatry, Joan Thornton.
EIN: 161414621

39592
Alan V. Iselin Family Foundation, Inc.
38 Fairway Ct.
Albany, NY 12208

Donor(s): Allan Iselin.
Financial data (yr. ended 12/31/01): Grants paid, $2,850; assets, $365 (M); gifts received, $1,000; expenditures, $4,408; qualifying distributions, $2,850.
Limitations: Applications not accepted. Giving primarily in NY.
Application information: Contributes only to pre-selected organizations.
Officers and Directors:* Alan V. Iselin,* Pres. and Treas.; Barbara H. Iselin,* V.P. and Secy.; Ralph Iselin.
EIN: 237009077

39593
Mardkha Family Charitable Foundation Trust
c/o Amir Mardkha
15 Hillcrest Dr.
Great Neck, NY 11021

Established in 1999 in NY.
Donor(s): Amir Mardkha.
Financial data (yr. ended 12/31/01): Grants paid, $2,850; assets, $1,122 (M); expenditures, $2,850; qualifying distributions, $2,850.
Officer: Amir Mardkha, Mgr.
EIN: 113477240

39594
Ringel Family Foundation
1750 44th St.
Brooklyn, NY 11204-1050

Established in 1991 in NY.
Donor(s): Abraham Ringel, Arye Ringel.
Financial data (yr. ended 04/30/02): Grants paid, $2,850; assets, $90,030 (M); expenditures, $3,151; qualifying distributions, $2,850.
Limitations: Applications not accepted. Giving primarily in Israel.
Application information: Contributes only to pre-selected organizations.
Trustees: Tyla Pshemish, Abraham Ringel, Arye Ringel, Chana Ringel, Moshe Ringel, Nathan Ringel.
EIN: 113083761

39595
Samuel & Lillian Greenberg Family Foundation, Inc.
c/o Kevin Mullins
336 West St.
White Plains, NY 10605

Financial data (yr. ended 12/31/01): Grants paid, $2,833; assets, $1 (M); expenditures, $3,425; qualifying distributions, $2,833.
Limitations: Applications not accepted. Giving primarily in New York, NY.
Application information: Contributes only to pre-selected organizations.
Officer: Aaron Greenberg, Pres.
EIN: 136271606

39596
The Haber Foundation
60 Wimbledon Dr.
Roslyn, NY 11576

Established in 1986 in NY.
Donor(s): Michael Haber.
Financial data (yr. ended 11/30/01): Grants paid, $2,832; assets, $21,977 (M); gifts received, $3,000; expenditures, $2,832; qualifying distributions, $2,832.
Limitations: Applications not accepted. Giving primarily in NY.
Application information: Contributes only to pre-selected organizations.
Trustees: Michael Haber, Chair.; Joyce Haber, Robert H. Haber.
EIN: 116329738

39597
Itto Willits Charitable Foundation
c/o Bessemer Trust Co., NA
630 5th Ave.
New York, NY 10111   (212) 708-9216

Established in 1997 in FL.
Donor(s): Itto A. Willits.
Financial data (yr. ended 12/31/99): Grants paid, $2,831; assets, $121,402 (M); expenditures, $4,406; qualifying distributions, $2,831.
Trustee: John C. Kelly.
EIN: 656235199

39598
Beatrice Vought Charitable Trust
c/o M&T Bank
1 M&T Plz., 8th Fl.
Buffalo, NY 14203

Established in 1999 in PA.
Financial data (yr. ended 12/31/00): Grants paid, $2,822; assets, $50,414 (M); expenditures, $4,169; qualifying distributions, $2,822.
Limitations: Applications not accepted.
Application information: Contributes only to pre-selected organizations.
Trustee: M&T Bank.
EIN: 237931055

39599
William & Phyllis Haft Foundation, Inc.
c/o Albert A. Chait
2001 Marcus Ave., Ste. N. 121
New Hyde Park, NY 11042

Financial data (yr. ended 04/30/02): Grants paid, $2,800; assets, $30,103 (M); expenditures, $3,477; qualifying distributions, $2,800.
Limitations: Applications not accepted.
Application information: Contributes only to pre-selected organizations.
Officer: William Haft, Pres.
EIN: 136217086

39600
The Meyer and Lillian Jacobowitz Foundation, Inc.
P.O. Box 367
Walden, NY 12586-0367   (845) 778-2121

Donor(s): Meyer Jacobowitz, Lillian Jacobowitz.
Financial data (yr. ended 12/31/01): Grants paid, $2,800; assets, $40,570 (M); expenditures, $3,579; qualifying distributions, $2,800.
Limitations: Giving limited to NY.
Officers and Directors:* Arthur Concors, Pres.; Gerald N. Jacobowitz,* V.P.; Joyce Concors, Secy.; Marlene Jacobowitz, Treas.; Andrew Concors, Bruce Concors, Leslie Concors, Marcia Jacobowitz.
EIN: 222515704

39601
Ruth W. & Alice I. Chamberlin Scholarship Trust
(Formerly Ruth W. Chamberlin Scholarship Trust)
c/o NBT Bank, N.A.
52 S. Broad St.
Norwich, NY 13815-1646
Application address: c/o Afton Central School, Afton, NY 13730
Contact: John Donlon, Guidance Dir.

Established in 1981 in NY.
Donor(s): Alice I. Chamberlin, Ruth W. Chamberlin.
Financial data (yr. ended 05/31/00): Grants paid, $2,750; assets, $78,737 (M); expenditures, $3,444; qualifying distributions, $3,230.
Limitations: Giving limited to Afton, NY.
Application information: Application form required.
Trustee: NBT Bank, N.A.
EIN: 166243756
Codes: GTI

39602
Alfonso L. DeMatteis Family Foundation
c/o Donald M. Schaeffer
102 EAB Plaza, 15th Fl., W. Tower
Uniondale, NY 11556

Established in 1991 in NY.
Donor(s): Alfonso L. DeMatteis.
Financial data (yr. ended 12/31/00): Grants paid, $2,750; assets, $2,520 (L); gifts received, $3,600; expenditures, $3,662; qualifying distributions, $2,750.
Limitations: Applications not accepted. Giving primarily in NY.
Application information: Contributes only to pre-selected organizations.
Directors: Richard L. Braunstein, Alfonso L. DeMatteis, Keith DeMatteis, Donald M. Schaeffer.
EIN: 113052224

39603
Diamond Jubilee Fund of King Solomon-Beethoven Lodge No. 232
c/o Robert Lippman
7 W. 96th St., Apt. 2A
New York, NY 10025   (212) 666-6021
Contact: Robert L. Lippmann, Chair.

Established in 1927 in NY.
Financial data (yr. ended 12/31/99): Grants paid, $2,750; assets, $155,580 (M); gifts received, $80; expenditures, $3,056; qualifying distributions, $3,056.
Limitations: Giving primarily in NY.
Application information: Application form required.
Officers and Trustees:* Robert L. Lippmann,* Chair. and Treas.; H. Harry Franklin,* Secy.; Martin L. Kay, Allan Schiller.
EIN: 136110395

39604
The Foundation for Neuromuscular Reconstruction, Inc.
425 W. 59th St., Ste. 5C-1
New York, NY 10019

Established in 2000 in NY.
Donor(s): Miriam Stern Foundation.
Financial data (yr. ended 12/31/00): Grants paid, $2,750; assets, $14,272 (M); gifts received, $17,000; expenditures, $2,768; qualifying distributions, $2,768.
Limitations: Applications not accepted.

39604—NEW YORK

Officers and Directors:* Andrew E. Price,* Pres. and Treas.; Jesse Kirsch,* V.P.; Dorothy Bergeron,* Secy.
EIN: 134093158

39605
Eugene & Gloria Goodman Foundation
c/o Prager and Fenton
675 3rd Ave.
New York, NY 10017

Established in 1996 in NY.
Donor(s): Gloria Goodman.
Financial data (yr. ended 12/31/01): Grants paid, $2,750; assets, $107,355 (M); expenditures, $4,801; qualifying distributions, $4,147.
Limitations: Applications not accepted.
Application information: Contributes only to pre-selected organizations.
Officers: Gloria Goodman, Pres.; Scott Goodman, Secy.; Frank Walters, Treas.
EIN: 113339382

39606
Joseph & Doris Jackler Family Foundation
221 S. Warren St.
Syracuse, NY 13202-1608

Donor(s): Joseph J. Jackler, Doris Jackler.
Financial data (yr. ended 12/31/01): Grants paid, $2,715; assets, $23,809 (M); gifts received, $3,000; expenditures, $2,840; qualifying distributions, $2,715.
Limitations: Applications not accepted. Giving primarily in FL.
Application information: Contributes only to pre-selected organizations.
Trustees: Doris Jackler, Jay L. Jackler, Joseph J. Jackler.
EIN: 222492985

39607
The Gregory Foundation Charitable Trust
39 Monroe Ave.
Larchmont, NY 10538 (914) 967-1188
Contact: Bruce Gregory, Tr.

Financial data (yr. ended 12/31/99): Grants paid, $2,700; assets, $139,228 (M); expenditures, $4,732; qualifying distributions, $4,732.
Limitations: Giving on a national basis.
Trustee: Bruce Gregory.
EIN: 521323628

39608
Anthony J. Luisi Memorial Foundation
265 Post Ave.
Westbury, NY 11590
Contact: Kathy A. Luisi, Tr.

Donor(s): Frances M. Luisi.
Financial data (yr. ended 11/30/99): Grants paid, $2,700; assets, $26,257 (M); gifts received, $1,000; expenditures, $2,808; qualifying distributions, $2,795.
Limitations: Giving primarily in NY.
Trustee: Kathy A. Luisi.
EIN: 136873972

39609
Retina Surgery Institute, Inc.
666 3rd Ave., 29th Fl.
New York, NY 10017-4011

Established in 1984 in NY.
Donor(s): Margaret De Neufville, Penguin Supermarkets, Inc.
Financial data (yr. ended 09/30/01): Grants paid, $2,700; assets, $90,913 (M); expenditures, $6,510; qualifying distributions, $2,700.
Limitations: Applications not accepted. Giving primarily in Cambridge, MA.
Application information: Contributes only to pre-selected organizations.
Officers and Directors:* Jesse L. Sigelman,* Pres. and Treas.; Alice R. Sigelman,* V.P.; Ronald Stein, Secy.
EIN: 133062780

39610
Reginald Rose Foundation, Inc.
c/o Plumer & Epstein
105-58 Flatlands 5th St.
Brooklyn, NY 11236-4636 (718) 241-5485
Application address: 20 Wedgewood Rd., Westport, CT 06880
Contact: Reginald Rose, Pres.

Donor(s): Reginald Rose.
Financial data (yr. ended 12/31/01): Grants paid, $2,700; assets, $20,728 (M); expenditures, $2,991; qualifying distributions, $2,700.
Officers: Reginald Rose, Pres.; Maurice Spanbock, Secy.
EIN: 136159249

39611
J. & H. Rubin Foundation
c/o Robert Rubin, Postner & Rubin
17 Battery Pl., Ste. 1914
New York, NY 10004

Financial data (yr. ended 12/31/01): Grants paid, $2,700; assets, $30,121 (M); expenditures, $2,700; qualifying distributions, $2,700.
Limitations: Applications not accepted. Giving primarily in NJ and NY.
Application information: Contributes only to pre-selected organizations.
Trustee: Robert A. Rubin.
EIN: 116005490

39612
Joseph M. Suozzi Foundation, Inc.
c/o Joseph A. Suozzi
9 September Pl.
Glen Cove, NY 11542

Established in 2000 in NY.
Donor(s): Deutsche Bank AG London, Meyer, Suozzi, English & Klein, P.C.
Financial data (yr. ended 12/31/01): Grants paid, $2,700; assets, $55,785 (M); gifts received, $3,148; expenditures, $3,728; qualifying distributions, $2,726.
Limitations: Applications not accepted.
Application information: Contributes only to pre-selected organizations.
Officers: Marea Suozzi, Chair.; Joseph A. Suozzi, Pres.; Thomas Suozzi, Secy.; Christopher Suozzi, Treas.
EIN: 113540762
Codes: CS

39613
The van Amerongen Charitable Trust
c/o LVA Enterprises
667 Madison Ave., 12th Fl.
New York, NY 10021

Established in 1986 in NY.
Donor(s): Lewis van Amerongen.
Financial data (yr. ended 12/31/01): Grants paid, $2,700; assets, $35,164 (M); expenditures, $5,959; qualifying distributions, $2,700.
Limitations: Applications not accepted. Giving primarily in New York, NY.
Application information: Contributes only to pre-selected organizations.
Trustee: Lewis van Amerongen.
EIN: 133385797

39614
Robert F. & Eva H. Dirkes Fund
c/o JPMorgan Chase Bank
P.O. Box 31412
Rochester, NY 14603-1412

Established in 1992 in CT.
Financial data (yr. ended 08/31/01): Grants paid, $2,682; assets, $108,157 (M); expenditures, $5,432; qualifying distributions, $2,962.
Limitations: Applications not accepted.
Application information: Contributes only to pre-selected organizations.
Trustee: JPMorgan Chase Bank.
EIN: 066387781

39615
Muriel & Felix Lilienthal Foundation, Inc.
930 5th Ave.
New York, NY 10021

Donor(s): Felix Lilienthal, Jr.
Financial data (yr. ended 12/31/01): Grants paid, $2,659; assets, $1,979 (M); gifts received, $2,480; expenditures, $3,026; qualifying distributions, $2,659.
Limitations: Giving primarily in New York, NY.
Officer: Felix Lilienthal, Pres.
EIN: 237065514

39616
B.L. Sharing Association
c/o Wrenn & Schmid
25A Chapel Pl.
Great Neck, NY 11021-1427

Donor(s): Robert A. Lewis.
Financial data (yr. ended 12/31/01): Grants paid, $2,650; assets, $54,033 (M); expenditures, $4,180; qualifying distributions, $2,650.
Limitations: Applications not accepted.
Application information: Contributes only to pre-selected organizations.
Officers: Robert A. Lewis, Pres. and Treas.; Peter I. Bermas, V.P.; Roger E. Bermas, Secy.
EIN: 116100982

39617
The Harold & Helen Gottlieb Foundation
c/o Lentz
19 Bridge St., Ste. 5
Glen Cove, NY 11542

Established in 2000 in NY.
Donor(s): Helen Gottlieb.
Financial data (yr. ended 06/30/01): Grants paid, $2,650; assets, $22,296 (M); gifts received, $25,576; expenditures, $3,280; qualifying distributions, $3,280.
Limitations: Applications not accepted.
Application information: Contributes only to pre-selected organizations.
Directors: Helen Gottlieb, Carole A. Lentz, Paul Marchese.
EIN: 113562280

39618
The Reichenthal Foundation
179-05 80th Rd.
Jamaica, NY 11432 (718) 969-9126
Contact: Steven Reichenthal, Chair.

Donor(s): Steven Reichenthal, Helen Silverman, Jeffrey Reichenthal, Gloria Reichenthal.
Financial data (yr. ended 12/31/01): Grants paid, $2,650; assets, $25,595 (M); expenditures, $2,650; qualifying distributions, $2,650.
Officers: Steven Reichenthal, Chair.; Harvey Reichenthal, Secy.-Treas.
EIN: 112604644

39619
Webster W. & Florence M. Stetson Foundation, Inc.
555 Madison Ave., 19th Fl.
New York, NY 10022

Financial data (yr. ended 12/31/01): Grants paid, $2,650; assets, $122,482 (M); expenditures, $2,650; qualifying distributions, $2,650.
Limitations: Applications not accepted. Giving primarily in NY and PA.
Application information: Contributes only to pre-selected organizations.
Officer: Roger Winston, Secy.-Treas.
EIN: 237092237

39620
Albert & Vickie Stein Foundation
c/o Shulman, Jones & Co.
200 E. Post Rd.
White Plains, NY 10601
Application address: 23 Pine Ridge Rd., Rye Brook, NY 10573, tel.: (914) 937-4520
Contact: Nancy Tunis, Secy.

Financial data (yr. ended 03/31/01): Grants paid, $2,635; assets, $8,739 (M); expenditures, $4,532; qualifying distributions, $2,635.
Limitations: Giving primarily in Rye, NY.
Application information: Application form not required.
Officer and Trustee:* Nancy Tunis,* Secy.
EIN: 237396017

39621
The Jock Hatfield Memorial Trust
c/o The Bank of New York
1 Wall St.
New York, NY 10286
Application address: 13 Old Point Rd., Quogue, NY 11959-1311
Contact: J.D. Hatfield, Pres.

Financial data (yr. ended 12/31/00): Grants paid, $2,600; assets, $45,249 (M); gifts received, $20,010; expenditures, $2,825; qualifying distributions, $2,600.
Limitations: Giving primarily in NY.
Officers: Elaine Hatfield, Chair.; Jason D. Hatfield, Pres.
EIN: 770126226

39622
Hurwitz Foundation, Inc.
c/o Michael A. Davis
21 Longleat Dr.
Buffalo, NY 14226-4113 (716) 834-0403

Financial data (yr. ended 12/31/01): Grants paid, $2,600; assets, $10,804 (M); expenditures, $3,121; qualifying distributions, $2,600.
Limitations: Applications not accepted. Giving primarily in western NY.
Application information: Contributes only to pre-selected organizations.
Trustee: Michael A. Davis.
EIN: 237442875

39623
Sara and Richard Koffman Charitable Foundation
c/o Piaker & Lyons, PC
P.O. Box 247
Vestal, NY 13851-0247

Financial data (yr. ended 12/31/01): Grants paid, $2,600; assets, $36,209 (M); gifts received, $31; expenditures, $2,631; qualifying distributions, $2,600.
Limitations: Applications not accepted. Giving primarily in NY.
Application information: Contributes only to pre-selected organizations.
Trustees: Richard E. Koffman, Sara Koffman.
EIN: 222701586

39624
Memorare Foundation, Inc.
2183 Jackson Ave.
Seaford, NY 11783-2607

Financial data (yr. ended 09/30/01): Grants paid, $2,600; assets, $28,380 (M); gifts received, $3,307; expenditures, $3,590; qualifying distributions, $2,600.
Limitations: Applications not accepted. Giving primarily in Bellmore, NY.
Application information: Contributes only to pre-selected organizations.
Officers: Michael J. Murphy, Pres.; J. Loester, Treas.
Trustees: C. Barbarello, J. Kaley, G. Parachini, R. Reale, T. Reyer.
EIN: 112680625

39625
The Gussie & Harry Lehr Foundation
444 E. 86th St.
New York, NY 10028-0957 (212) 288-6765
Contact: Lewis Lehr, Tr.

Financial data (yr. ended 04/30/01): Grants paid, $2,565; assets, $59,608 (M); expenditures, $4,396; qualifying distributions, $2,565.
Trustee: Lewis Lehr.
EIN: 136108328

39626
Abraham S. Guterman Foundation
c/o JPMorgan Chase Bank
1211 Ave. of the Americas, 34th Fl.
New York, NY 10036
Application address: c/o Loeb & Loeb, 345 Park Ave, New York, NY 10184
Contact: Abraham Guterman, Pres.

Established around 1963.
Financial data (yr. ended 03/31/01): Grants paid, $2,564; assets, $921,676 (M); gifts received, $1,367; expenditures, $9,401; qualifying distributions, $2,683.
Limitations: Giving primarily in NY.
Officers: Abraham Guterman, Pres.; Laurie S. Ruckel, Secy.
Director: Robert L. Pelz.
EIN: 136124873

39627
Briguglio Family Foundation
c/o Frank & Kyle Briguglio
75 Chestnut St.
Oneonta, NY 13820
Application address: c/o The Anthony N. Briguglio Scholarship, 13 College Park Dr., Oneonta, NY 13820

Established in 1991 in NY.
Donor(s): Members of the Briguglio family.
Financial data (yr. ended 12/31/99): Grants paid, $2,500; assets, $32,631 (M); gifts received, $25; expenditures, $2,687; qualifying distributions, $2,500.
Limitations: Giving limited to NY.
Application information: Application form required.
Trustees: Frank A. Briguglio, Jr., Kyle M. Briguglio, Martha B. Forgiano, Richard S. Woods.
EIN: 223098659

39628
CSP Foundation
1022 E. 23rd St.
Brooklyn, NY 11210 (718) 283-8544
Contact: Eric Paneth, Tr.

Established in 2001 in NY.
Financial data (yr. ended 12/31/01): Grants paid, $2,500; assets, $6,500 (M); gifts received, $9,000; expenditures, $2,500; qualifying distributions, $2,500.
Trustees: Eric Paneth, Sharon Paneth.
EIN: 316666898

39629
Joseph and Rose Cusimano Charitable Foundation
6 Winchester Dr.
Glen Head, NY 11545

Established in 1998 in NY.
Donor(s): Dominic Cusimano.
Financial data (yr. ended 06/30/00): Grants paid, $2,500; assets, $28,469 (M); expenditures, $4,158; qualifying distributions, $2,500.
Limitations: Applications not accepted.
Application information: Contributes only to pre-selected organizations.
Director: Dominic Cusimano.
EIN: 113385624

39630
Jerome Lowell De Jur Trust
c/o Engish Dept. Chair.
Convent Ave. & 138th St.
New York, NY 10031

Financial data (yr. ended 06/30/99): Grants paid, $2,500; assets, $81,042 (M); expenditures, $3,204; qualifying distributions, $2,500.
Limitations: Giving primarily in New York, NY.
Trustees: Marion De Jur, Leon Guilhamet, Yolanda T. Moses.
EIN: 136223537

39631
Dikaia Foundation, Inc.
P.O. Box 426
Syracuse, NY 13210-0426

Financial data (yr. ended 04/30/01): Grants paid, $2,500; assets, $295,915 (M); gifts received, $31,374; expenditures, $12,430; qualifying distributions, $12,430.
Limitations: Giving limited to Syracuse, NY.
Application information: Applicant must be enrolled at Syracuse University.
Officers: Rick Holldad, Pres.; James McKay, Secy.; Oswald C. Street, Treas.
EIN: 166044201

39632
Maurice & Judi Falk Foundation, Inc.
275 Hewlett Neck Rd.
Woodmere, NY 11598

Established in 1994 in NY.
Donor(s): Judi L. Falk, Maurice B. Falk.
Financial data (yr. ended 12/31/01): Grants paid, $2,500; assets, $1,072,382 (M); gifts received, $75,000; expenditures, $4,550; qualifying distributions, $2,500.
Limitations: Applications not accepted. Giving limited to RI.
Application information: Contributes only to pre-selected organizations.
Officers: Judi L. Falk, Mgr.; Maurice B. Falk, Mgr.
EIN: 113239050

39633
Foundation for the Re-Development of Individual Characters
c/o J. Silber
44 Blackberry Dr.
Brewster, NY 10509-4111

Financial data (yr. ended 12/31/01): Grants paid, $2,500; assets, $223,129 (M); gifts received, $100; expenditures, $13,016; qualifying distributions, $2,500.
Trustees: Lynn Abbott, Lucinda Moran, Jill Silber.
EIN: 141628128

39634
The Fund for Sephardic Communal Activities, Inc.
20 Cedar St., Ste. 101
New Rochelle, NY 10801

Donor(s): Joseph Caspi.
Financial data (yr. ended 06/30/01): Grants paid, $2,500; assets, $54,578 (M); expenditures, $3,050; qualifying distributions, $2,775.
Limitations: Applications not accepted. Giving primarily in NY.
Application information: Contributes only to pre-selected organizations.
Officers: Steven Caspi, Pres.; James H. Caspi, V.P.
EIN: 133102296

39635
David H. Gluck Foundation, Inc.
3935 Blackstone Ave., Ste. 4B
Bronx, NY 10471-3718

Established in 1961.
Donor(s): A. George Saks, Daniel Saks, Emanuel M. Gluck.‡
Financial data (yr. ended 12/31/01): Grants paid, $2,500; assets, $297,365 (M); gifts received, $30,275; expenditures, $4,340; qualifying distributions, $2,500.
Limitations: Applications not accepted. Giving primarily in the greater metropolitan New York, NY, area.
Application information: Contributes only to pre-selected organizations.
Officers: A. George Saks, Pres.; Daniel Saks, V.P.; Mark Saks, V.P.; Stephanie Saks, Secy.; David Saks, Treas.
EIN: 136161375

39636
William and Bertha Goldfinger Foundation, Inc.
c/o Myron Goldfinger
220 Mead St.
Waccabuc, NY 10597

Established in 1998 in NY.
Donor(s): Myron Goldfinger.
Financial data (yr. ended 12/31/01): Grants paid, $2,500; assets, $49,101 (M); expenditures, $2,653; qualifying distributions, $2,500.
Limitations: Applications not accepted.
Application information: Contributes only to pre-selected organizations.
Officers: Myron Goldfinger, Pres.; Djerba Goldfinger, V.P.; Thira Goldfinger, V.P.; June Goldfinger, Treas.
EIN: 133975051

39637
The P. & K. Iacovelli Charitable Foundation, Inc.
600 Old Country Rd.
Garden City, NY 11530

Established in 2000 in NY.
Donor(s): Peter Iacovelli, Karen Iacovelli.
Financial data (yr. ended 12/31/01): Grants paid, $2,500; assets, $528,504 (M); gifts received, $2,342; expenditures, $7,691; qualifying distributions, $2,500.
Limitations: Applications not accepted.
Application information: Contributes only to pre-selected organizations.
Officers: Peter Iacovelli, Pres.; Karen Iacovelli, V.P.; Todd Lineburger, Secy.; Louis P. Karol, Treas.
EIN: 113568113

39638
The William R. Larkin Memorial Foundation
28 Boylston St.
Garden City, NY 11530 (516) 742-1163
Contact: Eleanor Larkin, Tr.

Financial data (yr. ended 12/31/01): Grants paid, $2,500; assets, $51,500 (M); gifts received, $156; expenditures, $2,786; qualifying distributions, $2,483.
Limitations: Giving primarily in RI.
Application information: Limited to college students.
Trustees: Patricia Garone, Deborah Larkin, Edward Larkin, Eleanor Larkin.
EIN: 237109896

39639
Robert and Ruth Lewis Charitable Trust
130 Lovell Rd.
New Rochelle, NY 10804

Established in 1998 in NY.
Donor(s): Ruth Freeman, Robert Lewis.
Financial data (yr. ended 12/31/01): Grants paid, $2,500; assets, $44,060 (M); gifts received, $9,734; expenditures, $3,354; qualifying distributions, $2,500.
Limitations: Applications not accepted. Giving primarily in New York, NY; some giving also in Israel.
Application information: Contributes only to pre-selected organizations.
Trustees: Ruth Freeman, Robert Lewis.
EIN: 137123323

39640
M-W Rotary Foundation, Inc.
(also known as Monroe-Woodbury Rotary Foundation, Inc.)
c/o Isabel Babcock
P.O. Box 399
Monroe, NY 10950

Financial data (yr. ended 12/31/02): Grants paid, $2,500; assets, $40,044 (M); gifts received, $1,753; expenditures, $2,546; qualifying distributions, $2,500.
Limitations: Giving limited to the Monroe-Woodbury, NY, area.
Application information: Application form required.
Officers: Ray Hafenecker, Pres.; Martha Bill, Secy.; William H. Bollenbach, Treas.
EIN: 133387109

39641
The Masonic Guild of Suffern, Inc.
540 Haverstraw Rd.
Suffern, NY 10901

Established in 2001 in NY.
Financial data (yr. ended 12/31/01): Grants paid, $2,500; assets, $449,679 (M); gifts received, $455,387; expenditures, $25,803; qualifying distributions, $20,102.
Limitations: Applications not accepted.
Application information: Contributes only to pre-selected organizations.
Trustee: Provident Bank.
EIN: 316669440

39642
The MDC Charitable Foundation
c/o Wlody, Market Data Corp.
6 International Dr., 3rd Fl.
Rye Brook, NY 10573

Established in 1997 in NY.
Donor(s): Market Data Corp.
Financial data (yr. ended 12/31/01): Grants paid, $2,500; assets, $492 (M); expenditures, $2,500; qualifying distributions, $2,500.
Limitations: Applications not accepted.
Application information: Contributes only to pre-selected organizations.
Officers and Directors:* Rod Fisher,* Chair. and Pres.; Iris Cantor,* Vice-Chair.; Andrew Seidel,* Exec. V.P.; Franz Paasche,* Secy.; Michael Wlody,* Treas.
EIN: 133964416
Codes: CS, CD

39643
The Allen W. Mead Medical Foundation, Inc.
c/o Allen W. Mead
1 Lexington Ave.
New York, NY 10010-5515

Financial data (yr. ended 12/31/01): Grants paid, $2,500; assets, $67,061 (M); expenditures, $4,100; qualifying distributions, $2,500.
Limitations: Applications not accepted. Giving primarily in NY.
Application information: Contributes only to pre-selected organizations.
Officers: Allen W. Mead, M.D., Pres.; Allen W. Mead, Jr., V.P.; Anne S. Mead, Secy.-Treas.
EIN: 133792798

39644
Pauline R. Parker Trust
c/o Chemung Canal Trust Co.
P.O. Box 1522
Elmira, NY 14902-1522 (607) 737-3896
Contact: Richard F. Kuhnen, Tr.

Established in 1967 in NY.
Donor(s): Pauline R. Parker.‡
Financial data (yr. ended 12/31/01): Grants paid, $2,500; assets, $322,862 (M); expenditures, $11,502; qualifying distributions, $6,665; giving activities include $2,500 for loans to individuals.
Limitations: Giving limited to residents of Broome County, NY.
Application information: Application form required.
Trustee: Chemung Canal Trust Co.
EIN: 166095226
Codes: GTI

39645
Karol Pilarczyk Foundation, Inc.
6 Pepper Ln.
Albany, NY 12211 (518) 783-0545

Established in 1995 in NY.
Financial data (yr. ended 12/31/01): Grants paid, $2,500; assets, $207,746 (M); expenditures, $11,413; qualifying distributions, $2,500.
Limitations: Giving on an international basis, primarily to Canada.
Directors: Ian Pilarczyk, Karol Pilarczyk, Roman Z. Pilarczyk.
EIN: 141777374

39646
Raman and Lakshmi Foundation
216-07 Sawyer Ave.
Queens Village, NY 11427

Established in 1994.
Donor(s): Subramamiam Sundararaman.

Financial data (yr. ended 12/31/01): Grants paid, $2,500; assets, $27,541 (M); expenditures, $2,509; qualifying distributions, $2,500.
Limitations: Giving primarily in NY.
Officer: Subramamiam Sundararaman, Pres.
EIN: 113243819

39647
The Susan B. Oppenheimer Sassower and Philip S. Sassower Foundation, Inc.
135 E. 57th St., 12th Fl.
New York, NY 10022 (212) 759-1909
Contact: Philip S. Sassower, Pres.

Established in 1994 in NY.
Donor(s): Philip S. Sassower.
Financial data (yr. ended 12/31/01): Grants paid, $2,500; assets, $2,548 (M); expenditures, $2,500; qualifying distributions, $2,500.
Limitations: Giving primarily in New York, NY.
Officers: Philip S. Sassower, Pres.; Susan B. Sassower, Secy.; Herman Sassower, Treas.
EIN: 133802207

39648
Shah & Shah Foundation, Inc.
528 Old Country Rd.
Plainview, NY 11803

Established in 1998 in NY.
Donor(s): Surendra G. Shah, Mrudula Shah.
Financial data (yr. ended 12/30/01): Grants paid, $2,500; assets, $12,725 (M); expenditures, $3,008; qualifying distributions, $2,500.
Limitations: Applications not accepted.
Application information: Contributes only to pre-selected organizations.
Officers: Surendra G. Shah, Pres.; Mrudula Shah, Secy.-Treas.
EIN: 113420563

39649
Shelter Rock Foundation, Inc.
c/o Hertz, Herson & Co., LLP
2 Park Ave.
New York, NY 10016-5601

Established around 1945.
Financial data (yr. ended 06/30/02): Grants paid, $2,500; assets, $268,825 (M); expenditures, $11,265; qualifying distributions, $2,500.
Limitations: Applications not accepted. Giving primarily in New York, NY.
Application information: Contributes only to pre-selected organizations.
Officers: Robin Becker Maki, V.P.; Michael T. Incantalupo, Secy.-Treas.
Directors: Lynn Stralem, William B. Warren.
EIN: 136065516

39650
Marjorie Tallman Educational Foundation Trust
c/o Roberta Lobel
400 E. 56th St., Ste. 8N
New York, NY 10022-4147
Contact: Roberta Lobel, Tr.

Donor(s): Marjorie Tallman, Marjorie Tallman.
Financial data (yr. ended 12/31/01): Grants paid, $2,500; assets, $36,294 (M); expenditures, $3,351; qualifying distributions, $2,500.
Limitations: Giving limited to NY.
Application information: Application form not required.
Trustees: Robert Lobel, Marjorie Tallman.
EIN: 133887249

39651
The WCT III and JDT Family Foundation
(Formerly The Walter C. Teagle III Foundation)
c/o Rosen Seymour Shapss Martin & Co.
757 3rd Ave.
New York, NY 10017-2049

Established in 1999 in NY.
Financial data (yr. ended 11/30/01): Grants paid, $2,500; assets, $10,443 (M); expenditures, $8,616; qualifying distributions, $2,500.
Limitations: Giving primarily in MT.
Directors: Janet Teagle, Walter Teagle.
EIN: 134153121

39652
John Winslow Foundation, Inc.
P.O. Box 368
Millbrook, NY 12545 (845) 677-3400
Contact: Robert W. Gunther, Secy.-Treas.

Financial data (yr. ended 12/31/00): Grants paid, $2,500; assets, $3,832 (M); expenditures, $2,516; qualifying distributions, $2,500.
Limitations: Giving limited to residents of Washington, NY.
Application information: Applicant must be entering sophomore year in college. Application form required.
Officers: Helen I. Gunther, Pres.; Robert W. Gunther, Secy.-Treas.
EIN: 146030176
Codes: GTI

39653
Hulbert W. Tripp Scholarship Fund
c/o Citibank, N.A., Tax Dept.
1 Court Sq., 22nd Fl.
Long Island City, NY 11120
Application address: 153 E. 53rd St., New York, NY 10043
Contact: Donna Kostanz, Trust Off., Citibank, N.A.

Financial data (yr. ended 12/31/00): Grants paid, $2,485; assets, $53,981 (M); expenditures, $3,141; qualifying distributions, $2,560.
Trustee: Citibank, N.A.
EIN: 136327940

39654
Mohansic Foundation, Inc.
6 Xavier Dr., Rm. 311A
Yonkers, NY 10704

Donor(s): David Gildin, Marcus Gildin.
Financial data (yr. ended 12/31/99): Grants paid, $2,475; assets, $148,790 (M); expenditures, $3,552; qualifying distributions, $2,831.
Limitations: Applications not accepted. Giving primarily in New York City and Westchester County, NY, and CT.
Application information: Contributes only to pre-selected organizations.
Officers: Marcus Gildin, Pres.; Gertrude Gildin, Secy.
EIN: 136187890

39655
Rebecca & Victor Barocas Foundation, Inc.
58 W. 40th St., 11th Fl.
New York, NY 10018

Financial data (yr. ended 05/31/02): Grants paid, $2,474; assets, $171,377 (M); expenditures, $2,780; qualifying distributions, $2,474.
Limitations: Applications not accepted. Giving primarily in NY, and Sumter, SC.
Application information: Contributes only to pre-selected organizations.
Officers: Martin Barocas, Pres.; Leon Barocas, Secy.; Albert Barocas, Treas.
EIN: 136272700

39656
Gitel Siegel Foundation, Inc.
c/o Ritter & Co.
25 Smith St., No. 405
Nanuet, NY 10954 (845) 624-7400
Contact: Jacob Siegel

Donor(s): Jack Siegel, Sharon Siegel.
Financial data (yr. ended 07/31/02): Grants paid, $2,469; assets, $304 (M); gifts received, $2,250; expenditures, $2,971; qualifying distributions, $2,469.
Limitations: Giving primarily in the New York, NY, area.
Officers: Jack Siegel, Pres.; Miriam Siegel, V.P.; Sharon Siegel, Secy.-Treas.
EIN: 132832462

39657
Dede Emerson Foundation, Inc.
33 Noel Dr.
Ossining, NY 10562 (914) 941-1644
Contact: Dede Emerson, Pres.

Established in 1995.
Donor(s): Dede Emerson.
Financial data (yr. ended 12/31/00): Grants paid, $2,459; assets, $84,089 (M); gifts received, $9,719; expenditures, $3,146; qualifying distributions, $3,346.
Limitations: Giving primarily in the greater Grand Rapids, MN school district.
Application information: Applications are available through the Grand Rapids High School counselors' office. Application form required.
Officers: Dede Emerson, Pres and Treas.; Warren Emerson, V.P.; Bonnie Emerson, Secy.
EIN: 133794936

39658
The Starfish Group
c/o Anchin Block & Anchin
1375 Broadway
New York, NY 10018

Established in 2000 in NY.
Financial data (yr. ended 12/31/01): Grants paid, $2,437; assets, $243,992 (M); gifts received, $249,246; expenditures, $2,437; qualifying distributions, $2,413.
Limitations: Applications not accepted.
Application information: Contributes only to pre-selected organizations.
Officers: Virginia Anne Gilder, Pres.; Lynn Slaughter, V.P.
Directors: Margaret Mathews, Alan Preston.
EIN: 134128526

39659
Mitchell Family Foundation, Inc.
c/o Victoria Mitchell Robbins
3 Treetop Ln.
Pleasantville, NY 10570

Financial data (yr. ended 10/31/00): Grants paid, $2,426; assets, $32,742 (M); expenditures, $2,501; qualifying distributions, $2,426.
Limitations: Applications not accepted.
Application information: Contributes only to pre-selected organizations.
Officer: Victoria Mitchell Robbins, Pres.
EIN: 136161091

39660
Joseph, Lisa, and Heidi Delorenzo Foundation
102 Greenway N.
Forest Hills, NY 11375

Established in 1999 in NY.
Financial data (yr. ended 12/31/00): Grants paid, $2,415; assets, $61,071 (M); expenditures, $6,846; qualifying distributions, $2,415.
Officers: Joseph A. Delorenzo, Pres.; Lisa Delorenzo, V.P.
Director: Rod Tabriztchi.
EIN: 522207236

39661
David & Elaine Pearce Foundation
8855 Tibbitts Rd.
New Hartford, NY 13413-5230

Established in 1985 in NY.
Financial data (yr. ended 12/31/01): Grants paid, $2,413; assets, $17,144 (M); gifts received, $465; expenditures, $3,048; qualifying distributions, $2,413.
Limitations: Applications not accepted. Giving primarily in NY.
Application information: Contributes only to pre-selected organizations.
Trustees: David F. Pearce, Elaine Pearce.
EIN: 222682444

39662
Simon and Esther Geldwerth Foundation
c/o Wasser, Brettler, Klar & Lipstein
132 Nassau St., Ste. 300
New York, NY 10038

Donor(s): Simon Geldwerth, Esther Geldwerth.
Financial data (yr. ended 09/30/01): Grants paid, $2,410; assets, $87,042 (M); expenditures, $3,160; qualifying distributions, $3,160.
Limitations: Applications not accepted.
Application information: Contributes only to pre-selected organizations.
Trustees: Esther Geldwerth, Simon Geldwerth.
EIN: 112487307

39663
The Baruch Handler and Raizel Handler Charitable Foundation
1840 52nd St., Ste. 21
Brooklyn, NY 11204

Financial data (yr. ended 06/30/01): Grants paid, $2,400; assets, $33,998 (M); gifts received, $4,700; expenditures, $5,772; qualifying distributions, $5,772.
Trustees: Baruch Handler, Raizel Handler.
EIN: 116466236

39664
The Ronald S. and Susan D. Hummel Family Foundation
19 Edgewood Pkwy.
Fayetteville, NY 13066 (315) 637-9569
Contact: Ronald & Susan Hummel

Established in 1999 in NY.
Donor(s): Ronald S. Hummel, Susan D. Hummel.
Financial data (yr. ended 12/31/01): Grants paid, $2,400; assets, $71,451 (M); expenditures, $3,360; qualifying distributions, $2,400.
Officers: Susan D. Hummel, Pres.; Robert G. Hummel, V.P.; Cynthia H. Taylor, V.P.; Michael J. Byrne, Secy.; Ronald S. Hummel, Treas.
EIN: 161577002

39665
Fred M. Teel Charitable Trust
c/o NBT Bank, N.A., Trust Dept.
52 S. Broad St.
Norwich, NY 13815-1646
Application address: c/o Guidance Dept., Afton Central School, Afton, NY 13733

Established in 1976 in NY.
Donor(s): Fred M. Teel.
Financial data (yr. ended 12/31/01): Grants paid, $2,400; assets, $74,295 (M); expenditures, $3,052; qualifying distributions, $2,838.
Limitations: Giving limited to residents of Afton, NY.
Application information: Application form required.
Trustee: NBT Bank, N.A.
EIN: 156020508
Codes: GTI

39666
The Vaitulis Family Charitable Trust
2825 Curry Rd.
Schenectady, NY 12303-3462

Established in 1990 in NY.
Donor(s): Aldona Vaitulis.
Financial data (yr. ended 12/31/01): Grants paid, $2,400; assets, $35,735 (M); expenditures, $2,740; qualifying distributions, $2,740.
Limitations: Applications not accepted. Giving primarily in IA.
Application information: Contributes only to pre-selected organizations.
Trustees: Aldona Vaitulis, Vetto Vaitulis.
EIN: 146151663

39667
Weiner & Bauer Foundation, Inc.
c/o William Greene & Co., PC
55 Katonah Ave.
Katonah, NY 10536
Contact: Donald Song, Pres.

Financial data (yr. ended 11/30/01): Grants paid, $2,400; assets, $66,033 (M); expenditures, $6,008; qualifying distributions, $2,400.
Limitations: Giving primarily in NY.
Officers: Donald Song, Pres.; Betsy Song, Secy.-Treas.
EIN: 136095344

39668
Louis C. Backhus Memorial Funds
P.O. Box 31412
Rochester, NY 14603

Established in 2001 in CT.
Donor(s): Bachus Charity.
Financial data (yr. ended 12/31/01): Grants paid, $2,389; assets, $85,199 (M); gifts received, $91,995; expenditures, $3,449; qualifying distributions, $2,495.
Limitations: Applications not accepted.
Application information: Contributes only to pre-selected organizations.
Trustee: JPMorgan Chase Bank.
EIN: 166530311

39669
Francis J. Taylor Trust
c/o JPMorgan Chase Bank
P.O. Box 31412
Rochester, NY 14603-1412

Financial data (yr. ended 12/31/00): Grants paid, $2,389; assets, $197,314 (M); expenditures, $8,188; qualifying distributions, $5,845.
Limitations: Applications not accepted. Giving primarily in NY.
Application information: Contributes only to pre-selected organizations.
Trustee: JPMorgan Chase Bank.
EIN: 166240793

39670
AHEPA Rochester Foundation
100 Ahepa Cir.
Webster, NY 14580

Financial data (yr. ended 12/31/99): Grants paid, $2,371; assets, $151,360 (M); gifts received, $3,479; expenditures, $4,371; qualifying distributions, $0.
Officers: Nicholas Tzimas, Pres.; Michael Papapanu, V.P.; Demosthenes R. Kiriazides, Secy.; Stelios Vordonis, Treas.
EIN: 161448695

39671
Bernard & Florence Galkin Foundation, Inc.
211 Court St.
P.O. Box 1616
Binghamton, NY 13902-1616

Established in 1994 in NY.
Donor(s): Florence Galkin.
Financial data (yr. ended 12/31/01): Grants paid, $2,353; assets, $138 (M); gifts received, $2,776; expenditures, $3,118; qualifying distributions, $2,353.
Limitations: Applications not accepted. Giving on a national basis.
Application information: Contributes only to pre-selected organizations.
Officers: Florence Galkin, Pres.; Judith Galkin, Secy.-Treas.
EIN: 133738476

39672
Lewyt Foundation, Inc.
Lewyt St.
Port Washington, NY 11050

Financial data (yr. ended 12/31/01): Grants paid, $2,350; assets, $23,965 (M); expenditures, $4,813; qualifying distributions, $2,350.
Limitations: Applications not accepted.
Application information: Contributes only to pre-selected organizations.
Officer: Elisabeth Lewyt, Mgr.
EIN: 136077745

39673
The Benjamin and Ruth Perse Family Foundation, Inc.
c/o Benjamin Perse
200 W. 86th St.
New York, NY 10024

Established in 1997 in NY.
Donor(s): Ruth Perse.
Financial data (yr. ended 04/30/02): Grants paid, $2,350; assets, $127,154 (M); expenditures, $2,645; qualifying distributions, $2,350.
Limitations: Applications not accepted.
Application information: Contributes only to pre-selected organizations.
Officers and Directors:* Benjamin Perse,* Pres.; Harold E. Perse,* V.P.; Lawrence Perse,* V.P.; Victor S. Perse,* V.P.; Ruth Perse,* Secy.
EIN: 133949299

39674
Anna and Marvin Jaffe Family Foundation Trust
740 Eagle Dr.
Valley Stream, NY 11581-3540
(516) 791-3460
Contact: Marvin Jaffe, Tr.

Established in 1989 in NY.
Donor(s): Anna Jaffe, Marvin Jaffe.

Financial data (yr. ended 11/30/01): Grants paid, $2,346; assets, $1,738 (L); expenditures, $2,580; qualifying distributions, $2,346.
Limitations: Giving primarily in North Woodmere, NY.
Trustees: Anna Jaffe, Marvin Jaffe.
EIN: 116378706

39675
The Herbert L. Samuels & Elsie R. Schwartz Foundation, Inc.
c/o Dorothy Malett
851 Glen Dr.
Woodmere, NY 11598

Donor(s): S & S Industries, Inc.
Financial data (yr. ended 10/31/01): Grants paid, $2,315; assets, $26,694 (M); expenditures, $2,346; qualifying distributions, $2,315.
Limitations: Applications not accepted. Giving primarily in the metropolitan New York, NY, area.
Application information: Contributes only to pre-selected organizations.
Officers: Dorothy Malett, Pres.; Jerry Malett, V.P.; Rhoda Miller, V.P.; Alan Miller, Secy.-Treas.
EIN: 133471562
Codes: CS, CD

39676
Jacques M. Levy & Co. Foundation, Inc.
150 Great Neck Rd., Ste. 100
Great Neck, NY 11021

Donor(s): Jacques M. Levy & Co.
Financial data (yr. ended 03/31/02): Grants paid, $2,300; assets, $2,477 (M); expenditures, $2,300; qualifying distributions, $2,300.
Limitations: Applications not accepted. Giving primarily in NY.
Application information: Contributes only to pre-selected organizations.
Officers: Sol Greenbaum, Pres.; Sidney H. Greene, V.P.; Jerald B. Greenberg, Secy.
EIN: 136123188
Codes: CS, CD

39677
Radow Foundation
175-20 Wexford Terr., Apt. 14X
Jamaica, NY 11432
Contact: Roy B. Radow, Mgr.

Financial data (yr. ended 12/31/01): Grants paid, $2,300; assets, $24,888 (M); expenditures, $3,020; qualifying distributions, $2,300.
Limitations: Giving primarily in NY.
Officer: Roy B. Radow, Mgr.
EIN: 237052082

39678
White Family Trust
240 Old Montauk Hwy.
Montauk, NY 11954

Financial data (yr. ended 12/31/01): Grants paid, $2,300; assets, $49,076 (M); gifts received, $13,300; expenditures, $2,311; qualifying distributions, $2,300.
Limitations: Applications not accepted. Giving primarily in NY.
Application information: Contributes only to pre-selected organizations.
Officer and Trustees:* Eugene B. White,* Mgr.; Adam White, Claudia White.
EIN: 136089984

39679
The Mellinger Family Foundation
75 Inningwood Rd.
Millwood, NY 10546
Contact: Jerome D. Mellinger, Pres.

Donor(s): Barbara Mellinger, Jerome D. Mellinger.
Financial data (yr. ended 05/31/02): Grants paid, $2,250; assets, $6,801 (M); expenditures, $3,932; qualifying distributions, $2,250.
Limitations: Applications not accepted.
Application information: Contributes only to pre-selected organizations.
Officers: Jerome D. Mellinger, Pres.; Douglas K. Mellinger, V.P.; Gregory S. Mellinger, V.P.; Barbara Mellinger, Secy.; Paul L. Mellinger, Treas.
EIN: 134011007

39680
Newman W. Benson Foundation
c/o Chemung Canal Trust Co.
P.O. Box 1522
Elmira, NY 14902
Contact: Patti Crandell, Trust Off.

Established in 1990 in NY.
Donor(s): Newman W. Benson.
Financial data (yr. ended 12/31/01): Grants paid, $2,249; assets, $815,111 (M); expenditures, $60,905; qualifying distributions, $2,249.
Limitations: Giving primarily in Bradford and Towanda County, PA.
Trustee: Chemung Canal Trust Co.
EIN: 161387370

39681
Wingate Memorial Carillon Foundation
81 N. Main St.
Alfred, NY 14802 (607) 587-8118
Contact: Daniel E. Rase, Tr. or Margaret W. Rase, Tr.

Established in 1995 in NY.
Donor(s): Daniel E. Rase, Margaret Wingate Rase.
Financial data (yr. ended 12/31/01): Grants paid, $2,227; assets, $11,438 (M); gifts received, $3,100; expenditures, $2,491; qualifying distributions, $2,227.
Trustees: Daniel E. Rase, Margaret Wingate Rase.
EIN: 161483372

39682
Francis and Eve Barron Charitable Foundation
c/o Cravath, Swaine & Moore
825 8th Ave., 40th Fl.
New York, NY 10019-7416

Established in 1986 in NY.
Donor(s): Francis P. Barron.
Financial data (yr. ended 11/30/01): Grants paid, $2,225; assets, $34,555 (M); expenditures, $2,407; qualifying distributions, $2,225.
Limitations: Applications not accepted. Giving limited to NY.
Application information: Contributes only to pre-selected organizations.
Trustee: Francis P. Barron.
EIN: 133383346

39683
Joan & Barry Tucker Foundation, Inc.
c/o Joan Tucker
716 Old Post Rd.
Bedford, NY 10506-1212

Established in 1996 in NY.
Financial data (yr. ended 12/31/01): Grants paid, $2,225; assets, $348 (M); gifts received, $3,000; expenditures, $3,228; qualifying distributions, $2,225.

Limitations: Applications not accepted. Giving primarily in NY.
Application information: Contributes only to pre-selected organizations.
Officers: Barry Tucker, Pres.; Joan Tucker, Secy.-Treas.
EIN: 133395422

39684
War & Peace Foundation for Education, Inc.
20 E. 9th St., Ste 23E
New York, NY 10003

Established in 1993 in NY.
Donor(s): Selma Brackman.
Financial data (yr. ended 12/31/00): Grants paid, $2,220; assets, $28,614 (M); gifts received, $120,195; expenditures, $99,508; qualifying distributions, $99,508; giving activities include $99,508 for programs.
Limitations: Applications not accepted.
Application information: Contributes only to pre-selected organizations.
Officers: Selma Brackman, Pres.; Jessica Brackman, V.P.; Kevin Sanders, Secy.
EIN: 133599092

39685
Andrew J. Feldman Foundation
c/o Cornick, Garber & Sandler, LLP
630 3rd Ave.
New York, NY 10017

Established in 1996 in NY.
Donor(s): Andrew J. Feldman.
Financial data (yr. ended 06/30/01): Grants paid, $2,200; assets, $254,065 (M); gifts received, $45,000; expenditures, $3,853; qualifying distributions, $2,250.
Limitations: Applications not accepted. Giving on a national basis, with some emphasis on the East Coast.
Application information: Contributes only to pre-selected organizations.
Officers: Andrew J. Feldman, Pres.; Richard S. Zimmerman, V.P. and Secy.; Joshua Wesson, V.P.
EIN: 133886828

39686
Keith Educational Scholarship Fund
c/o Wyoming County Bank
55 N. Main St.
Warsaw, NY 14569
Application address: c/o Wyoming Central School District, Academy St., Wyoming, NY 14591, tel.: (716) 786-3131

Financial data (yr. ended 12/31/99): Grants paid, $2,200; assets, $32,897 (L); expenditures, $2,254; qualifying distributions, $2,254.
Limitations: Giving limited to residents of Middlebury, CT.
Application information: Application form required.
Officer and Scholarship Committee Members:* Kevin Maroney,* V.P. and Treas.; Rev. Stephen Calos, Rev. Andrew Chalmer, Jon Cooper, David Dinolfo, Rev. Douglas Evans, Malina Hannon.
EIN: 166027803

39687
The Carolyn Miles Spencer Foundation
39 Drohan St.
Huntington, NY 11743

Established in 2000 in NY.
Donor(s): William T. Margiotta, Jr., Joan C. Margiotta.
Financial data (yr. ended 08/31/01): Grants paid, $2,200; assets, $841 (M); gifts received, $6,750;

39687—NEW YORK

expenditures, $5,909; qualifying distributions, $2,200.
Limitations: Applications not accepted. Giving primarily in Seattle, WA.
Application information: Contributes only to pre-selected organizations.
Officers: William T. Margiotta, Jr., Pres.; Thomas C. Margiotta, V.P.; William J. Margiotta, V.P.; Joan C. Margiotta, Secy.-Treas.
EIN: 113567200

39688
Whole Earth Charitable Trust
2106 Bailey Rd.
Ontario, NY 14519-9612

Donor(s): Jason Bowman.
Financial data (yr. ended 12/31/01): Grants paid, $2,200; assets, $17,077 (M); gifts received, $7,053; expenditures, $5,014; qualifying distributions, $4,494.
Limitations: Applications not accepted.
Application information: Contributes only to pre-selected organizations.
Trustee: Jason Bowman.
EIN: 527090699

39689
Polyscope Action Fund
454 W. 46th St., Apt. 405
New York, NY 10036

Established in 1998 in NY.
Donor(s): Amy Conrad Stokes, Christopher M. Stokes.
Financial data (yr. ended 12/31/01): Grants paid, $2,195; assets, $64,386 (M); gifts received, $32,125; expenditures, $2,303; qualifying distributions, $2,195.
Limitations: Applications not accepted.
Application information: Contributes only to pre-selected organizations.
Officers and Directors:* Amy Conrad Stokes,* Pres.; Christopher M. Stokes,* Secy.-Treas.; Alison L. Paul.
EIN: 061533274

39690
The William and Edith Berger Foundation, Inc.
1407 46th St.
Brooklyn, NY 11219-2633

Established in 1992 in NY.
Donor(s): William Berger.
Financial data (yr. ended 12/31/01): Grants paid, $2,175; assets, $329,257 (M); expenditures, $3,639; qualifying distributions, $2,541.
Limitations: Applications not accepted.
Application information: Contributes only to pre-selected organizations.
Officers: William Berger, Pres.; Edith Berger, Secy.
Directors: David Berger, Harold Berger, Larry Berger, Richie Brown.
EIN: 113110041

39691
Aram Rahman Chowdhury Memorial Foundation
722 Montauk Hwy.
West Islip, NY 11795 (631) 587-3340
Contact: Dr. Faizur R. Chowdhury, Pres.

Established in 1995 in NY.
Financial data (yr. ended 12/31/99): Grants paid, $2,150; assets, $79,563 (M); gifts received, $10,359; expenditures, $2,808; qualifying distributions, $2,558.
Limitations: Giving primarily in Suffolk and Nassau counties, NY.
Application information: Application form not required.

Officers: Faizur R. Chowdhury, Pres.; Tamanna Pullman, V.P.; Ellen R. Chowdhury, Secy.-Treas.
EIN: 113241316

39692
Henry Plehn Foundation, Inc.
c/o P. Diener
425 E. 58th St., Ste. 16D
New York, NY 10022
Contact: Patricia Diener, Tr.

Financial data (yr. ended 12/31/01): Grants paid, $2,124; assets, $53,824 (M); expenditures, $2,599; qualifying distributions, $2,124.
Application information: Application form not required.
Trustee: Patricia Diener.
EIN: 136169146

39693
Audrey and Eli Weinberg Charitable Foundation
c/o Arthur Friedman
280 Madison Ave., Ste. 1007
New York, NY 10016

Established in 1986 in NY.
Donor(s): Eli Weinberg.
Financial data (yr. ended 12/31/00): Grants paid, $2,110; assets, $44,412 (M); gifts received, $111; expenditures, $2,230; qualifying distributions, $2,110.
Limitations: Applications not accepted. Giving limited to NY.
Application information: Contributes only to pre-selected organizations.
Officers and Directors:* Eli Weinberg,* Pres.; Audrey Weinberg,* V.P.; Paul Herman, Secy.; Arthur Friedman, Treas.
EIN: 112848291

39694
Cumming 2000 Charitable Trust
45 Lookout View Rd.
Fairport, NY 14450

Established in 2000 in NY.
Donor(s): Donald J. Cumming, Judith V. Cumming.
Financial data (yr. ended 12/31/01): Grants paid, $2,100; assets, $69,780 (M); gifts received, $38,713; expenditures, $2,100; qualifying distributions, $2,100.
Limitations: Applications not accepted. Giving primarily in Buffalo, NY.
Application information: Contributes only to pre-selected organizations.
Trustees: Donald J. Cumming, Judith V. Cumming.
EIN: 166513818

39695
Sean Q. Flynn Charitable Trust
328 W. 87th St., Ste. 3
New York, NY 10024

Financial data (yr. ended 12/31/00): Grants paid, $2,100; assets, $29,862 (M); expenditures, $2,100; qualifying distributions, $2,100.
Trustees: George Flynn, Sean Flynn.
EIN: 941737782

39696
The Patrick Halligan Foundation
164 E. 72nd St.
New York, NY 10021

Established in 1998 in NY.
Donor(s): Margaret Duffy.
Financial data (yr. ended 12/31/99): Grants paid, $2,100; assets, $41,266 (M); expenditures, $2,150; qualifying distributions, $2,100.
Limitations: Applications not accepted.

Application information: Contributes only to pre-selected organizations.
Officers and Trustees:* Margaret Duffy,* Pres.; Mary Travers, Secy.; Nancy Kelly,* Treas.
EIN: 134015187

39697
Philip Messinger Family Foundation, Inc.
c/o A. Fishman, H. Wolfson & Co.
370 7th Ave.
New York, NY 10001-3901

Established in 1987 in NY.
Donor(s): Philip Messinger.
Financial data (yr. ended 12/31/01): Grants paid, $2,100; assets, $20,444 (M); expenditures, $2,186; qualifying distributions, $2,100.
Limitations: Applications not accepted.
Application information: Contributes only to pre-selected organizations.
Officers and Directors:* Leticia Celenza,* Pres. and Secy.; Philip Messinger,* Treas.; Bruce Messinger, Caryl Taylor.
EIN: 133378588

39698
Louis M. Rabinowitz Foundation, Inc.
740 Broadway
New York, NY 10003

Financial data (yr. ended 12/31/01): Grants paid, $2,100; assets, $97,903 (M); expenditures, $3,212; qualifying distributions, $2,100.
Limitations: Giving primarily in the metropolitan New York, NY, area.
Application information: Application form not required.
Officer: Victor Rabinowitz, Pres.
EIN: 136093070

39699
Retired Transit Police Officers Foundation, Inc.
626 Elton St.
Brooklyn, NY 11208

Financial data (yr. ended 12/31/00): Grants paid, $2,100; assets, $7,193 (M); expenditures, $7,443; qualifying distributions, $0.
Limitations: Applications not accepted.
Application information: Contributes only to pre-selected organizations.
Officers: Frederick Bodie, Pres.; Leonard Alston, V.P.; Claude Henry, Secy.; Elwood Hazel, Treas.
EIN: 133168656

39700
The William D. Vogel Foundation, Inc.
c/o Clifford, Chance, Rogers & Wells
200 Park Ave.
New York, NY 10166
Application address: 45 E. End Ave., New York, NY 10028
Contact: William D. Vogel, Pres.

Established in 1999 in NY.
Donor(s): William D. Vogel II.
Financial data (yr. ended 12/31/01): Grants paid, $2,100; assets, $17,039 (M); expenditures, $7,123; qualifying distributions, $2,100.
Officers: William D. Vogel, Pres.; Ralph B. Vogel II, Secy.; Mary T. Vogel, Treas.
Directors: Diana G. Vogel, Mabel H. Vogel, Ralph B. Vogel.
EIN: 134037664

39701
Sylvia & Sidney Reznik Foundation
2630 Cropsey Ave.
Brooklyn, NY 11214

Donor(s): Sylvia Reznik, Sidney Reznik.

Financial data (yr. ended 02/28/01): Grants paid, $2,098; assets, $26,611 (M); expenditures, $2,114; qualifying distributions, $2,098.
Limitations: Applications not accepted. Giving primarily in NY.
Application information: Contributes only to pre-selected organizations.
Trustees: Sidney Reznik, Sylvia Reznik.
EIN: 112630818

39702
Walton Central School District Trust No. 1
c/o The National Bank of Delaware County
P.O. Box 389
Walton, NY 13856
Application address: c/o Guidance Dept., Walton High School, Walton, NY 13856

Financial data (yr. ended 12/31/00): Grants paid, $2,075; assets, $94,030 (M); expenditures, $2,715; qualifying distributions, $2,398.
Limitations: Giving limited to residents of Walton, NY.
Application information: Application form required.
Trustee: The National Bank of Delaware County.
EIN: 166280038
Codes: GTI

39703
Louise & Marvin Fenster Foundation, Inc.
535 E. 86th St.
New York, NY 10028-7533

Donor(s): Marvin Fenster.
Financial data (yr. ended 12/31/01): Grants paid, $2,061; assets, $19,683 (M); expenditures, $2,086; qualifying distributions, $2,061.
Limitations: Giving primarily in New York, NY.
Application information: Application form not required.
Officers: Julie Fenster, Secy.; Marvin Fenster, Mgr.
EIN: 136277914

39704
Nathan & Eva Treitel Foundation, Inc.
c/o N. Treitel & Co., Inc.
244 W. 30th St.
New York, NY 10001-4901 (212) 736-6138
Contact: Theodore Treitel, Tr.

Donor(s): N. Treitel & Co., Inc., Rudolf Treitel, Theodore Treitel.
Financial data (yr. ended 12/31/01): Grants paid, $2,060; assets, $46,973 (M); expenditures, $2,118; qualifying distributions, $2,060.
Trustees: Rudolf Treitel, Theodore Treitel.
EIN: 136219640

39705
The Vincent Kosuga & Pauline Kosuga Foundation, Inc.
P.O. Box 630
Warwick, NY 10990

Established in 1997 in NY.
Financial data (yr. ended 12/31/00): Grants paid, $2,056; assets, $52,483 (M); expenditures, $2,807; qualifying distributions, $2,056.
Limitations: Applications not accepted.
Application information: Contributes only to pre-selected organizations.
Directors: Pauline Kosuga, Vincent Kosuga, Mary Olsen.
EIN: 133947073

39706
Perkins Charitable Foundation
1494 Wendell Ave.
Schenectady, NY 12308 (518) 374-6815
Contact: Michael T. Brockbank, Tr.

Established in 1999 in NY.
Financial data (yr. ended 12/31/00): Grants paid, $2,037; assets, $617,620 (M); expenditures, $8,178; qualifying distributions, $8,178.
Limitations: Giving primarily in Schenectady, NY.
Trustee: Michael T. Brockbank.
EIN: 161531489

39707
Peter & Harold Lewison Foundation
c/o Kleinfeld
315 E. 69th St.
New York, NY 10021

Financial data (yr. ended 12/31/01): Grants paid, $2,026; assets, $33,521 (M); expenditures, $5,052; qualifying distributions, $2,026.
Application information: Application form not required.
Officers: Miriam Lewison, Pres.; Peggy Brenner, Secy.
EIN: 136174019

39708
Raymond and Ruth D. Laven Charitable Foundation, Inc.
134 Melrose Ave.
Albany, NY 12203 (518) 438-7026
Contact: Ruth D. Laven, Pres.

Established in 2001 in NY.
Donor(s): Ruth D. Laven.
Financial data (yr. ended 12/31/01): Grants paid, $2,005; assets, $214,440 (M); gifts received, $260,908; expenditures, $8,314; qualifying distributions, $8,314.
Application information: Application form required.
Officers and Directors:* Ruth D. Laven,* Pres.; Barbara L. Laven,* V.P.; Murray S. Carr,* Secy.; Michael B. Laven,* Treas.
EIN: 141821110

39709
AHEPA Syracuse Foundation, Inc.
100 Ahepa Cir.
Syracuse, NY 13215

Financial data (yr. ended 12/31/01): Grants paid, $2,000; assets, $2,879 (M); gifts received, $3,329; expenditures, $2,823; qualifying distributions, $2,000.
Officers: Peter Manolakos, Pres.; George Papageorge, V.P.; Bill Kousmonides, Secy.; Christ Lemonides, Treas.
EIN: 161538634

39710
The Aurelia Foundation, Inc.
303 E. 83rd St.
New York, NY 10028
Contact: Susan A. Gitelson, Pres.

Established in 1990 in NY.
Donor(s): Susan A. Gitelson.
Financial data (yr. ended 12/31/00): Grants paid, $2,000; assets, $1,918 (M); gifts received, $1,000; expenditures, $2,030; qualifying distributions, $2,000.
Limitations: Giving primarily in New York, NY.
Application information: Application form not required.
Officer: Susan A. Gitelson, Pres.
EIN: 133575971

39711
Jon Benedetto Memorial Scholarship Fund, Inc.
3120 Arthur Kill Rd.
Staten Island, NY 10309

Established in 1997 in NY.
Donor(s): Gar Benedetto & Sons Swere Contracting, Inc.
Financial data (yr. ended 03/31/00): Grants paid, $2,000; assets, $35,266 (M); gifts received, $304; expenditures, $2,150; qualifying distributions, $1,986.
Limitations: Applications not accepted.
Application information: Contributes only to pre-selected organizations.
Officer: Nancy Benedetto, Secy.
EIN: 133949269

39712
Kenneth and Mamie Phipps Clark Family Foundation, Inc.
17 Pinecrest Dr.
Hastings-on-Hudson, NY 10706

Financial data (yr. ended 11/30/00): Grants paid, $2,000; assets, $40,570 (M); expenditures, $6,237; qualifying distributions, $2,000.
Limitations: Applications not accepted. Giving primarily in New York, NY.
Application information: Contributes only to pre-selected organizations.
Officers: Kenneth B. Clark, Pres.; Hilton B. Clark, V.P.; Kate C. Harris, V.P.
EIN: 133573145

39713
Crystal Foundation
c/o Crystal Window & Door Systems Ltd.
31-10 Whitestone Expwy.
Flushing, NY 11354-2531

Established in 2000 in NY.
Donor(s): Crystal Window & Door Systems, Ltd.
Financial data (yr. ended 04/30/01): Grants paid, $2,000; assets, $47,584 (M); gifts received, $52,300; expenditures, $5,000; qualifying distributions, $26,297; giving activities include $21,300 for programs.
Limitations: Applications not accepted. Giving primarily in NJ and NY.
Application information: Contributes only to pre-selected organizations.
Officers and Directors:* Thomas Chen,* Pres.; Anna Chen,* Secy.; Jen-In Tsou.
EIN: 113540759
Codes: CS, CD

39714
DBM Charitable Trust
5218 14th Ave.
Brooklyn, NY 11219-3929

Established in 1998 in NY.
Donor(s): David Meisels.
Financial data (yr. ended 12/31/00): Grants paid, $2,000; assets, $195,836 (M); gifts received, $115,500; expenditures, $6,360; qualifying distributions, $2,000.
Limitations: Applications not accepted.
Application information: Contributes only to pre-selected organizations.
Trustees: David Meisels, Joseph Meisels.
EIN: 116509169

39715
The Virginia McDonald Delehanty Scholarship Fund
c/o John M. Delehanty
666 3rd Ave.
New York, NY 10017-4011
Application address: c/o Ray T. Granai, Asst. Principal, Weymouth High School, 1051 Commercial St., E. Weymouth, MA 02189

Financial data (yr. ended 07/31/01): Grants paid, $2,000; assets, $27,657 (M); expenditures, $3,260; qualifying distributions, $1,988.
Limitations: Giving limited to Weymouth, MA.
Application information: Application form required.
Trustees: Dennis M. Delehanty, Hugh J. Delehanty, John M. Delehanty.
EIN: 042681343

39716
The Joseph P. Ferrugio Family Charitable Trust
466 Lexington Ave., 18th Fl.
New York, NY 10017

Established in 1997 in NY.
Donor(s): Joseph P. Ferrugio, Jennison Associates, LLC.
Financial data (yr. ended 12/31/01): Grants paid, $2,000; assets, $44,344 (M); gifts received, $80; expenditures, $2,105; qualifying distributions, $2,000.
Limitations: Applications not accepted. Giving primarily in NY.
Application information: Contributes only to pre-selected organizations.
Trustees: Catherine Ferrugio, Joseph P. Ferrugio.
EIN: 066455282

39717
Ida Fink Memorial Association
1247 E. 8th St.
Brooklyn, NY 11230-5105
Contact: David Goldman, Pres.

Financial data (yr. ended 12/31/99): Grants paid, $2,000; assets, $10,671 (M); gifts received, $2,400; expenditures, $2,148; qualifying distributions, $2,000.
Limitations: Giving primarily in NY.
Officer: David Goldman, Pres.
EIN: 237259908

39718
Joseph Finkelstein and Nadia Ehrich Finkelstein Foundation
2416 Brookshire Dr.
Niskayuna, NY 12309-4855

Established in 1997.
Donor(s): Joseph F. Finkelstein, Nadia Ehrich Finkelstein.
Financial data (yr. ended 12/31/01): Grants paid, $2,000; assets, $0 (M); gifts received, $2,335; expenditures, $2,165; qualifying distributions, $2,000.
Limitations: Applications not accepted.
Application information: Contributes only to pre-selected organizations.
Officers: Joseph F. Finkelstein, Pres.; Nadia Ehrich Finkelstein, V.P.
EIN: 161527136

39719
Foundation for Intestinal and Nutritional Disorders
116 Carthage Rd.
Scarsdale, NY 10583-7202

Financial data (yr. ended 09/30/01): Grants paid, $2,000; assets, $17,419 (M); expenditures, $2,014; qualifying distributions, $2,000.
Limitations: Applications not accepted. Giving primarily in NY.
Application information: Contributes only to pre-selected organizations.
Trustees: Alan S. Pearce, David B. Pearce, Linda P. Rosensweig.
EIN: 132893324

39720
The Howard Gillman Foundation
c/o Wiener, Frushtick & Straub, PC
500 5th Ave., Ste. 2610
New York, NY 10110

Established in 1997 in CA.
Donor(s): Howard Gillman.
Financial data (yr. ended 12/31/00): Grants paid, $2,000; assets, $38,379 (M); expenditures, $2,080; qualifying distributions, $2,000.
Limitations: Applications not accepted.
Application information: Contributes only to pre-selected organizations.
Officers and Director:* Howard Gillman,* Pres.; Kathleen Gillman, Secy.-Treas.
EIN: 954633605

39721
Elsie S. Greathead Trust
c/o M&T Bank
1 M&T PLz., 8th Fl.
Buffalo, NY 14203
Application address: c/o M&T Bank, 14 N. Main St., Chambersburg, PA 17201, tel.: (717) 267-7625
Contact: John Schall, Tr.

Established in 1991.
Donor(s): Elsie Greathead.‡
Financial data (yr. ended 12/31/01): Grants paid, $2,000; assets, $42,175 (M); expenditures, $3,228; qualifying distributions, $1,974.
Limitations: Giving limited to residents of McConnellsburg, PA.
Application information: Application form required.
Trustee: M & T Bank.
EIN: 236263603

39722
The Sara Greco and Lucy Muffoletto Foundation
228 Linwood Ave.
Buffalo, NY 14209

Established in 1997 in NY.
Donor(s): Vincent J. Muffoletto.
Financial data (yr. ended 11/30/01): Grants paid, $2,000; assets, $29,804 (M); gifts received, $6,215; expenditures, $2,135; qualifying distributions, $2,000.
Limitations: Applications not accepted. Giving primarily in NY and TN.
Application information: Contributes only to pre-selected organizations.
Officers: Vincent J. Muffoletto, Pres.; Donna M. Campbell, V.P.; Michele Iversen, Treas.
EIN: 161541459

39723
Ada Janow Jacobs Scholarship Fund, Inc.
16 Deer Meadow Dr.
West Nyack, NY 10994

Financial data (yr. ended 12/31/01): Grants paid, $2,000; assets, $305 (M); gifts received, $516; expenditures, $2,028; qualifying distributions, $2,000.
Limitations: Applications not accepted. Giving primarily in New York, NY.
Application information: Unsolicited requests for funds not accepted.
Officer and Directors:* Hugh Janow,* Pres.; Glenn Jacobs, Linda Janow, Mildred Janow, Rony Kessler.
EIN: 133254147

39724
Senator Norman J. Levy and Joy Levy Charitable Foundation
c/o Davis & Gilbert
1740 Broadway
New York, NY 10019 (212) 468-4800
Contact: Jerry Saslow, Dir.

Financial data (yr. ended 06/30/02): Grants paid, $2,000; assets, $9,670 (M); expenditures, $2,921; qualifying distributions, $2,000.
Directors: Joy Levy, Jerry Saslow, Lisa Young.
EIN: 134031711

39725
Linda & Phyliss Malin Foundation
128 E. 7th St., 5th Fl.
New York, NY 10009-6100
Contact: Linda Malin, Tr.

Established in 1999.
Financial data (yr. ended 12/31/00): Grants paid, $2,000; assets, $95,375 (M); gifts received, $65,000; expenditures, $2,000; qualifying distributions, $2,100.
Trustee: Linda Malin.
EIN: 134051198

39726
George Barry Mallon Memorial Foundation
c/o E. Nobles Lowe
554 Gipsy Trail Rd.
Carmel, NY 10512-4206

Financial data (yr. ended 12/31/99): Grants paid, $2,000; assets, $19,717 (M); gifts received, $100; expenditures, $2,151; qualifying distributions, $2,135.
Officers and Directors: Edward Crane, Jr.,* Pres.; E. Nobles Lowe,* Secy.-Treas.; Jennifer Allen, Tom Bisky, Peter Brown, Ray Errol Fox, Wade Kirby.
EIN: 136133318

39727
Joseph and Esther Mandel Foundation, Inc.
742 Wilson St.
Valley Stream, NY 11581

Established in 1988 in NY.
Donor(s): Joseph Mandel, Esther Mandel.
Financial data (yr. ended 11/30/01): Grants paid, $2,000; assets, $82,316 (M); expenditures, $3,771; qualifying distributions, $2,000.
Limitations: Applications not accepted.
Application information: Contributes only to pre-selected organizations.
Directors: Fritzie Fink, Kenneth S. Fink.
EIN: 133494910

39728
M. Regina McCormick Memorial Scholarship Foundation
94 Melrose St.
Buffalo, NY 14220-1624 (716) 824-4512
Contact: James J. Brady, Tr.

Financial data (yr. ended 10/31/00): Grants paid, $2,000; assets, $9,273 (M); expenditures, $2,130; qualifying distributions, $2,055.
Limitations: Giving primarily in Buffalo, NY.
Application information: Application form required.
Trustee: James J. Brady.
EIN: 166120335

39729
J. A. Melnick Foundation, Inc.
c/o Young Stuff Apparel
1407 Broadway, Ste. 610
New York, NY 10018

Donor(s): Jacob A. Melnick.‡
Financial data (yr. ended 12/31/99): Grants paid, $2,000; assets, $1 (M); expenditures, $2,325; qualifying distributions, $2,000.
Limitations: Applications not accepted. Giving primarily in NY.
Application information: Contributes only to pre-selected organizations.
Officers: R.E. Melnick, Pres.; J.A. Miller, Secy.; K.J. Miller, Treas.
EIN: 136219137

39730
Louis G. Merritt Trust Education Fund
c/o HSBC Bank USA
P.O. Box 4203, 17th Fl.
Buffalo, NY 14240

Financial data (yr. ended 10/31/01): Grants paid, $2,000; assets, $43,758 (M); expenditures, $2,761; qualifying distributions, $2,000.
Limitations: Applications not accepted. Giving primarily in NY and PA.
Application information: Contributes only to pre-selected organizations.
Trustee: HSBC Bank USA.
EIN: 166021084

39731
Mildred R. Mulroy Scholarship Fund
c/o A.G. Edwards & Sons, Inc.
5786 Widewaters Pkwy.
Syracuse, NY 13214 (315) 449-4344
Contact: Bill Branson, Jr., Tr.

Established in 1996 in NY.
Donor(s): Bill Branson, Jr.
Financial data (yr. ended 12/31/99): Grants paid, $2,000; assets, $37,012 (M); gifts received, $2,038; expenditures, $5,573; qualifying distributions, $3,800.
Limitations: Giving limited to residents of Marcellus, NY.
Application information: Application form required.
Trustees: Bill Branson, Jr., Bruce Widger.
EIN: 166426024

39732
Sybil Trent Nieporent Foundation, Inc.
239 W. Broadway
New York, NY 10013
Contact: Tracy Nieporent, Dir.

Established in 2000 in NY.
Donor(s): Drew Nieporent, Tracy Nieporent.
Financial data (yr. ended 12/31/01): Grants paid, $2,000; assets, $18,500 (M); gifts received, $7,195; expenditures, $2,650; qualifying distributions, $2,080.
Directors: Drew Nieporent, Tracy Nieporent, Steven R. Wagner.
EIN: 134122820

39733
Bertram & Sally Nirenberg Foundation, Inc.
c/o Stulmaker, Kohn, and Richardson
524 Broadway
Albany, NY 12207

Financial data (yr. ended 12/31/01): Grants paid, $2,000; assets, $895 (M); expenditures, $2,355; qualifying distributions, $2,000.
Limitations: Applications not accepted. Giving primarily in NY.
Application information: Contributes only to pre-selected organizations.
Trustee: Kenneth M. Nirenberg.
EIN: 146033255

39734
Northrup Educational Foundation, Inc.
2485 County Line Rd.
Watkins Glen, NY 14891-9512
(607) 535-7438
Contact: Marilyn W. Cross, Secy.-Treas.

Established in 1942 in NY.
Financial data (yr. ended 08/31/01): Grants paid, $2,000; assets, $298,888 (M); expenditures, $7,648; qualifying distributions, $26,265; giving activities include $21,579 for loans to individuals.
Limitations: Giving limited to residents of Schuyler County, NY.
Application information: Application form required.
Officers and Directors:* William Ellison, Pres.; Anne Meehan,* V.P.; Marilyn W. Cross, Secy.-Treas.; Jean Argetsinger, Carol Boyce, Richard B. Corbett, Mary Ellen Correa, Marie Earl, Brian O'Donnell, Kenneth Wilson.
EIN: 156020359
Codes: GTI

39735
Martin Pinsley Neonatology Fund, Inc.
58 Washington St.
Saratoga Springs, NY 12866-4100
(518) 587-5111

Financial data (yr. ended 12/31/01): Grants paid, $2,000; assets, $51,614 (M); gifts received, $1,201; expenditures, $2,124; qualifying distributions, $2,000.
Limitations: Giving on a national basis, with emphasis on the Northeast.
Application information: Application form not required.
Officers: Barry Pinsley, Pres.; Carol L. Pinsley, Secy.
EIN: 510185953

39736
The Sabatine Foundation
110 E. 64th St.
New York, NY 10021

Established in 1999 in DE.
Donor(s): Matthew Sabatine.
Financial data (yr. ended 12/31/01): Grants paid, $2,000; assets, $38,880 (M); expenditures, $2,210; qualifying distributions, $2,000.
Limitations: Applications not accepted. Giving primarily in MA and NY.
Application information: Contributes only to pre-selected organizations.
Officers: Matthew Sabatine, Pres.; Marc Sabatine, V.P.; Natalie Sabatine, Secy.-Treas.
EIN: 133985372

39737
The Sandy Foundation
c/o Sayles & Evans
1 W. Church St.
Elmira, NY 14901

Established in 2000 in NY.
Donor(s): Joanie L. Dunham, Craig T. Dunham.
Financial data (yr. ended 04/30/01): Grants paid, $2,000; assets, $91,923 (M); gifts received, $101,207; expenditures, $3,557; qualifying distributions, $2,000.
Limitations: Applications not accepted. Giving primarily in IN and NY.
Application information: Contributes only to pre-selected organizations.
Officers and Trustees:* Joanie L. Dunham,* Pres.; Craig T. Dunham,* Secy.-Treas.; Pamela Mayes.
EIN: 161577947

39738
Judge Louis B. Scheinman Memorial Scholarship Fund Charitable Trust
Stangel Rd.
P.O. Box 27
Woodbourne, NY 12788
Contact: Robert B. Scheinman, Tr.

Financial data (yr. ended 08/31/01): Grants paid, $2,000; assets, $19,886 (M); gifts received, $1,475; expenditures, $2,000; qualifying distributions, $1,988.
Limitations: Giving limited to residents of Sullivan County, NY.
Application information: Application form required.
Trustees: Ava B. Kleinman, Robert B. Scheinman, Steven J. Scheinman.
EIN: 222684635

39739
Silbert Family Charitable Foundation
120 E. 81st St., Ste. 8F
New York, NY 10028

Established in 1998 in NY.
Donor(s): Jules Silbert, Nancy Silbert.
Financial data (yr. ended 12/31/01): Grants paid, $2,000; assets, $17,288 (M); gifts received, $13,329; expenditures, $2,000; qualifying distributions, $2,000.
Limitations: Applications not accepted.
Application information: Contributes only to pre-selected organizations.
Trustee: Jules Silbert.
EIN: 311603432

39740
Aime Simon Trust Fund
35 Cherry Tree Rd.
Loudonville, NY 12211

Established in 1995 in NY.
Financial data (yr. ended 12/31/00): Grants paid, $2,000; assets, $21,205 (M); gifts received, $1,325; expenditures, $2,416; qualifying distributions, $2,000.
Limitations: Applications not accepted.
Application information: Contributes only to pre-selected organizations.
Trustees: Barry Simon, Julie Simon.
EIN: 146184636

39741
The Leonard J. Sonnenberg Memorial Fund
c/o Harold Stangler
1 Old Country Rd.
Carle Place, NY 11514-1801 (516) 742-9200

Established in 1994 in NY.

39741 — NEW YORK

Donor(s): Eleanor Sonnenberg, Frida Stangler, Harold Stangler, Peter Berk, Susan Berk, Abraham Rapp, Ken Hirsch, Joanne Hirsch.
Financial data (yr. ended 12/31/01): Grants paid, $2,000; assets, $1 (M); gifts received, $8,000; expenditures, $2,024; qualifying distributions, $2,000.
Limitations: Applications not accepted. Giving primarily in NY.
Application information: Contributes only to pre-selected organizations.
Trustees: Abraham Rapp, Eleanor Sonnenberg, Harold Stangler.
EIN: 113242816

39742
David Tyson Foundation, Inc.
c/o James D. Miller & Co.
350 5th Ave., Ste. 5019
New York, NY 10118-0080

Donor(s): Carolyn Tyson.
Financial data (yr. ended 05/31/00): Grants paid, $2,000; assets, $183,776 (M); expenditures, $5,024; qualifying distributions, $3,475.
Limitations: Applications not accepted. Giving primarily in OH.
Application information: Contributes only to pre-selected organizations.
Officers and Trustees:* David Tyson,* Pres. and V.P.; Kathleen Tyson,* Secy.; John P. Volandes,* Treas.
EIN: 136130092

39743
Villchur Foundation
c/o Edgar Villchur
P.O. Box 306
Woodstock, NY 12498

Established in 1993 in NY.
Donor(s): Edgar Villchur.
Financial data (yr. ended 12/31/01): Grants paid, $2,000; assets, $26,386 (M); expenditures, $4,007; qualifying distributions, $2,000.
Limitations: Applications not accepted. Giving on a national basis.
Application information: Contributes only to pre-selected organizations.
Officers: Edgar Villchur, Pres. and Treas.; Rosemary M. Villchur, V.P. and Secy.
EIN: 141764435

39744
Wason Foundation
(Formerly Dolan Foundation)
101 S. Salina St., Ste. 600
P.O. Box 4967
Syracuse, NY 13221-4967
Contact: Jay W. Wason, Tr.

Financial data (yr. ended 12/31/01): Grants paid, $2,000; assets, $61,533 (M); expenditures, $2,542; qualifying distributions, $2,000.
Limitations: Giving primarily in Syracuse, NY.
Trustees: James Wason, Jay W. Wason, Martha Wason.
EIN: 156022925

39745
The Weeks Family Foundation
5355 Junction Rd.
Lockport, NY 14094 (716) 433-0965
FAX: (716) 433-0965
Contact: R. Thomas Weeks, Pres.

Established in 1989 in NY.
Donor(s): R. Thomas Weeks.
Financial data (yr. ended 12/31/00): Grants paid, $2,000; assets, $500 (M); gifts received, $2,000; expenditures, $2,907; qualifying distributions, $2,900.
Limitations: Giving limited to residents of NY.
Application information: Application form required.
Officers and Directors:* R. Thomas Weeks,* Pres.; Gerald S. Sacca,* V.P.; Charles Sauberan,* Secy.-Treas.
EIN: 222978143

39746
William J. Woerner Charitable Foundation
1482 North Rd.
Scottsville, NY 14546-9763

Financial data (yr. ended 12/31/01): Grants paid, $2,000; assets, $61,650 (M); expenditures, $2,574; qualifying distributions, $2,403.
Limitations: Applications not accepted. Giving limited to Rochester, NY.
Application information: Contributes only to pre-selected organizations.
Trustee: Donald Woerner, Jr.
EIN: 166051124

39747
Payne Street Foundation, Inc.
P.O. Box 179
Hamilton, NY 13346-0179

Established in 1994 in NY.
Donor(s): Paul J. Schupf, Lee Wothan.
Financial data (yr. ended 12/31/01): Grants paid, $1,974; assets, $5,255,431 (M); gifts received, $277,000; expenditures, $10,319; qualifying distributions, $60,319.
Limitations: Applications not accepted. Giving on a national basis.
Application information: Contributes only to pre-selected organizations.
Directors: Sanford E. Becker, Eric Rolfson, Paul J. Schupf, Lee Wothan.
EIN: 161466958

39748
Rudman Foundation, Inc.
975 E. 18th St.
Brooklyn, NY 11230-3802

Donor(s): Deborah N. Rudman.
Financial data (yr. ended 12/31/01): Grants paid, $1,970; assets, $46,143 (M); expenditures, $2,638; qualifying distributions, $1,970.
Limitations: Applications not accepted. Giving primarily in NY.
Application information: Contributes only to pre-selected organizations.
Officer: Reuben Rudman, V.P.
EIN: 112538541

39749
Msgr. Dermod C. Flinn Charitable Trust
(Formerly Flinn Trust)
c/o Fleet National Bank
159 E. Main St.
Rochester, NY 14638

Financial data (yr. ended 09/30/99): Grants paid, $1,956; assets, $201,887 (M); expenditures, $4,548; qualifying distributions, $3,667.
Limitations: Applications not accepted. Giving primarily in New York, NY.
Application information: Contributes only to pre-selected organizations.
Trustee: Fleet National Bank.
EIN: 166294438

39750
The Greer Family Foundation
c/o Estelle Greer
1010 5th Ave.
New York, NY 10028

Donor(s): Estelle Greer.
Financial data (yr. ended 12/31/01): Grants paid, $1,950; assets, $19,792 (M); gifts received, $2,502; expenditures, $2,559; qualifying distributions, $1,950.
Limitations: Applications not accepted.
Application information: Contributes only to pre-selected organizations.
Trustee: Estelle Greer.
EIN: 133973405

39751
Center for Contemporary Judaica
c/o Rabbi Jonathan D. Levine
304 E. 49th St., Ste. 2
New York, NY 10017

Donor(s): Rabbi Jonathan D. Levine.
Financial data (yr. ended 12/31/01): Grants paid, $1,918; assets, $63,097 (M); expenditures, $2,253; qualifying distributions, $1,918.
Limitations: Applications not accepted.
Application information: Contributes only to pre-selected organizations.
Officers: Rabbi Jonathan D. Levine, Pres.; Andrew Ansel, Treas.
Directors: Howard Rome, Joel Sharir, Rabbi Gerald Zelermyer.
EIN: 133737404

39752
Joseph F. Carlino Foundation, Inc.
c/o BSB Assocs.
201 Moreland Rd.
Hauppauge, NY 11788

Donor(s): Joseph F. Carlino.
Financial data (yr. ended 11/30/01): Grants paid, $1,870; assets, $2,138 (M); expenditures, $2,109; qualifying distributions, $1,870.
Limitations: Giving primarily in NY.
Trustee: Joseph F. Carlino.
EIN: 116009690

39753
Divre Josher Foundation
P.O. Box 190897
Brooklyn, NY 11219-0897

Established in 1986 in NY.
Donor(s): Eugen Vorhand.
Financial data (yr. ended 04/30/00): Grants paid, $1,870; assets, $22,410 (M); gifts received, $1,330; expenditures, $1,870; qualifying distributions, $1,870.
Limitations: Applications not accepted.
Application information: Contributes only to pre-selected organizations.
Trustee: Eugen Vorhand.
EIN: 133335158

39754
Dr. Sidney A. Rapp Memorial Scholarship Trust
c/o Amy Rapp
30 Mohegan Rd.
Larchmont, NY 10538-1448

Established in 1991 in NY.
Financial data (yr. ended 12/31/99): Grants paid, $1,860; assets, $8,267 (M); expenditures, $4,189; qualifying distributions, $3,084.
Limitations: Applications not accepted. Giving primarily in CT and NY.
Application information: Contributes only to pre-selected organizations.

Trustees: Howard Kahn, Meg Kahn.
EIN: 136975452

39755
Avery Scholarship Foundation
P.O. Box 772
Livingston Manor, NY 12758
Application address: c/o Guidance Dept., Livingston Manor Central School, Livingston Manor, NY 12758

Donor(s): Irving R. Avery.‡
Financial data (yr. ended 12/31/00): Grants paid, $1,850; assets, $80,109 (M); gifts received, $18,798; expenditures, $2,032; qualifying distributions, $16,850.
Limitations: Giving limited to residents of Livingston, NY.
Application information: Application form required.
Officers: Richard S. Sturdevant, Chair.; Patricia Ward, Secy.
Directors: Mary Fried, Debbie Lynker, George Silverman.
EIN: 141798357

39756
The Alfred L. Cohen Foundation, Inc.
400 E. 56th St., 32nd Fl.
New York, NY 10022 (212) 980-1884
Contact: Alfred L. Cohen, Pres.

Financial data (yr. ended 12/31/01): Grants paid, $1,850; assets, $8,473 (M); expenditures, $2,028; qualifying distributions, $1,850.
Officers: Alfred L. Cohen, Pres.; Jerome A. Manning, Secy.
EIN: 132621899

39757
Solomon Stern Foundation, Inc.
104 Hards Ln.
Lawrence, NY 11559

Donor(s): Jonas Stern.
Financial data (yr. ended 12/31/00): Grants paid, $1,807; assets, $43,836 (M); gifts received, $2,151; expenditures, $1,857; qualifying distributions, $1,857.
Limitations: Applications not accepted.
Application information: Contributes only to pre-selected organizations.
Officers: Andrew Stern, Pres.; Eli Mendlowitz, Treas.
EIN: 116036966

39758
Aronson Family Foundation, Inc.
1107 5th Ave., Ste. 9N
New York, NY 10128

Established in 1998 in NY.
Donor(s): Arnold Aronson, Sheila Aronson.
Financial data (yr. ended 12/31/01): Grants paid, $1,800; assets, $302 (M); expenditures, $2,484; qualifying distributions, $1,800.
Limitations: Applications not accepted.
Application information: Contributes only to pre-selected organizations.
Directors: Arnold Aronson, Sheila Aronson.
EIN: 311570649

39759
Books for Israel, Inc.
c/o J.A. Rednor
1979 Marcus Ave., Ste. E-146
New Hyde Park, NY 11042

Donor(s): Joshua A. Rednor, Rose W. Brooks Foundation.
Financial data (yr. ended 12/31/01): Grants paid, $1,800; assets, $5,436 (M); gifts received, $2,300; expenditures, $1,838; qualifying distributions, $1,838.
Limitations: Applications not accepted.
Application information: Contributes only to pre-selected organizations.
Officers: Joshua A. Rednor, Pres.; Fred R. Rednor, V.P.; Blanche F. Rednor, Secy.-Treas.
EIN: 112584720

39760
The Grafer Foundation
132 Country Club Dr.
Port Washington, NY 11050

Established in 2001 in NY.
Donor(s): H. Richard Grafer, Gloria G. Grafer.
Financial data (yr. ended 12/31/01): Grants paid, $1,800; assets, $157,750 (M); gifts received, $160,000; expenditures, $2,400; qualifying distributions, $1,800.
Limitations: Applications not accepted.
Application information: Contributes only to pre-selected organizations.
Trustees: Gloria G. Grafer, H. Richard Grafer.
EIN: 113631379

39761
Keren Chasdei Avos, Inc.
c/o M.J. Elias
1442 44th St.
Brooklyn, NY 11219

Established in 1999 in NY.
Donor(s): M.J. Elias.
Financial data (yr. ended 06/30/01): Grants paid, $1,800; assets, $28,675 (M); gifts received, $29,500; expenditures, $5,003; qualifying distributions, $1,800.
Limitations: Giving primarily in Brooklyn, NY.
Officer: M.J. Elias, Mgr.
EIN: 311676071

39762
Harley Northrop Family Foundation
1961 Tonawanda Creek Rd.
Amherst, NY 14228

Established in 1998 in NY.
Donor(s): Harley E. Northrop, Jon Northrop.
Financial data (yr. ended 05/31/02): Grants paid, $1,800; assets, $12,968 (M); gifts received, $61; expenditures, $2,336; qualifying distributions, $1,800.
Limitations: Applications not accepted.
Application information: Contributes only to pre-selected organizations.
Trustees: Harley E. Northrop, Jere Northrop, Jon Northrop.
EIN: 166480100

39763
John Saionz Memorial Dance Foundation
c/o Hy Allen & Co.
399 Knollwood Rd., Ste. 107
White Plains, NY 10603
Application address: 137 N. Larchmont Blvd., Los Angeles, CA 90004
Contact: Grace Saionz, Pres.

Financial data (yr. ended 11/30/01): Grants paid, $1,800; assets, $0 (M); expenditures, $2,230; qualifying distributions, $1,800.
Officer: Grace Saionz, Pres.
EIN: 133165758

39764
The Winterburn Foundation
30 Rockefeller Plz., Rm. 5600
New York, NY 10112

Established in 1991 in NY.
Donor(s): Rodman C. Rockefeller.‡
Financial data (yr. ended 12/31/99): Grants paid, $1,800; assets, $39 (M); expenditures, $1,800; qualifying distributions, $1,800.
Limitations: Applications not accepted. Giving primarily in New York, NY.
Application information: Contributes only to pre-selected organizations.
Trustees: Rodman C. Rockefeller, Sascha M. Rockefeller, Andrew Von Hirsch.
EIN: 136943521

39765
Rangjung Yeshe Institute
P.O. Box 2204
New York, NY 10163-2204

Established in 1988 in CA; funded in 1989.
Financial data (yr. ended 12/31/00): Grants paid, $1,765; assets, $5,962 (M); gifts received, $7,357; expenditures, $3,023; qualifying distributions, $3,023.
Limitations: Applications not accepted. Giving on a national and international basis.
Application information: Contributes only to pre-selected organizations.
Officers: Ian Saude, Pres.; James Gentry, V.P.; Michele Carrizales, Treas.
EIN: 943053869

39766
Herbert Ferber Foundation
44 MacDougal St.
New York, NY 10012-2920

Financial data (yr. ended 12/31/01): Grants paid, $1,750; assets, $112,337 (M); expenditures, $6,656; qualifying distributions, $5,238.
Limitations: Applications not accepted.
Application information: Contributes only to pre-selected organizations.
Officers: Edith Ferber, Pres.; Laurie Godfrey, V.P.; David L. Godfrey, Treas.
EIN: 132923712

39767
The Kirschbaum Family Foundation, Inc.
c/o Kay Collyer & Boose, LLP
1 Dag Hammarskjold Plz.
New York, NY 10017-2299

Established in 2000 in NY.
Donor(s): Herman Kirschbaum.‡
Financial data (yr. ended 12/31/01): Grants paid, $1,708; assets, $47,619 (M); gifts received, $1,000; expenditures, $6,070; qualifying distributions, $1,708.
Officers and Directors:* Robert Kirschbaum,* Pres.; Jacqueline Methany,* Secy.; Arthur Nager.
EIN: 134130880

39768
Madeline Beth Freedman Memorial Fund
127 Colonial Rd.
Great Neck, NY 11021-2713
Contact: Morris Freedman, Admin.

Financial data (yr. ended 12/31/00): Grants paid, $1,700; assets, $22,006 (M); gifts received, $246; expenditures, $1,700; qualifying distributions, $1,520.
Limitations: Giving primarily in NY.
Officers and Trustee:* David Freedman, Admin.; Morris Freedman,* Admin.; Nancy Freedman, Admin.
EIN: 112892446

39769
African Christian Teachers Association
135-38 226th St.
Laurelton, NY 11413-2432

Financial data (yr. ended 12/31/99): Grants paid, $1,650; assets, $10,102 (M); gifts received, $3,359; expenditures, $3,359; qualifying distributions, $1,650.
Limitations: Applications not accepted. Giving limited to New York, NY.
Officers: Vivian L. Ladson, Secy.; Edmond L. Ladson, Treas.
Director: Etta M. Ladson.
EIN: 237057127

39770
The Manheim Foundation, Inc.
c/o Barry Strauss Assocs., Ltd.
307 5th Ave., 8th Fl.
New York, NY 10016-6517

Donor(s): Paul E. Manheim.
Financial data (yr. ended 06/30/01): Grants paid, $1,650; assets, $116,735 (M); expenditures, $3,993; qualifying distributions, $3,252.
Limitations: Applications not accepted. Giving primarily in New York, NY.
Application information: Contributes only to pre-selected organizations.
Officers and Directors:* Anthony A. Manheim,* Pres.; Martha M. Green,* V.P.; Emily Goldman,* Secy.-Treas.
EIN: 136094022

39771
Pall Foundation
c/o The Bank of New York, Tax Dept.
1 Wall St., 28th Fl.
New York, NY 10286

Financial data (yr. ended 12/31/01): Grants paid, $1,629; assets, $33,195 (M); expenditures, $2,488; qualifying distributions, $1,629.
Limitations: Applications not accepted. Giving primarily in NY.
Application information: Contributes only to pre-selected organizations.
Trustee: The Bank of New York.
EIN: 136136793

39772
Jere & Lynn Northrop Family Foundation
1961 Tonawanda Creek Rd.
Amherst, NY 14228

Established in 1998 in NY.
Donor(s): Jere Northrop.
Financial data (yr. ended 08/31/01): Grants paid, $1,618; assets, $21,473 (M); gifts received, $2,118; expenditures, $2,168; qualifying distributions, $1,618.
Limitations: Applications not accepted.
Application information: Contributes only to pre-selected organizations.
Trustees: Jere Northrop, Lara Northrop, Lynn Northrop.
EIN: 166480101

39773
Achim Foundation
7302 137th St.
Flushing, NY 11367

Established in 2001 in NY.
Donor(s): David Solomon.
Financial data (yr. ended 12/31/01): Grants paid, $1,615; assets, $108,501 (M); gifts received, $112,500; expenditures, $4,397; qualifying distributions, $4,397.
Limitations: Applications not accepted.

Application information: Contributes only to pre-selected organizations.
Officer: David Solomon, Pres.
EIN: 113622409

39774
Leslie Arthur Rose, Sr. 2000 Trust
c/o Winston G. Rose
P.O. Box 1787
New York, NY 10163-1787

Financial data (yr. ended 12/31/01): Grants paid, $1,614; assets, $5,670 (M); gifts received, $8,592; expenditures, $1,764; qualifying distributions, $1,614.
Application information: Application form required.
Trustees: Kenroy A. Rose, Marjorie L. Rose, Wayne D. Rose, Winston G. Rose.
EIN: 137265627

39775
Catherine J. Hintz Foundation
4995 Beef St.
Syracuse, NY 13215-8659 (315) 673-2505
Contact: David C. Hintz, Chair.

Established in 1999 in NY.
Financial data (yr. ended 12/31/01): Grants paid, $1,600; assets, $12,007 (M); gifts received, $12,602; expenditures, $1,606; qualifying distributions, $1,606.
Limitations: Giving limited to residents of Auburn, Marcellus, and Solvay, NY.
Application information: Application form required.
Trustees: David C. Hintz, Chair.; Katherine A. Hintz, Allan J. Olson.
EIN: 161591024

39776
Joseph Rosenbach Foundation, Inc.
c/o Abraham Hendel
7922 21st Ave.
Brooklyn, NY 11214-1948 (718) 259-9398
Contact: Abraham Hendel, Tr.

Financial data (yr. ended 02/28/02): Grants paid, $1,600; assets, $32,124 (M); expenditures, $1,899; qualifying distributions, $1,600.
Limitations: Giving primarily in Brooklyn, NY.
Application information: Application form not required.
Officers: Bernard Rosenbach, Pres.; Myron Rosenbach, V.P.; Abraham Hendel, Secy.-Treas.
EIN: 136185748

39777
Sackett/Olean High School Scholarship Fund Trust
c/o The Bank of New York, Tax Dept.
1 Wall St., 28th Fl.
New York, NY 10286

Established in 1987 in NY.
Financial data (yr. ended 12/31/01): Grants paid, $1,600; assets, $30,265 (M); expenditures, $1,774; qualifying distributions, $1,638.
Limitations: Giving limited to Olean, NY.
Trustee: The Bank of New York.
EIN: 166031983

39778
Terra Nova Foundation
c/o Technical Services of N.A.
P.O. Box 4566
New York, NY 10163-4566

Established in 1997 in NY.
Donor(s): Charles P. Stevenson, Jr.
Financial data (yr. ended 12/31/00): Grants paid, $1,600; assets, $96,205 (M); gifts received, $1,600; expenditures, $1,700; qualifying distributions, $1,600.
Limitations: Applications not accepted.
Application information: Contributes only to pre-selected organizations.
Trustees: Inez E. D'Arcangelo, Charles P. Stevenson, Jr.
EIN: 133948138

39779
Rita Bhandari Memorial Foundation, Inc.
85 Deerfield Ln. N.
Pleasantville, NY 10570

Financial data (yr. ended 12/31/99): Grants paid, $1,570; assets, $76,519 (M); gifts received, $900; expenditures, $1,720; qualifying distributions, $1,570.
Limitations: Applications not accepted.
Application information: Contributes only to pre-selected organizations.
Officer and Directors:* Anil Bhandari,* Pres.; Giriraj Jadeja, Mslini Jadeja, R. Kaul.
EIN: 133462782

39780
The Joseph Shamma Foundation
620 Ave. W
Brooklyn, NY 11223

Established in 1999 in NY.
Donor(s): Joseph Shamma.
Financial data (yr. ended 12/31/00): Grants paid, $1,569; assets, $34,148 (M); gifts received, $30,000; expenditures, $3,226; qualifying distributions, $1,569.
Limitations: Applications not accepted.
Application information: Contributes only to pre-selected organizations.
Trustees: Joseph Shamma, Madal Shamma.
EIN: 113523647

39781
The Martin and Robert Peyser Family Foundation
c/o Robert J. Peyser
165 E. 32nd St., Ste. 11C
New York, NY 10016

Established in 1997 in NY.
Financial data (yr. ended 12/31/01): Grants paid, $1,557; assets, $538 (M); gifts received, $1,925; expenditures, $1,557; qualifying distributions, $1,557.
Officers: Robert J. Peyser, Pres. and Treas.; Ronald P. Carroccio, V.P.; Richard Kenyon, V.P.; Paul M. Scheib, Secy.
EIN: 133957753

39782
Sarah Rinker Memorial Scholarship Fund, Inc.
(also known as Sarah Rinker-Rita Robinson Memorial Scholarship Fund)
c/o Weiskotten Hall
750 E. Adams St., Rm. 2156
Syracuse, NY 13210
Application address: c/o Clinical Pathology, SUNY-HSC at Syracuse, 750 E. Adams St, Syracuse, NY 13210

Established in 1973 in NY.
Financial data (yr. ended 10/31/00): Grants paid, $1,550; assets, $22,606 (M); gifts received, $10,278; expenditures, $1,639; qualifying distributions, $1,639.
Limitations: Giving limited to Syracuse, NY.
Application information: Application form required.
Officers: Robert Sunheimer, Pres.; Elizabeth Palumbo, V.P.; Sharon Pulney, Secy.; DeForest Brooker, Treas.

EIN: 237260158

39783
Augusto Lou Memorial Foundation, Inc.
56-47 Oceania St.
Oakland Gardens, NY 11364-1736

Financial data (yr. ended 09/30/01): Grants paid, $1,530; assets, $47,550 (M); gifts received, $2,500; expenditures, $1,634; qualifying distributions, $1,530.
Limitations: Applications not accepted. Giving primarily in NY.
Application information: Contributes only to pre-selected organizations.
Officers: Theresa Gottlieb, Pres.; Sui Wah Lou, V.P.; Stephen Quigley, Secy.; Roger Begelman, Treas.; Roger Begelman, Treas.
EIN: 112737020

39784
Redwood Foundation
c/o Peter Slusser
901 Lexington Ave.
New York, NY 10021-5952

Financial data (yr. ended 12/31/01): Grants paid, $1,530; assets, $79,938 (M); gifts received, $3,689; expenditures, $1,660; qualifying distributions, $1,530.
Limitations: Applications not accepted. Giving primarily in New York, NY.
Application information: Contributes only to pre-selected organizations.
Officers and Directors:* W. Peter Slusser,* Pres.; Joanne Slusser,* V.P. and Secy.; Kathleen Mullen,* Treas.; Caroline Converse, Martin Slusser, Sarah Slusser, Wendy Slusser.
EIN: 237009841

39785
The Frances Goldin Foundation
c/o Frances Goldin
57 E. 117th St., Ste. 5B
New York, NY 10003

Established in 1997.
Donor(s): Frances Goldin.
Financial data (yr. ended 12/31/01): Grants paid, $1,525; assets, $16,739 (M); expenditures, $2,127; qualifying distributions, $1,525.
Director: Frances Goldin.
EIN: 133982512

39786
Paul O. and Joanne D. Stillman Charitable Foundation
c/o NBT Bank, N.A.
52 S. Broad St.
Norwich, NY 13815

Established in 1999 in NY.
Donor(s): Paul O. Stillman.
Financial data (yr. ended 05/31/02): Grants paid, $1,525; assets, $44,759 (M); gifts received, $10,000; expenditures, $2,067; qualifying distributions, $1,525.
Limitations: Applications not accepted. Giving primarily in NY.
Application information: Contributes only to pre-selected organizations.
Officers and Trustees:* Paul O. Stillman,* Pres.; Joanne D. Stillman,* V.P.
EIN: 161573234

39787
George and Corinne Greenspan Foundation
885 Park Ave.
New York, NY 10021-0325

Donor(s): George Greenspan.‡

Financial data (yr. ended 12/31/01): Grants paid, $1,518; assets, $161,824 (M); expenditures, $5,145; qualifying distributions, $1,518.
Limitations: Applications not accepted. Giving primarily in New York, NY.
Application information: Contributes only to pre-selected organizations.
Officer: Corinne Greenspan, Pres.
EIN: 136067458

39788
Donner Family Charitable Foundation
1282 E. 10th St.
Brooklyn, NY 11230

Donor(s): Avruhum Donner, Toby Donner.
Financial data (yr. ended 12/31/01): Grants paid, $1,508; assets, $194 (M); gifts received, $1,732; expenditures, $2,308; qualifying distributions, $1,508.
Limitations: Applications not accepted.
Application information: Contributes only to pre-selected organizations.
Officer: Avruhum Donner, Pres.
Directors: Chaim Donner, Toby Donner.
EIN: 061525059

39789
Valerie Anne Briehl Foundation, Inc.
c/o Robin Briehl
11 Powder Hill Rd.
Waccabuc, NY 10597

Established in 1985 in NY.
Donor(s): Robin W. Briehl, Marie Brichl.
Financial data (yr. ended 12/31/99): Grants paid, $1,500; assets, $136,111 (M); gifts received, $1,000; expenditures, $1,640; qualifying distributions, $1,640.
Limitations: Applications not accepted. Giving primarily in Managua, Nicaragua, and Boston, MA.
Application information: Contributes only to pre-selected organizations.
Officers and Directors:* Robin W. Briehl, M.D.,* Pres.; Sam Seifter, Ph.D.,* Secy.; Charlotte Cohen, M.D., Edith Tiger.
EIN: 133324859

39790
Ida J. Christie Fund for Music
2309 Emery Rd.
South Wales, NY 14139

Established in 2000 in NY.
Donor(s): William L. Christie.
Financial data (yr. ended 12/31/01): Grants paid, $1,500; assets, $46,339 (M); expenditures, $3,407; qualifying distributions, $1,500.
Limitations: Applications not accepted.
Application information: Contributes only to pre-selected organizations.
Trustees: Ida J. Christie, William L. Christie.
EIN: 166503938

39791
Peter Cooper Charity Fund
c/o Harry Freed
120-4 Benchley Pl., Bldg. 24, Apt. 4L
Bronx, NY 10475

Financial data (yr. ended 08/31/01): Grants paid, $1,500; assets, $3,673 (M); gifts received, $1,488; expenditures, $1,575; qualifying distributions, $75.
Limitations: Applications not accepted. Giving primarily in NY.
Application information: Contributes only to pre-selected organizations.
Officers: Samuel J. Prussak, Pres.; Harry Freed, Secy.-Treas.

EIN: 237202045

39792
Dent Foundation, Inc.
c/o The Bank of New York, Tax Dept.
1 Wall St., 28th Fl.
New York, NY 10286
Application address: 221 Montgomery Dr., Spartanburg, SC 29302
Contact: Frederick B. Dent, Tr.

Established in 1943 in NY.
Financial data (yr. ended 12/31/01): Grants paid, $1,500; assets, $1,830,383 (M); expenditures, $31,675; qualifying distributions, $2,966.
Trustee: Frederick B. Dent.
Directors: Frederick B. Dent, Jr., Magruder H. Dent.
EIN: 136108041

39793
The Giallanza Foundation
5653 Broadway
Lancaster, NY 14086
Contact: Elaine L. Giallanza, Pres.

Established in 1997 in NY.
Financial data (yr. ended 12/31/01): Grants paid, $1,500; assets, $19,223 (M); gifts received, $5,050; expenditures, $1,500; qualifying distributions, $1,484.
Officers: Elaine Giallanza, Pres.; Joseph Giallanza, V.P.; Philip Tantillo, V.P.; Mary Giallanza, Secy.; Michael Giallanza, Treas.
EIN: 166428986

39794
The Scott & Kelley Johnston Foundation
100 McLain St.
Bedford Corners, NY 10549

Established in 1999 in NY.
Donor(s): Scott Johnston, Kelley Johnston.
Financial data (yr. ended 12/31/01): Grants paid, $1,500; assets, $48,758 (M); expenditures, $15,906; qualifying distributions, $1,500.
Limitations: Applications not accepted.
Application information: Contributes only to pre-selected organizations.
Trustees: Kelley Johnston, Scott Johnston.
EIN: 134092715

39795
Margaret Ford Leonard & Marion E. McKinney Charitable Foundation
c/o Henry L. Hulbert
6 Ford Ave.
Oneonta, NY 13820 (607) 432-6720

Established in 2000 in NY.
Donor(s): Marion E. McKinney.
Financial data (yr. ended 12/31/01): Grants paid, $1,500; assets, $52,425 (M); gifts received, $25,000; expenditures, $1,525; qualifying distributions, $1,500.
Limitations: Giving primarily in Oneonta, NY.
Trustees: Henry L. Hulbert, Maureen P. Hulbert, Marion E. McKinney.
EIN: 161573609

39796
The Cameron and Hayden Lord Foundation
c/o Tim Lord
12 W. 96th St., Ste. 8C
New York, NY 10025 (212) 828-9512

Established in 2001 in NY.
Donor(s): Fred Whitemore, Marion Whitemore, Scott Taylor, Marjorie Taylor, Martha Spofford, Scott Spofford, Van Beuren Family Foundation.
Financial data (yr. ended 12/31/01): Grants paid, $1,500; assets, $491,349 (M); gifts received,

39796—NEW YORK

$505,042; expenditures, $18,574; qualifying distributions, $18,466.
Directors: Blyth T. Lord, Gay P. Lord, Thomas P. Lord, Evelyn M. Taylor.
EIN: 316653586

39797
The Brian F. Mullaney Charitable Foundation
c/o Brian F. Mullaney
292 Madison Ave., 23rd Fl.
New York, NY 10017

Established in 1998 in NY.
Donor(s): Brian F. Mullaney.
Financial data (yr. ended 12/31/01): Grants paid, $1,500; assets, $41,829 (M); expenditures, $1,550; qualifying distributions, $1,500.
Limitations: Applications not accepted.
Application information: Contributes only to pre-selected organizations.
Trustee: Brian F. Mullaney.
EIN: 134014312

39798
David Jacob Oransky Memorial Fund for Education
3 Rugby Rd.
New City, NY 10956 (845) 348-2533
Contact: Stanley Oransky, M.D., Pres.

Established in 1998 in NY.
Financial data (yr. ended 12/31/00): Grants paid, $1,500; assets, $32,752 (M); gifts received, $1,119; expenditures, $3,018; qualifying distributions, $1,492.
Limitations: Giving limited to residents of New City, NY.
Officers: Stanley Oransky, M.D., Pres.; Lesley Oransky, Secy.; Dennis Gaber, Treas.
EIN: 133810849

39799
The Pack Johnson Foundation
33 Franklin St.
Piermont, NY 10968

Established in 2000.
Donor(s): Jacqueline Pack-Johnson.
Financial data (yr. ended 11/30/00): Grants paid, $1,500; assets, $37,569 (M); gifts received, $89,028; expenditures, $44,045; qualifying distributions, $1,500.
Trustee: Jacqueline Pack-Johnson.
EIN: 134092174

39800
Larry Rivers Foundation, Inc.
c/o Richard Shebairo, PC
560 Broadway, Ste. 404A
New York, NY 10012-3945

Established in 1993 in DE and NY.
Donor(s): Larry Rivers.
Financial data (yr. ended 12/31/01): Grants paid, $1,500; assets, $32,635 (M); gifts received, $5,000; expenditures, $2,715; qualifying distributions, $1,500.
Limitations: Applications not accepted. Giving primarily in NY.
Application information: Contributes only to pre-selected organizations.
Officers and Directors:* Larry Rivers,* Pres.; Joan Gordon,* Secy.; Richard Shebairo,* Treas.; Earl McGrath, Diana Molinari.
EIN: 113137296

39801
The Serenbetz Family Foundation, Inc.
695 West St.
Harrison, NY 10528

Established in 1998 in NJ.
Donor(s): Warren L. Serenbetz.
Financial data (yr. ended 12/31/00): Grants paid, $1,500; assets, $828,401 (M); gifts received, $473,750; expenditures, $2,981; qualifying distributions, $1,500.
Limitations: Applications not accepted. Giving primarily in Phoenix, AZ.
Application information: Contributes only to pre-selected organizations.
Officers and Trustees:* Thelma R. Serenbetz,* Pres.; Jean B. Serenbetz,* Secy.-Treas.; Clay R. Serenbetz, Cynthia L. Serenbetz, Paul Serenbetz, Stuart W. Serenbetz, Warren L. Serenbetz, Warren L. Serenbetz, Jr.
EIN: 133993644

39802
Thomas J. Skuse Trust
c/o Silver & Brelia
2001 Palmer Ave., Ste. 207
Larchmont, NY 10538

Financial data (yr. ended 12/31/99): Grants paid, $1,500; assets, $34,339 (M); expenditures, $2,156; qualifying distributions, $1,486.
Limitations: Applications not accepted. Giving limited to New York, NY.
Application information: Contributes only to pre-selected organizations.
Trustee: Herbert H. Blau.
EIN: 136067557

39803
The E. Leo and Louise F. Spain Scholarship Foundation
83 Bay St., Box 785
Glens Falls, NY 12801 (518) 793-5173
Contact: Robert J. O'Brien, Tr.

Financial data (yr. ended 09/30/01): Grants paid, $1,500; assets, $99,012 (M); expenditures, $5,234; qualifying distributions, $4,458.
Limitations: Giving limited to residents of Glens Falls, NY.
Application information: Application form not required.
Trustees: Robert G. Landry, Michael Massiano, Thomas J. Murphy, Robert J. O'Brien, Daniel F. O'Keefe, M.D., George J. Zurlo.
EIN: 133354188
Codes: GTI

39804
Joshua Swartz Foundation, Inc.
7 Cobblestone Ct.
Centerport, NY 11721
Application address: 400 E. 66th St., New York, NY 10001, tel.: (646) 314-9826
Contact: Josh Swartz, Pres.

Established in 2000 in NY.
Financial data (yr. ended 12/31/00): Grants paid, $1,500; assets, $31,721 (M); gifts received, $35,000; expenditures, $4,578; qualifying distributions, $1,500.
Officers and Directors:* Josh Swartz,* Pres.; Alan Fell,* Secy.; Bruce A. Rosen,* Treas.
EIN: 113515925

39805
The Joseph & Mary Vasile Family Foundation
15 Tobey Woods
Pittsford, NY 14534-1823

Financial data (yr. ended 12/31/01): Grants paid, $1,500; assets, $33,997 (M); expenditures, $1,957; qualifying distributions, $1,500.
Limitations: Applications not accepted. Giving primarily in NY.
Application information: Contributes only to pre-selected organizations.
Officer: David Vasile, Mgr.
EIN: 222960850

39806
Westchester Mid Hudson Chapter American Institute of Architects Scholarship Fund
P.O. Box 611
Katonah, NY 10536

Established in 1996 in NY.
Financial data (yr. ended 12/31/00): Grants paid, $1,500; assets, $34,227 (M); gifts received, $5,000; expenditures, $1,500; qualifying distributions, $1,495.
Limitations: Giving primarily in NY.
Application information: Application form required.
Officers: Jerome Kerner, Pres.; Peter Gaito, V.P.; Charles Place, Secy.; Russell Davidson, Treas.
EIN: 133585407

39807
Dr. Nathan Young Memorial Scholarship Corporation
45-40 218th St.
Bayside, NY 11361-3538

Established in 1987 in NY.
Donor(s): Belle Young.
Financial data (yr. ended 12/31/00): Grants paid, $1,500; assets, $10,062 (M); expenditures, $1,560; qualifying distributions, $1,558.
Limitations: Applications not accepted. Giving primarily in NY.
Application information: Contributes only to pre-selected organizations.
Officers and Directors:* Dennis Young,* Chair.; Sidney Young,* Vice-Chair.; Stephen Young,* Secy.-Treas.
EIN: 112819375

39808
The Grace Fund
164-38 75th Ave., 2nd Fl.
Flushing, NY 11366

Established in 1999 in NY.
Financial data (yr. ended 11/30/01): Grants paid, $1,470; assets, $16,593 (M); gifts received, $520; expenditures, $12,756; qualifying distributions, $1,470.
Limitations: Applications not accepted.
Application information: Contributes only to pre-selected organizations.
Directors: Ana Chang, Canen Chang.
EIN: 113523667

39809
Kee Tov Foundation, Inc.
421 Arlingtong Rd.
Cedarhurst, NY 11516

Established in 1996 in NY.
Financial data (yr. ended 12/31/01): Grants paid, $1,460; assets, $24,161 (M); expenditures, $324,804; qualifying distributions, $1,460.
Limitations: Applications not accepted.
Application information: Contributes only to pre-selected organizations.
Officer: Samuel Schwebel, Mgr.
Directors: Barry Binik, Moshe Hallon, Eliezer Mendlowitz.
EIN: 113300875

39810
Teraskiewicz Foundation, Inc.
585 Stewart Ave., Rm. 409
Garden City, NY 11530

Established in 1985 in DE.
Donor(s): Edward Teraskiewicz.

Financial data (yr. ended 09/30/01): Grants paid, $1,460; assets, $7,748 (M); expenditures, $1,822; qualifying distributions, $1,460.
Limitations: Applications not accepted. Giving primarily in Wilmington, NC.
Application information: Contributes only to pre-selected organizations.
Officer: Edward Teraskiewicz, Pres.
EIN: 133349740

39811
Daniel C. Zuckerman Foundation
c/o A.R. Baum
556 Ave. Z, Apt. 6H
Brooklyn, NY 11223-6166   (718) 648-7238

Donor(s): Stanley Zuckerman.
Financial data (yr. ended 12/31/00): Grants paid, $1,450; assets, $40,727 (M); gifts received, $33,539; expenditures, $2,652; qualifying distributions, $1,450.
Limitations: Giving primarily in the San Francisco Bay Area, CA.
Officer: Stanley Zuckerman, Mgr.
EIN: 136201164

39812
Gregory S. Coleman Foundation
5909 N. Hempstead Tpke.
East Norwich, NY 11732-1612
Contact: Gregory S. Coleman, Pres.

Donor(s): Gregory S. Coleman.
Financial data (yr. ended 12/31/01): Grants paid, $1,400; assets, $2,042 (M); gifts received, $2,000; expenditures, $1,880; qualifying distributions, $1,400.
Limitations: Giving primarily in NY.
Application information: Application form not required.
Officer and Directors:* Gregory S. Coleman,* Pres.; Jack Bronston.
EIN: 116079403

39813
Irving & Rosalind Richards Foundation, Inc.
c/o Lois Broido
200 E. 66th St.
New York, NY 10021-6132

Donor(s): Irving Richards, Rosalind Richards.‡
Financial data (yr. ended 12/31/01): Grants paid, $1,400; assets, $46,263 (M); expenditures, $2,514; qualifying distributions, $1,400.
Limitations: Applications not accepted. Giving primarily in New York, NY.
Application information: Contributes only to pre-selected organizations.
Officers: Irving Richards, Pres.; Lois Broido, V.P.; Eric Richards, V.P.
EIN: 237024035

39814
The Helyn B. Reich Memorial Scholarship Fund, Inc.
633 3rd Ave.
New York, NY 10017

Established in 2000 in NY.
Financial data (yr. ended 12/31/00): Grants paid, $1,350; assets, $99,621 (M); gifts received, $103,104; expenditures, $2,350; qualifying distributions, $1,350.
Limitations: Applications not accepted.
Application information: Contributes only to pre-selected organizations.
Officers: Melvin Salberg, Pres.; Stuart Fischer, V.P.; Karen Rubinstein, V.P.; Seymour D. Reich, Secy.; Keith E. Reich, Treas.
EIN: 134084107

39815
Gerald Starr Family Foundation, Inc.
111 Ames Ct.
Plainview, NY 11803   (516) 349-0070
Contact: Gerald Starr, Dir.

Established in 1966 in NY.
Donor(s): Gerald Starr.
Financial data (yr. ended 12/31/00): Grants paid, $1,325; assets, $40,786 (M); expenditures, $1,417; qualifying distributions, $1,325.
Limitations: Giving primarily in New York, NY.
Directors: Joel S. Ehrenkranz, Gerald Starr.
EIN: 116080767

39816
Sunrise Foundation
c/o Gerald Schwebel
2302 Nostrand Ave., P.M.B. 4612
Brooklyn, NY 11210

Established in 1999 in NY.
Donor(s): Gerald Schwebel.
Financial data (yr. ended 12/31/01): Grants paid, $1,320; assets, $9,447 (M); expenditures, $1,435; qualifying distributions, $1,320.
Limitations: Applications not accepted.
Application information: Contributes only to pre-selected organizations.
Trustees: Gerald Schwebel, Sheila Schwebel.
EIN: 134091623

39817
David Himelberg Foundation
c/o B. Strauss Assoc., Ltd.
307 5th Ave., 8th Fl.
New York, NY 10016-6517

Established in 1998 in NY.
Donor(s): David Himelberg.
Financial data (yr. ended 08/31/01): Grants paid, $1,303; assets, $228,443 (M); gifts received, $99,673; expenditures, $4,421; qualifying distributions, $1,303.
Limitations: Applications not accepted.
Application information: Contributes only to pre-selected organizations.
Trustees: David Himelberg, Norman Himelberg.
EIN: 137200887

39818
Ruth Gardner Trust for Anna & Meyer Gardner Scholarship Fund
c/o HSBC Bank USA
1 HSBC Ctr., 17th Fl.
Buffalo, NY 14203

Donor(s): Ruth Gardner.‡
Financial data (yr. ended 05/31/99): Grants paid, $1,300; assets, $64,969 (M); expenditures, $2,219; qualifying distributions, $1,416.
Limitations: Applications not accepted. Giving primarily in NY.
Trustee: HSBC Bank USA.
EIN: 166071950

39819
Charles M. Kurtz Trust
KeyBank Towers
50 Fountain Plz., Ste. 301
Buffalo, NY 14202-2291

Established around 1989.
Financial data (yr. ended 11/30/01): Grants paid, $1,300; assets, $95,458 (M); expenditures, $3,508; qualifying distributions, $1,300.
Limitations: Applications not accepted. Giving primarily in New York, NY.
Application information: Contributes only to pre-selected organizations.
Trustee: E.W. Dann Stevens.

EIN: 166313958

39820
Katherine Lavelle-Hamilton Foundation
c/o Williams W. Hamilton
96 Magnolia Dr.
Dobbs Ferry, NY 10522-3510   (914) 693-0669

Established in 2001.
Donor(s): William W. Hamilton.
Financial data (yr. ended 12/31/01): Grants paid, $1,300; assets, $3,664 (M); gifts received, $7,512; expenditures, $3,862; qualifying distributions, $1,300.
Limitations: Giving limited to residents of Dobbs Ferry, NY.
Officers and Directors:* William W. Hamilton,* Pres. and Treas.; Mary L. Grein,* Clerk; Anne L. May.
EIN: 061623905

39821
New West 111th Street Block Association, Inc.
52 W. 111th St.
New York, NY 10026

Financial data (yr. ended 06/30/01): Grants paid, $1,300; assets, $0 (M); expenditures, $3,157; qualifying distributions, $1,671.
Officers: Catherine Gallop, Pres.; Anna Tiwoni, Secy.; Milas Foxworth, Treas.
EIN: 133046763

39822
Harry & Jennie Slayton Foundation, Inc.
2345 Jericho Tpke., 2nd Fl.
New Hyde Park, NY 11040
Contact: Paul Slayton, Mgr.

Donor(s): Roy L. Slayton, Paul R. Slayton.
Financial data (yr. ended 10/31/01): Grants paid, $1,300; assets, $29 (M); gifts received, $1,375; expenditures, $1,375; qualifying distributions, $1,300.
Limitations: Giving primarily in New York, NY.
Officer: Paul Slayton, Mgr.
EIN: 136160993

39823
The Bowers Foundation, Inc.
51 Nanticoke Rd.
Maine, NY 13802
Contact: Janet Bowers Bothwell, Pres.

Donor(s): Broome County Historical Society.
Financial data (yr. ended 12/31/01): Grants paid, $1,284; assets, $371,045 (M); expenditures, $19,389; qualifying distributions, $1,284.
Limitations: Giving primarily in NY.
Publications: Application guidelines.
Officers: Janet Bowers Bothwell, Pres.; R. Lee Mauk, V.P.; Charles Hathorn, Secy.; Douglas R. Johnson, Treas.
Directors: Bruce Pomeroy, Lawrence Rice.
EIN: 166092993

39824
Mr. and Mrs. Leo Considine Scholarship Trust
(Formerly Mr. and Mrs. Leo Considine Scholarship Trust f/b/o St. Joseph's Hospital School of Nursing)
P.O. Box 1522
Elmira, NY 14902-1522
Application address: c/o Dir., School of Nursing, St. Joseph's Hospital, 555 E. Market St., Elmira, NY 14901, tel.: (607) 733-6541

Financial data (yr. ended 12/31/01): Grants paid, $1,272; assets, $25,028 (M); expenditures, $1,405; qualifying distributions, $1,316.
Limitations: Giving limited to residents of Elmira, NY.

39824—NEW YORK

Application information: Requirements set by St. Joseph's Hospital School of Nursing.
Trustee: Chemung Canal Trust Co.
EIN: 166047968

39825
Leo E. Considine Scholarship Trust
(Formerly Considine Scholarship Trust f/b/o Notre Dame High School Scholarship Fund)
c/o Chemung Canal Trust Co.
P.O. Box 1522
Elmira, NY 14902-1522
Application address: c/o Chaplain and Principal, Notre Dame High School, Elmira, NY 14904, tel.: (607) 734-2267

Established in 1964 in NY.
Donor(s): Leo E. Considine.‡
Financial data (yr. ended 12/31/00): Grants paid, $1,267; assets, $26,614 (M); expenditures, $1,444; qualifying distributions, $1,314.
Limitations: Giving limited to Elmira, NY.
Application information: Recipient selected by Elmire H.S. Principal and Chaplain.
Trustee: Chemung Canal Trust Co.
EIN: 166047964

39826
Andrea Nadel Griffen Memorial Foundation, Inc.
433 Beechmont Dr.
New Rochelle, NY 10804-4617

Established in 1985 in NY.
Donor(s): Murray Nadel.
Financial data (yr. ended 12/31/00): Grants paid, $1,250; assets, $70,544 (M); gifts received, $2,720; expenditures, $2,445; qualifying distributions, $1,250.
Limitations: Applications not accepted.
Officers and Directors:* Murray Nadel,* Pres.; John Griffen,* V.P.; Sue M. Nadel,* Secy.-Treas.
EIN: 133258351

39827
Gisela Herzl Foundation, Inc.
411 Theodore Fremd Ave.
P.O. Box 569
Rye, NY 10580

Established in 1997 in NY.
Financial data (yr. ended 12/31/00): Grants paid, $1,250; assets, $15,080 (M); expenditures, $1,900; qualifying distributions, $1,250.
Limitations: Applications not accepted.
Application information: Contributes only to pre-selected organizations.
Trustees: Gisela Herzl, Joseph Winston.
EIN: 133902787

39828
Richard L. & Rita S. Porterfield Charitable Trust
c/o Deutsche Trust Co. of NY
P.O. Box 1297, Church St. Sta.
New York, NY 10008

Established in 2000 in CT.
Donor(s): Richard L. Porterfield, Rita S. Porterfield.
Financial data (yr. ended 12/31/00): Grants paid, $1,250; assets, $499,683 (M); gifts received, $500,000; expenditures, $1,250; qualifying distributions, $1,250.
Trustee: Deutsche Bank.
EIN: 527144659

39829
Barbara & Edward Schlussel Foundation, Inc.
333 Longwood Crossing
Lawrence, NY 11559

Established in 2000 in NY.
Donor(s): Edward Schlussel.

Financial data (yr. ended 12/31/01): Grants paid, $1,250; assets, $67,851 (M); gifts received, $25,109; expenditures, $1,516; qualifying distributions, $1,250.
Limitations: Applications not accepted.
Application information: Contributes only to pre-selected organizations.
Officers: Edward Schlussel, Pres.; Michael Schlussel, V.P.; Barbara Schlussel, Secy.
EIN: 113524899

39830
Max and Anna Pressner Foundation, Inc.
99 Gold St.
Brooklyn, NY 11201 (718) 858-1000
Contact: Jerry Pressner, Pres.

Donor(s): M. Pressner & Co.
Financial data (yr. ended 12/31/01): Grants paid, $1,238; assets, $25,446 (M); expenditures, $1,363; qualifying distributions, $1,238.
Application information: Application form not required.
Officers: Jerry Pressner, Pres.; Judith Pressner, Treas.
EIN: 136201539

39831
DSRS Fund
1437 President St.
Brooklyn, NY 11213

Established in 1999 in NY.
Financial data (yr. ended 12/31/01): Grants paid, $1,220; assets, $4,242 (M); expenditures, $1,745; qualifying distributions, $1,220.
Limitations: Applications not accepted.
Application information: Contributes only to pre-selected organizations.
Trustees: Dovie Sperlin, Ruthie Sperlin.
EIN: 113509471

39832
Leon and Symma Miller Memorial Trust
213 Glen St.
Glen Cove, NY 11542

Established in 1999 in NY.
Donor(s): Leon Miller.
Financial data (yr. ended 12/31/01): Grants paid, $1,202; assets, $14,031 (M); gifts received, $23,000; expenditures, $1,347; qualifying distributions, $1,202.
Limitations: Applications not accepted.
Application information: Contributes only to pre-selected organizations.
Trustees: Edward J. Miller, Howard Miller, Leon Miller, Sari S. Miller.
EIN: 137076144

39833
The Kenlou Foundation, Inc.
P.O. Box 25300
Rochester, NY 14625

Established in 2000 in NY.
Donor(s): Mary E. Swierkos, John K. Williams, Richard E. Williams, Robert M. Williams.
Financial data (yr. ended 12/31/01): Grants paid, $1,201; assets, $3,803,222 (M); expenditures, $31,800; qualifying distributions, $1,201.
Limitations: Applications not accepted.
Application information: Contributes only to pre-selected organizations.
Officers: Richard E. Williams, Pres.; John K. Williams, V.P.; Robert M. Williams, Secy.; Mary E. Swierkos, Treas.
EIN: 161596738

39834
Arnold Charitable Trust
2934 E. Lake Rd.
Dunkirk, NY 14048-9726

Established in OH in 1997.
Financial data (yr. ended 12/31/99): Grants paid, $1,200; assets, $17,199 (M); expenditures, $1,200; qualifying distributions, $1,200.
Limitations: Applications not accepted. Giving primarily in Tonawanda, NY.
Application information: Contributes only to pre-selected organizations.
Directors: James E. Arnold, Jean R. Arnold.
EIN: 166462837

39835
Erroll Garner Memorial Foundation, Inc.
c/o Martha Glaser
521 5th Ave., Ste. 1700
New York, NY 10175

Financial data (yr. ended 09/30/01): Grants paid, $1,200; assets, $7,231 (M); gifts received, $79; expenditures, $1,279; qualifying distributions, $1,274.
Officers: Martha Glaser, Pres.; Theodore Present, Treas.
EIN: 132937400

39836
The HHD Foundation
c/o L.H. Frishkoff & Co., LLP
529 Fifth Ave.
New York, NY 10017

Established in 1999 in NY.
Donor(s): Betsy Rothstein.
Financial data (yr. ended 12/31/01): Grants paid, $1,200; assets, $47,946 (M); gifts received, $35,000; expenditures, $1,201; qualifying distributions, $1,200.
Limitations: Applications not accepted.
Application information: Contributes only to pre-selected organizations.
Trustee: Betsy Rothstein.
EIN: 134076952

39837
Arlee Moore Scholarship Fund
c/o HSBC Bank USA
1 HSBC Ctr., 16th Fl.
Buffalo, NY 14203-2885

Financial data (yr. ended 12/31/01): Grants paid, $1,200; assets, $30,378 (M); expenditures, $1,343; qualifying distributions, $1,213.
Limitations: Applications not accepted.
Application information: Unsolicited requests for funds not accepted.
Trustee: HSBC Bank USA.
EIN: 166098349

39838
Jack & Jeanne Reinhardt Foundation
2750 Homecrest Ave.
Brooklyn, NY 11235
Contact: Paula B. Forman, Pres.

Financial data (yr. ended 12/31/00): Grants paid, $1,200; assets, $93,545 (M); expenditures, $3,127; qualifying distributions, $1,200.
Limitations: Giving primarily in New York, NY.
Application information: Application form not required.
Officers: Paula B. Forman, Pres.; Neil D. Forman, V.P.
EIN: 136156410

39839
The Abdallah & Francine Simon Foundation, Inc.
F.D.R. Station
P.O. Box 1148
New York, NY 10150-1148

Established in 1986 in NY.
Donor(s): Abdallah H. Simon.
Financial data (yr. ended 06/30/01): Grants paid, $1,200; assets, $214,856 (M); expenditures, $1,430; qualifying distributions, $1,430.
Limitations: Applications not accepted. Giving primarily in NY.
Application information: Contributes only to pre-selected organizations.
Officers: Abdallah H. Simon, Pres. and Treas.; Francine Simon, V.P. and Secy.
EIN: 133370159

39840
Sheldon & Ellen Tannen Charitable Trust
40 E. 66th St.
New York, NY 10022-1011
Contact: Sheldon Tannen, Tr., or Ellen Tannen, Tr.

Established in 1993 in NY.
Donor(s): Kreidler Burns Foundation.
Financial data (yr. ended 12/31/01): Grants paid, $1,200; assets, $38,776 (M); gifts received, $5,000; expenditures, $1,796; qualifying distributions, $1,200.
Limitations: Giving primarily in NY.
Trustees: Ellen Tannen, Sheldon Tannen.
EIN: 137008920

39841
The Peter Singer Foundation, Inc
c/o Singer, Netter, Dowd and Berman
745 Fifth Avenue, Ste. 603
New York, NY 10151-0013

Established in 2001 in NY.
Donor(s): Nell Singer, Peter Singer.
Financial data (yr. ended 12/31/01): Grants paid, $1,199; assets, $240,841 (M); gifts received, $249,844; expenditures, $1,199; qualifying distributions, $1,199.
Limitations: Applications not accepted.
Application information: Contributes only to pre-selected organizations.
Officer: Peter Singer, Pres.
Directors: Richard Netter, Nell Singer.
EIN: 134137010

39842
The Bloom Family Foundation
(Formerly Bloom-Hochberg Foundation, Inc.)
450 7th Ave.
New York, NY 10123-0001

Established in 1968.
Donor(s): Joseph J. Bloom,‡ Myron Bloom, Irwin Hochberg, Wendy Benjamin.
Financial data (yr. ended 12/31/01): Grants paid, $1,186; assets, $12 (M); gifts received, $460; expenditures, $1,226; qualifying distributions, $1,186.
Limitations: Applications not accepted. Giving primarily in NY.
Application information: Contributes only to pre-selected organizations.
Officers: Irwin Hochberg, V.P.; Myron Bloom, Secy.; Wendy B. Goldsmith, Treas.
EIN: 136198885

39843
Emily Howland Chauncey Trust Fund
c/o The Bank of New York, Tax Dept.
1 Wall St., 28th Fl.
New York, NY 10286

Financial data (yr. ended 08/31/01): Grants paid, $1,172; assets, $44,582 (M); expenditures, $1,490; qualifying distributions, $1,252.
Limitations: Applications not accepted. Giving primarily in NY.
Application information: Contributes only to pre-selected organizations.
Trustee: The Bank of New York.
EIN: 136080788

39844
Matthew R. Daw Scholarship Foundation
P.O. Box 730, Maple Row
Crompond, NY 10517
Contact: Thomas R. Daw, Pres.

Established in 1991 in NY.
Financial data (yr. ended 12/31/99): Grants paid, $1,160; assets, $24,148 (M); gifts received, $275; expenditures, $1,257; qualifying distributions, $1,145.
Limitations: Giving limited to Westchester County, NY.
Application information: Application form required.
Officers: Thomas R. Daw, Pres.; Gail Jencik, V.P.; David Schuman, V.P.; Ann Daw, Secy.-Treas.
Directors: Dan George, Barry Jencik, E. James Kissack, Joe Kolman, John Morten, Joe Wooley.
EIN: 223178461

39845
John C. Kleinert Foundation
c/o BCRS Assocs., LLC
67 Wall St., 8th Fl.
New York, NY 10005

Established in 1996 in NJ.
Donor(s): John C. Kleinert.
Financial data (yr. ended 10/31/01): Grants paid, $1,150; assets, $27,407 (M); expenditures, $1,150; qualifying distributions, $1,150.
Limitations: Applications not accepted. Giving primarily in Wyckoff, NJ.
Application information: Contributes only to pre-selected organizations.
Trustees: Janie A. Kleinert, John C. Kleinert.
EIN: 137103951

39846
Kenneth and Lois Lippmann Charitable Foundation, Inc.
Keeler Hill Farm
North Salem, NY 10560

Established in 1998 in NY.
Donor(s): Kenneth Lippmann, Lois Lippmann.
Financial data (yr. ended 12/31/01): Grants paid, $1,150; assets, $29,657 (M); gifts received, $10,500; expenditures, $1,700; qualifying distributions, $1,150.
Limitations: Applications not accepted. Giving primarily in North Salem, NY.
Application information: Contributes only to pre-selected organizations.
Officers and Directors:* Kenneth Lippmann,* Pres.; Lois Lippmann,* V.P.
Directors: Christopher Lippmann, Kenneth Lippmann, Jr.
EIN: 134009287

39847
John M. McMillin Foundation, Inc.
c/o M.R. Weiser & Co., LLP
3000 Marcus Ave.
Lake Success, NY 11042 (516) 873-1100
Contact: John M. McMillin III, Pres.

Financial data (yr. ended 12/31/01): Grants paid, $1,150; assets, $265,105 (M); expenditures, $8,566; qualifying distributions, $4,600.
Limitations: Giving primarily in NY.
Application information: Application form not required.
Officers: John M. McMillin III, Pres.; Ellen M. McMillin, Secy.; Terence L. Kelleher, Treas.
EIN: 136090795

39848
The Carlos R. Munoz Foundation
13 Club Pointe Dr.
White Plains, NY 10605

Established in 1997 in NY.
Donor(s): Carlos R. Munoz.
Financial data (yr. ended 12/31/01): Grants paid, $1,150; assets, $311,996 (M); gifts received, $40,000; expenditures, $3,121; qualifying distributions, $1,150.
Limitations: Applications not accepted.
Application information: Contributes only to pre-selected organizations.
Directors: Carlos R. Munoz, Kyle A. Munoz, Carla Munoz Slaughter.
EIN: 133986200

39849
The Myron M. Studner Foundation, Inc.
2 E. 61st St.
New York, NY 10021
Contact: Phyllis J. Grant, Pres.

Donor(s): Phyllis J. Grant.
Financial data (yr. ended 12/31/01): Grants paid, $1,150; assets, $64,299 (M); expenditures, $1,298; qualifying distributions, $1,150.
Limitations: Giving primarily in New York, NY.
Officer: Phyllis J. Grant, Pres.
EIN: 136100823

39850
The Pitman Educational Foundation, Inc.
170 E. 73rd St.
New York, NY 10021

Established in 1988 in NY.
Donor(s): Gerald Pitman.
Financial data (yr. ended 12/31/00): Grants paid, $1,125; assets, $5,276 (M); gifts received, $4,500; expenditures, $1,150; qualifying distributions, $1,150.
Limitations: Applications not accepted.
Application information: Contributes only to pre-selected organizations.
Directors: Robert Haber, Gerald Pitman, Charles Ramat.
EIN: 133491340

39851
The Gancfried Family Foundation
c/o Chava Intl.
6101 16th Ave.
Brooklyn, NY 11204
Application address: 1234 43rd St., Brooklyn, NY 11219
Contact: Isaac Gancfried, Tr.

Established in 1993 in NY.
Donor(s): Isaac Gancfried.
Financial data (yr. ended 12/31/99): Grants paid, $1,112; assets, $37,088 (M); gifts received, $700;

39851—NEW YORK

expenditures, $1,112; qualifying distributions, $1,112.
Trustee: Isaac Gancfried.
EIN: 113190101

39852
The Gerald and Linda Marsden Foundation
444 Madison Ave.
New York, NY 10022

Established in 1987 in NY.
Donor(s): Gerald Marsden, Linda Marsden.
Financial data (yr. ended 12/31/01): Grants paid, $1,111; assets, $13,509 (M); gifts received, $10,000; expenditures, $1,355; qualifying distributions, $1,111.
Limitations: Applications not accepted. Giving primarily in Roslyn, NY.
Application information: Contributes only to pre-selected organizations.
Officers and Directors:* Gerald Marsden,* Pres.; Linda Marsden,* V.P.
EIN: 133440549

39853
Herbert & Eileen Bernard Foundation
c/o American Express Tax and Business SVCS
1185 Ave. of the Americas
New York, NY 10036
Contact: Herbert Bernard, Manager

Financial data (yr. ended 12/31/01): Grants paid, $1,100; assets, $11,090 (M); gifts received, $15,000; expenditures, $3,950; qualifying distributions, $1,100.
Officer: Herbert C. Bernard, Pres.
EIN: 136227509

39854
Max M. Farash Tooling and Machinery Foundation
919 Winton Rd., S.
Rochester, NY 14618-1633 (716) 244-1886

Donor(s): Max M. Farash.
Financial data (yr. ended 12/31/01): Grants paid, $1,100; assets, $21,820 (M); expenditures, $1,718; qualifying distributions, $1,100.
Limitations: Applications not accepted. Giving limited to Rochester, NY.
Application information: Contributes only to pre-selected organizations.
Trustees: Max M. Farash, Michael W. Farash, S. Joseph Goodyear, John D. Hostutler, Lucien A. Morin, Thomas P. Ryan, Jr., Lynn Farash Tarbox.
EIN: 112558438

39855
Joseph E. Glickman Memorial Scholarship Fund, Inc.
187 Tumbleweed Dr.
Pittsford, NY 14534

Established in 1996 in NY.
Financial data (yr. ended 02/28/00): Grants paid, $1,100; assets, $39,514 (M); gifts received, $332; expenditures, $2,009; qualifying distributions, $1,054.
Limitations: Applications not accepted.
Officers: Loren J. Gibson, Pres.; John J. Kehrig, V.P.; John V. Jaun, Secy.-Treas.
Directors: Arthur M. English, Robert Prescott, Kevin M. Sullivan.
EIN: 161451784

39856
Andrew Goodman Foundation, Inc.
161 W. 86th St., Ste. 8A
New York, NY 10024

Established in 1966.

Donor(s): Carolyn Goodman Eisner, Time Warner, Inc.
Financial data (yr. ended 12/31/00): Grants paid, $1,100; assets, $111,811 (M); gifts received, $24,665; expenditures, $38,202; qualifying distributions, $38,089; giving activities include $25,521 for programs.
Limitations: Giving primarily in New York, NY.
Officers: Carolyn Goodman, Pres.; David Goodman, Secy.; Edward Lowenthal, Treas.
Trustees: Frances Boehm, Eli Lee, Jane Mark.
EIN: 136207568

39857
Michele E. Martin Memorial Trust
45 W. Bayberry Rd.
Glenmont, NY 12077-9693

Financial data (yr. ended 06/30/01): Grants paid, $1,100; assets, $21,044 (M); gifts received, $9,123; expenditures, $7,749; qualifying distributions, $6,740.
Limitations: Applications not accepted. Giving limited to Plattsburgh, NY.
Application information: Contributes only to pre-selected organizations.
Trustees: Elizabeth Martin, William Martin.
EIN: 222462913

39858
Sunrise-Laurelton Lodge Foundation, Inc.
(Formerly Laurelton Lodge Foundation, Inc.)
20 Bond Ln.
Hicksville, NY 11801-4511 (516) 571-7901
Contact: Richard Ryder, Treas.

Financial data (yr. ended 12/31/01): Grants paid, $1,100; assets, $17,112 (M); expenditures, $1,277; qualifying distributions, $1,100.
Limitations: Giving primarily in NY.
Officers: Oscar London, Chair.; Joseph T. Padawer, Pres.; William Ruthizer, Secy.; Richard Ryder, Treas.
EIN: 116036339

39859
Johan Maasbach World Mission Foundation, Inc.
c/o Johnson, Lauder & Savidge, LLP
P.O. Box 367
Endicott, NY 13761-0367

Financial data (yr. ended 06/30/00): Grants paid, $1,050; assets, $42,171 (M); gifts received, $1,335; expenditures, $2,684; qualifying distributions, $2,315; giving activities include $660 for programs.
Limitations: Applications not accepted. Giving on an international basis, with emphasis on the Netherlands.
Application information: Contributes only to pre-selected organizations.
Officers: David Maasbach, Pres.; Alida W. Klumper, V.P.; Theodoor G. Gieseler, Secy.; John T.L. Maasbach, Treas.
EIN: 237225516

39860
SJMS Humanities Arts & Sciences Charity, Inc.
20 Elkland Rd.
Melville, NY 11747-3302
Contact: Melvin Rosen, Pres.

Financial data (yr. ended 12/31/01): Grants paid, $1,050; assets, $25,677 (M); expenditures, $6,597; qualifying distributions, $1,050.
Officers: Melvin Rosen, Pres.; Hillegonda Rosen, Secy.
Director: Robert Katz.
EIN: 113027025

39861
North River Community Environmental Review Board, Inc.
c/o HGS
P.O. Box 605
New York, NY 10031-0605

Financial data (yr. ended 06/30/00): Grants paid, $1,025; assets, $10,081 (M); gifts received, $22,592; expenditures, $20,650; qualifying distributions, $0; giving activities include $20,650 for programs.
Officer and Trustees:* L. Annrocker,* Chair. and C.E.O.; Marilyn Alexander, James Capel, Cindre B. Demeteun.
EIN: 133614524

39862
American Friends of the Cambodia Trust, Inc.
c/o Peter V. Darrow
1675 Broadway
New York, NY 10019-5820

Financial data (yr. ended 06/30/01): Grants paid, $1,020; assets, $12,821 (M); gifts received, $22,425; expenditures, $14,862; qualifying distributions, $0.
Directors: Peter V. Darrow, Christine M.Y. Ho, Limor Nissan.
EIN: 521798613

39863
Shoshana Gad Z"L Foundation, Inc.
c/o Amerind
580 5th Ave., 24th Fl.
New York, NY 10036

Established in 2001 in NY.
Financial data (yr. ended 12/31/01): Grants paid, $1,017; assets, $20,425 (M); gifts received, $22,368; expenditures, $1,943; qualifying distributions, $1,943.
Limitations: Applications not accepted.
Application information: Contributes only to pre-selected organizations.
Officers: Solomon Gad, Pres.; Dalia Gad, V.P.; Ruth Hendelman, V.P.
EIN: 134150844

39864
Yasuo Kuniyoshi Fund, Inc.
c/o Bruce Currie
120 Boggs Hill
Woodstock, NY 12498-2712

Financial data (yr. ended 12/31/00): Grants paid, $1,007; assets, $20,012 (M); expenditures, $1,384; qualifying distributions, $1,007.
Limitations: Applications not accepted. Giving limited to Woodstock, NY.
Application information: Recipient artists are selected by panel of judges.
Officers: Sara M. Kuniyoshi, Chair.; Bruce Currie, Secy.
EIN: 141485217

39865
Carol A. Gregory and Angelo Calabrese Memorial Trust
c/o William Calabrese
403 Stage Rd.
Monroe, NY 10950-3331
Application address: c/o Carol A. Gregory, BOCES, Gibson Rd., Goshen, NY 10924

Financial data (yr. ended 06/30/99): Grants paid, $1,005; assets, $23,488 (M); expenditures, $1,005; qualifying distributions, $1,005.
Limitations: Giving primarily in Orange and Ulster counties, NY.

IN THIS SECTION, WITHIN EACH STATE, FOUNDATIONS ARE LISTED IN DESCENDING ORDER BY TOTAL GRANTS PAID

Application information: Application form required.
Directors and Trustees:* Myrna Calabrese, William Calabrese, Marguerite Flood, A. Paul Hackett, Judith G. Knight.
EIN: 141601579

39866
The Anatol & Arthur Charitable Foundation
2-4 Longview Ave., Ste. 201
White Plains, NY 10601
Contact: Dan Costin, Tr.

Established in 1999 in NY.
Donor(s): Dan Costin.
Financial data (yr. ended 12/31/01): Grants paid, $1,000; assets, $14,134 (M); gifts received, $9,731; expenditures, $7,712; qualifying distributions, $1,000.
Trustees: Dan Costin, Sandra Costin.
EIN: 134092833

39867
Elaine Elizabeth Barbiere Foundation
1892 Gerritsen Ave.
Brooklyn, NY 11229-2600

Financial data (yr. ended 10/31/01): Grants paid, $1,000; assets, $21,208 (M); gifts received, $1,160; expenditures, $1,190; qualifying distributions, $1,175.
Limitations: Giving limited to Corpus Christi, TX.
Officer: Mabel E. Barbiere, Pres.
EIN: 237098611

39868
J. Reid and Louise H. Barton Foundation
60 Cady Ave.
P.O. Box 11
Nichols, NY 13812
Contact: J. Reid Barton, Tr.

Established in 2000 in NY.
Financial data (yr. ended 12/31/01): Grants paid, $1,000; assets, $18,277 (M); gifts received, $641; expenditures, $1,640; qualifying distributions, $1,000.
Trustees: David R. Barton, J. Reid Barton, Elizabeth B. Kerr.
EIN: 161589089

39869
Barbara L. Becker and Jonathan C. Gallant Charitable Foundation
c/o S. Ditsky
733 3rd Ave., Ste. 1900
New York, NY 10017

Established in 1997.
Donor(s): Barbara Lynn Becker.
Financial data (yr. ended 12/31/99): Grants paid, $1,000; assets, $16,462 (M); expenditures, $1,000; qualifying distributions, $1,000.
Limitations: Applications not accepted.
Application information: Contributes only to pre-selected organizations.
Directors: Barbara L. Becker, Jack Becker, Marjorie Anne Becker, Jonathan C. Gallant.
EIN: 133949651

39870
Walter and Beatrice J. Beigel Scholarships Trust
c/o First Tier Bank and Trust
107 Main St.
Salamanca, NY 14779-1529
Application address: c/o Chuck Crist, Principal, Salamanca Central High School, 50 Iroquois Dr., Salamanca, NY 14779, tel.: (716) 945-2400

Financial data (yr. ended 12/31/99): Grants paid, $1,000; assets, $21,806 (M); expenditures, $1,264; qualifying distributions, $1,264.

Limitations: Giving limited to Salamanca, NY.
Application information: Interview required.
Trustee: First Tier Bank and Trust.
EIN: 166250187

39871
Brotherhood in Action, Inc.
c/o Becker, Ross, Stone, DeStefano & Klein
317 Madison Ave.
New York, NY 10017-5372

Donor(s): Joseph and Ceil Mazur Foundation.
Financial data (yr. ended 06/30/01): Grants paid, $1,000; assets, $9,739 (M); expenditures, $1,774; qualifying distributions, $1,524.
Limitations: Applications not accepted.
Officers: Jesse Margolin, Chair.; William J. Dean, Pres.; Myron Beldock, V.P.; Ruth Brooks, V.P.
EIN: 136098439

39872
John Butler Foundation, Inc.
c/o Siegel, Sachs, Press & Lacher
630 3rd Ave., 22nd Fl.
New York, NY 10017

Established in 1999 in NY.
Financial data (yr. ended 12/31/99): Grants paid, $1,000; assets, $55,065 (M); gifts received, $32,850; expenditures, $17,951; qualifying distributions, $1,000.
Limitations: Applications not accepted.
Application information: Contributes only to pre-selected organizations.
Officer and Directors:* Melvin Dwork,* Pres.; Judith Jamison, Scott Kemper, Stoner Winslett.
EIN: 133988194

39873
Capranica Foundation
c/o Tompkins County Trust Co.
P.O. Box 460
Ithaca, NY 14851-0460 (607) 273-3210
Contact: Robert R. Capranica, Chair.

Established in 1986 in NY.
Donor(s): Robert R. Capranica, Patricia A. Capranica.
Financial data (yr. ended 12/31/99): Grants paid, $1,000; assets, $24,250 (M); expenditures, $1,678; qualifying distributions, $1,093.
Limitations: Giving on a national basis.
Application information: Application form not required.
Directors: Robert R. Capranica, Chair.; Patricia A. Capranica, Peter M. Narins.
EIN: 222670921

39874
The Castner Family Foundation
c/o Tanton & Co.
37 W. 57th St.
New York, NY 10019

Established in 1998 in DE.
Donor(s): Alan G. Castner.
Financial data (yr. ended 05/31/01): Grants paid, $1,000; assets, $33,548 (M); gifts received, $11,938; expenditures, $1,319; qualifying distributions, $1,000.
Limitations: Applications not accepted.
Application information: Contributes only to pre-selected organizations.
Officers: Allen G. Castner, Pres. and Treas.; Erin M. Castner, V.P. and Secy.
EIN: 134010799

39875
Chapel Hill Foundation, Inc.
107 Salmon River Rd.
Plattsburgh, NY 12901

Donor(s): Martha B. Frost, Richard B. Frost.
Financial data (yr. ended 12/31/01): Grants paid, $1,000; assets, $21,944 (M); gifts received, $22,000; expenditures, $3,667; qualifying distributions, $3,667.
Limitations: Giving primarily in NY.
Trustees: Martha B. Frost, Richard B. Frost.
EIN: 141820272

39876
Chaverim Kol Yisrael/Jewish Life Network
(also known as Jewish Life Network)
6 E. 39th St., 10th Fl.
New York, NY 10016 (212) 279-2288

Established in 1993 in NY.
Financial data (yr. ended 08/31/00): Grants paid, $1,000; assets, $13,454,979 (M); gifts received, $13,188; expenditures, $1,907,875; giving activities include $1,250,913 for programs.
Officers: M. Steinhardt, Chair.; Rabbi Irving Greenberg, Pres.; Jonathan J. Greenberg, Secy.-Treas.
EIN: 133731980
Codes: CM

39877
DOS BFS Charitable Foundation Trust
100 Ring Rd. W.
Garden City, NY 11530

Established in 2000 in NY.
Financial data (yr. ended 12/31/00): Grants paid, $1,000; assets, $1,500 (M); gifts received, $2,500; expenditures, $1,000; qualifying distributions, $1,000.
Trustees: Bette Stein, Donald Stein.
EIN: 116548603

39878
Robert and Kathryn P. Fagliarone Foundation
2629 E. Lake Rd.
Skaneateles, NY 13152

Established in 2000 in NY.
Donor(s): Robert Fagliarone, Kathryn Fagliarone.
Financial data (yr. ended 12/31/01): Grants paid, $1,000; assets, $7,726 (M); gifts received, $1,000; expenditures, $1,500; qualifying distributions, $1,000.
Limitations: Applications not accepted. Giving primarily in Syracuse, NY.
Application information: Contributes only to pre-selected organizations.
Trustee: Kristin Fagliarone Burnett.
EIN: 161562158

39879
The Anthony & Vanda Ficalora Foundation
10 Castle Rd.
Irvington, NY 10533

Established in 1999 in NY.
Donor(s): Anthony Ficalora, Vanda Ficalora.
Financial data (yr. ended 12/31/01): Grants paid, $1,000; assets, $47,926 (M); gifts received, $24,975; expenditures, $1,121; qualifying distributions, $1,000.
Limitations: Applications not accepted. Giving primarily in NY.
Application information: Contributes only to pre-selected organizations.
Directors: Anthony Ficalora, Vanda Ficalora.
EIN: 134055679

39880
Phylis and James Fogelson Foundation
c/o B. Strauss Assoc., Ltd.
307 5th Ave., 8th Fl.
New York, NY 10016-6517

Established in 2000 in NY.
Donor(s): Phylis Fogelson.
Financial data (yr. ended 08/31/01): Grants paid, $1,000; assets, $174,441 (M); gifts received, $200,000; expenditures, $1,000; qualifying distributions, $1,000.
Limitations: Applications not accepted. Giving primarily in NY.
Application information: Contributes only to pre-selected organizations.
Officers and Directors:* Phylis Fogelson,* Pres.; Robert Fogelson,* Secy.; Matthew Fogelson,* Treas.
EIN: 061602427

39881
Fred Goldsmith Trust f/b/o Delhi Central School District
c/o Johanna Koenig
101 Harding Farm Rd.
Oneonta, NY 13820

Established in 1993 in NY.
Donor(s): Fred Goldsmith.‡
Financial data (yr. ended 06/30/01): Grants paid, $1,000; assets, $29,166 (M); expenditures, $1,780; qualifying distributions, $1,000.
Limitations: Applications not accepted. Giving limited to Delhi, NY.
Application information: Unsolicited requests for funds not accepted.
Trustees: Arthur C. Goldsmith, Johanna Koenig, Carlo Rodio.
EIN: 166380471

39882
The Jeffrey and Jamie Harris Family Foundation Trust
7 Oak Ln.
Scarsdale, NY 10583

Established in 2001 in NY.
Donor(s): Jeffrey A. Harris.
Financial data (yr. ended 11/30/01): Grants paid, $1,000; assets, $268,677 (M); gifts received, $268,591; expenditures, $1,650; qualifying distributions, $1,650.
Limitations: Applications not accepted. Giving primarily in New York, NY.
Application information: Contributes only to pre-selected organizations.
Trustee: Jeffrey A. Harris.
EIN: 137273247

39883
The Harris Foundation, Inc.
5700 Arlington Ave., Ste. 17X
Riverdale, NY 10471 (718) 601-0042
Contact: Adrienne C. Harris, Pres.

Established in 1996.
Donor(s): Adrienne C. Harris.
Financial data (yr. ended 07/31/02): Grants paid, $1,000; assets, $17,646 (M); expenditures, $1,217; qualifying distributions, $1,000.
Officers: Adrienne C. Harris, Pres. and Treas.; Trina Tuckett, V.P.; Dorothea V. Canty, Secy.
EIN: 133876324

39884
Ruth Haulenbeek St. John - Helena L. Cable Scholarship Fund
c/o Francis Cucciarre
25 Maple St.
Walton, NY 13856

Financial data (yr. ended 12/31/01): Grants paid, $1,000; assets, $285,657 (M); gifts received, $54,858; expenditures, $25,441; qualifying distributions, $1,441; giving activities include $24,000 for loans to individuals.
Application information: Application form required.
Officers: Francis Cucciarre, Pres.; Penny Tweedie, V.P.; Frederika Cranston, Secy.; Marian Budine, Treas.
EIN: 161372173

39885
Herbst Family Foundation, Inc.
42 Claire Ct.
West Babylon, NY 11704-7304

Established in 1997.
Financial data (yr. ended 12/31/01): Grants paid, $1,000; assets, $4,996 (M); expenditures, $1,375; qualifying distributions, $1,000.
Limitations: Giving primarily in NY.
Trustee: Janice Herbst.
EIN: 113405415

39886
John V. Jacobs Benevolent Fund
c/o NBT Bank, N.A.
52 S. Broad St.
Norwich, NY 13815-1646
Application address: c/o NBT Bank, N.A. Bainbridge, NY 13733, tel.: (607) 337-6193

Financial data (yr. ended 12/31/01): Grants paid, $1,000; assets, $20,642 (M); expenditures, $1,334; qualifying distributions, $1,178.
Limitations: Giving limited to Bainbridge, NY.
Trustee: NBT Bank, N.A.
EIN: 166043561

39887
Hannah & Robert Judelson Foundation, Inc.
270 Pepperidge Rd.
Hewlett, NY 11557

Donor(s): Robert Judelson, Marvin Tolkin.
Financial data (yr. ended 09/30/01): Grants paid, $1,000; assets, $50,854 (M); gifts received, $200; expenditures, $1,150; qualifying distributions, $1,000.
Limitations: Applications not accepted. Giving primarily in NY.
Application information: Contributes only to pre-selected organizations.
Officers: Marvin Tolkin, Pres.; David Tolkin, V.P.; Lawrence Tolkin, V.P.
EIN: 112648449

39888
David Kagan Foundation, Inc.
322 Central Park W.
New York, NY 10025 (212) 662-6693

Donor(s): Irving Kagan, Shirley Kagan.
Financial data (yr. ended 12/31/01): Grants paid, $1,000; assets, $41,346 (M); gifts received, $15,100; expenditures, $10,379; qualifying distributions, $1,000.
Limitations: Giving primarily in New York, NY.
Officers: Irving Kagan, Pres.; Shirley Kagan, Secy.
EIN: 133335496

39889
Louise and Peter Kaufman Charitable Foundation Trust
165 Duchess Ave.
Staten Island, NY 10304

Established in 2001.
Financial data (yr. ended 12/31/01): Grants paid, $1,000; assets, $10,921 (M); expenditures, $1,000; qualifying distributions, $1,000.
Trustees: Louise Kaufman, Peter Kaufman.
EIN: 137268662

39890
Donald Keene Foundation for Japanese Culture
c/o Noriku Fuku
310 Riverside Dr.
New York, NY 10025

Established in 2001.
Donor(s): Donald Keene.
Financial data (yr. ended 12/31/01): Grants paid, $1,000; assets, $11,726 (M); gifts received, $21,000; expenditures, $9,320; qualifying distributions, $1,000.
Limitations: Applications not accepted.
Application information: Contributes only to pre-selected organizations.
Directors: Donald Keene, Hugh Patrick, Barbara Ruch.
EIN: 311704871

39891
David J. Kelman Research Foundation, Inc.
220 Madison Ave.
New York, NY 10016

Donor(s): Charles D. Kelman, M.D.
Financial data (yr. ended 12/31/01): Grants paid, $1,000; assets, $759,962 (M); gifts received, $6,868; expenditures, $22,389; qualifying distributions, $12,242; giving activities include $11,242 for programs.
Officer: Charles D. Kelman, M.D., Pres.
Director: Diane Spiro.
EIN: 136274538

39892
Harry & Bella Koffman Charitable Foundation
c/o Piaker & Lyons, PC
P.O. Box 247
Vestal, NY 13851

Established in 1998.
Donor(s): Harry Koffman.
Financial data (yr. ended 12/31/01): Grants paid, $1,000; assets, $209,941 (M); gifts received, $200; expenditures, $1,459; qualifying distributions, $1,000.
Limitations: Applications not accepted.
Application information: Contributes only to pre-selected organizations.
Trustees: Burton I. Koffman, Richard E. Koffman.
EIN: 222932359

39893
Chris Larkin Memorial Fund, Inc.
3169 Lincoln Ave.
Oceanside, NY 11572 (516) 536-3069
Contact: Wilma Larkin, Secy.-Treas.

Established in 1987 in NY.
Financial data (yr. ended 12/31/01): Grants paid, $1,000; assets, $12,396 (M); expenditures, $1,427; qualifying distributions, $1,000.
Limitations: Giving primarily in Oceanside, NY.
Application information: Application form not required.
Officers: Peter Larkin, Pres.; Kim Larkin, V.P.; Wilma Larkin, Secy.-Treas.
EIN: 112894655

39894
Long Island Restaurant & Caterers Memorial Scholarship Foundation, Inc.
640 Fulton St., Ste. 4
Farmingdale, NY 11735 (516) 752-0707
Contact: Christine Nowak, Tr.

Established in 1987 in NY.
Financial data (yr. ended 12/31/01): Grants paid, $1,000; assets, $16,665 (M); gifts received, $1,350; expenditures, $1,695; qualifying distributions, $1,000.
Limitations: Giving limited to NY.
Trustees: Donald Lecompte, Jerry Marlowe, Robert McCarroll, Christine Nowak.
EIN: 112873153

39895
Major Family Charitable Trust
c/o Martin Major
25 Chestnut Hill Ln.
Briarcliff Manor, NY 10510

Established in 1999 in NY.
Donor(s): Martin Major, Sheila Major.
Financial data (yr. ended 06/30/00): Grants paid, $1,000; assets, $101,522 (M); gifts received, $100,000; expenditures, $1,500; qualifying distributions, $1,000.
Limitations: Applications not accepted.
Application information: Contributes only to pre-selected organizations.
Trustee: Martin Major.
EIN: 137221394

39896
Melone Foundation for Orthopedic Research of the Hand and Wrist
62 W. 12 St.
New York, NY 10011

Established in 1996 in NY.
Donor(s): Charles P. Melone, Jr.
Financial data (yr. ended 12/31/01): Grants paid, $1,000; assets, $17,903 (M); gifts received, $1,008; expenditures, $1,008; qualifying distributions, $1,000.
Directors: Charles P. Melone, Jr., Cherie Melone.
EIN: 133595667

39897
New York Drama Critics Circle, Inc.
c/o Rosenzweig & Maffia, LLP
845 3rd Ave., Ste. 1300
New York, NY 10022

Financial data (yr. ended 09/30/01): Grants paid, $1,000; assets, $23,446 (M); expenditures, $1,878; qualifying distributions, $1,000.
Limitations: Applications not accepted. Giving primarily in New York, NY.
Officers: Jacques Le Sourd, Pres.; Ken Mandelbaum, Secy.-Treas.
EIN: 132893085

39898
Newtown High School Teacher's Welfare League, Inc.
48-01 90th St.
Elmhurst, NY 11373

Established in 1988 in NY.
Financial data (yr. ended 12/31/01): Grants paid, $1,000; assets, $47,295 (M); expenditures, $1,716; qualifying distributions, $1,052.
Limitations: Giving limited to residents of Queens County, NY.
Officers: Howard Friedman, Pres.; Walter Kamlot, Treas.; Joel Roth, Secy.
EIN: 112897296

39899
William and Elizabeth Moot O'Hern Scholarship Fund
c/o The Central National Bank
24 Church St.
Canajoharie, NY 13317-1101

Established in 1978 in NY.
Financial data (yr. ended 12/31/01): Grants paid, $1,000; assets, $22,501 (M); expenditures, $1,484; qualifying distributions, $1,000.
Limitations: Applications not accepted. Giving primarily in Richmondville, NY.
Application information: Contributes only to pre-selected organizations.
Trustee: The Central National Bank.
EIN: 222368196

39900
Mary Jo Orzano Memorial Scholarship
436 Kinsley Ct.
Oceanside, NY 11572-1309
Application address: c/o Robert Ledlie, Asst. Principal, Oceanside High School, Brower Ave., Oceanside, NY 11572, tel.: (516) 678-8531

Financial data (yr. ended 12/31/01): Grants paid, $1,000; assets, $18,665 (M); expenditures, $1,139; qualifying distributions, $1,000.
Limitations: Giving limited to Oceanside, NY.
Application information: Applicant must submit high school grades and college acceptance.
Trustees: Grace Orzano Griffin, Elizabeth Kramer.
EIN: 116079935

39901
Steve Pearson Foundation, Inc.
c/o L. Wollin
350 5th Ave., Ste. 2822
New York, NY 10118

Established in 1998 in DE.
Donor(s): Gerald Pearson.
Financial data (yr. ended 03/31/02): Grants paid, $1,000; assets, $54,120 (M); expenditures, $1,195; qualifying distributions, $1,000.
Limitations: Applications not accepted.
Application information: Contributes only to pre-selected organizations.
Officer: Steve Pearson, Pres.
EIN: 510380635

39902
The Punia Foundation
c/o H.J. Behrman & Co., LLP
215 Lexington Ave., Ste. 202
New York, NY 10016

Donor(s): Charles Punia.‡
Financial data (yr. ended 10/31/01): Grants paid, $1,000; assets, $3,025 (M); expenditures, $1,100; qualifying distributions, $1,000.
Limitations: Applications not accepted. Giving primarily in MA, NJ, and NY.
Application information: Contributes only to pre-selected organizations.
Officers: Leonard Punia, Pres.; Herbert Punia, V.P.; Joseph Punia, Secy.; Jeffrey Punia, Treas.
EIN: 116020420

39903
Putnam Family Foundation, Inc.
120 N. Grand St.
Cobleskill, NY 12043

Established in 1998 in NY.
Financial data (yr. ended 12/31/01): Grants paid, $1,000; assets, $2,840,701 (M); gifts received, $2,612,790; expenditures, $14,685; qualifying distributions, $1,000.
Limitations: Applications not accepted.
Application information: Contributes only to pre-selected organizations.
Directors: Anne B. Putnam, Catherine M. Putnam, Thomas O. Putnam.
EIN: 141804783

39904
George Rickey Foundation, Inc.
76 Rte. 34
East Chatham, NY 12060

Established in 1994 in NY.
Donor(s): George Rickey.‡
Financial data (yr. ended 12/31/01): Grants paid, $1,000; assets, $498,503 (M); gifts received, $200,700; expenditures, $7,495; qualifying distributions, $1,000.
Limitations: Applications not accepted. Giving primarily in St. Paul, MN.
Application information: Contributes only to pre-selected organizations.
Directors: Max Davidson, Curtis Harnack, Ralph E. Lerner, Philip J. Rickey, Stuart R. Rickey, Nan Rosenthal.
EIN: 141768291

39905
The Riordan Fund
767 5th Ave., Ste. 4701
New York, NY 10153-4798

Established in 2001 in NY.
Donor(s): William J. Ruane.
Financial data (yr. ended 12/31/01): Grants paid, $1,000; assets, $5,021,050 (M); gifts received, $5,053,125; expenditures, $1,000; qualifying distributions, $1,000.
Limitations: Applications not accepted. Giving primarily in NY.
Application information: Contributes only to pre-selected organizations.
Trustee: Joyce C. Ruane.
EIN: 137298631

39906
Frank A. and Lulu Rose Foundation
c/o Vera Farrell
P.O. Box 1399
Livingston Manor, NY 12758

Established in 1992 in NY.
Financial data (yr. ended 12/31/00): Grants paid, $1,000; assets, $326 (M); gifts received, $1,000; expenditures, $1,263; qualifying distributions, $1,000.
Limitations: Giving limited to residents of Livingston Manor, NY.
Trustees: Vera Farrell, Charles L. Fontana, William R. Knipscher, Shirley Schwartz.
EIN: 141750606

39907
The Peggy and Ronald Schulhof Foundation
c/o Nathan Berkman & Co.
29 Broadway, Ste. 2900
New York, NY 10006-3296

Established in 1998 in NY.
Donor(s): Didi and King Hirsh Foundation.
Financial data (yr. ended 09/30/01): Grants paid, $1,000; assets, $312,474 (M); expenditures, $3,535; qualifying distributions, $1,000.
Limitations: Applications not accepted.
Application information: Contributes only to pre-selected organizations.
Trustees: Amy Schulhof, R. Dean Schulhof, R. Mark Schulhof.
EIN: 133987113

39908
The Sind Family Foundation, Inc.
c/o Robert H. Haines
405 Lexington Ave.
New York, NY 10174

Established in 1998 in NY.
Donor(s): Robert L. Sind.
Financial data (yr. ended 12/31/01): Grants paid, $1,000; assets, $30,472 (M); expenditures, $1,045; qualifying distributions, $1,000.
Limitations: Applications not accepted. Giving primarily in New York, NY.
Application information: Contributes only to pre-selected organizations.
Officers: Robert L. Sind, Pres.; William J. Sind, V.P.; Amy C. Sind, Treas.
EIN: 134033046

39909
Eric Sopracasa Memorial Scholarship Fund
33 Neil Dr.
Farmingville, NY 11738

Established in 1999 in NY.
Financial data (yr. ended 06/30/02): Grants paid, $1,000; assets, $7,523 (M); gifts received, $985; expenditures, $1,000; qualifying distributions, $1,000.
Director: Ernest Sopracasa.
EIN: 113502143

39910
Sovereign Senators Charity Fund, Inc.
488 7th Ave., Ste. 3E
New York, NY 10018-6806 (212) 868-3988
Contact: Malcolm Kravitz, Treas.

Financial data (yr. ended 04/30/02): Grants paid, $1,000; assets, $8,333 (M); gifts received, $2,800; expenditures, $1,081; qualifying distributions, $1,000.
Limitations: Giving primarily in NY.
Officers: Bernard Schneider, Pres.; Howard E. Good, V.P.; Ronald Bing, Secy.; Malcolm Kravitz, Treas.
EIN: 136161273

39911
The Spear Family Foundation, Inc.
184-51 Radnor Rd.
Jamaica, NY 11432

Financial data (yr. ended 10/31/01): Grants paid, $1,000; assets, $0 (M); gifts received, $1,000; expenditures, $1,000; qualifying distributions, $1,000.
Limitations: Applications not accepted.
Application information: Contributes only to pre-selected organizations.
Officer: Bernard Spear, Pres.
EIN: 113185266

39912
A. L. Stamm Foundation, Inc.
c/o J.D. Miller & Co., LLP
350 5th Ave., Ste. 5019
New York, NY 10118-0080

Financial data (yr. ended 06/30/02): Grants paid, $1,000; assets, $86,595 (M); expenditures, $2,941; qualifying distributions, $1,000.
Limitations: Applications not accepted. Giving primarily in FL and NY.
Application information: Contributes only to pre-selected organizations.
Officers: Robert C. Stamm, Pres.; Catherine Stamm, Treas.
Directors: John-Paul Stamm, Philip Stamm.
EIN: 136161146

39913
The Three Kings Foundation, Inc.
c/o Sol M. Israel
185 Madison Ave.
New York, NY 10016

Established in 1996 in NY.
Donor(s): Isaac Israel, Pauline Israel.
Financial data (yr. ended 05/31/01): Grants paid, $1,000; assets, $44,308 (M); expenditures, $2,817; qualifying distributions, $1,000.
Limitations: Applications not accepted.
Application information: Contributes only to pre-selected organizations.
Officers and Directors:* Isaac Israel,* Pres. and Treas.; Sol M. Israel,* V.P. and Secy.; Arthur R. Israel,* V.P.; Pauline Israel,* V.P.; Richard P. Israel,* V.P.
EIN: 113327433

39914
Moshe Willig Memorial Fund
c/o Herbert Willig
147-32 69th Rd.
Flushing, NY 11367-1732

Donor(s): Jerome Willig.
Financial data (yr. ended 03/31/01): Grants paid, $1,000; assets, $28,873 (M); gifts received, $1,000; expenditures, $1,160; qualifying distributions, $1,000.
Limitations: Applications not accepted. Giving primarily in New York, NY.
Application information: Contributes only to pre-selected organizations.
Trustees: Herbert Willig, Jerome Willig, Leonard Willig.
EIN: 237178699

39915
Tifereth Yaakov Foundation
857 E. 26th St.
Brooklyn, NY 11210
Contact: Eugene Lipschitz, Tr.

Financial data (yr. ended 07/31/02): Grants paid, $1,000; assets, $18,977 (M); expenditures, $4,526; qualifying distributions, $1,000.
Limitations: Giving primarily in NY.
Trustee: Eugene Lipschitz.
EIN: 113445073

39916
June & Irwin Katlowitz Foundation
110-20 71st Rd.
Forest Hills, NY 11375-4945

Donor(s): Irwin Katlowitz.
Financial data (yr. ended 12/31/00): Grants paid, $988; assets, $4,945 (M); expenditures, $1,428; qualifying distributions, $988.
Limitations: Applications not accepted. Giving primarily in New York, NY.
Application information: Contributes only to pre-selected organizations.
Officers: Irwin Katlowitz, Pres. and Secy.; June Katlowitz, V.P. and Treas.
EIN: 112672096

39917
The Dukoff-Toro Foundation
224 Everit Ave.
Hewlett Harbor, NY 11557-2225
Contact: Amy Dukoff-Toro, Tr.

Established in 1989 in NY.
Donor(s): Amy Dukoff-Toro.
Financial data (yr. ended 12/31/01): Grants paid, $961; assets, $32,727 (M); expenditures, $1,135; qualifying distributions, $961.
Limitations: Giving primarily in New York, NY.
Trustees: Marilyn Dukoff, Amy Dukoff-Toro.
EIN: 133510308

39918
Sheriff Michael A. Amico Law Enforcement Scholarship Trust
c/o M&T Bank
P.O. Box 22900
Rochester, NY 14692
Application address: c/o Michael A. Amico, Advisory Comm., 363 Dan Troy Dr., Williamsville, NY 14221, tel.: (716) 632-7772

Financial data (yr. ended 12/31/01): Grants paid, $956; assets, $51,705 (M); expenditures, $1,711; qualifying distributions, $956.
Limitations: Giving limited to Albany, NY.
Trustee: M&T Bank.
EIN: 166212229

39919
Judy Hokaj Memorial Scholarship Fund
9 James Pl.
Lancaster, NY 14086-2607
Contact: Edward L. Hokaj, Tr.

Established in 1997 in NY.
Financial data (yr. ended 05/31/00): Grants paid, $950; assets, $10,804 (M); gifts received, $750; expenditures, $950; qualifying distributions, $950.
Application information: Application form not required.
Trustees: Robert Dubel, Ronald F. Grazen, David J. Hokaj, Edward L. Hokaj, Paula J. Hokaj, Paul A. Kendall.
EIN: 161520237

39920
Alexander Levy Foundation, Inc.
29-03 Hunterspoint Ave.
Long Island City, NY 11101-3493
(718) 786-3760
Contact: Alexander Levy, Pres.

Donor(s): Alexander Levy.
Financial data (yr. ended 10/31/01): Grants paid, $940; assets, $8,291 (M); expenditures, $940; qualifying distributions, $940.
Limitations: Giving primarily in NY.
Officer and Director:* Alexander Levy,* Pres.
EIN: 116021729

39921
Michael Lowy Foundation, Inc.
c/o Alfred C. Lowy, M.D.
1036 Park Ave.
New York, NY 10028-0971 (212) 288-0015

Established in 1946 in NY.
Financial data (yr. ended 12/31/01): Grants paid, $925; assets, $15,808 (M); expenditures, $1,458; qualifying distributions, $925.
Limitations: Applications not accepted. Giving primarily in New York, NY.
Application information: Contributes only to pre-selected organizations.
Officer: Alfred C. Lowy, M.D., Pres.
EIN: 136113542

39922
Ida & Irving Allerhand Foundation, Inc.
704 Ave. I
Brooklyn, NY 11230-2712 (718) 252-5850
Contact: Irving Allerhand, Pres.

Donor(s): Irving Allerhand.
Financial data (yr. ended 12/31/01): Grants paid, $914; assets, $35,912 (M); expenditures, $1,096; qualifying distributions, $914.
Limitations: Giving primarily in NY.
Officers: Irving Allerhand, Pres.; Joseph Allerhand, Secy.; Hershel Allerhand, Treas.

EIN: 136120583

39923
The Nora Feury Scholarship Fund, Inc.
3515 Henry Hudson Pkwy., Ste. 4G
Bronx, NY 10463 (718) 409-1277
Contact: Nora Feury, Chair.

Financial data (yr. ended 12/31/99): Grants paid, $900; assets, $42,375 (M); gifts received, $174; expenditures, $1,200; qualifying distributions, $900.
Limitations: Giving limited to the Bronx, NY.
Application information: Application form required.
Officer: Nora Feury, Chair.
EIN: 133290390

39924
The Rottman Foundation
15 Bonnie Meadow Rd.
Scarsdale, NY 10583

Financial data (yr. ended 11/30/01): Grants paid, $900; assets, $14,744 (M); expenditures, $911; qualifying distributions, $900.
Limitations: Giving limited to NY.
Officer and Trustees: Hy Rottman,* Chair.; Karen Roth, Dana Rottman.
EIN: 133378305

39925
Striks Family Charitable Foundation
6 Wallenberg Cir.
Monsey, NY 10952

Financial data (yr. ended 12/31/01): Grants paid, $900; assets, $317,884 (M); expenditures, $10,398; qualifying distributions, $900.
Application information: Application form not required.
Officer: Sylvia Striks, Mgr.
Trustee: Jeffrey Striks.
EIN: 137156609

39926
Cecile & Walter Feder Family Foundation, Inc.
998 E. 8th St.
Brooklyn, NY 11230
Contact: Walter Feder, Pres.

Established in 1997 in NY.
Donor(s): Walter Feder.
Financial data (yr. ended 12/31/01): Grants paid, $883; assets, $1,699 (M); gifts received, $5,794; expenditures, $1,612; qualifying distributions, $1,612.
Officers: Walter Feder, Pres.; Roslyn Lipsky, V.P. and Secy.; Martin Feder, V.P.; Carol Simon, Treas.
EIN: 113312335

39927
Martin E. and Betty Z. Greif Charitable Trust
8 Sandy Ct.
Port Washington, NY 11050

Established in 1998 in NY.
Donor(s): Martin Greif.
Financial data (yr. ended 11/30/01): Grants paid, $875; assets, $7,015 (M); gifts received, $5; expenditures, $880; qualifying distributions, $875.
Limitations: Applications not accepted.
Application information: Contributes only to pre-selected organizations.
Officer: Martin E. Greif, Pres.
Director: Betty Z. Greif.
EIN: 116514724

39928
Laubich Family Foundation
4 Laura Ln.
Scarsdale, NY 10583

Established in 1986 in NY.
Donor(s): Arnold Laubich, Felicia G. Laubich.
Financial data (yr. ended 12/31/01): Grants paid, $870; assets, $8,793 (M); expenditures, $1,229; qualifying distributions, $870.
Limitations: Giving primarily in New York, NY.
Officers: Felicia G. Laubich, Pres.; Arnold Laubich, V.P.; Lori M. Laubich, Secy.-Treas.
EIN: 133387489

39929
Jeremy Wiesen Foundation
254 E. 68th St., Apt. 30F
New York, NY 10021-6001 (212) 734-4839
Contact: Jeremy Wiesen, Pres.

Financial data (yr. ended 01/31/02): Grants paid, $870; assets, $25,919 (M); expenditures, $1,616; qualifying distributions, $870.
Limitations: Giving primarily in West Palm Beach, FL, and New York, NY.
Officers: Jeremy Wiesen, Pres.; Jack Goldhaber, Secy.-Treas.
EIN: 133290373

39930
The Salomon Family Foundation
c/o Max Wasser
132 Nassau St., Ste. 300
New York, NY 10038

Established in 1997.
Financial data (yr. ended 06/30/01): Grants paid, $857; assets, $550 (M); gifts received, $1,000; expenditures, $1,617; qualifying distributions, $857.
Limitations: Applications not accepted.
Application information: Contributes only to pre-selected organizations.
Officer: Israel Salomon, Mgr.
EIN: 137120562

39931
George Blass Memorial Foundation, Inc.
82 Doral Greens Dr. W.
Rye Brook, NY 10573-5411 (914) 937-0885
Contact: Natalie Blass Greenberg, Pres.

Established in 1975 in NY.
Financial data (yr. ended 12/31/01): Grants paid, $850; assets, $11,596 (M); gifts received, $530; expenditures, $873; qualifying distributions, $873.
Limitations: Giving primarily in NY.
Officer: Natalie Blass Greenberg, Pres.
EIN: 912142405

39932
Mabel Bookstaver Scholarship Trust Fund
c/o HSBC Bank, USA
1 HSBC Ctr., 16th Fl.
Buffalo, NY 14203-2885

Established in 1987 in NY.
Financial data (yr. ended 12/31/01): Grants paid, $850; assets, $12,766 (M); expenditures, $1,040; qualifying distributions, $861.
Limitations: Applications not accepted.
Application information: Unsolicited requests for funds not accepted.
Trustee: HSBC Bank USA.
EIN: 166024196

39933
Esses Foundation, Inc.
c/o Leo Esses
2232 E. 4th St.
Brooklyn, NY 11223 (718) 645-1500

Donor(s): Leo Esses.
Financial data (yr. ended 12/31/99): Grants paid, $850; assets, $3,915 (M); gifts received, $2,000; expenditures, $1,445; qualifying distributions, $850.
Limitations: Applications not accepted. Giving primarily in NY.
Application information: Contributes only to pre-selected organizations.
Officer: Leo Esses, Pres.
EIN: 136101303

39934
E. R. Woelfel Memorial Scholarship Fund
c/o JPMorgan Chase Bank
P.O. Box 31412
Rochester, NY 14603-1412

Financial data (yr. ended 12/31/00): Grants paid, $850; assets, $23,640 (M); expenditures, $1,003; qualifying distributions, $937.
Limitations: Applications not accepted. Giving limited to Newark, NY.
Application information: Students are chosen by the Senior Guidance Committee of Newark Central School, NY.
Trustee: JPMorgan Chase Bank.
EIN: 166015366

39935
Flare Foundation for the Arts, Inc.
200 Central Park S., No. 21E
New York, NY 10019

Financial data (yr. ended 12/31/01): Grants paid, $829; assets, $24,561 (M); expenditures, $1,875; qualifying distributions, $829.
Limitations: Applications not accepted.
Officers: Louis D. Srybnik, Pres.; Knox Martin, V.P.
EIN: 237412320

39936
The Star-Gazette Fund, Inc.
201 Baldwin St.
Elmira, NY 14901

Financial data (yr. ended 12/31/00): Grants paid, $818; assets, $96,734 (M); expenditures, $1,307; qualifying distributions, $818.
Limitations: Applications not accepted. Giving primarily in NY.
Application information: Accepts only referrals from local charities.
Officers: Monte Tranner, Pres.; Dawn Bush, Secy.
Directors: Kathy Carpenter, April Semel.
EIN: 222268547

39937
The Marksohn Family Foundation
c/o Katz & Bloom
200 S. Service Rd., Ste. 208
Roslyn Heights, NY 11577

Established in 1998 in NY.
Financial data (yr. ended 09/30/01): Grants paid, $805; assets, $5,650 (M); gifts received, $1,000; expenditures, $805; qualifying distributions, $805.
Limitations: Applications not accepted.
Application information: Contributes only to pre-selected organizations.
Officers: Walter Marksohn, Pres. and Treas.; Edith Marksohn, V.P. and Secy.
EIN: 113458507

39938
Borchardt Family Foundation
430 E. 59th St.
New York, NY 10022

Established in 2000 in NY.
Donor(s): Thomas Georges Borchardt.
Financial data (yr. ended 12/31/01): Grants paid, $800; assets, $5,672 (M); gifts received, $9,000; expenditures, $1,116; qualifying distributions, $800.
Limitations: Giving primarily in New York, NY.
Officers: Thomas Georges Borchardt, Pres.; Anne Borchardt, V.P.; Valerie Borchardt, Treas.
EIN: 134112773

39939
Herbert J. Feuer Foundation
(Formerly Herbert J. Feuer, Helen Feuer and Leila D. Howard Foundation)
c/o Feuer, Orlando, Pye, & Co.
117 E. 29th St., 6th Fl., No.6
New York, NY 10016

Donor(s): Helen Feuer.
Financial data (yr. ended 10/31/01): Grants paid, $800; assets, $18,840 (M); gifts received, $18; expenditures, $939; qualifying distributions, $933.
Limitations: Applications not accepted.
Application information: Contributes only to pre-selected organizations.
Trustees: Edward S. Feuer, Helen Feuer.
EIN: 237000386

39940
Edward R. Kolevzon Foundation, Inc.
c/o Peter S. Kolevzon
919 3rd Ave.
New York, NY 10022-3904

Financial data (yr. ended 06/30/01): Grants paid, $800; assets, $5,826 (M); gifts received, $1,200; expenditures, $862; qualifying distributions, $800.
Officers: Peter S. Kolevzon, Pres.; Beatrice Kolevzon, V.P.; Michael Kolevzon, V.P.
EIN: 132879783

39941
Puppies for People, Inc.
645 Madison Ave., Ste. 500
New York, NY 10022

Established in 1997 in NY.
Financial data (yr. ended 12/31/01): Grants paid, $800; assets, $7,923 (M); gifts received, $2,000; expenditures, $1,621; qualifying distributions, $1,579.
Limitations: Applications not accepted.
Application information: Contributes only to pre-selected organizations.
Officers and Directors:* Barbara Chin,* C.E.O.; Elena Lusenta,* Pres.; Robert W. Lenthe,* V.P. and Secy.; James J. Doykos II,* V.P.; Seymour L. Wane, Treas.; Herbert M. Friedman.
EIN: 133951830

39942
The Gerard T. Ryan Foundation, Inc.
17 Westbury Rd.
Garden City, NY 11530 (516) 742-7851
Contact: Gerard T. Ryan, Pres.

Established in 1994 in NY.
Donor(s): Gerard T. Ryan.
Financial data (yr. ended 12/31/01): Grants paid, $800; assets, $5,011 (M); gifts received, $500; expenditures, $832; qualifying distributions, $800.
Limitations: Applications not accepted.
Officer: Gerard T. Ryan, Pres.
EIN: 113205451

39943
Toldos Shaya Vsara Foundation
c/o Jesse and Sara Elefant
1077 54th St.
Brooklyn, NY 11219

Established in 1999 in NY.
Donor(s): Jesse Elefant.
Financial data (yr. ended 12/31/01): Grants paid, $790; assets, $31,132 (M); expenditures, $790; qualifying distributions, $790.
Limitations: Applications not accepted.
Application information: Contributes only to pre-selected organizations.
Trustees: Jesse Elefant, Sara Elefant.
EIN: 113497107

39944
The Cummings-Goldman Foundation
c/o David Michael & Co.
7 Penn Plz., Ste. 316
New York, NY 10001

Established in 1991 in NY.
Donor(s): Eric Goldman.
Financial data (yr. ended 10/31/01): Grants paid, $763; assets, $21,847 (M); gifts received, $14,844; expenditures, $1,216; qualifying distributions, $763.
Limitations: Applications not accepted. Giving primarily in NY.
Application information: Contributes only to pre-selected organizations.
Trustees: Norma J. Cummings, Eric Goldman.
EIN: 133642159

39945
Michael Diamond Memorial Foundation
P.O. Box 511
Wurtsboro, NY 12790

Financial data (yr. ended 03/31/01): Grants paid, $760; assets, $16,590 (M); expenditures, $780; qualifying distributions, $780.
Limitations: Applications not accepted. Giving limited to Wurtsboro, NY.
Officers: Joann Salamone, Pres.; Marie Bryan, Secy.; Joseph Levine, Treas.
Directors: Barbara Semonite, Louise Traver, and 4 additional directors.
EIN: 141711268

39946
Angelo Calabrese Memorial Trust
9 Calabrese Dr.
Pine Bush, NY 12566
Application address: c/o BOCES, Gibson Rd., Goshen, NY 10924, tel.: (845) 291-0311

Financial data (yr. ended 06/30/01): Grants paid, $750; assets, $9,279 (M); expenditures, $775; qualifying distributions, $750.
Limitations: Giving primarily in NY.
Application information: Application form required.
Trustees: Myrna Calabrese, William Calabrese, Deborah Carr.
EIN: 146196716

39947
Chrysos, Ltd.
(Formerly The Chrysos Foundation, Ltd.)
2211 Broadway, Ste. 3B
New York, NY 10024
Contact: Wendy James, Dir.

Established in 1998 in NY.
Donor(s): Wendy James.
Financial data (yr. ended 12/31/99): Grants paid, $750; assets, $6,185 (M); gifts received, $9,158; expenditures, $10,233; qualifying distributions, $10,232; giving activities include $6,014 for programs.
Limitations: Giving primarily in MA and NY.
Director: Wendy James.
EIN: 133922434

39948
Ciechanover Foundation, Inc.
115 Central Park W., Rm. 9A
New York, NY 10023

Established in 1988 in NY.
Donor(s): Joseph Ciechanover.
Financial data (yr. ended 09/30/01): Grants paid, $750; assets, $39 (M); expenditures, $830; qualifying distributions, $750.
Limitations: Applications not accepted.
Application information: Contributes only to pre-selected organizations.
Officers: Joseph Cienhanover, Pres. and Treas.; Atara Cienhanover, V.P. and Secy.
EIN: 133498260

39949
Elf Foundation
P.O. Box 92505
Rochester, NY 14692-0505

Established in 2000 in NY.
Donor(s): Thomas H. Frauenhofer.
Financial data (yr. ended 12/31/01): Grants paid, $750; assets, $595,174 (M); expenditures, $3,218; qualifying distributions, $750.
Limitations: Applications not accepted.
Application information: Contributes only to pre-selected organizations.
Trustees: Erika L. Frauenhofer, Thomas H. Frauenhofer.
EIN: 166515844

39950
David Evan Hirsch Memorial Fund, Inc.
126 Kensington Oval
New Rochelle, NY 10805-2906

Donor(s): Armand Lerner, Marlene Hirsch Lerner.
Financial data (yr. ended 08/31/01): Grants paid, $750; assets, $14,298 (M); expenditures, $773; qualifying distributions, $750.
Limitations: Applications not accepted. Giving primarily in NY.
Application information: Contributes only to pre-selected organizations.
Officers and Directors:* Marlene Hirsch Lerner,* Pres.; Steven Hirsch,* Secy.; Armand Lerner.
EIN: 133096803

39951
Raymond C. Kennedy Foundation, Inc.
c/o R. Galluscio
21 N. 7th St.
Hudson, NY 12534

Donor(s): Raymond C. Kennedy.‡
Financial data (yr. ended 01/31/02): Grants paid, $750; assets, $516,990 (M); expenditures, $10,998; qualifying distributions, $750.
Limitations: Giving primarily in NY.
Officers and Directors:* Paul J. Zindell,* Pres. and Treas.; Deborah J. Zindell,* V.P. and Secy.; Michael D. Difabio, Rev. Hugh F. Hines, Meghan Zindell.
EIN: 222773896

39952
McLaughlin Family Foundation
2 Upper Dogwood Ln.
Rye, NY 10580

Established in 2000 in NY.
Donor(s): Vickie McLaughlin, Greg McLaughlin.

Financial data (yr. ended 12/31/01): Grants paid, $750; assets, $8,803 (M); gifts received, $1,500; expenditures, $2,250; qualifying distributions, $750.
Limitations: Applications not accepted.
Application information: Contributes only to pre-selected organizations.
Officers: Greg McLaughlin, Mgr.; Vickie McLaughlin, Mgr.
EIN: 061601986

39953
Mehta Family Foundation
c/o Dilip J. Mehta, M.D.
870 United Nations Plz.
New York, NY 10017

Established in 1999 in DE and NY.
Donor(s): Dilip J. Mehta, M.D., Carole Mehta.
Financial data (yr. ended 12/31/01): Grants paid, $750; assets, $31,759 (M); gifts received, $20,474; expenditures, $2,071; qualifying distributions, $750.
Limitations: Applications not accepted.
Application information: Contributes only to pre-selected organizations.
Officers: Dilip J. Mehta, M.D., Pres.; Carole Mehta, Secy.
EIN: 061560228

39954
Mount Kisco Junior Football League, Inc.
P.O. Box 181
Mount Kisco, NY 10549-0181
Contact: Ferdinand "Bud" Jobin, Pres.

Financial data (yr. ended 12/31/99): Grants paid, $750; assets, $57,150 (L); gifts received, $3,800; expenditures, $19,715; qualifying distributions, $730.
Limitations: Giving limited to Mount Kisco, NY.
Officers: Ferdinand "Bud" Jobin, Pres.; Charles Piergostini, Treas.
EIN: 237133627

39955
Sawyer Scholarship Foundation
c/o Fleet National Bank
River Rd.
Callicoon, NY 12723 (845) 887-4003
Contact: Ruth Brustman, Tr.

Financial data (yr. ended 12/31/99): Grants paid, $750; assets, $75,596 (M); expenditures, $1,254; qualifying distributions, $750.
Limitations: Giving limited to Sullivan County, NY.
Application information: Application form required.
Trustees: Ruth Brustman, Mary Curtis, Robert Curtis, Maurice Roche, Fred W. Stabbert III.
EIN: 136113938

39956
Shapiro-Viertel Foundation
180 S. Broadway
White Plains, NY 10605

Donor(s): Robert E. Shapiro, Joseph E. Viertel.
Financial data (yr. ended 05/31/02): Grants paid, $750; assets, $42,724 (M); expenditures, $1,687; qualifying distributions, $750.
Limitations: Applications not accepted. Giving primarily in NY.
Application information: Contributes only to pre-selected organizations.
Trustees: Robert E. Shapiro, Joseph E. Viertel, Thomas M. Viertel.
EIN: 136125388

39957
Kathleen A. Campion Foundation
13 Bittersweet Ln.
Clifton Park, NY 12065
Contact: Daniel Campion, Tr., or Linda Campion, Tr.

Established in 1993 in NY.
Donor(s): Daniel Campion, Linda Campion.
Financial data (yr. ended 12/31/01): Grants paid, $747; assets, $99,305 (M); gifts received, $100; expenditures, $7,157; qualifying distributions, $747.
Trustees: Daniel Campion, Linda Campion, Kristine M. Gleason.
EIN: 141764678

39958
The Hoover & Borgognoni Foundation, Inc.
1 Doncaster Rd.
Kenmore, NY 14217-2107

Established in 1997 in NY.
Donor(s): Bruce W. Hoover, Mary E. Borgognoni.
Financial data (yr. ended 10/31/01): Grants paid, $725; assets, $8,535 (M); expenditures, $725; qualifying distributions, $725.
Limitations: Applications not accepted. Giving primarily in NY.
Application information: Contributes only to pre-selected organizations.
Officers and Directors:* Mary Borgognoni,* Pres.; Bruce Hoover,* V.P.; Mary Beth Labate.
EIN: 161539529

39959
Jack Chutick Foundation, Inc.
c/o F.T. Kleiger & Co.
80 Cuttermill Rd., Ste. 302
Great Neck, NY 11021

Donor(s): Jack Chutick.
Financial data (yr. ended 12/31/99): Grants paid, $700; assets, $2,004 (M); expenditures, $2,593; qualifying distributions, $700.
Limitations: Applications not accepted.
Application information: Contributes only to pre-selected organizations.
Officers: Jack Chutick, Pres.; Ruth Chutick, Secy.-Treas.
EIN: 116014031

39960
The Golub Family Foundation
23 Morewood Oaks
Port Washington, NY 11050-1603

Established in 1987 in NY.
Donor(s): Daniel A. Golub, Judith V. Golub.
Financial data (yr. ended 09/30/01): Grants paid, $700; assets, $10,794 (M); gifts received, $300; expenditures, $1,000; qualifying distributions, $700.
Limitations: Applications not accepted.
Application information: Contributes only to pre-selected organizations.
Trustees: Daniel A. Golub, Judith V. Golub.
EIN: 136884894

39961
Bernard & Barbara Green Charitable Foundation, Inc.
c/o Friedman, Alpren & Green, LLP
1700 Broadway, 23rd Fl.
New York, NY 10019

Established in 1986 in NY.
Donor(s): Bernard R. Green.
Financial data (yr. ended 08/31/01): Grants paid, $700; assets, $345,180 (M); expenditures, $1,869; qualifying distributions, $700.
Limitations: Applications not accepted. Giving primarily in New York, NY.
Application information: Contributes only to pre-selected organizations.
Officers: Bernard R. Green, Pres.; Shirley Dembner, V.P.; Barbara Gordon Green, Secy.; Andrea Green, Treas.
EIN: 133374415

39962
Jerolamon Charitable Trust
1158 5th Ave., Ste. 5B
New York, NY 10029-6917

Established in 1999 in NY.
Donor(s): Robert J. Edmondson.
Financial data (yr. ended 12/31/01): Grants paid, $700; assets, $3,352 (M); gifts received, $2,000; expenditures, $700; qualifying distributions, $700.
Limitations: Giving primarily in IN.
Trustees: Robert J. Edmondson, Mary D. Edmondson.
EIN: 134084972

39963
Kurt Kaufmann Foundation Charitable Trust
147 Hillview Ave.
Yonkers, NY 10704
Contact: Ruth Kaufmann, Tr.

Established in 1999.
Financial data (yr. ended 12/31/00): Grants paid, $700; assets, $11,663 (M); expenditures, $700; qualifying distributions, $700.
Limitations: Giving primarily in Yonkers, NY.
Application information: Application form required.
Trustee: Ruth Kaufmann.
EIN: 134070863

39964
Kucera Family Foundation
c/o Brown Bros. Harriman Trust Co., LLC
63 Wall St.
New York, NY 10005

Established in 2000 in IL.
Donor(s): Lauren Kaplan, Barbara J. Kucera.
Financial data (yr. ended 12/31/01): Grants paid, $700; assets, $233,816 (M); expenditures, $3,174; qualifying distributions, $700.
Limitations: Applications not accepted.
Application information: Contributes only to pre-selected organizations.
Directors: Lauren Kaplan, Barbara J. Kucera, William R. Kucera.
EIN: 364408436

39965
David & Sadie Traum Foundation, Inc.
61 Broadway, 18th Fl.
New York, NY 10006-2794

Financial data (yr. ended 10/31/01): Grants paid, $700; assets, $25,767 (M); expenditures, $1,445; qualifying distributions, $1,198.
Limitations: Applications not accepted.
Application information: Contributes only to pre-selected organizations.
Officer: Alice T. Booth, Pres.
EIN: 136164157

39966
Lester Tanner Foundation
(Formerly Lester & Marcy Tanner Foundation)
99 Park Ave., 25th Fl.
New York, NY 10016-1643 (212) 476-0710
Contact: Lester J. Tanner, Tr.

Donor(s): Lester J. Tanner.

39966—NEW YORK

Financial data (yr. ended 12/31/00): Grants paid, $680; assets, $325 (M); expenditures, $680; qualifying distributions, $0.
Limitations: Giving primarily in New York, NY.
Trustee: Lester J. Tanner.
EIN: 136113762

39967
Melissa Wilson Scholarship Trust
c/o Kenneth J. & Mary W. Wilson
111 15th St.
Watkins Glen, NY 14891-1515
Application address: c/o Nancy Lorizlin, Watkins Glen Central School, 12th St., Watkins Glen, NY 14891

Financial data (yr. ended 09/30/00): Grants paid, $650; assets, $13,057 (M); gifts received, $190; expenditures, $687; qualifying distributions, $680.
Limitations: Giving limited to Watkins Glen, NY.
Application information: Students nominated by school faculty.
Trustees: Kenneth J. Wilson, Mary W. Wilson.
EIN: 161511672

39968
Donald Zucker Foundation
c/o Donald Zucker
101 W. 55th St.
New York, NY 10019-5343 (212) 977-4800

Established in 1985 in NY.
Donor(s): Donald Zucker.
Financial data (yr. ended 04/30/00): Grants paid, $650; assets, $1,700 (M); expenditures, $720; qualifying distributions, $720.
Limitations: Applications not accepted. Giving primarily in NY.
Application information: Contributes only to pre-selected organizations.
Officers: Donald Zucker, Pres.; Barbara Zucker Albinder, V.P.; Laurie Zucker Lederman, V.P.; Barbara Hrbek Zucker, Secy.-Treas.
EIN: 133269497

39969
Marcelle Picard White Foundation
c/o Mildred C. Brinn
570 Park Ave.
New York, NY 10021-7370

Donor(s): Lawrence E. Brinn,‡ Marcelle Picard White.‡
Financial data (yr. ended 12/31/01): Grants paid, $620; assets, $5,126 (M); expenditures, $1,361; qualifying distributions, $620.
Limitations: Applications not accepted.
Application information: Contributes only to pre-selected organizations.
Officers and Directors:* Mildred C. Brinn,* Pres. and Treas.; Peter F. DeGaetano,* Secy.
EIN: 237072759

39970
The Kenneth D. Pearlman Foundation
(Formerly S. & K. Pearlman Foundation)
c/o Norman Berg, C.P.A.
747 5th Ave., Ste. 709
New York, NY 10016

Financial data (yr. ended 12/31/00): Grants paid, $615; assets, $13,896 (M); expenditures, $674; qualifying distributions, $615.
Limitations: Applications not accepted. Giving primarily in CT and New York, NY.
Application information: Contributes only to pre-selected organizations.
Trustee: Kenneth D. Pearlman.
EIN: 136171205

39971
The Anna and Philip Kimmel Foundation, Inc.
237 Schenck Ave.
Great Neck, NY 11021
Contact: Howard B. Kimmel, Dir.

Established in 1994 in NY.
Donor(s): Howard B. Kimmel, Fred D. Kimmel, Gladys Hymanson.
Financial data (yr. ended 11/30/01): Grants paid, $611; assets, $660,346 (M); gifts received, $309,000; expenditures, $46,052; qualifying distributions, $42,420.
Limitations: Giving primarily in NY.
Application information: Application form not required.
Officers and Directors:* Howard B. Kimmel,* Pres.; Ronald Kisner,* V.P.; Sylvia Kimmel,* Secy.; Cynthia Poeggel,* Dir. of Finance; Mortimer F. Zimmerman, Treas.; John Mulrayan,* Exec. Dir.; Steve Boughner, Soul Katz, Wilbur Klatsky, Phil Schorr, Abe Seldin, Ed Simmons, Charles Vogeley, Evelyn Weinstein, Robert S. Widon.
EIN: 113267241

39972
Hess/Kaplan Charitable Fund
c/o Hect and Co., PC
111 W. 40th St.
New York, NY 10018

Established in 1998 in NY.
Donor(s): Anne Helen Hess.
Financial data (yr. ended 12/31/01): Grants paid, $600; assets, $1 (M); expenditures, $1,245; qualifying distributions, $600.
Limitations: Applications not accepted.
Application information: Contributes only to pre-selected organizations.
Trustees: Anne Helen Hess, Craig Kaplan.
EIN: 137142739

39973
The Pratt Family Foundation
c/o Dan Nolan, The Ayco Co., LP
P.O. Box 8009
Clifton Park, NY 12065-8009

Established in 1998 in NY.
Donor(s): Edmund T. Pratt.
Financial data (yr. ended 12/31/01): Grants paid, $600; assets, $10,253 (M); expenditures, $600; qualifying distributions, $600.
Limitations: Applications not accepted.
Application information: Contributes only to pre-selected organizations.
Officers: Edmund T. Pratt, Jr., Pres.; Keith T. Pratt, Secy.; Randolf R. Pratt, Treas.
EIN: 113457679

39974
Western Catskill Foundation
c/o Davidson, Fox & Co., LLP
53 Chenango St.
Binghamton, NY 13901
Application address: 89 Cross Hwy., West Redding, CT 06896-2403
Contact: James E. Bacon, Chair.

Established in 1995 in NY.
Donor(s): James Bacon.
Financial data (yr. ended 06/30/01): Grants paid, $600; assets, $5,420 (M); expenditures, $1,570; qualifying distributions, $1,072.
Limitations: Giving primarily in the Catskill region, NY.
Officers: James E. Bacon, Chair. and Pres.; Carolyn Bacon, V.P. and Treas.; C. Gordon Coughlin, Jr., Secy.
EIN: 222642833

39975
The Anne Anastasi Charitable Foundation
c/o J. Galente
Fordham University, Dealy Hall 345
Bronx, NY 10458

Financial data (yr. ended 12/31/01): Grants paid, $598; assets, $5,097 (M); gifts received, $225; expenditures, $598; qualifying distributions, $598.
Limitations: Applications not accepted. Giving primarily in New York, NY.
Application information: Contributes only to pre-selected organizations.
Officers: Jonathan Galente, Pres.; J. Francis Stroud, Secy.; Anthony J. DeVito, Treas.
EIN: 134013290

39976
Construction Technology Scholarship Fund
c/o NYC Technical College, Construction Dept.
186 Jay St.
Brooklyn, NY 11201-1937 (718) 260-5575
Contact: Prof. E. Colachamiro

Financial data (yr. ended 06/30/00): Grants paid, $592; assets, $20,153 (M); expenditures, $658; qualifying distributions, $637.
Limitations: Giving limited to Brooklyn, NY.
Application information: Application form required.
Officers: Seymour B. Foreman, Pres.; Frank Formica, V.P.; Anthony Cioffi, Secy.-Treas.
EIN: 116037673

39977
Leo and Rachel Sussman Foundation, Inc.
11 Riverside Dr.
New York, NY 10023

Financial data (yr. ended 12/31/01): Grants paid, $575; assets, $55,154 (M); expenditures, $575; qualifying distributions, $575.
Limitations: Applications not accepted. Giving primarily in NY.
Officer: Rachel Sussman, Pres.
EIN: 237009839

39978
Gershon J. & Beylah Feigon Foundation, Inc.
1761 50th St.
Brooklyn, NY 11204

Financial data (yr. ended 12/31/01): Grants paid, $565; assets, $11,549 (M); expenditures, $576; qualifying distributions, $565.
Limitations: Applications not accepted. Giving limited to NY.
Application information: Contributes only to pre-selected organizations.
Officers: Bernard Erlbaum, Pres.; Deborah Erlbaum, Secy.
EIN: 136161254

39979
Charles E. McDonnell Foundation, Inc.
c/o Mary Frances McDonnell
99 Biltmore Ave.
Rye, NY 10580-1837

Financial data (yr. ended 12/31/99): Grants paid, $565; assets, $962 (M); expenditures, $566; qualifying distributions, $565.
Limitations: Applications not accepted. Giving primarily in Rye, NY.
Application information: Contributes only to pre-selected organizations.
Officers: Mary F. McDonnell, Pres. and Treas.; James J. Beha, V.P.; Margaret M. George, Secy.
EIN: 136113573

39980
Millbrook Scholarship Fund
c/o The Bank of New York
1 Wall St., Tax Dept., 28th Fl.
New York, NY 10286
Application address: c/o Helen Grady,
Millbrook Central School District, P.O. Box A,
Millbrook, NY 12545

Established in 1994 in NY.
Financial data (yr. ended 12/31/01): Grants paid, $550; assets, $11,588 (M); expenditures, $610; qualifying distributions, $550.
Limitations: Applications not accepted. Giving limited to Millbrook, NY.
Trustee: The Bank of New York.
EIN: 146017689

39981
The A & H Foundation Trust
4819 13th Ave., Ste. 201
Brooklyn, NY 11219

Established in 2000.
Donor(s): Aron Kahan.
Financial data (yr. ended 12/31/01): Grants paid, $500; assets, $545 (M); gifts received, $1,000; expenditures, $500; qualifying distributions, $500.
Trustee: Aron Kahana.
EIN: 116545587

39982
The Bill Baldwin Fund, Inc.
P.O. Box 1602
Troy, NY 12181-1602

Financial data (yr. ended 12/31/00): Grants paid, $500; assets, $451 (M); gifts received, $173; expenditures, $3,381; qualifying distributions, $3,361.
Officers: Robert Rubin, Pres. and Treas.; John Rustin, Secy.
EIN: 146025770

39983
Rose Borowski Memorial Scholarship Fund, Inc.
c/o Edward J. Borowski
5 Hawk Ln.
Hauppauge, NY 11788

Established in 1999 in NY.
Financial data (yr. ended 12/31/01): Grants paid, $500; assets, $3,402 (M); gifts received, $2,616; expenditures, $4,773; qualifying distributions, $4,773.
Limitations: Applications not accepted.
Officers: Edward J. Borowski, Pres.; Robert J. Borowski, V.P.; Paul E. Borowski, Secy.; Janet M. Orlando, Treas.
EIN: 113517126

39984
Chesed Foundation
22 Washington Ave.
Spring Valley, NY 10977
Contact: Imrich Katz, Dir.

Established in 2000 in NY.
Donor(s): Imrich Katz.
Financial data (yr. ended 12/31/01): Grants paid, $500; assets, $8,761 (M); expenditures, $575; qualifying distributions, $500.
Director: Imrich Katz.
EIN: 134115596

39985
The Michael and Joan Dritz Charitable Trust
20 Cole Dr.
Armonk, NY 10504

Established in 1986 in NY.
Donor(s): Michael Dritz.
Financial data (yr. ended 12/31/00): Grants paid, $500; assets, $82,715 (L); expenditures, $764; qualifying distributions, $144.
Limitations: Applications not accepted. Giving primarily in NY.
Application information: Contributes only to pre-selected organizations.
Trustees: Joan Dritz, Michael Dritz, Susan Rapaport.
EIN: 136884604

39986
The Dynaton Foundation
c/o Robert Anthoine
1 Battery Park Plz., 28th Fl.
New York, NY 10004-1490

Donor(s): Robert Anthoine.
Financial data (yr. ended 06/30/01): Grants paid, $500; assets, $2,255 (M); expenditures, $520; qualifying distributions, $520.
Limitations: Applications not accepted. Giving primarily in NY.
Application information: Contributes only to pre-selected organizations.
Officers: Robert Anthoine, Pres.; Allen M. Singer, V.P.; Rubecia S. Rudnick, Secy.
EIN: 133470294

39987
The Fagenson Family Foundation
c/o Stephanie Fagenson
60 Broad St., 38th Fl.
New York, NY 10004

Established in 1997 in NY.
Donor(s): Robert Fagenson, Jennifer Fagenson, Stephanie Fagenson.
Financial data (yr. ended 12/31/01): Grants paid, $500; assets, $256,156 (M); expenditures, $670; qualifying distributions, $500.
Limitations: Applications not accepted.
Application information: Contributes only to pre-selected organizations.
Officers and Directors:* Robert Fagenson,* Pres.; Margaret Fagenson,* V.P.; Richard Kandel, Secy.-Treas.; Jennifer Fagenson, Stephanie Fagenson.
EIN: 133980456

39988
The FBR Foundation, Inc.
c/o Yohalem Gillman & Co., LLP
477 Madison Ave.
New York, NY 10022-5802

Established in 1998 in NY.
Donor(s): Fred B. Renwick.
Financial data (yr. ended 11/30/01): Grants paid, $500; assets, $48,257 (M); gifts received, $30,113; expenditures, $3,188; qualifying distributions, $500.
Limitations: Applications not accepted. Giving primarily in New York, NY.
Application information: Contributes only to pre-selected organizations.
Officers: Fred B. Renwick, Pres. and V.P.; Rodney Harris, Secy.
Director: Denise Lucille Harris Williams.
EIN: 061533446

39989
Festa Madonna Della Scala, Inc.
4 Spruce Ln.
Glen Cove, NY 11542

Financial data (yr. ended 05/31/02): Grants paid, $500; assets, $14,934 (M); expenditures, $25,723; qualifying distributions, $500.
Limitations: Applications not accepted. Giving primarily in Italy.

Application information: Contributes only to pre-selected organizations.
Officers: Sal Gaudio, Pres.; Giuseppe Tornicchio, V.P.; Pietra Belcastro, Secy.
EIN: 112970001

39990
Paul A. Flemma Scholarship Fund
16 Smithport Rd.
Utica, NY 13501   (315) 735-4009
Contact: M. David Flemma, Tr.

Financial data (yr. ended 12/31/01): Grants paid, $500; assets, $12,793 (M); expenditures, $493; qualifying distributions, $493.
Limitations: Giving limited to New Hartford, NY.
Trustee: M. David Flemma.
EIN: 161355208

39991
The Foundation for the Prevention of Child Abuse, Inc.
c/o G. Liebner
295 Starling Ct.
Manhasset, NY 11030
Contact: Robert Korval, Pres.

Financial data (yr. ended 12/31/01): Grants paid, $500; assets, $6,253 (M); expenditures, $500; qualifying distributions, $500.
Limitations: Giving primarily in Woodmere, NY.
Officers: Robert Korval, Pres.; George Leibner, Secy.-Treas.
EIN: 133495270

39992
Frishauf Family Charitable Foundation, Inc.
303 W. 103rd St.
New York, NY 10025
Contact: Peter Frishauf, Pres.

Established in 2000 in NY.
Donor(s): Stephen H. Frishauf.
Financial data (yr. ended 12/31/01): Grants paid, $500; assets, $45,143 (M); expenditures, $6,274; qualifying distributions, $500.
Officers: Peter Frishauf, Pres.; Stephen H. Frishauf, V.P.; Katharine C. Rice, Secy.; Ronald Berk, Treas.
EIN: 134147179

39993
The Grund Foundation
c/o Robin Grund
171 Chappaqua Rd.
Briarcliff Manor, NY 10510

Established in 1955.
Financial data (yr. ended 10/31/01): Grants paid, $500; assets, $12,734 (M); expenditures, $11,533; qualifying distributions, $500.
Limitations: Applications not accepted. Giving primarily in New York, NY.
Application information: Contributes only to pre-selected organizations.
Officers: Robin Grund, Pres.; Heloise Goodman, Secy.
Director: Ralph Zervi.
EIN: 136126346

39994
Jennie Bradley Hanford Education Fund
c/o The National Bank of Delaware County
P.O. Box 389
Walton, NY 13856

Financial data (yr. ended 12/31/99): Grants paid, $500; assets, $15,235 (M); expenditures, $597; qualifying distributions, $500.
Limitations: Applications not accepted. Giving limited to residents of Walton, NY.

Application information: Contributes only to pre-selected individuals.
Trustee: The National Bank of Delaware County.
EIN: 166056964

39995
Platt Mead Hanford Educational Fund
c/o The National Bank of Delaware County
P.O. Box 389
Walton, NY 13856 (607) 865-4126

Financial data (yr. ended 12/31/01): Grants paid, $500; assets, $11,333 (M); expenditures, $596; qualifying distributions, $577.
Limitations: Giving limited to Walton, NY.
Trustee: The National Bank of Delaware County.
EIN: 166056965

39996
Walter S. Hannan, et al. Trust for Gilbert Sykes Blakely Memorial Scholarship Trust Fund
c/o JPMorgan Chase Bank
P.O. Box 31412
Rochester, NY 14603-1412
Application address: c/o Scholarship Comm., Evander Childs High School, 800 E. Gunhill Rd., New York, NY 10467

Established around 1927 in NY.
Financial data (yr. ended 12/31/01): Grants paid, $500; assets, $8,751 (M); expenditures, $567; qualifying distributions, $526.
Limitations: Giving limited to residents of the New York, NY, area.
Application information: Contact high school for application. Application form required.
Trustee: JPMorgan Chase Bank.
EIN: 136044803

39997
Heart Education and Research Foundation, Inc.
10 Plaza St.
Brooklyn, NY 11238

Financial data (yr. ended 12/31/01): Grants paid, $500; assets, $10,503 (M); expenditures, $703; qualifying distributions, $500.
Limitations: Applications not accepted. Giving primarily in Brooklyn, NY.
Application information: Contributes only to pre-selected organizations.
Officer: Irving Kroop, Secy.-Treas.
EIN: 116042668

39998
The Horowitz Family Foundation
(Formerly Ben and Bess Horowitz Family Charitable Foundation)
c/o Levene, Gouldin & Thompson, LLP
P.O. Box F 1706
Binghamton, NY 13902-0106

Established in 1986 in NY.
Donor(s): Benjamin Horowitz.
Financial data (yr. ended 12/31/01): Grants paid, $500; assets, $36,248 (M); expenditures, $1,057; qualifying distributions, $500.
Limitations: Applications not accepted. Giving limited to the Binghamton, NY, area.
Application information: Contributes only to pre-selected organizations.
Trustees: Jerald I. Horowitz, Richard D. Horowitz.
EIN: 222776291

39999
Barbara J. Johnson Foundation, Inc.
8 Haven Ave., Ste. 203
Port Washington, NY 11050

Established in 2000 in NY.
Donor(s): Craig M. Johnson.

Financial data (yr. ended 12/31/01): Grants paid, $500; assets, $14,277 (M); gifts received, $80; expenditures, $605; qualifying distributions, $500.
Limitations: Applications not accepted.
Application information: Contributes only to pre-selected organizations.
Officers and Directors:* Craig M. Johnson,* Pres.; Elizabeth Kase Johnson, Secy.; Stuart M. Johnson,* Treas.; Karin H. Johnson.
EIN: 113545172

40000
Frank A. LaMonica Foundation, Inc.
P.O. Box 795
Oneonta, NY 13820
Application address: c/o 16 Dietz St., Oneonta, NY 13820, tel.: (607) 432-5530
Contact: Frank A. Getman, Dir.

Donor(s): Frank A. LaMonica, Jr.
Financial data (yr. ended 12/31/01): Grants paid, $500; assets, $93 (M); expenditures, $684; qualifying distributions, $500.
Limitations: Giving primarily in Oneonta, NY.
Officers and Directors:* Frank A. LaMonica, Jr.,* Pres.; JoAnn LaMonica,* V.P.; F.R. Blankenship, Frank A. Getman, Benjamin Nesbitt.
EIN: 222478901

40001
Morris Levy Charitable Foundation
c/o Sunnyview Farm
140 Arch Bridge Rd.
Ghent, NY 12075
Contact: Adam R. Levy, Tr.

Financial data (yr. ended 12/31/01): Grants paid, $500; assets, $36,331 (M); expenditures, $975; qualifying distributions, $500.
Application information: Application form not required.
Trustees: Adam R. Levy, Jules Weinstein.
EIN: 136945492

40002
Elise Mindy Lyons Foundation Trust
111 E. 30th St.
New York, NY 10016

Established in 1989 in OH.
Financial data (yr. ended 12/31/01): Grants paid, $500; assets, $8,017 (M); gifts received, $759; expenditures, $709; qualifying distributions, $500.
Limitations: Applications not accepted.
Application information: Contributes only to pre-selected organizations.
Trustee: Annette R. Lyons.
EIN: 316348468

40003
Mawar Foundation, Inc.
c/o William A. Warshaw
111 W. 40th St.
New York, NY 10018-2506

Financial data (yr. ended 11/30/01): Grants paid, $500; assets, $21,544 (M); expenditures, $558; qualifying distributions, $500.
Limitations: Applications not accepted.
Application information: Contributes only to pre-selected organizations.
Officers: Peter Warshaw, V.P. and Secy.; Hortence Warshaw, V.P.; William A. Warshaw, V.P.
EIN: 136121927

40004
The Kevin E. Parker Foundation
941 Park Ave.
New York, NY 10028-0318

Established in 1996 in NY.
Donor(s): Kevin E. Parker.

Financial data (yr. ended 11/30/01): Grants paid, $500; assets, $28,985 (M); gifts received, $1,375; expenditures, $1,875; qualifying distributions, $500.
Limitations: Applications not accepted. Giving primarily in New York, NY.
Application information: Contributes only to pre-selected organizations.
Directors: Dolores A. Parker, Kevin E. Parker.
EIN: 133923815

40005
Abraham & Rebecca Pokoik Foundation
575 Madison Ave.
New York, NY 10022-2511

Financial data (yr. ended 03/31/01): Grants paid, $500; assets, $38,216 (M); expenditures, $525; qualifying distributions, $500.
Limitations: Applications not accepted. Giving primarily in New York, NY.
Application information: Contributes only to pre-selected organizations.
Trustees: Harold Derfner, Helen Derfner, Leon Pokoik.
EIN: 136158569

40006
Rockette Alumnae Foundation
908 N. Broadway
Yonkers, NY 10701
Contact: Fern D. Weizner, Tr.

Donor(s): Luncheon Express.
Financial data (yr. ended 12/31/01): Grants paid, $500; assets, $208,380 (M); expenditures, $1,483; qualifying distributions, $500.
Limitations: Giving primarily in New York, NY.
Trustees: Percy Douglas, Kenneth Perko, Fern D. Weizner.
EIN: 116180006

40007
Sackett/Archbishop Walsh Scholarship Trust
c/o The Bank of New York, Tax Dept.
1 Wall St., 28th Fl.
New York, NY 10286

Financial data (yr. ended 12/31/00): Grants paid, $500; assets, $32,291 (M); expenditures, $691; qualifying distributions, $553.
Limitations: Applications not accepted. Giving limited to Olean, NY.
Trustee: The Bank of New York.
EIN: 166032562

40008
Sackler Foundation, Inc.
17 E. 62nd St.
New York, NY 10021

Established in 1967 in NY.
Donor(s): Mortimer D. Sackler, Raymond R. Sackler.
Financial data (yr. ended 12/31/01): Grants paid, $500; assets, $5,092 (M); expenditures, $500; qualifying distributions, $500.
Limitations: Applications not accepted.
Application information: Contributes only to pre-selected organizations.
Officers: Mortimer D. Sackler, Secy.; Raymond R. Sackler, Treas.
EIN: 237022477

40009
Ronald Seltzer Memorial Scholarship Foundation
c/o Berlin Kolin
1790 Broadway, Rm. 705
New York, NY 10019
Application address: c/o Principal, Bellport High School, Bellport, NY 11713

Financial data (yr. ended 11/30/00): Grants paid, $500; assets, $10,790 (M); expenditures, $585; qualifying distributions, $500.
Limitations: Applications not accepted. Giving limited to students in Bellport, NY.
Application information: Scholarship recipients selected by Bellport High School principal.
Officers: Regina Seltzer, Pres.; Ralph Weston, V.P. and Treas.
EIN: 112457979

40010
Harry & Vivian Silverson Foundation, Inc.
c/o Liss, Okun, Goldstein, Okun & Tancer
99 Cuttermill Rd., Ste. 422N
Great Neck, NY 11021

Financial data (yr. ended 10/31/01): Grants paid, $500; assets, $56,176 (M); expenditures, $1,564; qualifying distributions, $500.
Limitations: Applications not accepted.
Application information: Contributes only to pre-selected organizations.
Officer and Directors:* Jeffrey Silverson, Judith S. Sloan, Joan S. Wexler.
EIN: 136098833

40011
The Alan Vituli Foundation
968 James St.
Syracuse, NY 13203

Established in 1996 in NY.
Donor(s): Alan Vituli.
Financial data (yr. ended 12/31/01): Grants paid, $500; assets, $4,264 (M); expenditures, $500; qualifying distributions, $500.
Limitations: Applications not accepted. Giving primarily in New York, NY.
Application information: Contributes only to pre-selected organizations.
Trustees: Alan Asher, Alan Vituli, Nancy Vituli.
EIN: 161517434

40012
Michele and David Vozick Family Foundation
579 Bedford Dr.
Mount Kisco, NY 10549

Donor(s): David Vozick.
Financial data (yr. ended 11/30/01): Grants paid, $500; assets, $42,195 (M); expenditures, $559; qualifying distributions, $500.
Limitations: Applications not accepted. Giving primarily in NY.
Application information: Contributes only to pre-selected organizations.
Officers and Trustees:* David Vozick,* Pres.; Michele Vozick,* Secy.-Treas.
EIN: 133798068

40013
The Bernard M. Manuel Foundation
c/o Cygne Designs, Inc.
1372 Broadway
New York, NY 10018

Donor(s): Bernard M. Manuel.
Financial data (yr. ended 07/31/99): Grants paid, $490; assets, $10,880 (M); gifts received, $490; expenditures, $490; qualifying distributions, $490.
Application information: Application form not required.
Officer: Bernard M. Manuel, Mgr.
EIN: 133742131

40014
Abraham and Mildred Goldstein Charitable Trust
c/o Eisner & Lubin
444 Madison Ave.
New York, NY 10022

Established in 1997 in NY.
Donor(s): Abraham Goldstein,‡ Mildred Goldstein.
Financial data (yr. ended 12/31/00): Grants paid, $475; assets, $10,159 (M); gifts received, $675; expenditures, $550; qualifying distributions, $475.
Limitations: Applications not accepted.
Application information: Contributes only to pre-selected organizations.
Trustees: Abraham Goldstein, Mildred Goldstein, Hirschell E. Levine.
EIN: 137061296

40015
Melvin R. Lane Trust
c/o JPMorgan Chase Bank
P.O. Box 31412
Rochester, NY 14603 (800) 850-7222
Contact: Mary M. Koegel, Trust Off., JPMorgan Chase Bank

Financial data (yr. ended 12/31/01): Grants paid, $469; assets, $16,548 (M); expenditures, $548; qualifying distributions, $472.
Trustee: JPMorgan Chase Bank.
EIN: 136049509

40016
Harry S. Klavan Memorial Foundation, Inc.
(Formerly Rabbi Joshua & Fannie D. Klavan Memorial Foundation)
c/o Goldstein
137-16 72nd Rd.
Flushing, NY 11367

Established in 1962.
Donor(s): Harry S. Klavan,‡ Rena S. Klavan.
Financial data (yr. ended 12/31/01): Grants paid, $460; assets, $269,110 (M); expenditures, $1,048; qualifying distributions, $460.
Limitations: Applications not accepted. Giving primarily in Washington, DC and NY.
Application information: Contributes only to pre-selected organizations.
Directors: Shulamith K. Goldstein, David Klavan, Rabbi Hillel Klavan, Joshua Klavan, Rena S. Klavan, Miriam K. Meyers.
EIN: 526054006

40017
The Fellowship of Messiah Jesus, Inc.
P.O. Box 488
New Hampton, NY 10958

Financial data (yr. ended 12/31/01): Grants paid, $453; assets, $312 (M); gifts received, $3,140; expenditures, $2,882; qualifying distributions, $2,882.
Directors: Andrew L. Lowry, Jr., Marguerite Lowry.
EIN: 133782668

40018
The Ralph I. Gindi Foundation, Inc.
3611 Bedford Ave.
Brooklyn, NY 11210-5236

Established in 1992 in NY.
Financial data (yr. ended 12/31/01): Grants paid, $450; assets, $2,029 (M); gifts received, $2,500; expenditures, $2,028; qualifying distributions, $450.
Limitations: Applications not accepted. Giving primarily in the greater metropolitan New York, NY, area.
Application information: Contributes only to pre-selected organizations.
Trustees: Harris Gindi, Ralph I. Gindi, Randal Gindi, Zachary Gindi.
EIN: 113117510

40019
The Horeinu Foundation
c/o Mendel Vim
1561 E. 12th St.
Brooklyn, NY 11230

Established in 1996.
Donor(s): Mendel Vim, Pauline Vim.
Financial data (yr. ended 11/30/99): Grants paid, $433; assets, $31,093 (M); gifts received, $13,848; expenditures, $523; qualifying distributions, $433.
Limitations: Applications not accepted.
Application information: Contributes only to pre-selected organizations.
Officers: Mendel Vim, Pres.; Pauline Vim, Secy.-Treas.
EIN: 113380676

40020
Ellen Hanford Scholarship Fund
c/o The National Bank of Delaware County
P.O. Box 389
Walton, NY 13856
Application address: c/o Principal, Utica Free Academy, Utica, NY 13501

Financial data (yr. ended 12/31/00): Grants paid, $425; assets, $10,348 (M); expenditures, $515; qualifying distributions, $491.
Limitations: Giving limited to residents of Utica, NY.
Application information: Applicant must be a member of the Utica Free Academy.
Trustee: The National Bank of Delaware County.
EIN: 166056966

40021
Melamid International Foundation, Inc.
14 S. Bedford Rd.
Chappaqua, NY 10514-3423
Contact: Zev Melamid, Pres. or Estelle Melamid, Secy.

Donor(s): Zev Melamid, Estelle Melamid.
Financial data (yr. ended 11/30/01): Grants paid, $425; assets, $8,596 (M); expenditures, $512; qualifying distributions, $425.
Limitations: Giving primarily in the greater New York, NY, area.
Officers: Zev Melamid, Pres.; Diana Melamid, V.P.; Elan Melamid, V.P.; Estelle Melamid, Secy.
EIN: 133263278

40022
Zabronsky Family Foundation, Inc.
1980 Broadcast Plz.
Merrick, NY 11566

Financial data (yr. ended 06/30/02): Grants paid, $405; assets, $855 (M); expenditures, $485; qualifying distributions, $405.
Limitations: Applications not accepted. Giving primarily in NY.
Application information: Contributes only to pre-selected organizations.
Officers: Lester Zabronsky, Pres.; Alan Zabronsky, V.P.
EIN: 136270767

40023
Bressler Family Foundation, Inc.
520 8th Ave.
New York, NY 10018-4901

Financial data (yr. ended 12/31/99): Grants paid, $400; assets, $15,259 (M); expenditures, $558; qualifying distributions, $400.
Limitations: Applications not accepted. Giving primarily in New York, NY.
Application information: Contributes only to pre-selected organizations.
Officer: Alvin Bressler, Pres.
EIN: 136217692

40024
The Robert A. Certilman Family Foundation, Inc.
780 Middle Country Rd.
St. James, NY 11780

Established in 2000.
Donor(s): Robert A. Cerilman.
Financial data (yr. ended 08/31/01): Grants paid, $400; assets, $971,289 (M); gifts received, $912,269; expenditures, $440; qualifying distributions, $440.
Limitations: Applications not accepted. Giving primarily in New York, NY.
Application information: Contributes only to pre-selected organizations.
Officers: Robert A. Certilman, Pres.; Steven Certilman, V.P.; Lee Certilman, Secy.
EIN: 311734664

40025
Elbaum Family Foundation
c/o Hellen Elbaum
37 Riverside Dr., Ste. 11B
New York, NY 10023-8027

Established in 1995 in NY.
Financial data (yr. ended 12/31/01): Grants paid, $400; assets, $20,809 (M); expenditures, $936; qualifying distributions, $400.
Limitations: Applications not accepted.
Application information: Contributes only to pre-selected organizations.
Trustee: Helen Elbaum.
EIN: 133793215

40026
Forestville/Sackett Scholarship Fund Trust
c/o The Bank of New York
1 Wall St., 28th Fl.
New York, NY 10005-2500

Established in 1987 in NY.
Financial data (yr. ended 12/31/01): Grants paid, $400; assets, $10,615 (M); expenditures, $468; qualifying distributions, $400.
Limitations: Giving limited to the greater Olean and Cattaraugus, NY, areas.
Application information: Application form required.
Trustee: The Bank of New York.
EIN: 166031985

40027
The Jack Galef Arts Foundation, Inc.
c/o Golomb, Sindel & Dible, PC
16 E. 34th St., Ste. 1600
New York, NY 10016

Donor(s): Jack L. Galef II.
Financial data (yr. ended 12/31/01): Grants paid, $400; assets, $544 (M); gifts received, $520; expenditures, $504; qualifying distributions, $400.
Limitations: Giving primarily in New York, NY.
Officers and Directors:* Jack L. Galef II,* Pres. and Treas.; Sandra B. Sindel,* Secy.; Irving L. Golomb.
EIN: 133573140

40028
The Gail Godwin Foundation
237 Main St., Ste. 1100
Buffalo, NY 14203

Financial data (yr. ended 12/31/01): Grants paid, $400; assets, $29,673 (M); gifts received, $525; expenditures, $968; qualifying distributions, $705.
Trustee: Willard B. Saperston.
EIN: 161520147

40029
Emma Kiess Award Trust
c/o M&T Bank
1 M&T Plz., 8th Fl.
Buffalo, NY 14203
Application address: c/o Guidance Counselor, Williamsport Area High School, W. 4th St., Williamsport, PA 17701, tel.: (570) 323-8411

Financial data (yr. ended 12/31/01): Grants paid, $400; assets, $10,964 (M); expenditures, $1,491; qualifying distributions, $10,965.
Limitations: Applications not accepted. Giving limited to the Williamsport, PA, area.
Application information: Recipient selected by the faculty of Williamsport Area High School, PA.
Trustee: M & T Bank.
EIN: 236634511

40030
McRostie Foundation, Inc.
c/o Benson R. Frost, Jr.
21 Chestnut St.
Rhinebeck, NY 12572

Established in 1998 in NY.
Financial data (yr. ended 12/31/01): Grants paid, $400; assets, $18,335 (M); gifts received, $5,000; expenditures, $850; qualifying distributions, $400.
Limitations: Applications not accepted.
Application information: Contributes only to pre-selected organizations.
Officers and Directors:* Benson R. Frost, Jr.,* Pres.; Barbara V. Frost,* Secy.; Janet L. Cotting.
EIN: 141803911

40031
Sophie & David Rubin Foundation
1600 Hillside Ave., Ste. 203
New Hyde Park, NY 11040

Established in 2000 in NY.
Donor(s): David Rubin.
Financial data (yr. ended 12/31/01): Grants paid, $400; assets, $20,020 (M); gifts received, $14,289; expenditures, $600; qualifying distributions, $400.
Limitations: Applications not accepted.
Application information: Contributes only to pre-selected organizations.
Trustee: David Rubin.
EIN: 113565586

40032
Packin Family Foundation, Inc.
110 Varick Ave.
Brooklyn, NY 11237

Established in 2000.
Donor(s): David Packin, Joseph Packin, Eugene Packin.
Financial data (yr. ended 12/31/01): Grants paid, $399; assets, $259,705 (M); gifts received, $43,000; expenditures, $40,050; qualifying distributions, $40,009.
Trustee: David Packin.
EIN: 113550180

40033
J. Gordon Gill Trust
c/o Fleet National Bank
159 E. Main St.
Rochester, NY 14638

Financial data (yr. ended 02/28/99): Grants paid, $390; assets, $6,100 (M); expenditures, $471; qualifying distributions, $432.
Limitations: Applications not accepted. Giving primarily in NY.
Application information: Contributes only to pre-selected organizations.
Trustee: Fleet National Bank.
EIN: 146106161

40034
Joseph M. & Geraldine C. La Motta Charitable Trust
69 Black Brook Rd.
Pound Ridge, NY 10576

Established in 1993 in NY.
Donor(s): Geraldine C. La Motta, Joseph M. La Motta.
Financial data (yr. ended 12/31/01): Grants paid, $385; assets, $326,160 (M); expenditures, $485; qualifying distributions, $385.
Limitations: Applications not accepted.
Application information: Contributes only to pre-selected organizations.
Trustees: Geraldine C. La Motta, Joseph M. La Motta.
EIN: 137027896

40035
J. F. Schoellkopf Trust
c/o HSBC Bank USA
1 HSBC Ctr., 17th Fl.
Buffalo, NY 14240

Financial data (yr. ended 12/31/00): Grants paid, $353; assets, $16,627 (M); expenditures, $406; qualifying distributions, $355.
Limitations: Applications not accepted. Giving primarily in NY.
Application information: Contributes only to pre-selected organizations.
Trustee: HSBC Bank USA.
EIN: 166021841

40036
Jack Gluck Family Foundation, Inc.
524 Chauncey Ln.
Lawrence, NY 11559
Contact: Jack Gluck, Tr.

Established in 1995 in NY.
Donor(s): Jack Gluck.
Financial data (yr. ended 12/31/99): Grants paid, $340; assets, $5,930 (M); expenditures, $670; qualifying distributions, $670.
Limitations: Giving limited to Lawrence, NY.
Trustee: Jack Gluck.
EIN: 113304854

40037
Michael Mordechai & Pearl Inzlicht Foundation, Inc.
(Formerly Michael & Pearl Inzlicht Foundation, Inc.)
c/o Zell & Ettinger
3001 Ave. M
Brooklyn, NY 11210-4744

Established in 1990 in NY.
Donor(s): Michael Inzlicht.
Financial data (yr. ended 12/31/00): Grants paid, $340; assets, $6,218 (L); expenditures, $340; qualifying distributions, $340.

Limitations: Applications not accepted.
Application information: Contributes only to pre-selected organizations.
Officers: Michael Inzlicht, Pres.; Pearl Inzlicht, V.P.; Jack Basch, Co-Secy.; Jeffrey Zell, Co-Secy.
EIN: 133584775

40038
EMB Foundation, Ltd.
2621 Ave. N.
Brooklyn, NY 11210

Established in 1997 in NY.
Donor(s): Alex Gonter, Shlomo Gonter, Sam Tropper.
Financial data (yr. ended 12/31/01): Grants paid, $334; assets, $708 (M); gifts received, $450; expenditures, $555; qualifying distributions, $334.
Limitations: Applications not accepted.
Application information: Unsolicited requests for funds not accepted.
Officer: Alex Gonter, Mgr.
EIN: 113393489

40039
Susan Aberbach Charitable Foundation
41 E. 57th St., Ste. 1401
New York, NY 10022-1908

Established in 1996 in NY.
Donor(s): Susan Aberbach.
Financial data (yr. ended 12/31/01): Grants paid, $325; assets, $70,400 (M); gifts received, $1,028; expenditures, $1,435; qualifying distributions, $325.
Limitations: Applications not accepted.
Application information: Contributes only to pre-selected organizations.
Trustee: Susan Aberbach.
EIN: 137083486

40040
Richard and Elizabeth Boggio Foundation
c/o Joseph Lapatin
73-51 177th St.
Flushing, NY 11366

Established in 1996 in NY.
Financial data (yr. ended 12/31/01): Grants paid, $325; assets, $109,788 (M); expenditures, $4,080; qualifying distributions, $325.
Limitations: Giving primarily in NY.
Directors: James Feeley, Max Feinstein, Joseph Lapatin.
EIN: 133904367

40041
C.I.C. Development Corporation
150 Van Aucker St.
Rochester, NY 14608-2106

Financial data (yr. ended 12/31/00): Grants paid, $319; assets, $1,212 (M); expenditures, $472; qualifying distributions, $319.
Limitations: Giving limited to Rochester, NY.
Trustee: Alfred Robinson.
EIN: 160955951

40042
Edward T. Bedford Foundation
c/o Bessemer Trust Co., N.A., Tax Dept.
630 5th Ave.
New York, NY 10111

Established in 1995 in FL.
Donor(s): E.T. Bedford Davie.
Financial data (yr. ended 12/31/01): Grants paid, $308; assets, $4,353 (M); expenditures, $1,208; qualifying distributions, $308.
Trustees: E.T. Bedford Davie, Bessemer Trust Co., N.A.
EIN: 656164872

40043
Howard B. Dean Foundation
1035 Park Ave.
New York, NY 10028 (212) 876-4433
Contact: Howard B. Dean, Tr.

Donor(s): Howard B. Dean.
Financial data (yr. ended 12/31/01): Grants paid, $300; assets, $17,993 (M); expenditures, $314; qualifying distributions, $300.
Limitations: Giving primarily in NY.
Trustees: Andree N. Dean, Howard B. Dean.
EIN: 136109171

40044
Dean M. Graham Foundation
c/o Timothy J. Sweeney
5075 State Rte.
Cobleskill, NY 12043 (518) 234-7516

Established in 1992 in NY; funded in 1993.
Financial data (yr. ended 12/31/01): Grants paid, $300; assets, $2,881 (M); expenditures, $476; qualifying distributions, $300.
Limitations: Applications not accepted.
Trustees: Dean M. Graham, Victoria Graham, Timothy J. Sweeney.
EIN: 223211041

40045
The Mitch Foundation, Inc.
P.O. Box 267
Oneida, NY 13421

Established in 1995 in NY.
Financial data (yr. ended 12/31/01): Grants paid, $300; assets, $2,193 (M); gifts received, $850; expenditures, $532; qualifying distributions, $300.
Officers and Directors:* Richard W. Mitchell I,* Pres. and Treas.; Rosemary Mitchell,* V.P.; Joseph Wormworth,* Secy.; David L. Mitchell, Lynda M. Mitchell.
EIN: 161481016

40046
Reisler Family Foundation
P.O. Box 61
108 Woodcrest Terr.
Amawalk, NY 10501

Established in 2000 in NY.
Donor(s): Philip Brent, Mrs. Philip Brent.
Financial data (yr. ended 12/31/01): Grants paid, $300; assets, $143,312 (M); expenditures, $4,812; qualifying distributions, $300.
Limitations: Applications not accepted.
Application information: Contributes only to pre-selected organizations.
Officers and Directors:* Barry Reisler,* Pres. and Treas.; Laurie Reisler,* V.P. and Secy.; Rita Reisler.
EIN: 134150716

40047
American Friends of the Museum of the Mikveh, Inc.
1360 44th St.
Brooklyn, NY 11219

Financial data (yr. ended 12/31/99): Grants paid, $297; assets, $0 (M); gifts received, $45,372; expenditures, $57,796; qualifying distributions, $0; giving activities include $41,000 for programs.
Limitations: Applications not accepted.
Application information: Contributes only to pre-selected organizations.
Officers: Yaakov Singer, Chair.; Emmanuel Ravad, Pres.; Morris Weiser, Secy.
EIN: 112918759

40048
Council for Unity, Inc.
48 E. 21st St.
New York, NY 10010
Contact: Justine Lungo

Financial data (yr. ended 06/30/00): Grants paid, $295; assets, $94,647 (L); gifts received, $345,971; expenditures, $400,444; qualifying distributions, $0.
Officers: Thomas Butler, Chair.; Robert DeSena, Pres.; Barbara Santasiero, Secy.; William Serrao, Treas.
EIN: 112880221

40049
The Seidenfeld Family Foundation
c/o Aaron Seidenfeld
1551 59th St.
Brooklyn, NY 11219

Established in 1999 in NY.
Donor(s): Aaron Seidenfeld.
Financial data (yr. ended 12/31/00): Grants paid, $270; assets, $38,571 (M); gifts received, $1,000; expenditures, $320; qualifying distributions, $270.
Limitations: Applications not accepted. Giving primarily in Brooklyn, NY.
Application information: Contributes only to pre-selected organizations.
Trustees: Aaron Seidenfeld, Esther Seidenfeld.
EIN: 113412171

40050
Art Spirit, Inc
23 East 74th St., No. 6-B
New York, NY 10021

Donor(s): Marion Berrian Williams.
Financial data (yr. ended 12/31/01): Grants paid, $250; assets, $2,034 (M); gifts received, $36,537; expenditures, $34,881; qualifying distributions, $250; giving activities include $8,716 for programs.
Officers: Mira Burack, Secy-Treas.; Marion Berrian Williams, Exec. Dir.
EIN: 113276202

40051
The Davis Foundation, Inc.
(Formerly Martin S. and Luella Davis Foundation)
c/o Reminick, Aarons & Co., LLP
1430 Broadway
New York, NY 10018-3308

Established around 1988.
Donor(s): Martin S. Davis.
Financial data (yr. ended 12/31/01): Grants paid, $250; assets, $2,040,501 (M); expenditures, $2,150; qualifying distributions, $250.
Limitations: Applications not accepted. Giving primarily in NY.
Application information: Contributes only to pre-selected organizations.
Officer: F. Luella Davis, Pres.
Director: Andrew H. Weiss.
EIN: 061187647

40052
Abraham W. & Marion Geller Foundation, Inc.
c/o Amy Geller
11-15 45th Ave., 2C
Long Island City, NY 11101

Established in 1985.
Donor(s): Marion Geller.
Financial data (yr. ended 12/31/01): Grants paid, $250; assets, $18,616 (M); expenditures, $877; qualifying distributions, $250.

Limitations: Applications not accepted. Giving primarily in New York, NY.
Application information: Contributes only to pre-selected organizations.
Officer: Marion Geller, Pres. and Treas.
EIN: 237111848

40053
K. A. in V.C. Foundation, Inc.
c/o Sciarabba Walker
200 E. Buffalo St.
Ithaca, NY 14850
Application address: 3316 Chatham Pl., Media, PA 19063, tel.: (215) 382-9800
Contact: James L. Goldman, Treas.

Financial data (yr. ended 06/30/01): Grants paid, $250; assets, $6,262 (M); expenditures, $1,023; qualifying distributions, $650.
Limitations: Giving limited to Ithaca, NY.
Officers: John Fuller, Pres.; Joshua Koenig, Secy.; James L. Goldman, Treas.
EIN: 237053071

40054
One Point of Light Foundation, Inc.
28-53 45th St.
Astoria, NY 11103
Contact: Gary W. Weeks, Mgr.

Established in 1999 in NY.
Financial data (yr. ended 12/31/00): Grants paid, $250; assets, $4,660 (M); expenditures, $399; qualifying distributions, $250.
Limitations: Giving primarily in NY.
Officers: Karl A. Spahlinger, Pres.; Gary W. Weeks, Mgr.
Directors: Dominick Biondi, Michael Vietri.
EIN: 113490562

40055
Clarke Sanford Memorial Trust Fund
c/o The National Bank of Delaware County
P.O. Box 389
Walton, NY 13856-0389
Application address: c/o A. Omland, Franklin Central School, Franklin, NY 13775, tel.: (607) 829-3551

Financial data (yr. ended 12/31/01): Grants paid, $250; assets, $16,913 (M); expenditures, $374; qualifying distributions, $250.
Limitations: Giving limited to residents of Delaware County, NY.
Trustee: The National Bank of Delaware County.
EIN: 166099596

40056
Harry & Sylvia Schneider Foundation, Inc.
710 Beck Rd.
Far Rockaway, NY 11691-4827
(718) 471-9723
Contact: Harry Schneider, Pres.

Donor(s): Harry Schneider, Sylvia Schneider.
Financial data (yr. ended 12/31/00): Grants paid, $250; assets, $3,904 (M); expenditures, $550; qualifying distributions, $250.
Limitations: Giving primarily in New York, NY.
Officer: Harry Schneider, Pres.
EIN: 136198857

40057
The Dr. Allen Packer Foundation, Inc.
100 Dehaven Dr.
Yonkers, NY 10703
Contact: Allen Packer, Dir.

Established in 1999 in NY.
Donor(s): Allen Packer.
Financial data (yr. ended 12/31/01): Grants paid, $242; assets, $5,236 (M); expenditures, $242; qualifying distributions, $242.
Application information: Application form not required.
Directors: Bonnie Franklin Drazen, Amy Ann Franklin, Marc M. Franklin, Allen Packer, Michael Packer, Paul Packer.
EIN: 134088479

40058
The Esther Rose Packer Foundation, Inc.
100 Dehaven Dr.
Yonkers, NY 10703
Contact: Allen Packer, Dir.

Established in 1999 in NY.
Donor(s): Esther Rose Packer.
Financial data (yr. ended 12/31/01): Grants paid, $242; assets, $5,135 (M); expenditures, $242; qualifying distributions, $242.
Application information: Application form not required.
Directors: Phyllis Packer Franklin, Allen Packer, Martin Packer.
EIN: 134073105

40059
Robert L. Ungerer Foundation
4 Clinton Sq., Ste. 106
Syracuse, NY 13202-1034 (315) 476-0532
Contact: Robert V. Hunter, Tr.

Established in 1990 in NY.
Donor(s): Robert L. Ungerer.
Financial data (yr. ended 12/31/01): Grants paid, $231; assets, $17,680 (M); expenditures, $393; qualifying distributions, $231.
Limitations: Giving primarily in NY.
Trustees: Robert V. Hunter, Robert L. Ungerer.
EIN: 161319380

40060
Robin Chandler Duke Foundation
c/o Mrs. Robin Chandler Duke
435 E. 52nd St.
New York, NY 10022

Established in 2000 in NY.
Donor(s): Robin Chandler Duke.
Financial data (yr. ended 12/31/01): Grants paid, $225; assets, $3,570 (M); expenditures, $1,130; qualifying distributions, $225.
Limitations: Giving primarily in NY.
Trustee: Robin Chandler Duke.
EIN: 137202865

40061
The Edgar M. Bronfman Family Foundation, Inc.
c/o Mildred Kalik
425 Lexington Ave.
New York, NY 10017

Established in 1995 in NY.
Financial data (yr. ended 12/31/00): Grants paid, $207; assets, $5,242 (M); gifts received, $1,000; expenditures, $207; qualifying distributions, $207.
Officer: Edgar M. Bronfman, Pres.
Directors: Adam R. Bronfman, Edgar Bronfman, Jr., Matthew Bronfman, Samuel Bronfman II, Holly Bronfman Hoffman.
EIN: 133769022

40062
Council of American Artist Societies, Inc.
c/o Roland A. Anderson
577 Portland Ave.
Baldwin, NY 11510
Application address: 1550 N. Grand Ave., Baldwin, NY 11510
Contact: Leonard Benari, Treas.

Financial data (yr. ended 03/31/00): Grants paid, $200; assets, $39,274 (M); expenditures, $1,094; qualifying distributions, $200.
Limitations: Giving primarily in NY.
Officer: Leonard Benari, Treas.
EIN: 136173876

40063
The Y. & F. Grunwald Foundation
c/o Joseph Grunwald
1855 50th St.
Brooklyn, NY 11204

Established in 1993 in NY.
Donor(s): Joseph Grunwald.
Financial data (yr. ended 12/31/00): Grants paid, $200; assets, $767 (M); expenditures, $270; qualifying distributions, $270.
Limitations: Applications not accepted. Giving primarily in NJ and NY; some giving also in Israel.
Application information: Contributes only to pre-selected organizations.
Trustees: Frumi Grunwald, Joseph Grunwald.
EIN: 113181042

40064
Nancy Kalinsky Scholarship Fund, Inc.
11 Ivy Ln.
Pomona, NY 10970

Financial data (yr. ended 12/31/00): Grants paid, $200; assets, $880 (M); gifts received, $25; expenditures, $215; qualifying distributions, $215.
Limitations: Giving primarily in NY.
Officers: Marcie Kalinsky, Pres. and Treas.; Sidney Young, V.P.; Howard Kalinsky, Secy.
EIN: 112412466

40065
The Frederick P. Lenz Foundation for American Buddhism
c/o Ernst & Young
787 7th Ave.
New York, NY 10019

Established in 1998 in NY.
Financial data (yr. ended 12/31/00): Grants paid, $200; assets, $2,926 (M); gifts received, $10,754; expenditures, $12,659; qualifying distributions, $200.
Limitations: Applications not accepted.
Application information: Contributes only to pre-selected organizations.
Officer and Directors:* Norman Marcus,* Pres.; Frederick P. Lenz, Jr., Norman S. Oberstein.
EIN: 134014022

40066
Mount Moriah Benevolent Fund, Inc.
c/o Cecil Miller
114 W. James St.
Falconer, NY 14733

Financial data (yr. ended 12/31/99): Grants paid, $200; assets, $4,695 (M); expenditures, $211; qualifying distributions, $200.
Limitations: Giving primarily in NY.
Officers: Rockland Milne, Pres.; Leland Sperry, V.P.; Murray Marsh, Jr., Secy.; Cecil Miller, Treas.
EIN: 166030457

40067
The Daniel & Trudy Regan Foundation, Inc.
c/o R. Braunschweig
420 Lexington Ave., Ste. 336
New York, NY 10170-0399

Established in 1991 in NY.
Donor(s): Daniel Regan, Trudy Regan.
Financial data (yr. ended 12/31/01): Grants paid, $200; assets, $15,622 (M); gifts received, $679; expenditures, $10,010; qualifying distributions, $200.
Limitations: Applications not accepted. Giving primarily in NY.
Application information: Contributes only to pre-selected organizations.
Directors: H. Williamson Grinskey, Daniel Regan, Trudy Regan.
EIN: 133595312

40068
William C. Sonen Memorial Fund
18-75 Corporal Kennedy St., Apt. 6A
Bayside, NY 11360

Financial data (yr. ended 06/30/01): Grants paid, $200; assets, $3,860 (M); expenditures, $200; qualifying distributions, $200.
Limitations: Applications not accepted. Giving primarily in NY.
Officers: Herbert L. Plafker, Pres.; Beth Turano, V.P.; Marilyn Wanger, Secy.; Iris Plafker, Treas.
EIN: 112718593

40069
Sara M. Holzer Trust
c/o JPMorgan Chase Bank
P.O. Box 31412
Rochester, NY 14603-1412

Established in 1991 in NY.
Donor(s): Sara M. Holzer.‡
Financial data (yr. ended 12/31/01): Grants paid, $183; assets, $40,021 (M); expenditures, $829; qualifying distributions, $279.
Limitations: Giving limited to residents of Bridgeport, CT.
Application information: Contact local high school guidance office. Application form not required.
Trustee: JPMorgan Chase Bank.
EIN: 066032174

40070
The Eisner & Lubin Foundation
444 Madison Ave., 11th Fl
New York, NY 10022

Established in 1986 in NY.
Financial data (yr. ended 12/31/01): Grants paid, $180; assets, $2,278 (M); expenditures, $180; qualifying distributions, $180.
Limitations: Applications not accepted. Giving primarily in NY.
Application information: Contributes only to pre-selected organizations.
Trustees: Hirschell E. Levine, Gerald Marsden.
EIN: 136077722

40071
Martin Stern Family Foundation
1367 53rd St.
Brooklyn, NY 11219

Established in 1999 in NY.
Financial data (yr. ended 09/30/01): Grants paid, $180; assets, $16,265 (M); expenditures, $180; qualifying distributions, $177.
Directors: Samuel Gestetner, Fred Stern, Martin Stern.
EIN: 113513958

40072
Blachly Foundation
674 Deer Park Ave.
Dix Hills, NY 11746
Contact: David K. Blachly, Pres.

Established in 2000 in NY.
Donor(s): David Blachly, Henry Blachly.
Financial data (yr. ended 12/31/01): Grants paid, $175; assets, $450,123 (M); gifts received, $196,851; expenditures, $18,179; qualifying distributions, $175.
Officers: David K. Blachly, Pres.; Marjorie I. Blachly, V.P.; Gaye B. Iorio, Secy.; Henry D. Blachly, Treas.
Trustee: Fleet National Bank.
EIN: 113564067

40073
Charles J. Dunlap Endowment Fund
c/o The Bank of New York, Tax Dept.
1 Wall St., 28th Fl.
New York, NY 10286

Financial data (yr. ended 12/31/01): Grants paid, $167; assets, $3,498 (M); expenditures, $202; qualifying distributions, $189.
Limitations: Applications not accepted. Giving primarily in NY.
Application information: Contributes only to pre-selected organizations.
Trustee: The Bank of New York.
EIN: 136080615

40074
Onondaga Funding Facilities for the Handicapped, Inc.
600 S. Wilbur Ave.
Syracuse, NY 13204-2730

Financial data (yr. ended 04/30/00): Grants paid, $135; assets, $88,394 (M); expenditures, $4,631; qualifying distributions, $194.
Limitations: Applications not accepted. Giving primarily in Syracuse, NY.
Application information: Contributes only to pre-selected organizations.
Officers: Sharon Moran, Pres.; Fred Brissette, V.P.; Sharon Sullivan, Secy.; Peter Holmes, Treas.
Directors: Patricia Almeida, Carol Bullard, Joyce Carmen, and 12 additional directors.
EIN: 510204288

40075
Arielle Tepper Charitable Foundation, Inc.
645 5th Ave., Ste. 900
New York, NY 10022

Established in 1993 in NY & FL.
Donor(s): Susan J. Tepper Charitable Trust.
Financial data (yr. ended 11/30/00): Grants paid, $130; assets, $324,992 (M); gifts received, $100,000; expenditures, $123,959; qualifying distributions, $130.
Limitations: Applications not accepted.
Application information: Contributes only to pre-selected organizations.
Officers: Arielle Tepper, Pres.; Martin B. Tepper, V.P.; Len Grunstein, Secy.; Adam K. Levin, Treas.
EIN: 650454051

40076
The Martin F. Zorn Foundation
(Formerly Bodenheim Foundation, Inc.)
25 E. 86th St.
New York, NY 10028
Contact: Penny Zorn, Pres.

Financial data (yr. ended 01/31/02): Grants paid, $125; assets, $36,187 (M); expenditures, $1,321; qualifying distributions, $125.

Application information: Application form not required.
Officers: Penny Zorn, Pres.; Lynn Zorn, Secy.; Robin DeMaio, Treas.
EIN: 136120797

40077
The Word
c/o Michael Fitzpatrick
P.O. Box 11
Uniondale, NY 11553

Donor(s): Michael Fitzpatrick.
Financial data (yr. ended 12/31/01): Grants paid, $120; assets, $1,737 (M); gifts received, $235; expenditures, $312; qualifying distributions, $120.
Limitations: Applications not accepted. Giving on a national basis.
Application information: Contributes only to pre-selected organizations.
Officers: Michael Fitzpatrick, Pres.; Bradley Arrington, Exec. V.P.; Christine Kelly, V.P. and Secy.
EIN: 112422677

40078
New Rochelle Maennerchor
c/o Alfred Barsuhn
20 Vanderburgh Rd.
Poughquag, NY 12570-5206

Established in 1985 in NY.
Financial data (yr. ended 12/31/01): Grants paid, $105; assets, $48,493 (M); expenditures, $12,164; qualifying distributions, $7,063.
Limitations: Applications not accepted. Giving primarily in Westchester County, NY.
Application information: Contributes only to pre-selected organizations.
Officers: Johanna Janet Hammel, Pres.; Katherina Calabro, V.P.; Ruth Cameron, Secy.; Hedwig Albrecht, Fin. Secy.; Alfred Barsuhn, Treas.
EIN: 133255590

40079
David & Michele Cudmore Scholarship Fund
c/o Gary Cudmore
13 Evelyn Ave.
Amsterdam, NY 12010

Financial data (yr. ended 12/31/99): Grants paid, $100; assets, $9,410 (M); expenditures, $214; qualifying distributions, $214.
Limitations: Giving limited to Amsterdam, NY.
Application information: Application form not required.
Trustees: Bernice Archambeault, Gary Cudmore, Pansy Cudmore.
EIN: 510137302

40080
The Fogel Foundation, Inc.
(Formerly The Ralph and Rochelle Fogel Foundation, Inc.)
c/o William G. Peskoff, Spear, Leeds & Kellogg
120 Broadway
New York, NY 10271-0002

Established in 1985.
Donor(s): Ralph A. Fogel.
Financial data (yr. ended 11/30/00): Grants paid, $100; assets, $1,036 (M); gifts received, $2,000; expenditures, $2,962; qualifying distributions, $2,910.
Limitations: Applications not accepted. Giving primarily in NJ and NY.
Application information: Contributes only to pre-selected organizations.
Officers: Ralph A. Fogel, Pres.; Carl Hewitt, Secy.-Treas.
EIN: 133339954

40081
Kenny Foundation, Inc.
450 Park Ave.
New York, NY 10022-2605

Established in 1998 in NY.
Financial data (yr. ended 12/31/01): Grants paid, $100; assets, $1,655 (M); expenditures, $100; qualifying distributions, $100.
Officers: Finbar Kenny, Pres.; Marianne Kenny, Secy.
Director: Philip J. Michaels.
EIN: 133959549

40082
The MPF Trust
307 7th Ave.
New York, NY 10001

Established in 2000.
Donor(s): Miriam Friedman.
Financial data (yr. ended 05/31/01): Grants paid, $100; assets, $0 (M); gifts received, $33,600; expenditures, $8,202; qualifying distributions, $100.
Limitations: Giving primarily in Brooklyn, NY.
Trustees: Miriam Friedman, Morris Friedman.
EIN: 116524712

40083
Neal Pardo Memorial Scholarship Fund, Inc.
c/o Mitchell Pardo
1233 Beach St.
Atlantic Beach, NY 11509

Established in 1989 in NY.
Financial data (yr. ended 12/31/01): Grants paid, $100; assets, $6,475 (M); expenditures, $100; qualifying distributions, $100.
Limitations: Applications not accepted. Giving limited to NY.
Application information: Contributes only to pre-selected organizations.
Directors: Howard Bauman, Milly Pardo, Mitchell Pardo.
EIN: 113003431

40084
Sheldon N. Peck Memorial Scholarship Fund
P.O. Box 423
Windham, NY 12496-0423

Financial data (yr. ended 12/31/01): Grants paid, $100; assets, $614 (M); expenditures, $100; qualifying distributions, $100.
Limitations: Giving primarily in the Windham, NY, area.
Officers: Robert Ferris, Pres.; Patricia Ferris, V.P.; Ethel Peck, Secy.; George Davis, Treas.
EIN: 141615838

40085
PR Foundation
c/o Ruth M. Guffee
RR 2, Bullet Hole Rd.
Patterson, NY 12563

Established in 1999.
Donor(s): Ruth M. Guffee.
Financial data (yr. ended 12/31/99): Grants paid, $100; assets, $0 (M); gifts received, $100; expenditures, $100; qualifying distributions, $100.
Limitations: Applications not accepted.
Application information: Contributes only to pre-selected organizations.
Trustee: Ruth M. Guffee.
EIN: 141812111

40086
The Rock Family Foundation, Inc.
111 Lefurgy Ave.
Dobbs Ferry, NY 10522

Established in 1999 in NY.
Donor(s): Erwin Rock.
Financial data (yr. ended 12/31/01): Grants paid, $100; assets, $451 (M); expenditures, $100; qualifying distributions, $100.
Limitations: Applications not accepted.
Application information: Contributes only to pre-selected organizations.
Officer and Trustee:* Erwin Rock,* Pres.
EIN: 134059587

40087
Morris and Ruth Strickoff Charitable Foundation, Inc.
2284 Babylon Tpke.
Merrick, NY 11566-3829
Contact: Kive I. Strickoff, Mgr.

Established in 1998 in NY.
Financial data (yr. ended 12/31/01): Grants paid, $100; assets, $478 (M); gifts received, $500; expenditures, $287; qualifying distributions, $100.
Application information: Application form not required.
Officer and Directors:* Kive I. Strickoff,* Mgr.; Avery Strickoff, Carol Strickoff.
EIN: 113439647

40088
Rommel Wilson Memorial Fund, Inc.
3 Oak Tree Ln.
Shelter Island Heights, NY 11965

Financial data (yr. ended 12/31/01): Grants paid, $100; assets, $1,372 (M); gifts received, $400; expenditures, $100; qualifying distributions, $100.
Limitations: Applications not accepted.
Officers: Helen R. Wancura, Pres.; Paul F. Wancura, V.P.
Directors: Daniel Smith, Walter A. Smith.
EIN: 112109773

40089
Concerned Citizens for Creedmoor, Inc.
c/o Creedmoor State Hospital
80-45 Winchester Blvd., Bldg. 40, 2nd Fl.
Queens Village, NY 11427-2193
Contact: Josephine Nuzzo, Pres. or Michael Halpert, V.P.

Financial data (yr. ended 12/31/01): Grants paid, $75; assets, $17,598 (M); gifts received, $100; expenditures, $2,000; qualifying distributions, $75.
Limitations: Giving primarily in Queens Village, NY.
Application information: Application form not required.
Officers: Josephine Nuzzo, Pres.; Michael Halpert, V.P. and Treas.; Linda C. Louie, Secy.
EIN: 116037202

40090
Jamie Lehmann Memorial Foundation
910 5th Ave., Ste. 11A
New York, NY 10021 (212) 489-7676
Contact: Marcia Lehmann Herschmann, Pres.

Donor(s): Eugene Siegel, Barbara Siegel, B. Retter, Marcia Lehmann Herschmann, Manfred Lehmann, Karen Eisner, Ann Lehmann.
Financial data (yr. ended 05/31/02): Grants paid, $64; assets, $5,878 (M); gifts received, $1,118; expenditures, $2,902; qualifying distributions, $64.
Officers and Directors:* Marcia Lehmann Herschmann, Pres.; Ann Lehmann, V.P.; Karen Eisner,* Treas.; Barbara L. Siegel, Secy.; Eugene Siegel.
EIN: 133167374

40091
The Harvey and Elizabeth Prior Shriber Charitable Foundation Trust
c/o Levine, Gouldin & Thompson
P.O. Box F-1706
Binghamton, NY 13902-0106

Established in 1989 in NY.
Financial data (yr. ended 12/31/01): Grants paid, $64; assets, $606 (M); expenditures, $426; qualifying distributions, $64.
Limitations: Applications not accepted.
Application information: Contributes only to pre-selected organizations.
Trustees: Samuel K. Levine, Elizabeth Prior Shriber, Harvey Shriber.
EIN: 222970929

40092
The Wally Foundation, Inc.
c/o Walter Feldesman
805 3rd Ave.
New York, NY 10022-7513

Financial data (yr. ended 12/31/01): Grants paid, $58; assets, $743 (M); expenditures, $479; qualifying distributions, $58.
Limitations: Giving primarily in NY.
Officer: Walter Feldesman, Mgr.
EIN: 136213520

40093
Julia M. Cullen Foundation
15 Knoerl Ave.
Buffalo, NY 14210-2329 (716) 822-7186
Contact: M. Jane Dickman, Tr.

Established in 2000 in NY.
Donor(s): Julia M. Cullen.
Financial data (yr. ended 12/31/01): Grants paid, $50; assets, $15,329 (M); gifts received, $5,050; expenditures, $50; qualifying distributions, $50.
Trustees: Julia M. Cullen, M. Jane Dickman.
EIN: 161595352

40094
Rosenblatt Foundation
3225 Lighthouse Rd.
Southold, NY 11971 (631) 765-1409
Contact: James Pritchard

Established in 2000 in NY.
Donor(s): Daniel Rosenblatt.
Financial data (yr. ended 12/31/01): Grants paid, $50; assets, $47,503 (M); expenditures, $1,122; qualifying distributions, $50.
Director: Daniel Rosenblatt.
EIN: 113465430

40095
Trenton Falls Association, Inc.
c/o Henry Miller
235 Dover Rd.
Barneveld, NY 13304-3103

Financial data (yr. ended 12/31/01): Grants paid, $50; assets, $1 (M); gifts received, $1,260; expenditures, $306; qualifying distributions, $50.
Officers: Robert E. Welch, Pres.; Henry F. Miller, Secy.-Treas.
EIN: 237339642

40096
Von Rydingsvard and Greengard Foundation
362 E. 69th St.
New York, NY 10021

Established in 1996 in NY.
Financial data (yr. ended 12/31/01): Grants paid, $50; assets, $1,256 (M); expenditures, $435; qualifying distributions, $50.
Officers and Directors:* Ursula Von Rydingsard,* Pres.; Paul Greengard,* Secy.-Treas.
EIN: 133915986

40097
Marty & Iris Walshin Foundation, Inc.
634 N. Broadway
Yonkers, NY 10701

Established in 1999 in NY.
Financial data (yr. ended 12/31/01): Grants paid, $50; assets, $830 (M); gifts received, $600; expenditures, $50; qualifying distributions, $50.
Officers and Directors:* Marty Walshin,* Pres.; Iris Walshin,* Secy.; Jared Viarengo, Jason Viarengo.
EIN: 134090925

40098
C. P. Ward Charitable Foundation, Inc.
100 River Rd.
P.O. Box 900
Scottsville, NY 14546-0900 (716) 889-8800
Contact: Richard A. Ash, Pres.

Donor(s): C.P. Ward, Inc.
Financial data (yr. ended 12/31/00): Grants paid, $50; assets, $0 (M); expenditures, $65; qualifying distributions, $65.
Limitations: Giving limited to the Rochester, NY, area.
Officer: Richard A. Ash, Pres.
EIN: 166098244
Codes: CS, CD

40099
Hugh James Ashford, D.C. Memorial Scholarship Fund, Inc.
54 W. Millpage Dr.
Bethpage, NY 11714-4818

Financial data (yr. ended 12/31/01): Grants paid, $44; assets, $19,882 (M); gifts received, $44; expenditures, $44; qualifying distributions, $44.
Limitations: Applications not accepted. Giving primarily in NY.
Officers: Hugh F. Ashford, D.C., Pres.; Dennis M. Ashford, D.C., V.P.; Nancy Ashford Cypser, Secy.-Treas.
Trustee: William Harrison.
EIN: 112605373

40100
COBH Heritage Foundation
c/o Charles D. Mooney
88 Pine St., 21st Fl.
New York, NY 10005

Financial data (yr. ended 12/31/01): Grants paid, $40; assets, $256 (M); expenditures, $445; qualifying distributions, $40.
Limitations: Applications not accepted.
Application information: Contributes only to pre-selected organizations.
Officers and Directors:* A. Brian West, M.D.,* V.P.; Charles D. Mooney, Secy.; John Arthur David Bird,* Treas.; Paul S. Quinn, Robert Anthony Rutledge.
EIN: 133711111

40101
Howard Kanovitz Foundation, Inc.
c/o Howard Kanovitz
361 N. Seamecox Rd.
Southampton, NY 11968

Established in 1996 in NY.
Financial data (yr. ended 12/31/01): Grants paid, $25; assets, $1,451 (L); gifts received, $2,000; expenditures, $574; qualifying distributions, $574.
Limitations: Applications not accepted.
Application information: Contributes only to pre-selected organizations.
Officer: Howard Kanovitz, Pres.
EIN: 133859430

40102
Harvey G. Cook Memorial Trust
c/o JPMorgan Chase Bank
P.O. Box 31412
Rochester, NY 14603-1412

Financial data (yr. ended 12/31/00): Grants paid, $18; assets, $998 (M); expenditures, $53; qualifying distributions, $49.
Limitations: Applications not accepted. Giving limited to Newark, NY.
Application information: Recipient selected by the supervisor of the music department at the Newark public high schools.
Trustee: JPMorgan Chase Bank.
EIN: 166097901

40103
The David S. and Karen M. Zahner Family Foundation
848 Dickens St.
Woodmere, NY 11598

Donor(s): David Zahner.
Financial data (yr. ended 12/31/01): Grants paid, $18; assets, $6,298 (M); gifts received, $105; expenditures, $123; qualifying distributions, $18.
Limitations: Applications not accepted.
Application information: Contributes only to pre-selected organizations.
Officers and Directors:* David Zahner,* Pres. and Treas.; Karen Zahner,* V.P. and Secy.; Stanley Zahner.
EIN: 113012840

40104
Doyle Foundation
c/o George Bresler
675 Third Ave.
New York, NY 10017

Established in 1966.
Financial data (yr. ended 12/31/00): Grants paid, $1; assets, $566,967 (M); expenditures, $7,553; qualifying distributions, $4,732.
Limitations: Applications not accepted. Giving primarily in New York, NY.
Application information: Contributes only to pre-selected organizations.
Officer and Directors:* David Zack,* Treas.; George Bresler, Michael Doyle, Marguerite Jossel.
EIN: 136216198

40105
The Achleitner Family Foundation
c/o Goldman Sachs & Co.
85 Broad St., Tax Dept.
New York, NY 10004

Established in 1996 in MA.
Donor(s): Paul M. Achleitner.
Financial data (yr. ended 06/30/01): Grants paid, $0; assets, $35,052 (M); expenditures, $155; qualifying distributions, $115.
Limitations: Applications not accepted.

Application information: Contributes only to pre-selected organizations.
Trustees: Ann-Kristin Achleitner, Paul M. Achleitner.
EIN: 133923031

40106
Acorn Foundation, Inc.
c/o CPI Associates, Inc.
32 E. 57th St., 14th Fl.
New York, NY 10022

Established in 2000 in DE.
Donor(s): George F. Merck.
Financial data (yr. ended 12/31/01): Grants paid, $0; assets, $1,428,558 (M); gifts received, $5,180; expenditures, $23,686; qualifying distributions, $0.
Officer: George F. Merck, Pres.
EIN: 223768896

40107
Ruth & Ernest Adler Foundation, Inc.
c/o Joel Isaacson & Co., Inc.
516 5th Ave.
New York, NY 10036

Financial data (yr. ended 05/31/02): Grants paid, $0; assets, $184 (M); expenditures, $0; qualifying distributions, $0.
Officer: Ernest Adler, Pres.
EIN: 136269984

40108
Aitken Brain Trauma Foundation, Inc.
(Formerly Brain Trauma Foundation, Inc.)
523 E. 72nd St., 7th Fl.
New York, NY 10021 (212) 772-0608
Contact: Peter C. Quinn, Exec. Dir.

Established in 1986 in NY.
Donor(s): Annie-Laurie Aitken Charitable Trust.
Financial data (yr. ended 06/30/99): Grants paid, $0; assets, $20,460 (M); gifts received, $50,420; expenditures, $93,094; qualifying distributions, $23,141; giving activities include $23,182 for programs.
Limitations: Giving primarily in NY.
Publications: Informational brochure (including application guidelines), financial statement.
Application information: Application form not required.
Officers: Ala Isham, Pres.; George Morris Gurley, V.P.; Ralph Heyward Isham, Treas.; Peter C. Quinn, Exec. Dir.
Directors: Henry B. Betts, M.D., Deeda Blair, Jam Ghajar.
EIN: 133349779

40109
All the Way Washington Heights, Inc.
c/o Four M Corp.
115 Stevens Ave.
Valhalla, NY 10595

Financial data (yr. ended 06/30/01): Grants paid, $0; assets, $17,636 (M); gifts received, $120,900; expenditures, $112,351; qualifying distributions, $112,351; giving activities include $112,351 for programs.
Limitations: Giving primarily in NY.
Officers: Dennis Mehiel, Chair.; Harvey L. Friedman, Secy.; Anna Marie Cotter, Treas.
EIN: 133976407

40110
Allen Family Foundation, Inc.
c/o Abbe G. Shapiro, Dechert, Price, & Rhoads
30 Rockefeller Plz., 23rd Fl.
New York, NY 10112

Established in 1998 in DE.

Donor(s): Leon Allen.
Financial data (yr. ended 12/31/01): Grants paid, $0; assets, $193,488 (M); gifts received, $5,867; expenditures, $5,867; qualifying distributions, $0.
Limitations: Applications not accepted.
Application information: Contributes only to pre-selected organizations.
Officers and Directors:* Leon Allen,* Pres.; Benjamin Allen,* V.P.; Zulay M. Teran,* V.P.; Michael Allen,* Secy.-Treas.
EIN: 134010777

40111
Amagil Foundation, Inc.
1365 Carroll St.
Brooklyn, NY 11213 (718) 953-1133
Contact: Mordechai Gil, Pres.

Established in 1983.
Donor(s): Mordechai Gil, Adele Gil.
Financial data (yr. ended 11/30/01): Grants paid, $0; assets, $921,348 (M); gifts received, $10,000; expenditures, $2,902; qualifying distributions, $888.
Limitations: Giving primarily in Brooklyn, NY.
Officers: Mordechai Gil, Pres.; David Freedman, V.P.; Menachem M. Freedman, V.P.; Moshe Freedman, Treas.; Adele Gil, Secy.
EIN: 112730864

40112
The American Compassion Foundation
100 Hilton Ave., Ste. 410E
Garden City, NY 11530

Established in 2001 in NY.
Donor(s): Gary Bencivenga, Pauline Bencivenga.
Financial data (yr. ended 12/31/01): Grants paid, $0; assets, $500,000 (M); gifts received, $500,000; expenditures, $0; qualifying distributions, $0.
Limitations: Applications not accepted.
Application information: Contributes only to pre-selected organizations.
Directors: Gary Bencivenga, Mary Bencivenga, Pauline Bencivenga.
EIN: 113626440

40113
American Friends of Foundation Stone Israel
c/o Gary Fuchs
9 Holland Ln.
Monsey, NY 10952

Established in 2000.
Financial data (yr. ended 04/30/01): Grants paid, $0; assets, $440 (M); gifts received, $1,940; expenditures, $1,500; qualifying distributions, $0.
Limitations: Applications not accepted.
Application information: Contributes only to pre-selected organizations.
Officer: Gary Fuchs, Pres.
EIN: 311727132

40114
American Philanthropic Foundation
666 3rd Ave., 29th Fl.
New York, NY 10017-4011

Incorporated in 1929 in IL.
Donor(s): Nina Rosenwald, William Rosenwald,‡ Alice R. Sigelman, Elizabeth R. Varet.
Financial data (yr. ended 12/31/00): Grants paid, $0; assets, $1,201,042 (M); expenditures, $6,073; qualifying distributions, $0.
Limitations: Applications not accepted. Giving primarily in New York, NY.
Application information: Contributes only to pre-selected organizations.

Officers and Directors:* David P. Steinmann, Pres. and Treas.; Nina Rosenwald,* V.P.; Alice R. Sigelman,* V.P.; Elizabeth R. Varet,* Secy.
EIN: 136088097

40115
American Society for the Florence Academy of Art, Inc.
c/o CT Corp. System
P.O. Box 613
Lawrence, NY 11559-0613

Donor(s): Leonard A. Kestenbaum.
Financial data (yr. ended 12/31/01): Grants paid, $0; assets, $19,395 (M); gifts received, $500; expenditures, $0; qualifying distributions, $0.
Limitations: Applications not accepted.
Application information: Contributes only to pre-selected organizations.
Officers and Directors:* Christopher J. Braden,* Chair.; Leonard A. Kestenbaum,* Pres.; Daniel Graves,* Secy.; Carl Vissen,* Treas.
EIN: 541652548

40116
American-Russian Law Institute, Inc.
250 W. 57th St., Ste. 916
New York, NY 10107

Established in 2001 in NY.
Financial data (yr. ended 12/31/01): Grants paid, $0; assets, $1,280 (M); gifts received, $2,000; expenditures, $720; qualifying distributions, $0.
Directors: Alexander Fishkin, Vladimir Peisikoy, Emanuel E. Zeltser.
EIN: 134158309

40117
Julia Dyckman Andrus Memorial, Inc.
1156 N. Broadway
Yonkers, NY 10701

Established in 1972.
Financial data (yr. ended 06/30/00): Grants paid, $0; assets, $45,780,099 (M); gifts received, $961,611; expenditures, $13,051,742; qualifying distributions, $12,081,312; giving activities include $11,024,382 for programs.
Limitations: Applications not accepted.
Application information: Contributes only to pre-selected organizations.
Officers and Directors:* Lawrence S.C. Griffith, Chair.; Gary O. Carman, Ph.D.,* Pres. and C.E.O.; Conrad Harris,* V.P.; Sharlyn Carter,* Secy.; A. Tappen Soper,* Treas.; John Allen, Caroline P. Andrus, Elizabeth Andrus, John E. Andrus III, Ann Bernstein, Joseph T. Butler, and 11 additional directors.
EIN: 132793295
Codes: TN

40118
Animal Rescue & Rehabilitation Foundation, Ltd.
6435 Wolf Run Rd.
Savona, NY 14879-9749

Financial data (yr. ended 06/30/02): Grants paid, $0; assets, $171,733 (M); gifts received, $880; expenditures, $18,355; qualifying distributions, $0.
Officers: Florence Cooke, Pres.; Lester Cooke, V.P.
EIN: 113075233

40119
Frances Patrick Anthony Foundation
317 Overlook Dr.
Syracuse, NY 13207

Established in 1999 in NY.
Donor(s): Lawrence T. Ryan, Mary T. Ryan.

Financial data (yr. ended 12/31/01): Grants paid, $0; assets, $210,989 (M); expenditures, $590; qualifying distributions, $0.
Directors: Lawrence T. Ryan, Margaret Ryan, Mary Kay Ryan.
EIN: 522214351

40120
Susan B. Anthony Neighborhood Association, Inc.
26 Madison St.
Rochester, NY 14608

Financial data (yr. ended 12/31/01): Grants paid, $0; assets, $1 (M); gifts received, $16,656; expenditures, $10,711; qualifying distributions, $0.
Limitations: Applications not accepted.
Application information: Contributes only to pre-selected organizations.
Officers: Daniel Hoffman, Pres.; Maria Manley, V.P.; Mary Ellen Burley, Secy.; Frank Miccoli, Treas.
EIN: 161213228

40121
Peter & Rosanne Aresty Foundation
c/o Alfred Dunner, Inc.
1411 Broadway
New York, NY 10018

Established in 2001 in NY.
Donor(s): Joseph Aresty.
Financial data (yr. ended 12/31/01): Grants paid, $0; assets, $2,022,906 (M); gifts received, $2,000,000; expenditures, $0; qualifying distributions, $0.
Limitations: Applications not accepted.
Application information: Contributes only to pre-selected organizations.
Trustees: Peter Aresty, Rosanne Aresty.
EIN: 316666451

40122
Steven & Sheila Aresty Foundation
c/o Alfred Dunner, Inc.
1411 Broadway
New York, NY 10018

Established in 2001 in NY.
Donor(s): Joseph Aresty.
Financial data (yr. ended 12/31/01): Grants paid, $0; assets, $2,020,160 (M); gifts received, $2,000,000; expenditures, $0; qualifying distributions, $0.
Limitations: Applications not accepted.
Application information: Contributes only to pre-selected organizations.
Trustees: Sheila Aresty, Steven Aresty.
EIN: 316666392

40123
Armstead-Johnson Foundation for Theater Research, Inc.
300 Garden City Plz., Ste. 326
Garden City, NY 11530

Donor(s): Helen A. Johnson.
Financial data (yr. ended 12/31/01): Grants paid, $0; assets, $35 (M); gifts received, $1,800; expenditures, $120; qualifying distributions, $0.
Limitations: Applications not accepted.
Officers: Helen A. Johnson, Pres.; Edward Manowitz, Treas.
EIN: 237362775

40124
Art Matters, Inc.
c/o Ellenbosen, Rubenstein, Eisdorfer
440 Park Ave. S.
New York, NY 10016 (212) 539-3120
Application address: 187 E. 4th St., Ste. 5N,
New York, NY 10009
Contact: Marianne Weems, Pres.

Established in 1985 in NY.
Donor(s): Laura Donnelley.
Financial data (yr. ended 12/31/00): Grants paid, $0; assets, $45,256 (M); gifts received, $40,000; expenditures, $21,372; qualifying distributions, $0.
Limitations: Giving limited to the U.S.
Publications: Application guidelines.
Officers: Marianne Weems, Pres.; Cee Brown, Exec. V.P.
Directors: Alexander Gray, Esther McGowan, Naomi Meyer, Bonnie Reese, Barbara Roush, Mark Uhl.
EIN: 133271577

40125
Rukmini Arundale Charitable Society, Inc.
c/o Sellon Mgmt. Corp.
P.O. Box 800
Purchase, NY 10577-0800

Established in 1990 in NY.
Donor(s): John B. Sellon, Theosophical Society in America.
Financial data (yr. ended 12/31/01): Grants paid, $0; assets, $6,150 (M); expenditures, $585; qualifying distributions, $0.
Limitations: Applications not accepted.
Application information: Contributes only to pre-selected organizations.
Officers and Directors:* Peter J. Sellon,* Pres.; Krishna Hoffman,* V.P.; C.T. Nachiappan,* Secy.; John Kunz,* Treas.
EIN: 133532571

40126
Ezra and Sharyn Ashkenazi Foundation, Inc.
1902 Ocean Pkwy.
Brooklyn, NY 11223
NJ tel.: (732) 574-9000
Contact: Ezra S. Ashkenazi, Pres.

Established in 1987 in NY.
Donor(s): Ezra S. Ashkenazi.
Financial data (yr. ended 12/31/01): Grants paid, $0; assets, $33 (M); expenditures, $0; qualifying distributions, $0.
Limitations: Giving primarily in NJ.
Application information: Application form not required.
Officers: Ezra S. Ashkenazi, Pres.; Saul E. Ashkenazi, V.P. and Treas.; Sharyn Ashkenazi, Secy.
EIN: 133410527

40127
Ast Foundation, Inc.
c/o Ellen Levy
622 Greenwich St., Ste. 4F
New York, NY 10014

Established in 2001 in NY.
Donor(s): David E. Levy, Ellen K. Levy.
Financial data (yr. ended 12/31/01): Grants paid, $0; assets, $10,167 (M); gifts received, $11,000; expenditures, $833; qualifying distributions, $0.
Directors: David E. Levy, Ellen K. Levy, Michele Ruiz.
EIN: 134170959

40128
R. R. Atkins Foundation
c/o Bisset & Atkins
330 Madison Ave.
New York, NY 10017

Donor(s): Ronald R. Atkins.
Financial data (yr. ended 12/31/01): Grants paid, $0; assets, $6,450 (M); expenditures, $161; qualifying distributions, $0.
Limitations: Applications not accepted. Giving primarily in New York, NY.
Application information: Contributes only to pre-selected organizations.
Trustees: Mary Elizabeth Atkins, Ronald R. Atkins.
EIN: 237012074

40129
Atlasta Foundation Corporation
P.O. Box 140
Chateaugay, NY 12920

Donor(s): Margaret F. Danes.
Financial data (yr. ended 06/30/01): Grants paid, $0; assets, $0 (L); gifts received, $11,959; expenditures, $11,136; qualifying distributions, $11,136; giving activities include $11,136 for programs.
Officers: Betty S. Danes, Pres.; Margaret F. Danes, Secy.-Treas.
EIN: 141675578

40130
Donald E. Axinn Foundation
131 Jericho Tpke.
Jericho, NY 11753 (516) 333-8500
Contact: Donald E. Axinn, Tr.

Established in 1999 in NY.
Donor(s): Donald E. Axinn.
Financial data (yr. ended 12/31/01): Grants paid, $0; assets, $141,705 (M); gifts received, $25,000; expenditures, $1,648; qualifying distributions, $0.
Limitations: Giving primarily in NY.
Trustees: Donald Axinn, Joan F. Axinn, Mark W. Hamer, Kenneth B. Katzman, Jean Kelly.
EIN: 237165425

40131
John J. Babines Trust
c/o HSBC Bank USA
1 Marine Midland Ctr., 17th Fl.
Buffalo, NY 14240

Financial data (yr. ended 06/30/99): Grants paid, $0; assets, $6,478 (M); expenditures, $42; qualifying distributions, $4.
Limitations: Applications not accepted.
Application information: Contributes only to pre-selected organizations.
Trustee: HSBC Bank USA.
EIN: 146107535

40132
Jessie H. Baker Educational Fund
1 HSBC Center, 16th Fl.
Buffalo, NY 14203

Established in 1984 in NY.
Financial data (yr. ended 08/31/01): Grants paid, $0; assets, $3,262,232 (M); expenditures, $58,115; qualifying distributions, $85,902; giving activities include $83,000 for loans to individuals.
Limitations: Applications not accepted. Giving limited to residents of Broome County, NY.
Application information: Distributes funds only to pre-selected individuals.
Trustee: HSBC Bank USA.
EIN: 222478098
Codes: GTI

40133
The Artur Balsam Foundation for Chamber Music
825 W. End Ave., Apt. 2C
New York, NY 10025-5349
Contact: Dan Berlinghoff, Exec. Dir.

Donor(s): Ruth Balsam.‡
Financial data (yr. ended 12/31/00): Grants paid, $0; assets, $712,948 (M); gifts received, $685,973; expenditures, $57,790; qualifying distributions, $0.
Limitations: Giving primarily in New York, NY.
Officer: Ruth Balsam, Pres.
Directors: Dan Berlinghoff, Exec. Dir.; Edmond Battersby, Diana Boyle, Gregory Frydman, William A. Monroe, Linda Rosdeitcher.
EIN: 133809561

40134
Band Foundation
c/o U.S. Trust
114 W. 47th St., TaxVas
New York, NY 10036

Established in 1999 in NY.
Donor(s): Burks B. Lapham, Evergreen II Trust.
Financial data (yr. ended 12/31/01): Grants paid, $0; assets, $1,764,693 (M); gifts received, $54,178; expenditures, $10,330; qualifying distributions, $0.
Limitations: Applications not accepted. Giving in the U.S. to national organizations.
Application information: Contributes only to pre-selected organizations.
Trustees: Anthony A. Lapham, Burks B. Lapham, David A. Lapham, Nicholas P. Lapham.
EIN: 137210814

40135
Bandrowski Family Foundation
1150 Underhill Rd.
East Aurora, NY 14052

Established in 2000 in NY.
Financial data (yr. ended 12/31/00): Grants paid, $0; assets, $918 (M); expenditures, $150; qualifying distributions, $0.
Officers: Paul J. Bandrowski, Pres.; Barbara J. Bandrowski, V.P.; Glenn T. Koszka, Treas.
EIN: 161589953

40136
Arnold & Corrine Barsky Foundation, Inc.
c/o Rosen Seymour Shapss Martin & Co.
757 3rd Ave.
New York, NY 10017-2013

Established in 1988 in NY.
Donor(s): Arnold Barsky, Corrine Barsky.
Financial data (yr. ended 12/31/01): Grants paid, $0; assets, $39,229 (M); expenditures, $0; qualifying distributions, $0.
Limitations: Applications not accepted. Giving primarily in New York, NY.
Application information: Contributes only to pre-selected organizations.
Officers and Directors:* Corrine Barsky,* Pres.; Robyn Barsky,* V.P. and Treas.
EIN: 112930153

40137
Bath Rotary Student Fund, Inc.
14 Pulteney Sq.
Bath, NY 14810
Contact: Michael Wheeler, Secy.-Treas.

Financial data (yr. ended 12/31/00): Grants paid, $0; assets, $132,939 (M); expenditures, $2,168; qualifying distributions, $2,168; giving activities include $2,168 for loans to individuals.

Limitations: Giving limited to residents of the greater Bath, NY, area.
Officers and Directors:* Richard McCandless,* Chair.; Michael Wheeler,* Secy.-Treas.; Robert H. Cole, Donald Debolt, Peter Robbins, Marion Tunney.
EIN: 161109902

40138
Bauer Family Charitable Foundation, Inc.
c/o Bauer
1624 Webster Ave.
Bronx, NY 10457

Established in 2001 in NY.
Financial data (yr. ended 12/31/01): Grants paid, $0; assets, $51,010 (M); gifts received, $51,000; expenditures, $0; qualifying distributions, $0.
Directors: Bernard Bauer, Irving Bauer, Katalin Bauer.
EIN: 134197710

40139
Be a Buddy Foundation, Inc.
c/o Jacmel Jewelry
30-00 47th Ave.
Long Island City, NY 11101

Established in 1997 in NY.
Financial data (yr. ended 12/31/00): Grants paid, $0; assets, $65,491 (M); expenditures, $402; qualifying distributions, $0.
Limitations: Giving primarily in NY.
Officers: Evan Berkley, Pres.; Julian Krinsky, V.P.; Tom Mililo, Secy.; Jack Rahmey, Treas.
EIN: 113372720

40140
The Edward and Janet Beckler Foundation
535 Stone Bridge Rd.
Pottersville, NY 12860

Established in 2000 in TX.
Donor(s): Natural Stone Bridge and Caves, Inc.
Financial data (yr. ended 12/31/01): Grants paid, $0; assets, $10,419 (M); gifts received, $4,836; expenditures, $745; qualifying distributions, $745.
Limitations: Applications not accepted.
Application information: Contributes only to pre-selected organizations.
Directors: Edward Beckler, Janet J. Beckler, Philip A. Beckler.
EIN: 760581103
Codes: CS, CD

40141
William R. Bedell Broken Wing Foundation
c/o Morse, Zelnick, Rose & Lander
450 Park Ave., Ste. 902
New York, NY 10022
Application address: 55 Winding Road Farm, Ardsley, NY 10502
Contact: Eileen Bedell, Chair.

Established in 2000 in NY.
Financial data (yr. ended 12/31/00): Grants paid, $0; assets, $35,712 (M); gifts received, $233,357; expenditures, $0; qualifying distributions, $0.
Officer: Eileen Bedell, Chair.
Trustees: Jennifer Paternostro, Kenneth Rose.
EIN: 134110314

40142
Herbert R. Behrens Foundation
c/o FJC
130 E. 59th St., 14th Fl.
New York, NY 10155-1302

Donor(s): Herbert R. Behrens.
Financial data (yr. ended 12/31/00): Grants paid, $0; assets, $0 (M); expenditures, $0; qualifying distributions, $0.

Limitations: Applications not accepted.
Application information: Contributes only to pre-selected organizations.
Trustee: Herbert R. Behrens.
EIN: 116036252

40143
The Hal H. Beretz Foundation, Inc.
c/o Hal H. Beretz
48 South Dr.
Great Neck, NY 11021

Established in 1985 in NY.
Donor(s): Hal H. Beretz.
Financial data (yr. ended 06/30/02): Grants paid, $0; assets, $17,681 (M); gifts received, $3,333; expenditures, $3,254; qualifying distributions, $0.
Limitations: Applications not accepted. Giving primarily in NY.
Application information: Contributes only to pre-selected organizations.
Officers: Hal H. Beretz, Pres.; Henry A. Katz, Treas.
EIN: 133315591

40144
Berkman Fund
P.O. Box 40
Bellmore, NY 11710 (516) 679-0320
Contact: Andrew S. Berkman, Mgr.

Donor(s): Ingraham Bedell Corp.
Financial data (yr. ended 11/30/99): Grants paid, $0; assets, $16,274 (M); expenditures, $249; qualifying distributions, $249.
Officer and Trustees:* Andrew S. Berkman,* Mgr.; Alice B. Berkman.
EIN: 116021845

40145
Joyce & Stanley M. Berman Foundation, Inc.
20 E. 47th St.
New York, NY 10021

Established in 2001 in NY.
Financial data (yr. ended 12/31/01): Grants paid, $0; assets, $97,152 (M); expenditures, $2,500; qualifying distributions, $0.
Limitations: Applications not accepted.
Application information: Contributes only to pre-selected organizations.
Directors: Joyce Berman, Stanley M. Berman, Scott Sosnik.
EIN: 134158916

40146
Harold P. Bernstein Foundation
25 Melville Park Rd.
Melville, NY 11747-3109

Established in 1986 in NY.
Donor(s): Harold P. Bernstein.
Financial data (yr. ended 11/30/01): Grants paid, $0; assets, $7,243 (M); expenditures, $80; qualifying distributions, $0.
Limitations: Applications not accepted.
Application information: Contributes only to pre-selected organizations.
Directors: Gene M. Bernstein, Harold P. Bernstein, Jay Bernstein.
EIN: 581716360

40147
Beta Delta Foundation, Inc.
c/o Sciorobba Walker & Co.
200 E. Buffalo St.
Ithaca, NY 14850-4258

Financial data (yr. ended 06/30/01): Grants paid, $0; assets, $92 (M); expenditures, $24; qualifying distributions, $0.
Limitations: Giving primarily in Ithaca, NY.

EIN: 222438758

40148
Bhooplapur Foundation, Inc.
26 Princeton Dr.
Syosset, NY 11791

Established in 1999 in NY.
Financial data (yr. ended 12/31/99): Grants paid, $0; assets, $500 (L); expenditures, $3,800; qualifying distributions, $0.
Limitations: Applications not accepted.
Officer: Ravishankar Bhooplapur, Mgr.
Directors: Jayashella Bhooplapur, Prabhuraj Bhooplapur, Iswar Govda Patil.
EIN: 113515568

40149
Bie Family Foundation
1 Wall St., Tax Dept., 28th Fl.
New York, NY 10286

Established in 2001 in NY.
Financial data (yr. ended 01/31/02): Grants paid, $0; assets, $2,063,815 (M); gifts received, $2,327,199; expenditures, $16,604; qualifying distributions, $5,642.
Trustee: The Bank of New York.
EIN: 137290614

40150
The Birks Works Foundation, Inc.
c/o Ganer, Grossbach & Ganer
1995 Broadway, 16th Fl.
New York, NY 10023
Contact: Mark D. Zuckerman, Dir.

Established in 2000 in NY.
Financial data (yr. ended 12/31/01): Grants paid, $0; assets, $49,853 (M); expenditures, $1,837; qualifying distributions, $0.
Directors: Lorraine Gillespie, Jerrold B. Gold, Harris B. Straytner, M.D., Mark D. Zuckerman.
EIN: 134098578

40151
Dr. Maxwell L. & Florence C. Blumenriech Foundation, Inc.
1520 Northern Blvd.
Manhasset, NY 11030-3006
Contact: Fred Colin, Dir.

Established in 1987 in NY.
Donor(s): Fred Colin, Stephen Colin.
Financial data (yr. ended 04/30/02): Grants paid, $0; assets, $205,148 (M); gifts received, $53,896; expenditures, $776; qualifying distributions, $0.
Limitations: Giving primarily in New York, NY.
Application information: Application form not required.
Directors: Fred Colin, Eva Colin Usdan.
EIN: 133432280

40152
The Book Family Foundation
68 Carlton Rd.
Monsey, NY 10952

Established in 1999 in NY.
Donor(s): Henry Book.
Financial data (yr. ended 02/28/00): Grants paid, $0; assets, $50,000 (L); gifts received, $50,000; expenditures, $0; qualifying distributions, $0.
Trustee: Henry Book.
EIN: 137179283

40153
Joseph Israel Bookstaber Foundation, Inc.
c/o Berlack, et al
120 W. 45th St.
New York, NY 10036

Established in 2000 in NY.
Donor(s): Richard Bookstaber.
Financial data (yr. ended 12/31/01): Grants paid, $0; assets, $6,880 (M); gifts received, $7,500; expenditures, $10,583; qualifying distributions, $0.
Officers and Directors:* Richard Bookstaber,* Pres. and Treas.; Janice Horowitz,* V.P. and Secy.; David Bookstaber,* V.P.; Kenneth R. Asher.
EIN: 311729939

40154
Boswick-Cambre Family Foundation
68 Jane St., Ste. 5W
New York, NY 10014

Established in 2000 in NY.
Donor(s): Sean M. Morgan, Gina Cambre.
Financial data (yr. ended 12/31/00): Grants paid, $0; assets, $250,000 (M); gifts received, $250,000; expenditures, $0; qualifying distributions, $0.
Officers: Sean Morgan Boswick, Pres.; Gina Cambre, V.P. and Secy.
EIN: 134140078

40155
The Thomas & Regina Bradley Foundation, Inc.
85-12 87th St.
Woodhaven, NY 11421

Established in 1997 in NY.
Donor(s): Thomas Bradley.
Financial data (yr. ended 09/30/01): Grants paid, $0; assets, $245,722 (M); expenditures, $505; qualifying distributions, $0.
Limitations: Applications not accepted.
Application information: Contributes only to pre-selected organizations.
Officers: Thomas Bradley, Pres. and Treas.; Regina Bradley, V.P. and Secy.; Richard Bradley, V.P.
EIN: 133986715

40156
Bridge of Allen Foundation
c/o News America, Inc.
1211 Ave. of the Americas, 28th Fl.
New York, NY 10036
Contact: Anna Mann, Tr.

Established in 2000 in NY.
Donor(s): Anna Mann.
Financial data (yr. ended 09/30/01): Grants paid, $0; assets, $1,042,501 (M); gifts received, $1,094,473; expenditures, $8,989; qualifying distributions, $0.
Trustee: Anna Mann.
EIN: 134148389

40157
The Ruby Bridges Foundation
c/o Salans Hertzfield
620 5th Ave.
New York, NY 10020-2457
Application address: 10931 Harrow Rd., New Orleans, LA 70129
Contact: Ruby Bridges Hall, Pres.

Established in 1999 in NY.
Financial data (yr. ended 12/31/01): Grants paid, $0; assets, $35,413 (M); gifts received, $3,434; expenditures, $26,547; qualifying distributions, $0.
Application information: Application form not required.

Officers and Directors:* Ruby Bridges Hall, Pres.; Christina Turcic,* Secy.; David B. Blanchard.
EIN: 134059131

40158
Bright Horizon Foundation
c/o Jim Ledley, Kleinberg, Kaplan, Wolff & Cohen, PC
551 5th Ave.
New York, NY 10176

Established in 2000 in DE and NY.
Donor(s): Louis Salkind.
Financial data (yr. ended 12/31/00): Grants paid, $0; assets, $2,400,000 (M); gifts received, $2,402,924; expenditures, $2,924; qualifying distributions, $0.
Limitations: Applications not accepted.
Application information: Contributes only to pre-selected organizations.
Director: Louis Salkind.
EIN: 134121003

40159
Broadway Walk of Stars Foundation, Inc.
c/o Arlene Dahl
150 E. 72nd St.
New York, NY 10021

Established in 1999 in NY.
Donor(s): Marylou Whitney.
Financial data (yr. ended 12/31/99): Grants paid, $0; assets, $9,994 (M); gifts received, $10,000; expenditures, $21; qualifying distributions, $0.
Limitations: Applications not accepted.
Application information: Contributes only to pre-selected organizations.
Officers: Arlene Dahl, Pres.; Diahn McGrath, Secy.-Treas.; Alvin Cooperman, Exec. Dir.
EIN: 133994346

40160
The Brookdale Foundation
126 E. 56th St., 10th Fl.
New York, NY 10022 (212) 308-7355
E-mail: BkdlFdn@aol.com; URL: http://www.ewol.com/brookdale

Incorporated in 1950 in NY.
Donor(s): Henry L. Schwartz,‡ and his brothers.
Financial data (yr. ended 06/30/01): Grants paid, $0; assets, $6,363,625 (M); expenditures, $295,889; qualifying distributions, $185,623.
Limitations: Applications not accepted. Giving on a national basis.
Publications: Program policy statement.
Application information: Contributes only to pre-selected organizations.
Officers and Directors:* Stephen L. Schwartz,* Pres.; Mary Ann Van Clief,* V.P.; Katherine Burns, Stanley Epstein, Arthur Norman Field, Lois Juliber, Jeanette Pereira, Roy J. Zuckerberg.
EIN: 136076863

40161
The Brown Simpson Foundation, Inc.
152 W. 57th St.
New York, NY 10019

Established in 1999 in NY.
Donor(s): Brown Simpson Asset Management, LLC.
Financial data (yr. ended 12/31/01): Grants paid, $0; assets, $0 (M); expenditures, $14,920; qualifying distributions, $0.
Limitations: Applications not accepted.
Application information: Contributes only to pre-selected organizations.
Officers: Matthew C. Brown, Pres.; Mitchell D. Kaye, V.P.; Evan J. Levine, V.P.; James R. Simpson, Secy.

EIN: 133956144
Codes: CS

40162
L. M. Brown Trust f/b/o Lois M. Brown Scholarship Fund
(also known as Lois M. Brown Scholarship Fund)
c/o M&T Bank
101 S. Salina St., 3rd Fl.
Syracuse, NY 13202
Application address: c/o Principal's Off., Lansingburgh High School, North Troy, NY 12182

Financial data (yr. ended 12/31/01): Grants paid, $0; assets, $81,116 (M); expenditures, $1,059; qualifying distributions, $0.
Limitations: Giving limited to the Troy, NY, area.
Application information: Application form not required.
Trustee: M & T Bank.
EIN: 146083274

40163
Buffalo Sports Enterprises Foundation
651 Delaware Ave.
Buffalo, NY 14202

Financial data (yr. ended 12/31/01): Grants paid, $0; assets, $1 (M); expenditures, $71; qualifying distributions, $0.
Officers: Randall Clark, Chair.; Neal Miller, Vice-Chair.; Lisa Driscoll, Secy.; Mark E. Hamister, Treas.
EIN: 161547088

40164
D. Burger Trust
c/o M&T Bank
1 M&T Plz., 8th Fl.
Buffalo, NY 14203

Established in 2000 in PA.
Financial data (yr. ended 12/31/00): Grants paid, $0; assets, $778,585 (M); gifts received, $759,844; expenditures, $7,848; qualifying distributions, $0.
Trustee: M & T Bank.
EIN: 256679680

40165
Tony and Rose Buscaglia Family Foundation
2497 W. River Rd.
Grand Island, NY 14072

Established in 2001 in NY.
Donor(s): Anthony B. Buscaglia, Rose F. Buscaglia.
Financial data (yr. ended 12/31/01): Grants paid, $0; assets, $23,173 (M); gifts received, $23,312; expenditures, $0; qualifying distributions, $0.
Limitations: Applications not accepted.
Application information: Contributes only to pre-selected organizations.
Trustees: Anthony B. Buscaglia, Rose F. Buscaglia.
EIN: 161598742

40166
Edward "Doc" Butler Family Foundation
12 Kingsview Ct.
Amherst, NY 14221

Established in 2000 in NY.
Financial data (yr. ended 02/28/01): Grants paid, $0; assets, $10 (M); gifts received, $10; expenditures, $0; qualifying distributions, $0.
Trustees: Christopher A. Butler, Edward J. Butler, Karen J. Butler.
EIN: 912151289

40167
The Cahnman Foundation, Inc.
c/o Berlack, Israels & Liberman
120 W. 45th St.
New York, NY 10036

Established in 1982 in NY.
Donor(s): Gisella L. Cahnman.
Financial data (yr. ended 12/31/01): Grants paid, $0; assets, $392,544 (M); gifts received, $15,000; expenditures, $3,795; qualifying distributions, $0.
Limitations: Giving primarily in New York, NY.
Officers and Directors:* Joseph Maier,* Pres.; Ira H. Jolles,* V.P. and Secy.; Bobye List, V.P. and Treas.
EIN: 139234308

40168
Calf Island Foundation
c/o Bear Stearns Co.
245 Park Ave.
New York, NY 10167
Contact: William Jennings, Jr., Pres.

Established in 1987.
Donor(s): William M. Jennings, Jr., Elizabeth B. Dater.
Financial data (yr. ended 01/31/02): Grants paid, $0; assets, $278,574 (M); gifts received, $2,580; expenditures, $2,580; qualifying distributions, $0.
Limitations: Applications not accepted. Giving limited to NY.
Application information: Contributes only to pre-selected organizations.
Officer and Trustees:* William Mitchell Jennings, Jr.,* Pres.; Elizabeth B. Dater.
EIN: 066304990

40169
Camp Deerpark, Inc.
P.O. Box 394
Westbrookville, NY 12785

Financial data (yr. ended 12/31/99): Grants paid, $0; assets, $27,147 (M); gifts received, $77,019; expenditures, $214,080; qualifying distributions, $0.
Officer: Lowell Jantzi, Chair.
Director: Kenton Bontrager.
EIN: 223096390

40170
Campbell Foundation
26 Beckett Way
Ithaca, NY 14850

Established in 1997 in NY.
Financial data (yr. ended 12/31/01): Grants paid, $0; assets, $7 (M); gifts received, $200; expenditures, $200; qualifying distributions, $0.
Limitations: Applications not accepted. Giving primarily in NY.
Application information: Contributes only to pre-selected organizations.
Officers: T. Collin Campbell, Pres.; T. Nelson Campbell, V.P.; Karen L. C. Campbell, Secy.-Treas.
EIN: 161500454

40171
Michael Canty Memorial Fund, Inc.
719 Hampton Ave.
Schenectady, NY 12309 (518) 346-7138
Contact: Edward Canty, Treas.

Established in 2001 in NY.
Financial data (yr. ended 12/31/01): Grants paid, $0; assets, $180,003 (M); gifts received, $175,823; expenditures, $50; qualifying distributions, $226.
Limitations: Giving limited to residents of Schenectedy, NY.

Officers: Kathryn Canty, Pres.; William Canty, V.P.; Edward Canty, Treas.
EIN: 141835423

40172
Isadore A. Caputo, M.D. Memorial Fund, Inc.
184-26 Cambridge Rd.
Jamaica, NY 11432

Established in 1990 in NY.
Financial data (yr. ended 12/31/01): Grants paid, $0; assets, $32,191 (M); expenditures, $521; qualifying distributions, $0.
Limitations: Applications not accepted.
Application information: Contributes only to a pre-selected organization.
Officer: Anita Caputo, Pres.
EIN: 113008068

40173
Carbonel Foundation
c/o White & Case
1155 Ave. of the Americas
New York, NY 10036
Application address: c/o Sheehan & Co., 230 Park Ave., Ste. 416, New York, NY 10169, tel.: (212) 962-4470

Established in 1979 in NY and DE.
Donor(s): Antonia K. Fondaras, Charlotte S. Wyman.
Financial data (yr. ended 12/31/01): Grants paid, $0; assets, $864,456 (M); expenditures, $9,159; qualifying distributions, $3,979.
Limitations: Giving primarily in San Francisco, CA.
Officers and Directors:* Antonia K. Fondaras,* Pres.; Joseph Goffman,* V.P.; Adisa Douglas,* Secy.; Daniela Levine,* Treas.
EIN: 133006358

40174
Caregivers, Inc.
6323 7th Ave.
Brooklyn, NY 11220

Established in 1998 in NY.
Financial data (yr. ended 12/31/99): Grants paid, $0; assets, $5,798,892 (M); expenditures, $23,650,278; qualifying distributions, $0; giving activities include $20,086,460 for programs.
Limitations: Applications not accepted.
Application information: Contributes only to pre-selected organizations.
Officer: Eli S. Feldman, C.E.O.
Directors: Harold Cohen, Paul Finkelstein, Philip Geller, Michael Gerber, Charles Reiss, Martin Simon, Steven Topal.
EIN: 112838163

40175
Carey Industries Charitable Foundation
c/o JPMorgan Chase Bank
P.O. Box 31412
Rochester, NY 14603-1412

Donor(s): Carey Industries, Inc.
Financial data (yr. ended 05/31/02): Grants paid, $0; assets, $2,544 (M); expenditures, $3; qualifying distributions, $0.
Limitations: Applications not accepted. Giving primarily in Danbury, CT.
Application information: Contributes only to a pre-selected organization.
Trustee: JPMorgan Chase Bank.
EIN: 066121564
Codes: CS, CD

40176
The P. J. & Palmina Casella Foundation
c/o Pinker & Lyons
P.O. Box 247
Vestal, NY 13851-0247

Donor(s): Palmina Casella.
Financial data (yr. ended 12/31/01): Grants paid, $0; assets, $340,862 (M); gifts received, $20,000; expenditures, $846; qualifying distributions, $0.
Limitations: Applications not accepted. Giving primarily in Binghamton, NY.
Application information: Contributes only to pre-selected organizations.
Trustees: Palmina Casella, Michael H. Zuckerman.
EIN: 237032083

40177
Cavallo Family Foundation
630 Russet Rd.
Valley Cottage, NY 10989-1623

Established in 2001 in NY.
Financial data (yr. ended 12/31/01): Grants paid, $0; assets, $46,849 (M); gifts received, $46,883; expenditures, $45; qualifying distributions, $15.
Limitations: Applications not accepted.
Application information: Contributes only to pre-selected organizations.
Trustees: James Cavallo, Joanna Cavallo, Susan C. Visgilio.
EIN: 134149268

40178
The Center for Educational Studies, Inc.
475 Riverside Dr., Ste. 448
New York, NY 10115-0088

Established in 1995.
Donor(s): John Templeton Foundation, William H. Donner Foundation, John M. Olin Foundation, Smith Richardson Foundation.
Financial data (yr. ended 12/31/01): Grants paid, $0; assets, $66,458 (M); gifts received, $110,500; expenditures, $98,802; qualifying distributions, $86,548; giving activities include $98,822 for programs.
Limitations: Giving primarily in NY.
Application information: Unsolicited request for funds not accepted.
Officers: Gilbert T. Sewall, Pres.; H. Brooks Smith, Treas.
Director: Constance Lowenthal.
EIN: 133526469

40179
Ohel Shaya Chabot Foundation, Inc.
107 Broadway, Ste. 1810
New York, NY 10018
Contact: A. Bert Chabot, Pres.

Donor(s): A. Bert Chabot.
Financial data (yr. ended 12/31/01): Grants paid, $0; assets, $9,251 (M); expenditures, $108; qualifying distributions, $0.
Limitations: Giving limited to Brooklyn, NY.
Officer: A. Bert Chabot, Pres.
EIN: 136155656

40180
Changing Lives Foundation, Inc.
(Formerly Sterling Foster Foundation, Inc.)
66 S. Tyson Ave.
Floral Park, NY 11001 (516) 328-3800
Contact: Adam Lieberman, Pres.

Established in 1995 in NY.
Donor(s): Sterling Foster & Co., Inc.
Financial data (yr. ended 12/31/00): Grants paid, $0; assets, $2,534 (M); expenditures, $140; qualifying distributions, $0.

Limitations: Giving primarily in NY.
Officer and Directors:* Adam Lieberman,* Pres.; David Lieberman, Robert Lieberman.
EIN: 113287519

40181
The Chanos Family Charitable Foundation
c/o James Chanos
153 E. 53rd St., 43rd Fl.
New York, NY 10022

Established in 1999 in NY.
Donor(s): James Chanos.
Financial data (yr. ended 11/30/01): Grants paid, $0; assets, $39,583 (M); gifts received, $3,020; expenditures, $3,706; qualifying distributions, $0.
Limitations: Applications not accepted.
Application information: Contributes only to pre-selected organizations.
Directors: William Brown, Amy Chanos, James Chanos.
EIN: 134037093

40182
The Charugundla Foundation, Inc
60 E. 56th St., 9th Fl.
New York, NY 10022

Established in 2001 in NY.
Donor(s): Kent S. Charugundla.
Financial data (yr. ended 12/31/01): Grants paid, $0; assets, $150,000 (M); gifts received, $150,000; expenditures, $0; qualifying distributions, $0.
Limitations: Applications not accepted.
Application information: Contributes only to pre-selected organizations.
Officer and Directors:* Kent S. Charugundla,* Pres.; John Charugundla, Marguerite K. Charugundla.
EIN: 134149673

40183
The CHEER Foundation, Inc.
(Formerly Children's Hospital Education & Entertainment Readings, Inc.)
c/o Howard Menkes
90-18 153rd Ave.
Howard Beach, NY 11414

Established in 1995 in NY.
Donor(s): National Endowment for the Arts, Pfizer Pharmaceutical, Philip Morris, Avin Bakai.
Financial data (yr. ended 09/30/01): Grants paid, $0; assets, $1,260 (M); gifts received, $146,666; expenditures, $29,937; qualifying distributions, $29,937; giving activities include $16,739 for programs.
Limitations: Applications not accepted.
Application information: Contributes only to pre-selected organizations.
Officers: Howard Menkes, Pres.; Leslie Bildner, V.P.
EIN: 113184295

40184
The Chen-Josephson Foundation
40 W. 57th St., 16th Fl.
New York, NY 10019 (212) 556-5781

Established in 1991 in DE.
Donor(s): Marvin Josephson, Tina Chen-Josephson.
Financial data (yr. ended 12/31/01): Grants paid, $0; assets, $447 (M); expenditures, $210; qualifying distributions, $0.
Limitations: Applications not accepted.
Application information: Contributes only to pre-selected organizations.

Officers and Directors:* Tina Chen-Josephson,* Pres. and Secy.; Marvin Josephson,* Treas.; Yiling Chen-Josephson.
EIN: 133569004

40185
Chesed Ahavah Foundation
207 Harbor View South
Lawrence, NY 11559

Established in 2000 in NY.
Donor(s): Marc Preston.
Financial data (yr. ended 12/31/00): Grants paid, $0; assets, $275,000 (M); gifts received, $275,000; expenditures, $0; qualifying distributions, $0.
Limitations: Applications not accepted.
Application information: Contributes only to pre-selected organizations.
Officer: Marc Preston.
EIN: 113578475

40186
Chen Chi Foundation, Inc.
c/o Chen Chi
15 Gramercy Park
New York, NY 10003 (212) 473-7915

Donor(s): Chen Chi.
Financial data (yr. ended 11/30/01): Grants paid, $0; assets, $122,213 (M); expenditures, $1,978; qualifying distributions, $0.
Limitations: Applications not accepted. Giving on an international basis, with emphasis on Shanghai, China.
Application information: Contributes only to pre-selected organizations.
Officer: Chen Chi, Pres.
Director: Bradford Kelleher.
EIN: 133324068

40187
The Children's A.I.R. Foundation
101 W. 55th St.
New York, NY 10019

Established in 1999 in NY.
Donor(s): Helen Marx.‡
Financial data (yr. ended 12/31/99): Grants paid, $0; assets, $83,423 (M); gifts received, $89,625; expenditures, $1,894; qualifying distributions, $1,894.
Limitations: Applications not accepted.
Application information: Contributes only to pre-selected organizations.
Officers: Laurie Zucker Lederman, Pres.; Erin Escobar, V.P.; Herbert Schinderman, V.P.; Rick Albert, Secy.; Cynthia Marks, Treas.
EIN: 134045167

40188
Children's Development and Education Foundation
P.O. Box 498
Mount Kisco, NY 10549

Established in 1998 in NY.
Donor(s): Thomas J. Hilfiger.
Financial data (yr. ended 06/30/01): Grants paid, $0; assets, $89,832 (M); gifts received, $1,065; expenditures, $23,109; qualifying distributions, $10,725; giving activities include $10,746 for programs.
Limitations: Applications not accepted.
Application information: Contributes only to pre-selected organizations.
Officers: Susan Hilfiger, V.P.; Joan Lamport, Secy.-Treas.; Lydia H. Soifer, Ph.D., Exec. Dir.
Board Members: Herbert J. Cohen, M.D., Ruth Kaminer, M.D., Judith T. Moskowitz, Ph.D., Maris Rosenberg, M.D., Joann Toledano, M.D.

EIN: 134016985

40189
Nanny Chisholm/Winthrop Family Charitable Trust
c/o Owen J. Flanagan & Co.
60 E. 42nd St., Ste. 1536
New York, NY 10165

Established in 1991 in MA.
Donor(s): Euphemia Chisholm,‡ Iris Freeman, Angela Winthrop, Robert Winthrop, Grant Winthrop, Frederic Winthrop, Jonathan Winthrop.
Financial data (yr. ended 12/31/01): Grants paid, $0; assets, $380,968 (M); expenditures, $6,889; qualifying distributions, $0.
Limitations: Applications not accepted. Giving primarily in MA.
Application information: Contributes only to pre-selected organizations.
Trustees: Jonathan Winthrop, Robert Winthrop II.
EIN: 046673178

40190
The Robert J. & Susan L. Chrenc Family Foundation
18 Harbor Point Dr.
Northport, NY 11768

Established in 2001.
Donor(s): Robert J. Chrenc, Susan L. Chrenc.
Financial data (yr. ended 12/31/01): Grants paid, $0; assets, $395,436 (M); gifts received, $397,285; expenditures, $124; qualifying distributions, $0.
Trustees: Robert J. Chrenc, Susan L. Chrenc.
EIN: 100001595

40191
The Clair Family Foundation
(Formerly Sherry and Jerry Clair Foundation)
c/o Sherman Lawrence
1350 Ave. of Americas, 26th Fl.
New York, NY 10019

Donor(s): Venus Trimming & Binding, Venus Pleating Corp., Jerome Clair.
Financial data (yr. ended 10/31/01): Grants paid, $0; assets, $8,375 (M); expenditures, $81; qualifying distributions, $0.
Limitations: Applications not accepted. Giving primarily in Garden City, NY.
Application information: Contributes only to pre-selected organizations.
Officers and Directors:* Jerome Clair,* Pres.; Sherman Lawrence,* Secy.
EIN: 112512608

40192
Clinton-Henry Housing Development Fund Corp.
c/o Peoples Mutual Housing
209 E. 3rd St.
New York, NY 10009-7524

Established in 1996.
Financial data (yr. ended 12/31/00): Grants paid, $0; assets, $420,241 (M); expenditures, $73,932; qualifying distributions, $73,932; giving activities include $73,932 for programs.
Officers: Herman Hewitt, Pres.; Mana Perez, Secy.; Idaka Chavous, Treas.
Board Member: Alice Arnold.
EIN: 133619108

40193
Donald H. Cloudsley Foundation
1100 Liberty Blvd.
Buffalo, NY 14202-4405 (716) 856-9090
Contact: Patrick E. Martin, Tr.

Established in 1995.

40193—NEW YORK

Donor(s): Donald H. Cloudsley.
Financial data (yr. ended 12/31/01): Grants paid, $0; assets, $7,298 (M); expenditures, $7; qualifying distributions, $7.
Application information: Application form not required.
Trustee: Patrick E. Martin.
EIN: 166428422

40194
John E. Codina Foundation, Inc.
c/o Pavia & Hartcourt
600 Madison Ave., 12th Fl.
New York, NY 10022-1681

Donor(s): Rose O. Codina.
Financial data (yr. ended 12/31/01): Grants paid, $0; assets, $12,169 (M); expenditures, $5,953; qualifying distributions, $0.
Limitations: Applications not accepted.
Application information: Contributes only to pre-selected organizations.
Directors: Rose O. Codina, Mario Gazzola.
EIN: 133916623

40195
Abe M. Cohen Family Foundation, Inc.
c/o The Conway Organization
1333 Broadway, 3rd Fl.
New York, NY 10018
Contact: Abe M. Cohen, Pres.

Established in 1990.
Donor(s): The Conway Org.
Financial data (yr. ended 12/31/99): Grants paid, $0; assets, $16,649 (M); expenditures, $0; qualifying distributions, $0.
Application information: Application form not required.
Officers: Abe M. Cohen, Pres.; Morris Cohen, V.P.; Richard Cohen, Secy.; Jeffrey Cohen, Treas.
EIN: 112996463

40196
Richard L. Cohen Family Foundation
2233 Broadhollow Rd.
Farmingdale, NY 11735-1010

Established in 2000 in NY.
Financial data (yr. ended 12/31/00): Grants paid, $0; assets, $121,573 (M); gifts received, $125,000; expenditures, $9; qualifying distributions, $0.
Trustees: Cristina D. Cohen, Donna L. Cohen, Richard L. Cohen, Stephen M. Cohen, Inge A. Kowal, Jill S. Kornman.
EIN: 113573795

40197
Cohn & Tubetex Foundation, Inc.
c/o Cohn
150 E. 69th St., No. 14J
New York, NY 10021

Financial data (yr. ended 03/31/01): Grants paid, $0; assets, $660 (M); expenditures, $42; qualifying distributions, $0.
Limitations: Giving primarily in New York, NY.
Officers: Mae Cohn, Pres.; Lawrence B. Gutner, V.P.
EIN: 136028132

40198
The Frederick S. and Dorothy S. Coleman Foundation, Inc.
c/o Brown Rudnick
120 W. 45th St.
New York, NY 10036

Established in 2001 in NY.
Donor(s): Dorothy S. Coleman, Frederick S. Coleman.‡

Financial data (yr. ended 12/31/01): Grants paid, $0; assets, $1,251,619 (M); gifts received, $1,257,200; expenditures, $600; qualifying distributions, $0.
Limitations: Applications not accepted.
Application information: Contributes only to pre-selected organizations.
Officers: Dorothy S. Coleman, Pres.; Steven F. Wasserman, V.P.; Kenneth R. Asher, Secy.
EIN: 311781304

40199
The Paul Rykoff Coleman Foundation, Inc.
c/o Mark Burdett
26 Grove St., Ste. 2A
New York, NY 10014

Established in 1997 in NY.
Donor(s): Paul Coleman.‡
Financial data (yr. ended 06/30/01): Grants paid, $0; assets, $382,604 (M); expenditures, $2,645; qualifying distributions, $0.
Limitations: Applications not accepted.
Application information: Contributes only to pre-selected organizations.
Directors: Jeffrey Mark Burdett, Eric R. Coleman, Robin Murphy, Wendy Coleman Wood.
EIN: 133726090

40200
Coleman Student Fund, Inc.
P.O. Box 284
Trumansburg, NY 14886-0284

Financial data (yr. ended 07/31/01): Grants paid, $0; assets, $187,683 (M); gifts received, $8; expenditures, $377; qualifying distributions, $16,500; giving activities include $18,400 for loans to individuals.
Limitations: Giving limited to residents of Trumansburg, NY.
Application information: Application form required.
Officers: Lester Burns, Pres.; Rene Carver, Secy.-Treas.
Trustees: John Delaney, John Furey.
EIN: 222387137
Codes: GTI

40201
Community Action of Greene County, Inc.
2 Franklin St.
Catskill, NY 12414

Financial data (yr. ended 03/31/99): Grants paid, $0; assets, $1,475,779 (L); gifts received, $2,304,567; expenditures, $2,347,703; giving activities include $2,038,508 for programs.
Limitations: Giving primarily in Greene County, NY.
Board Members: Joseph Donohue, Guy Loughran, Kathy Myers, William Reich, Donna Rummo-Faulkner, Robert C. Schrock, Donald Spitz, Joanne Tuosto, Tom Yandeau.
EIN: 141498767
Codes: CM

40202
Community Workshop Scholarship & Aid Fund
c/o JPMorgan Chase Bank
P.O. Box 31412
Rochester, NY 14603-1412
Application address: c/o William Gusky, Chair., Scholarship Comm., Community Workshop, Inc., Sherman Medical, Waterbury, CT 06708

Financial data (yr. ended 01/31/02): Grants paid, $0; assets, $37,539 (M); expenditures, $989; qualifying distributions, $0.
Limitations: Giving limited to residents of CT.

Application information: Application form required.
Trustee: JPMorgan Chase Bank.
EIN: 066098834

40203
The Merrie Contillo Memorial Foundation
550 Brush Ave.
Bronx, NY 10465

Established in 2000 in NY.
Donor(s): Michael Contillo.
Financial data (yr. ended 04/30/02): Grants paid, $0; assets, $5,571 (M); expenditures, $105; qualifying distributions, $0.
Directors: Danielle Contillo, Micheal Contillo, Joseph Deglomini.
EIN: 134133269

40204
Coral Reef Foundation
745 5th Ave., Ste. 1210
New York, NY 10151

Established in 1978 in TX.
Donor(s): Jayne L. Wrightsman, Charles B. Wrightsman.‡
Financial data (yr. ended 12/31/01): Grants paid, $0; assets, $129,042 (M); expenditures, $2,524; qualifying distributions, $1,399.
Limitations: Applications not accepted. Giving primarily in New York, NY.
Application information: Contributes only to pre-selected organizations.
Officers and Directors:* Jayne L. Wrightsman,* Pres.; James F. Dolan,* Secy.-Treas.
EIN: 741969035

40205
The Joseph and Robert Cornell Memorial Foundation
c/o American Express, TBS
1185 Ave. of the Americas
New York, NY 10036-2602

Donor(s): Joseph Cornell.‡
Financial data (yr. ended 12/31/01): Grants paid, $0; assets, $67,158,779 (M); expenditures, $479,584; qualifying distributions, $0.
Limitations: Applications not accepted. Giving primarily in Washington, DC, and Annapolis, MD.
Application information: Contributes only to pre-selected organizations.
Trustees: Richard M. Ader, Donald Windham.
EIN: 133097502

40206
Corporate Angel Network, Inc.
(Formerly Chain Foundation, Inc.)
Westchester County Airport, Bldg. 1
White Plains, NY 10604-1206

Established in 1962 in NY.
Financial data (yr. ended 12/31/00): Grants paid, $0; assets, $632,937 (M); gifts received, $258,497; expenditures, $248,511; qualifying distributions, $234,542; giving activities include $234,542 for programs.
Limitations: Applications not accepted.
Publications: Financial statement, program policy statement.
Application information: Contributes only to pre-selected organizations.
Officers and Directors:* Richard A. Sporn,* Secy.; Arthur E. Ludwig, Jr., Treas.; Thomas Robertazzi, Exec. Dir.; Leonard M. Greene, Randall A. Greene, David C. Hurley, Wilson S. Leach.
EIN: 136143014

40207
The William J. and Dorothy H. Cox Foundation, Inc.
c/o William L. Tatro
2084 Hydesville Rd.
Newark, NY 14513-9729   (716) 218-9860

Established in 1989 in NY.
Donor(s): William J. Cox.
Financial data (yr. ended 12/31/99): Grants paid, $0; assets, $230,044 (M); expenditures, $1,823; qualifying distributions, $1,823.
Limitations: Applications not accepted. Giving limited to western NY.
Application information: Recipients are nominated by school principal.
Officer and Directors:* William L. Tatro,* V.P.; James Fantigrossi.
EIN: 161353302

40208
The Creative Process Fund, Inc.
c/o Graphic Solutions
424 W. 33rd St.
New York, NY 10001

Established in 1996 in NY.
Financial data (yr. ended 09/30/01): Grants paid, $0; assets, $13,198 (M); expenditures, $157; qualifying distributions, $0.
Limitations: Applications not accepted.
Application information: Contributes only to pre-selected organizations.
Officers and Directors:* Russell Patrick,* Pres.; Francine Stefanelli,* Secy.; Jeff Sander.
EIN: 133920548

40209
Cull Martin Foundation
c/o A. Jeffrey Cull
3365 Laurie Brook Dr.
Binghamton, NY 13903-3153

Established in 2001 in NY.
Financial data (yr. ended 12/31/01): Grants paid, $0; assets, $100 (M); gifts received, $100; expenditures, $0; qualifying distributions, $0.
Trustees: Jeffrey Cull, Marilyn Cull.
EIN: 161609981

40210
Anne Kathleen Cullen Foundation
66 Milton Rd., Apt. J11
Rye, NY 10580-3847
Contact: Nancy Hackett, Mgr.

Financial data (yr. ended 12/31/01): Grants paid, $0; assets, $250,942 (M); expenditures, $2,298; qualifying distributions, $0.
Officer: Nancy Hackett, Mgr.
EIN: 136167124

40211
Cunningham Education Memorial Fund
c/o JPMorgan Chase Bank
P.O. Box 31412
Rochester, NY 14603-1412

Financial data (yr. ended 12/31/00): Grants paid, $0; assets, $182,794 (M); expenditures, $1,912; qualifying distributions, $255.
Limitations: Applications not accepted. Giving limited to Newark, NY.
Trustee: JPMorgan Chase Bank.
EIN: 166015102

40212
The Bevan Daddino Foundation
c/o CSAM
466 Lexington Ave., 17th Fl.
New York, NY 10017
Contact: Anthony F. Daddino, Dist. Comm. Member

Established in 1995 in NY.
Donor(s): Anthony F. Daddino.
Financial data (yr. ended 12/31/01): Grants paid, $0; assets, $769,935 (M); gifts received, $311,255; expenditures, $2,915; qualifying distributions, $100.
Limitations: Giving primarily in New York, NY.
Application information: Application form not required.
Distribution Committee: Susan J. Bevan, Anthony F. Daddino.
Trustee: Winthrop Trust Co.
EIN: 137080449

40213
Dalet Foundation, Inc.
18 W. 70th St.
New York, NY 10023   (212) 874-0207
Contact: Judah L. Guedalia, Pres.

Financial data (yr. ended 12/31/01): Grants paid, $0; assets, $6,406 (M); expenditures, $82; qualifying distributions, $0.
Limitations: Giving primarily in NY.
Officers: Judah Leon Guedalia, Pres.; Selma Guedalia, Secy.; Harris Guedalia, Treas.
EIN: 133381297

40214
Dancing Tides Foundation, Inc.
c/o Frankel Loughran Starr & Vallone
404 Park Ave. S., 6th Fl.
New York, NY 10016

Established in 2001 in NJ.
Donor(s): Peter Muller.
Financial data (yr. ended 12/31/01): Grants paid, $0; assets, $3,761,314 (M); gifts received, $5,000; expenditures, $0; qualifying distributions, $0.
Limitations: Applications not accepted.
Application information: Contributes only to pre-selected organizations.
Trustees: Nathan E. Arnell, Peter Muller, Seth Starr.
EIN: 010553351

40215
The Dar-Ul-Tabligh Foundation
790 Summa Ave.
Westbury, NY 11590

Established in 1999 in NY.
Financial data (yr. ended 12/31/99): Grants paid, $0; assets, $11,642 (M); gifts received, $21,720; expenditures, $11,106; qualifying distributions, $8,986.
Trustees: Sadique M. Jaffer, Hasnain Walji.
EIN: 113503794

40216
John H. Darby Memorial Trust
c/o Gibson, Mcaskill & Crosby, LLP
69 Delaware Ave., Ste. 900
Buffalo, NY 14202-3866
Contact: Roger B. Simon, Tr.

Established in 1986 in NY.
Donor(s): Betty C. Darby, Fred W. Darby.
Financial data (yr. ended 11/30/01): Grants paid, $0; assets, $133,414 (M); expenditures, $1,329; qualifying distributions, $0.
Application information: Application form not required.
Trustees: Betty C. Darby, Fred W. Darby, Roger B. Simon.
EIN: 166293985

40217
The David Family Foundation, Inc.
c/o Jack David
210 W. 90th St.
New York, NY 10024

Established in 1999 in NY.
Financial data (yr. ended 12/31/01): Grants paid, $0; assets, $139,000 (M); expenditures, $1,785; qualifying distributions, $0.
Limitations: Applications not accepted.
Application information: Contributes only to pre-selected organizations.
Officers and Directors:* Jack David,* Pres. and Treas.; Melanie M. Kirkpatrick David,* V.P.; Nicole David Channing.
EIN: 134088264

40218
Leland Deane Foundation
c/o Perelson, Weiner, LLP
1 Dag Hammarskjold Plz., 42nd Fl.
New York, NY 10017

Established in 1998 in NY.
Donor(s): Leland M. Deane.
Financial data (yr. ended 05/31/02): Grants paid, $0; assets, $1 (M); expenditures, $80; qualifying distributions, $0.
Limitations: Applications not accepted.
Application information: Contributes only to pre-selected organizations.
Trustee: Leland M. Deane.
EIN: 137160165

40219
Dorothy Dehner Foundation for the Visual Arts
61 Broadway, 18th Fl.
New York, NY 10006-2794
Application address: 220 Madison Ave., New York, NY 10016, tel.: (212) 889-2315
Contact: Joan Marter, Pres.

Established in 1995 in NY.
Donor(s): Dorothy Mann Dehner.‡
Financial data (yr. ended 12/31/01): Grants paid, $0; assets, $1,694,109 (M); expenditures, $20,993; qualifying distributions, $0.
Limitations: Giving primarily in NY.
Officer and Directors:* Joan Marter,* Pres.; Ann Gibson, Sandra Lerner, David Levy, Martica Sawin, Melanie Thernstorm.
EIN: 133830526

40220
The Dennelisse Corporation
250 W. 57th St., Ste. 926
New York, NY 10107

Established in 1987.
Donor(s): City of NY-Human Resources Admin. for Homemaker Program, Medical Health & Research Assoc. for Case Mgmt. Program, Medicaid Mgmt. Information System for Case Mgmt. Program.
Financial data (yr. ended 06/30/01): Grants paid, $0; assets, $2,265,632 (M); gifts received, $7,425,067; expenditures, $7,676,823; qualifying distributions, $0; giving activities include $6,704,882 for programs.
Officers: Alston Gilliard, Pres.; Roberto Lewis, V.P.; Wilfredo Fernandez, Secy.; Facundo Pomar, Treas.; Luis Pons, Exec. Dir.
Directors: Lissette Fuentes, Casey McArdie, Paulette Racine.
EIN: 133224954

40221
Department of Radiology/Special Education Foundation
c/o E. Stephen Amis, Montefiore Hospital
111 E. 210th St.
Bronx, NY 10467

Established in 1989 in NY.
Financial data (yr. ended 12/31/01): Grants paid, $0; assets, $412,696 (M); expenditures, $29,957; qualifying distributions, $0.
Limitations: Applications not accepted.
Application information: Contributes only to pre-selected organizations.
Trustees: E. Stephen Amis, Milton Elkins, M.D., Melvin Zelefsky.
EIN: 237408432

40222
The Disosway Foundation
942 Old Liverpool Rd.
Liverpool, NY 13088

Established in 1999 in NY.
Financial data (yr. ended 12/31/01): Grants paid, $0; assets, $389,342 (M); expenditures, $2,938; qualifying distributions, $0.
Limitations: Applications not accepted.
Application information: Contributes only to pre-selected organizations.
Trustees: Jennifer J. Eddy, Dudley D. Johnson, Thomas E. Kruger.
EIN: 137198350

40223
The T. F. Dixon Family Foundation, Inc.
c/o Brown Brothers Harriman Trust Co. LLP
63 Wall St.
New York, NY 10005 (212) 493-8182
Contact: William F. Hibberd, Secy.

Established in 2000 in NY.
Donor(s): Thomas F. Dixon.
Financial data (yr. ended 12/31/00): Grants paid, $0; assets, $2,111,919 (M); gifts received, $268,198; expenditures, $47,674; qualifying distributions, $8,008.
Limitations: Applications not accepted.
Application information: Contributes only to pre-selected organizations.
Officers and Directors:* Thomas F. Dixon,* Pres.; Adam H. Dixon,* V.P.; Hillary A. Dixon,* V.P.; Linda F. Dixon,* V.P.; William F. Hibberd, Secy.; Anna T. Korniczky, Treas.
EIN: 134118192

40224
DJB Foundation
5042 Theall Rd.
Rye, NY 10580-1445

Established in 1960 in NY.
Donor(s): Carol B. Ferry.
Financial data (yr. ended 12/31/00): Grants paid, $0; assets, $3,877 (M); expenditures, $28; qualifying distributions, $25.
Limitations: Applications not accepted. Giving limited to Washington, DC, MA and New York, NY.
Application information: Contributes only to pre-selected organizations.
Officers: Carol B. Ferry, Pres.; Vincent F. McGee, V.P.; Stephen R. Abrams, Secy.-Treas.
EIN: 136105885

40225
The Katherine and Peter Dolan Family Foundation
c/o The Bank of New York- Tax Dept.
1 Wall St., 28th Fl.
New York, NY 10286

Established in 2001 in NY.
Donor(s): Peter R. Dolan, Katherine E. Dolan.
Financial data (yr. ended 12/31/01): Grants paid, $0; assets, $708,783 (M); gifts received, $719,105; expenditures, $0; qualifying distributions, $0.
Limitations: Applications not accepted.
Application information: Contributes only to pre-selected organizations.
Trustees: Katherine E. Dolan, Peter R. Dolan.
EIN: 470846774

40226
E. John Dolan Foundation
c/o Stella M. Dion
333 Bronx River Rd., Apt. 616
Yonkers, NY 10704

Donor(s): E. John Dolan, M.D.‡
Financial data (yr. ended 12/31/99): Grants paid, $0; assets, $545,062 (M); expenditures, $1,589; qualifying distributions, $0.
Limitations: Applications not accepted. Giving limited to Yonkers, NY.
Trustees: Elizabeth K. Blanchfield, Stella M. Dion.
EIN: 136271587

40227
Dollee Charitable Foundation Trust
P.O. Box 609
Manlius, NY 13104-0609
Contact: Marlene Costanzo Denney, Tr.

Established in 2000 in NY.
Donor(s): Marlene Costanzo Denney.
Financial data (yr. ended 12/31/00): Grants paid, $0; assets, $23,016 (M); gifts received, $23,000; expenditures, $0; qualifying distributions, $0.
Trustees: Lee Marie Denney, Marlene Costanzo Denney.
EIN: 161588072

40228
Henry Doneger Charitable Foundation
463 7th Ave.
New York, NY 10018

Established in 1996 in NY.
Donor(s): Henry Doneger Assoc., Inc.
Financial data (yr. ended 12/31/01): Grants paid, $0; assets, $5,575 (M); expenditures, $25; qualifying distributions, $0.
Trustee: Abraham L. Doneger.
EIN: 133866434

40229
The Patrice and Jack Dweck Family Foundation
(Formerly The Jack and Shari Dweck Family Foundation)
c/o Kamerman & Soniker, PC
885 2nd Ave.
New York, NY 10017

Established in 1992 in NY.
Donor(s): Jack Dweck, Patrice Dweck.
Financial data (yr. ended 12/31/01): Grants paid, $0; assets, $1,087 (M); gifts received, $77; expenditures, $0; qualifying distributions, $0.
Limitations: Applications not accepted. Giving limited to the metropolitan New York, NY, area.
Application information: Contributes only to pre-selected organizations.
Trustees: Jack Dweck, Patrice Dweck.
EIN: 136999773

40230
Ecovillage at Ithaca, Inc.
c/o Anabel Taylor Hall
Cornell Univ.
Ithaca, NY 14853

Established in 1996 in NY.
Financial data (yr. ended 06/30/01): Grants paid, $0; assets, $432,768 (M); gifts received, $20,800; expenditures, $16,592; qualifying distributions, $0.
Officers: John Schroeder, Chair.; Barry Adams, Secy.
Directors: Gil Gillespie, Pam Mackesey, Joe Nolan, Liz Walker, and 5 additional directors.
EIN: 161414876

40231
Bilquis Edhi Relief Foundation, Inc.
45-11 National St.
Corona, NY 11368

Established in 1998.
Financial data (yr. ended 12/31/01): Grants paid, $0; assets, $4,886,115 (M); gifts received, $1,136,918; expenditures, $719,046; qualifying distributions, $0; giving activities include $523,930 for programs.
Application information: Application form required.
Officers: Bilquis Edhi, Pres.; Abdul S. Edhi, V.P.; Qutub Edhi, Secy.
EIN: 113454067

40232
Educational Fund of the Rochester New York Branch of the American Association of University Women
494 East Ave.
Rochester, NY 14607-1911 (716) 244-8890
Contact: Jean Cleminson, Treas.

Financial data (yr. ended 06/30/01): Grants paid, $0; assets, $105,830 (M); gifts received, $181,500; expenditures, $405; qualifying distributions, $9,473; giving activities include $9,500 for loans to individuals.
Limitations: Giving limited to residents of Monroe County, NY.
Application information: Interviews and a loan guarantor required. Application form required.
Officers and Trustees:* Norma Astill,* Chair.; Grace Schlageter,* Secy.; Jean Cleminson,* Treas.; Bruna Evangelista, Elizabeth O'Neill.
EIN: 510204285
Codes: GTI

40233
The Educational Projects Foundation, Inc.
c/o David Cohen
720 Fort Washington Ave., Ste. 2C
New York, NY 10040-3708

Established in 1998 in NY.
Donor(s): Peter Cohn.
Financial data (yr. ended 08/31/01): Grants paid, $0; assets, $197,420 (M); expenditures, $1,055; qualifying distributions, $0.
Limitations: Applications not accepted. Giving primarily in New York, NY.
Application information: Contributes only to pre-selected organizations.
Officers and Directors:* David Cohn,* Pres. and Treas.; Peter Cohn,* V.P.; Carmela Cohn,* Secy.
EIN: 134027467

40234
Ehara Foundation
c/o Goldman Sachs & Co.
85 Broad St., Tax Dept.
New York, NY 10004

Established in 1989 in NY.
Financial data (yr. ended 06/30/01): Grants paid, $0; assets, $1,233,747 (M); expenditures, $1,289; qualifying distributions, $490.
Limitations: Applications not accepted. Giving on an international basis, with emphasis on Tokyo, Japan.
Application information: Contributes only to pre-selected organizations.
Trustees: Kayoko Ehara, Nobuyoshi John Ehara, Robert J. Katz.
EIN: 133543267

40235
The Edgar & Lucky Eisner Foundation
71 Wood Rd.
Bedford Hills, NY 10507

Established in 1997 in NY.
Donor(s): Edgar Eisner.
Financial data (yr. ended 04/30/01): Grants paid, $0; assets, $206,126 (M); gifts received, $2,316; expenditures, $3,350; qualifying distributions, $1,200.
Director: Edgar Eisner.
EIN: 133949131

40236
1185 Park Foundation, Inc.
122 E. 42nd. St., 24th Fl.
New York, NY 10168

Established in 1999 in NY.
Donor(s): David P. Steinmann.
Financial data (yr. ended 02/28/02): Grants paid, $0; assets, $145,116 (M); gifts received, $564; expenditures, $50; qualifying distributions, $0.
Limitations: Applications not accepted.
Application information: Contributes only to pre-selected organizations.
Officer: David P. Steinmann, Pres. and Treas.; Catherine Steinmann, V.P. and Secy.; Jennifer Steinmann, 2nd V.P.; Joshua Steinmann, 3rd V.P.; Gabriel Steinmann, 4th V.P.; Joel Steinmann.
EIN: 133997444

40237
Elizabethtown Social Center, Inc.
P.O. Box 373
Elizabethtown, NY 12932-0373

Established in 1940 in NY.
Donor(s): Cora Putnam Hale.‡
Financial data (yr. ended 12/31/01): Grants paid, $0; assets, $2,521,010 (M); gifts received, $110,400; expenditures, $233,399; qualifying distributions, $202,524; giving activities include $203,501 for programs.
Limitations: Applications not accepted. Giving limited to Elizabethtown, NY.
Application information: Contributes only to pre-selected organizations.
Officers and Board Members:* Paul Hooper,* Pres.; Marsha Fenimore,* V.P.; Hildegarde Moore,* Secy.; Marcella Denton,* Treas.; Brian Hume, Angus McPhail, Robert Sweatt.
Trustees: E.V. Hall, Richard W. Lawrence, Jr., Arthur V. Savage.
EIN: 141338389

40238
The Elsinore Foundation
c/o Mark Gasarch
40 W. 57th St., 33rd Fl.
New York, NY 10019

Established in 2000 in NY.
Donor(s): Innovative Diagnostics, LLC.
Financial data (yr. ended 12/31/01): Grants paid, $0; assets, $1,630 (M); expenditures, $470; qualifying distributions, $0.
Limitations: Giving primarily in Switzerland.
Officers and Director:* Mark Gasarch,* Pres. and Treas.; Francis J. Sanzillo, V.P. and Secy.
EIN: 134097331

40239
The Energy East Foundation, Inc.
605 Third Ave., 27th Fl.
New York, NY 10158
Application address: P.O. Box 3287, Ithaca, NY 14852-3287
Contact: Paul Karakantas, Treas.

Established in 2001 in DE.
Donor(s): The Union Water-Power Co., Energy East Corp.
Financial data (yr. ended 12/31/01): Grants paid, $0; assets, $4,609,863 (M); gifts received, $4,610,000; expenditures, $164; qualifying distributions, $0.
Application information: Application form required.
Officers: Angela Sparks Beddoe, Pres.; Leonard Blum, Secy.; Paul Karakantas, Treas.
Directors: Michael German, Wesley Von Schack.
EIN: 134200689
Codes: CS

40240
Eortc-USA Foundation, Inc.
c/o Mahoney Cohen
111 W. 40th St.
New York, NY 10018

Established in 2000.
Financial data (yr. ended 12/31/00): Grants paid, $0; assets, $10,000 (M); gifts received, $10,000; expenditures, $0; qualifying distributions, $0.
Limitations: Applications not accepted.
Application information: Contributes only to pre-selected organizations.
Officers: Vincent Mai, Pres.; Louise Ross, Secy.; Lisa Moore, Treas.
EIN: 521855076

40241
EPSD Foundation, Inc.
c/o Ethel Person
135 Central Park W.
New York, NY 10023

Established in 2000 in NY.
Donor(s): Nat Sherman Foundation.
Financial data (yr. ended 12/31/01): Grants paid, $0; assets, $29,138 (M); gifts received, $2,055; expenditures, $2,499; qualifying distributions, $0.
Officers: Ethel S. Person, Pres.; Stanley Diamond, Secy.
EIN: 223696549

40242
Edith K. Eyre-Ainsworth Scholarship Trust
(Formerly Edith K. Eyre-Ainsworth Scholarship Trust No. 2)
c/o Deutsche Bank Trust Co. of NY
P.O. Box 1297, Church St. Sta.
New York, NY 10008
Application address: Michael P. Mortell, Pres. or Anne Landers, Records, c/o University College Cork, Records/Exams Off., College Rd., Cork, Ireland; URL: http://www.UCC.IE; E-mail: Information@UCC.IE

Financial data (yr. ended 12/31/01): Grants paid, $0; assets, $655,938 (M); expenditures, $13,725; qualifying distributions, $4,904.
Limitations: Giving limited to Cork, Ireland.
Trustee: Deutsche Bank.
EIN: 136041720

40243
Aouni Faks Foundation
4302 Farragut Rd.
Brooklyn, NY 11203

Established in 2001 in NY.
Donor(s): World of Chantilly, Inc.
Financial data (yr. ended 12/31/01): Grants paid, $0; assets, $60,000 (M); gifts received, $60,000; expenditures, $0; qualifying distributions, $0.
Officers: Ibriham Faks, V.P.; Freddy Faks, Secy.; Daniel Faks, Treas.
EIN: 306004475
Codes: CS

40244
Michael David Falk Foundation, Inc.
188 E. 70th St., Apt. 29A
New York, NY 10021

Established in 1968 in NY.
Donor(s): Isidore Falk.
Financial data (yr. ended 12/31/00): Grants paid, $0; assets, $9,471,616 (M); expenditures, $10,584; qualifying distributions, $0.
Limitations: Applications not accepted. Giving primarily in New York, NY.
Application information: Contributes only to pre-selected organizations.
Officers: Isidore Falk, Mgr.; Maurice B. Falk, Mgr.
EIN: 136265854

40245
Robert D. Farber Foundation
c/o Richards and O'Neil
885 3rd Ave.
New York, NY 10022 (212) 207-1357
Contact: David Schaaf, Tr.

Established in 1996 in NY.
Donor(s): Leonard Farber, Robert D. Farber.‡
Financial data (yr. ended 12/31/01): Grants paid, $0; assets, $1 (M); expenditures, $0; qualifying distributions, $0.
Limitations: Giving primarily in Boston, MA, and New York, NY.
Trustees: Peggy Farber, Julie Garfield, Patrick Moore, David Schaaf, Tina Summerlin.
EIN: 133763399

40246
The Fassbinder Foundation, Inc.
c/o Pryor, Cashman, Sherman & Flynn LLP
410 Park Ave.
New York, NY 10022

Established in 1998 in NY.
Financial data (yr. ended 11/30/01): Grants paid, $0; assets, $1,644 (M); gifts received, $5,000; expenditures, $4,512; qualifying distributions, $0.
Limitations: Applications not accepted.

40246—NEW YORK

Application information: Contributes only to pre-selected organizations.
Officers and Directors:* Juliane Lorenz,* Pres.; Laurence Kardish,* Secy.; Ingrid Scheib-Rothbart,* Treas.
EIN: 134055562

40247
Fawzia Sultan Educational Corp.
c/o Loeb, Block & Partners
505 Park Ave.
New York, NY 10022

Established in 1997 in DE.
Financial data (yr. ended 08/31/01): Grants paid, $0; assets, $69,052 (M); gifts received, $70,000; expenditures, $6,926; qualifying distributions, $0.
Officers and Directors:* Yasmine S.M. Al-Saleh,* Pres.; Yasmine Al-Sabah,* V.P.; Carol Aslanian,* Secy.; Elizabeth Chaffee, Tarek Aziz Essa, Mina Ghattas.
EIN: 134027240

40248
The Dominic Ferraioli Foundation
c/o Mario Papa
6 Fremont St.
Gloversville, NY 12078

Established in 2000 in NY.
Donor(s): Dominic Ferraioli.‡
Financial data (yr. ended 06/30/01): Grants paid, $0; assets, $1,290,957 (M); gifts received, $1,289,297; expenditures, $4,021; qualifying distributions, $0.
Trustees: Robert F. Campbell, David L. Evans, Mario J. Papa, Louis M. Papandrea, M.D., Fred B. Wander.
EIN: 141829814

40249
Fesjian Foundation
661 Hillside Rd.
P.O. Box 889
Pelham, NY 10803-0889

Established in 1987 in NY.
Donor(s): Suren Fesjian, Mondial International Corp.
Financial data (yr. ended 12/31/01): Grants paid, $0; assets, $147,011 (M); expenditures, $337; qualifying distributions, $0.
Limitations: Applications not accepted. Giving on a national basis.
Application information: Contributes only to pre-selected organizations.
Officers: Suren Fesjian, Pres.; Richard Sarkisian, V.P.
EIN: 133453440

40250
The Robert L. Fine Cancer Research Laboratory Foundation, Inc.
650 W. 168th St., BB20-05
New York, NY 10032

Established in 1999 in NY.
Financial data (yr. ended 12/31/99): Grants paid, $0; assets, $125,000 (M); gifts received, $125,000; expenditures, $0; qualifying distributions, $0.
Limitations: Applications not accepted.
Application information: Contributes only to pre-selected organizations.
Directors: Abigail Fine, Barry Fine, Robert L. Fine, M.D.
EIN: 134091033

40251
Harry & Stella Fischbach Foundation
630 Park Ave.
New York, NY 10021-6544

Donor(s): Stella Fischbach.
Financial data (yr. ended 12/31/01): Grants paid, $0; assets, $31,588 (M); expenditures, $117; qualifying distributions, $101.
Limitations: Applications not accepted. Giving primarily in New York, NY.
Application information: Contributes only to pre-selected organizations.
Officer: Stella Fischbach, Pres. and Treas.
EIN: 136277889

40252
The Zachary & Elizabeth M. Fisher Medical Foundation, Inc.
c/o Fisher Brothers
299 Park Avenue
New York, NY 10017

Financial data (yr. ended 12/31/00): Grants paid, $0; assets, $4,272 (M); expenditures, $218; qualifying distributions, $0.
Limitations: Applications not accepted.
Application information: Contributes only to pre-selected organizations.
Officer and Directors:* Bijan Safai,* Pres.; Elizabeth Fisher.
EIN: 133738461

40253
The Fiske Family Foundation
10 Gregory Ave.
Binghamton, NY 13901

Established in 2001 in NY.
Financial data (yr. ended 12/31/01): Grants paid, $0; assets, $100 (M); gifts received, $100; expenditures, $1,000; qualifying distributions, $1,000.
Trustees: Leona Fiske, Nelson Fiske.
EIN: 161610727

40254
The Michael Flatley Foundation
c/o Gelfand, Rennert & Feldman, LLC
1330 Ave. of the Americas, 6th Fl.
New York, NY 10019
Application address: c/o Gipson, Hoffman & Panicone, 1901 Ave. of the Stars, Ste. 1100, Los Angeles, CA 90067

Established in 1998 in DE.
Donor(s): Michael Flatley, Bill Graham Enterprises, Inc.
Financial data (yr. ended 12/31/99): Grants paid, $0; assets, $144,781 (M); gifts received, $48,858; expenditures, $86; qualifying distributions, $86.
Directors: Michael Flatley, Robert E. Gipson.
EIN: 954672824

40255
Flux, Inc.
c/o C. Sackett
P.O. Box 31051
Rochester, NY 14603

Established in 2000 in DE.
Donor(s): Alison E. Sant.
Financial data (yr. ended 12/31/01): Grants paid, $0; assets, $204,375 (M); gifts received, $3,872; expenditures, $3,872; qualifying distributions, $0.
Limitations: Applications not accepted.
Application information: Contributes only to pre-selected organizations.
Officers and Directors:* Richard R. Johnson,* Chair. and Secy.; Alison E. Sant,* Pres. and Treas.; Peter G. Richards.
EIN: 161597310

40256
Fonzy Foundation, Inc.
c/o Greenberg
200 Madison Ave., Ste. 2225
New York, NY 10016

Established in 2001 in NY.
Financial data (yr. ended 12/31/01): Grants paid, $0; assets, $10,000 (M); gifts received, $10,000; expenditures, $0; qualifying distributions, $0.
EIN: 134161599

40257
The Theodore J. Forstmann Foundation, Inc.
(Formerly The Gustav Wurzweiler Foundation, Inc.)
c/o Forstmann Little and Co.
767 5th Ave., 44th Fl.
New York, NY 10153

Incorporated in 1950 in NY.
Donor(s): Gustav Wurzweiler,‡ Theodore J. Forstmann, Nicholas C. Forstmann, Frank Drendel.
Financial data (yr. ended 12/31/00): Grants paid, $0; assets, $8,508 (M); gifts received, $100; expenditures, $100; qualifying distributions, $0.
Limitations: Applications not accepted. Giving primarily in New York, NY.
Application information: Contributes only to pre-selected organizations.
Officers: Nicholas C. Forstmann, Pres.; Sarah Connell, Secy.; Kathleen Broderick, Treas.
EIN: 131945820

40258
Foundation Bnei Shlomo
5612 18th Ave.
Brooklyn, NY 11204

Established in 1999.
Financial data (yr. ended 12/31/00): Grants paid, $0; assets, $0 (M); gifts received, $1,500; expenditures, $77; qualifying distributions, $77.
Limitations: Applications not accepted.
Officer: Sigmond Schonfeld, Mgr.
EIN: 113462299

40259
The Foundation for Freedom and Justice
45 E. 25th St., Ste. 39B
New York, NY 10010

Established in 2000 in NY.
Donor(s): Robert Y. Gelfond.
Financial data (yr. ended 12/31/00): Grants paid, $0; assets, $1,190,213 (M); gifts received, $1,190,213; expenditures, $0; qualifying distributions, $0.
Limitations: Applications not accepted.
Application information: Contributes only to pre-selected organizations.
Trustees: Robert Y. Gelfond, Sandra Leong.
EIN: 134156644

40260
Foundation for Patient Advocacy, Inc.
26 S. Oxford St., Ste. 1B
Brooklyn, NY 11217

Established in 2000 in NY.
Donor(s): Patricia J.S. Simpson.
Financial data (yr. ended 03/31/01): Grants paid, $0; assets, $10,644 (M); gifts received, $10,922; expenditures, $278; qualifying distributions, $278.
Limitations: Applications not accepted. Giving primarily in NY.
Application information: Contributes only to pre-selected organizations.
Officers: Ella Shapiro, Pres.; Jennifer Boyd, V.P.; Joan Fleischman, Secy.-Treas.

EIN: 133841082

40261
Foundation to Advance Interfaith Trust and Harmony
(also known as F.A.I.T.H.)
c/o Greenberg Traurig
200 Park Ave., 15th Fl.
New York, NY 10166-1400

Established in 1995 in NY.
Donor(s): Conrad Plimpton, Ann Plimpton.
Financial data (yr. ended 12/31/01): Grants paid, $0; assets, $12,473 (M); expenditures, $320; qualifying distributions, $0.
Limitations: Applications not accepted. Giving on a national basis.
Application information: Contributes only to pre-selected organizations.
Officer: Mark L. Winer, Pres.
Director: Robert Goldstein, Conrad Plimpton.
EIN: 133846040
Codes: TN

40262
The Stephen C. Francis Charitable Foundation
c/o Charter Atlantic Corp.
200 Park Ave., 46th Fl.
New York, NY 10166 (212) 681-3018
Contact: Stephen C. Francis, Tr.

Donor(s): Stephen C. Francis.
Financial data (yr. ended 11/30/99): Grants paid, $0; assets, $16,737 (M); expenditures, $44; qualifying distributions, $37.
Limitations: Giving primarily in NY.
Application information: Application form not required.
Trustee: Stephen C. Francis.
EIN: 136881141

40263
Joseph and Constance Franklin Charitable Foundation, Inc.
c/o Inverness Counsel, Inc.
545 Madison Ave.
New York, NY 10022

Established in 1997 in MI and NY.
Financial data (yr. ended 12/31/01): Grants paid, $0; assets, $303,802 (M); expenditures, $4,913; qualifying distributions, $0.
Limitations: Applications not accepted. Giving primarily in NY.
Application information: Contributes only to pre-selected organizations.
Officers and Directors:* Constance Franklin,* Pres.; Joseph Franklin,* V.P.; William Franklin,* V.P.; Philip Franklin,* Secy.; Robert Maddock,* Treas.
EIN: 383352412

40264
Robert M. & Margaret Freeman Foundation
c/o American Express Tax & Business Svcs.
1185 Ave. of the Americas
New York, NY 10036-2602

Established in 1987 in NY.
Donor(s): Robert M. Freeman, Robert M. Freeman Charitable Lead Trust.
Financial data (yr. ended 06/30/01): Grants paid, $0; assets, $69,918 (M); expenditures, $2,500; qualifying distributions, $1,250.
Limitations: Applications not accepted.
Application information: Contributes only to pre-selected organizations.
Trustees: Margaret Freeman, Robert M. Freeman.
EIN: 133437919

40265
The Wayne D. Freihofer Family Foundation
147 Old Niskayuna Rd.
Loudonville, NY 12211
Contact: Wayne D. Freihofer, Tr.

Established in 1997.
Financial data (yr. ended 12/31/01): Grants paid, $0; assets, $97,659 (M); gifts received, $1,024; expenditures, $1,402; qualifying distributions, $0.
Trustee: Wayne D. Freihofer.
EIN: 166453351

40266
Freygish Foundation
c/o Bloom
292 Hicks St.
Brooklyn, NY 11201

Established in 2000 in NY.
Donor(s): Peter Bloom.
Financial data (yr. ended 07/31/01): Grants paid, $0; assets, $268,206 (M); gifts received, $328,826; expenditures, $1,087; qualifying distributions, $0.
Limitations: Applications not accepted.
Application information: Contributes only to pre-selected organizations.
Trustees: Peter Bloom, Janet Greenfield.
EIN: 113578290

40267
The Ruth & Arthur Friedman Family Foundation
111 Great Neck Rd., Ste. 408
Great Neck, NY 11021
Contact: Arthur Friedman, Pres.

Established in 2000 in NY.
Donor(s): Arthur Friedman, Ruth Friedman.
Financial data (yr. ended 12/31/00): Grants paid, $0; assets, $77,000 (M); gifts received, $76,500; expenditures, $0; qualifying distributions, $0.
Officers and Directors:* Arthur Friedman,* Pres.; Ruth Friedman,* V.P.
EIN: 113563658

40268
Gerald J. and Dorothy R. Friedman Medical Foundation, Inc.
c/o Peter W. Schmidt, Willkie Farr and Gallagher
787 7th Ave.
New York, NY 10019-6018

Established in 1992 in FL.
Donor(s): Gerald J. Friedman.
Financial data (yr. ended 06/30/01): Grants paid, $0; assets, $2,533,691 (M); expenditures, $29,718; qualifying distributions, $0.
Limitations: Giving primarily in the metropolitan New York, NY, area.
Application information: Application form not required.
Officers: Jane Friedman, Pres.; Louis Bernstein, Secy.-Treas.
EIN: 650416767

40269
Friends of FAI-Italian Environment Foundation
c/o Patterson, Belknap, Webb & Tyler, LLP
1133 Ave. of the Americas, Ste. 2200
New York, NY 10036-6710 (212) 336-2000
Contact: Dana W. Hiscock, Secy.

Established around 1991.
Financial data (yr. ended 12/31/01): Grants paid, $0; assets, $212,480 (M); gifts received, $171,000; expenditures, $2,686; qualifying distributions, $0.
Limitations: Giving primarily in Italy.

Officers and Directors:* Gulia Maria Crespi Mozzoni,* Pres.; Dana W. Hiscock, Secy.; Giorgio Poggiani,* Treas.; Marilyn Perry.
EIN: 133599581

40270
Friends of the Society for Coptic Archaeology, Inc.
c/o M. Raged-Whitma
200 Park Ave.
New York, NY 10166

Established in 1992 in NY.
Financial data (yr. ended 12/31/99): Grants paid, $0; assets, $1,324 (M); expenditures, $892; qualifying distributions, $892.
Directors: Selim F. Bakholm, Glen Bowersock, Nassif Boutros-Ghali, Nazeeh S. Habachy, Shaker A. Khayatt, Bentley Layton, Elaine Pagels.
EIN: 133610552

40271
William Froelich Foundation
c/o Rifkin & Lubcher, LLP
477 Madison Ave., 10th Fl.
New York, NY 10022
Contact: William Froelich, Pres.

Established in 1999 in NY.
Donor(s): William Froelich.
Financial data (yr. ended 05/31/00): Grants paid, $0; assets, $784,358 (M); expenditures, $3,000; qualifying distributions, $1,500.
Officer: William Froelich, Pres.
EIN: 137169965

40272
The Fryde-Verdiger Family Foundation, Inc.
c/o Middlegate Securities, Ltd.
8 W. 40th St., 4th Fl.
New York, NY 10018-3902
Contact: Esther Verdiger, Pres.

Established in 2000 in NY.
Donor(s): Esther Verdiger.
Financial data (yr. ended 12/31/01): Grants paid, $0; assets, $74,839 (M); gifts received, $137,563; expenditures, $3,583; qualifying distributions, $0.
Officers: Esther Verdiger, Pres.; Isaac Verdiger, V.P.; Moshe Verdiger, V.P.; Chavi Felsenberg, Secy.
EIN: 134037043

40273
Geds Help Fund Foundation
c/o Scott Rechler
225 Broadhollow Rd., CS 5341
Melville, NY 11747

Established in 2001 in NY.
Donor(s): Scott Rechler, Deborah Rechler.
Financial data (yr. ended 12/31/01): Grants paid, $0; assets, $484 (M); gifts received, $3,500; expenditures, $3,016; qualifying distributions, $258.
Directors: Jordan Heller, Deborah Rechler, Scott Rechler.
EIN: 113613923

40274
Georgian-Lehman Philanthropic Fund, Inc.
175 Varick St.
New York, NY 10014

Donor(s): The Georgian Press, Inc.
Financial data (yr. ended 11/30/01): Grants paid, $0; assets, $441 (M); expenditures, $0; qualifying distributions, $0.
Limitations: Applications not accepted. Giving primarily in NY.
Application information: Contributes only to pre-selected organizations.

40274—NEW YORK

Directors: Dana Lehman, Jesse J. Lehman, Jonathan Lehman.
EIN: 136059803

40275
Jerome Gevirman Foundation
c/o Gluckman & Gevirman
597 5th Ave., 9th Fl.
New York, NY 10017

Financial data (yr. ended 12/31/01): Grants paid, $0; assets, $1 (M); expenditures, $135; qualifying distributions, $0.
Limitations: Applications not accepted. Giving primarily in New York, NY.
Officer: Herbert H. Gevirman, Pres.
EIN: 136161520

40276
The Dorothy M. Gillespie Foundation, Inc.
c/o Siegel, Sacks, Press
630 3rd Ave.
New York, NY 10017

Established in 2000 in NY.
Donor(s): Dorothy M. Gillespie.
Financial data (yr. ended 12/31/00): Grants paid, $0; assets, $79,747 (M); gifts received, $79,000; expenditures, $53; qualifying distributions, $0.
Limitations: Applications not accepted.
Application information: Contributes only to pre-selected organizations.
Officers and Directors:* Dorothy M. Gillespie,* Pres. and Treas.; Joel Buchman,* Secy.; George Bolge.
EIN: 134138652

40277
Gilligan Family Foundation, Inc.
c/o Lonnie E. Wollin
350 5th Ave., Ste. 2822
New York, NY 10118

Established in 1987 in NY.
Donor(s): Gerard Gilligan, Madeline Gilligan, Mary Gilligan.
Financial data (yr. ended 09/30/01): Grants paid, $0; assets, $26,332 (M); expenditures, $290; qualifying distributions, $0.
Limitations: Applications not accepted. Giving primarily in Chicago, IL.
Application information: Contributes only to pre-selected organizations.
Officers: Gerard Filligan, Pres.; Lonnie E. Wollin, Secy. and Mgr.
EIN: 222842888

40278
The Eli Gindi Private Foundation
c/o G. Reji, LLC
2093 E. 3rd St.
Brooklyn, NY 11223

Established in 1999 in NY.
Donor(s): Eli Gindi.
Financial data (yr. ended 12/31/99): Grants paid, $0; assets, $386,250 (M); gifts received, $375,375; expenditures, $0; qualifying distributions, $0.
Limitations: Applications not accepted.
Application information: Contributes only to pre-selected organizations.
Officer: Eli Gindi, Pres.
EIN: 134100749

40279
The Girgenti Foundation
3312 Judith Dr.
Bellmore, NY 11710

Established in 2000 in NY.

Financial data (yr. ended 12/31/01): Grants paid, $0; assets, $259,139 (M); gifts received, $122,613; expenditures, $2,000; qualifying distributions, $0.
Limitations: Applications not accepted.
Application information: Contributes only to pre-selected organizations.
Trustees: Carrie Girgenti, Jody Girgenti.
EIN: 134084456

40280
Jane L. & Laurence C. Glazer Charitable Trust
35 Heatherstone Ln.
Rochester, NY 14618

Established in 1997 in NY.
Donor(s): Laurence C. Glazer.
Financial data (yr. ended 12/31/01): Grants paid, $0; assets, $47,170 (M); expenditures, $23; qualifying distributions, $0.
Limitations: Applications not accepted.
Application information: Contributes only to pre-selected organizations.
Trustees: Jane L. Glazer, Laurence C. Glazer.
EIN: 223418982

40281
The Richard and Kara Gnodde Foundation
c/o Goldman Sachs
85 Broad St., Tax Dept.
New York, NY 10004

Established in 1999 in NY.
Donor(s): Richard J. Gnodde.
Financial data (yr. ended 12/31/01): Grants paid, $0; assets, $349,325 (M); gifts received, $2,000; expenditures, $4,390; qualifying distributions, $0.
Limitations: Applications not accepted.
Application information: Contributes only to pre-selected organizations.
Trustees: Kara Gnodde, Richard J. Gnodde.
EIN: 134092816

40282
Steven & Lissa Goldberg Family Foundation
c/o Kamerman & Soniker, PC
655 3rd Ave.
New York, NY 10017

Established in 1995.
Donor(s): Lissa Goldberg, Steven Goldberg.
Financial data (yr. ended 12/31/01): Grants paid, $0; assets, $378 (M); expenditures, $144; qualifying distributions, $0.
Limitations: Applications not accepted.
Application information: Contributes only to pre-selected organizations.
Trustees: Lissa Goldberg, Steven Goldberg.
EIN: 133788004

40283
The Goldstone Family Foundation
570 Lexington Ave., 37th Fl.
New York, NY 10022

Established in 2000 in NY and DE.
Donor(s): Steven F. Goldstone, Elizabeth Goldstone.
Financial data (yr. ended 12/31/00): Grants paid, $0; assets, $22,030,052 (M); gifts received, $22,001,137; expenditures, $1,137; qualifying distributions, $0.
Limitations: Applications not accepted.
Application information: Contributes only to pre-selected organizations.
Officers and Directors:* Steven F. Goldstone,* Pres. and Treas.; Elizabeth Goldstone,* V.P. and Secy.
EIN: 061596255

40284
John L. Goldwater Foundation, Inc.
35 Sutton Pl.
New York, NY 10022-2464

Financial data (yr. ended 12/31/99): Grants paid, $0; assets, $2,046 (M); expenditures, $0; qualifying distributions, $0.
Limitations: Applications not accepted.
Application information: Contributes only to pre-selected organizations.
Officer: Gloria F. Goldwater, Pres.
EIN: 136160230

40285
Jean & Jula Goldwurm Memorial Foundation
c/o Schapiro, Wisan & Krassner, PC
122 E. 42nd St., Ste. 2500
New York, NY 10168-0057

Established in 1991 in NY.
Donor(s): Iva Goldwurm, Gordon S. Oppeheimer.
Financial data (yr. ended 09/30/01): Grants paid, $0; assets, $644,755 (M); expenditures, $5,297; qualifying distributions, $0.
Limitations: Applications not accepted. Giving primarily in New York, NY.
Application information: Contributes only to pre-selected organizations.
Trustees: Lotte Bilgrey, Iva Goldwurm, Gordon S. Oppenheimer.
EIN: 133635589

40286
The Robert and Phyllis Tishman Gonchar Family Foundation, Inc.
(Formerly The Robert & Phyllis Tishman Speyer Family Foundation)
10 Brayton Rd.
Scarsdale, NY 10583

Established in 1986.
Financial data (yr. ended 12/31/01): Grants paid, $0; assets, $13,222 (M); expenditures, $450; qualifying distributions, $0.
Limitations: Applications not accepted. Giving primarily in New York, NY.
Application information: Contributes only to pre-selected organizations.
Officers: Robert V. Tishman, Chair.; Lynne T. Speyer, Vice-Chair.; Jerry I. Speyer, Secy.-Treas.
EIN: 133348612

40287
Abraham Goodman Trust
c/o Sullivan & Cromwell
125 Broad St.
New York, NY 10004 (212) 558-3848

Established in 1988 in NJ.
Donor(s): Abraham Goodman.‡
Financial data (yr. ended 05/31/01): Grants paid, $0; assets, $32,003 (M); expenditures, $3,250; qualifying distributions, $1,625.
Limitations: Giving primarily in NY.
Application information: Application form not required.
Trustees: M. Bernard Aidinoff, Leonard Goodman.
EIN: 136910945

40288
Gottlieb Family Foundation
c/o Schwartz & Co.
2580 Sunrise Hwy.
Bellmore, NY 11710
Contact: Brian Gottlieb, Pres.

Established in 2000 in NY.
Financial data (yr. ended 12/31/00): Grants paid, $0; assets, $155,172 (M); gifts received,

$560,345; expenditures, $0; qualifying distributions, $0.
Application information: Application form not required.
Officers: Brian Gottlieb, Pres. and Treas.; Bethel Gottlieb, V.P. and Secy.
Director: Michael J. Schwartz.
EIN: 113572597

40289
George and Lenore Gottridge Foundation, Inc.
3 Vivian Pl.
Plainview, NY 11803

Established in 2001 in NY.
Donor(s): Members of the Gottridge family.
Financial data (yr. ended 12/31/01): Grants paid, $0; assets, $10,000 (M); gifts received, $10,000; expenditures, $0; qualifying distributions, $0.
Directors: George Gottridge, Lenore Gottridge, Marc Gottridge, Jo Anne Patrizi.
EIN: 113558022

40290
Goyal Family Foundation, Inc.
154-62 Powells Cove Blvd.
Whitestone, NY 11357
Contact: Shivlal Goyal, Pres.

Established in 2000 in NY.
Donor(s): Shivlal Goyal.
Financial data (yr. ended 12/31/01): Grants paid, $0; assets, $207,558 (M); expenditures, $175; qualifying distributions, $0.
Officer: Shivlal Goyal, Pres.
EIN: 113579353

40291
The Grand Foundation Trust
c/o Nancy Easton
123 W. 80th St., Apt. 3R
New York, NY 10024-7154 (212) 721-9003

Donor(s): Diane Kent.
Financial data (yr. ended 12/31/00): Grants paid, $0; assets, $26,753 (M); gifts received, $1,000; expenditures, $1,000; qualifying distributions, $0.
Trustees: Nancy Easton, Andrew Nippon.
EIN: 582330948

40292
Grand Street Foundation, Inc.
50 Riverside Dr.
New York, NY 10024-6504

Established in 1985 in NY.
Financial data (yr. ended 03/31/02): Grants paid, $0; assets, $463,297 (M); expenditures, $32,864; qualifying distributions, $0.
Limitations: Applications not accepted. Giving primarily in New York, NY.
Application information: Contributes only to pre-selected organizations.
Officers and Directors:* Benjamin Sonnenberg,* Pres. and Treas.; Dorothy Gallagher,* Secy.; Howard Sobel.
EIN: 133247663

40293
Great Mountain Forest Corporation
c/o S.W. Childs Mgmt. Corp.
15 Maiden Ln., Ste. 1001
New York, NY 10038
Contact: Robert N. Schmalz, Secy.

Donor(s): Edward C. Childs.
Financial data (yr. ended 03/31/02): Grants paid, $0; assets, $848,862 (M); gifts received, $5,000; expenditures, $33,412; qualifying distributions, $0.
Limitations: Giving primarily in New Haven, CT.
Officers: Starling W. Childs II, Chair. and Pres.; Charles H. Collins, Vice-Chair.; Edward Calder Childs, V.P.; Robert N. Schmalz, Secy.; Elisabeth C. Gill, Treas.
EIN: 132998991

40294
The Francis J. Greenburger Foundation, Inc.
c/o Time Equities, Inc.
55 5th Ave.
New York, NY 10003

Established in 1985.
Donor(s): Francis J. Greenburger, Winnick & Rich, P.C., Judith Willows.
Financial data (yr. ended 12/31/00): Grants paid, $0; assets, $5,414 (M); expenditures, $75; qualifying distributions, $0.
Limitations: Applications not accepted. Giving primarily in New York, NY.
Application information: Contributes only to pre-selected organizations.
Directors: Carol Frederick, Francis Greenburger, Robert Kantor.
EIN: 133406046

40295
Allen I. Gross Charitable Foundation
50 Broadway, 6th Fl.
New York, NY 10004-1607
Contact: E. Gross, Tr.

Established in 1987 in NY.
Donor(s): Allen I. Gross.
Financial data (yr. ended 11/30/01): Grants paid, $0; assets, $2,543,872 (M); gifts received, $2,500; expenditures, $19,710; qualifying distributions, $0.
Limitations: Giving primarily in NY.
Officer: Allen I. Gross, Pres.
Trustees: Brian Gross, Edie Gross, Jonathan Gross, Carolyn Weiser.
EIN: 112906887

40296
Max Gruber Foundation, Inc.
99 Powerhouse Rd.
Roslyn Heights, NY 11577-2021

Donor(s): Milton Levin,‡ Maurice Gruber.
Financial data (yr. ended 12/31/01): Grants paid, $0; assets, $764 (M); expenditures, $25; qualifying distributions, $0.
Limitations: Giving primarily in NY.
Officer: Maurice Gruber, Secy.-Treas.
EIN: 116021912

40297
Thomas V. Guarino Family Foundation
247 Scotchtown Rd.
Goshen, NY 10924 (845) 294-6127
Contact: Thomas V. Guarino, Pres.

Established in 2001 in NY.
Donor(s): Thomas V. Guarino.
Financial data (yr. ended 12/31/01): Grants paid, $0; assets, $141,450 (M); gifts received, $140,000; expenditures, $0; qualifying distributions, $0.
Officers: Thomas V. Guarino, Pres.; Gail Guarino, V.P.; Mary Jo Guarino, Secy.; Sandy Guarino, Treas.
EIN: 061617207

40298
Guinea Development Foundation, Inc.
c/o Sekou M. Sylla
140 West End Ave., Ste. 17G
New York, NY 10023 (212) 874-2911

Financial data (yr. ended 06/30/99): Grants paid, $0; assets, $21,676 (M); expenditures, $17,634; qualifying distributions, $17,634; giving activities include $17,634 for programs.
Officers: Sekou M. Sylla, M.D., Pres.; Koly Boiro, V.P.; Frank W. Booth, V.P.; Susan C. Brady, V.P.; Alfred Bush, V.P.; David M. French, M.D., V.P.; Samuel Hunter, Ph.D., V.P.; Mireill Sultan, V.P.
EIN: 133472572

40299
Hardingner/Norton Charitable Foundation
20 N. Moore St., Apt. 1E
New York, NY 10013

Established in 2001 in NY.
Donor(s): Ruth Hardinger.
Financial data (yr. ended 12/31/01): Grants paid, $0; assets, $10,000 (M); gifts received, $10,000; expenditures, $0; qualifying distributions, $0.
Limitations: Applications not accepted.
Application information: Contributes only to pre-selected organizations.
Officers: Ruth Hardingner, Pres.; C Michael Norton, Secy.
EIN: 137311943

40300
Gordon and Daniella Harris Foundation, Inc.
c/o Anchin, Block & Anchin LLP
1375 Broadway, 18th Fl.
New York, NY 10018

Established in 2001 in NJ.
Donor(s): Gordon J. Harris.
Financial data (yr. ended 12/31/01): Grants paid, $0; assets, $336,000 (M); gifts received, $336,625; expenditures, $0; qualifying distributions, $0.
Limitations: Applications not accepted.
Application information: Contributes only to pre-selected organizations.
Trustees: Ancell Harris, Daniella Harris, Gordon J. Harris, Janice Villiers.
EIN: 223850142

40301
Mortimer J. Harrison Article 11(B) Trust
c/o Torys
237 Park Ave.
New York, NY 10017
Application address: 810 S. Springfield Ave., Springfield, NJ 07081
Contact: Arthur E. Lashinsky, Tr.

Established in 1996 in NY.
Donor(s): Mortimer J. Harrison.‡
Financial data (yr. ended 12/31/00): Grants paid, $0; assets, $67,622 (M); gifts received, $50,000; expenditures, $6,068; qualifying distributions, $0.
Trustee: Arthur E. Lashinsky.
EIN: 137075861

40302
Mortimer J. Harrison Article 11(C) Trust
c/o Torys
237 Park Ave.
New York, NY 10017
Application address: 810 S. Springfield Ave., Springfield, NJ 07081
Contact: Arthur E. Lashinsky, Tr.

Established in 1996 in NY.
Donor(s): Mortimer J. Harrison,‡ Arthur E. Lashinsky.
Financial data (yr. ended 12/31/00): Grants paid, $0; assets, $94,433 (M); gifts received, $50,000; expenditures, $8,257; qualifying distributions, $0.
Trustee: Arthur E. Lashinsky.
EIN: 137075862

40303
Mortimer J. Harrison Article 11(E) Trust
c/o Torys
237 Park Ave.
New York, NY 10017
Application address: 810 S. Springfield Ave., Springfield, NJ 07081
Contact: Arthur E. Lashinsky, Tr.

Established in 1996 in NY.
Donor(s): Mortimer J. Harrison.‡
Financial data (yr. ended 12/31/00): Grants paid, $0; assets, $92,773 (M); gifts received, $50,000; expenditures, $6,899; qualifying distributions, $0.
Trustee: Arthur E. Lashinsky.
EIN: 137075864

40304
Huntington Hartford Family Fund Inc.
c/o Deforest & Duer
90 Broad St., 18th Fl.
New York, NY 10004 (212) 269-0230

Financial data (yr. ended 12/31/01): Grants paid, $0; assets, $12,873 (M); expenditures, $580; qualifying distributions, $0.
Limitations: Giving primarily in New York, NY.
Officers and Directors:* Huntington Hartford, Pres. and Treas.; John Mosler,* V.P.; Arthur A. Lane,* Secy.
EIN: 136092857

40305
The Robert V. Hauff & John F. Dreeland Foundation
c/o Paul Wood, Bleakley, Platt, and Remsen Millham
44 Wall St., 19th Fl.
New York, NY 10005-2407

Established in 2001 in NY.
Donor(s): Robert V. Hauff.‡
Financial data (yr. ended 12/31/01): Grants paid, $0; assets, $8,428 (M); gifts received, $10,000; expenditures, $1,600; qualifying distributions, $1,600.
Limitations: Applications not accepted.
Application information: Contributes only to pre-selected organizations.
Trustees: Robert E. Burke, Milton Gordon, Paul G. Wood.
EIN: 134168109

40306
Head Family Foundation
c/o Head Co.
1330 6th Ave., 12th Fl.
New York, NY 10019-5402

Established in 1997 in NY.
Financial data (yr. ended 12/31/01): Grants paid, $0; assets, $1,531,714 (M); expenditures, $4,705; qualifying distributions, $0.
Limitations: Giving primarily in Cambridge, MA.
Trustees: John C. Head III, Madie Ivy.
EIN: 133964593

40307
The Healing Lights Foundation
c/o Veronica Alloca
1200 Glen Curtiss Blvd.
Uniondale, NY 11553

Established in 1997 in NY.
Donor(s): Calvin Kleiman.
Financial data (yr. ended 12/31/00): Grants paid, $0; assets, $296 (M); expenditures, $0; qualifying distributions, $0.
Limitations: Applications not accepted.
Application information: Contributes only to pre-selected organizations.
Officers: Calvin Kleinman, Chair.; Marc Gellman, Vice-Chair.; Thomas Hartman, Vice-Chair.
EIN: 113377531

40308
Claudia Hearn & Edward Stern Foundation
c/o Bessemer Trust Co.
630 Fifth Ave., 37th Fl.
New York, NY 10111

Established in 2001 in CT.
Donor(s): Edward Stern.
Financial data (yr. ended 12/31/01): Grants paid, $0; assets, $214,400 (M); gifts received, $212,000; expenditures, $0; qualifying distributions, $0.
Limitations: Applications not accepted.
Application information: Contributes only to pre-selected organizations.
Trustees: Claudia Hearn, Edward Stern, Bessemer Trust Co.
EIN: 316675328

40309
Hegarty Family Foundation
177 Old Briarcliff Rd.
Briarcliff Manor, NY 10510

Established in 1998 in NY.
Donor(s): Anita Lise-Ingrid Hegarty, Michael Hegarty.
Financial data (yr. ended 06/30/01): Grants paid, $0; assets, $2,353,441 (M); gifts received, $3,545; expenditures, $48,574; qualifying distributions, $1,136.
Limitations: Applications not accepted. Giving primarily in NY and VA.
Application information: Contributes only to pre-selected organizations.
Trustees: Anita Lise-Ingrid Hegarty, Michael Hegarty.
EIN: 061532648

40310
Leona and Harry B. Helmsley Foundation, Inc.
(Formerly The Harry B. Helmsley Foundation, Inc.)
230 Park Ave., Ste. 659
New York, NY 10169

Incorporated in 1954 in NY.
Donor(s): Harry B. Helmsley.‡
Financial data (yr. ended 05/31/02): Grants paid, $0; assets, $10,869,078 (M); expenditures, $6,370; qualifying distributions, $0.
Limitations: Applications not accepted. Giving primarily in CT.
Application information: Contributes only to pre-selected organizations.
Officers and Directors:* Leona M. Helmsley,* Pres. and Treas.; Abe Wolf,* V.P.; Hubie Weyer,* Secy.
EIN: 136123336

40311
Luella Henkel Foundation, Inc.
c/o William J. Butler
280 Madison Ave., 11th Fl.
New York, NY 10016

Financial data (yr. ended 06/30/02): Grants paid, $0; assets, $95,006 (M); expenditures, $304; qualifying distributions, $0.
Limitations: Applications not accepted.
Application information: Contributes only to pre-selected organizations.
Officers: William J. Butler, Pres. and Treas.; Stanley Geller, Secy.
EIN: 136219943

40312
The Mary Henry Foundation
c/o Goldman Sachs & Co.
85 Broad St., Tax Dept.
New York, NY 10004

Established in 1997 in NY.
Donor(s): Mary C. Henry.
Financial data (yr. ended 12/31/99): Grants paid, $0; assets, $1,319,111 (M); gifts received, $1,072,232; expenditures, $257; qualifying distributions, $50.
Limitations: Applications not accepted.
Application information: Contributes only to pre-selected organizations.
Trustees: Mary C. Henry, Rajpal Sandhu.
EIN: 133936475

40313
The Jane Henson Foundation
c/o Prager and Fenton
675 3rd Ave., 3rd Fl.
New York, NY 10017

Established in 2000 in CT.
Donor(s): Brian Henson, Cheryl Henson, Heather Henson, John P. Henson, Lisa Henson, Jane Henson.
Financial data (yr. ended 12/31/00): Grants paid, $0; assets, $6,620,457 (M); gifts received, $6,740,925; expenditures, $1,417; qualifying distributions, $0.
Limitations: Applications not accepted.
Application information: Contributes only to pre-selected organizations.
Officer: Jane Henson, Pres.
EIN: 133818954

40314
The Jim Henson Legacy, Inc.
c/o Prager & Fenton
675 3rd. Ave., 3rd. Fl.
New York, NY 10017
Application address: 117 E. 69th St., New York, NY 10021, tel.: (212) 794-2400
Contact: Jane Henson, Pres.

Established in 1992 in NY.
Donor(s): Jane Henson.
Financial data (yr. ended 12/31/99): Grants paid, $0; assets, $128,698 (M); gifts received, $44,683; expenditures, $70,421; qualifying distributions, $69,747; giving activities include $57,411 for programs.
Limitations: Giving primarily in CT.
Officer: Jane Henson, Pres.
EIN: 133696981

40315
Frank and Helen Hermann Foundation, Inc.
64-07 77th Pl.
Middle Village, NY 11379

Established in 2001 in NY.
Donor(s): Helen Hermann.
Financial data (yr. ended 12/31/01): Grants paid, $0; assets, $5,000 (M); gifts received, $5,000; expenditures, $0; qualifying distributions, $0.
Limitations: Applications not accepted.
Application information: Contributes only to pre-selected organizations.
Officers and Directors:* Helen Hermann,* Pres.; Frank Osanitch, V.P.; Donald Magnotta.
EIN: 113618580

40316
The Lillian A. Hertlin Foundation
c/o Lillian A. Hertlin
283 Holbrook Ave.
Lake Ronkonkoma, NY 11779-1808

Established in 1999 in NY.
Financial data (yr. ended 12/31/01): Grants paid, $0; assets, $58,380 (M); gifts received, $22,300; expenditures, $3,175; qualifying distributions, $0.
Limitations: Applications not accepted.
Application information: Contributes only to pre-selected organizations.
Directors: Richard Altieri, Gloria Bender, Lillian A. Hertlin.
EIN: 113467681

40317
The Andrew R. Heyer and Mindy B. Heyer Foundation
55 Cushman Rd.
Scarsdale, NY 10583

Established in 2000 in NY.
Donor(s): Andrew R. Heyer, Mindy B. Heyer.
Financial data (yr. ended 09/30/01): Grants paid, $0; assets, $1,691,390 (M); gifts received, $1,724,932; expenditures, $0; qualifying distributions, $0.
Trustees: Andrew R. Heyer, Mindy B. Heyer.
EIN: 134146979

40318
Hibernian Festival Singers of Suffolk County
(Formerly The Bay Shore Irish American Choral Society)
15 N. Clinton Ave.
Bay Shore, NY 11706-7800

Financial data (yr. ended 12/31/99): Grants paid, $0; assets, $19,994 (M); gifts received, $5,175; expenditures, $26,287; qualifying distributions, $26,287; giving activities include $2,450 for programs.
Officers: Ronald Allen, Chair.; William Best, Secy.; Margaret Scheibel, Treas.
EIN: 112543482

40319
Hidden Ponds Foundation, Inc.
c/o Maier, Markey & Menashi
222 Bloomingdale Rd., Ste. 400
White Plains, NY 10605

Established in 2000 in NJ.
Donor(s): Carolyn J. Ferolito.
Financial data (yr. ended 07/31/01): Grants paid, $0; assets, $100,000 (M); gifts received, $100,000; expenditures, $0; qualifying distributions, $0.
Limitations: Applications not accepted.
Application information: Contributes only to pre-selected organizations.
Officers: Carolyn J. Ferolito, Pres.; John M. Ferolito, V.P.; Ciro Scalera, Secy.-Treas.
EIN: 223640312

40320
Charles and Eleanor Ho Foundation
4241 Marietta Dr.
Vestal, NY 13850

Established in 2001 in NY.
Financial data (yr. ended 12/31/01): Grants paid, $0; assets, $100 (M); gifts received, $100; expenditures, $0; qualifying distributions, $0.
Trustees: Charles S. Ho, Eleanor S. Ho.
EIN: 161613721

40321
The Hochberg Family Foundation, Inc.
176 Westview Ln.
Hewlett, NY 11557

Established in 2001 in NY.
Donor(s): Allen Hochberg.
Financial data (yr. ended 04/30/02): Grants paid, $0; assets, $943 (M); expenditures, $0; qualifying distributions, $0.
Limitations: Applications not accepted.
Application information: Contributes only to pre-selected organizations.
Officer: Allen Hochberg, Mgr.
EIN: 311722876

40322
Robert Hoe Foundation, Inc.
P.O. Box 69
Poughkeepsie, NY 12602-0069
(845) 454-4364
Contact: Robert Hoe, IV, Dir.

Donor(s): Marilyn C. Hoe.
Financial data (yr. ended 04/30/00): Grants paid, $0; assets, $89,102 (M); expenditures, $9,234; qualifying distributions, $2,397; giving activities include $18,058 for programs.
Limitations: Giving primarily in NY.
Officer and Directors:* Marilyn C. Hoe,* Pres.; Paul E. Bierley, Robert Hoe VI, Charles P. Irwin, John A. Johnson, Arthur W. Lehman, Polly Diane Hoe Mucci, William H. Rehrig.
EIN: 222587533

40323
Holcomb Family Foundation
124 Woodlawn Dr.
Gloversville, NY 12078
Application address: 11 Easterly St., Gloversville, NY, tel.: (518) 725-2374
Contact: Edward Holcomb, Tr.

Established in 2001 in NY.
Donor(s): Edward S. Holcomb.
Financial data (yr. ended 12/31/01): Grants paid, $0; assets, $20,000 (M); gifts received, $20,000; expenditures, $0; qualifying distributions, $0.
Trustees: Edward Holcomb, Nancy Holcomb.
EIN: 146211440

40324
Holiatric Foundation, Inc.
706 Madison Ave.
Albany, NY 12208

Financial data (yr. ended 12/31/01): Grants paid, $0; assets, $1,082 (M); expenditures, $800; qualifying distributions, $0.
Limitations: Applications not accepted. Giving primarily in Albany, NY.
Application information: Contributes only to pre-selected organizations.
Officers: Jonathan Harris, M.D., Pres.; Laura Harris Hirsh, V.P.; Alan M. Harris, Secy.; Sarah Harris, Treas.
EIN: 146018823

40325
John D. and Seana L. Holtz Foundation, Inc.
133 Kilbourn Rd.
Rochester, NY 14618

Established in 2001 in NY.
Donor(s): Holtz House of Vehicles Inc.
Financial data (yr. ended 12/31/01): Grants paid, $0; assets, $100,000 (M); gifts received, $100,000; expenditures, $0; qualifying distributions, $0.
Limitations: Applications not accepted.
Application information: Contributes only to pre-selected organizations.
Directors: John Holtz, Seana Holtz, William Kreienberg, James Latona, Sr.
EIN: 364490829
Codes: CS

40326
The Homeless in America Foundation
280 Park Ave., 24th Fl.
New York, NY 10017 (212) 451-3100
Additional tel.: (212) 451-3200
Contact: Peter W. May, Dir., or Nelson Pletz, Dir.

Established in 1988 in NY.
Donor(s): Peter W. May, Nelson Peltz.
Financial data (yr. ended 12/31/01): Grants paid, $0; assets, $57,376 (M); expenditures, $126; qualifying distributions, $0.
Limitations: Giving on a national basis.
Publications: Informational brochure.
Application information: Application form not required.
Directors: Peter W. May, Nelson Peltz.
EIN: 133572841

40327
The Horowitz Family Foundation
156 Taymil Rd.
New Rochelle, NY 10804

Established in 1999 in NY.
Donor(s): Bernard Horowitz, Marilyn Horowitz.
Financial data (yr. ended 06/30/01): Grants paid, $0; assets, $227,405 (M); gifts received, $106,200; expenditures, $6,554; qualifying distributions, $4,162.
Limitations: Applications not accepted.
Application information: Contributes only to pre-selected organizations.
Officers: Marilyn S. Horowitz, Pres.; Gregory M. Horowitz, V.P.; Stephen I. Horowitz, Secy.; Bernard Horowitz, Treas.
EIN: 134070878

40328
Frederick & Arlene Horowitz Family Foundation, Inc.
c/o Goldstein Golub Kessler & Co.
1185 Ave. of the Americas
New York, NY 10036

Established in 1996 in NY.
Donor(s): Frederick Horowitz.
Financial data (yr. ended 01/31/99): Grants paid, $0; assets, $374 (M); expenditures, $125; qualifying distributions, $0.
Limitations: Applications not accepted.
Application information: Contributes only to pre-selected organizations.
Directors: Blair P. Effron, Arlene Horowitz, Frederick Horowitz.
EIN: 133874517

40329
The Mr. and Mrs. Raymond J. Horowitz Foundation for the Arts, Inc.
c/o Raymond J. Horowitz
600 3rd Ave.
New York, NY 10016-2097

Financial data (yr. ended 12/31/01): Grants paid, $0; assets, $46,740 (M); expenditures, $18; qualifying distributions, $0.
Limitations: Applications not accepted.
Application information: Contributes only to pre-selected organizations.
Officers and Directors:* Raymond J. Horowitz,* Pres. and Treas.; Margaret Horowitz,* Secy.; Elaine M. Reich.
EIN: 133699100

40330
Hps Foundation
c/o Herman Steinmetz
60 Hewes St.
Brooklyn, NY 11211

Established in 2000 in NY.
Financial data (yr. ended 06/30/01): Grants paid, $0; assets, $500 (M); gifts received, $500; expenditures, $0; qualifying distributions, $0.
Trustees: Bluma Steinmetz, Herman Steinmetz.
EIN: 522300814

40331
The Sidney L. Huff & Onnolee D. Huff Charitable Foundation
c/o NBT Bank, N.A.
52 S. Broad St.
Norwich, NY 13815

Established in 2000 in NY.
Donor(s): Onnolee D. Huff, Sidney L. Huff.
Financial data (yr. ended 11/30/01): Grants paid, $0; assets, $117,133 (M); gifts received, $116,550; expenditures, $1,390; qualifying distributions, $1,212.
Limitations: Applications not accepted.
Application information: Contributes only to pre-selected organizations.
Trustees: Onnolee D. Huff, Sidney L. Huff, Peter V. Smith, NBT Bank, N.A.
EIN: 166523074

40332
HVB Americas Foundation, Inc.
150 E. 42nd St.
New York, NY 10017-4679

Established in 2001 in NY.
Donor(s): HVB America Inc.
Financial data (yr. ended 12/31/01): Grants paid, $0; assets, $500,000 (M); gifts received, $500,000; expenditures, $0; qualifying distributions, $0.
Limitations: Applications not accepted.
Application information: Contributes only to pre-selected organizations.
Directors: Stephan Bub, Richard Cerick, Gregor Medinger, Judith Samuels.
EIN: 134199169
Codes: CS

40333
The Raymond and Leigh Ingleby Family Foundation, Inc.
c/o Zukerman, Gore & Brandeis, LLP
900 3rd Ave.
New York, NY 10022
Contact: Raymond Ingleby, Pres.

Established in 1997 in NY.
Financial data (yr. ended 12/31/00): Grants paid, $0; assets, $19,916 (M); expenditures, $1,870; qualifying distributions, $1,870.
Limitations: Giving primarily in New York, NY.
Officers: Raymond Ingleby, Pres.; Jeffrey D. Zuckerman, V.P.; Leigh Ingleby, Secy.
EIN: 133983053

40334
Institute for Brain Initiatives
c/o White and Case, LLP
1155 6th Ave., Ste. 3436
New York, NY 10036-2787 (212) 819-8200

Established in 1995 in DE.
Financial data (yr. ended 12/31/01): Grants paid, $0; assets, $171,219 (M); expenditures, $149; qualifying distributions, $0.
Limitations: Applications not accepted.

Application information: Contributes only to pre-selected organizations.
Trustees: Hildegarde Mahoney, Edward Rover, Maureen Rover.
EIN: 133568413

40335
Institute for Ice Age Studies, Inc.
25 Waverly Pl.
New York, NY 10003-6759
Contact: Randall K. White, Exec. Dir.

Established in 1991 in NY.
Financial data (yr. ended 12/31/01): Grants paid, $0; assets, $7,001 (M); expenditures, $520; qualifying distributions, $0.
Officers and Directors:* Lynda M. Hughes,* Secy.-Treas.; Randall K. White,* Exec. Dir.; John Pfeiffer, Eileen S. Silvers, Ian Tattersal.
EIN: 133396112

40336
International Boxing Hall of Fame, Inc.
P.O. Box 425
Canastota, NY 13032-0425

Established in 1987 in NY.
Financial data (yr. ended 12/31/00): Grants paid, $0; assets, $352,083 (M); gifts received, $43,362; expenditures, $479,572; qualifying distributions, $67,590.
Officers: Donald S. Ackerman, Pres.; Donald F. Cerio, Sr., V.P.; Robert W. Moher, V.P.; Darryl Hughto, Secy.; Mike Milmoe, Treas.
Directors: Richard Bartlett, Paul Basilio, John Giamartino, Wynn Kintz, Bill LeMon, John S. Patane, Alex Rinaldi, John Rinaldi.
EIN: 161229381

40337
International Eastern European Heritage and Assistance Foundation
2126 Benson Ave., Apt. 1C
Brooklyn, NY 11214-5029

Established in 2000 in NY.
Donor(s): Nachrum Krashianski.
Financial data (yr. ended 04/30/01): Grants paid, $0; assets, $6,240 (M); gifts received, $46,000; expenditures, $40,180; qualifying distributions, $40,000; giving activities include $38,489 for programs.
Director: Nachrum Krashianski.
EIN: 113436654

40338
International Foundation for Arts & Culture, Inc.
100 United Nations Plz., Ste. 12B
New York, NY 10017

Established in 1996 in NY.
Donor(s): IFAC of Tokyo.
Financial data (yr. ended 03/31/01): Grants paid, $0; assets, $1,154,474 (M); gifts received, $220,134; expenditures, $158,502; qualifying distributions, $0.
Limitations: Applications not accepted.
Application information: Contributes only to pre-selected organizations.
Officers: Toshu Fukami, Pres.; Kathy Calhoun Hobbs, V.P.; Lloyd Rothenberg, Secy.
Directors: Masao Kunihiro, Naotado Osaki, Peter David Pedersen.
EIN: 133888511

40339
Italian Civic Association, Inc. Scholarship Trust Fund
(also known as I.C.A. Scholarship Trust Fund)
c/o Richard Lagatta
29 Springer Ave.
Yonkers, NY 10704-1509
Application address: c/o Italian Civic Assoc., N. 5th Ave. and North St., Mount Vernon, NY 10550
Contact: William C. Prattella, Chair.

Financial data (yr. ended 12/31/01): Grants paid, $0; assets, $26,942 (M); expenditures, $14; qualifying distributions, $14.
Limitations: Giving limited to residents of Mount Vernon, NY.
Application information: Application form required.
Officers: William C. Prattella, Chair.; Marge Longobueco, Secy.; Richard LaGatta, Treas.
EIN: 136315805

40340
The Brooke Jackman Foundation, Inc.
P.O. Box 354
Mill Neck, NY 11765

Established in 2001 in NY.
Donor(s): Robert Jackman, Daniel R. Delahanty, Daniel L. Keating, Todd Deutsch, Michael Deutsch, Gayle Steinberg, Charles Steinberg, Nathaniel Singer, Ross Jackman, Eileen Heuweller, Paul Heuweller, Barbara Jackman.
Financial data (yr. ended 12/31/01): Grants paid, $0; assets, $418,326 (M); gifts received, $417,649; expenditures, $0; qualifying distributions, $0.
Directors: Barbara Jackman, Erin Jackman, Robert Jackman, Ross Jackman, Charles Steinberg.
EIN: 113629289

40341
Michael I. Jacobs, M.D., Charitable Foundation
c/o Ganer, Grossback, & Ganer
1995 Broadway, 16th Fl.
New York, NY 10023
Contact: Michael I. Jacobs, Pres.

Established in 2001 in NY.
Donor(s): Michael I. Jacobs.
Financial data (yr. ended 12/31/01): Grants paid, $0; assets, $6,000 (M); gifts received, $6,500; expenditures, $500; qualifying distributions, $0.
Officers and Directors:* Michael I. Jacobs,* Pres.; Sophie Jacobs,* Secy.; Ira Grossbach,* Treas.
EIN: 134178135

40342
Melinda & Stanley R. Jaffe Foundation
c/o Eisman, Klein & Co.
2001 Palmer Ave., Ste. 104
Larchmont, NY 10538

Established in 1998 in NY.
Donor(s): Stanley R. Jaffe, Melinda Jaffe.
Financial data (yr. ended 12/31/01): Grants paid, $0; assets, $6,911 (M); expenditures, $381; qualifying distributions, $0.
Limitations: Applications not accepted. Giving primarily in NY.
Application information: Contributes only to pre-selected organizations.
Officers and Directors:* Stanley R. Jaffe,* Pres.; Melinda Jaffe,* V.P. and Secy.; Arthur E. Eisman, Treas.; Elizabeth Jaffe, Robert D. Jaffe.
EIN: 133974548

40343
The Jaskiel Family Foundation
1750 47th St.
Brooklyn, NY 11204

Established in 2000 in NY.
Financial data (yr. ended 09/30/01): Grants paid, $0; assets, $57,585 (M); expenditures, $698; qualifying distributions, $0.
Limitations: Applications not accepted.
Application information: Contributes only to pre-selected organizations.
Trustees: Sally Jaskiel, Wolf Jaskiel, Chani Pollack, Gita Schwartz.
EIN: 113513653

40344
The Jeffery Foundation
c/o RSM McGladrey, Inc.
380 Madison Ave.
New York, NY 10017

Established in 2001 in NY.
Donor(s): Reuben Jeffery III.
Financial data (yr. ended 12/31/01): Grants paid, $0; assets, $1,658,690 (M); gifts received, $1,672,200; expenditures, $0; qualifying distributions, $0.
Limitations: Applications not accepted.
Application information: Contributes only to pre-selected organizations.
Trustee: Reuben Jeffery III.
EIN: 980362226

40345
The JMC Foundation, Inc.
c/o Arthur V. Fox, C.P.A.
126 E. 56th St., 12th Fl.
New York, NY 10022

Established in 1985 in NY.
Donor(s): Jeremiah M. Callaghan, The Monterey Fund, Inc.
Financial data (yr. ended 09/30/01): Grants paid, $0; assets, $103,317 (M); expenditures, $0; qualifying distributions, $0.
Limitations: Applications not accepted. Giving primarily in New York, NY.
Application information: Contributes only to pre-selected organizations.
Officers and Directors:* Jeremiah M. Callaghan,* Pres.; Karen Callaghan,* V.P. and Secy.; Eugene Callaghan,* Treas.
EIN: 133320959

40346
The JMS Foundation for Children
c/o B. Strauss Assoc., Ltd.
307 5th Ave., 8th Fl.
New York, NY 10016-6517

Established in 1999 in NJ.
Donor(s): Jayne Stevlingson.
Financial data (yr. ended 08/31/01): Grants paid, $0; assets, $31,647 (M); expenditures, $590; qualifying distributions, $0.
Limitations: Applications not accepted.
Application information: Contributes only to pre-selected organizations.
Trustees: John Callaghan, Barbara Stevlingson, Deanna Stevlingson, Jayne Stevlingson.
EIN: 223677596

40347
The Leo H. Joachim Scholarship Fund
c/o Stanley Katz, Berenson & Co.
135 W. 50th St.
New York, NY 10020

Donor(s): Florence Joachim.‡

Financial data (yr. ended 06/30/00): Grants paid, $0; assets, $66,440 (M); expenditures, $127; qualifying distributions, $50.
Limitations: Giving primarily in NY.
Application information: Letter.
Trustee: Stanley Katz.
EIN: 133107081

40348
James Graham Johnston & Marcelle Launay Johnston Foundation
c/o Evan R. Dawson, Pres.
630 5th Ave., Ste. 1905
New York, NY 10111-0100

Established in 1963 in DE.
Donor(s): James Graham Johnston.‡
Financial data (yr. ended 12/31/01): Grants paid, $0; assets, $83,486 (M); expenditures, $1,736; qualifying distributions, $1,710.
Limitations: Applications not accepted. Giving primarily in Redlands, CA.
Application information: Contributes only to pre-selected organizations.
Officers and Directors:* Evan R. Dawson,* Pres.; E. Ward Smith,* V.P.; Sue A. Dawson,* Secy.-Treas.
EIN: 136167908

40349
Rebecca Joseph Memorial Foundation
c/o Raphael J. Joseph
1850 Ocean Pkwy, Ste. A-5
Brooklyn, NY 11223

Donor(s): Raphael J. Joseph.
Financial data (yr. ended 08/31/01): Grants paid, $0; assets, $7,931 (M); gifts received, $200; expenditures, $117; qualifying distributions, $0.
Limitations: Applications not accepted. Giving primarily in NY.
Application information: Contributes only to pre-selected organizations.
Officers: Raphael J. Joseph, Pres.; Joshua Leiman, V.P.; Ezra S. Nathan, Secy.-Treas.
EIN: 113346761

40350
Joy of Giving Foundation, Inc.
30 Hunt Ct.
Jericho, NY 11753

Established in 1999.
Financial data (yr. ended 12/31/01): Grants paid, $0; assets, $1,803 (M); expenditures, $0; qualifying distributions, $0.
Director: Mayur Dalal.
EIN: 113522231

40351
Ernest L. & Florence L. Judkins Scholarship Fund
P.O. Box 380
Schenectady, NY 12301-0380
Application address: c/o College Scholarship Comm., Union College, Schenectady, NY 12305, tel.: (518) 370-6123

Financial data (yr. ended 09/30/01): Grants paid, $0; assets, $165,566 (M); expenditures, $1,611; qualifying distributions, $0.
Limitations: Giving limited to Schenectady, NY.
Trustee: Trustco Bank Corp. NY.
EIN: 146015967

40352
The Louise and Gerald Kaiser Family Foundation, Inc.
131 Bethel Rd.
Albertson, NY 11507

Established in 2001 in NY.
Donor(s): Christina Kaiser.

Financial data (yr. ended 12/31/01): Grants paid, $0; assets, $2,000,000 (M); gifts received, $2,000,000; expenditures, $0; qualifying distributions, $0.
Limitations: Applications not accepted.
Application information: Contributes only to pre-selected organizations.
Director: Christina Kaiser.
EIN: 113640058

40353
Robert N. Kaplan Family Foundation
c/o Robert N. Kaplan
805 3rd Ave., 22nd Fl.
New York, NY 10022

Established in 1999 in NY.
Donor(s): Robert N. Kaplan.
Financial data (yr. ended 12/31/00): Grants paid, $0; assets, $90,581 (M); expenditures, $500; qualifying distributions, $500.
Limitations: Applications not accepted.
Application information: Contributes only to pre-selected organizations.
Officer: Robert N. Kaplan, Pres.
EIN: 134090904

40354
The Karan-Weiss Foundation
c/o Urban Zen, LLC
570 7th Ave.
New York, NY 10018-1603

Established in 1999.
Donor(s): Donna Karan, Stephan Weiss.
Financial data (yr. ended 12/31/99): Grants paid, $0; assets, $2,970,514 (M); gifts received, $635,659; expenditures, $0; qualifying distributions, $0.
Limitations: Applications not accepted.
Application information: Contributes only to pre-selected organizations.
Trustees: Donna Karan, Stephan Weiss.
EIN: 134084069

40355
The Muriel Linsky Karasik Foundation, Inc.
c/o Braunstein & Stern
60 E. 42nd St.
New York, NY 10165

Established in 1990 in NY.
Financial data (yr. ended 12/31/01): Grants paid, $0; assets, $822 (M); expenditures, $1,220; qualifying distributions, $0.
Limitations: Applications not accepted. Giving primarily in NY.
Application information: Contributes only to pre-selected organizations.
Officers: Muriel Linsky, Pres.; Victoria Benalloul, Secy.; Albert Benalloul, Treas.
EIN: 133581195

40356
The Kat Trust, Inc.
c/o Reminick, Aarons & Co., LLP
1430 Broadway, 17th Fl.
New York, NY 10017-4037

Established in 1986 in NY.
Financial data (yr. ended 12/31/01): Grants paid, $0; assets, $57,583 (M); expenditures, $519; qualifying distributions, $0.
Limitations: Applications not accepted. Giving primarily in NY.
Application information: Contributes only to pre-selected organizations.
Trustees: Katrina Vanden Heuvel, Wendy Vanden Heuvel, Gillian Walker.
EIN: 136874219

40357
The Arthur P. Keller Family Foundation, Inc.
131 Lakeledge Dr.
Williamsville, NY 14221-5751

Established in 2000 in NY.
Donor(s): Marie L. Keller.
Financial data (yr. ended 12/31/01): Grants paid, $0; assets, $348,324 (M); gifts received, $81,051; expenditures, $6,379; qualifying distributions, $0.
Limitations: Applications not accepted.
Application information: Contributes only to pre-selected organizations.
Officers: Arthur P. Keller, Jr., Pres.; Kathie A. Keller, V.P.; Michael A. Keller, V.P.; Peter J. Keller, V.P.; Edward J. Carland, Secy.; Daniel J. Dirrigl, Treas.
Directors: Marie L. Keller, Patricia H. Keller.
EIN: 161590699

40358
Keller-Shatanoff Foundation
c/o Ruth Sturm
18 Park Dr.
Chappaqua, NY 10514-3127

Established in 1993 in NY.
Donor(s): Betty S. Keller.
Financial data (yr. ended 12/31/01): Grants paid, $0; assets, $260,438 (M); expenditures, $2,550; qualifying distributions, $0.
Limitations: Applications not accepted. Giving primarily in New York, NY.
Application information: Contributes only to pre-selected organizations.
Officers and Directors:* Betty S. Keller,* Pres.; Ruth Sturm,* V.P.; Irving Gluck,* Secy.-Treas.
EIN: 133699801

40359
The M. J. Kelley Foundation
15 Stepping Stone Ln.
Orchard Park, NY 14127

Established in 1999 in NY.
Financial data (yr. ended 12/31/99): Grants paid, $0; assets, $2,005 (M); gifts received, $2,000; expenditures, $0; qualifying distributions, $0.
Limitations: Applications not accepted.
Application information: Contributes only to pre-selected organizations.
Trustees: Candace Kelley, Kathleen Kelley.
EIN: 161576418

40360
The Keluche-Fuller Foundation
c/o Weiss & Co.
22 W. 38th St.
New York, NY 10018-6269
Application address: 4620 Bradford Heights, Colorado Springs, CO 80906, tel.: (800) 483-6448
Contact: Eugene Keluche, Pres., or Frieta Fuller Keluche, Secy.

Established in 1990 in DE.
Donor(s): Freita Fuller Keluche, Gene Keluche.
Financial data (yr. ended 11/30/99): Grants paid, $0; assets, $20,293 (M); gifts received, $13,200; expenditures, $25,290; qualifying distributions, $25,290.
Limitations: Giving on a national basis.
Officers: Eugene Keluche, Pres.; Freita Fuller Keluche, Secy.
EIN: 931010170

40361
The Kenbe Foundation
383 5th Ave.
New York, NY 10016

Established in 2001 in NY.

Donor(s): Robert Lynch.
Financial data (yr. ended 12/31/01): Grants paid, $0; assets, $10,003 (M); gifts received, $10,000; expenditures, $0; qualifying distributions, $0.
Limitations: Applications not accepted.
Application information: Contributes only to pre-selected organizations.
Officers: Genevieve Lynch, Pres.; Robert Lynch, C.F.O.
Director: Terence Lohman.
EIN: 134200004

40362
The Kesser Foundation
c/o Spalter
1519 President St.
Brooklyn, NY 11213-4542

Established in 2000 in NY.
Financial data (yr. ended 12/31/01): Grants paid, $0; assets, $159 (M); expenditures, $0; qualifying distributions, $0.
Limitations: Applications not accepted.
Application information: Contributes only to pre-selected organizations.
Trustees: Ann Spalter, Joseph Spalter.
EIN: 113470046

40363
Kessler-Sachs Charitable Foundation
100 Marlborough Ct.
Rockville Centre, NY 11570

Established in 1999 in NY.
Donor(s): Jerome Kessler.
Financial data (yr. ended 12/31/01): Grants paid, $0; assets, $241,920 (M); gifts received, $71; expenditures, $1,179; qualifying distributions, $0.
Limitations: Applications not accepted. Giving primarily in New York, NY and Fairfax, VA.
Application information: Contributes only to pre-selected organizations.
Trustees: Jerome Kessler, Norma Sachs Kessler.
EIN: 116524719

40364
The Benjamin Kessner Foundation, Inc.
400 E. 56th St., Ste. 10-K
New York, NY 10022

Established in 2001 in NY.
Financial data (yr. ended 12/31/01): Grants paid, $0; assets, $459 (M); expenditures, $527; qualifying distributions, $0.
Officers and Directors:* Benjamin Kessner,* Chair. and Pres.; Deborah Peskin,* V.P. and Secy.-Treas.; Gale Gradus.
EIN: 134043510

40365
George J. King Foundation for Needy Children, Inc.
7219 3rd Ave.
Brooklyn, NY 11209-2198 (718) 238-3360
Contact: Harry G. English, Tr.

Financial data (yr. ended 06/30/01): Grants paid, $0; assets, $165,780 (M); expenditures, $2,531; qualifying distributions, $125.
Limitations: Giving primarily in NY.
Trustees: Muriel T. Dorff, Eileen E. English, Harry G. English.
EIN: 112635364

40366
B. King Productions, Inc.
c/o Starr & Co.
350 Park Ave.
New York, NY 10022

Financial data (yr. ended 02/28/02): Grants paid, $0; assets, $101,510 (M); expenditures, $0; qualifying distributions, $0.
Officer: Brenda Seimer, Pres.
EIN: 113121207

40367
Kingston Community Services Corp.
(Formerly K H Holding Co., Inc.)
396 Broadway
Kingston, NY 12401

Established in 1998.
Financial data (yr. ended 12/31/01): Grants paid, $0; assets, $1 (M); expenditures, $0; qualifying distributions, $0.
Officers: Peter E. Fallon, Pres.; Donald Katt, V.P.; Thomas Roach, Secy.; Christus J. Larios, Treas.
Directors: John Lawson, Amos Newcombe.
EIN: 141684383

40368
Kissaway County Foundation
c/o U.S. Trust Co.
114 W. 47th St.
New York, NY 10036

Established in 1997 in FL.
Donor(s): Allan J. McCorkle, Rosemary H. McCorkle.
Financial data (yr. ended 12/31/01): Grants paid, $0; assets, $414,978 (M); expenditures, $7,251; qualifying distributions, $0.
Limitations: Applications not accepted. Giving primarily in FL.
Application information: Unsolicited requests for funds not accepted.
Trustees: Allan J. McCorkle, Holly Jane McCorkle, Kimberly Rae McCorkle, Rosemary H. McCorkle.
EIN: 593452640

40369
The Jason Christopher Klein Foundation
c/o Jeanette Labarb
119 Murray Ave.
Port Washington, NY 11050

Established in 1998 in NY.
Financial data (yr. ended 12/31/01): Grants paid, $0; assets, $97,731 (M); expenditures, $1,001; qualifying distributions, $0.
Officers and Directors:* David Klein,* Secy.; Patricia Murphy,* Treas.
EIN: 113455167

40370
Stephen & Regina Klein Foundation
c/o Park Tower Reality Corp.
499 Park Ave.
New York, NY 10022-1240

Financial data (yr. ended 03/31/02): Grants paid, $0; assets, $11,969 (M); expenditures, $105; qualifying distributions, $0.
Limitations: Applications not accepted.
Application information: Contributes only to pre-selected organizations.
Trustee: George Klein.
EIN: 231025685

40371
The Lawrence Klosk Foundation, Inc.
(Formerly Michael Foundation, Inc.)
432 Zerega Ave.
Bronx, NY 10473-1211

Donor(s): Lawrence Klosk.
Financial data (yr. ended 12/31/99): Grants paid, $0; assets, $3,055 (M); expenditures, $1,770; qualifying distributions, $281.
Limitations: Applications not accepted. Giving primarily in NY.
Application information: Contributes only to pre-selected organizations.
Officer: Michael J. Klosk, Pres.
EIN: 136154546

40372
Betsy Koffman and Lorraine Bates Family Fund
c/o Piaker & Lyons, PC
P.O. Box 247
Vestal, NY 13851-0247

Established in 2001 in NY.
Donor(s): Elizabeth M. Koffman.
Financial data (yr. ended 12/31/01): Grants paid, $0; assets, $10,000 (M); gifts received, $10,000; expenditures, $0; qualifying distributions, $0.
Limitations: Applications not accepted.
Application information: Contributes only to pre-selected organizations.
Trustees: Lorraine L. Bates, Elizabeth M. Koffman.
EIN: 166527936

40373
The Karen E. Kohler Charitable Foundation
466 Lexington Ave., 18th Fl.
New York, NY 10017

Established in 1997 in NY.
Financial data (yr. ended 12/31/00): Grants paid, $0; assets, $67,686 (M); gifts received, $31,795; expenditures, $95; qualifying distributions, $95.
Limitations: Applications not accepted. Giving primarily in Norton, MA.
Application information: Contributes only to pre-selected organizations.
Trustee: Karen E. Kohler.
EIN: 133922666

40374
Paul L. Kohnstamm Family Charitable Trust
c/o The Bank of New York, Tax Dept.
1 Wall St., 28th Fl.
New York, NY 10286 (212) 635-1520
Contact: Kathryn Higgins, Trust Off. The Bank of New York

Financial data (yr. ended 12/31/01): Grants paid, $0; assets, $2,644 (M); expenditures, $23; qualifying distributions, $0.
Limitations: Giving primarily in NY.
Trustee: The Bank of New York.
EIN: 136078693

40375
The Komansky Foundation, Inc.
c/o John D. Dadakis, Clifford, Chance, Rogers, & Wells
200 Park Ave.
New York, NY 10166

Established in 1997 in NY.
Donor(s): David H. Komansky, Phyllis J. Komansky.
Financial data (yr. ended 12/31/01): Grants paid, $0; assets, $4,720,648 (M); gifts received, $1,552,000; expenditures, $34,106; qualifying distributions, $0.

Officers and Directors:* David H. Komansky,* Pres.; Phyllis J. Komansky,* Secy.; Evan Holod, Elyssa M. Komansky, Jennifer R. Komansky.
EIN: 133978765

40376
The Meyer G. and Ellen Goodstein Koplow Foundation
c/o Wachtell, Lipton, Rosen & Katz
51 W. 52nd St.
New York, NY 10019

Established in 1986 in NY.
Donor(s): Meyer G. Koplow, Ellen Goodstein Koplow.
Financial data (yr. ended 04/30/01): Grants paid, $0; assets, $689,485 (M); gifts received, $75,000; expenditures, $100; qualifying distributions, $0.
Limitations: Applications not accepted.
Application information: Contributes only to pre-selected organizations.
Officers and Directors:* Meyer G. Koplow,* Pres.; Ellen Goodstein Koplow,* V.P.; Kenneth B. Forrest.
EIN: 133388393

40377
Robert & Deborah Kopp Family Foundation
241 Westchester Dr., S.
Delmar, NY 12054-4234

Established in 2001 in NY.
Donor(s): Deborah Kopp.
Financial data (yr. ended 12/31/01): Grants paid, $0; assets, $49,372 (M); gifts received, $50,273; expenditures, $0; qualifying distributions, $0.
Limitations: Applications not accepted.
Application information: Contributes only to pre-selected organizations.
Officers: Robert Kopp, Pres. and Treas.; Deborah Kopp, Secy.
Director: John H. Lavelle.
EIN: 800006018

40378
The Charles Koppelman Family Foundation, Inc.
c/o Mason & Company, LLP
400 Park Ave., Ste. 1200
New York, NY 10022
Application address: 26 Glenwood Rd., Roslyn Harbor, NY 11576
Contact: Stacy Koppelman Fritz, Pres.

Established in 1997 in NY.
Financial data (yr. ended 12/31/00): Grants paid, $0; assets, $10,886 (M); expenditures, $121; qualifying distributions, $0.
Officers and Directors:* Stacy Koppelman Fritz,* Pres.; Jennifer Koppelman Hutt,* V.P.; Amy Koppelman,* V.P.; Brenda Koppelman,* Secy.-Treas.
EIN: 133959066

40379
Korean Language & Cultural Institute, Inc.
246 5th Ave., Ste. 500
New York, NY 10001

Financial data (yr. ended 04/30/02): Grants paid, $0; assets, $18,257 (M); gifts received, $54,952; expenditures, $47,745; qualifying distributions, $0.
Officer: Sang Ho Shin, Pres.
Directors: Joon Hong Cho, Kyong Ro Lee, Diana Park.
EIN: 133229829

40380
Sarah & Isidor Korein Charitable Trust
240 Central Park S., Ste. 1B
New York, NY 10019

Established in 2000 in NY.
Donor(s): Sara Korein.‡
Financial data (yr. ended 12/31/00): Grants paid, $0; assets, $10,173 (M); gifts received, $10,000; expenditures, $0; qualifying distributions, $0.
Director: Julius Korein.
EIN: 137180474

40381
Anne & Sidney Kriser Foundation
(Formerly Charles and Bertha Kriser Foundation)
211 E. 43rd St., Ste. 2304
New York, NY 10017

Established in 1958 in NY.
Donor(s): Sidney P. Kriser, Richard Feldstein, Judy Feldstein, R.C. Mahon & Co.
Financial data (yr. ended 05/31/02): Grants paid, $0; assets, $2,061,060 (M); expenditures, $7,899; qualifying distributions, $0.
Limitations: Applications not accepted. Giving primarily in NY.
Application information: Contributes only to pre-selected organizations.
Officer: Sidney P. Kriser, Pres.
EIN: 136188243

40382
Calliope & Manuel Kulukundis Foundation
c/o Grayson and Bock
74 Trinity Pl., Ste. 1500
New York, NY 10006

Established in 2000 in DE.
Financial data (yr. ended 12/31/01): Grants paid, $0; assets, $389,005 (M); expenditures, $215; qualifying distributions, $0.
Limitations: Applications not accepted.
Application information: Contributes only to pre-selected organizations.
Officers: Michael M. Kulukundis, Pres.; Albert Sigal, Secy.-Treas.
EIN: 522286126

40383
The Matthew G. L'Heureux Foundation
c/o Goldman Sachs & Co.
85 Broad St., Tax Dept.
New York, NY 10004

Established in 1999 in NY.
Donor(s): Matthew G. L'Heureux.
Financial data (yr. ended 10/31/01): Grants paid, $0; assets, $884,163 (M); gifts received, $3,500; expenditures, $18,400; qualifying distributions, $0.
Limitations: Applications not accepted.
Application information: Contributes only to pre-selected organizations.
Trustees: Matthew G. L'Heureux, Odell E. L'Heureux.
EIN: 134091391

40384
Lakeside Forest Preservation Trust
1 Blue Hill Plz.
Pearl River, NY 10965-3104

Financial data (yr. ended 12/31/01): Grants paid, $0; assets, $75,822 (M); expenditures, $10,201; qualifying distributions, $0.
Application information: Application form not required.
Trustees: Davis R. Chant, Kenneth Schultz, Benjamin Wechsler.
EIN: 136932248

40385
Lambert Family Foundation
c/o Bessemer Trust Co., N.A.
630 5th AVe.
New York, NY 10111
Contact: Bill & Sheila Lambert, Trustees

Established in 2001 in NY.
Donor(s): Bill Lambert, Sheila Lambert.
Financial data (yr. ended 12/31/01): Grants paid, $0; assets, $9,729,265 (M); gifts received, $9,821,250; expenditures, $8,586; qualifying distributions, $0.
Trustees: Bill Lambert, Sheila Lambert.
EIN: 316665497

40386
Ralph Landau Foundation
c/o Miller, Ellin & Co.
750 Lexington Ave.
New York, NY 10022

Financial data (yr. ended 12/31/01): Grants paid, $0; assets, $285 (L); expenditures, $285; qualifying distributions, $285.
Limitations: Applications not accepted.
Application information: Contributes only to pre-selected organizations.
Officers: Claire Landau, Pres.; Laurie J. Landau, V.P.; Edward F. Rover, Secy.-Treas.
EIN: 132895717

40387
Landmark Theatre Foundation
P.O. Box 1400
Syracuse, NY 13202-1400

Established in 1995 in NY.
Financial data (yr. ended 12/31/01): Grants paid, $0; assets, $1 (M); expenditures, $88; qualifying distributions, $0.
Limitations: Applications not accepted. Giving primarily in Syracuse, NY.
Application information: Contributes only to a pre-selected organization specified in the governing instrument.
Officers: Tarky Lombardi, Chair.; Joseph C. Maryak, Secy.-Treas.
EIN: 222773892
Codes: TN

40388
The Elaine and Robert Lang Foundation
c/o JPMorgan Chase Bank
1211 6th Ave., 34th Fl.
New York, NY 10036
Application address: P.O. Box 864, 900 S. Wapiti Rd., Wilson, WY 83014
Contact: George R. Harris, Secy.-Treas.

Established in 1989 in NJ.
Donor(s): Elaine Lang, Robert Lang.
Financial data (yr. ended 12/31/01): Grants paid, $0; assets, $346,506 (M); expenditures, $3,697; qualifying distributions, $0.
Limitations: Giving limited to NJ.
Application information: Application form not required.
Officers and Trustees:* Elaine Lang,* V.P.; Robert Lang,* V.P.; George R. Harris,* Secy.-Treas.; JPMorgan Chase Bank.
EIN: 521616109

40389
The Lillian & Ira N. Langsan Foundation, Inc.
605 3rd Ave.
New York, NY 10158-3698

Established about 1961 in NY.
Financial data (yr. ended 11/30/01): Grants paid, $0; assets, $1,253,919 (M); gifts received, $195,003; expenditures, $3,100; qualifying distributions, $0.
Limitations: Applications not accepted. Giving primarily in New York, NY.
Application information: Contributes only to pre-selected organizations.
Officers: Susan Black, V.P.; Lillian Langsan, Secy.
EIN: 136051637

40390
The Laub Family Foundation, Inc.
44 Neustadt Ln.
Chappaqua, NY 10514   (914) 238-4125

Financial data (yr. ended 12/31/01): Grants paid, $0; assets, $50 (M); gifts received, $300; expenditures, $80; qualifying distributions, $0.
Limitations: Applications not accepted. Giving primarily in Rye, NY.
Application information: Contributes only to pre-selected organizations.
Officers: Joseph Laub, Pres.; Allen Laub, Secy.; Michael Laub, Treas.
EIN: 222563750

40391
Bernard J. & Jeanne M. Lawler Family Charitable Foundation
c/o Scolaro
90 Presidential Plz.
Syracuse, NY 13202

Established in 1999 in NY.
Donor(s): Bernard J. Lawler.‡
Financial data (yr. ended 12/31/01): Grants paid, $0; assets, $93,615 (M); expenditures, $864; qualifying distributions, $0.
Limitations: Applications not accepted.
Application information: Contributes only to pre-selected organizations.
Trustees: Bernard J. Lawler, Jr., Jeanne M. Lawler, Sean M. Lawler, Catherine L. Levin, Richard S. Scolaro.
EIN: 166464903

40392
Jacob and Gwendolyn Lawrence Foundation
P.O. Box 5533
New York, NY 10027-5577

Established in 1999 in WA.
Donor(s): Jacob Lawrence, Gwendolyn Knight Lawrence.
Financial data (yr. ended 12/31/01): Grants paid, $0; assets, $476,763 (M); gifts received, $158,155; expenditures, $137,708; qualifying distributions, $0; giving activities include $79,326 for programs.
Limitations: Applications not accepted.
Application information: Contributes only to pre-selected organizations.
Officers and Directors:* Walter O. Evans,* Pres.; Thaddeus Spratlen,* V.P.; Michelle DuBois,* Secy.-Treas.; Gwendolyn Knight Lawrence, Jacob Lawrence, Peter T. Nesbett, John Reed, James Renick, Francince Seders.
EIN: 912015166

40393
Marie Lazare Foundation, Inc.
c/o Halper & Co.
331 Madison Ave., 8th Fl.
New York, NY 10017

Established around 1949 in NY.
Financial data (yr. ended 05/31/02): Grants paid, $0; assets, $1,903 (M); gifts received, $27; expenditures, $27; qualifying distributions, $0.
Limitations: Applications not accepted. Giving primarily in New York, NY.
Application information: Contributes only to pre-selected organizations.
Officer: Doriane Lazare, Secy.
EIN: 136066194

40394
Marie Lechesi Foundation for Charitable Purposes, Inc.
7219 3rd Ave.
Brooklyn, NY 11209
Contact: Harry G. English, Chair.

Established in 2001 in DC.
Donor(s): Maria E. Orr.
Financial data (yr. ended 12/31/01): Grants paid, $0; assets, $116,856 (M); expenditures, $739; qualifying distributions, $739.
Officers: Harry G. English, Chair.; Erica R. Brand, Secy.; Eileen E. English, Treas.
EIN: 522295717

40395
The Lefrak Family Foundation, Inc.
c/o Gerald Weinstein
97-77 Queens Blvd.
Rego Park, NY 11374-3317

Established in 1996 in DE and NY.
Financial data (yr. ended 11/30/99): Grants paid, $0; assets, $15,213 (M); expenditures, $770; qualifying distributions, $0.
Limitations: Applications not accepted.
Application information: Contributes only to pre-selected organizations.
Officer: Samuel J. Lefrak, Pres.
EIN: 113355562

40396
The Helen Dent Lenahan Foundation, Inc.
2316 Delaware Ave.
P.O. Box 115
Buffalo, NY 14216

Established in 2001 in NY.
Donor(s): Helen Dent Lenahan.
Financial data (yr. ended 12/31/01): Grants paid, $0; assets, $313,720 (M); gifts received, $319,376; expenditures, $0; qualifying distributions, $0.
Limitations: Applications not accepted.
Application information: Contributes only to pre-selected organizations.
Officers: Helen Dent Lenahan, Chair.; Christopher D. Lenahan, Pres.; John J. Lenahan II, Exec. V.P.; John J. Lenahan III, V.P.; Sharon G. O'Neill, Secy.; Susan Lenahan Kimberly, Treas.
EIN: 161606326

40397
The Leonora Foundation, Inc.
c/o Press Schonig & Co.
500 Bi-County Blvd., Ste. 201
Farmingdale, NY 11735

Established in 1993 in NY.
Donor(s): Emily Malino Scheuer.
Financial data (yr. ended 07/31/01): Grants paid, $0; assets, $42,370 (M); expenditures, $3,875; qualifying distributions, $0.
Application information: Application form not required.
Officers: Emily Malino Scheuer, Pres.; Laura L. Scheuer, V.P.; Elizabeth N. Scheuer, Secy.
EIN: 113176423

40398
Isabel & Russell Levin Foundation
c/o Fleischman & Co.
307 5th Ave., 13th Fl.
New York, NY 10016

Donor(s): Isabel E. Levin.

Financial data (yr. ended 10/31/01): Grants paid, $0; assets, $37,633 (M); expenditures, $1,348; qualifying distributions, $0.
Limitations: Applications not accepted. Giving on a national basis.
Application information: Contributes only to pre-selected organizations.
Trustees: Constance L. Devries, Isabel E. Levin, Peter M. Levin.
EIN: 136059071

40399
Levitt Family Foundation
c/o Barrie Levitt
16 Stone Wall Ln.
Mamaroneck, NY 10543

Established in 2001 in NY.
Donor(s): Barrie Levitt.
Financial data (yr. ended 12/31/01): Grants paid, $0; assets, $125,589 (M); gifts received, $125,590; expenditures, $0; qualifying distributions, $0.
Officer: Barrie Levitt, Mgr.
EIN: 137303430

40400
The Levy Foundation, Inc.
24 E. 84th St.
New York, NY 10028

Established in 1999 in NY.
Financial data (yr. ended 05/31/01): Grants paid, $0; assets, $10,502 (M); expenditures, $0; qualifying distributions, $0.
Limitations: Applications not accepted.
Application information: Contributes only to pre-selected organizations.
Directors: Bernard Levy, Frank Levy, S. Dean Levy.
EIN: 134090336

40401
George E. & Edith S. Lewis Foundation
c/o M&T Bank
P.O. Box 22900
Rochester, NY 14692

Donor(s): Edith S. Lewis.
Financial data (yr. ended 12/31/01): Grants paid, $0; assets, $72,372 (M); expenditures, $1,054; qualifying distributions, $0.
Limitations: Applications not accepted. Giving primarily in NY.
Application information: Contributes only to pre-selected organizations.
Trustees: Roberta L. Foreman, Edith S. Lewis, M&T Bank.
EIN: 166105764

40402
Ruth Aleine DeGraw Libertson & William Libertson Foundation
51 Lost Mountain Trail
Rochester, NY 14625

Established in 1998 in NY.
Donor(s): William Libertson.
Financial data (yr. ended 12/31/01): Grants paid, $0; assets, $872 (M); expenditures, $0; qualifying distributions, $0.
Limitations: Applications not accepted.
Application information: Contributes only to pre-selected organizations.
Trustee: William Libertson.
EIN: 166471887

40403
Liberty Legacy Foundation, Inc
c/o Neal Baker
244 Storer Ave.
New Rochelle, NY 10801

Established in 2001.
Financial data (yr. ended 12/31/01): Grants paid, $0; assets, $110,374 (M); gifts received, $110,500; expenditures, $126; qualifying distributions, $0.
Trustees: Neal Baker, Quina Baker.
EIN: 134194167

40404
The Lisette Model Foundation
c/o Gersen Wood & Blakeman, LLP
270 Madison Ave.
New York, NY 10016 (212) 683-6383
Contact: Daniel Gersen, Pres.

Established in 1996.
Financial data (yr. ended 12/31/01): Grants paid, $0; assets, $561,232 (M); expenditures, $15,465; qualifying distributions, $0.
Limitations: Giving primarily in New York, NY.
Application information: Application form not required.
Officer: Daniel Gersen, Pres.
EIN: 133591085

40405
Logo Foundation, Inc.
250 W. 85th St., Ste. 4D
New York, NY 10024

Donor(s): Logo Japan, Inc.
Financial data (yr. ended 06/30/02): Grants paid, $0; assets, $52,224 (M); gifts received, $100; expenditures, $56,082; qualifying distributions, $0.
Officers: Michael Temple, Pres.; Seymour Papert, Chair.
Director: Tessa R. Harvey.
EIN: 133629947

40406
The Long Family Foundation
c/o Robert Long
115 Central Park W.
New York, NY 10023

Established in 1998 in NY.
Donor(s): Robert D. Long.
Financial data (yr. ended 12/31/01): Grants paid, $0; assets, $88,398 (M); expenditures, $50; qualifying distributions, $0.
Limitations: Applications not accepted.
Application information: Contributes only to pre-selected organizations.
Directors: Susan Elizabeth Biondo, Randall Caudill, Robert D. Long.
EIN: 311634845

40407
Peter C. Lovenheim Charitable Trust
280 Sandringham Rd.
Rochester, NY 14610

Established in 1996 in NY.
Donor(s): Peter C. Lovenheim.
Financial data (yr. ended 12/31/01): Grants paid, $0; assets, $36 (M); expenditures, $0; qualifying distributions, $0.
Trustees: Peter C. Lovenheim, Robert J. Lovenheim.
EIN: 166438267

40408
Robert J. Lovenheim Charitable Trust
280 Sandringham Rd.
Rochester, NY 14610
Contact: Peter C. Lovenheim, Tr.

Established in 1996 in NY.
Financial data (yr. ended 12/31/01): Grants paid, $0; assets, $36 (M); expenditures, $0; qualifying distributions, $0.
Trustees: Peter C. Lovenheim, Robert J. Lovenheim.
EIN: 223418985

40409
MacAndrews & Forbes Foundation, Inc.
c/o MacAndrews & Forbes Holdings Inc.
38 E. 63rd St., Tax Dept.
New York, NY 10021

Established in 1982 in NY.
Donor(s): MacAndrews & Forbes Co., MacAndrews & Forbes Group, Inc., Technicolor, Inc., Wilbur Chocolate Co., RLL Corp.
Financial data (yr. ended 12/31/00): Grants paid, $0; assets, $57,626 (M); expenditures, $98; qualifying distributions, $0.
Limitations: Applications not accepted. Giving primarily in New York, NY.
Application information: Contributes only to pre-selected organizations.
Officers and Directors:* Ronald O. Perelman,* Chair. and C.E.O.; Donald Drapkin,* Vice-Chair.; Howard Gittis,* Vice-Chair.; Bruce Slovin,* Vice-Chair.; Richard E. Halperin, Pres.; Irwin Engelman, Exec. V.P. and C.F.O.; Barry F. Schwartz, Exec. V.P.; Glenn P. Dickes, V.P. and Secy.; Laurence Winoker, V.P. and Cont.; Gerry R. Kessel, V.P.; Marvin Schaffer, V.P.
EIN: 133116648
Codes: CS, CD

40410
Madison Charitable Fund, Inc.
200 Madison Ave., 5th Fl.
New York, NY 10016

Established in 1992 in NY and DE.
Donor(s): Sandra Priest Rose, Susan and Elihu Rose Foundation, Inc.
Financial data (yr. ended 12/31/00): Grants paid, $0; assets, $956 (M); gifts received, $1,000; expenditures, $207; qualifying distributions, $0.
Limitations: Applications not accepted. Giving on a national basis.
Application information: Contributes only to pre-selected organizations.
Officers and Director:* Elihu Rose,* Pres.; Daniel Rose, V.P.; Michael D. Sullivan, Secy.-Treas.
EIN: 133646262

40411
MAH Foundation
40 Windy Hill Rd.
Millbrook, NY 12545
Application address: R.R. 1, Box 132A, Kernals Rd., Millbrook, NY 12545, tel.: (914) 677-9292
Contact: Munir Abu-Haidar, Tr.

Established in 1996 in NY.
Donor(s): Munir Abu-Haidar.
Financial data (yr. ended 12/31/01): Grants paid, $0; assets, $595,058 (M); gifts received, $492,955; expenditures, $0; qualifying distributions, $0.
Trustees: Munir Abu-Haidar, Susan Abu-Haidar.
EIN: 133895871

40412
The Herbert Mahne Family Foundation
(Formerly The Lucy Wang Foundation)
c/o Bessemer Trust Co., N.A.
630 5th Ave., Tax Dept.
New York, NY 10111

Established in 2000 in CA.
Donor(s): Michael Aragon, Marlo Mahne Aragon.
Financial data (yr. ended 12/31/01): Grants paid, $0; assets, $121,605 (M); gifts received, $350; expenditures, $6,423; qualifying distributions, $0.
Limitations: Applications not accepted.
Application information: Contributes only to pre-selected organizations.
Officers and Directors:* Marlo Mahne Aragon,* Pres.; Michael Aragon,* V.P. and Treas.; Malin Coleridge,* Secy.; Christine M. Mills.
EIN: 954797008

40413
The Maimonides Trust
4611 12th Ave.
Brooklyn, NY 11219-2539

Established in 1993.
Donor(s): David Bistricer, Ester Bistricer.
Financial data (yr. ended 12/31/01): Grants paid, $0; assets, $130,063 (M); expenditures, $50; qualifying distributions, $0.
Limitations: Applications not accepted.
Application information: Contributes only to pre-selected organizations.
Trustees: David Bistricer, Ester Bistricer.
EIN: 116427321

40414
Maioglio-Blobel Foundation
c/o Rockefeller University
1230 York Ave.
New York, NY 10021

Established in 1999.
Financial data (yr. ended 06/30/01): Grants paid, $0; assets, $0 (M); expenditures, $30; qualifying distributions, $0.
Officers: Gunter Blobel, Pres.; Carl P. Blobel, V.P.; Laura Maioglio, Secy.
EIN: 134068267

40415
The Malevich Society
2 Park Ave., 21st Fl.
New York, NY 10016
Contact: Lawrence M. Kaye, Secy.

Established in 2001 in NY.
Donor(s): Clemens Toussaint.
Financial data (yr. ended 12/31/01): Grants paid, $0; assets, $998,107 (M); gifts received, $1,014,985; expenditures, $20,857; qualifying distributions, $16,740.
Officers: Charlotte Douglas, Pres.; Vivian Barnett, V.P.; Lawrence M. Kaye, Secy.; Clemens Toussaint, Treas.
Director: Christina Lodder.
EIN: 134181214

40416
Steven Malin Foundation for Creative Arts & Sciences
128 E. 7th St., Ste. 4
New York, NY 10009-6100

Established in 1999 in NY.
Donor(s): Steven Malin.
Financial data (yr. ended 12/31/99): Grants paid, $0; assets, $43,000 (M); gifts received, $41,520; expenditures, $0; qualifying distributions, $0.
Limitations: Applications not accepted.
Application information: Contributes only to pre-selected organizations.
Director: Steven Malin.
EIN: 134063223

40417
Eskandar Manocherian Foundation
c/o Mrs. Darel Benaim
135 Central Park W.
New York, NY 10023

Established in 2000 in NY.
Donor(s): Eskandar Manocherian.‡
Financial data (yr. ended 06/30/01): Grants paid, $0; assets, $726,993 (M); gifts received, $1,000,000; expenditures, $6,800; qualifying distributions, $0.
Trustees: Darel Benaim, Donald Manocherian, Jeffrey Manocherian.
EIN: 137251596

40418
Ralph C. Marcove Cancer Research Foundation, Inc.
c/o Marcove
517 E. 71st St.
New York, NY 10021-4871

Established in 1974.
Donor(s): Ralph C. Marcove.‡
Financial data (yr. ended 12/31/01): Grants paid, $0; assets, $1,151,648 (M); expenditures, $8,316; qualifying distributions, $0.
Limitations: Applications not accepted. Giving primarily in NY.
Application information: Contributes only to pre-selected organizations.
Officers: Nancy Marcove Nelson, V.P.; Christina Cherevko, Secy.
EIN: 237309316

40419
The Debbie and Jerry Marcus Foundation
c/o P. Vermont
60 E. 42nd St., Ste. 2918
New York, NY 10165
Application address: 84-09 Chevy Chase St., Jamaica Estates, NY 11432, tel.: (917) 776-0200
Contact: Jerome Marcus, Pres.

Established in 2000 in NY.
Donor(s): Jerome Marcus.
Financial data (yr. ended 12/31/00): Grants paid, $0; assets, $100,753 (M); gifts received, $100,613; expenditures, $0; qualifying distributions, $0.
Application information: Application form not required.
Officers: Jerome Marcus, Pres. and Treas.; Deborah S. Marcus, V.P.; Jaimie Marcus, Secy.
EIN: 113577656

40420
Donald B. Marron Charitable Trust
c/o Starr & Co.
350 Park Ave.
New York, NY 10022
Application address: 51 W. 52nd St., 23rd Fl., New York, NY 10019
Contact: Donald Marron, Tr.

Established in 2000 in NY.
Donor(s): Donald B. Marron.
Financial data (yr. ended 12/31/00): Grants paid, $0; assets, $16,592,452 (M); gifts received, $15,821,171; expenditures, $0; qualifying distributions, $0.
Trustee: Donald B. Marron.
EIN: 137260354

40421
The Catherine C. Marron Foundation
720 Park Ave.
New York, NY 10021
Application address: 1285 Ave. of the Americas, New York, NY 10019
Contact: Catherine C. Marron, Pres.

Donor(s): Donald B. Marron.
Financial data (yr. ended 12/31/00): Grants paid, $0; assets, $1,330,124 (M); gifts received, $1,268,311; expenditures, $344; qualifying distributions, $0.
Officer: Catherine C. Marron, Pres.
EIN: 133919083

40422
The Andrew H. Marshak Foundation
c/o Andrew H. Marshak
146 Duane St., Ste. 5C
New York, NY 10013

Established in 1999 in NY.
Donor(s): Andrew H. Marshak.
Financial data (yr. ended 05/31/99): Grants paid, $0; assets, $11,250 (M); gifts received, $1,502; expenditures, $1,500; qualifying distributions, $0.
Limitations: Applications not accepted.
Application information: Contributes only to pre-selected organizations.
Director: Andrew H. Marshak.
EIN: 134053947

40423
Maslow Foundation, Inc.
1633 Broadway
New York, NY 10019-6708 (212) 974-1100
Contact: Lester Maslow, Pres.

Established in 1953 in NY.
Donor(s): Best Mfg., Inc.
Financial data (yr. ended 12/31/01): Grants paid, $0; assets, $755 (M); expenditures, $0; qualifying distributions, $0.
Limitations: Applications not accepted. Giving primarily in New York, NY.
Application information: Contributes only to pre-selected organizations.
Officers: Lester Maslow, Pres.; Irving Miles, V.P.
EIN: 136128653

40424
Pierre and Maria-Gaetana Matisse Charitable Foundation
1 E. 53rd St.
New York, NY 10022

Established in 1995 in DE and NY.
Donor(s): Maria-Gaetana Matisse.
Financial data (yr. ended 12/31/00): Grants paid, $0; assets, $11,632 (M); gifts received, $210,000; expenditures, $195,093; qualifying distributions, $0; giving activities include $285 for programs.
Limitations: Applications not accepted.
Application information: Contributes only to pre-selected organizations.
Officers: Maria-Gaetana Matisse, Pres.; Robert H. Horowitz, Secy.
Directors: Janos Farkas, Eugene V. Thaw.
EIN: 133838457

40425
Max Foundation
c/o George V. Delson Assocs.
110 E. 59th St.
New York, NY 10022-1304

Financial data (yr. ended 06/30/01): Grants paid, $0; assets, $36,463 (M); expenditures, $1,832; qualifying distributions, $1,429.
Limitations: Applications not accepted.

Application information: Contributes only to pre-selected organizations.
Trustees: Darren K. Indyke, Ghislaine Maxwell.
EIN: 656194566

40426
Mayore Foundation, Ltd.
100 Henry St.
Brooklyn, NY 11201

Established in 2000 in NY.
Donor(s): Sholom Drizin.
Financial data (yr. ended 12/31/01): Grants paid, $0; assets, $1,336 (M); gifts received, $32; expenditures, $32; qualifying distributions, $0.
Limitations: Giving primarily in Brooklyn, NY.
Officers: Sholom Drizin, Pres.; Shoshana Drizin, Secy.; Moshe Drizin, Treas.
EIN: 113432602

40427
Charles V. McAdam, Jr. Charitable Foundation, Inc.
c/o M.J. Bernardo
444 Madison Ave., Ste. 2901
New York, NY 10022-6903

Established in 2000 in FL.
Financial data (yr. ended 12/31/01): Grants paid, $0; assets, $1,475 (M); expenditures, $380; qualifying distributions, $0.
Officers: Charles V. McAdam, Jr., Pres.; Frank Gannett McAdam, Secy.-Treas.
EIN: 311603603

40428
David McCall Foundation, Inc.
136 E. 64th St.
New York, NY 10021

Established in 1992 in NY.
Donor(s): David B. McCall.‡
Financial data (yr. ended 06/30/01): Grants paid, $0; assets, $117,566 (M); expenditures, $85; qualifying distributions, $0.
Limitations: Applications not accepted.
Application information: Contributes only to pre-selected organizations.
Directors: Anne Joyce, David B. McCall, Jr., John P. McCall, Peter C. McCall, Robert D. McCall, Thomas C. McCall, William D. McCall, Jerome S. Traum.
EIN: 133676098

40429
The McClean Family Foundation
87 Mill River Rd.
Upper Brookville, NY 11771-2737

Established in 2000 in NY.
Donor(s): Ferrel P. McClean.
Financial data (yr. ended 12/31/01): Grants paid, $0; assets, $389,979 (M); gifts received, $307,993; expenditures, $4,755; qualifying distributions, $0.
Limitations: Applications not accepted.
Application information: Contributes only to pre-selected organizations.
Trustees: Ferrell P. McClean, William C. McClean III, William C. McClean IV.
EIN: 113584337

40430
Anne O'Hare McCormick Memorial Fund, Inc.
c/o News Women's Club
15 Gramercy Park S., 2nd Fl.
New York, NY 10003 (212) 777-1610

Established in 1955 in NY.
Financial data (yr. ended 12/31/01): Grants paid, $0; assets, $2,543,262 (M); gifts received, $9,501; expenditures, $1,109; qualifying distributions, $1,109.
Limitations: Giving limited to New York, NY.
Publications: Application guidelines.
Application information: Send SASE (regular business-size). Application form required.
Officers: Joan O'Sullivan, Pres.; Judith Crist, V.P.; Sylvia Carter, Secy.; Amanda Harris, Treas.
EIN: 136144221
Codes: GTI

40431
Joseph and Martha Melohn Philanthropic Fund
1995 Broadway, 14th Fl.
New York, NY 10023-5882 (212) 787-2500
Contact: Alfons Melohn, Tr.

Established in 1986 in NY.
Donor(s): Alfons Melohn.
Financial data (yr. ended 11/30/01): Grants paid, $0; assets, $3 (M); expenditures, $0; qualifying distributions, $0.
Limitations: Giving primarily in New York, NY.
Trustee: Alfons Melohn.
EIN: 133395221

40432
Jill Metzler Foundation
c/o Charles Metzler
70 Cadman Ave.
Babylon, NY 11702

Established in 2001 in NY.
Donor(s): Charles Metzler, Arlene Metzler.
Financial data (yr. ended 12/31/01): Grants paid, $0; assets, $9,857 (M); gifts received, $9,857; expenditures, $150; qualifying distributions, $0.
Trustees: Patricia Brienzo, Arlene Metzler, Charles Metzler, Keith Metzler, Kurt Metzler, William Metzler.
EIN: 311814466

40433
Meyer Family Foundation
c/o Jankoff & Gabe, PC
575 Lexington Ave., 14th Fl.
New York, NY 10022
Contact: Eric Meyer, Dir.

Established in 2000 in NY.
Donor(s): Eric Meyer.
Financial data (yr. ended 12/31/00): Grants paid, $0; assets, $71,562 (M); gifts received, $175,000; expenditures, $0; qualifying distributions, $0.
Application information: Application form not required.
Directors: Donald Duffy, Eric Meyer, Mary Ellen Meyer.
EIN: 134120984

40434
The William & Theresa Meyerowitz Foundation, Inc.
c/o American Express Tax & Business Svcs. of NY, Inc.
1185 Ave. of the Americas
New York, NY 10036-2602

Established in 1978.
Donor(s): William Meyerowitz.‡
Financial data (yr. ended 12/31/00): Grants paid, $0; assets, $1,045,029 (M); expenditures, $24,983; qualifying distributions, $20,898.
Limitations: Applications not accepted. Giving limited to New York, NY.
Application information: Contributes only to pre-selected organizations.
Officer: Arthur S. Hoffman, Treas.
EIN: 133054669

40435
Mid-Hudson Preservation Alliance, Inc.
P.O. Box 500
Pine Plains, NY 12567

Established in 1997 in NY.
Financial data (yr. ended 12/31/00): Grants paid, $0; assets, $6,097 (M); gifts received, $12,050; expenditures, $10,735; qualifying distributions, $10,735; giving activities include $10,735 for programs.
Officers: Burt Diamond, Pres.; Karry Madigan, Secy.; Florence Diamond, Treas.
Directors: Jim Petrie, Joan Redmond, Neal Rosenthal, Connie Sayre, Connie Young.
EIN: 141729507

40436
Mika Sports Association, Inc.
96 Schermerhorn St.
Brooklyn, NY 11201-5039

Financial data (yr. ended 12/31/01): Grants paid, $0; assets, $5,208 (M); gifts received, $400; expenditures, $1,835; qualifying distributions, $0.
Directors: Matthew Cadeau, Barney Davis, Lawrence Major.
EIN: 113017715

40437
The MM & CTW Foundation, Inc.
c/o Alfred West
1657 49th St.
Brooklyn, NY 11204

Established in 2000 in NY.
Donor(s): Alfred West.
Financial data (yr. ended 12/31/00): Grants paid, $0; assets, $1,450,332 (M); gifts received, $1,450,332; expenditures, $0; qualifying distributions, $0.
Limitations: Applications not accepted.
Application information: Contributes only to pre-selected organizations.
EIN: 113540903

40438
Montgomerie Foundation
c/o Inverness Counsel
545 Madison Ave., 9th Fl.
New York, NY 10022

Established in 2001 in DE.
Donor(s): Patricia Montgomerie.
Financial data (yr. ended 12/31/01): Grants paid, $0; assets, $96,163 (M); gifts received, $98,061; expenditures, $0; qualifying distributions, $0.
Limitations: Applications not accepted.
Application information: Contributes only to pre-selected organizations.
EIN: 134195642

40439
Morasha Foundation, Inc.
750 Kappock St.
Riverdale, NY 10463

Established in 1996.
Financial data (yr. ended 12/31/99): Grants paid, $0; assets, $209,246 (M); expenditures, $41,461; qualifying distributions, $41,461; giving activities include $41,461 for programs.
Limitations: Applications not accepted.
Application information: Contributes only to pre-selected organizations.
Director: Haim Soloveichik.
EIN: 133354143

40440
The Tom Morgan & Erna J. McReynolds Charitable Foundation
c/o Henry L. Hulbert
6 Ford Ave.
Oneonta, NY 13820
Application address: 20 Clinton St., Oneonta, NY 13820
Contact: George Thomas Morgan, Tr.

Established in 1999 in NY.
Financial data (yr. ended 12/31/99): Grants paid, $0; assets, $5,011 (M); gifts received, $5,000; expenditures, $0; qualifying distributions, $0.
Limitations: Giving primarily in Oneonta, NY.
Trustees: Wendy M. Brown, Erna J. McReynolds, George Thomas Morgan.
EIN: 166494096

40441
Chelsea Morrison Foundation
19 E. 72nd St., Ste. 3B
New York, NY 10021

Established in 2001 in NY.
Financial data (yr. ended 12/31/01): Grants paid, $0; assets, $24,094 (M); gifts received, $26,000; expenditures, $1,906; qualifying distributions, $0.
Limitations: Applications not accepted.
Application information: Contributes to pre-selected organizations.
Directors: Joanne Morrison, Thomas Morrison.
EIN: 134159265

40442
Moynihan Charitable Foundation
3 Beechwood Dr.
Glen Oaks, NY 11004

Established in 2001 in NY.
Financial data (yr. ended 12/31/01): Grants paid, $0; assets, $168 (M); gifts received, $168; expenditures, $0; qualifying distributions, $0.
Trustee: Denis J. Moynihan.
EIN: 113586652

40443
MRF Foundation
1527 55th St.
Brooklyn, NY 11219-4314
Contact: Mark Frankel, Tr.

Established in 1995 in NY.
Donor(s): Mark Frankel, Martin Weissman.
Financial data (yr. ended 12/31/00): Grants paid, $0; assets, $386,992 (M); expenditures, $202; qualifying distributions, $0.
Limitations: Applications not accepted.
Application information: Contributes only to pre-selected organizations.
Trustees: Mark Frankel, Rachel Frankel.
EIN: 133864392

40444
The Albert R. and Margaret S. Mugel Foundation
12 Fountain Plz.
Buffalo, NY 14202

Established in 1999 in NY.
Financial data (yr. ended 12/31/01): Grants paid, $0; assets, $195,553 (M); expenditures, $5,233; qualifying distributions, $0.
Limitations: Applications not accepted.
Application information: Contributes only to pre-selected organizations.
Officers and Directors:* Albert R. Mugel,* Pres.; Christopher J. Mugel, V.P.; Richard L. Mugel,* Secy.-Treas.; Douglas N. Mugel, Jonathan A. Mugel.
EIN: 161575787

40445
John J. & Jane C. Muraco Foundation for Charity, Inc.
3001 James St., 2nd Fl.
Syracuse, NY 13206

Established in 1997 in NY.
Donor(s): Michael S. Muraco.
Financial data (yr. ended 12/31/00): Grants paid, $0; assets, $2,309 (M); expenditures, $578; qualifying distributions, $0.
Limitations: Applications not accepted.
Application information: Contributes only to pre-selected organizations.
Officers: Michael S. Muraco, Chair.; Lisa Muraco, Secy.
EIN: 161515930

40446
Jules and Susan Musinger Foundation
282 Ambassador Dr.
Rochester, NY 14610-3411

Established in 1986 in NY.
Donor(s): Jules Musinger, Susan S. Musinger.
Financial data (yr. ended 11/30/01): Grants paid, $0; assets, $15,604 (M); expenditures, $50; qualifying distributions, $0.
Limitations: Applications not accepted. Giving primarily in Rochester, NY.
Application information: Contributes only to pre-selected organizations.
Officer and Trustees:* Jules Musinger,* Chair.; Douglas S. Musinger, Susan S. Musinger.
EIN: 222775675

40447
The Nanwani Foundation, Inc.
1407 Broadway, Ste. 2300
New York, NY 10018-2666

Established in 1997 in NY; funded in 1998.
Donor(s): Suresh Nanwani.
Financial data (yr. ended 12/31/99): Grants paid, $0; assets, $680,181 (M); expenditures, $2,732; qualifying distributions, $2,466.
Limitations: Applications not accepted.
Application information: Contributes only to pre-selected organizations.
Officer: Suresh Nanwani, Pres.
Directors: Sheetal Nanwani, Edmund Schaffzin.
EIN: 133982507

40448
The Marie and Paul Napoli Foundation
1985-4 Cedar Swamp Rd.
Brookville, NY 11545

Established in 2000 in NY.
Donor(s): Paul Joseph Napoli, Marie Elizabeth Kaiser Napoli.
Financial data (yr. ended 12/31/00): Grants paid, $0; assets, $250,000 (M); gifts received, $250,000; expenditures, $0; qualifying distributions, $250,000.
Limitations: Applications not accepted.
Application information: Contributes only to pre-selected organizations.
Officers and Directors:* Marie Elizabeth Kaiser Napoli,* Pres. and Secy.-Treas.; Paul Joseph Napoli,* V.P.; Gerald J. Kaiser.
EIN: 113579283

40449
Morris & Rita Nass Foundation
6251 Asquith Crescent
Rego Park, NY 11374-3929 (718) 997-7133
Contact: Morris Nass, Pres.

Financial data (yr. ended 12/31/01): Grants paid, $0; assets, $1,521 (M); gifts received, $1,600; expenditures, $100; qualifying distributions, $0.
Limitations: Applications not accepted. Giving primarily in NY.
Officers: Morris Nass, Pres.; Howard Nass, Secy.-Treas.
EIN: 112289444

40450
The National Council for Research on Women
11 Hanover Sq., 20th Fl.
New York, NY 10005 (212) 785-7335
Contact: Donna Shavlik, Chair.

Financial data (yr. ended 09/30/99): Grants paid, $0; assets, $191,744 (M); gifts received, $531,115; expenditures, $494,589; qualifying distributions, $494,589; giving activities include $309,125 for programs.
Limitations: Giving limited to female residents of India and Bangladesh.
Officers and Directors:* Donna Shavlik,* Chair.; Heather Johnston Nicholson,* Vice-Chair.; Linda Basch, Exec. Dir.; Kathryn Rodgers, Exec. Dir.; Judith Saidel, Exec. Dir.; Electra Arenal, and 17 additional directors.
EIN: 133170956
Codes: TN

40451
Natsource Charitable Foundation
140 Broadway, 30th Fl.
New York, NY 10005

Established in 2001 in NY.
Donor(s): Natsource, LLC.
Financial data (yr. ended 12/31/01): Grants paid, $0; assets, $326,000 (M); gifts received, $326,000; expenditures, $0; qualifying distributions, $0.
Officers: Jack Cogen, Pres.; Marc G. Mellman, V.P. and Secy.-Treas.; Stephen Touchstone, V.P.
EIN: 522362637
Codes: CS

40452
Natures Plus Foundation
548 Broadhollow Rd.
Melville, NY 11747 (631) 293-0030
Contact: Marci Dunder

Financial data (yr. ended 11/30/01): Grants paid, $0; assets, $481,794 (M); expenditures, $1,735; qualifying distributions, $0.
Limitations: Giving primarily in Ynez, CA.
Application information: Application form required.
Trustee: Gerald Kessler.
EIN: 112670750

40453
The Navigation Trust
1 HSBC Ctr., 16th Fl.
Buffalo, NY 14203-2885

Established in 2001 in NY.
Donor(s): Howard Berman, Marilyn Berman.
Financial data (yr. ended 12/31/01): Grants paid, $0; assets, $95,835 (M); gifts received, $100,000; expenditures, $409; qualifying distributions, $41.
Trustees: Howard J. Berman, Marilyn Berman, HSBC Bank USA.
EIN: 161602590

40454
The Ne'eman Foundation, Inc.
495 S. Broadway
Yonkers, NY 10705

Established in 2000 in NY.
Financial data (yr. ended 12/31/00): Grants paid, $0; assets, $3,177 (L); gifts received, $3,450; expenditures, $1,749; qualifying distributions, $233; giving activities include $1,709 for programs.
Directors: Aryeh Jeselsohn, Natan Jeselsohn, Sura Jeselsohn.
EIN: 134039907

40455
The Neal-Schuman Foundation, Inc.
77 Fulton St., Ste. 13C
New York, NY 10038

Established in 2001.
Donor(s): John Vincent Neal, Patricia Glass Schuman.
Financial data (yr. ended 12/31/01): Grants paid, $0; assets, $20,163 (M); gifts received, $10,000; expenditures, $150; qualifying distributions, $0.
Directors: Nancy Keanick, John Vincent Neal, Patricia Glass Schuman.
EIN: 134163018

40456
Neff Family Charitable Trust
c/o Wachtell, Lipton, Rosen & Katz
51 W. 52nd St.
New York, NY 10019

Established in 1987 in NY.
Donor(s): Daniel A. Neff.
Financial data (yr. ended 12/31/01): Grants paid, $0; assets, $25,134 (M); expenditures, $30; qualifying distributions, $0.
Limitations: Applications not accepted. Giving primarily in New York, NY.
Application information: Contributes only to pre-selected organizations.
Trustees: Daniel A. Neff, Jodi J. Schwartz.
EIN: 133389914

40457
Leroy Neiman Foundation, Inc.
1 W. 67th St.
New York, NY 10023-6223
Contact: Jason Jacobs, Secy.-Treas.

Established in 1987 in NY.
Donor(s): Leroy Neiman, Janet Neiman.
Financial data (yr. ended 12/31/01): Grants paid, $0; assets, $4,326,122 (M); gifts received, $900,000; expenditures, $6,170; qualifying distributions, $0.
Limitations: Applications not accepted. Giving limited to NY.
Application information: Contributes only to pre-selected organizations.
Officers: Leroy Neiman, Pres.; Janet Neiman, V.P.; Jason Jacobs, Secy.-Treas.
EIN: 133385053

40458
Rona and Randolph M. Nelson Foundation
300 Central Park W., Ste. 5G
New York, NY 10024

Established in 2001 in NY.
Donor(s): Randolph M. Nelson, Ruth Nelson Family Foundation.
Financial data (yr. ended 12/31/01): Grants paid, $0; assets, $348,875 (M); gifts received, $254,117; expenditures, $505; qualifying distributions, $0.
Limitations: Applications not accepted.

Application information: Contributes only to pre-selected organizations.
Trustees: Randolph M. Nelson, Rona Nelson.
EIN: 134196469

40459
Win J. Neuger and Christie C. Neuger Family Foundation, Inc.
c/o American Express Tax Svcs.
1185 Ave. of the Americas
New York, NY 10038

Established in 1998 in NY.
Donor(s): Win J. Neuger.
Financial data (yr. ended 06/30/99): Grants paid, $0; assets, $285,388 (M); gifts received, $260,601; expenditures, $5,601; qualifying distributions, $4,201.
Limitations: Applications not accepted.
Application information: Contributes only to pre-selected organizations.
Directors: Christie C. Neuger, Win J. Neuger.
EIN: 364263404

40460
The Neuhauser Family Foundation, Inc.
c/o Brown Rudnick, et al.
120 W. 45th St.
New York, NY 10036

Established in 2001 in NY.
Donor(s): Stuart Neuhauser.
Financial data (yr. ended 12/31/01): Grants paid, $0; assets, $215,004 (M); gifts received, $215,000; expenditures, $0; qualifying distributions, $0.
Limitations: Applications not accepted.
Application information: Contributes only to pre-selected organizations.
Officers and Directors:* Stuart Neuhauser,* Pres.; Chani Neuhauser,* Secy.; Ben Neuhauser.
EIN: 010556235

40461
Maria I. New Children's Hormone Foundation, Inc.
525 E. 68th St., Box 103
New York, NY 10021

Established in 2001 in NY.
Donor(s): J.H. Weldon Foundation, Inc., Hecksher Foundation for Children.
Financial data (yr. ended 12/31/01): Grants paid, $0; assets, $10,000 (M); gifts received, $15,147; expenditures, $5,647; qualifying distributions, $500.
Limitations: Applications not accepted.
Application information: Contributes only to pre-selected organizations.
Officers and Directors:* Andrea Geisser,* Pres.; Frank Argenbright,* V.P.; Robert Toussie,* Secy.-Treas.; John Baxter, M.D., F. Randall Bigony, Meryl Erlanger, Rafael Garcia, Themis Hadjiyanis, Peter S. Kalikow, Maria I. New, M.D., Howard G. "Peter" Sloane, Colleen Kelleher Sorrentino, Arthur G. Tisi, June de H. Weldon.
EIN: 134200099

40462
New Jersey/New York Laborers' Research Foundation, Inc.
18 Corporate Woods Blvd.
Albany, NY 12211

Established in 1997 in NY.
Financial data (yr. ended 12/31/01): Grants paid, $0; assets, $32,415 (M); expenditures, $0; qualifying distributions, $0.
Officer and Director:* Raymond Pocino,* Pres.
EIN: 161530372

40463
The New York Eye and Ear Infirmary Foundation
310 E. 14th St.
New York, NY 10003

Established in 2000 in NY.
Donor(s): The New York Eye and Ear Infirmary.
Financial data (yr. ended 12/31/00): Grants paid, $0; assets, $2,741,078 (M); gifts received, $3,000,000; expenditures, $0; qualifying distributions, $0.
Limitations: Applications not accepted.
Application information: Contributes only to pre-selected organizations.
Officers: Peter Frelinghuysen, Pres.; Judith Zesiger, V.P.; Matthew J. Trachtenberg, Treas.
EIN: 134012469
Codes: CS

40464
The Newcomer Foundation, Inc.
388 Guard Hill Rd.
Bedford, NY 10506 (914) 234-9068
Contact: Nancy Newcomer Vick, Pres.

Established in 2001 in NY.
Donor(s): Nancy Newcomer Vick.
Financial data (yr. ended 12/31/01): Grants paid, $0; assets, $988,166 (M); gifts received, $11,115; expenditures, $0; qualifying distributions, $0.
Application information: Application form not required.
Officers: Nancy Newcomer Vick, Pres.; Judy Newcomer Birkett, V.P.; Linda Schoenthaler, Secy.-Treas.
EIN: 134199724

40465
The Wynn Newhouse Foundation, Inc.
c/o Paul Scherer & Co., LLP
335 Madison Ave., 9th Fl.
New York, NY 10017

Established in 1994 in NY.
Donor(s): Advance Publications, Inc.
Financial data (yr. ended 12/31/01): Grants paid, $0; assets, $106 (M); expenditures, $0; qualifying distributions, $0.
Limitations: Applications not accepted. Giving limited to the Northeast.
Application information: Contributes only to pre-selected organizations.
Officers: Wynn Newhouse, Pres.; Robert J. Miron, V.P.; Richard Diamond, Secy.-Treas.
EIN: 133780428
Codes: CS, CD

40466
The Newman Family Foundation, Inc.
c/o Bessember Trust Co., N.A.
630 5th Ave., Tax Dept.
New York, NY 10111

Established in 1999 in FL.
Donor(s): Charles W. Newman.
Financial data (yr. ended 12/31/01): Grants paid, $0; assets, $182,698 (M); gifts received, $185,801; expenditures, $3,254; qualifying distributions, $0.
Limitations: Applications not accepted.
Application information: Contributes only to pre-selected organizations.
Officers: Charles W. Newman, Pres.; Diane G. Newman, V. P.; Charles J. Newman, Secy.; Marc A. Newman, Treas.
EIN: 593560674

40467
The Kathryn J. & Theodore E. Nixon Family Foundation, Inc.
45 Sunset Blvd.
Pittsford, NY 14534

Established in 2001 in NY.
Donor(s): Theodore Nixon, Kathryn Nixon.
Financial data (yr. ended 12/31/01): Grants paid, $0; assets, $520,000 (M); gifts received, $520,000; expenditures, $0; qualifying distributions, $0.
Limitations: Applications not accepted.
Application information: Contributes only to pre-selected organizations.
Officer and Directors:* Theodore E. Nixon,* Pres.; Erik B. Nixon, Jessica Nixon, Kathryn J. Nixon.
EIN: 161614090

40468
The Nixon Foundation, Inc.
c/o Oberfest & Assoc.
287 King St.
Chappaqua, NY 10514

Donor(s): Plonia Nixon.
Financial data (yr. ended 09/30/01): Grants paid, $0; assets, $195,739 (M); gifts received, $200; expenditures, $2,896; qualifying distributions, $0.
Limitations: Applications not accepted. Giving primarily in CT.
Application information: Contributes only to pre-selected organizations.
Officers and Directors:* Plonia Nixon,* Pres.; Bruce D. Oberfest,* Secy.-Treas.; Fred Leuthasuur, Karl Van Horn.
EIN: 222488429

40469
Nina Norgaard Charitable Trust
c/o Fleet National Bank
159 E. Main St.
Rochester, NY 14638

Financial data (yr. ended 12/31/00): Grants paid, $0; assets, $122,097 (M); expenditures, $1,575; qualifying distributions, $960.
Limitations: Applications not accepted. Giving primarily in Auburn, NY.
Application information: Contributes only to pre-selected organizations.
Trustee: Fleet National Bank.
EIN: 166156459

40470
The Teddy and Bill Novak Foundation
P.O. Box 176
Hopewell Junction, NY 12533

Established in 1999 in NY.
Financial data (yr. ended 12/31/01): Grants paid, $0; assets, $311 (M); gifts received, $300; expenditures, $300; qualifying distributions, $0.
Officers and Directors:* William H. Novak,* Pres., Secy., and Treas.; Terese Novak,* V.P.; Timothy Novak.
EIN: 141805345

40471
NYBDC Charitable Foundation, Inc.
P.O. Box 738
Albany, NY 12201-0738

Established in 2000 in NY.
Donor(s): NYBDC - New York Business Development Corporation.
Financial data (yr. ended 09/30/01): Grants paid, $0; assets, $100,026 (M); gifts received, $100,000; expenditures, $0; qualifying distributions, $0.

Directors: H. Chorbajian, T. Goldrick, Jr., K. Hitchcock, E. Kailbourne, R. Lazar, J. Mack, W. Rich.
EIN: 141834499
Codes: CS

40472
James Charles O'Connor Foundation, Inc.
c/o Buchbinder, Tunick & Co., LLP
1 Pennsylvania Plz., No. 5335
New York, NY 10119

Financial data (yr. ended 12/31/01): Grants paid, $0; assets, $106,902 (M); expenditures, $2,333; qualifying distributions, $0.
Limitations: Giving limited to Dublin, Ireland.
Officers: James C. Grey, Pres.; Frederick I. Kahn, V.P.
EIN: 237224948

40473
The T. D. & M. A. O'Malley Foundation, Inc.
c/o David Berdon & Co., LLP
415 Madison Ave.
New York, NY 10017-1111

Established in 1985 in CT.
Donor(s): Thomas D. O'Malley.
Financial data (yr. ended 09/30/01): Grants paid, $0; assets, $8,770,234 (M); gifts received, $9,102,400; expenditures, $3,013; qualifying distributions, $0.
Limitations: Applications not accepted. Giving primarily in CT and New York, NY.
Application information: Contributes only to pre-selected organizations.
Officers: Thomas D. O'Malley, Pres. and Treas.; Mary Alice O'Malley, V.P. and Secy.
Director: Edwin J. O'Mara, Jr.
EIN: 061157580

40474
Charles Z. Offin Charitable Trust
c/o JPMorgan Private Bank
1211 Ave. of the Americas, 38th Fl.
New York, NY 10036 (212) 789-5679
FAX: (212) 596-3712; *E-mail:* elias_jacqueline@jpmorgan.com
Contact: Jacqueline Elias, V.P., JPMorgan Chase Bank

Established in 1990 in NY.
Financial data (yr. ended 11/30/01): Grants paid, $0; assets, $2,396,856 (M); expenditures, $39,587; qualifying distributions, $13,926.
Limitations: Giving limited to New York, NY.
Application information: Application guidelines available on request.
Trustee: JPMorgan Chase Bank.
EIN: 136944122

40475
The OGM Foundation, Inc.
c/o Edward Rappa
425 E. 58th St.
New York, NY 10022

Established in 1986 in NY.
Donor(s): Edward Rappa.
Financial data (yr. ended 11/30/01): Grants paid, $0; assets, $744 (M); expenditures, $0; qualifying distributions, $0.
Limitations: Applications not accepted. Giving primarily in NY and PA.
Application information: Contributes only to pre-selected organizations.
Officers: Edward Rappa, Pres.; Tamara Rappa, Secy.
EIN: 133387948

40476
Ohev Hesed Foundation, Inc.
703 Ave. I
Brooklyn, NY 112293

Donor(s): David Shalam.
Financial data (yr. ended 12/31/00): Grants paid, $0; assets, $463 (M); gifts received, $330; expenditures, $1,241; qualifying distributions, $1,241.
Officer: David Shalam, Pres.; Maurice Shalam, V.P.; Ruth Shalam, Secy.
EIN: 113408676

40477
Julian R. and Varue W. Oishei Foundation
424 Main St., Ste. 1100
Buffalo, NY 14202-3611
Contact: Patrick E. Martin, V.P.

Established in 1996 in NY.
Donor(s): Varue Whitten Oishei.
Financial data (yr. ended 12/31/01): Grants paid, $0; assets, $13,609 (M); expenditures, $582; qualifying distributions, $0.
Officers: Varue Whitten Oishei,* Pres.; Patrick E. Martin,* V.P. and Secy.-Treas.; Mary Kennedy Martin, Secy.-Treas.
EIN: 161490673

40478
Old Huntington Green, Inc.
c/o Russell C. Vollmer
P.O. Box 356
Greenlawn, NY 11740-0356

Financial data (yr. ended 12/31/01): Grants paid, $0; assets, $177,036 (M); expenditures, $27,046; qualifying distributions, $0.
Limitations: Applications not accepted. Giving primarily in NY.
Application information: Contributes only to pre-selected organizations.
Officers: Nicholas J. DeVito, Pres.; Charles T. Matthews, V.P.; Carol Matthews, Secy.; Russell C. Vollmer, Treas.
EIN: 116037166

40479
Oldenburg Van Bruggen Foundation, Inc.
556 Broome St.
New York, NY 10013

Established in 2000 in DE.
Donor(s): Claes Oldenburg, Coosje Van Bruggen.
Financial data (yr. ended 12/31/01): Grants paid, $0; assets, $8,167 (M); expenditures, $180; qualifying distributions, $0.
Limitations: Applications not accepted.
Application information: Contributes only to pre-selected organizations.
Officers and Directors:* Coosje Van Bruggen, Chair. and Pres.; Maartje Eslibeth Oldenburg, V.P. and Treas.; Claes Oldenburg,* V.P.; Michael Ward Stout,* Secy.
EIN: 134122015

40480
Omnificent Ink Productions, Inc.
626 Riverside Dr., Ste. 10J
New York, NY 10031

Established in 2000 in NY.
Financial data (yr. ended 12/31/01): Grants paid, $0; assets, $3,500 (M); expenditures, $25; qualifying distributions, $0.
Director: Laurence C. Halde.
EIN: 133747516

40481
Orange Housing, Inc.
249 Broadway
Newburgh, NY 12550-5420

Financial data (yr. ended 12/31/01): Grants paid, $0; assets, $1,044,984 (M); expenditures, $81,970; qualifying distributions, $0.
Officers: Regina Black, Pres.; Micheal Koniak, Treas.
EIN: 222363356

40482
Orbital Disease Education and Research Foundation, Inc.
(Formerly Sigmund Schutz Foundation, Inc.)
c/o Richard Dean Lisman, M.D.
635 Park Ave.
New York, NY 10021

Donor(s): Edna Blum.
Financial data (yr. ended 12/31/01): Grants paid, $0; assets, $1 (M); gifts received, $48,600; expenditures, $25,826; qualifying distributions, $0.
Limitations: Applications not accepted. Giving primarily in NY.
Officers: Richard Dean Lisman, M.D., Pres.; Michael Kazim, M.D., V.P.; Norman D. Medow, M.D., V.P.; James S. Schutz, M.D., V.P.; J. Frederick Berg, Jr., Secy.; Rene Rodriguez-Sains, M.D., Treas.
EIN: 136139636

40483
The Phyllis & Thomas Osterman Family Foundation
111 Great Neck Rd., Ste. 408
Great Neck, NY 11021
Contact: L. Thomas Osterman, Pres.

Established in 2000 in NY.
Donor(s): L. Thomas Osterman, Phyllis Osterman.
Financial data (yr. ended 12/31/00): Grants paid, $0; assets, $165,532 (M); gifts received, $164,475; expenditures, $18; qualifying distributions, $0.
Application information: Application form not required.
Officers and Directors:* L. Thomas Osterman,* Pres.; Phyllis Osterman,* Secy.-Treas.
EIN: 113563663

40484
Chaim and Dvora Ostreicher Foundation
67-42 180th St.
Fresh Meadows, NY 11365

Established in 2001 in NY.
Donor(s): Robert Ostreicher.
Financial data (yr. ended 12/31/01): Grants paid, $0; assets, $40,024 (M); gifts received, $40,600; expenditures, $600; qualifying distributions, $100.
Limitations: Applications not accepted.
Application information: Contributes only to pre-selected organizations.
Officers and Directors:* Robert Ostreicher,* Pres. and Treas.; Dvora Ostreicher,* Secy.; David Ostreicher, Michael Ostreicher.
EIN: 113637425

40485
Outside in July, Inc
c/o J.L. Rosenhouse, C.P.A.
250 W. 57 St., Ste. 2203
New York, NY 10019

Donor(s): James Dine.
Financial data (yr. ended 12/31/00): Grants paid, $0; assets, $10,351 (M); gifts received, $71,685; expenditures, $139,708; qualifying distributions, $136,323; giving activities include $139,708 for programs.
Limitations: Applications not accepted.
Application information: Contributes only to pre-selected organizations.
Officers and Directors:* Nancy Dine, Pres.; John Silberman,* V.P.; James Dine.
EIN: 133442712

40486
Packer Family Foundation
785 Addison St.
Woodmere, NY 11598

Established in 2001 in NY.
Donor(s): Paul Packer.
Financial data (yr. ended 12/31/01): Grants paid, $0; assets, $300,000 (M); gifts received, $300,000; expenditures, $0; qualifying distributions, $0.
Limitations: Applications not accepted.
Application information: Contributes only to pre-selected organizations.
Trustees: Jennifer Packer, Paul Packer.
EIN: 113640508

40487
Ann Palmer Foundation
282 Katonah Ave., Box 210
Katonah, NY 10536
Contact: Kathleen K. Johnson, Pres.

Established in 2000 in NY.
Financial data (yr. ended 12/31/00): Grants paid, $0; assets, $1,000,000 (M); gifts received, $1,000,000; expenditures, $0; qualifying distributions, $0.
Application information: Application form required.
Officers and Directors: Kathleen K. Johnson,* Pres.; Christine F. Watkins,* V.P.
EIN: 951731484

40488
Pamet River Foundation
c/o Bessemer Trust Co., N.A.
630 5th Ave.
New York, NY 10111

Established in 1998 in DE.
Donor(s): Peter W. Gilson.
Financial data (yr. ended 12/31/01): Grants paid, $0; assets, $855,556 (M); expenditures, $24,851; qualifying distributions, $0.
Limitations: Applications not accepted.
Application information: Contributes only to pre-selected organizations.
Trustees: Margaret W. Gilson, Peter W. Gilson.
EIN: 232962933

40489
Pan Am Historical Foundation, Inc.
(Formerly Flight Spectrum International, Inc.)
c/o Edward S. Trippe
230 Park Ave.
New York, NY 10169

Established around 1987.
Donor(s): Aware, Inc., Centenial Documents.
Financial data (yr. ended 12/31/99): Grants paid, $0; assets, $187,798 (M); gifts received, $39,857; expenditures, $106,966; qualifying distributions, $100,989.
Limitations: Applications not accepted.
Application information: Contributes only to pre-selected organizations.
Officers and Directors:* Edward S. Trippe,* Pres.; Paul Roitsch,* Exec. V.P.; David Abrams,* V.P.; Jerry O'Donnell,* V.P.; Kathleen M. Clair,* Secy.; Jennie D. Sefton,* Treas.; Jeffrey F. Kreindler, Exec. Dir.; Mary Goshgarian, James O. Leet, Charles W. Trippe.
EIN: 592653271

40490
Paragon Foundation, Inc.
c/o Joe DiSanto
1663 W. 7th St.
Brooklyn, NY 11223-1342

Financial data (yr. ended 12/31/01): Grants paid, $0; assets, $1 (M); expenditures, $1,854; qualifying distributions, $0.
Limitations: Giving primarily in FL and NY.
Officers: Sheldon Stachel, Pres.; Michell Falk, V.P.; Joseph DiSanto, Secy.-Treas.
EIN: 116037172

40491
Park West Foundation, Inc.
c/o H. Sussman
110 E. 59th St., 29th Fl.
New York, NY 10022

Established in 1999 in NY.
Financial data (yr. ended 11/30/01): Grants paid, $0; assets, $100 (M); expenditures, $0; qualifying distributions, $0.
Directors: Naomi Freilich, Chales Katz, Michelle Katz.
EIN: 133980788

40492
The Frank Pasquale Foundation
300 E. 42nd St.
New York, NY 10017

Established in 2000 in NY.
Financial data (yr. ended 12/31/01): Grants paid, $0; assets, $20,791 (M); expenditures, $1; qualifying distributions, $0.
Officers: Joseph Cassin, Pres.; Robert Dunn, V.P.; Robert Pasquale, Secy.-Treas.
EIN: 134095376

40493
Umeshchandra Patil Family Charitable Foundation
c/o Vijayalakshmi Patil
3321 E. Lake Rd.
Skaneateles, NY 13152   (315) 685-8421

Established in 2001 in NY.
Donor(s): Brindavan, Inc., Vijayalakshmi Patil, Umeshchandra Patil.
Financial data (yr. ended 12/31/01): Grants paid, $0; assets, $237,286 (M); gifts received, $183,401; expenditures, $7,900; qualifying distributions, $0.
Trustees: Neena M. Patil, Padmavathi Patil.
EIN: 161609271

40494
The John D. & Kate H. Payne Foundation, Inc.
c/o Kevin Shreve
118 Prospect St., Ste. 311
Ithaca, NY 14850

Established in 1999 in NY.
Financial data (yr. ended 12/31/01): Grants paid, $0; assets, $46,264 (M); gifts received, $26,673; expenditures, $1,723; qualifying distributions, $0.
Limitations: Applications not accepted.
Application information: Contributes only to pre-selected organizations.
Officers: Thomas Hanna, Pres.; Kevin Shreve, Secy.-Treas.
Director: Thomas Vanderzee.
EIN: 161560604

40495
Glenn and Carol Pearsall Adirondack Foundation, Inc.
1187 Garnet Lake Rd. N.
Johnsburg, NY 12843
Application address: P.O. Box 105, Johnsburg, NY 12843; URL: http://www.pearsallfoundation.org

Established in 2000 in NY.
Donor(s): Glenn L. Pearsall, Carol Pearsall.
Financial data (yr. ended 06/30/01): Grants paid, $0; assets, $198,023 (M); gifts received, $219,827; expenditures, $1,073; qualifying distributions, $0.
Limitations: Giving primarily in NY.
Application information: Application form required.
Officers: Glenn L. Pearsall, Pres.; Heather Pearsall, V.P.; Carol Pearsall, Secy.; Adam Pearsall, Treas.
EIN: 141827199

40496
The Irving Penn Trust
c/o Starr & Co.
350 Park Ave.
New York, NY 10022

Established in 1999 in NY.
Financial data (yr. ended 12/31/01): Grants paid, $0; assets, $174,057 (M); gifts received, $1,500; expenditures, $2,028; qualifying distributions, $0.
Limitations: Applications not accepted.
Application information: Contributes only to pre-selected organizations.
Trustees: Neale M. Albert, Irving Penn, Tom Penn.
EIN: 137081071

40497
Penthesilea Fund, Inc.
(Formerly Alexandra Stanton Foundation)
c/o World Wide Holdings Corp.
150 E. 58th St.
New York, NY 10155

Established in 1995 in NY.
Donor(s): Alexandra Stanton.
Financial data (yr. ended 12/31/00): Grants paid, $0; assets, $314,449 (M); expenditures, $3,781; qualifying distributions, $0.
Limitations: Applications not accepted.
Application information: Contributes only to pre-selected organizations.
Officer: Alexandra Stanton, Pres.
EIN: 133840632

40498
The Harry H. and Ann L. Perse Family Foundation, Inc.
c/o Edward Issacs & Co.
380 Madison Ave.
New York, NY 10017

Established in 1997 in NY.
Donor(s): Harry H. Perse.
Financial data (yr. ended 03/31/02): Grants paid, $0; assets, $155,576 (M); expenditures, $2,436; qualifying distributions, $0.
Limitations: Applications not accepted. Giving primarily in NY.
Application information: Contributes only to pre-selected organizations.
Officers and Directors:* Victor S. Rich, V.P. and Treas.; Ann L. Perse,* Secy.; Daniel S. Cohan.
EIN: 133946384

40499
Persistence Foundation, Inc.
Joslin Ln.
Buskirk, NY 12028

Established in 1998.
Donor(s): Constance Kheel.
Financial data (yr. ended 07/31/01): Grants paid, $0; assets, $854,250 (M); gifts received, $610,145; expenditures, $69,285; qualifying distributions, $568,405; giving activities include $499,120 for program-related investments.
Limitations: Applications not accepted.
Application information: Contributes only to pre-selected organizations.
Officers: Constance Kheel, Pres. and Treas.; Connie Madigan, V.P.; Dunja Marton, Secy.
EIN: 141797449

40500
Henry Peterson Foundation
c/o Warshaw Burstein, et al.
555 5th Ave.
New York, NY 10017

Donor(s): Feature Ring Co., Inc.
Financial data (yr. ended 02/28/02): Grants paid, $0; assets, $3,317 (M); expenditures, $217; qualifying distributions, $205.
Limitations: Applications not accepted.
Application information: Contributes only to pre-selected organizations.
Officers: Jerome Peterson, Pres.; Arline Brass, Secy.
Trustees: Joel Newman, Milton Warshaw.
EIN: 136161002

40501
The Carroll and Milton Petrie Foundation
c/o Jerome A. Manning, Stroock, Stroock & Lavan, LLP
180 Maiden Ln.
New York, NY 10038

Established in NY in 1998.
Financial data (yr. ended 12/31/01): Grants paid, $0; assets, $26,371,216 (M); gifts received, $26,102,493; expenditures, $32,353; qualifying distributions, $0.
Trustees: Dorothy Fink, Joseph H. Flom, Hilda Kirschbaum, Jerome A. Manning, Bernard Petrie, Carroll Petrie, Laurence A. Tisch, David Zack.
EIN: 311596433

40502
The John and Annamaria Phillips Foundation, Inc.
c/o Peter F. De Gaetano
488 Madison Ave.
New York, NY 10022

Established in 1993 in NY.
Financial data (yr. ended 12/31/00): Grants paid, $0; assets, $93,572 (M); expenditures, $4,698; qualifying distributions, $0.
Officers and Directors:* Andrea Cairone,* Pres.; Peter F. Degaetano,* Secy.; Francois Sicart,* Treas.
EIN: 013732915

40503
Hyman Podell Family Foundation
605 3rd Ave.
New York, NY 10158-0180

Established in 1984 in NY.
Financial data (yr. ended 12/31/01): Grants paid, $0; assets, $718 (M); expenditures, $25; qualifying distributions, $0.
Limitations: Applications not accepted. Giving primarily in NY.
Application information: Contributes only to pre-selected organizations.
Trustees: Berthram Podell, Herbert Podell.
EIN: 133247814

40504
John G. Popp Foundation, Inc.
1060 5th Ave., No. 2D
New York, NY 10128

Established in 1997 in DE and NY.
Donor(s): John G. Popp.
Financial data (yr. ended 11/30/01): Grants paid, $0; assets, $32,634 (M); expenditures, $530; qualifying distributions, $0.
Limitations: Applications not accepted.
Application information: Contributes only to pre-selected organizations.
Director: John G. Popp.
EIN: 133981557

40505
Robert & Hermine Popper Foundation, Inc.
486 Bedford Rd.
Armonk, NY 10504 (914) 273-3326
Contact: Ellen Popper, Pres.

Donor(s): Robert L. Popper.
Financial data (yr. ended 05/31/02): Grants paid, $0; assets, $39,652 (M); gifts received, $1,740; expenditures, $1,765; qualifying distributions, $0.
Limitations: Giving primarily in NY.
Application information: Application form not required.
Officer: Ellen Popper, Pres.
Trustees: Susan Berresford, Paul Gartner, Carol Isaacs, Maurice Russell.
EIN: 136115782

40506
Propane Education & Research of New York
c/o Richard Brescia
120 Washington Ave.
Albany, NY 12210

Established in 1998 in NY.
Financial data (yr. ended 12/31/01): Grants paid, $0; assets, $6,015 (M); expenditures, $13,202; qualifying distributions, $0.
Officers: Roland Penta, Pres.; Raymond Murray III, Treas.
EIN: 311585989

40507
Puchowitzer Society, Inc.
c/o M. Steinberg
1412 Remsen Ave.
Brooklyn, NY 11236

Financial data (yr. ended 12/31/01): Grants paid, $0; assets, $235,849 (M); expenditures, $4,841; qualifying distributions, $3,728.
Limitations: Applications not accepted. Giving primarily in New York, NY.
Application information: Contributes only to pre-selected organizations.
Officers: Randy Rosebaum, Pres.; Stephen Freinhar, V.P.; Judy Rudnick, Rec. Secy.; Morton Steinberg, Fin. Secy.; Betty Slobodow, Treas.
EIN: 112789328

40508
Pythagoras Charitable Fund, Inc.
c/o Lane & Lipton
2942 Allon St.
Oceanside, NY 11572

Financial data (yr. ended 09/30/01): Grants paid, $0; assets, $1,965 (M); gifts received, $500; expenditures, $80; qualifying distributions, $0.
Limitations: Applications not accepted.
Application information: Contributes only to pre-selected organizations.
Officer: Morris Lipton, Pres.

EIN: 510192365

40509
Thomas & Diane Quinlan Charitable Foundation
564 Bement Ave.
Staten Island, NY 10310
Contact: Thomas Quinlan, Tr.

Established in 1999 in NY.
Donor(s): Thomas Quinlan, Diane Quinlan.
Financial data (yr. ended 06/30/01): Grants paid, $0; assets, $10,702 (M); expenditures, $0; qualifying distributions, $0.
Limitations: Giving primarily in Staten Island, NY.
Trustees: Anne Quinlan, Diane Quinlan, Thomas Quinlan.
EIN: 134086820

40510
R.J.C. Fund
c/o John L. Casey
P.O. Box 999
Quogue, NY 11959-0999

Donor(s): John L. Casey.
Financial data (yr. ended 12/31/01): Grants paid, $0; assets, $104,686 (M); expenditures, $44; qualifying distributions, $0.
Limitations: Applications not accepted. Giving primarily in MA.
Application information: Contributes only to pre-selected organizations.
Trustees: Edward C. Casey, John L. Casey.
EIN: 136217326

40511
Raab Foundation
c/o Samuel Raab
1812 55th St.
Brooklyn, NY 11204

Established in 1993 in NY.
Donor(s): Samuel Raab.
Financial data (yr. ended 09/30/01): Grants paid, $0; assets, $265,662 (M); gifts received, $50,000; expenditures, $1,071; qualifying distributions, $0.
Limitations: Applications not accepted. Giving primarily in Brooklyn, NY.
Application information: Contributes only to pre-selected organizations.
Trustees: Samuel Raab, Soloman Raab, Zissie C. Raab.
EIN: 113185633

40512
The Dorothea and Leo Rabkin Foundation
c/o Leo Rabkin
218 W. 20th St.
New York, NY 10011

Established in 2000 in NY.
Donor(s): Leo Rabkin.
Financial data (yr. ended 11/30/01): Grants paid, $0; assets, $154,315 (M); gifts received, $55,000; expenditures, $3,448; qualifying distributions, $0.
Limitations: Applications not accepted. Giving primarily in Washington, DC and New York, NY.
Application information: Contributes only to pre-selected organizations.
Officers: Dorothy Rabkin, Pres. and Secy.; Leo Rabkin, V.P. and Treas.; Robert Prizer, V.P.
EIN: 134091650

40513
Charna Radbell Foundation
134 Harbor View South
Lawrence, NY 11559

Established in 2001 in NJ.
Donor(s): Charna Radbell.

Financial data (yr. ended 12/31/01): Grants paid, $0; assets, $234,623 (M); gifts received, $231,297; expenditures, $0; qualifying distributions, $0.
Limitations: Applications not accepted.
Application information: Contributes only to pre-selected organizations.
Trustees: Arlene Radbell, Laurence Radbell, Maria Onorato.
EIN: 226887924

40514
Raghavendran Foundation
680 5th Ave., 9th Fl.
New York, NY 10019 (212) 230-9264
Contact: Ramanan Raghavendran, Dir.

Established in 1999 in NY.
Donor(s): Ramanan Raghavendran.
Financial data (yr. ended 12/31/00): Grants paid, $0; assets, $558,750 (M); gifts received, $16,498; expenditures, $0; qualifying distributions, $0.
Directors: Wayne R. Landesman, Fubramanian Raghavendran, Ramanan Raghavendran.
EIN: 134091354

40515
Rahr Family Foundation
3 Croyden Ct.
Dix Hills, NY 11746-6143

Established in 1997 in NY.
Financial data (yr. ended 12/31/01): Grants paid, $0; assets, $167,221 (M); expenditures, $0; qualifying distributions, $0.
Limitations: Applications not accepted. Giving primarily in Brooklyn, NY.
Application information: Contributes only to pre-selected organizations.
Trustees: Carol Rahr, Felicia Rahr, Robert Rahr, Stewart Rahr.
EIN: 113374721

40516
Elias and Sonja Rand Charitable Foundation, Inc.
c/o Reminick Aarons & Co.
685 3rd Ave., 19th Fl.
New York, NY 10017

Established in 1999 in NY.
Donor(s): Sonja Rand.
Financial data (yr. ended 12/31/01): Grants paid, $0; assets, $6,832 (M); expenditures, $650; qualifying distributions, $0.
Limitations: Applications not accepted.
Application information: Contributes only to pre-selected organizations.
Officer: Jerry Glassman, Pres.
Directors: Russell Marlow, Nelson H. Willick.
EIN: 134074575

40517
Michael & Joseph Ratner Foundation, Inc.
c/o William Greene and Co.
55 Katonah Ave.
Katonah, NY 10536-2167
Contact: Joseph Ratner, Secy.-Treas.

Donor(s): Michael Ratner, Joseph Ratner.
Financial data (yr. ended 12/31/01): Grants paid, $0; assets, $23,739 (M); expenditures, $155; qualifying distributions, $0.
Limitations: Giving primarily in NY.
Application information: Application form not required.
Officers: Michael Ratner, Pres.; Joseph Ratner, Secy.-Treas.
EIN: 133006986

40518
The Melvin Rauch Foundation, Inc.
3 York St.
New York, NY 10013

Established in 2000 in NY.
Donor(s): Melvin Rauch, Angela Mary Rauch.
Financial data (yr. ended 12/31/00): Grants paid, $0; assets, $1,005,422 (M); gifts received, $1,000,000; expenditures, $0; qualifying distributions, $0.
Officers: Melvin Rauch, Pres.; Michael Meiselman, Secy.
Director: Angela Mary Rauch.
EIN: 134144529

40519
The Reel Family Foundation, Inc.
27 Virginia Pl.
Staten Island, NY 10314 (718) 668-9559
Contact: Joseph S. Reel, Pres.

Established in 2000 in NY.
Donor(s): Joseph S. Reel.
Financial data (yr. ended 12/31/00): Grants paid, $0; assets, $39,170 (M); gifts received, $50,514; expenditures, $915; qualifying distributions, $612.
Application information: Application form required.
Officers: Joseph S. Reel, Pres.; William J. Reel, V.P.; Suellen Reel, Secy.
Director: Ursula A. Reel.
EIN: 134124111

40520
Renu and Divyang Charitable Foundation
27 Foster Ave.
Staten Island, NY 10314-5609

Financial data (yr. ended 12/31/01): Grants paid, $0; assets, $123,407 (M); gifts received, $130,000; expenditures, $6,600; qualifying distributions, $0.
Trustees: Divyang Parikh, Renu Parikh.
EIN: 134176663

40521
Research and Social Service Foundation
153 E. 53rd St.
New York, NY 10043
Contact: Marie Giangolano

Donor(s): Walter J. Levy.
Financial data (yr. ended 09/30/01): Grants paid, $0; assets, $63,135 (M); expenditures, $322; qualifying distributions, $0.
Limitations: Giving primarily in NY.
Application information: Application form not required.
Officers: Eric Sondheimer, V.P.; Ann Joseph, Secy.
EIN: 136123707

40522
Research Associates for Defense Conversion, Inc.
10002 Hillside Terr.
Marcy, NY 13403

Financial data (yr. ended 01/31/01): Grants paid, $0; assets, $516,190 (M); expenditures, $1,213,340; qualifying distributions, $1,238,725; giving activities include $1,213,340 for programs.
Officers: Kenneth Stiefvater, Pres.; Henrietta Stiefvater, V.P. and Secy.-Treas.; Edward Stiefvater, Secy.
EIN: 161454486

40523
Louis & Mildred Resnick Foundation
124 S. Main St.
Ellenville, NY 12428

Established in 1977 in NY.
Donor(s): Louis Resnick, Mildred Resnick.
Financial data (yr. ended 08/31/01): Grants paid, $0; assets, $1,921 (M); expenditures, $0; qualifying distributions, $0.
Limitations: Applications not accepted. Giving primarily in Miami, FL, and southern NY.
Application information: Contributes only to pre-selected organizations.
Trustees: Louis Resnick, Mildred Resnick.
EIN: 132915626

40524
Betty Retter Foundation
210 Central Park S., Ste. 9D
New York, NY 10019 (212) 246-1115
Contact: Betty Retter, Tr.

Donor(s): Betty Retter.
Financial data (yr. ended 06/30/01): Grants paid, $0; assets, $300,564 (M); expenditures, $236; qualifying distributions, $0.
Limitations: Giving primarily in NY.
Trustees: Allen Retter, Betty Retter, Daniel Retter, David Retter.
EIN: 133938484

40525
Revlon Foundation, Inc.
c/o MacAndrews & Forbes Holdings, Inc.
38 E. 63rd St.
New York, NY 10021

Incorporated in 1955 in NY.
Donor(s): Revlon, Inc., and its subsidiaries.
Financial data (yr. ended 12/31/01): Grants paid, $0; assets, $1,487 (L); expenditures, $270; qualifying distributions, $0.
Limitations: Applications not accepted.
Application information: Contributes only to pre-selected organizations.
Officers and Directors:* Jeffrey M. Nugent,* Pres.; Wade H. Nichols III, Exec., V.P.; Robert K. Kretzman, Sr. V.P. and Secy.; Laurence Winoker, Sr. V.P., Treas. and Cont.; James T. Conroy, Sr. V.P.; Stanley B. Dessen, Sr. V.P.; Howard Gittis, Ronald O. Perelman.
EIN: 136126130
Codes: CS, CD

40526
The Dianne T. & Charles E. Rice Family Foundation, Inc.
c/o Bessemer Trust Co., N.A.
630 5th Ave.
New York, NY 10111
Application address: 801 Brickell Ave., Miami, FL 33131
Contact: Celeste Rice Donovan, C.E.O.

Established in 2001 in FL.
Donor(s): Charles E. Rice.
Financial data (yr. ended 12/31/01): Grants paid, $0; assets, $5,184,946 (M); gifts received, $5,154,498; expenditures, $134,565; qualifying distributions, $40,205.
Application information: Application form not required.
Officer and Directors:* Celeste Rice Donovan,* C.E.O.; C. Daniel Rice, Charles E. Rice, Dianne T. Rice, Julie F. Rice.
EIN: 593701678

40527
The M. A. M. Richardson Family Foundation, Inc.
5700 Arlington Ave., Ste. 19J
Riverdale, NY 10471 (718) 548-4883
Contact: Marion R. Thompson, Pres.

Financial data (yr. ended 06/30/02): Grants paid, $0; assets, $27,838 (M); expenditures, $668; qualifying distributions, $0.
Officers: Marion R. Thompson, Pres.; Adrienne C. Harris, V.P.; David H. Snipe, Secy.
EIN: 133911718

40528
E. R. Roberts Family Foundation
c/o Edward Roberts
575 Madison Ave., Ste. 1006
New York, NY 10022-2511

Established in 2000 in NY.
Donor(s): Edward R. Roberts, Marc Roberts.
Financial data (yr. ended 11/30/01): Grants paid, $0; assets, $739,292 (M); gifts received, $717,366; expenditures, $0; qualifying distributions, $0.
Limitations: Applications not accepted.
Application information: Contributes only to pre-selected organizations.
Directors: Edward R. Roberts, Marc Roberts, Nancy C. Roberts.
EIN: 311772701

40529
The Stephanie & Michael Robinson Foundation
1317 Everett Pl.
Hewlett, NY 11557-2728

Established in 1993 in NY.
Donor(s): Michael M. Robinson.
Financial data (yr. ended 12/31/00): Grants paid, $0; assets, $543 (M); gifts received, $176; expenditures, $75; qualifying distributions, $0.
Limitations: Applications not accepted.
Application information: Contributes only to pre-selected organizations.
Directors: Michael M. Robinson, Scott Alan Robinson, Stephanie Ann Robinson.
EIN: 113150310

40530
L. Robinson Trust
(Formerly Lewis Robinson Trust)
c/o HSBC Bank USA
P.O. Box 4203
Buffalo, NY 14240 (800) 284-5866

Established in 1986 in NY.
Financial data (yr. ended 12/31/01): Grants paid, $0; assets, $275,270 (M); expenditures, $5,429; qualifying distributions, $0.
Limitations: Applications not accepted. Giving primarily in Plattsburgh, NY.
Application information: Contributes only to pre-selected organizations.
Trustees: James E. Keable, HSBC Bank USA.
EIN: 510244640

40531
The Rochlis Family Foundation, Inc.
150 E. 69th St.
New York, NY 10021

Established in 2001 in NY.
Donor(s): James J. Rochlis.
Financial data (yr. ended 12/31/01): Grants paid, $0; assets, $1,971,693 (M); gifts received, $1,975,174; expenditures, $500; qualifying distributions, $500.
Limitations: Applications not accepted.
Application information: Contributes only to pre-selected organizations.
Directors: James J. Rochlis, Jeffrey Rochlis, Susan Rochlis.
EIN: 134200739

40532
Morris & Rose Rochman Foundation, Inc.
60 Tain Dr.
Great Neck, NY 11021
Contact: Morton Rochman, Pres.

Financial data (yr. ended 12/31/01): Grants paid, $0; assets, $428,363 (M); expenditures, $24,138; qualifying distributions, $24,138.
Limitations: Giving primarily in NY.
Application information: Application form not required.
Officers and Directors:* Morton Rochman,* Pres. and Secy; Toby Gorelick, Treas.
EIN: 116006655

40533
The William and Beverly Rockford Foundation, Inc.
110 Deepwood Dr.
Chappaqua, NY 10514

Established in 2000 in NY.
Donor(s): William Rockford, Beverly Rockford.
Financial data (yr. ended 12/31/00): Grants paid, $0; assets, $517,945 (M); gifts received, $483,363; expenditures, $8,843; qualifying distributions, $0.
Limitations: Applications not accepted.
Application information: Contributes only to pre-selected organizations.
Directors: May Gaynor, Beverly Rockford, William Rockford.
EIN: 134143364

40534
Rocky Foundation
c/o I.A. Piedilato
600 Forest Ave.
Staten Island, NY 10310

Established in 1993 in CA.
Financial data (yr. ended 12/31/00): Grants paid, $0; assets, $1,268,522 (L); expenditures, $521; qualifying distributions, $0.
Limitations: Giving on a national basis.
Application information: Application form required.
Officers: Tsu-Ku Lee, Pres.; Henry Chang, Secy.; Ken Chen, Treas.
EIN: 330291963
Codes: GTI

40535
Nicholas Roerich Museum, Inc.
319 W. 107th St.
New York, NY 10025-2799

Financial data (yr. ended 12/31/99): Grants paid, $0; assets, $833,845 (M); gifts received, $179,268; expenditures, $195,680; qualifying distributions, $187,062; giving activities include $54,045 for programs.
Limitations: Applications not accepted.
Application information: Contribute only to pre-selected organizations.
Officers: Edgar Lansbury, Pres.; Daniel Entin, Secy.-Treas.
EIN: 136161674

40536
Jack & Judith Rosenberg Foundation
c/o American Express TBS, Inc.
1185 Ave. of the Americas
New York, NY 10036-2602

Established in 2000.
Donor(s): Jack Rosenberg, Judith Rosenberg.
Financial data (yr. ended 12/31/00): Grants paid, $0; assets, $101,353 (M); gifts received, $95,412; expenditures, $0; qualifying distributions, $0.
Limitations: Applications not accepted.
Application information: Contributes only to pre-selected organizations.
Trustees: Jack Rosenberg, Judith Rosenberg.
EIN: 656355938

40537
The Herbert & Nannette Rothschild Memorial Fund
c/o Stapper & Van Doren
10 Rockefeller Plz., Ste. 919
New York, NY 10020

Established in 1979 in NY.
Donor(s): Judith Rothschild.‡
Financial data (yr. ended 12/31/01): Grants paid, $0; assets, $1,737 (M); expenditures, $1,875; qualifying distributions, $0.
Limitations: Applications not accepted.
Application information: Contributes only to pre-selected organizations.
Trustees: Harvey S. Shipley Miller, Erik J. Stapper.
EIN: 133020004

40538
The Irving L. Rousso Family Foundation
860 United Nations Plz.
New York, NY 10017

Established in 1997 in NY.
Financial data (yr. ended 12/31/01): Grants paid, $0; assets, $997 (M); expenditures, $0; qualifying distributions, $0.
Limitations: Applications not accepted.
Application information: Contributes only to pre-selected organizations.
Officer: Irving L. Rousso.
EIN: 113360900

40539
Carolyn C. & George R. Rowland Foundation
c/o Deutsche Trust Co. of NY
P.O. Box 1297, Church St. Sta.
New York, NY 10008

Established in 1996 in MA.
Donor(s): Carolyn C. Rowland, George R. Rowland.
Financial data (yr. ended 10/31/01): Grants paid, $0; assets, $1,439,529 (M); expenditures, $16,463; qualifying distributions, $8,214.
Limitations: Applications not accepted. Giving limited to VT.
Application information: Contributes only to pre-selected organizations.
Trustee: Deutsche Bank.
EIN: 137097149

40540
Guy G. Rutherfurd, Jr. Charitable Fund
c/o Morris & McVeigh, LLP
767 3rd Ave.
New York, NY 10017-2023

Established in 1997 in NY.
Donor(s): Guy G. Rutherfurd, Jr.
Financial data (yr. ended 12/31/99): Grants paid, $0; assets, $62,669 (M); expenditures, $567; qualifying distributions, $567.
Limitations: Applications not accepted.

Application information: Contributes only to pre-selected organizations.
Trustees: Guy Rutherfurd, Jr., Marie Rutherfurd.
EIN: 137137033

40541
The Richard & Ruthanne Ruzika Family Foundation
c/o Goldman Sachs & Co.
85 Broad St., Tax Dept.
New York, NY 10004

Established in 1999 in NY.
Donor(s): Richard Ruzika.
Financial data (yr. ended 10/31/01): Grants paid, $0; assets, $1,345,071 (M); gifts received, $3,500; expenditures, $28,900; qualifying distributions, $4,900.
Limitations: Applications not accepted. Giving primarily in MD and NY.
Application information: Contributes only to pre-selected organizations.
Trustees: Richard Ruzika, Ruthanne Ruzika.
EIN: 134090693

40542
Robert K. Ryan & Patricia A. Shea Ryan Foundation
39 Colonial Rd.
Plandome, NY 11030

Established in 2001 in NY.
Donor(s): Robert K. Ryan.
Financial data (yr. ended 12/31/01): Grants paid, $0; assets, $102,000 (M); gifts received, $102,025; expenditures, $0; qualifying distributions, $0.
Limitations: Applications not accepted.
Application information: Contributes only to pre-selected organizations.
Trustees: Robert K. Ryan, Patricia A. Shea-Ryan.
EIN: 260015500

40543
The Sack Foundation
730 5th Ave.
New York, NY 10022

Donor(s): Israel Sack, Inc.
Financial data (yr. ended 12/31/00): Grants paid, $0; assets, $968 (M); expenditures, $0; qualifying distributions, $0.
Limitations: Giving on a national basis, with emphasis on the Northeast.
Trustees: Albert M. Sack, Robert M. Sack.
EIN: 136211485

40544
Richard & Beth Sackler Foundation, Inc.
c/o Chadbourne & Parke, LLP
30 Rockefeller Plz., Ste. 3218
New York, NY 10112

Established in 1998 in DE.
Donor(s): Richard S. Sackler.
Financial data (yr. ended 12/31/01): Grants paid, $0; assets, $114,890 (M); gifts received, $111,681; expenditures, $1,525; qualifying distributions, $0.
Limitations: Applications not accepted.
Application information: Contributes only to pre-selected organizations.
Officers and Directors:* Richard S. Sackler, M.D.,* Pres. and Treas.; Beth Sackler,* V.P. and Secy.; Jonathan D. Sackler, V.P.; Michael Friedman.
EIN: 311577962

40545
Salice Family Charitable Trust
4 Lakeside Dr.
Rye, NY 10580

Established in 2001 in NY.

Donor(s): Thomas Salice, Susan Salice.
Financial data (yr. ended 12/31/01): Grants paid, $0; assets, $1,238,350 (M); gifts received, $1,195,061; expenditures, $0; qualifying distributions, $0.
Limitations: Applications not accepted.
Application information: Contributes only to pre-selected organizations.
Trustees: Susan Salice, Thomas Salice.
EIN: 226902474

40546
The Salm Family Foundation, Inc.
2277 N. Sea Rd.
Southampton, NY 11969

Established in 2000 in NY.
Financial data (yr. ended 12/31/01): Grants paid, $0; assets, $2,320 (M); expenditures, $580; qualifying distributions, $0.
Limitations: Applications not accepted.
Application information: Contributes only to pre-selected organizations.
Officers: Wiltraud Salm, Pres.; Maria Antonia Salm, V.P. and Secy.; Karl Ludwig Salm, Treas.
EIN: 113522197

40547
The Sarton Fund
967 South End
Woodmere, NY 11598

Established in 1995 in NY.
Financial data (yr. ended 12/31/99): Grants paid, $0; assets, $629,227 (M); gifts received, $489; expenditures, $65,636; qualifying distributions, $55,710.
Application information: Application form required.
Officer: Mark Meizler, Pres.
Directors: Joseph Meizler, Keith Meizler.
EIN: 113281507

40548
Sayare Whitehead Family Foundation, Inc.
c/o Shulman, Jones & Co.
200 E. Post Rd.
White Plains, NY 10601

Established in 2000 in DE.
Financial data (yr. ended 11/30/01): Grants paid, $0; assets, $0 (M); gifts received, $1,535; expenditures, $1,535; qualifying distributions, $0.
Officers and Directors:* Susan Whitehead,* Pres. and Treas.; Mitchel Sayare,* V.P. and Secy.
EIN: 133985747

40549
Schafler Foundation
944 5th Ave.
New York, NY 10021-2656

Financial data (yr. ended 05/31/02): Grants paid, $0; assets, $3,572 (M); expenditures, $80; qualifying distributions, $0.
Limitations: Giving primarily in New York, NY.
Trustees: Rubelle Schafler, Julie Schafler Yale.
EIN: 136162234

40550
Irwin S. Scherzer Foundation, Inc.
829 Park Ave.
New York, NY 10021

Established in 2001.
Donor(s): Irwin S. Scherzer.
Financial data (yr. ended 12/31/01): Grants paid, $0; assets, $410,046 (M); gifts received, $400,000; expenditures, $71; qualifying distributions, $0.
Directors: Chien-Cho Liu, Leonard Orkin, Irwin S. Scherzer.

EIN: 061619844

40551
Frederick and Amelia Schimper Foundation
509 Madison Ave., Ste. 1012
New York, NY 10022
Contact: Myles A. Cane, Pres.

Incorporated in 1943 in NY.
Donor(s): Amelia S. Ehrmann.‡
Financial data (yr. ended 12/31/01): Grants paid, $0; assets, $446,662 (M); expenditures, $60,891; qualifying distributions, $0.
Limitations: Applications not accepted. Giving primarily in NY.
Application information: Contributes only to pre-selected organizations.
Officer and Directors:* Myles A. Cane,* Pres.; Stanley S. Weithorn.
EIN: 136108507

40552
Jeannette F. Schlobach Article 4 Trust
c/o Teahan and Constantino
P.O. Box 1181
Millbrook, NY 12545

Established in 2001 in NY.
Financial data (yr. ended 12/31/01): Grants paid, $0; assets, $12,151,537 (M); expenditures, $14,199; qualifying distributions, $0.
Limitations: Applications not accepted. Giving primarily in NY.
Application information: Contributes only to pre-selected organizations.
Trustee: Mark V. Dennis.
EIN: 226863221

40553
Schloss Family Foundation
c/o CSAM
466 Lexington Ave., 17th Fl.
New York, NY 10017

Established in 1997 in NY.
Donor(s): Lawrence M. Schloss.
Financial data (yr. ended 12/31/01): Grants paid, $0; assets, $99,368 (M); gifts received, $5,000; expenditures, $560; qualifying distributions, $0.
Limitations: Applications not accepted. Giving primarily in New Orleans, LA and New York, NY.
Application information: Contributes only to pre-selected organizations.
Trustees: Laurie S. Schloss, Lawrence M. Schloss, Winthrop Trust Co.
EIN: 133952127

40554
Lisa and Michael Schultz Foundation, Inc.
10 Gracie Sq., Apt. 14F
New York, NY 10028

Established in 2001 in NY.
Donor(s): Lisa Schultz, Michael Schultz.
Financial data (yr. ended 12/31/01): Grants paid, $0; assets, $223,935 (M); gifts received, $225,500; expenditures, $110; qualifying distributions, $0.
Limitations: Applications not accepted.
Application information: Contributes only to pre-selected organizations.
Officers: Lisa Schultz, Pres.; Lawrence S. Blumberg, V.P.; Michael Schultz, Secy.
EIN: 134092871

40555
Schwartz-Marrow Foundation
2338 Hermany Ave.
Bronx, NY 10473-1130

Donor(s): Hermany Farms, Meadow Brook Farms.
Financial data (yr. ended 11/30/01): Grants paid, $0; assets, $235 (M); expenditures, $95; qualifying distributions, $0.
Limitations: Applications not accepted.
Trustees: Robert Marrow, William Schwartz.
EIN: 136144645

40556
The Schwarzman Charitable Foundation
c/o Barry Strauss Assocs., Ltd.
307 5th Ave., 8th Fl.
New York, NY 10016-6517

Established in 1986 in NY.
Donor(s): Stephen A. Schwarzman.
Financial data (yr. ended 11/30/01): Grants paid, $0; assets, $74,531 (M); gifts received, $25; expenditures, $90; qualifying distributions, $0.
Limitations: Applications not accepted. Giving primarily in Boston, MA, and New York, NY.
Application information: Contributes only to pre-selected organizations.
Trustees: Joseph Schwarzman, Stephen A. Schwarzman.
EIN: 133460672

40557
The Malik Sealy Foundation, Inc.
137 Clinton Ave.
Brooklyn, NY 11205

Established in 2000.
Financial data (yr. ended 12/31/01): Grants paid, $0; assets, $1 (M); gifts received, $22,000; expenditures, $53; qualifying distributions, $0.
Officers and Trustees:* Ragiba Sealy Bourne,* Pres.; Ann Sealy,* V.P.; Sidney Sealy,* Secy.
EIN: 223762432

40558
Second District Dental Society of the State of New York Benevolent Fund
c/o Callaghan
500 Merrick Rd.
Rockville Centre, NY 11570

Financial data (yr. ended 12/31/01): Grants paid, $0; assets, $7,535 (M); gifts received, $300; expenditures, $1,430; qualifying distributions, $0.
Limitations: Giving limited to NY.
Officer: Bernard W. Hackett, Exec. Dir.
EIN: 116113433

40559
The Segal Family Foundation
c/o Robert Segal
35 E. 85th St.
New York, NY 10028

Established in 1985.
Donor(s): Charles Segal.
Financial data (yr. ended 11/30/01): Grants paid, $0; assets, $274,145 (M); expenditures, $10,623; qualifying distributions, $0.
Limitations: Applications not accepted. Giving primarily in NY.
Application information: Contributes only to pre-selected organizations.
Director: Robert Lloyd Segal.
EIN: 136095933

40560
The Spiros Segalas Charitable Trust
466 Lexington Ave.
New York, NY 10017-3140

Established in 1984 in NY.
Donor(s): Jennison Assocs. Capital Corp., Spiros Segalas.
Financial data (yr. ended 12/31/01): Grants paid, $0; assets, $1,316,749 (M); expenditures, $5,039; qualifying distributions, $0.
Limitations: Applications not accepted.
Application information: Contributes only to pre-selected organizations.
Trustees: Diane Segalas, Spiros Segalas.
EIN: 136848308

40561
Novi Seher Foundation, Inc.
135 E. 96th St.
New York, NY 10128-2508

Financial data (yr. ended 12/31/00): Grants paid, $0; assets, $517 (M); expenditures, $75; qualifying distributions, $0.
Limitations: Applications not accepted.
Application information: Contributes only to pre-selected organizations.
Officer: Fr. Robert V. Lott, Pres.
Directors: Rev. Msgr. Oscar Aquino, Fr. Joso Orsolic.
EIN: 133811224

40562
Maurice Sendak Foundation, Inc.
c/o Sidley & Austin
875 3rd Ave.
New York, NY 10022

Established in 1995 in NY.
Donor(s): Maurice Sendak.
Financial data (yr. ended 12/31/01): Grants paid, $0; assets, $212,935 (M); expenditures, $5,198; qualifying distributions, $0.
Limitations: Applications not accepted.
Application information: Contributes only to pre-selected organizations.
Officers: Maurice Sendak, Pres.; Stephen K. Urice, Secy.; Ralph E. Lerner, Treas.
EIN: 133807627

40563
Senior Citizen Association of Taiwanese Christian in Greater New York
137-44 Northern Blvd.
Flushing, NY 11354

Financial data (yr. ended 07/31/99): Grants paid, $0; assets, $0 (L); gifts received, $13,625; expenditures, $42,261; qualifying distributions, $0.
Officers: Shueimei Chen, Pres.; Sheng Wei, V.P.; Shu Huei Wu, Treas.
EIN: 112943875

40564
The Sephardic Benevolent Society, Inc.
c/o Kamran Hakim
426 E. 61st St.
New York, NY 10021

Established in 1997 in NY.
Financial data (yr. ended 08/31/01): Grants paid, $0; assets, $261,284 (M); gifts received, $5,000; expenditures, $1,570; qualifying distributions, $0.
Limitations: Applications not accepted.
Application information: Contributes only to pre-selected organizations.
Officers: Scott Hakim, Pres.; Kamran Hakim, V.P.; Ellen Hakim, Secy.-Treas.
EIN: 133911530

40565
Noel and W. Sydnor Settle Foundation
c/o Geller & Co.
800 3rd Ave., 19th Fl.
New York, NY 10022
Contact: C. Pomo

Established in 1986 in NY.
Donor(s): Noel Settle, W. Sydnor Settle.

Financial data (yr. ended 12/31/01): Grants paid, $0; assets, $182,607 (M); gifts received, $4,000; expenditures, $4,871; qualifying distributions, $0.
Limitations: Applications not accepted. Giving primarily in NJ.
Application information: Contributes only to pre-selected organizations.
Director: W. Sydnor Settle.
EIN: 136894991

40566
Setton Family Foundation, Inc.
1411 Broadway, 8th Fl.
New York, NY 10018

Established in 1996 in NY.
Financial data (yr. ended 12/31/99): Grants paid, $0; assets, $128 (M); expenditures, $122; qualifying distributions, $0.
Officers: Marc Setton, Pres. and Treas.; Jack Setton, V.P. and Secy.
EIN: 133784749

40567
Seventeen Torah Foundation, Inc.
c/o Glass & Shiechel, LLP
110 Stewart Ave.
Hicksville, NY 11801
Application address: Jankoff and Gabe, P.C., 575 Lexington Ave., 14th Fl., New York, NY 10022, tel.: (212) 371-5700

Established in 2000 in NY.
Donor(s): Chaim Wachsman.
Financial data (yr. ended 12/31/00): Grants paid, $0; assets, $2,500,000 (M); gifts received, $2,500,000; expenditures, $0; qualifying distributions, $0.
Limitations: Applications not accepted.
Directors: Yitty Eichenstein, Chaya Shaindy Tauber, Benzion A. Wachsman, Boruch J. Wachsman, Chaim Wachsman, Naftali Wachsman.
EIN: 113529422

40568
The Shaar Family Foundation
5304 17th Ave.
Brooklyn, NY 11204

Established in 1997 in NY.
Donor(s): Moses Silver, Rachel Silver.
Financial data (yr. ended 12/31/99): Grants paid, $0; assets, $43,299 (M); expenditures, $1,344; qualifying distributions, $1,344.
Trustee: Moses Silver.
EIN: 113411309

40569
Rachel Bat Shulamit Foundation, Inc.
c/o Fleet Street, Ltd.
512 7th Ave.
New York, NY 10018

Established in 2000 in NY.
Financial data (yr. ended 04/30/01): Grants paid, $0; assets, $445 (M); gifts received, $1,376; expenditures, $935; qualifying distributions, $0.
Officers: Manny Haber, Pres.; Shari Haber, V.P.; Stephen Haber, Secy.; Raymond Haber, Treas.
EIN: 134122676

40570
The Sicherman Family Foundation, Inc.
1451 52nd St.
Brooklyn, NY 11219
Contact: Wolf Sicherman, Pres.

Established in 1995 in NY.
Financial data (yr. ended 02/28/01): Grants paid, $0; assets, $4,860 (M); expenditures, $812; qualifying distributions, $812.

Limitations: Giving on a national basis.
Officer: Wolf Sicherman, Pres.
EIN: 510365530

40571
The Jeffrey P. Siegel Charitable Trust
c/o Jennison Associates, LLC
466 Lexington Ave., 18th Fl.
New York, NY 10017

Established in 1999 in NY.
Donor(s): Jennison Associates, LLC.
Financial data (yr. ended 12/31/01): Grants paid, $0; assets, $97,224 (M); expenditures, $130; qualifying distributions, $0.
Limitations: Applications not accepted.
Application information: Contributes only to pre-selected organizations.
Trustees: Lola Panebianco, Jeffrey P. Siegel.
EIN: 134098788

40572
The Silver Family Foundation
1486 Carroll St.
Brooklyn, NY 11213

Established in 1996.
Donor(s): Abram J. Silver.
Financial data (yr. ended 12/31/00): Grants paid, $0; assets, $182,900 (M); gifts received, $20,000; expenditures, $138; qualifying distributions, $0.
Limitations: Applications not accepted.
Application information: Contributes only to pre-selected organizations.
Trustees: Abram J. Silver, Hindy Silver.
EIN: 113353200

40573
Lisa T. and Jeffrey S. Silverman Foundation
c/o Mahoney, Cohen & Co., C.P.A.
111 W. 40th St.
New York, NY 10018

Established in 1997 in CT.
Financial data (yr. ended 06/30/01): Grants paid, $0; assets, $57 (M); expenditures, $0; qualifying distributions, $0.
Officers and Directors:* Jefrey S. Silverman,* Pres.; Lonnie E. Wollin,* Secy.; Lisa Silverman.
EIN: 223531749

40574
The Simon Foundation
101 Brookline Ave.
Albany, NY 12203-1806
Contact: Marcia P. Simon, Tr.

Donor(s): Marcia P. Simon.
Financial data (yr. ended 12/31/01): Grants paid, $0; assets, $28,924 (M); expenditures, $75; qualifying distributions, $0.
Limitations: Giving primarily in the Albany, NY, area.
Trustee: Marcia P. Simon.
EIN: 146017796

40575
Herbert T. Singer Foundation, Inc.
c/o Washburn, et al.
P.O. Box 1219
Gloversville, NY 12078-0354

Donor(s): Herbert T. Singer.‡
Financial data (yr. ended 12/31/01): Grants paid, $0; assets, $14,172 (M); expenditures, $32; qualifying distributions, $0.
Limitations: Applications not accepted. Giving primarily in Amsterdam, NY.
Application information: Contributes only to pre-selected organizations.
Officers: Donald Singer, Pres.; Judith Bercuvitz, V.P.; David Singer, Secy.-Treas.

EIN: 146017581

40576
Singla Charitable Foundation, Inc
60 Hanson Ln.
New Rochelle, NY 10804-1705

Established in 2001.
Financial data (yr. ended 12/31/01): Grants paid, $0; assets, $2,350 (M); gifts received, $4,000; expenditures, $1,650; qualifying distributions, $0.
Trustee: Sudarshan K. Singla.
EIN: 134166984

40577
Sky Meadow Fund, Inc.
200 Madison Ave., 5th Fl.
New York, NY 10016

Established in 1992 in NY.
Donor(s): Susan and Elihu Rose Foundation, Inc.
Financial data (yr. ended 12/31/00): Grants paid, $0; assets, $14,420 (M); expenditures, $275; qualifying distributions, $0.
Limitations: Applications not accepted. Giving primarily in New York, NY.
Application information: Contributes only to pre-selected organizations.
Officers: Amy Rose, Pres.; Isabel Rose, V.P.; Abigail Rose, Secy.-Treas.
EIN: 133646264

40578
Michael & Ruth Slade Foundation
114 Piping Rock Rd.
Matinecock, NY 11560-2507

Established in 2000 in NY.
Donor(s): Michael Slade, Ruth Slade.
Financial data (yr. ended 12/31/01): Grants paid, $0; assets, $12,087 (M); expenditures, $0; qualifying distributions, $0.
Limitations: Giving primarily in NY.
Officer: Michael Slade, Mgr.
EIN: 113478088

40579
The Ethel M. & Orville A. Slutzky Family Foundation
P.O. Box 295
Hunter, NY 12442

Established in 1999 in NY.
Donor(s): Orvet Partners, LLP.
Financial data (yr. ended 12/31/99): Grants paid, $0; assets, $122,903 (M); gifts received, $122,903; expenditures, $0; qualifying distributions, $0.
Trustees: Ethel Slutzky, Gary Slutzky, Orville Slutzky, Paul Slutzky, Carol Slutzky Tenerowicz.
EIN: 141818230

40580
David H. Smith Foundation
c/o Lachman & Lachman
444 Madison Ave.
New York, NY 10022

Established in 1994 in DE.
Financial data (yr. ended 12/31/00): Grants paid, $0; assets, $26,898,188 (M); gifts received, $5,199,032; expenditures, $247,987; qualifying distributions, $90,125.
Limitations: Applications not accepted. Giving primarily in NY.
Application information: Contributes only to pre-selected organizations.
Officers: Joan M. Smith, Pres.; Andrea L. Smith, V.P.; Jennifer L. Smith, Secy.; Rachel A. Smith, Treas.
EIN: 133601934

40581
Albert C. Snell Memorial Fund, Inc.
c/o Stephen Snell
228 Oakdale Dr.
Rochester, NY 14618

Established in 1998 in NY.
Financial data (yr. ended 12/31/01): Grants paid, $0; assets, $4,817 (M); expenditures, $712; qualifying distributions, $0.
Limitations: Applications not accepted. Giving primarily in Rochester, NY.
Application information: Contributes only to pre-selected organizations.
Officers and Directors:* Steven S. Ching, M.D.,* Chair.; Stephen C. Snell,* Treas.; Bernard Donovan, M.D., Donald A. Grover, M.D., Robert E. Kennedy, M.D., Sandra J. Kennedy, Sarah Snell Singal, M.D.
Board Member: Albert C. Snell, Jr., M.D.
EIN: 166026840

40582
Andres Soriano Cancer Research Fund
c/o Sullivan & Cromwell
125 Broad St.
New York, NY 10004-2498
Contact: Donald R. Osborn, Tr.

Established in 1965 in CT.
Financial data (yr. ended 12/31/01): Grants paid, $0; assets, $22,555 (M); expenditures, $2,762; qualifying distributions, $0.
Limitations: Giving on an international basis.
Trustees: Donald R. Osborn, Andres Soriano III.
EIN: 136183838

40583
Kathryn E. Spence Family Foundation
c/o Kathryn E. Spence
5 Governors Rd.
Bronxville, NY 10708

Established in 2000 in NY.
Donor(s): Kathryn E. Spence.
Financial data (yr. ended 07/31/01): Grants paid, $0; assets, $183,419 (M); gifts received, $201,804; expenditures, $4,420; qualifying distributions, $0.
Limitations: Applications not accepted.
Application information: Contributes only to pre-selected organizations.
Trustee: Kathryn E. Spence.
EIN: 137202870

40584
A. J. Spiegel Foundation
c/o Marks Paneth, et al.
622 3rd Ave.
New York, NY 10017-6701

Established in 2000 in NJ.
Donor(s): Allen J. Spiegel.
Financial data (yr. ended 12/31/01): Grants paid, $0; assets, $499,449 (M); gifts received, $509,375; expenditures, $0; qualifying distributions, $0.
Limitations: Applications not accepted.
Application information: Contributes only to pre-selected organizations.
Trustee: Allen J. Spiegel.
EIN: 134201621

40585
Spirit of Hope Foundation, Inc.
31-00 47th Ave., 4th Fl.
Long Island City, NY 11101

Financial data (yr. ended 04/30/01): Grants paid, $0; assets, $4,402 (M); gifts received, $100; expenditures, $190; qualifying distributions, $0.

Limitations: Applications not accepted. Giving limited to residents of Thailand.
Application information: Contributes only to a pre-selected organization.
Directors: David W. Doyle, Jonathan M. Fox, Herbert Lee Martin, Sr., Larry Weinman.
EIN: 113378813

40586
Zita Spiss Research Trust
c/o Rosen
16 Secor Rd.
Scarsdale, NY 10583

Established in 1994 in NY.
Financial data (yr. ended 12/31/00): Grants paid, $0; assets, $320,174 (M); expenditures, $0; qualifying distributions, $0.
Trustee: Norman Rosen.
EIN: 133707557

40587
Margaret W. Spofford Foundation
c/o White & Case
1155 Ave. of the Americas, Ste. 3702
New York, NY 10036

Established in 1994 in DE.
Donor(s): Margaret W. Spofford.
Financial data (yr. ended 12/31/01): Grants paid, $0; assets, $445,729 (M); gifts received, $232,179; expenditures, $9,312; qualifying distributions, $0.
Limitations: Applications not accepted. Giving primarily in NY.
Application information: Contributes only to pre-selected organizations.
Officers and Directors:* Margaret W. Spofford,* Pres.; John S.W. Spofford,* V.P. and Secy.; C. Nicholas Spofford,* V.P. and Treas.
EIN: 133803322

40588
Dick Stack Memorial Scholarship Fund
c/o Michael D. Sherwood
P.O. Box 426
Vestal, NY 13851-0426

Established in 2000 in NY.
Donor(s): Dick's Sporting Goods, Inc.
Financial data (yr. ended 09/30/01): Grants paid, $0; assets, $26,467 (M); gifts received, $44,689; expenditures, $0; qualifying distributions, $0.
Trustees: Nancy Heichemer, Kim Myers.
EIN: 161555913
Codes: CS

40589
Theodoros Stamos Foundation Trust
132 W. 70th St.
New York, NY 10023

Established in 1999 in NY.
Donor(s): Georgianna Savas.
Financial data (yr. ended 12/31/99): Grants paid, $0; assets, $4,429 (M); gifts received, $34,710; expenditures, $30,281; qualifying distributions, $0.
Officer: Georgianna Savas, Mgr.
EIN: 137203091

40590
Steele Foundation
c/o Richard J. DioGuardi, C.P.A.
555 Pleasantville Rd., No. Bldg., 120
Briarcliff Manor, NY 10510-1955
Application address: P.O. Box 1063, East Hampton, NY 11937-0801

Established in 1973 in NY.
Donor(s): Louis Thornton Steele.

Financial data (yr. ended 08/31/01): Grants paid, $0; assets, $39,728 (M); gifts received, $1,107; expenditures, $1,110; qualifying distributions, $803.
Limitations: Applications not accepted.
Application information: Contributes only to pre-selected organizations.
Trustees: Victor G. Bloede III, Kevin Crowley, William Duggan, Margaret N. Jewett, Louis Thornton Steele, Mildred M. Steele, Lois E. Womer.
EIN: 510163773

40591
Toby R. Stein Foundation, Inc.
c/o Stanley & Caroline Stein
45 W. 67th St.
New York, NY 10023

Established in 2000 in NY.
Donor(s): Mt. Sinai Hospital.
Financial data (yr. ended 12/31/00): Grants paid, $0; assets, $225,146 (M); gifts received, $225,000; expenditures, $0; qualifying distributions, $0.
Trustees: Richard Rose, Caroline Stein, Stanley Stein.
EIN: 134143500

40592
Edward L. & Judith Steinberg Charitable Foundation
c/o Scott Langstein, C.P.A.
263 W. Walnut St.
Long Beach, NY 11561-3214 (516) 889-7707

Established in 1991 in NY.
Donor(s): Edward L. Steinberg, Judith Steinberg.
Financial data (yr. ended 09/30/01): Grants paid, $0; assets, $3,591 (M); gifts received, $1,025; expenditures, $1,086; qualifying distributions, $0.
Limitations: Applications not accepted. Giving primarily in NY.
Application information: Contributes only to pre-selected organizations.
Officers: Edward L. Steinberg, Pres.; Judith Steinberg, Secy.-Treas.
EIN: 133630818

40593
Thomas D. & Denise R. Stern Family Foundation
c/o Yohalem Gillman & Co.
477 Madison Ave.
New York, NY 10022

Established in 2001 in NY.
Donor(s): Thomas D. Stern.
Financial data (yr. ended 12/31/01): Grants paid, $0; assets, $1,420,012 (M); gifts received, $1,400,130; expenditures, $30,000; qualifying distributions, $0.
Limitations: Applications not accepted.
Application information: Contributes only to pre-selected organizations.
Trustees: Denise R. Stern, Thomas D. Stern.
EIN: 134195656

40594
The Harry M. Stevens Family Foundation, Inc.
186 Riverside Dr., Apt. 16D
New York, NY 10024 (212) 580-1709
Contact: William M. Hunt, Pres.

Established in 1994 in DE and NY.
Donor(s): Harry M. Stevens, Inc.
Financial data (yr. ended 06/30/01): Grants paid, $0; assets, $374,960 (M); expenditures, $2,237; qualifying distributions, $0.
Officers: William M. Hunt, Pres.; William H. Stevens III, Secy.; Joseph B. Stevens, Treas.
Trustee: James G. Titus.
EIN: 133801734

40595
Stirling Foundation
c/o Bessemer Trust Co., N.A.
630 5th Ave., 37th Fl.
New York, NY 10111
Application address: P.O. Box 381213, Cambridge, MA 02238-1213
Contact: Jennifer Boyd, Tr.

Established in 1999 in MA.
Donor(s): Patricia K. Boyd.
Financial data (yr. ended 12/31/01): Grants paid, $0; assets, $311,537 (M); gifts received, $363; expenditures, $7,151; qualifying distributions, $0.
Trustees: Cameron B. Boyd, David A. Boyd, Jennifer Boyd, Patricia K. Boyd.
EIN: 912058002

40596
Sayles E. Stone Foundation
c/o James E. Mackin, Bond, Schoeneck & King
1 Lincoln Ctr.
Syracuse, NY 13202

Established in 1997 in NY.
Financial data (yr. ended 12/31/01): Grants paid, $0; assets, $211,631 (M); expenditures, $2,828; qualifying distributions, $0.
Limitations: Applications not accepted.
Application information: Contributes only to pre-selected organizations.
Trustee: James E. Mackin.
EIN: 166438884

40597
Hyman and Rose Strum Foundation, Inc.
c/o Anita S. Gluck
60 East End Ave.
New York, NY 10028

Financial data (yr. ended 06/30/02): Grants paid, $0; assets, $40,644 (M); expenditures, $301; qualifying distributions, $0.
Limitations: Applications not accepted. Giving limited to New York, NY.
Application information: Contributes only to pre-selected organizations.
Officer and Directors:* Anita S. Gluck,* Secy.; Elias Strum, William Strum.
EIN: 136086985

40598
Student Agencies Foundation, Inc.
c/o Student Agencies, Inc.
409 College Ave.
Ithaca, NY 14850-4697
Contact: Dan Kathan, Treas.

Donor(s): Student Agencies Properties, Inc.
Financial data (yr. ended 12/31/01): Grants paid, $0; assets, $17,300 (M); gifts received, $1,000; expenditures, $0; qualifying distributions, $0.
Limitations: Giving primarily in Ithaca, NY.
Publications: Newsletter, program policy statement.
Officers and Trustees:* Sharon Dauk,* Chair.; Joe Cook, Pres.; Dan Kathan, Treas. and Mgr.; Louis D'Agrosa, Richard Highfield, Nancy Humphries, John Jaquette, Michael Karangelen.
EIN: 150461439

40599
Sundheimer Foundation
c/o Richard Schneyer, Jenkens & Gilchris
405 Lexington Ave.
New York, NY 10174

Donor(s): Margot Sundheimer.‡
Financial data (yr. ended 12/31/00): Grants paid, $0; assets, $446,816 (M); expenditures, $3,089; qualifying distributions, $0.
Limitations: Applications not accepted.
Application information: Contributes only to pre-selected organizations.
Officer: Richard E. Schneyer, Pres.
Director: Otto R. Walter.
EIN: 133857970

40600
The Robert F. Sutner Foundation, Inc.
3 Richard Hill
Irvington, NY 10533
Contact: Robert F. Sutner, Pres.

Financial data (yr. ended 12/31/01): Grants paid, $0; assets, $2,791 (M); expenditures, $0; qualifying distributions, $0.
Officer: Robert F. Sutner, Pres.
EIN: 136213515

40601
Alexandra and Martin Symonds Foundation, Inc.
320 W. 86th St. Apt. 7B
New York, NY 10024

Established in 1995 in DE.
Donor(s): Martin Symonds.
Financial data (yr. ended 06/30/01): Grants paid, $0; assets, $75,451 (M); expenditures, $636; qualifying distributions, $0.
Limitations: Applications not accepted.
Application information: Contributes only to pre-selected organizations.
Directors: Joann Gerardi, Jeffrey Rubin, Martin Symonds.
EIN: 133866604

40602
Ensign Lionel J. Tachna Memorial Fund
c/o Gordon S. Oppemheimer
50 Howell Ave.
Larchmont, NY 10538-3249
Application address: P.O. Box 197, Larchmont, NY 10538-0197
Contact: Ruth Tachna, Tr.

Financial data (yr. ended 12/31/01): Grants paid, $0; assets, $50,374 (M); expenditures, $822; qualifying distributions, $0.
Limitations: Giving primarily in NY.
Application information: Application form not required.
Trustees: Gordon S. Oppenheimer, Ruth Tachna.
EIN: 136125027

40603
Tarriff Family Trust
c/o Anchin, Block & Anchin
1375 Broadway, 18th Fl.
New York, NY 10018

Established in 2001 in NJ.
Donor(s): Scott L. Tarriff, Marsha L. Tarriff.
Financial data (yr. ended 12/31/01): Grants paid, $0; assets, $155,981 (M); gifts received, $157,607; expenditures, $81; qualifying distributions, $81.
Limitations: Applications not accepted.
Application information: Contributes only to pre-selected organizations.
Trustees: Marsha L. Tariff, Scott L. Tariff.
EIN: 226902821

40604
The Tawfik Family Charitable Trust
36 Waterford Dr.
Wheatley Heights, NY 11798

Established in 2000 in NY.
Financial data (yr. ended 12/31/00): Grants paid, $0; assets, $98,064 (M); expenditures, $0; qualifying distributions, $0.
Trustee: Mohamed Tawfik.
EIN: 066505204

40605
Kenneth and Caroline Taylor Family Foundation
c/o Brown Brothers Harriman Trust Co., LLC
63 Wall St., 31st Fl.
New York, NY 10005

Established in 2000 in PA.
Donor(s): Caroline E. Taylor, Kenneth H. Taylor, Jr.
Financial data (yr. ended 12/31/00): Grants paid, $0; assets, $253,484 (M); gifts received, $23,897; expenditures, $0; qualifying distributions, $0.
Limitations: Applications not accepted.
Application information: Contributes only to pre-selected organizations.
Trustees: Caroline E. Taylor, Kenneth H. Taylor, Jr.
EIN: 256742004

40606
Clark Taylor Legacy Care to Live Foundation
c/o Rocky Mountain Productions, Inc.
P.O. Box 1296, Cathedral Sta.
New York, NY 10025-1296

Established in 1995.
Financial data (yr. ended 12/31/01): Grants paid, $0; assets, $1,493 (M); expenditures, $473; qualifying distributions, $0.
Officer: Judy M. Collins, Mgr.
EIN: 133791099

40607
Technology Colleges Trust Foundation
c/o Loeb, Block
505 Park Ave.
New York, NY 10022

Established in 1999 in DE.
Financial data (yr. ended 12/31/99): Grants paid, $0; assets, $10,000 (M); expenditures, $0; qualifying distributions, $0.
Officers: Peter Tcherepnine, Pres.; George Blumenthal, V.P.; Russell Taylor, V.P.; Benjamin Davenport, Secy.; Sir Cyril Taylor, Treas.
EIN: 061559758

40608
Telesford Eistrup Miller Family Foundation, Inc.
409 Edgecombe Ave., Ste. 4A
New York, NY 10032-8026
Contact: Cecile A. Eistrup, Pres.

Established around 1996.
Donor(s): Rudy A. Telesford, Daphne R. Miller, Cecile Eistrup.
Financial data (yr. ended 06/30/02): Grants paid, $0; assets, $6,961 (M); expenditures, $1,172; qualifying distributions, $0.
Officers: Cecile A. Eistrup, Pres. and Treas.; Michelle Eistrup, V.P.; Claire Tomlinson, Secy.
EIN: 133872650

40609
The Tepper Family Foundation
111 Great Neck Rd., Ste. 408
Great Neck, NY 11021
Contact: Marvin B. Tepper, Pres.

Established in 2000 in NY.
Donor(s): Marvin B. Tepper, Elise C. Tepper.
Financial data (yr. ended 12/31/00): Grants paid, $0; assets, $484,390 (M); gifts received, $541,316; expenditures, $51; qualifying distributions, $0.
Officers: Marvin B. Tepper, Pres.; Elise C. Tepper, V.P. and Secy.-Treas.; Jacqueline G. Tepper, V.P.; Edward M. Tepper, V.P.
EIN: 113563659

40610
Think First of New York, Inc.
c/o Ann Burton- Sunnyview
1270 Belmont Ave.
Schenectady, NY 12308

Financial data (yr. ended 12/31/01): Grants paid, $0; assets, $6,941 (M); expenditures, $2,406; qualifying distributions, $0.
Officers: Richard J. Cummings, Pres.; David Resseguie, V.P.; Paul T. Hogan, Secy.; Cathy Flanagan, Treas.
Director: Ann Burton.
EIN: 141743794

40611
The Thorofare Foundation
12 Meadow Ln.
Brookhaven, NY 11719
Contact: George Cole, Dir.

Established in 1999 in NY.
Donor(s): George W. Cole.
Financial data (yr. ended 12/31/01): Grants paid, $0; assets, $404,678 (M); gifts received, $164,648; expenditures, $0; qualifying distributions, $0.
Director: George W. Cole.
EIN: 113522682

40612
The Andrew H. Tisch Family Foundation
c/o Mark J. Krinsky, C.P.A.
655 Madison Ave., 8th Fl.
New York, NY 10021

Established in 1998 in NY.
Donor(s): Laurence A. Tisch.
Financial data (yr. ended 12/31/01): Grants paid, $0; assets, $34 (M); expenditures, $0; qualifying distributions, $0.
Limitations: Applications not accepted.
Application information: Contributes only to pre-selected organizations.
Trustee: Laurence A. Tisch.
EIN: 134037379

40613
The Daniel R. Tisch Family Foundation
c/o Mark J. Krinsky, C.P.A.
655 Madison Ave., 8th Fl.
New York, NY 10021

Established in 1998 in NY.
Donor(s): Laurence A. Tisch.
Financial data (yr. ended 12/31/01): Grants paid, $0; assets, $34 (M); expenditures, $0; qualifying distributions, $0.
Limitations: Applications not accepted.
Application information: Contributes only to pre-selected organizations.
Trustee: Laurence A. Tisch.
EIN: 134037381

40614
The James S. Tisch Family Foundation
c/o Mark J. Krinsky, C.P.A.
655 Madison Ave., 8th Fl.
New York, NY 10021

Established in 1998 in NY.
Donor(s): Laurence A. Tisch.
Financial data (yr. ended 12/31/01): Grants paid, $0; assets, $34 (M); expenditures, $0; qualifying distributions, $0.
Limitations: Applications not accepted.
Application information: Contributes only to pre-selected organizations.
Trustee: Laurence A. Tisch.
EIN: 134037380

40615
The Jonathan M. Tisch Family Foundation
c/o Mark J. Krinsky, C.P.A.
655 Madison Ave., 8th Fl.
New York, NY 10021

Established in 1998 in NY.
Donor(s): Preston R. Tisch.
Financial data (yr. ended 12/31/01): Grants paid, $0; assets, $34 (M); expenditures, $0; qualifying distributions, $0.
Limitations: Applications not accepted.
Application information: Contributes only to pre-selected organizations.
Trustee: Preston R. Tisch.
EIN: 134037382

40616
The Steven E. Tisch Family Foundation
c/o Mark J. Krinsky, C.P.A.
655 Madison Ave, 8th Fl.
New York, NY 10021-0000

Established in 1998 in NY.
Donor(s): Preston R. Tisch.
Financial data (yr. ended 12/31/01): Grants paid, $0; assets, $34 (M); expenditures, $0; qualifying distributions, $0.
Trustee: Preston R. Tisch.
EIN: 134037377

40617
Thomas J. Tisch Family Foundation
c/o Mark J. Krinsky, C.P.A.
655 Madison Ave., 8th Fl.
New York, NY 10021

Established in 1998 in NY.
Donor(s): Laurence A. Tisch.
Financial data (yr. ended 12/31/01): Grants paid, $0; assets, $34 (M); expenditures, $0; qualifying distributions, $0.
Limitations: Applications not accepted.
Application information: Contributes only to pre-selected organizations.
Trustee: Laurence A. Tisch.
EIN: 134037378

40618
The William S. & Frances B. Todman Foundation
c/o Donald Scheier
40 W. 57th St., 26th Fl.
New York, NY 10019

Established in 1980 in NY.
Donor(s): Frances B. Todman, William S. Todman, Jr.
Financial data (yr. ended 11/30/01): Grants paid, $0; assets, $832 (M); expenditures, $21; qualifying distributions, $0.
Limitations: Applications not accepted. Giving primarily in FL and NY.
Application information: Contributes only to pre-selected organizations.
Trustees: Lisa Todman Plough, Frances B. Todman, William S. Todman, Jr.
EIN: 133064427

40619
Town of Amherst Development Corporation
130 John Muir Dr.
Buffalo, NY 14228-1148 (716) 688-9000
Contact: James J. Allen, Exec. Dir.

Donor(s): New York State Urban Development Corp., Niagara Mohawk Power Corp.
Financial data (yr. ended 12/31/01): Grants paid, $0; assets, $349,735 (M); gifts received, $8,875; expenditures, $15,349; qualifying distributions, $0.
Limitations: Giving limited to Amherst, NY.

Officers: Edward F. Stachura, Chair.; John P. Deluca, Vice-Chair.; Frederick A. Vilonen, Secy.; Paula A. Quebral, Treas.; James J. Allen, Exec. Dir.
EIN: 222867364

40620
Marguerite Traphagen Foundation
c/o Fleet National Bank
45 East Ave.
Rochester, NY 14604
Contact: Laura Weisenfluh, Trust Off., Fleet National Bank

Established in 1995 in NY.
Financial data (yr. ended 06/30/00): Grants paid, $0; assets, $154,232 (M); expenditures, $1,098; qualifying distributions, $602.
Trustee: Fleet National Bank.
EIN: 223374618

40621
The Trautschold Family Foundation
c/o John L. Cady
46 Summit Ave.
Bronxville, NY 10708

Established in 2000 in NY.
Donor(s): Jerome F. Trautschold, Jr.
Financial data (yr. ended 12/31/00): Grants paid, $0; assets, $181,852 (M); gifts received, $192,946; expenditures, $0; qualifying distributions, $0.
Limitations: Applications not accepted.
Application information: Contributes only to pre-selected organizations.
Officers: Jerome F. Trautschold, Jr., Pres.; John L. Cady, Secy.; Carol M. Trautschold, Treas.
EIN: 134140093

40622
The Traveler Fund
c/o Skydell
30 Fiddlers Green Dr.
Lloyd Harbor, NY 11743

Established in 2001 in NY.
Donor(s): Vicki Skydell.
Financial data (yr. ended 12/31/01): Grants paid, $0; assets, $26,879 (M); gifts received, $26,295; expenditures, $426; qualifying distributions, $1,852.
Limitations: Applications not accepted.
Application information: Contributes only to pre-selected organizations.
Trustees: Paul Skydell, Vicki Skydell.
EIN: 116567697

40623
Joel H. and Marjorie J. Treisman Foundation
c/o B. Strauss Associate Ltd.
307 5th Ave., 8th Fl.
New York, NY 10016-6517

Established in 2001 in CT.
Donor(s): Joel H. Treisman.
Financial data (yr. ended 04/30/02): Grants paid, $0; assets, $26,963 (M); gifts received, $26,250; expenditures, $0; qualifying distributions, $0.
Limitations: Applications not accepted.
Application information: Contributes only to pre-selected organizations.
Trustees: Joel H. Treisman, Marjorie J. Treisman.
EIN: 061618348

40624
Fred C. Trump Foundation
c/o Durben & Tosti, LLP
200 Garden City Plz.
Garden City, NY 11530-3303
Contact: Fred C. Trump, Dir.

Incorporated in 1952 in NY.

Donor(s): Beach Haven Apartments, Inc., Green Park Essex, Inc., Shore Haven Apartments, Inc., Trump Village Construction Corp.
Financial data (yr. ended 12/31/01): Grants paid, $0; assets, $13,387 (M); expenditures, $75; qualifying distributions, $0.
Limitations: Giving primarily in NJ and NY.
Application information: Application form not required.
Directors: Irwin Durben, Donald J. Trump, Fred C. Trump.
EIN: 116015006

40625
Tulip Tree Foundation
c/o Bessemer Trust Co., N.A.
630 5th Ave., Tax Dept.
New York, NY 10111

Established in 2000 in NY.
Donor(s): Alastair B. Martin.
Financial data (yr. ended 12/31/01): Grants paid, $0; assets, $460,359 (M); gifts received, $330,200; expenditures, $218; qualifying distributions, $0.
Limitations: Applications not accepted.
Application information: Contributes only to pre-selected organizations.
Trustees: Lawrence Bukzin, Norman Volk.
EIN: 137248063

40626
Tung Family Foundation
1158 5th Ave., Ste. 11B
New York, NY 10029

Established in 2000 in DE.
Donor(s): Marion S. Heydt.
Financial data (yr. ended 12/31/00): Grants paid, $0; assets, $760,541 (M); gifts received, $1,006,288; expenditures, $0; qualifying distributions, $0.
Limitations: Applications not accepted.
Application information: Contributes only to pre-selected organizations.
Officers: Alison A. Tung, Pres. and Treas.; K. Yung Tung, Secy.
EIN: 134120754

40627
Turobiner Foundation, Inc.
c/o Harold Turobiner
262 Central Park W., Apt. 11E
New York, NY 10024

Established in 1986 in DE.
Donor(s): Harold Turobiner, Alice Turobiner.‡
Financial data (yr. ended 11/30/01): Grants paid, $0; assets, $422 (M); gifts received, $218; expenditures, $618; qualifying distributions, $0.
Limitations: Applications not accepted. Giving primarily in NY.
Application information: Contributes only to pre-selected organizations.
Officer: Harold Turobiner, V.P.
Directors: Ann Dachs, Carol Finley.
EIN: 133177174

40628
Tutunjian Family Foundation
12 Bluff Rd.
Glen Cove, NY 11542

Established in 2001 in NY.
Donor(s): John P. Tutunjian.
Financial data (yr. ended 12/31/01): Grants paid, $0; assets, $50,000 (M); gifts received, $50,000; expenditures, $0; qualifying distributions, $0.
Limitations: Applications not accepted.
Application information: Contributes only to pre-selected organizations.

Director: John P. Tutunjian.
EIN: 010564658

40629
Joseph Tzvi Foundation
c/o Max Wasser
132 Nassau St., Ste. 300
New York, NY 10038-2416

Established in 1999.
Financial data (yr. ended 07/31/01): Grants paid, $0; assets, $87,426 (M); gifts received, $60,000; expenditures, $356,854; qualifying distributions, $1,562.
Limitations: Applications not accepted.
Application information: Contributes only to pre-selected organizations.
Trustees: Esther Konig, Michael Konig.
EIN: 137153248

40630
U.S. Friends of Shine
365 Whipoorwill Rd.
Chappaqua, NY 10514

Established in 2000 in NY.
Donor(s): Paul Tudor Jones, Peter Gerhard, Mark Heffernan.
Financial data (yr. ended 12/31/01): Grants paid, $0; assets, $127,654 (M); gifts received, $127,500; expenditures, $2; qualifying distributions, $0.
Limitations: Applications not accepted.
Application information: Contributes only to pre-selected organizations.
Officer: Lisa Endlich, Pres.
Trustees: Mark Heffernan, Sherry Kronenfeld.
EIN: 134141607

40631
L. Caroline Underwood Historical Museum
P.O. Box 397
Penn Yan, NY 14527

Established in 2000 in NY.
Financial data (yr. ended 12/31/00): Grants paid, $0; assets, $99,824 (M); gifts received, $107,235; expenditures, $11,537; qualifying distributions, $11,537; giving activities include $11,537 for programs.
Trustee: Philip L. Bailey.
EIN: 166510492

40632
The Unicorn Foundation
c/o M. Gilder
201 E. 79th St., Ste. 15C
New York, NY 10021

Established in 2000 in NY.
Donor(s): Richard Gilder, Jr.
Financial data (yr. ended 12/31/01): Grants paid, $0; assets, $180,022 (M); gifts received, $0; qualifying distributions, $0.
Officer: Margaret Gilder.
EIN: 134132474

40633
Union State-ICBA Disaster Relief Fund, Inc.
c/o Steven Sabatini
100 Ditch Hill Rd.
Orangeburg, NY 10962

Established in 2001 in NY.
Donor(s): Union State Bank, Independent Community Bankers of America, Tomkins Trust Co., Kalamazoo County State Bank, Citizens Bank, Community State Bank, Goldstein Family Foundation, Lea County State Bank.
Financial data (yr. ended 12/31/01): Grants paid, $0; assets, $133,260 (M); gifts received, $133,523; expenditures, $263; qualifying distributions, $0.
Limitations: Applications not accepted.
Application information: Contributes only to pre-selected organizations.
Directors: Lynne Allan, Raymond J. Crotty, Thomas E. Hales, Steven T. Sabatini.
EIN: 134189458
Codes: CS

40634
United Vision Foundation
34 State St.
Ossining, NY 10562

Established in 1998 in NY.
Donor(s): Yann Sandt.
Financial data (yr. ended 07/31/00): Grants paid, $0; assets, $536,656 (M); gifts received, $489,947; expenditures, $3,962; qualifying distributions, $0.
Limitations: Applications not accepted.
Application information: Contributes only to pre-selected organizations.
Officers and Directors:* Hyun Jin Moon,* Pres.; Teruaki Nakai,* V.P.; Michael Sommer,* Secy.-Treas.
EIN: 911924248

40635
Unity Foundation
60 E. 42nd St., Ste. 2217
New York, NY 10164-2217
Contact: Norton W. Mailman, Tr.

Donor(s): Norton Mailman.
Financial data (yr. ended 12/31/01): Grants paid, $0; assets, $108,771 (M); expenditures, $617; qualifying distributions, $0.
Limitations: Giving primarily in NY.
Trustee: Norton W. Mailman.
EIN: 237003479

40636
University Neurosurgeons and Research Foundation
c/o Paul R. Cooper, M.D., NY Univ. Medical Ctr.
550 1st Ave.
New York, NY 10016

Established in 2000 in NY.
Financial data (yr. ended 12/31/01): Grants paid, $0; assets, $316,038 (M); gifts received, $302,182; expenditures, $182,717; qualifying distributions, $0.
Officers: Paul Cooper, M.D., Pres.; Pat Kelly, M.D., Secy.; John Golfinos, M.D., Treas.
Trustees: Jafar Jafar, M.D., Max Koslow, M.D., Howard Weiner, M.D.
EIN: 137221539

40637
Up-Wingers, Inc.
c/o C. Sarowitz Grayman & Co.
169 W. End Ave.
Brooklyn, NY 11235-4808

Established in 1986 in NY.
Donor(s): Flora Schnall.
Financial data (yr. ended 06/30/99): Grants paid, $0; assets, $710 (M); expenditures, $60; qualifying distributions, $60.
Limitations: Applications not accepted. Giving primarily in New York, NY.
Officers: Flora Schnall, Pres.; John C. Nelson, Secy.
EIN: 132923707

40638
Brocho V'Chesed, Inc.
66 Penn St., Ste. 3B
Brooklyn, NY 11211

Established in 2000 in NY.
Donor(s): David Klein, Jacob Klein.
Financial data (yr. ended 12/31/00): Grants paid, $0; assets, $132,084 (M); gifts received, $132,005; expenditures, $172; qualifying distributions, $0.
Officers: Jacob Klein, Pres.; David Klein, Secy.; Miriam Klein, Treas.
EIN: 133571013

40639
Gerard A. & Isabel Natalie Varlotta Foundation, Inc.
P.O. Box 4484
Great Neck, NY 11023-4484

Financial data (yr. ended 05/31/01): Grants paid, $0; assets, $1,857 (M); expenditures, $0; qualifying distributions, $0.
Limitations: Giving primarily in the New York, NY, area.
Application information: Application form not required.
Directors: Gerard DiSenso, Gerard A. Varlotta, Isabel N. Varlotta.
EIN: 112514199

40640
Vegari Foundation, Inc.
c/o Citrin Cooperman & Co., LLP
529 5th Ave., 10th Fl.
New York, NY 10017-4608
Application address: 400 Millercreek Rd., Gladwyne, PA 19035, tel.: (610) 658-0702
Contact: Matt Vegari, Pres.

Established in 1991.
Donor(s): Matt Vegari, Sheila Vegari.
Financial data (yr. ended 12/31/00): Grants paid, $0; assets, $22,303 (M); expenditures, $167; qualifying distributions, $0.
Officers: Matt Vegari, Co-Pres.; Sheila Vegari, Co-Pres.
EIN: 223082557

40641
The Velocity Foundation
667 Madison Ave., 25th Fl.
New York, NY 10021
Application address: 25 Stratford Rd., Harrison, NY 10528
Contact: Richard E. Halperin, Tr.

Established in 2000 in NY.
Financial data (yr. ended 12/31/00): Grants paid, $0; assets, $118,361 (M); gifts received, $7,500; expenditures, $500; qualifying distributions, $0.
Application information: Application form not required.
Trustees: Lucy Landesman Halperin, Richard E. Halperin.
EIN: 137237236

40642
Edward H. Vick Foundation, Inc.
501 Guard Hill Rd.
Bedford, NY 10506 (914) 234-6617

Established in 2001 in NY.
Donor(s): Edward H. Vick.
Financial data (yr. ended 12/31/01): Grants paid, $0; assets, $988,166 (M); gifts received, $11,115; expenditures, $0; qualifying distributions, $0.
Officers: Edward H. Vick, Pres.; Joshua D. Vick, V.P.; Linda Schoenthaler, Secy.-Treas.
EIN: 134199723

40643
The Jeffrey K. Vogel Family Foundation, Inc.
1 Meadow Dr.
Lawrence, NY 11559-2811

Established in 1999 in NY.
Financial data (yr. ended 12/31/00): Grants paid, $0; assets, $21,539 (M); expenditures, $0; qualifying distributions, $0.
Limitations: Applications not accepted.
Application information: Contributes only to pre-selected organizations.
Trustees: Jeffrey K. Vogel, Marjorie Vogel.
EIN: 113522518

40644
The Walker Foundation, Inc.
22 W. 66th St.
New York, NY 10023-0016

Established in 2000 in NY.
Financial data (yr. ended 12/31/00): Grants paid, $0; assets, $319,030 (M); expenditures, $282; qualifying distributions, $0.
Officers: Dale R. Walker, Chair. and Treas.; Linda L. Walker, V.P.; Virginia Ashley Walker, V.P.; Whitney Beaumont Walker, V.P.
EIN: 134143838

40645
The Honore T. Wamsler Foundation, Inc.
c/o Robert Morse, Mgr.
230 Park Ave., Ste. 1635
New York, NY 10169

Established in 1998 in DE.
Donor(s): Honore T. Wamsler.
Financial data (yr. ended 03/31/01): Grants paid, $0; assets, $1,048,884 (M); gifts received, $502,000; expenditures, $20,351; qualifying distributions, $885.
Limitations: Applications not accepted.
Application information: Contributes only to pre-selected organizations.
Officer: Robert Morse, Mgr.
Directors: Pauline Joerger, Susanne Redetzki, Caroline Wamsler, Irene Wamsler-Snow, Bettina Wamsler-Weithauer.
EIN: 134011655

40646
Paul M. Warburg Fund
c/o JPMorgan Chase Bank
P.O. Box 31412, Tr. Tax Dept.
Rochester, NY 14603

Financial data (yr. ended 12/31/01): Grants paid, $0; assets, $20,047 (M); expenditures, $562; qualifying distributions, $0.
Limitations: Applications not accepted. Giving on a national basis.
Application information: Unsolicited request for funds not accepted.
Trustee: JPMorgan Chase Bank.
EIN: 136218156

40647
Stanford S. Warshawsky Family Foundation
20 Exchange Pl.
New York, NY 10005-3201 (212) 269-8628
Contact: Stanford S. Warshawsky, Pres.

Established in 1986 in NY.
Donor(s): Stanford S. Warshawsky.
Financial data (yr. ended 12/31/01): Grants paid, $0; assets, $20,001 (M); expenditures, $1,920; qualifying distributions, $0.
Officers: Stanford S. Warshawsky, Pres.; Sandra Warshawsky, V.P.; Deborah Warshawsky, Secy.; Susan Warshawsky, Treas.
EIN: 222853594

40648
James D. Watson Family Foundation
c/o U.S. Trust
P.O. Box 2004
New York, NY 10109-1910

Established in 2000 in NY.
Donor(s): James Dewey Watson.
Financial data (yr. ended 12/31/00): Grants paid, $0; assets, $400,625 (M); gifts received, $50; expenditures, $0; qualifying distributions, $0.
Officer: James Dewey Watson, Pres.
EIN: 113576477

40649
Bettina Weary, Ph.D. Charitable Trust
2495 Kensington Ave.
Amherst, NY 14226
Application address: P.O. Box 339, Kent, CT 06757
Contact: Jeannette Marlow, Tr.

Established in 2001 in NY.
Financial data (yr. ended 12/31/01): Grants paid, $0; assets, $2,540,945 (M); expenditures, $19,646; qualifying distributions, $1,103.
Trustee: Jeannette Marlow.
EIN: 311684811

40650
Robert B. Wegman Charitable Foundation
1500 Brooks Ave.
P.O. Box 30844
Rochester, NY 14603-0844

Established in 1993 in NY.
Donor(s): Daniel R. Wegman.
Financial data (yr. ended 12/31/01): Grants paid, $0; assets, $1,926,481 (M); gifts received, $500; expenditures, $250; qualifying distributions, $0.
Limitations: Applications not accepted.
Application information: Contributes only to pre-selected organizations.
Officers: Robert B. Wegman, Chair. and Treas.; Daniel R. Wegman, Pres.; Margaret F. Wegman, V.P.; Paul S. Speranza, Jr., Secy.
EIN: 223247037

40651
William Wegman Foundation, Inc.
c/o Davis & Grutman, LLP
275 Madison Ave., Ste. 1614
New York, NY 10016-1101

Established in 1999 in DE.
Financial data (yr. ended 12/31/01): Grants paid, $0; assets, $1,621 (M); expenditures, $713; qualifying distributions, $0.
Trustee: William Wegman.
EIN: 133878893

40652
The Weinstein Foundation
c/o Ark Restaurants
85 5th Ave., 14th Fl.
New York, NY 10024

Donor(s): Michael Weinstein.
Financial data (yr. ended 06/30/02): Grants paid, $0; assets, $13 (M); expenditures, $25; qualifying distributions, $0.
Limitations: Applications not accepted.
Application information: Contributes only to pre-selected organizations.
Trustee: Michael Weinstein.
EIN: 133139097

40653
Welles Family Foundation, Inc.
1 W. Church St.
Elmira, NY 14901
Application address: 482 Crane Rd., P.O. Box 448, Horseheads, NY 14845
Contact: Paddy S. Welles, Pres.

Established in 2000 in NY.
Donor(s): Gillett Welles III.
Financial data (yr. ended 12/31/01): Grants paid, $0; assets, $276,440 (M); gifts received, $101,969; expenditures, $9,339; qualifying distributions, $0.
Officers and Directors:* Paddy S. Welles,* Pres.and Mgr.; Gillett Welles III,* V.P. and Treas.; John R. Alexander,* Secy.
EIN: 161594021

40654
The WEMGO Charitable Trust
92 Pearl St.
Staten Island, NY 10304-2165

Established in 2000 in NY.
Donor(s): Mildred Olsen.
Financial data (yr. ended 12/31/00): Grants paid, $0; assets, $59,500 (M); gifts received, $59,500; expenditures, $0; qualifying distributions, $0.
Officers: Mildred Olsen, Pres.; Eric William Olsen, V.P.; Warren Richard Olsen, Secy.-Treas.
EIN: 137282175

40655
Westchester Health Fund
3010 Westchester Ave.
Purchase, NY 10577-2524 (914) 694-6428
FAX: (914) 694-2768
Contact: Harry L. Staley, Exec. Dir.

Established in 1969 in NY.
Financial data (yr. ended 12/31/01): Grants paid, $0; assets, $2,549,161 (M); expenditures, $18,548; qualifying distributions, $0.
Limitations: Giving limited to Westchester County, NY.
Publications: Application guidelines.
Application information: Application form not required.
Officers and Directors:* Ross M. Weale,* Chair.; Richard Finucane, M.D.,* Pres.; Joseph L. Staley, Secy.; Harry L. Staley, Treas. and Exec. Dir.; Steven Galef, Raymond M. Plannell.
EIN: 237071929

40656
The Weston Charitable Foundation
199 Pinesbridge Rd.
Ossining, NY 10562

Established in 1997 in NY.
Donor(s): Emma R. Weston.
Financial data (yr. ended 12/31/99): Grants paid, $0; assets, $2,112,413 (M); gifts received, $1,140,000; expenditures, $480,627; qualifying distributions, $347,699; giving activities include $480,627 for programs.
Limitations: Applications not accepted.
Application information: Contributes only to pre-selected organizations.
Officers and Director:* Rev. Jordan Peck,* Chair.; Sue Morrow Flanagan, Pres.; Emma R. Weston, Secy-Treas.
EIN: 133967969

40657
The Nina and Gary Wexler Foundation
100 Jericho Quadrangle, No. 106
Jericho, NY 11753

Established in 1998 in NY.
Donor(s): G. Martin Wexler, Nina Wexler.
Financial data (yr. ended 12/31/01): Grants paid, $0; assets, $20,702 (M); expenditures, $605; qualifying distributions, $0.
Limitations: Applications not accepted. Giving primarily in New York, NY.
Application information: Contributes only to pre-selected organizations.
Trustees: G. Martin Wexler, Nina Wexler.
EIN: 113441913

40658
The Wharton Foundation, Inc.
c/o Marks Panneth & Shron
111 Great Neck Rd.
Great Neck, NY 11021

Donor(s): Irving L. Wharton.
Financial data (yr. ended 07/31/01): Grants paid, $0; assets, $26,664 (M); expenditures, $40; qualifying distributions, $0.
Limitations: Applications not accepted.
Application information: Contributes only to pre-selected organizations.
Officer: Irving L. Wharton, Pres.
EIN: 116037013

40659
The Wheeler Family Foundation
c/o Goldman Sachs & Co.
85 Broad St., Tax Dept.
New York, NY 10004

Established in 1996 in NY.
Donor(s): Peter S.W. Wheeler.
Financial data (yr. ended 07/31/01): Grants paid, $0; assets, $29,819 (M); expenditures, $58; qualifying distributions, $0.
Limitations: Applications not accepted.
Application information: Contributes only to pre-selected organizations.
Trustees: Peter S.W. Wheeler, Susan E.M. Wheeler.
EIN: 133921101

40660
The Judith C. White Foundation, Inc.
57 Barkers Point Rd.
Sands Point, NY 11050 (516) 883-5531
Contact: Jeffrey Kovner, Dir.

Established in 2000 in NY.
Donor(s): Judith C. White.
Financial data (yr. ended 12/31/01): Grants paid, $0; assets, $6,833 (M); gifts received, $3,250; expenditures, $3,047; qualifying distributions, $0.
Application information: Application form not required.
Directors: Amy Kovner, Jeffrey Kovner, David White.
EIN: 113548952

40661
B. Belle Whitney Scholarship Trust
c/o JPMorgan Chase Bank
P.O. Box 31412
Rochester, NY 14603-1412
Application addresses: c/o Guidance Dept., Danbury High School, Clapboard Ridge Rd., Danbury, CT 06811, or c/o Financial Aid Off, Vassar College, 124 Raymond Ave., Poughkeepsie, NY 12604

Financial data (yr. ended 12/31/01): Grants paid, $0; assets, $257,511 (M); expenditures, $6,374; qualifying distributions, $1,108.
Limitations: Giving limited to residents of Danbury, CT.
Trustee: JPMorgan Chase Bank.
EIN: 066022861
Codes: GTI

40662
Whitten Arts Foundation
424 Main St., Ste. 1100-Lib. Bldg.
Buffalo, NY 14202-3611 (716) 856-9090
Contact: Patrick E. Martin, Secy.-Treas.

Established in 1996 in NY.
Donor(s): Varue Whitten Oishei.
Financial data (yr. ended 12/31/01): Grants paid, $0; assets, $12,569 (M); expenditures, $582; qualifying distributions, $0.
Officers and Directors:* Varue Whitten Oishei,* Pres.; Patrick E. Martin,* V.P.; Mary Kennedy Martin,* Secy.-Treas.
EIN: 161511476

40663
Hans & Dorothy Widenmann Fund
c/o KPMG, LLP
345 Park Ave., 38th Fl.
New York, NY 10154

Financial data (yr. ended 11/30/01): Grants paid, $0; assets, $497,353 (M); expenditures, $10,526; qualifying distributions, $5,230.
Limitations: Applications not accepted.
Application information: Contributes only to pre-selected organizations.
Trustees: Fred A. Allardyce, Judith A. Boylan, Francis K. Decker, Jr.
EIN: 136085602

40664
The Wieder Family Charitable Trust
c/o Roth & Co., LLP
5612 18th Ave.
Brooklyn, NY 11204

Established in 1996.
Donor(s): Abraham Wieder, Tzirel Wieder.
Financial data (yr. ended 11/30/01): Grants paid, $0; assets, $32,148 (M); expenditures, $0; qualifying distributions, $0.
Limitations: Giving primarily in NY.
Officer: Abraham Wieder, Mgr.
EIN: 116466023

40665
Wild Waters Foundation
c/o Myer, Greene & Degge
P.O. Box 930
Pearl River, NY 10965

Established in 1996 in DE and CO.
Donor(s): Ann R. McAlpin, David H. McAlpin, Jr., Joan R. McAlpin Charitable Lead Trust, Wild Wings Foundation.
Financial data (yr. ended 11/30/01): Grants paid, $0; assets, $872,267 (M); gifts received, $109,505; expenditures, $18,982; qualifying distributions, $0.
Limitations: Applications not accepted.
Application information: Contributes only to pre-selected organizations.
Officers: Ann R. McAlpin, Pres. and Treas.; Janet U. McAlpin, Secy.
Director: Timothy L. Sampsel.
EIN: 133928203

40666
William & Rachel Foundation
c/o Max Glauber
25 Satmar Dr., Ste. 301
Monroe, NY 10950

Established in 1997 in NY.
Financial data (yr. ended 12/31/99): Grants paid, $0; assets, $1,809 (M); expenditures, $1,021; qualifying distributions, $0.
Limitations: Applications not accepted.

Application information: Contributes only to pre-selected organizations.
Officers: Peter Glauber, Pres.; Max Glauber, Secy.; Meshulem Jacobowitz, Treas.
EIN: 133948170

40667
The Craig E. Wishman Foundation
180 West End Ave., Apt. 20D
New York, NY 10023-4910

Donor(s): Craig E. Wishman.
Financial data (yr. ended 12/31/01): Grants paid, $0; assets, $18,042 (M); gifts received, $2,575; expenditures, $72; qualifying distributions, $0.
Trustees: Fern Wishman, Harvey B. Wishman.
EIN: 133963942

40668
The Alfred Wohl Foundation, Inc.
c/o B.R. Glickman
105 S. Bedford Rd., Ste. 320
Mount Kisco, NY 10549

Established in 1955 in NY.
Donor(s): Sheila Wohl.
Financial data (yr. ended 03/31/02): Grants paid, $0; assets, $844 (M); gifts received, $500; expenditures, $152; qualifying distributions, $0.
Limitations: Applications not accepted. Giving primarily in Miami, FL.
Application information: Contributes only to pre-selected organizations.
Officers: Sheila Wohl, Pres.; Michael Wohl, V.P.; Donna Rubin-Bishop, Secy.-Treas.
EIN: 116012485

40669
World Community Foundation
c/o Bonnie Fields
315 W. 70th St., Apt. 9B
New York, NY 10023

Established in 1991 in NY.
Donor(s): Judith Fields, Norma Grabler, Bonnie Ann Fields.
Financial data (yr. ended 12/31/00): Grants paid, $0; assets, $21,270 (M); gifts received, $10,000; expenditures, $423; qualifying distributions, $423.
Limitations: Applications not accepted.
Application information: Contributes only to pre-selected organizations.
Officer: Bonnie Ann Fields, Pres. and Secy.
Directors: Eloy Anello, John Huddleston, Ruhiyyih Huddleston, Jeremy Martin.
EIN: 133612343

40670
WUCWO Foundation USA, Inc.
c/o Barbara W. Gallagher
P.O. Box 1435
Scarsdale, NY 10583-9435

Established in 1999.
Donor(s): Barbara Gallagher.
Financial data (yr. ended 12/31/01): Grants paid, $0; assets, $38,538 (M); gifts received, $32,079; expenditures, $7,867; qualifying distributions, $6,890.
Limitations: Applications not accepted.
Application information: Contributes only to pre-selected organizations.
Directors: Barbara Gallagher, Terrance Gallagher, Maria Nigro Parker.
EIN: 134074527

40671
The Wyckoff Family Foundation, Inc.
159 Maxwell Ave.
Geneva, NY 14456

Established in 2001 in NY.
Donor(s): Margaret H. Wyckoff.
Financial data (yr. ended 12/31/01): Grants paid, $0; assets, $91,598 (M); gifts received, $88,173; expenditures, $0; qualifying distributions, $0.
Limitations: Applications not accepted.
Application information: Contributes only to pre-selected organizations.
Officers and Directors:* Margaret H. Wyckoff,* Pres.; Stephen G. Wyckoff,* V.P.; Peter B. Wyckoff,* V.P.; James H. Wyckoff,* V.P.; Andrew W. Wyckoff,* V.P.; Katherine G. Wyckoff,* Secy.; Janet R. Wyckoff,* Treas.
EIN: 100001401

40672
Fan & Sig Wyler Foundation, Inc.
122 E. 42nd St., Ste. 616
New York, NY 10168-0113 (212) 687-0050
Contact: Wilfred Wyler, Pres.

Financial data (yr. ended 06/30/02): Grants paid, $0; assets, $4,736 (M); expenditures, $0; qualifying distributions, $0.
Limitations: Giving primarily in New York, NY.
Application information: Application form not required.
Officer: Wilfred Wyler, Pres.
EIN: 136188027

40673
Divrei Yitzchok Foundation
1165 E. 24th St.
Brooklyn, NY 11210 (718) 283-8544

Established in 2001 in NY.
Financial data (yr. ended 12/31/01): Grants paid, $0; assets, $7,503 (M); gifts received, $10,000; expenditures, $2,500; qualifying distributions, $2,500.
Trustees: Esther Beinhorn, Marvin Beinhorn.
EIN: 113603802

40674
Raymond Zeph Foundation
c/o William Kitchell
235 Logue St.
North Bellmore, NY 11710

Financial data (yr. ended 12/31/99): Grants paid, $0; assets, $60,061 (M); expenditures, $1,225; qualifying distributions, $1,183.

Limitations: Applications not accepted. Giving primarily in NY.
Application information: Contributes only to pre-selected organizations.
Officers: Michael G. Reichert, Pres.; Charles P. Peterson, V.P.; Leonard Robertson, Jr., Secy.; William R. Kitchell, Treas.; Paul A. Combes, Mgr.
Directors: Bruce S. Brandt, Stanley R. Butterworth, Bradford W. Ferguson, Herbert H. Klare, Arthur P. Molkentin, Henry R. Pekarek, Allyn N. Richards, Frederick A. Rogers, Bruce Testut, Ernest N. Thilesen, Donald A. Woolnough, and 4 additional directors.
EIN: 116103934

40675
Zichron Aaron Charitable Foundation
147 7th St.
Brooklyn, NY 11215-3106
Contact: Gabor Gluck, Tr.

Established in 1998 in NY.
Financial data (yr. ended 10/31/01): Grants paid, $0; assets, $74,630 (M); gifts received, $22,466; expenditures, $500; qualifying distributions, $0.
Limitations: Giving primarily in Brooklyn, NY.
Trustees: Esther Guttman, Martin Guttman.
EIN: 113453187

40676
Zichron Alter Meir Wilamowsky Foundation
49 Sealy Dr.
Lawrence, NY 11559

Established in 2001 in NY.
Donor(s): David Rybak, Eli Wilamowsky.
Financial data (yr. ended 12/31/01): Grants paid, $0; assets, $3,216,000 (M); gifts received, $3,216,000; expenditures, $0; qualifying distributions, $0.
Limitations: Applications not accepted.
Application information: Contributes only to pre-selected organizations.
Directors: Eli Wilamowsky, Rhone Wilamowsky, Steven Wilamowsky.
EIN: 311795391

40677
The Zichron Libby Charitable Foundation
1364 47th St.
Brooklyn, NY 11219

Established in 2000 in NY.
Donor(s): Chaim Herman.
Financial data (yr. ended 12/31/00): Grants paid, $0; assets, $106,217 (M); gifts received, $100,000; expenditures, $0; qualifying distributions, $0.
Officer: Chaim Herman.
EIN: 113512542

NORTH CAROLINA

40678
The Duke Endowment
100 N. Tryon St., Ste. 3500
Charlotte, NC 28202-4012 (704) 376-0291
FAX: (704) 376-9336; E-mail:
droberson@tde.org; URL: http://
www.dukeendowment.org
Contact: Elizabeth H. Locke, Ph.D., Pres.

Trust established in 1924 in NJ.
Donor(s): James Buchanan Duke.‡
Financial data (yr. ended 12/31/01): Grants paid, $105,192,627; assets, $2,489,158,509 (M); expenditures, $121,976,034; qualifying distributions, $109,687,661.
Limitations: Giving limited to NC and SC.
Publications: Annual report (including application guidelines), informational brochure (including application guidelines), grants list, occasional report.
Application information: Application form not required.
Officers and Trustees:* Russell M. Robinson II,* Chair.; Mary D.B.T. Semans,* Chair. Emeritus; Hugh M. Chapman,* Vice-Chair.; Louis C. Stephens, Jr.,* Vice-Chair.; Elizabeth H. Locke, Ph.D., Pres. and Dir., Education Div.; Eugene W. Cochrane, Jr., V.P. and Dir., Health Care Div.; Terri W. Honeycutt, Secy.; Janice C. Walker, C.F.O. and Treas.; Stephanie S. Lynch, C.I.O.; William G. Anlyan, M.D., John Hope Franklin, Ph.D., Constance F. Gray, Richard H. Jenrette, Mary D.T. Jones, Thomas S. Kenan III, Juanita M. Kreps, Ph.D., John G. Medlin, Jr., Minor M. Shaw, Jean G. Spaulding, M.D., L. Neil Williams, Jr.
EIN: 560529965
Codes: FD, FM

40679
Bank of America Foundation, Inc.
100 N. Tryon St., NC1-007-18-01
Charlotte, NC 28255-0001
URL: http://www.bankofamerica.com/foundation
Contact: Mike Sweeney, Dir.

Established under current name in 1998 following the merger of NationsBank Corporation and BankAmerica Corporation.
Donor(s): Bank of America Corp., and subsidiaries.
Financial data (yr. ended 12/31/00): Grants paid, $85,755,841; assets, $2,212,307 (M); gifts received, $85,737,445; expenditures, $82,431,561; qualifying distributions, $85,755,841.
Limitations: Giving limited to areas of major company operations, including 21 states and Washington, DC, and other select areas where there is a company presence.
Application information: Application information available on foundation Web site.
EIN: 582429625
Codes: CS, FD, CD, FM

40680
Burroughs Wellcome Fund
21 T. W. Alexander Dr.
P.O. Box 13901
Research Triangle Park, NC 27709-3901
(919) 991-5100
FAX: (919) 991-5160; E-mail: info@bwfund.org.;
URL: http://www.bwfund.org
Contact: Mirinda Kossoff, Comm. Off.

Incorporated in 1955 in NY.
Donor(s): Burroughs Wellcome Co., The Wellcome Trust.
Financial data (yr. ended 08/31/01): Grants paid, $34,106,187; assets, $698,876,247 (M); expenditures, $44,333,800; qualifying distributions, $37,752,678.
Limitations: Giving limited to the U.S. and Canada.
Publications: Annual report (including application guidelines), newsletter, occasional report, informational brochure (including application guidelines).
Application information: Application form required.
Officers and Directors:* Enriqueta C. Bond, Ph.D.,* Pres.; Scott G. Schoedler, V.P., Finance; Gail H. Cassell, Ph.D., Stephen D. Corman, Mary Anne Fox, Henry G. Friesen, M.D., Phil Gold, M.D., Ph.D., Albert James Hudspeth, M.D., Ph.D., I. George Miller, M.D., Mary Lou Pardue, Ph.D., Jerome F. Strauss III, M.D., Ph.D., Judith Swain, M.D., Philip R. Tracy, Jean D. Wilson, M.D.
EIN: 237225395
Codes: FD, FM, GTI

40681
Kate B. Reynolds Charitable Trust
128 Reynolda Village
Winston-Salem, NC 27106-5123
(336) 723-1456
FAX: (336) 723-7765; URL: http://www.kbr.org
Contact: E. Ray Cope, Pres.; John H. Frank, Dir., Health Care Div.; or Joyce T. Adger, Dir., Poor and Needy Div.

Established in 1947 in NC.
Donor(s): Kate B. Reynolds.‡
Financial data (yr. ended 08/31/02): Grants paid, $26,506,244; assets, $451,008,874 (M); expenditures, $27,788,005; qualifying distributions, $26,506,244.
Limitations: Giving limited to NC; social welfare grants limited to Winston-Salem and Forsyth County; health care giving, statewide.
Publications: Annual report (including application guidelines), application guidelines, informational brochure, newsletter.
Application information: Applicant should contact the trust staff to discuss the proposal prior to submitting a written application. Advance consultation is required before an application can be accepted for consideration. Applications will not be accepted electronically. Application form required.
Officer: E. Ray Cope, Pres.
Trustee: Wachovia Bank, N.A.
EIN: 566036515
Codes: FD, FM

40682
Foundation for the Carolinas
217 South Tryon St.
Charlotte, NC 28202 (704) 973-4500
Additional tel.: (888) 335-9541; FAX: (704) 973-4599; URL: http://www.fftc.org
Contact: Don Jonas, Sr. V.P., Community Philanthropy

Incorporated in 1958 in NC.

Financial data (yr. ended 12/31/00): Grants paid, $26,405,093; assets, $250,975,459 (M); gifts received, $36,441,020; expenditures, $33,769,360.
Limitations: Giving primarily to organizations serving the citizens of NC and SC, with emphasis on the greater Charlotte, NC, region.
Publications: Annual report (including application guidelines), newsletter, application guidelines.
Application information: The foundation is currently undertaking an internal study and review of grantmaking program areas. Applications are not being accepted at this time. Application form required.
Officers and Directors:* Peter B. Ridder,* Chair.; Michael Marsicano, Pres.; McCray V. Benson, Sr. V.P., Regional Initiatives; Don Jonas, Sr. V.P., Community Philanthropy; Judy L. Kerns, Sr. V.P., Finance and Admin.; C. Barton Landess, J.D., Sr. V.P., Devel. and Donor Svcs.; Charity L. Perkins,* V.P., Comm. and Donor Svcs.; Holly K. Welch, V.P., Devel. and Legal Affairs; and 17 additional directors.
EIN: 566047886
Codes: CM, FD, FM, GTI

40683
The First Union Foundation
c/o Wachovia Corp.
301 S. Tryon St., TW-11
Charlotte, NC 28288-0143 (704) 374-6649
Local bank addresses: CT, NJ, NY: Yvonne Calcagno, 370 Scotch Rd., Trenton, NJ 08628, tel.: (609) 530-7357, FL: Connie Smith, 225 Water St., 7th Fl., FL0670, Jacksonville, FL 32202, tel.: (904) 489-3268, DC, GA, MD, NC, SC, VA: Robby Russell, 310 S. Tryon St., Charlotte, NC 28288-0143, tel.: (704) 374-4912, DE, PA: Kevin Dow, 1339 Chestnut St., 13th Fl., Philadelphia, PA 19107, tel.: (267) 321-7664, First Union Securities, Inc.: Tim Holtz, 10700 Wheat 1st Dr., Glen Allen, VA 23060, tel.: (804) 965-2415; FAX: (704) 374-2484; URL: http://www.wachovia.com/inside/page/0,,139_414_431,00.html
Contact: Shannon McFadden, Dir.

Established in 1987 in NC.
Donor(s): First Union Corp., Wachovia Corp.
Financial data (yr. ended 12/31/00): Grants paid, $23,933,599; assets, $892,746 (M); gifts received, $13,170,918; expenditures, $25,188,322; qualifying distributions, $24,685,171.
Limitations: Giving limited to CT, Washington, DC, DE, FL, GA, MD, NC, NJ, NY, PA, SC, TN, and VA.
Publications: Annual report, informational brochure.
Application information: Application form not required.
Directors: Edward E. Barr, G. Alex Bernhardt, Sr., Erskine B. Bowles, W. Waldo Bradley, Robert J. Brown, Edward E. Crutchfield, A. Dano Davis, Norwood H. Davis, Jr., Beverly F. Dolan, Roddy Dowd, Sr., William H. Goodwin, Jr., Frank M. Henry, Ernest E. Jones, Herbert Lotman, Radford D. Lovett, Mackey J. McDonald, Shannon McFadden, Patricia A. McFate, Joseph Neubauer, James M. Seabrook, Sr., Ruth G. Shaw, Lanty L. Smith, Ken Thompson.
Trustee: First Union National Bank.
EIN: 566288589
Codes: CS, FD, FM

40684
The Sabbah Family Foundation, Inc.
109 Muirs Chapel Rd.
P.O. Box 19608
Greensboro, NC 27419 (336) 294-4494

Established in 1987 in NC.
Donor(s): Maurice D. Sabbah, Zmira Sabbah, Leeor Sabbah.
Financial data (yr. ended 10/31/00): Grants paid, $21,845,347; assets, $23,124,978 (M); gifts received, $1,066,616; expenditures, $21,974,963; qualifying distributions, $21,829,711.
Limitations: Applications not accepted.
Application information: Contributes only to pre-selected organizations.
Officers and Directors:* Maurice D. Sabbah,* Pres. and Treas.; Zmira Sabbah,* Secy.; Leeor Sabbah.
EIN: 561603860
Codes: FD, FM

40685
Z. Smith Reynolds Foundation, Inc.
14 S. Cherry St., Ste. 200
Winston-Salem, NC 27101-5287
(336) 725-7541
Additional tel.: (800) 443-8319; FAX: (336) 725-6069; E-mail: info@zsr.org; URL: http://www.zsr.org
Contact: Thomas W. Ross, Exec. Dir.

Incorporated in 1936 in NC.
Donor(s): Nancy S. Reynolds,‡ Mary Reynolds Babcock,‡ Richard J. Reynolds, Jr.,‡ William N. Reynolds.‡
Financial data (yr. ended 12/31/01): Grants paid, $20,066,550; assets, $410,838,777 (M); gifts received, $24,279,926; expenditures, $22,064,251; qualifying distributions, $22,108,676; giving activities include $575,359 for programs.
Limitations: Giving limited to NC.
Publications: Annual report (including application guidelines), occasional report, informational brochure.
Application information: Application form required.
Officers and Trustees:* Lloyd P. Tate, Jr.,* Pres.; Mary Mountcastle,* V.P.; Thomas W. Ross, Secy. and Exec. Dir.; Jane S. Patterson,* Treas.; Nancy R. Bagley, Smith W. Bagley, Daniel G. Clodfelter, Anita Brown Graham, R. Darrell Hancock, Hubert Humphrey, John O. McNairy, Katharine B. Mountcastle, Stephen L. Neal, Zachary T. Smith.
EIN: 586038145
Codes: FD, FM, GTI

40686
The Winston-Salem Foundation
860 W. 5th St.
Winston-Salem, NC 27101-2506
(336) 725-2382
FAX: (336) 727-0581; E-mail: info@wsfoundation.org; URL: http://www.wsfoundation.org
Contact: Scott F. Wierman, Pres.

Established in 1919 in NC by declaration of trust.
Financial data (yr. ended 12/31/01): Grants paid, $17,941,763; assets, $179,938,414 (M); gifts received, $17,573,597; expenditures, $20,280,252; giving activities include $20,000 for loans to organizations and $121,000 for loans to individuals.
Limitations: Giving primarily in the greater Forsyth County, NC, area.
Publications: Annual report (including application guidelines), newsletter, grants list, application guidelines.
Application information: Application form required for student aid or student loans only and includes $20 application fee.
Officer: Scott F. Wierman, Pres.
Foundation Committee: Richard P. Budd, Chair.; Rence Callahan, Greg Cox, Richard Janeway, M.D., James T. Lambie, Dr. Harold L. Martin, John G. Medlin, Jr., T. David Neill, L. Glenn Orr, Jr., Ann C. Ring, Vivian L. Turner, Robert C. Vaughn, Jr., Jane B. Williams.
Trustees: Bank of America, B.B. & T., Central Carolina Bank & Trust Co., First Citizens Bank, First Union National Bank of North Carolina, Wachovia Bank of North Carolina, N.A.
EIN: 566037615
Codes: CM, FD, FM, GTI

40687
The Community Foundation of Western North Carolina, Inc.
1 W. Park Sq., Ste. 1600
Asheville, NC 28802 (828) 254-4960
Mailing address: P.O. Box 1888, Asheville, NC 28802; FAX: (828) 251-2258; URL: http://www.cfwnc.org
Contact: Pat Smith, Exec. Dir.

Incorporated in 1978 in NC as the Community Foundation of Greater Asheville, Inc.
Financial data (yr. ended 06/30/02): Grants paid, $11,160,708; assets, $85,739,721 (M); gifts received, $16,594,262; expenditures, $17,759,185.
Limitations: Giving limited to western NC.
Publications: Annual report, newsletter, application guidelines, informational brochure (including application guidelines).
Application information: Application form required.
Officers and Directors:* James B. Powell II,* Chair.; Eleanor Owen,* Vice-Chair.; Isabel Nichols,* Secy.; Charles Nesbitt,* Treas.; Pat Smith, Exec. Dir.; and 30 additional directors.
EIN: 561223384
Codes: CM, FD, GTI

40688
Duke Energy Foundation
(Formerly Duke Power Company Foundation)
526 S. Church St., M.C. ECO6G-FC
P.O. Box 1009
Charlotte, NC 28201-1009 (704) 373-7930
FAX: (704) 382-7600; URL: http://www.duke-energy.com

Established in 1984 in NC.
Donor(s): Duke Power Co., Duke Energy Corp.
Financial data (yr. ended 12/31/00): Grants paid, $10,052,743; assets, $5,258,123 (M); gifts received, $3,679,890; expenditures, $10,058,268; qualifying distributions, $10,052,768.
Limitations: Giving primarily in the company's headquarters and service areas in NC and SC.
Application information: Unsolicited requests for funds are discouraged.
Officers and Directors:* Richard B. Priory,* Chair.; Ruth G. Shaw,* Pres.; Roberta B. Bowman, V.P.; Christopher E. Carter, Secy. and Exec. Dir.; Richard W. Blackburn, William A. Coley, Fred J. Fowler, Richard J. Osborne, Harvey J. Padewer.
EIN: 581586283
Codes: CS, FD, CD, FM, GTI

40689
The Wachovia Foundation, Inc.
c/o Wachovia Bank of North Carolina, N.A.
P.O. Box 3099
Winston-Salem, NC 27150-7131
Application addresses: GA: c/o Ben Boswell, P.O. Box 4148, M.C.-1102, Atlanta, GA 30302; VA: c/o Kenneth L. Flemins, 1021 E. Cary St., Richmond, VA 23219; and FL: c/o Teresa Weaver, 100 N. Tampa St., Ste. 4100, Tampa, FL 33609; URL: http://www.wachovia.com/inside/page/0,,139_414_430,00.html
Contact: Ed Loflin, Asst. Treas.

Incorporated in 1982 in NC.
Donor(s): Wachovia Corp.
Financial data (yr. ended 12/31/00): Grants paid, $9,929,899; assets, $8,789,718 (M); gifts received, $1,000; expenditures, $9,975,991; qualifying distributions, $9,937,240.
Limitations: Giving primarily in FL, GA, NC, SC, and VA.
Application information: Applications available at local Wachovia branch office. Application form required.
Directors: L.M. Baker, Jr., Chair.; James C. Cherry, Jean E. Davis, Stanhope A. Kelly, Paula Robinson, Will B. Spence, D. Gary Thompson.
EIN: 581485946
Codes: CS, FD, CD, FM

40690
The Cannon Foundation, Inc.
P.O. Box 548
Concord, NC 28026-0548 (704) 786-8216
URL: http://www.thecannonfoundationinc.org
Contact: Frank Davis, Exec. Dir.

Incorporated in 1943 in NC.
Donor(s): Charles A. Cannon,‡ Cannon Mills Co.
Financial data (yr. ended 09/30/01): Grants paid, $9,822,749; assets, $182,177,724 (M); expenditures, $10,621,784; qualifying distributions, $10,005,341.
Limitations: Giving primarily in NC, with emphasis on the Cabarrus County area.
Publications: Application guidelines, informational brochure (including application guidelines).
Application information: Application form required.
Officers and Directors:* Mariam C. Hayes,* Pres.; W.S. Fisher,* V.P.; Dan L. Gray,* Secy.-Treas.; Frank Davis, Exec. Dir.; G.A. Batte, Jr., W.C. Cannon, Jr., T.M. Grady, R.C. Hayes, T.C. Haywood, Elizabeth L. Quick.
EIN: 566042532
Codes: FD, FM

40691
Janirve Foundation
1 N. Pack Sq., Ste. 416
Asheville, NC 28801 (828) 258-1877
FAX: (828) 258-1837
Contact: Met R. Poston, Chair.

Established in 1954 in FL.
Donor(s): Irving J. Reuter,‡ Jeannett M. Reuter.‡
Financial data (yr. ended 12/31/00): Grants paid, $8,373,665; assets, $82,462,214 (M); expenditures, $9,123,688; qualifying distributions, $8,471,057.
Limitations: Giving primarily in western NC.
Publications: Annual report, application guidelines.
Application information: Applicants should contact Asheville, NC, office for application procedures. Application form required.

Directors: Met R. Poston, Chair.; E. Charles Dyson, John W. Erichson, James Woolcott, Richard B. Wynne.
Trustee: First National in Palm Beach.
EIN: 596147678
Codes: FD, FM

40692
Community Foundation of Greater Greensboro, Inc.
(Formerly The Foundation of Greater Greensboro, Inc.)
100 S. Elm St., Ste. 307
Greensboro, NC 27401-2638 (336) 379-9100
FAX: (336) 378-0725; E-mail: info@cfgg.org, or wsanders@cfgg.org; URL: http://www.cfgg.org
Contact: H. Walker Sanders, Pres.

Established in 1983.
Financial data (yr. ended 06/30/01): Grants paid, $7,504,703; assets, $65,423,885 (M); gifts received, $12,865,622; expenditures, $8,709,321.
Limitations: Giving primarily in the greater Greensboro, NC, area.
Publications: Annual report, application guidelines, program policy statement, newsletter, financial statement, grants list, informational brochure.
Application information: Call or write for guidelines. Application form required.
Officers and Directors:* Albert Lineberry, Jr.,* Chair.; Van King,* Chair. Elect; H. Walker Sanders, Pres.; Lewis Ritchie,* Secy.; Michael Cashwell,* Treas.; Tara M. Sandercock, Mary W. Stebbins, and 26 additional directors.
EIN: 561380249
Codes: CM, FD, GTI

40693
Progress Energy Foundation, Inc.
(Formerly CP & L Foundation, Inc.)
P.O. Box 2591
Raleigh, NC 27602-2591 (919) 546-6441
URL: http://www.progress-energy.com/community/foundation.html
Contact: Merrilee Jacobson, Contrib. Specialist

Established in 1990 in NC.
Donor(s): Carolina Power & Light Co., Progress Energy, Inc.
Financial data (yr. ended 12/31/01): Grants paid, $7,340,106; assets, $8,593,262 (M); gifts received, $14,559,252; expenditures, $7,380,523; qualifying distributions, $7,338,265.
Limitations: Giving primarily in Progress Energy service areas of NC, SC, and FL.
Publications: Application guidelines, annual report.
Application information: Grant proposal required. Application form required.
Officers and Directors:* William Cavanaugh III, Pres.; William "Skip" Orser,* V.P.; Tammy S. Brown, Secy.; Fred Day, Wm. Habermeyer, Robert McGehee, Peter Scott.
Trustee: Wachovia Bank of North Carolina, N.A.
EIN: 561720636
Codes: CS, FD, CD, FM

40694
C. D. Spangler Foundation, Inc.
P.O. Box 36007
Charlotte, NC 28236-6007 (704) 372-4500
Contact: W.D. Cornwell, Jr., V.P. and Secy.-Treas.

Established in 1956.
Donor(s): C.D. Spangler,‡ PTI Investments Inc., Delcap, Inc., C.D. Spangler Construction Co.
Financial data (yr. ended 12/31/01): Grants paid, $7,138,225; assets, $196,247,235 (M); gifts received, $885,000; expenditures, $7,227,290; qualifying distributions, $7,148,860.
Limitations: Applications not accepted. Giving primarily in NC.
Application information: Unsolicited requests for funds not considered.
Officers and Directors:* Meredith R. Spangler,* Chair.; C.D. Spangler, Jr.,* Pres.; W.D. Cornwell, Jr.,* V.P. and Secy.-Treas.; Denise E. Gardner, V.P.; Anna Spangler Nelson,* V.P.; Abigail R. Spangler.
EIN: 566061548
Codes: FD, FM

40695
Triangle Community Foundation
100 Park Offices, Ste. 209
P.O. Box 12834
Research Triangle Park, NC 27709
(919) 549-9840
FAX: (919) 990-9066; E-mail: info@trianglecf.org; E-mail for application: jan@trianglecf.org; URL: http://www.trianglecf.org
Contact: Polly Guthrie, Prog. Dir.

Incorporated in 1983 in NC.
Financial data (yr. ended 06/30/99): Grants paid, $6,061,202; assets, $74,563,651 (M); gifts received, $14,822,360; expenditures, $6,925,941.
Limitations: Giving limited to Durham, Orange, Chatham and Wake counties, NC.
Publications: Annual report (including application guidelines), newsletter, application guidelines, financial statement, grants list.
Application information: Application form required.
Officers and Directors:* Stephen D. Corman, Pres.; Sara Brooks Creagh,* V.P.; Thomas F. Keller, Secy.; Shannon E. St. John, Exec. Dir.; and 14 additional directors.
EIN: 561380796
Codes: CM, FD, GTI

40696
BB&T Charitable Foundation
c/o BB&T, Trust Dept.
P.O. Box 2907
Wilson, NC 27894

Established in 1998 in NC.
Donor(s): BB&T Corporation.
Financial data (yr. ended 12/31/00): Grants paid, $5,871,950; assets, $2,513,066 (M); gifts received, $5,500,000; expenditures, $5,896,062; qualifying distributions, $5,869,033.
Limitations: Applications not accepted. Giving primarily in NC.
Application information: Contributes only to pre-selected organizations.
Trustee: BB&T.
EIN: 562093089
Codes: CS, FD, CD, FM

40697
Mary Reynolds Babcock Foundation, Inc.
2920 Reynolda Rd.
Winston-Salem, NC 27106-3016
(336) 748-9222
FAX: (336) 777-0095; E-mail: info@mrbf.org; URL: http://www.mrbf.org
Contact: Gayle Williams, Exec. Dir.

Incorporated in 1953 in NC.
Donor(s): Mary Reynolds Babcock,‡ Charles H. Babcock.‡
Financial data (yr. ended 12/31/01): Grants paid, $5,582,225; assets, $115,115,832 (M); expenditures, $7,428,219; qualifying distributions, $6,586,209.
Limitations: Giving in the southeastern U.S., with emphasis on eastern AL, AR, GA, LA, MS, NC, SC, TN, north and central FL, and the Appalachian regions of KY and WV.
Publications: Annual report (including application guidelines).
Application information: Application form required.
Officers and Directors:* Mary Mountcastle,* Pres.; Otis S. Johnson,* V.P.; David Dodson,* Secy.; Akosva Barthwell Evans,* Treas.; Gayle Williams, Exec. Dir.; Bruce M. Babcock, Sybil J. Hampton, Nathaniel Irvin III, Barbara B. Millhouse, Katharine B. Mountcastle, Katherine R. Mountcastle, Kenneth F. Mountcastle III, Laura L. Mountcastle, L. Richardson Preyer, Zachary T. Smith, Carol P. Zippert.
EIN: 560690140
Codes: FD, FM

40698
The John Motley Morehead Foundation
P.O. Box 690
Chapel Hill, NC 27514-0690
FAX: (919) 962-1615; URL: http://www.moreheadfoundation.org
Contact: Charles E. Lovelace, Jr., Exec. Dir.

Trust established in 1945 in NY.
Donor(s): John Motley Morehead III.‡
Financial data (yr. ended 06/30/01): Grants paid, $4,956,693; assets, $116,608,732 (M); expenditures, $6,916,740; qualifying distributions, $6,229,923.
Limitations: Giving primarily in NC and selected secondary schools.
Publications: Annual report, informational brochure.
Application information: Nomination form required.
Officers: Charles W. Johnston, Jr., Treas.; Charles E. Lovelace, Jr., Exec. Dir.
Trustees: Alan Thomas Dickson, Chair.; Lucy Hanes Chatham,* Vice-Chair.; Timothy Brooks Burnett, Robert Cluett, Jean Morehead Larkin, Russell M. Robinson II.
EIN: 560599225
Codes: FD, FM, GTI

40699
The Joseph M. Bryan Foundation of Greater Greensboro, Inc.
P.O. Box 21927
Greensboro, NC 27420
Contact: Carole W. Bruce, Secy.-Treas.

Established in 1986 in NC.
Donor(s): Joseph M. Bryan.
Financial data (yr. ended 12/31/01): Grants paid, $4,801,376; assets, $107,953,725 (M); expenditures, $5,447,785; qualifying distributions, $5,940,137; giving activities include $342,871 for programs.
Limitations: Applications not accepted. Giving limited to NC.
Application information: Contributes only to pre-selected organizations.
Officers and Directors:* E.S. Melvin,* Pres.; H. Mike Weaver,* V.P.; Carole W. Bruce,* Secy.-Treas.; David DeVries, Shirley Frye, Mike W. Haley.
EIN: 561548051
Codes: FD

40700—NORTH CAROLINA

40700
The Leon Levine Foundation
P.O. Box 1017
Charlotte, NC 28201-1017
Contact: Leon Levine, Pres. and Treas.

Established in 1981 in NC.
Donor(s): Leon Levine.
Financial data (yr. ended 06/30/01): Grants paid, $4,465,960; assets, $154,966,342 (M); gifts received, $29,285,746; expenditures, $5,109,827; qualifying distributions, $4,465,960.
Limitations: Applications not accepted. Giving primarily in Charlotte, NC.
Application information: Contributes only to pre-selected organizations.
Officers: Leon Levine, Pres. and Treas.; Sandra Levine, V.P. and Secy.; Lori Levine Sklut, V.P.
EIN: 581427515
Codes: FD, FM

40701
The Blumenthal Foundation
P.O. Box 34689
Charlotte, NC 28234 (704) 377-9237
Additional tel.: (704) 377-6555, ext. 2305
Contact: Philip Blumenthal, Tr.

Trust established in 1953 in NC.
Donor(s): I.D. Blumenthal,‡ Herman Blumenthal, Radiator Specialty Co.
Financial data (yr. ended 12/31/00): Grants paid, $3,746,900; assets, $20,276,145 (M); expenditures, $4,026,367; qualifying distributions, $3,746,900.
Limitations: Giving primarily in NC, with emphasis on Charlotte and Mecklenburg County.
Publications: Annual report, multi-year report, grants list, application guidelines.
Application information: Application form not required.
Trustees: Alan Blumenthal, Anita Blumenthal, Herman Blumenthal, Philip Blumenthal, Samuel Blumenthal, Ph.D.
EIN: 560793667
Codes: FD

40702
The North Carolina GlaxoSmithKline Foundation
(Formerly The Glaxo Wellcome Foundation)
5 Moore Dr.
Research Triangle Park, NC 27709
(919) 483-2140
FAX: (919) 315-3015; *URL:* http://www.glaxowellcome.com/gwfound/index.html
Contact: Cathy Smith, Coord., Fdn. Svcs.; or Marilyn Foote-Hudson, Exec. Dir.

Established in 1986 in NC.
Donor(s): Glaxo Wellcome Americas Inc., GlaxoSmithKline Holdings (Americas) Inc.
Financial data (yr. ended 12/31/00): Grants paid, $3,410,567; assets, $66,455,220 (M); expenditures, $3,944,003; qualifying distributions, $3,917,135.
Limitations: Giving limited to NC.
Publications: Annual report, informational brochure (including application guidelines).
Application information: Application form not required.
Officers and Directors:* Robert A. Ingram,* Chair.; Margaret B. Dardess,* Pres.; Paul Holcombe, Secy.; Adrian Hennah, Treas.; Marilyn Foote-Hudson,* Exec. Dir.; George Abercrombie, W. Robert Connor, Shirley T. Frye, Thomas R. Haber, George Morrow, Timothy D. Proctor, Joseph J. Ruvane, Jr., Charles A. Sanders, M.D.
EIN: 581698610
Codes: CS, FD, CD

40703
The Sunshine Lady Foundation, Inc.
P.O. Box 1074
Morehead City, NC 28557-1074
(252) 240-2788
Contact: Doris B. Bryant, Pres.

Established in 1996 in NC.
Donor(s): Doris B. Bryant.
Financial data (yr. ended 12/31/01): Grants paid, $3,355,316; assets, $5,355,896 (M); gifts received, $516; expenditures, $3,702,061; qualifying distributions, $3,338,304.
Limitations: Applications not accepted. Giving on a national basis.
Application information: Unsolicited requests for funds not accepted.
Officers: Doris B. Bryant, Pres.; Alfred S. Bryant, V.P. and Secy.; Diane Grimsley, Treas.
EIN: 561977987
Codes: FD

40704
Louis M. Plansoen Charitable Trust
c/o First Union National Bank
401 S. Tryon St., NC 1159
Charlotte, NC 28288-1159 (704) 715-3896
Contact: Ms. Geri J. Weintraub, Asst. V.P.

Established in 1991 in PA.
Donor(s): Louis Plansoen.‡
Financial data (yr. ended 12/31/01): Grants paid, $2,992,500; assets, $15,744,456 (M); expenditures, $3,141,106; qualifying distributions, $2,983,060.
Limitations: Giving primarily on the East Coast, with emphasis on NJ.
Application information: Application form not required.
Trustees: John L. Plansoen, Helen Post, First Union National Bank.
EIN: 226322826
Codes: FD

40705
The Belk Foundation
2801 W. Tyvola Rd.
Charlotte, NC 28217-4500 (704) 357-1000
Contact: Paul B. Wyche, Jr., Tr.

Trust established in 1928 in NC.
Donor(s): The Belk Department Stores, Matthews Belk, Belk Enterprises, Belk, Inc.
Financial data (yr. ended 05/31/01): Grants paid, $2,813,004; assets, $57,019,809 (M); gifts received, $595,651; expenditures, $3,052,381; qualifying distributions, $2,786,891.
Limitations: Giving primarily in NC.
Trustees: Paul B. Wyche, Jr., First Union National Bank of North Carolina.
Advisors: Claudia W. Belk, Katherine M. Belk, James K. Glenn, Jr., B. Frank Matthews, Katherine B. Morris, Leroy Robinson.
EIN: 566046450
Codes: CS, FD, CD

40706
Cape Fear Memorial Foundation
2508 Independence Blvd., Ste. 200
Wilmington, NC 28412
FAX: (910) 452-5879; *E-mail:* Shelvie@cfmfdn.org
Contact: Garry A. Garris, Pres.

Established in 1996 in NC; converted from the sale of Cape Fear Memorial Hospital to Columbia/HCA.
Donor(s): Cape Fear Memorial Health Care Corp.
Financial data (yr. ended 06/30/02): Grants paid, $2,728,830; assets, $50,287,000; expenditures, $3,261,850; qualifying distributions, $2,728,830.
Limitations: Giving limited to southeastern NC, generally within a 50-mile radius of Wilmington, NC.
Publications: Informational brochure (including application guidelines).
Application information: Application form required.
Officers and Directors:* R.T. Sinclair, Jr., M.D.,* Chair.; Garry A. Garris,* Pres. and Treas.; Agnes R. Beane,* Secy.; William H. Cameron, J. Richard Corbett, M.D., W. Carter Mebane III, Robert F. Warwick, Richard L. Woodbury.
EIN: 561974747
Codes: FD

40707
The William Kenan, Jr. Fund
Kenan Ctr.
P.O. Box 3808, Bowles Dr.
Chapel Hill, NC 27515-3808 (919) 962-8150
Contact: Richard M. Krasno, Pres.

Established in 1983 in NC.
Donor(s): Frank H. Kenan,‡ William R. Kenan, Jr. Charitable Trust, Thomas S. Kenan III.
Financial data (yr. ended 06/30/01): Grants paid, $2,691,366; assets, $59,670,127 (M); gifts received, $840; expenditures, $3,722,559; qualifying distributions, $2,900,145.
Limitations: Applications not accepted.
Application information: Contributes only to pre-selected organizations.
Officers and Directors:* Richard M. Krasno,* Pres.; Thomas S. Kenan III,* V.P.; Braxton Schell,* Secy.-Treas.; J. Haywood Davis, Daniel W. Drake, Elizabeth Price Kenan, Owen G. Kenan, Thomas J. Sweeney.
EIN: 570757568
Codes: FD

40708
Community Foundation of Gaston County, Inc.
P.O. Box 123
Gastonia, NC 28053
FAX: (704) 869-0222; *E-mail:* cfgaston@perigee.net
Contact: John A. Edgerton, Exec. Dir.

Incorporated in 1978 in NC.
Financial data (yr. ended 12/31/01): Grants paid, $2,681,844; assets, $63,495,654 (M); gifts received, $18,187,585; expenditures, $3,387,055.
Limitations: Giving primarily in Gaston County, NC.
Publications: Annual report, informational brochure, newsletter.
Application information: Application form required.
Officers and Directors:* Tom D. Efird,* Pres.; Joseph P. Pearson,* V.P.; Pamela K. Warlick,* Secy.; Ben R. Rudisill,* Treas.; John A. Edgerton, Exec. Dir.
EIN: 581340834
Codes: CM, FD

40709
Jefferson-Pilot Foundation
P.O. Box 21008, Dept. 3602
Greensboro, NC 27420-1008 (336) 691-3313
Contact: Paul Mason

Established in 1951 in NC.
Donor(s): Jefferson-Pilot Corp.
Financial data (yr. ended 11/30/00): Grants paid, $2,571,905; assets, $1,929,217 (M); gifts received, $1,840,000; expenditures, $2,601,817; qualifying distributions, $2,576,056.
Limitations: Giving primarily in the southeastern U.S.

Application information: Application form not required.
Trustees: John C. Ingram, Ken Mlekush, Hoyt Phillips, Russell C. Simpson, David A. Stonecipher.
EIN: 566040780
Codes: CS, FD, CD

40710
John M. Belk Foundation
2801 W. Tyvola Rd.
Charlotte, NC 28217-4500
Contact: Paul B. Wyche, Jr., Tr.

Established in 1959.
Financial data (yr. ended 12/31/00): Grants paid, $2,510,100; assets, $251,211 (M); expenditures, $2,521,457; qualifying distributions, $2,501,717.
Limitations: Applications not accepted. Giving primarily in NC and SC.
Application information: Unsolicited requests for funds not accepted.
Trustee: Paul B. Wyche, Jr.
Advisory Committee: Claudia W. Belk, Luther T. Moore, Leroy Robinson.
EIN: 566046453
Codes: FD

40711
North Carolina Community Foundation
200 S. Salisbury St.
Raleigh, NC 27602-2828 (919) 828-4387
FAX: (919) 828-5495; E-mail: general@nccommf.org; Western Regional Office: P.O. Box 2148, Sylva, NC 28779, tel.: (828) 586-4616, FAX: (828) 631-3951, E-mail: slelivre@earthlink.net; Northeastern Regional Office: Harbinger Ctr., Ste. 4, Point Harbor, NC 27964, tel.: (252) 491-8166, FAX: (252) 491-5714, E-mail: pbirknccommf@mindspring.com; Hickory, NC office: P.O. Box 2851, Hickory, NC 28603, tel.: (828) 328-1237, FAX: (828) 328-3948, E-mail: cvcf@earthlink.net; URL: http://www.nccommf.org
Contact: Elizabeth C. Fentress, Exec. Dir.

Established in 1985 in NC.
Financial data (yr. ended 03/31/02): Grants paid, $2,432,779; assets, $7,731,099 (M); gifts received, $7,731,099; expenditures, $3,974,655.
Limitations: Applications not accepted. Giving primarily in NC.
Publications: Annual report, informational brochure, newsletter.
Officers and Directors:* Lewis R. Holding,* Pres.; Charles W. Gaddy,* V.P.; Billy T. Woodard, Secy.; C. Ronald Scheeler, Treas.; Elizabeth C. Fentress, Exec. Dir.; J.F. Allen, and 34 additional directors.
EIN: 581661700
Codes: CM, FD

40712
The Dickson Foundation, Inc.
301 S. Tyron St., Ste. 1800
Charlotte, NC 28202 (704) 372-5404
Contact: Alan T. Dickson, Pres. or Susan W. Patterson, Secy-Treas.

Incorporated in 1944 in NC.
Donor(s): American and Efird Mills, Inc.
Financial data (yr. ended 12/31/00): Grants paid, $2,284,617; assets, $34,885,198 (M); expenditures, $2,411,469; qualifying distributions, $2,352,022.
Limitations: Giving primarily in NC.
Officers and Directors:* R. Stuart Dickson,* Chair.; Alan T. Dickson,* Pres.; Rush S. Dickson III,* V.P.; Thomas W. Dickson,* V.P.; Susan W. Patterson, Secy.-Treas.
EIN: 566022339

Codes: FD

40713
The Community Foundation of Henderson County, Inc.
401 N. Main St., 3rd Fl.
P.O. Box 1108
Hendersonville, NC 28793 (828) 697-6224
FAX: (828) 696-4026; E-mail: cfhc@ioa.com; URL: http://www.cfhendersoncounty.org
Contact: Priscilla Cantrell, Exec. Dir., or Crystal Reese, Fin. Dir.

Incorporated in 1982 in NC.
Financial data (yr. ended 06/30/02): Grants paid, $2,251,599; assets, $45,787,246 (M); gifts received, $17,507,813; expenditures, $3,086,398.
Limitations: Giving limited to the Henderson County, NC, area.
Publications: Annual report, newsletter, application guidelines, informational brochure.
Application information: Scholarship availability is announced in Nov. Application form required.
Officers and Directors:* Sherri Metzger,* Pres.; Bill Smith,* V.P., Distrib.; Sue Ballard Gilliam,* V.P., Development; Ronald Rosenburger,* Secy.; F. Lee Thomas,* Treas.; Priscilla Cantrell,* Exec. Dir.; Sally Boyd, Katie Hunter, Fair Johnson, Sam Leftwich, Bernie Linder, Bob Ogden, David Reeves, Jan Shefter, Alice Soder, Art Stuenkel, and 4 additional directors.
EIN: 561330792
Codes: CM, FD, GTI

40714
The William R. Kenan, Jr. Fund for Engineering, Technology and Science
P.O. Box 3808
Chapel Hill, NC 27515
Contact: Richard M. Krasno, Pres.

Established in 1991 in NC.
Financial data (yr. ended 06/30/01): Grants paid, $2,173,500; assets, $30,747,449 (M); expenditures, $2,350,762; qualifying distributions, $2,235,089.
Limitations: Applications not accepted. Giving primarily in Raleigh, NC.
Application information: Contributes only to pre-selected organizations.
Officers and Directors:* Richard M. Krasno,* Pres.; Thomas S. Kenan III,* V.P.; Braxton Schell,* Secy.-Treas.; J. Haywood Davis, Daniel W. Drake, Elizabeth Price Kenan, Owen G. Kenan, Thomas J. Sweeney.
EIN: 561761145
Codes: FD

40715
The Cemala Foundation, Inc.
122 N. Elm St., Ste. 816
Greensboro, NC 27401 (336) 274-3541
FAX: (336) 272-8153; E-mail: Cemala@aol.com
Contact: Ms. Priscilla P. Taylor, Exec. Dir.

Established in 1986 in NC.
Donor(s): Martha A. Cone,‡ Ceasar Cone II.‡
Financial data (yr. ended 12/31/99): Grants paid, $2,063,693; assets, $46,769,863 (M); expenditures, $2,449,443; qualifying distributions, $2,320,605.
Limitations: Giving limited to Guilford County, NC, and projects with statewide benefit.
Publications: Application guidelines, grants list.
Application information: Application form required.
Officers and Directors:* Martha C. Wright,* Chair.; Ceasar Cone III,* Vice-Chair.; John A. Richmond, Secy.; Walter Cone,* Treas.; Priscilla P. Taylor, Exec. Dir.; Janet G. Cone, William L.

Hemphill, Mathew D. Richmond, William R. Rogers.
EIN: 561528982
Codes: FD

40716
Hillsdale Fund, Inc.
P.O. Box 20124
Greensboro, NC 27420-0124 (336) 274-5471
Contact: Edward E. Doolan, Admin. V.P.

Incorporated in 1963 in NC.
Donor(s): The L. Richardson family.
Financial data (yr. ended 12/31/00): Grants paid, $2,023,600; assets, $2,526,792 (M); gifts received, $1,556,478; expenditures, $2,395,632; qualifying distributions, $2,119,823.
Limitations: Giving primarily in NC and the Eastern Seaboard.
Application information: Application form required.
Officers and Trustees:* Lunsford Richardson, Jr.,* Pres.; Edward E. Doolan, Admin. V.P.; Sion A. Boney,* Secy.-Treas.; Sion A. Boney III, Laurinda Lowenstein Douglas, Barbara E. Evans, J. Peter Gallagher, Margaret W. Gallagher, Louise Boney McCoy, Eudora L. Richardson, James Lunsford Richardson, L.R. Smith, Molly R. Smith, Richard G. Smith III, Margaret R. White.
EIN: 566057433
Codes: FD

40717
The Anonymous Fund
c/o Joseph M. Bryan, Jr.
P.O. Box 9908
Greensboro, NC 27429

Established in 1995 in NC.
Financial data (yr. ended 12/31/01): Grants paid, $1,952,500; assets, $22,398,659 (M); expenditures, $2,099,490; qualifying distributions, $2,053,395.
Limitations: Applications not accepted. Giving on a national basis, with emphasis on NC.
Application information: Contributes only to pre-selected organizations.
Officers: Joseph M. Bryan, Jr., Pres.; Ronald P. Johnson, Secy.
Trustee: William P. Massey.
EIN: 562152734
Codes: FD

40718
John and Mary Franklin Foundation, Inc.
Bank of America Plz., NC1-002-11-18
Charlotte, NC 28255
Additional address: 3350 Riverwood Pkwy., Ste. 2140, Atlanta, GA 30339
Contact: Dr. Marilu McCarty, Secy.

Incorporated in 1955 in GA.
Donor(s): John Franklin,‡ Mary O. Franklin.‡
Financial data (yr. ended 12/31/01): Grants paid, $1,943,200; assets, $34,711,872 (M); expenditures, $2,232,280; qualifying distributions, $2,056,282.
Limitations: Giving primarily in GA, with emphasis on the metropolitan Atlanta area.
Application information: Application form not required.
Officers and Trustees:* L. Edmund Rast,* Chair.; Marilu H. McCarty,* Secy.; Virlyn B. Moore, Jr., Secy.; Richard W. Courts II, Maj. Genl. George T. Duncan, John B. Ellis, Frank M. Malone, Jr., Walter W. Sessoms, Alexander W. Smith, Jr., William M. Suttles.
EIN: 586036131
Codes: FD

40719
Broyhill Family Foundation, Inc.
P.O. Box 500, Golfview Park
Lenoir, NC 28645-0472
Contact: Paul H. Broyhill, Chair., or Mrs. Lee E. Pritchard, Asst. Secy.-Treas.

Incorporated in 1945 in NC.
Donor(s): Broyhill Furniture Industries, Inc., James E. Broyhill, and family.
Financial data (yr. ended 12/31/00): Grants paid, $1,881,133; assets, $45,785,412 (M); expenditures, $2,217,641; qualifying distributions, $2,050,370.
Limitations: Giving primarily in NC.
Officers and Directors:* Paul H. Broyhill,* Chair.; M. Hunt Broyhill,* Pres.; Mrs. Lee E. Pritchard,* Secy.-Treas.; Faye A. Broyhill.
EIN: 566054119
Codes: FD

40720
The Goodrich Foundation, Inc.
(Formerly The B.F.Goodrich Foundation, Inc.)
c/o 4 Coliseum Ctr.
2730 W. Tyvola Rd.
Charlotte, NC 28217-4578 (704) 423-7080
FAX: (704) 423-7127; E-mail: mviser@corp.bfg.com
Contact: Marty Viser, Mgr., Community Rels.

Established in 1989 in OH.
Donor(s): The B.F.Goodrich Co., Goodrich Corp.
Financial data (yr. ended 12/31/00): Grants paid, $1,858,726; assets, $14,150,924 (M); expenditures, $1,915,676; qualifying distributions, $1,852,317.
Limitations: Giving on a national basis.
Publications: Informational brochure, application guidelines.
Application information: Contributes mostly to pre-selected organizations. Limited funds for unsolicited grant requests. Application form not required.
Officers: Terrence G. Linnert, Pres.; Marshall Larsen, V.P.; Ernie Schaub, V.P.; Rick Schmidt, V.P.; Patty Meinecke, Secy.; Scott Kuechle, Treas.
EIN: 341601879
Codes: CS, FD, CD

40721
The Stewards Fund
P.O. Box 6575
Raleigh, NC 27628
Contact: Joyce Adler, Asst. Secy.

Established in 1986 in NC.
Financial data (yr. ended 12/31/00): Grants paid, $1,801,923; assets, $39,013,616 (M); expenditures, $1,862,116; qualifying distributions, $1,751,938.
Limitations: Applications not accepted. Giving limited to Wake, Durham, and Orange counties, NC.
Application information: Contributes only to pre-selected organizations. Unsolicited requests for funds not accepted.
Trustees: Marian Bergdolt, David Dodson, Martin Eakes, Anne B. Faircloth, Thomas H. McGuire, Wyndham Robertson, Art Ross.
EIN: 561482138
Codes: FD

40722
A. E. Finley Foundation, Inc.
P.O. Box 98266
Raleigh, NC 27624 (919) 782-0565
Additional tel.: (919) 782-0529; FAX: (919) 782-6978
Contact: Robert C. Brown, Pres.

Incorporated in 1957 in NC.
Donor(s): A.E. Finley.‡
Financial data (yr. ended 11/30/00): Grants paid, $1,727,625; assets, $37,323,173 (M); expenditures, $2,250,819; qualifying distributions, $1,694,590.
Limitations: Giving primarily in NC.
Publications: Informational brochure.
Application information: Application form not required.
Officers and Directors:* Robert C. Brown,* Pres. and Treas.; Ben G. Nottingham,* V.P.; A. Earle Finley II,* Secy.; David A. Goodwin, A.E. Howard, C.D. Nottingham II.
EIN: 566057379
Codes: FD

40723
The Morgan Foundation, Inc.
10421 Old Wire Rd.
Laurel Hill, NC 28351 (910) 462-2016
Additional address: P.O. Box 1167, Laurel Hill, NC 28351; FAX: (910) 462-2019
Contact: James L. Morgan, Sr., Chair.

Established in 1992 in NC as successor to Morgan Trust for Charity, Religion, and Education which was established in 1949.
Donor(s): Edwin Morgan,‡ Elise McK. Morgan,‡ Morgan Mills, Inc., The Morgan Co. of Laurel Hill, Inc., Morgan Farms, Inc., Walden Court, Inc.
Financial data (yr. ended 04/30/01): Grants paid, $1,717,750; assets, $11,400,731 (M); gifts received, $89,823; expenditures, $1,795,742; qualifying distributions, $1,779,978.
Limitations: Giving primarily in the Laurel Hill, NC, area.
Publications: Financial statement.
Application information: Application form not required.
Officers and Trustees:* James L. Morgan, Sr.,* Chair. and Pres.; James L. Morgan, Jr.,* Vice-Chair.; Elizabeth E. Morgan,* V.P.; William C. Fitzgerald,* Secy.-Treas.; Susan Farrell.
EIN: 561790979
Codes: FD

40724
Cumberland Community Foundation, Inc.
P.O. Box 2345
Fayetteville, NC 28302-2171 (910) 483-4449
FAX: (910) 483-2905; E-mail: ccfnd@infi.net, ccf3@infi.net, or ccfadmin@infi.net; URL: http://www.cumberlandcf.org
Contact: Monika Simmons, Grants and Scholarship Mgr.

Established in 1980 in NC.
Donor(s): Lucile Hutaff.‡
Financial data (yr. ended 06/30/01): Grants paid, $1,705,792; assets, $18,457,598 (M); gifts received, $3,526,196; expenditures, $2,245,897.
Limitations: Giving limited to southeastern NC.
Publications: Annual report, informational brochure, application guidelines, occasional report, financial statement, grants list, newsletter, program policy statement.
Application information: Competitive grants are awarded in the county of the donor. Application form required.
Officers and Directors:* Ramon L. Yarborough,* Pres.; Leslie A. Griffin,* V.P.; Sammy Short,* Secy.; Anthony G. Chavonne,* Treas.; Kamal M. Bakri, Mildred Braxton, Mary Lynn M. Bryan, Elaine M. Bryant, Alfred E. Cleveland, Margaret H. Dickson, Robert W. Drake, Ellie Fleishman, John T. Henley, Jr., J. Wes Jones, Robert O. McCoy, Jr., J.S. McFadyen, Jr., Samuel H. Meares, Donald Porter, Robert G. Ray, Dot Wyatt.
EIN: 581406831
Codes: CM, FD

40725
Henry Nias Foundation, Inc.
277 Glendale Dr.
Carthage, NC 28327 (910) 824-4413
Contact: Richard Edelman, Treas.

Incorporated in 1955 in NY.
Donor(s): Henry Nias.‡
Financial data (yr. ended 11/30/99): Grants paid, $1,697,000; assets, $33,108,721 (M); expenditures, $1,904,476; qualifying distributions, $1,795,671.
Limitations: Giving limited to the metropolitan New York, NY, area.
Application information: Applications by invitation only. Unsolicited requests for funds not accepted.
Officers and Directors:* Stanley Edelman, M.D.,* Chair.; Charles D. Fleischman,* Pres.; William F. Rosenberg,* Secy.; Richard J. Edelman,* Treas.
EIN: 136075785
Codes: FD

40726
The John P. McConnell Foundation
c/o Wachovia Bank of North Carolina, N.A.
P.O. Box 3099
Winston-Salem, NC 27150-7131

Established in 1997 in NC.
Financial data (yr. ended 12/31/00): Grants paid, $1,558,150; assets, $2,646,637 (M); expenditures, $1,606,437; qualifying distributions, $1,545,129.
Limitations: Applications not accepted. Giving primarily in VA.
Application information: Contributes only to pre-selected organizations.
Officer and Director:* John P. McConnell,* Pres.
Trustee: Wachovia Bank of North Carolina, N.A.
EIN: 562051268
Codes: FD

40727
The Blanche and Julian Robertson Family Foundation, Inc.
P.O. Box 4242
Salisbury, NC 28145-4242 (704) 637-0511
FAX: (704) 637-0177
Contact: David Setzer, Exec. Dir.

Established in 1997 in NC.
Donor(s): Julian H. Robertson, Jr., Wyndham Robertson.
Financial data (yr. ended 12/31/01): Grants paid, $1,526,590; assets, $14,061,210 (M); expenditures, $1,577,687; qualifying distributions, $1,564,760.
Limitations: Giving limited to Salisbury, NC, and its surrounding area.
Publications: Occasional report, application guidelines, grants list, informational brochure (including application guidelines).
Application information: Application form required.
Officers and Directors:* James F. Hurley,* Chair.; James G. Whitton,* Vice-Chair.; Margaret H. Kluttz,* Secy.; J. Fred Corriher, Jr., Catrelia Hunter, B. Clay Lindsay, Jr., R. Scott Maddox, Lillian L. Morgan, Spencer Robertson, Wyndham Robertson, Fred J. Stanback, Jr.

EIN: 562027907
Codes: FD

40728
Richmond Community Foundation, Inc.
217 S. Tryon St.
Charlotte, NC 28202   (704) 973-4500

Established in 2001.
Donor(s): Richmond Memorial Hospital Foundation, First Union National Bank.
Financial data (yr. ended 12/31/01): Grants paid, $1,525,143; assets, $29,265,791 (M); gifts received, $30,120,773; expenditures, $2,450,935; qualifying distributions, $1,693,930.
Limitations: Giving primarily in Richmond County, NC.
Application information: Application form required.
Board Of Directors: Russelle E. Bennett, Jr., Raymond E. "Gene" Burrell, R. Larry Campbell, Bett Dorsett, Robert E. Hutchinson, John J. Jackson, Franklin Clay Jenkins, John D. Price, Paul R. Smart, Roger Staley, Bruce Stanback, Bill M. Thompson.
EIN: 562168849
Codes: FD

40729
William R. Kenan, Jr. Fund for the Arts
P.O. Box 3808
Chapel Hill, NC 27515
Contact: Richard M. Krasno, Pres.

Established in 1991 in NC.
Donor(s): William R. Kenan, Jr. Charitable Trust.
Financial data (yr. ended 06/30/01): Grants paid, $1,481,875; assets, $31,161,775 (M); expenditures, $1,685,905; qualifying distributions, $1,552,051.
Limitations: Applications not accepted. Giving primarily in NC.
Application information: Contributes only to pre-selected organizations.
Officers and Directors:* Richard M. Krasno,* Pres.; Thomas S. Kenan III,* V.P.; Braxton Schell,* Secy.-Treas.; J. Haywood Davis, Daniel W. Drake, Elizabeth Price Kenan, Owen G. Kenan, Thomas J. Sweeney.
EIN: 581976597
Codes: FD

40730
The John W. and Anna H. Hanes Foundation
c/o Wachovia Bank N.A.
P.O. Box 3099, MC-NC6732
Winston-Salem, NC 27150   (336) 732-5372
Contact: Linda G. Tilley, Sr. V.P., Wachovia Bank, N.A.

Trust established in 1947 in NC.
Financial data (yr. ended 12/31/01): Grants paid, $1,447,902; assets, $28,253,555 (M); expenditures, $1,582,075; qualifying distributions, $1,470,184.
Limitations: Giving limited to NC, with emphasis on Forsyth County.
Publications: Program policy statement, application guidelines.
Application information: Application form required.
Trustees: Frank Borden Hanes, Sr., Frank Borden Hanes, Jr., R. Philip Hanes, Jr., Drewry H. Nostitz, Ralph H. Womble, Wachovia Bank, N.A.
EIN: 566037589
Codes: FD

40731
Van Houten Charitable Trust
c/o First Union National Bank
401 S. Tyron St., TH-4, NC1159
Charlotte, NC 28288-1159

Established in 1991 in NJ.
Financial data (yr. ended 11/30/00): Grants paid, $1,441,270; assets, $21,803,344 (M); expenditures, $1,631,816; qualifying distributions, $1,386,405.
Limitations: Giving primarily in NJ.
Application information: Application form not required.
Trustee: First Union National Bank.
EIN: 226311441
Codes: FD

40732
CCB Foundation, Inc.
P.O. Box 51489
Durham, NC 27717   (919) 683-7602
Application address: P.O. Box 931, Durham, NC 27702
Contact: John D. Ramsey, Pres.

Established in 1985 in NC.
Donor(s): CCB Financial Corp., Central Carolina Bank and Trust.
Financial data (yr. ended 12/31/00): Grants paid, $1,414,563; assets, $1,420,847 (M); gifts received, $1,661,125; expenditures, $1,431,624; qualifying distributions, $1,414,339.
Limitations: Giving primarily in NC.
Officer: John D. Ramsey, Pres.
Board Members: Roy Abercrombie, William L. Burns, Jr., Richard Furr, David Jordan, Steve Pike.
EIN: 581611223
Codes: CS, FD, CD

40733
Mermans Foundation, Inc.
14051 Island Dr.
Huntersville, NC 28078   (704) 992-0705
Contact: Cornelis A.M. Mermans, Pres.

Established in 1989 in NC.
Donor(s): Cornelis A.M. Mermans, Johanna J. Mermans.
Financial data (yr. ended 12/31/01): Grants paid, $1,343,147; assets, $21,156,729 (M); expenditures, $1,351,753; qualifying distributions, $1,341,198.
Limitations: Giving primarily in the Charlotte, NC, area.
Application information: Application form not required.
Officers: Cornelis A.M. Mermans, Pres.; Johanna J. Mermans, Secy.
Directors: Andy Mermans, Bryan K. Mermans, Jennifer E. Mermans, Nicole A. Mermans, Tasha B. Mermans.
EIN: 561677733
Codes: FD

40734
Lynn R. and Karl E. Prickett Fund
P.O. Box 20124
Greensboro, NC 27420

Established in 1964 in NC.
Donor(s): Lynn R. Prickett.‡
Financial data (yr. ended 06/30/00): Grants paid, $1,319,300; assets, $27,797,010 (M); expenditures, $3,491,817; qualifying distributions, $1,340,844.
Limitations: Giving on a national basis.
Application information: Application form not required.

Trustees: Charles S. Chapin, Chester F. Chapin, Samuel C. Chapin, C.W. Cheek, Lynn C. Gunzenhauser, Lisa V. Prochnow.
EIN: 566064788
Codes: FD

40735
The Dover Foundation, Inc.
P.O. Box 208
Shelby, NC 28151   (704) 487-8888
FAX: (704) 482-6818; E-mail: doverfnd@shelby.net
Contact: Hoyt Q. Bailey, Pres.

Incorporated in 1944 in NC.
Financial data (yr. ended 08/31/01): Grants paid, $1,317,675; assets, $25,823,307 (M); expenditures, $1,636,939; qualifying distributions, $1,400,956.
Limitations: Giving primarily in Cleveland County, NC.
Publications: Informational brochure (including application guidelines).
Application information: Application form not required.
Officers and Directors:* Hoyt Q. Bailey,* Pres.; Kathleen D. Hamrick,* V.P.; Harvey B. Hamrick,* Secy.; J. Linton Suttle,* Treas.; Nancy T. Moore, Exec. Dir.; Cynthia B. Buckingham, Harvey B. Hamrick, Jr., Melanie A. Knight, Kathleen H. Wilson.
EIN: 560769897
Codes: FD

40736
Warner Foundation
(Formerly The D. Michael Warner Foundation, Inc.)
501 Washington St., Ste. D.
Durham, NC 27701   (919) 530-8842
FAX: (919) 530-8852; E-mail: info@thewarnerfoundation.org; URL: http://www.thewarnerfoundation.org
Contact: Tony Pipa, Dir.

Established in 1996 in NC.
Donor(s): D. Michael Warner.
Financial data (yr. ended 12/31/01): Grants paid, $1,306,656; assets, $11,580,399 (M); gifts received, $3,000,000; expenditures, $1,863,164; qualifying distributions, $1,801,147.
Limitations: Giving limited to NC.
Publications: Application guidelines, grants list, annual report.
Application information: Contact foundation for application guidelines, or visit website. Application form not required.
Officers and Directors:* D. Michael Warner,* Pres.; Elizabeth Craven,* Secy.; Daryl Lester, Tony Pipa.
EIN: 561969171
Codes: FD

40737
Grace Jones Richardson Trust
c/o Piedmont Financial Co.
P.O. Box 20124
Greensboro, NC 27420-0124
Contact: P.L. Richardson, Tr.

Trust established in 1962 in CT.
Donor(s): Grace Jones Richardson.‡
Financial data (yr. ended 12/31/01): Grants paid, $1,306,000; assets, $59,949,928 (M); gifts received, $1,462,190; expenditures, $1,841,201; qualifying distributions, $1,539,870.
Limitations: Giving on a national basis.
Trustees: P.L. Richardson, S.S. Richardson.
EIN: 066023003
Codes: FD

40738
The Cowan Foundation, Inc.
c/o Cherry Bekaert & Holland, LLP
525 N. Tryon St., Ste. 1800
Charlotte, NC 28202 (704) 940-2678

Established around 1969.
Financial data (yr. ended 12/31/01): Grants paid, $1,284,174; assets, $217,411 (M); expenditures, $1,292,220; qualifying distributions, $1,284,174.
Limitations: Giving primarily in VA.
Application information: Application form required.
Officers: Bishop Michael J. Begley, Pres.; Kathleen Potter, V.P.; Hon. Robert D. Potter, Secy.-Treas.
EIN: 237027181
Codes: FD

40739
The Neal Family Foundation
P.O. Box 561109
Charlotte, NC 28256

Established in 1994 in NC.
Donor(s): Tobianne M. Neal, Thomas C. Neal.
Financial data (yr. ended 12/31/01): Grants paid, $1,280,024; assets, $17,259,017 (M); expenditures, $1,345,254; qualifying distributions, $1,280,024.
Limitations: Applications not accepted. Giving on a national basis.
Application information: Contributes only to pre-selected organizations.
Officers: Tobianne M. Neal, Pres.; Peter C. Neal, V.P.; Thomas C. Neal, V.P.; William T. Barnes, Secy.-Treas.
EIN: 582081294
Codes: FD

40740
Janet H. and T. Henry Wilson, Jr. Foundation
c/o T. Henry Wilson, Jr.
411 Tremont Cir.
Lenoir, NC 28645

Established in 1997 in NC.
Donor(s): Janet Wilson, Henry Wilson.
Financial data (yr. ended 12/31/00): Grants paid, $1,271,350; assets, $24,798,058 (M); gifts received, $20,806,975; expenditures, $1,276,473; qualifying distributions, $1,271,350.
Limitations: Applications not accepted. Giving primarily in NC.
Application information: Contributes only to pre-selected organizations.
Officers: T. Henry Wilson, Pres. and Treas.; Janet Wilson, V.P. and Secy.
EIN: 562042058
Codes: FD

40741
The Lindback Foundation
(also known as Christian R. and Mary F. Lindback Foundation)
c/o First Union National Bank
401 S. Tryon, NC1159
Charlotte, NC 28288-1159
Application address: 1500 1 Franklin Plz., Philadelphia, PA 19109
Contact: Roland Morris, Tr.

Trust established in 1955, registered in NJ.
Donor(s): Mary F. Lindback,‡ Christian R. Lindback.‡
Financial data (yr. ended 12/31/01): Grants paid, $1,255,804; assets, $23,190,175 (M); expenditures, $1,551,902; qualifying distributions, $1,256,426.
Limitations: Giving primarily in NJ and PA.
Application information: Application form not required.
Trustees: Martin Heckscher, Roland Morris, First Union National Bank.
EIN: 236290348
Codes: FD

40742
James G. Hanes Memorial Fund
(Formerly James G. Hanes Memorial Fund/Foundation)
c/o First Union National Bank
301 S. Tryon St., T-11
Charlotte, NC 28288-1159 (704) 383-6937
FAX: (704) 374-2242
Contact: Mary Logan, V.P., First Union National Bank

Established in 1957 in NC. The James G. Hanes Memorial Fund reincorporated under its current name following the formal merger and transfer of all foundation assets to the fund in Dec. 1991. The foundation terminated in 1992.
Financial data (yr. ended 10/31/01): Grants paid, $1,222,378; assets, $21,654,051 (M); expenditures, $1,408,171; qualifying distributions, $1,213,767.
Limitations: Giving primarily in NC, with emphasis on Winston-Salem.
Publications: Informational brochure, application guidelines.
Application information: Application form required.
Distribution Committee: Eldridge C. Hanes, Chair.; Edward K. Crawford, James G. Hanes III, Douglas R. Lewis, Drewry Hanes Nostitz, Frank F. Willingham.
Trustee: First Union National Bank.
EIN: 566036987
Codes: FD

40743
E. A. Morris Charitable Foundation
3802 Swarthmore Rd.
Durham, NC 27707
Contact: John S. Thomas, Pres.

Established in 1980.
Donor(s): E.A. Morris, Mrs. E.A. Morris.
Financial data (yr. ended 12/31/00): Grants paid, $1,209,000; assets, $21,692,543 (M); expenditures, $1,581,450; qualifying distributions, $1,198,384.
Officers and Directors:* John S. Thomas,* Pres.; Mary C. Morris,* V.P.; K. Barry Morgan,* Treas.; Joseph E. Morris, Dorothy S. Shaw, Katharine Thomas.
EIN: 581413060
Codes: FD

40744
Lowe's Charitable and Educational Foundation
c/o Lowe's Cos., Inc.
P.O. Box 1111
North Wilkesboro, NC 28656 (336) 658-5481
Application address: c/o Lowe's Cos., Inc., 1605 Curtis Bridge Rd., Wilkesboro, NC 28697
Contact: Robert Egleston

Established in 1957.
Donor(s): Lowe's Cos., Inc.
Financial data (yr. ended 10/31/01): Grants paid, $1,177,996; assets, $11,684,333 (M); gifts received, $792,381; expenditures, $1,185,126; qualifying distributions, $1,183,517.
Limitations: Giving primarily in NC.
Application information: Application form not required.
Officers: Larry D. Stone, Chair.; N. Brian Peace, Secy.; Larry Stanley, Treas.
Trustees: Darryl K. Henderson, Perry G. Jennings, Dale C. Pond.
EIN: 566061689
Codes: CS, FD, CD

40745
Weaver Foundation, Inc.
324 W. Wendover, Ste. 300
Greensboro, NC 27408 (336) 378-7910
Application address: P.O. Box 26040, Greensboro, NC 27420-6040; FAX:(336) 275-9602; E-mail: RLM@weaverfoundation.com; URL: http://www.weaverfoundation.com
Contact: Richard L. Moore, Pres.

Incorporated in 1967 in NC.
Donor(s): W.H. Weaver,‡ E.H. Weaver, H. Michael Weaver.
Financial data (yr. ended 12/31/01): Grants paid, $1,167,904; assets, $22,795,336 (M); gifts received, $151,770; expenditures, $1,565,640; qualifying distributions, $1,413,806.
Limitations: Applications not accepted. Giving limited to the greater Greensboro, NC, area.
Publications: Annual report, grants list, informational brochure.
Application information: Unsolicited requests for funds not accepted.
Officers and Trustees:* H.M. Weaver,* Chair.; Richard L. Moore, Pres.; Ashley W. Hodges,* V.P.; Michele W. Shutter,* V.P.; Katherine Weaver,* V.P.; William Stone, Treas.
EIN: 566093527
Codes: FD

40746
The Mary Duke Biddle Foundation
1044 W. Forest Hills Blvd.
Durham, NC 27707 (919) 493-5591
Contact: James H. Semans, M.D., Chair.; or Douglas C. Zinn, Exec. Dir.

Trust established in 1956 in NY.
Donor(s): Mary Duke Biddle.‡
Financial data (yr. ended 12/31/01): Grants paid, $1,151,724; assets, $28,035,275 (M); expenditures, $1,594,667; qualifying distributions, $1,151,724.
Limitations: Giving limited to NC and New York, NY.
Publications: Annual report.
Application information: Application form not required.
Officers and Trustees:* James H. Semans, M.D.,* Chair.; Mary D.B.T. Semans,* Vice-Chair.; Thomas S. Kenan III,* Secy.-Treas.; Mary T. Jones, John G. Mebane, James D.B.T. Semans.
EIN: 136068883
Codes: FD

40747
Arthur F. and Alice E. Adams Charitable Foundation
c/o First Union National Bank of Florida
401 S. Tryon St., NC1159
Charlotte, NC 28288
Application address: c/o First Union National Bank of Florida, Attn.: Susan Best, 200 S. Biscayne Blvd., 14th Fl., Miami, FL 33131

Established in 1987 in FL.
Donor(s): Alice E. Adams.‡
Financial data (yr. ended 09/30/01): Grants paid, $1,145,600; assets, $22,970,690 (M); expenditures, $1,515,742; qualifying distributions, $1,173,335.
Limitations: Giving primarily in FL and TN.
Governors: R. Grady Barrs, Virginia Clark, Renee Clark Guibao.
Trustees: William B. Warren, First Union National Bank of Florida.

EIN: 656003785
Codes: FD

40748
Nickel Producers Environmental Research Association, Inc.
2605 Meridian Pkwy., Ste. 200
Durham, NC 27713-2203 (919) 544-7722
FAX: (919) 544-7724
Contact: Hudson K. Bates, Exec. Dir.

Established in 1980.
Financial data (yr. ended 12/31/01): Grants paid, $1,139,192; assets, $2,212,191 (M); gifts received, $1,943,564; expenditures, $2,226,286; qualifying distributions, $2,157,717.
Limitations: Giving primarily in the U.S., Europe, Canada, and Japan.
Officers: Bert Swennen, Chair.; Philippe Panier, Vice-Chair.; Toshiharu Kanai, Secy.; Vanessa Guthrie, Treas.; Hudson K. Bates, Exec. Dir.
EIN: 133070077
Codes: FD, GTI

40749
James J. and Angelia M. Harris Foundation
P.O. Box 220427
Charlotte, NC 28222 (704) 364-6046
Contact: Sherri McDaniel Harrell, Exec. Dir.

Established as a trust in 1984 in NC.
Donor(s): James J. Harris.‡
Financial data (yr. ended 11/30/01): Grants paid, $1,127,650; assets, $16,548,630 (M); expenditures, $1,570,050; qualifying distributions, $1,114,088.
Limitations: Giving limited to Clarke County, GA, and Mecklenburg County, NC (except where otherwise provided in trust agreement).
Publications: Application guidelines, informational brochure.
Application information: Application form not required.
Officers and Managers:* Cameron M. Harris,* Chair.; Sherri McDaniel Harrell, Exec. Dir.; Sara H. Bissell, John W. Harris, James E.S. Hynes, James E. Johnson, Jr.
EIN: 561465696
Codes: FD

40750
Charlotte Merchants Foundation
c/o Wachovia Bank, N.A.
P.O. Box 3099
Winston-Salem, NC 27150-7131

Established in 1994 in NC.
Financial data (yr. ended 12/31/01): Grants paid, $1,096,271; assets, $18,349,185 (M); expenditures, $1,212,126; qualifying distributions, $1,095,078.
Limitations: Applications not accepted.
Application information: Contributes only to pre-selected organizations.
Officers and Directors:* Malcolm T. Murray, Jr.,* Chair.; Gene Williams,* Vice-Chair.; Harold Hoak,* Secy.; Lee O. Creede,* Treas.; and 11 additional directors.
EIN: 561853632
Codes: FD

40751
Holdeen Fund 47-10
c/o First Union National Bank
401 S. Tryon St., NC 1159
Charlotte, NC 28288-1159

Financial data (yr. ended 12/31/01): Grants paid, $1,047,709; assets, $18,147,599 (M); expenditures, $1,138,041; qualifying distributions, $1,045,228.
Limitations: Applications not accepted. Giving limited to Boston, MA.
Application information: Contributes only to a pre-selected organization specified in the governing instrument.
Trustee: First Union National Bank.
EIN: 146018147
Codes: TN

40752
Margaret C. Woodson Foundation, Inc.
201 W. Council St.
Salisbury, NC 28145-0829 (704) 633-5000
Application address: P.O. Box 829, Salisbury, NC 28145-0829
Contact: Beulah Hillard, Dir.

Incorporated in 1954 in NC.
Donor(s): Margaret C. Woodson.‡
Financial data (yr. ended 12/31/01): Grants paid, $1,036,200; assets, $1,021,973 (M); gifts received, $1,034,890; expenditures, $1,089,341; qualifying distributions, $1,086,466.
Limitations: Giving primarily in Davie and Rowan counties, NC.
Application information: Application form not required.
Officers and Directors:* Mary H. Woodson,* Pres.; Mary Anne Woodson,* V.P.; Paul B. Woodson, Jr.,* Secy.; Donald D. Sayers,* Treas.; Paul Leake Bernhardt, John B.E. Cunningham, Beulah H. Hillard, William G. Johnson.
EIN: 566064938
Codes: FD

40753
Philip L. Van Every Foundation
c/o Bank of America
101 S. Tryon St, NC1-002-11-18
Charlotte, NC 28255 (704) 554-1421

Established in 1961 in NC.
Donor(s): Philip Van Every.
Financial data (yr. ended 12/31/01): Grants paid, $1,025,060; assets, $16,150,609 (M); expenditures, $1,066,810; qualifying distributions, $1,035,242.
Limitations: Applications not accepted. Giving primarily in NC and SC.
Application information: Contributes only to pre-selected organizations.
Officer: Zean Jamison, Jr., Secy.-Treas.
Directors: J.W. Disher, James S. Howell, Willie Royal, Albert F. Sloan, Paul A. Stroup.
Trustee: Bank of America.
EIN: 566039337
Codes: FD

40754
The Allergan Foundation
c/o Wachovia Bank, N.A.
P.O. Box 3099
Winston-Salem, NC 27150-7131

Established in 1998 in GA.
Financial data (yr. ended 12/31/01): Grants paid, $1,016,208; assets, $18,740,225 (M); expenditures, $1,103,395; qualifying distributions, $1,012,321.
Limitations: Applications not accepted.
Application information: Contributes only to pre-selected organizations.
Agent: Wachovia Bank, N.A.
EIN: 330794475
Codes: FD

40755
Lori L. Sklut Foundation
c/o Bank of America
101 S. Tryon St., NC-1-002-11-18
Charlotte, NC 28255-0001
Contact: Karen Morris, V.P. and Relationship Mgr.

Established in 1995 in NC.
Donor(s): Lori L. Sklut.
Financial data (yr. ended 12/31/01): Grants paid, $936,279; assets, $11,984,413 (M); expenditures, $942,068; qualifying distributions, $928,388.
Limitations: Applications not accepted. Giving primarily in NC.
Application information: Contributes only to pre-selected organizations.
Directors: Leon Levine, Eric R. Sklut, Lori Levine Sklut.
Trustee: Bank of America.
EIN: 561904190
Codes: FD

40756
Tannenbaum-Sternberger Foundation, Inc.
(Formerly Sigmund Sternberger Foundation, Inc.)
600 Bank of America Bldg.
P.O. Box 3112
Greensboro, NC 27402 (336) 373-1500
Contact: Robert O. Klepfer, Jr., Exec. Dir.

Incorporated in 1957 in NC.
Donor(s): Sigmund Sternberger,‡ Rosa Sternberger Williams.‡
Financial data (yr. ended 03/31/01): Grants paid, $918,650; assets, $17,178,525 (M); expenditures, $1,100,325; qualifying distributions, $945,557.
Limitations: Giving primarily in Guilford County, NC.
Publications: Application guidelines.
Application information: Application form required.
Officers and Directors:* Leah Louise B. Tannenbaum, Chair.; Sigmund I. Tannenbaum,* Chair., Scholarship; John T. Warmath, Jr., Chair., Invest.; Charles M. Reid,* Secy.-Treas.; Robert O. Klepfer, Jr., Exec. Dir.; William L. Hemphill, Jeanne L. Tannenbaum, Nancy B. Tannenbaum, Susan M. Tannenbaum.
EIN: 566045483
Codes: FD, GTI

40757
William R. Kenan, Jr. Fund for Ethics
P.O. Box 3808
Chapel Hill, NC 27515-4150
Contact: Richard M. Krasno, Pres.

Established in 1995 in NC.
Donor(s): William R. Kenan, Jr. Charitable Trust.
Financial data (yr. ended 06/30/01): Grants paid, $899,500; assets, $10,758,549 (M); gifts received, $2,262,000; expenditures, $989,365; qualifying distributions, $951,337.
Limitations: Applications not accepted. Giving primarily in Durham, NC.
Application information: Contributes only to pre-selected organizations.
Officers: Elizabeth Price Kenan, Chair.; Richard M. Krasno, Pres.; Thomas S. Kenan III, V.P.; Braxton Schell, Secy.
Directors: J. Haywood Davis, Daniel W. Drake, Owen G. Kenan, Thomas J. Sweeney.
EIN: 561919423
Codes: FD

40758
The R. P. Holding Foundation, Inc.
(Formerly The Robert P. Holding Foundation)
P.O. Box 1377
Smithfield, NC 27577-1377

Incorporated in 1955 in NC.
Donor(s): Robert Holding,‡ Maggie B. Holding.
Financial data (yr. ended 12/31/00): Grants paid, $895,662; assets, $16,441,418 (M); expenditures, $901,777; qualifying distributions, $893,128.
Limitations: Applications not accepted. Giving primarily in NC.
Application information: Contributes only to pre-selected organizations and individuals.
Officers: Frank B. Holding, Pres.; Lewis R. Holding, V.P. and Secy.; Doris T. Allen, Treas.
EIN: 566044205
Codes: FD

40759
George & Harriet Woodward
c/o First Union National Bank
401 S. Tryon Street, 4th Fl.
Charlotte, NC 28288-1159

Financial data (yr. ended 11/30/01): Grants paid, $893,095; assets, $34,052,010 (M); expenditures, $1,696,716; qualifying distributions, $1,181,595.
Limitations: Applications not accepted.
Application information: Contributes only to pre-selected organizations.
Trustees: James Stevens, Richard Stevens, First Union National Bank.
EIN: 237750367
Codes: FD

40760
Richard J. Reynolds III and Marie Mallouk Reynolds Foundation
370 Knollwood St., Ste. 600
Winston-Salem, NC 27103-1815

Established in 1995 in NC.
Donor(s): Richard J. Reynolds III.‡
Financial data (yr. ended 06/30/01): Grants paid, $859,810; assets, $19,041,302 (M); gifts received, $192,382; expenditures, $981,481; qualifying distributions, $865,296.
Limitations: Applications not accepted.
Application information: Contributes only to pre-selected organizations.
Committee Members: Hon. Robert Collier, Robinson & Lawing, LLP.
Trustee: Mercantile-Safe Deposit & Trust Co.
EIN: 561925457
Codes: FD

40761
Provident Benevolent Foundation
(Formerly Providence Charitable Foundation)
c/o Wachovia Bank, N.A.
P.O. Box 3099
Winston-Salem, NC 27150-7131
Application address: 4500 Cameron Valley Pkwy., Ste. 450, Charlotte, NC 28211
Contact: Jesse J. Thompson

Established in 1989 in NC.
Donor(s): Jesse J. Thompson.
Financial data (yr. ended 06/30/01): Grants paid, $851,000; assets, $14,913,814 (M); expenditures, $908,741; qualifying distributions, $846,392.
Limitations: Giving limited to NC.
Trustees: Jesse J. Thompson, Wachovia Bank, N.A.
EIN: 581881092
Codes: FD

40762
The Royal & SunAlliance Insurance Foundation, Inc.
(Formerly The Royal Insurance Foundation, Inc.)
9300 Arrowpoint Blvd.
Charlotte, NC 28273
Contact: Fred E. Dabney II, Exec. Dir.

Established in 1989 in NC.
Donor(s): Royal Group, Inc.
Financial data (yr. ended 12/31/00): Grants paid, $847,955; assets, $647,556 (M); gifts received, $1,000,000; expenditures, $1,286,906; qualifying distributions, $1,286,392.
Limitations: Giving limited to the U.S. in the areas of company operations where the largest concentration of employees and customers reside.
Publications: Informational brochure (including application guidelines).
Application information: Capital funding requests considered once a year at annual meeting, with priority given to industry-related projects. Telephone or direct mail marketing solicitation not considered. Application form required.
Officers and Directors:* Elizabeth J. McLaughlin,* Pres.; Frederick E. Dabney II,* V.P. and Exec. Dir.; Joyce Wheeler,* Secy.; Sean A. Beatty,* Treas.; Terry Broderick, Alan T. Dickson, Micheal E. Goodwine, Wendy Harrigan, Debra A. Wright.
EIN: 561658178
Codes: CS, FD, CD

40763
Roanoke-Chowan Foundation, Inc.
500 S. Academy St.
Ahoskie, NC 27910 (252) 209-3175
Contact: Peter N. Geilich, Pres.

Established in 1997 in NC; converted from the Roanoke-Chowan hospital.
Financial data (yr. ended 09/30/02): Grants paid, $840,000; assets, $15,000,000 (M); expenditures, $900,000; qualifying distributions, $840,000.
Limitations: Giving limited to Bertie, Gates, Hertford, or Northampton counties, NC.
Publications: Annual report, occasional report, application guidelines, informational brochure, program policy statement.
Application information: Application form required.
Officers: Robert C. Kahn, M.D., Chair.; Ernest L. Evans, Vice-Chair.; Peter N. Geilich, Pres.; J.S. Almario, M.D., Secy.-Treas.
Directors: Eugene Brown, Ernest Carter, Yvonne C. Flood, Reba Green-Holley, Charles Hughes, James W. Mason, Carl D. Taylor.
EIN: 561535057
Codes: FD

40764
Champion McDowell Davis Charitable Foundation
P.O. Box 2342
Wilmington, NC 28402 (910) 763-4565
Contact: William O.J. Lynch, Secy.

Established in 1963 in NC.
Donor(s): Champion McDowell Davis.‡
Financial data (yr. ended 12/31/01): Grants paid, $825,000; assets, $15,383,326 (M); expenditures, $896,893; qualifying distributions, $732,522.
Limitations: Giving primarily in Wilmington, NC.
Application information: Application form not required.
Officers and Trustees:* R.T. Sinclair, Jr., M.D.,* Chair.; William O.J. Lynch,* Secy.; William H. Cameron, Thomas L. Dodson, Cyrus D. Hogue, Jr., John R. Murchinson.
EIN: 566055716
Codes: FD

40765
Randleigh Foundation Trust
c/o Thomas S. Kenan III
P.O. Box 4150
Chapel Hill, NC 27515

Established in 1984 in NC.
Donor(s): William R. Kenan, Jr.‡
Financial data (yr. ended 03/31/01): Grants paid, $787,500; assets, $17,568,496 (M); expenditures, $800,822; qualifying distributions, $780,247.
Limitations: Applications not accepted. Giving primarily in KY and NC.
Application information: Contributes only to pre-selected organizations.
Trustees: James G. Kenan III, Owen G. Kenan, Thomas S. Kenan III, Garrett Kirk, Jr.
EIN: 136207897
Codes: FD

40766
The Polk County Community Foundation, Inc.
(Formerly Polk Community Foundation)
255 S. Trade St.
Tryon, NC 28782-3707 (828) 859-5314
FAX: (828) 859-6122; *E-mail:* foundation@polkccf.org; *URL:* http://www.polkccf.org
Contact: Elizabeth Nager, Exec. Dir.

Incorporated in 1975 in NC.
Financial data (yr. ended 12/31/01): Grants paid, $785,279; assets, $16,633,301 (M); gifts received, $1,143,112; expenditures, $1,536,746.
Limitations: Giving limited to Polk County, NC, and its surrounding areas.
Publications: Annual report, application guidelines, newsletter, financial statement, informational brochure (including application guidelines).
Application information: Application form required.
Officers and Directors:* Betty Knopp,* Pres.; Larry Wassong,* V.P.; Cathie A. Campbell,* Secy.; Peggy C. Woodward,* Treas.; Elizabeth Nager, Exec. Dir.; Holland Brady, Jr., Arthur Brown, Donald Eifert, Laura Fields, Ann McCown, Renee McDermott, David Slater, Alice Tennant, B.G. Woodham, Robert Worsnop.
EIN: 510168751
Codes: CM, FD

40767
Horatio B. Ebert Charitable Foundation
P.O. Box 830
Mooresville, NC 28115-0830
Contact: Mark B. Edwards, Admin. Tr.

Established in 1985.
Donor(s): Lyda G. Ebert,‡ Robert O. Ebert.
Financial data (yr. ended 12/31/01): Grants paid, $783,400; assets, $14,303,257 (M); expenditures, $1,045,184; qualifying distributions, $781,911.
Limitations: Applications not accepted. Giving primarily in FL, KY, MD, NC, OH, and TN.
Application information: Unsolicited requests for funds not accepted.
Trustees: Catherine G. Ebert, Cecile G. Ebert, Robert O. Ebert, Mark B. Edwards, Adrienne E. Miller.
EIN: 592602801
Codes: FD

40768
Sall Family Foundation, Inc.
201 Vineyard Ln.
Cary, NC 27513-3067 (919) 677-8000
Contact: John Phillip Sall, Pres.

Established in 1993.
Donor(s): John Phillip Sall, Virginia B. Sall.

Financial data (yr. ended 12/31/00): Grants paid, $768,000; assets, $8,673,026 (M); gifts received, $374,675; expenditures, $804,862; qualifying distributions, $779,058.
Limitations: Giving on a national basis.
Officers: John Phillip Sall, Pres.; Virginia B. Sall, Treas.
EIN: 582016050
Codes: FD

40769
Nucor Foundation
2100 Rexford Rd.
Charlotte, NC 28211-3418 (704) 366-7000
Contact: James M. Coblin, Dir.

Established in 1973 in NC.
Donor(s): Nucor Corp.
Financial data (yr. ended 12/31/01): Grants paid, $764,406; assets, $145,920 (M); gifts received, $750,000; expenditures, $766,106; qualifying distributions, $766,065.
Limitations: Giving limited to children of company employees.
Application information: Application form required.
Directors: James M. Coblin, Daniel R. Dimilco, Terry S. Lisenby.
EIN: 237318064
Codes: CS, FD, CD, GTI

40770
Brody Brothers Foundation, Inc.
703 N. Queen St.
Kinston, NC 28501

Established in 1966.
Donor(s): David Brody, J.S. Brody, Leo Brody, J. & S. Investment Co.
Financial data (yr. ended 07/31/01): Grants paid, $763,139; assets, $6,543,268 (M); gifts received, $483,163; expenditures, $807,600; qualifying distributions, $761,593.
Limitations: Applications not accepted. Giving primarily in NC.
Application information: Contributes only to pre-selected organizations.
Officers: David S. Brody, Pres.; Leo Brody, V.P.; Hyman J. Brody, Secy.; Morris Brody, Treas.
EIN: 560858144
Codes: FD

40771
Fieldcrest Cannon Foundation
(Formerly Fieldcrest Foundation)
c/o Dir., Fieldcrest Cannon
1 Lake Circle Dr.
Kannapolis, NC 28081-3435 (704) 939-2775
Contact: Karen Cobb

Incorporated in 1959 in NC.
Donor(s): Fieldcrest Cannon, Inc.
Financial data (yr. ended 12/31/00): Grants paid, $762,510; assets, $2,224,273 (M); gifts received, $153,809; expenditures, $767,857; qualifying distributions, $759,707.
Limitations: Giving primarily in plant communities in NC and SC.
Application information: Application form required.
Officers and Directors:* Anthony T. Williams, V.P. and C.F.O.; Jamie Vasquez,* V.P. and Treas.; Brenda A. Sanders, Secy.
EIN: 566046659
Codes: CS, FD, CD, GTI

40772
The Seby B. Jones Family Foundation, Inc.
P.O. Box 19067
Raleigh, NC 27619-9067 (919) 829-2498
Contact: Anne M. Rogers, Secy.-Treas.

Established in 1983 in NC.
Donor(s): Seby B. Jones, Christina B. Jones.‡
Financial data (yr. ended 06/30/01): Grants paid, $755,700; assets, $10,097,688 (M); gifts received, $3,853,000; expenditures, $763,987; qualifying distributions, $754,793.
Limitations: Giving primarily in NC.
Application information: Application form not required.
Officers: Robert L. Jones, Chair. and V.P.; James R. Jones, Pres.; Anne M. Rogers, Secy.-Treas.
EIN: 311578859
Codes: FD

40773
Robert Lee Stowe, Jr. Foundation, Inc.
100 N. Main St.
P.O. Box 351
Belmont, NC 28012-0351 (704) 825-5314
Contact: Robert L. Stowe, III, Pres., or Daniel Harding Stowe, V.P.

Incorporated in 1945 in NC.
Donor(s): Robert Lee Stowe, Jr.,‡ Robert Lee Stowe III, R.L. Stowe Mills, Inc.
Financial data (yr. ended 12/31/00): Grants paid, $752,237; assets, $1,847,524 (M); gifts received, $1,000; expenditures, $761,826; qualifying distributions, $752,469.
Limitations: Giving primarily in NC, with emphasis on the Charlotte area.
Officers: Robert Lee Stowe III, Pres.; Daniel Harding Stowe, V.P.; Richmond H. Stowe, V.P.; Jean H. Gibson, Secy.-Treas.
EIN: 566034773
Codes: FD

40774
F. W. Symmes Foundation
c/o Wachovia Bank, N.A.
P.O. Box 3099
Winston-Salem, NC 27150-7131
Application address: c/o Wachovia Bank, N.A., 1401 Main St., Columbia, SC 29226, tel.: (803) 765-3671
Contact: C. Gerald Lane, V.P.

Trust established in 1954 in SC.
Donor(s): F.W. Symmes.‡
Financial data (yr. ended 03/31/01): Grants paid, $744,000; assets, $15,885,753 (M); expenditures, $830,207; qualifying distributions, $754,585.
Limitations: Giving primarily in the Greenville, SC, area.
Publications: Application guidelines, informational brochure.
Application information: Application form not required.
Trustees: M. Donavan Bessinger, O. Perry Earle III, Eleanor Welling, F. McKinnon Wilkinson, Wachovia Bank, N.A.
EIN: 576017472
Codes: FD

40775
Cape Fear Community Foundation, Inc.
P.O. Box 119
Wilmington, NC 28402-0119 (910) 251-3911
FAX: (910) 251-1040; E-mail: bbecka@bellsouth.net
Contact: Betsey H. Young, Exec. Dir.

Incorporated in 1987 in NC.

Financial data (yr. ended 09/30/01): Grants paid, $727,285; assets, $1,746,938 (M); gifts received, $958,823; expenditures, $805,271.
Limitations: Giving limited to the Cape Fear, NC, area, including New Hanover, Columbus, Brunswick, Bladen, and Pender counties for discretionary giving.
Publications: Annual report, application guidelines, newsletter, informational brochure (including application guidelines).
Application information: Application form required.
Officers and Directors:* Todd J. Toconis, Chair., Property Comm.; William O. McMillan, Jr., M.D.,* Pres.; Shirley Hart Berry,* V.P. and Dist. Chair.; William N. Smith,* Secy.; William E. Perdew,* Treas.; John Codington, Stephen C. Coogins, Neill A. Currie, Hannah Dawson Gage, Frank Gibson, Joyce A. Grant, Herbert J. McDuffie, John Moore, William A. Raney, Carolyn Simmons, Ph.D., Jane C. Sullivan, R. Bertram Williams III.
EIN: 561560364
Codes: CM, FD

40776
The Simpson Foundation
c/o Wachovia Bank of South Carolina, N.A.
P.O. Box 3099
Winston-Salem, NC 27102-3099
Application address: 1401 Main St., Columbia, SC 29226, tel.: (803) 765-3671
Contact: C. Gerald Lane, V.P. and Trust Off., Wachovia Bank of South Carolina, N.A.

Trust established in 1956 in SC.
Donor(s): W.H.B. Simpson,‡ Mrs. W.H.B. Simpson.
Financial data (yr. ended 12/31/01): Grants paid, $716,350; assets, $10,221,031 (M); gifts received, $150,039; expenditures, $733,273; qualifying distributions, $715,471.
Limitations: Giving primarily in SC.
Application information: Application form not required.
Directors: Wilma Johnson, J.A. Kuhne, Nell M. Rice, Claire Russo.
Trustee: Wachovia Bank of South Carolina, N.A.
EIN: 576017451
Codes: FD

40777
Atlanta Foundation
c/o Wachovia Bank, N.A.
P.O. Box 3099
Winston-Salem, NC 27150-7131
Application address: 191 Peachtree St. N.E., Atlanta, GA 30303-1102, tel.: (404) 332-6074
Contact: Bennie Boswell, Jr., Comm. Member

Established in 1921 in GA by bank resolution and declaration of trust.
Financial data (yr. ended 12/31/01): Grants paid, $714,511; assets, $19,078,507 (M); gifts received, $82,877; expenditures, $983,658; qualifying distributions, $846,863.
Limitations: Giving limited to Fulton and DeKalb counties, GA.
Publications: Application guidelines.
Application information: Application form required.
Officers and Directors:* Isaiah Tidwell, Chair.; Beverly Blake, Secy.; Juanita Eber, Edward C. Harris, Thomas D. Hills, Dom H. Wyant.
Trustee: Wachovia Bank, N.A.
EIN: 586026879
Codes: FD

40778
The Graham Foundation
c/o Bank of America
101 S. Tryon St.
Charlotte, NC 28280

Established in 1985 in SC.
Donor(s): Allen J. Graham, Frances G. MacIlwinen.
Financial data (yr. ended 08/31/01): Grants paid, $704,000; assets, $11,834,010 (M); gifts received, $1,626,351; expenditures, $785,209; qualifying distributions, $722,656.
Limitations: Applications not accepted. Giving limited to Asheville, NC, and Greenville, SC.
Application information: Contributes only to pre-selected organizations.
Trustees: Wilbur Bridges, William Bridges, Allen J. Graham, Frances G. MacIlwinen, Susan B. Roberson.
Agent: Bank of America.
EIN: 570805774
Codes: FD

40779
Dowd Foundation, Inc.
P.O. Box 35430
Charlotte, NC 28235

Established in 1951.
Donor(s): Charlotte Pipe and Foundry Co.
Financial data (yr. ended 12/31/01): Grants paid, $699,316; assets, $10,433,535 (M); gifts received, $2,000,000; expenditures, $766,846; qualifying distributions, $699,316.
Limitations: Applications not accepted. Giving limited to NC and VA.
Application information: Contributes only to pre-selected organizations.
Officers: Edward H. Hardison, Pres.; W. Frank Dowd IV, V.P.; E. Hooper Hardison, Secy.-Treas.
EIN: 566061389
Codes: FD

40780
Burlington Industries Foundation
3330 W. Friendly Ave.
P.O. Box 21207
Greensboro, NC 27420 (336) 379-2303
Contact: Delores C. Sides, Exec. Dir.

Established in 1943 in NC.
Donor(s): Burlington Industries, Inc., and subsidiary companies.
Financial data (yr. ended 09/30/01): Grants paid, $691,212; assets, $2,810,901 (M); expenditures, $718,502; qualifying distributions, $696,811.
Limitations: Giving primarily in areas of company operations in NC, SC, and VA.
Publications: Application guidelines.
Application information: Application form not required.
Officer and Trustees:* Delores C. Sides,* Exec. Dir.; Park R. Davidson, George W. Henderson III, Charles A. McLendon, Jr.
EIN: 566043142
Codes: CS, FD, CD, GTI

40781
Thomas Austin Finch Foundation
c/o Wachovia Bank, N.A.
P.O. Box 3099, MC-NC6732
Winston-Salem, NC 27150-7131
(336) 732-5372
Contact: Linda G. Tilley, Sr. V.P.

Trust established in 1944 in NC.
Donor(s): Ernestine L. Finch Mobley,‡ Thomas Austin Finch, Jr.‡

Financial data (yr. ended 12/31/01): Grants paid, $689,539; assets, $11,153,122 (M); expenditures, $775,472; qualifying distributions, $701,583.
Limitations: Giving limited to Thomasville, NC.
Publications: Informational brochure (including application guidelines).
Application information: Application form required.
Foundation Committee: David Finch, Chair.; Kermit Cloninger, John L. Finch, Sumner Finch, Meredith Slane Person.
Trustee: Wachovia Bank, N.A.
EIN: 566037907
Codes: FD

40782
George Foundation, Inc.
P.O. Box 800
Hickory, NC 28603
Contact: Boyd George, Pres.

Established in 1980 in NC.
Donor(s): Boyd George, G. Lee George,‡ Merchants Distributors, Inc., Lowe's Food Stores, Inc., Institution Food House, Inc.
Financial data (yr. ended 11/30/01): Grants paid, $671,450; assets, $4,030,909 (M); gifts received, $717,814; expenditures, $696,374; qualifying distributions, $667,955.
Limitations: Giving primarily in Hickory, NC.
Officers and Trustees:* Boyd George,* Pres.; John B. Orgain, Secy.; Ron Knedlik,* Treas.; Joyce George Corbett, William R. Waddell.
EIN: 561282417
Codes: FD

40783
Walrath Trust
c/o First Union National Bank
401 S. Tryon St., 4th Fl.
Charlotte, NC 28288-1159

Established in 2000 in PA.
Financial data (yr. ended 12/31/01): Grants paid, $669,516; assets, $6,640,886 (L); expenditures, $710,172; qualifying distributions, $675,203.
Limitations: Applications not accepted. Giving primarily in Wilmington, DE.
Application information: Contributes only to pre-selected organizations.
Trustee: First Union National Bank.
EIN: 516179755
Codes: FD

40784
James J. and Mamie R. Perkins Memorial Fund
c/o Bank of America, Private Client Group
1 Hanover Sq., Ste. 306
Raleigh, NC 27601-1754
Application address: P.O. Box 20067, Greenville, NC 27858, tel.: (252) 756-8888
Contact: James G. Sullivan, Chair.

Established in 1989 in NC.
Financial data (yr. ended 09/30/01): Grants paid, $667,512; assets, $12,957,240 (M); expenditures, $799,024; qualifying distributions, $722,242.
Limitations: Giving limited to Pitt County, NC.
Application information: Application form required.
Officer and Director:* James Sullivan,* Chair.
Members: Danny McNally, Thomas Midyette.
Trustee: Bank of America.
EIN: 566325764
Codes: FD

40785
Allene Broyhill Heilman Foundation, Inc.
c/o Allene B. Heilman
153 Hillhaven Pl. S.E.
Lenoir, NC 28645

Established in 1993 in NC.
Donor(s): Satie L. Broyhill.‡
Financial data (yr. ended 12/31/99): Grants paid, $666,667; assets, $1,763,192 (M); gifts received, $2,098,444; expenditures, $675,670; qualifying distributions, $664,400.
Limitations: Applications not accepted. Giving primarily in Boone, NC.
Application information: Contributes only to pre-selected organizations.
Officers: Allene Broyhill Heilman, Pres.; Robert E. Heilman, V.P.; Betty T. Johnson, Secy.-Treas.
EIN: 561824646
Codes: FD

40786
Nancy Sayles Day Foundation
c/o First Union National Bank
401 S. Tryon St., NC1159
Charlotte, NC 28288-1159
Application address: c/o First Union National Bank, 10 State House Sq., 2nd Fl., Hartford, CT 06103
Contact: John Small

Trust established in 1964 in CT.
Donor(s): Nancy Sayles Day,‡ Mrs. Lee Day Gillespie.
Financial data (yr. ended 09/30/01): Grants paid, $665,000; assets, $14,659,681 (M); expenditures, $762,412; qualifying distributions, $666,147.
Limitations: Giving primarily in MA.
Application information: Application form not required.
Trustee: First Union National Bank.
EIN: 066071254
Codes: FD

40787
The Bailey Wildlife Foundation
10223 Bushveld Ln.
Raleigh, NC 27612
Application address: 30 Gray Rd., Andover, MA 01810, tel.: (978) 901-3471
Contact: H. Whitney Bailey, Tr.

Established in 1987.
Financial data (yr. ended 12/31/00): Grants paid, $650,620; assets, $5,983,891 (M); expenditures, $714,392; qualifying distributions, $640,570.
Limitations: Giving primarily in the eastern U.S.
Trustees: Gordon M. Bailey, H. Whitney Bailey, Merritt P. Bailey, William H. Bailey, Margaret B. Barbabella.
EIN: 546037402
Codes: FD

40788
R. B. Terry Charitable Foundation, Inc.
P.O. Box 1009
High Point, NC 27261-1009
Contact: Randall B. Terry, Jr., Pres.

Established in 1998 in NC.
Financial data (yr. ended 12/31/00): Grants paid, $647,230; assets, $41,233,310 (M); gifts received, $1,754,493; expenditures, $777,658; qualifying distributions, $620,845.
Limitations: Giving primarily in Raleigh, NC and Woodberry Forest, VA.
Publications: Annual report.
Officers and Directors:* Randall B. Terry, Jr.,* Pres.; Walter Craigie, Secy.; Charles L. Odom,* Treas.
EIN: 562066238

Codes: FD

40789
First Gaston Foundation, Inc.
(Formerly Myers-Ti-Caro Foundation, Inc.)
P.O. Box 2696
Gastonia, NC 28053 (704) 864-9242
Contact: Albert G. Myers III, Chair.

Incorporated in 1950 in NC.
Donor(s): Textiles, Inc., Threads, Inc.
Financial data (yr. ended 09/30/01): Grants paid, $638,917; assets, $10,422,725 (M); expenditures, $759,440; qualifying distributions, $675,347.
Limitations: Giving limited to Gaston County, NC.
Application information: Application form required for scholarships.
Officers and Trustees:* Albert G. Myers III,* Chair.; B. Frank Matthews II,* Vice-Chair.; Mary Adams,* Secy.; Tom D. Efird,* Treas.; A. Leonel Brunnemer, Robert P. Caldwell, Jr., Albert G. Myers, Jr., Charlton Torrence.
EIN: 560770083
Codes: FD, GTI

40790
The Julian Price Family Foundation
c/o Wachovia Bank, N.A.
P.O. Box 3099, NC6732
Winston-Salem, NC 27150-6732

Established in 1996 in NC.
Financial data (yr. ended 12/31/01): Grants paid, $626,500; assets, $20,923,677 (M); expenditures, $3,849,503; qualifying distributions, $720,928.
Limitations: Applications not accepted.
Application information: Contributes only to pre-selected organizations.
Trustees: Laura Deboisfeuillet Edwards, Susan Jarrell Edwards, Melaine Taylor Farland, Mary P.T. Harrison, J.M. Bryan Taylor, John Guest Taylor, Ray Howard Taylor III.
EIN: 311665269
Codes: FD

40791
Center for the Public Domain
(Formerly Red Hat Center)
2525 Meridian Pkwy., Ste. 200
Durham, NC 27713
FAX: (919) 549-8449; E-mail: grantmaking@centerpd.org; URL: http://www.centerforthepublicdomain.org

Established in 2000 in NC.
Donor(s): Bob Young, Marc Ewing.
Financial data (yr. ended 12/31/00): Grants paid, $620,000; assets, $4,614,347 (M); gifts received, $290,532; expenditures, $1,369,028; qualifying distributions, $1,316,016.
Limitations: Applications not accepted. Giving on a national and international basis.
Application information: Contributes only to pre-selected organizations.
Officers and Directors:* Robert Young,* Chair.; Sim Sitkin,* Secy.; Laurie Racine,* Exec. Dir.; James Boyle, John Seely Brown, Marc Ewing, John Gilmore, Lawrence Lessig.
EIN: 562179420
Codes: FD

40792
The Ray M. and Mary Elizabeth Lee Foundation, Inc.
Bank of America Plz., NC1-002-11-18
Charlotte, NC 28255
Application address: 3414 Peachtree Rd., Ste. 722, Atlanta, GA 30326, tel.: (404) 842-1870
Contact: Larry B. Hooks, Admin. Mgr.

Incorporated in 1966 in GA.
Donor(s): Ray M. Lee,‡ Mary Elizabeth Lee.‡
Financial data (yr. ended 09/30/01): Grants paid, $613,500; assets, $11,388,973 (M); expenditures, $786,109; qualifying distributions, $689,363.
Limitations: Giving limited to the metropolitan Atlanta, GA, area.
Publications: Application guidelines.
Application information: Application form not required.
Officer: William B. Stark, Pres.
Trustees: Ronald Gann, Donald D. Smith.
EIN: 586049441
Codes: FD

40793
Elmer R. Deaver Foundation
c/o First Union National Bank
401 S. Tryon St., NC1159
Charlotte, NC 28288-1159

Established in 1996 in PA.
Financial data (yr. ended 12/31/01): Grants paid, $607,416; assets, $12,742,578 (M); gifts received, $65,000; expenditures, $725,058; qualifying distributions, $624,496.
Limitations: Applications not accepted. Giving primarily in PA.
Application information: Contributes only to pre-selected organizations.
Trustees: Berthold W. Levy, First Union National Bank.
EIN: 237830263
Codes: FD

40794
The Palin Foundation
808-104 Salem Woods Dr.
Raleigh, NC 27615
Contact: Dr. John F. Philips, V.P.

Established in 1985 in NC.
Donor(s): Clifton L. Benson, Jr.
Financial data (yr. ended 12/31/01): Grants paid, $605,660; assets, $2,021,455 (M); gifts received, $35,000; expenditures, $791,617; qualifying distributions, $605,660.
Limitations: Giving primarily in NC.
Application information: Application form not required.
Officers and Trustees:* Clifton L. Benson, Jr.,* Pres.; John F. Philips,* V.P.; Margaret P. Benson,* Secy.
EIN: 561490228
Codes: FD

40795
Philip and Irene Toll Gage Foundation
Bank of America Plz., NC1-002-11-18
Charlotte, NC 28255
Application address: 3414 Peachtree Rd., Ste. 722, Atlanta, GA 30326, tel.: (404) 842-1870
Contact: Larry B. Hooks, Tr.

Established in 1985 in GA.
Donor(s): Betty G. Holland.
Financial data (yr. ended 11/30/01): Grants paid, $603,180; assets, $10,124,427 (M); gifts received, $132,578; expenditures, $680,618; qualifying distributions, $638,685.
Limitations: Giving limited to Atlanta, GA.
Publications: Application guidelines.
Application information: Application form not required.
Trustees: Larry Hooks, Bank of America.
EIN: 581727394
Codes: FD

40796
Martin Marietta Philanthropic Trust
(Formerly Martin Marietta Materials, Inc. Philanthropic Trust)
c/o First Union National Bank
401 S. Tryon St., 4th Fl.
Charlotte, NC 28288-1159

Trust established in 1952 in NC.
Donor(s): Martin Marietta Materials, Inc., Superior Stone Co.
Financial data (yr. ended 12/31/01): Grants paid, $598,249; assets, $527,398 (M); expenditures, $609,950; qualifying distributions, $600,452.
Limitations: Giving limited to areas of company operations in 13 states in the Southeast and the Midwest.
Application information: Application form not required.
Trustee: First Union National Bank.
EIN: 566035971
Codes: CS, FD, CD

40797
The Jeff Gordon Foundation
c/o Robert B. Brannan, III
P.O. Box 880
Harrisburg, NC 28075

Established in 2000 in NC.
Donor(s): Jeff M. Gordon, Jennifer B. Gordon.
Financial data (yr. ended 12/31/01): Grants paid, $586,800; assets, $256,946 (M); gifts received, $731,424; expenditures, $715,995; qualifying distributions, $657,428.
Limitations: Applications not accepted. Giving on a national basis.
Application information: Contributes only to pre-selected organizations.
Officers: Jeff M. Gordon, Pres. and Treas.; Jennifer B. Gordon, V.P. and Secy.
Director: Kathey Boyd.
EIN: 562174163
Codes: FD

40798
The Ellis Foundation
101 S. Tryon, NC1-002-11-18
Charlotte, NC 28255
Application address: c/o Tom Crews, Bank of America, 600 Peachtree St., Ste., Atlanta, GA 30308, tel.: (404) 607-6257

Established in 1997 in GA.
Financial data (yr. ended 12/31/01): Grants paid, $581,500; assets, $1,919,136 (M); gifts received, $394,898; expenditures, $587,391; qualifying distributions, $580,095.
Trustee: Bank of America.
EIN: 586362281
Codes: FD

40799
The Jolley Foundation
c/o Wachovia Bank N.A.
P.O. Box 3099
Winston-Salem, NC 27150-6732
Application address: c/o Wachovia Bank, N.A., 1426 Main St., 16th Fl., Columbia, SC 29226, tel.: (803) 765-3671
Contact: C. Gerald Lane, V.P. and Trust Off.

Established in 1947.
Donor(s): R.A. Jolley, Jr., James E. Jolley, Mamie J. Bruce.
Financial data (yr. ended 12/31/01): Grants paid, $550,000; assets, $13,286,289 (M); gifts received, $368,264; expenditures, $611,658; qualifying distributions, $552,237.
Limitations: Giving primarily in the Greenville, SC, area.

Trustees: Mamie J. Bruce, James E. Jolley, R.A. Jolley, Jr.
EIN: 576024996
Codes: FD

40800
Priscilla J. Schneller Scholarship Trust
c/o First Union National Bank
401 S. Tryon St., 4th Fl.
Charlotte, NC 28288-1159

Established in 1995 in FL.
Donor(s): Priscilla J. Schneller.‡
Financial data (yr. ended 12/31/01): Grants paid, $548,285; assets, $5,631,570 (M); expenditures, $610,808; qualifying distributions, $546,972.
Limitations: Applications not accepted. Giving primarily in Miami, FL.
Application information: Contributes only to pre-selected organizations.
Trustee: First Union National Bank.
EIN: 656163293
Codes: FD

40801
CTF, Inc.
(Formerly Christian Training Foundation)
2004 Valencia Terr.
Charlotte, NC 28226

Established in 1972 in MN.
Donor(s): C. Wilbur Peters, Bessie Peters.
Financial data (yr. ended 01/31/01): Grants paid, $532,338; assets, $14,979,209 (M); gifts received, $1,716; expenditures, $596,229; qualifying distributions, $532,338.
Limitations: Applications not accepted. Giving primarily in Charlotte, NC.
Application information: Contributes only to pre-selected organizations.
Officer: C. Wilbur Peters, Pres.
EIN: 237167181
Codes: FD

40802
Price Gilbert, Jr. Charitable Fund
c/o Wachovia Bank, N.A.
P.O. Box 3099
Winston-Salem, NC 27150-7131
Application address: c/o Wachovia Bank, N.A., 191 Peachtree St., N.E., MC-GA31214, Atlanta, GA 30303, tel.: (404) 332-6074
Contact: Bennie Boswell, Jr., Comm. Member

Established in 1973 in GA.
Financial data (yr. ended 05/31/01): Grants paid, $527,000; assets, $10,421,081 (M); expenditures, $687,020; qualifying distributions, $618,324.
Limitations: Giving limited to the Atlanta, GA, area.
Application information: Application form required.
Distribution Committee: Isaiah Tidwell, Chair.; Beverly Blake, Secy.; Bennie Boswell, Jr., D. Gary Thompson.
Trustee: Wachovia Bank, N.A.
EIN: 582064640
Codes: FD

40803
Edward C. Smith, Jr. & Christopher B. Smith Foundation, Inc.
P.O. Box 1527
Greenville, NC 27835
Contact: Edward C. Smith, Jr., Dir.

Established in 1993 in NC.
Donor(s): Edward C. Smith, Jr., Christopher B. Smith, C & E Enterprises.

Financial data (yr. ended 06/30/01): Grants paid, $515,984; assets, $11,447,387 (M); expenditures, $622,888; qualifying distributions, $491,716.
Limitations: Applications not accepted. Giving primarily in NC.
Application information: Contributes only to pre-selected organizations.
Directors: Christopher B. Smith, Edward C. Smith, Jr., Jo A. Smith.
EIN: 561844198
Codes: FD

40804
Thomas R. & Elizabeth E. McLean Foundation, Inc.
P.O. Box 58329
Fayetteville, NC 28305
Application address: P.O. Box 87009, Fayetteville, NC 28304-7009, tel.: (910) 483-8104
Contact: Alfred Cleveland, Tr.

Established in 1998 in NC.
Donor(s): Tom McLean.
Financial data (yr. ended 12/31/01): Grants paid, $515,000; assets, $15,743,578 (M); gifts received, $6,267,474; expenditures, $646,050; qualifying distributions, $515,000.
Limitations: Giving limited to NC.
Trustees: Alfred Cleveland, Harry Shaw.
EIN: 311470721
Codes: FD

40805
Alice Butler Foundation
(Formerly J. D. and Alice Butler Memorial Scholarship Foundation)
c/o First Union National Bank
401 S. Tryon St., NC 1159
Charlotte, NC 28288-1159
Application address: c/o Principal, Deerfield Beach Senior High School, 910 S.W. 15th St., Deerfield Beach, FL 33461

Established in 1987 in FL.
Financial data (yr. ended 08/31/01): Grants paid, $512,661; assets, $10,408,392 (M); expenditures, $625,471; qualifying distributions, $527,445.
Limitations: Giving limited to Deerfield Beach, FL.
Application information: Application form required.
Trustee: First Union National Bank.
EIN: 596878169
Codes: FD

40806
Alex Hemby Foundation
2633 Richardson Dr.
Charlotte, NC 28211
Contact: T.E. Hemby, Jr., Tr.

Established in 1950 in NC.
Donor(s): Hemby Investment Co.
Financial data (yr. ended 12/31/01): Grants paid, $512,400; assets, $5,796,097 (M); expenditures, $515,443; qualifying distributions, $509,609.
Limitations: Giving primarily in NC.
Trustees: Alexa H. Amick, Sandy D. Burnett, T.E. Hemby, Jr., Beverly H. Leahy, Beverly H. Sheaff.
EIN: 566046767
Codes: FD

40807
Goodnight Educational Foundation
c/o Wachovia Bank, N.A.
P.O. Box 3099
Winston-Salem, NC 27150-7153

Established in 1998 in NC.

Financial data (yr. ended 12/31/00): Grants paid, $510,000; assets, $10,285,949 (M); expenditures, $552,216; qualifying distributions, $505,586.
Limitations: Applications not accepted.
Application information: Contributes only to pre-selected organizations.
Directors: Susan G. Ellis, Ann Baggett Goodnight, James H. Goodnight, Leah A. Goodnight.
EIN: 566533546
Codes: FD

40808
Tom Davis Fund
P.O. Box 25864
Winston-Salem, NC 27114-5864
FAX: (336) 768-6996
Contact: Cheryl Hartman, Exec. Dir.

Established in 1988 in NC.
Donor(s): Thomas H. Davis.‡
Financial data (yr. ended 12/31/01): Grants paid, $504,450; assets, $8,108,466 (M); gifts received, $4,983,472; expenditures, $619,979; qualifying distributions, $516,859.
Limitations: Giving primarily in NC.
Directors: G. Franklin T. Davis, Thomas H. Davis, Jr.
EIN: 581813100
Codes: FD

40809
William and Patricia Gorelick Family Foundation
P.O. Box 35129
Charlotte, NC 28235-5129
Contact: William Gorelick, Pres.

Established in 1990 in NC.
Donor(s): William Gorelick.
Financial data (yr. ended 06/30/01): Grants paid, $504,041; assets, $3,890,888 (M); expenditures, $521,604; qualifying distributions, $500,310.
Limitations: Applications not accepted. Giving primarily in NC.
Application information: Contributes only to pre-selected organizations.
Officers and Trustees: William Gorelick,* Pres. and Treas.; Patricia Gorelick, V.P.; Todd A. Gorelick, Secy.
EIN: 561743190
Codes: FD

40810
Stonecutter Foundation, Inc.
300 Dallas St.
Spindale, NC 28160
Application address: P.O. Box 157, Spindale, NC 28160
Contact: Van H. Lonon, Treas.

Incorporated in 1944 in NC.
Donor(s): Stonecutter Mills Corp., Ivy Cowan.
Financial data (yr. ended 03/31/01): Grants paid, $503,175; assets, $9,448,650 (M); expenditures, $593,554; qualifying distributions, $585,714; giving activities include $50,041 for loans to individuals.
Limitations: Giving primarily in NC; student loans restricted to Rutherford and Polk County, NC, area residents.
Application information: Application forms provided for student loans.
Officers: Z.E. Dobbins, Pres.; James R. Cowan, V.P.; James M. Perry, V.P.; Thomas P. Walker, Secy.; Van H. Lonon, Treas.
Directors: D. Daniel Briscoe, Dillard Morrow, James T. Strickland, M.L. Summey, K.S. Tanner.
EIN: 566044820
Codes: CS, FD, CD, GTI

40811
Deichman-Lerner Foundation
(Formerly Deichman U.S. Foundation)
Charlotte Plz.
8310 Technology Dr.
Charlotte, NC 28262-3387

Established in 1985.
Financial data (yr. ended 02/03/01): Grants paid, $500,000; assets, $37,056 (M); gifts received, $500,000; expenditures, $500,023; qualifying distributions, $500,000.
Limitations: Applications not accepted. Giving on a national and international basis.
Application information: Contributes only to pre-selected organizations.
Officers and Directors:* Heinz H. Deichman,* Chair. and Pres.; Heinrich O. Deichman, V.P.; James Y. Preston,* Secy.-Treas.
EIN: 581615694
Codes: FD

40812
The Lucille P. and Edward C. Giles Foundation
(Formerly The Edward C. Giles Foundation)
P.O. Box 830
Mooresville, NC 28115
Contact: Bernard R. Fitzgerald, Pres.

Established in 1981 in NC.
Donor(s): Lucille P. Giles.‡
Financial data (yr. ended 12/31/01): Grants paid, $497,385; assets, $13,980,085 (M); expenditures, $622,165; qualifying distributions, $5,239,751.
Limitations: Applications not accepted. Giving primarily in the Charlotte, NC, area.
Application information: Unsolicited requests for funds not accepted.
Officers: Bernard Fitzgerald, Pres.; Van L. Weatherspoon, V.P.; Mark B. Edwards, Secy.-Treas.
EIN: 581450874
Codes: FD, GTI

40813
Chapin Foundation of Myrtle Beach, South Carolina
c/o Bank of America
1 NationsBank Plz., T09-1
Charlotte, NC 28255 (843) 449-7284
Application address: P.O. Box 70248, Myrtle Beach, SC 29572; FAX: (843) 449-3895; E-mail: csprouse@chapinfoundation.org
Contact: Claire C. Sprouse, Exec. Dir.

Trust established in 1943 in SC.
Donor(s): S.B. Chapin.‡
Financial data (yr. ended 07/31/01): Grants paid, $492,400; assets, $26,414,566 (M); expenditures, $540,699; qualifying distributions, $505,333.
Limitations: Giving limited to the Myrtle Beach, SC, area.
Publications: Application guidelines.
Application information: Application form required.
Officers and Directors:* Claude M. Epps,* Chair.; Harold D. Clardy,* Chair. Emeritus; Ruth T. Gore, V.P.; Claire Chapin Epps, Secy.; Lawton Benton, Treas.; Clair Louise Sprouse, Exec. Dir.; Harold Hartshorne, Jr., Howell Vaught Bellamey, Jr.
Trustee: Bank of America.
EIN: 566039453
Codes: FD

40814
Irwin Belk Educational Foundation
6100 Fairview Rd., Ste. 640
Charlotte, NC 28210-3277 (704) 553-8296
Contact: Carl G. Belk, Dir.

Established in 1992.
Donor(s): Carl G. Belk, Irwin Belk.
Financial data (yr. ended 12/31/01): Grants paid, $467,015; assets, $683,655 (M); gifts received, $483,509; expenditures, $483,642; qualifying distributions, $462,120.
Limitations: Giving primarily in NC.
Application information: Application form required.
Directors: Bill Belk, Carl G. Belk, Irene Belk Miltimore, Marilyn Belk Wallis.
EIN: 561783301
Codes: FD

40815
J. F. Hurley Foundation
P.O. Box 4354
Salisbury, NC 28145-4354 (704) 633-3603
FAX: (704) 633-1961
Contact: Gordon P. Hurley, Pres.

Established in 1982 in NC.
Donor(s): Gordon P. Hurley, J.F. Hurley III.
Financial data (yr. ended 12/31/01): Grants paid, $453,564; assets, $5,353,384 (M); expenditures, $555,026; qualifying distributions, $453,196.
Limitations: Giving primarily in Rowan County, NC, with emphasis on Salisbury.
Application information: Application form not required.
Officers and Directors:* J.F. Hurley III,* Chair. and Secy.-Treas.; Gordon P. Hurley,* Pres.; Elizabeth V. Rankin, Exec. V.P.
EIN: 561318937
Codes: FD

40816
The Hartquist Foundation
c/o Wachovia Bank, N.A.
P.O. Box 3099
Winston-Salem, NC 27150-7131

Established in 1998 in NC.
Financial data (yr. ended 12/31/00): Grants paid, $450,000; assets, $3,103,484 (M); expenditures, $482,570; qualifying distributions, $446,566.
Limitations: Applications not accepted.
Application information: Contributes only to pre-selected organizations.
Trustee: Wachovia Bank, N.A.
EIN: 911912805
Codes: FD

40817
John C. Slane Foundation
1210 Westwood Ave.
High Point, NC 27262 (336) 883-2334
Contact: John C. Slane, Pres.

Established in 1984 in NC.
Donor(s): John C. Slane.
Financial data (yr. ended 12/31/00): Grants paid, $448,652; assets, $6,846,302 (M); gifts received, $15,850; expenditures, $555,036; qualifying distributions, $448,652.
Limitations: Giving primarily in High Point, NC.
Officers and Directors:* John C. Slane,* Pres. and Treas.; Marsha B. Slane,* Secy.; Charles E. Lynch, Jr.
EIN: 581599165
Codes: FD

40818
Baird Foundation
c/o Wachovia Bank, N.A.
P.O. Box 3099
Winston-Salem, NC 27150-7131

Established in 1994 in GA.
Financial data (yr. ended 12/31/01): Grants paid, $443,940; assets, $8,097,486 (M); expenditures, $500,680; qualifying distributions, $443,060.
Limitations: Applications not accepted. Giving limited to GA.
Application information: Contributes only to pre-selected organizations.
Trustee: Wachovia Bank, N.A.
EIN: 586307787
Codes: FD

40819
The Covenant Foundation
c/o Wachovia Charitable Funds Mgmt.
P.O. Box 3099
Winston-Salem, NC 27150-6732

Established in 1989 in GA.
Donor(s): Dennis M. Chorba, Lavon L. Chorba.
Financial data (yr. ended 12/31/01): Grants paid, $440,495; assets, $383,502 (M); expenditures, $445,579; qualifying distributions, $443,258.
Limitations: Applications not accepted. Giving primarily in GA.
Application information: Contributes only to pre-selected organizations. Unsolicited requests for funds not considered.
Trustees: Dennis M. Chorba, Lavon L. Chorba, Wachovia Bank, N.A.
EIN: 586241819
Codes: FD

40820
P & B Foundation
2004 Valencia Terr.
Charlotte, NC 28226

Established in 1970.
Donor(s): C. Wilbur Peters, Eli Scholarship Fund.
Financial data (yr. ended 08/31/01): Grants paid, $437,598; assets, $24,036,744 (M); gifts received, $9,617,373; expenditures, $555,260; qualifying distributions, $437,598.
Limitations: Applications not accepted. Giving on a national basis.
Application information: Unsolicited requests for funds not accepted.
Officer: C. Wilbur Peters, Pres.
EIN: 237083912
Codes: FD

40821
Harvest Charities
(Formerly Belk-Simpson Foundation)
c/o Wachovia Bank, N.A.
P.O. Box 3099
Winston-Salem, NC 27150-7131
Application address: c/o Wachovia Bank, N.A., 1426 Main St., Columbia, SC 29226, tel.: (803) 765-3677
Contact: C. Gerald Lane, V.P. and Trust Off.

Trust established in 1944 in SC.
Donor(s): Belk-Simpson Co.
Financial data (yr. ended 12/31/01): Grants paid, $435,100; assets, $10,827,610 (M); expenditures, $450,669; qualifying distributions, $440,848.
Limitations: Giving primarily in SC.
Trustee: Wachovia Bank, N.A.
Board of Advisors: Claire Efird, John A. Kuhn, Lucy S. Kuhn, Nell M. Rice, Caroline Schmitt, Kate M. Simpson.
EIN: 576020261
Codes: CS, FD, CD

40822
Beaver Family Foundation, Inc.
(Formerly Donald C. Beaver Family Foundation, Inc.)
2425 N. Center St., No. 227
Hickory, NC 28601
E-mail: margaretglaze@twave.net

Established in 1997 in NC.

40822—NORTH CAROLINA

Donor(s): Donald C. Beaver.
Financial data (yr. ended 04/30/02): Grants paid, $434,540; assets, $9,128,337 (M); gifts received, $4,199; expenditures, $499,181; qualifying distributions, $430,765.
Limitations: Applications not accepted.
Application information: Contributes only to pre-selected organizations.
Officers: Donald C. Beaver, Pres.; Angela B. Simmons, Secy.; Patricia A. Beaver, Treas.
Directors: Deborah E. Beaver, Donna B. Beaver.
EIN: 562028723
Codes: FD

40823
The Coffey Foundation, Inc.
P.O. Box 1170
Lenoir, NC 28645
Application address: 406 Norwood St. S.W., Lenoir, NC 28645
Contact: Harriet Hailey

Established about 1979 in NC.
Donor(s): Harold F. Coffey Trust.
Financial data (yr. ended 11/30/01): Grants paid, $434,250; assets, $8,916,791 (M); expenditures, $543,828; qualifying distributions, $446,878.
Limitations: Giving primarily in Caldwell County, NC; scholarships limited to residents of Caldwell County.
Application information: Application forms for student grants available at high schools in Caldwell County. Application form required.
Trustees: Gary W. Bradford, Charles E. Dobbin, Leslie D. Hines, Jr., Betty Lou Miller, Wayne J. Miller, Jr.
EIN: 566047501
Codes: FD, GTI

40824
Blue Cross and Blue Shield of North Carolina Foundation
c/o Grant Review Comm.
P.O. Box 2291
Durham, NC 27702 (919) 765-4104

Established in 2000 in NC.
Donor(s): Blue Cross and Blue Shield of NC.
Financial data (yr. ended 06/30/01): Grants paid, $432,323; assets, $14,462,798 (M); gifts received, $14,999,928; expenditures, $1,661,826; qualifying distributions, $456,348; giving activities include $29,846 for programs.
Limitations: Giving primarily in NC.
Application information: Application form required.
Officers: Robert J. Greczyn, Jr., Pres.; Kathy Higgins, V.P.; Maureen O'Connor, Secy.; Steve Cherrier, Treas.
Trustees: Lynne Garrison, Daniel E. Glaser, John T. Roos, Rhone Sasser, J. Bradley Wilson.
EIN: 562226009
Codes: FD

40825
D. F. Halton Foundation
(Formerly Pepsi-Cola of Charlotte Foundation, Inc.)
P.O. Box 241167
Charlotte, NC 28224-1167 (704) 523-6761
Contact: Dale F. Halton, Pres.

Established in 1987 in NC.
Donor(s): Pepsi-Cola Bottling Co. of Charlotte.
Financial data (yr. ended 12/31/01): Grants paid, $430,625; assets, $354,176 (M); gifts received, $500,000; expenditures, $430,625; qualifying distributions, $430,613.
Limitations: Giving limited to the seven-county franchise area in Cabarrus, Cleveland, Gaston, Lincoln, Mecklenburg, Stanly, and Union counties, NC.
Application information: Applications from outside the Charlotte, NC, area are generally not accepted. Application form not required.
Officers: Dale F. Halton, Pres.; Phil Halton, V.P. and Treas.; Darrell Holland, Secy.
EIN: 561591985
Codes: CS, FD, CD

40826
Stephen Ross Angel Private Charitable Foundation
1608 Spring Garden St.
Greensboro, NC 27403
Contact: B. Ross Angel, Chair.

Established in 1997.
Donor(s): B. Ross Angel.
Financial data (yr. ended 04/30/01): Grants paid, $429,000; assets, $1,294,231 (M); expenditures, $436,238; qualifying distributions, $425,895.
Limitations: Giving primarily in NC.
Officers: B. Ross Angel, Chair.; Richard C. Forman, Secy.-Treas.
EIN: 562013753
Codes: FD

40827
Clanseer & Anna Johnson Scholarship Fund
c/o First Union National Bank
401 S. Tyron St., NC 1159
Charlotte, NC 28288-1159

Established in 1993 in NJ.
Donor(s): Clanseer Johnson.‡
Financial data (yr. ended 09/30/00): Grants paid, $427,057; assets, $15,232 (M); expenditures, $432,325; qualifying distributions, $427,976.
Limitations: Giving limited to residents of NJ.
Trustee: First Union National Bank.
EIN: 237749026

40828
Mildred Sheffield Wells Charitable Trust
c/o Bank of America
1 Hanover Sq., Ste. 600
Raleigh, NC 27601-1754
Application address: 600 Lynndale Ct., Ste. F, P.O. Box 20067, Greenville, NC 27858, tel.: (252) 756-8888
Contact: James G. Sullivan, Chair.

Established in 1997 in NC.
Financial data (yr. ended 09/30/01): Grants paid, $421,710; assets, $6,842,016 (M); expenditures, $509,591; qualifying distributions, $455,604.
Limitations: Giving primarily in Pitt County, NC.
Application information: Application form required.
Officer: James G. Sullivan, Chair.
Trustee: Bank of America.
Members: Danny D. McNally, C. Thomas Midyette.
EIN: 566505336
Codes: FD

40829
The C. Felix Harvey Foundation, Inc.
P.O. Box 189
Kinston, NC 28502

Established around 1970 in NC.
Donor(s): Felix Harvey, Margaret B. Harvey, Dixie Denning Supply Co.
Financial data (yr. ended 08/31/99): Grants paid, $421,575; assets, $9,449,650 (M); gifts received, $770,757; expenditures, $438,123; qualifying distributions, $413,822.
Limitations: Applications not accepted. Giving primarily in NC.
Application information: Contributes only to pre-selected organizations.
Officers: Margaret B. Harvey, Pres.; Robert Lee Burrows, Jr., V.P.; C. Felix Harvey, V.P.; Sunny Harvey Burrows, Secy.-Treas.
EIN: 237038942
Codes: FD

40830
The Family Foundation
(Formerly The Cash Family Foundation)
c/o F.A. Cash, Jr.
1601 Queens Rd. W.
Charlotte, NC 28207

Established in 1991 in NC.
Donor(s): F.A. Cash.
Financial data (yr. ended 12/31/01): Grants paid, $415,400; assets, $1,013,963 (M); gifts received, $709,469; expenditures, $417,962; qualifying distributions, $417,962.
Limitations: Giving primarily in Charlotte, NC.
Officers: F.A. Cash, Jr., Pres.; Barbara Cash, Secy.
EIN: 566382881
Codes: FD

40831
Collins & Aikman Foundation
(Formerly The Wickes Foundation)
701 McCullough Dr.
Charlotte, NC 28262-3318

Established in 1987 in CA.
Donor(s): Collins & Aikman Corp.
Financial data (yr. ended 12/31/01): Grants paid, $411,370; assets, $2,649,813 (M); expenditures, $416,229; qualifying distributions, $415,101.
Limitations: Applications not accepted. Giving primarily in NC and the eastern states.
Application information: Contributes only to pre-selected organizations.
Officers and Directors:* Thomas E. Evans,* Pres.; Jonathan L. Pelsner,* V.P. and Secy.; Ronald T. Lindsey, V.P.; Eugene A. White,* V.P.
EIN: 954085655
Codes: CS, FD, CD

40832
Rostan Family Foundation
P.O. Box 970
Valdese, NC 28690-0970

Established in 1995 in NC.
Donor(s): John P. Rostan, Jr.,‡ Naomi B. Rostan.
Financial data (yr. ended 12/31/01): Grants paid, $411,000; assets, $7,363,039 (M); expenditures, $443,370; qualifying distributions, $409,220.
Limitations: Applications not accepted. Giving limited to NC, wih emphasis on Burke County.
Application information: Contributes only to pre-selected organizations. Unsolicited requests for funds not accepted.
Officers and Trustees:* Mrs. John P. Rostan, Jr.,* C.E.O. and Pres.; John P. Rostan III,* V.P. and Secy.; James H. Rostan,* V.P. and Treas.
EIN: 561901626
Codes: FD

40833
The Carrie E. & Lena V. Glenn Foundation
1552 Union Rd., Ste. D
Gastonia, NC 28054-5582 (704) 867-0296
FAX: (704) 867-4496; E-mail: glennfnd@bellsouth.net
Contact: Barbara H. Voorhees, Exec. Dir.

Established in 1971 in NC.
Donor(s): Carrie Eugenia Glenn,‡ Lena Viola Glenn.‡

Financial data (yr. ended 09/30/02): Grants paid, $403,877; assets, $7,006,000 (M); expenditures, $546,128; qualifying distributions, $460,670.
Limitations: Giving limited to Gaston County, NC.
Publications: Application guidelines, grants list.
Application information: Application form required.
Officers and Directors:* W. Alex Hall,* Chair.; Ernest W. Sumner,* Vice-Chair.; Caroline H. Garrison,* Secy.; George L. Hodges III,* Treas.; David Stoker, Mayor Jennifer T. Stultz.
Trustee: B.B. & T.
EIN: 237140170
Codes: FD

40834
Harry Kramer Memorial Fund
c/o First Union National Bank
401 S. Tryon, 4th Fl.
Charlotte, NC 28202-1934
Application address: c/o First Union National Bank, 200 S. Biscayne Blvd., Miami, FL 33131-2310
Contact: Susan Best

Established in 1982 in FL.
Financial data (yr. ended 12/31/01): Grants paid, $402,233; assets, $7,350,299 (M); expenditures, $505,971; qualifying distributions, $402,225.
Limitations: Giving primarily in the southern FL, area; some giving also in Israel.
Application information: Application form not required.
Trustees: Leslie J. August, First Union National Bank.
EIN: 596644290
Codes: FD

40835
The Bolick Foundation
P.O. Box 307
Conover, NC 28613

Established in 1967 in NC.
Donor(s): Southern Furniture Co. of Conover, Inc.
Financial data (yr. ended 06/30/01): Grants paid, $400,000; assets, $9,149,148 (M); gifts received, $295,524; expenditures, $471,855; qualifying distributions, $394,015.
Limitations: Applications not accepted. Giving primarily in NC.
Application information: Contributes only to pre-selected organizations.
Trustee: Jerome W. Bolick.
EIN: 566086348
Codes: CS, FD, CD

40836
Southern Bank Foundation
P.O. Box 729
Mount Olive, NC 28365-0729
(919) 658-7007
Contact: David A. Bean, Treas.

Established in 1996 in NC.
Donor(s): Southern Bank and Trust Co.
Financial data (yr. ended 12/31/01): Grants paid, $393,485; assets, $5,342,558 (M); gifts received, $225; expenditures, $403,622; qualifying distributions, $388,892.
Limitations: Giving primarily in NC.
Application information: Application form required.
Officers: Frank B. Holding, Pres.; John N. Walker, V.P.; John E. Pegram, Jr., Secy.; David A. Bean, Treas.
Directors: Hope Holding Connell, Charles L. Revelle, Jr.
EIN: 562002871
Codes: CS, FD

40837
Tanner Foundation, Inc.
P.O. Box 1139
Rutherfordton, NC 28139-2115
Contact: George Clayton, Dir.

Established around 1975.
Donor(s): Tanner Companies.
Financial data (yr. ended 12/31/01): Grants paid, $392,202; assets, $106,394 (M); gifts received, $353,758; expenditures, $392,277; qualifying distributions, $392,100.
Limitations: Giving primarily in NC, with emphasis on Rutherford County.
Application information: Application form required.
Officers: James T. Tanner, Pres.; Chapman Johnston, V.P.; Michael S. Tanner, Secy.; George Clayton, Treas.
Directors: Sharon Decker, Bud Oates, Pell Tanner.
EIN: 510151695
Codes: CS, FD, CD

40838
Slick Family Foundation
P.O. Box 5958
Winston-Salem, NC 27113

Established in 1997 in NC.
Donor(s): Earl F. Slick.
Financial data (yr. ended 12/31/00): Grants paid, $385,000; assets, $9,388,515 (M); gifts received, $202,641; expenditures, $453,495; qualifying distributions, $414,405.
Limitations: Applications not accepted. Giving primarily in NC.
Application information: Contributes only to pre-selected organizations.
Officers and Directors:* Earl F. Slick,* Pres.; Phyllis S. Cowell,* V.P.; Jane P. Slick,* V.P.; Mary Caroline Gamble,* Secy.-Treas.; John Cowell, Lynn C. Ives.
EIN: 311500854
Codes: FD

40839
Holdeen Fund 55-10
c/o First Union National Bank
401 S. Tryon, NC1159
Charlotte, NC 28288-1159

Financial data (yr. ended 12/31/01): Grants paid, $379,922; assets, $6,473,795 (M); expenditures, $410,330; qualifying distributions, $379,052.
Limitations: Applications not accepted. Giving limited to Boston, MA.
Application information: Contributes only to pre-selected organizations.
Trustee: First Union National Bank.
EIN: 146018155
Codes: TN

40840
Henningsen Family Foundation
4401 City of Oaks Wynd
Raleigh, NC 27612

Established in 1998 in NC.
Donor(s): Lee A. Henningsen.
Financial data (yr. ended 12/31/99): Grants paid, $375,000; assets, $4,611,565 (M); expenditures, $413,162; qualifying distributions, $375,000.
Limitations: Applications not accepted.
Application information: Contributes only to pre-selected organizations.
Officers and Directors:* Lee A. Henningsen,* Pres. and Treas.; Brenda J. Henningsen,* V.P. and Secy.; Eric Henningsen.
EIN: 311623193

40841
Harry L. Dalton Foundation, Inc.
736 Wachovia Ctr.
Charlotte, NC 28285 (704) 332-5380
FAX: (704) 378-5320
Contact: R. Alfred Brand III, V.P.

Established about 1979 in NC.
Financial data (yr. ended 07/31/01): Grants paid, $373,058; assets, $5,645,734 (M); expenditures, $402,164; qualifying distributions, $370,233.
Limitations: Giving primarily in Mecklenburg County, NC.
Publications: Annual report.
Application information: Application form not required.
Officers and Directors:* Elizabeth D. Brand,* Pres.; R. Alfred Brand III, V.P. and Treas.; Deeda M. Coffey,* Secy.
EIN: 566061267
Codes: FD

40842
The Pratt Family Foundation, Inc.
300 S. Westgate Dr., Ste. A
Greensboro, NC 27407

Established in 1999 in NC.
Donor(s): William J. Pratt, Jeanne M. Pratt.
Financial data (yr. ended 12/31/01): Grants paid, $371,150; assets, $4,596,140 (M); expenditures, $462,768; qualifying distributions, $371,150.
Limitations: Applications not accepted. Giving primarily in NC.
Application information: Contributes only to pre-selected organizations.
Officers: William J. Pratt, Pres.; Jeanne Anne Pratt, V.P.; Jeanne M. Pratt, Secy.; William H. Pratt, Treas.
EIN: 311677890
Codes: FD

40843
Thomasville Furniture Industries Foundation
c/o Wachovia Bank of North Carolina, N.A.
P.O. Box 3099
Winston-Salem, NC 27150-1022
(336) 732-6010
Application address: c/o Vickie Holder, Thomasville Furniture Industries, Inc., P.O. Box 339, Thomasville, NC 27360
Contact: Sherald Cratch

Trust established in 1960 in NC.
Donor(s): Thomasville Furniture Industries, Inc.
Financial data (yr. ended 12/31/01): Grants paid, $367,423; assets, $4,483,081 (M); expenditures, $409,788; qualifying distributions, $368,336.
Limitations: Giving primarily in NC.
Administrative Committee: Frederick B. Starr, Chair.; Carlyle A. Nance, Jr., Secy.; Frank B. Burr, Charles G. O'Brien.
Trustee: Wachovia Bank of North Carolina, N.A.
EIN: 566047870
Codes: CS, FD, CD, GTI

40844
Dr. Arthur J. & Helen M. Horvat Foundation
c/o First Union National Bank
401 S. Tryon St.
Charlotte, NC 28288
Application address: c/o David Glickman, First Union National Bank, 123 S. Broad St., Philadelphia, PA 19109

Established in 1987 in PA.
Financial data (yr. ended 12/31/00): Grants paid, $365,923; assets, $6,719,063 (M); expenditures, $437,892; qualifying distributions, $391,902.
Limitations: Giving limited to Duryea, PA, and surrounding areas.

Publications: Informational brochure (including application guidelines).
Application information: Application form required.
Trustees: Edward Neureuter, Nicholas D. Tellie, First Union National Bank.
EIN: 236846849
Codes: FD, GTI

40845
Robert Lee Chastain and Thomas M. Chastain Charitable Foundation
c/o First Union National Bank
401 S. Tryon St., 4th Fl.
Charlotte, NC 28202-1934

Trust established in 1966 in FL.
Donor(s): Robert Lee Chastain.‡
Financial data (yr. ended 12/31/01): Grants paid, $358,922; assets, $3,744,466 (L); expenditures, $397,657; qualifying distributions, $358,924.
Limitations: Applications not accepted. Giving primarily in the Palm Beach and Martin County, FL, area.
Application information: Contributes only to pre-selected organizations.
Trustee: First Union National Bank.
EIN: 596171294
Codes: FD

40846
The Mary Lynn Richardson Fund
P.O. Box 20124
Greensboro, NC 27420 (336) 274-5471
Contact: Betsy B. Mead, Tr.

Trust established in 1940 in NC.
Donor(s): Mary Lynn Richardson.‡
Financial data (yr. ended 12/31/99): Grants paid, $358,903; assets, $9,021,479 (M); expenditures, $432,776; qualifying distributions, $377,511.
Limitations: Giving limited to Guilford County, NC, for domestic programs; giving also on an international basis.
Application information: No new grants to individuals will be awarded. Application form not required.
Trustees: Eric R. Calhoun, Betsy Boney Mead, Janet Mermey, Cary R. Paynter, William Y. Preyer, Jr.
EIN: 066025946
Codes: FD

40847
The Beattie Foundation
(Formerly Frances and William H. Beattie Foundation)
c/o Wachovia Bank, N.A.
P.O. Box 3099
Winston-Salem, NC 27150-6732

Donor(s): William H. Beattie.‡
Financial data (yr. ended 12/31/01): Grants paid, $358,200; assets, $6,939,682 (M); expenditures, $389,126; qualifying distributions, $364,769.
Limitations: Applications not accepted. Giving primarily in the Greenville, SC, area.
Application information: Contributes only to pre-selected organizations.
Trustee: Wachovia Bank, N.A.
Advisory Committee: Dorothy B. Hamill, Chair.; Joel B. Adams, Jr., Mrs. Joel B. Adams, Jr.
EIN: 576113645
Codes: FD

40848
Gandy Family Foundation
P.O. Box 2218
Cornelius, NC 28031-2218 (704) 892-0015
Contact: Quinton M. Gandy, Dir.

Established in 1997 in NC.
Donor(s): Phil M. Gandy, Jr., Quinton M. Gandy.
Financial data (yr. ended 07/31/01): Grants paid, $357,000; assets, $14,965 (M); gifts received, $61,000; expenditures, $358,450; qualifying distributions, $356,964.
Application information: Application form not required.
Directors: Phil M. Gandy, Jr., Quinton M. Gandy.
EIN: 562056507
Codes: FD

40849
Lance Foundation
c/o Bank of America
101 S. Tryon St., NC1-002-11-18
Charlotte, NC 28255
Application address: c/o Lance, Inc., P.O. Box 32368, Charlotte, NC 28232
Contact: Zean Jamison, Dir.

Trust established in 1956 in NC.
Donor(s): Lance, Inc., and members of the Van Every family.
Financial data (yr. ended 06/30/01): Grants paid, $355,950; assets, $4,414,843 (M); expenditures, $404,770; qualifying distributions, $367,962.
Limitations: Giving primarily in NC and SC.
Application information: Application form not required.
Directors: Zean Jamison, Jr., Earl D. Leake, Clyde Preslar, Paul A. Stroup III, Richard G. Tucker.
Trustee: Bank of America.
EIN: 566039487
Codes: CS, FD, CD

40850
The Edward M. Armfield, Sr. Foundation, Inc.
P.O. Box 9436
Greensboro, NC 27429

Established in 2000 in NC.
Donor(s): Edward M. Armfield, Sr.‡
Financial data (yr. ended 12/31/01): Grants paid, $355,227; assets, $14,716,760 (M); gifts received, $4,062,408; expenditures, $535,862; qualifying distributions, $420,750.
Limitations: Applications not accepted. Giving primarily in NC.
Application information: Contributes only to pre-selected organizations.
Directors: Adair P. Armfield, W.J. Armfield, Bedford Cannon, Steve Joyce.
EIN: 562156876
Codes: FD

40851
David L. Lieb Foundation, Inc.
244 Pine Ridge
Boone, NC 28607
Contact: Charles H. Lieb, Pres.

Established in 1959.
Donor(s): David L. Lieb.‡
Financial data (yr. ended 12/31/01): Grants paid, $354,938; assets, $9,881,462 (M); expenditures, $406,301; qualifying distributions, $362,303.
Limitations: Applications not accepted. Giving primarily in NY.
Application information: Contributes only to pre-selected organizations.
Officers: Charles H. Lieb, Pres.; Barbara Lieb Baumstein, V.P.; Toby Lieb, Secy.; Richard Baumstein, Treas.
EIN: 136077728

Codes: FD

40852
O'Herron Foundation, Inc.
6827-C Fairview Rd.
Charlotte, NC 28210 (704) 364-6531
Contact: Edward M. O'Herron, Jr., Pres.

Established in 1962 in NC.
Donor(s): Edward M. O'Herron, Jr.
Financial data (yr. ended 12/31/01): Grants paid, $354,200; assets, $7,307,926 (M); expenditures, $422,237; qualifying distributions, $354,200.
Limitations: Giving primarily in Palm Beach County, FL, Mecklenburg and Wake counties, NC, and Horry County, SC.
Officers: Edward M. O'Herron, Jr., Pres. and Treas.; Margaret B. O'Herron, V.P.; Patricia Norman, Secy.
Directors: Kenneth Coe, Kennedy O'Herron, William O'Herron.
EIN: 566061256
Codes: FD

40853
Ferguson Family Foundation
2495 Barker Rd.
Oxford, NC 27565 (252) 438-2097
Contact: Jack E. Ferguson, Pres.

Established in 1997 in NC.
Donor(s): Debra B. Ferguson, Jack E. Ferguson.
Financial data (yr. ended 12/31/01): Grants paid, $353,775; assets, $482,355 (M); gifts received, $236,663; expenditures, $355,758; qualifying distributions, $353,563.
Limitations: Giving primarily in NC, with emphasis on Oxford.
Officers: Jack E. Ferguson, Pres.; Debra B. Ferguson, V.P.; Thomas L. Robinson, Jr., Secy.
EIN: 562050757
Codes: FD

40854
The Chandran Family Foundation, Inc.
c/o Wachovia Bank, N.A.
P.O. Box 3099
Winston-Salem, NC 27150-7131

Established in 2000 in NC.
Donor(s): Clarence J. Chandran.
Financial data (yr. ended 12/31/01): Grants paid, $350,535; assets, $610,365 (M); expenditures, $359,354; qualifying distributions, $350,535.
Limitations: Applications not accepted.
Application information: Contributes only to pre-selected organizations.
Trustee: Wachovia Bank, N.A.
EIN: 562190350

40855
The Loftis Foundation, Inc.
4704 Greenpoint Ln.
Holly Springs, NC 27540
Contact: Richard A. Hart

Established around 1994.
Financial data (yr. ended 07/31/01): Grants paid, $347,500; assets, $4,248,512 (M); gifts received, $31,325; expenditures, $440,425; qualifying distributions, $381,081.
Limitations: Giving on a national basis.
Application information: Application form not required.
Officer: Robert W. Loftis, Pres.
EIN: 582110528
Codes: FD

40856
BIN Charitable Foundation
P.O. Box 3127
Durham, NC 27715
Contact: Bond Anderson III, Secy.

Established in 1999 in NC.
Donor(s): Barbara Newborg.
Financial data (yr. ended 12/31/01): Grants paid, $347,000; assets, $2,681,125 (M); gifts received, $634,595; expenditures, $388,657; qualifying distributions, $347,000.
Officers: Barbara Newborg, Pres.; Bond Anderson III, Secy.; Sarah F. Preyer, Treas.
EIN: 562111550
Codes: FD

40857
ABC Foundation
c/o Bank of America
Bank of America Plz., NC1-002-08-12
Charlotte, NC 28255
Application address: Cone Mills Corp., 804 Green Valley Rd., Ste. 300, Greensboro, NC 27408, tel.: (336) 379-6220
Contact: Carolyn Hines, Mgr., Comm.

Trust established in 1944 in NC.
Donor(s): Cone Mills Corp.
Financial data (yr. ended 10/31/01): Grants paid, $345,604; assets, $4,462,837 (M); expenditures, $330,996; qualifying distributions, $311,451.
Limitations: Giving limited to areas of company operations in NC.
Officers and Directors:* John L. Bakane,* Pres.; Terry L. Weatherford,* Secy.-Treas.; Michael K. Horrigan, Gary L. Smith, Dewey L. Trogdon.
Trustee: Bank of America.
EIN: 581504894
Codes: CS, FD, CD

40858
The Shelton Foundation
4201 Congress St., Ste. 470
Charlotte, NC 28209

Established in 1985 in NC.
Donor(s): The Shelton Companies, Charles M. Shelton, R. Edwin Shelton, Ballard G. Norwood.
Financial data (yr. ended 12/31/01): Grants paid, $345,476; assets, $2,356,083 (M); expenditures, $429,961; qualifying distributions, $341,756.
Limitations: Applications not accepted. Giving primarily in NC.
Application information: Contributes only to pre-selected organizations.
Officers: Charles M. Shelton, Pres.; R. Edwin Shelton, V.P.; Ballard G. Norwood, Secy.-Treas.
EIN: 581596729
Codes: CS, FD, CD

40859
Betty J. & Robert P. Williams Family Foundation
P.O. Box 26262
Greensboro, NC 27420

Established in 1999 in NC.
Donor(s): Robert P. Williams.
Financial data (yr. ended 06/30/01): Grants paid, $344,050; assets, $929,792 (M); gifts received, $21,200; expenditures, $380,205; qualifying distributions, $342,928.
Limitations: Applications not accepted. Giving primarily in Greensboro, NC.
Application information: Contributes only to pre-selected organizations.
Officers: Robert P. Williams, Pres. and Treas.; Betty Jane F. Williams, V.P. and Secy.
EIN: 562170735
Codes: FD

40860
Davis Hospital Foundation, Inc.
P.O. Box 908
Statesville, NC 28687-0908

Established in 1983 in NC; converted from the sale of Davis Hospital.
Financial data (yr. ended 06/30/01): Grants paid, $343,040; assets, $7,369,682 (M); expenditures, $419,179; qualifying distributions, $340,133.
Limitations: Applications not accepted. Giving primarily in Boiling Springs and Statesville, NC.
Application information: Contributes only to pre-selected organizations.
Officers and Board Members:* John N. Gilbert, Jr.,* Chair.; John S. Steele,* Vice-Chair.; Sammy Black,* Secy. and Chair., Nominating Comm.; F. Anderson Sherrill, Jr.,* Treas. and Chair., Investment Mng. Comm.; Ralph Bentley,* Chair., Prog. Review Comm.; Doug Hendrix,* Chair., Financial Assistance Comm.; H. Brown Kimball,* Chair., Bylaws Comm.; William A. Long,* Mgr.; Marie Brendle, Maxine Middlesworth, John L. West, Hoyle L. Whiteside, Margaret Wilhide.
EIN: 581528127
Codes: FD

40861
James E. and Mary Z. Bryan Foundation, Inc.
c/o First Citizens Bank
P.O. Box 29522
Raleigh, NC 27626-0522
Application address: 125 Overbrook Rd., Goldsboro, NC 27534, tel.: (919) 735-3820
Contact: Dr. James M. Zealy, Pres.

Incorporated in 1954 in NC.
Donor(s): James E. Bryan,‡ Mary Z. Bryan.‡
Financial data (yr. ended 06/30/01): Grants paid, $340,000; assets, $6,465,313 (M); expenditures, $369,898; qualifying distributions, $347,554.
Limitations: Giving limited to NC.
Publications: Financial statement.
Application information: Application form not required.
Officers: James M. Zealy, Pres.; William H. Bryan, V.P.; Lewis R. Holding, Secy.-Treas.
EIN: 566034567
Codes: FD

40862
The Lichtin Family Foundation
3110 Edwards Mill Rd., Ste. 200
Raleigh, NC 27612

Established in 1998 in NC.
Donor(s): Harold S. Lichtin.
Financial data (yr. ended 12/31/01): Grants paid, $333,734; assets, $5,300 (M); gifts received, $88,900; expenditures, $344,416; qualifying distributions, $343,721.
Limitations: Applications not accepted. Giving primarily in NC.
Application information: Contributes only to pre-selected organizations.
Officers: Harold S. Lichtin, Pres. and Treas.; Noel A. Lichtin, V.P. and Secy.
EIN: 311639979
Codes: FD

40863
O. Temple Sloan, Jr. Foundation
P.O. Box 26006
Raleigh, NC 27611 (919) 573-3000
Contact: Carol Sloan, Tr.

Established in 1994 in NC.
Donor(s): O. Temple Sloan, Jr., O. Temple Sloan, Jr. Charitable Lead Trust.
Financial data (yr. ended 12/31/00): Grants paid, $333,122; assets, $40,497 (M); gifts received, $254,265; expenditures, $335,133; qualifying distributions, $330,915.
Limitations: Giving primarily in NC.
Application information: Application form required.
Trustees: Malcolm C. Graham, Carson S. Henline, Carol C. Sloan, W. Gerald Thornton, George C. Turner.
EIN: 561870844
Codes: FD

40864
The General William A. Smith Trust
c/o B.B. & T., Trust Dept.
P.O. Box 2907
Wilson, NC 27894-2907
Application address: 200 S. College St., Charlotte, NC 28202-2005
Contact: Judy Micha

Trust established in 1940 in NC.
Donor(s): Genl. William A. Smith.
Financial data (yr. ended 12/31/01): Grants paid, $331,365; assets, $6,032,813 (M); expenditures, $420,022; qualifying distributions, $328,194.
Limitations: Giving primarily in Anson County, NC.
Application information: Application form not required.
Trustees: Joe E. Gaddy, James A. Hardison, Jr., Frank F. Mills, B.B. & T.
EIN: 566042630
Codes: FD

40865
Melba Bayers Meyer Charitable Trust
c/o First Union National Bank
401 S. Tryon St., NC1159
Charlotte, NC 28288
Application address: c/o First Union National Bank, 21 E. Garden St., Pensacola, FL 32501
Contact: Connie Cox

Established in 1995 in PA.
Donor(s): Melba Bayers Meyer.‡
Financial data (yr. ended 05/31/01): Grants paid, $331,200; assets, $6,163,525 (M); expenditures, $372,184; qualifying distributions, $326,349.
Limitations: Giving primarily in Pensacola, FL.
Application information: Application form not required.
Trustee: First Union National Bank.
EIN: 656192782
Codes: FD

40866
The Dee and Rick Ray Foundation, Inc.
c/o Neuray Holdings LLC
P.O. Box 37149
Charlotte, NC 28237 (704) 332-1153

Financial data (yr. ended 12/31/01): Grants paid, $330,756; assets, $69,496 (M); expenditures, $333,476; qualifying distributions, $333,077.
Limitations: Giving primarily in Charlotte, NC.
Trustees: Delores K. Ray, William E. Ray.
EIN: 593444525
Codes: FD

40867
R. A. Bryan Foundation, Inc.
400 Patetown Rd.
P.O. Drawer 919
Goldsboro, NC 27533-0919 (919) 734-8400
Contact: R.A. Bryan, Jr., Pres.

Established in 1956 in NC.
Donor(s): R.A. Bryan, Jr., Ruby M. Bryan,‡ Aviation Fuel Terminals, Inc., Ridgewood, Inc., T.A. Loving Co.

40867—NORTH CAROLINA

Financial data (yr. ended 12/31/01): Grants paid, $327,500; assets, $15,926,435 (M); gifts received, $174,640; expenditures, $405,333; qualifying distributions, $338,725.
Limitations: Applications not accepted. Giving primarily in NC.
Application information: Contributes only to pre-selected organizations.
Officers: R.A. Bryan, Jr., Pres.; Stephen C. Bryan, V.P.; Thomas R. Howell, Treas.
EIN: 566044320
Codes: FD

40868
Tina Guzzardi/Guzzardi Memorial Foundation
401 S. Tryon St.
Charlotte, NC 28288-1159

Established in 1988 in PA.
Financial data (yr. ended 12/31/01): Grants paid, $327,000; assets, $493 (M); expenditures, $331,555; qualifying distributions, $326,795.
Limitations: Applications not accepted. Giving primarily in PA.
Application information: Contributes only to pre-selected organizations.
Trustees: Michael Guzzardi, Robert Guzzardi, First Union National Bank.
EIN: 226453591
Codes: FD

40869
Glenn Family Foundation
P.O. Box 2736
Winston-Salem, NC 27102-2736
Application address: 1540 Silas Creek Pkwy., Winston-Salem, NC 27107, tel.: (336) 772-3441
Contact: J. Kirk Glen, Jr., V.P.

Established in 1987.
Donor(s): James K. Glenn, James K. Glenn, Jr.
Financial data (yr. ended 12/31/01): Grants paid, $325,875; assets, $6,936,222 (M); gifts received, $10,910; expenditures, $603,856; qualifying distributions, $332,761.
Limitations: Giving primarily in Winston-Salem, NC.
Officers and Directors:* James K. Glenn,* Pres. and Treas.; James K. Glenn, Jr.,* V.P. and Secy.; Frances G. Porter, Salley G. Williams.
EIN: 581748268
Codes: FD

40870
Anna Oschwald Trust
c/o First Union National Bank
401 S. Tryon St., 4th Fl.
Charlotte, NC 28288-1159

Established in 2000 in NJ.
Financial data (yr. ended 12/31/01): Grants paid, $322,439; assets, $7,702,836 (M); gifts received, $919,074; expenditures, $398,593; qualifying distributions, $322,439.
Limitations: Applications not accepted. Giving primarily in Red Bank, NJ; funding also in Washington, DC, New York, NY, and Harrisburg, PA.
Application information: Contributes only to pre-selected organizations.
Trustees: Stephen J. Oppenheim, First Union National Bank.
EIN: 256626923
Codes: FD

40871
E. H. Barnard Charitable Trust
P.O. Box 51489
Durham, NC 27717

Established in 1988 in NC.
Donor(s): E.H. Barnard.‡
Financial data (yr. ended 05/31/01): Grants paid, $322,000; assets, $6,020,610 (M); expenditures, $360,482; qualifying distributions, $313,022.
Limitations: Applications not accepted. Giving primarily in Yadkin County, NC.
Application information: Contributes only to pre-selected organizations.
Trustee: Central Carolina Bank & Trust Co.
EIN: 566299574
Codes: FD

40872
Alice Gibson Brock Trust
c/o First Union National Bank
401 S. Tryon St., NC1159
Charlotte, NC 28288-1159

Established in 1995 in PA.
Financial data (yr. ended 12/31/00): Grants paid, $321,108; assets, $4,656,012 (M); expenditures, $332,123; qualifying distributions, $316,660.
Limitations: Applications not accepted. Giving primarily in PA.
Application information: Contributes only to pre-selected organizations.
Trustees: Betsy Zubrow Cohen, Herbert Riband, Jr., First Union National Bank.
EIN: 236219064
Codes: FD

40873
North Carolina Foam Foundation
c/o Bank of America
1 Bank of America Plz., NC1-002-11-18
Charlotte, NC 28255
Contact: Robert H. Perkins, Dir.

Established in 1965.
Donor(s): North Carolina Foam Industries, Inc.
Financial data (yr. ended 12/31/01): Grants paid, $320,050; assets, $5,677,260 (M); gifts received, $171,116; expenditures, $373,742; qualifying distributions, $330,753.
Limitations: Applications not accepted. Giving primarily in Mount Airy and Surry County, NC.
Application information: Contributes only to pre-selected organizations.
Directors: Jake Barnhardt, Swanson Snow.
Trustee: Bank of America.
EIN: 566068247
Codes: CS, FD, CD

40874
Fox Family Foundation, Inc.
2726 Croasdaile Dr., Ste. 102
Durham, NC 27705-2500 (919) 383-5575
FAX: (919) 383-5577; *E-mail:* dbeischer@mindspring.com
Contact: David D. Beischer, Exec. Dir.

Established in 1991 in NC.
Donor(s): Frances Hill Fox.
Financial data (yr. ended 12/31/01): Grants paid, $320,000; assets, $5,683,374 (M); expenditures, $398,487; qualifying distributions, $319,523.
Limitations: Giving limited to Durham, Orange, and Wake counties, NC.
Publications: Grants list, application guidelines.
Application information: Application form required.
Officers and Directors:* Frances Hill Fox,* Pres.; Susan Fox Beischer,* V.P.; Randolph Dudley Fox,* V.P.; A. William Kennon,* Secy.; J. David Ross,* Treas.; David D. Beischer,* Exec. Dir.; John W. Mallard.
EIN: 561756144
Codes: FD

40875
Newton B. Shingleton Trust
c/o First Union National Bank
401 S. Tryon St., NC1159
Charlotte, NC 28288-1159

Established in 1990 in VA.
Financial data (yr. ended 09/30/01): Grants paid, $319,665; assets, $5,510,933 (M); expenditures, $419,102; qualifying distributions, $353,392.
Limitations: Applications not accepted.
Application information: Contributes only to pre-selected organizations.
Trustees: Harold Spurling, First Union National Bank.
EIN: 546184224
Codes: FD

40876
Vivian S. West-West Memorial Fund
c/o Bank of America
1 Hanover Sq.
Raleigh, NC 27601
Application address: P.O. Box 20067, Greenville, NC 27858
Contact: James G. Sullivan, Chair.

Established in 1998 in NC.
Financial data (yr. ended 03/31/00): Grants paid, $315,053; assets, $10,630,960 (M); expenditures, $433,922; qualifying distributions, $315,053.
Limitations: Giving primarily in Greenville, NC.
Application information: Application form required.
Officer and Trustees:* James G. Sullivan,* Chair; Bank of America.
Directors: Dottie W. Brooks, Danny D. McNally.
EIN: 566520255

40877
Kellenberger Historical Foundation
(Formerly May Gordon Latham Kellenberger Historical Foundation)
P.O. Box 908
New Bern, NC 28563 (252) 514-4900
Contact: Dee Sage

Established in 1979.
Donor(s): May Gordon Latham Kellenberger.‡
Financial data (yr. ended 11/30/01): Grants paid, $314,793; assets, $3,150,697 (M); expenditures, $367,529; qualifying distributions, $342,334.
Limitations: Giving limited to Craven County and New Bern, NC.
Application information: Application form required.
Officer and Trustees:* Jeffrey J. Crow,* Chair.; Bank of America, and 11 additional trustees.
EIN: 581360279
Codes: FD

40878
O'H. Rankin Foundation, Inc.
2611 Richardson Dr.
Charlotte, NC 28211-3397 (704) 571-3245
Application address: c/o Betty Hechenbleikner, 601 Colville Rd., Charlotte, NC 28207; *E-mail:* SamRankin@aol.com
Contact: Samuel B. Rankin, Pres.

Established in 1976.
Financial data (yr. ended 05/31/01): Grants paid, $313,238; assets, $3,391,866 (M); expenditures, $382,580; qualifying distributions, $310,614.
Limitations: Giving primarily in the Charlotte, NC, area.
Application information: Application form not required.
Officers and Directors:* David H. Rankin,* Chair.; Samuel B. Rankin,* Pres.; Nancy O'H.

Rankin,* V.P.; Betty R. Hechenbleikner, Secy.-Treas.; Michael O'H. Rankin.
EIN: 237005335
Codes: FD

40879
Henrietta Tower Wurts Memorial Foundation
c/o First Union National Bank
401 S. Tryon St., 4th Fl.
Charlotte, NC 28288-1159
Application address: Broad and Walnut Sts. PA 1308, Philadelphia, PA 19109-1199
Contact: Diane Stables

Incorporated in 1934 in PA.
Donor(s): Henrietta Tower Wurts.‡
Financial data (yr. ended 12/31/01): Grants paid, $312,616; assets, $5,680,013 (M); expenditures, $350,987; qualifying distributions, $310,492.
Limitations: Giving limited to Philadelphia, PA.
Publications: Application guidelines, annual report (including application guidelines).
Application information: Application form required.
Trustee: First Union National Bank.
EIN: 236297977
Codes: FD

40880
Adelaide Worth Daniels Foundation, Inc.
298 Webb Cove Rd.
Asheville, NC 28804   (828) 251-0515
Contact: Adelaide Worth Daniels Key, Pres.

Established in 1989 in NC.
Donor(s): Adelaide Worth Daniels Key.
Financial data (yr. ended 11/30/01): Grants paid, $308,875; assets, $532,780 (M); gifts received, $7,979; expenditures, $330,914; qualifying distributions, $314,770.
Limitations: Giving primarily in western NC.
Officers: Adelaide Worth Daniels Key, Pres. and Treas.; Gilbert Russell Key II, V.P.
Director: Robert J. Robinson.
EIN: 561706623
Codes: FD

40881
Albert & Helen C. Meserve Memorial Fund
c/o First Union National Bank
401 S. Tryon St., NC1159
Charlotte, NC 28288

Established in 1983 in CT; grant program administered through the Fairfield County Community Foundation.
Donor(s): Albert W. Meserve,‡ Helen C. Meserve.‡
Financial data (yr. ended 08/31/01): Grants paid, $303,325; assets, $4,497,571 (M); expenditures, $367,833; qualifying distributions, $327,674.
Limitations: Applications not accepted. Giving primarily in Bethel, Bridgewater, Brookfield, Danbury, New Fairfield, New Milford, Newton, Redding, Ridgefield, and Sherman, CT.
Application information: Contributes only to pre-selected organizations.
Trustees: David C. Murphy, First Union National Bank.
EIN: 066254956
Codes: FD, GTI

40882
Leeolou Family Foundation
c/o U.S. Trust
4000 WestChase Blvd., Ste. 350
Raleigh, NC 27607
Contact: Robert E. Mallernee, Asst. Secy.

Established in 1998 in NC.
Donor(s): Mary Denise Leeolou, Stephen R. Leeolou.
Financial data (yr. ended 12/31/01): Grants paid, $301,333; assets, $1,691,719 (M); expenditures, $301,333; qualifying distributions, $301,333.
Limitations: Applications not accepted.
Application information: Contributes only to pre-selected organizations.
Officers: Stephen R. Leeolou, Pres.; Mary Denise Leeolou, V.P.
EIN: 562114229
Codes: FD

40883
The Medic Educational Foundation
c/o Wachovia Bank, N. A.
P. O. Box 3099
Winston-Salem, NC 27150-6732

Established in 1997 in NC.
Donor(s): The John McConnel Foundation, The Roth Foundation, Lightfoot H. Goddin.
Financial data (yr. ended 12/31/01): Grants paid, $298,500; assets, $930,698 (M); expenditures, $1,200,126; qualifying distributions, $303,286.
Limitations: Applications not accepted. Giving on a national basis.
Application information: Unsolicited requests for funds not accepted.
Officer: Luanne Roth, Exec. Dir.
Directors: John McConnell, Alan Winchester.
EIN: 582391110
Codes: FD

40884
The A. Pat and Kathryne L. Brown Foundation, Inc.
c/o Thomas F. Foster
P.O. Box 1550
High Point, NC 27261-1550   (889) 873-3181

Established in 1991 in NC.
Donor(s): Kathryne L. Brown.‡
Financial data (yr. ended 12/31/01): Grants paid, $295,000; assets, $5,452,221 (M); gifts received, $5,581,241; expenditures, $302,692; qualifying distributions, $293,841.
Limitations: Applications not accepted. Giving primarily in NC.
Application information: Contributes only to pre-selected organizations.
Officers and Directors:* David L. Maynard,* Pres.; W. Calvin Reynolds,* V.P.; Norma Smith,* Secy.; Thomas F. Foster,* Treas.; Tom Blount, John Hamilton, Jeff Horney.
EIN: 561761750
Codes: FD

40885
Kulynych Family Foundation I, Inc.
(Formerly Petro Kulynych Foundation, Inc.)
450 Shady Ln.
Wilkesboro, NC 28697

Established in 1992 in NC.
Donor(s): Petro Kulynych.
Financial data (yr. ended 06/30/01): Grants paid, $289,050; assets, $6,899,683 (M); gifts received, $375,099; expenditures, $292,312; qualifying distributions, $284,724.
Limitations: Applications not accepted. Giving primarily in NC.
Officers: Petro Kulynych, Chair. and Treas.; Brenda Cline, Pres.; Dale Cline, V.P.; Roena B. Kulynych, Secy.
EIN: 237335353
Codes: FD

40886
William G. & Helen Hoffman Foundation
c/o First Union National Bank
401 S. Tyron, Ste. NC 1159
Charlotte, NC 28211
Application address: 190 River Rd., Summit, NJ 07901; FAX: (973) 598-3583
Contact: Tamara I. Morales, Trust Assoc.

Established in 1998 in NJ.
Financial data (yr. ended 12/31/01): Grants paid, $287,700; assets, $5,798,181 (M); expenditures, $336,134; qualifying distributions, $268,450.
Limitations: Giving primarily in NJ or NJ chapters of national organizations.
Application information: FAX or hand-delivered proposals are not accepted. Application form required.
Trustee: First Union National Bank.
EIN: 237981677
Codes: FD

40887
J. H. & R. H. Rumbaugh Foundation
c/o First Union National Bank
401 S. Tryon St., NC1159
Charlotte, NC 28288

Established in 1986 in FL.
Financial data (yr. ended 03/31/02): Grants paid, $285,539; assets, $7,229,816 (M); expenditures, $361,898; qualifying distributions, $265,539.
Limitations: Applications not accepted. Giving primarily in PA.
Application information: Contributes only to pre-selected organizations.
Trustee: First Union National Bank.
EIN: 596851866
Codes: FD

40888
William R. and Jeanne H. Jordan Family Foundation
c/o William R. Jordan
2014 Litho Pl.
Fayetteville, NC 28304-2518

Established in 1995 in NC.
Donor(s): William R. Jordan, Jeanne H. Jordan Revocable Trust.
Financial data (yr. ended 12/31/01): Grants paid, $284,116; assets, $291,779 (M); expenditures, $295,764; qualifying distributions, $284,116.
Limitations: Applications not accepted. Giving primarily in NC; some giving also in FL.
Application information: Contributes only to pre-selected organizations.
Officers: Jeanne H. Jordan, Pres.; William R. Jordan, V.P.
EIN: 561893648
Codes: FD

40889
Whitener Foundation
1941 English Rd., Box E
High Point, NC 27261-1941

Established in 1973.
Financial data (yr. ended 12/31/00): Grants paid, $280,000; assets, $5,057,957 (M); expenditures, $293,362; qualifying distributions, $276,475.
Limitations: Applications not accepted. Giving primarily in NC.
Application information: Contributes only to pre-selected organizations.
Officers and Directors:* Marshall Pittman,* Pres.; Edgar Whitener,* V.P.; Lorene Ward,* Secy.-Treas.
EIN: 521467548
Codes: FD

40890
Triangle Bancorp Foundation
134 N. Church St.
Rocky Mount, NC 27804
Contact: Michael S. Patterson, Pres.

Established in NC in 1998.
Donor(s): Triangle Bancorp.
Financial data (yr. ended 12/31/99): Grants paid, $278,599; assets, $1,772 (M); gifts received, $161,750; expenditures, $278,642; qualifying distributions, $278,598.
Officers and Directors:* Michael S. Patterson,* Pres.; Alexander M. Donaldson, V.P.; Debra L. Lee,* V.P.; Diana M. Morde, Secy.; Lisa F. Campbell, Treas.; Steven R. Ogburn, Edward O. Wessell.
EIN: 562075242
Codes: CS

40891
O. Leonard Moretz Foundation Trust, Inc.
c/o First Union National Corp.
401 S. Tryon St., Ste. NC1159
Charlotte, NC 28288-1159

Established in 1980.
Financial data (yr. ended 07/31/01): Grants paid, $276,000; assets, $4,160,131 (M); expenditures, $315,354; qualifying distributions, $267,230.
Limitations: Applications not accepted. Giving primarily in NC.
Application information: Contributes only to pre-selected organizations.
Trustee: First Union National Corp.
EIN: 580012117
Codes: FD

40892
Michael and Laura Brader-Araje Foundation
2530 Meridian Pkwy., 3rd Fl.
Durham, NC 27713

Established in 2000 in NC.
Donor(s): Michael Brader-Araje, Laura Brader-Araje.
Financial data (yr. ended 12/31/01): Grants paid, $266,500; assets, $4,622,756 (M); expenditures, $764,305; qualifying distributions, $264,706.
Limitations: Applications not accepted. Giving on a national basis.
Application information: Contributes only to pre-selected organizations.
Officers: Michael Brader-Araje, Pres. and Secy.; Laura Brader-Araje, V.P. and Treas.
EIN: 562205579
Codes: FD

40893
C. Hamilton Sloan Foundation
P.O. Box 26006
Raleigh, NC 27611
Contact: Ann C. Sloan, Tr.

Established in 1994 in NC.
Financial data (yr. ended 12/31/01): Grants paid, $264,300; assets, $381,529 (M); gifts received, $246,880; expenditures, $277,737; qualifying distributions, $268,065.
Limitations: Applications not accepted. Giving on a national basis.
Application information: Unsolicited requests for funds not accepted.
Trustees: Ann C. Sloan, O. Temple Sloan, Jr., W. Gerald Thornton.
EIN: 561870847
Codes: FD

40894
G. Gregory Smith Family Foundation, Inc.
5201 Hedrick Dr.
Greensboro, NC 27410
Contact: John R. Perkinson, Jr.

Established in 1994 in NC.
Donor(s): George Gregory Smith.
Financial data (yr. ended 09/30/01): Grants paid, $263,140; assets, $2,580,215 (M); gifts received, $200,000; expenditures, $271,553; qualifying distributions, $262,730.
Limitations: Giving primarily in Greensboro, NC.
Officers: George Gregory Smith, Pres.; George Gregory Smith, Jr., V.P.; Carol Belk Smith, Secy.-Treas.
EIN: 561902026
Codes: FD

40895
L. Robertson Foundation
c/o Bank of America
Bank of America Plz., NC1-002-11-18
Charlotte, NC 28255
Application address: 7 N. Laurens St., Greenville, SC 29601
Contact: William A. Bridges

Established in 1997 in SC.
Donor(s): Linda M. Robertson.
Financial data (yr. ended 12/31/01): Grants paid, $259,006; assets, $791,496 (M); expenditures, $278,385; qualifying distributions, $269,857.
Limitations: Giving primarily in SC.
Trustee: Bank of America.
EIN: 582307536
Codes: FD

40896
The Doak Finch Foundation
c/o Lula Cook, Bank of America
380 Knollwood St.
Winston-Salem, NC 27103 (336) 386-7581
Application address: 10 Welloskie Dr., Thomasville, NC 27360
Contact: Mr. J.C. Dorety

Trust established in 1961 in NC.
Donor(s): Doak Finch.‡
Financial data (yr. ended 10/31/01): Grants paid, $257,100; assets, $4,170,154 (M); expenditures, $291,153; qualifying distributions, $265,155.
Limitations: Giving limited to the Thomasville, NC, area.
Application information: Application form not required.
Trustee Bank: Bank of America.
EIN: 566042823
Codes: FD

40897
The Wilson L. Smith Family Foundation
113 Canteberry Dr.
Salisbury, NC 28144 (704) 636-9142
Contact: Ronald L. Smith

Established in 1989 in NC.
Donor(s): Ronald L. Smith, Wilson L. Smith.
Financial data (yr. ended 12/31/01): Grants paid, $253,035; assets, $5,651,949 (M); gifts received, $116,288; expenditures, $269,219; qualifying distributions, $253,035.
Limitations: Giving primarily in Salisbury, NC.
Officers: Ronald L. Smith, Pres.; Wilson L. Smith, V.P.; Timothy R. Smith, Treas.
EIN: 561658247
Codes: FD

40898
Edwin B. Garrigues Trust
401 S. Tryon St., 4th Fl.
Charlotte, NC 28288-1159
Application address: c/o Duane Morris, LLP, 1 Liberty Pl., Philadelphia, PA 19103
Contact: Seymour Wagner

Established in 1922 in PA.
Financial data (yr. ended 12/31/01): Grants paid, $252,250; assets, $4,583,820 (M); expenditures, $275,027; qualifying distributions, $252,426.
Limitations: Giving primarily in the Philadelphia, PA, area.
Trustees: Robert W. Denious, First Union National Bank.
EIN: 236220616
Codes: FD

40899
Kenan Family Foundation
P.O. Box 4150
Chapel Hill, NC 27515-4150

Established in 1984 in NC.
Donor(s): Frank H. Kenan.‡
Financial data (yr. ended 12/31/01): Grants paid, $249,500; assets, $4,729,553 (M); expenditures, $261,631; qualifying distributions, $258,976.
Limitations: Applications not accepted. Giving primarily in NC.
Application information: Contributes only to pre-selected organizations.
Officers and Directors:* Elizabeth Kenan Howell,* Pres.; Thomas S. Kenan III,* V.P. and Treas.; Annice Hawkins Kenan,* V.P.; Braxton Schell,* Secy.; Owen Gwyn, Jr., Elizabeth Price Kenan, Owen G. Kenan.
EIN: 581587972
Codes: FD

40900
Sarah H. Sutherland Charitable Trust
c/o B.B. & T., Trust Dept.
P.O. Box 1270
Winston-Salem, NC 27102-1270
E-mail: rhand@BBTnet.com
Contact: Ray Hand, V.P., B.B. & T.

Established in 1995 in NC.
Financial data (yr. ended 12/31/00): Grants paid, $248,829; assets, $5,940,398 (M); expenditures, $291,478; qualifying distributions, $244,863.
Limitations: Applications not accepted. Giving primarily in NC.
Application information: Contributes only to pre-selected organizations.
Trustee: B.B. & T.
EIN: 566456377
Codes: FD

40901
Thomas & Kate Fonville Trust Account
1018 Harvey St.
Raleigh, NC 27608-2332

Established in 1995 in NC.
Donor(s): Thomas L. Fonville.
Financial data (yr. ended 12/31/01): Grants paid, $239,700; assets, $783,537 (M); gifts received, $257,293; expenditures, $241,988; qualifying distributions, $239,700.
Limitations: Applications not accepted. Giving primarily in NC.
Application information: Contributes only to pre-selected organizations.
Officer: Thomas L. Fonville, Chair.
Trustees: John C. Morisey, Jr., Frank L. Robuck, Jr.
EIN: 566460501
Codes: FD2

40902
Windmill Foundation
c/o First Union National Bank
401 S. Tryon St., Ste. NC 1159
Charlotte, NC 28288-1159

Established in 2000 in PA.
Financial data (yr. ended 12/31/00): Grants paid, $234,750; assets, $1,363,770 (M); expenditures, $239,663; qualifying distributions, $234,750.
Limitations: Applications not accepted.
Application information: Contributes only to pre-selected organizations.
Agent: First Union National Bank.
EIN: 256707437
Codes: FD2

40903
Smith Family Foundation
(Formerly Liberty Hosiery Mills Foundation)
c/o Trust Co. of the South
3041 S. Church St.
Burlington, NC 27215
Contact: John H. Slayton, Pres. and C.E.O., Trust Co. of the South

Established in 1952 in NC.
Financial data (yr. ended 06/30/01): Grants paid, $234,350; assets, $4,299,323 (M); gifts received, $3,695; expenditures, $332,545; qualifying distributions, $231,434.
Limitations: Applications not accepted. Giving limited to Alamance, Orange, Guilford, Durham, Caswell, Chatham, Randolph, Montgomery, and Moore counties, NC.
Application information: Contributes only to pre-selected organizations.
Trustees: J. Harold Smith, Sr., Trust Co. of the South.
EIN: 566040787
Codes: FD2

40904
Trent Ragland, Jr. Trust
c/o First Union National Bank
401 S. Tryon St., 4th Fl.
Charlotte, NC 28288-1159
Contact: Carolyn M. Hoke

Established in 1959 in NC.
Donor(s): W. Trent Ragland, Jr.
Financial data (yr. ended 12/31/01): Grants paid, $233,559; assets, $3,151,452 (M); expenditures, $247,489; qualifying distributions, $230,142.
Limitations: Applications not accepted. Giving primarily in FL, NC, and VA.
Application information: Contributes only to pre-selected organizations.
Trustee: First Union National Bank.
EIN: 566035980
Codes: FD2

40905
W. H. Brady Foundation, Inc.
P.O. Box 610
Maggie Valley, NC 28751 (828) 926-1413
Shipping address: 1461 Soco Rd., Maggie Valley, NC 28751; FAX: (828) 926-0167; URL: http://www.bradyfoundation.org
Contact: Elizabeth P. Pungello, Pres.

Incorporated in 1956 in WI.
Financial data (yr. ended 06/30/02): Grants paid, $233,500; assets, $19,891,554 (M); expenditures, $552,684; qualifying distributions, $441,452.
Limitations: Giving on a national basis.
Application information: See Web site for information.
Officers and Directors:* Elizabeth P. Pungello,* Pres.; Peter J. Lettenberger,* V.P.; Elizabeth Haynes, Secy. and Prog. Off.; Phillip M. McGoohan,* Treas.; Kimberly O. Dennis, Heather R. Higgins, Sherry K. Hoel.
EIN: 396064733
Codes: FD2

40906
J. K. Gholston Trust
Bank of America Plz., NC1-002-11-18
Charlotte, NC 28255
Application address: c/o Bank of America, 600 Peachtree St., Ste. 1100, Atlanta, GA 30308-2214, tel.: (404) 607-5307
Contact: Amber Gratwick, V.P., Bank of America

Established in 1967 in GA.
Donor(s): J. Knox Gholston.‡
Financial data (yr. ended 02/28/01): Grants paid, $229,774; assets, $7,068,467 (M); gifts received, $12,999; expenditures, $277,847; qualifying distributions, $249,085.
Limitations: Giving limited to the Comer, GA, area.
Application information: Scholarship applicants must be graduates of Comer Elementary School and Madison County High School. Application form required.
Trustee: Bank of America.
EIN: 586056879
Codes: FD2

40907
George & Frances London Educational Foundation
P.O. Box 20389
Raleigh, NC 27619-0389 (919) 787-8880
Contact: Howard E. Manning, Sr., Tr.

Established in 1996 in NC.
Donor(s): Frances P. London.
Financial data (yr. ended 12/31/01): Grants paid, $228,748; assets, $838,034 (M); gifts received, $79,361; expenditures, $235,942; qualifying distributions, $228,747.
Limitations: Giving limited to Bertie, Graham, Hertford, Northampton, Pasquotank, Perquimans, Swain, and Warren counties, NC.
Application information: Application form required.
Trustees: David D. Dahl, Frances P. London, Howard E. Manning, Sr.
EIN: 582233144
Codes: FD2, GTI

40908
The Marion Stedman Covington Foundation
P.O. Box 29304
Greensboro, NC 27429-9304 (336) 282-0480
Contact: Alexa Aycock, Grants Coord.

Established in 1986 in NC.
Donor(s): Marion Stedman Covington.
Financial data (yr. ended 12/31/00): Grants paid, $225,035; assets, $4,963,848 (M); expenditures, $291,568; qualifying distributions, $270,465.
Limitations: Giving primarily in NC, with emphasis on Guilford and Randolph counties, for human services.
Publications: Informational brochure (including application guidelines), grants list.
Application information: Application form required.
Officer and Trustees:* Stephen C. Hassenfelt,* Chair.; Kathleen Crockett, Jane C. Hilderbrand, J. Myrick Howard.
EIN: 566286555
Codes: FD2

40909
Thomas Henry Wilson & Family Foundation
3709 Brandon Dr.
High Point, NC 27265

Established in 1967.
Donor(s): Thomas Henry Wilson, Jr., James Douglas Wilson, Janet H. Wilson, and members of the Wilson family.
Financial data (yr. ended 12/31/00): Grants paid, $224,658; assets, $3,936,064 (M); gifts received, $5,974; expenditures, $242,677; qualifying distributions, $209,018.
Limitations: Applications not accepted. Giving on a national basis.
Application information: Contributes only to pre-selected organizations.
Trustees: Dorothy Wilson Chappell, Anne Wilson Payne, Katherine Wilson Singleton, Daniel Culp Wilson, James D. Wilson, Jr., John B. Wilson, Sr., John B. Wilson, Jr.
Agents: Barbara Bullin, James Douglas Wilson, Sr.
EIN: 566125766
Codes: FD2

40910
The Donald & Elizabeth Cooke Foundation
P.O. Box 1940
Southern Pines, NC 28388-1940
Contact: Sandy G. Patterson, Pres.

Established in 1980 in NC.
Donor(s): Elizabeth G. Cooke.‡
Financial data (yr. ended 12/31/01): Grants paid, $223,700; assets, $4,769,604 (M); expenditures, $267,599; qualifying distributions, $220,934.
Limitations: Applications not accepted. Giving primarily in NC.
Application information: Unsolicited requests for funds not accepted.
Officers and Directors:* Sandy G. Patterson,* Pres.; Mary McLauchlin Pope,* V.P. and Secy.; Debbie Riley Hobbs.
EIN: 581408721
Codes: FD2

40911
John and Frances Morisey Trust Account
3601 Williamsborough Ct.
Raleigh, NC 27609

Established around 1993.
Donor(s): John C. Morisey.
Financial data (yr. ended 12/31/01): Grants paid, $220,950; assets, $1,071,938 (M); gifts received, $349,902; expenditures, $222,150; qualifying distributions, $220,950.
Limitations: Applications not accepted. Giving on a national basis, with emphasis on NC.
Application information: Contributes only to pre-selected organizations.
Trustees: Frances D. Morisey, John C. Morisey, Jr., John C. Morisey III.
EIN: 566419428
Codes: FD2

40912
Edward E. Crutchfield Family Foundation
401 S. Tryon St., Ste. 2880
Charlotte, NC 28288

Established in 2000 in NC.
Donor(s): Edward E. Crutchfield.
Financial data (yr. ended 12/31/01): Grants paid, $220,000; assets, $4,307,577 (M); gifts received, $580,757; expenditures, $231,799; qualifying distributions, $223,748.
Limitations: Applications not accepted. Giving primarily in NC.
Application information: Contributes only to pre-selected organizations.

40912—NORTH CAROLINA

Officers: Edward E. Crutchfield, Chair. and Pres.; Sarah Crutchfield Davis, V.P.; Edward E. Crutchfield, Jr., Secy.-Treas.
EIN: 562220389

40913
Mary Norris Preyer Fund
c/o Piedmont Financial Co. Inc.
P.O. Box 20124
Greensboro, NC 27420-0124 (336) 274-5471
Contact: Jane Preyer, Admin.

Established in 1965 in NC.
Donor(s): members of the Preyer family.
Financial data (yr. ended 06/30/01): Grants paid, $220,000; assets, $4,563,372 (M); expenditures, $261,704; qualifying distributions, $226,033.
Limitations: Giving primarily in NC.
Application information: Application form not required.
Trustees: Elizabeth P. Adamson, Ellen Preyer Davis, Mary Norris Preyer Oglesby, Frederick L. Preyer, Kelly A. Preyer, Norris W. Preyer, Sr., Norris W. Preyer, Jr., Robert O. Preyer.
EIN: 566068167
Codes: FD2

40914
The Harkey Foundation, Inc.
1043 E. Morehead St., Ste. 300
Charlotte, NC 28204-2800

Established in 1989 in NC.
Donor(s): Elizabeth A. Harkey.
Financial data (yr. ended 12/31/00): Grants paid, $218,550; assets, $1,155,123 (M); expenditures, $231,094; qualifying distributions, $219,269.
Limitations: Applications not accepted. Giving primarily in NC.
Application information: Contributes only to pre-selected organizations.
Officers: Henry A. Harkey, Pres.; Averill C. Harkey, V.P.
EIN: 561643562
Codes: FD2

40915
Gambrell Family Foundation
6100 Fairview Rd., Ste. 640
Charlotte, NC 28211 (704) 553-8296
Contact: Sarah Belk Gambrell, Pres.

Established in 1998 in NC.
Donor(s): Sarah Belk Gambrell.
Financial data (yr. ended 12/31/01): Grants paid, $215,000; assets, $110,571 (M); gifts received, $208,089; expenditures, $218,415; qualifying distributions, $215,000.
Limitations: Giving primarily in Charlotte, NC.
Officers: Sarah Belk Gambrell, Pres.; Sarah Gambrell Knight, V.P.; Larry Estridge, Secy.
EIN: 562120679
Codes: FD2

40916
The Katherine And Thomas Belk Foundation, Inc.
2801 W. Tyvola Rd.
Charlotte, NC 28217-4500
Contact: Paul B. Wyche, Jr.

Established in 2001 in NC.
Donor(s): Katherine M. Belk.
Financial data (yr. ended 12/31/01): Grants paid, $213,078; assets, $3,265,876 (M); expenditures, $223,451; qualifying distributions, $211,790.
Limitations: Giving primarily in NC.
Officers and Directors:* Katherine Belk Morris,* Pres.; H. W. McKay Belk,* V.P.; Thomas M. Belk, Jr.,* V.P.; Katherine M. Belk,* Secy.; John R. Belk,* Treas.

EIN: 562220828
Codes: FD2

40917
Gambrill Foundation
c/o Wachovia Bank of North Carolina, N.A.
P.O. Box 3099
Winston-Salem, NC 27150-7153
Application address: c/o Wachovia Bank of North Carolina, N.A., 1401 Main St., Ste. 501, Columbia, SC 29226-9365, tel.: (803) 765-3671
Contact: Jerry Lane, Tr. Off., Wachovia Bank of North Carolina, N.A.

Established in 1967.
Donor(s): Anne J. Gambrill.‡
Financial data (yr. ended 12/31/01): Grants paid, $212,935; assets, $4,674,321 (M); expenditures, $253,679; qualifying distributions, $216,552.
Limitations: Giving limited to Anderson, SC.
Trustees: Lila F. Albergotti, Harry W. Findley, Robert M. Rainey, William L. Watkins, F. McKinnon Wilkinson, Wachovia Bank of North Carolina, N.A.
EIN: 576029520
Codes: FD2

40918
James H. and Jesse E. Millis Foundation, Inc.
c/o Wachovia Bank, N.A.
P.O. Box 3099
Winston-Salem, NC 27150-1022
(336) 732-5372
Application address: P.O. Box 5186, High Point, NC 27262, tel.: (336) 885-6585
Contact: Linda G. Tilley, Sr. V.P.

Established in 1988 in NC.
Donor(s): Jesse E. Millis, James H. Millis, Sr.
Financial data (yr. ended 12/31/01): Grants paid, $212,750; assets, $6,538,891 (M); expenditures, $247,380; qualifying distributions, $245,497.
Limitations: Giving limited to High Point and Guilford counties, NC.
Application information: Application form required.
Officer and Directors:* James H. Millis, Sr.,* Chair.; Molly M. Hedgecock, Emily M. Hiatt, James H. Millis, Jr., Jesse E. Millis, William B. Millis, Jean S. Stockton.
EIN: 581811274
Codes: FD2

40919
The Leonard G. Herring Family Foundation, Inc.
310 Coffey St.
North Wilkesboro, NC 28659
Contact: Leonard G. Herring, Pres.

Established in 1994 in NC.
Donor(s): Leonard G. Herring.
Financial data (yr. ended 12/31/01): Grants paid, $210,920; assets, $8,750,058 (M); gifts received, $647,200; expenditures, $213,753; qualifying distributions, $210,920.
Limitations: Applications not accepted.
Application information: Contributes only to pre-selected organizations.
Officers: Leonard G. Herring, Pres.; Rozelia S. Herring, V.P.; Sandra Herring Gaddy, Secy.; Albert Lee Herring, Treas.
EIN: 561881015
Codes: FD2

40920
William Harold Smith Charitable Trust
1105 Airport Rd.
Marion, NC 28752 (828) 652-9443
Contact: Matt Smith, Tr.

Established in 1998 in NC.

Financial data (yr. ended 12/31/01): Grants paid, $210,501; assets, $4,129,194 (M); expenditures, $221,877; qualifying distributions, $217,028.
Limitations: Giving primarily in McDowell County, NC.
Application information: Applications are available in McDowell High School guidance office. Application form required.
Trustee: Matt Smith.
EIN: 566526359
Codes: FD2, GTI

40921
The Yeargan Foundation Charitable Trust
7777 White Oak Rd.
Garner, NC 27529-8808

Established in 1998.
Financial data (yr. ended 12/31/01): Grants paid, $209,849; assets, $3,880,595 (M); gifts received, $245,458; expenditures, $219,272; qualifying distributions, $208,405.
Limitations: Applications not accepted. Giving primarily in NC.
Application information: Contributes only to pre-selected organizations.
Trustees: Flora A. Yeargan, Rowann Yeargan, Sherman Yeargan.
EIN: 581846281
Codes: FD2

40922
Clark and Ruby Baker Foundation
c/o Bank of America
Bank of America Plz., NC1-002-11-18
Charlotte, NC 28255
Application address: c/o Bank of America, 600 Peachtree St., Ste. 1100, Atlanta, GA 30308
Contact: Amber Gratwick, Secy.

Established in 1974 in GA.
Donor(s): Clark A. Baker.‡
Financial data (yr. ended 12/31/01): Grants paid, $209,740; assets, $3,028,456 (M); expenditures, $223,498; qualifying distributions, $209,640.
Limitations: Giving limited to GA.
Application information: GA residents must apply through college or university for scholarships.
Officers: Virlyn B. Moore, Jr., Chair.; Amber Gratwick, Secy.
Trustee: Bank of America.
EIN: 581429097
Codes: FD2, GTI

40923
J. William Gholston Trust
c/o Bank of America
Bank of America Plz., NC1-002-11-18
Charlotte, NC 28255

Financial data (yr. ended 12/31/01): Grants paid, $209,135; assets, $3,656,373 (M); expenditures, $231,855; qualifying distributions, $216,115.
Limitations: Applications not accepted. Giving primarily in GA.
Application information: Contributes only to pre-selected organizations.
Trustee: Bank of America.
EIN: 586027903
Codes: FD2

40924
The Donald H. & Barbara K. Bernstein Family Foundation
3723 Foxcroft Rd.
Charlotte, NC 28211-3752
Contact: Donald H. Bernstein, Pres.

Established in 1988 in NC.
Donor(s): Donald H. Bernstein, Barbara K. Bernstein.

Financial data (yr. ended 12/31/01): Grants paid, $208,381; assets, $932,882 (M); gifts received, $118; expenditures, $218,819; qualifying distributions, $208,811.
Limitations: Applications not accepted. Giving primarily in Charlotte, NC.
Application information: Contributes only to pre-selected organizations.
Officers: Donald H. Bernstein, Pres.; Barbara K. Bernstein, Mgr.
EIN: 581804268
Codes: FD2

40925
Harold M. Cole Scholarship Trust
c/o Branch Banking and Trust Co.
P.O. Drawer 1149
Pinehurst, NC 28374 (910) 215-2620

Established in 1987 in NC.
Donor(s): Harold M. Cole.‡
Financial data (yr. ended 03/31/02): Grants paid, $206,367; assets, $1,828,203 (M); expenditures, $242,007; qualifying distributions, $206,367.
Limitations: Giving limited to Moore County, NC, residents.
Application information: Application form required.
Trustees: Scott A. Brewer, Patrice Cain, Frankie Page, Jr.
EIN: 586212292
Codes: FD2, GTI

40926
Michael W. Haley Foundation, Inc.
c/o Mike Winnig
228 W. Market St.
Greensboro, NC 27401-2504

Established in 1990 in NC.
Financial data (yr. ended 10/31/99): Grants paid, $204,773; assets, $5,295,780 (M); expenditures, $213,471; qualifying distributions, $204,773.
Limitations: Applications not accepted. Giving primarily in Greensboro, NC.
Application information: Contributes only to pre-selected organizations.
Officers and Directors:* Michael W. Haley,* Pres. and Treas.; Lynn C. Haley,* Secy.; Leigh H. Jones, Elizabeth L. Stanley.
EIN: 561720197
Codes: FD2

40927
Flowers Charitable Foundation
c/o First Union National Bank
401 S. Tryon, NC1159
Charlotte, NC 28288-1159

Established around 1982.
Donor(s): Frank S. Flowers.‡
Financial data (yr. ended 12/31/01): Grants paid, $203,331; assets, $3,729,605 (M); expenditures, $231,914; qualifying distributions, $202,862.
Limitations: Giving primarily in NJ, with emphasis on Gloucester and Salem counties, and the boroughs of Paulsboro and Wenonah; some giving also in Philadelphia, PA.
Application information: Application form not required.
Trustee: First Union National Bank.
EIN: 226318172
Codes: FD2

40928
Dornick Foundation, Inc.
(Formerly Cross Creek Foundation, Inc.)
18 Hilltop Rd.
Asheville, NC 28803

Established in 1997 in NC.
Donor(s): William Idema.
Financial data (yr. ended 12/31/01): Grants paid, $202,599; assets, $12,454,468 (M); expenditures, $241,015; qualifying distributions, $202,599.
Limitations: Applications not accepted. Giving primarily in NC.
Application information: Contributes only to pre-selected organizations.
Officers: Robert C. Pew III, Pres. and Treas.; Susan H. Taylor, Secy.
Board Member: Kate Wolters.
EIN: 562057825
Codes: FD2

40929
Karl and Anna Ginter Foundation
c/o Bank of America
101 S. Tryon St., NC1-002-22-22
Charlotte, NC 28255 (704) 386-9189
Contact: David Hughes

Established in 1968 in NC.
Donor(s): Karl Ginter,‡ Anna Ginter.‡
Financial data (yr. ended 12/31/01): Grants paid, $202,585; assets, $2,777,158 (M); expenditures, $207,377; qualifying distributions, $203,308.
Limitations: Giving limited to Mecklenburg County, NC.
Application information: Funds are mostly committed. Application form not required.
Directors: Esley O. Anderson, Joseph W. Grier, Jr., Don Sanders.
Trustee: Bank of America.
EIN: 566094355
Codes: FD2

40930
The Rauch Family Foundation
P.O. Box 1970
Southern Pines, NC 28388

Established in 1989 in NC.
Donor(s): Dudley A. Rauch, Cecilia B. Rauch, Henry E. Rauch.‡
Financial data (yr. ended 12/31/01): Grants paid, $202,000; assets, $2,805,460 (M); gifts received, $300,000; expenditures, $288,252; qualifying distributions, $202,000.
Limitations: Applications not accepted. Giving primarily in CA and Washington, DC.
Application information: Contributes only to pre-selected organizations.
Officers and Directors:* Dudley A. Rauch,* Pres. and Treas.; Cecilia B. Rauch,* V.P. and Secy.; Heather B.R. Watkins,* V.P.
EIN: 581888280

40931
The Betty J. and J. Stanley Livingstone Charitable Foundation, Inc.
119 Chestnut Tree Rd.
Mooresville, NC 28117-7328

Established in 1986 in NC.
Donor(s): Betty J. Livingstone.‡
Financial data (yr. ended 05/31/01): Grants paid, $201,733; assets, $3,433,384 (M); expenditures, $258,431; qualifying distributions, $212,003.
Limitations: Applications not accepted. Giving primarily in Charlotte, NC.
Application information: Contributes only to pre-selected organizations.
Officers: Margaret D. Callen, Pres.; David M. Bishop, Secy.; Mary S. Stokes, Treas.
EIN: 566233211
Codes: FD2

40932
Kulynych Family Foundation II, Inc.
450 Shady Ln.
Wilkesboro, NC 28697

Established in 1996 in NC.
Donor(s): Petro Kulynych.
Financial data (yr. ended 06/30/01): Grants paid, $201,600; assets, $5,743,117 (M); gifts received, $1,127,147; expenditures, $204,271; qualifying distributions, $198,635.
Limitations: Applications not accepted.
Application information: Contributes only to pre-selected organizations.
Officers: Petro Kulynych, Chair. and Treas.; Janice Story, Pres.; Thomas E. Story, V.P.; Roena Kulynych, Secy.
EIN: 561982360
Codes: FD2

40933
The Anne Shuford McBryde Family Foundation
P.O. Box 1768
Laurinburg, NC 28353-1768
Application address: 8200 X-Way Rd., Gibson, NC 28343
Contact: Anne S. McBryde, Pres.

Established in 1994 in NC.
Donor(s): Anne S. McBryde.
Financial data (yr. ended 12/31/01): Grants paid, $200,665; assets, $2,029,997 (M); gifts received, $156,489; expenditures, $206,662; qualifying distributions, $198,625.
Limitations: Giving primarily in NC.
Officers: Anne S. McBryde, Pres.; Anne S. McKenzie, V.P.; Barbara M. Scott, Secy.; Charles D. Smith, Treas.
EIN: 561876412
Codes: FD2

40934
Martha and Spencer Love Foundation
c/o First Union National Bank
401 S. Tryon St., 4th Fl.
Charlotte, NC 28288-1159

Trust established in 1947 in NC.
Donor(s): J. Spencer Love,‡ Martha E. Love Ayers.
Financial data (yr. ended 12/31/01): Grants paid, $200,000; assets, $2,583,562 (M); expenditures, $219,875; qualifying distributions, $199,366.
Limitations: Applications not accepted. Giving primarily in NC.
Application information: Contributes only to pre-selected organizations.
Trustee: First Union National Bank.
EIN: 566040789
Codes: FD2

40935
The Cary Foundation, Inc.
(Formerly The Bray Cary Foundation, Inc.)
301 S. Tryon St., Ste. 35127
Charlotte, NC 28202-1915 (704) 348-9667
Contact: A. Bray Cary, Jr., Pres.

Established in 1996.
Donor(s): A. Bray Cary, Jr.
Financial data (yr. ended 12/31/00): Grants paid, $199,350; assets, $4,634,873 (M); gifts received, $30,000; expenditures, $210,749; qualifying distributions, $197,232.
Officers and Directors:* A. Bray Cary, Jr.,* Pres. and Treas.; Dianne S. Cary,* V.P.; A. Stuart McKaig III,* Secy.
EIN: 562002202
Codes: FD2

40936
Blue Bell Foundation
c/o Wachovia Bank, N.A.
P.O. Box 3099
Winston-Salem, NC 27150-7153
(336) 373-3580
Application address: P.O. Box 21488, Greensboro, NC 27420, tel.: (910) 373-3412
Contact: Charles Conkin, V.P., Human Resources

Trust established in 1944 in NC.
Donor(s): Blue Bell, Inc., Wrangler.
Financial data (yr. ended 12/31/01): Grants paid, $198,587; assets, $6,274,401 (M); expenditures, $249,231; qualifying distributions, $200,587.
Limitations: Giving primarily in areas where corporation has plants.
Advisory Committee: D.P. Laws, Robert H. Matthews, T.L. Weatherford.
Trustee: Wachovia Bank, N.A.
EIN: 566041057
Codes: CS, FD2, CD

40937
Almena C. & Malcolm P. McLean Trust
P.O. Box 1368
Lumberton, NC 28359-1368

Established in 1964.
Donor(s): John L. McLean, John P. McLean.
Financial data (yr. ended 12/31/01): Grants paid, $196,158; assets, $3,760,504 (M); gifts received, $311,301; expenditures, $217,409; qualifying distributions, $195,786.
Limitations: Giving primarily in NC.
Trustees: Isabelle G. McLean, John L. McLean, John P. McLean.
EIN: 566065281
Codes: FD2

40938
The Munther and Janet Qubain Foundation
7405 Spyglass Way
Raleigh, NC 27615-5480

Established in 2000 in NC.
Donor(s): Munther E. Qubain, Janet A. Qubain.
Financial data (yr. ended 12/31/01): Grants paid, $194,356; assets, $1,357,462 (M); expenditures, $249,959; qualifying distributions, $194,650.
Limitations: Applications not accepted. Giving primarily in NC.
Application information: Contributes only to pre-selected organizations.
Officers and Directors:* Munther E. Qubain,* Pres.; Janet A. Qubain,* V.P. and Secy.-Treas.
EIN: 562207553
Codes: FD2

40939
High Point Community Foundation
P.O. Box 1371
High Point, NC 27261-1371

Financial data (yr. ended 06/30/00): Grants paid, $193,065; assets, $9,660,917 (M); gifts received, $1,434,287; expenditures, $301,311.
Limitations: Giving limited to the High Point, NC, area.
Officers and Trustees:* James F. Morgan,* Chair.; George Erath,* Vice-Chair.; Bill Horney,* Vice-Chair.; Bill McGuinn,* Vice-Chair.; Jim Millis, Sr.,* Vice-Chair.; Phil Phillips,* Vice-Chair.; Nido Qubein,* Vice-Chair.; Marsha Slane,* Vice-Chair.; Charles A. Green,* Secy.; Charles L. Odom,* Treas.; Paul Lessard, Exec. Dir.; Bob Amos, Jr., and 23 additional trustees.
EIN: 561695787
Codes: CM, FD2

40940
Oscar & Mona Sokol Foundation
c/o Bank of America
Bank of America Plz., NC1-002-11-18
Charlotte, NC 28255
Application address: c/o Charles S. Goldberg, 61 Broad St., Charleston, SC 29401, tel.: (803) 720-2800

Established in 1994 in SC.
Financial data (yr. ended 12/31/00): Grants paid, $189,181; assets, $4,162,065 (M); expenditures, $283,591; qualifying distributions, $208,771.
Limitations: Giving on a national basis.
Trustees: Charles S. Goldberg, Ivan N. Nossokoff, Maurice N. Weintraub, M.D., Bank of America.
EIN: 576139525
Codes: FD2

40941
Nicholas Bunn Boddie, Sr. and Lucy Mayo Boddie Foundation
c/o Boddie-Noell Enterprises, Inc.
P.O. Box 1908
Rocky Mount, NC 27802-1908
Contact: B. Mayo Boddie, Pres.

Established in 1996 in NC.
Donor(s): B. Mayo Boddie.
Financial data (yr. ended 12/31/01): Grants paid, $188,827; assets, $2,897,595 (M); expenditures, $223,410; qualifying distributions, $189,418.
Limitations: Giving primarily in the South.
Officers: B. Mayo Boddie, Pres.; William L. Boddie, V.P.; Michael W. Boddie, Secy.; B. Mayo Boddie, Jr., Treas.
EIN: 561678893
Codes: FD2

40942
The Ellis Charitable Foundation, Inc.
2596 Youngs Rd.
P.O. Box 2570
Southern Pines, NC 28388
Hillsboro, NC tel.: (919) 692-7246
Contact: M. Nixon Ellis, Tr.

Established in 1997 in NC.
Donor(s): M. Nixon Ellis.
Financial data (yr. ended 12/31/00): Grants paid, $188,816; assets, $1,852 (M); expenditures, $188,816; qualifying distributions, $188,816.
Limitations: Giving primarily in SC.
Trustees: Andrew Chew Ellis, Josephine T. Ellis, Lesley Taylor Ellis, M. Nixon Ellis.
EIN: 562056686
Codes: FD2

40943
Greensboro Jaycees Charitable Foundation, Inc.
401 N. Greene St.
Greensboro, NC 27401

Established in 1967.
Financial data (yr. ended 04/30/00): Grants paid, $187,827; assets, $119,158 (M); gifts received, $205,380; expenditures, $188,033; qualifying distributions, $187,827.
Limitations: Applications not accepted.
Application information: Contributes only to pre-selected organizations.
Officers: Leigh Ann Good, Chair.; Barbara Esquibel, Pres.; Randy Harris, V.P.; Krista McEachern, Secy.; Teresa Tebbs, Treas.
EIN: 566085407
Codes: FD2

40944
Charles and Irene Nanney Foundation
c/o D.P. Nanney
P.O. Box 935
Gastonia, NC 28053-0935

Established in 1961 in NC.
Donor(s): Charles P. Nanney,‡ Irene B. Nanney.‡
Financial data (yr. ended 12/31/01): Grants paid, $187,255; assets, $4,153,021 (M); expenditures, $200,273; qualifying distributions, $193,306.
Limitations: Applications not accepted. Giving primarily in NC.
Application information: Contributes only to pre-selected organizations.
Officer and Trustees:* D. Powell Nanney,* Pres.; Charles D. Gray III, David P. Nanney, Jr.
EIN: 566046763
Codes: FD2

40945
William Bruce Hutchison Charitable Trust
1341 E. Morehead St., Ste. 102
Charlotte, NC 28204

Financial data (yr. ended 12/31/00): Grants paid, $186,750; assets, $305,695 (M); expenditures, $189,249; qualifying distributions, $189,118.
Limitations: Applications not accepted.
Application information: Contributes only to pre-selected organizations.
Trustee: Allen A. Bailey.
EIN: 581368867
Codes: FD2

40946
Guzenhauser-Chapin Fund
c/o Piedmont Financial Co., Inc.
P.O. Box 20124
Greensboro, NC 27420
Contact: Chester F. Chapin, V.P.

Established in 1998 in NC.
Financial data (yr. ended 12/31/00): Grants paid, $186,100; assets, $7,542,776 (M); gifts received, $4,015,954; expenditures, $209,077; qualifying distributions, $179,991.
Limitations: Giving primarily in CA.
Officers and Directors:* Charles S. Chapin,* Pres.; Chester F. Chapin,* V.P.; Lynn R. Chapin Guzenhauser,* V.P.; Lisa Vinson Beaman,* Secy.; Samuel C. Chapin,* Treas.
EIN: 562089195
Codes: FD2

40947
The Florence Rogers Charitable Trust
P.O. Box 36006
Fayetteville, NC 28303-1006 (910) 484-2033
Contact: Nolan P. Clark, Tr.

Trust established in 1961 in NC.
Donor(s): Florence L. Rogers.‡
Financial data (yr. ended 03/31/02): Grants paid, $186,093; assets, $4,687,481 (M); expenditures, $371,462; qualifying distributions, $241,334.
Limitations: Giving primarily in Fayetteville, Cumberland County, and southeastern NC.
Publications: Informational brochure (including application guidelines).
Application information: Application form required.
Trustees: Nolan P. Clark, John C. Tally.
EIN: 566074515
Codes: FD2

40948
R. E. & Joan S. Allen Foundation, Inc.
401 S. Tryon St., 4th Fl.
Charlotte, NC 28288-1159
Contact: Dr. Karen Allen, Secy.

Established in 1991 in FL.
Donor(s): R.E. Allen.
Financial data (yr. ended 12/31/01): Grants paid, $185,000; assets, $0 (M); expenditures, $215,042; qualifying distributions, $199,750.
Limitations: Giving limited to residents of Kenton, OH.
Application information: Application form required.
Officers: R.E. Allen, Pres.; Rex Allen, V.P.; Richard Allen, V.P.; Karen Allen, Ph.D., Secy.
EIN: 650225533
Codes: FD2, GTI

40949
Charles Russell Wellons Foundation
3620 Cape Center Dr.
Fayetteville, NC 28304
Application address: P.O. Box 52328, Durham, NC 27717
Contact: William T. Allen, Pres.

Established in 1995 in NC.
Donor(s): Charles R. Wellons.
Financial data (yr. ended 12/31/00): Grants paid, $181,535; assets, $3,323,077 (M); expenditures, $334,628; qualifying distributions, $179,632.
Application information: Application form required.
Officers: William T. Allen, Pres.; Charles B. Nye, V.P.; Charlene Hamlett, Secy.-Treas.
EIN: 561889755
Codes: FD2

40950
The Griffin Endowment
1333 Queens Rd., No. 103
Charlotte, NC 28207
FAX: (704) 375-8691
Contact: Clarence A. Griffin, Jr., Pres.

Established in 1990 in NC.
Donor(s): Clarence A. Griffin, Elizabeth S. Griffin.
Financial data (yr. ended 06/30/01): Grants paid, $181,305; assets, $3,799,665 (M); expenditures, $242,737; qualifying distributions, $181,305.
Limitations: Applications not accepted. Giving on a national basis, with some emphasis on Charlotte, NC.
Application information: Unsolicited applications not reviewed.
Officers and Directors:* Clarence A. Griffin, Jr.,* Pres.; Clarence A. Griffin III,* V.P.; Elizabeth S. Griffin,* Secy.; Haynes G. Griffin,* Treas.
EIN: 561687879
Codes: FD2

40951
Percy B. Ferebee Endowment
c/o Wachovia Bank of North Carolina, N.A.
P.O. Box 3099
Winston-Salem, NC 27150-7131
(336) 732-6090
Contact: Erich Hamm

Established in 1973 in NC.
Donor(s): Percy Ferebee.‡
Financial data (yr. ended 12/31/00): Grants paid, $181,200; assets, $4,551,244 (M); expenditures, $223,145; qualifying distributions, $183,019.
Limitations: Giving primarily in Cherokee, Clay, Graham, Jackson, Macon, and Swain counties, NC, and the Cherokee Indian Reservation.
Publications: Informational brochure (including application guidelines).
Application information: Scholarship application forms can be obtained from and submitted to local high schools in specified NC counties. Application form required.
Trustee: Wachovia Bank of North Carolina, N.A.
EIN: 566118992
Codes: FD2, GTI

40952
The Midgard Foundation
P.O. Box 7286
Asheville, NC 28802
Contact: Philip C. Broughton, Pres.

Established in 1968 in NY.
Donor(s): Richard W. Weatherhead.‡
Financial data (yr. ended 12/31/00): Grants paid, $180,900; assets, $3,887,450 (M); expenditures, $193,214; qualifying distributions, $181,464.
Limitations: Applications not accepted. Giving primarily in the eastern U.S.
Application information: Unsolicited requests for funds not accepted.
Officers and Director:* Philip C. Broughton,* Pres. and Treas.; Philip C. Broughton, Jr., V.P.; C. Hardiman, Secy.
EIN: 136206619
Codes: FD2

40953
The Trexler Foundation
P.O. Box 32486
Charlotte, NC 28232
Contact: C. Brent Trexler, Jr., Tr.

Established in 1986 in NC.
Donor(s): Alice E. Trexler, C. Brent Trexler, Jr., Charles B. Trexler,‡ James Henry Trexler, John F. Trexler, Mary Margaret Trexler.
Financial data (yr. ended 12/31/01): Grants paid, $180,000; assets, $5,378,985 (M); expenditures, $184,687; qualifying distributions, $177,150.
Limitations: Applications not accepted. Giving primarily in Charlotte, NC.
Application information: Contributes only to pre-selected organizations.
Trustees: Alice E. Trexler, C. Brent Trexler, Jr., James Henry Trexler, John F. Trexler, Mary Margaret Trexler.
EIN: 561546464
Codes: FD2

40954
Shuford Industries Foundation, Inc.
(Formerly Century Foundation, Inc.)
c/o Richard Reese
401 11th St. N.W.
Hickory, NC 28601-4750 (828) 326-8365

Established in 1978.
Donor(s): Shuford Industries, Inc., Valdese Weavers, Inc.
Financial data (yr. ended 12/31/01): Grants paid, $177,000; assets, $424 (M); gifts received, $200,000; expenditures, $177,832; qualifying distributions, $176,988.
Limitations: Applications not accepted. Giving primarily in Catawba County, NC.
Application information: Contributes only to pre-selected organizations.
Officers: H.F. Shuford, Sr., Pres.; N.S. Dowdy, V.P.; A.A. Shuford II, V.P.; H.F. Shuford, Jr., V.P.; R.L. Reese, Secy.-Treas.
EIN: 581394774
Codes: CS, FD2, CD

40955
Solon E. & Espie Watts Little Scholarship Loan Fund, Inc.
43 Union St. S.
Concord, NC 28025 (704) 786-8173
Contact: Webster S. Medlin, Pres.

Incorporated in 1982 in NC.
Donor(s): Espie Watts Little.‡
Financial data (yr. ended 12/31/01): Grants paid, $176,237; assets, $3,305,926 (M); expenditures, $311,297; qualifying distributions, $284,804; giving activities include $176,237 for loans to individuals.
Limitations: Giving limited to Alexander County, NC high school graduates.
Application information: Applicant must have resided in Alexander County for at least 1 year. Application form required.
Officers: Webster S. Medlin, Pres. and Treas.; Steve L. Medlin, V.P. and Secy.
EIN: 581491453
Codes: FD2, GTI

40956
The Michel Family Foundation
c/o Albert J. Michel
1113 Hammel Rd.
Greensboro, NC 27408

Established in 1994 in NC.
Donor(s): Albert J. Michel, Margaret A. Michel.
Financial data (yr. ended 12/31/00): Grants paid, $175,100; assets, $4,945,322 (M); expenditures, $251,140; qualifying distributions, $177,231.
Limitations: Applications not accepted. Giving primarily in NC, with emphasis on the Greensboro area.
Application information: Contributes only to pre-selected organizations.
Officers: Margaret A. Michel, Pres.; Albert J. Michel, V.P. and Secy.-Treas.
Directors: Joe Michel, Susan Michel, Mary R. Temoche.
EIN: 561853139
Codes: FD2

40957
Kevin and Peggy Roche Family Foundation
7700 Baltusrol Ln.
Charlotte, NC 28210-4030 (704) 552-7191
Contact: Kevin J. Roche, Pres.

Established in 1998 in NC.
Donor(s): Kevin J. Roche, Peggy Roche.
Financial data (yr. ended 12/31/00): Grants paid, $175,000; assets, $355,863 (M); expenditures, $182,223; qualifying distributions, $175,000.
Limitations: Giving primarily in NC.
Officers: Kevin J. Roche, Pres.; Peggy Roche, V.P. and Secy.
EIN: 562116040
Codes: FD2

40958
1st State Bank Foundation, Inc.
P.O. Box 1797
Burlington, NC 27216

Established in 1999 in NC.
Financial data (yr. ended 12/31/01): Grants paid, $174,650; assets, $4,606,222 (M); expenditures, $178,435; qualifying distributions, $167,334.
Officers and Directors:* James C. McGill,* Pres.; James A. Barnwell,* Secy.; Richard C. Keziah.
EIN: 562150853
Codes: FD2

40959
Magee Christian Education Foundation
P.O. Box 754
Lake Junaluska, NC 28745   (828) 452-5427
E-mail: etullis@iopener.net
Contact: Edward L. Tullis, Secy.-Treas.

Established in 1938 in KY.
Donor(s): Ella G. Magee,‡ Magee Carpet Company.
Financial data (yr. ended 12/31/01): Grants paid, $174,500; assets, $4,064,310 (M); gifts received, $6,511; expenditures, $226,908; qualifying distributions, $198,522.
Limitations: Giving on a national basis.
Publications: Annual report (including application guidelines).
Application information: Application form required.
Officers and Directors:* James Magee,* Pres.; Otis W. Erisman,* V.P.; Edward L. Tullis,* Secy.-Treas.; Glen S. Bagby, David Hilton, William R. Jennings, Mrs. Myles Katerman, Robert H. Spain.
EIN: 616034760
Codes: FD2

40960
Oscar C. Rixson Foundation, Inc.
5 Pintail Ln.
Hendersonville, NC 28792-2839
Contact: Thomas J. Elliott, Sr., Pres.

Incorporated in 1925 in NY.
Donor(s): Oscar C. Rixson,‡ Mary Rixson,‡ Eleanor Rixon Cannon,‡ Ulrika Rixon Booth.‡
Financial data (yr. ended 12/31/01): Grants paid, $174,487; assets, $3,053,117 (M); gifts received, $190,155; expenditures, $229,497; qualifying distributions, $174,487.
Limitations: Giving throughout the U.S., Canada, Africa, Europe, South America, and the Far East.
Officers and Directors:* Thomas J. Elliott, Sr.,* Pres.; Allan L. Mojonnier,* V.P. and Treas.; Richard Yeskoo, Secy.; Donald Dunkerton, Nathan Dunkerton, RADM. Thomas J. Elliott, Jr., James M. Gilbert, Joseph Giordano, William R. Kusche, Jr., Timothy Van Wyck.
EIN: 136129767
Codes: FD2, GTI

40961
The Toleo Foundation
(Formerly The Kaplan Family Foundation)
604 Green Valley Rd., Ste. 400
Greensboro, NC 27408

Established in 1982 in NC.
Donor(s): Leonard J. Kaplan, Tobee W. Kaplan.
Financial data (yr. ended 12/31/01): Grants paid, $174,137; assets, $4,357,082 (M); gifts received, $7,000; expenditures, $269,335; qualifying distributions, $251,877.
Limitations: Applications not accepted. Giving primarily in NC.
Application information: Contributes only to pre-selected organizations.
Officers: Leonard J. Kaplan, Pres. and Treas.; Tobee W. Kaplan, V.P. and Secy.
EIN: 581496345
Codes: FD2

40962
Mark A. and Rena R. Norcross Family Foundation
1049 Rockford Rd.
High Point, NC 27262

Established in 2000 in NC.
Financial data (yr. ended 04/30/02): Grants paid, $171,325; assets, $193,163 (M); gifts received, $182,000; expenditures, $171,390; qualifying distributions, $171,325.
Limitations: Applications not accepted.
Application information: Contributes only to pre-selected organizations.
Officers: Mark A. Norcross, Chair., Pres. and Treas.; Rena R. Norcross, V.P. and Secy.
EIN: 562191282

40963
Brown F. Finch Foundation
c/o Wachovia Bank, N.A.
P.O. Box 3099
Winston-Salem, NC 27150-6090
(336) 732-6351
Contact: Nola G. Miller, Asst. V.P., Wachovia Bank, N.A.

Established in 1961 in NC.
Financial data (yr. ended 12/31/01): Grants paid, $171,293; assets, $2,298,359 (M); expenditures, $199,815; qualifying distributions, $177,142.
Limitations: Giving primarily in NC.
Application information: Application form not required.
Trustee: Wachovia Bank of North Carolina, N.A.
EIN: 566037909
Codes: FD2

40964
Nora and William Smith Foundation
c/o Bank of America
Bank of America Plz., NC1-002-11-18
Charlotte, NC 28255
Application address: c/o Bank of America, P.O. Box 608, Greenville, SC 29602
Contact: Bill Bridges

Established in 1986 in SC.
Financial data (yr. ended 05/31/02): Grants paid, $170,198; assets, $3,464,748 (M); expenditures, $198,232; qualifying distributions, $177,661.
Limitations: Giving primarily in GA and SC.
Application information: Contributes mostly to pre-selected organizations. Trustees may make discretionary grants.
Trustee: Bank of America.
EIN: 576110584
Codes: FD2

40965
The Bradshaw Charitable Foundation
75 Brookhaven Rd.
Pinehurst, NC 28374
Contact: Stanley J. Bradshaw, Pres.

Donor(s): Jean M. Bradshaw, Stanley J. Bradshaw.
Financial data (yr. ended 12/31/01): Grants paid, $169,040; assets, $828,249 (M); gifts received, $35,020; expenditures, $170,140; qualifying distributions, $169,040.
Application information: Application form not required.
Officers: Stanley J. Bradshaw, Pres.; Jean M. Bradshaw, V.P.
EIN: 431781113

40966
American Schlafhorst Foundation, Inc.
c/o American Schlafhorst Co.
P.O. Box 240828
Charlotte, NC 28224   (704) 554-0800
Contact: Dan W. Loftis, Pres.

Established in 1987 in NC.
Donor(s): American Schlafhorst Co.
Financial data (yr. ended 12/31/00): Grants paid, $163,500; assets, $3,462,323 (M); expenditures, $199,710; qualifying distributions, $163,500.
Limitations: Giving primarily in Charlotte, NC.
Application information: Application form not required.
Officer: Dan W. Loftis, Pres.
Directors: Frank Paetzold, Charles B. Park III, Tracy E. Tindal.
EIN: 561590110
Codes: CS, FD2, CD

40967
J. Leonard & Dorothy B. Moore Foundation
c/o Wachovia Bank, NA
P.O. Box 3099
Winston-Salem, NC 27150-7131

Established in 2000 in NC.
Financial data (yr. ended 12/31/00): Grants paid, $161,190; assets, $6,707,770 (M); gifts received, $4,540,271; expenditures, $231,125; qualifying distributions, $161,692.
Limitations: Applications not accepted. Giving primarily in Richmond, VA.
Application information: Contributes only to pre-selected organizations.
Trustee: Wachovia Bank, N.A.
EIN: 566558952
Codes: FD2

40968
Robert C. and Sadie G. Anderson Foundation
c/o Bank of America
1 Bank of America Plz., NC1-002-22-22
Charlotte, NC 28255
Contact: Leslie McIver, V.P., Private Bank

Trust established in 1952 in NC.
Donor(s): Robert C. Anderson,‡ Sadie Gaither Anderson.‡
Financial data (yr. ended 12/31/01): Grants paid, $160,000; assets, $3,374,063 (M); expenditures, $208,188; qualifying distributions, $167,114.
Limitations: Giving limited to NC.
Publications: Program policy statement.
Application information: Application form not required.
Directors: William M.M. Barnhardt, Katherine McKay Belk, Paul Bell, William Maynard Fountain, Jr., Bryan Ives III, Jennifer Richey, Ralph S. Robinson, Jr.
Trustee: Bank of America.
EIN: 566065233
Codes: FD2

40969
Bobbie Bailey Foundation, Inc.
c/o Bank of America
Bank of America Plz.
Charlotte, NC 28255
Application address: c/o Bank of America, P.O. Box 4446, Atlanta, GA 30302, tel.:(404) 607-6219
Contact: Michael Stogner

Established in 1994 in GA.
Donor(s): Bobbie Bailey.
Financial data (yr. ended 12/31/01): Grants paid, $159,000; assets, $2,836,245 (M); expenditures, $173,290; qualifying distributions, $155,858.
Limitations: Giving primarily in GA.
Trustee: Bank of America.
EIN: 582085849
Codes: FD2

40970
Morris and Gertrude Brenner Foundation
2110 Cloverdale Ave., Ste. 1A
Winston-Salem, NC 27103

Established in 1993 in NC.
Financial data (yr. ended 12/31/01): Grants paid, $159,000; assets, $3,222,005 (M); expenditures, $178,839; qualifying distributions, $158,704.

Limitations: Applications not accepted. Giving primarily in Winston-Salem, NC.
Application information: Contributes only to pre-selected organizations.
Officers: Anita Sue Brenner Kurtz, Pres.; Lynn Brenner Eisenburg, V.P.
Directors: Barry A. Eisenberg, Brian Adam Eisenberg, Jennifer E. Grosswald, Arthur H. Kurtz, David Alex Kurtz, Jon Brenner Kurtz.
EIN: 582072507
Codes: FD2

40971
Grace Richardson Fund
c/o Piedmont Financial Co., Inc.
P.O. Box 20124
Greensboro, NC 27420-0124 (336) 274-5471

Established in 1965 in NC.
Financial data (yr. ended 06/30/01): Grants paid, $155,314; assets, $2,955,586 (M); expenditures, $181,374; qualifying distributions, $160,170.
Limitations: Applications not accepted. Giving on a national basis.
Application information: Contributes only to pre-selected organizations.
Trustees: R.R. Richardson, Grace R. Stetson.
EIN: 566067849
Codes: FD2

40972
The Jack Levin Foundation, Inc.
(Formerly The Levin Foundation)
10 Postbridge Ct.
Greensboro, NC 27409-7890

Established in 1975 in NC.
Donor(s): Jack Levin, Seymour Levin, United Metal Recyclers.
Financial data (yr. ended 12/31/01): Grants paid, $154,909; assets, $554,280 (M); gifts received, $5,702; expenditures, $155,322; qualifying distributions, $154,591.
Limitations: Applications not accepted. Giving primarily in NC and New York, NY.
Application information: Contributes only to pre-selected organizations.
Officers and Directors:* Jack Levin,* Pres. and Treas.; Freddy H. Robinson,* V.P. and Secy.; Janis L. Fields.
EIN: 561116935
Codes: FD2

40973
Gilmer-Smith Foundation
P.O. Box 251
Mount Airy, NC 27030

Established in 1982 in NC.
Financial data (yr. ended 11/30/01): Grants paid, $152,113; assets, $4,241,602 (M); expenditures, $381,780; qualifying distributions, $299,157; giving activities include $84,166 for programs.
Limitations: Applications not accepted. Giving primarily in Mount Airy and Chapel Hill, NC.
Application information: Contributes only to pre-selected organizations.
Officers: Edward N. Swanson, Pres.; P.M. Sharpe, Secy.
Trustees: David Beal, George T. Fawcett, Jr., Betty B. Patterson.
EIN: 581463411
Codes: FD2

40974
The C. M. Herndon Foundation
6606 Barbee Rd.
Durham, NC 27713-8538

Established in 1992 in NC.
Donor(s): C. M. Herndon.‡
Financial data (yr. ended 10/31/01): Grants paid, $152,000; assets, $3,791,067 (M); gifts received, $12,000; expenditures, $201,333; qualifying distributions, $173,931.
Limitations: Applications not accepted. Giving primarily in Durham, NC.
Application information: Contributes only to pre-selected organizations.
Trustees: Robert F. Bailey, Gus Godwin, Marshall T. Sears.
EIN: 582018112
Codes: FD2

40975
Maye Morrison Abernethy Testamentary Charitable Trust
c/o Claude S. Abernethy, Jr.
P.O. Box 700
Newton, NC 28658-0700

Established in 1985 in NC.
Donor(s): Maye M. Abernethy.‡
Financial data (yr. ended 02/28/02): Grants paid, $151,600; assets, $2,712,819 (M); expenditures, $167,159; qualifying distributions, $152,211.
Limitations: Applications not accepted. Giving primarily in NC.
Application information: Contributes only to pre-selected organizations.
Trustee: Claude S. Abernethy, Jr.
EIN: 566257481
Codes: FD2

40976
Accel Foundation
c/o James M. Strathmeyer
9012 Carrington Ridge Dr.
Raleigh, NC 27615

Established around 1995.
Financial data (yr. ended 08/31/01): Grants paid, $150,950; assets, $1,645,565 (M); expenditures, $155,387; qualifying distributions, $150,672.
Limitations: Applications not accepted. Giving limited to Lancaster, PA.
Application information: Unsolicited requests for grants are not accepted.
Officer: James M. Strathmeyer, Pres.
EIN: 561900007
Codes: FD2, GTI

40977
Proctor Foundation
c/o Wachovia Bank of North Carolina, N.A.
P.O. Box 3099
Winston-Salem, NC 27150-7153
(336) 732-6996
Contact: Erich Hamm

Established in 1974 in NC.
Donor(s): Lucile S. Proctor.‡
Financial data (yr. ended 12/31/01): Grants paid, $150,695; assets, $2,621,850 (M); expenditures, $182,231; qualifying distributions, $155,865.
Limitations: Giving primarily in Rowan County, NC.
Application information: Application form not required.
Directors: F. Rivers Lawther, Jr., Edward P. Norvell, Lucile P. Norvell, Patricia P. Rendleman, Richard J. Rendleman.
Agent: Wachovia Bank of North Carolina, N.A.
EIN: 237398904
Codes: FD2

40978
Aiken Foundation, Inc.
c/o B.B. & T.
P.O. Box 2907
Wilson, NC 27894-2907

Incorporated in 1947 in SC.
Donor(s): Members of the Aiken family.
Financial data (yr. ended 12/31/01): Grants paid, $150,000; assets, $2,907,629 (M); expenditures, $157,793; qualifying distributions, $152,711.
Limitations: Applications not accepted. Giving primarily in Florence, SC.
Application information: Contributes only to pre-selected organizations.
Directors: Boone Aiken, J.B. Aiken III, Sandy Aiken, Thomas B. Aiken, Dina Jordan, Peg McLeod, Cornelia Owens, Elizabeth A. Rabun, Lyles Stone, Laurie A. Tiller.
Agent: B.B. & T.
EIN: 576019769
Codes: FD2

40979
Wilson Foundation
190 Wilson Park Rd.
Statesville, NC 28625 (704) 872-2411
FAX: (704) 872-8281; E-mail: foundation@glwilson.com
Contact: Thomas L. Wilson, Pres.

Established in 1981 in NC.
Donor(s): G.L. Wilson Building Co.
Financial data (yr. ended 12/31/01): Grants paid, $150,000; assets, $2,646,301 (M); expenditures, $181,066; qualifying distributions, $148,527.
Limitations: Giving primarily in NC.
Publications: Application guidelines, program policy statement.
Application information: Application form not required.
Officers: Thomas L. Wilson, Pres.; James D. Wilson, V.P.; William W. Wilson, V.P.; Elizabeth W. Norton, Secy.-Treas.
EIN: 561262432
Codes: FD2

40980
Pearl Dixon Balthis Foundation
c/o First Union National Bank
401 S. Tryon St., NC 1159
Charlotte, NC 28288-1159
Application address: c/o Kenneth R. Brown, First Union National Bank of NC, Trust Tax, CMG-10-1159, Charlotte, NC 28288-1159, tel.: (704) 374-6593

Established in 1957 in NC.
Donor(s): W.L. Balthis.‡
Financial data (yr. ended 06/30/02): Grants paid, $149,734; assets, $1,589,788 (M); expenditures, $158,070; qualifying distributions, $149,734.
Limitations: Giving limited to NC, with emphasis on the western Piedmont area.
Application information: Application form not required.
Trustee: First Union National Bank.
EIN: 566041570
Codes: FD2

40981—NORTH CAROLINA

40981
Cecelia Hand Nelson and Morgan Hand II Memorial Scholarship Fund
c/o First Union National Bank
401 S. Tryon St., NC1159
Charlotte, NC 28288-1159
Application address: c/o First Union National Bank, Cuthbert Rd. and MacArthur Blvd., Haddon Township, NJ 08033
Contact: Shep Millar, Trust Off., First Union National Bank

Established in 1994 in PA.
Donor(s): Cecelia Hand Nelson.‡
Financial data (yr. ended 07/31/01): Grants paid, $149,498; assets, $2,173,027 (M); expenditures, $168,980; qualifying distributions, $149,383.
Limitations: Giving primarily in Ocean City, NJ.
Application information: Contact guidance counselor. Application form required.
Trustees: William J. Hughes, First Union National Bank.
EIN: 237790152
Codes: FD2, GTI

40982
H. H. Webb and Nora Midkiff Webb Benevolent Trust
c/o Lowe & Williams, PLLC
P.O. Box 1463
Mount Airy, NC 27030
Contact: Raleigh Cooley, Tr.

Established in 1995 in NC.
Financial data (yr. ended 12/31/01): Grants paid, $149,258; assets, $2,267,225 (M); expenditures, $191,483; qualifying distributions, $148,465.
Limitations: Giving primarily in Surry County, NC, and Carroll and Patrick counties, VA.
Publications: Annual report.
Application information: Application form not required.
Officer: Sharon Lowe, Secy.
Trustees: Raleigh Cooley, Howard Morris, Myrtle Morris.
EIN: 566467466
Codes: FD2

40983
Ruth Anderson Foundation
c/o First Union National Bank
401 S. Tryon, NC 1159
Charlotte, NC 28288-1159
Contact: Jack G. Admire, Gov.

Established in 1989 in FL.
Donor(s): Ruth Anderson.‡
Financial data (yr. ended 04/30/01): Grants paid, $149,000; assets, $2,462,676 (M); gifts received, $5,864; expenditures, $196,679; qualifying distributions, $154,807.
Limitations: Giving primarily in Miami, FL.
Publications: Application guidelines.
Application information: Application form not required.
Governor: Jack G. Admire.
Trustee Bank: First Union National Bank.
EIN: 656027700
Codes: FD2

40984
W. W. Burgiss Charities, Inc.
c/o Wachovia Bank of South Carolina, N.A.
P.O. Box 3099
Winston-Salem, NC 27150-6732
Application address: c/o Gerald C. Lane, Wachovia Bank of South Carolina, N.A., 1426 Main St., Ste. 501, Columbia, SC 29226, tel.: (803) 765-3671

Incorporated in 1952 in SC.
Donor(s): W.W. Burgiss.
Financial data (yr. ended 12/31/01): Grants paid, $149,000; assets, $2,526,258 (M); expenditures, $170,812; qualifying distributions, $154,100.
Limitations: Giving primarily in SC, with emphasis on Greenville.
Application information: Application form not required.
Trustees: O. Perry Earle III, Arthur C. McCall, Jr., Wachovia Bank of South Carolina, N.A.
EIN: 576020262
Codes: FD2

40985
William A. Stern Foundation
1002 Dover Rd.
Greensboro, NC 27408 (336) 274-3027
Contact: Albert J. Jacobson, Dir.

Established in 1993 in NC.
Donor(s): William A. Stern.
Financial data (yr. ended 12/31/00): Grants paid, $148,850; assets, $2,644,860 (M); expenditures, $157,294; qualifying distributions, $148,623.
Limitations: Giving primarily in the Guilford County and Piedmont, NC, area.
Application information: Application form required.
Officers and Directors:* Katherine G. Stern,* Pres. and Treas.; Sidney J. Stern, Jr.,* V.P.; Susan Stern,* V.P.; Albert J. Jacobson.
EIN: 561841856
Codes: FD2

40986
The Gutterman Foundation
604 Waycross Dr.
Greensboro, NC 27410
FAX: (336) 294-8720; E-mail: nansea3@aol.com
Contact: Bernard Gutterman, Pres.

Established in 1988 in NC.
Donor(s): Bernard Gutterman, Nancy Gutterman.
Financial data (yr. ended 12/31/01): Grants paid, $148,075; assets, $2,267,683 (M); gifts received, $140,654; expenditures, $162,402; qualifying distributions, $147,216.
Limitations: Applications not accepted. Giving primarily in NC, PA, and WI.
Application information: Contributes only to pre-selected organizations.
Officers and Directors:* Bernard Gutterman,* Pres.; Nancy Gutterman,* V.P.; David D. Gutterman, Donna L. Gutterman, Deborah A. Rovner.
EIN: 561588363
Codes: FD2

40987
Hermes Family Foundation
c/o Ernst & Young, LLP
202 Centreport Dr., Ste. 200
Greensboro, NC 27409 (336) 662-6600
Contact: Steve Tutor

Established in 1975 in VA.
Financial data (yr. ended 09/30/01): Grants paid, $148,050; assets, $1,559,672 (M); expenditures, $187,877; qualifying distributions, $144,328.
Limitations: Giving primarily in NC and VA.
Officers: Sally S. Hermes-Flanagan, Pres.; Irma Smart, V.P.; Adrienne Hermes, Secy.
Directors: Doris H. Crumpler, Gwendolyn Smith.
EIN: 510172567
Codes: FD2

40988
J. W. Burress Foundation
380 Knollwood St., Ste. 610
Winston-Salem, NC 27103
Contact: John W. Burress III, Pres.

Established in 1986 in NC.
Donor(s): J.W. Burress, Inc., John W. Burress III, Mary Louise Walker Burress.
Financial data (yr. ended 12/31/01): Grants paid, $147,000; assets, $1,066,445 (M); expenditures, $155,106; qualifying distributions, $147,000.
Limitations: Giving primarily in NC.
Application information: Application form not required.
Officers: John W. Burress III, Pres. and Treas.; Sue Burress Wall, Secy.
EIN: 561554131
Codes: CS, FD2, CD

40989
Huffman-Cornwell Foundation
c/o Wachovia Bank of North Carolina, N.A.
P.O. Box 3099
Winston-Salem, NC 27150-7131
Application address: P.O. Box 1113, Morganton, NC 28680-1113
Contact: Mary Louise McCombs, Dir.

Established in 1960 in NC.
Financial data (yr. ended 12/31/01): Grants paid, $144,488; assets, $3,000,806 (M); gifts received, $309,402; expenditures, $185,830; qualifying distributions, $159,482.
Limitations: Giving primarily in NC; scholarships limited to students of Freedom High School, Morganton, NC.
Application information: Application form required for scholarships and grants.
Directors: Richard C. Avery, Anna Avery-Leagan, Lou N. Crouch, Julie M. Garner, Mary Lou M. Hudspeth, J.H. McCombs, Jr., James McCombs III, Mary Louise McCombs, Tom McCombs, Barbara C. Norvell, Brad Norvell, Jay T. Norvell, Jerry T. Norvell, Jr., Jan N. Stephanides.
Trustee: Wachovia Bank of North Carolina, N.A.
EIN: 566065286
Codes: FD2, GTI

40990
Green Printing Foundation
P.O. Box 0727
Lexington, NC 27293-0727

Established in 1995 in NC.
Donor(s): Green Printing Co., Inc.
Financial data (yr. ended 06/30/00): Grants paid, $144,450; assets, $3,693 (M); expenditures, $144,596; qualifying distributions, $144,410.
Limitations: Applications not accepted. Giving primarily in areas of company operations.
Application information: Contributes only to pre-selected organizations.
Directors: Leonard Beck, J.Z. Green, Harold Mabry.
EIN: 561973232
Codes: CS, FD2, CD

40991
Robert E., Jr. & Kathryn Scott Long Family Foundation
P.O. Box 26262
Greensboro, NC 27420

Established in 1998 in NC.
Donor(s): Robert E. Long, Jr.
Financial data (yr. ended 12/31/01): Grants paid, $144,000; assets, $264,466 (M); expenditures, $146,438; qualifying distributions, $144,378.
Limitations: Applications not accepted. Giving primarily in Greensboro, NC.

Application information: Contributes only to pre-selected organizations.
Officers: Robert E. Long, Jr., Pres.; Kathryn Scott Long, V.P.
EIN: 562114613
Codes: FD2

40992
Alexander Worth McAlister Foundation, Inc.
c/o Wachovia Bank, N.A.
P.O. Box 3099
Winston-Salem, NC 27150-7131
(336) 732-5763
Contact: Blake Hardin

Established in 1968 in NC.
Donor(s): Sarah L. McAlister.
Financial data (yr. ended 12/31/01): Grants paid, $143,800; assets, $2,736,218 (M); expenditures, $177,983; qualifying distributions, $145,920.
Limitations: Giving primarily in NC, with emphasis on Greensboro and Charlotte.
Publications: Informational brochure.
Application information: Application form required.
Officers: John W. McAlister, Jr., Pres.; Margaret M. Sealy, V.P.
Board Members: Alexander M. Flora, Lacey L. Flora, Mary W. McAlister Flora, Elizabeth M. Groves, Cynthia V. McAlister, John W. McAlister II, R. Vaughn McAlister, Sarah L. McAlister, John B. Sealy III, Josephine Sealy Zuray.
Agent: Wachovia Bank, N.A.
EIN: 566095754
Codes: FD2

40993
John R. and Carolyn J. Maness Family Foundation
c/o U.S. Trust Co. of North Carolina
P.O. Box 26262
Greensboro, NC 27402

Established in 1995 in NC.
Donor(s): John R. Maness, Carolyn J. Maness.
Financial data (yr. ended 12/31/01): Grants paid, $142,616; assets, $2,957,484 (M); gifts received, $40,353; expenditures, $164,869; qualifying distributions, $147,398.
Limitations: Applications not accepted. Giving primarily in NC.
Application information: Contributes only to pre-selected organizations.
Officers: John R. Maness, Pres.; Carolyn J. Maness, Secy.
EIN: 561949954
Codes: FD2

40994
Thomas S. Kenan III Foundation, Inc.
P.O. Box 4150
Chapel Hill, NC 27515-4150

Established in 1993 in NC.
Donor(s): Thomas S. Kenan III.
Financial data (yr. ended 06/30/01): Grants paid, $142,500; assets, $2,727,117 (M); gifts received, $382,492; expenditures, $170,995; qualifying distributions, $145,403.
Limitations: Applications not accepted. Giving primarily in NC.
Application information: Contributes only to pre-selected organizations.
Officers and Directors:* Thomas S. Kenan III,* Pres.; William W. Gantt,* Secy.-Treas.; Christopher A. Shuping, Phyllis P. Snow.
EIN: 561816652
Codes: FD2

40995
Ralph S. Robinson Family Foundation
P.O. Box 959
Gastonia, NC 28053-0959
Contact: Ralph S. Robinson, Jr., Mgr.

Established in 1955 in NC.
Financial data (yr. ended 12/31/01): Grants paid, $141,933; assets, $2,924,764 (M); expenditures, $144,630; qualifying distributions, $139,878.
Limitations: Giving primarily in NC.
Application information: Application form not required.
Officer and Trustees:* Ralph S. Robinson, Jr.,* Mgr.; Ann R. Black, Leigh R. Finley, Charlotte C. Robinson, Russell M. Robinson.
EIN: 566049912
Codes: FD2

40996
Rauch Foundation
3824 Sherwood Cir.
Gastonia, NC 28056 (704) 867-5333
Contact: Marshall A. Rauch, Dir.

Established in 1993 in NC.
Donor(s): Rauch Industries, Inc., Marc Rauch, Elaine Lyerly Rauch, Marshall A. Rauch.
Financial data (yr. ended 12/31/01): Grants paid, $141,762; assets, $861,878 (M); gifts received, $100; expenditures, $143,876; qualifying distributions, $141,762.
Limitations: Giving primarily in NC.
Directors: Jeanne G. Rauch, Marshall A. Rauch.
EIN: 561854850
Codes: FD2

40997
Daniel R. Hoover Trust Fund
c/o First Union National Bank of North Carolina
3 First Union Ctr., 401 S. Tryon St.
Charlotte, NC 28288-1159 (877) 500-5655
Contact: Matthew A. Johnson, V.P. and Trust Off., First Union National Bank of North Carolina

Established in 1991 in NC.
Donor(s): Ray C. Hoover.‡
Financial data (yr. ended 06/30/01): Grants paid, $141,551; assets, $1,162,432 (M); expenditures, $153,067; qualifying distributions, $141,209.
Limitations: Giving limited to residents of Cabarrus, NC.
Application information: Application form required.
Trustee: First Union National Bank of North Carolina.
EIN: 566034863
Codes: FD2, GTI

40998
Ruth B. & George T. Huff Fund
c/o Wachovia Bank
P.O. Box 3099
Winston-Salem, NC 27150-7131
Application address: c/o Wachovia Bank, 1021 E. Cary St., 4th Fl., Richmond, VA 23219, tel.: (804) 697-6901
Contact: Mary Jo Tull, V.P.

Established in 1966 in VA.
Donor(s): George T. Huff.‡
Financial data (yr. ended 09/30/01): Grants paid, $141,347; assets, $1,943,688 (M); expenditures, $155,128; qualifying distributions, $141,347.
Limitations: Giving limited to the City of Charlottesville, and Floyd, Greene, Patrick, and Albemarle counties, VA.
Publications: Annual report.
Application information: Scholarships awarded to institutions on behalf of named individual recipients. Applications accepted only through public schools in designated localities. Application form required.
Trustee: Wachovia Bank, N.A.
EIN: 546088063
Codes: FD2, GTI

40999
Youth Ministry, Inc.
3827 Lillie St.
High Point, NC 27265-9334 (336) 288-5853
Contact: Jerry H. Knox, Pres.

Established in 1978.
Donor(s): Fil Anderson, Lucie Anderson, William Preyer, Jr., National Christian Charitable Foundation, Inc., Scott & Stringfellow, Inc.
Financial data (yr. ended 12/31/01): Grants paid, $141,330; assets, $30,858 (M); gifts received, $160,698; expenditures, $145,110; qualifying distributions, $141,330.
Application information: Written application containing academic standing, church affiliation and academic cost. Application form required.
Officers: Jerry H. Knox, Pres.; Johnny McConnell, V.P.; Bob Thompson, V.P.; Sarah K. Bash, Secy.-Treas.
EIN: 581366662
Codes: FD2, GTI

41000
Emily Monk Davidson Foundation, Inc.
c/o Betty Langston
P.O. Box 148
Farmville, NC 27828-0148 (252) 753-8249

Established in 1997 in NC.
Donor(s): Emily Monk Davidson.
Financial data (yr. ended 08/31/01): Grants paid, $141,078; assets, $1,206,766 (M); gifts received, $48,033; expenditures, $145,931; qualifying distributions, $138,638.
Limitations: Giving primarily in MD and NC.
Officers: Emily Monk Davidson, Pres.; Robert T. Monk, Jr., V.P.; Frances Joyner Monk, Secy.
EIN: 562029548
Codes: FD2

41001
James McKeen Cattell Fund
c/o Duke Univ., Dept. of Psychology
Box 90086
Durham, NC 27708-0086
FAX: (919) 660-5726; *E-mail:* williams@psych.duke.edu
Contact: Dr. Christina Williams, Secy.-Treas.

Trust established in 1942 in NY.
Donor(s): James McKeen Cattell.‡
Financial data (yr. ended 12/31/01): Grants paid, $140,753; assets, $2,676,239 (M); expenditures, $175,971; qualifying distributions, $145,974.
Limitations: Giving in the U.S.
Publications: Annual report, application guidelines.
Application information: Must be a tenured academic psychologist to apply. Application form required.
Officers and Trustees:* Christina L. Williams,* Secy.-Treas.; Lyle V. Jones,* Mgr.; Marcia K. Johnson, Gregory A. Kimble, Janet T. Spence.
EIN: 136129600
Codes: FD2, GTI

41002
Myrtle C. Chaley Trust
c/o Wachovia Bank, N.A.
P.O. Box 3099
Winston-Salem, NC 27150-6732

Established in 1995 in SC.

Financial data (yr. ended 12/31/01): Grants paid, $140,511; assets, $3,109,552 (M); expenditures, $171,088; qualifying distributions, $147,938.
Limitations: Applications not accepted. Giving primarily in SC.
Application information: Contributes only to pre-selected organizations.
Trustee: Wachovia Bank, N.A.
EIN: 586325609
Codes: FD2

41003
Margaret W. & Lorimer W. Midgett Trust
c/o Centura Bank
P.O. Box 1220
Rocky Mount, NC 27802

Financial data (yr. ended 12/31/00): Grants paid, $140,492; assets, $3,082,595 (M); expenditures, $157,848; qualifying distributions, $140,992.
Limitations: Applications not accepted.
Application information: Contributes only to pre-selected organizations.
Trustee: Centura Bank.
EIN: 527100207
Codes: FD2

41004
Joseph M. Wright Charitable Foundation
P.O. Box 208
Shelby, NC 28151 (704) 487-8888
Application address: 27 E. Randolph St., Shelby, NC 28150
Contact: Hoyt O. Bailey

Established in 1992.
Financial data (yr. ended 12/31/01): Grants paid, $140,300; assets, $2,824,931 (M); gifts received, $11,445; expenditures, $198,277; qualifying distributions, $140,095.
Limitations: Giving primarily in OH.
Trustee: Wachovia Bank of North Carolina, N.A.
EIN: 561872992
Codes: FD2

41005
Erwin Bauer Charitable Trust
c/o First Union National Bank
401 S. Tryon St., 4th Fl.
Charlotte, NC 28288-1159

Established in 1997 in CT.
Donor(s): Erwin Bauer.‡
Financial data (yr. ended 10/31/01): Grants paid, $139,960; assets, $2,072,789 (M); expenditures, $168,602; qualifying distributions, $139,431.
Limitations: Applications not accepted.
Application information: Contributes only to pre-selected organizations.
Trustee: Catherine Carroll Petroni.
Agent: First Union National Bank.
EIN: 256620895
Codes: FD2

41006
Frank J. Michaels Scholarship Fund
c/o First Union National Bank
401 S. Tryon St., NC 1159
Charlotte, NC 28288-1159
Application address: c/o First Union National Bank, 123 S. Broad St., Philadelphia, PA 19109
Contact: Vicki Hills, Asst. V.P.

Established in 1977 in PA.
Donor(s): Frank J. Michaels.‡
Financial data (yr. ended 01/31/02): Grants paid, $139,139; assets, $2,158,310 (M); expenditures, $161,979; qualifying distributions, $145,290.
Limitations: Giving limited to Oxford, PA, area residents.

Application information: Application forms available from First Union National Bank. Application form required.
Trustee: First Union National Bank.
EIN: 236680399
Codes: FD2, GTI

41007
Citizens Savings Bank S.S.B. Foundation
c/o B.B. & T., Trust Dept.
P.O. Box 2907
Wilson, NC 27894-2907

Established in 1994.
Financial data (yr. ended 12/31/01): Grants paid, $138,678; assets, $101,066 (M); expenditures, $143,605; qualifying distributions, $138,678.
Limitations: Applications not accepted. Giving primarily in NC.
Application information: Contributes only to pre-selected organizations.
Trustee: B.B. & T.
EIN: 566436047

41008
The Charles E. & Pauline Hayworth Foundation
c/o Wachovia Bank, N.A.
P.O. Box 3099
Winston-Salem, NC 27150-7131
Contact: Pauline Lewis Hayworth, Pres.

Established in 1986 in NC.
Donor(s): David R. Hayworth, Charles E. Hayworth, Jr.,‡ The Hayworth Foundation.
Financial data (yr. ended 12/31/01): Grants paid, $138,500; assets, $3,243,124 (M); expenditures, $175,789; qualifying distributions, $144,208.
Limitations: Giving primarily in NC.
Officers and Directors:* Pauline L. Hayworth,* Pres.; David R. Hayworth,* V.P.; Elizabeth L. Quick,* Treas.; Linwood Davis.
EIN: 570834648
Codes: FD2

41009
Senah C. and C. A. Kent Foundation
c/o Wachovia Bank of North Carolina, N.A.
P.O. Box 3099
Winston-Salem, NC 27150-7131
Application addresses: c/o Wayne E. Johnson, Asst. Dir., Student Fin. Aid, P.O. Box 7305, Winston-Salem, NC 27109, tel.: (336) 761-5265; c/o Pamela Butts, Assoc. Dir. of Fin. Aid, Salem College, P.O. Box 10548, Winston-Salem, NC 27108-0548, tel.: (336) 721-2808; or c/o Ginger Klock, Student Dir., NC School of the Arts, P.O. Box 12189, Winston-Salem, NC 27117-2189, tel.: (336) 770-3297

Established in 1971 in NC.
Donor(s): Senah C. Kent.‡
Financial data (yr. ended 12/31/00): Grants paid, $137,842; assets, $3,095,308 (M); expenditures, $175,070; qualifying distributions, $139,637.
Limitations: Giving limited to NC.
Application information: Scholarships are limited to Wake Forest University, North Carolina School of the Arts, and Salem College. Contact individual schools for application information. Application form required.
Trustee: Wachovia Bank of North Carolina, N.A.
EIN: 566037248
Codes: FD2, GTI

41010
Effie Allen Little Foundation
P.O. Box 340
Wadesboro, NC 28170-0340 (704) 694-2213
Contact: Henry Little, Pres.

Established in 1954 in NC.
Donor(s): Charles L. Little, Sr.,‡ Hal W. Little.‡
Financial data (yr. ended 12/31/01): Grants paid, $136,988; assets, $2,349,360 (M); expenditures, $165,321; qualifying distributions, $137,400.
Limitations: Applications not accepted. Giving limited to Anson County, NC.
Application information: Contributes only to pre-selected organizations.
Officers and Board Members:* Henry W. Little III,* Pres.; Mary Louise Little,* Secy.; Mrs. Charles L. Little,* Treas.
Director: Effie Little Richert.
Agent: B.B. & T.
EIN: 566048449
Codes: FD2

41011
Continental General Tire Foundation
1800 Continental Blvd.
Charlotte, NC 28273 (704) 583-3900
Contact: J.C. Curry, Tr.

Established in 1996 in NC.
Donor(s): Continental General Tire, Inc., Continental Tire North America, Inc.
Financial data (yr. ended 12/31/01): Grants paid, $135,890; assets, $215,152 (M); gifts received, $8,784; expenditures, $136,155; qualifying distributions, $136,156.
Limitations: Giving primarily in NC.
Trustees: J.C. Curry, B. Frangenberg, D.L. Hollnagel.
EIN: 561960645
Codes: CS, FD2

41012
Stephen Knight Pond Foundation
P.O. Box 10499
Greensboro, NC 27404-0499

Established in 1985 in NC.
Donor(s): Stephen Knight Pond.
Financial data (yr. ended 12/31/01): Grants paid, $135,500; assets, $1,511,364 (M); expenditures, $153,587; qualifying distributions, $138,757.
Limitations: Applications not accepted. Giving primarily in NC.
Application information: Contributes only to pre-selected organizations.
Officers and Directors:* Stephen Knight Pond,* Pres.; James T. Williams, Jr.,* Secy.; Gary P. Sherrill.
EIN: 581648777
Codes: FD2

41013
Hagan Family Fund
P.O. Box 3463
Greensboro, NC 27402 (336) 373-1600
Contact: Charles T. Hagan III, V.P.

Established in 1994.
Donor(s): Charles T. Hagan, Jr.
Financial data (yr. ended 12/31/01): Grants paid, $135,000; assets, $2,039,440 (M); expenditures, $152,380; qualifying distributions, $134,786.
Limitations: Applications not accepted. Giving primarily in NC.
Application information: Unsolicited requests for funds not accepted.
Officers and Directors:* Charles T. Hagan, Jr.,* Pres.; Charles T. Hagan III,* V.P. and Secy.-Treas.; Anne B. Hagan,* V.P.; David B. Hagan,* V.P.; Henry G. Hagan,* V.P.; John C. Hagan,* V.P.
EIN: 561905696

Codes: FD2

41014
Jack H. & Ruth C. Campbell Foundation
c/o Wachovia Bank of North Carolina, N.A.
P.O. Box 3099
Winston-Salem, NC 27150-7131
Application address: c/o Nola Miller, Charitable Funds Management, Wachovia, 301 N. Main St., Winston-Salem, NC 27150

Established in 1994 in NC.
Financial data (yr. ended 12/31/01): Grants paid, $133,708; assets, $1,207,215 (M); expenditures, $146,990; qualifying distributions, $133,698.
Limitations: Giving primarily in NC.
Application information: Application form not required.
Officers: Ruth C. Campbell, Vice-Chair.; Jack H. Campbell, Sr., Pres.; Jack H. Campbell, Jr., Secy.-Treas.
Director: Jenny C. Ross.
Trustee: Wachovia Bank of North Carolina, N.A.
EIN: 561887261
Codes: FD2

41015
The Winston Family Foundation, Inc.
2209 Century Dr., Ste. 300
Raleigh, NC 27612
Application address: 2626 Glenwood Ave., No. 200, Raleigh, NC 27608
Contact: Charles M. Winston, Chair.

Established in 1997 in NC.
Donor(s): Charles M. Winston, Florence B. Winston.
Financial data (yr. ended 12/31/01): Grants paid, $133,175; assets, $1,928,818 (M); gifts received, $388,170; expenditures, $163,248; qualifying distributions, $140,846.
Officers: Charles M. Winston, Chair. and Pres.; Charles M. Winston, Jr., V.P.; Florence B. Winston, V.P.; Marion T. Winston, Secy.; Robert W. Winston III, Treas.
EIN: 562058027
Codes: FD2

41016
The Hurley-Trammell Foundation
P.O. Box 4354
126 W. Innes St.
Salisbury, NC 28145-4354 (704) 633-3603
Contact: Elizabeth V. Rankin, Exec. V.P.

Established in 1987 in NC.
Donor(s): James F. Hurley, Geraldine T. Hurley.
Financial data (yr. ended 12/31/01): Grants paid, $133,000; assets, $1,281,717 (M); expenditures, $166,455; qualifying distributions, $133,000.
Limitations: Giving primarily in Salisbury, NC.
Application information: Application form not required.
Officers and Directors:* Geraldine T. Hurley,* Pres.; Elizabeth V. Rankin,* Exec. V.P.; James F. Hurley,* Secy.-Treas.; Gordon P. Hurley, Linda Alexander Weaver, Mark Wineka.
EIN: 561576470
Codes: FD2

41017
Larson Foundation
2 Quail Ct.
Foxfire, NC 27281

Established in 2000 in NC.
Donor(s): Darwin A. Larson.
Financial data (yr. ended 12/31/01): Grants paid, $133,000; assets, $1,711,832 (M); gifts received, $13,755; expenditures, $148,980; qualifying distributions, $122,196.

Limitations: Applications not accepted.
Application information: Contributes only to pre-selected organizations.
Officers and Directors:* Darwin A. Larson,* Pres. and Treas.; Susan J. Larson,* V.P.; Jennifer B. Garner, Secy.; Linda L. Barko, Mary L. Stitt.
EIN: 311736010

41018
Mary Koons Trust
c/o First Union National Bank
401 S. Tryon St. NC1159
Charlotte, NC 28288

Established in 1995 in PA.
Financial data (yr. ended 12/31/00): Grants paid, $132,846; assets, $2,752,009 (M); expenditures, $151,211; qualifying distributions, $131,293.
Limitations: Applications not accepted.
Application information: Contributes only to pre-selected organizations.
Trustee: First Union National Bank.
EIN: 236445183
Codes: FD2

41019
W. S. Wellons Foundation
P.O. Box 766
Spring Lake, NC 28390
Contact: W.S. Wellons, Jr., Chair.

Donor(s): W.S. Wellons, Sr., Florence Wellons, William S. Wellons, Jr., David Wellons.
Financial data (yr. ended 12/31/00): Grants paid, $132,053; assets, $2,767,335 (M); gifts received, $1,360,000; expenditures, $223,988; qualifying distributions, $131,354.
Limitations: Giving primarily in Fayetteville, NC.
Application information: Letter.
Officers: W.S. Wellons, Jr., Chair.; Florence C. Wellons, Secy.-Treas.
EIN: 581537766

41020
S.D.R. Foundation, Inc.
8704 Highhill Rd.
Raleigh, NC 27615

Established in 1999 in NC.
Donor(s): David S. Rendall, Suganthi E. Rendall.
Financial data (yr. ended 12/31/00): Grants paid, $132,000; assets, $995,563 (M); gifts received, $75,000; expenditures, $144,384; qualifying distributions, $144,384.
Limitations: Applications not accepted. Giving primarily in NC, with some giving in TN and TX.
Application information: Contributes only to pre-selected organizations.
Directors: David S. Rendall, Suganthi Rendall.
EIN: 562170889
Codes: FD2

41021
Outer Banks Community Foundation, Inc.
P.O. Box 1100
Kill Devil Hills, NC 27948-1100
(252) 261-8839
FAX: (252) 261-0371; E-mail: info@obcf.org;
URL: http://www.obcf.org
Contact: Barbara A. Bingham, Exec. Dir.

Incorporated in 1982 in NC.
Donor(s): David Stick, Andy Griffith, Edward Greene, W. Ray White, Jack Adams, George S. Crocker,‡ Martin Kellogg, Jr.‡
Financial data (yr. ended 12/31/01): Grants paid, $131,450; assets, $2,549,732 (M); gifts received, $143,435; expenditures, $197,158.
Limitations: Giving limited to the Outer Banks, NC, area.

Publications: Annual report, financial statement, informational brochure, newsletter, grants list, application guidelines.
Application information: Application form required.
Officers and Directors:* T. Olin Davis,* Pres.; Bob Oakes,* V.P.; Nonie Booth,* Secy.; Helen Ford,* Treas.; Barbara A. Bingham, Exec. Dir.; Marcelle Brenner, Cashar Evans, William J. Fields, John F. Hughes, Michael Kelly, Ken Mann, Dorothy Toolan, Sterling Webster.
EIN: 581516313
Codes: CM, FD2

41022
Anna & Isidore Roseman Foundation
c/o First Union National Bank
401 S. Tryon St., Ste. NC 1159
Charlotte, NC 28288-1159

Donor(s): Anna Roseman,‡ Isidore Roseman.‡
Financial data (yr. ended 04/30/01): Grants paid, $131,367; assets, $772,593 (M); expenditures, $141,004; qualifying distributions, $129,861.
Limitations: Applications not accepted. Giving primarily in NY and PA.
Application information: Contributes only to pre-selected organizations.
Trustees: Morris P. Baran, Leonard I. Korman, Nathan Phillips, First Union National Bank.
EIN: 236676499
Codes: FD2

41023
The Bowles Family Foundation
c/o U.S. Trust Co. of NC
P.O. Box 26262
Greensboro, NC 27420
Contact: Kim D. Garcia, Asst. Secy.

Established in 1985 in NC.
Donor(s): R. Kelly Bowles, Louise H. Bowles, Laura B. Warren, James D. Warren.
Financial data (yr. ended 12/31/01): Grants paid, $131,320; assets, $882,158 (M); expenditures, $142,979; qualifying distributions, $133,662.
Limitations: Applications not accepted.
Application information: Contributes only to pre-selected organizations.
Officers: R. Kelly Bowles, Pres.; Louise H. Bowles, Secy.
Directors: Donna B. Schweers, Laura B. Warren.
EIN: 581681913
Codes: FD2

41024
W. Lester Brooks Foundation, Inc.
1914 Brunswick Ave., Ste. 2B
Charlotte, NC 28207-1892 (704) 334-7271
Contact: W. Lester Brooks, Jr., Pres.

Established around 1960.
Donor(s): W. Lester Brooks.
Financial data (yr. ended 11/30/01): Grants paid, $131,000; assets, $2,575,858 (M); gifts received, $5,085; expenditures, $144,907; qualifying distributions, $129,107.
Limitations: Giving primarily in NC.
Application information: Application form not required.
Officers: W. Lester Brooks, Jr., Pres. and Treas.; Patty F. Brooks, V.P.
EIN: 566060695
Codes: FD2

41025
Thomas H. and Mary H. C. Leath Foundation
c/o B.B. & T., Trust Dept
P.O. Box 2907
Wilson, NC 27894-2907
Application address: P.O. Drawer 1149, Pinehurst, NC 28374, tel.: (910) 215-2627
Contact: Patrice Cain

Established in 1989 in NC.
Donor(s): Mary Headley Leath.‡
Financial data (yr. ended 07/31/01): Grants paid, $130,310; assets, $2,591,676 (M); expenditures, $171,407; qualifying distributions, $130,310.
Limitations: Giving primarily in Richmond County, NC.
Application information: Application form required.
Trustees: Judy S. Blount, Robert Hutchinson, F. Brent Neal, B.B. & T.
EIN: 566294400
Codes: FD2, GTI

41026
Brewer Foundation, Inc.
P.O. Box 7906
Rocky Mount, NC 27804
Contact: Joseph B. Brewer, Jr., Pres.

Established in 1969 in NC.
Donor(s): Joseph B. Brewer, Jr., Lucy Ann Brewer.‡
Financial data (yr. ended 08/31/01): Grants paid, $130,019; assets, $954,147 (M); gifts received, $177,929; expenditures, $132,091; qualifying distributions, $130,019.
Limitations: Giving limited to NC.
Application information: Application form not required.
Officer: Joseph B. Brewer, Jr., Pres.
EIN: 560941242
Codes: FD2, GTI

41027
Turner B. Bunn, Jr. and Catherine E. Bunn Foundation, Inc.
P.O. Box 3299
Wilson, NC 27895

Established in 2000 in NC.
Financial data (yr. ended 12/31/01): Grants paid, $130,000; assets, $1,865,833 (M); expenditures, $155,020; qualifying distributions, $130,000.
Limitations: Applications not accepted.
Application information: Contributes only to pre-selected organizations.
Directors: Fred M. Bunn, Joseph E. Bunn, Turner B. Bunn III.
EIN: 561692623

41028
The Donald D. Lynch Family Foundation
108 Artillery Ln.
Raleigh, NC 27615
Contact: Donald Lynch, Exec. Dir.

Established in 1997 in NC.
Donor(s): Donald D. Lynch.
Financial data (yr. ended 06/30/01): Grants paid, $129,227; assets, $1,401,383 (M); expenditures, $141,321; qualifying distributions, $129,227.
Limitations: Giving on a national basis.
Application information: Application form required.
Officers and Directors:* Susan Lynch Campbell,* Secy.; Donald D. Lynch,* Exec. Dir.
EIN: 562053851
Codes: FD2

41029
Charles L. & Doris M. Fonville Foundation
P.O. Box 241477
Charlotte, NC 28224-1477

Established around 1995.
Donor(s): Fonville & Co.
Financial data (yr. ended 12/31/01): Grants paid, $129,000; assets, $708,638 (M); gifts received, $150,000; expenditures, $129,810; qualifying distributions, $128,820.
Limitations: Applications not accepted. Giving primarily in Charlotte, NC.
Application information: Contributes only to pre-selected organizations.
Officer and Trustees: Charles L. Fonville,* Chair.; Doris Fonville.
EIN: 561896989
Codes: CS, FD2, CD

41030
Elizabeth City Foundation
P.O. Box 574
Elizabeth City, NC 27907-0574
(252) 335-7850
Contact: Ray S. Jones, Jr., Exec. Dir.

Established in 1959 in NC.
Financial data (yr. ended 07/31/01): Grants paid, $128,604; assets, $3,603,495 (M); gifts received, $10,335; expenditures, $170,666; qualifying distributions, $155,694.
Limitations: Giving limited to the Albemarle area of northeastern NC for general grants, and Camden County, NC, for scholarships.
Publications: Application guidelines, informational brochure, financial statement.
Application information: Scholarship application forms available at Wachovia Bank and Trust Co. and Camden High School for Camden County, NC, residents only. Application form required.
Officer: Ray S. Jones, Jr., Exec. Dir.
Trustee Banks: B.B. & T., Centura Bank, First Citizens National Bank, First Union National Bank of North Carolina, Wachovia Bank of North Carolina, N.A.
Committee Members: Donald W. Baker, Jack A. Cooper, Levin B. Culpepper, and 4 additional members:.
EIN: 237076018
Codes: FD2, GTI

41031
The Charis Foundation, Inc.
(also known as The Judith E. & Joseph C. Cook, Jr. Foundation)
26 Timber Park Dr.
Black Mountain, NC 28711
Contact: Joseph C. Cook, Jr., Pres.

Established in 1997 in IN.
Donor(s): Joseph C. Cook, Jr., Judith E. Cook.
Financial data (yr. ended 12/31/01): Grants paid, $128,340; assets, $2,752,377 (M); gifts received, $458,322; expenditures, $158,412; qualifying distributions, $128,363.
Limitations: Applications not accepted. Giving primarily in the southeastern U.S.
Application information: Contributes only to pre-selected organizations.
Officer: Joseph C. Cook, Jr., Pres.
EIN: 352006656
Codes: FD2

41032
Barcalounger Foundation, Inc.
(Formerly Furniture Comfort Foundation, Inc.)
P.O. Box 6157
Rocky Mount, NC 27801
Application address: c/o Phil Chamberlain, 1450 Atlantic Ave., Rocky Mount, NC 27801, tel.: (252) 977-6395

Incorporated in 1945 in NY; formerly, Mohasco Memorial Fund, Inc.
Donor(s): Consolidated Furniture Corp.
Financial data (yr. ended 12/31/01): Grants paid, $127,135; assets, $582,448 (M); expenditures, $161,608; qualifying distributions, $126,668.
Limitations: Giving primarily in areas of company operations in the South.
Application information: Application form not required.
Officers: John B. Sganga, Chair. and Secy.; Wayne Stevens, Pres.
EIN: 146019132
Codes: CS, FD2, CD

41033
Chatham Foundation, Inc.
c/o Wachovia Bank of North Carolina, N.A.
P.O. Box 3099
Winston-Salem, NC 27150-7153
Application address: P.O. Box 151, Elkin, NC 28621, tel.: (336) 835-2155
Contact: David H. Cline, Secy.-Treas.

Incorporated in 1943 in NC.
Donor(s): Members of the Chatham family, members of the Hanes family, and Chatham/Hanes-affiliated corporations.
Financial data (yr. ended 12/31/00): Grants paid, $127,000; assets, $3,712,588 (M); expenditures, $165,781; qualifying distributions, $143,259.
Limitations: Giving primarily in the Elkin, NC, area.
Application information: Application form required for scholarships.
Officers: Lucy Chatham, Pres.; Barbara F. Chatham, V.P.; David H. Cline, Secy.-Treas.
Director: Alex Chatham, Jr.
EIN: 560771852
Codes: CS, FD2, CD

41034
Harley W. Howell Charitable Foundation
c/o First Union National Bank
401 S. Tryon St., 4th Fl.
Charlotte, NC 28288-1159
Application address: c/o First Union National Bank, P.O. Box 17034, Baltimore, MD 21203
Contact: Vicki Novak

Established in 1961 in MD.
Donor(s): Harley W. Howell.
Financial data (yr. ended 12/31/01): Grants paid, $126,000; assets, $1,778,682 (M); expenditures, $136,832; qualifying distributions, $126,750.
Limitations: Giving primarily in the Baltimore, MD, area.
Application information: Application form not required.
Trustee: First Union National Bank.
EIN: 526033554
Codes: FD2

41035
Paulsen Family Foundation
c/o North Carolina Trust Co.
P.O. Box 26262
Greensboro, NC 27402-1108

Established in 1998 in NC.

Financial data (yr. ended 12/31/01): Grants paid, $125,977; assets, $1,684,481 (M); expenditures, $149,540; qualifying distributions, $125,977.
Limitations: Applications not accepted.
Application information: Contributes only to pre-selected organizations.
Directors: Katharine C. Paulsen, William F. Paulsen, Laura E. Taft.
EIN: 311604299
Codes: FD2

41036
W. T. Anderson Trust
Bank of America Plz., NC1-002-11-18
Charlotte, NC 28255
Application address: c/o Bank of America, 487 Cherry St., Ste. 200, Macon, GA 31201
Contact: John Carter

Established in 1996 in GA.
Financial data (yr. ended 10/31/01): Grants paid, $125,000; assets, $2,524,538 (M); expenditures, $151,271; qualifying distributions, $130,093.
Limitations: Giving primarily in GA.
Trustee: Bank of America.
EIN: 586331063
Codes: FD2

41037
Carter Foundation, Inc.
P.O. Box 29093
Greensboro, NC 27429
Application address: P.O. Box 26000, Greensboro, NC 27420, tel.: (336) 373-8850
Contact: Erwin Fuller

Established in 1948 in NC.
Financial data (yr. ended 12/31/01): Grants paid, $125,000; assets, $2,331,347 (M); expenditures, $128,625; qualifying distributions, $124,155.
Limitations: Giving primarily in NC, with emphasis on Greensboro.
Application information: Application form required.
Officers: W.J. Carter, Jr., Pres.; Natalie C. Freeman, V.P.; W. Erwin Fuller, Jr., Secy.-Treas.
EIN: 566060796
Codes: FD2

41038
J. Richard & Sybel Hayworth Foundation
c/o Wachovia Bank, N.A.
P.O. Box 3099
Winston-Salem, NC 27150-7131

Donor(s): Sybel F. Hayworth.
Financial data (yr. ended 12/31/00): Grants paid, $125,000; assets, $1,956,441 (M); expenditures, $144,042; qualifying distributions, $125,244.
Limitations: Giving primarily in NC.
Trustee: Wachovia Bank of North Carolina, N.A.
EIN: 586269128
Codes: FD2

41039
Carrie B. DeWitt Family Foundation
3298 N. U.S. Hwy. 220
Ellerbe, NC 28338

Established in 1997 in NC.
Donor(s): Carrie B. DeWitt.
Financial data (yr. ended 05/31/01): Grants paid, $123,250; assets, $269,329 (M); gifts received, $190,000; expenditures, $125,960; qualifying distributions, $121,244.
Limitations: Applications not accepted.
Application information: Contributes only to pre-selected organizations.
Directors: Carrie B. DeWitt, Nancy Lee DeWitt-Daugherty, Jo DeWitt-Wilson.
EIN: 562061017
Codes: FD2

41040
Durham Merchants Association Charitable Foundation
P.O. Box 52016
Durham, NC 27717 (919) 489-7921
Contact: Frank Ward, Pres.; or M.W. Lynam, Exec. Dir.

Established in 1989 in NC.
Donor(s): Durham Merchants Assn., Inc.
Financial data (yr. ended 12/31/01): Grants paid, $123,200; assets, $3,639,199 (M); expenditures, $196,800; qualifying distributions, $176,698.
Limitations: Giving limited to Durham County, NC.
Publications: Application guidelines.
Application information: Application form required.
Officers and Directors:* Frank Ward,* Pres.; Cynthia F. Barnes, V.P.; Evelyn D. Schmidt, Secy.; Steve Hancock,* Treas.; M.W. Lynam, Exec. Dir.; Nancy Brown, N. Wayne Campbell, Jefferson Clark, Susan Cranford Ross, Charles J. Stewart.
EIN: 561651068
Codes: FD2

41041
Mary and Elliott Wood Foundation
(Formerly Elliott S. Wood Foundation)
c/o Wachovia Bank of North Carolina, N.A.
P.O. Box 3099
Winston-Salem, NC 27150-7153
Application address: P.O. Box 2448, High Point, NC 27261, tel.: (336) 885-5051
Contact: Elliott S. Wood, Committee Member

Donor(s): Elliott S. Wood, Mary W. Wood.
Financial data (yr. ended 12/31/00): Grants paid, $122,563; assets, $2,971,770 (M); expenditures, $151,582; qualifying distributions, $127,390.
Limitations: Giving primarily in NC.
Trustee: Wachovia Bank of North Carolina, N.A.
Committee Members: Elliott S. Wood, Mary W. Wood, William Pennuel Wood.
EIN: 566055686
Codes: FD2

41042
George W. and Ruth R. Baxter Foundation, Inc.
(Formerly George W. Baxter Foundation, Inc.)
6525 Morrison Blvd., Ste. 501
Charlotte, NC 28211-3530
Contact: George W. Baxter, Sr., Dir.

Established about 1970 in NC.
Donor(s): George W. Baxter, Sr.
Financial data (yr. ended 06/30/01): Grants paid, $122,498; assets, $12,528,965 (M); gifts received, $12,102; expenditures, $225,650; qualifying distributions, $186,673.
Limitations: Applications not accepted. Giving primarily in NC.
Application information: Contributes only to pre-selected organizations.
Officers and Directors:* Nolan D. Pace, Jr.,* Chair.; Ruth R. Baxter, Vice-Chair.; G. Steven Baxter,* Pres.; Mark B. Edwards,* Secy.; George W. Baxter, Sr.
EIN: 560949547
Codes: FD2

41043
Lawrence Saunders Fund
c/o First Union National Bank
401 S. Tryon St., Ste. NC 1159
Charlotte, NC 28202
Contact: Camie Morrison, V.P., First Union National Bank

Established in 1970 in PA.
Financial data (yr. ended 12/31/00): Grants paid, $122,044; assets, $2,269,252 (M); expenditures, $134,587; qualifying distributions, $123,341.
Limitations: Giving primarily in Philadelphia and in Chester and Montgomery counties, PA.
Application information: Application form required.
Trustees: Isaac H. Clothier IV, Kenneth W. Gemmilln, Anne B. Kellett, First Union National Bank.
EIN: 236488524
Codes: FD2

41044
Kittie M. Fairey Educational Fund
c/o Wachovia Bank of North Carolina, N.A.
P.O. Box 3099
Winston-Salem, NC 27150-7153
SC tel.: (803) 765-3677
Scholarship application address: c/o Sandra Lee, Dir., P.O. Box 1465, Taylors, SC 29687-1465, tel.: (803) 268-3363

Trust established in 1967 in SC.
Donor(s): Kittie Moss Fairey.‡
Financial data (yr. ended 09/30/01): Grants paid, $122,024; assets, $3,066,564 (M); expenditures, $145,416; qualifying distributions, $128,580.
Limitations: Giving limited to SC.
Application information: Applicants for scholarships must attend a four-year college or university in the state of SC. Application form required.
Trustee: Wachovia Bank of North Carolina, N.A.
EIN: 576037140
Codes: FD2, GTI

41045
McColl Foundation
1508 Biltmore Dr.
P.O. Box 6144
Charlotte, NC 28207
Contact: Jane McColl Lockwood, Pres.

Established in 1996 in NC.
Donor(s): Hugh L. McColl, Jr.
Financial data (yr. ended 12/31/01): Grants paid, $121,098; assets, $2,882,228 (M); expenditures, $129,915; qualifying distributions, $126,924.
Limitations: Giving primarily in GA and NC.
Publications: Application guidelines.
Officers: Jane S. McColl, Chair.; Jane McColl Lockwood, Pres.; Hugh L. McColl III, V.P.; John S. McColl, Secy.-Treas.
EIN: 562002906
Codes: FD2

41046
The Randall R. Kaplan Family Foundation
P.O. Box 19608
Greensboro, NC 27419

Established in 1995 in NC.
Donor(s): Randall R. Kaplan.
Financial data (yr. ended 12/31/01): Grants paid, $120,888; assets, $178 (M); gifts received, $117,413; expenditures, $120,888; qualifying distributions, $120,887.
Limitations: Applications not accepted.
Application information: Contributes only to pre-selected organizations.

41046—NORTH CAROLINA

Officers and Directors:* Randall R. Kaplan,* Pres.; Kathy E. Manning,* V.P.
EIN: 561933212
Codes: FD2

41047
James B. Powell Foundation
c/o U.S. Trust Co. of North Carolina
P.O. Box 26262
Greensboro, NC 27420-6262

Established in 1987 in NC.
Donor(s): James B. Powell.
Financial data (yr. ended 06/30/01): Grants paid, $120,662; assets, $1,712,580 (M); expenditures, $150,152; qualifying distributions, $125,661.
Limitations: Applications not accepted.
Application information: Contributes only to pre-selected organizations.
Trustees: Daphne Powell Markcrow, Anne E. Powell, James B. Powell, John S. Powell, U.S. Trust Co. of North Carolina.
EIN: 581773026

41048
The Medic Foundation
(Formerly Medic Computer Systems Foundation)
c/o Wachovia Bank, N.A.
P.O. Box 3099
Winston-Salem, NC 27150-7131
(336) 732-5252

Established in 1997 in NC.
Financial data (yr. ended 12/31/00): Grants paid, $120,000; assets, $2,829,620 (M); expenditures, $138,998; qualifying distributions, $121,308.
Limitations: Applications not accepted.
Application information: Contributes only to pre-selected organizations.
Trustee: Wachovia Bank, N.A.
EIN: 058239110
Codes: FD2

41049
The Sprinkle Family Foundation, Inc.
c/o U.S. Trust Co. of North Carolina
P.O. Box 26262
Greensboro, NC 27420

Established in 1994 in NC.
Donor(s): R. David Sprinkle.
Financial data (yr. ended 12/31/00): Grants paid, $119,350; assets, $973,449 (M); gifts received, $62,188; expenditures, $123,349; qualifying distributions, $117,580.
Limitations: Applications not accepted.
Application information: Contributes only to pre-selected organizations.
Officers and Directors:* R. David Sprinkle,* Pres.; Pamela P. Sprinkle,* V.P. and Secy.-Treas.; David Phelps Sprinkle, Ellen Sprinkle Thomas.
EIN: 561900911
Codes: FD2

41050
Carlyle & Co. Foundation
4615 Dundas Dr.
Greensboro, NC 27407-1613 (336) 294-2450
Contact: Russell L. Cohen, Vice-Chair.

Established around 1969.
Donor(s): Carlyle & Co. Jewelers.
Financial data (yr. ended 12/31/00): Grants paid, $118,710; assets, $8,946 (M); gifts received, $91,270; expenditures, $120,789; qualifying distributions, $118,710.
Limitations: Giving primarily in Greensboro, NC.
Officers: Lawrence M. Cohen, Chair.; Russell L. Cohen, Vice-Chair.; John K. Cohen, Pres.
EIN: 237062047
Codes: CS, FD2, CD

41051
Charles K. Smith, Jr. Trust
c/o First Union National Bank
401 S. Tryon St., Ste. NC 1159
Charlotte, NC 28288-1159

Established in 1995 in NJ.
Financial data (yr. ended 05/31/01): Grants paid, $118,386; assets, $3,763,249 (M); expenditures, $138,031; qualifying distributions, $118,766.
Limitations: Applications not accepted. Giving primarily in Philadelphia, PA.
Application information: Contributes only to pre-selected organizations.
Trustee: First Union National Bank.
EIN: 236218805
Codes: FD2

41052
The Katherine H. Daveler and David R. Hayworth Foundation
c/o Wachovia Bank of North Carolina, N.A.
P.O. Box 3099, NC6732
Winston-Salem, NC 27150-6732
Application address: 800 Rockford Rd., High Point, NC 27262-4653, tel.: (336) 889-4439
Contact: David Hayworth, Dir.

Established in 1986.
Financial data (yr. ended 12/31/01): Grants paid, $115,000; assets, $6,094,153 (M); gifts received, $160,800; expenditures, $130,821; qualifying distributions, $120,982.
Limitations: Giving limited to NC, with emphasis on High Point.
Application information: Application form not required.
Directors: David R. Hayworth, John C. Slane, Marsha B. Slane.
Custodian: Wachovia Bank, N.A.
EIN: 581705607
Codes: FD2

41053
The H. English and Ermine Carter Robinson Foundation
c/o Wachovia Bank of North Carolina, N.A.
P.O. Box 3099
Winston-Salem, NC 27150-0001
Application address: c/o Phillip Millians, 191 Peachtree St. N.E., Atlanta, GA 30303, tel.: (404) 332-1422

Established in 1991 in NC.
Donor(s): H. English Robinson.
Financial data (yr. ended 12/31/00): Grants paid, $114,400; assets, $2,255,168 (M); expenditures, $133,680; qualifying distributions, $114,804.
Limitations: Giving limited to Atlanta, GA.
Advisory Committee: Harry English Robinson, Jr., Peyton Carter Robinson.
Trustee: Wachovia Bank of North Carolina, N.A.
EIN: 581981556
Codes: FD2

41054
Holdeen Fund 50-10
c/o First Union National Bank, 4th Fl.
401 S. Tryon St., NC1159
Charlotte, NC 28288-1159
Contact: Eugene Williams

Established about 1982 in PA.
Financial data (yr. ended 12/31/01): Grants paid, $114,393; assets, $1,969,562 (M); expenditures, $122,009; qualifying distributions, $113,902.
Limitations: Giving limited to Boston, MA.
Trustee: First Union National Bank.
EIN: 146018148
Codes: TN

41055
The Robinson Foundation, Inc.
P.O. Box 19608
Greensboro, NC 27419-9608

Established in 1966 in NC.
Donor(s): Bernard Robinson, Joseph Robinson, Gloria Robinson, Freddy Robinson.
Financial data (yr. ended 12/31/01): Grants paid, $113,805; assets, $437,622 (M); gifts received, $64,227; expenditures, $115,066; qualifying distributions, $113,805.
Limitations: Applications not accepted. Giving primarily in NC.
Application information: Contributes only to pre-selected organizations.
Officers and Directors:* Gloria Robinson,* Pres.; Freddy Robinson,* V.P.; Joyce Shuman,* Secy.
EIN: 560857643
Codes: FD2

41056
Mitsubishi Semiconductor America, Inc. Funds
3 Diamond Ln.
Durham, NC 27704-9409 (919) 479-3333
Contact: Gary Edge, V.P.

Established in 1988 in NC.
Donor(s): Mitsubishi Semiconductor America, Inc.
Financial data (yr. ended 12/31/01): Grants paid, $113,000; assets, $1,568,931 (M); expenditures, $120,200; qualifying distributions, $113,000.
Limitations: Giving limited to NC.
Publications: Application guidelines.
Application information: Application form required.
Officers: Osamu Tomisawa, Pres.; Gary Edge, V.P.; Pat Hefferan, Secy.; Hoyt Robinson, Treas.
EIN: 561637250
Codes: CS, FD2, CD

41057
Elizabeth Burns Yost Trust
c/o B.B. & T., Trust Dept.
P.O. Box 2907
Wilson, NC 27894-2907
Application address: c/o B.B. & T., P.O. Box 149, Pinehurst, NC 28374, tel.: (910) 215-2627
Contact: Patrice Cain

Established in 1989 in NC.
Donor(s): Elizabeth Burns Yost.‡
Financial data (yr. ended 12/31/01): Grants paid, $112,850; assets, $3,570,594 (M); expenditures, $156,660; qualifying distributions, $112,850.
Limitations: Giving limited to Anson County, NC.
Application information: Application form required.
Trustee: B.B. & T.
EIN: 566355993
Codes: FD2

41058
The Reese Foundation
P.O. Box 69
Hickory, NC 28603 (828) 465-3431
Contact: Thomas W. Reese, Pres.

Established in 1985 in NC.
Donor(s): Thomas W. Reese.
Financial data (yr. ended 09/30/01): Grants paid, $112,500; assets, $362,853 (M); expenditures, $113,899; qualifying distributions, $112,323.
Limitations: Applications not accepted. Giving primarily in NC.
Officers: Thomas W. Reese, Pres.; Elizabeth Watts, V.P.; Sallie A. Martin, Secy.; Jeffrey A. Hale, Treas.
Director: Darrell Smith.
EIN: 581627279
Codes: FD2

41059
Sarah Belk Gambrell Foundation
6100 Fairview Rd., Ste. 640
Charlotte, NC 28210
Contact: Sarah Gambrell Knight, Board Member

Established in 1960.
Financial data (yr. ended 12/31/01): Grants paid, $112,250; assets, $2,005,105 (M); expenditures, $118,420; qualifying distributions, $110,799.
Limitations: Giving primarily in NC.
Advisory Board Members: Larry D. Estridge, Sarah Gambrell Knight, Rachel McClain.
Trustee: Paul B. Wyche, Jr.
EIN: 566046451
Codes: FD2

41060
The L. B. Lane Family Foundation, Inc.
1006 4th Ave. Dr. N.W.
Hickory, NC 28601-3453   (828) 328-5014
Contact: Landon B. Lane, Jr., Pres.

Established in 1988 in NC.
Donor(s): Landon B. Lane, Jr., Connie L. Vucurevich.
Financial data (yr. ended 12/31/01): Grants paid, $111,729; assets, $1,538,585 (M); expenditures, $119,096; qualifying distributions, $115,913.
Limitations: Applications not accepted.
Application information: Contributes only to pre-selected organizations.
Officers: Landon B. Lane, Jr., Pres. and Treas.; Connie L. Vucurevich, Secy.-Treas.; Nila P. Lane, Secy.
EIN: 561622837
Codes: FD2

41061
Alex & Agnes O. McIntosh Foundation
c/o First Union Bank
401 S. Tryon St., 4th Fl.
Charlotte, NC 28288-1159
Application address: 200 S. Biscayne Blvd., Miami, FL 33131
Contact: Jack G. Admire, Tr.

Established in 1981 in FL.
Donor(s): Agnes McIntosh.‡
Financial data (yr. ended 04/30/01): Grants paid, $111,500; assets, $1,329,577 (M); expenditures, $149,660; qualifying distributions, $112,291.
Limitations: Giving primarily in the Miami and Dade County, FL, area.
Application information: Application form not required.
Trustees: Jack G. Admire, First Union National Bank of Florida.
EIN: 592082319
Codes: FD2

41062
Edward R. Welsh Trust
c/o First Union National Bank
401 S. Tryon St. TH-4, Ste. NC 1159
Charlotte, NC 28288-1159
Application address: 631 Market St., Camden, NJ 08102
Contact: William J. Murray

Established in 1996 in NJ.
Financial data (yr. ended 11/30/00): Grants paid, $111,500; assets, $1,673,997 (M); gifts received, $11,405; expenditures, $128,137; qualifying distributions, $1,102,277.
Limitations: Giving limited to residents of Camden County, NJ.
Trustee: First Union National Bank.
EIN: 237899951
Codes: FD2

41063
Berea Foundation, Inc.
3921 Columbine Cir.
Charlotte, NC 28211
Contact: Ernest C. Bourne, Dir.

Established in 1998 in NC.
Donor(s): Benjamin Ernest Bourne, Ernest C. Bourne, Raymond Fairbanks Bourne.
Financial data (yr. ended 12/31/01): Grants paid, $111,350; assets, $2,276,737 (M); expenditures, $122,211; qualifying distributions, $111,350.
Limitations: Giving primarily in TN.
Directors: Benjamin Ernest Bourne, Ernest C. Bourne, Raymond Fairbanks Bourne.
EIN: 562125412
Codes: FD2

41064
Helen McBee Irrevocable Trust
c/o First Union National Bank
401 S. Tryon St., 4th Fl.
Charlotte, NC 28288-1159

Established in 1995 in NC.
Donor(s): Helen McBee.
Financial data (yr. ended 12/31/01): Grants paid, $110,768; assets, $2,777,994 (M); expenditures, $137,946; qualifying distributions, $109,929.
Limitations: Applications not accepted. Giving primarily in Bakersville, NC.
Application information: Contributes only to pre-selected organizations.
Trustee: First Union National Bank.
EIN: 566453865
Codes: FD2

41065
Neisler Foundation
c/o First Union National Bank
3 First Union Ctr., 401 S. Tryon St., TN-2
Charlotte, NC 28288-1159
Contact: Stella N. Putnam

Established in 1952 in NC.
Financial data (yr. ended 12/31/01): Grants paid, $110,705; assets, $2,288,098 (M); expenditures, $124,807; qualifying distributions, $110,981.
Limitations: Giving primarily in the South.
Application information: Unsolicited requests for funds not accepted. Application form not required.
Trustee: First Union National Bank.
EIN: 566042484
Codes: FD2

41066
The Deal Foundation
c/o Wachovia Bank of North Carolina, N.A.
P.O. Box 3099
Winston-Salem, NC 27150-7151
Application address: P.O. Drawer G, High Point, NC 27261, tel.: (336) 887-7300

Established in 1989 in NC.
Financial data (yr. ended 12/31/00): Grants paid, $110,500; assets, $3,027,839 (M); expenditures, $180,154; qualifying distributions, $112,229.
Limitations: Giving primarily in NC.
Officers: Doris P. Deal, Secy.; R.L. Deal, Treas.
Trustee: Wachovia Bank of North Carolina, N.A.
EIN: 581842530
Codes: FD2

41067
Eloise Strother Wyly Scholarship Trust
c/o Wachovia Bank of North Carolina, N.A.
P.O. Box 3099
Winston-Salem, NC 27150-7131
Scholarship application address: c/o John Hostetler, Walhalla High School, Razorback Ln., Walhalla, SC 29691

Established in 1976 in SC.
Financial data (yr. ended 07/31/01): Grants paid, $110,250; assets, $2,003,992 (M); expenditures, $126,300; qualifying distributions, $112,364.
Limitations: Giving limited to SC.
Application information: Scholarship application available through Walhalla High School.
Trustee: Wachovia Bank of North Carolina, N.A.
EIN: 570640726
Codes: FD2, GTI

41068
Hopeman Memorial Fund
c/o Wachovia Bank of North Carolina, N.A.
P.O. Box 3099
Winston-Salem, NC 27150-7131

Incorporated in 1980 in VA.
Donor(s): Hopeman Bros., Inc., Royston Manufacturing Corp.
Financial data (yr. ended 12/31/01): Grants paid, $109,000; assets, $1,979,330 (M); expenditures, $132,011; qualifying distributions, $109,663.
Limitations: Applications not accepted. Giving primarily in VA.
Application information: Contributes only to pre-selected organizations.
Officers: Henry W. Hopeman, Pres. and Treas.; Harriet M. Hopeman, V.P.; Ray R. Brown, Secy.
Directors: Lynn G. Hopeman, David M. Lascell.
EIN: 541156930
Codes: FD2

41069
Strickland Family Foundation
2 Piedmont Plz., Ste. 604
2000 W. 1st St.
Winston-Salem, NC 27104
Contact: Robert L. Strickland, Secy.

Established around 1995.
Donor(s): Robert L. Strickland.
Financial data (yr. ended 07/31/01): Grants paid, $108,840; assets, $2,510,526 (M); expenditures, $123,583; qualifying distributions, $108,571.
Limitations: Giving primarily in Winston-Salem, NC.
Officers: Elizabeth Miller Strickland, Pres.; Cynthia Anne Strickland, V.P.; Robert E.M. Strickland, V.P.; Robert L. Strickland, Secy.
EIN: 561900147
Codes: FD2

41070
Owens Scholarship Trust Co.
c/o B.B. & T., Trust Dept.
P.O. Box 2907
Wilson, NC 27894-2907
Application address: c/o Superintendent, Wilson County schools, P.O. Box 2048, Wilson, NC 27893
Contact: Larry Price, Committee Member

Established in 1998 in NC.
Donor(s): PeeWee Owens,‡ Myrtle Owens.
Financial data (yr. ended 08/31/01): Grants paid, $108,414; assets, $3,005,895 (M); gifts received, $1,350; expenditures, $152,329; qualifying distributions, $106,452.
Publications: Application guidelines.

41070—NORTH CAROLINA

Application information: Applications available from high school guidance counselors in Wilson County, NC. Application form required.
Trustees: Will Winslow, B.B. & T.
Committee Members: Thomas Evans, Christine L. Fitch, Larry Price, Jimmy Tillman, Bill Williamson.
EIN: 566532306
Codes: FD2, GTI

41071
The Perry-Griffin Foundation
P.O. Box 82
Oriental, NC 28571-0082 (252) 249-2879
Contact: Joseph R. Hudnell, Secy.

Established in 1987 in NC.
Financial data (yr. ended 08/31/01): Grants paid, $108,100; assets, $2,582,095 (M); expenditures, $217,900; qualifying distributions, $173,600; giving activities include $14,000 for loans to individuals and $25,104 for programs.
Limitations: Giving limited to Pamlico and Jones counties, NC.
Application information: Application form required.
Officers and Directors:* Ned E. Delamar,* Vice-Chair.; Joseph R. Hudnell,* Secy.; Edward D. Lupton, Mgr.; Cynthia L. Delamar.
EIN: 560860864
Codes: FD2

41072
Marguerite Carl Smith Foundation
c/o First Union National Bank
401 S. Tryon St., Ste. NC 1159
Charlotte, NC 28288-1159

Established in 1989 in PA.
Donor(s): Marguerite Carl Smith.
Financial data (yr. ended 05/31/01): Grants paid, $108,000; assets, $3,145,700 (M); expenditures, $132,798; qualifying distributions, $115,078.
Limitations: Giving primarily in Jersey Shore, PA.
Trustees: Ralph Kuhns, Mrs. Ralph Kuhns, Shirley Loud, Lee Smith, Mary Tuefel.
EIN: 232564406
Codes: FD2, GTI

41073
William G. & Margaret B. Frasier Charitable Foundation
c/o Wachovia Bank of North Carolina, N.A.
P.O. Box 3099
Winston-Salem, NC 27150-1022
(336) 732-5991
Scholarship application address: c/o Business Mgr., Southeastern Baptist Theological Seminary, Wake Forest, NC 27587
Contact: Paula Johnson

Established in 1972 in NC.
Financial data (yr. ended 12/31/01): Grants paid, $107,890; assets, $1,936,588 (M); expenditures, $137,043; qualifying distributions, $117,135.
Limitations: Giving limited to NC.
Application information: Application forms not required for scholarships.
Trustee: Wachovia Bank of North Carolina, N.A.
EIN: 566144594
Codes: FD2, GTI

41074
Argo Foundation
c/o Bank of America
Bank of America Plz., NC1-002-11-18
Charlotte, NC 28255
Application address: c/o John F. Oglesby, 287 Springdale Dr. N.E., Atlanta, GA 30305, tel.: (404) 237-9472
Contact: Richard A. Oglesby, Jr., Exec. Dir.

Donor(s): Mrs. Lamar Oglesby, Richard A. Oglesby, Sr.
Financial data (yr. ended 12/31/01): Grants paid, $107,750; assets, $2,104,716 (M); gifts received, $239,486; expenditures, $126,734; qualifying distributions, $106,144.
Limitations: Giving limited to GA.
Officers: John F. Oglesby, Secy.-Treas.; Richard A. Oglesby, Jr., Exec. Dir.
EIN: 582020943
Codes: FD2

41075
Marsh Foundation, Inc.
P.O. Box 35329
Charlotte, NC 28235
Contact: Gretchen M. Johnston, V.P.

Established in 1954.
Donor(s): Marsh Assocs., Marsh Realty Co., Marsh Mortgage Co.
Financial data (yr. ended 12/31/01): Grants paid, $107,100; assets, $2,482,467 (M); gifts received, $280,699; expenditures, $124,504; qualifying distributions, $110,182.
Limitations: Giving primarily in NC.
Officers: Betty H. Marsh, Pres.; Gretchen M. Johnston, V.P.; G. Alex Marsh III, V.P.; Hunter Johnston McLawhorn, V.P.; James McLawhorn, V.P.
EIN: 566056515
Codes: CS, FD2, CD

41076
The Blanc Fund
150 N. Avalon Rd.
Winston-Salem, NC 27104

Established in 1998 in NC.
Financial data (yr. ended 12/31/00): Grants paid, $106,500; assets, $1,732,552 (M); expenditures, $120,357; qualifying distributions, $106,500.
Limitations: Applications not accepted. Giving primarily in VA.
Application information: Contributes only to pre-selected organizations.
Trustees: Charles B. Campbell, Nancy I. Campbell, Williamson Ghirskey.
EIN: 562099316
Codes: FD2

41077
Survival in Freedom (SURFREE)
4480 Springmoor Cir.
Raleigh, NC 27615-5708

Established in 1970 in NY.
Donor(s): Elizabeth Morse, John W. Morse.
Financial data (yr. ended 12/31/01): Grants paid, $106,000; assets, $680,311 (M); expenditures, $115,215; qualifying distributions, $107,509.
Trustees: Elizabeth Morse, John W. Morse.
EIN: 237087207
Codes: TN

41078
Charles & Charlotte Falk Foundation, Inc.
P.O. Box 35103
Greensboro, NC 27425-5103
Contact: Michael Falk, Exec. V.P.

Established around 1969 in NC.
Donor(s): Harry Falk, Charlotte Falk.
Financial data (yr. ended 12/31/00): Grants paid, $105,210; assets, $1,515,822 (M); expenditures, $109,218; qualifying distributions, $105,460.
Limitations: Giving primarily in Greensboro, NC.
Officers and Directors:* Michael Falk,* Exec. V.P.; Charlotte Falk,* V.P.
EIN: 237055636
Codes: FD2

41079
Poole Foundation, Inc.
c/o W. Roy Poole
4206 W. Vernon Ave.
Kinston, NC 28504

Established in 1996 in NC.
Financial data (yr. ended 12/31/01): Grants paid, $104,195; assets, $1,890,683 (M); expenditures, $113,882; qualifying distributions, $146,701.
Limitations: Applications not accepted. Giving primarily in Kinston, NC.
Application information: Contributes only to pre-selected organizations.
Officers and Directors:* Walter R. Poole, Jr.,* Pres.; Elizabeth B. Askew,* Secy.; J. Gregory Poole.
EIN: 561890954
Codes: FD2

41080
George Smedes Poyner Foundation, Inc.
4412 Delta Lake Dr.
Raleigh, NC 27612

Established around 1961.
Donor(s): James M. Poyner,‡ James M. Poyner III.
Financial data (yr. ended 06/30/02): Grants paid, $103,468; assets, $1,250,777 (M); expenditures, $136,708; qualifying distributions, $103,468.
Limitations: Applications not accepted. Giving primarily in NC.
Application information: Contributes only to pre-selected organizations.
Officers: Edythe P. Poyner, Chair.; James M. Poyner III, Pres.; Florence C. Poyner, V.P.
EIN: 566061776

41081
Mike Brenner Foundation, Inc.
P.O. Box 76
Winston-Salem, NC 27102

Established in 1997 in NC.
Donor(s): Mike Brenner.
Financial data (yr. ended 06/30/01): Grants paid, $102,978; assets, $311,171 (M); expenditures, $104,479; qualifying distributions, $102,478.
Limitations: Applications not accepted. Giving primarily in Winston-Salem, NC.
Application information: Contributes only to pre-selected organizations.
Officers and Directors:* Mike Brenner, Pres. and Treas.; Susan Brenner,* V.P. and Secy.; Frances Brenner, Frank Brenner.
EIN: 562059999
Codes: FD2

41082
Lucius Wade Edwards Private Foundation, Inc.
714 St. Mary's St.
Raleigh, NC 27605 (919) 856-9233
URL: http://www.wade.org
Contact: Sarah Lowder, Dir.

Established in 1997 in NC.
Donor(s): Elizabeth Anania, John R. Edwards, David F. Kirby.
Financial data (yr. ended 12/31/00): Grants paid, $102,450; assets, $3,829,343 (M); expenditures, $220,382; qualifying distributions, $214,876.

Limitations: Applications not accepted. Giving primarily in NC.
Publications: Newsletter, informational brochure.
Application information: Contributes only to pre-selected organizations.
Officers and Directors:* Elizabeth Anania,* Pres.; John R. Edwards,* V.P.; David F. Kirby,* Secy.-Treas.; Sarah Lowder.
EIN: 562026070
Codes: FD2

41083
Hope Through Life Foundation
P.O. Box 4150
Chapel Hill, NC 27515-4150

Established in 1998 in NC.
Donor(s): Elizabeth Kenan Howell.
Financial data (yr. ended 06/30/01): Grants paid, $102,000; assets, $2,144,834 (M); gifts received, $120,000; expenditures, $110,548; qualifying distributions, $109,876.
Limitations: Applications not accepted. Giving primarily in NC.
Application information: Contributes only to pre-selected organizations.
Officer and Directors:* Dennis Andrew Howell,* Pres. and Treas.; Elizabeth Kenan Howell,* V.P. and Secy.
EIN: 562114270
Codes: FD2

41084
George Shinn Foundation, Inc.
100 Hive Dr.
Charlotte, NC 28217 (704) 357-0252
Contact: J.L. Brooks

Established in 1973.
Donor(s): The Charlotte Hornets, George Shinn, George Shinn & Assocs., Inc.
Financial data (yr. ended 12/31/01): Grants paid, $101,932; assets, $84,596 (M); gifts received, $100,633; expenditures, $147,211; qualifying distributions, $140,151.
Limitations: Giving primarily in Charlotte, NC.
Officers: George Shinn, Pres.; Wayne DeBlander, Secy.-Treas.
EIN: 561083525
Codes: FD2

41085
Carstarphen Family Foundation, Inc.
(Formerly William J. & Catherine Stowe Pharr Foundation, Inc.)
P.O. Box 1939
McAdenville, NC 28101-1939
Application address: 100 Main St., McAdenville, NC 28101, tel.: (704) 824-3551
Contact: Catherine P. Carstarphen, Pres.

Established around 1953 in NC.
Financial data (yr. ended 12/31/00): Grants paid, $101,338; assets, $677,737 (M); gifts received, $149,992; expenditures, $102,479; qualifying distributions, $101,338.
Limitations: Giving primarily in the Gaston County, NC, area.
Application information: Application form not required.
Officers: Catherine Pharr Carstarphen, Pres.; J.M. Carstarphen, V.P.
EIN: 560769476
Codes: FD2

41086
Wilson Family Memorial Scholarship
c/o First Union National Bank
401 S. Tryon St., 4th Fl.
Charlotte, NC 28288-1159

Donor(s): Harvey C. Leroy Wilson,‡ Wilson Unitrust.
Financial data (yr. ended 12/31/01): Grants paid, $100,605; assets, $2,649,646 (M); expenditures, $109,394; qualifying distributions, $100,039.
Limitations: Applications not accepted.
Application information: Contributes only to pre-selected organizations.
Trustee: First Union National Bank.
EIN: 237787902
Codes: FD2

41087
Robert A. Mills Foundation
c/o First Union National Bank
401 S. Tryon St., NC1159
Charlotte, NC 28288-1159

Established in 1979 in NJ.
Donor(s): Robert A. Mills.‡
Financial data (yr. ended 11/30/01): Grants paid, $100,500; assets, $1,559,770 (M); expenditures, $111,170; qualifying distributions, $100,807.
Limitations: Giving primarily in NJ.
Publications: Application guidelines.
Application information: Application form not required.
Trustee: First Union National Bank.
EIN: 226311439

41088
Dennis Foundation
c/o Wachovia Bank of North Carolina, N.A.
P.O. Box 3099
Winston-Salem, NC 27150-7153
Wachovia Bank of VA tel.: (804) 697-6901
Contact: Mary Jo Tull

Established in 1966 in VA.
Donor(s): Benjamin Dennis, Jr.,‡ O.D. Dennis, Sr.‡
Financial data (yr. ended 12/31/00): Grants paid, $100,000; assets, $2,484,113 (M); expenditures, $115,815; qualifying distributions, $101,741.
Limitations: Giving primarily in Richmond, VA.
Application information: Application form not required.
Manager: Wayne Oplinger.
Trustees: James W. Dennis, Wachovia Bank, N.A.
EIN: 546061431
Codes: FD2

41089
Steven Erlbaum Foundation
401 S. Tryon St., NC 1159
Charlotte, NC 28288-1159

Established in 2000 in PA.
Financial data (yr. ended 12/31/00): Grants paid, $98,500; assets, $2,151,429 (M); gifts received, $2,200,000; expenditures, $102,809; qualifying distributions, $98,500.
Limitations: Applications not accepted. Giving primarily in Philadelphia, PA.
Application information: Contributes only to pre-selected organizations.
Trustee: First Union National Bank.
EIN: 256722771
Codes: FD2

41090
USFreightways Corporation
(also known as The TNT North America Foundation Charitable Trust)
c/o Bank of America
401 S. Tryon St., 4th Fl.
Charlotte, NC 28288
Application address: c/o TNT Freightways Corp., 9700 Higgins Rd., Ste. 570, Rosemont, IL 60018
Contact: Stephen D. Gill, V.P.

Donor(s): TNT Freightways Corp., USFreightways Corporation, TNT North America Inc.
Financial data (yr. ended 11/30/01): Grants paid, $98,050; assets, $63,758 (M); expenditures, $101,389; qualifying distributions, $99,157.
Limitations: Giving primarily in IL.
Application information: Application form not required.
Directors: J.G. Carruth, Christopher L. Ellis, Neil H. Ulsh.
Trustee: Bank of America.
EIN: 566038358
Codes: CS, CD

41091
William B. McGuire, Jr. Family Foundation
309 E. Morehead St., Ste. 125
Charlotte, NC 28202

Established in 1996 in NC.
Donor(s): William B. McGuire, Jr.
Financial data (yr. ended 12/31/00): Grants paid, $98,000; assets, $2,722,003 (M); gifts received, $770,238; expenditures, $108,732; qualifying distributions, $98,000.
Limitations: Applications not accepted.
Application information: Contributes only to pre-selected organizations.
Officer and Directors:* William B. McGuire, Jr.,* Chair.; Molly L. McGuire, Susanne H. McGuire.
EIN: 561988052
Codes: FD2

41092
The Dillard Fund, Inc.
3900 Spring Garden St.
Greensboro, NC 27407 (336) 299-1211
Contact: Newell F. Holt, Chair.

Established in 1964 in NC.
Financial data (yr. ended 12/31/01): Grants paid, $97,987; assets, $1,847,759 (M); expenditures, $103,138; qualifying distributions, $109,563.
Limitations: Giving primarily in NC.
Officers and Directors:* Newell F. Holt,* Chair.; Harrison Stewart,* Secy.-Treas.; Tom Rose.
EIN: 566065838
Codes: FD2

41093
Percy & Elizabeth Meekins Charitable Trust
2 Hannover Pl., Ste. 2200
Raleigh, NC 27601 (919) 743-2200
Application address: 201 Ananias Dare St., Manteo, NC 27954-9576

Established in 1996 in NC.
Financial data (yr. ended 12/31/99): Grants paid, $97,500; assets, $2,006,019 (M); gifts received, $283,407; expenditures, $103,121; qualifying distributions, $96,525.
Limitations: Giving limited to Dare County, NC.
Application information: Application form not required.
Trustees: Myrtle E. Alexander, William Alexander, Charles Evans.
EIN: 566484256
Codes: FD2

41094
The Howe Foundation, Inc.
P.O. Box 227
Belmont, NC 28012-0749
Application address: P.O. Box 749, Belmont, NC 28012
Contact: Henry Howe, Treas.

Established in 1966 in NC.
Donor(s): Knitcraft, Inc., Beltax Corp.
Financial data (yr. ended 10/31/01): Grants paid, $97,400; assets, $2,753,958 (M); expenditures, $102,143; qualifying distributions, $101,281.
Limitations: Giving limited to the Belmont, NC, area.
Officers: Isaac E. Howe, Pres.; George M. Howe, Jr., Secy.; H.T. Howe, Treas.
Directors: Dave Hall, David J. Howe, H.R. Howe, Jr.
EIN: 566070727
Codes: CS, FD2, CD

41095
Needles Foundation
c/o First Union National Bank
401 S. Tryon St., Ste. NC1159
Charlotte, NC 28288

Established in 1984 in VA.
Financial data (yr. ended 12/31/01): Grants paid, $97,088; assets, $1,319,357 (M); expenditures, $103,907; qualifying distributions, $98,191.
Limitations: Applications not accepted. Giving primarily in VA.
Application information: Contributes only to pre-selected organizations.
Officers and Committee Members:* Karl A. Vandergriff,* V.P.; Raleigh Campbell,* Exec. Dir.; William S. Bainter, Larry D. Carter, Robert Kulinski.
Trustee: First Union National Bank.
EIN: 521390124
Codes: FD2, GTI

41096
Arrow International, Inc. Scholarship Fund
c/o First Union National Bank
401 S. Tryon St., Rm. TH-4
Charlotte, NC 28288-1159
Application address: c/o First Union National Bank, 600 Penn St., P.O.Box 1102, Reading, PA 19603
Contact: Andrew Melzer, V.P.

Established in 1994 in PA.
Donor(s): Robert L. McNeil, Jr.
Financial data (yr. ended 11/30/01): Grants paid, $96,762; assets, $1,855,663 (M); expenditures, $118,110; qualifying distributions, $97,168.
Limitations: Giving primarily in Berks County, PA.
Application information: Application form required.
Trustees: Lee Fredericks, Frederick Gaige, Kendall Teselle, First Union National Bank.
EIN: 232801942
Codes: FD2

41097
Wide Waters Fund, Inc.
117 Sheffield Cir.
Chapel Hill, NC 27514
Contact: James Bernstein, Pres.

Established in 1959.
Financial data (yr. ended 05/31/01): Grants paid, $96,500; assets, $1,983,708 (M); expenditures, $123,889; qualifying distributions, $97,819.
Limitations: Giving primarily in the East.
Application information: Application form not required.
Officer: James Bernstein, Pres. and Treas.
EIN: 136161392

Codes: FD2

41098
Smith M. U. - Lankenau Trust
401 S. Tryon St., 4th Fl.
Charlotte, NC 28288-1159

Established in 1997 in PA.
Financial data (yr. ended 05/31/01): Grants paid, $96,292; assets, $1,616,209 (M); expenditures, $100,483; qualifying distributions, $94,229.
Limitations: Applications not accepted. Giving primarily in Bryn Mawr, PA.
Application information: Contributes only to pre-selected organizations.
Trustee: First Union Corp.
EIN: 236789237
Codes: FD2

41099
Strowd Roses, Inc.
1526 E. Franklin St., Ste. 5-202
Chapel Hill, NC 27514-2827
Application address: P.O. Box 3558, Chapel Hill, NC 27515-3558
Contact: Jennifer B. Boger, Pres.

Established in 2001 in NC.
Donor(s): Irene H. Strowd,‡ Gladis H. Adams Charitable Trust.
Financial data (yr. ended 12/31/01): Grants paid, $95,027; assets, $5,059,231 (M); gifts received, $5,010,139; expenditures, $103,714; qualifying distributions, $103,714.
Limitations: Giving primarily in Orange County, NC.
Application information: Application form required.
Officers: Jennifer B. Boger, Pres.; Sydynham B. Alexander, V.P.; Stephen B. Mileler, Secy.; Donald A. Williams, Treas.
Board Members: Doris L. Hicks, Edward A. Norfleet.
EIN: 562241874
Codes: FD2

41100
Linus R. Gilbert Foundation
c/o First Union National Bank
401 S. Tryon St., 4th Fl.
Charlotte, NC 28288-1159
Application address: c/o First Union National Bank, 600 Cuthbert Blvd., Haddon Twp., NJ 08108
Contact: Shep Millar, Trust Off., First Union National Bank

Established around 1965.
Financial data (yr. ended 12/31/01): Grants paid, $95,000; assets, $1,395,202 (M); expenditures, $107,089; qualifying distributions, $94,703.
Limitations: Giving primarily in NJ.
Application information: Contact foundation for application information.
Trustees: Norma G. Farr, B. Judith Gilbert, First Union National Bank.
EIN: 226067331
Codes: FD2

41101
Community Savings Charitable Foundation, Inc.
P.O. Box 1837
Burlington, NC 27215 (336) 229-2768
Contact: William Gilliam, Pres.

Established in 1999 in NC.
Financial data (yr. ended 12/31/01): Grants paid, $94,250; assets, $1,402,572 (M); expenditures, $97,661; qualifying distributions, $93,689.
Limitations: Giving primarily in NC.

Officers: Willliam R. Gilliam, Pres.; Julian Griffin, Secy.; J.D. Moser, Jr., Treas.
EIN: 562145115
Codes: FD2

41102
Craven Charitable Trust
c/o First Union National Bank
401 S. Tryon St., NC1159
Charlotte, NC 28288

Financial data (yr. ended 12/31/01): Grants paid, $93,406; assets, $1,446,301 (M); expenditures, $105,617; qualifying distributions, $93,406.
Limitations: Applications not accepted.
Application information: Contributes only to pre-selected organizations.
Trustees: Arthur Ford III, First Union National Bank.
EIN: 237749022

41103
Loomis Foundation, Inc.
c/o Central Carolina Bank & Trust Co.
P.O. Box 51489
Durham, NC 27717-1489

Established in 1993 in NC.
Donor(s): William L. Burns, Jr.
Financial data (yr. ended 12/31/01): Grants paid, $93,167; assets, $2,159,143 (M); gifts received, $203,704; expenditures, $107,341; qualifying distributions, $91,327.
Limitations: Applications not accepted.
Application information: Contributes only to pre-selected organizations.
Officers: William L. Burns, Jr., Pres.; Dorothy Dillard Burns, V.P.; William Loomis Burns III, V.P.; Joseph Eugene Burns, Secy.; Charlton Spotswood Burns, Treas.
EIN: 561849009
Codes: FD2

41104
Clifford A. and Lillian C. Peeler Family Foundation, Inc.
P.O. Box 697
Salisbury, NC 28145-0697

Established in 1997 in NC.
Donor(s): Clifford A. Peeler.
Financial data (yr. ended 06/30/01): Grants paid, $93,000; assets, $1,942,959 (M); expenditures, $95,155; qualifying distributions, $92,157.
Limitations: Applications not accepted. Giving primarily in NC.
Application information: Contributes only to pre-selected organizations.
Officers: Shirley Ritchie, Pres.; Nancy Keppel, V.P.; Rebecca Parsons, Secy.; Larry Peeler, Treas.
EIN: 562060988
Codes: FD2

41105
Centura First Savings Foundation of Rutherford County, Inc.
c/o Centura Banks, Inc.
P.O. Box 388
Forest City, NC 28043 (828) 248-4160
FAX: (828) 248-4165
Contact: David Whilden; or Juanita Newton

Established in 1993 in NC.
Donor(s): Centura Banks, Inc., RBC Centura Banks, Inc.
Financial data (yr. ended 12/31/01): Grants paid, $92,800; assets, $1,680,610 (M); expenditures, $113,152; qualifying distributions, $93,252.
Limitations: Giving primarily in Rutherford County, NC.

Application information: Application forms available in Nov. Application form required.
Trustee: Centura Bank.
EIN: 561832201
Codes: CS, FD2, CD

41106
Knier Family Foundation
114 Edinburgh St. S., Ste. 102
Cary, NC 27511
Contact: Steve Knier, Dir.

Established in 1998 in NC.
Donor(s): Steve Knier.
Financial data (yr. ended 12/31/01): Grants paid, $92,670; assets, $1,852,512 (M); gifts received, $2,300; expenditures, $109,766; qualifying distributions, $82,460.
Director: Bonnie Knier, Steve Knier.
EIN: 562061224
Codes: FD2

41107
Jonathan Havens Charitable Trust
1 Hanover Sq., Ste. 306
Raleigh, NC 27601-1754
Application address: 600 Lyndale Ct., Ste. F, Greenville, NC 27858, tel.: (252) 756-8888
Contact: James G. Sullivan, Chair.

Established in 1992.
Financial data (yr. ended 06/30/01): Grants paid, $92,526; assets, $1,863,221 (M); expenditures, $118,416; qualifying distributions, $101,045.
Limitations: Giving limited to Beaufort County, NC.
Application information: Application form required.
Officers and Directors:* James G. Sullivan,* Chair.; Dottie Brooks,* Secy.; Edward N. Rodman.
Trustee: Bank of America.
EIN: 566378684
Codes: FD2

41108
Chou Family Foundation
13300 Durant Rd.
Raleigh, NC 27614
Contact: Alice S. Chou, Tr.

Established in 1997.
Donor(s): Alice Chou, Paul C. Chou.
Financial data (yr. ended 12/31/01): Grants paid, $92,500; assets, $3,213,472 (M); expenditures, $253,484; qualifying distributions, $92,500.
Limitations: Giving on a national basis.
Application information: Application form required.
Trustees: Alice Chou, Paul C. Chou.
EIN: 621720872
Codes: FD2

41109
Robertshaw Controls Company Foundation
c/o Wachovia Bank, N.A.
P.O. Box 3099
Winston-Salem, NC 27102-3099
Application address: c/o Robertshaw Controls Co., 2809 Emerywood Pkwy., Richmond, VA 23294-3743, tel.: (804) 289-4200
Contact: Crystal Schoof

Established in 1958 in VA.
Donor(s): Robertshaw Controls Co.
Financial data (yr. ended 12/31/01): Grants paid, $92,138; assets, $429 (M); gifts received, $31,000; expenditures, $92,163; qualifying distributions, $92,126.
Limitations: Giving primarily in VA, with emphasis on Richmond.

Application information: Application form not required.
Manager: Michael Light.
Trustee: Wachovia Bank, N.A.
EIN: 546033124
Codes: CS, FD2, CD

41110
William C. Ethridge Foundation, Inc.
2634 Dover Rd.
Raleigh, NC 27608 (919) 328-1532
Application address: c/o Jim A. King, P.O. Box 3470, Topsail Beach, NC 28445-9831
Contact: William C. Ethridge, Pres.

Established in 1992 in NC.
Donor(s): William C. Ethridge.
Financial data (yr. ended 12/31/99): Grants paid, $92,000; assets, $2,112,968 (M); expenditures, $94,584; qualifying distributions, $92,239.
Limitations: Giving primarily in NC.
Publications: Annual report.
Application information: Application form not required.
Officers and Trustees:* William C. Ethridge,* Chair. and Pres.; R. Peyton Woodson,* V.P.; Jim A. King,* Secy.-Treas.; R. Dan Edwards, James Frank Scott.
EIN: 582000825
Codes: FD2

41111
Horace L. Young Trust
c/o First Union National Bank
401 S. Tryon St., 4th Fl.
Charlotte, NC 28288-1159

Established in 1985 in PA.
Donor(s): Horace L. Young.‡
Financial data (yr. ended 12/31/01): Grants paid, $91,956; assets, $881,799 (M); expenditures, $100,043; qualifying distributions, $92,460.
Limitations: Giving on a national basis.
Trustee: First Union National Bank.
EIN: 236218857
Codes: FD2, GTI

41112
Bobby G. & Glenda C. Biggerstaff Foundation, Inc.
P.O. Box 41196
Greensboro, NC 27404-1196 (336) 282-4338
Contact: Bobby G. Biggerstaff, Dir.

Established in 1997 in NC.
Donor(s): Bobby G. Biggerstaff, Glenda C. Biggerstaff.
Financial data (yr. ended 12/31/00): Grants paid, $91,800; assets, $93,183 (M); expenditures, $98,495; qualifying distributions, $91,718.
Limitations: Giving primarily in Greensboro, NC.
Directors: Bobby G. Biggerstaff, Glenda C. Biggerstaff, Paula B. Salmon.
EIN: 562030960
Codes: FD2

41113
The Schechter Foundation, Inc.
1204 Perry Park Dr.
Kinston, NC 28501
Application address: P.O. Box 614, Kinston, NC 28502-0614, tel.: (252) 527-1128
Contact: Sol Schechter, Pres.

Established in 1982 in NC.
Donor(s): Sol Schechter.
Financial data (yr. ended 12/31/01): Grants paid, $91,465; assets, $1,753,155 (M); expenditures, $97,502; qualifying distributions, $91,465.
Limitations: Giving primarily in NC.

Application information: Application form not required.
Officers: Sol Schechter, Pres. and Treas.; Arielle C. Schechter, V.P.; Arnold M.C. Schechter, V.P.; Pearl F. Schechter, Secy.
EIN: 561318527
Codes: FD2

41114
Challenge Fund
c/o Piedmont Financial Co.
P.O. Box 20124
Greensboro, NC 27420-0124
Contact: Karen E. Brown, Acct. Admin.

Established in 1964 in NC.
Financial data (yr. ended 12/31/00): Grants paid, $91,250; assets, $246,302 (M); expenditures, $94,664; qualifying distributions, $91,200.
Limitations: Giving primarily in CA and NC.
Application information: Application form not required.
Directors: Cary R. Paynter, H. Smith Richardson III, Page Richardson.
EIN: 566059951
Codes: FD2

41115
The B. N. & W. L. Jordan Scholarship Fund
c/o Wachovia Bank of North Carolina, N.A.
P.O. Box 3099
Winston-Salem, NC 27150-6732
Contact: Ed Loflin, Admin.

Established in 1997 in NC.
Financial data (yr. ended 12/31/01): Grants paid, $91,002; assets, $1,435,388 (M); expenditures, $108,269; qualifying distributions, $92,643.
Limitations: Giving limited to Henderson County, NC.
Application information: Application form required.
Trustee: Wachovia Bank of North Carolina, N.A.
EIN: 566487341
Codes: FD2

41116
Stuart and Margaret L. Forbes Foundation, Inc.
216 Pacolet St.
Tryon, NC 28782

Established in 1998 in NC.
Financial data (yr. ended 02/28/02): Grants paid, $90,961; assets, $854,384 (M); gifts received, $354,228; expenditures, $103,515; qualifying distributions, $90,961.
Officer: Margaret L. Forbes, Chair.
EIN: 562079528

41117
The Miller Family Foundation
100 Kemp Rd. W.
Greensboro, NC 27410

Established in 1988 in NC.
Donor(s): Kenneth J. Miller, Deborah W. Miller.
Financial data (yr. ended 12/31/01): Grants paid, $90,784; assets, $163,424 (M); gifts received, $65,548; expenditures, $93,708; qualifying distributions, $90,784.
Limitations: Applications not accepted. Giving primarily in Greensboro, NC.
Application information: Contributes only to pre-selected organizations.
Officers: Kenneth J. Miller, Pres. and Treas.; Deborah W. Miller, V.P. and Secy.
Directors: Stacey M. Gorelick, C. Davis Miller.
EIN: 581776784
Codes: FD2

41118
Lucas Family Foundation
c/o Wachovia Bank of North Carolina, N.A.
P.O. Box 3099
Winston-Salem, NC 27150-7153
Application address: P.O. Box 3931, Florence, SC 29501, tel.: (843) 662-2300
Contact: Marion D. Lucas, Jr., Tr.

Established in 1992 in NC.
Donor(s): Marion D. Lucas, Jr.
Financial data (yr. ended 12/31/00): Grants paid, $90,745; assets, $2,080,668 (M); expenditures, $114,188; qualifying distributions, $90,745.
Limitations: Giving primarily in SC.
Trustees: Finley P. Lucas, Marion D. Lucas, Jr., Marion D. Lucas III, Ruth E. Lucas.
Agent: Wachovia Bank of North Carolina, N.A.
EIN: 570966153
Codes: FD2

41119
The Harold & Margaret Deal Foundation
1460 6th St. Cir. N.W.
Hickory, NC 28601 (828) 324-7466
Contact: Ronald E. Deal, V.P.

Established in 1994 in NC.
Donor(s): Margaret S. Deal.
Financial data (yr. ended 12/31/01): Grants paid, $90,000; assets, $823,547 (M); gifts received, $4,434; expenditures, $102,375; qualifying distributions, $90,000.
Limitations: Giving limited to NC.
Officers and Directors:* Margaret S. Deal,* Pres.; Suzanne D. Wells,* V.P. and Secy.; Ronald E. Deal,* V.P. and Treas.
EIN: 561896328

41120
L. Jack & Ella Shaw Spiers Foundation
c/o Wachovia Bank of North Carolina, N.A.
P.O. Box 3099
Winston-Salem, NC 27150-7153

Established in 1995 in NC.
Financial data (yr. ended 12/31/00): Grants paid, $90,000; assets, $698,761 (M); expenditures, $98,710; qualifying distributions, $90,523.
Limitations: Applications not accepted.
Application information: Contributes only to pre-selected organizations.
Trustee: Wachovia Bank of North Carolina, N.A.
EIN: 582241078
Codes: FD2

41121
The Ardizzone Charitable Foundation, Inc.
5416 Challisford Ln.
Charlotte, NC 28226

Established in 1998 in NC.
Donor(s): Ramon D. Ardizzone.
Financial data (yr. ended 12/31/01): Grants paid, $89,525; assets, $2,958 (M); gifts received, $92,255; expenditures, $89,606; qualifying distributions, $89,525.
Limitations: Applications not accepted.
Application information: Contributes only to pre-selected organizations.
Officers and Directors:* Ramon D. Ardizzone,* Pres.; Carole K. Ardizzone,* V.P.; Dale S. Ardizzone,* Secy.; Kristen K. Ardizzone,* Treas.; Barbara Ardizzone.
EIN: 562105490

41122
Esther McDonald Foundation
c/o First Union National Bank
401 S. Tryon St., Ste. 4th Fl.
Charlotte, NC 28288-1159

Established in 1998 in DE.
Financial data (yr. ended 12/31/01): Grants paid, $89,280; assets, $529,742 (M); expenditures, $97,320; qualifying distributions, $89,931.
Limitations: Applications not accepted. Giving primarily in Wilmington, DE, and New York, NY.
Application information: Contributes only to pre-selected organizations.
Trustee: First Union National Bank.
EIN: 516191503
Codes: FD2

41123
F. R. Robuck Family Foundation, Inc.
P.O. Box 17102
Raleigh, NC 27619-7102
Contact: Franklin L. Robuck, Jr., Pres.

Established in 1995 in NC.
Donor(s): Franklin L. Robuck, Jr.
Financial data (yr. ended 12/31/00): Grants paid, $89,275; assets, $1,892,065 (M); gifts received, $222,000; expenditures, $93,466; qualifying distributions, $89,275.
Limitations: Applications not accepted.
Application information: Contributes only to pre-selected organizations.
Officers: Franklin L. Robuck, Jr., Pres. and Treas.; Linda J. Robuck, Secy.
EIN: 581692303
Codes: FD2

41124
Lemma M. Apple & Ben R. Apple Foundation
1876 Hagers Point Ln.
Denver, NC 28037 (704) 483-5387
Contact: Ben T. Vernon, Tr.

Established in 1988 in NC.
Donor(s): Lemma M. Apple.‡
Financial data (yr. ended 12/31/99): Grants paid, $89,168; assets, $1,940,142 (M); expenditures, $131,226; qualifying distributions, $89,168.
Limitations: Applications not accepted. Giving limited to eastern Stokes and western Rockingham counties, NC.
Application information: Contributes only to pre-selected organizations.
Trustees: J. Michael Cumberland, James F. McMichael, Benjamin T. Vernon, S.J. Webster, Jr.
EIN: 581750755
Codes: FD2

41125
Edward A. Arditti Charitable Foundation
P.O. Box 221
Hickory, NC 28603 (828) 322-5870
Contact: Edward A. Arditti, Pres.

Established in 1992 in NC.
Donor(s): Edward A. Arditti.
Financial data (yr. ended 04/30/01): Grants paid, $89,014; assets, $1,335,240 (L); gifts received, $25,000; expenditures, $90,188; qualifying distributions, $87,841.
Limitations: Giving primarily in NC.
Application information: Application form not required.
Officers and Directors:* Edward A. Arditti,* Pres.; Jeffrey Arditti,* V.P.; Omega Starnes,* Secy.-Treas.; Martin C. Pannell, Charles M. Snipes.
EIN: 561777663
Codes: FD2

41126
Blystone Foundation
13515 Ballantyne Corp. Pl.
Charlotte, NC 28277

Established in 1997 in MI.
Donor(s): John B. Blystone.
Financial data (yr. ended 12/31/01): Grants paid, $88,980; assets, $86,714 (M); gifts received, $150,520; expenditures, $90,912; qualifying distributions, $90,855.
Limitations: Applications not accepted. Giving primarily in Muskegon, MI and South Bend, IN.
Application information: Contributes only to pre-selected organizations.
Officers and Directors:* John B. Blystone,* Pres. and Treas.; Julie A. Blystone,* Secy.; Christopher J. Kearney, James M. Sheridan.
EIN: 383381956
Codes: FD2

41127
The Grace and Hope Foundation, Inc.
504 S. Trade St.
Matthews, NC 28105

Established in 1997 in NC.
Donor(s): Aana Lisa Johnson Whatley.
Financial data (yr. ended 12/31/00): Grants paid, $88,953; assets, $1,803,568 (M); gifts received, $1,000,000; expenditures, $110,143; qualifying distributions, $88,447.
Limitations: Applications not accepted. Giving primarily in NC.
Application information: Contributes only to pre-selected organizations.
Officer and Board Members:* Aana Lisa Johnson Whatley,* Chair.; James Lee Johnson, Jon Stephen Johnson, Aana Lisa Kane, James Edward Whatley, Jr.
EIN: 582303901
Codes: FD2

41128
Karl M. and Ruth W. Linville Memorial Foundation
c/o Wachovia Bank, N.A.
P. O. Box 3099
Winston-Salem, NC 27150-6732

Donor(s): Karl Linville, Ruth Linville.
Financial data (yr. ended 12/31/01): Grants paid, $88,924; assets, $2,209,717 (M); gifts received, $920,762; expenditures, $104,068; qualifying distributions, $90,924.
Limitations: Applications not accepted.
Application information: Contributes only to pre-selected organizations.
Trustee: Wachovia Bank, N.A.
EIN: 566570414
Codes: FD2

41129
Winn Foundation Trust
c/o First Union National Bank
401 S. Tryon St., 4th Fl.
Charlotte, NC 28288-1159
Application address: c/o First Union National Bank, 123 Broad St., Philadelphia, PA 19109-9989

Established in 1967.
Donor(s): Mary E. Winn.
Financial data (yr. ended 12/31/01): Grants paid, $88,600; assets, $1,950,727 (M); expenditures, $98,304; qualifying distributions, $88,196.
Application information: Application form not required.
Trustee: First Union National Bank.
EIN: 596194105
Codes: FD2

41130
Cooley Family Foundation
2548 Roswell Ave.
Charlotte, NC 28209
Application address: c/o Bank of America, NC1-007-57-02, 100 N. Tryon St., Charlotte, NC 28202
Contact: Nancy D. Dry, Tr.

Established in 1997 in NC.
Donor(s): Charles J. Cooley.
Financial data (yr. ended 12/31/01): Grants paid, $88,345; assets, $817,186 (M); expenditures, $99,184; qualifying distributions, $81,421.
Limitations: Giving primarily in Charlotte, NC.
Application information: Application form not required.
Officers and Directors:* Bernadette K. Cooley,* Pres.; Charles Jennings Cooley II,* Exec. V.P.; Christopher Young Cooley,* Exec. V.P.; Kathryn Cooley Heiser,* Exec. V.P.; Charles J. Cooley,* Secy.-Treas.
Trustee: Nancy D. Dry.
EIN: 562026137
Codes: FD2

41131
The Stubblefield Foundation, Inc.
8525 Double Eagle Gateway
Charlotte, NC 28210
Application address: P.O. Box 7500, Charlotte, NC 28241, tel.: (704) 588-3030
Contact: Fred Stubblefield, Jr., Pres.

Established in 1991 in NC.
Donor(s): Fred Stubblefield, Jr.
Financial data (yr. ended 12/31/01): Grants paid, $88,250; assets, $1,339,441 (M); expenditures, $89,029; qualifying distributions, $88,250.
Limitations: Giving primarily in NC.
Officers and Directors:* Fred Stubblefield, Jr.,* Pres.; Nancy K. Stubblefield,* V.P.; Fred Stubblefield III,* Secy.; Lisa S. Ballard,* Treas.
EIN: 561760217
Codes: FD2

41132
Robert E. Bryan, Jr. Foundation
P.O Box 53557
Fayetteville, NC 28305
Contact: Robert E. Bryan, Jr., Pres.

Established in 1998 in NC.
Donor(s): Robert E. Bryan, Jr.
Financial data (yr. ended 12/31/01): Grants paid, $87,750; assets, $1,086,931 (M); gifts received, $153,490; expenditures, $88,570; qualifying distributions, $87,750.
Limitations: Giving primarily in NC.
Officer: Robert E. Bryan, Jr., Pres.
EIN: 311623195
Codes: FD2

41133
Evelyn B. Pope & Ruth P. Pope Charitable Foundation
216 E. Chatham St., Ste. 106
Cary, NC 27511

Established in 1999 in NC.
Donor(s): Ruth P. Pope.
Financial data (yr. ended 12/31/01): Grants paid, $87,500; assets, $1,000,413 (M); gifts received, $5,209; expenditures, $180,021; qualifying distributions, $87,500.
Limitations: Applications not accepted. Giving primarily in NC.
Application information: Contributes only to pre-selected organizations.
Trustees: James D. Cox, Stanley L. Dalton.
EIN: 561941321

Codes: FD2

41134
Louise H. Haeseler Memorial Fund
c/o First Union National Bank
401 S. Tryon St., 4th Fl.
Charlotte, NC 28288-1159
Application address: c/o Philadelphia High School for Girls, Bread and Olney Sts., Philadelphia, PA 19141
Contact: Judith Brindle, Tr.

Financial data (yr. ended 12/31/01): Grants paid, $87,276; assets, $793,623 (M); expenditures, $95,284; qualifying distributions, $87,117.
Limitations: Giving limited to the Philadelphia, PA, area.
Application information: Application form required.
Officers and Trustees:* Eva F. Fidler,* Chair.; Mervin Krimins,* Treas.; Judith Brindle, Frances Conway, Eva F. Fidler, Albert I. Glassman, Doris T. Johnson, Fannie Kendall, Cora Robinson, Mary H. Wright, First Union National Bank.
EIN: 236428035
Codes: FD2, GTI

41135
The Hudson Foundation
c/o Thomas W. Hudson, Jr.
10730 Governors Dr.
Chapel Hill, NC 27514-8405

Established in 1991 in NY.
Donor(s): Thomas W. Hudson, Jr.
Financial data (yr. ended 01/31/01): Grants paid, $86,500; assets, $4,048,704 (M); gifts received, $415,000; expenditures, $97,417; qualifying distributions, $97,017.
Limitations: Applications not accepted. Giving primarily in NC.
Application information: Contributes only to pre-selected organizations.
Trustees: John A. Gerson, Mary J. Hudson, Thomas W. Hudson, Jr.
EIN: 136968093
Codes: FD2

41136
John S. Carpenter Trust
c/o First Union National Bank
101 S. Tryon St., NC1159
Charlotte, NC 28288
Application address: c/o First Union National Bank, Broad and Walnut Sts., Philadelphia, PA 19109

Established in 1995 in NJ.
Financial data (yr. ended 12/31/00): Grants paid, $86,398; assets, $1,214,874 (M); expenditures, $96,831; qualifying distributions, $87,736.
Limitations: Giving on a national basis.
Trustee: First Union National Bank.
EIN: 226501059
Codes: FD2, GTI

41137
Sverdrup Corporation Charitable Trust
(Formerly Sverdrup & Parcel, Inc. Charitable Trust)
c/o First Union National Bank
401 S. Tryon St., 4th Fl.
Charlotte, NC 28288-1159

Established in 1951 in MO.
Donor(s): Sverdrup Corp.
Financial data (yr. ended 12/31/01): Grants paid, $85,200; assets, $241,151 (M); expenditures, $85,283; qualifying distributions, $85,200.
Limitations: Applications not accepted. Giving primarily in St. Louis, MO.

Application information: New requests for support are not being considered; the trust will fulfill its previous multi-year contribution commitments.
Board of Control: R.J. Messey, J.S. Raeder, H.G. Schwartz.
Trustee: First Union National Bank.
EIN: 436023499
Codes: TN

41138
Alwinell Foundation
c/o Bank of America
1 Bank of America Plz., NC1002-11-18
Charlotte, NC 28255

Established in 1951 in NC.
Donor(s): Allison-Erwin Co., Industrial & Textile Supply Co.
Financial data (yr. ended 05/31/01): Grants paid, $85,000; assets, $1,381,629 (M); expenditures, $91,079; qualifying distributions, $85,000.
Limitations: Applications not accepted. Giving primarily in Charlotte, NC.
Application information: Contributes only to pre-selected organizations.
Officers: Henry J. Allison, Jr., Secy.; James R. Allison, Mgr.; R.K. Allison, Mgr.
Trustee: Bank of America.
EIN: 566039491
Codes: FD2

41139
Nash Family Foundation, Inc.
P.O. Box 2870
Asheville, NC 28802 (828) 684-2747
Contact: Thomas E. Nash, Jr., Dir.

Established in 2000 in NC.
Donor(s): Thomas E. Nash, Jr.
Financial data (yr. ended 12/31/01): Grants paid, $85,000; assets, $794,515 (M); gifts received, $385,000; expenditures, $94,987; qualifying distributions, $85,000.
Limitations: Giving primarily in NC.
Directors: Brenda G. Nash, Thomas E. Nash, Jr.
EIN: 561923903

41140
The Robert H. and Kathryne B. Tharpe Foundation
(Formerly The Tharpe Foundation)
c/o Wachovia Bank of North Carolina, N.A.
P.O. Box 3099
Winston-Salem, NC 27150-0001

Established in 1989 in GA.
Donor(s): Robert H. Tharpe, Sr., Kathryne Brook Tharpe.
Financial data (yr. ended 12/31/01): Grants paid, $84,500; assets, $1,448,412 (M); expenditures, $100,592; qualifying distributions, $86,152.
Limitations: Applications not accepted. Giving primarily in GA.
Application information: Unsolicited requests for funds not accepted.
Trustee: Wachovia Bank of North Carolina, N.A.
Directors: Linda Tharpe, Mercer McCall Tharpe, Patrice J. Tharpe, Robert H. Tharpe, Jr.
EIN: 581858404
Codes: FD2, GTI

41141—NORTH CAROLINA

41141
The Marc and Mattye Silverman Family Foundation
(Formerly The Silverman Foundation)
6707-C Fairview Rd.
Charlotte, NC 28210
FAX: (704) 362-2279
Contact: Mattye B. Silverman, Pres.

Established in 1989 in NC.
Donor(s): Marc H. Silverman, Mattye B. Silverman.
Financial data (yr. ended 03/31/01): Grants paid, $84,472; assets, $2,209,939 (M); gifts received, $124,865; expenditures, $116,895; qualifying distributions, $84,472.
Limitations: Giving primarily in Charlotte, NC.
Application information: Application form required.
Officer and Directors:* Mattye B. Silverman,* Pres.; Lorin L. Silverman, Shara K. Silverman, Fred C. Thompson.
EIN: 561678118
Codes: FD2

41142
The Thomas B. and Robertha K. Coleman Foundation, Inc.
P.O. Box 1169
New Bern, NC 28563

Established in 1998 in NC.
Donor(s): Robertha K. Coleman.
Financial data (yr. ended 12/31/00): Grants paid, $84,435; assets, $2,745,739 (M); expenditures, $127,300; qualifying distributions, $84,435.
Limitations: Applications not accepted. Giving primarily in New Bern, NC.
Application information: Contributes only to pre-selected organizations.
Officers: Katherine C. Haroldson, Pres. and Secy.; Robertha K. Coleman, V.P.; Thomas Brooks Coleman III, V.P.; John O. Haroldson, Treas.
EIN: 562086113
Codes: FD2

41143
Christian International and Domestic Services, Inc.
P.O. Box 1033
Lincolnton, NC 28093
Application address: 1379 S. Aspen St., Lincolnton, NC 28092, tel.: (704) 735-1421 or (704) 732-1108
Contact: William D. Beutel, Pres.

Established around 1994.
Donor(s): William D. Beutel.
Financial data (yr. ended 12/31/99): Grants paid, $84,327; assets, $7,020 (M); gifts received, $84,261; expenditures, $86,424; qualifying distributions, $86,325.
Officers: William D. Beutel, Pres.; Nancy A. Beutel, V.P.; Rev. Oliver Perry, Secy.-Treas.
Directors: Kay Reynolds, Ned Reynolds, Mendall Smith.
EIN: 561788014
Codes: FD2

41144
The Lookout Foundation
c/o U.S. Trust
P.O. Box 26262
Greensboro, NC 27420

Established in 1999 in NC.
Donor(s): Stephen C. Hassenfelt, Pamela H. Hassenfelt.
Financial data (yr. ended 06/30/01): Grants paid, $83,425; assets, $702,665 (M); gifts received, $4,342; expenditures, $93,509; qualifying distributions, $83,425.
Limitations: Applications not accepted.
Application information: Contributes only to pre-selected organizations.
Officers: Stephen C. Hassenfelt, Pres. and Treas.; Pamela H. Hassenfelt, V.P. and Secy.
EIN: 562173641
Codes: FD2

41145
Walter D. Dunn Memorial Trust
c/o First Union National Bank
401 S. Tryon., Ste. TH-4
Charlotte, NC 28288-1159

Established in 1995 in PA.
Financial data (yr. ended 04/30/01): Grants paid, $83,248; assets, $1,728,130 (M); expenditures, $97,536; qualifying distributions, $80,905.
Limitations: Applications not accepted. Giving primarily in Philadelphia, PA.
Application information: Contributes only to pre-selected organizations.
Trustee: First Union National Bank.
EIN: 236609806
Codes: FD2

41146
Helen M. Clabough Charitable Foundation
P.O. Box 434
Blowing Rock, NC 28605-0434
(828) 295-5054
Contact: Carole Spainhour, Tr.

Established in 1999 in NC.
Donor(s): Helen M. Clabough.
Financial data (yr. ended 12/31/01): Grants paid, $83,000; assets, $9,624 (M); gifts received, $30,000; expenditures, $99,069; qualifying distributions, $83,000.
Trustees: Helen M. Clabough, Frank B. Gibb III, Carole Spainhour.
EIN: 566527710

41147
Victoria Susan Sutton Charitable Trust
c/o Grier & Grier, PA
101 N. Tryon St., Ste. 1240
Charlotte, NC 28246-0001

Established in 1990 in NC.
Donor(s): Victoria Susan Sutton.
Financial data (yr. ended 12/31/00): Grants paid, $82,925; assets, $2,357 (M); gifts received, $50,807; expenditures, $86,936; qualifying distributions, $82,925.
Limitations: Applications not accepted. Giving primarily in NC.
Application information: Contributes only to pre-selected organizations.
Officers and Trustees:* Victoria Susan Sutton,* Chair.; Kathryn Lynn Ridge,* Vice-Chair.; Elizabeth Sutton Spratt,* Secy.; Charles Davis Bing, Catherine Sutton Bryant.
EIN: 566376395
Codes: FD2

41148
The Seymour Levin Foundation, Inc.
6 New Bern Sq.
Greensboro, NC 27408-3835

Established in 1990 in NC.
Donor(s): Levin Investment Co.
Financial data (yr. ended 12/31/00): Grants paid, $82,908; assets, $1,850,434 (M); expenditures, $95,544; qualifying distributions, $82,908.
Limitations: Applications not accepted. Giving primarily in NC.
Application information: Contributes only to pre-selected organizations.
Officers and Directors:* Seymour Levin,* Pres. and Treas.; Carol Levin,* V.P. and Secy.; Freddy Robinson.
EIN: 581898093
Codes: FD2

41149
Charles Preston Lunsford & Marion Garrett Lunsford Charitable Trust
c/o First Union National Bank
401 S. Tryon St., 4th Fl.
Charlotte, NC 28288-1159
Application address: c/o First Union National Bank, P.O. Box 14061, Roanoke, VA 24040, tel.: (703) 563-7887
Contact: Charles I. Lunsford II, Tr.

Established in 1978 in VA.
Financial data (yr. ended 12/31/01): Grants paid, $82,838; assets, $1,563,197 (M); expenditures, $98,576; qualifying distributions, $83,724.
Limitations: Giving primarily in Roanoke, VA.
Trustees: Charles I. Lunsford II, First Union National Bank.
EIN: 546166191
Codes: FD2

41150
Burning Bush Foundation
P.O. Box 81
Montreat, NC 28757
Contact: James W. Taylor, Pres.

Established in 1999 in NC.
Donor(s): James W. Taylor, Letta Jean Taylor.
Financial data (yr. ended 12/31/00): Grants paid, $82,760; assets, $300,877 (M); gifts received, $176; expenditures, $84,472; qualifying distributions, $80,958.
Officers: James W. Taylor, Jr., Pres.; Letta Jean Taylor, V.P. and Secy.-Treas.
Directors: Steven T. Aceto, Katherine T. Condon, Stephen L. Condon.
EIN: 582407717

41151
The Fast Foundation, Inc.
8812 Lake Challis Ln.
Charlotte, NC 28226

Established in 1994.
Donor(s): Anthony S. Johnson, Shelley M. Johnson.
Financial data (yr. ended 12/31/00): Grants paid, $82,310; assets, $160,345 (M); gifts received, $80,000; expenditures, $88,577; qualifying distributions, $82,310.
Limitations: Applications not accepted. Giving on a national basis.
Application information: Contributes only to pre-selected organizations.
Officers: Anthony S. Johnson, Pres.; Shelley M. Johnson, Secy.-Treas.
EIN: 351913602
Codes: FD2

41152
Bank of Granite Foundation
c/o Bank of Granite Corp.
23 N. Main St.
Granite Falls, NC 28630-1401

Established around 1966 in NC.
Donor(s): Bank of Granite Corp.
Financial data (yr. ended 12/31/01): Grants paid, $82,260; assets, $249,055 (M); gifts received, $72,000; expenditures, $83,858; qualifying distributions, $82,260.

Limitations: Applications not accepted. Giving limited to NC.
Application information: Contributes only to pre-selected organizations.
Trustees: John A. Forlines, Charles M. Snipes.
EIN: 566075867
Codes: CS, CD

41153
Bailey Endowment, Inc.
27 E. Randolph Rd.
Shelby, NC 28150 (704) 487-8888
Contact: Hoyt Q. Bailey, Dir.

Established in 1992 in NC.
Donor(s): Hoyt Q. Bailey.
Financial data (yr. ended 12/31/00): Grants paid, $82,175; assets, $2,383,306 (M); gifts received, $45,173; expenditures, $87,172; qualifying distributions, $82,175.
Limitations: Giving primarily in Shelby, NC.
Officers and Directors:* Hoyt G. Tessener,* Pres. and Secy.; Cynthia B. Bailey,* V.P.; Melanie A. Bailey,* V.P.; Hoyt Q. Bailey.
EIN: 561802700
Codes: FD2

41154
Rocky Mount Community Foundation, Inc.
P.O. Box 7608
Rocky Mount, NC 27804
Application address: 1100 N. Wesleyan Blvd., Rocky Mount, NC 27804, tel.: (252) 446-6131
Contact: J. Buckley Strandberg, Pres.

Established in 1997 in NC.
Donor(s): Rocky Mount Merchants Association.
Financial data (yr. ended 12/31/01): Grants paid, $81,926; assets, $3,693,840 (M); gifts received, $671,138; expenditures, $112,262; qualifying distributions, $81,926.
Limitations: Giving limited to the Rocky Mount, NC, area.
Officers: J. Buckley Strandberg, Pres. and Secy.; Eugene F. Holland, Jr., Treas.
Directors: Bill Daughtridge, John B. Kincheloe, Jr., Charles Penny, Cindy Stewart.
EIN: 562055212
Codes: FD2

41155
Cleon W. Mauldin Foundation
c/o First Union National Bank
401 S. Tryon St., 4th Fl.
Charlotte, NC 28288-1159

Established in 1999 in GA.
Financial data (yr. ended 03/31/02): Grants paid, $80,500; assets, $1,550,839 (M); expenditures, $93,039; qualifying distributions, $80,931.
Limitations: Applications not accepted.
Application information: Contributes only to pre-selected organizations.
Trustee: First Union National Bank.
EIN: 656290702
Codes: FD2

41156
Southland Charitable Trust
P.O. Box 20409
Raleigh, NC 27619

Established in 1986.
Donor(s): Gordon Smith, Jr., Jean P. Smith.
Financial data (yr. ended 06/30/01): Grants paid, $80,500; assets, $1,772,083 (M); expenditures, $106,600; qualifying distributions, $575,500; giving activities include $495,000 for loans.
Limitations: Applications not accepted. Giving primarily in NC and VA.

Application information: Contributes only to pre-selected organizations.
Trustees: Clark Smith, Gordon Smith.
EIN: 566268422
Codes: FD2

41157
The Sadie Bernstine and Henrietta Harris Scholarship Fund
c/o First Union National Bank
401 S. Tryon St., NC 1159
Charlotte, NC 28288-1159
Application address: c/o Principal, Atlantic City High School, 1400 N. Albany Ave., Atlantic City, NJ 08401-1208

Donor(s): Sadie Bernstine,‡ Henrietta Harris.‡
Financial data (yr. ended 09/30/01): Grants paid, $80,250; assets, $1,495,114 (M); expenditures, $96,710; qualifying distributions, $83,007.
Limitations: Giving limited to residents of Atlantic City, NJ.
Application information: Application form required.
Trustees: Harvey Elfman, First Union National Bank.
EIN: 226347842
Codes: FD2, GTI

41158
Wilma R. McCurdy Memorial Trust Fund
c/o First Union National Bank
301 S. Tryon St.
Charlotte, NC 28288-1159 (704) 383-6937
Contact: Mary Logan, V.P., First Union National Bank

Established in 1973 in NC.
Financial data (yr. ended 06/30/01): Grants paid, $80,250; assets, $1,464,531 (M); expenditures, $96,806; qualifying distributions, $80,043.
Limitations: Giving primarily in NC.
Trustees: Rev. Harold L. McDonald, Jerry E. McGee, First Union National Bank.
EIN: 566169358
Codes: FD2

41159
The Borden Fund, Inc.
(Formerly Borden Manufacturing Company Fund, Inc.)
P.O. Drawer P
Goldsboro, NC 27533-9715

Established in 1952 in NC.
Donor(s): Borden Manufacturing Co.
Financial data (yr. ended 12/31/01): Grants paid, $80,101; assets, $2,074,537 (M); expenditures, $127,956; qualifying distributions, $110,281.
Limitations: Applications not accepted. Giving primarily in Goldsboro, NC, and areas of company operations.
Application information: Contributes only to pre-selected organizations.
Officers: W. Lee Borden, Pres. and Treas.; Robert H. Borden, V.P.; Edwin B. Borden III, Secy.
EIN: 566045689
Codes: CS, FD2, CD

41160
Ephraim Bloch Charitable Trust
4500 Cameron Valley Pkwy., Ste. 130
Charlotte, NC 28211-3552

Established in 1999 in CT.
Donor(s): Ephraim Bloch, Michelle Bloch.
Financial data (yr. ended 12/31/99): Grants paid, $80,000; assets, $903,324 (M); gifts received, $1,000,000; expenditures, $80,000; qualifying distributions, $80,000.

Limitations: Applications not accepted. Giving primarily in FL.
Application information: Contributes only to pre-selected organizations.
Trustee: Michelle Bloch.
EIN: 656274062
Codes: FD2

41161
Frances V. Holton Foundation
c/o Donald F. Fontes
4300 Six Forks, Ste. 400
Raleigh, NC 27609

Established in 1998 in NC.
Donor(s): Frances V. Holton.
Financial data (yr. ended 12/31/01): Grants paid, $80,000; assets, $2,458,245 (M); gifts received, $1,842,945; expenditures, $179,685; qualifying distributions, $80,000.
Limitations: Applications not accepted. Giving primarily in NC.
Application information: Contributes only to pre-selected organizations.
Officers and Directors:* Frances V. Holton,* Pres.; Donald F. Fontes,* Secy.; William J. Blanton,* Treas.
EIN: 562091275

41162
George T. Lewis, Jr. & Betty G. Lewis Educational Foundation
9405 Arrowpoint Blvd.
Charlotte, NC 28273-8110

Established in 1993 in NC.
Financial data (yr. ended 12/31/01): Grants paid, $80,000; assets, $1,133,875 (M); expenditures, $105,200; qualifying distributions, $80,000.
Limitations: Giving primarily in NC.
Officers: James E. Lewis, Pres.; David J. Lewis, Secy.-Treas.
Director: William J. Boardman.
EIN: 561851327

41163
Willis Family Foundation
3522 Niblock Ct.
Denver, NC 28037 (704) 483-1997
Contact: Jennie Willis List, Secy.

Established in 1997 in NC.
Donor(s): James Richard Willis.
Financial data (yr. ended 12/31/00): Grants paid, $79,500; assets, $1,404,489 (M); expenditures, $125,064; qualifying distributions, $79,500.
Limitations: Giving primarily in NC.
Officers and Directors:* James Richard Willis, Pres.; Evelyn R. Willis,* V.P.; Jennie Willis List,* Secy.; Michael Willis Good, Jeffrey Ledward.
EIN: 562055841
Codes: FD2

41164
A. Alex Shuford Foundation
P.O. Box 2228
Hickory, NC 28603-0608
Tel.: (828) 328-2141, Ext. 8500; E-mail: hshuford@shurtape.com
Contact: C. Hunt Shuford, Jr., Secy.-Treas.

Established in 1952 in NC.
Financial data (yr. ended 12/31/01): Grants paid, $78,000; assets, $121,140 (M); expenditures, $78,000; qualifying distributions, $78,000.
Limitations: Applications not accepted. Giving primarily in NC, with an emphasis on Hickory.
Application information: Contributes only to pre-selected organizations.
Officers: Peggy B. Shuford, Pres.; C. Hunt Shuford, Jr., Secy.-Treas.

41164—NORTH CAROLINA

Directors: Dorothy S. Lanier, A. Pope Shuford, James B. Shuford, Stephenson P. Shuford.
EIN: 566039449
Codes: FD2

41165
Earl Johnson, Jr. & Margery Scott Johnson Endowment Trust
P.O. Box 26262
Greensboro, NC 27402

Established in 1960 in NC.
Donor(s): Margery Scott Johnson, Earl Johnson, Jr.
Financial data (yr. ended 12/31/00): Grants paid, $77,750; assets, $874,789 (M); expenditures, $86,135; qualifying distributions, $79,771.
Limitations: Applications not accepted. Giving primarily in Raleigh, NC.
Application information: Contributes only to pre-selected organizations.
Trustees: Earl Johnson, Jr., Margery Scott Johnson.
EIN: 546048452
Codes: FD2

41166
The Dragon Foundation, Inc.
c/o Wachovia Bank N.A.
P.O. Box 3099
Winston-Salem, NC 27150-7131

Established in 1999 in GA.
Financial data (yr. ended 12/31/00): Grants paid, $77,500; assets, $361,336 (M); gifts received, $6,387; expenditures, $92,143; qualifying distributions, $77,500.
Limitations: Applications not accepted.
Application information: Contributes only to pre-selected organizations.
Director: David S. Golden.
Trustee: Wachovia Bank, N.A.
EIN: 566554615
Codes: FD2

41167
Roderick J. & Gertrude B. Jordan Charitable Trust
P.O Box 448
Murfreesboro, NC 27855-0448
(252) 398-4171
Contact: J. Guy Revelle, Jr., Tr.

Financial data (yr. ended 03/31/01): Grants paid, $77,500; assets, $1,155,046 (M); expenditures, $111,665; qualifying distributions, $107,342.
Limitations: Giving limited to residents of Northampton County, NC.
Application information: Applications available at Northampton County, NC, high schools. Application form required.
Trustees: Elizabeth P. Barnes, L. Frank Burleson, Ben I. Mann, J. Guy Revelle, Jr., Linwood E. Ward.
EIN: 566302665
Codes: FD2, GTI

41168
The Halstead Foundation, Inc.
P.O. Box 9983
Greensboro, NC 27429
Contact: Peggy Robertson, V.P.

Established in 1988 in NC.
Donor(s): Halstead Industries, Inc.
Financial data (yr. ended 12/31/00): Grants paid, $77,100; assets, $1,997,318 (M); expenditures, $115,000; qualifying distributions, $99,187.
Limitations: Giving primarily in Greensboro, NC.
Officers: Bill Halstead, Chair.; Martha Halstead, Pres.; Leroy Lintz, V.P.; Peggy Robertson, V.P.
EIN: 581821220
Codes: CS, FD2, CD

41169
Gipson Family Foundation
7340 Six Forks Rd.
Raleigh, NC 27615
Contact: Thomas L. Gipson, Tr.

Established in 1996.
Financial data (yr. ended 12/31/01): Grants paid, $77,000; assets, $2,638,059 (M); expenditures, $78,025; qualifying distributions, $54,763.
Limitations: Giving primarily in NC.
Application information: Application form required.
Trustees: Elizabeth Cheatham, Cary Gipson, Clay Gipson, Donald Gipson, Patricia Gipson, Thomas L. Gipson.
EIN: 562001414
Codes: FD2

41170
The Guilford Foundation
P.O. Box 26969
Greensboro, NC 27419-6969 (336) 316-4000
Application address: 4925 W. Market St., Greensboro, NC 27409
Contact: Charles A. Hayes, Pres.

Established in 1992 in NC.
Donor(s): Guilford Mills, Inc.
Financial data (yr. ended 06/30/01): Grants paid, $77,000; assets, $2,037,189 (M); expenditures, $77,809; qualifying distributions, $77,000.
Limitations: Giving limited to NC.
Officers: Charles A. Hayes, Pres.; J. Douglas Galyon, V.P.; Robert A. Emken, Secy.; Kim A. Thompson, Treas.
EIN: 561797269
Codes: CS, FD2, CD

41171
The J. E. and Mildred Waggoner Foundation, Inc.
536 Torrence Dr.
Gastonia, NC 28054
Contact: Ruth Waggoner, Treas.

Established in 1993 in NC.
Donor(s): J.E. Waggoner,‡ Mildred W. Waggoner.
Financial data (yr. ended 03/31/01): Grants paid, $77,000; assets, $1,445,813 (M); expenditures, $90,692; qualifying distributions, $77,000.
Limitations: Giving limited to NC.
Application information: Application form not required.
Officers and Directors:* Mildred W. Waggoner,* Pres.; Jacqueline W. Darken,* V.P.; Joyce W. Forman,* V.P.; Dorothy W. Hager,* Secy.; Ruth W. Waggoner,* Treas.
EIN: 561847923
Codes: FD2

41172
Arthur and Irene Cash Charitable Trust
c/o First Union National Bank
401 S. Tryon St., Ste. NC 1159
Charlotte, NC 28288-1159

Established in 1985 in FL.
Financial data (yr. ended 09/30/01): Grants paid, $76,469; assets, $956,027 (M); expenditures, $93,249; qualifying distributions, $76,097.
Limitations: Applications not accepted. Giving primarily in Sarasota, FL.
Application information: Contributes only to pre-selected organizations.
Trustee: First Union National Bank.
EIN: 596832340
Codes: FD2

41173
Lucile W. Kerr Trust
c/o Wachovia Bank, N.A.
P.O. Box 3099
Winston-Salem, NC 27150-7153

Financial data (yr. ended 12/31/01): Grants paid, $76,348; assets, $1,220,436 (M); expenditures, $85,158; qualifying distributions, $79,052.
Limitations: Applications not accepted. Giving primarily in GA and SC.
Application information: Contributes only to pre-selected organizations.
Trustee: Wachovia Bank of South Carolina, N.A.
EIN: 576079684
Codes: FD2

41174
Guffey Family Foundation
6908 Matthews Mint Hill Rd.
PMB 256, Ste. 340
Charlotte, NC 28227-4406

Established in 1997 in NC.
Donor(s): John W. Guffey, Jr.
Financial data (yr. ended 12/31/00): Grants paid, $76,000; assets, $312,503 (M); expenditures, $79,957; qualifying distributions, $73,148.
Limitations: Applications not accepted. Giving primarily in Charlotte, NC.
Application information: Contributes only to pre-selected organizations.
Directors: Laurie R. Davis, John W. Guffey, Jr., Mark R. Guffey, Paula D. Guffey, Terri L. Potter.
EIN: 562060549
Codes: FD2

41175
The Wellman Family Foundation
101 Richelieu Dr.
Cary, NC 27511-8634

Established in 2000 in NC.
Financial data (yr. ended 12/31/00): Grants paid, $76,000; assets, $2,522,595 (M); gifts received, $3,042,082; expenditures, $76,000; qualifying distributions, $76,000.
Officers: F. Selby Wellman, Jr., Pres. and Treas.; Donna Bias Wellman, V.P. and Secy.; Brent Alan Wellman, V.P.; Brian Ashley Wellman, V.P.
EIN: 562210377
Codes: FD2

41176
The Allen Tate Foundation
6620 Fairview Rd.
Charlotte, NC 28210-3322 (704) 367-7303
Contact: H. Allen Tate, Jr., Tr.

Established in 1997 in NC.
Donor(s): H. Allen Tate, Jr.
Financial data (yr. ended 12/31/01): Grants paid, $75,350; assets, $133,765 (M); gifts received, $98,490; expenditures, $76,445; qualifying distributions, $75,350.
Limitations: Giving primarily in Charlotte, NC.
Trustees: Patrick Riley, H. Allen Tate, Jr., H. Allen Tate III.
EIN: 562044322
Codes: FD2

41177
Mills Family Foundation, Inc.
P.O. Box 8100
Asheville, NC 28814-8100
Contact: Pamela M. Turner, Pres.

Established around 1963.
Financial data (yr. ended 05/31/01): Grants paid, $75,264; assets, $752,594 (M); expenditures, $79,511; qualifying distributions, $76,214.

Limitations: Applications not accepted. Giving primarily in Asheville, Buncomebe, and Madison counties, NC.
Application information: Unsolicited requests for funds not accepted.
Officers and Directors:* Pamela M. Turner,* Pres.; James W. Turner,* V.P.; Robin Turner Oswald, Brian Mills Turner.
EIN: 566060644
Codes: FD2

41178
E. Boyd Family Foundation, Inc.
7009 Harps Mill Rd.
Raleigh, NC 27615-3225

Established in 1999 in NC.
Donor(s): Elbert M. Boyd, Jr.
Financial data (yr. ended 12/31/01): Grants paid, $75,000; assets, $351,939 (M); expenditures, $76,271; qualifying distributions, $74,912.
Limitations: Giving primarily in Raleigh, NC.
Officers: Elbert M. Boyd, Jr., Pres.; Ann C. Boyd, Secy.-Treas.
EIN: 562108418

41179
The Joanne K. Pegram Foundation, Inc.
P.O. Box 3189
Cary, NC 27519

Established in 2000 in NC.
Donor(s): Terry Pegram, PBM Graphics, Inc.
Financial data (yr. ended 12/31/00): Grants paid, $75,000; assets, $13,974 (M); gifts received, $126,687; expenditures, $148,410; qualifying distributions, $75,000.
Limitations: Applications not accepted. Giving primarily in NC.
Application information: Contributes only to pre-selected organizations.
Officers: Terry Pegram, Pres.; Garry Pegram, V.P.; Larry Pegram, Secy.-Treas.
EIN: 311724168

41180
The J. L. Suttle, Jr. Family Foundation
(Formerly Suttle Family Foundation)
1232 Brookwood Dr.
Shelby, NC 28150

Established in 1997 in NC.
Donor(s): J.L. Suttle, Jr.
Financial data (yr. ended 12/31/01): Grants paid, $75,000; assets, $756,117 (M); expenditures, $76,888; qualifying distributions, $75,000.
Limitations: Giving primarily in Boiling Springs, NC.
Directors: Carol Suttle Arey, J. Linton Suttle, J.V. Suttle.
EIN: 562024708

41181
The Weatherspoon Foundation
135 Perrin Pl.
Charlotte, NC 28207

Established in 1999 in NC.
Donor(s): Van L. Weatherspoon.
Financial data (yr. ended 12/31/01): Grants paid, $75,000; assets, $2,071,357 (M); gifts received, $50,000; expenditures, $91,299; qualifying distributions, $74,800.
Limitations: Applications not accepted.
Application information: Contributes only to pre-selected organizations.
Board Members: Martha Kay Massey Weatherspoon, Van L. Weatherspoon.
EIN: 562154056
Codes: FD2

41182
The Whichard Family Foundation
c/o U.S. Trust Co. of North Carolina
P.O. Box 26262
Greensboro, NC 27420

Established in 1998 in NC.
Financial data (yr. ended 12/31/01): Grants paid, $74,668; assets, $926,817 (M); expenditures, $82,093; qualifying distributions, $74,668.
Limitations: Applications not accepted.
Application information: Contributes only to pre-selected organizations.
Trustee: U.S. Trust Co. of North Carolina.
EIN: 562135508

41183
Josephine Stevenson Charitable Trust
c/o Wachovia Bank, N.A.
P.O. Box 3099
Winston-Salem, NC 27150-7131
Application address: c/o Wachovia Bank, N.A., 1426 Main St., 16th Fl., Columbia, SC 29226, tel.: (803) 765-3671

Established in 1997 in SC.
Financial data (yr. ended 01/31/01): Grants paid, $74,662; assets, $1,483,179 (M); expenditures, $87,311; qualifying distributions, $77,722.
Limitations: Giving primarily in SC.
Trustee: Wachovia Bank, N.A.
EIN: 586358122

41184
Dorothy Holder Charitable Trust
c/o First Union National Bank
401 S. Tryon St., NC 1159
Charlotte, NC 28288-1159

Established in 2000 in NC.
Financial data (yr. ended 12/31/01): Grants paid, $74,617; assets, $3,020,794 (M); gifts received, $68,848; expenditures, $85,846; qualifying distributions, $74,617.
Limitations: Applications not accepted.
Application information: Contributes only to pre-selected organizations.
Trustee: First Union National Bank.
EIN: 316639989

41185
The Ladane Foundation, Ltd.
c/o Ladane Williamson
9686 Scenic Dr. S.W.
Calabash, NC 28467

Established in 2000 in NC.
Donor(s): Ladane Williamson.
Financial data (yr. ended 12/31/00): Grants paid, $74,589; assets, $2,755 (M); gifts received, $89,000; expenditures, $86,351; qualifying distributions, $86,164.
Limitations: Applications not accepted.
Application information: Contributes only to pre-selected organizations.
Officers: Ladane Williamson, Pres.; Sanford J. Schlesinger, V.P.; Mark G. Bosswick, Secy.-Treas.
EIN: 134105176

41186
Hunt Family Foundation
P.O. Drawer 2440
Burlington, NC 27216

Established in 1998 in NC.
Donor(s): R. Samuel Hunt, Victoria S. Hunt.
Financial data (yr. ended 12/31/01): Grants paid, $74,250; assets, $321,216 (M); expenditures, $76,850; qualifying distributions, $74,250.
Limitations: Applications not accepted.

Application information: Contributes only to pre-selected organizations.
Trustees: R. Samuel Hunt III, Victoria S. Hunt.
EIN: 562115931

41187
Riegelwood Community Foundation, Inc.
865 John Reigel Rd.
Riegelwood, NC 28456 (910) 655-6202

Financial data (yr. ended 12/31/00): Grants paid, $73,771; assets, $256,207 (M); expenditures, $126,795; qualifying distributions, $78,852.
Limitations: Applications not accepted. Giving limited to Riegelwood, NC, and communities located within a 35-mile radius.
Application information: Contributes only to pre-selected organizations.
Officers: J. Scott Grimes, Pres.; Don Devlin, Secy.
EIN: 560712178

41188
The Butler Family Foundation
c/o Wachovia Bank, N.A.
P.O. Box 3099
Winston-Salem, NC 27150-7131

Established in 1999 in GA.
Financial data (yr. ended 12/31/01): Grants paid, $73,500; assets, $1,022,542 (M); expenditures, $82,639; qualifying distributions, $75,272.
Limitations: Applications not accepted.
Application information: Contributes only to pre-selected organizations.
Trustee: Wachovia Bank, N.A.
EIN: 566547924

41189
The Pate Fund
c/o Wachovia Bank, N.A.
P.O. Box 3099
Winston-Salem, NC 27150-7131
Application address: c/o Wachovia Bank, N.A., 1401 Main St., Ste. 501, Columbia, SC 29226, tel.: (803) 765-3677

Established in 1944 in SC.
Financial data (yr. ended 12/31/99): Grants paid, $73,000; assets, $1,198,941 (M); expenditures, $140,054; qualifying distributions, $76,382.
Limitations: Giving limited to SC.
Application information: Application form not required.
Trustee: Wachovia Bank of North Carolina, N.A.
Advisory Committee: John M. Pate, Wallace F. Pate, Jr., William W. Pate, Jr.
EIN: 576017422

41190
J. & J. Neely Foundation
c/o Wachovia Bank, N.A.
P.O. Box 3099, MC-NC6732
Winston-Salem, NC 27150-7153
(336) 732-5372
Contact: Linda Tilley, Sr. V.P., Wachovia Bank, N.A.

Established in 1997 in NC.
Donor(s): Joe Neely.
Financial data (yr. ended 12/31/01): Grants paid, $72,590; assets, $1,136,546 (M); expenditures, $82,860; qualifying distributions, $73,714.
Limitations: Applications not accepted. Giving primarily in NC.
Application information: Contributes only to pre-selected organizations.
Trustee: Wachovia Bank, N.A.
EIN: 566505854

41191
Donnie Royal Foundation
c/o William T. Allen
3620 Cape Center Dr.
Fayetteville, NC 28304

Established in 2001 in NC.
Donor(s): Donnie M. Royal.
Financial data (yr. ended 12/31/01): Grants paid, $72,500; assets, $1,809,583 (M); gifts received, $1,868,670; expenditures, $73,178; qualifying distributions, $72,500.
Limitations: Giving primarily in NC.
Officers: William T. Allen, Pres. and Secy.; Dorothy T. Royal, V.P. and Treas.
EIN: 912052930

41192
The Curtis Foundation
P.O. Box 20443
Raleigh, NC 27619-0443 (919) 781-6119
Contact: Barbara H. Curtis, Secy.-Treas.

Donor(s): Donald W. Curtis.
Financial data (yr. ended 11/30/01): Grants paid, $72,150; assets, $1,260,512 (M); gifts received, $1,000,000; expenditures, $80,901; qualifying distributions, $71,861.
Limitations: Giving primarily in NC.
Officers and Trustees:* Donald W. Curtis,* Pres.; Barbara H. Curtis,* Secy.-Treas.; J.D. Longfellow, Donna C. McClatchey.
EIN: 561257146

41193
Joseph & Gerald Quina Endowment Fund
c/o First Union National Bank
401 S. Tryon St., NC1159
Charlotte, NC 28288-1935
Application address: 818 Highway A1a, Ste. 102, Ponte Verdra Beach, FL 32080, tel.: (904) 361-7514; FAX: (904) 361-7475; E-mail: Nina.Hunter1@FirstUnion.com
Contact: Nina D. Hunter, V.P.

Established in 1998 in FL.
Financial data (yr. ended 12/31/01): Grants paid, $72,114; assets, $1,348,382 (M); expenditures, $92,376; qualifying distributions, $71,696.
Limitations: Applications not accepted. Giving primarily in Pensacola, FL.
Application information: Contributes only to pre-selected organizations.
Trustee: First Union National Bank.
EIN: 596474315

41194
Ficklen Fund, Inc.
c/o Wachovia Bank, N.A.
P.O. Box 3099
Winston-Salem, NC 27150-1022
(336) 732-6478
Application addresses: c/o L.S. Ficklen, Pres., 520 W. Long Meadow Rd., Greenville, NC 27858; c/o J.S. Ficklen, V.P., P.O. Box 2017, ECU Station, Greenville, NC 27834
Contact: Jim Gallaher, V.P., Wachovia Bank, N.A.

Established in 1953.
Financial data (yr. ended 04/30/02): Grants paid, $72,000; assets, $110,830 (M); expenditures, $72,997; qualifying distributions, $72,000.
Limitations: Giving primarily in NC and VA.
Application information: Application form not required.
Officers and Directors:* L.S. Ficklen,* Pres. and Treas.; J.S. Ficklen,* V.P. and Secy.; James S. Ficklen, Jr., Louis S. Fincklen.
EIN: 566048106

41195
Josephus Daniels Pell Foundation
c/o First Union National Bank
401 S. Tryon St., NC1159
Charlotte, NC 28288
Application address: c/o Beth Downs, P.O. Box 11367, Richmond, VA 23230, tel.: (804) 359-9451

Established in 1997 in VA.
Financial data (yr. ended 12/31/01): Grants paid, $72,000; assets, $1,338,790 (M); expenditures, $82,565; qualifying distributions, $72,752.
Application information: Application form required.
Trustee: First Union National Bank.
EIN: 541476076

41196
The Share Foundation
(Formerly The Edge Foundation)
c/o Wachovia Bank, N.A.
P.O. Box 3099
Winston-Salem, NC 27150-7131
Application address: c/o Wayne and Deborah Edge, 9000 Winged Bourne, Charlotte, NC 28210

Established in 1991 in NC as The Edge Foundation.
Donor(s): Wayne Edge, Deborah Edge.
Financial data (yr. ended 12/31/01): Grants paid, $72,000; assets, $1,226,828 (M); expenditures, $86,746; qualifying distributions, $74,000.
Limitations: Giving primarily in NC.
Trustee: Wachovia Bank, N.A.
EIN: 561761396

41197
E. J. Snyder Family Foundation
c/o Edward J. Snyder, Jr.
221 Snuggs St.
Albemarle, NC 28001

Established in 1968 in NC.
Donor(s): E.J. Snyder & Company, Inc., Edward J. Snyder, Jr., Margaret Snyder,‡ Michael E. Snyder, Roger F. Snyder.
Financial data (yr. ended 12/31/00): Grants paid, $71,500; assets, $1,950,365 (M); gifts received, $20,711; expenditures, $98,037; qualifying distributions, $71,500.
Limitations: Applications not accepted. Giving primarily in NC.
Application information: Contributes only to pre-selected organizations.
Officers: Edward J. Snyder, Jr., Pres.; Michael E. Snyder, V.P.; Roger F. Snyder, Secy.-Treas.
EIN: 237011326
Codes: CS, CD

41198
Louise C. Nacca Trust
c/o First Union National Bank
401 S. Tryon St., NC1159
Charlotte, NC 28288-1159

Established in 1993 in NJ.
Donor(s): Stella Nacca.‡
Financial data (yr. ended 04/30/01): Grants paid, $71,368; assets, $2,845,201 (M); expenditures, $86,474; qualifying distributions, $71,402.
Limitations: Applications not accepted.
Application information: Contributes only to a pre-selected organization specified in the governing instrument. Scholarships only to the disabled.
Trustee: First Union National Bank.
EIN: 222265900
Codes: GTI

41199
Goodman Foundation, Inc.
P.O. Box 1040
Salisbury, NC 28145-1040 (704) 633-5982
Contact: Jeffrey V. Goodman, V.P.

Established in 1952 in NC.
Donor(s): E.A. Goodman, Jr., B.V. Hedrick Gravel and Sand Co., Cumberland Gravel and Sand Co., Material Sales Co., Southern Concrete Materials, Inc.
Financial data (yr. ended 12/31/01): Grants paid, $71,100; assets, $829,552 (M); gifts received, $120,053; expenditures, $71,999; qualifying distributions, $71,465.
Limitations: Giving limited to NC.
Application information: Application form not required.
Officers: E.A. Goodman, Jr., Pres.; Jeffrey V. Goodman, V.P. and Treas.; Gail Settle, V.P.; Michael A. Goodman, Secy.
EIN: 566034757

41200
The Jim & Carollee Balloun Charitable
c/o Wachovia Bank, N.A.
P.O. Box 3099
Winston-Salem, NC 27150-7131

Established in 1999 in GA.
Financial data (yr. ended 12/31/01): Grants paid, $71,000; assets, $1,133,364 (M); expenditures, $83,161; qualifying distributions, $72,733.
Limitations: Applications not accepted. Giving primarily in GA.
Application information: Contributes only to pre-selected organizations.
Trustee: Wachovia Bank, N.A.
EIN: 586381081

41201
Dorothy Friend Trust
c/o Wachovia Bank, N.A.
P.O. Box 3099
Winston-Salem, NC 27150-7131
Application address: c/o Wachovia Bank, N.A., Main St., Columbia, SC 29226, tel.: (803) 765-3671
Contact: C. Gerald Lane

Established in 1992 in SC.
Financial data (yr. ended 12/31/01): Grants paid, $70,674; assets, $1,618,827 (M); expenditures, $85,305; qualifying distributions, $74,390.
Limitations: Giving primarily in Oconee County, SC.
Trustee: Wachovia Bank, N.A.
EIN: 576139022

41202
Cameron Charitable Trust
c/o Wachovia Bank of North Carolina, N.A.
P.O. Box 3099
Winston-Salem, NC 27150-7131
(800) 462-7159

Established in 1992 in NC; funded in 1993.
Donor(s): Edward Alexander Cameron.
Financial data (yr. ended 12/31/00): Grants paid, $70,500; assets, $1,614,060 (M); expenditures, $86,712; qualifying distributions, $71,985.
Limitations: Giving primarily in NC.
Trustee: Wachovia Bank of North Carolina, N.A.
EIN: 582051729

41203
J. P. Riddle Charitable Foundation, Inc.
P.O. Box 53646
Fayetteville, NC 28305-3646 (910) 864-3232
Contact: March F. Riddle, Tr.

Established in 1976 in NC.
Donor(s): Joseph P. Riddle, Jr.
Financial data (yr. ended 12/31/01): Grants paid, $70,500; assets, $3,795,090 (M); expenditures, $127,617; qualifying distributions, $70,500.
Limitations: Giving primarily in NC.
Trustees: Carolyn R. Armstrong, Joseph P. Riddle III, March F. Riddle, Sharlene R. Williams.
EIN: 561152362

41204
The Lovett Foundation
10 Stump Tree Ln.
Winston-Salem, NC 27106
E-mail: clovett@triad.rr.com; *URL:* http://www.aznet.co.uk/clovett/pages/foundation.html
Contact: Charles C. Lovett, Pres.

Established in 1994 in NC.
Financial data (yr. ended 12/31/01): Grants paid, $70,200; assets, $1,293,564 (M); expenditures, $92,008; qualifying distributions, $70,200.
Limitations: Giving primarily in the southeastern U.S., with emphasis on NC.
Application information: Application form available on website. Application form required.
Officers and Trustees:* Charles C. Lovett,* Pres.; Karl Douglas Vass,* Treas.; Mark Blakeman, Janice T. Lovett, Stephanie Lovett, Lisa Newham, Howard Skillington.
EIN: 561795876

41205
Tom Barnhardt Family Foundation
600 Llewellyn Pl.
Charlotte, NC 28207

Established in 1998 in NC.
Donor(s): Thomas M. Barnhardt III.
Financial data (yr. ended 12/31/01): Grants paid, $70,000; assets, $396,862 (M); gifts received, $6,000; expenditures, $79,847; qualifying distributions, $71,200.
Limitations: Applications not accepted.
Application information: Contributes only to pre-selected organizations.
Officers: Thomas M. Barnhardt III, Pres.; Robert S. Barnhardt, V.P.; Lee B. Hatling, V.P.; Lewis B. Barnhardt, Secy.; Thomas L. Barnhardt, Treas.
EIN: 562060263

41206
Gravely Foundation, Inc.
P.O. Box 291
Rocky Mount, NC 27802

Financial data (yr. ended 12/31/01): Grants paid, $70,000; assets, $1,305,163 (M); expenditures, $74,520; qualifying distributions, $70,000.
Limitations: Applications not accepted. Giving primarily in NC.
Application information: Contributes only to pre-selected organizations.
Officer and Trustees:* Elizabeth G. Lea,* Chair.; Cynthia Cope, Lanny Shuff.
EIN: 566044106

41207
Visiontech Partners Scholarship Foundation
2000 Regency Pkwy., Ste. 285
Cary, NC 27511

Established in 2000 in NC.
Financial data (yr. ended 12/31/00): Grants paid, $70,000; assets, $271 (M); gifts received, $72,000; expenditures, $72,848; qualifying distributions, $70,000.
Limitations: Applications not accepted.
Application information: Contributes only to pre-selected organizations.
Directors: Donald Piper, Philip Santoni.
EIN: 562172475

41208
Dacotah Foundation, Inc.
3 E. 1st St.
Lexington, NC 27292

Financial data (yr. ended 11/30/01): Grants paid, $69,775; assets, $313,355 (M); expenditures, $70,900; qualifying distributions, $69,775.
Limitations: Applications not accepted. Giving primarily in NC.
Application information: Contributes only to pre-selected organizations.
Officers: John Moore, Pres.; Robert Hedrick, Secy.; Ron Evans, Treas.
Director: Felix O. Gee.
EIN: 566061268

41209
C. L. Kelly Charitable Trust
c/o Centura Bank
P.O. Box 1220
Rocky Mount, NC 27802-1220
FAX: (252) 454-4446; *E-mail:* cbmoore@centura.com
Contact: Claudia Moore, Trust Rep., Centura Bank

Established in 1980 in NC.
Donor(s): C.L. Kelly, Sr.‡
Financial data (yr. ended 01/31/02): Grants paid, $69,752; assets, $1,365,563 (M); expenditures, $86,691; qualifying distributions, $74,196; giving activities include $44,552 for loans to individuals.
Limitations: Giving limited to Halifax County, NC.
Application information: Application form required.
Trustee: Centura Bank.
EIN: 566218777
Codes: GTI

41210
The John G. B., Jr. and Jane R. Ellison Family Foundation, Inc.
P.O. Box 29027
Greensboro, NC 27429-9027

Established in 1996 in NC.
Financial data (yr. ended 12/31/01): Grants paid, $69,546; assets, $2,806,518 (M); expenditures, $69,741; qualifying distributions, $69,546.
Limitations: Applications not accepted. Giving primarily in NC.
Application information: Contributes only to pre-selected organizations.
Officers: John G.B. Ellison, Jr., Pres. and Treas.; Jane R. Ellison, Secy.
EIN: 561981120

41211
Orders/Smith Foundation
c/o Wachovia Bank, NA
P.O. Box 3099
Winston-Salem, NC 27150-7153
(336) 732-5252

Financial data (yr. ended 11/30/01): Grants paid, $69,193; assets, $391,227 (M); expenditures, $75,504; qualifying distributions, $69,193.
Trustees: Carolyn L. Orders, William H. Orders, C. Michael Smith, Nancy O. Smith.
EIN: 582361437

41212
The Polsky Family Foundation
c/o Bank of America
Bank of America Plz., NC1-002-11-18
Charlotte, NC 28255

Established in 1997 in NC.
Financial data (yr. ended 12/31/01): Grants paid, $69,123; assets, $283,733 (M); gifts received, $49,208; expenditures, $72,858; qualifying distributions, $69,123.
Limitations: Applications not accepted.
Application information: Contributes only to pre-selected organizations.
Officers and Directors:* Laurence H. Polsky,* Pres.; Dale S. Polsky,* Secy.; Jonathan S. Polsky,* Treas.; Anne K. Polsky.
Trustee: Bank of America.
EIN: 562061159

41213
The Edna Hughes Davis Scholarship Fund
c/o Wachovia Bank of North Carolina, N.A.
P.O. Box 3099
Winston-Salem, NC 27150-7131
Application address: c/o C. Gerald Lane, Wachovia Bank, N.A, 1401 Main St., Columbia, SC 29226, tel.: (803) 765-3671

Established in 1998 in SC.
Financial data (yr. ended 12/31/01): Grants paid, $69,006; assets, $964,868 (M); expenditures, $81,611; qualifying distributions, $69,006.
Limitations: Giving primarily in SC.
Application information: Application form required.
Trustee: Wachovia Bank, N.A.
EIN: 582433135

41214
DeLeon Carter Foundation
P.O. Box 8386
Rocky Mount, NC 27804 (252) 937-2294
Contact: George G. Whitaker, Tr.

Financial data (yr. ended 12/31/01): Grants paid, $69,000; assets, $1 (M); expenditures, $87,184; qualifying distributions, $69,000.
Limitations: Giving primarily in NC.
Directors: W.O. Baker, Jr., B. Mayo Boddle, Joe Edwards, Sr., George M. Moore, Matthew T. Strickland, Augustas Tullos.
Trustee: George G. Whitaker.
EIN: 581771815

41215
Holdeen Fund 54-120
(Formerly Holdeen Fund 54-50)
c/o First Union National Bank
401 S. Tryon St., NC1159
Charlotte, NC 28288-1159

Financial data (yr. ended 12/31/01): Grants paid, $68,369; assets, $1,130,794 (M); expenditures, $73,163; qualifying distributions, $68,209.
Limitations: Applications not accepted. Giving limited to Boston, MA.
Application information: Contributes only to a pre-selected organization specified in the governing instrument.
Trustee: First Union National Bank.
EIN: 146018154
Codes: TN

41216
The Swimmer Family Foundation
455 Providence Rd. S.
Waxhaw, NC 28173
Contact: Harry S. Swimmer, Pres.

Established in 1997 in NC.

41216—NORTH CAROLINA

Donor(s): Harry S. Swimmer.
Financial data (yr. ended 12/31/01): Grants paid, $68,300; assets, $584,827 (M); gifts received, $58,500; expenditures, $77,269; qualifying distributions, $68,300.
Application information: Application form not required.
Officer: Harry S. Swimmer, Pres.
Director: Marilyn B. Swimmer.
EIN: 562029896

41217
The Talmidim Foundation
407 Rutherglen Dr.
Cary, NC 27511

Established in 2000 in NC.
Donor(s): Carsie K. Denning, Jr., Thomas E. Knox, Jerry H. Knox, Jane Knox, Daniel S. Knox.
Financial data (yr. ended 12/31/01): Grants paid, $68,142; assets, $169,010 (M); gifts received, $3,000; expenditures, $63,294; qualifying distributions, $68,142.
Limitations: Applications not accepted. Giving on an international basis.
Application information: Contributes only to pre-selected organizations.
Officers: Thomas E. Knox, Pres.; Carsie K. Denning, Jr., V.P.; Karen F. Knox, Secy.; Angela B. Denning, Treas.
EIN: 562187596

41218
Shelton Gorelick Family Foundation
6060 JA Jones Dr., No. 516
Charlotte, NC 28289
FAX: (704) 553-7291
Contact: Shelton Gorelick, Pres.

Established in 1990; funded in 1991.
Donor(s): Shelton Gorelick.
Financial data (yr. ended 06/30/01): Grants paid, $67,930; assets, $3,736,556 (M); expenditures, $82,843; qualifying distributions, $68,775.
Limitations: Applications not accepted. Giving limited to Charlotte, NC.
Application information: Contributes only to pre-selected organizations.
Officers: Shelton Gorelick, Pres. and Treas.; Scott Gorelick, V.P. and Secy.; Jeff Gorelick, V.P.; Pamela Gorelick, V.P.
EIN: 561743194

41219
Ann Lewallen Spencer Family Foundation
c/o Wachovia Bank, N.A.
P.O. Box 3099
Winston-Salem, NC 27150-7153
(336) 732-5372
Contact: Linda Tilley

Established in 1997 in NC.
Financial data (yr. ended 12/31/01): Grants paid, $67,601; assets, $1,052,281 (M); expenditures, $80,064; qualifying distributions, $67,601.
Limitations: Giving primarily in Winston-Salem, NC.
Application information: Application form required.
Trustee: Wachovia Bank, N.A.
EIN: 566507018

41220
Cashion Family Foundation, Inc.
c/o James T. Cashion, Sr.
1303 E. Broad St.
Statesville, NC 28677

Established in 1994 in NC.
Donor(s): James T. Cashion, Sr.
Financial data (yr. ended 03/31/02): Grants paid, $67,380; assets, $408,550 (M); gifts received, $69,779; expenditures, $75,508; qualifying distributions, $67,380.
Limitations: Applications not accepted. Giving primarily in NC.
Application information: Contributes only to pre-selected organizations.
Officers: James T. Cashion, Sr., Pres.; Elizabeth B. Cashion, V.P.; Robert B. Cashion, V.P.; James T. Cashion, Jr., Secy.; Julia C. Johnson, Treas.
EIN: 561891858

41221
Lundy Foundation, Inc.
208 Fox Lake Dr.
Clinton, NC 28328

Established in 1966 in NC.
Financial data (yr. ended 11/30/01): Grants paid, $66,850; assets, $1,369,426 (M); expenditures, $116,486; qualifying distributions, $66,850.
Limitations: Giving primarily in NC.
Officers: Annabelle L. Fetterman, Pres.; Lewis M. Fetterman, Jr., V.P.; Mabel F. Held, Secy.-Treas.
EIN: 566093241

41222
O. Max Gardner Foundation, Inc.
P.O. Box 277
Shelby, NC 28151
Application address: P.O. Box 2286, Shelby, NC 28151, tel.: (704) 487-5361
Contact: John Mull Gardner III, Pres.

Established in 1946 in NC.
Financial data (yr. ended 07/31/01): Grants paid, $66,150; assets, $1,592,308 (M); expenditures, $71,786; qualifying distributions, $68,468.
Application information: Application form not required.
Officers and Directors:* John Mull Gardner III,* Pres.; O. Max Gardner III,* V.P.; Katharine S. Gardner, Secy.; Kathleen G. Hunt, Treas.; James Webb Gardner, Jr., O. Max Gardner IV, Sylvia L. Gardner, Victoria H. Gardner, Julian W. Hamrick.
EIN: 560490704

41223
Vera Holland Memorial Community Fund
P.O. Box 507
Eden, NC 27289-0507

Established in 1994 in NC.
Financial data (yr. ended 09/30/01): Grants paid, $66,146; assets, $571,051 (M); expenditures, $84,281; qualifying distributions, $66,146.
Limitations: Giving primarily in NC.
Trustees: William E. Crews, Joseph Maddrey.
EIN: 566455540

41224
Kathleen C. Spicer Scholarship Fund
c/o Bank of America
101 S. Tryon St.
Charlotte, NC 28255 (704) 989-6103
Application address: c/o Kim Sexton, Bank of America, N.A., 600 Peachtree St., N.E., 11th Fl., Atlanta, GA 30308

Established around 1980 in GA.
Donor(s): Kathleen C. Spicer.‡
Financial data (yr. ended 06/30/01): Grants paid, $66,000; assets, $1,181,280 (M); expenditures, $81,728; qualifying distributions, $73,501.
Limitations: Giving primarily to residents of Cobb County, GA.
Publications: Application guidelines.
Application information: Application form required.
Trustees: Howard Sheely, Dan Walls, Bank of America.
EIN: 586180927

41225
Cary Oil Foundation, Inc.
c/o Craig Stephenson
P.O. Box 4649
Cary, NC 27519-4649

Established in 1996 in NC.
Donor(s): Cary Oil Company, Inc.
Financial data (yr. ended 12/31/01): Grants paid, $65,280; assets, $1,499,219 (M); gifts received, $220,262; expenditures, $81,170; qualifying distributions, $65,280.
Limitations: Applications not accepted. Giving primarily in NC.
Application information: Contributes only to pre-selected organizations.
Officers and Directors:* Harry D. Stephenson,* Pres.; Thomas C. Stephenson,* V.P.; Anthony Craig Stephenson,* Secy.-Treas.
EIN: 561950150
Codes: CS, CD

41226
Dixie Foundation, Inc.
c/o Lexington Furniture Industries
P.O. Box 1008
Lexington, NC 27293

Established in 1958.
Donor(s): Lexington Furniture Industries.
Financial data (yr. ended 09/30/99): Grants paid, $65,065; assets, $15,765 (M); gifts received, $71,000; expenditures, $65,209; qualifying distributions, $65,064.
Application information: Application form required.
Officers: Jeff Young, Pres.; Donald K. Crotts, Secy.-Treas.
EIN: 566042530
Codes: CS, CD, GTI

41227
The Underdown Family Foundation, Inc.
c/o Wachovia Bank, N.A.
P.O. Box 3099
Winston-Salem, NC 27150-7131

Established in 1994 in NC.
Donor(s): P.C. Underdown, Jr., Joanne F. Underdown.
Financial data (yr. ended 12/31/01): Grants paid, $65,000; assets, $1,082,617 (M); gifts received, $441; expenditures, $77,150; qualifying distributions, $65,000.
Limitations: Applications not accepted. Giving primarily in NC.
Application information: Contributes only to pre-selected organizations.
Officers: P.C. Underdown, Jr., Pres.; Joanne F. Underdown, V.P. and Treas.; Susan Underdown, Secy.
Agent: Wachovia Bank, N.A.
EIN: 561827986

41228
Hans Klaussner Foundation, Inc.
c/o Dave Bryant
P.O. Box 220
Asheboro, NC 27204-0220

Established in 1987.
Financial data (yr. ended 12/31/01): Grants paid, $64,525; assets, $24,642 (M); expenditures, $64,660; qualifying distributions, $64,660.
Limitations: Giving primarily in NC.
Directors: J.B. Davis, Hans J. Klaussner.
EIN: 581781767

41229
Graham Music Fund
c/o First Union National Bank
401 S. Tryon St., Ste. NC1159
Charlotte, NC 28288-1159

Established in 1998 in PA.
Donor(s): Bessie Graham Unitrust.
Financial data (yr. ended 07/31/01): Grants paid, $64,300; assets, $1,547,843 (M); expenditures, $79,476; qualifying distributions, $63,790.
Limitations: Applications not accepted. Giving primarily in Allentown, PA.
Application information: Contributes only to pre-selected organizations.
Trustees: Charles T. Noonan, First Union National Bank.
EIN: 256620864

41230
Fred W. Davis Memorial Foundation
c/o First Union National Bank
401 S. Tryon St., NC1159
Charlotte, NC 28288-1159

Financial data (yr. ended 08/31/01): Grants paid, $64,250; assets, $805,877 (M); expenditures, $83,705; qualifying distributions, $67,396.
Application information: Applicants must be recommended by Dean of their Episcopalian seminary.
Trustee: First Union National Bank.
EIN: 596717509
Codes: GTI

41231
James G. K. McClure Educational and Development Fund, Inc.
11 Sugar Hollow Rd.
Fairview, NC 28730 (828) 628-2114

Incorporated in 1944 in NC.
Financial data (yr. ended 06/30/00): Grants paid, $63,996; assets, $3,749,023 (M); gifts received, $1,655; expenditures, $130,479; qualifying distributions, $135,198.
Limitations: Giving limited to western NC.
Publications: Biennial report, application guidelines, informational brochure.
Application information: Application form required.
Officers: Martha Guy, Pres.; Richard G. Jennings, Jr., V.P.; Annie Clarke Ager, Secy.
Trustee: Edwin C. Graham.
EIN: 560690982
Codes: GTI

41232
Carl Herbert Myerley Trust
c/o First Union National Bank
401 S. Tryon St., NC1159
Charlotte, NC 28288

Established in 1997 in PA.
Financial data (yr. ended 06/30/02): Grants paid, $63,934; assets, $562,925 (M); expenditures, $69,211; qualifying distributions, $63,934.
Limitations: Applications not accepted. Giving primarily in Ephrata, PA and Charlottesville, VA.
Application information: Contributes only to pre-selected organizations.
Trustee: First Union National Bank.
EIN: 236221636

41233
Ferree Educational & Welfare Fund
P.O. Box 2207
Asheboro, NC 27204-2207 (336) 629-2998
Application address: P.O. Box 2207, Asheboro, NC 27204-2207; E-mail: sprouse@asheboro.com
Contact: Linda R. Cranford, Exec. Dir.

Established in 1953 in NC.
Donor(s): Mabel P. Ferree,‡ A.I. Ferree.‡
Financial data (yr. ended 12/31/00): Grants paid, $63,250; assets, $2,650,032 (M); expenditures, $115,440; qualifying distributions, $127,601; giving activities include $53,000 for loans to individuals.
Limitations: Giving limited to residents of Randolph County, NC.
Application information: Loans are for one year only; students must reapply each spring. Application form required.
Officers and Trustees:* Michael C. Miller,* Pres. and Treas.; Linda R. Cranford,* Exec. Dir.; Worth Hatley, Phil Kemp, Martha Sheriff, Greg Spainhour, W. Joe Trogdon, Charles Tyson.
EIN: 566062560
Codes: GTI

41234
Irmgard Johanna Laszig Trust
c/o First Union National Bank
401 S. Tryon St., NC1159
Charlotte, NC 28288
Application address: c/o First Union National Bank, 10 State House Sq., 2nd Fl., Hartford, CT 06103, tel.: (860) 692-7232

Financial data (yr. ended 05/31/02): Grants paid, $63,000; assets, $1,164,594 (M); expenditures, $72,724; qualifying distributions, $63,000.
Limitations: Giving primarily in Ridgefield, CT.
Application information: Application form not required.
Trustee: First Union National Bank.
EIN: 066235627

41235
The R. Y. and Eileen L. Sharpe Foundation
5210 Bermuda Village
Advance, NC 27006
Application address: c/o Ernst & Young, LLP, Winston-Salem, NC 27111, tel.: (336) 725-0611
Contact: Danny R. Newcomb, Dir.

Established in 1986.
Financial data (yr. ended 12/31/01): Grants paid, $62,917; assets, $924,678 (M); expenditures, $79,381; qualifying distributions, $62,917.
Limitations: Giving primarily in Winston-Salem, NC.
Directors: Shirley S. Duncan, Lynn Sharpe Hill, Danny R. Newcomb, Eileen L. Sharpe, Keith Y. Sharpe.
EIN: 581722771

41236
The Ireland Family Foundation
1434 Arboretum Dr.
Chapel Hill, NC 27514 (919) 932-3556
Contact: Lori Ireland, Pres.

Established in 2000 in NC.
Donor(s): Lori Ireland, Gregg Elden Ireland.
Financial data (yr. ended 12/31/01): Grants paid, $62,000; assets, $847,272 (M); gifts received, $400,000; expenditures, $69,996; qualifying distributions, $62,000.
Officers: Lori Ireland, Pres.; Gregg Elden Ireland, V.P.
EIN: 562227048

41237
Helen Kimberly Jones Charitable Trust
c/o Wachovia Bank, N.A.
P.O. Box 3099
Winston-Salem, NC 27150-7153

Established in 1995 in NC.
Financial data (yr. ended 12/31/01): Grants paid, $62,000; assets, $1,117,824 (M); expenditures, $76,118; qualifying distributions, $62,000.
Limitations: Applications not accepted. Giving primarily in NC.
Trustees: William C. Morris, Jr., Wachovia Bank, N.A.
EIN: 566447979

41238
The Z. V. Pate Foundation, Inc.
9120 Morgan St.
P.O. Box 159
Laurel Hill, NC 28351-0157
Contact: David L. Burns, Chair.

Established about 1984.
Donor(s): Z.V. Pate, Inc., Scottish Food Systems, Inc., Swink-Quality Oil Co., Inc.
Financial data (yr. ended 06/30/01): Grants paid, $62,000; assets, $341,578 (M); gifts received, $61,758; expenditures, $62,353; qualifying distributions, $62,000.
Limitations: Giving limited to the southeastern U.S., with emphasis on NC.
Officers and Trustees:* David L. Burns,* Chair. and Pres.; Carolyn P. Paul,* Secy.; Thomas A. Wilson,* Treas.
EIN: 561469816

41239
Perry Foundation, Inc.
920 Water St.
Wrightsville Beach, NC 28480-3146
(910) 256-3433

Established in 1943 in NC.
Financial data (yr. ended 06/30/01): Grants paid, $62,000; assets, $1,591,044 (M); expenditures, $63,635; qualifying distributions, $63,125.
Limitations: Applications not accepted.
Application information: Contributes only to pre-selected organizations.
Officer: A. Frazier Perry, Treas.
Director: Jane P. Liles.
EIN: 566047784

41240
Wren Foundation, Inc.
P.O. Box 447
Siler City, NC 27344-0447 (919) 663-3838
Contact: Marion G. Wren, Pres.

Donor(s): William M. Wren.
Financial data (yr. ended 12/31/01): Grants paid, $61,835; assets, $1,842,497 (M); expenditures, $70,181; qualifying distributions, $61,835.
Limitations: Giving primarily in NC.
Officers and Directors:* Marion G. Wren,* Pres.; Margaret de St. Aubin,* V.P. and Secy.-Treas.
EIN: 566063055

41241
Harry K. Garrett Trust
c/o First Union National Bank
401 S. Tryon St. TH-4, Ste. NC1159
Charlotte, NC 28288-1159

Established in 1995.
Financial data (yr. ended 09/30/01): Grants paid, $61,573; assets, $1,463,751 (M); expenditures, $80,379; qualifying distributions, $61,261.
Limitations: Applications not accepted. Giving primarily in PA.

41241—NORTH CAROLINA

Application information: Contributes only to pre-selected organizations.
Trustee: First Union National Bank.
EIN: 236789195

41242
Clarence D. Senseman Fund
c/o First Union National Bank
401 S. Tryon St., NC1159
Charlotte, NC 28288

Financial data (yr. ended 05/31/02): Grants paid, $61,508; assets, $1,284,572 (M); expenditures, $76,505; qualifying distributions, $61,508.
Limitations: Applications not accepted. Giving primarily in Cambridge, MA and Philadelphia, PA.
Application information: Contributes only to pre-selected organizations.
Trustee: First Union National Bank.
EIN: 236492978

41243
Germantown Relief Society Foundation
c/o First Union National Bank
401 S. Tryon St., NC 1159
Charlotte, NC 28288-1159
Application address: c/o First Union National Bank, 123 S. Broad St., Philadelphia, PA 19109, tel.: (215) 965-7952
Contact: Shep Millar

Established in 1947 in PA.
Financial data (yr. ended 09/30/01): Grants paid, $61,500; assets, $1,055,640 (M); expenditures, $70,247; qualifying distributions, $62,242.
Limitations: Giving primarily in Philadelphia, PA.
Application information: Contact foundation for information.
Trustee: First Union National Bank.
EIN: 236215778

41244
The B-G Foundation
c/o Wachovia Bank of North Carolina, N.A.
P.O. Box 3099
Winston-Salem, NC 27150-7153
(336) 732-5912
Contact: Nicole B. Bryan

Established in 1989 in VA.
Donor(s): W. Turner Lundy.
Financial data (yr. ended 12/31/99): Grants paid, $61,390; assets, $1,549,686 (M); expenditures, $61,905; qualifying distributions, $61,390.
Limitations: Applications not accepted. Giving limited to VA.
Officers and Directors:* W. Turner Lundy,* Pres. and Treas.; Louise B. Lundy,* Secy.
Trustee: Wachovia Bank of North Carolina, N.A.
EIN: 541526783
Codes: GTI

41245
George Prall Trust Fund
c/o First Union National Bank
401 S. Tryon, NC1159
Charlotte, NC 28288-1159

Established around 1995.
Financial data (yr. ended 12/31/01): Grants paid, $61,107; assets, $786,932 (M); expenditures, $71,220; qualifying distributions, $61,107.
Limitations: Applications not accepted. Giving primarily in Lambertville, NJ.
Committee Members: Helen Jane Baker, Alfred Richard Coleman, Bambi Kuhl, Rev. William Thompson.
Trustee: First Union National Bank.
EIN: 226453036

41246
Hanes Companies Foundation
P.O. Box 202
Winston-Salem, NC 27102-0202

Established in 1986 in NC.
Donor(s): Hanes Companies, Inc.
Financial data (yr. ended 12/31/01): Grants paid, $60,931; assets, $106,075 (M); gifts received, $50,000; expenditures, $61,617; qualifying distributions, $60,931.
Limitations: Applications not accepted. Giving primarily in NC.
Application information: Contributes only to pre-selected organizations.
Officers: Ralph H. Womble, Pres.; David S. Haffner, V.P.; Mark V. Linville, Secy.-Treas.
Director: Michael A. Glauber.
EIN: 581658698
Codes: CS, CD

41247
Karl M. Brawner Charitable Trust
c/o Bank of America
101 S. Tryon St.
Charlotte, NC 28255

Financial data (yr. ended 12/31/01): Grants paid, $60,810; assets, $1,313,350 (M); gifts received, $582,970; expenditures, $72,329; qualifying distributions, $60,810.
Limitations: Applications not accepted. Giving primarily in Atlanta, GA.
Application information: Contributes only to pre-selected organizations.
Trustee: Bank of America.
EIN: 527091643

41248
Bane Charitable Foundation
c/o First Union National Bank
401 S. Tryon St., 4th Fl.
Charlotte, NC 28288-1159
Application address: 213 S. Jefferson St., Roanoke, VA 24011

Established in 1990 in VA.
Donor(s): Eugene M. Bane.‡
Financial data (yr. ended 12/31/01): Grants paid, $60,165; assets, $3,054,958 (M); gifts received, $300,314; expenditures, $82,880; qualifying distributions, $60,925.
Limitations: Giving primarily in VA.
Trustee: First Union National Bank.
EIN: 546293471

41249
Croydon Foundation
4201 Congress St., Ste. 135
Charlotte, NC 28209
Application address: 2500 Charlotte Plz., Charlotte, NC 28244, tel.: (704) 372-9000; E-mail: jyp@parkerpac.com
Contact: James Y. Preston, Pres.

Established in 1997 in NC.
Donor(s): Ethel T. Dickson.‡
Financial data (yr. ended 12/31/01): Grants paid, $60,000; assets, $971,182 (M); expenditures, $72,145; qualifying distributions, $60,000.
Limitations: Giving primarily in Charlotte and Mecklenburg County, NC.
Application information: Application form not required.
Officers and Directors:* James Y. Preston,* Pres.; Robert G. Sanford,* V.P.; Debra C. Correll,* Secy.; John T. Bartley, Jr.,* Treas.; C.C. Dickson, Jr., Robert T. Dickson, Cecelia D. Stewart.
EIN: 562023468

41250
Bertha McQueen Fortune Foundation
c/o B.B. & T., Trust Dept.
P.O. Box 2907
Wilson, NC 27894-2907

Established in 2000 in SC.
Financial data (yr. ended 07/31/01): Grants paid, $60,000; assets, $874,602 (M); gifts received, $839,115; expenditures, $68,156; qualifying distributions, $60,000.
Limitations: Applications not accepted.
Application information: Contributes only to pre-selected organizations.
Trustee: B.B. & T.
EIN: 586386865

41251
Paula Steinbach Trust
c/o First Union National Bank
401 S. Tryon St., 4th Fl.
Charlotte, NC 28288-1159

Financial data (yr. ended 12/31/01): Grants paid, $60,000; assets, $1,126,090 (M); expenditures, $62,890; qualifying distributions, $59,656.
Limitations: Applications not accepted. Giving primarily in PA.
Application information: Contributes only to pre-selected organizations.
Trustee: First Union National Bank.
EIN: 236574129

41252
The Zelnak Private Foundation
c/o U.S. Trust Co.
P.O. Box 2626
Greensboro, NC 27420
Contact: Stephen P. Zelnak, Jr., Tr.

Established in 1998 in NC.
Donor(s): Stephen P. Zelnak, Jr.
Financial data (yr. ended 12/31/01): Grants paid, $60,000; assets, $763,121 (M); expenditures, $66,784; qualifying distributions, $61,209.
Limitations: Applications not accepted. Giving primarily in NC.
Application information: Contributes only to pre-selected organizations.
Trustees: Judy D. Zelnak, Stephen P. Zelnak, Jr.
EIN: 562115096

41253
Griffin Family Foundation
c/o US Trust Co. of North Carolina
P.O. Box 26262
Greensboro, NC 27420

Established in 1998 in NC.
Donor(s): Haynes Griffin.
Financial data (yr. ended 12/31/01): Grants paid, $59,679; assets, $1,576,132 (M); expenditures, $76,248; qualifying distributions, $59,679.
Limitations: Applications not accepted. Giving primarily in Woodberry Forest, VA.
Application information: Contributes only to pre-selected organizations.
Officers: Haynes G. Griffin, Pres.; Virginia R. Griffin, V.P.
EIN: 562114288

41254
The Mutual Savings Bank of Rockingham County, SSB Foundation
c/o B.B. & T., Trust Dept.
P.O. Box 2887
Wilson, NC 27894-2887

Established in 1994 in NC.
Donor(s): Mutual Savings Bank of Rockingham County, SSB.

Financial data (yr. ended 12/31/99): Grants paid, $59,417; assets, $212 (M); expenditures, $63,420; qualifying distributions, $59,438.
Limitations: Applications not accepted. Giving primarily in Rockingham County, NC.
Application information: Contributes only to pre-selected organizations.
Trustee: B.B. & T.
EIN: 566457034
Codes: CS, CD

41255
Johnston Family Foundation
c/o Wachovia Bank, N.A.
P.O. Box 3099
Winston-Salem, NC 27150-7131

Established in 1998 in NC.
Financial data (yr. ended 12/31/01): Grants paid, $59,250; assets, $595,111 (M); expenditures, $70,576; qualifying distributions, $60,619.
Limitations: Applications not accepted.
Application information: Contributes only to pre-selected organizations.
Trustees: Emily Drummond, Amanda Fitzgerald, James Johnston.
EIN: 911876318

41256
Simon Guggenheim Scholarship Fund
c/o First Union National Bank
401 S. Tryon St, 4th Fl.
Charlotte, NC 28288-1159
Application address: c/o Pres., Central High School, Ogontz Ave., Philadelphia, PA 19122

Established in 1985 in PA.
Financial data (yr. ended 12/31/01): Grants paid, $59,208; assets, $1,192,994 (M); gifts received, $15,000; expenditures, $66,347; qualifying distributions, $59,549.
Limitations: Giving limited to Philadelphia, PA.
Application information: Application form required.
Trustee: First Union National Bank.
EIN: 236219173
Codes: GTI

41257
Leroy von der Tan Foundation
c/o First Union National Bank
401 S. Tryon St., TH-4, NC1159
Charlotte, NC 28288

Established in 1999 in NJ.
Donor(s): Leroy von der Tan.‡
Financial data (yr. ended 12/31/01): Grants paid, $59,010; assets, $1,710,360 (M); expenditures, $87,362; qualifying distributions, $61,953.
Limitations: Applications not accepted. Giving primarily in NJ.
Application information: Contributes only to pre-selected organizations.
Trustees: Thurston von der Tan, Yvonne D. Wolf, First Union National Bank.
EIN: 256612851

41258
Gillings Family Foundation
4825 Creekstone Dr., Ste. 130
Durham, NC 27703
Contact: Cynthia M. Roberts, Secy.-Treas.

Established in 2000 in NC.
Donor(s): Dennis Gillings.
Financial data (yr. ended 12/31/01): Grants paid, $59,000; assets, $886,812 (M); gifts received, $870,925; expenditures, $60,387; qualifying distributions, $59,000.
Limitations: Giving primarily in NC and Chatham, VA.

Officers: Dennis Gillings, Pres.; Joan H. Gillings, V.P.; Cynthia M. Roberts, Secy.-Treas.
EIN: 562197561

41259
Wiegand Family Foundation, Inc.
230 Old Keller Farm Rd.
Boone, NC 28607
Contact: William L. Sax, Treas.

Established in 1997 in FL.
Donor(s): Joseph P. Wiegand.
Financial data (yr. ended 02/28/02): Grants paid, $59,000; assets, $1,117,563 (M); expenditures, $69,238; qualifying distributions, $59,000.
Limitations: Applications not accepted. Giving primarily in FL.
Application information: Contributes only to pre-selected organizations.
Officers and Directors:* Joseph Wiegand,* Pres.; Ligia Wiegand,* V.P.; Marilyn McAuliffe,* Secy.; William Sax, Treas.
EIN: 650734395

41260
Ella Ann L. and Frank B. Holding Foundation
1723 Canterbury Rd.
Raleigh, NC 27608-1109

Established in 1997 in NC.
Donor(s): Ella Holding, Frank B. Holding.
Financial data (yr. ended 12/31/00): Grants paid, $58,500; assets, $2,675,779 (M); expenditures, $65,157; qualifying distributions, $57,571.
Limitations: Giving primarily in NC.
Application information: Contributes mostly to pre-selected organizations; grants for education-specific scholarships are limited to individuals in financial need.
Officers: Olivia B. Holding, Pres.; Frank B. Holding, Jr., V.P.; Hope Holding Connell, Secy.-Treas.
EIN: 562002528

41261
The Howard Foundation
c/o Wachovia Bank, N. A.
P. O. Box 3099
Winston-Salem, NC 27150-6732

Established in 2001 in NC.
Financial data (yr. ended 12/31/01): Grants paid, $58,300; assets, $1,263,878 (M); gifts received, $329,882; expenditures, $68,968; qualifying distributions, $60,380.
Limitations: Applications not accepted. Giving primarily in NC.
Application information: Contributes only to pre-selected organizations.
Officer: Martha B. Howard, Exec. Dir.
EIN: 562050997

41262
Hayden-Harman Foundation
2058 Hatchery Rd.
Burlington, NC 27215-8843

Established in 2000 in NC.
Financial data (yr. ended 12/31/01): Grants paid, $58,275; assets, $1,371,999 (M); expenditures, $64,792; qualifying distributions, $58,275.
Limitations: Applications not accepted.
Application information: Contributes only to pre-selected organizations.
Directors: David L. Harman, John P. Harman, Phoebe Harman.
EIN: 562180022

41263
Bramble Charitable Foundation
7244 Blaney Bluffs Ln.
Raleigh, NC 27606-9018
Contact: J. David Bramble, Tr.

Established in 1993 in DE.
Donor(s): Sybil Bundek.‡
Financial data (yr. ended 12/31/00): Grants paid, $57,821; assets, $1,678,745 (M); gifts received, $21,396; expenditures, $143,198; qualifying distributions, $57,821.
Limitations: Giving on a national basis.
Trustees: J. David Bramble, Susan Trionfo.
EIN: 650455531

41264
The McMichael Family Foundation
505 Murphy St.
Madison, NC 27025

Established in 1992 in NC.
Donor(s): Dalton L. McMichael, Sr.
Financial data (yr. ended 12/31/01): Grants paid, $57,500; assets, $330,565 (M); gifts received, $260,262; expenditures, $71,595; qualifying distributions, $57,500.
Limitations: Applications not accepted. Giving primarily in NC.
Application information: Contributes only to pre-selected organizations.
Officers and Directors:* Dalton L. McMichael, Jr.,* Pres.; Gail McMichael Drew,* V.P.; Flavel McMichael Godfrey,* V.P.; Dalton L. McMichael,* V.P.; Louise McMichael Miracle, Secy.-Treas.
EIN: 561774976

41265
The J. Alex and Vivian G. Mull Foundation
(Formerly Mull Foundation)
c/o Wachovia Bank, N.A.
P.O. Box 3099, MC 37131
Winston-Salem, NC 27150-7131
Application address: P.O. Box 923, Morganton, NC 28655, tel.: (828) 437-0921
Contact: Rev. Robert E. Roach, Comm. Chair.

Established in 1982 in NC.
Donor(s): John Alexander Mull.‡
Financial data (yr. ended 12/31/01): Grants paid, $57,500; assets, $1,492,492 (M); expenditures, $76,209; qualifying distributions, $57,500.
Limitations: Giving primarily in Burke County, NC.
Officer and Distribution Comm.:* Robert E. Roach,* Chair.; Truman H. Brown, Susan C. Fenter.
Trustee: Wachovia Bank, N.A.
EIN: 586170608

41266
Emma Fanny Dietrich Trust
240 3rd Ave. W.
Hendersonville, NC 28739-4308
(828) 692-2595
Contact: Boyd B. Massagee, Jr., Tr.

Financial data (yr. ended 12/31/00): Grants paid, $57,250; assets, $1,628,799 (M); expenditures, $64,653; qualifying distributions, $57,250.
Limitations: Giving primarily in NC.
Application information: Application form required.
Trustees: Boyd B. Massagee, Jr., Hugh H. Randall, Alex Viola.
EIN: 566152201
Codes: GTI

41267
Moore County Charitable Foundation, Inc.
P.O. Box 591
Southern Pines, NC 28388-0591
(910) 692-7219
Contact: Michael R. Holden, Treas.

Donor(s): Lawrence Johnson, John Camp, Mary Camp, Campbell Foundation.
Financial data (yr. ended 12/31/00): Grants paid, $57,180; assets, $621,272 (M); gifts received, $28,131; expenditures, $60,763; qualifying distributions, $60,763.
Limitations: Giving limited to NC, with emphasis on Moore County.
Officers: Norris Hodgkins, Pres.; Lawrence Johnson, Secy.; Michael R. Holden, Treas.
Directors: Beth Duncan, Linda Duncan, Juanita Harbour, Sherwood Lapping, Doris Moon.
EIN: 566092613

41268
The Dolores & Donald Burnett Foundation
P.O. Box 1437
Flat Rock, NC 28731-1437 (828) 692-8836

Donor(s): Donald R. Burnett, Dondel Corp.
Financial data (yr. ended 06/30/01): Grants paid, $56,699; assets, $1,226,675 (M); gifts received, $75,209; expenditures, $58,574; qualifying distributions, $56,472.
Limitations: Giving limited to Urbana, IL.
Application information: Application form not required.
Trustees: Dolores B. Burnett, Donald R. Burnett, Richard Burnett, Nancy Gorski, Donna Vanderbok.
EIN: 943034358

41269
Waste Industries Foundation
c/o Carol J. Poole
3301 Benson Dr., Ste. 601
Raleigh, NC 27609-7362

Established in 1998 in NC.
Donor(s): Carol J. Poole.
Financial data (yr. ended 12/31/00): Grants paid, $55,250; assets, $632,984 (L); expenditures, $64,565; qualifying distributions, $55,250.
Limitations: Applications not accepted. Giving on a national basis, with emphasis on NC and TX.
Application information: Contributes only to pre-selected organizations.
Officers and Directors:* Carol J. Poole,* Pres.; Robert H. Hall,* Secy.-Treas.
EIN: 562087730

41270
Miles J. Smith Family Foundation
507 W. Innes St., Ste. 235
Salisbury, NC 28144-4233 (704) 633-4296

Donor(s): Miles J. Smith, Jr., Angela S. Harrison, Ernest Hayes Smith.
Financial data (yr. ended 12/31/01): Grants paid, $55,000; assets, $1,004,261 (M); expenditures, $60,044; qualifying distributions, $54,452.
Limitations: Applications not accepted. Giving primarily in Salisbury, NC.
Application information: Contributes only to pre-selected organizations.
Officers: Miles J. Smith, Jr., Pres.; Robert G. Smith, V.P.; Ernest Hayes Smith, Secy.-Treas.
EIN: 581574762

41271
Plastic Packaging Foundation, Inc.
c/o Plastic Packaging, Inc.
1246 Main Ave. S.E.
Hickory, NC 28602-1238

Established about 1969.
Donor(s): Plastic Packaging, Inc.
Financial data (yr. ended 09/30/01): Grants paid, $54,848; assets, $46,518 (M); gifts received, $50,000; expenditures, $54,886; qualifying distributions, $54,865.
Limitations: Giving primarily in NC.
Application information: Unsolicited request for funds not accepted.
Officers: Joseph Mercer, Pres.; Jim Roane, V.P.; Bert Brinkley, Treas.
EIN: 237009918
Codes: CS, CD

41272
Ernest G. Arps Memorial Fund
c/o B.B. & T.
P.O. Box 2907
Wilson, NC 27894-2907
Application address: c/o Samuel J. Styons, P.O. Box 127, Plymouth, NC 27962

Established in 1988 in NC.
Donor(s): Ernest G. Arps.‡
Financial data (yr. ended 09/30/01): Grants paid, $54,750; assets, $894,071 (M); expenditures, $69,289; qualifying distributions, $56,973.
Limitations: Applications not accepted. Giving limited to residents of Washington County, NC.
Application information: Unsolicited requests for funds not accepted. Funds only available to seniors in Washington County, NC high schools. These seniors are made aware of available funds through individual guidance counselors.
Trustee: B.B. & T.
EIN: 566228126
Codes: GTI

41273
Edwards-Hobgood Foundation, Inc.
P.O. Box 1499
Kinston, NC 28503

Established in 1992.
Donor(s): Pauline G. Edwards.‡
Financial data (yr. ended 12/31/00): Grants paid, $54,625; assets, $713,906 (M); expenditures, $61,429; qualifying distributions, $54,625.
Limitations: Applications not accepted. Giving primarily in NC.
Publications: Annual report.
Application information: Contributes only to pre-selected organizations.
Officers and Directors:* Elizabeth H. Wellons,* Pres.; A.L. Hobgood III,* V.P. and Secy.; W.E. Parham,* Treas.; Kenneth E. Hobgood, Thomas A. Hobgood.
EIN: 561789818

41274
Iona M. Allen Music Scholarship Fund
c/o Wachovia Bank of North Carolina, N.A.
P.O. Box 3099
Winston-Salem, NC 27150-7153
(336) 732-5912
Contact: Nicole B. Bryan

Financial data (yr. ended 12/31/99): Grants paid, $53,875; assets, $1,429,324 (M); expenditures, $64,952; qualifying distributions, $55,060.
Limitations: Giving limited to Cherokee, Clay, Graham, Macon, Swain, Haywood, Transylvania, Henderson, Polk, Jackson, Buncombe, and Madison counties, NC.
Trustee: Wachovia Bank of North Carolina, N.A.

Advisory Committee: James Dooley, Joyce Dorr, Walter Gray, Henry Janiac, Robert W. Kehrberg, Ruth Paddison.
EIN: 586189987
Codes: GTI

41275
Morgan Hand II Memorial Scholarship Fund
c/o First Union National Bank
401 S. Tryon St., NC1159
Charlotte, NC 28288

Established in 1998 in PA.
Financial data (yr. ended 12/31/01): Grants paid, $53,400; assets, $735,141 (M); expenditures, $60,309; qualifying distributions, $53,400.
Limitations: Giving primarily in PA.
Trustees: William J. Hughes, First Union National Bank.
EIN: 237873028

41276
Lucy Daniels Foundation, Inc.
c/o Heather Craige, Clinical Coord.
9001 Weston Pkwy.
Cary, NC 27513 (919) 677-9888
FAX: (919) 677-0095; E-mail: info@ldf.org; URL: http://www.ldf.org

Established in 1989 in NC.
Donor(s): Lucy D. Inman.
Financial data (yr. ended 09/30/01): Grants paid, $53,220; assets, $7,526,173 (M); gifts received, $128,750; expenditures, $873,335; qualifying distributions, $970,561.
Limitations: Giving primarily in the Raleigh, Durham, and Chapel Hill, NC, areas.
Publications: Informational brochure, application guidelines.
Application information: Application information available on Web site. Application form required.
Officers and Directors:* Lucy D. Inman, Ph.D.,* Chair. and Treas.; Melvin G. Shimm,* Vice-Chair.; Landrum S. Tucker, Jr., M.D.,* Secy.; and 7 additional directors.
EIN: 581854794
Codes: GTI

41277
Ernest Wooler Memorial Scholarship Fund
c/o First Union National Bank
401 S. Tryon St., NC1159
Charlotte, NC 28288

Established in 1985 in FL.
Financial data (yr. ended 06/30/02): Grants paid, $53,073; assets, $877,708 (M); expenditures, $54,798; qualifying distributions, $53,073.
Limitations: Applications not accepted. Giving limited to Broward County, FL.
Application information: Contributes only to pre-selected organizations.
Trustee: First Union National Bank.
EIN: 596517267

41278
Stephenson Pope Babcock Foundation
2000 Frontis Plz. Blvd., Ste. 106
Winston-Salem, NC 27103

Established in 1996 in NC.
Donor(s): Bruce Babcock, Anne Babcock, Luke Babcock.
Financial data (yr. ended 09/30/01): Grants paid, $52,500; assets, $1,051,097 (M); gifts received, $97,806; expenditures, $56,310; qualifying distributions, $52,500.
Limitations: Giving primarily in NY and VA.
Officer: Bruce M. Babcock, Pres.
EIN: 562000456

41279
Coats North American Educational Foundation
(Formerly American Thread Educational Foundation, Inc.)
c/o Coats American
4135 S. Stream Blvd.
Charlotte, NC 28217
Contact: Wade Bowman, V.P.

Donor(s): Coats American.
Financial data (yr. ended 12/31/00): Grants paid, $52,500; assets, $1,414,897 (M); gifts received, $6,936; expenditures, $62,510; qualifying distributions, $53,996.
Limitations: Giving primarily in areas of company operations to children of employees at Coats American and Coats and Clark.
Application information: Application form required.
Officers: Richard C. Norman, Pres.; Wade Bowman, V.P. and Secy.; Alan DeMello, Treas.
EIN: 566093510
Codes: CS, CD, GTI

41280
Todd and Stacy Gorelick Foundation
P.O. Box 35129
Charlotte, NC 28235-5129

Established in 1999 in NC.
Donor(s): Todd A. Gorelick.
Financial data (yr. ended 06/30/01): Grants paid, $51,982; assets, $19,220 (M); gifts received, $35,000; expenditures, $53,797; qualifying distributions, $51,850.
Limitations: Applications not accepted.
Application information: Contributes only to pre-selected organizations.
Officers: Todd A. Gorelick, Pres. and Treas.; Stacy M. Gorelick, V.P. and Secy.
EIN: 562150337

41281
Gorrell Family Foundation
P.O. Box 26262
Greensboro, NC 27420

Established in 1998 in NC.
Donor(s): Robert P. Gorrell.
Financial data (yr. ended 12/31/01): Grants paid, $51,408; assets, $980,302 (M); expenditures, $61,922; qualifying distributions, $51,408.
Limitations: Applications not accepted.
Application information: Contributes only to pre-selected organizations.
Officers: Robert P. Gorrell, Pres.; Sarah Swain Gorrell, Secy.
EIN: 562089597

41282
The Weeks Foundation, Inc.
c/o Wachovia Bank, N.A.
P.O. Box 3099
Winston-Salem, NC 27150-7131

Established in 1997 in GA.
Financial data (yr. ended 12/31/01): Grants paid, $51,250; assets, $71,133 (M); expenditures, $72,598; qualifying distributions, $51,250.
Limitations: Applications not accepted.
Application information: Contributes only to pre-selected organizations.
Trustee: Wachovia Bank, N.A.
EIN: 582328331

41283
Boyles-Eidson Family Foundation
P.O. Box 625
Elkin, NC 28621-0625

Established in 1998 in NC.

Financial data (yr. ended 12/31/01): Grants paid, $51,000; assets, $996,527 (M); expenditures, $53,310; qualifying distributions, $51,000.
Officers: Rachel S. Boyles, Pres.; Jane B. Eidson, V.P. and Secy.; Fred G. Eidson, V.P. and Treas.
EIN: 562088318

41284
Ketner Foundation, Inc.
P.O. Box 1308
Salisbury, NC 28145-1308   (704) 633-4971
Contact: Glenn E. Ketner, Jr., V.P.

Established in 1956.
Financial data (yr. ended 03/31/02): Grants paid, $51,000; assets, $1,049,059 (M); gifts received, $7,950; expenditures, $54,446; qualifying distributions, $51,000.
Limitations: Giving primarily in Salisbury, NC.
Application information: Application form not required.
Officers: Glenn E. Ketner, Sr., Pres.; Glenn E. Ketner, Jr., V.P.; Addie G. Ketner, Secy.-Treas.
EIN: 566061068

41285
Clyde R. Potter Charitable Foundation
c/o Central Carolina Bank & Trust Co.
P.O. Box 30010
Durham, NC 27702

Financial data (yr. ended 03/31/02): Grants paid, $51,000; assets, $811,881 (M); expenditures, $61,192; qualifying distributions, $51,000.
Limitations: Applications not accepted. Giving primarily in NC.
Application information: Contributes only to pre-selected organizations.
Trustee: Central Carolina Bank & Trust Co.
EIN: 566267552

41286
The Brent Milgrom Family Foundation, Inc.
(Formerly The Milgrom Brothers Foundation, Inc.)
5970 Fairview Rd., Ste. 414
Charlotte, NC 28210-3103

Established in 1986 in NC.
Donor(s): Brent Milgrom, Brent Milgrom, Jr., Milgrom Properties.
Financial data (yr. ended 12/31/01): Grants paid, $50,858; assets, $972,478 (M); gifts received, $55,758; expenditures, $53,652; qualifying distributions, $50,858.
Limitations: Applications not accepted. Giving primarily in NC.
Application information: Contributes only to pre-selected organizations.
Officers: Brent Milgrom, Pres. and Treas.; Brent Milgrom, Jr., V.P. and Secy.
Director: Joe Lawrance.
EIN: 561497294

41287
Robert & John Appleby Foundation
401 S. Tryon St., 4th Fl.
Charlotte, NC 28288
Application address: c/o Robert S. Appleby, 18 E. 3rd St., New Castle, DE 19720, tel.: (302) 328-6275

Established in 1997 in DE.
Donor(s): Joan Appleby, Robert S. Appleby.
Financial data (yr. ended 12/31/01): Grants paid, $50,500; assets, $455,962 (L); expenditures, $53,425; qualifying distributions, $50,463.
Limitations: Giving primarily in DE.
Trustee: First Union National Bank.
EIN: 526841078

41288
Kassner Family Foundation
(Formerly Fred E. Kassner Family Foundation)
c/o First Union National Bank
401 S. Tryon St., NC1159
Charlotte, NC 28288-1159

Established in 1998 in PA.
Donor(s): Fred Kassner,‡ Sanford C. Bernstein & Co.
Financial data (yr. ended 12/31/01): Grants paid, $50,500; assets, $1,215,733 (M); gifts received, $315,756; expenditures, $66,010; qualifying distributions, $51,250.
Limitations: Applications not accepted. Giving limited to NY.
Application information: Contributes only to pre-selected organizations.
Trustee: First Union National Bank.
EIN: 223594386

41289
Darrell and Patricia Steagall Family Foundation
3731 St. Regis Dr.
Gastonia, NC 28056-7543   (704) 865-5389
Contact: Darrell C. Steagall, Pres. and Patricia C. Steagall, Secy.

Established in 1997 in NC.
Donor(s): Darrell Steagall, Patricia Steagall.
Financial data (yr. ended 12/31/01): Grants paid, $50,300; assets, $1,028,563 (M); expenditures, $59,584; qualifying distributions, $50,300.
Officers: Darrell C. Steagall, Pres. and Treas.; Darrell P. Steagall, V.P.; Gabriel J. Steagall, V.P.; Holly G. Steagall, V.P.; Patricia C. Steagall, Secy.
EIN: 562061059

41290
Peabody Foundation
c/o First Union National Bank
401 S. Tryon St., NC1159
Charlotte, NC 28288-1159
Application address: 1212 Haywood Rd., No. 200, Greenville, SC 29615, tel.: (864) 675-0250
Contact: Nancy Howard

Established in 1997 in SC.
Donor(s): Alan M. Peabody, M.D.
Financial data (yr. ended 12/31/00): Grants paid, $50,256; assets, $1,896,193 (M); expenditures, $154,836; qualifying distributions, $142,948.
Limitations: Giving primarily in NC and SC.
Officer and Directors:* Alan M. Peabody, M.D.,* Pres.; Carl Burton, M.D.; William Caine, Clifton Galloway, James Hergner.
Trustee: First Union National Bank.
EIN: 571060450

41291
Robert C. White Trust for School Boy Rowing
c/o First Union National Bank
401 S. Tryon St. TH-4, NC1159
Charlotte, NC 28288
Contact: Tom Praiss, V.P., First Union National Bank

Established in 1987 in PA.
Donor(s): Robert C. White.‡
Financial data (yr. ended 08/31/01): Grants paid, $50,200; assets, $885,716 (M); expenditures, $61,876; qualifying distributions, $50,904.
Limitations: Giving primarily in PA.
Trustee: First Union National Bank.
EIN: 236878917

41292
BB&T Foundation of Wilson County
P.O. Box 2907
Wilson, NC 27894-2907

Financial data (yr. ended 12/31/01): Grants paid, $50,000; assets, $497,477 (M); expenditures, $62,051; qualifying distributions, $50,000.
Limitations: Applications not accepted. Giving limited to Wilson County, NC.
Application information: Contributes only to pre-selected organizations.
Trustee: B.B. & T.
EIN: 566474894

41293
Christian and Teresa M. Dingler Foundation
c/o David W. Carr
102 Wild Oak Ln.
Carrboro, NC 27510

Financial data (yr. ended 04/30/01): Grants paid, $50,000; assets, $885,000 (M); expenditures, $63,670; qualifying distributions, $40,000.
Limitations: Applications not accepted. Giving limited to NJ.
Application information: Grants are paid to NJ institutions of higher education on behalf of residents of Essex County.
Trustees: Carol A. Carr, David W. Carr, Harold M. George, Jr.
EIN: 237026897

41294
Harrison Charitable Foundation
(also known as Claude and Anne Nelson Harrison Charitable Foundation)
c/o First Union National Bank
401 S. Tryon St., NC1159
Charlotte, NC 28288

Established in 1991 in VA.
Donor(s): Claude Harrison.‡
Financial data (yr. ended 12/31/01): Grants paid, $50,000; assets, $973,944 (M); expenditures, $62,026; qualifying distributions, $50,000.
Limitations: Applications not accepted.
Application information: Contributes only to pre-selected organizations.
Trustee: First Union National Bank.
EIN: 546248184

41295
King Family Foundation
2641 Les Ln.
Denver, NC 28037 (704) 483-5470
Contact: S. J. King, Dir.

Established in 1998 in NC.
Financial data (yr. ended 12/31/01): Grants paid, $50,000; assets, $547,234 (M); gifts received, $1,000; expenditures, $67,516; qualifying distributions, $50,000.
Directors: Marie M. King, S. J. King.
EIN: 562029682

41296
Orr Family Foundation
c/o U.S. Trust
P.O. Box 26262
Greensboro, NC 27420 (336) 272-5100

Established in 1996 in NC.
Donor(s): Donald F. Orr, Mary Hart Orr.
Financial data (yr. ended 12/31/01): Grants paid, $50,000; assets, $35,263 (M); expenditures, $51,809; qualifying distributions, $50,000.
Limitations: Applications not accepted.
Application information: Contributes only to pre-selected organizations.

Officers: Donald F. Orr, Pres.; Mary Hart Orr, Secy.-Treas.
Director: Stephen C. Hassenfelt.
EIN: 566488503

41297
John Garland Plunkett Endowment Fund
c/o Wachovia Bank
P.O. Box 3099
Winston-Salem, NC 27150-6732

Established in 1998 in VI.
Donor(s): L.M. Plunkett.‡
Financial data (yr. ended 12/31/00): Grants paid, $50,000; assets, $1,328,972 (M); gifts received, $2,622; expenditures, $62,449; qualifying distributions, $50,000.
Limitations: Applications not accepted. Giving primarily in Blacksburg, VA.
Application information: Contributes only to pre-selected organizations.
Trustee: Wachovia Bank, N.A.
EIN: 226905332

41298
Schoenith Foundation
c/o Bank of America
Bank of America Pl., NC1-002-11-18
Charlotte, NC 28255 (800) 401-2635

Established in 1960 in NC.
Financial data (yr. ended 12/31/01): Grants paid, $50,000; assets, $1,220,089 (M); expenditures, $60,139; qualifying distributions, $50,000.
Limitations: Applications not accepted. Giving on a national basis.
Application information: Contributes only to pre-selected organizations.
Directors: Charles E. Knox, Sr., Dorothy K. McMillan, Holly L. McMillan, James L. McMillan, Thomas M. McMillan.
Trustee: Bank of America.
EIN: 566039185

41299
State Employees Association of North Carolina Scholarship Fund, Inc.
P.O. Drawer 27727
Raleigh, NC 27611 (919) 833-6436
E-mail: mleonard@seanc.org
Contact: Mitch Leonard, Dir.

Established in 1974 in NC.
Donor(s): State Employees Association of North Carolina, Inc., Edward Jones.
Financial data (yr. ended 09/30/01): Grants paid, $50,000; assets, $363,378 (M); gifts received, $18,199; expenditures, $74,885; qualifying distributions, $56,787.
Limitations: Giving limited to NC.
Publications: Informational brochure (including application guidelines).
Officers and Directors:* Donna Sexton, Schol. Chair.; Karan Rose,* Treas.; Michael T.W. Bell, Gary Carter, Kim Glover, Mickey Jernigan, Mitch Leonard, Kodell Loftis, Brenda Nicholas, Sidney Sandy, Ray Stone, Linda R. Sutton, Emily Walls, Don Whitaker.
EIN: 561436745
Codes: GTI

41300
Diana Gayle Wortham Foundation, Inc.
c/o Wachovia Bank, N.A.
P.O. Box 3099
Winston-Salem, NC 27150-6732
(336) 732-6090
Contact: Nola Miller

Established in 1995 in NC.

Financial data (yr. ended 12/31/01): Grants paid, $50,000; assets, $2,116,792 (M); expenditures, $75,043; qualifying distributions, $53,935.
Limitations: Giving limited to Buncombe County, NC.
Application information: Application form not required.
Directors: Lyndall Booher, Susan Kosma, Tina McGuire, Edward Allen Skeens, Diana Skeens Smith, Diana Gayle Wortham.
EIN: 581995071

41301
The John C. Harmon Family Foundation, Inc.
P.O. Box 26262
Greensboro, NC 27402-1108

Established in 1996 in NC.
Financial data (yr. ended 12/31/01): Grants paid, $49,840; assets, $1,125,808 (M); expenditures, $55,982; qualifying distributions, $49,840.
Limitations: Applications not accepted.
Application information: Contributes only to pre-selected organizations.
Officer: John C. Harmon, Pres.
EIN: 561999363

41302
The Eleanor Hayes Barnhardt Charitable Trust
2032 Princeton Ave.
Charlotte, NC 28207
Contact: Sadler H. Barnhardt, Tr.

Established in 1986.
Donor(s): James H. Barnhardt, Sr., Eleanor Hayes Barnhardt, Deborah K. Barnhardt, Sadler H. Barnhardt, James H. Preston.
Financial data (yr. ended 12/31/01): Grants paid, $49,550; assets, $1,459,408 (M); gifts received, $2,564; expenditures, $50,764; qualifying distributions, $49,550.
Limitations: Giving primarily in NC.
Trustees: Deborah K. Barnhardt, Dorothy Barnhardt, Eleanor Hayes Barnhardt, James H. Barnhardt, Jr., Sadler H. Barnhardt.
EIN: 566269136

41303
William B. Lake Foundation
c/o First Union National Bank
401 S. Tryon St., NC119
Charlotte, NC 28288
Application address: c/o Elizabeth K. Deegan, 214 W. Maury St., Chester, PA, 19013

Financial data (yr. ended 05/31/01): Grants paid, $49,474; assets, $1,079,663 (M); expenditures, $52,929; qualifying distributions, $50,180.
Limitations: Giving limited to residents of Philadelphia, PA.
Publications: Application guidelines.
Directors: Baldo M. Carnecchia, Jr., Camie Morrison, Thomas F. Prestel, Jr., M.D., Susan J. Sink, Linda Smith.
Trustee: First Union National Bank.
EIN: 236266137
Codes: GTI

41304
Brady Foundation, Inc.
P.O. Box 1040
Salisbury, NC 28145-1040 (704) 633-5982
Contact: Jane B. Arnold, Pres.

Financial data (yr. ended 12/31/00): Grants paid, $49,406; assets, $47,195 (M); gifts received, $59,413; expenditures, $49,830; qualifying distributions, $49,479.
Limitations: Giving primarily in NC.
Application information: Application form not required.

Officers: Jane B. Arnold, Pres.; Alma H. Brady, V.P.; Margaret R. Brady, V.P.; Charles E. Brady, Secy.; Burl H. Brady, Treas.
Board Members: Margaret R. Brady, Susan M. Brady.
EIN: 561705736

41305
Williamson Family Foundation
P.O. Drawer 848
Fayetteville, NC 28302-0848

Established in 1986 in NC.
Donor(s): Harrison H. Williamson, Jane D. Williamson.
Financial data (yr. ended 12/31/01): Grants paid, $49,347; assets, $1,082,196 (M); gifts received, $25,000; expenditures, $83,900; qualifying distributions, $49,347.
Limitations: Applications not accepted.
Application information: Contributes only to pre-selected organizations.
Trustees: Harrison H. Williamson, Jane D. Williamson.
EIN: 581744883

41306
Morgan & Mary G. Hand II Memorial Scholarship Fund
c/o First Union National Bank
401 S. Tryon St., NC1159
Charlotte, NC 28288-1159

Established in 1998 in PA.
Donor(s): Morgan Hand II.
Financial data (yr. ended 12/31/01): Grants paid, $49,150; assets, $725,809 (M); expenditures, $57,491; qualifying distributions, $49,150.
Limitations: Giving primarily in DE, MD, NC, NJ, PA, and VA.
Trustees: William J. Hughes, First Union National Bank.
EIN: 237873029

41307
George S. & Sally T. Blackwelder Foundation, Inc.
P.O. Box 3366
Hickory, NC 28603-3366

Established in 1980 in NC.
Donor(s): George S. Blackwelder, Jr., Sally T. Blackwelder.
Financial data (yr. ended 12/31/01): Grants paid, $49,087; assets, $107,881 (M); gifts received, $106,000; expenditures, $50,613; qualifying distributions, $49,087.
Limitations: Applications not accepted. Giving primarily in NC.
Application information: Contributes only to pre-selected organizations.
Officers: George S. Blackwelder, Jr., Pres. and Treas.; Sally T. Blackwelder, V.P.; George S. Blackwelder III, Secy.
EIN: 581416771

41308
The Eleanor A. and Bernard H. Breedlove Foundation
(Formerly Breedlove Foundation)
Bank of America
101 S. Tyron St.
Charlotte, NC 28255-0001
Application address: 8 Cougar, Hilton Head Island, SC 29926-1952
Contact: William K. Mackey, Jr., Treas.

Established in 1994 in SC.
Financial data (yr. ended 09/30/01): Grants paid, $49,000; assets, $682,912 (M); expenditures, $58,315; qualifying distributions, $51,471.

Officers: Eleanor A. Breedlove, Chair.; Bernard H. Breedlove, Pres.; William S. Rose, Jr., Secy.; William K. Mackey, Jr., Treas.
Trustee: Bank of America.
EIN: 571005761

41309
The Bernard Foundation, Inc.
301 Cascade Dr.
High Point, NC 27265-8486

Established in 1965 in NC.
Donor(s): Herman W. Bernard.
Financial data (yr. ended 12/31/01): Grants paid, $48,950; assets, $351,267 (M); expenditures, $54,953; qualifying distributions, $48,950.
Limitations: Applications not accepted. Giving primarily in NC.
Application information: Contributes only to pre-selected organizations.
Officers and Directors:* Zelda Bernard,* Pres.; Rose B. Ackermann,* Secy.
EIN: 566064833

41310
McSpadden Family Foundation, Inc.
6100 W. Friendly Ave., No. 3105
Greensboro, NC 27410   (336) 299-0965

Financial data (yr. ended 03/31/01): Grants paid, $48,841; assets, $1 (M); expenditures, $50,743; qualifying distributions, $48,841.
Officers and Directors:* Jane A. McSpadden,* Pres.; George E. McSpadden,* Secy.-Treas.; G. David McSpadden, J. David McSpadden, J. Steven McSpadden, Robert A. McSpadden, Thomas E. McSpadden.
EIN: 562029918

41311
Tom & Elaine Wright Family Foundation, Inc.
32 Sturbridge Ln.
Greensboro, NC 27408-3842
Contact: Thomas E. Wright, Chair.

Established in 1994 in NC.
Donor(s): Thomas E. Wright.
Financial data (yr. ended 12/31/01): Grants paid, $48,500; assets, $811,233 (M); gifts received, $10,519; expenditures, $52,038; qualifying distributions, $48,500.
Limitations: Giving primarily in Guilford County, NC.
Officers and Directors:* Thomas E. Wright,* Chair. and Pres.; Elaine R. Wright,* V.P. and Treas.; Michael H. Godwin, Secy.
EIN: 561901006

41312
CBT Charitable Trust
c/o C. Brent Trexler, Jr.
P.O. Box 32486
Charlotte, NC 28232

Established in 1990 in NC.
Financial data (yr. ended 12/31/01): Grants paid, $48,450; assets, $1,892,347 (M); expenditures, $53,971; qualifying distributions, $48,450.
Limitations: Applications not accepted. Giving primarily in NC.
Application information: Contributes only to pre-selected organizations.
Trustees: C. Brent Trexler, Jr., Claire W. Trexler.
EIN: 566370754

41313
Grimley Scholarship Trust
c/o First Union National Bank
401 S. Tryon St., 4th Fl.
Charlotte, NC 28288-1159

Donor(s): Isaac C. Grimley.‡

Financial data (yr. ended 12/31/01): Grants paid, $48,148; assets, $577,210 (M); expenditures, $50,803; qualifying distributions, $48,267.
Limitations: Applications not accepted. Giving primarily in PA.
Application information: Unsolicited requests for funds not accepted.
Trustee: First Union National Bank.
EIN: 236408183
Codes: GTI

41314
Felicite B. Latane Endowment Fund
c/o Central Carolina Bank & Trust Co.
P.O. Box 51489
Durham, NC 27707

Established in 1999 in NC.
Donor(s): Felicite Latane Trust.
Financial data (yr. ended 07/31/01): Grants paid, $48,002; assets, $1,034,846 (M); expenditures, $59,449; qualifying distributions, $48,002.
Limitations: Applications not accepted. Giving primarily in Orange County, NC.
Application information: Contributes only to pre-selected organizations.
Trustee: Central Carolina Bank & Trust Co.
EIN: 566544480

41315
The Babies Hospital Foundation, Inc.
c/o Wachovia Bank of North Carolina, N.A.
P.O. Box 3099
Winston-Salem, NC 27150-1022
Application address: P.O. Box 1229, Wilmington, NC 28402
Contact: Raymond H. Holland, Jr., Treas.

Financial data (yr. ended 09/30/99): Grants paid, $48,000; assets, $1,090,833 (M); expenditures, $62,691; qualifying distributions, $49,363.
Limitations: Giving primarily in Wilmington, NC.
Officers and Directors:* Walker Taylor III,* Pres.; William H. Joyner, Jr.,* V.P.; Robert A. Little, Jr.,* Secy.; Raymond H. Holland, Jr.,* Treas.; Harold D. Alexius, William O.J. Lynch, William A. Raney.
Trustee: Wachovia Bank of North Carolina, N.A.
EIN: 560547500

41316
The Macamor Foundation
813 Logan Trail
Rocky Mount, NC 27803-1592

Established around 1957.
Financial data (yr. ended 06/30/02): Grants paid, $47,877; assets, $958,729 (M); expenditures, $63,701; qualifying distributions, $47,877.
Limitations: Applications not accepted. Giving primarily in the East, with emphasis on Washington, DC, and NC.
Application information: Contributes only to pre-selected organizations.
Directors: Michael Galberith, James M. Smith, Jr., Jim Smith.
EIN: 546052444

41317
The E. Merle & Ollie M. Edwards Foundation, Inc.
2697 Hwy. 258 N.
Kinston, NC 28504   (252) 527-3178
Contact: Thomas L. Edwards, Pres.

Established in 2000 in NC.
Donor(s): Edwards Investment Group, C. Felix Harvey, Carolina Ice Co., John R. Farley.
Financial data (yr. ended 12/31/01): Grants paid, $47,788; assets, $234,114 (M); gifts received, $47,500; expenditures, $48,856; qualifying distributions, $48,793.

41317—NORTH CAROLINA

Limitations: Giving primarily in Kinston, NC.
Application information: Application form not required.
Officers and Directors:* Thomas L. Edwards,* Pres.; Merle W. Edwards,* V.P.; David C. Edwards, Secy.-Treas.; Edwin M. Edwards, Stuart M. Edwards, Thomas L. Edwards, Jr.
EIN: 562166688
Codes: CS

41318
James E. Hoyle Charitable Trust
c/o First Union National Bank
401 S. Tryon St., NC1159
Charlotte, NC 28288

Established in 1998 in VA.
Financial data (yr. ended 12/31/01): Grants paid, $47,534; assets, $2,649,619 (M); gifts received, $23,360; expenditures, $62,599; qualifying distributions, $47,534.
Limitations: Applications not accepted. Giving primarily in VA.
Application information: Contributes only to pre-selected organizations.
Trustee: First Union National Bank.
EIN: 237931413

41319
John H. Wellons Foundation, Inc.
(Formerly Wellons Foundation, Inc.)
P.O. Box 1254
Dunn, NC 28335-1254 (910) 892-0436
Contact: John H. Wellons, Sr., Pres.

Established in 1950 in NC.
Financial data (yr. ended 12/31/99): Grants paid, $47,154; assets, $3,634,822 (M); gifts received, $366,047; expenditures, $794,568; qualifying distributions, $47,154.
Limitations: Giving limited to the Dunn, NC, area.
Application information: Student loans limited to students of local area high schools and universities. Application form required.
Officers and Directors:* John H. Wellons, Sr.,* Pres.; John H. Wellons, Jr.,* V.P.; Llewellyn Jernigan, Secy.; Sylvia W. Craft, Gene T. Jernigan, Donald McCoy.
EIN: 566061476
Codes: GTI

41320
Ola Warren & John W. Patterson, Jr. Scholarship Fund
c/o First Union National Bank
401 S. Tryon, NC1159
Charlotte, NC 28288-1159

Established in 1995 in NC.
Donor(s): John W. Patterson, Jr.‡
Financial data (yr. ended 12/31/00): Grants paid, $47,090; assets, $1,163,955 (M); expenditures, $70,363; qualifying distributions, $46,930.
Limitations: Applications not accepted. Giving primarily in NC and SC.
Application information: Contributes only to pre-selected organizations.
Trustee: First Union National Bank.
EIN: 586314688

41321
Dicey Foundation
P.O. Box 1090
Shelby, NC 28151
Contact: Henry P. Neisler, Sr., Dir.

Established in 1995.
Financial data (yr. ended 11/30/01): Grants paid, $46,600; assets, $434,874 (M); gifts received, $30,000; expenditures, $48,484; qualifying distributions, $46,600.

Limitations: Giving primarily in IN.
Application information: Application form not required.
Directors: C. Andrew Neisler, Charles A. Neisler, Sr., Henry P. Neisler, Sr., William Hayne Neisler.
EIN: 561442950

41322
CCBCC Relief Foundation, Inc.
P.O. Box 31487
Charlotte, NC 28231-1487
Application address: c/o Coca-Cola Bottling Co. Consolidated, 4115 Coca-Cola Plz., Charlotte, NC 28211-3400, tel.: (704) 557-4425
Contact: Caroline S. Umberger, Secy.

Established in 1995 in NC.
Donor(s): Coca-Cola Bottling Co. Consolidated, and employees.
Financial data (yr. ended 12/31/01): Grants paid, $46,500; assets, $302,496 (M); gifts received, $12,309; expenditures, $46,924; qualifying distributions, $46,500.
Limitations: Giving to employees and former employees, primarily in the South (FL, NC, SC, and TN).
Application information: Application form required.
Officers: Robert D. Pettus, Jr., Pres.; Umesh Kasbekar, V.P.; T. Fred Melton, V.P.; Lauren C. Steele, V.P.; Caroline S. Umberger, Secy.; Clifford M. Deal III, Treas.
Directors: William B. Elmore, J. Frank Harrison III.
EIN: 561927278
Codes: CS, CD

41323
The Stephen D. Falkenbury, Jr. Foundation
810 Shetland Pl., N.W.
Concord, NC 28027-7578

Established in 2000 in NC.
Donor(s): Stephen D. Falkenbury, Jr.‡
Financial data (yr. ended 12/31/01): Grants paid, $46,000; assets, $840,135 (M); gifts received, $100; expenditures, $70,167; qualifying distributions, $50,000.
Limitations: Applications not accepted. Giving primarily in NC.
Application information: Contributes only to pre-selected organizations.
Officers: John Falkenbury, Pres.; Jeane Falkenbury, V.P.; Pamela Albright, Secy.
Board Members: Paul Falkenbury, Stephen D. Falkenbury III.
EIN: 562201996

41324
Ralph C. Sadler Foundation Trust
c/o B.B. & T., Trust Dept.
P.O. Box 632
Whiteville, NC 28472 (910) 642-1420
Contact: Susan McKeithan

Established in 1967.
Financial data (yr. ended 12/31/01): Grants paid, $46,000; assets, $1,080,522 (M); expenditures, $55,780; qualifying distributions, $46,000.
Limitations: Giving primarily in NC.
Application information: Application form not required.
Trustee: B.B. & T.
EIN: 566122933

41325
Anna L. Way Trust
c/o First Union National Bank
401 S. Tryon St., NC 1159
Charlotte, NC 28288-1159

Financial data (yr. ended 08/31/01): Grants paid, $46,000; assets, $257,613 (M); expenditures, $49,551; qualifying distributions, $46,800.
Limitations: Applications not accepted. Giving limited to Philadelphia, PA.
Application information: Restricted by the trust instrument to admission fees for aged persons to non-profit homes for the aged.
Trustee: First Union National Bank.
EIN: 236222000

41326
Mary Doyle Memorial Fund
(Formerly Dr. Edgar Clay Doyle and Mary Cherry Doyle Memorial Fund)
c/o Wachovia Bank of North Carolina, N.A.
P.O. Box 3099
Winston-Salem, NC 27150-7131
Application address: c/o South Carolina Foundation of Independent Colleges, P.O. Box 1465, Taylors, SC 29687-1465, tel.: (803) 268-4002
Contact: Sandra H. Lee

Established in 1973 in SC.
Donor(s): Edgar Clay Doyle,‡ Mary Cherry Doyle.‡
Financial data (yr. ended 01/31/00): Grants paid, $45,870; assets, $1,279,435 (M); expenditures, $58,983; qualifying distributions, $48,241.
Limitations: Giving limited to residents of Oconee County, SC.
Publications: Annual report.
Application information: Applications available at high schools in Oconee County, SC. Application form required.
Trustee: Wachovia Bank of North Carolina, N.A.
EIN: 576019447
Codes: GTI

41327
Kent Foundation
79 Forest at Duke Dr.
Durham, NC 27705 (919) 419-1859

Donor(s): Ralph E. Kent.
Financial data (yr. ended 08/31/01): Grants paid, $45,800; assets, $996,863 (M); expenditures, $52,066; qualifying distributions, $45,800.
Limitations: Giving primarily in the East.
Application information: Application form not required.
Officers: Ralph E. Kent, Pres.; Betty K. Kent, V.P.; William L. Stanford, Secy.
Directors: Gary A. Kent, Gregory D. Kent.
EIN: 136126351

41328
The Joanna Foundation
1957 Prestwick Ln.
Wilmington, NC 28405
Application address: 1975 Prestwick Ln., Wilmington, NC 28405, tel.: (910) 256-6808
Contact: Lynn Regnery, Pres.

Established in 1991 in IL.
Financial data (yr. ended 12/31/01): Grants paid, $45,079; assets, $975,983 (M); expenditures, $65,680; qualifying distributions, $45,079.
Limitations: Giving primarily in AZ.
Application information: Application form not required.
Officers and Directors:* Lynn Regnery,* Pres. and Treas.; Eddie Keith, Secy.; Gretchen Regnery Wallerich.

EIN: 363666551

41329
Lillie E. Norket Charitable Unitrust
339 N. Greenbriar Rd.
Statesville, NC 28677

Financial data (yr. ended 12/31/01): Grants paid, $45,000; assets, $181,812 (M); expenditures, $45,325; qualifying distributions, $45,000.
Limitations: Applications not accepted.
Application information: Contributes only to pre-selected organizations.
Trustees: Richard Boyd, David Hendry, John West.
EIN: 566269715

41330
The Stephens Endowment
P.O. Drawer 1507
Morganton, NC 28680-1507

Established in 1988 in NC.
Donor(s): Gerald K. Stephens.
Financial data (yr. ended 10/31/01): Grants paid, $45,000; assets, $1,014,681 (M); gifts received, $7,000; expenditures, $59,384; qualifying distributions, $45,000.
Limitations: Applications not accepted. Giving limited to Morganton, NC.
Application information: Contributes only to pre-selected organizations.
Officers: Gerald K. Stephens, Pres.; G. Kenneth Stephens, Jr., V.P.; Jean T. Stephens, Secy.
EIN: 560633355

41331
Spivey Scholarship Trust
c/o First Citizens Bank & Trust Dept.
P.O. Box 29522
Raleigh, NC 27626
Application address: Rte. 1, Box 95, Hobbsville, NC 27946, tel.: (919) 357-0720
Contact: Linda F. Hofler, Tr.

Financial data (yr. ended 11/30/01): Grants paid, $44,810; assets, $909,226 (M); expenditures, $52,429; qualifying distributions, $45,238.
Limitations: Giving limited to Gates County, NC.
Publications: Annual report.
Application information: Application form required.
Trustees: Linda F. Hofler, Sidney Earl Stallings, Dennis Trotman.
EIN: 566235902
Codes: GTI

41332
Ralph N. Jones Foundation, Inc.
2316 South Blvd.
Charlotte, NC 28203-5008
Contact: Ralph N. Jones, Jr., Pres.

Financial data (yr. ended 06/30/01): Grants paid, $44,560; assets, $629,871 (M); expenditures, $69,326; qualifying distributions, $44,560.
Limitations: Giving primarily in NC.
Application information: Application form not required.
Officers: Ralph N. Jones, Jr., Pres. and Secy.; Wristen Jones, V.P. and Treas.
EIN: 566061169

41333
Frank & Sallie Borden Foundation Trust
c/o Wachovia Bank, N.A.
P.O. Box 3099
Winston-Salem, NC 27150-7131
(336) 732-6478

Donor(s): Wilmer K. Borden.
Financial data (yr. ended 12/31/99): Grants paid, $44,500; assets, $1,196,798 (M); gifts received, $25; expenditures, $57,099; qualifying distributions, $44,822.
Limitations: Giving limited to Wayne County and Goldsboro, NC.
Application information: Applications available from principal and Chair. of Goldsboro High School, NC. Application form required.
Trustee: Wachovia Bank of North Carolina, N.A.
Scholarship Committee: Mrs. E.B. Borden III, Robert H. Borden, Frank B. Hanes, Jr., Georgia C. Joyner, Sallie Walker.
EIN: 566035962
Codes: GTI

41334
The Jonas Foundation
P.O. Box 1650
Lenoir, NC 28645-6427
Application address: 401 Kincaid St., Lenoir, NC 28645, tel.: (704) 728-3271
Contact: Myron L. Moore, Jr., Secy.-Treas.

Established in 1984 in NC.
Donor(s): Lenoir Mirror Co., A.G. Jonas, Sr.
Financial data (yr. ended 06/30/01): Grants paid, $44,500; assets, $814,513 (M); expenditures, $45,204; qualifying distributions, $44,325.
Limitations: Giving primarily in Caldwell County, NC.
Officers: A.G. Jonas, Jr., Pres.; Myron L. Moore, Jr., Secy.-Treas.
EIN: 561459346

41335
Martha and William Murray Charitable Foundation
(Formerly The James M. Hornaday Charitable Foundation II)
c/o U.S. Trust
P.O. Box 26262
Greensboro, NC 27420

Established in 1986 in NC.
Financial data (yr. ended 09/30/01): Grants paid, $44,000; assets, $811,339 (M); expenditures, $55,042; qualifying distributions, $46,070.
Limitations: Applications not accepted. Giving primarily in NC.
Application information: Contributes only to pre-selected organizations.
Trustees: Martha H. Murray, William G. Murray, U.S. Trust.
EIN: 566293527

41336
Bauman Family Foundation, Inc.
16 Elm Ridge Ln.
Greensboro, NC 27408

Established in 1999 in NC.
Donor(s): Edward J. Bauman, Vivien K. Bauman.
Financial data (yr. ended 12/31/01): Grants paid, $43,775; assets, $289,533 (M); gifts received, $8,247; expenditures, $43,862; qualifying distributions, $43,775.
Limitations: Applications not accepted. Giving primarily in NC.
Application information: Contributes only to pre-selected organizations.
Officers: Edward J. Bauman, Pres. and Treas.; Vivien K. Bauman, V.P. and Secy.
EIN: 562168228

41337
The Blanchard Foundation
3343 Alamance Dr.
Raleigh, NC 27609 (919) 787-1631
Contact: Charles F. Blanchard, Pres.

Established in 1988 in NC.
Donor(s): Charles F. Blanchard.
Financial data (yr. ended 12/31/01): Grants paid, $43,581; assets, $1,009,192 (M); expenditures, $45,502; qualifying distributions, $43,581.
Limitations: Giving primarily in NC.
Application information: Application form not required.
Officers: Charles F. Blanchard, Pres. and Treas.; Bernard B. Blanchard, V.P.; Anna Neal Blanchard, Secy.
EIN: 581837158

41338
The Mealy Family Foundation, Inc.
c/o U.S. Trust
P.O. Box 26262
Greensboro, NC 27420

Established in 1998 in NC.
Donor(s): Mark W. Mealy.
Financial data (yr. ended 12/31/01): Grants paid, $43,000; assets, $678,459 (M); gifts received, $60,030; expenditures, $50,501; qualifying distributions, $43,000.
Limitations: Applications not accepted.
Application information: Contributes only to pre-selected organizations.
Directors: Mark W. Mealy, Rose Patrick Mealy.
EIN: 562109869

41339
Ralph Wilson Plastics Scholarship Fund, Inc.
P.O. Box 1118
Fletcher, NC 28732-1118

Donor(s): Ralph Wilson Plastics Co., Service America Corp.
Financial data (yr. ended 12/31/00): Grants paid, $42,921; assets, $727,473 (M); gifts received, $26,976; expenditures, $45,908; qualifying distributions, $44,597; giving activities include $1,676 for programs.
Limitations: Applications not accepted. Giving limited to NC.
Officers: Scott Schnell, Pres.; Cheryl Crosby, V.P.; Damion Brookshire, Secy.; Terri Elliott, Treas.
EIN: 581576914
Codes: CS, CD, GTI

41340
Hurshell and Gerrie Keener Family Foundation
P.O. Box 3349
Hickory, NC 28603 (828) 328-4053
Contact: Hurshell H. Keener, Pres.

Established in 2000 in NC.
Donor(s): Hurshell H. Keener, Geraldine F. Keener.
Financial data (yr. ended 12/31/01): Grants paid, $42,905; assets, $28,345 (M); gifts received, $69,488; expenditures, $42,906; qualifying distributions, $42,905.
Limitations: Giving primarily in NC.
Officers and Directors:* Hurshell H. Keener,* Pres. and Treas.; Geraldine F. Keener,* V.P. and Secy.; Staley Cates Keener, Caroline Keener North.
EIN: 562177063

41341
The Rexam Foundation
(Formerly Rexam Corporation Foundation)
4201 Congress St., Ste. 340
Charlotte, NC 28209

Established in 1958 in DE and NY.
Donor(s): Rexam Inc.
Financial data (yr. ended 12/31/01): Grants paid, $42,845; assets, $3,453 (M); gifts received, $45,589; expenditures, $43,318; qualifying distributions, $43,318.
Limitations: Giving primarily in the Southeast, with emphasis on NC and SC.

41341—NORTH CAROLINA

Application information: Application form required for employee-related scholarships, which are administered by the National Merit Scholarship Corp.
Officers: Frank C. Brown, Pres.; Lisa R. Larmore-Hysko, V.P.; Clinton H. Tumlin, Treas.
EIN: 136165669
Codes: CS, CD, GTI

41342
Grace D. Dreher Memorial Scholarship Fund
c/o First Union National Bank
401 S. Tryon St., NC1159
Charlotte, NC 28288-1159

Financial data (yr. ended 04/30/01): Grants paid, $42,500; assets, $829,191 (M); expenditures, $53,481; qualifying distributions, $42,299.
Limitations: Giving limited to residents of Monroe County, PA.
Trustee: First Union National Bank.
EIN: 236478635
Codes: GTI

41343
Bluethenthal Family Fund
10 New Bern Sq.
Greensboro, NC 27408

Established in 1997 in NC.
Donor(s): Arthur Bluethenthal, Joanne K. Bluethenthal.
Financial data (yr. ended 12/31/01): Grants paid, $42,356; assets, $348,787 (M); expenditures, $53,455; qualifying distributions, $42,356.
Limitations: Applications not accepted. Giving primarily in Greensboro, NC.
Application information: Contributes only to pre-selected organizations.
Directors: Ruth B. Appel, Anne Bluethenthal, Arthur Bluethenthal, Arthur Bluethenthal, Jr., Joanne K. Bluethenthal.
EIN: 562026234

41344
Joseph Dave Foundation
c/o Wachovia Bank, N.A.
P.O. Box 3099
Winston-Salem, NC 27150
Application address: P.O. Box 2630, Asheville, NC 28802
Contact: A. Jerome Dave, Chair.

Financial data (yr. ended 12/31/01): Grants paid, $42,250; assets, $157,515 (M); gifts received, $50,000; expenditures, $45,159; qualifying distributions, $42,250.
Limitations: Giving primarily in NC.
Officer and Trustees:* A. Jerome Dave,* Chair. and Secy.; Hyman Dave, Jeffrey E. Dave, William N. Lewin, Wachovia Bank, N.A.
EIN: 566035045

41345
Ida W. Browning Audio-Visual Trust
c/o First Union National Bank
401 S. Tryon St.
Charlotte, NC 28288-1159
Application address: 30 N. 3rd St., P.O. Box 1071, Harrisburg, PA 17101-1703
Contact: Pamela Nothstein, V.P., First Union National Bank

Established in 1964 in PA.
Donor(s): Ida W. Browning.‡
Financial data (yr. ended 09/30/01): Grants paid, $42,182; assets, $882,509 (M); expenditures, $48,420; qualifying distributions, $42,182.
Limitations: Giving primarily in parts of Cumberland County, and the Dauphin County and greater Harrisburg, PA, areas.

Application information: Application form required.
Director: Charles R. Carnes, Jr.
Trustee: First Union National Bank.
EIN: 236271540

41346
Thomasville Community Foundation
P.O. Box 2283
Thomasville, NC 27361
Contact: Marti Baity, Secy.-Treas.

Community foundation established in 1949 in NC.
Financial data (yr. ended 12/31/00): Grants paid, $42,171; assets, $327,308 (M); gifts received, $23,450; expenditures, $46,498.
Limitations: Applications not accepted. Giving limited to Thomasville, NC.
Publications: Financial statement.
Officers: E. Thompson Smith, Pres.; Paul Albertson, V.P.; Marti Baity, Secy.-Treas.
Directors: Conley Abrams, Joe Bennett, Linda Berrier, Shirley F. Cecil, James C. Dorety, Simon Downs, Charlie Hall, Sue Hunter, Cindy Ingram, Stuart Kennedy, William B. Mills, Swope Montgomery, Charles O'Brien, Aldeen Robbins, Colin Starrett, David Williams.
EIN: 566056287
Codes: CM

41347
Olin Foundation of Asheville
4 Cedar Chine
Asheville, NC 28803-3048

Established in 1997 in NC.
Donor(s): Ronald G. Olin, Sandra D. Olin.
Financial data (yr. ended 12/31/00): Grants paid, $42,000; assets, $411,294 (M); expenditures, $47,582; qualifying distributions, $41,869.
Limitations: Applications not accepted.
Application information: Contributes only to pre-selected organizations.
Officers and Directors:* Sandra D. Olin,* Secy.; Ronald G. Olin,* C.F.O.
EIN: 562029426

41348
Ernest B. Albat and Rose A. Albat Foundation for Cancer Research
c/o First Union National Bank
401 S. Tryon St., NC 1159
Charlotte, NC 28288

Established in 1988 in NC.
Financial data (yr. ended 08/31/01): Grants paid, $41,623; assets, $707,144 (M); expenditures, $51,710; qualifying distributions, $41,408.
Limitations: Applications not accepted. Giving primarily in MD and NC.
Application information: Contributes only to pre-selected organizations.
Trustee: First Union National Bank.
EIN: 566312891

41349
B. B. Walker Foundation
P.O. Drawer 1167
Asheboro, NC 27204-1167 (336) 625-1380
Contact: Edna A. Walker, Pres.

Established in 1963.
Financial data (yr. ended 06/30/01): Grants paid, $41,575; assets, $975,275 (M); expenditures, $51,507; qualifying distributions, $46,677.
Limitations: Giving primarily in NC.
Application information: Application form not required.
Officers and Director:* Edna A. Walker,* Pres.; James P. McDermott, Secy.-Treas.
EIN: 566061441

41350
Ruth P. Seruga Lehigh County Charities Trust
c/o First Union National Bank
401 S. Tryon St., 4th Fl.
Charlotte, NC 28288-1159

Established in 1988 in PA.
Financial data (yr. ended 12/31/01): Grants paid, $41,500; assets, $826,947 (M); expenditures, $43,749; qualifying distributions, $41,666.
Limitations: Applications not accepted. Giving limited to Lehigh County, PA.
Application information: Contributes only to pre-selected organizations.
Trustee: First Union National Bank.
EIN: 236908392

41351
Donna & Norman Levin Family Foundation
225 King Owen Ct.
Charlotte, NC 28211-4097

Established in 1999 in NC.
Donor(s): Sadie Levin.‡
Financial data (yr. ended 12/31/01): Grants paid, $41,471; assets, $248,411 (M); expenditures, $44,280; qualifying distributions, $41,471.
Limitations: Applications not accepted.
Application information: Contributes only to pre-selected organizations.
Officers and Directors:* Norman Levin,* Pres.; Donna Levin,* Secy.; Rabbi Frank S. Levin, Ross C. Levin.
EIN: 562113238
Codes: TN

41352
Snyder Watchorn Foundation, Inc.
1316 Brigham Ct.
Chapel Hill, NC 27514

Established in 1992.
Financial data (yr. ended 12/31/01): Grants paid, $41,300; assets, $825,125 (M); expenditures, $42,489; qualifying distributions, $41,300.
Limitations: Applications not accepted. Giving primarily in NC.
Application information: Contributes only to pre-selected organizations.
Officer: Philip M. Snyder III, Pres.
EIN: 561748840

41353
The Talbert Family Foundation
12 Water St.
Wrightsville Beach, NC 28480

Established in 1988 in NC.
Donor(s): John Talbert, Hanes Companies Foundation, Inc.
Financial data (yr. ended 12/31/01): Grants paid, $41,090; assets, $915,194 (M); expenditures, $41,692; qualifying distributions, $41,090.
Limitations: Applications not accepted. Giving limited to Winston-Salem, NC.
Application information: Contributes only to pre-selected organizations.
Officers: John B. Talbert, Jr., Pres. and Treas.; Judy Blackwelder Talbert, V.P. and Secy.
EIN: 581807228

41354
The Faith Foundation
213 Shady Circle Dr.
Rocky Mount, NC 27803-1710

Established in 1989 in NC.
Donor(s): Anne B. Lewis, John W. Lewis.
Financial data (yr. ended 12/31/01): Grants paid, $41,000; assets, $672,646 (M); gifts received,

$6,840; expenditures, $43,972; qualifying distributions, $41,000.
Limitations: Applications not accepted. Giving primarily in NC.
Application information: Contributes only to pre-selected organizations.
Directors: J.C.D. Bailey, Anne B. Lewis, Anne W. Lewis, John W. Lewis, Lynn L. White.
EIN: 561636192

41355
Will Paul Bateman Scholarship Fund Trust
c/o First Union National Bank
401 S. Tryon St., NC1159
Charlotte, NC 28288

Financial data (yr. ended 04/30/01): Grants paid, $40,791; assets, $890,350 (M); expenditures, $54,189; qualifying distributions, $40,343.
Limitations: Giving limited to FL.
Application information: Application available at Florida colleges and universities. Application form required.
Trustee: First Union National Bank.
EIN: 596149634
Codes: GTI

41356
Victor Bates Foundation, Inc.
P.O. Box 19608
Greensboro, NC 27419-9608

Established in 1956.
Donor(s): Emma Bates, Victor Bates.
Financial data (yr. ended 09/30/01): Grants paid, $40,785; assets, $349,662 (M); expenditures, $42,886; qualifying distributions, $40,785.
Limitations: Applications not accepted. Giving primarily in NC.
Application information: Contributes only to pre-selected organizations.
Officers and Directors:* Louis Bates,* Pres.; Laurence A. Bates,* Secy.; Freddy Robinson,* Treas.
EIN: 566060716

41357
Wayne Foundation, Inc.
644 N. Spence Ave.
Goldsboro, NC 27534   (919) 778-1379
Contact: Alan Weil, Treas.

Established around 1943 in NC.
Donor(s): Betty Fischer, Alan Weil.
Financial data (yr. ended 12/31/01): Grants paid, $40,730; assets, $727,399 (M); gifts received, $5,766; expenditures, $48,752; qualifying distributions, $40,730.
Limitations: Giving primarily in Goldsboro and Greenville, NC.
Application information: Application form not required.
Officers: Louis Weil, Pres.; Alan Weil, Treas.
EIN: 566044387

41358
Ely J. Perry Foundation, Inc.
518 Plaza Blvd.
Kinston, NC 28501

Financial data (yr. ended 08/31/01): Grants paid, $40,564; assets, $38,270 (M); gifts received, $46,849; expenditures, $42,155; qualifying distributions, $40,564.
Limitations: Applications not accepted.
Application information: Contributes only to pre-selected organizations.
Officers: Ely J. Perry, Jr., Pres.; Dan E. Perry, V.P. and Treas.; Warren S. Perry, Secy.
EIN: 237076030

41359
Lang Family Foundation, Inc.
712 Radburn Pl.
Raleigh, NC 27615

Financial data (yr. ended 12/31/01): Grants paid, $40,228; assets, $641,585 (M); expenditures, $66,107; qualifying distributions, $40,228.
Limitations: Applications not accepted. Giving on a national basis.
Application information: Contributes only to pre-selected organizations.
Officers: Linda L. Lang, Chair., Pres. and Treas.; F. Jordan Lang, Secy.
Directors: J. Christopher Lang, Philip C. Lang.
EIN: 582130410

41360
Joseph J. Miller Foundation
c/o Wachovia Bank, N.A.
P.O. Box 3099
Winston-Salem, NC 27150-7131
Application address: c/o Wachovia Bank, N.A., 1426 Main St., Columbia, SC 29226-9365, tel.: (803) 765-3677
Contact: C. Gerald Lane, V.P. and Trust Off., Wachovia Bank, N.A.

Financial data (yr. ended 12/31/01): Grants paid, $40,200; assets, $1,061,771 (M); expenditures, $53,454; qualifying distributions, $40,200.
Limitations: Giving primarily in the Orangeburg-Elloree, SC, area.
Directors: Ralph T. Crim, Sue Daniels, Sylvia D. Steinberg.
Trustee: Wachovia Bank, N.A.
EIN: 576055700

41361
Hogan Family Foundation, Inc.
2835 Willowbrook Rd.
Lenoir, NC 28645

Established in 2001 in NC.
Financial data (yr. ended 12/31/01): Grants paid, $40,000; assets, $971,572 (M); gifts received, $1,014,240; expenditures, $40,011; qualifying distributions, $40,011.
Officers and Directors:* Janis P. Hogan,* Pres.; Walter J. Hogan,* V.P.; Marie B. Hogan,* Secy.; John C. Hogan,* Treas.; James B. Hogan, Margaret P. Hogan.
EIN: 562255419

41362
The Annie Jack Foundation
P.O. Box 2652
Surf City, NC 28445-9821   (910) 328-5182
Contact: Kenneth W. Arnold, Pres.

Established in 1995 in NC.
Financial data (yr. ended 12/31/01): Grants paid, $40,000; assets, $1,019,343 (M); expenditures, $52,642; qualifying distributions, $9,231.
Limitations: Giving limited to Raleigh, NC.
Officers: Kenneth W. Arnold, Pres.; Frances K. Arnold, V.P.; Nettie L. Peterson, Secy.
EIN: 561931383

41363
Stephen R. Kerrigan and Maureen W. Kerrigan Family Foundation, Inc.
7300 Governors Hill Ln.
Charlotte, NC 28211

Established in 1998 in NC.
Donor(s): Stephen R. Kerrigan, Maureen W. Kerrigan.
Financial data (yr. ended 12/31/01): Grants paid, $40,000; assets, $5,100 (M); gifts received, $1,050; expenditures, $41,050; qualifying distributions, $40,000.
Limitations: Applications not accepted. Giving primarily in VA.
Application information: Contributes only to pre-selected organizations.
Officer and Directors:* Stephen R. Kerrigan,* Pres.; Ronald S. Brody, Daniel J. Kerrigan, Maureen W. Kerrigan.
EIN: 562099706

41364
Revell Memorial Mission
60 Patton Ave.
Asheville, NC 28801-3312

Financial data (yr. ended 12/31/01): Grants paid, $39,975; assets, $63,635 (M); gifts received, $12,542; expenditures, $45,803; qualifying distributions, $39,975.
Limitations: Applications not accepted. Giving primarily in Asheville, NC.
Application information: Contributes only to pre-selected organizations.
Trustees: Edgar J. Duckworth, W.T. Duckworth, Jr., Douglas E. Holcombe, Phillip D. Ray.
EIN: 581573191

41365
The Eplee Foundation, Inc.
9059 Walkers Ferry Rd.
Charlotte, NC 28214-3339

Established in 1991 in NC.
Donor(s): Herbert W. Eplee, Sr., Shirley J. Eplee.
Financial data (yr. ended 12/31/01): Grants paid, $39,500; assets, $147,542 (M); gifts received, $90,000; expenditures, $39,892; qualifying distributions, $39,500.
Limitations: Applications not accepted. Giving primarily in NC.
Application information: Contributes only to pre-selected organizations.
Officers: Herbert W. Eplee, Sr., Pres.; Shirley J. Eplee, Secy.
Directors: Gordon Kelly Eplee, Herbert W. Eplee, Jr., Melvin Glen Eplee.
EIN: 561761082

41366
Helen Lancaster Minton Educational Trust
c/o Centura Bank, Trust Dept.
P.O. Box 1220
Rocky Mount, NC 27802-1220
(252) 454-4017
Contact: Sharon Stephens, Trust Off., Centura Bank

Donor(s): Helen Lancaster Minton.
Financial data (yr. ended 03/31/02): Grants paid, $39,500; assets, $793,946 (M); expenditures, $48,827; qualifying distributions, $43,412.
Limitations: Giving limited to residents of Edgecombe and Nash counties, NC.
Application information: Application form required.
Trustee: Centura Bank.
EIN: 566180453
Codes: GTI

41367
The Hedrick Family Foundation, Inc.
P.O. Box 1040
Salisbury, NC 28145   (704) 633-5982
Contact: Frances H. Johnson, Pres.

Established in 1997 in NC.
Financial data (yr. ended 12/31/01): Grants paid, $39,495; assets, $29,650 (M); gifts received, $57,767; expenditures, $39,894; qualifying distributions, $39,863.

41367—NORTH CAROLINA

Limitations: Giving on a national basis.
Officers: Frances H. Johnson, Pres.; Jeffrey V. Goodman, V.P.; F. Joanne Johnson, Secy.; Alma H. Brady, Treas.
EIN: 561994087

41368
Lilienthal Investment Foundation
138 Clearwater Ln.
Mooresville, NC 28117-7529

Established in 1999 in NC.
Financial data (yr. ended 12/31/01): Grants paid, $39,168; assets, $2,314,386 (M); expenditures, $104,290; qualifying distributions, $39,168.
Officer: Robert David Lilienthal, Pres.
EIN: 562131918

41369
Colchamiro Family Foundation, Inc.
6 Roundtree Ct.
Greensboro, NC 27410

Established in 1994 in NC.
Donor(s): Harvey Colchamiro.
Financial data (yr. ended 12/31/01): Grants paid, $39,064; assets, $622,863 (M); gifts received, $109,725; expenditures, $40,337; qualifying distributions, $39,064.
Limitations: Applications not accepted.
Application information: Contributes only to pre-selected organizations.
Officer: Harvey Colchamiro, Pres.
EIN: 561890531

41370
The Stiver Foundation
P.O. Box 956
Linville, NC 28646
Contact: Jeanine B. Rush, Tr.

Donor(s): Verna Revitis.
Financial data (yr. ended 11/30/01): Grants paid, $39,000; assets, $724,095 (M); expenditures, $41,370; qualifying distributions, $39,000.
Limitations: Giving on a national basis.
Trustees: Fred L. Rush, Jeanine B. Rush.
EIN: 136076808

41371
Carlton Daley Christian Trust
(Formerly Daley Adair Family Trust)
5325 Orange Grove Rd.
Hillsborough, NC 27278 (919) 969-9290
Contact: H. Mark Daley, Jr., Tr.

Established in 1971.
Donor(s): Rev. Jerome T. Daley, Bryan D. Adair, H. Mark Daley, Jr.
Financial data (yr. ended 06/30/01): Grants paid, $38,910; assets, $121,666 (M); gifts received, $46,606; expenditures, $40,224; qualifying distributions, $38,910.
Limitations: Giving primarily in NC.
Trustee: H. Mark Daley, Jr.
EIN: 566099732

41372
Windsor Foundation
104 Ronsard Ln.
Cary, NC 27511-6019

Established in 2000 in NC.
Donor(s): Laura M. Stealey.
Financial data (yr. ended 12/31/00): Grants paid, $38,899; assets, $984,848 (M); gifts received, $1,031,162; expenditures, $38,923; qualifying distributions, $38,923.
Directors: Alyson M. Stealey, John W. Stealey, Laura M. Stealey.
EIN: 562226375

41373
Ella Mount Burr Trust
c/o First Union National Bank
401 S. Tyron St., NC 1159
Charlotte, NC 28288-1159

Financial data (yr. ended 07/31/01): Grants paid, $38,875; assets, $603,571 (M); expenditures, $42,157; qualifying distributions, $38,494.
Limitations: Applications not accepted.
Application information: Unsolicited requests for funds not accepted.
Trustee: First Union National Bank.
EIN: 223527315

41374
Ann Sherman Charitable Trust
c/o First Union National Bank
401 S. Tryon St., 4th Fl.
Charlotte, NC 28288-1159

Established in 1995 in VA.
Financial data (yr. ended 12/31/01): Grants paid, $38,822; assets, $1,421,456 (L); expenditures, $47,772; qualifying distributions, $40,418.
Limitations: Applications not accepted. Giving primarily in VA.
Application information: Contributes only to pre-selected organizations.
Trustee: First Union National Bank.
EIN: 546305592

41375
Tex Williams Foundation, Inc.
P.O. Box 41198
Greensboro, NC 27404
Application address: c/o Richard J. Williams, 4246 McConnell Rd., Greensboro, NC 27406-9012

Established in 1993 in NC.
Financial data (yr. ended 12/31/01): Grants paid, $38,306; assets, $156,236 (M); expenditures, $41,007; qualifying distributions, $38,306.
Limitations: Giving primarily in NC.
Directors: Chris Williams, David B. Williams, Richard J. Williams.
EIN: 561900949

41376
Leona Gruber Catholic & Community Charities of the Lehigh Valley
c/o First Union National Bank
401 S. Tryon St., NC1159
Charlotte, NC 28288-1159

Established in 1995 in PA.
Financial data (yr. ended 10/31/01): Grants paid, $38,230; assets, $837,820 (M); expenditures, $53,023; qualifying distributions, $38,230.
Limitations: Applications not accepted. Giving primarily in PA.
Application information: Contributes only to pre-selected organizations.
Trustees: John Labukas, Jr., First Union National Bank.
EIN: 237831170

41377
Samuel L. Phillips Family Foundation
P.O. Box 400
Spruce Pine, NC 28777

Established in 2000 in NC.
Financial data (yr. ended 12/31/01): Grants paid, $38,200; assets, $662,243 (M); gifts received, $489,000; expenditures, $49,597; qualifying distributions, $38,200.
Officers and Directors:* Samuel L. Phillips, Chair., Pres., and Treas.; Jewel M. Phillips,* V.P.; G. Byron Phillips,* Secy.

EIN: 562225556

41378
The Mary D. B. T. Semans Foundation
1044 W. Forest Hills Blvd.
Durham, NC 27707-1625
Contact: James D.B.T. Semans, Secy.-Treas.

Donor(s): James H. Semans, Mary D.B.T. Semans.
Financial data (yr. ended 12/31/01): Grants paid, $38,000; assets, $582,967 (M); expenditures, $50,602; qualifying distributions, $38,000.
Limitations: Giving primarily in NC.
Application information: Application form not required.
Officers and Trustees:* James H. Semans,* Pres.; Melvin Larence Thrash,* V.P.; James D.B.T. Semans,* Secy.-Treas.; Thomas S. Kenan III, Jenny Semans Koortbojian, Douglas C. Zinn.
EIN: 581484629

41379
Woodson Family Foundation, Inc.
505 Oberlin Rd., Ste. 210
Raleigh, NC 27605-1345 (919) 833-2882
Contact: R. Peyton Woodson III, Tr.

Established in 1986 in NC.
Donor(s): R. Peyton Woodson III.
Financial data (yr. ended 12/31/01): Grants paid, $38,000; assets, $815,657 (M); expenditures, $45,250; qualifying distributions, $38,000.
Limitations: Giving primarily in NC.
Application information: Application form not required.
Trustees: Martha Auison Woodson, R. Peyton Woodson III, Richard P. Woodson IV.
EIN: 561544614

41380
Gordon H. & Ruth A. Clark Educational Fund
c/o College Foundation, Inc.
P.O. Box 12100
Raleigh, NC 27605-2100 (919) 834-2893

Financial data (yr. ended 06/30/99): Grants paid, $37,764; assets, $573,027 (M); expenditures, $43,693; qualifying distributions, $37,518; giving activities include $37,764 for loans to individuals.
Limitations: Giving limited to residents of Moore County, NC.
Application information: Application form required.
Trustee: College Foundation, Inc.
EIN: 566045119

41381
Lewis A. Sikes Foundation
200 S. Lewis St.
Tabor City, NC 28463

Donor(s): Harriet Lewis Sikes.‡
Financial data (yr. ended 12/31/01): Grants paid, $37,600; assets, $1,153,441 (M); gifts received, $8,000; expenditures, $45,579; qualifying distributions, $44,359.
Limitations: Giving primarily in NC.
Officers: John E. Coles, Pres.; James Craigle, V.P.; O. Richard Wright, Jr., Secy.; Puckette W. Wooten, Treas.
Directors: Harold Hughes, Sterling Koonce, Naomi W. Ward.
EIN: 561947091

41382
Ruth T. Farrow Trust
c/o First Union National Bank
401 S. Tryon St., 4th Fl.
Charlotte, NC 28288-1159
Application address: 765 Broad St., Newark, NJ 07101
Contact: Andrew Davis, Trust Off., First Union National Bank

Financial data (yr. ended 12/31/01): Grants paid, $37,498; assets, $65,881 (M); expenditures, $38,516; qualifying distributions, $38,228.
Limitations: Giving limited to residents of Hunterdon County, NJ.
Trustee: First Union National Bank.
EIN: 226298532
Codes: GTI

41383
Hugh Morson Memorial Scholarship Fund
c/o Wachovia Bank, N.A.
100 N. Main St.
Winston-Salem, NC 27150-7153
(336) 732-4090
Contact: Chris Spaugh, Trust Off., Charitable Svcs., Wachovia Bank, N.A.

Financial data (yr. ended 12/31/01): Grants paid, $37,400; assets, $830,267 (M); expenditures, $44,901; qualifying distributions, $38,998.
Limitations: Giving primarily in Chapel Hill, NC.
Application information: Application form required.
Trustee: Wachovia Bank, N.A.
Selection Committee: Walter K. Joyner, John Weems.
EIN: 237418060
Codes: GTI

41384
Henry N. Brawner, Jr. Foundation
1802 Fairway Dr.
Reidsville, NC 27320-5416
Contact: Margaret A. Cooke, Pres.

Financial data (yr. ended 12/31/01): Grants paid, $37,000; assets, $712,604 (M); expenditures, $42,064; qualifying distributions, $37,000.
Limitations: Applications not accepted. Giving primarily in Washington, DC.
Application information: Contributes only to pre-selected organizations.
Officers: Margaret A. Cooke, Pres.; Edgar N. Brawner III, V.P.; Rodney H. Becker, Treas.
Directors: Richard A. Bechwith, Sally Beckwith.
EIN: 526047194

41385
First Citizens Foundation, Inc.
P.O. Box 1377
Smithfield, NC 27577-1377

Established in 1957 in NC.
Donor(s): First Citizens BancShares, Inc.
Financial data (yr. ended 12/31/00): Grants paid, $37,000; assets, $265,195 (M); expenditures, $40,957; qualifying distributions, $36,303.
Limitations: Applications not accepted. Giving primarily in NC.
Application information: Contributes only to pre-selected organizations.
Officers: Frank B. Holding, Pres.; Lewis R. Holding, V.P. and Secy.; Doris T. Allen, Treas.
EIN: 566044206
Codes: CS, CD

41386
John B. & Olive S. Cook Foundation
c/o Scott E. Lebensburger
211 N. Main St.
Hendersonville, NC 28792-5072

Established in 1998 in NC.
Financial data (yr. ended 12/31/01): Grants paid, $36,396; assets, $952,454 (M); expenditures, $74,822; qualifying distributions, $36,396.
Limitations: Applications not accepted.
Application information: Contributes only to pre-selected organizations.
Officers: Brenda Lebensburger, Secy.; Gerald Baggish, Treas.
Director: Scott E. Lebensburger.
EIN: 562066916

41387
George Hess Educational Fund
(also known as Hazel Porter Hess and George R. Hess Educational Trust)
c/o First Union National Bank
401 S. Tryon St., NC1159
Charlotte, NC 28288-1159

Financial data (yr. ended 12/31/01): Grants paid, $36,250; assets, $586,402 (M); expenditures, $42,978; qualifying distributions, $36,687.
Limitations: Giving limited to Loudoun County, VA.
Application information: Recipients are selected by faculty and administration at 2 high schools.
Trustee: First Union National Bank.
EIN: 546200977
Codes: GTI

41388
Daniel R. Miller Trust Fund for Education
c/o First Union National Bank
401 S. Tryon St., NC1159
Charlotte, NC 28288-1159

Financial data (yr. ended 12/31/01): Grants paid, $36,025; assets, $691,439 (M); expenditures, $42,808; qualifying distributions, $36,306.
Limitations: Applications not accepted. Giving primarily to residents of the Borough of Pinegrove, PA; secondarily to residents of the Township of Pinegrove, PA; and thirdly to residents of Clear Spring in Washington County, MD.
Trustee: First Union National Bank.
EIN: 236246260
Codes: GTI

41389
The Marks Family Foundation
5239 Winding Brook Rd.
Charlotte, NC 28226

Financial data (yr. ended 12/31/01): Grants paid, $36,000; assets, $586,688 (M); expenditures, $39,389; qualifying distributions, $36,000.
Limitations: Applications not accepted.
Application information: Contributes only to pre-selected organizations.
Trustees: Lora M. Bamauer, Barbara L. Marks, Daniel C. Marks, Jason M. Marks, John H. Marks, Melissa M. Marks.
EIN: 562114037

41390
Acme-McCrary and Sapona Foundation, Inc.
(Formerly McCrary-Acme Foundation, Inc.)
c/o Acme-McCrary Corp.
159 North St.
Asheboro, NC 27203-5411
Application address: P.O. Box 1287, Asheboro, NC 27204
Contact: Fred M. Kearns, Jr., Pres.

Established in 1953.
Donor(s): Acme-McCrary Corp., Sapona Manufacturing Co., Inc.
Financial data (yr. ended 12/31/01): Grants paid, $35,700; assets, $1,242,779 (M); expenditures, $61,324; qualifying distributions, $35,700.
Limitations: Giving primarily in Randolph County, NC.
Application information: Application form not required.
Officers: Fred M. Kearns, Jr., Pres.; C.W. McCrary, Jr., V.P.; S. Steele Redding, V.P.; W.H. Redding, Jr., V.P.; John O.H. Toledano, V.P.; John O.H. Toledano, Jr., V.P.; Bruce Patram, Secy.-Treas.
Directors: C.W. McCrary III, John O.H. Toledano, Jr.
EIN: 566047739
Codes: CS, CD

41391
Donald R. & Carol P. Lovett Charitable Trust
c/o Donald R. Lovett
10 Thornapple Dr.
Hendersonville, NC 28739-7049

Established in 1992.
Donor(s): Donald R. Lovett, Carol P. Lovett.
Financial data (yr. ended 07/31/01): Grants paid, $35,525; assets, $497,854 (M); expenditures, $36,416; qualifying distributions, $35,525.
Limitations: Applications not accepted. Giving primarily in NC.
Application information: Contributes only to pre-selected organizations.
Trustees: Carol P. Lovett, Donald R. Lovett, Joan E. Tripp.
EIN: 363846863

41392
The Hooper Foundation
c/o First Union National Bank
401 S. Tryon, NC1159
Charlotte, NC 28288-1159
Application address: 4 Claybrook Rd., Dover, MA 02030
Contact: James F. Hooper III, Tr.

Financial data (yr. ended 12/31/01): Grants paid, $35,500; assets, $339,721 (M); expenditures, $39,397; qualifying distributions, $35,500.
Limitations: Giving on a national basis, with emphasis on Baltimore, MD.
Trustee: First Union National Bank.
EIN: 236233576

41393
Blowing Rock Community Foundation
P.O. Box 525
Blowing Rock, NC 28605

Financial data (yr. ended 06/30/01): Grants paid, $35,250; assets, $534,376 (M); expenditures, $55,000.
Limitations: Giving primarily in Blowing Rock, NC.
Officers: Barbara Ball, Pres.; Susan Craig, Treas.
Trustees: Welborn E. Alexander, Jr., Susan Greene, Terry D. Lentz, Herbert Miller, Sandra S. Miller, David Rankin, Daniel H. Wolfe.
EIN: 561515818
Codes: CM

41394
The Paul and Margaret Porter Charitable Foundation
(Formerly Porter Brothers Foundation)
P.O. Box 1939
Shelby, NC 28151-1939

Donor(s): Porter Corporation, Paul B. Porter.
Financial data (yr. ended 11/30/01): Grants paid, $35,232; assets, $787,688 (M); expenditures, $78,882; qualifying distributions, $35,232.
Limitations: Applications not accepted. Giving primarily in NC.
Application information: Contributes only to pre-selected organizations.
Officer: Paul B. Porter, Pres.
EIN: 591750571
Codes: CS, CD

41395
Philip & Christa Santoni Foundation
111 Richelieu Dr.
Cary, NC 27511

Established in 2000 in NC.
Donor(s): Philip A. Santoni, Christa M. Santoni.
Financial data (yr. ended 12/31/01): Grants paid, $35,206; assets, $1,849 (M); gifts received, $25,000; expenditures, $36,710; qualifying distributions, $35,206.
Limitations: Applications not accepted. Giving primarily in Fairfield, IA, St. Louis, MO, and NC.
Application information: Contributes only to pre-selected organizations.
Officers: Philip A. Santoni, Pres. and Treas.; Crista M. Santoni, V.P. and Secy.
Directors: Joan R. Madden, William L. Madden, Albert R. Santoni, Catherine R. Santoni.
EIN: 562184127

41396
Shugart Family Foundation
4004 Long Meadow Ln.
Winston-Salem, NC 27106

Established in 2000 in NC.
Donor(s): Shugart Enterprises, LLC.
Financial data (yr. ended 04/30/02): Grants paid, $35,000; assets, $354,793 (M); gifts received, $312,234; expenditures, $39,047; qualifying distributions, $35,000.
Limitations: Applications not accepted.
Application information: Contributes only to pre-selected organizations.
Directors: Grover F. Shugart, Jr., Kay W. Shugart.
EIN: 562230054
Codes: CS

41397
Eleanor Cameron van Clief Foundation
c/o Wachovia Bank, N.A.
P.O. Box 3099
Winston-Salem, NC 27150
Contact: Faith Munro-Kerr, Tr.

Financial data (yr. ended 12/31/01): Grants paid, $35,000; assets, $345,462 (M); expenditures, $37,570; qualifying distributions, $35,000.
Limitations: Giving primarily in NC.
Trustees: Faith Munro-Kerr, Wachovia Bank, N.A.
EIN: 546030149

41398
Corabelle Chappell Memorial Fund
c/o First Union National Bank
401 S. Tryon, 4th Fl.
Charlotte, NC 28288-1159
Application address: 130 Wyoming Ave., Scranton, PA 18503

Established in 1993 in PA.

Donor(s): G.L. Chappell.‡
Financial data (yr. ended 12/31/01): Grants paid, $34,956; assets, $188,448 (M); expenditures, $47,291; qualifying distributions, $34,956.
Limitations: Giving limited to La Plume, PA.
Trustee: First Union National Bank.
EIN: 237710777
Codes: GTI

41399
Robert and Cora Peeples Foundation
c/o Wachovia Bank, N.A.
P.O. Box 3099
Winston-Salem, NC 27150-7153

Established in 1998 in SC.
Financial data (yr. ended 12/31/01): Grants paid, $34,890; assets, $836,166 (M); expenditures, $38,911; qualifying distributions, $34,890.
Limitations: Applications not accepted.
Application information: Contributes only to pre-selected organizations.
Trustee: Wachovia Bank, N.A.
Directors: Cora McKenzie Peeples, Robert E. H. Peeples, Robert E. Warner.
EIN: 582433751

41400
Hendricks Foundation
c/o W.E. Hendricks
953 Sandswood Dr.
Gastonia, NC 28054-1513

Donor(s): W.E. Hendricks.
Financial data (yr. ended 12/31/01): Grants paid, $34,800; assets, $895,695 (M); expenditures, $35,495; qualifying distributions, $34,800.
Limitations: Applications not accepted. Giving primarily in Gaston County, NC.
Application information: Contributes only to pre-selected organizations.
Officers: W.E. Hendricks, Pres. and Treas.; Shirley H. Cox, V.P.; Dema P. Hendricks, Secy.
EIN: 566046966

41401
Merritt J. Crawford Trust
c/o First Union National Bank
401 S. Tryon St., NC1159
Charlotte, NC 28288-1159

Donor(s): Merritt J. Crawford.‡
Financial data (yr. ended 10/31/01): Grants paid, $34,792; assets, $867,519 (M); expenditures, $40,462; qualifying distributions, $34,792.
Limitations: Applications not accepted.
Application information: Contributes only to pre-selected organizations.
Trustee: First Union National Bank.
EIN: 656290694

41402
Canterbury Foundation, Inc.
519 Senlac Rd.
Chapel Hill, NC 27514

Established in 1998 in NC.
Donor(s): Charles W. Browning.
Financial data (yr. ended 12/31/01): Grants paid, $34,535; assets, $206,652 (M); expenditures, $37,181; qualifying distributions, $34,535.
Limitations: Applications not accepted.
Application information: Contributes only to pre-selected organizations.
Officer: Charles W. Browning, Pres.
EIN: 562039923

41403
Kyser Foundation
504 E. Franklin St.
Chapel Hill, NC 27514-3708

Financial data (yr. ended 12/31/01): Grants paid, $34,500; assets, $891,326 (M); expenditures, $39,148; qualifying distributions, $34,500.
Limitations: Applications not accepted.
Application information: Contributes only to pre-selected organizations.
Trustee: Georgia K. Kyser.
EIN: 566061070

41404
Doris Floyd Moore Scholarship Fund
(Formerly J. W. and Doris Floyd Moore Scholarships)
c/o Wachovia Bank, N.A.
P.O. Box 3099
Winston-Salem, NC 27150-1022

Financial data (yr. ended 05/31/01): Grants paid, $34,500; assets, $535,938 (M); expenditures, $41,348; qualifying distributions, $36,017.
Limitations: Applications not accepted. Giving limited to residents of Dillon County, SC.
Trustee: Wachovia Bank, N.A.
EIN: 576094970
Codes: GTI

41405
The Shiloh Fund
1216 W. Haven Blvd.
Rocky Mount, NC 27803

Established in 1999 in NC.
Donor(s): Thomas Looney, Peggy Looney.
Financial data (yr. ended 12/31/00): Grants paid, $34,500; assets, $586,048 (M); gifts received, $5,500; expenditures, $34,589; qualifying distributions, $34,500.
Trustees: Stuart L. Allen, Ashlin L. Graveley, Peggy Looney, Thomas Looney, Elizabeth L. McGuire.
EIN: 566532288

41406
David & Elizabeth Nimocks Foundation
P.O. Box 87128
Fayetteville, NC 28304

Established in 1995 in NC.
Donor(s): David R. Nimocks, Jr., Elizabeth B. Nimocks.
Financial data (yr. ended 12/31/01): Grants paid, $34,488; assets, $644,821 (M); expenditures, $41,529; qualifying distributions, $34,488.
Limitations: Applications not accepted. Giving primarily in Fayetteville, NC.
Application information: Contributes only to pre-selected organizations.
Officers: David R. Nimocks, Jr., Pres.; Elizabeth B. Nimocks, Secy.
EIN: 582203214

41407
Ganatra Family Foundation
6523 Ashdale Pl.
Charlotte, NC 28215

Established in 2000 in NC.
Donor(s): Tansukh V. Ganatra, Sarlaben T. Ganatra.
Financial data (yr. ended 12/31/01): Grants paid, $34,233; assets, $632,662 (M); gifts received, $611,688; expenditures, $36,567; qualifying distributions, $34,233.
Limitations: Applications not accepted. Giving primarily in Charlotte, NC.
Application information: Contributes only to pre-selected organizations.

Officers: Tansukh V. Ganatra, Pres.; Sarlaben T. Ganatra, V.P.
Director: Rajesh T. Ganatra.
EIN: 562195283

41408
Thompson Family Foundation
555 Hempstead Pl.
Charlotte, NC 28207
Contact: James W. Thompson, Chair.

Established in 1999 in NC.
Donor(s): James W. Thompson.
Financial data (yr. ended 12/31/01): Grants paid, $34,200; assets, $867,851 (M); expenditures, $34,200; qualifying distributions, $34,200.
Officer and Directors:* James W. Thompson,* Chair. and Pres.; Ann T. Brock, James W. Thompson, Jr., Lucy G. Thompson, Meredith C. Thompson.
EIN: 562170932

41409
John M. Cook, Jr. Charitable Trust
c/o First Union National Bank
401 S. Tryon St., 4th Fl.
Charlotte, NC 28288-1159

Established in 2000 in NC.
Financial data (yr. ended 12/31/01): Grants paid, $34,102; assets, $1,210,153 (M); expenditures, $41,652; qualifying distributions, $33,578.
Limitations: Applications not accepted. Giving primarily in Concord, NC.
Application information: Contributes only to pre-selected organizations.
Trustee: First Union National Bank.
EIN: 566092900

41410
Jared C. Fox Family Foundation
P.O. Box 2143
Wilmington, NC 28402-2143

Financial data (yr. ended 12/31/01): Grants paid, $34,000; assets, $799,107 (M); expenditures, $36,510; qualifying distributions, $34,000.
Limitations: Applications not accepted. Giving primarily in NC.
Application information: Contributes only to pre-selected organizations.
Trustees: Charlotte Fox, James C. Fox.
EIN: 566075573

41411
Jenkins-Tapp Foundation, Inc.
P.O. Box 667
Kinston, NC 28502-0667
Contact: Elizabeth C. Jenkins, Pres.

Incorporated in 1961 in NC.
Financial data (yr. ended 12/31/01): Grants paid, $34,000; assets, $768,441 (M); expenditures, $64,346; qualifying distributions, $34,000.
Limitations: Giving primarily in NC.
Application information: Application form not required.
Officers: Elizabeth C. Jenkins, Pres., Treas., and Mgr.; Lee B. Jenkins, V.P. and Secy.; Coleman T. Hardy, V.P.; John T. Jenkins, Jr., V.P.
EIN: 560845817

41412
Battle Foundation, Inc.
c/o Centura Bank, Tax Dept.
P.O. Box 1220
Rocky Mount, NC 27802-1220
Application address: P.O. Box 1240, Rocky Mount, NC 27802-1240, tel.: (252) 442-1145
Contact: Thomas R. Battle, Pres.

Financial data (yr. ended 11/30/01): Grants paid, $33,780; assets, $668,311 (M); expenditures, $40,369; qualifying distributions, $33,780.
Limitations: Giving primarily in eastern and central NC.
Officer: Thomas R. Battle, Pres.
Trustee: Centura Bank.
EIN: 566060618

41413
The Toccoa W. Switzer Foundation, Inc.
3215 Champaign St.
Charlotte, NC 28210

Established in 2000 in NC.
Donor(s): Toccoa W. Switzer.
Financial data (yr. ended 12/31/01): Grants paid, $33,526; assets, $322,961 (M); gifts received, $47,446; expenditures, $40,155; qualifying distributions, $33,526.
Directors: James L. Switzer, Jr., Paul Kent Switzer III, Toccoa Bailey Switzer.
EIN: 562198047

41414
Eastern Scientific & Education Foundation
c/o First Union National Bank
401 S. Tryon St., 4th Fl.
Charlotte, NC 28288-1159

Established in 1983 in PA.
Financial data (yr. ended 12/31/01): Grants paid, $33,250; assets, $699,018 (M); expenditures, $39,989; qualifying distributions, $34,000.
Limitations: Applications not accepted. Giving primarily in PA.
Trustee: First Union National Bank.
EIN: 236738070
Codes: GTI

41415
Bob & Kay Timberlake Foundation
c/o Bob Timberlake
1660 E. Center St.
Lexington, NC 27292

Established in 1994 in NC.
Financial data (yr. ended 12/31/01): Grants paid, $33,154; assets, $27,520 (M); expenditures, $34,581; qualifying distributions, $33,154.
Limitations: Applications not accepted. Giving primarily in NC.
Application information: Contributes only to pre-selected organizations.
Officers: Kay M. Timberlake, Co-Chair.; Roberts E. Timberlake, Co-Chair.; Kelly T. Ellis, Secy.; R.E. Timberlake, Jr., Treas.
EIN: 561874500

41416
Florence H. Maxwell Foundation
c/o Bank of America
Bank of America Plz., NC1-002-11-18
Charlotte, NC 28255
Application address: c/o Kim Sexton, 600 Peach Tree St. N.E., 11th Fl., Atlanta, GA 30308

Established in 1988 in GA.
Financial data (yr. ended 04/30/02): Grants paid, $33,000; assets, $1,172,341 (M); expenditures, $45,679; qualifying distributions, $33,000.
Limitations: Giving primarily in GA.

Trustee: Bank of America.
EIN: 586220417

41417
Ronald J. Midura Foundation, Inc.
P.O. Box 25088
Winston-Salem, NC 27114 (336) 760-8100
Contact: Robert L. Watson, Jr., Secy.-Treas.

Established in 1994 in NC.
Donor(s): Jan P. Midura, Ronald J. Midura.
Financial data (yr. ended 12/31/01): Grants paid, $33,000; assets, $642,799 (M); expenditures, $36,614; qualifying distributions, $33,000.
Limitations: Giving primarily in NC.
Officers: Ronald J. Midura, Pres.; Jan P. Midura, V.P; Robert L. Watson, Jr., Secy.-Treas.
Directors: April M. Holder, Jacqueline M. Midura, R. Andrew Midura.
EIN: 561901127

41418
Joe L. & Hester M. Sims Family Foundation, Inc.
1015 W. Innes St.
Salisbury, NC 28144-4038

Established in 1995 in NC.
Donor(s): Joe L. Sims, Hester M. Sims.
Financial data (yr. ended 06/30/02): Grants paid, $32,800; assets, $590,611 (M); gifts received, $100; expenditures, $34,860; qualifying distributions, $32,800.
Limitations: Giving primarily in Salisbury, NC.
Officers: Joe I. Sims, Pres.; Hester M. Sims, V.P.
EIN: 561941864

41419
The Montag Family Foundation
3900 Seminole Ct.
Charlotte, NC 28210-4902

Financial data (yr. ended 12/31/01): Grants paid, $32,789; assets, $474,358 (M); expenditures, $36,355; qualifying distributions, $32,643.
Limitations: Applications not accepted.
Application information: Contributes only to pre-selected organizations.
Directors: Mark R. Bernstein, Emily Montag, Ethel Montag, James Montag.
EIN: 561546268

41420
Ruth Z. Fleishman Foundation, Inc.
P.O. Box 90522
Durham, NC 27708-0522

Donor(s): Joel L. Fleishman.
Financial data (yr. ended 12/31/01): Grants paid, $32,637; assets, $621,057 (M); gifts received, $41,500; expenditures, $39,987; qualifying distributions, $36,470.
Limitations: Applications not accepted. Giving primarily in NC.
Application information: Contributes only to pre-selected organizations.
Director: Joel L. Fleishman.
EIN: 560897935

41421
Jack & Viola Bess Charitable Foundation
c/o First Union National Bank
401 S. Tryon St., NC1159
Charlotte, NC 28288-1159

Established in 2000 in VA.
Financial data (yr. ended 03/31/01): Grants paid, $32,500; assets, $646,697 (M); gifts received, $57,688; expenditures, $40,057; qualifying distributions, $32,500.
Limitations: Applications not accepted.
Application information: Contributes only to pre-selected organizations.

41421—NORTH CAROLINA

Trustee: First Union National Bank.
EIN: 316639312

41422
Kemp Foundation, Inc.
102 N. Andrews Ave.
Goldsboro, NC 27530-5218
Contact: William P. Kemp, Jr., Pres.

Donor(s): William P. Kemp, Jr.
Financial data (yr. ended 12/31/01): Grants paid, $32,500; assets, $518,394 (M); expenditures, $35,733; qualifying distributions, $32,498.
Limitations: Giving primarily in NC.
Officer: William P. Kemp, Jr., Pres.
Director: Betty S. Kemp.
EIN: 560630681

41423
Berkeley and George Harris Charitable Foundation
(Formerly The James M. Hornaday Charitable Foundation I)
c/o U.S. Trust
P.O. Box 26262
Greensboro, NC 27420

Established in 1986 in NC.
Financial data (yr. ended 09/30/01): Grants paid, $32,400; assets, $638,529 (M); expenditures, $40,475; qualifying distributions, $33,998.
Limitations: Applications not accepted. Giving primarily in NC.
Application information: Contributes only to pre-selected organizations.
Trustees: Berkeley H. Harris, George Harris, U.S. Trust.
EIN: 566297219

41424
The Grace Foundation
3620 Cape Center Dr.
Fayetteville, NC 28304
Application address: P.O. Box 52328, Durham, NC 27717
Contact: Charlene Hamlett, Pres.

Established in 1996 in NC.
Donor(s): Charlene Hamlett.
Financial data (yr. ended 12/31/01): Grants paid, $32,280; assets, $320,711 (M); gifts received, $9,700; expenditures, $32,427; qualifying distributions, $32,280.
Limitations: Giving limited to Durham, NC.
Officer: Charlene Hamlett, Pres.
EIN: 562006078

41425
S. McKay Smith Trust
P.O. Box 7
St. Pauls, NC 28384
Contact: Paul Truett Canady, Tr.

Financial data (yr. ended 12/31/01): Grants paid, $32,209; assets, $219,575 (M); expenditures, $33,514; qualifying distributions, $32,209.
Limitations: Giving on a national basis, with some emphasis on the South.
Trustees: Hazel Canady, Paul Truett Canady, Linda F. West.
EIN: 566061553

41426
Salisbury-Rowan Merchants Association Foundation
P.O. Box 1907
Salisbury, NC 28145-1907
Tel.: (704) 636-3629, ext. 226; FAX: (704) 633-4970; E-mail: SRMA@salisburysource.com
Contact: Richard Perkins, Exec. Dir.

Established in 1998 in NC.
Financial data (yr. ended 12/31/01): Grants paid, $32,162; assets, $660,024 (M); expenditures, $41,854; qualifying distributions, $32,038.
Limitations: Giving primarily in Salisbury and Rowan County, NC.
Publications: Application guidelines.
Application information: Application form required.
Officers: C. A. Hoffman, Pres.; Jerry L. Sides, V.P.; Bonzie H. Everson, Secy.; Robert S. Setzer, Treas.; Richard Perkins, Exec. Dir.
Directors: Summie Carter, Charles Deadwyler, Jr., Lillian Morgan.
EIN: 562024652

41427
Sara N. & E. J. Evans Foundation, Inc.
P.O. Box 2252
Durham, NC 27702-2252

Established in 1996 in NC.
Donor(s): E.J. Evans.
Financial data (yr. ended 06/30/01): Grants paid, $32,000; assets, $396,100 (M); expenditures, $35,169; qualifying distributions, $33,979.
Limitations: Applications not accepted. Giving primarily in Atlanta, GA.
Application information: Contributes only to pre-selected organizations.
Directors: Eli N. Evans, Robert M. Evans.
EIN: 561668528

41428
Eliz S. Taylor Trust
c/o First Union National Bank
401 S. Tryon St., NC 1159
Charlotte, NC 28288-1159

Financial data (yr. ended 05/31/02): Grants paid, $31,863; assets, $655,222 (M); expenditures, $42,434; qualifying distributions, $31,863.
Limitations: Applications not accepted. Giving primarily in AZ and PA.
Application information: Contributes only to pre-selected organizations.
Trustee: First Union National Bank.
EIN: 236628470

41429
Garvie O. and Kathleen Chambers Family Foundation
P.O. Box 16166
Greensboro, NC 27416-0166

Established in 1999 in NC.
Donor(s): Garvie O. Chambers, Kathleen Chambers.
Financial data (yr. ended 12/31/01): Grants paid, $31,800; assets, $94,302 (M); gifts received, $50,000; expenditures, $33,694; qualifying distributions, $31,800.
Limitations: Applications not accepted.
Application information: Contributes only to pre-selected organizations.
Directors: Garvie O. Chambers, Kathleen Chambers.
EIN: 566507267

41430
Henry & Sidney T. Davenport Educational Family Foundation
(Formerly Henry & Sidney T. Davenport Educational Fund)
c/o Centura Bank
P.O. Box 1220
Rocky Mount, NC 27803 (252) 454-4017
Contact: Sharon M. Stephens, Trust Off., Centura Bank

Established in 1960 in NC.
Donor(s): Henry N. Davenport,‡ Sidney T. Davenport.
Financial data (yr. ended 06/30/00): Grants paid, $31,800; assets, $785,164 (M); expenditures, $38,377; qualifying distributions, $31,255; giving activities include $31,800 for loans to individuals.
Limitations: Giving limited to residents of Nash and Edgecombe Counties, NC.
Application information: Application form required.
Trustee: Centura Bank.
EIN: 237422939
Codes: GTI

41431
Martha W. Davis Trust
c/o B.B. & T.
P.O. Box 2887
Wilson, NC 27894-2887

Established in 2001 in NC.
Donor(s): Martha Woodard Davis.‡
Financial data (yr. ended 12/31/01): Grants paid, $31,766; assets, $583,185 (M); gifts received, $568,133; expenditures, $36,713; qualifying distributions, $31,766.
Limitations: Applications not accepted.
Application information: Contributes only to pre-selected organizations.
Trustee: B.B. & T.
EIN: 566574243

41432
Jane Vonderleith Testamentary Charitable Trust
c/o First Union National Bank
401 S. Tryon St., NC1159
Charlotte, NC 28288-1159

Financial data (yr. ended 12/31/01): Grants paid, $31,748; assets, $1,178,335 (M); expenditures, $40,041; qualifying distributions, $31,748.
Limitations: Applications not accepted. Giving limited to Mount Pulaski, IL.
Application information: Contributes only to pre-selected organizations.
Trustees: Howard G. Wachenfeld, First Union National Bank.
EIN: 226130513

41433
Barbara C. Breazeale Trust
c/o First Union National Bank
401 S. Tryon St., NC1159
Charlotte, NC 28288

Financial data (yr. ended 05/31/02): Grants paid, $31,712; assets, $601,453 (M); expenditures, $36,144; qualifying distributions, $31,712.
Limitations: Applications not accepted. Giving primarily in Murray, KY.
Application information: Contributes only to pre-selected organizations.
Trustee: First Union National Bank.
EIN: 596858257

41434
Robert Monroe Carlisle Trust
c/o First Citizens Bank, Trust Dept.
P.O. Box 29522
Raleigh, NC 27626
Application address: c/o William C. Harper, Comm. Chair., First Citizens Bank, Hickory, NC, 28601, tel.: (704) 326-1100

Established in 1995 in NC.
Financial data (yr. ended 12/31/01): Grants paid, $31,070; assets, $577,212 (M); expenditures, $37,678; qualifying distributions, $31,070.
Limitations: Giving limited to Catawba County, NC.
Trustee: First Citizens Bank.

EIN: 566455126

41435
Edward L. Ballard Memorial Scholarship Fund
c/o First Union National Bank
401 S. Tryon St., NC1159
Charlotte, NC 28288-1159
Application address: c/o Guidance Dept., Ridgefield High School, N. Salem Rd., Ridgefield, CT 06877

Financial data (yr. ended 09/30/01): Grants paid, $31,000; assets, $523,918 (M); expenditures, $39,250; qualifying distributions, $31,248.
Limitations: Giving limited to residents of Ridgefield, CT.
Application information: Application form available at Ridgefield High School guidance department or family aid room. Application form required.
Trustee: First Union National Bank.
EIN: 066042949
Codes: GTI

41436
McHenry Foundation, Inc.
2313 Vernon Dr.
Charlotte, NC 28211-1829

Donor(s): Wade Dean McHenry.‡
Financial data (yr. ended 11/30/01): Grants paid, $31,000; assets, $710,733 (M); gifts received, $4,900; expenditures, $31,467; qualifying distributions, $31,000.
Limitations: Applications not accepted. Giving primarily in Charlotte, NC.
Application information: Contributes only to pre-selected organizations.
Officers and Directors:* Richard I. McHenry,* Pres. and Treas.; Marilyn Joyce McHenry,* V.P. and Secy.
EIN: 560790399

41437
Oscar B. Teague and Mossie S. Teague Foundation, Inc.
P.O. Box 2801
Greensboro, NC 27402-2801

Financial data (yr. ended 12/31/01): Grants paid, $30,900; assets, $581,436 (M); expenditures, $36,750; qualifying distributions, $30,900.
Limitations: Applications not accepted. Giving primarily in NC.
Application information: Contributes only to pre-selected organizations.
Officers: John E. Teague, Pres.; Tommy L. Teague, V.P.; Brantley Teague, Secy.
EIN: 581758771

41438
Carson Family Foundation
c/o U.S. Trust
P.O. Box 26262
Greensboro, NC 27420

Established in 1997.
Financial data (yr. ended 12/31/01): Grants paid, $30,530; assets, $223,787 (M); expenditures, $33,382; qualifying distributions, $30,530.
Limitations: Applications not accepted. Giving primarily in NC.
Application information: Contributes only to pre-selected organizations.
Officers: Patricia L. Carson, Pres.; Stephen T. Carson, Secy.-Treas.
EIN: 561953678

41439
Esse Quam Videre Foundation, Inc.
c/o Howard G. Clark III
4600 Troys Mountain Ave.
Durham, NC 27705 (919) 489-4900

Established in 1998 in NC.
Donor(s): Howard Clark, Julia Evans Clark.
Financial data (yr. ended 12/31/01): Grants paid, $30,500; assets, $775,079 (M); expenditures, $31,883; qualifying distributions, $30,500.
Limitations: Applications not accepted. Giving primarily in NC.
Application information: Contributes only to pre-selected organizations.
Officers: Howard G. Clark III, Chair. and Pres.; Julia Evans Clark, Secy.-Treas.
Directors: Susan Clark Bissett, Elaine Clark Blake, Howard G. Clark IV.
EIN: 562089202

41440
Meg Foundation, Inc.
920 D-5 Paverstone Dr.
Raleigh, NC 27615

Established in 1999 in NC.
Donor(s): M. Elizabeth Gant.
Financial data (yr. ended 12/31/01): Grants paid, $30,500; assets, $542,177 (M); expenditures, $49,521; qualifying distributions, $30,500.
Limitations: Applications not accepted. Giving primarily in NC.
Application information: Contributes only to pre-selected organizations.
Officers: M. Elizabeth Gant, Pres. and Treas.; Esther Hall, Secy.
EIN: 562130580

41441
Chief John Alfred Tahquette Education Trust
(also known as Amy Critzer Trust)
c/o First Citizens Bank, Trust Dept.
P.O. Box 29522
Raleigh, NC 27626
Application address: c/o First Citizens Bank, Hickory, NC 28601, tel.: (704) 326-1100
Contact: William C. Harper, Chair.

Established in 1999.
Financial data (yr. ended 12/31/01): Grants paid, $30,500; assets, $1,074,991 (M); expenditures, $38,274; qualifying distributions, $30,500.
Limitations: Giving primarily in NC.
Trustee: First Citizens Bank.
EIN: 566529542

41442
Rudolph Williams Charitable Trust
c/o First Union National Bank
401 S. Tryon St., 4th Fl.
Charlotte, NC 28288-1159
Application address: c/o First Union National Bank, 765 Broad St., Newark, NJ 07102
Contact: Andrew Davis

Established in 1988 in NJ.
Donor(s): Rudolph Williams.‡
Financial data (yr. ended 12/31/01): Grants paid, $30,500; assets, $424,424 (M); expenditures, $33,815; qualifying distributions, $31,138.
Application information: Application form not required.
Trustee: First Union National Bank.
EIN: 226422164

41443
Raleigh Kiwanis Foundation, Inc.
2923 Hostetler St.
Raleigh, NC 27609
Application address: 1614 Brookrun Dr., Raleigh, NC 27614
Contact: A. Kent Pittman, V.P.

Donor(s): Kiwanis Club of Raleigh, N.C., Inc.
Financial data (yr. ended 12/31/00): Grants paid, $30,441; assets, $403,320 (M); gifts received, $7,435; expenditures, $41,664; qualifying distributions, $30,441.
Limitations: Giving limited to Raleigh, NC.
Officers: H. Hugh Stevens, Jr., Pres.; A. Kent Pittman, V.P.; Sam B. Carruthers, Secy.; Nancy B. Essex, Treas.
Directors: Alice D. Garland, Clarence A. Goins.
EIN: 566045235

41444
The Haworth Foundation, Inc.
P.O. Box 15369
Charlotte, NC 28211-0601 (704) 332-7666
Contact: Howard H. Haworth, Pres.

Established in 1984 in NC.
Donor(s): Howard H. Haworth.
Financial data (yr. ended 12/31/01): Grants paid, $30,325; assets, $41,286 (M); gifts received, $65,555; expenditures, $30,460; qualifying distributions, $30,325.
Limitations: Giving primarily in NC.
Officers: Howard H. Haworth, Pres.; Patricia G. Haworth, V.P. and Secy.
Directors: Ellen Haworth Boardman, Lucy H. Shorthouse.
EIN: 581574743

41445
Lutz Foundation, Inc.
P.O. Box 277
Shelby, NC 28151-0277
Application address: 727 E. Main St., Forest City, NC 28043, tel.: (828) 245-0402
Contact: Jack L. Lutz, Pres.

Established in 1989.
Financial data (yr. ended 12/31/01): Grants paid, $30,280; assets, $394,081 (M); gifts received, $6,481; expenditures, $32,498; qualifying distributions, $32,498.
Application information: Application form not required.
Officers and Trustees:* Jack L. Lutz,* Pres.; Betty L. Bowling,* V.P.; Forrest D. Bridges, Secy.; Robert H. Lutz,* Treas.; Richard F. Bowling II, Sherri L. Curtis, Carolyn M. Lutz, John Ray Lutz II, William D. Lutz, Betsy L. McPherson, Adelyn L. Parker, William R. Parker.
EIN: 561073160

41446
Atwood Family Foundation, Inc.
837 Harvard Pl.
Charlotte, NC 28207

Established in 1994 in NC.
Donor(s): Robert T. Atwood, Pauletta Y. Atwood, Molly Atwood Taylor.
Financial data (yr. ended 12/31/01): Grants paid, $30,145; assets, $56,559 (M); expenditures, $31,485; qualifying distributions, $30,145.
Limitations: Applications not accepted.
Directors: Pauletta Y. Atwood, Robert T. Atwood, Molly Atwood Taylor.
EIN: 561898696

41447
William Cooper Trust
c/o First Union National Bank
401 S. Tryon St., NC1159
Charlotte, NC 28288

Financial data (yr. ended 12/31/00): Grants paid, $30,062; assets, $1,504,909 (M); expenditures, $46,736; qualifying distributions, $30,812.
Limitations: Applications not accepted.
Trustee: First Union National Bank.
EIN: 386029952

41448
The Asheville Jaycee Foundation, Inc.
c/o Robert A. Freeman III
P.O. Box 7625
Asheville, NC 28802

Established in 1997 in NC.
Financial data (yr. ended 12/31/01): Grants paid, $30,000; assets, $560,129 (M); expenditures, $44,802; qualifying distributions, $30,000.
Limitations: Giving primarily in NC.
Officers: Larry Wright, Pres.; Jim Reed, Secy.
Directors: Steve Harrington, David Levitch.
EIN: 561903541

41449
Mary R. Gilbert Memorial Fund
c/o First Union National Bank
401 S. Tryon St., 4th Fl.
Charlotte, NC 28288-1159

Established in 1997 in PA.
Financial data (yr. ended 12/31/01): Grants paid, $30,000; assets, $940,410 (M); expenditures, $37,800; qualifying distributions, $30,000.
Limitations: Applications not accepted. Giving limited to PA.
Application information: Contributes only to pre-selected organizations.
Trustee: First Union National Bank.
EIN: 237879665

41450
The Laughery Foundation
120 N. Franklin St., Ste. E
Rocky Mount, NC 27804-5448
Application address: 1730 Hunter Hill Rd., Rocky Mount, NC 27804, tel.: (252) 443-6778
Contact: Jack A. Laughery, Pres.

Established in 1988 in NC.
Donor(s): Jack A. Laughery.
Financial data (yr. ended 04/30/01): Grants paid, $30,000; assets, $258,860 (M); expenditures, $31,283; qualifying distributions, $30,406.
Limitations: Giving primarily in NC, with emphasis on Rocky Mount.
Application information: Application form not required.
Officers: Jack A. Laughery, Pres.; Helen H. Laughery, V.P.; Kelly Laughery Winstead, Secy.
EIN: 581839447

41451
Ken A. & Gail B. Miller Family Foundation
c/o U.S. Trust
P.O. Box 26262
Greensboro, NC 27420

Established in 1998 in NC.
Donor(s): Kenneth D. Miller.
Financial data (yr. ended 12/31/01): Grants paid, $30,000; assets, $968,348 (M); gifts received, $227,978; expenditures, $33,486; qualifying distributions, $30,000.
Limitations: Applications not accepted.
Application information: Contributes only to pre-selected organizations.
Officers: Kenneth D. Miller, Pres.; Gail B. Miller, V.P.
EIN: 562113226

41452
J. Smith & Helen W. Young Family Foundation
521 E. Center St., Rm. B
Lexington, NC 27292-4111

Established in 1996 in NC.
Financial data (yr. ended 12/31/01): Grants paid, $30,000; assets, $272,673 (M); expenditures, $30,869; qualifying distributions, $30,000.
Limitations: Applications not accepted. Giving primarily in Lexington, NC.
Application information: Contributes only to pre-selected organizations.
Officers: J. Smith Young, Jr., Pres.; Charles Jeffery Young, V.P.; Sydney Y. Beck, Secy.
EIN: 561977282

41453
Helen R. Van Rensselaer Charitable Foundation
c/o First Union National Bank
401 S. Tryon St., NC 1159
Charlotte, NC 28288-1159

Established in 1984 in VA.
Financial data (yr. ended 12/31/01): Grants paid, $29,713; assets, $557,711 (M); expenditures, $33,289; qualifying distributions, $30,261.
Limitations: Giving primarily in Roanoke, VA.
Trustee: First Union National Bank.
EIN: 521327967

41454
Mary Y. Berman Charitable Trust
Exchange W.
1414 Raleigh Rd., Ste. 150
Chapel Hill, NC 27517
Application address: c/o Bethel Synagogue, 1004 Watts St., Durham, NC 27701, tel.: (919) 683-1238
Contact: Emmanuel J. Evans

Established in 1987 in NC.
Financial data (yr. ended 06/30/01): Grants paid, $29,661; assets, $575,352 (M); expenditures, $35,866; qualifying distributions, $29,047.
Limitations: Giving primarily in NC.
Application information: Application form not required.
Advisory Committee: Emmanuel J. Evans, Bernard G. Greenberg, Earl Seigel.
Trustee: Central Carolina Bank & Trust Co.
EIN: 566095536

41455
The Page and George Bradham Family Foundation
2736 Cherry Ln.
Denver, NC 28037

Established in 1999 in NC.
Donor(s): Page Bradham.
Financial data (yr. ended 12/31/01): Grants paid, $29,500; assets, $935,073 (M); expenditures, $41,883; qualifying distributions, $29,500.
Officers: Page B. Kizer, Chair.; R. Edward Kizer, Jr., Secy.
EIN: 562155753

41456
Bloch-Selinger Educational Trust Fund
c/o First Union National Bank
401 S. Tryon St., 4th Fl.
Charlotte, NC 28288-1159
Application address: c/o Superintendent of Danville Schools, P.O. Box 139, Danville, PA 17821

Financial data (yr. ended 12/31/01): Grants paid, $29,351; assets, $460,888 (M); expenditures, $34,251; qualifying distributions, $29,259.
Limitations: Giving limited to Danville, PA.
Application information: Application form required.
Trustee: First Union National Bank.
EIN: 236558579
Codes: GTI

41457
The Dudley Foundation
c/o Cowles Liipfert
1080 Old Greensboro Rd.
Kernersville, NC 27284-8488 (336) 993-8800
Contact: Eunice M. Dudley, Secy.-Treas.

Established in 1997 in NC.
Donor(s): Dudley Products, Inc.
Financial data (yr. ended 12/31/00): Grants paid, $29,181; assets, $0 (M); gifts received, $30,298; expenditures, $30,046; qualifying distributions, $29,230.
Officers and Directors:* Joe L. Dudley, Sr.,* Pres.; Terrie L. Clawson,* V.P.; Joe L. Dudley, Jr.,* V.P.; Laska H. Jones,* V.P.; Ursula D. Oglesby,* V.P.; Eunice M. Dudley,* Secy.-Treas.; Cowles Liipfert.
EIN: 562026106
Codes: GTI

41458
Wesley Smith Charitable Trust
c/o Bank of America Plaza
401 S. Tryon St., NC1-002-11-18
Charlotte, NC 28255-0001

Established in 1998 in GA.
Donor(s): Wesley Smith.
Financial data (yr. ended 03/31/02): Grants paid, $29,138; assets, $599,120 (M); expenditures, $35,481; qualifying distributions, $29,138.
Limitations: Applications not accepted.
Application information: Contributes only to pre-selected organizations.
Trustee: Bank of America.
EIN: 586284321

41459
Charles Cecil McKinney Foundation
1006 Harvey St.
Raleigh, NC 27608 (919) 834-1317

Established in 1997 in NC.
Donor(s): Charles C. McKinney.
Financial data (yr. ended 12/31/99): Grants paid, $29,046; assets, $968,149 (M); expenditures, $38,371; qualifying distributions, $29,003.
Application information: Application form not required.
Trustees: Charles Cecil McKinney, Marc Jason McKinney, Robin Ashley McKinney, Suzanne Reeves McKinney, Emry McKinney Olson.
EIN: 562026410

41460
Sumas Foundation
c/o First Union National Bank, N.A.
401 S. Tryon St., 4th Fl.
Charlotte, NC 28288-1159

Financial data (yr. ended 08/31/01): Grants paid, $29,030; assets, $293,055 (M); expenditures, $31,328; qualifying distributions, $28,822.
Limitations: Applications not accepted. Giving limited to NJ.
Application information: Contributes only to pre-selected organizations.
Trustee: First Union National Bank.
EIN: 226107899

41461
Edgar A. Brown Foundation
c/o Bank of America
101 S. Tryon St.
Charlotte, NC 28255

Financial data (yr. ended 12/31/01): Grants paid, $29,000; assets, $869,726 (M); expenditures, $38,976; qualifying distributions, $31,785.
Limitations: Applications not accepted. Giving limited to Clemson, SC.
Application information: Contributes only to a pre-selected organization.
Officer: Robert C. Edwards, Chair.
Trustee: Bank of America.
EIN: 237045556
Codes: GTI

41462
Holdeen Fund 46-10
c/o First Union National Bank
401 S. Tryon, NC1159
Charlotte, NC 28288-1159

Financial data (yr. ended 12/31/01): Grants paid, $28,927; assets, $485,988 (M); expenditures, $31,042; qualifying distributions, $28,860.
Limitations: Applications not accepted. Giving limited to Boston, MA.
Application information: Contributes only to a pre-selected organization.
Trustee: First Union National Bank.
EIN: 146018146
Codes: TN

41463
Annie Gray Sprunt Charitable Trust
c/o L.G. Sprunt
P.O. Box 3625
Wilmington, NC 28406-0625

Donor(s): K.M. Sprunt, L.G. Sprunt.
Financial data (yr. ended 12/31/01): Grants paid, $28,900; assets, $533,268 (M); gifts received, $14,096; expenditures, $32,076; qualifying distributions, $28,900.
Limitations: Applications not accepted. Giving primarily in NC.
Application information: Contributes only to pre-selected organizations.
Trustees: K.M. Sprunt, L.G. Sprunt.
EIN: 566068294

41464
The Wesley Family Foundation
c/o Wachovia Bank, N.A.
P.O. Box 3099
Winston-Salem, NC 27150-7131
(336) 732-5763
Contact: Patrick Weiner

Established in 1986 in NC.
Donor(s): Robert N. Wesley, Jr.
Financial data (yr. ended 12/31/01): Grants paid, $28,802; assets, $542,712 (M); expenditures, $37,075; qualifying distributions, $28,802.
Limitations: Giving primarily in NC and OH.
Trustee: Wachovia Bank of North Carolina, N.A.
EIN: 561542728

41465
Gertrude Marion Ruskin Trust
c/o Wachovia Bank, N.A.
P.O. Box 3099
Winston-Salem, NC 27150-1022
Application address: Shane Thomas c/o Wachovia Bank, N.A., 100 N. Main St., Winston-Salem, NC 27150-6732, tel.: (332) 732-5912

Established in 1986 in GA.
Donor(s): Gertrude M. Ruskin.‡
Financial data (yr. ended 01/31/02): Grants paid, $28,800; assets, $472,651 (M); expenditures, $34,537; qualifying distributions, $30,800.
Limitations: Giving limited to Buncombe, Haywood, and Madison counties, and Cherokee Indian Reservation, NC.
Application information: Application form required.
Trustee: Wachovia Bank, N.A.
EIN: 586187363
Codes: GTI

41466
Elizabeth H. Soeder Scholarship Trust
c/o First Union National Bank
401 S. Tryon St.
Charlotte, NC 28288
Application address: First Union National Bank, Broad and Walnut Sts., PA1308, Philadelphia, PA 19109-1199, tel.: (215) 670-4240

Established around 1964.
Donor(s): Elizabeth H. Soeder.‡
Financial data (yr. ended 04/30/01): Grants paid, $28,750; assets, $612,874 (M); expenditures, $33,720; qualifying distributions, $28,551.
Limitations: Giving limited to residents of Cape May County, NJ.
Application information: Application form required.
Trustee: First Union National Bank.
EIN: 226082438
Codes: GTI

41467
The Emily B. Andrews Memorial Foundation
P.O. Box 1908
Boone, NC 28607
Application address: 2124 Blowing Rock Rd., Boone, NC 28607
Contact: Theodore J. Mackorell, Jr., Chair.

Financial data (yr. ended 12/31/99): Grants paid, $28,700; assets, $1,609,080 (M); expenditures, $43,118; qualifying distributions, $42,335.
Limitations: Giving primarily in NC, with some giving in SC.
Application information: Application form not required.
Officers and Trustees:* Theodore J. Mackorell, Jr., Chair.; Vickie B. Owens, Secy.; Stacy A. Conn, Treas.; Kenneth E. Hester, Patricia O. Ragland, Iris Work.
EIN: 561667607

41468
Associated Foundation Incorporated
P.O. Box 707
Belmont, NC 28012

Financial data (yr. ended 09/30/01): Grants paid, $28,500; assets, $647,334 (M); expenditures, $30,953; qualifying distributions, $35,107.
Limitations: Applications not accepted. Giving primarily in NC.
Application information: Contributes only to pre-selected organizations.
Officers: S.P. Stowe III, Pres.; C.J. Deitz, Sr. V.P.; R.P. Hall, Jr., V.P.; J.C. Stowe, V.P.; R. White, Secy.; H.D. Stowe, Treas.
EIN: 566043197

41469
Saperstein Foundation, Inc.
c/o Paul Saperstein
P.O. Box 847
High Point, NC 27261

Established in 1984 in NC.
Donor(s): Paul Saperstein.
Financial data (yr. ended 03/31/02): Grants paid, $28,206; assets, $3,496 (M); gifts received, $9,111; expenditures, $29,360; qualifying distributions, $28,206.
Limitations: Applications not accepted. Giving primarily in NC.
Application information: Contributes only to pre-selected organizations.
Officers: Paul Saperstein, Pres.; Sara Saperstein, Secy.-Treas.
EIN: 581623244

41470
Clyde Nartowicz Private Foundation
c/o First Union National Bank
401 S. Tryon St., NC1159
Charlotte, NC 28288

Established in 2000 in PA.
Donor(s): Clyde Nartowicz.
Financial data (yr. ended 12/31/01): Grants paid, $28,200; assets, $381,148 (M); expenditures, $35,183; qualifying distributions, $28,200.
Limitations: Applications not accepted.
Application information: Contributes only to pre-selected organizations.
Trustee: First Union National Bank.
EIN: 256722573

41471
Victor E. Bell, Jr. & Jane McNair Bell Family Foundation
P.O. Box 17274
Raleigh, NC 27619-7274

Established in 1997 in NC.
Donor(s): Victor E. Bell, Jr., Bell Investments Limited Partnership, Jane McNair Bell.
Financial data (yr. ended 12/31/01): Grants paid, $28,000; assets, $877,014 (M); gifts received, $162,000; expenditures, $28,247; qualifying distributions, $28,000.
Limitations: Applications not accepted. Giving primarily in NC.
Application information: Contributes only to pre-selected organizations.
Officers: Victor E. Bell III, Pres. and Treas.; John McNair Bell, V.P.; Fairley Bell Cook, Secy.
EIN: 562019191

41472
The Futch Foundation, Inc.
481 Blue Heron Rd.
Mars Hill, NC 28754-9412

Established in 1998.

41472—NORTH CAROLINA

Financial data (yr. ended 12/31/01): Grants paid, $27,750; assets, $448,333 (M); expenditures, $36,079; qualifying distributions, $29,844.
Director: Judith Futch.
EIN: 311611588

41473
The Ackermann Foundation
214 Manchester Pl.
Greensboro, NC 27410

Established in 1986 in NC.
Donor(s): Rose Ackermann, Victor Ackermann.
Financial data (yr. ended 12/31/01): Grants paid, $27,660; assets, $55,858 (M); gifts received, $26,054; expenditures, $28,814; qualifying distributions, $27,660.
Limitations: Applications not accepted. Giving primarily in NC.
Application information: Contributes only to pre-selected organizations.
Officers and Directors:* Victor Ackermann,* Pres.; Rose Ackermann,* Secy.-Treas.; Joseph Robinson.
EIN: 581711772

41474
Eugene R. Matthews Memorial Fund
P.O. Box 3737
Gastonia, NC 28054

Established in 1984 in NC.
Financial data (yr. ended 05/31/01): Grants paid, $27,500; assets, $681,003 (M); expenditures, $47,287; qualifying distributions, $27,500.
Limitations: Applications not accepted. Giving primarily in NC.
Application information: Contributes only to pre-selected organizations.
Trustee: B. Frank Matthews II.
EIN: 581580753

41475
Hambrick Memorial Foundation, Inc.
P.O. Box 2089
Hickory, NC 28603-2587

Financial data (yr. ended 09/30/01): Grants paid, $27,200; assets, $505,457 (M); expenditures, $31,390; qualifying distributions, $27,200.
Limitations: Applications not accepted. Giving primarily in Hickory, NC.
Application information: Contributes only to pre-selected organizations.
Directors: Margaret H. Glaze, Mrs. Robert T. Hambrick, Sr., Mrs. Robert T. Hambrick, Jr., Robert T. Hambrick III, Suzanne H. Hambrick, Carl L. Matheson.
EIN: 560670674

41476
Patricia Richard Scholarship Fund
c/o First Union National Bank
401 S. Tryon St., NC 1159
Charlotte, NC 28288-1159

Established in 2000 in NC.
Financial data (yr. ended 12/31/00): Grants paid, $27,171; assets, $86,818 (M); expenditures, $27,527; qualifying distributions, $27,140.
Limitations: Applications not accepted.
Application information: Contributes only to pre-selected organizations.
Trustee: First Union National Bank.
EIN: 256711492

41477
Tuscarora Foundation, Inc.
2442 Sunset Ave.
Rocky Mount, NC 27804
Application address: Becky Butler, P.O. Box 912, Rocky Mount, NC 27802, tel.: (919) 443-7041

Established in 1995 in NC.
Financial data (yr. ended 11/30/01): Grants paid, $27,100; assets, $276,710 (M); expenditures, $27,768; qualifying distributions, $27,100.
Application information: Application form not required.
EIN: 561853955

41478
Georgia S. Downing Trust
c/o Wachovia Bank of North Carolina, N.A.
P.O. Box 3099
Winston-Salem, NC 27150-7131

Financial data (yr. ended 11/30/99): Grants paid, $27,000; assets, $655,576 (M); expenditures, $37,231; qualifying distributions, $27,827.
Limitations: Applications not accepted. Giving primarily in GA.
Application information: Contributes only to pre-selected organizations.
Trustee: Wachovia Bank of North Carolina, N.A.
EIN: 586026643

41479
Diane Swift Modaff Foundation, Inc.
124 Stuyvesant Rd.
Asheville, NC 28803

Established in 2000 in NC.
Donor(s): John Modaff.
Financial data (yr. ended 04/30/02): Grants paid, $27,000; assets, $1,950 (M); gifts received, $1,000; expenditures, $27,000; qualifying distributions, $27,000.
Limitations: Applications not accepted.
Application information: Contributes only to pre-selected organizations.
Officers and Directors:* John Modaff,* Pres. and Treas.; David Modaff,* Secy.; Lynda Modaff.
EIN: 562200480

41480
P. L. & J. Luther, Ada Warren Fund
c/o First Union National Bank
401 S. Tryon St., NC 1159
Charlotte, NC 28288

Financial data (yr. ended 12/31/01): Grants paid, $26,645; assets, $666,867 (M); expenditures, $35,316; qualifying distributions, $26,645.
Limitations: Applications not accepted. Giving primarily in GA.
Application information: Contributes only to pre-selected organizations.
Trustee: First Union National Bank.
EIN: 237755718

41481
Philippians 4:19 Foundation
2109 Prescott Pl.
Raleigh, NC 27615

Established in 1999 in NC.
Donor(s): David Demski, Vaneetha Demski.
Financial data (yr. ended 12/31/00): Grants paid, $26,500; assets, $423,038 (M); gifts received, $320,750; expenditures, $28,240; qualifying distributions, $26,500.
Limitations: Applications not accepted.
Application information: Contributes only to pre-selected organizations.
Directors: David Demski, Vaneetha Demksi.
EIN: 562172891

41482
John V. and Teri L. Sutton Private Foundation
135 Shallotte Blvd.
Ocean Isle Beach, NC 28469
Contact: John Sutton, Pres.

Established in 1999 in NC.
Donor(s): John V. Sutton.
Financial data (yr. ended 12/31/01): Grants paid, $26,488; assets, $209,691 (M); expenditures, $39,986; qualifying distributions, $26,488.
Officers: John Sutton, Pres.; Teri Sutton, Secy.-Treas.
EIN: 311471960

41483
The KGR Foundation, Inc.
P.O. Box 1915
Wake Forest, NC 27588-1915

Established in 1993 in NC.
Donor(s): Kathleen M. Lake.
Financial data (yr. ended 12/31/01): Grants paid, $26,139; assets, $446,881 (M); expenditures, $29,029; qualifying distributions, $26,047.
Limitations: Applications not accepted. Giving primarily in NC.
Application information: Contributes only to pre-selected organizations.
Officers: Kathleen M. Lake, Pres.; James Mackie, V.P.; George C. Mackie, Jr., Secy.-Treas.
EIN: 561852393

41484
The McMillan Foundation
c/o U.S. Trust
P.O. Box 26262
Greensboro, NC 27420

Established in 1996 in NC.
Donor(s): Alex McMillan.
Financial data (yr. ended 12/31/01): Grants paid, $26,040; assets, $24,230 (M); expenditures, $27,149; qualifying distributions, $26,040.
Limitations: Applications not accepted. Giving primarily in NC and VA.
Application information: Contributes only to pre-selected organizations.
Directors: Elizabeth M. Hagood, Charlotte H. McMillan, J. Alex McMillan III, John A. McMillan IV.
EIN: 561951552

41485
The Samuel Ernest Douglass, Jr. Foundation
P.O. Box 10480
Wilmington, NC 28404-0480

Established in 1997 in NC.
Donor(s): Katharine D. Hesmer.
Financial data (yr. ended 12/31/01): Grants paid, $26,000; assets, $444,270 (M); expenditures, $28,142; qualifying distributions, $26,000.
Limitations: Applications not accepted. Giving primarily in NC.
Application information: Contributes only to pre-selected organizations.
Officers and Directors:* Katharine D. Hesmer,* Pres. and Treas.; Ronald G. Hesmer,* V.P. and Secy.
EIN: 562059723

41486
Foscue Foundation
c/o Wachovia Bank of North Carolina, N.A.
P.O. Box 3099
Winston-Salem, NC 27150-0001
Application address: 2671 Del Mar Dr., Gulf Breeze, FL 32961
Contact: Henry A. Foscue, Jr., Chair., Administrative Comm.

Donor(s): Valworth M. Foscue.
Financial data (yr. ended 12/31/01): Grants paid, $26,000; assets, $474,869 (M); expenditures, $32,539; qualifying distributions, $27,881.
Limitations: Giving primarily in NC.
Administrative Committee: Henry A. Foscue, Jr., Chair.; Ellen F. Johnson.
Trustee: Wachovia Bank, N.A.
EIN: 566044947

41487
Nalle Clinic Foundation
c/o Wachovia Bank, N.A.
P.O. Box 3099
Winston-Salem, NC 27150-7153
Application address: 1350 S. Kings Dr., Charlotte, NC 28207, tel.: (704) 372-8750
Contact: Suzanne Savard, Dir.

Financial data (yr. ended 11/30/01): Grants paid, $26,000; assets, $464,788 (M); expenditures, $38,976; qualifying distributions, $26,000.
Limitations: Giving limited to Mecklenburg County, NC.
Application information: Application form not required.
Officers and Directors:* Ted Lucas,* Chair.; Fred Thies, Jr.,* Vice-Chair.; Suzanne Savard.
Trustee: Wachovia Bank, N.A.
EIN: 566039686

41488
Dr. Zack D. Owens and Martha Anderson Owens Trust
108 Riverview Ave.
Camden, NC 27921

Established in 1998 in NC.
Financial data (yr. ended 12/31/01): Grants paid, $26,000; assets, $1,738,635 (M); expenditures, $30,646; qualifying distributions, $26,000.
Limitations: Applications not accepted. Giving primarily in Elizabeth City, NC.
Application information: Contributes only to pre-selected organizations.
Trustees: Kimberly Chalot, Marie B. Jones.
EIN: 566501010

41489
Winchester Foundation Trust
c/o First Union National Bank
401 S. Tryon St., Ste. TH-4
Charlotte, NC 28288-1159

Financial data (yr. ended 09/30/01): Grants paid, $25,700; assets, $194,676 (M); expenditures, $28,381; qualifying distributions, $25,700.
Limitations: Applications not accepted. Giving primarily in PA.
Application information: Contributes only to pre-selected organizations.
Trustee: First Union National Bank.
EIN: 236215528

41490
George A. Moretz Family Foundation, Inc.
1296 9th St. N.W.
Hickory, NC 28601 (828) 324-1386

Established in 1997 in NC.
Donor(s): George Moretz.
Financial data (yr. ended 12/31/01): Grants paid, $25,500; assets, $3,334 (M); gifts received, $24,000; expenditures, $25,895; qualifying distributions, $25,500.
Limitations: Applications not accepted. Giving primarily in NC.
Application information: Contributes only to pre-selected organizations.
Officers: George A. Moretz, Pres. and Treas.; Carolyn S. Morets, V.P.
EIN: 562006438

41491
The Timberlake Foundation, Inc.
339 S. Main St.
Lexington, NC 27292-3256

Established in 1986 in NC.
Donor(s): Casper H. Timberlake, Sr.‡
Financial data (yr. ended 05/31/02): Grants paid, $25,172; assets, $114,114 (M); expenditures, $25,695; qualifying distributions, $25,172.
Limitations: Applications not accepted. Giving primarily in Lexington, NC.
Application information: Contributes only to pre-selected organizations.
Officer and Directors:* Casper H. Timberlake, Jr.,* Pres.; Mary Craig Brown, Camey T. Dillon, Casper H. Timberlake III, Daniel Timberlake, Margaret Timberlake, Tricia T. Welch.
EIN: 561527386

41492
Sallie B. Dubbs Fellowship Fund
c/o First Union National Bank
401 S. Tyron St., NC1159
Charlotte, NC 28288-1159

Established in 1993 in PA.
Financial data (yr. ended 11/30/01): Grants paid, $25,000; assets, $451,177 (M); expenditures, $29,494; qualifying distributions, $25,607.
Limitations: Applications not accepted.
Application information: Contributes only to a pre-selected organization.
Trustee: First Union National Bank.
EIN: 237767079

41493
The Hudson 1992 Charitable Trust
c/o Thomas W. Hudson, Jr.
10730 Governors Dr.
Chapel Hill, NC 27514-8405

Established in 1992 in NY.
Donor(s): Thomas W. Hudson, Jr.
Financial data (yr. ended 04/30/02): Grants paid, $25,000; assets, $19,771 (M); gifts received, $2,000; expenditures, $27,138; qualifying distributions, $25,000.
Limitations: Applications not accepted. Giving primarily in the eastern U.S.
Application information: Contributes only to pre-selected organizations.
Trustee: Thomas W. Hudson, Jr.
EIN: 136994372

41494
Michael J. Kosloski Foundation
c/o First Union National Bank
401 S. Tryon St., NC 1159
Charlotte, NC 28288-1159

Established in 2000 in NC.
Financial data (yr. ended 12/31/00): Grants paid, $25,000; assets, $708,481 (M); gifts received, $750,000; expenditures, $30,514; qualifying distributions, $24,875.
Limitations: Applications not accepted. Giving primarily in NJ.

Application information: Contributes only to pre-selected organizations.
Trustee: First Union National Bank.
EIN: 226900804

41495
Albert & Nan Gray Monk Foundation
c/o U.S. Trust
P.O. Box 26262
Greensboro, NC 27420
Contact: Robert E. Mallernee, Asst. Secy.

Established in 1996 in NC.
Donor(s): Albert Monk, Nan Gray Atkins Monk.
Financial data (yr. ended 12/31/01): Grants paid, $25,000; assets, $596,245 (M); gifts received, $100,505; expenditures, $27,690; qualifying distributions, $25,000.
Limitations: Applications not accepted. Giving primarily in NC and VA.
Application information: Contributes only to pre-selected organizations.
Officers: Albert C. Monk, Pres. and Treas.; Nan Gray Atkins Monk, V.P. and Secy.
EIN: 566473877

41496
Fred L. and Myrtle R. Proctor Charitable Trust
3200 Northline Ave., Ste. 145
Greensboro, NC 27408 (336) 855-1872
Contact: Coak J. May, Tr.

Established in 1988 in NC.
Financial data (yr. ended 12/31/01): Grants paid, $25,000; assets, $428,549 (M); expenditures, $30,606; qualifying distributions, $25,000.
Limitations: Giving limited to SC.
Application information: Application form required.
Trustees: C. Allen Foster, Coak J. May.
EIN: 581706141

41497
The V. C. and Mary A. Puckett Foundation
c/o Wachovia Bank, N.A.
P.O. Box 3099
Winston-Salem, NC 27150-6732

Established in 2001 in GA.
Financial data (yr. ended 12/31/01): Grants paid, $25,000; assets, $475,188 (M); gifts received, $1,000; expenditures, $26,326; qualifying distributions, $25,000.
Limitations: Applications not accepted.
Application information: Contributes only to pre-selected organizations.
Trustee: Wachovia Bank, N.A.
EIN: 566587328

41498
Zimmerman Scholarship Fund
(Formerly Martin H. Zimmerman Scholarship Trust)
c/o First Union National Bank
401 S. Tryon St., NC 1159
Charlotte, NC 28288-1159 (704) 383-5589
Application address: 4259 W. Swamp Rd., Ste. 310, Doylestown, PA 18901

Financial data (yr. ended 06/30/01): Grants paid, $25,000; assets, $521,297 (M); expenditures, $29,436; qualifying distributions, $25,439.
Limitations: Giving limited to residents of the municipalities and townships of Pennridge in southeast PA.
Application information: Application form required.
Officers: Donald B. Smith, Jr., Chair.; Aaron Landis, Jr., Vice-Chair.; William H. Kantner, Secy.
Trustee: First Union National Bank.
EIN: 236688479

41498—NORTH CAROLINA

Codes: GTI

41499
The Helton Family Foundation
1015 Marlowe Rd.
Raleigh, NC 27609

Established in 1998 in NC.
Donor(s): W. Charles Helton.
Financial data (yr. ended 06/30/01): Grants paid, $24,500; assets, $316,120 (M); gifts received, $205,283; expenditures, $25,747; qualifying distributions, $25,119.
Limitations: Applications not accepted. Giving primarily in NC.
Application information: Contributes only to pre-selected organizations.
Officers: W. Charles Helton, Pres.; Thomas Dale Helton, V.P.; Barbara S. Helton, Secy.; Laura Elaine Helton, Treas.
EIN: 562094702

41500
M & J Foundation, Inc.
1504 E. Walnut St.
Goldsboro, NC 27530-5240 (919) 735-1651
Contact: Marcellus J. Best, Pres.

Donor(s): Best Distributing Co.
Financial data (yr. ended 12/31/01): Grants paid, $24,480; assets, $1,249,573 (M); expenditures, $28,766; qualifying distributions, $24,480.
Limitations: Giving primarily in Wayne County, NC.
Application information: Application form not required.
Officer: Marcellus J. Best, Pres.
EIN: 566050267
Codes: CS, CD

41501
Robert B. Lee and Ruth K. Lee Foundation
c/o Wachovia Bank, NA
P.O. Box 3099
Winston-Salem, NC 27150-7131
Application address: c/o C. Gerald Lane, Wachovia Bank, N.A., 1426 Main St. Columbia, SC 29226, tel: (803) 765-3671

Established in 2000 in SC.
Donor(s): Ruth K. Lee.
Financial data (yr. ended 12/31/01): Grants paid, $24,370; assets, $879,755 (M); expenditures, $34,666; qualifying distributions, $24,370.
Application information: Application form not required.
Directors: John J. Fuller, Jr., Ruth K. Lee.
Trustee: Wachovia Bank, N.A.
EIN: 566562309

41502
Marie J. Kister Trust
c/o First Union National Bank
401 S. Tryon St., NC 1159
Charlotte, NC 28288-1159

Established in 1997 in PA.
Financial data (yr. ended 05/31/00): Grants paid, $24,085; assets, $447,661 (M); expenditures, $28,186; qualifying distributions, $23,884.
Limitations: Applications not accepted.
Application information: Contributes only to pre-selected organizations.
Trustee: First Union National Bank.
EIN: 237991810

41503
H.J.B. Foundation, Inc.
740 Greenville Blvd., Ste. 400-168
Greenville, NC 27858

Established in 1986 in NC.
Donor(s): Morris Brody.
Financial data (yr. ended 11/30/01): Grants paid, $24,071; assets, $432,952 (M); expenditures, $29,998; qualifying distributions, $23,982.
Limitations: Applications not accepted. Giving primarily in Pitt County, NC.
Application information: Contributes only to pre-selected organizations.
Officers: Hyman I. Brody, Pres.; Martin Gable, V.P.; Lorraine Brody, Secy.; Morris Brody, Treas.
EIN: 561547030

41504
Patton Foundation, Inc.
3201 S. Blvd.
Charlotte, NC 28209

Donor(s): John C. Patton, Jimmie W. Patton.
Financial data (yr. ended 07/31/01): Grants paid, $24,055; assets, $461,194 (M); gifts received, $1,000; expenditures, $24,190; qualifying distributions, $24,055.
Limitations: Applications not accepted. Giving primarily in the Southeast, with emphasis on NC and SC.
Application information: Contributes only to pre-selected organizations.
Officers: John C. Patton, Pres.; Michael S. Cranford, V.P.; Joe D. Pool, Secy.-Treas.
EIN: 237026742

41505
Edwin Gilbert Trust - Georgetown School Fund
c/o First Union National Bank
401 S. Tryon St., 4th Fl.
Charlotte, NC 28288-1159
Application address: c/o James C. Driscoll III, P.O. Box 248, Bethel, CT 06801, tel.: (203) 744-5000

Financial data (yr. ended 12/31/01): Grants paid, $24,000; assets, $421,417 (L); expenditures, $36,329; qualifying distributions, $28,707.
Limitations: Giving limited to residents of Georgetown, CT.
Application information: Request for application. Application form required.
Trustees: Serena Nazzao, Charles Pfahl, Jr., Carl B. Rosendahl, First Union National Bank.
EIN: 066044834
Codes: GTI

41506
Norris Foundation
c/o Wachovia Bank, N.A.
P.O. Box 3099
Winston-Salem, NC 27150-1022
Application address: c/o Wachovia Bank, N.A., 1401 Main St., Ste. 501, Columbia, SC 29226-9365, tel.: (803) 765-3677

Financial data (yr. ended 12/31/01): Grants paid, $24,000; assets, $669,850 (M); expenditures, $33,043; qualifying distributions, $24,000.
Limitations: Giving limited to SC.
Directors: H. Neel Hipp, Jr., Edgar M. Norris, Sr., Edgar M. Norris, Jr.
Trustee: Wachovia Bank, N.A.
EIN: 576034086

41507
Racing for a Reason
18917 Peninsula Pt. Rd.
Cornelius, NC 28031

Established in 1997 in NC.
Donor(s): Jeffrey M. Gordon.
Financial data (yr. ended 12/31/01): Grants paid, $23,800; assets, $93,110 (M); gifts received, $16,470; expenditures, $25,521; qualifying distributions, $25,320.
Limitations: Applications not accepted.
Application information: Contributes only to pre-selected organizations.
Officer: Raymond D. Evernham, Jr., Pres.
EIN: 562053289

41508
Practical Christian Services, Inc.
3773 Boy Scout Camp Rd.
Kannapolis, NC 28081

Financial data (yr. ended 12/31/01): Grants paid, $23,600; assets, $105,339 (M); gifts received, $110; expenditures, $29,344; qualifying distributions, $23,600.
Limitations: Applications not accepted.
Application information: Contributes only to pre-selected organizations.
Officer: H. Russell, Pres.
EIN: 561808886

41509
The J. W. & D. B. Wyatt Foundation
311 Summertime Rd.
Fayetteville, NC 28303

Established in 2000 in NC.
Donor(s): J.W. Wyatt, D.B. Wyatt.
Financial data (yr. ended 12/31/01): Grants paid, $23,500; assets, $716,224 (M); gifts received, $76,363; expenditures, $23,650; qualifying distributions, $23,500.
Limitations: Applications not accepted. Giving primarily in NC.
Application information: Contributes only to pre-selected organizations.
Officers: J.W. Wyatt, Pres.; D.B. Wyatt, V.P. and Secy.; Melanie Jenkins, V.P. and Treas.; J.W. Wyatt III, V.P.
EIN: 311721276

41510
The Leon Algernon Dunn, Jr. & Pattie McCay Dunn Family Foundation
P.O. Box 7397
Rocky Mount, NC 27804-0397
Application address: c/o Board of Directors, 3801 Sunset Ave. W., Rocky Mount, NC 27804-3106

Established in 1990 in NC.
Donor(s): Guardian Corp.
Financial data (yr. ended 12/31/01): Grants paid, $23,422; assets, $10 (M); gifts received, $23,497; expenditures, $23,527; qualifying distributions, $23,527.
Limitations: Giving primarily in areas of company operations.
Application information: Application form required.
Officers and Directors:* Eugenie Dunn Andracchio,* Pres.; Jane M. Pittman,* V.P.; Wilma J. Morin, Secy.; Debra W. Williams, Treas.; Vincent C. Andracchio II, Pattie McCay Dunn, Leon Algernon Dunn, Jr.
EIN: 561711109
Codes: CS, CD

41511
Michael Harasimik Education Foundation
c/o First Union National Bank
401 S. Tryon St., NC 1159
Charlotte, NC 28288-1159
Application address: c/o Pastor, St. Vladimer Ukranian Catholic Church, 425 Grier Ave., Elizabeth, NJ 07202, tel.: (908) 352-8823

Established in 1988 in NJ.
Financial data (yr. ended 07/31/01): Grants paid, $23,400; assets, $1,678,384 (M); expenditures, $40,228; qualifying distributions, $23,400.

Limitations: Giving limited to residents of NJ.
Trustee: First Union National Bank.
EIN: 226362831

41512
Lawrence C. Fuller, Jr. Memorial Diabetic Foundation
(Formerly Fuller Memorial Diabetic Foundation)
c/o First Union National Bank
401 S. Tryon St., NC1159
Charlotte, NC 28288-1159

Established in 1991 in PA.
Financial data (yr. ended 12/31/01): Grants paid, $23,250; assets, $1,006,328 (M); expenditures, $34,692; qualifying distributions, $23,250.
Limitations: Giving primarily in Philadelphia, PA.
Application information: Application form not required.
Trustee: First Union National Bank.
EIN: 232663503

41513
Tri-County Telephone Foundation
P.O. Box 91
Belhaven, NC 27810 (252) 964-4211
Contact: Dennis Wallace, Exec. Dir.

Established around 1994 in NC.
Financial data (yr. ended 09/30/01): Grants paid, $23,245; assets, $1,353,543 (M); expenditures, $124,190; qualifying distributions, $23,245.
Limitations: Giving limited to Beaufort, Hyde and Washington counties, NC.
Application information: Application form not required.
Officers: Edwin M. Baldree, Pres.; Charlie F. Wallace, 1st V.P.; Jack Arliss Mason, 2nd V.P.; Clarence E. Tetterton, Secy.-Treas.; Dennis Wallace, Exec. Dir.
Directors: C. Wayne Black, Gary Respess, Charles E. Slade, Cecil O. Smith, Frank Waters.
EIN: 561742130

41514
George Walter & Violet C. Edmonds Scholarship Trust
c/o First Union National Bank
401 S. Tryon St., NC1159
Charlotte, NC 28288-1159
Application address: c/o Herb Tschappat, Principal, Palmetto High School, Palmetto, FL 34221, tel.: (941) 722-4848

Financial data (yr. ended 09/30/01): Grants paid, $23,225; assets, $295,360 (M); expenditures, $28,152; qualifying distributions, $23,073.
Limitations: Giving limited to the Palmetto, FL, area.
Trustee: First Union National Bank.
EIN: 596804593
Codes: GTI

41515
TASCA
(also known as Taller de Salud Compesina)
3609 Swift Dr.
Raleigh, NC 27606-2541

Established in 1999 in NC.
Donor(s): Robert Harvey.
Financial data (yr. ended 12/31/99): Grants paid, $23,035; assets, $44,844 (M); gifts received, $54,204; expenditures, $47,850; qualifying distributions, $47,850.
Limitations: Applications not accepted.
Officers and Directors:* Jacqueline Talley,* Secy.; Evelyn Caldwell, Treas.; Robert Harvey, Exec. Dir.; Maria Fraser-Molina, Maria Garcia-Moll, Frederick Richard Jacob, Joseph Ryan.
EIN: 561855167

41516
Cozart Foundation, Inc.
1005 Harvey St.
Raleigh, NC 27608 (919) 782-6317
Application address: 2309 Fairview Rd., Raleigh CT, 27608
Contact: William C. Cozart, Dir.

Established in 1960.
Financial data (yr. ended 12/31/01): Grants paid, $23,000; assets, $662,847 (M); expenditures, $25,302; qualifying distributions, $23,000.
Limitations: Giving primarily in NC.
Application information: Generally contributes only to pre-selected organizations. Application form not required.
Directors: David L. Cozart III, Elizabeth L. Cozart, Rosa Lee Cozart, William C. Cozart.
EIN: 566044443

41517
The Howard and Margie Coble Horney Foundation, Inc.
P.O. Box 785
Siler City, NC 27344

Established in 1999 in NC.
Donor(s): William H. Horney, Margie Coble Horney.
Financial data (yr. ended 05/31/02): Grants paid, $23,000; assets, $388,539 (M); expenditures, $24,643; qualifying distributions, $23,000.
Limitations: Applications not accepted. Giving primarily in NC.
Application information: Contributes only to pre-selected organizations.
Officers: William H. Horney, Pres.; Margie Coble Horney, Secy.
Director: Jeanette C. Thomas.
EIN: 562151466

41518
Lillie M. Bennett Memorial Foundation
c/o Branch Banking & Trust
P.O. Box 2907
Wilson, NC 27894-2907
Application address: 402 W. Wade St., Wadesboro, NC 28170, tel.: (704) 694-3094
Contact: James A. Hardison, Jr., Tr.

Established in 1985 in NC.
Financial data (yr. ended 12/31/01): Grants paid, $22,300; assets, $538,522 (M); expenditures, $31,515; qualifying distributions, $22,081.
Limitations: Giving limited to Charlotte, NC.
Trustees: James A. Hardison, Jr., Robert W. Huntley, J.D. McLeod, Eugene M. Ward.
EIN: 566128334

41519
The Fennie Family Foundation
P.O. Box 540
Greensboro, NC 27402

Established in 2000 in NC.
Financial data (yr. ended 12/31/01): Grants paid, $22,000; assets, $318,217 (M); expenditures, $25,307; qualifying distributions, $22,000.
Limitations: Applications not accepted.
Application information: Contributes only to pre-selected organizations.
Officers and Directors:* Walter A. Fennie,* Pres.; Gary J. Fennie,* V.P.; Dirk H. Fennie,* Secy.; Scott B. Fennie,* Treas.
EIN: 562215230

41520
Betty & Kan Isaac Scholarship Foundation, Inc.
3234 Weidner Rd.
Newton, NC 28658 (828) 464-0920
Contact: Betty D. Isaac, Secy.

Established in 1994 in NC.
Donor(s): Theodore R. Brewer, Jr., William D. Holloway, Betty D. Isaac, Kenneth C. Isaac, Ned M. Jarrett, W. Gregory Terry.
Financial data (yr. ended 12/31/00): Grants paid, $22,000; assets, $273,569 (M); gifts received, $60,000; expenditures, $24,460; qualifying distributions, $24,448.
Limitations: Giving limited to residents of Catawba County, NC.
Application information: Application form required.
Officers and Directors:* Kenneth C. Isaac, Pres.; Betty D. Isaac,* Secy.; William D. Holloway,* Treas.; Theodore R. Brewer, Jr., Ned M. Jarrett, W. Gregory Terry.
EIN: 561875423
Codes: GTI

41521
Miller Family Foundation of Wake County
1916 Torrey Pines Pl.
Raleigh, NC 27615

Donor(s): J. Fielding Miller, Kimberly G. Miller.
Financial data (yr. ended 12/31/01): Grants paid, $22,000; assets, $76,325 (M); gifts received, $196,748; expenditures, $25,560; qualifying distributions, $22,000.
Limitations: Applications not accepted. Giving primarily in Raleigh, NC.
Application information: Contributes only to pre-selected organizations.
Officers: J. Fielding Miller, Pres.; Kimberly G. Miller, Secy.
EIN: 562136458

41522
The Pharmacy Network Foundation, Inc.
4000 Old Wake Forest Rd., Ste. 102
Raleigh, NC 27609 (919) 876-4642
Contact: J. Andrew Barrett, Exec. V.P.

Donor(s): Pharmacy Network Nat'l Corp., United Pharmacy Cooperative, Inc.
Financial data (yr. ended 12/31/00): Grants paid, $22,000; assets, $438,601 (M); gifts received, $137,699; expenditures, $33,490; qualifying distributions, $22,000.
Limitations: Giving limited to NC.
Officers: Mitchell W. Watts, Pres.; J. Andrew Barrett, Exec. V.P.; Jimmy S. Jackson, V.P. and Secy.; Julian E. Upchurch, V.P.; Jonathan A. Hill, Treas.
EIN: 561690027

41523
Ella & Les Swindell Foundation
c/o Robert Swindell
2208 Granville Rd.
Greensboro, NC 27408

Financial data (yr. ended 12/31/01): Grants paid, $22,000; assets, $552,972 (M); expenditures, $31,809; qualifying distributions, $22,000.
Limitations: Applications not accepted.
Application information: Contributes only to pre-selected organizations.
Trustees: Jeffrey L. Bradley, Priscilla Swindell Raleigh, Anne R. Swindell, Robert B. Swindell, and 3 additional trustees.
EIN: 566042828

41524
The Hatcher Family Foundation
220 Midland Rd.
P.O. Box 2340
Pinehurst, NC 28374-2340
Contact: Alton P. Hatcher, Jr., Tr.

Established in 1990 in NC.
Donor(s): Alton P. Hatcher, Jr., Nell H. Hatcher.
Financial data (yr. ended 12/31/01): Grants paid, $21,700; assets, $498,685 (M); expenditures, $23,653; qualifying distributions, $21,700.
Limitations: Giving on a national basis, with emphasis on NC.
Trustees: Hayley Hatcher Dettor, Alton P. Hatcher, Jr., Barbara Ann Hatcher, John Howell Hatcher, Nell H. Hatcher, Tere H. Smart.
EIN: 256358588

41525
Edgar and Lois Reich Education Foundation
c/o Wachovia Bank, N.A.
P.O. Box 3099
Winston-Salem, NC 27150-7131

Established in 1996 in NC.
Financial data (yr. ended 12/31/99): Grants paid, $21,592; assets, $753,520 (M); expenditures, $28,625; qualifying distributions, $22,471.
Limitations: Applications not accepted.
Trustee: Wachovia Bank, N.A.
EIN: 582245280

41526
The Willy Beuthahn Charitable Foundation
c/o First Union National Bank
401 S. Tyron St., NC1159
Charlotte, NC 28288-1159
Application address: c/o Andrew Davis, First Union National Bank, 765 Broad St., Newark, NJ 07102, tel.: (201) 430-4721

Established in 1993 in NJ.
Donor(s): Willy Beuthahn.
Financial data (yr. ended 11/30/01): Grants paid, $21,590; assets, $438,968 (M); expenditures, $23,289; qualifying distributions, $21,590.
Limitations: Giving limited to Passaic, NJ.
Trustees: First Union National Bank.
EIN: 223264646

41527
Edwin G. W. Ruge Education Foundation
c/o First Union National Bank
401 S. Tryon St., NC1159
Charlotte, NC 28288-1159

Established in 1989 in FL.
Financial data (yr. ended 12/31/00): Grants paid, $21,550; assets, $456,843 (M); expenditures, $28,731; qualifying distributions, $21,453.
Limitations: Giving limited to residents of FL, with preference to residents of Apalachicola.
Application information: Application form required.
Trustee: First Union National Bank.
EIN: 596527097
Codes: GTI

41528
Japajag Foundation
6926 Finian Dr.
Wilmington, NC 28409-2685 (910) 313-0321
Contact: Charles D. Pierce, Admin.

Donor(s): Jeffrey B. Henriques, Sr.‡
Financial data (yr. ended 08/31/02): Grants paid, $21,500; assets, $210,676 (M); gifts received, $275; expenditures, $25,421; qualifying distributions, $21,500.
Limitations: Giving primarily in CT.

Officer: Charles D. Pierce, Admin.
Trustees: Jeffrey B. Henriques, Peter R. Henriques, Gloria H. Patterson, Judith R. Pierce.
EIN: 136212462

41529
Fritz and Lavinia Jensen Foundation
c/o C. Land Hite
Bank of America Plz.
Charlotte, NC 28255-0001

Established in 1999 in NC.
Donor(s): Lavinia J. Jenson.
Financial data (yr. ended 12/31/01): Grants paid, $21,500; assets, $180,820 (M); gifts received, $1,275; expenditures, $58,736; qualifying distributions, $21,500.
Limitations: Applications not accepted. Giving on a national basis.
Application information: Singers are required to supply 2 letters of recommendation from reputable teachers, conductors or coaches.
Officers: Lavinia J. Jensen, Chair.; Richard Benjamin Leaptrott, Jr., V.P.; Lendon Todd Munday, V.P.; Danielle Noies Goldin Munday, Secy.-Treas.
Director: Oliver Wendell Worthington II.
EIN: 562107412

41530
RCC Foundation
c/o Ken Shabbaz
P.O. Box 4528
Greensboro, NC 27404-0493

Established around 1994.
Donor(s): Rachel C. Camp.
Financial data (yr. ended 06/30/01): Grants paid, $21,500; assets, $268,873 (M); expenditures, $21,500; qualifying distributions, $21,500.
Limitations: Applications not accepted. Giving limited to Wilmington, NC.
Application information: Contributes only to pre-selected organizations.
Officers and Directors:* Rachel C. Camp,* Pres.; Rachel MacRae,* V.P.; Hugh MacRae III,* Secy.; Nelson MacRae,* Treas.
EIN: 561801410

41531
The Walker Crow Families Foundation
415 W. Cameron Ave.
Chapel Hill, NC 27516

Established in 2000 in NC.
Donor(s): James Crow.
Financial data (yr. ended 12/31/01): Grants paid, $21,438; assets, $82,135 (M); gifts received, $1,134; expenditures, $22,572; qualifying distributions, $21,438.
Officers: James Crow, Pres.; Eric H. Geiger, Secy.
Directors: Stephen D. Coggins, Rev. Stephen Elkins-Williams.
EIN: 562196671

41532
Flora Y. Hatcher Trust
c/o First Union National Bank
401 S. Tryon St., 4th Fl.
Charlotte, NC 28288-1159

Established in 2000 in VA.
Financial data (yr. ended 12/31/01): Grants paid, $21,192; assets, $1,137,032 (M); expenditures, $44,723; qualifying distributions, $21,917.
Limitations: Applications not accepted.
Application information: Contributes only to pre-selected organizations.
Trustee: First Union National Bank.
EIN: 316670506

41533
Maria Veg Wyatt Trust
P.O. Box 51
Lake Lure, NC 28746-0051 (828) 625-2222
Contact: Betty Cashion Zieger

Financial data (yr. ended 02/28/02): Grants paid, $21,162; assets, $480,795 (M); expenditures, $30,478; qualifying distributions, $21,162.
Limitations: Giving limited to Bat Cave, Bills Creek, Chimney Rock, Gerton and Lake Lure, NC.
Application information: Application form required for scholarships.
Officer: Syble Freeman, Chair.
Trustees: Red Anderson, Wallace Earley, Steve Lackey, Rev. Mickey Mugan.
EIN: 561200714
Codes: GTI

41534
Fred H. DuVall Scholarship Fund
c/o First Union National Bank
401 S. Tryon St., NC1159
Charlotte, NC 28288-1159
Application address: P.O. Box 782, Bryson City, NC 28713
Contact: Steve Cooper, Exec. Mgr., First Union National Bank

Established in 1992 in NC.
Donor(s): Fred DuVall.‡
Financial data (yr. ended 08/31/01): Grants paid, $21,100; assets, $369,535 (M); gifts received, $564; expenditures, $23,098; qualifying distributions, $21,870.
Limitations: Giving limited to residents of Swain County, NC.
Application information: Written nomination by high school counselor or teacher required. Application form not required.
Trustee: First Union National Bank.
EIN: 566415001
Codes: GTI

41535
Perry N. Rudkins Foundation, Inc.
28 Hunters Ln.
Hendersonville, NC 28791

Established in 1994, funded in 2001.
Financial data (yr. ended 12/31/01): Grants paid, $21,000; assets, $3,729,292 (M); gifts received, $3,619,039; expenditures, $21,398; qualifying distributions, $21,000.
Application information: Application form required.
Officers: Peggy Judkins, Pres. and Tres.; Steven A. Jackson, V.P. and Sec.
EIN: 561903174

41536
Perry Memorial Scholarship Fund
(Formerly Frank H. & Annie Belle Whilhelm Perry Memorial Scholarships)
c/o Bank of America
Bank of America Plz., NC1-002-11-18
Charlotte, NC 28255-0001
Application address: 101 S. Tyron St., NC1-002-22-22, Charlotte, NC 28255
Contact: Nancy Truitt, V.P., Bank of America

Established in 1987 in NC.
Financial data (yr. ended 01/31/01): Grants paid, $20,893; assets, $546,420 (M); expenditures, $27,244; qualifying distributions, $24,783.
Limitations: Giving limited to NC and TN.
Application information: Application form not required.
Trustee: Bank of America.
EIN: 566290640
Codes: GTI

41537
Philpott Foundation, Inc.
P.O. Box 1205
Lexington, NC 27293-1205

Financial data (yr. ended 09/30/01): Grants paid, $20,600; assets, $472,945 (M); expenditures, $21,868; qualifying distributions, $20,600.
Limitations: Applications not accepted. Giving primarily in NC.
Application information: Contributes only to pre-selected organizations.
Directors: Ben Philpott, H. Cloyd Philpott, Hubert J. Philpott.
EIN: 566044474

41538
National Society of the Daughters of the American Revolution
(also known as National Society of the DAR)
c/o Wachovia Bank, N.A.
P.O. Box 3099
Winston-Salem, NC 27150-7131
Application address: 509 Redbud Rd., Chapel Hill, NC 27514, tel.: (919) 942-7898
Contact: Betty Manning

Financial data (yr. ended 12/31/00): Grants paid, $20,555; assets, $530,982 (M); expenditures, $27,919; qualifying distributions, $22,637.
Limitations: Giving limited to NC residents of Orange County and that part of Chatham County lying north of U.S. Hwy. 64 and NC Hwy. 87.
Trustee: Wachovia Bank, N.A.
EIN: 566484835

41539
Olive A. Stokes Scholarship Trust
c/o RBC Centura Bank
P.O. Box 1220
Rocky Mount, NC 27802

Established in 2001 in NC.
Financial data (yr. ended 09/30/01): Grants paid, $20,310; assets, $524,830 (M); expenditures, $23,087; qualifying distributions, $20,715.
Limitations: Giving primarily in NC.
Trustee: RBC Centura Bank.
EIN: 316646001

41540
Martha E. Yerkes Scholarship Trust
(Formerly Martha E. Yerkes Scholarship Foundation)
c/o First Union National Bank
401 S. Tryon St., NC1159
Charlotte, NC 28288

Established in 1986 in PA.
Financial data (yr. ended 12/31/01): Grants paid, $20,167; assets, $211,688 (M); expenditures, $23,121; qualifying distributions, $20,167.
Limitations: Giving limited to Chester County, PA.
Application information: Application form required.
Trustee: First Union National Bank.
EIN: 236441277

41541
Glass Family Foundation, Inc.
1 N. Pack Sq., Ste. 410
Asheville, NC 28801

Established in 2000 in NC.
Donor(s): Kenneth E. Glass.
Financial data (yr. ended 12/31/01): Grants paid, $20,000; assets, $784,769 (M); gifts received, $562,020; expenditures, $40,165; qualifying distributions, $20,000.
Limitations: Applications not accepted.

Application information: Contributes only to pre-selected organizations.
Officers: Kenneth E. Glass, Pres.; Nancy J. Glass, V.P.; Lara Nolletti, Secy.
Director: David Nolletti.
EIN: 562196225

41542
Wesley Walls Foundation, Inc.
8711 Lake Challis Ln.
Charlotte, NC 28226-2666

Donor(s): Wesley Walls, Christine Walls.
Financial data (yr. ended 12/31/00): Grants paid, $19,940; assets, $0 (M); expenditures, $21,610; qualifying distributions, $21,460.
Officers: Wesley Walls, Pres.; Christine Walls, V.P. and Secy.-Treas.
Directors: Gordon B. Grigg, Todd Christian Richter.
EIN: 562020061

41543
Allan C. Mims & Margaret L. Mims Charitable Trust
c/o Centura Bank
P.O. Box 1220
Rocky Mount, NC 27802

Established in 2000 in NC.
Financial data (yr. ended 12/31/01): Grants paid, $19,750; assets, $1,659,648 (M); expenditures, $62,294; qualifying distributions, $19,750.
Limitations: Applications not accepted. Giving primarily in Rocky Mount, NC.
Application information: Contributes only to pre-selected organizations.
Trustee: Centura Bank.
EIN: 566207750

41544
The Lerner Foundation
5009 Monroe Rd., Ste. 200
Charlotte, NC 28205

Donor(s): Harry Lerner.
Financial data (yr. ended 10/31/01): Grants paid, $19,665; assets, $380,471 (M); expenditures, $20,675; qualifying distributions, $19,665.
Limitations: Applications not accepted.
Application information: Contributes only to pre-selected organizations.
Officers and Directors:* Harry Lerner,* Pres.; Mark Lerner,* Secy.
EIN: 581416326

41545
Hunt Scholarship Trust
c/o First Union National Bank
401 S. Tryon St., NC 1159
Charlotte, NC 28288
Application address: c/o First Union National Bank, Broad and Walnut Sts., Philadelphia, PA 19109, tel.: (215) 670-7320

Established in 1992 in NJ.
Donor(s): Todd B. Hunt.‡
Financial data (yr. ended 06/30/01): Grants paid, $19,625; assets, $371,099 (M); expenditures, $23,209; qualifying distributions, $20,800.
Limitations: Giving limited to residents of Auburn, Gloucester, Penns Grove, Salem, and Swedesboro counties, NJ.
Trustee: First Union National Bank.
EIN: 226452371
Codes: GTI

41546
The Sing Foundation, Inc.
c/o Kenneth F. Essex
1701 South Blvd.
Charlotte, NC 28203
Application address: P.O. Box 11398, Winslow, WA 98110, Attn. Dr. J.M. Sing
Contact: Jeanne Marie Sing, Pres.

Established in 1988 in NC.
Donor(s): Jeanne Marie Sing, Robert L. Sing, Jr.
Financial data (yr. ended 03/31/99): Grants paid, $19,500; assets, $488,002 (M); gifts received, $14; expenditures, $19,955; qualifying distributions, $19,500.
Limitations: Giving primarily in CA.
Officers and Directors:* Jeanne Marie Sing,* Pres.; Robert L. Sing, Jr.,* V.P. and Treas.; Kenneth F. Essex, Secy.; Ethan Robert Sing, Graham H. Sing, Gregory Morris Sing, Janelle Fay Sing.
EIN: 561309711

41547
Hummel Family Foundation, Inc.
c/o Bradley L. Jacobs
1907 Rosecrest Dr.
Greensboro, NC 27408-6215

Donor(s): Anne D. Hummel.
Financial data (yr. ended 03/31/02): Grants paid, $19,475; assets, $407,334 (M); gifts received, $156,880; expenditures, $20,169; qualifying distributions, $19,475.
Limitations: Applications not accepted.
Application information: Contributes only to pre-selected organizations.
Officers and Directors:* Sam D. Hummel,* Pres.; Anne D. Hummel,* Secy.-Treas.; Amelia H. Hummel, Elizabeth H. Hummel.
EIN: 562035183

41548
E. J. Pope & Son Foundation
c/o E.J. Pope, Jr.
P.O. Drawer 649
Mount Olive, NC 28365
E-mail: buddy-pope@ejpope&son.com

Established in 1995 in NC.
Donor(s): E.J. Pope & Son, Inc.
Financial data (yr. ended 08/31/02): Grants paid, $19,249; assets, $176,633 (M); expenditures, $19,848; qualifying distributions, $19,249.
Limitations: Applications not accepted. Giving limited to NC.
Application information: Contributes only to pre-selected organizations.
Officers: E.J. Pope, Jr., Pres.; E.J. Pope III, V.P.; Kaye Thompson, Secy.
EIN: 561939755

41549
The T. A. and Mollie P. Brooks Trust
(Formerly Timothy A. Brooks Trust)
c/o Bank of America
101 S. Tryon St.
Charlotte, NC 28255

Established in 1988 in NC.
Financial data (yr. ended 12/31/01): Grants paid, $19,240; assets, $501,034 (M); expenditures, $21,947; qualifying distributions, $19,240.
Limitations: Applications not accepted. Giving primarily in NC.
Application information: Contributes only to pre-selected organizations.
Trustee: Bank of America.
EIN: 566060315

41550
JJM Family Foundation
c/o J. Verne McKenzie
60152 Burton
Chapel Hill, NC 27514-8470

Established in 1989 in NE.
Donor(s): John Verne McKenzie, Janet McKenzie, Berkshire Hathaway, Inc.
Financial data (yr. ended 07/31/01): Grants paid, $18,928; assets, $1 (M); gifts received, $2,700; expenditures, $19,056; qualifying distributions, $18,928.
Limitations: Applications not accepted. Giving primarily in NE.
Application information: Contributes only to pre-selected organizations.
Officers: John Verne McKenzie, Pres.; Janet McKenzie, V.P.; Sara McKenzie, V.P.
EIN: 470729940

41551
Estes Winn Blomberg Foundation, Inc.
P.O. Box 6854
Asheville, NC 28804-1931 (828) 253-7651

Donor(s): S.M. Patton, Barbara Blomberg, Marilyn B. Patton.
Financial data (yr. ended 10/31/01): Grants paid, $18,789; assets, $92,856 (M); gifts received, $8,494; expenditures, $44,263; qualifying distributions, $18,789.
Limitations: Applications not accepted. Giving primarily in NC.
Application information: Contributes only to pre-selected organizations.
Officers and Directors:* S.M. Patton,* Pres.; Marilyn B. Patton,* V.P. and Secy.; Barbara Blomberg,* V.P. and Treas.
EIN: 566094477

41552
The Edmondson Foundation
P.O. Box 1616
Goldsboro, NC 27533-1615

Established in 1999 in NC.
Donor(s): Gail B. Edmondson.
Financial data (yr. ended 12/31/99): Grants paid, $18,726; assets, $0 (M); gifts received, $18,726; expenditures, $18,726; qualifying distributions, $18,726.
Limitations: Applications not accepted. Giving primarily in Goldsboro, NC.
Application information: Contributes only to pre-selected organizations.
Officers: Gail B. Edmondson, Pres.; Judy C. Tart, V.P.; Charles Vernon Braswell, Secy.
EIN: 562057241

41553
The Furr Foundation
7855 Live Oaks Dr.
Denver, NC 28037 (704) 394-2229
Contact: William P. Furr, Pres.

Donor(s): William P. Furr.
Financial data (yr. ended 10/31/01): Grants paid, $18,400; assets, $149,767 (M); gifts received, $99,839; expenditures, $31,501; qualifying distributions, $18,400.
Officers: William P. Furr, Pres. and Treas.; Emily R. Furr, Exec. V.P. and Secy.; Laura Furr, V.P.; Thomas Furr, V.P.; Elizabeth Furr Hammond, V.P.
EIN: 562066688

41554
William S. & Arthur R. Stambaugh Scholarship Foundation
c/o First Union National Bank
401 S. Tryon St.
Charlotte, NC 28288-1159
Application address: 39 N. 3rd St., P.O. Box 1071, Harrisburg, PA 17108
Contact: Pamela C. Nothstein

Established in 1999 in PA.
Financial data (yr. ended 10/31/01): Grants paid, $18,400; assets, $362,015 (M); expenditures, $24,511; qualifying distributions, $18,400.
Trustee: First Union National Bank.
EIN: 256634174

41555
The New Earth Private Foundatiion
1675 Lake Country Dr.
Asheboro, NC 27203

Financial data (yr. ended 12/31/01): Grants paid, $18,258; assets, $9,604 (M); gifts received, $19,975; expenditures, $23,013; qualifying distributions, $18,258.
Limitations: Applications not accepted.
Application information: Contributes only to pre-selected organizations.
Trustees: Gary L. Cameron, Michael F. Pearl.
EIN: 562084337

41556
Margaret W. Midgett Charitable Trust
c/o Centura Bank
P.O. Box 1220
Rocky Mount, NC 27802

Established in 2000 in NC.
Financial data (yr. ended 12/31/01): Grants paid, $18,126; assets, $360,509 (M); expenditures, $24,578; qualifying distributions, $18,156.
Limitations: Applications not accepted.
Application information: Contributes only to pre-selected organizations.
Trustee: RBC Centura Bank.
EIN: 316648798

41557
The Richter Foundation, Inc.
1712 East Blvd.
Charlotte, NC 28203 (704) 377-9335
Contact: Lloyd Richter, V.P.

Donor(s): Moses Richter.‡
Financial data (yr. ended 11/30/01): Grants paid, $18,020; assets, $2,624 (M); gifts received, $17,000; expenditures, $18,288; qualifying distributions, $18,020.
Limitations: Giving primarily in Charlotte, NC.
Application information: Application form not required.
Officers: Sherry Richter, Pres.; Benjamin Richter, V.P. and Secy.; Lloyd Richter, V.P. and Treas.
EIN: 566057552

41558
The Susan N. Adams Charitable Foundation
1602 Lakeshore Dr.
Dunn, NC 28334

Established in 1998 in NC.
Donor(s): Susan N. Adams.
Financial data (yr. ended 12/31/01): Grants paid, $18,000; assets, $127,065 (M); expenditures, $18,153; qualifying distributions, $18,000.
Limitations: Applications not accepted. Giving primarily in GA.
Application information: Contributes only to pre-selected organizations.
Trustee: Susan N. Adams.
EIN: 566537575

41559
Glad Tithings Foundation
401 Sweeten Way
Asheville, NC 28803 (828) 274-8506
Contact: Don Deibert, Mgr.

Established in 1997 in NC.
Donor(s): Barbara D. Deibert, Irvin E. Deibert.
Financial data (yr. ended 12/31/01): Grants paid, $18,000; assets, $397,256 (M); gifts received, $30,420; expenditures, $38,706; qualifying distributions, $18,000.
Limitations: Giving primarily in Asheville, NC.
Officer: Don Deibert, Mgr.
Directors: Barbara D. Deibert, Irvin E. Deibert.
EIN: 597109741

41560
Gail and Harry Grim Foundation
1104 Dilworth Cresent Row
Charlotte, NC 28203
Contact: Harry J. Grim, Chair.

Established in 1997.
Donor(s): Gail R. Grim, Harry J. Grim.
Financial data (yr. ended 12/31/01): Grants paid, $18,000; assets, $567,203 (M); expenditures, $27,362; qualifying distributions, $18,000.
Limitations: Giving primarily in Charlotte, NC.
Officers and Directors:* Harry J. Grim,* Chair., V.P. and Secy.; Gail R. Grim,* Vice-Chair., Pres. and Treas.
EIN: 562011081

41561
Thomas Leonard Umphlet Charitable Trust
P.O. Box 362
Raleigh, NC 27602

Established in 1995 in NC.
Financial data (yr. ended 12/31/01): Grants paid, $18,000; assets, $241,247 (M); expenditures, $19,519; qualifying distributions, $18,000.
Limitations: Applications not accepted.
Application information: Contributes only to pre-selected organizations.
Trustee: Thomas Griffin Douglas.
EIN: 566451375

41562
Dr. Robert A. Team Scholarship Fund
604 Peachtree St.
Lexington, NC 27292

Donor(s): Robert A. Team.
Financial data (yr. ended 12/31/01): Grants paid, $17,959; assets, $121,738 (M); gifts received, $100; expenditures, $18,661; qualifying distributions, $17,959.
Officers: Robert A. Team, Pres.; John H. Frank, V.P.; Ann McMurray, Secy.
EIN: 561872786

41563
The United Brass Foundation, Inc.
714 S. Main St.
Randleman, NC 27317-2100

Donor(s): United Brass Works, Inc.
Financial data (yr. ended 12/31/01): Grants paid, $17,950; assets, $83,017 (M); expenditures, $17,955; qualifying distributions, $17,950.
Limitations: Applications not accepted. Giving primarily in Greensboro, NC.
Application information: Contributes only to pre-selected organizations.
Directors: Edward Benson, Michael Berkelhammer.
EIN: 581489756
Codes: CS, CD

41564
Word Ministry of Charlotte
2100 Walnut Ln.
Monroe, NC 28112-7334

Financial data (yr. ended 09/30/01): Grants paid, $17,939; assets, $4,302 (M); gifts received, $21,197; expenditures, $20,205; qualifying distributions, $17,939.
Limitations: Applications not accepted. Giving primarily in NC.
Application information: Contributes only to pre-selected organizations.
Directors: Donald C. Hagler, Jr., Ramona B. Hagler, Betty Smith, Rev. J. Arlen Smith, Betty Stone, Richard Stone.
EIN: 561343039

41565
A. L. Johnson Charity Trust
c/o First Union National Bank, NC 1159
401 N. Tryon St., NC1159
Charlotte, NC 28288
Application address: c/o First Union National Bank, Broad and Walnut Sts., Philadelphia, PA 19109

Donor(s): Alice L. Johnson.‡
Financial data (yr. ended 08/31/01): Grants paid, $17,915; assets, $597,835 (M); expenditures, $19,712; qualifying distributions, $17,915.
Limitations: Giving limited to Bristol, PA.
Trustee: First Union National Bank.
EIN: 236222364
Codes: GTI

41566
Dan D. Davenport Fund
c/o B.B. & T., Trust Dept.
P.O. Box 2907
Wilson, NC 27894-2907

Financial data (yr. ended 12/31/01): Grants paid, $17,900; assets, $256,328 (M); expenditures, $22,119; qualifying distributions, $17,900.
Limitations: Applications not accepted. Giving primarily in NC.
Application information: Contributes only to pre-selected organizations.
Trustee: B.B. & T.
EIN: 576020148

41567
Grover C. and Jane C. McNair Charitable Foundation Trust
128 S. Tryon St.
1st Citizen Plz., No. 1800
Charlotte, NC 28202-5001 (704) 375-0057

Financial data (yr. ended 12/31/01): Grants paid, $17,800; assets, $128,023 (M); gifts received, $500; expenditures, $18,493; qualifying distributions, $17,800.
Limitations: Applications not accepted. Giving primarily in Winston-Salem, NC.
Application information: Contributes only to pre-selected organizations.
Trustees: Grover C. McNair, Jane C. McNair, William H. McNair.
EIN: 566285721

41568
Leroy & Charlotte Martin Foundation
3504 Carlton Square Pl.
Raleigh, NC 27612

Established in 1999 in NC.
Donor(s): Leroy B. Martin, Jr.
Financial data (yr. ended 12/31/01): Grants paid, $17,575; assets, $22,726 (M); gifts received, $32,487; expenditures, $18,319; qualifying distributions, $17,575.
Limitations: Giving primarily in Raleigh, NC.
Officers: Leroy B. Martin, Jr., Pres.; Charlotte Martin, Treas.
Directors: Christopher H. Martin, Eric M. Martin, Leroy B. Martin III.
EIN: 562115174

41569
Patrick Beaver Scholarship Foundation, Inc.
2421 N. Center St., Ste. 227
Hickory, NC 28601

Established in 1998.
Financial data (yr. ended 08/31/00): Grants paid, $17,500; assets, $1,058,995 (M); gifts received, $205; expenditures, $27,540; qualifying distributions, $17,500.
Officers: Donald C. Beaver, Pres.; Patricia A. Beaver, V.P. and Treas.; Angela B. Simmons, Secy.
Directors: Deborah E. Beaver, Donna B. Hadley.
EIN: 562048446

41570
Eugene G. Blackford and Margaret M. Blackford Memorial Scholarship Fund
c/o First Union National Bank
401 S. Tryon St., NC1159
Charlotte, NC 28288

Financial data (yr. ended 12/31/01): Grants paid, $17,198; assets, $506,142 (M); expenditures, $23,763; qualifying distributions, $17,198.
Limitations: Applications not accepted. Giving primarily in FL.
Application information: Contributes only to pre-selected organizations.
Trustee: First Union National Bank.
EIN: 596709347

41571
Sigmund and Ellen Tannenbaum Foundation, Inc.
1004 Dover Rd.
Greensboro, NC 27408-7312

Established in 1992 in NC.
Donor(s): Sigmund I. Tannenbaum.
Financial data (yr. ended 07/31/01): Grants paid, $17,075; assets, $453,422 (M); expenditures, $21,680; qualifying distributions, $17,075.
Limitations: Applications not accepted.
Application information: Contributes only to pre-selected organizations.
Directors: James N. Duggins, Jr., Ellen V. Tannenbaum, Sigmund I. Tannenbaum.
EIN: 561787404

41572
Wingaris Scholarship Fund
c/o First Union National Bank
401 S. Tryon St., NC 1159
Charlotte, NC 28288-1159

Financial data (yr. ended 06/30/02): Grants paid, $17,050; assets, $253,016 (M); expenditures, $18,564; qualifying distributions, $16,969.
Limitations: Applications not accepted. Giving primarily in PA.
Application information: Unsolicited requests for funds not accepted.
Trustee: First Union National Bank.
EIN: 236790141

41573
Edward Nixon McKay Memorial Scholarship Fund
c/o First Union National Bank
401 S. Tryon St., NC1159
Charlotte, NC 28288
Application address: c/o First Union National Bank, P.O. Box 1193, 501 Broad St., Rome, GA 30162

Financial data (yr. ended 04/30/01): Grants paid, $17,000; assets, $340,392 (M); expenditures, $20,920; qualifying distributions, $17,621.
Limitations: Giving limited to GA.
Application information: Students nominated by high school principal's recommendation only. Application form not required.
Trustee: First Union National Bank.
EIN: 586161795
Codes: GTI

41574
Gladys P. & Augustus G. Roycroft Charitable Foundation
c/o Central Carolina Bank & Trust Co.
P.O. Box 30010
Durham, NC 27701

Established in 1999 in NC.
Financial data (yr. ended 12/31/01): Grants paid, $16,980; assets, $376,149 (M); expenditures, $21,243; qualifying distributions, $16,980.
Limitations: Applications not accepted.
Application information: Contributes only to pre-selected organizations.
Trustee: Central Carolina Bank & Trust Co.
EIN: 566541210

41575
North Carolina Fenton Foundation
123 Newby Ct.
Rocky Mount, NC 27804-3322
(252) 443-1951
Contact: Caroline H. High, Pres.

Financial data (yr. ended 12/31/01): Grants paid, $16,875; assets, $264,781 (M); expenditures, $18,798; qualifying distributions, $16,739.
Limitations: Giving primarily in NC.
Officer: Caroline H. High, Pres.
Trustees: John H. High, Jr., Robert M. High.
EIN: 311468487

41576
The Paddison Family Foundation No.11
c/o Wachovia Bank, N.A.
P.O. Box 3099
Winston-Salem, NC 27150-7131

Established in 1996 in NC.
Financial data (yr. ended 12/31/01): Grants paid, $16,875; assets, $625,649 (M); expenditures, $26,056; qualifying distributions, $16,875.
Limitations: Applications not accepted.
Application information: Contributes only to pre-selected organizations.
Trustee: Wachovia Bank, N.A.
EIN: 566493042

41577
Holiday Home Foundation, Inc. of Petersburg
7606 Doe Run Trail
Staley, NC 27355

Donor(s): Catherine A. Dunigan, Kenneth I. Dunigan.
Financial data (yr. ended 09/30/01): Grants paid, $16,850; assets, $63,832 (M); gifts received, $1,827; expenditures, $17,446; qualifying distributions, $16,822.

41577—NORTH CAROLINA

Limitations: Applications not accepted. Giving limited to Petersburg, IN.
Application information: Contributes only to pre-selected organizations.
Officers: Kenneth I. Dunigan, Pres.; Helen Dunigan, V.P.; Catherine A. Dunigan, Secy.-Treas.
EIN: 310971615

41578
Jack M. Taylor & Ulma Q. Taylor Charitable Trust
c/o B.B. & T. Trust Dept.
P.O. Box 2907
Wilson, NC 27894-2907

Established in 1987 in NC.
Financial data (yr. ended 12/31/01): Grants paid, $16,619; assets, $336,629 (M); expenditures, $21,441; qualifying distributions, $16,619.
Limitations: Applications not accepted.
Application information: Contributes only to pre-selected organizations.
Trustee: B.B. & T.
EIN: 566243085

41579
James Hickey Rumbough Fund
c/o First Union National Bank
401 S. Tryon St.
Charlotte, NC 28288-1159
Application address: c/o Supreme Court Bldg., 101 N. 8th St., Richmond, VA 23219
Contact: Jane D. Hickey, Advisory Comm. Member

Financial data (yr. ended 12/31/01): Grants paid, $16,531; assets, $298,766 (M); expenditures, $21,749; qualifying distributions, $17,198.
Limitations: Giving limited to the Lynchburg, VA, area.
Application information: Application form required.
Trustee: First Union National Bank.
Advisory Committee Members: Beverly R. Crosby, Fred Hickey, Jane D. Hickey.
EIN: 546113973
Codes: GTI

41580
Sabates Foundation
4201 Congress St., Ste. 470
Charlotte, NC 28209 (704) 372-9527
Contact: Dominic Cappelli, Dir.

Established in 1986 in NC.
Financial data (yr. ended 11/30/01): Grants paid, $16,400; assets, $3,164 (M); gifts received, $16,000; expenditures, $16,447; qualifying distributions, $16,447.
Limitations: Giving primarily in Charlotte, NC.
Application information: Request application form 6 months prior to date needed. Application form required.
Directors: Dominic Cappelli, Barbara W. Darden, Carolyn P. Sabates.
EIN: 561542930

41581
The William Sturgis Family Foundation
c/o Wachovia Bank, N.A.
P.O. Box 3099
Winston-Salem, NC 27150-7131

Established in 1996 in SC.
Financial data (yr. ended 12/31/01): Grants paid, $16,185; assets, $367,164 (M); gifts received, $11,000; expenditures, $22,033; qualifying distributions, $16,185.
Limitations: Applications not accepted.
Application information: Contributes only to pre-selected organizations.

Trustees: Martha E. Sturgis, William B. Sturgis.
EIN: 570946293

41582
H.E.L.P. Center, Inc.
1700 Secrest Shortcut Rd.
Monroe, NC 28110-2454

Established in 1994 in NC.
Financial data (yr. ended 12/31/01): Grants paid, $16,179; assets, $435,766 (M); gifts received, $118,202; expenditures, $95,839; qualifying distributions, $16,179.
Limitations: Applications not accepted.
Application information: Contributes only to pre-selected organizations.
Officers and Trustees:* Tara Quinn,* Pres.; Larry Quinn,* V.P.; Linda Privette,* Secy.; Carolyn Newton,* Treas.; Jim Holmes, Lonnie Riley.
EIN: 582096778

41583
The Roth Family Foundation
c/o Wachovia Bank, N.A.
P.O. Box 3099
Winston-Salem, NC 27150-7131

Established in 1997 in NC.
Financial data (yr. ended 12/31/01): Grants paid, $16,138; assets, $410,726 (M); gifts received, $79,288; expenditures, $20,737; qualifying distributions, $18,151.
Limitations: Applications not accepted.
Application information: Contributes only to pre-selected organizations.
Officer: Robert Roth, Exec. Dir.
Trustee: Wachovia Bank, N.A.
EIN: 562065972

41584
J. Vance & Regina Crowder Suttle Foundation, Inc.
P.O. Box 730
Shelby, NC 28151

Donor(s): J. Vance Suttle.
Financial data (yr. ended 12/31/01): Grants paid, $16,050; assets, $166,765 (M); expenditures, $17,512; qualifying distributions, $16,050.
Limitations: Giving primarily in Shelby, NC.
Officers: J. Vance Suttle, Pres. and Treas.; Regina C. Suttle, V.P. and Secy.
EIN: 562024618

41585
Rudolph Ellis Gratuity Fund
c/o First Union National Bank
401 S. Tryon St., 4th Fl.
Charlotte, NC 28288-1159

Established in 1954 in PA.
Financial data (yr. ended 12/31/01): Grants paid, $16,000; assets, $2,294,324 (M); expenditures, $26,943; qualifying distributions, $17,500.
Limitations: Giving primarily in PA.
Trustee: First Union National Bank.
EIN: 236220273
Codes: GTI

41586
The Peters Family Foundation
c/o Bank of America
101 S. Tryon St., NC1-002-11-18
Charlotte, NC 28255

Established in 1999 in NC.
Donor(s): Raymond R. Peters, Nancy M. Peters.
Financial data (yr. ended 12/31/01): Grants paid, $16,000; assets, $253,011 (M); gifts received, $44,284; expenditures, $30,041; qualifying distributions, $16,000.

Limitations: Applications not accepted. Giving primarily in NC.
Application information: Contributes only to pre-selected organizations.
Directors: Angel Peters Barba, Matthew Peters, Nancy M. Peters, Raymond R. Peters, Raymond R. Peters, Jr.
Trustee: Bank of America.
EIN: 562169466

41587
The Wellons Family Foundation
P.O. Box 1018
Morehead City, NC 28557

Established in 2000.
Donor(s): Calvin G. Wellons.
Financial data (yr. ended 12/31/01): Grants paid, $16,000; assets, $129,956 (M); gifts received, $15,000; expenditures, $17,201; qualifying distributions, $16,000.
Officers: Calvin G. Wellons, Pres.; Jean R. Wellons, V.P.; Gaye W. Mashburn, Secy.; Mary W. Moore, Treas.
Director: Kathryn W. Todd.
EIN: 562190192

41588
Alexander M. Worth Fund
c/o Wachovia Bank, N.A.
P.O. Box 3099
Winston-Salem, NC 27150-7131
Application address: P.O. Box 10012; Greensboro, NC 27404
Contact: Alexander McAlister Worth, Jr., Pres.

Established in 1997 in NC.
Donor(s): Alexander McAlister Worth, Jr.
Financial data (yr. ended 12/31/01): Grants paid, $16,000; assets, $186,709 (M); expenditures, $20,104; qualifying distributions, $16,000.
Officers and Directors:* Alexander McAlister Worth, Jr.,* Pres.; Robert Preston Worth,* Secy.-Treas.
Trustee: Wachovia Bank, N.A.
EIN: 562025181

41589
The Knott Family Foundation, Inc.
3210 Medford Rd.
Durham, NC 27705-2752 (919) 383-9308
Contact: Bruce W. Knott, Dir.

Established in 1996 in NC.
Donor(s): Bruce W. Knott, Janet C. Knott.
Financial data (yr. ended 12/31/01): Grants paid, $15,955; assets, $479,611 (M); gifts received, $73,020; expenditures, $24,125; qualifying distributions, $16,054.
Limitations: Giving primarily in Durham, NC.
Directors: Bruce W. Knott, Janet C. Knott.
EIN: 562003192

41590
Carl W. Meares Foundation, Inc.
P.O. Box 187
Fair Bluff, NC 28439
Contact: Carl W. Meares, Jr., Tr.

Established in 1986 in NC.
Donor(s): Carl W. Meares, Sr., Carl W. Meares, Jr., Margaret B. Meares.
Financial data (yr. ended 12/31/01): Grants paid, $15,900; assets, $263,153 (M); expenditures, $18,499; qualifying distributions, $15,900.
Application information: Application form not required.
Trustees: Carl W. Meares, Jr., Carolyn M. Meares, Margaret B. Meares.
EIN: 561544084

41591
Louis Lavitt Foundation, Inc.
c/o Wachovia Bank, N.A.
P.O. Box 3099
Winston-Salem, NC 27150-7131
Contact: Linda Tilley

Financial data (yr. ended 12/31/00): Grants paid, $15,770; assets, $300 (M); expenditures, $21,918; qualifying distributions, $17,288.
Limitations: Giving on a national basis.
Trustees: John Stephen Singer, Wachovia Bank, N.A.
EIN: 566040608

41592
Albert and Jessie D. Martin Scholarship Trust Fund
c/o Elizabeth Martin
8016 NC Hwy. 601
Boonville, NC 27011
Application address: P.O. Box 91, Boonville, NC 27011, tel.: (919) 367-7582
Contact: Robert E. Adams, Sr., Tr.

Established in 1989 in NC.
Donor(s): Jay Martin, S.W. Martin.
Financial data (yr. ended 12/31/01): Grants paid, $15,750; assets, $218,866 (M); gifts received, $25,000; expenditures, $16,420; qualifying distributions, $16,390.
Limitations: Giving limited to residents of Boonville, NC.
Application information: Recipients are nominated by Starmount High School staff. Application form required.
Officer and Trustees:* Brad Storie,* Chair.; Robert E. Adams, Sr., Christy Brown, Frank Brown, Edward Lakey.
EIN: 586241009

41593
The Fruit Bearing Foundation
3620 Cape Center Dr.
Fayetteville, NC 28304
Application address: P.O. Box 52328, Durham, NC 27717
Contact: Miriam Wellons, Pres.

Established in 1996 in NC.
Donor(s): Miriam Wellons.
Financial data (yr. ended 12/31/01): Grants paid, $15,665; assets, $201,662 (M); gifts received, $1,000; expenditures, $15,676; qualifying distributions, $15,665.
Limitations: Giving limited to Durham, NC.
Officer: Miriam Wellons, Pres.
EIN: 562006076

41594
Allentown Area Foundation
c/o First Union National Bank
401 S. Tryon St., NC 1159
Charlotte, NC 28288-1159

Financial data (yr. ended 06/30/02): Grants paid, $15,523; assets, $256,593 (M); expenditures, $16,555; qualifying distributions, $15,523.
Limitations: Applications not accepted. Giving limited to Allentown, PA.
Application information: Contributes only to pre-selected organizations.
Trustee: First Union National Bank.
EIN: 236573326

41595
David & Sheila Perkins Foundation
916 Stone Falls Trl.
Raleigh, NC 27614

Established in 1999 in NC.
Donor(s): David B. Perkins.
Financial data (yr. ended 12/31/01): Grants paid, $15,523; assets, $161,701 (M); gifts received, $110,000; expenditures, $18,004; qualifying distributions, $15,523.
Limitations: Applications not accepted.
Application information: Contributes only to pre-selected organizations.
Officers: David B. Perkins, Pres.; Sheila F. Perkins, Secy.
EIN: 562171597

41596
The Earl N. Phillips, Jr. Family Foundation
101 S. Main St.
P.O. Box 890
High Point, NC 27261
Contact: Earl N. Philips, Pres.

Established in 1998 in NC.
Donor(s): Earl N. Phillips, Jr.
Financial data (yr. ended 12/31/01): Grants paid, $15,500; assets, $401,852 (M); expenditures, $16,452; qualifying distributions, $15,500.
Limitations: Applications not accepted. Giving primarily in High Point, NC.
Application information: Contributes only to pre-selected organizations.
Officers and Directors:* Earl N. Phillips, Jr.,* Pres. and Treas.; Sarah B. Phillips,* V.P.; Courtney D. Phillips,* Secy.
EIN: 911941861

41597
Plato S. & Susan Elizabeth Wilson Foundation
908 Parkwood Cir.
High Point, NC 27262-7419

Established in 1996 in NC.
Donor(s): Plato S. Wilson, Susan E. Wilson.
Financial data (yr. ended 12/31/01): Grants paid, $15,424; assets, $307,918 (M); expenditures, $15,641; qualifying distributions, $15,424.
Officers and Trustees:* Plato S. Wilson,* Chair.; Mark Pierce,* Secy.; David L. Sledge,* Treas.; Bill Harris, Susan Wilson.
EIN: 311529864

41598
Edward E. Hale Trust
c/o First Union National Bank
401 S. Tryon St., 4th Fl.
Charlotte, NC 28288-1159

Established in 1999 in FL.
Financial data (yr. ended 12/31/01): Grants paid, $15,407; assets, $529,382 (M); expenditures, $23,919; qualifying distributions, $16,493.
Limitations: Applications not accepted. Giving primarily in Charleston, WV.
Application information: Contributes only to pre-selected organizations.
Trustee: First Union National Bank.
EIN: 596645432

41599
Laura C. Weyher Foundation
1108 W. Vernon Ave.
Kinston, NC 28501-3616   (252) 523-3895
Contact: Ella Green Weyher, Pres.

Established in 1991 in NC.
Donor(s): Harry F. Weyher.
Financial data (yr. ended 12/31/01): Grants paid, $15,340; assets, $307,752 (M); gifts received, $10,000; expenditures, $15,489; qualifying distributions, $15,340.
Limitations: Giving primarily in NC.
Officers and Directors:* Ella Green Weyher,* Pres.; Harry F. Weyher,* Secy.
EIN: 581942796

41600
Jesse David & Katie B. Bundy Scholarship Trust
c/o Bank of America
380 Knollwood St.
Winston-Salem, NC 27103
Contact: Lula Cook, Trust Off., Bank of America

Established in 1996 in NC.
Donor(s): William L. Bundy.
Financial data (yr. ended 08/31/00): Grants paid, $15,307; assets, $195,580 (M); expenditures, $16,717; qualifying distributions, $15,583.
Limitations: Giving limited to Wilkes County, NC.
Application information: Application form required.
Trustee: Bank of America.
EIN: 566501861

41601
Virginia C. Warrington Memorial Trust
c/o Doctors Park Bldg.
501 Paladin Drive
Greenville, NC 27834-7826   (252) 752-1520
Contact: Thomas S. Burkart, Secy.

Financial data (yr. ended 06/30/01): Grants paid, $15,258; assets, $54,462 (M); gifts received, $4,008; expenditures, $16,173; qualifying distributions, $15,258.
Limitations: Applications not accepted. Giving limited to the Greenville, NC, area.
Application information: Recipients are referred by the Dept. of Social Services; foundation operates program of assistance for end stage renal disease patients.
Officers: Graham Byrum, Pres.; Thomas E. Burkart, M.D., Secy.; Walter J. Newman, M.D., Treas.
EIN: 561586624

41602
Stanley & Mary Mahalick Scholarship Fund
c/o First Union National Bank
401 S. Tryon St., NC1159
Charlotte, NC 28288-1159

Established in 1998 in PA.
Financial data (yr. ended 11/30/01): Grants paid, $15,250; assets, $249,861 (M); expenditures, $18,273; qualifying distributions, $15,902.
Limitations: Applications not accepted. Giving limited to the Mahanoy City, PA, area.
Trustee: First Union National Bank.
EIN: 256643477

41603
The Surtman Foundation
2326 Ferncliff Rd.
Charlotte, NC 28211-2638   (704) 366-2282
Contact: Irene S. Chanter, Tr.

Established in 1952 in NC.
Donor(s): J.R. Surtman.‡
Financial data (yr. ended 07/31/00): Grants paid, $15,200; assets, $1,890,833 (M); expenditures, $23,902; qualifying distributions, $15,200.
Limitations: Giving primarily in Charlotte and Mecklenburg County, NC; giving for research on a national basis.
Application information: Application form not required.
Trustee: Irene S. Chanter.
EIN: 566056565

41604
John J. and Mildred M. Beattie Scholarship Fund
c/o First Union National Bank
401 S. Tryon St., 4th Fl.
Charlotte, NC 28288-1159

Established in 1988 in PA.

41604—NORTH CAROLINA

Financial data (yr. ended 12/31/01): Grants paid, $15,000; assets, $322,376 (M); expenditures, $16,391; qualifying distributions, $15,202.
Limitations: Applications not accepted. Giving primarily in PA.
Application information: Unsolicited requests for funds not accepted.
Trustee: First Union National Bank.
EIN: 236851059

41605
The Boyd-Glenn Foundation, Inc.
P.O. Box 762
Lincolnton, NC 28093 (704) 735-3092
Contact: William G. Boyd, Tr.

Established in 1993 in NC.
Financial data (yr. ended 12/31/01): Grants paid, $15,000; assets, $618,565 (M); expenditures, $15,885; qualifying distributions, $15,000.
Application information: Application form not required.
Trustees: Dan M. Boyd III, William G. Boyd, Mary B. Hornbaker.
EIN: 561855689

41606
H. Loren Clements Scholarship Fund
c/o First Union National Bank
401 S. Tryon St., 4th Fl.
Charlotte, NC 28288-1159

Financial data (yr. ended 12/31/01): Grants paid, $15,000; assets, $360,000 (M); expenditures, $19,907; qualifying distributions, $16,059.
Limitations: Giving primarily in PA.
Trustee: First Union National Bank.
EIN: 236523865
Codes: GTI

41607
Julia Ellen Crump Foundation, Inc.
P.O. Box 1990
Raleigh, NC 27602-1990

Established in 1999 in NC.
Financial data (yr. ended 12/31/01): Grants paid, $15,000; assets, $162,094 (M); gifts received, $87,333; expenditures, $15,147; qualifying distributions, $15,000.
Limitations: Applications not accepted. Giving primarily in Raleigh, NC.
Application information: Contributes only to pre-selected organizations.
Officers: Robert Daniel Boyce, Pres.; Laura Boyce Isley, Secy.-Treas.; Patricia A. Boyce, Treas.
Director: Gordon Eugene Boyce.
EIN: 562077857

41608
Harry J. and Mollie S. Dilcher Student Loan Fund
c/o First Union National Bank
401 S. Tryon St., 4th Fl.
Charlotte, NC 28288-1159

Established in 1990 in PA.
Financial data (yr. ended 12/31/01): Grants paid, $15,000; assets, $299,930 (M); expenditures, $16,478; qualifying distributions, $15,377.
Limitations: Applications not accepted. Giving limited to Allentown, PA.
Application information: Unsolicited requests for funds not considered or acknowledged.
Trustee: First Union National Bank.
EIN: 236955204
Codes: GTI

41609
Mount Olive Pickle Company Foundation
c/o Mount Olive Pickle Co., Inc.
812 N. Chestnut St.
Mount Olive, NC 28365

Established in 1994 in NC.
Donor(s): Mount Olive Pickle Co., Inc.
Financial data (yr. ended 04/30/02): Grants paid, $15,000; assets, $600,157 (M); gifts received, $2,488; expenditures, $17,488; qualifying distributions, $15,000.
Limitations: Applications not accepted. Giving primarily in Mount Olive and Wayne County, NC.
Application information: Contributes only to pre-selected organizations.
Officers and Directors:* William A. Potts,* Pres.; William H. Bryan,* V.P.; Larry Graham,* Secy.-Treas.
EIN: 561888088
Codes: CS, CD

41610
Nunnally Foundation
c/o Wachovia Bank, N.A.
P.O. Box 3099
Winston-Salem, NC 27150-1022
Application address: P.O. Box 12312, Richmond VA 23241
Contact: Wayne F. Oplinger, Trust Off., Wachovia Bank, N.A.

Financial data (yr. ended 06/30/01): Grants paid, $15,000; assets, $357,654 (M); expenditures, $16,810; qualifying distributions, $15,850.
Limitations: Giving primarily in the metropolitan Richmond, VA, area.
Trustees: Dianne N. Collins, F. Alton Garrett, Wayne F. Oplinger, Wachovia Bank, N.A.
EIN: 237083249

41611
Mary Goddard Pickens Foundation, Inc.
3004 Cool Spring Dr.
Chapel Hill, NC 27514

Established in 1996 in NC.
Donor(s): Peter M. Pickens.
Financial data (yr. ended 12/31/01): Grants paid, $15,000; assets, $412,467 (M); gifts received, $110,438; expenditures, $15,000; qualifying distributions, $15,000.
Limitations: Applications not accepted.
Application information: Contributes only to pre-selected organizations.
Officer and Director:* Peter M. Pickens,* Pres.
EIN: 562012519

41612
Larus Educational Trust
250 Tranquility Pl.
Hendersonville, NC 28739-8314
(828) 693-1984
Contact: Charles T. Larus, Tr.

Donor(s): Charles T. Larus, Mrs. Charles T. Larus.
Financial data (yr. ended 12/31/01): Grants paid, $14,937; assets, $253,521 (M); gifts received, $253,521; expenditures, $15,118; qualifying distributions, $15,004.
Limitations: Giving limited to residents of Henderson County, NC.
Application information: Application form required.
Trustees: Charles T. Larus, B.B. Massagee III.
EIN: 566324591
Codes: GTI

41613
The John H. Maxheim Foundation, Inc.
P.O. Box 33068
Charlotte, NC 28233-3068
Contact: John H. Maxheim, Pres.

Established in 1998 in NC.
Donor(s): John H. Maxheim.
Financial data (yr. ended 12/31/01): Grants paid, $14,900; assets, $272,887 (M); gifts received, $45,921; expenditures, $17,809; qualifying distributions, $14,900.
Officers: John H. Maxheim, Pres.; Ware Schiefer, V.P.; Ray Killough, Secy.
EIN: 562096475

41614
Murphy, Cox and Mills Foundation
7 Laurel Forest Dr.
Horse Shoe, NC 28742 (828) 891-9691

Established in 1998.
Donor(s): J. Mason Cox, Linda W. Cox.
Financial data (yr. ended 12/31/99): Grants paid, $14,884; assets, $420,504 (M); expenditures, $15,134; qualifying distributions, $14,884.
Limitations: Applications not accepted. Giving primarily in NC.
Application information: Contributes only to pre-selected organizations.
Trustee: J. Mason Cox.
EIN: 566529610

41615
Stella J. Stasiak Trust
c/o First Union National Bank
401 S. Tryon St.
Charlotte, NC 28288-1159

Financial data (yr. ended 12/31/01): Grants paid, $14,729; assets, $250,547 (M); gifts received, $135,513; expenditures, $16,508; qualifying distributions, $14,729.
Limitations: Applications not accepted.
Application information: Contributes only to pre-selected organizations.
Trustee: First Union National Bank.
EIN: 256730664

41616
Furniture Library Association
c/o Carl Vuncannon
1009 N. Main St.
High Point, NC 27262 (336) 883-4011

Established in 1983 as a private foundation.
Financial data (yr. ended 06/30/99): Grants paid, $14,500; assets, $4,594,541 (M); gifts received, $8,825; expenditures, $188,639; qualifying distributions, $138,476; giving activities include $76,232 for programs.
Limitations: Giving on a national basis.
Officers: J. Thomas Gooding, Pres. and Treas.; Benjamin G. Philpott, V.P.; L. Paul Brayton, V.P., Education; Richard Barentine, V.P., Facilities; Joseph T. Frye, V.P., Membership; Charles Sutton, V.P., Permanent Collections; Charles A. Greene, Secy.
Directors: Richard R. Bennington, Barton Blenenstock, Russell Blenenstock, and 33 additional directors.
EIN: 237249036

NORTH CAROLINA—41629

41617
William S. Little Scholarship Foundation
c/o First Union National Bank
401 S. Tyron St., Ste. NC1159
Charlotte, NC 28288-1159
Application address: c/o William S. Little, 206 Wind Hollow Ct., Mahwah, NJ 07430

Donor(s): William S. Little.
Financial data (yr. ended 07/31/01): Grants paid, $14,400; assets, $267,198 (M); expenditures, $17,359; qualifying distributions, $14,293.
Limitations: Giving limited to Ridgewood and Rutherford, NJ.
Application information: Application form required.
Trustee: First Union National Bank.
EIN: 237411024

41618
Robert R. & Carrie M. Machmer Charitable Trust
c/o First Union National Bank
401 S. Tryon St., NC1159
Charlotte, NC 28288-1159

Established in 1995 in PA.
Financial data (yr. ended 12/31/01): Grants paid, $14,295; assets, $335,917 (M); expenditures, $22,261; qualifying distributions, $15,553.
Limitations: Applications not accepted. Giving primarily in FL and PA.
Application information: Contributes only to pre-selected organizations.
Trustee: First Union National Bank.
EIN: 237838787

41619
Rixstine Charitable Trust
(Formerly Mary Amanda Hawke Rixstine Charitable Trust)
c/o First Union National Bank
401 S. Tryon St., 4th Fl.
Charlotte, NC 28288-1159
Application address: c/o First Union National Bank, Trust Dept., 123 S. Broad St., Philadelphia, PA 19109-9989

Donor(s): Mary Amanda Hawke Rixstine.‡
Financial data (yr. ended 12/31/01): Grants paid, $14,000; assets, $200,113 (M); expenditures, $16,048; qualifying distributions, $15,457.
Limitations: Giving limited to the Phoenixville, PA, area.
Application information: Application form not required.
Trustee: First Union National Bank.
EIN: 236242481

41620
The Steward Foundation
3620 Cape Center Dr.
Fayetteville, NC 28304
Contact: William T. Allen, Pres.

Established in 1997 in NC.
Financial data (yr. ended 12/31/01): Grants paid, $14,000; assets, $248,304 (M); expenditures, $14,000; qualifying distributions, $14,000.
Officer: William T. Allen, Pres.
EIN: 311511801

41621
Dunvegan Foundation of the Clan MacLeod Society, U.S.A., Inc.
c/o MacLeod Society USA, Inc.
P.O. Box 17303
Raleigh, NC 27619 (919) 782-7010
Contact: James Blount MacLeod, Treas.

Established in 1956 in NY.
Donor(s): MacLeod Stewardship Foundation.
Financial data (yr. ended 12/31/01): Grants paid, $13,940; assets, $455,449 (M); gifts received, $29,036; expenditures, $29,788; qualifying distributions, $13,940.
Limitations: Giving primarily in the United Kingdom.
Publications: Informational brochure.
Application information: Application form required.
Officers and Trustees:* William F. MacLeod, Chair.; Lt. Col. John B. MacLeod,* Vice-Chair.; Gloria McLeod,* Secy.; James Blount MacLeod,* Treas.; Olive Bell, Charlene J. Boyes, Coralane M. Boyes, Gordon A. Lewis, N. Donald B. MacLeod, N. Douglas MacLeod, Jr., Roderick K. MacLeod, James S. McLeod, Katherine McLeod, Sarah Piepgrass, Larry R. Sears, Jack McLeod Stephens.
EIN: 136161583

41622
Charles F. Stevens Trust
c/o First Union National Bank
401 S. Tryon St., NC1159
Charlotte, NC 28288-1159

Financial data (yr. ended 12/31/01): Grants paid, $13,928; assets, $573,235 (M); expenditures, $19,175; qualifying distributions, $13,928.
Limitations: Applications not accepted.
Application information: Contributes only to pre-selected organizations.
Trustee: First Union National Bank.
EIN: 226279016

41623
Florence W. & Albert J. Jacobson Family Foundation
1002 Dover Rd.
Greensboro, NC 27408-7312

Established in 1998 in NC.
Donor(s): Albert J. Jacobson, Beryl M. Zander.
Financial data (yr. ended 12/31/00): Grants paid, $13,856; assets, $131,553 (M); gifts received, $52,415; expenditures, $14,147; qualifying distributions, $13,856.
Limitations: Applications not accepted.
Application information: Contributes only to pre-selected organizations.
Trustees: Albert J. Jacobson, Michael Jacobson, Steven Jacobson, Beryl Zander.
EIN: 526936436

41624
Buehler Memorial Trust
(Formerly Buehler Memorial Fund)
c/o First Union National Bank
401 S. Tryon St., NC1159
Charlotte, NC 28288-1159

Established in 2000 in PA.
Financial data (yr. ended 04/30/02): Grants paid, $13,814; assets, $269,884 (M); expenditures, $25,567; qualifying distributions, $13,814.
Limitations: Applications not accepted. Giving primarily in Allentown, PA.
Application information: Contributes only to pre-selected organizations.
Trustee: First Union National Bank.
EIN: 236442917

41625
The Strickland Family Foundation
777 Three Wood Dr.
Fayetteville, NC 28301-8721
Contact: Joseph Strickland, Pres.

Established in 1995 in NC.
Donor(s): Joseph Strickland.
Financial data (yr. ended 12/31/01): Grants paid, $13,800; assets, $509,680 (M); gifts received, $15,000; expenditures, $24,196; qualifying distributions, $13,800.
Application information: Application form not required.
Officer: Joseph Strickland, Pres.
EIN: 561951984

41626
William Cullen Colburn Memorial Fund
c/o First Union National Bank
401 S. Tryon St., NC1159
Charlotte, NC 28288-1159
Application address: P.O. Box 2450, Asheville, NC 28802

Financial data (yr. ended 12/31/01): Grants paid, $13,750; assets, $441,433 (M); expenditures, $18,193; qualifying distributions, $14,500.
Limitations: Giving limited to residents of Buncombe County, NC.
Application information: Application form required.
Trustee: First Union National Bank.
EIN: 566049108
Codes: GTI

41627
Joan & Robert Huntley Charitable Foundation
P.O. Box 190
Chapel Hill, NC 27514

Established in 1997 in MA.
Donor(s): Angel M. Garcia, Joan Huntley, Robert Huntley.
Financial data (yr. ended 12/31/01): Grants paid, $13,750; assets, $321,319 (M); expenditures, $18,183; qualifying distributions, $13,750.
Limitations: Applications not accepted.
Application information: Contributes only to pre-selected organizations.
Trustees: Angel M. Garcia, Joan Huntley, Robert Huntley.
EIN: 311556907

41628
Katherine Ann Greene Foundation
216 Fairway Ln.
Wilkesboro, NC 28697-8543

Donor(s): Edward F. Greene.
Financial data (yr. ended 06/30/01): Grants paid, $13,700; assets, $269,057 (M); gifts received, $11,000; expenditures, $26,723; qualifying distributions, $13,700.
Limitations: Applications not accepted. Giving primarily in Wilkesboro, NC.
Application information: Contributes only to pre-selected organizations.
Directors: Edward F. Greene, Frances C. Greene, Richard E. Greene, Stephen P. Greene.
EIN: 581450129

41629
Lerner Family Foundation, Inc.
945 Confederate Ave.
Salisbury, NC 28144

Established in 1990 in NC.
Donor(s): Bernice L. Lerner, Morton S. Lerner.
Financial data (yr. ended 09/30/01): Grants paid, $13,585; assets, $12,460 (M); expenditures, $13,811; qualifying distributions, $13,585.
Limitations: Applications not accepted. Giving primarily in New York, NY.
Application information: Contributes only to pre-selected organizations.
Officer and Directors:* Bernice L. Lerner,* Pres., V.P., and Secy.-Treas.; Dena P. Lerner, Mark H. Lerner, Richard I. Lerner.

41629—NORTH CAROLINA

EIN: 561720870

41630
Frances Galey Foundation
c/o F. Michael Persson
2208 Black Walnut Ct.
Raleigh, NC 27606-9014 (919) 821-7022
Contact: Mary E. Persson, Secy.

Established in 1997 in NC.
Donor(s): F. Michael Persson.
Financial data (yr. ended 12/31/99): Grants paid, $13,500; assets, $279,072 (M); expenditures, $13,500; qualifying distributions, $13,500.
Limitations: Giving primarily in GA, MO, and NC.
Application information: Application form required.
Officer and Trustees:* Mary E. Persson,* Secy.; F. Michael Persson.
EIN: 364263661

41631
Robert B. Taylor III Foundation
P.O. Box 9694
Greensboro, NC 27429-0694

Established in 1997 in NC.
Donor(s): Robert B. Taylor, Jr.
Financial data (yr. ended 12/31/01): Grants paid, $13,400; assets, $246,209 (M); gifts received, $900; expenditures, $13,871; qualifying distributions, $13,400.
Officers: Robert B. Taylor, Jr., Pres.; David D. Taylor, V.P.; Joseph W. Taylor, V.P.; Rebecca W. Taylor, Secy.
EIN: 562075719

41632
Fitzgerald Family Foundation, Inc.
1612 Jarvis St.
Raleigh, NC 27608-2213

Donor(s): F. Owen Fitzgerald, Mary O. Fitzgerald.
Financial data (yr. ended 12/31/01): Grants paid, $13,384; assets, $398,268 (M); expenditures, $13,901; qualifying distributions, $13,455.
Limitations: Applications not accepted. Giving primarily in NC.
Application information: Contributes only to pre-selected organizations.
Officers: F. Owen Fitzgerald, Pres.; Anne T. Fitzgerald, V.P.; Frank O. Fitzgerald, V.P.; Mary O. Fitzgerald, Secy.-Treas.
EIN: 561844444

41633
Thomas C. Meredith, Jr. Foundation
c/o Wachovia Bank, N.A.
P.O. Box 3099
Winston-Salem, NC 27150-7153
Application address: c/o Sandra Lee, Dir., Thomas C. Meredith, Jr. Scholarship Program, P.O. Box 1465, Taylors, SC 29687, tel.: (803) 268-3363

Established in 1994 in SC.
Financial data (yr. ended 12/31/01): Grants paid, $13,360; assets, $109,657 (M); expenditures, $14,959; qualifying distributions, $13,360.
Application information: Application form required.
Committee: Judy M. Bessinger, Steven E. Holtschlag, Louise Rogers Slater.
Trustee: Wachovia Bank, N.A.
EIN: 566455071

41634
The Lowrance Family Foundation
1410 Scotland Ave.
Charlotte, NC 28207

Established in 1999 in NC.
Donor(s): Sallie Lowrance, Fred Lowrance.
Financial data (yr. ended 12/31/01): Grants paid, $13,335; assets, $193,009 (M); expenditures, $17,080; qualifying distributions, $13,335.
Limitations: Applications not accepted.
Application information: Contributes only to pre-selected organizations.
Officers: Sallie Lowrance, Pres.; Fred Lowrance, Jr., V.P.; Sallie P. Lowrance, V.P.; Shannon Lowrance, V.P.; Fred Lowrance, Secy.-Treas.
EIN: 562169197

41635
The Ingrid Reynolds Avera Charitable Trust
c/o Wachovia Bank of North Carolina, N.A.
P.O. Box 3099
Winston-Salem, NC 27150-7153

Established in 1995 in NC.
Financial data (yr. ended 12/31/01): Grants paid, $13,228; assets, $122,407 (M); expenditures, $17,066; qualifying distributions, $15,202.
Limitations: Applications not accepted.
Application information: Contributes only to pre-selected organizations.
Trustee: Wachovia Bank of North Carolina, N.A.
EIN: 582241034

41636
R. L. Davis Charitable Trust Fund, Inc.
P.O. Box 806
Farmville, NC 27828-0112
Application address: 112 W. Wilson St., Ste. 170, Farmville, NC 27828, tel.: (252) 753-4520
Contact: Cedric Davis, Secy.

Donor(s): R.L. Davis.‡
Financial data (yr. ended 10/31/01): Grants paid, $13,200; assets, $684,062 (M); expenditures, $30,904; qualifying distributions, $30,341.
Limitations: Giving limited to the Farmville, NC, area.
Application information: Application form not required.
Officer: Cedric Davis, Secy.
EIN: 566045863
Codes: GTI

41637
The Nancy and Udean Burke Foundation, Inc.
P.O. Box 880
Newton, NC 28658-0880
Application address: 4643 Hwy. 16 S., Maiden, NC 28650
Contact: Udean Burke, Pres.

Established in 1995 in NC.
Donor(s): Nancy Burke, Udean Burke.
Financial data (yr. ended 12/31/01): Grants paid, $13,000; assets, $227,260 (M); gifts received, $50; expenditures, $15,251; qualifying distributions, $13,000.
Limitations: Giving primarily in NC.
Officers: Udean Burke, Pres.; Nancy Burke, Secy.-Treas.
Directors: Aaron Burke, Tim Burke, Heather Owenby, Mellanee Owenby.
EIN: 561914059

41638
Sophie Einstein Loan Fund
c/o Wachovia Bank, N.A.
P.O. Box 3099
Winston-Salem, NC 27150-6732
Application address: 227 N. Tryon St., Charlotte, NC 28202
Contact: Irving Brenner, Chair.

Financial data (yr. ended 12/31/01): Grants paid, $13,000; assets, $225,531 (M); expenditures, $17,661; qualifying distributions, $17,000.
Limitations: Giving limited to NC.
Application information: Application form required.
Trustees: Irving Brenner, Chair.; Wachovia Bank, N.A.
EIN: 566036006

41639
Moore & Van Allen Foundation, Inc.
100 N. Tryon St., Fl. 47
Charlotte, NC 28202-4000

Established in 1991 in NC.
Donor(s): Moore & Van Allen.
Financial data (yr. ended 12/31/00): Grants paid, $12,904; assets, $1,211 (M); gifts received, $14,764; expenditures, $16,180; qualifying distributions, $16,180.
Limitations: Applications not accepted. Giving primarily in Raleigh, NC.
Application information: Contributes only to pre-selected organizations.
Officer and Directors:* W.B. Hawfield, Jr.,* Chair. and Pres.; James W. Hovis, Reich L. Welborn.
EIN: 581940952
Codes: CS, CD

41640
Lawrence and Sandra Davis Family Foundation
c/o Lawrence E. Davis, III
2628 Tatton Dr.
Raleigh, NC 27608-2053 (919) 834-8496

Established in 1998 in NC.
Donor(s): Egbert L. Davis, Jr. Charitable Lead Trust.
Financial data (yr. ended 12/31/01): Grants paid, $12,900; assets, $381 (M); gifts received, $10,746; expenditures, $13,170; qualifying distributions, $12,900.
Limitations: Giving primarily in NC.
Officers: Lawrence Davis, Pres.; Sandra Davis, V.P.; Alexandra Davis Hipps, Secy.; Egbert L. Davis, Treas.
EIN: 562075692

41641
Clodfelter Family Foundation
3620 Cape Center Dr.
Fayetteville, NC 28304-4405
Contact: William Temple Allen

Established in 1996.
Donor(s): Dean Clodfelter.
Financial data (yr. ended 12/31/00): Grants paid, $12,810; assets, $36,507 (M); expenditures, $22,850; qualifying distributions, $12,809.
Officers: Dean Clodfelter, Pres. and Treas.; Sue Clodfelter, V.P. and Secy.
EIN: 561949761

41642
Doris Whisnant Memorial Foundation, Inc.
P.O. Box 15
Hickory, NC 28603
Contact: Alfred N. Whisnant, Dir.

Financial data (yr. ended 06/30/01): Grants paid, $12,700; assets, $237,997 (M); expenditures, $13,671; qualifying distributions, $13,380.
Limitations: Giving primarily in NC.
Application information: Application form required.
Directors: Alfred N. Whisnant, Betty J. Whisnant.
EIN: 237318076
Codes: GTI

NORTH CAROLINA—41656

41643
Dwight H. Harrelson Memorial Scholarship Trust
c/o Bank of America
P.O. Box 1091
Charlotte, NC 28255   (704) 388-3150

Financial data (yr. ended 12/31/01): Grants paid, $12,650; assets, $288,494 (M); expenditures, $15,722; qualifying distributions, $13,907.
Limitations: Giving limited to Lincolnton, NC.
Application information: Application form not required.
Trustee: Bank of America.
EIN: 237159114
Codes: GTI

41644
Warshauer Charitable Trust
2917 Hydrangea Pl.
Wilmington, NC 28403-4015

Established in 1997 in NC.
Donor(s): Samuel E. Warshauer, Miriam Warshauer.
Financial data (yr. ended 12/31/01): Grants paid, $12,635; assets, $30,536 (M); gifts received, $3,243; expenditures, $12,758; qualifying distributions, $12,635.
Limitations: Applications not accepted.
Application information: Contributes only to pre-selected organizations.
Trustees: Maxine Warshauer, Miriam Warshauer.
EIN: 566488709

41645
Leonard Carlton Peckitt Scholarship
c/o First Union National Bank
401 S. Tryon St., NC1159
Charlotte, NC 28288-1159

Donor(s): CoreStates Bank, N.A.
Financial data (yr. ended 12/31/01): Grants paid, $12,600; assets, $290,755 (M); expenditures, $13,894; qualifying distributions, $13,200.
Limitations: Applications not accepted. Giving limited to Catasauqua, PA.
Trustee: First Union National Bank.
EIN: 236611993
Codes: GTI

41646
Jordan Family Foundation
1701 W. Ehringhaus St.
Elizabeth City, NC 27909-4553
Application address: 98 Small Dr., Elizabeth City, NC 27909
Contact: Robert C. Jordan, Pres.

Established in 1991 in NC.
Donor(s): Earldine Jordan.
Financial data (yr. ended 06/30/01): Grants paid, $12,500; assets, $160,288 (M); gifts received, $15,000; expenditures, $13,651; qualifying distributions, $12,500.
Limitations: Giving primarily in NC.
Officers: Robert C. Jordan, Pres.; Earldine D. Jordan, Secy.; Louise P. Jordan, Treas.
EIN: 581959119

41647
Reemprise Fund
c/o U.S. Trust
P.O. Box 26262
Greensboro, NC 27420

Established in 1999 in NC.
Donor(s): Robert E. Elberson.
Financial data (yr. ended 12/31/01): Grants paid, $12,500; assets, $214,413 (M); expenditures, $13,352; qualifying distributions, $12,500.

Limitations: Applications not accepted.
Application information: Contributes only to pre-selected organization.
Director: Robert E. Elberson.
EIN: 562175220

41648
James and Adele Bedrick Foundation
c/o James and Adele Bedrick
2025 Delpond Ln.
Charlotte, NC 28226

Established in 1986 in NC.
Donor(s): James Bedrick, Adele Bedrick.
Financial data (yr. ended 12/31/01): Grants paid, $12,474; assets, $26,796 (M); expenditures, $13,791; qualifying distributions, $12,474.
Limitations: Applications not accepted. Giving primarily in Charlotte, NC.
Application information: Contributes only to pre-selected organizations.
Directors: Adele Bedrick, James Bedrick.
EIN: 566293862

41649
The Jerry R. Licari Foundation
8204 Bar Harbor Ln.
Charlotte, NC 28210   (704) 335-5311
Contact: Jerry R. Licari, Pres.

Established in 1998 in NC.
Donor(s): Jerry R. Licari.
Financial data (yr. ended 12/31/01): Grants paid, $12,150; assets, $594,338 (M); gifts received, $160,220; expenditures, $12,215; qualifying distributions, $12,150.
Officers: Jerry R. Licari, Pres.; Mark S. Licari, V.P.; Teresa M. Licari, Secy.; Brian T. Licari, Treas.
Director: Gina M. Licari.
EIN: 562145169

41650
The Harold H. Bate Foundation, Inc.
3405 Trent Rd.
New Bern, NC 28562   (252) 638-1998

Financial data (yr. ended 12/31/00): Grants paid, $12,000; assets, $35,109,400 (M); gifts received, $34,630,958; expenditures, $21,146; qualifying distributions, $19,584.
Limitations: Giving limited to NC.
Officers: Silas B. Seymour, Pres.; Donald K. Brinkley, V.P.; Berleen B. Burnette, Secy.; Gary H. Baldree, Sr., Treas.; Dennis W. Ball, Exec. Dir.
Directors: James L. Lanier, Robert L. Mattocks II, Marvin B. Mullinix.
EIN: 562121302

41651
The Robert E. Mason Foundation
1550 Queens Rd.
Charlotte, NC 28207   (704) 376-1722
Contact: Robert E. Mason III, Dir.

Established in 2000 in NC.
Donor(s): Robert E. Mason, III.
Financial data (yr. ended 12/31/01): Grants paid, $12,000; assets, $258,753 (M); gifts received, $15,627; expenditures, $22,345; qualifying distributions, $12,000.
Application information: Application form not required.
Directors: Esten B. Mason, Robert E. Mason, III.
EIN: 311737728

41652
Ralph Larosh Trust
c/o First Union National Bank
401 S. Tryon St., NC 1159
Charlotte, NC 28288-1159

Established in 1993 in PA.

Financial data (yr. ended 08/31/01): Grants paid, $11,778; assets, $564,898 (M); expenditures, $14,975; qualifying distributions, $11,778.
Limitations: Applications not accepted.
Application information: Contributes only to pre-selected organizations.
Trustee: First Union National Bank.
EIN: 236681110

41653
The C. Munroe Best, Jr. Foundation
c/o Jack Best
809 Mill Rd.
Goldsboro, NC 27534

Established in 1995 in NC.
Donor(s): C. Munroe Best, Jr.
Financial data (yr. ended 12/31/01): Grants paid, $11,550; assets, $16,567 (M); expenditures, $11,883; qualifying distributions, $11,550.
Limitations: Applications not accepted. Giving primarily in NC.
Application information: Contributes only to pre-selected organizations.
Officers: C. Munroe Best, Jr., Pres.; C. Munroe Best III, Treas.
EIN: 561949712

41654
Kimberly S. Bates Foundation
P.O. Box 19608
Greensboro, NC 27419-9608   (336) 299-2752

Established in 1987 in NC.
Donor(s): Louis Bates.
Financial data (yr. ended 12/31/01): Grants paid, $11,529; assets, $278,923 (M); expenditures, $11,693; qualifying distributions, $11,529.
Limitations: Applications not accepted. Giving primarily in Greensboro, NC.
Application information: Contributes only to pre-selected organizations.
Officers: Louis Bates, Pres.; Joan W. Bates, V.P.; Laurence A. Bates, Secy.
EIN: 581745901

41655
Good Shepherd Foundation, Inc.
6244 Hwy. 55 W.
Kinston, NC 28504-7435   (252) 569-3241
Contact: Sue White, Secy.-Treas.

Donor(s): The Good Shepherd Foundation Trust.
Financial data (yr. ended 11/30/01): Grants paid, $11,500; assets, $11,356 (M); gifts received, $10,000; expenditures, $13,700; qualifying distributions, $13,509.
Limitations: Giving primarily in Kinston, NC.
Application information: Application form required.
Officers: Wiley Jones, Jr., Pres.; Marietta Elmore, V.P.; Sue White, Secy.-Treas.
EIN: 510175676
Codes: GTI

41656
Dale & Gwen Orred Family Foundation, Inc.
c/o Wachovia Bank, N.A.
P.O. Box 3099
Winston-Salem, NC 27150-7131

Established in 2000 in GA.
Donor(s): Dale Orred, Gwen Orred.
Financial data (yr. ended 12/31/01): Grants paid, $11,500; assets, $262,313 (M); gifts received, $1,193; expenditures, $15,724; qualifying distributions, $11,500.
Limitations: Applications not accepted.
Application information: Contributes only to pre-selected organizations.

41656—NORTH CAROLINA

Trustees: Dale Orred, Gwen Orred, Wachovia Bank, N.A.
EIN: 566577919

41657
The Rauch Rainoff Foundation, Inc.
P.O. Box 1970
Southern Pines, NC 28388-1970

Financial data (yr. ended 12/31/01): Grants paid, $11,400; assets, $189,899 (M); expenditures, $11,865; qualifying distributions, $11,400.
Limitations: Applications not accepted.
Application information: Contributes only to pre-selected organizations.
Officers: Elizabeth Ferris Rainoff, Pres.; George R. Rainoff, V.P.; John H. Ferris, Secy.-Treas.
EIN: 561842949

41658
R. M. & Hattie L. Waldroup Educational Fund
c/o Wachovia Bank, N.A.
P.O. Box 3099
Winston-Salem, NC 27150-7153

Established in 1958 in NC.
Financial data (yr. ended 12/31/99): Grants paid, $11,385; assets, $307,947 (M); expenditures, $14,259; qualifying distributions, $12,114.
Limitations: Applications not accepted. Giving primarily in Brevard, NC.
Trustee: Wachovia Bank, N.A.
Scholarship Committee: Rev. James Armstrong, Rev. Chris Thore.
EIN: 566035401

41659
W. C., Jr. & K. M. Cullen Trust
c/o First Union National Bank
401 S. Tryon St., 4th Fl.
Charlotte, NC 28288-1159

Established in 2001 in VA.
Donor(s): Calvert Cullen.‡
Financial data (yr. ended 12/31/01): Grants paid, $11,200; assets, $394,767 (L); gifts received, $400,000; expenditures, $17,296; qualifying distributions, $13,130.
Limitations: Applications not accepted. Giving primarily in VA.
Application information: Contributes only to pre-selected organizations.
Trustee: First Union National Bank.
EIN: 586432618

41660
Dewey C. Duncan Trust
c/o First Union National Bank
401 S. Tryon St., NC1159
Charlotte, NC 28288-1159

Established in 1990 in VA.
Donor(s): Anne Duncan.‡
Financial data (yr. ended 12/31/01): Grants paid, $11,127; assets, $315,172 (M); expenditures, $16,347; qualifying distributions, $11,327.
Limitations: Giving limited to Grundy and Pulaski, VA.
Application information: Unsolicited requests for funds not accepted.
Trustee: First Union National Bank.
EIN: 546066637
Codes: GTI

41661
Whipple Marlboro Foundation
c/o Wachovia Bank, N.A.
P.O. Box 3099
Winston-Salem, NC 27150-7153
Application address: 1426 Main St., Columbia, SC 29226, tel.: (803) 765-3671
Contact: C. Gerald Lane

Financial data (yr. ended 06/30/01): Grants paid, $11,000; assets, $206,365 (M); gifts received, $6,000; expenditures, $15,945; qualifying distributions, $12,184.
Limitations: Giving limited to Marlboro County, SC.
Distribution Committee: Harry R. Easterling, Tracy Kea, Jr., W.L. Kinney, Jr., D.H. McQuade, J.W. Walker, Jr.
Trustee: Wachovia Bank, N.A.
EIN: 576054865

41662
Norman B. & Gabriella W. Smith Charitable Trust
3502 Madison Ave.
Greensboro, NC 27403-1030

Financial data (yr. ended 12/31/01): Grants paid, $10,950; assets, $41,055 (M); gifts received, $6,000; expenditures, $10,959; qualifying distributions, $10,950.
Limitations: Applications not accepted.
Application information: Contributes only to pre-selected organizations.
Trustees: Gabriella W. Smith, Norman B. Smith.
EIN: 566472170

41663
Ballard Family Foundation
4506 Monck Ct.
New Bern, NC 28562
Contact: Harry Ballard, Pres.

Donor(s): Harry Ballard, Dolly Ballard.
Financial data (yr. ended 12/31/01): Grants paid, $10,931; assets, $237,797 (M); expenditures, $18,150; qualifying distributions, $10,931.
Limitations: Giving primarily in NC.
Officers: Harry Ballard, Pres. and Treas.; Dolly Ballard, Secy.
EIN: 562025731

41664
Unifour Foundation, Inc.
P.O. Box 1727
Hickory, NC 28603-1727 (704) 328-2323
Contact: Betty Allen, Exec. Dir.

Established in 1997 in NC.
Financial data (yr. ended 08/31/01): Grants paid, $10,799; assets, $220,316 (M); expenditures, $13,001; qualifying distributions, $10,799.
Limitations: Giving primarily in Alexander, Burke, Caldwell, and Catawba counties, NC.
Application information: Application form required.
Officers: Hal Huffman, Pres.; Nancy Fritz, V.P.; Clinton Annas, Secy.; Charles Snipes, Treas.; Betty Allen, Exec. Dir.
Trustees: Kathy Greathouse, Paul Kercher.
EIN: 561992426

41665
John F. McNair Memorial Fund Trust
c/o Wachovia Bank, N.A.
100 N. Main St.
Winston-Salem, NC 27150
Application address: c/o Scholarship Coordinator, Scotland High School, 1000 W. Church St., Laurinburg, NC 28352, tel.: (919) 276-7370

Financial data (yr. ended 12/31/01): Grants paid, $10,650; assets, $163,974 (M); expenditures, $11,456; qualifying distributions, $10,761.
Limitations: Giving limited to residents of Laurinburg, NC.
Application information: Application form required.
Trustee: Wachovia Bank, N.A.
EIN: 566035967

41666
Diamond Trust
310 Earlwood Rd.
Statesville, NC 28677-5412

Financial data (yr. ended 11/30/01): Grants paid, $10,645; assets, $285,472 (M); expenditures, $11,598; qualifying distributions, $10,645.
Limitations: Applications not accepted.
Application information: Contributes only to pre-selected organizations.
Trustees: Anne R. Scott, G. Rhyne Scott, Gordon P. Scott, Jr.
EIN: 566056460

41667
Robert L. Jones Charitable Foundation
P.O. Box 19067
Raleigh, NC 27619-9067

Established in 1999 in NC.
Donor(s): Robert L. Jones.
Financial data (yr. ended 12/31/01): Grants paid, $10,600; assets, $165,436 (M); gifts received, $105,000; expenditures, $10,735; qualifying distributions, $10,600.
Limitations: Applications not accepted.
Application information: Contributes only to pre-selected organizations.
Officers: Robert L. Jones, C.E.O. and Pres.; Seby R. Jones, Secy.
EIN: 562172548

41668
The Eugene S. and Gail M. LeBauer Family Foundation, Inc.
104 Kemp Rd. W.
Greensboro, NC 27410

Established in 1999 in NC.
Donor(s): Eugene S. LeBauer.
Financial data (yr. ended 12/31/01): Grants paid, $10,600; assets, $34,795 (M); expenditures, $10,750; qualifying distributions, $10,600.
Limitations: Applications not accepted. Giving primarily in Greensboro, NC.
Application information: Contributes only to pre-selected organizations.
Officers and Trustees:* Eugene S. LeBauer,* Pres. and Treas.; Gail M. LeBauer,* Exec. V.P. and Secy.; Courtney E. LeBauer,* V.P.; Michael J. LeBauer,* V.P.; Scott A. LeBauer,* V.P.
EIN: 562169160

41669
Christine B. Stevenson Charitable Trust
c/o Wachovia Bank, N.A.
P.O. Box 3099
Winston-Salem, NC 27150-7153
Application address: c/o Wachovia Bank, N.A., 1401 Main St., Columbia, SC 29226, tel.: (803) 765-3671
Contact: C. Gerald Lane, Trust Off., Wachovia Bank, N.A.

Established in 1997 in SC.
Financial data (yr. ended 01/31/02): Grants paid, $10,600; assets, $159,060 (M); expenditures, $16,856; qualifying distributions, $10,600.
Trustee: Wachovia Bank, N.A.
EIN: 586358120

41670
McCutchen Family Foundation
c/o Wachovia Bank, N.A.
P.O. Box 3099
Winston-Salem, NC 27150-7153
Application address: 1401 Main St., Columbia, SC, tel.: (803) 765-3671
Contact: C. Gerald Lane, Trust Off., Wachovia Bank, N.A.

Established in 1993 in SC.
Financial data (yr. ended 12/31/00): Grants paid, $10,586; assets, $107,715 (M); expenditures, $11,906; qualifying distributions, $10,586.
Trustee: Wachovia Bank, N.A.
EIN: 582118744

41671
Mary Grey Burney Estate Trust
c/o B.B. & T., Trust Tax Dept.
P.O. Box 2907
Wilson, NC 27894-2907
Application address: Susan McKeithan, Trust Off., c/o B.B. & T., Trust Tax Dept., 115 N. 3rd St., Wilmington, NC 28401, tel.: (910) 815-2803

Financial data (yr. ended 12/31/01): Grants paid, $10,500; assets, $212,751 (M); expenditures, $13,706; qualifying distributions, $10,325.
Limitations: Applications not accepted. Giving primarily in NC.
Application information: Contributes only to pre-selected organizations.
Trustee: B.B. & T.
EIN: 566074098

41672
The Clark-Foute Foundation
(Formerly The Clark-Foute Trust)
c/o Wachovia Bank, N.A.
P.O. Box 3099
Winston-Salem, NC 27150-6732

Established in 1997 in GA.
Financial data (yr. ended 12/31/01): Grants paid, $10,500; assets, $199,029 (M); expenditures, $13,200; qualifying distributions, $11,222.
Limitations: Applications not accepted.
Application information: Contributes only to pre-selected organizations.
Trustee: Wachovia Bank of North Carolina, N.A.
EIN: 586335618

41673
The Clark-Foute Trust
c/o Wachovia Bank, N.A.
P.O. Box 3099, NC6732
Winston-Salem, NC 27150-6732

Financial data (yr. ended 12/31/01): Grants paid, $10,500; assets, $199,029 (M); expenditures, $13,200; qualifying distributions, $11,222.

Limitations: Applications not accepted. Giving primarily in GA.
Application information: Contributes only to pre-selected organizations.
Trustee: Benjamin C. Clark, Ph.D.
EIN: 586351800

41674
Drs. Henley & Smith Memorial Fund
c/o First Union National Bank
401 S. Tryon St., NC1159
Charlotte, NC 28288-1159

Established in 1984 in DC.
Financial data (yr. ended 12/31/00): Grants paid, $10,500; assets, $183,036 (M); expenditures, $14,167; qualifying distributions, $11,175.
Limitations: Giving limited to Washington, DC.
Application information: Scholarship recipients are recommended by the College of Medicine at Howard University.
Trustee: First Union National Bank.
EIN: 526061059

41675
The Jane R. McBryde Family Charitable Trust
2216 Selwyn Ave.
Charlotte, NC 28207

Established in 1998.
Donor(s): Jane R. McBryde.
Financial data (yr. ended 12/31/01): Grants paid, $10,500; assets, $108,167 (M); gifts received, $55,621; expenditures, $12,442; qualifying distributions, $10,500.
Limitations: Applications not accepted.
Application information: Contributes only to pre-selected organizations.
Trustees: Angus Murdoch McBryde III, Jane Holland McBryde, Jane R. McBryde, John Peter Rostan McBryde, Mary Gregory McBryde.
EIN: 566533822

41676
The Hall Foundation, Inc.
5618 Camilla Dr.
Charlotte, NC 28226 (704) 362-1939
Contact: Kenneth E. Hall, Pres.

Donor(s): Hall Contracting Corporation.
Financial data (yr. ended 11/30/01): Grants paid, $10,460; assets, $212,423 (M); gifts received, $37,500; expenditures, $12,296; qualifying distributions, $10,485.
Limitations: Giving primarily in KY.
Officers and Trustee:* Kenneth E. Hall, Pres.; Irene S. Hall, V.P.; K. Michael Hall,* Secy.; Patricia H. Burd, Treas.
EIN: 610996178
Codes: CS, CD

41677
Ernest E. Mahoney Hospital Trust
(Formerly Ernest E. Mahoney Trust)
c/o First Union National Bank
401 S. Tryon St., NC1159
Charlotte, NC 28288-1159
Application address: c/o Waldo County Hospital, Camden, ME 04915

Established in 1988 in FL.
Financial data (yr. ended 12/31/01): Grants paid, $10,409; assets, $80,637 (M); expenditures, $13,258; qualifying distributions, $10,401.
Limitations: Giving limited to the residents of the Lincolnville, ME, area.
Trustee: First Union National Bank.
EIN: 596811062

41678
Dickinson-Kline Trust
401 S. Tryon St., 4th Fl.
Charlotte, NC 28288-1159

Financial data (yr. ended 12/31/01): Grants paid, $10,240; assets, $68,241 (M); expenditures, $10,951; qualifying distributions, $10,523.
Limitations: Applications not accepted. Giving primarily in Carlisle, PA.
Application information: Contributes only to pre-selected organizations.
Trustee: First Union National Bank.
EIN: 232072607

41679
Samet Foundation
c/o Norman G. Samet
P.O. Box 8050
Greensboro, NC 27419

Established in 1992 in NC.
Donor(s): Norman G. Samet, Sylvia L. Samet.
Financial data (yr. ended 12/31/01): Grants paid, $10,202; assets, $285,703 (M); expenditures, $13,654; qualifying distributions, $10,202.
Limitations: Applications not accepted. Giving limited to Greensboro, NC.
Application information: Contributes only to pre-selected organizations.
Officers: Norman G. Samet, Pres. and Treas.; Sylvia L. Samet, Secy.
EIN: 582010052

41680
Sherwood Anderson Foundation
202 Avonwood Dr.
Jamestown, NC 27282-9318 (336) 294-2014
Contact: Karlyn Shankland, Dir.

Financial data (yr. ended 12/31/00): Grants paid, $10,200; assets, $370,456 (M); expenditures, $12,908; qualifying distributions, $10,200.
Directors: Elizabeth Anderson, John Anderson, Hilbert Campbell, Martha Copenhaver, Don Francis, Charles Modlin, Karlyn Shankland, Margo Shankland, Paul Shankland, Michael M. Spear, Susie Spear, Margaret Stuart, Anna Spear Sturm, W. D. Taylor, Kenny Williams.
EIN: 581717970

41681
Murray Foundation, Inc.
161 Bermuda Run Dr.
Advance, NC 27006

Donor(s): M.H. Murray.
Financial data (yr. ended 12/31/99): Grants paid, $10,200; assets, $132,060 (M); expenditures, $10,464; qualifying distributions, $10,200.
Limitations: Applications not accepted.
Application information: Contributes only to pre-selected organizations.
Officer and Directors:* M.H. Murray,* Pres.; Chiquita M. Gughemli.
EIN: 237001826

41682
Carrie M. Rothenberger Trust
c/o First Union National Bank
401 S. Tryon St., NC1159
Charlotte, NC 28288

Financial data (yr. ended 12/31/01): Grants paid, $10,184; assets, $389,218 (M); expenditures, $21,063; qualifying distributions, $12,644.
Limitations: Applications not accepted. Giving primarily in Reading, PA.
Application information: Contributes only to pre-selected organizations.
Trustee: First Union National Bank.

41682—NORTH CAROLINA

EIN: 256643488

41683
James E. Harris, Jr. Charitable Foundation
P.O. Box 11408
Charlotte, NC 28220-1408

Established in 1989.
Donor(s): James E. Harris, Jr.
Financial data (yr. ended 12/31/01): Grants paid, $10,154; assets, $375,046 (M); expenditures, $15,829; qualifying distributions, $10,154.
Limitations: Applications not accepted. Giving primarily in NC.
Application information: Contributes only to pre-selected organizations.
Directors: Georgia K. Harris, James E. Harris, Jr., James E. Harris III, Jocelyn E. Harris, Dennis L. Thompson.
EIN: 581821215

41684
Carrie & Luther Huffines Educational Fund
c/o Centura Bank
P.O. Box 1220
Rocky Mount, NC 27802-1220
Contact: Sharon Stephens, Trust Off., Centura Bank

Established in 1955 in NC.
Donor(s): Robert L. Huffines, Jr.
Financial data (yr. ended 06/30/01): Grants paid, $10,050; assets, $110,398 (M); expenditures, $13,189; qualifying distributions, $10,761.
Limitations: Giving limited to Edgecombe and Nash counties, NC.
Application information: Application form required.
Trustee: Centura Bank.
EIN: 566046187

41685
Bill Beck Memorial Foundation
c/o Phyllis Nance
5141 E. Independence Blvd.
Charlotte, NC 28212 (704) 535-6400

Established in NC in 1996.
Donor(s): Patricia Q. Beck.
Financial data (yr. ended 12/31/00): Grants paid, $10,000; assets, $75,140 (M); gifts received, $2,068; expenditures, $10,018; qualifying distributions, $9,997.
Trustees: Patricia Q. Beck, Charles V. Ricks.
EIN: 562005985

41686
Castelloe Family Foundation, Inc.
3950 Blue Ridge Rd.
Raleigh, NC 27612 (919) 571-8863
Contact: Paul E. Castelloe, Pres.

Established in 1999 in NC.
Financial data (yr. ended 12/31/01): Grants paid, $10,000; assets, $183,145 (M); expenditures, $11,511; qualifying distributions, $10,000.
Limitations: Giving primarily in Raleigh, NC.
Officers: Paul E. Castelloe, Pres.; Ann P. Castelloe, V.P. and Secy.-Treas.; Blair Castelloe Vanhook, V.P.
EIN: 562148069

41687
Graham Family Foundation
c/o Graham Associates, Ltd.
100 Europa Dr., Ste. 190
Chapel Hill, NC 27517

Established in 1999 in NC.
Donor(s): A.H. Graham, Jr., Laura Pinner Graham.
Financial data (yr. ended 12/31/01): Grants paid, $10,000; assets, $338,016 (M); expenditures, $21,091; qualifying distributions, $13,021.
Limitations: Applications not accepted. Giving primarily in NC.
Application information: Contributes only to pre-selected organizations.
Officers and Directors:* John P. Graham,* Pres. and Treas.; A.H. Graham II,* V.P.; Laura Graham Whedon,* V.P.; Margaret Graham Campbell,* Secy.
Directors: A.H. Graham, Jr., Laura Pinner Graham.
EIN: 562152871

41688
The Haidt Foundation, Inc.
c/o Harold Haidt
24203 Cherry
Chapel Hill, NC 27514

Established in 1994.
Donor(s): Harold Haidt.
Financial data (yr. ended 06/30/02): Grants paid, $10,000; assets, $101,917 (M); expenditures, $10,737; qualifying distributions, $10,000.
Limitations: Applications not accepted.
Application information: Contributes only to pre-selected organizations.
Officers: Harold Haidt, Pres.; Elaine Haidt, V.P. and Treas.; Frances Haidt, V.P.; Samantha E. Haidt Davenport, Secy.
Directors: Jonathan Haidt, Rebecca Haidt.
EIN: 133787045

41689
The Deborah S. Harris Foundation
2700 Richardson Dr.
Charlotte, NC 28211
Contact: Deborah S. Harris, Dir.

Established in 2001 in NC.
Donor(s): Deborah S. Harris.
Financial data (yr. ended 12/31/01): Grants paid, $10,000; assets, $76,062 (M); gifts received, $85,386; expenditures, $10,192; qualifying distributions, $10,000.
Limitations: Giving primarily in WA.
Director: Deborah S. Harris.
EIN: 311795384

41690
The Harriss & Covington Foundation
P.O. Box 1909
High Point, NC 27261

Financial data (yr. ended 12/31/99): Grants paid, $10,000; assets, $138,163 (M); gifts received, $75,000; expenditures, $10,064; qualifying distributions, $10,000.
Limitations: Applications not accepted. Giving primarily in NC.
Application information: Contributes only to pre-selected organizations.
Officers and Directors:* Edward H. Covington,* Pres.; Darrell L. Frye,* Secy.
EIN: 582037679

41691
JDSW Family Foundation
1525 W. W.T. Harris Blvd.
Charlotte, NC 28288-1159

Established in 2001.
Financial data (yr. ended 12/31/01): Grants paid, $10,000; assets, $502,902 (M); gifts received, $506,366; expenditures, $10,069; qualifying distributions, $10,000.
Limitations: Applications not accepted.
Application information: Contributes only to pre-selected organizations.
Trustee: First Union National Bank.
EIN: 226898336

41692
Barbara and Jerry Levin Charitable Foundation
5019 Carmel Park Dr.
Charlotte, NC 28226

Established in 2000 in NC.
Donor(s): Jerry Levin.
Financial data (yr. ended 12/31/01): Grants paid, $10,000; assets, $155,111 (M); gifts received, $5,000; expenditures, $10,000; qualifying distributions, $10,000.
Limitations: Applications not accepted.
Application information: Contributes only to pre-selected organizations.
Officers and Directors:* Barbara Levin,* Pres.; Jerry Levin,* Secy.-Treas.; Linda Goldsmith, Nancy L. Kipis, Bruce Levin.
EIN: 562227885

41693
June and Sherrill Shaw Foundation
209 Shaw St.
Randleman, NC 27317

Established in 1999 in NC.
Donor(s): June Shaw, Sherrill Shaw.
Financial data (yr. ended 04/30/02): Grants paid, $10,000; assets, $433 (M); gifts received, $10,000; expenditures, $10,072; qualifying distributions, $10,000.
Limitations: Giving primarily in NC.
Officers: Sherrill Shaw, Pres. and Treas.; Ella June Shaw, V.P. and Secy.
EIN: 311693804

41694
Lottie D. Stoudenmire Education Fund
c/o Wachovia Bank, N.A.
P.O. Box 3099
Winston-Salem, NC 27150
Application address: c/o Financial Aid Dir., Newberry College, Newberry, SC 29108

Financial data (yr. ended 04/30/01): Grants paid, $10,000; assets, $247,092 (M); expenditures, $14,683; qualifying distributions, $10,000.
Limitations: Giving limited to Newberry, SC.
Trustee: Wachovia Bank, N.A.
EIN: 576087466

41695
Dudley R. West Memorial Scholarship Foundation
c/o First Union National Bank
401 S. Tryon St., 4th Fl.
Charlotte, NC 28288-1159
Application address: c/o First Union National Bank, Box 26311, Richmond, VA, 23260, tel.: (804) 771-7069

Established in 1993 in VA.
Donor(s): Dudley R. West.‡
Financial data (yr. ended 12/31/01): Grants paid, $10,000; assets, $206,531 (M); expenditures, $11,614; qualifying distributions, $10,634.
Limitations: Giving limited to residents of Buckingham County, VA.
Application information: Application form required.
Scholarship Committee: Elsie N. Bryan, Allen Gooden, Jr., Joseph Scruggs.
Trustee: First Union National Bank.
EIN: 541672687
Codes: GTI

41696
The William M. Gilfillin Foundation
c/o Wachovia Bank of North Carolina, N.A.
P.O. Box 3099
Winston-Salem, NC 27150-7131
Application address: 1426 Main St., Columbia, SC 29226, tel.: (803) 765-3677
Contact: Gerald Lane, Trust Off., Wachovia Bank of North Carolina, N.A.

Established in 1996 in SC.
Financial data (yr. ended 12/31/01): Grants paid, $9,978; assets, $167,934 (M); gifts received, $25; expenditures, $13,489; qualifying distributions, $9,978.
Trustee: Wachovia Bank of North Carolina, N.A.
EIN: 586336932

41697
Bossong Trust Fund
c/o Wachovia Bank of North Carolina, N.A.
P.O. Box 3099
Winston-Salem, NC 27150-7153
Application address: c/o Bossong Hosiery Mills, Inc., P.O. Box 789, Asheboro, NC 27023
Contact: Joseph C. Bossong, V.P.

Established around 1977 in NC.
Donor(s): Bossong Hosiery Mills, Inc.
Financial data (yr. ended 11/30/01): Grants paid, $9,975; assets, $256,341 (M); expenditures, $14,754; qualifying distributions, $10,575.
Limitations: Giving limited to NC.
Application information: Application form not required.
Officer: Joseph C. Bossong, V.P.
Trustee: Wachovia Bank of North Carolina, N.A.
EIN: 136028097
Codes: CS, CD

41698
The Good Shepherd Fund, Inc.
(also known as The Good Shepherd Home, Inc.)
P.O. Box 1625
Whiteville, NC 28472-1625

Financial data (yr. ended 12/31/01): Grants paid, $9,960; assets, $195,257 (M); expenditures, $11,583; qualifying distributions, $9,960.
Limitations: Giving limited to Bladen, Brunswick, Columbus, New Hanover, and Robeson counties, NC.
Publications: Informational brochure.
Application information: Application form required.
Officers: Kevin Page, Chair.; Deborah Cigary, Secy.; Marie Tutwiler, Treas.
EIN: 560934854

41699
Egerton Family Foundation, Inc.
312 Irving Pl.
Greensboro, NC 27408-6512

Established in 1997.
Donor(s): Doris I. Egerton.
Financial data (yr. ended 04/30/02): Grants paid, $9,850; assets, $191,032 (M); expenditures, $14,542; qualifying distributions, $9,850.
Limitations: Applications not accepted.
Application information: Contributes only to pre-selected organizations.
Officers: Doris Egerton Kiser, Pres.; Catherine T. Egerton, Secy.
EIN: 562030939

41700
Lenoir Community Foundation, Inc.
P.O. Box 740
Lenoir, NC 28645
Contact: William F. Howard III, Secy.-Treas.

Financial data (yr. ended 10/31/01): Grants paid, $9,830; assets, $535,448 (M); gifts received, $40,000; expenditures, $10,503.
Limitations: Giving limited to Caldwell County, NC.
Application information: Application form not required.
Officers: Dan Wortman, Pres.; A.G. Jones, V.P.; William F. Howard III, Secy.-Treas.
EIN: 510202755
Codes: CM

41701
Augustine Family Foundation
c/o Wachovia Bank, N.A.
P.O. Box 3099
Winston-Salem, NC 27150-7131

Established in 1999 in NC.
Donor(s): William A. Augustine.
Financial data (yr. ended 12/31/01): Grants paid, $9,703; assets, $150,224 (M); expenditures, $12,515; qualifying distributions, $9,703.
Limitations: Applications not accepted.
Application information: Contributes only to pre-selected organizations.
Trustee: Wachovia Bank, N.A.
EIN: 562182084

41702
Lee Industries Educational Foundation, Inc.
P.O. Box 26
Newton, NC 28658 (828) 464-8318
Contact: Scholarship Comm.

Established in 1997.
Donor(s): Lee Industries, Inc.
Financial data (yr. ended 12/31/01): Grants paid, $9,665; assets, $33,591 (M); gifts received, $20,000; expenditures, $9,665; qualifying distributions, $9,665.
Limitations: Giving limited to residents of NC.
Application information: Application form required.
Officers: Bill G. Coley, Pres.; Dorcas B. Coley, V.P.; Charles D. Robinson, Secy.-Treas.
EIN: 562046037
Codes: GTI

41703
Ann F. and John W. Copeland Charitable Foundation, Inc.
8300 Bar Harbor Ln.
Charlotte, NC 28210 (704) 556-1233
Contact: John W. Copeland, Pres.

Established in 1990 in NC.
Donor(s): John W. Copeland, Ann F. Copeland.
Financial data (yr. ended 12/31/00): Grants paid, $9,573; assets, $88,707 (M); expenditures, $9,573; qualifying distributions, $0.
Limitations: Giving primarily in NC.
Officers: John W. Copeland, Pres. and Treas.; Ann F. Copeland, V.P. and Secy.
EIN: 561674347

41704
Frank R. Palmer Foundation
c/o First Union National Bank
401 S. Tryon St., NC1159
Charlotte, NC 28288-1159

Financial data (yr. ended 12/31/01): Grants paid, $9,550; assets, $200,581 (M); expenditures, $10,153; qualifying distributions, $9,452.
Limitations: Applications not accepted. Giving primarily in PA.
Application information: Contributes only to pre-selected organizations.
Trustee: First Union National Bank.
EIN: 236263954

41705
Tabitha M. DeVisconti Scholarship Fund
P.O. Box 647
Farmville, NC 27828-0004
Application address: 112 Lakewood Dr., Greenville, NC 27834
Contact: Elizabeth B. Ward, Tr.

Established around 1983.
Financial data (yr. ended 12/31/00): Grants paid, $9,500; assets, $85,177 (M); expenditures, $11,032; qualifying distributions, $9,468.
Limitations: Giving limited to residents of Farmville, NC.
Application information: Application form required.
Trustee: Elizabeth B. Ward.
EIN: 581737093

41706
Marie Palmer Stewart Scholarship Trust
c/o Wachovia Bank, N.A.
P.O. Box 3099
Winston-Salem, NC 27150-7131
Application address: c/o Guidance Counselor, 23 School Dr., Franklin High School, Franklin, NC 28734, tel.: (828) 524-6467
Contact: Carolyn Patillo, Counselor

Financial data (yr. ended 12/31/99): Grants paid, $9,465; assets, $244,152 (M); expenditures, $12,429; qualifying distributions, $10,208.
Limitations: Giving primarily in western NC.
Trustee: Wachovia Bank, N.A.
EIN: 566194108

41707
Area Scholastic Awards Trust Fund
c/o First Union National Bank
401 S. Tryon St., 4th Fl.
Charlotte, NC 28288-1159

Established in 1996 in PA.
Financial data (yr. ended 12/31/01): Grants paid, $9,350; assets, $222,245 (M); gifts received, $6,498; expenditures, $11,153; qualifying distributions, $9,350.
Limitations: Applications not accepted.
Application information: Contributes only to pre-selected organizations.
Trustee: First Union National Bank.
EIN: 237056712

41708
1104 Foundation
6000 Monroe Rd., Ste. 101
Charlotte, NC 28212-6119
Contact: Charles V. Ricks, Tr.

Established in 1994 in NC.
Donor(s): Charles V. Ricks.
Financial data (yr. ended 12/31/00): Grants paid, $9,320; assets, $109,836 (M); gifts received, $25,000; expenditures, $9,360; qualifying distributions, $9,320.
Trustee: Charles V. Ricks.
EIN: 566419561

41709
James McAllister Christmas Fund
P.O. Box 53758
Fayetteville, NC 28305-3758   (910) 323-0350
Contact: Brownie D. Schaeffer, Tr.

Financial data (yr. ended 12/31/99): Grants paid, $9,100; assets, $82,147 (M); expenditures, $9,436; qualifying distributions, $9,100.
Limitations: Giving limited to the Fayetteville, NC, area.
Trustees: Charles Broadwell, Crawford B. Mackethan, Jr., Brownie D. Schaeffer.
EIN: 566063083

41710
Alton Bridges Memorial Scholarship
c/o Carroll Tedder Bass
324 Boswell Rd.
Kenly, NC 27542

Established in 1997.
Financial data (yr. ended 12/31/99): Grants paid, $9,000; assets, $290,426 (M); expenditures, $10,361; qualifying distributions, $10,205.
Limitations: Giving limited to residents of Wilson County, NC.
Trustee: Carroll Tedder Bass.
EIN: 566486563

41711
Chapin Foundation of North Carolina
c/o Bank of America
101 S. Tryon St.
Charlotte, NC 28255
Application address: P.O. Box 309, Sanford, NC 27330
Contact: Jimmy L. Love, Secy.

Financial data (yr. ended 05/31/02): Grants paid, $9,000; assets, $105,017 (M); expenditures, $10,850; qualifying distributions, $9,000.
Officer and Trustees:* Jimmy L. Love,* Secy.; Bank of America.
EIN: 566039452

41712
Mary S. Groff Scholarship Trust
c/o First Union National Bank
401 S. Tryon St., 4th Fl.
Charlotte, NC 28288-1159

Financial data (yr. ended 12/31/01): Grants paid, $9,000; assets, $209,041 (M); expenditures, $10,686; qualifying distributions, $9,254.
Limitations: Applications not accepted. Giving primarily to residents of PA.
Trustee: First Union National Bank.
EIN: 236479982
Codes: GTI

41713
Mooresville Foundation for Excellence in Education
P.O. Box 119
308 N. Main St.
Mooresville, NC 28115

Established in 2001 in NC.
Financial data (yr. ended 06/30/02): Grants paid, $9,000; assets, $81,082 (M); expenditures, $10,520; qualifying distributions, $9,000.
EIN: 561757904

41714
The Helms Family Private Foundation
117 Royal Oaks Ln.
Gastonia, NC 28056

Financial data (yr. ended 12/31/01): Grants paid, $8,960; assets, $10,000 (M); expenditures, $9,027; qualifying distributions, $8,960.
Limitations: Applications not accepted.
Application information: Contributes only to pre-selected organizations.
Trustees: Betty G. Helms, Billy R. Helms.
EIN: 566533993

41715
Huffines Trust for Calvary Lutheran Church
c/o Central Carolina Bank & Trust Co., Trust Dept.
P.O. Box 30010
Durham, NC 27702-3010

Established in 1997 in NC.
Financial data (yr. ended 12/31/01): Grants paid, $8,953; assets, $198,486 (M); expenditures, $9,886; qualifying distributions, $8,953.
Limitations: Applications not accepted.
Application information: Contributes only to pre-selected organizations.
Trustee: Central Carolina Bank & Trust Co.
EIN: 566196023

41716
Carol J. Ledward Memorial Foundation
(Formerly J. Dehaven Ledward Memorial Foundation)
c/o First Union National Bank
401 S. Tryon St., NC1159
Charlotte, NC 28288
Application address: c/o Dean of Admissions, Univ. of PA, 34th & Market Sts., Philadelphia, PA 19104

Financial data (yr. ended 06/30/01): Grants paid, $8,937; assets, $327,725 (M); expenditures, $12,085; qualifying distributions, $9,687.
Limitations: Giving limited to residents of Delaware County, PA.
Trustee: First Union National Bank.
EIN: 232112337

41717
John Stephen Singer Foundation
c/o Wachovia Bank, N.A.
P.O. Box 3099
Winston-Salem, NC 27150-0001
(336) 732-5252
Application address: c/o J.S. Singer & Co., Inc., 535 Madison Ave., 22nd Fl., New York, NY 10022
Contact: John Stephen Singer, Comm. Member

Financial data (yr. ended 12/31/01): Grants paid, $8,925; assets, $501,631 (M); gifts received, $1,568; expenditures, $17,582; qualifying distributions, $8,925.
Limitations: Giving primarily in Palm Beach, FL, and New York, NY.
Committee Member: John Stephen Singer.
Trustee: Wachovia Bank, N.A.
EIN: 510203748

41718
Hunneke Family Foundation
c/o Fred E. Hunneke
1100 Hardee Rd.
Kinston, NC 28501-2529

Established in 1992 in NC.
Donor(s): Fred E. Hunneke.
Financial data (yr. ended 12/31/01): Grants paid, $8,775; assets, $47,562 (M); expenditures, $8,796; qualifying distributions, $8,775.
Limitations: Applications not accepted.
Application information: Contributes only to pre-selected organizations.
Officers: Fred E. Hunneke, Pres.; Anneliese E. Hunneke, Secy.; Roy A. Cohen, Treas.
EIN: 561806223

41719
Serfco, Inc.
125 Williams White Rd.
Zebulon, NC 27597-7790

Established around 1973 in NC.
Donor(s): Carl D. Southard.
Financial data (yr. ended 12/31/01): Grants paid, $8,702; assets, $109,141 (M); gifts received, $8,123; expenditures, $10,634; qualifying distributions, $8,702.
Limitations: Applications not accepted.
Application information: Contributes only to pre-selected organizations.
Officer and Directors:* Carl D. Southard,* Secy.-Treas.; Merle Maris, Rev. Roy Smith.
EIN: 237328056

41720
Amy Muse Trust f/b/o W. H. Muse Scholarship
(also known as W. H. Muse Scholarship Trust)
c/o Wachovia Bank, N.A.
P.O. Box 3099
Winston-Salem, NC 27150-7153
(336) 732-5252
Application address: c/o Leonard Arnold, Principal, Triton High School, Rte. 1, Box 210, Erwin, NC 28339, tel.: (910) 897-8121

Financial data (yr. ended 12/31/99): Grants paid, $8,610; assets, $200 (M); expenditures, $9,161; qualifying distributions, $8,610.
Limitations: Giving limited to Erwin, NC.
Trustee: Wachovia Bank, N.A.
EIN: 566064235

41721
J. C. Flexer Fund
(Formerly E. J. C. Flexer Scholarship Fund)
c/o First Union National Bank
401 S. Tryon St., NC1159
Charlotte, NC 28288-1159

Financial data (yr. ended 12/31/01): Grants paid, $8,568; assets, $160,473 (M); expenditures, $9,385; qualifying distributions, $8,568.
Limitations: Applications not accepted. Giving limited to Kutztown, PA.
Application information: Contributes only to pre-selected organizations.
Trustee: First National Bank.
EIN: 236510544

41722
Krupa Family Foundation, Inc.
3190 Woodview Dr.
Winston-Salem, NC 27106
Contact: Bansi P. Shah, Pres.

Established in 2000 in NC.
Donor(s): Bansi P. Shah.
Financial data (yr. ended 12/31/01): Grants paid, $8,525; assets, $762,454 (M); gifts received, $402,212; expenditures, $14,270; qualifying distributions, $8,525.
Application information: Application form required.
Officers: Bansi P. Shah, Pres.; Sumati B. Shah, V.P. and Secy.
EIN: 562223942

41723
Harry J. Erbe Trust
c/o First Union National Bank
401 S. Tryon St., NC 1159
Charlotte, NC 28288-1159

Financial data (yr. ended 12/31/01): Grants paid, $8,500; assets, $298,719 (M); expenditures, $14,968; qualifying distributions, $8,500.
Limitations: Applications not accepted.

Application information: Contributes only to pre-selected organizations.
Trustee: First Union National Bank.
EIN: 236515628

41724
The Wesley Mancini Foundation
P.O. Box 35509
Charlotte, NC 28235

Established in 2000 in NC.
Donor(s): Wesley Mancini.
Financial data (yr. ended 12/31/01): Grants paid, $8,500; assets, $59 (M); expenditures, $12,839; qualifying distributions, $8,500.
Officer: Wesley Mancini, Pres.
EIN: 311740091

41725
McIntire Foundation
3608 Smokerise Hill Dr.
Charlotte, NC 28277

Established in 2000.
Donor(s): Clifton McIntire, Carrol McIntire, Lisa McIntire.
Financial data (yr. ended 12/31/01): Grants paid, $8,500; assets, $190,952 (M); gifts received, $133,000; expenditures, $9,444; qualifying distributions, $8,500.
Limitations: Applications not accepted. Giving primarily in Charleston, SC.
Application information: Contributes only to pre-selected organizations.
Officers: Clifton McIntire, Pres.; Lisa McIntire, V.P.; Carrol McIntire, Treas.
EIN: 562200747

41726
Robert T. and Suellen G. Monk Family Foundation
c/o M. Jo Brooks
P.O. Box 1108
Greensboro, NC 27402

Established in 1997 in NC.
Donor(s): Robert T. Monk, Suellen G. Monk.
Financial data (yr. ended 12/31/01): Grants paid, $8,500; assets, $493,286 (M); expenditures, $11,255; qualifying distributions, $8,500.
Limitations: Applications not accepted.
Application information: Contributes only to pre-selected organizations.
Officers: Robert T. Monk, Pres. and Treas.; Suellen G. Monk, Secy.
EIN: 562018406

41727
The Richard and Carol Weingarten Foundation
P.O. Box 370
Tryon, NC 28782

Established in 1997 in DE.
Donor(s): Richard Weingarten, Carol Weingarten.
Financial data (yr. ended 12/31/99): Grants paid, $8,392; assets, $80,810 (M); expenditures, $9,731; qualifying distributions, $8,392.
Limitations: Applications not accepted.
Application information: Contributes only to pre-selected organizations.
Officer: Richard Weingarten, Chair.
EIN: 582267858

41728
Elizabeth W. Purcell Educational Trust
c/o First Union National Bank
401 S. Tryon St., NC1159
Charlotte, NC 28288-1159

Established in 1997 in GA.

Financial data (yr. ended 09/30/01): Grants paid, $8,247; assets, $363,528 (M); expenditures, $11,750; qualifying distributions, $8,247.
Limitations: Applications not accepted. Giving primarily in Columbus, GA.
Application information: Contributes only to pre-selected organizations.
Trustee: First Union National Bank.
EIN: 656327927

41729
Christian Mission Foundation
P.O. Box 153
Oakboro, NC 28129-0153 (704) 485-3339
Contact: Don M. Russell, Pres.

Established in 2000.
Donor(s): Rusco Fixture Co., Inc.
Financial data (yr. ended 07/31/01): Grants paid, $8,200; assets, $284,990 (M); gifts received, $301,690; expenditures, $9,604; qualifying distributions, $8,541.
Officers: Don M. Russell, Pres.; Virginia W. Russell, Secy.-Treas.
EIN: 562229925
Codes: CS

41730
The Milford R. & Reba S. Quinn Family Foundation
526 Works Farm Rd.
Warsaw, NC 28398

Established in 1998 in NC.
Donor(s): members of the Quinn family.
Financial data (yr. ended 12/31/01): Grants paid, $8,200; assets, $154,192 (M); expenditures, $8,768; qualifying distributions, $8,200.
Limitations: Applications not accepted.
Application information: Contributes only to pre-selected organizations.
Officers: Terry C. Quinn, Pres.; Milford C. Quinn, V.P.; Robin S. Quinn, Secy.; Kimberly Quinn, Treas.; Milford R. Quinn, Mgr.
EIN: 562089449

41731
Stickley Foundation, Inc.
5950 Fairview Rd., Ste. 418
Charlotte, NC 28210

Donor(s): John L. Stickley, Sr.
Financial data (yr. ended 11/30/01): Grants paid, $8,075; assets, $104,211 (M); expenditures, $21,960; qualifying distributions, $8,075.
Limitations: Giving primarily in NC.
Officers: John L. Stickley, Jr., Pres. and Treas.; Jennie M. Stickley, V.P. and Secy.; Michael T. Stickley, V.P.
EIN: 566061870

41732
Prescott Family Charitable Trust
2008 Aurora Dr.
Raleigh, NC 27615 (919) 828-7722

Donor(s): John F. Prescott.‡
Financial data (yr. ended 12/31/01): Grants paid, $8,050; assets, $252,318 (M); expenditures, $8,855; qualifying distributions, $8,050.
Limitations: Applications not accepted.
Application information: Contributes only to pre-selected organizations.
Trustee: Mollie W. Prescott.
EIN: 566492251

41733
The Jorman and Sue Fields Foundation
c/o Jorman W. Fields
P.O. Box 35527
Greensboro, NC 27425

Financial data (yr. ended 12/31/00): Grants paid, $8,000; assets, $22,428 (M); expenditures, $9,668; qualifying distributions, $9,668.
Limitations: Applications not accepted.
Application information: Contributes only to pre-selected organizations.
Trustees: Jorman W. Fields, Sue B. Field.
EIN: 562002938

41734
The Robert & Marjorie Froeber Foundation
c/o Felix McDaniel
2101 Coleman Pl.
Henderson, NC 27536

Established in 1995 in NC.
Donor(s): Robert J. Froeber, Sr., Marjorie Froeber.
Financial data (yr. ended 12/31/01): Grants paid, $8,000; assets, $271,235 (M); gifts received, $3,000; expenditures, $8,765; qualifying distributions, $8,080.
Limitations: Applications not accepted.
Application information: Contributes only to pre-selected organizations.
Officers and Directors:* Marjorie H. Froeber,* Pres.; Joseph H. Froeber,* V.P.; Robert J. Froeber, Jr.,* V.P.; Sarah M. Froeber,* V.P.; Judith F. Rizzo,* V.P.; Robert J. Froeber, Sr.
EIN: 561910966

41735
Jared Eben McEachern Scholarship Trust
c/o Wachovia Bank, N.A.
P.O. Box 3099
Winston-Salem, NC 27150-3099

Financial data (yr. ended 06/30/01): Grants paid, $8,000; assets, $185,460 (M); expenditures, $11,025; qualifying distributions, $8,939.
Limitations: Applications not accepted. Giving limited to Kershaw, SC.
Application information: Unsolicited requests for funds not accepted.
Trustee: Wachovia Bank, N.A.
EIN: 576107369

41736
Richie Family Foundation, Inc.
c/o Robert A. Richie
12 Cedar Chine
Asheville, NC 28803

Established in 2000 in NC.
Donor(s): Robert A. Richie, Cherie H. Richie, Therman L. Richie II, Elizabeth Richie.
Financial data (yr. ended 12/31/01): Grants paid, $8,000; assets, $427,409 (M); expenditures, $23,838; qualifying distributions, $8,000.
Limitations: Applications not accepted. Giving primarily in Asheville, NC.
Application information: Contributes only to pre-selected organizations.
Officers and Directors:* Robert A. Richie,* Pres. and Treas.; Cherie H. Richie,* V.P. and Secy.; Elizabeth Richie, Therman L. Richie II.
EIN: 562223574

41737
Whitener Family Foundation, Inc.
P.O. Drawer 398
Morganton, NC 28680 (828) 437-6244
Contact: John W. Whitener, Pres.

Established in 1998 in NC.
Donor(s): John W. Whitener.

41737—NORTH CAROLINA

Financial data (yr. ended 12/31/01): Grants paid, $8,000; assets, $171,749 (M); gifts received, $5,000; expenditures, $8,630; qualifying distributions, $8,000.
Limitations: Giving primarily in NC.
Application information: Application form not required.
Officers and Directors:* John W. Whitner,* Pres. and Treas.; Elizabeth W. Whitener,* V.P. and Secy.; Mary Martha Beecy, Steven J. Beecy.
EIN: 562060428

41738
The Winchester Foundation
c/o Wachovia Bank, N.A.
P.O. Box 3099
Winston-Salem, NC 27150

Established in 1997 in NC.
Donor(s): Alex Brown and Sons Inc., Chase.
Financial data (yr. ended 12/31/01): Grants paid, $8,000; assets, $424,002 (M); gifts received, $136,810; expenditures, $12,873; qualifying distributions, $8,180.
Limitations: Applications not accepted. Giving primarily in Salisbury, NC.
Application information: Contributes only to pre-selected organizations.
Officer: Alan Winchester, Exec. Dir.
Trustee: Wachovia Bank, N.A.
EIN: 562074822
Codes: CS

41739
Peden Foundation, Inc.
P.O. Box 40489
Raleigh, NC 27629 (919) 832-2081
Application address: 1815 Capital Blvd., Raleigh, NC 27604
Contact: James M. Peden, Jr., Pres.

Financial data (yr. ended 12/31/99): Grants paid, $7,972; assets, $22,383 (M); expenditures, $9,633; qualifying distributions, $7,971.
Limitations: Giving primarily in Raleigh, NC.
Officer and Director:* James M. Peden, Jr.,* Pres.
EIN: 566075560

41740
The Barry Charitable Foundation, Inc.
1810 S. Lakeshore Dr.
Chapel Hill, NC 27514-6735

Established in 1997 in NC.
Donor(s): David W. Barry.
Financial data (yr. ended 12/31/01): Grants paid, $7,821; assets, $281,920 (M); gifts received, $158,595; expenditures, $7,821; qualifying distributions, $7,821.
Limitations: Applications not accepted.
Application information: Contributes only to pre-selected organizations.
Officers and Trustees:* David W. Barry,* Pres.; Gracia Chin Barry,* Secy.-Treas.; Christopher Meng Barry, Jennifer Ming Barry.
EIN: 562017439

41741
Althouse Foundation
c/o First Union National Bank
401 S. Tryon St., 4th Fl.
Charlotte, NC 28288-1159

Financial data (yr. ended 12/01/01): Grants paid, $7,800; assets, $143,433 (M); expenditures, $8,325; qualifying distributions, $7,755.
Limitations: Applications not accepted. Giving primarily in Reading, PA.
Application information: Contributes only to pre-selected organizations.
Trustee: First Union National Bank.

EIN: 236461059

41742
Beach Family Foundation Trust
c/o U.S. Trust
P.O. Box 26262
Greensboro, NC 27420

Established in 1998 in NC.
Donor(s): Lamar Beach.
Financial data (yr. ended 12/31/01): Grants paid, $7,666; assets, $122,433 (M); expenditures, $10,156; qualifying distributions, $7,666.
Limitations: Applications not accepted. Giving primarily in NC.
Application information: Contributes only to pre-selected organizations.
Officers and Director:* Lamar Beach,* Pres.; Gladys C. Beach, V.P.
EIN: 566522423

41743
The Donald Hughes Family Foundation, Inc.
3 New Bern Sq.
Greensboro, NC 27408 (336) 379-2981
Contact: Donald Hughes, Chair.

Established in 1998 in NC.
Donor(s): Donald Hughes.
Financial data (yr. ended 12/31/01): Grants paid, $7,500; assets, $199,872 (M); gifts received, $75,000; expenditures, $9,118; qualifying distributions, $7,500.
Limitations: Giving primarily in Greensboro, NC.
Application information: Application form not required.
Officers: Donald Hughes, Chair.; Agnes Hughes, V.P.; Suzanne H. Sullivan, Secy.; Elizabeth Hughes, Treas.
EIN: 562239763

41744
Kirby & Holt Foundation
P.O. Box 31665
Raleigh, NC 27622

Established in 1999 in NC.
Financial data (yr. ended 12/31/01): Grants paid, $7,500; assets, $7,574 (M); gifts received, $304; expenditures, $8,411; qualifying distributions, $8,304.
Limitations: Applications not accepted.
Application information: Contributes only to pre-selected organizations.
Officers and Directors:* David F. Kirby,* Pres. and Treas.; C. Mark Holt, V.P.; William B. Bystrynski, Secy.; Isaac L. Thorp.
EIN: 562169714

41745
White Oak Foundation
2416 White Oak Rd.
Raleigh, NC 27609-7612

Established in 1986 in NC.
Donor(s): Karl G. Hudson, Jr., Annie Catherine W. Hudson.
Financial data (yr. ended 12/31/01): Grants paid, $7,500; assets, $298,075 (M); expenditures, $9,448; qualifying distributions, $7,500.
Limitations: Applications not accepted. Giving primarily in Raleigh, NC.
Application information: Contributes only to pre-selected organizations.
Trustees: Annie Catherine W. Hudson, Karl G. Hudson, Jr.
EIN: 561539057

41746
Ben F. & Hugh Burgess Trust Fund
(Formerly B. Hugh Burgess Foundation)
c/o Bank of America
101 S. Tyron St.
Charlotte, NC 28255-0001

Financial data (yr. ended 06/30/02): Grants paid, $7,360; assets, $248,404 (M); expenditures, $16,952; qualifying distributions, $7,360.
Limitations: Applications not accepted. Giving primarily in GA.
Application information: Contributes only to pre-selected organizations.
Trustee: Bank of America.
EIN: 586103644

41747
James Ewing Mitchell Foundation
c/o First Union National Bank
401 S. Tryon St., NC1159
Charlotte, NC 28288-1159
Application address: c/o First Union National Bank, N.A., 765 Broad St., Newark, NJ 07101

Financial data (yr. ended 12/31/01): Grants paid, $7,350; assets, $94,154 (M); expenditures, $9,976; qualifying distributions, $7,725.
Limitations: Giving primarily in NY.
Trustee: First Union National Bank.
EIN: 226041479

41748
Schug Foundation
c/o Phillip M. Bragg
7013 Erin Ct.
Charlotte, NC 28210-4906

Established in 2001.
Donor(s): Peggy C. Schug.
Financial data (yr. ended 12/31/01): Grants paid, $7,293; assets, $483,404 (M); gifts received, $505,575; expenditures, $13,657; qualifying distributions, $7,293.
Limitations: Giving limited to residents of NC.
Application information: Application form required.
Trustees: John B. Schug, Peggy C. Schug.
EIN: 566583795

41749
The Kodali Family Private Foundation
577 Broyhill Rd.
Fayetteville, NC 28314

Established in 1999 in NC.
Donor(s): Valli P. Kodali.
Financial data (yr. ended 12/31/01): Grants paid, $7,234; assets, $192,567 (M); gifts received, $1,264; expenditures, $8,950; qualifying distributions, $7,234.
Limitations: Applications not accepted. Giving primarily in NC.
Application information: Contributes only to pre-selected organizations.
Trustees: Usha Kodali, Valli P. Kodali.
EIN: 562094126

41750
TTR Foundation
4629 Herter Rd.
Lincolnton, NC 28092

Established in 1998 in NC.
Financial data (yr. ended 12/31/99): Grants paid, $7,225; assets, $4,964 (M); gifts received, $1,675; expenditures, $7,225; qualifying distributions, $7,225.
Limitations: Applications not accepted.
Application information: Contributes only to pre-selected organizations.

Trustees: David T. Seaford, Elva Seaford.
EIN: 562029983

41751
Carole Shapiro Memorial Foundation, Inc.
P.O. Box 7625
Asheville, NC 28802

Donor(s): Eugene N. Shapiro, Ellaine F. Shapiro.
Financial data (yr. ended 04/30/02): Grants paid, $7,205; assets, $236,050 (M); expenditures, $8,449; qualifying distributions, $7,205.
Limitations: Applications not accepted.
Application information: Contributes only to pre-selected organizations.
Officers and Directors:* Ellaine F. Shapiro,* Pres.; Eugene N. Shapiro,* V.P.
EIN: 566060223

41752
Israel K. Gorelick Foundation
P.O. Box 35129
Charlotte, NC 28235

Established in 2000 in NC.
Financial data (yr. ended 06/30/01): Grants paid, $7,187; assets, $2,995 (M); gifts received, $10,000; expenditures, $7,327; qualifying distributions, $7,187.
Officer: Israel K. Gorelick, Pres.
EIN: 562204181

41753
Ed & Lois Reich-Davidson County Trust
c/o Wachovia Bank, N.A.
P.O. Box 3099
Winston-Salem, NC 27150-7131

Donor(s): Lois Reich.‡
Financial data (yr. ended 12/31/01): Grants paid, $7,038; assets, $152,208 (M); expenditures, $10,442; qualifying distributions, $7,038.
Limitations: Applications not accepted. Giving primarily in Lexington, NC.
Application information: Contributes only to pre-selected organizations.
Trustee: Wachovia Bank, N.A.
EIN: 566482956

41754
Holden Family Charitable Foundation
3620 Cape Center Dr.
Fayetteville, NC 28304
Application address: 3852 Holden Rd. S.W., Shallotte, NC 28470
Contact: Ronald C. Holden, Pres.

Established in 2000 in NC.
Donor(s): Ronald C. Holden, Clarice Holden.
Financial data (yr. ended 12/31/01): Grants paid, $7,000; assets, $53,378 (M); gifts received, $30,000; expenditures, $7,028; qualifying distributions, $7,000.
Officers: Ronald C. Holden, Pres.; Clarice Holden, Secy.-Treas.
EIN: 562227887

41755
The Warren P. Reynolds Charitable Trust
c/o Wachovia Bank, N.A.
P.O. Box 3099
Winston-Salem, NC 27150-7153

Established in 1995 in NC.
Financial data (yr. ended 12/31/01): Grants paid, $7,000; assets, $122,482 (M); expenditures, $10,849; qualifying distributions, $8,974.
Limitations: Applications not accepted.
Application information: Contributes only to pre-selected organizations.
Trustee: Wachovia Bank, N.A.
EIN: 582241074

41756
Sigma Chi Memorial Foundation
(Formerly Gary Lindsay Dana Memorial Foundation)
2304 Beechridge Rd.
Raleigh, NC 27608-1430
Application address: 5151 Glenwood Ave., Ste. 100, Raleigh, NC 27612-3267
Contact: John L. Hughes, Secy.

Financial data (yr. ended 12/31/99): Grants paid, $7,000; assets, $123,895 (M); gifts received, $1,190; expenditures, $7,140; qualifying distributions, $7,140.
Limitations: Giving primarily in Raleigh, NC.
Application information: Application form required.
Officers: Robert Wright, Chair.; O. Franklin Smith, Vice-Chair.; John L. Hughes, Secy.; George H. Ellinwood, Treas.
EIN: 237413002

41757
Hekler Family Fund
1117 Kensington Dr.
High Point, NC 27262-4502

Established in 1999 in NC.
Donor(s): Norman N. Hekler.
Financial data (yr. ended 12/31/01): Grants paid, $6,990; assets, $123,314 (M); expenditures, $7,628; qualifying distributions, $6,990.
Directors: Donald L. Hekler, Hedy Y. Hekler, Norman N. Hekler, Ursula S. Hekler, Erica H. Herman.
EIN: 562116947

41758
Alan M. Zimmer Family Foundation
111 Princess St.
P.O. Box 2628
Wilmington, NC 28402

Established in 1997 in NC.
Financial data (yr. ended 12/31/01): Grants paid, $6,883; assets, $21,171 (M); gifts received, $8,000; expenditures, $6,883; qualifying distributions, $6,883.
Limitations: Applications not accepted.
Application information: Contributes only to pre-selected organizations.
Officer: Alan Zimmer.
EIN: 562034209

41759
Lossie Grist Clark Memorial Trust Fund
c/o B.B. & T., Trust Dept.
P.O. Box 2907
Wilson, NC 27894-2907
Application address: c/o Florence James, B.B. & T. Trust Dept., P.O. Box 2907, Wilson, NC 27894-2907, tel.: (252) 246 4821
Contact: Mahlon W. DeLoatch, Jr., V.P., B.B. & T.

Financial data (yr. ended 12/31/01): Grants paid, $6,861; assets, $124,900 (M); expenditures, $11,800; qualifying distributions, $6,861.
Limitations: Giving limited to residents of Edgecombe County, NC.
Trustee: B.B. & T.
EIN: 566175848

41760
Bill Rogers Bonitz Scholarship Fund
c/o Wachovia Bank, N.A.
P.O. Box 3099
Winston-Salem, NC 27150-7131
Application address: c/o Wachovia Bank, N.A., 1426 Main St., Columbia, SC 26226, tel.: (803) 765-3671
Contact: C. Gerald Lane

Established in 1999 in SC.
Donor(s): Bonitz of South Carolina, Inc., and subsidiaries and affiliates.
Financial data (yr. ended 06/30/01): Grants paid, $6,793; assets, $212,779 (M); gifts received, $75,000; expenditures, $9,636; qualifying distributions, $7,216.
Limitations: Giving limited to residents of SC.
Application information: Application form required.
Trustee: Wachovia Bank, N.A.
EIN: 566549889
Codes: CS, CD

41761
Munroe Best Foundation, Inc.
809 Mill Rd.
Goldsboro, NC 27534
Contact: C. Munroe Best, Jr., Pres.

Financial data (yr. ended 12/31/01): Grants paid, $6,750; assets, $210,747 (M); expenditures, $7,303; qualifying distributions, $6,750.
Limitations: Giving primarily in NC.
Application information: Unsolicited request for funds not accepted.
Officer: C. Munroe Best, Jr., Pres.
EIN: 566061641

41762
Weathers Family Foundation
c/o First National Bank, Trust Dept.
P.O. Box 168
Shelby, NC 28151-0168 (704) 484-6200

Established in 1998.
Financial data (yr. ended 12/31/01): Grants paid, $6,750; assets, $293,628 (M); gifts received, $20,000; expenditures, $11,003; qualifying distributions, $6,750.
Officers: Henry L. Weathers, Mgr.; Pearl A. Weathers, Mgr.
Trustee: First National Bank.
EIN: 566501028

41763
Patla, Straus, Robinson & Moore Foundation, Inc.
(Formerly Patla Straus Family Foundation)
P.O. Box 7625
Asheville, NC 28802-7625

Donor(s): Karl H. Straus.
Financial data (yr. ended 11/30/01): Grants paid, $6,705; assets, $5,253 (M); gifts received, $7,600; expenditures, $6,728; qualifying distributions, $6,705.
Limitations: Applications not accepted. Giving limited to Asheville, NC.
Application information: Contributes only to pre-selected organizations.
Officers: Robert J. Robinson, Pres.; Steven I. Goldstein, V.P. and Treas.; Richard S. Daniels, Secy.
EIN: 566074652

41764—NORTH CAROLINA

41764
Goldthorpe Foundation, Inc.
2420-104 Roswell Ave.
Charlotte, NC 28209 (704) 333-6872
Contact: Theodore F. Goldthorpe, Tr.

Established in 1988 in SC.
Donor(s): Ted F. Goldthorpe, Mrs. Ted F. Goldthorpe.
Financial data (yr. ended 12/31/01): Grants paid, $6,652; assets, $31,707 (M); gifts received, $10,517; expenditures, $7,078; qualifying distributions, $6,652.
Limitations: Giving primarily in NC and SC.
Trustees: Itice R. Goldthorpe, Theodore F. Goldthorpe, Donald B. Scott.
EIN: 570879223

41765
Zeno and Mattie S. Edwards Charitable Foundation
4 Allwood Ct.
Greensboro, NC 27410

Established in 1985 in NC.
Donor(s): Zeno Edwards, Mattie S. Edwards, Ephraim Z. Edwards.
Financial data (yr. ended 11/30/01): Grants paid, $6,639; assets, $72,799 (M); expenditures, $7,004; qualifying distributions, $6,639.
Limitations: Applications not accepted.
Application information: Contributes only to pre-selected organizations.
Officers: Ephraim Z. Edwards, Pres.; Mattie S. Edwards, V.P.
EIN: 061199425

41766
Wishart, Norris, Henninger & Pittman Charitable Foundation, Inc.
3120 S. Church St.
Burlington, NC 27215

Established in 2001 in NC.
Donor(s): Wishart, Norris, Henninger & Pittman, P.A.
Financial data (yr. ended 12/31/01): Grants paid, $6,513; assets, $32,744 (M); gifts received, $36,599; expenditures, $6,600; qualifying distributions, $6,513.
Limitations: Applications not accepted.
Application information: Contributes only to pre-selected organizations.
Officer: Jan Shepherd, Chair.
EIN: 562243215
Codes: CS

41767
Mary A. Croll Educational Trust
c/o First Union National Bank
401 S. Tryon St., NC1159
Charlotte, NC 28288-1159

Financial data (yr. ended 09/30/00): Grants paid, $6,500; assets, $163,327 (M); expenditures, $8,594; qualifying distributions, $7,175.
Limitations: Applications not accepted. Giving limited to PA.
Trustee: First Union National Bank.
EIN: 236687104

41768
The George W. Henderson III Family Foundation, Inc.
c/o U.S. Trust
P.O. Box 26262
Greensboro, NC 27420

Established in 1996 in NC.
Donor(s): George W. Henderson III.
Financial data (yr. ended 12/31/01): Grants paid, $6,500; assets, $127,147 (M); expenditures, $8,540; qualifying distributions, $6,500.
Limitations: Applications not accepted. Giving limited to Greensboro, NC.
Application information: Contributes only to pre-selected organizations.
Officers: George W. Henderson III, Pres.; Lindsay C. Henderson, V.P.
EIN: 561993026

41769
The Korschun Foundation
c/o Wachovia Bank, N.A.
P.O. Box 3099
Winston-Salem, NC 27150-7131

Established in 2000 in NC.
Financial data (yr. ended 12/31/00): Grants paid, $6,500; assets, $462,331 (M); gifts received, $494,000; expenditures, $9,148; qualifying distributions, $6,500.
Limitations: Applications not accepted. Giving on a national basis.
Application information: Contributes only to pre-selected organizations.
Trustee: Wachovia Bank, N.A.
EIN: 566566455

41770
Marbut Foundation
c/o First Union National Bank
401 S. Tyron St., NC1159
Charlotte, NC 28288-1159
Application address: c/o Bennett Yort, Trust Off., First Union National Bank, P.O. Box 1211, Augusta, GA 30901

Financial data (yr. ended 06/30/01): Grants paid, $6,500; assets, $113,814 (M); expenditures, $9,351; qualifying distributions, $7,134.
Limitations: Giving primarily in Augusta, GA.
Trustee: First Union National Bank.
EIN: 586037711

41771
H. L. and K. G. Ryan County Scholarship Fund
(Formerly Katherine G. Ryan County Scholarship Fund)
c/o First Union National Bank
401 S. Tryon St.
Charlotte, NC 28288-1559
Contact: Mrs. Dean K. Schleicher

Financial data (yr. ended 03/31/02): Grants paid, $6,500; assets, $115,947 (M); expenditures, $9,359; qualifying distributions, $7,733.
Limitations: Giving limited to residents of Bucks County, PA.
Application information: Application form required.
Trustee: First Union National Bank.
EIN: 232164671
Codes: GTI

41772
William E. Stroud Trust
c/o Wachovia Bank, N.A.
P.O. Box 3099
Winston-Salem, NC 27150-6732

Established in 1959 in NC.
Financial data (yr. ended 12/31/01): Grants paid, $6,498; assets, $133,985 (M); expenditures, $9,154; qualifying distributions, $7,565.
Limitations: Applications not accepted. Giving limited to the Goldsboro, NC, area.
Application information: Contributes to 3 pre-selected organizations specified in the trust instrument; scholarships restricted to graduates of Goldsboro High School.
Trustee: Wachovia Bank, N.A.
Scholarship Committee: Ray Brayboy, Gerald Whitely, Rector, St. Stephen's Episcopal Church.
EIN: 566035825

41773
Crown-Salwen Foundation
P.O. Box 610
Claremont, NC 28610

Donor(s): Jesse L. Salwen.
Financial data (yr. ended 11/30/01): Grants paid, $6,450; assets, $27,735 (M); expenditures, $6,462; qualifying distributions, $6,450.
Limitations: Applications not accepted.
Application information: Contributes only to pre-selected organizations.
Officer: Jesse L. Salwen, Mgr.
EIN: 236297440

41774
Mary Jane Pierson Trust
c/o Bank of America
1 Bank of America Plz., NC1-002-11-18
Charlotte, NC 28255 (800) 401-2635

Financial data (yr. ended 12/31/01): Grants paid, $6,446; assets, $171,651 (M); expenditures, $9,426; qualifying distributions, $6,446.
Limitations: Applications not accepted.
Application information: Contributes only to pre-selected organizations.
Trustee: Bank of America.
Directors: Carolyn P. Sherrill, Everette P. Sherrill.
EIN: 566064339

41775
The Shepherd Foundation
316 Buncombe St.
Raleigh, NC 27609-6312

Established in 1996 in NC.
Donor(s): Lee A. Whitehurst.
Financial data (yr. ended 11/30/01): Grants paid, $6,439; assets, $161,132 (M); expenditures, $8,073; qualifying distributions, $6,439.
Limitations: Applications not accepted. Giving primarily in NC.
Application information: Contributes only to pre-selected organizations.
Officers: Lee A. Whitehurst, Pres.; Ann D. Whitehurst, Secy.-Treas.
EIN: 562010297

41776
Education Now Advances Change Tomorrow
(also known as ENACT)
6005 Castlebrook Dr.
Raleigh, NC 27604-5972 (919) 870-4822
Contact: Carolyn S. Leith, Chair.

Established in 1991 in NC.
Donor(s): Carolyn S. Leith.
Financial data (yr. ended 12/31/01): Grants paid, $6,350; assets, $167,862 (M); expenditures, $8,144; qualifying distributions, $6,350.
Limitations: Giving primarily in Raleigh, NC.
Officers: Carolyn S. Leith, Chair.; Judie L. Cipriani, Secy.
Trustees: Christopher M. Leith, Linda J. Leith.
EIN: 581923658

41777
Henry D. & Stella O. Gray Scholarship Fund
c/o B.B. & T., Trust Dept.
P.O. Box 2907
Wilson, NC 27894-2907
Application address: c/o Principal, Jones Central High School, Wilson, NC 27893

Financial data (yr. ended 06/30/99): Grants paid, $6,325; assets, $165,392 (M); expenditures, $7,906; qualifying distributions, $6,275.
Limitations: Giving limited to residents of Jones County, NC.
Trustee: B.B. & T.
EIN: 566114935

41778
Leona Bedient Crouchley Trust
c/o First Union National Bank
401 S. Tryon St., 4th Fl.
Charlotte, NC 28288-1159

Established in 1996 in CT.
Financial data (yr. ended 06/30/01): Grants paid, $6,250; assets, $123,023 (M); expenditures, $9,712; qualifying distributions, $6,250.
Limitations: Giving primarily in CO and CT.
Application information: Application form not required.
Trustee: First Union National Bank.
EIN: 066042093

41779
Matheson Lecture Foundation
c/o Bank of America
101 S. Tryon St.
Charlotte, NC 28255

Donor(s): J.P. Matheson.‡
Financial data (yr. ended 12/31/00): Grants paid, $6,200; assets, $139,434 (M); expenditures, $7,117; qualifying distributions, $6,835.
Limitations: Applications not accepted. Giving primarily in Charlotte, NC.
Application information: Contributes only to pre-selected organizations.
Trustee: Bank of America.
EIN: 566050070

41780
Wilson Memorial Scholarship Fund
c/o Bank of America
101 S. Tryon St., NC1-002-11-18
Charlotte, NC 28255 (800) 401-2635

Financial data (yr. ended 12/31/01): Grants paid, $6,056; assets, $189,300 (M); expenditures, $8,402; qualifying distributions, $7,026.
Limitations: Applications not accepted. Giving primarily in NC.
Application information: Contributes only to pre-selected organizations.
Trustee: Bank of America.
EIN: 566204069

41781
The Greenhoot Family Foundation, Inc.
640 Colville Rd.
Charlotte, NC 28207
Contact: Kathryn Greenhoot, Dir.

Established in 1996 in NC.
Donor(s): Jerry Greenhoot, Kathryn Greenhoot.
Financial data (yr. ended 12/31/99): Grants paid, $6,000; assets, $126,310 (M); gifts received, $47,696; expenditures, $6,680; qualifying distributions, $6,303.
Directors: Jerry Greenhoot, Kathryn Greenhoot.
EIN: 561980147

41782
The McCormack Foundation, Inc.
c/o J. Parrish McCormack
1009 Bearmore Dr.
Charlotte, NC 28211

Established in 2000 in NC.
Donor(s): J. Parrish McCormack, H. Suzanne McCormack.
Financial data (yr. ended 11/30/01): Grants paid, $6,000; assets, $92,563 (M); gifts received, $10,000; expenditures, $8,602; qualifying distributions, $6,000.
Limitations: Applications not accepted.
Application information: Contributes only to pre-selected organizations.
Officers: J. Parrish McCormack, Chair. and Pres.; H. Suzanne McCormack, Secy.-Treas.
Director: Elayne P. McCormack.
EIN: 311677370

41783
Charles E. Erb Foundation
c/o Wachovia Bank, N.A.
P.O. Box 3099
Winston-Salem, NC 27150-7131
Application address: c/o Wachovia Bank, N.A., 1401 N. Main St., Columbia, SC 29226, tel.: (803) 765-3671
Contact: Jerry Lane, Trust Off., Wachovia Bank

Established in 1997 in IL and SC.
Donor(s): Charles E. Erb.
Financial data (yr. ended 10/31/01): Grants paid, $5,957; assets, $108,093 (M); expenditures, $12,120; qualifying distributions, $5,957.
Application information: Application form not required.
Trustees: Charles E. Erb, Wachovia Bank of South Carolina, N.A.
EIN: 367207751

41784
Harriet Marks Scholarship Fund
c/o B.B. & T., Trust Dept.
P.O. Box 2907
Wilson, NC 27894-2907

Financial data (yr. ended 03/31/00): Grants paid, $5,900; assets, $203,880 (M); expenditures, $7,580; qualifying distributions, $5,934.
Limitations: Giving limited to NC.
Application information: Application form not required.
Trustee: B.B. & T.
EIN: 566115020

41785
Edna C. Koons Trust
c/o First Union National Bank
401 S. Tryon St., Ste. NC1159
Charlotte, NC 28288

Financial data (yr. ended 07/31/02): Grants paid, $5,849; assets, $121,009 (M); expenditures, $6,121; qualifying distributions, $5,849.
Limitations: Applications not accepted. Giving primarily in PA.
Application information: Contributes only to pre-selected organizations.
Trustee: First Union National Bank.
EIN: 236611873

41786
Scott and Dana Gorelick Family Foundation
6060 JA Jones Dr., Ste. 516
Charlotte, NC 28287

Established in 1999 in NC.
Donor(s): Scott R. Gorelick.

Financial data (yr. ended 06/30/01): Grants paid, $5,800; assets, $304,969 (M); expenditures, $7,478; qualifying distributions, $6,850.
Limitations: Applications not accepted. Giving primarily in NC.
Application information: Contributes only to pre-selected organizations.
Officers: Scott R. Gorelick, Pres. and Treas.; Dana S. Gorelick, V.P. and Secy.
EIN: 562170948

41787
H. E. Woodward Trust
c/o First Union National Bank
401 S. Tryon St., NC1159
Charlotte, NC 28288-1159

Financial data (yr. ended 12/31/01): Grants paid, $5,731; assets, $102,568 (M); expenditures, $211,538; qualifying distributions, $7,150.
Limitations: Applications not accepted.
Application information: Contributes only to pre-selected organizations.
Trustee: First Union National Bank.
EIN: 236960096

41788
Charles B. Loflin Educational Foundation
c/o High Point Bank & Trust Co.
P.O. Box 2278
High Point, NC 27261-2278
Contact: Elizabeth Allen, Trust Off., High Point Bank and Trust Co.

Financial data (yr. ended 12/31/00): Grants paid, $5,696; assets, $118,130 (M); expenditures, $6,175; qualifying distributions, $5,696.
Limitations: Giving limited to High Point, NC.
Officers: Richard Budd, Mgr.; Charles Green, Mgr.; Jeff Horney, Mgr.
Trustee: High Point Bank & Trust Co.
EIN: 237035432
Codes: GTI

41789
Eleanor Starkey Scholarship Fund
c/o First Union National Bank
401 S. Tryon St.
Charlotte, NC 28288-1159
Application address: c/o First Union National Bank, Williamsport, PA 17703-1268

Financial data (yr. ended 12/31/01): Grants paid, $5,600; assets, $121,897 (M); expenditures, $6,736; qualifying distributions, $5,600.
Limitations: Giving limited to the townships of Brookfield, Chatham, Clymer, Deerfield, Westfield, and the boroughs of Knoxville and Westfield in Tioga County, PA.
Application information: Applicants are recommended by school's principal, guidance counselor, and music supervisor.
Trustee: First Union National Bank.
EIN: 236640683

41790
John Shaw Tillman and Anna Walters Tillman Scholarship Trust
1870 NC Hwy. 49 S.
Asheboro, NC 27203-8910

Established in 1991 in NC.
Donor(s): Nina T. Vaughn.‡
Financial data (yr. ended 04/30/00): Grants paid, $5,600; assets, $128,243 (M); gifts received, $5,000; expenditures, $6,001; qualifying distributions, $5,940; giving activities include $401 for programs.
Limitations: Applications not accepted. Giving limited to residents of Asheboro, NC.
Trustee: Carol Tillman Bullins.

41790—NORTH CAROLINA

EIN: 561735521

41791
Boldon Foundation, Inc.
601 Montevista Ave.
Marion, NC 28752-5376 (828) 659-9707
Contact: Frank L. Boldon, Pres.

Established in 1993 in NC.
Donor(s): Frank L. Boldon.
Financial data (yr. ended 12/31/01): Grants paid, $5,530; assets, $116,268 (M); expenditures, $6,268; qualifying distributions, $5,530.
Officers: Frank L. Boldon, Pres.; Debra J. Boldon, V.P.
EIN: 561852852

41792
The Rallis Richner Foundation, Inc.
104 N. Devimy Ct.
Cary, NC 27511 (919) 461-0988
Contact: Chris A. Rallis, Pres.

Established in 1999 in NC.
Donor(s): Chris A. Rallis.
Financial data (yr. ended 12/31/01): Grants paid, $5,527; assets, $63,200 (M); gifts received, $740; expenditures, $6,267; qualifying distributions, $5,527.
Officer: Chris A. Rallis, Pres.
EIN: 562167465

41793
Helen S. and Julius L. Goldman Scholarship Fund, Inc.
205 Wachovia Bank Bldg.
130 S. Main St., Ste. 205
Salisbury, NC 28144-4942
Application address: 1350 Potneck Rd., Salisbury, NC 28147, tel.: (704) 636-3895
Contact: Judy Grissom, V.P.

Established in 1995 in NC.
Financial data (yr. ended 06/30/01): Grants paid, $5,500; assets, $331,276 (M); gifts received, $410; expenditures, $14,975; qualifying distributions, $14,953.
Limitations: Giving limited to residents of Rowan County, NC.
Application information: Application form required.
Officers: Ann Medlin, Pres.; Judy Grissom, V.P.; Carolyn Blackman, Secy.; Hilda Foreman, Treas.
Directors: Thomas Caddell, Norma Goldman, Bonnie Hodges, Catrelia Hunter, Alyce H. Lanier, Mark Perry.
EIN: 561941869

41794
Karyae Benevolent Foundation
P.O. Box 37169
Charlotte, NC 28237-7169
Scholarship address: c/o Selection Committee, P.O. Box 37169, Charlotte, NC 28236

Financial data (yr. ended 12/31/01): Grants paid, $5,500; assets, $364,426 (M); expenditures, $7,295; qualifying distributions, $6,706; giving activities include $4,000 for loans to individuals.
Limitations: Giving limited to residents of Karyae, Greece.
Application information: Application form required.
Officers: D.G. Kaperonis, Pres.; John Hondros, V.P.; Jon Couchell, Secy.; Jimmy Kaperonis, Treas.
EIN: 566058576
Codes: GTI

41795
Louis B. & Ida K. Orlowitz Variety Club Scholarship
c/o First Union National Bank
401 S. Tryon St., NC1159
Charlotte, NC 28288

Financial data (yr. ended 12/31/01): Grants paid, $5,396; assets, $98,654 (M); expenditures, $7,341; qualifying distributions, $5,396.
Limitations: Applications not accepted. Giving primarily in Philadelphia, PA.
Application information: Contributes only to pre-selected organizations.
Trustee: First Union National Bank.
EIN: 236272773

41796
Richard W. Treleaven Private Foundation
7908-A Industrial Village Dr.
Greensboro, NC 27409-9691
Contact: Carl W. Treleaven, Pres.

Established in 1977 in IL.
Donor(s): Westlake Industries, Inc.
Financial data (yr. ended 06/30/02): Grants paid, $5,380; assets, $155,628 (M); expenditures, $10,785; qualifying distributions, $5,380.
Limitations: Giving primarily in NC.
Application information: Application form not required.
Officers and Directors:* Carl W. Treleaven,* Pres.; Lina Z. Treleaven,* Secy.; Thomas J. Schultz,* Treas.
EIN: 362944336

41797
Frances Morgan Roberson Charitable Trust
c/o Bank of America
101 S. Tryon St.
Charlotte, NC 28255

Established in 1996 in NC.
Financial data (yr. ended 12/31/01): Grants paid, $5,378; assets, $101,344 (M); expenditures, $6,449; qualifying distributions, $5,378.
Limitations: Applications not accepted.
Application information: Contributes only to pre-selected organizations.
Trustee: Bank of America.
EIN: 566482081

41798
R. & C. Whedbee Scholarship Trust
c/o Bank of America
401 S. Tryon St., NC1-002-11-18
Charlotte, NC 28202

Established in 2000 in NC.
Financial data (yr. ended 12/31/01): Grants paid, $5,374; assets, $394,082 (M); expenditures, $12,505; qualifying distributions, $5,374.
Limitations: Applications not accepted. Giving primarily in Chapel Hill, NC.
Application information: Contributes only to pre-selected organizations.
Trustee: Bank of America.
EIN: 566499755

41799
Institut Francais de Washington
234 Dey Hall, CB 3170 UNC-CH
Chapel Hill, NC 27599-3170 (919) 962-2032
Contact: Catherine A. Maley, Pres.

Financial data (yr. ended 12/31/01): Grants paid, $5,300; assets, $104,729 (M); gifts received, $7,840; expenditures, $6,816; qualifying distributions, $6,816.
Limitations: Giving primarily in Europe; giving also on a national basis.
Officers: Catherine A. Maley, Pres.; Sarah Maza, V.P.; Lloyd Kramer, Secy.; Jean J. Wilson, Treas.
EIN: 526052929
Codes: GTI

41800
North Carolina Dietetic Association Foundation, Inc.
300 Connie Cir.
Goldsboro, NC 27530
Application address: c/o Meredith College, Dept. of Human Environmental Sciences, 3800 Hillsborough St., Raleigh, N.C. 27607-5298
Contact: Susan G. Munroe

Established in 1987 in NC.
Financial data (yr. ended 05/31/00): Grants paid, $5,300; assets, $87,484 (M); gifts received, $7,366; expenditures, $7,632; qualifying distributions, $5,300.
Limitations: Giving limited to residents of NC.
Application information: Application form required.
Officers and Directors:* Lesley Stanford,* Chair.; Beverly Warner,* 1st Vice-Chair.; Janet Bryan,* 2nd Vice-Chair.; Kris Rumps,* Secy.; Nancy Williams,* Treas.
EIN: 561538250

41801
Woltz Charitable Trust
c/o J. Samuel Gentry
P.O. Box 1707
Mount Airy, NC 27030

Established around 1967.
Donor(s): Edward O. Woltz, Jr., John E. Woltz.
Financial data (yr. ended 12/31/01): Grants paid, $5,300; assets, $104,198 (M); expenditures, $7,550; qualifying distributions, $5,300.
Limitations: Applications not accepted. Giving primarily in Mount Airy, NC.
Application information: Contributes only to pre-selected organizations.
Trustee: J. Samuel Gentry, Jr.
Directors: Edwin M. Woltz, Howard O. Woltz, Jr., James L. Woltz, Patricia G. Woltz.
EIN: 237034704

41802
Hummel Hodges Foundation, Inc.
2511-A Miller Park Cir.
Winston-Salem, NC 27103

Established in 2001 in NC.
Donor(s): Amelia Hummel Hodges.
Financial data (yr. ended 12/31/01): Grants paid, $5,280; assets, $90,887 (M); gifts received, $96,418; expenditures, $7,090; qualifying distributions, $5,280.
Limitations: Applications not accepted.
Application information: Contributes only to pre-selected organizations.
Officer and Director:* Amelia Hummel Hodges.*
EIN: 562254766

41803
Janet K. Hintenlang Trust
c/o First Union National Bank
401 S. Tryon St., NC1159
Charlotte, NC 28288-1159

Established in 2001 in PA.
Financial data (yr. ended 12/31/01): Grants paid, $5,252; assets, $281,871 (M); gifts received, $289,951; expenditures, $6,956; qualifying distributions, $5,252.
Limitations: Applications not accepted. Giving primarily in PA.
Application information: Contributes only to pre-selected organizations.

Trustee: First Union National Bank.
EIN: 586437500

41804
Gwyn Family Foundation, Inc.
P.O. Box 1004
North Wilkesboro, NC 28659

Established in 1997 in NC.
Donor(s): W. Blair Gwyn.
Financial data (yr. ended 12/31/01): Grants paid, $5,227; assets, $139,633 (M); gifts received, $1,000; expenditures, $6,487; qualifying distributions, $5,227.
Limitations: Applications not accepted. Giving primarily in North Wilkesboro, NC.
Application information: Contributes only to pre-selected organizations.
Officers: W. Blair Gwyn, Pres.; Michael P. Gwyn, V.P.; W.B. Gwyn, Jr., V.P.; Florence G. Gwyn, Secy.-Treas.
EIN: 562014836

41805
Sullivan Foundation, Inc.
911 Harvard Pl.
Charlotte, NC 28207

Financial data (yr. ended 11/30/01): Grants paid, $5,150; assets, $111,150 (M); expenditures, $7,262; qualifying distributions, $5,150.
Limitations: Applications not accepted. Giving primarily in NC.
Application information: Contributes only to pre-selected organizations.
Officer: Kathy Sullivan, Pres.
EIN: 237004267

41806
Caris Foundation
2200 W. Main St., Ste. 800
Durham, NC 27705 (919) 286-8000

Established in NC in 1997.
Donor(s): Charles Holton.
Financial data (yr. ended 12/31/01): Grants paid, $5,100; assets, $6,048 (M); gifts received, $12,575; expenditures, $11,252; qualifying distributions, $11,232.
Limitations: Applications not accepted. Giving primarily in Honduras.
Application information: Contributes only to pre-selected organizations.
Officers: Charles Holton, Pres. and Treas.; Janice M. Massey, V.P.; Robert H. Jones, Secy.
EIN: 562060822

41807
The Britton Foundation
6745 N. Baltusrol Ln.
Charlotte, NC 28210-7300

Established in 1992 in CT.
Donor(s): Arthur M. Britton, William R. Britton, Jr.
Financial data (yr. ended 12/31/01): Grants paid, $5,000; assets, $141,952 (M); gifts received, $9,695; expenditures, $5,720; qualifying distributions, $5,000.
Limitations: Applications not accepted.
Application information: Contributes only to pre-selected organizations.
Officers: William R. Britton, Jr., Pres.; Arthur M. Britton, Secy.
Director: Margaret M. Britton.
EIN: 582024189

41808
A. L. Crump Family Foundation
(Formerly Crump Family Foundation)
8157 Rowe Dr.
Longisland, NC 28609 (828) 478-5558

Donor(s): A.L. Crump, Constance Rammer, Carol Crump.
Financial data (yr. ended 12/31/01): Grants paid, $5,000; assets, $97,436 (M); expenditures, $5,465; qualifying distributions, $5,000.
Limitations: Applications not accepted.
Application information: Contributes only to pre-selected organizations.
Officers: Constance Rammer, Pres.; Carol L. Crump, Secy.-Treas.
EIN: 363933230

41809
Sadie and Hobert Fouts Scholarship Fund
c/o High Point Bank & Trust Co.
P.O. Box 2278
High Point, NC 27261-2278

Established in 1997 in NC.
Financial data (yr. ended 12/31/99): Grants paid, $5,000; assets, $208,875 (M); expenditures, $7,466; qualifying distributions, $4,888.
Trustee: High Point Bank & Trust Co.
EIN: 566481132

41810
Howard D. and Rose E. Goodwin Scholarship Trust
c/o First Union National Bank
402 S. Tryon St., 4th Fl.
Charlotte, NC 28288-1159

Financial data (yr. ended 12/31/01): Grants paid, $5,000; assets, $111,516 (M); expenditures, $5,743; qualifying distributions, $5,256.
Limitations: Applications not accepted. Giving primarily in PA.
Application information: Unsolicited requests for funds not accepted.
Trustee: First Union National Bank.
EIN: 236476039
Codes: GTI

41811
Kooken Family Foundation
227 W. 5th St., Ste. 1
Winston-Salem, NC 27101 (336) 773-1344
Contact: Ruth D. Kooken, Secy.-Treas.

Established in 1998 in NC.
Donor(s): Keith R. Kooken, Ruth D. Kooken.
Financial data (yr. ended 12/31/01): Grants paid, $5,000; assets, $178,253 (M); expenditures, $8,627; qualifying distributions, $5,000.
Limitations: Giving primarily in NC.
Officers and Directors:* Katherine K. Carr, Kara K. Cochran, Kelly K. Hane, Keith R. Kooken,* Pres.; Kevin L. Kooken,* V.P.; Ruth D. Kooken,* Secy.-Treas.
EIN: 911938062

41812
Maness Family Foundation, Inc.
538 Woodland Dr.
Greensboro, NC 27408-7532

Established in 1999 in NC.
Donor(s): A.K. Maness, Jr.
Financial data (yr. ended 04/30/01): Grants paid, $5,000; assets, $77,148 (M); expenditures, $5,975; qualifying distributions, $5,000.
Officers: A. Kelly Maness, Jr., Pres.; Caroline G. Maness, Secy.
Directors: Alexander N. Maness, Archibald K. Maness III, Peter G. Maness.

EIN: 562090779

41813
Ernest and Ruby Mcswain Charitable Foundation, Inc.
P.O. Box 70
Sanford, NC 27331-0070

Established in 1999 in NC.
Financial data (yr. ended 04/30/02): Grants paid, $5,000; assets, $100,692 (M); expenditures, $5,586; qualifying distributions, $5,000.
Limitations: Applications not accepted.
Application information: Contributes only to pre-selected organizations.
Officers: W. Woods Doster, Pres.; S. Wilson Cox, Treas.
EIN: 562083620

41814
North Carolina State Grange Foundation, Inc.
2751 Patterson St.
Greensboro, NC 27407

Established in 1999 in NC.
Donor(s): Oakview Grange No. 1034, Guilford Pomona Grange, Farmer Grange, Elm City Grange.
Financial data (yr. ended 12/31/01): Grants paid, $5,000; assets, $54,060 (M); gifts received, $2,532; expenditures, $5,016; qualifying distributions, $5,000.
Limitations: Applications not accepted. Giving primarily in NC.
Application information: Contributes only to pre-selected organizations.
Officers: Robert Caldwell, Pres.; Ned Hudson, V.P.; Margie Spivey, Secy.; Jack McKee, Treas.
Director: LuAnne Brock.
EIN: 562125884

41815
The James R. Smith Family Charitable Foundation
c/o Wachovia Bank, N.A.
P.O. Box 3099
Winston-Salem, NC 27150-7131

Established in 2000 in VA.
Financial data (yr. ended 12/31/00): Grants paid, $5,000; assets, $55,603 (M); gifts received, $66,925; expenditures, $5,000; qualifying distributions, $5,000.
Limitations: Applications not accepted.
Application information: Contributes only to pre-selected organizations.
Trustee: Wachovia Bank, N.A.
EIN: 566577908

41816
William & Jacqueline Warwick Foundation, Inc.
2004 Balmoral Pl.
Wilmington, NC 28405-6212
Contact: William Warwick, Dir.

Established in 1999 in NC.
Donor(s): William Warwick, Jacqueline Warwick.
Financial data (yr. ended 06/30/01): Grants paid, $5,000; assets, $466,893 (M); gifts received, $5,000; expenditures, $10,571; qualifying distributions, $5,385.
Limitations: Giving primarily in Wilmington, NC.
Directors: Jacqueline Warwick, William Warwick.
EIN: 562170837

41817
The Whaley Endowment Fund
P.O. Box 51099
Durham, NC 27717-1099

Established in 2000 in NC.
Donor(s): Lloyd M. Whaley.

41817—NORTH CAROLINA

Financial data (yr. ended 12/31/01): Grants paid, $5,000; assets, $41,490 (M); gifts received, $24,568; expenditures, $5,915; qualifying distributions, $4,957.
Limitations: Applications not accepted.
Application information: Contributes only to pre-selected organizations.
Officers: Lloyd M. Whaley, Pres.; Gary M. Whaley, Secy.; Donald M. Whaley, Treas.
Director: Jason M. Whaley.
EIN: 562196964

41818
Kermit G. Phillips II Foundation, Inc.
1400 Battleground Ave., Ste. 201
Greensboro, NC 27408-8028

Established in 1991 in NC.
Donor(s): Kermit G. Phillips II.
Financial data (yr. ended 12/31/01): Grants paid, $4,950; assets, $1,503,376 (M); expenditures, $6,908; qualifying distributions, $4,950.
Limitations: Applications not accepted. Giving primarily in Greensboro, NC.
Application information: Contributes only to pre-selected organizations.
Officer: D. Wade Doggett, Secy.
Directors: Keith P. Phillips, Kermit G. Phillips II, Kermit G. Phillips III.
EIN: 561721385

41819
Minor Foundation, Inc.
1914 Brunswick Ave., Ste. 2B
Charlotte, NC 28207-1891
Contact: Kathreen M. Minor, Chair.

Financial data (yr. ended 09/30/01): Grants paid, $4,910; assets, $101,936 (M); expenditures, $5,226; qualifying distributions, $4,910.
Limitations: Giving primarily in NC.
Application information: Application form not required.
Officers: Kathreen M. Minor, Chair.; Kathreen R. Minor, Secy.
EIN: 566047752

41820
William P. & Tondra W. Milgrom Foundation
c/o William Milgrom
7001 Thames Ct.
Matthews, NC 28105

Financial data (yr. ended 12/31/01): Grants paid, $4,860; assets, $49,058 (M); gifts received, $4,000; expenditures, $4,869; qualifying distributions, $4,860.
Limitations: Applications not accepted.
Application information: Contributes only to pre-selected organizations.
Officers: William Milgrom, Pres.; Craig Milgrom, V.P. and Treas.; Jenifer Beek, Secy.
EIN: 561716551

41821
Willie Poovey Calton Foundation, Inc.
3205 Clark Ave.
Raleigh, NC 27607-7031

Financial data (yr. ended 10/31/01): Grants paid, $4,850; assets, $25,990 (M); expenditures, $4,878; qualifying distributions, $4,850.
Limitations: Applications not accepted. Giving primarily in NC.
Application information: Contributes only to pre-selected organizations.
Officers: Mary H. Calton, Pres. and Treas.; W.C. Calton, Jr., V.P.; Mary Fernandez DeCastro, Secy.
Directors: Philip B. Calton, R.J. Calton.
EIN: 566060799

41822
H. E. "Gene" Rayfield, Jr. Foundation
6330 Quadrangle Dr., Ste. 340
Chapel Hill, NC 27514

Established in 1997 in NC.
Donor(s): H.E. Rayfield, Jr.
Financial data (yr. ended 12/31/01): Grants paid, $4,850; assets, $58,465 (M); expenditures, $5,991; qualifying distributions, $4,850.
Limitations: Applications not accepted.
Application information: Contributes only to pre-selected organizations.
Officer: Gayle S. Rayfield, Secy.
Trustee: H.E. Rayfield, Jr.
EIN: 562032126

41823
Reef C. Ivey II Foundation
3216 Sussex Rd.
Raleigh, NC 27607-6639

Established in 1989 in PA.
Donor(s): Reef C. Ivey II.
Financial data (yr. ended 04/30/02): Grants paid, $4,825; assets, $42,087 (M); gifts received, $40,000; expenditures, $5,974; qualifying distributions, $4,825.
Limitations: Applications not accepted. Giving primarily in NC and PA.
Application information: Contributes only to pre-selected organizations.
Officers: Reef C. Ivey II, Pres.; Ethel Ivey, Secy.; R.C. Ivey, Treas.
EIN: 232570292

41824
Richards Family Private Foundation
317 Country Club Dr.
Durham, NC 27712-2423

Established in 1998 in NC.
Donor(s): John Richards.
Financial data (yr. ended 12/31/01): Grants paid, $4,825; assets, $11,089 (M); expenditures, $5,090; qualifying distributions, $4,825.
Limitations: Applications not accepted.
Application information: Contributes only to pre-selected organizations.
Officer: John Richards, Pres.
EIN: 562024158

41825
Marvin Courtney Memorial Scholarship Fund
c/o Ruby L. Courtney
3275 Playmore Beach Rd.
Morganton, NC 28655-8568
Scholarship application address: c/o Superintendent, Caldwell County Schools, Lenoir, NC 28645, tel.: (828) 728-8407

Established in 1990 in NC.
Donor(s): Robert Marvin Courtney.‡
Financial data (yr. ended 12/31/01): Grants paid, $4,775; assets, $104,054 (M); expenditures, $7,156; qualifying distributions, $6,861.
Limitations: Giving limited to residents of Caldwell County, NC.
Application information: Application form required.
Trustee: Ruby L. Courtney.
EIN: 566360424

41826
Albert Leibenguth Charitable Trust
c/o First Union National Bank
401 S. Tryon St., NC1159
Charlotte, NC 28288-1159

Financial data (yr. ended 12/31/01): Grants paid, $4,681; assets, $89,057 (M); expenditures, $5,417; qualifying distributions, $4,659.
Limitations: Applications not accepted.
Application information: Contributes only to pre-selected organizations.
Trustee: First Union National Bank.
EIN: 236746106

41827
The Langson Family Foundation
c/o Bank of America
101 S. Tryon St., Ste. 3601
Charlotte, NC 28280

Established in 1999 in NC.
Donor(s): Seth H. Langson, Bridgett Langson.
Financial data (yr. ended 12/31/01): Grants paid, $4,600; assets, $22,128 (M); gifts received, $4,100; expenditures, $27,508; qualifying distributions, $4,600.
Officers and Directors:* Seth H. Langson,* Chair.; Bridgett Langson,* V.P. and Secy.; Victor A. Way.
EIN: 562170810

41828
Martha Tovell Von Gunten Scholarship Fund
c/o First Union National Bank
401 S. Tryon St., NC1159
Charlotte, NC 28288
Application address: c/o Franklin Senior High School, 12000 Reisterstown Rd., Reisterstown, MD 21136, tel.: (410) 833-0580
Contact: Kenneth Flickinger

Financial data (yr. ended 12/31/01): Grants paid, $4,492; assets, $164,350 (M); expenditures, $8,088; qualifying distributions, $4,492.
Limitations: Giving limited to the Baltimore and Reisterstown, MD, areas.
Application information: Application form not required.
Trustee: First Union National Bank.
EIN: 526195912

41829
Hilton Charitable Trust
(Formerly Helen Reber Hilton Charitable Trust)
c/o First Union National Bank
401 S. Tryon St., 4th Fl.
Charlotte, NC 28288-1158

Established in 1996 in PA.
Financial data (yr. ended 12/31/01): Grants paid, $4,491; assets, $148,723 (M); expenditures, $5,118; qualifying distributions, $4,791.
Limitations: Applications not accepted. Giving primarily in Pottsville, PA.
Application information: Contributes only to pre-selected organizations.
Trustee: First Union National Bank.
EIN: 237831172

41830
Beasley Foundation
(Formerly Beasley, Gibbs & Kemp Foundation)
P.O. Box 12242
New Bern, NC 28560-2242

Established in 1997 in NC.
Donor(s): Clarence B. Beasley.
Financial data (yr. ended 12/31/01): Grants paid, $4,400; assets, $73,599 (M); expenditures, $8,776; qualifying distributions, $4,400.
Limitations: Applications not accepted.

Application information: Contributes only to pre-selected organizations.
Director: Clarence B. Beasley.
EIN: 562059794

41831
C. Haley Foundation, Inc.
c/o Mike Winnig
228 W. Market St.
Greensboro, NC 27401

Financial data (yr. ended 10/31/01): Grants paid, $4,400; assets, $70,006 (M); expenditures, $4,498; qualifying distributions, $4,400.
Limitations: Applications not accepted. Giving primarily in NC.
Application information: Contributes only to pre-selected organizations.
Officers and Directors:* Clifford E. Haley, Jr.,* Pres. and Treas.; Mary E. Haley,* Secy.; Clifford E. Haley III, Winder Pell.
EIN: 561726958

41832
Paulina and Stephen Cepreghy Charitable Foundation
c/o First Union National Bank
401 S. Tryon St., NC1159
Charlotte, NC 28288-1159

Established in 2000 in NC.
Financial data (yr. ended 12/31/01): Grants paid, $4,386; assets, $58,723 (M); expenditures, $12,613; qualifying distributions, $4,386.
Trustee: First Union National Bank.
EIN: 256699332

41833
Wayne and Carolyn Jones Charitable Foundation
3620 Cape Center Dr.
Fayetteville, NC 28304
Application address: 5 Northbrook Way, Greenville, SC 29615-6046
Contact: Wayne Jones, Pres. and Carolyn Jones, Treas.

Established in 2000 in NC.
Donor(s): Carolyn Jones, Wayne Jones.
Financial data (yr. ended 12/31/01): Grants paid, $4,355; assets, $405,436 (M); gifts received, $303,400; expenditures, $5,376; qualifying distributions, $4,355.
Officers: Wayne Jones, Pres.; William T. Allen, Secy.; Carolyn Jones, Treas.
EIN: 311738970

41834
Praise Broadcasting Network, Inc.
c/o McAnderson's Plz.
P.O. Box 3992
Wilmington, NC 28406-0992

Donor(s): Dennis Anderson.
Financial data (yr. ended 12/31/00): Grants paid, $4,315; assets, $175,108 (M); gifts received, $44,664; expenditures, $228,370; qualifying distributions, $149,187.
Limitations: Applications not accepted.
Application information: Contributes only to pre-selected organizations.
Officers and Directors:* Dennis Anderson,* Pres. and V.P.; Michael Escalante,* Secy.-Treas.
EIN: 561465080

41835
NCITE Foundation, Inc.
P.O. Box 469
Raleigh, NC 27602

Donor(s): NCITE Association Inc.

Financial data (yr. ended 12/31/01): Grants paid, $4,306; assets, $32,461 (M); gifts received, $21,500; expenditures, $21,425; qualifying distributions, $4,306.
Limitations: Applications not accepted.
Application information: Contributes only to pre-selected organizations.
Officer: Philip Fowler, Secy.-Treas.
EIN: 561948555

41836
Boyd Family Foundation
c/o Pascal Boyd II
3916 Chippenham Rd.
Durham, NC 27707

Established in 1999 in NC.
Financial data (yr. ended 12/31/01): Grants paid, $4,300; assets, $91,392 (M); expenditures, $6,610; qualifying distributions, $4,300.
Limitations: Applications not accepted. Giving primarily in Durham, NC.
Application information: Contributes only to pre-selected organizations.
Officers: Pascal S. Boyd II, Pres.; Jetta Boyd, Secy.-Treas.
Directors: Pascal S. Boyd III, Sarah Elizabeth Debruyne.
EIN: 562146331

41837
Clara J. & Harvey Moody Memorial Scholarship Fund
c/o Wachovia Bank, N.A.
P.O. Box 3099
Winston-Salem, NC 27150-7131

Established in 1999 in NC.
Donor(s): M. Ada Moody.‡
Financial data (yr. ended 12/31/01): Grants paid, $4,298; assets, $494,971 (M); expenditures, $12,117; qualifying distributions, $4,298.
Limitations: Applications not accepted.
Application information: Contributes only to pre-selected organizations.
Trustee: Wachovia Bank, N.A.
EIN: 566558951

41838
Susong Family Foundation, Inc.
321 S. Elm St., Ste. 309
Greensboro, NC 27401
Contact: Kirk Susong

Established in 1998 in GA.
Donor(s): Adrienne Susong, Andrew Kirk Susong.
Financial data (yr. ended 12/31/99): Grants paid, $4,225; assets, $11,016 (M); gifts received, $9,851; expenditures, $4,225; qualifying distributions, $4,225.
Officer: Adrienne Susong, Pres. and Secy.-Treas.
Board Member: Andrew Kirk Susong.
EIN: 582408605

41839
Byerly Foundation, Inc.
1446 6th St., Circle Ct., N.W.
Hickory, NC 28601

Donor(s): W. Grimes Byerly, W. Grimes Byerly, Jr.
Financial data (yr. ended 12/31/01): Grants paid, $4,200; assets, $56,854 (M); gifts received, $2,750; expenditures, $4,964; qualifying distributions, $4,200.
Limitations: Applications not accepted. Giving primarily in NC.
Application information: Contributes only to pre-selected organizations.
Officers: W. Grimes Byerly, Jr., Pres. and Treas.; Wesley G. Byerly III, V.P.; Andrew B. Byerly, Secy.
EIN: 561156811

41840
Miriam E. Alsobrooks Educational Fund
c/o Wachovia Bank of South Carolina, N.A.
P.O. Box 3099
Winston-Salem, NC 27150-7153
Application address: c/o Dir. of Guidance, Marlboro County High School, 951 Fayettvile Ave. EXT., Bennettsville, SC 29512

Financial data (yr. ended 06/30/01): Grants paid, $4,000; assets, $191,442 (M); expenditures, $5,694; qualifying distributions, $4,390.
Limitations: Giving limited to Marlboro County, SC.
Application information: Application form required.
Trustee: Wachovia Bank of South Carolina, N.A.
EIN: 576037000
Codes: GTI

41841
Donahue Charitable Foundation
c/o Edward C. Donahue
2919 Somerset Dr.
Charlotte, NC 28209-1433

Established in 1997.
Donor(s): Edward C. Donahue.
Financial data (yr. ended 12/31/01): Grants paid, $4,000; assets, $77,456 (M); gifts received, $15,000; expenditures, $4,549; qualifying distributions, $4,089.
Officers: Edward C. Donahue, Mgr.; Theresa D. Donahue, Mgr.; Michelle Dudley, Mgr.
EIN: 043368096

41842
Evans Family Foundation, Inc.
c/o Bank of America
101 S. Tryon St., NC1-002-11-18
Charlotte, NC 28255-0002

Established in 1996 in NC.
Donor(s): David S. Evans, Yvonne Willer Evans.
Financial data (yr. ended 12/31/01): Grants paid, $4,000; assets, $70,687 (M); expenditures, $5,628; qualifying distributions, $4,000.
Limitations: Applications not accepted.
Application information: Contributes only to pre-selected organizations.
Officers and Directors:* Yvonne Willer Davis,* Pres.; David S. Evans,* Secy.
Trustee: Bank of America.
EIN: 561977040

41843
Robert L. Smith, Jr. Memorial Education Fund
308 Buncombe St.
Raleigh, NC 27609-6312 (919) 881-9571
Application address: c/o Ms. Peadin, Farmville Central High School, P.O. Box 209, Farmville, NC 27828

Established in 1990 in NC.
Donor(s): Robert L. Smith, Jr.
Financial data (yr. ended 12/31/01): Grants paid, $4,000; assets, $105,758 (M); expenditures, $4,858; qualifying distributions, $4,146.
Limitations: Giving limited to residents of Pitt, Green, and Edgecombe counties, NC.
Application information: Application form required.
Selection Committee Members: Carl W. Blackwood, Bill Davis, Tommy Lang.
Trustee: David L. Smith.
EIN: 561709175

41844
Stone Family Foundation
c/o Bank of America
Bank of America Plz., NC1-002-11-18
Charlotte, NC 28255
Application address: 4200 Clinard Rd.,
Clemmons, NC 27012
Contact: Sandra R. Linker, Pres.

Established 1999 in NC.
Donor(s): Sandra R. Linker.
Financial data (yr. ended 04/30/01): Grants paid, $4,000; assets, $193,299 (M); gifts received, $602; expenditures, $16,373; qualifying distributions, $11,992.
Officers and Director:* Sandra R. Linker,* Pres.; Jeffrey W. Andrews, V.P.; Kimberly A. Ebert, Secy.; Suzanna A. Ray.
EIN: 571093407

41845
Wayne Memorial Hospital Auxiliary Endowment, Inc.
3300 Cashwell Dr., Ste. 1
Goldsboro, NC 27534-4456
Contact: John B. Parker

Established in 1990 in NC.
Donor(s): Wayne Memorial Hospital Auxiliary.
Financial data (yr. ended 12/31/00): Grants paid, $4,000; assets, $59,821 (M); expenditures, $4,522; qualifying distributions, $4,000.
Limitations: Giving limited to residents of Wayne County, NC.
Application information: Application form required.
Officer: Jane Franklin, Pres.
EIN: 581893466

41846
The Ramsay Family Foundation, Inc.
1409 Westmont Cir.
Asheboro, NC 27205

Established in 1999.
Donor(s): Julius M. Ramsay, Jr., Winifred P. Ramsay.
Financial data (yr. ended 01/31/02): Grants paid, $3,989; assets, $164,860 (M); expenditures, $5,181; qualifying distributions, $3,989.
Limitations: Applications not accepted. Giving on a national basis.
Application information: Contributes only to pre-selected organizations.
Officers: Julius M. Ramsay, Jr., Pres.; Winifred P. Ramsay, Secy.-Treas.
Directors: Benjamin H. Ramsay, James M. Ramsay III.
EIN: 562126602

41847
Providence Foundation
3515 Foxcroft Rd.
Charlotte, NC 28211-3719
Contact: Hugh A. Cathey, Chair.

Established in 1945 in NC.
Financial data (yr. ended 12/31/01): Grants paid, $3,900; assets, $898,558 (M); expenditures, $5,377; qualifying distributions, $3,900.
Officers: Hugh A. Cathey, Chair. and Pres.; Mary A. Cathey, V.P.; C.C. Burgston, Secy.; Hugh A. Cathey, Jr., Treas.
EIN: 566063503

41848
Charles Brantley Strickland Scholarship Foundation, Inc.
P.O. Box 8010
Goldsboro, NC 27533
Application address: c/o V.P., Employee Relations, P.O. Drawer 2027, Goldsboro, NC 27533

Donor(s): Strickland Insurance Group.
Financial data (yr. ended 11/30/00): Grants paid, $3,898; assets, $80,772 (M); gifts received, $1,300; expenditures, $3,898; qualifying distributions, $3,898.
Application information: Application form required.
Officers: Richard Yarbrough, Pres.; Robert E. Watson, Secy.-Treas.
EIN: 561848330

41849
Culler Foundation
c/o Wachovia Bank, N.A.
P.O. Box 3099
Winston-Salem, NC 27150-7153
Application address: 1223 Westwood Ave., High Point, NC 27262, tel.: (336) 886-7525
Contact: Roy B. Culler, Jr., Admin. Comm.

Donor(s): Roy B. Culler, Jr., Roy B. Culler, Jr.
Financial data (yr. ended 06/30/01): Grants paid, $3,890; assets, $70,555 (M); expenditures, $6,885; qualifying distributions, $5,641.
Limitations: Giving primarily in NC.
Application information: Application form not required.
Administrative Committee: Iola D. Culler, Robert A. Culler, Roy B. Culler, Jr.
Trustee: Wachovia Bank, N.A.
EIN: 566072011

41850
Lirtie L. and Sarah Clark Memorial Endowment Fund
c/o Wachovia Bank of North Carolina, N.A.
P.O. Box 3099
Winston-Salem, NC 27150-7131

Financial data (yr. ended 12/31/01): Grants paid, $3,889; assets, $121,197 (M); expenditures, $7,236; qualifying distributions, $3,889.
Limitations: Applications not accepted. Giving limited to VA.
Application information: Contributes only to pre-selected organizations.
Officer: Belinda Pullen, Mgr.
Trustee: Wachovia Bank of North Carolina, N.A.
EIN: 546211495

41851
Coppedge Foundation
c/o Karen C. Coppedge
918 Bayshore Dr.
Wilmington, NC 28405

Established in 1987 in NC.
Financial data (yr. ended 12/31/01): Grants paid, $3,840; assets, $37,625 (M); expenditures, $4,481; qualifying distributions, $3,840.
Limitations: Applications not accepted. Giving primarily in Wilmington, NC.
Application information: Contributes only to pre-selected organizations.
Trustee: Karen C. Coppedge.
EIN: 566289525

41852
Closer to the Stars Foundation
P.O. Box 7965
Rocky Mount, NC 27804-0965

Established in 2000 in NC.
Donor(s): Mack B. Pearsall, Janice J. Pearsall.
Financial data (yr. ended 12/31/00): Grants paid, $3,678; assets, $31,934 (M); gifts received, $31,643; expenditures, $4,628; qualifying distributions, $3,634.
Limitations: Applications not accepted. Giving primarily in NC.
Application information: Contributes only to pre-selected organizations.
Trustees: Janice J. Pearsall, Mack B. Pearsall.
EIN: 562179410

41853
Mid-Atlantic Foundation
P.O. Box 2063
Goldsboro, NC 27533-2063 (919) 734-1111
Contact: David Weil, Dir.

Established in 1998 in NC.
Donor(s): Charles B. Ellis.
Financial data (yr. ended 12/31/01): Grants paid, $3,650; assets, $6,173 (M); gifts received, $7,000; expenditures, $5,324; qualifying distributions, $3,650.
Limitations: Giving limited to the Mid-Atlantic region, with emphasis on NC.
Directors: David Weil, Emily Weil.
EIN: 562026040

41854
William W. Flowers Trust f/b/o Durham Charities
c/o Wachovia Bank, N.A.
P.O. Box 3099
Winston-Salem, NC 27150-7153
Contact: Jim Gallaher

Financial data (yr. ended 12/31/01): Grants paid, $3,533; assets, $92,503 (M); expenditures, $5,029; qualifying distributions, $3,533.
Limitations: Giving limited to Durham, NC.
Trustee: Wachovia Bank, N.A.
EIN: 566040174

41855
R. C. Hines, Jr. and Viola D. Hines Foundation
233 Bellewood Dr.
Henderson, NC 27536

Financial data (yr. ended 12/31/01): Grants paid, $3,500; assets, $103,473 (M); gifts received, $927; expenditures, $4,211; qualifying distributions, $3,500.
Limitations: Applications not accepted. Giving primarily in VA.
Application information: Contributes only to pre-selected organizations.
Officers: Michael G. Harper, Pres.; Lynn H. Harper, Secy.; Melissa N. Hines, Treas.
EIN: 561889610

41856
The Mustard Seed Foundation
3620 Cape Center Dr.
Fayetteville, NC 28304
Application address: P.O. Box 52328, Durham, NC 27717
Contact: Miriam Wellons, Pres.

Established in 1997 in NC.
Financial data (yr. ended 12/31/01): Grants paid, $3,500; assets, $38,338 (M); gifts received, $5,000; expenditures, $3,500; qualifying distributions, $3,500.
Officer: Miriam Wellons, Pres.

EIN: 311519267

41857
C. & D. VanDeusen Foundation, Inc.
621 Laurel Lane Dr.
Tryon Estates, Apt. B110
Columbus, NC 28722-7420
Contact: Courtland VanDeusen III, Pres.

Financial data (yr. ended 07/31/01): Grants paid, $3,500; assets, $73,467 (M); gifts received, $4,211; expenditures, $4,611; qualifying distributions, $3,500.
Limitations: Giving on a national basis.
Officers: Courtland VanDeusen III, Pres. and Treas.; Lawrence VanDeusen, V.P.; Roy F. Mahlberg, Secy.
Directors: Bill Gibbs, Greg Sperry, C. VanDeusen IV, D.S. VanDeusen, E. VanDeusen.
EIN: 161264422

41858
Joan and Stanley Fox Foundation
P.O. Box 1206
Oxford, NC 27565-2741

Established in 1989 in NC.
Donor(s): Stanley Fox.
Financial data (yr. ended 12/31/01): Grants paid, $3,350; assets, $5,218 (M); expenditures, $3,460; qualifying distributions, $3,350.
Limitations: Applications not accepted. Giving primarily in NC.
Application information: Contributes only to pre-selected organizations.
Officers: Stanley Fox, Pres. and Treas.; Susan F. Robinson, Secy.
EIN: 561666689

41859
Frederick L. Block Foundation, Inc.
6266 Hawksbill Dr.
Wilmington, NC 28409

Financial data (yr. ended 12/31/01): Grants paid, $3,275; assets, $59,784 (M); expenditures, $4,276; qualifying distributions, $3,275.
Limitations: Applications not accepted.
Application information: Contributes only to pre-selected organizations.
Officer: F.L. Block, Pres.
Director: D.E. Block.
EIN: 581968575

41860
David E. Block Foundation, Inc.
P.O. Box 1848
Wilmington, NC 28402-1848

Established in 1992 in FL.
Financial data (yr. ended 12/31/01): Grants paid, $3,250; assets, $72,371 (M); expenditures, $3,573; qualifying distributions, $3,250.
Limitations: Applications not accepted.
Application information: Contributes only to pre-selected organizations.
Directors: David E. Block, F.L. Block.
EIN: 581958227

41861
The James T. and Natalie A. Beckert Family Foundation
2722 Chessel Pl.
Charlotte, NC 28226-4352

Established in 2000 in NC.
Donor(s): James T. Beckert, Natalie A. Beckert.
Financial data (yr. ended 12/31/01): Grants paid, $3,200; assets, $5,415 (M); gifts received, $5,045; expenditures, $5,877; qualifying distributions, $3,200.

Officers: James T. Beckert, Pres. and Treas.; Natalie A. Beckert, Secy.
Directors: Jason M. Beckert, Joseph M. Beckert, Juliane Beckert, Suzanne Hindes.
EIN: 562228339

41862
The Flynn Foundation, Inc.
97 Overlook Dr.
Cullowhee, NC 28723
Contact: Paul S. Flynn, Secy.

Financial data (yr. ended 12/31/99): Grants paid, $3,200; assets, $136,785 (M); gifts received, $2,207; expenditures, $3,736; qualifying distributions, $5,809; giving activities include $2,400 for loans to individuals.
Limitations: Giving limited to NC.
Officers: Jim W. Meredith, Pres.; Charles L. Ricketts, V.P.; Paul S. Flynn, Secy.; Pat White, Treas.
EIN: 510173869
Codes: GTI

41863
The George Muller Foundation
175 Davidson Hwy.
Concord, NC 28025
Contact: John E. Littlefield, Exec. Dir.

Established in 1999 in NC.
Financial data (yr. ended 05/31/01): Grants paid, $3,200; assets, $21,645 (M); gifts received, $2,439; expenditures, $3,200; qualifying distributions, $3,189.
Limitations: Giving limited to residents of NC.
Application information: Application form required.
Officer: John E. Littlefield, Exec. Dir.
Directors: David Drye, Jr., Jennifer Drye Jewell, James K. Jewell, Leann Drye Littlefield.
EIN: 562145464

41864
Domestic Industries Foundation
c/o Fred E. Hunneke
1100 Hardee Rd.
Kinston, NC 28501-2529

Financial data (yr. ended 12/31/01): Grants paid, $3,150; assets, $26,177 (M); expenditures, $3,170; qualifying distributions, $3,150.
Limitations: Applications not accepted. Giving primarily in Greenville, NC.
Application information: Contributes only to pre-selected organizations.
Officers: Fred E. Hunneke, Pres.; Anneliese E. Hunneke, Secy.; Roy A. Cohen, Treas.
EIN: 561806743

41865
Jean Koch Evangelistic Association
c/o Rev. Jean Koch
8812 Windjammer Dr.
Raleigh, NC 27615

Financial data (yr. ended 12/31/01): Grants paid, $3,041; assets, $140 (M); gifts received, $4,046; expenditures, $4,001; qualifying distributions, $3,041.
Officers: Rev. Jean A. Koch, Pres.; William C. Koch, Jr., V.P.; Annette R. Williams, Treas.
Director: Hilda Killian Smith.
EIN: 582018290

41866
Robert J. Alander Scholarship Fund
P.O. Box 472654
Charlotte, NC 28247-2654
Application address: P.O. Box 32368, Charlotte, NC 28232
Contact: Robert Teague, Chair.

Financial data (yr. ended 06/30/01): Grants paid, $3,000; assets, $38,511 (M); expenditures, $3,447; qualifying distributions, $3,000.
Limitations: Giving limited to residents of Charlotte, NC.
Application information: Application form required.
Officers and Trustees: Robert Teague,* Chair.; David Miller,* Pres.; Margaret Fisher, Jeanne F. Reynolds.
EIN: 566235792
Codes: GTI

41867
Classic Foundation, Inc.
c/o Classic Leather, Inc.
P.O. Box 2404
Hickory, NC 28603-2404

Established in 1976 in NC.
Donor(s): Classic Leather, Inc.
Financial data (yr. ended 10/31/01): Grants paid, $3,000; assets, $25,598 (M); gifts received, $5,000; expenditures, $4,700; qualifying distributions, $4,700.
Limitations: Applications not accepted. Giving limited to NC.
Application information: Contributes only to pre-selected organizations.
Officers: Thomas H. Shores, Sr., Pres. and Treas.; Charles D. Dixon, Secy.
EIN: 581351062
Codes: CS, CD

41868
Kimberly F. Crews Foundation, Inc.
5517 Shadowbrook Dr.
Raleigh, NC 27612

Established in 1996.
Financial data (yr. ended 12/31/01): Grants paid, $3,000; assets, $264,049 (M); expenditures, $11,244; qualifying distributions, $3,000.
Limitations: Applications not accepted.
Application information: Contributes only to pre-selected organizations.
Officers: Alan Crews, Pres. and Treas.; Melissa Johnson, V.P.; Denise Everett, Secy.
EIN: 561961615

41869
J. H. & Janet E. Fields Family Private Foundation
2226 Meadow Wood Rd.
Fayetteville, NC 28303-5303

Established in 1997.
Donor(s): J.H. Fields, Janet E. Fields.
Financial data (yr. ended 12/31/01): Grants paid, $3,000; assets, $62,926 (M); expenditures, $3,137; qualifying distributions, $3,000.
Limitations: Applications not accepted.
Application information: Contributes only to pre-selected organizations.
Trustee: Janet E. Fields.
EIN: 566504617

41870
Braswell Gorham Foundation
6000 Monroe Rd., Ste. 101
Charlotte, NC 28212
Application address: c/o Becky Butler, P.O. Box 912, Rocky Mount, NC 27802, tel.: (252) 443-7041

Financial data (yr. ended 12/31/00): Grants paid, $3,000; assets, $32,770 (M); expenditures, $3,000; qualifying distributions, $3,000.
Limitations: Giving primarily in NC.
Application information: Application form not required.
Trustee: Robert D. Gorham, Jr.
EIN: 566090283

41871
Mildred B. Hoopes and Lydia Y. Hoopes Scholarship Fund
c/o First Union National Bank
401 S. Tryon St, NC 1159
Charlotte, NC 28288
Application address: c/o Principal, Pennwood Senior High School, Lansdowne, PA 19050

Financial data (yr. ended 08/31/01): Grants paid, $3,000; assets, $54,131 (M); expenditures, $3,966; qualifying distributions, $3,730.
Limitations: Giving limited to Landsdowne, PA.
Application information: Application form not required.
Trustee: First Union National Bank.
EIN: 236221158

41872
Eleanor Craig Kline Scholarship Fund
c/o Wachovia Bank, N.A.
P.O. Box 3099
Winston-Salem, NC 27150-8732

Established in 1991 in NC.
Financial data (yr. ended 12/31/01): Grants paid, $3,000; assets, $66,503 (M); gifts received, $2,900; expenditures, $4,575; qualifying distributions, $3,723.
Limitations: Giving limited to residents of Charleston, SC.
Trustees: Eva Lou Sherrod Costa, Barbara Gilchrist, Neal Golden, Jr., Wachovia Bank, N.A.
EIN: 570935398

41873
Tompkins Family Foundation
c/o James R. and Myra D. Tompkins
2161 Ash Little River Rd. N.W.
Ash, NC 28420

Established in 2001 in NC.
Donor(s): James R. Tompkins, Myra D. Tompkins.
Financial data (yr. ended 12/31/01): Grants paid, $2,999; assets, $25,811 (M); gifts received, $30,000; expenditures, $4,000; qualifying distributions, $2,999.
Officers: James R. Tompkins, Pres.; C. Tompkins, V.P.; Myra D. Tompkins, Secy.; N. Tompkins, Treas.
EIN: 562232102

41874
The Micah Foundation
4120 Dresden Dr.
Winston-Salem, NC 27104
Contact: Nancy H. Southard, Pres.

Established in 1999 in NC.
Donor(s): Nancy H. Southard, John K. Southard.
Financial data (yr. ended 12/31/01): Grants paid, $2,915; assets, $53,457 (M); gifts received, $10,558; expenditures, $5,433; qualifying distributions, $2,915.

Limitations: Giving primarily in Winston-Salem, NC.
Application information: Application form required.
Officers: Nancy H. Southard, Pres.; Timothy K. Southard, Secy.-Treas.
EIN: 911984388

41875
The Breeden Family Foundation
100 Europa Dr., Ste. 200
Chapel Hill, NC 27514
Application address: 721 E. Franklin St., Chapel Hill, NC 27514
Contact: Douglas T. Breeden, Pres.

Donor(s): Douglas T. Breeden.
Financial data (yr. ended 12/31/01): Grants paid, $2,907; assets, $272 (M); gifts received, $2,500; expenditures, $2,937; qualifying distributions, $2,907.
Officers: Douglas T. Breeden, Pres.; Josie C. Breeden, V.P.; Russell Breeden III, V.P.; Annabelle T. Breeden, Secy.-Treas.
EIN: 562006787

41876
Seaman's Outreach Services, Inc.
P.O. Box 68
Sealevel, NC 28577-0068
Contact: Robert E.L. Taylor, Pres.

Financial data (yr. ended 12/31/00): Grants paid, $2,800; assets, $1,029 (M); gifts received, $3,720; expenditures, $3,697; qualifying distributions, $3,697.
Officers: Robert E.L. Taylor, Pres.; Marie P. Taylor, Secy.-Treas.
Director: Nancy Cox Taylor.
EIN: 592263586

41877
The Kern Foundation, Inc.
c/o David R. McCoy, C.P.A.
723 W. Innes St.
Salisbury, NC 28144-4690 (704) 638-0431
Contact: Thomas Kern, Pres.

Donor(s): Thomas W. Kern.
Financial data (yr. ended 12/31/00): Grants paid, $2,650; assets, $200,942 (M); expenditures, $3,279; qualifying distributions, $0.
Limitations: Giving primarily in Salisbury, NC.
Officers: Thomas W. Kern, Pres.; George Kluttz, V.P.
EIN: 561215343

41878
The Sanders Family Foundation
P.O. Box 37
Tabor City, NC 28463-0037

Established in 1999 in NC.
Donor(s): Annie M. Sanders.
Financial data (yr. ended 12/31/01): Grants paid, $2,596; assets, $128,098 (M); gifts received, $64,545; expenditures, $3,687; qualifying distributions, $2,596.
Officer: Roderick Sanders, Pres.
Directors: Anne Mallard Sanders, Daniel Sanders.
EIN: 562169104

41879
Blythe Brothers Foundation
1415 E. Westinghouse Blvd.
Charlotte, NC 28273
Contact: F.J. Blythe, Jr., Pres.

Financial data (yr. ended 12/31/01): Grants paid, $2,500; assets, $46,816 (M); expenditures, $2,542; qualifying distributions, $2,500.
Limitations: Giving primarily in Charlotte, NC.

Officers: F.J. Blythe, Jr., Pres.; L.J. Blythe, V.P.; F.W. Blythe, Secy.
EIN: 566075607

41880
Colonial Foundation, Inc.
228 Sudley Cir.
Salisbury, NC 28144-2961 (704) 633-8248
Contact: John F. Lipe, Jr., Pres.

Financial data (yr. ended 12/31/01): Grants paid, $2,500; assets, $76,044 (M); expenditures, $3,111; qualifying distributions, $2,500.
Application information: Application form required.
Officer: John F. Lipe, Jr., Pres. and Treas.
EIN: 566047503

41881
Matthews Foundation of Asheville, Inc.
615 High Ridge Rd.
Waynesville, NC 28786-9138

Financial data (yr. ended 11/30/01): Grants paid, $2,500; assets, $75,145 (M); expenditures, $3,941; qualifying distributions, $2,500.
Limitations: Applications not accepted. Giving primarily in Asheville, NC.
Application information: Contributes only to pre-selected organizations.
Officers: Mildred Matthews Dillard, Pres.; Deborah R. Wilson, V.P.; John L. Robinson, Secy.; Raymond Eley Robinson, Treas.
EIN: 566066291

41882
Sammy and Michele Martin Foundation
306 Waterside Dr.
Carrboro, NC 27510-1289

Financial data (yr. ended 12/31/00): Grants paid, $2,450; assets, $57,688 (M); expenditures, $3,308; qualifying distributions, $2,450.
Limitations: Applications not accepted.
Application information: Contributes only to pre-selected organizations.
Trustees: Michele Martin, Sammy Martin.
EIN: 562117256

41883
Louise L. Tuller Trust
c/o J. Allen Harrington
1410 Elm St.
Sanford, NC 27330
Application address: P.O. Box 1766, Sanford, NC 27331-1766
Contact: Harry Miller, Tr.

Financial data (yr. ended 12/31/01): Grants paid, $2,400; assets, $451,658 (M); expenditures, $12,854; qualifying distributions, $7,505; giving activities include $2,400 for loans to individuals.
Limitations: Giving limited to residents of Lee County, NC.
Application information: Application form required.
Trustees: J. Allen Harrington, Kenneth R. Hoyle, Elaine Hylwa, Harry Miller, Margaret Wicker.
EIN: 566225205
Codes: GTI

41884
Bob and Sharlene Williams Charitable Foundation
104 Great Oaks Rd.
Fayetteville, NC 28303 (910) 864-3232
Contact: Robert J. Williams IV, Pres.

Established in 2000 in NC.
Donor(s): Robert J. Williams IV, Sharlene R. Williams.

Financial data (yr. ended 12/31/01): Grants paid, $2,400; assets, $7,502 (M); expenditures, $2,400; qualifying distributions, $2,400.
Application information: Application form not required.
Officers: Robert J. Williams IV, Pres. and Treas.; Sharlene R. Williams, V.P. and Secy.
EIN: 562121671

41885
Eldred and Sarah Wooten Prince Foundation
c/o B.B. & T., Trust Dept.
P.O. Box 632
Whiteville, NC 28472
Application address: P.O. Box 6676, Florence, SC 29502, tel.: (843) 664-1010

Established in 1993 in NC.
Financial data (yr. ended 06/30/02): Grants paid, $2,380; assets, $44,023 (M); expenditures, $3,662; qualifying distributions, $2,380.
Trustee: B.B. & T.
EIN: 566429281

41886
Five Star Foundation, Inc.
101 E. Center St.
Mebane, NC 27302
Application address: P.O. Box 10, Mebane, NC 27302
Contact: William R. Hupman, Jr., Dir.

Established in 1998 in NC.
Donor(s): William R. Hupman, Jr.
Financial data (yr. ended 06/30/00): Grants paid, $2,352; assets, $5,292 (M); gifts received, $18,300; expenditures, $14,537; qualifying distributions, $17,395.
Limitations: Giving limited to NC.
Directors: Charles Bateman, Lynn Briggs, Jo Anne Hayes, Anne Honeycutt, Mary M. Hupman, William R. Hupman, Jr., Kim Mellor, Amy Walker.
EIN: 562087249

41887
William A. & Eleanor R. Nichols Foundation
4500 Cameron Valley Pkwy., Ste. 130
Charlotte, NC 28211
Contact: William A. Nichols, Jr., Pres.

Established in 1998 in NC.
Donor(s): William A. Nichols, Eleanor R. Nichols.
Financial data (yr. ended 12/31/01): Grants paid, $2,310; assets, $26,312 (M); gifts received, $15,414; expenditures, $11,830; qualifying distributions, $10,750.
Limitations: Giving primarily in Charlotte, NC.
Officer and Directors:* William A. Nichols, Jr.,* Pres.; Henry Nichols, Jackson Nichols, Mark Nichols.
EIN: 571066131

41888
Amelia & Ben Solomon Fund
c/o Wachovia Bank, N.A.
P.O. Box 3099
Winston-Salem, NC 27150-1022
(336) 732-5372
Contact: Linda Tilley

Financial data (yr. ended 01/31/02): Grants paid, $2,303; assets, $61,927 (M); expenditures, $3,350; qualifying distributions, $2,303.
Limitations: Giving limited to Wilmington, NC.
Trustee: Wachovia Bank, N.A.
EIN: 566040673

41889
Columbus County Community Foundation
c/o B.B. & T., Trust Dept.
P.O. Box 632
Whiteville, NC 28472 (910) 642-1420

Financial data (yr. ended 08/31/00): Grants paid, $2,300; assets, $56,489 (M); expenditures, $4,851; qualifying distributions, $2,300.
Trustee: B.B. & T.
EIN: 566094482

41890
Association of Capitular Masons, Inc.
7515 Timber Ridge Dr.
Charlotte, NC 28227-4012 (704) 545-3748

Financial data (yr. ended 12/31/01): Grants paid, $2,251; assets, $191,669 (M); expenditures, $2,842; qualifying distributions, $2,251.
Limitations: Giving primarily in NC.
Officers: A.G. Bartlett, Pres.; Allen Hagler, V.P.; N. Peter Hansen, Secy.-Treas.
Directors: Harry Benfield, Mike Davis, Ralph Heedick, Charles W. Smith.
EIN: 560858000

41891
Joppa Foundation, Inc.
c/o David L. Lollar
812 Ascot Ln.
Raleigh, NC 27615-1901 (919) 847-0577

Established in 1991 in NC.
Donor(s): David Lollar, Beverly B. Lollar.
Financial data (yr. ended 12/31/01): Grants paid, $2,250; assets, $61,311 (M); expenditures, $2,696; qualifying distributions, $2,250.
Limitations: Applications not accepted.
Application information: Contributes only to pre-selected organizations.
Officers and Directors:* David Lollar,* Pres.; Beverly B. Lollar,* Secy.
EIN: 561759539

41892
William M. York Benevolence Fund
507 Jackson St.
Greensboro, NC 27403-2462

Financial data (yr. ended 12/31/01): Grants paid, $2,201; assets, $30,650 (M); expenditures, $3,132; qualifying distributions, $2,201.
Limitations: Applications not accepted.
Application information: Contributes only to pre-selected organizations.
Trustees: Frank W. York, William M. York, Jr.
EIN: 566061489

41893
War Memorial Scholarship of the National League of Women's Service
c/o First Union National Bank
401 S. Tryon St.
Charlotte, NC 28288-1159
Application address: Guidance Dept., c/o Ridgefield High School, Ridgefield, CT 06877

Financial data (yr. ended 12/31/00): Grants paid, $2,200; assets, $38,387 (M); expenditures, $5,219; qualifying distributions, $3,033.
Limitations: Giving limited to residents of Ridgefield, CT.
Application information: Applications are available from Ridgefield High School, Ridgefield, CT.
Trustee: First Union National Bank.
EIN: 066042954

41894
Peter Joseph Cusano Foundation, Inc.
P.O. Box 472474
Charlotte, NC 28247-6474

Established around 1987 in NC.
Financial data (yr. ended 12/31/01): Grants paid, $2,171; assets, $119,801 (M); expenditures, $2,881; qualifying distributions, $2,171.
Limitations: Applications not accepted.
Application information: Contributes only to pre-selected organizations.
Officers: Michael R. Cusano, Pres.; Antoinette M. Cusano, V.P.; Karen E. Cusano, Secy.; Thomas M. Cusano, Treas.
EIN: 561582389

41895
Katharine Andrews Foundation
604 Laurel Hill Rd.
Chapel Hill, NC 27514 (919) 967-4620
Contact: Katharine A. Browne, Pres.

Established in 1996 in NC and VA.
Donor(s): Katharine A. Browne.
Financial data (yr. ended 12/31/01): Grants paid, $2,134; assets, $156,235 (M); gifts received, $12,804; expenditures, $3,848; qualifying distributions, $2,134.
Officer and Director:* Katharine A. Browne,* Pres.
EIN: 522006320

41896
Child Like Faith Foundation
3620 Cape Center Dr.
Fayetteville, NC 28304
Application address: P.O. Box 52328, Durham, NC 27717
Contact: Charlene Hamlett, Pres.

Established in 1997 in NC.
Financial data (yr. ended 12/31/01): Grants paid, $2,100; assets, $39,749 (M); gifts received, $6,000; expenditures, $2,177; qualifying distributions, $2,100.
Limitations: Giving primarily in Durham, NC.
Officer: Charlene Hamlett, Pres.
EIN: 311521635

41897
First Union National Bank of South Carolina Scholarship Fund for South Carolina State College
c/o First Union National Bank
401 S. Tryon St., NC1159
Charlotte, NC 28288-1159
Additional address: c/o SC Foundation of Independent Colleges, P.O. Box 1465, Taylors, SC 29687

Established in 1990 in SC.
Donor(s): First Union National Bank of South Carolina, First Union Corp., Wachovia Corp.
Financial data (yr. ended 10/31/01): Grants paid, $2,028; assets, $55,840 (M); expenditures, $2,778; qualifying distributions, $2,746.
Limitations: Giving limited to SC.
Application information: Application form required.
Trustee: First Union National Bank.
EIN: 586239696
Codes: CS, CD

41898
Ethel M. Heina Educational Fund
c/o College Foundation, Inc.
P.O. Box 12100
Raleigh, NC 27605-2100 (919) 821-4771

Financial data (yr. ended 06/30/99): Grants paid, $2,003; assets, $261,539 (M); expenditures, $9,179; qualifying distributions, $2,003; giving activities include $2,003 for loans to individuals.
Limitations: Giving limited to residents of NC.
Application information: Application form required.
Trustee: College Foundation, Inc.
EIN: 566114717

41899
Dora Austin & Lois Gillespie Foundation
422-A Fisher Park Cir.
Greensboro, NC 27401-1615 (336) 574-2942
Contact: Maurice E. Schwartz, Pres.

Established in 2000 in NC.
Financial data (yr. ended 12/31/01): Grants paid, $2,000; assets, $48,764 (M); expenditures, $2,000; qualifying distributions, $2,000.
Limitations: Giving primarily in NC.
Application information: Application form not required.
Officers: Maurice E. Schwartz, Pres.; Eugenia S. Schwartz, Secy.-Treas.
EIN: 311685343

41900
Bradley Creek Extension Homemakers Club
235 Peiffer Ave.
Wilmington, NC 28409-4771

Financial data (yr. ended 12/31/01): Grants paid, $2,000; assets, $13,173 (M); expenditures, $2,918; qualifying distributions, $2,000.
Limitations: Applications not accepted. Giving primarily in Wilmington, NC.
Application information: Contributes only to pre-selected organizations.
Officers: Beatrice Beasley, Co-Pres.; Ann Levesque, Co-Pres.; Betty Myer, Secy.; Eugie Daniels, Treas.
EIN: 561717788

41901
The Thomas L. Coble Foundation, Inc.
2461 Anthony Rd.
Burlington, NC 27215

Financial data (yr. ended 10/31/01): Grants paid, $2,000; assets, $17 (M); expenditures, $2,025; qualifying distributions, $2,000.
Limitations: Applications not accepted.
Application information: Contributes only to pre-selected organizations.
Officers and Directors:* Thomas L. Coble,* Pres.; Matthew Coble, V.P. and Exec. Dir.; Misty Coble, V.P. and Exec. Dir.; Deborah T. Coble,* Secy.-Treas.; P.J. Coble.
EIN: 581758251

41902
The Cotter Foundation
P.O. Box 3099
Winston-Salem, NC 27150-7131

Established in 2000 in NC.
Donor(s): Thomas G. Cotter, Patricia A. Cutter.
Financial data (yr. ended 12/31/01): Grants paid, $2,000; assets, $709,524 (M); expenditures, $8,384; qualifying distributions, $2,000.
Limitations: Applications not accepted.
Application information: Contributes only to pre-selected organizations.
Trustee: Wachovia Bank, N.A.
EIN: 566577903

41903
The Gaston County Medical Society and Auxiliary Foundation, Inc.
2555 Court Dr., Ste. 150
Gastonia, NC 28054 (704) 864-4378
Contact: Richard Akers, M.D., Mgr.

Financial data (yr. ended 12/31/01): Grants paid, $2,000; assets, $64,024 (M); gifts received, $5,000; expenditures, $2,896; qualifying distributions, $2,000.
Limitations: Giving limited to residents of Gaston County, NC.
Officer: Richard Akers, M.D., Mgr.
EIN: 561301782

41904
Bobby R. Harold Family Charitable Trust
P.O. Box 1304
Mount Airy, NC 27030-1304
Application address: 116 Kennesaw Ln., Mounty Airy, NC 27030, tel.: (336) 786-4364
Contact: Bobby R. Harold, Chair.

Established in 1997 in NC.
Donor(s): Bobby R. Harold.
Financial data (yr. ended 03/31/02): Grants paid, $2,000; assets, $112,435 (M); expenditures, $2,145; qualifying distributions, $2,000.
Trustees: Bobby R. Harold, Chair.; Gary L. Harold, Sylvia M. Harold, Susan Harold Thomas.
EIN: 566500009

41905
Moore Family Foundation
1128 W. U.S. Hwy. 70
Garner, NC 27529 (919) 772-2121
Contact: Joan S. Moore, Secy.-Treas.

Established in 1998 in NC.
Financial data (yr. ended 12/31/01): Grants paid, $2,000; assets, $26,673 (M); gifts received, $12,000; expenditures, $2,741; qualifying distributions, $2,000.
Officers: R.W. Moore, Pres.; Joan S. Moore, Secy.-Treas.
Director: Jason Daniel Moore.
EIN: 562111657

41906
Pearl Foundation
c/o Peter S. Galloway
18806 Halyard Point Ln.
Cornelius, NC 28031-5238

Established in 2000 in NC.
Donor(s): Peter S. Galloway.
Financial data (yr. ended 12/31/01): Grants paid, $2,000; assets, $85,423 (M); gifts received, $87,465; expenditures, $3,183; qualifying distributions, $3,163.
Limitations: Applications not accepted.
Application information: Contributes only to pre-selected organizations.
Officers and Directors:* Peter S. Galloway,* Pres.; Arlis Galloway,* V.P.; Peter M. Galloway, Kristin G. Kelly, Kary G. Rafizadeh.
EIN: 562172887

41907
The Raftelis Foundation
511 East Blvd.
Charlotte, NC 28203 (704) 373-1199

Donor(s): George Raftelis, Eva Raftelis.
Financial data (yr. ended 12/31/01): Grants paid, $2,000; assets, $92,482 (M); gifts received, $7,815; expenditures, $2,221; qualifying distributions, $2,000.
Directors: Eva Raftelis, George Raftelis.
EIN: 562105040

41908
Ora B. Smith Charity Fund
c/o Whitman E. Smith, Jr.
1005 Pee Dee Ave.
Albemarle, NC 28001

Financial data (yr. ended 12/31/01): Grants paid, $2,000; assets, $108,125 (M); expenditures, $3,552; qualifying distributions, $2,000.
Limitations: Applications not accepted. Giving primarily in NC.
Application information: Contributes only to pre-selected organizations.
Trustees: Leonard W. Mabry, Whitman E. Smith, Jr.
EIN: 566045947

41909
Tomar Foundation, Inc.
c/o Phillips E. Rominger
100 Willow Dr., Ste. 70
Chapel Hill, NC 27514-2945

Established in 2001 in NC.
Donor(s): Phil Rominger.
Financial data (yr. ended 12/31/01): Grants paid, $2,000; assets, $9,041 (M); gifts received, $25,000; expenditures, $16,044; qualifying distributions, $2,000.
Officers: Phillip E. Rominger, Pres.; Dean A. Richards, Jr., V.P.; Thomas J. Rhodes, Secy.; Linda Whitaker, Treas.
EIN: 562253755

41910
Richard Douglas Turk Charitable Trust
1113 Sherwood Dr.
Burlington, NC 27215-3525

Established in 1996 in NC.
Financial data (yr. ended 12/31/01): Grants paid, $2,000; assets, $17,031 (M); expenditures, $2,137; qualifying distributions, $1,995.
Limitations: Applications not accepted.
Application information: Contributes only to pre-selected organizations.
Trustee: Jill Brinkley.
EIN: 566492079

41911
White Stone Foundation
c/o R. Gary Dorian
P.O. Box 1367
Flat Rock, NC 28731
Contact: R. Gary Dorian, Tr.

Established in 1998 in NC.
Donor(s): R. Gary Dorian, Teresa Dorian.
Financial data (yr. ended 12/31/99): Grants paid, $2,000; assets, $856,041 (M); gifts received, $22,834; expenditures, $75,971; qualifying distributions, $1,985.
Trustees: R. Gary Dorian, Teresa H. Dorian.
EIN: 566519103

41912
Kenneth W. Whitney & Ora P. Whitney Foundation
400 Avinger Ln., Apt. 406
Davidson, NC 28036

Donor(s): Kenneth W. Whitney, Ora P. Whitney.
Financial data (yr. ended 12/31/01): Grants paid, $2,000; assets, $32,838 (M); expenditures, $2,000; qualifying distributions, $2,000.
Limitations: Applications not accepted. Giving primarily in NC.
Application information: Contributes only to pre-selected organizations.
Trustees: Kenneth W. Whitney, Ora P. Whitney.
EIN: 222464657

41913
Murrill Foundation, Inc.
P.O. Box 1109
Monroe, NC 28111-1109 (704) 289-5438
Contact: Mary A. Hargette, V.P.

Financial data (yr. ended 12/31/01): Grants paid, $1,932; assets, $2,464,552 (M); gifts received, $1,484,287; expenditures, $1,947; qualifying distributions, $1,932.
Application information: Application form not required.
Officer: Mary A. Hargette, V.P. and Treas.
EIN: 566068245

41914
Ken Hubbs Foundation
c/o Joe E. Hubbs, Jr.
10104 Grafton Rd.
Raleigh, NC 27615-1141
Application address: 6121 Geremander, Rialto, CA 92376, tel.: (949) 874-1086
Contact: Keith Hubbs, Pres.

Financial data (yr. ended 12/31/01): Grants paid, $1,927; assets, $22,169 (M); gifts received, $1,260; expenditures, $2,127; qualifying distributions, $1,927.
Limitations: Giving limited to southern CA.
Officers: Keith Hubbs, Pres.; Joe E. Hubbs, Jr., Secy.-Treas.
Directors: Paul Brown, Kirk L. Hubbs, Kraig M. Hubbs, Ray Hubbs, Max J. Lofy, Harold Preece, and 6 additional directors.
EIN: 956102451

41915
Arthur Lloyd & Mildred Morris Brown Memorial Scholarship Fund
c/o Wachovia Bank, N.A.
P.O. Box 3099
Winston-Salem, NC 27150-7131
Application addresses: c/o Virginia Theological Seminary, 3737 Seminary Rd., Alexandria, VA 22304; c/o Union Theological Seminary, 3401 Brook Rd., Richmond, VA 23227; or c/o University of Richmond, 23 Westhampton Way, Richmond, VA 23173

Financial data (yr. ended 09/30/01): Grants paid, $1,926; assets, $53,955 (M); expenditures, $3,015; qualifying distributions, $1,926.
Limitations: Giving limited to residents of VA.
Application information: Application form not required.
Trustee: Wachovia Bank, N.A.
EIN: 546125386

41916
Francis F. Rainey Education Foundation
c/o Rick Smith
3395 Airport Rd.
Pinehurst, NC 28374

Established in 1973 in NC.
Donor(s): Robert C. Fisher, Mrs. Robert C. Fisher.
Financial data (yr. ended 04/30/01): Grants paid, $1,865; assets, $59,917 (M); expenditures, $2,660; qualifying distributions, $2,636.
Limitations: Giving limited to Southern Pines, NC.
Application information: Application form required.
Trustee: Sandhills Comm. College Foundation.
EIN: 566164909

41917
The Paul Ciener Botanical Gardens Foundation
101 S. Main St.
Kernersville, NC 27284

Established in 1999 in NC.
Financial data (yr. ended 12/31/01): Grants paid, $1,850; assets, $655,983 (M); gifts received, $306,589; expenditures, $2,168; qualifying distributions, $1,850.
Officers: Gregory M. Ciener, Pres.; David B. Ciener, V.P.; John G. Wolfe III, Secy.; Michael K. Hayes, Treas.
EIN: 562105544

41918
Earle W. Webb, Jr. Memorial & Civic Center, Inc.
812 Evans St.
Morehead City, NC 28557-4223
(252) 726-3012
Contact: Gloria Fleming

Established around 1933 in NC.
Financial data (yr. ended 12/31/99): Grants paid, $1,850; assets, $458,676 (M); gifts received, $2,110; expenditures, $70,449; qualifying distributions, $69,730.
Limitations: Giving limited to NC.
Application information: Application form required.
Officers: Earle Webb Moffitt, Jr., Pres.; Everette A. Webb, Jr., V.P.; F. Brower Moffitt, Secy.-Treas.
EIN: 135581041

41919
John V. R. Stehman Scholarship Fund
c/o First Union National Bank
401 S. Tryon St.
Charlotte, NC 28288-1159

Financial data (yr. ended 12/31/00): Grants paid, $1,839; assets, $36,610 (M); expenditures, $4,078; qualifying distributions, $3,874.
Limitations: Applications not accepted. Giving primarily in Reading, PA.
Trustee: First Union National Bank.
EIN: 236246328

41920
Oakview Community Service Corporation
1419 Olde Eden Dr.
High Point, NC 27265
Contact: F. Ray Williard, Treas.

Financial data (yr. ended 05/31/99): Grants paid, $1,800; assets, $17,239 (M); expenditures, $2,214; qualifying distributions, $1,795.
Limitations: Giving limited to High Point, NC.
Application information: Application form required.
Officers: W.D. Dawkins, Pres.; John W. Wells, V.P.; Ernest L. Galloway, Secy.; F. Ray Williard, Treas.
EIN: 566088560

41921
Bruce and Lena Kennedy Family Foundation
c/o Joseph B. Kennedy
7832 Seton House Ln.
Charlotte, NC 28277

Established in 1998 in NC.
Donor(s): Bruce Kennedy, Lena Kennedy.
Financial data (yr. ended 03/31/01): Grants paid, $1,746; assets, $24,135 (M); expenditures, $2,382; qualifying distributions, $1,746.
Limitations: Applications not accepted.
Application information: Contributes only to pre-selected organizations.
Officers: Bruce Kennedy, Pres.; Joseph B. Kennedy, Secy.; Lena Kennedy, Treas.
EIN: 911911439

41922
The Gail Phillips Family Foundation
c/o Chatham County Board of Education
P.O. Box 128
Pittsboro, NC 27312-0128
Application address: c/o Principal, Chatham Central High School, P.O. Box 80, Bear Creek, NC 27207, tel.: (919) 837-2251

Financial data (yr. ended 06/30/01): Grants paid, $1,700; assets, $30,656 (M); expenditures, $1,735; qualifying distributions, $1,700.
Limitations: Giving limited to Bear Creek, NC.
Application information: Application form required.
Trustee: Chatham County Board of Education.
EIN: 566284193

41923
Crossley Family Foundation, Inc.
802 Sunset Dr.
Greensboro, NC 27408

Established in 1997 in NC.
Donor(s): James J. Crossley.
Financial data (yr. ended 12/31/01): Grants paid, $1,600; assets, $44,437 (M); gifts received, $150; expenditures, $3,044; qualifying distributions, $1,600.
Limitations: Applications not accepted. Giving primarily in NC.
Application information: Contributes only to pre-selected organizations.
Officers and Directors:* James J. Crossley, Pres.; Elizabeth W. Crossley, Secy.; Patricia W. Crossley, Secy.; Catherine M. Crossley, Virginia W. Dries.
EIN: 562056125

41924
Rebecca and Walker Rucker Family Fund
309 Kimberly Dr.
Greensboro, NC 27408

Established in 1994 in NC.
Donor(s): Walker F. Rucker.
Financial data (yr. ended 12/31/01): Grants paid, $1,550; assets, $56,903 (M); gifts received, $500; expenditures, $1,550; qualifying distributions, $1,550.
Limitations: Applications not accepted.
Application information: Contributes only to pre-selected organizations.
Officers and Directors:* Walker F. Rucker,* Pres.; Ann R. Leonard,* Secy.; Rebecca Frazer Rucker, James G. Rucker.
EIN: 561901989

41925
Oscar C. Vatz Charitable Trust
c/o First Citizens Bank
P.O. Box 29522
Raleigh, NC 27626

Financial data (yr. ended 12/31/99): Grants paid, $1,529; assets, $52,971 (M); expenditures, $2,351; qualifying distributions, $1,529.
Limitations: Applications not accepted. Giving primarily in NC.
Application information: Contributes only to pre-selected organizations.
Trustee: First Citizens Bank.
EIN: 566100051

41926
Lincoln County Farmer Terracing Association Scholarship Fund
c/o Bank of America, NC 1-002-22-22
P.O. Box 2408
Charlotte, NC 28255-0001 (704) 326-1250
Contact: Nancy Truitt, Trust Off., Bank of America

Financial data (yr. ended 03/31/01): Grants paid, $1,500; assets, $43,532 (M); expenditures, $2,136; qualifying distributions, $1,500.
Limitations: Giving limited to Lincoln County, NC.
Application information: Application form required.
Trustee: Bank of America.
EIN: 581457946

41927
Ernest Earl Mahoney Scholarship Trust
c/o First Union National Bank
401 S. Tryon St., NC1159
Charlotte, NC 28288-1159
Application address: c/o First Union National Bank, 214 Hogan St., Jacksonville, FL 32202

Established in 1988.
Financial data (yr. ended 12/31/01): Grants paid, $1,500; assets, $100,725 (M); expenditures, $4,601; qualifying distributions, $1,500.
Limitations: Giving limited to residents of Lincolnville, ME.
Application information: Application form not required.
Trustee: First Union National Bank.
EIN: 596811061

41928
The Gerald H. & Rita S. Quinn Family Foundation
526 Works Farm Rd.
Warsaw, NC 28398

Established in 1998 in NC.
Donor(s): Gerald H. Quinn, Sr.
Financial data (yr. ended 12/31/01): Grants paid, $1,500; assets, $23,802 (M); expenditures, $1,799; qualifying distributions, $1,500.
Officers and Directors:* Gerald H. Quinn, Jr.,* Pres.; Carla Q. Rouse,* V.P.; Rita S. Quinn,* Treas.; Gerald H. Quinn, Patricia T. Quinn, Richard L. Rouse.
EIN: 562089450

41929
Edison D. Wright Trust Fund
c/o Centura Bank
P.O. Box 1220
Rocky Mount, NC 27802

Financial data (yr. ended 03/31/01): Grants paid, $1,500; assets, $97,814 (M); expenditures, $3,365; qualifying distributions, $1,500.
Limitations: Giving primarily in NC and SC.
Trustee: Centura Bank.
EIN: 566302698

41930
Cove Creek High School Class of 1955 Memorial Scholarship Fund
P.O. Box 234
Sugar Grove, NC 28679
Application address: c/o Watauga County High School, Guidance Office, 400 High School Dr., Boone, NC 28607, tel.: (828) 264-2407

Donor(s): Members from the Class of 1955.
Financial data (yr. ended 12/31/00): Grants paid, $1,400; assets, $7,707 (M); gifts received, $520; expenditures, $1,400; qualifying distributions, $1,400.

Limitations: Giving limited to residents of Grove Creek, NC.
Application information: Application form required.
Trustees: Lowell Cable, James Hagaman, Barbara Lawrence, William H. Mast, Jerry Shull.
EIN: 561472606

41931
Henson-Long Family Foundation
27415 Walker, Governor's Club
Chapel Hill, NC 27514-8318

Donor(s): Donald L. Henson, Alexandra Long-Henson.
Financial data (yr. ended 12/31/01): Grants paid, $1,300; assets, $15,077 (M); gifts received, $5,000; expenditures, $3,188; qualifying distributions, $1,300.
Limitations: Applications not accepted. Giving primarily in Raleigh, NC.
Application information: Contributes only to pre-selected organizations.
Trustees: Donald L. Henson, Alexandra Long-Henson.
EIN: 562112523

41932
Maynard Family Foundation
c/o Investment Mgmt. Corp.
P.O. Box 29502
Raleigh, NC 27626

Established in 1992 in NC.
Donor(s): James H. Maynard, Connie M. Maynard.
Financial data (yr. ended 12/31/01): Grants paid, $1,300; assets, $87,380 (M); expenditures, $1,343; qualifying distributions, $1,300.
Limitations: Applications not accepted.
Application information: Contributes only to pre-selected organizations.
Officer and Directors:* James H. Maynard,* Pres.; Connie M. Maynard, Easter Ann Maynard.
EIN: 561768062

41933
Florida Foundation for the Advancement of Medical Research
c/o First Union National Bank
401 S. Tryon St., NC1159
Charlotte, NC 28288
Application address: c/o Shands Teaching Hospital, Gainesville, FL 32610
Contact: Eloise Harmon, M.D., Pres.

Financial data (yr. ended 12/31/00): Grants paid, $1,293; assets, $126,128 (M); gifts received, $205; expenditures, $3,043; qualifying distributions, $1,293.
Limitations: Giving limited to Alachua County, FL.
Officers: Eloise Harmon, M.D., Pres.; John W. Robertson, V.P.
Trustee: First Union National Bank.
EIN: 592189649

41934
Joseph H. Myers Trust
c/o First Union National Bank
401 S. Tryon St., NC1159
Charlotte, NC 28288-1159
Application address: 56 Beach Ave., Pennsville, NJ 08070
Contact: Mrs. George Reichwein

Financial data (yr. ended 12/31/01): Grants paid, $1,250; assets, $63,113 (M); expenditures, $2,313; qualifying distributions, $2,000.
Limitations: Giving limited to NJ.
Application information: Application form required.

Trustee: First Union National Bank.
EIN: 226339093

41935
Smyre Foundation, Inc.
P.O. Box 3508
Gastonia, NC 28053
Contact: F.L. Smyre III, Pres.

Financial data (yr. ended 08/31/01): Grants paid, $1,250; assets, $32,231 (M); gifts received, $150; expenditures, $1,513; qualifying distributions, $1,250.
Limitations: Giving primarily in NC.
Officers: Fred L. Smyre III, Pres.; W.G. Anderson, V.P.; Fred L. Smyre, Jr., Secy.-Treas.
EIN: 566047839

41936
Harriett & George Thorpe Foundation
P.O. Box 2545
Rocky Mount, NC 27802-2545
Contact: George W. Thorpe, Pres.

Established in 1999 in NC.
Donor(s): George W. Thorpe.
Financial data (yr. ended 12/31/00): Grants paid, $1,216; assets, $85,421 (M); gifts received, $41,995; expenditures, $2,233; qualifying distributions, $1,216.
Officers: George W. Thorpe, Pres.; Harriett D. Thorpe, V.P.
Directors: Sara C. Thorpe Bastian, Sallie C. Cahill, Sarah A. Peterson.
EIN: 562120806

41937
Nancy Bagwell Gabriel Scholarship Trust
c/o Bank of America
101 S. Tryon St.
Charlotte, NC 28255 (704) 388-3150
Contact: Nancy Truitt, Trust Off., Bank of America

Financial data (yr. ended 12/31/01): Grants paid, $1,200; assets, $38,321 (M); expenditures, $1,757; qualifying distributions, $1,458.
Limitations: Giving limited to residents of Mooresville, NC.
Application information: Application form not required.
Trustee: Bank of America.
EIN: 566200441

41938
John O. Reynolds III Memorial Scholarship Fund, Inc.
P.O. Box 198
Salisbury, NC 28145-0198
Application address: 23 Hanover Ct., Salisbury, NC 28144, tel.: (704) 637-2426
Contact: Patricia M. Reynolds, Secy.-Treas.

Established around 1993.
Donor(s): John O. Reynolds, Jr., Patricia M. Reynolds.
Financial data (yr. ended 12/31/99): Grants paid, $1,200; assets, $24,267 (M); gifts received, $50; expenditures, $1,200; qualifying distributions, $1,189.
Limitations: Giving limited to residents of Salisbury, NC.
Application information: Application form not required.
Officers and Directors:* John O. Reynolds, Jr.,* Pres.; Patricia M. Reynolds,* Secy.-Treas.; Thomas M. Caddell.
EIN: 561758692

41939
Andrew M. Campbell Memorial Scholarship Fund
10300 Balmoral Cir.
Charlotte, NC 28210

Established in 1998 ion NC.
Financial data (yr. ended 12/31/99): Grants paid, $1,000; assets, $7,495 (M); gifts received, $1,725; expenditures, $1,000; qualifying distributions, $1,000.
Limitations: Giving primarily in NC.
Trustees: Thomas F. Carroll, Jr., R. Allen Hewett, Jr., Laurence E. Oliphant III.
EIN: 562086954

41940
The Peggy Lepley Foundation
14539 Ballantyne Country Club Dr.
Charlotte, NC 28277-2788
Application address: 100 N. Tryon St., Ste. 5400, Charlotte, NC 28202, tel.: (704) 344-7516
Contact: Erman E. Lepley, Jr., Pres.

Established in 1997 in NC.
Financial data (yr. ended 12/31/00): Grants paid, $1,000; assets, $16,020 (M); expenditures, $1,026; qualifying distributions, $1,000.
Limitations: Giving limited to Charlotte, NC.
Application information: Application form required.
Officers and Directors:* Erman E. Lepley, Jr.,* Pres.; Robert D. Lyerly, Jr.,* Secy.-Treas.; Michael A. Bradley.
EIN: 562017949

41941
Lew H. Foundation
c/o Lewis R. Holding
P.O. Box 29549
Raleigh, NC 27626-0549

Established in 1997 in NC.
Donor(s): Lewis R. Holding.
Financial data (yr. ended 12/31/01): Grants paid, $1,000; assets, $263,162 (M); expenditures, $1,332; qualifying distributions, $1,000.
Limitations: Giving primarily in NC.
Officers: Lewis R. Holding, Pres.; Carmen P. Holding, Secy.-Treas.
EIN: 582346981

41942
Len McLendon Memorial Fund
P.O. Box 3365
Greensboro, NC 27402-3365

Financial data (yr. ended 12/31/99): Grants paid, $1,000; assets, $14,991 (M); expenditures, $1,524; qualifying distributions, $997.
Limitations: Applications not accepted. Giving primarily in Greensboro, NC.
Application information: Scholarships recipients are nominated by the administrators of Page High School, NC.
Trustees: Charles A. McLendon, W.W. McLendon, A.L. Meyland.
EIN: 566086772

41943
James C. & Geraldine H. Plyler, Jr. Foundation
102 Dogwood Cir.
Monroe, NC 28110

Established in 2000 in NC.
Donor(s): James C. Plyler, Jr.
Financial data (yr. ended 12/31/01): Grants paid, $1,000; assets, $29,597 (M); gifts received, $1,250; expenditures, $1,763; qualifying distributions, $1,000.

Directors: Geraldine H. Plyler, Jr., James C. Plyler, Jr.
EIN: 562252623

41944
The David P. Riggins Foundation
2108 Sherwood Dr.
Charlotte, NC 28207

Established in 1996 in NC.
Donor(s): David P. Riggins.
Financial data (yr. ended 12/31/01): Grants paid, $1,000; assets, $775 (M); gifts received, $1,000; expenditures, $1,144; qualifying distributions, $1,000.
Limitations: Applications not accepted.
Application information: Contributes only to pre-selected organizations.
Officers and Directors:* David P. Riggins,* Pres.; Barbara L. Riggins,* V.P.; Stanley Riggins,* Secy.-Treas.
EIN: 561947898

41945
Seaman Scholarship Fund Trust
c/o First Union National Bank
401 S. Tryon St., NC 1159
Charlotte, NC 28288-1159

Established in 1999 in PA.
Financial data (yr. ended 12/31/00): Grants paid, $1,000; assets, $9,234 (M); expenditures, $1,133; qualifying distributions, $1,077.
Limitations: Applications not accepted.
Application information: Contributes only to pre-selected organizations.
Trustee: First Union National Bank.
EIN: 236435542

41946
William G. Sirrine High School Fund
c/o Wachovia Bank, N.A.
P.O. Box 3099
Winston-Salem, NC 27150-1022
Application address: 1401 Main St., Columbia, SC 29226, tel.: (803) 765-3671
Contact: C. Gerald Lane, Trust Off., Wachovia Bank, N.A.

Financial data (yr. ended 12/31/99): Grants paid, $1,000; assets, $18,468 (M); expenditures, $1,932; qualifying distributions, $1,000.
Limitations: Giving limited to Greenville, SC.
Application information: Application form required.
Trustee: Wachovia Bank of North Carolina, N.A.
EIN: 576017456

41947
TKB Foundation
1600 Morganton Rd., Lot K5
Pinehurst, NC 28374-6849 (910) 692-7553
Contact: Thomas C. Boucherle, Tr.

Financial data (yr. ended 12/31/01): Grants paid, $1,000; assets, $38,119 (M); expenditures, $1,419; qualifying distributions, $1,000.
Limitations: Giving primarily in CA.
Application information: Application form not required.
Trustee: Thomas C. Boucherle.
EIN: 346779395

41948
VVV Athletic Association Sports Fund
First Union National Bank
401 S. Tryon St., 4th Fl.
Charlotte, NC 28288-1159

Financial data (yr. ended 12/31/01): Grants paid, $1,000; assets, $19,358 (M); expenditures, $1,435; qualifying distributions, $993.

Limitations: Applications not accepted. Giving limited to Reading, PA.
Application information: Contributes only to pre-selected organizations.
Trustee: First Union National Bank.
EIN: 236668400

41949
James Walker Memorial Hospital
5113 Woods Edge Rd.
Wilmington, NC 28409 (910) 392-2634
Contact: Lillian Newton, Mgr.

Financial data (yr. ended 12/31/00): Grants paid, $1,000; assets, $41,250 (M); gifts received, $250; expenditures, $1,667; qualifying distributions, $1,667.
Limitations: Giving primarily in Wilmington, NC.
Officers: Mae McInnis, Secy.; Sarah Devlin, Treas.; Lillian Newton, Mgr.
Trustees: Dorothy Ballard, Carol Dusenbury, Frances O'Neil.
EIN: 237035430

41950
T. Sherwin Cook Foundation
c/o Wachovia Bank, N.A.
P.O. Box 3099
Winston-Salem, NC 27150-7131

Established in 2000 in VA.
Financial data (yr. ended 12/31/01): Grants paid, $996; assets, $175,065 (M); expenditures, $6,496; qualifying distributions, $996.
Limitations: Applications not accepted.
Application information: Contributes only to pre-selected organizations.
Trustee: Wachovia Bank, N.A.
EIN: 566562320

41951
Waldroop Blind Trust Fund
P.O. Box 1252
Franklin, NC 28734-1252
Contact: Everett Stiles, Tr.

Financial data (yr. ended 12/31/01): Grants paid, $980; assets, $52,954 (M); expenditures, $1,465; qualifying distributions, $980.
Limitations: Giving limited to Macon and Swain counties, NC.
Application information: Application form required.
Trustees: Daryl Gossett, Everett Stiles, Jim Thomas.
EIN: 566243993

41952
R. H. Taliaferro Scholarship Fund
c/o First Union National Bank
401 S. Tryon St., 4th Fl.
Charlotte, NC 28288-1159
Application address: c/o First Union National Bank of North Carolina, 101 13th St., Columbus, GA 31993

Financial data (yr. ended 12/31/00): Grants paid, $958; assets, $18,149 (M); expenditures, $2,458; qualifying distributions, $1,791.
Limitations: Giving limited to Columbus, GA.
Trustee: First Union National Bank.
EIN: 586057583

41953
James B. Neely Foundation
101 Sunset Ave.
Asheboro, NC 27203 (336) 626-8326

Financial data (yr. ended 12/31/01): Grants paid, $840; assets, $14,500 (M); expenditures, $859; qualifying distributions, $840.
Officers and Trustees:* James M. Culberson, Jr.,* Chair.; Jerry A. Little, Treas.; James M. Campbell,

41953—NORTH CAROLINA

Jr., W.L. Hancock, Thomas A. Jordan, Michael C. Miller, R. Reynolds Neely, Jr., Richard K. Pugh, J.M. Ramsey III, Charles W. Stout, Earlene V. Ward.
EIN: 560190785

41954
John R. Paddison, Jr. and Mary Paddison Student Aid Fund
c/o Wachovia Bank, N.A.
P.O. Box 3099
Winston-Salem, NC 27150-7153

Financial data (yr. ended 08/31/01): Grants paid, $820; assets, $6,187 (M); expenditures, $847; qualifying distributions, $816.
Limitations: Applications not accepted. Giving limited to NC.
Trustee: Wachovia Bank, N.A.
EIN: 566072485

41955
The Bailey Foundation
P.O. Box 312
Rocky Mount, NC 27802-0312

Established in 1988 in NC.
Donor(s): J.C.D. Bailey.
Financial data (yr. ended 09/30/01): Grants paid, $800; assets, $168,381 (M); gifts received, $800; expenditures, $1,177; qualifying distributions, $800.
Limitations: Applications not accepted. Giving primarily in NC and TN.
Application information: Contributes only to pre-selected organizations.
Officers and Directors:* J.C.D. Bailey,* Pres. and Treas.; Anne Neal Bailey,* V.P.; Susan B. Bailey,* Secy.; Sara Camden Hodges, John W. Lewis, Anne Duncan Weaver.
EIN: 561636112

41956
PIP Foundation
c/o William P. Wuehrmann
180 Doubleday Rd.
Tryon, NC 28782 (828) 859-9394

Donor(s): William P. Wuenrmann.
Financial data (yr. ended 10/31/01): Grants paid, $800; assets, $570 (M); gifts received, $900; expenditures, $800; qualifying distributions, $800.
Limitations: Applications not accepted. Giving limited to IA.
Application information: Contributes only to pre-selected organizations.
Officer and Trustee:* William P. Wuehrmann,* Pres.
EIN: 237044673

41957
Annas Foundation, Inc.
2415 Vine St. S.W.
Lenoir, NC 28645
Application address: P.O. Box 314, Hudson, NC 28638
Contact: J.C. Sullivan, Pres.

Financial data (yr. ended 01/31/01): Grants paid, $750; assets, $15,451 (M); expenditures, $805; qualifying distributions, $797.
Limitations: Giving primarily in Caldwell County, NC.
Officers: J.C. Sullivan, Pres.; Howard Annas, Secy.-Treas.
EIN: 566073351

41958
Simpson Foundation
204 E. McDowell St.
Morganton, NC 28655-3545

Financial data (yr. ended 09/30/01): Grants paid, $750; assets, $16,389 (M); gifts received, $500; expenditures, $1,106; qualifying distributions, $750.
Limitations: Applications not accepted. Giving primarily in Alpine, NC.
Application information: Contributes only to pre-selected organizations.
Trustee: James Reid Simpson II.
EIN: 566244644

41959
L. E. Hassell, Sr. Memorial Scholarship Fund
c/o B.B. & T., Trust Dept.
P.O. Box 2907, MC100-01-02-20
Wilson, NC 27894-2907
Application address: c/o Superintendent of Public Schools, Washington, NC 27889

Financial data (yr. ended 06/30/02): Grants paid, $740; assets, $10,931 (M); expenditures, $876; qualifying distributions, $740.
Application information: Application form not required.
Trustee: B.B. & T.
EIN: 566041654

41960
William Edward Starnes Educational Fund
c/o College Foundation, Inc.
P.O. Box 12100
Raleigh, NC 27605-2100 (919) 834-2893

Financial data (yr. ended 06/30/99): Grants paid, $707; assets, $39,622 (M); expenditures, $6,992; qualifying distributions, $707; giving activities include $707 for loans to individuals.
Limitations: Giving limited to residents of Moore County, NC.
Application information: Application form required.
Trustee: College Foundation, Inc.
EIN: 566099413

41961
John M. Jordan Foundation
P.O. Box 128
Saxapahaw, NC 27340-0128 (336) 376-3132
Contact: Margaret C. Jordan, Secy.

Donor(s): John M. Jordan.
Financial data (yr. ended 12/31/99): Grants paid, $690; assets, $55,252 (M); gifts received, $3,870; expenditures, $2,449; qualifying distributions, $690.
Limitations: Giving limited to the Saxapahaw, NC, area.
Application information: Application form required.
Officers: John M. Jordan, Pres.; Margaret C. Jordan, Secy.; Earlene Morris, Treas.
EIN: 561529446

41962
Peter Ho and Patricia King Family Private Foundation
c/o Peter Ho
409 Golfview Ct.
Lenoir, NC 28645 (828) 757-3095

Established in 1997 in NC.
Donor(s): Peter Ho, Patricia King.
Financial data (yr. ended 12/31/01): Grants paid, $675; assets, $35,618 (M); gifts received, $13; expenditures, $1,872; qualifying distributions, $675.

Trustees: Peter Ho, Patricia King.
EIN: 562058268

41963
Stafford Family Trust
c/o Wachovia Bank, N.A.
P.O. Box 3099
Winston-Salem, NC 27150-7131

Established in 2000 in NC.
Donor(s): Ivan B. Stafford, Melba S. Stafford.
Financial data (yr. ended 12/31/01): Grants paid, $653; assets, $566,374 (M); gifts received, $459,403; expenditures, $6,457; qualifying distributions, $653.
Limitations: Applications not accepted.
Application information: Contributes only to pre-selected organizations.
Trustee: Wachovia Bank, N.A.
EIN: 566570127

41964
David J. Toman Foundation
325 Queens Rd., Ste. 10
Charlotte, NC 28204-3256

Established in 1998 in IL.
Financial data (yr. ended 12/31/01): Grants paid, $650; assets, $12,714 (M); expenditures, $731; qualifying distributions, $650.
Limitations: Applications not accepted. Giving primarily in DE.
Application information: Contributes only to pre-selected organizations.
Trustees: Andrea Peterson, Gary J. Toman, Judith Tomen.
EIN: 376348816

41965
Sally Pestcoe Trust
c/o First Union National Bank
401 S. Tryon St., NC1159
Charlotte, NC 28288
Application address: c/o Pres., Central High School, Philadelphia, PA 19109

Financial data (yr. ended 05/31/01): Grants paid, $625; assets, $12,021 (M); expenditures, $1,465; qualifying distributions, $1,363.
Limitations: Giving limited to Philadelphia, PA.
Application information: Application form not required.
Trustee: First Union National Bank.
EIN: 236423254

41966
The Foundation for Good News
110 E. Main St.
Clinton, NC 28328-4029

Established in 1988 in NC.
Donor(s): George E. Wilson.
Financial data (yr. ended 12/31/01): Grants paid, $600; assets, $114,643 (M); gifts received, $4,000; expenditures, $4,508; qualifying distributions, $1,838.
Limitations: Applications not accepted. Giving primarily in Falcon, NC.
Application information: Unsolicited requests for funds not accepted.
Officers: George E. Wilson, Pres.; Jeffrey S. Wilson, V.P.; Regina W. Parker, Secy.; Sharlene W. Tew, Treas.
EIN: 561635295

41967
The Harrison Family Foundation, Inc.
2505 King Arthur Dr.
Monroe, NC 28110

Established in 1997 in NC.

Financial data (yr. ended 12/31/01): Grants paid, $600; assets, $1,557 (M); expenditures, $968; qualifying distributions, $600.
Limitations: Applications not accepted.
Application information: Contributes only to pre-selected organizations.
Officers: Margaret K. Harrison, Pres.; Robert K. Harrison, Treas.
Directors: Margaret H. Bergman, Catherine H. Frye, Robert Keith Harrison, Jr., Susan H. Hock.
EIN: 562031747

41968
The I. J. Quinn Family Foundation
526 Works Farm Rd.
Warsaw, NC 28398

Established in 1998 in NC.
Donor(s): I.J. Quinn, Sr.
Financial data (yr. ended 12/31/01): Grants paid, $550; assets, $11,376 (M); expenditures, $818; qualifying distributions, $550.
Limitations: Applications not accepted.
Application information: Contributes only to pre-selected organizations.
Officers: I.J. Quinn, Sr., Pres. and Treas.; I.J. Quinn, Jr., V.P.; Kimberly Quinn, Secy.
EIN: 562089451

41969
Jane Cothran High School Fund
c/o Wachovia Bank, N.A.
P.O. Box 3099
Winston-Salem, NC 27150-7131
Application address: c/o Wachovia Bank, N.A., 1041 Main St., Columbia, SC 29266, tel.: (803) 765-3671
Contact: C. Gerald Lane, V.P. and Trust Off., Wachovia Bank, N.A.

Established in 1956 in SC.
Donor(s): Jane Cothran.
Financial data (yr. ended 12/31/00): Grants paid, $500; assets, $18,691 (M); expenditures, $1,350; qualifying distributions, $1,163.
Limitations: Giving limited to Greenville, SC.
Application information: Application form required.
Trustee: Wachovia Bank, N.A.
EIN: 576017257

41970
Charles C. Hoover Scholarship
c/o High Point Bank & Trust Co.
P.O. Box 2278
High Point, NC 27261-2278
Application address: c/o Principal, South Davidson High School, Rte. 2, Box 2000, Denton, NC 27239

Financial data (yr. ended 12/31/01): Grants paid, $500; assets, $12,466 (M); expenditures, $800; qualifying distributions, $500.
Limitations: Giving limited to Denton, NC.
Trustee: High Point Bank & Trust Co.
EIN: 566193152

41971
Catherine M. Mahady Scholarship Fund
c/o First Union National Bank
401 S. Tryon St., NC1159
Charlotte, NC 28288-1159

Established in 1999 in NJ.
Financial data (yr. ended 12/31/00): Grants paid, $500; assets, $18,962 (M); expenditures, $985; qualifying distributions, $893.
Limitations: Applications not accepted. Giving limited to residents of NJ.
Trustee: First Union National Bank.
EIN: 226501060

41972
Larry and Herman Mixon Scholarship Fund, Inc.
4223 Farlow Dr.
Greensboro, NC 27406-9051
Contact: Enola Mixon, Dir.

Established around 1986 in NC.
Financial data (yr. ended 12/31/01): Grants paid, $500; assets, $24,165 (M); gifts received, $2,468; expenditures, $1,586; qualifying distributions, $1,586.
Directors: William J. Blake, Alfrema Chambers, Cynthia Crawford-Greene, Enola Mixon, Lori S. Mixon.
EIN: 581727396

41973
Shining Acres Foundation
(Formerly Alternative Charitable Foundation)
240 Renn Rd.
Stokesdale, NC 27357 (336) 548-2020
Contact: Gerald L. Helfrey, Secy.-Treas.

Donor(s): Janet Dellosa, Gerald L. Helfrey.
Financial data (yr. ended 12/31/01): Grants paid, $500; assets, $312,477 (M); gifts received, $1,005; expenditures, $5,014; qualifying distributions, $500.
Limitations: Giving primarily in NC.
Officers: Janet B. Dellosa, Pres.; Gerald L. Helfrey, Secy.-Treas.
EIN: 562043300

41974
George G. Woelpper Trust
c/o First Union National Bank
401 S. Tryon St., NC1159
Charlotte, NC 28288
Application address: c/o Robert L. Ross, 223 Woodlyn Ave., Pitman, NJ 08071

Financial data (yr. ended 08/31/01): Grants paid, $459; assets, $7,071 (M); expenditures, $1,231; qualifying distributions, $1,205.
Application information: Application form not required.
Trustee: First Union National Bank.
EIN: 236208800

41975
Armat Foundation, Inc.
900 Greenhill Rd.
Mount Airy, NC 27030

Established in 1998 in NC.
Donor(s): Hylton Wright, Betty Wright.
Financial data (yr. ended 12/31/01): Grants paid, $400; assets, $11,014 (M); gifts received, $14; expenditures, $1,406; qualifying distributions, $400.
Limitations: Applications not accepted.
Application information: Contributes only to pre-selected organizations.
Officers: Hylton Wright, Pres.; Betty Wright, Secy.
EIN: 562045002

41976
Hunter-Jenkins Foundation
c/o Isabel Bader
P.O. Box 32127
Charlotte, NC 28232-2127

Established in 2001 in NC.
Donor(s): John Edwards Jenkins, Sr.
Financial data (yr. ended 12/31/01): Grants paid, $400; assets, $55,974 (M); gifts received, $50,000; expenditures, $895; qualifying distributions, $854.
Officers: Margaret J. Hunter, Pres.; Richard G. Hunter III, V.P.; Isabel J. Badez, Secy.
EIN: 562203887

41977
William L. Medlin Trust f/b/o Selected Graduates of Roanoke Rapids High School
c/o Centura Bank
P.O. Box 1220
Rocky Mount, NC 27802-1220
Application address: c/o Roanoke Rapids High School, P.O. Box 340, Roanoke Rapids, NC 27870, tel.: (252) 537-8563
Contact: Velna Hux, Counselor

Established in 1974 in NC.
Financial data (yr. ended 10/31/00): Grants paid, $400; assets, $34,408 (M); expenditures, $840; qualifying distributions, $457.
Limitations: Giving limited to Roanoke Rapids, NC.
Trustee: Centura Bank.
EIN: 510197343

41978
R. F. Paddison Student Aid Fund
c/o Wachovia Bank, N.A.
P.O. Box 3099
Winston-Salem, NC 27150-6732

Financial data (yr. ended 08/31/01): Grants paid, $400; assets, $6,620 (M); expenditures, $428; qualifying distributions, $396.
Limitations: Applications not accepted. Giving limited to NC.
Trustee: Wachovia Bank, N.A.
EIN: 566072487

41979
Daniel Jonathan Stowe Foundation, Inc.
P.O. Box 1046
Belmont, NC 28012-1046
Contact: Shirley S. Rankin, Secy.

Established around 1955 in NC.
Donor(s): Daniel J. Stowe.
Financial data (yr. ended 12/31/01): Grants paid, $382; assets, $404,381 (M); gifts received, $8,079; expenditures, $16,073; qualifying distributions, $382.
Limitations: Giving primarily in NC.
Application information: Application form not required.
Officers and Directors:* Daniel J. Stowe, Pres.; Robert L. Stowe III, V.P.; Shirley S. Rankin,* Secy.; James B. Garland, Alene N. Stowe.
EIN: 560769870

41980
Jennie H. Smith Testamentary Trust f/b/o Mills Home
c/o Wachovia Bank, N.A.
P.O. Box 3099
Winston-Salem, NC 27150-7153

Financial data (yr. ended 12/31/99): Grants paid, $373; assets, $30,565 (M); expenditures, $923; qualifying distributions, $681.
Limitations: Applications not accepted. Giving limited to NC.
Application information: Recipients selected from list of qualified candidates provided by the scholarship committee of Chowan College.
Trustee: Wachovia Bank of North Carolina, N.A.
EIN: 566035973

41981
Daniel and Marcelle Peck Foundation
P.O. Box 35129
Charlotte, NC 28235

Established in 2000 in NC.
Donor(s): William and Patrick Family Fdn.
Financial data (yr. ended 06/30/01): Grants paid, $350; assets, $8,842 (M); gifts received, $10,000;

41981—NORTH CAROLINA

expenditures, $1,527; qualifying distributions, $1,217.
Limitations: Applications not accepted.
Application information: Contributes only to pre-selected organizations.
Officers: Daniel Peck, Pres.; Marcelle Peck, V.P.
EIN: 562205948

41982
The Presbyterian Journal Foundation, Inc.
P.O. Box 2330
Asheville, NC 28802-3075

Financial data (yr. ended 06/30/01): Grants paid, $321; assets, $6,920 (M); expenditures, $321; qualifying distributions, $321.
Limitations: Applications not accepted. Giving primarily in Asheville, NC.
Application information: Contributes only to pre-selected organizations.
Officers: Joel Belz, C.E.O.; Robert Singleton, Chair.; John White, Vice-Chair.; Stephen Lutz, V.P., Sales/Marketing; Eric Zetterholm, V.P., Finance/Administration; Nelson Somerville, Secy.; Kevin Cusack, Treas.
Directors: Miriam Bell, Robert Case II, William F. Joseph, James S. Morgan, Jr., William H. Newton III, Bentley B. Rayburn, David Strassner, Raymond F. Thompson, Jack Williamson.
EIN: 580850649

41983
Bright W. & Lucille W. Beck Trust Award in American History
c/o First Union National Bank
401 S. Tryon St., NC1159
Charlotte, NC 28288-1159

Financial data (yr. ended 04/30/99): Grants paid, $300; assets, $12,094 (M); expenditures, $379; qualifying distributions, $300.
Limitations: Applications not accepted. Giving primarily in Kutztowm, PA.
Application information: Contributes only to pre-selected organizations.
Trustee: First Union National Bank.
EIN: 236511969

41984
Ellen Madeira Scholastic Award Fund
c/o First Union National Bank
401 S. Tryon St., NC1159
Charlotte, NC 28288-1159

Financial data (yr. ended 12/31/01): Grants paid, $300; assets, $8,066 (M); expenditures, $671; qualifying distributions, $596.
Limitations: Applications not accepted. Giving primarily in PA.
Application information: Unsolicited requests for funds not accepted.
Trustee: First Union National Bank.
EIN: 236573590

41985
The Suffolk Foundation
c/o Wachovia Bank, N.A.
P.O. Box 3099
Winston-Salem, NC 27150-7131
Application address: c/o Beth Barnhill, Wachovia Bank, N.A., 999 Waterside Dr., Ste. 2500, Norfolk, VA 23510

Financial data (yr. ended 12/31/99): Grants paid, $300; assets, $48,400 (M); expenditures, $1,767; qualifying distributions, $658.
Limitations: Giving limited to the Suffolk, VA, area.
Application information: Application form required.
Directors: Cecil Gwaltney, Jr., Mrs. Robert Jillette, Betty Luse, Martha Saunders, Steven D. Woodyard.
Trustee: Wachovia Bank of North Carolina, N.A.
EIN: 546116367

41986
Lurene R. Brown Memorial Scholarship Fund
c/o Halifax Electric Membership Corp., Scholarship Comm.
P.O. Box 667
Enfield, NC 27823-0667   (252) 445-5113

Donor(s): Fred J. Brown.
Financial data (yr. ended 12/31/01): Grants paid, $250; assets, $9,927 (M); expenditures, $259; qualifying distributions, $250.
Limitations: Giving limited to residents of NC.
Application information: Application form required.
Trustees: Sanders P. Cox, Michael E. Finney.
EIN: 561542813

41987
Carl Painter, Jr. Scholarship Fund
1465 Lakeshore Dr.
Lake Junaluska, NC 28745-8773

Donor(s): Ruth E.M. Painter.
Financial data (yr. ended 12/31/01): Grants paid, $250; assets, $7,421 (M); expenditures, $250; qualifying distributions, $245.
Limitations: Giving limited to Cullowhee, NC.
Officer: Ruth E.M. Painter, Pres. and Secy.-Treas.
EIN: 561897793

41988
The Viser Family Fund, Inc.
305 Inverness Rd.
Clinton, NC 28328

Established in 2000 in NC.
Donor(s): Paul Viser.
Financial data (yr. ended 12/31/01): Grants paid, $250; assets, $13,771 (M); gifts received, $5,000; expenditures, $609; qualifying distributions, $250.
Limitations: Applications not accepted. Giving primarily in Clinton, NC.
Application information: Contributes only to pre-selected organizations.
Director: Paul Viser.
EIN: 562168703

41989
Community Resource Council Polk Youth Institute
1001 Veazy Rd.
Butner, NC 27509-1649

Established in 1999.
Financial data (yr. ended 12/31/01): Grants paid, $243; assets, $750 (M); gifts received, $50; expenditures, $243; qualifying distributions, $243.
Officers: Pat Ford, Chair.; John W. Wimbush, Treas.
EIN: 582000094

41990
Legatus Foundation
200 W. 2nd St., Ste. 1700
Winston-Salem, NC 27101

Established in 2000 in NC.
Financial data (yr. ended 12/31/01): Grants paid, $100; assets, $86 (M); expenditures, $100; qualifying distributions, $100.
Officers and Director:* Ranlet S. Bell,* Pres.; Frank M. Bell, Jr., Secy.-Treas.
EIN: 311737683

41991
Louise & Harry M. Solomon Fund
c/o Wachovia Bank, N.A.
P.O. Box 3099
Winston-Salem, NC 27150-7153

Financial data (yr. ended 12/31/01): Grants paid, $84; assets, $2,148 (M); expenditures, $145; qualifying distributions, $84.
Limitations: Applications not accepted. Giving primarily in Wilmington, NC.
Application information: Contributes only to pre-selected organizations.
Trustee: Wachovia Bank of North Carolina, N.A.
EIN: 566050315

41992
The Stephen H. Millender Foundation Charitable Trust
P.O. Box 1843
Burlington, NC 27216

Established in 1999 in NC.
Financial data (yr. ended 12/31/01): Grants paid, $35; assets, $641 (M); expenditures, $65; qualifying distributions, $35.
Limitations: Applications not accepted.
Application information: Contributes only to pre-selected organizations.
Trustees: Margaret M. Holmes, Stephen H. Millender.
EIN: 621800963

41993
Lynn Campbell Charitable Foundation
P.O. Box 18135
Raleigh, NC 27619

Financial data (yr. ended 12/31/00): Grants paid, $8; assets, $210 (M); gifts received, $614; expenditures, $383; qualifying distributions, $8.
Limitations: Applications not accepted. Giving primarily in Raleigh, NC.
Application information: Contributes only to pre-selected organizations.
Trustees: Van B. Bottomley, Frank C. Campbell, Stanley L. Dalton.
EIN: 562095394

41994
The Alphin Family Foundation
c/o Jesse C. Alphin
3489 U.S. 301 S.
Dunn, NC 28334

Established in 1999 in NC.
Financial data (yr. ended 12/31/01): Grants paid, $0; assets, $49,298 (M); expenditures, $0; qualifying distributions, $0.
Limitations: Applications not accepted.
Application information: Contributes only to pre-selected organizations.
Trustee: Jesse C. Alphin.
EIN: 562108036

41995
The Arbor Charitable Foundation, Inc.
c/o Wachovia Bank, N.A.
P.O. Box 31608
Charlotte, NC 28231

Established in 1996.
Donor(s): Edward W. Cook, Jr.
Financial data (yr. ended 12/31/01): Grants paid, $0; assets, $31,934 (M); expenditures, $2,930; qualifying distributions, $0.
Limitations: Applications not accepted.
Application information: Contributes only to pre-selected organizations.

Officers and Directors:* Edward W. Cook, Jr.,* Pres.; William Andrew Tullis,* Secy.-Treas.; C. Wells Hall III.
EIN: 561882080

41996
The Arndt Foundation
c/o Wachovia Bank of North Carolina, N.A.
P.O. Box 3099
Winston-Salem, NC 27150-7131

Established in 1997 in GA.
Financial data (yr. ended 12/31/01): Grants paid, $0; assets, $3,640 (M); expenditures, $4,638; qualifying distributions, $885,787.
Limitations: Applications not accepted.
Application information: Contributes only to pre-selected organizations.
Officer: John D. Arndt, Pres.
Trustee: Wachovia Bank of North Carolina, N.A.
EIN: 581109386

41997
The Marvin L. Baker Family Foundation, Inc.
531 Hertford St.
Raleigh, NC 27609

Established in 2001 in FL.
Donor(s): Martha B. Capps.
Financial data (yr. ended 12/31/01): Grants paid, $0; assets, $1,071,197 (M); gifts received, $1,941,996; expenditures, $6,751; qualifying distributions, $0.
Limitations: Applications not accepted.
Application information: Contributes only to pre-selected organizations.
Officers: Harold E. Blondeau, Pres.; Neal W. Knight, Jr., V.P.
EIN: 651138658

41998
Henry Bane Memorial Foundation
c/o Wachovia Bank, N.A.
P.O. Box 3099
Winston-Salem, NC 27150-7131

Established in 1999 in NC.
Financial data (yr. ended 12/31/99): Grants paid, $0; assets, $1,939,676 (M); gifts received, $1,659,740; expenditures, $3,345; qualifying distributions, $48.
Limitations: Applications not accepted.
Application information: Contributes only to pre-selected organizations.
Trustee: Wachovia Bank, N.A.
EIN: 566539645

41999
William I. Barbour Trust
c/o College Foundation, Inc.
P.O. Box 12100
Raleigh, NC 27605-2100 (919) 834-2893

Financial data (yr. ended 06/30/01): Grants paid, $0; assets, $6,398 (M); expenditures, $1,035; qualifying distributions, $730; giving activities include $730 for loans to individuals.
Limitations: Giving limited to residents of Southern Pines, NC.
Application information: Application form required.
Trustee: College Foundation, Inc.
EIN: 566085068

42000
BB&T Foundation of Robeson County
c/o B.B. & T., Trust Dept.
P.O. Box 2907
Wilson, NC 27894-2907

Established in 1996 in NC.

Financial data (yr. ended 12/31/01): Grants paid, $0; assets, $200,131 (M); expenditures, $4,925; qualifying distributions, $0.
Limitations: Applications not accepted.
Application information: Contributes only to pre-selected organizations.
Trustee: B.B. & T.
EIN: 566474893

42001
John M. Belk Educational Endowment
2801 W. Tyvola Rd.
Charlotte, NC 28217 (704) 357-1000
Contact: John M. Belk, Pres.

Established in 1996 in NC.
Donor(s): John M. Belk.
Financial data (yr. ended 12/31/01): Grants paid, $0; assets, $111,840 (M); expenditures, $1,564; qualifying distributions, $0.
Officers: John M. Belk, Pres. and Treas.; Claudia W. Belk, V.P. and Secy.
Directors: Katherine Belk Morris, Leroy Robinson.
EIN: 561954114

42002
Belk Research Foundation
7310 Walkup Rd.
Waxhaw, NC 28173-8602
Contact: William Henry Belk, III, Tr.

Established in 1989 in NC.
Donor(s): W.H. Belk, Jr.
Financial data (yr. ended 06/30/00): Grants paid, $0; assets, $95,257 (M); gifts received, $10,000; expenditures, $25,647; qualifying distributions, $0.
Limitations: Giving on a national basis.
Trustees: Diane Belk, William Henry Belk III.
EIN: 136188004

42003
The Blackburn Family Foundation
314 Polk St.
Raleigh, NC 27604

Established in 2000 in NC.
Donor(s): Shelmer D. Blackburn, Jr.
Financial data (yr. ended 12/31/01): Grants paid, $0; assets, $59,694 (M); expenditures, $128; qualifying distributions, $0.
Limitations: Applications not accepted.
Application information: Contributes only to pre-selected organizations.
Officers: Shelmer D. Blackburn, Jr., Pres.; Paul T. Flick, V.P.; Terry J. Carlton, Secy.-Treas.
EIN: 562190094

42004
The George & Ida Wood Blanton Endowment Trust
P.O. Box 168
Shelby, NC 28151-0168

Financial data (yr. ended 12/31/01): Grants paid, $0; assets, $160,268 (M); gifts received, $200; expenditures, $2,312; qualifying distributions, $0.
Limitations: Applications not accepted. Giving primarily in Shelby, NC.
Application information: Contributes only to pre-selected organizations.
Trustee: First National Bank of Shelby.
EIN: 581914208

42005
Bradford T. Blauvelt Memorial Trust Fund
c/o First Union National Bank
401 S. Tryon St., 4th Fl.
Charlotte, NC 28288-1159

Established in 1988 in NJ.

Financial data (yr. ended 12/31/01): Grants paid, $0; assets, $166,758 (M); gifts received, $28,340; expenditures, $1,596; qualifying distributions, $750.
Limitations: Applications not accepted. Giving primarily in the Toms River, NJ, area.
Application information: Contributes only to pre-selected organizations.
Trustee: First Union National Bank.
EIN: 226304441

42006
The Bodford Family Foundation
3400 Edgefield Ct.
Greensboro, NC 27409-9663

Established in 1998 in NC.
Donor(s): Epes Carriers, Inc.
Financial data (yr. ended 04/30/02): Grants paid, $0; assets, $197,800 (M); gifts received, $50,000; expenditures, $2,195; qualifying distributions, $0.
Officers: Amy Bodford Poteat, Pres.; Alvin M. Bodford, Secy.-Treas.
Directors: Brenda S. Bodford, Jason Bodford.
EIN: 562099865

42007
James R. and Bronnie L. Braswell Trust
c/o Poisson, Poisson, Bower & Clodfelter
300 E. Wade St.
Wadesboro, NC 28170
Contact: George L. Bower, Jr.

Established in 2001 in NC.
Donor(s): James R. Braswell.‡
Financial data (yr. ended 12/31/01): Grants paid, $0; assets, $11,600 (M); gifts received, $10,000; expenditures, $0; qualifying distributions, $0.
Limitations: Applications not accepted.
Application information: Contributes only to pre-selected organizations.
Trustee: George L. Bower, Jr.
EIN: 736339730

42008
James T. & Louise R. Broyhill Foundation, Inc.
c/o Robert T. Beach
P.O. Box 25427
Winston-Salem, NC 27114-5427
(336) 768-7230
Contact: James T. Broyhill, Pres.

Established in 1994 in NC.
Donor(s): James T. Broyhill, Louise R. Broyhill, Satie L. Broyhill.
Financial data (yr. ended 12/31/01): Grants paid, $0; assets, $2,276,628 (M); gifts received, $32,346; expenditures, $6,183; qualifying distributions, $0.
Limitations: Giving primarily in NC.
Application information: Application form not required.
Officers: James T. Broyhill, Pres.; Louise R. Broyhill, V.P.; James Edgar Broyhill II, Secy.; Robert T. Beach, Treas.
Directors: Marilyn Broyhill Beach, Philip R. Broyhill.
EIN: 561853094

42009
J. Phil Carlton Foundation, Inc.
P.O. Box 67
Pinetops, NC 27864

Financial data (yr. ended 06/30/01): Grants paid, $0; assets, $332,681 (M); gifts received, $31,000; expenditures, $2,055; qualifying distributions, $0.
Limitations: Applications not accepted. Giving limited to NC.
Application information: Contributes only to pre-selected organizations.

42009—NORTH CAROLINA

Officers and Directors:* J. Phil Carlton,* Pres.; Dean D. Carlton,* V.P.; W. Deanna Carlton Drescher,* V.P.; Elizabeth H. Carlton Trathen,* V.P.
EIN: 561545913

42010
Carolina Girls Family Foundation
P.O. Box 573
Sanford, NC 27331

Established in 2001 in NC.
Financial data (yr. ended 12/31/01): Grants paid, $0; assets, $15,022 (M); gifts received, $15,022; expenditures, $0; qualifying distributions, $0.
Trustee: Terese C. Nixon.
EIN: 562278066

42011
Carolina Motor Club Foundation for Traffic Safety, Inc.
6600 AAA Dr.
Charlotte, NC 28212

Established in 1999 in NC.
Financial data (yr. ended 09/30/01): Grants paid, $0; assets, $55 (M); expenditures, $0; qualifying distributions, $0.
Limitations: Giving primarily in NC.
Officer: Dave Parsons, C.E.O. and Pres.
Directors: Tom Crosby, Jess Davis.
EIN: 562139475

42012
Carringer Family Charitable Foundation
1003 Palace Ct.
Apex, NC 27502

Established in 2000.
Financial data (yr. ended 10/31/01): Grants paid, $0; assets, $10,000 (M); gifts received, $10,000; expenditures, $0; qualifying distributions, $0.
Trustees: Richard D. Carringer, Sandra J. Carringer, Elizabeth B. Godfrey.
EIN: 562223130

42013
Jack and Mary Cartwright Foundation
c/o Richard Tuggle
1040 Cantering Rd.
High Point, NC 27262-4506

Donor(s): Jack Cartwright, Mary Cartwright.
Financial data (yr. ended 03/31/02): Grants paid, $0; assets, $10,065 (M); expenditures, $0; qualifying distributions, $0.
Limitations: Applications not accepted.
Application information: Contributes only to pre-selected organizations.
Officers and Directors:* Jack Cartwright,* Chair., Pres. and Treas.; Mary F. Cartwright,* V.P. and Secy.; Mary Annette Bibee,* V.P.; Mary Elizabeth Sutton,* V.P.
EIN: 561790677

42014
Margaret Cline Foundation
c/o First Union National Bank
401 S. Tryon St., 4th Fl.
Charlotte, NC 28288-1159

Established in 2001.
Financial data (yr. ended 12/31/01): Grants paid, $0; assets, $252,288 (M); gifts received, $250,000; expenditures, $1,659; qualifying distributions, $0.
Limitations: Applications not accepted.
Application information: Contributes only to pre-selected organizations.
Trustee: First Union National Bank.
EIN: 256758495

42015
Cobb Family Foundation
231 Perrin Pl.
Charlotte, NC 28207

Established in 2001 in NC.
Donor(s): Ruth M. Cobb.
Financial data (yr. ended 12/31/01): Grants paid, $0; assets, $316,618 (M); gifts received, $52,064; expenditures, $0; qualifying distributions, $0.
Limitations: Applications not accepted.
Application information: Contributes only to pre-selected organizations.
Officers and Directors:* Ruth M. Cobb,* Pres. and Treas.; Ruth Mills Cobb,* V.P. and Secy.; James T. Cobb, Jr., Roger M. Cobb.
EIN: 562278436

42016
The Copwood Hill Foundation
166 Woodwinds Dr.
Banner Elk, NC 28604-7912

Established in 2001 in NC.
Donor(s): Kathryn Copley.
Financial data (yr. ended 12/31/01): Grants paid, $0; assets, $34,966 (M); gifts received, $21,097; expenditures, $0; qualifying distributions, $0.
Limitations: Applications not accepted.
Application information: Contributes only to pre-selected organizations.
Director: Kathryn W. Copley.
EIN: 562275567

42017
Frank Deaton and McBride Alexander Deaton Christian Memorial Foundation
P.O. Box 9327
Charlotte, NC 28299-9327

Donor(s): Frank A. Deaton.
Financial data (yr. ended 06/30/01): Grants paid, $0; assets, $583,186 (M); gifts received, $400; expenditures, $21,861; qualifying distributions, $21,861.
Limitations: Applications not accepted. Giving primarily in the South, with emphasis on NC.
Application information: Contributes only to pre-selected organizations.
Officers: Frank A. Deaton, Pres. and Treas.; Carolyn S. Deaton, Secy.
EIN: 561542624

42018
Clyde C. & Dorothy C. Dickson Foundation
2633 Richardson Dr.
Charlotte, NC 28211

Established in 2001 in NC.
Donor(s): C. C. Dickson, Jr.
Financial data (yr. ended 12/31/01): Grants paid, $0; assets, $4,739 (M); gifts received, $5,100; expenditures, $361; qualifying distributions, $0.
Limitations: Applications not accepted.
Application information: Contributes only to pre-selected organizations.
Officers: C. C. Dickson, Jr., Pres.; Dorothy C. Dickson, V.P.
Director: James Y. Preston.
EIN: 562262387

42019
Dorcas Foundation
158 Bingham & Parks Rd.
Advance, NC 27006 (336) 998-4829

Established in 2001.
Donor(s): William A. Long.
Financial data (yr. ended 12/31/01): Grants paid, $0; assets, $6,015 (M); gifts received, $6,000; expenditures, $0; qualifying distributions, $0.

Officers: William A. Long, Pres.; Kim R. Beauchamp, V.P.; Peggy R. Long, Secy.; Kimberly R. Beauchamp, Treas.
Directors: R. Scott Cranfill, Matthew McKnight, Howard Wilburn.
EIN: 562232813

42020
The Eason Foundation
c/o Stephen A. Eason
1824 Bristol Rd.
Durham, NC 27707

Established in 2001 in NC.
Donor(s): Stephen A. Eason.
Financial data (yr. ended 12/31/01): Grants paid, $0; assets, $212,357 (M); gifts received, $206,550; expenditures, $0; qualifying distributions, $0.
Limitations: Applications not accepted.
Application information: Contributes only to pre-selected organizations.
Directors: Kathryn E. Eason, Stephen A. Eason.
EIN: 562276733

42021
Endtime Ministries, Inc.
6676 Styers Ferry Rd.
Clemmons, NC 27012-8074

Financial data (yr. ended 12/31/00): Grants paid, $0; assets, $14,324 (M); gifts received, $10,902; expenditures, $12,485; qualifying distributions, $11,493; giving activities include $11,496 for programs.
Limitations: Applications not accepted.
Application information: Contributes only to pre-selected organizations.
Officers: Dwight M. Jester, Pres.; Martha W. Jester, Secy.-Treas.
Directors: Tim Key, Eddie Ritenour, David Stewart.
EIN: 561150470

42022
David Farmer Family Foundation
8701 Old Tom Way
Raleigh, NC 27613

Established in 2000 in NC.
Financial data (yr. ended 06/30/01): Grants paid, $0; assets, $79,164 (M); expenditures, $1,812; qualifying distributions, $0.
Officers: David L. Farmer, Pres.; Ann M. Farmer, Secy.
Directors: Katie M. Farmer, Shelly L. Farmer.
EIN: 562203097

42023
Forbes Foundation, Inc.
c/o Joseph W. Forbes, Jr.
203 Smyrna Church Rd.
Robbins, NC 27325

Established in 2000 in NC.
Donor(s): Joseph W. Forbes, Jr., Suzanne Forbes.
Financial data (yr. ended 12/31/00): Grants paid, $0; assets, $787,729 (M); gifts received, $800,249; expenditures, $0; qualifying distributions, $0.
Limitations: Applications not accepted.
Application information: Contributes only to pre-selected organizations.
Officers: Joseph W. Forbes, Jr., Pres. and Treas.; Joseph W. Forbes, Sr., V.P. and Secy.; Suzanne Forbes, V.P.
EIN: 582587780

42024
Gafner Family Foundation
c/o Barry J. Gafner
516 Tharps Ln.
Raleigh, NC 27614-9466

Established in 2001 in NC.
Donor(s): Barry J. Gafner, Annette B. Gafner.
Financial data (yr. ended 12/31/01): Grants paid, $0; assets, $280,379 (M); gifts received, $319,540; expenditures, $0; qualifying distributions, $0.
Officers: Barry J. Gafner, Pres. and Treas.; Annette B. Gafner, V.P. and Secy.
EIN: 562236053

42025
The Jimmy Woodard Garrell Foundation
P.O. Box 771
Tabor City, NC 28463

Established in 2000 in NC.
Donor(s): Jimmy Woodard Garrell.
Financial data (yr. ended 12/31/01): Grants paid, $0; assets, $305,286 (M); expenditures, $666; qualifying distributions, $0.
Limitations: Giving primarily in NC.
Officer and Directors:* Jimmy Woodard Garrell,* Pres.; Gloria Fowler, Terray Suggs.
EIN: 562174021

42026
Greensboro Generals Foundation, Inc.
208 W. Wendover Ave.
Greensboro, NC 27401

Established in 1999 in NC.
Donor(s): Arthur J. Donaldson.
Financial data (yr. ended 12/31/01): Grants paid, $0; assets, $224 (M); expenditures, $162; qualifying distributions, $0.
Officers: Arthur J. Donaldson, Pres.; James C. Roscetti, Secy.-Treas.
EIN: 311676405

42027
John D. Gruwell Trust
c/o First Union National Bank
401 S. Tryon St., NC1159
Charlotte, NC 28288-1159

Established in 2000 in NC.
Financial data (yr. ended 12/30/00): Grants paid, $0; assets, $3,750 (M); expenditures, $3,750; qualifying distributions, $0.
Trustee: First Union National Bank.
EIN: 256699434

42028
Miriam S. & William T. Hall, Jr. Foundation
c/o James B. Garland
P.O. Box 1657
Gastonia, NC 28053

Established in 2001 in AK and NC.
Financial data (yr. ended 06/30/01): Grants paid, $0; assets, $533,732 (M); expenditures, $4,119; qualifying distributions, $0.
Trustees: Richard K. Boyce, Jesse B. Caldwell III, James B. Garland.
EIN: 566563541

42029
Hamlin-Goddard Foundation, Inc.
c/o Wachovia Bank, N.A.
P.O. Box 3099
Winston-Salem, NC 27150-7131

Established in 2000 in GA.
Donor(s): Billy Hamlin, Karen Hamlin.
Financial data (yr. ended 12/30/00): Grants paid, $0; assets, $1,047,295 (M); gifts received, $1,000,016; expenditures, $0; qualifying distributions, $0.
Limitations: Applications not accepted.
Application information: Contributes only to pre-selected organizations.
Trustees: Billy Hamlin, Karen Hamlin, Wachovia Bank, N.A.
EIN: 582544384

42030
Betty Mallory Harkness Foundation
c/o Wachovia Bank, N.A.
P.O. Box 3099
Winston-Salem, NC 27150-7131

Established in 1999 in NC.
Donor(s): Betty Mallory Harkness.‡
Financial data (yr. ended 12/31/99): Grants paid, $0; assets, $590,658 (M); gifts received, $350,000; expenditures, $3,300; qualifying distributions, $0.
Trustee: Wachovia Bank, N.A.
EIN: 541945462

42031
The Havelock Senior Citizens Club
c/o Eddie Turner
P.O. Box 655
Havelock, NC 28532-0655

Financial data (yr. ended 12/31/01): Grants paid, $0; assets, $1 (M); expenditures, $0; qualifying distributions, $0.
Officers: Bernice Rudder, Pres.; Penay Young, V.P.; Marcille Johnson, Secy.; Elizabeth Smith, Treas.
EIN: 581835340

42032
Charles F. Herman Educational Fund
c/o College Foundation, Inc.
P.O. Box 12100
Raleigh, NC 27605-2100 (919) 834-2893

Financial data (yr. ended 06/30/01): Grants paid, $0; assets, $50,166 (M); expenditures, $2,898; qualifying distributions, $2,380; giving activities include $489 for loans to organizations and $1,933 for loans to individuals.
Limitations: Giving limited to residents of Moore County, NC.
Application information: Application form required.
Trustee: College Foundation, Inc.
EIN: 566090151

42033
Holliday Cemetery Trust
c/o RBC Centura Bank
P.O. Box 1220
Rocky Mount, NC 27802

Financial data (yr. ended 01/31/01): Grants paid, $0; assets, $34,264 (M); expenditures, $608; qualifying distributions, $15.
Trustee: RBC Centura Bank.
EIN: 566410975

42034
Torry Holt Foundation
c/o Wachovia Bank, N.A.
P.O. Box 3099
Winston-Salem, NC 27150-7131

Established in 2000 in NC.
Donor(s): Torry Holt.
Financial data (yr. ended 12/31/00): Grants paid, $0; assets, $6,174 (M); gifts received, $6,834; expenditures, $660; qualifying distributions, $660.
Limitations: Applications not accepted.
Application information: Contributes only to pre-selected organizations.
Officers and Directors:* Torry Holt,* Pres.; Charles T. Francis,* Secy.-Treas.; Gregory Williams.
EIN: 566570426

42035
The Jarrell-Snipes Foundation
P.O. Box 3472
Wilmington, NC 28406-3472

Financial data (yr. ended 12/31/01): Grants paid, $0; assets, $133,965 (M); expenditures, $757; qualifying distributions, $0.
Limitations: Applications not accepted.
Application information: Contributes only to pre-selected organizations.
Officers and Directors:* Esther Snipes,* Pres.; Priscilla Soto,* V.P.; Linda Soto,* Secy.; Joseph Soto,* Treas.
EIN: 562111292

42036
Johnson Foundation
P.O. Box 1040
Salisbury, NC 28145-1040 (704) 633-5982
Contact: Frances H. Johnson, Pres.

Established in 1954 in NC.
Donor(s): B.V. Hedrick Gravel and Sand Co., Frances H. Johnson.
Financial data (yr. ended 12/31/01): Grants paid, $0; assets, $565,529 (M); gifts received, $70,071; expenditures, $904; qualifying distributions, $495.
Limitations: Giving limited to Salisbury, NC.
Application information: Application form not required.
Officers: Frances H. Johnson, Pres.; F. Joanne Johnson, V.P.; Judith H. Johnson, Secy.; Kathryn H. Johnson, Treas.
EIN: 566034758

42037
Jordan Foundation, Inc.
P.O. Box 2021
Raleigh, NC 27602-0709

Donor(s): John R. Jordan, Jr.
Financial data (yr. ended 11/30/00): Grants paid, $0; assets, $27,993 (L); gifts received, $11,500; expenditures, $9,288; qualifying distributions, $9,288; giving activities include $9,038 for programs.
Limitations: Applications not accepted.
Application information: Contributes only to pre-selected organizations.
Officers and Directors:* John R. Jordan, Jr.,* Pres.; J. Richard Jordan III,* V.P.; Steven R. Dolan,* Secy.; Ellen J. McCarren,* Treas.
EIN: 561316249

42038
The J. A. Joseph Family Foundation
c/o American Embassy-Pretoria
60140 Davie
Chapel Hill, NC 27514

Established in 1996 in VA.
Donor(s): James A. Joseph, Mary B. Joseph.
Financial data (yr. ended 12/31/99): Grants paid, $0; assets, $79,891 (M); gifts received, $2,190; expenditures, $169; qualifying distributions, $0.
Limitations: Applications not accepted.
Application information: Contributes only to pre-selected organizations.
Officers: James A. Joseph, Pres.; Jeffrey A. Joseph, V.P. and Treas.; Denise A. Joseph, Secy.
Trustee: Mary B. Joseph.
EIN: 541782686

42039
The Joseph Project
191 Azalea Rd.
Mooresville, NC 28115

Established in 1998.
Donor(s): Dean A. Stein, Jennifer Stein.
Financial data (yr. ended 12/31/01): Grants paid, $0; assets, $1 (M); gifts received, $7; expenditures, $27; qualifying distributions, $0.
Officers: Dean A. Stein, Pres. and Treas.; Jennifer E. Stein, Secy.
EIN: 562104196

42040
Kel Foundation, Inc.
2601 Reynolds Dr.
Winston-Salem, NC 27104 (336) 725-2946
Contact: J. Leon Rumley, Secy.-Treas.

Established in 1997 in NC.
Financial data (yr. ended 06/30/02): Grants paid, $0; assets, $1,864 (M); expenditures, $24; qualifying distributions, $0.
Officers: Katherine F. Rumley, Pres.; J. Leon Rumley, Secy.-Treas.
EIN: 562038048

42041
The Leith Foundation
P.O. Box 40110
Raleigh, NC 27629

Financial data (yr. ended 12/31/01): Grants paid, $0; assets, $174 (M); expenditures, $105; qualifying distributions, $0.
Officers and Trustee:* Michael J. Leith,* Pres.; Linda J. Leith, Secy.-Treas.
Director: David H. Leithead.
EIN: 561690119
Codes: TN

42042
A. Alexander Lewis Scholarship Trust
c/o First Union National Bank
401 S. Tryon St., NC 1159
Charlotte, NC 28288-1159

Established in 2000 in NJ.
Financial data (yr. ended 12/31/00): Grants paid, $0; assets, $118,990 (M); gifts received, $11,042; expenditures, $1,888; qualifying distributions, $1,451.
Limitations: Applications not accepted.
Application information: Contributes only to pre-selected organizations.
Trustee: First Union National Bank.
EIN: 256699459

42043
The Mangum Fund, Inc.
(Formerly Paraclete Foundation, Inc.)
c/o William E. Mangum
3141 John Humphries Wynd
Raleigh, NC 27612

Established in 1994 in NC.
Donor(s): William E. Mangum, Michael D. Mangum, Jim Anthony.
Financial data (yr. ended 12/31/01): Grants paid, $0; assets, $65,402 (M); expenditures, $920; qualifying distributions, $0.
Limitations: Applications not accepted. Giving primarily in NC.
Application information: Contributes only to pre-selected organizations.
Officers and Directors:* William E. Mangum,* Pres.; Merl E. Mangum,* V.P.; Jeanne M. Andrus,* Secy.-Treas.; Tom Andrus, Christopher Mangum, Geraldine Mangum, Michael Mangum, Pat Mangum, Tal Mangum.

EIN: 561880871

42044
J. Marshall & L. Powell Charitable Trust
c/o Bank of America
Bank of America Plz.
Charlotte, NC 28255
Application address: c/o Bank of America, 600 Peachtree St. N.E., Atlanta, GA 30308
Contact: Bank of America

Established in 2000.
Donor(s): Lucille G. Powell.‡
Financial data (yr. ended 09/30/01): Grants paid, $0; assets, $1,665,349 (M); gifts received, $2,359,188; expenditures, $18,722; qualifying distributions, $5,805.
Trustee: Bank of America.
EIN: 527106649

42045
William Kemp & Mary S. Mauney Foundation, Inc.
P.O. Box 1279
Kings Mountain, NC 28086-1279
(704) 739-3621
Contact: William K. Mauney, Jr., Pres.

Financial data (yr. ended 10/31/99): Grants paid, $0; assets, $64,052 (M); expenditures, $15; qualifying distributions, $0.
Officer: William K. Mauney, Jr., Pres.
EIN: 566047270

42046
MCM Foundation
702 Oberlin Rd.
P.O. Box 12317
Raleigh, NC 27605

Established in 1966 in NC.
Financial data (yr. ended 12/31/99): Grants paid, $0; assets, $20 (M); expenditures, $145; qualifying distributions, $0.
Officer and Trustees:* Cecilia Taylor,* Treas.; Kevin J. Hamm, George E. King, Stephen L. Stephano.
EIN: 566075561

42047
C. O. & Luella T. McNiel Memorial Educational Fund, Inc.
P.O. Box 242
North Wilkesboro, NC 28659-0242
(336) 838-2171
Contact: Leonard L. Brooks, Jr., Dir.

Financial data (yr. ended 12/31/01): Grants paid, $0; assets, $36,268 (M); expenditures, $4,209; qualifying distributions, $0.
Limitations: Giving limited to the Wilkesboro, NC, area.
Application information: Application form required.
Directors: Phyllis Blair, Elizabeth A. Brooks, Leonard L. Brooks, Jr., David D. Deal, Marsh Lyall, Jerry McGuire, Ronald S. Shoemaker.
EIN: 566068237

42048
Melton Foundation
4406 Rock Creek Rd.
Hays, NC 28635

Established in 2001 in NC.
Donor(s): Doris W. Melton.
Financial data (yr. ended 12/31/01): Grants paid, $0; assets, $99,841 (M); gifts received, $100,724; expenditures, $0; qualifying distributions, $0.
Limitations: Applications not accepted.
Application information: Contributes only to pre-selected organizations.

Officers: Doris W. Melton, Pres.; Randy L. Melton, V.P.; Steven E. Melton, Secy.-Treas.
EIN: 562276922

42049
Merritt Memorial Fund, Inc.
P.O. Box 1425
Mount Airy, NC 27030-1425 (336) 789-7848
Contact: H. Lee Merritt, Jr., Chair.

Financial data (yr. ended 12/31/01): Grants paid, $0; assets, $886 (M); expenditures, $26; qualifying distributions, $0.
Officer: H. Lee Merritt, Jr., Chair.
EIN: 566047729

42050
Joe D. Moore Foundation, Inc.
36 Springmoor Ct.
Raleigh, NC 27615-4324 (919) 848-7036
Contact: Joe D. Moore, Pres.

Established in 1986 in NC.
Donor(s): Joe D. Moore.
Financial data (yr. ended 12/31/01): Grants paid, $0; assets, $147,309 (M); expenditures, $362; qualifying distributions, $0.
Limitations: Giving primarily in NC and SC.
Application information: Application form not required.
Officers and Directors:* Joe D. Moore,* Pres. and Treas.; Virgilia C. Moore,* Secy.; James Y. Preston.
EIN: 561518712

42051
The Moritz Foundation
c/o Wachovia Bank, N.A.
P.O. Box 3099
Winston-Salem, NC 27150-7131

Established in 2000 in CT.
Donor(s): Kenneth N. Musen.
Financial data (yr. ended 12/31/00): Grants paid, $0; assets, $150,293 (M); gifts received, $150,000; expenditures, $0; qualifying distributions, $0.
Limitations: Applications not accepted.
Application information: Contributes only to pre-selected organizations.
Trustees: Dieter Feddersen, Andrea M.L. Goelkel, Ester Carola Goelkel, Judith Sonja Goelkel, Kenneth N. Musen, Wachovia Bank, N.A.
EIN: 066504115

42052
M. Edward Morris Foundation, Inc.
c/o First Union National Bank
401 S. Tryon, NC1159
Charlotte, NC 28288-1159

Established in 2000 in NJ.
Financial data (yr. ended 12/31/01): Grants paid, $0; assets, $1,553,369 (M); expenditures, $13,539; qualifying distributions, $0.
Limitations: Applications not accepted.
Application information: Contributes only to pre-selected organizations.
Trustees: Victor Walcoff, First Union National Bank.
EIN: 223469302

42053
NC Children's and Young Adult's Clinical Research Foundation
109 Conner Dr., Ste. 107-B
Chapel Hill, NC 27514
Contact: Dr. Charles Shaeffer, M.D., Exec. Dir.

Established in 1997 in NC.
Financial data (yr. ended 12/31/01): Grants paid, $0; assets, $180,435 (M); expenditures, $1,449,394; qualifying distributions, $0.

Officers: Floyd W. Denny, M.D., Chair. and Pres.; Campbell W. McMillan, M.D., Vice Chair. and V.P.; Don A. Williams, M.D., Secy.; Carolyn S. Schroeder, Ph.D., Treas.; Charles Shaeffer, M.D., Exec. Dir.
EIN: 561937207

42054
Nordling Family Foundation
12717 Waterman Dr.
Raleigh, NC 27614

Established in 2000 in NC.
Donor(s): Anne-Berit Nordling, Karl Nordling.
Financial data (yr. ended 06/30/01): Grants paid, $0; assets, $153,452 (M); gifts received, $152,244; expenditures, $2,244; qualifying distributions, $0.
Limitations: Applications not accepted.
Application information: Contributes only to pre-selected organizations.
Directors: Anne-Berit Nordling, Karl Nordling.
EIN: 943382637

42055
Janet and Jack O'Loughlin Foundation, Inc.
P.O. Box 3579
Pinehurst, NC 28374-3579

Established in 1986 in IL.
Donor(s): Jack K. O'Loughlin, Janet T. O'Loughlin.
Financial data (yr. ended 12/31/00): Grants paid, $0; assets, $14,435 (M); expenditures, $0; qualifying distributions, $0.
Limitations: Applications not accepted. Giving primarily in IL.
Application information: Contributes only to pre-selected organizations.
Officers: Janet T. O'Loughlin, Pres.; Jack K. O'Loughlin, V.P.; Robert K. O'Loughlin, Secy.-Treas.
EIN: 363484549

42056
Tolly Vinik-Bascom Palmer Charitable Trust 2
c/o First Union National Bank
401 S. Tryon St., NC1159
Charlotte, NC 28288-1159

Established in 1995 in FL.
Financial data (yr. ended 12/31/01): Grants paid, $0; assets, $1,261,485 (M); expenditures, $23,363; qualifying distributions, $0.
Limitations: Applications not accepted.
Application information: Contributes only to pre-selected organizations.
Trustee: First Union National Bank.
EIN: 596979686

42057
Plumtree Foundation, Inc.
c/o W.W. Avery Jr.
P.O. Box 101
Plumtree, NC 28664

Financial data (yr. ended 12/31/01): Grants paid, $0; assets, $69,711 (M); gifts received, $300; expenditures, $268; qualifying distributions, $0.
Officers: W.W. Avery, Pres.; D. Calloway, V.P.; Addie Barrier, Secy.-Treas.
Directors: Edna Aldridge, Bob Loven.
EIN: 561150568

42058
Norris & Kathryn Preyer Fund
c/o Piedmont Financial Co., Inc.
P.O. Box 20124
Greensboro, NC 27420-0124
Contact: Norris W. Preyer, Tr.

Established in 1988 in NC.

Financial data (yr. ended 06/30/01): Grants paid, $0; assets, $425,296 (M); expenditures, $4,340; qualifying distributions, $0.
Limitations: Giving primarily in Charlotte, NC.
Trustees: Janet Preyer Nelson, Kathryn C. Preyer, Norris W. Preyer, Sr., Norris W. Preyer, Jr.
EIN: 561637436

42059
Quickel Scholarship Foundation
c/o Bank of America
1 Bank of America Plz.
Charlotte, NC 28255 (704) 386-5731

Financial data (yr. ended 12/31/01): Grants paid, $0; assets, $10,182 (M); expenditures, $532; qualifying distributions, $0.
Limitations: Giving primarily in NC.
Application information: Application form not required.
Trustee: Bank of America.
EIN: 566069263

42060
William M. & Betty J. Ragland Foundation
c/o Wachovia Bank, N.A.
P.O. Box 3099
Winston-Salem, NC 27150-7131

Established in 1994 in NC.
Financial data (yr. ended 12/31/01): Grants paid, $0; assets, $4,602 (M); expenditures, $303; qualifying distributions, $0.
Limitations: Applications not accepted.
Application information: Contributes only to pre-selected organizations.
Trustee: Wachovia Bank, N.A.
EIN: 566393570

42061
Renfro Family Foundation, Inc.
15 Greenwood Rd.
Asheville, NC 28803-3110 (828) 684-2747
Contact: George D. Renfro, Tr.

Donor(s): George D. Renfro.
Financial data (yr. ended 12/31/01): Grants paid, $0; assets, $478 (M); expenditures, $15; qualifying distributions, $0.
Limitations: Giving limited to western NC.
Trustees: Donna H. Renfro, George D. Renfro.
EIN: 561896568

42062
Hubert A. Ritchie Foundation
c/o Wachovia Bank, N.A.
P.O. Box 3099
Winston-Salem, NC 27150-7131

Established in 2000 in NC.
Financial data (yr. ended 12/31/00): Grants paid, $0; assets, $24,178 (M); gifts received, $23,913; expenditures, $0; qualifying distributions, $0.
Limitations: Applications not accepted.
Application information: Contributes only to pre-selected organizations.
Trustees: Barbar E. Brown, Tim Erwin, Donald Menius, Wachovia Bank, N.A.
EIN: 546481375

42063
Emmet and Mary Robinson Trust Foundation
c/o Wachovia Bank, N.A.
P.O. Box 3099
Winston-Salem, NC 27150-6732

Established in 2001 in NC.
Donor(s): Mary R. Norwood.
Financial data (yr. ended 12/31/01): Grants paid, $0; assets, $499,976 (M); gifts received, $466,593; expenditures, $2,999; qualifying distributions, $0.

Limitations: Giving primarily in Wayne County, NC.
Trustee: Wachovia Bank, N.A.
EIN: 566582132

42064
The Rogers Family Foundation
40 Cheswick St.
Durham, NC 27707

Established in 2001 in NC.
Donor(s): Ralph P. Rogers, Elizabeth S. Rogers.
Financial data (yr. ended 12/31/01): Grants paid, $0; assets, $111,336 (M); gifts received, $104,340; expenditures, $3,135; qualifying distributions, $0.
Limitations: Applications not accepted.
Application information: Contributes only to pre-selected organizations.
Officers and Directors:* Ralph P. Rogers,* Pres. and Treas.; Elizabeth S. Rogers,* V.P. and Secy.; Jean R. Flowers, Dewitt R. Rogers.
EIN: 562270372

42065
Bettey & Karl Search Scholarship Fund
c/o First Union National Bank
401 S. Tryon St., NC 1159
Charlotte, NC 28288-1159

Established in 2000 in PA.
Financial data (yr. ended 12/31/00): Grants paid, $0; assets, $757,514 (M); gifts received, $812,254; expenditures, $6,115; qualifying distributions, $0.
Limitations: Applications not accepted.
Application information: Contributes only to pre-selected organizations.
Trustee: First Union National Bank.
EIN: 256699396

42066
Shaman Charitable Foundation
c/o First Union National Bank
401 S. Tryon St., 4th Fl.
Charlotte, NC 28288-1159

Established in 2001 in DC.
Donor(s): Louis Shaman.
Financial data (yr. ended 12/31/01): Grants paid, $0; assets, $781,186 (M); gifts received, $768,389; expenditures, $9,653; qualifying distributions, $0.
Trustee: First Union National Bank.
EIN: 586433772

42067
Vivian Holmes Shamotulski Trust
c/o First Union National Bank
401 S. Tryon St., 4th Fl.
Charlotte, NC 28288-1159

Financial data (yr. ended 12/31/00): Grants paid, $0; assets, $2,326,244 (M); expenditures, $9,161; qualifying distributions, $91,104.
Limitations: Applications not accepted. Giving limited to residents of GA.
Trustee: First Union National Bank.
EIN: 586026202

42068
Sheldon Scholarship Trust Fund
c/o College Foundation, Inc.
P.O. Box 12100
Raleigh, NC 27605-2100 (919) 834-2893

Financial data (yr. ended 06/30/01): Grants paid, $0; assets, $110,139 (M); expenditures, $8,977; qualifying distributions, $7,634; giving activities include $7,634 for loans to individuals.
Limitations: Giving limited to residents of Moore County, NC.

Application information: Application form required.
Trustee: College Foundation, Inc.
EIN: 566045116

42069
Silly Putty Charitable Trust
c/o Wachovia Bank, N.A.
P.O. Box 3099
Winston-Salem, NC 27150-7131
Application address: c/o C. Gerlad Lane, Trust Off., Wachovia Bank, N.A., 1401 Main St., Columbia, SC 29226, tel.: (803) 765-3671

Donor(s): Binney & Smith, Inc., F.R. Buckley.
Financial data (yr. ended 12/31/01): Grants paid, $0; assets, $107,059 (M); gifts received, $3,100; expenditures, $2,166; qualifying distributions, $1,250.
Limitations: Giving limited to the Camden, SC, area.
Officer and Directors:* F. Reid Buckley,* Chair.; Claude Langford Buckley, William Hunting Buckley, Elizabeth Buckley Riley.
Trustee: Wachovia Bank, N.A.
EIN: 576071454
Codes: CS, CD

42070
Slosman Family Foundation, Inc.
c/o E. Benson Slosman
P.O. Box 3019
Asheville, NC 28802

Financial data (yr. ended 02/28/02): Grants paid, $0; assets, $34,413 (M); expenditures, $248; qualifying distributions, $0.
Limitations: Applications not accepted.
Application information: Contributes only to pre-selected organizations.
Officers: Frederick N. Slosman, Pres. and Treas.; Jean Quayle, Secy.
EIN: 566094138

42071
Staton Foundation
c/o B.B. & T., Trust Dept.
P.O. Box 2907
Wilson, NC 27894-2907

Established in 1993 in NC.
Donor(s): Phillip Staton, Ingeborg Staton.
Financial data (yr. ended 12/31/00): Grants paid, $0; assets, $6,459,860 (M); gifts received, $898,281; expenditures, $28,025; qualifying distributions, $0.
Limitations: Applications not accepted. Giving primarily in NC.
Application information: Contributes only to pre-selected organizations.
Trustee: Philip A.R. Staton, B.B. & T.
EIN: 566436381

42072
The W. David Stedman and Sarah White Stedman Foundation
(Formerly The Stedman Foundation)
P.O. Box 21927
Greensboro, NC 27420-1927

Established in 1986 in NC.
Donor(s): W. David Stedman.
Financial data (yr. ended 12/31/01): Grants paid, $0; assets, $114,538 (M); expenditures, $4,810; qualifying distributions, $0.
Limitations: Applications not accepted. Giving primarily in NC.
Application information: Contributes only to pre-selected organizations.
Trustees: Sarah W. Stedman, W. David Stedman.
EIN: 561547595

42073
Lee & Tammy Storms Family Foundation, Inc.
828 East Blvd.
Charlotte, NC 28207
Application address: c/o Debra M. Haigler, P.O. Box 981, Pineville, NC 28134, tel.: (704) 571-1234

Donor(s): Tamela K. Storms.
Financial data (yr. ended 12/31/01): Grants paid, $0; assets, $1,505 (M); expenditures, $0; qualifying distributions, $0.
Directors: Donald L. Storms, Gordon Lee Storms, Tamela K. Storms.
EIN: 593284032

42074
Kathleen Clay Taylor Foundation
c/o Wachovia Bank, N.A.
P.O. Box 3099
Winston-Salem, NC 27150-6732

Established in 2001 in NC.
Donor(s): Kathleen Bryan Edwards.
Financial data (yr. ended 12/31/01): Grants paid, $0; assets, $2,976,337 (M); gifts received, $2,960,086; expenditures, $8,235; qualifying distributions, $7,500.
Limitations: Applications not accepted.
Application information: Contributes only to pre-selected organizations.
Trustees: Kathleen Clay Taylor, Wachovia Bank, N.A.
EIN: 226905334

42075
The Taylor Grant Joss Foundation
P.O. Box 51280
Durham, NC 27717-1280

Established in 1992 in NC.
Donor(s): James F. Taylor.
Financial data (yr. ended 12/31/01): Grants paid, $0; assets, $1 (M); gifts received, $1,000; expenditures, $542; qualifying distributions, $0.
Limitations: Applications not accepted. Giving limited to NC.
Application information: Contributes only to pre-selected organizations.
Officers and Directors:* James F. Taylor,* Pres. and Treas.; Janet E. Taylor,* Secy.; Richard E. Jenkins, John M. Joss, Harold Taylor.
EIN: 581978626

42076
Taylor Home of Charlotte, Inc.
401 S. Independence Blvd., Ste. 644
Charlotte, NC 28204

Established in 1996.
Financial data (yr. ended 09/30/99): Grants paid, $0; assets, $307,799 (M); expenditures, $19,251; qualifying distributions, $0; giving activities include $19,251 for programs.
Officers: Stephen Kelley, Pres.; Patty Stogner, V.P.; Joel Bently, Secy.; James Dearman, Treas.; A. Jack Wall, Exec. Dir.
Directors: Michael Page, Frank Stevens, William Stogner, Beth Tate, Miles Ware, Stana Ware, Tina Weinberg.
EIN: 561781744
Codes: TN

42077
Harvey Thomas Estate Student Aid Trust
c/o First Union National Bank
401 S. Tryon St., NC1159
Charlotte, NC 28288
Application address: P.O. Box 7558, PA 1308, Philadelpha, PA 19101
Contact: David Glickman, Trust Off., First Union National Bank

Financial data (yr. ended 09/30/01): Grants paid, $0; assets, $1,285,050 (M); expenditures, $17,086; qualifying distributions, $46,291; giving activities include $46,291 for loans to individuals.
Limitations: Giving limited to residents of Chester County, PA.
Trustee: First Union National Bank.
EIN: 236215693
Codes: GTI

42078
The Thomas Foundation
3475 N. Hwy. 109
Thomasville, NC 27360 (336) 476-3294
Contact: Patsy Schmidlin

Established in 1976 in NC.
Donor(s): Thomas Built Buses, Inc.
Financial data (yr. ended 12/31/01): Grants paid, $0; assets, $425,401 (M); expenditures, $7,818; qualifying distributions, $0.
Limitations: Giving primarily in High Point, NC.
Officers: P.A. Thomas, Chair. and Pres.; J.W. Thomas III, Vice-Chair. and V.P.; P.T. Schmidlin, Secy.-Treas.
Trustees: L.T. Gayle, Douglas M. Harrison, R.A. Price, B.L. Thomas, John W. Thomas, Jr.
EIN: 510189803
Codes: CS, CD

42079
Thorpe Private Foundation
P.O. Box 631
Rocky Mount, NC 27802

Established in 2001 in NC.
Donor(s): Thorpe & Company.
Financial data (yr. ended 12/31/01): Grants paid, $0; assets, $78 (M); gifts received, $250; expenditures, $172; qualifying distributions, $0.
Officers: Alexander P. Thorpe III, Pres.; Alexander P. Thorpe IV, V.P.; Annie Gray Thorpe Dixon, Secy.
EIN: 562233985

42080
Triangle Orthopaedic Research & Education Foundation
120 William Penn Plz.
Durham, NC 27704

Established in 2000 in NC.
Donor(s): Pfizer Inc, G.D. Searle & Co., Pharmacia & Upjohn Co.
Financial data (yr. ended 06/30/01): Grants paid, $0; assets, $46,140 (M); gifts received, $79,799; expenditures, $33,659; qualifying distributions, $33,455.
Limitations: Applications not accepted.
Application information: Contributes only to pre-selected organizations.
Officers: Kyle Black, V.P.; Richard Bruch, V.P.; Thomas A. Dimmig, V.P.; Lawrence Frank, V.P.; Peter W. Gilmer, V.P.; Ralph A. Liebelt, V.P.; William Mallon, V.P.
Director: Edwin T. Preston.
EIN: 562206061

42081
Rusty Wallace Charitable Foundation
c/o Richard A. Paysor
136 Knob Hill Rd.
Mooresville, NC 28115

Established in 1996 in NC.
Donor(s): NASCAR.
Financial data (yr. ended 12/31/01): Grants paid, $0; assets, $17,401 (M); gifts received, $2,500; expenditures, $503; qualifying distributions, $0.
Limitations: Applications not accepted.
Application information: Contributes only to pre-selected organizations.
Officers: Rusty Wallace, Pres.; Patricia Wallace, V.P.; Richard A. Paysor, Mgr.
EIN: 561938326

42082
The Ward Family Charitable Trust
c/o Wachovia Bank, N.A.
P.O. Box 3099
Winston-Salem, NC 27150-6732

Established in 2001 in NC and GA.
Donor(s): John F. Ward.
Financial data (yr. ended 12/31/01): Grants paid, $0; assets, $122,426 (M); gifts received, $126,540; expenditures, $15,141; qualifying distributions, $14,970.
Trustee: Wachovia Bank, N.A.
EIN: 586110277

42083
Earl Watson Family Trust
c/o Wachovia Bank, N.A.
P.O. Box 3099
Winston-Salem, NC 27150-7131
Application addresses: c/o Rev. Philip R. Byrum, Christ Episcopal Church, Stanley County, P.O. Box 657, Albemarle, NC 28001, tel.: (704) 982-1428, c/o Thomas W. Acker, County Extension Dir., P.O. Box 1797, Anderson, SC 29622, tel.: (843) 226-1581

Financial data (yr. ended 12/31/99): Grants paid, $0; assets, $11,126 (M); expenditures, $2,695; qualifying distributions, $546.
Limitations: Giving limited to Stanley County, NC, and Anderson, SC.
Trustee: Wachovia Bank, N.A.
EIN: 581402071

42084
Edgar S. Welborn, Jr. Endowment
c/o Wachovia Bank, N.A.
P.O. Box 3099
Winston-Salem, NC 27150-7131

Established in 2000 in NC.
Donor(s): Frances M. Welborn.
Financial data (yr. ended 12/31/00): Grants paid, $0; assets, $1,043,641 (M); gifts received, $1,076,401; expenditures, $0; qualifying distributions, $0.
Limitations: Applications not accepted. Giving primarily in Dividson and Moore counties, NC.
Application information: Contributes only to pre-selected organizations.
Trustee: Wachovia Bank, N.A.
EIN: 566566462

42085
The Brian White Foundation
2709 Commerce Rd.
Jacksonville, NC 28546

Established in 1998 in NC.
Donor(s): Trans Global Communications, Inc., Michael E. White, Shirley Ann White.
Financial data (yr. ended 12/31/01): Grants paid, $0; assets, $1,481,566 (M); gifts received, $600,000; expenditures, $338; qualifying distributions, $0.
Limitations: Applications not accepted.
Application information: Contributes only to pre-selected organizations.
Directors: Michael E. White, Shirley Ann White.
EIN: 562116081

42086
Wings Over Jordan Foundation, Inc.
P.O. Box 1573
Winterville, NC 28590

Financial data (yr. ended 12/31/99): Grants paid, $0; assets, $5,854 (M); gifts received, $23,618; expenditures, $17,844; qualifying distributions, $0.
Officers and Trustees:* Samuel Barber,* Pres.; James K. Rice,* Secy.; Dwight Lynch.
EIN: 510162230

42087
Lavina Michl Wright Scholarship
c/o First Union National Bank
401 S. Tryon St., 4th Fl.
Charlotte, NC 28288-1159

Established in 2001 in FL.
Donor(s): Lavina Wright.‡
Financial data (yr. ended 12/31/01): Grants paid, $0; assets, $168,471 (M); gifts received, $168,862; expenditures, $3,225; qualifying distributions, $2,039.
Limitations: Applications not accepted.
Application information: Contributes only to pre-selected organizations.
Trustee: First Union National Bank.
EIN: 586449065

42088
Ena Zucchi Charitable Trust
c/o First Union National Bank
401 S. Tryon St., 4th Fl.
Charlotte, NC 28288-1159
Application address: c/o First Union National Bank, Glen Rock, NJ 07102, tel.: (201) 251-4467

Established in 1990 in NJ.
Financial data (yr. ended 05/31/02): Grants paid, $0; assets, $441,973 (M); expenditures, $4,509; qualifying distributions, $740.
Limitations: Giving primarily in NJ.
Application information: Application form not required.
Trustee: First Union National Bank.
EIN: 232667612

NORTH DAKOTA

42089
Fargo-Moorhead Area Foundation
609 1st Ave. N., Ste. 205
Fargo, ND 58102-4997 (701) 234-0756
FAX: (701) 234-9724; E-mail: office@areafoundation.org; URL: http://www.areafoundation.org
Contact: Jan Ulferts Stewart, Exec. Dir.

Established in 1960 in ND.
Financial data (yr. ended 12/31/01): Grants paid, $1,625,564; assets, $33,305,528 (M); gifts received, $4,121,667; expenditures, $2,098,439.
Limitations: Giving limited to Clay County, MN, and Cass County, ND.
Publications: Program policy statement, application guidelines, informational brochure, annual report, newsletter.
Application information: Use the Fargo-Moorhead Area Foundation (FMAF) Application or the Minnesota Common Application Form. Application form required.
Officers, Distribution Committee and Directors:* Mitch Olson, Pres.; Michael Hannaher,* V.P.; Jan Ulferts Stewart, Exec. Dir.; Susan Andrews, Gale Chapman, William Guy III, Phyllis May-Machunda, Jim Stenerson, Mary Timmons, Samuel Wai.
Trustee Banks: Community First National Bank, Alerus Financial, Heartland Trust Co., Wells Fargo Bank, N.A., U.S. Bank, N.A.
EIN: 456010377
Codes: CM, FD

42090
North Dakota Community Foundation
P.O. Box 387
Bismarck, ND 58502-0387 (701) 222-8349
E-mail: kdvorak@ndcf.net; URL: http://www.ndcf.net
Contact: Kevin J. Dvorak, Pres.

Established in 1977 in ND.
Financial data (yr. ended 12/31/01): Grants paid, $1,050,706; assets, $18,720,439 (L); gifts received, $1,729,429; expenditures, $1,514,775.
Limitations: Giving primarily in ND.
Publications: Annual report, newsletter, informational brochure.
Application information: Foundation will contact applicant by Oct. 1 for additional materials. Application form not required.
Officers and Directors:* Frank P. Keogh, Chair.; Linda Steve,* Vice-Chair.; Kevin J. Dvorak,* Pres.; Orlin Backes, George Cox, Joe Hauer, Tara Holt, Dennis Johnson, Lynn Nelson, Lowell Overbo, Chad Peterson, Marlys Prince, Russell Stegman.
EIN: 450336015
Codes: CM, FD, GTI

42091
North Dakota Natural Resources Trust, Inc.
(Formerly North Dakota Wetlands Trust, Inc.)
1605 E. Capitol Ave. Ste. 101
Bismarck, ND 58501-2102 (701) 223-8501
Contact: Keith Trego

Established in 1987 in ND.
Financial data (yr. ended 12/31/01): Grants paid, $838,463; assets, $16,049,115 (M); gifts received, $12,612,986; expenditures, $1,090,451; qualifying distributions, $323,702.
Limitations: Applications not accepted. Giving limited to ND.
Application information: Contributes only to pre-selected organizations.
Officers: Dick Kroger, V.P.; Scott Peterson, Secy.-Treas.
Directors: Bruce Adams, Dean Hildebrand, Duane Liffring, Jack Olin, Genevieve Thompson.
EIN: 363512179
Codes: FD

42092
Tom and Frances Leach Foundation, Inc.
P.O. Box 1136
Bismarck, ND 58502-1136 (701) 255-0479
Contact: Delanis M. Eckroth, Grants Coord.

Established in 1955 in ND.
Donor(s): Thomas W. Leach,‡ Frances V. Leach.‡
Financial data (yr. ended 12/31/01): Grants paid, $729,250; assets, $12,367,654 (M); expenditures, $947,387; qualifying distributions, $741,471.
Limitations: Giving primarily in ND, particularly in Bismarck and Mandan, and the upper Midwest.
Publications: Annual report, informational brochure, application guidelines.
Application information: Application form required.
Officers and Directors:* Gilbert N. Olson,* Chair.; Frank J. Bavendick,* Pres.; Brian R. Bjella,* V.P.; William L. Daniel,* Secy.-Treas.; Russell R. Mather, John T. Roswick, Paul D. Schliesman, James P. Wachter.
EIN: 456012703
Codes: FD

42093
MDU Resources Foundation
P.O. Box 5650
Bismarck, ND 58506-5650
FAX: (701) 222-7607
Contact: Robert E. Wood, Pres.

Established in 1983 in ND.
Donor(s): MDU Resources Group, Inc., WBI Holdings, Inc., Knife River Corp., Montana Dakota Utilities Co.
Financial data (yr. ended 12/31/01): Grants paid, $525,897; assets, $2,009,633 (M); gifts received, $674,445; expenditures, $531,237; qualifying distributions, $530,537.
Limitations: Giving primarily in areas of company operations of MDU Resources Group and its utility division and subsidiaries.
Publications: Annual report.
Application information: Application form required.
Officers and Directors:* Robert E. Wood,* Pres.; Douglas C. Kane,* V.P.; Warren L. Robinson,* Secy.-Treas.; John C. Castleberry, Terry D. Hildestad, Ronald D. Tipton.
EIN: 450378937
Codes: CS, FD, CD

42094
Alex Stern Family Foundation
Bill Stern Bldg., Ste. 205
609 1/2 1st Ave., N.
Fargo, ND 58102
Contact: Donald Scott, Exec. Dir.

Established in 1964 in ND.
Donor(s): William Stern,‡ Sam Stern,‡ Edward A. Stern.‡
Financial data (yr. ended 12/31/01): Grants paid, $465,730; assets, $9,864,546 (M); expenditures, $538,310; qualifying distributions, $473,341.
Limitations: Giving limited to the Moorhead, MN, and Fargo, ND areas.
Publications: Application guidelines, annual report.
Application information: Application form required.
Officer and Trustees:* Donald L. Scott,* Exec. Dir.; Dan Carey, H. Michael Hardy.
EIN: 456013981
Codes: FD

42095
The R. B. Nordick Foundation
675 12th Ave. N.
West Fargo, ND 58078-3500

Established in 1995 in ND.
Donor(s): Ralph B. Nordick.
Financial data (yr. ended 12/31/01): Grants paid, $368,000; assets, $12,700,455 (M); gifts received, $2,550,000; expenditures, $380,054; qualifying distributions, $366,099.
Limitations: Applications not accepted. Giving limited to ND.
Application information: Contributes only to pre-selected organizations.
Officers: Ralph B. Nordick, Pres.; Brett A. Nordick, V.P.; Douglas R. Geeslin, Secy.-Treas.
Director: Yvonne Nordick.
EIN: 450442920
Codes: FD

42096
L. W. Huncke Foundation
P.O. Box 5008
Bismarck, ND 58502-5008

Established in 1980 in KS.
Donor(s): L.W. Huncke.
Financial data (yr. ended 09/30/01): Grants paid, $285,000; assets, $6,284,291 (M); gifts received, $735,000; expenditures, $363,329; qualifying distributions, $274,194.
Limitations: Applications not accepted. Giving primarily in IA and ND.
Application information: Contributes only to pre-selected organizations.
Trustee: Otto W. Dohn.
EIN: 480912892
Codes: FD

42097
William O. and Elizabeth H. Nilles Charitable Trust
220 8th St. S.
Fargo, ND 58103-1881

Established in 1987 in ND.
Donor(s): Elizabeth H. Nilles, William O. Nilles.
Financial data (yr. ended 12/31/01): Grants paid, $233,105; assets, $146,148 (M); expenditures, $234,309; qualifying distributions, $233,105.
Limitations: Applications not accepted. Giving on a national basis.
Application information: Contributes only to pre-selected organizations.
Trustees: Elizabeth H. Nilles, William O. Nilles.
EIN: 456070299

42098
Noel and Judith Fedje Foundation
2429 E. Country Club Dr.
Fargo, ND 58103

Established in 1990.
Donor(s): Noel I. Fedje, Judith A. Fedje.
Financial data (yr. ended 12/31/01): Grants paid, $207,900; assets, $3,631,074 (M); gifts received, $33,885; expenditures, $207,900; qualifying distributions, $206,162.
Limitations: Applications not accepted. Giving primarily in MN and ND.
Application information: Contributes only to pre-selected organizations.

Officers and Trustees: Noel I. Fedje,* Pres.; Judith A. Fedje,* V.P.; Jill Fedje Johnson, Julie Fedje Johnston, Lori Fedje Paulson, Kari Fedje Rasmus.
EIN: 450418868
Codes: FD2

42099
Myra Foundation
P.O. Box 13536
Grand Forks, ND 58208-3536

Incorporated in 1941 in ND.
Donor(s): John E. Myra.‡
Financial data (yr. ended 12/31/00): Grants paid, $193,131; assets, $2,326,262 (M); gifts received, $25; expenditures, $293,331; qualifying distributions, $193,131.
Limitations: Giving limited to Grand Forks County, ND.
Publications: Informational brochure (including application guidelines).
Application information: Application form not required.
Officers: John Botsford, Pres.; Donna J. Gillig, V.P.; Robert F. Hansen, Secy.-Treas.
EIN: 450215088
Codes: FD2

42100
Devils Lake Area Foundation
P.O. Box 160
Devils Lake, ND 58301-0160

Financial data (yr. ended 11/20/00): Grants paid, $177,678; assets, $3,137,127 (M); gifts received, $508,051; expenditures, $502,859.
Limitations: Giving limited to the Devils Lake, ND, area.
Distribution Committee: Darwin Brokke, Deb Carlson, Mike Connor, Ray Frohlich, Donovan Herman, Joe Smith, Duane Tabert.
Trustee: Ramsey National Bank & Trust.
EIN: 466040496
Codes: CM, FD2

42101
C. F. Martell Memorial Foundation
c/o First International Bank & Trust
P.O. Box 1088
Williston, ND 58802-1088
Scholarship loan application address: P.O. Box 546, Watford City, ND 58854
Contact: William W. McLees, Jr.

Established in 1962.
Financial data (yr. ended 07/31/01): Grants paid, $110,097; assets, $1,003,823 (M); expenditures, $125,784; qualifying distributions, $115,704.
Limitations: Giving limited to residents of Williams and McKenzie counties, ND.
Application information: Applications available from district judge of Williams County, county judge of McKenzie County, and pastor of St. Joseph's Church in Williston. Application form required.
Officers: Frances Olson, Chair.; Gerald Rustad, Vice-Chair.; William McLees, Secy.
Directors: Fr. John Guthrie, Kevin Keenaghan.
Trustee: First International Bank & Trust.
EIN: 456010183
Codes: FD2, GTI

42102
Gabriel J. Brown Trust Loan Fund
112 Ave. E.W.
Bismarck, ND 58501 (701) 223-5916
Contact: Susan Lundberg, Tr.

Established in 1969 in ND.
Donor(s): Gabriel J. Brown,‡ Susan Lundberg.
Financial data (yr. ended 03/31/02): Grants paid, $104,900; assets, $1,322,989 (M); expenditures, $27,400; qualifying distributions, $121,221; giving activities include $104,900 for loans to individuals.
Limitations: Giving limited to residents of ND.
Application information: Application form required.
Trustee: Susan Lundberg.
EIN: 237086880
Codes: FD2, GTI

42103
North Dakota Masonic Foundation
201 14th Ave. N.
Fargo, ND 58102 (701) 223-7960
Contact: Virgil Carmichael

Financial data (yr. ended 06/30/01): Grants paid, $90,106; assets, $2,108,395 (M); gifts received, $8,522; expenditures, $154,629; qualifying distributions, $135,607.
Limitations: Giving primarily in ND.
Trustees: C. Christianson, M. Farbo, D. Jensen, C. Mondahl, G. Nelson, J. Nelson, R. Webb.
EIN: 237304386
Codes: FD2

42104
Forum Communications Foundation
(also known as Norman Black Foundation)
P.O. Box 2020
Fargo, ND 58107-2020
Contact: Lloyd G. Case, Secy.-Treas.

Financial data (yr. ended 07/31/00): Grants paid, $84,184; assets, $1,237,742 (M); expenditures, $87,279; qualifying distributions, $87,279.
Limitations: Giving primarily in Moorhead, MN, and Fargo, ND.
Application information: Application form required.
Officers: William C. Marcil, Pres.; Jane B. Marcil, V.P.; Lloyd G. Case, Secy.-Treas.
Director: William C. Marcil, Jr.
EIN: 456012365
Codes: FD2, GTI

42105
Ralph Boone Charitable Foundation
c/o Steve Boone
1704 Lincoln Ave.
Devils Lake, ND 58301
Application address: 15009 County Rd. 9, Grafton, ND 58237
Contact: Ralph Boone, Pres.

Established in 1998 in ND.
Financial data (yr. ended 12/31/01): Grants paid, $80,000; assets, $1,578,764 (M); expenditures, $93,834; qualifying distributions, $80,975.
Limitations: Giving primarily in ND.
Officers: Ralph Boone, Pres.; Stephen Boone, Secy.-Treas.
Director: Douglas Christensen.
EIN: 911789781

42106
Dr. Henry Hobert Ruger Trust
P.O. Box 838
Devils Lake, ND 58301
Application address: 509 5th St., Devils Lake, ND 58301, tel.: (701) 662-4077
Contact: John T. Traynor, Tr.

Established in 1988 in ND.
Financial data (yr. ended 12/31/01): Grants paid, $80,000; assets, $1,337,255 (M); expenditures, $117,859; qualifying distributions, $96,340.
Limitations: Giving limited to students at the University of North Dakato in Grand Forks, ND, and the Park District of the city of to Devils Lake, ND.
Trustee: John T. Traynor.
EIN: 456071291
Codes: GTI

42107
Plains Art Museum Foundation
P.O. Box 2338
Fargo, ND 58108-2338

Established in 1999 in ND.
Donor(s): Plains Art Museum.
Financial data (yr. ended 06/30/02): Grants paid, $40,000; assets, $942,654 (M); gifts received, $200; expenditures, $41,173; qualifying distributions, $40,000.
Limitations: Applications not accepted. Giving primarily in Fargo, ND.
Application information: Contributes only to pre-selected organizations.
Officers: Richard Brown, Pres.; Gary Wolsky, V.P.; Terry Jelsing, Secy.-Treas.
Board Members: John Bennett, Kathleen Enz Finken, Angie McCarthy, Tim McLarnan.
EIN: 450453162

42108
Vickers Foundation
205 11th St. E.
Williston, ND 58801-5125 (701) 572-7109
Contact: Rollin C. Vickers, Pres.

Donor(s): Patricia C. Vickers, Rollin C. Vickers.
Financial data (yr. ended 12/31/01): Grants paid, $37,414; assets, $679,397 (M); gifts received, $2,056; expenditures, $38,881; qualifying distributions, $37,414.
Limitations: Applications not accepted. Giving on a national basis.
Application information: Contributes only to pre-selected organizations.
Officers: Rollin C. Vickers, Pres.; Jeffrey P. Vickers, V.P.; Patricia C. Vickers, Secy.
Director: Deborah L. Maxey.
EIN: 450339038

42109
Theodore H. Sedler Scholarship Fund
c/o Community First Bank
Main at Broadway
Fargo, ND 58124-0001 (701) 293-2326

Established in 1995 in ND.
Financial data (yr. ended 12/31/01): Grants paid, $36,250; assets, $747,449 (M); expenditures, $52,511; qualifying distributions, $37,477.
Limitations: Giving primarily in MN and ND.
Application information: Applicant must supply letters of reference. Application form not required.
Advisory Committee: Chris Johnson, Earl Staltenow.
Trustee: Community First Bank & Trust.
EIN: 456091443
Codes: GTI

42110
The Julius and Bertha Orth Foundation
P.O. Box 1618
Bismarck, ND 58502 (701) 255-6832
Contact: Perry Bohl, Dir.

Established in 1997 in ND.
Donor(s): Bertha Orth.
Financial data (yr. ended 03/31/02): Grants paid, $36,000; assets, $612,668 (M); expenditures, $44,669; qualifying distributions, $36,000.
Directors: Perry Bohl, Barbara Foss, Bertha Orth, Chuck Stroup, Faye Williamson.
EIN: 450427503

42111—NORTH DAKOTA

42111
Minot Rotary Scholarship Foundation
P.O. Box 1584
Minot, ND 58702   (701) 852-7006
Contact: Thomas Hinzpeter, Secy.

Established charter in 1918 in ND.
Financial data (yr. ended 12/31/01): Grants paid, $35,000; assets, $157,500 (M); gifts received, $24,843; expenditures, $35,244; qualifying distributions, $35,000.
Limitations: Giving limited to residents of Minot, ND.
Officers: Kenneth R. Williams, Chair.; Thomas Hinzpeter, Secy.
Directors: Daniel Feist, Kathleen Helming.
EIN: 363369060
Codes: GTI

42112
Leland Stenehjem Family Foundation
100 N. Main St.
Watford City, ND 58854-7100
Contact: Stephen Stenehjem, Dir.

Established in 1996 in ND.
Financial data (yr. ended 12/31/01): Grants paid, $33,600; assets, $664,457 (M); expenditures, $39,720; qualifying distributions, $33,600.
Directors: Joan Rustvang, Judith Stenehjem, Leland Stenehjem, Jr., Stephen Stenehjem.
Trustee: First International Bank & Trust.
EIN: 450446602

42113
John A. Kozel Charitable Trust
5551 175th Ave. N.W.
Bismarck, ND 58501
Contact: William J. Kozel, Tr.

Established in 1985 in ND.
Donor(s): William J. Kozel.
Financial data (yr. ended 12/31/01): Grants paid, $30,830; assets, $491,879 (M); gifts received, $5,000; expenditures, $31,407; qualifying distributions, $30,830.
Limitations: Giving primarily in ND.
Trustees: Julie M. Kozel, Lisa Kozel, William J. Kozel, William L. Kozel.
EIN: 363412610

42114
Aldis Folson Trust
c/o Alerus Financial
2401 Demers Ave.
Grand Forks, ND 58201

Financial data (yr. ended 12/31/00): Grants paid, $30,000; assets, $123,340 (M); expenditures, $32,157; qualifying distributions, $30,448.
Directors: Leonard Gumlia, Roxy Gumlia Klein, Julie Gumlia Marvel, Jody Gumlia Parker.
Trustee: Alerus Financial.
EIN: 456028046

42115
H. M. & C. M. Iverson Charitable Trust
c/o Wells Fargo Bank North Dakota, N.A.
406 Main Ave.
Fargo, ND 58126-7032

Financial data (yr. ended 12/31/01): Grants paid, $29,967; assets, $486,095 (M); expenditures, $38,009; qualifying distributions, $29,967.
Limitations: Applications not accepted.
Application information: Contributes only to pre-selected organizations.
Trustees: Joseph Knutson, Nelson Mervin, Lorraine Rylander, Wells Fargo Bank North Dakota, N.A.
EIN: 456061996

42116
United Telephone Educational Foundation, Inc.
P.O. Box 729
Langdon, ND 58249   (701) 256-5156
Contact: Kenneth Carlson, Secy.-Treas.

Established in 1991 in ND.
Donor(s): United Telephone Mutual Aid Corporation.
Financial data (yr. ended 12/31/01): Grants paid, $29,800; assets, $579,531 (M); expenditures, $36,102; qualifying distributions, $35,107.
Limitations: Giving limited to areas of company operations.
Application information: Application form required.
Officers: Allyn Hart, Pres.; Bernard Schommer, V.P.; Kenneth Carlson, Secy.-Treas.
Directors: William Brooks, Arlaine Delebo, Nancy Haraseth, Stacie Metelmann, Guy Mitchell, Gene Narum, Marlin Swanson.
EIN: 450414760
Codes: CS, CD, GTI

42117
Elmer & Kaya Berg Foundation No. 2
c/o Northern Capitol Trust Co.
P.O. Box 829
Fargo, ND 58107-0829   (701) 282-1901
Contact: Paul Sather

Established in 1990 in ND.
Donor(s): Elmer H. Berg.
Financial data (yr. ended 12/31/01): Grants paid, $26,100; assets, $968,393 (M); gifts received, $75,000; expenditures, $31,342; qualifying distributions, $26,100.
Limitations: Giving primarily in Fargo, ND.
Directors: David R. Berg, Gerald M. Berg, Richard N. Berg.
EIN: 363668256

42118
Vera Ellsworth & Bea Cox Charitable Trust
212 N. 4th St.
P.O. Box 2796
Bismarck, ND 58502-2796
Contact: Thecla Ohlhauser, Trust Off., Trust Center of America

Established in 2000 in IA.
Financial data (yr. ended 12/31/01): Grants paid, $25,901; assets, $475,949 (M); expenditures, $29,891; qualifying distributions, $25,739.
Limitations: Giving primarily in Council Bluffs, IA.
Application information: Application form required.
Directors: Leonard Cox, Betty Davis, Gretchen Johnson, Richard Miller, Philip Willson, Trust Center of America.
EIN: 421499303

42119
Dawson Foundation
c/o Deb Dawson
P.O. Box 1958
Fargo, ND 58107-1958

Financial data (yr. ended 12/31/01): Grants paid, $25,165; assets, $160,051 (M); expenditures, $27,216; qualifying distributions, $25,165.
Limitations: Applications not accepted. Giving primarily in MN and ND.
Application information: Contributes only to pre-selected organizations.
Trustees: Deb Dawson, Edith Dawson, Tom Dawson.
EIN: 456013294

42120
Arthur Moore Trust Fund
c/o Bremer Bank, N.A.
424 5th St.
Devils Lake, ND 58301   (701) 662-1276
Contact: Laurie Walski, Trust Off., Bremer Bank

Financial data (yr. ended 12/31/99): Grants paid, $21,564; assets, $693,191 (M); expenditures, $27,076; qualifying distributions, $21,564.
Application information: Application form not required.
Trustees: Laurie Walski, Bremer Bank, N.A.
EIN: 456066375

42121
Max & Anne Goldberg Foundation
1700 S. 9th St.
Fargo, ND 58103-4910   (701) 232-4741
Contact: Ruth G. Landfield, Tr.

Financial data (yr. ended 12/31/01): Grants paid, $20,800; assets, $417,231 (M); expenditures, $26,976; qualifying distributions, $21,391.
Limitations: Giving primarily in MA and MD.
Trustees: Marc E. Goldberg, Ray A. Goldberg, Ruth G. Landfield.
EIN: 456011859

42122
The Heart & Lung Clinic Foundation
P.O. Box 2698
Bismarck, ND 58502-2698
Application address: 311 N. 9th St., Bismarck, ND 58501, tel.: (701) 224-7564
Contact: Karen Hagel, Secy.-Treas.

Established in 1993 in ND.
Financial data (yr. ended 12/31/01): Grants paid, $19,550; assets, $2,739 (M); gifts received, $22,020; expenditures, $19,898; qualifying distributions, $19,550.
Limitations: Giving primarily in Bismarck, ND.
Officer: Karen Hagel, Secy.-Treas.
Directors: Michael Booth, M.D., Hugh Carlson, M.D., James Hughes, M.D.
EIN: 450431923

42123
Maude M. Schuetze Foundation
c/o American State Bank & Trust Co.
P.O. Box 1446
Williston, ND 58802-1446   (701) 774-4120

Donor(s): Maude M. Schuetze.
Financial data (yr. ended 04/30/00): Grants paid, $14,025; assets, $323,379 (M); expenditures, $19,447; qualifying distributions, $14,025.
Limitations: Giving limited to Bainville, Culbertson, Froid, Medicine Lake, Plentywood, and Westby, MT.
Trustees: Louise Cooper, American State Bank & Trust Co.
EIN: 456063398
Codes: GTI

42124
SBL Foundation, Inc.
P.O. Box 628
Lakota, ND 58344

Donor(s): State Bank of Lakota.
Financial data (yr. ended 12/31/01): Grants paid, $13,700; assets, $163 (M); expenditures, $13,710; qualifying distributions, $13,700.
Limitations: Applications not accepted. Giving primarily in ND.
Application information: Contributes only to pre-selected organizations.
Officers: Aron D. Anderson, Pres.; Bruce A. Anderson, V.P.; Jeffry D. Anderson, Secy.

EIN: 450436454

42125
C. P. & Irene Olson Trust
c/o Bremer Bank, N.A.
P.O. Box 1548
Minot, ND 58702-1548

Established in 1992.
Financial data (yr. ended 12/31/99): Grants paid, $12,900; assets, $254,922 (M); expenditures, $14,897; qualifying distributions, $12,708.
Limitations: Applications not accepted. Giving limited to residents of MN and ND.
Trustee: Bremer Bank, N.A.
EIN: 456076668

42126
Lucille Coghlan McCormick Memorial Trust
902 3rd Ave. S.
Fargo, ND 58103-1707
Application address: 502 1st Ave. N., Fargo, ND 58103, tel.: (701) 237-6893
Contact: Maurice G. McCormick, Tr.

Donor(s): John L. McCormick.
Financial data (yr. ended 12/31/01): Grants paid, $12,800; assets, $253,666 (M); expenditures, $15,937; qualifying distributions, $12,800.
Limitations: Giving primarily in ND.
Trustees: John L. McCormick, Maurice G. McCormick, Steve McCormick, Thomas McCormick.
EIN: 366874755

42127
North Dakota Eastern Star Home Corporation
c/o Ella Mae Rowe
P.O. Box 42
Bathgate, ND 58216

Established in 1989 in ND.
Financial data (yr. ended 04/30/02): Grants paid, $12,000; assets, $234,880 (M); expenditures, $13,898; qualifying distributions, $12,000.
Limitations: Applications not accepted. Giving primarily in the Midwest.
Application information: Contributes only to pre-selected organizations.
Officers: Douglas Woodall, Chair.; Tom Swinland, Vice-Chair.; Phyllis Campbell, Secy.; Ella Mae Rowe, Treas.
Trustee: Mayo Hanson.
EIN: 450213284

42128
George E. Haggart Foundation, Inc.
c/o Jerry Larson
P.O. Box 2189
Fargo, ND 58108-2189
Application address: P.O. Box 1962, Fargo, ND 58107
Contact: John E. Haggart, Pres.

Donor(s): John E. Haggart.
Financial data (yr. ended 12/31/01): Grants paid, $10,500; assets, $133,733 (M); expenditures, $10,770; qualifying distributions, $10,500.
Limitations: Giving primarily in Fargo, ND.
Officers and Directors:* John E. Haggart,* Pres.; Elizabeth Larson,* V.P. and Treas.; Ronald W. Moen, Secy.
EIN: 456013475

42129
The G. E. and Virginia R. Satrom Family Foundation
2000 Belmont Rd.
Grand Forks, ND 58201

Established in 1997 in ND.
Donor(s): Gale E. Satrom.
Financial data (yr. ended 12/31/00): Grants paid, $8,368; assets, $164,536 (M); gifts received, $20,000; expenditures, $9,815; qualifying distributions, $8,368.
Limitations: Applications not accepted.
Application information: Contributes only to pre-selected organizations.
Officers: Gale E. Satrom, Pres.; Barbara G. Nunn, Secy.; John C. Satrom, Treas.
EIN: 911783971

42130
Walter and Barbara E. Reishus Pedersen Lutheran Foundation
P.O. Box 5267
Grand Forks, ND 58206-5267
Contact: Kirk Tingum, V.P.

Donor(s): Barbara E. Pedersen.
Financial data (yr. ended 12/31/01): Grants paid, $8,272; assets, $157,167 (M); gifts received, $15,000; expenditures, $8,875; qualifying distributions, $8,272.
Limitations: Giving primarily in Grand Forks, ND.
Officers: Barbara E. Pedersen, Pres.; Kirk Tingum, V.P.; Judy Pettit, Secy.-Treas.
EIN: 363421204

42131
Knute & Blenda Hagen Scholarship Trust
P.O. Box 1088
Williston, ND 58801

Established in 1999 in ND.
Financial data (yr. ended 12/31/00): Grants paid, $8,200; assets, $190,679 (M); expenditures, $10,808; qualifying distributions, $7,941.
Limitations: Giving primarily in ND.
Application information: Application form required.
Trustee: First International Bank & Trust.
EIN: 450451739

42132
John A. and Yvonne S. Cronquist Midway Scholarship Trust
c/o Mike Porter
P.O. Box 13118
Grand Forks, ND 58208-3118 (701) 795-4502
Contact: Mike Porter, Chair.

Established in 1990 in ND.
Donor(s): John A. Cronquist, Yvonne S. Cronquist.
Financial data (yr. ended 12/31/99): Grants paid, $8,100; assets, $106,135 (M); expenditures, $8,241; qualifying distributions, $8,100.
Limitations: Giving limited to residents of ND.
Officer and Trustees:* Mike Porter,* Chair.; Tom Durkin, Kenneth Reed.
EIN: 450418794

42133
Gerald C. Ryan and Suzanne H. Ryan Family Foundation
c/o Mark Hall
P.O. Box 6001
Grand Forks, ND 58206-6001

Established in 1995 in ND.
Financial data (yr. ended 12/31/01): Grants paid, $8,094; assets, $147,423 (M); expenditures, $10,562; qualifying distributions, $8,094.
Limitations: Applications not accepted. Giving primarily in ND.
Application information: Contributes only to pre-selected organizations.
Officers: Suzanne H. Ryan, Pres.; Casey Ryan, V.P.; J. Patrick Ryan, Secy.-Treas.
EIN: 363977373

42134
Harold & Dorothy Madson Foundation
2441 E. Country Club Dr.
Fargo, ND 58103 (701) 232-4734

Financial data (yr. ended 12/31/01): Grants paid, $8,000; assets, $277,292 (M); gifts received, $32,098; expenditures, $9,040; qualifying distributions, $8,000.
Officer and Trustee:* Harold L. Madson,* Chair.
EIN: 450450400

42135
Helen R. Ernst Charitable Trust
c/o Ramsey National Bank & Trust Co.
P.O. Box 160
Devils Lake, ND 58301-0160
Application address: c/o Higher Educ. Off., Spirit Lake Nation, P.O. Box 359, Fort Totten, ND 58375, tel.: (701) 766-1263
Contact: Joanne Crosswhite, Comm. Member

Financial data (yr. ended 06/30/02): Grants paid, $7,403; assets, $106,077 (M); expenditures, $10,674; qualifying distributions, $9,115.
Limitations: Giving limited to Fort Totten, ND.
Application information: Application form required.
Committee Members: Joanne Crosswhite, Helen Foughty, Allen Hanson, Duane Olson.
Trustee: Ramsey National Bank & Trust Co.
EIN: 456050423
Codes: GTI

42136
W. R. Haggart Foundation, Inc.
c/o Russell Freeman
1800 Radisson Tower
Fargo, ND 58108
Application address: P.O. Box 2001, Fargo, ND 58107, tel.: (701) 235-9712
Contact: William L. Haggart, Pres.

Financial data (yr. ended 12/31/01): Grants paid, $7,100; assets, $144,889 (M); expenditures, $8,159; qualifying distributions, $7,100.
Limitations: Giving primarily in Fargo, ND.
Officers: William L. Haggart, Pres.; Marjorie Haggart, Secy-Treas.
EIN: 456011075

42137
Peter & Anna Kostenko Trust
c/o Bremer Bank, N.A.
P.O. Box 1548
Minot, ND 58702-1548

Financial data (yr. ended 08/31/00): Grants paid, $6,350; assets, $106,312 (M); expenditures, $7,874; qualifying distributions, $6,297.
Limitations: Applications not accepted. Giving limited to Butte, ND.
Application information: Contributes only to pre-selected organizations.
Trustee: Bremer Bank, N.A.
EIN: 450404341

42138
Urdahl, Inc.
c/o Ruth E. Urdahl
1411 7th Ave. S.W.
Jamestown, ND 58401-5234 (701) 252-2783
Contact: Kenneth N. Urdahl, Pres.

Established in 1991 in ND.
Donor(s): Kenneth N. Urdahl, Ruth E. Urdahl.
Financial data (yr. ended 03/31/02): Grants paid, $6,224; assets, $159,479 (M); gifts received, $21,400; expenditures, $9,147; qualifying distributions, $6,224.
Limitations: Giving on a national basis.

42138—NORTH DAKOTA

Officers: Kenneth N. Urdahl, Pres.; Kevin B. Urdahl, V.P.; Ruth E. Urdahl, Secy.-Treas.
EIN: 450422833

42139
Vincent Gaffney Foundation
c/o American State Bank & Trust Co.
P.O. Box 1446
Williston, ND 58802-1446 (701) 774-4121
Contact: Noel Hanson, V.P. and Trust Off., American State Bank & Trust Co.

Established in 1987 in ND.
Donor(s): Vincent Gaffney.‡
Financial data (yr. ended 06/30/02): Grants paid, $6,189; assets, $219,840 (M); expenditures, $9,112; qualifying distributions, $6,189.
Limitations: Giving primarily in ND.
Publications: Annual report.
Application information: Application form required.
Advisory Committee: Stanley Lund.
Trustee: American State Bank & Trust Co.
EIN: 363507945
Codes: GTI

42140
McKenzie County Education Trust
11520 11th St. N.E.
Aneta, ND 58212 (701) 797-3383
Application address: R.R. 2, Box 25, Aneta, ND 58212
Contact: Carolyn Dekker, Tr.

Established in 1997 in ND.
Donor(s): Nora Lanz.‡
Financial data (yr. ended 12/31/99): Grants paid, $6,000; assets, $191,620 (M); expenditures, $11,534; qualifying distributions, $7,221; giving activities include $6,000 for loans to individuals.
Limitations: Giving limited to residents of McKenzie County, ND.
Application information: Application form required.
Trustee: Carolyn Dekker.
EIN: 311490129

42141
The Clairmont Family Foundation
P.O. Box 1074
Bismarck, ND 58502-1074
Application address: 1720 Burnt Boat Dr., Box 1074, Bismarck, ND 58502
Contact: William Clairmont, Dir.

Established in 2001 in ND.
Donor(s): William Clairmont.
Financial data (yr. ended 12/31/01): Grants paid, $5,300; assets, $254,700 (M); gifts received, $260,000; expenditures, $5,300; qualifying distributions, $5,300.
Directors: Patricia Clairmont, William Clairmont, Cynthia Larson.
EIN: 450462427

42142
Bottrell/Dolan Family Foundation
3100 13th Ave. S.W., Ste. 202
Fargo, ND 58103

Established in 1999 in ND.
Financial data (yr. ended 12/31/00): Grants paid, $4,500; assets, $0 (M); gifts received, $4,500; expenditures, $4,500; qualifying distributions, $4,500.
Limitations: Giving primarily in Cavalier and Towner counties, ND.
Officers and Directors:* Donald G. Bottrell,* Pres.; Teresa Bottrell,* V.P.; Marnie Bennett,* Secy.; James Bennett,* Treas.; Lowell P. Bottrell.
EIN: 450453811

42143
VFW Charitable Trust
4605 E. Roundup Rd.
Bismarck, ND 58501 (701) 258-5016
Contact: Wallace Bolte, Dir.

Donor(s): West Fargo V.F.W. Post, and 12 other V.F.W. Posts.
Financial data (yr. ended 06/30/01): Grants paid, $4,450; assets, $57,733 (M); gifts received, $12,050; expenditures, $7,015; qualifying distributions, $4,450.
Limitations: Giving limited to ND.
Directors: Wallace Bolte, Harold Gustafson, Joe Shoman.
EIN: 456056378
Codes: GTI

42144
Greenleaf Foundation
c/o W.A. Greenleaf
P.O. Box 891
Devils Lake, ND 58301-0891

Donor(s): Doris A. Greenleaf, W.A. Greenleaf.
Financial data (yr. ended 12/31/01): Grants paid, $4,131; assets, $1 (M); gifts received, $4,131; expenditures, $4,131; qualifying distributions, $4,131.
Limitations: Applications not accepted. Giving primarily in Devils Lake, ND.
Application information: Contributes only to pre-selected organizations.
Trustees: Elizabeth A. Gitter, Doris A. Greenleaf, W.A. Greenleaf.
EIN: 363792877

42145
Howard and Lois Crummy Educational Trust
908 3rd St.
Langdon, ND 58249 (701) 256-3717
Contact: Cameron D. Sillers, Tr.

Established in 1996 in ND.
Financial data (yr. ended 12/31/01): Grants paid, $4,000; assets, $86,996 (M); expenditures, $4,321; qualifying distributions, $4,000.
Limitations: Giving limited to residents of Cavalier County, ND.
Application information: Application form required.
Trustee: Cameron D. Sillers.
EIN: 456088874

42146
Myrtle Bloedow Memorial Foundation
c/o Wells Fargo Bank North Dakota, N.A.
406 Main Ave.
Fargo, ND 58126-7032

Financial data (yr. ended 12/31/00): Grants paid, $3,400; assets, $105,346 (M); expenditures, $5,199; qualifying distributions, $4,336.
Limitations: Applications not accepted. Giving limited to the Edgeley, ND, area.
Application information: Scholarships awarded on merit.
Trustee: Wells Fargo Bank North Dakota, N.A.
EIN: 456015458

42147
The Philip B. Vogel Law Partners Memorial Trust
5012 1st Ave. N.
P.O. Box 1389
Fargo, ND 58107-1389
Contact: C. Nicholas Vogel, Tr.

Financial data (yr. ended 12/31/00): Grants paid, $3,212; assets, $53,265 (M); expenditures, $3,222; qualifying distributions, $3,212.

Limitations: Giving limited to the Fargo-Moorhead, ND, area.
Trustees: C. Nicholas Vogel, H. Patrick Weir.
EIN: 450345746

42148
Paul Hoghaug Scholarship Fund
(Formerly Paul Hoghaug Scholarship Trust)
c/o Ramsey National Bank & Trust Co.
P.O. Box 160
Devils Lake, ND 58301-0160

Donor(s): Paul Hoghaug.
Financial data (yr. ended 12/31/99): Grants paid, $2,800; assets, $73,962 (M); gifts received, $365; expenditures, $3,162; qualifying distributions, $2,800.
Limitations: Giving limited to the Devils Lake and Lake Region, ND, areas.
Application information: Application form required.
Directors: Randy Fixen, Harold Ovre, Steve Swiontek.
Trustee: Ramsey National Bank & Trust Co.
EIN: 456014582

42149
Emmons County Sports Alumni, Inc.
c/o Terry Gimbel
420 N. Broadway
Linton, ND 58552

Financial data (yr. ended 12/31/01): Grants paid, $2,000; assets, $7,943 (M); gifts received, $9,049; expenditures, $5,783; qualifying distributions, $5,783.
Limitations: Giving limited to Emmons County, ND.
Application information: Application form required.
Officers: Al Dosch, Pres.; Tom Weisser, Secy.; Terry Gimbel, Treas.
EIN: 363442049
Codes: GTI

42150
Medina Community Services, Inc.
5772 40th St. S.E.
Medina, ND 58467
Application address: 305 College St. E., Medina, ND 58467
Contact: LuVerne Dockter, Secy.

Financial data (yr. ended 12/31/01): Grants paid, $2,000; assets, $30,287 (M); expenditures, $2,155; qualifying distributions, $2,000.
Limitations: Giving limited to Medina, ND.
Officers and Directors:* Brenda Guthmiller,* Pres.; Betty Klundt,* V.P.; LuVerne Dockter,* Secy.; Bruce Rau,* Treas.; Elmer Heupel, Lorraine Meadows, Ernest Moser, Alice Opp, Neal Rau.
EIN: 450386861

42151
The Halverson Family Foundation
14521 County Rd. 19
P.O. Box 38
Forest River, ND 58233
Contact: Gregg Halverson, Pres. and Dir.

Established in 2000 in ND.
Donor(s): Gregg Halverson.
Financial data (yr. ended 12/31/01): Grants paid, $1,500; assets, $101,699 (M); gifts received, $1,991; expenditures, $2,871; qualifying distributions, $1,500.
Officers and Directors:* Gregg Halverson,* Pres.; John Halverson,* V.P.; Leah Halverson,* Secy.; Eric Halverson,* Treas.
EIN: 450458134

42152
The Greater Grand Forks Community Foundation
11 S. 4th St.
Grand Forks, ND 58201 (701) 795-3429
Contact: P. Lazarus, Exec. Dir.

Established in 1998 in ND.
Financial data (yr. ended 12/31/99): Grants paid, $1,402; assets, $472,916 (M); gifts received, $200,000; expenditures, $264,788; giving activities include $1,402 for programs.
Limitations: Giving limited to the northwest MN and northeast ND.
Publications: Annual report, informational brochure (including application guidelines).
Application information: Application form required.
Officers: Mike Maidenberg, Pres.; Darrell E. Larson, V.P.; Mark Hall, Secy.-Treas.; Patti Lazarus, Exec. Dir.
Directors: Pat Berger, Duaine Espegard, Maury Finney, Jim Gjerset, Randy Newman, Diane Odegaard, Marijo Shide.
EIN: 450448088
Codes: CM

42153
Abrahamson Foundation
1614 8th St. S.
Fargo, ND 58103-4240

Established around 1973.
Financial data (yr. ended 12/31/01): Grants paid, $1,000; assets, $32,512 (M); expenditures, $1,497; qualifying distributions, $1,000.
Limitations: Applications not accepted. Giving limited to ND.
Application information: Contributes only to pre-selected organizations.
Officers: Paul R. Abrahamson, Pres.; Connie Abrahamson, V.P.; M. Jeanette Abrahamson, Treas.
EIN: 510161368

42154
Nierling-Anne Carlson Center Trust
301 7th Ave. N.W.
Jamestown, ND 58401

Established in 1999 in ND.
Donor(s): Richard B. Nierling.
Financial data (yr. ended 12/31/01): Grants paid, $675; assets, $53,108 (M); expenditures, $675; qualifying distributions, $675.
Limitations: Applications not accepted.
Application information: Contributes only to pre-selected organizations.
Trustee: Richard B. Nierling.
EIN: 912004887

42155
Legal Education Fund, Inc.
655 1st Ave. N., Ste. 340
Fargo, ND 58102-4952 (701) 297-7261

Financial data (yr. ended 12/31/01): Grants paid, $600; assets, $1,627 (M); gifts received, $600; expenditures, $1,101; qualifying distributions, $600.
Officers: Richard J. Henderson, Pres.; Suzanne Morrison, V.P.; Lana Jo Schultz, Secy.-Treas.
Director: Myron H. Bright.
EIN: 450372710

42156
Charles Hurley Memorial Fund
1124 Belmont Rd.
Grand Forks, ND 58201

Established in 1986 in ND.
Financial data (yr. ended 12/31/01): Grants paid, $532; assets, $8,893 (M); gifts received, $350; expenditures, $532; qualifying distributions, $532.
Limitations: Applications not accepted. Giving limited to ND.
Application information: Contributes only to pre-selected organizations.
Officers: Joann Hurley, Pres.; Patrick Hurley, V.P.; Timothy Hurley, Secy.-Treas.
EIN: 363465773

42157
Mark Werre Community Service Trust
c/o Wahpeton Chamber of Commerce
118 6th St. N.
Wahpeton, ND 58075-4327

Financial data (yr. ended 12/31/01): Grants paid, $444; assets, $5,861 (M); expenditures, $444; qualifying distributions, $444.
Limitations: Applications not accepted.
Application information: Contributes only to pre-selected organizations.
Director: Jim Oliver.
EIN: 456076434

42158
Burke-Divide Memorial Foundation
P.O. Box 6
Columbus, ND 58727-0006
Contact: Keith Berg, Tr.

Established in 2001.
Financial data (yr. ended 12/31/01): Grants paid, $402; assets, $9,103 (M); gifts received, $240; expenditures, $410; qualifying distributions, $410.
Limitations: Giving limited to residents of ND.
Trustees: Keith Berg, Dennis Bratlien, Iola Rosenquist, Robert Stauffer.
EIN: 456014666

42159
Dorothy M. Cross Scholarship Foundation
c/o Morris O. Cross
Rte. 1 Box 19
Alexander, ND 58831

Financial data (yr. ended 12/31/99): Grants paid, $300; assets, $5,021 (M); expenditures, $307; qualifying distributions, $307.
Limitations: Giving primarily in ND.
Trustee: Morris O. Cross.
EIN: 450423724

42160
Dakota Foundation
c/o Janet L. Holaday
P.O. Box 1535
Jamestown, ND 58402-1535
Application address: c/o Lynn B. Villella, Exec. Dir., 46 Camino Barranca, Placitas, NM 87043-9314

Established in 1997 in IL and NM.
Donor(s): A. Bart Holaday.
Financial data (yr. ended 12/31/00): Grants paid, $0; assets, $6,561,213 (M); gifts received, $1,673,280; expenditures, $78,028; qualifying distributions, $116,948; giving activities include $115,000 for loans.
Limitations: Giving primarily in ND and NM.
Application information: Contributes only to organizations. Prefers to make Program-related Investments (PRIs). Application form not required.
Officers: A. Bart Holaday, Chair.; Janet L. Holaday, Treas.; Lynn B. Villella, Exec. Dir.
Advisory Committee: Alberta B. Holaday, Brett C. Holaday, Jerry Villella, Patrick B. Holaday, Paul S. Villella, Peter B. Villella.
EIN: 367213554

42161
Dale & Martha Hawk Foundation
(Formerly Dakota Hawk Foundation)
P.O. Box 100
Rolla, ND 58367-0100

Financial data (yr. ended 12/31/99): Grants paid, $0; assets, $1,035,537 (M); gifts received, $39,315; expenditures, $47,396; qualifying distributions, $0; giving activities include $34,126 for programs.
Officer: Oscar Solberg, Pres.
EIN: 450365556

42162
Lillibridge-Grimson Rainbow Memorial Loan Fund Trust
P.O. Box 263
Wahpeton, ND 58074-0263 (701) 642-6533
Contact: Eugene Plummer, Secy.-Treas.

Financial data (yr. ended 12/31/00): Grants paid, $0; assets, $65,662 (L); expenditures, $83; qualifying distributions, $2,500; giving activities include $2,500 for loans to individuals.
Limitations: Giving limited to residents of ND.
Officers: Thomas J. Clifford, Pres.; James A. Schnable, V.P.; Eugene Plummer, Secy.-Treas.
EIN: 450355619

42163
Muthu Family Foundation
c/o Kanagasabai Muthu
2849 Lilac Ln.
Fargo, ND 58102

Established in 1997 in ND.
Financial data (yr. ended 12/31/01): Grants paid, $0; assets, $4,161 (M); expenditures, $469; qualifying distributions, $0.
Limitations: Applications not accepted.
Application information: Contributes only to pre-selected organizations.
Directors: Kanagasabai Muthu, Mrs. Kanagasabai Muthu.
EIN: 911815958

42164
The Leonard Rydell Foundation
2700 S. Washington St.
Grand Forks, ND 58208-3398
Application address: c/o Mark Hall, Alerus Financial, 401 Demers Ave., Grand Forks, ND 58201

Established in 2000 in ND.
Donor(s): Rydell Chevrolet Oldsmobile Cadillac, Ivan Gandrud Chevrolet, Inc., Gilleland Chevrolet, Inc., Lunde Lincoln Mercury, Minot Chrysler Center Inc., Ressler Chevrolet Inc., Saturn of St. Paul, Inc., Sioux Falls Ford, Inc., Rydell Chevrolet of Waterloo, Sheboygan Chevy.
Financial data (yr. ended 12/31/01): Grants paid, $0; assets, $373,277 (M); gifts received, $125,000; expenditures, $6,130; qualifying distributions, $686.
Application information: Application form required.
Officers and Directors:* Wes Rydell,* Pres.; Dennis Lunde,* V.P.; Randy Newring,* Secy.; Ivan Gandrud,* Treas.; Connie Mondry, Jim Rydell.
EIN: 450459133
Codes: CS

42165
Sheridan County Memorial Educational Trust
P.O. Box 1827
Williston, ND 58802-1827
Application address: P.O. Box 697, Blaine, WA 98230
Contact: Weldon Richardson, Tr., Donald Hedges, Tr. or Betty Jean Olson, Tr.

Established in 1988 in ND.
Financial data (yr. ended 12/31/99): Grants paid, $0; assets, $60,995 (M); gifts received, $110,265; expenditures, $550; qualifying distributions, $0.
Limitations: Giving limited to Sheridan County, MT.
Application information: Application form required.
Trustees: Donald Hedges, Stan Lund, Weldon Richardson, First National Bank & Trust Co.
EIN: 363479962

42166
Tisdale Foundation
c/o First National Bank
2401 Demers Ave.
Grand Forks, ND 58201-4183
Application address: c/o First National Bank, P.O. Box 6001, Grand Forks, ND 58206-6001
Contact: Douglas Carpenter, Trust Off., First National Bank

Established in 1981.
Financial data (yr. ended 08/31/02): Grants paid, $0; assets, $1 (M); expenditures, $92,525; qualifying distributions, $0.
Limitations: Giving limited to Drayton, ND.
Application information: Application form not required.
Advisory Committee Members: Pete Anderson, Jon Brosseau, Raymond Hoselton.
Trustee: Alerus Financial.
EIN: 450366901

42167
Tuttle Area Development Corp.
P.O. Box 168
Tuttle, ND 58488

Financial data (yr. ended 12/31/01): Grants paid, $0; assets, $448,086 (M); expenditures, $23,707; qualifying distributions, $0.
Officers: Jack Spah, Pres.; Roxanne Miller, Secy.; Norman Bickel, Treas.
Director: Terry Landerbarger.
EIN: 450444605

OHIO

42168
The Cleveland Foundation
1422 Euclid Ave., Ste. 1300
Cleveland, OH 44115-2001 (216) 861-3810
FAX: (216) 589-9039; *TTY:* (216) 861-3806;
E-mail: ldunford@clevefdn.org; URL: http://www.clevelandfoundation.org
Contact: Steven A. Minter, Pres.

Established in 1914 in OH by bank resolution and declaration of trust.
Financial data (yr. ended 12/31/01): Grants paid, $62,276,948; assets, $1,499,767,419 (M); gifts received, $34,112,542; expenditures, $79,447,195; giving activities include $2,000,000 for program-related investments.
Limitations: Giving limited to the greater Cleveland, OH, area, with primary emphasis on Cleveland, Cuyahoga, Lake, and Geauga counties, unless specified by donor.
Publications: Annual report (including application guidelines), newsletter, occasional report, application guidelines, financial statement, informational brochure.
Application information: Application available on foundation's Web site. Application form required.
Officers: Steven A. Minter, Pres.; J.T. Mullen, Sr. V.P., Treas. and C.F.O.; Richard Batyko, V.P., Comm.; Marlene Casini, V.P., Gift Planning and Donor Rels.; Robert E. Eckardt, V.P., Prog.; Lynn M. Sargi, V.P. Admin. and Human Resources; Leslie A. Dunford, Corp. Secy., and C.O.S.
Directors: Catherine Monroe Lewis, Chair.; John Sherwin, Jr., Vice-Chair.; James E. Bennett III, Terri Hamilton Brown, Tana N. Carney, David Goldberg, Ric Harris, Benson Lee, Alex Machaskee, Rev. Otis Moss, Jr., Maria Jose Pujana, M.D., Alayne L. Reitman, Jerry Sue Thorton, Jacqueline F. Woods.
Trustees: Bank One, Cleveland, N.A., FirstMerit Bank, N.A., The Huntington National Bank, KeyBank, N.A., National City Bank.
EIN: 340714588
Codes: CM, FD, FM

42169
The Columbus Foundation and Affiliated Organizations
(Formerly The Columbus Foundation)
1234 E. Broad St.
Columbus, OH 43205-1453 (614) 251-4000
FAX: (614) 251 4009; E-mail: info@columbusfoundation.org, rbiddisc@columbusfoundation.org; URL: http://www.columbusfoundation.org
Contact: Raymond J. Biddiscombe, V.P., Finance and Admin.

Established in 1943 in OH by resolution and declaration of trust.
Financial data (yr. ended 12/31/01): Grants paid, $55,372,561; assets, $656,714,613 (M); gifts received, $52,242,344; expenditures, $61,403,160.
Limitations: Giving limited to Franklin County, OH, from unrestricted and other discretionary funds.
Publications: Annual report, application guidelines, newsletter, informational brochure (including application guidelines).
Application information: Grant requests to the Columbus Youth Foundation must be submitted by the 1st Fri. in Feb. and Oct. for consideration at meetings held in Apr. and Dec.; requests to the Ingram-White Castle Foundation must be submitted by the 1st Fri. in Feb. and Sept. for consideration in Apr. and Nov. Application form required.
Officers: Douglas F. Kridler, Pres.; Raymond J. Biddiscombe, V.P., Finance and Admin.; Philip T. Schavone, V.P., Advancement.
Governing Committee: Abigail Wexner, Chair.; Dimon McFerson, Vice-Chair.; Donald B. Shackelford, Vice-Chair.; Bill Ingram, John G. McCoy, David R. Meuse, Ann Pizzuti, Lewis R. Smott, Sr., Ann Isaly Wolfe.
Trustee Banks: Bank One Ohio Trust Co., N.A., The Huntington National Bank, KeyBank, N.A., National City Bank, Columbus.
EIN: 316044264
Codes: CM, FD, FM

42170
PLACE Fund
c/o Peter B. Lewis
6300 Wilson Mills Rd.
Cleveland, OH 44143-2182
Contact: Betty J. Powers

Established in 1986 in OH.
Donor(s): Peter B. Lewis.
Financial data (yr. ended 12/31/01): Grants paid, $38,093,997; assets, $17,084,699 (M); expenditures, $38,136,653; qualifying distributions, $38,134,620.
Limitations: Giving on a national basis, with some emphasis on OH.
Publications: Occasional report.
Application information: Application form not required.
Officers and Trustees:* Peter B. Lewis,* Pres.; Adam L. Lewis,* V.P.; John D. Garson,* Secy.
EIN: 341532635
Codes: FD

42171
The Dayton Foundation
2100 Kettering Tower
Dayton, OH 45423-1395 (937) 222-0410
Toll-free tel.: (877) 222-0410; *FAX:* (937) 222-0636; E-mail: info@daytonfoundation.org; URL: http://www.daytonfoundation.org
Contact: Michael M. Parks, Pres.

Established in 1921 in OH by resolution and declaration of trust.
Financial data (yr. ended 06/30/01): Grants paid, $36,239,465; assets, $232,344,104 (M); gifts received, $66,828,049; expenditures, $56,085,157.
Limitations: Giving limited to the greater Dayton and Miami Valley, OH, area.
Publications: Annual report (including application guidelines), newsletter, program policy statement, application guidelines, informational brochure (including application guidelines).
Application information: Application form required.
Officers and Governing Board:* Robert S. Neff,* Chair.; Michael M. Parks, Pres. and Secy.; Robert J. Bruggeman, C.F.O.; John N. Taylor, Jr.,* Treas.; Thomas G. Breitenbach, Douglas L. Hawthorne, Franz J. Hoge, Charles A. Jones, Paula J. MacIlwaine, Judy D. McCormick, Laura Pannier, Caryl D. Philips, Fred C. Setzer, Jr., Estus Smith, Fred E. Weber, Betsy B. Whitney.
Trustees: Bank One Ohio Trust Co., N.A., Fifth Third Bank, KeyBank, N.A., Merrill Lynch Pierce Fenner & Smith, National City Bank, PNC Bank Ohio, N.A.
EIN: 316027287
Codes: CM, FD, GTI

42172
The Greater Cincinnati Foundation
200 W. 4th St.
Cincinnati, OH 45202-2602 (513) 241-2880
FAX: (513) 852-6888; E-mail: info@greatercincinnatifdn.org; URL: http://www.greatercincinnatifdn.org
Contact: E. Miles Wilson, V.P., Grants and Progs.

Established in 1963 in OH by bank resolution and declaration of trust.
Financial data (yr. ended 12/31/01): Grants paid, $27,748,981; assets, $388,586,880 (M); gifts received, $26,808,991; expenditures, $32,228,911.
Limitations: Giving limited to southeastern IN, northern KY, and the greater Cincinnati, OH area.
Publications: Annual report (including application guidelines), newsletter, informational brochure (including application guidelines), application guidelines.
Application information: Common Grant Application form used after invitation. Application form required.
Officers: Kathryn E. Merchant, C.E.O. and Pres.; Amy L. Cheney, V.P., Advancement; Lawrence D. Graziani, V.P., Oper.; E. Miles Wilson, V.P., Grants and Progs.; Michael Cheney, C.F.O.
Governing Board: John A. Stith, Chair.; Barbara Lewis, Vice-Chair.; Richard J. Ruebel, Legal Counsel; Thomas A. Brennan, Lee A. Carter, Paul W. Chellgren, Jennifer M. Dauer, Elizabeth D. Goldsmith, Johnathan M. Holifield, Bert Huff, David B. O'Maley, William C. Portman III, Myrtis Powell, Ph.D., Marvin H. Rorick, M.D., Merri Gaither Smith.
Trustee Banks: Bank One Ohio Trust Co., N.A., Fifth Third Bank, The Huntington National Bank, KeyBank, N.A., The Lebanon Citizens National Bank, North Side Bank & Trust Co., PNC Bank, N.A., The Provident Bank, Star Bank, N.A.
EIN: 310669700
Codes: CM, FD, FM

42173
The F. J. O'Neill Charitable Corporation
3550 Lander Rd.
Cleveland, OH 44124 (216) 464-2121

Established in 1979 in OH.
Donor(s): Francis J. O'Neill.‡
Financial data (yr. ended 12/31/00): Grants paid, $27,102,000; assets, $27,277,713 (M); expenditures, $27,663,971; qualifying distributions, $27,052,160.
Limitations: Applications not accepted. Giving primarily in greater Cleveland, OH.
Application information: Contributes only to pre-selected organizations. Unsolicited requests for funds not accepted.
Officers: Hugh O'Neill, Pres.; Nancy M. O'Neill, V.P.; Rev. E.P. Joyce, Secy.-Treas.
EIN: 341286022
Codes: FD, FM

42174
The Procter & Gamble Fund
P.O. Box 599
Cincinnati, OH 45201 (513) 983-2173
Inf. line: (513) 945-8454; *FAX:* (513) 983-2147;
E-mail: pgfund.im@pg.com
Contact: Carol G. Talbot, V.P.

Incorporated in 1952 in OH.
Donor(s): The Procter & Gamble Co.
Financial data (yr. ended 06/30/01): Grants paid, $25,814,046; assets, $31,020,998 (M); gifts received, $44,400,000; expenditures, $21,868,835; qualifying distributions, $21,865,133.

42174—OHIO

Limitations: Giving primarily in areas in the U.S. where the company and its subsidiaries have large concentrations of employees; national giving for higher education and economic and public affairs.
Publications: Corporate giving report.
Application information: Do not call for guidelines. Grant requests from colleges and universities are discouraged, as most grants are initiated by the trustees within specified programs. Application form not required.
Officers and Trustees:* C.R. Otto, Pres.; C.G. Talbot,* V.P.; C.C. Daley, Jr., Treas.; J.E. Pepper, A.R. Sempowski.
EIN: 316019594
Codes: CS, FD, CD, FM

42175
The George Gund Foundation
1845 Guildhall Bldg.
45 Prospect Ave., W.
Cleveland, OH 44115-1018 (216) 241-3114
FAX: (216) 241-6560; URL: http://www.gundfdn.org
Contact: David Abbott, Exec. Dir.

Incorporated in 1952 in OH.
Donor(s): George Gund.‡
Financial data (yr. ended 12/31/01): Grants paid, $20,345,592; assets, $424,502,237 (M); expenditures, $24,125,437; qualifying distributions, $21,121,817; giving activities include $19,683 for program-related investments.
Limitations: Giving primarily in northeastern OH and the greater Cleveland, OH, area.
Publications: Annual report (including application guidelines), application guidelines.
Application information: Proposals sent by FAX not considered. Application form not required.
Officers and Trustees:* Geoffrey Gund,* Pres. and Treas.; Llura A. Gund,* V.P.; Ann L. Gund,* Secy.; David Abbott, Exec. Dir.; Marjorie M. Carlson, Catherine Gund, George Gund III, Robert D. Storey.
EIN: 346519769
Codes: FD, FM

42176
Wexner Foundation
6525 W. Campus Oval, Ste. 110
New Albany, OH 43054 (614) 939-6060
Contact: Rabbi Elka Abrahamson, Dir.

Established in 1973.
Donor(s): Abigail Wexner, Leslie H. Wexner.
Financial data (yr. ended 12/31/00): Grants paid, $17,726,179; assets, $16,492,171 (M); expenditures, $20,544,213; qualifying distributions, $20,357,506.
Limitations: Giving primarily in North America.
Publications: Informational brochure, program policy statement.
Application information: Contributes only to pre-selected organizations; applications accepted for fellowship programs. Contact the foundation for complete application information. Application form required.
Officers and Trustees:* Leslie H. Wexner,* Chair.; Larry S. Moses, Pres.; Jeffrey Epstein.
EIN: 237320631
Codes: FD, FM, GTI

42177
Key Foundation
(Formerly Society Foundation)
127 Public Sq., MC-OH-01-27-0705
Cleveland, OH 44114-1306 (216) 689-3546
FAX: (216) 689-3865; E-mail:
key_foundation@keybank.com
Contact: Margot Copeland, Chair.

Established about 1969 in OH.
Donor(s): Society Corp., Society Capital Corp., KeyCorp., N.A.
Financial data (yr. ended 12/31/01): Grants paid, $16,716,370; assets, $37,499,287 (M); gifts received, $10,291,000; expenditures, $16,872,670; qualifying distributions, $16,716,370.
Limitations: Giving primarily in primarily in areas of company operations in AL; CO; ID; IN; MA; ME; MI; NY; OH; UT; VA; and WA.
Publications: Annual report, application guidelines.
Application information: Application form required.
Officers and Trustees:* Margot Copeland,* Chair.; Robert B. Heisler, Jr.,* Pres.; Patrick V. Auletta, John Burnmaster, Tom Helfrich, Robert G. Jones, Karen Kaefling, Jack Kopinsky, John Mancuso, Mike Monroe, Bruce Murphy.
EIN: 237036607
Codes: CS, FD, CD

42178
NCC Charitable Foundation II
c/o National City Bank
1900 E. 9th St., LOC 2157
Cleveland, OH 44114 (216) 222-2994
E-mail: bruce.mccrodden@nationalcity.com or joanne.clark@nationalcity.com
Contact: Joanne Clark, V.P.

Established in 1993.
Donor(s): National City Bank of Kentucky.
Financial data (yr. ended 06/30/01): Grants paid, $16,484,703; assets, $33,017,534 (M); gifts received, $1,369; expenditures, $16,536,652; qualifying distributions, $16,464,086.
Limitations: Giving primarily in the northeastern U.S., with emphasis on OH.
Publications: Corporate giving report.
Officers: Bruce McCrodden, Off.; David A. Daberko, Off.; William E. McDonald, Off.
Trustee: National City Bank.
EIN: 347050989
Codes: CS, FD, CD, FM

42179
Mathile Family Foundation
P.O. Box 13615
Dayton, OH 45413-0615 (937) 264-4600
FAX: (937) 264-4635; E-mail:
brenda.carnal@cymi.com
Contact: Brenda Carnal, Asst. to the Exec. Dir.

Established in 1987 in OH.
Donor(s): Clayton Lee Mathile, MaryAnn Mathile.
Financial data (yr. ended 11/30/01): Grants paid, $15,471,325; assets, $289,593,560 (M); gifts received, $9,555,297; expenditures, $18,952,352; qualifying distributions, $17,793,313; giving activities include $500,000 for program-related investments.
Limitations: Giving primarily in the Dayton, OH, area.
Publications: Annual report (including application guidelines).
Application information: Mass mailings not accepted. Application form not required.
Officers and Trustees: MaryAnn Mathile,* Chair and C.E.O.; Clayton Lee Mathile,* Pres.; Leslie S. Banwart,* Vice-Pres.; Richard J. Chernesky,* Secy.; Jeanine Hufford, Exec. Dir.
EIN: 311257219
Codes: FD, FM

42180
Nationwide Foundation
(Formerly Nationwide Insurance Enterprise Foundation)
1 Nationwide Plz.
Columbus, OH 43215-2220 (614) 249-5095
Additonal tel.: (614) 249-4310; URL: http://www.nationwide.com/about_us/involve/fndatn.htm
Contact: Stephen A. Rish, Pres.

Incorporated in 1959 in OH.
Donor(s): Nationwide Mutual Insurance Co., and affiliates.
Financial data (yr. ended 12/31/01): Grants paid, $12,828,624; assets, $51,901,311 (M); gifts received, $10,797,028; expenditures, $13,153,885; qualifying distributions, $13,140,502.
Limitations: Giving primarily in OH, with emphasis on Columbus, and other communities where the company maintains offices.
Publications: Informational brochure (including application guidelines).
Application information: The foundation has a specific format for requests for funding, which is listed in the Guidelines for Grant Consideration brochure. Application form not required.
Officers and Trustees:* W.G. Jurgensen, Chair. and C.E.O.; Stephen A. Rish, Pres.; Robert A. Oakley, Exec. V.P., and C.F.O.; Robert J. Woodward, Jr., Exec. V.P., and C.I.O.; Edwin P. McCausland, Jr., Sr. V.P., Fixed Income Securities; Glenn W. Soden, V.P. and Secy.; Carol L. Dove, V.P. and Treas.; Alan A. Todryk, V.P., Taxation; Yvonne M. Curl, Keith W. Eckel, David O. Miller, James F. Patterson, Arden L. Shisler.
EIN: 316022301
Codes: CS, FD, CD, FM

42181
Federated Department Stores Foundation
7 W. 7th St.
Cincinnati, OH 45202
FAX: (513) 579-7185; URL: http://www.federated-fds.com/community/report/chapter2/index_1_4.asp
Contact: Dixie Barker, Fdn. Admin.

Established in 1995 in OH.
Donor(s): Federated Department Stores, Inc.
Financial data (yr. ended 02/03/01): Grants paid, $11,808,076; assets, $21,679,054 (M); gifts received, $11,700,200; expenditures, $11,929,810; qualifying distributions, $11,949,275.
Limitations: Giving primarily in areas of company operations.
Publications: Corporate giving report, annual report, informational brochure (including application guidelines), application guidelines.
Application information: Application form required.
Officers and Trustees:* Thomas G. Cody,* Pres.; Klaus M. Ziermaier, Secy.; Susan R. Robinson, Treas.; Ronald W. Tysoe, James M. Zimmerman.
EIN: 311427325
Codes: CS, FD, CD, FM

42182
The Martha Holden Jennings Foundation
The Halle Bldg.
1228 Euclid Ave. Ste. 710
Cleveland, OH 44115 (216) 589-5700
FAX: (216) 589-5730; Business office: 20620 N. Park Blvd., No. 215, Cleveland, OH 44118, tel.: (216) 932-7337; FAX: (216) 932-0331; URL: http://www.mhjf.org
Contact: Dr. William T. Hiller, Exec. Dir.

Incorporated in 1959 in OH.
Donor(s): Martha Holden Jennings.‡
Financial data (yr. ended 12/31/01): Grants paid, $10,885,188; assets, $103,079,737 (M); expenditures, $11,877,477; qualifying distributions, $11,574,123.
Limitations: Giving limited to OH.
Publications: Annual report, newsletter, program policy statement, application guidelines.
Application information: Application form required for Grants-to-Educators Program available on Web site.
Officers and Trustees:* George B. Milbourn,* Chair. and Pres.; Arthur S. Holden, Jr.,* Chair. Emeritus; William T. Hiller, Exec. Dir.; David Abbott, Jeanette Grasselli Brown, George B. Chapman, Jr., Roy Church, Russell Gifford, Karen Nestor, Jon Outcalt, Deborah Read.
EIN: 340934478
Codes: FD, FM, GTI

42183
Timken Foundation of Canton
200 Market Ave. N., Ste. 210
Canton, OH 44702 (330) 452-1144
Contact: Don D. Dickes, Secy.-Treas.

Incorporated in 1934 in OH.
Donor(s): members of the Timken family.
Financial data (yr. ended 09/30/01): Grants paid, $10,606,938; assets, $132,416,565 (M); expenditures, $10,911,505; qualifying distributions, $10,685,641.
Limitations: Giving primarily in local areas of Timken Co. domestic operations in Ashland, Bucyrus, Canton, Columbus, Eaton, New Philadelphia, Wauseon, and Wooster, OH; Ashboro, Columbus, and Lincolnton, NC; Concord, Keene, and Lebanon, NH; Latrobe, PA; Gaffney, SC; and Altavista, VA. Giving also in local areas in Australia, Brazil, Canada, France, Great Britain, Italy, Poland, Romania, and South Africa where Timken Co. has manufacturing facilities.
Application information: Application form not required.
Officers and Trustees:* Ward J. Timken,* Pres.; W.R. Timken, Jr.,* V.P.; Don D. Dickes,* Secy.-Treas.
EIN: 346520254
Codes: FD, FM

42184
Jack N. and Lilyan Mandel Foundation
2829 Euclid Ave.
Cleveland, OH 44115 (216) 875-6523
Contact: Jack N. Mandel, Tr.

Established in 1963 in OH.
Donor(s): Jack N. Mandel, Lilyan Mandel.‡
Financial data (yr. ended 12/31/00): Grants paid, $10,363,688; assets, $190,064,870 (M); gifts received, $4,735,700; expenditures, $13,729,775; qualifying distributions, $9,875,638.
Limitations: Giving primarily in Cleveland, OH.
Application information: Application form not required.
Officer and Trustees:* Karen A. Vereb,* Secy.; Jack N. Mandel, Joseph C. Mandel.
EIN: 346546418
Codes: FD

42185
Second Foundation
1111 Superior Ave., Ste. 1000
Cleveland, OH 44114-2507 (216) 696-4200
FAX: (212) 696-7303
Contact: Dorothy Yoder, Asst. Secy.

Established in 1984 in OH.
Donor(s): 1525 Foundation.
Financial data (yr. ended 12/31/01): Grants paid, $8,856,955; assets, $3,389,996 (M); expenditures, $8,960,524; qualifying distributions, $8,933,187.
Limitations: Giving primarily in OH, with emphasis on the Cleveland area.
Application information: Application form not required.
Officers and Trustees:* Thelma G. Smith,* Pres.; William B. LaPlace,* V.P.; Phillip A. Ranney,* Secy.-Treas.
EIN: 341436198
Codes: FD, FM

42186
Greater Wayne County Foundation, Inc.
133 S. Market St.
P.O. Box 201
Wooster, OH 44691 (330) 262-3877
FAX: (330) 262-8057; E-mail: gwcf@bright.net; URL: http://www.gwcf.net
Contact: B. Diane Gordon, Exec. Dir.

Established in 1978 in OH.
Financial data (yr. ended 06/30/02): Grants paid, $8,424,441; assets, $21,243,917 (M); gifts received, $6,907,587; expenditures, $8,669,525.
Limitations: Giving limited to Wayne County, OH.
Publications: Annual report, informational brochure (including application guidelines), financial statement, application guidelines.
Application information: Application form required.
Officer: B. Diane Gordon, Exec. Dir.
EIN: 341281026
Codes: CM, FD

42187
The Lerner Foundation
c/o Charles P. Malitz
23240 Chagrin Blvd., Ste. 400
Beachwood, OH 44122 (216) 831-4343

Established in 1993 in OH.
Donor(s): Alfred Lerner.
Financial data (yr. ended 12/31/00): Grants paid, $7,145,556; assets, $10,387,935 (M); expenditures, $7,145,756; qualifying distributions, $7,103,974.
Trustees: Nancy Beck, Alfred Lerner, Norma Lerner, Randolf Lerner.
EIN: 341744726
Codes: FD, FM

42188
Barberton Community Foundation
104 3rd St. N.W., Ste. 202
Barberton, OH 44203-8226 (330) 745-5995
FAX: (330) 745-3990; URL: http://www.bcfcharity.org
Contact: Thomas L. Harnden, Exec. Dir.

Established in 1996 in OH; converted from the sale of Barberton Citizens Hospital to Quorum Health Group, Inc.
Financial data (yr. ended 12/31/01): Grants paid, $7,046,527; assets, $98,131,868 (M); gifts received, $8,040,065; expenditures, $7,920,301.
Limitations: Giving primarily in Barberton, OH.
Publications: Annual report, informational brochure (including application guidelines), application guidelines, newsletter.
Application information: Application forms available on foundation Web site. Application form required.
Officers and Trustees:* Kenneth R. Cox,* Chair.; Walter Ritzman,* Vice-Chair.; Esther Sarb,* Secy.; Thomas D. Doak,* Treas.; Thomas L. Harnden, Exec. Dir.; Robert J. Genet, Randy Hart, Daniel C. Knoor, Milan Pavkov, and 7 additional trustees.
EIN: 341846432
Codes: CM, FD, GTI

42189
The Elisabeth Severance Prentiss Foundation
c/o National City Bank
1900 E. Ninth St., Loc. 2066
Cleveland, OH 44114 (216) 222-2760
Contact: Frank M. Rizzo, Secy.

Trust established in 1944 in OH.
Donor(s): Elisabeth Severance Prentiss,‡ Luther L. Miller,‡ Kate W. Miller.‡
Financial data (yr. ended 12/31/01): Grants paid, $6,865,749; assets, $99,771,484 (M); expenditures, $7,036,284; qualifying distributions, $6,942,851.
Limitations: Giving primarily in the greater Cleveland, OH, area.
Publications: Annual report (including application guidelines).
Application information: Proposals should be accompanied by six copies of an executive summary. Application form not required.
Officers and Managers:* Quentin Alexander,* Pres.; Frank M. Rizzo, Secy.; Elisabeth H. Alexander, Pamela A. Alexander, Harry J. Bolwell, William R. Robertson.
Trustee: National City Bank.
EIN: 346512433
Codes: FD, FM

42190
The GAR Foundation
50 S. Main St.
P.O. Box 1500
Akron, OH 44309-1500 (330) 643-0201
E-mail: RBriggs@BDBlaw.com; URL: http://www.garfdn.org
Contact: Robert W. Briggs, Exec. Dir.

Trust established in 1967 in OH.
Donor(s): Ruth C. Roush,‡ Galen Roush.‡
Financial data (yr. ended 12/31/01): Grants paid, $6,821,126; assets, $167,850,596 (M); expenditures, $9,091,779; qualifying distributions, $7,976,153.
Limitations: Giving primarily in the Akron-Summit County area and secondarily in Cuyahoga, Stark, Medina, Portage and Wayne counties, OH.
Publications: Application guidelines.
Application information: Application form required.
Officer and Trustees:* Robert W. Briggs,* Exec. Dir.; National City Bank.
Distribution Committee: Richard A. Chenoweth, Joseph Clapp, John L. Tormey, S.R. Werner, Douglas A. Wilson.
EIN: 346577710
Codes: FD, FM

42191
The Weatherhead Foundation
730 Ohio Savings Plz.
1801 E. 9th St.
Cleveland, OH 44114-3103 (216) 771-4000
FAX: (216) 771-0422
Contact: Thomas F. Allen, Treas.

Incorporated in 1953 in OH; foundation is income beneficiary of a perpetual trust; assets reflect assets of both feeder trust and foundation.
Donor(s): Albert J. Weatherhead, Jr.‡
Financial data (yr. ended 12/31/00): Grants paid, $6,732,427; assets, $10,974,815 (M); gifts received, $6,095,234; expenditures, $6,855,818; qualifying distributions, $6,803,862.
Limitations: Giving on a national basis.
Publications: Application guidelines, informational brochure.
Application information: Grants are initiated by the trustees. Unsolicited applications are not encouraged.
Officers and Trustees:* Albert J. Weatherhead III,* Pres.; Frank M. Rasmussen,* V.P.; Henry Rosovsky,* V.P.; Charles E. Sheedy,* V.P.; Celia J. Weatherhead,* V.P.; John P. Weatherhead,* V.P.; Thomas F. Allen,* Treas.
EIN: 132711998
Codes: FD, FM

42192
The Fifth Third Foundation
c/o Fifth Third Bank
38 Foundation Sq. Plz., M D 109017
Cincinnati, OH 45263 (513) 534-7001
Contact: Lawra J. Baumann, Fdn. Off., Fifth Third Bank

Trust established in 1948 in OH.
Donor(s): Fifth Third Bank.
Financial data (yr. ended 09/30/01): Grants paid, $6,715,761; assets, $4,334,782 (M); expenditures, $7,006,305; qualifying distributions, $6,797,639.
Limitations: Giving primarily in the Cincinnati, OH, area, and other operating areas of the corporation.
Publications: Annual report, application guidelines.
Application information: Application form not required.
Trustee: Fifth Third Bank.
EIN: 316024135
Codes: CS, FD, CD, FM

42193
Scripps Howard Foundation
P.O. Box 5380
312 Walnut St., 28th Fl.
Cincinnati, OH 45202 (513) 977-3035
FAX: (513) 977-3800; E-mail: clabes@scripps.com or cottingham@scripps.com; URL: http://www.scripps.com/foundation
Contact: Judith G. Clabes, Pres.; or Patty Cottingham, Exec. Dir.

Incorporated in 1962 in OH.
Donor(s): The E.W. Scripps Co., and employees of the company and friends of the foundation.
Financial data (yr. ended 12/31/00): Grants paid, $6,676,715; assets, $85,838,950 (M); gifts received, $4,566,622; expenditures, $8,694,444; qualifying distributions, $7,714,613.
Limitations: Giving primarily in areas of company operations for scholarships, internships and literary grants, and nationally for special grants and awards.
Publications: Annual report (including application guidelines).

Application information: Application form not required.
Officers and Trustees:* Judith G. Clabes,* C.E.O. and Pres.; Patty Cottingham,* Secy. and Exec. Dir.; J. Robert Routt,* Treas.; Drew Berry, Colleen C. Conant, Clyde Gray, Julia Scripps Heidt, Pamela Howard, John Lansing, Angus McEachran, Susan Packard, Susan J. Porter, Edward Scripps, Jr., Maggie Scripps, Paul K. Scripps, Robert P. Scripps.
EIN: 316025114
Codes: CS, FD, CD, FM, GTI

42194
The Kelvin and Eleanor Smith Foundation
26380 Curtiss Wright Pkwy., Ste. 105
Cleveland, OH 44143 (216) 289-5789
FAX: (216) 289-5948
Contact: Carol W. Zett, Mgr.

Incorporated in 1955 in OH.
Donor(s): Kelvin Smith.‡
Financial data (yr. ended 10/31/01): Grants paid, $6,664,650; assets, $145,547,213 (M); gifts received, $34,221,838; expenditures, $7,311,627; qualifying distributions, $6,860,550.
Limitations: Giving primarily in the greater Cleveland, OH, area.
Publications: Application guidelines.
Application information: Application form not required.
Officers and Trustees:* Lucia S. Nash,* Co-Chair.; Cara S. Stirn,* Co-Chair.; Ellen S. Mavec,* Pres.; Andrew L. Fabens III, Secy.; William B. LaPlace,* Treas.; Carol W. Zett, Grants Mgr.; Charles P. Bolton, Michael D. Eppig, M.D., William J. O'Neill, Jr.
EIN: 346555349
Codes: FD, FM

42195
Fred A. Lennon Charitable Trust
25101 Chagrin Blvd., Ste. 310
Beachwood, OH 44122 (216) 831-4433

Established in 1993 in OH.
Donor(s): Fred A. Lennon.‡
Financial data (yr. ended 12/31/00): Grants paid, $6,651,167; assets, $65,495,748 (M); expenditures, $7,611,530; qualifying distributions, $6,877,674.
Limitations: Applications not accepted. Giving primarily in OH, with emphasis on Cleveland.
Application information: Contributes only to pre-selected organizations.
Trustees: F.J. Callahan, T. Janoch, E.P. Mansour, A. Malachi Mixon, N. Tobbe.
EIN: 341761181
Codes: FD

42196
Harry and Violet Turner 95 Charitable Trust
4 W. Main St.
Springfield, OH 45502
Contact: John Landess

Established in 2001 in OH.
Donor(s): Harry M. Turner 97 Trust.
Financial data (yr. ended 12/31/01): Grants paid, $6,094,297; assets, $34,602,013 (M); gifts received, $42,605,250; expenditures, $6,805,666; qualifying distributions, $6,648,039.
Application information: Application form required.
Trustees: Sara Landess, Security National Bank.
EIN: 311711190
Codes: FD

42197
Akron Community Foundation
345 W. Cedar St.
Akron, OH 44307-2407 (330) 376-8522
FAX: (330) 376-0202; E-mail: adfmail@akroncommunityfdn.com or acfmail@akroncommunityfdn.org; URL: http://www.akroncommunityfdn.org
Contact: Jody Bacon, Pres.

Incorporated in 1955 in OH.
Financial data (yr. ended 03/31/02): Grants paid, $5,836,784; assets, $96,436,000 (M); gifts received, $5,723,000; expenditures, $7,154,000.
Limitations: Giving primarily in Akron, Summit, and Medina counties, OH.
Publications: Annual report (including application guidelines), application guidelines, newsletter.
Application information: No more than 1 grant to an organization in a 12-month period. Application form not required.
Officers and Trustees:* Marc Merklin,* Chair.; Scott A. Lyons, Jr., Vice Chair. and Treas.; Jody Bacon, Pres.; Patricia Graves,* Secy.; Rennick Andreoli, Mark Bober, Cynthia Capers, Marie Covington, James Crutchfield, George Daverio, William F. Demas, M.D., Kathryn Dindo, Ernest Estep, Clifford Isroff, Mary Ann Jackson, Mike Lewis, Gregory McDermott, Robert Merzweiler, Virginia Robinson, George Sarkis, Bill Sharp, Hoyt Wells.
Trustee Banks: Bank One, N.A., Brandes Investment Partners, Clover Capital Mgmt., FirstMerit Bank, N.A., Frontier Capital Mgmt., National City Bank, Oak Assocs., Osprey Investment Partners.
EIN: 341087615
Codes: CM, FD

42198
The Hamilton Community Foundation, Inc.
319 N. 3rd St.
Hamilton, OH 45011-1624 (513) 863-1389
FAX: (513) 863-2868; E-mail: John@HamiltonFoundation.org; URL: http://www.hamiltonfoundation.org
Contact: John Guidugli, C.E.O. and Pres.

Incorporated in 1951 in OH.
Financial data (yr. ended 12/31/01): Grants paid, $5,791,743; assets, $62,324,425 (M); gifts received, $5,791,743; expenditures, $6,701,422.
Limitations: Giving limited to Butler County, OH.
Publications: Annual report, newsletter, application guidelines.
Application information: Application form not required.
Officers and Trustees:* Mary Pat Essman, Chair.; Jack Rhodes, Vice-Chair.; John Guidugli, C.E.O. and Pres.; Cynthia V. Parrish, Exec. Dir.; David L. Belew, Donald M. Cisle, William Groth, Gerald Hammond, Lee H. Parrish, Stanley Pontius, John Reister, Craig Wilks.
Trustee Banks: First Financial Bank, KeyBank, N.A., Star Bank, N.A.
EIN: 316038277
Codes: CM, FD

42199
The Burton D. Morgan Foundation
50 S. Main St., 10th Fl.
P.O. Box 1500
Akron, OH 44309-1500 (330) 258-6512
Contact Marie Erb for questions regarding grant application guidelines, TL: (330) 643-0219;
FAX: (330) 258-6559; E-mail: admin@bdmorganfdn.org; URL: http://www.bdmorganfdn.org
Contact: John V. Frank, Pres.

Established in 1967 in OH.
Donor(s): Burton D. Morgan.
Financial data (yr. ended 12/31/01): Grants paid, $5,554,900; assets, $76,514,025 (M); gifts received, $200,011; expenditures, $6,280,753; qualifying distributions, $5,699,339.
Limitations: Giving primarily in northeastern OH.
Publications: Annual report (including application guidelines), application guidelines.
Application information: The foundation will not be accepting grant requests form new applicants for at least one year. The next possible opportunity for review of new applicant projects will be at the foundation's January 2004 meeting. Application form not required.
Officers and Trustees:* John V. Frank,* Pres.; J. Martin Erbaugh, V.P.; Richard A. Chenoweth,* Secy.-Treas.; Keith A. Brown, Stanley C. Gault, Mark D. Robeson, Richard N. Seaman.
EIN: 346598971
Codes: FD

42200
The MeadWestvaco Foundation
(Formerly The Mead Corporation Foundation)
Courthouse Plz. N.E.
Dayton, OH 45463 (937) 495-3031
URL: http://www.mead.com/am/cc_frset.html
Contact: Kathryn A. Strawn, V.P. and Exec. Dir.

Trust established in 1957 in OH; reincorporated in 2003 following merger of Mead and Westvaco Corps.
Donor(s): The Mead Corp.
Financial data (yr. ended 12/31/01): Grants paid, $5,492,529; assets, $32,628,081 (M); expenditures, $5,785,172; qualifying distributions, $5,762,512.
Limitations: Giving primarily in areas of company operations.
Publications: Application guidelines.
Application information: All foundation proposals must be submitted to local Mead management for their review and recommendation to the foundation.
Officers and Governing Committee:* Kathryn A. Strawn, V.P. and Exec. Dir.; P.C. Norris, Secy.; L.M. Sheffield,* Treas.; J.C. Dutton, A.R. Rosenberger, S.R. Scherger, W.A. Wendell.
Trustee: Mellon Trust.
EIN: 061652243
Codes: CS, FD, CD, FM

42201
The Agnes Gund Foundation
c/o Agnes Gund
517 Broadway, 3rd Fl.
East Liverpool, OH 43920 (330) 385-3400

Established in 1988 in OH.
Donor(s): Agnes Gund.
Financial data (yr. ended 09/30/01): Grants paid, $5,280,154; assets, $245,705 (M); gifts received, $5,175,735; expenditures, $5,329,992; qualifying distributions, $5,232,726.
Limitations: Giving primarily in New York, NY.
Trustees: Agnes Gund, Daniel Shapiro.
EIN: 341606084

Codes: FD, FM

42202
The Kettering Fund
1560 Kettering Tower
Dayton, OH 45423 (937) 228-1021
FAX: (973) 228-2399; E-mail: ketteringfund@aol.com
Contact: Terri Hurd

Established in 1958 in OH.
Donor(s): Charles F. Kettering.‡
Financial data (yr. ended 06/30/01): Grants paid, $5,245,952; assets, $93,884,453 (M); gifts received, $8,492; expenditures, $5,688,568; qualifying distributions, $5,304,095.
Limitations: Giving primarily in OH.
Publications: Application guidelines.
Application information: Application form not required.
Distribution Committee: Susan K. Beck, Virginia W. Kettering, Jane K. Lombard, Susan K. Williamson.
Trustee: Bank One, Dayton, N.A.
EIN: 316027115
Codes: FD, FM

42203
The Reinberger Foundation
27600 Chagrin Blvd.
Cleveland, OH 44122 (216) 292-2790
FAX: (216) 292-4466
Contact: Robert N. Reinberger, Dir.

Established in 1968 in OH.
Donor(s): Clarence T. Reinberger,‡ Louise F. Reinberger.‡
Financial data (yr. ended 12/31/00): Grants paid, $5,201,505; assets, $94,823,407 (M); expenditures, $6,069,029; qualifying distributions, $5,382,369.
Limitations: Giving primarily in the Cleveland and Columbus, OH, metropolitan areas.
Publications: Grants list, informational brochure (including application guidelines), application guidelines.
Application information: Application form not required.
Officer: Richard H. Oman, Secy.
Directors: Sara R. Dyer, Karen R. Hooser, Robert N. Reinberger, William C. Reinberger.
Agent: The Glenmede Trust Co.
EIN: 346574879
Codes: FD, FM

42204
Stranahan Foundation
4159 Holland-Sylvania Rd., Ste. 206
Toledo, OH 43623-2590 (419) 882-5575
FAX: (419) 882-2072; E-mail: mail@stranahanfoundation.org; URL: http://www.stranahanfoundation.org
Contact: Pamela G. Roberts, Prog. Off.

Trust established in 1944 in OH.
Donor(s): Robert A. Stranahan,‡ Frank D. Stranahan,‡ and others.
Financial data (yr. ended 12/31/01): Grants paid, $5,150,000; assets, $87,728,211 (M); gifts received, $1,000; expenditures, $5,759,301; qualifying distributions, $5,218,786.
Limitations: Giving primarily in Toledo, OH.
Publications: Annual report, informational brochure (including application guidelines).
Application information: Application form not required.
Officer and Trustees:* Stephen Stranahan,* Pres.; Charles G. Yeager,* C.F.O.; Diana Foster, Michael Foster, William Foster, Frances Parry, Roberta Pawlak, Marcia Piper, Duane Stranahan, Jr., Mark Stranahan.
EIN: 346514375
Codes: FD, FM

42205
Toledo Community Foundation, Inc.
608 Madison Ave., Ste. 1540
Toledo, OH 43604-1151 (419) 241-5049
FAX: (419) 242-5549; E-mail: phbtcf@yahoo.com; URL: http://www.pgdc.net/TOLEDO
Contact: Pam Howell-Beach, Dir.

Established in 1924 in OH by trust agreement; reactivated in 1973.
Financial data (yr. ended 12/31/01): Grants paid, $4,986,954; assets, $90,931,276 (M); gifts received, $8,885,670; expenditures, $6,114,496.
Limitations: Giving primarily in northwestern OH, with emphasis on the greater Toledo area.
Publications: Annual report (including application guidelines), newsletter.
Application information: Application form not required.
Officer and Trustees:* Patricia Wise,* Pres.; Richard P. Anderson, Sara Jane DeHoff, William Foster, Frank D. Jacobs, Dennis Johnson, Susan Morgan, Charles Oswald, William Rose, Elizabeth Ruppert.
Director: Pamela Howell-Beach.
EIN: 237284004
Codes: CM, FD

42206
The Eaton Charitable Fund
c/o Eaton Corp.
1111 Superior Ave.
Cleveland, OH 44114-2584 (216) 523-4944
FAX: (216) 479-7013; E-mail: jamesmason@eaton.com; URL: http://www.eaton.com
Contact: James L. Mason, V.P., Public and Community Affairs

Trust established in 1953 in OH.
Donor(s): Eaton Corp.
Financial data (yr. ended 12/31/00): Grants paid, $4,974,167; assets, $9,851,946 (M); gifts received, $12,475; expenditures, $5,042,439; qualifying distributions, $4,967,534.
Limitations: Giving primarily in areas of company operations.
Publications: Annual report, corporate giving report, application guidelines.
Application information: Eaton employee involvement with requesting organization is a key consideration in deciding to fund a request. Contribution requests should be made through a local Eaton manager wherever possible. Application form not required.
Corporate Contributions Committee: James L. Mason, Chair.; Kristen M. Bihary, Stephen M. Buente, Donald Bullock, Jr., Susan J. Cook, Alexander M. Cutler, Thomas W. O'Boyle, Ken D. Semelsberger.
Trustee: KeyBank, N.A.
EIN: 346501856
Codes: CS, FD, CD, FM

42207
Cinergy Foundation, Inc.
(Formerly PSI Foundation, Inc.)
139 E. 4th St.
2801 Atrium II
Cincinnati, OH 45202 (513) 287-1251
Additional tel.: (800) 262-3000, ext. 1251; URL: http://www.cinergy.com/foundation
Contact: Karol King, Mgr.

Established in 1991. The Cinergy Foundation was created as a result of the merger between PSI Resources and Cincinnati Gas & Electric Co.
Donor(s): Cinergy Corp., Vernley R. Rehnstrom.
Financial data (yr. ended 12/31/99): Grants paid, $4,638,685; assets, $0 (M); gifts received, $4,678,483; expenditures, $4,748,590; qualifying distributions, $4,746,288.
Limitations: Giving limited to areas of company operations in IN, southwestern OH, and northern KY.
Publications: Application guidelines, annual report.
Application information: The foundation only accepts online applications. Paper copies will not be accepted.
Officers and Directors:* James E. Rogers,* Chair.; J. Joseph Hale, Jr.,* Pres.; Julia S. Janson, Secy.; Wendy Aumiller, Treas.; Philip R. Cox, Kenneth M. Duberstein, John A. Hillenbrand II, George C. Juilfs, James L. Turner, R. Foster Duncan, Douglas F. Esamann, Gregory C. Ficke, Mary Shapiro, Philip R. Sharp, Jerome A. Vennemann.
EIN: 351755088
Codes: CS, FD, CD

42208
The Jewish Foundation of Cincinnati
8044 Montgomery Rd., Ste. 700
Cincinnati, OH 45236 (513) 792-2715
FAX: (513) 792-2716; E-mail: jfdncin@supern.com
Contact: Connie Hinitz, Admin.

Established in 1995 in OH; created when the Jewish Hospital of Cincinnati's capital assets were sold to the Health Alliance of Cincinnati.
Financial data (yr. ended 10/31/01): Grants paid, $4,637,217; assets, $77,871,938 (M); gifts received, $14,769; expenditures, $5,052,305; qualifying distributions, $4,612,515.
Limitations: Giving limited to Cincinnati, OH.
Publications: Annual report, application guidelines.
Application information: Application form required.
Officers and Trustees:* Robert Kanter,* Chair.; Gloria S. Haffer,* Pres.; Phyllis S. Sewell,* V.P.; Warren C. Falberg, Secy.; Gary Heiman,* Treas.; Philip T. Cohen, Bernard L. Dave, Benjamin Gettler, Sidney A. Peerless, M.D., Robert W. Walsh.
EIN: 311451489
Codes: FD, FM

42209
The Nord Family Foundation
347 Midway Blvd., Ste. 210
Elyria, OH 44035 (440) 324-2822
Additional tel.: (800) 745-8946; FAX: (440) 324-6427; E-mail: execdir@nordff.org; URL: http://www.nordff.org
Contact: John Mullaney, Exec. Dir.

Trust established in 1952 in OH; reorganized in 1988 under current name.
Donor(s): Walter G. Nord,‡ Mrs. Walter G. Nord,‡ Nordson Corp.
Financial data (yr. ended 12/31/00): Grants paid, $4,615,035; assets, $83,133,887 (M); expenditures, $5,770,329; qualifying distributions, $5,137,169; giving activities include $115,236 for programs.
Limitations: Giving primarily in the Lorain and Cuyahoga County, OH, areas; also gives secondarily in Denver, CO, Boston, MA, and Columbia, SC.
Publications: Annual report (including application guidelines), informational brochure (including application guidelines).
Application information: Application form required.
Officers and Trustees:* Joseph N. Ignat,* Pres.; Cynthia W. Nord,* V.P.; Emma Mason, Secy.; Samuel Berk,* Treas.; Sharon White, Cont.; John J. Mullaney, Exec. Dir.; Randall Barbato, Elizabeth I. Bausch, John R. Clark, Brenda Grier-Miller, Pam Ignat, Eric Thomas Nord, Richard Nord, Shannon Nord.
EIN: 341595929
Codes: FD, FM

42210
The Huntington Foundation
41 S. High St., HC 3413
Columbus, OH 43215 (614) 480-3898
Contact: Elfi DiBella, Pres.

Established in 1999 in OH.
Donor(s): Huntington Bancshares Incorporated, The Huntington National Bank.
Financial data (yr. ended 12/31/01): Grants paid, $4,439,953; assets, $888,866 (M); gifts received, $5,059,454; expenditures, $4,481,759; qualifying distributions, $4,382,381.
Limitations: Giving primarily in OH.
Officers and Trustees:* Elfi DiBella,* Pres.; John Van Flert,* V.P.; John W. Liebersbach,* Secy.
EIN: 311681542
Codes: CS, FD, CD

42211
Wolfe Associates, Inc.
34 S. 3rd St.
Columbus, OH 43215 (614) 460-3782
Contact: Rita J. Wolfe Hoag, V.P.

Incorporated in 1973 in OH.
Donor(s): The Dispatch Printing Co., The Ohio Co., WBNS-TV, Inc., RadiOhio, Inc., Video Indiana, Inc.
Financial data (yr. ended 12/31/01): Grants paid, $4,436,887; assets, $8,118,703 (M); gifts received, $2,967,935; expenditures, $4,520,338; qualifying distributions, $4,425,596.
Limitations: Giving primarily in central OH.
Publications: Program policy statement, application guidelines.
Application information: Application form not required.
Officers: John F. Wolfe, Chair. and Pres.; James H. Gilmour, V.P. and Secy.-Treas.; Michael Curtin, V.P.; Rita J. Wolfe Hoag, V.P.; Nancy Wolfe Lane, V.P.; Sara Wolfe Perrini, V.P.
EIN: 237303111
Codes: CS, FD, CD, FM

42212
H.C.S. Foundation
1801 E. 9th St., Ste. 1035
Cleveland, OH 44114-3103 (216) 781-3502
Contact: Trustees

Trust established in 1959 in OH.
Donor(s): Harold C. Schott.‡
Financial data (yr. ended 12/31/00): Grants paid, $4,309,333; assets, $93,831,430 (M); expenditures, $4,929,105; qualifying distributions, $4,600,399.
Limitations: Giving limited to OH.
Application information: Application form not required.
Trustees: Francie S. Hiltz, L. Thomas Hiltz, Betty Jane Mulcahy, William Dunne Saal, Milton B. Schott, Jr.
EIN: 346514235
Codes: FD, FM

42213
The Community Foundation of Greater Lorain County
1865 N. Ridge Rd. E., Ste. A
Lorain, OH 44055 (440) 277-0142
Additional tel.: (440) 323-4445; FAX: (440) 277-6955; E-mail: Foundation@cfglc.org; URL: http://www.cfglc.org
Contact: Brian R. Frederick, C.E.O. and Pres.

Incorporated in 1980 in OH.
Financial data (yr. ended 12/31/00): Grants paid, $4,147,054; assets, $70,536,753 (M); gifts received, $1,751,751; expenditures, $5,088,118.
Limitations: Giving limited to Lorain County, OH, and immediate vicinity.
Publications: Annual report (including application guidelines), informational brochure (including application guidelines), application guidelines, newsletter, program policy statement.
Application information: Application form required.
Officers and Directors:* Susan Schaeffer,* Chair.; Rita Canfield, Vice-Chair.; Brian R. Frederick,* C.E.O. and Pres.; Marilyn Jenne, Secy.; Nelson Bour,* Treas.; Larry Alderman, Don Arnold, Bob Bowman, Leonard DeLuca, Kevin Flanigan, Jack Gaudry, Terry Goode, Michael Goodman, Charles Horton, Judy Lozano, Jim Pank, Thomas Pillari, Rigo Reveron.
EIN: 341322781
Codes: CM, FD, FM, GTI

42214
The Raymond John Wean Foundation
P.O. Box 760
Warren, OH 44482-0760 (330) 394-5600
Additional address: 108 Main Ave. SW, Ste. 1005, Warren, OH, 44481; FAX: (330) 394-5601; E-mail: rjweanfdn@aol.com
Contact: Raymond John Wean, Jr., Chair.

Trust established in 1949 in OH.
Donor(s): Raymond J. Wean, Sr.‡
Financial data (yr. ended 12/31/01): Grants paid, $4,042,318; assets, $83,990,931 (M); expenditures, $4,227,184; qualifying distributions, $4,188,784.
Limitations: Giving primarily in Allegheny County, PA, and northeast OH, with emphasis on Cuyahoga, Mahoning, and Trumbull counties.
Publications: Application guidelines, financial statement.
Application information: Application form required.
Administrators: Raymond John Wean, Jr., Chair.; Jennie Dennison-Budak, John L. Pogue, Patricia Sweet, Gordon B. Wean, Raymond John Wean III.
Trustee: Second National Bank of Warren.
EIN: 346505038
Codes: FD, FM

42215
Eva L. and Joseph M. Bruening Foundation
627 Hanna Building
1422 Euclid Ave.
Cleveland, OH 44115-1901 (216) 621-2632
FAX: (216) 621-8198; URL: http://www.fmscleveland.com/bruening
Contact: Janet E. Narten, Exec. Dir.

Established in 1987 in OH.

Donor(s): Joseph M. Bruening,‡ Eva L. Bruening.‡
Financial data (yr. ended 12/31/01): Grants paid, $4,028,578; assets, $66,694,994 (M); expenditures, $4,970,158; qualifying distributions, $4,335,902.
Limitations: Giving limited to the greater Cleveland, OH, area.
Publications: Annual report (including application guidelines).
Application information: The foundation does not respond to mass mailings or annual campaign appeals. Application form not required.
Officer: Janet E. Narten, Exec. Dir.
Distribution Committee: Marilyn A. Cunin, Chair.; Douglas Bannerman, John A. Favret, E. Lorrie Robertson, Anne B. Springer.
Trustee: KeyBank, N.A.
EIN: 341584378
Codes: FD, FM

42216
The Jay L. and Jean Schottenstein Foundation
(Formerly Jay L. Schottenstein Foundation)
1800 Moler Rd.
Columbus, OH 43207-1698

Donor(s): Jay Schottenstein.
Financial data (yr. ended 12/31/00): Grants paid, $3,987,264; assets, $12,210,316 (M); expenditures, $3,987,674; qualifying distributions, $3,987,674.
Limitations: Applications not accepted. Giving limited to NY and OH.
Application information: Contributes only to pre-selected organizations.
Officers: Jay L. Schottenstein, Pres.; Geraldine Schottenstein, V.P.; Saul Schottenstein, Secy.-Treas.
EIN: 311111955
Codes: FD, FM

42217
Stark Community Foundation
(Formerly The Stark County Foundation, Inc.)
The Saxton House
331 Market Ave. S.
Canton, OH 44702-2107 (330) 454-3426
FAX: (330) 454-5855; E-mail: jbower@starkcf.org; Additional E-mail: cmlazer@starkcf.org; URL: http://www.starkcommunityfoundation.org
Contact: James A. Bower, Pres., and Cynthia M. Lazor, V.P.

Established in 1963 in OH by resolution and declaration of trust.
Financial data (yr. ended 12/31/02): Grants paid, $3,790,413; assets, $110,454,507 (M); gifts received, $3,615,457; expenditures, $7,191,285.
Limitations: Giving limited to Stark County, OH.
Publications: Annual report (including application guidelines), program policy statement, application guidelines, financial statement, grants list, newsletter, informational brochure.
Application information: Application form required only for student aid; applicants may telephone foundation for form. Application form not required.
Officers: James A. Bower, Pres.; Cynthia M. Lazor, V.P., Progs.; Christine E. Kruman, V.P., Devel.; Patricia C. Quick, Treas.
Distribution Committee: Paul R. Bishop, Chair; Paralee W. Compton, Lynne S. Dragomier, Jeffrey A. Fisher, Thomas W. Schervish, Candy Wallace, John R. Werren.
Trustee Banks: Bank One Ohio Trust Co., N.A., FirstMerit Bank, N.A., KeyBank, N.A., National City Bank, Northeast, Univan Bank, Sky Bank.
EIN: 340943665
Codes: CM, FD, GTI

42218
Morton and Barbara Mandel Family Foundation
(Formerly Morton and Barbara Mandel Foundation)
2829 Euclid Ave.
Cleveland, OH 44115 (216) 875-6523
Contact: Morton L. Mandel, Tr.

Established in 1963 in OH.
Donor(s): Morton L. Mandel, Barbara A. Mandel.
Financial data (yr. ended 12/31/00): Grants paid, $3,705,021; assets, $66,877,193 (M); gifts received, $5,997,725; expenditures, $5,081,984; qualifying distributions, $3,551,610.
Limitations: Giving primarily in Cleveland, OH; giving also in MA and NY.
Application information: Application form not required.
Officers and Trustees:* Jack N. Mandel,* Pres.; Barbara A. Mandel, Joseph C. Mandel, Morton L. Mandel, Karen A. Vereb.
EIN: 346546420
Codes: FD, FM

42219
The Youngstown Foundation
P.O. Box 1162
Youngstown, OH 44501 (330) 744-0320
FAX: (330) 758-4663
Contact: G.M. Walsh, Exec. Dir.

Established in 1918 in OH by bank resolution.
Financial data (yr. ended 12/31/99): Grants paid, $3,652,050; assets, $68,387,256 (M); gifts received, $1,648,351; expenditures, $4,116,482.
Limitations: Giving limited to Mahoning County, OH, with emphasis on Youngstown.
Publications: Annual report.
Application information: Application form not required.
Officer: G.M. Walsh, Exec. Dir.
Distribution Committee: Cynthia Anderson, Phillip B. Dennison, Thomas R. Hollern, Joseph S. Nohra, William Powell.
Trustee: National City Bank, Northeast.
EIN: 346515788
Codes: CM, FD

42220
Jacob G. Schmidlapp Trust No. 1 and No. 2
(Formerly Jacob G. Schmidlapp Trust No. 1)
c/o Fifth Third Bank
38 Fountain Sq. Plz., MD 1090C7
Cincinnati, OH 45263 (513) 534-7001
Contact: Lawra J. Baumann, Fdn. Off., Fifth Third Bank

Trust established in 1927 in OH.
Donor(s): Jacob G. Schmidlapp.‡
Financial data (yr. ended 09/30/01): Grants paid, $3,617,166; assets, $66,552,672 (M); expenditures, $4,203,929; qualifying distributions, $3,779,059.
Limitations: Giving primarily in the greater Cincinnati, OH, area.
Publications: Annual report, application guidelines.
Application information: Application form not required.
Trustee: Fifth Third Bank.
Codes: FD, FM

42221
The Hoover Foundation
101 E. Maple St.
North Canton, OH 44720 (330) 499-9200
Contact: Lawrence R. Hoover, Chair.

Trust established in 1945 in OH.
Donor(s): Members of the Hoover family.

Financial data (yr. ended 12/31/00): Grants paid, $3,557,400; assets, $60,985,981 (M); expenditures, $3,983,581; qualifying distributions, $3,571,703.
Limitations: Giving primarily in Stark County, OH.
Application information: Application form not required.
Trust Committee: Lawrence R. Hoover, Chair.; Ronald K. Bennington, Thomas H. Hoover, M.D., Joyce U. Niffeneggar, Timothy D. Schlitz.
Trustee: United National Bank.
EIN: 346510994
Codes: FD

42222
The Generation Trust
c/o Fifth Third Bank Northwestern Ohio, N.A.
606 Madison Ave., 3rd Fl., M.D. 292933
Toledo, OH 43604 (419) 259-6806
Contact: J. Philip Ruyle, Esq., V.P., Fifth Third Bank Northwestern Ohio, N.A.

Established in 1985 in OH.
Donor(s): John D. Beckett, The R.W. Beckett Corp., and members of the Beckett family.
Financial data (yr. ended 12/31/00): Grants paid, $3,402,500; assets, $0 (M); gifts received, $331,082; expenditures, $3,500,809; qualifying distributions, $3,386,051.
Limitations: Giving on a national and international basis.
Application information: Application form not required.
Advisory Committee Members: John D. Beckett, Wendy D. Beckett, Robert S. Cook.
EIN: 346850815
Codes: FD, FM

42223
John P. Murphy Foundation
c/o Terminal Tower
50 Public Sq., Ste. 924
Cleveland, OH 44113-2203 (216) 623-4770
FAX: (216) 623-4773; URL: http://fdncenter.org/grantmaker/jpmurphy
Contact: Allan J. Zambie, Exec. V.P.

Incorporated in 1960 in OH.
Donor(s): John P. Murphy.‡
Financial data (yr. ended 12/31/01): Grants paid, $3,397,626; assets, $57,225,734 (M); expenditures, $4,140,308; qualifying distributions, $3,692,618.
Limitations: Giving primarily in the greater Cleveland, OH, area.
Publications: Informational brochure, application guidelines.
Application information: Application form required.
Officers and Trustees:* Nancy W. McCann,* Pres. and Treas.; Allan J. Zambie,* Exec. V.P. and Secy.; Robert R. Broadbent,* V.P.; R. Bruce Campbell,* V.P.; Marie S. Strawbridge,* V.P.
EIN: 346528308
Codes: FD, FM

42224
The Piqua Community Foundation
P.O. Box 613
Piqua, OH 45356

Financial data (yr. ended 12/31/00): Grants paid, $3,294,140; assets, $4,779,430 (M); gifts received, $3,197,691; expenditures, $3,320,561.
Limitations: Giving limited to the Piqua, OH, area.
Officers: Mimi A. Crawford, Pres.; L. Edward Fry, V.P.; Neill H. Haas, Secy.-Treas.
Directors: John S. Alexander, Leesa A. Baker, James W. Brown, Cheryl L. Burkhardt, Jerry L. Clark, Lucinda L. Fess, Daniel P. French, Elmer V.

42224—OHIO

Harris, R. Charles Hemm, Jr., Ray L. Loffer, Steven K. Staley, Tom Wendlen, Michael P. Yannucci.
EIN: 311391908
Codes: CM, FD

42225
The Kroger Co. Foundation
1014 Vine St.
Cincinnati, OH 45202-1100 (513) 762-4000
FAX: (513) 762-1295
Contact: Lynn Marmer, Pres.

Established in 1987 in OH.
Donor(s): The Kroger Co.
Financial data (yr. ended 12/31/00): Grants paid, $3,266,708; assets, $12,957,218 (M); expenditures, $3,283,215; qualifying distributions, $3,281,732.
Limitations: Giving primarily in areas of company operations; certain national and regional groups will also be supported, but only to the extent to which they provide services to areas of company operations.
Publications: Application guidelines.
Application information: Application form not required.
Officers: Lynn Marmer, Pres.; Lawrence Turner, V.P. and Secy.-Treas.
EIN: 311192929
Codes: CS, FD, CD

42226
Joseph and Florence Mandel Foundation
2829 Euclid Ave.
Cleveland, OH 44115 (216) 875-6523
Contact: Joseph C. Mandel, Tr.

Established in 1963 in OH.
Donor(s): Florence Mandel,‡ Joseph C. Mandel.
Financial data (yr. ended 12/31/00): Grants paid, $3,204,227; assets, $58,170,505 (M); gifts received, $573,325; expenditures, $4,416,029; qualifying distributions, $3,062,155.
Limitations: Giving primarily in OH.
Application information: Application form not required.
Officers and Trustees:* Joseph C. Mandel,* Pres.; Patrick F. Sullivan,* V.P. and Treas.; Karen A. Vereb, Secy.; Michele Beyer, Jack N. Mandel, Morton L. Mandel, Penni Weinberg.
EIN: 346546419
Codes: FD

42227
John J. and Mary R. Schiff Foundation
P.O. Box 145496
Cincinnati, OH 45250-5496

Established in 1983 in OH.
Donor(s): John J. Schiff, Mary R. Schiff.
Financial data (yr. ended 06/30/01): Grants paid, $3,078,236; assets, $78,570,033 (M); gifts received, $22,648,123; expenditures, $3,119,018; qualifying distributions, $3,105,436.
Limitations: Applications not accepted. Giving primarily in Cincinnati, OH.
Application information: Contributes only to pre-selected organizations.
Officer: John J. Schiff, Jr., Chair.
Trustees: Suzanne Reid, Thomas R. Schiff.
EIN: 311077222
Codes: FD

42228
Louis D. Kacalieff Foundation
1111 Superior Ave., Ste. 1000
Cleveland, OH 44114-2507

Established in 1994 in OH.
Donor(s): Louis D. Kacalieff.

Financial data (yr. ended 12/31/01): Grants paid, $3,000,000; assets, $239,053 (M); gifts received, $1,550,000; expenditures, $3,024,751; qualifying distributions, $3,010,138.
Limitations: Applications not accepted. Giving primarily in Cleveland, OH.
Application information: Contributes only to pre-selected organizations.
Officers and Trustees:* James N. Dietrich,* Pres.; Phillip A. Ranney,* V.P. and Secy.; Charles F. Adler,* Treas.
EIN: 341726699
Codes: FD

42229
The Hood/Meyerson Foundation
791 Wye Rd.
Akron, OH 44333-2268

Established in 1997 in OH.
Financial data (yr. ended 12/31/01): Grants paid, $2,998,281; assets, $99,718 (M); gifts received, $1,774,250; expenditures, $3,143,256; qualifying distributions, $3,025,194.
Limitations: Giving limited to southwest FL and northeast OH.
Application information: Application form not required.
Officers and Trustees:* Robert F. Meyerson,* Chair.; Alex L. Csiszar, Pres.; Elizabeth S. Murphy,* V.P. and Secy.; Andrew S. Meyerson,* V.P.; Elinor M. Culotta, Treas.
EIN: 311559249
Codes: FD

42230
Dana Corporation Foundation
P.O. Box 1000
Toledo, OH 43697 (419) 535-4500
Contact: Ed McNeal

Incorporated in 1956 in OH.
Donor(s): Dana Corp.
Financial data (yr. ended 03/31/01): Grants paid, $2,879,492; assets, $10,760,175 (M); expenditures, $2,943,552; qualifying distributions, $2,871,131.
Limitations: Giving primarily in areas of company operations.
Publications: Informational brochure (including application guidelines).
Application information: Application form not required.
Officers and Directors:* Joe Magliochetti, Pres.; Tony Shelbourn,* V.P.; Joe Stancati,* Secy.; Rebecca Judis,* Treas.; Bob Fesenmyer, Cheryl Kline, Mike Laisure, Anne Marie Riley.
EIN: 346544909
Codes: CS, FD, CD

42231
Western-Southern Enterprise Fund
(Formerly Western-Southern Foundation, Inc.)
400 Broadway
Cincinnati, OH 45202 (513) 629-2121
Contact: Richard K. Taulbee

Established in 1988 in OH.
Donor(s): Western & Southern Life Insurance Co., Columbus Life.
Financial data (yr. ended 12/31/00): Grants paid, $2,855,962; assets, $62,345,188 (M); gifts received, $7,900; expenditures, $2,892,308; qualifying distributions, $2,892,308.
Trustees: John F. Barrett, Thomas L. Williams, William J. Williams.
EIN: 311259670
Codes: CS, FD, CD

42232
The John Huntington Fund for Education
20620 N. Park Blvd., Ste. 215
Cleveland, OH 44118 (216) 321-7185
Contact: Ann O. Pinkerton, Treas.

Incorporated in 1954 in OH.
Donor(s): John Huntington.‡
Financial data (yr. ended 12/31/01): Grants paid, $2,790,000; assets, $45,043,149 (M); expenditures, $2,960,959; qualifying distributions, $2,817,671.
Limitations: Giving limited to Cuyahoga County, OH.
Application information: Application form not required.
Officers and Trustees:* Peter W. Adams,* Pres.; Oakley Andrews,* Secy.; Ann O. Pinkerton,* Treas.; Albert J. Abramovitz, Chandler Everett, Robert M. Ginn, Karen R. Nestor, Leigh H. Perkins, Lyman Treadway.
EIN: 340714434
Codes: FD

42233
FirstEnergy Foundation
(Formerly Centerior Energy Foundation)
76 S. Main St.
Akron, OH 44308 (330) 761-4246
URL: http://www.firstenergycorp.com/community
Contact: Donna Valentine, Mgr.

Incorporated in 1961 in OH.
Donor(s): The Cleveland Electric Illuminating Co., Centerior Energy Corp., FirstEnergy Corp., The Toledo Edison Co.
Financial data (yr. ended 12/31/01): Grants paid, $2,699,470; assets, $62,311,815 (M); expenditures, $2,705,993; qualifying distributions, $2,698,465.
Limitations: Giving limited to areas served in NJ, OH, and PA.
Publications: Program policy statement, informational brochure.
Application information: Application form not required.
Officer and Trustees:* Mary Beth Carroll,* Pres.; H. Pete Burg, Earl T. Carey, Richard Marsh.
EIN: 346514181
Codes: CS, FD, CD

42234
Blankemeyer Foundation, Inc.
524 Hunters Run
Bluffton, OH 45817-1233

Established in 1994 in OH.
Donor(s): James C. Blankemeyer.
Financial data (yr. ended 12/31/00): Grants paid, $2,695,859; assets, $12,050,968 (M); gifts received, $1,420,000; expenditures, $2,734,714; qualifying distributions, $2,695,859.
Limitations: Applications not accepted. Giving on a national basis.
Application information: Contributes only to pre-selected organizations.
Officers and Directors:* James Blankemeyer,* Pres. and Treas.; Carolyn Blankemeyer, V.P.; Julie Breidenbaugh,* Secy.; Bruce Blankemeyer, Janelle Blankemeyer, Jeff Blankemeyer, Keith Blankemeyer, Kevin Blankemeyer, Mark J. Blankemeyer, Sarah Blankemeyer, Shanna Blankemeyer, Gary Bridenbaugh, Dewayne Brinkman, Mary Brinkman, Amy J. Cox, Michael Cox.
EIN: 582086417
Codes: FD

42235
Charles H. Dater Foundation, Inc.
302 Gwynne Bldg.
602 Main St., Ste. 302
Cincinnati, OH 45202 (513) 241-2658
E-mail: info@DaterFoundation.org; URL: http://www.daterfoundation.org
Contact: Bruce A. Krone, Secy.

Established in 1985 in OH.
Financial data (yr. ended 08/31/01): Grants paid, $2,633,500; assets, $51,474,475 (M); expenditures, $3,830,800; qualifying distributions, $3,283,849.
Limitations: Giving primarily in the greater Cincinnati, OH, area.
Publications: Multi-year report, application guidelines.
Application information: Application form required.
Officers and Directors:* David L. Olberding,* Pres.; Dorothy G. Krone,* V.P.; John D. Silvati,* V.P.; Bruce A. Krone,* Secy.; Stanley J. Frank, Jr.,* Treas.
EIN: 311150951
Codes: FD

42236
The Ireland Foundation
c/o H & I Advisors
1030 Hanna Bldg., 1422 Euclid Ave.
Cleveland, OH 44115-2004 (216) 363-1033
Contact: Louise Ireland Humphrey, Pres.

Incorporated in 1951 in OH.
Donor(s): Margaret Allen Ireland,‡ R. Livingston Ireland,‡ Kate Ireland, and members of the Ireland family.
Financial data (yr. ended 12/31/01): Grants paid, $2,627,000; assets, $1,797,270 (M); expenditures, $2,741,928; qualifying distributions, $2,626,459.
Limitations: Giving on a national basis.
Application information: Funds committed to the same charities each year; foundation rarely considers new appeals.
Officers and Trustees:* Louise Ireland Humphrey,* Pres.; Kate Ireland, V.P.; R.L. Ireland, Jr., V.P.; Carole M. Nowak, Secy.; R.L. Ireland III,* Treas.
EIN: 346525817
Codes: FD

42237
The Olive Branch Foundation, Inc.
P.O. Box 20881
Canton, OH 44701 (330) 456-7900

Established in 1998 in OH.
Donor(s): Marshall B. Belden, Jr.
Financial data (yr. ended 12/31/01): Grants paid, $2,561,660; assets, $4,524,640 (M); gifts received, $2,252,850; expenditures, $2,601,362; qualifying distributions, $2,550,576.
Limitations: Applications not accepted. Giving primarily in OH.
Application information: Unsolicited requests for funds not accepted.
Trustees: Diana Davis Belden, Marshall B. Belden, Jr., James Bagnola.
EIN: 341862239
Codes: FD

42238
Marietta Community Foundation
215 5th St.
P.O. Box 77
Marietta, OH 45750-0077 (740) 376-4380
FAX: (740) 376-4490; E-mail: mcf@marietta.edu; URL: http://www.mariettacommunityfoundation.org
Contact: Bret N. Bicoy, C.E.O.

Established in 1974 in OH.
Donor(s): Lillian Strecker Smith,‡ Mrs. William Mildren, Sr.,‡ Carl L. Broughton,‡ William Mildren, Sr., Jane McCoy Peterson, Susan Marsch.
Financial data (yr. ended 12/31/01): Grants paid, $2,555,735; assets, $6,581,189 (L); gifts received, $794,107; expenditures, $2,670,962.
Limitations: Giving limited to the Marietta, OH, area, including Washington County, OH, and Wood County, WV.
Publications: Annual report, application guidelines, occasional report, informational brochure (including application guidelines), newsletter.
Application information: Application form required.
Officers and Directors:* Teri Ann Zide,* Chair.; John Moberg,* Vice-Chair.; Bret N. Bicoy, C.E.O. and Pres.; William Fields,* Secy.; Mark Schwendeman,* Treas.; David Barrett, Ron Bishop, Michael Iaderosa, Robert E. Kirkbride, Karen Osborne, William Thompson, Bonnie Witten.
EIN: 237359721
Codes: CM, FD, GTI

42239
Kulas Foundation
50 Public Sq., Terminal Tower, Ste. 924
Cleveland, OH 44113-2203 (216) 623-4770
FAX: (216) 623-4773; URL: http://fdncenter.org/grantmaker/kulas
Contact: Allan J. Zambie, V.P. and Secy.

Incorporated in 1937 in OH.
Donor(s): Fynette H. Kulas,‡ E.J. Kulas.‡
Financial data (yr. ended 12/31/01): Grants paid, $2,518,135; assets, $37,246,781 (M); gifts received, $404,619; expenditures, $2,919,979; qualifying distributions, $2,704,873.
Limitations: Giving limited to Cuyahoga County, OH, and its contiguous counties.
Publications: Application guidelines, informational brochure (including application guidelines).
Application information: Special policy on Music Therapy - telephone for information. Application form required.
Officers and Trustees:* Richard W. Pogue,* Chair.; Nancy McCann,* Pres. and Treas.; Allan J. Zambie, V.P. and Secy.; Patrick F. McCartan,* V.P.
EIN: 340770687
Codes: FD

42240
John F. and Doris E. Ernsthausen Charitable Foundation
c/o Citizens National Bank
12 E. Main St.
Norwalk, OH 44857-1542
Application address: 13 E. Main St., Ste. B, Norwalk, OH 44857, tel.: (419) 668-2067
Contact: Frederick F. Waugh

Trust established in 1956 in OH.
Donor(s): John F. Ernsthausen, Doris E. Ernsthausen.
Financial data (yr. ended 06/30/01): Grants paid, $2,462,381; assets, $9,555,338 (M); expenditures, $2,508,840; qualifying distributions, $2,439,929.
Limitations: Giving primarily in OH.
Application information: Application form not required.
Trustee: Citizens National Bank.
EIN: 346501908
Codes: FD

42241
The Abington Foundation
c/o Foundation Mgmt. Svcs., Inc.
1422 Euclid Ave., Ste. 627
Cleveland, OH 44115-1952 (216) 621-2901
FAX: (216) 621-8198; E-mail: cstarkey@fmscleveland.com; URL: http://www.fmscleveland.com/abington
Contact: Janet E. Narten, Consultant

Established in 1983 in OH.
Donor(s): David Knight Ford,‡ Elizabeth Brooks Ford.‡
Financial data (yr. ended 12/31/01): Grants paid, $2,455,087; assets, $39,935,046 (M); expenditures, $2,836,364; qualifying distributions, $2,577,416.
Limitations: Giving primarily in Cleveland, OH.
Publications: Annual report (including application guidelines).
Application information: Application form not required.
Officers and Trustees:* Amasa B. Ford, M.D.,* Pres.; Allen H. Ford,* V.P. and Treas.; David Kingsley Ford,* V.P.; Oliver M. Ford,* V.P.; David Ford, Jr., Hope Ford Murphy, Katharine Ford, Ned Ford.
EIN: 341404854
Codes: FD

42242
The Harry C. Moores Foundation
100 S. 3rd St.
Columbus, OH 43215 (614) 227-8884
Contact: Mary B. Cummins

Trust established in 1961 in OH.
Donor(s): Harry C. Moores.‡
Financial data (yr. ended 09/30/00): Grants paid, $2,432,577; assets, $45,879,158 (M); expenditures, $2,516,422; qualifying distributions, $2,385,977.
Limitations: Giving primarily in the Columbus, OH, area.
Publications: Application guidelines.
Application information: Application form required.
Trustees: John P. Beavers, Neil B. Distelhorst, Cris J. Gillespie, Ronald D. Rardon, Kristen Sydney.
EIN: 316035344
Codes: FD

42243
Manuel D. & Rhoda Mayerson Foundation
312 Walnut St., Ste. 3600
Cincinnati, OH 45202 (513) 621-7500
FAX: (513) 621-2864; E-mail: applications@mayersonfoundation.org; URL: http://www.mayersonfoundation.org
Contact: Dr. Neal H. Mayerson, Pres.

Established in 1986 in FL.
Donor(s): Manuel D. Mayerson, Rhoda Mayerson.
Financial data (yr. ended 10/31/01): Grants paid, $2,423,028; assets, $20,919,827 (M); gifts received, $7,528,774; expenditures, $2,897,204; qualifying distributions, $2,821,482.
Limitations: Giving primarily in Cincinnati, OH.
Publications: Informational brochure (including application guidelines).
Application information: Greater Cincinnati Common Grant Application Form preferred. Application form required.

42243—OHIO

Officer and Trustees:* Neal H. Mayerson, Ph.D.,* Pres.; Arlene B. Mayerson, Donna Mayerson, Ph.D., Frederic H. Mayerson, Manuel D. Mayerson, Rhoda Mayerson.
EIN: 311310431
Codes: FD

42244
The American Foundation Corporation
720 National City Bank Bldg.
Cleveland, OH 44114 (216) 241-6664

Incorporated in 1974 as successor to trust established in 1944 in OH.
Donor(s): Members of the Corning family, and members of the Murfey family.
Financial data (yr. ended 12/31/01): Grants paid, $2,373,755; assets, $36,566,052 (M); gifts received, $24,736; expenditures, $2,545,608; qualifying distributions, $2,415,615.
Limitations: Applications not accepted. Giving primarily in CA and in the Cleveland, OH, area.
Publications: Annual report.
Application information: Contributes only to pre-selected organizations. Funds presently committed.
Officers and Trustees:* William W. Murfey,* Pres.; Spencer L. Murfey, Jr., V.P.; Maria G. Muth, Secy.-Treas.; Dwight B. Corning, Spencer Murfey.
EIN: 237348126
Codes: FD

42245
The Stocker Foundation
559 Broadway Ave., 2nd Fl.
Lorain, OH 44052 (440) 246-5719
FAX: (440) 246-5720; E-mail: pobrien@stockerfoundation.org or mwilson@stockerfoundation.org; URL: http://www.stockerfoundation.org
Contact: Patricia O'Brien, Exec. Dir.

Incorporated in 1979 in OH.
Donor(s): Beth K. Stocker.
Financial data (yr. ended 09/30/01): Grants paid, $2,331,696; assets, $39,420,343 (M); gifts received, $858,908; expenditures, $2,725,523; qualifying distributions, $2,293,269.
Limitations: Giving primarily in southern AZ (Cochise, Pima, and Santa Cruz counties), Dona Ana County, NM, and Lorain County, OH.
Publications: Annual report (including application guidelines), informational brochure.
Application information: Proposals received by FAX not considered; proposals exceeding 10 pages will not be reviewed. Cover sheet required.
Officers and Trustees:* Beth K. Stocker,* Pres.; Jane Norton,* Secy.-Treas.; Sue Woodling, Secy.; Patricia O'Brien, Exec. Dir.; Mary Ann Dobras, Benjamin P. Norton, Bradley S. Norton, Brent Norton, Anne Woodling, Nancy Elizabeth Woodling.
Corporate Trustee: KeyBank, N.A.
EIN: 341293603
Codes: FD

42246
The Wolfson Charitable Foundation
20707 Chagrin Blvd., Ste. 100
Shaker Heights, OH 44122

Established in 1998 in OH.
Donor(s): Warren L. Wolfson.
Financial data (yr. ended 11/30/00): Grants paid, $2,300,458; assets, $0 (M); gifts received, $58,119; expenditures, $2,301,259; qualifying distributions, $2,300,458.
Limitations: Applications not accepted. Giving primarily in Cleveland, OH.
Application information: Contributes only to pre-selected organizations.
Trustees: Kimberly Wolfson, Ruth Wolfson, Warren L. Wolfson.
EIN: 341879658
Codes: FD

42247
The Parker-Hannifin Foundation
6035 Parkland Blvd.
Cleveland, OH 44124 (216) 896-3000
Contact: Thomas A. Piraino, V.P.

Incorporated in 1953 in OH.
Donor(s): Parker-Hannifin Corp.
Financial data (yr. ended 06/30/01): Grants paid, $2,279,492; assets, $211,558 (M); gifts received, $2,280,497; expenditures, $2,279,573; qualifying distributions, $2,279,492.
Limitations: Applications not accepted. Giving primarily in areas of company operations.
Officers and Trustees:* Duane E. Collins, Chair.; D.E. Washkewicz,* C.E.O. and Pres.; Thomas A. Piraino,* V.P., Secy. and Genl. Counsel.
EIN: 346555686
Codes: CS, FD, CD

42248
El-An Foundation
1800 Moler Rd.
Columbus, OH 43207-1680

Incorporated in 1957 in OH.
Donor(s): Schottenstein Stores Corp., Value City Furniture, Inc., W.M. Whitney & Co., Elyria City, Inc., Geraldine Schottenstein.
Financial data (yr. ended 12/31/00): Grants paid, $2,274,052; assets, $6,839,341 (M); gifts received, $1,962,566; expenditures, $2,274,452; qualifying distributions, $2,274,452.
Limitations: Giving primarily in OH, with emphasis on Columbus.
Officers: Geraldine Schottenstein, Chair.; Saul Schottenstein, Vice-Chair.; Jay L. Schottenstein, Secy.-Treas.
EIN: 316050597
Codes: FD

42249
Montgomery Foundation
Roscoe Village
Coshocton, OH 43812
Application address: 365 N. Whitewoman St., Coshocton, OH 43812; FAX: (740) 622-4838
Contact: Linda M. Scott

Established in 1972 in OH.
Donor(s): Edward E. Montgomery,‡ Frances B. Montgomery.‡
Financial data (yr. ended 12/31/01): Grants paid, $2,259,000; assets, $28,222,000 (M); expenditures, $2,515,783; qualifying distributions, $2,259,000.
Limitations: Giving primarily in Coshocton, OH.
Publications: Application guidelines.
Application information: Application form not required.
Officers and Trustees:* Richard E. Corbett,* Pres.; Suzanne Bowen,* V.P.; William Dutton, Secy.; Robert Simpson, Treas.; Joseph S. Montgomery, Scott Montgomery.
EIN: 237165768
Codes: FD, FM

42250
James M. Cox, Jr. Foundation, Inc.
4th and Ludlow Sts.
Dayton, OH 45402 (678) 645-0602
Application address: c/o Cox Enterprises, Inc., P.O. Box 105720, Atlanta, GA 30348
Contact: Leigh Ann Launius, Asst. Secy.

Established in 1969 in GA.
Donor(s): James M. Cox, Jr.‡
Financial data (yr. ended 12/31/01): Grants paid, $2,234,000; assets, $47,141,019 (M); expenditures, $2,424,348; qualifying distributions, $2,234,000.
Limitations: Giving limited to cities where Cox Enterprises does business.
Publications: Application guidelines.
Application information: Application form not required.
Officers and Trustees:* Barbara Cox Anthony,* Chair.; Timothy W. Hughes,* V.P.; Andrew A. Merdek, Secy.; John G. Bayette, Treas.; Richard Braunstein, James Cox Kennedy, Leigh Ann Launius.
EIN: 237256190
Codes: FD

42251
Bremer Foundation
c/o James E. Mitchell
Mahoning Bank Bldg., Ste. 1200
Youngstown, OH 44503

Incorporated in 1953 in OH.
Donor(s): Richard P. Bremer.‡
Financial data (yr. ended 12/31/01): Grants paid, $2,200,000; assets, $338,856 (M); expenditures, $2,229,663; qualifying distributions, $2,180,390.
Limitations: Applications not accepted. Giving primarily in OH.
Application information: Contributes only to pre-selected organizations.
Officers: Joan L. McCoy, Pres.; Henry G. Cramblett, M.D., V.P.; James E. Mitchell, Secy.; George Woodman, Secy.-Treas.
Trustee: Jeffery Bremer, George J. Limbert, Neil H. Maxwell.
EIN: 346514168
Codes: FD

42252
The Sapirstein-Stone-Weiss Foundation
(Formerly The Jacob Sapirstein Foundation of Cleveland)
1 American Rd.
Cleveland, OH 44144 (216) 252-7300
Contact: Gary Weiss, V.P. and Secy.

Incorporated in 1952 in OH.
Donor(s): Jacob Sapirstein.‡
Financial data (yr. ended 05/31/01): Grants paid, $2,157,426; assets, $25,277,107 (M); expenditures, $2,465,201; qualifying distributions, $2,157,426.
Officers and Trustees:* Morry Weiss,* Pres.; Gary Weiss,* V.P. and Secy.; Zev Weiss, Treas.; Gary Lippe, Steven Tatar, Ellie Weiss, Jeffrey Weiss, Judith Weiss.
EIN: 346548007
Codes: FD

42253
Psalms Foundation
49 E. 4th St., Ste. 521
Cincinnati, OH 45202

Established in 1995 in OH.
Financial data (yr. ended 12/31/99): Grants paid, $2,137,000; assets, $857,271 (M); gifts received, $4,397; expenditures, $2,162,895; qualifying distributions, $2,119,971.

Limitations: Applications not accepted.
Application information: Contributes only to pre-selected organizations.
Officers and Trustees:* Carl H. Lindner III,* Pres. and Treas.; Martha S. Lindner,* V.P. and Secy.; Michael S. Cambron, John T. Lawrence.
EIN: 311404734
Codes: FD

42254
The Murdough Foundation
(Formerly Thomas G. & Joy P. Murdough Foundation)
P.O. Box 2134
Hudson, OH 44236-0134
Application address: 195 S. Main St., Ste. 300, Akron, OH 44308-1314, tel.: (330) 762-7377
Contact: William M. Oldham, Tr.

Established in 1984.
Donor(s): Thomas G. Murdough, Jr.
Financial data (yr. ended 12/31/01): Grants paid, $2,123,000; assets, $8,581,447 (M); expenditures, $2,186,107; qualifying distributions, $2,121,257.
Limitations: Giving primarily in OH, with emphasis on northeastern OH.
Application information: Application form not required.
Officers and Trustees:* Thomas G. Murdough, Jr.,* Pres. and Treas.; Joy P. Murdough,* Secy.; William M. Oldham.
EIN: 341454379
Codes: FD

42255
Kenneth A. Scott Charitable Trust
c/o KeyBank, N.A.
127 Public Sq., 17th Fl.
Cleveland, OH 44114-1306 (216) 556-4062
Contact: H. Richard Obermanns, Exec. Dir.

Established in 1995 in OH.
Financial data (yr. ended 08/31/01): Grants paid, $2,116,330; assets, $19,653,772 (M); expenditures, $2,358,906; qualifying distributions, $2,183,299.
Limitations: Giving primarily in OH for local organizations; giving outside OH only for national organizations.
Publications: Application guidelines, annual report.
Trustee: KeyBank, N.A.
EIN: 347034544
Codes: FD

42256
The Jochum-Moll Foundation
P.O. Box 368022
Cleveland, OH 44136-9722

Incorporated in 1961 in OH.
Donor(s): MTD Products, Inc., and its subsidiaries.
Financial data (yr. ended 07/31/01): Grants paid, $2,112,500; assets, $28,403,541 (M); gifts received, $129,399; expenditures, $2,313,389; qualifying distributions, $2,106,484.
Limitations: Applications not accepted. Giving primarily in Cleveland, OH.
Application information: Contributes only to pre-selected organizations.
Officers and Trustees:* Carol B. Manning,* Pres.; Theo S. Moll,* V.P.; David J. Hessler,* Secy.; Curtis E. Moll,* Treas.; Emil Jochum, Darrell Moll.
EIN: 346538304
Codes: CS, FD, CD

42257
Forest City Enterprises Charitable Foundation, Inc.
1100 Terminal Tower, 50 Public Sq., Ste. 1100
Cleveland, OH 44113 (216) 621-6060
Contact: Allan Krulak, Dir., Community Affairs

Trust established in 1976 in OH.
Donor(s): Forest City Enterprises, Inc.
Financial data (yr. ended 01/31/01): Grants paid, $2,110,549; assets, $255,813 (M); gifts received, $2,208,500; expenditures, $2,110,634; qualifying distributions, $2,110,634.
Limitations: Giving primarily in OH.
Application information: Application form not required.
Officers and Trustees:* Charles Ratner,* Pres.; Samuel H. Miller, V.P. and Treas.; Thomas G. Smith, Secy.; J. Struchun.
EIN: 341218895
Codes: CS, FD, CD

42258
The Lubrizol Foundation
29400 Lakeland Blvd., No. 053A
Wickliffe, OH 44092 (440) 347-5080
FAX: (440) 347-1858; *E-mail:* Kmi@lubrizol.com; *URL:* http://www.lubrizol.com/foundation/default.htm
Contact: K.M. Iwashita, Pres., Secy., and C.O.O.

Incorporated in 1952 in OH.
Donor(s): The Lubrizol Corp.
Financial data (yr. ended 12/31/01): Grants paid, $2,106,556; assets, $18,308,413 (M); expenditures, $2,169,380; qualifying distributions, $2,040,670.
Limitations: Giving primarily in areas of major company operations, particularly the greater Cleveland, OH, and Houston, TX, areas.
Publications: Annual report (including application guidelines).
Application information: Application form not required.
Officers and Trustees:* George R. Hill,* Chair. and C.E.O.; Kenneth M. Iwashita,* Pres., Secy., and C.O.O.; Kenneth J. Marr, Treas.; W.G. Bares, Stephen A. DiBiase, Joe E. Hodge, Kenneth H. Hopping, C.W. Jones, Mark W. Meister, L.K. Naylor, J.L. Petric, J. Robinson, M.F. Salomon, D.H. Sheets, J.M. Sutherland.
EIN: 346500595
Codes: CS, FD, CD

42259
Richland County Foundation
(Formerly The Richland County Foundation of Mansfield, Ohio)
24 W. 3rd St., Ste. 100
Mansfield, OH 44902-1209 (419) 525-3020
FAX: (419) 525-1590; *E-mail:* info@rcfoundation.org; *URL:* http://www.rcfoundation.org
Contact: Pamela H. Siegenthaler, C.E.O.

Incorporated in 1945 in OH.
Financial data (yr. ended 12/31/01): Grants paid, $2,080,697; assets, $57,517,585 (M); gifts received, $1,451,661; expenditures, $2,468,172.
Limitations: Giving primarily in Richland County, OH.
Publications: Annual report (including application guidelines), application guidelines, newsletter, informational brochure.
Application information: Scholarship applications available on website. Application form required.
Officers and Trustees:* Richard S. Cummins,* Chair.; Rev. Clifford Schutjer,* Vice-Chair.; Pamela H. Siegenthaler, C.E.O. and Pres.; J. Jeffrey Heck,* Secy.; Deborah M. Schenk,* Treas.; Col. Daniel G. Arnold, Suzanne C. Davis, Thomas A. Depler, Gary D. Feagin, Katherine N. Fernyak, Gayle Gorman Freeman, Lawrence L. Gibson, M.D., Catherine D. Goldman, William J. Hartnett, Lt. Col. Michael Howard, Edith B. Humphrey, E. William McCarrick, Carol E. Payton, Linda H. Smith, Rev. Wray C. Smith, D.D., Rick B. Taylor, John W. Welsh, J. George Williams.
Trustee Banks: Bank One, Mansfield, N.A., KeyBank, N.A., National City Bank, Columbus, Richland Bank, Mansfield.
EIN: 340872883
Codes: CM, FD, GTI

42260
Lois and Richard Rosenthal Foundation
123 E. Liberty St.
Cincinnati, OH 45208
Application address: 1507 Dana Ave., Cincinnati, OH 45207, tel.: (513) 531-2222
Contact: Richard Rosenthal, Tr.

Established in 1986 in OH.
Donor(s): Richard Rosenthal, Lois Rosenthal.
Financial data (yr. ended 12/31/00): Grants paid, $2,043,833; assets, $5,671,338 (M); gifts received, $4,097,898; expenditures, $2,081,564; qualifying distributions, $2,027,302.
Limitations: Giving primarily in the Cincinnati, OH, area.
Trustees: Jennie D. Berliant, David S. Rosenthal, Lois R. Rosenthal, Richard H. Rosenthal.
EIN: 311203666
Codes: FD

42261
Paul P. Tell Foundation, Inc.
195 S. Main St., Ste. 200
Akron, OH 44308 (330) 434-8355
Contact: David J. Schipper, Exec. Dir.

Incorporated in 1952 in OH.
Donor(s): Anne P. Tell, David J. Schipper, Michael Tell, Tell family members, and their business interests.
Financial data (yr. ended 12/31/00): Grants paid, $2,027,000; assets, $24,807,998 (M); expenditures, $2,224,654; qualifying distributions, $2,027,000.
Limitations: Giving on a national basis.
Application information: Application form not required.
Officers: David J. Schipper, Pres. and Exec. Dir.; Peter Keslar, V.P.; Jean Anne Schipper, Secy.-Treas.
Trustees: David Fair, Terry Hollister, Anne P. Tell, Michael Tell, Brenda Unruh.
EIN: 346537201
Codes: FD

42262
OMNOVA Solutions Foundation Inc.
175 Ghent Rd.
Fairlawn, OH 44333-3300 (330) 869-4289
FAX: (330) 869-4345; *E-mail:* theresa.carter@omnova.com; *URL:* http://www.omnova.com/commfr.htm
Contact: Theresa Carter, Dir.

Established in 1999.
Financial data (yr. ended 11/30/01): Grants paid, $2,000,089; assets, $30,714,659 (M); expenditures, $2,331,145; qualifying distributions, $2,097,989.
Limitations: Giving primarily in areas of company operations in AL, GA, MA, MS, NC, NH, OH, PA, SC, and WI.
Publications: Annual report, application guidelines.
Application information: Application form not required.

42262—OHIO

Officers and Trustees:* Gregory T. Troy,* Pres.; Kristine C. Syrvalin,* Secy.; Frank Robers,* Treas.; Michael E. Hicks, Sandra Klaasse, Barry Rosenbaum.
Director: Theresa Carter, Dir.
EIN: 341909350
Codes: CS, FD, CD

42263
The Foundation for the Continuity of Mankind
71963 Lodge Rd.
Freeport, OH 43973-8908

Established in 1989 in OH.
Donor(s): Floyd E. Kimble.‡
Financial data (yr. ended 12/31/01): Grants paid, $1,900,000; assets, $48,301,798 (M); expenditures, $2,366,989; qualifying distributions, $2,186,424; giving activities include $233,525 for programs.
Limitations: Applications not accepted. Giving primarily in OH.
Application information: Contributes only to pre-selected organizations.
Trustees: Doris Kimble, Greg Kimble, Phillip Raber.
EIN: 341622273
Codes: FD

42264
National Machinery Foundation, Inc.
161 Greenfield St.
P.O. Box 747
Tiffin, OH 44883 (419) 447-5211
Contact: Don Bero, Admin.

Incorporated in 1948 in OH.
Donor(s): National Machinery Co.
Financial data (yr. ended 12/31/00): Grants paid, $1,871,700; assets, $15,114,580 (M); expenditures, $718,429; qualifying distributions, $1,924,334.
Limitations: Giving primarily in Seneca County and Tiffin, OH.
Application information: Application form not required.
Officers: A.H. Kalnow, Chair.; P.N. Aley, Pres.; L.F. Baker, V.P.; D.B. Bero, Secy.-Treas.
Trustees: M.P. Hilmer, C.F. Kalnow, N.E. Martin.
EIN: 346520191
Codes: CS, FD, CD, GTI

42265
The Nordson Corporation Foundation
28601 Clemens Rd.
Westlake, OH 44145-1119 (440) 892-1580
Additional tel.: (440) 988-9411; FAX: (216) 892-9253; URL: http://www.nordson.com/corporate/grants.html
Contact: Constance T. Haqq, Exec. Dir.

Established in 1988 in OH.
Donor(s): Nordson Corp.
Financial data (yr. ended 10/31/00): Grants paid, $1,862,460; assets, $4,776,224 (M); gifts received, $800,000; expenditures, $1,932,038; qualifying distributions, $1,880,375.
Limitations: Giving limited to San Diego County, CA, Atlanta, GA, northern OH, and the Providence, RI, area.
Publications: Annual report (including application guidelines), grants list, corporate giving report.
Application information: Application form required.
Officer: Constance T. Haqq, Exec. Dir.
Trustees: Edward P. Campbell, Beverly J. Coen, Peter S. Hellman, Donald J. McLane.
EIN: 341596194
Codes: CS, FD, CD

42266
Britton Fund
c/o Advisory Svcs., Inc.
1422 Euclid Ave., 1010 Hanna Bldg.
Cleveland, OH 44115-2078 (216) 363-6489
Contact: Nick Valentino, Treas.

Incorporated in 1952 in OH.
Donor(s): Gertrude H. Britton,‡ Charles S. Britton II,‡ Brigham Britton.‡
Financial data (yr. ended 12/31/01): Grants paid, $1,818,600; assets, $25,610,926 (L); expenditures, $1,955,688; qualifying distributions, $1,835,232.
Limitations: Giving primarily in OH.
Publications: Annual report.
Application information: Funds substantially committed. Application form not required.
Officers and Trustees:* Lynda R. Britton,* Pres.; Terence B. Britton,* V.P.; Timothy C. Britton,* V.P.; Gloria Kirkwood, Secy.; Nick Valentino, Treas.
EIN: 346513616
Codes: FD, FM

42267
The Harold and Helen McMaster Foundation, Inc.
c/o SJS Investment Consulting
6711 Monroe St., Bldg. 4, Ste. A
Sylvania, OH 43560 (419) 885-2626
Contact: Scott Savage or Patricia Lopez

Established in 1988 in OH.
Donor(s): Harold A. McMaster, Helen E. McMaster.
Financial data (yr. ended 11/30/00): Grants paid, $1,800,282; assets, $8,949,297 (M); expenditures, $1,909,772; qualifying distributions, $1,784,698.
Limitations: Giving primarily in OH.
Publications: Application guidelines.
Application information: Application form required.
Officers: Harold A. McMaster, Pres. and Treas.; Helen E. McMaster, V.P. and Secy.
Trustee: Nancy Cobie, Jeanine Dunn, Frank Jacobs, Alan McMaster, Ronald A. McMaster.
EIN: 341576110
Codes: FD

42268
The Dayton Power and Light Company Foundation
Courthouse Plz., S.W.
P.O. Box 1247
Dayton, OH 45401 (937) 259-7131
FAX: (937) 259-7245
Contact: Ginny Strausburg, Admin.

Established in 1984 in OH.
Donor(s): The Dayton Power and Light Co.
Financial data (yr. ended 12/31/00): Grants paid, $1,797,879; assets, $45,408,169 (M); gifts received, $12,504,041; expenditures, $1,931,117; qualifying distributions, $1,857,622.
Limitations: Giving primarily in west central OH.
Publications: Informational brochure (including application guidelines).
Application information: Application form not required.
Officers and Trustees:* Stephen F. Kozair,* Pres.; Judy W. Lansaw,* Secy.; Thomas M. Jenkins,* Treas.
EIN: 311138883
Codes: CS, FD, CD

42269
Charlotte R. Schmidlapp Fund
(Formerly C. Schmidlapp Fund)
38 Fountain Sq. Plz., M.D. 109067
Cincinnati, OH 45263 (513) 534-7001
Contact: Lawra J. Baumann, Fdn. Off., Fifth Third Bank

Trust established in 1908 in OH.
Donor(s): Jacob G. Schmidlapp.‡
Financial data (yr. ended 09/30/01): Grants paid, $1,778,753; assets, $30,286,186 (M); expenditures, $2,021,433; qualifying distributions, $1,861,996.
Limitations: Giving primarily in Cincinnati, OH.
Publications: Annual report, application guidelines.
Application information: Application form not required.
Trustee: Fifth Third Bank.
EIN: 310532641
Codes: FD

42270
Edward M. Wilson Family Foundation
c/o National City Bank of Indiana
P.O. Box 94651
Cleveland, OH 44101-4651
Application address: c/o National City Bank of Indiana, P.O. Box 110, Fort Wayne, IN 46801, tel.: (219) 461-6218
Contact: Teresa Tracey

Established around 1980 in IN.
Donor(s): William Telfer.
Financial data (yr. ended 09/30/00): Grants paid, $1,759,441; assets, $41,227,885 (M); expenditures, $2,056,867; qualifying distributions, $1,825,414.
Limitations: Giving primarily in Fort Wayne, IN.
Trustee: National City Bank of Indiana.
EIN: 310976337
Codes: FD

42271
Carl H. Lindner Foundation
49 E. 4th St., Ste. 521
Cincinnati, OH 45202-3808

Established in 1993 in OH.
Donor(s): Carl H. Lindner, Jr.
Financial data (yr. ended 12/31/01): Grants paid, $1,752,500; assets, $15,976,400 (M); gifts received, $2,378; expenditures, $1,759,397; qualifying distributions, $1,750,437.
Limitations: Applications not accepted. Giving primarily in Cincinnati, OH.
Application information: Contributes only to pre-selected organizations.
Officers and Trustees:* Carl H. Lindner, Jr.,* Pres.; Edyth B. Lindner,* V.P.; Joseph A. Pedoto,* Secy.
EIN: 310738034
Codes: FD

42272
The Perkins Charitable Foundation
1030 Hanna Bldg.
1422 Euclid Ave.
Cleveland, OH 44115 (216) 621-0465
Contact: Marilyn Best, Secy.-Treas.

Trust established in 1950 in OH.
Donor(s): Leigh H. Perkins, Sallie Sullivan, Members of the Perkins family.
Financial data (yr. ended 12/31/01): Grants paid, $1,735,750; assets, $29,832,061 (M); expenditures, $1,822,978; qualifying distributions, $1,739,004.
Limitations: Giving on a national basis.
Application information: Application form not required.

Officer: Marilyn Best, Secy.-Treas.
Trustees: George Oliva III, Leigh H. Perkins, Sallie P. Sullivan.
EIN: 346549753
Codes: FD

42273
The Louise H. and David S. Ingalls Foundation, Inc.
301 Tower E.
20600 Chagrin Blvd.
Shaker Heights, OH 44122   (216) 921-6000
Contact: Jane W. Watson

Incorporated in 1953 in OH.
Donor(s): Louise H. Ingalls,‡ Edith Ingalls Vignos, Louise Ingalls Brown,‡ David S. Ingalls,‡ David S. Ingalls, Jr.,‡ Jane I. Davison, Anne I. Lawrence.
Financial data (yr. ended 12/31/01): Grants paid, $1,704,625; assets, $30,040,199 (M); expenditures, $1,798,973; qualifying distributions, $1,745,308.
Limitations: Giving on a national basis, primarily in Cleveland, OH.
Application information: Application form not required.
Officers and Trustees:* Barbara Brown,* Pres.; Nina S. Ingalls,* V.P.; Caren V. Sturges,* Secy.; John T. Lawrence III, Treas.; E.P. Davison, Jr., Anne I. Lawrence.
EIN: 346516550
Codes: FD

42274
The George H. Deuble Foundation
5757 Mayfair Rd.
P.O. Box 2288
North Canton, OH 44720   (330) 455-0610
Contact: Andrew H. Deuble, Secy.

Established in 1995 in OH.
Financial data (yr. ended 12/31/00): Grants paid, $1,690,061; assets, $32,582,412 (M); expenditures, $1,867,049; qualifying distributions, $1,708,965.
Officers and Trustees:* Steven G. Deuble,* Pres.; Andrew H. Deuble,* Secy.; Walter C. Deuble, Walter J. Deuble, Charles A. Morgan, Jr.
EIN: 341806245
Codes: FD

42275
The Thomas H. White No. 1 Trust
(also known as Thomas H. White Foundation)
c/o Foundation Mgmt. Svcs., Inc.
1422 Euclid Ave., Ste. 627
Cleveland, OH 44115-1952   (216) 696-7273
FAX: (216) 621-8198
Contact: Susan Althans, Exec. Dir.

Trust established in 1913 in OH; became active in 1939.
Donor(s): Thomas H. White.‡
Financial data (yr. ended 12/31/01): Grants paid, $1,673,554; assets, $22,551,720 (M); expenditures, $1,850,845; qualifying distributions, $1,726,393.
Limitations: Giving limited to Cuyahoga County, OH.
Publications: Annual report (including application guidelines).
Application information: Mass mailings not accepted. Application form not required.
Distribution Committee: Richard Buffett, Margot James Copeland, Linda Grandstaff, Ruben L. Holloway, Cindy Koury.
Trustee: KeyBank, N.A.
EIN: 346505722
Codes: FD

42276
George Edward Durell Foundation
623-J Park Meadow Rd.
Westerville, OH 43081-2873

Established in 1985 in VA.
Donor(s): George Edward Durell.‡
Financial data (yr. ended 12/31/01): Grants paid, $1,672,000; assets, $33,854,464 (M); expenditures, $909,134; qualifying distributions, $1,836,454.
Limitations: Applications not accepted. Giving on a national basis, with some emphasis on Columbus, OH, and VA.
Application information: Contributes only to pre-selected organizations. Unsolicited requests for funds not considered.
Officer and Trustees:* David A. Durell,* Chair.; James Landaker, Elizabeth Racer, Paul A. Schoonover, Alson H. Smith, William S. Weiant.
EIN: 311111800
Codes: FD

42277
R.T. Foundation
(Formerly Tomsich Foundation)
6140 Parkland Blvd.
Mayfield Heights, OH 44124-4187
(440) 461-6000

Donor(s): Robert J. Tomsich.
Financial data (yr. ended 12/31/99): Grants paid, $1,629,610; assets, $4,282,853 (M); expenditures, $1,707,151; qualifying distributions, $1,626,487.
Limitations: Applications not accepted. Giving primarily in Cleveland, OH.
Application information: Contributes only to pre-selected organizations.
Officer: Robert J. Tomsich, Pres.
EIN: 341537777
Codes: FD

42278
R. Templeton Smith Foundation
3001 Fairmount Blvd.
Cleveland Heights, OH 44118

Established in 1997 in OH.
Donor(s): Kennedy Smith, Jr.
Financial data (yr. ended 12/31/00): Grants paid, $1,611,700; assets, $5,623,868 (M); expenditures, $1,714,530; qualifying distributions, $1,668,758; giving activities include $60,000 for programs.
Limitations: Applications not accepted.
Application information: Contributes only to pre-selected organizations.
Officers: Frederick A. Smith, Pres.; Mark T. Smith, V.P.; Edward C. Smith, Secy.-Treas.
Trustees: Mary Smith Podles, Ann T. Seabright, Kennedy Smith, Jr.
EIN: 341823830
Codes: FD

42279
Licking County Foundation
25 Walnut St.
P.O. Box 4212
Newark, OH 43058-4212   (740) 349-3863
FAX: (740) 345-8138; E-mail: lcf@msmisp.com
Contact: Melynda R. Bagley, Exec. Dir.

Established in 1956 in OH.
Financial data (yr. ended 10/31/01): Grants paid, $1,569,163; assets, $27,634,745 (M); gifts received, $3,027,508; expenditures, $1,873,383.
Limitations: Giving limited to Licking County, OH.
Publications: Annual report (including application guidelines), informational brochure, newsletter.
Application information: Grant follow-up due in 90 days from check issue. Application form required.

Officers and Governing Committee:* Frank B. Murphy,* Chair.; Barbara M. Hammond,* Vice-Chair.; William S. Moore,* Secy. and Treas.; Melynda R. Bagley, Exec. Dir.; Ronald B. Alford, Robert A. Barnes, Robert H. Flory, Jr., J. Michael King, William T. McConnell, Christine Warner, James T. Young.
Trustee Banks: Bank One, N.A., National City Bank, The Park National Bank.
EIN: 316018618
Codes: CM, FD, GTI

42280
Paul & Maxine Frohring Foundation, Inc.
c/o R.A. Bumblis
1900 E. 9th St., Ste. 3200
Cleveland, OH 44114-3485
Contact: William W. Falsgraf, Secy.

Established in 1958 in OH.
Donor(s): Paul R. Frohring,‡ Maxine A. Frohring.‡
Financial data (yr. ended 12/31/01): Grants paid, $1,498,948; assets, $32,130,596 (M); expenditures, $1,551,860; qualifying distributions, $1,531,731.
Limitations: Giving primarily in OH.
Application information: Application form not required.
Officer and Trustees:* William W. Falsgraf,* Secy.; James Kushlan, Paula Frohring Kushlan.
EIN: 346513729
Codes: FD

42281
The Longaberger Foundation
1500 E. Main St.
Newark, OH 43055-8847   (740) 322-5039
FAX: (740) 322-5616
Contact: Matthew Elli, Dir.

Established in 1997 in OH.
Donor(s): The Longaberger Co.
Financial data (yr. ended 12/31/01): Grants paid, $1,474,072; assets, $10,188,062 (M); gifts received, $133,429; expenditures, $1,520,276; qualifying distributions, $1,485,759.
Limitations: Giving on a regional and national basis.
Officer: Rachel Longaberger, Pres.
EIN: 311575931
Codes: FD

42282
The NCR Foundation
(Formerly AT&T Global Information Solutions Foundation)
1700 S. Patterson Blvd.
Dayton, OH 45479   (937) 445-2577
Contact: M. Karr, V.P.

Incorporated in 1953 in OH.
Donor(s): NCR Corp.
Financial data (yr. ended 12/31/01): Grants paid, $1,472,800; assets, $3,943,398 (M); gifts received, $3,412,500; expenditures, $1,479,604; qualifying distributions, $1,472,800.
Limitations: Applications not accepted. Giving primarily in areas of company operations, with emphasis on Dayton, OH.
Application information: Contributes only to pre-selected organizations.
Officers and Trustees:* Earl Shanks,* Pres.; Mary Karr,* V.P.; Laura K. Nyquist,* Secy.; Bo Sawyer,* Treas.; Shelley Bird, Jonathan Hoak, Keith Taylor.
EIN: 316030860
Codes: CS, FD, CD

42283
The Springfield Foundation
4 W. Main St., Ste. 825
Springfield, OH 45502-1323 (937) 324-8773
FAX: (937) 324-1836; URL: http://www.springfieldfoundation.org
Contact: Robin Atwood Pfeil, Exec. Dir.

Incorporated in 1948 in OH.
Financial data (yr. ended 03/31/02): Grants paid, $1,465,215; assets, $25,106,331 (M); gifts received, $3,244,161; expenditures, $1,687,569.
Limitations: Giving limited to Clark County, OH.
Publications: Annual report, financial statement, newsletter, grants list, informational brochure (including application guidelines), program policy statement, application guidelines.
Application information: Application form required.
Officers and Directors:* Charlie Brougher,* Pres.; Pete Noonan, V.P.; Gus Geil,* Treas.; Robin Atwood Pfeil, Exec. Dir.; and 22 additional directors.
EIN: 316030764
Codes: CM, FD, GTI

42284
Charities Foundation
1 Seagate, 5-OSG
Toledo, OH 43666 (419) 247-2929

Trust established in 1937 in OH.
Donor(s): Owens-Illinois, Inc., William E. Levis,‡ Harold Boeschenstein,‡ and others.
Financial data (yr. ended 12/31/01): Grants paid, $1,457,012; assets, $1,834,327 (M); gifts received, $1,371,781; expenditures, $1,469,752; qualifying distributions, $1,456,457.
Limitations: Applications not accepted. Giving primarily in OH, with emphasis on Toledo.
Publications: Annual report.
Application information: Contributes only to pre-selected organizations. All funds presently committed.
Trustees: Jeffrey Denker, Henry Page, Carter Smith, Lee A. Wesselmann.
EIN: 346554560
Codes: CS, FD, CD

42285
Castellini Foundation
312 Elm St., Ste. 2600
Cincinnati, OH 45202
Contact: Christopher L. Fister, Secy.-Treas.

Established in 1991 in OH.
Donor(s): Robert Castellini, Susan Castellini.
Financial data (yr. ended 03/31/01): Grants paid, $1,436,885; assets, $13,555,191 (M); gifts received, $975; expenditures, $1,591,008; qualifying distributions, $1,425,388.
Limitations: Giving limited to the greater Cincinnati, OH, area.
Application information: Application form not required.
Officers and Trustees:* Robert H. Castellini,* Chair. and Pres.; Christopher L. Fister,* Secy.-Treas.; Susan F. Castellini.
Agent: Fifth Third Bank.
EIN: 316429763
Codes: FD

42286
The Harry & Violet Turner Charitable Foundation, Inc.
2525 N. Limestone St.
Springfield, OH 45503

Established in 1987 in OH.
Donor(s): Harry M. Turner.
Financial data (yr. ended 11/30/00): Grants paid, $1,419,512; assets, $5,345 (M); expenditures, $1,421,346; qualifying distributions, $1,419,128.
Limitations: Applications not accepted. Giving limited to Springfield, OH.
Application information: Contributes only to pre-selected organizations.
Trustees: John T. Landess, Sara Jane Turner Landess, Judith Ann Turner Lorman.
EIN: 311224184
Codes: FD

42287
The Louise Taft Semple Foundation
312 Walnut St., Ste. 3560
Cincinnati, OH 45202 (513) 421-9090
FAX: (513) 421-7107; E-mail: benefactors@fuse.net
Contact: Penny Friedman

Incorporated in 1941 in OH.
Donor(s): Louise Taft Semple.‡
Financial data (yr. ended 12/31/01): Grants paid, $1,393,524; assets, $22,624,236 (M); expenditures, $1,566,946; qualifying distributions, $1,409,024.
Limitations: Giving primarily in the Cincinnati and Hamilton County, OH, area.
Publications: Application guidelines.
Application information: Application form required.
Officers and Trustees:* Dudley S. Taft,* Chair.; James R. Bridgeland, Jr.,* Secy.; John T. Lawrence III,* Treas.; William O. DeWitt, Mrs. John T. Lawrence, Jr., Mrs. Robert A. Taft II, John B. Tytus.
EIN: 310653526
Codes: FD

42288
AK Steel Foundation
703 Curtis St.
Middletown, OH 45043
Contact: Brian Coughlin, Exec. Dir.

Established in 1989 in OH.
Donor(s): AK Steel Corp., Kawasaki Steel Investments, Inc.
Financial data (yr. ended 12/31/00): Grants paid, $1,383,333; assets, $20,930,361 (M); expenditures, $2,202,088; qualifying distributions, $1,393,496.
Limitations: Giving primarily in OH.
Officers: Richard M. Wardrop, Jr., Chair.; Alan H. McCoy, Vice-Chair.; Brian Coughlin, Exec. Dir.
Trustees: Brenda Harmon, John G. Hirtz, Gary McDaniel, Richard E. Newsted, James Wainscott.
EIN: 311284344
Codes: CS, FD, CD

42289
William & Mary Mitchell Foundation
c/o National City Bank of Indiana
P.O. Box 94651
Cleveland, OH 44101-4651

Established in 1991 in IN.
Donor(s): William Mitchell Family Trust, Mary Elizabeth Mitchell Irrevocable Trust.
Financial data (yr. ended 06/30/01): Grants paid, $1,373,194; assets, $13,806,825 (M); gifts received, $991,641; expenditures, $1,449,988; qualifying distributions, $1,409,484.
Limitations: Applications not accepted. Giving primarily in FL and NJ.
Application information: Contributes only to pre-selected organizations.
Trustee: National City Bank of Indiana.
EIN: 356536740
Codes: FD

42290
The Thomas J. Emery Memorial
c/o PNC Bank
P.O. Box 1198
Cincinnati, OH 45201-1198 (513) 651-8377
Contact: Lee Crooks, Fdn. Admin.

Incorporated in 1925 in OH.
Donor(s): Mary Muhlenberg Emery.‡
Financial data (yr. ended 12/31/01): Grants paid, $1,350,633; assets, $29,854,500 (M); expenditures, $1,605,706; qualifying distributions, $1,428,761.
Limitations: Giving primarily in Cincinnati, OH.
Publications: Application guidelines.
Application information: Request of guidelines. Application form required.
Officers and Trustees:* Lee A. Carter,* Pres.; John T. Lawrence, Jr.,* V.P.; James S. Wachs,* Secy.; John F. Barrett,* Treas.; Thomas L. Williams.
EIN: 310536711
Codes: FD

42291
The Austin Memorial Foundation
251 W. Garfield Rd., Ste. 230
Aurora, OH 44202-8856
Contact: Donald G. Austin, Jr., Pres.

Incorporated in 1961 in OH.
Donor(s): Members of the Austin family.
Financial data (yr. ended 12/31/01): Grants paid, $1,348,709; assets, $12,894,931 (M); gifts received, $1,497,562; expenditures, $1,505,028; qualifying distributions, $1,409,401.
Limitations: Applications not accepted.
Application information: Contributes only to pre-selected organizations. Unsolicited requests for funds not accepted.
Officers and Trustees:* Donald G. Austin, Jr.,* Pres.; Colette F. Mylott, Secy.; David A. Rodgers,* Treas.; James W. Austin, John C. Austin, Paul W. Austin, Richard C. Austin, Samuel H. Austin, Stewart G. Austin, Sr., Stewart G. Austin, Jr., Thomas G. Austin, Winifred N. Austin, Margaret C. Chiles, Sarah R. Cole, Gretchen Cole-Corona, Alexandra R. Loeffler, Ann R. Loeffler, Ellen Austin Smith.
EIN: 346528879
Codes: FD

42292
The Paul & Carol David Foundation
(Formerly The David Family Foundation)
6283 Frank Ave., N.W.
North Canton, OH 44720 (330) 490-2600
FAX: (330) 497-4499
Contact: Jospeh P. Belloni, D.C., Tr.

Established in 1980 in OH.
Donor(s): Paul David.
Financial data (yr. ended 12/31/01): Grants paid, $1,336,067; assets, $26,706,756 (M); expenditures, $1,584,062; qualifying distributions, $1,341,342.
Limitations: Giving limited to Stark County, OH.
Application information: Application form required.
Officer and Trustees:* Paul David,* Pres.; Joseph P. Belloni, Jeff David, Tom Knoll.
EIN: 341319236
Codes: FD, GTI

42293
Robert C. & Adele R. Schiff Foundation
1 W. 4th St., Ste. 1300
Cincinnati, OH 45202

Established in 1983.
Donor(s): Adele R. Schiff, Robert C. Schiff.

Financial data (yr. ended 11/30/01): Grants paid, $1,311,783; assets, $34,408,126 (M); expenditures, $1,366,836; qualifying distributions, $1,325,975.
Limitations: Applications not accepted. Giving primarily in OH.
Application information: Contributes only to pre-selected organizations.
Trustees: Adele R. Schiff, Robert C. Schiff.
EIN: 311080947
Codes: FD

42294
Virginia Toulmin Charitable Foundation II
c/o Key Trust Co.
34 N. Main St.
Dayton, OH 45401
Contact: Kevin McDonald, V.P., Key Trust Co.

Established in 1999 in OH.
Financial data (yr. ended 03/31/00): Grants paid, $1,294,400; assets, $1,084,744 (M); gifts received, $497,954; expenditures, $1,295,490; qualifying distributions, $1,294,400.
Limitations: Applications not accepted. Giving primarily in FL, NY, and OH.
Trustee: KeyBank, N.A.
EIN: 311642248
Codes: FD

42295
The George W. Codrington Charitable Foundation
c/o Key Trust Co. of Ohio, N.A.
800 Superior Ave., 4th Fl.
Cleveland, OH 44114
Application address: 3900 Society Ctr., 127 Public Sq., 17th Fl. Cleveland, OH 44114-1216
Contact: Raymond T. Sawyer, Chair.

Trust established in 1955 in OH.
Donor(s): George W. Codrington.‡
Financial data (yr. ended 12/31/00): Grants paid, $1,292,000; assets, $22,867,114 (M); expenditures, $1,489,398; qualifying distributions, $1,268,593.
Limitations: Giving limited to Cuyahoga County, OH, and the surrounding area.
Publications: Annual report (including application guidelines).
Application information: Application form not required.
Officers and Supervisory Board:* Raymond T. Sawyer, Chair.; John J. Dwyer,* Vice-Chair.; Keith A. Ashmus,* Secy.; William E. McDonald, Curtis E. Moll, William Seelbach.
Trustee: KeyBank, N.A.
EIN: 346507457
Codes: FD

42296
The Corbett Foundation
127 W. 9th St., Ste. 3
Cincinnati, OH 45202 (513) 241-3320
Contact: Karen P. McKim, Exec. Dir.

Incorporated in 1958 in OH.
Donor(s): J. Ralph Corbett,‡ Patricia A. Corbett.
Financial data (yr. ended 04/30/01): Grants paid, $1,279,936; assets, $24,103,851 (M); expenditures, $2,885,709; qualifying distributions, $1,402,443.
Limitations: Giving primarily in the greater Cincinnati, OH, area.
Officers: Patricia A. Corbett, Chair. and Pres.; Jean S. Reis, V.P. and Treas.; Karen P. McKim, Secy. and Exec. Dir.
Trustees: Thomas R. Corbett, James A. Markley, Jr., Melvin L. Schulman, Nancy Walker.
EIN: 316050360

Codes: FD

42297
The Diggs Family Foundation
1630 Kettering Tower
Dayton, OH 45423

Established in 1994 in OH.
Donor(s): Matthew O. Diggs, Jr.
Financial data (yr. ended 11/30/01): Grants paid, $1,246,000; assets, $1,532,087 (M); gifts received, $1,500,000; expenditures, $1,275,140; qualifying distributions, $1,245,573.
Limitations: Applications not accepted. Giving primarily in OH.
Application information: Contributes only to pre-selected organizations.
Trustees: Elizabeth Diehl, Matthew A. Diggs, Jr., Judith Keenan, Joan Townsend.
EIN: 311423026
Codes: FD

42298
The Richard and Marcy Horvitz Foundation
6095 Parkland Blvd., Ste. 300
Cleveland, OH 44124-4184

Established in 1997 in OH.
Donor(s): Marcy R. Horvitz, Richard A. Horvitz.
Financial data (yr. ended 12/31/00): Grants paid, $1,231,937; assets, $2,911,490 (M); gifts received, $2,838,875; expenditures, $1,243,157; qualifying distributions, $1,240,411.
Limitations: Applications not accepted. Giving primarily in OH, with emphasis on Cleveland.
Application information: Contributes only to pre-selected organizations. Unsolicited requests for funds not accepted.
Officers: Richard A. Horvitz, Pres.; Marcy R. Horvitz, V.P.
Trustee: Mark F. Polzin.
EIN: 311533634
Codes: FD

42299
The Cincinnati Foundation for the Aged
2100 Fourth and Vine Twr.
5 W. 4th St.
Cincinnati, OH 45202 (513) 381-6859
Contact: Ruth Avram, Secy.

Established in 1891 in OH.
Donor(s): Oscar Cohrs,‡ Otto Luedeking.‡
Financial data (yr. ended 03/31/01): Grants paid, $1,228,324; assets, $20,136,596 (M); gifts received, $103,462; expenditures, $1,268,028; qualifying distributions, $1,220,457.
Limitations: Giving limited to the greater Cincinnati, OH, area.
Application information: Disbursements limited to the foundation's single mission described in "Purpose & activities"; funding requests for studies or any other activity not eligible for consideration. Application form required.
Officers: Robert C. Porter, Jr., Pres.; Jon Hoffheimer, 1st V.P.; Gene Weber, 2nd V.P.; Ruth Avram, Secy.; Bernice Gartrell, Treas.
Trustees: Guido Gores, Jack Greer, Heather Hoefinghoff, Richard Hoefinghoff, Robert Keefer, William Dock Meyer, Robert Porter III, Philip Walters.
EIN: 310536971
Codes: FD

42300
Gerlach Foundation, Inc.
37 W. Broad St., 5th Fl.
Columbus, OH 43215 (614) 224-7141

Incorporated in 1953 in OH.

Donor(s): Pauline Gerlach,‡ John J. Gerlach, John B. Gerlach.
Financial data (yr. ended 11/30/01): Grants paid, $1,209,730; assets, $26,418,242 (M); expenditures, $1,237,432; qualifying distributions, $1,205,317.
Limitations: Applications not accepted. Giving primarily in OH, with emphasis on Columbus.
Application information: Contributes only to pre-selected organizations.
Officers: Susan Douglass, V.P.; David P. Gerlach, V.P.; John B. Gerlach, Jr., Treas.
EIN: 316023912
Codes: FD

42301
John F. and Mary A. Geisse Foundation
(Formerly The Geisse Foundation)
38050 Jackson Rd.
Chagrin Falls, OH 44022-2025
(216) 595-1700
FAX: (216) 595-1707; E-mail: timgeisse@aol.com
Contact: Tim Geisse, Tr.

Established in 1970.
Donor(s): John F. Geisse,‡ Mary A. Geisse.‡
Financial data (yr. ended 12/31/01): Grants paid, $1,203,016; assets, $16,152,235 (M); expenditures, $1,440,127; qualifying distributions, $1,248,185; giving activities include $250,000 for loans.
Limitations: Giving primarily on an international basis.
Publications: Occasional report, informational brochure (including application guidelines).
Application information: Application form not required.
Trustees: Lawrence J. Geisse, M.D., Timothy F. Geisse.
EIN: 237049780
Codes: FD

42302
Great Commission Foundation, Inc.
7045 T.R. 94
Findlay, OH 45840 (419) 423-3688
Contact: Jack W. Ridge, Pres.

Established in 1989 in OH.
Donor(s): Gary M. Harpst, Vern Strong, Jack W. Ridge.
Financial data (yr. ended 11/30/01): Grants paid, $1,199,402; assets, $1,933 (M); gifts received, $1,095,020; expenditures, $1,204,773; qualifying distributions, $1,198,523.
Limitations: Giving primarily in OH.
Application information: Application form required.
Officers and Trustees:* Jack W. Ridge,* Pres.; Larry Hoover,* V.P.; Gary M. Harpst,* Secy.-Treas.
EIN: 341648111
Codes: FD, GTI

42303
The Evenor Armington Fund
c/o The Huntington National Bank
917 Euclid Ave.
Cleveland, OH 44115 (216) 515-6798
E-mail: bill.babis@huntington.com
Contact: William E. Babis, V.P. and Trust Off.

Established in 1954 in OH.
Donor(s): Everett Armington, and members of the Armington family.
Financial data (yr. ended 06/30/01): Grants paid, $1,185,054; assets, $7,106,229 (M); expenditures, $1,263,551; qualifying distributions, $1,208,252.
Limitations: Applications not accepted. Giving on a national basis.

Application information: Contributes only to pre-selected organizations. Unsolicited requests for funds not considered or acknowledged.
Advisors: David E. Armington, Paul Armington, Peter Armington.
Trustee: The Huntington National Bank.
EIN: 346525508
Codes: FD

42304
NFG Foundation
c/o Mark D. Senff
65 E. State St., Ste. 2100
Columbus, OH 43215-4215
Contact: Chris Fidler

Established around 1993.
Donor(s): Mildred George, Noel George Trust.
Financial data (yr. ended 12/31/00): Grants paid, $1,174,660; assets, $3,034,775 (M); gifts received, $69,579; expenditures, $1,180,443; qualifying distributions, $1,167,631.
Limitations: Giving primarily in Oklahoma City, OK.
Application information: Application form not required.
Officers: James N. George, Pres.; Rebecca Q. Morgan, Secy.-Treas.
EIN: 311387062
Codes: FD

42305
Levin Family Foundation
111 W. 1st St., Ste. 848
Dayton, OH 45402
E-mail: levinfamilyfound@ameritech.net
Contact: Karen Levin, Exec. Dir.

Established around 1992.
Donor(s): Allen Levin, Louis Levin, Barbara Levin, Karen Levin, Ryan Levin, Darrell Murphy.
Financial data (yr. ended 12/31/01): Grants paid, $1,173,675; assets, $23,987,601 (M); expenditures, $1,566,904; qualifying distributions, $1,153,872.
Limitations: Giving primarily in the Cincinnati and Dayton, OH, areas.
Publications: Application guidelines.
Application information: Application form required.
Officer and Trustees:* Karen Levin,* Exec. Dir.; Allen Levin, Barbara Levin, Louis Levin, Ryan Levin, Darrell Murphy.
EIN: 311327847
Codes: FD

42306
Community Foundations, Inc.
1234 E. Broad St.
Columbus, OH 43205-1463 (614) 251-4000
Contact: Raymond J. Biddiscomse, V.P., Fin. and Admin.

Established in 1985 in OH.
Financial data (yr. ended 12/31/01): Grants paid, $1,159,335; assets, $19,644,746 (M); gifts received, $2,295,428; expenditures, $1,255,738.
Limitations: Applications not accepted. Giving primarily in OH.
Publications: Annual report.
Application information: Unsolicited requests for funds not accepted.
Officers and Trustees:* Abigail S. Wexner,* Chair.; Dimon R. McFerson, Vice-Chair.; Donald Shackelford, Vice-Chair.; Douglas F. Kridler, Pres.; James I. Luck, Pres.; Raymond J. Biddiscombe, V.P., Fin. and Admin.; Philip T. Schavone, V.P., Advancement; Bill Ingram, John G. McCoy, David R. Meuse, Ann Pizzuti, Lewis R. Smoot, Sr., Ann Isaly Wolfe.

EIN: 311197385
Codes: CM, FD

42307
The 1525 Foundation
1111 Superior Ave., Ste. 1000
Cleveland, OH 44114-2507 (216) 696-4200
FAX: (216) 696-7303
Contact: Dorothy Yoder, Asst. Secy.

Incorporated in 1971 in OH.
Donor(s): Kent H. Smith.‡
Financial data (yr. ended 12/31/01): Grants paid, $1,151,515; assets, $5,163,089 (M); expenditures, $1,256,801; qualifying distributions, $1,256,801.
Limitations: Giving primarily in OH, with emphasis on Cuyahoga County.
Application information: Application form not required.
Officers and Trustees:* Thelma G. Smith,* Pres.; William B. LaPlace,* V.P.; Phillip A. Ranney,* Secy.-Treas.
EIN: 341089206
Codes: FD

42308
Middletown Community Foundation
36 Donham Plz.
Middletown, OH 45042 (513) 424-7369
FAX: (513) 424-7555; *E-mail:* info@mcfoundation.org; *URL:* http://www.mcfoundation.org
Contact: Kay Wright, Exec. Dir.

Incorporated in 1976 in OH.
Financial data (yr. ended 12/31/01): Grants paid, $1,137,000; assets, $17,145,582 (M); gifts received, $1,856,805; expenditures, $1,966,775.
Limitations: Giving limited to the greater Middletown, OH, area.
Publications: Annual report, newsletter, application guidelines, informational brochure (including application guidelines), financial statement.
Application information: Application form not required.
Officers and Trustees:* Joseph Lyons,* Pres.; William Schaefer,* V.P.; Vickie Frazer, Secy.; John Venturella, Treas.; Kay Wright, Exec. Dir.; John Burley, Sue Butcher, Sarah Campbell, Doug Casper, Joe Cristo, David Daugherty, Michael Dickenson, Ron Ely, Carl Esposito, Michael Governanti, Kathleen Gramke, Gregg Grimes, David Haft, Loretta Harrison, Carolyn Henderson, Seth Johnston, Ronald Olson, Jack O'Neill, Mary Jane Palmer, Elmon Prier, Michael J. Sanders, Gary Shupe, Molly Williams.
EIN: 310898380
Codes: CM, FD, GTI

42309
Hemingway Foundation
c/o KeyBank, N.A.
800 Superior Ave., 4th Fl.
Cleveland, OH 44114

Established in 1987 in UT.
Donor(s): Rev. Richard K. Hemingway.
Financial data (yr. ended 12/31/01): Grants paid, $1,126,461; assets, $15,974,073 (M); gifts received, $1,917; expenditures, $1,389,609; qualifying distributions, $1,152,113.
Limitations: Applications not accepted. Giving primarily in Salt Lake City, UT.
Application information: Contributes only to pre-selected organizations.
Trustees: Ann Hemingway, Hallie Hemingway, Katie Hemingway, Richard Hemingway, Jane Mason, KeyBank, N.A.
EIN: 876205846

Codes: FD

42310
Marge & Charles J. Schott Foundation
30 E. Central Pkwy., Ste. 300
Cincinnati, OH 45202-1147 (513) 721-8400
Contact: Phyllis J. Cartwright, Secy.-Treas.

Established around 1980.
Donor(s): Margaret U. Schott.
Financial data (yr. ended 06/30/01): Grants paid, $1,123,055; assets, $9,530,420 (M); gifts received, $5,309; expenditures, $1,128,459; qualifying distributions, $1,123,055.
Limitations: Giving primarily in Cincinnati, OH.
Officers: Margaret U. Schott, Pres.; Phyllis J. Cartwright, Secy.-Treas.
EIN: 316063407
Codes: FD

42311
Wodecroft Foundation
1900 Chemed Ctr.
255 E. 5th St.
Cincinnati, OH 45202 (513) 977-8236
Contact: J. Michael Cooney, Chair.

Established in 1958 in OH.
Donor(s): Roger Drackett.‡
Financial data (yr. ended 12/31/01): Grants paid, $1,117,000; assets, $18,747,502 (M); expenditures, $1,221,761; qualifying distributions, $1,127,000.
Limitations: Giving primarily in southwestern FL, and southwestern OH.
Application information: Few unsolicited applications granted. Application form not required.
Officers: J. Michael Cooney, Chair.; H. Truxton Emerson, Secy.-Treas.
Trustee: Jeanne Drackett.
EIN: 316047601
Codes: FD

42312
The Slemp Foundation
c/o U.S. Bank
P.O. Box 1118
Cincinnati, OH 45201
Application address: P.O. Box 5208, ML. 7155
Cincinnati, OH 45201-5208
Contact: Patricia L. Durbin

Trust established in 1943 in VA.
Donor(s): C. Bascom Slemp.‡
Financial data (yr. ended 06/30/01): Grants paid, $1,096,665; assets, $22,113,065 (M); gifts received, $1,000; expenditures, $1,307,878; qualifying distributions, $1,147,203.
Limitations: Giving primarily in Lee and Wise counties, VA.
Application information: Application forms provided for scholarship applicants.
Trustees: Mary Virginia Edmonds, Pamela S. Edmonds, John A. Reid, Melissa S. Smith Sircy, James C. Smith, Nancey E. Smith.
Agent: U.S. Bank.
EIN: 316025080
Codes: FD, GTI

42313
Elizabeth Ring Mather and William Gwinn Mather Fund
1111 Superior Ave., Ste. 1000
Cleveland, OH 44114 (216) 696-4200
FAX: (216) 861-4908
Contact: Kathleen K. Riley

Incorporated in 1954 in OH.
Donor(s): Elizabeth Ring Mather.‡

Financial data (yr. ended 12/31/01): Grants paid, $1,088,644; assets, $9,711,729 (M); gifts received, $315,713; expenditures, $1,218,425; qualifying distributions, $1,155,750.
Limitations: Giving primarily in OH, with emphasis on the greater Cleveland area.
Application information: The foundation does not encourage new requests for grants. Application form not required.
Officers and Trustees:* James D. Ireland III,* Pres.; Lucy I. Weller,* V.P.; Cornelia I. Hallinan,* Secy.; George R. Ireland,* Treas.
EIN: 346519863
Codes: FD

42314
Cincinnati Bell Foundation, Inc.
201 E. 4th St., Rm. 102-890
Cincinnati, OH 45202-2301
Application address: 201 E. 4th St., ML 102-560, Cincinnati, OH 45202, tel.: (513) 397-7545
Contact: Robert Horine, Public Affairs Dir.

Established in 1984 in OH.
Donor(s): Cincinnati Bell Inc., Broadwing Inc.
Financial data (yr. ended 12/31/00): Grants paid, $1,056,772; assets, $183,060 (M); expenditures, $531,633; qualifying distributions, $1,062,184.
Limitations: Giving primarily in northern KY, the greater Cincinnati, OH, area, and in other cities in which the company has a significant corporate presence.
Publications: Informational brochure (including application guidelines).
Application information: Application form not required.
Officers and Trustees:* Richard G. Ellenberger,* Pres.; Jeffrey C. Smith, Corp. Secy. and C.A.O.; Mark W. Peterson, Treas.; Kevin W. Mooney.
EIN: 311125542
Codes: CS, FD, CD

42315
The Mellen Foundation
c/o John D. Drinko
3200 National City Ctr., 1900 E. 9th St.
Cleveland, OH 44114-3485

Established in 1963 in OH.
Donor(s): Edward J. Mellen.
Financial data (yr. ended 12/31/01): Grants paid, $1,036,200; assets, $4,196,675 (M); expenditures, $1,122,077; qualifying distributions, $1,071,923.
Limitations: Applications not accepted. Giving primarily in Cleveland, OH.
Application information: Contributes only to pre-selected organizations.
Officers and Trustees:* John D. Drinko,* Chair. and Pres.; Elizabeth G. Drinko,* V.P.; Lloyd F. Loux, Jr.,* Secy.; J. Richard Hamilton,* Treas.; J. Raymond Barry, John R. Burlingame, James A. Cullen, J. Randall Drinko, Jay Deaver Drinko, John J. Dwyer, R. Steven Kestner, Diana Lynn Martin.
EIN: 346560874
Codes: FD

42316
The Van Wert County Foundation
138 E. Main St.
Van Wert, OH 45891 (419) 238-1743
FAX: (419) 238-3374; E-mail: vwcf@bright.net
Contact: Larry L. Wendel, Exec. Secy.

Incorporated in 1925 in OH.
Donor(s): Charles F. Wassenberg,‡ Gaylord Saltzgaber,‡ John D. Ault,‡ Kernan Wright,‡ Richard L. Klein,‡ Hazel Gleason,‡ Constance Eirich.‡

Financial data (yr. ended 12/31/01): Grants paid, $1,034,937; assets, $29,144,954 (M); gifts received, $717,956; expenditures, $1,317,624; qualifying distributions, $1,160,903; giving activities include $106,638 for programs.
Limitations: Giving limited to Van Wert and Paulding counties, OH.
Publications: Application guidelines, informational brochure.
Application information: The foundation has discontinued its loans to individuals program. Previous commitments will be honored. Application form required.
Officers and Trustees:* Robert C. Young,* Pres.; F.W. Purmort III,* V.P.; Larry L. Wendel, Exec. Secy.; Michael T. Cross, Secy.; D.L. Brumback III, William S. Derry, Clair Dudgeon, Bruce C. Kennedy, Watson Ley, Paul W. Purmort, Jr., C. Allan Runser, Donald C. Sutton, Gerald Thatcher, Roger K. Thompson, Hon. Sumner J. Walters, Michael R. Zedaker.
EIN: 340907558
Codes: FD, GTI

42317
The LaValley Foundation
5800 Monroe St., Bldg. F
Sylvania, OH 43560-2207

Established in 1992 in OH.
Donor(s): Richard G. LaValley.
Financial data (yr. ended 12/31/01): Grants paid, $1,028,750; assets, $19,508,745 (M); gifts received, $900; expenditures, $1,032,850; qualifying distributions, $1,028,750.
Limitations: Applications not accepted. Giving primarily in Toledo, OH.
Application information: Contributes only to pre-selected organizations.
Officers and Trustees:* Richard G. LaValley,* Pres.; Daniel J. LaValley,* V.P.; Richard G. LaValley, Jr.,* V.P.
EIN: 341722402
Codes: FD

42318
The Sisler McFawn Foundation
P.O. Box 149
Akron, OH 44309-0149 (330) 849-8887
FAX: (330) 996-6215
Contact: Charlotte M. Stanley, Grants Mgr.

Trust established in 1959 in OH.
Donor(s): Lois Sisler McFawn.‡
Financial data (yr. ended 12/31/01): Grants paid, $1,020,904; assets, $20,345,715 (M); expenditures, $1,187,175; qualifying distributions, $1,017,299.
Limitations: Giving primarily in Summit County, OH.
Publications: Application guidelines, grants list.
Application information: Application form not required.
Distribution Committee: Jon V. Heider, Chair.; H. Peter Burg, Michael J. Connor, Howard L. Flood, Patricia A. Kemph, John L. Macso, Justin T. Rogers, Jr.
Trustee: KeyBank, N.A.
EIN: 346508111
Codes: FD

42319
The Sherwin-Williams Foundation
101 Prospect Ave., N.W., 12th Fl.
Cleveland, OH 44115 (216) 566-2000
Contact: Barbara Gadosik, Dir., Corp. Contribs.

Incorporated in 1964 in OH.
Donor(s): The Sherwin-Williams Co.

Financial data (yr. ended 12/31/01): Grants paid, $1,015,720; assets, $14,727,501 (M); expenditures, $1,034,020; qualifying distributions, $1,004,474.
Limitations: Giving primarily in areas of company headquarters and plants; most grants are in Cleveland, OH.
Application information: Application form not required.
Trustees: C.M. Connor, Chair.; John G. Breen, T.E. Hopkins, L.J. Pitorak, J.M. Scaminace.
EIN: 346555476
Codes: CS, FD, CD

42320
Brentwood Foundation
1400 McDonald Investment Ctr.
800 Superior Ave.
Cleveland, OH 44114-2688
Application address: c/o Terri Kovach, PMB 303, 3593 Medina Rd., Medina, OH 44256, tel.: (330) 239-6405; FAX: (330) 239-6205; E-mail: terrik@apk.net; URL: http://www.southpointegme.com/frames_pages
Contact: John D. Wheeler, Secy.

Established in 1994 in OH; converted following the merger of Brentwood Hospital, which was an osteopathic hospital, with Meridia Suburban Hospital.
Financial data (yr. ended 12/31/00): Grants paid, $957,796; assets, $30,493,084 (M); gifts received, $6,000,000; expenditures, $7,435,531; qualifying distributions, $1,125,013.
Limitations: Giving limited to OH, with strong emphasis on the northeast OH, area.
Publications: Annual report (including application guidelines), financial statement, newsletter, informational brochure (including application guidelines).
Application information: Grant requests submitted within the Meridia Health System must follow MSPH internal grant application procedures. Application form required.
Officers: Theodore F. Classen, Pres.; John D. Wheeler, Secy.; Parry Keller, Treas.
Trustees: Vincent F. Decrane, Thomas J. Ebner, Daniel L. Ekelman, Raymond J. Grabow, John A. Howells, Charles E. Hugus, David Krahe, Gregory P. Kurtz, Alex P. Mekedis, Lucille Reed Narducci, Thomas A. Peter, Jr.
EIN: 341783117
Codes: FD

42321
Farmer Family Foundation
c/o Summer Hill Inc.
P.O. Box 625737
Cincinnati, OH 45262-5737
Contact: Amy F. Joseph, V.P.

Established in 1988 in OH.
Donor(s): Brynne F. Coletti, Richard T. Farmer, Amy F. Joseph.
Financial data (yr. ended 12/31/00): Grants paid, $950,000; assets, $33,355,183 (M); gifts received, $7,673,592; expenditures, $1,004,420; qualifying distributions, $950,000.
Limitations: Giving primarily in Cincinnati, OH.
Officers and Trustees:* Brynne F. Coletti,* Pres. and Treas.; Amy F. Joseph,* V.P. and Secy.; Robert E. Coletti.
EIN: 311256614
Codes: FD

42322
Mary S. & David C. Corbin Foundation
910 Key Bldg.
159 S. Main St.
Akron, OH 44308 (330) 762-6427
FAX: (330) 762-6428; E-mail:
corbin@nls.netURL: http://fdncenter.org/grantmaker/corbin
Contact: Joseph M. Holden, Pres.

Established about 1970.
Donor(s): David C. Corbin.‡
Financial data (yr. ended 12/31/01): Grants paid, $945,823; assets, $21,719,138 (M); expenditures, $1,184,050; qualifying distributions, $971,776.
Limitations: Giving primarily in Akron, OH.
Publications: Application guidelines.
Application information: Application form required.
Officers and Trustees:* Joseph M. Holden,* Pres. and Secy.; James S. Hartenstein,* V.P. and Treas.; Sophie E. Albrecht, Robert M. Bonchack, Louis A. Maglione, Roger T. Read, Raymond R. Wernig.
EIN: 237052280
Codes: FD

42323
Cooper Tire & Rubber Foundation
Lima & Western Aves.
Findlay, OH 45840 (419) 423-1321
Contact: Philip G. Weaver, V.P., Cooper Tire & Rubber Co.

Established in 1953 in OH.
Donor(s): Cooper Tire & Rubber Co.
Financial data (yr. ended 12/31/01): Grants paid, $944,743; assets, $149,608 (M); gifts received, $38,919; expenditures, $946,551; qualifying distributions, $946,551.
Limitations: Giving on a national basis.
Trustees: W.C. Hattendorf, P.G. Weaver, E.B. White.
EIN: 237025013
Codes: CS, FD, CD

42324
Vesper Foundation
6950 S. Edgerton Rd.
Brecksville, OH 44141-3184

Established in 1961 in OH.
Donor(s): Vesper Corp.
Financial data (yr. ended 12/31/01): Grants paid, $943,116; assets, $7,186,347 (M); gifts received, $2,250,000; expenditures, $950,607; qualifying distributions, $950,607.
Limitations: Applications not accepted. Giving on a national basis, with emphasis on the Northeast.
Application information: Contributes only to pre-selected organizations.
Trustees: James Benenson, Jr., James Benenson III, John V. Curci.
EIN: 236251198
Codes: CS, FD, CD

42325
Ruth and Lovett Peters Foundation
(Formerly Lovett Peters Foundation)
1500 Chiquita Ctr.
250 E. 5th St.
Cincinnati, OH 45202
Contact: Dan Peters, Pres.

Established in 1992 in MA.
Donor(s): Lovett C. Peters.
Financial data (yr. ended 12/31/01): Grants paid, $942,250; assets, $4,967,751 (M); expenditures, $1,495,650; qualifying distributions, $1,557,725.
Limitations: Applications not accepted. Giving primarily in MA.
Officer and Trustees:* Daniel S. Peters,* Pres.; Lovett C. Peters, Ruth Stott Peters.
EIN: 046748820
Codes: FD

42326
Lafe P. Fox Family Foundation, Inc.
c/o National City Trust Co.
P.O. Box 94651
Cleveland, OH 44101-4651

Established in 1995 in FL.
Donor(s): Rita D. Fox.
Financial data (yr. ended 12/31/99): Grants paid, $941,274; assets, $4,264,169 (M); expenditures, $982,427; qualifying distributions, $939,070.
Limitations: Applications not accepted. Giving on a national basis.
Application information: Contributes only to pre-selected organizations.
Board Members: Carol F. DeJoy, William DeJoy, Richard P. Fox, Patricia Fox Miron.
Trustee: First Union National Bank.
EIN: 656160649
Codes: FD

42327
Robert and Patricia Switzer Foundation
(Formerly Switzer Foundation)
127 Public Sq.
3900 Key Ctr.
Cleveland, OH 44114-1291

Established in 1985 in CA.
Donor(s): Members of the Switzer family.
Financial data (yr. ended 06/30/01): Grants paid, $940,054; assets, $18,063,634 (M); expenditures, $1,174,288; qualifying distributions, $1,028,187.
Limitations: Applications not accepted. Giving limited to CA, MA, ME, NH, and VT.
Application information: Contributes only to pre-selected organizations.
Officer and Trustees:* Thomas K. Wessels,* Chair.; Lissa Widoff, Exec. Dir.; Cynthia R. Robinson, Shawna Switzer Saaty, Debbie Swander, Ann P. Switzer, Patricia D. Switzer, Paul E. Switzer.
EIN: 341504501

42328
A. Malachi Mixon III & Barbara W. Mixon Foundation
25 W. Prospect Ave., Ste.1400
Cleveland, OH 44113

Established in 1991 in OH.
Donor(s): A. Malachi Mixon III, Barbara W. Mixon.
Financial data (yr. ended 11/30/99): Grants paid, $939,388; assets, $878,078 (M); expenditures, $954,095; qualifying distributions, $935,325.
Limitations: Applications not accepted. Giving primarily in Cleveland, OH.
Application information: Contributes only to pre-selected organizations.
Officer: A. Malachi Mixon III, Pres.
Trustees: Robert N. Gudbranson, Barbara W. Mixon.
EIN: 341692992
Codes: FD

42329
The Jon & Susan Diamond Family Foundation
320 S. Parkview Ave.
Columbus, OH 43209
E-mail: Jond@safeauto.com or SSDiamond2@aol.com
Contact: Susan Diamond, Pres.

Established in 1997 in OH.
Donor(s): Susan Diamond, Jon Diamond, Schottenstein Stores Corp.
Financial data (yr. ended 12/31/00): Grants paid, $929,361; assets, $5,474,730 (M); gifts received, $1,106,250; expenditures, $929,688; qualifying distributions, $929,688.
Limitations: Giving primarily in NY and OH.
Officers: Susan Diamond, Pres.; Jon Diamond, V.P.; Ann Deshe, Secy.; Geraldine Schottenstein, Treas.
EIN: 311523574
Codes: FD

42330
The Spaulding Foundation
(Formerly Joseph H. Spaulding Foundation)
c/o John E. Prather
8260 N. Creek Dr., Ste. 340
Cincinnati, OH 45236-6114 (513) 936-0101
Contact: Lisa Prather, V.P.

Established in 1997 in OH.
Donor(s): Ruth E. Spaulding Trust.
Financial data (yr. ended 02/28/02): Grants paid, $917,597; assets, $28,340,336 (M); gifts received, $175,000; expenditures, $1,341,746; qualifying distributions, $1,059,809.
Limitations: Giving limited to the greater Cincinnati, OH, area.
Publications: Application guidelines.
Application information: Application form required.
Officers: John E. Prather, Pres. and Treas.; Linda Marlow, V.P.; Lisa Prather, V.P.; James R. Marlow, Secy.
EIN: 311096254
Codes: FD

42331
Randolph J. & Estelle M. Dorn Foundation
165 E. Washington Row
Sandusky, OH 44870-2610 (419) 625-8324
Contact: M.J. Stauffer, Pres.

Established around 1971.
Donor(s): Estelle M. Dorn.
Financial data (yr. ended 04/30/01): Grants paid, $904,369; assets, $25,296,875 (M); expenditures, $1,196,587; qualifying distributions, $1,006,485.
Limitations: Giving limited to northern OH, with strong emphasis on Sandusky.
Application information: Application form not required.
Officers and Trustees:* M.J. Stauffer,* Pres.; Mary Jane Hill,* V.P. and Secy.; David F. Reid,* V.P.; Bobbie J. Hummel,* Treas.; John O. Bacon.
EIN: 237099592
Codes: FD

42332
The Herbert W. Hoover Foundation
Unizan Plz.
220 Market Ave. S.
Canton, OH 44702 (330) 453-5555
FAX: (330) 453-5622; E-mail:
herbertwhoover@neo.rr.com
Contact: Ellen Beidler, Exec. Dir.

Established in 1990 in OH.
Donor(s): The Hoover Foundation.
Financial data (yr. ended 12/31/01): Grants paid, $902,811; assets, $22,692,939 (M); expenditures, $1,249,063; qualifying distributions, $1,091,498.
Limitations: Giving primarily in Stark County, OH.
Publications: Application guidelines.
Trust Committee: Elizabeth Lacey Hoover, Chair.; Mrs. Carl Good Hoover, Vice-Chair.; Ruth H. Basner, Robert S. O'Brien, Blair C. Woodside, Jr.
Trustee: KeyBank, N.A.
EIN: 346905388

Codes: FD

42333
Owens Corning Foundation
c/o Owens Corning World Headquarters
1 Owens Corning Pkwy.
Toledo, OH 43659 (419) 248-6719
FAX: (419) 248-5689
Contact: Emerson J. Ross, Pres. and Treas.

Donor(s): Owens Corning.
Financial data (yr. ended 12/31/01): Grants paid, $887,648; assets, $6,983,482 (M); gifts received, $277,546; expenditures, $929,782; qualifying distributions, $887,648.
Limitations: Giving primarily in major corporate manufacturing locations.
Publications: Annual report, program policy statement, informational brochure (including application guidelines).
Application information: Application form not required.
Officers: Mike Thaman, Chair.; Emerson J. Ross, Pres. and Treas.; William F. Dent, V.P.; Rod Nowland, Secy.
Directors: George E. Kiemle, Terry L. Priestap, Bill Rossiter, Jeremiah M. Sullivan, Karel Vose.
Trustee: KeyBank, N.A.
EIN: 341270856
Codes: CS, FD, CD

42334
The Payne Fund
1770 Huntington Bldg.
925 Euclid Ave.
Cleveland, OH 44115 (216) 696-1621
Contact: Irene R. Roberts

Incorporated in 1929 in OH.
Donor(s): Frances P. Bolton.‡
Financial data (yr. ended 12/31/00): Grants paid, $872,206; assets, $4,959,849 (M); gifts received, $1,339,276; expenditures, $1,061,062; qualifying distributions, $986,905; giving activities include $141,506 for programs.
Limitations: Applications not accepted. Giving primarily in San Francisco, CA, Atlanta, GA, Boston, Cambridge, and Milton, MA, and Cleveland and Gambier, OH.
Application information: Contributes only to pre-selected organizations.
Officers and Directors:* Barbara Bolton Gratry,* Pres.; Kenyon C. Bolton III,* V.P.; Thomas C. Bolton,* V.P.; William B. Bolton,* V.P.; Mary Bolton Hooper, V.P.; Charles P. Bolton,* Secy.-Treas.; John B. Bolton, Philip P. Bolton, Frederick B. Taylor.
EIN: 135563006
Codes: FD

42335
Mary K. Peabody Foundation
c/o National City Bank of Indiana
P.O. Box 94651
Cleveland, OH 44101-4651

Established in 1991 in IN.
Financial data (yr. ended 07/31/01): Grants paid, $869,675; assets, $5,390,512 (M); expenditures, $948,280; qualifying distributions, $904,907.
Limitations: Applications not accepted. Giving primarily in Conway and East Jordan, MI, and Poughkeepsie, NY.
Application information: Contributes only to pre-selected organizations.
Trustees: Frances H. Fisher, National City Bank of Indiana.
Distribution Committee: Robert Wagner.
EIN: 356546371
Codes: FD

42336
The William J. and Dorothy K. O'Neill Foundation, Inc.
30195 Chagrin Blvd., Ste. 250
Cleveland, OH 44124 (216) 831-9667
FAX: (216) 831-3779; *E-mail:* oneillfdn@aol.com; *URL:* http://www.oneillfdn.org
Contact: William J. O'Neill, Jr., Pres., and Christine E. Henry, Dir.

Established in 1987 in OH.
Donor(s): Dorothy K. O'Neill.‡
Financial data (yr. ended 12/31/00): Grants paid, $863,753; assets, $15,498,109 (M); gifts received, $9,882,796; expenditures, $1,019,201; qualifying distributions, $921,582.
Limitations: Giving primarily in the Cleveland, OH, area, and cities where family members reside, including Washington DC, Upper Keys, FL, Big Island, HI, New Orleans, LA, Baltimore/Annapolis, MD, Ann Arbor, MI, New York, NY, Cincinnati and Columbus, OH, Richmond and Virginia Beach, VA, and Houston, TX.
Publications: Annual report (including application guidelines), occasional report, grants list.
Application information: Will review no more than 1 proposal from the same organization in the same year. Check website or telephone for exact deadlines. Application form not required.
Officers and Trustees:* William J. O'Neill, Jr.,* Pres.; Krishne I. Sadlo, Secy.; Douglas J. Smorag, Treas.; John E. Kohl, John H. O'Neill.
Director: Christine E. Henry.
Grantmaking Committee: William M. France, Jr., Chair.
EIN: 341560893
Codes: FD

42337
Salem Community Foundation, Inc.
713 E. State St.
Salem, OH 44460-2911 (330) 332-4021
FAX: (330) 337-3474; *E-mail:* scf@salemohio.com
Contact: John E. Tonti, Pres.

Established about 1966.
Financial data (yr. ended 12/31/01): Grants paid, $861,718; assets, $11,463,563 (M); expenditures, $921,153.
Limitations: Giving primarily in Salem and Perry Township, OH.
Publications: Annual report, newsletter.
Application information: Application form required.
Officers and Trustees:* John E. Tonti,* Pres.; Bruce P. Gordon,* V.P.; Salvatore C. Apicella, M.D.,* Secy.; Joe Sedzmak,* Treas.; David Brobeck, Larry G. Cecil, Wayne T. Darling, Geoffrey Goll, Robert Guehl, Brian Jensen, Joseph Julian, Deb McCulloch, Gary E. Moffett, Wilma Navyosky, Robert E. Pond, William Stevenson, M.D., Nancy Willeman.
EIN: 341001130
Codes: CM, FD, GTI

42338
The Kettering Family Foundation
1560 Kettering Twr.
Dayton, OH 45423
Application address: 2833 S. Colorado Blvd., Ste. 2415, Denver, CO 80222; *E-mail:* Ketteringfamilyf@aol.com; *URL:* http://www.ketteringfamilyfoundation.org
Contact: Charles F. Kettering III, Pres.

Incorporated in 1956 in IL; reincorporated in 1966 in OH.
Donor(s): E.W. Kettering,‡ Virginia W. Kettering, Jane K. Lombard, S.K. Williamson, P.D. Williamson, M.D., Richard D. Lombard,‡ B. Weiffenbach,‡ Charles F. Kettering III, Lisa S. Kettering, M.D., Leslie G. Williamson, Douglas E. Williamson, M.D., Susan S. Kettering, Kyle W. Cox, Mark A. Cox, Douglas J. Cushnie, Karen W. Cushnie, Linda K. Danneberg, William H. Danneberg, Jean S. Kettering, Richard J. Lombard, Debra L. Williamson, Nathalie R. Lombard.
Financial data (yr. ended 12/31/01): Grants paid, $851,070; assets, $13,027,470 (M); gifts received, $6,000; expenditures, $890,500; qualifying distributions, $859,787.
Limitations: Giving on a national basis.
Publications: Informational brochure (including application guidelines).
Application information: Unsolicited proposals considered after trustee-sponsored requests. Trustee-sponsored requests get priority. Trustees may sponsor requests from generally excluded areas. Only trustee-sponsored requests will be considered for international giving. Grants list available on the foundation's website. Application form not required.
Officers and Trustees:* Charles F. Kettering III, Pres.; Susan S. Kettering,* V.P.; Debra L. Williamson,* V.P.; Richard J. Lombard,* Secy.-Treas.; Kyle W. Cox, Karen W. Cushnie, Linda K. Danneberg, Jean S. Kettering, Lisa S. Kettering, M.D., Virginia W. Kettering, Jane K. Lombard, Douglas E. Williamson, M.D., P.D. Williamson, M.D., Susan K. Williamson.
EIN: 310727384
Codes: FD

42339
Berry Family Foundation
(Formerly Loren M. Berry Foundation)
3055 Kettering Blvd., Ste. 418
Dayton, OH 45439 (937) 293-0398
Contact: William T. Lincoln, Treas.

Incorporated in 1960 in OH.
Donor(s): Loren M. Berry,‡ George W. Berry.
Financial data (yr. ended 12/31/01): Grants paid, $848,100; assets, $16,163,977 (M); expenditures, $937,358; qualifying distributions, $840,697.
Limitations: Giving primarily in Dayton, OH; giving on a national basis for education.
Officers and Trustees:* John W. Berry, Jr.,* Pres.; William T. Lincoln,* Treas.; Charles D. Berry, David L. Berry, George W. Berry, Martha B. Fraim, William L. Fraim, Elizabeth B. Gray, Leland W. Henry, James O. Payne.
EIN: 316026144
Codes: FD

42340
Harley C. & Mary Hoover Price Foundation
c/o KeyBank, N.A.
800 Superior Ave., 4th Fl.
Cleveland, OH 44114-2601
Application address: c/o Brian Hostettler, KeyBank, N.A., 126 Central Plz., Canton, OH 44702, tel.: (330) 489-5427

Financial data (yr. ended 12/31/01): Grants paid, $844,170; assets, $14,305,342 (M); expenditures, $950,784; qualifying distributions, $882,101.
Limitations: Giving limited to KY, NY, and OH.
Trustee: KeyBank, N.A.
EIN: 346510993
Codes: FD

42341
Lester E. & Kathleen A. Coleman Foundation
14849 Trappers Trail
Novelty, OH 44072-9543 (216) 861-1148
Contact: Lester E. Coleman, Tr.

Established in 1994 in OH.
Donor(s): Lester E. Coleman.
Financial data (yr. ended 12/31/01): Grants paid, $838,500; assets, $1,744,191 (M); expenditures, $894,394; qualifying distributions, $851,136.
Limitations: Giving primarily in OH.
Trustees: Kathleen A. Coleman, Kenneth J. Coleman, Lester E. Coleman, Mark W. Meister.
EIN: 341788395
Codes: FD

42342
The Timken Company Charitable Trust
c/o Bank One
101 Central Plz., S.
Canton, OH 44702
Application address: c/o The Timken Co., 1835 Dueber Ave. S.W., Canton, OH 44706

Trust established in 1947 in OH.
Donor(s): The Timken Co.
Financial data (yr. ended 12/31/01): Grants paid, $833,358; assets, $1,982,811 (M); expenditures, $845,610; qualifying distributions, $836,553.
Limitations: Giving primarily in OH.
Application information: Application form not required.
Trustees: Gene Little, John J. Schubach, Ward J. Timken.
EIN: 346534265
Codes: CS, FD, CD

42343
Lois U. Horvitz Foundation
(Formerly HRH Family Foundation)
c/o Parkland Mgmt. Co.
1001 Lakeside Ave., Ste. 900
Cleveland, OH 44114-1151 (216) 479-2200
FAX: (216) 479-2222
Scholarship application address: c/o Dr. Nyles C. Ayers, Scholarship Prog. Admin., 3314 W. End Ave., Nashville, TN 37203-1022, tel.: (615) 292-4379
Contact: Thomas H. Oden

Established in 1988 in OH.
Financial data (yr. ended 12/31/00): Grants paid, $822,375; assets, $8,378,844 (M); expenditures, $831,763; qualifying distributions, $823,174.
Application information: Application form required for scholarships.
Officers and Trustees:* Lois U. Horvitz,* Pres.; Leo M. Krulitz,* Secy. and Exec. Dir.; Thomas H. Oden,* Treas.
EIN: 341594655
Codes: FD, GTI

42344
The Hershey Foundation
10229 Prouty Rd.
Concord, OH 44077 (440) 256-6003
FAX: (440) 256-0233; *URL:* http://fdncenter.org/grantmaker/hershey
Contact: Debra Hershey Guren, Pres.

Established in 1986 in OH.
Donor(s): Jo Hershey Selden,‡ Loren W. Hershey, Debra Hershey Guren, Carole Hershey Walters.
Financial data (yr. ended 12/31/01): Grants paid, $818,000; assets, $16,762,673 (M); expenditures, $844,365; qualifying distributions, $818,000.
Limitations: Giving primarily in northeastern OH.
Publications: Annual report, multi-year report, informational brochure (including application guidelines), grants list.

Application information: No new proposals will be accepted in 2003 to allow for strategic planning. Application form not required.
Officers and Trustees:* Debra Hershey Guren,* Pres.; Carole Hershey Walters,* V.P. and Secy.; Loren W. Hershey,* Treas.; Georgia A. Froelich.
EIN: 341525626
Codes: FD

42345
L. and L. Nippert Charitable Foundation, Inc.
c/o The Randolph Co.
8255 Spooky Hollow Rd.
Cincinnati, OH 45242-6518 (513) 891-7144
E-mail: crandolph@green-acres.org
Contact: Carter Randolph, V.P.

Established in 1992 in OH as successor to L. and L. Nippert Charitable Foundation.
Donor(s): Louis Nippert,‡ Louise D. Nippert.
Financial data (yr. ended 12/31/01): Grants paid, $818,000; assets, $13,053,521 (M); expenditures, $905,568; qualifying distributions, $813,955.
Limitations: Giving primarily in Hamilton County, OH.
Application information: Application form not required.
Officers and Trustees:* Louise D. Nippert,* Pres.; Carter Randolph,* V.P.; Marie Eberhard,* Secy.-Treas.; Tim Johnson, Lawrence Kyte, Guy Randolph, Jane Randolph.
EIN: 311351011
Codes: FD

42346
Findlay Hancock County Community Foundation
101 W. Sandusky St., Ste. 207
Findlay, OH 45840 (419) 425-1100
FAX: (419) 425-9339; *E-mail:* commfdn@bright.net; *URL:* http://www.community-foundation.com
Contact: Barbara Deerhake, Exec. Dir.

Established in 1992 in OH as a supporting organization of the Cleveland Foundation; became a community foundation independent of the Cleveland Foundation in Feb. 1999.
Financial data (yr. ended 12/31/01): Grants paid, $817,940; assets, $22,136,224 (M); gifts received, $975,908; expenditures, $1,361,025.
Limitations: Giving limited to the greater Hancock County, OH, area.
Publications: Annual report, financial statement, application guidelines, informational brochure (including application guidelines).
Application information: See foundation website for full application guidelines and requirements. Proposals submitted by facsimile or e-mail not accepted. Application form not required.
Officers and Trustees:* G. Norman Nicholson,* Chair.; Charles J. Younger,* Vice-Chair.; Barbara M. Deerhake,* Pres. and Exec. Dir.; Charles F. Stumpp, Jr.,* Treas.; Karl L. Heminger, Jennifer Payne-White, Patrick R. Rooney, Judy M. Rower, Ralph D. Russo, Hon. John P. Stozich.
EIN: 341713261
Codes: CM, FD

42347
The Frances R. Luther Charitable Trust
c/o Fifth Third Bank
38 Fountain Sq. Plz., Trust Tax Dept., MD 1COM44
Cincinnati, OH 45263
Contact: Paula Wharton, Trust Off., Fifth Third Bank

Established in 2000 in OH.
Donor(s): Frances R. Luther Trust.

Financial data (yr. ended 12/31/00): Grants paid, $813,000; assets, $52,620,466 (M); gifts received, $50,524,334; expenditures, $945,620; qualifying distributions, $829,783.
Trustees: Narley L. Haley, Fifth Third Bank.
EIN: 316646985

42348
The Ashtabula Foundation, Inc.
510 W. 44th St.
Ashtabula, OH 44004 (440) 992-6818
Scholarship application address: c/o Gary Ensign, Ashtabula Campus, Kent State University, 3325 W. 13th St., Ashtabula, OH 44004, tel.: (440) 964-3322

Incorporated in 1922 in OH.
Financial data (yr. ended 12/31/01): Grants paid, $791,694; assets, $17,395,366 (M); gifts received, $754,738; expenditures, $971,924; qualifying distributions, $801,582.
Limitations: Giving limited to the Ashtabula, OH, area.
Publications: Annual report, application guidelines.
Application information: Application guidelines for scholarship funds available. Application form required.
Officers and Trustees:* William W. Hill,* Pres.; Eleanor A. Jammal,* Secy.-Treas.; Thomas D. Anderson, Roy H. Bean, Jerry Brockway, Liz Campbell, Rick Coblitz, Thad Hague, Glen W. Warner, Barbara P. Wiese.
EIN: 346538130
Codes: FD, GTI

42349
The Wuliger Foundation, Inc.
28601 Chagrin Blvd., Ste. 410
Beachwood, OH 44122 (216) 999-8922
Contact: Timothy F. Wuliger, Secy.-Treas.

Incorporated in 1956 in OH.
Donor(s): Ernest M. Wuliger.‡
Financial data (yr. ended 12/31/01): Grants paid, $784,024; assets, $15,475,392 (M); expenditures, $1,327,515; qualifying distributions, $768,136.
Limitations: Giving primarily in northeastern OH.
Application information: Application form not required.
Officers and Directors:* E. Jeffrey Wuliger,* Pres.; Gregory Wuliger,* V.P.; Timothy F. Wuliger,* Secy.-Treas.
EIN: 346527281
Codes: FD

42350
The Mercer County Civic Foundation, Inc.
P.O. Box 439
Celina, OH 45822 (419) 586-9950
E-mail: mccf@bright.net
Contact: Rita S. Bair, Dir.

Incorporated in 1960 in OH.
Financial data (yr. ended 12/31/01): Grants paid, $780,233; assets, $4,572,796 (M); gifts received, $197,048; expenditures, $853,727; giving activities include $20,200 for loans to individuals.
Limitations: Giving limited to Mercer County, OH.
Publications: Annual report (including application guidelines), application guidelines, informational brochure, newsletter.
Application information: Application form required.
Director: Rita S. Bair.
EIN: 346539139
Codes: CM, FD

42351
Midland Company Foundation
c/o John I. Von Lehman
7000 Midland Blvd.
Amelia, OH 45102

Established in 1998 in OH.
Donor(s): The Midland Co.
Financial data (yr. ended 12/31/00): Grants paid, $778,847; assets, $875,228 (M); gifts received, $1,340,050; expenditures, $782,578; qualifying distributions, $778,847.
Limitations: Applications not accepted. Giving primarily in Cincinnati, OH.
Application information: Contributes only to pre-selected organizations.
Officers: Joseph P. Hayden III, Chair.; John W. Hayden, Pres.; John I. Von Lehman, V.P. and Secy.; W. Todd Gray, Treas.
EIN: 311580326
Codes: CS, FD, CD

42352
Community Foundation of Mount Vernon & Knox County
(Formerly The Mount Vernon/Knox County Community Trust)
c/o The First-Knox National Bank
1 S. Main St., P.O. Box 1270
Mount Vernon, OH 43050 (740) 392-3270
FAX: (740) 399-5296; E-mail: thefoundation@firstknox.com
Contact: Sam Barone, Exec. Dir.

Established in 1944 in OH by declaration of trust.
Financial data (yr. ended 12/31/01): Grants paid, $765,004; assets, $22,413,891 (M); expenditures, $1,000,189.
Limitations: Giving primarily in Knox County, OH.
Publications: Annual report, informational brochure, occasional report, application guidelines.
Application information: Application form required.
Officers: Mark A. Ramser, Chair.; John D. Ellis, Vice-Chair.; Robert L. Rauzi, Secy.; Sally A. Nelson, Treas.
Board Members: Douglas O. Brenneman, E. LeBron Fairbanks, Thomas R. Fosnaught, Ronald G. Godfrey, Joan E. Jones, L. Bruce Levering, Deborah J. Reeder, Dennis L. Snyder.
Trustee: The First-Knox National Bank.
EIN: 311768219
Codes: CM, FD

42353
The Lincoln Electric Foundation
c/o KeyBank, N.A.
800 Superior Ave., Ste. 0420
Cleveland, OH 44114-2601
Application address: 22801 St. Clair Ave., Cleveland, OH 44117, tel.: (216) 481-8100
Contact: Paul Beddia

Trust established in 1952 in OH.
Donor(s): The Lincoln Electric Co.
Financial data (yr. ended 09/13/01): Grants paid, $761,000; assets, $2,386,796 (M); gifts received, $851,000; expenditures, $768,605; qualifying distributions, $761,938.
Limitations: Giving primarily in OH, with emphasis on Cleveland.
Application information: Application form not required.
Trustee: KeyBank, N.A.
EIN: 346518355
Codes: CS, FD, CD

42354
The Jesse and Caryl Philips Foundation
3870 Honey Hill Ln.
Dayton, OH 45405

Established in 1990 in OH.
Donor(s): Jesse Philips.‡
Financial data (yr. ended 06/30/01): Grants paid, $760,000; assets, $7,574,424 (M); expenditures, $822,907; qualifying distributions, $754,708.
Limitations: Applications not accepted. Giving primarily in Dayton, OH.
Application information: Contributes only to pre-selected organizations.
Officer and Trustees:* Caryl Philips,* Pres.; Benjamin M. Beatty, Mary Dombrowsky Beatty, Milton Roisman.
EIN: 341656718
Codes: FD

42355
Frank Mangano Foundation
2020 S. Union Ave.
Alliance, OH 44601

Established in 1988 in OH.
Donor(s): Frank J. Mangano.‡
Financial data (yr. ended 12/31/01): Grants paid, $753,069; assets, $12,559,176 (M); expenditures, $769,870; qualifying distributions, $755,670.
Limitations: Applications not accepted. Giving primarily in OH, VA, and WV.
Application information: Contributes only to pre-selected organizations.
Trustees: M.S. Hoover, Margaret E. Mangano.
EIN: 341600651
Codes: FD

42356
Joseph J. Schott Foundation
6650 Miralake Dr.
Cincinnati, OH 45243 (859) 431-5544
Contact: L. Thomas Hiltz, V.P.

Established in 1960 in OH.
Donor(s): Joseph J. Schott.‡
Financial data (yr. ended 12/31/00): Grants paid, $750,067; assets, $15,288,860 (M); expenditures, $767,054; qualifying distributions, $750,067.
Limitations: Giving primarily in the OH.
Officers: L. Thomas Hiltz, V.P.; William D. Saal, Secy.
EIN: 346513748
Codes: FD

42357
Bicknell Fund
c/o Advisory Svcs., Inc.
1422 Euclid Ave., Rm. 1010
Cleveland, OH 44115-2078 (216) 363-6482
FAX: (216) 363-6488
Contact: Robert G. Acklin, Secy.-Treas.

Incorporated in 1949 in OH.
Donor(s): Kate H. Bicknell,‡ Warren Bicknell, Jr.,‡ Warren Bicknell III, Kate B. Kirkham.
Financial data (yr. ended 12/31/01): Grants paid, $750,000; assets, $8,853,247 (M); expenditures, $783,133; qualifying distributions, $756,149.
Limitations: Giving primarily in the greater Cleveland, OH, area.
Publications: Application guidelines.
Application information: Multi-year grants not awarded. Application form not required.
Officers and Trustees:* Kate B. Kirkham,* Pres.; Warren Bicknell III,* V.P.; Robert G. Acklin, Secy.-Treas.; Wendy H. Bicknell, Donald J. Hofman, Henry L. Meyer III, Alexander S. Taylor II, Lyman H. Treadway III.
EIN: 346513799
Codes: FD

42358
The Murch Foundation
830 Hanna Bldg.
Cleveland, OH 44115

Incorporated in 1956 in OH.
Donor(s): Maynard H. Murch.‡
Financial data (yr. ended 12/31/01): Grants paid, $750,000; assets, $17,726,081 (M); expenditures, $772,019; qualifying distributions, $750,000.
Limitations: Applications not accepted. Giving primarily in OH.
Application information: Contributes only to pre-selected organizations.
Officers and Trustees:* Maynard H. Murch IV,* Pres. and Treas.; Creighton B. Murch,* V.P. and Secy.; Robert B. Murch,* V.P.; Maynard H. Murch V.
EIN: 346520188
Codes: FD

42359
LKC Foundation
1 Walsh Pl.
Cincinnati, OH 45208

Established in 1996 in DE.
Financial data (yr. ended 12/31/00): Grants paid, $744,770; assets, $14,158,641 (M); expenditures, $890,521; qualifying distributions, $740,916.
Limitations: Applications not accepted. Giving primarily in OH.
Application information: Contributes only to pre-selected organizations.
Officers and Directors:* Lucille K. Carothers,* Pres. and Treas.; Paula K. Oppenheim,* V.P. and Secy.; Ellen Stern Kerr, V.P.
EIN: 311490185
Codes: FD

42360
M. I. Schottenstein Homes Foundation
3 Easton Oval, Ste. 500
Columbus, OH 43219 (614) 418-8000
Contact: Irving E. Schottenstein, Pres.

Established in 1989 in OH.
Financial data (yr. ended 12/31/00): Grants paid, $743,564; assets, $3,386,140 (M); gifts received, $1,950,000; expenditures, $747,459; qualifying distributions, $743,564.
Limitations: Giving primarily in Columbus, OH.
Officers and Trustees:* Irving E. Schottenstein,* Pres.; Gary Schottenstein,* V.P.; Paul S. Coppel,* Secy.; William A. Roberts, Treas.; Phillip Creek, Linda Fisher, Robert Schottenstein, Steven Schottenstein.
EIN: 311254013
Codes: FD

42361
Reeves Foundation
232-4 W. 3rd St.
P.O. Box 441
Dover, OH 44622-0441 (330) 364-4660
Contact: Don A. Ulrich, Exec. Dir.

Trust established in 1966 in OH.
Donor(s): Margaret J. Reeves,‡ Helen F. Reeves,‡ Samuel J. Reeves.‡
Financial data (yr. ended 12/31/01): Grants paid, $742,745; assets, $23,622,428 (M); expenditures, $954,514; qualifying distributions, $796,948.
Limitations: Giving primarily in OH, with emphasis on the Dover area.
Application information: Application form not required.
Officers and Trustees:* W.E. Lieser,* Pres.; Thomas J. Patton,* V.P.; Jeffrey Wagner,* Secy.-Treas.; Don A. Ulrich, Exec. Dir.; Ronald L. Pissocra, Peter F. Wagner.

42361—OHIO

EIN: 346575477
Codes: FD

42362
The Fran and Warren Rupp Foundation
c/o KeyBank, N.A.
42 N. Main St.
Mansfield, OH 44902 (419) 525-7667
FAX: (419) 525-7666
Contact: Nick Gesouras

Established in 1977.
Donor(s): Fran R. Christian, Warren Rupp,‡ Suzanne R. Hartung.
Financial data (yr. ended 12/31/01): Grants paid, $719,003; assets, $20,133,053 (M); gifts received, $36,000; expenditures, $819,596; qualifying distributions, $792,026.
Limitations: Giving primarily in Mansfield and Richland County, OH.
Publications: Informational brochure (including application guidelines).
Application information: Application form required.
Officers and Trustees:* Frances R. Christian,* Co-Chair.; Sharon A. Rupp,* Co-Chair.; Suzanne R. Hartung,* Pres.; Sheila York, Secy.; B. Gene Hahn,* Treas.; Arnold Haring.
EIN: 341230690
Codes: FD

42363
Home Savings Charitable Foundation
c/o Home Savings and Loan Co.
P.O. Box 1111
Youngstown, OH 44501-1111 (330) 742-0500
Additional tel.: (330) 742-0571
Contact: Darlene Pavlock, Prog. Admin.

Established in 1991 in OH.
Donor(s): Home Savings and Loan Co.
Financial data (yr. ended 12/31/00): Grants paid, $715,292; assets, $19,072,328 (M); expenditures, $771,800; qualifying distributions, $750,070.
Limitations: Giving primarily in Mahoning, Trumbull, and Columbiana counties, OH.
Application information: Grant application furnished upon request. Application form not required.
Trustee: Butler Wick Trust Co.
EIN: 341695319
Codes: CS, FD, CD

42364
Jesse Philips Foundation
3870 Honey Hill Ln.
Dayton, OH 45405

Incorporated in 1960 in OH.
Donor(s): Tomkins Industries, Inc., and subsidiaries, Jesse Philips.‡
Financial data (yr. ended 02/28/01): Grants paid, $710,840; assets, $24,149,250 (M); expenditures, $941,475; qualifying distributions, $739,048.
Limitations: Applications not accepted. Giving primarily in Dayton, OH.
Application information: Contributes only to pre-selected organizations.
Officers: Caryl Philips, Pres.; Milton Roisman, V.P.; Mary D. Beatty, Secy.; Benjamin M. Beatty, Treas.
EIN: 316023380
Codes: CS, FD, CD

42365
The Andrew Jergens Foundation
c/o PNC Bank
P.O. Box 1198
Cincinnati, OH 45201-1198 (513) 651-8377
Contact: Lee D. Crooks, Fdn. Admin.

Incorporated in 1962 in OH.
Donor(s): Andrew N. Jergens.‡
Financial data (yr. ended 08/31/01): Grants paid, $703,712; assets, $11,726,852 (M); expenditures, $818,521; qualifying distributions, $710,051.
Limitations: Giving limited to the greater Cincinnati, OH, area.
Publications: Application guidelines.
Application information: Proposal must meet requirements outlined in proposal guidelines. Application form required.
Officers and Trustees:* Rev. Andrew M. Jergens,* Chair.; Andrew W. Jergens,* Pres.; Michael B. Hays,* V.P.; Peter H. Jergens,* Secy.; Thomas C. Hays,* Treas.; Consuelo W. Harris, Mary Ann Hays, Linda Busken Jergens, Eric H. Kearney, Joyce J. Keeshin, Jennifer H. Morris.
EIN: 316038702
Codes: FD

42366
John Hauck Foundation
c/o Fifth Third Bank
38 Fountain Sq. Plz.
Cincinnati, OH 45263
Contact: Paula Wharter

Established in 1989 in OH.
Donor(s): Frederick Hauck.
Financial data (yr. ended 09/30/01): Grants paid, $702,500; assets, $12,236,063 (M); expenditures, $781,037; qualifying distributions, $719,503.
Limitations: Applications not accepted. Giving primarily in Cincinnati, OH.
Application information: Contributes only to pre-selected organizations.
Trustees: E. Allen Elliott, Narley L. Haley, John W. Hauck, Fifth Third Bank.
EIN: 316366846
Codes: FD

42367
Milacron Foundation
(Formerly Cincinnati Milacron Foundation)
2090 Florence Ave.
Cincinnati, OH 45206 (513) 487-5912
FAX: (513) 487-5586
Contact: John C. Francy, Asst. Treas.

Incorporated in 1951 in OH.
Donor(s): Cincinnati Milacron Inc., Milacron Inc.
Financial data (yr. ended 12/31/01): Grants paid, $694,645; assets, $137,118 (M); gifts received, $650,000; expenditures, $705,125; qualifying distributions, $705,125.
Limitations: Giving primarily in Detroit, MI, and OH.
Publications: Application guidelines.
Application information: Application form not required.
Officer and Trustees:* Daniel J. Meyer,* Pres. and Treas.; D.F. Allen, N.A. Armstrong, R.D. Brown, J. Francy, B.G. Kasting, R.I. Lienesch.
EIN: 316030682
Codes: CS, FD, CD

42368
The William Bingham Foundation
20325 Center Ridge Rd., Ste. 629
Rocky River, OH 44116 (440) 331-6350
E-mail: info@WBinghamFoundation.org; *URL:* http://fdncenter.org/grantmaker/bingham
Contact: Laura H. Gilbertson, Dir.

Incorporated in 1955 in OH.
Donor(s): Elizabeth B. Blossom.‡
Financial data (yr. ended 12/31/01): Grants paid, $693,175; assets, $20,830,856 (M); expenditures, $928,306; qualifying distributions, $814,239.
Limitations: Giving primarily in the eastern U.S. and the West Coast, with emphasis on communities in which the trustees reside.
Publications: Informational brochure (including application guidelines).
Application information: Full proposals accepted only by request in response to applicant's initial letter; many of the grant proposals are initiated by trustees. FAX and E-mail proposals not accepted. Application form not required.
Officers and Trustees:* C. Bingham Blossom,* Pres.; Robin Dunn Blossom,* V.P.; Thomas F. Allen, Secy.; C. Perry Blossom,* Treas.; Jonathan B. Blossom, Laurel Blossom, Virginia O. Blossom, Elizabeth B. Heffernan, Rebecca B. Kovacik.
Director: Laura H. Gilbertson.
EIN: 346513791
Codes: FD

42369
Charles E. Schell Foundation for Education
c/o Fifth Third Bank
38 Fountain Sq. Plz., MD 1090L7
Cincinnati, OH 45263 (513) 534-7001
Contact: Lawra J. Baumann, Fdn. Off., Fifth Third Bank

Established in 1939 OH.
Donor(s): Charles E. Schell.‡
Financial data (yr. ended 09/30/01): Grants paid, $685,501; assets, $2,710,812 (M); gifts received, $1,696,723; expenditures, $710,940; qualifying distributions, $692,887.
Limitations: Giving limited to IN, KY, OH, WV, and adjoining states.
Publications: Annual report, application guidelines.
Application information: Application form required.
Trustee: Fifth Third Bank.
EIN: 316019720
Codes: FD

42370
John McIntire Educational Fund
c/o Unizan Fin. Svcs. Group
422 Main St., P.O. Box 2307
Zanesville, OH 43702-2307 (740) 455-7060
Contact: Neana Butler, Admin. Asst.

Established about 1937.
Donor(s): John McIntire.‡
Financial data (yr. ended 06/30/01): Grants paid, $684,541; assets, $13,676,757 (M); expenditures, $737,337; qualifying distributions, $698,360.
Limitations: Giving limited to Zanesville, OH, residents.
Application information: Application form required.
Officers and Directors:* Milman H. Linn III,* Pres.; Charles A. Gorsuch,* V.P.; Frederic Grant,* Secy.; Nelson McCoy, Jr.,* Treas.; William Brown, Michael Leplante, William Stewart.
EIN: 316021239
Codes: FD, GTI

42371
The LaMacchia Family Foundation
7800 Deer Crossing
Cincinnati, OH 45243 (513) 621-8210
Contact: Elizabeth H. LaMacchia, Tr.

Established in 1999 in OH.
Donor(s): John T. LaMacchia.
Financial data (yr. ended 12/31/00): Grants paid, $669,000; assets, $534,132 (M); gifts received, $1,061,585; expenditures, $676,447; qualifying distributions, $662,306.
Limitations: Giving primarily in OH.
Trustees: Charles R. LaMacchia, Elizabeth E. LaMacchia, Elizabeth H. LaMacchia, John P. LaMacchia, John T. LaMacchia, Mary E. LaMacchia, Thomas F. LaMacchia.
EIN: 311645287
Codes: FD

42372
The Kim and Gary Heiman Family Foundation
c/o Edward M. Frankel
P.O. Box 371805
Cincinnati, OH 45222-1805

Established in 1998 in OH.
Donor(s): Gary Heiman, Kim Heiman.
Financial data (yr. ended 12/31/00): Grants paid, $667,005; assets, $228,965 (M); gifts received, $681,386; expenditures, $668,705; qualifying distributions, $668,402.
Limitations: Applications not accepted.
Application information: Contributes only to pre-selected organizations.
Officers: Gary Heiman, Pres.; Kim Heiman, V.P.; Edward M. Frankel, Secy.-Treas.
EIN: 316605176
Codes: FD

42373
The Ohio Valley Foundation
c/o Fifth Third Bank
38 Fountain Sq. Plz., MD 1090L7
Cincinnati, OH 45263 (513) 534-7001
Contact: Lawra J. Baumann, Fdn. Off., Fifth Third Bank

Incorporated in 1946 in OH.
Donor(s): John J. Rowe,‡ Wm. L. McGrath,‡ John W. Warrington.‡
Financial data (yr. ended 09/30/01): Grants paid, $666,667; assets, $8,318,653 (M); expenditures, $772,251; qualifying distributions, $686,699.
Limitations: Giving primarily in the greater Cincinnati, OH, area.
Publications: Annual report, application guidelines.
Application information: Application form not required.
Board Members: Phillip C. Long, George A. Schaefer, Jr., Dudley S. Taft.
Trustee: Fifth Third Bank.
EIN: 316008508
Codes: FD

42374
LZ Francis Foundation
c/o Mark Mihalik
3550 Lander Rd., Ste. 200
Pepper Pike, OH 44124

Established in 1992 in OH as partial successor to the Nason Foundation.
Donor(s): The Nason Foundation, Katharine Nason Tipper.
Financial data (yr. ended 12/31/01): Grants paid, $661,000; assets, $13,776,649 (M); gifts received, $13,115; expenditures, $769,315; qualifying distributions, $710,855.
Limitations: Applications not accepted. Giving primarily in FL and VT.
Application information: Contributes only to pre-selected organizations.
Officers: Katharine Nason Tipper, Pres. and Treas.; Charles F. Tipper, V.P. and Secy.; Jessica A. Oski, V.P.
EIN: 341721860
Codes: FD

42375
The Sidney Frohman Foundation
c/o Muehlhauser & Moore
P.O. Box 790
Sandusky, OH 44871-0790

Trust established in 1952 in OH.
Donor(s): Sidney Frohman,‡ Blanche P. Frohman.‡
Financial data (yr. ended 12/31/01): Grants paid, $659,008; assets, $11,385,666 (M); expenditures, $692,407; qualifying distributions, $668,648.
Limitations: Applications not accepted. Giving primarily in OH, with emphasis on Erie County.
Application information: Contributes only to pre-selected organizations.
Trustees: Daniel C. Frohman, George T. Henderson, Donald G. Koch.
EIN: 346517809
Codes: FD

42376
The Convergys Foundation, Inc.
201 E. 4th St., Ste. 102-1960
Cincinnati, OH 45202 (513) 784-5937
Contact: Joseph B. Curry

Established in 1999 in OH.
Financial data (yr. ended 12/31/01): Grants paid, $655,390; assets, $133,719 (M); gifts received, $250,000; expenditures, $456,582; qualifying distributions, $656,660.
Limitations: Giving primarily in Cincinnati, OH; some giving in Salt Lake City, UT.
Trustees: Cheryl N. Campbell, David F. Dougherty, Robert J. Marino, James F. Orr, Steven G. Rolls.
EIN: 311619871
Codes: FD

42377
Ann and Ari Deshe Foundation
c/o Ari Deshe
75 S. Robinwood
Whitehall, OH 43213

Established in 1997 in OH.
Donor(s): Ann Deshe, Ari Deshe.
Financial data (yr. ended 12/31/00): Grants paid, $654,187; assets, $3,815,675 (M); expenditures, $654,496; qualifying distributions, $654,496.
Limitations: Giving primarily in Columbus, OH.
Officers: Ann Deshe, Pres.; Ari Deshe, V.P.
EIN: 311499050
Codes: FD

42378
Pulley Foundation
(Formerly L. L. Browning Memorial Fund)
c/o U.S. Bank
P.O. Box 1118
Cincinnati, OH 45201-1118

Established in 1969.
Donor(s): L.L. Browning, Jr. Charitable Lead Unitrust.
Financial data (yr. ended 12/31/01): Grants paid, $650,500; assets, $11,879,068 (M); gifts received, $1,003,898; expenditures, $689,348; qualifying distributions, $650,760.
Limitations: Applications not accepted. Giving primarily in Maysville, KY, and St. Louis, MO.
Application information: Contributes only to pre-selected organizations. Unsolicited requests for funds are not accepted.
Officers and Trustees:* Virginia J. Browning,* Pres.; Dorothy W. Browning,* Secy.-Treas.; Kathryn B. Hendrickson, Virginia B. Illick.
Agent: U.S. Bank.
EIN: 237009545
Codes: FD

42379
Sankey Family Foundation
4040 Embassy Pkwy., Ste. 100
Akron, OH 44333-8354 (330) 668-6500
Contact: Alan J. Tobin, Secy.

Established in 1999 in OH.
Donor(s): James K. Sankey.
Financial data (yr. ended 12/31/01): Grants paid, $643,600; assets, $8,726,137 (M); gifts received, $7,760; expenditures, $652,540; qualifying distributions, $647,657.
Limitations: Giving on a national basis, with some emphasis on OH.
Application information: Application form not required.
Officers: James K. Sankey, Pres.; Beth H. Sankey, V.P and Treas.; Alan J. Tobin, Secy.
Trustee: Richard W. Sankey.
EIN: 341909797
Codes: FD

42380
George W. & Mary F. Ritter Charitable Trust
c/o KeyBank, N.A.
P.O. Box 10099
Toledo, OH 43699-0099 (419) 259-8655
Contact: Diane Ohns, V.P., KeyBank, N.A.

Established in 1982 in OH.
Donor(s): George W. Ritter.‡
Financial data (yr. ended 11/30/01): Grants paid, $641,367; assets, $12,066,207 (M); expenditures, $677,749; qualifying distributions, $641,685.
Limitations: Giving primarily in the Toledo, OH, area.
Application information: Application form required for scholarships.
Trustee: KeyBank, N.A.
EIN: 346781636
Codes: FD

42381
Leonard C. & Mildred F. Ferguson Foundation
c/o FirstMerit Bank, N.A.
121 S. Main St., Ste. 200
Akron, OH 44308 (330) 384-7304
Contact: Joseph Wojcik

Established in 1998 in FL.
Donor(s): Mildred F. Ferguson Irrevocable Trust.
Financial data (yr. ended 01/31/01): Grants paid, $638,048; assets, $13,703,702 (M); gifts received, $15,447,345; expenditures, $707,726; qualifying distributions, $656,695.
Limitations: Giving primarily in IL.
Officers: Nancy Seeley, Pres.; Lynne Seeley, V.P.
Trustee Banks: FirstMerit Bank, N.A., Northern Trust Bank of Florida, N.A.
EIN: 656245247
Codes: FD

42382
The Reynolds and Reynolds Company Foundation
P.O. Box 2608
Dayton, OH 45402-2608 (937) 485-4409
Contact for proposal information: Alice Davisson, Admin., tel.: (937) 485-8138, E-mail: alice_davisson@reyrey.com; Additional contact: Cathy Ponitz, tel.: (937) 485-8140, E-mail: cathy_ponitz@reyrey.com; URL: http://www.reyrey.com/about/community.asp

Established in 1986 in OH.
Donor(s): The Reynolds and Reynolds Co.
Financial data (yr. ended 09/30/01): Grants paid, $636,195; assets, $792,114 (M); expenditures, $638,956; qualifying distributions, $638,760.
Limitations: Giving in the areas of Dayton and Celina, OH.
Publications: Application guidelines.
Application information: All proposals must be submitted electronically. See website for application guidelines. Application form required.
Trustees: Kim Brown, Catherine Ponitz, Scott Schafer, Mike Stoner, Gillis West.
EIN: 311168299
Codes: CS, FD, CD

42383
Covenant Foundation, Inc.
5807 McCray Ct.
Cincinnati, OH 45224
Contact: Timothy E. Johnson, Tr.

Established in 1987 in OH.
Financial data (yr. ended 12/31/01): Grants paid, $628,140; assets, $12,959,447 (M); gifts received, $1,000,000; expenditures, $638,252; qualifying distributions, $628,140.
Limitations: Applications not accepted. Giving on a national basis.
Application information: Unsolicited requests for grants not accepted. Grants only to organizations known to trustees.
Trustees: Janet L. Johnson, Paul T. Johnson, Timothy E. Johnson, David C. Tedford.
EIN: 311225037
Codes: FD

42384
Coshocton Foundation
220 S. 4th St.
P.O. Box 55
Coshocton, OH 43812 (740) 622-0010
Additional tel.: (740) 622-0212; FAX: (740) 622-1660; E-mail: Jamesg@coshoctonfoundation.org; URL: http://www.coshoctonfoundation.org
Contact: James Gauerke, Exec. Dir.

Established in 1966 in OH.
Donor(s): Adolph Golden,‡ Fred Johnston, Edward E. Montgomery,‡ Edith Schooler,‡ Seward Schooler,‡ Mary F. Taylor, Robert M. Thomas, Willard Baughman,‡ Willard S. Breon, James E. Wilson,‡ Herbert E. Carlson,‡ Ralph Wisenburg, Richard Barthebaug, Mrs. Richard Barthebaug, Ed Mulligan, Marion Mulligan Sutton.
Financial data (yr. ended 09/30/01): Grants paid, $619,225; assets, $14,016,237 (M); gifts received, $346,519; expenditures, $848,103.
Limitations: Giving limited to Coshocton County, OH.
Publications: Annual report, newsletter, application guidelines, financial statement, occasional report, informational brochure (including application guidelines), application guidelines (including application guidelines).

Application information: Scholarships granted directly to college or university. Application form required.
Officers and Trustees:* Dan Erb, Pres.; Sheila Packhill, V.P.; Carolyn Holls, Secy.; James Gauerke,* Treas. and Exec. Dir.; Willard S. Breon, Sally Bullens, Samuel C. Clow.
Distribution Committee: Don Packhill, Chair., Distrib. Comm.; Tom Edwards, William Given, Tom Thompson, Barbara Warren.
Investment Committee: Ralph Wisenburg, Chair., Invest. Comm.; Dick Baker, Richard Corbett, Orville Fuller, Fred Johnston.
EIN: 316064567
Codes: CM, FD

42385
Albert G. and Olive H. Schlink Foundation
49 Benedict Ave., Ste. C
Norwalk, OH 44857 (419) 668-8211
FAX: (419) 668-2813
Contact: Robert A. Wiedemann, Pres.

Established in 1966 in OH.
Donor(s): Albert G. Schlink,‡ Olive H. Schlink.‡
Financial data (yr. ended 12/31/01): Grants paid, $618,767; assets, $14,353,030 (M); expenditures, $806,772; qualifying distributions, $722,870.
Limitations: Giving primarily in OH.
Application information: Application form not required.
Officers and Trustees:* Robert A. Wiedemann,* Pres. and Secy.; Curtis J. Koch,* V.P.; John D. Allton,* Treas.; Michael N. Clemens, Dorothy E. Wiedemann.
EIN: 346574722
Codes: FD

42386
The S. K. Wellman Foundation
P.O. Box 32554
Euclid, OH 44132-0554 (216) 261-7250
Contact: Ethel Pearson, Secy.

Incorporated in 1951 in OH.
Donor(s): S.K. Wellman.‡
Financial data (yr. ended 12/31/01): Grants paid, $613,800; assets, $8,073,587 (M); expenditures, $750,874; qualifying distributions, $652,655.
Limitations: Giving primarily in OH.
Publications: Application guidelines, grants list.
Application information: Application form not required.
Officers: John M. Wilson, Jr., Pres.; Ethel Pearson, Secy.
Trustees: Franklin B. Floyd, Susanne Wellman O'Gara, Patricia Wellman Wilson.
EIN: 346520032
Codes: FD

42387
Iddings Benevolent Trust
(also known as Iddings Foundation)
Ketting Twr., Ste. 1620
Dayton, OH 45401 (937) 224-1773
FAX: (937) 224-1871
Contact: Maribeth A. Graham, Admin.

Established in 1973 in OH.
Donor(s): Roscoe C. Iddings,‡ Andrew S. Iddings.‡
Financial data (yr. ended 12/31/00): Grants paid, $612,585; assets, $14,476,846 (M); expenditures, $906,928; qualifying distributions, $694,880.
Limitations: Giving limited to OH, with emphasis on the Dayton metropolitan area.
Publications: Informational brochure (including application guidelines).
Application information: Application form not required.
Trustee: Bank One Trust Co., N.A.

EIN: 316135058
Codes: FD

42388
George M. and Pamela S. Humphrey Fund
c/o Advisory Svcs., Inc.
1010 Hanna Bldg., 1422 Euclid Ave.
Cleveland, OH 44115-2078 (216) 363-6483
Contact: Jackie A. Horning, Secy.-Treas.

Incorporated in 1951 in OH.
Donor(s): George M. Humphrey,‡ Pamela S. Humphrey.‡
Financial data (yr. ended 12/31/01): Grants paid, $612,370; assets, $13,433,192 (M); expenditures, $657,500; qualifying distributions, $621,263.
Limitations: Giving primarily in OH, with emphasis on Cleveland.
Publications: Annual report.
Application information: Application form not required.
Officers and Trustees:* Pamela B. Keefe,* Pres.; Stephen T. Keefe, V.P.; Jackie A. Horning, Secy.-Treas.; Peter W. Adams, Alice B. Burnham.
EIN: 346513798
Codes: FD

42389
John E. & Sue M. Jackson Charitable Trust
c/o National City Bank of Pennsylvania
P.O. Box 94651
Cleveland, OH 44101-4651
Application address: 20 Stanwix St, Pittsburgh, PA 15222, tel.: (412) 644-6005; FAX: (412) 644-6176
Contact: John M. Dodson

Established in 1950.
Financial data (yr. ended 12/31/01): Grants paid, $609,000; assets, $10,845,502 (M); expenditures, $640,405; qualifying distributions, $615,415.
Limitations: Giving primarily in Washington, DC, FL, MD, and VA.
Trustee: National City Bank of Pennsylvania.
EIN: 256019484
Codes: FD

42390
The Josephine Schell Russell Charitable Trust
c/o PNC Bank, N.A.
P.O. Box 1198
Cincinnati, OH 45201-1198 (513) 651-8377
Contact: Lee D. Crooks, Fdn. Admin.

Trust established in 1976 in OH.
Donor(s): Josephine Schell Russell.‡
Financial data (yr. ended 06/30/02): Grants paid, $608,100; assets, $10,961,744 (M); expenditures, $631,350; qualifying distributions, $628,836.
Limitations: Giving limited to the greater Cincinnati, OH, area.
Publications: Application guidelines.
Application information: Application form required.
Trustee: PNC Bank, N.A.
EIN: 316195446
Codes: FD

42391
John and Shirley Davies Foundation
(Formerly Bishopric Foundation)
8044 Montgomery Rd., Ste. 163
Cincinnati, OH 45236-2923
Contact: S. John Davies, Jr., Pres.

Established in 1991 in OH.
Donor(s): S. John Davies, Jr.
Financial data (yr. ended 12/31/00): Grants paid, $607,095; assets, $1,952,975 (M); gifts received, $219,125; expenditures, $663,614; qualifying distributions, $635,600.

Limitations: Giving primarily in Cincinnati, OH.
Application information: Scholarship awards limited to Goshen school district students and are paid directly to the college or university on behalf of the named recipient. Application form not required.
Officers: S. John Davies, Jr., Pres.; Ashley Davies, V.P.; Shirl Moran, Secy.; Darla Davies, Treas.
EIN: 311335126
Codes: FD

42392
Conrad & Caroline Jobst Foundation
c/o KeyBank, N.A.
P.O. Box 10099
Toledo, OH 43699-0099 (419) 259-8655
Contact: Diane Ohns, V.P., KeyBank, N.A.

Established in 1986.
Financial data (yr. ended 12/31/01): Grants paid, $600,000; assets, $11,312,489 (M); expenditures, $674,037; qualifying distributions, $657,141.
Limitations: Giving primarily in Toledo, OH; some giving also in MI.
Trustees: John M. Curphey, Douglas Metz, Orval Seydlitz, KeyBank, N.A.
EIN: 346872214
Codes: FD

42393
Fairfield County Foundation
109 N. Broad St.
P.O. Box 2450
Lancaster, OH 43130-2450 (740) 654-8451
FAX: (614) 653-7074
Contact: W. Thomas Leckrone, Exec. Dir.

Established in 1989 in OH.
Financial data (yr. ended 12/31/00): Grants paid, $595,034; assets, $9,336,505 (M); gifts received, $1,095,657; expenditures, $840,998.
Limitations: Giving limited to Fairfield County, OH.
Publications: Annual report, application guidelines, informational brochure.
Application information: Application form required.
Officer: W. Thomas Leckrone, Exec. Dir.
EIN: 341623983
Codes: CM, FD

42394
The Ohio National Foundation
1 Financial Way
Cincinnati, OH 45242 (513) 559-6493
Contact: Anthony Esposito, Secy.

Established in 1987 in OH.
Donor(s): The Ohio National Life Insurance Co., Ohio National Financial Svcs.
Financial data (yr. ended 12/31/01): Grants paid, $592,871; assets, $2,009,598 (M); gifts received, $1,002,675; expenditures, $593,604; qualifying distributions, $592,697.
Limitations: Giving primarily in Cincinnati, OH.
Application information: Application form not required.
Officers and Trustees:* David B. O'Maley,* Pres.; Joseph P. Brom,* V.P.; Anthony Esposito, Secy.; Roylene Broadwell, Treas.; Howard C. Becker, Chris A. Carlson, Ronald J. Dolan, Stuart G. Summers.
EIN: 311230164
Codes: CS, FD, CD

42395
Nathan Rothschild Foundation
c/o National City Bank of Indiana
P.O. Box 94651
Cleveland, OH 44101-4651

Financial data (yr. ended 10/31/00): Grants paid, $591,003; assets, $19,383 (M); expenditures, $593,486; qualifying distributions, $587,512.
Limitations: Applications not accepted. Giving primarily in Fort Wayne, IN.
Application information: Contributes only to pre-selected organizations.
Trustee: National City Bank of Indiana.
EIN: 356022675
Codes: FD

42396
Fred F. Silk Charitable Foundation
900 Bank One Tower
Canton, OH 44702-1498
Contact: Paul J. Helmuth, Tr.

Established in 1990 in OH.
Donor(s): Fred F. Silk.‡
Financial data (yr. ended 09/30/01): Grants paid, $590,668; assets, $15,305,510 (M); expenditures, $734,067; qualifying distributions, $714,955.
Limitations: Applications not accepted. Giving primarily in Canton, OH.
Application information: Contributes only to pre-selected organizations.
Trustees: Dennis J. Fox, Paul J. Helmuth.
EIN: 341651258
Codes: FD

42397
Samuel H. Miller Family Fund, Inc.
c/o Samuel H. Miller, Forest City Enterprises
1170 Terminal Tower, 50 Public Sq.
Cleveland, OH 44113

Established in 1989 in OH.
Donor(s): Samuel H. Miller.
Financial data (yr. ended 12/31/01): Grants paid, $589,991; assets, $652,702 (M); gifts received, $395,862; expenditures, $681,506; qualifying distributions, $589,052.
Limitations: Applications not accepted. Giving primarily in Cleveland, OH.
Application information: Contributes only to pre-selected organizations.
Officers and Trustees:* Samuel H. Miller,* Pres.; Abraham Miller,* V.P.; Eleanor Fanslau,* Secy.-Treas.; Bruce W. Lang, Maria Miller.
EIN: 341482231
Codes: FD

42398
The Andrews Foundation
13111 Shaker Sq., Ste. 208
Cleveland, OH 44120 (216) 751-2115
FAX: (216) 751-2105
Contact: Laura Baxter-Heuer, Pres.

Incorporated in 1951 in OH.
Donor(s): Mrs. Matthew Andrews.‡
Financial data (yr. ended 12/31/01): Grants paid, $589,500; assets, $10,175,836 (M); expenditures, $665,636; qualifying distributions, $618,611.
Limitations: Giving limited to northeastern OH.
Application information: Application form not required.
Officers and Trustees:* Laura Baxter-Heuer,* Pres.; James H. Dempsey, Jr.,* Secy.; Thomas DeVan,* Treas.
EIN: 346515110
Codes: FD

42399
Diebold Foundation
5995 Mayfair Rd.
North Canton, OH 44720

Established in 1993 in OH.
Donor(s): Diebold, Inc.
Financial data (yr. ended 12/31/01): Grants paid, $583,515; assets, $8,299,778 (M); expenditures, $613,655; qualifying distributions, $583,735.
Limitations: Applications not accepted. Giving primarily in OH.
Application information: Contributes only to pre-selected organizations.
Officers: W.W. O'Dell, Pres.; G. Geswein, V.P. and Treas.; Charles B. Scheurer, Secy.
EIN: 341757351
Codes: CS, FD, CD

42400
Muskingum County Community Foundation
534 Putnam Ave.
Zanesville, OH 43701 (740) 453-5192
Mailing address: P.O. Box 3042, Zanesville, OH 43702-3042; FAX: (740) 453-5734; E-mail: giving@mccf.org; URL: http://www.mccf.org
Contact: Dr. David Mitzel, Exec. Dir.

Established in 1985 in OH.
Financial data (yr. ended 12/31/00): Grants paid, $578,520; assets, $12,400,000 (M); gifts received, $985,000; expenditures, $1,244,691.
Limitations: Applications not accepted. Giving limited to Muskingum County, OH.
Publications: Annual report, newsletter, informational brochure, grants list.
Application information: Unsolicited requests for funds not accepted.
Officers and Trustee:* Douglas Mock,* Pres.; James McDonald,* V.P.; Sondra Kopf,* Secy.; Frank Dosch,* Treas.
EIN: 311147022
Codes: CM, FD

42401
Helen G., Henry F. & Louise T. Dornette Foundation
c/o Fifth Third Bank
38 Fountain Sq. Plz.
Cincinnati, OH 45263

Established in 1991 in OH.
Donor(s): Helen G. Dornette.
Financial data (yr. ended 03/31/01): Grants paid, $577,600; assets, $12,274,752 (M); expenditures, $659,108; qualifying distributions, $602,081.
Limitations: Applications not accepted. Giving primarily in OH.
Application information: Contributes only to pre-selected organizations.
Trustee: Fifth Third Bank.
EIN: 316425317

42402
Woodruff Foundation
1422 Euclid Ave., Ste. 627
Cleveland, OH 44115 (216) 566-1853
FAX: (216) 621-8198; URL: http://www.FMSCleveland.com/woodruff
Contact: Janet E. Narten, Exec. Dir.

Established in 1986 in OH; converted with proceeds from the sale of Woodruff Hospital.
Financial data (yr. ended 12/31/01): Grants paid, $577,009; assets, $12,159,572 (M); expenditures, $771,960; qualifying distributions, $653,722.
Limitations: Giving limited to Cuyahoga County, OH.
Publications: Annual report.
Application information: Application form not required.

42402—OHIO

Officers and Trustees:* Steven Neuhaus, Ph.D.,* Pres.; Hon. Carolyn Friedland,* V.P.; L. Douglas Lenkoski, Secy.-Treas.; Hon. Patricia Ann Blackmon, Oliver C. Henkel, Jr., Lenora A. Kola, Ph.D., Adrian Maldonado, Paul Omelsy, M.D., Mario Tonti.
EIN: 237425631
Codes: FD

42403
Robert and Mary Weisbrod Foundation
c/o National City Bank of Pennsylvania
P.O. Box 94651
Cleveland, OH 44101-4651
Application address: c/o National City Bank, P.O. Box 837, Pittsburgh, PA 15230, tel.: (412) 644-8114
Contact: The Distrib. Comm.

Established in 1968 in PA.
Donor(s): Mary E. Weisbrod,‡ Mary Weisbrod Unitrust.
Financial data (yr. ended 12/31/01): Grants paid, $567,520; assets, $14,230,352 (M); gifts received, $83,105; expenditures, $657,846; qualifying distributions, $612,832.
Limitations: Giving primarily in the Pittsburgh, PA, area.
Application information: Application form not required.
Trustee: National City Bank of Pennsylvania.
EIN: 256105924
Codes: FD

42404
Orleton Trust Fund
c/o Anne Greene
4365 Delco Dell Rd.
Dayton, OH 45429

Trust established in 1944 in OH.
Donor(s): Mary E. Johnston.‡
Financial data (yr. ended 12/31/01): Grants paid, $564,125; assets, $8,361,245 (M); expenditures, $579,620; qualifying distributions, $558,264.
Limitations: Applications not accepted. Giving primarily in San Mateo County, CA, and Dayton, OH.
Application information: Contributes only to pre-selected organizations.
Trustee: Anne Greene.
EIN: 316024543
Codes: FD

42405
The Hauss-Helms Foundation, Inc.
P.O. Box 25
Wapakoneta, OH 45895

Incorporated in 1965 in OH.
Donor(s): Besse Hauss Helms,‡ W.B. Helms.‡
Financial data (yr. ended 12/31/01): Grants paid, $563,092; assets, $10,008,958 (M); expenditures, $636,720; qualifying distributions, $635,760.
Limitations: Applications not accepted. Giving limited to residents of Auglaize and Allen counties, OH.
Application information: Unsolicited requests for funds not accepted.
Officers: James E. Weger, Pres.; Douglas Jauert, Secy.
Trustees: N. Thomas Cornell, John C. Haehn, Robert C. Lietz, James S. West.
EIN: 340975903
Codes: FD, GTI

42406
Clement O. Miniger Memorial Foundation
709 Madison Ave., Rm. 205
P.O. Box 1985
Toledo, OH 43603-1985

Incorporated in 1952 in OH.
Donor(s): George M. Jones, Jr.,‡ Eleanor Miniger Jones.‡
Financial data (yr. ended 12/31/01): Grants paid, $559,950; assets, $12,278,083 (M); expenditures, $689,542; qualifying distributions, $598,824.
Limitations: Giving primarily in northwestern OH.
Application information: Application form not required.
Officers and Trustees:* George M. Jones III,* Pres.; John A. Morse,* V.P.; Thomas DeVilbiss, Exec. Secy. and Treas.; William F. Buckley, Severn Joyce, Mark Schaffer, Steve Staellin, Edward Weber.
EIN: 346523024
Codes: FD

42407
Frederick J. Pfeiffer Foundation
c/o National City Bank of Indiana
P.O. Box 94651
Cleveland, OH 44101-4651

Established in 1994 in IN.
Donor(s): Frederick J. Pfeiffer.‡
Financial data (yr. ended 06/30/01): Grants paid, $558,121; assets, $11,474,529 (M); expenditures, $676,958; qualifying distributions, $584,251.
Limitations: Applications not accepted. Giving primarily in Chicago, IL, Fort Wayne, IN, and Philadelphia, PA.
Application information: Contributes only to pre-selected organizations.
Trustee: National City Bank of Indiana.
EIN: 356593983
Codes: FD

42408
The Richard R. Hallock Foundation
291 Morgan St.
Oberlin, OH 44074
Contact: David W. Clark, Fdn. Mgr.

Established in 1999 in OH.
Donor(s): Richard R. Hallock.‡
Financial data (yr. ended 12/31/01): Grants paid, $550,926; assets, $11,267,337 (M); expenditures, $673,606; qualifying distributions, $565,384.
Limitations: Applications not accepted. Giving primarily in Lorain County, OH.
Application information: Contributes only to pre-selected organizations.
Officers and Directors:* Myriam L. Hallock, Pres.; Robert O. Sawyer,* Secy.; David W. Clark, Mgr.
EIN: 341901406

42409
Richard M. & Yvonne Hamlin Foundation
3560 W. Market St., Ste. 300
Akron, OH 44333
Contact: Rosemary Lombardi

Donor(s): McDowell Manufacturing.
Financial data (yr. ended 12/31/01): Grants paid, $548,900; assets, $4,221,895 (M); gifts received, $121,404; expenditures, $584,853; qualifying distributions, $549,618.
Limitations: Giving primarily in OH.
Application information: Application form required.
Trustees: R. Mark Hamlin, Richard M. Hamlin, Yvonne F. Hamlin.
EIN: 341812974
Codes: FD

42410
The Murphy Family Foundation
25800 Science Park Dr., Ste. 200
P.O. Box 22747
Beachwood, OH 44122 (216) 831-7320
FAX: (216) 831-2296; E-mail: mff@apk.net
Contact: Rita M. Carfagna, Pres.

Established in 1986 in OH.
Donor(s): Members of the Murphy family.
Financial data (yr. ended 12/31/01): Grants paid, $544,576; assets, $4,805,962 (M); gifts received, $550,473; expenditures, $551,402; qualifying distributions, $535,815.
Limitations: Giving primarily in the greater Cleveland, OH, area.
Publications: Informational brochure (including application guidelines), financial statement.
Application information: Application form not required.
Officers and Trustees:* Rita Murphy Carfagna,* Pres.; Paul J. Murphy,* V.P. and Secy.-Treas.; Brian F. Murphy, Margaret S. Murphy, Murlan J. Murphy, Sr., Murlan J. Murphy, Jr., Raymond M. Murphy.
EIN: 341526161
Codes: FD

42411
The Warrington Foundation
c/o Fifth Third Bank
38 Fountain Sq. Plz., MD 1COM31
Cincinnati, OH 45263
Contact: Lawra Baumann, Dir.

Established in 1997 in OH.
Donor(s): Elsie H. Warrington.
Financial data (yr. ended 12/31/00): Grants paid, $542,466; assets, $10,318,693 (M); expenditures, $603,140; qualifying distributions, $526,185.
Trustees: Dan Bailey, John Bailey, Lesley Bailey, Sam Bailey.
Agent: Fifth Third Bank.
EIN: 311582067
Codes: FD

42412
The Wohlgemuth-Herschede Foundation
c/o Fifth Third Bank
38 Fountain Square Plz.
Cincinnati, OH 45263
Contact: Elizabeth D. Wohlgemuth, Trust Off., Fifth Third Bank

Established in 1994 in OH.
Financial data (yr. ended 12/31/01): Grants paid, $539,500; assets, $9,651,981 (M); expenditures, $614,394; qualifying distributions, $552,791.
Limitations: Giving primarily in the greater Cincinnati, OH, area.
Application information: Application form not required.
Officers and Trustees:* Nelson Schwab, Jr.,* Pres.; Steven Monder,* V.P.; John G. Slauson,* Secy.; William F. Bahl,* Treas.; Joseph P. Rouse, Elizabeth D. Wohlgemuth.
Bank Trustee: Fifth Third Bank.
EIN: 311409317
Codes: FD

42413
The Katherine Kenyon Lippitt Foundation
c/o National City Bank
P.O. Box 94651
Cleveland, OH 44101-4651
Application address: c/o Tom Gilchrist, National City Bank, P.O. Box 5756, LOC 2020, Cleveland, OH 44101, tel.: (216) 222-9272

Established in 1987 in OH.
Donor(s): Esther McEwan Black.‡

Financial data (yr. ended 12/31/01): Grants paid, $537,500; assets, $6,726,790 (M); expenditures, $604,281; qualifying distributions, $546,114.
Limitations: Giving primarily in Richland County, OH.
Application information: Generally contributes only to pre-selected organizations. Application form not required.
Officers: John B. Black, Pres.; Peter M. Black, V.P. and Treas.; Kenneth G. Hochman, Secy.
EIN: 341571383
Codes: FD

42414
France Stone Foundation
608 Madison Ave., Ste. 1000
Toledo, OH 43604 (419) 241-2201
Contact: Joseph S. Heyman, Pres.

Established in 1952 in OH.
Donor(s): George A. France,‡ The France Stone Co., and subsidiaries.
Financial data (yr. ended 12/31/01): Grants paid, $536,100; assets, $13,177,532 (M); expenditures, $628,168; qualifying distributions, $544,740.
Limitations: Giving primarily in IN, MI, and northwestern OH.
Application information: Application form not required.
Officers and Trustees:* Joseph S. Heyman,* Pres.; Ollie J. Risner,* V.P.; Andrew E. Anderson,* Secy.-Treas.
EIN: 346523033
Codes: FD

42415
The M. G. O'Neil Foundation
P.O. Box 3409
Cuyahoga Falls, OH 44223
Contact: M.G. O'Neil, Pres.

Incorporated in 1953 in OH.
Donor(s): M.G. O'Neil.
Financial data (yr. ended 06/30/01): Grants paid, $535,200; assets, $2,799,636 (M); expenditures, $553,703; qualifying distributions, $537,461.
Limitations: Giving primarily in OH.
Application information: Application form not required.
Officers: M.G. O'Neil, Pres. and Treas.; T.M. Haidnick, V.P.; E.R. Dye, Secy.
Trustees: Joe Leydon, Jean O'Neil.
EIN: 346516968
Codes: FD

42416
Walter Henry Freygang Foundation
2794 Forestview Dr.
Akron, OH 44333

Incorporated in 1949 in NJ.
Donor(s): Walter Henry Freygang,‡ Marie A. Freygang.‡
Financial data (yr. ended 08/31/01): Grants paid, $532,543; assets, $9,417,491 (M); expenditures, $589,510; qualifying distributions, $526,578.
Limitations: Applications not accepted. Giving on a national basis.
Application information: Contributes only to pre-selected organizations.
Officers: Dale G. Freygang, Pres. and Treas.; Dorothea F. Drennan, V.P.; David B. Freygang, Secy.
Trustees: Joseph A. Drennan, Gustav G. Freygang, Katherine A. Freygang, W. Nicholas F. Freygang.
EIN: 226027952
Codes: FD

42417
The Arthur B. McBride, Sr. Family Foundation
2069 W. 3rd St.
Cleveland, OH 44113

Established in 1989 in OH.
Donor(s): Arthur B. McBride, Jr.
Financial data (yr. ended 12/31/99): Grants paid, $529,000; assets, $9,473,486 (M); gifts received, $410,941; expenditures, $534,673; qualifying distributions, $532,203.
Limitations: Applications not accepted. Giving primarily in the Cleveland, OH, area.
Application information: Contributes only to pre-selected organizations.
Trustees: Arthur B. McBride, Jr., Brian A. McBride, Maureen McBride, Rita McBride, Kathleen McBride Plum.
EIN: 341612197
Codes: FD

42418
Sam Williams Foundation
c/o Spieth, Bell McCurdy & Nowell Co.
925 Euclid Ave., Ste. 2000
Cleveland, OH 44115-1496

Established in 1997 in MI.
Donor(s): Sam B. Williams.
Financial data (yr. ended 12/31/01): Grants paid, $528,979; assets, $85,374 (M); gifts received, $3,825; expenditures, $545,470; qualifying distributions, $528,712.
Limitations: Applications not accepted.
Application information: Contributes only to pre-selected organizations.
Trustee: Sam B. Williams.
EIN: 316565449
Codes: FD

42419
Gardner Family Foundation
P.O. Box 625737
Cincinnati, OH 45262-5737
Contact: James J. Gardner, Pres.

Established in 1994 in OH.
Donor(s): Joan A. Gardner, Margaret M. Johns, Linda G. Mueller, Lorraine G. Sommer, Spencer J. Gardner, Patricia F. Gardner, James J. Gardner, Gardner Family 2000 Charitable Trust.
Financial data (yr. ended 12/31/00): Grants paid, $522,000; assets, $18,838,175 (M); gifts received, $4,542,174; expenditures, $543,917; qualifying distributions, $535,861.
Limitations: Giving primarily in Cincinnati, OH; giving also in Denver, CO, and Orlando, FL.
Officers and Trustees:* James J. Gardner,* Pres.; Joan J. Gardner,* V.P.; Margaret M. Johns,* Secy.; Linda G. Mueller,* Treas.; Patricia F. Gardner, Spencer J. Gardner, Gary D. Johns, Thomas J. Mueller, Lorraine G. Sommer.
EIN: 311397164
Codes: FD

42420
Anderson Foundation
480 W. Dussel Dr.
P.O. Box 119
Maumee, OH 43537-0119 (419) 891-6404
Application address: 608 Madison Ave., Ste. 1540, Toledo, OH 43604, tel.: (419) 243-1706
Contact: Ms. Fredi Heywood, Fdn. Svcs. Admin.

Trust established in 1949 in OH.
Donor(s): Partners in The Andersons, Inc.
Financial data (yr. ended 12/31/00): Grants paid, $520,103; assets, $5,121,168 (M); gifts received, $50; expenditures, $573,911; qualifying distributions, $540,202.
Limitations: Giving primarily in the greater Toledo, OH, area, including Maumee and Columbus. Giving also to organizations located within the areas of the Anderson plants in the following cities: Champaign, IL, Delphi and Dunkirk, IN, and Albion, Potterville, Webberville, and White Pigeon, MI.
Publications: Application guidelines.
Application information: Application form not required.
Officer and Trustees:* Thomas H. Anderson,* Chair.; Charles W. Anderson, Jeffrey W. Anderson, Matthew C. Anderson, Richard M. Anderson, Martha A. Corcoran, Dale W. Fallat, John P. Kraus.
EIN: 346528868
Codes: FD

42421
The Frost-Parker Foundation
165 E. Washington Row, Ste. 206
Sandusky, OH 44870-2610 (419) 625-8324
Contact: Melvyn J. Stauffer, Secy.

Established in 1986 in OH.
Donor(s): Ruth F. Parker.
Financial data (yr. ended 04/30/01): Grants paid, $518,950; assets, $1,063,690 (M); gifts received, $472,139; expenditures, $582,037; qualifying distributions, $536,550.
Limitations: Giving limited to northern OH, with emphasis on Sandusky.
Application information: Application form not required.
Officers and Trustees:* Ruth F. Parker,* Pres. and Treas.; Melvyn J. Stauffer,* Secy.; Mary Beth Carroll, Richard B. Fuller.
EIN: 341515319
Codes: FD

42422
M. E. & F. J. Callahan Foundation
25101 Chagrin Blvd., Ste. 310
Beachwood, OH 44122-7311

Established in 1975 in OH.
Donor(s): F.J. Callahan.
Financial data (yr. ended 12/31/00): Grants paid, $516,634; assets, $4,349,835 (M); gifts received, $547,969; expenditures, $636,523; qualifying distributions, $516,862.
Limitations: Applications not accepted. Giving primarily in Cleveland, OH.
Application information: Contributes only to pre-selected organizations.
Officers: F.J. Callahan, Pres.; T.J. Callahan, V.P.; Ernest P. Mansour, Secy.
EIN: 510164320
Codes: FD

42423
The Jack J. Smith, Jr. Charitable Trust
c/o PNC Bank
P.O. Box 1198
Cincinnati, OH 45201-1198 (513) 651-8377
Contact: Lee D. Crooks, Fdn. Admin.

Established in 1972 in OH.
Donor(s): Jack J. Smith, Jr.‡
Financial data (yr. ended 09/30/01): Grants paid, $516,120; assets, $8,927,055 (M); expenditures, $633,055; qualifying distributions, $539,878.
Limitations: Giving limited to the greater Cincinnati, OH, area.
Publications: Application guidelines.
Application information: Application form required.
Trustees: James S. Wachs, PNC Bank.
EIN: 310912146
Codes: FD

42424
DJ Foundation
545 Hanna Bldg.
1422 Euclid Ave., Ste. 545
Cleveland, OH 44115-1901
Contact: James S. Reid, Jr., Pres.

Established in 1984.
Financial data (yr. ended 12/31/01): Grants paid, $514,750; assets, $5,994,861 (M); expenditures, $537,464; qualifying distributions, $513,217.
Limitations: Applications not accepted. Giving primarily in Cambridge, MA, and Cleveland, OH.
Application information: Contributes only to pre-selected organizations.
Officers and Trustees:* James S. Reid, Jr.,* Pres. and Treas.; Donna S. Reid,* V.P.; R. Steven Kestner,* Secy.
EIN: 341454506
Codes: FD

42425
Edward L. Hutton Foundation
2600 Chemed Ctr.
255 E. 5th St.
Cincinnati, OH 45202

Established in 1991 in OH.
Donor(s): Edward L. Hutton, Kathryn Jane Hutton.
Financial data (yr. ended 12/31/01): Grants paid, $511,449; assets, $5,081,990 (M); gifts received, $1,314,584; expenditures, $541,683; qualifying distributions, $517,250.
Limitations: Applications not accepted. Giving on a national basis, with emphasis on IN, OH, and PA.
Application information: Contributes only to pre-selected organizations.
Officers: Edward L. Hutton, Pres.; Edward A. Hutton, V.P.; Kathryn Jane Hutton, V.P.; Thomas C. Hutton, V.P.; Jennie Hutton Jacoby, V.P.
EIN: 311334189
Codes: FD

42426
J. B. Wilson & Garnet A. Wilson Charitable Trust
P.O. Box 686
Waverly, OH 45690-0686 (740) 947-2727
Contact: Billy S. Moore, Tr.

Established in 1980.
Donor(s): Garnet A. Wilson.‡
Financial data (yr. ended 12/31/00): Grants paid, $506,835; assets, $6,925,401 (M); expenditures, $537,130; qualifying distributions, $537,130.
Limitations: Giving limited to residents and graduates of Pike County, OH, schools.
Application information: Application form required.
Trustees: William Foster, Billy S. Moore, Glenda Williams.
EIN: 310983188
Codes: FD, GTI

42427
Fox Foundation, Inc.
1445 Cincinnati-Zanesville Rd., S.W.
Lancaster, OH 43130
Contact: Dorothy B. Fox, Dir.

Established in 1953 in OH.
Donor(s): Robert K. Fox.
Financial data (yr. ended 11/30/01): Grants paid, $501,207; assets, $7,796,422 (M); expenditures, $518,024; qualifying distributions, $501,447.
Limitations: Giving primarily in OH.
Application information: Application form not required.
Directors: Dorothy B. Fox, Robert L. Fox.
EIN: 316029306
Codes: FD

42428
The Helen Steiner Rice Foundation
221 E. 4th St., Ste. 2100, Atrium 2
P.O. Box 0236
Cincinnati, OH 45201-0236 (513) 451-9241
Contact: Andrea Cornett, Grant Coord.

Established in 1980 in OH.
Donor(s): Helen Steiner Rice.‡
Financial data (yr. ended 06/30/02): Grants paid, $496,000; assets, $8,829,048 (M); gifts received, $760; expenditures, $737,589; qualifying distributions, $572,686.
Limitations: Giving limited to the greater Cincinnati area and Lorain, OH.
Publications: Annual report (including application guidelines), application guidelines, informational brochure, program policy statement.
Application information: Application form required.
Trustees: Willis D. Gradison, Jr., Gregory Ionna, Gary Johnston, Eugene P. Ruehlmann, Donald E. Weston.
EIN: 310978383
Codes: FD

42429
Brennan Family Foundation
1200 Sunset View Dr.
Akron, OH 44313 (330) 864-5528
E-mail: annamer@aol.com
Contact: Ann Brennan, Pres.

Established in 1995 in OH.
Donor(s): David L. Brennan, Mrs. David L. Brennan, Hayes Industrial Brake, Inc.
Financial data (yr. ended 12/31/99): Grants paid, $488,080; assets, $13,007,600 (M); expenditures, $543,372; qualifying distributions, $488,080.
Limitations: Giving primarily in northeastern OH, with emphasis on Summit County.
Application information: Application form not required.
Officers: Ann Brennan, Pres.; David Brennan, V.P.; Nancy Brennan, Secy.-Treas.
EIN: 341812978
Codes: FD

42430
Hartzell-Norris Charitable Trust
c/o Fifth Third Bank
P.O. Box 630858
Cincinnati, OH 45263

Established in 1943 in OH.
Donor(s): Hartzell Industries, Inc.
Financial data (yr. ended 10/31/01): Grants paid, $485,187; assets, $6,565,337 (M); expenditures, $531,389; qualifying distributions, $488,819.
Limitations: Applications not accepted. Giving primarily in OH.
Application information: Unsolicited requests for funds not accepted.
Trustee: Fifth Third Bank.
EIN: 316024521
Codes: CS, FD, CD

42431
Jasam Foundation, Inc.
P.O. Box 494
Worthington, OH 43085

Established in 1953 in OH.
Donor(s): Samuel S. Davis.‡
Financial data (yr. ended 12/31/99): Grants paid, $483,333; assets, $23,299,378 (M); expenditures, $548,814; qualifying distributions, $548,814.
Limitations: Applications not accepted. Giving primarily in Franklin County, OH.
Application information: Contributes only to pre-selected organizations.
Officers: Joan Guylas, Pres.; Jane Ferger, Secy.
Trustee: Samuel B. Davis.
EIN: 316036574
Codes: FD

42432
Kenneth L. Calhoun Charitable Trust
c/o KeyBank, N.A.
800 Superior Ave., 4th Fl.
Cleveland, OH 44114-2601
Application address: c/o KeyBank, N.A., 157 S. Main St., Akron, OH 44308, tel.: (330) 379-1647
Contact: Karen Krino, Sr. Trust Off., KeyBank, N.A.

Established in 1982 in OH.
Donor(s): Kenneth Calhoun.‡
Financial data (yr. ended 07/31/01): Grants paid, $481,033; assets, $6,355,413 (M); expenditures, $536,173; qualifying distributions, $486,878.
Limitations: Giving limited to the greater Akron, OH, area with emphasis on Summit County.
Application information: Application form not required.
Trustee: KeyBank, N.A.
EIN: 341370330
Codes: FD

42433
The Molly Bee Fund
c/o Thomas F. Allen
20325 Center Ridge Rd., Ste. 629
Rocky River, OH 44116 (440) 331-8220

Established in 1995 in OH.
Donor(s): Elizabeth B. Blossom.
Financial data (yr. ended 12/31/01): Grants paid, $480,646; assets, $6,262,710 (M); expenditures, $506,662; qualifying distributions, $491,043.
Limitations: Applications not accepted. Giving on a national basis.
Application information: Contributes only to pre-selected organizations.
Officers and Trustees:* Mary E. Gale,* Pres.; Benjamin Gale,* V.P.; Thomas F. Allen, Secy.-Treas.; Thomas H. Gale, Kevin R. Kneisly.
EIN: 341812998
Codes: FD

42434
George & Betty Schaefer Foundation
c/o Fifth Third Bank
38 Foundation Sq. Plz.
Cincinnati, OH 45263
Contact: Lawra Baumann, Dir.

Established in 1997 in OH.
Donor(s): Betty Schaefer, George Schaefer.
Financial data (yr. ended 12/31/01): Grants paid, $475,655; assets, $2,854,515 (M); gifts received, $14,186; expenditures, $478,892; qualifying distributions, $473,258.
Limitations: Giving limited to Cincinnati, OH.
Officers and Trustees:* George A. Schaefer, Jr.,* Pres.; Betty Ann Schaefer,* V.P. and Secy.-Treas.; George A. Schaefer III, Fifth Third Bank.
Director: Lawra Baumann.
EIN: 311532097
Codes: FD

42435
Paul F. and Margaret M. Wutz Foundation
72 Brandywine Dr.
Hudson, OH 44236

Established in 2000 in OH.
Donor(s): Paul F. Wutz, Margaret M. Wutz.
Financial data (yr. ended 12/31/01): Grants paid, $475,000; assets, $3,370,956 (M); expenditures, $560,429; qualifying distributions, $475,000.
Limitations: Applications not accepted.

Application information: Contributes only to pre-selected organizations.
Officers and Trustees:* Paul F. Wutz,* Pres.; Laura A. Wutz,* Secy.; Margaret M. Wutz,* Treas.
EIN: 341939673

42436
Harold & Ivalou Bordner Private Charitable Foundation
(Formerly Harold, Ivalou & Hazel Bordner Private Charitable Foundation)
15160 Range Line Rd.
Weston, OH 43569

Donor(s): Harold Bordner,‡ Ivalou Bordner.‡
Financial data (yr. ended 11/30/01): Grants paid, $470,000; assets, $1,555,561 (M); expenditures, $473,898; qualifying distributions, $470,000.
Limitations: Applications not accepted. Giving primarily in Bowling Green, Perrysburg, and Pemberville, OH.
Application information: Contributes only to pre-selected organizations.
Officer and Trustees:* Harold Bateson,* Chair.; Ken Hoot, Hugh Sheline.
EIN: 341334646
Codes: FD

42437
The Sage Cleveland Foundation
(Formerly The Standard Products Foundation)
c/o John D. Drinko
3200 National City Ctr.
Cleveland, OH 44114

Incorporated in 1953 in OH.
Donor(s): The Standard Products Co.
Financial data (yr. ended 06/30/01): Grants paid, $462,000; assets, $8,865,682 (M); expenditures, $599,849; qualifying distributions, $471,944.
Limitations: Applications not accepted. Giving primarily in Cleveland, OH.
Application information: Contributes only to pre-selected organizations.
Officers and Trustees:* J.S. Reid, Jr.,* Pres.; J. Richard Hamilton,* Secy.; John D. Drinko,* Treas.; Edward B. Brandon, John D. Sigel.
EIN: 346525047
Codes: CS, FD, CD

42438
The Triple T Foundation
c/o KeyBank, N.A.
800 Superior Ave., 4th Fl.
Cleveland, OH 44114-2601

Established in 1996 in OH.
Donor(s): Edith J. Bastian, Alison C. Jones, Ellen W. Jones, Theodore T. Jones, Warren Tanner Jones.
Financial data (yr. ended 12/31/01): Grants paid, $461,751; assets, $8,108,381 (M); gifts received, $101,885; expenditures, $469,602; qualifying distributions, $468,544.
Limitations: Applications not accepted.
Application information: Contributes only to pre-selected organizations.
Trustee: KeyBank, N.A.
EIN: 341811968
Codes: FD

42439
The Cleveland-Cliffs Foundation
1100 Superior Ave., Ste. 1800
Cleveland, OH 44114-2589 (216) 694-5700
Contact: Dana Byrne, V.P.

Established in 1960 in OH.
Donor(s): Cleveland-Cliffs, Inc., Tilden Mining Co., Empire Iron Mining Partnership, Hibbing Taconite Co., Northshore Mining Co.
Financial data (yr. ended 12/31/01): Grants paid, $461,005; assets, $638,000 (M); gifts received, $200,000; expenditures, $461,256; qualifying distributions, $460,936.
Limitations: Giving primarily in areas of company operations, with emphasis on MI, MN, and Cleveland, OH.
Publications: Application guidelines.
Application information: Application form not required.
Officers and Trustees:* J.S. Brinzo,* Chair. and C.E.O.; T.J. O'Neill,* Pres. and C.O.O.; W.R. Calfee,* Exec. V.P., Commercial; Cynthia B. Bezik,* Sr. V.P., Finance.
EIN: 346525124
Codes: CS, FD, CD

42440
The Motorists Insurance Group Foundation
(Formerly The Motorists Insurance Company)
c/o John J. Bishop
471 E. Broad St.
Columbus, OH 43215-3861 (614) 255-8613

Established in 2000 in OH.
Donor(s): Motorists Mutual Insurance Company.
Financial data (yr. ended 12/31/01): Grants paid, $459,494; assets, $80,229 (M); gifts received, $67,990; expenditures, $464,451; qualifying distributions, $461,094.
Limitations: Applications not accepted. Giving primarily in Columbus, OH, Indianapolis, IN, and Arlington, VA.
Application information: Contributes only to pre-selected organizations.
Trustees: John J. Bishop, Thomas C. Ogg, Robert E.H. Rabold, Michael L. Wiseman.
EIN: 311712343
Codes: CS, FD, CD

42441
Firman Fund
c/o H & I Advisors
1422 Euclid Ave., 1030 Hanna Bldg.
Cleveland, OH 44115-2078 (216) 363-1030
Contact: Royal Firman, III, Pres.

Incorporated in 1951 in OH.
Donor(s): Pamela H. Firman.‡
Financial data (yr. ended 12/31/01): Grants paid, $458,700; assets, $12,386,089 (M); expenditures, $537,970; qualifying distributions, $466,173.
Limitations: Giving primarily in Denver, CO, Tallahassee, FL, Thomasville, GA, and Cleveland, OH.
Officers and Trustees:* Royal Firman III, Pres.; Cynthia F. Webster,* V.P.; Neil A. Brown, Secy.; Carole M. Nowak, Treas.; Stephanie Firman, Robert Webster, Jr.
EIN: 346513655
Codes: FD

42442
H & H Foundation
P.O. Box 1888
Lima, OH 45802-1888
Contact: Leo J. Hawk, Chair.

Established in 1989 in OH.
Donor(s): Henry J. Hawk, Jr., Beverly Ann Hawk, Leo Hawk, Arlene F. Hawk.
Financial data (yr. ended 12/31/01): Grants paid, $456,235; assets, $872,903 (M); gifts received, $421,000; expenditures, $494,155; qualifying distributions, $455,407.
Limitations: Giving limited to Allen County, OH, including Lima.
Officers: Leo J. Hawk, Chair.; Arlene F. Hawk, V.P.; Beverly Ann Hawk, V.P.; Diane L. Drennan, Secy.-Treas.
EIN: 341625352
Codes: FD

42443
M/B Foundation
1011 Sandusky St., Ste. L
Perrysburg, OH 43551

Established in 1986 in OH.
Donor(s): William W. Boeschenstein, Elizabeth M. Boeschenstein.
Financial data (yr. ended 12/31/01): Grants paid, $453,922; assets, $663,672 (M); expenditures, $478,047; qualifying distributions, $457,148.
Limitations: Applications not accepted. Giving primarily in Toledo, OH; some giving also on the East Coast.
Application information: Contributes only to pre-selected organizations.
Trustees: Josephine M. Boeschenstein, William W. Boeschenstein.
EIN: 311195114
Codes: FD

42444
The Williams Foundation
212 E. 3rd St., Ste. 300
Cincinnati, OH 45202-5500

Established in 1938 in OH.
Donor(s): Harriette R. Downey, William J. Williams, Helen D. Williams, Mary Frances W. Clauder.
Financial data (yr. ended 12/31/01): Grants paid, $450,939; assets, $6,452,191 (M); gifts received, $55,915; expenditures, $478,293; qualifying distributions, $455,633.
Limitations: Applications not accepted. Giving primarily in Cincinnati, OH.
Application information: Contributes only to pre-selected organizations.
Trustees: Mary W. Clauder, Sharon W. Frisbie, Carol W. Jodar, Lawrence H. Kyte, Jr., Helen D. Williams, Thomas L. Williams, William J. Williams, W. Joseph Williams, Jr.
EIN: 316032504
Codes: FD

42445
Edward and Betty Sloat Foundation
3065 Fairfax Rd.
Cleveland Heights, OH 44118 (216) 321-7159
E-mail: mektra@aol.com
Contact: Anne Unverzagt, Pres.

Established in 1990 in OH.
Donor(s): Edward Sloat.
Financial data (yr. ended 12/31/00): Grants paid, $450,000; assets, $6,495,645 (M); expenditures, $496,873; qualifying distributions, $450,000.
Limitations: Giving primarily in Cleveland, OH.
Publications: Application guidelines, multi-year report, financial statement, grants list.
Application information: Application form not required.
Officers and Directors:* Anne Unverzagt,* Pres.; Richard P. Goddard,* Secy.; Joseph F. Ciulla,* Treas.; Patricia Ciulla.
EIN: 341657230
Codes: FD

42446
Crossroads Foundation
c/o Blossom Business Office, Inc.
20325 Center Ridge Rd., Ste. 629
Rocky River, OH 44116 (440) 331-8220

Established in 1995 in OH.
Financial data (yr. ended 12/31/01): Grants paid, $449,980; assets, $6,423,730 (M); expenditures, $505,796; qualifying distributions, $456,474.

Limitations: Giving primarily in OH.
Application information: Application form not required.
Officers and Trustees:* Dudley S. Blossom,* Pres.; Kathryn F. Blossom,* V.P.; Thomas F. Allen,* Secy.; Kirk A. Linn,* Treas.
EIN: 341811495
Codes: FD

42447
The Steris Foundation
5960 Heisley Rd.
Mentor, OH 44060

Established in 1995 in OH.
Financial data (yr. ended 03/31/00): Grants paid, $447,053; assets, $217,214 (M); gifts received, $220,000; expenditures, $448,001; qualifying distributions, $447,675.
Limitations: Applications not accepted. Giving limited to OH.
Application information: Contributes only to pre-selected organizations.
Officers: Gerard J. Reis, Pres.; Laurie Brlas, V.P. and Treas.; Les C. Vinney, V.P.; Jane A. Steger, Secy.
Trustee: Bill R. Sanford.
EIN: 341807803

42448
Sky Foundation
221 S. Church St.
Bowling Green, OH 43402-0428
(419) 327-6300
Contact: Ebbony Page Hamilton

Established in 1998 in OH.
Donor(s): Sky Financial Group, Inc.
Financial data (yr. ended 12/31/01): Grants paid, $445,868; assets, $2,077,781 (M); gifts received, $1,091,575; expenditures, $452,199; qualifying distributions, $438,409.
Limitations: Giving limited to areas of company operations in IN, MI, OH, PA, and WV.
Application information: Application form required.
Trustees: Marty E. Adams, Debra Bish, Jennifer L. Iliff, Darlene Minnick, Edward J. Reiter, Curtis E. Shepherd, Eric C. Stachler, Kevin T. Thompson.
EIN: 341886344
Codes: CS, FD, CD

42449
The S. N. Ford and Ada Ford Fund
c/o KeyBank, N.A.
P.O. Box 10099
Toledo, OH 43699-0099
Application address: 42 N. Main St., Mansfield, OH 44902, tel.: (419) 525-7665
Contact: David Irvin, Trust Off., KeyBank, N.A.

Established in 1947 in OH.
Donor(s): Ada Ford, M.D.‡
Financial data (yr. ended 12/31/00): Grants paid, $442,782; assets, $12,624,848 (M); gifts received, $150; expenditures, $530,515; qualifying distributions, $480,025.
Limitations: Giving primarily in Richland County, OH.
Publications: Annual report.
Application information: Application form required.
Officers: W. Thomas Ross, Pres.; Stephen B. Bogner, V.P.; John W. Welsh, Secy.
Distribution Committee: Edwin M. Cook, Deborah M. Schenk.
Trustee: KeyBank, N.A.
EIN: 340842282
Codes: FD, GTI

42450
The Ratner, Miller, Shafran Foundation
50 Public Sq., Ste. 1600
Cleveland, OH 44113-2295 (216) 267-1200
Application address: 1100 Terminal Tower, 50 Public Sq., Cleveland, OH 44113-2203
Contact: Albert Ratner, Secy.

Incorporated in 1952 in OH.
Donor(s): Max Ratner,‡ Albert Ratner, Sam Miller.
Financial data (yr. ended 11/30/01): Grants paid, $442,770; assets, $606,647 (M); expenditures, $443,813; qualifying distributions, $443,813.
Limitations: Giving on a national and international basis.
Application information: Application form required for scholarships.
Officers: Sam Miller, V.P.; Albert Ratner, Secy.
EIN: 346521216
Codes: FD, GTI

42451
Robert A. Stranahan, Jr. Charitable Trust
c/o KeyBank, N.A.
P.O. Box 10099
Toledo, OH 43699-0099
Contact: Diane Ohns, V.P., KeyBank, N.A.

Established in 1959.
Donor(s): Robert A. Stranahan, Jr., Nancy S. Jones, Lynn S. Butler.
Financial data (yr. ended 12/31/00): Grants paid, $435,250; assets, $9,468,015 (M); expenditures, $450,419; qualifying distributions, $440,248.
Limitations: Applications not accepted. Giving primarily in Toledo, OH.
Application information: Contributes only to pre-selected organizations.
Advisors: Robert Brotje, Gerald W. Miller, Roberta M. Pawlak, Francis G. Pletz.
Trustee: KeyBank, N.A.
EIN: 346504818
Codes: FD

42452
Bernie J. Kosar Charitable Trust
755 Boardman-Canfield Rd., No. K1
Youngstown, OH 44512
Contact: Bernie J. Kosar, Sr., Mgr.

Established in 1991 in OH.
Donor(s): Bernie J. Kosar, Jr.
Financial data (yr. ended 12/31/01): Grants paid, $435,150; assets, $1,320,213 (M); expenditures, $593,128; qualifying distributions, $437,942; giving activities include $2,792 for programs.
Limitations: Applications not accepted. Giving primarily in OH.
Application information: Contributes only to pre-selected organizations.
Officer: Bernie J. Kosar, Sr., Mgr.
Trustee: Bernie J. Kosar, Jr.
EIN: 341673013
Codes: FD

42453
100 Times Foundation
c/o Joseph A. Pedoto
49 E. 4th St., Ste. 521
Cincinnati, OH 45202-3808

Established in 1998 in OH.
Donor(s): Keith E. Lindner.
Financial data (yr. ended 12/31/01): Grants paid, $433,325; assets, $149,840 (M); gifts received, $3,756; expenditures, $436,822; qualifying distributions, $429,705.
Limitations: Applications not accepted. Giving primarily in OH.
Application information: Contributes only to pre-selected organizations.

Officers and Trustees:* Keith E. Lindner,* Pres.; Courtney O'Neil Lindner,* Secy.; Joseph A. Pedoto, Treas.; Christopher B. Hewett.
EIN: 311611064
Codes: FD

42454
First Place Bank Community Foundation
(Formerly First Federal of Warren Community Foundation)
P.O. Box 551
Warren, OH 44482-0551 (330) 373-1230
Additional tel.: (800) 995-2646, ext. 2273
Contact: David J. Jenkins, Exec. Dir.

Established in 1998 in OH.
Donor(s): First Place Financial Corp.
Financial data (yr. ended 06/30/01): Grants paid, $429,904; assets, $10,102,486 (M); expenditures, $451,760; qualifying distributions, $414,503.
Limitations: Giving limited to the Mahoning Valley, OH, area and contiguous localities.
Application information: Telephone solicitations not accepted or considered. Application form required.
Officers and Directors:* Richard P. Cowin,* Chair.; Steven R. Lewis,* Pres.; David J. Jenkins, Secy. and Exec. Dir.; Bruce R. Downie, Treas.; Robert S. McGeough, E.J. Rossi.
EIN: 341879025
Codes: CS, FD, CD

42455
Susan and John Turben Foundation
c/o John F. Turben
2550 Som Ctr. Rd., Ste. 105
Willoughby, OH 44094

Established in 1992 in OH.
Donor(s): John F. Turben, Susan H. Turben.
Financial data (yr. ended 12/31/99): Grants paid, $426,552; assets, $1,440,938 (M); gifts received, $590,381; expenditures, $464,161; qualifying distributions, $423,612.
Limitations: Applications not accepted. Giving primarily in OH.
Application information: Contributes only to pre-selected organizations.
Officers and Trustees:* Susan H. Turben,* Pres.; John F. Turben,* V.P.; Debra Bowman, Treas.; James H. Kimberly, Newton S. Kimberly, Jr., Mary K. Prien, David C. Turben, Nicholas A. Turben.
EIN: 341725277
Codes: FD

42456
Community Foundation of Union County, Inc.
126 N. Main St.
P.O. Box 608
Marysville, OH 43040-0608 (937) 642-9618
FAX: (937) 642-7376; *E-mail:* commfounduc@midohio.net
Contact: David A. Vollrath, Exec. Dir.

Established in 1962 in OH.
Financial data (yr. ended 12/31/01): Grants paid, $425,059; assets, $1,600,027 (M); gifts received, $109,646; expenditures, $453,761.
Limitations: Giving limited to Union County, OH.
Publications: Annual report, informational brochure, application guidelines.
Application information: Application form required.
Officers: Bob Conklin, Chair; Patricia J. Nuckles, Vice-Chair.; Richard L. Bump, Secy.-Treas.; David Vollrath, Exec. Dir.; David F. Allen, Counsel.
Trustees: Daniel Behrens, Jennifer Brill, Robert Buckley, Phillip Connolly, Gerald E. Dackin, Myron W. Gallogly, Nancy Hoffman, Kevin Kern, Frank Miller, Dorothy Mudgett, Barbara Timmons.

EIN: 310628641
Codes: CM

42457
Downing Foundation
7 Grandin Ln.
Cincinnati, OH 45208-3363 (513) 321-2230
Contact: W. Charles Blum, Secy.

Established in 1994 in OH.
Donor(s): Jack G. Downing.
Financial data (yr. ended 05/31/01): Grants paid, $423,533; assets, $8,072,747 (M); expenditures, $484,578; qualifying distributions, $423,533.
Limitations: Giving primarily in Cincinnati, OH.
Officers: Mary J. Blum, Chair.; W. Charles Blum, Secy.
EIN: 311416687
Codes: FD

42458
Daniel and Susan Pfau Foundation
c/o PNC Bank, N.A.
P.O. Box 1198
Cincinnati, OH 45201-1198 (513) 651-8377
Contact: Lee D. Crooks, Fdn. Admin.

Established in 1994 in OH.
Donor(s): Daniel A. Pfau, Susan L. Pfau.
Financial data (yr. ended 12/31/01): Grants paid, $423,337; assets, $9,493,686 (M); gifts received, $563,615; expenditures, $445,146; qualifying distributions, $445,146.
Limitations: Giving primarily in the greater Cincinnati, OH, area.
Publications: Application guidelines.
Application information: Application form required.
Advisory Board: David Brill, Steve Brill, Daniel A. Pfau, Susan L. Pfau.
Trustee: PNC Bank, N.A.
EIN: 311411794
Codes: FD

42459
Carol Ann and Ralph V. Haile, Jr. Foundation, Inc.
c/o U.S. Bank
P.O. Box 1118
Cincinnati, OH 45201-1118

Established in 1997 in OH.
Donor(s): Carol Ann Haile, Ralph V. Haile, Jr.
Financial data (yr. ended 12/31/01): Grants paid, $423,000; assets, $377,160 (M); gifts received, $423,000; expenditures, $423,518; qualifying distributions, $423,000.
Limitations: Applications not accepted. Giving primarily in KY and OH.
Application information: Contributes only to pre-selected organizations.
Officers: Carol Ann Haile, Pres.; Ralph V. Haile, Jr., V.P.; Jennie P. Carlson, Secy.
Trustees: Jerry A. Grundhofer, Timothy J. Maloney, David M. Moffett.
EIN: 311492387

42460
Richard J. Fasenmyer Foundation
3875 Embassy Pkwy., Ste. 110
Fairlawn, OH 44333-8330

Established in 1989 in OH.
Donor(s): RJF International Corp.
Financial data (yr. ended 12/31/01): Grants paid, $422,600; assets, $478,815 (M); gifts received, $300,100; expenditures, $423,569; qualifying distributions, $422,485.
Limitations: Applications not accepted. Giving primarily in OH.

Application information: Contributes only to pre-selected organizations.
Officers and Trustees:* Richard J. Fasenmyer,* Pres. and Treas.; Haven J. Hood,* V.P. and Secy.; Lawrence N. Schultz.
EIN: 341627457
Codes: FD

42461
The Grant Munro Scholarship Trust
c/o National City Bank
P.O. Box 94651
Cleveland, OH 44101-4651
Application address: c/o Fairfield Foundation, 109 N. Broad St., Lancaster, OH 43130
Contact: Charles H. Hodson, Chair.

Established in 1995.
Donor(s): Grant Munro.
Financial data (yr. ended 05/31/02): Grants paid, $422,074; assets, $5,662,839 (M); expenditures, $455,248; qualifying distributions, $438,356.
Limitations: Giving primarily in Fairfield County, OH.
Application information: Application form required.
Trustee: National City Bank.
EIN: 316517313
Codes: FD

42462
The Elizabeth G. & John D. Drinko Charitable Foundation
(Formerly Cleveland Institute of Electronics Charitable Foundation)
3200 National City Ctr.
Cleveland, OH 44114

Established in 1982 in OH.
Donor(s): John D. Drinko, Elizabeth G. Drinko.
Financial data (yr. ended 11/30/01): Grants paid, $422,000; assets, $1,263,844 (M); expenditures, $428,980; qualifying distributions, $421,640.
Limitations: Applications not accepted. Giving primarily in OH, PA, and WV.
Application information: Contributes only to pre-selected organizations.
Officers and Trustees:* John D. Drinko,* Pres.; Elizabeth G. Drinko,* V.P.; J. Randall Drinko,* V.P.; Lloyd F. Loux, Jr., Secy.; J. Richard Hamilton,* Treas.; John H. Burlingame, Jay Deaver Drinko, R. Steven Kestner, Diana Lynn Martin, Elizabeth D. Sullivan.
EIN: 341391069
Codes: FD

42463
Carleton F. & Ruth T. Davidson Trust
285 Ridge Mall
Springfield, OH 45504
Contact: Norma Dillon, Tr.

Established in 1987 in OH.
Donor(s): Carleton F. Davidson.
Financial data (yr. ended 12/31/01): Grants paid, $421,330; assets, $8,448,864 (M); expenditures, $464,738; qualifying distributions, $421,330.
Limitations: Giving primarily in Springfield, and Clark County, OH.
Trustees: Norma Dillon, Ed Rice.
EIN: 316328010
Codes: FD

42464
Ridgecliff Foundation, Inc.
4169 Story Rd.
Fairview Park, OH 44126 (440) 333-1803
FAX: (440) 331-6361; *E-mail:* michaelaminelli@ameritech.net
Contact: Michael A. Minelli, Grant Review Chair.

Established in 1991 in OH; converted from sale of Laurelwood Hospital to Mount Sinai Medical Center.
Donor(s): Mount Sinai Medical Ctr., Laurelwood Hospital.
Financial data (yr. ended 12/31/01): Grants paid, $420,229; assets, $8,787,183 (M); expenditures, $482,496; qualifying distributions, $436,687.
Limitations: Giving primarily in Ashtabula, Cuyahoga, Geauga, Lake, Lorain, Mahoning, Medina, Portage, Summit, and Trumbull counties, OH.
Publications: Application guidelines.
Application information: Awards limited to 1 grant per organization in a 12-month period. Application form not required.
Officers and Trustees:* C.Y. Liu,* Pres.; Dorothea King,* V.P.; Joseph Meissner,* Secy.; Thomas Kaung,* Treas.; Bob Gutin, Michael A. Minelli, Manny Schor.
EIN: 341671405
Codes: FD

42465
Robbins & Myers Foundation
1400 Kettering Twr.
Dayton, OH 45423
Contact: Gerald L. Connelly, Chair.

Incorporated in 1966 in OH.
Donor(s): Robbins & Myers, Inc.
Financial data (yr. ended 08/31/01): Grants paid, $418,815; assets, $55,211 (M); gifts received, $418,815; expenditures, $418,815; qualifying distributions, $418,815.
Limitations: Giving primarily in areas of company operations, including Fairfield and Goleta, CA, Eden Prairie, MN, and Springfield and Gallipolis, OH.
Application information: Application form not required.
Officers: G.L. Connelly, Pres.; Kevin J. Brown, V.P. and Treas.; Hugh E. Becker, Secy.
EIN: 316064597
Codes: CS, FD, CD

42466
Thomas H. and Barbara W. Gale Foundation
20325 Center Ridge Rd., Ste. 629
Rocky River, OH 44116

Established in 1995 in OH.
Donor(s): Elizabeth B. Blossom, The William Bingham Foundation.
Financial data (yr. ended 12/31/01): Grants paid, $413,425; assets, $6,397,864 (M); expenditures, $437,510; qualifying distributions, $420,770.
Limitations: Applications not accepted. Giving primarily in CT, Washington, DC, MD, and NY.
Application information: Contributes only to pre-selected organizations.
Officers and Trustees:* Barbara W. Gale,* Pres.; Thomas H. Gale,* 1st V.P.; Alicia W. Gale,* 2nd V.P.; Jennifer L. Gale,* Secy.; Elizabeth A. Gale,* Treas.
EIN: 341813012
Codes: FD

42467
The DBJ Foundation
(Formerly The David H. and Barbara M. Jacobs Foundation)
127 Public Sq., Ste. 2500
Cleveland, OH 44114-1303
Contact: Patrick S. Mullin, Tr.

Established in 1990 in OH.
Donor(s): David H. Jacobs, Barbara M. Jacobs.
Financial data (yr. ended 12/31/01): Grants paid, $413,000; assets, $14,966,021 (M); expenditures, $489,070; qualifying distributions, $418,500.
Limitations: Giving primarily in Cleveland, OH.
Trustees: Barbara M. Jacobs, Patrick S. Mullin.
EIN: 341661482
Codes: FD

42468
The Rieveschl Foundation
c/o Fifth Third Bank
38 Fountain Sq. Plz., Dept. 630858, M D 1090C8
Cincinnati, OH 45263
Contact: Lawra Baumann, Dir.

Established in 1997 in OH.
Financial data (yr. ended 12/31/00): Grants paid, $410,309; assets, $8,644,961 (M); expenditures, $494,231; qualifying distributions, $424,960.
Limitations: Giving primarily in the greater Cincinnati, OH area.
Trustees: Gary T. Rieveschl, George Rieveschl, Jr., Jan L. Rieveschl.
Director: Lawra Baumann.
Agent: Fifth Third Bank.
EIN: 311515801
Codes: FD

42469
The Park National Corp. Foundation
(Formerly The Park National Bank Foundation)
P.O. Box 3500
Newark, OH 43058-3500

Established in 1983 in OH.
Donor(s): Park National Bank, Fairfield National Bank, The Richland Trust Co.
Financial data (yr. ended 12/31/00): Grants paid, $409,560; assets, $8,993,307 (M); gifts received, $150,000; expenditures, $406,334; qualifying distributions, $405,211.
Limitations: Applications not accepted. Giving primarily in OH, with emphasis on Newark.
Application information: Contributes only to pre-selected organizations.
Officers: William T. McConnell, Chair.; Dan Delawder, Pres.; Stuart N. Parsons, Secy.-Treas.
Trustees: David C. Bowers, H. David Shuman.
EIN: 316249406
Codes: CS, FD, CD

42470
Louise Kramer Foundation
c/o KeyBank, N.A.
34 N. Main St., P.O. Box 1809
Dayton, OH 45401-1809
Contact: Kevin McDonald, V.P. and Trust Off., KeyBank, N.A.

Established in 1965 in OH.
Donor(s): Louise Kramer.‡
Financial data (yr. ended 12/31/01): Grants paid, $406,500; assets, $6,941,487 (M); expenditures, $456,409; qualifying distributions, $404,327.
Limitations: Giving primarily in Dayton, OH.
Application information: Application form not required.
Trustees: W.T. Lincoln, Hugh Wall, Jr., KeyBank, N.A.
EIN: 316055729

Codes: FD

42471
The Timken Company Educational Fund, Inc.
P.O. Box 6927, BIC 18
Canton, OH 44706-0927 (330) 471-3933
E-mail: rankine@timken.com
Contact: Debra J. Rankine

Established in 1957.
Donor(s): The Timken Co.
Financial data (yr. ended 12/31/00): Grants paid, $404,004; assets, $1,637,635 (M); gifts received, $100,000; expenditures, $425,619; qualifying distributions, $421,544.
Publications: Informational brochure, application guidelines.
Application information: Application form required.
Officers and Trustees:* Ward J. Timken,* Pres.; R.L. Leibensperger,* V.P.; G.E. Little,* Secy.-Treas.
EIN: 346520257
Codes: CS, FD, CD, GTI

42472
Honda of America Foundation
c/o Comm. Dept., Marysville Motorcycle Plant
24000 Honda Pkwy.
Marysville, OH 43040-9251 (937) 645-8785
E-mail: rene_hoy@ham.honda.com
Contact: Lourene Hoy, Asst. Mgr.

Established in 1981 in OH.
Donor(s): Honda of America Mfg., Inc.
Financial data (yr. ended 12/31/01): Grants paid, $403,705; assets, $6,863,027 (M); expenditures, $454,186; qualifying distributions, $401,645.
Limitations: Giving primarily in OH, where Honda of America facilities are located and associates reside.
Application information: Application form required.
Officers and Trustees:* Rick Schostek,* Pres.; Shaun McCloskey,* Treas.; John Adams, Larry Jutte, Kay Miller, Ted Noguchi.
EIN: 311006130
Codes: CS, FD, CD

42473
Ferro Foundation
1000 Lakeside Ave.
Cleveland, OH 44114-1183 (216) 641-8580
Contact: D.E. Katchman, Secy.-Treas.

Incorporated in 1959 in OH.
Donor(s): Ferro Corp.
Financial data (yr. ended 04/30/01): Grants paid, $402,710; assets, $379,812 (M); expenditures, $404,043; qualifying distributions, $402,710.
Limitations: Giving primarily in OH.
Application information: Application form not required.
Officers and Trustees:* H.R. Ortino,* Pres.; P.V. Richard, V.P.; D.E. Katchman, Secy.-Treas.; R.J. Finch, H.K. Lee.
EIN: 346554832
Codes: CS, FD, CD

42474
The Gerhard Foundation, Inc.
c/o David J. Hessler
6055 Rockside Woods Blvd., Ste. 200
Cleveland, OH 44131

Established in 1990 OH.
Donor(s): Emma L. Gerhard.‡
Financial data (yr. ended 12/31/01): Grants paid, $400,000; assets, $7,421,719 (M); expenditures, $482,110; qualifying distributions, $432,844.
Limitations: Applications not accepted. Giving primarily in IN and OH.
Application information: Contributes only to pre-selected organizations.
Officers: David J. Hessler, Pres.; Keith Vanderburg, Secy.; Peter A. Hessler, Treas.
EIN: 341659675
Codes: FD

42475
The C. Carlisle and Margaret M. Tippit Charitable Trust
925 Euclid Ave., Ste. 2000
Cleveland, OH 44115-1496

Established in 1989 in OH.
Financial data (yr. ended 08/31/01): Grants paid, $400,000; assets, $7,195,871 (M); gifts received, $40,000; expenditures, $428,577; qualifying distributions, $407,909.
Limitations: Applications not accepted. Giving primarily in OH.
Application information: Contributes only to pre-selected organizations.
Trustees: James R. Bright, Carl J. Tippit.
EIN: 341627297
Codes: FD

42476
Waite-Brand Foundation
c/o KeyBank, N.A.
P.O. Box 10099
Toledo, OH 43699-0099
Application address: c/o Shumaker, Loop & Kendrick, 1000 Jackson Blvd., Toledo, OH 43624, tel.: (419) 241-9000
Contact: Gregory G. Alexander, Esq., Tr.

Established in 1965 in OH.
Financial data (yr. ended 02/28/02): Grants paid, $400,000; assets, $4,157,672 (M); expenditures, $461,829; qualifying distributions, $445,673.
Limitations: Giving primarily in the Toledo, OH, area.
Application information: Application form not required.
Trustees: Gregory G. Alexander, Gregory S. Shumaker, Hope J. Welles, Philip H. Wolf, KeyBank, N.A.
EIN: 346563471
Codes: FD

42477
E. Kenneth & Esther Marie Hatton Foundation
c/o James Menniger
7015 Rembald St.
Cincinnati, OH 45227

Established in 1997 in OH.
Donor(s): Esther Marie Hatton, Kenneth Hatton.
Financial data (yr. ended 12/31/99): Grants paid, $398,856; assets, $19,470,516 (M); gifts received, $12,472,313; expenditures, $447,445; qualifying distributions, $398,856.
Limitations: Applications not accepted. Giving primarily in OH.
Application information: Contributes only to pre-selected organizations.
Officers: Kenneth E. Hatton, Pres.; Walter R. Lunsford, V.P. and Treas.; James F. Menniger, Secy.
EIN: 311533046
Codes: FD

42478
The Phil Wagler Charitable Foundation
3730 Tabs Dr.
Uniontown, OH 44685-9562

Established in 1988 in OH.
Donor(s): Phil Wagler.
Financial data (yr. ended 12/31/01): Grants paid, $397,025; assets, $7,492,031 (M); gifts received,

$350,108; expenditures, $405,158; qualifying distributions, $393,625.
Limitations: Applications not accepted. Giving primarily in OH.
Application information: Contributes only to pre-selected organizations.
Trustee: Phil Wagler.
EIN: 346886145
Codes: FD

42479
Stuart Rose Family Foundation
2875 Needmore Rd.
Dayton, OH 45414

Established in 1988 in OH.
Donor(s): Stuart A. Rose, Christy Rose.
Financial data (yr. ended 11/30/01): Grants paid, $396,875; assets, $3,064,392 (M); expenditures, $419,165; qualifying distributions, $414,202.
Limitations: Applications not accepted. Giving limited to Dayton, OH.
Application information: Contributes only to pre-selected organizations.
Officers and Director:* Stuart A. Rose, Pres.; Christine Rose,* V.P.; Jaqueline T. Rose, Secy.; Eugene S. Rose, Treas.
EIN: 311274967
Codes: FD

42480
Arnold M. & Sydell L. Miller Foundation
30575 Bainbridge Rd., Ste. 130
Solon, OH 44139-2275
Contact: Sydell L. Miller, Pres.

Established in 1984 in OH.
Donor(s): Arnold M. Miller,‡ Sydell L. Miller.
Financial data (yr. ended 06/30/01): Grants paid, $395,929; assets, $9,763,904 (M); gifts received, $500,000; expenditures, $411,730; qualifying distributions, $399,306.
Limitations: Giving limited to OH.
Publications: Financial statement.
Application information: Application form required.
Officers: Sydell L. Miller, Pres. and Treas.; Lauren B. Spilman, V.P.; Stacie L. Halpern, Secy.
EIN: 341460324
Codes: FD, GTI

42481
The Thomas J. Evans Foundation
36 N. 2nd St.
Newark, OH 43055
Contact: J. Gilbert Reese, Chair.

Established in 1965 in OH.
Donor(s): Thomas J. Evans.‡
Financial data (yr. ended 10/31/01): Grants paid, $395,292; assets, $21,886,153 (M); expenditures, $580,517; qualifying distributions, $589,070.
Limitations: Giving primarily in Licking County, OH.
Application information: Application form not required.
Officers: J. Gilbert Reese, Chair. and C.E.O.; Sarah R. Wallace, Pres. and Secy.; Louella H. Reese, V.P. and Treas.
EIN: 316055767
Codes: FD

42482
Donald J. Foss Memorial Employees Trust
604 Madison Ave.
Wooster, OH 44691-4764
Contact: Woodrow J. Zook, Tr.

Established in 1956 in OH.
Donor(s): Donald J. Foss,‡ Mrs. Donald J. Foss,‡ Walter R. Foss.‡
Financial data (yr. ended 04/30/02): Grants paid, $393,264; assets, $7,082,683 (M); expenditures, $393,464; qualifying distributions, $389,268.
Limitations: Applications not accepted. Giving primarily in Wooster, OH.
Application information: Unsolicited requests for funds not accepted.
Trustees: Robert L. Weiss, Thomas W. Zook, Woodrow J. Zook.
EIN: 346517801
Codes: FD, GTI

42483
The Heimann Family Foundation
9000 Kugler Mill Rd.
Cincinnati, OH 45243 (513) 831-2161
Contact: Robert A. Heimann, Pres.

Established in 1986 in OH.
Financial data (yr. ended 05/31/01): Grants paid, $391,730; assets, $5,880,278 (M); expenditures, $391,946; qualifying distributions, $391,730.
Limitations: Giving primarily in Cincinnati, OH.
Officers and Trustees:* Robert Heimann,* Pres.; Sandra Heimann,* V.P.; William F. Woeste.
EIN: 311197600
Codes: FD

42484
The Gilbert Reese Family Foundation
36 N. 2nd St.
Newark, OH 43055-5610

Established in 1994.
Donor(s): J. Gilbert Reese, Everett D. Reese.‡
Financial data (yr. ended 12/31/01): Grants paid, $391,162; assets, $8,046,465 (M); expenditures, $396,865; qualifying distributions, $388,545.
Limitations: Applications not accepted. Giving primarily in Newark, OH; some giving also on a national basis.
Application information: Contributes only to pre-selected organizations.
Officers: Louella H. Reese, Chair.; Gilbert H. Reese, Pres.; Joyce H. McCreary, Secy.; Megan R. Edwards, Treas.
EIN: 311421173
Codes: FD

42485
Miriam G. Knoll Charitable Foundation
c/o First Financial Bank
300 High St.
Hamilton, OH 45011-6078 (513) 425-7532
Application address: P.O. Box 220, Middletown, OH 45044
Contact: Advisory Comm.

Established in 1985 in OH.
Financial data (yr. ended 10/31/01): Grants paid, $390,224; assets, $7,632,517 (M); expenditures, $443,489; qualifying distributions, $409,223.
Limitations: Giving limited to OH, primarily in Middletown.
Application information: Application form not required.
Officer: Roland P. Ely, Exec. Dir.
Trustee: First Financial Bank.
EIN: 316282842
Codes: FD

42486
The Frank M. Tait Foundation
Courthouse Plz., S.W., 7th Fl.
Dayton, OH 45402 (937) 222-2401
FAX: (937) 224-6015
Contact: Susan T. Rankin, Exec. Dir.

Incorporated in 1955 in OH.
Donor(s): Frank M. Tait,‡ Mrs. Frank M. Tait.‡
Financial data (yr. ended 12/31/01): Grants paid, $389,508; assets, $7,419,232 (L); expenditures, $424,058; qualifying distributions, $415,474.
Limitations: Giving limited to Montgomery County, OH.
Publications: Grants list, informational brochure (including application guidelines).
Application information: Application form not required.
Officers and Trustees:* Peter H. Forster,* Pres.; Alexander J. Williams,* V.P.; Susan T. Rankin, Secy.-Treas. and Exec. Dir.; Thomas G. Breitenbach, David R. Holmes, Robert J. Kegerreis.
EIN: 316037499
Codes: FD

42487
William P. Anderson Foundation
c/o PNC Bank, Ohio, N.A.
P.O. Box 1198
Cincinnati, OH 45273-9631
Contact: Paul D. Myers, Secy.

Incorporated in 1941 in OH.
Financial data (yr. ended 10/31/01): Grants paid, $387,000; assets, $6,716,991 (M); expenditures, $447,597; qualifying distributions, $396,649.
Limitations: Giving primarily in Cincinnati, OH.
Application information: The foundation no longer awards scholarships to individual students; existing commitments will be paid out. Application form required.
Officers and Trustees:* William P. Anderson V,* Pres.; Vachael Anderson Coombe,* V.P.; Harry W. Whittaker,* V.P.; Paul D. Myers,* Secy.; Grenville Anderson,* Treas.; Eva Jane Coombe, Michael A. Coombe, Tucker J. Coombe, James A. Myers, Polly W. Rosenkrantz.
EIN: 316034059
Codes: FD

42488
Gries Family Foundation
1801 E. 9th St., Ste. 1600
Cleveland, OH 44114-3100 (216) 861-1146
Contact: Robert D. Gries, Pres.

Established in 1986.
Donor(s): Robert D. Gries, Ellen G. Cole.
Financial data (yr. ended 12/31/01): Grants paid, $382,581; assets, $4,244,639 (M); gifts received, $119,738; expenditures, $470,353; qualifying distributions, $381,321.
Limitations: Giving primarily in the greater Cleveland, OH, area.
Application information: Contributes only to charities of interest to the trustees. Application form not required.
Officers and Trustees:* Robert D. Gries,* Pres.; David G. Cole,* V.P.; Sally P. Gries,* Secy.-Treas.
EIN: 341536795
Codes: FD

42489
The Invacare Foundation
1 Invacare Way
Elyria, OH 44035 (440) 329-6102
Application address: 1 Invacare Way, Elyria, OH 44036
Contact: Debra Warden, Asst. Secy.

Established in 1992 in OH.
Donor(s): Invacare Corp.
Financial data (yr. ended 06/30/01): Grants paid, $379,500; assets, $1,330,494 (M); expenditures, $390,252; qualifying distributions, $379,141.
Limitations: Giving primarily in OH.
Publications: Application guidelines.
Application information: Application form required.

Officers and Trustees:* Thomas R. Kroeger, Pres.; David T. Williams, V.P.; Jerome E. Fox, Jr., Secy.-Treas.; Gerald B. Blough, A. Malachi Mixon III.
EIN: 341726060
Codes: CS, FD, CD

42490
Charles M. & Thelma M. Pugliese Foundation
c/o U.S. Bank
P.O. Box 479
Youngstown, OH 44501-0479

Established in 1998 in OH.
Donor(s): Charles M. Pugliese, Thelma M. Pugliese.
Financial data (yr. ended 12/31/01): Grants paid, $379,167; assets, $7,723,750 (M); expenditures, $462,116; qualifying distributions, $383,124.
Limitations: Giving primarily in Steubenville, OH.
Officers and Trustees:* William W. McElwain,* Chair.; Douglas C. Naylor, Sr.,* Secy.; H. Lee Kinney, U.S. Bank.
EIN: 341784660
Codes: FD

42491
Austin-Bailey Health and Wellness Foundation
2719 Fulton Rd., N.W., Ste. D
Canton, OH 44718 (330) 580-2380
FAX: (330) 580-2381; E-mail: abfdn@cannet.com; URL: http://fdncenter.org/grantmaker/austinbailey
Contact: Gerald L. Meck, Pres.; or Don A. Sultzbach, Exec. Dir.

Established in 1996 in OH. Foundation received proceeds converted from the sale of Doctors Hospital in Massillon to Quorum.
Financial data (yr. ended 06/30/02): Grants paid, $378,977; assets, $8,000,000 (M); expenditures, $504,855; qualifying distributions, $378,977.
Limitations: Giving primarily in Holmes, Stark, Tuscarawas, and Wayne counties, OH.
Publications: Annual report, informational brochure, application guidelines, informational brochure (including application guidelines).
Application information: Application form required.
Officers and Trustees:* William G. Bittle,* Chair.; Gerald L. Meck,* Pres.; Charles R. Conklin,* Secy.; Peter Kopko,* Treas.; Don A. Sultzbach,* Exec. Dir.; James S. Gwin, Stephen S. Higley, Candace Lautenschleger, Elton D. Lehman, Daniel N. Moretta, John L. Muhlbach, Jr., Virginia Neutzling, Frederick W. Rohrig.
EIN: 341845584
Codes: FD

42492
The Rock Foundation
7660 Twin Lakes Trail
Chagrin Falls, OH 44022

Established in 1989 in OH.
Donor(s): Arthur S. Holmes.
Financial data (yr. ended 12/31/01): Grants paid, $377,000; assets, $78,458 (M); expenditures, $378,100; qualifying distributions, $378,100.
Limitations: Applications not accepted. Giving on a national basis, with some emphasis on VA.
Application information: Contributes only to pre-selected organizations.
Trustees: Arthur S. Holmes, Christine H. Holmes, Julie C. Holmes.
EIN: 341636792
Codes: FD

42493
Emma and Laura Bahmann Family Foundation
8041 Hosbrook Rd., Ste. 210
Cincinnati, OH 45236-2907
E-mail: info@bahmann.org; URL: http://www.bahmann.org
Contact: John T. Gatch, Exec. Dir.

Established in 1984 in OH.
Donor(s): Emma Leah Bahmann, Laura Belle Bahmann.
Financial data (yr. ended 12/31/01): Grants paid, $374,224; assets, $9,973,341 (M); expenditures, $715,496; qualifying distributions, $603,191.
Limitations: Applications not accepted. Giving primarily in the greater Cincinnati, OH, area.
Application information: Unsolicited requests for funds not accepted.
Officer: John T. Gatch, Exec. Dir.
Trustee: Lewis G. Gatch.
EIN: 316369498
Codes: FD

42494
The Fred E. Scholl Charitable Foundation
c/o Bernard L. Karr
600 Superior Ave., E., Ste. 2100
Cleveland, OH 44114

Established in 1997 in OH.
Donor(s): Fred R. School Declaration of Trust.
Financial data (yr. ended 12/31/01): Grants paid, $366,610; assets, $5,558,757 (M); expenditures, $511,140; qualifying distributions, $366,610.
Limitations: Applications not accepted. Giving primarily in Cleveland, OH.
Application information: Contributes only to pre-selected organizations.
Officers and Trustees:* Bernard L. Karr,* Pres.; Thomas F. Kirchendorfer,* V.P.; Nancy Karr,* Secy.; Jeffrey D. Consolo,* Treas.
EIN: 311520141
Codes: FD

42495
The Eric and Jane Nord Foundation
P.O. Box 457
Oberlin, OH 44074

Established in 1984 in OH.
Donor(s): Eric T. Nord, Jane B. Nord.
Financial data (yr. ended 06/30/01): Grants paid, $365,918; assets, $9,749,231 (M); gifts received, $110,000; expenditures, $374,531; qualifying distributions, $370,406.
Limitations: Applications not accepted. Giving primarily in OH.
Application information: Contributes only to pre-selected organizations.
Officers: Eric T. Nord, Pres. and Treas.; Jane B. Nord, V.P.; William D. Ginn, Secy.
EIN: 341465569
Codes: FD

42496
George B. Quatman Foundation
c/o Fifth Third Bank
38 Fountain Sq. Plz., M.D. 1COM31
Cincinnati, OH 45263
FAX: (937) 335-8374
Contact: Peter Klosterman, Trust Off., Fifth Third Bank of Western Ohio, N.A.

Established in 1994 in OH.
Financial data (yr. ended 12/31/01): Grants paid, $365,166; assets, $5,342,889 (M); expenditures, $400,442; qualifying distributions, $372,643.
Application information: Application form required.
Trustee: Fifth Third Bank.
EIN: 316068296
Codes: FD

42497
Schooler Family Foundation
P.O. Box 1300
Coshocton, OH 43812
E-mail: sff@coshoctonfoundation.org, or sffo@att6i.com
Contact: Christine Cugliari, Prog. Mgr.

Established in Dec. 1985 in OH.
Donor(s): Seward D. Schooler,‡ Edith Schooler.‡
Financial data (yr. ended 12/31/01): Grants paid, $364,752; assets, $6,866,795 (M); expenditures, $543,738; qualifying distributions, $421,525.
Limitations: Giving primarily in OH.
Publications: Annual report (including application guidelines), financial statement, grants list.
Application information: Application form not required.
Officers and Trustees:* Dean Schooler,* Pres. and Treas.; Willard S. Breon,* V.P.; David R. Schooler,* V.P.; C. Fenning Pierce,* Secy.; Steven J. Barr, Heather L. Schooler.
Program Staff: Christine Cugliari.
EIN: 311157433
Codes: FD

42498
The Thomas F. Peterson Foundation
3200 National City Ctr.
Cleveland, OH 44114
Contact: John D. Drinko, V.P.

Established in 1953 in OH.
Donor(s): Ethel B. Peterson.‡
Financial data (yr. ended 10/31/01): Grants paid, $364,000; assets, $3,541,830 (M); expenditures, $444,069; qualifying distributions, $398,711.
Limitations: Applications not accepted. Giving primarily in OH.
Application information: Contributes only to pre-selected organizations.
Officers and Trustees:* Barbara P. Ruhlman,* Pres.; John D. Drinko,* V.P.; R. Steven Kestner,* Secy.; J. Richard Hamilton,* Treas.
EIN: 346524958
Codes: FD

42499
Heed Ophthalmic Foundation
c/o F.A. Gutman, M.D., Cleveland Clinic Foundation
9500 Euclid Ave., Desk I-32
Cleveland, OH 44195 (216) 445-8145
Contact: Connie Gast

Trust established in 1946 in IL.
Donor(s): Thomas D. Heed,‡ Mrs. Thomas D. Heed,‡ Society of Heed Fellows.
Financial data (yr. ended 12/31/01): Grants paid, $360,000; assets, $5,205,436 (M); gifts received, $15,000; expenditures, $472,664; qualifying distributions, $371,968.
Limitations: Giving limited to U.S. citizens.
Publications: Application guidelines, program policy statement.
Application information: Application form required.
Officers and Trustees:* Lee Jampol, M.D.,* Chair.; Froncie A. Gutman, M.D.,* Exec. Secy.; Stuart Fine, M.D., Morton F. Goldberg, M.D., Steve Kramer, M.D.
EIN: 366012426
Codes: FD, GTI

42500
Bryan Area Foundation, Inc.
102 N. Main St.
P.O. Box 651
Bryan, OH 43506 (419) 633-1156
E-mail: baf@williams-net.com
Contact: Michael Wolfe, Exec. Dir.

Established in 1969 in OH.
Financial data (yr. ended 06/30/00): Grants paid, $358,283; assets, $9,231,178 (M); gifts received, $825,653; expenditures, $523,392.
Limitations: Giving limited to the Bryan, OH, area.
Publications: Application guidelines, occasional report.
Application information: Scholarships are paid directly to universities on behalf of recipient. Application form required.
Officers: Thomas Herman, Pres.; C. Gregory Spangler, V.P.; Craig L. Roth, Secy.; Albert Horn, Treas.
Trustees: Kay Jackson, Gregory Spangler, George Stockman, and 5 additional directors.
EIN: 237041310
Codes: CM, FD

42501
Turn 2 Foundation, Inc.
IMG Ctr., Ste. 100
1360 E. 9th St.
Cleveland, OH 44114-1782
Application address: 350 E. Michigan Ave., Ste. 205, Kalamazoo MI 49007-5807, tel.: (269) 349-0819

Established in 1997 MI.
Donor(s): Derek S. Jeter.
Financial data (yr. ended 12/30/00): Grants paid, $358,154; assets, $588,299 (M); gifts received, $502,619; expenditures, $484,192; qualifying distributions, $480,747.
Limitations: Giving limited to Kalamazoo, MI, and New York City.
Officers: Derek S. Jeter, Pres.; Sanderson Charles Jeter, V.P.; Dorothy Jeter, Secy.-Treas.
Director: Sharlee Jeter.
EIN: 341847687
Codes: FD

42502
Harold C. & Marjorie Q. Rosenberry Tuscarawas County Foundation
c/o Belmont National Bank
P.O. Box 249
St. Clairsville, OH 43950-0249
Application address: Att: Selection Committee, c/o Larry Gibbs, P.O. Box 1003, New Philadelphia, OH 44663, tel.: (330) 343-5518

Established in 1994 in OH.
Financial data (yr. ended 12/30/00): Grants paid, $353,949; assets, $7,312,676 (M); expenditures, $385,422; qualifying distributions, $362,053.
Limitations: Giving limited to Tuscarawas County, OH.
Application information: Application form required.
Trustee: Belmont National Bank.
EIN: 341772635
Codes: FD

42503
Fred & Alice Wallace Charitable Memorial Foundation, Inc.
34 N. Main St.
Dayton, OH 45402 (937) 609-9048
Contact: Dennis Hanaghan, Exec. Dir.

Established in 1978.
Financial data (yr. ended 12/31/01): Grants paid, $353,662; assets, $13,669,483 (M); expenditures, $527,998; qualifying distributions, $406,193.
Limitations: Giving limited to OH, with emphasis on the Miami Valley area.
Publications: Financial statement, informational brochure (including application guidelines), program policy statement.
Application information: Application form required.
Officers: Dennis Hanaghan, Pres.; Jacob Warner, V.P.; J.R. Hochwalt, Secy.-Treas.
EIN: 310944135
Codes: FD

42504
The Brush Foundation
3135 Euclid Ave., Ste. 102
Cleveland, OH 44115 (216) 881-5121
FAX: (216) 881-1834
Contact: Lee Minto, Pres.

Trust established in 1928 in OH.
Donor(s): Charles F. Brush,‡ Maurice Perkins.‡
Financial data (yr. ended 12/31/01): Grants paid, $352,012; assets, $6,716,439 (M); expenditures, $410,409; qualifying distributions, $383,621.
Limitations: Giving in the U.S., with some emphasis on northeastern OH, and Third World countries.
Publications: Application guidelines, multi-year report (including application guidelines).
Application information: The foundation does not accept unsolicited proposals. Organizations that meet the foundation's stated goals will be invited to submit proposals; contact foundation for application guidelines.
Officers and Managers:* Lee Minto,* Pres.; Virginia P. Carter, Ph.D.,* V.P.; Gita P. Gidwani, M.D.,* Secy.; Barbara Brush-Wright,* Treas.; Ellen Rome Asbeck, M.D., Cindie Carroll-Pankhurst, Ph.D., Henry Foster, Meacham Hitchcock, Jane Perkins Moffett, Daniel E. Pellegrom, Mark Salo.
Trustee Bank: KeyBank, N.A.
EIN: 346000445
Codes: FD

42505
Edith C. Justus Trust
P.O. Box 94651
Cleveland, OH 44101-4651
Application address: P.O. Box 374, Oil City, PA 16301, tel.: (814) 677-5085
Contact: Stephen P. Kosak, Consultant

Trust established in 1931 in PA.
Donor(s): Edith C. Justus.‡
Financial data (yr. ended 12/31/01): Grants paid, $351,109; assets, $6,236,652 (M); expenditures, $398,969; qualifying distributions, $382,426.
Limitations: Giving primarily in Venango County, PA, with emphasis on Oil City.
Publications: Application guidelines, grants list.
Application information: Application form required.
Trustee: National City Bank of Pennsylvania.
EIN: 256031057
Codes: FD

42506
Ruth J. & Robert A. Conway Foundation, Inc.
2897 Alpine Terr.
Cincinnati, OH 45208-3439
Contact: Robert A. Conway, Sr., V.P.

Established in 1998 in OH.
Donor(s): Robert A. Conway, Sr., Ruth J. Conway.
Financial data (yr. ended 12/31/01): Grants paid, $351,025; assets, $5,734,613 (M); expenditures, $387,795; qualifying distributions, $351,025.
Officers: Ruth J. Conway, Pres.; Robert A. Conway, Sr., V.P.; Thomas H. Clark, Secy.-Treas.
EIN: 311575184

42507
William & Aileen Whiting Foundation
c/o U.S. Bank
P.O. Box 1118
Cincinnati, OH 45201-1118
Application address: c/o Harold Klink, 425 Walnut St., Cincinnati, OH 45202
Contact: Aileen O. Whiting, Tr.

Established in 1994 in OH.
Donor(s): Aileen O. Whiting.
Financial data (yr. ended 12/31/01): Grants paid, $350,623; assets, $489,370 (M); gifts received, $201,108; expenditures, $359,247; qualifying distributions, $350,623.
Limitations: Giving primarily in OH.
Trustees: Aileen O. Whiting, U.S. Bank.
EIN: 311394946

42508
SCOA Foundation, Inc.
41 S. High St., Rm. 3310
Columbus, OH 43215
Contact: Patricia S. Hershorin, Pres.

Established in 1969 in OH.
Donor(s): SCOA Industries, Inc., Hills Stores Co.
Financial data (yr. ended 12/31/01): Grants paid, $350,000; assets, $4,057,801 (M); expenditures, $369,099; qualifying distributions, $350,000.
Limitations: Giving on a national basis with emphasis on NY and OH.
Officer and Trustees:* Patricia Hershorin,* Pres.; Eugene Bankers, David H. Lissy, Mark von Mayrhauser.
EIN: 237002220
Codes: CS, FD, CD

42509
Lloyd L. and Louise K. Smith Foundation
c/o FirstMerit Bank, N.A.
121 S. Main St., Ste. 200
Akron, OH 44308 (330) 384-7320
FAX: (330) 849-8992; *E-mail:* brenda.moubray@firstmerit.com
Contact: R.B. Tynan, Sr., V.P. and Trust Off., FirstMerit Bank, N.A.

Established in 1992 in OH.
Donor(s): Lloyd L. Smith Trust.
Financial data (yr. ended 08/31/01): Grants paid, $350,000; assets, $6,331,647 (M); expenditures, $392,920; qualifying distributions, $358,967.
Limitations: Giving primarily in Summit County, OH.
Application information: Application form not required.
Trustees: Robert M. Bonchack, Allan Johnson, Charles E. Pierson, FirstMerit Bank, N.A.
EIN: 341717038
Codes: FD

42510
Hugo H. and Mabel B. Young Foundation
c/o JPMorgan Chase Bank
109 S. Market St.
Loudonville, OH 44842
Contact: Michael C. Bandy

Incorporated in 1963 in OH.
Financial data (yr. ended 04/30/01): Grants paid, $348,977; assets, $5,957,479 (M); expenditures, $397,434; qualifying distributions, $347,719.
Limitations: Giving limited to Ashland and Holmes counties, OH.
Application information: Application form not required.

Officers and Trustees:* James J. Dudte,* Pres.; Richard D. Mayer,* V.P.; James Lingenfelter, Secy.-Treas.; Jon H. Cooperrider II, William B. LaPlace, Phillip A. Ranney.
EIN: 346560664
Codes: FD

42511
Jazwa Family Foundation, Inc.
12500 Elmwood Ave.
Cleveland, OH 44111 (216) 941-8100
Contact: John J. Jazwa, Pres.

Established in 1994 in OH.
Donor(s): John Jazwa.
Financial data (yr. ended 12/31/99): Grants paid, $347,000; assets, $1,030,815 (M); expenditures, $357,889; qualifying distributions, $354,146.
Officer: John J. Jazwa, Pres.
Trustees: Dolores Jazwa, Jeffrey Jazwa, Jerry Jazwa, Cindy Wagner.
EIN: 341792693
Codes: FD

42512
The William O. and Gertrude Lewis Frohring Foundation, Inc.
3200 Natl. City Ctr.
Cleveland, OH 44114 (216) 621-0200
Additional address: 1900 E. 9th St., Cleveland, OH 44114
Contact: William W. Falsgraf, Tr.

Trust established in 1958 in OH; incorporated in 1963.
Donor(s): William O. Frohring,‡ Gertrude L. Frohring.‡
Financial data (yr. ended 12/31/01): Grants paid, $346,800; assets, $5,691,101 (M); expenditures, $474,336; qualifying distributions, $359,320.
Limitations: Applications not accepted. Giving primarily in Geauga, Lake, and Cuyahoga counties, OH.
Application information: Unsolicited requests for funds not accepted.
Officers and Trustees:* Glenn H. Frohring,* Chair.; Elaine A. Szilagyi,* Secy.; William W. Falsgraf, Evelyn Frohring.
EIN: 346516526
Codes: FD

42513
The Spahr Foundation
(Formerly The Spahr Family Foundation)
c/o Thomas F. Allen
1801 E. 9th St., Ste. 730
Cleveland, OH 44114-3103 (216) 771-4000

Established in 1990 in OH.
Donor(s): Charles E. Spahr, Mary Jane Spahr.
Financial data (yr. ended 12/31/00): Grants paid, $345,814; assets, $8,072,587 (M); gifts received, $110,000; expenditures, $395,619; qualifying distributions, $361,994.
Limitations: Giving primarily in Cleveland, OH.
Application information: Application form not required.
Officers and Trustees:* Charles E. Spahr,* Chair. and Pres.; Mary Jane Spahr,* V.P.; Thomas F. Allen,* Secy.-Treas.; J. Donald Cairns, Cynthia S. Moran, Stephanie J. Spahr, Stephen D. Spahr, John C. Whitlow.
EIN: 341673582
Codes: FD

42514
Lucile and Robert H. Gries Charity Fund
1600 Ohio Saving Plz.
1801 E. 9th St., Ste. 1600
Cleveland, OH 44114 (216) 861-1146
Contact: Robert D. Gries, Member, Distrib. Comm.

Trust established in 1968 in OH.
Donor(s): Lucile D. Gries.‡
Financial data (yr. ended 12/31/01): Grants paid, $344,250; assets, $2,524,570 (M); gifts received, $17,500; expenditures, $379,113; qualifying distributions, $345,533.
Limitations: Giving primarily in the greater Cleveland, OH, area.
Application information: Contributes only to charities of interest to the trustees. Application form not required.
Distribution Committee: David G. Cole, Robert D. Gries.
Trustee: KeyBank, N.A.
EIN: 346507593
Codes: FD

42515
The Harry K. & Emma R. Fox Charitable Foundation
c/o Frank M. Rizzo, Sr. V.P., National City Bank
1900 E. 9th St., LOC 2066
Cleveland, OH 44101-2146 (216) 222-2507
FAX: (216) 222-2410; *Additional address:* c/o Harold E. Friedman, Penton Media Bldg., 1300 E. 9th St., Cleveland, OH 44114-1583, tel.: (216) 902-8931, FAX: (216) 621-7488; Nancy S. Friedman, 23149 Laureldale Rd., Shaker Heights, OH, 44122; E-mail: hfriedman@ulmer.com
Contact: Harold E. Friedman, Secy.

Trust established in 1959 in OH.
Donor(s): Emma R. Fox.‡
Financial data (yr. ended 12/31/01): Grants paid, $343,800; assets, $9,440,966 (M); expenditures, $402,555; qualifying distributions, $379,612.
Limitations: Giving primarily in northeastern OH, with emphasis on the greater Cleveland area.
Publications: Application guidelines.
Application information: 1 copy of each proposal must be sent to each of the trustees. Application form not required.
Officers and Trustees:* Nancy S. Friedman,* Chair.; Harold E. Friedman, Secy.; Frank M. Rizzo, National City Bank.
EIN: 346511198
Codes: FD

42516
Berlin Family Foundation, Inc.
(Formerly Berlin Family Charitable Corporation)
1795 Brookwood Dr.
Akron, OH 44313
Application address: c/o Robin Berlin Kane, 7450 Main St., Gates Mill, OH 44040
Contact: Judi Roman

Established in 1990 in FL and OH.
Donor(s): Tire Centers, Inc.
Financial data (yr. ended 10/31/01): Grants paid, $343,783; assets, $2,224,606 (M); gifts received, $1,084,704; expenditures, $351,958; qualifying distributions, $343,783.
Limitations: Giving primarily in Boca Raton, FL, and Akron and Cleveland, OH.
Officers: Madeline Berlin, Pres.; Robin Berlin Kane, V.P.
EIN: 650230453
Codes: FD

42517
The Gale Foundation
c/o T.F. Allen; Blossom Business Office
20325 Center Ridge Rd., Ste. 629
Rocky River, OH 44116 (440) 331-8220

Established in 1995 in OH.
Donor(s): Elizabeth B. Blossom, The William Bingham Foundation.
Financial data (yr. ended 12/31/01): Grants paid, $343,130; assets, $6,398,998 (M); expenditures, $370,205; qualifying distributions, $353,464.
Limitations: Applications not accepted. Giving on a national basis.
Application information: Contributes only to pre-selected organizations.
Officers and Trustees:* Benjamin Gale,* Pres.; Deborah B. Gale,* V.P.; Thomas F. Allen, Secy.-Treas.; Charles L. Freer, Deborah G. Freer, Mary B. Gale, Thomas V. Gale.
EIN: 341812999
Codes: FD

42518
The Ellie Fund
(Formerly Gerson-Margolis Foundation)
c/o Foundation Mgmt. Svcs., Inc.
1422 Euclid Ave., No. 627
Cleveland, OH 44115-1952 (216) 621-2901
FAX: (216) 621-8198; URL: http://www.fmscleveland.com/ellie
Contact: Kimberly S. Cowan, Consultant

Established in 1997 in OH.
Financial data (yr. ended 12/31/01): Grants paid, $343,100; assets, $1,196,396 (M); gifts received, $250,000; expenditures, $378,069; qualifying distributions, $343,100.
Limitations: Giving primarily in Cuyahoga County, OH.
Publications: Grants list, informational brochure (including application guidelines).
Application information: Grants are limited to 4 consecutive years. Applicants from outside the Cuyahoga County, OH, area will not be considered unless a trustee has pre-approved the application. Application form not required.
Officers and Trustees:* Margaret G. Margolis,* Pres.; Daniel M. Margolis,* V.P.; James A. Margolis,* V.P.; Richard D. Margolis,* Secy.-Treas.
EIN: 311491821
Codes: FD

42519
The David and Lura Lovell Foundation
1 Exmoor
Toledo, OH 43615
Application address: 8400 N. National Dr., Tucson, AZ 85742, tel.: (520) 575-1108, E-mail: lmlovell@earthlink.net
Contact: Lura M. Lovell, Pres.

Established in 1993 in OH.
Donor(s): Lura M. Lovell, David C. Lovell.‡
Financial data (yr. ended 12/31/01): Grants paid, $342,964; assets, $7,064,857 (M); gifts received, $84,521; expenditures, $441,965; qualifying distributions, $342,964.
Limitations: Applications not accepted. Giving primarily in AZ and OH.
Application information: Unsolicited requests for funds not accepted.
Officers and Trustees:* Lura M. Lovell,* Pres.; Ann Moushey,* Secy.; Stephen J. Lovell, Jodee Robertson.
EIN: 341733685
Codes: FD

42520
The Gardner Foundation
304 S. Highview
Middletown, OH 45044
Contact: Martha Sorrell, Business Mgr.

Incorporated in 1952 in OH.
Financial data (yr. ended 05/31/01): Grants paid, $342,100; assets, $5,903,121 (M); expenditures, $398,278; qualifying distributions, $341,713.
Limitations: Giving limited to Middletown and Cincinnati, OH.
Publications: Program policy statement, application guidelines.
Application information: Application forms available only from high school guidance counselors. Grant payments made to school of applicant's choice. Application form required.
Officers and Trustees:* E.T. Gardner III,* Pres.; Robert Q. Millan,* V.P.; Ames Gardner, Jr., Secy.-Treas.; Eugenie G. Campbell, Colin Gardner IV, Stephen V. Gardner, Mary Gates.
EIN: 316050604
Codes: FD, GTI

42521
The Charles E. and Mabel M. Ritchie Memorial Foundation
c/o FirstMerit Bank, N.A.
121 S. Main St., Ste. 200
Akron, OH 44308 (330) 384-7320
FAX: (330) 849-8992; E-mail: brenda.moubray@firstmerit.com
Contact: Ronald B. Tynan, Sr., V.P. and Trust Off., FirstMerit Bank, N.A.

Trust established in 1954 in OH.
Donor(s): Mabel M. Ritchie.‡
Financial data (yr. ended 12/31/01): Grants paid, $340,643; assets, $8,085,388 (M); expenditures, $401,866; qualifying distributions, $409,239.
Limitations: Giving limited to Summit County, OH.
Application information: Application form not required.
Advisory Committee: Edward F. Carter, Jon Heider, Kathryn M. Hunter.
Trustee: FirstMerit Bank, N.A.
EIN: 346500802
Codes: FD

42522
The Beaverson Foundation
1474 Ramblewood Dr.
Wooster, OH 44691-3038

Established in 1992 in OH.
Donor(s): Audrey L. Beaverson.
Financial data (yr. ended 09/30/01): Grants paid, $336,000; assets, $1,122,913 (M); gifts received, $175,000; expenditures, $350,254; qualifying distributions, $336,000.
Limitations: Applications not accepted. Giving primarily in Wayne County, OH.
Application information: Contributes only to pre-selected organizations.
Officers: Audrey L. Beaverson, Chair.; Robert E. Mapes, V.P.; John C. Johnston III, Secy.
EIN: 341722868
Codes: FD

42523
The Leonard and Joan Horvitz Foundation
6095 Parkland Blvd., Ste. 300
Mayfield Heights, OH 44124

Established in 2000 in OH.
Donor(s): Leonard C. Horvitz, Joan L. Horvitz.
Financial data (yr. ended 12/31/00): Grants paid, $336,000; assets, $296,656 (M); gifts received, $628,438; expenditures, $336,059; qualifying distributions, $334,333.
Limitations: Applications not accepted. Giving limited to OH.
Application information: Contributes only to pre-selected organizations.
Officers: Leonard C. Horvitz, Pres.; Joan L. Horvitz, V.P.; Mark F. Polzin, Secy.-Treas.
EIN: 341894055

42524
Webster H. Sturdivant Charitable Trust
c/o KeyBank, N.A.
P.O. Box 10099
Toledo, OH 43699-0099

Established in 1990 in OH.
Financial data (yr. ended 12/31/01): Grants paid, $334,976; assets, $3,666,460 (M); expenditures, $374,024; qualifying distributions, $340,719.
Limitations: Applications not accepted. Giving primarily in OH.
Application information: Contributes only to pre-selected organizations.
Trustee: KeyBank, N.A.
EIN: 346905144
Codes: FD

42525
Clarence L. & Edith B. Schust Foundation
c/o National City Bank of Indiana
P.O. Box 94651
Cleveland, OH 44101-4651
Application address: P.O. Box 110, Fort Wayne, IN 46801, tel.: (219) 461-6218
Contact: Teresa Tracey

Established in 1983 in IN.
Financial data (yr. ended 04/30/01): Grants paid, $334,249; assets, $7,365,268 (M); expenditures, $372,684; qualifying distributions, $349,422.
Limitations: Giving primarily in IN, with emphasis on Fort Wayne.
Trustee: National City Bank of Indiana.
EIN: 311064803
Codes: FD

42526
Lancaster Lens, Inc.
c/o Clarence Clapham
37 W. Broad St., Rm. 530
Columbus, OH 43215

Established in 1953.
Financial data (yr. ended 07/31/01): Grants paid, $334,200; assets, $6,443,184 (M); expenditures, $354,804; qualifying distributions, $336,833.
Limitations: Applications not accepted. Giving primarily in Columbus, OH.
Application information: Contributes only to pre-selected organizations.
Officers: Bruce L. Rosa, Pres.; Clarence Clapham, Secy.; Joseph E. Schmidhammer, Treas.
EIN: 316023927
Codes: FD

42527
W. Henry Hoover Trust Fund
c/o KeyBank, N.A.
800 Superior Ave., Trust Tax, M/C OH-01-0
Cleveland, OH 44114
Application address: 4495 Everhard Rd. N.W., Canton, OH 44718
Contact: Chuck Wondra

Established in 1945 in OH.
Donor(s): W. Henry Hoover.‡
Financial data (yr. ended 12/31/00): Grants paid, $332,000; assets, $6,209,004 (M); expenditures, $377,431; qualifying distributions, $338,813.
Limitations: Giving primarily in Canton, OH.
Trustee: KeyBank, N.A.
EIN: 346573738
Codes: FD

42528
The Louis and Sandra Berkman Foundation
330 N. 7th St.
P.O. Box 576
Steubenville, OH 43952-2249
Application address: P.O. Box 820, Steubenville, OH 43952
Contact: John R. Koren

Incorporated in 1952 in OH.
Donor(s): Louis Berkman, Sr.,‡ Mrs. Louis Berkman, The Louis Berkman Co., Follansbee Steel Corp.
Financial data (yr. ended 12/31/01): Grants paid, $328,928; assets, $14,004,765 (M); expenditures, $329,061; qualifying distributions, $329,061.
Limitations: Giving primarily in OH and PA.
Officers and Trustees:* Louis Berkman,* Pres. and Treas.; Robert A. Paul,* V.P.; Linda L. Pirkle,* Secy.; Donna Berkman Paul.
EIN: 346526694
Codes: FD

42529
Lippman Kanfer Family Foundation
(Formerly Jerome Lippman Family Foundation)
P.O. Box 991
Akron, OH 44309-0991 (330) 255-6205
Contact: Sharon Guten, Secy.

Established in 1991 in OH.
Donor(s): Gojo Industries, Inc.
Financial data (yr. ended 12/31/01): Grants paid, $326,750; assets, $771,497 (M); gifts received, $600,000; expenditures, $328,129; qualifying distributions, $326,457.
Limitations: Giving primarily in OH.
Publications: Informational brochure.
Application information: Application form not required.
Officers: Jerome Lippman, Pres.; Sharon Guten, Secy.
Directors: Stan Bober, Marcella Kanfer, Paul Sobel, Phillip Nabors.
EIN: 340974875
Codes: FD

42530
Nelson Mead Fund
c/o Rend & Co.
500 Lincoln Park Blvd., Ste. 322
Kettering, OH 45429
FAX: (937) 395-3568
Contact: Ruth C. Mead, Tr.

Established in 1965 in OH.
Donor(s): Ioka Fund, Ruth C. Mead.
Financial data (yr. ended 11/30/01): Grants paid, $325,209; assets, $5,705,070 (M); expenditures, $356,784; qualifying distributions, $323,915.
Limitations: Applications not accepted. Giving on a national basis.
Application information: Contributes only to pre-selected organizations. Unsolicited requests for funds not considered.
Trustee: Ruth C. Mead.
EIN: 316064591
Codes: FD

42531
Gordon & Llura Gund 1993 Charitable Foundation
925 Euclid Ave., Ste. 2000
Cleveland, OH 44115

Established in 1993 in OH.

42531—OHIO

Donor(s): Gordon and Llura Liggett Gund Charitable Lead Annuity Trust.
Financial data (yr. ended 12/31/00): Grants paid, $325,000; assets, $2,785 (M); gifts received, $318,000; expenditures, $325,147; qualifying distributions, $324,997.
Limitations: Applications not accepted. Giving primarily in MD and VT.
Application information: Contributes only to pre-selected organizations.
Trustee: Richard T. Watson.
EIN: 341730494
Codes: FD

42532
Reuter Foundation
7700 Clinton Rd.
Cleveland, OH 44144 (216) 961-1141
FAX: (216) 651-1777; E-mail: mail@ReuterFdn.org (general) or Proposals@ReuterFdn.org (proposals); URL: http://www.reuterfdn.org
Contact: Bob Reuter, Pres.

Established in 1987 in OH.
Donor(s): Robert Reuter.
Financial data (yr. ended 11/30/01): Grants paid, $321,503; assets, $7,674,597 (M); expenditures, $339,588; qualifying distributions, $321,503.
Limitations: Giving primarily in Cleveland, OH and Dallas, TX.
Publications: Application guidelines, informational brochure (including application guidelines).
Application information: Application guideline available on website. Application form not required.
Officers and Trustees:* Robert A. Reuter, Pres.; Gretchen Reuter Bowen,* V.P.; Heidi Reuter Paul,* Secy.; Christopher R. Reuter,* Treas.; Matthew J. Bowen, Holly K. Gigante, Dana F. Paul, Richard F. Sofka.
EIN: 341766081
Codes: FD

42533
Paul R. Gingher State Auto Insurance Companies Foundation
518 E. Broad St.
Columbus, OH 43215-3976

Established in 1989 in OH.
Donor(s): State Automobile Mutual Insurance Co.
Financial data (yr. ended 12/31/01): Grants paid, $319,686; assets, $3,466,166 (M); gifts received, $250,052; expenditures, $320,714; qualifying distributions, $319,987.
Limitations: Applications not accepted. Giving primarily in Columbus, OH.
Application information: Contributes only to pre-selected organizations.
Trustees: Mark Blackburn, Noreen Johnson, Steven J. Johnston, John R. Lowther, Robert H. Moone.
EIN: 311257265
Codes: CS, FD

42534
Johnson Family Foundation
c/o U.S. Bank
P.O. Box 1118, ML CN-WN-07IV
Cincinnati, OH 45201-1118 (513) 632-4633
Contact: Terry K. Crilley, Dir.

Established in 1997 in OH.
Donor(s): Arlyn T. Johnson, Samuel J. Johnson IV.
Financial data (yr. ended 04/30/01): Grants paid, $318,400; assets, $6,099,913 (M); expenditures, $319,829; qualifying distributions, $315,876.
Limitations: Giving primarily in OH and MA.
Trustees: Arlyn T. Johnson, Gwendolyn Kess Johnson, Samuel J. Johnson IV, Samuel J. Johnson V, Jesse Lipcon, Patricia L. Johnson Lipcon.
Directors: Terry K. Crilley, David S. Hamilton.
EIN: 311542859
Codes: FD

42535
The Jeffrey Horvitz Foundation
28601 Chagrin Blvd., Ste. 550
Cleveland, OH 44122

Established in 1995 in OH.
Donor(s): Jeffrey E. Horvitz.
Financial data (yr. ended 12/31/99): Grants paid, $318,000; assets, $1,193,507 (M); gifts received, $1,000,000; expenditures, $379,630; qualifying distributions, $348,812.
Limitations: Applications not accepted. Giving primarily in MA.
Application information: Contributes only to pre-selected organizations.
Officers and Trustees:* Jeffrey E. Horvitz,* Pres.; Richard A. Horvitz,* Secy.-Treas.; Carol Sunday.
EIN: 341817950
Codes: FD

42536
The Scioto County Area Foundation
National City Bank Bldg., Ste. 801
800 Gallia St.
Portsmouth, OH 45662 (740) 354-4612
FAX: (740) 354-4612
Contact: Sallie C. Schisler, Chair.

Established in 1974 in OH.
Financial data (yr. ended 12/31/99): Grants paid, $307,708; assets, $12,700,000 (M); gifts received, $706,250; expenditures, $452,963.
Limitations: Giving limited to Scioto County, OH.
Publications: Application guidelines, annual report, informational brochure.
Application information: Grants accepted on a quarterly basis. Application form required.
Officer: Sallie C. Schisler, Chair.
EIN: 510157026
Codes: CM, FD

42537
Dorothy T. & Myron Seifert Charitable Trust
c/o National City Bank
P.O. Box 94651
Cleveland, OH 44101-4651

Established in 1996 in OH.
Financial data (yr. ended 12/31/00): Grants paid, $305,498; assets, $5,941,885 (M); gifts received, $201; expenditures, $350,710; qualifying distributions, $320,102.
Limitations: Applications not accepted. Giving limited to OH.
Application information: Contributes only to pre-selected organizations.
Trustee: National City Bank.
EIN: 316535424
Codes: FD

42538
Hayfields Foundation
4001 Carew Twr.
Cincinnati, OH 45202 (513) 621-1384
Contact: Eric B. Yeiser, Pres.

Established in 1946.
Donor(s): Louise F. Tate,‡ Charles F. Yeiser.
Financial data (yr. ended 12/31/01): Grants paid, $305,000; assets, $6,186,002 (M); gifts received, $72; expenditures, $318,374; qualifying distributions, $301,034.
Limitations: Giving primarily in the greater Cincinnati, OH, area.
Application information: Application form not required.
Officers: Eric B. Yeiser, Pres.; Charles F. Yeiser, V.P.; Robert E. Rich, Secy.
EIN: 316025518
Codes: FD

42539
The Laub Foundation
c/o Katherine C. Wolk
19655 Parklane Dr.
Rocky River, OH 44116 (440) 331-4028
Application addresses: 5 Ocean Ave., South Harwich, MA 02661, or P.O. Box 194, South Harwich, MA 02661

Incorporated in 1958 in OH.
Donor(s): Herbert J. Laub,‡ Elsie K. Laub.‡
Financial data (yr. ended 10/31/01): Grants paid, $304,670; assets, $5,039,947 (M); expenditures, $358,131; qualifying distributions, $305,364.
Limitations: Giving primarily in Cuyahoga County, OH, and adjacent counties.
Publications: Annual report.
Application information: Distribution of grants made at Aug. meeting. Application form not required.
Officers and Trustees:* Malcolm D. Campbell, Jr.,* Pres. and Treas.; Katherine C. Wolk,* V.P.; Lisa Robert Mamone,* Secy.; Laurence A. Bartell, Amie M. Campbell, Thomas C. Westropp.
EIN: 346526087
Codes: FD

42540
Hubert Foundation
7929 Okeana Drewersburg Rd.
Okeana, OH 45053-9500

Established in 1984 in OH.
Donor(s): Edward Hubert, Hubert Enterprises.
Financial data (yr. ended 06/30/01): Grants paid, $304,236; assets, $11,719,557 (M); gifts received, $65,100; expenditures, $353,316; qualifying distributions, $766,796; giving activities include $444,857 for program-related investments.
Limitations: Applications not accepted. Giving primarily in Cincinnati, OH.
Application information: Contributes only to pre-selected organizations.
Trustees: Edward Hubert, George Hubert, Jr., Sharon Hubert, Howard Thomas.
EIN: 311129121
Codes: FD

42541
Broussard Charitable Foundation Trust
c/o Fifth Third Bank
38 Fountain Sq. Plz.
Cincinnati, OH 45263

Established in 1996.
Financial data (yr. ended 12/31/01): Grants paid, $304,000; assets, $6,798,587 (M); gifts received, $333,591; expenditures, $351,979; qualifying distributions, $303,827.
Limitations: Giving primarily in IN.
Trustee: Fifth Third Bank.
EIN: 356634227
Codes: FD

42542
Highfield Foundation
c/o Fifth Third Bank, Trust Tax Dept.
38 Fountain Sq. Plz., MD 1COM31
Cincinnati, OH 45263
Contact: Paula Wharton

Established in 1990 in OH.
Donor(s): Samuel Benedict.

Financial data (yr. ended 09/30/01): Grants paid, $302,509; assets, $3,938,585 (M); expenditures, $332,458; qualifying distributions, $311,509.
Limitations: Giving on a national basis.
Application information: Application form not required.
Trustee: Fifth Third Bank.
EIN: 316391904
Codes: FD

42543
The Walter and Jean Kalberer Foundation
1259 W. Hill Dr.
Gates Mills, OH 44040

Established in 1995 in OH.
Donor(s): Walter E. Kalberer, Jean C. Kalberer, Peter Scheid.
Financial data (yr. ended 12/31/00): Grants paid, $302,394; assets, $10,603,550 (M); gifts received, $1,627,298; expenditures, $307,718; qualifying distributions, $302,599.
Limitations: Applications not accepted. Giving primarily in Cleveland, OH.
Application information: Contributes only to pre-selected organizations.
Trustees: Jean C. Kalberer, Lori Kalberer, Walter E. Kalberer, Gwenn S. Winkhaus.
EIN: 341817179
Codes: FD

42544
George and Deborah Mehl Family Foundation, Inc.
c/o W. Stuart Dornette
1800 Firstar Tower, 425 Walnut St.
Cincinnati, OH 45202

Established in 1999 in OH.
Donor(s): George & Deborah Mehl Family Trust.
Financial data (yr. ended 12/31/01): Grants paid, $301,208; assets, $8,451,263 (M); gifts received, $200,000; expenditures, $356,753; qualifying distributions, $324,180.
Limitations: Applications not accepted. Giving on a national basis.
Application information: Contributes only to pre-selected organizations.
Officers and Trustees:* W. Stuart Dornette,* Pres.; Bonnie Mehl,* V.P.; Martha Dornette,* Secy.; David Mehl,* Treas.
EIN: 311679603
Codes: FD

42545
Roan Foundation
1001 Lakeside Ave. E., Ste. 1400
Cleveland, OH 44114-1152

Established around 1977.
Donor(s): William A. Rawlings, Jr.
Financial data (yr. ended 12/31/00): Grants paid, $300,600; assets, $15,325 (M); expenditures, $325,270; qualifying distributions, $300,575.
Limitations: Applications not accepted. Giving primarily in Cleveland, OH.
Application information: Contributes only to pre-selected organizations.
Trustee: Joan Rawlings.
EIN: 341201202
Codes: FD

42546
The Thendara Foundation, Inc.
3333 Burnett Ave.
Cincinnati, OH 45229
Contact: James M. Anderson, Tr.

Established in 1984 in OH.
Donor(s): C. Lawson Reed,‡ Dorothy W. Reed.
Financial data (yr. ended 12/31/01): Grants paid, $298,178; assets, $7,447,483 (M); expenditures, $351,772; qualifying distributions, $315,143.
Limitations: Giving primarily in CA, with emphasis on San Francisco, and OH.
Trustees: James M. Anderson, Janet Reed Goss, C.L. Reed III, Foster A. Reed.
EIN: 311126072
Codes: FD

42547
William M. Shinnick Educational Fund
58 N. 5th St.
Zanesville, OH 43701-3504 (740) 452-2273
Contact: Barbara Cornell, Admin. Asst.

Established in 1923 in OH.
Donor(s): William M. Shinnick, Eunice Hale Buckingham.
Financial data (yr. ended 06/30/01): Grants paid, $296,750; assets, $3,538,216 (M); gifts received, $92,985; expenditures, $354,223; qualifying distributions, $328,557; giving activities include $86,750 for loans to individuals.
Limitations: Giving limited to residents of Muskingum County, OH.
Application information: Application form not required.
Officers and Trustees:* Hazel L. Butterfield,* Pres.; William S. Barry, William D. Joseph, Norma Littick, Thomas Price.
EIN: 314394168
Codes: FD, GTI

42548
Klock Kingston Foundation
(Formerly Jay E. Klock and Lucia De L. Klock Kingston Foundation)
c/o KeyBank, N.A.
800 Superior Ave.
Cleveland, OH 44114
Application address: c/o KeyBank, N.A., 2637 Wall St., Kingston, NY 12401

Established in 1966 in NY.
Financial data (yr. ended 12/31/01): Grants paid, $296,650; assets, $5,045,804 (M); expenditures, $333,699; qualifying distributions, $290,959.
Limitations: Giving limited to Kingston and Ulster County, NY.
Trustee: KeyBank, N.A.
EIN: 146038479
Codes: FD

42549
Florence B. Kilworth Charitable Foundation
c/o KeyBank, N.A.
800 Superior Ave., 4th Fl.
Cleveland, OH 44114
Application address: c/o KeyBank, N.A., WA-31-01-0310, 1101 Pacific Ave., 3rd Fl., P.O. Box 11500, Tacoma, WA 98411-5052
Contact: Mollie C. Determan, V.P., KeyBank, N.A.

Established in 1977.
Financial data (yr. ended 12/31/01): Grants paid, $296,000; assets, $5,957,120 (M); expenditures, $351,445; qualifying distributions, $305,932.
Limitations: Giving primarily in the Tacoma and Pierce counties, WA, area.
Application information: Application form required.
Trustee: KeyBank, N.A.
EIN: 916221495
Codes: FD

42550
Tomkins Corporation Foundation
(Formerly Philips Industries Foundation)
4801 Springfield St.
Dayton, OH 45431-1084

Established in 1986 in OH.
Donor(s): Tomkins Industries, Inc.
Financial data (yr. ended 04/30/01): Grants paid, $294,443; assets, $7,543,434 (M); expenditures, $303,672; qualifying distributions, $294,443.
Limitations: Applications not accepted. Giving primarily in OH.
Application information: Contributes only to pre-selected organizations.
Officers and Trustees:* Anthony J. Reading,* Pres.; Daniel J. Disser,* V.P.; Gregory F. Kirchhoff,* V.P.; George S. Pappayliou, Secy.
EIN: 311207183
Codes: CS, FD, CD

42551
George Lee Miller Memorial Trust
c/o KeyBank, N.A.
800 Superior Ave.
Cleveland, OH 44114
Application address: c/o KeyBank, N.A., P.O. Box 9950, Trust Dept., Canton, OH 44711-0950, tel.: (330) 497-3600
Contact: Brian Cherkala, Trust Admin., KeyBank, N.A.

Established about 1982 in OH.
Financial data (yr. ended 12/31/01): Grants paid, $293,922; assets, $4,646,576 (M); expenditures, $342,383; qualifying distributions, $298,983.
Limitations: Giving primarily in the Canton, OH, area.
Trustee: KeyBank, N.A.
EIN: 346748261
Codes: FD

42552
Bardes Fund
4730 Madison Rd.
Cincinnati, OH 45227-1426 (513) 871-4000
Contact: Rebecca Autry, Secy.-Treas.

Established in 1955 in OH.
Donor(s): Bardes Corp.
Financial data (yr. ended 12/31/00): Grants paid, $292,599; assets, $4,915,820 (M); expenditures, $325,212; qualifying distributions, $292,559.
Limitations: Giving on a national basis.
Officer: Rebecca Autry, Secy.-Treas.
EIN: 316036206
Codes: CS, FD, CD

42553
Cecil I. Walker Machinery Company Charitable Trust
c/o Bank One, Trust Tax Dept.
774 Park Meadow Rd.
Westerville, OH 43081

Donor(s): Cecil I. Walker Machinery Co.
Financial data (yr. ended 05/31/01): Grants paid, $292,500; assets, $2,009,506 (M); expenditures, $311,828; qualifying distributions, $292,713.
Limitations: Applications not accepted. Giving limited to areas of company operations.
Application information: Contributes only to pre-selected organizations.
Trustees: D. Stephen Walker, Richard B. Walker, Bank One, N.A.
EIN: 556050733
Codes: CS, FD, CD

42554—OHIO

42554
The Foster Family Foundation
c/o National City Bank
P.O. Box 94651
Cleveland, OH 44101-4651
Application address: c/o National City Bank, P.O. Box 5756, Cleveland, OH 44101-0756, tel.: (216) 575-2420
Contact: Bonita Rowbotham

Established in 1992 in OH.
Donor(s): The Clyde T. and Lyla C. Foster Foundation.
Financial data (yr. ended 12/31/01): Grants paid, $291,616; assets, $2,435,844 (M); expenditures, $322,010; qualifying distributions, $292,223.
Limitations: Giving primarily in OH and WI.
Trustees: Byron T. Foster, Coleman A. Foster.
Agent: National City Bank.
EIN: 346968228
Codes: FD

42555
Warren Brown Family Foundation
c/o Janice J. Brown
2493 Cummins Hill Dr.
Marion, OH 43302

Established in 1996 in OH.
Donor(s): D. Warren Brown.‡
Financial data (yr. ended 12/31/99): Grants paid, $290,324; assets, $7,260,100 (M); gifts received, $5,095,532; expenditures, $324,839; qualifying distributions, $290,324.
Limitations: Giving primarily in Marion, OH.
Application information: Application form not required.
Officers: Janice J. Brown, Pres.; Douglas W. Brown, Secy.; Joe D. Donithen, Treas.
Trustees: Katherine B. Shepherd, James H. Wyland.
EIN: 341811779
Codes: FD

42556
Horace & Letitia Newton Scholarship Fund
c/o KeyBank, N.A.
P.O. Box 10099
Toledo, OH 43699-0099 (419) 259-8218
E-mail: Marilyn_brown@keybank.com
Contact: Marilyn Brown

Established in 1991 in OH.
Financial data (yr. ended 12/31/01): Grants paid, $288,574; assets, $5,578,349 (M); expenditures, $341,840; qualifying distributions, $299,977.
Limitations: Giving primarily in Toledo, OH.
Application information: Application form required.
Trustee: KeyBank, N.A.
EIN: 346502592
Codes: FD, GTI

42557
Ar-Hale Family Foundation, Inc.
(Formerly Ar-Hale Foundation, Inc.)
P.O. Box 1507
Lima, OH 45802
Application address: 2301 Baton Rouge Ave., Lima, OH 45805
Contact: Leo Hawk, Pres.

Established in 1990 in OH; funded in 1991.
Donor(s): Superior Metal Products, Inc.
Financial data (yr. ended 12/31/01): Grants paid, $286,490; assets, $108,802 (M); gifts received, $305,000; expenditures, $287,190; qualifying distributions, $286,490.
Officers: Leo Hawk, Pres.; Arlene F. Hawk, V.P.
EIN: 341644337
Codes: FD

42558
John C. and Sally S. Morley Family Foundation
c/o Richard T. Watson
925 Euclid Ave., Ste. 2000
Cleveland, OH 44115
Contact: Tina Leneghan, Admin. Asst.

Established in OH in 1998.
Donor(s): John C. Morley, Sally C. Morley.
Financial data (yr. ended 12/31/01): Grants paid, $285,250; assets, $422,845 (M); gifts received, $326,448; expenditures, $281,159; qualifying distributions, $285,022.
Limitations: Applications not accepted. Giving primarily in OH.
Application information: Contributes only to pre-selected organizations.
Trustee: Richard T. Watson.
EIN: 347065759
Codes: FD

42559
The S. Livingston Mather Charitable Trust
10401 Griswold Rd.
Mentor, OH 44060-8214 (440) 255-8447
Additional tel.: (440) 255-5143; FAX: (440) 255-6485
Contact: Thomas W. Offutt III, Secy.

Trust established in 1953 in OH.
Donor(s): S. Livingston Mather.‡
Financial data (yr. ended 12/31/00): Grants paid, $285,000; assets, $5,822,436 (M); expenditures, $316,059; qualifying distributions, $295,387.
Limitations: Giving primarily in northeastern OH.
Publications: Application guidelines.
Application information: Mass mail solicitations not considered. Application form not required.
Officers and Distribution Committee:* Elizabeth M. McMillan, M.D.,* Pres.; Thomas W. Offutt III,* Secy.; Katharine M. Jeffrey, Ph.D., Elizabeth H. McMillan, S. Sterling McMillan, Ph.D., S. Sterling McMillan III.
EIN: 346505619
Codes: FD

42560
Mary C. & Perry F. Spencer Foundation
c/o National City Bank of Indiana
P.O. Box 94651
Cleveland, OH 44101-4651
Application address: c/o Michele Delaney, National City Bank of Indiana; P.O. Box 110, Fort Wayne, IN 46801, tel.: (219) 461-6199

Established in 1981.
Donor(s): Mary Spencer.‡
Financial data (yr. ended 12/31/01): Grants paid, $284,339; assets, $4,700,049 (M); expenditures, $304,646; qualifying distributions, $293,432.
Limitations: Giving primarily in Fort Wayne, IN.
Directors: D.J. Brandenberger, Homer Harper, Connie Sowers.
Trustee: National City Bank of Indiana.
EIN: 311016213
Codes: FD

42561
Haskell Fund
c/o Advisory Svcs., Inc.
1422 Euclid Ave., 1010 Hanna Bldg.
Cleveland, OH 44115-2078 (216) 363-6481
Contact: James Sekerak, Treas.

Incorporated in 1955 in OH.
Donor(s): Melville H. Haskell,‡ Coburn Haskell, Melville H. Haskell, Jr., Mark Haskell.
Financial data (yr. ended 12/31/01): Grants paid, $282,500; assets, $4,888,675 (M); expenditures, $322,118; qualifying distributions, $290,344.
Limitations: Giving on a national basis for education; giving primarily in Cleveland, OH for community services.
Application information: Application form not required.
Officers and Trustees:* Coburn Haskell,* Pres.; Schuyler A. Haskell,* V.P.; Paulette Kitko, Secy.; James C. Sekerak, Treas.; Sarah Haskell Greene, Eric T. Haskell, Mark Haskell, Mary E. Haskell, Melville H. Haskell, Jr., Mary H. Walker.
EIN: 346513797
Codes: FD

42562
The Ruby Hughes Memorial Fund
c/o KeyBank, N.A.
800 Superior Ave., OH-01-02-0420
Cleveland, OH 44114

Established in 1999 in OH.
Financial data (yr. ended 12/31/00): Grants paid, $281,822; assets, $4,214,807 (M); expenditures, $337,260; qualifying distributions, $296,547.
Limitations: Applications not accepted. Giving primarily in MN, New York, NY, and Cleveland, OH.
Application information: Contributes only to pre-selected organizations.
Trustee: KeyBank, N.A.
EIN: 526956586
Codes: FD

42563
Eleanora C. U. Alms Trust
(Formerly Eleanora Alms Trust)
c/o Fifth Third Bank
38 Fountain Sq. Plz., M.D. 109OL7
Cincinnati, OH 45263 (513) 534-7001
Contact: Lawra J. Baumann, Fdn. Off., Fifth Third Bank

Trust established in 1939 in OH.
Donor(s): Eleanora C.U. Alms.‡
Financial data (yr. ended 09/30/01): Grants paid, $280,000; assets, $5,381,270 (M); expenditures, $338,742; qualifying distributions, $297,550.
Limitations: Giving limited to Cincinnati, OH.
Publications: Annual report, application guidelines.
Application information: Application form not required.
Trustee: Fifth Third Bank.
EIN: 316019723
Codes: FD

42564
Robert E. Browning Fund
c/o U.S. Bank
P.O. Box 1118
Cincinnati, OH 45201-1118

Financial data (yr. ended 12/31/01): Grants paid, $280,000; assets, $2,023,658 (M); expenditures, $289,727; qualifying distributions, $279,586.
Limitations: Applications not accepted. Giving limited to Wellesley, MA, Exeter, NH, and Columbus, OH.
Application information: Contributes only to pre-selected organizations.
Officers: Louis N. Browning, Pres.; Robert E. Browning, V.P.; L.L. Browning, Jr., Secy.; Virginia J. Browning, Treas.
Agent: U.S. Bank.
EIN: 311238149
Codes: FD

42565
McGinty Family Foundation
(Formerly Alice and Patrick McGinty Foundation, Inc.)
2 Commerce Park Sq., Ste. 325
23220 Chagrin Blvd.
Beachwood, OH 44122-5403 (216) 831-5000
FAX: (216) 464-9531; E-mail: thosmcg@aol.com
Contact: T.P. McGinty, Exec. Dir.

Established in 1989 in OH.
Donor(s): Thomas E. McGinty, June T. McGinty.
Financial data (yr. ended 10/31/01): Grants paid, $279,896; assets, $4,177,771 (M); expenditures, $624,210; qualifying distributions, $279,896.
Limitations: Giving limited to Cuyahoga and surrounding counties in northeastern OH.
Publications: Annual report (including application guidelines), newsletter, occasional report, informational brochure (including application guidelines), application guidelines.
Application information: Endorsement from supervisor or school superintendent required. Application form required.
Officer and Trustees:* Thomas P. McGinty,* Exec. Dir.; June T. McGinty, Matthew J. McGinty, Michael J. McGinty, Thomas E. McGinty.
EIN: 341643124
Codes: FD, GTI

42566
Carl Jacobs Foundation
c/o Fifth Third Bank, Trust Dept.
38 Fountain Sq. Plz., MD 1COM31
Cincinnati, OH 45263
Contact: Robert Erickson, V.P., Fifth Third Bank

Established in 1997 in DE.
Donor(s): Carl Jacobs.
Financial data (yr. ended 12/31/01): Grants paid, $279,715; assets, $5,879,331 (M); expenditures, $373,418; qualifying distributions, $288,724.
Limitations: Giving primarily in New York, NY.
Trustee: Fifth Third Bank.
EIN: 133933000
Codes: FD

42567
August A. Rendigs, Jr. Foundation
c/o Fifth Third Bank
38 Fountain Sq. Plz., Dept. 1090C4
Cincinnati, OH 45263
Application address: c/o Rendigs, Fry, Kiley & Dennis, 4th & Vine Sts., Cincinnati, OH 45202, tel.: (513) 381-9206
Contact: W. Roger Fry

Established in 1989 in OH.
Financial data (yr. ended 12/31/01): Grants paid, $278,600; assets, $4,814,393 (M); expenditures, $368,485; qualifying distributions, $286,942.
Limitations: Giving primarily in Cincinnati, OH.
Application information: Application form required.
Agent: Fifth Third Bank.
EIN: 311093339
Codes: FD

42568
J. G. Bell Foundation
18519 Detroit Ave.
Lakewood, OH 44107 (216) 221-0800

Established in 1969 in OH.
Donor(s): Jess A. Bell, Bonne Bell, Inc.
Financial data (yr. ended 06/30/01): Grants paid, $276,869; assets, $859,002 (M); gifts received, $621,360; expenditures, $278,986; qualifying distributions, $277,009.
Limitations: Giving primarily in OH.
Officer: Jess A. Bell, Chair.
EIN: 341018779
Codes: FD

42569
James R. Duncan Trust
c/o Fifth Third Bank
P.O. Box 630858
Cincinnati, OH 45263
Contact: Julie Smith, Admin. Asst., Fifth Third Bank

Established in 1973 in IN.
Donor(s): James Duncan,‡ Adelaide Duncan.‡
Financial data (yr. ended 12/31/01): Grants paid, $275,265; assets, $5,996,173 (M); expenditures, $328,633; qualifying distributions, $279,794.
Limitations: Applications not accepted. Giving primarily in Evansville, IN.
Application information: Contributes only to pre-selected organizations.
Trustee: Fifth Third Bank.
EIN: 356028034
Codes: FD

42570
Blade Foundation
541 N. Superior St.
Toledo, OH 43660 (419) 245-6210
Contact: William Block, Jr., Pres.

Established in 1969 in OH.
Donor(s): Blade Communications, Inc.
Financial data (yr. ended 12/31/00): Grants paid, $273,129; assets, $243,497 (M); gifts received, $275,000; expenditures, $273,487; qualifying distributions, $273,483.
Limitations: Giving primarily in OH.
Officers: William Block, Jr., Pres.; Allan Block, V.P.; John Block, V.P.; William Block, Sr., V.P.; Lanetta Goings, V.P.; Sandy J. Chavez, Secy.; Gary J. Blair, Treas.
EIN: 346559843
Codes: CS, FD, CD

42571
The Community Foundation of Sidney and Shelby County
(Formerly Sidney Community Foundation)
P.O. Box 4186
Sidney, OH 45365-4186 (937) 497-7800
FAX: (937) 497-7799; E-mail: commfoun@bright.net; URL: http://www.commfoun.com
Contact: Marian Spicer, Exec. Dir.

Incorporated in 1952 in OH.
Financial data (yr. ended 12/31/00): Grants paid, $270,450; assets, $4,425,570 (M); gifts received, $864,781; expenditures, $356,251.
Limitations: Giving limited to Shelby County, OH, and surrounding areas.
Publications: Informational brochure, newsletter.
Application information: Application form required.
Officers and Trustees:* Patrick Milligan,* Pres.; Sandra Shoemaker,* V.P.; Raymond Koenig,* Secy.; Edward Borchers, Treas.; Marian Spicer, Exec. Dir.; Bruce Boyd, John Dunlap, Judy Westerheide.
EIN: 346565194
Codes: CM, FD, GTI

42572
The Sutphin Family Foundation
c/o PNC Bank
P.O. Box 1198
Cincinnati, OH 45201-1198 (513) 651-8377
Contact: Lee Crooks, Fdn. Admin.

Established in 1994 in OH.
Donor(s): Jean Webber Sutphin, Richard H. Sutphin, Mary W. Parker.
Financial data (yr. ended 12/31/01): Grants paid, $270,300; assets, $6,065,651 (M); expenditures, $280,442; qualifying distributions, $266,470.
Limitations: Giving primarily in Cincinnati, OH.
Publications: Application guidelines.
Application information: Application form required.
Officers and Trustees:* Jean W. Sutphin,* Pres.; Christine S. Kohnen,* V.P.; Stuart B. Sutphin III,* V.P.; Richard H. Sutphin,* Secy.-Treas.
EIN: 311423164
Codes: FD

42573
Jessee Eyman Trust
132 1/2 E. Court St.
Washington Court House, OH 43160
(740) 335-2480
Contact: Robert S. Sanderson, Jr., Tr.

Trust established in 1924 in OH.
Donor(s): Jesse Eyman.‡
Financial data (yr. ended 12/31/01): Grants paid, $269,134; assets, $6,063,110 (M); expenditures, $314,386; qualifying distributions, $280,428.
Limitations: Giving limited to Fayette County, OH.
Application information: Funds are disbursed only to support organizations.
Trustees: Jessee Persinger, R.S. Sanderson, Jr.
EIN: 316040007
Codes: FD

42574
Weil Foundation
4224 Conklin Ct.
New Albany, OH 43054
Contact: Kenneth M. Weil, Secy.-Treas.

Established in 1998 in OH.
Donor(s): Kenneth M. Weil, Audrey York Weil.
Financial data (yr. ended 06/30/01): Grants paid, $269,100; assets, $4,279,516 (M); gifts received, $1,321,082; expenditures, $279,846; qualifying distributions, $263,225.
Limitations: Giving primarily in OH.
Officers: Audrey York Weil, Pres.; Kenneth M. Weil, Secy.-Treas.
EIN: 311627660
Codes: FD

42575
Walter E. and Caroline H. Watson Foundation
c/o National City Bank
P.O. Box 94651
Cleveland, OH 44101
Contact: Myra L. Vitto

Trust established in 1964 in OH.
Donor(s): Walter E. Watson.‡
Financial data (yr. ended 12/31/01): Grants paid, $268,813; assets, $8,195,521 (M); expenditures, $317,756; qualifying distributions, $293,992.
Limitations: Giving primarily in OH, including the Youngstown and Mahoning Valley areas.
Application information: Application form not required.
Trustee: National City Bank.
EIN: 346547726
Codes: FD

42576
The E. F. Wildermuth Foundation
1014 Dublin Rd.
Columbus, OH 43215-1116 (614) 487-0040
Contact: Robert W. Lee, Treas.

Established in 1962.

42576—OHIO

Financial data (yr. ended 12/31/01): Grants paid, $268,500; assets, $6,015,231 (M); expenditures, $344,972; qualifying distributions, $274,957.
Limitations: Giving primarily in OH and contiguous states.
Application information: Application form not required.
Officers: J. Patrick Campbell, Chair. and Pres.; Bettie A. Kalb, Pres.; David T. Patterson, V.P. and Secy.; Karl Borton, V.P.; Genevieve Connable, V.P.; Robert W. Lee, Treas.
Trustees: Thomas Borton, Phillip N. Phillipson, Harriet Slaughter.
EIN: 316050202
Codes: FD

42577
F. T. and Anna C. Manley Memorial Fund
c/o KeyBank, N.A.
800 Superior Ave.
Cleveland, OH 44114

Established in 1987 in NY.
Financial data (yr. ended 12/31/01): Grants paid, $268,000; assets, $3,558,331 (M); expenditures, $298,285; qualifying distributions, $268,250.
Limitations: Applications not accepted. Giving limited to organizations in Allegheny and Cattaraugus counties, NY.
Application information: Contributes only to pre-selected organizations.
Trustee: KeyBank, N.A.
EIN: 136905221
Codes: FD

42578
The F. & J. Kloenne Foundation
c/o Fifth Third Bank
600 Vine St., Ste. 402
Cincinnati, OH 45263 (513) 579-5498
Contact: Paula Wharton

Established in 1999 in OH.
Financial data (yr. ended 12/31/00): Grants paid, $267,000; assets, $4,774,976 (M); expenditures, $302,056; qualifying distributions, $276,153.
Limitations: Giving primarily in OH.
Trustees: Narley L. Haley, Fifth Third Bank.
EIN: 311629236
Codes: FD

42579
Patsie and Jenee Campana Foundation Charitable Trust
2115 W. Park Dr.
Lorain, OH 44053

Established in 1995 in OH.
Donor(s): Dolores J. Campana.
Financial data (yr. ended 12/31/01): Grants paid, $264,537; assets, $402,688 (M); gifts received, $266,500; expenditures, $265,373; qualifying distributions, $265,196.
Limitations: Applications not accepted. Giving primarily in OH.
Application information: Contributes only to pre-selected organizations.
Trustees: Dolores J. Campana, Patricia A. Campana.
EIN: 341810114
Codes: FD

42580
Henry H. Geary, Jr. Memorial Foundation
c/o KeyBank, N.A.
800 Superior, Trust Tax
Cleveland, OH 44114

Established in 1995 in OH.
Donor(s): H.H. Geary, Jr. Irrevocable Trust.
Financial data (yr. ended 12/31/01): Grants paid, $262,766; assets, $7,014,475 (M); expenditures, $337,180; qualifying distributions, $258,384.
Limitations: Applications not accepted. Giving primarily in Fostoria, OH.
Application information: Contributes only to pre-selected organizations.
Trustee: KeyBank, N.A.
EIN: 341594662
Codes: FD

42581
Sandra L. and Dennis B. Haslinger Family Foundation, Inc.
2524 Ira Rd.
Akron, OH 44333
Application address: c/o Seikel & Co., Inc., 686 W. Market St., OH 44303, tel.: (330) 761-1040
Contact: Sandra L. Haslinger, Pres.

Established in 1997 in OH.
Donor(s): Sandra L. Haslinger.
Financial data (yr. ended 12/31/01): Grants paid, $262,000; assets, $6,267,576 (M); gifts received, $300,000; expenditures, $506,629; qualifying distributions, $260,483.
Limitations: Giving primarily in OH.
Officers and Trustees:* Sandra L. Haslinger,* Pres.; Douglas S. Haslinger,* Secy.; Jennifer S. Lenox,* Treas.; Benjamin G. Haslinger, Kimberly M. Haslinger, Melissa A. Haslinger, Myriam Eve Haslinger.
EIN: 341848698
Codes: FD

42582
The Miller Family Foundation
30575 Bainbridge Rd., Ste. 130
Solon, OH 44139

Established in 1999 in OH.
Donor(s): Sydell L. Miller Charitable Lead Annuity Trust.
Financial data (yr. ended 12/31/01): Grants paid, $260,500; assets, $817,612 (M); gifts received, $500,000; expenditures, $262,700; qualifying distributions, $260,500.
Limitations: Applications not accepted. Giving primarily in Cleveland, OH.
Application information: Contributes only to pre-selected organizations.
Trustees: Stacie L. Halpern, Dennis E. Lubin, Lauren B. Spilman.
EIN: 341855841
Codes: FD

42583
R. C. and Katharine M. Musson Charitable Foundation
Box 7038
Akron, OH 44306-0038 (330) 773-7651
Contact: Ben D. Segers, Tr.

Established in 1984 in OH as R. C. and Katharine M. Musson Charitable Trust; successor foundation established in 1988.
Donor(s): R.C. Musson.‡
Financial data (yr. ended 06/30/01): Grants paid, $259,813; assets, $4,672,273 (M); expenditures, $302,964; qualifying distributions, $270,327.
Limitations: Giving primarily in Summit County, OH.
Application information: Application form not required.
Trustees: Irvin J. Musson, Jr., Irvin J. Musson III, Ben Segers, Robert S. Segers.
EIN: 341549070
Codes: FD

42584
The Carol and Charles A. Rini, Sr. Family Foundation
19050 Lorain Rd.
Fairview Park, OH 44126-1915

Established in 1996 in OH.
Donor(s): Charles A. Rini, Sr.
Financial data (yr. ended 12/31/01): Grants paid, $259,550; assets, $1,269,803 (M); gifts received, $123,445; expenditures, $268,403; qualifying distributions, $258,768.
Limitations: Applications not accepted.
Application information: Contributes only to pre-selected organizations.
Trustees: Nicole A. Rini Bebie, Carol Ann Rini, Charles A. Rini, Sr., Charles A. Rini, Jr., Theresa A. Rini Sims, Christine A. Rini Slyman.
EIN: 341847507
Codes: FD

42585
Kenny King Foundation, Inc.
c/o Paragon Advisors, Inc.
20600 Chagrin Blvd. Tower E., Ste. 600
Shaker Heights, OH 44122
Contact: Kenneth J. King, Jr., Pres.

Established in 1986 in OH.
Donor(s): The Kenny King Corp., Kenneth J. King, Jr., Mary Anne King.
Financial data (yr. ended 12/31/01): Grants paid, $257,820; assets, $768,952 (M); expenditures, $267,152; qualifying distributions, $257,820.
Limitations: Giving primarily in Cleveland, OH.
Officers and Trustees:* Kenneth J. King, Jr.,* Pres. and Treas.; Mary Anne King,* Secy.; Jennifer Crichter, Steven Gariepy, Craig T. King, Michael S. King, Terence C. Sullivan.
EIN: 341479088
Codes: FD

42586
The Kangesser Foundation
(Formerly The Robert E., Harry A., and M. Sylvia Kangesser Foundation)
10 Daisy Ln.
Pepper Pike, OH 44124
Contact: Helen Kangesser, Pres.

Incorporated in 1947 in OH.
Donor(s): Robert E. Kangesser,‡ Harry A. Kangesser,‡ M. Sylvia Kangesser.‡
Financial data (yr. ended 12/31/01): Grants paid, $257,300; assets, $4,416,342 (M); expenditures, $341,287; qualifying distributions, $265,673.
Limitations: Applications not accepted. Giving primarily in the greater Cleveland, OH, area.
Application information: Contributes only to pre-selected organizations.
Officers and Trustees:* Helen G. Kangesser,* Pres.; David G. Kangesser,* V.P.; Hedy Kangesser Adler,* Secy.-Treas.
EIN: 346529478
Codes: FD

42587
J. Ford Crandall Memorial Foundation
26 Market St., Rm. 904
Youngstown, OH 44503 (330) 744-2125
Contact: R.J. Christian, Counsel

Trust established in 1975 in OH.
Donor(s): J. Ford Crandall.‡
Financial data (yr. ended 12/31/01): Grants paid, $257,199; assets, $5,686,376 (M); expenditures, $260,232; qualifying distributions, $254,767.
Limitations: Giving limited to Mahoning County, OH.
Publications: Annual report.

Application information: Application form not required.
Officers and Trustees:* Amy H. Gambrel,* Chair.; William G. Marshall,* Vice-Chair.; Andrew Bresko,* 2nd Vice-Chair.; Robert J. Christian, Counsel.
EIN: 346513634
Codes: FD

42588
Avrum Katz Foundation
c/o Avrum Katz
3681 Green Rd., Ste. 302
Beachwood, OH 44122-5716

Donor(s): Avrum S. Katz.
Financial data (yr. ended 12/31/01): Grants paid, $256,964; assets, $4,106,504 (M); expenditures, $275,386; qualifying distributions, $256,166.
Limitations: Applications not accepted. Giving primarily in, but not limited to, OH.
Application information: Contributes only to pre-selected organizations.
Officer: Avrum S. Katz, Pres.
EIN: 341471066
Codes: FD

42589
Leonora H. Knowles Trust B
c/o KeyBank, N.A., Trust Div.
800 Superior Ave., 4th Fl.
Cleveland, OH 44114-2601

Established in 1987 in ME.
Financial data (yr. ended 12/31/01): Grants paid, $256,888; assets, $6,384,418 (M); expenditures, $338,187; qualifying distributions, $253,891.
Limitations: Applications not accepted. Giving primarily in MA and ME.
Application information: Contributes only to pre-selected organizations.
Trustee: KeyBank, N.A.
EIN: 222789214
Codes: FD, GTI

42590
The Soo Foundation, Inc.
10810 Reservoir Rd.
Ada, OH 45810
Application address: c/o Liang Yee Soo, 1 Friday Ln., Chapel Hill, NC 27514; FAX: (419) 649-7544
Contact: Susan Hunsaker, Secy.-Treas.

Established in 1985 in OH.
Donor(s): Liang Yee Soo, M.D., Dixie L.B. Soo, M.D.
Financial data (yr. ended 12/31/00): Grants paid, $256,040; assets, $3,613,372 (M); gifts received, $498,802; expenditures, $321,592; qualifying distributions, $274,943.
Limitations: Giving primarily in NC.
Officers: Liang Yee Soo, M.D., Pres.; Dixie L.B. Soo, M.D., V.P.; Susan Hunsaker, Secy.-Treas.
Directors: Catherine E. Nerantzis, Jeffrey D. Soo, Kenneth Alexander Soo, Michael L. Soo.
EIN: 341481699
Codes: FD

42591
Baker & Hostetler Founders' Trust
c/o John D. Drinko
3200 National City Ctr., 1900 E. 9th St.
Cleveland, OH 44114-3485

Established in 1965.
Donor(s): Baker & Hostetler, John D. Drinko, Hazel P. Hostetler.‡
Financial data (yr. ended 12/31/01): Grants paid, $255,000; assets, $919,271 (M); gifts received, $67,700; expenditures, $260,525; qualifying distributions, $256,063.
Limitations: Applications not accepted. Giving primarily in OH.
Application information: Contributes only to pre-selected organizations.
Officer: John D. Drinko, Exec. Dir.
Trustees: Gary L. Bryenton, John H. Burlingame, George W. Hairston.
EIN: 346570132
Codes: CS, FD, CD

42592
Loeb Foundation
c/o Lebanon Citizens National Bank
P.O. Box 59
Lebanon, OH 45036-0059 (513) 932-1414
FAX: (513) 932-1492; *E-mail:* bwright@lcnb.com
Contact: B.H. Wright, Jr., Tr.

Established in 1992 in OH.
Donor(s): Justus H. Loeb.‡
Financial data (yr. ended 09/30/01): Grants paid, $253,810; assets, $7,661,502 (M); expenditures, $359,113; qualifying distributions, $288,847.
Limitations: Giving limited to Warren County, OH.
Application information: Application form not required.
Trustees: Michael E. Foley, Bernard H. Wright, Jr., The Lebanon Citizens National Bank.
EIN: 316225986
Codes: FD, GTI

42593
Louis S. and Mary Myers Foundation
1293 S. Main St.
Akron, OH 44301 (330) 253-5592
Contact: Stephen E. Myers, Tr.

Established in 1956 in OH.
Donor(s): Louis S. Myers, Myers Industries, Inc., Mary S. Myers.
Financial data (yr. ended 12/31/00): Grants paid, $251,624; assets, $3,676,904 (M); expenditures, $255,099; qualifying distributions, $251,624.
Limitations: Applications not accepted. Giving primarily in OH; some giving in New York, NY.
Application information: Unsolicited requests for funds not accepted.
Trustees: Kathryn Myers, Mary S. Myers, Stephen E. Myers.
EIN: 346555862
Codes: FD

42594
Boles Family Foundation
2750 Crafton Park
Columbus, OH 43221-3629
Contact: E. Thomas Boles, Jr., Pres. and Treas.

Established in 1991 in OH.
Donor(s): E. Thomas Boles, Jr.
Financial data (yr. ended 12/31/01): Grants paid, $250,000; assets, $4,317,265 (M); expenditures, $336,809; qualifying distributions, $255,618.
Limitations: Applications not accepted. Giving primarily in OH.
Application information: Contributes only to pre-selected organizations.
Officers: E. Thomas Boles, Jr., Pres. and Treas.; Mark D. Senff, Secy.
Trustees: Charles Blake, Janice A. Boles, Robert S. Boles, Stephen T. Boles, Katherine B. Smith.
EIN: 311334948
Codes: FD

42595
Hope for Cleveland's Children
c/o Brennan Industrial Group
159 S. Main St., No. 725
Akron, OH 44308

Established in 1995 in OH.
Donor(s): David L. Brennan, Mrs. David L. Brennan.
Financial data (yr. ended 06/30/01): Grants paid, $250,000; assets, $1 (M); gifts received, $250,000; expenditures, $273,890; qualifying distributions, $250,000.
Limitations: Applications not accepted.
Application information: Contributes only to pre-selected organizations.
Officers: John D. Helline, Pres.; Joseph R. Weber, Secy.; Nancy Kepley, Treas.
EIN: 341805456

42596
Alice & Leslie Lancy Foundation
c/o National City Bank of Pennsylvania
P.O. Box 94651
Cleveland, OH 44101-4651
Contact: Craig Kelsey

Donor(s): Leslie E. Lancy.‡
Financial data (yr. ended 12/31/01): Grants paid, $250,000; assets, $3,561,982 (M); expenditures, $278,709; qualifying distributions, $263,580.
Limitations: Giving primarily in CA.
Trustee: National City Bank of Pennsylvania.
EIN: 251371367
Codes: FD

42597
The Llewellyn Foundation
c/o Hugh Barnett
1 S. Limestone St., Ste. 800
Springfield, OH 45501

Established in 1997.
Financial data (yr. ended 02/28/02): Grants paid, $250,000; assets, $3,159,313 (M); expenditures, $257,563; qualifying distributions, $249,181.
Limitations: Applications not accepted. Giving primarily in MT and OH.
Application information: Contributes only to pre-selected organizations.
Officers and Trustees:* Sarah H. Lupfer,* Pres.; Caroline Lupfer Kurtz,* Secy. and Mng. Dir.; Jonathan B. Lupfer,* Treas.
EIN: 311534056
Codes: FD

42598
The Harold W. & Mary Louise Shaw Foundation
113 Katharine Terr.
Dayton, OH 45419

Established in 1997 in OH.
Donor(s): Harold Shaw, Louise Shaw.
Financial data (yr. ended 11/30/01): Grants paid, $250,000; assets, $4,702,070 (M); gifts received, $5,000,000; expenditures, $268,284; qualifying distributions, $250,000.
Limitations: Applications not accepted.
Application information: Contributes only pre-selected organizations.
Officers: Harold W. Shaw, Pres.; Mary Louise Shaw, V.P.; Sally Louise Veitch, Secy.
EIN: 311577890
Codes: FD

42599
The Scott & Fetzer Foundation
c/o The Scott Fetzer Co.
28800 Clemens Rd.
Westlake, OH 44145 (440) 892-3000
Contact: Edie DeSantis

Established in 1967 in OH.
Donor(s): The Scott Fetzer Co.
Financial data (yr. ended 12/31/00): Grants paid, $249,764; assets, $385,573 (M); gifts received, $333,067; expenditures, $250,167; qualifying distributions, $249,764.
Limitations: Giving primarily in OH, with emphasis on Cleveland.
Publications: Program policy statement.
Application information: Application form not required.
Officers: Kenneth J. Semelsberger, Pres.; William W.T. Stephans, V.P. and Treas.; Patricia M. Scanlon, Secy.
EIN: 346596076
Codes: CS, FD, CD

42600
P. K. Ranney Foundation
111 Superior Ave., Ste. 1000
Cleveland, OH 44114-2507 (216) 696-4200
Application address: 13881 Lake Ave., Lakewood, OH 44107-1424; FAX: (216) 696-7303; E-mail: pranney@ssrl.com
Contact: Phillip A. Ranney, Secy.

Incorporated in 1973 in OH.
Financial data (yr. ended 12/31/01): Grants paid, $249,000; assets, $6,705,847 (M); expenditures, $284,651; qualifying distributions, $261,492.
Limitations: Giving primarily in the greater Cleveland, OH, area.
Application information: Application form not required.
Officers: Peter K. Ranney, Pres. and Treas.; Robert K. Bissell, V.P.; Phillip A. Ranney, Secy.
EIN: 237343201
Codes: FD

42601
H. Fort Flowers Foundation, Inc.
219 S. Main St.
Findlay, OH 45840
Contact: R. W. Flowers, V.P.

Incorporated in 1951 in DE.
Donor(s): Flowers Trust.
Financial data (yr. ended 12/31/01): Grants paid, $247,800; assets, $649,393 (M); gifts received, $231,445; expenditures, $254,014; qualifying distributions, $249,838.
Application information: Application form not required.
Officers and Trustees:* D.F. Flowers,* Pres.; R.W. Flowers,* V.P. and Secy.; D.F. Flowers, Jr.,* V.P. and Treas.; S.M. Beall,* V.P.; S.F. Paschall Dodd, J.W. Donaldson, J.R. Murray, Jr., and 4 additional trustees.
EIN: 346513672
Codes: FD

42602
Robert Gould Foundation, Inc.
P.O. Box 44338
Cincinnati, OH 45244-0338 (513) 231-0872
Application address: c/o Susan Beckman, 5071 Signal Hill Ln., Cincinnati, OH 45244

Established about 1973.
Donor(s): Robert Gould.‡
Financial data (yr. ended 12/31/01): Grants paid, $247,190; assets, $8,746,758 (M); expenditures, $463,516; qualifying distributions, $247,190.
Limitations: Giving primarily in Aspen, CO, and Cincinnati, OH.
Trustees: Susan Beckman, Thomas Beckman.
EIN: 316064275

42603
HCR Manor Care Foundation
(Formerly Manor Care Foundation, Inc.)
333 N. Summit St.
P.O. Box 10086
Toledo, OH 43699-0086 (419) 252-5989
FAX: (419) 252-5521; E-mail: jsteiner@hcr-manorcare.com; URL: http://www.hcr-manorcare.org
Contact: Jennifer Steiner, Exec. Dir.; or Amy Kautz, Asst.

Established in 1997 in MD.
Donor(s): Manor Care, Inc., HCR Manor Care, Inc.
Financial data (yr. ended 05/31/01): Grants paid, $247,189; assets, $3,676,606 (M); expenditures, $404,440; qualifying distributions, $396,321.
Limitations: Giving restricted to the states in which Manor Care operates (currently in 32 states).
Publications: Annual report (including application guidelines), grants list, application guidelines.
Application information: Visit the foundation's website. Application form required.
Officers and Directors:* Susan Harless,* Chair. and Pres.; Rick Rump,* Secy.; John Huber,* Treas.; Karen Bell, Kathy Hutchinson, Larry Lester, Meredith Pasco.
EIN: 522031975
Codes: CS, FD, CD

42604
Alfred C. Mahan Charitable Trust
c/o KeyBank, N.A.
800 Superior Ave., 4th Fl.
Cleveland, OH 44114

Established in 1996 in OH.
Financial data (yr. ended 12/31/01): Grants paid, $247,000; assets, $4,366,274 (M); expenditures, $290,924; qualifying distributions, $282,506.
Limitations: Applications not accepted. Giving primarily in OH.
Application information: Contributes only to pre-selected organizations.
Trustee: KeyBank, N.A.
EIN: 347034403
Codes: FD

42605
Louise Kling Trust
1392 Collinswood Ln.
Marion, OH 43302-0499
Contact: Vickie Davidson, Tr.

Established in 1986 in OH.
Financial data (yr. ended 12/31/00): Grants paid, $245,871; assets, $3,524,432 (M); expenditures, $277,258; qualifying distributions, $243,809.
Limitations: Giving limited to Marion County, OH.
Application information: Generally contributes only to pre-selected organizations. Scholarship applicants must be graduating from Harding High School and pursuing studies in music or medicine and should submit a written application.
Trustee: Vickie Davidson.
EIN: 346841720
Codes: FD2, GTI

42606
Kate Ireland Foundation
1422 Euclid Ave., Ste. 1030
Cleveland, OH 44115-2004 (216) 363-1034
Contact: Kate Ireland, Pres.

Established in 1994 in OH.
Donor(s): Kate Ireland Charitable Lead Trust No. 1, Ireland Foundation.
Financial data (yr. ended 12/31/01): Grants paid, $245,290; assets, $1,677,987 (M); gifts received, $1,696,964; expenditures, $245,291; qualifying distributions, $245,290.
Officers and Trustees:* Kate Ireland,* Pres.; Carole M. Nowak, Secy.; Neil A. Brown, Treas.; DuBose Ausley, Thomas Barron, Richard T. Watson.
EIN: 341786209
Codes: FD2

42607
The Crowell Educational Foundation
c/o Douglas Neary
800 Superior Ave.
Cleveland, OH 44114-2688

Established in 1997.
Donor(s): Robert J. Crowell.
Financial data (yr. ended 12/31/00): Grants paid, $245,000; assets, $167,744 (M); gifts received, $2,078; expenditures, $247,203; qualifying distributions, $247,167.
Limitations: Applications not accepted. Giving primarily in MA.
Application information: Contributes only to pre-selected organizations.
Officers: Robert J. Crowell, Pres. and Treas.; Lynn Eilertson Crowell, V.P. and Secy.
Trustee: Douglas A. Neary.
EIN: 311528634
Codes: FD2

42608
Renner Foundation
505 N. Wooster Ave.
P.O. Box 8
Dover, OH 44622-0008

Incorporated in 1947 in OH as Renner Clinic Foundation.
Donor(s): R. Richard Renner, M.D.‡
Financial data (yr. ended 05/31/01): Grants paid, $245,000; assets, $4,894,042 (M); expenditures, $339,788; qualifying distributions, $256,767.
Limitations: Applications not accepted. Giving primarily in CA and MS.
Application information: Contributes only to pre-selected organizations.
Officer: Richard R. Renner, Treas.
Trustees: Brett Percy, David Percy, Jennifer Percy, Kevin Percy, Ruth A. Percy, Daniel S. Renner, Debra Renner, John W. Renner, Karen Renner, Mary Renner, Robert Renner, Steven Renner, Tamara Renner, Tara Renner, Carlton B. Schnell, Jane Renner See, Ann Stillwater.
EIN: 340684303
Codes: FD2

42609
Elizabeth Firestone-Graham Foundation
c/o Bank One Trust Co., N.A.
P.O. Box 1308
Westerville, OH 43081

Established in 1983 in Ohio.
Financial data (yr. ended 11/30/01): Grants paid, $244,500; assets, $5,130,574 (M); expenditures, $313,035; qualifying distributions, $286,539.
Limitations: Applications not accepted. Giving on a national basis.
Application information: Contributes only to pre-selected organizations.
Trustees: Barbara F. Graham, Ray A. Graham III.
Agent: Bank One Ohio Trust Co., N.A.
EIN: 341388252
Codes: FD2

42610
The Iott Family Foundation
3402 Chapel Dr.
Toledo, OH 43615

Established in 1991 in OH.
Donor(s): W.D. Iott.
Financial data (yr. ended 08/31/01): Grants paid, $243,850; assets, $4,892,863 (M); expenditures, $260,686; qualifying distributions, $243,850.
Limitations: Applications not accepted. Giving primarily in Toledo, OH.
Application information: Contributes only to pre-selected organizations.
Trustees: Constance Heider, Jeanette M. Iott, Richard B. Iott, W.D. Iott.
EIN: 341695607
Codes: FD2

42611
The Williams Family Foundation
925 Euclid Ave., Ste. 2000
Cleveland, OH 44115-1496 (216) 696-4700
Contact: Clyde E. Williams, Jr., Tr.

Established in 1997 in OH.
Donor(s): Ruth V. Williams, The William Investment Co.
Financial data (yr. ended 12/31/01): Grants paid, $242,458; assets, $2,758,211 (M); expenditures, $306,593; qualifying distributions, $241,370.
Limitations: Giving primarily in OH.
Trustees: Clyde E. Williams, Jr., Sam B. Williams, Thomas J. Williams.
EIN: 311532483
Codes: FD2

42612
Second Bancorp Foundation
c/o The Second National Bank of Warren
108 Main Ave. S.W.
Warren, OH 44481

Established in 1997 in OH.
Donor(s): Second Bancorp, Inc.
Financial data (yr. ended 12/31/00): Grants paid, $241,305; assets, $601,504 (M); expenditures, $242,855; qualifying distributions, $240,849.
Limitations: Applications not accepted. Giving primarily in OH.
Application information: Contributes only to pre-selected organizations.
Officers and Trustees:* Diane C. Bastic,* Pres.; Darryl E. Mast,* V.P.; Jennice Zymaris, Secy.; Thomas Allen, Rick Blossom, Karen A. Herrman.
EIN: 311519129
Codes: CS, FD2, CD

42613
Commercial Intertech Foundation
(Formerly Commercial Shearing Foundation)
P.O. Box 239
Youngstown, OH 44501 (330) 746-8011
Contact: Shirley M. Shields, Secy.

Trust established in 1953 in OH.
Donor(s): Commercial Intertech Corp., Parker-Hannifin Corp.
Financial data (yr. ended 10/31/01): Grants paid, $240,985; assets, $595,288 (M); gifts received, $240,000; expenditures, $243,739; qualifying distributions, $240,731.
Limitations: Giving limited to areas of company operations.
Application information: Application form not required.
Officers and Trustees:* Paul J. Powers,* Pres.; Bruce C. Wheatley, V.P.; Shirley M. Shields,* Secy.; Kenneth W. Marcum, Treas.; William J. Bresnahan, Charles B. Cushwa III, William W. Cushwa, John M. Galvin, Richard J. Hill, Neil D. Humphrey, William E. Kassling, Gilbert M. Manchester, Gerald C. McDonough, C. Edward Midgely, George M. Smart, Don E. Tucker.
EIN: 346517437
Codes: CS, FD2

42614
The Provident Foundation
c/o Provident Bank, Trust
P.O. Box 2176
Cincinnati, OH 45201 (513) 639-5480
Contact: Chris White

Established in 1980 in OH.
Financial data (yr. ended 12/31/01): Grants paid, $240,550; assets, $33,350 (M); gifts received, $210,000; expenditures, $242,097; qualifying distributions, $241,660.
Limitations: Giving primarily in the Sarasota, FL, area and in the greater Cincinnati, Cleveland, and Dayton OH, areas.
Application information: Application form not required.
Trustees: John Farrenkopf, Phillip Myers.
EIN: 310999986
Codes: FD2

42615
The Hankins Foundation
c/o R.A. Bumblis, C.P.A.
1900 E. 9th St., Ste.3200
Cleveland, OH 44114-3485 (216) 861-7623
Contact: Richard R. Hollington Jr.

Trust established in 1952 in OH.
Donor(s): Edward R. Hankins,‡ Ann H. Long,‡ Jane H. Lockwood,‡ Ruth Leale Hankins.
Financial data (yr. ended 12/31/01): Grants paid, $240,500; assets, $8,026,188 (M); expenditures, $291,336; qualifying distributions, $262,050.
Limitations: Giving primarily in AZ and OH.
Application information: Application form not required.
Trustees: Ruth Leale Hankins, Richard R. Hollington, Jr., Edward G. Lockwood, Gordon Long, Janet L. Tarwater.
EIN: 346565426
Codes: FD2

42616
The Sherman-Standard Register Foundation
626 Albany St.
P.O. Box 1167
Dayton, OH 45408

Incorporated in 1955 in OH.
Donor(s): The Standard Register Co.
Financial data (yr. ended 11/30/01): Grants paid, $239,412; assets, $1,511,144 (M); gifts received, $200,000; expenditures, $244,030; qualifying distributions, $239,412.
Limitations: Applications not accepted. Giving primarily in OH.
Application information: Contributes only to pre-selected organizations.
Officers: John Q. Sherman, Pres.; Craig J. Brown, V.P. and Treas.; Kathryn A. Lamme, Secy.
Trustees: Roy W. Begley, Jr., Dennis L. Rediker, Robert F. Smith.
EIN: 316026027
Codes: CS, FD2, CD

42617
Chemed Foundation
255 E. 5th St., Ste. 2600
Cincinnati, OH 45202
Contact: Sandra E. Laney, Pres.

Established in 1991 in OH.
Donor(s): Chemed Corp.
Financial data (yr. ended 12/31/01): Grants paid, $238,464; assets, $3,500,717 (M); gifts received, $242,785; expenditures, $269,898; qualifying distributions, $260,964.
Limitations: Giving primarily in OH.
Publications: Annual report.
Officers and Directors:* Sandra E. Laney,* Pres.; Kevin J. McNamara,* Secy.; David J. Lohbeck, Treas.; Thomas C. Hutton.
EIN: 311326421
Codes: CS, FD2, CD

42618
Saint Gerard Foundation
c/o William E. Reichard
25109 Detroit Rd., Ste. 300
Westlake, OH 44145

Established in 1966 in OH.
Donor(s): Mooney Chemicals, Inc., and members of the Mooney family.
Financial data (yr. ended 12/31/00): Grants paid, $236,375; assets, $178,743 (M); expenditures, $239,646; qualifying distributions, $237,914.
Limitations: Applications not accepted. Giving on a national basis.
Application information: Contributes only to pre-selected organizations.
Officers and Trustees:* William E. Reichard, Secy.; Elizabeth C. Mooney,* Treas.; Brian G. Mooney.
EIN: 346574667
Codes: FD2

42619
Joseph L. & Sarah S. Marcum Foundation
1275 Stephanie Dr.
Hamilton, OH 45013

Established in 1987 in OH.
Donor(s): Joseph L. Marcum.
Financial data (yr. ended 12/31/01): Grants paid, $234,090; assets, $6,062,388 (M); gifts received, $3,000; expenditures, $245,442; qualifying distributions, $234,090.
Limitations: Applications not accepted. Giving primarily in OH.
Application information: Contributes only to pre-selected organizations.
Officer and Trustees:* Joseph L. Marcum,* Chair.; Catherine M. Lowe, M. Christina Manchester, Sarah S. Marcum, Stephen S. Marcum, Sarah S. Shuffield.
EIN: 311190243
Codes: FD2

42620
The Albert J. Weatherhead III Foundation
c/o Thomas F. Allen
1801 E. 9th St., Ste. 730
Cleveland, OH 44114-3103

Established in 1975 in OH.
Donor(s): Albert J. Weatherhead III.
Financial data (yr. ended 12/31/01): Grants paid, $234,021; assets, $3,244,339 (M); gifts received, $199,138; expenditures, $253,656; qualifying distributions, $241,028.
Limitations: Applications not accepted. Giving primarily in Houston, TX.
Application information: Contributes only to pre-selected organizations.
Officers and Trustees:* Albert J. Weatherhead III,* Pres.; Celia J. Weatherhead,* V.P.; Thomas F. Allen,* Secy.-Treas.; Frank M. Rasmussen, Charles E. Sheedy.
EIN: 510137950
Codes: FD2

42621
The Reid Foundation
Chagrin N. 1
34900 Chardon Rd., Ste. 206
Willoughby Hills, OH 44094-9161

Established in 1989 in OH.
Donor(s): Alan J. Reid, Corinne M. Reid.
Financial data (yr. ended 10/31/01): Grants paid, $233,700; assets, $4,189,805 (M); gifts received, $300; expenditures, $305,063; qualifying distributions, $233,300.
Limitations: Applications not accepted. Giving primarily in Cleveland, OH.
Application information: Contributes only to pre-selected organizations.
Trustees: Alan J. Reid, Corinne M. Reid.
EIN: 346924704
Codes: FD2

42622
Edward A. Lozick Foundation
29425 Chagrin Blvd., Ste. 201
Beachwood, OH 44122-4602
Contact: Edward A. Lozick, Tr.

Established in 1983.
Donor(s): Nerts, Inc., Whitney Research Tool Co.
Financial data (yr. ended 12/31/01): Grants paid, $233,180; assets, $1,410,094 (M); gifts received, $500,000; expenditures, $273,391; qualifying distributions, $233,180.
Limitations: Applications not accepted. Giving primarily in Cleveland, OH.
Application information: Contributes only to pre-selected organizations.
Trustees: John F. Fant, Jr., Catherine L. Lozick, Edward A. Lozick.
EIN: 341386776
Codes: FD2

42623
The Grimes Foundation
166 Tanglewood Dr.
Urbana, OH 43078
Contact: Lewis B. Moore, Tr.

Incorporated about 1951 in OH.
Donor(s): Warren G. Grimes.
Financial data (yr. ended 12/31/01): Grants paid, $232,050; assets, $2,796,868 (M); expenditures, $266,275; qualifying distributions, $246,776.
Limitations: Giving limited to Delray Beach, FL, and Champaign County, OH.
Application information: Application form not required.
Trustees: Clarence J. Brown, Jr., James S. Mihori, Gregory Moore, Lewis B. Moore, Steven Polsley.
EIN: 346528288
Codes: FD2

42624
The Camden Foundation
c/o Fifth Third Bank
38 Fountain Square Plz., Trust Tax Dept.
Cincinnati, OH 45263 (513) 579-5472
Contact: David Garber

Established in 1952 in OH.
Financial data (yr. ended 09/30/01): Grants paid, $232,000; assets, $3,128,927 (M); expenditures, $258,617; qualifying distributions, $239,549.
Limitations: Giving primarily in the Cincinnati, OH, area.
Application information: Application form required.
Trustee: Fifth Third Bank.
EIN: 316024141
Codes: FD2

42625
The Wagnalls Memorial
P.O. Box 217
Lithopolis, OH 43136 (614) 833-4767
E-mail: jneff@wagnalls.org; URL: http://www.wagnalls.org
Contact: Jerry W. Neff, Exec. Dir.

Incorporated in 1924 in OH.
Donor(s): Mabel Wagnalls-Jones.‡
Financial data (yr. ended 08/31/01): Grants paid, $231,881; assets, $20,712,248 (M); gifts received, $21,410; expenditures, $1,918,834; qualifying distributions, $1,523,283; giving activities include $1,265,672 for programs.
Limitations: Giving limited to the Bloom Township and Fairfield County, OH, areas.
Publications: Annual report, newsletter, application guidelines, financial statement.
Application information: Application forms required for scholarships. Application form required.
Officers and Trustees:* Edwin A. Wisner, J.D.,* Chair.; William M. Hayes,* Vice-Chair.; John R. Watkins,* Secy.-Treas.; Jerry W. Neff, Exec. Dir.; Gary Griggs, William M. Haynes, D.V.M., Robert O. Jepsen, D.V.M., Scott R. Phillips, M.D., David L. Wynkoop.
EIN: 314379589
Codes: FD2, GTI

42626
Dale & Alyce Sheely Family Foundation
c/o Sky Trust, N.A.
P.O. Box 479
Youngstown, OH 44501 (330) 742-7035
Contact: David Sabine, Sr. V.P. and Sr. Trust Off., Sky Trust, N.A.

Established in 1994 in OH.
Donor(s): Dale R. Sheely, Sr.
Financial data (yr. ended 12/31/01): Grants paid, $231,000; assets, $1,231,855 (M); gifts received, $59,579; expenditures, $242,632; qualifying distributions, $233,688.
Limitations: Giving limited to Mahoning Valley, OH.
Application information: Application form not required.
Officer: Dale R. Sheely, Sr., Chair.
Directors: Albert Ortenzio, Alyce Sheely, Linda Cappelli Sladick.
Trustee: Sky Trust, N.A.
EIN: 347012061
Codes: FD2

42627
Thomas R. Gross Family Foundation
1241 Gibbard Ave.
Columbus, OH 43219
Contact: Thomas R. Gross, Tr.

Established in 1997 in OH.
Financial data (yr. ended 12/31/01): Grants paid, $230,750; assets, $3,688,625 (M); expenditures, $255,959; qualifying distributions, $230,102.
Limitations: Giving primarily in the greater Columbus, OH, area.
Application information: Application form required.
Trustees: David B. Gross, Michael L. Gross, Thomas R. Gross, Thomas R. Gross, Jr.
EIN: 311529104
Codes: FD2

42628
The Craig Young Family Foundation
400 Technecenter Dr., Ste. 410
Milford, OH 45150-2746

Established in 1994.
Donor(s): Craig S. Young.
Financial data (yr. ended 12/31/99): Grants paid, $230,400; assets, $5,799,848 (M); expenditures, $231,175; qualifying distributions, $228,721.
Trustees: Craig S. Young, Margaret S. Young, Mary E. Young.
EIN: 311423879
Codes: FD2

42629
Kamm Foundation
P.O. Box 16248
Rocky River, OH 44116

Established in 1961.
Donor(s): J.O. Kamm, J.S. Kamm.
Financial data (yr. ended 12/31/01): Grants paid, $230,080; assets, $4,322,529 (M); expenditures, $247,544; qualifying distributions, $228,191.
Limitations: Applications not accepted. Giving primarily in the midwestern states, with emphasis on IL and OH.
Application information: Contributes only to pre-selected organizations.
Officers and Trustees:* J.S. Kamm,* Pres.; J.O. Kamm II,* V.P. and Secy.; C.P. Kamm,* V.P. and Treas.
EIN: 346533601
Codes: FD2

42630
Lowe-Marshall Trust
c/o C. Marshall Lowe
5301 C. Huffman Ln.
Chesterhill, OH 43728-9021
E-mail: mblowe@morganco.net
Contact: C. Marshall Lowe, Tr.

Established in 1968.
Donor(s): James T. Lowe,‡ Constance M. Lowe.‡
Financial data (yr. ended 12/31/01): Grants paid, $230,000; assets, $5,361,051 (M); expenditures, $264,413; qualifying distributions, $252,342.
Limitations: Applications not accepted. Giving primarily in the Appalachian region and developing countries.
Publications: Program policy statement.
Application information: Contributes only to pre-selected organizations.
Officer and Trustees:* C. Marshall Lowe,* Chair.; Betty M. Lowe, Peter A. Lowe.
EIN: 316084154
Codes: FD2

42631
George J. Record School Foundation
P.O. Box 581
Conneaut, OH 44030 (440) 599-8283
Contact: Charles N. Lafferty, Exec. Dir.

Incorporated in 1958 in OH.
Donor(s): George J. Record.‡
Financial data (yr. ended 12/31/00): Grants paid, $229,341; assets, $3,908,351 (M); expenditures, $313,679; qualifying distributions, $267,273.
Limitations: Giving limited to residents of Ashtabula County, OH.
Application information: Formal interview at foundation is required. Application form required.
Officers and Trustees:* Charles N. Lafferty,* Pres. and Exec. Dir.; Harold M. Ladner,* V.P.; Howard T. Glover,* Secy.-Treas.; Angela Nelson, Mgr.; William H. Gerdes, William N. Runion.
EIN: 340830818
Codes: FD2, GTI

42632
Ralph M. and Ella M. Eccles Foundation
c/o National City Bank of Pennsylvania
P.O. Box 94651
Cleveland, OH 44101-4651
Application address: c/o National Bank of PA, 20 Stanwix St., Pittsburgh, PA 15222
Contact: Emily Eisenman

Established in 1972 in PA.
Financial data (yr. ended 12/31/01): Grants paid, $229,203; assets, $4,208,697 (M); expenditures, $262,400; qualifying distributions, $249,232.
Limitations: Giving limited to Clarion County, PA.
Publications: Application guidelines.
Application information: Application form required.
Trustee: National City Bank of Pennsylvania.
EIN: 237261807
Codes: FD2

42633
Jane and Jon Outcalt Foundation
(Formerly Outcalt Charitable Fund)
3201 Enterprise Pkwy., Ste. 220
Beachwood, OH 44122

Donor(s): Jon H. Outcalt, Jane Q. Outcalt.
Financial data (yr. ended 12/31/01): Grants paid, $228,100; assets, $3,245,260 (M); gifts received, $126,930; expenditures, $230,761; qualifying distributions, $222,059.
Limitations: Applications not accepted. Giving primarily in Cleveland, OH.
Application information: Contributes only to pre-selected organizations.
Officers: Jane Q. Outcalt, Pres.; Jon H. Outcalt, Jr., V.P.; David B. Outcalt, Secy.; Robin M. Outcalt, Treas.
EIN: 311194069
Codes: FD2

42634
The Miriam & Stanley Schwartz, Jr. Philanthropic Foundation
268 N. Parkview Ave.
Columbus, OH 43209-1438

Established in NY in 1998.
Financial data (yr. ended 12/31/01): Grants paid, $227,000; assets, $9,089 (M); gifts received, $226,500; expenditures, $232,004; qualifying distributions, $227,075.
Limitations: Applications not accepted. Giving primarily in FL, MA, MO, and OH.
Application information: Contributes only to pre-selected organizations.
Officers: Bruce A. Schwartz, Chair.; James M. Schwartz, Pres.; Robert S. Schwartz, V.P. and Secy.-Treas.
EIN: 311577991

42635
Helen & Louis Stolier Family Foundation
20102 Chagrin Blvd.
Shaker Heights, OH 44122-4947
(216) 991-6892
Contact: Carl J. Monastra, Tr.

Established in 1995 in OH.
Donor(s): Helen Stolier.‡
Financial data (yr. ended 12/31/01): Grants paid, $225,470; assets, $3,759,797 (M); expenditures, $307,220; qualifying distributions, $225,470.
Limitations: Giving limited to OH, primarily in Cleveland.
Application information: Application form not required.
Trustees: Louis P. Castellarin, Carl J. Monastra, Ruth Stolier.
EIN: 346991709

Codes: FD2

42636
The Della Selsor Trust
P.O. Box 1488
Springfield, OH 45501 (937) 324-5541
Contact: Glenn W. Collier, Tr. or Walter A. Wildman, Tr.

Established in 1966 in OH.
Donor(s): Della Selsor.‡
Financial data (yr. ended 12/31/01): Grants paid, $225,120; assets, $140,005 (M); expenditures, $259,614; qualifying distributions, $249,528.
Limitations: Giving primarily in the Springfield, OH, area.
Trustees: Glenn W. Collier, Walter A. Wildman.
EIN: 510163338
Codes: FD2

42637
The Leo Yassenoff Foundation
51 N. Hight St., Ste. 003
Columbus, OH 43215 (614) 221-4315
Contact: Frederick E. Dauterman, Jr., Chair.

Incorporated in 1947 in DE.
Donor(s): Leo Yassenoff.‡
Financial data (yr. ended 12/31/00): Grants paid, $225,100; assets, $2,048,120 (M); gifts received, $7,060; expenditures, $254,367; qualifying distributions, $236,251.
Limitations: Giving limited to Franklin County, OH.
Publications: Application guidelines.
Application information: Proposal must follow foundation guidelines. Application form not required.
Officers: Frederick E. Dauterman, Jr., Chair.; Benjamin L. Zox, Vice-Chair.; Cynthia A. Cecil-Lazarus, Secy.; Mary J. Hoover, Treas.
EIN: 310829426
Codes: FD2

42638
Ruth M. Hughes Scholarship Trust
c/o Unizan Financial Svcs. Group, N.A.
P.O. Box 2307
Zanesville, OH 43702-2307 (740) 455-7060

Established in 1995 in OH.
Financial data (yr. ended 12/31/01): Grants paid, $225,000; assets, $5,774,051 (M); expenditures, $254,567; qualifying distributions, $225,714.
Limitations: Giving limited to Muskingum County, OH.
Application information: Application form required.
Trustee: Unizan Financial Services Group, N.A.
EIN: 316442501
Codes: FD2, GTI

42639
E & H Foundation
c/o KeyBank, N.A.
800 Superior Ave., 4th Fl.
Cleveland, OH 44114

Established in 1994 in OH.
Donor(s): Helen Gratzer.
Financial data (yr. ended 12/31/99): Grants paid, $224,027; assets, $494 (M); gifts received, $1,000; expenditures, $235,599; qualifying distributions, $232,515.
Limitations: Applications not accepted. Giving primarily in Cleveland, OH.
Application information: Contributes only to pre-selected organizations.
Trustee: KeyBank, N.A.
EIN: 347030481
Codes: FD2

42640
Walter L. Gross, Jr. Family Foundation
312 Walnut St., Ste. 3150
Cincinnati, OH 45202 (513) 721-5086
Contact: Jeffrey H. Gross, Tr.

Established in 1997 in OH.
Donor(s): Walter L. Gross, Jr.
Financial data (yr. ended 12/31/00): Grants paid, $224,000; assets, $3,782,828 (M); expenditures, $242,011; qualifying distributions, $224,200.
Limitations: Giving primarily in the greater Cincinnati, OH, area.
Trustees: Barbara Gross, Jeffrey H. Gross, Sandra L. Gross, Walter L. Gross III.
EIN: 311571716
Codes: FD2

42641
John D. Finnegan Foundation
c/o Sky Trust, N.A.
P.O. Box 479
Youngstown, OH 44501 (330) 742-7035
Contact: David Sabine, Sr. V.P. and Sr. Trust Off., Sky Trust, N.A.

Trust established in 1957 in OH.
Donor(s): John D. Finnegan.‡
Financial data (yr. ended 12/31/01): Grants paid, $221,000; assets, $5,665,538 (M); expenditures, $265,226; qualifying distributions, $233,270.
Limitations: Giving primarily in Youngstown, OH.
Application information: Application form not required.
Officers and Directors:* John M. Newman,* Chair.; W.W. Bresnahan,* Vice-Chair.; William J. Mullen, Gregory L. Ridler.
Trustee: Sky Trust, N.A.
EIN: 346516439
Codes: FD2

42642
The Howland Memorial Fund
2080 Stockbridge Rd.
Akron, OH 44313 (330) 258-6512
Contact: John V. Frank, Tr.

Established in 1974 in OH.
Donor(s): Mame E. Howland.‡
Financial data (yr. ended 12/31/01): Grants paid, $220,800; assets, $3,942,888 (M); expenditures, $299,539; qualifying distributions, $235,429.
Limitations: Applications not accepted. Giving primarily in Akron, OH.
Application information: Majority of funding initiated by trustees. Unsolicited requests for funds not accepted.
Trustee: John V. Frank.
EIN: 346709057
Codes: FD2

42643
Florence M. and Paul M. Staehle Foundation
c/o National City Bank of Indiana
P.O. Box 94651
Cleveland, OH 44101-4651
Application address: P.O. Box 110, Fort Wayne, IN 46801, tel.: (219) 461-6218
Contact: Tersesa Tracey

Established in 1980 in IN.
Financial data (yr. ended 12/31/01): Grants paid, $220,191; assets, $5,094,662 (M); expenditures, $251,910; qualifying distributions, $236,365.
Limitations: Giving primarily in Fort Wayne, IN.
Application information: Contributes two-thirds of giving to pre-selected organizations.
Trustee: National City Bank of Indiana.
EIN: 356255328
Codes: FD2

42644
Willard E. Smucker Foundation
c/o The J.M. Smucker Co.
Strawberry Ln.
Orrville, OH 44667

Established in 1968 in OH.
Donor(s): The J.M. Smucker Co., and members of the Smucker family.
Financial data (yr. ended 12/31/01): Grants paid, $220,165; assets, $7,583,436 (M); gifts received, $83,333; expenditures, $222,916; qualifying distributions, $220,915.
Limitations: Applications not accepted. Giving primarily in OH.
Application information: Contributes only to pre-selected organizations.
Officers and Trustees:* Timothy P. Smucker,* Pres.; Marcella S. Clark,* Exec. V.P.; Lorraine E. Smucker,* V.P.; Steven J. Ellcessor, Secy.; Richard K. Smucker, Treas.
EIN: 346610889
Codes: CS, FD2, CD

42645
The Schwebel Family Foundation
P.O. Box 6018
Youngstown, OH 44501-6018
Contact: Paul Schwebel, Tr.

Established in 1989 in OH.
Donor(s): Frances Solomon, Schwebel Baking Co.
Financial data (yr. ended 12/31/00): Grants paid, $220,074; assets, $8,433,624 (M); gifts received, $532,909; expenditures, $255,537; qualifying distributions, $220,074.
Limitations: Applications not accepted. Giving primarily in Youngstown, OH.
Application information: Contributes only to pre-selected organizations.
Trustees: Joseph Schwebel, Paul Schwebel, Frances Solomon, Alyson Winick.
EIN: 341600311
Codes: FD2

42646
Edward and Ruth Wilkof Foundation
116 Cleveland Ave. N.W., Ste. 525
Canton, OH 44702 (330) 452-9788
Contact: Harry Mestel, Pres.

Established in 1986 in OH.
Donor(s): Edward Wilkof, Ruth Wilkof.
Financial data (yr. ended 06/30/01): Grants paid, $219,684; assets, $1,958,975 (M); gifts received, $28,000; expenditures, $229,011; qualifying distributions, $218,585.
Limitations: Giving primarily in Sarasota, FL, and Canton, OH.
Application information: Application form not required.
Officers: Harry Mestel, Pres.; Michael Sweeney, Secy.-Treas.
Trustee: Richard Wilkof.
EIN: 341536119
Codes: FD2

42647
Associated Charities of Findlay, Ohio
233 S. Main St.
Findlay, OH 45840-3395 (419) 423-2021
Contact: Peggy Wood

Established in 1918 in OH.
Financial data (yr. ended 12/31/00): Grants paid, $219,487; assets, $4,728,985 (M); gifts received, $18,654; expenditures, $635,658; qualifying distributions, $237,891.
Limitations: Giving limited to Findlay and the surrounding Hancock County, OH, area.
Publications: Annual report.

Application information: Application form not required.
Officers: Harry Cross, Pres.; Betty McBride, V.P.; Jim Brannigan, Secy.; Mary Coughlin, Treas.
Directors: Norma Calvert, Clair Davis, Jay Edel, Kathy Grant, Robert Hollister, Jack MacGregor, Bill Miller, Sterling Pfeiffer, Nancy Wilkins, Richard Zunkiewicz.
EIN: 346400067
Codes: FD2, GTI

42648
James P. McCready Family Foundation
670 W. Market St.
Akron, OH 44303-1414 (330) 849-6503
Contact: Linda Martin

Established in 1986 in OH.
Donor(s): James P. McCready, Gail J. McCready.
Financial data (yr. ended 12/31/99): Grants paid, $216,882; assets, $37,001 (M); gifts received, $36,000; expenditures, $217,927; qualifying distributions, $216,882.
Limitations: Giving primarily in Akron, OH.
Application information: Application form required.
Trustees: Gail J. McCready, James P. McCready.
EIN: 346866439

42649
Focus Foundation
30400 Detroit Ave., Ste. 203
Westlake, OH 44145 (440) 892-5022
Contact: Keith A. Brown, Pres.

Established in 1997 in OH.
Donor(s): Keith A. Brown.
Financial data (yr. ended 12/31/01): Grants paid, $215,170; assets, $3,233,463 (M); expenditures, $246,080; qualifying distributions, $215,170.
Officer: Keith A. Brown, Pres.
EIN: 311526199

42650
The Tetlak Foundation
c/o R.A. Bumblis, C.P.A.
1900 E. 9th St., Ste. 3200
Cleveland, OH 44114-3485

Established in 1998 in OH.
Donor(s): Joseph F. Tetlak.
Financial data (yr. ended 12/31/01): Grants paid, $215,000; assets, $3,707,118 (M); expenditures, $229,690; qualifying distributions, $218,238.
Limitations: Applications not accepted. Giving primarily in OH.
Application information: Contributes only to pre-selected organizations.
Officers and Trustees:* Joseph F. Tetlak,* Pres.; Jane T. Haylor,* Secy.; Edward G. Ptaszek, Jr.,* Treas.
EIN: 341880531
Codes: FD2

42651
Barry Foundation
P.O. Box 129
Columbus, OH 43216-0129

Incorporated in 1963 in OH.
Donor(s): Florence Melton, R.G. Barry Corp.
Financial data (yr. ended 12/31/00): Grants paid, $214,996; assets, $2,523 (M); gifts received, $200,000; expenditures, $216,299; qualifying distributions, $216,291.
Limitations: Applications not accepted. Giving primarily in Columbus, OH; funding also in Hanover, NH.
Publications: Financial statement.
Application information: Contributes only to pre-selected organizations.

Officers: Gordon Zacks, Chair. and Pres.; Richard L. Burrell, Secy.-Treas.
Trustee: Roger Lautzenhiser.
EIN: 316051086
Codes: CS, FD2, CD

42652
The Cotswold Foundation
c/o Fifth Third Bank
38 Fountain Sq. Plz., Dept. 630858
Cincinnati, OH 45263 (513) 579-6034

Established in 1998 in OH.
Donor(s): Beth B. Jones.
Financial data (yr. ended 12/31/01): Grants paid, $214,000; assets, $3,925,210 (M); expenditures, $224,201; qualifying distributions, $217,626.
Limitations: Giving primarily in OH, with some giving in FL and MT.
Trustees: Catherine J. Bournstein, Martha L. Burchenal, Beth B. Jones, Fifth Third Bank.
EIN: 316611702
Codes: FD2

42653
MJH Foundation
c/o Parkland Mgmt. Co.
1001 Lakeside Ave., Ste. 900
Cleveland, OH 44114-1151 (216) 479-2200
Contact: Thomas H. Oden, Treas.

Established in 1998 in OH as a follow-up to the Lois U. Horvitz Foundation.
Donor(s): Lois U. Horvitz Foundation.
Financial data (yr. ended 12/31/99): Grants paid, $213,800; assets, $11,293,063 (M); expenditures, $225,215; qualifying distributions, $213,800.
Limitations: Giving primarily in CA and OH.
Application information: Application form required.
Officers and Trustee:* Michael J. Horvitz,* Pres.; Jane R. Horvitz, V.P.; Leo M. Krulitz, Secy. and Exec. Dir.; Thomas H. Oden, Treas.
EIN: 341853843

42654
The Waddell Ladies Home Association
1101 E. Barks Rd.
P.O. Box 358
Marion, OH 43302-0358
Contact: James Waddell, Pres.

Established in 1901 in OH.
Donor(s): Benjamin Waddell.‡
Financial data (yr. ended 05/31/01): Grants paid, $213,128; assets, $3,486,243 (M); expenditures, $225,097; qualifying distributions, $221,659.
Limitations: Giving primarily in Marion County, OH, and adjacent counties.
Publications: Annual report.
Application information: Application form not required.
Officers: James P. Waddell, Pres.; William Dunn, V.P.; William Payette, Secy.; Tim Waddell, Treas.
Trustees: Betty Dendinger, David Williamson.
EIN: 314386851
Codes: FD2

42655
The Cayuga Foundation
c/o KeyBank, N.A.
P.O. Box 10099
Toledo, OH 43699-0099 (419) 259-8372
Contact: Erwin Diener

Established in 1960 in OH.
Financial data (yr. ended 12/31/00): Grants paid, $212,000; assets, $3,960,001 (M); expenditures, $249,917; qualifying distributions, $213,903.
Limitations: Giving primarily in NY.

Application information: Application form not required.
Trustee: KeyBank, N.A.
Advisors: Sandra Fritch, Donald J. Keune, Elizabeth M. Pfenninger.
EIN: 346504822
Codes: FD2

42656
The Orvis-Perkins Foundation
(Formerly The Leigh H. Perkins Foundation)
1030 Hanna Bldg.
1422 Euclid Ave.
Cleveland, OH 44115 (216) 621-0465
Contact: Marilyn Best, Secy.-Treas.

Established in 1985 in OH.
Donor(s): The Orvis Co., Inc.
Financial data (yr. ended 12/31/00): Grants paid, $212,000; assets, $3,627,650 (M); expenditures, $260,781; qualifying distributions, $217,293.
Application information: Application form not required.
Officers and Directors:* Leigh H. Perkins,* Pres.; Romi M. Perkins,* V.P.; Marilyn Best, Secy.-Treas.; John D. Drinko, David D. Perkins, Leigh H. Perkins, Jr., Mary B. Perkins, Melissa M. Perkins.
EIN: 341496755
Codes: CS, FD2, CD

42657
Scotford Foundation
211 S. Main St.
Poland, OH 44514
Contact: John Scotford, Jr., Tr.

Established in 1978 in OH.
Donor(s): John Scotford, Judy Scotford, John Scotford, Jr., Laura Scotford, Stephen L. Scotford.
Financial data (yr. ended 12/31/01): Grants paid, $211,180; assets, $3,349,454 (M); gifts received, $50,000; expenditures, $226,816; qualifying distributions, $214,786.
Limitations: Giving primarily in OH.
Application information: Application form not required.
Trustees: John P. Scotford, John Scotford, Jr., Judith Scotford, Laura Scotford, Stephen Scotford.
EIN: 341278622
Codes: FD2

42658
Homan Foundation
7609 Coldstream Dr.
Cincinnati, OH 45255-3932
Application address: P.O. Box 76548, Cold Spring, KY 41076-0548
Contact: Walter E. Homan, Tr.

Established in 1969 in OH.
Financial data (yr. ended 12/31/01): Grants paid, $211,150; assets, $1,400,481 (M); gifts received, $22,000; expenditures, $221,181; qualifying distributions, $211,110.
Limitations: Giving primarily in the Cincinnati, OH area.
Publications: Annual report.
Application information: Application form not required.
Trustees: Frank X. Homan, Margo S. Homan, Walter E. Homan.
EIN: 237038734
Codes: FD2

42659
The Carol and James Besl Family Foundation
c/o Force Control
P.O. Box 18366
Fairfield, OH 45018
Application address: 6 Cogswell Grant, Fairfield, OH 45014, tel.: (513) 860-9221
Contact: Carol Besl, Pres.

Established in 1991 in OH.
Donor(s): James L. Besl, Force Control Industries, Inc.
Financial data (yr. ended 06/30/01): Grants paid, $210,500; assets, $1,923,127 (M); gifts received, $75,000; expenditures, $224,303; qualifying distributions, $210,111.
Limitations: Giving primarily in Cincinnati, OH.
Application information: Application form required.
Officers: Carol Besl, Pres.; Joseph E. Besl, V.P.; Timothy A. Garry, Secy.
Trustees: James C. Besl, Michael Besl, Karen Besl Murrell.
EIN: 311332002
Codes: FD2

42660
The George Foundation
P.O. Box 21609
Columbus, OH 43221-0609
Contact: Jack George, Pres.

Established in 1982 in OH.
Donor(s): Kaplan Trucking Co., Noel George Trust.
Financial data (yr. ended 12/31/01): Grants paid, $210,320; assets, $4,318,205 (M); gifts received, $68,845; expenditures, $217,821; qualifying distributions, $208,021.
Limitations: Giving on a national basis, with some emphasis on Columbus, OH.
Application information: Application form not required.
Officers and Trustees:* Jack George,* Pres.; Mildred George,* V.P.; Joan George,* Secy.-Treas.; Carol George, Sarah George.
EIN: 311030194
Codes: FD2

42661
Ralph and Lucille Schey Foundation
(Formerly The Schey Foundation)
195 Dunbar Ct.
Aurora, OH 44202-8540

Established in 1985 in OH.
Donor(s): Ralph E. Schey, Walter A. Rajki.
Financial data (yr. ended 06/30/01): Grants paid, $210,115; assets, $5,485,198 (M); gifts received, $500,000; expenditures, $231,425; qualifying distributions, $210,115.
Limitations: Applications not accepted. Giving primarily in Cleveland, OH.
Application information: Contributes only to pre-selected organizations.
Officer and Trustees:* Ralph Schey,* Pres.; David E. Cook, Lucille L. Schey.
EIN: 341502219
Codes: FD2

42662
Dr. Louis Sklarow Memorial Fund
c/o KeyBank, N.A., Trust Tax Dept.
800 Superior Ave., 4th Fl.
Cleveland, OH 44114
Application address: c/o Henry Z. Urban, Jr., KeyBank, N.A., Key Ctr., 50 Fountain Plz., Buffalo, NY 14202, tel.: (716) 847-2226

Established in 1975 in NY.
Donor(s): Louis Sklarow.‡

Financial data (yr. ended 05/31/01): Grants paid, $210,000; assets, $2,264,692 (M); expenditures, $236,871; qualifying distributions, $208,779.
Limitations: Giving primarily in NY.
Trustee: KeyBank, N.A.
EIN: 166201243
Codes: FD2

42663
Charles F. High Foundation
1520 Melody Ln.
Bucyrus, OH 44820 (419) 562-2074
Contact: John R. Clime, Admin.

Established in 1939 in OH.
Donor(s): Charles F. High.‡
Financial data (yr. ended 12/31/01): Grants paid, $209,392; assets, $4,744,761 (M); expenditures, $229,823; qualifying distributions, $217,392.
Limitations: Giving limited to OH.
Application information: Application form required.
Officer and Trustees:* John R. Clime,* Admin.; F.J. Farmer, L.R. Likins, J.R. Miller II, D.J. Wingate.
EIN: 346527860
Codes: FD2, GTI

42664
Herbert G. Feldman Charitable Foundation
c/o National City Bank of Pennsylvania
P.O. Box 94651
Cleveland, OH 44101-4651

Established in 1999 in PA.
Donor(s): Herbert G. Feldman,‡ Mary M. Zielinski.
Financial data (yr. ended 12/31/01): Grants paid, $209,000; assets, $4,641,407 (M); gifts received, $118,000; expenditures, $288,207; qualifying distributions, $255,024.
Limitations: Applications not accepted. Giving primarily in Pittsburgh, PA.
Application information: Contributes only to pre-selected organizations.
Officers: Mary M. Zielinski, Pres.; David Rothbart, Secy.; Clara Verbin, Treas.
EIN: 251832024
Codes: FD2

42665
The John C. Bates Foundation
2401 Front St.
Toledo, OH 43605

Established in 1993 in OH.
Donor(s): Heidtman Steel Products, Inc., Centaur, Inc., HS Processing, LP.
Financial data (yr. ended 03/31/01): Grants paid, $208,558; assets, $1,429 (M); gifts received, $190,000; expenditures, $209,431; qualifying distributions, $209,418.
Limitations: Applications not accepted. Giving primarily in MI and OH.
Application information: Contributes only to pre-selected organizations.
Officers and Trustees:* Darlene B. Dotson,* Pres.; John M. Carey,* Secy.; Mark E. Ridenour,* Treas.
EIN: 341749094
Codes: FD2

42666
Lester J. Besl Family Foundation
P.O. Box 18335
Fairfield, OH 45018 (513) 868-0900
Application address: 250 E. 5th St., 29th Fl., Cincinnati, OH 45202, tel.: (513) 784-8012
Contact: Dennis Doyle, Secy.

Established in 1981 in OH.
Donor(s): Lester J. Besl, Force Control Industries, Inc.

42666

Financial data (yr. ended 12/31/00): Grants paid, $207,400; assets, $2,232,218 (M); gifts received, $22,500; expenditures, $225,220; qualifying distributions, $206,649.
Limitations: Giving primarily in OH.
Application information: Application form required.
Officers: James C. Besl, Pres.; Dennis M. Doyle, Secy.; Michael L. Besl, Treas.
Trustees: Joseph E. Besl, Alvin B. Dennig, Karen M. Murrell.
EIN: 311016859
Codes: FD2

42667
Schumacher Foundation
c/o Porter, Wright, Morris & Arthur
41 S. High St.
Columbus, OH 43215

Donor(s): Frederick W. Schumacher Trust.
Financial data (yr. ended 12/31/01): Grants paid, $207,256; assets, $3,342,936 (M); gifts received, $80,209; expenditures, $267,522; qualifying distributions, $227,184.
Limitations: Applications not accepted. Giving primarily in Columbus, OH; some giving also in Canada.
Application information: Contributes only to pre-selected organizations.
Trustees: Leslie Blanchard, Carter H. Finnell, Hunter Finnell.
EIN: 316022954
Codes: FD2

42668
The Huffy Foundation, Inc.
225 Byers Rd.
Miamisburg, OH 45342
Contact: Pamela Booher, Secy.

Established in 1959 in OH as Huffman Foundation; name changed in 1978.
Donor(s): Huffy Corp.
Financial data (yr. ended 12/31/01): Grants paid, $206,644; assets, $112,572 (M); gifts received, $150,000; expenditures, $207,331; qualifying distributions, $206,726.
Limitations: Giving primarily in areas of company operations in OH and WI.
Publications: Informational brochure (including application guidelines).
Application information: Application form not required.
Officers and Trustees:* Fred C. Smith,* Chair.; Don R. Graber,* Pres.; Pamela K. Booher, Secy.; Nancy A. Michaud.
EIN: 316023716
Codes: CS, FD2, CD

42669
Meshech Frost Testamentary Trust
c/o National City Bank
P.O. Box 94651
Cleveland, OH 44101-4651
Application address: 155 E. Broad St., Columbus, OH 43151, tel.: (614) 463-8331
Contact: Jim S. Deyo

Established in 1922 in OH.
Donor(s): Meshech Frost.‡
Financial data (yr. ended 12/31/01): Grants paid, $206,500; assets, $4,581,925 (M); expenditures, $227,649; qualifying distributions, $214,703.
Limitations: Giving limited to Tiffin, OH.
Trustee: National City Bank.
EIN: 316019431
Codes: FD2, GTI

42670
Four Winds Foundation
c/o Joseph A. Pedoto
49 E. 4th St., Ste. 521
Cincinnati, OH 45202

Established in 1994 in OH.
Donor(s): S. Craig Lindner.
Financial data (yr. ended 12/31/01): Grants paid, $206,101; assets, $2,143,877 (M); gifts received, $1,867; expenditures, $209,866; qualifying distributions, $206,101.
Limitations: Applications not accepted. Giving primarily in OH.
Application information: Contributes only to pre-selected organizations.
Officers and Trustees:* S. Craig Lindner,* Pres. and Treas.; Frances Lindner,* V.P. and Secy.
EIN: 311420130

42671
The Linnemann Family Foundation
312 Walnut St., Ste. 3150
Cincinnati, OH 45202-4059
Contact: Beth Troendly

Established in 1995 in OH.
Donor(s): Patricia G. Linnemann, Calvin C. Linnemann.
Financial data (yr. ended 12/31/00): Grants paid, $206,000; assets, $4,571,074 (M); expenditures, $222,160; qualifying distributions, $204,006.
Limitations: Giving on a national basis.
Application information: Application form not required.
Officers: Calvin C. Linnemann, Pres.; Patricia G. Linnemann, Secy.-Treas.
Trustees: Catherine A. Linnemann, Mark D. Linnemann.
EIN: 311394291
Codes: FD2

42672
Sedgwick Family Charitable Trust
c/o KeyBank, N.A.
800 Superior Ave., 4th Fl.
Cleveland, OH 44114
Additional address: 105 W. Hill Dr., Farmville, VA 23901

Established in 1991 in OH.
Donor(s): Ellery Sedgwick, Jr.‡
Financial data (yr. ended 12/31/00): Grants paid, $205,000; assets, $4,680,682 (M); expenditures, $205,000; qualifying distributions, $205,000.
Limitations: Applications not accepted. Giving primarily in south GA.
Application information: Contributes only to pre-selected organizations. Unsolicited requests for funds not accepted.
Trustees: Irene Sedgwick Briedis, Elizabeth W. Sedgwick, Ellery Sedgwick III, Theodore Sedgwick, Walter Cabot Sedgwick, KeyBank, N.A.
EIN: 346958569
Codes: FD2

42673
Robert Rogan Burchenal Foundation
c/o Fifth Third Bank
38 Fountain Sq. Plz.
Cincinnati, OH 45263
Contact: Lawra Baumann, Fdn. Off.

Established in 1972.
Donor(s): Robert R. Burchenal.
Financial data (yr. ended 11/30/01): Grants paid, $204,400; assets, $2,933,360 (M); expenditures, $215,159; qualifying distributions, $207,326.
Limitations: Giving primarily in MO, MT, and OH.
Trustees: Catherine J. Bournstein, Cooper L. Burchenal, James J. Burchenal, Martha L. Burchenal, Beth B. Jones, William H. Kreidler II.
EIN: 237231471
Codes: FD2

42674
Landman-Goldman Foundation
c/o Weber & Sterling
1721 Indian Wood Cir., Ste. 1
Maumee, OH 43537-4008

Established in 1987 in OH.
Financial data (yr. ended 12/31/01): Grants paid, $203,650; assets, $4,898,795 (M); expenditures, $226,484; qualifying distributions, $213,017.
Limitations: Applications not accepted. Giving limited to northwest OH.
Application information: Contributes only to pre-selected organizations.
Trustees: Leslie F. Sterling, Robert V. Sterling, Alice H. Weber, Edward F. Weber.
EIN: 341543174
Codes: FD2

42675
Norman & Carol Traeger Foundation, Inc.
1317 E. Broad St.
Columbus, OH 43205 (614) 258-3191
Contact: Norman L. Traeger, Tr.

Established in 1980 in OH.
Donor(s): Carol Traeger, Norman L. Traeger.
Financial data (yr. ended 04/30/01): Grants paid, $203,600; assets, $4,237,832 (M); gifts received, $96,321; expenditures, $228,515; qualifying distributions, $200,369.
Limitations: Giving primarily in FL.
Application information: Application form not required.
Trustees: Carol Traeger, Norman L. Traeger, Alan Wasserstrom.
EIN: 310988108
Codes: FD2

42676
T. R. Murphy Residuary Trust
50 N. 4th St.
P.O. Box 1030
Zanesville, OH 43702-1030
Contact: R. William Geyer, Tr.

Established in 1985.
Financial data (yr. ended 06/30/01): Grants paid, $203,493; assets, $4,294,292 (M); expenditures, $264,789; qualifying distributions, $212,687.
Limitations: Giving limited to Muskingum County, OH.
Application information: Application form required for scholarships.
Trustee: R. William Geyer.
Committee Members: Pat Greenwood, David E. Morland, Perry Robinson, Jeff Zellers.
EIN: 316285970
Codes: FD2, GTI

42677
The Kaplan Foundation
312 Walnut St., Ste. 3150
Cincinnati, OH 45202 (513) 721-5086
Contact: Stanley M. Kaplan, M.D., Pres., and Myran J. Kaplan, Secy.

Established in 1994 in OH.
Financial data (yr. ended 12/31/00): Grants paid, $202,444; assets, $5,186,222 (M); expenditures, $314,732; qualifying distributions, $202,444.
Limitations: Giving primarily in the greater Cincinnati, OH, area.
Officers: Stanley M. Kaplan, M.D., Pres. and Treas.; Myran Kaplan, Secy.

Trustees: Barbara S. Kaplan, M.D., Richard M. Kaplan, Steven J. Kaplan.
EIN: 311423392
Codes: FD2

42678
NiSource Charitable Foundation
(Formerly Columbia Gas Foundation)
200 Civic Center Dr.
Columbus, OH 43215   (614) 460-4207
Application address: 801 E. 86th Ave., Merriville IN, 46410; tel.: (219) 647-6215

Established in 1990 in DE.
Donor(s): The Columbia Gas System, Inc., and its affiliated companies.
Financial data (yr. ended 12/31/01): Grants paid, $201,930; assets, $1,230,814 (M); gifts received, $22,071; expenditures, $204,287; qualifying distributions, $201,930.
Limitations: Giving limited to areas of company operations.
Application information: Application form required.
Officers and Directors:* Gary Neagle,* Chair.; Julie Basich, Exec. Dir.; Stephen Adik, Vince DeVito, Maria Hibba, Kathie A. Mole, Michael O'Donnell, Louis A. Ortiz, Gary W. Pottorff.
EIN: 510324200
Codes: CS, FD2

42679
John N. Browning Family Fund C
c/o U.S. Bank
P.O. Box 1118, ML 6190
Cincinnati, OH 45201-1118

Established in 1992.
Financial data (yr. ended 04/30/01): Grants paid, $201,500; assets, $4,014,520 (M); expenditures, $235,499; qualifying distributions, $200,874.
Limitations: Applications not accepted. Giving primarily in KY.
Application information: Contributes only to pre-selected organizations.
Officers: Carlisle B. Van Meter, Pres.; George M. Van Meter, Jr., Secy.
Trustee: Laurance Van Meter.
Agent: U.S. Bank.
EIN: 311284450
Codes: FD2

42680
Benjamin S. Gerson Family Foundation
c/o Foundation Mgmt. Svcs., Inc.
1422 Euclid Ave., Ste. 627
Cleveland, OH 44115-1952   (216) 621-2901
FAX: (216) 621-8198; *URL:* http://www.fmscleveland.com/gerson
Contact: Kimberly S. Cowan, Consultant

Established in 1968 in OH.
Donor(s): Benjamin S. Gerson.‡
Financial data (yr. ended 12/31/01): Grants paid, $200,550; assets, $3,306,594 (M); gifts received, $166,666; expenditures, $256,907; qualifying distributions, $191,020.
Limitations: Giving primarily in the greater Cleveland, OH, area.
Publications: Grants list, informational brochure (including application guidelines).
Application information: Application form not required.
Officer and Trustees:* Thomas E. Gerson,* Pres. and Treas.; Judith Gerson, Sue Gerson, Jessica Gurbst, Jill G. Parker, Robert Parker.
EIN: 311491817
Codes: FD2

42681
The Jacob Family Foundation Corporation
2600 Far Hills Bldg., Ste. 307
Dayton, OH 45419-1514
Contact: Richard Jacob, Tr.

Established in 1987 in OH.
Financial data (yr. ended 12/31/01): Grants paid, $200,482; assets, $1,140,792 (M); gifts received, $496,795; expenditures, $202,385; qualifying distributions, $200,198.
Limitations: Giving primarily in Palm Beach, FL, and Dayton, OH.
Application information: Application form not required.
Trustees: Arnold M. Jacob, Louise M. Jacob, Richard J. Jacob, Patricia Vanartsdalen.
EIN: 311214668
Codes: FD2

42682
Leonard & Cecelia Polster Family Foundation
11 Hyde Park
Cleveland, OH 44122-7520

Established in 1998 in OH.
Donor(s): Leonard Polster, Cecelia Polster.
Financial data (yr. ended 12/31/00): Grants paid, $200,400; assets, $312,706 (M); gifts received, $55,900; expenditures, $205,234; qualifying distributions, $200,500.
Limitations: Applications not accepted. Giving primarily in Cleveland, OH.
Application information: Contributes only to pre-selected organizations.
Trustees: Cecelia Polster, Keith A. Polster, Leonard Polster, Scott H. Polster, Pamela E. Tepper.
Agent: KeyBank, N.A.
EIN: 341864680
Codes: FD2

42683
The Van Meter/Barnhart Family Fund
(Formerly John N. Browning Family Fund L, Inc.)
c/o U.S. Bank
P.O. Box 1118, ML CN-WN-06TX
Cincinnati, OH 45201-1118

Financial data (yr. ended 04/30/01): Grants paid, $200,100; assets, $5,133,928 (M); expenditures, $240,727; qualifying distributions, $200,270.
Limitations: Applications not accepted. Giving primarily in KY.
Application information: Contributes only to pre-selected organizations.
Officers: Florence V. Barnhart, Pres.; John Van Meter, Secy.
Manager: Isaac C. Van Meter, Jr.
Agent: U.S. Bank.
EIN: 311284451
Codes: FD2

42684
The Bower-Suhrheinrich Foundation
c/o Fifth Third Bank
Trust Tax Dept., MD 1COM31
Cincinnati, OH 45263

Established in 1997 in IN.
Financial data (yr. ended 12/31/01): Grants paid, $200,000; assets, $2,866,247 (M); expenditures, $217,192; qualifying distributions, $201,497.
Limitations: Giving primarily in Evansville, IN.
Trustee: Fifth Third Bank.
EIN: 352031773

42685
The Pruina Corporation
c/o Thomas F. Allen
1801 E. 9th St., Ste. 1300
Cleveland, OH 44114-3103

Established in 1963.
Donor(s): Andrew H. Kalnow, Loretta K. Kalnow, Gertrude K. Chisholm, Carl F. Kalnow.
Financial data (yr. ended 12/31/01): Grants paid, $200,000; assets, $3,135,942 (M); gifts received, $1,064; expenditures, $203,949; qualifying distributions, $202,204.
Limitations: Applications not accepted. Giving primarily in Forrest, IL, and Tiffin, OH.
Application information: Contributes only to pre-selected organizations.
Officers and Trustees:* Loretta K. Kalnow,* Pres. and Treas.; Gertrude K. Chisholm,* V.P.; Andrew H. Kalnow,* Secy.; Carl F. Kalnow.
EIN: 346596908
Codes: FD2

42686
Irving I. Stone Foundation
1 American Rd.
Cleveland, OH 44144

Established in 1999 in OH.
Donor(s): Irving I. Stone.
Financial data (yr. ended 12/31/01): Grants paid, $200,000; assets, $7,644,438 (M); gifts received, $4,200,000; expenditures, $226,362; qualifying distributions, $210,026.
Limitations: Applications not accepted. Giving primarily in New York, NY.
Application information: Contributes only to pre-selected organizations.
Officers: Gary Weiss, Pres.; Judith Stone Weiss, Secy.-Treas.
Trustees: Hensha Gansbourg, Helen Stone, Myrna Tatar, Elle Weiss, Jeffrey Weiss, Morry Weiss, Zev Weiss.
EIN: 341892327
Codes: FD2

42687
Danaher Foundation
5335 Avion Park Dr.
Highland Heights, OH 44143-1916

Established in 1952 in IL.
Donor(s): Joslyn Corp., Steven M. Rales.
Financial data (yr. ended 12/31/00): Grants paid, $199,990; assets, $2,361,126 (M); expenditures, $206,517; qualifying distributions, $199,668.
Limitations: Applications not accepted. Giving primarily in areas of company operations.
Application information: Contributes only to pre-selected organizations.
Officers and Directors:* Patrick W. Allender,* Pres.; Christopher C. McMahon,* Secy.; James H. Ditkoff,* Treas.
EIN: 366042871
Codes: CS, FD2

42688
Goerlich Family Foundation, Inc.
National City Bank Bldg.
405 Madison Ave., Ste. 1900
Toledo, OH 43604-1207
Contact: William F. Bates, Pres.

Incorporated in 1965 in OH.
Donor(s): John Goerlich,‡ Selma E. Goerlich.‡
Financial data (yr. ended 12/31/01): Grants paid, $199,625; assets, $3,737,070 (M); expenditures, $221,359; qualifying distributions, $205,364.
Limitations: Applications not accepted. Giving primarily in Toledo, OH.

42688—OHIO

Application information: Contributes only to pre-selected organizations.
Officers and Directors:* William F. Bates,* Pres. and Treas.; Paul Putman,* V.P.; Sandrea Sue Goerlich Alexander,* Secy.; Edward H. Alexander, William S. Miller, Selma Goerlich Putman.
EIN: 340970919
Codes: FD2

42689
Elisha-Bolton Foundation
c/o Advisory Svcs., Inc.
1422 Euclid Ave., 1010 Hanna Bldg.
Cleveland, OH 44115-2078
Contact: James C. Sekerak, Treas.

Established in 1986 in OH.
Donor(s): Betsy Bolton Schafer.
Financial data (yr. ended 12/31/01): Grants paid, $199,000; assets, $5,345,519 (M); expenditures, $255,129; qualifying distributions, $208,219.
Application information: Application form not required.
Officers and Trustees:* Betsy Bolton Schafer,* Pres.; Kenneth G. Hochman,* V.P.; Gilbert P. Schafer III,* V.P.; Paulette Kitko, Secy.; James C. Sekerak, Treas.
EIN: 341500135
Codes: FD2

42690
Albert W. and Edith V. Flowers Charitable Foundation
c/o FirstMerit Bank, N.A.
121 S. Main St., Ste. 200
Akron, OH 44308 (330) 384-7320
FAX: (330) 849-8992; E-mail: brenda.moubray@firstmerit.com
Contact: Ronald B. Tynan, Chair.

Trust established in 1968 in OH.
Donor(s): Albert W. Flowers,‡ Edith V. Flowers.‡
Financial data (yr. ended 12/31/01): Grants paid, $197,430; assets, $3,096,667 (M); expenditures, $223,724; qualifying distributions, $200,057.
Limitations: Giving primarily in Stark County, OH.
Distribution Committee: Ronald B. Tynan, Chair.; F.E. McCullough, Charles J. Tyburski.
Trustee: FirstMerit Bank, N.A.
EIN: 346608643
Codes: FD2

42691
The Joseph L. Steiner and Marjorie S. Steiner Foundation
7300 Wood Meadow Dr.
Cincinnati, OH 45243

Established in 1994 in OH.
Donor(s): Joseph Steiner.
Financial data (yr. ended 12/31/01): Grants paid, $197,077; assets, $2,742,083 (M); gifts received, $60,000; expenditures, $278,382; qualifying distributions, $241,690.
Limitations: Applications not accepted.
Application information: Contributes only to pre-selected organizations.
Trustee: John A. Steiner.
EIN: 311420608
Codes: FD2

42692
The Cochran Foundation Agency
c/o National City Bank, Kentucky
P.O. Box 94651
Cleveland, OH 44101-4651
Application address: 513 Country Ln., Louisville, KY 40207, tel.: (507) 895-1282
Contact: Lee Cochran, Pres.

Established in 1960.

Financial data (yr. ended 12/31/01): Grants paid, $196,828; assets, $5,032 (M); expenditures, $201,650; qualifying distributions, $196,828.
Limitations: Giving limited to Jefferson City, KY.
Officers and Trustees:* Lee Cochran,* Pres.; Polly C. Blakemore,* V.P.
EIN: 616023382

42693
The Clara Weiss Fund
2225 Marks Rd.
Valley City, OH 44280-9370 (330) 225-8514
Contact: David C. Weiss, Mgr.

Established in 1955 in OH.
Donor(s): L.C. Weiss, Mrs. L.C. Weiss.
Financial data (yr. ended 12/31/00): Grants paid, $196,500; assets, $4,072,316 (M); expenditures, $251,678; qualifying distributions, $205,109.
Limitations: Giving primarily in the Cleveland, OH, area.
Application information: Application form not required.
Officer and Trustees:* David C. Weiss,* Mgr.; Arthur D. Weiss, Robert L. Weiss.
EIN: 346556158
Codes: FD2

42694
The Allyn Foundation
2211 S. Dixie Ave., Ste. 302
Dayton, OH 45409 (937) 299-2295
E-mail: csafdn@ix.netcom.com
Contact: Charles S. Allyn, Jr., Pres.

Incorporated in 1955 in OH.
Donor(s): S.C. Allyn.‡
Financial data (yr. ended 12/31/00): Grants paid, $195,000; assets, $4,359,625 (M); expenditures, $250,259; qualifying distributions, $216,480.
Limitations: Giving primarily in southern OH, with the exception of certain schools and universities.
Publications: Annual report (including application guidelines).
Application information: Application form not required.
Officers and Trustees:* Charles S. Allyn, Jr.,* Pres.; Mary Louise Sunderland,* V.P.; Compton Allyn,* Secy.-Treas.; Sarah Allyn Bahlman, Elizabeth A. Lowsley-Williams, Anne Reed Sunderland, Louise Allyn Sunderland, Mary Compton Sunderland.
EIN: 316030791
Codes: FD2

42695
Edward W. Powers Charitable Fund
c/o National City Bank
P.O. Box 94651
Cleveland, OH 44101-4651
Application address: c/o Myra Vitto, National City Bank, 20 Federal Plaza W., Youngstown, OH 44503, tel.: (330) 742-4289
Contact: Thomas Orr, Trust Off., National City Bank

Established in 1966.
Donor(s): Edward W. Powers.‡
Financial data (yr. ended 12/31/00): Grants paid, $194,880; assets, $2,334,430 (M); expenditures, $201,046; qualifying distributions, $198,122.
Limitations: Giving limited to Youngstown, OH.
Appointing Committee: Franklin I. Powers, John W. Powers, Jeanne D. Tyler.
Trustee: National City Bank.
EIN: 346577350
Codes: FD2

42696
Central Soya Foundation
c/o National City Bank of Indiana
P.O. Box 94651
Cleveland, OH 44101-4051
Application address: c/o National City Bank of Indiana, P.O. Box 110, Fort Wayne, IN 46801-0110, tel.: (219) 461-6218
Contact: Theresa J. Tracey

Trust established in 1954 in IN.
Donor(s): Central Soya Co., Inc.
Financial data (yr. ended 12/31/01): Grants paid, $194,236; assets, $258,299 (M); gifts received, $200,000; expenditures, $195,830; qualifying distributions, $194,692.
Limitations: Giving primarily in Fort Wayne, IN.
Trustee: National City Bank of Indiana.
EIN: 356020624
Codes: CS, FD2, CD

42697
The American Electric Power System Educational Trust Fund
c/o AEP, Tax Dept.
P.O Box 16428
Columbus, OH 43216-0428
Scholarship application address: c/o American Electric Power System, Personnel Svcs. and EEO, 1 Riverside Plz., Columbus, OH 43215, tel.: (614) 223-1000

Donor(s): American Electric Power Co., Inc., Columbus Southern Power Co., Ohio Power Co.
Financial data (yr. ended 02/28/01): Grants paid, $194,000; assets, $4,193,271 (M); expenditures, $213,223; qualifying distributions, $197,452.
Limitations: Giving primarily in areas of company operations, including IN, OH, and VA.
Publications: Program policy statement, application guidelines.
Application information: Application form required.
Trustees: Mary G. Cofer, Henry W. Fayne, W.J. Lhota, J.H. Vipperman.
EIN: 237418083
Codes: CS, FD2, CD, GTI

42698
McDonald Investments Foundation
(Formerly McDonald & Company Securities Foundation)
800 Superior Ave.
Cleveland, OH 44114-2603 (216) 689-4776
FAX: (216) 689-3865; E-mail: karen_a_white@keybank.com
Contact: Karen A. White, Secy.-Treas.

Established in 1983 in OH.
Donor(s): McDonald & Co. Investments, Inc., McDonald Investments, Inc.
Financial data (yr. ended 12/31/01): Grants paid, $193,916; assets, $770,376 (M); expenditures, $198,885; qualifying distributions, $194,144.
Limitations: Giving primarily in areas of company operations in the U.S., with emphasis on Cleveland, OH.
Publications: Informational brochure (including application guidelines).
Application information: Support for higher education only through contributions to the Ohio Foundation for Independent Colleges and Cleveland, OH, area colleges not affiliated with the OFIC; religious and welfare support is restricted to local arms of United Way, United Jewish Welfare Fund, and Catholic Charities. Application form not required.
Officers and Trustees:* Pamela Burke,* Chair.; Karen A. White,* Secy.-Treas.; Jonathan Crane, Fred Cummings, William Grove, Robert G. Jones,

Thomas J. McDonald, John O'Brien, Mark H. Summers, Rebecca Talley.
EIN: 341386528
Codes: CS, FD2, CD

42699
Ada & Helen Rank Charitable Trust
c/o KeyBank, N.A.
800 Superior Ave., 4th Fl.
Cleveland, OH 44114
Application address: 4495 Everhard Rd. N.W., Canton, OH 44718, tel.: (330) 497-3603
Contact: Charles Wondra

Established in 1950 in OH.
Financial data (yr. ended 09/30/01): Grants paid, $193,272; assets, $2,961,371 (M); expenditures, $231,065; qualifying distributions, $213,050.
Limitations: Giving primarily in Canton, OH.
Trustee: KeyBank, N.A.
EIN: 346576279
Codes: FD2

42700
Fishel Foundation
c/o The Fishel Co.
1810 Arlingate Ln.
Columbus, OH 43228

Established in 1993 in OH.
Donor(s): The Fishel Co.
Financial data (yr. ended 02/28/01): Grants paid, $192,925; assets, $2,966,659 (M); gifts received, $1,550,000; expenditures, $203,181; qualifying distributions, $192,925.
Limitations: Applications not accepted. Giving primarily in Columbus, OH.
Application information: Contributes only to pre-selected organizations.
Trustees: Diane L. Keeler, J.F. Keeler, Jr.
EIN: 316063414
Codes: CS, FD2, CD

42701
The Sears-Swetland Family Foundation
(Formerly The Sears-Swetland Foundation)
2700 Eaton Rd.
Cleveland, OH 44118
FAX: (216) 932-2745
Contact: Ruth Swetland Eppig, Tr.

Trust established in 1949 in OH.
Donor(s): Anna L. Sears,‡ Lester M. Sears,‡ Ruth P. Sears,‡ Mary Ann Swetland.‡
Financial data (yr. ended 12/31/01): Grants paid, $192,500; assets, $3,420,916 (M); gifts received, $401; expenditures, $224,314; qualifying distributions, $197,969.
Limitations: Giving primarily in the Cleveland, OH, area.
Publications: Grants list, application guidelines.
Application information: Application form not required.
Trustees: Ruth Swetland Eppig, David Sears Swetland, David W. Swetland.
EIN: 346522143
Codes: FD2

42702
Charles Pagella Charitable Trust
c/o KeyBank, N.A.
800 Superior Ave.
Cleveland, OH 44114
Contact: Stanley Lepkowski, Trust Off., KeyBank, N.A.

Established in 2000 in ME.
Financial data (yr. ended 12/31/01): Grants paid, $192,389; assets, $1,422,640 (M); gifts received, $19,719; expenditures, $213,432; qualifying distributions, $192,389.
Trustee: KeyBank, N.A.
EIN: 912107324

42703
The Klein Foundation
24200 Chagrin Blvd., Rm. 242
Beachwood, OH 44122 (216) 464-5105
Contact: G. Robert Klein, Chair.

Established in 1979 in OH.
Donor(s): George R. Klein, George R. Klein, Jr.
Financial data (yr. ended 09/30/01): Grants paid, $191,210; assets, $10,654 (M); gifts received, $190,718; expenditures, $193,832; qualifying distributions, $189,862.
Limitations: Giving primarily in Cleveland, OH.
Application information: Application form not required.
Officers: George R. Klein, Chair.; George R. Klein, Jr., Pres.; Marilyn E. Brown, Secy.
EIN: 341288590
Codes: FD2

42704
The Sutowski Foundation
9301 Allen Dr.
Valley View, OH 44125
E-mail: JDelaney@freewaycorp.com
Contact: Judie Scherler-Delaney, V.P.

Established in 1985 in OH.
Donor(s): Walter Sutowski, Sut-Scher, Inc.
Financial data (yr. ended 12/31/01): Grants paid, $190,300; assets, $3,028,125 (M); gifts received, $100,000; expenditures, $211,722; qualifying distributions, $190,300.
Limitations: Applications not accepted. Giving primarily in OH.
Application information: Contributes only to pre-selected organizations.
Officers: Walter Sutowski, Pres.; Judie Scherler-Delaney, V.P. and Secy.; Pat Flynn, Treas.
EIN: 341501376
Codes: FD2

42705
The William M. & A. Cafaro Family Foundation
c/o The Cafaro Co.
2445 Belmont Ave.
Youngstown, OH 44504-0186

Established in 1998 in OH.
Donor(s): Anthony Cafaro.
Financial data (yr. ended 03/31/01): Grants paid, $190,188; assets, $6,970,295 (M); gifts received, $1,869,146; expenditures, $227,845; qualifying distributions, $212,912.
Limitations: Giving limited to OH.
Trustees: Anthony Cafaro, Flora M. Cafaro, Joseph S. Nohra.
EIN: 311550874
Codes: FD2

42706
Cornerstone Foundation
765 Hedgerow Ln.
Cincinnati, OH 45246-4611 (513) 554-1600
Contact: Ronald H. McSwain, Tr.

Established in 1987 in OH.
Donor(s): Ronald H. McSwain.
Financial data (yr. ended 12/31/01): Grants paid, $190,030; assets, $3,322,584 (M); gifts received, $14,483; expenditures, $217,372; qualifying distributions, $189,407.
Limitations: Giving primarily in Cincinnati, OH.
Application information: Giving restricted to inner-city projects among the poor in which board members take an active role.
Trustees: Jason McSwain, Phyllis McSwain, Ronald H. McSwain.
EIN: 311220787
Codes: FD2

42707
Harvey Foundation
(also known as Arthur Harvey Charitable Foundation)
c/o First Financial Bank
300 High St.
Hamilton, OH 45011-6078

Established in 1964 in OH.
Donor(s): Arthur Harvey.
Financial data (yr. ended 10/31/01): Grants paid, $189,161; assets, $3,479,327 (M); gifts received, $525; expenditures, $209,717; qualifying distributions, $188,608.
Limitations: Applications not accepted. Giving primarily in Middletown, OH.
Application information: Contributes only to pre-selected organizations.
Trustees: S.R. Campbell, Willard H. Campbell, Stuart A. Schloss, Jr., First Financial Bank.
EIN: 316053064
Codes: FD2

42708
Laura B. Frick Trust
c/o Wayne County National Bank
P.O. Box 757
Wooster, OH 44691 (330) 264-7111
E-mail: aliggett@wcnb.com
Contact: Arianna Liggett, Trust Off., Wayne County National Bank

Established in 1959 in OH.
Financial data (yr. ended 12/31/01): Grants paid, $188,524; assets, $3,666,231 (M); expenditures, $206,886; qualifying distributions, $194,776.
Limitations: Giving limited to Wayne or Holmes counties, OH.
Application information: Application form required.
Trustee: Wayne County National Bank.
EIN: 346513247
Codes: FD2

42709
Florence Simon Beecher Foundation
c/o Sky Trust, N.A.
P.O. Box 479
Youngstown, OH 44501 (330) 742-7035
Contact: David Sabine, Sr. V.P. and Sr. Trust Off., Sky Trust, N.A.

Established in 1969 in OH.
Donor(s): Florence Simon Beecher.
Financial data (yr. ended 12/31/01): Grants paid, $186,766; assets, $9,028,198 (M); expenditures, $286,911; qualifying distributions, $205,292.
Limitations: Giving limited to Youngstown, OH.
Application information: Application form not required.
Directors: Eleanor Beecher Flad, Erle L. Flad, Ward Beecher Flad, Gregory L. Ridler, J. David Sabine.
Trustee: Sky Trust, N.A.
EIN: 346613413
Codes: FD2

42710
English Family Foundation
(Formerly Walter and Marian English Foundation)
1300 Fountaine Dr.
Columbus, OH 43221-1522 (614) 451-6434
Contact: Ellen W. Julian, Tr.

Established about 1978 in Ohio.
Donor(s): Walter English.

42710—OHIO

Financial data (yr. ended 12/31/01): Grants paid, $186,400; assets, $2,731,812 (M); expenditures, $218,648; qualifying distributions, $186,490.
Limitations: Giving limited to Franklin County, OH.
Application information: Application form not required.
Trustees: Mari W. Deminski, Ellen W. Julian.
EIN: 310921799
Codes: FD2

42711
Ladislas & Vilma Segoe Family Foundation
c/o Lewis G. Gatch
8050 Hosbrook Rd., Ste. 210
Cincinnati, OH 45236 (513) 984-3587
Additional address: c/o David Ellis, 580 Walnut, Cincinnati, OH 45202, tel.: (513) 579-5941

Established in 1991 in OH.
Donor(s): Vilma Segoe.‡
Financial data (yr. ended 12/31/01): Grants paid, $185,000; assets, $3,873,276 (M); expenditures, $301,662; qualifying distributions, $252,621.
Limitations: Giving limited to the greater Cincinnati, OH, area.
Trustees: David W. Ellis III, Lewis G. Gatch.
EIN: 316369499
Codes: FD2

42712
Richard B. Sneed Foundation
715 Hawthorne Dr.
Circleville, OH 43113
Contact: Robert B. Sneed, Pres.

Established in 1998 in MI and OH.
Donor(s): Richard B. Sneed Charitable Trust.
Financial data (yr. ended 12/31/01): Grants paid, $184,300; assets, $1,276,838 (M); gifts received, $232,352; expenditures, $221,510; qualifying distributions, $183,328.
Limitations: Applications not accepted. Giving on a national basis, with emphasis on OH and MO.
Application information: Contributes only to pre-selected organizations.
Officers: Robert B. Sneed, Pres.; Jennifer D. Sneed, V.P.; Richard C. Sneed, Secy.; Nancy S. Sneed, Treas.
EIN: 311627480
Codes: FD2

42713
Joyce and Paul Heiman Foundation
(Formerly Heiman Family Charitable Foundation)
P.O. Box 371805
Cincinnati, OH 45222-1805
Contact: Edward M. Frankel, Treas.

Established in 1994 in OH.
Donor(s): Paul L. Heiman, Joyce E. Heiman.
Financial data (yr. ended 12/31/01): Grants paid, $184,240; assets, $246,608 (M); gifts received, $50,000; expenditures, $185,951; qualifying distributions, $185,701.
Limitations: Applications not accepted.
Application information: Unsolicited requests for funds not accepted.
Officers and Trustees:* Paul L. Heiman,* Pres.; Joyce E. Heiman,* Exec. V.P.; Gary Lee Heiman,* V.P.; Mark J. Heiman,* V.P.; Harry J. Heiman,* Secy.; Edward M. Frankel,* Treas.
EIN: 311423877
Codes: FD2

42714
E. S. & M. L. Jones Charitable Foundation
c/o National City Bank
P.O. Box 94651
Cleveland, OH 44101-4651

Established in 1999 in OH.
Donor(s): Mary L. Jones.‡
Financial data (yr. ended 12/31/01): Grants paid, $183,370; assets, $1,945,588 (M); gifts received, $1,031,085; expenditures, $196,350; qualifying distributions, $189,338.
Limitations: Applications not accepted. Giving primarily in FL.
Application information: Contributes only to pre-selected organizations.
Trustee: National City Bank.
EIN: 341893799
Codes: FD2

42715
Stern Special Fund
(Formerly The Stern Family Charitable Trust)
c/o Ronald Greenfeld, CPA
P.O. Box 221257
Beachwood, OH 44122-0996

Established in 1993 in OH.
Donor(s): Israel Stern.
Financial data (yr. ended 12/31/00): Grants paid, $182,911; assets, $409,014 (M); gifts received, $304,130; expenditures, $185,667; qualifying distributions, $180,630.
Limitations: Applications not accepted. Giving primarily in Cleveland, OH.
Application information: Contributes only to pre-selected organizations.
Trustees: Feige Stern, Israel Stern.
EIN: 341721862
Codes: FD2

42716
Walter W. Bettinger, II Foundation
c/o Walter W. Bettinger II
3551 W. Galloway Dr.
Richfield, OH 44286

Established in 1999 in OH.
Donor(s): Walter W. Bettinger II, James McCool.
Financial data (yr. ended 12/31/00): Grants paid, $181,670; assets, $550,643 (M); gifts received, $115,500; expenditures, $192,594; qualifying distributions, $181,639.
Limitations: Applications not accepted. Giving primarily in OH.
Application information: Contributes only to pre-selected organizations.
Officer: Walter W. Bettinger II, Pres. and Secy.-Treas.
Trustee: James McCool.
EIN: 341907847
Codes: FD2

42717
Sandusky/Erie County Community Foundation
165 E. Washington Row, Ste. 304
Sandusky, OH 44870 (419) 621-9690
FAX: (419) 621-9691; E-mail: info@sanduskyfound.com; URL: http://www.sanduskyfoundation.org
Contact: Dee Leibersberger, Pres.

Established in 1996 in OH.
Financial data (yr. ended 12/31/01): Grants paid, $181,550; assets, $8,272,805 (M); gifts received, $2,422,375; expenditures, $339,508.
Limitations: Giving primarily in Erie County, OH.
Publications: Annual report, informational brochure (including application guidelines), financial statement, grants list, newsletter, occasional report, application guidelines.

Application information: Application form required.
Officers and Directors:* John O. Bacon,* Chair.; Mary Jane Hill, Vice-Chair.; Dee Leibersberger, Pres.; Mel Stauffer, Secy.; Eugene Koby, Treas.; Laurence Bettcher, George Mylander, Ruth Parker, Charles W. Rainger, and 10 additional directors.
EIN: 341792862
Codes: CM, FD2

42718
John K. Saxman, Jr. Charitable Trust
c/o National City Bank of Pennsylvania
P.O. Box 94651
Cleveland, OH 44101-4651

Established in 1989 in PA.
Financial data (yr. ended 12/31/01): Grants paid, $181,430; assets, $3,609,433 (M); expenditures, $212,736; qualifying distributions, $195,450.
Limitations: Applications not accepted. Giving primarily in PA.
Application information: Contributes only to pre-selected organizations. Unsolicited requests for funds not accepted.
Trustee: National City Bank of Pennsylvania.
EIN: 256577111
Codes: FD2

42719
The Davey Company Foundation
1500 N. Mantua St.
P.O. Box 5193
Kent, OH 44240-5193 (330) 673-9511
FAX: (330) 673-7089
Contact: Marjorie L. Conner, Secy.

Established in 1957 in OH.
Donor(s): The Davey Tree Expert Co.
Financial data (yr. ended 12/31/00): Grants paid, $180,708; assets, $1,025,040 (M); gifts received, $50,000; expenditures, $201,375; qualifying distributions, $180,708.
Limitations: Giving primarily in the U.S.; some giving also in Canada.
Application information: Scholarship grants made only to students who are children of employees of the Davey Tree Expert Co. and who have academic qualifications and financial need. Application form not required.
Officers: R. Douglas Cowan, Pres.; Howard Bowles, V.P.; C. Kenneth Celmer, V.P.; Roger C. Funk, V.P.; Richard Ramsey, V.P.; Karl J. Warnke, V.P.; Marjorie L. Conner, Secy.; David E. Adante, Treas.
EIN: 346555132
Codes: CS, FD2, CD

42720
The Troy Foundation
c/o U.S. Bank Building
910 W. Main St.
Troy, OH 45373 (937) 335-8513
FAX: (937) 332-8305; E-mail: info@thetroyfoundation.org
Contact: Melissa A. Kleptz, Exec. Dir.

Established in 1924 in OH by bank resolution and declaration of trust.
Donor(s): Nannie Kendall,‡ A.G. Stouder,‡ J.M. Spencer.‡
Financial data (yr. ended 12/31/01): Grants paid, $180,599; assets, $36,983,960 (M); gifts received, $2,124,741; expenditures, $3,091,932.
Limitations: Giving limited to the Troy City, OH, School District.
Publications: Annual report, informational brochure (including application guidelines), application guidelines, informational brochure.

Application information: Application form required.
Trustees: Thomas B. Atikinson, R. Daniel Sadlier, Ronald B. Scott.
Distribution Committee: Cindy Meeker, Chair.; Steve M. Baker, Elizabeth A. Earhart, Arthur D. Haddad, Joan C. Heidelburg.
EIN: 316018703
Codes: CM, FD2

42721
Dr. R. S. Hosler Memorial Educational Fund
P.O. Box 5
Ashville, OH 43103-0005 (740) 983-2557
Application address: 50 Bortz St., Ashville, OH 43103
Contact: Leo J. Hall, Tr.

Established in 1982 in OH.
Financial data (yr. ended 12/31/01): Grants paid, $180,426; assets, $4,679,735 (M); expenditures, $276,268; qualifying distributions, $223,191.
Limitations: Giving limited to graduates of Teays Valley and Amanda Clearcreek, OH, high schools.
Application information: Scholarship application available upon request. Application form required.
Trustee: Leo J. Hall.
EIN: 311073939
Codes: FD2, GTI

42722
Kathryn & Vishnoo Shahani Charitable Trust
1217 Beechwood Dr.
Wyoming, OH 45215-2011

Established in 1996 in OH.
Donor(s): Kathryn Shahani, Vishnoo Shahani.
Financial data (yr. ended 12/31/99): Grants paid, $178,004; assets, $345,107 (M); gifts received, $500; expenditures, $180,511; qualifying distributions, $179,533.
Limitations: Applications not accepted.
Application information: Contributes only to pre-selected organizations.
Trustees: Kathryn Shahani, Vishnoo Shahani.
EIN: 311486562
Codes: FD2

42723
The Sauerland Foundation
P.O. Box 621
Chagrin Falls, OH 44022
Contact: Franz L. Sauerland, Tr.

Established in 1994 in OH.
Donor(s): Franz L. Sauerland.
Financial data (yr. ended 12/31/01): Grants paid, $178,000; assets, $3,441,951 (M); expenditures, $180,635; qualifying distributions, $180,082.
Limitations: Giving primarily in OH.
Trustees: Elizabeth I. Sauerland, Franz L. Sauerland, Paul E. Sauerland.
EIN: 341787952
Codes: FD2

42724
The Cyrus Eaton Foundation
24200 Chagrin Blvd., Ste. 233
Beachwood, OH 44122-5531 (216) 360-9550
URL: http://www.deepcove.org
Contact: Henry W. Gulick, Treas.

Established in 1955 in DE.
Financial data (yr. ended 12/31/01): Grants paid, $177,300; assets, $3,702,842 (M); expenditures, $255,935; qualifying distributions, $203,022.
Limitations: Giving primarily in OH, with emphasis on Cleveland.
Application information: Application form required.

Officers and Trustees:* Raymond Szabo,* Pres.; Mary Stephens Eaton,* V.P.; Alice J. Gulick,* V.P.; Ralph P. Higgins,* Secy.; Henry W. Gulick,* Treas.; Barring Coughlin, Catherine I. Eaton.
EIN: 237440277
Codes: FD2

42725
Spencer Education Foundation
(Formerly George and Marie G. Spencer Education Foundation and Trust)
c/o National City Bank of Indiana
P.O. Box 94651
Cleveland, OH 44101-4651
Scholarship application addresses: c/o Tipton High School, 619 S. Main St., Tipton, IN 46072, tel.: (765) 675-7431, c/o Tri-Central High School, R.R. No. 2, Sharpesville, IN 46068, tel.: (765) 963-2560

Established in 1967 in IN.
Financial data (yr. ended 12/31/00): Grants paid, $175,748; assets, $4,229,703 (M); expenditures, $199,048; qualifying distributions, $185,682.
Limitations: Giving limited to residents of Tipton County, IN.
Application information: Application form required.
Trustee: National City Bank of Indiana.
EIN: 356072759
Codes: FD2, GTI

42726
The William H. Albers Foundation, Inc.
P.O. Box 58360
Cincinnati, OH 45258-0360
Contact: Board of Trustees

Incorporated in 1982 in OH.
Donor(s): J.H. Dornheggen,‡ Irene A. Dornheggen.‡
Financial data (yr. ended 04/30/01): Grants paid, $175,200; assets, $2,824,416 (M); expenditures, $202,098; qualifying distributions, $175,727.
Limitations: Giving primarily in Cincinnati, OH.
Application information: Application form not required.
Officers and Trustees:* Timothy J. Leonard,* Pres.; Luke J. Leonard,* V.P.; Anna M.D. Kallaher,* Secy.-Treas.; Daniel Bonn, David Dornheggen, J. Harry Dornheggen, Jill Leonard.
EIN: 316023881
Codes: FD2

42727
The Edwards Foundation, Inc.
(Formerly J. T. Edwards Company Foundation)
c/o Edwards Industries, Inc.
495 S. High St., Ste. 150
Columbus, OH 43215

Established in 1964 in OH.
Donor(s): Edwards Industries, Inc., Ross Willoughby Co., Edwards Insulation, Duffy Homes, Swan Manufacturing Co., Mooney and Moses of Ohio, Inc.
Financial data (yr. ended 06/30/01): Grants paid, $175,175; assets, $27,567 (M); gifts received, $138,516; expenditures, $177,444; qualifying distributions, $177,444.
Limitations: Applications not accepted. Giving primarily in OH, with emphasis on Columbus.
Application information: Contributes only to pre-selected organizations.
Officer: John A. Leibold, Treas.
Trustees: Paula Cochran, Jeffrey W. Edwards, Peter H. Edwards, Sr., Judith Sandbo.
EIN: 237447588
Codes: CS, FD2, CD

42728
Salem Lutheran Foundation
750 Northlawn Dr.
Columbus, OH 43214 (614) 863-3124
Contact: Rev. Marc Schroeder, Tr.

Established in 1968 in OH.
Donor(s): Homewood Corp., George A. Skestos.
Financial data (yr. ended 12/31/00): Grants paid, $175,150; assets, $4,274,555 (M); expenditures, $190,036; qualifying distributions, $179,459.
Limitations: Giving on a national basis.
Application information: Application form required.
Officers and Trustees:* George A., Skestos, Pres.; Terrie Rice, Secy.; John Bain,* Treas.; Rev. Marc Schroeder, Andrew Schut.
EIN: 316084166
Codes: CS, FD2, CD, GTI

42729
The Oliver Family Foundation
c/o Fifth Third Bank
38 Fountain Sq. Plz. MD 1090L7
Cincinnati, OH 45263-3191 (513) 579-6034
Contact: Lawra Baumann, Fdn. Off., Fifth Third Bank

Established in 1992 in OH.
Donor(s): Gertrude M. Oliver, Richard D. Oliver.
Financial data (yr. ended 12/31/01): Grants paid, $175,000; assets, $3,684,048 (M); gifts received, $74,684; expenditures, $208,576; qualifying distributions, $182,737.
Limitations: Giving primarily in Cincinnati, OH.
Trustees: Vere W. Gaynor, John J. Kropp, Gertrude M. Oliver, John C. Oliver, Richard D. Oliver, Fifth Third Bank.
EIN: 311365209
Codes: FD2

42730
The O'Brien-VRBA Scholarship Trust
c/o National City Bank
P.O. Box 94651
Cleveland, OH 44101-4651
Application addresses: c/o National City Bank, Attn: Jo Ann Harlen, P.O. Box 749, Peoria, IL 61110-0128, tel.: (815) 987-2014, or c/o NC Illinois Trust Co., 120 West Slate St., Rockford, IL 61110-0128, tel.: (815) 987-2104

Established in 1991.
Financial data (yr. ended 12/31/01): Grants paid, $174,000; assets, $4,069,026 (M); expenditures, $215,879; qualifying distributions, $191,127.
Limitations: Giving primarily to residents of IA, IL, IN, MI, and WI.
Application information: Application form required for scholarship program. Application form required.
Trustee: National City Bank.
EIN: 376277500
Codes: FD2

42731
The Rockwern Charitable Foundation
30 Garfield Pl., Ste. 1030
Cincinnati, OH 45202-4322
Contact: Benjamin Gettler, Tr.

Established in 1998 in OH.
Donor(s): S. Sumner Rockwern.‡
Financial data (yr. ended 05/31/02): Grants paid, $173,339; assets, $8,376,850 (M); gifts received, $134,566; expenditures, $355,715; qualifying distributions, $173,339.
Limitations: Giving primarily in Cincinnati, OH.
Trustees: Stephanie R. Amlung, Benjamin Gettler, Gloria S. Haffer.
EIN: 311590504

42731—OHIO

Codes: FD2

42732
Margaret and Irwin Lesher Foundation
c/o National City Bank of Pennsylvania, Trust Tax
P.O. Box 94651
Cleveland, OH 44101-4651
Application address: 35 Fisher Ave., Oil City, PA 16301, tel: (814) 677-5085
Contact: Stephen P. Kosak, Consultant

Trust established in 1963 in PA.
Donor(s): Margaret W. Lesher.‡
Financial data (yr. ended 12/31/01): Grants paid, $170,950; assets, $3,118,747 (M); expenditures, $202,442; qualifying distributions, $188,735.
Limitations: Giving limited to Union Joint School District of Clarion County, PA.
Publications: Application guidelines.
Application information: Application form required.
Trustee: National City Bank of Pennsylvania.
EIN: 256067843
Codes: FD2, GTI

42733
Gretel B. Bloch Charitable Trust
5910 Landerbrook Dr., Ste. 200
Mayfield Heights, OH 44124
Contact: Sanford Shore, Tr.

Established in 1988 in OH.
Financial data (yr. ended 12/31/01): Grants paid, $170,083; assets, $1,828,850 (M); expenditures, $201,126; qualifying distributions, $168,564.
Limitations: Giving primarily in OH.
Trustee: Sanford Shore.
EIN: 316566082
Codes: FD2

42734
Fibus Family Foundation
190 N. Meridian Rd.
Youngstown, OH 44509

Established in 1982.
Donor(s): Steel City Corp., C. Kenneth Fibus, M. Fibus,‡ Dinesol Plastics, Inc.
Financial data (yr. ended 05/31/01): Grants paid, $169,708; assets, $1,420,470 (M); gifts received, $147,000; expenditures, $192,481; qualifying distributions, $169,485.
Limitations: Applications not accepted. Giving limited to Youngstown, OH.
Application information: Contributes only to pre-selected organizations.
Trustees: C. Kenneth Fibus, Stuart A. Strasfeld, Robert Wagmiller.
EIN: 341340458
Codes: FD2

42735
Pysht Foundation
(Formerly Weller Charitable Trust)
c/o Charles Weller
12521 Lake Shore Blvd.
Bratenahl, OH 44108

Established in 1996 in OH.
Financial data (yr. ended 12/31/00): Grants paid, $169,574; assets, $379,480 (M); expenditures, $174,247; qualifying distributions, $169,502.
Limitations: Applications not accepted. Giving primarily in Cleveland, OH.
Application information: Contributes only to pre-selected organizations.
Trustees: Charles Weller, Lucy Ireland Weller.
EIN: 311549202
Codes: FD2

42736
Baird Brothers Company Foundation
c/o The Huntington National Bank
P.O. Box 1558
Columbus, OH 43216 (614) 480-5453
Application address: 41 S. High St., Columbus, OH 43215
Contact: Donna Auten, V.P., The Huntington National Bank

Established in 1977 in OH.
Donor(s): Baird Bros. Company.
Financial data (yr. ended 06/30/01): Grants paid, $169,561; assets, $3,988,811 (M); expenditures, $215,333; qualifying distributions, $181,343.
Limitations: Giving limited to Nelsonville, OH.
Application information: Application form not required.
Directors: David S. Fraedrich, Jane E. Harmony, Wilbert W. Warren.
Trustee: The Huntington National Bank.
EIN: 316194844
Codes: CS, FD2

42737
Hubert A. & Gladys C. Estabrook Charitable Trust
c/o Bruce Snyder
P.O. Box 1805
Dayton, OH 45401-1805

Established in 1977 in OH.
Donor(s): Gladys C. Estabrook Charitable Remainder Unitrust.
Financial data (yr. ended 03/31/02): Grants paid, $169,398; assets, $3,018,114 (M); expenditures, $207,694; qualifying distributions, $178,725.
Limitations: Applications not accepted. Giving limited to OH, with an emphasis on Dayton.
Application information: Contributes only to pre-selected organizations.
Trustee: R. Bruce Snyder.
EIN: 310909737
Codes: FD2

42738
Joseph H. Thompson Fund
c/o C.E. Bartter, C.P.A.
440 Old Reservoir Rd.
Berea, OH 44017-2561

Incorporated in 1957 in OH.
Donor(s): Joseph H. Thompson.
Financial data (yr. ended 12/31/01): Grants paid, $169,250; assets, $2,710,195 (M); expenditures, $192,121; qualifying distributions, $180,686.
Limitations: Applications not accepted. Giving on a national basis.
Application information: Contributes only to pre-selected organizations.
Officers and Trustees:* Catherine Clark Shopneck,* Pres.; Robert A. Toepfer,* V.P. and Secy.; Elizabeth N. Armstrong,* V.P. and Treas.; Lacey Neuhaus Dorn,* V.P.; William J. Clark, Jr., Joan T. Neuhaus, Mary Clark Talbot.
EIN: 346520252
Codes: FD2

42739
Virginia Gay Fund
c/o National City Bank, Columbus
P.O. Box 94651
Cleveland, OH 44101-4651
Application address: 750 Brooksedge Blvd., Ste. 104, Westerville, OH 43081

Established in 1914 in OH.
Financial data (yr. ended 12/31/00): Grants paid, $168,528; assets, $2,234,009 (M); expenditures, $185,634; qualifying distributions, $168,000.
Limitations: Giving limited to OH.
Application information: Application form required.
Officers: George D. Norris, Pres.; L.D. Shuter, Pres. Emeritus; Orin E. Morris, V.P.; Joseph Endry, Secy.-Treas.
Trustees: Marjorie Ater, Mary Ellen Meredith, J. Richard Zimmerman.
EIN: 314379588
Codes: FD2, GTI

42740
Sightless Children Club, Inc.
3700 Braddock St.
Dayton, OH 45420 (937) 426-2538
E-mail: vagabriel@frognet.net or MFLOHRE@prodigy.net; *URL:* http://www.words.org/scc/index.html
Contact: Randy Phipps, Treas.

Established in 1958 in OH.
Financial data (yr. ended 10/31/01): Grants paid, $168,513; assets, $2,560,771 (M); gifts received, $300; expenditures, $762,892; qualifying distributions, $73,115.
Limitations: Giving limited to the Dayton, OH, area.
Publications: Informational brochure (including application guidelines), newsletter.
Application information: Application form required.
Officer: Randy Phipps, Treas.
Directors: Joyce Culbertson, Harvey Schroeder.
EIN: 316006092
Codes: FD2, GTI

42741
The Louise and Leonard Fletcher Foundation
c/o National City Bank
P.O. Box 94651
Cleveland, OH 44101-4651

Established in 1991 in OH.
Donor(s): Leonard H. Fletcher, Louise A. Fletcher.
Financial data (yr. ended 11/30/01): Grants paid, $168,000; assets, $2,793,780 (M); expenditures, $186,260; qualifying distributions, $174,857.
Limitations: Applications not accepted. Giving primarily in OH.
Application information: Contributes only to pre-selected organizations.
Trustees: Susan K. Salo, National City Bank.
EIN: 341694479
Codes: FD2

42742
Christopher Foundation
100 7th Ave., Ste. 150
Chardon, OH 44024-1067 (440) 285-2242
Contact: Paul J. Dolan, Secy.

Established in 1952 in OH.
Financial data (yr. ended 12/31/01): Grants paid, $167,756; assets, $18,946 (M); expenditures, $171,466; qualifying distributions, $167,756.
Limitations: Giving primarily in OH.
Application information: Application form not required.
Officer: Paul J. Dolan, Secy.
Trustees: Lou Alexander, Helen Dolan, Smith Barney, Inc.
EIN: 340961579

42743
Ohio Savings Association Charitable Foundation
1801 E. 9th St., No. 200
Cleveland, OH 44114

Established around 1970.
Donor(s): Ohio Savings Bank.
Financial data (yr. ended 11/30/01): Grants paid, $167,217; assets, $3,437,211 (M); gifts received,

$250,000; expenditures, $167,597; qualifying distributions, $167,027.
Limitations: Applications not accepted. Giving primarily in Cleveland, OH.
Application information: Contributes only to pre-selected organizations.
Officer: Robert Goldberg, Chair.
Trustee: David Goldberg.
EIN: 237055858
Codes: CS, FD2, CD

42744
The Harry Stensen Memorial Trust Fund
c/o KeyBank, N.A.
P.O. Box 10099
Toledo, OH 43699-0099 (419) 259-8655
Contact: Diane H. Ohns, V.P., KeyBank, N.A.

Established in 1986 in OH.
Financial data (yr. ended 05/31/01): Grants paid, $166,835; assets, $3,124,770 (M); expenditures, $183,639; qualifying distributions, $169,139.
Limitations: Giving limited to the Port Clinton, OH, area.
Application information: Information available upon request.
Trustee: KeyBank, N.A.
EIN: 346619471
Codes: FD2

42745
Ann McConahay Educational Foundation
c/o United National Bank & Trust Co., Trust Dept.
P.O. Box 24190
Canton, OH 44701
Application address: c/o Guidance Counselor, Alliance High School, Alliance, OH 44601

Established in 1987 in OH.
Financial data (yr. ended 12/31/01): Grants paid, $166,223; assets, $1,655,195 (M); expenditures, $182,720; qualifying distributions, $170,486.
Limitations: Giving limited to Alliance, OH.
Application information: Recipients must be enrolled at Alliance High School and selection is made at the discretion of the trustees. Application form required.
Officers and Trustees:* Marjorie Brainard,* Pres.; Mark Henschen,* V.P.; Michael Hoover,* V.P.
EIN: 341550065
Codes: FD2, GTI

42746
Charles Moerlein Foundation
c/o Fifth Third Bank
38 Fountain Sq., MD 10927
Cincinnati, OH 45263 (513) 534-7001
Contact: Lawra J. Baumann, Fdn. Off., Fifth Third Bank

Established in 1966 in OH.
Donor(s): Charles Moerlein.‡
Financial data (yr. ended 09/30/01): Grants paid, $166,000; assets, $2,349,530 (M); expenditures, $206,537; qualifying distributions, $176,290.
Limitations: Giving limited to the greater Cincinnati, OH, area.
Publications: Annual report, application guidelines.
Application information: Application form not required.
Trustee: Fifth Third Bank.
EIN: 316020341
Codes: FD2

42747
Mirapaul Foundation
1687 Brookwood Dr.
Akron, OH 44313
Application address: 411 Wolf Ledges, Ste. 301B, Akron, OH 44311
Contact: Walter Mirapaul, Tr.

Established in 1988 in OH.
Donor(s): Members of the Mirapaul family.
Financial data (yr. ended 09/30/01): Grants paid, $165,128; assets, $2,759,966 (M); gifts received, $17,558; expenditures, $178,539; qualifying distributions, $162,736.
Limitations: Giving primarily in IL, OH, and PA.
Trustees: Evan D. Mirapaul, Matthew B. Mirapaul, Walter N. Mirapaul.
EIN: 341602913
Codes: FD2

42748
Skyler Foundation
780 Ivy Ln.
Cincinnati, OH 45246
E-mail: schiff@one.net
Contact: Marguerite Gieseke, Tr.

Established in 1994 in OH.
Donor(s): John J. Schiff, Jr.
Financial data (yr. ended 09/30/01): Grants paid, $165,000; assets, $5,036,459 (M); gifts received, $414,688; expenditures, $165,225; qualifying distributions, $165,000.
Limitations: Applications not accepted. Giving primarily in Cincinnati, OH.
Application information: Unsolicited requests for funds not accepted.
Trustees: Marguerite Gieske, Charles O. Schiff, John J. Schiff III.
EIN: 311420623
Codes: FD2

42749
The Wolfe Family Charitable Foundation
c/o Health Care Peit, Inc.
1 Seagate, Ste. 1960
Toledo, OH 43603-2165

Established in 1993.
Donor(s): Frederic D. Wolfe.
Financial data (yr. ended 12/31/99): Grants paid, $164,196; assets, $1,223,820 (M); gifts received, $655; expenditures, $172,198; qualifying distributions, $164,196.
Limitations: Applications not accepted. Giving primarily in OH.
Application information: Contributes only to pre-selected organizations.
Trustees: James M. Morton, Jr., Elizabeth T. Wolfe, Frederic D. Wolfe, Mary T. Wolfe.
EIN: 341756997
Codes: FD2

42750
The MLM Charitable Foundation
3131 Executive Pkwy., No. 102
Toledo, OH 43606-1327

Established in 1967 in OH.
Donor(s): Charles A. McKenny,‡ Mary L. McKenny.
Financial data (yr. ended 12/31/01): Grants paid, $164,120; assets, $5,206,881 (M); gifts received, $369,734; expenditures, $195,688; qualifying distributions, $164,120.
Limitations: Applications not accepted. Giving primarily in MI, NY, and OH.
Application information: Contributes only to pre-selected organizations.
Officers: Mary L. McKenny, Pres. and Treas.; Anne E. McKenny, V.P. and Secy.
Trustees: Ivan Kurtz, Arthur E. McKenny, Thomas C. McKenny.
EIN: 341018519
Codes: FD2

42751
Kenridge Fund
c/o Advisory Svcs., Inc.
1422 Euclid Ave., 1010 Hanna Bldg.
Cleveland, OH 44115-2078
Contact: Jackie Horning, Treas.

Established in 1989 in OH as partial successor to Bolton Foundation.
Donor(s): Fanny H. Bolton, Claire H.B. Jonklaas.
Financial data (yr. ended 12/31/01): Grants paid, $164,000; assets, $3,741,622 (M); expenditures, $207,660; qualifying distributions, $174,829.
Application information: Application form not required.
Officers and Trustees:* Claire H.B. Jonklaas,* Pres.; Kenneth G. Hochman,* V.P.; Paulette Kitko, Secy.; J.A. Horning, Treas.; Claire Hanna Buckley, Anthony Jonklaas.
EIN: 341616683
Codes: FD2

42752
The Simmons Charitable Trust
c/o National City Bank
P.O. Box 450
Youngstown, OH 44501-0450 (330) 742-4289
Contact: Myra L. Vitto

Established in 1977 in OH.
Financial data (yr. ended 05/31/01): Grants paid, $163,758; assets, $3,101,655 (M); expenditures, $180,726; qualifying distributions, $169,186.
Limitations: Giving primarily in Jefferson County, OH, with emphasis on Steubenville.
Application information: Application form not required.
Trustee: National City Trust Co.
EIN: 346743541
Codes: FD2, GTI

42753
Charles O'Bleness Foundation No. 3
c/o The Huntington National Bank, Trust Dept.
P.O. Box 1558 HC-0534
Columbus, OH 43216
Application address: Donna Auten, V.P. c/o The Huntington National Bank, 41 S. High St., Columbus, OH 43215, tel.: (614) 480-5453

Established in 1963 in OH.
Donor(s): Charles O'Bleness,‡ Charles O'Bleness Foundation No. 1.
Financial data (yr. ended 06/30/01): Grants paid, $163,652; assets, $3,566,394 (M); expenditures, $195,176; qualifying distributions, $170,542.
Limitations: Giving limited to Athens County, OH.
Application information: Application form not required.
Advisors: John M. Jones, David Vogt.
Trustee: The Huntington National Bank.
EIN: 316042978
Codes: FD2

42754
Richard J. Fitton Family Foundation
c/o First Financial Bank
300 High St.
Hamilton, OH 45011

Established in 1999 in OH.
Donor(s): Richard J. Fitton.
Financial data (yr. ended 12/31/01): Grants paid, $163,500; assets, $1,804 (M); gifts received, $75; expenditures, $165,720; qualifying distributions, $162,997.

42754

Limitations: Applications not accepted. Giving primarily in OH.
Application information: Contributes only to pre-selected organizations.
Trustee: First Financial Bank.
EIN: 311653186
Codes: FD2

42755
Gilbert W. & Louise Ireland Humphrey Foundation
1422 Euclid Ave., Ste. 1030
Cleveland, OH 44115-2004 (216) 363-1033
Contact: Louise Ireland Humphrey, Pres.

Incorporated in 1951 in OH.
Donor(s): Gilbert W. Humphrey,‡ Louise Ireland Humphrey.
Financial data (yr. ended 12/31/01): Grants paid, $163,200; assets, $1,742,656 (M); gifts received, $43,022; expenditures, $175,438; qualifying distributions, $162,431.
Limitations: Giving primarily in OH.
Application information: Funds committed to the same charities each year; foundation rarely considers new appeals. Application form not required.
Officers and Trustees:* Louise Ireland Humphrey,* Pres.; Margaret H. Bindhardt,* V.P.; Carole M. Nowak,* Secy.; George M. Humphrey II,* Treas.
EIN: 346525832
Codes: FD2

42756
The Abner and Esther Yoder Charitable Foundation
P.O. Box 80469
Canton, OH 44708-0469
Contact: Esther Yoder, Secy.

Established in 1991 in OH.
Donor(s): Stark Truss Co., Inc.
Financial data (yr. ended 12/31/01): Grants paid, $163,200; assets, $230,191 (M); gifts received, $150,000; expenditures, $164,366; qualifying distributions, $163,200.
Limitations: Giving primarily in OH, OK, and TX.
Application information: Application form not required.
Officers: Abner Yoder, Pres.; Esther Yoder, Secy.; Wendy Jo Spillman, Treas.
EIN: 341677646
Codes: FD2

42757
Zaring Family Foundation
c/o PNC Bank, N.A.
P.O. Box 1198
Cincinnati, OH 45201-1198 (513) 651-8377
Contact: Lee Crooks, Fdn. Admin.

Established in 1992 in OH.
Donor(s): Allen G. Zaring III.
Financial data (yr. ended 12/31/01): Grants paid, $162,690; assets, $2,802,972 (M); expenditures, $178,272; qualifying distributions, $163,671.
Limitations: Applications not accepted. Giving limited to New York, NY, and to Cincinnati, OH.
Application information: Contributes only to pre-selected organizations.
Officers and Trustees:* Anne M. Zaring, Pres.; Mark Zaring,* 1st V.P.; Heather Zaring Vecellio,* 2nd V.P.; Allen G. Zaring III,* Secy.; Allen G. Zaring IV,* Treas.; Martin E. Mooney, Andrew Vecellio.
Agent: PNC Bank, N.A.
EIN: 311354230
Codes: FD2

42758
YSI Foundation, Inc.
P.O. Box 279
Yellow Springs, OH 45387 (937) 767-7241
E-mail: dturner@ysi.com
Contact: Deb Stottlemyer, Treas.

Established in 1990 in OH.
Donor(s): YSI Inc.
Financial data (yr. ended 12/31/01): Grants paid, $161,975; assets, $31,578 (M); gifts received, $185,000; expenditures, $163,225; qualifying distributions, $161,975.
Limitations: Giving primarily in OH.
Publications: Informational brochure, application guidelines.
Application information: Application form not required.
Officers: Sarah Harris, Chair.; Susan Miller, Secy.; Deb Stottlemyer, Treas.
EIN: 311292180
Codes: CS, FD2, CD

42759
The Cardinal Foundation
3055 Kettering Blvd., Ste. 310
Dayton, OH 45439

Established in 1998 in OH.
Donor(s): Thomas D. MacLeod.
Financial data (yr. ended 11/30/00): Grants paid, $160,750; assets, $3,322,036 (M); gifts received, $3,713,462; expenditures, $223,854; qualifying distributions, $143,361.
Limitations: Applications not accepted.
Application information: Contributes only to pre-selected organizations.
Officers and Trustees:* Thomas D. MacLeod, Pres.; William J. Leibold,* Secy.; Barbara B. MacLeod.
EIN: 311681353

42760
M. J. Zahniser Memorial Trust
c/o National City Bank
P.O. Box 94651
Cleveland, OH 44101-4651

Financial data (yr. ended 12/31/00): Grants paid, $160,000; assets, $3,565,934 (M); expenditures, $194,252; qualifying distributions, $175,944.
Limitations: Applications not accepted.
Application information: Contributes only to pre-selected organizations.
Trustee: National City Bank.
EIN: 256231572

42761
M. J. Zanhniser Memorial Trust
c/o National City Bank
P.O. Box 94651
Cleveland, OH 44101-4651

Established in 2000 in PA.
Financial data (yr. ended 12/31/01): Grants paid, $160,000; assets, $3,043,084 (M); expenditures, $205,716; qualifying distributions, $172,664.
Limitations: Applications not accepted. Giving primarily in OH.
Application information: Contributes only to pre-selected organizations.
Trustee: National City Bank.
EIN: 341961084
Codes: FD2

42762
William Dauch Foundation
(Formerly Believers Foundation)
1570 Dutch Hollow Rd.
Lima, OH 45807 (419) 339-4441
Contact: Thomas E. Brown, Pres.

Established in 1986 in OH.
Donor(s): Gladys Dauch, Thomas E. Brown, Marilyn Brown, Brown Supply Co.
Financial data (yr. ended 12/31/01): Grants paid, $159,450; assets, $4,702,937 (M); gifts received, $64,445; expenditures, $362,502; qualifying distributions, $159,450.
Limitations: Giving on a national and international basis, with emphasis on Canada, the Philippines, Korea, South Africa, and India.
Officers and Trustees:* Thomas E. Brown,* Pres.; Marilyn Brown,* Secy.; Debra Grant,* Treas.; Tamara Brown LeRoux.
EIN: 341516486
Codes: FD2

42763
The Roberts Foundation
124 Forrer Rd.
Dayton, OH 45419

Established in 1985 in OH.
Donor(s): Burnell R. Roberts.
Financial data (yr. ended 11/30/01): Grants paid, $159,000; assets, $2,097,533 (M); gifts received, $17,667; expenditures, $207,133; qualifying distributions, $196,539.
Limitations: Applications not accepted. Giving primarily in OH.
Application information: Contributes only to pre-selected organizations.
Trustees: Richard F. Carlile, Burnell R. Roberts, Karen Ragatz Roberts.
EIN: 316299228
Codes: FD2

42764
Justin F. Coressel Charitable Trust
101 Clinton St., Ste. 2000
Defiance, OH 43512
Application address: 500 E. High St., Defiance, OH 43512, tel.: (419) 782-6677
Contact: Justin F. Coressel, Dir.

Established around 1969.
Donor(s): Justin F. Coressel.
Financial data (yr. ended 12/31/01): Grants paid, $157,100; assets, $2,994,116 (M); expenditures, $156,435; qualifying distributions, $155,143.
Limitations: Giving primarily in Defiance, OH.
Application information: Application form not required.
Director: Justin F. Coressel.
Trustees: Mark Hench, Terry L. Melton, Paul L. Moser.
EIN: 237022234
Codes: FD2

42765
The V. C. Campanella Family Charitable Trust
c/o Phillip J. Campanella
800 Superior Ave., Ste. 1400
Cleveland, OH 44114

Established in 1999 in OH.
Donor(s): Vincent C. Campanella.
Financial data (yr. ended 12/31/01): Grants paid, $157,000; assets, $1,196,673 (M); expenditures, $171,568; qualifying distributions, $157,000.
Trustees: Phillip J. Campanella, Vincent C. Campanella, William R. Plato.
EIN: 341906131

42766
Lori Schottenstein Foundation
1800 Moler Rd.
Columbus, OH 43207-1680

Established in 1997 in OH.
Donor(s): Lori Schottenstein.
Financial data (yr. ended 12/31/00): Grants paid, $156,800; assets, $2,487,968 (M); expenditures, $158,769; qualifying distributions, $158,769.
Limitations: Giving primarily in NY and Columbus, OH.
Officers: Geraldine Schottenstein, Pres.; Jay Schottenstein, V.P.; Susan Diamond, Secy.; Ann Deshe, Treas.
EIN: 311533377
Codes: FD2

42767
The Grace High Washburn Trust
1520 Melody Ln.
Bucyrus, OH 44820
Application address: P.O. Box 389, Bucyrus, OH 44820
Contact: John R. Clime, Secy.-Treas.

Established in 1949 in OH.
Financial data (yr. ended 12/31/01): Grants paid, $156,433; assets, $3,059,545 (M); expenditures, $169,381; qualifying distributions, $159,338.
Limitations: Giving limited to residents of the Bucyrus, OH, area.
Application information: Provide cover letter with application. Application form required.
Officers: John R. Miller II, Pres.; Donald D. Fishpaw, V.P.; John R. Clime, Secy.-Treas.
EIN: 346521078
Codes: FD2, GTI

42768
The Brian H. & Jill R. Rowe Family Foundation
c/o Fifth Third Bank
38 Fountain Sq. Plz., MD 1090L7
Cincinnati, OH 45263
Contact: Lawra Baumann, Trust Off., Fifth Third Bank

Established in 1994 in OH.
Financial data (yr. ended 12/31/01): Grants paid, $156,000; assets, $1,523,380 (M); gifts received, $663; expenditures, $170,242; qualifying distributions, $154,423.
Limitations: Giving primarily in Cincinnati, OH.
Trustee: Fifth Third Bank.
EIN: 311425728
Codes: FD2

42769
Glenn R. and Alice V. Boggess Memorial Foundation
c/o FirstMerit Bank, N.A.
121 S. Main St., Ste. 200
Akron, OH 44308-1440 (330) 384-7320
FAX: (330) 849-8992; E-mail: bjmobray@firstmerit.com
Contact: Ronald B. Tynan, V.P. and Tr. Off., FirstMerit Bank, N.A.

Established in 1988 in OH.
Donor(s): Alice V. Boggess.‡
Financial data (yr. ended 12/31/01): Grants paid, $155,400; assets, $2,398,855 (M); expenditures, $183,921; qualifying distributions, $160,082.
Limitations: Giving limited to Summit County, OH.
Application information: Application form not required.
Distribution Committee: Joel R. Aberth, Donald A. Brott, Ronald B. Tynan, Sr.
EIN: 346890256
Codes: FD2

42770
Dudley Taft Charitable Foundation
c/o Fifth Third Bank
38 Fountain Sq. Plz., MD 1090 C8
Cincinnati, OH 45263
Additional address: 312 Walnut St., Ste. 3550, Cincinnati, OH 45202
Contact: Dudley Taft, Pres.

Established in 1997 in OH.
Financial data (yr. ended 12/31/01): Grants paid, $155,060; assets, $2,157,999 (M); expenditures, $166,408; qualifying distributions, $155,091.
Limitations: Giving primarily in the greater Cincinnati, OH, area.
Officers: Dudley S. Taft, Pres.; David A. Kohnen, Secy.; Lee A. Carter, Treas.
Agent: Fifth Third Bank.
EIN: 311532283
Codes: FD2

42771
Dale Jr. & Elizabeth McMillen Foundation
c/o National City Bank of Indiana
P.O. Box 94651
Cleveland, OH 44101-4651
Application address: c/o Michele Delaney, P.O. Box 110, Fort Wayne, IN 46801, tel.: (219) 461-6199

Established in 1962 in IN.
Financial data (yr. ended 12/31/01): Grants paid, $155,000; assets, $2,768,868 (M); expenditures, $170,128; qualifying distributions, $157,970.
Limitations: Giving primarily in Fort Wayne, IN.
Application information: Application form not required.
Trustee: National City Bank of Indiana.
EIN: 356020615
Codes: FD2

42772
The Otto M. Budig Family Foundation
6705 Wyman La.
Cincinnati, OH 45243-2729 (513) 621-6111
Contact: Otto M. Budig, Jr., Pres.

Established in 1994 in OH.
Donor(s): Otto M. Budig, Jr.
Financial data (yr. ended 12/31/01): Grants paid, $154,494; assets, $639 (M); gifts received, $142,317; expenditures, $154,644; qualifying distributions, $154,492.
Limitations: Giving primarily in Cincinnati, OH.
Publications: Occasional report.
Application information: Application form not required.
Officer and Trustees:* Otto M. Budig, Jr.,* Pres.; David H. Budig, Mark E. Budig, Sandra F. Budig, Julie B. Held.
EIN: 311411132
Codes: FD2

42773
The William O. Purdy, Jr. Foundation
c/o PNC Bank, N.A.
P.O. Box 1198
Cincinnati, OH 45201-1198 (513) 651-8377
Contact: Lee D. Crooks, Fdn. Admin.

Established in 1988 in OH.
Donor(s): William O. Purdy, Jr.‡
Financial data (yr. ended 12/31/01): Grants paid, $154,216; assets, $2,878,868 (M); expenditures, $203,482; qualifying distributions, $160,370.
Limitations: Giving primarily in Cincinnati, OH.
Publications: Application guidelines.
Application information: Application form required.
Trustees: Joseph P. Mellen, Jim S. Wachs, PNC Bank, N.A.

EIN: 311256644
Codes: FD2

42774
Margaret Sage Unitrust
c/o Bank One Ohio Trust Co., N.A.
6 Federal Plaza W.
Youngstown, OH 44503

Established in 1986 in OH.
Financial data (yr. ended 12/31/01): Grants paid, $153,846; assets, $1,383,025 (M); expenditures, $172,982; qualifying distributions, $154,871.
Limitations: Applications not accepted. Giving primarily in PA.
Application information: Contributes only to pre-selected organizations.
Trustee: Bank One Ohio Trust Co., N.A.
EIN: 346854365
Codes: FD2

42775
The O'Neill Brothers Foundation
3550 Lander Rd., Ste. 140
Cleveland, OH 44124
Contact: Robert K. Healey, Pres.

Incorporated in 1953 in MI.
Donor(s): William J. O'Neill,‡ P.J. O'Neill,‡ H.M. O'Neill,‡ Francis J. O'Neill,‡ George C. Fortner,‡ Robert K. Healey, Mrs. Robert K. Healey.
Financial data (yr. ended 12/31/01): Grants paid, $153,387; assets, $759,765 (M); expenditures, $170,645; qualifying distributions, $162,286.
Limitations: Giving primarily in Cleveland, OH.
Application information: Application form required.
Officers and Trustees:* Robert K. Healey,* Pres.; Hugh O'Neill,* Secy.
EIN: 346545084
Codes: FD2

42776
Austin E. Knowlton Foundation, Inc.
1800 Star Bank Ctr.
425 Walnut St.
Cincinnati, OH 45202-3957
Contact: Charles D. Lindberg, Tr.

Established in 1982.
Donor(s): Austin E. Knowlton.
Financial data (yr. ended 12/31/01): Grants paid, $153,300; assets, $3,025,960 (M); expenditures, $165,508; qualifying distributions, $155,066.
Limitations: Giving primarily in OH.
Application information: Application form not required.
Trustees: Austin E. Knowlton, Charles D. Lindberg.
EIN: 311044475
Codes: FD2

42777
Michael Pender Memorial Foundation
c/o KeyBank, N.A.
800 Superior Ave., OH-01-02-0420, 4th Fl.
Cleveland, OH 44114
Application address: P.O. Box 248, Gates Mills, OH 44040, tel.: (440) 423-1858; FAX: (440) 423-0133
Contact: Katherine Pender, Pres.

Established in 1998 in OH.
Financial data (yr. ended 12/31/00): Grants paid, $153,097; assets, $2,731,480 (M); expenditures, $153,497; qualifying distributions, $152,062.
Limitations: Giving primarily in OH.
Application information: Application form not required.
Officer and Trustees:* Katherine C. Pender,* Pres.; Katherine P. Clark, Oliver C. Henkel, James Robert Pender, Marc Pender, KeyBank, N.A.

42777—OHIO

EIN: 341861675
Codes: FD2

42778
Zenith Foundation, Inc.
405 Madison Ave., Ste. 1900
Toledo, OH 43604-1207

Established in 1967.
Donor(s): Richard H. Peters.
Financial data (yr. ended 12/31/01): Grants paid, $153,050; assets, $3,106,712 (M); expenditures, $161,238; qualifying distributions, $159,759.
Limitations: Applications not accepted. Giving primarily in Toledo, OH.
Application information: Contributes only to pre-selected organizations.
Officers and Trustees:* Richard H. Peters,* Pres. and Treas.; William F. Bates,* V.P. and Secy.; Carol J. Middleton.
EIN: 341018513
Codes: FD2

42779
Montauk Foundation
236 3rd St. S.W.
Canton, OH 44702-1622
Contact: Barbara C. Timken, Pres.

Established in 1983 in OH.
Donor(s): Barbara C. Timken, Louise B. Timken.
Financial data (yr. ended 09/30/01): Grants paid, $152,000; assets, $2,620,017 (M); gifts received, $80,000; expenditures, $154,926; qualifying distributions, $152,055.
Limitations: Giving on a national basis.
Officers and Trustees:* Barbara C. Timken,* Pres.; Polly M. Timken,* V.P.; Don D. Dickes,* Secy.; W.R. Timken, Jr.,* Treas.
EIN: 341411177
Codes: FD2

42780
The South Waite Foundation
c/o KeyBank, N.A.
800 Superior Ave., 4th Fl., MC OH-01-02-040
Cleveland, OH 44114-1306
Contact: Richard H. Buffett

Incorporated in 1953 in OH.
Donor(s): Francis M. Sherwin,‡ Margaret H. Sherwin.‡
Financial data (yr. ended 12/31/01): Grants paid, $152,000; assets, $2,913,552 (M); expenditures, $170,169; qualifying distributions, $153,679.
Limitations: Giving limited to the Cleveland, OH, area.
Application information: Trustees normally make grants only to charities with which they are familiar. Application form not required.
Officers: Brian Sherwin, Pres.; Donald W. Gruetner, Secy.-Treas.
Board Members: Sherman Dye, Dennis Sherwin, Peter Sherwin.
Agent: KeyBank, N.A.
EIN: 346526411
Codes: FD2

42781
Wood Foundation
(also known as Robert S. Wood Foundation)
P.O. Box 575
154 N. High St.
Canal Winchester, OH 43110

Established in 1987 in OH.
Financial data (yr. ended 12/31/00): Grants paid, $151,500; assets, $2,977,580 (M); gifts received, $98,250; expenditures, $165,929; qualifying distributions, $150,429.

Limitations: Applications not accepted. Giving primarily in OH.
Application information: Contributes only to pre-selected organizations.
Officers: Robert S. Wood, Chair.; Kitty I. Argobright, V.P.; Robert S. Wood II, V.P.; Cheryl E. Mathias, Secy.; Vicki M. Wood, Treas.
EIN: 311217729
Codes: FD2

42782
Murray and Agnes Seasongood Good Government Foundation
15 E. 8th St., Ste. 200W
Cincinnati, OH 45202 (513) 721-2181
Application address: 414 Walnut St., Ste. 1006, Cincinnati, OH 45202
Contact: D. David Altman, Exec. Secy.

Established in 1987 in OH.
Financial data (yr. ended 12/31/01): Grants paid, $151,291; assets, $5,824,739 (M); expenditures, $325,171; qualifying distributions, $276,907.
Limitations: Giving primarily in Cincinnati, OH.
Publications: Informational brochure.
Application information: Application form required.
Officers: Travis L. Kubale, Pres.; Dean Jay Chatterjee, 1st V.P.; David D. Black, 2nd V.P.; D. David Altman, Exec. Secy.; Henry R. Winkler, Secy.; William T. Bahlman, Jr., Treas.
Board Members: Mary Asbury, Arnold L. Bortz, Michelle E. Busch, Janet Hoffheimer, Jon Hoffheimer, Bruce I. Petrie, Sr., Bruce I. Petrie, Jack Sherman, Jr.
EIN: 311220827
Codes: FD2

42783
Sullivan Family Fund
(Formerly The Sullivan Family Foundation, Inc.)
800 Superior Ave., Ste. 1800
Cleveland, OH 44114-2601

Established in 1986 in OH.
Donor(s): Pine Fund Corp.
Financial data (yr. ended 12/31/00): Grants paid, $150,970; assets, $335,752 (M); gifts received, $50,000; expenditures, $154,172; qualifying distributions, $150,465.
Limitations: Applications not accepted. Giving primarily in OH.
Application information: Contributes only to pre-selected organizations.
Trustees: Joseph D. Sullivan, Joseph D. Sullivan, Jr., Sandra H. Sullivan.
EIN: 341537311
Codes: FD2

42784
Joseph and Eva Hurwitz Charitable Trust
1800 Moler Rd.
Columbus, OH 43207

Established in 1995.
Financial data (yr. ended 12/31/99): Grants paid, $150,735; assets, $1,632,419 (M); gifts received, $20,125; expenditures, $151,979; qualifying distributions, $149,695.
Limitations: Applications not accepted. Giving primarily in NY.
Application information: Contributes only to pre-selected organizations.
Trustees: Mark Hurwitz, Geraldine Schottenstein.
EIN: 311358933
Codes: FD2

42785
The John C. Markey Charitable Fund
P.O. Box 623
Bryan, OH 43506
Contact: John C. Markey II, Treas.

Established in 1966 in OH.
Donor(s): John C. Markey.‡
Financial data (yr. ended 06/30/01): Grants paid, $150,550; assets, $3,565,392 (M); expenditures, $186,315; qualifying distributions, $156,607.
Limitations: Giving primarily in OH.
Application information: Application form not required.
Officers: Carl T. Anderson, Pres. and Secy.; Lorance W. Lisle, V.P.; John Clifton Markey II, Treas.
Trustee: Larry D. Lisle.
EIN: 346572724
Codes: FD2

42786
The Halcyon Foundation
c/o IAI, IMG Center, Ste. 100
1360 E. 9th St.
Cleveland, OH 44114-1782

Established in 1991 in NY.
Donor(s): Ray C. Cave.
Financial data (yr. ended 12/31/00): Grants paid, $150,523; assets, $578,481 (M); expenditures, $151,663; qualifying distributions, $150,523.
Limitations: Applications not accepted. Giving primarily in Boothbay Harbor, ME, and New York, NY.
Application information: Contributes only to pre-selected organizations.
Trustees: Jon T. Cave, Ray C. Cave, Catherine Christine Hatfield, Patricia Ryan.
EIN: 346961975
Codes: FD2

42787
The Veale Foundation
(Formerly V and V Foundation)
30195 Chagrin Blvd., Ste. 310-N
Pepper Pike, OH 44124
Contact: Mary C. Farrar, Admin. Dir.

Established in 1965.
Donor(s): Tinkham Veale II, Harriet Ernst Veale.‡
Financial data (yr. ended 12/31/01): Grants paid, $150,489; assets, $3,935,286 (M); expenditures, $170,835; qualifying distributions, $160,489.
Limitations: Applications not accepted. Giving primarily in OH, with emphasis on Cleveland.
Application information: Contributes only to pre-selected organizations.
Officers and Trustees:* Tinkham Veale II,* Chair.; Daniel Harrington,* Secy.; John Kennedy, Jane Kober, Thomas McCann, John Vaughan.
EIN: 346565830
Codes: FD2

42788
Blanche and Thomas Hope Memorial Fund
P.O. Box 94651
Cleveland, OH 44101-4651
Application address: c/o Cordell Lawrence, National City Bank, 101 S. 5th St., Louisville, KY 40233, tel.: (502) 581-5107

Established in 1969 in KY.
Donor(s): Blanche Hope,‡ Thomas Hope.‡
Financial data (yr. ended 12/31/01): Grants paid, $150,402; assets, $3,633,086 (M); expenditures, $171,539; qualifying distributions, $152,851.
Limitations: Giving limited to Boyd and Greenup counties, KY, and Lawrence County, OH, residents.

Application information: Application form available from high school guidance counselors. Application form required.
Trustee: National City Bank, Kentucky.
EIN: 616067105
Codes: FD2, GTI

42789
The Anderson Foundation, Inc.
925 Euclid Ave, Ste. 1995
Cleveland, OH 44115

Established in 2000 in OH.
Donor(s): Brian Anderson, Anna Anderson.
Financial data (yr. ended 12/31/01): Grants paid, $150,075; assets, $296,511 (M); gifts received, $244,364; expenditures, $151,697; qualifying distributions, $150,075.
Limitations: Applications not accepted.
Application information: Contributes only to pre-selected organizations.
Officers: Brian Anderson, Pres. and Treas.; Anna Anderson, V.P.; Phillip A. Ciano, Secy.
EIN: 341922586
Codes: FD2

42790
Rhein Family Foundation
c/o Robert C. Rhein
7265 Kenwood Rd., Ste. 220
Cincinnati, OH 45236

Established in 1999 in OH.
Donor(s): Marilyn S. Rhein, Robert C. Rhein.
Financial data (yr. ended 12/31/00): Grants paid, $150,028; assets, $155,900 (M); gifts received, $103,613; expenditures, $151,547; qualifying distributions, $150,020.
Limitations: Applications not accepted. Giving primarily in Boston, MA, and Cincinnati, OH.
Application information: Contributes only to pre-selected organizations.
Trustees: Adam Rhein, Amanda Rhein, Marilyn S. Rhein, Robert C. Rhein.
EIN: 311682674
Codes: FD2

42791
Howard A. Drescher Foundation
c/o KeyBank, N.A.
800 Superior Ave., 4th Fl.
Cleveland, OH 44114

Established in 1995.
Financial data (yr. ended 11/30/01): Grants paid, $150,000; assets, $2,762,936 (M); expenditures, $171,439; qualifying distributions, $150,250.
Limitations: Applications not accepted.
Application information: Contributes only to pre-selected organizations.
Trustee: KeyBank, N.A.
EIN: 146178336
Codes: FD2

42792
Edwin D. Northrup II Fund Trust
c/o National City Bank
P.O. Box 94651
Cleveland, OH 44193 (216) 575-2736
Contact: Michael Galland, V.P., National City Bank

Established in 1984 in OH.
Donor(s): Edwin Northrup II.‡
Financial data (yr. ended 12/31/01): Grants paid, $150,000; assets, $3,248,833 (M); expenditures, $170,274; qualifying distributions, $160,288.
Limitations: Giving primarily in NY and OH.
Application information: Application form not required.
Trustee: National City Bank.
EIN: 346829894
Codes: FD2

42793
Marion G. Resch Foundation
c/o Harrington, Hoppe & Mitchell, Ltd.
1200 Mahoning Bank Bldg.
Youngstown, OH 44503
Application address: c/o Butler Wick Trust Co., City Centre One, Ste. 700, Youngstown, OH 44503, tel.: (330) 744-4351
Contact: James H. Sisek, Tr.

Established in 1997 in OH.
Donor(s): Marion G. Resch.
Financial data (yr. ended 12/31/01): Grants paid, $150,000; assets, $1,659,000 (M); gifts received, $1,417,416; expenditures, $172,330; qualifying distributions, $160,843.
Limitations: Giving limited within 100 miles of Youngstown, OH.
Trustees: Neil H. Maxwell, James E. Mitchell, George B. Pugh, Marion G. Resch, James H. Sisek, George B. Woodman, Eldon S. Wright.
Agent: Butler Wick Trust Co.
EIN: 341853367
Codes: FD2

42794
The Trzcinski Foundation
8050 Corporate Cir., Rm. 2
North Royalton, OH 44133 (440) 237-8083
Contact: Ronald Trzcinski, Pres.

Established in 1997 in OH.
Donor(s): Ronald Trzcinski.
Financial data (yr. ended 06/30/01): Grants paid, $150,000; assets, $5,976,504 (M); gifts received, $3,000,000; expenditures, $169,380; qualifying distributions, $150,000.
Limitations: Giving primarily in OH.
Officer: Ronald Trzcinski, Pres.
EIN: 341852993
Codes: FD2

42795
Richman Brothers Foundation
P.O. Box 657
Chagrin Falls, OH 44022
Contact: Richard R. Moore, Pres.

Incorporated in 1932 in OH.
Donor(s): Nathan G. Richman,‡ Charles L. Richman,‡ Henry C. Richman.‡
Financial data (yr. ended 12/31/01): Grants paid, $149,445; assets, $2,860,614 (M); expenditures, $175,597; qualifying distributions, $149,925.
Limitations: Giving primarily in OH, with emphasis on Cleveland.
Application information: Application form not required.
Officers and Trustees:* Richard R. Moore,* Pres.; Ernest J. Marvar,* V.P.; Raymond J. Novack, Treas.; Frank Harding.
EIN: 346504927
Codes: FD2

42796
Community Foundation of Delaware County
P.O. Box 261
40 N. Sandusky, Ste. 202
Delaware, OH 43015 (740) 369-0095
FAX: (740) 369-1140; *E-mail:* cfdc@midohio.net; *URL:* http://www.delawarecf.com
Contact: Robert A. Holm, Pres.

Established in 1995 in OH.
Financial data (yr. ended 12/31/00): Grants paid, $149,315; assets, $1,721,658 (M); gifts received, $213,665; expenditures, $185,473.
Limitations: Giving limited to Delaware County, OH.
Publications: Financial statement, grants list, informational brochure (including application guidelines), program policy statement.
Application information: Application form required.
Officers: E. Jane Van Fossen, Chair.; Rozella Miller, Vice-Chair.; Robert A. Holm, Pres.; Stephen D. Martin, Secy.; William D. Rogers, Treas.
Trustees: Thomas B. Courtice, D.G. Edgerton, Dee Ketterling, Richard Lombardi, Peter Manos, William McCartney, Bradley N. Scott, Michael Shade.
EIN: 311450786
Codes: CM, FD2

42797
O'Rourke-Schof Family Foundation
c/o National City Bank of Indiana
P.O. Box 94651
Cleveland, OH 44101-4651
Application address: P.O. Box 110, Fort Wayne, IN 46801, tel.: (219) 461-6199
Contact: Michele Herald

Established in 1985 in IN.
Donor(s): Rejean O'Rourke.‡
Financial data (yr. ended 04/30/02): Grants paid, $149,000; assets, $4,834,013 (M); expenditures, $173,703; qualifying distributions, $160,226.
Limitations: Giving primarily in Fort Wayne, IN.
Application information: Application form not required.
Officers: Marlene Buesching, Chair.; Marjorie Motherwell, Vice-Chair; Daniel Nieter, Secy.
Trustee: National City Bank of Indiana.
EIN: 356437238
Codes: FD2

42798
Katherine & Lee Chilcote Foundation
c/o KeyBank, N.A.
800 Superior Ave., Ste. 420
Cleveland, OH 44114
Application address: 2322 Delamere Dr., Cleveland Heights, OH 44106
Contact: Lee A. Chilcote

Established in 1998 in OH.
Financial data (yr. ended 12/31/01): Grants paid, $148,625; assets, $1,852,482 (M); gifts received, $9,600; expenditures, $169,735; qualifying distributions, $156,734.
Limitations: Giving limited to OH, primarily in Cleveland.
Trustee: KeyBank, N.A.
EIN: 341856511
Codes: FD2

42799
The Ames Family Foundation
c/o Cornerstone Family Office
5885 Landerbrook Dr., Ste. 210
Mayfield Heights, OH 44124

Established in 1995 in OH.
Donor(s): B. Charles Ames, Mrs. B. Charles Ames.
Financial data (yr. ended 12/31/01): Grants paid, $148,400; assets, $5,037,287 (M); gifts received, $2,887,125; expenditures, $152,441; qualifying distributions, $148,295.
Limitations: Applications not accepted. Giving primarily in Cleveland, OH.
Application information: Contributes only to pre-selected organizations.
Officers: B. Charles Ames, Pres.; Richard S. Ames, V.P.; Cynthia Ames Hoge, V.P.; Paula A. Ames Redman, V.P.; Joyce G. Ames, Secy.-Treas.
EIN: 341809978

42799—OHIO

Codes: FD2

42800
Joseph H. Kanter Foundation
9792 Windisch Rd.
West Chester, OH 45069-3808
Contact: Robert E. Wildermuth, Tr.

Established in 1964.
Donor(s): Joseph H. Kanter.
Financial data (yr. ended 09/30/01): Grants paid, $148,245; assets, $1,419,789 (M); gifts received, $12,500; expenditures, $154,969; qualifying distributions, $152,647.
Limitations: Giving primarily in Los Angeles, CA, Miami, FL, and Cincinnati, OH.
Application information: Application form not required.
Officers and Trustees:* Joseph H. Kanter,* Pres.; Amy Gulleman-Miller, Secy.; Nancy R. Kanter,* Treas.; Robert E. Wildermuth.
EIN: 237075058
Codes: FD2

42801
David Meade Massie Trust
65 E. 2nd St.
Chillicothe, OH 45601 (740) 772-5070
Application address: P.O. Box 41, Chillicothe, OH 45601

Established in 1979 in OH.
Financial data (yr. ended 12/31/00): Grants paid, $148,101; assets, $5,527,885 (M); expenditures, $324,936; qualifying distributions, $186,059.
Limitations: Giving limited to Chillicothe and Ross County, OH.
Publications: Program policy statement, application guidelines.
Application information: Application form required.
Trustees: Joseph G. Kear, Thomas M. Spetnagel, Joseph P. Sulzer.
EIN: 316022292
Codes: FD2

42802
Kibble Foundation
P.O. Box 723
Pomeroy, OH 45769

Established in 1976.
Financial data (yr. ended 12/31/00): Grants paid, $148,100; assets, $3,794,233 (M); expenditures, $172,545; qualifying distributions, $164,831.
Limitations: Giving limited to Meigs County, OH.
Application information: Application form required.
Trustee: Bernard V. Fultz.
EIN: 316175971
Codes: FD2, GTI

42803
Ranch Foundation
1400 N. Point Twr.
1001 Lakeside Ave.
Cleveland, OH 44114-1152

Established in 1977 in OH.
Donor(s): George F. Wasmer, Lake Erie Screw Corp.
Financial data (yr. ended 12/31/00): Grants paid, $147,931; assets, $1,685,644 (M); gifts received, $44,165; expenditures, $163,944; qualifying distributions, $147,931.
Limitations: Applications not accepted. Giving primarily in Cleveland, OH.
Application information: Contributes only to pre-selected organizations.
Trustee: George F. Wasmer.
EIN: 341200521

Codes: FD2

42804
Ward Beecher Foundation
c/o Sky Trust, N.A.
P.O. Box 479
Youngstown, OH 44501 (330) 742-7035
Contact: J. David Sabine, Sr. V.P. and Sr. Trust Off., Sky Trust, N.A.

Established in 1958 in OH.
Donor(s): Ward Beecher.‡
Financial data (yr. ended 12/31/01): Grants paid, $147,800; assets, $4,100,498 (M); expenditures, $204,292; qualifying distributions, $157,221.
Limitations: Giving limited to the Youngstown, OH, area.
Application information: Application form not required.
Directors: Eleanor Beecher Flad, Erle L. Flad, Ward Beecher Flad, Gregory L. Ridler, J. David Sabine.
Trustee: Sky Trust, N.A.
EIN: 346516441
Codes: FD2

42805
Danis Foundation, Inc.
P.O. Box 725
Dayton, OH 45401-0725
Contact: Michael N. Matzko

Established in 1957 in OH.
Donor(s): Danis Industries Corp.
Financial data (yr. ended 12/31/00): Grants paid, $147,400; assets, $738,737 (M); gifts received, $140,000; expenditures, $150,455; qualifying distributions, $147,400.
Limitations: Giving primarily in the Dayton, OH, area.
Application information: Application form required for scholarships.
Officers: John Danis, Pres. and Secy.-Treas.; Thomas P. Hammelrath, V.P.
EIN: 316041012
Codes: CS, FD2, CD

42806
Williamson Family Foundation
8399 Tippecanoe Rd.
Canfield, OH 44406

Donor(s): WKBN Broadcasting Corp.
Financial data (yr. ended 12/31/00): Grants paid, $147,261; assets, $2,268,238 (M); expenditures, $167,388; qualifying distributions, $152,111.
Limitations: Applications not accepted. Giving primarily in OH.
Application information: Contributes only to pre-selected organizations.
Officers: Warren P. Williamson III, Pres.; John D. Williamson II, V.P.; Doris J. Saloom, Secy.-Treas.
EIN: 346568495
Codes: CS, FD2, CD

42807
Charles Westheimer Family Fund
36 E. 4th St., Ste. 905
Cincinnati, OH 45202-3810
FAX: (513) 421-9343
Contact: Charles Westheimer, Pres.; or May O. Westheimer, V.P.

Established in 1980 in OH.
Donor(s): Charles Westheimer, Irwin F. Westheimer,‡ May O. Westheimer.
Financial data (yr. ended 12/31/01): Grants paid, $146,493; assets, $313,202 (M); gifts received, $328,930; expenditures, $148,798; qualifying distributions, $144,268.
Limitations: Giving primarily in Cincinnati, OH.

Application information: Application form not required.
Officers: Charles Westheimer, Pres.; May O. Westheimer, V.P. and Treas.; John R. Westheimer, Secy.
EIN: 311016766
Codes: FD2

42808
Neils A. Lundgard and Ruth Lundgard Foundation
c/o Fifth Third Bank
P.O. Box 703
Piqua, OH 45356-0703 (937) 227-6532
Contact: Peter M. Klosterman

Established in 1990 in OH.
Financial data (yr. ended 12/31/01): Grants paid, $146,475; assets, $4,724,215 (M); expenditures, $192,087; qualifying distributions, $158,761.
Limitations: Giving limited to Miami County, OH.
Application information: Application form required.
Trustee: Fifth Third Bank.
EIN: 316375418
Codes: FD2

42809
Charles & Charlotte Bissell Smith Scholarship
c/o KeyBank, N.A.
800 Superior Ave., 4th Fl.
Cleveland, OH 44114
Application address: c/o KeyBank, N.A., P.O. Box 1965, Albany, NY 12201

Financial data (yr. ended 02/28/01): Grants paid, $146,250; assets, $2,859,456 (M); expenditures, $168,715; qualifying distributions, $146,500.
Limitations: Giving limited to the Oneonta, NY, area.
Trustee: KeyBank, N.A.
EIN: 146105261
Codes: FD2, GTI

42810
Lewis J. & Nelle A. Davis Foundation
c/o National City Bank
P.O. Box 94651
Cleveland, OH 44101-4651
Application address: c/o Superintendent of Schools, Galion School District, Galion, OH 44833, tel.: (419) 468-3432

Established in 1991 in OH.
Donor(s): Nelle A. Davis.‡
Financial data (yr. ended 11/30/01): Grants paid, $146,000; assets, $2,627,232 (M); expenditures, $210,715; qualifying distributions, $159,466.
Limitations: Giving limited to Galion, OH.
Trustee: National City Bank.
EIN: 346942736
Codes: FD2, GTI

42811
The Taj Foundation
3000 Burrwood Dr.
Springfield, OH 45503
Contact: Tajuddin Ahmed, Tr.

Established in 1987 in OH.
Donor(s): Tajuddin Ahmed, Shahana Ahmed, Satiad H. Siddiqi, Edith Siddiqi.
Financial data (yr. ended 12/31/01): Grants paid, $145,179; assets, $2,600,788 (M); gifts received, $121,530; expenditures, $159,738; qualifying distributions, $144,620.
Limitations: Giving on a national basis.
Application information: Application form required.
Trustees: Afshan Ahmed, Shahana Ahmed, Tajuddin Ahmed.

EIN: 311191104
Codes: FD2

42812
Walter E. & Marilyn L. Bartlett Family Foundation
c/o U.S. Bank
P.O. Box 1118, ML CN-WN-06TX
Cincinnati, OH 45201-1118

Established in 1999 in OH.
Financial data (yr. ended 12/31/01): Grants paid, $145,000; assets, $176,823 (M); gifts received, $100,000; expenditures, $152,062; qualifying distributions, $145,000.
Limitations: Giving limited to Cincinnati, OH.
Application information: Application form not required.
Trustees: John P. Bartlett, Marilyn L. Bartlett, Robert C. Bartlett, Walter E. Bartlett, Lawrence H. Kyte, Jr., Suzanne Bartlett Solimine, U.S. Bank.
EIN: 311650192

42813
R. G. Laha Foundation
c/o The Huntington National Bank
P.O. Box 1558, HC-0534
Columbus, OH 43216

Established in 2000 in OH.
Donor(s): R. Laha.‡
Financial data (yr. ended 12/31/01): Grants paid, $144,989; assets, $1,221,960 (M); expenditures, $156,879; qualifying distributions, $144,989.
Limitations: Applications not accepted.
Application information: Contributes only to pre-selected organizations.
Trustee: The Huntington National Bank.
EIN: 912071253

42814
Ashland County Community Foundation
P.O. Box 733
Ashland, OH 44805 (419) 281-4733
FAX: (419) 281-4733
Contact: Lucille G. Ford, Pres.

Established in 1995 in OH.
Financial data (yr. ended 06/30/01): Grants paid, $144,052; assets, $3,595,677 (M); gifts received, $675,495; expenditures, $144,052.
Limitations: Giving limited to Ashland County, OH.
Publications: Annual report, newsletter, informational brochure, application guidelines.
Application information: Application form required.
Officer: Lucille G. Ford, Ph.D., Pres.
EIN: 341812908
Codes: CM, FD2

42815
Ben S. & Gerome R. Stefanski Charitable Foundation
c/o Mark S. Allio
7007 Broadway Ave.
Cleveland, OH 44105-1490
Contact: Marc A. Stefanski, Pres.

Established in 1991 in OH.
Donor(s): Monica Martines, Paul Stefanik, Third Federal S&L Assoc. of Cleveland.
Financial data (yr. ended 12/31/01): Grants paid, $143,500; assets, $176,220 (M); gifts received, $198,838; expenditures, $145,323; qualifying distributions, $145,323.
Limitations: Giving limited to the greater Cleveland, OH, area.
Application information: Application form not required.

Officers and Trustees:* Marc A. Stefanski,* Pres.; Bernard Kobak,* V.P.; Mark S. Allio,* Treas.
EIN: 341691023
Codes: FD2

42816
Ohio Casualty Foundation, Inc.
9450 Seward Rd.
Fairfield, OH 45014 (513) 603-2035
FAX: (513) 603-3181; *E-mail:* debby.jordan@ocas.com
Contact: Debbie Jordan

Established in 1992 in OH.
Donor(s): Ohio Casualty Corp.
Financial data (yr. ended 09/30/01): Grants paid, $143,450; assets, $2,313,957 (M); expenditures, $144,698; qualifying distributions, $143,675.
Limitations: Giving limited to headquarters city and major operating areas.
Publications: Informational brochure.
Application information: Application form required.
Officers and Trustees:* William Woodall,* Chair.; John E. Bade, Jr.,* Vice-Chair.; Howard Sloneker III,* Secy.; Richard Kelly,* Treas.; Debra K. Crane.
EIN: 311357883
Codes: CS, FD2, CD

42817
Samuel Reese Willis Foundation, Inc.
57 Baker Blvd.
Akron, OH 44333-3640 (330) 836-7040
Contact: James R. Graves, Tr.

Established in 1991 in OH.
Financial data (yr. ended 09/30/01): Grants paid, $143,347; assets, $3,477,951 (M); expenditures, $185,687; qualifying distributions, $163,974.
Limitations: Giving limited to Akron and Canton, OH.
Trustees: Janet Beruset, James R. Graves, Michele R. Smith.
EIN: 341662189
Codes: FD2

42818
Midmark Foundation
P.O. Box 286
Versailles, OH 45380
Scholarship application address: c/o Midmark Corp., Human Resources Dept., 60 Vista Dr., Versailles, OH 45380, tel.: (937) 526-3662

Established in 1969 in OH.
Donor(s): Midmark Corp.
Financial data (yr. ended 12/31/00): Grants paid, $143,080; assets, $731,290 (M); expenditures, $150,517; qualifying distributions, $143,080.
Limitations: Giving primarily in OH, with emphasis on Greenville.
Application information: Application form required for employee-related scholarships.
Officers: Mitchell Eiting, Pres.; Polly Grow, V.P.; Shirley Magoteaux, Secy. and Treas.
EIN: 237068805
Codes: CS, FD2, CD

42819
Entelco Foundation
132 W. 2nd St., Ste. B
Perrysburg, OH 43551
Contact: Stephen Stranahan, Tr.

Established in 1979 in OH.
Donor(s): Stephen Stranahan.
Financial data (yr. ended 12/31/01): Grants paid, $142,725; assets, $4,228,408 (M); expenditures, $156,473; qualifying distributions, $144,611.
Limitations: Giving primarily in the Toledo and northwestern OH area.

Publications: Application guidelines.
Application information: Application form not required.
Trustees: Ann A. Stranahan, Stephen Stranahan.
Director: Dawn Knisel.
EIN: 341288595
Codes: FD2

42820
Wasserstrom Foundation
477 S. Front St.
Columbus, OH 43215-5677 (614) 226-6525
Contact: Rodney Wasserstrom, Tr.

Established in 1963 in OH.
Donor(s): Rodney Wasserstrom, N. Wasserstrom & Sons, Quadra-Tech, The Wasserstrom Co., Amtekco Industries.
Financial data (yr. ended 09/30/01): Grants paid, $142,600; assets, $2,574,613 (M); gifts received, $179,700; expenditures, $151,331; qualifying distributions, $143,588.
Limitations: Giving limited to central OH.
Trustees: Alan Wasserstrom, Rodney Wasserstrom.
EIN: 316041116
Codes: FD2

42821
Cole National Foundation
5915 Landerbrook Dr., Ste. 300
Mayfield Heights, OH 44124-4041
(440) 449-4100
Contact: Jeffrey A. Cole, Pres.

Established in 1981 in OH.
Donor(s): Cole National Corp.
Financial data (yr. ended 12/31/00): Grants paid, $142,560; assets, $894,539 (M); expenditures, $146,207; qualifying distributions, $145,060.
Limitations: Giving primarily in the Cleveland, OH, area.
Application information: Application form not required.
Officer: Jeffrey A. Cole, Pres. and Treas.
Trustees: Joseph Gaglioti, Matthew Selvaggio.
EIN: 341341165
Codes: CS, FD2, CD

42822
Arnold C. Dienstberger Foundation, Inc.
302 W. 1st St.
Delphos, OH 45833 (419) 692-0060
Contact: Paula Minzing, Tr.

Established in 1999 in OH.
Financial data (yr. ended 12/31/00): Grants paid, $142,500; assets, $5,522,710 (M); expenditures, $150,879; qualifying distributions, $141,615.
Limitations: Giving primarily in the Delphos, OH, school district.
Officers: Paula Minzing, Pres.; Robert Scherger, V.P.; Rosemary Wolery, Secy.; Richard Thompson, Sr., Treas.
Directors: Douglas Harter, Ruth Michael, Edna Jane Sadler.
EIN: 346539337
Codes: FD2

42823
The Hillier Family Foundation
(Formerly Robert E. Hillier Family Charitable Trust)
P.O. Box 517
Sharon Center, OH 44274-0517
(330) 239-2711
FAX: (330) 239-4535
Contact: Robert C. Bolon, Exec. Dir.

Established in 1974 in OH.
Donor(s): Pleadis Hillier,‡ Colon C. Hillier,‡ Ruth E. Hillier.‡

Financial data (yr. ended 12/31/01): Grants paid, $142,426; assets, $10,067,199 (M); expenditures, $544,247; qualifying distributions, $1,219,042; giving activities include $172,993 for programs.
Limitations: Giving primarily in Medina, Summit and Tuscarawus counties, OH.
Publications: Informational brochure (including application guidelines).
Application information: Application form not required.
Officers: Robert C. Bolon, Pres.; Robert J. Wyatt, V.P. and Secy.; Floyd H. Blaine, Treas.
Trustee: Robert C. Jagger.
EIN: 341818989
Codes: FD2

42824
The Don M. Casto Foundation
209 E. State St.
Columbus, OH 43215-4309

Incorporated in 1962 in OH.
Donor(s): Members of the Casto family and family-related businesses.
Financial data (yr. ended 12/31/00): Grants paid, $142,350; assets, $821,449 (M); gifts received, $129,860; expenditures, $151,915; qualifying distributions, $151,576.
Limitations: Giving primarily in OH.
Application information: Generally does not consider unsolicited applications.
Trustees: Frank S. Benson III, Don M. Casto III, Dan J. Kerscher.
EIN: 316049506
Codes: FD2

42825
Harold K. & Catherine F. Folk Charitable Foundation
(also known as Folk Charitable Foundation)
c/o Hausser & Taylor
1001 Lakeside Ave. E, Ste. 1400
Cleveland, OH 44114-1152

Established in 1982 in OH.
Donor(s): Harold K. Folk, Dutch Folk Corp.
Financial data (yr. ended 06/30/01): Grants paid, $141,833; assets, $2,384,799 (M); expenditures, $174,706; qualifying distributions, $140,319.
Limitations: Applications not accepted. Giving primarily in Cleveland, OH.
Application information: Contributes only to pre-selected organizations.
Officers and Trustees:* George D. Vaul,* Pres.; George W. Daverio, Jr.,* V.P.; John J. Webster.
EIN: 341373593
Codes: FD2

42826
J. Bowman Proper Charitable Trust
c/o National City Bank of Pennsylvania
P.O. Box 94651
Cleveland, OH 44101-4651
Application address: c/o Stephen J. Kosak, P.O. Box 374, Oil City, PA 16301, tel.: (814) 677-5085

Established in 1991 in PA.
Donor(s): J. Bowman Proper.‡
Financial data (yr. ended 09/30/01): Grants paid, $141,523; assets, $2,347,471 (M); expenditures, $166,124; qualifying distributions, $156,135.
Limitations: Giving for scholarships limited to West Forest County, PA; giving for organizations limited to the Tionesta, PA, area.
Application information: Application form required.
Trustee: National City Bank of Pennsylvania.
EIN: 251670828
Codes: FD2

42827
The Maynard Family Foundation
3200 Gilchrist Rd.
Mogadore, OH 44260-0277 (330) 733-6291
Contact: Pamela E. Loughry

Established in 1993.
Donor(s): Philip H. Maynard, Les Radwany.
Financial data (yr. ended 12/31/00): Grants paid, $140,377; assets, $2,576,393 (M); gifts received, $372,759; expenditures, $158,672; qualifying distributions, $140,377.
Limitations: Giving primarily in OH.
Application information: Application form not required.
Officers: Amy Griffith, Mgr.; Emily Maynard, Mgr.; Peter E. Maynard, Mgr.; Philip H. Maynard, Mgr.; Susan Maynard, Mgr.
EIN: 341750527
Codes: FD2

42828
Toby and Morton J. Gross Family Foundation
14300 Ridge Rd., Ste. 100
North Royalton, OH 44133

Established in 1992 in OH.
Donor(s): Morton J. Gross.
Financial data (yr. ended 12/31/01): Grants paid, $140,300; assets, $397,371 (M); expenditures, $142,179; qualifying distributions, $140,020.
Limitations: Applications not accepted. Giving primarily in NY and OH.
Application information: Contributes only to pre-selected organizations.
Officers: Morton J. Gross, Pres.; Gary L. Gross, V.P.; Toby Gross, Secy.; Harley I. Gross, Treas.
EIN: 341717060

42829
Edward M. Barr Charitable Trust
c/o Sky Trust, N.A.
23 Federal Plz., P.O. Box 479
Youngstown, OH 44501 (330) 742-7035
Contact: Carol Chamberlain, V.P. and Trust Off., Sky Trust, N.A.

Established in 1973 in OH.
Financial data (yr. ended 12/31/01): Grants paid, $140,000; assets, $2,855,236 (M); expenditures, $176,275; qualifying distributions, $149,708.
Limitations: Giving primarily in Youngstown, OH.
Application information: Application form not required.
Trustee: Sky Trust, N.A.
Members: Ralph A. Beard, Frank Hierro.
EIN: 346687006
Codes: FD2

42830
Bert and Ann Shearer Foundation
c/o U.S. Bank
P.O. Box 1118
Cincinnati, OH 45201-1118

Established in 1999 in OH.
Donor(s): Bert Shearer, Ann Shearer.
Financial data (yr. ended 12/31/01): Grants paid, $140,000; assets, $164,413 (M); gifts received, $140,000; expenditures, $143,726; qualifying distributions, $140,000.
Limitations: Applications not accepted. Giving primarily in Charleston, WV.
Application information: Contributes only to pre-selected organizations.
Officers and Trustees:* Bert Shearer,* Pres. and Treas.; Dennis L. Manes,* Secy.; Harold A. Klink, U.S. Bank.
EIN: 311681324

42831
Count Your Blessings Foundation
1604 Madison Pl.
Wapakoneta, OH 45895
Contact: Kay E. Nolte, Tr.

Established in 1989 in OH.
Financial data (yr. ended 12/31/01): Grants paid, $139,700; assets, $1,261,116 (M); expenditures, $171,742; qualifying distributions, $147,027.
Limitations: Giving limited to OH.
Trustees: David Cheney, Janet Dice, Craig A. Nolte, Jay T. Nolte, Kay E. Nolte, Donald A. Rodden.
EIN: 311286688
Codes: FD2

42832
C. David Snyder Family Foundation
1940 E. 6th St., Ste. 200
Cleveland, OH 44114
Application address: 17216 Edgewater Dr., Lakewood, OH 44107
Contact: C. David Snyder, Tr.

Established in 1998 in OH.
Financial data (yr. ended 12/31/01): Grants paid, $139,643; assets, $362,839 (M); expenditures, $143,944; qualifying distributions, $142,102.
Limitations: Giving primarily in OH.
Application information: Application form not required.
Trustees: Charles D. Snyder, Michelle P. Snyder, Lee C. Weingart.
EIN: 341870322
Codes: FD2

42833
Jasper H. Sheadle Trust
c/o KeyBank, N.A., Trust Tax Dept.
800 Superior Ave., 4th Fl.
Cleveland, OH 44114

Established in 1917 in OH.
Donor(s): Jasper H. Sheadle.‡
Financial data (yr. ended 12/31/01): Grants paid, $139,480; assets, $2,526,020 (M); expenditures, $158,397; qualifying distributions, $139,680.
Limitations: Applications not accepted. Giving limited to residents of Cuyahoga and Mahoning counties, OH.
Application information: Unsolicited requests for funds not considered or acknowledged.
Managers: Tony Blossom, Hon. John J. Donnelly, Bishop J. Clark Grew.
Trustee: KeyBank, N.A.
EIN: 346506457
Codes: FD2, GTI

42834
Douglas Q. and Melinda P. Holmes Foundation Annuity Trust
P.O. Box 553
Gates Mills, OH 44040-0553

Established in 1998 in OH.
Donor(s): Douglas Q. Holmes.
Financial data (yr. ended 12/31/00): Grants paid, $138,010; assets, $103,606 (M); gifts received, $100; expenditures, $159,591; qualifying distributions, $145,263.
Limitations: Applications not accepted. Giving primarily in NY and OH.
Application information: Contributes only to pre-selected organizations.
Trustees: David C. Fulton, Jr., Douglas Q. Holmes, Melinda P. Holmes.
EIN: 341880329
Codes: FD2

42835
Kennebec Foundation
c/o KeyBank, N.A.
800 Superior Ave., 4th Fl.
Cleveland, OH 44114

Established in 1985 in ME.
Financial data (yr. ended 12/31/01): Grants paid, $136,021; assets, $2,116,727 (M); expenditures, $147,298; qualifying distributions, $130,107.
Limitations: Applications not accepted. Giving limited to the Kennebec County, ME, area.
Application information: Contributes only to pre-selected organizations.
Trustee: KeyBank, N.A.
EIN: 222624600
Codes: FD2

42836
Corinne F. O'Neill Charitable Trust
3550 Lander Rd.
Cleveland, OH 44124

Established in 1988 in OH.
Financial data (yr. ended 12/31/00): Grants paid, $136,000; assets, $881,408 (M); expenditures, $159,241; qualifying distributions, $145,207.
Limitations: Applications not accepted. Giving primarily in Cleveland, OH.
Application information: Contributes only to pre-selected organizations.
Trustees: Robert K. Healey, Hugh O'Neill, Alice O'Neill Powers.
EIN: 346732464
Codes: FD2

42837
Tuscora Park Health & Wellness Foundation
104 3rd St. N.W., Ste. 204
Barberton, OH 44203-8226 (330) 753-4607
Additional tel. for nursing scholarships: (330) 745-1611; FAX: (330) 745-3990
Contact: Frances D. Rice, Dir.

Established in 1996 in OH; converted from the merger of the Barberton Citizens Auxiliary and the Barberton Citizens Hospital Foundation.
Financial data (yr. ended 12/31/01): Grants paid, $135,950; assets, $4,136,898 (M); gifts received, $4,656; expenditures, $301,365; qualifying distributions, $175,751.
Limitations: Giving primarily in Barberton, OH, and surrounding communities.
Application information: Contact foundation for application guidelines and materials. Application form required.
Officers and Trustees:* Pat McGrath,* Chair.; Duane L. Isham,* Vice-Chair.; Cathy Vukovich, M.D.,* Secy.; Willard P. Roderick,* Treas.; Laurette Bradnick, Karen Burnette, Jack Deuber, Brenda J. Farrell, Nancy Francis, Sharyn McCaulley, Barb Parks, Steven D. Poholski, Jim Stonkus, Emil Voelz, Daniel G. Warder.
Director: Frances D. Rice.
EIN: 341193807
Codes: FD2, GTI

42838
Arthur & Ermille Ehlers Foundation
c/o Fifth Third Bank
38 Fountain Sq. Plz., 1COM31
Cincinnati, OH 45263

Financial data (yr. ended 09/30/01): Grants paid, $135,438; assets, $1,970,279 (M); expenditures, $156,781; qualifying distributions, $138,859.
Limitations: Applications not accepted. Giving limited to FL, KY, OH, and NY, with emphasis on Cincinnati, OH.
Application information: Contributes only to pre-selected organizations.
Trustee: Fifth Third Bank.
EIN: 316093842
Codes: FD2

42839
Fisher-Renkert Foundation
(Formerly Herman G. and Suzanne G. Fisher Foundation)
925 Euclid Ave., Ste. 2000
Cleveland, OH 44115-1407
Contact: Rebecca H. Dent, Tr.

Established in 1969 in MA.
Financial data (yr. ended 08/31/01): Grants paid, $135,000; assets, $3,183,238 (M); expenditures, $157,671; qualifying distributions, $135,730.
Limitations: Applications not accepted. Giving limited to Buffalo, NY, and OH.
Application information: Contributes only to pre-selected organizations.
Trustees: Rebecca H. Dent, John B. Fisher, Judith Fisher, Gordon A. MacLeod, Amelia S. Renkert, Rachel F. Renkert, Boston Safe Deposit & Trust Co.
EIN: 046198798
Codes: FD2

42840
Frances and Jane S. Lausche Foundation
1942 Brushview Dr.
Richmond Heights, OH 44143
(216) 943-0989
Contact: Madeline D. Debevec, Secy.

Established in 1990 in OH.
Financial data (yr. ended 12/31/00): Grants paid, $135,000; assets, $2,633,064 (M); expenditures, $168,682; qualifying distributions, $160,012.
Officers: James V. Debevec, Pres.; Madeline D. Debevec, Secy.
Director: John M. Urbancich.
EIN: 341585461
Codes: FD2

42841
The Patricia and J. Harvey Graves Family Foundation
P.O. Box 249
Akron, OH 44309-0249

Established in 1997 in OH.
Donor(s): J. Harvey Graves.
Financial data (yr. ended 12/31/01): Grants paid, $134,986; assets, $975,489 (M); expenditures, $154,290; qualifying distributions, $136,385.
Limitations: Applications not accepted. Giving primarily in OH, with some giving in FL and TX.
Application information: Contributes only to pre-selected organizations.
Officers: J. Harvey Graves, Pres.; Patricia L. Graves, V.P. and Treas.; John H. Graves, Jr., Secy.
Trustees: Dianne Graves Dickey, Mary Ann Graves.
EIN: 311545374
Codes: FD2

42842
John Q. Shunk Association
P.O. Box 625
Bucyrus, OH 44820-0625
FAX: (740) 386-6134; *E-mail:* pepspatch@marion.net
Scholarship application address: 1201 Timber Ln., Marion, OH 43302-5739
Contact: Jane C. Peppard, Secy.-Treas.

Established in 1938 in OH.
Donor(s): John Q. Shunk.‡
Financial data (yr. ended 12/31/01): Grants paid, $134,950; assets, $2,096,885 (M); expenditures, $193,630; qualifying distributions, $187,117.
Limitations: Giving primarily in Bucyrus and Crawford counties, OH; scholarships limited to graduates of four high schools in Crawford County.
Application information: Applications available from foundation or high school guidance offices. Application form required.
Officers: John Kennedy, Pres.; Phil Gerker, V.P.; Jane C. Peppard, Secy.-Treas. and Mgr.; Jim Gillenwater, Mgr.; Paul Kennedy, Mgr.
EIN: 340896477
Codes: FD2, GTI

42843
Molyneaux Foundation
c/o First Financial Bank
300 High St.
Hamilton, OH 45011 (513) 867-4818
Contact: Dennis G. Walsh, Trust Off., First Financial Bank

Established in 1975 in OH.
Donor(s): Kendle Molyneaux, Mrs. Kendle Molyneaux.
Financial data (yr. ended 06/30/02): Grants paid, $134,645; assets, $2,785,731 (M); gifts received, $5,667; expenditures, $157,413; qualifying distributions, $132,976.
Limitations: Giving limited to Butler County, OH, with emphasis on Oxford.
Trustee: First Financial Bank.
EIN: 510154432
Codes: FD2

42844
Wimmer Scholarship Fund
(Formerly George G., Elma & Ruth M. Wimmer Scholarship Fund)
c/o National City Bank
P.O. Box 94651
Cleveland, OH 44101-4651
Scholarship application address: 533 Warren St., Huntington, IN 46750-2723, tel.: (219) 356-4100
Contact: William S. Gordon, Sr.

Established in 1981 in IN.
Donor(s): Ruth M. Wimmer.‡
Financial data (yr. ended 08/31/01): Grants paid, $134,200; assets, $2,602,851 (M); gifts received, $150; expenditures, $150,701; qualifying distributions, $142,872.
Limitations: Giving limited to Fort Wayne and Huntington, IN.
Application information: Scholarship applications are made through guidance offices of Fort Wayne, Elmhurst, and Huntington North high schools. A committee outside of the foundation selects recipients. Application form required.
Trustee: National City Bank of Indiana.
EIN: 311036448
Codes: FD2, GTI

42845
Cleveland Automobile Club Orphans Outing Fund
5700 Brecksville Rd.
Independence, OH 44131
Contact: Jean Ziemba, Corp. Secy.

Established in 1945 in OH.
Financial data (yr. ended 12/31/01): Grants paid, $133,970; assets, $2,457,617 (M); expenditures, $154,659; qualifying distributions, $135,500.
Limitations: Giving primarily in the greater Cleveland, OH, area.
Application information: Application form not required.
Officers: Peter C. Ohlheiser, Chair.; Jean Ziemba, Corp. Secy.; Michael R. Pratt, Treas.

42845—OHIO

Trustees: Edward Coaxum, Gary S. Cowling, Mary Jane Fabish, Jane B. Sheats, David Stashower.
EIN: 346515142
Codes: FD2

42846
The C. C. Hobart Foundation
P.O. Box 1024
Troy, OH 45373 (937) 339-8417
Contact: JoAnn W. Howell, Chair.

Established in 1942 in OH.
Donor(s): Members of the Hobart family.
Financial data (yr. ended 12/31/99): Grants paid, $133,000; assets, $1,641,577 (M); expenditures, $156,658; qualifying distributions, $132,034.
Limitations: Giving primarily in Troy, OH.
Application information: The scholarship program has been discontinued. Application form not required.
Officers and Trustees:* JoAnn W. Howell,* Chair.; Richard L. Cultice, Pres. and Treas.; Shirley M. Miller, Secy.; W. Busser Howell, and 3 additional trustees.
EIN: 316030834
Codes: FD2

42847
Chiquita Brands International Foundation
(Formerly United Brands Foundation)
250 E. 5th St., 27th Fl., Tax Dept.
Cincinnati, OH 45202
Contact: Stephanie Krummert, Corp. Affairs

Incorporated in 1954 in IL.
Donor(s): Chiquita Brands International, Inc.
Financial data (yr. ended 12/31/01): Grants paid, $132,960; assets, $95,940 (M); gifts received, $228,920; expenditures, $132,980; qualifying distributions, $132,980.
Limitations: Giving on a national basis.
Application information: Application form not required.
Officers and Directors:* Steven G. Warshaw,* Pres.; Joseph W. Bradley, V.P.; James B. Riley, V.P.; Jeffrey M. Zalla,* V.P.; Robert W. Olson, Secy.; William A. Tsacalis,* Treas.
EIN: 366051081
Codes: CS, FD2, CD

42848
Arthur Rhodes Mackley Memorial Scholarship Fund Trust
(also known as Dorothy M. Corson Testamentary Trust)
c/o National City Bank, Columbus
P.O. Box 94651
Cleveland, OH 44101-4651
Scholarship application address: c/o Tom Slater, Principal, Jackson High School, 21 Tropic St., Jackson, OH 45640, tel.: (740) 286-7575

Established in 1975.
Financial data (yr. ended 12/31/00): Grants paid, $132,513; assets, $1,740,308 (M); expenditures, $143,103; qualifying distributions, $136,809.
Limitations: Giving limited to residents of Jackson County, OH.
Application information: Application form required.
Trustee: National City Bank, Columbus.
Advisors: Lucinda Eubanks, Randy Layton, Kevin Rice.
EIN: 316177708
Codes: FD2, GTI

42849
The Richard H. and Ann Shafer Foundation
8 E. Long St., Rm. 400
Columbus, OH 43215 (614) 224-8111
Contact: Fannie L. Shafer, Mgr.

Donor(s): Richard A. Shafer,‡ Ohio Road Paving Co.
Financial data (yr. ended 12/31/01): Grants paid, $132,500; assets, $2,736,923 (M); gifts received, $5,000; expenditures, $135,751; qualifying distributions, $132,725.
Limitations: Giving limited to OH, with emphasis on Columbus.
Application information: Application form not required.
Officer: Fannie L. Shafer, Mgr.
EIN: 316029095
Codes: FD2

42850
J. Harrington & Marie E. Glidden Foundation
c/o KeyBank, N.A.
800 Superior Ave.
Cleveland, OH 44114-2601

Established in 1998 in OH.
Donor(s): Marie E. Glidden.‡
Financial data (yr. ended 12/31/00): Grants paid, $131,500; assets, $87 (M); gifts received, $135,111; expenditures, $135,144; qualifying distributions, $135,142.
Limitations: Applications not accepted. Giving primarily in Cleveland, OH.
Application information: Contributes only to pre-selected organizations.
Officers: Robert J. Cleary, Jr., Pres. and Treas.; Loretta C. Cleary, V.P.; Anne C. Grevey, Secy.
EIN: 341881366
Codes: FD2

42851
Children's Family Care, Inc.
245 Locust St.
Akron, OH 44302

Established in 1999 in OH.
Donor(s): Maxene D. Darrah Revocable Trust.
Financial data (yr. ended 12/31/00): Grants paid, $131,000; assets, $5,736,982 (M); gifts received, $270,699; expenditures, $193,623; qualifying distributions, $129,676.
Limitations: Applications not accepted. Giving primarily in OH.
Application information: Contributes only to pre-selected organizations.
Officers: Sheldon W. Barlette, Jr., Pres.; Dana Zahuranec, Secy.; Michael G. Soful, Treas.
Trustees: John Blickle, Robert Bobbitt, Steve Cox, Dale G. Freygang, Richard Heidman, Emily B. Petrarca, John Shaffer, Donald D. Shook, John P. Stoner, Jim Stroble, Nedra Yamokoski.
EIN: 341405958
Codes: FD2

42852
RLB Foundation
16121 Rd. 17 N.
Fort Jennings, OH 45844 (419) 532-3498
Contact: Robert L. Blankemeyer, Pres.

Established in 1995 in OH.
Donor(s): Robert L. Blankemeyer.
Financial data (yr. ended 12/31/99): Grants paid, $131,000; assets, $141,444 (M); gifts received, $100,000; expenditures, $135,149; qualifying distributions, $130,914.
Limitations: Giving primarily in Orlando, FL.
Officers: Robert L. Blankemeyer, Pres.; Judith M. Blankemeyer, V.P.; Kathleen A. Blankemeyer, Secy.
EIN: 341816839

42853
The KRW Foundation
1400 N. Point Twr.
1001 Lakeside Ave.
Cleveland, OH 44114-1152

Established in 1976 in OH.
Donor(s): George J. Durkin.
Financial data (yr. ended 12/31/00): Grants paid, $130,750; assets, $33,444 (M); gifts received, $100,359; expenditures, $159,283; qualifying distributions, $130,750.
Limitations: Applications not accepted. Giving primarily in OH.
Application information: Contributes only to pre-selected organizations.
Trustee: George J. Durkin.
EIN: 341201133
Codes: FD2

42854
Kingdom Resources Foundation
460 Club Dr.
Aurora, OH 44202
Contact: Thomas M. Yancy, Pres.

Established in 1997 in OH.
Financial data (yr. ended 12/31/01): Grants paid, $130,217; assets, $434,191 (M); gifts received, $33,500; expenditures, $132,128; qualifying distributions, $131,364.
Limitations: Applications not accepted.
Application information: Contributes only to pre-selected organizations.
Officers: Thomas M. Yancy, Pres.; Susan Yancy, Secy.
Trustee: Mary Beth Ott.
EIN: 311531668
Codes: FD2

42855
Anderton Bentley Fund
c/o Fifth Third Bank
P.O. Box 1868
Toledo, OH 43603
Contact: Phil Ruyle, V.P. and Trust Off., Fifth Third Bank of Northwestern Ohio, N.A.

Financial data (yr. ended 10/31/01): Grants paid, $130,000; assets, $347,512 (M); expenditures, $133,329; qualifying distributions, $130,909.
Limitations: Giving primarily in Toledo, OH.
Application information: Application form not required.
Trustee: Fifth Third Bank.
EIN: 346509881
Codes: FD2

42856
Thomas C. Sullivan Family Foundation, Inc.
P.O. Box 777
Medina, OH 44258-0777
Application address: 2628 Pearl Rd., Medina, OH 44258-9909, tel.: (330) 273-5090
Contact: Thomas C. Sullivan, V.P.

Established in 1986 in OH.
Donor(s): Margaret Sullivan, Thomas C. Sullivan.
Financial data (yr. ended 10/31/01): Grants paid, $130,000; assets, $3,557,589 (M); gifts received, $663,556; expenditures, $142,963; qualifying distributions, $130,529.
Limitations: Giving primarily in northwestern OH.
Officers: Sandra S. Sullivan, Pres.; Thomas C. Sullivan, V.P.; Mary K. Hall, Secy.-Treas.
EIN: 341537658
Codes: FD2

42857
R. G. Dunbar Foundation, Inc.
5333 Monroe St.
Toledo, OH 43623

Established in 1993 in OH.
Donor(s): R.G. Dunbar, Inc., Roger G. Dunbar.
Financial data (yr. ended 12/31/99): Grants paid, $129,950; assets, $2,389,478 (M); expenditures, $131,602; qualifying distributions, $131,602.
Limitations: Applications not accepted.
Application information: Contributes only to pre-selected organizations.
Officers and Directors:* Roger G. Dunbar,* Pres.; Frank A. Szymanski,* V.P.; Daniel A. Worline,* Secy.; Bob Schnapp, Treas.; Dale Graber, Miles O'Malia.
EIN: 341756363
Codes: FD2

42858
Sandfair Foundation
32400 Fairmount Blvd.
Pepper Pike, OH 44124-4830
FAX: (440) 442-7693; *E-mail:* dadd050@aol.com
Contact: William E. Conway, Pres.

Established in 1995 in OH.
Donor(s): William E. Conway, Mary French Conway.
Financial data (yr. ended 12/31/01): Grants paid, $129,800; assets, $1,395,516 (M); expenditures, $132,572; qualifying distributions, $129,800.
Limitations: Giving primarily in northern NM and northeastern OH.
Application information: Application form required.
Officers: William E. Conway, Pres.; Mary French Conway, V.P.; Anne Conway Juster, Secy.-Treas.
EIN: 341815135
Codes: FD2

42859
Ralph R. and Grace B. Jones Foundation
225 N. Market St.
Wooster, OH 44691
Contact: J. Douglas Drushal, Tr.

Established in 1997 in OH.
Financial data (yr. ended 12/31/01): Grants paid, $129,022; assets, $1,413,347 (M); expenditures, $129,854; qualifying distributions, $127,868.
Limitations: Giving primarily in OH.
Application information: Application form not required.
Trustees: J. Douglas Drushal, Kathryn G. Long.
EIN: 311508706
Codes: FD2

42860
The Norman Nitschke Foundation
c/o R.G. Lavalley, Jr.
5800 Monroe St., Ste. F
Perrysburg, OH 43551

Established in 2000 in OH.
Donor(s): Norman C. Nitschke.
Financial data (yr. ended 12/31/01): Grants paid, $128,275; assets, $394,076 (M); expenditures, $130,247; qualifying distributions, $128,087.
Limitations: Applications not accepted. Giving primarily in OH.
Application information: Contributes only to pre-selected organizations.
Officers and Trustees:* Norman C. Nitschke,* Pres.; John S. Nitschke,* V.P.; Richard G. Lavalley, Jr.,* Secy.
EIN: 341941074
Codes: FD2

42861
United Bank Charitable Trust
c/o United National Bank
P.O. Box 24190
Canton, OH 44701-4190

Established in 1993 in OH.
Donor(s): United National Bank & Trust Co.
Financial data (yr. ended 12/31/01): Grants paid, $128,075; assets, $349,058 (M); gifts received, $200,000; expenditures, $133,524; qualifying distributions, $129,205.
Limitations: Applications not accepted. Giving primarily in Canton, OH.
Application information: Contributes only to pre-selected organizations.
Officer: Lang D'Atri, Chair.
Directors: Roger Mann, Abner Yoder, United National Bank.
EIN: 347028857
Codes: CS, FD2

42862
The McCormack Foundation
c/o Roberta J. Lemmo
IMG Center, 1360 E. 9th St., Ste. 100
Cleveland, OH 44114-1782

Established in 1986 in OH.
Donor(s): Mark H. McCormack.
Financial data (yr. ended 12/31/00): Grants paid, $127,900; assets, $1,105,101 (M); gifts received, $674,425; expenditures, $132,048; qualifying distributions, $128,179.
Limitations: Applications not accepted.
Application information: Contributes only to pre-selected organizations.
Trustees: Peter A. Carfagna, Mark H. McCormack, Mary Leslie McCormack, Scott B. McCormack, Todd H. McCormack.
EIN: 341536692
Codes: FD2

42863
Corinne L. Dodero Trust for The Arts and Sciences
37 Pepper Creek Dr.
Pepper Pike, OH 44124

Established in 1998 in FL.
Donor(s): Samuel J. Frankino.
Financial data (yr. ended 03/31/01): Grants paid, $127,575; assets, $6,236,224 (M); expenditures, $219,654; qualifying distributions, $183,414.
Limitations: Applications not accepted. Giving primarily in OH, with emphasis on Cleveland.
Application information: Contributes only to pre-selected organizations.
Trustees: Robert J. Bronchetti, Corinne L. Dodero, Lorraine C. Dodero, Samuel J. Frankino.
EIN: 656239071
Codes: FD2

42864
Terry Lee Fuller Foundation
c/o KeyBank, N.A.
157 S. Main St.
Akron, OH 44308
Contact: K.M. Kedno, Trust Off., KeyBank, N.A.

Established in 1999 in OH.
Financial data (yr. ended 12/31/01): Grants paid, $127,500; assets, $770,350 (M); expenditures, $138,101; qualifying distributions, $130,177.
Publications: Informational brochure.
Application information: Application form not required.
Trustee: KeyBank, N.A.
EIN: 316628591
Codes: FD2

42865
The Norweb Foundation
c/o KeyBank, N.A.
800 Superior Ave., 4th Fl.
Cleveland, OH 44114
Contact: R. Henry Norweb III, Pres.

Established in 1952 in OH.
Donor(s): Eliz Norweb, R. Henry Norweb, Jr.‡
Financial data (yr. ended 12/31/01): Grants paid, $127,075; assets, $1,898,073 (M); gifts received, $50,000; expenditures, $145,250; qualifying distributions, $129,947.
Limitations: Applications not accepted. Giving primarily in Cleveland, OH.
Application information: Contributes only to pre-selected organizations.
Trustee: KeyBank, N.A.
EIN: 346517914
Codes: FD2

42866
Dicke Family Foundation
1700 Courthouse Plz. N.E.
Dayton, OH 45402-1788

Established in 1984 in OH.
Donor(s): Members of the Dicke family, Crown Equipment Corp., James F. Dicke II, James Dicke, Sr., Eileen W. Dicke.
Financial data (yr. ended 11/30/01): Grants paid, $126,350; assets, $889,228 (M); gifts received, $900,550; expenditures, $134,041; qualifying distributions, $126,350.
Limitations: Applications not accepted. Giving on a national basis.
Application information: Contributes only to pre-selected organizations.
Trustees: Eileen W. Dicke, James Dicke, Sr., James F. Dicke II.
EIN: 341446513
Codes: FD2

42867
Borra Family Foundation
2298 June Dr.
Lima, OH 45805

Established in 1997 in OH.
Donor(s): Pier C. Borra.
Financial data (yr. ended 12/31/00): Grants paid, $125,000; assets, $1,569,733 (M); expenditures, $126,679; qualifying distributions, $123,920.
Limitations: Applications not accepted. Giving primarily in Lima, OH.
Application information: Contributes only to pre-selected organizations.
Officers: Renee A. Borra, Pres.; Pier C. Borra, V.P.
Trustee: Pier C. Borra, Jr.
EIN: 311533388
Codes: FD2

42868
Wallace F. and Sally E. Krueger Foundation
c/o Wallace F. Krueger
4401 Merriweather Rd.
Toledo, OH 43623

Established in 1996 in OH.
Donor(s): Wallace F. Krueger.
Financial data (yr. ended 12/31/01): Grants paid, $125,000; assets, $177,551 (M); gifts received, $121,000; expenditures, $127,306; qualifying distributions, $126,438.
Limitations: Applications not accepted. Giving primarily in Toledo, OH.
Application information: Contributes only to pre-selected organizations.
Trustee: Wallace F. Krueger.
EIN: 341848224
Codes: FD2

42869
Sarah C. Hirsh Foundation
c/o KeyBank, N.A.
800 Superior Ave., 4th Fl.
Cleveland, OH 44114 (216) 828-9562

Established in 1997 in OH.
Financial data (yr. ended 12/31/00): Grants paid, $124,500; assets, $878,188 (M); expenditures, $137,864; qualifying distributions, $124,500.
Limitations: Applications not accepted. Giving primarily in Cleveland, OH.
Application information: Contributes only to pre-selected organizations.
Trustee: KeyBank, N.A.
EIN: 311533904
Codes: FD2

42870
Shelby Foundation
142 N. Gamble St.
Shelby, OH 44875 (419) 342-3686
E-mail: administrator@shelbyfoundation.com
Contact: Thomas A. Depler, Pres.

Established in 1985 in OH.
Financial data (yr. ended 12/31/01): Grants paid, $124,343; assets, $2,903,253 (M); gifts received, $480,399; expenditures, $171,370; qualifying distributions, $123,855.
Limitations: Giving limited to the Shelby, OH, area.
Application information: Application form required.
Officers: Thomas A. Depler, Pres.; Mark Reed, V.P.; Cheryl Schumacher, Secy.; Jeff Green, Treas.
Board Members: Dave Brown, Denny Curry, Jim Kehoe, Ralph Phillips, J. George Williams.
EIN: 346710288
Codes: FD2, GTI

42871
Case Western Reserve University Department of Surgery Foundation
(also known as CWRU Department of Surgery Foundation)
2074 Abington Rd.
Cleveland, OH 44106

Established around 1989.
Financial data (yr. ended 12/31/99): Grants paid, $124,041; assets, $67,627 (M); gifts received, $5,750; expenditures, $127,101; qualifying distributions, $127,101.
Limitations: Applications not accepted. Giving primarily in Cleveland, OH.
Application information: Contributes only to pre-selected organizations.
Officers and Trustees:* Jerry M. Shuck, M.D.,* Pres.; Edward Luce, M.D.,* V.P.; Mark Malangoni, M.D.,* V.P.; Thomas A. Stellato, M.D.,* V.P.
EIN: 341583598

42872
Howe Family Foundation
c/o Roger L. Howe
2120 Star Bank Ctr., 425 Walnut St., Ste. 2120
Cincinnati, OH 45245

Established in 1991 in OH.
Donor(s): Roger L. Howe, Karen C. Howe, R. Edwin Howe, Mary H. Davis.
Financial data (yr. ended 12/31/01): Grants paid, $124,000; assets, $1,797,249 (M); expenditures, $139,132; qualifying distributions, $137,085.
Limitations: Applications not accepted. Giving primarily in Cincinnati, OH.
Application information: Contributes only to pre-selected organizations.
Officers: Karen C. Howe, Pres.; Mary H. Davis, Secy.; R. Edwin Howe, Treas.

Trustees: Joyce L. Howe, Roger L. Howe.
EIN: 311339302
Codes: FD2

42873
The Alpaugh Foundation
525 Vine St., 21st Fl.
Cincinnati, OH 45202

Established in 1986 in OH.
Donor(s): Peter A. Alpaugh.
Financial data (yr. ended 06/30/01): Grants paid, $123,722; assets, $2,328,338 (M); gifts received, $55,107; expenditures, $126,334; qualifying distributions, $125,521.
Limitations: Giving on a national basis.
Officer: Peter A. Alpaugh, Mgr.
EIN: 316314074
Codes: FD2

42874
The Lamson & Sessions Foundation
c/o KeyBank, N.A.
800 Superior Ave., 4th Fl.
Cleveland, OH 44114-2601
Application address: c/o The Lamson & Sessions Co., 25701 Science Dr., Cleveland, OH 44122, tel.: (216) 464-3400
Contact: James J. Abel

Trust established in 1951 in OH.
Donor(s): The Lamson & Sessions Co.
Financial data (yr. ended 06/30/01): Grants paid, $123,048; assets, $30,161 (M); gifts received, $150,000; expenditures, $124,578; qualifying distributions, $123,078.
Limitations: Giving primarily in OH.
Application information: Application form not required.
Trustee: KeyBank, N.A.
EIN: 346501823
Codes: CS, FD2, CD

42875
The Community Health Foundation
1237 Lincoln Way E.
Massillon, OH 44646-6992 (330) 837-6864
FAX: (330) 837-3639; *E-mail:* cameron@chfoundation.org or jud.@chfoundation.org or chfoundation@chfoundation.org; *URL:* http://www.chfoundation.org
Contact: Jack Cameron, Exec. Dir.

Established in 1997 in OH; converted in April 1999 from a merger between Akron General Medical Center and Massillon Community Hospital.
Donor(s): The Health Group, Massillon Community Hospital.
Financial data (yr. ended 12/31/01): Grants paid, $122,942; assets, $7,190,461 (M); expenditures, $335,869; qualifying distributions, $249,258.
Limitations: Giving limited to Western Stark, Wayne, and Tuscarawos counties, OH.
Application information: Application form not required.
Officers and Board Members:* Charles Clark,* Pres.; John Ferrero, Jr.,* V.P.; John J. McGrath,* Secy.; William Schumacher,* Treas.; Dominic V. Belloni, Katherine M. Catazaro, R.N., Gayle Gamble, Robert Gessner, Edward Hill, M.D., Geoffrey A. Jollay, Alan Osler, Judith Paquelet, Eugene D. Pogorelec, Nanette Ream, Vanessa Stergios, Marion "Stu" Stewart.
EIN: 311516370
Codes: FD2

42876
Charles H. and Fannie M. Giles Memorial Foundation
627 W. St. Clair Ave.
Cleveland, OH 44113-1204
Contact: Michael J. O'Brien, Secy.

Established in 1959 in OH.
Financial data (yr. ended 12/31/01): Grants paid, $122,800; assets, $1,605,239 (M); expenditures, $210,023; qualifying distributions, $122,800.
Limitations: Giving limited to OH, with emphasis on Chagrin Falls and the Cleveland area.
Officers: Linda K. Fenn, Pres. and Treas.; Michael J. O'Brien, Secy.
Trustee: Richard H. Brown.
EIN: 346554844
Codes: FD2

42877
The Bahl Family Foundation
212 E. 3rd St., Ste. 200
Cincinnati, OH 45202
Contact: William F. Bahl, Tr.

Established in 1998 in OH.
Donor(s): William F. Bahl.
Financial data (yr. ended 12/31/00): Grants paid, $122,706; assets, $604,361 (M); gifts received, $449,400; expenditures, $123,407; qualifying distributions, $122,706.
Limitations: Giving primarily in Cincinnati, OH.
Trustees: Katherine C. Bahl, W. Jeffrey Bahl, William F. Bahl.
EIN: 311621821
Codes: FD2

42878
John T. and Ada Diederich Educational Trust Fund
c/o National City Bank, Kentucky
P.O. Box 94651
Cleveland, OH 44101-4651
Application address: P.O. Box 1919, Ashland, KY 41105-1919, tel.: (606) 836-8186
Contact: Jenny Templeton, Exec. Dir.

Established in 1985 in KY.
Financial data (yr. ended 12/31/01): Grants paid, $122,018; assets, $5,207,885 (M); expenditures, $170,726; qualifying distributions, $134,302.
Limitations: Giving limited to residents of Boyd, Greenup, Martin, Lawrence, and Carter counties, KY.
Application information: Application form required.
Trustee: National City Bank, Kentucky.
EIN: 316271680
Codes: FD2, GTI

42879
Stay Fast Foundation, Inc.
505 Lake Shore Blvd.
Painesville, OH 44077 (440) 357-5546

Established in 1985 in OH.
Donor(s): Stafast Products, Inc., Donald Selle, Joan Selle.
Financial data (yr. ended 12/31/01): Grants paid, $121,938; assets, $198,862 (M); gifts received, $50,000; expenditures, $124,408; qualifying distributions, $124,408.
Limitations: Giving primarily in Lake County, OH.
Application information: Application form required.
Trustees: Donald S. Selle, Joan M. Selle, James Steicher.
EIN: 341485142
Codes: CS, FD2, CD

42880
The Nicholson Foundation
2930 Forest Lake Dr.
Westlake, OH 44145-1782

Established in 1976 in OH.
Donor(s): John C. Wasmer, Jr.
Financial data (yr. ended 12/31/01): Grants paid, $121,889; assets, $955,882 (M); gifts received, $10,000; expenditures, $126,345; qualifying distributions, $121,374.
Limitations: Applications not accepted. Giving primarily in Cleveland, OH.
Application information: Contributes only to pre-selected organizations.
Trustee: John C. Wasmer, Jr.
EIN: 341201203
Codes: FD2

42881
The Beerman Foundation, Inc.
11 W. Monument Bldg., 8th Fl.
Dayton, OH 45402
Contact: William S. Weprin, V.P.

Incorporated in 1945 in OH.
Donor(s): Arthur Beerman,‡ Jessie Beerman.
Financial data (yr. ended 12/31/00): Grants paid, $121,238; assets, $9,308,618 (M); gifts received, $400,587; expenditures, $374,230; qualifying distributions, $183,463.
Limitations: Giving primarily in the Dayton, OH, area.
Publications: Annual report.
Officers: Barbara B. Weprin, Pres.; William S. Weprin, V.P. and Secy.; Vicki L. Adams, Treas.
EIN: 316024369
Codes: FD2

42882
Pearce Foundation
c/o Sky Trust, N.A.
23 Federal Plz., P.O. Box 479
Youngstown, OH 44501-0479 (330) 742-7035
Contact: Carol Chamberlain, V.P. and Trust Off., Sky Trust, N.A.

Established in 1966.
Financial data (yr. ended 12/31/01): Grants paid, $120,886; assets, $2,555,646 (M); expenditures, $147,001; qualifying distributions, $126,252.
Limitations: Giving primarily in OH, with emphasis on Salem.
Application information: Application form not required.
Directors: Marjorie Barnes, Carol Chamberlain, Robert McCulloch III.
Trustee: Sky Trust, N.A.
EIN: 346572300
Codes: FD2, GTI

42883
Friedlander Family Fund
36 E. 4th St., Ste. 400
Cincinnati, OH 45202-3810
Contact: Melissa LaCorte, Secy.

Established in 1968 in OH.
Donor(s): William A. Friedlander, Susan S. Friedlander, Jane K. Steinfirst, Ellen Friedlander.
Financial data (yr. ended 12/31/01): Grants paid, $120,537; assets, $3,108,892 (M); gifts received, $926,430; expenditures, $137,551; qualifying distributions, $115,203.
Limitations: Giving limited to the greater Cincinnati, OH, area.
Application information: Application form not required.
Officers: William A. Friedlander, Pres. and Secy.; Susan S. Friedlander, V.P. and Treas.; Melissa M. LaCorte, Secy.

EIN: 316023791
Codes: FD2

42884
Lewis and Dorothy Tamplin Trust
600 S. Main St.
West Mansfield, OH 43358
Contact: Valarie Stanley, Tr.

Established in 1996 in OH.
Financial data (yr. ended 12/31/01): Grants paid, $120,365; assets, $1,596,798 (M); expenditures, $149,316; qualifying distributions, $120,365.
Limitations: Giving limited to OH.
Trustee: Valarie Stanley.
EIN: 347044702
Codes: FD2

42885
Robert T. Keller Foundation
c/o Ronald C. Christian
1800 Firstar Tower, 425 Walnut St.
Cincinnati, OH 45202-3957

Established in 2001 in OH.
Donor(s): Robert T. Keeler.
Financial data (yr. ended 12/31/01): Grants paid, $120,300; assets, $5,410,526 (M); gifts received, $5,553,840; expenditures, $123,454; qualifying distributions, $123,045.
Limitations: Applications not accepted. Giving primarily in OH.
Application information: Contributes only to pre-selected organizations.
Officers and Trustees:* Margaret P. Keeler,* Pres.; Ronald C. Christian,* Secy.; Mary L. Rust,* Treas.
EIN: 311420552

42886
The Fleischmann Foundation
4001 Carew Tower
441 Vine St.
Cincinnati, OH 45202 (513) 621-1384
Contact: Charles Fleischmann III, Pres.

Incorporated in 1931 in OH.
Donor(s): Julius Fleischmann.‡
Financial data (yr. ended 12/31/01): Grants paid, $120,205; assets, $2,962,060 (M); expenditures, $134,629; qualifying distributions, $119,250.
Limitations: Giving primarily in OH.
Officers: Charles Fleischmann III, Pres. and Treas.; Eric P. Yeiser, V.P.; Blair S. Fleischmann, Secy.
Trustee: Noah Fleischmann.
EIN: 316025516
Codes: FD2

42887
The Oliver & Peg Amos Foundation, Inc.
1841 W. Cisco Rd.
Sidney, OH 45365

Established in 1998 in OH.
Donor(s): Margaret Amos.
Financial data (yr. ended 12/31/99): Grants paid, $120,000; assets, $1,217,830 (M); expenditures, $128,061; qualifying distributions, $119,867.
Officers: John O. Amos, Pres.; Carolyn Amos, V.P.; Margaret Francis, V.P.; J. Daniel Francis, Secy.-Treas.
EIN: 311616624

42888
Marguerite M. Wilson Foundation
c/o Carol Donaldson, Doug Horner, et al.
23811 Chagrin Blvd., Ste. LL10
Beachwood, OH 44122 (216) 292-5730
Contact: Patricia Ziats, Tr.

Established in 1953 in OH.
Donor(s): Frederic S. Remington, Henri Eugene LeSidaner.
Financial data (yr. ended 12/31/00): Grants paid, $120,000; assets, $3,291,351 (M); expenditures, $142,574; qualifying distributions, $126,663.
Limitations: Giving primarily in OH.
Application information: Application form not required.
Officers and Trustees:* Carol Horner Donaldson,* Pres. and Treas.; James H. Dempsey, Jr.,* Secy.; Holly Munger Book, Lawrence W. Hatch, Douglas M. Horner, James A. Horner, Jr., Jeffrey Munger, Patricia Ziats.
EIN: 346521259
Codes: FD2

42889
John K. and Alice O'Neill Powers Foundation
1406 W. 6th St., 3rd Fl.
Cleveland, OH 44113-1300

Established in 1986 in OH.
Donor(s): Alice O'Neill Powers.
Financial data (yr. ended 12/31/01): Grants paid, $119,462; assets, $391,176 (M); expenditures, $122,921; qualifying distributions, $117,965.
Limitations: Applications not accepted. Giving primarily in OH.
Application information: Contributes only to pre-selected organizations.
Trustees: Alice O'Neill Powers, John K. Powers, Jr.
EIN: 346589966
Codes: FD2

42890
Helen McCalla Foundation
c/o KeyBank, N.A.
P.O. Box 10099
Toledo, OH 43699-0099
Application address: P.O. Box 8612, Ann Arbor, MI 48107
Contact: Bill Dunlap, Admin.

Established in 1995 in MI.
Donor(s): Helen McCalla.‡
Financial data (yr. ended 12/31/01): Grants paid, $119,248; assets, $2,334,192 (M); expenditures, $137,853; qualifying distributions, $122,855.
Limitations: Giving limited to the Washtenaw County, MI, area.
Trustee: KeyBank, N.A.
EIN: 383195451
Codes: FD2

42891
Taylor-McHenry Memorial Fund
(Formerly Richard M. & Lydia McHenry Taylor Trust)
c/o Unizam Financial Svcs. Group, N.A.
P.O. Box 2307
Zanesville, OH 43702-2307 (740) 455-7060

Established in 1964 in OH.
Financial data (yr. ended 12/31/01): Grants paid, $118,843; assets, $3,618,868 (M); expenditures, $135,972; qualifying distributions, $121,096.
Limitations: Giving limited to Muskingum County, OH.
Application information: Application form required.
Trustee: First National Bank.
EIN: 316063772
Codes: FD2

42892
W. E. Mikhail Foundation
4203 Shamley Green Dr.
Toledo, OH 43623-3234

Established in 1985 in OH.
Donor(s): W.E. Mikhail.
Financial data (yr. ended 12/31/00): Grants paid, $118,477; assets, $359,649 (M); gifts received,

$25,000; expenditures, $118,898; qualifying distributions, $117,795.
Limitations: Applications not accepted. Giving primarily in Toledo, OH.
Application information: Contributes only to pre-selected organizations.
Trustees: Michael Mikhail, Salma O. Mikhail, W.E. Mikhail.
EIN: 341474820
Codes: FD2

42893
The Milliron Foundation
103 S. Diamond St.
P.O. Box 1026
Mansfield, OH 44901
Contact: Grant Milliron, Pres.

Established in 1997 in OH.
Donor(s): Grant Milliron.
Financial data (yr. ended 12/31/99): Grants paid, $118,100; assets, $2,212,775 (M); expenditures, $124,822; qualifying distributions, $122,406.
Limitations: Applications not accepted. Giving primarily in Mansfield, OH.
Application information: Contributes only to pre-selected organizations.
Officers and Trustees:* Grant Milliron,* Pres.; Thomas F. Allen,* Secy.; Roger E. Shank,* Treas.
EIN: 311541621

42894
Hazelbaker Foundation
1661 Old Henderson Rd.
Columbus, OH 43220

Established in 1985 in OH.
Donor(s): Ralph E. Hazelbaker, Billie E. Hazelbaker.
Financial data (yr. ended 02/28/01): Grants paid, $117,734; assets, $1,471,840 (M); expenditures, $124,130; qualifying distributions, $117,734.
Limitations: Applications not accepted. Giving primarily in Columbus, OH.
Officers: Ralph E. Hazelbaker, Pres.; Billie E. Hazelbaker, Secy.; R. Brian Hazelbaker, Treas.
EIN: 311131197
Codes: FD2

42895
The McGinness Foundation
7012 Union Ave.
Cleveland, OH 44105-1382

Established about 1961.
Donor(s): H.J. McGinness, Jr.
Financial data (yr. ended 12/31/00): Grants paid, $117,500; assets, $1,802,826 (M); gifts received, $10,000; expenditures, $125,160; qualifying distributions, $117,500.
Limitations: Applications not accepted. Giving primarily in OH.
Application information: Contributes only to pre-selected organizations.
Officer: Henry McGinness.
EIN: 346527701
Codes: FD2

42896
The Ahuja Charitable Foundation
c/o Transtar Industries, Inc.
7350 Young Dr.
Walton Hills, OH 44146

Donor(s): Thomas Khoury, Monte Ahuja, Transtar Industries, Inc.
Financial data (yr. ended 12/31/00): Grants paid, $117,000; assets, $1,212,280 (M); gifts received, $430,000; expenditures, $118,150; qualifying distributions, $116,863.
Limitations: Giving primarily in Cleveland, OH.
Trustees: Monte Ahuja, Usha Ahuja, Vir K. Sundi.
EIN: 341685088
Codes: FD2

42897
RELTEC Charitable Foundation
c/o Marconi Communications Inc.
5900 Landerbrook Dr., Ste. 300
Cleveland, OH 44124
Contact: Craig S. Richter, Tax Mgr.

Established in 1997 in OH.
Donor(s): RELTEC Communications Inc., Marconi Communications Inc.
Financial data (yr. ended 12/31/01): Grants paid, $116,172; assets, $249,436 (M); gifts received, $250,000; expenditures, $120,611; qualifying distributions, $116,172.
Limitations: Applications not accepted. Giving on a national basis.
Application information: Contributes only to pre-selected organizations.
Officers and Trustees:* Dudley P. Sheffler,* Pres.; Scott A. Fine,* V.P.; David G. Phelps,* V.P.; Susan M. Clark,* Secy.; John L. Wilson,* Treas.
EIN: 311524328
Codes: CS, FD2, CD

42898
Hugh A. Fraser Fund
c/o The Huntington National Bank
P.O. Box 1558, HC0534
Columbus, OH 43216
Application address: c/o New Philadelphia Lions Club, 206 W. High Ave., New Philadelphia, OH 44663
Contact: Richard L. Stephenson, Chair.

Financial data (yr. ended 06/30/01): Grants paid, $115,683; assets, $2,172,183 (M); expenditures, $145,325; qualifying distributions, $120,134.
Limitations: Giving limited to Tuscarawas County, OH.
Application information: Application form not required.
Officer: Richard L. Stephenson, Chair.
Trustee: The Huntington National Bank.
EIN: 346622461
Codes: FD2, GTI

42899
LeBlond Foundation
7680 Innovation Way
Mason, OH 45040
Contact: Beverly J. Bowser

Established in 1952 in OH.
Donor(s): LeBlond Makino Machine Tool Co.
Financial data (yr. ended 12/31/00): Grants paid, $115,100; assets, $905,309 (M); expenditures, $126,682; qualifying distributions, $114,304.
Limitations: Giving primarily in the greater Cincinnati, OH, area.
Application information: Application form not required.
Officers: Daniel W. LeBlond, Chair.; Donald D. Lane, Vice-Chair.; James M. McVicker, Secy.
EIN: 316036274
Codes: CS, FD2, CD

42900
Bishop Fund
c/o KeyBank, N.A.
127 Public Sq., 17th Fl.
Cleveland, OH 44114 (216) 689-4651
Contact: Cyndi Clifton

Established about 1964.
Financial data (yr. ended 12/31/00): Grants paid, $115,000; assets, $2,434,980 (M); expenditures, $138,366; qualifying distributions, $119,234.
Limitations: Applications not accepted. Giving on a national basis.
Application information: Contributes only to pre-selected organizations. Unsolicited requests for funds not considered or acknowledged.
Director: Jonathan S. Bishop.
Trustee: KeyBank, N.A.
EIN: 346513612
Codes: FD2

42901
Mervin B. and Berenice R. France Foundation
c/o Foundations & Endowments
P.O. Box 10099
Toledo, OH 43699-0099 (419) 259-8218
Contact: KeyBank, N.A., Agent

Donor(s): Berenice R. France.‡
Financial data (yr. ended 11/30/00): Grants paid, $115,000; assets, $1,151,584 (M); expenditures, $121,793; qualifying distributions, $115,104.
Limitations: Giving on a national basis.
Trustees: Elizabeth France Dunn, William M. France, Ralph P. Higgins, Jr.
EIN: 341298875
Codes: FD2

42902
The G2 R2 Foundation
250 E. 5th St., Ste. 285
Cincinnati, OH 45202

Established in 1998 in OH.
Donor(s): Ronald G. Joseph.
Financial data (yr. ended 12/31/00): Grants paid, $115,000; assets, $594,439 (M); expenditures, $115,950; qualifying distributions, $115,000.
Limitations: Applications not accepted. Giving primarily in Cincinnati, OH.
Application information: Contributes only to pre-selected organizations.
Directors: Greg Joseph, Ronald G. Joseph.
EIN: 311493073
Codes: FD2

42903
Michael & Lois Russell Family Foundation
1240 Boardman-Canfield Rd.
Youngstown, OH 44512

Financial data (yr. ended 12/31/00): Grants paid, $115,000; assets, $744,861 (M); expenditures, $123,561; qualifying distributions, $114,663.
Trustee: Thomas J. Stabi.
EIN: 347084133
Codes: FD2

42904
Henry A. True Trust
146 E. Center St.
Marion, OH 43302 (740) 387-6000
Contact: John Kline Bartram, Tr.

Established in 1964 OH.
Financial data (yr. ended 12/31/00): Grants paid, $115,000; assets, $3,756,869 (M); expenditures, $229,653; qualifying distributions, $190,480.
Limitations: Giving limited to the Marion, OH, area.
Trustees: John C. Bartram, John Kline Bartram, Joe D. Donithen.
EIN: 310679235
Codes: FD2

42905
The Lampl Family Foundation
30799 Pinetree Rd., Unit 409
Pepper Pike, OH 44124
FAX: (216) 491-3995
Contact: Jack W. Lampl III, Pres.

Established in 1988 in OH.

Financial data (yr. ended 12/31/01): Grants paid, $114,750; assets, $1,843,083 (M); expenditures, $142,738; qualifying distributions, $120,786.
Limitations: Applications not accepted. Giving primarily in Cleveland, OH.
Application information: Unsolicited requests for funds not accepted.
Officer and Trustees:* Jack W. Lampl III,* Pres.; Carolyn C. Lampl, Joshua C. Lampl.
EIN: 341499838
Codes: FD2

42906
The Dennis M. and Lois A. Doyle Family Foundation
7757 Hopper Rd.
Cincinnati, OH 45255-4626
Contact: Dennis M. Doyle, Chair.

Established in 1989 in OH.
Donor(s): Dennis M. Doyle.
Financial data (yr. ended 12/31/01): Grants paid, $114,650; assets, $1,291,234 (M); expenditures, $118,253; qualifying distributions, $113,387.
Limitations: Giving primarily in Cincinnati, OH.
Application information: Application form required.
Officers and Trustees:* Dennis M. Doyle,* Chair.; Lois A. Doyle,* Pres. and Secy.-Treas.; Brian J. Doyle.
EIN: 311309829
Codes: FD2

42907
Maxwell C. Weaver Foundation
c/o U.S. Bank
P.O. Box 1118, M.L. 6190
Cincinnati, OH 45201
Contact: Terry Crilley

Established in 1985 in OH.
Financial data (yr. ended 12/31/01): Grants paid, $114,400; assets, $1,491,248 (M); expenditures, $125,691; qualifying distributions, $114,082.
Limitations: Giving primarily in Cincinnati, OH.
Application information: Application form not required.
Trustee: U.S. Bank.
EIN: 316275346
Codes: FD2

42908
The Schmitz Family Foundation
P.O. Box 248
Perrysburg, OH 43551
Contact: David L. Schmitz, Treas.

Established in 1990 in OH.
Donor(s): Martha D. Schmitz-Wealleans, David L. Schmitz, William W. Rogers, S & R Equipment Co., Inc.
Financial data (yr. ended 12/31/01): Grants paid, $114,388; assets, $2,045,001 (M); expenditures, $128,428; qualifying distributions, $114,388.
Limitations: Applications not accepted. Giving limited to northwest OH.
Application information: Unsolicited requests for funds not accepted.
Officers and Trustees:* Martha D. Schmitz-Wealleans,* Pres.; William L. Rogers,* Secy.; David L. Schmitz,* Treas.
EIN: 341665968
Codes: FD2

42909
St. Mary's Community Foundation
146 E. Spring St.
St. Marys, OH 45885 (419) 394-5693
E-mail: smcf@bright.net
Contact: Darwin D. Zeigler, Admin.

Established in 1974 in OH.
Financial data (yr. ended 06/30/01): Grants paid, $114,374; assets, $2,802,330 (M); gifts received, $283,468; expenditures, $137,640; giving activities include $83,500 for loans to individuals.
Limitations: Applications not accepted. Giving limited to the St. Mary's, OH, area.
Publications: Annual report, informational brochure, occasional report.
Application information: Contributes only to pre-selected organizations.
Officers and Members:* Edward S. Noble,* Pres.; Norman Kuhlman,* V.P.; Larry Shelby,* Secy.; Alma Kuffer, Michael Lynch, Ed Pierce, Maryann Sheaks, and 35 additional members.
EIN: 237372270
Codes: CM, FD2, GTI

42910
The McConnell Educational Foundation
150 E. Wilson Bridge Rd., Ste. 230
Worthington, OH 43085

Established in 1992 in OH.
Donor(s): John P. McConnell.
Financial data (yr. ended 12/31/01): Grants paid, $114,000; assets, $2,081,061 (M); expenditures, $117,516; qualifying distributions, $112,771.
Limitations: Applications not accepted. Giving primarily in CO, OH, and WV.
Application information: Contributes only to pre-selected organizations.
Officers and Trustees:* John P. McConnell,* Pres.; Michael A. Priest,* Secy.-Treas.; John S. Christie, George N. Corey.
EIN: 311365344
Codes: FD2

42911
PAS Foundation
c/o Howard S. Essner
1140 Terex Rd.
Hudson, OH 44236-3771

Established in 1994.
Donor(s): Peter A. Spitalieri, Celeste M. Spitalieri.
Financial data (yr. ended 12/31/01): Grants paid, $114,000; assets, $1,007,899 (M); gifts received, $198,000; expenditures, $125,178; qualifying distributions, $114,000.
Limitations: Applications not accepted. Giving primarily in OH.
Application information: Contributes only to pre-selected organizations.
Trustees: Howard S. Essner, Celeste M. Spitalieri, Peter A. Spitalieri.
EIN: 341766667
Codes: FD2

42912
The Alvin and Laura Siegal Foundation
28950 S. Woodland Rd.
Pepper Pike, OH 44124-5662

Established in 1998 in OH.
Donor(s): Alvin Siegal, Laura Siegal.
Financial data (yr. ended 12/31/00): Grants paid, $113,014; assets, $2,293,621 (M); gifts received, $15,000; expenditures, $121,052; qualifying distributions, $121,052.
Limitations: Applications not accepted. Giving primarily in Cleveland, OH.
Application information: Contributes only to pre-selected organizations.

Officers and Trustees:* Alvin Siegal,* Pres.; Kirk Schneider,* V.P.; Michael Siegal,* V.P.; Laura Siegal,* Secy.; Raj Patel,* Treas.
EIN: 341885840
Codes: FD2

42913
The Charles M. and Helen M. Brown Memorial Foundation
c/o KeyBank, N.A.
800 Superior Ave.
Cleveland, OH 44114

Established in 1999 in OH.
Donor(s): Helen M. Brown Crut, Helen Brown.‡
Financial data (yr. ended 12/31/01): Grants paid, $113,000; assets, $4,892,659 (M); gifts received, $2,018,122; expenditures, $140,468; qualifying distributions, $121,104.
Limitations: Applications not accepted. Giving primarily in Cleveland, OH.
Application information: Contributes only to pre-selected organizations.
Trustees: Raymond L. Pianka, KeyBank, N.A.
EIN: 347104901
Codes: FD2

42914
The I. J. Van Huffel Foundation
c/o William Hanshaw, Butler Wick Trust Dept.
425 Niles Cortland Rd. S.E., Bldg. A, Ste. 202
Warren, OH 44484-2478

Trust established in 1951 in OH.
Donor(s): Van Huffel Tube Corp.
Financial data (yr. ended 12/31/01): Grants paid, $113,000; assets, $3,359,681 (M); gifts received, $600; expenditures, $131,007; qualifying distributions, $117,178.
Limitations: Giving primarily in OH.
Directors: Kareen Klier, Evelyn M. Lawlor, Cheryle Remley, Ruth A. Van Huffel.
Trustees: Butler Wick Trust Dept., Second National Bank, Trust Dept.
EIN: 346516726
Codes: FD2

42915
Figgie Family Foundation
c/o Phillips Management
23550 Chagrin Blvd., Ste. 320
Beachwood, OH 44122 (216) 514-4777
Contact: Julie Brandow

Established in 1968.
Donor(s): Harry E. Figgie, Jr.
Financial data (yr. ended 12/31/00): Grants paid, $112,400; assets, $2,919,814 (M); gifts received, $25,000; expenditures, $165,808; qualifying distributions, $127,068.
Limitations: Giving primarily in OH.
Officers and Trustees:* Harry E. Figgie, Jr.,* Pres.; Richard S. Tomer,* Treas.; Mark P. Figgie, Nancy F. Figgie.
EIN: 346606657
Codes: FD2

42916
Genesis Foundation
(Formerly The Monarch Machine Tool Company Foundation)
2600 Kettering Tower
Dayton, OH 45423

Trust established in 1952 in OH.
Donor(s): The Monarch Machine Tool Co.
Financial data (yr. ended 12/31/00): Grants paid, $112,220; assets, $3,940,023 (M); expenditures, $97,917; qualifying distributions, $113,255.
Limitations: Applications not accepted. Giving primarily in OH, with some emphasis on Sidney.

42916—OHIO

Application information: Contributes only to pre-selected organizations.
Officers: Richard Clemens, Pres.; Timothy Gibson, V.P.; Karl Frydryk, Secy.-Treas.
Trustee: Nicholas Bergman.
EIN: 346556088
Codes: CS, FD2, CD

42917
The J. Colin Campbell Scholarship Fund
123 S. Broad St., Ste. 211
Lancaster, OH 43130-4304
Application address: 4307 Bauman Hill Rd., Lancaster, OH 43130-9455
Contact: William J. Sitterley, Tr.

Established in 1995 in OH.
Donor(s): The J. Colin Campbell Inter Vivos Trust.
Financial data (yr. ended 08/31/01): Grants paid, $112,000; assets, $1,638,531 (M); expenditures, $115,158; qualifying distributions, $113,867.
Limitations: Giving limited to residents of Fairfield County, OH.
Application information: Application form required.
Trustee: William J. Sitterley.
EIN: 316204632
Codes: FD2, GTI

42918
Nelson Talbott Foundation
Hanna Bldg., Ste. 1044
1422 Euclid Ave.
Cleveland, OH 44115
Contact: Nelson Talbott, Tr.

Established in 1947 in OH.
Donor(s): Nelson S. Talbott.
Financial data (yr. ended 09/30/01): Grants paid, $111,880; assets, $2,941,293 (M); expenditures, $155,089; qualifying distributions, $129,507.
Limitations: Applications not accepted. Giving primarily in Washington, DC, and Cleveland, OH.
Application information: Contributes only to pre-selected organizations.
Trustees: Malvin Banks, Josephine L. Talbott, Nelson S. Talbott.
EIN: 316039441
Codes: FD2

42919
The Joseph H. & Ellen B. Thomas Foundation, Inc.
2692 Wadsworth Rd.
Shaker Heights, OH 44122-2010
Contact: Joseph H. Thomas, Tr.

Established in 1988 in OH.
Donor(s): Joseph H. Thomas, Ellen B. Thomas.
Financial data (yr. ended 12/31/99): Grants paid, $111,825; assets, $1,099,442 (M); gifts received, $198,124; expenditures, $115,001; qualifying distributions, $110,593.
Limitations: Giving primarily in OH.
Application information: Application form not required.
Trustees: Elizabeth H. Leathery, Ellen B. Thomas, Joseph H. Thomas, Richard L. Thomas, Virginia H. Thomas.
EIN: 341615922

42920
Father James M. Fitzgerald Scholarship Trust
c/o National City Bank
P.O. Box 94651
Cleveland, OH 44101-4651
Application address: 301 S.W. Adams, Peoria, IL 61652, tel.: (309) 655-5322

Trust established in 1964 in IL.
Donor(s): Fr. James M. Fitzgerald.‡
Financial data (yr. ended 12/31/01): Grants paid, $111,312; assets, $2,794,654 (M); expenditures, $138,580; qualifying distributions, $117,342.
Limitations: Giving limited to residents of IL.
Application information: Application form not required.
Trustees: Msgr. Albert Hallin, National City Bank.
EIN: 376050189
Codes: FD2, GTI

42921
The Stephen and Joan McEwen Foundation
1503 Pinewood Ct.
Bowling Green, OH 43402

Donor(s): Stephen McEwen, Joan McEwen.
Financial data (yr. ended 12/31/01): Grants paid, $111,000; assets, $33,547 (M); expenditures, $112,251; qualifying distributions, $111,000.
Limitations: Applications not accepted.
Application information: Contributes only to pre-selected organizations.
Officers and Trustees:* Stephen McEwen,* Pres.; Joan McEwen,* V.P.; Richard G. LaValley, Jr.,* Secy.
EIN: 311627964

42922
Taiho Kogyo Tribology Research Foundation
194 Heritage Dr.
Tiffin, OH 44883

Established in 2000 in IL.
Donor(s): Taiho Kohyo Co., Ltd.
Financial data (yr. ended 12/31/01): Grants paid, $110,888; assets, $69,350 (M); gifts received, $100,000; expenditures, $198,180; qualifying distributions, $110,888.
Limitations: Giving on a national basis.
Application information: Scholarships application available at graduate schools of engineering. Application form required.
Officers: Senjiro Shibata, Pres.; DeAnn Krauss, V.P.; Keiichi Shimasaki, Secy.; Yasuji Sugisaki, Treas.
Directors: Herbert S. Cheng, Nobuo Fukuma, Masaru Funai, Yoshitsugu Kimura, Ward O. Winer.
EIN: 364399285

42923
Dr. Frank Vecchio and Helen Williams Vecchio Foundation
925 Euclid Ave., Ste. 1100
Cleveland, OH 44115-1475 (216) 696-4087
Contact: Robert B. Tamaro, Tr.

Established in 1983.
Donor(s): Helen Williams Vecchio.‡
Financial data (yr. ended 12/31/01): Grants paid, $110,667; assets, $1,708,582 (M); expenditures, $147,979; qualifying distributions, $110,667.
Limitations: Giving primarily in northeastern OH.
Trustees: Michael E. Elliott, Charles O'Toole, Robert B. Tamaro.
EIN: 341422252
Codes: FD2

42924
The Meyers Foundation
c/o Bartlett & Co.
35 E. 4th St.
Cincinnati, OH 45202

Established in 1949 in OH.
Financial data (yr. ended 12/31/01): Grants paid, $110,500; assets, $2,340,764 (M); expenditures, $136,391; qualifying distributions, $111,828.
Limitations: Applications not accepted. Giving primarily in OH.
Application information: Contributes only to pre-selected organizations.
Officers: Philip M. Meyers III, Pres.; Ann Meyers, Secy.
Trustees: Susan Falk, Lynne Gordon.
EIN: 316023945
Codes: FD2

42925
Browne Agape Family Foundation, Inc
4615 MacDonald Ct.
Mason, OH 45040

Established in 1998 in OH.
Donor(s): David Browne.
Financial data (yr. ended 09/30/01): Grants paid, $110,000; assets, $1,017,052 (M); gifts received, $50,037; expenditures, $116,511; qualifying distributions, $116,122.
Limitations: Applications not accepted.
Application information: Contributes only to pre-selected organizations.
Officers: David Browne, Pres.; Debbie Browne, Secy.; Mike Ellison, Treas.
EIN: 311622025
Codes: FD2

42926
The Tuck & Ham-Hi Lee Foundation, Inc.
1200 Edison Plz.
300 Madison Ave.
Toledo, OH 43604

Established in 1997 in OH.
Donor(s): Ham-Hi Lee, Tuck B. Lee.
Financial data (yr. ended 12/31/99): Grants paid, $110,000; assets, $220,260 (M); expenditures, $115,546; qualifying distributions, $111,990.
Limitations: Applications not accepted.
Application information: Contributes only to pre-selected organizations.
Directors: Ham-Hi Lee, Tuck B. Lee, Daniel A. Worline.
EIN: 341851792
Codes: FD2

42927
The O'Neill Foundation
c/o Robert E. O'Neill
1445 W. Main St.
Newark, OH 43055

Established in 1997 in OH.
Donor(s): John J. O'Neill, John J. O'Neill.
Financial data (yr. ended 12/31/00): Grants paid, $110,000; assets, $2,557,440 (M); gifts received, $34,895; expenditures, $120,767; qualifying distributions, $108,765.
Limitations: Applications not accepted. Giving primarily in OH.
Application information: Contributes only to pre-selected organizations.
Officers: Robert E. O'Neill, Pres.; Martha J. Morrison, Secy.; John J. O'Neill, Treas.
EIN: 311530980
Codes: FD2

42928
The Susan Scherer Charitable Foundation, Inc.
P.O. Box 163602
Columbus, OH 43216
Contact: Susan Scherer, Pres.

Established in 1998 in OH.
Donor(s): Susan Scherer.
Financial data (yr. ended 11/30/00): Grants paid, $110,000; assets, $1,084,760 (M); expenditures, $118,799; qualifying distributions, $110,000.
Application information: Application form not required.
Officers and Trustees:* Susan Scherer,* Pres.; Michael R. Weed, Ph.D,* Secy.; Stephen T. Weed, M.S.,* Treas.; Michael Bishop, Robert Blalock,

Susan Brooks, Beverly G. Gottschalk, Priscilla D. Mead, Lanah M. Miller, Aron Ross, Todd S. Scherer.
EIN: 311628446
Codes: FD2

42929
Edward E. Meyer Educational Trust
c/o Fifth Third Bank
38 Fountain Square Plz.
Cincinnati, OH 45263

Financial data (yr. ended 12/31/00): Grants paid, $109,652; assets, $2,538,831 (M); expenditures, $129,143; qualifying distributions, $108,821.
Limitations: Applications not accepted. Giving limited to residents of Vanderburgh County, IN.
Application information: Unsolicited requests for funds not accepted.
Trustee: Fifth Third Bank.
EIN: 356259567
Codes: FD2, GTI

42930
The Heffner Fund
c/o National City Bank
P.O. Box 5756
Cleveland, OH 44101 (216) 575-2742
Application address: c/o National City Bank, 1900 E. 9th St., Cleveland, OH 44114-3484

Established in 1965 in OH.
Financial data (yr. ended 12/31/00): Grants paid, $109,500; assets, $1,847,520 (M); gifts received, $77,428; expenditures, $125,403; qualifying distributions, $114,340.
Limitations: Giving primarily in OH.
Trustee: National City Bank.
EIN: 346568632
Codes: FD2

42931
The Bares Foundation
468 Bentleyville Rd.
Chagrin Falls, OH 44022-2416

Established in 1977 in OH.
Donor(s): Milbar Corp., Jack A. Bares.
Financial data (yr. ended 06/30/01): Grants paid, $109,480; assets, $2,693,682 (M); gifts received, $45,000; expenditures, $114,925; qualifying distributions, $113,087.
Limitations: Applications not accepted. Giving primarily in OH.
Application information: Contributes only to pre-selected organizations.
Officer and Trustees:* Jack A. Bares,* Pres. and Secy.; Alice W. Bares, Charles C. Bares, John E. Bares, Kent K. Bares, Lori Northrup.
EIN: 341211995
Codes: FD2

42932
The Arnovitz Foundation
6105 N. Dixie Dr.
Dayton, OH 45413
Application address: 22 S. Jefferson St., Dayton, OH 45402
Contact: Matthew Arnovitz, Treas.

Donor(s): Theodore M. Arnovitz.
Financial data (yr. ended 03/31/01): Grants paid, $108,858; assets, $148,533 (M); gifts received, $77,113; expenditures, $110,408; qualifying distributions, $108,858.
Limitations: Giving primarily in OH.
Officers: Theodore M. Arnovitz, Pres.; Beverly A. Saeks, V.P.; Matthew E. Arnovitz, Treas.
EIN: 316063400
Codes: FD2

42933
The John and Joan Jackson Foundation
1802 Carew Tower
441 Vine St.
Cincinnati, OH 45202 (513) 721-6521
Contact: Albert T. Metz, Exec. Dir.

Established in 1998 in OH.
Donor(s): John Jackson, Joan Jackson.
Financial data (yr. ended 12/31/00): Grants paid, $108,288; assets, $10,625 (M); gifts received, $92,850; expenditures, $186,481; qualifying distributions, $108,288.
Limitations: Giving on a national basis.
Officers: John Jackson, Pres.; Richard L. Katz, Secy.; Joan Jackson, Treas.; Albert T. Metz, Exec. Dir.
EIN: 311588051
Codes: FD2

42934
Helen L. & Marie F. Rotterman Trust
1300 Courthouse Plz., N.E.
P.O. Box 220
Dayton, OH 45402-0220 (937) 222-2500
Contact: Jeffrey B. Shulman, Tr.

Established in 1982 in OH.
Financial data (yr. ended 07/31/01): Grants paid, $108,000; assets, $3,618,846 (M); expenditures, $144,600; qualifying distributions, $125,241.
Limitations: Giving to organizations on a national basis; scholarships given primarily to residents of Dayton, OH.
Application information: Individual applicants should include Trinity College application and a copy of high school record and certification of Catholic church affiliation.
Trustees: John O. Hubler, Jan S. Scheid, Jeffrey B. Shulman.
EIN: 316236156
Codes: FD2, GTI

42935
The Donald E. & Eydie R. Garlikov Family Foundation
41 S. High St., Ste. 2710
Columbus, OH 43215

Donor(s): Donald E. Garlikov.
Financial data (yr. ended 12/31/01): Grants paid, $107,599; assets, $2,705,224 (M); expenditures, $109,261; qualifying distributions, $107,599.
Limitations: Applications not accepted.
Application information: Contributes only to pre-selected organizations.
Officer and Trustee:* Donald E. Garlikov,* Pres.
EIN: 311487317

42936
Phyllis & Sidney Reisman Foundation
P.O. Box 22688
Beachwood, OH 44122-0688

Established in 1999 in OH.
Donor(s): Sidney Reisman.
Financial data (yr. ended 11/30/00): Grants paid, $106,800; assets, $987,827 (M); expenditures, $111,518; qualifying distributions, $106,800.
Limitations: Applications not accepted. Giving primarily in Cleveland, OH.
Application information: Contributes only to pre-selected organizations.
Trustees: Allen T. Reisman, Peter J. Reisman, Sidney Reisman.
EIN: 341881441
Codes: FD2

42937
Gould Inc. Foundation
c/o Gould Inc., Scholarship Dir.
34929 Curtis Blvd.
Eastlake, OH 44095 (440) 953-5000
Application address: c/o Dir., Gould Inc. Fdn. Scholarship Prog., 35129 Curtis Blvd., Eastlake, OH 44095

Incorporated in 1951 in OH.
Donor(s): Gould Electronics Inc.
Financial data (yr. ended 12/31/01): Grants paid, $106,560; assets, $2,422,748 (M); expenditures, $108,332; qualifying distributions, $106,560.
Limitations: Giving primarily in areas of company operations: Chandler, AZ, Newburyport, MA, Glen Burnie, MD, and Cleveland, Eastlake, and McConnelsville, OH.
Publications: Application guidelines.
Application information: Write to principal manager of local Gould facility; application required for scholarship program.
Officers and Directors:* C.D. Ferguson,* Pres.; M.C. Veysey,* V.P. and Secy.; J.L. Monaco, V.P. and Treas.; L.J. Huss,* V.P.
EIN: 346525555
Codes: CS, FD2, CD, GTI

42938
Richard I. and Arline J. Landers Foundation
590 Lexington Ave.
Mansfield, OH 44907
Contact: Richard V. Kleshinski, Tr.

Established in 1989 in OH.
Donor(s): Arline J. Landers, Richard I. Landers.‡
Financial data (yr. ended 12/31/01): Grants paid, $106,400; assets, $2,795,158 (M); gifts received, $90,000; expenditures, $145,400; qualifying distributions, $115,162.
Limitations: Giving primarily in OH.
Trustees: Richard M. Kleshinski, Richard V. Kleshinski, Arline J. Landers.
EIN: 341623986
Codes: FD2

42939
Helene P. Kaighin Charitable Trust
c/o Second National Bank of Warren
108 Main St., S.W.
Warren, OH 44481

Financial data (yr. ended 12/31/01): Grants paid, $106,370; assets, $1,358,841 (M); expenditures, $123,560; qualifying distributions, $106,370.
Limitations: Giving primarily in Warren, OH.
Application information: Application form not required.
Directors: Marilyn K. Townsend, Nancy K. VanFossan.
Trustee: Second National Bank of Warren.
EIN: 346582182

42940
Frederick Melvin Douglas Foundation
c/o Fifth Third Bank
P.O. Box 630858
Cincinnati, OH 45263
Application address: P.O. Box 1868, Toledo, OH 43603-1868, tel.: (419) 259-6851
Contact: R.G. Papenfus

Donor(s): Frederick Melvin Douglas.‡
Financial data (yr. ended 12/31/01): Grants paid, $106,353; assets, $1,806,426 (M); expenditures, $129,620; qualifying distributions, $110,860.
Limitations: Giving limited to Toledo, OH, and in adjacent areas.
Application information: Research project applications supplied by hospital. Application form required.

42940—OHIO

Trustee: Fifth Third Bank.
EIN: 346518567
Codes: FD2

42941
Premix Foundation
3365 E. Center St.
North Kingsville, OH 44068
Contact: B. Webster, Secy.

Established in 1986 in OH.
Donor(s): Premix, Inc.
Financial data (yr. ended 12/31/01): Grants paid, $106,305; assets, $78,897 (M); gifts received, $30,184; expenditures, $108,102; qualifying distributions, $51,727.
Limitations: Giving primarily in OH, with emphasis on Ashtabula.
Officers and Trustees:* W. Shenk, Pres.; F.M. Davey,* V.P.; E.T. Warren,* Secy.-Treas.; K.W. Lazo, N. McCarthy.
EIN: 341530598
Codes: CS, FD2, CD

42942
Wightman-Wieber Consolidate STCA
c/o Keybank, N.A.
P.O. Box 10099
Toledo, OH 43699-0099 (419) 259-8655
Contact: Dian Ohns, Trust Off., Keybank, N.A.

Established in 1999 in OH.
Financial data (yr. ended 12/31/01): Grants paid, $106,187; assets, $5,166,718 (M); expenditures, $150,453; qualifying distributions, $131,710.
Limitations: Giving primarily in OH.
Officers and Trustees:* George L. Mylander,* Pres.; Nelson Alward,* Secy.; Keybank, N.A.
EIN: 341831533

42943
David E. Toomey Trust
c/o Huntington National Bank
P.O. Box 1558
Columbus, OH 43216

Established in 1999 in OH.
Financial data (yr. ended 06/30/01): Grants paid, $105,812; assets, $3,649,321 (M); expenditures, $137,237; qualifying distributions, $112,218.
Limitations: Applications not accepted.
Application information: Contributes only to pre-selected organizations.
Trustee: The Huntington National Bank.
EIN: 316630556

42944
Pizzuti Family Foundation
250 E. Broad St., Ste. 1900
Columbus, OH 43215-3708
Contact: Linda G. Readey, Dir. of Comm. Affairs

Established in 1985 in OH.
Donor(s): Ronald A. Pizzuti, Ann L. Pizzuti.
Financial data (yr. ended 12/31/01): Grants paid, $105,455; assets, $141,734 (M); gifts received, $118,062; expenditures, $118,062; qualifying distributions, $105,236.
Limitations: Applications not accepted. Giving limited to Columbus, OH.
Application information: Contributes only to pre-selected organizations.
Officers: Ronald A. Pizzuti, Pres.; Ann L. Pizzuti, Treas.
Trustee: Fredric L. Smith.
Director: John W. Elam.
EIN: 311144793
Codes: FD2

42945
L. R. Moffitt & L. Q. Moffitt Foundation
c/o FirstMerit Bank, N.A.
121 S. Main St., Ste. 200
Akron, OH 44308 (330) 384-7320
FAX: (330) 849-8992; E-mail: bjmobray@firstmerit.com
Contact: R.B. Tynan, Sr., V.P. and Trust Off., FirstMerit Bank, N.A.

Established in 1967 in OH.
Donor(s): Lucian Q. Moffitt.‡
Financial data (yr. ended 12/31/01): Grants paid, $105,335; assets, $1,909,449 (M); expenditures, $121,480; qualifying distributions, $103,123.
Limitations: Giving limited to Akron and Summit County, OH.
Application information: Application form not required.
Trustees: Allan Johnson, Charles E. Pierson, FirstMerit Bank, N.A.
EIN: 346597380
Codes: FD2

42946
Lawrence Selhorst Charitable Foundation
26300 Miles Rd.
Bedford Heights, OH 44146
Contact: Sandra Gibbons, Pres.

Established in 1999 in OH.
Donor(s): Lawrence O. Selhorst.
Financial data (yr. ended 12/31/00): Grants paid, $105,250; assets, $241,781 (M); gifts received, $200,156; expenditures, $113,833; qualifying distributions, $106,983.
Limitations: Giving on a national basis, with emphasis on OH.
Officers and Trustees:* Sandra S. Gibbons,* Pres.; Kathryn A. Klindera,* V.P.; Timothy W. Selhorst,* Secy.-Treas.; Lawrence O. Selhorst.
EIN: 341906163

42947
Estelle S. Campbell Charitable Foundation
c/o National City Bank of Pennsylvania
P.O. Box 94651
Cleveland, OH 44101-4651
Application address: c/o William M. Schmidt, National City Bank of Pennsylvania, 20 Stanwix St., Pittsburgh, PA 15222, tel.: (412) 644-8332

Established in 1998 in PA.
Financial data (yr. ended 12/31/01): Grants paid, $105,000; assets, $1,042,674 (M); gifts received, $320,000; expenditures, $122,732; qualifying distributions, $107,512.
Limitations: Giving primarily in Pittsburgh, PA.
Trustee: National City Bank of Pennsylvania.
EIN: 251809360
Codes: FD2

42948
Scherr Foundation
(Formerly Joseph W. Scherr, Jr. Foundation No. 2)
c/o Fifth Third Bank
38 Fountain Sq. Plz., Dept. 00858
Cincinnati, OH 45263 (513) 579-6034
Contact: Lawra J. Baumann, Fdn. Off., Fifth Third Bank

Established in 1989 in OH.
Donor(s): Joseph W. Scherr, Jr.‡
Financial data (yr. ended 12/31/00): Grants paid, $105,000; assets, $1,556,048 (M); expenditures, $136,850; qualifying distributions, $102,055.
Limitations: Giving on a national basis.
Application information: Application form required.
Trustee: Fifth Third Bank.
EIN: 316195447

Codes: FD2

42949
Vista Foundation
3557 Bayard Dr.
Cincinnati, OH 45208 (513) 321-6999
Contact: Helen K. Heekin, Pres.

Established in 1998 in OH.
Financial data (yr. ended 12/31/01): Grants paid, $104,945; assets, $2,317,501 (M); gifts received, $751,286; expenditures, $154,431; qualifying distributions, $104,945.
Limitations: Giving primarily in CA.
Officers and Trustees:* Helen K. Heekin,* Pres.; Charles L. Heekin III,* V.P.; R. McShane Heekin,* V.P.; Peter K. Heekin,* Secy.; Micaela K. Heekin,* Treas.
EIN: 311347794

42950
Pastore Foundation
1925 30th St. N.E.
Canton, OH 44705-2598

Established in 1981 in OH.
Donor(s): Anthony M. Pastore, James A. Pastore, Myrna A. Pastore, East Beeson Farm, Inc., Reeder Poultry, Inc., St. Peter's Farm, Inc.
Financial data (yr. ended 04/30/01): Grants paid, $104,900; assets, $704,984 (M); gifts received, $90,000; expenditures, $106,552; qualifying distributions, $106,139.
Limitations: Applications not accepted. Giving primarily in OH.
Application information: Contributes only to pre-selected organizations.
Trustees: Anthony M. Pastore, James A. Pastore, James A. Pastore, Jr., Michael G. Pastore.
EIN: 341333219
Codes: FD2

42951
Donald E. and Alice M. Noble Charitable Foundation, Inc.
2345 Gateway Dr.
Wooster, OH 44691 (330) 264-8066
Contact: Donald E. Noble, Secy.

Established in 1990 in OH.
Donor(s): Donald E. Noble, Alice M. Noble.
Financial data (yr. ended 12/31/01): Grants paid, $104,700; assets, $4,255,287 (M); gifts received, $2,500,000; expenditures, $111,107; qualifying distributions, $104,700.
Limitations: Giving primarily in Wooster, OH.
Application information: Application form not required.
Officers and Trustees:* Alice M. Noble,* Pres.; Donald E. Noble,* Secy.; Nancy L. Holland, Jeanne M. Langford, David D. Noble, Richard S. Noble.
EIN: 341665641
Codes: FD2

42952
Joseph E. and Mary E. Keller Foundation
105 Collingwood Ave.
Dayton, OH 45419
Contact: John C. Keyes, Tr.

Established in 1991 in OH.
Donor(s): Joseph E. Keller, Mary E. Keller.
Financial data (yr. ended 12/31/01): Grants paid, $104,200; assets, $784,647 (M); expenditures, $140,868; qualifying distributions, $104,200.
Limitations: Applications not accepted. Giving on a national basis.
Application information: Contributes only to pre-selected organizations.

Trustees: W. Michael Conway, Mary E. Keller, John C. Keyes.
EIN: 316411369
Codes: FD2

42953
Raymond Rosenberger Award Foundation
c/o National City Bank of Indiana
P.O. Box 94651
Cleveland, OH 44101-4651

Established in 1996 in IN.
Financial data (yr. ended 06/30/01): Grants paid, $103,927; assets, $1,620,052 (M); expenditures, $111,338; qualifying distributions, $108,028.
Limitations: Applications not accepted. Giving primarily in Fort Wayne, IN.
Application information: Contributes only to pre-selected organizations.
Trustee: National City Bank of Indiana.
EIN: 356627244
Codes: FD2

42954
The Gladys and Ralph Lazarus Foundation
(Formerly Ralph Lazarus Foundation)
c/o Frost, Brown, & Todd
2200 PNC Ctr., 201 E. 5th St.
Cincinnati, OH 45202-2803

Established in 1994 in OH.
Financial data (yr. ended 06/30/01): Grants paid, $103,000; assets, $2,557,919 (M); expenditures, $128,482; qualifying distributions, $103,979.
Limitations: Applications not accepted. Giving on a national basis, with emphasis on CA and TX.
Application information: Contributes only to pre-selected organizations.
Trustees: Kathryn Lazarus Baron, James Lazarus, John R. Lazarus.
EIN: 316018922
Codes: FD2

42955
Owen and Jean Pritchard Foundation
P.O. Box 94651
Cleveland, OH 44101-4651
Application address: c/o National City Bank of Indiana, P.O. Box 110, Ft. Wayne, IN 46801, tel.: (219) 461-6199
Contact: Michele Herald

Established in 1997 in IN.
Financial data (yr. ended 03/31/01): Grants paid, $102,850; assets, $1,875,164 (M); expenditures, $112,037; qualifying distributions, $103,545.
Limitations: Giving primarily in Fort Wayne, IN.
Trustee: National City Bank of Indiana.
EIN: 352016378
Codes: FD2

42956
Zapis Charitable Foundation, Inc.
P.O. Box 5728
Cleveland, OH 44101-0728

Established in 1999 in FL.
Financial data (yr. ended 06/30/01): Grants paid, $102,806; assets, $2,263,748 (M); expenditures, $138,674; qualifying distributions, $89,403.
Limitations: Applications not accepted. Giving primarily in OH.
Application information: Contributes only to pre-selected organizations.
Officers and Trustees:* Xenophon Zapis,* Pres.; Smaragda Zapis,* V.P.; Donna Z. Thomas,* Secy.; Leon X. Zapis,* Treas.; Renee Z. Seybert, Maria A. Wymer.
EIN: 311681569
Codes: FD2

42957
The Morse Family Foundation
824 Sun Ridge Ln.
Chagrin Falls, OH 44022-4256
Contact: Bradish G. Morse, Pres.

Established in 1996 in OH.
Donor(s): A. Reynolds Morse, Eleanor R. Morse.
Financial data (yr. ended 12/31/01): Grants paid, $102,800; assets, $246 (M); gifts received, $104,750; expenditures, $105,105; qualifying distributions, $105,093.
Limitations: Applications not accepted. Giving primarily in FL and OR.
Application information: Contributes only to pre-selected organizations.
Officers and Trustees:* Bradish G. Morse,* Pres.; Jayne Morse,* Secy.-Treas.; Eleanor R. Morse.
EIN: 341802971
Codes: FD2

42958
Don and Virginia Wolf Charitable Foundation
c/o National City Bank of Indiana
P.O. Box 94651
Cleveland, OH 44101-4651

Established in 1990 in IN.
Donor(s): Don A. Wolf, Hagerman Construction.
Financial data (yr. ended 12/31/01): Grants paid, $102,425; assets, $1,952,188 (M); expenditures, $123,220; qualifying distributions, $100,301.
Limitations: Applications not accepted. Giving primarily in IN.
Application information: Contributes only to pre-selected organizations.
Officer and Directors:* Don A. Wolf,* Pres.; Virginia Wolf.
EIN: 351799317
Codes: FD2

42959
Meisel Family Foundation
2444 Madison Rd., Ste. 105
Cincinnati, OH 45208
Application address: 7915 Willowridge Ln., Cincinnati, OH 45237
Contact: Alvin Meisel, Pres.

Established in 1997 in OH.
Financial data (yr. ended 11/30/01): Grants paid, $102,308; assets, $1,630,475 (M); expenditures, $105,354; qualifying distributions, $102,308.
Officer and Trustees:* Alvin Z. Meisel,* Pres.; Nancy Meisel,* Secy.-Treas.; Mark H. Berliant.
EIN: 311581846
Codes: FD2

42960
Robert S. Morrison Foundation
P.O. Box 370
Ashtabula, OH 44005 (440) 992-1549
Contact: Marge Bien

Donor(s): Robert S. Morrison.
Financial data (yr. ended 12/31/00): Grants paid, $101,700; assets, $1,591,527 (M); expenditures, $105,474; qualifying distributions, $100,882.
Limitations: Giving limited to within 100 miles of Ashtabula, OH.
Trustees: Rick Coblitz, Stuart W. Cordell, Douglas A. Hedberg, Robert S. Morrison, Louise Raffa.
EIN: 237246162
Codes: FD2

42961
Christ Foundation
P.O. Box 1180
Hartville, OH 44632-1180 (330) 877-1155
Contact: Patricia P. Moore, Secy.

Established in 1971 in OH.
Donor(s): Jerry Moore.
Financial data (yr. ended 12/31/00): Grants paid, $101,536; assets, $3,314,758 (M); gifts received, $48,698; expenditures, $114,319; qualifying distributions, $110,419.
Limitations: Giving primarily in OH.
Officers: Jerry Moore, Pres.; Patricia P. Moore, Secy.; Lewis Yoder, Treas.
EIN: 237121546
Codes: FD2

42962
Charles W. & Sarah Jane Syak Foundation
P.O. Box 429
124 Hopewell Dr.
Girard, OH 44420
Contact: Sally J. Williams, Tr.

Established in 1993 in OH.
Donor(s): Charles W. Syak, Sarah Jane Syak.
Financial data (yr. ended 12/31/01): Grants paid, $101,315; assets, $762,328 (M); expenditures, $104,127; qualifying distributions, $101,715.
Limitations: Giving primarily in Youngstown, OH.
Application information: Application form not required.
Trustees: Charles W. Syak, Harry A. Syak, Sarah Jane Syak, Sally J. Williams.
EIN: 346992766
Codes: FD2

42963
The W. E. Bliss Foundation
c/o Bank One Ohio Trust Co., N.A.
P.O. Box 359
Youngstown, OH 44501 (330) 742-6743

Established in 1954 in OH.
Financial data (yr. ended 12/31/00): Grants paid, $101,025; assets, $863,969 (M); expenditures, $113,647; qualifying distributions, $102,526.
Limitations: Giving primarily in Youngstown, OH.
Trustee: Bank One Ohio Trust Co., N.A.
Appointing Committee: Alice Mae Schmutz.
EIN: 346514091
Codes: FD2

42964
Richard & Patricia Alderson Foundation
c/o PNC Advisors
P.O. Box 1198
Cincinnati, OH 45201-1198 (513) 651-8377
Contact: Lee D. Crooks, Fdn. Admin.

Established in 1996 in OH.
Donor(s): Patricia F. Alderson, Richard L. Alderson.
Financial data (yr. ended 12/31/01): Grants paid, $101,000; assets, $1,165,495 (M); expenditures, $111,097; qualifying distributions, $101,000.
Limitations: Applications not accepted. Giving primarily in OH.
Application information: Contributes only to pre-selected organizations.
Officers and Trustees:* Richard L. Alderson,* Pres. and Treas.; Patricia F. Alderson,* V.P. and Secy.; Amanda Lin Alderson, Michelle Ruth Alderson.
EIN: 311487519

42965
Clinton County Foundation
P.O. Box 831
Wilmington, OH 45177
E-mail: tlamke@erinet.com
Contact: Tony Lamke, Exec. Secy.

Established in 1972 in OH.
Financial data (yr. ended 12/31/99): Grants paid, $100,659; assets, $439,894 (M); gifts received, $123,558; expenditures, $106,568.
Limitations: Giving limited to Clinton County, OH.
Application information: Application form not required.
Officer and Trustees:* Tony Lamke,* Exec. Secy.; Mark Williams.
EIN: 311140087
Codes: CM

42966
George Isaac Foundation
P.O. Box 667
Bryan, OH 43506-0667

Established in 1993 in OH.
Donor(s): George A. Isaac, Jr.
Financial data (yr. ended 12/31/00): Grants paid, $100,100; assets, $1,879,931 (M); gifts received, $149,455; expenditures, $126,669; qualifying distributions, $100,100.
Limitations: Applications not accepted.
Application information: Contributes only to pre-selected organizations.
Officer: George A. Isaac, Jr., Pres.
EIN: 341724575
Codes: FD2

42967
Warren and Zoann Little Dusenbury Charitable Trust
32481 Meadowlark Way
Pepper Pike, OH 44124 (216) 591-0367
Contact: Zoann Dusenbury, Tr.

Established in 1986.
Donor(s): Warren Dusenbury,‡ Zoann Dusenbury.
Financial data (yr. ended 12/31/01): Grants paid, $100,000; assets, $486,509 (M); gifts received, $7,982; expenditures, $112,484; qualifying distributions, $100,000.
Limitations: Giving primarily in Cleveland, OH.
Trustee: Zoann Dusenbury.
EIN: 346847641
Codes: TN

42968
The Fedeli Family Charitable Foundation
P.O. Box 318003
Independence, OH 44131

Established in 2000 in OH.
Donor(s): Umberto Fedeli, Jr.
Financial data (yr. ended 12/31/00): Grants paid, $100,000; assets, $299,565 (M); gifts received, $531,738; expenditures, $100,000; qualifying distributions, $100,000.
Limitations: Applications not accepted. Giving primarily in Cleveland, OH.
Application information: Contributes only to pre-selected organizations.
Trustees: Jeffrey P. Consolo, Umberto Fedeli, Jr., Albert N. Salvatore.
EIN: 311740537

42969
The Thomas Lord Charitable Trust
c/o National City Bank of Pennsylvania
P.O. Box 94651
Cleveland, OH 44101-4651
Contact: C.A. Junter

Established in 1955.
Donor(s): Thomas Lord.
Financial data (yr. ended 12/31/01): Grants paid, $100,000; assets, $3,107,278 (M); expenditures, $114,212; qualifying distributions, $102,620.
Limitations: Giving primarily in NY and PA.
Application information: Application form not required.
Trustee: National City Bank of Pennsylvania.
EIN: 256028793
Codes: FD2

42970
The Nason Foundation
127 Public Sq., Ste. 2500
Cleveland, OH 44114
Contact: Emrie Thoresen, Dir.

Established in 1981 in WY.
Donor(s): Katherine H. Nason.‡
Financial data (yr. ended 11/30/00): Grants paid, $100,000; assets, $1,194,459 (M); expenditures, $119,855; qualifying distributions, $108,563.
Limitations: Applications not accepted. Giving primarily in OH.
Application information: Contributes only to pre-selected organizations.
Officers: John D. Merwin, Pres.; John Baird, V.P. and Secy.; Emrie Thoresen, Treas.
Director: Lynn Shaw.
EIN: 742226170
Codes: FD2

42971
The Richey Family Foundation
1 Invacare Way
Elyria, OH 44035

Established in 1997 in OH.
Donor(s): Joseph B. Richey.
Financial data (yr. ended 12/31/01): Grants paid, $100,000; assets, $687,826 (M); expenditures, $106,909; qualifying distributions, $100,000.
Limitations: Applications not accepted. Giving primarily in Cleveland, OH.
Application information: Contributes only to pre-selected organizations.
Officers: J.B. Richey, Pres.; James P. Oliver, Treas.
EIN: 341830501

42972
Jane Hard Russell No. 2 Fund B
c/o KeyBank, N.A.
800 Superior Ave., 4th Fl.
Cleveland, OH 44114-2601

Financial data (yr. ended 12/31/01): Grants paid, $100,000; assets, $1,655,248 (M); expenditures, $116,660; qualifying distributions, $104,925.
Limitations: Applications not accepted. Giving primarily in ME and OH.
Application information: Contributes only to pre-selected organizations.
Trustees: Gordon D. Russell, Joseph G. Russell, KeyBank, N.A.
EIN: 346507961
Codes: FD2

42973
Tony & Gladys Teramana Charitable Foundation
4110 Sunset Blvd.
Steubenville, OH 43952-3616
Contact: William F. Blake, Jr., Tr.

Established in 1992 in OH.
Donor(s): Tony Teramana.
Financial data (yr. ended 09/30/01): Grants paid, $100,000; assets, $321,627 (M); expenditures, $101,075; qualifying distributions, $99,958.
Limitations: Giving primarily in Steubenville, OH.
Trustees: William F. Blake, Jr., Albert B. Teramana, Anthony J. Teramana, Jr.
EIN: 341721203
Codes: FD2

42974
The John and Lillian E. Tymkewicz Family Foundation
1406 W. 6th St., 3rd Fl.
Cleveland, OH 44113-1300

Established in 1995 in OH.
Donor(s): John Tymkewicz, Lillian Tymkewicz.
Financial data (yr. ended 12/31/00): Grants paid, $100,000; assets, $255,004 (M); gifts received, $850; expenditures, $100,950; qualifying distributions, $100,907.
Limitations: Applications not accepted.
Application information: Contributes only to pre-selected organizations.
Trustees: Vivian A. Coticchia, Allen R. Tymkewicz, Lillian Tymkewicz.
EIN: 341818112
Codes: FD2

42975
The Zukowski Foundation
2590 Chagrin River Rd.
Chagrin Falls, OH 44022
Contact: Raymond J. Zukowski, Pres.

Established in 1995 in OH.
Donor(s): Raymond Zukowski.
Financial data (yr. ended 12/31/01): Grants paid, $100,000; assets, $1,733,260 (M); gifts received, $386,525; expenditures, $108,901; qualifying distributions, $99,802.
Officers and Trustees:* Raymond J. Zukowski,* Pres. and Treas.; Mary Ann Zukowski,* V.P. and Secy.; Michael R. Canty, Michele Alexis Canty, Ann Marie Wakeen, Kenneth A. Wakeen, Christine O. Zukowski.
EIN: 341818002
Codes: FD2

42976
Anthony D. Bullock III Foundation, Inc.
1 W. 4th St., Ste. 1400
Cincinnati, OH 45202
Contact: Kyle C. Brooks

Established in 1997 in OH.
Donor(s): Eleine H. Brooks, Kyle C. Brooks.
Financial data (yr. ended 05/31/01): Grants paid, $99,980; assets, $813,240 (M); gifts received, $1,120; expenditures, $102,871; qualifying distributions, $99,980.
Limitations: Giving primarily in TX.
Application information: Application form not required.
Officers: Eleine H. Brooks, Kyle C. Brooks.
EIN: 311580767
Codes: FD2

42977
The Sendzimir Foundation, Inc.
c/o Clark, Schaefer, Hackett & Co.
105 E. 4th St., Ste. 1600
Cincinnati, OH 45202 (513) 241-3111
Contact: Jan Sendzimir, Pres.

Established in 1994 in MA.
Donor(s): Sendzimir Charitable Lead Trust.
Financial data (yr. ended 06/30/01): Grants paid, $99,812; assets, $415,322 (M); gifts received, $134,071; expenditures, $125,877; qualifying distributions, $116,908.
Limitations: Giving in the U.S. and Eastern Europe, with emphasis on Poland.
Officers: Jan Sendzimir, Pres.; Gisela Bosch, Mgr.
Director: Stanley Sendzimir.
EIN: 223309860
Codes: FD2

42978
J. B. Firestone Charitable Trust
c/o FirstMerit Bank, N.A.
105 Court St.
Elyria, OH 44035-5525 (440) 329-3000
Contact: Michael E. Yanick, V.P. and Sr. Trust Off., FirstMerit Bank, N.A.

Established in 1966 in OH.
Financial data (yr. ended 12/31/01): Grants paid, $99,624; assets, $1,895,758 (M); expenditures, $114,225; qualifying distributions, $121,196; giving activities include $5,500 for loans to individuals.
Limitations: Giving limited to the Spencer, OH area.
Application information: Application form not required.
Trustee: FirstMerit Bank, N.A.
EIN: 346577308
Codes: FD2, GTI

42979
Belford Family Charitable Trust
(Formerly David A. Belford Charitable Trust)
2372 E. Main St.
Columbus, OH 43209-2478

Established in 1993 in OH.
Donor(s): David A. Belford.
Financial data (yr. ended 12/31/01): Grants paid, $99,620; assets, $2,314,241 (M); gifts received, $114,490; expenditures, $108,198; qualifying distributions, $108,198.
Limitations: Applications not accepted. Giving primarily in Columbus, OH.
Application information: Contributes only to pre-selected organizations.
Trustee: David A. Belford.
EIN: 311396819
Codes: FD2

42980
Chambers Foundation of Johnstown, Ohio
200 E. Coshocton St.
Johnstown, OH 43031-0486 (740) 967-9015
Contact: Michael R. Chambers, Tr.

Established in 1994 in OH.
Donor(s): Pauline C. Yost.
Financial data (yr. ended 12/31/00): Grants paid, $99,250; assets, $365,050 (M); gifts received, $100,000; expenditures, $100,184; qualifying distributions, $99,250.
Limitations: Giving primarily in the Johnstown, OH, area.
Trustees: Michael R. Chambers, Cheryl C. Poulton, Pauline C. Yost.
EIN: 311409343
Codes: FD2

42981
Worner Trust
c/o National City Bank
P.O. Box 94651
Cleveland, OH 44101-4651
Application address: 301 S.W. Adams St., Peoria, IL 61652, tel.: (309) 655-5385
Contact: Jo Ann Harlan

Established in 1996 in IL.
Financial data (yr. ended 03/31/01): Grants paid, $99,209; assets, $2,405,602 (M); expenditures, $110,917; qualifying distributions, $100,954.
Limitations: Giving primarily in IL.
Application information: Application form not required.
Trustee: National City Bank.
EIN: 376337761
Codes: FD2

42982
ICF Foundation
4000 Embassy Pkwy., Ste. 330
Akron, OH 44333

Established in 1998 in OH.
Donor(s): John Ong.
Financial data (yr. ended 12/31/01): Grants paid, $99,052; assets, $2,356,422 (M); expenditures, $123,973; qualifying distributions, $115,535.
Limitations: Giving primarily in OH and western PA.
Publications: Application guidelines.
Application information: Application form not required.
Officers: John D. Ong, Pres.; Mary Lee Ong, Secy.-Treas.
Trustees: M. Katherine Landini, John F.H. Ong, Richard P.B. Ong.
EIN: 341826821
Codes: FD2

42983
The Lang Foundation
c/o R.A. Bumblis
1900 E. 9th St., Ste. 3200
Cleveland, OH 44114-3485

Established in 1987 in OH.
Donor(s): Frances Wise Lang.
Financial data (yr. ended 12/31/01): Grants paid, $98,600; assets, $678,805 (M); gifts received, $50,735; expenditures, $105,880; qualifying distributions, $98,800.
Limitations: Applications not accepted. Giving primarily in New York, NY.
Application information: Contributes only to pre-selected organizations.
Officers and Trustees:* John A. Lang,* Pres.; Wendy F. Lang,* V.P.; Oakley V. Andrews,* Secy.
EIN: 341540723
Codes: FD2

42984
The Osterman Foundation
c/o Stan Bazan, Jr.
4807 Rockside Rd., Ste. 330
Cleveland, OH 44131
Application address: 10 Canyon Creek, Rancho Mirage, CA 92270, tel.: (619) 328-0913
Contact: William Osterman, Tr.

Established in 1988 in OH.
Donor(s): William Osterman.
Financial data (yr. ended 12/31/01): Grants paid, $98,500; assets, $1,133,822 (M); expenditures, $110,664; qualifying distributions, $100,449.
Limitations: Giving primarily in CA, NY, and OH.
Application information: Application form not required.
Trustees: Cydney Osterman, William Osterman.

EIN: 346890382
Codes: FD2

42985
Flora Dale Krouse Foundation
c/o National City Bank of Indiana
P.O. Box 94651
Cleveland, OH 44101-4651
Application address: c/o National City Bank of Indiana, P.O. Box 110, Fort Wayne, IN 46801
Contact: Teresa Tracey

Financial data (yr. ended 09/30/01): Grants paid, $98,340; assets, $1,810,224 (M); expenditures, $97,133; qualifying distributions, $104,863.
Limitations: Giving primarily in Fort Wayne, IN.
Trustee: National City Bank of Indiana.
EIN: 310902923
Codes: FD2

42986
The Stanley & Susan Chesley Foundation
c/o Fifth Third Bank
38 Fountain Sq. Plz.
Cincinnati, OH 45263
Contact: Lawra Baumann, Fdn. Dir., Dir.

Established in 1996 in OH.
Financial data (yr. ended 12/31/00): Grants paid, $98,215; assets, $2,457,695 (M); expenditures, $121,872; qualifying distributions, $103,216.
Limitations: Giving limited to the greater Cincinnati, OH, area.
Application information: Application form not required.
Trustees: Richard A. Chesley, Stanley M. Chesley, Lauren Chesley Cohen.
Bank Trustee: Fifth Third Bank.
EIN: 311490928
Codes: FD2

42987
Biery Family Foundation, Inc.
P.O. Box 214
Louisville, OH 44641-9524 (330) 875-3381
Contact: Dennis Biery, V.P.

Established in 1984 in OH.
Donor(s): Fern M. Biery, Harold N. Biery, Biery Cheese Co., Homestead Leasing Co., and members of the Biery family.
Financial data (yr. ended 09/30/01): Grants paid, $98,191; assets, $2,766,733 (M); gifts received, $82,400; expenditures, $117,127; qualifying distributions, $98,191.
Limitations: Giving primarily in OH.
Officers: Fern M. Biery, Pres.; Dennis H. Biery, V.P. and Treas.; Judith L. Biery, Secy.
EIN: 341453162
Codes: FD2

42988
A. K. Stephenson Foundation Charitable Trust
c/o First Financial Bank
300 High St.
Hamilton, OH 45011 (513) 867-4838
Contact: Thomas E. Humbach, Tr.

Established in 1994 in OH.
Financial data (yr. ended 12/31/01): Grants paid, $97,910; assets, $1,438,102 (M); gifts received, $1,860; expenditures, $156,096; qualifying distributions, $98,410.
Limitations: Giving primarily in OH.
Trustees: Thomas E. Humbach, First Financial Bank.
EIN: 311386444
Codes: FD2, GTI

42989
Robert & Ruth Westheimer Family Fund
(Formerly Robert Westheimer Family Fund)
36 E. 4th St., Ste. 905
Cincinnati, OH 45202
Application address: 2525 Rookwood Pl.,
Cincinnati, OH 45208
Contact: Ruth W. Westheimer, Pres.

Established in 1981 in OH.
Donor(s): Robert Westheimer, Ruth W. Westheimer.
Financial data (yr. ended 12/31/00): Grants paid, $97,626; assets, $1,185,967 (M); expenditures, $119,321; qualifying distributions, $97,826.
Limitations: Giving primarily in Cincinnati, OH.
Application information: Application form not required.
Officers: Ruth W. Westheimer, Pres.; Richard L. Westheimer, V.P. and Secy.; Ann W. Williams, V.P. and Treas.; Sallie E. Westheimer, V.P.
EIN: 311016777
Codes: FD2

42990
Harry W. Salon Foundation
c/o National City Bank of Indiana
P.O. Box 94651
Cleveland, OH 44101-4651
Application address: c/o National City Bank of Indiana, P.O. Box 110, Fort Wayne, IN 46801, tel.: (219) 461-6199
Contact: Michele Herald

Established in 1989 in IN.
Donor(s): Harry W. Salon.‡
Financial data (yr. ended 07/31/01): Grants paid, $97,479; assets, $1,810,871 (M); expenditures, $132,520; qualifying distributions, $112,955.
Limitations: Giving primarily in Allen County and Fort Wayne, IN.
Trustees: Lawrence E. Shine, Pearl Shonfield, National City Bank of Indiana.
EIN: 356512443
Codes: FD2

42991
The Morris Friedman and Phyllis Friedman Charitable Foundation
20 Federal Plz. W., Ste. 600
Youngstown, OH 44503 (330) 744-0247
Contact: Jay M. Skolnick, Tr.

Established in 1999 in OH.
Donor(s): Morris I. Friedman, Phyllis J. Friedman.
Financial data (yr. ended 12/31/01): Grants paid, $97,406; assets, $259,896 (M); expenditures, $99,196; qualifying distributions, $97,406.
Limitations: Giving primarily in Youngstown, OH.
Application information: Application form required.
Trustees: Morris I. Friedman, Phyllis J. Friedman, Jay M. Skolnick.
EIN: 341895014
Codes: FD2

42992
Shouvlin Foundation
P.O. Box 1503
Springfield, OH 45501-1503

Financial data (yr. ended 12/31/00): Grants paid, $97,350; assets, $1,906,711 (M); expenditures, $100,375; qualifying distributions, $98,266.
Limitations: Applications not accepted. Giving on a national basis.
Application information: Contributes only to pre-selected organizations.
Trustees: J.B. Riley, Daniel R. Shouvlin, Joseph P. Shouvlin, M. Kirk Shouvlin, Michael P. Shouvlin.
EIN: 316033067
Codes: FD2

42993
The Lippy Foundation
3915 E. Market St.
Warren, OH 44484 (330) 856-7092
Contact: Stephen R. Lippy, Tr.

Donor(s): William H. Lippy.
Financial data (yr. ended 12/31/01): Grants paid, $97,280; assets, $610,862 (M); gifts received, $100; expenditures, $109,434; qualifying distributions, $97,280.
Limitations: Giving primarily in OH.
Trustees: Sandra Lippy, Stephen R. Lippy, William H. Lippy.
EIN: 237003982

42994
Jackie & Bruce Davey Family Foundation
39 Public Sq.
Medina, OH 44256
Contact: W. Bruce Davey, Mgr.

Donor(s): Bruce Davey, Jackie Davey, Peter B.W. Davey.
Financial data (yr. ended 12/31/01): Grants paid, $97,125; assets, $823,011 (M); expenditures, $103,061; qualifying distributions, $97,393.
Limitations: Giving in the U.S., primarily in OH; some giving also in Canada.
Application information: Application form not required.
Officers: Jacqueline E. Davey, Mgr.; W. Bruce Davey, Mgr.
Trustee: FirstMerit Bank, N.A.
EIN: 346941084
Codes: FD2

42995
Northeastern New York Community Trust
c/o KeyBank, N.A.
800 Superior, Trust Tax
Cleveland, OH 44114-2601
Application address: c/o KeyBank, N.A., 54 State St., Albany, NY 12207, tel.: (518) 486-8734; FAX: (518) 436-1013

Established in 1955 in NY.
Financial data (yr. ended 12/31/01): Grants paid, $97,000; assets, $2,257,362 (M); expenditures, $117,714; qualifying distributions, $90,149.
Limitations: Giving limited to northeastern NY residents.
Application information: Scholarship awards administered by each college. Application form not required.
Trustees: Stan Lepkowski, KeyBank, N.A.
EIN: 146030063
Codes: FD2

42996
Irene C. Shea Charitable Foundation
c/o National City Bank of Pennsylvania
P.O. Box 94651
Cleveland, OH 44101-4651
Application address: P.O. Box 8050, Pittsburgh, PA 15216
Contact: Thomas J. Hickey, Tr.

Established in 1993 in PA.
Donor(s): Irene C. Shea.
Financial data (yr. ended 07/31/01): Grants paid, $97,000; assets, $1,926,238 (M); gifts received, $360,000; expenditures, $120,057; qualifying distributions, $110,102.
Limitations: Giving primarily in PA.
Trustees: Thomas J. Hickey, National City Bank of Pennsylvania.
EIN: 256410108
Codes: FD2

42997
Toy Run, Inc.
496 Tallmadge Rd.
Kent, OH 44240-7336 (330) 677-3465
Contact: Paul P. Dill, Pres.

Financial data (yr. ended 12/31/00): Grants paid, $96,692; assets, $187,002 (M); gifts received, $3,240; expenditures, $187,281; qualifying distributions, $96,692.
Limitations: Giving primarily in OH.
Officers: Paul P. Dill, Pres.; Dave Davis, V.P.
Director: Richard Kato.
EIN: 341769873

42998
The Charis Foundation
4544 Kipling Rd.
Columbus, OH 43220

Established in 1998 in OH.
Donor(s): Raymond D. Johnston, Mrs. Raymond D. Johnston.
Financial data (yr. ended 12/31/01): Grants paid, $96,500; assets, $102,512 (M); gifts received, $105,000; expenditures, $100,176; qualifying distributions, $97,527.
Limitations: Applications not accepted. Giving on a national basis.
Application information: Contributes only to pre-selected organizations.
Trustee: Raymond James Trust Company.
EIN: 311590961
Codes: FD2

42999
Alice Louise Ridenour Wood Scholarship Fund
c/o National City Bank
P.O. Box 94651
Cleveland, OH 44101

Established in 1994 in OH.
Financial data (yr. ended 12/31/00): Grants paid, $96,452; assets, $1,942,860 (M); expenditures, $118,382; qualifying distributions, $102,638.
Limitations: Giving limited to Columbus, OH.
Application information: Application form required.
Trustee: National City Bank, Columbus.
EIN: 316395426
Codes: FD2, GTI

43000
Collacott Foundation
13415 Shaker Blvd., No. 9J5
Cleveland, OH 44120 (216) 283-0560
Contact: May Targett, Tr.

Established in 1951 in OH.
Financial data (yr. ended 12/31/01): Grants paid, $96,000; assets, $1,928,404 (M); expenditures, $119,428; qualifying distributions, $98,050.
Limitations: Giving primarily in the Cleveland, OH, area.
Application information: Application form not required.
Trustees: Malvin E. Bank, May C. Targett, Robert S. Targett.
EIN: 346530833
Codes: FD2

43001
William O. and Margaret H. DeWitt Foundation
300 Main St.
Cincinnati, OH 45202-4173 (513) 241-8716

Established around 1967 in OH.
Financial data (yr. ended 12/31/01): Grants paid, $96,000; assets, $1,355,035 (M); expenditures, $107,469; qualifying distributions, $96,223.

Limitations: Applications not accepted. Giving primarily in OH.
Application information: Contributes only to pre-selected organizations.
Officers and Trustees:* William O. DeWitt, Jr., Pres. and Treas.; Katherine C. DeWitt,* Secy.; William O. DeWitt III.
EIN: 316078890
Codes: FD2

43002
Mueller-Scherger Foundation
c/o National City Bank of Indiana
P.O. Box 94651
Cleveland, OH 44101-4651
Application address: c/o Michelle Delaney, P.O. Box 110, Fort Wayne, IN 46801, tel.: (219) 461-6199

Established in 1983 in IN.
Financial data (yr. ended 11/30/01): Grants paid, $96,000; assets, $1,635,637 (M); expenditures, $96,000; qualifying distributions, $99,659.
Limitations: Giving limited to the Huntington, IN, and Van Wert, OH, areas.
Trustee: National City Bank of Indiana.
EIN: 311087759
Codes: FD2

43003
Philip G. Steiner Family Foundation
c/o Richard H. Steiner
4044 Rose Hill Ave.
Cincinnati, OH 45229 (513) 281-0867

Established in 1991 in OH.
Donor(s): Philip H. Steiner, Richard H. Steiner.
Financial data (yr. ended 12/31/00): Grants paid, $96,000; assets, $2,473,326 (M); expenditures, $99,484; qualifying distributions, $96,000.
Limitations: Applications not accepted. Giving primarily in OH.
Application information: Contributes only to pre-selected organizations.
Trustees: Philip H. Steiner, Richard H. Steiner.
EIN: 311335514
Codes: FD2

43004
The Frederick E. and Julia G. Nonneman Foundation
18816 N. Valley Dr.
Fairview Park, OH 44126

Established in 1998 in OH.
Donor(s): Frederick E. Nonneman.
Financial data (yr. ended 12/31/00): Grants paid, $95,985; assets, $2,503,594 (M); gifts received, $341,880; expenditures, $101,226; qualifying distributions, $95,702.
Limitations: Applications not accepted.
Application information: Contributes only to pre-selected organizations.
Officers: Frederick E. Nonneman, Pres.; Julia G. Nonneman, V.P.; Lois E. Nonneman, Secy.-Treas.
Trustee: Anita C. Nonneman.
EIN: 341881601
Codes: FD2

43005
The Metropolitan Foundation
c/o Robert M. Kaye
6001 Landerhaven Dr.
Mayfield Heights, OH 44124

Established in 1993 in OH.
Donor(s): Robert M. Kaye, Alexander J. Vytell.
Financial data (yr. ended 12/31/01): Grants paid, $95,500; assets, $96,237 (M); gifts received, $59,480; expenditures, $95,698; qualifying distributions, $95,500.
Limitations: Applications not accepted. Giving limited to Cleveland, OH.
Application information: Contributes only to pre-selected organizations.
Officers and Trustees:* Robert M. Kaye,* Pres.; Malvin E. Bank,* Secy.; Robert R. Broadbent, Ralph D. Ketchum, David P. Miller.
EIN: 341735508

43006
Lewis & Marjorie Daniel Foundation
c/o Fifth Third Bank
38 Fountain Sq. Plz.
Cincinnati, OH 45263 (513) 579-6034
Contact: Lawra Baumann

Established in 1998 in OH.
Financial data (yr. ended 12/31/00): Grants paid, $95,000; assets, $2,111,188 (M); expenditures, $102,659; qualifying distributions, $95,566.
Limitations: Giving primarily in OH.
Officers: Deborah D. Long, Pres.; Marjorie G. Daniel, V.P.; Bruce C. Long, Secy.-Treas.
Agent: Fifth Third Bank.
EIN: 311595386
Codes: FD2

43007
Wildflower Foundation
c/o Donald A. Brott
P.O. Box 1163
Bath, OH 44210-1163

Established in 1983 in OH.
Donor(s): Hanna O. Rice.
Financial data (yr. ended 06/30/01): Grants paid, $95,000; assets, $2,267,818 (M); expenditures, $130,087; qualifying distributions, $92,477.
Limitations: Applications not accepted. Giving primarily in Akron, OH.
Application information: Contributes only to pre-selected organizations.
Trustee: Robert R. Rice.
EIN: 341436725
Codes: FD2

43008
Women's Project Foundation
c/o KeyBank, N.A.
800 Superior Ave., 4th Fl.
Cleveland, OH 44114 (216) 689-4651
Application address: c/o KeyBank, N.A., 127 Public Sq., 17th Fl., Cleveland, OH 44114-1306
Contact: Cyndi Clifton, Trust Off., KeyBank, N.A.

Established in 1986.
Financial data (yr. ended 11/30/01): Grants paid, $95,000; assets, $31,464,769 (M); expenditures, $194,740; qualifying distributions, $95,000.
Limitations: Giving on a national basis, with emphasis on New York, NY.
Trustees: Louise L. Gund, KeyBank, N.A.
EIN: 133417304
Codes: FD2

43009
Crawford Family Foundation
5774 Hendrickson Rd.
Franklin, OH 45005

Established in 1999 in OH.
Financial data (yr. ended 12/31/00): Grants paid, $94,800; assets, $4,113 (M); expenditures, $96,953; qualifying distributions, $94,800.
Limitations: Applications not accepted. Giving primarily in OH.
Application information: Contributes only to pre-selected organizations.
Officers: James K. Crawford, Pres. and Treas.; Linda Crawford, V.P. and Secy.
Trustee: Jason W. Crawford.
EIN: 311682860
Codes: FD2

43010
The Heymann Foundation
c/o Trust Co. of Toledo, N.A.
6135 Trust Dr.
Holland, OH 43528

Established in 1955 in OH.
Donor(s): Ohio Plate Glass.
Financial data (yr. ended 12/31/00): Grants paid, $94,144; assets, $1,788,994 (M); expenditures, $101,869; qualifying distributions, $97,951.
Limitations: Applications not accepted. Giving primarily in Toledo, OH.
Application information: Contributes only to pre-selected organizations.
Trustee: Trust Co. of Toledo, N.A.
EIN: 346518714
Codes: FD2

43011
Miami County Foundation
(Formerly Piqua-Miami County Foundation)
9 Marymount Dr.
Piqua, OH 45356

Established in 1985 in OH.
Donor(s): Richard E. Hunt.
Financial data (yr. ended 12/31/01): Grants paid, $94,130; assets, $3,366,512 (M); gifts received, $1,294,124; expenditures, $119,856; qualifying distributions, $93,694.
Limitations: Giving limited to Miami County, OH.
Publications: Informational brochure.
Application information: Application form required.
Officers and Trustees:* Richard E. Hunt,* Chair.; Douglas R. Murray,* Pres.; Richard N. Adams, V.P.; Joanna Hill Heitzman,* V.P. and Secy.; George Ashton, Richard A. Goater, J. Richard Harris, William Posey, Kenneth Rupp.
EIN: 311142558
Codes: FD2

43012
Showers Family Foundation
c/o David M. Showers
9839 Strausser St.
Canal Fulton, OH 44614

Incorporated in 1998 in OH with assets transferred from the terminated trust Showers Family Foundation (EI 34-1854843).
Financial data (yr. ended 07/31/01): Grants paid, $94,000; assets, $2,215,720 (M); expenditures, $109,842; qualifying distributions, $94,000.
Limitations: Applications not accepted. Giving primarily in OH.
Application information: Contributes only to pre-selected organizations.
Officers and Trustees:* David M. Showers,* Pres. and Secy.-Treas.; Martha A. Showers,* V.P.; Tracy Johnson, Michelle Martina, James D. Showers.
EIN: 341865312
Codes: FD2

43013
The Thomas L. and Catherine R. Carlisle Private Foundation
11671 S.R. 776
Jackson, OH 45640
Contact: Joan C. Greathouse, Pres.

Established in 1993 in OH.
Donor(s): Thomas L. Carlisle, Catherine R. Carlisle.
Financial data (yr. ended 12/31/01): Grants paid, $93,833; assets, $8,984 (M); expenditures, $94,852; qualifying distributions, $93,833.

43013—OHIO

Limitations: Giving limited to residents of OH.
Officers and Trustees:* Joan C. Greathouse,* Pres.; Thomas A. Carlisle,* V.P.; Jill L. Hale,* Secy.; Gwyn L. Carlisle,* Treas.
EIN: 311394692

43014
Marian Foundation
9050 Turfway Bend
Powell, OH 43065
Application address: P.O. Box 21748, Columbus, OH 43221
Contact: Norm Hausfeld, Pres.

Established in 1954 in OH.
Financial data (yr. ended 04/30/02): Grants paid, $93,800; assets, $2,070,069 (M); expenditures, $106,921; qualifying distributions, $105,333.
Limitations: Giving primarily in Columbus, OH.
Officers: Stephen A. Mitchell, Pres.; Msgr. J. Colby Grimes, V.P.; Pat Foley, Secy.; Jack Morrison, Treas.
EIN: 316050535
Codes: FD2

43015
Fred N. VanBuren Scholarship Fund
719 W. Market St.
Baltimore, OH 43105-1124 (740) 862-4191
Contact: Richard Miller, Dir., James Keller, Dir., and G. Gene Jackson, Dir.

Established in 1984 in OH.
Donor(s): Fred N. VanBuren.
Financial data (yr. ended 06/30/01): Grants paid, $93,000; assets, $1,589,355 (M); expenditures, $113,507; qualifying distributions, $93,000.
Limitations: Giving limited to the Liberty Township, OH, area.
Application information: Application form required.
Trustees: G. Gene Jackson, James L. Keller, Richard Miller.
EIN: 311117779
Codes: FD2, GTI

43016
Colin Gardner Foundation
c/o First Financial Bank
300 High St.
Hamilton, OH 45011 (513) 425-7566

Financial data (yr. ended 12/31/01): Grants paid, $92,885; assets, $832,695 (M); gifts received, $6,040; expenditures, $98,761; qualifying distributions, $93,087.
Limitations: Applications not accepted. Giving on a national basis.
Application information: Unsolicited requests for funds not accepted.
Trustees: Ames Gardner, Colin Gardner IV, Stephen V. Gardner, Eleanor Lashley, Eugenie G. Millan.
EIN: 316026289

43017
Evelyn E. Walter Foundation
116 S. Main St.
Marion, OH 43302-3702 (740) 387-9093
Contact: Ronald Cramer, Tr.

Established in 1987 in OH.
Financial data (yr. ended 12/31/00): Grants paid, $92,829; assets, $1,715,400 (M); expenditures, $113,771; qualifying distributions, $91,722.
Limitations: Giving primarily in Marion County, OH.
Trustees: Ronald D. Cramer, George F. Kennedy, William T. Rogers.
EIN: 311171927
Codes: FD2

43018
The Fairfax Foundation
2840 Lander Rd.
Pepper Pike, OH 44124-4820 (216) 595-9665
Application address: 30195 Chagrin Blvd., Ste. 350W., Cleveland, OH 44124
Contact: Gerald A. Conway, Tr.; Kevin C. Conway, Tr.; or Martine V. Conway, Tr.

Established in 1986 in OH.
Donor(s): Gerald A. Conway, Martine V. Conway.
Financial data (yr. ended 12/31/01): Grants paid, $92,600; assets, $2,649,860 (M); expenditures, $143,482; qualifying distributions, $92,600.
Limitations: Giving primarily in OH.
Application information: Contributes primarily to pre-selected organizations. Application form required.
Officer and Trustees:* Gerald A. Conway,* Chair.; Gerald A. Conway, Jr., Kevin C. Conway, Martine V. Conway.
EIN: 341553708
Codes: FD2

43019
The William W. and Margaret L. Bresnahan Foundation
c/o Sky Trust, N.A.
P.O. Box 479
Youngstown, OH 44501 (330) 742-7035
Contact: Carol Chamberlain

Donor(s): Hynes Industries, Inc., William W. Bresnahan.
Financial data (yr. ended 12/31/00): Grants paid, $92,550; assets, $337,560 (M); gifts received, $107,975; expenditures, $99,771; qualifying distributions, $93,213.
Limitations: Giving primarily in OH.
Application information: Application form not required.
Trustees: David L. Bresnahan, Michael J. Bresnahan, Patrick C. Bresnahan, Timothy T. Bresnahan, William J. Bresnahan, William M. Bresnahan.
EIN: 341791494

43020
Second Abraham S. and Fannie B. Levey Foundation
c/o KeyBank, N.A.
800 Superior Ave., 4th Fl.
Cleveland, OH 44114

Established in 1957 in ME.
Financial data (yr. ended 10/31/01): Grants paid, $92,250; assets, $1,048,643 (M); expenditures, $124,088; qualifying distributions, $91,953.
Limitations: Applications not accepted. Giving primarily in the northeastern U.S., including MA, MD, ME, and NY.
Application information: Contributes only to pre-selected organizations.
Trustee: KeyBank, N.A.
EIN: 016007022
Codes: FD2

43021
Charles W. Saunders Charitable Trust
c/o KeyBank, N.A.
800 Superior Ave., 4th Fl., Ste. 420
Cleveland, OH 44114-2601

Established in 1994 in OH.
Donor(s): Charles W. Saunders.‡
Financial data (yr. ended 12/31/01): Grants paid, $92,175; assets, $1,019,475 (M); expenditures, $112,148; qualifying distributions, $91,306.
Limitations: Applications not accepted. Giving primarily in Washington, DC, NY, and OH.
Application information: Contributes only to pre-selected organizations.
Trustee: KeyBank, N.A.
EIN: 346996841
Codes: FD2

43022
Diana K. and Lawrence T. Foster Charitable Foundation
c/o Lawrence T. Foster
132 W. 2nd St., Ste. A
Perrysburg, OH 43551

Established in 1988 in OH.
Donor(s): Diana K. Foster, Lawrence T. Foster.
Financial data (yr. ended 12/31/01): Grants paid, $92,100; assets, $2,326,538 (M); expenditures, $97,839; qualifying distributions, $92,100.
Limitations: Applications not accepted. Giving primarily in OH.
Application information: Contributes only to pre-selected organizations.
Trustees: Diana K. Foster, Lawrence T. Foster.
EIN: 346883855
Codes: FD2

43023
James A. Jackson Trust
(Formerly James A. Jackson and Beatrice D. Jackson Scholarship Trust)
c/o KeyBank, N.A.
800 Superior Ave., 4th Fl.
Cleveland, OH 44114
Contact: Superintendent of the Oxford County School District

Established in 1994 in ME.
Donor(s): James Jackson.‡
Financial data (yr. ended 06/30/01): Grants paid, $91,476; assets, $2,369,665 (M); expenditures, $119,104; qualifying distributions, $91,476.
Limitations: Giving limited to residents of West Paris, ME.
Trustee: KeyBank, N.A.
EIN: 016128257
Codes: FD2, GTI

43024
Ohio Turfgrass Research Trust, Inc.
P.O. Box 3388
Zanesville, OH 43702-3388

Established in 1999 in OH.
Financial data (yr. ended 01/31/02): Grants paid, $91,470; assets, $56,946 (M); gifts received, $92,710; expenditures, $92,973; qualifying distributions, $91,457.
Limitations: Giving primarily in Columbus, OH.
Directors: Kevin Thompson, Exec. Dir.; Doug Halterman, Paul Jacquemin, Bob O'Brien, Gene Probasco, Randy Tischer.
EIN: 311411216
Codes: FD2

43025
Sam & Esther Friedman Foundation
23215 Commerce Park Dr., Ste.111
Beachwood, OH 44122

Established in 1954 in OH.
Donor(s): Richard K. Friedman, S.M. Friedman.
Financial data (yr. ended 06/30/01): Grants paid, $91,430; assets, $1,571,511 (M); expenditures, $96,372; qualifying distributions, $92,382.
Limitations: Applications not accepted. Giving primarily in OH.
Application information: Contributes only to pre-selected organizations.
Officers and Trustees:* Richard K. Friedman,* Pres.; Amy Friedman Benbadis,* Secy.; Josh Friedman,* Treas.

EIN: 346554839
Codes: FD2

43026
Letha E. House Foundation
c/o FirstMerit Bank, N.A.
39 Public Sq.
Medina, OH 44256 (330) 764-7251
Contact: Catherine M. Carmany

Established in 1967 in OH.
Financial data (yr. ended 06/30/01): Grants paid, $91,384; assets, $1,757,633 (M); expenditures, $173,483; qualifying distributions, $156,306.
Limitations: Giving primarily in the Medina County, OH, area.
Application information: Application form not required.
Trustees: Charles Clark Griesinger, Paul M. Jones, Jr., FirstMerit Bank, N.A.
EIN: 237025122
Codes: FD2

43027
S. W. & Doris Caplan Foundation
9880 Sweet Valley Dr.
Valley View, OH 44125

Established in 1999.
Donor(s): Sidney W. Caplan.
Financial data (yr. ended 12/31/01): Grants paid, $91,045; assets, $204,336 (M); expenditures, $94,488; qualifying distributions, $90,955.
Trustee: Sidney W. Caplan.
EIN: 341911676
Codes: FD2

43028
Stertzer Family Charitable Foundation
1710 Abbotsford Green Dr.
Powell, OH 43065

Established in 1997 in OH.
Financial data (yr. ended 12/31/00): Grants paid, $91,000; assets, $1,609,695 (M); expenditures, $102,580; qualifying distributions, $90,077.
Limitations: Applications not accepted. Giving on a national and international basis.
Application information: Contributes only to pre-selected organizations.
Trustees: Brian R. Stertzer, Carol W. Stertzer, Robert E. Warwick.
EIN: 311576310
Codes: FD2

43029
Charles B. & Margaret E. Cushwa Foundation
c/o KeyBank, N.A.
800 Superior Ave., 4th Fl.
Cleveland, OH 44114
Application address: 126 Central Plz. N., Canton, OH 44702, tel.: (330) 489-5434
Contact: Kim Mayle, Trust Off., KeyBank, N.A.

Established in 1994 in OH.
Donor(s): Margaret E. Cushwa.
Financial data (yr. ended 12/31/01): Grants paid, $90,901; assets, $1,769,775 (M); expenditures, $106,536; qualifying distributions, $91,834.
Limitations: Giving primarily in OH.
Advisors: Charles B. Cushwa III, William W. Cushwa, Nicholas Wolsonovich.
Trustee: KeyBank, N.A.
EIN: 341787513
Codes: FD2

43030
Robert D. Lindner Foundation
3955 Montgomery Rd.
Cincinnati, OH 45212-3798

Established in 1967 in OH.
Donor(s): Robert D. Lindner, Sr.
Financial data (yr. ended 12/31/01): Grants paid, $90,200; assets, $934,288 (M); gifts received, $1,365; expenditures, $91,915; qualifying distributions, $90,200.
Limitations: Applications not accepted. Giving primarily in Cincinnati, OH.
Application information: Contributes only to pre-selected organizations.
Officers and Trustees:* Robert D. Lindner, Sr.,* Pres.; Betty R. Lindner,* V.P. and Treas.; Joseph A. Pedoto,* Secy.
EIN: 310738035

43031
Marie D. Berry Funds H and H-1
c/o KeyBank, N.A.
800 Superior Ave., 4th Fl.
Cleveland, OH 44114-1306

Established in 1981 in OH.
Donor(s): Marie D. Berry.‡
Financial data (yr. ended 12/31/01): Grants paid, $90,000; assets, $2,586,811 (M); expenditures, $130,487; qualifying distributions, $116,399.
Limitations: Giving limited to Findlay, OH.
Application information: Application form required.
Directors: Bradley Cox, Hon. Robert Walker.
Trustee: KeyBank, N.A.
EIN: 346506704
Codes: FD2, GTI

43032
Maplewood Foundation, Inc.
c/o National City Bank, Kentucky
P.O. Box 94651
Cleveland, OH 44101-4651
Application address: 4025 Leland Rd., Louisville, KY 40207, tel.: (502) 899-1719
Contact: George W. Rue, III, Secy.

Established in 1997 in KY.
Donor(s): Lee Hancock.
Financial data (yr. ended 12/31/00): Grants paid, $90,000; assets, $1,774,400 (M); gifts received, $29,117; expenditures, $98,140; qualifying distributions, $90,000.
Limitations: Giving primarily in KY.
Officers and Directors:* Lee A. Hancock,* Pres.; W. Mitchell Rue, Jr., V.P.; George W. Rue III,* Secy. and Treas.; David B. Rue.
Trustee: National City Bank, Kentucky.
EIN: 626333498
Codes: FD2

43033
David F. & Sara K. Weston Fund
1900 Chemed Ctr.
255 E. 5th St.
Cincinnati, OH 45202-4797 (513) 977-8269
FAX: (513) 977-8141
Contact: Harris K. Weston, Pres.

Established in 1952 in OH.
Donor(s): David F. Weston,‡ Sara K. Weston,‡ Harris K. Weston.
Financial data (yr. ended 12/31/00): Grants paid, $89,911; assets, $1,879,784 (M); expenditures, $91,976; qualifying distributions, $89,911.
Limitations: Giving primarily in Cincinnati, OH.
Publications: Financial statement.
Application information: Application form not required.
Officers and Trustees:* Harris K. Weston,* Pres. and Treas.; Alice F. Weston,* V.P. and Secy.; Carol W. Roberts, Barbara W. Sasser.
EIN: 316026109
Codes: FD2

43034
Miraldi Family Private Foundation
800 Superior Ave., 4th Fl.
Cleveland, OH 44114

Established in 1999 in OH.
Donor(s): David P. Miraldi, James L. Miraldi.
Financial data (yr. ended 12/31/01): Grants paid, $89,600; assets, $1,214 (M); gifts received, $50,668; expenditures, $90,969; qualifying distributions, $89,600.
Limitations: Applications not accepted. Giving on a national basis.
Application information: Contributes only to pre-selected organizations.
Officers: Mary K. Miraldi, Pres.; James L. Miraldi, V.P.; Leslee W. Miraldi, Secy.; David P. Miraldi, Treas.
EIN: 341889399

43035
The Norton Family Foundation
3535 E. Erie Ave.
Lorain, OH 44052

Established in 1997 in OH.
Donor(s): Sara Jane Norton.
Financial data (yr. ended 12/31/00): Grants paid, $88,876; assets, $1,495,992 (M); gifts received, $1,582; expenditures, $106,661; qualifying distributions, $88,876.
Limitations: Applications not accepted. Giving primarily in Lorain County, OH.
Application information: Contributes only to pre-selected organizations.
Trustees: Amy L. Norton, Benjamin G. Norton, Benjamin P. Norton, Bradley S. Norton, Brenda D. Norton, Brent A. Norton, Deborah R. Norton, Sara Jane Norton.
EIN: 341874344
Codes: FD2

43036
The Epstein/Zuckerman Family Foundation
3100 Bremerton Rd.
Pepper Pike, OH 44124

Established in 1996 on OH.
Donor(s): Ethel D. Zuckerman.
Financial data (yr. ended 12/31/99): Grants paid, $88,530; assets, $570,633 (M); expenditures, $95,524; qualifying distributions, $90,819.
Limitations: Applications not accepted. Giving primarily in Cleveland, OH.
Application information: Contributes only to pre-selected organizations.
Officers: Natalie Z. Epstein, Pres.; Morton G. Epstein, V.P.; Jonathan A. Epstein, Secy.; Howard G. Epstein, M.D., Treas.
EIN: 346850627

43037
James Worthington Willmott Memorial Trust II
P.O. Box 94651
Cleveland, OH 44101
Application address: 301 E. Main St., Lexington, KY 40507, tel.: (859) 281-5248
Contact: John Cheshire

Established in 1990 in KY.
Financial data (yr. ended 12/31/01): Grants paid, $88,500; assets, $2,232,114 (M); expenditures, $110,938; qualifying distributions, $97,502.
Limitations: Giving limited to residents of Bourbon County, KY, and adjacent counties.
Application information: Application form required.
Trustee: National City Bank, Kentucky.
EIN: 616174229
Codes: FD2, GTI

43038
Graham and Carol Hall Family Foundation
c/o Peter A. DeMarco
1100 Superior Ave., Ste. 1100
Cleveland, OH 44114-2518

Established in 1993 in OH.
Donor(s): Graham Hall, Carol Hall.
Financial data (yr. ended 12/31/00): Grants paid, $88,000; assets, $830,598 (M); gifts received, $4,284; expenditures, $96,345; qualifying distributions, $88,660.
Limitations: Applications not accepted. Giving limited to Cleveland, OH.
Application information: Contributes only to pre-selected organizations.
Trustees: Carol Hall, Graham Hall, Helen I. Hall.
EIN: 341757618
Codes: FD2

43039
William & Ann Jean Cushwa Foundation
c/o KeyBank, N.A.
800 Superior Ave., 4th Fl.
Cleveland, OH 44114

Established in 1997 in OH.
Financial data (yr. ended 12/31/01): Grants paid, $87,750; assets, $1,764,845 (M); expenditures, $103,957; qualifying distributions, $89,653.
Limitations: Applications not accepted. Giving primarily in IL, IN, OH, and NY.
Application information: Contributes only to pre-selected organizations.
Trustee: KeyBank, N.A.
EIN: 341849990
Codes: FD2

43040
Scherr Charitable Foundation
c/o Fifth Third Bank
38 Fountain Sq. Plz. MD 1090C7
Cincinnati, OH 45263
Contact: Lawra J. Baumann, Fdn. Off., Fifth Third Bank

Established in 1993 in OH.
Financial data (yr. ended 12/31/00): Grants paid, $87,750; assets, $1,388,295 (M); expenditures, $120,409; qualifying distributions, $83,625.
Limitations: Giving primarily in Cincinnati, OH.
Application information: Application form required.
Trustees: Mildred M. Dyer, Elizabeth M. Gaudet, Elinor S. Mosher, Frederic Mosher, Jr., Susan V. Mosher.
EIN: 311385225
Codes: FD2

43041
Wright Foundation
5200 3 Villager Dr., PH-E
Lyndhurst, OH 44124
Contact: Bernadine D. Wright, Pres.

Incorporated in 1953 in OH.
Donor(s): J.D. Wright, Bernadine D. Wright.
Financial data (yr. ended 12/31/00): Grants paid, $87,750; assets, $2,355,770 (M); expenditures, $111,820; qualifying distributions, $94,700.
Limitations: Giving primarily in OH.
Officers: Bernadine D. Wright, Pres.; John D. Wright, Jr., V.P.; Evelyn Mann, Secy.
EIN: 346520282
Codes: FD2

43042
Brian A. Bass Charitable Trust
P.O. Box 844
Lorain, OH 44052

Established in 1986.
Donor(s): Michael J. Bass, Barbara H. Bass.
Financial data (yr. ended 12/31/00): Grants paid, $87,672; assets, $2,331,627 (M); gifts received, $626,873; expenditures, $96,048; qualifying distributions, $87,672.
Limitations: Applications not accepted.
Application information: Contributes only to pre-selected organizations.
Trustees: Barbara H. Bass, Michael J. Bass.
EIN: 341501672
Codes: FD2

43043
Will Ptak Foundation, Inc.
c/o Island Estates
43075 N. Ridge Rd.
Elyria, OH 44035

Financial data (yr. ended 12/31/00): Grants paid, $87,570; assets, $183,531 (M); expenditures, $89,390; qualifying distributions, $87,636.
Officer: Wilbur F. Ptak, Pres. and Treas.
Trustees: Madonna Ptak, Merrill Lynch.
EIN: 237161341
Codes: FD2

43044
Clement and Ann Buenger Foundation
c/o Fifth Third Bank
38 Fountain Sq. Plz., MD 1090C8
Cincinnati, OH 45263
Contact: Lawra J. Baumann, Fdn. Off.

Established in 1988 in OH.
Donor(s): Clement L. Buenger, Ann Buenger.
Financial data (yr. ended 09/30/01): Grants paid, $87,500; assets, $2,456,629 (M); expenditures, $118,372; qualifying distributions, $91,285.
Limitations: Giving primarily in KY and Cincinnati, OH.
Application information: Application form required.
Officers: Ann Buenger, Pres.; George A. Schaefer, Jr., Secy.-Treas.
EIN: 311259480
Codes: FD2

43045
Robert C. & Betty A. Forchheimer Foundation
7 Hanover Ln.
Beachwood, OH 44122-7521
Contact: Robert C. Forchheimer, Pres.

Established in 1997 in OH.
Donor(s): Betty A. Forchheimer, Robert C. Forchheimer.
Financial data (yr. ended 12/31/01): Grants paid, $87,500; assets, $1,756,085 (M); expenditures, $88,921; qualifying distributions, $87,921.
Limitations: Applications not accepted. Giving primarily in New York, NY.
Application information: Contributes only to pre-selected organizations.
Officers: Robert C. Forchheimer, Pres.; Melanie Kutnick, Secy.; Betty A. Forchheimer, Treas.
EIN: 311530820
Codes: FD2

43046
Beck Foundation
199 S. 5th St.
Columbus, OH 43215-5299 (614) 221-9223
Contact: Charles T. Kaps, C.E.O.

Established in 1984 in OH.
Financial data (yr. ended 12/31/01): Grants paid, $87,250; assets, $1,881,242 (M); gifts received, $57,888; expenditures, $142,997; qualifying distributions, $87,250.
Limitations: Giving primarily in Columbia, OH.
Officers and Trustees:* Charles T. Kaps,* C.E.O.; Shirley M. Beck,* Pres.; Charles G. Kaps,* Secy.; Dennis O. Kaps, Virginia E. Kaps.
EIN: 311103484

43047
Frankel Family Foundation
9643 Ash Ct.
Cincinnati, OH 45242

Established in 1998 in OH.
Donor(s): Allison O. Frankel, Erna Frankel, Edward M. Frankel, Norman A. Frankel.
Financial data (yr. ended 12/31/00): Grants paid, $86,704; assets, $42,122 (M); gifts received, $84,496; expenditures, $87,004; qualifying distributions, $86,457.
Limitations: Applications not accepted. Giving limited to Cincinnati, OH.
Application information: Contributes only to pre-selected organizations.
Officers and Trustees:* Edward M. Frankel,* Pres. and Treas.; Norman A. Frankel,* V.P. and Secy.; Allison O. Frankel, Rebecca A. Frankel.
EIN: 311572982
Codes: FD2

43048
The Abundant Life Foundation
9624 Cincinnati - Columbus Rd.
Cincinnati, OH 45241

Established in 1998.
Financial data (yr. ended 12/31/01): Grants paid, $86,500; assets, $2,986,561 (M); gifts received, $800; expenditures, $99,781; qualifying distributions, $85,180.
Limitations: Applications not accepted. Giving primarily in MA.
Application information: Contributes only to pre-selected organizations.
Trustees: Robert Dukes, Timothy Johnson, John Pierce, Lois Pierce.
EIN: 311562299

43049
Green Family Foundation
c/o Gumbleton & Co.
9902 Carver Rd., Ste. 110
Cincinnati, OH 45242
Application address: 2700 Date Palm Rd., Boca Raton, FL 33432
Contact: Louis B. Green, Tr.

Established in 1969 in OH.
Donor(s): Louis B. Green.
Financial data (yr. ended 12/31/00): Grants paid, $86,406; assets, $13,376 (M); gifts received, $100,000; expenditures, $89,335; qualifying distributions, $87,623.
Limitations: Giving primarily in FL and NY; some giving also in OH.
Trustees: Laurence Bergman, Andrew J. Green, Anne W. Green, Louis B. Green.
EIN: 316087315
Codes: FD2

43050
Edward F. Knight Family Foundation
c/o Fifth Third Bank
P.O. Box 1868
Toledo, OH 43604 (419) 259-6804
Contact: Anthony A. Zugay, Jr.

Financial data (yr. ended 12/31/00): Grants paid, $86,400; assets, $697,705 (M); expenditures, $95,475; qualifying distributions, $86,484.
Limitations: Giving on a national basis.
Trustee: Fifth Third Bank.
EIN: 346510131
Codes: FD2

43051
Tom H. Barrett Foundation
2135 Stockbridge Rd.
Akron, OH 44313

Established in 1997 in OH.
Donor(s): Tom Barrett.
Financial data (yr. ended 12/31/00): Grants paid, $86,390; assets, $788,170 (M); expenditures, $106,574; qualifying distributions, $86,390.
Limitations: Applications not accepted. Giving primarily in OH.
Application information: Contributes only to pre-selected organizations.
Trustees: Tom H. Barrett, Ronald D. Glosser, John F. Rasnick.
EIN: 311534905

43052
The Margaret Clark Morgan Foundation
50 S. Main St.
Akron, OH 44308
Application address: 10 W. Streetsboro St.; Hudson, OH 44236, tel.: (330) 653-3916
Contact: Deborah D. Hoover, Exec. Dir.

Established in 2001 in OH.
Donor(s): Margaret Clark Morgan.
Financial data (yr. ended 12/31/01): Grants paid, $86,000; assets, $446,167 (M); gifts received, $540,000; expenditures, $99,187; qualifying distributions, $92,441.
Limitations: Giving primarily in NJ and OH.
Officers and Trustees:* Margaret C. Morgan,* Pres.; Burton D. Morgan,* V.P. and Treas.; Deborah D. Hoover, Secy. and Exec. Dir.; William H. Fellows, Suzanne Morgan, Mary Ann Winders.
EIN: 341948246
Codes: FD2

43053
Robert M. Butler Memorial Foundation
c/o Paul L. Hehman
P.O. Box 75020
Cincinnati, OH 45275

Donor(s): Corporex Cos., Inc.
Financial data (yr. ended 09/30/01): Grants paid, $85,781; assets, $850,722 (M); gifts received, $268,050; expenditures, $97,463; qualifying distributions, $85,781.
Limitations: Giving limited to northern KY.
Trustees: Christa Butler, Kevin Butler, Marty Butler, Mary Sue Butler, William P. Butler, Barbara Schaefer.
EIN: 310981683
Codes: FD2

43054
Amcast Industrial Foundation
7887 Washington Village Dr.
Dayton, OH 45459 (937) 291-7021
Mailing address: P.O. Box 98, Dayton, OH 45401; FAX: (937) 291-7007
Contact: Sue Smith

Incorporated in 1952 in OH.
Donor(s): Amcast Industrial Corp.
Financial data (yr. ended 08/31/01): Grants paid, $85,610; assets, $346,045 (M); expenditures, $91,321; qualifying distributions, $85,610.
Limitations: Giving primarily in areas of company operations in Fayetteville, AR; Elkhart, Geneva, Richmond, Gas City, and Fremont, IN; Southfield, MI; Wapakoneta and Dayton, OH; Washington, PA; Cedarburg, WI; and Ontario, Canada.
Publications: Informational brochure.
Application information: Letters to the foundation are routed to the different divisions which then make grant recommendations to the foundation. Applicants may write to the division in their area directly. Application form not required.
Officers and Trustees: Byron O. Pond, Jr., Pres.; Francis J. Drew, V.P.; Samuel Reese, Secy.; Michael R. Higgins, Treas.
EIN: 316016458
Codes: CS, FD2, CD

43055
CLH Foundation
201 E. 5th St., Ste. 2500
Cincinnati, OH 45202-4104 (513) 651-6832
Contact: Christine H. Heekin, Pres.

Established in 1998 in OH.
Financial data (yr. ended 12/31/01): Grants paid, $85,500; assets, $2,341,396 (M); gifts received, $751,286; expenditures, $134,780; qualifying distributions, $85,500.
Limitations: Giving primarily in Cincinnati, OH.
Officers and Trustees:* Christine H. Heekin,* Pres.; Christopher J. Heekin,* V.P.; Albert Heekin,* Treas.; James K. Heekin,* Secy.
EIN: 311346007

43056
Restoration Foundation
515 Wyoming Ave.
Cincinnati, OH 45215

Established in 2000.
Financial data (yr. ended 12/31/01): Grants paid, $85,500; assets, $0 (M); gifts received, $15,000; expenditures, $87,694; qualifying distributions, $85,500.
Limitations: Giving primarily in OH.
Officers: Mike Fremont, Pres.; Marilyn Wall, V.P.
Trustee: D. David Altman.
EIN: 311694359

43057
Acker Foundation Charitable Trust
1422 Euclid Ave., Ste. 1104
Cleveland, OH 44115

Established in 1998 in OH.
Financial data (yr. ended 12/31/00): Grants paid, $85,000; assets, $25,272 (M); gifts received, $76,742; expenditures, $86,035; qualifying distributions, $84,992.
Limitations: Applications not accepted.
Application information: Contributes only to pre-selected organizations.
Directors: Thomas S. Acker, Patricia A. Basista.
EIN: 311522488
Codes: FD2

43058
Helen Greene Perry Charitable Trust
c/o KeyBank, N.A.
800 Superior Ave., 4th Fl.
Cleveland, OH 44114-2601
Application address: 127 Public Sq., 17th Fl., Cleveland, OH 44114

Established in 1996 in OH.
Financial data (yr. ended 12/31/00): Grants paid, $85,000; assets, $1,478,567 (M); expenditures, $103,276; qualifying distributions, $84,771.
Limitations: Giving primarily in Cleveland, OH.
Trustee: KeyBank, N.A.
EIN: 347045202
Codes: FD2

43059
Sophia Foundation
c/o George H. Vincent
P.O. Box 9442
Cincinnati, OH 45209-0442

Established in 1999 in OH.
Financial data (yr. ended 12/31/00): Grants paid, $85,000; assets, $360,133 (M); gifts received, $62,785; expenditures, $92,722; qualifying distributions, $83,355.
Trustees: George H. Vincent, Marcy R. Wydman, Mary Florence Witt Wydman.
EIN: 311575600
Codes: FD2

43060
Solomon Spector Foundation
c/o KeyBank, N.A.
800 Superior Ave., 4th Fl.
Cleveland, OH 44114
Application address: c/o Joseph Spector, 2507 S.W. 23rd Cranbrook Dr., Boynton Beach, Fl 33436

Established in 1991.
Financial data (yr. ended 12/31/01): Grants paid, $85,000; assets, $1,701,789 (M); expenditures, $97,491; qualifying distributions, $85,250.
Limitations: Giving primarily in NY.
Trustees: Elaine Spector, Joseph Spector, KeyBank, N.A.
EIN: 156018859
Codes: FD2

43061
Harry A. Logan, Jr. Foundation
c/o National City Bank of Pennsylvania
P.O. Box 94651
Cleveland, OH 44101
Application address: 20 Stanwix St., Pittsburgh, PA, 15222, tel.: (814) 723-5300
Contact: Edward A. Kavanaugh

Established in 1985 in PA.
Financial data (yr. ended 12/31/00): Grants paid, $84,719; assets, $316,002 (M); expenditures, $87,669; qualifying distributions, $85,526.
Limitations: Giving primarily in western PA.
Application information: Application form required.
Trustee: National City Bank of Pennsylvania.
EIN: 251514648
Codes: FD2

43062
Ervin and Marie Wilkof Foundation
116 Cleveland Ave. N.W., Ste. 525
Canton, OH 44702 (330) 452-9788
Contact: David Schroder, Pres. and Treas.

Established in 1986 in OH.

Financial data (yr. ended 06/30/01): Grants paid, $84,300; assets, $1,341,938 (M); expenditures, $90,781; qualifying distributions, $83,750.
Limitations: Giving primarily in Canton, OH.
Officers: David Schroder, Pres. and Treas.; Marie Wilkof, V.P.; Ronald Wilkof, Secy.
EIN: 341536116
Codes: FD2

43063
The Brotherhood Foundation
c/o Sky Trust, N.A.
P.O. Box 479
Youngstown, OH 44501-0479 (330) 742-7035

Established in 1987 in OH.
Donor(s): Mary M. Evans.
Financial data (yr. ended 12/31/01): Grants paid, $84,288; assets, $1,761,085 (M); expenditures, $103,892; qualifying distributions, $84,288.
Limitations: Giving limited to the Youngstown, OH, area.
Directors: Dolores E. Beck, Mary Evans, Janet E. Harmon.
Trustee: Sky Trust, N.A.
EIN: 346883645

43064
The Teri & Dan German Family Foundation, Inc.
(Formerly The Daniel S. German Foundation, Inc.)
55 N. Main St.
Centerville, OH 45459

Established in 1999 in OH.
Donor(s): Daniel S. German.
Financial data (yr. ended 12/31/01): Grants paid, $84,279; assets, $194,061 (M); gifts received, $45,085; expenditures, $89,455; qualifying distributions, $84,279.
Limitations: Applications not accepted. Giving primarily in Dayton, OH.
Application information: Contributes only to pre-selected organizations.
Trustees: Stephen P. Burke, Bill German, James G. Kordik.
EIN: 311648563
Codes: FD2

43065
The Bokom Foundation
24200 Chagrin Blvd., Ste. 242
Beachwood, OH 44122-5531
Contact: George R. Klein, Pres.

Established in 1993 in OH.
Financial data (yr. ended 12/31/00): Grants paid, $84,125; assets, $2,564,024 (M); expenditures, $87,134; qualifying distributions, $84,125.
Officers: George R. Klein, Pres. and Treas.; Susan A. Klein, V.P.
EIN: 341760423
Codes: FD2

43066
The Paintstone Foundation
7373 Production Dr.
P.O. Box 780
Mentor, OH 44060

Established in 1986 in OH.
Donor(s): Aexcel Corp.
Financial data (yr. ended 12/31/00): Grants paid, $84,100; assets, $833,712 (M); gifts received, $35,000; expenditures, $96,964; qualifying distributions, $84,100.
Limitations: Applications not accepted. Giving primarily in the Cleveland, OH, area.
Application information: Contributes only to pre-selected organizations.

Trustees: Andrew Milgram, John S. Milgram, Joseph B. Milgram, Margaretta S.C. Milgram, Thomas Milgram.
EIN: 341538822
Codes: CS, FD2, CD

43067
Alma A. & Harry R. Templeton Medical Research Foundation
c/o KeyBank, N.A., Trust Tax Dept.
127 Public Sq., 17th Fl.
Cleveland, OH 44114 (216) 689-5972
Contact: Kathryn D. Blaszak, V.P., KeyBank, N.A.

Donor(s): Alma Templeton, Harry Templeton.‡
Financial data (yr. ended 12/31/01): Grants paid, $84,000; assets, $1,398,368 (M); expenditures, $108,117; qualifying distributions, $83,209.
Limitations: Giving limited to OH.
Application information: Application form not required.
Trustee: KeyBank, N.A.
EIN: 346598526
Codes: FD2

43068
Jane E. Hunter Test Trust
c/o KeyBank N.A. Tax Dept.
800 Superior Ave., 4th Fl.
Cleveland, OH 44114

Established in 2001 in OH.
Financial data (yr. ended 12/31/01): Grants paid, $82,967; assets, $2,400,310 (M); gifts received, $2,314,666; expenditures, $106,813; qualifying distributions, $90,614.
Limitations: Applications not accepted.
Application information: Unsolicited requests for funds not accepted.
Trustee: KeyBank, N.A.
EIN: 346699212
Codes: FD2

43069
Skestos Family Foundation
750 Northlawn Dr.
Columbus, OH 43214

Established in 2000 in OH.
Donor(s): George A. Skestos, Jason Skestos, Alexandra Skestos, Stephanie K. Skestos.
Financial data (yr. ended 12/31/00): Grants paid, $82,500; assets, $7,850,361 (M); gifts received, $7,606,686; expenditures, $89,846; qualifying distributions, $88,975.
Limitations: Giving primarily in Columbus, OH.
Officers: George Arthur Skestos, Pres.; Terrie L. Rice, Secy.-Treas.
Trustees: Alexandra Skestos Block, George Anthony Skestos, Stephanie K. Skestos.
EIN: 311721314
Codes: FD2

43070
The McKeever Foundation, Inc.
2289 Chatfield Dr.
Cleveland Heights, OH 44106
Contact: Jerome McKeever, Tr.

Established in 1993 in OH.
Donor(s): Catherine McKeever.
Financial data (yr. ended 12/31/01): Grants paid, $82,286; assets, $672,664 (M); gifts received, $2,800; expenditures, $101,161; qualifying distributions, $85,286.
Limitations: Giving primarily in OH.
Application information: Funds fully committed for the next 6 years. Application form not required.
Trustees: Catherine Denton, Catherine McKeever, Jerome McKeever.
EIN: 311367070

Codes: FD2

43071
Mooney Family Foundation
c/o William E. Reichard
25109 Detroit Rd., Ste. 300
Westlake, OH 44145

Established in 1989 in OH.
Donor(s): James P. Mooney, Janet M. Mooney, St. Gerard Foundation.
Financial data (yr. ended 12/31/00): Grants paid, $82,166; assets, $580,926 (M); expenditures, $85,296; qualifying distributions, $82,166.
Limitations: Applications not accepted. Giving primarily in OH.
Application information: Contributes only to pre-selected organizations.
Trustees: James P. Mooney, Janet M. Mooney, Michael X. Mooney.
EIN: 346921500
Codes: FD2

43072
The Henry and Eugenia Green Family Foundation, Inc.
15975 Shaker Blvd.
Shaker Heights, OH 44120-1657
Contact: Andrew Green, Pres.

Established in 1991 in OH.
Donor(s): Henry Green.‡
Financial data (yr. ended 06/30/02): Grants paid, $81,750; assets, $743,382 (M); expenditures, $81,850; qualifying distributions, $81,750.
Limitations: Giving primarily in Cleveland, OH.
Officers: Andrew Green, Pres.; Judy K. Green, Secy.; Joseph F. Ciulla, Treas.
EIN: 341695272
Codes: FD2

43073
Robert Kutz Charitable Trust
c/o KeyBank, N.A.
157 S. Main St.
Akron, OH 44308
Contact: K.M. Krino, Sr. Trust. Off.

Established in 1987 in OH.
Donor(s): Robert A. Kutz.‡
Financial data (yr. ended 12/31/01): Grants paid, $81,700; assets, $2,170,431 (M); expenditures, $114,102; qualifying distributions, $89,145.
Limitations: Giving limited to Summit County, OH.
Application information: Application form required.
Trustees: W. Paul Jeffrey, Joseph G. Miller, KeyBank, N.A.
EIN: 346977068
Codes: FD2

43074
The Ruth H. Beecher Charitable Trust
c/o National City Bank, Northeast
P.O. Box 450
Youngstown, OH 44501-0450 (330) 742-4289
Contact: Myra Vitto, National City Bank

Established in 1986 in OH.
Financial data (yr. ended 09/30/01): Grants paid, $81,500; assets, $2,205,416 (M); expenditures, $94,793; qualifying distributions, $91,332.
Limitations: Giving primarily in Youngstown, OH.
Application information: Application form not required.
Trustees: John Weed Powers, National City Bank, Northeast.
EIN: 346861417
Codes: FD2

43075
Hieronymus Family Fund, Inc.
1278 Maue Rd.
Miamisburg, OH 45342

Established in 1993 in OH.
Donor(s): Harriet Hieronymus.
Financial data (yr. ended 12/31/00): Grants paid, $81,500; assets, $1,520,371 (M); expenditures, $92,282; qualifying distributions, $81,500.
Limitations: Applications not accepted. Giving primarily in OH.
Application information: Contributes only to pre-selected organizations.
Trustees: Harriet Hieronymus, Lee Hieronymus, Theodore Hieronymus.
EIN: 311381301
Codes: FD2

43076
Edward Lamb Foundation, Inc.
P.O. Box 155
Maumee, OH 43537
Contact: Priscilla L. Schwier, Pres.

Established in 1948.
Financial data (yr. ended 12/31/00): Grants paid, $81,350; assets, $1,641,498 (M); expenditures, $96,883; qualifying distributions, $83,854.
Limitations: Giving primarily in OH.
Application information: Application form not required.
Officers and Trustees:* Priscilla L. Schwier,* Pres.; Hugh J. Morgan,* V.P.; Caroline M. Partin, Secy.-Treas.; Edward H. Lamb, Prudence H. Lamb, Robert R. Metz, Frederick W. Schwier.
EIN: 340463131
Codes: FD2

43077
Gosiger Foundation
c/o G. Haley
108 McDonough St.
Dayton, OH 45402

Established in 1992 in OH.
Donor(s): Gosiger, Inc.
Financial data (yr. ended 12/31/01): Grants paid, $80,800; assets, $411,885 (M); gifts received, $250,000; expenditures, $82,531; qualifying distributions, $81,049.
Limitations: Applications not accepted. Giving primarily in Dayton, OH.
Application information: Contributes only to pre-selected organizations.
Officers and Trustees:* Jane Haley,* Pres.; Jerry Gecowets,* Exec. V.P.; John Haley,* V.P.; Pete Haley,* V.P.; Hugh E. Wall III,* Secy.; Jerry Pressel,* Treas.
EIN: 311365457
Codes: CS, FD2, CD

43078
The Wapakoneta Area Community Foundation
10 W. Auglaize St.
P.O. Box 1957
Wapakoneta, OH 45895-1957
(419) 738-9274
Additional tels.: (419) 738-8121 or (419) 739-9223; FAX: (419) 738-3403 or (419) 739-9220; E-mail: jauertds@bright.net or LTESTERWACF@brightohio.net; URL: http://www.wapakacf.org
Contact: Douglas S. Jauert, Pres.

Established in 1989 in OH.
Financial data (yr. ended 12/31/01): Grants paid, $80,515; assets, $1,175,008 (M); gifts received, $114,510; expenditures, $84,192.
Limitations: Giving limited to the Wapakoneta, OH, area.

Publications: Newsletter.
Application information: Application form not required.
Officer: Douglas S. Jauert, Pres.
EIN: 341615229
Codes: CM, FD2, GTI

43079
Paul & Dina W. Block Foundation
541 N. Superior St.
Toledo, OH 43660
Application address: c/o Pittsburgh Post-Gazette, 34 Blvd. of the Allies, Pittsburgh, PA 15222
Contact: William Block, Jr., Secy.

Established in 1957.
Financial data (yr. ended 12/31/00): Grants paid, $80,500; assets, $1,460,013 (M); expenditures, $88,747; qualifying distributions, $80,500.
Limitations: Giving primarily in PA.
Application information: Application form not required.
Officers: William Block, Sr., Pres.; Allan Block, V.P.; William Block, Jr., Secy.; John Block, Treas.
EIN: 136083017
Codes: FD2

43080
New Orphan Asylum Scholarship Foundation
2340 Victory Pkwy., No. 1
Cincinnati, OH 45206 (513) 961-6626
Contact: Melody Sparks

Established in 1942 in OH.
Financial data (yr. ended 12/31/00): Grants paid, $80,461; assets, $3,798,943 (M); gifts received, $4,363; expenditures, $155,373; qualifying distributions, $121,543.
Limitations: Giving limited to organizations and residents of the greater Cincinnati, OH, area.
Application information: Limited support for postgraduate studies available through Samuel Bullock Scholarships; payments are made directly to the educational institution. Application form required.
Officers: Penni Tibbs, Pres.; Louis Patrick, Secy.; Willie Carden, Jr., Treas.
Trustees: C. Jude Johnson, Blanche Kalfus.
EIN: 310536683
Codes: FD2, GTI

43081
The Leslie C. Mapp Foundation
6024 Mad River Rd.
Centerville, OH 45459-1508

Established in 2000 in OH.
Donor(s): Leslie C. Mapp.
Financial data (yr. ended 12/31/01): Grants paid, $80,130; assets, $399,865 (M); gifts received, $240,000; expenditures, $84,068; qualifying distributions, $80,130.
Officer: Leslie C. Mapp, Pres.
EIN: 316647864

43082
William M. Weiss Foundation
c/o William M. Weiss
24920 Sittinghouse Ln.
Beachwood, OH 44122

Established in 1994.
Donor(s): William M. Weiss.
Financial data (yr. ended 12/31/01): Grants paid, $80,000; assets, $1,927,942 (M); gifts received, $407,951; expenditures, $80,000; qualifying distributions, $80,000.
Limitations: Applications not accepted. Giving primarily in NJ, New York, NY, Cleveland, OH, and Dallas, TX.

Application information: Contributes only to pre-selected organizations.
Trustees: David Weiss, Jeffrey Weiss, William M. Weiss.
EIN: 341787366
Codes: FD2

43083
William S. Rowe Foundation
c/o Fifth Third Bank
38 Fountain Sq. Plz. MD 1COM31
Cincinnati, OH 45263 (513) 579-6034

Established in 1988 in OH.
Financial data (yr. ended 09/30/01): Grants paid, $79,500; assets, $1,524,612 (M); expenditures, $99,643; qualifying distributions, $84,642.
Limitations: Giving limited to the greater Cincinnati, OH, area.
Application information: Application form required.
Officers: Martha P. Rowe, Pres.; Phillip C. Long, Secy.-Treas.
EIN: 311255004
Codes: FD2

43084
Galion Community Foundation
135 Harding Way W.
Galion, OH 44833
Contact: Steven J. Erlsten, Chair.

Established in 1957.
Donor(s): Chester E. Zimmerman,‡ Steven J. Erlsten.
Financial data (yr. ended 06/30/01): Grants paid, $79,354; assets, $1,584,355 (M); gifts received, $2,500; expenditures, $98,247; qualifying distributions, $81,985.
Limitations: Giving limited to the Galion, OH, area.
Application information: Application form not required.
Board of Advisors: Steven J. Erlsten, Chair.; J. William Stepro, Secy.; Bruce Angell, Sam Buehrer, Margaret Cagle, Tyler K. Huggins, Becky Miller, Ed Rieke, Dan W. Shealy, John Shuler, David Spraw.
EIN: 316023104
Codes: FD2, GTI

43085
Henry Towne Scholarship Fund
c/o KeyBank, N.A.
800 Superior Ave., 4th Fl.
Cleveland, OH 44114-2601
Application address: c/o Human Resources Dept., Eaton Corp., Eaton Ctr., Cleveland, OH 44114, tel.: (216) 534-4353
Contact: Melanie Maloney

Donor(s): Eaton Corp.
Financial data (yr. ended 12/31/00): Grants paid, $79,260; assets, $838,029 (M); expenditures, $90,227; qualifying distributions, $80,560.
Limitations: Giving primarily in areas of company operations.
Application information: Application form required.
Trustees: Susan J. Cooks, J.R. Horst, Billie Rawot, KeyBank, N.A.
EIN: 136104340
Codes: CS, FD2, CD

43086
The Benjamin Family Foundation
3550 Lander Rd., Ste. 200
Pepper Pike, OH 44124

Financial data (yr. ended 12/31/00): Grants paid, $78,605; assets, $668,348 (M); expenditures, $827,288; qualifying distributions, $81,288.

Limitations: Applications not accepted. Giving primarily in OH.
Application information: Contributes only to pre-selected organizations.
Officers and Trustees:* Stanley S. Benjamin,* Pres.; Jeanne R. Benjamin,* V.P.; Barry J. Benjamin,* Secy.; David N. Benjamin,* Treas.; John E. Burns, David E. Griffiths.
EIN: 650828804
Codes: FD2

43087
The Bascom Little Fund
34750 Cedar Rd.
Gates Mills, OH 44040-9788
Application address: c/o Andrew L. Fabens III, 127 Public Sq., Ste. 3900, Cleveland, OH 44114
Contact: Richard A. Manuel, Tr.

Established in 1965 in OH.
Donor(s): Sue L. Little,‡ Mrs. Calvin A. Lohmiller.‡
Financial data (yr. ended 06/30/01): Grants paid, $78,576; assets, $1,131,839 (M); expenditures, $88,103; qualifying distributions, $76,604.
Limitations: Giving limited to the Cleveland, OH, area.
Application information: Application form required.
Trustees: Richard H. Bole, Andrew L. Fabens III, Richard A. Manuel, Dixon Morgan, Jr., Stanley W. Morgenstern, Harry D. Weller III.
Advisory Board: Linda Allen, Ronald Bishop, Rudolph Bubalo, Margaret Brouwer, Loris O. Chobanian, Dennis Eberhard, Margaret Griebling-Haigh, Richard A. Manuel, Dwight Oltman, Jeffrey Quick, Klaus C. Roy, Thomas Shellhammer, Jean Geis Stell, Frank E. Wiley.
EIN: 346572279
Codes: FD2, GTI

43088
John F. Savage Family Foundation, Inc.
c/o Scott J. Savage
6711 Monroe St., Ste. A
Sylvania, OH 43560-9806

Established in 1988 in OH.
Donor(s): John F. Savage.
Financial data (yr. ended 12/31/01): Grants paid, $78,550; assets, $840,878 (M); expenditures, $81,776; qualifying distributions, $77,863.
Limitations: Applications not accepted. Giving limited to OH, with emphasis on Toledo.
Application information: Contributes only to pre-selected organizations.
Trustees: John M. Savage, Mary K. Savage, Scott J. Savage.
EIN: 341612056
Codes: FD2

43089
Windows of Heaven Foundation
4465 Fulton Dr., N.W., Ste. 100
Canton, OH 44718 (330) 492-9602
Contact: Frederick E. Berndt, Treas.

Established in 1988 in OH.
Donor(s): Gail L. Harmelink, Robert A. Harmelink.
Financial data (yr. ended 12/31/00): Grants paid, $78,500; assets, $1,427,148 (M); expenditures, $96,242; qualifying distributions, $78,500.
Limitations: Giving primarily in OH.
Application information: Application form not required.
Officers: Robert A. Harmelink, Chair. and Pres.; Gail L. Harmelink, Secy.; Frederick E. Berndt, Treas.
EIN: 341590288
Codes: FD2

43090
The Sussen Foundation
7460 Markell Rd.
Waite Hill, OH 44094

Established in 1988 in OH.
Donor(s): Daniel C. Sussen, Sr., Joseph J. Sussen, Sr.
Financial data (yr. ended 12/31/00): Grants paid, $78,137; assets, $546,114 (M); gifts received, $62,672; expenditures, $95,092; qualifying distributions, $78,889.
Limitations: Applications not accepted. Giving primarily in Cleveland, OH.
Application information: Contributes only to pre-selected organizations.
Trustee: Daniel C. Sussen, Sr.
EIN: 341617964

43091
The Bush Foundation
511 Walnut St., Ste. 1900
Cincinnati, OH 45202
Contact: G. Kenner Bush, Secy.

Established in 1997 in OH.
Donor(s): G. Kenner Bush, Margene G. Bush.
Financial data (yr. ended 12/31/01): Grants paid, $78,000; assets, $1,038,832 (M); gifts received, $59,112; expenditures, $87,112; qualifying distributions, $78,561.
Limitations: Applications not accepted. Giving primarily in OH.
Application information: Contributes only to pre-selected organizations.
Officers: Margene G. Bush, Pres.; G. Kenner Bush, Secy.
Trustee: Frederick G. Bush.
EIN: 311579626
Codes: FD2

43092
The Marnick Foundation
c/o PNC Bank, N.A., Trust Tax Dept.
P.O. Box 1198
Cincinnati, OH 45201-1198
Application address: 10 Grandin Ln., Cincinnati, OH 45208, tel.: (513) 271-3300
Contact: H. Nicholas Ragland III

Established in 1996 in OH.
Donor(s): Martha H. Ragland.
Financial data (yr. ended 12/31/01): Grants paid, $78,000; assets, $13,283,234 (M); gifts received, $1,041,200; expenditures, $82,182; qualifying distributions, $78,900.
Limitations: Giving primarily in OH.
Application information: Application form not required.
Trustees: H.N. Ragland III, H. Nicholas Ragland IV, John J. Ragland, Joseph A. Ragland, Martha H. Ragland, Peter D. Ragland.
EIN: 311493613
Codes: FD2

43093
Nutis Foundation, Inc.
P.O. Box 27248
Columbus, OH 43227-1125 (614) 237-8626
Application address: 3540 E. Fulton St., Columbus, OH 43227
Contact: Frank R. Nutis, Pres.

Established in 1965.
Donor(s): Frank Nutis, Nutis Press, Inc.
Financial data (yr. ended 12/31/01): Grants paid, $77,910; assets, $660,681 (M); gifts received, $30,000; expenditures, $78,895; qualifying distributions, $77,910.
Application information: Application form not required.

Officer: Frank R. Nutis, Pres.
EIN: 316065584

43094
Henry L. Morse Charitable Trust
c/o KeyBank, N.A., Trust Div.
P.O. Box 10099, Ste. 0330
Toledo, OH 43699-0099

Donor(s): Henry L. Morse.
Financial data (yr. ended 12/31/01): Grants paid, $77,622; assets, $916,968 (M); expenditures, $82,329; qualifying distributions, $79,379.
Limitations: Applications not accepted. Giving limited to OH.
Application information: Contributes only to pre-selected organizations.
Trustee: KeyBank, N.A.
EIN: 346813860
Codes: FD2

43095
Alice Kindler Charitable Fund
123 S. Broad St., Ste. 211
Lancaster, OH 43130
Application address: 4307 Bauman Hill Rd., Lancaster, OH 43130
Contact: William J. Sitterley

Established in 1996 in OH.
Donor(s): Alice Kindler.‡
Financial data (yr. ended 08/31/01): Grants paid, $77,450; assets, $1,257,608 (M); expenditures, $80,612; qualifying distributions, $78,850.
Limitations: Giving primarily in Fairfield County, OH.
Application information: Application form required.
Trustees: Christine A. Sitterley, William J. Sitterley.
EIN: 311337515
Codes: FD2

43096
CRL Foundation
c/o R.K. Smith & Assocs., Inc.
24803 Detroit Rd.
Westlake, OH 44145-2512 (440) 835-9450
Contact: Robert K. Smith, Tr.

Financial data (yr. ended 12/31/00): Grants paid, $77,000; assets, $212,680 (M); expenditures, $78,366; qualifying distributions, $77,000.
Limitations: Giving primarily in OH.
Trustees: Miles C. Durfey, Hon. Donald Nugent, Hon. John T. Patton, Wayne Reese, Robert K. Smith, William K. Suter, James Weisbarth.
EIN: 341499058
Codes: FD2

43097
DeBartolo Family Foundation
100 DeBartolo Pl., Ste. 300
P.O. Box 9430
Youngstown, OH 44513

Established in 2001 in OH.
Donor(s): Edward J. DeBartolo, Jr., The DeBartolo Family Foundation, Edward J. DeBartolo Memorial Scholarship Foundation.
Financial data (yr. ended 01/31/02): Grants paid, $77,000; assets, $879,098 (M); gifts received, $1,145,977; expenditures, $81,689; qualifying distributions, $76,867.
Limitations: Applications not accepted. Giving primarily in OH.
Application information: Contributes only to pre-selected organizations.
Directors: Edward J. DeBartolo, Jr., Lisa Marie DeBartolo, Tiffanie L. DeBartolo, Nicole Ann DeBartolo Heldfond, Edward Muransky.
EIN: 311739677

43098
Gene & Neddie Mae Elkus Family Foundation
c/o Fifth Third Bank
Trust Tax Dept. M/D 1COM31
Cincinnati, OH 45202-3191
Contact: Frank Fisher

Established in 1996 in OH.
Financial data (yr. ended 12/31/01): Grants paid, $77,000; assets, $1,347,217 (M); expenditures, $87,993; qualifying distributions, $77,000.
Limitations: Giving primarily in Cincinnati, OH.
Trustees: Michael Elkus, Richard Elkus, Fifth Third Bank.
EIN: 311487336

43099
Mussel Mitigation Trust Fund
139 E. 4th St., Ste. 260
Cincinnati, OH 45202 (513) 287-3884
Contact: Bernard L. Huff, Tr.

Established in 1987 in OH.
Financial data (yr. ended 12/31/01): Grants paid, $76,863; assets, $166,029 (M); expenditures, $86,421; qualifying distributions, $78,178.
Limitations: Giving primarily in KY, MO, OH, and TN.
Officers: Robert C. Schnelle, Chair.; Randall E. Sanders, Secy.
Trustees: C. Thomas Bennett, Michael J. Budzik, Wayne L. Davis, Bernard L. Huff.
EIN: 311222484
Codes: FD2

43100
Joseph and Helen Skilken Foundation
P.O. Box 1148
Columbus, OH 43216-1148
Application address: 383 S. 3rd. St., Columbus, OH 43216, tel.: (614) 221-4547
Contact: Helen R. Skilken, Dir., Lynne E. Skilken, Dir., or Steven A. Skilken, Dir.

Established in 1962 in OH.
Donor(s): Steven A. Skilken, Lynne E. Skilken.
Financial data (yr. ended 12/31/01): Grants paid, $76,675; assets, $1,363,591 (M); expenditures, $240,858; qualifying distributions, $76,675.
Limitations: Giving on a national basis.
Application information: Application form not required.
Directors: Helen R. Skilken, Lynne E. Skilken, Steven A. Skilken.
EIN: 316050827

43101
The Joseph and Mollie Mendes Family Charitable Fund
23800 Commerce Park, Ste. L
Beachwood, OH 44122-5828

Established in 1989 in OH.
Donor(s): Mrs. Joseph Mendes.‡
Financial data (yr. ended 12/31/00): Grants paid, $76,515; assets, $1,042,923 (M); expenditures, $78,637; qualifying distributions, $78,487.
Limitations: Applications not accepted. Giving limited to OH.
Application information: Contributes only to pre-selected organizations.
Officers and Trustees:* Harold B. Mendes,* Pres.; Morton R. Mendes,* Secy.; Faye D. Kaplan,* Treas.
EIN: 341622034
Codes: FD2

43102
The Jerome Kobacker Charities Foundation
41 S. High St., Ste. 3610
Columbus, OH 43215

Established in 1949 in OH.
Donor(s): Nan Delaubadere, Jeffrey M. Kobacker, John S. Kobacker, Marvin Kobacker,‡ Mrs. Marvin Kobacker,‡ Marlenko, Inc.
Financial data (yr. ended 12/31/01): Grants paid, $76,500; assets, $1,913,086 (M); gifts received, $60,000; expenditures, $81,892; qualifying distributions, $77,496.
Limitations: Applications not accepted. Giving primarily in CO and OH.
Application information: Contributes only to pre-selected organizations.
Trustees: James M. Kobacker, Jeffrey M. Kobacker, John S. Kobacker.
EIN: 346522097
Codes: FD2

43103
Duff Family Foundation
956 S. Broadway
Lima, OH 45804 (419) 222-5050
Contact: L. Eugene Duff, V.P.

Established in 1965.
Donor(s): L. Eugene Duff, Duff Warehouses, Inc.
Financial data (yr. ended 06/30/01): Grants paid, $76,320; assets, $1,050,780 (M); expenditures, $77,797; qualifying distributions, $75,833.
Limitations: Giving primarily in Lima, OH.
Application information: Application form not required.
Officers and Trustees:* Bonnie J. Duff,* Pres.; L. Eugene Duff,* V.P.
EIN: 346529813
Codes: FD2

43104
Joe Busam Foundation
795 Kingfisher Ln.
Cincinnati, OH 45246-4711
Contact: Claire M. Busam, Pres.

Established in 1997 in OH.
Financial data (yr. ended 07/31/01): Grants paid, $76,293; assets, $1,313,068 (M); expenditures, $97,301; qualifying distributions, $75,898.
Limitations: Applications not accepted.
Application information: Contributes only to pre-selected organizations.
Officers and Trustees:* Claire M. Busam,* Chair. and Pres.; Michele M. Ulrich,* V.P.; Barbara B. Kelly,* Secy.; Claire B. Corcoran,* Treas.; John A. Busam, Joseph Charles Busam, Molly A. Busam, Thomas Jeffrey Corcoran, Mary B. Cornwell, Helene B. Gruber, Robert J. Gruber, Timothy P. Kelly, Stephanie Sudbrack-Busam, David W. Ulrich.
EIN: 311568776
Codes: FD2

43105
Woodward Family Charitable Foundation
c/o U.S. Bank
P.O. Box 1118, CN-WN-10TX
Cincinnati, OH 45201-1118

Established in 1993 in OH.
Donor(s): Marianna M. Woodward.
Financial data (yr. ended 12/31/01): Grants paid, $76,000; assets, $1,373,813 (M); expenditures, $85,694; qualifying distributions, $75,798.
Limitations: Applications not accepted. Giving on a national basis, with emphasis on IL and OH.
Application information: Contributes only to pre-selected organizations.
Trustees: Jeanette Bunn, Anthony Woodward.
Agent: U.S. Bank.
EIN: 367015446
Codes: FD2

43106
The Peterloon Foundation
c/o Gradison Div., McDonald & Co.
580 Walnut St.
Cincinnati, OH 45202 (513) 579-5886
Contact: Paul G. Sittenfeld, Secy.

Established in 1958.
Donor(s): John J. Emery.‡
Financial data (yr. ended 12/31/01): Grants paid, $75,836; assets, $6,397,070 (M); expenditures, $329,300; qualifying distributions, $184,692.
Limitations: Giving primarily in the metropolitan Cincinnati, OH, area.
Application information: Application form not required.
Officers: Lela Emery Steele, Pres. and Treas.; Melissa Emery Lanier, V.P.; Paul G. Sittenfeld, Secy.
Trustees: John L. Campbell, Ethan Emery, Irene Emery Goodale, Elizabeth Hinkley Hoyt, Judith M. Mitchell.
EIN: 316037801
Codes: FD2

43107
Edgerton Area Foundation
P.O. Box 399
Edgerton, OH 43517-0399
Contact: Roger D. Strup, Pres.

Established in 1993 in OH.
Financial data (yr. ended 06/30/00): Grants paid, $75,808; assets, $910,117 (M); gifts received, $149,398; expenditures, $107,605.
Limitations: Giving limited to the Edgerton, OH, area.
Officer and Trustees:* Roger D. Strup,* Pres.; Dan Clark, Christine Dietsch, Dale Mathys, Wayne Wilson.
EIN: 341593384
Codes: CM

43108
Catanzarite Family Foundation
c/o Lamrite West, Inc.
21160 Drake Rd.
Strongsville, OH 44136

Established in 1998 in OH.
Donor(s): Patsy G. Catanzarite.
Financial data (yr. ended 12/31/00): Grants paid, $75,050; assets, $406,718 (M); gifts received, $200,000; expenditures, $80,976; qualifying distributions, $75,028.
Limitations: Applications not accepted.
Application information: Contributes only to pre-selected organizations.
Officers and Trustees:* Patsy G. Catanzarite,* Pres.; Sharon Kilbane,* V.P. and Secy.; Michael A. Catanzarite,* V.P. and Treas.; Patrice Alberty,* V.P.; David Catanzarite,* V.P.; Beatrice Catanzarite.
EIN: 341868367
Codes: FD2

43109
The Larmis Foundation
c/o National City Bank
P.O. Box 94651
Cleveland, OH 44101-4651

Established in 1998 in OH.
Donor(s): Robert W. McChesney.
Financial data (yr. ended 05/31/02): Grants paid, $75,000; assets, $85,013 (M); expenditures, $77,672; qualifying distributions, $75,000.
Limitations: Applications not accepted. Giving primarily in Chicago, IL, and Madison, WI.

43109—OHIO

Application information: Contributes only to pre-selected organizations.
Trustee: National City Bank.
EIN: 341878789

43110
Longview Foundation
2501 Arlington Rd.
Cleveland Heights, OH 44118
FAX: (216) 861-1861; E-mail: lgs@xa.com
Contact: Charles Stack, Treas.

Established in 1997 in OH.
Donor(s): Charles Stack, Laura Stack.
Financial data (yr. ended 12/31/01): Grants paid, $75,000; assets, $145,951 (M); expenditures, $76,192; qualifying distributions, $75,000.
Officers: Laura Stack, Pres.; Camille Tillman, Secy.; Charles Stack, Treas.
EIN: 311533391

43111
The Dudley P. and Barbara K. Sheffler Foundation
25109 Detroit Rd., Ste. 300
Westlake, OH 44145

Established in 1991 in OH.
Donor(s): Dudley P. Sheffler, Barbara K. Sheffler.
Financial data (yr. ended 12/31/00): Grants paid, $75,000; assets, $2,024,297 (M); gifts received, $264,360; expenditures, $94,012; qualifying distributions, $74,227.
Limitations: Applications not accepted. Giving primarily in OH.
Application information: Contributes only to pre-selected organizations.
Trustees: Barbara K. Sheffler, Dudley P. Sheffler.
EIN: 346959040
Codes: FD2

43112
Sherwood Foundation
2700 E. Main St., Ste. 107
Columbus, OH 43209

Established in 1985.
Donor(s): Dorothea H. Ulrich.
Financial data (yr. ended 06/30/01): Grants paid, $75,000; assets, $1,345,676 (M); expenditures, $89,723; qualifying distributions, $74,434.
Limitations: Applications not accepted. Giving primarily in Winona, MN, and Constable, NY.
Application information: Contributes only to pre-selected organizations.
Trustees: Kiehner Johnson, Dorothea H. Ulrich.
EIN: 311151549

43113
Towering Pines Foundation
405 Madison Ave., Ste. 1900
Toledo, OH 43604-1207
Contact: Jay L. Peters, Pres.

Established in 1997 in OH.
Donor(s): Jay L. Peters.
Financial data (yr. ended 12/31/00): Grants paid, $75,000; assets, $1,871,372 (M); expenditures, $79,125; qualifying distributions, $78,754.
Limitations: Applications not accepted. Giving primarily in Durham, NC.
Application information: Contributes only to pre-selected organizations.
Officers and Trustees:* Jay L. Peters,* Pres.; Kathryn H. Peters,* V.P.; William F. Bates,* Secy.-Treas.
EIN: 311534802

43114
Agnes Nordloh Charitable Trust
900 Central Trust Tower
Cincinnati, OH 45202 (513) 381-9200
Application address: 900 4th & Vine Tower, Cincinnati, OH 45202
Contact: J. Kenneth Meagher, Tr.

Established in 1990 in OH.
Financial data (yr. ended 12/31/01): Grants paid, $74,750; assets, $1,289,531 (M); expenditures, $113,785; qualifying distributions, $112,823.
Limitations: Giving primarily in Cincinnati, OH.
Trustee: J. Kenneth Meagher.
EIN: 316368067

43115
Wayne R. Hellman Foundation
32000 E. Aurora Rd.
Cleveland, OH 44139-2814

Established in 1997.
Financial data (yr. ended 12/31/00): Grants paid, $74,730; assets, $440,913 (M); expenditures, $151,764; qualifying distributions, $74,730.
Limitations: Applications not accepted. Giving primarily in Cleveland, OH.
Application information: Contributes only to pre-selected organizations.
Officers: Wayne R. Hellman, Pres.; Gerald W. Cowden, Secy.
EIN: 311545138

43116
Weston Family Foundation
(Formerly Eugene J. & Rose H. Weston Foundation)
c/o Gradison & Co.
580 Bldg.
Cincinnati, OH 45202

Established in 1961 in OH.
Donor(s): Alan E. Weston, Donald E. Weston, Paul J. Weston.
Financial data (yr. ended 08/31/01): Grants paid, $74,700; assets, $746,636 (M); gifts received, $25,118; expenditures, $77,607; qualifying distributions, $72,772.
Limitations: Applications not accepted. Giving primarily in OH.
Application information: Contributes only to pre-selected organizations.
Officers: Donald E. Weston, Pres.; Alan E. Weston, V.P.; Paul J. Weston, Treas.
EIN: 316040827

43117
Kenneth & Joan L. Campbell Foundation
4564 Morris Ct.
Mason, OH 45040

Established in 1990 in OH.
Donor(s): Kenneth R. Campbell, Joan L. Campbell.
Financial data (yr. ended 12/31/01): Grants paid, $74,629; assets, $1,616,622 (M); gifts received, $150,000; expenditures, $88,916; qualifying distributions, $74,629.
Limitations: Applications not accepted. Giving primarily in Cincinnati, OH.
Application information: Contributes only to pre-selected organizations.
Trustees: Joan L. Campbell, Kenneth R. Campbell, Daniel O'Brien.
EIN: 311314448

43118
Seaman Family Foundation
1000 Venture Blvd.
Wooster, OH 44691-9358 (330) 262-1111
Contact: Richard N. Seaman, Tr.

Established in 1993 in OH.
Donor(s): Richard N. Seaman, Judith Seaman.
Financial data (yr. ended 12/31/00): Grants paid, $74,532; assets, $1,366,375 (M); expenditures, $109,429; qualifying distributions, $7,432.
Limitations: Giving primarily in the Wooster, OH, area.
Trustee: Richard N. Seaman.
EIN: 341770650

43119
The Russell Family Foundation
c/o Wayland J. Russell
467 Hickory Hollow Dr.
Canfield, OH 44406

Donor(s): Wayland J. Russell.
Financial data (yr. ended 12/31/00): Grants paid, $74,450; assets, $207,636 (M); gifts received, $70,100; expenditures, $74,711; qualifying distributions, $74,450.
Limitations: Applications not accepted.
Application information: Contributes only to pre-selected organizations.
Officers and Trustees:* Wayland J. Russell,* Pres.; Michael Pecchia, Secy.; Donna Russell,* Treas.
EIN: 341885760

43120
St. Clair Foundation
c/o Eaton National Bank & Trust Co.
110 W. Main St.
Eaton, OH 45320-1746 (937) 456-5544
Contact: Myra Frame

Established in 1971 in OH.
Financial data (yr. ended 12/31/01): Grants paid, $74,000; assets, $373,730 (M); gifts received, $82,109; expenditures, $178,198.
Limitations: Giving limited to OH.
Officers: Dale Harrison, Pres.; Thomas Kline, Secy.-Treas.
EIN: 237126102
Codes: CM

43121
The Osherow Family Foundation
c/o Bober, Markey, Fedorovich & Co.
411 Wolf Ledges Pkwy., Ste. 400
Akron, OH 44311-1054

Established in 1957 in OH.
Donor(s): Carl Osherow, Gary Osherow, James Osherow, Michael Osherow, Thelma Osherow.
Financial data (yr. ended 12/31/00): Grants paid, $73,750; assets, $314,552 (M); gifts received, $35,269; expenditures, $74,087; qualifying distributions, $73,750.
Limitations: Applications not accepted. Giving primarily in Akron, OH.
Application information: Contributes only to pre-selected organizations.
Officers: Carl Osherow, Pres.; Thelma Osherow, V.P.; Michael Osherow, Secy.-Treas.
Trustees: Gary Osherow, James Osherow.
EIN: 346557733

43122
Mitchel L. Fromm Family Foundation
122 N. Hayden Pkwy.
Hudson, OH 44236-3152 (330) 650-6073
Contact: Mitchel L. Fromm, Tr.

Established in 1999 in OH.
Donor(s): Mitchel L. Fromm, Simone G. Fromm.

Financial data (yr. ended 12/31/00): Grants paid, $73,500; assets, $718,958 (M); expenditures, $82,281; qualifying distributions, $60,656.
Limitations: Giving primarily in OH.
Trustee: Mitchel L. Fromm.
EIN: 341909603

43123
Melvin G. & Mary F. Keller Scholarship Fund
c/o National City Bank of Pennsylvania
P. O. Box 94651
Cleveland, OH 44101-4651
Application address: 315 2nd Ave., Warren, PA 16365, tel.: (814) 871-1279
Contact: Chris Junker, Trust Off., National City Bank of Pennsylvania

Established in 1989 in PA.
Financial data (yr. ended 12/31/01): Grants paid, $73,500; assets, $1,257,508 (M); expenditures, $83,216; qualifying distributions, $77,830.
Limitations: Giving primarily to residents of Warren, PA.
Application information: Application form required.
Trustee: National City Bank of Pennsylvania.
EIN: 256344325
Codes: GTI

43124
Neil, Tressie, & Neil J. Delong Charitable Remainder Trust
7597 Tenbury Dr.
Dublin, OH 43017-7622
Contact: Jon P. Riegel, Tr.

Established in 1995.
Financial data (yr. ended 12/31/00): Grants paid, $73,377; assets, $1,444,205 (M); expenditures, $89,490; qualifying distributions, $73,377.
Limitations: Giving primarily in Columbus, OH.
Application information: Application form not required.
Trustees: James C. DeBoard, Jon P. Riegel.
EIN: 311403596

43125
N. & S. Bruns Foundation, Inc.
3481 Central Pkwy., Ste. 101
Cincinnati, OH 45223-3398
Contact: Robert F. Uhrig, Secy.-Treas.

Established in 1999 in OH.
Financial data (yr. ended 11/30/01): Grants paid, $73,350; assets, $806,288 (M); gifts received, $435,994; expenditures, $73,919; qualifying distributions, $73,350.
Officers: Anthony Bruns, Pres.; Janet Bruns, V.P.; Robert F. Uhrig, Secy.-Treas.
EIN: 311682493

43126
XTEK Foundation
c/o U.S. Bank
P.O. Box 1118
Cincinnati, OH 45201
Application address: 114151 Reading Rd., Cincinnati, OH 45241, tel.: (513) 733-7800
Contact: James E. Schwab, Secy.-Treas.

Incorporated in 1962 in OH.
Donor(s): XTEK, Inc., James D. Kiggen.
Financial data (yr. ended 12/31/01): Grants paid, $73,055; assets, $148,267 (M); gifts received, $100,000; expenditures, $75,093; qualifying distributions, $73,155.
Limitations: Giving primarily in the greater Cincinnati, OH, area.
Application information: Application form not required.

Officers: James D. Kiggen, Pres.; James E. Schwab, Secy.-Treas.
Agent: U.S. Bank.
EIN: 316029606
Codes: CS, CD

43127
Barr Foundation
7260 Drake Rd.
Cincinnati, OH 45243 (513) 561-6001
Contact: Roderick W. Barr, Pres.

Established in 1982 in OH.
Donor(s): Roderick W. Barr.
Financial data (yr. ended 07/31/01): Grants paid, $73,008; assets, $560,422 (M); expenditures, $95,708; qualifying distributions, $73,008.
Limitations: Giving primarily in Cincinnati, OH.
Officers and Trustees:* Roderick W. Barr,* Pres.; Barbara B. Barr,* Secy.; Daniel A. Barr,* Treas.
EIN: 311078948

43128
Rachel Fiero Clarke Trust
c/o KeyBank, N.A.
800 Superior Ave., 4th Fl.
Cleveland, OH 44114-1306
Application address: c/o Catskill Board of Education, Catskill, NY 12414

Financial data (yr. ended 06/30/01): Grants paid, $73,000; assets, $1,665,406 (M); expenditures, $89,410; qualifying distributions, $73,250.
Limitations: Giving limited to residents of Catskill, NY.
Trustee: KeyBank, N.A.
EIN: 237122166
Codes: GTI

43129
PAV Foundation
c/o Bank One Trust Co., N.A.
P.O. Box 1103
Dayton, OH 45401-1103

Established in 1957 in OH.
Financial data (yr. ended 12/31/00): Grants paid, $73,000; assets, $317,759 (M); expenditures, $83,543; qualifying distributions, $73,287.
Limitations: Applications not accepted. Giving on a national basis.
Application information: Contributes only to pre-selected organizations.
Officers: Albert F. Polk, Sr., Pres. and Mgr.; Patricia Polk, V.P. and Mgr.
Trustee: Bank One Trust Co., N.A.
EIN: 316029349

43130
Nesalis Foundation
8614 Twilight Tear Ln.
Cincinnati, OH 45249
Contact: N. Sundermann, Tr.

Donor(s): N. Sundermann.
Financial data (yr. ended 12/31/00): Grants paid, $72,735; assets, $247,182 (M); gifts received, $114,579; expenditures, $73,808; qualifying distributions, $72,735.
Application information: Application form not required.
Trustees: N. Sundermann, S. Sundermann.
EIN: 311485061

43131
The Hurd Charitable Trust
c/o National City Bank
P.O. Box 94651
Cleveland, OH 44101-4651

Financial data (yr. ended 12/31/01): Grants paid, $72,574; assets, $1,994,460 (M); expenditures, $74,975; qualifying distributions, $74,074.
Limitations: Applications not accepted. Giving primarily in OH.
Application information: Contributes only to pre-selected organizations.
Trustee: National City Bank.
EIN: 346904248

43132
Diehl Family Foundation
24 N. Clinton St.
Defiance, OH 43512-1835
Contact: William A. Diehl, Tr.

Established in 1985 in OH.
Donor(s): William A. Diehl, Helen R. Diehl.
Financial data (yr. ended 12/31/01): Grants paid, $72,556; assets, $746,208 (M); gifts received, $201,400; expenditures, $79,532; qualifying distributions, $72,556.
Limitations: Giving on a national basis, with some emphasis on Defiance, OH.
Application information: Application form not required.
Trustees: Helen R. Diehl, William A. Diehl.
EIN: 341396754

43133
Maurice Perkins Trust No. 1
c/o KeyBank, N.A.
800 Superior Ave., 4th Fl.
Cleveland, OH 44114

Financial data (yr. ended 12/31/00): Grants paid, $72,500; assets, $1,062,934 (M); expenditures, $81,974; qualifying distributions, $70,152.
Limitations: Applications not accepted. Giving on a national basis, with emphasis on Washington, DC, New York, NY, and Cleveland, OH.
Application information: Contributes only to pre-selected organizations.
Trustee: KeyBank, N.A.
EIN: 346505958

43134
Aimee and Lulu Seidel Trust
c/o Hammond & Hammond
904 Mahoning Bank Bldg.
Youngstown, OH 44503 (330) 744-2125
Contact: Robert Christian

Established in 1997 in OH.
Donor(s): Lulu C. Seidel.‡
Financial data (yr. ended 12/31/01): Grants paid, $72,500; assets, $1,418,881 (M); expenditures, $91,908; qualifying distributions, $72,494.
Limitations: Giving primarily in Mahoning County, OH.
Trustees: Rand Becker, Amy H. Gambrel, Robert M. Hammond.
EIN: 347064419

43135
Sledd Foundation Discretionary
c/o National City Bank of Indiana
P.O. Box 94651
Cleveland, OH 44101-4651
Application address: c/o Teresa Tracey, P.O. Box 110, Fort Wayne, IN 46802, tel.: (219) 461-6218

Established in 1960 in IN.

43135—OHIO

Financial data (yr. ended 07/31/01): Grants paid, $72,500; assets, $1,543,169 (M); expenditures, $94,471; qualifying distributions, $76,004.
Limitations: Giving limited to Fort Wayne, IN.
Trustee: National City Bank.
EIN: 356270529

43136
Frank J. Smith Foundation
c/o National City Bank of Indiana
P.O. Box 94651
Cleveland, OH 44101-4651
Application address: P.O. Box 110, Fort Wayne, IN 46801, tel.: (219) 461-7114
Contact: Dama Arnold

Established in 1994 in IN.
Donor(s): Frank J. Smith.
Financial data (yr. ended 01/31/02): Grants paid, $72,465; assets, $1,314,911 (M); expenditures, $83,349; qualifying distributions, $74,035.
Limitations: Giving primarily in Fort Wayne, IN.
Trustee: National City Bank of Indiana.
EIN: 356598564

43137
The Gettler Family Foundation
30 Garfield Pl., Ste. 1000
Cincinnati, OH 45202
Contact: Benjamin Gettler, Chair.

Established in 1993 in OH.
Donor(s): Benjamin Gettler.
Financial data (yr. ended 02/28/01): Grants paid, $72,061; assets, $1,029,389 (M); gifts received, $201,626; expenditures, $76,915; qualifying distributions, $72,061.
Limitations: Applications not accepted.
Application information: Unsolicited requests for funds not accepted.
Officers: Benjamin Gettler, Chair. and Treas.; Delian A. Gettler, Pres. and Secy.; Benjamin R. Gettler, V.P.
Trustee: Thomas D. Gettler.
EIN: 311374350

43138
The Gracia Foundation
c/o KeyBank, N.A.
800 Superior Ave., 4th Fl.
Cleveland, OH 44114

Donor(s): Molly D. White.
Financial data (yr. ended 12/31/01): Grants paid, $72,000; assets, $1,291,120 (M); expenditures, $85,905; qualifying distributions, $71,521.
Limitations: Applications not accepted. Giving on an international basis.
Application information: Contributes only to pre-selected organizations.
Officers: Molly D. White, Pres.; Arthur C. White, V.P. and Secy.; John Montgomery, Treas.
Director: Timothy Dearborn.
EIN: 911263322

43139
Smith Family Foundation
745 Lakengren Cove
Eaton, OH 45320

Established in 1998 in OH.
Donor(s): Joseph R. Smith.
Financial data (yr. ended 12/31/00): Grants paid, $71,800; assets, $1,093,112 (M); expenditures, $72,515; qualifying distributions, $71,800.
Limitations: Applications not accepted. Giving primarily in OH.
Application information: Contributes only to pre-selected organizations.
Trustee: Joseph R. Smith.
EIN: 311603487

43140
G. P. & H. E. Longabaugh Charitable Trust
c/o National City Bank of Pennsylvania
P.O. Box 94651
Cleveland, OH 44101-4651

Established in 1980 in OH.
Financial data (yr. ended 12/31/01): Grants paid, $71,592; assets, $2,227,411 (M); expenditures, $92,936; qualifying distributions, $73,983.
Limitations: Applications not accepted. Giving primarily in FL and McKeesport, PA.
Application information: Contributes only to pre-selected organizations.
Trustee: National City Bank of Pennsylvania.
EIN: 256582681

43141
The Morris & Fannie Skilken Family Foundation
P.O. Box 875
Columbus, OH 43216
Contact: B. Lee Skilen, Treas.

Established in 1985 in OH.
Financial data (yr. ended 12/31/00): Grants paid, $71,500; assets, $2,509,966 (M); gifts received, $43,460; expenditures, $82,067; qualifying distributions, $81,122.
Officers: Stanley B. Skilken, Pres.; Herbert Wolman, Secy.; B. Lee Skilken, Treas.
Trustees: Tobi Gold, Daniel Skilken.
EIN: 311172421

43142
H. D. Jones Charitable Trust
c/o National City Bank
P.O. Box 94651
Cleveland, OH 44101-4651

Established in 1989 in PA.
Financial data (yr. ended 12/31/01): Grants paid, $71,000; assets, $1,381,479 (M); expenditures, $100,318; qualifying distributions, $76,587.
Limitations: Applications not accepted. Giving limited to PA, with emphasis on Titusville.
Application information: Contributes only to pre-selected organizations.
Trustee: National City Bank.
EIN: 256119452

43143
George A. Avril Family Fund
4445 Kings Run Dr.
Cincinnati, OH 45232-1401

Financial data (yr. ended 12/31/99): Grants paid, $70,946; assets, $770,758 (M); expenditures, $72,533; qualifying distributions, $70,192.
Limitations: Giving primarily in Cincinnati, OH.
Officers and Trustees:* Thomas B. Avril,* Pres.; John G. Avril,* Secy.
EIN: 316056635

43144
Leroy Erickson Scholarship Fund
c/o National City Bank of Pennsylvania
P. O. Box 94651
Cleveland, OH 44101-4651
Application address: c/o Pennbank, Leroy G. Erickson Scholarship Committee, Trust Dept., 71 Main St., Bradford, PA 16701
Contact: John Frey

Established in 1991 in PA.
Financial data (yr. ended 10/31/01): Grants paid, $70,584; assets, $951,844 (M); expenditures, $79,419; qualifying distributions, $74,302.
Limitations: Giving primarily in PA.
Application information: Application form required.
Trustee: National City Bank of Pennsylvania.

EIN: 256358243
Codes: GTI

43145
Hunter Fund
c/o Advisory Services, Inc.
1010 Hanna Bldg., 1422 Euclid Ave.
Cleveland, OH 44115-2078 (216) 363-6483
Contact: Jackie A. Horning, Treas.

Established in 1956 in OH.
Financial data (yr. ended 12/31/00): Grants paid, $70,350; assets, $1,190,616 (M); expenditures, $80,827; qualifying distributions, $72,757.
Limitations: Giving primarily in AZ, GA, and KY.
Publications: Annual report.
Application information: Application form not required.
Officers and Trustees:* Barbara Hunter,* Pres.; J. Rukin Jelks, Jr.,* V.P.; R.S. St. John, Secy.; Jackie A. Horning, Treas.; Carolyn G. Jelks.
EIN: 346513679

43146
The Norbert Gazin Educational Foundation
c/o KeyBank, N.A.
800 Superior Ave., 4th Fl.
Cleveland, OH 44114

Established in 2000 in NY.
Donor(s): Norbert L. Gazin.‡
Financial data (yr. ended 12/31/01): Grants paid, $70,250; assets, $1,928,046 (M); gifts received, $15,000; expenditures, $85,856; qualifying distributions, $70,250.
Limitations: Applications not accepted.
Application information: Contributes only to pre-selected organizations.
Trustee: KeyBank, N.A.
EIN: 527124691

43147
Frederick W. and Janet P. Dorn Foundation
629 Euclid Ave., Ste. 1525
Cleveland, OH 44114-3066 (216) 696-4200
Contact: Phillip A. Ranney, Secy.-Treas.

Established in 1990 in OH.
Donor(s): Janet D. Heil.
Financial data (yr. ended 12/31/00): Grants paid, $70,095; assets, $1,497,668 (M); gifts received, $71,000; expenditures, $81,894; qualifying distributions, $73,795.
Limitations: Giving primarily in the Cleveland, OH, area.
Officers and Trustees:* Janet D. Heil,* Pres.; Robert F. Dorn,* V.P.; Phillip A. Ranney,* Secy.-Treas.; Charles F. Adler, Deborah K. Dorn.
EIN: 341653306

43148
The Robert H. Brethen Foundation
1730 Kettering Twr.
Dayton, OH 45423-1730
Contact: Robert H. Brethen, Pres.

Established in 1988 in OH.
Donor(s): Robert H. Brethen.
Financial data (yr. ended 10/31/01): Grants paid, $70,035; assets, $408,571 (M); gifts received, $75,000; expenditures, $77,240; qualifying distributions, $70,035.
Limitations: Giving primarily in the Dayton, OH, area.
Application information: Application form not required.
Officers and Trustees:* Robert H. Brethen,* Pres.; Alma H. Brethen,* Secy.; David Brethen.
EIN: 311213173

43149
The M. Roger and Anne Melby Clapp Foundation
9100 Billings Rd.
Kirtland, OH 44094
Contact: Anne Melby Clapp, Secy.

Established in 1988 in OH.
Donor(s): Anne Melby Clapp, M. Roger Clapp.
Financial data (yr. ended 12/31/00): Grants paid, $70,000; assets, $1,440,169 (M); gifts received, $100,000; expenditures, $85,303; qualifying distributions, $76,718.
Limitations: Giving primarily in OH.
Officers: M. Roger Clapp, Pres.; Anne Melby Clapp, Secy.
Trustees: Mrs. John Munn, Mrs. John Roediger, Mrs. Robert Sedgwick.
EIN: 341543994

43150
Solot Family Foundation
c/o National City Bank
P.O. Box 94651
Cleveland, OH 44101-4651

Established in 1998 in PA.
Donor(s): Howard L. Solot.
Financial data (yr. ended 12/31/00): Grants paid, $70,000; assets, $875,183 (M); expenditures, $81,867; qualifying distributions, $72,303.
Limitations: Applications not accepted. Giving primarily in IL.
Application information: Contributes only to pre-selected organizations.
Trustees: Marsha B. Karp, Robert N. Karp, Howard L. Solot, Janet Solot, Julie E. Solot, Michael J. Solot.
EIN: 237933630

43151
The Georgine E. Bates Memorial Fund, Inc.
P.O. Box 808
Urbana, OH 43078 (937) 653-7186
Contact: Joyce Reinhart, Treas.

Established in 1979 in OH.
Financial data (yr. ended 10/31/01): Grants paid, $69,810; assets, $1,604,110 (M); expenditures, $84,938; qualifying distributions, $69,810.
Limitations: Giving limited to Champaign County, OH.
Application information: Application form not required.
Officers: James R. Wilson, Pres.; Judy A. Markin, Secy.; Joyce Reinhart, Treas.
EIN: 341296531

43152
The Peninsula Foundation
517 Broadway, 3rd Fl.
East Liverpool, OH 43920

Established in 1997 in OH.
Donor(s): Agnes Gund.
Financial data (yr. ended 11/30/01): Grants paid, $69,681; assets, $11,477,400 (M); expenditures, $392,618; qualifying distributions, $94,731; giving activities include $24,850 for programs.
Limitations: Applications not accepted. Giving primarily in NY.
Application information: Contributes only to pre-selected organizations.
Trustees: Agnes Gund, Daniel Shapiro.
EIN: 347070871

43153
Bill & Edith Walter Foundation
6711 Elmers Ct.
Worthington, OH 43085

Donor(s): William Walter Trust, Edith Walter Trust.
Financial data (yr. ended 12/31/01): Grants paid, $69,444; assets, $328,469 (M); expenditures, $84,270; qualifying distributions, $69,444.
Limitations: Applications not accepted. Giving primarily in Columbus, OH.
Application information: Contributes only to pre-selected organizations.
Trustees: Fredrick L. Fisher, Betty B. Lane, James E. Lane.
EIN: 311102570

43154
Brighten Your Future
188 W. Main St.
Logan, OH 43138-1606
Application address: 30436 Hideaway Hills Rd., Logan, OH 43138; tel.: (740) 385-8561
Contact: Larry Kienzle, Tr.

Established in 1994 in OH.
Donor(s): Roberta A. Child Foundation.
Financial data (yr. ended 06/30/01): Grants paid, $69,288; assets, $1,167,305 (M); gifts received, $85,137; expenditures, $111,993; qualifying distributions, $111,993.
Limitations: Giving limited to Logan, OH.
Application information: Application form required.
Trustees: Dick Brandt, Van Cardaras, Valerie Daubenmire, Lorus Davidson, Brian Hawk, Bill Heath, Lee Howdyshell, and 10 additional trustees.
EIN: 311255015
Codes: GTI

43155
The Jeanette Hajjar Foundation
2422 Manoa Ln. N.
Toledo, OH 43615-2432

Established in 1999 in OH.
Financial data (yr. ended 12/31/01): Grants paid, $69,119; assets, $420,423 (M); expenditures, $120,196; qualifying distributions, $100,319.
Limitations: Giving primarily in Beirut, Lebanon.
Application information: Application form required.
Trustee: Sami I. Sayegh.
EIN: 341893921

43156
The Marshall L. and Deborah L. Berkman Family Charitable Trust
1801 E. 9th St., Ste. 1425
Cleveland, OH 44114-3199

Established in 1996 in OH.
Donor(s): Deborah L. Berkman.
Financial data (yr. ended 12/31/01): Grants paid, $69,100; assets, $1,559,325 (M); gifts received, $111,375; expenditures, $77,097; qualifying distributions, $69,100.
Limitations: Applications not accepted. Giving primarily in NM.
Application information: Contributes only to pre-selected organizations.
Trustees: Deborah L. Berkman, Ellen F. Berkman, Laura B. Coleman, Martha B. Winfield.
EIN: 341845200

43157
Edwin P. Kell Charitable Trust
c/o KeyBank, N.A.
P.O. Box 10099
Toledo, OH 43699-0099

Established in 1998 in OH.
Donor(s): Edwin P. Kell Trust.
Financial data (yr. ended 12/31/01): Grants paid, $68,861; assets, $1,177,818 (M); expenditures, $77,818; qualifying distributions, $68,861.
Limitations: Applications not accepted. Giving primarily in OH.
Application information: Contributes only to pre-selected organizations.
Trustee: KeyBank, N.A.
EIN: 341882259

43158
Springfield Faith Ministries
5765 Yeazell Rd.
Springfield, OH 45503

Established in 1999 in OH.
Donor(s): M. K. Hufford.
Financial data (yr. ended 11/30/01): Grants paid, $68,700; assets, $689,938 (M); expenditures, $73,928; qualifying distributions, $71,520.
Limitations: Applications not accepted. Giving primarily in Springfield, OH.
Application information: Contributes only to pre-selected organizations.
Officers: M. K. Hufford, Pres.; Sherri L. Hufford, V.P.; Sheryl Wagner, Secy.-Treas.
EIN: 311682843

43159
The Marla and Joseph Shafran Foundation
2720 Van Aken Blvd., Ste. 200
Cleveland, OH 44120

Established in 1989 in OH.
Donor(s): Joseph M. Shafran.
Financial data (yr. ended 12/31/01): Grants paid, $68,423; assets, $11,316 (M); gifts received, $75,285; expenditures, $68,436; qualifying distributions, $68,423.
Limitations: Applications not accepted. Giving primarily in Cleveland, OH.
Application information: Contributes only to pre-selected organizations.
Trustees: Joseph M. Shafran, Marla M. Shafran.
EIN: 341613094

43160
Electric Furnace Foundation
435 W. Wilson St.
Salem, OH 44460-2767

Donor(s): Electric Furnace Company.
Financial data (yr. ended 09/30/01): Grants paid, $68,250; assets, $483,822 (M); expenditures, $68,757; qualifying distributions, $68,250.
Limitations: Applications not accepted. Giving primarily in OH.
Application information: Contributes only to pre-selected organizations.
Officers and Trustees:* C.P. Kamm,* Pres.; J.O. Kamm II,* V.P.; Patricia A. Simonsic,* Treas.; J.S. Kamm.
EIN: 346520768
Codes: CS, CD

43161
Howard P. Arnold Foundation, Inc.
c/o National City Bank of Indiana
P.O. Box 94651
Cleveland, OH 44101-4651 (216) 575-2934
Application address: P.O. Box 110, Fort Wayne, IN 46801
Contact: Michele Delaney, V.P.

Established in 1987 in IN.
Financial data (yr. ended 12/31/01): Grants paid, $68,166; assets, $1,382,650 (M); expenditures, $75,874; qualifying distributions, $68,914.
Limitations: Giving primarily in Fort Wayne, IN.
Officers: Kim Stacey, Chair.; Lawrence Shine, V.P.; Maclyn Parker, Secy.
Trustee: National City Bank of Indiana.
EIN: 311202969

43162
The V. E. & Betty Phillips Scholarship Fund
c/o National City Bank of Pennsylvania
P.O. Box 94651
Cleveland, OH 44101-4651
Application address: c/o Michael L. Stahlman, Corry Area High School, 534 E. Pleasant St., Corry, PA 16407, tel.: (814) 665-8297

Financial data (yr. ended 04/30/01): Grants paid, $68,150; assets, $11,444,927 (M); expenditures, $80,670; qualifying distributions, $74,224.
Limitations: Giving limited to the Corry, PA, area.
Application information: Application form required.
Trustee: National City Bank.
EIN: 237418046
Codes: GTI

43163
The Kenneth and Luanne P. Lashutka Foundation
3555 Eldorado Dr.
Rocky River, OH 44116

Established in 1999 in OH.
Donor(s): Kenneth Lashutka.
Financial data (yr. ended 12/31/01): Grants paid, $68,000; assets, $354,902 (M); expenditures, $70,242; qualifying distributions, $68,000.
Limitations: Applications not accepted.
Application information: Contributes only to pre-selected organizations.
Trustees: Amy L. Lashutka, Anne P. Lashutka, Kenneth Lashutka, Luanne P. Lashutka.
EIN: 341899564

43164
The Cassner Foundation
835 S. High St.
Hillsboro, OH 45133-9602 (937) 393-3426
Scholarship application address: c/o Frederick Slater, Superintendent, Hillsboro City School, 358 W. Main St., Hillsboro, OH 45133, tel.: (937) 939-3475
Contact: Alvin B. Cassner, Pres.

Established in 1961.
Donor(s): Rotary Forms Press, Inc., Computer Stock Forms, Inc., Unit Sets, Alvin B. Cassner.
Financial data (yr. ended 03/31/01): Grants paid, $67,890; assets, $1,343,663 (M); gifts received, $41,634; expenditures, $73,261; qualifying distributions, $67,109.
Limitations: Giving for scholarships limited to residents of Highland County, OH.
Officers: Alvin B. Cassner, Pres.; Alice Cassner, V.P.
EIN: 386090665
Codes: GTI

43165
R. Gordon & Agnes K. Black Family Foundation
P.O. Box 3775
Mansfield, OH 44907-0775

Established in 1998 in OH.
Financial data (yr. ended 12/31/01): Grants paid, $67,715; assets, $338,008 (M); expenditures, $70,543; qualifying distributions, $67,715.
Limitations: Applications not accepted.
Application information: Contributes only to pre-selected organizations.
Officer: R. Gordon Black, Pres.
EIN: 311582261

43166
William G. Schmoeger Residuary Trust
c/o National City Bank of Pennsylvania
P.O. Box 94651
Cleveland, OH 44101-4651

Established around 1990 in IL.
Financial data (yr. ended 12/31/00): Grants paid, $67,696; assets, $63,819 (M); expenditures, $69,489; qualifying distributions, $68,559.
Limitations: Applications not accepted. Giving primarily in Peoria, IL.
Application information: Contributes only to pre-selected organizations.
Trustee: National City Bank.
EIN: 376114468

43167
Hughes-Keenan Foundation
143 Willow Brook Way S.
Delaware, OH 43015-3860 (740) 363-0411
Contact: Harry A. Humes, Pres.

Financial data (yr. ended 10/31/01): Grants paid, $67,675; assets, $411,704 (M); expenditures, $68,677; qualifying distributions, $67,675.
Limitations: Giving primarily in central OH.
Application information: Application form not required.
Officers: Harry A. Humes, Pres. and Treas.; Pauline Way, V.P.; Mary Jo Humes, Secy.
EIN: 316026601

43168
Akron Jaycee Foundation
1745 W. Market St.
Akron, OH 44313 (330) 867-8055
FAX: (330) 867-7842
Contact: Shirley Foster, Mgr.

Established in 1975 in OH.
Donor(s): NEC World Series of Golf/Akron Golf Charities Foundation.
Financial data (yr. ended 12/31/00): Grants paid, $67,665; assets, $130,997 (M); gifts received, $300; expenditures, $99,950; qualifying distributions, $67,665.
Limitations: Giving primarily in Akron, OH.
Application information: Application form required.
Officers and Directors:* Paula Masuga-Adam,* Chair.; Kevin Harris,* Pres.; Kevin K. Crum,* V.P.; Paula Harman,* Treas.
EIN: 510163841

43169
The Brisben Family Foundation
7800 E. Kemper Rd.
Cincinnati, OH 45249

Established in 1999 in OH.
Financial data (yr. ended 12/31/01): Grants paid, $67,500; assets, $8,181 (M); expenditures, $67,500; qualifying distributions, $67,500.
Limitations: Applications not accepted. Giving primarily in Cincinnati, OH.
Application information: Contributes only to pre-selected organizations.
Trustees: Brent W. Brisben, Chad R. Brisben, William O. Brisben, Tara J. Brisben-Nelson.
EIN: 311538179

43170
J. P. Crain Family Scholarship Fund
c/o KeyBank, N.A.
P.O. Box 10099
Toledo, OH 43699-0099 (419) 259-8218
E-mail: marilyn_brown@keybank.com
Contact: Marilyn Brown, Tr. Assoc.

Established in 1993 in OH.
Donor(s): Glendine L. Crain.‡
Financial data (yr. ended 03/31/01): Grants paid, $67,500; assets, $1,084,753 (M); expenditures, $112,636; qualifying distributions, $82,155.
Limitations: Giving limited to residents of Paulding, OH.
Trustee: KeyBank, N.A.
Scholarship Committee: David Bagley, Ken Doseck, William Shugars.
EIN: 346985380
Codes: GTI

43171
Simson First Foundation
4300 E. Broad St.
Columbus, OH 43213

Established in 1978 in OH.
Donor(s): Theodore R. Simson.
Financial data (yr. ended 12/31/01): Grants paid, $67,210; assets, $180,715 (M); gifts received, $12,281; expenditures, $69,871; qualifying distributions, $67,210.
Limitations: Applications not accepted. Giving primarily in Washington, DC, New York, NY, and Columbus, OH.
Application information: Contributes only to pre-selected organizations.
Officers and Trustees:* Theodore R. Simson,* Pres.; Douglas A. Simson,* V.P.; Sherran S. Blair,* Secy.; Bevlyn A. Simson.
EIN: 310935291

43172
H.O.P.E. Foundation of Darke County
c/o Jeffrey R. Lewis
324 E. 3rd St.
Greenville, OH 45331

Established in 1986 in OH.
Financial data (yr. ended 06/30/01): Grants paid, $67,150; assets, $1,203,559 (M); gifts received, $25,536; expenditures, $83,032; qualifying distributions, $73,602.
Limitations: Giving limited to residents of Darke County, OH.
Application information: Application form required.
Officers and Directors:* Eileen Litchfield,* Pres.; Bob Lantz,* V.P.; John Montogomery,* Secy.; Jeff Lewis,* Treas.; Richard Baker, Gary Brown, Steve Burns, Marvin Stammen, and 13 additional directors.
EIN: 311177601
Codes: GTI

43173
The Eden Family Foundation
3120 E. Galbraith Rd.
Cincinnati, OH 45236

Established in 2000 in OH.
Donor(s): Norman N. Eden.
Financial data (yr. ended 12/31/01): Grants paid, $67,149; assets, $176,912 (M); gifts received,

$66,106; expenditures, $73,842; qualifying distributions, $67,149.
Limitations: Applications not accepted.
Application information: Contributes only to pre-selected organizations.
Officers and Trustees:* Norman N. Eden,* Pres.; Shulamith Eden,* V.P.; Avi D. Eden.
EIN: 311703667

43174
Nellie Leaman Taft Charitable Foundation, Inc.
c/o CSH
105 E. 4th St., Ste. 1600
Cincinnati, OH 45202
Application address: c/o Symantha Gates, Grants Mgmt. Assocs., 77 Summer St., 8th Fl., Boston, MA 02110, tel.: (617) 426-7172; E-mail: pzinn@grantsmanagement.com
Contact: Prentice Zinn, Prog. Off.

Established in 1997 in MA.
Financial data (yr. ended 12/31/01): Grants paid, $67,143; assets, $1,318,656 (M); expenditures, $79,904; qualifying distributions, $67,143.
Limitations: Giving primarily in Boston, MA and ME.
Publications: Application guidelines.
Officer: Nellie L. Taft, Pres. and Treas.
Trustee: Dudley S. Taft.
EIN: 043361704

43175
The Neyer Foundation
3800 Red Bank Rd.
Cincinnati, OH 45227-3406
Contact: John R. Neyer, Chair.

Established in 1991 in OH.
Donor(s): Donald Neyer, Al Neyer, Inc.
Financial data (yr. ended 12/31/01): Grants paid, $66,865; assets, $878,452 (M); gifts received, $446; expenditures, $74,914; qualifying distributions, $71,740.
Limitations: Giving primarily in Cincinnati, OH and other areas of company operations.
Application information: Contributes primarily to employee sponsored organizations. Application form not required.
Officers: John R. Neyer, Chair.; Thomas Neyer, Sr., Vice-Chair.; Thomas Neyer, Jr., Secy.
EIN: 311315708

43176
The Gradison & Company Foundation
580 Bldg.
Cincinnati, OH 45202 (513) 579-5000
Contact: Richard M. Curry, Tr.

Established in 1981 in OH.
Donor(s): Gradison & Co., Inc., McDonald & Co. Investments, Inc., McDonald Investments, Inc.
Financial data (yr. ended 12/31/01): Grants paid, $66,634; assets, $249,051 (M); gifts received, $22,250; expenditures, $80,921; qualifying distributions, $66,934.
Limitations: Giving primarily in the greater Cincinnati, OH, area.
Application information: Application form not required.
Trustees: Richard M. Curry, David Ellis III, Mary Beth Martin, Paul Sittenfeld, Stephen Wesselkamper.
EIN: 311018948
Codes: CS, CD

43177
The Sullivan Family Foundation
3 Tremore Way
Holland, OH 43528

Financial data (yr. ended 12/31/00): Grants paid, $66,500; assets, $900,471 (M); expenditures, $73,658; qualifying distributions, $65,947.
Limitations: Applications not accepted. Giving primarily in IN and OH.
Application information: Contributes only to pre-selected organizations.
Officers and Trustees:* Frank E. Sullivan, Jr.,* Pres.; Mary Colette Sullivan,* V.P.; Anne Sullivan Kaminski,* Secy.; Robert A. Sullivan,* Treas.
EIN: 223109302

43178
W. R. Timken, Jr. Foundation
(Formerly Suzanne & W. R. Timken, Jr. Family Foundation)
200 Market Ave. N. Ste. 210
Canton, OH 44702-1437
Contact: Don D. Dickes, Secy.-Treas.

Established in 1985 in OH.
Donor(s): Mary J. Timken, L. B. Timken, W.R. Timken, W.R. Timken, Jr.
Financial data (yr. ended 09/30/01): Grants paid, $66,315; assets, $1,027,517 (M); gifts received, $1,000; expenditures, $68,443; qualifying distributions, $66,984.
Limitations: Applications not accepted. Giving in the U.S., with emphasis on Naples, FL, and Canton, OH.
Officers and Trustees:* W.R. Timken, Jr.,* Pres.; W.R. Timken III,* V.P.; Don D. Dickes,* Secy.-Treas.
EIN: 341524592

43179
Flagship Foundation
405 Madison Ave., Ste. 1900
Toledo, OH 43604-1207
Contact: Todd M. Peters, Pres.

Established in 1997 in OH.
Donor(s): Todd M. Peters.
Financial data (yr. ended 12/31/01): Grants paid, $66,000; assets, $1,486,667 (M); expenditures, $67,741; qualifying distributions, $68,112.
Limitations: Applications not accepted. Giving primarily in MA.
Application information: Contributes only to pre-selected organizations.
Officers and Trustees:* Todd M. Peters,* Pres.; Jeanne M. Peters,* V.P.; William F. Bates,* Secy.-Treas.
EIN: 311534898

43180
Charles Loehr Charitable Trust
c/o Wayne County National Bank
1776 Beall Ave.
Wooster, OH 44691 (330) 264-7111
Contact: Stephen Kitchen, Tr.

Established in 1997 in OH.
Financial data (yr. ended 12/31/01): Grants paid, $66,000; assets, $821,757 (M); expenditures, $71,157; qualifying distributions, $67,956.
Limitations: Giving limited to Holmes and Wayne County, OH.
Application information: Application form not required.
Trustee: Stephen Kitchen.
EIN: 346792962

43181
Olaf S. Wessel Trust
c/o The Huntington National Bank
P.O. Box 1558, HC 1012
Columbus, OH 43216

Established in 1992.
Financial data (yr. ended 03/31/02): Grants paid, $65,834; assets, $1,418,215 (M); expenditures, $81,312; qualifying distributions, $65,834.
Limitations: Applications not accepted. Giving primarily in OH.
Application information: Contributes only to pre-selected organizations.
Trustee: The Huntington National Bank.
EIN: 316445639

43182
Helen & Ronald Ross Family Foundation
1960 County Line Rd.
Gates Mills, OH 44040 (440) 423-3157
Contact: Ronald Ross, Pres.

Established in 1997 in OH.
Donor(s): Ronald Ross.
Financial data (yr. ended 12/31/01): Grants paid, $65,650; assets, $32,268 (M); expenditures, $65,852; qualifying distributions, $65,685.
Limitations: Giving primarily in Cleveland, OH.
Application information: Application form not required.
Officers: Ronald Ross, Pres.; Helen Ross, V.P. and Secy.-Treas.
EIN: 311534678

43183
Bertha Werner Scholarship Fund
c/o Fifth Third Bank
38 Fountain Sq. Plz., Dept. 00858
Cincinnati, OH 45263 (513) 579-6034
Contact: Lawra Baumann, Trust Off., Fifth Third Bank

Financial data (yr. ended 03/31/01): Grants paid, $65,250; assets, $1,525,588 (M); expenditures, $83,511; qualifying distributions, $70,962.
Limitations: Giving limited to Cincinnati, OH.
Application information: Applications processed by Art Academy of Cincinnati and University of Cincinnati. Application form required.
Trustee: Fifth Third Bank.
EIN: 316129456

43184
Auburn Foundry Foundation
c/o National City Bank, Indiana
P.O. Box 94651
Cleveland, OH 44101-4651
Application address: c/o James Westerfield, National City Bank of Indiana, P.O. Box 110, Fort Wayne, IN 46801, tel.: (219) 461-7126

Established in 1955.
Donor(s): Auburn Foundry, Inc.
Financial data (yr. ended 02/28/01): Grants paid, $65,000; assets, $1,346,850 (M); expenditures, $91,066; qualifying distributions, $69,147.
Limitations: Giving primarily in IN.
Application information: Contact foundation for scholarship application form. Application form required.
Trustees: Walt Bienz, William E. Fink, National City Bank of Indiana.
EIN: 356019220
Codes: CS, CD

43185
Sam S. & Rose Stein Foundation
165 E. Washington Row
Sandusky, OH 44870 (419) 625-8324
Contact: M.J. Stauffer, Secy.-Treas.

Financial data (yr. ended 12/31/01): Grants paid, $65,000; assets, $5,417,824 (M); gifts received, $10,111; expenditures, $113,104; qualifying distributions, $65,000.
Officers and Trustees:* Jerome P. Stein,* Pres.; Marcia L. Goff,* V.P.; M.J. Stauffer,* Secy.-Treas.; Sam S. Stein.
EIN: 341406795

43186
The Blaha Family Foundation
c/o George R. Blaha
18500 Lake Rd., Ste. 220
Rocky River, OH 44116

Established in 1998 in OH.
Donor(s): George R. Blaha, Mary Terese Blaha.
Financial data (yr. ended 12/31/01): Grants paid, $64,625; assets, $80,385 (M); gifts received, $64,625; expenditures, $23,044; expenditures, $23,044; expenditures, $65,895; qualifying distributions, $64,625.
Limitations: Applications not accepted. Giving primarily in OH.
Application information: Contributes only to pre-selected organizations.
Trustees: George R. Blaha, Mary Terese Blaha.
EIN: 341861615

43187
Orpha J. McGarvey Charitable Trust
c/o National City Bank Of Pennsylvania
P.O. Box 94651
Cleveland, OH 44101-4651

Established in 1999 in PA.
Donor(s): Orpha J. McGarvey.
Financial data (yr. ended 08/31/01): Grants paid, $64,571; assets, $3,285,971 (M); gifts received, $13,512; expenditures, $89,534; qualifying distributions, $81,797.
Limitations: Applications not accepted. Giving primarily in PA and WV.
Application information: Contributes only to pre-selected organizations.
Trustee: National City Bank Of Pennsylvania.
EIN: 527056703

43188
Tallman Boys Fund Trust
c/o National City Bank
P.O. Box 94651
Cleveland, OH 44101-4651 (216) 575-2630
Application address: P.O. Box 749, 301 S.W. Adams St., Peoria, IL 61652-0749, tel.: (309) 655-5000

Established in 1956 in IL.
Financial data (yr. ended 01/31/02): Grants paid, $64,300; assets, $1,509,055 (M); expenditures, $69,492; qualifying distributions, $67,194.
Limitations: Giving limited to organizations benefiting male residents of Kankakee County, IL.
Application information: Application form required.
Trustee: National City Bank.
EIN: 366024917

43189
Milton A. and Charlotte R. Kramer Charitable Foundation
Halle Bldg.
1228 Euclid Ave., Ste. 310
Cleveland, OH 44115
Contact: Charlotte R. Kramer, Tr.

Established in 1984 in OH.
Donor(s): Charlotte R. Kramer.
Financial data (yr. ended 11/30/01): Grants paid, $64,244; assets, $1,047,107 (M); expenditures, $85,705; qualifying distributions, $64,244.
Limitations: Giving primarily in the Cleveland, OH, area.
Application information: Application form not required.
Trustees: Michael J. Horvitz, Charlotte R. Kramer, Mark R. Kramer, David G. Stiller.
EIN: 341467089

43190
Clarence & Judith Lapedes Family Foundation, Inc.
c/o D & T
1700 Courthouse Plz. N.E.
Dayton, OH 45402

Established in 1997 in OH.
Donor(s): Clarence Lapedes, Judith Lapedes.
Financial data (yr. ended 12/31/99): Grants paid, $64,200; assets, $476,654 (M); gifts received, $50,000; expenditures, $64,698; qualifying distributions, $64,200.
Limitations: Applications not accepted. Giving primarily in Dayton, OH.
Application information: Contributes only to pre-selected organizations.
Trustees: Clarence Lapedes, Judith Lapedes, Richard Lapedes, Debra Schwartz.
EIN: 311570785

43191
Springman Scholarship Fund
c/o Fifth Third Bank
38 Fountain Sq. Plz., Dept. 00858
Cincinnati, OH 45263-3191 (513) 579-5237
Contact: Kristina Baldwin, Trust Off., Fifth Third Bank

Established in 1992 in OH.
Donor(s): Edgar Springman.‡
Financial data (yr. ended 09/30/01): Grants paid, $64,000; assets, $1,096,392 (M); expenditures, $78,884; qualifying distributions, $68,173.
Limitations: Applications not accepted. Giving limited to Clermont County, OH.
Application information: Unsolicited requests for funds not accepted.
Trustee: Fifth Third Bank.
EIN: 316455677
Codes: GTI

43192
Merle & Peg Hamilton Charitable Foundation
116 S. Main St.
Marion, OH 43302 (740) 387-9093
Contact: Ronald D. Cramer, Tr.

Established in 1999 in OH.
Financial data (yr. ended 12/31/00): Grants paid, $63,879; assets, $1,205,408 (M); expenditures, $68,094; qualifying distributions, $67,402.
Limitations: Giving primarily in Marion, OH.
Trustees: Ronald D. Cramer, A. Merle Hamilton.
EIN: 311650890

43193
Bernhard-Wentz Scholarship Fund
c/o The Huntington National Bank
P.O. Box 1558, HC 1012
Columbus, OH 43216-1558
Application address: c/o Advisory Committee, Dover High School Administrative Bldg., 219 W. 6th St., Dover, OH 44622, tel.: (216) 343-7746

Established in 1988 in OH.
Financial data (yr. ended 12/31/99): Grants paid, $63,600; assets, $1,700,321 (M); expenditures, $79,538; qualifying distributions, $67,146.
Limitations: Giving limited to Dover, OH.
Trustee: The Huntington National Bank.
EIN: 316334477
Codes: GTI

43194
SIFCO Foundation
970 E. 64th St.
Cleveland, OH 44103 (216) 881-8600
Contact: Jeffrey P. Gotschall, Pres.

Donor(s): SIFCO Industries, Inc.
Financial data (yr. ended 08/31/01): Grants paid, $63,327; assets, $252,852 (M); expenditures, $65,371; qualifying distributions, $63,247.
Limitations: Giving primarily in areas of company operations, with some emphasis on Cleveland, OH.
Application information: Application form not required.
Officers: Jeffrey P. Gotschall, Pres.; Hudson D. Smith, Secy.; Frank Cappello, Treas.
EIN: 346531019
Codes: CS, CD

43195
The Gaynor Family Foundation
c/o U.S. Bank
P.O. Box 1118, M
Cincinnati, OH 45201-1118

Financial data (yr. ended 12/31/01): Grants paid, $63,125; assets, $864,315 (M); gifts received, $33,095; expenditures, $71,872; qualifying distributions, $63,125.
Limitations: Applications not accepted. Giving primarily in OH, with some giving in NY and RI.
Application information: Contributes only to pre-selected organizations.
Officers and Trustees:* Vere W. Gaynor,* Pres.; John J. Kropp,* V.P.; Wendy Kroner,* Secy.-Treas.; Rosemary Gaynor, William C.T. Gaynor, U.S. Bank.
EIN: 311581372

43196
Wood-Byer Foundation
c/o Robert A. Wood
4182 Fox Hollow Dr.
Cincinnati, OH 45241

Established in 1994 in OH.
Donor(s): Herbert I. Byer.
Financial data (yr. ended 12/31/99): Grants paid, $63,100; assets, $1,526,915 (M); expenditures, $74,891; qualifying distributions, $62,415.
Limitations: Applications not accepted. Giving primarily in OH.
Application information: Contributes only to pre-selected organizations.
Officers and Trustees:* Herbert I. Byer,* Pres.; Priscilla Wood-Byer,* Secy.; Robert A. Wood,* Treas.
EIN: 311433019

43197
John F. and Loretta A. Hynes Foundation
c/o Sky Trust, N.A.
23 Federal Plz., P.O. Box 479
Youngstown, OH 44501 (330) 742-7035
Contact: David Sabine, Sr. V.P. and Trust Off., Sky Trust, N.A.

Established in 1957 in OH.
Financial data (yr. ended 12/31/01): Grants paid, $63,000; assets, $2,422,200 (M); expenditures, $85,057; qualifying distributions, $69,372.
Limitations: Giving primarily in the Youngstown, OH, area.
Application information: Application form not required.
Officers and Members:* John M. Newman,* Chair.; W.W. Bresnahan,* Vice-Chair.; William J. Mullen, Gregory L. Ridler.
Trustee: Sky Trust, N.A.
EIN: 346516440

43198
Marilyn & Charles Krehbiel Foundation
c/o Fifth Third Bank
38 Foundation Sq. Plz.
Cincinnati, OH 45263

Established in 1997 in OH.
Donor(s): Marilyn Krehbiel McBride.
Financial data (yr. ended 12/31/01): Grants paid, $63,000; assets, $1,107,550 (M); expenditures, $77,860; qualifying distributions, $63,000.
Limitations: Giving primarily in Cincinnati, OH.
Agent: Fifth Third Bank.
EIN: 311533052

43199
M & M Osterman Foundation
c/o Stan Bazan
4807 Rockside Rd., Ste. 330
Cleveland, OH 44131
Application address: 1251 Pintail Cir., Boulder, CO 80303-1465
Contact: Michael J. Osterman, Tr.

Established in 1997 in OH.
Financial data (yr. ended 12/31/01): Grants paid, $62,500; assets, $1,024,193 (M); expenditures, $70,723; qualifying distributions, $62,500.
Limitations: Giving primarily in NJ and OH.
Application information: Application form not required.
Trustees: Michael J. Osterman, Michelle Osterman, William Osterman.
EIN: 311535572

43200
Jeanne Reed Foundation, Inc.
1643 Creek Run Dr.
Toledo, OH 43614
Contact: Jeanne Reed, Pres.

Established in 1992 in OH.
Donor(s): Jeanne Reed.
Financial data (yr. ended 12/31/01): Grants paid, $62,400; assets, $748,935 (M); expenditures, $76,089; qualifying distributions, $62,400.
Limitations: Giving limited to Toledo, OH.
Application information: Application form not required.
Officers and Trustees:* Jeanne Reed,* Pres. and Treas.; John F. Reed,* V.P.; Ruth Culbertson,* Secy.
EIN: 341717922

43201
Stella M. Buerger Charitable Trust
1 W. 4th St., Ste. 900
Cincinnati, OH 45202-3609 (513) 381-9200
Contact: W. Roger Fry, Tr.

Established in 1992 in OH.
Financial data (yr. ended 12/31/01): Grants paid, $62,375; assets, $1,667,889 (M); expenditures, $108,173; qualifying distributions, $108,173.
Limitations: Giving primarily in OH.
Trustee: W. Roger Fry.
EIN: 316436462

43202
MLP Charitable Trust
c/o Elisabeth L. Zehnder
5500 Frantz Rd., Ste. 105
Dublin, OH 43017-3545

Established in 1996 in OH.
Donor(s): Marcia L. Patterson.‡
Financial data (yr. ended 12/31/01): Grants paid, $62,370; assets, $286,203 (M); gifts received, $7,114; expenditures, $67,008; qualifying distributions, $62,370.
Limitations: Applications not accepted. Giving limited to Providence, RI.
Application information: Contributes only to pre-selected organizations.
Trustee: E.L. Zehnder.
EIN: 311453098

43203
The Albert K. Murray Fine Arts Educational Fund
9665 Young America Rd.
Adamsville, OH 43802 (740) 796-4797
Contact: Marion C. Gilliland, Tr.

Established in 1995 in OH.
Donor(s): Albert K. Murray Irrevocable Trust, Ruth Haupert, Laurance S. Rockefeller, Rockefeller Financial Services, C. Herbert Gilliland, Musk County Community Foundation, Wilma Bongi, Julianne Wilhelm.
Financial data (yr. ended 12/31/00): Grants paid, $62,350; assets, $2,174,438 (M); expenditures, $159,781; qualifying distributions, $62,350.
Limitations: Giving on a national basis.
Application information: Application form required.
Trustees: Wendel E. Dreve, Marion C. Gilliland.
EIN: 311404573

43204
Paulstan, Inc.
P.O. Box 921
Cuyahoga Falls, OH 44223

Established in 1984 in OH.
Donor(s): Stanley Myers,‡ Pauline W. Myers.
Financial data (yr. ended 12/31/00): Grants paid, $62,300; assets, $16,673 (M); expenditures, $63,812; qualifying distributions, $62,326.
Limitations: Applications not accepted. Giving primarily in CO, GA, and OH.
Application information: Contributes only to pre-selected organizations.
Officers and Directors:* David P. Myers,* Pres.; Scott D. Myers,* V.P.; Seth J. Myers,* Secy.; Dana S. Myers,* Treas.
EIN: 341462129

43205
Ralph E. Boyd Foundation
c/o KeyBank, N.A.
P.O. Box 10099
Toledo, OH 43699-0099

Financial data (yr. ended 12/31/01): Grants paid, $62,000; assets, $1,460,604 (M); expenditures, $76,123; qualifying distributions, $62,000.
Limitations: Applications not accepted. Giving primarily in Galion, OH.
Application information: 75 percent of the distributions are made to Gallion Community Center.
Advisors: Lonnie Eagle, C.E. McDonald, John A. McDonald, Fred E. Smith.
Trustee: KeyBank, N.A.
EIN: 340907473

43206
A. B. Cord Charitable Foundation
c/o North Side Bank & Trust Co.
4125 Hamilton Ave, P.O. Box 23128
Cincinnati, OH 45223-0128 (513) 542-7800
FAX: (513) 541-6941
Contact: Mary W. Johnson

Established in 1959 in OH.
Donor(s): Albert B. Cord.
Financial data (yr. ended 11/30/01): Grants paid, $62,000; assets, $1,427,411 (M); expenditures, $98,616; qualifying distributions, $64,893.
Limitations: Applications not accepted. Giving primarily in Cincinnati, OH.
Application information: Contributes only to pre-selected organizations.
Officer: Albert B. Cord, Mgr.
Trustee: North Side Bank & Trust Co.
EIN: 316016786

43207
Richard S. Hoover Charitable Trust 1956
c/o KeyBank, N.A.
800 Superior Ave., 4th Fl., OH 01 02 0421
Cleveland, OH 44114-2601
Application address: c/o Chuck Wondra, Trust Off., KeyBank, N.A., 4495 Everhard Rd. N.W., Canton, OH 44718, tel.: (330) 497-3603

Financial data (yr. ended 12/31/01): Grants paid, $62,000; assets, $1,165,348 (M); expenditures, $69,513; qualifying distributions, $62,000.
Limitations: Giving primarily in Canton, OH.
Trustee: KeyBank, N.A.
EIN: 346511001

43208
J. Frederick & Helen B. Vogel Trust
900 4th & Vine Twr.
Cincinnati, OH 45202 (513) 381-9200
Contact: W. Roger Fry, Tr.

Established in 1996 in OH.
Financial data (yr. ended 12/31/01): Grants paid, $62,000; assets, $1,432,775 (M); expenditures, $78,399; qualifying distributions, $62,000.
Limitations: Giving primarily in OH.
Trustee: W. Roger Fry.
EIN: 311484185

43209
Margaret C. Thompson Foundation
c/o National City Bank
P.O. Box 94651
Cleveland, OH 44101-4651

Established in 1986 in MI.
Donor(s): Margaret C. Thompson.
Financial data (yr. ended 12/31/01): Grants paid, $61,454; assets, $1,608,384 (M); expenditures, $75,205; qualifying distributions, $61,454.

43209—OHIO

Limitations: Applications not accepted. Giving limited to MI.
Application information: Contributes only to pre-selected organizations.
Trustee: National City Bank.
EIN: 386500422

43210
Brown Foundation
3500 Carew Twr.
441 Wine St.
Cincinnati, OH 45202

Financial data (yr. ended 12/31/01): Grants paid, $61,000; assets, $447,838 (M); expenditures, $66,091; qualifying distributions, $61,000.
Limitations: Applications not accepted. Giving primarily in Cincinnati, OH.
Application information: Contributes only to pre-selected organizations.
Trustees: Robert S. Brown, Guy M. Hild, Louise Scheard.
EIN: 316030537

43211
The Lawson Christian Foundation
1983 Wyndham Rd.
Akron, OH 44313

Established in 1962.
Financial data (yr. ended 12/31/01): Grants paid, $61,000; assets, $1,191,363 (M); expenditures, $69,803; qualifying distributions, $61,000.
Limitations: Applications not accepted. Giving primarily in Akron, OH.
Application information: Contributes only to pre-selected organizations.
Officers: Norman Lawson, Pres. and Treas.; Frances Lawson, Secy.
EIN: 346537427

43212
Philip R. & Julia P. Myers Family Foundation
8600 Bridgewater Ln.
Cincinnati, OH 45243 (513) 579-2276
Contact: Philip R. Myers, Tr.

Established in 1999 in OH.
Donor(s): Philip R. Myers.
Financial data (yr. ended 12/31/01): Grants paid, $60,845; assets, $1,043,661 (M); expenditures, $61,458; qualifying distributions, $58,529.
Limitations: Giving primarily in OH.
Trustees: Julia P. Myers, Philip R. Myers.
EIN: 311628971

43213
The Minster Machine Company Foundation
c/o Minster Machine Company Foundation
240 W. 5th St.
Minster, OH 45865-1027
Contact: Robert Sudhoff, V.P.

Donor(s): Minster Machine Co.
Financial data (yr. ended 11/30/01): Grants paid, $60,800; assets, $854,991 (M); gifts received, $16,100; expenditures, $61,601; qualifying distributions, $60,636.
Limitations: Giving primarily in OH.
Officers: Nancy E. Winch, Pres.; John Winch, V.P.; Heather R. Winch, Secy.; David C. Winch, Treas.
EIN: 346559271
Codes: CS, CD

43214
Mary R. McGaw Charitable Trust
c/o National City Bank of Pennsylvania
P.O. Box 94651
Cleveland, OH 44101-4651

Established in 1998 in PA.

Financial data (yr. ended 06/30/02): Grants paid, $60,549; assets, $1,132,304 (M); expenditures, $73,605; qualifying distributions, $60,549.
Limitations: Applications not accepted. Giving primarily in Pittsburgh, PA.
Application information: Contributes only to pre-selected organizations.
Trustee: National City Bank of Pennsylvania.
EIN: 256577115

43215
Perciak Family Foundation, Inc.
17429 Falmouth Dr.
Strongsville, OH 44136 (440) 846-0386
Contact: Thomas Perciak, Pres.

Established in 1999 in OH.
Financial data (yr. ended 12/31/01): Grants paid, $60,333; assets, $584,423 (M); expenditures, $61,033; qualifying distributions, $60,333.
Application information: Application form required.
Officers and Trustees:* Thomas Perciak,* Pres.; Patricia Perciak,* Secy.; Deborah Perciak,* Treas.
EIN: 341910059

43216
Ralph Kroehle Foundation
c/o Second National Bank of Warren
108 Main St., S.W.
Warren, OH 44481-0982 (330) 841-0128

Financial data (yr. ended 12/31/01): Grants paid, $60,100; assets, $1,223,899 (M); expenditures, $70,545; qualifying distributions, $60,100.
Limitations: Giving primarily in OH.
Trustee: Second National Bank of Warren.
EIN: 346505031

43217
Scott Technologies Foundation
(Formerly Figgie International Foundation)
2000 Auburn Dr., Ste. 400
Cleveland, OH 44122-4314
Application address: 1 Stanton St., Marinette, WI 54143; E-mail: sgerhartz@tycoint.com
Contact: Scott Gerhartz, Secy.

Established in 1979 in OH.
Donor(s): Figgie International Inc., Rawlings Sporting Goods Co., Inc., Scott Technologies, Inc.
Financial data (yr. ended 12/31/00): Grants paid, $60,050; assets, $1,458,153 (M); gifts received, $14,548; expenditures, $79,315; qualifying distributions, $60,301.
Limitations: Giving primarily in Cleveland, OH.
Application information: Application form not required.
Officer and Trustees:* Scott Gerhartz,* Secy.; Mark Bonaguru, Paul Gregoire.
EIN: 341304712
Codes: CS, CD

43218
The Blair Family Foundation
1701 Brookwood Dr.
Akron, OH 44313-5065

Established in 1999 in OH.
Donor(s): Tom B. Blair.
Financial data (yr. ended 12/31/01): Grants paid, $60,009; assets, $509,514 (M); expenditures, $73,233; qualifying distributions, $60,009.
Trustees: Faye A. Blair, Tom B. Blair.
EIN: 341910573

43219
William J. Bruder Charitable Trust
108 Main Ave., S.W.
Warren, OH 44481

Established in 1988 in OH.

Financial data (yr. ended 12/31/00): Grants paid, $60,000; assets, $1,300,134 (M); expenditures, $76,803; qualifying distributions, $64,342.
Limitations: Giving limited to Warren, OH.
Trustees: Porter B. Hall, Mary Ellen Riehm, Anthony G. Rossi, Guarnieri & Secrest.
EIN: 346557110

43220
William H. Drackett Family Foundation
c/o U.S. Bank
P.O. Box 1118, M.L. CN-WN
Cincinnati, OH 45201

Established in 1998 in OH.
Donor(s): William H. Drackett.
Financial data (yr. ended 12/31/01): Grants paid, $60,000; assets, $908,802 (M); expenditures, $39,702; qualifying distributions, $60,000.
Limitations: Giving primarily in Terrace Park, OH.
Application information: Application form not required.
Officers and Trustees:* William H. Drackett,* Pres. and Treas.; Mary H. Drackett,* Secy.; Ann Russell, U.S. Bank.
EIN: 311602084

43221
John M. Gilbertson Foundation
c/o KeyBank, N.A.
800 Superior Ave., 4th Fl.
Cleveland, OH 44114
Application address: P.O. Box 11500, WA-31-01-0310, Tacoma, WA 98411-5052
Contact: Michael Steadman, Trust Off., KeyBank, N.A.

Established in 1978.
Donor(s): John M. Gilbertson.‡
Financial data (yr. ended 06/30/02): Grants paid, $60,000; assets, $1,163,966 (M); expenditures, $77,348; qualifying distributions, $60,000.
Limitations: Giving primarily in WA.
Trustee: KeyBank, N.A.
EIN: 911086750

43222
The Mead Foundation
c/o KeyBank, N.A.
P.O. Box 10099
Toledo, OH 43615-0099 (419) 259-8372
Contact: Erwin Diener, Trust Off., KeyBank, N.A.

Established in 1998 in OH.
Donor(s): Elsie Hawkins.‡
Financial data (yr. ended 03/31/01): Grants paid, $60,000; assets, $1,812,596 (M); gifts received, $588,225; expenditures, $76,461; qualifying distributions, $60,000.
Limitations: Giving primarily in OH.
Application information: Application form not required.
Trustee: KeyBank, N.A.
Advisors: David J. Hawkins, James B. King, Susan B. King.
EIN: 341865129

43223
The Carney Foundation
2001 Crocker Rd., Ste. 440
Cleveland, OH 44145

Established in 1992 in OH.
Donor(s): James M. Carney, Sr., James M. Carney, Jr., Sally A. Carney, Howard W. Broadbent.
Financial data (yr. ended 12/31/00): Grants paid, $59,935; assets, $2,617,451 (M); gifts received, $1,413; expenditures, $71,553; qualifying distributions, $59,935.
Limitations: Applications not accepted. Giving on a national basis.

Application information: Contributes only to pre-selected organizations.
Trustee: James M. Carney, Jr.
EIN: 341667110

43224
Hildreth Foundation, Inc.
41 S. High St.
Columbus, OH 43215-3406
Contact: Mark Merkle, V.P.

Established in 1949.
Donor(s): Helen R. Davies.
Financial data (yr. ended 12/31/01): Grants paid, $59,750; assets, $1,246,392 (M); expenditures, $84,856; qualifying distributions, $59,750.
Limitations: Giving primarily in Columbus, OH, and MI.
Officers: Louis H. Sanford, Pres.; Louis Hildreth II, V.P. and Secy.; Mark Merkle, V.P. and Treas.
EIN: 316026444

43225
Windward Corporation Foundation
c/o National City Bank Of Indiana
P.O. Box 94651
Cleveland, OH 44101-4651
Application address: 10808 Lacabreah Ave., Fort Wayne, IN 46845, tel.: (260) 489-7950
Contact: Ric Zehr, Dir.

Donor(s): Joe Zehr.
Financial data (yr. ended 12/31/01): Grants paid, $59,698; assets, $548,707 (M); gifts received, $200,026; expenditures, $61,093; qualifying distributions, $59,807.
Limitations: Giving primarily in El Cajon, CA and Fort Wayne, IN.
Directors: Michelle Baldwin, Amy Mcintosh, Lisa Morlan, Joe Zehr, Ric Zehr.
EIN: 352095281

43226
Stephen H. Wilder Foundation
525 Vine St., 16th Fl.
Cincinnati, OH 45202
Contact: Eric Kearney, Dir.

Established in 1943 in OH.
Financial data (yr. ended 12/31/01): Grants paid, $59,384; assets, $89,063 (M); gifts received, $49,073; expenditures, $61,430; qualifying distributions, $59,384.
Limitations: Giving primarily in Lake Forest, IL.
Application information: Application form not required.
Officer: Charles M. Judd, Pres.
Directors: John Gilligan, Betty F. Johnson, Eric H. Kearney, Zane Miller, Beth Sullebarger.
EIN: 237086411

43227
Roddick Fund
390 Mentor Ave.
Painesville, OH 44077
Contact: R. Johnson, Tr.

Established in 1981 in OH.
Financial data (yr. ended 12/31/99): Grants paid, $59,061; assets, $1,223,791 (M); expenditures, $61,553; qualifying distributions, $59,890.
Limitations: Giving limited to the greater Painesville, OH, area.
Application information: Application form required.
Trustees: Shirley Green, Jeanne Gurley, George Hobbs, Richard Johnson, Patricia LaMuth.
EIN: 346793439
Codes: GTI

43228
Mitchell S. & Jacqueline P. Meyers Foundation
1041 Celestial St.
Cincinnati, OH 45202

Donor(s): Sidney S. Meyers.
Financial data (yr. ended 12/31/99): Grants paid, $59,011; assets, $2,456 (M); gifts received, $60,216; expenditures, $60,450; qualifying distributions, $59,011.
Limitations: Applications not accepted. Giving primarily in Cincinnati, OH.
Application information: Contributes only to pre-selected organizations.
Trustees: Mark Berliant, Jacqueline P. Meyers, Mitchell S. Meyers.
EIN: 316087639

43229
John & Betty Meyer Family Foundation
c/o Reiser & Marx
130 W. 2nd St., Ste. 1520
Dayton, OH 45402 (937) 224-4128
Contact: John Paul Rieser, Secy.

Established in 1998 in OH.
Donor(s): John E. Meyer.
Financial data (yr. ended 12/31/01): Grants paid, $59,000; assets, $1,208,164 (M); expenditures, $67,924; qualifying distributions, $59,000.
Limitations: Giving limited to Miami Valley, OH.
Officer: John Paul Rieser, Secy.
Trustees: John E. Meyer, Patricia Meyer, Marcia Meyer O'Rourke.
EIN: 311603720

43230
William P. & Suzanne W. Patterson Family Charitable Foundation
(also known as Patterson Family Charitable Foundation)
c/o U.S. Bank
P.O. Box 1118
Cincinnati, OH 45201

Established in 1998 in OH.
Financial data (yr. ended 12/31/01): Grants paid, $59,000; assets, $812,555 (M); expenditures, $66,227; qualifying distributions, $59,000.
Limitations: Applications not accepted.
Application information: Contributes only to pre-selected organizations.
Trustee: Suzanne Patterson.
Agent: U.S. Bank.
EIN: 311603127

43231
The Clinic Foundation
90 Jackson Pike
Gallipolis, OH 45631-9833
Contact: Janice Henry

Established in 1994 in OH and WV.
Donor(s): Holzer Clinic, Inc.
Financial data (yr. ended 12/31/01): Grants paid, $58,851; assets, $7,018 (M); gifts received, $58,650; expenditures, $60,311; qualifying distributions, $58,851.
Limitations: Giving primarily in OH and WV.
Officers: J. Craig Strafford, Pres.; T. Wayne Munro, V.P.; Robert E. Daniel, Admin.
EIN: 311073552

43232
Park Foundation
c/o The Huntington National Bank
P.O. Box 1558, HC0534
Columbus, OH 43216
Application address: c/o Park Foundation, P.O. Box 428, Corning, OH 43730

Financial data (yr. ended 06/30/01): Grants paid, $58,665; assets, $1,193,222 (M); expenditures, $72,600; qualifying distributions, $63,574.
Limitations: Giving limited to Monroe Township, Perry County, OH.
Application information: Application form required.
Advisors: Leo Altier, Louis Altier, Craig Axline, Kathy Colvin, Virginia Hull.
Trustee: The Huntington National Bank.
EIN: 316207775
Codes: GTI

43233
Hilda M. Padgett Charitable Trust
c/o National City Bank
P.O. Box 94651
Cleveland, OH 44101-4651
Application address: 301 S.W. Adams St., Peoria, IL 61652-0749
Contact: Jo Ann Harlan, Trust Off., National City Bank

Established in 1996 in IL.
Financial data (yr. ended 12/31/01): Grants paid, $58,500; assets, $998,900 (M); gifts received, $342,126; expenditures, $61,039; qualifying distributions, $58,500.
Limitations: Giving primarily in IL.
Trustee: National City Bank.
EIN: 371338566

43234
Bucyrus Area Community Foundation
231 S. Poplar St.
P.O. Box 387
Bucyrus, OH 44820 (419) 562-3958
FAX: (419) 562-9311; E-mail: bacf@cybrtown.com; URL: http://www.bacfoundation.org
Contact: John T. Bridges, Exec. Secy.

Established in 1985 in OH.
Financial data (yr. ended 12/31/00): Grants paid, $58,357; assets, $3,097,634 (M); gifts received, $982,333; expenditures, $226,493; giving activities include $109,312 for programs.
Limitations: Giving limited to the Crawford County, OH, area (except for the Galion area including Polk Township).
Publications: Multi-year report, informational brochure (including application guidelines).
Application information: See foundation Web site for full application guidelines. Application form not required.
Officers and Directors:* Phillip W. Gerber,* Pres.; Janet P. Pry,* V.P.; Phyllis Fowler,* Secy.; Roger R. Miller,* Treas.
EIN: 341465822
Codes: CM

43235
Pierre McBride Fund
(also known as Porcelain Metals Foundation)
c/o National City Bank, Kentucky
P.O. Box 94651
Cleveland, OH 44101-4651
Application address: c/o Porcelain Metals, 1400 S. 3rd St., Louisville, KY 40210, tel.: (502) 635-7421
Contact: John McBride, Pres.

Financial data (yr. ended 12/31/01): Grants paid, $58,012; assets, $1,060,703 (M); expenditures, $59,653; qualifying distributions, $58,133.
Limitations: Giving primarily in KY.
Application information: Application form not required.
Officers: John McBride, Pres.; O. Grant Burton, Secy.
Trustee: National City Bank, Kentucky.
Board Member: Carolyn McBride.
EIN: 616022899

43236
James E. Evans Foundation
c/o Provident Bank, Capital Mgmt. Group
P.O. Box 2176, Mail Stop 652A
Cincinnati, OH 45201-2176
Application address: 1 E. 4th St., Ste. 919, Cincinnati, OH 45202, tel.: (513) 579-2536
Contact: James E. Evans, Tr.

Established in 1989 in OH.
Donor(s): James E. Evans.
Financial data (yr. ended 12/31/01): Grants paid, $57,800; assets, $780,662 (M); expenditures, $72,738; qualifying distributions, $58,119.
Limitations: Giving limited to Cincinnati, OH.
Trustees: James E. Evans, J. David Rosenberg, Joseph P. Rouse.
EIN: 311262207

43237
Electric Power Equipment Company Foundation
60 E. Spring St.
Columbus, OH 43215-2583 (614) 224-5215
Contact: James C. McAtee, Chair.

Established in 1956 in OH.
Donor(s): Electric Power Equipment Co.
Financial data (yr. ended 09/30/01): Grants paid, $57,750; assets, $463,143 (M); expenditures, $62,741; qualifying distributions, $57,750.
Limitations: Giving primarily in Columbus, OH.
Trustees: Larry R. Brown, J.S. Coppel, J.B. Feibel, J.K. Jansen, James C. McAtee.
EIN: 316035112
Codes: CS, CD

43238
T. Raymond Gregory Family Foundation
c/o KeyBank, N.A.
800 Superior Ave., 4th Fl.
Cleveland, OH 44114-2601
Application address: c/o T. Raymond Gregory, Gregory Galvanizing & Metal Process, 4100 13th St., S.W., Canton, OH 44710

Established in 1991 in OH.
Donor(s): Gregory Galvanizing & Metal Processing, Inc.
Financial data (yr. ended 12/31/01): Grants paid, $57,635; assets, $1,113,455 (M); expenditures, $66,942; qualifying distributions, $59,760.
Limitations: Giving primarily in Canton and North Canton, OH.
Trustee: KeyBank, N.A.
EIN: 341685584
Codes: CS

43239
Robert & Carrie Steck Foundation
c/o National City Bank of Indiana
P.O. Box 94651
Cleveland, OH 44101-4651
Application address: P.O. Box 110, Fort Wayne, IN 46801, tel.: 219-461-7114
Contact: Dama Arnold, Trust Off., National City Bank of Indiana

Established in 1997 in IN.
Donor(s): E. Roberta Steck.
Financial data (yr. ended 12/31/01): Grants paid, $57,592; assets, $1,137,115 (M); expenditures, $70,836; qualifying distributions, $57,592.
Trustee: National City Bank of Indiana.
EIN: 352015863

43240
The Elizabeth Dole Charitable Foundation, Inc.
c/o IMG Ctr.
1360 E. 9th St., No. 100
Cleveland, OH 44114

Established in 1997 in VA.
Donor(s): Elizabeth H. Dole.
Financial data (yr. ended 12/31/99): Grants paid, $57,512; assets, $1,339,132 (M); expenditures, $73,855; qualifying distributions, $62,316.
Limitations: Applications not accepted. Giving on a national basis.
Application information: Contributes only to pre-selected organizations.
Officers and Directors:* Elizabeth H. Dole,* Pres.; Robert P. Davis,* Secy.; John Heubusch.
EIN: 522071982

43241
Patrick J. Calhoun, Jr. Charitable Trust
c/o U.S. Bank
P.O. Box 1118, ML CN-WN
Cincinnati, OH 45201

Established in 1986 in KY.
Financial data (yr. ended 12/31/00): Grants paid, $57,500; assets, $1,443,493 (M); expenditures, $72,612; qualifying distributions, $56,403.
Limitations: Applications not accepted. Giving primarily in Louisville, KY.
Application information: Contributes only to pre-selected organizations.
Administrative Committee: James Amik, William G. Duncan, Jr., Oma Jordan.
Trustee: U.S. Bank.
EIN: 616129304

43242
The Foundation of the Cincinnati Academy of Medicine
(Formerly The Medical Foundation of Cincinnati)
320 Broadway
Cincinnati, OH 45202 (513) 421-7010
E-mail: academy@fuse.net
Contact: Nancy Coomer, Staff Coord.

Established in 1959 in OH.
Financial data (yr. ended 12/31/01): Grants paid, $57,250; assets, $1,705,582 (M); gifts received, $4,425; expenditures, $104,040; qualifying distributions, $57,250.
Limitations: Giving primarily in Cincinnati, OH.
Publications: Application guidelines.
Application information: Application form required.
Officers: Robert Maltz, M.D., Pres.; Robert Smyth, M.D., V.P.; Jamie Scott, Secy.; John Wallace, Treas.
Trustees: Suzanne Costandi, Russell C. Dean, Jr., Andrew T. Filak, Jr., M.D., Jeanette Fisher, Joe N. Hackworth, M.D., Marlene Irvin, Andrew F. Robbins, Jr., M.D., Marvin H. Rorick, M.D., Barry Webb.
EIN: 310623960
Codes: TN

43243
Department of Medicine Research & Education Fund of Youngstown, Ohio
1044 Belmont Ave.
Youngstown, OH 44501-1006 (330) 480-3089

Established in 1984 in OH.
Financial data (yr. ended 06/30/01): Grants paid, $57,200; assets, $268,770 (M); gifts received, $972; expenditures, $68,198; qualifying distributions, $67,853.
Limitations: Giving limited to Youngstown, OH.
Officers: Charles E. Wilkens, Pres.; Thomas P. Marnejon, Treas.
EIN: 341433058
Codes: GTI

43244
Lillian M. Troutman Charitable Trust
c/o National City Bank of PA
P.O. Box 94651
Cleveland, OH 44101-4651

Established in 1998 in PA.
Financial data (yr. ended 12/31/01): Grants paid, $57,063; assets, $1,759,270 (M); expenditures, $83,032; qualifying distributions, $57,063.
Limitations: Applications not accepted. Giving primarily in PA.
Application information: Contributes only to pre-selected organizations. Unsolicited requests for funds not accepted.
Trustee: National City Bank.
EIN: 256583757

43245
Landon and Cynthia Knight Family Foundation
4793 Rolling View Dr.
Akron, OH 44313
Application address: c/o Brouse & McDowell, 500 1st National Tower, 106 S. Main St., Akron, OH 44308, tel.: (330) 535-5711
Contact: Michael A. Sweeney, Tr.

Established in 1998 in OH.
Financial data (yr. ended 12/31/01): Grants paid, $57,000; assets, $461,014 (M); expenditures, $62,253; qualifying distributions, $57,000.
Limitations: Giving primarily in OH.
Trustees: Cynthia Knight, Michael Sweeney.
EIN: 341848968

43246
John & Orlena Marsh Foundation
c/o The Huntington National Bank
P.O. Box 1558, HC1012
Columbus, OH 43216
Application address: P.O. Box 100, Dover, OH 44622; FAX: (330) 364-7492
Contact: John J. Marsh, Sr., Grant Comm. Member

Established in 1989 in OH.
Financial data (yr. ended 06/30/01): Grants paid, $57,000; assets, $9,625,212 (M); expenditures, $64,895; qualifying distributions, $57,240.
Limitations: Giving limited to Tuscarawas County, OH.
Application information: Application form not required.
Trustee: The Huntington National Bank.
Grant Committee: John J. Marsh, Jr., Marjorie M. Quicksall.
EIN: 316363890

43247
The E. Perry & Grace Beatty Memorial Foundation
c/o National City Bank, Northeast
P.O. Box 94651
Cleveland, OH 44101-4651

Financial data (yr. ended 12/31/99): Grants paid, $56,900; assets, $1,145,119 (M); expenditures, $67,768; qualifying distributions, $62,546.
Limitations: Applications not accepted. Giving primarily to residents of Youngstown, OH.
Trustee: National City Bank, Northeast.
EIN: 346515791
Codes: GTI

43248
Haman Family Foundation
c/o The Huntington National Bank
P.O. Box 1558, HC1012
Columbus, OH 43216
Application address: Lawrence Markworth, V.P., c/o The Huntington National Bank, 232 W. 3rd St., Dover, OH 44622; FAX: (330) 364-7492

Established in 1997 in OH.
Donor(s): Robert L. Haman,‡ Freda I. Haman.‡
Financial data (yr. ended 03/31/02): Grants paid, $56,891; assets, $1,188,421 (M); expenditures, $68,405; qualifying distributions, $56,891.
Limitations: Giving limited to Tuscarawas County, OH.
Application information: Application form required.
Trustee: The Huntington National Bank.
EIN: 316565640

43249
Oxford Community Foundation
52 E. Park Pl., Ste. 4
Oxford, OH 45056-1884 (513) 523-0623
FAX: (513) 524-1026; E-mail: oxcomfdn@ix.netcom.com
Contact: K.E. Smith, Exec. Dir.

Established in 1996 in OH.
Financial data (yr. ended 06/30/02): Grants paid, $56,816; assets, $2,453,859 (M); gifts received, $971,338; expenditures, $167,297.
Limitations: Giving limited to the Oxford, OH, area.
Publications: Financial statement, grants list, newsletter, informational brochure (including application guidelines).
Application information: Eight copies required for any proposal over 5 pages. Application form not required.
Officers and Trustees:* Jim Robinsom,* Pres.; Linda Balogh, V.P.; Ed Demske,* Treas.; K.E. Smith, Exec. Dir.; Biz Campbell, Tom Collins, Sondra Engel, Tom Fey, John Kirsch, Roberta L. Norman, Harry Ogle, Tom Peterson, Judy Ramsey, Judith Schiller, Phil Shriver, Suzanne H. Summers.
EIN: 311428999
Codes: CM

43250
The Michelson Foundation Charitable Trust
705 Merriman Rd.
Akron, OH 44303
Contact: Richard A. Michelson, Jr., Tr.

Established in 1968 in OH.
Donor(s): Albert S. Michelson,‡ Richard A. Michelson, Sr.
Financial data (yr. ended 12/31/01): Grants paid, $56,550; assets, $562,025 (M); expenditures, $68,617; qualifying distributions, $56,550.
Limitations: Giving primarily in the Akron, OH, area.

Application information: Application form not required.
Officer: Richard A. Michelson, Sr., Mgr.
Trustee: Richard A. Michelson, Jr.
EIN: 346616858

43251
Hawkes Scholarship Fund
c/o KeyBank, N.A.
800 Superior Ave., 4th Fl.
Cleveland, OH 44114-1306

Established in 1988 in ME.
Donor(s): John Hawkes Trust.
Financial data (yr. ended 07/31/01): Grants paid, $56,455; assets, $1,627,217 (M); expenditures, $72,651; qualifying distributions, $56,455.
Limitations: Applications not accepted.
Application information: Contributes only to pre-selected individuals.
Trustee: KeyBank, N.A.
EIN: 010441158
Codes: GTI

43252
Peter M. & Betty J. Brezovsky Charitable Trust
c/o KeyBank, N.A.
800 Superior Ave., 4th Fl.
Cleveland, OH 44114

Established in 2000 in OH.
Donor(s): Peter M. Brezovsky, Betty J. Brezovsky.
Financial data (yr. ended 12/31/01): Grants paid, $56,106; assets, $955,481 (M); gifts received, $20,492; expenditures, $75,414; qualifying distributions, $56,106.
Limitations: Applications not accepted.
Application information: Contributes only to pre-selected organizations.
Trustee: KeyBank, N.A.
EIN: 347131374

43253
William Courtney Family Foundation
c/o Sky Trust, N.A.
P.O. Box 479
Youngstown, OH 44501-0479 (330) 742-7039

Established in 1999 in OH.
Donor(s): William F. Courtney.
Financial data (yr. ended 12/31/00): Grants paid, $56,000; assets, $1,579,038 (M); gifts received, $122,259; expenditures, $68,935; qualifying distributions, $56,000.
Director: William F. Courtney.
Trustee: Sky Trust, N.A.
EIN: 341905199

43254
Steel Valley Charities
702 Twp. Hwy. 266
Bloomingdale, OH 43910-7854

Donor(s): Sam Davis, Willard Davis.
Financial data (yr. ended 09/30/01): Grants paid, $55,939; assets, $972,259 (M); gifts received, $92,589; expenditures, $57,276; qualifying distributions, $55,939.
Limitations: Applications not accepted. Giving on a national basis.
Application information: Contributes only to pre-selected organizations.
Trustees: Sam Davis, Willard Davis.
EIN: 341365357

43255
Mauger Insurance Fund
c/o National City Bank, Columbus
P.O. Box 94651
Cleveland, OH 44101-4651
Application address: c/o Mauger Scholarship Fund, Guidance Office, Watkins High School, 8808 Watkins Rd., Pataskala, OH 43062

Financial data (yr. ended 12/31/01): Grants paid, $55,850; assets, $1,082,031 (M); expenditures, $78,664; qualifying distributions, $66,366.
Limitations: Giving limited to southeastern Licking County, OH.
Application information: Application form required.
Trustee: National City Bank, Columbus.
EIN: 316198377
Codes: GTI

43256
Defiance Area Foundation, Inc.
Box 351
Defiance, OH 43512 (419) 782-3130
FAX: (419) 782-3174
Contact: Linda L. Brose, Exec. Dir.

Established in 1979 in OH.
Financial data (yr. ended 06/30/02): Grants paid, $55,555; assets, $2,545,298 (M); gifts received, $18,742; expenditures, $83,555.
Limitations: Giving limited to the Defiance, OH area.
Publications: Annual report, informational brochure (including application guidelines), financial statement.
Application information: Application form required.
Officers and Trustees:* Mark Hench, Pres.; Michael Walz, V.P.; Greg Reineke,* Secy.; James Gillis,* Treas.; Cynthia Beane, Steve Boomer, Barbara Callen, Walter Chaput, Bea Gonzales, Bruce Guilford, Philip Hoag, William Hughes, Glenn Kuhn, Terry Melton, Mary Reeves, Steve VanDemark, Steve Walker, Marc Warnke, Larry Woods.
EIN: 341278087
Codes: CM

43257
Gorski Family Foundation, Inc.
2261 Tracy Rd.
Northwood, OH 43619-1326

Established in 1994 in OH.
Financial data (yr. ended 12/31/00): Grants paid, $55,542; assets, $630,116 (M); gifts received, $133,168; expenditures, $55,624; qualifying distributions, $55,542.
Limitations: Applications not accepted.
Application information: Contributes only to pre-selected organizations.
Trustees: William V. Coulacous, Lucille F. Gorski, Cater Neff, Jane A. Schwartz.
EIN: 341783570

43258
Figgie Educational Foundation
c/o Phillips Mgmt.
25550 Chagrin Blvd., Ste. 320
Beachwood, OH 44122
Contact: Julie Brandow

Established in 1991 in OH.
Donor(s): Harry E. Figgie, Jr.
Financial data (yr. ended 12/31/00): Grants paid, $55,510; assets, $1,365,516 (M); gifts received, $35,000; expenditures, $73,339; qualifying distributions, $55,510.
Limitations: Giving primarily in OH.

43258—OHIO

Application information: Application form not required.
Officers and Trustees:* Harry E. Figgie, Jr.,* Pres.; David Carpenter, Secy.; Richard S. Tomer, Treas.; Nancy F. Figgie, Frances Rose.
EIN: 341199229

43259
The Vernay Foundation
P.O. Box 184
Yellow Springs, OH 45387
Contact: Elaine Szulewski, Tr.

Established in 1953 in OH.
Donor(s): Deborah J. Vernet, Serge A. Vernet, Vernay Laboratories, Inc.
Financial data (yr. ended 12/31/01): Grants paid, $55,500; assets, $73,803 (M); gifts received, $39,350; expenditures, $56,722; qualifying distributions, $55,500.
Limitations: Giving limited to Springfield, Xenia, and Yellow Springs, OH.
Application information: Application form not required.
Trustees: George Asakawa, Ruth B. Aschbacher, Elaine Szulewski.
Board Members: Glenn Collier, Jewell Graham.
EIN: 316050156
Codes: GTI

43260
Ella Weiss Educational Fund
c/o FirstMerit Bank, N.A.
121 S. Main St., Ste. 200
Akron, OH 44308 (330) 384-7320
Contact: Ronald B. Tynan, V.P., FirstMerit Bank, N.A.

Financial data (yr. ended 11/30/01): Grants paid, $55,500; assets, $847,774 (M); expenditures, $72,335; qualifying distributions, $61,408.
Limitations: Giving limited to residents of OH.
Application information: Application form required.
Trustee: FirstMerit Bank, N.A.
EIN: 237133041
Codes: GTI

43261
Evelyn C. Carter Trust
c/o Bank One Ohio Trust Co., N.A.
774 Park Meadow
Westerville, OH 43081
Application address: c/o Guidance Counselor, Bridgeport Senior High School, Bridgeport, WV 26330, tel.: (304) 842-3693

Established in 1996 in WV.
Donor(s): Evelyn C. Carter.‡
Financial data (yr. ended 12/31/00): Grants paid, $55,494; assets, $1,904,747 (M); expenditures, $70,585; qualifying distributions, $56,035.
Limitations: Giving limited to Bridgeport, WV.
Application information: Application form required.
Trustee: Bank One Ohio Trust Co., N.A.
EIN: 556129783
Codes: GTI

43262
The Robert H. Jentes Scholarship Fund
c/o FirstMerit Bank, N.A.
P.O. Box 36059
Canton, OH 44735 (330) 479-4300
Contact: Dana Vargo, Admin. Asst.

Established in 1990 in OH.
Donor(s): Fleming Co. Inc., Robert H. Jentes,‡ Fleming Foods Co.

Financial data (yr. ended 12/31/01): Grants paid, $55,000; assets, $1,094,015 (M); expenditures, $69,832; qualifying distributions, $57,684.
Limitations: Giving limited to OH.
Application information: Application form required.
Trustees: Robert W. McLain, Paul Von Gunten, William Wenger, FirstMerit Bank, N.A.
EIN: 346779406
Codes: GTI

43263
Arthur L. Parker Foundation
c/o Key Bank, N.A., Trust Div.
800 Superior Ave., 4th Fl.
Cleveland, OH 44114

Established in 1963.
Financial data (yr. ended 12/31/01): Grants paid, $55,000; assets, $958,883 (M); expenditures, $68,831; qualifying distributions, $55,000.
Limitations: Applications not accepted. Giving primarily in OH.
Application information: Contributes only to pre-selected organizations.
Officers and Directors:* Patrick S. Parker,* Pres.; Cynthia P. Matthews,* V.P.; Ralph P. Higgins,* Secy.-Treas.
EIN: 340690528

43264
The Jake and Jeanne Sweeney Foundation
440 Glendale Ave.
Glendale, OH 45246-3815
Application address: c/o Munninghoff, Lange, 430 Reading Rd., Cincinnati, OH 45202, tel.: (513) 241-2522
Contact: Mary S. Sweeney, Secy.-Treas.

Donor(s): C. Jeanne Sweeney.
Financial data (yr. ended 12/31/01): Grants paid, $55,000; assets, $146,381 (M); expenditures, $57,571; qualifying distributions, $55,000.
Officers and Trustees:* C. Jeanne Sweeney,* Pres.; Deborah Cassinelli,* V.P.; Susan S. Kreuzmann,* V.P.; Elizabeth S. Loper,* V.P.; Pamela S. Schneider,* V.P.; Gregory Sweeney,* V.P.; Mary S. Sweeney,* Secy.-Treas.
EIN: 311601553

43265
Molyneaux Charitable Foundation
c/o First Financial Bank
300 High St.
Hamilton, OH 45011
Application address: c/o Kevin P. Kuenzle, Secy., 777 Main St., Ste. 1300, Fort Worth, TX 76102
Contact: John P. Molyneaux, Pres.

Established in 1998 in OH and TX.
Financial data (yr. ended 12/31/01): Grants paid, $54,940; assets, $1,034,462 (M); expenditures, $65,779; qualifying distributions, $57,949.
Limitations: Giving limited to Fort Worth, TX.
Officers: John P. Molyneaux, Pres.; Kevin D. Kuenzli, Secy.-Treas.
Directors: N. David Moore, Judy Needham.
Trustee: First Financial Bank.
EIN: 752768418

43266
The Sogg Foundation, Inc.
164 Pheasant Run
Mayfield Heights, OH 44124-4174
Contact: Carol S. Markey, Pres.

Donor(s): Carol S. Markey.
Financial data (yr. ended 12/31/00): Grants paid, $54,300; assets, $953,527 (M); gifts received, $20,300; expenditures, $75,739; qualifying distributions, $54,300.

Limitations: Giving primarily in the greater Cleveland, OH, area.
Officers: Carol S. Markey, Pres.; Susan S. Stewart, V.P.
EIN: 346537192

43267
Ward Family Foundation
(Formerly Ashley F. Ward Foundation, Inc.)
210 E. Sharon Rd.
Cincinnati, OH 45246-4500

Donor(s): Ashley F. Ward II.
Financial data (yr. ended 01/31/02): Grants paid, $54,300; assets, $272,758 (M); expenditures, $54,927; qualifying distributions, $54,300.
Limitations: Applications not accepted. Giving primarily in OH.
Application information: Contributes only to pre-selected organizations.
Officer: Ashley F. Ward, Pres. and Secy.
EIN: 311039467

43268
Victor C. Laughlin, M.D. Memorial Foundation Trust
5910 Landerbrook Dr., No. 200
Mayfield Heights, OH 44124 (440) 446-1100
Contact: Irwin J. Dinn, Tr.

Established in 1985 in OH.
Donor(s): Victor C. Laughlin,‡ Lyda White Laughlin.‡
Financial data (yr. ended 12/31/01): Grants paid, $54,250; assets, $1,044,443 (M); expenditures, $76,473; qualifying distributions, $54,250.
Limitations: Giving primarily in northern OH.
Application information: Application form not required.
Trustee: Irwin J. Dinn.
EIN: 346815233

43269
The Albert M. Covelli Foundation
3900 E. Market St.
Warren, OH 44484-4723

Donor(s): Albert M. Covelli.
Financial data (yr. ended 12/31/01): Grants paid, $54,075; assets, $1,513,353 (M); expenditures, $55,477; qualifying distributions, $54,075.
Limitations: Applications not accepted. Giving primarily in Warren, OH.
Application information: Contributes only to pre-selected organizations.
Officers: Albert M. Covelli, Pres.; Josephine Covelli, V.P.; Annette Ricci, Secy.
Trustee: Michael Marando.
EIN: 341383117

43270
Chesterman Family Foundation
c/o Kenneth W. Chesterman
563 Locust Run Rd.
Cincinnati, OH 45245

Established in 1998 in OH.
Donor(s): Kenneth W. Chesterman.
Financial data (yr. ended 03/31/02): Grants paid, $54,000; assets, $826,628 (M); expenditures, $61,917; qualifying distributions, $54,000.
Limitations: Applications not accepted. Giving on a national basis, with emphasis on Cincinnati, OH.
Application information: Contributes only to pre-selected organizations.
Trustee: Kenneth W. Chesterman.
EIN: 311524334

43271
Edward T. Gardner Foundation
50 E. 3rd St.
Dayton, OH 45402

Donor(s): Elizabeth Paxton Gardner.
Financial data (yr. ended 12/31/01): Grants paid, $54,000; assets, $802,748 (M); expenditures, $59,678; qualifying distributions, $54,000.
Limitations: Applications not accepted. Giving primarily in OH.
Application information: Contributes only to pre-selected organizations.
Officers: Elizabeth Paxton Gardner, Pres.; Gloria Gardner, V.P.
EIN: 316026290

43272
The William P. and Amanda C. Madar Foundation
c/o William P. Madar
13515 Shaker Blvd., Ste. 5-B
Cleveland, OH 44120

Established in 1999 in OH.
Donor(s): William P. Madar, Amanda C. Madar.
Financial data (yr. ended 12/31/01): Grants paid, $53,900; assets, $180,984 (M); expenditures, $54,568; qualifying distributions, $53,900.
Limitations: Applications not accepted.
Application information: Contributes only to pre-selected organizations.
Officers: William P. Madar, Pres.; Amanda C. Madar, V.P., Secy.-Treas.; Josiah Russell Madar, V.P.; William Chase Madar, V.P.
EIN: 341892784

43273
Clayman Family Foundation, Inc.
P.O. Box 200
Canfield, OH 44406

Established in 1991 in OH.
Donor(s): William B. Clayman.
Financial data (yr. ended 06/30/01): Grants paid, $53,867; assets, $926,478 (M); expenditures, $55,036; qualifying distributions, $53,207.
Limitations: Applications not accepted. Giving primarily in Niles, OH.
Officers: William B. Clayman, Pres.; Gary A. Clayman, V.P.; Joel A. Clayman, Secy.; Michael S. Clayman, Treas.
EIN: 341685923
Codes: GTI

43274
Robert & Elizabeth Fergus Foundation
c/o Bank One Ohio Trust Co., N.A.
774 Park Meadow Rd.
Westerville, OH 43081
Application address: c/o Midwestern Enterprises, 5100 Post Rd., Dublin, OH 43017, tel.: (614) 889-2276
Contact: Robert E. Fergus, Tr.

Established in 1989 in OH.
Financial data (yr. ended 12/31/99): Grants paid, $53,600; assets, $5,658,468 (M); gifts received, $3,148; expenditures, $136,875; qualifying distributions, $57,676.
Limitations: Giving on a national basis.
Application information: Application form not required.
Trustees: Corwin Fergus, Elizabeth Fergus, Robert E. Fergus, Sylvia Fergus, Catherine Garber, Bank One Ohio Trust Co., N.A.
EIN: 316087932

43275
John C. Enk Charitable Residual Trust
c/o KeyBank, N.A.
800 Superior Ave., 4th Fl.
Cleveland, OH 44114
Scholarship application address: c/o Mrs. Cook, KeyBank, N.A., P.O. Box 1054, Augusta, ME 04332-1054, tel.: (207) 623-5527

Financial data (yr. ended 08/31/01): Grants paid, $53,380; assets, $1,108,955 (M); expenditures, $65,132; qualifying distributions, $53,228.
Limitations: Giving limited to ME.
Application information: Applications accepted for scholarships only. Contributes only to pre-selected organizations specified in the trust instrument.
Trustee: KeyBank, N.A.
EIN: 016056431

43276
Cambridge Kiwanis Foundation
P.O. Box 1757
Cambridge, OH 43725-6757 (740) 439-5513
Contact: Jeffrey T. Tucker, Pres.

Established in 1994 in OH.
Financial data (yr. ended 09/30/01): Grants paid, $53,145; assets, $975,751 (M); gifts received, $4; expenditures, $54,447; qualifying distributions, $53,145.
Limitations: Giving primarily in Cambridge, OH.
Application information: Application form required.
Officers: Jeffrey T. Tucker, Pres.; Richard A. Baker, V.P.; Kari A. Hitzel, Secy.-Treas.
Trustees: William H. Hartley, Don Huston.
EIN: 311425056

43277
August W. and J. Belle Bowman Fund
2080 Stockbridge Rd.
Akron, OH 44313
Contact: John V. Frank, Tr.

Established in 1994 in OH.
Financial data (yr. ended 06/30/01): Grants paid, $53,000; assets, $1,093,802 (M); expenditures, $58,900; qualifying distributions, $58,300.
Limitations: Giving primarily in Barberton, OH.
Trustees: John V. Frank, Michael L. Stark.
EIN: 347012477

43278
E.K. Foundation
c/o Fifth Third Bank
P.O. Box 630858
Cincinnati, OH 45263
Application address: 1800 Port Jefferson Rd., Sidney, OH 45365
Contact: Ella M. Kuck, Pres.

Established in 1986 in OH.
Financial data (yr. ended 10/31/01): Grants paid, $53,000; assets, $280,905 (M); expenditures, $55,902; qualifying distributions, $53,549.
Limitations: Giving primarily in OH.
Application information: Application form not required.
Officer and Trustees:* Ella M. Kuck,* Pres.; Fifth Third Bank.
EIN: 311201864

43279
Melvin R. & Ada C. Greiser Foundation
c/o PNC Advisors
P.O. Box 1198
Cincinnati, OH 45201-1198
Application address: 1330 Hill Crest Rd., Cincinnati, OH 45224-3226
Contact: R. Alan Greiser, Secy.

Donor(s): Melvin R. Greiser, Ada C. Greiser.
Financial data (yr. ended 11/30/01): Grants paid, $53,000; assets, $814,010 (M); expenditures, $59,801; qualifying distributions, $54,952.
Limitations: Giving on a national basis.
Officers: M. Neil Greiser, Pres.; R. Alan Greiser, Secy.
Trustees: Rhea G. Barrett, Lyra G. Brown, Ronald E. Greiser.
EIN: 510190031

43280
Edith Grace Reynolds Estate
(Formerly Edith Grace Reynolds Estate Residuary Trust)
c/o KeyBank, N.A.
800 Superior Ave., 4th Fl.
Cleveland, OH 44114-1306
Application address: c/o Stanley Lepkowski, Trust Off., KeyBank, N.A., 33 State St., Albany, NY 12207

Established in 1971 in NY.
Donor(s): Edith Grace Reynolds.‡
Financial data (yr. ended 03/31/02): Grants paid, $52,950; assets, $1,335,371 (M); expenditures, $65,707; qualifying distributions, $53,200.
Limitations: Giving limited to School District No. 1 in Rensselaer County, NY.
Trustee: KeyBank, N.A.
EIN: 237170056
Codes: GTI

43281
The Carmel Family Foundation
340 Darbys Run
Bay Village, OH 44140-2968
Contact: Willard E. Carmel, Pres.

Established in 1997 in OH.
Donor(s): Willard E. Carmel.
Financial data (yr. ended 12/31/01): Grants paid, $52,927; assets, $412,979 (M); expenditures, $53,093; qualifying distributions, $52,927.
Application information: Application form not required.
Officers and Trustees:* Willard E. Carmel,* Pres.; Donna J. Carmel,* Treas.; Donn H. Carmel, Todd R. Carmel, Amy Quintero.
EIN: 311511098

43282
The Hook Foundation
435 Bates Dr.
Bay Village, OH 44140-1422

Established in 1997 in OH.
Donor(s): David J. Hook, Georgia D. Hook, John B. Hook.
Financial data (yr. ended 12/31/01): Grants paid, $52,845; assets, $100,561 (M); expenditures, $53,137; qualifying distributions, $53,137.
Limitations: Applications not accepted. Giving primarily in OH.
Application information: Contributes only to pre-selected organizations.
Trustees: David J. Hook, Georgia D. Hook, John D. Hook.
EIN: 341852116

43283
Yellow Springs Community Foundation
P.O. Box 55
Yellow Springs, OH 45387 (937) 767-2655
E-mail: yscf@juno.com
Contact: Francine Rickenbach, Pres.

Chartered in 1974 in OH.
Financial data (yr. ended 12/31/01): Grants paid, $52,677; assets, $1,654,675 (L); gifts received, $77,808; expenditures, $73,593.
Limitations: Giving limited to the Yellow Springs and Greene County, OH, areas.
Publications: Annual report, informational brochure, grants list, application guidelines.
Application information: Application form required.
Officers and Trustees:* Francine Rickenbach,* Pres.; Bruce Bradtmiller,* V.P.; Evelyn LaMers,* Secy.; Larry Gerthoffer,* Treas.; Jane Baker, Staffan Erickson, John Gudgel, Dorothy O. Scott, Saul Young.
EIN: 237372791
Codes: CM

43284
Charity School of Kendal
4809 Munson St., N.W.
Canton, OH 44718
Contact: Richard C. Brunn, Secy.-Treas.

Financial data (yr. ended 12/31/01): Grants paid, $52,638; assets, $1,239,710 (M); expenditures, $59,784; qualifying distributions, $58,792.
Limitations: Giving limited to OH.
Application information: Resume, family information and qualifying factors.
Officers and Trustees:* Robert McClain,* Pres.; Maria Snively,* V.P.; Richard C. Brunn,* Secy.-Treas.; Paul Von Gunten, Margy Vogt, Nancy Welch.
EIN: 340905021

43285
Fairbanks-Horix Charitable Trust
c/o National City Bank of PA
P.O. Box 94651
Cleveland, OH 44101-4651
Application address: c/o Charles R. Dees, Jr., Assoc. Dir. of Student Aid, Univ. of Pittsburgh, 119 Schenley Hall, Pittsburgh, PA 15213
Contact: Joanna M. Mayo, V.P., National City Bank of PA

Established in 1965 in PA.
Donor(s): Horix Manufacturing Company.
Financial data (yr. ended 12/31/01): Grants paid, $52,592; assets, $715,377 (M); expenditures, $56,572; qualifying distributions, $54,181.
Limitations: Giving primarily in western PA and areas of company operations.
Trustees: Bryan Fairbanks, Frank Fairbanks, National City Bank of Pennsylvania.
EIN: 256084211
Codes: CS, CD, GTI

43286
Harry D. Stephens Memorial Trust, Inc.
c/o Flinn & Munteen Co.
429 Memorial Dr.
Greenville, OH 45331 (937) 548-0324

Established in 1990 in OH.
Donor(s): Harry D. Stephens Charitable Trust II.
Financial data (yr. ended 09/30/01): Grants paid, $52,558; assets, $12,722 (M); gifts received, $64,256; expenditures, $55,045; qualifying distributions, $52,558.
Limitations: Giving limited to Darke County, OH.
Application information: Application forms available from the Darke County Chamber of Commerce. Application form required.
Trustees: Virgil R. Boli, Alan W. Greiner, Peter F. Hemer, Mrs. William E. Hole, Jr., Mrs. John W. Spidel.
EIN: 316393086

43287
F. W. Albrecht Family Foundation
500 1st National Tower
Akron, OH 44308-1471
Application address: c/o Sue Guthier, 2700 Gilchrist Rd., P.O. Box 1910, Akron, OH 44310, tel.: (330) 733-2861

Established in 1990 in OH.
Donor(s): The Fred W. Albrecht Grocery Co., Inc.
Financial data (yr. ended 12/31/01): Grants paid, $52,550; assets, $712,080 (M); gifts received, $96,585; expenditures, $55,058; qualifying distributions, $52,550.
Limitations: Giving primarily in areas of company operations.
Trustees: F. Steven Albrecht, Richard H. Harris, Gary Myers, Joseph D. Parsons, Henry Saalfield, James H. Trout.
EIN: 341663626
Codes: CS, CD

43288
Coppock-Hole Trust
6469 Westfall Rd., Box 122
Greenville, OH 45331
Contact: William E. Hole, Jr., Pres.

Established in 1963 in OH.
Financial data (yr. ended 12/31/01): Grants paid, $52,500; assets, $1,324,851 (M); expenditures, $59,605; qualifying distributions, $52,500.
Limitations: Applications not accepted. Giving primarily in Greenville, OH.
Application information: Contributes only to pre-selected organizations.
Officer: William E. Hole, Jr., Pres.
Trustees: Barbara Hole Brewer, Susan Hole Brewer.
Agent: The Huntington National Bank.
EIN: 346557121

43289
George E. and Agnes M. Schael Trust Fund
c/o Fifth Third Bank, Trust Tax Dept.
38 Fountain Sq. Plz.
Cincinnati, OH 45263

Financial data (yr. ended 07/31/01): Grants paid, $52,364; assets, $358,350 (M); expenditures, $58,283; qualifying distributions, $52,364.
Limitations: Applications not accepted. Giving limited to Chicago, IL.
Trustee: Fifth Third Bank.
EIN: 356383161

43290
The N. J. Gregorich Foundation Living Trust
c/o KeyBank, N.A.
800 Superior Ave., 4th Fl.
Cleveland, OH 44114-2601
Application address: c/o Norbert J. Gregorich, P.O. Box 16983, Rocky River, OH 44116

Established in 1988 in OH.
Financial data (yr. ended 11/30/01): Grants paid, $52,069; assets, $1 (M); expenditures, $62,378; qualifying distributions, $52,069.
Limitations: Giving limited to Cleveland, OH.
Application information: Application form not required.
Trustee: KeyBank, N.A.
EIN: 346900255

43291
University Radiation Medicine Foundation
11100 Euclid Ave.
Cleveland, OH 44106
Contact: Timothy Kinsella, M.D., Tr.

Established in 2000.
Financial data (yr. ended 12/31/01): Grants paid, $51,930; assets, $246,459 (M); gifts received, $240,000; expenditures, $53,153; qualifying distributions, $51,930.
Trustee: Timothy Kinsella.
EIN: 341883187

43292
Marianne R. Rowe & Wood Family Foundation
c/o U.S. Bank
P.O. Box 1118
Cincinnati, OH 45201-1118

Established in 1999 in OH.
Financial data (yr. ended 12/31/01): Grants paid, $51,750; assets, $211,794 (M); gifts received, $14,627; expenditures, $64,132; qualifying distributions, $51,750.
Limitations: Giving primarily in Cincinnati, OH.
Trustees: William J. Baechtold, Vere E. Gaynor, Marianne R. Rowe, U.S. Bank.
EIN: 311679973

43293
Archeological Networks, Inc.
7322 Pettibone Rd.
Chagrin Falls, OH 44023-4939
Contact: Carl Jagatich, Dir.

Established in 1995.
Donor(s): Carl Jagatich.
Financial data (yr. ended 06/30/01): Grants paid, $51,518; assets, $850,099 (M); gifts received, $300,799; expenditures, $61,072; qualifying distributions, $51,518.
Limitations: Giving primarily in OH.
Director: Carl Jagatich.
EIN: 341804107

43294
Arthur Albert Smith Memorial Fund
c/o KeyBank, N.A.
800 Superior Ave. E, 4th Fl.
Cleveland, OH 44114-2601
Application address: c/o Mrs. Brown, KeyBank, N.A., P.O. Box 1054, Augusta, ME 04332-1054

Financial data (yr. ended 08/31/01): Grants paid, $51,432; assets, $253,769 (M); expenditures, $55,129; qualifying distributions, $51,189.
Limitations: Giving limited to the Freeport, ME, area.
Trustee: Keybank, N.A.
EIN: 016079294

43295
Harold L. & Phyllis V. Gardner Memorial Fund
c/o National City Bank
P.O. Box 94651
Cleveland, OH 44101-4651

Financial data (yr. ended 12/31/01): Grants paid, $51,148; assets, $982,538 (M); expenditures, $59,131; qualifying distributions, $55,069.
Limitations: Applications not accepted. Giving primarily in IL.
Application information: Contributes only to pre-selected organizations.
Trustee: National City Bank.
EIN: 366777457

43296
Fred C. Rutz Foundation
127 Public Sq., 17th Fl.
Cleveland, OH 44114-1306

Established in 1947.
Financial data (yr. ended 12/31/01): Grants paid, $51,050; assets, $1,208,889 (M); expenditures, $66,873; qualifying distributions, $51,050.
Limitations: Applications not accepted. Giving primarily in the Midwest.
Application information: Contributes only to pre-selected organizations.
Officers: Walter A. Maier, Mgr.; Fred L. Rutz, Mgr.; Miriam E. Rutz, Mgr.
Trustee: KeyBank, N.A.
EIN: 346521496

43297
Mervin Britton Memorial Scholarship Fund
c/o Security National Bank
40 S. Limestone
Springfield, OH 45502
Application address: c/o Clark County Board of Education, 1115 N. Limestone St., Springfield, OH 45503, tel.: (937) 325-7671

Established in 1995 in OH.
Financial data (yr. ended 12/31/01): Grants paid, $51,000; assets, $1,121,520 (M); expenditures, $62,182; qualifying distributions, $51,516.
Limitations: Giving limited to residents of Clark County, OH.
Application information: Application form required.
Trustee: Security National Bank.
EIN: 316511170
Codes: GTI

43298
Cincinnati Enquirer Foundation
312 Elm St.
Cincinnati, OH 45202-2739

Established in 1959.
Donor(s): The Cincinnati Enquirer.
Financial data (yr. ended 06/30/01): Grants paid, $51,000; assets, $4,802 (M); gifts received, $34,000; expenditures, $51,049; qualifying distributions, $51,000.
Limitations: Applications not accepted. Giving primarily in OH.
Application information: Scholarship applicants must be children of an employee of the Cincinnati Enquirer, who has completed at least five years of continuous, full-time employment as of Mar. 25 of each year. Children of retired or deceased employees are also eligible if the parent had completed five years of continuous, full-time employment at time of retirement or death; grant contributions to pre-selected organizations.
Officers: Harry M. Whipple, Pres.; Martha L. Flanagan, Secy.; Thomas E. Yunker, Cont.
EIN: 316037926
Codes: CS, CD

43299
Helmer Rabild Charitable Trust
c/o National City Bank of Pennsylvania
P. O. Box 94651
Cleveland, OH 44101-4651
Application address: c/o Lynette A. Pedensky, Trust Off., National City Bank of Pennsylvania, 127 W. Spring St., Titusville, PA 16354, tel.: (814) 827-5972

Financial data (yr. ended 12/31/01): Grants paid, $51,000; assets, $1,062,460 (M); expenditures, $58,672; qualifying distributions, $52,519.
Limitations: Giving primarily in the Titusville, PA, area.

Trustee: National City Bank.
EIN: 256013302

43300
Reuben B. Robertson Foundation
c/o George W. Robertson
P.O. Box 6464
Cincinnati, OH 45201-6464
Application address: 10140 Parkwood Dr., No. 1, Cupertino, CA 95014, tel.: (408) 257-1383
Contact: Daniel H. Robertson, Tr.

Financial data (yr. ended 12/31/01): Grants paid, $51,000; assets, $935,177 (M); expenditures, $56,818; qualifying distributions, $51,000.
Limitations: Giving primarily in Cincinnati, OH.
Application information: Application form not required.
Trustees: Beverly A. Everhart, Daniel H. Robertson, George W. Robertson.
EIN: 316028029

43301
Ward & Mary Wooddell Scholarship Trust
c/o National Bank & Trust Co.
P.O. Box 711
Wilmington, OH 45177-2212 (937) 382-1441
Contact: Sarah E. Barker, Trust Off., National Bank and Trust Co.

Established in 1989 in OH.
Financial data (yr. ended 09/30/01): Grants paid, $50,721; assets, $287,128 (M); expenditures, $54,529; qualifying distributions, $50,409.
Limitations: Giving limited to Clinton County, OH.
Application information: Application form required.
Trustee: National Bank & Trust Co.
EIN: 316368376
Codes: GTI

43302
MLFB Foundation
3536 Raymar Blvd.
Cincinnati, OH 45208

Established in 1994 in OH.
Donor(s): Joseph E. Brinkmeyer.
Financial data (yr. ended 12/31/01): Grants paid, $50,717; assets, $297,023 (M); gifts received, $110,981; expenditures, $51,687; qualifying distributions, $50,717.
Limitations: Applications not accepted. Giving primarily in Cincinnati, OH.
Application information: Contributes only to pre-selected organizations.
Trustees: Joseph E. Brinkmeyer, Mary F. Brinkmeyer.
EIN: 311449071

43303
The Brandon Family Foundation
c/o R.A. Bumblis, C.P.A.
1900 E. 9th St., Ste. 3200
Cleveland, OH 44114-3485

Established in 1994 in OH.
Donor(s): Edward B. Brandon.
Financial data (yr. ended 12/31/01): Grants paid, $50,621; assets, $1,229,723 (M); expenditures, $54,230; qualifying distributions, $50,621.
Limitations: Applications not accepted. Giving primarily in Cleveland, OH.
Application information: Contributes only to pre-selected organizations.
Officers and Trustees:* Edward B. Brandon,* Pres.; Phyllis P. Brandon,* V.P.; Beth A. Brandon,* Secy.-Treas.; E. Matthew Brandon, Robert P. Brandon, William M. Brandon, Beverly A. Marzullo.
EIN: 341786777

43304
Ruth A. & W. O. Mashburn, Jr. Charitable Foundation
c/o Richard A. Mashburn
3766 Ashworth Dr., No. 3
Cincinnati, OH 45208

Financial data (yr. ended 08/31/01): Grants paid, $50,500; assets, $839,106 (M); expenditures, $55,960; qualifying distributions, $50,500.
Limitations: Applications not accepted. Giving primarily in OH.
Application information: Contributes only to pre-selected organizations.
Trustees: Richard A. Mashburn, W.O. Mashburn.
EIN: 316041876

43305
The Jerome and Geraldine Schottenstein Foundation
c/o Jim Gesler
1800 Moler Rd.
Columbus, OH 43207-1680

Established in 1995 in OH.
Donor(s): Geraldine Schottenstein.
Financial data (yr. ended 12/31/00): Grants paid, $50,500; assets, $1,426 (M); gifts received, $50,000; expenditures, $50,665; qualifying distributions, $50,665.
Limitations: Giving primarily in NY.
Officers: Geraldine Schottenstein, Pres.; Jay Schottenstein, V.P.; Ann Deshe, Secy.; Susan Diamond, Treas.
EIN: 311442823

43306
Norma Green Family Foundation
c/o National City Bank
1900 E. 9th St.
Cleveland, OH 44114
Contact: Kathleen Honohan, V.P., National City Bank

Established in 1988 in OH.
Donor(s): Norma Green.‡
Financial data (yr. ended 12/31/01): Grants paid, $50,400; assets, $1,012,078 (M); expenditures, $59,816; qualifying distributions, $56,348.
Limitations: Applications not accepted. Giving primarily in NM, NY, and OH.
Application information: Contributes only to pre-selected organizations.
Trustee: National City Bank.
EIN: 346901968

43307
Strange Family Foundation
c/o Steven Cox
222 S. Main St.
Akron, OH 44308

Established in 2000 in OH.
Donor(s): Doris C. Strange.
Financial data (yr. ended 12/31/01): Grants paid, $50,300; assets, $12,087 (M); gifts received, $10,816; expenditures, $50,300; qualifying distributions, $50,290.
Limitations: Applications not accepted. Giving primarily in Kent and Ravenna, OH.
Application information: Contributes only to pre-selected organizations.
Officers: Doris C. Strange, Pres.; Steven A. Strange, V.P. and Treas.; Lee J. Strange, Secy.
EIN: 341914050

43308
Kahl Family Foundation
32432 Nottingham Dr.
Avon Lake, OH 44012-2192

Established in 1985 in OH.
Donor(s): John J. Kahl, Jr., Manco, Inc.
Financial data (yr. ended 12/31/01): Grants paid, $50,033; assets, $38,294 (M); expenditures, $52,133; qualifying distributions, $50,033.
Limitations: Applications not accepted. Giving primarily in Cleveland, OH.
Application information: Contributes only to pre-selected organizations.
Trustees: Robert E. Dorfmeyer, J. Michael Kahl, John J. Kahl, Jr., Margaret Kahl, William Edward Kahl.
EIN: 341517236

43309
The Boyer Family Foundation
7800 Big Creek Pkwy.
Middleburg Heights, OH 44130
(440) 234-9748
Contact: Duane O. Boyer, Pres.

Established in 1997 in OH.
Donor(s): Duane O. Boyer.
Financial data (yr. ended 12/31/01): Grants paid, $50,000; assets, $871,477 (M); expenditures, $54,115; qualifying distributions, $50,000.
Officers: Duane O. Boyer, Pres.; Penelope J. Boyer, V.P.; K. Page Boyer, Secy.; Shereen Boyer, Treas.
EIN: 311531786

43310
Victor M. & Harriet J. Goldberg Foundation
1710 Country Line Rd.
P.O. Box 578
Gates Mills, OH 44040 (440) 844-5900
Contact: Victor M. Goldberg, Pres.

Established in 1998 in OH.
Donor(s): Victor M. Goldberg, Harriet J. Goldberg.
Financial data (yr. ended 12/31/00): Grants paid, $50,000; assets, $582,056 (M); gifts received, $39,166; expenditures, $52,488; qualifying distributions, $49,161.
Limitations: Giving primarily in OH.
Application information: Application form not required.
Officers: Victor M. Goldberg, Pres. and Treas.; Harriet J. Goldberg, V.P. and Secy.
EIN: 311490083

43311
KeyBank of Maine Foundation
c/o KeyBank, N.A., Trust Div.
800 Superior Ave., 4th Fl.
Cleveland, OH 44114
Application address: c/o Cristina Cook, 286 Water St., Key Plz., 3rd Fl., Augusta, ME 04330, tel.: (207) 623-5527

Established in 1954 in ME.
Donor(s): Key Bank of Maine, KeyBank, N.A.
Financial data (yr. ended 11/30/01): Grants paid, $50,000; assets, $1,117,782 (M); expenditures, $68,056; qualifying distributions, $50,000.
Limitations: Giving primarily in VA.
Officers: Kathryn Underwood, Pres. and Secy.; Jeffrey Stone, Treas.
Director: Susan Snowden.
Trustee: KeyBank, N.A.
EIN: 016017321
Codes: CS, CD, GTI

43312
Land Family Foundation
1429 Wood River Blvd.
Beavercreek, OH 45434

Established in 1999 in OH.
Donor(s): Irene Land.
Financial data (yr. ended 12/31/01): Grants paid, $50,000; assets, $925,093 (M); expenditures, $63,550; qualifying distributions, $50,000.
Limitations: Applications not accepted. Giving primarily in OH.
Application information: Contributes only to pre-selected organizations.
Trustee: Irene Land.
EIN: 311647695

43313
Fred Lazarus, Jr. Foundation
2800 Cincinnati Commerce Ctr.
600 Vine St., 28th Fl.
Cincinnati, OH 45202-2409
Contact: Stuart A. Schloss, Jr., Tr.

Financial data (yr. ended 12/31/01): Grants paid, $50,000; assets, $781,919 (M); expenditures, $53,740; qualifying distributions, $50,000.
Limitations: Giving primarily in MA and MD.
Application information: Application form not required.
Trustees: Carol Lazarus, Fred Lazarus IV, John R. Lazarus, Stuart A. Schloss, Jr.
EIN: 316021207

43314
Almera Biddulph Reitz Foundation
4545 Hinckley Pkwy.
Cleveland, OH 44109-6009

Established in 2001 in OH.
Donor(s): Almera Reitz.‡
Financial data (yr. ended 12/31/01): Grants paid, $50,000; assets, $1,055,793 (M); gifts received, $1,071,945; expenditures, $51,625; qualifying distributions, $50,525.
Limitations: Giving primarily in OH.
Trustees: Steven H. Eccleston, Alice R. Scheeff.
EIN: 347127426

43315
A. L. Spencer Foundation
c/o National City Bank of Pennsylvania
P.O. Box 94651
Cleveland, OH 44101-4651
Application address: 1815 Washington Rd., Pittsburgh, PA 15241
Contact: A. Lawrence Spencer, Pres.

Established in 1999 in PA.
Donor(s): A. Lawrence Spencer.
Financial data (yr. ended 12/31/01): Grants paid, $50,000; assets, $804,109 (M); expenditures, $57,495; qualifying distributions, $50,000.
Limitations: Giving primarily in western PA.
Officers and Directors:* A. Lawrence Spencer,* Pres.; Kathleen M. Spencer,* Secy.-Treas.
EIN: 251843761

43316
The Sukenik Family Foundation
3323 Bremerton Rd.
Pepper Pike, OH 44124-5312

Established in 1994 in OH.
Donor(s): Will Sukenik.
Financial data (yr. ended 12/31/01): Grants paid, $50,000; assets, $1,548,436 (M); gifts received, $693,338; expenditures, $65,271; qualifying distributions, $50,000.
Limitations: Applications not accepted.
Application information: Contributes only to pre-selected organizations.
Officers and Trustees:* William Sukenik,* Pres.; Janet Sukenik,* Secy.; Ellen Sukenik.
EIN: 341786200

43317
Jane M. Timken Foundation
200 Market Ave. N., Ste. 210
Canton, OH 44702
Contact: Don D. Dickes, Secy.-Treas.

Incorporated in 1985 in OH.
Donor(s): Jane M. Timken.
Financial data (yr. ended 09/30/01): Grants paid, $50,000; assets, $1,094,920 (M); expenditures, $51,786; qualifying distributions, $50,555.
Limitations: Giving primarily in the New York, NY, area.
Application information: Application form not required.
Officers and Trustees:* Jane M. Timken,* Pres.; Don D. Dickes,* Secy.-Treas.; Barbara C. Timken.
EIN: 341526564

43318
Young Wood Foundation
c/o National City Bank of Pennsylvania
P.O. Box 94651
Cleveland, OH 44101-4651

Donor(s): Julia Wood Smith.‡
Financial data (yr. ended 12/31/01): Grants paid, $50,000; assets, $584,924 (M); gifts received, $7,030; expenditures, $52,167; qualifying distributions, $51,083.
Limitations: Applications not accepted. Giving primarily in PA.
Application information: Contributes only to pre-selected organizations.
Trustee: National City Bank of Pennsylvania.
EIN: 912140478

43319
J. Brannon Hull Scholarship Fund, Inc.
c/o Superintendent's Office
91 S. Buckeye St.
Crooksville, OH 43731 (740) 982-7040

Established in 1987 in OH.
Financial data (yr. ended 12/31/01): Grants paid, $49,830; assets, $798,490 (M); expenditures, $50,359; qualifying distributions, $52,059.
Limitations: Giving primarily in Crooksville, OH.
Application information: Application form required.
Officers: Bill Moore, Chair.; John Allen, Pres.; Douglas Cannon, V.P.; Mike Hankinson, Secy.
EIN: 311090015
Codes: GTI

43320
William K. Davis Trust
116 S. Main St.
Marion, OH 43302

Financial data (yr. ended 12/31/99): Grants paid, $49,618; assets, $962,247 (M); expenditures, $61,588; qualifying distributions, $52,467.
Trustees: Ronald D. Cramer, Harry L. Dowler, Jr.
EIN: 346955006

43321
The Huggett Foundation
c/o SES, Inc.
P.O. Box 479
Richfield, OH 44286

Established in 1995 in OH.
Donor(s): T. Virgil Huggett.
Financial data (yr. ended 12/31/01): Grants paid, $49,600; assets, $335,088 (M); gifts received,

$130,000; expenditures, $50,370; qualifying distributions, $49,600.
Limitations: Applications not accepted.
Application information: Contributes only to pre-selected organizations.
Trustees: Carol Huggett, Richard M. Huggett, Scott N. Huggett, T. Virgil Huggett.
EIN: 341824120

43322
T. M. & N. A. O'Donnell Foundation
19111 Detroit Ave., Ste. 201
Rocky River, OH 44116
Contact: Thomas M. O'Donnell, Mgr.

Donor(s): Thomas M. O'Donnell.
Financial data (yr. ended 12/31/00): Grants paid, $49,524; assets, $1,232,323 (M); expenditures, $64,384; qualifying distributions, $49,524.
Limitations: Giving primarily in greater Cleveland, OH.
Officer and Trustees:* Thomas M. O'Donnell,* Mgr.; George J. Durkin, Nancy A. O'Donnell.
EIN: 341095843

43323
Bert and Elizabeth Wolinsky Charitable Trust
1000 United Bank Plz.
Canton, OH 44702
Contact: Rabbi Armond E. Cohen, Tr.

Established in 1990 in OH.
Financial data (yr. ended 12/31/01): Grants paid, $49,500; assets, $943,659 (M); expenditures, $60,794; qualifying distributions, $49,500.
Limitations: Giving primarily in OH.
Application information: Application form required.
Trustee: Rabbi Armond E. Cohen.
EIN: 346889055

43324
Victor Mohr Memorial Trust
c/o Fifth Third Bank
38 Fountain Sq. Plz.
Cincinnati, OH 45263
Application address: c/o Principal, South Spencer High School, Rockport, IN 47635

Financial data (yr. ended 12/31/01): Grants paid, $49,484; assets, $1,218,863 (M); expenditures, $70,501; qualifying distributions, $52,288.
Limitations: Giving primarily in IN.
Application information: Application form required.
Trustee: Fifth Third Bank.
EIN: 356225418
Codes: GTI

43325
Shepherd's Foundation, Inc.
1500 McKinley Ave.
Niles, OH 44446

Financial data (yr. ended 12/31/99): Grants paid, $49,108; assets, $1,159,577 (M); gifts received, $136,409; expenditures, $139,674; qualifying distributions, $49,108.
Limitations: Applications not accepted.
Application information: Contributes only to a pre-selected organization.
Trustees: Edward Bellin, Fremont Camerino, Yt Chiu, Jack Ritter, Gail Seekins.
EIN: 341758384
Codes: TN

43326
Robert L. Rhoad Testamentary Trust
c/o Drake, Phillips, Kuenzli & Clark
301 S. Main St., Ste. 3
Findlay, OH 45840 (419) 423-0242
Contact: William E. Clark, Tr.

Established in 1994 in OH.
Financial data (yr. ended 12/31/00): Grants paid, $49,000; assets, $1,019,840 (M); expenditures, $96,164; qualifying distributions, $48,684.
Limitations: Giving limited to residents of Hancock County, OH.
Application information: Applicants must reside in Hancock County, OH, and be pursuing post-secondary education at qualified institutions. Applicants should include information regarding scholastic and extracurricular activities.
Trustees: Jim Barnhill, William E. Clark, Richard J. Rinebolt, James Shrader.
EIN: 346959896

43327
Robert M. & Lori B. Campana Charitable Foundation Trust
5905 Rosecliff Dr.
Lorain, OH 44053
Application address: 2115 W. Park Dr., Lorain, OH 44053
Contact: Patricia A. Campana, Tr.

Established in 1998 in OH.
Donor(s): Robert M. Campana, Lori B. Campana.
Financial data (yr. ended 12/31/99): Grants paid, $48,995; assets, $12,214 (M); gifts received, $30,748; expenditures, $48,995; qualifying distributions, $48,995.
Limitations: Giving primarily in OH.
Trustees: Lori B. Campana, Patricia A. Campana.
EIN: 341863772

43328
Gardiner Family Foundation
31200 Bainbridge Rd.
Solon, OH 44139 (440) 248-3400
Contact: William H. Gardiner, Tr.

Established in 1989 in OH.
Donor(s): William H. Gardiner.
Financial data (yr. ended 12/31/01): Grants paid, $48,850; assets, $181,780 (M); gifts received, $48,000; expenditures, $50,459; qualifying distributions, $50,453.
Limitations: Applications not accepted. Giving primarily in the greater Cleveland, OH, area.
Application information: Contributes only to pre-selected organizations.
Trustees: Gary Gardiner, Todd Gardiner, William H. Gardiner.
EIN: 341633714

43329
Gerald M. and Carole A. Miller Family Foundation
c/o Miller Valentine Group
1 Prestige Plz., Ste. 580
Miamisburg, OH 45342-3767
Contact: Kathy A. Alpeter, Treas.

Donor(s): Gerald Miller.
Financial data (yr. ended 06/30/01): Grants paid, $48,800; assets, $898,228 (M); gifts received, $200,000; expenditures, $70,644; qualifying distributions, $48,302.
Limitations: Giving primarily in Dayton, OH.
Officers and Trustees:* Carole A. Miller,* Pres.; Gerald M. Miller, Jr.,* V.P.; Matthew T. Miller,* V.P.; Laurie Miller-D'Arcangelo,* Secy.; Kathy A. Alpeter,* Treas.; David E. Alpeter, Christine Miller.
EIN: 311153159

43330
Louis & Mary J. Abstine College Scholarship Fund
c/o National City Bank of Indiana
P.O. Box 94651
Cleveland, OH 44101-4651
Application address: c/o National City Bank of Indiana, P.O. Box 5031, Indianapolis, IN 46255, tel.: (317) 267-7031
Contact: Sandy Haynes, Trust Off., National City Bank of Indiana

Established in 1990 in IN.
Donor(s): Mary J. Abstine.‡
Financial data (yr. ended 02/28/01): Grants paid, $48,750; assets, $1,327,845 (M); expenditures, $65,997; qualifying distributions, $56,159.
Limitations: Giving limited to residents of Shelby County, IN.
Application information: Application form required.
Trustee: National City Bank of Indiana.
EIN: 351787469
Codes: GTI

43331
Isaac & Esther Jarson - Stanley & Mickey Kaplan Foundation
(Formerly Isaac N. and Esther N. Jarson Charitable Trust)
312 Walnut St., Ste. 3150
Cincinnati, OH 45202
Application address: 105 E. 4th St., Ste. 710, Cincinnati, OH 45202, tel.: (513) 721-5086
Contact: Stanley M. Kaplan, Tr. or Myron J. Kaplan, Tr.

Trust established in 1955 in OH.
Financial data (yr. ended 12/31/01): Grants paid, $48,740; assets, $2,025,496 (M); expenditures, $68,368; qualifying distributions, $48,840.
Limitations: Giving primarily in the greater Cincinnati, OH, area.
Trustees: Myron J. Kaplan, Stanley M. Kaplan.
EIN: 316033453

43332
Dorothy Ames Trust
c/o KeyBank, N.A.
800 Superior Ave., 4th Fl.
Cleveland, OH 44114
Application address: P.O. Box 1054, Augusta, ME 04332-1054, tel.: (216) 828-9535
Contact: Cristina Cook, Trust Off., KeyBank, N.A.

Financial data (yr. ended 08/31/01): Grants paid, $48,240; assets, $715,264 (M); expenditures, $59,360; qualifying distributions, $47,425.
Limitations: Giving primarily in MA and ME.
Trustee: KeyBank, N.A.
EIN: 016065594
Codes: GTI

43333
Ward J. Timken Family Foundation
200 Market Ave. N., Ste. 210
Canton, OH 44702-1437
Contact: Don D. Dickes, Secy.-Treas.

Established in 1985 in OH.
Donor(s): Elizabeth Blyth Timken, Joy A. Timken, Mary J. Timken, Robert R. Timken, W.R. Timken,‡ Ward J. Timken, Ward J. Timken, Jr., Louise B. Timken.
Financial data (yr. ended 09/30/01): Grants paid, $48,034; assets, $1,205,996 (M); expenditures, $51,392; qualifying distributions, $49,676.
Limitations: Applications not accepted. Giving primarily in Canton, OH.
Application information: Contributes only to pre-selected organizations.

43333—OHIO

Officers and Trustees:* Ward J. Timken,* Pres.; Joy A. Timken,* V.P.; Don D. Dickes,* Secy.-Treas.
EIN: 341527256

43334
The Mary E. Babcock Foundation
c/o Jean Wright
9889 Hollow Rd.
Pataskala, OH 43062
Application address: 146 Granville St., Ste. C, Gahanna, OH 43230, tel.: (614) 337-2773
Contact: Thomas E. Gibson, Treas.

Financial data (yr. ended 03/31/00): Grants paid, $47,924; assets, $2,622,008 (M); gifts received, $1,078,113; expenditures, $52,589; qualifying distributions, $47,924.
Limitations: Giving primarily in the Johnstown, OH area.
Application information: Application form required.
Officers: Steven H. Williams, Pres.; Frederick W. Walker, V.P.; Mary C. Thomas, Secy.; Thomas E. Gibson, Treas.
Director: Richard Scovell.
EIN: 311170451

43335
Wayne County National Bank Foundation
c/o Stephen Kitchen
1776 Beall Ave.
Wooster, OH 44691

Established in 1997 in OH.
Donor(s): Wayne County National Bank.
Financial data (yr. ended 09/30/01): Grants paid, $47,832; assets, $462,473 (M); gifts received, $70,000; expenditures, $48,632; qualifying distributions, $47,788.
Limitations: Applications not accepted. Giving primarily in OH.
Application information: Contributes only to pre-selected organizations.
Officers: David Christopher, Chair.; David Boyle, Pres.; John C. Johnston III, Secy.; Stephen Kitchen, Treas.
EIN: 311540371
Codes: CS

43336
Carlisle B. Van Meter Family Foundation
c/o U.S. Bank
P.O. Box 1118
Cincinnati, OH 45201-1118

Established in 1998 in OH.
Donor(s): Carlisle B. Van Meter.
Financial data (yr. ended 04/30/02): Grants paid, $47,500; assets, $768,535 (M); expenditures, $57,678; qualifying distributions, $47,500.
Limitations: Applications not accepted. Giving primarily in KY.
Application information: Contributes only to pre-selected organizations.
Officers and Trustees:* Carlisle Van Meter,* Pres.; George Van Meter, Jr.,* V.P.; Carlisle V. Mayer,* V.P.; Laurance Van Meter,* Secy.; Thomas F. Van Meter II,* Treas.; U.S. Bank.
EIN: 311613369

43337
Paul Motry Memorial Fund
c/o Dean S. Lucal
P.O. Box 929
Sandusky, OH 44870-0357 (419) 625-0515
Application address: P.O. Box 387, Sandusky, OH 44870

Established in 1950.
Financial data (yr. ended 12/31/00): Grants paid, $47,373; assets, $568,494 (M); gifts received, $9,625; expenditures, $54,250; qualifying distributions, $53,518.
Limitations: Giving limited to Erie and eastern Ottawa counties, OH.
Officer: Judith Bakewell, Mgr.
Trustees: Darrel L. Legg, Marian Motry, Clarence E. Nagle, Kathryn M. Slackford, Grant W. Walls.
EIN: 237420173
Codes: GTI

43338
The McCall Foundation
c/o Julien L. McCall
115 Quail Ln.
Hunting Valley, OH 44022

Established in 1986 in OH.
Donor(s): Julien L. McCall, Janet J. McCall.
Financial data (yr. ended 12/31/01): Grants paid, $47,350; assets, $1,718,680 (M); gifts received, $175,130; expenditures, $49,350; qualifying distributions, $47,970.
Limitations: Applications not accepted. Giving primarily in OH.
Application information: Contributes only to pre-selected organizations.
Officers: Julien L. McCall, Jr., Chair.; Julien L. McCall, Pres. and Treas.; Janet J. McCall, V.P.
EIN: 341543993

43339
The Doll Family Foundation
3159 Van Aken Blvd.
Shaker Heights, OH 44120

Established in 1992 in OH.
Donor(s): Henry C. Doll.
Financial data (yr. ended 12/31/01): Grants paid, $47,170; assets, $935,921 (M); gifts received, $115,240; expenditures, $53,458; qualifying distributions, $47,170.
Limitations: Applications not accepted. Giving primarily in Cleveland, OH.
Application information: Contributes only to pre-selected organizations.
Officers and Trustees:* Henry C. Doll,* Pres.; Mary M. Doll,* Secy.; Sarah V. Doll.
EIN: 341725981

43340
The Eugene and Eleanor Harms Foundation
c/o Richard G. LaValley, Jr.
5800 Monroe St., Bldg. F
Sylvania, OH 43560-2207

Donor(s): Eugene Harms, Eleanor Harms.
Financial data (yr. ended 12/31/01): Grants paid, $47,000; assets, $664,636 (M); gifts received, $135,888; expenditures, $52,286; qualifying distributions, $46,760.
Limitations: Applications not accepted. Giving primarily in Perrysburg, OH.
Application information: Contributes only to pre-selected organizations.
Officers and Trustees:* Eugene Harms,* Pres.; Eleanor Harms,* V.P.; Richard G. LaValley, Jr.,* Secy.
EIN: 311627962

43341
Claire & Charles Phillips Foundation
c/o U.S. Bank
P.O. Box 1118 M.L. 6190
Cincinnati, OH 45201
Application address: c/o Cincinnati Scholarship Foundation, 652 Main St., Cincinnati, OH 45202

Established in 1998 in OH.
Donor(s): Charles A. Phillips, Claire B. Phillips.
Financial data (yr. ended 12/31/01): Grants paid, $46,964; assets, $1,242,303 (M); gifts received, $440; expenditures, $50,803; qualifying distributions, $46,964.
Officers and Trustees:* Claire B. Phillips,* Pres.; Charles A. Phillips,* V.P.; Peggy Greenberg,* Secy.; Pamela Rossmann,* Treas.
EIN: 311634128

43342
The Lorain Foundation
c/o Lorain National Bank
457 Broadway
Lorain, OH 44052

Established in 1947 in OH.
Donor(s): Edward J. Gould.‡
Financial data (yr. ended 12/31/99): Grants paid, $46,766; assets, $2,025,084 (M); gifts received, $15,000; expenditures, $72,039; qualifying distributions, $47,362.
Limitations: Giving limited to the Lorain, OH, area.
Application information: Application form required.
Trustees: Richard Colella, Nicholas Hutlock, Jane Kolczun, Eugene Sofranko, David Wiersma.
EIN: 341022034
Codes: GTI

43343
Richard D. Hannan Family Foundation
c/o Fifth Third Bank
38 Fountain Sq. Plz., Trust Tax Dept.
Cincinnati, OH 45263
Contact: Lawra Baumann, Trust Off., Fifth Third Bank

Established in 1996 in OH.
Donor(s): Richard D. Hannan.
Financial data (yr. ended 12/31/01): Grants paid, $46,510; assets, $391,907 (M); gifts received, $8,610; expenditures, $52,992; qualifying distributions, $46,510.
Limitations: Giving on a national basis.
Officers and Trustees:* Richard D. Hannan,* Pres.; Jeanne M. Hannan,* V.P.; James R. Marlow, Secy.; Kenneth R. Wurtenberger,* Treas.; Fifth Third Bank.
Advisory Committee Members: Hollie J. Hannan, Lauren Hannan Hudson.
EIN: 311482697

43344
The King Foundation
c/o Alexander S. Taylor
30050 Chagrin Blvd., Ste. 150
Pepper Pike, OH 44124-5774

Established in 1986 in OH.
Donor(s): Theodore E. Gordon, Jane B. King.
Financial data (yr. ended 06/30/02): Grants paid, $46,500; assets, $534,845 (M); expenditures, $48,234; qualifying distributions, $46,500.
Limitations: Applications not accepted. Giving primarily in FL.
Application information: Contributes only to pre-selected organizations.
Trustees: Jane B. King, Ralph T. King, Alexander S. Taylor.
EIN: 341567999

43345
The Michel Family Foundation
c/o Thomas F. Allen
1801 E. 9th St., Ste. 730
Cleveland, OH 44114-3103

Established in 1996 in OH.
Donor(s): Beno Michel, Elaine M. Michel.
Financial data (yr. ended 12/31/01): Grants paid, $46,500; assets, $731,248 (M); gifts received,

$2,606; expenditures, $48,957; qualifying distributions, $46,500.
Limitations: Applications not accepted.
Application information: Contributes only to pre-selected organizations.
Officers and Trustees:* Beno Michel,* Pres.; Elaine M. Michel,* V.P.; Marc H. Michel,* Secy.; Loren S. Michel,* Treas.; Lee K. Michel.
EIN: 341846021

43346
The Montei Foundation
1399 Brookwood Pl.
Columbus, OH 43209-2814

Established in 2000 in OH.
Financial data (yr. ended 12/31/01): Grants paid, $46,500; assets, $956,433 (M); expenditures, $58,458; qualifying distributions, $46,500.
Limitations: Applications not accepted. Giving primarily in OH.
Application information: Contributes only to pre-selected organizations.
Trustees: William K. Burton, Jo Ellen Montei, Julia Kimberly Gibson Montei, Todd Ross Montei, Tom Ross Montei.
EIN: 311736155

43347
Parrot Charitable Foundation
c/o National City Bank of Indiana
P.O. Box 94651
Cleveland, OH 44101-4651

Established in 1994.
Financial data (yr. ended 10/31/01): Grants paid, $46,500; assets, $755,292 (M); gifts received, $25; expenditures, $48,962; qualifying distributions, $46,500.
Limitations: Applications not accepted. Giving primarily in Fort Wayne, IN.
Application information: Contributes only to pre-selected organizations.
Trustee: National City Bank.
EIN: 356598565

43348
The Schuler-Walter Foundation
6 Perry St.
P.O. Box 369
Wapakoneta, OH 45895

Established in 1999 in OH.
Financial data (yr. ended 08/31/01): Grants paid, $46,450; assets, $0 (M); gifts received, $53,000; expenditures, $50,850; qualifying distributions, $46,450.
Trustees: Gail E. Walter, Stephen C. Walter.
EIN: 341885789

43349
Redwing Foundation
c/o Ethel W. Gast
2726 W. State Rte. 63
Lebanon, OH 45036

Established in 1997 in OH.
Donor(s): Ethel W. Gast.
Financial data (yr. ended 12/31/99): Grants paid, $46,284; assets, $9 (M); gifts received, $42,000; expenditures, $46,933; qualifying distributions, $46,284.
Limitations: Applications not accepted.
Application information: Contributes only to pre-selected organizations.
Officer and Trustee:* Ethel W. Gast,* Pres.
EIN: 311526551

43350
Kathryn Peters Schoeller Trust
c/o National City Bank of Pennsylvania
P.O. Box 94651
Cleveland, OH 44101-4651

Established in 1999 in PA.
Financial data (yr. ended 12/31/01): Grants paid, $46,280; assets, $930,253 (M); expenditures, $54,273; qualifying distributions, $46,280.
Limitations: Applications not accepted. Giving primarily in PA.
Application information: Contributes only to pre-selected organizations.
Trustee: National City Bank.
EIN: 256369182

43351
Stanley-Higgins Trust
c/o KeyBank, N.A.
800 Superior Ave. E., 4th Fl.
Cleveland, OH 44114-2601

Established in 1985 in ME.
Financial data (yr. ended 08/31/01): Grants paid, $46,180; assets, $1,319,783 (M); expenditures, $57,484; qualifying distributions, $46,180.
Limitations: Applications not accepted. Giving limited to Bangor, ME.
Application information: Contributes only to pre-selected organizations.
Trustee: KeyBank, N.A.
EIN: 016078824

43352
The Henry B. Kreuzman Family Foundation
7877 Calderwood Ln.
Cincinnati, OH 45243

Established in 1998 in OH.
Donor(s): Dorothy R. Kreuzman, Henry B. Kreuzman.
Financial data (yr. ended 12/31/01): Grants paid, $46,000; assets, $1,145,155 (M); gifts received, $1,397; expenditures, $50,060; qualifying distributions, $46,000.
Limitations: Applications not accepted.
Application information: Contributes only to pre-selected organizations.
Officers and Trustees:* Deborah A. Gladstone,* Pres.; Denise K. Lorenz,* Secy.; Dianne K. Hill,* Treas.; Henry B. Kreuzman III, Joseph L. Kreuzman.
EIN: 311604785

43353
LaRue Foundation
(Formerly Patrick S. Palmer Foundation)
c/o KeyBank, N.A., Trust Div.
800 Superior Ave., 4th Fl.
Cleveland, OH 44114 (216) 828-9770

Established in 1967.
Donor(s): Patrick S. Parker.
Financial data (yr. ended 12/31/01): Grants paid, $46,000; assets, $877,036 (M); expenditures, $59,060; qualifying distributions, $46,000.
Limitations: Applications not accepted. Giving limited to the Cleveland, OH, area.
Application information: Contributes only to pre-selected organizations.
Director: Ralph P. Higgins.
Trustee: KeyBank, N.A.
EIN: 956193293

43354
Daniel L. & Sophie K. Reiber Charitable Trust
874 Beechers Brook Rd.
Cleveland, OH 44143-3411

Established in 2000 in OH.
Financial data (yr. ended 12/31/01): Grants paid, $46,000; assets, $705,084 (M); gifts received, $750; expenditures, $59,959; qualifying distributions, $46,000.
Trustees: Gaye Laurell, Daniel J. Reiber, Evan Mattoon Reiber.
EIN: 226823891

43355
Harry J. & Claire S. Dworkin Foundation
101 Park Ave.
Box 187
Amherst, OH 44001-2229

Established in 1985 in OH.
Donor(s): Harry J. Dworkin.
Financial data (yr. ended 12/31/01): Grants paid, $45,952; assets, $86,889 (M); expenditures, $47,393; qualifying distributions, $45,952.
Limitations: Applications not accepted. Giving primarily in Cleveland, OH.
Trustee: Jonathan Dworkin.
EIN: 346540579

43356
The Helen T. Andrews Foundation
c/o Fifth Third Bank
38 Fountain Sq. Plz., Dept. 00858
Cincinnati, OH 45263

Established in 1992 in OH.
Donor(s): Helen T. Andrews.
Financial data (yr. ended 09/30/01): Grants paid, $45,350; assets, $410 (M); gifts received, $6,359; expenditures, $46,197; qualifying distributions, $45,350.
Limitations: Giving primarily in Cincinnati, OH.
Trustee: Fifth Third Bank.
EIN: 316453990

43357
Ralph and Rose Marie DeMange Charitable Trust
6870 Adamwald Ct.
Dayton, OH 45459-1350

Established in 1999 in OH.
Financial data (yr. ended 12/31/99): Grants paid, $45,100; assets, $5,967 (M); gifts received, $50,497; expenditures, $45,271; qualifying distributions, $46,814.
Limitations: Applications not accepted.
Application information: Contributes only to pre-selected organizations.
Trustee: Rose Marie DeMange.
EIN: 311480578

43358
The Percy Edwards Browning Foundation, Inc.
c/o U.S. Bank, ML CN-WN-07IV
P.O. Box 1118
Cincinnati, OH 45201

Established in 2000 in OH.
Donor(s): Priscilla E. Browning.
Financial data (yr. ended 12/31/01): Grants paid, $45,000; assets, $149,935 (M); gifts received, $77,135; expenditures, $49,062; qualifying distributions, $45,000.
Limitations: Applications not accepted.
Application information: Contributes only to pre-selected organizations.
Officers and Trustees:* Janet L. Houston,* Pres.; Patricia K. Wolf,* Secy.; James McNeal,* Treas.
EIN: 311691436

43359
Deupree Family Foundation
1242 E. Lytle-Five Points Rd.
Dayton, OH 45458 (937) 885-1682
Contact: Caleb T. Deupree, Treas.

Established in 2000 in OH.
Donor(s): Ann T. Deupree.
Financial data (yr. ended 06/30/01): Grants paid, $45,000; assets, $2,531,997 (M); gifts received, $2,701,427; expenditures, $50,566; qualifying distributions, $45,166.
Limitations: Giving primarily in the Midwest.
Application information: Application form required.
Officers and Trustees:* Ann T. Deupree,* Pres.; Susan D. Jones,* V.P.; Thomas R. Deupree,* Secy.; Caleb T. Deupree,* Treas.; Richard R. Deupree III.
EIN: 311746946

43360
The Edward and Elizabeth Gardner Foundation
c/o Elizabeth Paxton Gardner
50 E. 3rd St.
Dayton, OH 45402

Established in 1991 in OH.
Donor(s): Elizabeth Paxton Gardner.
Financial data (yr. ended 12/31/01): Grants paid, $45,000; assets, $660,704 (M); expenditures, $49,790; qualifying distributions, $44,848.
Limitations: Applications not accepted. Giving on a national basis, with emphasis on the Northeast.
Application information: Contributes only to pre-selected organizations.
Officers and Trustees:* Elizabeth Paxton Gardner,* Pres.; Edward T. Gardner,* V.P.; Ames Gardner, Jr.,* Secy.-Treas.
EIN: 311338344

43361
James H. Hader & Evelyn E. Hader Trust
c/o U.S. Bank
P.O. Box 1118
Cincinnati, OH 45201-1118

Established in 1997 in OH.
Financial data (yr. ended 12/31/01): Grants paid, $45,000; assets, $731,290 (M); expenditures, $49,639; qualifying distributions, $45,000.
Limitations: Applications not accepted. Giving primarily in Cincinnati, OH.
Application information: Contributes only to pre-selected organizations.
Trustees: Evelyn E. Hader, James E. Hader, Frederic J. Robbins.
EIN: 311579517

43362
C. Raymond Selker Charitable Foundation
c/o National City Bank of Pennsylvania
P.O. Box 94651
Cleveland, OH 44101-4651

Established in 1998 in PA.
Financial data (yr. ended 12/31/01): Grants paid, $45,000; assets, $933,712 (M); expenditures, $53,177; qualifying distributions, $45,000.
Limitations: Applications not accepted. Giving primarily in Clarion, PA.
Application information: Contributes only to pre-selected organizations.
Trustee: National City Bank.
Committee Members: Richard L. Lewis, Keith McFadden, Henry Ray Pope III, James Rutkowski, Thomas A. Wenner.
EIN: 237934113

43363
Kertesz Family Foundation
c/o Ronnie M. Kertesz
3435 W. Brainard Rd., Ste. 260
Woodmere, OH 44122

Established in 1994 in OH.
Financial data (yr. ended 12/31/01): Grants paid, $44,830; assets, $987,344 (M); expenditures, $53,449; qualifying distributions, $44,830.
Limitations: Applications not accepted.
Application information: Contributes only to pre-selected organizations.
Directors: Alex Kertesz, Randy Kertesz, Ronnie Kertesz.
EIN: 341700552

43364
The Carl H. Rosner Foundation
c/o Keybank, N.A.
800 Superior Ave., 4th Fl.
Cleveland, OH 44146

Established in 2000 in NY.
Donor(s): Carl H. Rosner.
Financial data (yr. ended 12/31/01): Grants paid, $44,750; assets, $1,829 (M); gifts received, $46,586; expenditures, $44,757; qualifying distributions, $44,750.
Limitations: Applications not accepted.
Application information: Contributes only to pre-selected organizations.
Trustees: Carl H. Rosner, Keybank, N.A.
EIN: 527156143

43365
Taylor-Winfield Foundation
c/o Second National Bank of Warren
108 Main St. S.W.
Warren, OH 44481-1058
Application address: c/o Taylor-Winfield Corp., Hubbard, OH 44425

Financial data (yr. ended 12/31/01): Grants paid, $44,750; assets, $902,514 (M); expenditures, $54,604; qualifying distributions, $44,750.
Limitations: Giving primarily in Warren and Columbus, OH.
Trustee: Second National Bank of Warren.
EIN: 346505032

43366
Henry, Bertha & Edward Rothman Foundation
2496 Beachwood Blvd.
Beachwood, OH 44122-1547
Contact: Jordan Lefko, Tr.

Financial data (yr. ended 12/31/00): Grants paid, $44,700; assets, $811,072 (M); expenditures, $49,128; qualifying distributions, $44,700.
Limitations: Giving primarily in New York, NY.
Application information: Application form not required.
Trustees: Jordan Lefko, Bernard Rothman, Henry Rothman.
EIN: 316030079

43367
Monroe Sturgell Towler Educational Foundation
c/o Banknorth Investment Management Group, N.A.
138 Putnam St.
Marietta, OH 45750

Established in 2001 in KY.
Donor(s): Ethel Lynn Monroe.‡
Financial data (yr. ended 12/31/01): Grants paid, $44,667; assets, $1,030,102 (M); gifts received, $1,297,626; expenditures, $76,932; qualifying distributions, $74,667.
Scholarship Committee: Mary Graham Burton, James Lyon, Jr., Michael C. Wilson.
Trustee: Banknorth Investment Management Group, N.A.
EIN: 611355728

43368
The Elson Family Charitable Trust
3645 Whitehouse Spencer Rd.
Swanton, OH 43558

Established in 1995.
Financial data (yr. ended 12/31/00): Grants paid, $44,200; assets, $1,543,410 (M); expenditures, $100,010; qualifying distributions, $44,200.
Limitations: Applications not accepted.
Application information: Contributes only to pre-selected organizations.
Trustee: Donald Croy.
EIN: 346855820

43369
Harry and Anne Mestel Foundation
116 Cleveland Ave. N.W., Ste. 525
Canton, OH 44702 (330) 452-9788
Contact: Harry Mestel, Pres.

Financial data (yr. ended 12/31/01): Grants paid, $44,175; assets, $577,216 (M); expenditures, $47,547; qualifying distributions, $44,175.
Limitations: Giving primarily in Canton, OH.
Officers: Harry Mestel, Pres.; Anne Mestel, Secy.-Treas.
Trustee: Clifford Mestel.
EIN: 341756960

43370
The Lair Family Foundation
5405 Meese Rd. N.E.
Louisville, OH 44641-9504

Established in 1987 in OH.
Donor(s): Edwin C. Lair, Esther S. Lair.‡
Financial data (yr. ended 11/30/01): Grants paid, $44,067; assets, $3,469 (M); gifts received, $23,850; expenditures, $45,012; qualifying distributions, $44,067.
Limitations: Applications not accepted. Giving primarily in OH.
Application information: Contributes only to pre-selected organizations.
Trustees: Edwin C. Lair, Pamela J. Lair.
EIN: 341574532

43371
Agnew Foundation
P.O. Box 820
Cambridge, OH 43725-0820 (614) 439-6688
Contact: H. William Davis, Pres.

Financial data (yr. ended 12/31/01): Grants paid, $44,000; assets, $634,137 (M); expenditures, $44,403; qualifying distributions, $43,835.
Limitations: Giving limited to Guernsey County, OH.
Application information: Application form required.
Officers: H. William Davis, Pres.; Fred Shimp, Secy.; Maribeth Wright, Treas.
EIN: 316077699
Codes: GTI

43372
The Herzog Family Foundation
P.O. Box 55
Ashtabula, OH 44005-0055
Contact: William R. Herzog, Treas.

Established in 1998 in OH.
Donor(s): Francis A. Herzog, Elinor M. Herzog.

Financial data (yr. ended 03/31/02): Grants paid, $44,000; assets, $866,328 (M); expenditures, $57,286; qualifying distributions, $44,000.
Limitations: Giving primarily in Ashtabula, OH.
Officers and Trustees:* Francis A. Herzog,* Chair.; Elinor M. Herzog,* Secy.; William R. Herzog,* Treas.; Francis A. Herzog, Jr., Mary L. Herzog-Andrews, John R. Lowther, Charlotte F. Osborne, Vicki M. Tyson.
EIN: 341867760

43373
The Mary and Oliver F. Emerson Foundation
21120 Brantley Rd.
Cleveland, OH 44122-1934

Established in 1988 in OH.
Donor(s): Mary Emerson.
Financial data (yr. ended 12/31/01): Grants paid, $43,985; assets, $13,271 (M); gifts received, $51,716; expenditures, $44,853; qualifying distributions, $43,531.
Limitations: Applications not accepted.
Application information: Contributes only to pre-selected organizations.
Officers: Mary Emerson, Pres.; Oliver F. Emerson, V.P. and Treas.; Scott Emerson, Secy.
EIN: 341575218

43374
The William & Virginia Stilson Foundation
7305 Stump Hollow Ln.
Chagrin Falls, OH 44022

Established in 1996 in OH.
Donor(s): Virginia A. Stilson, William C. Stilson.
Financial data (yr. ended 12/31/01): Grants paid, $43,700; assets, $225,465 (M); gifts received, $50,578; expenditures, $45,093; qualifying distributions, $43,700.
Limitations: Applications not accepted.
Application information: Contributes only to pre-selected organizations.
Officers: William C. Stilson, Pres.; Virginia A. Stilson, Secy.; William C. Stilson, Jr., Treas.
EIN: 311500615

43375
The Boymel Family Charitable Foundation
12100 Reed Hartman Hwy.
Cincinnati, OH 45241

Established in 1995 in OH.
Donor(s): Steven Boymel.
Financial data (yr. ended 12/31/99): Grants paid, $43,667; assets, $35,349 (M); gifts received, $25,000; expenditures, $44,189; qualifying distributions, $43,664.
Limitations: Applications not accepted.
Application information: Contributes only to pre-selected organizations.
Trustees: Carol Ann Boymel, Rachel Boymel, Samuel Boymel, Steven Boymel.
EIN: 316528155

43376
The Friedman-Klarreich Family Foundation
c/o SFB-Zinner & Co.
29125 Chagrin Blvd.
Beachwood, OH 44122
Application address: 551 Tyndall St., Los Altos, CA 94022; FAX: (650) 948-3148; E-mail: bkohn@aol.com; URL: http://members.aol.com/KlarFF
Contact: Susan Klarreich, Tr.

Established in 1992 in OH and CA.
Donor(s): Susan Klarreich.
Financial data (yr. ended 12/31/01): Grants paid, $43,580; assets, $497,654 (M); gifts received, $300; expenditures, $58,930; qualifying distributions, $43,580.
Limitations: Giving primarily in the San Francisco Bay Area, CA, the greater Miami, FL, area, Westchester County, NY, and the greater Cleveland, OH, area.
Trustees: Beth Klarreich Corwin, Karin Klarreich, Kathie Klarreich, Susan Klarreich, Betsy Klarreich Kohn.
EIN: 341713262

43377
John N. Browning Oregon Foundation
c/o U.S. Bank
P.O. Box 1118, ML CN-WN-10TX
Cincinnati, OH 45201-1118

Established in 1997.
Financial data (yr. ended 09/30/01): Grants paid, $43,500; assets, $633,546 (M); expenditures, $52,359; qualifying distributions, $43,707.
Limitations: Applications not accepted.
Application information: Contributes only to pre-selected organizations.
Officers and Trustees:* Florence V.M. Barnhart,* Pres.; Philip N. Barnhart,* V.P.; Laura T. Barnhart,* Treas.; Terry K. Crilley, U.S. Bank.
EIN: 311582892

43378
The Kenoyer Foundation
2544 River Rd.
Willoughby, OH 44094
Contact: Marleah J. Kenayer, Secy.

Established in 1995 in OH.
Donor(s): Quentin Kenoyer, Marleah Kenoyer.
Financial data (yr. ended 12/31/01): Grants paid, $43,500; assets, $655,871 (M); gifts received, $44,635; expenditures, $47,194; qualifying distributions, $43,500.
Limitations: Applications not accepted. Giving limited to Cleveland, OH.
Application information: Contributes only to pre-selected organizations.
Officers: Quentin Kenoyer, Pres.; Marleah J. Kenoyer, Secy.; David H. Baier, Treas.
Trustees: Kay Baier, David Hangosky, Linda Hangosky, Ann Tucker, George Tucker.
EIN: 341794082

43379
Alicia M. & William A. Miller Foundation
600 Superior Ave. E.
2100 Bank One Ctr.
Cleveland, OH 44114-2653
Application address: 39 Camino de Valle, Santa Fe, NM 87501, tel.: (505) 986-8210
Contact: William A. Miller, Pres.

Established in 2000 in OH.
Donor(s): William A. Miller, Alicia M. Miller.
Financial data (yr. ended 12/31/01): Grants paid, $43,400; assets, $392,252 (M); expenditures, $47,082; qualifying distributions, $43,400.
Officers: William A. Miller, Pres. and Treas.; Alicia M. Miller, V.P. and Secy.
EIN: 341954211

43380
The D. M. Schneider Foundation
c/o Kevin G. Robertson
1900 E. 9th St., Ste. 3200
Cleveland, OH 44114-3485

Established in 1998 in OH.
Donor(s): David M. Schneider.
Financial data (yr. ended 12/31/01): Grants paid, $43,300; assets, $733,945 (M); expenditures, $52,634; qualifying distributions, $43,300.
Limitations: Applications not accepted. Giving primarily in Cleveland, OH.
Application information: Contributes only to pre-selected organizations.
Officers and Trustees: David M. Schneider,* Pres.; Betty Schneider,* Secy.-Treas.; R. Steven Kestner.
EIN: 341866961

43381
Kinder Charitable Foundation
1340 Stonington Dr.
Youngstown, OH 44504

Financial data (yr. ended 12/31/01): Grants paid, $43,250; assets, $621,689 (M); expenditures, $43,737; qualifying distributions, $43,250.
Limitations: Applications not accepted. Giving primarily in Youngstown, OH.
Application information: Contributes only to pre-selected organizations.
Trustees: Edith Peskin, Gerald Peskin, Marvin Peskin.
EIN: 341500608

43382
The CBC Foundation
2550 Som Center Rd., Ste. 370
Willoughby, OH 44094

Established in 1999 in OH.
Donor(s): Michael Sherwin.
Financial data (yr. ended 12/31/01): Grants paid, $43,000; assets, $772,348 (M); expenditures, $50,609; qualifying distributions, $43,000.
Limitations: Applications not accepted. Giving on a national basis, with emphasis on OH.
Application information: Contributes only to pre-selected organizations.
Officers and Trustees:* Michael Sherwin,* Pres.; Roberta W. Laps, Secy.-Treas.; Carol L. Sherwin, Martha S. Sherwin, Michael J. Sherwin.
EIN: 341904019

43383
Thomas E. Reynolds Charitable Trust
c/o Citizens National Bank of Norwalk
12 E. Main St.
Norwalk, OH 44857
Contact: David Nocjar, V.P. and Trust Off., Citizens National Bank of Norwalk

Financial data (yr. ended 12/31/01): Grants paid, $43,000; assets, $852,941 (M); expenditures, $52,285; qualifying distributions, $43,000.
Limitations: Giving primarily in OH.
Advisory Committee Members: Dennis Doughty, Charles J. Hipp, Roland Reed.
Trustee: Citizens National Bank.
EIN: 346656480

43384
Charles A. Rini Charitable Trust
c/o KeyBank, N.A.
800 Superior Ave., 4th Fl.
Cleveland, OH 44114

Established in 1997 in OH.
Donor(s): Charles A. Rini.
Financial data (yr. ended 12/31/01): Grants paid, $43,000; assets, $713,317 (M); expenditures, $52,197; qualifying distributions, $45,510.
Limitations: Applications not accepted. Giving primarily in Cleveland, OH.
Application information: Contributes only to pre-selected organizations.
Trustees: Charles A. Rini, Martha Rini, KeyBank, N.A.
EIN: 316563675

43385
Marbeach Foundation
30201 Aurora Rd.
Solon, OH 44139

Financial data (yr. ended 12/31/01): Grants paid, $42,900; assets, $1,048,687 (M); expenditures, $45,078; qualifying distributions, $42,900.
Officers: Albert Gordon, Pres.; Lillian Gordon, V.P.; Debra Gordon Hoffmann, Secy.
EIN: 311604466

43386
Thomas L., Myrtle R., Arch and Eva Alexander Scholarship Fund
c/o Fifth Third Bank
MD 1COM31
Cincinnati, OH 45263
Application address: c/o Posey County School Districts, Posey County, IN 47620-0543, tel.: (812) 838-4333

Financial data (yr. ended 02/28/02): Grants paid, $42,800; assets, $1,137,949 (M); expenditures, $59,488; qualifying distributions, $47,258.
Limitations: Giving limited to Posey County, IN.
Application information: Recipients are selected by their respective high schools. Application form required.
Trustees: Hawley, Hudson & Hawley, Citizens Trust Co.
EIN: 356333739
Codes: GTI

43387
The Dupps Company Charitable Foundation
548 N. Cherry St.
P. O. Box 189
Germantown, OH 45327

Established in 1996 in OH.
Donor(s): Dupps Co.
Financial data (yr. ended 12/31/01): Grants paid, $42,654; assets, $109,400 (M); gifts received, $10,000; expenditures, $44,455; qualifying distributions, $42,606.
Limitations: Applications not accepted. Giving primarily in OH.
Application information: Contributes only to pre-selected organizations.
Trustees: David M. Dupps, Frank N. Dupps, John A. Dupps, Jr.
EIN: 311450495
Codes: CS, CD

43388
The Floyd A. Day and Gladys I. Day Family Foundation
3300 BP America Bldg.
200 Public Sq.
Cleveland, OH 44114

Established in 1987 in OH.
Donor(s): Gladys I. Day.
Financial data (yr. ended 12/31/01): Grants paid, $42,500; assets, $714,496 (M); expenditures, $56,329; qualifying distributions, $42,500.
Limitations: Applications not accepted. Giving primarily in OH.
Application information: Contributes only to pre-selected organizations.
Officers and Trustees:* Ralph P. Day,* V.P.; Raymond A. Day,* V.P.; Marilyn J. Jones,* Secy.; Myron R. Day,* Treas.; Virginia L. Walker.
EIN: 341533500

43389
The Gallia County Charitable Foundation
2219 E. Bethel Church Rd.
Gallipolis, OH 45631

Donor(s): Cynthia Eubanks,‡ John M. Weed.‡
Financial data (yr. ended 12/31/00): Grants paid, $42,500; assets, $860,275 (M); gifts received, $1,000; expenditures, $1,719; qualifying distributions, $0.
Limitations: Applications not accepted. Giving primarily in Gallipolis, OH.
Application information: Contributes only to pre-selected organizations.
Officers: William H. Lloyd, Pres.; Thomas S. Moulton, Secy.; Henrietta C. Evans, Treas.
Director: D. Dean Evans.
EIN: 912048725

43390
Pathfinder Fund
c/o T.L. Goudvis
43075 N. Ridge Rd.
Elyria, OH 44035

Financial data (yr. ended 12/31/01): Grants paid, $42,400; assets, $456,970 (M); expenditures, $43,671; qualifying distributions, $42,400.
Limitations: Applications not accepted. Giving primarily in CO.
Application information: Contributes only to pre-selected organizations.
Trustee: T.L. Goudvis.
EIN: 346536633

43391
Mattlin Foundation
2980 Linkbury Ln.
Columbus, OH 43221-2549 (614) 488-3226
Contact: Jane E. Mattlin, Tr.

Donor(s): Betty L. Mattlin.
Financial data (yr. ended 12/31/01): Grants paid, $42,151; assets, $863,495 (M); gifts received, $53,020; expenditures, $46,976; qualifying distributions, $42,151.
Limitations: Giving primarily in Columbus, OH.
Trustees: Betty L. Mattlin, Jane E. Mattlin, Richard I. Mattlin.
EIN: 316027872

43392
Art Iron Foundation
P.O. Box 364
Toledo, OH 43697-0964

Established in 1951 in OH.
Donor(s): Herman H. Schlatter.
Financial data (yr. ended 12/31/01): Grants paid, $42,000; assets, $960,052 (M); expenditures, $48,423; qualifying distributions, $42,000.
Limitations: Applications not accepted. Giving primarily in Toledo, OH.
Application information: Contributes only to pre-selected organizations.
Trustees: Melvin F. Retcher, Donald A. Schlatter, Herman H. Schlatter.
EIN: 346516469

43393
The Robert F. Busbey Charitable Foundation, Inc.
6350 Eastland Rd., Ste. B
Brookpark, OH 44142
Contact: Thomas P. Meehan, Secy.

Established in 1999 in OH. Funded in 2000.
Financial data (yr. ended 12/31/01): Grants paid, $42,000; assets, $695,250 (M); expenditures, $43,760; qualifying distributions, $42,000.
Application information: Application form not required.
Officers and Trustees:* Robert F. Busbey,* Pres.; Joseph D. Kaderabek,* V.P.; Thomas P. Meehan,* Secy.; George W. Morton,* Treas.
EIN: 341908504

43394
The Myron Fishel Scholarship Trust
c/o U.S. Bank
P.O. Box 400
Cambridge, OH 43725-0400 (740) 432-1334
Application address: 819 Wheeling Ave., Cambridge, OH 43725
Contact: Jeffrey C. East, Tr.

Financial data (yr. ended 09/30/01): Grants paid, $42,000; assets, $650,259 (M); gifts received, $151,977; expenditures, $44,630; qualifying distributions, $44,630.
Limitations: Giving limited to residents of OH.
Application information: Recipients are recommended to the trustees, or are selected by the trustees personally. Application form required.
Trustees: Jeffrey C. East, C. Keith Plummer, Blaise Urbanowicz.
EIN: 237407789
Codes: GTI

43395
Edward V. and Jessie L. Peters Charitable Trust
c/o National City Bank of Pennsylvania
P.O. Box 94651
Cleveland, OH 44101-4651
Application address: P.O. Box 318, Oil City Trust Off., PA 16301, tel.: (814) 678-3625
Contact: Susan K. Betz, Trust Off., National City Bank of Pennsylvania

Established in 1990 in PA.
Donor(s): Jessie L. Peters.
Financial data (yr. ended 12/31/01): Grants paid, $42,000; assets, $6,346,664 (M); gifts received, $2,754,181; expenditures, $55,383; qualifying distributions, $42,000.
Limitations: Giving primarily in PA.
Trustees: Joyce I. Hughes, Michael F. Hughes, National City Bank.
EIN: 256358729

43396
Edith M. Timken Family Foundation
200 Market Ave. N., Ste. 210
Canton, OH 44702-1437 (330) 452-1144
Contact: Don D. Dickes, Secy.-Treas.

Established in 1985 in OH.
Donor(s): Edith M. Timken, Mary J. Timken, W.R. Timken.‡
Financial data (yr. ended 09/30/01): Grants paid, $42,000; assets, $939,728 (M); expenditures, $43,991; qualifying distributions, $42,650.
Limitations: Giving primarily in Pomfret, CT.
Application information: Application form not required.
Officers and Trustees:* Edith M. Timken,* Pres.; W.R. Timken, Jr.,* V.P.; Don D. Dickes,* Secy.-Treas.
EIN: 341524586

43397
The Dorjac Foundation
6255 Sodom-Hutchings Rd.
Girard, OH 44420

Established in 1987 in OH.
Financial data (yr. ended 12/31/01): Grants paid, $41,682; assets, $299,795 (M); expenditures, $41,937; qualifying distributions, $40,930.
Limitations: Applications not accepted. Giving primarily in OH.

Application information: Contributes only to pre-selected organizations.
Officers: Jack B. Tamarkin, Pres.; Jerry P. Tamarkin, V.P.; Doris O. Tamarkin, Secy.-Treas.
EIN: 341540019

43398
Jane Friedman Anspach Family Foundation, Inc.
405 Madison Ave., Ste. 2100
Toledo, OH 43604
Contact: Jane Friedman Anspach, Dir.

Established in 1999 in OH.
Financial data (yr. ended 12/31/01): Grants paid, $41,500; assets, $977,300 (M); expenditures, $47,299; qualifying distributions, $41,500.
Directors: Jane Friedman Anspach, Robert M. Anspach, Robert G. Friedman.
EIN: 582462405

43399
The Roy and Patricia Begley Foundation
c/o Roy William Begley, Jr.
34 N. Main St., 11th Fl.
Dayton, OH 45402

Established in 1999 in OH.
Donor(s): Patricia Begley, Roy Begley.
Financial data (yr. ended 12/31/01): Grants paid, $41,500; assets, $675,599 (M); gifts received, $150,000; expenditures, $45,965; qualifying distributions, $41,500.
Limitations: Applications not accepted. Giving primarily in Dayton, OH.
Application information: Contributes only to pre-selected organizations.
Officers and Trustees:* Roy W. Begley,* Pres.; Patricia L. Begley,* V.P.; Roy William Begley, Jr., Secy.-Treas.
EIN: 311682886

43400
The Raymond and Rita Foos Family Charitable Foundation
30972 Pinehurst Dr.
Westlake, OH 44145
Florida tel.: (941) 598-2310
Contact: Raymond A. Foos, Pres.

Established in OH in 1997.
Donor(s): Raymond A. Foos.
Financial data (yr. ended 12/31/01): Grants paid, $41,000; assets, $736,888 (M); gifts received, $9,500; expenditures, $44,772; qualifying distributions, $40,960.
Officers: Raymond A. Foos, Pres.; Rita Foos, V.P.; Catherine M. Tasi, Secy.; Kevin C. Foos, Treas.
EIN: 311529311

43401
Nabama Foundation
c/o Barbara Mather Stross
P.O. Box 54233
Cincinnati, OH 45254-0233

Donor(s): Neil H. McElroy,‡ Camilla F. McElroy.‡
Financial data (yr. ended 01/31/02): Grants paid, $40,993; assets, $785,210 (M); expenditures, $43,036; qualifying distributions, $40,993.
Limitations: Applications not accepted. Giving primarily in Cincinnati, OH.
Application information: Contributes only to pre-selected organizations.
Trustees: Nancy McElroy Folger, Lori W. McElroy, Malcolm N. McElroy.
EIN: 316033919

43402
The Hayden Foundation
7000 Midland Blvd.
Amelia, OH 45102-2607

Financial data (yr. ended 12/31/01): Grants paid, $40,930; assets, $812,989 (M); expenditures, $46,373; qualifying distributions, $39,732.
Limitations: Applications not accepted. Giving primarily in Cincinnati, OH.
Application information: Contributes only to pre-selected organizations.
Officers: Joseph P. Hayden, Jr., Pres.; Mark E. Burke, Secy.
Trustees: Michael J. Conaton, John I. Von Lehman.
EIN: 316024537

43403
Ada M. Rogers Trust
(also known as Bruce & Mary Rogers Memorial Student Loan Fund)
c/o Sky Trust, N.A., Trust Dept.
P.O. Box 479
Youngstown, OH 44501-0479
Application address: c/o Rev. James L. Unger, Western Reserve Baptist Church, 8590 Hitchcock Rd., Youngstown, OH 44512

Donor(s): Ada M. Rogers.‡
Financial data (yr. ended 08/31/01): Grants paid, $40,779; assets, $375,291 (M); expenditures, $47,681; qualifying distributions, $40,779.
Limitations: Giving primarily in OH.
Application information: Application form required.
Officer: Rev. James L. Unger, Mgr.
Trustee: Sky Trust, N.A.
EIN: 346631957
Codes: GTI

43404
The Knight Family Foundation
c/o MAI, IMG Ctr.
1360 E. 9th St., Ste. 100
Cleveland, OH 44114-1782

Established in 1999 in OH.
Donor(s): Lester B. Knight III.
Financial data (yr. ended 12/31/01): Grants paid, $40,600; assets, $836,649 (M); expenditures, $40,968; qualifying distributions, $40,600.
Limitations: Applications not accepted.
Application information: Contributes only to pre-selected organizations.
Officers: Rebecca Knight, Pres.; Lester B. Knight III, V.P. and Treas.; Anthony Decello, Secy.
EIN: 341911247

43405
The Welty Family Foundation
3595 N. Fork Dr.
Akron, OH 44333

Established in 1999 in OH.
Donor(s): Jerry H. Welty.
Financial data (yr. ended 12/31/01): Grants paid, $40,416; assets, $1,241,749 (M); expenditures, $69,177; qualifying distributions, $40,416.
Limitations: Applications not accepted.
Application information: Contributes only to pre-selected organizations.
Officers: Jerry H. Welty, Pres.; Emily C. Welty, V.P.; Jeffrey T. Heintz, Secy.-Treas.
Trustees: Richard C. Feddrovich, Chad C. Welty, Monica D. Welty, Joseph Wojcik.
EIN: 341908053

43406
Lena P. Frederick Trust Fund
c/o KeyBank, N.A., Trust Div.
800 Superior Ave., 4th Fl.
Cleveland, OH 44114
Application address: c/o Christina Cook, KeyBank, N.A., 286 Water St., Augusta, ME 04330

Donor(s): Lena P. Frederick.‡
Financial data (yr. ended 04/30/01): Grants paid, $40,343; assets, $548,142 (M); expenditures, $48,842; qualifying distributions, $39,906.
Limitations: Giving limited to residents of Belfast, ME.
Trustee: KeyBank, N.A.
EIN: 016010164
Codes: GTI

43407
The Jack Family Foundation, Inc.
22225 Parnell Rd.
Shaker Heights, OH 44122

Established in 1989 in OH.
Donor(s): Donald M. Jack, Jr.
Financial data (yr. ended 12/31/01): Grants paid, $40,230; assets, $354,940 (M); gifts received, $50,951; expenditures, $40,740; qualifying distributions, $40,587.
Limitations: Applications not accepted. Giving primarily in Cleveland, OH.
Application information: Contributes only to pre-selected organizations.
Officers: Donald M. Jack, Jr., Pres.; Craig M. Jack, V.P.; Marta L. Jack, Secy.; Douglas L. Jack, Treas.
EIN: 346919621

43408
Dallas W. Bowyer Trust
c/o Fifth Third Bank
38 Fountain Sq. Plz., Ste. ICOM31
Cincinnati, OH 45263
Contact: Lawra Baumann, Trust Off., Fifth Third Bank

Financial data (yr. ended 09/30/01): Grants paid, $40,040; assets, $639,544 (M); expenditures, $50,486; qualifying distributions, $42,499.
Limitations: Giving limited to the greater Cincinnati, OH, area.
Application information: Application form not required.
Trustee: Fifth Third Bank.
EIN: 316450751

43409
The Edward J. DeBartolo Memorial Scholarship Foundation
7620 Market St.
P.O. Box 9128
Youngstown, OH 44513-9128 (330) 965-2000
Contact: Cindy Miller, Appl. Secy.

Established in 1998 in OH.
Donor(s): Edward J. DeBartolo, Jr., Marie Denise DeBartolo-York.
Financial data (yr. ended 12/31/00): Grants paid, $40,000; assets, $488,157 (M); gifts received, $141,571; expenditures, $83,685; qualifying distributions, $39,731.
Limitations: Giving limited to Youngstown, OH.
Application information: Application form required.
Trustees: Edward J. DeBartolo, Jr., Marie Denise DeBartolo-York, A. W. Liberati, F. Ronald Mastriana.
EIN: 311527910

43410
Descanso Foundation
c/o Chess Financial
30050 Chagrin Blvd., Ste. 100
Pepper Pike, OH 44124

Established in 2000 in OH.
Donor(s): Nancy P. Keithley.
Financial data (yr. ended 12/31/00): Grants paid, $40,000; assets, $5,912,359 (M); gifts received, $950,172; expenditures, $43,294; qualifying distributions, $40,000.
Limitations: Applications not accepted.
Application information: Contributes only to pre-selected organizations.
Officers and Trustee:* Elizabeth M. Keithley,* Pres.; James B. Griswold, Secy.; John D. Olsen, Treas.
EIN: 341927735

43411
James W. & Kitty Lee Hardin Foundation
c/o PNC Advisors
201 E. 5th St.
Cincinnati, OH 45201-1198 (513) 651-8413
Contact: James D. Huizenga, V.P. and Trust Off., PNC Advisors

Established in 1997 in GA.
Donor(s): James W. Hardin, Kitty Lee Hardin.
Financial data (yr. ended 12/31/01): Grants paid, $40,000; assets, $666,093 (M); expenditures, $46,592; qualifying distributions, $40,000.
Officers: James W. Hardin, Pres. and Treas.; Kitty Lee Hardin, V.P. and Secy.
EIN: 582317866

43412
Kuhns Brothers Company Foundation
1173 E. Lyons Rd.
Dayton, OH 45458

Donor(s): Kuhns Investment Co.
Financial data (yr. ended 12/31/01): Grants paid, $40,000; assets, $786,387 (M); expenditures, $50,899; qualifying distributions, $47,627.
Limitations: Applications not accepted. Giving primarily in the Montgomery County, OH, area.
Application information: Generally, continued support of prior assisted organizations before assisting additional new organizations.
Trustees: J.M. Johnson, C.L. Scheibert, J.A. Stanton.
EIN: 316023926
Codes: CS, CD

43413
Mann Family Foundation
c/o Sterling
3550 Lander Rd.
Pepper Pike, OH 44124

Established in 2000 in FL.
Donor(s): Frances M. Mann, Marvin L. Mann.
Financial data (yr. ended 12/31/01): Grants paid, $40,000; assets, $96,619 (M); gifts received, $76,062; expenditures, $40,483; qualifying distributions, $39,487.
Limitations: Applications not accepted. Giving primarily in AL, CT, and FL.
Application information: Contributes only to pre-selected organizations.
Trustees: Frances M. Mann, Marvin L. Mann.
EIN: 597182150

43414
Mack Snyder Rau Foundation
c/o R.A. Bumblis
1900 E. 9th St., Ste. 3200
Cleveland, OH 44114-3485
Contact: Peter W. Vogt, Treas.

Established in 1985 in OH.
Donor(s): Mark Snyder Rau Charitable Lead Trust.
Financial data (yr. ended 12/31/00): Grants paid, $40,000; assets, $1,106,170 (M); gifts received, $201,887; expenditures, $40,000; qualifying distributions, $40,000.
Limitations: Applications not accepted. Giving primarily in CA and FL.
Application information: Contributes only to pre-selected organizations.
Officers and Trustees:* Alice W. Bott,* Pres.; Susan W. Pangborn,* Secy.; Peter W. Vogt,* Treas.; David A. Rau, Norman Dean Rau, Edward Weil.
EIN: 341489556

43415
Brauchler-Collins Charitable Foundation
c/o John Collins
4100 Cleveland Ave., N.W.
Canton, OH 44709

Established in 1995 in OH.
Donor(s): John Collins.
Financial data (yr. ended 12/31/01): Grants paid, $39,940; assets, $874,228 (M); expenditures, $48,963; qualifying distributions, $39,940.
Limitations: Applications not accepted. Giving primarily in OH.
Application information: Contributes only to pre-selected organizations.
Trustees: Elizabeth Collins, John Collins, Katherine Collins.
EIN: 341785330

43416
Hardin County Community Foundation
c/o William D. Hart
P.O. Box 343
Kenton, OH 43326-0343

Established in 1991 in OH.
Donor(s): Victor Colmey, Virginia Colmey, J. Thomas Stout, Eula D. Hirsch.
Financial data (yr. ended 12/31/00): Grants paid, $39,937; assets, $832,916 (M); gifts received, $17,797; expenditures, $47,198.
Limitations: Giving primarily in Hardin County, OH.
Officers: John F. Jester, Pres.; C. Richard Hubbard, V.P.; Russell E. Berger, Secy.-Treas.
EIN: 311335053
Codes: CM

43417
Alpha & Inez Philbin Memorial Charitable Trust
c/o KeyBank, N.A., Trust Div.
P.O. Box 10099
Toledo, OH 43699-0099

Established in 1999 in OH.
Donor(s): Philbin Annuity Trust.
Financial data (yr. ended 03/31/02): Grants paid, $39,762; assets, $861,459 (M); expenditures, $44,991; qualifying distributions, $39,762.
Limitations: Applications not accepted. Giving primarily in Bucyrus, OH.
Application information: Contributes only to pre-selected organizations.
Trustee: KeyBank, N.A.
EIN: 341909146

43418
The Grimm Family Foundation
2675 Som Ctr. Rd.
Hunting Valley, OH 44022
Contact: Richard S. Grimm, Pres.

Established in 1997 in OH.
Donor(s): Richard S. Grimm.
Financial data (yr. ended 12/31/01): Grants paid, $39,700; assets, $860,231 (M); expenditures, $40,833; qualifying distributions, $39,700.
Officers: Richard S. Grimm, Pres.; Susan M. Grimm, Secy.-Treas.
Trustees: Jonathon L. Grimm, Scott S. Grimm, Thomas A. Grimm, Christine G. Hill, Scott R. Hill, Kathryn Wilson.
EIN: 311532275

43419
Steven and Jacqueline Miller Family Foundation
P.O. Box 37429
Cincinnati, OH 45222-0429

Financial data (yr. ended 12/31/00): Grants paid, $39,525; assets, $640,195 (M); expenditures, $41,083; qualifying distributions, $39,525.
Limitations: Applications not accepted.
Application information: Contributes only to pre-selected organizations.
Directors: Jacqueline Miller, Steven Miller.
EIN: 316308801

43420
George R. Gardner Foundation, Inc.
c/o U.S. Bank
910 W. Main St.
Troy, OH 45373
Contact: Thomas J. Kleptz, Tr.

Established in 1991 in OH.
Donor(s): George R. Gardner.‡
Financial data (yr. ended 09/30/01): Grants paid, $39,500; assets, $566,709 (M); expenditures, $46,886; qualifying distributions, $41,610.
Limitations: Giving on a national basis.
Officers: John R. Gardner, Pres.; Bruce A. Gardner, Treas.
Trustee: Kathleen S. Helle, Thomas J. Kleptz.
EIN: 311340457

43421
Alfaretta Young Trust
c/o National City Bank
P.O. Box 94651
Cleveland, OH 44101-4651

Established in 2001 in IL.
Financial data (yr. ended 12/31/01): Grants paid, $39,500; assets, $1,022,979 (M); expenditures, $41,125; qualifying distributions, $40,320.
Limitations: Applications not accepted. Giving primarily in IL, VA, and WI.
Application information: Contributes only to pre-selected organizations.
Trustee: National City Bank.
EIN: 366777452

43422
Lydia Schauer Memorial Trust Fund
507 S. Broadway
Greenville, OH 45331 (937) 548-1157
Contact: Thomas C. Hanes, Tr.

Established in 1989 in OH.
Donor(s): Lydia Schaurer.‡
Financial data (yr. ended 09/30/01): Grants paid, $39,444; assets, $1,064,203 (M); expenditures, $52,372; qualifying distributions, $39,444.
Limitations: Giving limited to Darke County, OH.
Trustees: James L. Bixler, Robert L. Fowble, Thomas C. Hanes.

EIN: 341651151

43423
Robert O. and AnnaMae Orr Family Foundation
c/o FirstMerit Bank, N.A.
121 S. Main St., Ste. 200
Akron, OH 44308-1418
Contact: Philip N. Murray, Attorney, FirstMerit Bank, N.A.

Established in 1998 in OH.
Donor(s): Robert Orr.
Financial data (yr. ended 05/31/01): Grants paid, $39,405; assets, $742,927 (M); expenditures, $61,257; qualifying distributions, $44,470.
Limitations: Giving primarily in OH.
Officer and Trustees:* Robert Orr,* Chair.; Bruce H. Buchholzer, Philip W. Murray, FirstMerit Bank, N.A.
EIN: 341867983

43424
Feckley Charitable Foundation
c/o FirstMerit Bank, N.A.
P.O. Box 725
Medina, OH 44258 (330) 722-5555
Contact: Donald M. Mikscho, Trust Off., FirstMerit Bank, N.A.

Established in 1990 in OH.
Donor(s): Dorothy Feckley Trust.
Financial data (yr. ended 12/31/01): Grants paid, $39,231; assets, $750,438 (M); expenditures, $49,389; qualifying distributions, $39,231.
Limitations: Giving limited to Medina County, OH.
Advisory Committee: Medina Noon Kiwanis, Pres.; William B. Young.
Trustee: FirstMerit Bank, N.A.
EIN: 341666103

43425
Tempa F. Bevington Adult Education
c/o National City Bank
P.O. Box 94651
Cleveland, OH 44101-4651
Application address: 301 S.W. Adams St., Peoria, IL 61602-1500, tel.: (309) 655-5385
Contact: Jo Ann Harlan

Established in 2001 in IL.
Financial data (yr. ended 12/31/01): Grants paid, $39,097; assets, $169,187 (M); expenditures, $40,120; qualifying distributions, $39,616.
Limitations: Giving limited to residents of Danvers, IL.
Trustee: National City Bank.
EIN: 367189588

43426
Evelyn W. Dunn Charitable Trust
900 Central Trust Tower
Cincinnati, OH 45202 (513) 381-9200
Contact: J. Kenneth Meagher, Tr.

Established in 1995 in OH.
Financial data (yr. ended 12/31/01): Grants paid, $39,000; assets, $778,226 (L); expenditures, $56,025; qualifying distributions, $55,905.
Limitations: Giving primarily in Cincinnati, OH.
Trustee: J. Kenneth Meagher.
EIN: 311418808

43427
Fisher Foundation
7711 Creekwood Ln.
Cincinnati, OH 45237-1713

Established in 1998 in OH.
Donor(s): members of the Fisher family.
Financial data (yr. ended 12/31/01): Grants paid, $38,907; assets, $1,185,539 (M); gifts received, $254,671; expenditures, $58,457; qualifying distributions, $38,907.
Officers: Melvyn Fisher, Pres. and Secy.-Treas.; David Fisher, V.P.; Marc Fisher, V.P.; Michael Fisher, V.P.; Robert Fisher, V.P.; Roberta Fisher, V.P.
EIN: 311625356

43428
Gibson Foundation, Inc.
c/o Mary Kay Icandela
1 American Rd.
Cleveland, OH 44144 (216) 252-7300

Established in 1988 in OH.
Financial data (yr. ended 12/31/00): Grants paid, $38,750; assets, $437,201 (M); expenditures, $39,303; qualifying distributions, $38,750.
Limitations: Giving primarily in Cincinnati, OH.
Application information: Application form not required.
Officers and Directors:* Morry Weiss,* Pres.; William S. Meyer,* V.P.; Patricia L. Ripple, V.P.; Erwin Weiss, V.P.; Jon Groetzinger, Secy.; Dale Cable,* Treas.
EIN: 311264728

43429
Cecil Mauger Charitable Trust
c/o Bank One Trust Co., N.A.
P.O. Box 710192
Westerville, OH 43081 (614) 248-4557
Contact: Clark Nyberg

Established in 1986 in OH.
Donor(s): Cecil L. Mauger.‡
Financial data (yr. ended 04/30/00): Grants paid, $38,685; assets, $2,268,883 (M); expenditures, $59,457; qualifying distributions, $40,012.
Limitations: Giving primarily in Licking County, OH.
Publications: Informational brochure (including application guidelines).
Application information: Annual requests for funding are discouraged.
Trustees: Earl Hawkins, Molly Ingold, Thomas E. Norpell, John Weaver, James T. Young, Bank One Trust Co., N.A.
EIN: 316313464

43430
The Richard and Dorothy Pandorf Foundation
c/o Dennis L. Manes
441 Vine St., Ste. 2900
Cincinnati, OH 45202

Established in 1997 in OH.
Donor(s): Dorothy D. Pandorf, Richard A. Pandorf.
Financial data (yr. ended 12/31/01): Grants paid, $38,600; assets, $677,751 (M); expenditures, $46,820; qualifying distributions, $38,600.
Limitations: Applications not accepted.
Application information: Contributes only to pre-selected organizations.
Officers and Trustees:* Richard A. Pandorf,* Pres. and Treas.; Dorothy D. Pandorf,* V.P. and Treas.; Dennis L. Manes,* Secy.
EIN: 311532336

43431
Timken Family Charitable Trust
236 3rd St. S.W.
Canton, OH 44702 (330) 455-5281
Contact: Don D. Dickes, Tr.

Established in 1989 in OH.
Donor(s): Peter T. Toot, Alexander C. Timken, Elizabeth Burnham Timken, Robert Ringen Timken, Mary J. Timken, W.R. Timken, Sandra M. Timken, Kristen T. Kingery, Robert F. Kingery.
Financial data (yr. ended 09/30/01): Grants paid, $38,550; assets, $639,430 (M); gifts received, $24,873; expenditures, $40,928; qualifying distributions, $38,550.
Limitations: Giving on a national basis.
Application information: Application form not required.
Trustees: Don D. Dickes, Ward J. Timken, W.R. Timken, Jr.
EIN: 346922439

43432
Robert C. & Susan M. Savage Family Foundation
4427 Talmadge Rd.
Toledo, OH 43623

Established in 1997 in OH.
Donor(s): Robert C. Savage.
Financial data (yr. ended 11/30/01): Grants paid, $38,346; assets, $637,481 (M); expenditures, $38,722; qualifying distributions, $38,346.
Limitations: Applications not accepted. Giving limited to the northwest OH, area.
Application information: Contributes only to pre-selected organizations.
Officers and Trustees:* Robert C. Savage,* Pres.; Susan M. Savage,* Secy.; Michelle K. Savage.
EIN: 311488119

43433
The Thomas V. and Corrine R. Francis Foundation, Inc.
c/o Thomas V. Francis
214 W. Main St.
Russia, OH 45363

Established in 1995 in OH.
Donor(s): Thomas V. Francis.
Financial data (yr. ended 12/31/01): Grants paid, $38,263; assets, $920,911 (M); gifts received, $20,000; expenditures, $39,839; qualifying distributions, $39,078.
Limitations: Applications not accepted. Giving primarily in OH.
Application information: Contributes only to pre-selected organizations.
Officers and Trustees:* Bradley J. Francis,* Pres.; David J. Francis,* V.P.; Kathleen S. Nichols,* Secy.-Treas.; Patrick A. Francis, Thomas V. Francis, William T. Francis, A. Renee Purpus, Shirley F. Shenk.
EIN: 311448010

43434
Dr. Carl T. Hoop Testamentary Trust
c/o National City Bank
P.O. Box 94651
Cleveland, OH 44101-4651

Financial data (yr. ended 07/31/02): Grants paid, $38,261; assets, $328,647 (M); expenditures, $43,077; qualifying distributions, $38,261.
Limitations: Applications not accepted. Giving primarily in Coshocton, OH.
Application information: Contributes only to pre-selected organizations.
Trustee: National City Bank.
EIN: 316473020

43435
Cathy J. King Trust
5 Daisy Ln.
Pepper Pike, OH 44124

Established in 1999 in OH.
Donor(s): Robert J. King, Jr.
Financial data (yr. ended 06/30/01): Grants paid, $38,190; assets, $397,615 (M); gifts received, $112,820; expenditures, $40,576; qualifying distributions, $38,190.
Limitations: Applications not accepted.

43435—OHIO

Application information: Contributes only to pre-selected organizations.
Trustees: Cathy J. King, Robert J. King, Jr., John P. Stockwell.
EIN: 347106580

43436
The B.F.L. Charitable Foundation
5450 Deerfield Ave., NW
North Lawrence, OH 44666

Established in 1997 in OH.
Donor(s): Carolyn A. Bartley.
Financial data (yr. ended 11/30/01): Grants paid, $38,000; assets, $403,341 (M); gifts received, $24,159; expenditures, $43,091; qualifying distributions, $38,000.
Limitations: Applications not accepted. Giving primarily in AZ and OH.
Application information: Contributes only to pre-selected organizations.
Trustees: Carolyn A. Bartley, David W. Bartley II, John C. Bartley.
EIN: 341852322

43437
Morris Family Foundation
7875 Tecumseh Trail
Cincinnati, OH 45243-4003
Application address: 6302 Crest Creek Ct., Louisville, KY 40222
Contact: John Richard Morris

Donor(s): John Richard Morris, John Ryan Morris, Glendolyn M. Morris.
Financial data (yr. ended 12/31/01): Grants paid, $37,898; assets, $498,671 (M); gifts received, $21,000; expenditures, $43,773; qualifying distributions, $43,773.
Limitations: Giving on a national basis.
Officer: Glendolyn M. Morris, Mgr.
EIN: 237125352

43438
S.E.C. Charitable Corp.
1041 Catawba Valley Dr.
Cincinnati, OH 45226

Established in 1997 in OH.
Donor(s): Susan Castleberry.
Financial data (yr. ended 12/31/01): Grants paid, $37,700; assets, $241,395 (M); expenditures, $39,326; qualifying distributions, $37,700.
Limitations: Applications not accepted.
Application information: Contributes only to pre-selected organizations.
Trustees: Christine Castleberry, Edward F. Castleberry, Kelly Castleberry, Susan Castleberry, Elizabeth Driscoll, Anne Pund.
EIN: 311529509

43439
The Tanis Foundation
1082 Lake Point Dr.
Lakewood, OH 44107-1033
Contact: John J. Tanis, Pres.

Donor(s): John Tanis.
Financial data (yr. ended 12/31/01): Grants paid, $37,700; assets, $262,979 (M); expenditures, $38,900; qualifying distributions, $37,700.
Limitations: Giving primarily in OH.
Officers and Directors:* John J. Tanis,* Pres. and Treas.; Nancy Tanis,* Secy.; T.A. Quintrell, John Warner Tanis.
EIN: 341847957

43440
Equimark Corporation Merit Scholarship Program
c/o National City Bank of Pennsylvania
P.O. Box 94651
Cleveland, OH 44101
Application address: c/o W.M. Schmidt, National City Bank of Pennsylvania, 20 Stanwix St., Pittsburgh, PA 15222

Donor(s): Equimark Corp.
Financial data (yr. ended 12/31/99): Grants paid, $37,651; assets, $0 (M); expenditures, $37,819; qualifying distributions, $37,778.
Limitations: Giving limited to areas of company operations.
Publications: Application guidelines.
Application information: Application form required.
Trustee: National City Bank.
EIN: 251284959
Codes: CS, CD

43441
Fairfield Community Foundation
5350 Pleasant Ave.
Fairfield, OH 45014 (513) 829-6355
FAX: (513) 867-5310; E-mail: foundation@fairfield-city.org
Contact: Betsy Dockery, Exec. Dir.

Established in 1999 in OH.
Financial data (yr. ended 06/30/01): Grants paid, $37,650; assets, $697,307 (M); gifts received, $199,340; expenditures, $50,226.
Limitations: Giving limited to Fairfield, OH.
Officers: Howard R. Dirksen, Pres.; Joan C. Bomaminio, V.P.; Evelyn J. Jones, Secy.; James G. Miller, Treas.
Board Members: Sandy Becker, Sally Braun, John H. Clemmons, Bruce S. Crutcher, Pam Elick, John M. Gleeson, Robert Wolterman.
EIN: 311625750
Codes: CM

43442
H. T. Mead Foundation
650 W. David Rd.
Dayton, OH 45429-1339

Donor(s): George Mead Foundation, Jr.
Financial data (yr. ended 02/28/02): Grants paid, $37,650; assets, $756,678 (M); expenditures, $67,733; qualifying distributions, $37,650.
Limitations: Applications not accepted. Giving on a national basis.
Application information: Contributes only to pre-selected organizations.
Trustee: Daniel Mead, Dudley H. Mead, George Mead, Mary G. Mead-Hagen, Whitaker W. Mead.
EIN: 311002350

43443
The Herbert C. Ziegler Foundation
4150 Millennium Blvd. S.E.
Massillon, OH 44646-7449 (330) 834-3332
Contact: William C. Ziegler, Tr.

Donor(s): Herbert C. Ziegler, William C. Ziegler.
Financial data (yr. ended 11/30/01): Grants paid, $37,600; assets, $799,363 (M); expenditures, $39,929; qualifying distributions, $39,713.
Limitations: Giving limited to OH.
Application information: Application form required.
Trustees: Harold E. Ziegler, Jr., Norman J. Ziegler, William C. Ziegler.
EIN: 341381823
Codes: GTI

43444
I.O.O.F. No. 107 and No. 379 Charitable Trust
c/o National City Bank
P.O. Box 94651
Cleveland, OH 44101-4651
Application address: Pottertown Advisory Committee, c/o Ms. Myra Vitto, National City Bank, P.O. Box 450, Youngstown, OH 44501, tel.: (330) 742-4289

Established in 1997 in OH.
Financial data (yr. ended 12/31/01): Grants paid, $37,500; assets, $453,630 (M); expenditures, $38,326; qualifying distributions, $37,500.
Limitations: Giving primarily in East Liverpool, OH.
Trustee: National City Bank.
EIN: 316571749

43445
Ronald D. and Lily H. Glosser Foundation
43 Twin Oaks Rd.
Akron, OH 44313

Financial data (yr. ended 12/31/01): Grants paid, $37,450; assets, $377,583 (M); expenditures, $38,400; qualifying distributions, $37,450.
Limitations: Applications not accepted.
Application information: Contributes only to pre-selected organizations.
Trustee: Ronald D. Glosser.
EIN: 311528195

43446
The Dr. John W. Flory Foundation
141 Balmoral Dr.
Dayton, OH 45429

Established in 1991 in OH.
Donor(s): John W. Flory.
Financial data (yr. ended 01/31/02): Grants paid, $37,300; assets, $926,100 (M); gifts received, $73,652; expenditures, $42,711; qualifying distributions, $37,300.
Limitations: Applications not accepted. Giving primarily in OH.
Application information: Contributes only to pre-selected organizations.
Officers: Jane Ellen Schwartz, Pres.; John W. Flory, V.P. and Treas.; Jennifer Schwartz, Secy.
Trustees: David L. Flory, Juliet Radcliffe Flory, Mary Eleanor Flory.
EIN: 311337519

43447
PDR Foundation
1 Park Centre Dr., Ste. 301A
Wadsworth, OH 44281

Established in 1998 in OH.
Donor(s): Patrick L. Ryan.
Financial data (yr. ended 12/31/01): Grants paid, $37,250; assets, $1,153,397 (M); gifts received, $300,000; expenditures, $48,508; qualifying distributions, $37,250.
Application information: Application form required.
Officers: Patrick L. Ryan, Pres. and Treas.; Debra D. Ryan, V.P. and Secy.
Director: Christopher G. Cook.
EIN: 341881438

43448
Charles & Isabel Hall Foundation
c/o Fifth Third Bank
P.O. Box 630858, M/D 1090L7
Cincinnati, OH 45263
Contact: Lawra Baumann, Trust Off., Fifth Third Bank

Established in 2000 in OH.

Donor(s): Isabel Hall.
Financial data (yr. ended 12/31/01): Grants paid, $37,095; assets, $382,288 (M); expenditures, $53,508; qualifying distributions, $37,095.
Officer: Isabel Hall, Pres.
Trustees: Timothy Rodgers, Frank J. Seurkamp.
EIN: 311745217

43449
The Murray Family Boy Scouts of America Endowment
9665 Young America Rd.
Adamsville, OH 43802-9721

Established in 1995 in OH.
Financial data (yr. ended 12/31/01): Grants paid, $37,005; assets, $508,167 (M); expenditures, $56,163; qualifying distributions, $37,005.
Limitations: Applications not accepted.
Application information: Contributes only to pre-selected organizations.
Trustees: Wendel E. Dreve, Jr., Marion C. Gilliland.
EIN: 311404570

43450
Fariways Foundation
c/o Fifth Third Bank, Trust Dept.
38 Fountain Sq. Plz., MD 1COM31
Cincinnati, OH 45263 (513) 579-6034
Contact: Lawra Baumann

Established in 1998 in OH.
Donor(s): Alexandra H. Elliott.
Financial data (yr. ended 09/30/01): Grants paid, $37,000; assets, $705,738 (M); gifts received, $21,204; expenditures, $41,391; qualifying distributions, $37,000.
Limitations: Giving primarily in Cincinnati, OH.
Application information: Application form required.
Trustees: Narley L. Haley, Fifth Third Bank.
EIN: 311628541

43451
Zembrodt Family Foundation, Inc.
3023 E. Kemper Rd., Bldg. 9
Cincinnati, OH 45241

Established in 1986 in OH and KY.
Donor(s): Cyril Zembrodt, Joe Zembrodt, John Zembrodt, Jerry Zembrodt.
Financial data (yr. ended 06/30/01): Grants paid, $37,000; assets, $4,316,050 (M); expenditures, $52,851; qualifying distributions, $37,223.
Limitations: Applications not accepted. Giving primarily in KY.
Application information: Contributes only to pre-selected organizations.
Officers and Directors:* Cyril C. Zembrodt,* Pres.; Joseph A. Zembrodt,* V.P.; John A. Zembrodt,* Secy.; Gerald L. Zembrodt,* Treas.
EIN: 611108902

43452
Lambur-Glorioso Foundation
c/o KeyBank, N.A., Trust Div.
800 Superior Ave., 4th Fl.
Cleveland, OH 44114

Established in 1999 in OH.
Donor(s): Glorioso P. Rita.
Financial data (yr. ended 12/31/01): Grants paid, $36,812; assets, $695,148 (M); expenditures, $41,788; qualifying distributions, $36,812.
Limitations: Applications not accepted. Giving primarily in OH.
Application information: Contributes only to pre-selected organizations.
Trustee: KeyBank, N.A.
EIN: 341891478

43453
Lida M. Ferguson Trust
34 N. Main St., 4th Fl.
Dayton, OH 45401

Financial data (yr. ended 12/31/01): Grants paid, $36,665; assets, $1,002,811 (M); expenditures, $56,362; qualifying distributions, $41,766.
Limitations: Giving primarily in Dayton, OH.
Trustee: KeyBank, N.A.
EIN: 316118804

43454
Athens Foundation
P.O. Box 366
Athens, OH 45701-0366 (740) 592-3338
FAX: (740) 592-3341
Contact: Richard Abel, Pres.

Established in 1980 in OH; reincorporated in 1999.
Financial data (yr. ended 09/30/00): Grants paid, $36,397; assets, $1,932,047 (M); gifts received, $1,215,674; expenditures, $38,854.
Limitations: Giving limited to Athens County, OH.
Officers: Richard Abel, Pres.; James Bruning, V.P.; Avi McWilliams, Secy.; William L. Kennard, Treas.
EIN: 311040215
Codes: CM

43455
Charles T. Mentzer Memorial Trust
c/o KeyBank, N.A., Trust Div.
800 Superior Ave., 4th Fl.
Cleveland, OH 44111
Application address: c/o KeyBank, N.A., Trust Client Svcs., 127 Public Sq., Cleveland, OH 44114, tel.: (800) 999-9658

Established in 1985 in WA.
Financial data (yr. ended 12/31/00): Grants paid, $36,324; assets, $534,188 (M); expenditures, $44,039; qualifying distributions, $37,795.
Trustee: KeyBank, N.A.
EIN: 916273732
Codes: GTI

43456
N. & P. Bruns Foundation, Inc.
c/o Clark, Schaefer, Hackett & Co.
105 E. 4th St.
Cincinnati, OH 45202
Contact: Robert F. Uhrig, Secy.-Treas.

Established in 1999 in OH.
Donor(s): Norbert Bruns.
Financial data (yr. ended 11/30/01): Grants paid, $36,275; assets, $665,254 (M); gifts received, $243,910; expenditures, $36,893; qualifying distributions, $36,275.
Officers: Thomas A. Bruns, Pres.; Jane A. Haslem Bruns, V.P.; Robert F. Uhrig, Secy.-Treas.
EIN: 311628492

43457
Irving J. Olson and Ruth B. Olson Foundation
c/o KeyBank, N.A.
800 Superior Ave.
Cleveland, OH 44114
Application address: c/o Karen M. Krino, KeyBank, N.A., 157 S. Main St., Akron, OH 44308, tel.: (330) 379-1647

Established in 1991 in OH.
Donor(s): Irving J. Olson, Ruth B. Olson.
Financial data (yr. ended 12/31/01): Grants paid, $36,202; assets, $360,517 (M); gifts received, $36,202; expenditures, $39,617; qualifying distributions, $36,202.
Limitations: Giving primarily in Akron, OH.
Committee Member: Irving J. Olson.

Trustee: KeyBank, N.A.
EIN: 341696795

43458
Marion C. Tyler Foundation
c/o KeyBank, N.A.
800 Superior Ave., Ste. 420
Cleveland, OH 44114-2601
Application address: c/o Don Whitehouse, 3200 Bessemer City Rd., Box 8900, Gastonia, NC 28053, tel.: (704) 629-2214

Established in 1931 in OH.
Donor(s): W.S. Tyler, Inc.
Financial data (yr. ended 12/31/00): Grants paid, $36,157; assets, $1,353,028 (M); expenditures, $49,282; qualifying distributions, $31,524.
Application information: Application form required.
Trustee: KeyBank, N.A.
EIN: 346525274
Codes: CS, CD, GTI

43459
The Sekerak Family Foundation
c/o William E. Reichard
25109 Detroit Rd., Ste. 300
Westlake, OH 44145

Established in 1991 in OH.
Donor(s): Jean Sekerak.
Financial data (yr. ended 12/31/00): Grants paid, $36,050; assets, $53,819 (M); gifts received, $39,647; expenditures, $36,515; qualifying distributions, $36,050.
Limitations: Applications not accepted. Giving primarily in OH.
Application information: Contributes only to pre-selected organizations.
Trustees: William E. Reichard, Jean Sekerak, Robert Sekerak.
EIN: 341688811

43460
Infinity Trust
c/o Raymond R. Chapin
7 Jennifer Way
Norwalk, OH 44857-9565
Application address: c/o Dennis C. Camp, 257 Benedict Ave., Bldg. D, Norwalk, OH 44857

Established in 1992 in OH.
Donor(s): Raymond R. Chapin, Marjorie S. Chapin.
Financial data (yr. ended 12/31/01): Grants paid, $36,000; assets, $790,469 (M); gifts received, $81,511; expenditures, $36,642; qualifying distributions, $36,000.
Limitations: Giving primarily in OH.
Trustees: Marjorie S. Chapin, Raymond R. Chapin.
EIN: 341712605

43461
The Mifsud Family Foundation
(Formerly OJM Family Foundation)
1 Park Centre Dr., Ste. 301A
Wadsworth, OH 44281

Established in OH in 1998.
Donor(s): Oscar J. Mifsud.
Financial data (yr. ended 12/31/01): Grants paid, $36,000; assets, $1,214,025 (M); gifts received, $300,000; expenditures, $45,761; qualifying distributions, $36,000.
Limitations: Applications not accepted.
Officers: Oscar J. Mifsud, Pres. and Treas.; Judith D. Mifsud, V.P. and Secy.
Directors: Caryl T. Loncar, Ryan S. Mifsud, Shelly A. Mifsud, Marcia J. Wexberg.
EIN: 341881436

43462
Galen Miller Foundation
901 Lakeside Ave.
Cleveland, OH 44114-1116 (216) 586-1078
Contact: Ellen E. Halfon, Secy.

Financial data (yr. ended 12/31/01): Grants paid, $36,000; assets, $655,208 (M); expenditures, $43,871; qualifying distributions, $36,000.
Limitations: Giving primarily in Cleveland, OH.
Officers and Trustees:* Joan M. Lynn,* Pres.; Elizabeth Miller Williams,* V.P.; Ellen E. Halfon, Secy.; James T. Lynn,* Treas.
EIN: 346551899

43463
Harry Ratner Foundation
1600 Terminal Tower
50 Public Sq.
Cleveland, OH 44113-2203 (216) 621-6060
Contact: Albert B. Ratner, Pres.

Financial data (yr. ended 01/31/02): Grants paid, $36,000; assets, $574,417 (M); expenditures, $36,921; qualifying distributions, $36,000.
Limitations: Giving primarily in Cleveland, OH.
Application information: Application form not required.
Officers and Trustees:* Albert B. Ratner,* Pres.; Charles A. Ratner,* Secy.
EIN: 346541541

43464
William & Anna Smith Foundation
(also known as W. F. & Anna Smith Foundation)
c/o KeyBank, N.A.
800 Superior Ave., 4th Fl.
Cleveland, OH 44114

Financial data (yr. ended 12/31/01): Grants paid, $35,787; assets, $743,229 (M); expenditures, $42,991; qualifying distributions, $36,824.
Limitations: Applications not accepted. Giving limited to the Wendover, UT, area.
Application information: Contributes only to pre-selected organizations.
Trustee: KeyBank, N.A.
EIN: 942728399
Codes: GTI

43465
Agnes Cecelia J. Siebenthal Scholarship Charitable Trust
c/o National City Bank
P.O. Box 94651
Cleveland, OH 44101-4651
Application address: c/o Principal, Manual High School, 811 S. Griswold, Peoria, IL 61605, tel.: (309) 672-6600

Financial data (yr. ended 09/30/01): Grants paid, $35,634; assets, $691,254 (M); expenditures, $39,418; qualifying distributions, $36,030.
Limitations: Giving limited to Peoria, IL.
Application information: Write for application information and deadlines.
Trustee: National City Bank.
EIN: 376193766
Codes: GTI

43466
Community Foundation of Jefferson County
(Formerly Fort Steuben Community Foundation, Inc.)
630 Market St.
P.O. Box 1822
Steubenville, OH 43952 (740) 284-9700
FAX: (740) 284-9701; E-mail: CFJC@1ST.net;
URL: http://www.jeffersoncountyohio.org/cfjc
Contact: Vicki Cummiskey, Exec. Dir.

Established in 1986 in OH.
Financial data (yr. ended 12/31/01): Grants paid, $35,627; assets, $38,942 (M); gifts received, $34,295; expenditures, $42,177.
Limitations: Giving limited to Jefferson County, OH.
Officers: Robert Hargrave, Pres.; Robert Filby, V.P.; Christine Hargrave, Secy.; David Skiviat, Treas.; Vicki Cummiskey, Exec. Dir.
Members: Gary Cain, William Chesson, Alan Hall, H. Lee Kinney, John Madigan, Tim McCoy, Duke Rakich.
EIN: 341530373
Codes: CM

43467
The Bardons & Oliver Foundation
5800 Harper Rd.
Solon, OH 44139

Financial data (yr. ended 12/31/01): Grants paid, $35,500; assets, $139,030 (M); expenditures, $35,784; qualifying distributions, $35,784.
Limitations: Applications not accepted. Giving primarily in Cleveland, OH.
Application information: Contributes only to pre-selected organizations.
Trustees: James S. Dalton, Heath Oliver.
EIN: 346527407

43468
The Birchtree Foundation, Inc.
580 N. 4th St., Ste. 620
Columbus, OH 43215

Established in 1997 in OH.
Donor(s): Robert D. Murtha, Ann E. Murtha.
Financial data (yr. ended 12/31/00): Grants paid, $35,404; assets, $142,073 (M); gifts received, $26,297; expenditures, $37,882; qualifying distributions, $35,404.
Limitations: Applications not accepted. Giving primarily in OH.
Application information: Contributes only to pre-selected organizations.
Trustees: Brent Danielson, Ann E. Murtha, Robert D. Murtha.
EIN: 311524003

43469
The Christian Legacy Foundation
P.O. Box 371
Hudson, OH 44236

Established in 1998 in OH.
Financial data (yr. ended 12/31/00): Grants paid, $35,400; assets, $715,051 (M); expenditures, $45,068; qualifying distributions, $35,400.
Limitations: Applications not accepted.
Application information: Contributes only to pre-selected organizations.
Trustees: Gerald H. Nuzum, Jason Nuzum, Lisa Nuzum, Mary Nuzum.
EIN: 341881154

43470
The Gerald F. and Susanne F. Schroer Family Foundation
20700 Beachcliff Blvd.
Rocky River, OH 44116-1323

Established in 1997 in OH.
Donor(s): Susanne F. Schroer, Gerald F. Schroer.
Financial data (yr. ended 06/30/02): Grants paid, $35,041; assets, $248,048 (M); gifts received, $30,000; expenditures, $36,503; qualifying distributions, $35,041.
Limitations: Applications not accepted. Giving primarily in OH.
Application information: Contributes only to pre-selected organizations.
Officers and Trustees:* Susanne F. Schroer,* Pres.; Gerald F. Schroer,* Secy.; Gerald F. Schroer, Jr.,* Treas.
EIN: 311599321

43471
The Essi Family Charitable Foundation
1406 W. 6th St., 3rd Fl.
Cleveland, OH 44113

Established in 1995 in OH.
Donor(s): Vernon P. Essi.
Financial data (yr. ended 12/31/01): Grants paid, $35,000; assets, $451,559 (M); gifts received, $55,410; expenditures, $39,159; qualifying distributions, $35,000.
Limitations: Applications not accepted. Giving primarily in OH.
Application information: Contributes only to pre-selected organizations.
Trustees: Brian Joseph Essi, Mark Stephen Essi, Paul Russell Essi, Vernon P. Essi, Vernon Paul Essi, Jr., Michelle Ann Norehad.
EIN: 341818158

43472
The Lott-Conlon Foundation
(Formerly Lott School for Handicapped Children)
c/o KeyBank, N.A., Trust Div.
P.O. Box 10099
Toledo, OH 43699-0099 (419) 259-8391
Contact: Diane Omns, Trust Off., KeyBank, N.A.

Financial data (yr. ended 08/31/02): Grants paid, $35,000; assets, $571,237 (M); expenditures, $37,277; qualifying distributions, $35,000.
Limitations: Giving primarily in Toledo, OH.
Officers: John T. Witte, Pres.; P. Richard Day, V.P.; Paul W. Hankins, 2nd V.P.; Joseph F. Drepps, Secy.; Henry A. Page, Treas.
Director: George S. Wade.
Trustee: KeyBank, N.A.
EIN: 346557797

43473
Lowe Family Foundation, Inc.
2940 Grandin Rd.
Cincinnati, OH 45208

Established in 2000 in OH.
Donor(s): Kenneth W. Lowe, Mary E. Lowe.
Financial data (yr. ended 12/31/01): Grants paid, $35,000; assets, $1,553,074 (M); gifts received, $937,367; expenditures, $41,843; qualifying distributions, $35,000.
Limitations: Applications not accepted. Giving primarily in OH.
Application information: Contributes only to pre-selected organizations.
Officers and Trustees:* Kenneth W. Lowe,* Pres. and Treas.; Mary E. Lowe,* V.P. and Secy.; William Burleigh.
EIN: 311739056

43474
Norton-White-Gale Trust
2550 Som Center Rd., No. 370
Willoughby, OH 44094

Established in 1955 in OH.
Donor(s): Robert I. Gale, Jr.,‡ Laurence H. Norton,‡ Robert C. Norton,‡ Fred R. White, Jr.,‡ Miriam N. White.‡
Financial data (yr. ended 12/31/01): Grants paid, $35,000; assets, $1,096,603 (M); expenditures, $43,869; qualifying distributions, $35,000.
Limitations: Applications not accepted. Giving primarily in Cleveland, OH.
Application information: Contributes only to pre-selected organizations.
Trustees: Carolyn W. Barr, Frances White Gale, Robert T. Gale III.
EIN: 346521422

43475
Scotts Miracle-Gro Foundation
c/o Rob McMahon
14111 Scottslawn Rd.
Marysville, OH 43041-0001

Established in 2001 in OH.
Donor(s): The Hagedorn Family Foundation, Inc.
Financial data (yr. ended 12/31/01): Grants paid, $35,000; assets, $4,793 (M); gifts received, $40,000; expenditures, $35,207; qualifying distributions, $35,207.
Limitations: Applications not accepted.
Application information: Contributes only to pre-selected organizations.
Officers and Directors:* Sue Hagedorn,* Pres.; Patrick J. Norton,* V.P.; Rob McMahon,* Secy.-Treas.; David Aronowitz, Arnold Donald, Jim Hagedorn, Paul Hagedorn.
EIN: 311799491

43476
George & Sandy Smart Family Foundation
1754 Turnberry Cir. N.W.
Canton, OH 44708

Established in 1997 in OH.
Donor(s): George M. Smart.
Financial data (yr. ended 12/31/01): Grants paid, $35,000; assets, $1,178,406 (M); gifts received, $442,500; expenditures, $38,258; qualifying distributions, $35,000.
Limitations: Giving primarily in Canton, OH.
Officers: George M. Smart, Pres.; Bruce Hunt, V.P.; Stacy Hunt, V.P.; Sandy Smart, V.P.; Shelly Smart, V.P.
EIN: 311513622

43477
Mildred L. Herzberger Charitable Trust
c/o William J. Sitterley
4307 Bauman Hill Rd. S.E.
Lancaster, OH 43130-9455

Established in 1998 in OH.
Donor(s): Mary Margaret Ackers,‡ Alice Kindler,‡ J. Colin Campbell.‡
Financial data (yr. ended 08/31/00): Grants paid, $34,733; assets, $499,669 (M); expenditures, $36,127; qualifying distributions, $35,695.
Limitations: Giving limited to residents of Fairfield County, OH.
Application information: Application form required.
Trustee: William Sitterley.
EIN: 311435269

43478
George P. Ballas Foundation
5715 W. Central Ave.
Toledo, OH 43615

Donor(s): George P. Ballas.
Financial data (yr. ended 12/31/01): Grants paid, $34,704; assets, $16,940 (M); gifts received, $32,000; expenditures, $35,273; qualifying distributions, $34,704.
Limitations: Applications not accepted. Giving primarily in OH.
Application information: Contributes only to pre-selected organizations.
Trustees: George P. Ballas, Peter G. Ballas II.
EIN: 341476413

43479
Harold Weber Charitable Trust
c/o KeyBank, N.A.
P.O. Box 10099
Toledo, OH 43699-0099

Donor(s): Harold Weber.‡
Financial data (yr. ended 12/31/01): Grants paid, $34,672; assets, $555,659 (M); expenditures, $36,005; qualifying distributions, $34,897.
Limitations: Applications not accepted. Giving limited to OH.
Application information: Contributes only to pre-selected organizations.
Trustee: KeyBank, N.A.
EIN: 346685817

43480
Brashares Family Foundation
2205 Wingate
Delaware, OH 43015-9270

Established in 2001 in OH.
Donor(s): Jeffrey Brashares.
Financial data (yr. ended 12/31/01): Grants paid, $34,669; assets, $980,346 (M); gifts received, $1,000,000; expenditures, $44,679; qualifying distributions, $34,669.
Limitations: Applications not accepted.
Application information: Contributes only to pre-selected organizations.
Officer and Trustees:* Jeffrey Brashares,* Pres.; Eileen J. Brashares, Margrit Ann Brashares.
EIN: 311758243

43481
Alfred C. & Ersa S. Arbogast Foundation
P.O. Box 94651
Cleveland, OH 44101-4651
Application address: c/o National City Bank of Indiana, 110 W. Berry, Fort Wayne, IN 46802, tel.: (219) 461-7126
Contact: Jim Westerfield

Financial data (yr. ended 12/31/01): Grants paid, $34,500; assets, $507,650 (M); expenditures, $37,882; qualifying distributions, $34,500.
Limitations: Giving primarily in IN.
Officers: A. Bruce Arbogast, Co.-Chair.; Beatrice Anne Stanaway, Co-Chair.; Linda K. Arbogast, Secy.
Trustee: Susan Stanaway.
EIN: 356026067

43482
JAF Charitable Foundation, Inc.
(Formerly Indiana Educational Cultrual & Fine Arts Foundation, Inc.)
7290 Green Farms Dr.
Cincinnati, OH 45224-1602   (513) 729-1819
Contact: Suzanne A. Joiner, Pres.

Financial data (yr. ended 12/31/01): Grants paid, $34,500; assets, $628,340 (M); gifts received, $40,000; expenditures, $37,042; qualifying distributions, $34,500.
Officers: Suzanne A. Joiner, Pres.; William C. Joiner, Secy.-Treas.
Director: William J. Joiner.
EIN: 351118578

43483
Chester H. & Roberta K. Mindling Memorial Church Fund
c/o Banknorth Investment Management Group, N.A.
P.O. Box 738
Marietta, OH 45750

Established in 1988 in OH.
Financial data (yr. ended 06/30/02): Grants paid, $34,474; assets, $742,023 (M); expenditures, $41,022; qualifying distributions, $34,474.
Limitations: Applications not accepted. Giving limited to OH.
Application information: Contributes only to pre-selected organizations.
Trustee: Banknorth Investment Management Group, N.A.
EIN: 316296253

43484
The Pilliod Foundation
413 Broadway Ave.
Swanton, OH 43558-1341
Contact: Peter P. Pilliod, Pres.

Donor(s): Peter P. Pilliod, William J. Pilliod, Thomas J. Pilliod.
Financial data (yr. ended 12/31/01): Grants paid, $34,250; assets, $442,767 (M); expenditures, $36,071; qualifying distributions, $34,250.
Limitations: Applications not accepted. Giving primarily in South Bend, IN, and Swanton, OH.
Application information: Contributes only to pre-selected organizations.
Officers: Peter P. Pilliod, Pres.; William J. Pilliod, Secy.; Thomas J. Pilliod, Treas.
EIN: 341762896

43485
The Weikel Family Charitable Foundation
c/o National City Bank, Northwest
P.O. Box 94651
Cleveland, OH 44101-4651

Established in 1994 in OH.
Donor(s): M. Keith Weikel.
Financial data (yr. ended 12/31/01): Grants paid, $34,100; assets, $227,705 (M); expenditures, $35,545; qualifying distributions, $34,100.
Limitations: Applications not accepted. Giving primarily in Toledo, OH.
Application information: Contributes only to pre-selected organizations.
Trustees: James M. Morton, Jr., Barbara Weikel, Kristen Weikel, M. Keith Weikel, Richard Weikel, National City Bank.
EIN: 341795038

43486
Clara Louise Kiser Memorial Fund
c/o National City Bank
P.O. Box 94651
Cleveland, OH 44101-4651
Application address: c/o Stephen P. Kosak, P.O. Box 374, Oil City, PA 16301, tel.: (814) 677-5085

Financial data (yr. ended 12/31/01): Grants paid, $34,043; assets, $674,667 (M); expenditures, $41,843; qualifying distributions, $38,487.
Limitations: Giving limited to Clarion, PA.
Application information: Application form required.

Trustee: National City Bank.
EIN: 256191759
Codes: GTI

43487
The Kaufmann Family Foundation
c/o Sheldon M. Lewin
6685 Beta Dr.
Mayfield Village, OH 44143

Established in 1999 in OH.
Donor(s): Katherine S. Kaufmann.
Financial data (yr. ended 12/31/01): Grants paid, $34,000; assets, $853,769 (M); expenditures, $43,435; qualifying distributions, $34,000.
Limitations: Applications not accepted.
Application information: Contributes only to pre-selected organizations.
Trustees: Amy E. Kaufmann, Andrew S. Kaufmann, John W. Kaufmann, Katherine S. Kaufmann.
EIN: 311624517

43488
Mikesell-Wade Foundation
c/o National City Bank
P.O. Box 94651
Cleveland, OH 44101-4651
Application address: c/o The Reuben Co., 1 Seagate, No. 1100, Toledo, OH 43604, tel.: (419) 247-5700
Contact: George Wade

Financial data (yr. ended 12/31/01): Grants paid, $34,000; assets, $785,130 (M); expenditures, $38,493; qualifying distributions, $34,000.
Limitations: Giving primarily in Toledo, OH.
Trustee: National City Bank.
EIN: 346518852

43489
Ward W. and Norabelle Wester Memorial Charitable Foundation
c/o National City Bank
P.O. Box 94651
Cleveland, OH 44101-4651
Application address: c/o Youngstown Shrine Club, P.O. Box 302, North Lima, OH 44452

Established in 1993 in OH.
Financial data (yr. ended 09/30/00): Grants paid, $33,748; assets, $1,256,818 (M); expenditures, $55,950; qualifying distributions, $41,991.
Limitations: Giving primarily in OH.
Trustees: Leonard A. Olson, Rev. Jerry Wester, National City Bank.
EIN: 346998992
Codes: GTI

43490
Butler-Wells Scholarship Fund
c/o Fifth Third Bank
38 Fountain Square Plz., MC 1COM31
Cincinnati, OH 45263 (513) 579-6034
Contact: Lawra Baumann

Established in 1998 in OH.
Financial data (yr. ended 12/31/01): Grants paid, $33,650; assets, $512,677 (M); expenditures, $41,743; qualifying distributions, $33,650.
Limitations: Giving limited to residents of the greater Cincinnati, OH, area.
Trustee: Fifth Third Bank.
EIN: 316019693

43491
Ruth & Elmer Babin Foundation
3645 Warrensville Ctr. Rd., Ste. 218
Shaker Heights, OH 44122-5245
Financial data (yr. ended 01/31/02): Grants paid, $33,225; assets, $473,212 (M); expenditures, $33,953; qualifying distributions, $33,225.
Limitations: Applications not accepted. Giving primarily in the Cleveland, OH, area.
Application information: Contributes only to pre-selected organizations.
Officers: Anthony W. Babin, Pres.; Judith B. Kaufman, Secy.
Trustees: Marilyn S. Babin, Jack Kaufman.
EIN: 346510523

43492
Louis N. Browning Fund
c/o U.S. Bank
P.O. Box 1118
Cincinnati, OH 45201-1118

Established around 1988.
Financial data (yr. ended 12/31/01): Grants paid, $33,200; assets, $1,070,294 (M); expenditures, $35,703; qualifying distributions, $33,200.
Limitations: Applications not accepted. Giving primarily in Maysville, KY.
Application information: Contributes only to pre-selected organizations.
Officers: Louis N. Browning, Pres.; Robert E. Browning, V.P.; L.L. Browning, Jr., Secy.; Virginia J. Browning, Treas.
Trustee: U.S. Bank.
EIN: 311238147

43493
The Granville Foundation
P.O. Box 321
Granville, OH 43023-0321 (740) 587-2812
Contact: Douglas Plunkett, Exec. Dir.

Established in 1971.
Financial data (yr. ended 12/31/01): Grants paid, $33,141; assets, $559,230 (M); gifts received, $61,408; expenditures, $36,136.
Limitations: Giving limited to Granville, OH.
Publications: Annual report.
Application information: Unsolicited requests for funds not accepted. Application form required.
Officer: Douglas Plunkett, Exec. Dir.
EIN: 237241045
Codes: CM

43494
International Institute Foundation of Youngstown, Inc.
c/o National City Bank
P.O. Box 94651
Cleveland, OH 44101-4651
Application address: c/o National City Bank, P.O. Box 450, Youngstown, OH 44501, tel.: (330) 742-4289
Contact: Myra Vitto

Established in 1986 in OH.
Financial data (yr. ended 12/31/01): Grants paid, $33,100; assets, $623,162 (M); expenditures, $34,641; qualifying distributions, $33,417.
Limitations: Giving limited to the Youngstown, OH, area.
Application information: Application form required.
Advisory Committee: Vera E. Friedman, Chair.; Virginia Schrum, Secy.; Anna Jean Cushwa, C. Gilbert James, Herbert Pridham, Dolores A. Strollo, Betty Szabo, Jean Tavolario, Sr. Teresa Winsen.
Trustee: National City Bank.
EIN: 346852663

43495
Robbins Foundation
c/o National City Bank
P.O. Box 14651
Cleveland, OH 44101-4651

Financial data (yr. ended 12/31/00): Grants paid, $33,000; assets, $746,950 (M); expenditures, $44,055; qualifying distributions, $33,000.
Limitations: Applications not accepted. Giving on a national basis.
Application information: Contributes only to pre-selected organizations.
Officer: Tyler B. Robbins, Pres. and Treas.
Trustee: National City Bank.
EIN: 346529567

43496
J. B. & D. E. McCutchan Scholarship Trust
c/o Fifth Third Bank
P.O. Box 630858
Cincinnati, OH 45263

Established in 1997 in IN.
Financial data (yr. ended 12/31/01): Grants paid, $32,977; assets, $614,771 (M); expenditures, $40,499; qualifying distributions, $32,977.
Limitations: Applications not accepted.
Application information: Contributes only to pre-selected organizations.
Trustee: Fifth Third Bank.
EIN: 356663006

43497
Guy and Rosa Lee Mabry Foundation
3150 N. Republic Blvd., Ste. 2
Toledo, OH 43615
Contact: Sandra Haessler

Established in 1990 in OH.
Donor(s): Guy O. Mabry.
Financial data (yr. ended 12/31/01): Grants paid, $32,910; assets, $262,528 (M); expenditures, $41,483; qualifying distributions, $32,910.
Limitations: Applications not accepted. Giving primarily in KS and OH.
Application information: Contributes only to pre-selected organizations.
Officers and Trustees:* Guy O. Mabry,* Pres.; Rose Lee Mabry, Secy.-Treas.; Richard C. Glowacki, R. Scott Trumbull.
EIN: 341664564

43498
Helen and Joseph Skilken Foundation
P.O. Box 1148
Columbus, OH 43216-1148
Application address: 383 S. 3rd St., Columbus, OH 43215, tel.: (614) 221-4547
Contact: Steven A. Skilken, Dir.

Established in 1988 in OH.
Donor(s): Joseph Skilken, Helen R. Skilken.
Financial data (yr. ended 12/31/01): Grants paid, $32,834; assets, $748,684 (M); expenditures, $35,563; qualifying distributions, $32,834.
Limitations: Giving primarily in OH.
Application information: Application form not required.
Directors: Helen R. Skilken, Lynne E. Skilken, Steven A. Skilken.
EIN: 311221036

43499
The Robert I. Gale III Family Foundation
2550 Som Center Rd., Ste. 370
Willoughby, OH 44094

Established in 1999 in OH.
Donor(s): Robert I. Gale III.

Financial data (yr. ended 12/31/01): Grants paid, $32,750; assets, $986,990 (M); expenditures, $39,468; qualifying distributions, $32,750.
Limitations: Applications not accepted. Giving primarily in OH.
Application information: Contributes only to pre-selected organizations.
Officers: Cathy M. Gale, Pres.; Elizabeth G. Kennedy, V.P.; Stephanie D. Gale, Secy.; Robert T. Gale, Treas.
Trustee: Robert I. Gale III.
EIN: 311679716

43500
Americana Arts Foundation
4357 Simca Ln.
Cincinnati, OH 45211
Contact: Robert S. Trach, Tr.

Established in 1997 in OH.
Donor(s): Edward Trach.
Financial data (yr. ended 12/31/01): Grants paid, $32,744; assets, $900,648 (M); expenditures, $55,773; qualifying distributions, $32,744.
Limitations: Giving on a national basis.
Trustees: Edward Trach, Michael J. Trach, Robert S. Trach, William E. Trach.
EIN: 311535209

43501
The Patricia A. Vance Foundation
8430 Willow Run Ct.
Cincinnati, OH 45243

Financial data (yr. ended 12/31/01): Grants paid, $32,350; assets, $23,065 (M); gifts received, $39,826; expenditures, $33,623; qualifying distributions, $32,350.
Trustees: Robert C. Martin, Sara M. Vance, Michelle Waddell.
EIN: 311696627

43502
George C. Beinke Scholarship Fund
c/o KeyBank, N.A.
P.O. Box 10099
Toledo, OH 43699-0099 (419) 259-8218
Contact: Marilyn Brown, Trust Off., KeyBank, N.A.

Financial data (yr. ended 08/31/01): Grants paid, $32,325; assets, $578,579 (M); expenditures, $40,113; qualifying distributions, $32,511.
Limitations: Giving limited to Lucas County, OH.
Application information: Application form required.
Advisory Committee Members: Gerald W. Miller, Rev. Stanley C. Schneider.
Trustee: KeyBank, N.A.
EIN: 346542089
Codes: GTI

43503
Marlboro 2465 Foundation
44 Laurel Lake Dr.
Hudson, OH 44236-2159
Contact: John L. Dampeer, Pres.

Established in 1986 in OH.
Donor(s): John L. Dampeer, Lucie K. Dampeer.‡
Financial data (yr. ended 12/31/01): Grants paid, $32,165; assets, $171,079 (M); gifts received, $1,004; expenditures, $33,493; qualifying distributions, $32,165.
Limitations: Giving primarily in Cuyahoga County, OH, and MA.
Application information: Application form not required.
Officers and Trustees:* John L. Dampeer,* Pres. and Secy.-Treas.; David K. Dampeer,* V.P.; G. Geoffrey Dampeer,* V.P.; Lyell B. Dampeer,* V.P.
EIN: 341536602

43504
The Volk Family Foundation
2880 Park Ave. W.
Mansfield, OH 44906 (419) 529-2578
Contact: Helen Volk, Tr.

Established in 1999 in OH.
Donor(s): Michael Volk, Helen Volk.
Financial data (yr. ended 12/31/00): Grants paid, $32,050; assets, $366,198 (M); expenditures, $32,700; qualifying distributions, $31,887.
Trustees: Helen Volk, Michael Volk.
EIN: 341904938

43505
Flerlage Foundation, Inc.
312 Walnut St., Ste. 1000
P.O. Box 5734
Cincinnati, OH 45202 (513) 651-9200
Contact: Michael J. Fitzgerald, Treas.

Financial data (yr. ended 12/31/01): Grants paid, $32,000; assets, $604,436 (M); expenditures, $34,367; qualifying distributions, $34,067.
Limitations: Giving primarily in Cincinnati, OH.
Application information: Application form required.
Officers and Trustees:* J. David Cummings,* Pres.; Sue Flerlage,* Secy.; Michael J. Fitzgerald,* Treas.; Daniel B. Flerlage, S. Thomas Flerlage, Donald W. Martin.
EIN: 311066269

43506
The O'Toole Family Charitable Foundation
c/o Charles J. O'Toole
925 Euclid Ave., Ste. 1100
Cleveland, OH 44115-1475

Established in 1996 in OH.
Donor(s): Charles J. O'Toole.
Financial data (yr. ended 12/31/01): Grants paid, $32,000; assets, $111,289 (M); gifts received, $12,041; expenditures, $33,848; qualifying distributions, $32,000.
Limitations: Applications not accepted. Giving primarily in OH.
Application information: Contributes only to pre-selected organizations.
Trustees: Carolyn A. O'Toole, Charles J. O'Toole.
EIN: 341838707

43507
Andree T. & Gladys E. Everhart Scholarship Fund Trust
c/o KeyBank, N.A., Trust Div.
800 Superior Ave., 4th Fl.
Cleveland, OH 44114
Application address: c/o KeyBank, N.A., 1211 S.W. 5th Ave., Ste. 560, Portland, OR 97204

Established in 1988 in OR.
Financial data (yr. ended 12/31/00): Grants paid, $31,832; assets, $858,551 (M); expenditures, $46,110; qualifying distributions, $34,946.
Limitations: Giving limited to OR.
Trustee: KeyBank, N.A.
EIN: 936212186
Codes: GTI

43508
Joel F. Gemunder Foundation
c/o Fifth Third Bank
38 Fountain Sq. Plz., M/D 1COM31
Cincinnati, OH 45263
Contact: Frank Fisher, Trust Off., Fifth Third Bank

Established in 1997 in OH.

Financial data (yr. ended 12/31/01): Grants paid, $31,750; assets, $374,037 (M); expenditures, $33,855; qualifying distributions, $31,750.
Limitations: Giving primarily in OH.
Trustees: Joel Gemunder, Fifth Third Bank.
EIN: 311534042

43509
Ruth R. Peters Scholarship B Fund
c/o Sky Trust, N.A.
P.O. Box 479
Youngstown, OH 44501-0479
Application address: c/o Superintendent, Brookfield High School, 7000 Grove St., Brookfield, OH 44403-9505

Established in 1997 in PA.
Financial data (yr. ended 12/31/01): Grants paid, $31,653; assets, $337,364 (M); expenditures, $35,517; qualifying distributions, $31,653.
Limitations: Giving limited to Oberlin, OH.
Application information: Application form required.
Trustee: Sky Trust, N.A.
EIN: 237872473

43510
Van Devere Charitable Foundation, Inc.
300 W. Market St.
Akron, OH 44303 (330) 253-6137
Contact: Joseph C. Van Devere, Tr.

Established in 1986 in OH.
Donor(s): Joseph C. Van Devere.
Financial data (yr. ended 12/31/01): Grants paid, $31,600; assets, $640,070 (M); gifts received, $70,000; expenditures, $38,791; qualifying distributions, $31,600.
Limitations: Giving on a national basis.
Trustee: Joseph C. Van Devere.
EIN: 341538755

43511
Fink Foundation
c/o National City Bank of Indiana
P.O. Box 94651
Cleveland, OH 44101-4651
Application address: c/o James Westerfield, National City Bank of Indiana, P.O. Box 110, Fort Wayne, IN 46801, tel.: (219) 461-7126

Established in 1997 in IN.
Financial data (yr. ended 03/31/02): Grants paid, $31,500; assets, $882,794 (M); gifts received, $18,050; expenditures, $32,811; qualifying distributions, $29,118.
Limitations: Giving primarily in Aubern, IN.
Officers: Gloria D. Fink, Pres.; Richard Fink, Secy.
EIN: 356640978

43512
Hauck Family Foundation
c/o Robison, Curphey & O'Connell
4622 Beaconsfield
Toledo, OH 43623

Established in 1992 in OH.
Donor(s): Charles Peter Hauck.
Financial data (yr. ended 12/31/01): Grants paid, $31,500; assets, $421,789 (M); expenditures, $33,734; qualifying distributions, $31,402.
Limitations: Applications not accepted. Giving primarily in OH.
Application information: Contributes only to pre-selected organizations.
Trustees: Charles Peter Hauck, Paula M. Hauck, Thomas C. Hauck, Nancy H. McMahon.
EIN: 341724374

43513—OHIO

43513
Frank C. and Norma J. Watson Foundation
c/o Butler Wick Trust Co.
City Ctr. 1, No. 700
Youngstown, OH 44503 (330) 744-4351

Financial data (yr. ended 12/31/01): Grants paid, $31,250; assets, $594,161 (M); expenditures, $38,431; qualifying distributions, $31,250.
Limitations: Giving primarily in Youngstown, OH.
Application information: Application form not required.
Advisory Committee: Frank C. Watson, Norma J. Watson.
Trustee: Butler Wick Trust Co.
EIN: 341559908

43514
Robert C. Neff Sinclair Trust f/b/o YMCA
c/o National City Bank
P.O. Box 94651
Cleveland, OH 44101-4651

Financial data (yr. ended 12/31/01): Grants paid, $31,234; assets, $598,101 (M); expenditures, $39,994; qualifying distributions, $31,234.
Limitations: Applications not accepted. Giving limited to Dayton, OH.
Application information: Contributes only to pre-selected organizations.
Trustee: National City Bank.
EIN: 316584210

43515
Lois C. & Thomas G. Stauffer Foundation
19 Warwick Ln.
Rocky River, OH 44116-2305

Established in 1998 in OH.
Donor(s): Thomas Stauffer.
Financial data (yr. ended 12/31/01): Grants paid, $31,140; assets, $614,120 (M); expenditures, $32,886; qualifying distributions, $31,140.
Officer: Thomas G. Stauffer, Pres.
Trustees: Jill Campsey Miller, Lois C. Stauffer.
EIN: 341860034

43516
The C. Walder Parke Family Foundation
c/o Richard W. Parke
18829 Fairmount Blvd.
Shaker Heights, OH 44118 (216) 575-2284
Application address: c/o National City Bank, 1900 E. 9th St., Cleveland, OH 44114-3484, tel.: (216) 575-2284
Contact: Mark W. Buxton

Established in 1997 in OH.
Donor(s): Gloria P. Parke.
Financial data (yr. ended 12/31/01): Grants paid, $31,109; assets, $713,703 (M); expenditures, $35,450; qualifying distributions, $31,109.
Limitations: Giving primarily in Cleveland, OH.
Trustees: Elizabeth P. MacIntyre, Caroline P. Oldenburg, Gloria P. Parke, Richard W. Parke.
EIN: 311535130

43517
Lucille M. Potter Charitable Trust
c/o KeyBank, N.A.
800 Superior Ave., 4th Fl.
Cleveland, OH 44114

Established in 1999 in ME.
Financial data (yr. ended 01/31/02): Grants paid, $31,096; assets, $526,805 (M); expenditures, $38,922; qualifying distributions, $31,096.

Limitations: Applications not accepted.
Application information: Contributes only to pre-selected organizations.
Trustee: KeyBank, N.A.
EIN: 316630121

43518
John Milton Costello Foundation
55 Public Sq., Ste. 1900
Cleveland, OH 44113
Application address: 2595 Fenwick Rd., University Heights, OH, 44118, tel.: (216) 932-5235
Contact: Mary Jane Cole, Pres.

Financial data (yr. ended 12/31/01): Grants paid, $31,000; assets, $674,439 (M); expenditures, $40,904; qualifying distributions, $35,869.
Limitations: Giving limited to the greater Cleveland, OH, area.
Application information: Application form not required.
Officers and Trustees:* Mary Jane Cole,* Pres.; Elizabeth B. McKegney,* V.P.; Bernard H. Niehaus,* Secy.; Lynn Kraty.
EIN: 346738800

43519
Edwin L. and Louis B. McCallay Educational Trust Fund
c/o First Financial Bank
300 High St.
Hamilton, OH 45011
Application address: c/o Trust Off., 815 Breiel Blvd., Middletown, OH 45042, tel.: (513) 425-7548

Financial data (yr. ended 02/28/02): Grants paid, $31,000; assets, $575,914 (M); expenditures, $38,047; qualifying distributions, $34,495.
Limitations: Giving primarily in OH.
Application information: Application form required.
Trustee: First Financial Bank.
EIN: 316111939
Codes: GTI

43520
Phyllis H. Steigler Trust
c/o KeyBank, N.A.
800 Superior Ave., 4th Fl.
Cleveland, OH 44114-2601
Application address: c/o KeyBank, N.A., Cristina Cook, Trust Off., P.O. Box 1054, Augusta, ME 04330

Established in 1991 in ME.
Financial data (yr. ended 06/30/01): Grants paid, $31,000; assets, $649,575 (M); expenditures, $38,758; qualifying distributions, $31,000.
Limitations: Giving limited to residents of ME.
Trustee: KeyBank, N.A.
EIN: 016109107
Codes: GTI

43521
The Smiley Family Charitable Foundation
35415 Solon Rd.
Solon, OH 44139-2415

Established in 1997 in OH.
Donor(s): Raymond E. Smiley.
Financial data (yr. ended 12/31/01): Grants paid, $30,762; assets, $1,019,591 (M); expenditures, $32,162; qualifying distributions, $30,762.
Limitations: Applications not accepted.

Application information: Contributes only to pre-selected organizations.
Officers: Raymond E. Smiley, Pres. and Treas.; Eleanor M. Smiley, Secy.
EIN: 311543239

43522
B.L. Family Foundation
901 Lakeside Ave., N. Point
Cleveland, OH 44114-1116 (216) 586-7189
Contact: Irvin A. Leonard, Pres.

Established in 1985 in OH.
Donor(s): Irvin A. Leonard, Elin L. Leonard, Live Partners Limited Partnership.
Financial data (yr. ended 10/31/01): Grants paid, $30,730; assets, $85,269 (M); gifts received, $19,358; expenditures, $31,914; qualifying distributions, $30,730.
Limitations: Giving primarily in FL, NY, and OH.
Trustees: Martin Barmack, Rebecca Barmack, Elin L. Leonard, Irvin A. Leonard.
EIN: 341499583

43523
The Valerian Family Foundation
c/o William E. Reichard
25109 Detroit Rd., Ste. 300
Westlake, OH 44145-2544

Established in 1997 in OH.
Financial data (yr. ended 12/31/00): Grants paid, $30,720; assets, $77,726 (M); expenditures, $35,031; qualifying distributions, $29,720.
Limitations: Applications not accepted. Giving primarily in Cleveland, OH.
Application information: Contributes only to pre-selected organizations.
Trustees: Diane C. Valerian, William A. Valerian.
EIN: 341851168

43524
Wing-Benjamin Trust Fund
c/o KeyBank, N.A.
800 Superior Ave., 4th Fl.
Cleveland, OH 44114-1306
Application address: 286 Water St., Augusta, ME 04330
Contact: Cris Cook, Trust Off., KeyBank, N.A.

Financial data (yr. ended 04/30/02): Grants paid, $30,550; assets, $923,858 (M); expenditures, $38,971; qualifying distributions, $30,550.
Limitations: Giving primarily in ME.
Trustee: KeyBank, N.A.
EIN: 016007288
Codes: GTI

43525
Evans Foundation, Inc.
c/o Fifth Third Bank
P.O. Box 630858
Cincinnati, OH 45263
Application address: 940 Portage Trl., Cuyahoga Falls, OH 44221-3048
Contact: William H. Evans, Tr.

Financial data (yr. ended 12/31/01): Grants paid, $30,200; assets, $588,121 (M); expenditures, $33,010; qualifying distributions, $30,200.
Limitations: Giving limited to northern OH.
Trustees: Betty G. Evans Carney, David G. Evans, Kenneth J. Evans, William H. Evans III, Howard W. Myers.
EIN: 346526309

43526
Helen Johnston Family Foundation
c/o Fifth Third Bank
38 Fountain Sq. Plz., Dept. 630858, M/D 1COM31
Cincinnati, OH 45263
Contact: Lawra Baumann, Trust Off., Fifth Third Bank

Established in 1997 in OH.
Financial data (yr. ended 12/31/01): Grants paid, $30,200; assets, $335,194 (M); expenditures, $34,245; qualifying distributions, $30,200.
Trustees: Helen R. Johnston, John Johnston, Laurie Johnston, Fifth Third Bank.
EIN: 311530591 @RH1 = 43527—OHIO

43527
Ellen E. & Victor J. Cohn Foundation
29225 Chagrin Blvd.
Beachwood, OH 44122-4629

Established in 1997 in OH.
Donor(s): Ellen E. Cohn.
Financial data (yr. ended 09/30/01): Grants paid, $30,170; assets, $256,336 (M); expenditures, $35,242; qualifying distributions, $30,170.
Limitations: Applications not accepted. Giving on a national basis.
Application information: Contributes only to pre-selected organizations.
Officers: Ellen E. Cohn, Pres. and Treas.; Victor J. Cohn, V.P. and Secy.
EIN: 341874449

43528
Marjorie and Alexander Hover Charitable Trust
c/o KeyBank, N.A., Trust Div.
800 Superior Ave., 4th Fl.
Cleveland, OH 44114

Established in 1999 in NY.
Financial data (yr. ended 12/31/01): Grants paid, $30,125; assets, $543,224 (M); expenditures, $37,383; qualifying distributions, $30,125.
Limitations: Applications not accepted. Giving primarily in NY and OH.
Application information: Contributes only to pre-selected organizations.
Trustee: KeyBank, N.A.
EIN: 141814056

43529
Lena A. & Paul F. Addison Trust
c/o Fifth Third Bank
P.O. Box 630858
Cincinnati, OH 45263
Application address: c/o Guidance Counselor, Mount Vernon Senior High School, 700 Harriett St., Mount Vernon, IN 47620

Established in 1997 in IN.
Financial data (yr. ended 12/31/01): Grants paid, $30,100; assets, $614,628 (M); expenditures, $43,637; qualifying distributions, $33,607.
Limitations: Giving limited to Mount Vernon, IN.
Application information: Application form required.
Trustee: Fifth Third Bank.
EIN: 356639866
Codes: GTI

43530
The Marilyn and Peter Tsivitse Foundation
3030 Roundwood Rd.
Hunting Valley, OH 44022-6632

Established in 1997 in OH.
Financial data (yr. ended 12/31/01): Grants paid, $30,077; assets, $577,025 (M); expenditures, $32,567; qualifying distributions, $30,077.
Limitations: Applications not accepted.
Application information: Contributes only to pre-selected organizations.
Officers and Trustees:* Peter J. Tsivitse,* Pres. and Treas.; Marilyn J. Tsivitse, Secy.; Paul T. Tsivitse.
EIN: 311546865

43531
The Brentlinger Foundation
50 Public Sq., Ste. 2700
Cleveland, OH 44113

Established in 1986 in OH.
Donor(s): Paul S. Brentlinger, Marilyn E. Brentlinger.
Financial data (yr. ended 12/31/01): Grants paid, $30,050; assets, $41,435 (M); gifts received, $38,090; expenditures, $31,300; qualifying distributions, $30,050.
Limitations: Applications not accepted. Giving limited to Cleveland, OH.
Application information: Contributes only to pre-selected organizations.
Officers and Trustees:* Paul S. Brentlinger,* Pres.; Marilyn E. Brentlinger,* V.P.; Sara I. Brentlinger Walters,* Secy.; David A. Brentlinger,* Treas.; Paula E. Brentlinger.
EIN: 346864391

43532
Blakney Foundation
One Park Centre Dr., Ste. 301A
Wadsworth, OH 44281

Established in 1998 in OH.
Donor(s): David B. Smith.
Financial data (yr. ended 12/31/01): Grants paid, $30,000; assets, $985,769 (M); gifts received, $200,000; expenditures, $31,800; qualifying distributions, $30,000.
Limitations: Applications not accepted. Giving primarily in Beaufort County, SC.
Application information: Contributes only to pre-selected organizations.
Officers: David B. Smith, Pres. and Treas.; Paticia J. Smith, V.P. and Secy.
Trustee: Paul M. Ostergard.
EIN: 341881439

43533
John & Pearl Conard Foundation Trust
Richland Bank Bldg.
3 N. Main St.
Mansfield, OH 44902-1715 (419) 525-8705
Contact: Jack Stewart

Established in 1984 in OH.
Financial data (yr. ended 06/30/01): Grants paid, $30,000; assets, $3,149,978 (M); expenditures, $65,140; qualifying distributions, $180,381.
Limitations: Giving limited to OH, with emphasis on Richland County.
Application information: Application form required.
Officers: William P. Jilek, Chair.; Thomas H. Bloor, Vice.-Chair.; Harold Davis, Secy.-Treas.; John P. Stewart, Rec. Secy.
Trustee: The Richland Trust Co.
Distribution Committee: Richard Adams, James R. Bierly, JoAnne McCarron, Grant Milliron.
EIN: 346777250

43534
Otto & Isabel Frings Memorial Scholarship Fund
c/o Fifth Third Bank
P.O. Box 630858
Cincinnati, OH 45263
Application address: c/o Fifth Third Bank of Western Ohio, Dayton, OH 45402, tel.: (937) 227-6532

Established in 2000 in OH.
Donor(s): Otto Frings,‡ Isabel Frings.‡
Financial data (yr. ended 12/31/01): Grants paid, $30,000; assets, $907,554 (M); gifts received, $259,240; expenditures, $40,511; qualifying distributions, $30,000.
Trustee: Fifth Third Bank.
EIN: 316641964

43535
James L. Hagle Foundation
c/o Lawrence L. Fisher
P.O. Box 1008
Columbus, OH 43216-1008
Application address: 9124 Hollyoak Dr., Bethesda, MD 20817, tel.: (301) 469-7159
Contact: Bette Rose Kovin, Pres.

Established in 1989 in OH.
Financial data (yr. ended 06/30/02): Grants paid, $30,000; assets, $425,666 (M); expenditures, $30,533; qualifying distributions, $30,000.
Limitations: Giving primarily in Washington, DC, and MA.
Officers and Trustees:* Bette Rose Kovin,* Pres.; Barbara L. Slonaker,* V.P. and Treas.; Lawrence L. Fisher,* Secy.
EIN: 311490983

43536
Gertrude Mead Ott Charitable Fund
236 3rd St., S.W.
Canton, OH 44702 (330) 455-5281
Contact: Gertrude Mead Ott, Pres.

Donor(s): Gertrude Mead Ott.
Financial data (yr. ended 09/30/01): Grants paid, $30,000; assets, $341,408 (M); expenditures, $31,355; qualifying distributions, $30,000.
Limitations: Giving limited to New London, CT.
Application information: Application form not required.
Officers and Trustees:* Gertrude Mead Ott,* Pres.; Don D. Dickes,* Secy.-Treas.; Barbara C. Timken, Jane M. Timken, John M. Timken, Jr.
EIN: 341323185

43537
C. D. Winning Scholarship Fund
(Formerly Kiwanis Scholarship Fund)
c/o National City Bank
P.O. Box 94651
Cleveland, OH 44101-4651
Application address: c/o Edward Hack, Egert, Schneider, Mayer, & Hack, Lakewood Ctr. N., 14600 Detroit Ave., Ste. 1300, Lakewood, OH 44107, tel.: (216) 228-4400

Established in 1988 in OH.
Donor(s): Charles D. Winning.
Financial data (yr. ended 12/31/01): Grants paid, $30,000; assets, $379,949 (M); expenditures, $24,089; qualifying distributions, $31,350.
Limitations: Giving limited to Lakewood, OH.
Application information: Application form required.
Trustee: National City Bank.
EIN: 346902315
Codes: GTI

43538
The Beverage Distributors, Inc. Foundation
3800 King Ave.
Cleveland, OH 44114

Established in 2001 in OH.
Donor(s): Beverage Distributors, Inc.
Financial data (yr. ended 12/31/01): Grants paid, $29,900; assets, $30,650 (M); gifts received, $23,684; expenditures, $32,850; qualifying distributions, $30,390.

43538—OHIO

Limitations: Applications not accepted. Giving primarily in Cleveland, OH.
Application information: Contributes only to pre-selected organizations.
Officers and Trustees:* James V. Conway,* Pres.; Patrick M. Flanagan,* Secy.; Michelle A. Bates,* Treas.
EIN: 341964921
Codes: CS

43539
Willard Stephenson Foundation
c/o FirstMerit Bank, N.A.
P.O. Box 725
Medina, OH 44258-0725
Application address: c/o FirstMerit Bank, N.A., 39 Public Sq., Medina, OH 44256

Established in 1990 in OH.
Donor(s): Willard A. Stephenson.
Financial data (yr. ended 12/31/00): Grants paid, $29,885; assets, $586,374 (M); gifts received, $42,156; expenditures, $36,797; qualifying distributions, $29,885.
Limitations: Giving primarily in OH.
Trustee: FirstMerit Bank, N.A.
EIN: 341635094

43540
The Krause Family Foundation
1100 Eaton Ctr.
Cleveland, OH 44114

Established in 1968.
Donor(s): Harold Krause, Alan M. Krause.
Financial data (yr. ended 12/31/01): Grants paid, $29,812; assets, $741,799 (M); expenditures, $32,206; qualifying distributions, $29,812.
Limitations: Applications not accepted. Giving primarily in Cleveland, OH.
Application information: Contributes only to pre-selected organizations.
Officers: Alan Krause, Mgr.; Harold Krause, Mgr.
EIN: 346611350

43541
Scallan Family Foundation
c/o Robert D. Scallan
4925 Willow Hills Ln.
Cincinnati, OH 45245

Established in 1999 in OH.
Donor(s): Robert D. Scallan.
Financial data (yr. ended 12/31/01): Grants paid, $29,575; assets, $191,810 (M); gifts received, $35,877; expenditures, $33,011; qualifying distributions, $29,575.
Limitations: Applications not accepted.
Application information: Contributes only to pre-selected organizations.
Director: Robert D. Scallan.
EIN: 311638335

43542
Charles & Dorothy Wein Charitable Fund
c/o National City Bank of Pennsylvania
P.O. Box 94651
Cleveland, OH 44101-4651
Application address: P.O. Box 374, Oil City, PA 16301, tel.: (814) 676-1600
Contact: Steven P. Kosak, Trust Off., National City Bank of Pennsylvania

Donor(s): Dorothy Wein.
Financial data (yr. ended 06/30/01): Grants paid, $29,550; assets, $771,811 (M); expenditures, $35,036; qualifying distributions, $34,004.
Limitations: Giving limited to residents of Clarion County, PA.
Application information: Application form required.

Trustee: National City Bank.
EIN: 256225347
Codes: GTI

43543
The Kurt E. & Lois J. Wallach Foundation
7501 Paragon Rd.
Dayton, OH 45459
Contact: John Ruffolo, Tr.

Established in 1999 in OH.
Financial data (yr. ended 12/31/01): Grants paid, $29,500; assets, $389,725 (M); expenditures, $33,107; qualifying distributions, $29,500.
Limitations: Giving primarily in Dayton, OH.
Application information: Application form required.
Trustee: John Ruffolo.
EIN: 311622765

43544
The Hinchman Foundation
c/o National City Bank
P.O. Box 94651
Cleveland, OH 44101-4651

Established in 1998 in PA.
Donor(s): Margaret E. Hinchman.
Financial data (yr. ended 12/31/01): Grants paid, $29,494; assets, $619,592 (M); expenditures, $32,849; qualifying distributions, $30,511.
Limitations: Applications not accepted. Giving primarily in Pittsburgh, PA.
Application information: Contributes only to pre-selected organizations.
Trustee: National City Bank.
EIN: 256581645

43545
The Semi J. & Ruth W. Begun Foundation
(Formerly The Begun Foundation)
1379 Burlington Rd.
Cleveland Heights, OH 44118-1270

Established in 1988 in OH.
Donor(s): Semi J. Begun.
Financial data (yr. ended 12/31/00): Grants paid, $29,336; assets, $819,764 (M); expenditures, $39,923; qualifying distributions, $29,336.
Limitations: Applications not accepted. Giving limited to Cleveland, OH.
Application information: Contributes only to pre-selected organizations.
Trustees: Peter Baldi, Ruth Weltmann Begun, Ronald L. Garman, Alan D. Gross, Peter A. Holmes, Carl F. Nardone, Allan Steinhardt.
EIN: 341594565

43546
The Jehm Foundation, Inc.
c/o Fifth Third Bank
P.O. Box 630858, Trust Dept. 00858
Cincinnati, OH 45263   (513) 579-6034
Contact: Lawra Baumann, Dir.

Established in 1998 in OH.
Financial data (yr. ended 12/31/00): Grants paid, $29,327; assets, $54,402 (M); gifts received, $295; expenditures, $31,149; qualifying distributions, $29,831.
Limitations: Giving primarily in OH.
Trustees: Phil Borack, Fifth Third Bank.
EIN: 347085205

43547
David Barron Foundation
(Formerly David & Carole Barron Foundation)
c/o U.S. Bank
P.O. Box 1118, CN-WN-07PT
Cincinnati, OH 45201-1118
Contact: Hal Klink, Sr. V.P., U.S. Bank

Established in 1997 in OH.
Donor(s): David Barron.
Financial data (yr. ended 12/31/01): Grants paid, $29,300; assets, $281,783 (M); gifts received, $10,000; expenditures, $34,630; qualifying distributions, $30,084.
Limitations: Applications not accepted. Giving primarily in OH.
Application information: Contributes only to pre-selected organizations.
Trustees: David Barron, Dennis L. Manes, U.S. Bank.
EIN: 311521552

43548
Louis T. Block Family Foundation
255 E. 5th St.
2400 Chemed Ctr.
Cincinnati, OH 45202-4724

Financial data (yr. ended 12/31/01): Grants paid, $29,300; assets, $524,963 (M); expenditures, $38,987; qualifying distributions, $29,300.
Limitations: Applications not accepted. Giving primarily in Cincinnati, OH.
Application information: Contributes only to pre-selected organizations.
Officers: Thomas Block, Pres.; Susan B. Litvak, V.P. and Treas.; Barbara Cohen, V.P.; Richard Block, Secy.
EIN: 310738544

43549
Glenn B. Fordyce Foundation
210 Hobart Dr.
Hillsboro, OH 45133

Established in 1998 in OH.
Donor(s): Glenn B. Fordyce.
Financial data (yr. ended 12/31/01): Grants paid, $29,110; assets, $475,780 (M); expenditures, $29,116; qualifying distributions, $29,110.
Limitations: Giving primarily in Hillsboro, OH.
Officers: Glenn B. Fordyce, Pres.; Dennis L. Manes, Secy.
Trustee: David M. Hollingsworth.
EIN: 311628371

43550
The Kent Family Foundation
c/o National City Bank
P.O. Box 94651
Cleveland, OH 44101-4651

Established in 1997 in IN.
Donor(s): Jeannette Kent.
Financial data (yr. ended 05/31/02): Grants paid, $29,073; assets, $599,134 (M); expenditures, $26,963; qualifying distributions, $29,073.
Director: Jeannette Kent.
Trustee: National City Bank.
EIN: 352016376

43551
C. James Burke Trust
c/o National City Bank of Indiana
P.O. Box 94651
Cleveland, OH 44101-4651

Financial data (yr. ended 12/31/01): Grants paid, $28,971; assets, $772,731 (M); expenditures, $84,030; qualifying distributions, $31,141.

Limitations: Applications not accepted. Giving primarily in IN.
Application information: Contributes only to pre-selected organizations.
Trustee: National City Bank of Indiana.
EIN: 356313928

43552
Richard S. Morrison Foundation
P.O. Box 675
Ashtabula, OH 44005-0675

Established in 1987 in OH.
Donor(s): Richard S. Morrison.
Financial data (yr. ended 12/31/01): Grants paid, $28,848; assets, $655,289 (M); expenditures, $46,407; qualifying distributions, $28,848.
Limitations: Applications not accepted.
Application information: Contributes only to pre-selected organizations.
Officer: Richard S. Morrison, Pres.
Trustee: William H. Kane.
EIN: 341535819

43553
The Olin Family Foundation
21925 McCauley Rd.
Shaker Heights, OH 44122

Established in 1992 in OH.
Donor(s): Gail Olin.
Financial data (yr. ended 12/31/01): Grants paid, $28,800; assets, $211,515 (M); gifts received, $513; expenditures, $33,517; qualifying distributions, $28,800.
Limitations: Applications not accepted. Giving primarily in Cleveland, OH.
Application information: Contributes only to pre-selected organizations.
Trustees: Gail Cowin, William Spring.
EIN: 341725337

43554
Summer Mission for Sick Children, Inc.
c/o National City Bank of Indiana
P.O. Box 94651
Cleveland, OH 44101-4651

Financial data (yr. ended 12/31/01): Grants paid, $28,800; assets, $643,847 (M); expenditures, $35,863; qualifying distributions, $28,800.
Limitations: Applications not accepted. Giving primarily in IN.
Application information: Contributes only to pre-selected organizations.
Officer: Stanley M. Harris, Secy.-Treas.
Trustee: National City Bank.
EIN: 351433187

43555
Alverta E. Schopene Charitable Trust
c/o National City Bank of Pennsylvania
P.O. Box 94651
Cleveland, OH 44101-4651

Financial data (yr. ended 12/31/01): Grants paid, $28,762; assets, $600,492 (M); expenditures, $32,292; qualifying distributions, $28,762.
Trustee: National City Bank.
EIN: 256583112

43556
Frank Foster Skillman Scholarship
c/o PNC Advisors
P.O. Box 1198
Cincinnati, OH 45201-1198 (513) 651-8413
Contact: James D. Huizenga, Trust Off., PNC Advisors

Financial data (yr. ended 09/30/01): Grants paid, $28,668; assets, $514,774 (M); expenditures, $48,293; qualifying distributions, $38,123.

Limitations: Giving limited to residents of Cincinnati, OH.
Application information: Application form required.
Trustee: PNC Bank, N.A.
EIN: 316018084
Codes: GTI

43557
The Hageman Family Foundation
c/o Kent D. Hageman
3431 E. Erie Ave.
Lorain, OH 44052

Established in 2000.
Donor(s): Virginia Hageman.
Financial data (yr. ended 12/31/01): Grants paid, $28,550; assets, $543,342 (M); expenditures, $43,266; qualifying distributions, $28,550.
Officers: Kent D. Hageman, Pres.; Virginia Hageman, V.P.; Wendy Hageman, Secy.
EIN: 311695028

43558
Downtown Catholic Club
2132 E. 9th St.
Cleveland, OH 44115 (216) 771-4811
Contact: Frank Kelley, Secy.

Financial data (yr. ended 12/31/01): Grants paid, $28,500; assets, $31,596 (M); gifts received, $12,000; expenditures, $28,519; qualifying distributions, $28,501.
Limitations: Giving limited to the Cleveland, OH, area.
Officers: Phillip Adams, Pres.; Leo McIntyre, V.P.; Frank Kelley, Secy.; Ray Pipak, Treas.
EIN: 346563156

43559
Maxon Foundation
c/o U.S. Bank
P.O. Box 1118, ML CN-NN-10TX
Cincinnati, OH 45201-1118

Donor(s): Glenway W. Maxon, Jr.
Financial data (yr. ended 12/31/01): Grants paid, $28,500; assets, $845,135 (M); expenditures, $36,847; qualifying distributions, $28,700.
Limitations: Applications not accepted. Giving primarily in Vero Beach, FL.
Application information: Contributes only to pre-selected organizations.
Trustee: Glenway W. Maxon, Jr.
Agent: U.S. Bank.
EIN: 316045992

43560
The I. B. Goodman Foundation
314 John St.
Cincinnati, OH 45202

Established in 1983 in OH.
Donor(s): Goodman Manufacturing Co., Inc.
Financial data (yr. ended 12/31/99): Grants paid, $28,495; assets, $58,840 (M); gifts received, $25,000; expenditures, $28,495; qualifying distributions, $28,495.
Limitations: Applications not accepted. Giving primarily in New York, NY.
Application information: Contributes only to pre-selected organizations.
Trustees: Jane Goodman Baum, Babette Goodman Cohen.
EIN: 311082135

43561
Joseph and Nancy Keithley Foundation
c/o Chess Financial Corp.
30050 Chagrin Blvd., Ste. 100
Pepper Pike, OH 44124

Established in 2000 in OH.
Donor(s): Joseph P. Keithley.
Financial data (yr. ended 12/31/00): Grants paid, $28,490; assets, $5,771,653 (M); gifts received, $958,586; expenditures, $31,802; qualifying distributions, $28,490.
Limitations: Applications not accepted. Giving primarily in Cleveland, OH.
Application information: Contributes only to pre-selected organizations.
Officers: Joseph P. Keithley, Pres.; James B. Griswold, Secy.; Nancy F. Keithley, Treas.
EIN: 341926208

43562
French Oil Mill Machinery Company Charitable Trust
c/o Fifth Third Bank
110 N. Main St., M.D. 332952
Dayton, OH 45402

Donor(s): French Oil Mill Machinery Co.
Financial data (yr. ended 11/30/01): Grants paid, $28,420; assets, $662,871 (M); expenditures, $36,381; qualifying distributions, $29,772.
Limitations: Applications not accepted. Giving primarily in OH.
Application information: Contributes only to pre-selected organizations.
Trustee: Fifth Third Bank.
EIN: 316024511
Codes: CS, CD

43563
Henry F. Koch Residual Trust
c/o Fifth Third Bank
39 Fountain Sq. Plz., 1COM31
Cincinnati, OH 45263

Financial data (yr. ended 12/31/01): Grants paid, $28,350; assets, $607,029 (M); expenditures, $38,212; qualifying distributions, $28,338.
Limitations: Giving primarily in IN.
Application information: Application form not required.
Trustee: Fifth Third Bank.
EIN: 356011881

43564
Louise Foley Conservation Fund
c/o KeyBank, N.A., Trust Div.
800 Superior Ave., 4th Fl.
Cleveland, OH 44114

Established in 1994 in WA.
Financial data (yr. ended 12/31/01): Grants paid, $28,200; assets, $742,809 (M); expenditures, $40,986; qualifying distributions, $30,857.
Limitations: Applications not accepted. Giving primarily in OR and WA.
Application information: Contributes only to pre-selected organizations.
Trustee: KeyBank, N.A.
EIN: 916369102

43565
W. B. Lockwood Fund
c/o National City Bank N.E.
P.O. Box 450
Youngstown, OH 44501-0450

Financial data (yr. ended 12/31/01): Grants paid, $28,100; assets, $716,889 (M); expenditures, $30,942; qualifying distributions, $28,100.
Limitations: Giving primarily in CT, NY, and OH.

43565—OHIO

Trustees: John H. Lockwood, W.B. Lockwood, Jr., National City Bank, Northeast.
EIN: 346515733

43566
The College Club of Cleveland Foundation
c/o Scholarship Comm.
2348 E. Overlook Rd.
Cleveland Heights, OH 44106-2398

Established in 1987 in OH.
Financial data (yr. ended 12/31/99): Grants paid, $28,000; assets, $662,444 (M); gifts received, $24,912; expenditures, $35,789; qualifying distributions, $29,209.
Limitations: Giving limited to Cleveland, OH.
Application information: Application form required.
Officers: Ruth Anderson, Pres.; Ruth Jenks, V.P.; Gloria Hastings, Secy.; Margery Nokes, Treas.
EIN: 341569601

43567
Robert L. Munger, Jr. Foundation
1 Cedar Point Dr.
Sandusky, OH 44870-5259
Application addresses: c/o Valleyfair Park, Personnel Dept., 1 Valleyfair Dr., Shakopee, MN 55379; c/o Dorney Park, Personnel Dept., 3830 Dorney Park Rd., Allentown, PA 18104; Cedar Point, Personnel Dept., 1 Cedar Point Dr., Sandusky, OH 44870-5259
Contact: Richard L. Kinzel, V.P.

Established in 1988 in OH.
Donor(s): Members of the Munger family, Cedar Farr, LP, Lazard Freres & Co., Pearson, Inc.
Financial data (yr. ended 12/31/01): Grants paid, $28,000; assets, $511,197 (M); expenditures, $34,935; qualifying distributions, $30,778.
Limitations: Giving limited to Shakopee, MN, Sandusky, OH, and Allentown, PA.
Application information: Application form required.
Officers and Trustees:* Holly Munger Book,* Pres. and Treas.; Richard L. Kinzel,* V.P. and Secy.; Jeffrey Munger, Marguerite Munger, Myron Munger.
EIN: 341599255
Codes: GTI

43568
John B. Van Meter Charitable Foundation, Inc.
c/o Ronald C. Christian
1800 Firstar Tower, 425 Walnut St.
Cincinnati, OH 45202-3957

Established in 1994 in KY.
Donor(s): John B. Van Meter.
Financial data (yr. ended 12/31/01): Grants paid, $28,000; assets, $447,071 (M); expenditures, $33,308; qualifying distributions, $28,614.
Limitations: Applications not accepted. Giving primarily in KY.
Application information: Contributes only to pre-selected organizations.
Officers and Trustees:* John B. Van Meter,* Pres.; Isaac C. Van Meter, Jr.,* Treas.; Terry K. Crilley.
EIN: 611274104

43569
The Shuree Abrams Foundation
25550 Chagrin Blvd., No. 310
Beachwood, OH 44122-5628

Donor(s): Shuree Abrams.
Financial data (yr. ended 05/31/00): Grants paid, $27,867; assets, $1,065,660 (M); expenditures, $30,578; qualifying distributions, $28,067.
Limitations: Applications not accepted. Giving primarily in FL and OH.

Application information: Contributes only to pre-selected organizations.
Officers: Shuree Abrams, Pres. and Treas.; Sydney Friedman, V.P. and Secy.
Trustee: Vivein Abrams.
EIN: 346555203

43570
Dix Foundation
c/o Wooster Daily Record, Inc.
212 E. Liberty St.
Wooster, OH 44691-4348 (330) 264-1125
Contact: Robert C. Dix, Jr., Tr.

Donor(s): The Defiance Publishing Co., Wooster Republican Printing Co.
Financial data (yr. ended 12/31/01): Grants paid, $27,860; assets, $1,265 (M); gifts received, $24,500; expenditures, $28,019; qualifying distributions, $28,018.
Limitations: Giving limited to the Defiance, OH, area.
Trustees: Albert E. Dix, David E. Dix, G. Charles Dix II, R. Victor Dix, Robert C. Dix, Jr.
EIN: 346554966
Codes: CS

43571
The Thomas J. Gruber and Judith Fay Gruber Charitable Foundation
9870 Hobart Rd.
Waite Hill, OH 44094 (440) 247-8100
Contact: Judith Fay Gruber, Tr.

Established in 1993 in OH.
Donor(s): Thomas J. Gruber, Judith Fay Gruber.
Financial data (yr. ended 06/30/01): Grants paid, $27,825; assets, $390,036 (M); expenditures, $29,747; qualifying distributions, $27,825.
Limitations: Giving primarily in Cleveland, OH.
Application information: Application form not required.
Trustees: Judith Fay Gruber, Thomas J. Gruber.
EIN: 341769361

43572
The Robert Kaplan Family Foundation, Inc.
200 Public Sq.
2300 BP America Bldg.
Cleveland, OH 44114-2378 (216) 363-4500
Contact: Howard A. Steindler, Secy.

Established in 1988 in OH.
Financial data (yr. ended 12/31/01): Grants paid, $27,700; assets, $453,230 (M); expenditures, $46,310; qualifying distributions, $27,700.
Limitations: Giving primarily in Cleveland, OH.
Application information: Application form not required.
Officers and Trustees:* Robert Alan Kaplan,* Pres. and Treas.; Linda Kaplan,* V.P.; Howard A. Steindler,* Secy.
EIN: 341613151

43573
Harley Ernest Foundation
2436 Streetsboro Rd.
Peninsula, OH 44264

Established in 1999 in OH.
Donor(s): Judith Ernest, John W. Harley.
Financial data (yr. ended 06/30/00): Grants paid, $27,550; assets, $421,365 (M); gifts received, $5,500; expenditures, $38,628; qualifying distributions, $34,101; giving activities include $6,551 for programs.
Limitations: Applications not accepted. Giving primarily in Cleveland, OH.
Application information: Contributes only to pre-selected organizations.

Trustees: Judith Ernest, John W. Harley, Walter S. Harley.
EIN: 341864155

43574
Blue Coats of Louisville, Inc.
c/o National City Bank, Kentucky
P.O. Box 94651
Cleveland, OH 44101-4651
Application address: c/o Arthur C. Peters, P.O. Box 32760, Louisville, KY 40232, tel.: (502) 895-8858
Contact: David J. Matton, Pres.

Financial data (yr. ended 12/31/99): Grants paid, $27,526; assets, $659,620 (M); expenditures, $29,978; qualifying distributions, $28,526.
Limitations: Giving limited to Louisville, KY.
Application information: Application form not required.
Officers: David J. Matton, Pres.; James S. Welch, V.P.; John McBride, Secy.
Trustee: National City Bank, Kentucky.
EIN: 616022331

43575
Conalin Family Foundation, Inc.
3560 Bayard Dr.
Cincinnati, OH 45208
Contact: Constance H. Miller, Treas.

Established in 1992 in FL.
Financial data (yr. ended 12/31/01): Grants paid, $27,500; assets, $350,310 (M); expenditures, $35,816; qualifying distributions, $27,456.
Officer and Trustees:* Constance H. Miller,* Treas.; Albert Halverstadt, Jr., Linda MacDuffie.
EIN: 656087042

43576
Edgar E. Kessel Scholarship Fund
(Formerly Edgar E. Kessel Trust)
c/o KeyBank, N.A.
800 Superior Ave., 4th Fl.
Cleveland, OH 44114-1306
Application address: 127 Public Sq., 18th Fl., Cleveland, OH 44114-1306
Contact: Kate Blaszak, Trust Off., KeyBank, N.A.

Financial data (yr. ended 09/30/01): Grants paid, $27,500; assets, $443,072 (M); expenditures, $35,061; qualifying distributions, $27,176.
Limitations: Giving primarily in Euclid, OH.
Trustee: KeyBank, N.A.
EIN: 346505938
Codes: GTI

43577
Rego Family Foundation
c/o Anthony C. Rego
75 Kensington Oval
Rocky River, OH 44116

Donor(s): Anthony C. Rego.
Financial data (yr. ended 12/31/01): Grants paid, $27,500; assets, $449,632 (M); expenditures, $47,312; qualifying distributions, $27,500.
Officer: Donna K. Rego, Pres.
EIN: 311530385

43578
Worthington Foods Foundation
430 E. Granville Rd.
Worthington, OH 43085 (614) 885-4426
Contact: Allan R. Buller, Tr.

Donor(s): Allan R. Buller, George T. Harding IV, Worthington Foods, Inc.
Financial data (yr. ended 06/30/02): Grants paid, $27,500; assets, $883,524 (M); gifts received, $65,000; expenditures, $61,369; qualifying distributions, $27,500.

Limitations: Giving primarily in Loma Linda, CA, Berrien Springs, MI, and Columbus, OH.
Trustees: Allan R. Buller, George T. Harding IV, Dale E. Twomley.
EIN: 311286538

43579
Chickesaw Foundation
c/o Provident Bank Capital Mgmt. Group
6815 Rapid Run Rd.
Cincinnati, OH 45233-1427 (513) 941-6549
Contact: Sherwood W. McIntire, Tr.

Established in 1984 in OH.
Donor(s): Sherwood W. McIntire, Shirley M. McIntire.
Financial data (yr. ended 12/31/01): Grants paid, $27,400; assets, $638,447 (M); expenditures, $32,089; qualifying distributions, $27,400.
Limitations: Giving primarily in OH.
Trustees: Sherwood W. McIntire, Shirley M. McIntire, Joseph P. Rouse.
EIN: 311122410

43580
Edwin J. Thomas Foundation
c/o National City Bank, N.E.
P.O. Box 94651
Cleveland, OH 44101-4651

Donor(s): Edwin J. Thomas.
Financial data (yr. ended 12/31/01): Grants paid, $27,400; assets, $976,022 (M); expenditures, $31,591; qualifying distributions, $27,400.
Limitations: Applications not accepted. Giving primarily in Akron, OH.
Application information: Contributes only to pre-selected organizations.
Trustees: James Mercer, Jean T. Mercer, Edwin John Thomas.
EIN: 346523110

43581
Siavosh Bozorgi Family Foundation
2612 Pine Shore Dr.
Lima, OH 45806-1355

Established in 1993 in OH.
Donor(s): Siavosh Bozorgi.
Financial data (yr. ended 12/31/01): Grants paid, $27,300; assets, $588,690 (M); expenditures, $35,773; qualifying distributions, $27,300.
Limitations: Applications not accepted. Giving limited to Dayton, OH.
Application information: Contributes only to pre-selected organizations.
Trustee: Siavosh Bozorgi.
EIN: 316458739

43582
Louis L. Manes Foundation
441 Wolf Ledges Pkwy., Ste. 400
P.O. Box 79
Akron, OH 44309-0079
Application address: 7301 N. 16th St., No. 103, Phoenix, AZ 85020
Contact: Stephen Manes, Tr.

Financial data (yr. ended 12/31/01): Grants paid, $27,300; assets, $523,587 (M); expenditures, $29,894; qualifying distributions, $27,300.
Limitations: Giving primarily in Akron, OH.
Application information: Application form not required.
Trustees: Bruce Manes, Louis L. Manes, Marvin G. Manes, Stephen Manes.
EIN: 346555169

43583
Oscar and Hildegard Thiele Scholarship Fund
c/o FirstMerit Bank, N.A.
P.O. Box 725, 39 Public Sq.
Medina, OH 44258 (330) 722-5555
Contact: Scholarship Comm.

Established in 1986 in OH.
Financial data (yr. ended 12/31/99): Grants paid, $27,285; assets, $292,857 (M); gifts received, $11,370; expenditures, $31,609; qualifying distributions, $28,656.
Limitations: Giving limited to Medina, OH.
Application information: Application form required.
Trustee: FirstMerit Bank, N.A.
Scholarship Committee: John Oberholtzer, Michael Thiele.
EIN: 346854105

43584
Dr. Alvin H. & Alva J. Crawford Family Foundation
3963 Winding Way
Cincinnati, OH 45229

Established in 1999 in OH.
Donor(s): Alvin H. Crawford, M.D.
Financial data (yr. ended 12/31/01): Grants paid, $27,120; assets, $21,419 (M); gifts received, $27,894; expenditures, $30,616; qualifying distributions, $27,120.
Limitations: Applications not accepted.
Application information: Contributes only to pre-selected organizations.
Officers and Trustees:* Alvin H. Crawford, M.D.,* Pres.; Richard M. Schwartz,* V.P.; Alva Jamison Crawford,* Secy.
EIN: 311674850

43585
The Hendrix Charitable Foundation
30050 Chagrin Blvd., Ste. 100
Pepper Pike, OH 44124
Application address: 106 W. Washington St., Chagrin Falls, OH 44022
Contact: Pamela M. Hendrix

Established in 1997 in OH.
Donor(s): Leon J. Hendrix, Jr.
Financial data (yr. ended 12/31/00): Grants paid, $27,100; assets, $568,517 (M); gifts received, $843; expenditures, $32,357; qualifying distributions, $27,100.
Limitations: Giving primarily in OH.
Officers: Pamela M. Hendrix, Pres.; Leon J. Hendrix, Jr., Secy.-Treas.
Trustee: Jill H. Buckenmeyer.
EIN: 311533515

43586
The Christine and Guido Di Geronimo Foundation
c/o Lee Di Geronimo
33325 Chagrin Blvd.
Moreland Hills, OH 44022

Established in 1994 in OH.
Donor(s): Guido E. Di Geronimo.
Financial data (yr. ended 11/30/01): Grants paid, $27,000; assets, $1,461,599 (M); gifts received, $75,000; expenditures, $39,145; qualifying distributions, $27,000.
Limitations: Applications not accepted.
Application information: Contributes only to pre-selected organizations.
Trustees: Lee Di Geronimo, Lynn Di Geronimo House.
EIN: 341788087

43587
J. William & Mary Helen Straker Charitable Foundation
925 Military Rd.
Zanesville, OH 43701
Contact: Susan Straker Henderson, Pres.

Established in 1994.
Donor(s): J. Wm. Straker, Mary H. Straker.
Financial data (yr. ended 12/31/01): Grants paid, $27,000; assets, $2,570,670 (M); expenditures, $114,293; qualifying distributions, $27,000.
Limitations: Giving primarily in Muskingum County, OH.
Application information: Application form required.
Officers and Board Members:* Susan Straker Henderson,* Pres. and Treas.; John W. Straker, Jr.,* Secy.; Anne Straker Plosser, J.W. Straker, Jane Straker, M.H. Straker.
EIN: 311396841

43588
Rachel Boyce Lang Charitable Trust
c/o National City Bank
P.O. Box 94651
Cleveland, OH 44101-4651

Established in 1998 in OH.
Donor(s): Rachel Boyce Lang.
Financial data (yr. ended 12/31/01): Grants paid, $26,969; assets, $525,739 (M); gifts received, $125,000; expenditures, $25,719; qualifying distributions, $26,884.
Limitations: Applications not accepted.
Application information: Contributes only to pre-selected organizations.
Trustees: Charles B. Lang, James R. Lang, Mary Sue Lang, Rachel Boyce Lang.
EIN: 311603385

43589
Envirosafe Services of Ohio, Inc. Foundation
c/o Sky Trust
P.O. Box 479
Youngstown, OH 44501-0479
Application address: c/o Mike McGrail, Trust Off., Sky Trust, 519 Madison Ave., Toledo, OH 43604, tel.: (419) 249-3310

Established in 1989 in OH.
Donor(s): Envirosafe Services of Ohio, Inc.
Financial data (yr. ended 12/31/01): Grants paid, $26,928; assets, $36,039 (M); expenditures, $29,295; qualifying distributions, $27,959.
Limitations: Giving limited to the following regions of OH: Lucas County; school districts of Bowling Green, Eastwood Lake, Northwood Otsego, Penta, Rossford, and Perrysburg in Wood County; and school districts of Genoa, Oak Harbor, and Woodmere in Ottawa County.
Trustee: Sky Trust.
EIN: 236956505
Codes: CS, CD, GTI

43590
The Kingsbury Family Foundation
c/o Steven Kingsbury
697 Watch Hill Ln.
Cincinnati, OH 45230

Established in 2001 in OH.
Donor(s): Steven R. Kinsgbury.
Financial data (yr. ended 12/31/01): Grants paid, $26,800; assets, $765,806 (M); gifts received, $300,000; expenditures, $34,494; qualifying distributions, $26,631.
Limitations: Applications not accepted. Giving primarily in KS and OH.
Application information: Contributes only to pre-selected organizations.

Trustees: Steven R. Kingsbury, Frederic J. Robinson, William D. Sherman.
EIN: 311742218

43591
The Joehlin Family Foundation
c/o Richard G. LaValley
5800 Monroe St., Bldg. F
Sylvania, OH 43560-2207

Donor(s): Stanley W. Joehlin, Dolores A. Joehlin.
Financial data (yr. ended 12/31/01): Grants paid, $26,740; assets, $297,400 (M); gifts received, $103,661; expenditures, $28,859; qualifying distributions, $26,740.
Limitations: Applications not accepted.
Officers and Trustees:* Stanley W. Joehlin,* Pres.; Dolores A. Joehlin,* V.P.; Richard G. LaValley, Jr.,* Secy.
EIN: 311627963

43592
Leigh and Mary Carter Family Foundation
c/o Paragon Advisors
20600 Chagrin Blvd., Ste. 600
Shaker Heights, OH 44122

Established in 1997 in OH.
Donor(s): Leigh Carter.
Financial data (yr. ended 12/31/01): Grants paid, $26,671; assets, $370,495 (M); gifts received, $14,946; expenditures, $26,780; qualifying distributions, $26,671.
Limitations: Applications not accepted. Giving primarily in OH.
Application information: Contributes only to pre-selected organizations.
Officers and Trustees:* Leigh Carter,* Pres.; Mary W. Carter,* Secy.; Terence C. Sullivan,* Treas.
EIN: 311530963

43593
The Marguerite Gambill Lyons Scholarship Fund
c/o National City Bank of Kentucky
P.O. Box 94651
Cleveland, OH 44101-4651
Application address: c/o National City Bank, P.O. Box 1270, Ashland, KY 41105, tel.: (502) 581-5107

Financial data (yr. ended 12/31/99): Grants paid, $26,667; assets, $363,953 (M); expenditures, $31,619; qualifying distributions, $28,331.
Limitations: Giving limited to Boyd and surrounding counties, KY.
Application information: Application form required.
Trustee: National City Bank.
EIN: 611121801

43594
Diebold Employees Charitable Fund
c/o KeyBank, N.A.
800 Superior Ave., 4th Fl.
Cleveland, OH 44114-1306

Established around 1977.
Donor(s): Diebold, Inc.
Financial data (yr. ended 10/31/01): Grants paid, $26,625; assets, $272,370 (M); gifts received, $39,974; expenditures, $31,018; qualifying distributions, $26,625.
Limitations: Applications not accepted. Giving primarily in Canton, OH.
Application information: Contributes only to pre-selected organizations.
Trustee: KeyBank, N.A.
EIN: 346734175
Codes: CS, CD

43595
Sara McDowell Trust f/b/o First Presbyterian Church
P.O. Box 94651
Cleveland, OH 44101-4651

Financial data (yr. ended 12/31/01): Grants paid, $26,623; assets, $589,066 (M); expenditures, $33,990; qualifying distributions, $26,623.
Trustee: National City Bank of Pennsylvania.
EIN: 237910303

43596
John A. Thiele Foundation
P.O. Box 1659
Dayton, OH 45401-1659

Financial data (yr. ended 08/31/01): Grants paid, $26,584; assets, $480,595 (M); expenditures, $32,635; qualifying distributions, $26,584.
Limitations: Applications not accepted. Giving primarily in OH.
Application information: Contributes only to pre-selected organizations.
Officers: Kenneth W. Thiele, Pres.; Mary Bippus, V.P.; Jane Higgins, Secy.; Elizabeth Leland, Treas.
EIN: 316023417

43597
Charles A. Huck Memorial Trust
c/o Fifth Third Bank
38 Fountain Square Plz.
Cincinnati, OH 45263

Established in 1999 in IN.
Financial data (yr. ended 12/31/01): Grants paid, $26,068; assets, $675,682 (M); gifts received, $838; expenditures, $35,060; qualifying distributions, $26,068.
Limitations: Applications not accepted. Giving primarily in OH.
Application information: Contributes only to pre-selected organizations.
Trustee: Fifth Third Bank.
EIN: 352069801

43598
Leighton A. Rosenthal Family Foundation
1228 Euclid Ave., Ste. 310
Cleveland, OH 44115
Contact: Leighton A. Rosenthal, Mgr.

Established in 1986 in OH.
Donor(s): Leighton A. Rosenthal.
Financial data (yr. ended 10/31/01): Grants paid, $26,011; assets, $538,289 (M); expenditures, $34,690; qualifying distributions, $26,011.
Limitations: Giving primarily in FL, NY, and OH.
Officer and Trustees:* Leighton A. Rosenthal,* Mgr.; Cynthia R. Boardman, Jane R. Horvitz, Honey R. Rosenthal.
EIN: 136877098

43599
Helene L. Bowley Scholarship Fund
c/o National City Bank of Pennsylvania
P.O. Box 94651
Cleveland, OH 44101-4651
Application address: 248 Seneca St., Oil City, PA 16301
Contact: Lynn Pedensky, Trust Off., National City Bank of Pennsylvania

Established in 1994 in PA.
Donor(s): Helene L. Bowley.‡
Financial data (yr. ended 08/31/01): Grants paid, $26,000; assets, $505,737 (M); expenditures, $30,831; qualifying distributions, $26,086.
Limitations: Giving limited to residents of Elk County, PA.
Application information: Application form required.
Trustee: National City Bank of Pennsylvania.
EIN: 256440187
Codes: GTI

43600
C. Blake, Jr. and Beatrice K. McDowell Foundation
c/o Brouse McDowell
500 First National Tower, Ste. 500
Akron, OH 44308

Established in 1998 in OH.
Donor(s): Beatrice K. McDowell.
Financial data (yr. ended 12/31/01): Grants paid, $26,000; assets, $1,090,164 (M); gifts received, $450,000; expenditures, $35,446; qualifying distributions, $26,000.
Limitations: Applications not accepted. Giving primarily in Akron, OH.
Application information: Contributes only to pre-selected organizations.
Officers and Trustees:* Beatrice K. McDowell,* Pres.; Margaret Lloyd,* Secy.; C. Blake McDowell III,* Treas.
EIN: 341873355

43601
Marilyn W. O'Neill Foundation
3550 Lander Rd., Ste. 140
Cleveland, OH 44124-5727

Established in 1994 in OH.
Financial data (yr. ended 12/31/01): Grants paid, $26,000; assets, $11,080 (M); expenditures, $26,984; qualifying distributions, $26,000.
Limitations: Applications not accepted. Giving primarily in Cleveland, OH.
Application information: Contributes only to pre-selected organizations.
Trustees: Brian C. O'Neill, Daniel J. O'Neill, John M O'Neill, Marilyn W. O'Neill, Michael T. O'Neill, Patrick J. O'Neill, Stephen J. O'Neill.
EIN: 341787953

43602
Over-the-Rhine Recreation Foundation
c/o Emery Group, Inc.
2300 Carew Tower
Cincinnati, OH 45202

Financial data (yr. ended 03/31/02): Grants paid, $26,000; assets, $13,011 (M); expenditures, $26,913; qualifying distributions, $26,000.
Limitations: Applications not accepted.
Application information: Contributes only to pre-selected organizations.
Trustees: Anthony G. Covatta, Addison Lanier II, Melissa E. Lanier Murphy.
EIN: 316061422

43603
Emily Waters Foundation
10 Center. St., Ste. G
Chagrin Falls, OH 44022-3168
(440) 247-9100
FAX: (440) 247-9109; *E-mail:* dpbrown@ameritech.com
Contact: Don P. Brown, Exec. Dir.

Established in 1984 in OH.
Financial data (yr. ended 12/31/00): Grants paid, $26,000; assets, $614,601 (M); expenditures, $40,136; qualifying distributions, $39,490.
Limitations: Giving primarily in OH.
Application information: Application form not required.
Officer: Don P. Brown, Exec. Dir.
EIN: 341475809

43604
Katherine G. Thomas Trust XI
c/o National City Bank
P.O. Box 94651
Cleveland, OH 44101-4651

Financial data (yr. ended 11/30/01): Grants paid, $25,981; assets, $320,769 (M); expenditures, $29,622; qualifying distributions, $25,981.
Limitations: Applications not accepted. Giving primarily in OH.
Application information: Contributes only to pre-selected organizations.
Trustee: National City Bank.
EIN: 346674388

43605
Killgallon Foundation
805 Noble Dr.
Bryan, OH 43506 (419) 636-3141
Contact: William C. Killgallon, Tr.

Established around 1969.
Donor(s): William C. Killgallon, The Ohio Art Co.
Financial data (yr. ended 12/31/01): Grants paid, $25,920; assets, $192,186 (M); gifts received, $10,000; expenditures, $25,950; qualifying distributions, $25,885.
Limitations: Giving primarily in VA.
Trustee: William C. Killgallon.
EIN: 237024236

43606
Allan and Millicent Kleinman Family Foundation
90 Easton Ln.
Moreland Hills, OH 44022
Contact: Allan Kleinman, Tr. or Millicent Kleinman, Tr.

Established in 1990 in OH.
Financial data (yr. ended 10/31/01): Grants paid, $25,905; assets, $238,274 (M); expenditures, $27,518; qualifying distributions, $25,905.
Trustees: Allan Kleinman, Millicent Kleinman, Reed Kleinman.
EIN: 341681024

43607
The Cannaley Foundation
c/o Gregory A. Hendel
1700 Woodlands Dr., Ste. 120
Maumee, OH 43537-4043

Established in 1995 in OH.
Donor(s): James R. Cannaley.
Financial data (yr. ended 12/31/01): Grants paid, $25,797; assets, $10,099 (M); gifts received, $25,672; expenditures, $25,805; qualifying distributions, $25,797.
Limitations: Applications not accepted. Giving primarily in OH.
Application information: Contributes only to pre-selected organizations.
Trustees: James R. Cannaley, Linda A. Cannaley, Gregory A. Hendel.
EIN: 341818455

43608
The Keene Foundation
95 W. Juniper Ln.
Moreland Hills, OH 44022

Established in 1998 in OH.
Financial data (yr. ended 12/31/01): Grants paid, $25,554; assets, $26,617 (M); gifts received, $17,825; expenditures, $37,074; qualifying distributions, $25,554.
Trustee: Kevin C. Keene.
EIN: 341880042

43609
Charles L. Suhr Charitable Trust
c/o National City Bank of Pennsylvania
P.O. Box 94651
Cleveland, OH 44101-4651
Application address: P.O. Box 374, Oil City, PA 16301, tel.: (814) 677-5085
Contact: Stephen P. Kosak

Financial data (yr. ended 12/31/01): Grants paid, $25,545; assets, $717,436 (M); expenditures, $33,125; qualifying distributions, $25,545.
Limitations: Giving limited to Oil City and Venango County, PA.
Trustee: National City Bank.
EIN: 256063178

43610
Cutter Family Foundation
22200 Lake Rd.
Rocky River, OH 44116-1011

Established in 1991 in OH.
Donor(s): Thomas A. Cutter.
Financial data (yr. ended 12/31/01): Grants paid, $25,445; assets, $4,578 (M); gifts received, $24,269; expenditures, $26,348; qualifying distributions, $25,445.
Limitations: Applications not accepted.
Application information: Contributes only to pre-selected organizations.
Officers and Trustees:* Thomas A. Cutter,* Pres.; Margaret S. Cutter,* Secy.-Treas.; Mary Margaret Cutter, Matthew A. Cutter, Michael T. Cutter.
EIN: 341694626

43611
Jocelyne K. and Frank N. Linsalata Family Foundation
3550 Lander Rd., Ste. 200
Pepper Pike, OH 44124

Established in 1999 in DE.
Donor(s): Frank N. Linsalata.
Financial data (yr. ended 12/31/01): Grants paid, $25,425; assets, $460,696 (M); gifts received, $2,000; expenditures, $31,819; qualifying distributions, $25,425.
Limitations: Applications not accepted.
Application information: Contributes only to pre-selected organizations.
Officers: Frank N. Linsalata, Pres.; Jocelyne K. Linsalata, Secy.-Treas.
EIN: 341910990

43612
Pegasus Foundation
1422 Euclid Ave., Ste. 1030
Cleveland, OH 44115 (216) 363-1034
Contact: Melville H. Ireland, Pres.

Established in 2001 in OH.
Donor(s): Ireland Foundation.
Financial data (yr. ended 12/31/01): Grants paid, $25,300; assets, $1,116,997 (M); gifts received, $1,058,970; expenditures, $25,553; qualifying distributions, $24,837.
Officers: Melville H. Ireland, Pres.; Carole M. Nowak, Secy.; Neil A. Brown, Treas.
EIN: 347137513

43613
James Forsythe Milroy Foundation
c/o Citizens Federal Bldg.
110 N. Main St.
Bellefontaine, OH 43311
Contact: Charles Earick, Tr.

Established in 1952 in OH.
Donor(s): Robert Milroy.‡

Financial data (yr. ended 12/31/01): Grants paid, $25,264; assets, $1,033,802 (M); expenditures, $45,484; qualifying distributions, $36,064.
Limitations: Giving limited to residents of Logan County, OH.
Application information: Application form not required.
Trustees: Tammy Dobbels, Charles Earick, Robert B. Fulton.
EIN: 346516844
Codes: GTI

43614
Otto F. Sharp & Thelma Sharp Scholarship Trust
c/o Robert B. Will, Jr.
P.O. Box 460
McArthur, OH 45651-0460
Application address: c/o Superintendent of Vinton County Schools, Memorial Bldg., 112 N. Market St., McArthur, OH 45651
Contact: John L. Simmons, Tr.

Established in 1992 in OH.
Donor(s): Thelma Sharp.‡
Financial data (yr. ended 12/31/01): Grants paid, $25,224; assets, $198,386 (M); expenditures, $26,242; qualifying distributions, $25,142.
Limitations: Giving limited to residents of Vinton County, OH.
Application information: Application form required.
Trustees: Jeffrey Simmons, John L. Simmons, Robert B. Will, Jr.
EIN: 311363401
Codes: GTI

43615
Leon A. McDermott Charitable Trust
c/o KeyBank, N.A.
P.O. Box 10099
Toledo, OH 43699-0099

Established in 1995 in MI.
Financial data (yr. ended 12/31/99): Grants paid, $25,212; assets, $938,994 (M); expenditures, $34,958; qualifying distributions, $25,235.
Limitations: Applications not accepted. Giving limited to Mount Pleasant, MI.
Application information: Contributes only to pre-selected organizations.
Trustee: KeyBank, N.A.
EIN: 341832860

43616
E & E Scholarship Trust
c/o KeyBank, N.A.
800 Superior Ave., 4th Fl.
Cleveland, OH 44114

Established in 2000 in ME.
Financial data (yr. ended 12/31/01): Grants paid, $25,200; assets, $688,158 (M); gifts received, $266,055; expenditures, $32,630; qualifying distributions, $25,200.
Limitations: Applications not accepted.
Application information: Contributes only to pre-selected organizations.
Trustee: KeyBank, N.A.
EIN: 527115055

43617
Semantic Foundation, Inc.
1293 S. Main St.
Akron, OH 44301 (330) 253-5592
Contact: Stephen E. Myers, Pres.

Established in 1994 in OH.
Donor(s): Stephen E. Myers.
Financial data (yr. ended 12/31/01): Grants paid, $25,200; assets, $344,713 (M); expenditures, $25,500; qualifying distributions, $25,200.

43617—OHIO

Limitations: Giving primarily in OH.
Officers: Stephen E. Myers, Pres.; Celeste B. Myers, V.P.
Trustee: Jeffrey L. Weiler.
EIN: 341787248

43618
The Phillips Family Foundation
P.O. Box 42036
Middletown, OH 45042-0036

Established in 1998 in OH.
Donor(s): Ralph H. Phillips.
Financial data (yr. ended 12/31/01): Grants paid, $25,087; assets, $536,101 (M); gifts received, $30,000; expenditures, $38,400; qualifying distributions, $25,087.
Limitations: Applications not accepted. Giving primarily in Shelby and Mansfield, OH.
Application information: Contributes only to pre-selected organizations.
Officer: Ralph H. Phillips, Pres.
EIN: 311544453

43619
Purnima & Ajeet Kothari Family Foundation
c/o Rustom D. Bhathena
5455 Broadview Rd.
Parma, OH 44134

Financial data (yr. ended 12/31/01): Grants paid, $25,001; assets, $545,381 (M); expenditures, $25,282; qualifying distributions, $25,001.
Limitations: Applications not accepted. Giving primarily in OH.
Application information: Contributes only to pre-selected organizations.
Trustees: Ajeet Kothari, Purnima Kothari, Jigar Shah.
EIN: 341850611

43620
Phyllis H. & William H. Evans Charitable Foundation
c/o KeyBank, N.A.
800 Superior Ave., 4th Fl.
Cleveland, OH 44114-1306
Application address: P.O. Box 30486, Cleveland, OH 44130-2301
Contact: William H. Evans, Tr.

Financial data (yr. ended 12/31/01): Grants paid, $25,000; assets, $567,498 (M); expenditures, $29,430; qualifying distributions, $25,000.
Limitations: Giving primarily in OH.
Trustees: Phyllis Evans, William H. Evans, KeyBank, N.A.
EIN: 346512852

43621
Grimes Aerospace Foundation
(Formerly Midland-Ross Foundation)
1710 Waltjam Rd.
Columbus, OH 43221
Additional address: 550 Rte. 55, Urbana, OH 43078

Incorporated in 1957 in OH.
Donor(s): Grimes Aerospace.
Financial data (yr. ended 12/31/00): Grants paid, $25,000; assets, $2,352 (M); gifts received, $23,900; expenditures, $25,000; qualifying distributions, $25,000.
Limitations: Applications not accepted. Giving limited to areas of company operations.
Application information: Contributes only to pre-selected organizations.
Director: John R. Huneck.
EIN: 346556087
Codes: CS, CD

43622
The Katherine E. Larose Charitable Foundation, Inc.
3535 Shade Rd.
Akron, OH 44333

Established in 2000 in OH.
Donor(s): Thomas Larose.
Financial data (yr. ended 12/31/01): Grants paid, $25,000; assets, $19,481 (M); gifts received, $16,017; expenditures, $25,954; qualifying distributions, $25,000.
Trustees: Richard W. Burke, Thomas G. Knoll, Thomas Larose.
EIN: 341942780

43623
Motch Corporation Foundation
(Formerly Oerlikon Motch Corporation Foundation)
1250 E. 222nd St.
Euclid, OH 44117-1190
Contact: Richard J. Schulz, Treas.

Donor(s): Motch Corp.
Financial data (yr. ended 12/31/01): Grants paid, $25,000; assets, $456,257 (M); expenditures, $25,134; qualifying distributions, $25,134.
Limitations: Giving primarily in Cleveland, OH.
Application information: Application form not required.
Officers and Trustees:* J. Hunter Banbury,* Pres.; Kirt Babuder,* V.P.; D. Marrapodi,* Secy.; Richard Schulz,* Treas.; A. Kuhar.
EIN: 346555823
Codes: CS, CD

43624
NCR Scholarship Foundation
WHQ 1
1700 S. Patterson Blvd.
Dayton, OH 45479
E-mail: jeanne.bauer@ncr.com
Application address: c/o Educational Testing Svc. (ETS), P.O. Box 6730, Princeton, NJ 08541-6730
Contact: Jeanne Bauer, Secy.

Established around 1975.
Donor(s): NCR Corporation.
Financial data (yr. ended 12/31/01): Grants paid, $25,000; assets, $383,668 (M); expenditures, $31,526; qualifying distributions, $25,000.
Limitations: Giving in areas of company operations.
Publications: Informational brochure (including application guidelines).
Application information: Application form required.
Officers and Directors:* Kenneth Williams, Pres.; Virginia Bell, V.P.; Jeane Bauer, Secy.; Bo Sawyer,* Treas.; W. Buiter, M.A. Janik, L.K. Nyquist.
EIN: 237431180
Codes: CS, CD, GTI

43625
The Private Foundation
500 1st National Tower
Akron, OH 44308

Established in 1990 in OH.
Donor(s): James Ott, Ellen Ott.
Financial data (yr. ended 12/31/00): Grants paid, $25,000; assets, $515,051 (M); expenditures, $26,051; qualifying distributions, $25,000.
Limitations: Applications not accepted. Giving primarily in Dallas, TX.
Application information: Contributes only to pre-selected organizations.
Officer and Trustees:* James Ott,* Pres.; Ellen Ott.
EIN: 341639720

43626
Kathryn L. Reichelderfer Foundation
c/o The Huntington National Bank
P.O. Box 1558, HC1012
Columbus, OH 43216

Established in 2000 in OH.
Donor(s): Kathryn L. Reichelderfer.‡
Financial data (yr. ended 12/31/01): Grants paid, $25,000; assets, $478,777 (M); expenditures, $32,414; qualifying distributions, $25,000.
Limitations: Applications not accepted. Giving limited to OH.
Application information: Contributes only to pre-selected organizations.
Trustee: The Huntington National Bank.
EIN: 311707332

43627
Ropchan Foundation
c/o National City Bank of Indiana
P.O. Box 94651
Cleveland, OH 44101-4651

Established in 1977 in IN.
Financial data (yr. ended 10/31/01): Grants paid, $25,000; assets, $573,336 (M); gifts received, $500; expenditures, $22,525; qualifying distributions, $25,487.
Limitations: Applications not accepted. Giving limited to within a 75-mile radius of Fort Wayne, IN.
Application information: Contributes only to pre-selected organizations.
Officer and Advisory Committee Members:* Robert C. Weber,* Chair.; Ted Heemstra, James Kindraka, Frank A. Webster.
Trustee: National City Bank.
EIN: 310922221

43628
The Scholtz Family Foundation
3425 Service Rd.
Cleveland, OH 44111 (216) 941-6115
Contact: Chet B. Scholtz, Pres.

Established in 1999 in OH.
Financial data (yr. ended 12/31/01): Grants paid, $25,000; assets, $267,602 (M); gifts received, $45,000; expenditures, $29,263; qualifying distributions, $25,000.
Limitations: Giving primarily in OH.
Officers: Chet B. Scholtz, Pres.; Bradley K. Scholtz, V.P.; Jane A. Scholtz, Secy.; David K. Scholtz, Treas.
EIN: 341900522

43629
The Snow Family Foundation
P.O. Box 147
Berea, OH 44017-0147
Contact: Glenn W. Snow, Tr.

Established in 2000.
Donor(s): Glenn Snow, Jean Snow, Peter Snow, Betsy Snow.
Financial data (yr. ended 12/31/01): Grants paid, $25,000; assets, $763,117 (M); gifts received, $390,000; expenditures, $25,300; qualifying distributions, $25,300.
Trustees: Betsy S. Snow, Glenn W. Snow, Jean A. Snow, Peter G. Snow.
EIN: 311675559

43630
The Vanderhorst Family Foundation
c/o Deloitte & Touche, LLP
1700 Courthouse Plz. N.E.
Dayton, OH 45402

Established in 1996 in OH.

Donor(s): Janet Vanderhorst, Jerome Vanderhorst.
Financial data (yr. ended 11/30/01): Grants paid, $25,000; assets, $489,196 (M); expenditures, $32,455; qualifying distributions, $25,000.
Limitations: Applications not accepted. Giving primarily in OH.
Application information: Contributes only to pre-selected organizations.
Trustees: Janet A. Vanderhorst, Jerome Vanderhorst, Richard Vanderhorst.
EIN: 311455345

43631
Warman Scholarship Trust
c/o KeyBank, N.A.
800 Superior Ave., 4th Fl.
Cleveland, OH 44114

Established in 1993 in ME.
Financial data (yr. ended 03/31/02): Grants paid, $25,000; assets, $538,639 (M); expenditures, $31,853; qualifying distributions, $25,000.
Limitations: Applications not accepted. Giving limited to residents of ME.
Application information: Contributes only to pre-selected organizations.
Trustee: KeyBank, N.A.
EIN: 046731724
Codes: GTI

43632
M. Mark Weaver Memorial Foundation, Inc.
7281 Button Rd.
Mentor, OH 44060
Contact: Timothy H. Weaver, Pres.

Established in 1999 in OH.
Donor(s): Timothy M. Weaver.
Financial data (yr. ended 12/31/01): Grants paid, $25,000; assets, $517,915 (M); gifts received, $198,000; expenditures, $29,712; qualifying distributions, $25,000.
Limitations: Giving primarily in northeastern OH.
Officers: Timothy H. Weaver, Pres.; Helen H. Weaver, Secy.; Bernard J. Sikon, Treas.
Trustee: Jeffrey M. Weaver.
EIN: 341911729

43633
The Winmax Foundation, Inc.
c/o U.S. Bank
425 Walnut St.
Cincinnati, OH 45202

Established in 1999 in OH.
Donor(s): Dorothy W. Browning.
Financial data (yr. ended 12/31/01): Grants paid, $25,000; assets, $459,770 (M); gifts received, $94,522; expenditures, $33,684; qualifying distributions, $25,000.
Limitations: Applications not accepted. Giving primarily in Maysville, KY.
Application information: Contributes only to pre-selected organizations.
Officers and Trustees:* Janet L. Houston,* Pres.; Patricia K. Wolf,* Secy.; James A. McNeal,* Treas.
EIN: 311677020

43634
The Butkin Foundation
The Village
9 Dorset Ct.
Beachwood, OH 44122

Donor(s): Muriel S. Butkin.
Financial data (yr. ended 11/30/01): Grants paid, $24,750; assets, $9,400 (M); gifts received, $28,000; expenditures, $27,035; qualifying distributions, $24,750.
Limitations: Applications not accepted. Giving primarily in Cleveland, OH.

Application information: Contributes only to pre-selected organizations.
Officers and Trustees:* Muriel S. Butkin,* Pres. and Treas.; Robert M. Brucken,* Secy.; Rita M. Wisney.
EIN: 346554958

43635
The Pavey Family Foundation Trust
c/o The Private Trust Co.
1422 Euclid Ave., Ste. 1130
Cleveland, OH 44115-2001

Established in 1999 in OH.
Donor(s): Robert Pavey, Patricia Pavey.
Financial data (yr. ended 12/31/01): Grants paid, $24,750; assets, $496,171 (M); expenditures, $32,925; qualifying distributions, $24,750.
Limitations: Applications not accepted.
Application information: Contributes only to pre-selected organizations.
Trustees: Patricia Pavey, Robert Pavey.
EIN: 347105279

43636
The Stillwagon Family Foundation
8295 Maplevale Dr.
Canfield, OH 44406

Established in 1994 in OH.
Donor(s): Franklin K. Stillwagon, Nancy J. Stillwagon.
Financial data (yr. ended 08/31/01): Grants paid, $24,746; assets, $471,762 (M); expenditures, $26,916; qualifying distributions, $24,285.
Limitations: Applications not accepted. Giving primarily in Youngstown, OH, and York, PA.
Application information: Contributes only to pre-selected organizations.
Trustees: Nancy Carstensen, Frederick J. Stillwagon, Nancy J. Stillwagon, Paul K. Stillwagon.
EIN: 341784044

43637
Alice A. Andrus Foundation
c/o National City Bank, Northeast
P.O. Box 94651
Cleveland, OH 44101-4651
c/o Principal of Wellington High School, 629 Main St., Wellington, OH 44090, tel.: (440) 647-3734

Financial data (yr. ended 03/31/01): Grants paid, $24,500; assets, $417,118 (M); expenditures, $27,706; qualifying distributions, $25,350.
Limitations: Applications not accepted. Giving limited to residents of Wellington, OH.
Trustee: National City Bank, Northeast.
EIN: 346653271
Codes: GTI

43638
G.A.F. Foundation
30195 Chagrin Blvd., No. 210N
Cleveland, OH 44124

Donor(s): Members of the Files family, Robert A. Files.
Financial data (yr. ended 09/30/01): Grants paid, $24,500; assets, $603,256 (M); expenditures, $25,704; qualifying distributions, $25,500.
Limitations: Applications not accepted. Giving primarily in the Cleveland, OH, area.
Application information: Contributes only to pre-selected organizations.
Trustees: Marc A. Files, Robert A. Files.
EIN: 346881707

43639
Gladys & Evelyn Rickert Memorial Scholarship Fund
c/o National City Bank of Pennsylvania
P.O. Box 94651
Cleveland, OH 44101-4651
Application address: c/o Principal of the Greenville Area High School, 9 Donation Rd., Greenville, PA 16125

Financial data (yr. ended 12/31/01): Grants paid, $24,500; assets, $323,074 (M); expenditures, $29,664; qualifying distributions, $26,322.
Limitations: Giving limited to residents of PA.
Trustee: National City Bank.
EIN: 237876237

43640
The Toots Foundation
8110 Plainfield Rd.
Cincinnati, OH 45236

Established in 1999 in OH.
Donor(s): Henry W. Schneider.
Financial data (yr. ended 12/31/00): Grants paid, $24,488; assets, $205,739 (M); expenditures, $27,998; qualifying distributions, $22,747.
Limitations: Applications not accepted. Giving primarily in Cincinnati, OH.
Application information: Contributes only to pre-selected organizations.
Officers: Henry W. Schneider, Pres. and Treas.; Anita R. Schneider, V.P.; Benjamin A. Schneider, Secy.
EIN: 311679841

43641
Paul E. Maher Charitable Foundation
c/o KeyBank, N.A., Trust Div.
34 N. Main St., 4th Fl.
Dayton, OH 45401

Established in 1992 in OH.
Financial data (yr. ended 12/31/01): Grants paid, $24,485; assets, $586,921 (M); expenditures, $33,136; qualifying distributions, $24,685.
Limitations: Applications not accepted. Giving primarily in Dayton, OH.
Application information: Contributes only to pre-selected organizations.
Trustee: KeyBank, N.A.
EIN: 316443896

43642
Edith B. & Joseph E. Humphrey Family Foundation
P.O. Box 3775
Mansfield, OH 44907-0775

Established in 1998 in OH.
Financial data (yr. ended 12/31/01): Grants paid, $24,450; assets, $471,517 (M); expenditures, $27,300; qualifying distributions, $24,450.
Officer: Edith B. Humphrey, Pres.
EIN: 311582254

43643
Franklin P. Greene Educational Loan Fund
c/o Grand Chief Engineer, Standard Bldg.
1370 Ontario St., Mezz.
Cleveland, OH 44113-1702 (216) 241-2630

Financial data (yr. ended 12/31/00): Grants paid, $24,442; assets, $107,949 (M); expenditures, $24,889; qualifying distributions, $24,440; giving activities include $24,442 for loans to individuals.
Trustee: Edward Dubroski.
EIN: 346538928

43644
Bob & Jewell Evans Foundation, Inc.
229 Colonial Dr.
Bidwell, OH 45614-9216

Established in OH in 1998.
Donor(s): Robert L. Evans.
Financial data (yr. ended 12/31/01): Grants paid, $24,425; assets, $521,879 (M); gifts received, $208; expenditures, $29,445; qualifying distributions, $24,425.
Limitations: Applications not accepted. Giving primarily in OH, some giving also in WV.
Application information: Contributes only to pre-selected organizations.
Officers and Trustees:* Robert L. Evans,* Pres.; Edward M. Vollborn,* Secy.; Jewell V. Evans,* Treas.; Deborah Donskov, Robert S. Evans.
EIN: 311588190

43645
The Altman Family Foundation
(Formerly Norman & Nettie Altman Foundation)
1251 Fairwood Ave.
Columbus, OH 43206-3313

Donor(s): The Altman Co.
Financial data (yr. ended 12/31/00): Grants paid, $24,300; assets, $247 (M); gifts received, $21,000; expenditures, $24,300; qualifying distributions, $24,300.
Limitations: Applications not accepted.
Application information: Contributes only to pre-selected organizations.
Trustees: James P. Altman, Jon Altman, Norman E. Altman, Jr., Norman J. Altman III, Judith Briley, Dorothy J. Gordon.
EIN: 311052997

43646
Harold C. Schilling Foundation
c/o Fifth Third Bank
38 Fountain Sq. Plz., Tax Dept. 1090C8
Cincinnati, OH 45263 (513) 579-5498
Contact: Paula Wharton, Mgr., Fifth Third Bank

Established in 1994 in OH.
Financial data (yr. ended 12/31/01): Grants paid, $24,252; assets, $450,230 (M); expenditures, $30,717; qualifying distributions, $24,252.
Limitations: Giving limited to Cincinnati, OH.
Trustee: Fifth Third Bank.
EIN: 311486667

43647
Lucille McComb Memorial Scholarship Fund
105 W. Main St.
Napoleon, OH 43545-1781
Application address: c/o Napoleon High School, 701 Briarheath, Napoleon, OH 43545, tel.: (419) 592-0010
Contact: Jeffrey Schlade, Principal

Financial data (yr. ended 12/31/01): Grants paid, $24,151; assets, $547,706 (M); expenditures, $34,650; qualifying distributions, $27,606.
Limitations: Giving limited to residents of Henry County, OH, with emphasis on Napoleon.
Application information: Application form required.
Scholarship Committee Members: Betsy Redd, Jeffrey Schlade.
Trustees: John I. Bisher, John A. Dietrick, Ronald P. Lankenau.
EIN: 346875773
Codes: GTI

43648
Scholarship Fund, Inc.
c/o J. A. Brunner
3312 Corey Rd.
Toledo, OH 43615

Financial data (yr. ended 12/31/01): Grants paid, $24,113; assets, $631,422 (M); expenditures, $36,716; qualifying distributions, $26,511.
Limitations: Giving limited to northwest OH.
Application information: Application form required.
Officers and Trustees:* Hon. Robert V. Franklin, Jr.,* Pres.; Hon. Jack R. Puffenberger,* V.P.; Ernest W. Weaver, Jr.,* Secy.; James A. Brunner,* Treas.; and 7 additional trustees.
EIN: 346533380
Codes: GTI

43649
The Harbert Foundation
c/o Norman C. Harbert
11292 Garfield Rd.
Hiram, OH 44234

Established in 1998 in OH.
Donor(s): Norman C. Harbert.
Financial data (yr. ended 12/31/01): Grants paid, $24,100; assets, $255,096 (M); gifts received, $6,000; expenditures, $24,506; qualifying distributions, $24,100.
Officers: Norman C. Harbert, Chair; Donna Harbert, Pres.; Carl J. Harbert, Secy.; Ann L. Harbert, Treas.
EIN: 341868292

43650
The Leland Foundation, Inc.
1210 Brittany Hills Dr.
Dayton, OH 45459

Financial data (yr. ended 08/31/02): Grants paid, $24,000; assets, $604,693 (M); expenditures, $39,540; qualifying distributions, $24,000.
Limitations: Applications not accepted. Giving primarily in OH.
Application information: Contributes only to pre-selected organizations.
Trustees: Gerald H. Leland, Harold E. Leland, Robert G. Leland, Virginia Palmatier, Ocie M. Paul, Margaret Russell.
EIN: 316049567

43651
Norman B. Williams Charitable Trust
c/o National City Bank
P.O. Box 94651
Cleveland, OH 44101-4651

Established in 1997 in IL.
Donor(s): Norman B. Williams.‡
Financial data (yr. ended 03/31/02): Grants paid, $23,883; assets, $666,688 (M); expenditures, $28,014; qualifying distributions, $25,492.
Limitations: Applications not accepted.
Application information: Contributes only to pre-selected organizations.
Trustee: National City Bank.
EIN: 367201494

43652
Kenneth W. & Jean S. Maxfield Charitable Trust
c/o National City Bank of Indiana
P.O. Box 94651
Cleveland, OH 44101-4651
Application address: P.O. Box 110, Fort Wayne, IN 46801, tel.: (219) 461-7117
Contact: Rhoda Miller, Trust Off., National City Bank of Indiana

Established in 1989 in IN.
Financial data (yr. ended 12/31/01): Grants paid, $23,750; assets, $189,341 (M); expenditures, $24,819; qualifying distributions, $23,750.
Limitations: Giving primarily in Fort Wayne, IN.
Trustee: National City Bank of Indiana.
EIN: 356512448

43653
Mildred Engel Nurse Scholarship Fund
c/o Levy J. Newman
125 Churchill Hubbard Rd.
Youngstown, OH 44505
Application address: c/o Nurse Scholarship Comm., 517 Gypsy Ln., Youngstown, OH 44501, tel.: (330) 746-1076

Financial data (yr. ended 12/31/99): Grants paid, $23,727; assets, $494,236 (M); expenditures, $28,302; qualifying distributions, $24,027.
Limitations: Giving primarily to residents of OH.
Trustee: J. Newman Levy.
EIN: 346987176

43654
Bowling Green Community Foundation, Inc.
P.O. Box 1175
Bowling Green, OH 43402-1175
(419) 354-5521
FAX: (419) 354-5435; *E-mail:* jhgordon@dacor.net; *URL:* http://www.wcnet.org/~bgcf
Contact: Donald Zajac, Pres.

Established in 1994 in OH.
Financial data (yr. ended 06/30/00): Grants paid, $23,587; assets, $841,181 (M); gifts received, $513,947; expenditures, $30,049.
Limitations: Giving limited to the Bowling Green, OH, area.
Publications: Annual report (including application guidelines), informational brochure.
Application information: Application form required.
Officer and Trustees:* Donald Zajac,* Pres.; Roger Anderson, Marilyn Beattie, John Bick, Ashel Bryan, Suzanne Crawford, Tim Dunn, Joan Gordon, Allen Green, Janet Knape, Marjorie Peatee, Charlotte Scherer, Jeff Snook, Fred Uhlman, Jr., William Welling.
EIN: 341790526
Codes: CM

43655
Lenora Ford Bland and W. Jennings Bland Scholarship Trust
402 Main St.
Coshocton, OH 43812-1511 (740) 622-0130
Contact: Van Blanchard II, Tr.

Financial data (yr. ended 12/31/01): Grants paid, $23,557; assets, $409,270 (M); expenditures, $57,537; qualifying distributions, $30,789.
Limitations: Giving limited to residents of Coshocton County, OH.
Application information: Application form required.
Trustee: Van Blanchard II.
EIN: 316430828
Codes: GTI

43656
John B. and Graceann H. Reese Foundation
15554 Country Rd., Ste. M-1
Napoleon, OH 43545

Established in 1986 in OH.
Donor(s): John B. Reese, Graceann H. Reese.
Financial data (yr. ended 12/31/01): Grants paid, $23,509; assets, $236,173 (M); gifts received, $25,000; expenditures, $25,400; qualifying distributions, $23,509.

Officers: John B. Reese, Pres.; Graceann H. Reese, Secy.-Treas.
Trustees: Emily G. Collins, Sara J. Luzny, Jane B. Reese.
EIN: 341563590

43657
Annabel W. Gasaway Trust
(Formerly Gasaway Educational Fund)
c/o National City Bank of Indiana
P.O. Box 94651
Cleveland, OH 44101-4651
Application address: P.O. Box 110, Fort Wayne, IN 46802, tel.: (210) 461-6218
Contact: Theresa Tracey, Trust Off., National City Bank of Indiana

Established in 1994 in IN.
Financial data (yr. ended 12/31/99): Grants paid, $23,500; assets, $362,076 (M); expenditures, $26,298; qualifying distributions, $23,975.
Limitations: Giving limited to IN.
Trustee: National City Bank of Indiana.
EIN: 351909932

43658
The Gregory Hackett Family Foundation
3268 Waterside Dr.
Akron, OH 44319

Established in 2000 in OH.
Donor(s): Gregory P. Hackett.
Financial data (yr. ended 12/31/01): Grants paid, $23,500; assets, $440,213 (M); expenditures, $24,885; qualifying distributions, $23,500.
Limitations: Applications not accepted.
Application information: Contributes only to pre-selected organizations.
Trustees: Elizabeth E. Brumbaugh, Gregory P. Hackett, Maria Quinn.
EIN: 341931870

43659
Perry Scholarship Foundation
(Formerly Nathan F. & Edna L. Perry Scholarship)
c/o KeyBank, N.A., Trust Div.
800 Superior Ave., 4th Fl.
Cleveland, OH 44114

Financial data (yr. ended 05/31/02): Grants paid, $23,500; assets, $465,298 (M); expenditures, $29,495; qualifying distributions, $23,500.
Limitations: Applications not accepted. Giving limited to ME.
Application information: Unsolicited requests for funds not accepted.
Trustee: KeyBank, N.A.
EIN: 510158963
Codes: GTI

43660
C.Y., Inc.
P.O. Box 118581
Cincinnati, OH 45211-8581

Financial data (yr. ended 04/30/02): Grants paid, $23,450; assets, $3,020 (M); gifts received, $23,485; expenditures, $23,807; qualifying distributions, $23,450.
Limitations: Giving primarily in OH.
Officers: Fred Bibstedt, Pres.; Charles Cummings, Jr., V.P.; Janet Cummings, Secy.; Jean Manning, Treas.
EIN: 316049746

43661
Mary Mansfield Fund for the Aged
c/o Fifth Third Bank
Dept. 00858
Cincinnati, OH 45263
Application address: 269 W. Main St., Lexington, KY 40507

Financial data (yr. ended 12/31/00): Grants paid, $23,356; assets, $415,838 (M); expenditures, $29,116; qualifying distributions, $23,271.
Limitations: Giving limited to Bourbon County, KY.
Application information: Application form required.
Trustee: Fifth Third Bank.
EIN: 616021948
Codes: GTI

43662
Fred & Anne Rzepka Family Foundation
25250 Rockside Rd.
Bedford Heights, OH 44146

Established in 1997 in OH.
Donor(s): Fred Rzepka.
Financial data (yr. ended 12/31/01): Grants paid, $23,300; assets, $634,500 (M); gifts received, $7,500; expenditures, $23,652; qualifying distributions, $23,300.
Limitations: Applications not accepted.
Application information: Contributes only to pre-selected organizations.
Trustee: David Rzepka.
EIN: 311532652

43663
Andrew Kaul Foundation, Inc.
c/o National City Bank
P.O. Box 94651
Cleveland, OH 44101-4651
Application address: c/o National City Bank of Pennsylvania, Oil City Trust Off., 20 Stanwix St., Pittsburgh, PA 15222, tel.: (814) 678-3649

Financial data (yr. ended 12/31/01): Grants paid, $23,200; assets, $537,552 (M); expenditures, $29,224; qualifying distributions, $23,200.
Limitations: Giving limited to the Elk County, PA, area.
Officers and Directors:* Andrew Kaul IV,* Pres.; Edward H. Kuntz,* Secy.-Treas.; William Keating.
Trustee: National City Bank.
EIN: 251112032

43664
The Karen and Paul Schaefer Foundation
7750 W. Bancroft St.
Toledo, OH 43617

Established in 1998 in OH.
Donor(s): Paul L. Schaefer, Karen A. Schaefer.
Financial data (yr. ended 12/31/01): Grants paid, $23,150; assets, $1 (M); gifts received, $17,597; expenditures, $23,857; qualifying distributions, $23,150.
Limitations: Applications not accepted.
Application information: Contributes only to pre-selected organizations.
Officers: Paul L. Schaefer, Pres. and Treas.; Karen A. Schaefer, Secy.
Trustee: Arthur M. Clendenin, Jr.
EIN: 341879639

43665
John F. Hynes and John D. Finnegan Foundation
(also known as Hynes Finnegan Foundation)
c/o Sky Bank
P.O. Box 479
Youngstown, OH 44501-0479 (330) 742-7035
Contact: Patrick A. Sebastiano, Sr. V.P., Sky Bank

Financial data (yr. ended 12/31/01): Grants paid, $23,120; assets, $453,127 (M); expenditures, $29,097; qualifying distributions, $24,834.
Limitations: Giving primarily in Youngstown, OH.
Officers and Directors:* John M. Newman,* Chair.; William W. Bresnahan,* Vice-Chair.; William J. Mullen, Gregory L. Ridler.
Trustee: Sky Bank.
EIN: 346554850

43666
The Marie C. and Charles L. Grossman Family Foundation
16900 Lake Ave.
Lakewood, OH 44107

Established in 1998 in OH.
Donor(s): Charles L. Grossman, Marie C. Grossman.
Financial data (yr. ended 12/31/00): Grants paid, $23,050; assets, $477,676 (M); gifts received, $48,395; expenditures, $27,395; qualifying distributions, $23,050.
Limitations: Applications not accepted.
Application information: Contributes only to pre-selected organizations.
Officers: Marie C. Grossman, Pres.; Charles L. Grossman, V.P.; Joseph L. Grossman, Secy.; Charles L. Grossman, Jr., Treas.
EIN: 311544403

43667
Ralph & Mary Simmons Welfare Fund
c/o KeyBank, N.A.
800 Superior Ave., 4th Fl.
Cleveland, OH 44114-2601
Application address: P.O. Box 1054, Augusta, ME 04332-1054
Contact: Mr. Mulford, Trust Off., KeyBank, N.A.

Financial data (yr. ended 08/31/01): Grants paid, $23,031; assets, $555,710 (M); expenditures, $25,981; qualifying distributions, $23,031.
Limitations: Giving limited to residents of Kingfield, ME.
Trustee: KeyBank, N.A.
EIN: 016007242
Codes: GTI

43668
Ficks Family Foundation
c/o PNC Advisors
P.O. Box 1198
Cincinnati, OH 45201-1198 (513) 651-8413
Application address: 201 E. 5th St., Cincinnati, OH 45201
Contact: James Huizenga, V.P., PNC Advisors

Established in 1998 in OH.
Donor(s): Katharine S. Ficks.
Financial data (yr. ended 12/31/01): Grants paid, $23,000; assets, $90,714 (M); expenditures, $25,070; qualifying distributions, $23,584.
Limitations: Giving primarily in Cincinnati, OH.
Officers and Trustees:* Katharine S. Ficks,* Pres.; Gerald J. Ficks, Jr.,* Secy.-Treas.; John S. Ficks, Philip L. Ficks.
EIN: 311572801

43669
John M. Timken, Jr. Family Foundation
236 3rd St. S.W.
Canton, OH 44702 (330) 455-5281
Contact: Don D. Dickes, Secy-Treas.

Established in 1986 in OH.
Donor(s): John M. Timken, Jr., Polly M. Timken.
Financial data (yr. ended 09/30/01): Grants paid, $23,000; assets, $551,179 (M); expenditures, $24,521; qualifying distributions, $23,000.
Application information: Application form not required.
Officers and Trustees:* John M. Timken, Jr.,* Pres.; Polly M. Timken,* V.P.; Don D. Dickes,* Secy.-Treas.
EIN: 341532625

43670
David B. & Gretchen W. Black Family Foundation
P.O. Box 3775
Mansfield, OH 44907-0775

Established in 1998 in OH.
Donor(s): Elizabeth T. Black.
Financial data (yr. ended 12/31/01): Grants paid, $22,850; assets, $500,280 (M); expenditures, $25,784; qualifying distributions, $22,850.
Limitations: Applications not accepted.
Application information: Contributes only to pre-selected organizations.
Officer: David B. Black, Pres.
EIN: 311582258

43671
William Corley Foundation of the Westlake-Bay Village Rotary Club, Inc.
24500 Center Ridge Rd., Ste. 425
Westlake, OH 44145-4113
Application address: 24113 Beechwood Dr., Westlake, OH 44145
Contact: Layton K. Washburn, Secy.

Financial data (yr. ended 12/31/01): Grants paid, $22,701; assets, $97,993 (M); gifts received, $2,071; expenditures, $23,615; qualifying distributions, $22,701.
Limitations: Giving limited to northeastern OH.
Officers: Mark Musial, Pres.; Doug Harper, V.P.; Layton K. Washburn, Secy.; Douglas D. Newcomb, Treas.
EIN: 341271287

43672
The Harry Cobey Foundation
P.O. Box 258
Iberia, OH 43325-0258

Donor(s): Eagle Crusher Co., Inc.
Financial data (yr. ended 11/30/01): Grants paid, $22,629; assets, $771,644 (M); gifts received, $20,000; expenditures, $41,163; qualifying distributions, $22,629.
Limitations: Applications not accepted.
Application information: Contributes only to pre-selected organizations.
Officers: Ralph Cobey, Pres.; Hortense Cobey, Secy.-Treas.
EIN: 346523175

43673
L. Kanhofer Trust f/b/o Lee McKinney Scholarship
(also known as Lee McKinney Scholarship Trust)
c/o National City Bank
P.O. Box 94651
Cleveland, OH 44101-4651
Application address: c/o Ronald Joyce, Guidance Dir., Titusville Area High School, Guidance Ctr., 302 E. Walnut St., Titusville, PA 16354, tel.: (814) 827-9687

Financial data (yr. ended 12/31/01): Grants paid, $22,500; assets, $359,723 (M); expenditures, $24,631; qualifying distributions, $23,298.
Limitations: Giving limited to benefit residents of Titusville, PA.
Application information: Application form required.
Trustee: National City Bank.
EIN: 256227057

43674
Alfred J. Loser Memorial Scholarship Fund
c/o Lorain National Bank
457 Broadway
Lorain, OH 44052-1769

Donor(s): E.G. Koury.
Financial data (yr. ended 12/31/01): Grants paid, $22,500; assets, $702,951 (M); expenditures, $60,025; qualifying distributions, $22,500.
Limitations: Giving limited to residents of Lorain, OH.
Application information: Personal interview may be required. Application form required.
Directors: P. Biber, C. Catanzarite, Y. Fernandez, E.G. Koury, F. Mosley.
EIN: 346742325
Codes: GTI

43675
The Ruth B. and Thomas F. Mackey Foundation
c/o Barbara Mackey
727 S. High St.
Urbana, OH 43078

Established in 1998.
Donor(s): Ruth B. Mackey.
Financial data (yr. ended 12/31/01): Grants paid, $22,500; assets, $185,911 (M); gifts received, $50,000; expenditures, $23,175; qualifying distributions, $22,500.
Limitations: Applications not accepted. Giving primarily in NY, with some giving also in MA.
Application information: Contributes only to pre-selected organizations.
Trustees: Barbara Mackey, Ruth B. Mackey.
EIN: 226765660

43676
Gerzeny World Missions Fund
10723 Greenhaven Pkwy.
Brecksville, OH 44141

Financial data (yr. ended 12/31/00): Grants paid, $22,450; assets, $197,420 (M); gifts received, $13,815; expenditures, $42,060; qualifying distributions, $23,537.
Limitations: Giving on a national basis.
Officers: Dorothy Gerzeny, Treas.; Ernest Gerzeny, Exec. Dir.
EIN: 346608942

43677
Ryan Bunch, Inc.
c/o Jon M. Derhodes
2514 River Rd.
Newton Falls, OH 44444-8730

Established in 1993 in OH.
Financial data (yr. ended 12/31/99): Grants paid, $22,400; assets, $125,255 (M); expenditures, $22,400; qualifying distributions, $22,400; giving activities include $21,900 for programs.
Limitations: Applications not accepted.
Application information: Contributes only to pre-selected organizations.
Officers: Timothy Ryan, Pres.; Susan Ryan, V.P.; Pamela Plasky, Secy.-Treas.
EIN: 341735121

43678
Sollie Rosen Memorial Foundation
c/o Katherine Rena Rosen
20 Stonehill Ln.
Moreland Hills, OH 44022

Established in 1994 in OH.
Donor(s): Kenneth Rosen, Rena Rosen.
Financial data (yr. ended 12/31/00): Grants paid, $22,264; assets, $431,076 (M); expenditures, $33,849; qualifying distributions, $22,264.
Limitations: Applications not accepted. Giving limited to OH.
Application information: Contributes only to pre-selected organizations.
Trustees: Tab A. Keplinger, Katherine Rena Rosen, Kenneth R. Rosen.
EIN: 341788999

43679
Virginia E. Stauffer Scholarship Fund
c/o KeyBank, N.A.
800 Superior Ave., 4th Fl.
Cleveland, OH 44114-2601

Financial data (yr. ended 08/31/00): Grants paid, $22,250; assets, $520,792 (M); expenditures, $29,437; qualifying distributions, $21,888.
Limitations: Giving limited to Olean, NY.
Application information: Application form required.
Trustee: KeyBank, N.A.
EIN: 133143537
Codes: GTI

43680
Zarnick Family Foundation
52 Collver Rd.
Rocky River, OH 44116
Contact: Genevieve Zarnick, Pres.

Donor(s): Bernard Zarnick, Genevieve Zarnick.
Financial data (yr. ended 10/31/01): Grants paid, $22,210; assets, $79,574 (M); gifts received, $25,000; expenditures, $22,311; qualifying distributions, $22,210.
Officer and Trustees:* Genevieve Zarnick,* Pres.; Laura Grabowsky, Lisa Zarnick, Molly Zarnick.
EIN: 341807961

43681
Abe & Ida Goldman Memorial Trust
c/o Sky Trust, N.A.
P.O. Box 479
Youngstown, OH 44501-0479

Established in 1994 in OH.
Financial data (yr. ended 12/31/01): Grants paid, $22,154; assets, $837,193 (M); expenditures, $34,873; qualifying distributions, $25,512.
Limitations: Applications not accepted. Giving primarily in Youngstown, OH.
Application information: Contributes only to pre-selected organizations.
Trustees: George Woodman, Sky Trust, N.A.
EIN: 346973293

43682
Skaneateles Central School Endowment Foundation
c/o KeyBank, N.A.
800 Superior Ave., 4th Fl.
Cleveland, OH 44114

Financial data (yr. ended 12/31/01): Grants paid, $22,150; assets, $652,600 (M); expenditures, $29,719; qualifying distributions, $22,250.
Limitations: Applications not accepted. Giving limited to Skaneateles, NY.
Trustee: KeyBank, N.A.
EIN: 166076528
Codes: GTI

43683
The Simonds Foundation Trust
c/o National Bank & Trust
P.O. Box 711
Wilmington, OH 45177-2212

Established in 1981 in OH.
Financial data (yr. ended 09/30/01): Grants paid, $22,050; assets, $338,952 (M); expenditures, $25,433; qualifying distributions, $21,992.
Limitations: Applications not accepted. Giving primarily in Clinton County, OH.
Application information: Contributes only to pre-selected organizations.
Trustee: National Bank & Trust.
EIN: 316229424

43684
Florence G. Hall Foundation
c/o The Huntington National Bank
P.O. Box 1558, HC1012
Columbus, OH 43216
Application address: 140 Fair Ave. N.W., New Philadelphia, OH 44663
Contact: Donald W. Zimmerman, Chair.

Financial data (yr. ended 12/31/99): Grants paid, $22,033; assets, $509,064 (M); expenditures, $28,004; qualifying distributions, $23,341.
Limitations: Giving limited to New Philadelphia, OH.
Application information: Application form required.
Officer and Trustees:* Donald W. Zimmerman,* Chair.; The Huntington National Bank.
EIN: 346521352

43685
The Aitken Family Foundation, Inc.
P.O. Box 151
Geneva, OH 44041

Established in 2000 in OH.
Donor(s): Madeline Aitken.
Financial data (yr. ended 12/31/00): Grants paid, $22,000; assets, $2,488 (M); gifts received, $25,000; expenditures, $22,512; qualifying distributions, $22,000.
Limitations: Applications not accepted.
Application information: Contributes only to pre-selected organizations.
Officers and Trustees:* Suzanne Aitken Shannon,* Pres.; Madeline Aitken,* Secy.; Joseph F. Ciulla.
EIN: 341904178

43686
John E. Bakes Scholarship Trust Fund
c/o National City Bank of Indiana
P.O. Box 94651
Cleveland, OH 44101-4651
Application addresses: c/o Guidance Counselor, Switzerland County High School, Venuay, IN 47043; c/o Guidance Counselor, Ohio County Rising Sun High School, Rising Sun, IN 47040

Financial data (yr. ended 12/31/01): Grants paid, $22,000; assets, $353,651 (M); expenditures, $25,189; qualifying distributions, $23,159.
Limitations: Giving limited to residents of Switzerland County and Rising Sun, IN.
Trustee: National City Bank of Indiana.
EIN: 356406002
Codes: GTI

43687
Lorenz Family Charitable Foundation
9341 Jerome Rd.
Dublin, OH 43017

Established in 1998 in OH.
Donor(s): Members of the Lorenz Family.
Financial data (yr. ended 12/31/01): Grants paid, $22,000; assets, $69,073 (M); gifts received, $500; expenditures, $23,004; qualifying distributions, $22,000.
Limitations: Applications not accepted. Giving primarily in Dublin, OH.
Application information: Contributes only to pre-selected organizations.
Trustee: Daniel E. Lorenz.
EIN: 311627926

43688
John and Cree Marshall Foundation
700 Ackerman Rd., Ste. 400
Columbus, OH 43202 (614) 267-2600
Contact: James Wyland, Tr.

Established in 1997 in OH.
Donor(s): John Marshall, Cree Marshall.
Financial data (yr. ended 12/31/01): Grants paid, $22,000; assets, $380,118 (M); gifts received, $9,000; expenditures, $28,357; qualifying distributions, $22,000.
Limitations: Giving primarily in OH.
Officers: John F. Marshall, Pres.; Carolyn C. Marshall, Secy.-Treas.
Trustees: Christine C. Girard, James H. Hyland.
EIN: 316589811

43689
John Otis and Nelle Evangeline Lamb Foundation, Inc.
(Formerly John Otis Lamb Foundation, Inc.)
6586 Wyndwatch Dr.
Cincinnati, OH 45230

Established in 1966 in OH.
Donor(s): Jane C. Lamb, Cincinnati Screen Process Supplies, Inc., Cincinnati Sign Supplies, Inc., Cincinnati Screen Printing Equipment Co.
Financial data (yr. ended 12/31/01): Grants paid, $21,990; assets, $232,972 (M); gifts received, $3,600; expenditures, $26,078; qualifying distributions, $21,990.
Limitations: Applications not accepted. Giving on a national basis.
Application information: Contributes only to pre-selected organizations.
Officers and Trustees:* John K. Lamb,* Pres. and Treas.; David A. Lamb,* V.P.; Susan M. Lamb,* Secy.
EIN: 316065265

43690
Gibbs Investment Fund Irrevocable Trust
c/o KeyBank, N.A., Trust Div.
800 Superior Ave., 4th Fl.
Cleveland, OH 44114

Financial data (yr. ended 12/31/00): Grants paid, $21,823; assets, $452,364 (M); expenditures, $24,916; qualifying distributions, $22,411.
Limitations: Applications not accepted. Giving limited to Canton, OH.
Application information: Contributes only to a pre-selected organization.
Trustee: KeyBank, N.A.
EIN: 346576283
Codes: TN

43691
Oglebay Norton Foundation
P.O. Box 6508
Cleveland, OH 44101-1508 (216) 861-8734
FAX: (216) 861-2399; E-mail: rwalk@oglebay.cleveland
Contact: Rochelle F. Walk, Secy.

Trust established in 1952 in OH; incorporated in 1959.
Donor(s): Oglebay Norton Co.
Financial data (yr. ended 12/31/01): Grants paid, $21,725; assets, $213 (M); expenditures, $21,904; qualifying distributions, $21,725.
Limitations: Giving primarily in Cleveland, OH.
Publications: Application guidelines.
Application information: Application form not required.
Officers and Trustees:* John N. Lauer,* Chair., C.E.O., and Pres.; David H. Kelsey, V.P. and Treas.; Rochelle F. Walk, Secy.; Michael F. Biehl, Ronald J. Compiseno.
EIN: 346513722
Codes: CS, TN

43692
Southside Community Health Association
c/o Education Comm.
1430 S. High St.
Columbus, OH 43207 (614) 443-0583

Established in 1991 in OH.
Financial data (yr. ended 12/31/00): Grants paid, $21,700; assets, $2,264,382 (M); expenditures, $222,652; qualifying distributions, $21,700.
Limitations: Giving limited to Columbus, OH.
Application information: Application form required.
Officers: Won G. Song, M.D., Chair. and Pres.; Miriam Knorr, Pres.; Lenore Housand, Secy.; Theresa Middleton, Treas.
Directors: Maheswora Baidya, M.D., Donald L. Feinstein, Fred W. Kreutz, Eunice F. McMullen, Ned McNamara, Cahit Palantekin, M.D., Nancy Schleppi, Rev. William L. Snider, Stewart F. Stock, M.D., Chi Weber.
EIN: 311124341
Codes: GTI

43693
The Jack and Madge Peters Foundation
705 Overlook Dr.
Alliance, OH 44601

Established in 1986 in OH.
Donor(s): John F. Peters, Madge A. Peters.
Financial data (yr. ended 12/31/01): Grants paid, $21,600; assets, $144,714 (M); expenditures, $22,791; qualifying distributions, $21,600.
Limitations: Applications not accepted. Giving primarily in Alliance, OH.
Application information: Contributes only to pre-selected organizations.

43693—OHIO

Trustees: Suzanne P. Clark, John F. Peters, Madge A. Peters, George K. Weimer, Jr.
EIN: 341535575

43694
The Coleman Foundation
148 S. Franklin St.
Chagrin Falls, OH 44022-3233

Donor(s): William H. Coleman, Sr.
Financial data (yr. ended 12/31/01): Grants paid, $21,586; assets, $89,733 (M); expenditures, $22,819; qualifying distributions, $21,586.
Limitations: Applications not accepted.
Application information: Contributes only to pre-selected organizations.
Trustees: Michael F. Coleman, T. Kelley Coleman.
EIN: 346610651

43695
Muriel Gilbert Memorial Scholarship Fund
c/o KeyBank, N.A.
P.O. Box 10099
Toledo, OH 43699-0099
Application addresses: c/o Eastern Michigan Univ., Music Dept., 1215 Huron River Dr., Ypsilanti, MI 48197, or c/o Superintendant of Schools, Milan Area Schools, 920 North St., Milan, MI 48160
Contact: James Hause, Prof.

Established in 1988 in MI.
Financial data (yr. ended 09/30/01): Grants paid, $21,552; assets, $467,352 (M); expenditures, $27,381; qualifying distributions, $22,908.
Limitations: Giving limited to the Milan, MI, area.
Application information: Application form required.
Trustee: KeyBank, N.A.
EIN: 386525706
Codes: GTI

43696
Philip F. Lattavo Family Foundation
2230 Shepler Church Rd.
P.O. Box 6270
Canton, OH 44706 (330) 456-4571

Established in 1987 in OH.
Donor(s): Philip E. Lattavo.
Financial data (yr. ended 12/31/01): Grants paid, $21,540; assets, $581,697 (M); gifts received, $32,583; expenditures, $22,999; qualifying distributions, $21,540.
Limitations: Giving primarily in Canton, OH.
Application information: Application form not required.
Trustees: Thomas W. Edwards IV, Judith A. Lattavo, Philip E. Lattavo.
EIN: 346883818

43697
Mary Margaret Ackers Charitable Trust
123 S. Broad St.
Lancaster, OH 43130
Application address: 4307 Bauman Hill Rd., Lancaster, OH 43130
Contact: William J. Sitterley, Tr.

Established in 1991 in OH.
Financial data (yr. ended 08/31/01): Grants paid, $21,500; assets, $344,490 (M); expenditures, $23,112; qualifying distributions, $23,012.
Limitations: Giving limited to residents of Fairfield County, OH.
Application information: Application form required.
Trustees: Christine A. Sitterley, William J. Sitterley.
EIN: 311327096

43698
The E. Thomas Arington Family Foundation
105 E. 4th St., Ste. 300
Cincinnati, OH 45202

Established in 1994 in OH.
Donor(s): E. Thomas Arington.
Financial data (yr. ended 12/31/01): Grants paid, $21,500; assets, $477,818 (M); expenditures, $21,750; qualifying distributions, $21,500.
Limitations: Applications not accepted. Giving primarily in KY and OH.
Application information: Contributes only to pre-selected organizations.
Officers: E. Thomas Arington, Pres. and Treas.; Bettye M. Arington, V.P.; Robert W. Buechner, Secy.
EIN: 311417811

43699
The Echement Family Foundation
c/o National City Bank of Pennsylvania
P.O. Box 94651
Cleveland, OH 44101-4651

Established in 1999 in PA.
Donor(s): John R. Echement.
Financial data (yr. ended 04/30/02): Grants paid, $21,500; assets, $74,949 (M); expenditures, $23,525; qualifying distributions, $21,500.
Limitations: Applications not accepted. Giving primarily in PA.
Application information: Contributes only to pre-selected organizations.
Trustee: National City Bank of Pennsylvania.
EIN: 256636811

43700
Edward and Linda Reiter Family Foundation
P.O. Box 479
Youngstown, OH 44501-0479
Application address: 20660 Carter Rd., Bowling Green, OH 43402
Contact: Mark Reiter, Tr. or Kelly Lum, Tr.

Established in 1999 in OH.
Financial data (yr. ended 12/31/01): Grants paid, $21,450; assets, $350,700 (M); expenditures, $23,861; qualifying distributions, $21,450.
Trustees: Kelly Lum, Mark Reiter, Sky Trust, N.A.
EIN: 347089394

43701
Geraldine Moss Charitable Trust
c/o Fifth Third Bank
P.O. Box 1868, Trust Tax Dept.
Toledo, OH 43603-0001
Application address: c/o Dir. of Financial Aid, Findlay College, 1000 Main St., Findlay, OH 45840, tel.: (419) 422-8313

Financial data (yr. ended 09/30/01): Grants paid, $21,438; assets, $463,567 (M); expenditures, $22,631; qualifying distributions, $20,963.
Limitations: Giving limited to the Findlay, OH, area.
Application information: Recipient chosen by scholarship committee. Application form required.
Trustee: Fifth Third bank.
EIN: 346812616
Codes: GTI

43702
The Hadley Family Foundation
c/o National City Bank
P.O. Box 94651
Cleveland, OH 44101-4651

Donor(s): Jack Hadley.
Financial data (yr. ended 12/31/01): Grants paid, $21,400; assets, $367,508 (M); gifts received, $20,000; expenditures, $22,847; qualifying distributions, $21,400.
Limitations: Applications not accepted.
Application information: Contributes only to pre-selected organizations.
Officer: Jack Hadley, Pres.
Distribution Committee: Jeanne Hadley.
Trustee: National City Bank.
EIN: 251783304

43703
Ethel M. Tyler Trust
c/o FirstMerit Bank, N.A.
105 Court St.
Elyria, OH 44035-5525 (440) 329-3000
Contact: Michael Yanick, V.P. and Sr. Trust Off., FirstMerit Bank, N.A.

Financial data (yr. ended 12/31/01): Grants paid, $21,360; assets, $517,452 (M); expenditures, $26,796; qualifying distributions, $21,360.
Limitations: Giving limited to Lorain County, OH.
Application information: Application form not required.
Trustee: FirstMerit Bank, N.A.
EIN: 346524600

43704
Niles I. Livingston Charitable Trust
c/o FirstMerit Bank, N.A.
121 S. Main St., Ste. 200
Akron, OH 44308-1440

Established in 1998 in OH.
Donor(s): Niles I. Livingston.‡
Financial data (yr. ended 01/31/00): Grants paid, $21,300; assets, $510,026 (M); expenditures, $28,167; qualifying distributions, $22,841.
Limitations: Applications not accepted. Giving primarily in Akron and Ravenna, OH.
Application information: Contributes only to pre-selected organizations.
Trustee: FirstMerit Bank, N.A.
EIN: 341873273

43705
The J.M.S. Foundation
1756 Dunbarton Dr. N.W.
Canton, OH 44708-1807

Financial data (yr. ended 12/31/01): Grants paid, $21,289; assets, $397,273 (M); expenditures, $22,218; qualifying distributions, $21,289.
Limitations: Applications not accepted. Giving primarily in OH.
Application information: Contributes only to pre-selected organizations.
Officers: Joanne A. Schauer, Pres.; Thomas A. Schauer, V.P.
Trustees: Alan T. Schauer, David T. Schauer, Susan F. Schauer, William T. Schauer.
EIN: 237000456

43706
Glenna Joyce Vernon (MAD) Foundation
c/o National City Bank of Indiana
P.O. Box 94651
Cleveland, OH 44101-4651

Established in 1996 in IN.
Financial data (yr. ended 12/31/01): Grants paid, $21,266; assets, $409,780 (M); expenditures, $24,370; qualifying distributions, $21,266.
Limitations: Applications not accepted.
Application information: Contributes only to pre-selected organizations.
Trustee: National City Bank.
EIN: 356473375

43707
Katharine L. Hageman Charitable Trust
c/o KeyBank, N.A.
800 Superior Ave., 4th Fl.
Cleveland, OH 44114

Financial data (yr. ended 12/31/00): Grants paid, $21,215; assets, $630,434 (M); expenditures, $21,215; qualifying distributions, $21,215.
Limitations: Applications not accepted. Giving primarily in OH.
Application information: Contributes only to pre-selected organizations.
Trustee: KeyBank, N.A.
EIN: 916530950

43708
Arthur H. Keeney Ophthalmic Fund
c/o National City Bank
P.O. Box 94651
Cleveland, OH 44101-4651
Application address: 54 Tepec Rd., Louisville, KY 40207
Contact: L. Douglas Keeney, Advisory Comm. Member

Established in 1988 in KY.
Financial data (yr. ended 12/31/01): Grants paid, $21,210; assets, $268,493 (M); expenditures, $22,770; qualifying distributions, $21,210.
Limitations: Giving primarily in Louisville, KY.
Investment Officer: Marshall Sellers.
Advisory Committee: L. Douglas Keeney, Virginia D. Keeney.
Trustee: National City Bank, Kentucky.
EIN: 341596929

43709
Judith Gerson Charitable Trust
c/o J.T. Young
1801 E. 9th St., Ste. 1425
Cleveland, OH 44114-3199

Established in 2001 in OH.
Donor(s): Judith Gerson, Eleanor Gerson Trust.
Financial data (yr. ended 12/31/01): Grants paid, $21,200; assets, $310,968 (M); gifts received, $333,833; expenditures, $24,641; qualifying distributions, $21,200.
Limitations: Applications not accepted. Giving primarily in Cleveland, OH.
Application information: Contributes only to pre-selected organizations.
Trustees: Judith Gerson, J. Talbot Young, Jr.
EIN: 912120410

43710
Edward J. & Lavelette Rockwell Sheil Memorial Fund
c/o National City Bank of Pennsylvania
P. O. Box 94651
Cleveland, OH 44101-4651
Application address: c/o Paul N. Shaler, Head Counselor, Coronado High School, 650 D Ave., Coronado, CA 92118, tel.: (714) 435-3172

Financial data (yr. ended 12/31/01): Grants paid, $21,167; assets, $263,208 (M); expenditures, $23,508; qualifying distributions, $22,167.
Limitations: Giving limited to residents of Coronado, CA.
Application information: Application form required.
Trustee: National City Bank.
EIN: 256081887
Codes: GTI

43711
The E. & E. Davis Foundation
P.O. Box 24731
Mayfield Heights, OH 44124
Contact: Edward B. Davis, Tr.

Established in 1997 in OH.
Financial data (yr. ended 12/31/01): Grants paid, $21,050; assets, $418,656 (M); gifts received, $45,955; expenditures, $27,560; qualifying distributions, $21,050.
Trustees: Edward B. Davis, Eileen K. Davis, James B. Davis, Robert A. Davis, Barbara D. Fleischman.
EIN: 341849861

43712
Living Memorial Scholarship Fund, Inc.
401 Main St.
Coshocton, OH 43812
Contact: Robert Hamilton, Dir.

Financial data (yr. ended 06/30/00): Grants paid, $21,000; assets, $256,429 (M); gifts received, $700; expenditures, $21,661; qualifying distributions, $20,879.
Limitations: Giving limited to OH.
Application information: Application form required.
Directors: Robert Hamilton, M. Schlarb, D. Shurtz, Jack Shurtz.
EIN: 341321980

43713
Aimee and Frank Mishou Scholarship Trust
c/o KeyBank, N.A., Trust Div.
800 Superior Ave., 4th Fl.
Cleveland, OH 44114
Application address: c/o Principal, Sumner High School, Sumner, ME 04607

Donor(s): Aimee Mishou,‡ Frank Mishou.‡
Financial data (yr. ended 04/30/01): Grants paid, $21,000; assets, $416,879 (M); expenditures, $26,532; qualifying distributions, $20,578.
Limitations: Giving limited to students at Sumner High School, or residents of Sullivan, Gouldsboro, or Winter Harbor, ME.
Application information: Application form required.
Trustee: KeyBank, N.A.
EIN: 016070062
Codes: GTI

43714
A. F. Robertson Family Memorial Fund
c/o National City Bank of Indiana
P.O. Box 94651
Cleveland, OH 44101-4651
Application addresses: c/o Seymour National Bank, Trust Dept., P.O. Box 5031, Indianapolis, IN 46255, tel.: (812) 265-5121; c/o Brownstown Central High School, Brownstown, IN; c/o Seymour High School, Seymour, IN
Contact: J. Muessel

Financial data (yr. ended 12/31/01): Grants paid, $20,825; assets, $596,658 (M); expenditures, $24,726; qualifying distributions, $22,456.
Limitations: Giving limited to Seymour, IN.
Application information: Application form required.
Trustee: National City Bank.
EIN: 356057077
Codes: GTI

43715
T. Spencer Shore Foundation
900 Central Ave.
Cincinnati, OH 45202
Application address: 900 4th & Vine Tower, Cincinnati, OH 45202
Contact: Thomas S. Shore, Jr., Tr.

Financial data (yr. ended 12/31/01): Grants paid, $20,600; assets, $163,602 (M); expenditures, $20,940; qualifying distributions, $20,600.
Limitations: Giving on a national basis, with emphasis on Rye, NY, and Cincinnati, OH.
Application information: Application form not required.
Trustees: Harriet S. Burke, Janet S. Kindel, Thomas S. Shore, Jr.
EIN: 316030086

43716
Dorothy S. Neff YWCA Gift Fund Charitable Trust
c/o National City Bank
P.O. Box 94651
Cleveland, OH 44101-4651

Established in 2000 in OH.
Financial data (yr. ended 12/31/01): Grants paid, $20,565; assets, $367,752 (M); expenditures, $29,050; qualifying distributions, $20,565.
Limitations: Applications not accepted. Giving primarily in Dayton, OH.
Application information: Contributes only to pre-selected organizations.
Trustee: National City Bank.
EIN: 316584209

43717
Thomas and Theresa Coury Charitable Foundation
2 Berea Commons, Ste. 1
Berea, OH 44017

Established in 1998 in OH.
Donor(s): Thomas J. Coury, Teri Coury Strimpel, Traci A. Ade.
Financial data (yr. ended 09/30/01): Grants paid, $20,500; assets, $58,636 (M); expenditures, $23,138; qualifying distributions, $20,500.
Limitations: Applications not accepted. Giving limited to OH.
Application information: Contributes only to pre-selected organizations.
Officers: Teri Coury Strimpel, Pres.; Theresa A. Coury, Treas.; Traci A. Ade, Secy.
EIN: 341877605

43718
The J. V. McNicholas Foundation
1500 Trumbull Ave.
Girard, OH 44420

Financial data (yr. ended 12/31/01): Grants paid, $20,500; assets, $412,779 (M); expenditures, $25,327; qualifying distributions, $20,500.
Limitations: Applications not accepted.
Application information: Contributes only to pre-selected organizations.
Trustees: D. Joseph Fleming, Thomas J. Fleming.
EIN: 341246079

43719
Charles & Salome Reymann Foundation
c/o Bank One Trust Co., N.A.
774 Park Meadow Rd.
Westerville, OH 43081

Financial data (yr. ended 12/31/01): Grants paid, $20,500; assets, $454,835 (M); gifts received, $452; expenditures, $67,335; qualifying distributions, $20,500.

43719—OHIO

Limitations: Applications not accepted. Giving primarily in Akron, OH.
Application information: Contributes only to pre-selected organizations.
Officers: Rosemary Reymann, Pres.; Vincent Reymann, V.P.; Kim Kovesci, Secy.; Barry M. Ward, Treas.
Trustee: Bank One Trust Co., N.A.
EIN: 346596966

43720
Mae Ward Educational Trust
c/o Fifth Third Bank
38 Fountain Sq. Plz.
Cincinnati, OH 45263
Application address: c/o Fifth Third Bank, P.O. Box 1730, Ashland, KY 41105-1730, tel.: (606) 329-9797

Financial data (yr. ended 12/31/01): Grants paid, $20,449; assets, $725,230 (M); expenditures, $32,334; qualifying distributions, $20,449.
Limitations: Giving limited to residents of KY.
Trustee: Fifth Third Bank.
EIN: 616246093

43721
Alfred H. Billstein Foundation
29685 Shelbourne Rd.
Perrysburg, OH 43551-3454
Contact: Robert A. Billstein, Pres.

Financial data (yr. ended 12/31/01): Grants paid, $20,257; assets, $399,894 (M); expenditures, $20,659; qualifying distributions, $20,257.
Limitations: Giving primarily in Toledo, OH.
Officers: Robert A. Billstein, Pres. and Treas.; Robert A. Billstein, Jr., V.P. and Secy.
EIN: 346531828

43722
Herbert W. Wunderlin Foundation
c/o National City Bank of Indiana
P.O. Box 94651
Cleveland, OH 44101-4651
Application address: P.O. Box 110, Fort Wayne, IN 46802, tel.: (219) 461-6199
Contact: Michele Herald

Established in 1996 in IN.
Donor(s): Herbert W. Wunderlin Irrevocable Trust.
Financial data (yr. ended 07/31/01): Grants paid, $20,172; assets, $721,824 (M); expenditures, $24,751; qualifying distributions, $21,822.
Limitations: Giving primarily in IN.
Trustee: National City Bank.
EIN: 356630203

43723
Roderick H. Dillon, Jr. Foundation
46 E. Sycamore St.
Columbus, OH 43206

Established in 1992 in OH.
Donor(s): Roderick H. Dillon, Jr.
Financial data (yr. ended 12/31/00): Grants paid, $20,150; assets, $527,181 (M); expenditures, $25,010; qualifying distributions, $20,150.
Limitations: Applications not accepted. Giving primarily in OH.
Application information: Contributes only to pre-selected organizations.
Trustee: Roderick H. Dillon, Jr.
EIN: 383056226

43724
The H. Willis and Anna A. Ratledge Foundation
441 Vine St., Ste. 2900
Cincinnati, OH 45202
Contact: Dennis L. Manes, Secy.

Established in 1997 in OH.
Donor(s): H. Willis Ratledge, Anna A. Ratledge.
Financial data (yr. ended 12/31/01): Grants paid, $20,140; assets, $560,459 (M); gifts received, $127,296; expenditures, $28,825; qualifying distributions, $20,140.
Limitations: Applications not accepted. Giving on a national basis, with emphasis on Cincinnati, OH.
Application information: Contributes only to pre-selected organizations.
Officers and Trustees:* H. Willis Ratledge,* Pres.; Anna A. Ratledge,* V.P.; Dennis L. Manes,* Secy.
EIN: 311572542

43725
Dr. Louis A. and Anne B. Schneider Foundation Trust
c/o National City Bank of Indiana
P.O. Box 94651
Cleveland, OH 44101-4651
Application address: 9512 Camberwell Dr., Fort Wayne, IN 46804
Contact: Louis A. Schneider, Tr.

Established in 1986 in IN.
Financial data (yr. ended 11/30/01): Grants paid, $20,136; assets, $374,156 (M); expenditures, $24,342; qualifying distributions, $20,136.
Limitations: Giving primarily in Fort Wayne, IN.
Trustees: Louis A. Schneider, National City Bank.
EIN: 311193706

43726
Carole Barron Foundation
4336 Ashley Meadow Ct.
Cincinnati, OH 45227

Established in 2000 in OH.
Donor(s): Carole Barron.
Financial data (yr. ended 12/31/01): Grants paid, $20,000; assets, $283,256 (M); gifts received, $2,197; expenditures, $25,534; qualifying distributions, $20,000.
Limitations: Applications not accepted.
Application information: Contributes only to pre-selected organizations.
Officer and Trustees:* Carole Barron,* Pres.; Jessica Barron, Guy M. Hild.
EIN: 311695570

43727
C.Y., Inc. Over 70
c/o Rev. Ernest A. Toth
1722 Larch Ave., Ste. 405
Cincinnati, OH 45224

Financial data (yr. ended 04/30/02): Grants paid, $20,000; assets, $16,866 (M); gifts received, $23,485; expenditures, $20,177; qualifying distributions, $20,000.
Limitations: Giving primarily in the greater Cincinnati, OH, area.
Officers: Rev. Herman Helfrich, Pres.; Rev. Ernest A. Toth, V.P.; Marilyn J. Kiefer, Treas.
Trustee: Delmar Hugo.
EIN: 311306434

43728
The Conn Family Foundation
11385 Montgomery Rd., Ste. 220
Cincinnati, OH 45249

Established in 2001 in OH.
Donor(s): Raymond Conn, Joan Conn.
Financial data (yr. ended 12/31/01): Grants paid, $20,000; assets, $780,282 (M); gifts received, $780,000; expenditures, $21,004; qualifying distributions, $20,000.
Limitations: Applications not accepted.
Application information: Contributes only to pre-selected organizations.

Officers: Raymond A. Conn, Pres.; Joan D. Conn, V.P.; Alan R. Trenz, Secy.-Treas.
EIN: 311784407

43729
The Rev. H. W. Hargett Scholarship Fund
c/o FirstMerit Bank, N.A.
121 S. Main St., Ste. 200
Akron, OH 44308-1426

Established in 1994 in OH.
Donor(s): Marion H. Allen Trust.
Financial data (yr. ended 09/30/01): Grants paid, $20,000; assets, $312,461 (M); expenditures, $25,776; qualifying distributions, $21,162.
Limitations: Applications not accepted. Giving primarily in Delaware, OH.
Application information: Contributes only to pre-selected organizations.
Trustee: FirstMerit Bank, N.A.
EIN: 341783357

43730
Henry P. Huber Scholarship Trust
c/o The Huntington National Bank
P.O. Box 1558, HC1012
Columbus, OH 43216
Application address: c/o Scholarship Comm., 101 N. Elizabeth, Lima, OH 45801

Financial data (yr. ended 06/30/01): Grants paid, $20,000; assets, $202,166 (M); expenditures, $24,116; qualifying distributions, $20,448.
Limitations: Giving limited to residents of the Bluffton, OH, area.
Trustee: The Huntington National Bank.
EIN: 346766601
Codes: GTI

43731
Helen Hart Hurlbert Foundation, Inc.
c/o Bank One of Eastern Ohio, N.A.
9250 King Graves Rd., N.E.
Warren, OH 44484

Financial data (yr. ended 11/30/01): Grants paid, $20,000; assets, $362,739 (M); expenditures, $31,075; qualifying distributions, $20,000.
Limitations: Applications not accepted. Giving primarily in OH.
Publications: Annual report.
Application information: Contributes only to pre-selected organizations.
Officers: Griswald H. Draz, V.P. and Treas.; Christian Draz, Secy.; Fred J. Schomer, Exec. Dir. and Mgr.
EIN: 346558853

43732
Ove W. Jorgensen Foundation, Inc.
c/o National City Bank of Indiana
P.O. Box 94651
Cleveland, OH 44101-4651

Established in 1998 in IN.
Donor(s): Ove W. Jorgensen.
Financial data (yr. ended 01/31/00): Grants paid, $20,000; assets, $1,468,883 (M); gifts received, $3,526; expenditures, $27,655; qualifying distributions, $20,888.
Officers: Ove W. Jorgensen, Pres.; Jay O. Jorgensen, V.P.; Winifred M. Jorgensen, Secy.
EIN: 352050475

43733
Kinnaird Foundation
c/o Mellott & Mellott
36 E. 4th St., Ste. 600
Cincinnati, OH 45202
Contact: William B. Davis, Tr.

Financial data (yr. ended 12/31/01): Grants paid, $20,000; assets, $349,847 (M); expenditures, $23,749; qualifying distributions, $20,000.
Limitations: Giving primarily in Oxford, OH.
Trustees: G. Scott Davis, William B. Davis, Mary Soldati.
EIN: 316089236

43734
The Frederick William Kruse Testamentary Trust
c/o Diana Thimmig
925 Euclid Ave., Ste. 1100
Cleveland, OH 44115-1475

Established in 1992 in OH.
Donor(s): Frederick William Kruse.‡
Financial data (yr. ended 12/31/01): Grants paid, $20,000; assets, $172,715 (M); expenditures, $22,491; qualifying distributions, $20,000.
Limitations: Applications not accepted. Giving on an international basis, with emphasis on Germany.
Application information: Contributes only to pre-selected organizations.
Trustee: Diana Thimmig.
EIN: 346981260

43735
Maradele Foundation
c/o Thomas F. Allen
1801 E. 9th St.
Cleveland, OH 44114

Donor(s): Douglas Wick, Allayne E. Wick.
Financial data (yr. ended 12/31/01): Grants paid, $20,000; assets, $225,935 (M); gifts received, $17,535; expenditures, $21,310; qualifying distributions, $21,279.
Limitations: Applications not accepted. Giving primarily in OH.
Application information: Contributes only to pre-selected organizations.
Trustees: Thomas F. Allen, Mary Wick Bole, Adele Ernst Wick, Douglas Wick.
EIN: 346539442

43736
Robert and Charline Moyer Foundation
519 Smith Rd.
Fremont, OH 43420-8865

Established in 1998 in OH.
Donor(s): Robert Moyer, Charline Moyer.
Financial data (yr. ended 12/31/00): Grants paid, $20,000; assets, $659,729 (M); gifts received, $404,453; expenditures, $25,088; qualifying distributions, $20,855.
Limitations: Applications not accepted. Giving primarily in Fremont, OH.
Application information: Contributes only to pre-selected organizations.
Officers: Robert H. Moyer, Pres.; Charline F. Moyer, V.P.; Charles Moyer, Secy.-Treas.
EIN: 341880794

43737
Northern Indiana Fuel and Light Company, Inc. Fund and Trust, Inc.
c/o National City Bank of Indiana
P.O. Box 94651
Cleveland, OH 44101-4651
Application address: c/o National City Bank of Indiana, P.O. Box 110, Fort Wayne, IN 46801, tel.: (219) 461-6199
Contact: Michele Delaney, Trust Off., National City Bank of Indiana

Donor(s): Northern Indiana Fuel and Light Co., Inc.
Financial data (yr. ended 12/31/01): Grants paid, $20,000; assets, $343,302 (M); expenditures, $20,442; qualifying distributions, $20,159.
Limitations: Giving primarily in areas of company operations.
Application information: Application form required.
Trustee: National City Bank of Indiana.
EIN: 311030243
Codes: CS, CD, GTI

43738
The Phillips Family Charitable Foundation
3410 Oyster Bay Ct.
Cincinnati, OH 45244

Established in 1996 in OH.
Donor(s): David C. Phillips.
Financial data (yr. ended 12/31/01): Grants paid, $20,000; assets, $306,343 (M); gifts received, $60,419; expenditures, $26,664; qualifying distributions, $20,000.
Limitations: Applications not accepted. Giving primarily in Cincinnati, OH.
Application information: Contributes only to pre-selected organizations.
Officers: David C. Phillips, Chair.; Liane Phillips, Pres.; Scott D. Phillips, V.P.; Brett P. Phillips, Secy.; Todd A. Phillips, Treas.
EIN: 311468818

43739
Eliza Kennedy Smith Foundation
3001 Fairmount Blvd.
Cleveland Heights, OH 44118

Established in 1995 in OH.
Donor(s): Kennedy Smith, Jr.
Financial data (yr. ended 12/31/00): Grants paid, $20,000; assets, $417,049 (M); expenditures, $20,515; qualifying distributions, $20,000.
Limitations: Applications not accepted.
Application information: Contributes only to pre-selected organizations.
Officers and Trustees:* Frederick A. Smith,* Pres.; Mark T. Smith,* V.P.; Edward C. Smith, Secy.-Treas.; Mary Smith Podles, Ann Seabright, Kennedy Smith, Jr.
EIN: 341823829

43740
Donald E. Bush & Barbara Ann Bush Charitable Foundation
161 E. Mohawk Dr.
Malvern, OH 44644

Established in 1989 in OH.
Donor(s): B & H Machine, Inc.
Financial data (yr. ended 12/31/01): Grants paid, $19,800; assets, $222,431 (M); expenditures, $24,240; qualifying distributions, $20,300.
Limitations: Applications not accepted. Giving primarily in OH.
Application information: Contributes only to pre-selected organizations.
Trustee: Barbara Ann Bush Hochstetler.
EIN: 346904600

43741
Lawrence Standish Scholarship Trust
c/o KeyBank, N.A.
800 Superior Ave., 4th Fl.
Cleveland, OH 44114

Established in 1992 in ME.
Financial data (yr. ended 06/30/01): Grants paid, $19,720; assets, $760,131 (M); expenditures, $35,100; qualifying distributions, $19,060.
Limitations: Applications not accepted. Giving limited to residents of ME.
Application information: Scholarship awarded by university faculty.
Trustee: KeyBank, N.A.
EIN: 016115928
Codes: GTI

43742
Harry Cagin Fund
23215 Commerce Park Dr., No. 316
Beachwood, OH 44122-5843

Established in 1965.
Donor(s): Harry Cagin.
Financial data (yr. ended 09/30/01): Grants paid, $19,590; assets, $46,552 (M); expenditures, $20,267; qualifying distributions, $19,565.
Limitations: Applications not accepted. Giving primarily in NY and OH.
Application information: Contributes only to pre-selected organizations.
Officers: Harry Cagin, Pres.; Meyer J. Kohn, Secy.; Ronna Sherman, Treas.
EIN: 346577985

43743
Apple Foundation
c/o Fifth Third Bank
Dept. 00858
Cincinnati, OH 45263

Financial data (yr. ended 12/31/01): Grants paid, $19,500; assets, $273,979 (M); gifts received, $250; expenditures, $21,433; qualifying distributions, $19,500.
Limitations: Applications not accepted. Giving primarily in OH.
Application information: Contributes only to pre-selected organizations.
Trustee: Fifth Third Bank.
EIN: 316086244

43744
The John & Mary Coyne Charitable Foundation
1428 Hamilton Ave.
Cleveland, OH 44114

Established in 1998 in OH.
Donor(s): John Coyne, Mary Coyne.
Financial data (yr. ended 12/31/01): Grants paid, $19,300; assets, $227,566 (M); gifts received, $14,150; expenditures, $20,934; qualifying distributions, $19,300.
Limitations: Applications not accepted.
Application information: Contributes only to pre-selected organizations.
Officers: John Coyne, Pres.; Mary Coyne, Secy.; Cathleen Coyne, Treas.
EIN: 341882946

43745
Jaffe Charitable Foundation
29555 Shaker Blvd.
Pepper Pike, OH 44124-5032

Donor(s): Samuel Jaffe, Myron Jaffe.‡
Financial data (yr. ended 06/30/02): Grants paid, $19,300; assets, $481,940 (M); gifts received, $500; expenditures, $21,581; qualifying distributions, $19,300.

Limitations: Applications not accepted.
Application information: Contributes only to pre-selected organizations.
Trustees: Anne Jacobs, Daniel Jaffe, David Jaffe, Marc Jaffe, Samuel Jaffe.
EIN: 346520456

43746
Newman Foundation, Inc.
2101 Ross Ave.
Cincinnati, OH 45212-2001

Donor(s): James O. Newman.
Financial data (yr. ended 12/31/01): Grants paid, $19,300; assets, $417,692 (M); gifts received, $58,560; expenditures, $21,546; qualifying distributions, $19,300.
Limitations: Applications not accepted. Giving primarily in OH.
Application information: Contributes only to pre-selected organizations.
Officer and Trustee:* James O. Newman,* Pres.
EIN: 316061954

43747
The Susan H. Walter and Paul W. Walter Charitable Trust
20725 Shaker Blvd.
Shaker Heights, OH 44122

Established in 1997 in OH.
Financial data (yr. ended 12/31/99): Grants paid, $19,280; assets, $105,240 (M); expenditures, $20,685; qualifying distributions, $19,173.
Limitations: Applications not accepted.
Application information: Contributes only to pre-selected organizations.
Trustees: Heather Cargile, Susan Cargile, Paul Walter, Jr.
EIN: 347031725

43748
Women's Benevolent Society
c/o Marcia Mason
1372 N. Westwood Dr.
Zanesville, OH 43701-5693

Financial data (yr. ended 12/31/01): Grants paid, $19,258; assets, $0 (M); gifts received, $15,916; expenditures, $19,848; qualifying distributions, $19,258.
Limitations: Giving limited to Muskingum and Zanesville counties, OH.
Officers: Flora Martin, Pres.; Elizabeth Burrier, V.P.; Anita Thompson, Secy.; Marcia Mason, Treas.
EIN: 346522598

43749
DeWine Family Foundation, Inc.
P.O. Box 68
Yellow Springs, OH 45387-0068

Established in 1996 in OH.
Donor(s): Jean L. DeWine, Richard L. DeWine.
Financial data (yr. ended 07/31/01): Grants paid, $19,250; assets, $499,282 (M); gifts received, $27,206; expenditures, $23,628; qualifying distributions, $19,250.
Limitations: Applications not accepted.
Application information: Contributes only to pre-selected organizations.
Trustees: Jill E. DeWine Darling, R. Patrick DeWine.
EIN: 311483132

43750
Anna Randle Truog Memorial Foundation Trust
c/o Richard C. Fedorovich
411 Wolf Ledges, Ste. 400
Akron, OH 44311-1040
Contact: William R. Truog, Tr.

Financial data (yr. ended 12/31/01): Grants paid, $19,195; assets, $243,186 (M); expenditures, $25,964; qualifying distributions, $19,195.
Limitations: Giving primarily in OH.
Trustee: J. Martin Erbaugh, Burton D. Morgan, William R. Truog.
EIN: 346696528

43751
Helen B. & Charles M. White Charitable Trust
c/o KeyBank, N.A.
800 Superior Ave., 4th Fl.
Cleveland, OH 44114-1306

Financial data (yr. ended 12/31/00): Grants paid, $19,150; assets, $490,468 (M); expenditures, $24,232; qualifying distributions, $18,161.
Limitations: Applications not accepted. Giving primarily in Cleveland, OH.
Application information: Contributes only to pre-selected organizations.
Director: Jean White Moseley.
Trustee: KeyBank, N.A.
EIN: 346505730

43752
Robert F. Heran, Jr. and Jean S. Heran Charitable Foundation, Inc.
c/o Jean S. Heran
1842 Donna Dr.
Westlake, OH 44145

Established in 1998 in OH.
Donor(s): Robert F. Heran, Jr., Jean S. Heran.
Financial data (yr. ended 12/31/01): Grants paid, $19,125; assets, $515,212 (M); expenditures, $19,125; qualifying distributions, $19,125.
Limitations: Applications not accepted.
Application information: Contributes only to pre-selected organizations.
Officers and Trustees:* Robert F. Heran,* Pres.; Jean S. Heran,* Secy.-Treas.; Lester T. Tolt.
EIN: 341724743

43753
Berlin Family Educational Foundation
37500 Eagle Rd.
Willoughby, OH 44094-6957

Established in 1995.
Donor(s): Thomas Berlin.
Financial data (yr. ended 12/31/01): Grants paid, $19,100; assets, $270,567 (M); expenditures, $23,047; qualifying distributions, $18,978.
Limitations: Applications not accepted. Giving primarily in OH.
Application information: Contributes only to pre-selected organizations.
Officers and Trustees:* Thomas G. Berlin,* Pres.; Scott Berlin,* Secy.; Joy L. Berlin,* Treas.
EIN: 341817284
Codes: GTI

43754
Tod Foundation
c/o Sky Trust N.A.
P.O. Box 479
Youngstown, OH 44501-0479 (330) 742-7000
Contact: Fred Tod, Jr., Pres.

Donor(s): Fred Tod, Jr., David Tod.
Financial data (yr. ended 12/31/01): Grants paid, $19,100; assets, $301,538 (M); gifts received, $576; expenditures, $20,861; qualifying distributions, $19,100.
Limitations: Giving primarily in FL and OH.
Officers: Fred Tod, Jr., Pres.; David Tod, V.P.
Director: James E. Mitchell.
Agent: Sky Trust, N.A.
EIN: 346557813

43755
Alfred E. Tonti Trust
20 E. Dominion Blvd.
Columbus, OH 43214-2796 (614) 263-8821
Contact: Rev. Kenneth Grimes, Tr.

Financial data (yr. ended 11/30/01): Grants paid, $19,021; assets, $230,253 (M); expenditures, $19,310; qualifying distributions, $19,021.
Limitations: Giving primarily in Columbus, OH.
Trustee: Rev. Kenneth Grimes.
EIN: 316277525

43756
The James W. Gettelfinger Family Foundation
1400 Provident Tower
1 E. 4th St.
Cincinnati, OH 45202

Established in 1999 in OH.
Financial data (yr. ended 12/31/00): Grants paid, $19,000; assets, $1,673,623 (M); gifts received, $843,929; expenditures, $26,093; qualifying distributions, $18,667.
Limitations: Applications not accepted. Giving primarily in OH.
Application information: Contributes only to pre-selected organizations.
Trustees: Marcia Burke, Michael J. Burke, Patrick J. Burke.
EIN: 311659080

43757
Noonan Foundation
34 N. Main St.
P.O. Box 1809
Dayton, OH 45401

Financial data (yr. ended 06/30/02): Grants paid, $19,000; assets, $268,983 (M); expenditures, $22,087; qualifying distributions, $19,000.
Limitations: Applications not accepted. Giving limited to Springfield, OH.
Application information: Contributes only to pre-selected organizations.
Officers: Mary Lu Noonan, Pres.; Peter Noonan, V.P.; Glen Collier, Secy.-Treas.
Trustees: Liz Cole, Ed Levanthal, Peggy Noonan.
EIN: 237085040

43758
Thomas Hughes Trust
c/o Richard H. Ward
323 Circlewood Ln.
Cincinnati, OH 45215
Application address: c/o Principal, Hughes High School, 2515 Clifton Ave., Cincinnati, OH 45219, tel.: (513) 559-3000

Financial data (yr. ended 12/31/99): Grants paid, $18,766; assets, $224,230 (M); expenditures, $21,977; qualifying distributions, $21,707.
Limitations: Giving primarily in Cincinnati, OH.
Application information: Application form required.
Officer and Trustees:* Robert Boeh,* Treas.; Kenneth Keller, Robert McCormick, Richard Ward, Carr W. Wright.
EIN: 316303782

43759
Castele Family Foundation
16103 Lake Ave.
Lakewood, OH 44107-1247

Donor(s): Theodore J. Castele, Mrs. Theodore J. Castele.
Financial data (yr. ended 12/31/00): Grants paid, $18,750; assets, $12,539 (M); gifts received, $30,000; expenditures, $19,690; qualifying distributions, $19,690.
Limitations: Applications not accepted. Giving primarily in Cleveland, OH.
Application information: Contributes only to pre-selected organizations.
Officers: Theodore J. Castele, Chair.; Richard T. Castele, Pres. and Treas.; John T. Castele, V.P. and Secy.
EIN: 341836479

43760
Eagle Foundation
232 N. 3rd St.
Columbus, OH 43215-2513
Contact: Todd A. Anglin, Tr.

Established in 1993 in OH.
Financial data (yr. ended 12/31/00): Grants paid, $18,623; assets, $242,978 (M); expenditures, $22,836; qualifying distributions, $18,623.
Trustee: Todd A. Anglin.
EIN: 311384474

43761
Ruchman Family Foundation
1 Dayton Ctr.
1 S. Main St., Ste. 1700
Dayton, OH 45402

Financial data (yr. ended 12/31/01): Grants paid, $18,600; assets, $233,913 (M); expenditures, $19,822; qualifying distributions, $18,600.
Limitations: Applications not accepted. Giving primarily in OH.
Application information: Contributes only to pre-selected organizations.
Officers: Minnette Ruchman, Pres.; Harriet R. Cohen, V.P.; Louise R. Warshauer, V.P.; Marshall D. Ruchman, Secy.-Treas.
EIN: 311021617

43762
Mary E. Becker Charitable Trust
c/o Fifth Third Bank
P.O. Box 630858
Cincinnati, OH 45263
Application address: c/o Fifth Third Bank of Western Ohio, N.A., Main and Ash Streets, Piqua, OH 45356
Contact: Joanne Townsend

Established in 1994 in OH.
Donor(s): Mary E. Becker.‡
Financial data (yr. ended 12/31/01): Grants paid, $18,570; assets, $561,530 (M); expenditures, $23,884; qualifying distributions, $18,570.
Limitations: Giving primarily in Piqua, OH.
Trustee: Fifth Third Bank.
EIN: 316500654

43763
The John & Barbara Burns Foundation
c/o Catherine C. Veres
3550 Lander Rd., Ste. 200
Pepper Pike, OH 44124

Established in 1997 in OH.
Donor(s): John Burns, Barbara Burns.
Financial data (yr. ended 12/31/01): Grants paid, $18,555; assets, $360,737 (M); expenditures, $18,866; qualifying distributions, $18,555.

Limitations: Applications not accepted. Giving on a national basis.
Application information: Contributes only to pre-selected organizations.
Trustees: Barbara M. Burns, John Burns, Scott J. Burns, Tracy A. Burns, Catherine C. Veres.
EIN: 341853086

43764
The Kriegel Family Foundation
P.O. Box 752
Van Wert, OH 45891

Established in 1989 in OH.
Donor(s): Kriegel Holding Co., Inc.
Financial data (yr. ended 12/31/01): Grants paid, $18,550; assets, $194,034 (M); expenditures, $19,052; qualifying distributions, $18,550.
Limitations: Applications not accepted. Giving primarily in Lima and Cincinnati, OH.
Application information: Contributes only to pre-selected organizations.
Officers: David L. Kriegel, Mgr.; Shirley C. Kriegel, Mgr.
EIN: 346907740

43765
The McConnell Foundation
P.O. Box 3500
Newark, OH 43058-3500

Established in 2000 in OH.
Donor(s): William T. McConnell.
Financial data (yr. ended 06/30/01): Grants paid, $18,550; assets, $295,086 (M); gifts received, $302,265; expenditures, $18,645; qualifying distributions, $18,590.
Limitations: Applications not accepted. Giving limited to OH.
Application information: Contributes only to pre-selected organizations.
Officers: Jane C. McConnell, Pres.; Jennifer W. McConnell, V.P.; William T. McConnell, Secy.-Treas.
EIN: 311717945

43766
The Mosier Family Foundation
1111 Superior Ave., Ste. 785
Cleveland, OH 44114

Established in 1995 in OH.
Donor(s): F.E. Mosier.
Financial data (yr. ended 12/31/00): Grants paid, $18,545; assets, $164,552 (M); expenditures, $20,076; qualifying distributions, $18,545.
Limitations: Applications not accepted. Giving primarily in Cleveland, OH.
Application information: Contributes only to pre-selected organizations.
Trustees: Frank E. Mosier, Terry F. Mosier, James P. Oliver.
EIN: 341795660

43767
Montpelier Area Foundation, Inc.
P.O. Box 161
Montpelier, OH 43543
Contact: John T. Ressler, Pres.

Established in 1988 in OH.
Financial data (yr. ended 06/30/00): Grants paid, $18,527; assets, $457,932 (L); gifts received, $457,932; expenditures, $18,527.
Limitations: Giving limited to the Montpelier, OH, area.
Publications: Informational brochure.
Application information: Application form not required.
Officers: John T. Ressler, Pres.; Barbara Fisher, Secy.; Laura E. Gray, Treas.

EIN: 341577486
Codes: CM

43768
The Stone Ledges Charitable Trust
210 Westgate Ave.
Wadsworth, OH 44281-1129

Established in OH in 1998.
Donor(s): Melvin L. Smith.
Financial data (yr. ended 12/31/01): Grants paid, $18,500; assets, $356,337 (M); gifts received, $5,000; expenditures, $20,484; qualifying distributions, $18,500.
Limitations: Applications not accepted.
Trustee: Melvin L. Smith.
EIN: 347079328

43769
Russell and Mary Gimbel Foundation
P.O. Box 1223
Mansfield, OH 44901

Established in 1989 in OH.
Donor(s): Russell Gimbel, Mary Gimbel.
Financial data (yr. ended 12/31/01): Grants paid, $18,477; assets, $2,985,310 (M); gifts received, $2,553,294; expenditures, $19,553; qualifying distributions, $18,477.
Limitations: Giving primarily in Mansfield, OH.
Application information: Application form required.
Trustees: Donald L. Dewald, John Hancock, Robert Kerst, Roger Renwick.
EIN: 341626310

43770
The Murel Grove, Carol J. Grove, and Charles D. Grove Family Foundation
c/o A. Edward Moss
P.O. Box 36963
Canton, OH 44735-6963

Donor(s): Charles D. Grove.
Financial data (yr. ended 12/31/01): Grants paid, $18,325; assets, $76,981 (M); expenditures, $19,411; qualifying distributions, $18,325.
Limitations: Applications not accepted. Giving primarily in Alliance, OH.
Application information: Contributes only to pre-selected organizations.
Trustees: Carol J. Grove, Charles D. Grove.
EIN: 341757241

43771
Sarvodaya Foundation
5455 Broadview Rd.
Parma, OH 44134

Donor(s): M. Mehtas, H. Mehtas.
Financial data (yr. ended 12/31/01): Grants paid, $18,301; assets, $27,006 (M); gifts received, $17,000; expenditures, $18,355; qualifying distributions, $18,301.
Limitations: Applications not accepted.
Application information: Contributes only to pre-selected organizations.
Officer: Niti Mehta, Pres.
EIN: 341813007

43772
T. L. & Debra Schwartz Fund
c/o Star Trust, N.A.
P.O. Box 1118
Cincinnati, OH 45201-1118

Established in 1996 in OH.
Donor(s): T.L. Schwartz, Debra Schwartz.
Financial data (yr. ended 01/31/01): Grants paid, $18,200; assets, $363,436 (M); expenditures, $20,543; qualifying distributions, $18,200.
Limitations: Applications not accepted.

Application information: Contributes only to pre-selected organizations.
Trustees: Andrew G. Schwartz, Stephen A. Schwartz, Theodore L. Schwartz.
EIN: 311477766

43773
William Weimar Foundation
c/o KeyBank, N.A., Trust Div.
800 Superior Ave., 4th Fl.
Cleveland, OH 44114
Application address: 1101 Pacific Ave., 3rd Fl., Tacoma, WA 98402, tel.: (253) 305-7203
Contact: Michael Steadman, Asst. V.P., KeyBank, N.A.

Financial data (yr. ended 12/31/01): Grants paid, $18,200; assets, $371,974 (M); expenditures, $24,041; qualifying distributions, $18,200.
Limitations: Giving primarily in Enumclaw, WA.
Trustee: KeyBank, N.A.
EIN: 916032377

43774
Marjorie Hart Trust
c/o Roy Gilliland
P.O. Box 284, 23 E. Broadway
Wellston, OH 45692

Established in 1996 in OH.
Financial data (yr. ended 12/31/01): Grants paid, $18,185; assets, $402,610 (L); expenditures, $27,405; qualifying distributions, $17,984.
Limitations: Giving primarily to residents of Wellston, OH.
Trustees: Kyle Gilliland, James Riepenhoff, Robert Willis.
EIN: 311428420

43775
Logan Holl Foundation
c/o Logan Clay Products Co.
P.O. Box 698
Logan, OH 43138 (740) 385-2184
Contact: Richard H. Brandt, Secy.-Treas.

Donor(s): Barton S. Holl, Mrs. Barton S. Holl.
Financial data (yr. ended 12/31/01): Grants paid, $18,065; assets, $544,744 (M); gifts received, $5,250; expenditures, $24,470; qualifying distributions, $18,065.
Limitations: Giving limited to Hocking County, OH.
Officers: Don Russell, Pres.; Richard H. Holl, V.P.; Richard H. Brandt, Secy.-Treas.
EIN: 316079573

43776
Bluegrass Foundation, Inc.
c/o Fifth Third Bank
38 Fountain Sq. Plz.
Cincinnati, OH 45263
Application address: P.O. Box 413021, Naples, FL 34101
Contact: John D. Ware, Chair., Fifth Third Bank

Established in 1999 in FL.
Donor(s): John Ware, Alice Ware.
Financial data (yr. ended 06/30/01): Grants paid, $18,000; assets, $259,044 (M); gifts received, $124,799; expenditures, $20,362; qualifying distributions, $18,457.
Limitations: Giving primarily in FL.
Trustees: Gary Brown, John D. Gast, John D. Ware, Fifth Third Bank.
EIN: 593584274

43777
Mark Goodwin Memorial Trust
c/o KeyBank, N.A., Trust Div.
800 Superior Ave., 4th Fl.
Cleveland, OH 44114

Established in 1991 in ME.
Donor(s): Cole Haan Holdings, Inc.
Financial data (yr. ended 08/31/01): Grants paid, $18,000; assets, $210,856 (M); gifts received, $1,172; expenditures, $23,646; qualifying distributions, $17,797.
Limitations: Applications not accepted. Giving limited to areas of company operations.
Application information: Unsolicited requests for funds not accepted.
Trustee: KeyBank, N.A.
EIN: 222256331
Codes: CS, GTI

43778
Ketrow Foundation
507 S. Broadway
Greenville, OH 45331 (937) 548-1157
Contact: Thomas H. Graber II, Tr.

Established in 1990 in OH.
Donor(s): Ketrow Trust No. 2.
Financial data (yr. ended 09/30/01): Grants paid, $18,000; assets, $458,602 (M); expenditures, $22,263; qualifying distributions, $18,000.
Limitations: Giving limited to Darke County, OH.
Trustee: Thomas H. Graber II.
EIN: 341667300

43779
C. Paul Palmer Memorial Scholarship Fund
P.O. Box 120
Findlay, OH 45839-0120 (419) 422-4341
Contact: Anita Schoonover

Established in 1993 in OH.
Financial data (yr. ended 12/31/01): Grants paid, $18,000; assets, $214,094 (M); expenditures, $19,736; qualifying distributions, $18,000.
Limitations: Giving primarily in Carey, OH.
Application information: Application form required.
Officers and Trustees:* John C. Gordon,* Pres.; Ronald W. Kruse, Secy.; Richard W. Flowers, Carleton P. Palmer, Thomas W. Palmer.
EIN: 341759012
Codes: GTI

43780
Panzica Family Foundation
490 N. Applecross
Highland Heights, OH 44143
Contact: Nacy A. Panzica, Pres.

Established in 1996 in OH.
Donor(s): Nacy A. Panzica.
Financial data (yr. ended 12/31/01): Grants paid, $18,000; assets, $597,053 (M); gifts received, $145,532; expenditures, $18,807; qualifying distributions, $18,000.
Limitations: Giving primarily in OH.
Officers: Nacy A. Panzica, Pres.; Mary Beth Link, Secy.; Anthony M. Panzica, Treas.
Trustee: Laura King.
EIN: 341844574

43781
Nancy J. and Charles J. Pilliod, Jr. Foundation
494 St. Andrews Dr.
Akron, OH 44303

Established in 1997 in OH.
Donor(s): Charles J. Pilliod, Jr., Nancy J. Pilliod.
Financial data (yr. ended 12/31/01): Grants paid, $18,000; assets, $142,427 (M); gifts received, $1,350; expenditures, $21,662; qualifying distributions, $18,000.
Limitations: Applications not accepted. Giving primarily in Akron, OH.
Application information: Contributes only to pre-selected organizations.
Trustees: Ronald D. Glosser, Charles J. Pilliod, Jr., Nancy J. Pilliod.
EIN: 311534559

43782
Harriet & Fred Pomeroy Scholarship Fund Trust
c/o KeyBank, N.A.
800 Superior Ave., 4th Fl.
Cleveland, OH 44114-1306
Application address: c/o Bates College, Lewiston, ME 04240

Financial data (yr. ended 06/30/01): Grants paid, $18,000; assets, $413,113 (M); expenditures, $23,008; qualifying distributions, $18,000.
Trustee: KeyBank, N.A.
EIN: 016008640
Codes: GTI

43783
The TKBW Private Foundation
7550 Coder Rd.
Maumee, OH 43537
Contact: Bruce W. Wetzel, Tr.

Established in 1999 in OH.
Donor(s): Toy D. Keeble, Bruce W. Wetzel.
Financial data (yr. ended 12/31/01): Grants paid, $18,000; assets, $317,353 (M); gifts received, $107,250; expenditures, $20,866; qualifying distributions, $18,000.
Limitations: Giving primarily in OH.
Trustees: Amy C. Wetzel, Bruce W. Wetzel, Stacy L. Wetzel.
EIN: 341903674

43784
Women's Christian Association
c/o Eleanor Cousins
125 Finsbury Ln.
Troy, OH 45373
Application address: c/o Eleanor Cousins, 125 Finsbury Ln., Troy, OH 45373
Contact: Sally Stein, Treas.

Donor(s): Robert J. Tweed, Nannie Sheets.‡
Financial data (yr. ended 12/31/01): Grants paid, $18,000; assets, $1,986 (M); gifts received, $18,000; expenditures, $18,081; qualifying distributions, $18,000.
Limitations: Giving limited to Troy, OH.
Application information: Application form not required.
Officers: Mildred Lenox, Pres.; Dorothea Hartley, V.P.; Mary Ann Ording, Secy.; Eleanor Cousins, Treas.
EIN: 316033394

43785
Beane Family Foundation
502 Holgate Ave.
Defiance, OH 43512
Contact: Evan J. Beane, Dir.

Established in 1991 in OH.
Donor(s): Evan J. Beane.
Financial data (yr. ended 12/31/99): Grants paid, $17,859; assets, $608,226 (M); gifts received, $65,000; expenditures, $18,117; qualifying distributions, $17,890.
Limitations: Giving primarily in Defiance, OH.
Application information: Application form not required.
Directors: Adam Beane, Cynthia Beane, Evan J. Beane, Jon Beane.

EIN: 341662821

43786
Herman M. & Myrtle Katz Foundation
c/o Renee Levine
7 Stonegate Village Dr.
Columbus, OH 43212-3270 (614) 486-1141
Contact: Renee Levine, Tr.

Established about 1959.
Financial data (yr. ended 07/31/01): Grants paid, $17,810; assets, $132,215 (M); expenditures, $18,316; qualifying distributions, $17,479.
Limitations: Giving primarily in Columbus, OH.
Application information: Application form not required.
Trustee: Renee Levine.
EIN: 316030723

43787
Glenn M. Weaver Foundation
250 William Howard Taft
Cincinnati, OH 45219

Established in 1997 in OH.
Donor(s): Glenn M. Weaver.
Financial data (yr. ended 12/31/01): Grants paid, $17,793; assets, $502,799 (M); gifts received, $120,670; expenditures, $23,861; qualifying distributions, $17,793.
Limitations: Applications not accepted.
Application information: Contributes only to pre-selected organizations.
Trustees: Corwin R. Dunn, Glenn M. Weaver, Glen Weissenberger, Star Trust, N.A.
EIN: 311534961

43788
The Michael and Nancy Baker Foundation
1239 Greenery Ln.
Cincinnati, OH 45233

Established in 2000 in OH.
Donor(s): Michael D. Baker.
Financial data (yr. ended 12/31/01): Grants paid, $17,678; assets, $106,644 (M); gifts received, $4,824; expenditures, $22,503; qualifying distributions, $17,678.
Limitations: Applications not accepted.
Application information: Contributes only to pre-selected organizations.
Officers and Trustees:* Michael D. Baker,* Pres. and Treas.; Nancy M. Baker,* V.P. and Secy.; Thomas J. Breed.
EIN: 311744250

43789
The Chilcote Company Charitable Trust
2160 Superior Ave.
Cleveland, OH 44114-2102 (216) 781-6000
Contact: Robert J. Marn, Tr.

Established in 1989 in OH.
Donor(s): The Chilcote Co.
Financial data (yr. ended 12/31/01): Grants paid, $17,625; assets, $141,181 (M); gifts received, $15,000; expenditures, $17,782; qualifying distributions, $17,579.
Limitations: Giving primarily in Cleveland and Cuyahoga County, OH.
Trustee: Robert J. Marn.
EIN: 341637597
Codes: CS, CD

43790
William J. Best Family Foundation
c/o Nancy Selm
4973 Pebblevalley Dr.
Cincinnati, OH 45252-2111

Established in 1994 in OH.
Donor(s): William J. Best.
Financial data (yr. ended 12/31/01): Grants paid, $17,500; assets, $125,056 (M); gifts received, $2,547; expenditures, $22,346; qualifying distributions, $17,500.
Limitations: Applications not accepted. Giving primarily in OH.
Application information: Contributes only to pre-selected organizations.
Trustees: William J. Best, Carol Ann Monahan, Nancy M. Selm.
EIN: 311423876

43791
Makulinski Family Foundation
203 Matzinger Rd.
Toledo, OH 43612 (419) 476-6572
Contact: Mark A. Makulinski, Pres.

Established in 1996 in OH.
Donor(s): Raka Corp.
Financial data (yr. ended 12/31/01): Grants paid, $17,500; assets, $542,973 (M); gifts received, $212,355; expenditures, $24,253; qualifying distributions, $17,500.
Limitations: Giving primarily in Toledo, OH.
Application information: Application form not required.
Officers: Mark A. Makulinski, Pres. and Treas.; Rosemary Makulinski, V.P. and Secy.
Trustee: Jennifer Agnes Krueger.
EIN: 341826533

43792
Semelsberger Foundation
19326 Ivywood Trail
Strongsville, OH 44136-3144

Donor(s): Kenneth J. Semelsberger.
Financial data (yr. ended 06/30/02): Grants paid, $17,500; assets, $7,742 (M); expenditures, $19,171; qualifying distributions, $17,500.
Limitations: Applications not accepted. Giving primarily in Cleveland, OH.
Application information: Contributes only to pre-selected organizations.
Officers and Trustees:* Kenneth J. Semelsberger,* Pres.; Marian L. Semelsberger, Secy.-Treas.; Kenneth D. Semelsberger.
EIN: 341502221

43793
Mary and Paul Heller Foundation
116 Cleveland Ave. N.W., Ste. 525
Canton, OH 44702
Application address: 234 Park Ln., Athewton, CA 94027, tel.: (650) 326-1718
Contact: William Heller, Pres.

Established in 1988 in OH.
Financial data (yr. ended 06/30/02): Grants paid, $17,400; assets, $168,597 (M); expenditures, $20,501; qualifying distributions, $17,400.
Limitations: Giving primarily in CA and OH.
Officers: William Heller, Pres.; Maurice Heller, Secy.; Harry Mestel, Treas.
EIN: 341593911

43794
Webster Foundation, Inc.
c/o Webster Industries, Inc.
325 Hall St.
Tiffin, OH 44883-1419
Contact: C.D. English, Tr.

Established in 1975 in OH.
Donor(s): Webster Industries, Inc.
Financial data (yr. ended 12/31/01): Grants paid, $17,356; assets, $11,170 (M); gifts received, $10,000; expenditures, $17,544; qualifying distributions, $17,544.
Limitations: Giving primarily in Seneca County, OH.
Trustees: C.D. English, Jim Getz, Brent Howard, J.F. Riedel, Fred C. Spurck, G.K. Tolford.
EIN: 237460923
Codes: CS, CD

43795
Dreamcatcher Fund
204 Walnut St.
Archbold, OH 43502-1150

Established in 1996 in OH.
Donor(s): Kenneth Bedell, Kathryn Bedell.
Financial data (yr. ended 12/31/01): Grants paid, $17,275; assets, $331,111 (M); gifts received, $200; expenditures, $18,887; qualifying distributions, $18,867.
Limitations: Applications not accepted. Giving on a national basis.
Application information: Contributes only to pre-selected organizations.
Officers: Kenneth B. Bedell, Pres.; Kathryn M. Bedell, V.P.
EIN: 311464399

43796
Howell and Lois Williams Memorial Fund
c/o National City Bank of PA
P.O. Box 94651
Cleveland, OH 44101-4651
Application address: c/o Lincoln High School, 501 Crescent Ave., Ellwood City, PA 16117
Contact: Donald E. Hollerman

Established in 1990 in PA.
Financial data (yr. ended 04/30/01): Grants paid, $17,200; assets, $340,875 (M); expenditures, $20,507; qualifying distributions, $18,649.
Limitations: Giving limited to residents of the Ellwood City, PA.
Application information: Application form required.
Trustee: National City Bank.
EIN: 251671119
Codes: GTI

43797
Barrand & Bradford Scholarship Foundation
c/o National City Bank of Indiana
P.O. Box 94651
Cleveland, OH 44101-4651
Application address: c/o Taylor University, Dir. of Financial Aid, 1025 W. Rudisill Blvd., Fort Wayne, IN 46807, tel.: (219) 456-2111

Established in 1995 in IN.
Donor(s): Blanche E. Bradford.‡
Financial data (yr. ended 07/31/00): Grants paid, $17,182; assets, $1,003,238 (M); expenditures, $20,958; qualifying distributions, $19,138.
Limitations: Giving limited to IN.
Application information: Application form required.
Trustee: National City Bank of Indiana.
EIN: 356615379
Codes: GTI

43798
The Dolores Douglas Foundation
c/o Scott J. Savage
6711 Monroe St., Ste. A
Sylvania, OH 43560-9806

Established in 1987 in OH.
Donor(s): Bruce Douglas.
Financial data (yr. ended 12/31/01): Grants paid, $17,100; assets, $237,188 (M); gifts received, $20,000; expenditures, $21,476; qualifying distributions, $17,100.

43798—OHIO

Limitations: Applications not accepted. Giving primarily in Columbus and Toledo, OH.
Application information: Contributes only to pre-selected organizations.
Officers and Trustees:* Bruce Douglas,* Pres. and Treas.; Dolores A. Douglas,* Secy.; Peter Douglas, Scott J. Savage.
EIN: 341569677

43799
Willard Thomas and Margaret Rose Plogsterth Foundation
c/o National City Bank of Indiana
P.O. Box 94651
Cleveland, OH 44101-4651
Application address: P.O. Box 110, Fort Wayne, IN 46802, tel.: (219) 461-7115
Contact: Jim Westerfield, Trust Off., NCB of Indiana

Established in 1986 in IN.
Financial data (yr. ended 07/31/01): Grants paid, $17,043; assets, $321,627 (M); expenditures, $18,630; qualifying distributions, $17,535.
Limitations: Giving primarily in Fort Wayne, IN.
Trustee: National City Bank.
EIN: 311206807

43800
1002 Foundation
5 Grandin Ln.
Cincinnati, OH 45208

Established in 1997 in OH.
Financial data (yr. ended 12/31/01): Grants paid, $17,033; assets, $348,091 (M); gifts received, $45,016; expenditures, $25,459; qualifying distributions, $17,033.
Limitations: Applications not accepted. Giving primarily in Cincinnati, OH.
Application information: Contributes only to pre-selected organizations.
Officers and Trustees:* Gates T. Richards,* Pres.; Margaret Mary K. Richards,* Secy.-Treas.; Gates T. Richards, Jr., L. Brady Richards, Margaret Mary Richards.
EIN: 311518488

43801
Nathalie and James Andrews Foundation
P.O. Box 5250
Poland, OH 44514

Established in 1986 in OH.
Donor(s): Nathalie M. Andrews.
Financial data (yr. ended 12/31/01): Grants paid, $17,000; assets, $287,734 (M); expenditures, $20,858; qualifying distributions, $17,224.
Limitations: Applications not accepted. Giving primarily in OH.
Application information: Contributes only to pre-selected organizations.
Officers and Trustees:* James H. Andrews,* Pres.; Nathalie M. Andrews,* V.P.; James H. Heyward.
EIN: 341535715

43802
The Babcox Family Foundation, Inc.
711 Delaware Ave.
Akron, OH 44313

Established in 1994 in OH.
Donor(s): Tom B. Babcox.‡
Financial data (yr. ended 12/31/01): Grants paid, $17,000; assets, $366,326 (M); expenditures, $21,509; qualifying distributions, $17,000.
Limitations: Applications not accepted. Giving primarily in Akron, OH.
Application information: Contributes only to pre-selected organizations.

Trustees: Mary L. Babcox, Mary Rebecca Babcox, Tom B. Babcox, Jr., William Edward Babcox, Sarah Babcox Harrity, Lucy B. Morris.
EIN: 341787178

43803
Pugh Family Charitable Trust
61 Oriole Dr.
Youngstown, OH 44505

Established in 1989 in OH.
Donor(s): George B. Pugh, Virginia W. Pugh.
Financial data (yr. ended 12/31/01): Grants paid, $17,000; assets, $178,882 (M); gifts received, $307; expenditures, $17,486; qualifying distributions, $17,000.
Limitations: Applications not accepted. Giving primarily in Youngstown, OH.
Application information: Contributes only to pre-selected organizations.
Trustees: David F. Bulkley, George B. Pugh, Virginia W. Pugh.
EIN: 341632294

43804
Raccoon Ridge Foundation
c/o National City Bank of Indiana
P.O. Box 94651
Cleveland, OH 44101-4651
Application address: c/o Dama Arnold, P. O. Box 110, Fort Wayne, IN 46801, tel.: (219) 461-7114

Financial data (yr. ended 12/31/01): Grants paid, $16,900; assets, $242,829 (M); expenditures, $18,063; qualifying distributions, $16,900.
Limitations: Giving primarily in IN.
Trustee: National City Bank.
EIN: 356073716

43805
George Justin Musekamp Foundation
c/o Fifth Third Bank
38 Fountain Sq.
Cincinnati, OH 45202
Contact: Lawra Baumann, Trust Off., Fifth Third Bank

Established in 1996 in OH.
Donor(s): George Musekamp.
Financial data (yr. ended 12/31/01): Grants paid, $16,856; assets, $286,186 (M); expenditures, $21,046; qualifying distributions, $16,856.
Director: Lawra Baumann.
Trustees: Helene J. McNerney, Eric R. Musekamp, George H. Musekamp, Jean Musekamp, Fifth Third Bank.
EIN: 311481411

43806
The Herbert A. Middendorff Foundation
8455 Kugler Mill Rd.
Cincinnati, OH 45243
Application address: 7633 Silver Fern Blvd., Sarasota, FL 34241
Contact: Herbert A. Middendorff, Pres.

Donor(s): Herbert A. Middendorff.
Financial data (yr. ended 12/31/01): Grants paid, $16,820; assets, $218,771 (M); expenditures, $22,033; qualifying distributions, $16,820.
Limitations: Giving primarily in Cincinnati, OH.
Officers and Trustees:* Herbert A. Middendorff,* Pres.; Suzanne B. Middendorff, V.P. and Treas.; J. Michael Cooney, Secy.; Robert V. Barnes.
EIN: 311189832

43807
Ralph E. and Orpha H. Towers Foundation
c/o Sky Trust, N.A.
P.O. Box 479
Youngstown, OH 44501-0479 (330) 742-7039

Established in 1992 in OH.
Donor(s): Orpha H. Towers.
Financial data (yr. ended 12/31/01): Grants paid, $16,800; assets, $195,293 (M); expenditures, $19,922; qualifying distributions, $16,800.
Limitations: Giving on a national basis.
Directors: Julia Towers Kline, David Slack, Natalie Towers Slack.
Trustee: Sky Trust, N.A.
EIN: 341706663

43808
Eileen Jean Luce Charitable Trust
c/o National City Bank of Pennsylvania
P.O. Box 94651
Cleveland, OH 44101-4651
Application address: P.O Box 374, Oil City, PA 16301, tel.: (814) 677-5085
Contact: Stephen P. Kosak

Established in 1992 in PA.
Donor(s): Eileen Jean Luce.‡
Financial data (yr. ended 10/31/01): Grants paid, $16,750; assets, $424,166 (M); expenditures, $22,459; qualifying distributions, $16,750.
Limitations: Giving primarily in Venango County, PA.
Trustee: National City Bank of Pennsylvania.
EIN: 256394192

43809
The Murray & Murray Charitable Foundation
111 E. Shoreline Dr.
Sandusky, OH 44870

Established in 1994 in OH.
Donor(s): Margaret A. Murray, Dennis E. Murray, Charles M. Murray.
Financial data (yr. ended 12/31/01): Grants paid, $16,710; assets, $328,516 (M); gifts received, $72,163; expenditures, $20,531; qualifying distributions, $16,710.
Limitations: Applications not accepted. Giving primarily in Sandusky, OH.
Application information: Contributes only to pre-selected organizations.
Trustees: Dennis E. Murray, Margaret A. Murray.
EIN: 341746379

43810
The Susan D. and Richard A. Van Auken Foundation
c/o Richard A. Van Auken
3588 Sparrow Pond Cir.
Fairlawn, OH 44333-1767

Donor(s): Richard A. Van Auken, Susan D. Van Auken.
Financial data (yr. ended 12/31/01): Grants paid, $16,510; assets, $21,343 (M); gifts received, $5,000; expenditures, $16,711; qualifying distributions, $16,510.
Limitations: Applications not accepted. Giving primarily in IN and OH.
Application information: Contributes only to pre-selected organizations.
Officers: Richard A. Van Auken, Pres.; Susan D. Van Auken, Secy.-Treas.
EIN: 311532439

43811
Bernowski Scholarship Trust Fund
c/o National City Bank of Pennsylvania
P.O. Box 94651
Cleveland, OH 44101-4651
Application address: 20 Stanwix St., LOC 09-066, Pittsburgh, PA 15222, tel.: (412) 644-8002
Contact: Joanna Mayo, Trust Off., National City Bank of PA

Established in 1996 in PA.
Financial data (yr. ended 12/31/01): Grants paid, $16,500; assets, $358,259 (M); expenditures, $19,603; qualifying distributions, $17,915.
Limitations: Giving limited to residents of Will-Charlevoix, Ringgold, and Belle Vernon, PA.
Application information: Application form required.
Trustee: National City Bank of Pennsylvania.
EIN: 256534799
Codes: GTI

43812
Elton B. and Joan Katz Foundation
(Formerly Elton B. Katz Foundation)
2 Laurel Hill Ln.
Pepper Pike, OH 44124

Established in 1991 in OH.
Donor(s): Elton B. Katz.‡
Financial data (yr. ended 09/30/01): Grants paid, $16,500; assets, $64,944 (M); expenditures, $17,520; qualifying distributions, $16,500.
Limitations: Applications not accepted. Giving limited to Pittsburgh, PA and OH.
Application information: Contributes only to pre-selected organizations.
Officers and Trustee:* Joan Katz,* Pres.; Mitchell Katz, V.P.; David Katz, Secy.
EIN: 341695399

43813
The Naomi and James I. FitzGibbon Family Foundation
21565 Aberdeen Rd.
Rocky River, OH 44116

Established in 1994 in OH.
Donor(s): Naomi FitzGibbon.
Financial data (yr. ended 12/31/00): Grants paid, $16,431; assets, $132,415 (M); expenditures, $16,582; qualifying distributions, $16,431.
Limitations: Applications not accepted. Giving primarily in Cleveland, OH.
Application information: Contributes only to pre-selected organizations.
Officers and Trustees:* Naomi FitzGibbon,* Pres.; Matthew FitzGibbon,* Secy.; Michael FitzGibbon,* Treas.
EIN: 341787933

43814
Virginia W. Van Hyning Scholarship Fund
c/o The Huntington National Bank
P.O. Box 1558
Columbus, OH 43216

Financial data (yr. ended 12/31/01): Grants paid, $16,400; assets, $295,204 (M); expenditures, $21,188; qualifying distributions, $17,671.
Limitations: Applications not accepted. Giving limited to Columbia, OH.
Application information: Contributes only to pre-selected organizations.
Trustee: The Huntington National Bank.
EIN: 316258749
Codes: GTI

43815
Donald W. and Marguerite J. Paul Foundation
c/o Donald W. Paul
2231 Augusta Dr.
Fremont, OH 43420-9130

Established in 1998 in OH.
Financial data (yr. ended 12/31/00): Grants paid, $16,300; assets, $283,954 (M); expenditures, $19,269; qualifying distributions, $16,204.
Limitations: Applications not accepted.
Application information: Contributes only to pre-selected organizations.
Officers: Donald W. Paul, Pres.; Marguerite J. Paul, Secy.
Trustee: Hugh J. Morgan.
EIN: 341881146

43816
The MFG Foundation
1601 W. 29th St.
Ashtabula, OH 44005-0675

Established in 1994 in OH.
Financial data (yr. ended 08/31/01): Grants paid, $16,250; assets, $425,890 (M); expenditures, $26,354; qualifying distributions, $16,250.
Limitations: Applications not accepted. Giving primarily in Ashtabula, OH.
Application information: Contributes only to pre-selected organizations.
Officers and Trustees:* Louise M. Raffa,* Pres.; Nancy S. Warner,* Secy.; William H. Kane, Treas.; Richard S. Morrison.
EIN: 341787987

43817
Luebbe Foundation
P.O. Box 141196
Cincinnati, OH 45250-1196 (513) 598-9424
Contact: Ralph A. Luebbe, Pres.

Established in 1991 in OH.
Donor(s): Ralph A. Luebbe.
Financial data (yr. ended 12/31/01): Grants paid, $16,240; assets, $207,563 (M); expenditures, $19,639; qualifying distributions, $16,240.
Limitations: Giving primarily in Cincinnati, OH.
Officers: Ralph A. Luebbe, Pres.; Mary B. Luebbe, V.P.; Janice Luebbe, Secy.
EIN: 311289981

43818
Ruth R. Peters Scholarship A Fund
Sky Trust, N.A.
P.O. Box 479
Youngstown, OH 44501-0479
Application address: c/o Guidance Office, West Middlesex Area High School, Sharon-New Castle Rd., West Middlesex, PA 16159, tel.: (724) 528-2002

Established in 1997 in PA.
Financial data (yr. ended 12/31/01): Grants paid, $16,090; assets, $337,534 (M); expenditures, $19,957; qualifying distributions, $16,090.
Limitations: Giving limited to Elon College, NC.
Application information: Application form required.
Trustee: Sky Trust, N.A.
EIN: 237872472

43819
Peter J. Blosser Student Loan Fund
(also known as Peter J. Blosser Scholarship Trust)
P.O. Box 6160
Chillicothe, OH 45601-6160 (740) 773-0043
Contact: Marie Rosebrook, Admin.

Established in 1977 in OH.
Donor(s): Katheryn Blosser.‡
Financial data (yr. ended 12/31/99): Grants paid, $16,000; assets, $2,240,617 (M); expenditures, $40,285; qualifying distributions, $204,730; giving activities include $162,900 for loans to individuals.
Limitations: Giving limited to residents of Ross County, OH.
Publications: Annual report, informational brochure, application guidelines.
Application information: Application form required.
Trustees: Donald C. Gatchell, Timothy Nusbaum, Lorene C. Washington.
EIN: 310629687
Codes: GTI

43820
Harry & Edna Husman Foundation
c/o Fifth Third Bank
38 Fountain Sq. Plz., Trust Dept. 00858
Cincinnati, OH 45263

Financial data (yr. ended 12/31/00): Grants paid, $16,000; assets, $314,110 (M); expenditures, $22,472; qualifying distributions, $16,862.
Limitations: Applications not accepted.
Application information: Contributes only to pre-selected organizations.
Trustee: Fifth Third Bank.
EIN: 316040670

43821
The Robert J. & Bernadette Kane Foundation
488 Lynden Dr.
Highland Heights, OH 44143

Established in 1999 in OH.
Donor(s): Robert J. Kane.
Financial data (yr. ended 12/31/01): Grants paid, $16,000; assets, $841,337 (M); expenditures, $26,760; qualifying distributions, $16,000.
Limitations: Applications not accepted.
Application information: Contributes only to pre-selected organizations.
Officers and Trustees:* Robert J. Kane,* Pres. and Treas.; Bernadette Kane,* V.P. and Secy.; Kelly M. Kane.
EIN: 341880930

43822
Ruth E. Roach Memorial Scholarship Fund
1150 S. McCord Rd., Ste. 601
Holland, OH 43528 (419) 865-4480
Contact: Rochelle Bartlett, Chair.

Established in 1995 in OH.
Donor(s): Frank J. Roach.
Financial data (yr. ended 12/31/99): Grants paid, $16,000; assets, $282,646 (M); expenditures, $18,478; qualifying distributions, $16,732.
Application information: Application form required.
Selection Committee Member: Rochelle Bartlett, Chair.
Trustee: Frank J. Roach.
EIN: 341799826

43823
Sharbek Family Foundation
c/o Mohammed F. Sharbek, M.D.
1930 Reid Ave.
Lorain, OH 44052

Established in 1993 in OH.
Donor(s): Mohammed F. Sharbek.
Financial data (yr. ended 12/31/01): Grants paid, $16,000; assets, $235,017 (M); expenditures, $17,247; qualifying distributions, $16,000.
Limitations: Applications not accepted. Giving primarily in OH.

43823—OHIO

Application information: Contributes only to pre-selected organizations.
Officers and Trustees:* Mohammed F. Sharbek, M.D.,* Pres. and Treas.; Armi Charbek,* V.P.; Abdel Rehim Charbek,* Secy.
EIN: 341757088

43824
The Paul and Adelyn C. Shumaker Foundation
c/o Bank One Trust Co., N.A.
774 Park Meadow Rd.
Westerville, OH 43081-1034
Application address: c/o Paul Shumaker, 28 Park Ave. W., Mansfield, OH 44901-1616, tel.: (419) 525-5517

Financial data (yr. ended 12/31/99): Grants paid, $16,000; assets, $1,602,928 (M); expenditures, $33,951; qualifying distributions, $16,885.
Limitations: Giving limited to Richland County, OH.
Application information: Application form required.
Trustee: Bank One Trust Co., N.A.
EIN: 346621245
Codes: GTI

43825
The Mark Heiman Family Foundation
c/o Edward Frankel
P.O. Box 371805
Cincinnati, OH 45222-1805

Established in 1996 in OH.
Donor(s): Mark Heiman.
Financial data (yr. ended 12/31/01): Grants paid, $15,900; assets, $5,532 (M); expenditures, $17,737; qualifying distributions, $15,900.
Limitations: Applications not accepted.
Application information: Contributes only to pre-selected organizations.
Officers and Trustees:* Mark J. Heiman,* Pres.; Paul L. Heiman,* V.P.; Edward Frankel, Secy.-Treas.; Joyce E. Heiman.
EIN: 911825292

43826
The Rev. Robert V. Tobin Education Trust
c/o Jack H. Adam
2100 Kettering Twr.
Dayton, OH 45423

Financial data (yr. ended 12/31/01): Grants paid, $15,900; assets, $319,632 (M); gifts received, $16,950; expenditures, $15,900; qualifying distributions, $15,900.
Limitations: Applications not accepted. Giving primarily in Maryknoll, NY.
Application information: Contributes only to pre-selected organizations.
Trustee: Jack H. Adam.
EIN: 316406859

43827
Industrial Nut Foundation
c/o Industrial Nut Corp.
1425 Tiffin Ave.
Sandusky, OH 44870-7338
Contact: J. William Springer, Pres.

Financial data (yr. ended 12/31/01): Grants paid, $15,771; assets, $28,384 (M); gifts received, $14,214; expenditures, $16,129; qualifying distributions, $15,771.
Limitations: Giving primarily in northwestern OH.
Application information: Application form not required.
Officer and Trustees:* J. William Springer,* Pres.; Stephen R. Springer, John Moffit.
EIN: 346512105

43828
Friend & B. Kerr Trust
c/o National City Bank of Pennsylvania
P.O. Box 94651
Cleveland, OH 44101-4651
Application address: c/o Ronald Joyce, Titusville Area High School, Guidance Ctr., 302 E. Walnut, Titusville, PA 16354, tel.: (814) 827-9687

Established in 1987 in PA.
Financial data (yr. ended 12/31/01): Grants paid, $15,750; assets, $202,652 (M); expenditures, $19,122; qualifying distributions, $16,833.
Limitations: Giving limited to residents of the Titusville, PA, area.
Application information: Application form required.
Trustee: National City Bank of Pennsylvania.
EIN: 256086650

43829
The Freedlander Foundation
c/o Meaden & Moore, Ltd.
201 E. Liberty St., Ste. 101
Wooster, OH 44691-4890 (330) 264-7307
Contact: Lois R. Freedlander, V.P.

Financial data (yr. ended 12/31/01): Grants paid, $15,700; assets, $59,415 (M); expenditures, $17,021; qualifying distributions, $15,835.
Limitations: Giving primarily in Wooster, OH.
Officers: Harold H. Freedlander, Pres. and Treas.; Lois R. Freedlander, V.P.
EIN: 346527162

43830
Timmons Foundation, Inc.
1681 Knob Hill Dr.
Coshocton, OH 43812
Contact: Robert T. Timmons, Pres.

Financial data (yr. ended 11/30/01): Grants paid, $15,700; assets, $279,298 (M); expenditures, $16,783; qualifying distributions, $15,700.
Limitations: Giving primarily in Coshocton, OH.
Application information: Application form not required.
Officers: Robert T. Timmons, Pres.; William D. Timmons, V.P.; Joseph Timmons, Secy.-Treas.
EIN: 316051732

43831
G. & M. White Scholarship Fund
c/o KeyBank, N.A.
800 Superior Ave., 4th Fl.
Cleveland, OH 44114
Application address: c/o Cooperstown High School, Cooperstown, NY 13326

Donor(s): Minnie M. White.‡
Financial data (yr. ended 12/31/01): Grants paid, $15,700; assets, $215,630 (M); expenditures, $18,215; qualifying distributions, $15,646.
Limitations: Giving primarily in Cooperstown, NY.
Application information: Application form required.
Trustee: KeyBank, N.A.
EIN: 156026002
Codes: GTI

43832
Paul E. Martin Scholarship Fund
c/o Second National Bank of Warren
P.O. Box 1311, 108 Main St.
Warren, OH 44482

Established in 1991 in OH.
Donor(s): Paul E. Martin.

Financial data (yr. ended 12/31/01): Grants paid, $15,659; assets, $424,699 (M); expenditures, $18,810; qualifying distributions, $15,659.
Limitations: Applications not accepted. Giving limited to OH.
Application information: Contributes only to pre-selected organizations.
Trustee: Second National Bank of Warren.
EIN: 346952913

43833
Frank & Virginia Jordan Marshall Foundation
(Formerly The C. F. & V. J. Marshall Foundation)
c/o FirstMerit Bank, N.A.
121 S. Main St., Ste. 200
Akron, OH 44308-1417

Financial data (yr. ended 12/31/01): Grants paid, $15,600; assets, $184,639 (M); expenditures, $17,777; qualifying distributions, $15,600.
Limitations: Applications not accepted. Giving primarily in the Akron, OH, area.
Application information: Contributes only to pre-selected organizations.
Trustee: FirstMerit Bank, N.A.
EIN: 346509476

43834
John R. Campbell Memorial Fund
c/o National City Bank of Pennsylvania
P. O. Box 94651
Cleveland, OH 44101-4651

Financial data (yr. ended 12/31/01): Grants paid, $15,400; assets, $301,896 (M); expenditures, $18,233; qualifying distributions, $16,271.
Limitations: Applications not accepted. Giving limited to PA.
Application information: Contributes only to pre-selected organizations.
Trustee: National City Bank of Pennsylvania.
EIN: 256030821

43835
Nussbaum Charitable Trust
c/o U.S. Bank
P.O. Box 1118, ML: CN-WN-06TX
Cincinnati, OH 45201
Application address: Janet Loewy, 1220 Marion Rd., Bucyrus, OH 44820, tel.: (419) 562-6307

Financial data (yr. ended 04/30/02): Grants paid, $15,304; assets, $538,256 (M); expenditures, $26,217; qualifying distributions, $15,304.
Limitations: Giving on a national basis.
Application information: Application form not required.
Trustees: Susan L. Agger, John H. Loewy, U.S. Bank.
EIN: 316021739

43836
Zelczer Family Foundation
c/o Alex Zelczer
3840 Severn Rd.
Cleveland Heights, OH 44118

Donor(s): Alex Zelczer, Ruth Zelczer.
Financial data (yr. ended 12/31/00): Grants paid, $15,257; assets, $409,311 (M); gifts received, $275,541; expenditures, $19,717; qualifying distributions, $15,257.
Limitations: Applications not accepted.
Application information: Contributes only to pre-selected organizations.
Trustees: Lisa Schneck, Alex Zelczer, Ruth Zelczer.
EIN: 341852921

43837
The Flood Family Foundation
590 Lexington Ave.
Mansfield, OH 44907-1505
Contact: Richard V. Kleshinski, Treas.

Established in 1994 in OH.
Donor(s): Jon P. Flood, Ellen Flood.
Financial data (yr. ended 12/31/01): Grants paid, $15,191; assets, $1,516,180 (M); gifts received, $1,094; expenditures, $18,388; qualifying distributions, $15,161.
Application information: Application form not required.
Officers and Trustees:* Ellen Flood,* Pres.; Jon Flood,* V.P.; William D. Heichel,* Secy.; Richard V. Kleshinski,* Treas.; Erik Flood, Jon Patrick Flood.
EIN: 341764048

43838
Max E. & Maude M. Dinger Scholarship Fund
c/o National City Bank of Pennsylvania
P.O. Box 94651
Cleveland, OH 44101-4651
Application address: c/o Punxsutawney Area High School, Guidance Dept., Punxsutawney, PA 15767

Financial data (yr. ended 12/31/01): Grants paid, $15,100; assets, $211,563 (M); expenditures, $16,145; qualifying distributions, $15,380.
Limitations: Giving limited to residents of Punxsutawney, PA.
Application information: Application form required.
Trustee: National City Bank of Pennsylvania.
EIN: 256291080

43839
E. E. Connelly Family Foundation, Inc.
3481 Central Pkwy., Ste. 101
Cincinnati, OH 45223-3398
Contact: John Connelly, Pres.

Established in 1999 in OH.
Donor(s): Edward G. Connelly.
Financial data (yr. ended 05/31/02): Grants paid, $15,043; assets, $216,051 (M); gifts received, $50,000; expenditures, $18,368; qualifying distributions, $15,043.
Limitations: Giving primarily in IN and OH.
Officers and Trustees:* John Connelly,* Pres.; Laura Connelly,* Treas.; Catherine Connelly Sharif.
EIN: 311680764

43840
Jessie D. DeGraw Benevolent Trust
c/o National City Bank
P.O. Box 94651
Cleveland, OH 44101-4651

Financial data (yr. ended 06/30/99): Grants paid, $15,000; assets, $460,736 (M); expenditures, $17,855; qualifying distributions, $16,378.
Limitations: Applications not accepted. Giving primarily in Columbus, OH.
Application information: Contributes only to pre-selected organizations.
Trustee: National City Bank.
EIN: 316159028

43841
Maribel Finnell Foundation for Nantucket
c/o Edward M. Segelken
41 S. High St., 32nd Fl., Ste. 288
Columbus, OH 43215-6101
Application address: 625 Fair Oaks Ave., Ste. 288, South Pasadena, CA 91030
Contact: Michael H. Finnell, Tr.

Financial data (yr. ended 12/31/01): Grants paid, $15,000; assets, $292,617 (M); expenditures, $17,475; qualifying distributions, $15,000.
Limitations: Giving limited to Nantucket, MA.
Trustees: Lesley Blanchard, Carter Finnell, Hunter Finnell, Michael H. Finnell.
EIN: 311077635

43842
Mary Gonter & Sara O'Brien Scholarship Foundation
c/o The Huntington National Bank
P.O. Box 1558, HC 1012
Columbus, OH 43216
Application address: Larry Markworth, V.P., c/o The Huntington National Bank, P.O. Box 232, Dover, OH 44622, tel.: (330) 364-7421

Financial data (yr. ended 06/30/01): Grants paid, $15,000; assets, $394,280 (M); expenditures, $20,450; qualifying distributions, $16,118.
Limitations: Giving limited to residents of OH.
Application information: Application form required.
Trustee: The Huntington National Bank.
EIN: 316317421
Codes: GTI

43843
Hardee Foundation
c/o KeyBank, N.A., Trust Div.
P.O. Box 10099
Toledo, OH 43699-0099 (419) 259-8391
Contact: Imogene Ripps, Trust Off., KeyBank, N.A.

Financial data (yr. ended 12/31/99): Grants paid, $15,000; assets, $636,549 (M); expenditures, $25,951; qualifying distributions, $23,825.
Trustee: KeyBank, N.A.
EIN: 346504819

43844
Jeg's Quarter Mile Charities
101 Jegs Pl.
Delaware, OH 43015

Established in 2000 in OH.
Donor(s): Jeg's Automotive, Inc.
Financial data (yr. ended 12/31/00): Grants paid, $15,000; assets, $26,353 (M); gifts received, $53,416; expenditures, $31,889; qualifying distributions, $15,000.
Limitations: Applications not accepted. Giving on a national basis.
Application information: Contributes only to pre-selected organizations.
Officers and Trustees:* Phillip Troy Coughlin,* Pres.; Edward John Coughlin,* Secy.-Treas.; Jeg Anthony Coughlin, Michael Allen Coughlin.
EIN: 311731261
Codes: CS, CD

43845
Ramona D. Kinsey Charitable Foundation
c/o National City Bank
P.O. Box 94651
Cleveland, OH 44101-4651
Application address: c/o Jack Crogan, National City Bank of Pennsylvania, 20 Stanwix St., Pittsburgh, PA 15222, tel.: (412) 644-6233
Scholarship application address: c/o Victor Mayhugh, Guidance Dir., 251 McMahon Rd. North Huntingdon, PA 15642

Established in 2000 in PA.
Donor(s): Ramona D. Kinsey.
Financial data (yr. ended 02/28/01): Grants paid, $15,000; assets, $456,662 (M); gifts received, $500,000; expenditures, $19,698; qualifying distributions, $17,338.
Limitations: Giving limited to PA.
Application information: Completion of application form required for scholarships. Application form required.
Trustees: Ramona D. Kinsey, National City Bank.
EIN: 256725533

43846
Kraak Charitable Foundation
c/o Glenn Cunningham
250 W. Main St.
Bellevue, OH 44811

Established in 2001 in OH.
Donor(s): Myron L. Kraak.
Financial data (yr. ended 12/31/01): Grants paid, $15,000; assets, $1,017,817 (M); gifts received, $1,015,402; expenditures, $15,000; qualifying distributions, $15,000.
Limitations: Applications not accepted.
Application information: Contributes only to pre-selected organizations.
Officers: Myron L. Kraak, Pres.; Richard Stein, V.P.; Glenn Cunningham, Secy.-Treas.
EIN: 341960643

43847
The Elwin and Doris Lackman Foundation
c/o Eileen Fern
24834 Lorain Rd.
North Olmsted, OH 44070

Established in 2001 in OH.
Donor(s): Doris E. Lackman.
Financial data (yr. ended 12/31/01): Grants paid, $15,000; assets, $103,981 (M); gifts received, $125,000; expenditures, $15,000; qualifying distributions, $15,000.
Limitations: Giving primarily in OH.
Trustee: Doris E. Lackman.
EIN: 347133693

43848
Eugene A. & Connie J. Leber Family Foundation
c/o Star Bank, N.A., Trust Tax 6190
P.O. Box 1118
Cincinnati, OH 45201

Established in 1995 in OH.
Financial data (yr. ended 12/31/01): Grants paid, $15,000; assets, $314,606 (M); expenditures, $24,167; qualifying distributions, $15,000.
Limitations: Applications not accepted. Giving primarily in OH.
Application information: Contributes only to pre-selected organizations.
Officer: Eugene A. Leber, Pres.
Trustees: Gregory T. Holtz, Connie J. Leber.
EIN: 311452941

43849
Joseph L. Marcum Scholarship Fund, Inc.
9450 Seward Rd.
Fairfield, OH 45014-5456
Application address: c/o Hamilton Community Fdn., 319 N. 3rd St., Hamilton, OH 45011, tel.: (513) 863-1389

Established in 1994 in OH.
Donor(s): Ohio Casualty Corporation.
Financial data (yr. ended 12/31/01): Grants paid, $15,000; assets, $142,197 (M); gifts received, $8,848; expenditures, $16,276; qualifying distributions, $15,965.
Limitations: Giving limited to OH.
Application information: Application form required.
Officers and Trustees:* Dan R. Carmichael,* Chair. and Pres.; John E. Bade, Jr., Exec. V.P.; Debra K. Crane,* V.P.; Howard Sloneker III,* Secy.; Richard B. Kelly,* C.F.O.
EIN: 311425290
Codes: CS, CD, GTI

43850
A.J. "IKE" Misali Family Charitable Foundation, Inc.
P.O. Box 1558, HC1012
Columbus, OH 43216

Established in 2000 in OH.
Financial data (yr. ended 12/31/01): Grants paid, $15,000; assets, $24 (M); gifts received, $15,000; expenditures, $15,000; qualifying distributions, $15,000.
Limitations: Applications not accepted. Giving primarily in OH.
Application information: Contributes only to pre-selected organizations.
Trustee: The Huntington National Bank.
EIN: 311604942

43851
The James B. and Ruth E. Morgan Foundation
3800 Perkins Ave.
Cleveland, OH 44114

Established in 1986 in OH.
Financial data (yr. ended 12/31/01): Grants paid, $15,000; assets, $79,909 (M); expenditures, $15,742; qualifying distributions, $15,000.
Limitations: Applications not accepted. Giving primarily in Cleveland, OH.
Application information: Contributes only to pre-selected organizations.
Officers and Trustees:* James B. Morgan, Sr.,* Pres.; Ruth E. Morgan,* V.P.; Thomas A. Morgan,* V.P.; James B. Morgan, Jr.,* Secy.
EIN: 341540933

43852
Pastoral Assistance Foundation
11377 Montgomery Rd.
Cincinnati, OH 45202-2312

Established in 1989 in OH.
Donor(s): Allen Davis, Richard D. Lindner, S. Craig Lindner, Philip R. Myers, Ronald F. Walker.‡
Financial data (yr. ended 12/31/01): Grants paid, $15,000; assets, $186,038 (M); expenditures, $20,139; qualifying distributions, $15,000.
Limitations: Applications not accepted. Giving primarily in Cincinnati, OH.
Application information: Contributes only to pre-selected organizations.
Trustees: Allen Davis, S. Craig Lindner, Philip R. Myers.
EIN: 311284937

43853
Saxby Family Foundation
5565 Citation Rd. N.
Toledo, OH 43615

Established in 1990 in OH.
Donor(s): Lewis W. Saxby, Jr.
Financial data (yr. ended 12/31/01): Grants paid, $15,000; assets, $230,520 (M); expenditures, $16,341; qualifying distributions, $15,000.
Limitations: Applications not accepted. Giving primarily in Toledo, OH.
Application information: Contributes only to pre-selected organizations.
Trustee: Lewis W. Saxby, Jr.
EIN: 346928394

43854
The White Family Foundation
(Formerly James F. White Family Foundation)
2 Riverplace, Ste. 444
Dayton, OH 45405
Contact: Timothy L. White, V.P.

Established in 1987 in OH.
Donor(s): Jim White Toyota.
Financial data (yr. ended 12/31/00): Grants paid, $15,000; assets, $438,699 (M); expenditures, $15,858; qualifying distributions, $15,000.
Limitations: Giving primarily in OH.
Application information: Application form required.
Officers and Trustees:* H. David White, Sr.,* Pres.; James F. White, Jr.,* V.P. and Secy.; Timothy L. White,* V.P. and Treas.
EIN: 341472286

43855
Zeiser Family Foundation
3200 Warsaw Ave.
Cincinnati, OH 45205

Established in 2000 in OH.
Donor(s): John A. Zeiser.
Financial data (yr. ended 12/31/01): Grants paid, $15,000; assets, $265,598 (M); gifts received, $62,000; expenditures, $15,000; qualifying distributions, $15,000.
Limitations: Applications not accepted.
Application information: Contributes only to pre-selected organizations.
Trustees: Daniel G. Pessler, David W. Zeiser, John A. Zeiser.
EIN: 316654782

43856
The Thomas and Susan Gerson Foundation
2992 Fontenay Rd.
Shaker Heights, OH 44120
Contact: Thomas E. Gerson, Pres. or Susan R. Gerson, V.P.

Established in 2000 in OH.
Donor(s): Thomas E. Gerson, Susan R. Gerson.
Financial data (yr. ended 12/31/01): Grants paid, $14,900; assets, $321,394 (M); gifts received, $333,333; expenditures, $16,496; qualifying distributions, $14,900.
Officers and Trustees:* Thomas E. Gerson,* Pres.; Susan R. Gerson,* V.P.; Frederick N. Widen,* Secy.
EIN: 341930482

43857
Sabety Family Foundation
P.O. Box 14227
Columbus, OH 43214
Contact: Pari Sabety, Tr.

Established in 1997 in OH.
Donor(s): Adrian M. Sabety, Mrs. Adrian M. Sabety.
Financial data (yr. ended 12/31/01): Grants paid, $14,867; assets, $34,535 (M); gifts received, $12,055; expenditures, $15,372; qualifying distributions, $14,867.
Officers and Trustees:* Adrian Sabety,* Pres.; Dorothy Sabety,* Secy.; Eric Sabety, Marian Sabety, Pari Sabety, Ted Sabety.
EIN: 311510929

43858
Electronic Image Systems, Inc. Employees Scholarship Fund
600 Bellbrook Ave.
Xenia, OH 45385 (937) 372-7597

Established in 1995 in OH.
Donor(s): Electronic Image Systems, Inc., Carole C. Holmes, Richard E. Holmes, Sr., Joe A. Mays.
Financial data (yr. ended 06/30/00): Grants paid, $14,775; assets, $99,161 (M); expenditures, $17,356; qualifying distributions, $14,775.
Limitations: Giving limited to the residents of OH.
Application information: Application form required.
Officers: Richard E. Holmes, Sr., Chair.; Carole C. Holmes, Secy.
Trustee: Joe A. Mays.
EIN: 311451475

43859
Adele and Thomas Keaney Charitable Foundation
c/o National City Bank
P.O. Box 94651
Cleveland, OH 44101-4651
Application address: 20 Stanwix St., Pittsburgh, PA 15222
Contact: Joanna Mayo

Established in 1998 in PA.
Financial data (yr. ended 09/30/00): Grants paid, $14,750; assets, $891,233 (M); gifts received, $13,874; expenditures, $26,483; qualifying distributions, $17,983.
Application information: Application form required.
Trustee: National City Bank.
EIN: 256583867

43860
Linda Novak Memorial Foundation
106 E. Market, Ste. 400
Warren, OH 44481-1103

Donor(s): Richard E. Novak.
Financial data (yr. ended 12/31/01): Grants paid, $14,700; assets, $307,780 (M); gifts received, $50; expenditures, $21,443; qualifying distributions, $14,700.
Limitations: Applications not accepted. Giving primarily in FL and OH.
Application information: Contributes only to pre-selected organizations.
Officers: Richard E. Novak, Pres., Treas. and Mgr.; Vilma B. Novak, V.P.
EIN: 341500436

43861
Albaugh Ann Wherry Charitable Foundation
300 Sinclair Bldg.
Steubenville, OH 43952
Application address: P.O. Box 1506, Steubenville, OH 43952
Contact: G. Daniel Spahn

Established in 1992 in OH.
Donor(s): Patricia W. Albaugh.
Financial data (yr. ended 12/31/99): Grants paid, $14,668; assets, $301,732 (M); expenditures, $17,042; qualifying distributions, $14,694.
Limitations: Giving primarily in Steubenville, OH.

Application information: Application form not required.
Trustees: Thomas L. Grimm, H. Lee Kinney, Frank B. Sinclair, G. Daniel Spahn.
EIN: 341707844

43862
The Capuano Foundation
c/o Terry D. Capuano
140 Greentree Rd.
Moreland Hills, OH 44022

Established in 2000 in OH.
Donor(s): Terry D. Capuano.
Financial data (yr. ended 12/31/01): Grants paid, $14,593; assets, $251,630 (M); expenditures, $47,575; qualifying distributions, $14,593.
Limitations: Applications not accepted.
Application information: Contributes only to pre-selected organizations.
Officers: Terry D. Capuano, Pres.; Sharon M. Capuano, Treas.
Director: William Capuano.
Trustees: Glenn Brown, Jenny Brown.
EIN: 341939755

43863
Helen F. Smucker Memorial Scholarship Trust
c/o Wayne County National Bank
1776 Beall Ave.
Wooster, OH 44691
Application address: c/o Guidance Dir., Orrville High School, 841 N. Ella, Orrville, OH 44667, tel.: (330) 682-4661

Financial data (yr. ended 12/31/01): Grants paid, $14,572; assets, $316,775 (M); expenditures, $17,840; qualifying distributions, $16,051.
Limitations: Giving limited to Orrville, OH.
Application information: Application form not required.
Trustee: Wayne County National Bank.
EIN: 341296818
Codes: GTI

43864
Nellie L. Ball Trust
P.O. Box 106
Wellston, OH 45692 (740) 384-3659
Contact: Peggy Murdock, Secy.

Financial data (yr. ended 12/31/00): Grants paid, $14,500; assets, $245,397 (M); expenditures, $14,895; qualifying distributions, $14,323.
Limitations: Giving primarily in Wellston, OH.
Application information: Application form required.
Officers and Directors:* Jackie Lockard,* Pres.; Peggy Murdock,* Secy.; Joan Ward,* Treas.; Virginia Ackerman, Vivian Pelletier.
EIN: 316543187

43865
Carfagna Family Foundation
2881 S. Park Blvd.
Shaker Heights, OH 44120

Established in 2000 in OH.
Donor(s): Rita M. Carfagna.
Financial data (yr. ended 12/31/01): Grants paid, $14,500; assets, $950,812 (M); gifts received, $496,374; expenditures, $43,860; qualifying distributions, $14,500.
Limitations: Applications not accepted.
Application information: Contributes only to pre-selected organizations.
Officers and Trustees:* Rita M. Carfagna,* Chair.; Peter A. Carfagna,* Pres.; Peter E. Carfagna,* Secy.; Michael J. Carfagna,* Treas.
EIN: 341940734

43866
The Kohl Foundation
32035 Oxgate Ln.
Chagrin Falls, OH 44022

Established in 1999 in OH.
Financial data (yr. ended 12/31/01): Grants paid, $14,500; assets, $277,451 (M); expenditures, $15,484; qualifying distributions, $14,500.
Trustees: Jennifer Griffiths, John E. Kohl, Kathleen Kohl, Kristie T. Kohl, Laurel Kohl.
EIN: 347106988

43867
The Walsh Family Foundation
39 S. Shore Dr.
Boardman, OH 44512-5926

Donor(s): G.M. Walsh, J.C. Walsh.
Financial data (yr. ended 10/31/01): Grants paid, $14,500; assets, $238,222 (M); expenditures, $14,700; qualifying distributions, $14,500.
Limitations: Applications not accepted. Giving primarily in Youngstown, OH.
Application information: Contributes only to pre-selected organizations.
Trustees: G.M. Walsh, J.C. Walsh.
EIN: 341399912

43868
Horace Williams Memorial Fund
c/o KeyBank, N.A.
800 Superior Ave., 4th Fl.
Cleveland, OH 44114-2601
Application address: P.O. Box 108, Augusta, ME 04330
Contact: William Pelletier, Trust Off., Kennebec Savings Bank

Financial data (yr. ended 08/31/01): Grants paid, $14,500; assets, $282,760 (M); expenditures, $16,983; qualifying distributions, $14,500.
Limitations: Giving primarily in ME.
Trustee: KeyBank, N.A.
EIN: 016008547
Codes: GTI

43869
CWRU Department of Ophthalmology Foundation
11100 Euclid Ave.
Cleveland, OH 44106

Established around 1993.
Donor(s): Web P. Chamberlin, Hiram Hardesty, Humphrey Fund.
Financial data (yr. ended 12/31/00): Grants paid, $14,385; assets, $66,420 (M); gifts received, $15,364; expenditures, $28,635; qualifying distributions, $14,385; giving activities include $3,902 for programs.
Limitations: Applications not accepted. Giving primarily in Cleveland, OH.
Application information: Contributes only to pre-selected organizations.
Officer: Jonathan H. Lass, M.D., Pres.
Trustee: Edward N. Burney, M.D.
EIN: 341728888

43870
Pumpkin Hill Foundation
c/o Fifth Third Bank, Trust Tax Dept.
38 Fountain Sq. Plz.
Cincinnati, OH 45263
Application address: 27 Burkehaven Ln., Sunapee, NH 03782
Contact: William N. & Elizabeth B. Peabody

Established in 1998 in NH.

Financial data (yr. ended 12/31/01): Grants paid, $14,312; assets, $483,551 (M); expenditures, $18,451; qualifying distributions, $14,312.
Limitations: Giving on a national basis.
Officer and Trustees: William N. Peabody,* Pres.; Elizabeth B. Peabody, Fifth Third Bank.
EIN: 020500977

43871
David Neufeld Memorial Foundation
c/o Fifth Third Bank
38 Fountain Sq., Trust Tax Dept.
Cincinnati, OH 45263
Contact: Mary Ann Michel

Financial data (yr. ended 12/31/01): Grants paid, $14,300; assets, $316,197 (M); gifts received, $1,400; expenditures, $17,060; qualifying distributions, $14,300.
Limitations: Giving on a national basis, with emphasis on CA, NY, and OH.
Trustee: Fifth Third Bank.
EIN: 237236188

43872
The Dr. H. S. & Florence Wang Family Charity Foundation
4329 Fountain Valley Ct.
Canfield, OH 44406-9591

Established in 1996 in OH.
Donor(s): H.S. Wang.
Financial data (yr. ended 12/31/01): Grants paid, $14,295; assets, $118,120 (M); expenditures, $15,541; qualifying distributions, $14,295.
Limitations: Applications not accepted.
Application information: Contributes only to pre-selected organizations.
Trustees: Florence Wang, H.S. Wang.
EIN: 341847717

43873
Blanchard Foundation
P.O. Box 816
Ashtabula, OH 44005
Contact: Douglas Blanchard, Secy.-Treas.

Donor(s): Bey Blanchard.
Financial data (yr. ended 11/30/01): Grants paid, $14,200; assets, $365,043 (M); expenditures, $14,343; qualifying distributions, $14,200.
Limitations: Giving primarily in Ashtabula, OH.
Officers: Bey Blanchard, Pres.; Phyllis Blanchard, V.P.; Douglas Blanchard, Secy.-Treas.; E. Terry Warren, Secy.
Trustees: Terry Blanchard, Carol Matson.
EIN: 341420823

43874
Grace M. Harvie Trust
5 W. 4th St.
900 4th and Vine Tower
Cincinnati, OH 45202 (513) 381-9200
Contact: W. Roger Fry, Tr.

Financial data (yr. ended 12/31/01): Grants paid, $14,200; assets, $357,848 (M); expenditures, $20,609; qualifying distributions, $20,516.
Limitations: Giving primarily in Cincinnati, OH.
Application information: Application form not required.
Trustee: W. Roger Fry.
EIN: 316301759

43875
Grace G. Appleton Student Loan Fund
c/o KeyBank, N.A.
800 Superior Ave., 4th Fl.
Cleveland, OH 44114
Application address: c/o Dir. of Financial Aid, State University of New York at Plattsburgh, 101 Broad St., Plattsburgh, NY 12901

Donor(s): Grace G. Appleton.‡
Financial data (yr. ended 12/31/01): Grants paid, $14,167; assets, $106,494 (M); expenditures, $16,165; qualifying distributions, $14,091; giving activities include $14,167 for loans to individuals.
Limitations: Giving limited to Plattsburgh, NY.
Trustee: KeyBank, N.A.
EIN: 237416731

43876
Phyllis Gulliver Charitable Foundation
c/o KeyBank, N.A.
800 Superior Ave., 4th Fl.
Cleveland, OH 44114

Established in 1999 in ME.
Financial data (yr. ended 08/31/01): Grants paid, $14,112; assets, $316,903 (M); expenditures, $34,557; qualifying distributions, $13,604.
Limitations: Applications not accepted.
Application information: Contributes only to pre-selected organizations.
Trustee: KeyBank, N.A.
EIN: 527006918

43877
John T. Rusher Scholarship Trust
c/o National City Bank
P.O. Box 94651
Cleveland, OH 44101-4651

Donor(s): Robert N. Hagemeyer.
Financial data (yr. ended 12/31/01): Grants paid, $14,103; assets, $270,814 (M); expenditures, $14,780; qualifying distributions, $14,103.
Limitations: Applications not accepted. Giving primarily in IL.
Application information: Contributes only to pre-selected organizations.
Trustee: National City Bank.
EIN: 376029969

43878
The Quatkemeyer Foundation
7817 Manor Dr.
West Chester, OH 45069
Contact: Robert Quatkemeyer, Jr., Pres.

Established in 1988 in OH.
Donor(s): Robert Quatkemeyer, Jr.
Financial data (yr. ended 12/31/01): Grants paid, $14,075; assets, $1 (M); expenditures, $6,694; qualifying distributions, $14,075.
Application information: Application form not required.
Officers: Robert Quatkemeyer, Jr., Pres.; Nancy Quatkemeyer, V.P.; Robert W. Buechner, Secy.
EIN: 311214850

43879
The Edward F. Crawford Foundation
23000 Euclid Ave.
Euclid, OH 44117

Financial data (yr. ended 12/31/01): Grants paid, $14,050; assets, $156,049 (M); gifts received, $25,000; expenditures, $17,389; qualifying distributions, $14,050.
Limitations: Applications not accepted.
Application information: Contributes only to pre-selected organizations.

Officers: Edward F. Crawford, Pres.; Mary M. Crawford, V.P.; Matthew V. Crawford, Secy.; Deborah A. Crawford, Treas.
EIN: 341870890

43880
The Burgett Family/Kokosing Foundation
c/o William B. Burgett
17531 Waterford Rd., P.O. Box 226
Fredericktown, OH 43019
Application address: 2922 Lost Run Rd., Fredericktown, OH 43019, tel.: (419) 522-7508
Contact: Shirley Burgett, Pres.

Established in 1992 in OH.
Donor(s): William B. Burgett, Shirley Burgett.
Financial data (yr. ended 12/31/01): Grants paid, $14,000; assets, $94,715 (M); gifts received, $55,267; expenditures, $14,052; qualifying distributions, $14,000.
Limitations: Giving limited to OH.
Officers and Trustees:* Shirley Burgett,* Pres.; William Barth Burgett,* V.P.; William Brian Burgett, V.P.; Marsha Rinehart,* Secy.; Valerie Matusik,* Treas.; Janenne Burgett, William B. Burgett.
EIN: 311367299

43881
Alex Foldvary Scholarship Fund
c/o Robert Foldvary
1886 Redwood Dr.
Defiance, OH 43512

Financial data (yr. ended 12/31/01): Grants paid, $14,000; assets, $235,723 (M); gifts received, $200; expenditures, $21,747; qualifying distributions, $14,000.
Trustees: Marilyn Foldvary, Robert Foldvary, Douglas Gildenmeister, Joseph O'Neil.
EIN: 341788596

43882
Italian American Cultural Foundation
3659 Green Rd., Ste. 124
Beachwood, OH 44122

Established in 1977.
Financial data (yr. ended 03/31/01): Grants paid, $14,000; assets, $63,455 (M); expenditures, $50,453; qualifying distributions, $14,000.
Limitations: Giving limited to residents of Cleveland, OH.
Application information: Unsolicited requests for funds not considered or acknowledged. Application form required.
Officers: Robert Bernadelli, Chair.; Nick Nardi, Pres.; Lou Amoroso, V.P.; Marie Monroe, Secy.; Dominic M. D'Amore, Jr., Treas.
EIN: 341213061
Codes: GTI

43883
The Revely Family Foundation
c/o Fifth Third Bank
38 Fountain Sq. Plz.
Cincinnati, OH 45263
Application address: c/o Thomas Revely, III, 3755 Fawnrun Dr., Cincinnati, OH 45241

Established in 2000 in OH.
Financial data (yr. ended 12/31/01): Grants paid, $14,000; assets, $36,605 (M); expenditures, $14,927; qualifying distributions, $14,000.
Application information: Application available upon request. Application form required.
Trustee: Fifth Third Bank.
EIN: 311752033

43884
Ralph L. & Florence A. Bernard Foundation
P.O. Box 8176
Akron, OH 44320

Established in 1998 in OH.
Donor(s): Ralph L. Bernard.
Financial data (yr. ended 04/30/02): Grants paid, $13,950; assets, $1,643,182 (M); expenditures, $20,176; qualifying distributions, $13,950.
Limitations: Giving primarily in OH.
Application information: Application form not required.
Trustees: Ralph L. Bernard, Ralph L. Bernard, Jr., Regina A. Dain.
EIN: 341867382

43885
Emch Family Charitable Foundation
3728 Sulphur Springs Rd.
Toledo, OH 43606-2626

Established in 1997 in OH.
Donor(s): A. Willard Emch.
Financial data (yr. ended 06/30/02): Grants paid, $13,950; assets, $277,751 (M); gifts received, $193,724; expenditures, $16,649; qualifying distributions, $13,950.
Limitations: Applications not accepted.
Application information: Contributes only to pre-selected organizations.
Trustees: Thomas A. Baither, A. Willard Emch, A. Willard Emch, Jr., Douglas H. Emch, Sharon M. Emch.
EIN: 341852946

43886
Arline & Thomas Patton Foundation
c/o The Huntington National Bank
P.O. Box 1558, HC-0534
Columbus, OH 43216
Application address: c/o The Huntington National Bank, 917 Euclid Ave., Cleveland, OH 44115, tel.: (216) 515-6533

Financial data (yr. ended 06/30/01): Grants paid, $13,950; assets, $291,757 (M); expenditures, $18,151; qualifying distributions, $14,569.
Limitations: Giving primarily in Cleveland, OH.
Application information: Application form not required.
Trustee: The Huntington National Bank.
EIN: 346521593

43887
The Johnson Charitable Trust
10979 Strausser St. N.W.
Canal Fulton, OH 44614-9483

Financial data (yr. ended 12/31/99): Grants paid, $13,935; assets, $246,689 (L); expenditures, $13,935; qualifying distributions, $13,935.
Limitations: Applications not accepted.
Application information: Contributes only to pre-selected organizations.
Directors: Dorothy Johnson, Vernon Johnson.
EIN: 341814366

43888
The E. Mandell and Betsy de Windt Foundation
c/o Eaton Corp.
Eaton Ctr.
Cleveland, OH 44114

Established in 1986 in OH.
Donor(s): E.M. de Windt.
Financial data (yr. ended 12/31/99): Grants paid, $13,850; assets, $616,741 (M); expenditures, $14,050; qualifying distributions, $13,950.
Limitations: Applications not accepted. Giving primarily in FL.

Application information: Contributes only to pre-selected organizations.
Officers: E. Mandell de Windt, Pres. and Treas.; Pamela Burke, V.P.; Dana de Windt, Secy.
EIN: 341536552

43889
Robert R. and Gay C. Cull Family Foundation
3500 Carnegie Ave.
Cleveland, OH 44115-2641 (216) 361-2100
Contact: Gay C. Cull, V.P.

Established in 1996 in OH.
Donor(s): Robert R. Cull.
Financial data (yr. ended 12/31/01): Grants paid, $13,750; assets, $549,494 (M); gifts received, $21,720; expenditures, $20,884; qualifying distributions, $13,750.
Limitations: Giving primarily in Cleveland, OH.
Officers: Robert R. Cull, Pres.; Gay C. Cull, V.P. and Treas.; Peter Kuhn, V.P.; Robert A. Toepfer, Secy.
Trustees: Ted Miller, Raymond L. Scherry.
EIN: 341847504

43890
Orlene Drobisch Moore Charitable Trust
c/o National City Bank
P.O. Box 94651
Cleveland, OH 44101-4651
Contact: Jo Ann Harlan

Established in 1995 in IL.
Financial data (yr. ended 06/30/01): Grants paid, $13,750; assets, $280,724 (M); expenditures, $16,299; qualifying distributions, $15,250.
Limitations: Giving limited to residents of Williamsville, IL.
Application information: Application form required.
Trustee: National City Bank.
EIN: 371316048
Codes: GTI

43891
The Hanna Dougherty Family Charitable Trust
c/o KeyBank, N.A.
800 Superior Ave., 4th Fl.
Cleveland, OH 44114

Established in 1998 in OH.
Financial data (yr. ended 12/31/00): Grants paid, $13,674; assets, $528,431 (M); expenditures, $22,231; qualifying distributions, $13,874.
Limitations: Applications not accepted. Giving primarily in Cleveland, OH.
Application information: Unsolicited requests for funds not accepted.
Trustees: Donald R. Beran, Marcus A. Hanna, KeyBank, N.A.
EIN: 341871363

43892
Shirley Rudman Trust
c/o National City Bank
P.O. Box 94651
Cleveland, OH 44101-4651

Financial data (yr. ended 12/31/00): Grants paid, $13,667; assets, $131,569 (M); expenditures, $15,454; qualifying distributions, $14,968.
Limitations: Applications not accepted. Giving primarily in IL and NY.
Application information: Contributes only to pre-selected organizations.
Trustee: National City Bank.
EIN: 366814300

43893
William Philbrick Charitable Trust No. 4
(Formerly William Philbrick Irrevocable Trust)
c/o KeyBank, N.A., Trust Div.
800 Superior Ave., 4th Fl.
Cleveland, OH 44114
Application address: c/o Principal, Skowhegan High School, Skowhegan, ME 04976

Financial data (yr. ended 04/30/00): Grants paid, $13,600; assets, $916,976 (M); expenditures, $23,656; qualifying distributions, $13,600.
Limitations: Giving limited to ME.
Application information: Application form required.
Trustee: KeyBank, N.A.
EIN: 016027550

43894
The Portage Foundation
(Formerly Greater Portage Area Visiting Nurses Association)
143 Gougler Ave.
Kent, OH 44240 (330) 676-1110
FAX: (330) 676-1106; E-mail: portagefound@mindspring.com

Established in 1976 in OH.
Financial data (yr. ended 12/31/00): Grants paid, $13,528; assets, $485,009 (M); gifts received, $18,672; expenditures, $121,204.
Limitations: Giving limited to the greater Portage, OH area.
Officer: Margaret Mascio, Exec. Dir.
EIN: 341176817
Codes: CM

43895
The Brown Family Foundation, Inc.
300 W. Main St.
Greenville, OH 45331-1432
Application address: 323 S. Broadway, Greenville, OH 45331, tel.: (937) 547-2261
Contact: Richard T. Brown, Tr.

Established in 1990 in OH; funded in 1992.
Financial data (yr. ended 12/31/01): Grants paid, $13,500; assets, $332,358 (M); expenditures, $14,418; qualifying distributions, $13,500.
Limitations: Giving limited to Darke County, OH.
Application information: Application form not required.
Trustees: Linda D. Brown, Mary C. Brown, Richard T. Brown.
EIN: 311308516

43896
C. W. & M. Ensminger Educational Fund
c/o Fifth Third Bank
38 Fountain Sq. Plz., M.D. 1COM31
Cincinnati, OH 45263
Application address: c/o Fifth Third Bank, Foundation Office, Dept. 00864, Cincinnati, OH 45263

Established in 1995.
Donor(s): C.W. Ensminger.‡
Financial data (yr. ended 09/30/01): Grants paid, $13,500; assets, $195,449 (M); gifts received, $488; expenditures, $13,835; qualifying distributions, $13,500.
Limitations: Giving primarily in Cincinnati, OH.
Trustee: Fifth Third Bank.
EIN: 316509994

43897
Hollington Family Foundation
c/o Richard R. Hollington
1900 E. 9th St., Ste. 3200
Cleveland, OH 44114-3485

Established in 1999 in OH.
Donor(s): Richard R. Hollington, Jr., Sally S. Hollington.
Financial data (yr. ended 12/31/01): Grants paid, $13,500; assets, $219,899 (M); gifts received, $67,068; expenditures, $14,241; qualifying distributions, $13,600.
Limitations: Applications not accepted.
Application information: Contributes only to pre-selected organizations.
Officers and Trustees:* Richard R. Hollington, Jr.,* Pres.; Sally S. Hollington,* Secy.-Treas.; Julie H. Grimm, Peter S. Hollington, Richard R. Hollington III, Lorie H. Smith.
EIN: 341910474

43898
Beatrice L. Miller Foundation
c/o United National Bank, Alliance
2 W. State St.
Alliance, OH 44601-4714

Financial data (yr. ended 12/31/01): Grants paid, $13,500; assets, $363,336 (M); expenditures, $18,625; qualifying distributions, $13,500.
Limitations: Applications not accepted. Giving primarily in Alliance, OH.
Application information: Contributes only to pre-selected organizations.
Officers: John A. Burnquist, Pres.; Connie Brodzinski, V.P. and Secy.-Treas.
Trustees: Marilyn Bower, Carl F. Wachsman.
EIN: 346522426

43899
The Jefferson Memorial Foundation
c/o Second National Bank of Warren
108 Main St. S.W.
Warren, OH 44481

Established in 1991 in OH.
Financial data (yr. ended 12/31/99): Grants paid, $13,450; assets, $363,179 (M); expenditures, $26,060; qualifying distributions, $17,914.
Limitations: Applications not accepted. Giving limited to Ashtabula and Jefferson County, OH.
Trustee: Second National Bank of Warren.
EIN: 346968316

43900
The Ginn Family Fund
3900 Key Ctr.
127 Public Sq.
Cleveland, OH 44114-1216
Contact: William D. Ginn, Tr.

Established in 1994 in OH.
Donor(s): William D. Ginn, Arlene D. Ginn.
Financial data (yr. ended 12/31/01): Grants paid, $13,350; assets, $444,210 (M); expenditures, $22,290; qualifying distributions, $13,350.
Limitations: Giving primarily in OH.
Trustees: Arlene D. Ginn, William D. Ginn, Roy L. Turnell.
EIN: 341790863

43901
Robert E. Mathews Family Foundation
16800 S. Park Blvd.
Cleveland, OH 44120-1642

Established in 1988 in OH.
Donor(s): Robert E. Mathews II.

Financial data (yr. ended 12/31/01): Grants paid, $13,350; assets, $196,455 (M); expenditures, $14,623; qualifying distributions, $14,205.
Limitations: Applications not accepted. Giving primarily in Cleveland, OH.
Application information: Contributes only to pre-selected organizations.
Officers and Trustees:* Robert E. Mathews II,* Pres.; Wanda Jean Mathews,* V.P.; William F. Snyder,* Secy.
EIN: 341598059

43902
Sandusky International Foundation
(Formerly Sandusky Foundry & Machine Company Foundation)
615 W. Market St.
P.O. Box 5012
Sandusky, OH 44871-5012

Established in 1967 in OH.
Donor(s): Sandusky Foundry & Machine Co., Sandusky International Inc.
Financial data (yr. ended 12/31/01): Grants paid, $13,350; assets, $5,481 (M); gifts received, $8,000; expenditures, $13,381; qualifying distributions, $13,345.
Limitations: Applications not accepted. Giving primarily in Erie and Sandusky counties, OH.
Application information: Contributes only to pre-selected organizations.
Trustees: R.A. Hargrave, E.R. Ryan.
EIN: 346596951
Codes: CS, CD

43903
Sara C. Cassidy Trust
c/o National City Bank of Kentucky
P.O. Box 94651
Cleveland, OH 44101-4651

Established in 1991 in KY.
Financial data (yr. ended 02/28/01): Grants paid, $13,329; assets, $384,288 (M); expenditures, $15,501; qualifying distributions, $14,553.
Limitations: Applications not accepted.
Application information: Contributes only pre-selected organizations.
Trustees: National City Bank, Kentucky.
EIN: 616192446

43904
The George L. Heldman Foundation
415 Bond Pl.
Cincinnati, OH 45206-1872

Financial data (yr. ended 12/31/01): Grants paid, $13,310; assets, $110,753 (M); gifts received, $882; expenditures, $14,185; qualifying distributions, $13,310.
Limitations: Applications not accepted. Giving primarily in Cincinnati, OH.
Application information: Contributes only to pre-selected organizations.
Officer: George Heldman, Pres.
EIN: 237003377

43905
The Matt Dudon Memorial Soccer Fund, Inc.
725 Lilac Ave.
Dayton, OH 45427
Application address: c/o Mutual Tool & Die, Inc., Matt Dudon Scholarship, P.O. Box 2, Paul Lawrence Dunbar Sta., Dayton, OH 45417, tel.: (937) 268-6713
Contact: Anthony Dudon, Tr.

Established in 1995.
Financial data (yr. ended 12/31/99): Grants paid, $13,282; assets, $147,982 (M); gifts received, $11,563; expenditures, $37,461; qualifying distributions, $13,282.
Limitations: Giving primarily in Dayton, OH.
Application information: Application form required.
Trustees: Anthony Dudon, David A. Dudon, Michelle Dudon, Rudy Dudon, Jr., Teresa Dudon, Amy M. O'Loughlin, Rebecca S. Tracey.
EIN: 311455620

43906
Associated Charities, Inc.
(Formerly Van Wert Associated Charities, Inc.)
Court House, Rm. 100
Van Wert, OH 45891
Contact: Keith E. Harman, Exec. Dir.

Incorporated in 1917 in OH.
Financial data (yr. ended 12/31/01): Grants paid, $13,230; assets, $382,936 (M); expenditures, $24,724.
Limitations: Giving limited to Van Wert County, OH.
Publications: Informational brochure.
Application information: Application form required.
Officers and Trustees:* Bryce L. Beckman,* Pres.; Michael Gearhart,* V.P.; Jane Harris, Secy.; Merle Brady, Treas.; Keith E. Harman, Exec. Dir.; Nancy Dixon, Charles Koch.
EIN: 346542013
Codes: CM

43907
Archbold Area Foundation
P.O. Box 224
Archbold, OH 43502

Financial data (yr. ended 12/31/99): Grants paid, $13,192; assets, $395,939 (M); gifts received, $10,025; expenditures, $13,666.
Limitations: Giving limited to the Archbold, OH, area.
Officers: Harold Plassman, Pres.; Marvin Miller, V.P.; Toni Vajen, Secy.; Timothy Yoder, Treas.
Board Members: Margaret Keim, Dale Kern, Claire Morton, Fannie Nofziger, Bill Phelps, Lowell E. Rupp, Joe Staudt, Mary Ann Thatcher.
EIN: 341452403
Codes: CM

43908
Schulzinger-Frankel Family Foundation
(Formerly Joseph N. Schulzinger Memorial Foundation)
8355 Crestdale Ct.
Cincinnati, OH 45236 (513) 891-5522
Contact: Peninah T. Frankel, Pres.

Established in 1970.
Donor(s): Ruth Schulzinger.‡
Financial data (yr. ended 12/31/01): Grants paid, $13,175; assets, $177,380 (M); expenditures, $23,271; qualifying distributions, $13,175.
Limitations: Giving primarily in Cincinnati, OH.
Officers and Trustees:* Peninah T. Frankel,* Pres. and Treas.; Naftali Frankel,* V.P. and Secy.; Steven Frankel.
EIN: 316180254

43909
Mary E. Higgins Educational Fund
c/o KeyBank, N.A.
800 Superior Ave., 4th Fl.
Cleveland, OH 44114
Application address: c/o Guidance Dept., Gray-Gloucester High School, Lobby Hill Rd., Gray, ME 04034

Donor(s): Mary E. Higgins.‡

Financial data (yr. ended 06/30/01): Grants paid, $13,050; assets, $180,031 (M); expenditures, $15,598; qualifying distributions, $12,847.
Limitations: Giving limited to residents of Gray, ME.
Trustee: KeyBank, N.A.
EIN: 016067064
Codes: GTI

43910
William Powell Company Foundation
2535 Spring Grove Ave.
Cincinnati, OH 45214

Donor(s): William Powell Co.
Financial data (yr. ended 11/30/99): Grants paid, $13,050; assets, $361,392 (M); expenditures, $13,475; qualifying distributions, $13,050.
Limitations: Applications not accepted. Giving primarily in Cincinnati, OH.
Application information: Contributes only to pre-selected organizations.
Trustees: Vachael Anderson Coombe, R.S. Dunham.
EIN: 316043487
Codes: CS, CD

43911
Draime Family Foundation
400 Hunters Hollow
Warren, OH 44484 (330) 856-2443

Financial data (yr. ended 12/31/01): Grants paid, $13,000; assets, $265,338 (M); expenditures, $14,349; qualifying distributions, $12,993.
Limitations: Applications not accepted.
Application information: Contributes only to pre-selected organizations.
Trustees: Cecile M. Draime, David M. Draime, Jeffrey P. Draime, Scott N. Draime, Rebecca M. Draime Gang.
EIN: 341853228

43912
The Stone Foundation
c/o Sheldon M. Lewin
6685 Beta Dr.
Mayfield Village, OH 44143

Established in 1985 in FL.
Donor(s): Linda S. Stone, Sheldon M. Lewin.
Financial data (yr. ended 12/31/01): Grants paid, $13,000; assets, $592,322 (M); expenditures, $21,113; qualifying distributions, $13,000.
Limitations: Applications not accepted.
Application information: Contributes only to pre-selected organizations.
Trustees: N. Herschel Koblenz, Sheldon M. Lewin, Lee Metzendorf, Linda A. Stone.
EIN: 592247155

43913
Jadetree Two Foundation
2000 Huntington Bldg., Attn: Red
925 Euclid Ave., Ste. 2000
Cleveland, OH 44115-1496

Established in 1998 in OH.
Donor(s): Barbara Briggs-Letson.
Financial data (yr. ended 07/31/01): Grants paid, $12,986; assets, $89,052 (M); expenditures, $14,615; qualifying distributions, $12,986.
Trustees: Barbara Briggs-Letson, David D. Watson, Richard T. Watson.
EIN: 341883234

43914
Stockbridge Foundation
c/o Brian K. Gorris
25845 Butternut Ridge Rd.
North Olmsted, OH 44070-4510

Established in 1999 in OH.
Donor(s): The Midwest Foundation.
Financial data (yr. ended 01/31/02): Grants paid, $12,935; assets, $119,216 (M); gifts received, $440; expenditures, $14,424; qualifying distributions, $12,921.
Limitations: Applications not accepted. Giving primarily in OH.
Application information: Contributes only to pre-selected organizations.
Trustees: Annette T. Gorris, Brian K. Gorris, Brian K. Gorris II, Matthew S. Gorris, Tony C. Gorris.
EIN: 341899572

43915
New Albany Community Foundation
220 Market St., Ste. 200
P.O. Box 772
New Albany, OH 43054
Contact: J. Craig Mohre, Exec. Dir.

Financial data (yr. ended 12/31/01): Grants paid, $12,894; assets, $18,282 (M); gifts received, $19,550; expenditures, $18,446.
Limitations: Giving limited to New Albany, OH.
Officers: John W. Kessler, Pres.; Ellen Bachmann, V.P.; Ralph Johnson, Secy.; J. Craig Mohre, Exec. Dir.
Board Member: Jonathan York.
EIN: 311409264
Codes: CM

43916
Leonora H. Knowles Trust A
c/o KeyBank, N.A.
800 Superior Ave., 4th Fl.
Cleveland, OH 44114-2601

Financial data (yr. ended 12/31/01): Grants paid, $12,797; assets, $297,170 (M); expenditures, $17,921; qualifying distributions, $12,797.
Limitations: Applications not accepted. Giving primarily in ME.
Application information: Contributes only to pre-selected organizations.
Trustee: KeyBank, N.A.
EIN: 222789211

43917
Charles L. Wright Foundation
c/o National City Bank of PA
P.O. Box 94651
Cleveland, OH 44101-4651 (800) 628-8151
Application address: c/o Cindy Lang, National City Bank, 1900 E. 9th St., Cleveland, OH 44114

Financial data (yr. ended 12/31/01): Grants paid, $12,750; assets, $119,499 (M); expenditures, $13,892; qualifying distributions, $13,152.
Limitations: Giving limited to New Brighton, PA.
Application information: Application form required.
Trustee: National City Bank.
EIN: 256217209
Codes: GTI

43918
Mary M. McGee Foundation
c/o Fifth Third Bank
38 Foundation Sq. Plz., Ste. ICOM31
Cincinnati, OH 45263

Established in 1992 in OH.
Donor(s): Mary M. McGee.‡
Financial data (yr. ended 09/30/01): Grants paid, $12,700; assets, $174,448 (M); expenditures, $16,113; qualifying distributions, $13,403.
Limitations: Giving limited to the greater Cincinnati, OH, area.
Application information: Application form required.
Trustee: Fifth Third Bank.
EIN: 316449572

43919
Voice Foundation
c/o Kathryn A. Derry
3719 Lake Rd.
Sheffield Lake, OH 44054-1026

Established in 1995 in VA.
Donor(s): Brian J. Derry, Kathryn A. Derry.
Financial data (yr. ended 12/31/01): Grants paid, $12,700; assets, $111,598 (M); gifts received, $5,626; expenditures, $15,147; qualifying distributions, $12,700.
Limitations: Applications not accepted. Giving primarily in OH.
Application information: Contributes only to pre-selected organizations.
Directors: Aaron J. Derry, Brian J. Derry, Joel B. Derry, Kathryn A. Derry.
EIN: 541781429

43920
Ross Foundation, Inc.
36790 Giles Rd.
Grafton, OH 44044-9752

Established in 1984 in OH.
Donor(s): Ross Environmental Services, Inc.
Financial data (yr. ended 05/31/02): Grants paid, $12,550; assets, $2,097 (M); gifts received, $13,306; expenditures, $12,834; qualifying distributions, $12,550.
Limitations: Applications not accepted. Giving limited to OH, with preference to Lorain County.
Application information: Contributes only to pre-selected organizations.
Officers and Trustees:* Maureen M. Cromling,* Pres. and Treas.; John Rybarczyk, Secy.; William E. Cromling, William E. Cromling II, James Rykaceski.
EIN: 341442262
Codes: CS, CD

43921
Jane Jackson Trust Foundation
c/o National City Bank
P.O. Box 94651
Cleveland, OH 44101-4651

Established in 1987 in OH.
Financial data (yr. ended 12/31/01): Grants paid, $12,540; assets, $229,806 (M); expenditures, $14,556; qualifying distributions, $12,540.
Limitations: Applications not accepted. Giving primarily in OH and PA.
Application information: Contributes only to pre-selected organizations.
Trustee: National City Bank.
EIN: 346515637

43922
John & Ellen Burnham Educational Trust
c/o KeyBank, N.A.
800 Superior Ave., 4th Fl.
Cleveland, OH 44114

Established in 1995 in ME.
Financial data (yr. ended 12/31/00): Grants paid, $12,500; assets, $155,334 (M); expenditures, $14,191; qualifying distributions, $12,358.
Limitations: Applications not accepted. Giving primarily in ME.
Application information: Unsolicited requests for funds not accepted.
Trustee: KeyBank, N.A.
EIN: 016131036

43923
George A. & Carolynn B. Mitchell Charitable Trust
1364 Meadowood Cir.
Poland, OH 44514

Established in 1999 in OH.
Financial data (yr. ended 12/31/01): Grants paid, $12,500; assets, $91,439 (M); gifts received, $112; expenditures, $12,612; qualifying distributions, $12,500.
Limitations: Applications not accepted.
Application information: Contributes only to pre-selected organizations.
Trustees: Carolynn B. Mitchell, George A. Mitchell.
EIN: 347099166

43924
Pollack Family Foundation
2510 Blossom Ln.
Beachwood, OH 44122

Established in 1997 in OH.
Donor(s): Michael Pollack.
Financial data (yr. ended 12/31/00): Grants paid, $12,500; assets, $477,494 (M); expenditures, $19,259; qualifying distributions, $12,500.
Limitations: Applications not accepted. Giving primarily in New York, NY and Cleveland, OH.
Application information: Contributes only to pre-selected organizations.
Officer: Michael Pollack, Pres.
EIN: 311571880

43925
Lorraine M. Taylor Scholarship Fund
c/o The Huntington National Bank
P.O. Box 1558, HC-0534
Columbus, OH 43216
Application address: c/o Eastview United Methodist Church, 1045 Ross Rd., Columbus, OH 43227
Contact: Rev. C. Richard Frasure, Tr.

Established in 1995 in OH.
Financial data (yr. ended 12/31/01): Grants paid, $12,500; assets, $237,732 (M); expenditures, $15,770; qualifying distributions, $12,500.
Limitations: Giving limited to Columbus, OH.
Trustee: The Huntington National Bank.
EIN: 311445924

43926
Frank W. & Mary M. Sullivan Foundation, Inc.
21315 Lalemant Rd.
University Heights, OH 44118-4503

Established in 1983.
Financial data (yr. ended 12/31/01): Grants paid, $12,470; assets, $115,258 (M); expenditures, $18,757; qualifying distributions, $12,470.
Limitations: Applications not accepted. Giving primarily in OH.
Application information: Contributes only to pre-selected organizations.
Trustees: Mary S. Power, Frank W. Sullivan, Joseph D. Sullivan, Michael M. Sullivan.
EIN: 341286873

43927
The Glockner Family Foundation, Inc.
4368 U.S. Rte. 23 N.
P.O. Box 1308
Portsmouth, OH 45662

Established in 1995 in OH.

Donor(s): Quality Car & Truck Leasing, Inc., Andrew M. Glockner.
Financial data (yr. ended 10/31/01): Grants paid, $12,457; assets, $277,437 (M); gifts received, $80,000; expenditures, $12,557; qualifying distributions, $11,756.
Limitations: Applications not accepted. Giving primarily in OH and IN.
Application information: Contributes only to pre-selected organizations.
Officers and Trustees:* Andrew M. Glockner,* Chair. and Treas.; Susan G. Fitzer,* Vice-Chair. and Secy.; Edward L. Glockner, Joanne K. Glockner.
EIN: 311453824

43928
Richard H. Siegel Philanthropic Fund for the Arts, Inc.
20133 Farnsleigh Rd.
Shaker Heights, OH 44122 (216) 991-6200
Contact: Michael Siegel, Secy.-Treas.

Established in 1996 in OH.
Donor(s): Madeleine E. Siegel.
Financial data (yr. ended 12/31/00): Grants paid, $12,389; assets, $26,758 (M); gifts received, $11,838; expenditures, $12,443; qualifying distributions, $12,389.
Application information: Application form not required.
Officers and Trustees:* Madeleine Siegel,* Pres.; Randy Siegel,* V.P.; Michael Siegel,* Secy.-Treas.; Peter Siegel, William Siegel.
EIN: 341839629

43929
Vietnam Veterans of America Ohio State Council, Inc.
P.O. Box 21578
Columbus, OH 43221

Established in 1997 in OH. Classified as a company-sponsored operating foundation in 2000.
Donor(s): American Trade & Convention Publications, Inc.
Financial data (yr. ended 12/31/01): Grants paid, $12,324; assets, $53,261 (M); gifts received, $24,973; expenditures, $14,710; qualifying distributions, $12,324.
Limitations: Giving primarily in OH.
Application information: Unsolicited request for funds not accepted.
Officers: Douglas Lay, Pres.; David Bradley, V.P.; Kelly Boyer, Secy.; Dana Harold, Treas.
EIN: 311437071

43930
Senkfor Family Foundation
c/o Precision Gear Co.
1900 Midway Dr.
Twinsburg, OH 44087

Established in 1994 in OH.
Financial data (yr. ended 12/31/01): Grants paid, $12,250; assets, $535,029 (M); gifts received, $61,701; expenditures, $16,076; qualifying distributions, $12,250.
Limitations: Applications not accepted.
Application information: Contributes only to pre-selected organizations.
Officers: Leonard Senkfor, Pres.; David Senkfor, V.P.; Steven Senkfor, V.P.
EIN: 341788305

43931
The Hendricks Family Foundation
c/o Lawrence S. Hendricks
2928 Whispering Pines
Canfield, OH 44406

Established in 1998 in OH.
Donor(s): Lawrence S. Hendricks.
Financial data (yr. ended 12/31/01): Grants paid, $12,200; assets, $69,476 (M); gifts received, $16,697; expenditures, $12,314; qualifying distributions, $12,200.
Limitations: Applications not accepted.
Application information: Contributes only to pre-selected organizations.
Officers: Lawrence S. Hendricks, Pres.; Sharon E. Hendricks, Secy.-Treas.; Michael Pecchia, Secy.
EIN: 341884896

43932
The Fortview Foundation
36 E. 4th St., Ste. 905
Cincinnati, OH 45202 (513) 651-1110
Contact: Richard L. Westheimer

Established in 2000 in OH.
Donor(s): Duffie Westheimer, Mary Helen Westheimer, Thomas Westheimer, William Westheimer.
Financial data (yr. ended 07/31/01): Grants paid, $12,176; assets, $443,075 (M); gifts received, $483,312; expenditures, $24,191; qualifying distributions, $12,176.
Limitations: Giving on a national basis, with emphasis on AZ, NH, and NY.
Trustees: Duffie Westheimer, John R. Westheimer, Mary Helen Westheimer, Thomas Westheimer, William Westheimer.
EIN: 311747284

43933
Edith A. Langdale Scholarship Fund
c/o National City Bank of Pennsylvania
P.O. Box 94651
Cleveland, OH 44101-4651
Application address: c/o Guidance Office, Warren Area High School, 345 E. 5th Ave., Warren, PA 16365, tel.: (814) 723-5300

Financial data (yr. ended 08/31/01): Grants paid, $12,175; assets, $239,715 (M); expenditures, $14,807; qualifying distributions, $13,510.
Limitations: Giving limited to residents of the Warren, PA, area.
Application information: Application form required.
Trustee: National City Bank of Pennsylvania.
EIN: 256164317

43934
Dayton Ahepa Philanthropic Foundation
4601 Fayette Ct.
Dayton, OH 45415-3205

Financial data (yr. ended 12/31/01): Grants paid, $12,100; assets, $359,780 (M); expenditures, $17,290; qualifying distributions, $12,100.
Officers: Harry G. Lake, Pres.; Nick Protos, V.P.; Perry Kirbabas, Secy.
EIN: 311329939

43935
The Printing Industries Education Fund, Inc.
(Formerly Printing Industry Scholarship Fund)
P.O. Box 819
Westerville, OH 43086-0819 (614) 794-2300
Contact: William L. Stickney, Tr.

Financial data (yr. ended 12/31/01): Grants paid, $12,100; assets, $334,378 (M); gifts received, $104,531; expenditures, $12,100; qualifying distributions, $12,100.
Limitations: Giving limited to residents of Columbus, OH.
Application information: Personal interview required.
Trustees: Don Campbell, William L. Stickney, Don Watkins.
EIN: 311020921

43936
Richard Vasak Memorial Trust
c/o KeyBank, N.A.
800 Superior Ave., 4th Fl.
Cleveland, OH 44114

Financial data (yr. ended 12/31/99): Grants paid, $12,080; assets, $304,260 (M); expenditures, $15,819; qualifying distributions, $12,302.
Limitations: Applications not accepted. Giving limited to Ashton, ID.
Application information: Contributes only to pre-selected organizations.
Trustee: KeyBank, N.A.
EIN: 826063361

43937
Shenk Family Foundation
27705 W. Chester Pkwy.
Westlake, OH 44145
Application address: c/o Lancaster Institute for Health Education, 143 E. Lemon St., Lancaster, PA 17602

Donor(s): F. Paul Shenk.
Financial data (yr. ended 12/31/01): Grants paid, $12,050; assets, $210,415 (M); expenditures, $13,599; qualifying distributions, $11,999.
Limitations: Giving primarily in Lancaster, PA.
Application information: Application form required.
Officer: F. Paul Shenk, Pres.
Directors: Carol Gress, Paul Gress, A. Ruth Shenk.
EIN: 341930425

43938
The Fred J. Heigel Foundation
2850 Firelands Blvd.
P.O. Box 261
Port Clinton, OH 43452-0261 (419) 797-2090
Contact: Vicki N. Heigel, Pres.

Established in 1994 in OH.
Donor(s): Vicki N. Heigel.
Financial data (yr. ended 12/31/01): Grants paid, $12,039; assets, $292,585 (M); expenditures, $13,958; qualifying distributions, $12,039.
Limitations: Giving limited to Ottawa County, OH, with emphasis on Port Clinton.
Application information: Application form not required.
Officers: Vicki N. Heigel, Pres. and Treas.; Jennifer Heigel, V.P. and Secy.; Jonathan Heigel, V.P. and Treas.
EIN: 341782057

43939
Don Conrad Family Scholarship Trust
c/o The Huntington National Bank
P.O. Box 1558
Columbus, OH 43216

Established in 1997 in KY.
Donor(s): Don Conrad.
Financial data (yr. ended 12/31/01): Grants paid, $12,000; assets, $448,665 (M); expenditures, $19,213; qualifying distributions, $12,000.
Limitations: Applications not accepted.
Application information: Contributes only to pre-selected organizations.
Trustee: The Huntington National Bank.

OHIO—43951

EIN: 311538763

43940
Edna & Harvey Eagle Scholarship Trust
c/o U.S. Bank
P.O. Box 1118
Cincinnati, OH 45201
Contact: William Klenk, Trust Off., U.S. Bank

Established in 1996 in OH.
Financial data (yr. ended 09/30/01): Grants paid, $12,000; assets, $210,707 (M); expenditures, $16,065; qualifying distributions, $12,113.
Limitations: Giving limited to Columbus, OH.
Application information: Application form required.
Trustees: Edward Whipps, U.S. Bank.
EIN: 316546256
Codes: GTI

43941
Nils and Janet Johnson Foundation, Inc.
12 W. Main St.
Canfield, OH 44406

Established in 1997 in OH.
Donor(s): Janet Johnson, Nils P. Johnson.
Financial data (yr. ended 12/31/00): Grants paid, $12,000; assets, $354,602 (M); expenditures, $12,222; qualifying distributions, $12,000.
Limitations: Applications not accepted.
Application information: Contributes only to pre-selected organizations.
Officers: Eric C. Johnson, Pres.; Rebecca J. Heikkinen, Secy.; Nils P. Johnson, Jr., Treas.
EIN: 311531914

43942
Joya Charitable Foundation
c/o Michael Oestreicher
312 Walnut St., Ste. 1400
Cincinnati, OH 45202

Established in 1997 in OH.
Donor(s): Gary Ross.
Financial data (yr. ended 06/30/01): Grants paid, $12,000; assets, $267,273 (M); gifts received, $40,000; expenditures, $15,048; qualifying distributions, $13,911.
Limitations: Applications not accepted.
Application information: Contributes only to pre-selected organizations.
Officers and Trustees:* Michael R. Oestreicher,* Pres.; Ed Ross,* Secy. and Treas.; Molly Ross.
EIN: 311585984

43943
Leslie Scholarship Fund
c/o Wells Fargo Bank Ohio, N.A.
114 E. Main St.
Van Wert, OH 45891
Application address: c/o Van Wert City Schools, Van Wert, OH 45891
Contact: Steve Farnsworth

Financial data (yr. ended 07/31/00): Grants paid, $12,000; assets, $279,869 (M); gifts received, $4,150; expenditures, $14,922; qualifying distributions, $11,392.
Limitations: Giving primarily in OH.
Application information: Application form required.
Trustee: Wells Fargo Bank Indiana, N.A.
EIN: 346566216

43944
John R. & Jean D. McClester Charitable Foundation
c/o National City Bank of Pennsylvania
P.O. Box 94651
Cleveland, OH 44101-4651
Application address: c/o William M. Schmidt, National City Bank of PA, 20 Stanwix St., Pittsburgh, PA 15222, tel.: (412) 644-8332

Established in 1998 in PA.
Donor(s): Jean D. McClester.
Financial data (yr. ended 12/31/01): Grants paid, $12,000; assets, $253,143 (M); expenditures, $14,373; qualifying distributions, $12,000.
Limitations: Giving primarily in PA.
Trustee: National City Bank of Pennsylvania.
EIN: 256579609

43945
MCD Foundation
John D. McDonald & Margaret O. Cottee
265 Glengarry Dr.
Aurora, OH 44202-8582

Established in 1990 in OH.
Donor(s): John G. McDonald, Mrs. John McDonald.
Financial data (yr. ended 11/30/01): Grants paid, $12,000; assets, $102,053 (M); expenditures, $13,000; qualifying distributions, $12,000.
Limitations: Giving primarily in Cleveland, OH.
Officers: John G. McDonald, Pres.; Margaret O. McDonald, V.P.
EIN: 341661960

43946
Gilbert and Evelyn Nolley Educational Scholarship Fund
c/o KeyBank, N.A., Trust Div.
800 Superior Ave., 4th Fl.
Cleveland, OH 44114
Application address: P.O. Box 9950, Canton, OH 44711-0950, tel.: (330) 489-5422
Contact: Brian Cherkala, Trust Off., KeyBank, N.A.

Financial data (yr. ended 12/31/00): Grants paid, $12,000; assets, $220,329 (M); expenditures, $15,516; qualifying distributions, $12,608.
Limitations: Giving limited to residents of Manchester, OH.
Trustee: KeyBank, N.A.
EIN: 346981666
Codes: GTI

43947
Willis H. Park Technical Student Fund
c/o National City Bank
P.O. Box 94651
Cleveland, OH 44101-4651
Application address: P.O. Box 450, Youngstwon, OH 44501, tel.: (330) 742-4289
Contact: Myra Vitto, Trust Off., National City Bank

Financial data (yr. ended 12/31/01): Grants paid, $12,000; assets, $116,735 (M); expenditures, $12,989; qualifying distributions, $12,433.
Limitations: Giving limited to residents of Youngstown, OH.
Application information: Application form required.
Trustee: National City Bank.
EIN: 346515519
Codes: GTI

43948
The Alexander Shashaty Family Foundation, Inc.
c/o Alexander Shashaty
41562 Lodge Rd.
Leetonia, OH 44431

Established in 1993 in OH.
Financial data (yr. ended 12/31/00): Grants paid, $12,000; assets, $234,345 (M); expenditures, $14,400; qualifying distributions, $12,000.
Limitations: Applications not accepted. Giving primarily in Youngstown, OH.
Application information: Contributes only to pre-selected organizations.
Officers: Alexander Shashaty, Pres.; Mildred Shashaty, V.P.; Yolanda Shashaty, Secy.-Treas.
EIN: 341667193

43949
W. E. Smith Family Charitable Trust Fund
c/o First Financial Bank
300 High St.
Hamilton, OH 45011 (513) 867-4818
Contact: Dennis G. Walsh, Tr.

Established in 1997 in OH.
Donor(s): Joseph W. Smith.
Financial data (yr. ended 12/31/01): Grants paid, $12,000; assets, $208,581 (M); gifts received, $10,200; expenditures, $15,859; qualifying distributions, $12,933.
Limitations: Giving limited to OH.
Application information: Application form required.
Trustees: Dennis G. Walsh, First Financial Bank.
EIN: 311438321

43950
The Tim and Joni Woofter Family Foundation
8845 State Rd. N.E.
Kinsman, OH 44428

Established in 1999 in OH.
Financial data (yr. ended 12/31/01): Grants paid, $12,000; assets, $331,749 (M); gifts received, $120,387; expenditures, $12,237; qualifying distributions, $12,000.
Limitations: Applications not accepted. Giving primarily in OH.
Application information: Contributes only to pre-selected organizations.
Trustees: Richard A. Pachuck, Joni Woofter, Timothy Woofter.
EIN: 341892080

43951
Claire Adair Hendrickson Foundation, Inc.
c/o U.S. Bank
P.O. Box 1118
Cincinnati, OH 45202-1118

Established in 1999 in OH.
Donor(s): Douglas A. Hendrickson, Kathryn B. Hendrickson.
Financial data (yr. ended 12/31/01): Grants paid, $11,965; assets, $536,962 (M); gifts received, $88,203; expenditures, $18,377; qualifying distributions, $11,965.
Limitations: Giving primarily in Maysville, KY.
Officers and Trustees:* Douglas A. Hendrickson,* Pres.; Janet L. Houston,* Secy.; James A. McNeal,* Treas.
EIN: 311677017

43952
Walter E. & Mary C. Beyer Fund
c/o National City Bank of Indiana
P.O. Box 94651
Cleveland, OH 44101-4651

Financial data (yr. ended 12/31/01): Grants paid, $11,937; assets, $345,876 (M); expenditures, $25,117; qualifying distributions, $11,937.
Limitations: Applications not accepted. Giving primarily in IN.
Application information: Contributes only to pre-selected organizations.
Trustee: National City Bank of Indiana.
EIN: 311018088

43953
Ambrose Middleton Trust
c/o KeyBank, N.A.
800 Superior Ave., 4th Fl.
Cleveland, OH 44114
Application address: c/o Distrib. Comm., First National Bank, McConnellsville, OH 43756, tel.: (614) 962-3911
Contact: Billy T. White

Established in 1984 in OH.
Financial data (yr. ended 08/31/01): Grants paid, $11,910; assets, $301,099 (M); expenditures, $13,320; qualifying distributions, $11,646.
Limitations: Giving limited to Morgan County, OH.
Application information: Application form not required.
Trustee: KeyBank, N.A.
EIN: 346513420
Codes: GTI

43954
Thomas S. & Mildred Dougherty Foundation
c/o KeyBank, N.A.
800 Superior Ave., 4th Fl.
Cleveland, OH 44114

Financial data (yr. ended 12/31/01): Grants paid, $11,803; assets, $449,479 (M); expenditures, $19,347; qualifying distributions, $12,706.
Limitations: Applications not accepted.
Application information: Contributes only to pre-selected organizations.
Trustees: Andrew S. Hanna, Marcus A. Hanna, KeyBank, N.A.
EIN: 346507206

43955
Anderson-Huffman Scholarship
c/o National City Bank of Indiana
P.O. Box 94651
Cleveland, OH 44101-4651

Financial data (yr. ended 12/31/99): Grants paid, $11,750; assets, $221,966 (M); expenditures, $13,840; qualifying distributions, $12,370.
Limitations: Applications not accepted. Giving primarily in IN.
Trustee: National City Bank of Indiana.
EIN: 356599183

43956
William H. Koptis, Jr. Christian Foundation, Inc.
9150 S. Hills Blvd.
Broadview Heights, OH 44147-3506
(440) 526-2525

Established in 1988 in OH.
Donor(s): William H. Koptis.
Financial data (yr. ended 12/31/01): Grants paid, $11,710; assets, $195,132 (M); gifts received, $12,160; expenditures, $12,374; qualifying distributions, $11,710.
Officers and Trustees:* William H. Koptis,* Pres.; Ruth D. Koptis,* V.P.; Gail Tanner, Secy.; Ray Culbertson, Karen Koptis, Marylee Koptis-Urman, Gail Tanner.
EIN: 341408058

43957
The Irving and Gloria Fine Foundation
38500 Chagrin Blvd.
Chagrin Falls, OH 44022

Established in 1994 in OH.
Donor(s): Irving Fine.
Financial data (yr. ended 12/31/01): Grants paid, $11,660; assets, $900,305 (M); gifts received, $400,825; expenditures, $16,262; qualifying distributions, $11,660.
Limitations: Applications not accepted. Giving primarily in Cleveland, OH.
Application information: Contributes only to pre-selected organizations.
Trustees: Gloria Fine, Irving Fine.
EIN: 341785414

43958
Ferndale Foundation, Inc.
P.O. Box 3906
Boardman, OH 44512

Established in 2001 in OH.
Financial data (yr. ended 12/31/01): Grants paid, $11,656; assets, $155,558 (M); gifts received, $33,662; expenditures, $13,537; qualifying distributions, $11,656.
Officer: H. William Trigg, Pres.
EIN: 341953950

43959
Anna Marie & Russel Waldron Scholarship Fund
c/o The Huntington National Bank
P.O. Box 1558, HC1012
Columbus, OH 43216

Established in 1994 in OH.
Financial data (yr. ended 06/30/00): Grants paid, $11,631; assets, $229,772 (M); expenditures, $16,269; qualifying distributions, $12,256.
Limitations: Giving limited to residents of OH.
Application information: Application form not required.
Advisory Committee Members: Barbara Coolhan, Michael Grote, James P. Peterson.
Trustee: The Huntington National Bank.
EIN: 311415607

43960
Harry A. Winter Family Foundation
National City Bank
P.O. Box 94651
Cleveland, OH 44101-4651
Application address: 4000 Logangate, Apt. 30, Youngstown, OH 44505, tel: (330) 759 8515
Contact: Harrold A. Winter, Advisory Member

Established in 1992 in OH.
Donor(s): Harold A. Winter.
Financial data (yr. ended 07/31/01): Grants paid, $11,621; assets, $7,217 (M); gifts received, $11,000; expenditures, $12,857; qualifying distributions, $12,146.
Limitations: Giving primarily in OH; some giving also in Jerusalem, Israel.
Application information: Application form required.
Advisory Committee: Harold A. Winter, Jerold L. Winter.
Trustee: National City Bank.
EIN: 346973688
Codes: GTI

43961
Adams Charitable Trust
95 Highmeadows Cir.
Powell, OH 43065-9432

Established in 1998 in OH.
Donor(s): Adams Asset Management Co.
Financial data (yr. ended 12/31/01): Grants paid, $11,612; assets, $11,338 (M); gifts received, $10,500; expenditures, $11,612; qualifying distributions, $11,588.
Limitations: Applications not accepted. Giving primarily in OH.
Application information: Contributes only to pre-selected organizations.
Directors: Cindi Adams, William Adams.
EIN: 367089752
Codes: CS, CD

43962
Lerner Family Foundation
c/o H. Jerome Lerner
7149 Knoll Rd.
Cincinnati, OH 45237

Established in 1995 in OH.
Donor(s): H. Jerome Lerner, Minna K. Lerner.
Financial data (yr. ended 01/31/02): Grants paid, $11,580; assets, $253,923 (M); gifts received, $6,189; expenditures, $11,894; qualifying distributions, $11,580.
Limitations: Applications not accepted. Giving primarily in OH.
Application information: Contributes only to pre-selected organizations.
Officers: H. Jerome Lerner, Pres. and Treas.; Minna K. Lerner, V.P. and Secy.; Andrew M. Lerner, V.P.; Julie S. Lerner, V.P.; Karen B. Lerner, V.P.
EIN: 311450170

43963
Carlton B. & Gail R. Coen Family Foundation
P.O. Box 9022
Canton, OH 44711-9022

Donor(s): Members of the Coen family, Coen Oil Co.
Financial data (yr. ended 12/31/01): Grants paid, $11,538; assets, $126,825 (M); expenditures, $14,852; qualifying distributions, $11,538.
Limitations: Applications not accepted. Giving primarily in Canton, OH.
Application information: Contributes only to pre-selected organizations.
Trustees: Donald C. Coen, Gail R. Coen, Jeanne B. Coen.
EIN: 346574575

43964
Jeanne Souers Garcia Foundation
c/o The Huntington National Bank
P.O. Box 1558, HC-0534
Columbus, OH 43216
Application address: 405 Chauncey Ave. N.W., New Philadelphia, OH 44663-1232

Established in 1994 in OH.
Financial data (yr. ended 06/30/02): Grants paid, $11,525; assets, $162,950 (M); expenditures, $13,863; qualifying distributions, $11,525.
Limitations: Giving limited to Tuscarawas County, OH.
Application information: Application form not required.
Trustee: The Huntington National Bank.
Advisory Committee: William Kyler, Wilford Miller, James Pringle.
EIN: 316496563

43965
Bocholt Foundation, Inc.
95 Elmwood Dr.
Versailles, OH 45380
Contact: Mitchell Eiting, Pres.

Established in 1990 in OH.
Donor(s): James Eiting, Esther Eiting.
Financial data (yr. ended 12/31/01): Grants paid, $11,508; assets, $273,195 (M); gifts received, $46,721; expenditures, $14,592; qualifying distributions, $11,508.
Limitations: Giving primarily in OH.
Officers: Mitchell Eiting, Pres.; Anne Eiting, V.P. and Treas.; Polly Grow, Secy.
EIN: 311313755

43966
The Banks Baldwin Foundation
P.O. Box 18678
Cleveland Heights, OH 44118
Contact: P. Jeffrey Lucier, Pres.

Established in 1994 in OH.
Donor(s): P. Jeffrey Lucier.
Financial data (yr. ended 12/31/00): Grants paid, $11,500; assets, $26,579 (M); expenditures, $13,990; qualifying distributions, $11,500.
Limitations: Giving limited to OH, primarily Cleveland.
Application information: Application form not required.
Officers: P. Jeffrey Lucier, Pres.; Craig W. Fraser, V.P.; Ronald C. Allan, Secy.
Trustees: W.H. Drane, Richard P. Stovsky.
EIN: 344006013

43967
Standard Steel Specialty Company Foundation
c/o National City Bank
P.O. Box 94651
Cleveland, OH 44101-4651
Application address: R.E. Conley, c/o Standard Steel Specialty Co., P.O. Box 20, Beaver Falls, PA 15010

Donor(s): Standard Steel Specialty Co.
Financial data (yr. ended 12/31/01): Grants paid, $11,500; assets, $77,429 (M); expenditures, $12,478; qualifying distributions, $11,950.
Limitations: Giving primarily in Beaver Falls and Monaca, PA, and Spartanburg, SC.
Application information: Application form not required.
Trustee: National City Bank.
EIN: 256038268
Codes: CS, CD

43968
Michael and Pearl Summerfield Charitable Trust
5910 Landerbrook Dr., Ste. 200
Cleveland, OH 44124 (440) 446-1100
Contact: Karen Shoss, Tr.

Established in 2000 in OH.
Financial data (yr. ended 12/31/01): Grants paid, $11,500; assets, $225,443 (M); gifts received, $87,508; expenditures, $14,608; qualifying distributions, $11,500.
Limitations: Giving primarily in Denver, CO and Houston, TX.
Trustees: Irwin J. Dinn, Karen Shoss.
EIN: 347119869

43969
The Whiston Foundation
231 N. Main St.
Mount Gilead, OH 43338-1114
Contact: Howard E. Whiston, Pres.

Donor(s): Howard E. Whiston.
Financial data (yr. ended 12/31/01): Grants paid, $11,486; assets, $266,703 (M); gifts received, $7,600; expenditures, $12,589; qualifying distributions, $11,486.
Limitations: Giving limited to Morrow County, OH.
Application information: Application form not required.
Officers: Howard E. Whiston, Pres.; Thomas E. Whiston, V.P.; Pauline M. Whiston, Secy.-Treas.
EIN: 316035458

43970
Rhineland Foundation
(Formerly Consolidated Graphic Foundation, Inc.)
443 Morgan St.
Cincinnati, OH 45206-2391

Financial data (yr. ended 10/31/01): Grants paid, $11,275; assets, $144,273 (M); expenditures, $12,178; qualifying distributions, $11,275.
Limitations: Applications not accepted. Giving limited to KY and OH.
Application information: Contributes only to pre-selected organizations.
Officers: John W. Steinman, Pres.; John W. Steinman III, V.P.; Joyce L. Steinman, Secy.; Steven C. Steinman, Treas.
EIN: 316034433

43971
The Huttenbauer Foundation, Inc.
44 Eswin Dr., Ste. A
Cincinnati, OH 45218-1402

Donor(s): Samuel Huttenbauer, Sr.‡
Financial data (yr. ended 12/31/01): Grants paid, $11,260; assets, $111,973 (M); expenditures, $17,902; qualifying distributions, $11,260.
Limitations: Applications not accepted. Giving primarily in Cincinnati, OH.
Application information: Contributes only to pre-selected organizations.
Officers: Samuel Huttenbauer, Jr., Pres.; Rita Ritter, Secy.-Treas.
EIN: 316026188

43972
Betty J. Blower Trust
c/o J.B. Yanity, Jr.
P.O. Box 748
Athens, OH 45701

Financial data (yr. ended 08/31/01): Grants paid, $11,200; assets, $206,087 (L); expenditures, $14,427; qualifying distributions, $11,070.
Limitations: Applications not accepted. Giving primarily in Gloucester, OH.
Application information: Contributes only to pre-selected organizations.
Trustee: J.B. Yanity, Jr.
EIN: 316368267

43973
Loretta Mae Hausmann Holmes Foundation
12025 Wintergreen Dr.
Chardon, OH 44024

Established in 2000 in OH.
Donor(s): Loretta Mae Hausmann Holmes.
Financial data (yr. ended 12/31/01): Grants paid, $11,142; assets, $193,913 (M); expenditures, $16,645; qualifying distributions, $11,142.
Limitations: Applications not accepted. Giving limited to OH.
Application information: Contributes only to pre-selected organizations.
Trustee: Loretta Mae Holmes.
EIN: 347113218

43974
The Baruth Charitable Trust
12674 Moss Pt. Rd.
Strongsville, OH 44136-3507

Established in 1996 in OH.
Donor(s): Baruth Asset Management.
Financial data (yr. ended 12/31/00): Grants paid, $11,040; assets, $1,052 (L); gifts received, $11,465; expenditures, $11,592; qualifying distributions, $11,040.
Trustees: Jain E. Baruth, John J. Baruth.
EIN: 341832399

43975
Sara M. Leki Trust
c/o National City Bank
P.O. Box 94651
Cleveland, OH 44101-4651

Established in 1999 in MI.
Financial data (yr. ended 12/31/01): Grants paid, $11,019; assets, $426,545 (M); expenditures, $15,079; qualifying distributions, $11,019.
Limitations: Applications not accepted. Giving primarily in MI.
Application information: Contributes only to pre-selected organizations.
Trustee: National City Bank.
EIN: 386703010

43976
Cohen Community Foundation
1300 E. 9th St.
Cleveland, OH 44114
Contact: Ronald B. Cohen, Chair. and Tr.

Established in 1999 in OH.
Financial data (yr. ended 12/31/01): Grants paid, $11,000; assets, $43,033 (M); gifts received, $5,745; expenditures, $11,285; qualifying distributions, $10,979.
Officers and Trustees:* Ronald B. Cohen,* Chair.; Randall S. Myeroff,* Pres.; Philip R. Light,* Secy.-Treas.; Henry C. Doll.
EIN: 341896053

43977
Linda M. Dunbar Charitable Foundation
88 N. 5th St.
Columbus, OH 43215

Established in 1995.
Donor(s): Linda Dunbar.
Financial data (yr. ended 06/30/00): Grants paid, $11,000; assets, $1,381,735 (M); gifts received, $1,500,000; expenditures, $148,680; qualifying distributions, $124,510; giving activities include $108,962 for programs.
Limitations: Applications not accepted.
Application information: Contributes only to pre-selected organizations.
Trustees: Jim Albers, Linda Dunbar.
EIN: 311449871

43978
Francies Scholarship Fund
c/o Bank One Trust Co., N.A.
774 Park Meadow Rd.
Westerville, OH 43081
Application address: 50 S. Main St., Akron, OH 44308, tel.: (216) 972-1594
Contact: Delores Dukes, Admin., Bank One Trust Co., N.A.

Established in 1991 in OH.
Financial data (yr. ended 04/30/00): Grants paid, $11,000; assets, $257,589 (M); expenditures, $17,497; qualifying distributions, $11,374.
Limitations: Giving primarily in OH.

43978—OHIO

Application information: Application form not required.
Trustee: Bank One Trust Co., N.A.
EIN: 316415216

43979
Geisen-Scheper Charitable Foundation
c/o U.S. Bank
P.O. Box 1118
Cincinnati, OH 45201

Established in 1997 in KY and OH.
Financial data (yr. ended 12/31/01): Grants paid, $11,000; assets, $174,747 (M); expenditures, $11,939; qualifying distributions, $11,000.
Limitations: Applications not accepted. Giving primarily in KY.
Application information: Contributes only to pre-selected organizations.
Directors: Scott Grosser, Charles R. Scheper, Julie Geisen Scheper.
Trustee: U.S. Bank.
EIN: 311532441

43980
Haag Foundation
c/o John A. Haag
41 Industry Rd.
Tallmadge, OH 44278

Established in 1998 in OH.
Donor(s): John A. Haag.
Financial data (yr. ended 12/31/01): Grants paid, $11,000; assets, $199,535 (M); expenditures, $12,589; qualifying distributions, $11,000.
Limitations: Giving primarily in OH.
Officers: John A. Haag, Pres.; Ann M. Haag, V.P.; Kathleen A. Edwards, Secy.
EIN: 341852785

43981
KS Foundation
5453 E. Blvd. N.W.
Canton, OH 44718

Established in 1997 in OH.
Donor(s): J. Kevin Ramsey.
Financial data (yr. ended 04/30/02): Grants paid, $11,000; assets, $187,566 (M); gifts received, $13,289; expenditures, $13,579; qualifying distributions, $11,000.
Limitations: Applications not accepted.
Application information: Contributes only to pre-selected organizations.
Trustees: J. Kevin Ramsey, Shirley M. Ramsey.
EIN: 316564245

43982
The Ernest & Maxine Wingett Memorial Education Trust
P.O. Box 78
Syracuse, OH 45779-0078
Contact: Robert Wingett, Tr.

Established in 1991; funded in fiscal 1993.
Donor(s): Ernest Wingett.
Financial data (yr. ended 06/30/01): Grants paid, $11,000; assets, $232,013 (M); gifts received, $9,464; expenditures, $13,397; qualifying distributions, $11,000.
Limitations: Giving limited to residents of OH.
Application information: Application form required.
Directors: Fred W. Crow III, A.E. Lee, Douglas Little, Robert Wingett.
EIN: 316411166
Codes: GTI

43983
Dr. L. G. Wisner & Winfred T. Wisner Scholarship Trust Fund
c/o National City Bank
P.O. Box 94651
Cleveland, OH 44101-4651
Application address: c/o Wisner Selection Board, Herscher C.U.S.D. No. 2 Office, P.O. Box 504, Herscher, IL 60941-0504

Established in 1996 in MI.
Donor(s): Winifred T. Wisner.‡
Financial data (yr. ended 04/30/00): Grants paid, $11,000; assets, $221,656 (M); expenditures, $13,056; qualifying distributions, $11,990.
Application information: Application form required.
Trustee: National City Bank.
EIN: 366872997
Codes: GTI

43984
George S. Case, Jr. Family Charitable Trust
2847 Broxton Rd.
Shaker Heights, OH 44120

Financial data (yr. ended 12/31/01): Grants paid, $10,970; assets, $116,584 (M); expenditures, $11,664; qualifying distributions, $10,970.
Limitations: Applications not accepted. Giving primarily in OH.
Application information: Contributes only to pre-selected organizations.
Trustee: Lucien H. Case.
EIN: 346527421

43985
William & Antonia Frank Foundation, Inc.
c/o William H. Frank
1695 Acreview Dr.
Cincinnati, OH 45240-3409

Established in 1997 in OH.
Financial data (yr. ended 12/31/01): Grants paid, $10,929; assets, $193,144 (M); expenditures, $19,280; qualifying distributions, $10,929.
Limitations: Giving primarily in Cincinnati, OH.
Trustees: Georgeanne Bender, James P. Frank, Thomas R. Frank, William H. Frank.
EIN: 311582089

43986
Sandusky County Bar Association
211 S. Park Ave.
Fremont, OH 43420
Application address: c/o Barry Luse, Trust Off., Croghan Colonial Bank, 323 Croghan St., Fremont, OH 43420, tel.: (419) 332-7301

Established in 1998 in OH.
Financial data (yr. ended 10/31/00): Grants paid, $10,920; assets, $225,123 (M); expenditures, $11,930; qualifying distributions, $11,930.
Limitations: Giving primarily in Sandusky, OH.
Application information: Application form required.
Trustees: William R. Bowlus, C. Wesley Bristley, Nancy Haley, Jon M. Ickes, John L. Zinkand.
EIN: 341894555

43987
Almeda Leake Toomey Trust f/b/o Dover High School & Central Catholic High School
P.O. Box 1558, Ste. HC1012
Columbus, OH 43216
Application address: c/o The Huntington National Bank, 41 S. High St., Columbus, OH 43215, tel.: (614) 480-0030

Established in 1999 in OH.
Financial data (yr. ended 06/30/00): Grants paid, $10,800; assets, $319,612 (M); gifts received, $246,857; expenditures, $12,565; qualifying distributions, $11,241.
Limitations: Applications not accepted. Giving limited to OH.
Application information: Contributes only to pre-selected organizations.
Trustee: The Huntington National Bank.
EIN: 316630558

43988
Z/G Foundation
c/o A.B. Glickman
17051 Shaker Blvd.
Shaker Heights, OH 44120

Established in 1999 in OH.
Donor(s): A.B. Glickman, Joyce S. Glickman.
Financial data (yr. ended 12/31/01): Grants paid, $10,750; assets, $145,455 (M); expenditures, $14,006; qualifying distributions, $10,750.
Limitations: Applications not accepted. Giving primarily in OH.
Application information: Contributes only to pre-selected organizations.
Officer: Joyce S. Glickman, Pres.
Trustees: Andrea J. Glickman, Matthew N. Glickman, Samantha L. Glickman.
EIN: 341906964

43989
The Hermes Foundation
13600 Shaker Blvd., Ste. 802
Cleveland, OH 44120-1571 (216) 751-1100
Contact: Eric J. Nilson, Tr.

Established in 1990 in OH.
Donor(s): Eric J. Nilson.
Financial data (yr. ended 12/31/01): Grants paid, $10,645; assets, $146,254 (M); gifts received, $18,046; expenditures, $12,136; qualifying distributions, $10,645.
Limitations: Giving primarily in Cleveland, OH.
Trustees: Jeffrey Mostade, Eric J. Nilson.
EIN: 346930405

43990
Alfred A. Moore Foundation
3000 Carew Tower
Cincinnati, OH 45202-2803

Donor(s): Alfred A. Moore.
Financial data (yr. ended 05/31/02): Grants paid, $10,561; assets, $576 (M); gifts received, $11,000; expenditures, $10,694; qualifying distributions, $10,561.
Limitations: Applications not accepted. Giving primarily in Cincinnati, OH.
Application information: Contributes only to pre-selected organizations.
Trustees: Janice R. Johnson, Alfred A. Moore, Betty Moore.
EIN: 316049604

43991
The Martino Family Foundation
37067 Shaker Blvd.
Hunting Valley, OH 44022
Contact: Mary Ann Martino, Pres.

Established in 1997 in OH.
Financial data (yr. ended 12/31/01): Grants paid, $10,550; assets, $19,467 (M); gifts received, $7,004; expenditures, $10,554; qualifying distributions, $10,550.
Officers: Mary Ann Martino, Pres.; Lana Martino, Secy.; Robert J. Martino, Treas.
EIN: 311494280

43992
Huenefeld Family Endowment Fund
c/o Fifth Third Bank
38 Fountain Sq. Plz., Dept. 00858
Cincinnati, OH 45263

Established in 1990 in OH.
Donor(s): Clara M. Huenefeld.‡
Financial data (yr. ended 09/30/01): Grants paid, $10,531; assets, $177,026 (M); expenditures, $13,243; qualifying distributions, $11,266.
Limitations: Applications not accepted. Giving primarily in Cincinnati, OH.
Application information: Contributes only to pre-selected organizations.
Trustee: Fifth Third Bank.
EIN: 316391898

43993
John G. Ozanich Crippled and Burned Children's Scholarship Fund Charitable Foundation
c/o Sky Trust, N.A.
P.O. Box 479
Youngstown, OH 44501-0479
Application address: c/o Dickey Electric, 180 W. South Range Rd., North Lima, OH 44452-9578
Contact: Joseph Dickey, Dir.

Established in 1989 in OH.
Donor(s): John G. Ozanich.‡
Financial data (yr. ended 12/31/01): Grants paid, $10,528; assets, $94,026 (M); expenditures, $12,400; qualifying distributions, $10,528.
Limitations: Giving limited to Cincinnati, OH, and Erie, PA.
Directors: David Collins, Joseph Dickey.
Trustee: Sky Trust, N.A.
EIN: 346851444

43994
The Benson Family Foundation
Gemini Tower I
1991 Crocker Rd., Ste. 430
Westlake, OH 44145

Established in 1996 in OH.
Donor(s): Michael D. Benson.
Financial data (yr. ended 12/31/01): Grants paid, $10,500; assets, $32,465 (M); gifts received, $10,825; expenditures, $10,627; qualifying distributions, $10,500.
Limitations: Applications not accepted.
Application information: Contributes only to pre-selected organizations.
Officers: Michael D. Benson, Pres.; Shirley J. Benson, Secy.-Treas.
EIN: 341847664

43995
The Byers Charitable Trust
c/o George Byers Sons, Inc.
390 E. Broad St.
Columbus, OH 43215 (614) 228-5111
Contact: Beth Sells

Established in 1986 in OH.
Financial data (yr. ended 12/31/01): Grants paid, $10,500; assets, $467,979 (M); expenditures, $14,446; qualifying distributions, $10,500.
Limitations: Giving primarily in Columbus, OH.
Application information: Application form required.
Trustee: The Huntington National Bank.
EIN: 316291142

43996
Grace W. Goodridge Trust f/b/o John Williams Scholarship
c/o National City Bank
P.O. Box 94651
Cleveland, OH 44101-4651
Application address: c/o Principal or Guidance Counselor, Struthers High School, 111 Euclid Ave., Struthers, OH 44471, tel.: (330) 750-1061

Established in 1985 in OH.
Financial data (yr. ended 06/30/01): Grants paid, $10,500; assets, $187,197 (M); expenditures, $11,734; qualifying distributions, $10,500.
Limitations: Giving limited to Struthers, OH.
Application information: Applications available at Struthers High School. Application form required.
Trustee: National City Bank.
EIN: 346838034

43997
Max and Jane Krantz Foundation
c/o Robert Klopper
400 E. 14th St., Box 469
Dover, OH 44622-1136

Established in 1994 in OH.
Donor(s): Max Krantz, Jane Krantz.
Financial data (yr. ended 12/31/00): Grants paid, $10,500; assets, $3,387 (M); gifts received, $100; expenditures, $11,868; qualifying distributions, $10,500.
Limitations: Applications not accepted. Giving primarily in OH.
Application information: Contributes only to pre-selected organizations.
Officers and Directors:* Max Krantz,* Chair.; Jane Krantz,* Vice-Chair.; Catherine Dindo, Robert Gorgas, Robert Klopper, John Ostapuck, Ben Smallridge.
EIN: 341757577

43998
The Dale E. & Bernice E. Mansperger Foundation, Inc.
23681 Effingham Blvd.
Euclid, OH 44117-2106
Contact: Dale E. Mansperger, Pres.

Donor(s): Dale E. Mansperger, Bernice E. Mansperger.
Financial data (yr. ended 12/31/01): Grants paid, $10,500; assets, $89,536 (M); expenditures, $11,436; qualifying distributions, $10,500.
Officers: Bernice E. Mansperger, V.P. and Treas.; Clare W. Mansperger, Secy.
EIN: 341262519

43999
Lily E. Drake Scholarship Trust
c/o KeyBank, N.A.
800 Superior Ave., 4th Fl.
Cleveland, OH 44114

Established in 1990 in OR.
Financial data (yr. ended 12/31/01): Grants paid, $10,477; assets, $248,894 (M); expenditures, $14,155; qualifying distributions, $11,330.
Limitations: Applications not accepted. Giving limited to female residents of OR.
Application information: Unsolicited requests for funds not accepted.
Trustee: KeyBank, N.A.
EIN: 936131516

44000
Searles Family Foundation
P.O. Box 818
Sylvania, OH 43560-0818

Established in 2000 in OH.
Donor(s): Edwards J. Searles.
Financial data (yr. ended 12/31/01): Grants paid, $10,474; assets, $773,455 (M); expenditures, $11,934; qualifying distributions, $10,474.
Limitations: Applications not accepted.
Application information: Contributes only to pre-selected organizations.
Officers and Trustees:* Edward J. Searles,* Pres.; William D. Searles,* V.P.; Richard G. Lavalley, Jr.,* Secy.-Treas.
EIN: 341915489

44001
L. Carl Bean Scholarship Fund
c/o KeyBank, N.A.
800 Superior Ave., 4th Fl.
Cleveland, OH 44114

Financial data (yr. ended 04/30/01): Grants paid, $10,400; assets, $282,071 (M); expenditures, $13,729; qualifying distributions, $10,400.
Limitations: Giving primarily in ME.
Application information: Unsolicited requests for funds not accepted.
Trustee: KeyBank, N.A.
EIN: 016068112

44002
Frank F. Bentley Trust
c/o KeyBank, N.A.
800 Superior Ave., 4th Fl.
Cleveland, OH 44114
Application address: c/o Joyce A. May, Turner & May, 800 Second National Bank Bldg., 108 Main Ave. S.W., Ste, 800, Warren, OH 44481, tel.: (330) 399-8801

Financial data (yr. ended 09/30/01): Grants paid, $10,375; assets, $368,212 (M); expenditures, $26,733; qualifying distributions, $15,491.
Limitations: Giving limited to Trumbull County, OH.
Application information: Application form not required.
Trustees: Nicholas Angelo, Clifford Johnson, Joyce A. May, KeyBank, N.A.
EIN: 346508762
Codes: GTI

44003
The Ann W. and Peter Williams Family Fund
1 Grandin Terr.
Cincinnati, OH 45208 (513) 871-1259
Contact: Ann W. Williams, Tr.

Established in 1999 in OH.
Donor(s): Ann W. Williams.
Financial data (yr. ended 07/31/01): Grants paid, $10,370; assets, $216,836 (M); expenditures, $11,120; qualifying distributions, $10,370.
Trustees: Ann W. Williams, Jennifer Williams, Peter Williams.
EIN: 311628724

44004
Jacob's Ladder
61 W. 2nd Ave., Ste. 201
Columbus, OH 43201 (614) 291-8247
Contact: Richard Jacob, Pres.

Established in 1995 in OH.
Financial data (yr. ended 12/31/01): Grants paid, $10,337; assets, $9,703 (M); gifts received, $16,700; expenditures, $11,022; qualifying distributions, $10,337.
Officer: Richard Jacob, Pres.
EIN: 311445365

44005
Frank R. "Bo" Dunlap Foundation, Inc.
4701 Hickory Bend Rd.
Circleville, OH 43113

Established in 1997 in OH.
Donor(s): Frank R. Dunlap.
Financial data (yr. ended 12/31/99): Grants paid, $10,303; assets, $837,586 (M); expenditures, $56,695; qualifying distributions, $10,303.
Limitations: Giving limited to Wayne and Union Township, OH.
Application information: Application form required.
Officers: Roger Davis, Pres.; Connie Kiser, Secy.; Frank R. Dunlap, Treas.
EIN: 311496488

44006
Josephine F. Rollman Charitable Remainder Trust
c/o Rollridge Farms
7680 Ridge Rd.
Cincinnati, OH 45237
Contact: Henry Rollman, II, Tr.

Established in 1989 in OH.
Financial data (yr. ended 12/31/00): Grants paid, $10,283; assets, $189,565 (M); expenditures, $10,419; qualifying distributions, $10,419.
Limitations: Giving primarily in Cincinnati, OH.
Application information: Application form not required.
Trustees: Joan Rollman Musekamp, Henry Rollman II.
EIN: 316249615

44007
The Berry Foundation
80 Farwood Dr.
Moreland Hills, OH 44022-6850

Established in 1997.
Financial data (yr. ended 12/31/01): Grants paid, $10,250; assets, $17,116 (M); gifts received, $15,500; expenditures, $10,279; qualifying distributions, $10,250.
Limitations: Applications not accepted. Giving on a national basis.
Application information: Contributes only to pre-selected organizations.
Trustees: Kathleen E. Berry, Philip C. Berry, Philip K. Berry.
EIN: 311538611

44008
Klink Charitable Trust
719 17th St. S.W.
Massillon, OH 44647-7401

Donor(s): Klink Asset Management Company, Timothy Klink.
Financial data (yr. ended 12/31/00): Grants paid, $10,145; assets, $0 (M); gifts received, $11,010; expenditures, $10,637; qualifying distributions, $10,145.
Limitations: Applications not accepted.
Application information: Contributes only to pre-selected organizations.
Trustees: Barbara Klink, Timothy Klink.
EIN: 341844928

44009
David-Edward-Margaret Davis Trust
c/o Fifth Third Bank
38 Fountain Sq. Plz.
Cincinnati, OH 45263

Financial data (yr. ended 09/30/01): Grants paid, $10,132; assets, $195,388 (M); expenditures, $14,367; qualifying distributions, $11,338.

Limitations: Applications not accepted. Giving limited to the Oak Hill, OH, area.
Application information: Contributes only to pre-selected organizations.
Trustee: Fifth Third Bank.
EIN: 316020260

44010
Carolyn Walker Scholarship Fund
c/o Sky Trust, N.A.
P.O. Box 479
Youngstown, OH 44501-0479
Application address: c/o Sky Bank, N.A., 6515 Tippecanoe Rd., Ste. B, Canfield, OH 44406

Established in 1998 in OH.
Donor(s): Carolyn Walker.
Financial data (yr. ended 12/31/00): Grants paid, $10,100; assets, $154,512 (M); expenditures, $12,482; qualifying distributions, $11,087.
Limitations: Giving primarily in Wheeling, OH.
Application information: Applicants must be graduating seniors of Wheeling Park High School who participated in sports. Application form not required.
Director: Bonnie Ritz.
Trustee: Sky Trust, N.A.
EIN: 347072088

44011
J. J. and F. M. Lutsch Memorial Fund
c/o National City Bank, Northeast
P.O. Box 94651
Cleveland, OH 44101-4651

Financial data (yr. ended 05/31/02): Grants paid, $10,074; assets, $313,663 (M); expenditures, $12,656; qualifying distributions, $10,074.
Limitations: Applications not accepted. Giving primarily in OH.
Application information: Contributes only to pre-selected organizations.
Trustee: National City Bank, Northeast.
EIN: 346997685

44012
Albers Family Foundation
7102 Knoll Rd.
Cincinnati, OH 45237 (513) 531-3512
Contact: Jennifer S. Albers, Tr.

Established in 2000 in OH.
Donor(s): Jennifer S. Albers, F. Gerard Albers.
Financial data (yr. ended 12/31/01): Grants paid, $10,000; assets, $155,586 (M); gifts received, $60,023; expenditures, $10,271; qualifying distributions, $9,025.
Limitations: Giving primarily in New York, NY and Cincinnati, OH.
Trustees: F. Gerard Albers, Jennifer S. Albers, Kathleen R. Mitts.
EIN: 311744357

44013
Anderson Family Foundation
10365 Pinecrest Rd.
Concord, OH 44077

Established in 1998 in OH.
Donor(s): Robert Anderson, Joanne Anderson.
Financial data (yr. ended 12/31/99): Grants paid, $10,000; assets, $418,016 (M); gifts received, $4,000; expenditures, $12,132; qualifying distributions, $21,815.
Limitations: Applications not accepted.
Application information: Contributes only to pre-selected organizations.
Officers and Trustee:* Robert L. Anderson,* Pres.; Douglas L. Anderson, V.P.; Cynthia L. Anderson, Secy.; Joanne L. Anderson, Treas.
EIN: 341877125

44014
The George and Millie Brown Family Foundation
3453 Mautz Yager Rd.
Marion, OH 43302

Established in 1988 in OH.
Financial data (yr. ended 12/31/00): Grants paid, $10,000; assets, $121 (L); gifts received, $10,110; expenditures, $10,150; qualifying distributions, $10,150.
Limitations: Applications not accepted. Giving primarily in Marion, OH.
Application information: Contributes only to pre-selected organizations.
Officers: Brooks Brown, Pres.; Catherine Ferguson, Secy.-Treas.
Trustees: Robert Ludwig, John McDaniel.
EIN: 311258061

44015
Dr. R. A. Gandy, Jr./Mercy Hospital Medical Staff, Inc. Scholarship Fund
2148 Evergreen Rd.
Toledo, OH 43606
Contact: Yvonne M. Gandy, Pres.

Established in 1997 in OH.
Donor(s): Yvonne M. Gandy.
Financial data (yr. ended 12/31/00): Grants paid, $10,000; assets, $131,801 (M); gifts received, $7,140; expenditures, $10,065; qualifying distributions, $9,874.
Limitations: Giving limited to Toledo, OH.
Application information: Application form required.
Officer: Yvonne M. Gandy, Pres.
Directors: Robyn A. Gandy, Roland A. Gandy III.
EIN: 311491102

44016
Thaddeus Garrett, Jr. Foundation
c/o Nicholas T. George
P.O. Box 1500
Akron, OH 44309-1500

Established in 2000 in OH.
Donor(s): Thaddeus A. Garrett, Jr.‡
Financial data (yr. ended 12/31/01): Grants paid, $10,000; assets, $706,112 (M); gifts received, $2,854; expenditures, $23,462; qualifying distributions, $10,000.
Limitations: Applications not accepted.
Application information: Contributes only to pre-selected organizations.
Trustees: Nicholas T. George, Thomas A. Haught, Constance E. Lykes.
EIN: 341898440

44017
The Gillespie Family Foundation
c/o KeyBank, N.A.
800 Superior Ave., 4th Fl.
Cleveland, OH 44114

Established in 1996 in OH.
Donor(s): Ann L. Gillespie, Robert W. Gillespie, Jr.
Financial data (yr. ended 12/31/01): Grants paid, $10,000; assets, $774,734 (M); gifts received, $312; expenditures, $16,854; qualifying distributions, $16,854.
Limitations: Applications not accepted. Giving primarily in Cleveland, OH.
Application information: Contributes only to pre-selected organizations.
Officers: Robert W. Gillespie, Jr., Chair.; Ann L. Gillespie, Secy.-Treas.
Trustees: Gwen E. Gillespie, Laura A. Gillespie.
Agent: KeyBank, N.A.
EIN: 041841679

44018
David N. Hall Foundation for Jazz
8200 Brill Rd.
Cincinnati, OH 45243 (513) 556-3557
Contact: Phillip A. Delong, Tr.

Established in 1998 in OH.
Donor(s): David N. Hall.
Financial data (yr. ended 12/31/01): Grants paid, $10,000; assets, $147,202 (M); expenditures, $11,782; qualifying distributions, $9,945.
Limitations: Giving primarily in Cincinnati, OH.
Trustees: Phillip A. DeGreg, David N. Hall, Douglas D. Thomson.
EIN: 311627805

44019
Jenbek Foundation
c/o Gradison McDonald Trust
580 Walnut St.
Cincinnati, OH 45202

Donor(s): Neil McElroy.‡
Financial data (yr. ended 12/31/01): Grants paid, $10,000; assets, $279,782 (M); expenditures, $15,165; qualifying distributions, $10,000.
Limitations: Applications not accepted. Giving primarily in Cincinnati, OH.
Application information: Contributes only to pre-selected organizations.
Trustees: Rebecca Dimling Cochran, Elizabeth Dimling, Jennifer Dimling Lippert.
EIN: 316065560

44020
Koscielny Family Foundation, Inc.
23535 Quail Hollow
Westlake, OH 44145 (440) 356-4544
Contact: Carole D. Koscielny, Tr.

Established in 1998.
Donor(s): Robert M. Koscielny, Carole D. Koscielny.
Financial data (yr. ended 12/31/01): Grants paid, $10,000; assets, $149,585 (M); gifts received, $37,288; expenditures, $10,157; qualifying distributions, $10,000.
Application information: Application form not required.
Trustees: Cindy L. Finley, Carole D. Koscielny, Gary M. Koscielny, Robert M. Koscielny, Cheri Koscielny-Maneri.
EIN: 341871438

44021
Joe and Jan Mollmann Foundation
2467 Tremont Rd.
Columbus, OH 43221

Established in 1998 in OH.
Donor(s): Joseph Mollmann, Jan Mollmann.
Financial data (yr. ended 12/31/99): Grants paid, $10,000; assets, $166,189 (M); gifts received, $9,588; expenditures, $12,873; qualifying distributions, $10,000.
Limitations: Applications not accepted.
Application information: Contributes only to pre-selected organizations.
Officer and Trustee:* Joseph M. Mollman,* Pres.
EIN: 311627925

44022
Barry and Nancy Phillips Family Foundation
403 Hillcrest Dr. N.E.
New Philadelphia, OH 44663
Contact: Barry L. Phillips, Tr.

Established in 1999 in OH.
Donor(s): Barry L. Phillips.
Financial data (yr. ended 12/31/01): Grants paid, $10,000; assets, $120,770 (M); expenditures, $11,125; qualifying distributions, $10,000.
Limitations: Giving primarily in Lewisburg, KY.
Application information: Application form not required.
Trustees: Amy A. Arseneau, Andrea M. Phillips, Barry L. Phillips, Matthew G. Phillips.
EIN: 341896112

44023
Joseph Rawson Scientific Trust
c/o Star Trust, N.A.
P.O. Box 1118, M.L. 6190
Cincinnati, OH 45201-1118
Application address: c/o Carol Foster, Trust Off., Star Trust, N.A., 425 Walnut St., M.L. 7129, Cincinnati, OH 45201, tel.: (513) 632-4421

Financial data (yr. ended 12/31/01): Grants paid, $10,000; assets, $270,839 (M); expenditures, $14,691; qualifying distributions, $10,000.
Limitations: Giving primarily in OH.
Trustee: Star Trust, N.A.
EIN: 316053727

44024
Preston & Katherine Robertson Foundation
c/o FirstMerit Bank, N.A.
P.O. Box 725
Medina, OH 44258
Contact: Robert J. Bux, Mgr.

Established in 1997 in OH.
Financial data (yr. ended 12/31/01): Grants paid, $10,000; assets, $171,338 (M); expenditures, $12,651; qualifying distributions, $10,000.
Limitations: Giving primarily in OH.
Officers: Robert J. Bux, Mgr.; Robert Fahrland, Mgr.; P.M. Jones, Mgr.; Jack Morrison, Mgr.
Trustee: FirstMerit Bank, N.A.
EIN: 311562256

44025
Lillian L. Root Scholarship Fund
c/o Third Fifth Bank
38 Fountain Sq. Plz.
Cincinnati, OH 45263

Financial data (yr. ended 12/31/00): Grants paid, $10,000; assets, $303,049 (M); expenditures, $14,083; qualifying distributions, $10,896.
Limitations: Applications not accepted.
Trustee: Third Fifth Bank.
EIN: 351901966

44026
220 Charitable Trust
220 S. Rose Blvd.
Akron, OH 44313-7827
Application address: KeyBank Bldg., 159 S. Main St., Ste. 520, Akron, OH 44308
Contact: John L. Tormey, Dir.

Established in 2000 in OH.
Donor(s): John L. Tormey.
Financial data (yr. ended 12/31/01): Grants paid, $10,000; assets, $208,153 (M); gifts received, $107,861; expenditures, $13,255; qualifying distributions, $10,000.
Directors: Michael L. Stark, James N. Tormey, John L. Tormey, Thomas A. Tormey.
EIN: 347122159

44027
Leatherman Family Foundation
200 Smokerise Dr., Ste. 300
Wadsworth, OH 44281

Established in 1992 in OH.
Donor(s): Robert Leatherman, American Health Care Centers.
Financial data (yr. ended 12/31/01): Grants paid, $9,930; assets, $290,318 (M); gifts received, $6,000; expenditures, $12,337; qualifying distributions, $9,930.
Limitations: Applications not accepted. Giving primarily in NY.
Application information: Contributes only to pre-selected organizations.
Officers and Trustees:* Robert Leatherman,* Pres. and Treas.; Phyllis Leatherman,* V.P. and Secy.; Karen Friedt, William Koptis, Robert J. Leatherman, Jr., Sean Leatherman, Robin Wenger.
EIN: 346981592

44028
Nora S. Wilder Trust
c/o FirstMerit Bank, N.A.
105 Court St.
Elyria, OH 44035-5525 (440) 329-3000
Contact: Michael Yanick, V.P. and Sr. Trust Off., FirstMerit Bank, N.A.

Financial data (yr. ended 12/31/01): Grants paid, $9,865; assets, $295,321 (M); expenditures, $13,453; qualifying distributions, $9,865.
Limitations: Giving primarily in Lorain County, OH.
Application information: Application form not required.
Trustee: FirstMerit Bank, N.A.
EIN: 346524605

44029
The Roe Green Foundation
925 Euclid Ave., Ste. 2000
Cleveland, OH 44115

Established in 1999 in OH.
Financial data (yr. ended 12/31/01): Grants paid, $9,700; assets, $1,073,178 (M); gifts received, $984,735; expenditures, $16,052; qualifying distributions, $9,700.
Trustees: Roe Green, Eugene A. Kratus.
EIN: 341886405

44030
Richards Charitable Trust
815 Weaver St. S.W.
Canton, OH 44706-4661

Donor(s): Richards Management.
Financial data (yr. ended 12/31/99): Grants paid, $9,695; assets, $1,986 (M); gifts received, $10,327; expenditures, $9,695; qualifying distributions, $9,695.
Limitations: Applications not accepted. Giving primarily in OH.
Application information: Contributes only to pre-selected organizations.
Trustee: Everett Richards.
EIN: 341808858

44031
The Deer Valley Foundation
5114 Hamilton Ave.
Cleveland, OH 44114

Established in 2000 in OH.
Donor(s): Christopher W. Horsburgh.
Financial data (yr. ended 12/31/01): Grants paid, $9,665; assets, $114,805 (M); expenditures, $15,522; qualifying distributions, $9,665.
Limitations: Applications not accepted. Giving primarily in OH.
Application information: Contributes only to pre-selected organizations.
Officers: Christopher W. Horsburgh, Pres.; Christopher W. Horsburgh, Jr., Secy.; Christine M. Horsburgh, Treas.
EIN: 341922743

44032
The Paula and George Buckingham Foundation
c/o William E. Reichard
25109 Detroit Rd., Ste. 300
Westlake, OH 44145

Established in 1991 in OH.
Donor(s): Paula Buckingham, George Buckingham.
Financial data (yr. ended 12/31/00): Grants paid, $9,640; assets, $8,218 (M); expenditures, $9,640; qualifying distributions, $9,639.
Limitations: Applications not accepted. Giving primarily in IL and IN.
Application information: Contributes only to pre-selected organizations.
Trustees: George Buckingham, Paula Buckingham, William E. Reichard.
EIN: 341694810

44033
Wanda K. Ganyard Scholarship Trust
(Formerly The Lyle B. & Wanda K. Ganyard Scholarship Trust)
c/o FirstMerit Bank, N.A.
121 S. Main St., Ste. 200
Akron, OH 44308 (330) 384-7302
Application addresses: c/o Copley High School, 3807 Ridgewood Rd., Copley, OH 44321-1697, tel.: (330) 668-3227, or c/o Revere High School, 3420 Everett Rd., Richfield, OH 44286, tel.: (330) 659-6111

Financial data (yr. ended 09/30/01): Grants paid, $9,543; assets, $839,364 (M); expenditures, $66,634; qualifying distributions, $55,763.
Limitations: Giving limited to OH.
Application information: Application form required.
Trustee: FirstMerit Bank, N.A.
EIN: 346820819
Codes: GTI

44034
The Smith-Prochaska Charitable Foundation, Inc.
1842 Hines Hill Rd.
Hudson, OH 44236-1714

Donor(s): Walter E. Smith, Carole P. Smith.
Financial data (yr. ended 12/31/01): Grants paid, $9,500; assets, $165,516 (M); gifts received, $10,000; expenditures, $10,418; qualifying distributions, $9,500.
Limitations: Applications not accepted. Giving primarily in OH.
Application information: Contributes only to pre-selected organizations.
Officers: Carole P. Smith, Pres.; Walter E. Smith, V.P.
EIN: 341577260

44035
R. K. North Charitable Trust
(Formerly R. S. Slack Charitable Trust)
408 Grandin Ridge Dr.
Maineville, OH 45039

Donor(s): R.K. North Asset Management Co.
Financial data (yr. ended 12/31/99): Grants paid, $9,422; assets, $181,551 (L); gifts received, $190,000; expenditures, $10,583; qualifying distributions, $9,422.
Limitations: Applications not accepted.
Application information: Contributes only to pre-selected organizations.
Trustees: Karen W. North, R. Bradley North.
EIN: 347072993

44036
East Liverpool Fawcett Community Foundation
P.O. Box 458
East Liverpool, OH 43920

Financial data (yr. ended 06/30/01): Grants paid, $9,400; assets, $409,302 (M); gifts received, $131,026; expenditures, $9,737.
Limitations: Giving primarily in East Liverpool, OH.
Officers and Trustees:* Marc D. Hoffrichter,* Pres.; Glenn Waight,* V.P.; Jackman S. Vodrey,* Secy.; Robert K. Gardner, Treas.; Lois Beals, J. David Buzzard, William Thomas Jarrett, Doris McKinnon, Charles W. Parry, William Sutherland, Rev. H. Gene Toot, Burl D. Warrick.
EIN: 341717593
Codes: CM

44037
Martha Selle Memorial Scholarship Trust
c/o National City Bank of Pennsylvania
P. O. Box 94651
Cleveland, OH 44101-4651
Application address: c/o Guidance Dir. or Principal, St. Mary's High School, 977 S. St. Mary's Rd., St. Mary's, PA 15857

Established in 1996 in PA.
Financial data (yr. ended 01/31/02): Grants paid, $9,400; assets, $197,368 (M); gifts received, $10; expenditures, $12,679; qualifying distributions, $9,400.
Application information: Application form required.
Trustee: National City Bank.
EIN: 256546515

44038
The Panevin Foundation
c/o KeyBank, N.A.
800 Superior Ave., 4th Fl.
Cleveland, OH 44114

Established in 1998 in OH.
Financial data (yr. ended 12/31/00): Grants paid, $9,396; assets, $388,241 (M); expenditures, $14,272; qualifying distributions, $9,762.
Limitations: Applications not accepted.
Application information: Contributes only to pre-selected organizations.
Trustee: KeyBank, N.A.
EIN: 341894112

44039
Walter G. and Ella M. Peak Scholarship Fund
c/o FirstMerit Bank, N.A.
105 Court St.
Elyria, OH 44035

Established in 1994 in OH.
Donor(s): Ella M. Peak Trust.
Financial data (yr. ended 12/31/01): Grants paid, $9,375; assets, $131,340 (M); expenditures, $13,670; qualifying distributions, $10,414.
Limitations: Giving limited to residents of Elyria, OH.
Application information: Application form required.
Trustee: FirstMerit Bank, N.A.
EIN: 341776865
Codes: GTI

44040
The Malley Foundation
13400 Brookpark Rd.
Cleveland, OH 44135

Established in 2000 in OH.
Donor(s): Daniel Malley, Melissa Malley.
Financial data (yr. ended 12/31/01): Grants paid, $9,334; assets, $5,515 (M); gifts received, $14,485; expenditures, $10,678; qualifying distributions, $9,334.
Limitations: Applications not accepted.
Application information: Contributes only to pre-selected organizations.
Trustees: Adele Malley, Daniel Malley, Melissa Malley.
EIN: 522282684

44041
Moon Family Foundation
c/o Henry G. Alexander, Jr.
511 Walnut St., Ste. 1900
Cincinnati, OH 45202
Application address: 3093-A Pinehurst Dr., Las Vegas, NV 89109
Contact: David D. Moon, Tr.

Established in 1994 in OH.
Donor(s): David D. Moon, Karen S. Moon.
Financial data (yr. ended 12/31/01): Grants paid, $9,313; assets, $141,629 (M); gifts received, $3,000; expenditures, $10,474; qualifying distributions, $9,313.
Limitations: Giving primarily in OH.
Application information: Application form not required.
Trustee: David D. Moon.
EIN: 311423751

44042
Lillian M. Jones Memorial Foundation Trust
c/o National City Bank
P.O. Box 94651
Cleveland, OH 44101-4651

Financial data (yr. ended 12/31/99): Grants paid, $9,300; assets, $269,397 (M); expenditures, $10,142; qualifying distributions, $9,786.
Limitations: Giving limited to residents of Ohio County, KY.
Trustee: National City Bank.
EIN: 616022770

44043
Jean P. Wade Foundation
c/o Rory O'Neil
7171 Greenwich Rd.
Seville, OH 44273-9125

Established in 1993 in OH.
Donor(s): Rory O'Neil.
Financial data (yr. ended 12/31/00): Grants paid, $9,250; assets, $242,201 (M); expenditures, $9,250; qualifying distributions, $9,250.
Limitations: Giving primarily in Akron, OH.
Trustees: Diane O'Neil, Rory O'Neil, Shannon K. O'Neil.
EIN: 341738755

44044
The Bock Foundation
P.O. Box 20053
Columbus, OH 43220-0001

Established in 1986 in OH.
Donor(s): J. John Bock, M.D.
Financial data (yr. ended 12/31/01): Grants paid, $9,218; assets, $484,303 (M); expenditures, $18,527; qualifying distributions, $9,218.
Limitations: Applications not accepted. Giving primarily in OH.
Application information: Contributes only to pre-selected organizations.
Trustees: J. John Bock, M.D., Janet L. Bock, Jennifer F. Bock, Sara E. Bock.
EIN: 311197029

44045
AEI Scholarship Fund
c/o KeyBank, N.A.
P.O. Box 10099
Toledo, OH 43699-0099
Appliction address: 100 Main St, Ann Arbor, MI 48104
Contact: Veena Khana, Trust Off., KeyBank

Financial data (yr. ended 06/30/02): Grants paid, $9,000; assets, $270,386 (M); expenditures, $11,778; qualifying distributions, $9,833.
Limitations: Giving on a national basis.
Application information: Application form required.
Trustee: KeyBank, N.A.
EIN: 382088329
Codes: GTI

44046
William M. and Louise O. Allen Scholarship Fund
c/o National City Bank of Indiana
P.O. Box 94651
Cleveland, OH 44101-4651
Application address: P.O. Box 5031, Indianapolis, IN 46201, tel.: (317) 267-7085
Contact: Mark Smiley, Trust Off., National City Bank of Indiana

Financial data (yr. ended 12/31/01): Grants paid, $9,000; assets, $159,559 (M); expenditures, $10,926; qualifying distributions, $9,889.
Limitations: Giving limited to Montgomery County, IN.
Trustee: National City Bank of Indiana.
EIN: 356033947
Codes: GTI

44047
Cleveland Alumnae Panhellenic Endowment Fund, Inc.
c/o Patricia O. Barta
10049 Bissell Dr.
Twinsburg, OH 44087
Application address: c/o Mary Chase, 7655 Isaac Ave., Middelburg Heights, OH 44130, tel.: (440) 243-1922

Established in 1985.
Financial data (yr. ended 05/31/01): Grants paid, $9,000; assets, $197,098 (M); gifts received, $7,175; expenditures, $9,974; qualifying distributions, $9,641.
Limitations: Giving limited to the metropolitan Cleveland, OH, area.
Application information: Application form required.
Officers: Priscilla Goodger, Pres.; Nina Wilhelm, Secy.; Louise Thomas, Treas.
EIN: 341476473
Codes: GTI

44048
G. Russell and Constance B. Lincoln Family Foundation Trust
c/o Republic Bldg.
25 W. Prospect Ave., Ste. 1400
Cleveland, OH 44115-1048

Donor(s): G. Russell Lincoln.
Financial data (yr. ended 12/31/01): Grants paid, $9,000; assets, $717,090 (M); expenditures, $12,475; qualifying distributions, $9,000.
Limitations: Applications not accepted.
Application information: Contributes only to pre-selected organizations.
Committee Members: Brinton C. Lincoln, Constance P. Lincoln, G. Russell Lincoln, James D. Lincoln.
Trustee: Robert N. Gudbranson.

EIN: 383471702

44049
George & Ida Mestel Foundation
220 E. Tuscarawas St.
Canton, OH 44702 (330) 452-9788
Contact: Harry Mestel, Pres.

Established in 1995 in FL.
Financial data (yr. ended 12/31/01): Grants paid, $9,000; assets, $190,490 (M); expenditures, $9,926; qualifying distributions, $9,000.
Limitations: Giving on a national basis, with emphasis on Los Angeles, CA.
Officers: Harry Mestel, Pres. and Treas.; Elaine Rich, Secy.
Trustee: Stanley Mestel.
EIN: 650559509

44050
The Mitchell Family Foundation
c/o Daniel J. LaValley
5800 Monroe St., Bldg. F
Sylvania, OH 43560
Application address: 3150 N. Republic Blvd., Ste. 3, Toledo, OH 43615
Contact: William C. Mitchell, Pres.

Established in 1995.
Donor(s): William C. Mitchell.
Financial data (yr. ended 12/31/01): Grants paid, $9,000; assets, $207,857 (M); expenditures, $10,271; qualifying distributions, $9,000.
Limitations: Giving primarily in northwest OH and southeast MI.
Officers and Trustees:* William C. Mitchell,* Pres.; Stephen R. Mitchell,* V.P.; Daniel J. LaValley,* Secy.
EIN: 311422869

44051
Price Family Foundation, Inc.
99 W. Main St.
Norwalk, OH 44857

Established in 1998 in OH.
Financial data (yr. ended 04/30/00): Grants paid, $9,000; assets, $465,863 (M); gifts received, $185,866; expenditures, $21,574; qualifying distributions, $9,787; giving activities include $10,473 for programs.
Limitations: Applications not accepted.
Application information: Contributes only to pre-selected organizations.
Trustees: Patricia Price Baker, Susan Price Blake, Molly Price Downey.
EIN: 341857959

44052
Mary Watson Trust
c/o Sky Trust, N.A.
P.O. Box 479
Youngstown, OH 44501-0479

Established in 1991 in OH.
Donor(s): Mary Watson.‡
Financial data (yr. ended 12/31/99): Grants paid, $9,000; assets, $192,180 (M); expenditures, $10,900; qualifying distributions, $9,577.
Trustee: Sky Trust, N.A.
EIN: 556046729

44053
The Robert J. Woodward Education Foundation
c/o Corporate Secy.
1200 Steelwood Rd.
Columbus, OH 43212

Established in 1997 in OH.
Financial data (yr. ended 12/31/01): Grants paid, $9,000; assets, $91,774 (M); gifts received,

$36,853; expenditures, $9,181; qualifying distributions, $9,000.
Officers: Robert J. Woodward, Jr., Chair.; Ronald E. Calhoun, Secy.; Robyn Pogany-Pollina, Treas.
EIN: 311471450

44054
Alfred R. Hughes Family Fund for Religious, Charitable, Scientific, Literary, and Educational Corporations and Organizations
851 Wildwood Dr. N.E.
Warren, OH 44483-4459 (330) 372-5335
Contact: Alfred R. Hughes II, Tr.

Financial data (yr. ended 12/31/01): Grants paid, $8,978; assets, $169,353 (M); expenditures, $12,703; qualifying distributions, $8,978.
Limitations: Giving primarily in Warren, OH.
Trustee: Alfred R. Hughes II.
EIN: 346550693

44055
The Skyline Chili Neighborhood Foundation
4180 Thunderbird Ln.
Fairfield, OH 45014

Established in 2000 in OH.
Donor(s): Skyline Chili, Inc.
Financial data (yr. ended 12/31/01): Grants paid, $8,955; assets, $2,509 (M); gifts received, $3,077; expenditures, $9,055; qualifying distributions, $8,955.
Limitations: Applications not accepted. Giving primarily in Cincinnati, OH.
Application information: Contributes only to pre-selected organizations.
Officers and Trustees:* Thomas L. Allen,* Pres.; Jeffrey W. Shelton,* V.P. and Treas.; Mark J. Zummo,* Secy.
EIN: 311668952

44056
Mary S. Enk Trust
c/o KeyBank, N.A., Trust Div.
800 Superior Ave., 4th Fl.
Cleveland, OH 44114

Financial data (yr. ended 04/30/02): Grants paid, $8,942; assets, $280,067 (M); expenditures, $12,608; qualifying distributions, $8,942.
Limitations: Applications not accepted. Giving limited to residents of Belfast, ME.
Application information: Unsolicited requests for funds not accepted.
Trustee: KeyBank, N.A.
EIN: 016047725

44057
Rev. Richard H. Ackerman Trust
c/o The Huntington National Bank
P.O. Box 1558
Columbus, OH 43216-1558

Established in 1993 in KY.
Financial data (yr. ended 12/31/01): Grants paid, $8,905; assets, $167,388 (M); expenditures, $10,998; qualifying distributions, $8,905.
Limitations: Applications not accepted. Giving primarily in Walton, KY.
Application information: Contributes only to pre-selected organizations.
Trustee: The Huntington National Bank.
EIN: 611279311

44058
Evan and Suzanne Morris Family Foundation
12459 Reeder N.E.
Alliance, OH 44601

Established in 1998 in OH.
Donor(s): Evan Morris, Suzanne Morris.

44058—OHIO

Financial data (yr. ended 12/31/01): Grants paid, $8,900; assets, $49,411 (M); expenditures, $10,298; qualifying distributions, $8,900.
Limitations: Applications not accepted.
Application information: Contributes only to pre-selected organizations.
Trustees: Evan Morris, Suzanne Morris.
EIN: 341858643

44059
Thomas B. Rentschler Family Foundation
(Formerly Walter A. Rentschler Family Foundation)
1030 New London Rd.
Hamilton, OH 45013

Financial data (yr. ended 12/31/01): Grants paid, $8,900; assets, $184,686 (M); expenditures, $10,173; qualifying distributions, $8,900.
Limitations: Applications not accepted. Giving primarily in OH and PA.
Application information: Contributes only to pre-selected organizations.
Officers: Thomas B. Rentschler, Pres.; Dorothy G. Rentschler, Treas.
Trustee: Merrill Lynch.
EIN: 316034715

44060
Nora Greenwalt Trust
(Formerly Nora Greenwalt Foundation)
c/o The Huntington National Bank
P.O. Box 1558, HC1012
Columbus, OH 43216
Application address: 140 E. Fair Ave., New Philadelphia, OH 44663, tel.: (216) 364-1614
Contact: Don Zimmerman, Chair.

Financial data (yr. ended 06/30/01): Grants paid, $8,878; assets, $175,471 (M); expenditures, $10,201; qualifying distributions, $9,040.
Limitations: Giving limited to the New Philadelphia, OH, area.
Application information: Application form required.
Officer: Don W. Zimmerman, Chair.
Trustee: The Huntington National Bank.
EIN: 346521347

44061
Abraham & Sarah Eiser Foundation
3524 Kenwood Blvd.
Toledo, OH 43606-2809 (419) 536-0890
Contact: Mendel Eiser

Donor(s): Abraham Eiser, Sarah Eiser.
Financial data (yr. ended 09/30/01): Grants paid, $8,869; assets, $167,102 (M); expenditures, $9,402; qualifying distributions, $8,869.
Limitations: Giving primarily in Toledo, OH.
Trustees: Sharon Beth Eiser Ackerman, Marcia Ruth Elser.
EIN: 510192713

44062
Charles D. "Bud" Hering, Jr. Foundation
c/o Michael Kerschner
634 W. Market St.
Tiffin, OH 44883-2516
Application address: 189 Gross St., Tiffin, OH 44883
Contact: William C. Felton, Chair

Financial data (yr. ended 12/31/99): Grants paid, $8,837; assets, $239,528 (M); gifts received, $8,836; expenditures, $9,290; qualifying distributions, $9,290.
Application information: Application form not required.

Officers: William C. Felton, Chair; Fred Spurk, Vice Chair; Brent Howard, Secy.; Michael J. Kerschner, Treas.
EIN: 341702565

44063
F. A. & J. S. Klaine Family Foundation
c/o Fifth Third Bank
38 Fountain Sq. Plz., Dept. 99858, MD 1090C8
Cincinnati, OH 45263

Established in 1998 in OH.
Donor(s): Janet S. Klaine.
Financial data (yr. ended 12/31/00): Grants paid, $8,800; assets, $326,825 (M); gifts received, $20,434; expenditures, $11,311; qualifying distributions, $8,118.
Trustees: Franklin A. Klaine, Jr., Janet S. Klaine, Louise Trapp, Fifth Third Bank.
EIN: 311650342

44064
Martin Education Trust
c/o Bank One Trust Co., N.A.
774 Park Meadow Rd.
Westerville, OH 43081
Application address: c/o Bank One Trust Co., N.A., 101 Central Plz. S., Canton, OH 44711, tel.: (330) 438-8354

Financial data (yr. ended 04/30/00): Grants paid, $8,800; assets, $523,064 (M); expenditures, $15,913; qualifying distributions, $9,133.
Limitations: Giving limited to Wayne and Wooster counties, OH.
Application information: Application form not required.
Trustee: Bank One Trust Co., N.A.
EIN: 346742103
Codes: GTI

44065
McCarthy, Lebit, Crystal & Haiman Foundation
101 Prospect Ave. W., Ste. 1800
Cleveland, OH 44115

Established in 1996 in OH.
Financial data (yr. ended 12/31/01): Grants paid, $8,797; assets, $3 (M); gifts received, $8,800; expenditures, $8,797; qualifying distributions, $8,797.
Limitations: Applications not accepted.
Application information: Contributes only to pre-selected organizations.
Officers: Kenneth B. Liffman, Pres.; Mark B. Conn, V.P.; Larry Crystal, Secy.; Thomas F. Adomaitis, Treas.
EIN: 341823004

44066
James P. & Peter R. Rentschler Foundation
8702 Sturbridge Dr.
Cincinnati, OH 45236

Financial data (yr. ended 11/30/01): Grants paid, $8,755; assets, $90,713 (M); expenditures, $12,926; qualifying distributions, $8,755.
Limitations: Applications not accepted. Giving primarily in MI and OH.
Application information: Contributes only to pre-selected organizations.
Trustees: James P. Rentschler, Peter R. Rentschler, Stephen P. Rentschler.
EIN: 316030870

44067
Frank T. Black Family Foundation
P.O. Box 3775
Mansfield, OH 44907-0775

Established in 1998 in OH.
Donor(s): Elizabeth T. Black.

Financial data (yr. ended 12/31/01): Grants paid, $8,750; assets, $486,041 (M); expenditures, $11,684; qualifying distributions, $8,750.
Limitations: Applications not accepted.
Application information: Contributes only to pre-selected organizations.
Officer: Elizabeth M. Black, Pres.
EIN: 311582253

44068
Pendleton Foundation, Inc.
(Formerly Warren Tool Foundation, Inc.)
c/o H. Alexander Pendleton
768 E. North St.
Akron, OH 44305-1164

Established around 1975 in OH.
Donor(s): Summit Tool Company.
Financial data (yr. ended 12/31/01): Grants paid, $8,617; assets, $432 (M); gifts received, $8,700; expenditures, $8,860; qualifying distributions, $8,860.
Limitations: Applications not accepted. Giving primarily in OH.
Application information: Contributes only to pre-selected organizations.
Officers and Directors:* H. Alexander Pendleton,* Chair. and Treas.; Scott C. Meyer,* Pres.; Tamara B. Pendleton,* Secy.
EIN: 347254279
Codes: CS, CD

44069
The James Foundation
c/o Fifth Third Bank
P.O. Box 1868
Toledo, OH 43603 (419) 259-6803
Contact: Marsha A. Manahan, Trust Off., Fifth Third Bank of Northwestern Ohio, N.A.

Established in 1992 in OH.
Donor(s): Jean M. Areddy.
Financial data (yr. ended 12/31/01): Grants paid, $8,600; assets, $331,360 (M); expenditures, $10,143; qualifying distributions, $8,600.
Limitations: Giving primarily in Toledo, OH.
Advisory Committee: Jean M. Areddy.
Trustee: Fifth Third Bank.
EIN: 346969288

44070
R. G. K. Strobel Charitable Trust
7305 Thompson Rd.
Cincinnati, OH 45247

Established in 1996 in OH.
Donor(s): Josefine Strobel, Rudolf Strobel.
Financial data (yr. ended 12/31/00): Grants paid, $8,600; assets, $213,303 (M); expenditures, $9,420; qualifying distributions, $8,600.
Limitations: Applications not accepted. Giving primarily in FL and OH.
Application information: Contributes only to pre-selected organizations.
Trustees: Josefine Strobel, Rudolf Strobel.
EIN: 316533622

44071
David M. Whitmore & Glenna M. Whitmore Memorial Scholarship Endowment Fund
c/o Robert P. Fite
P.O. Box 910
Piqua, OH 45356-0910
Application address: c/o Upper Valley Joint Vocational School, 8811 Career Dr., Piqua, OH 45356, tel.: (937) 778-1980
Contact: Larry Householder, Superintendent

Established in 1982 in OH.

Financial data (yr. ended 04/30/01): Grants paid, $8,583; assets, $111,099 (M); expenditures, $10,307; qualifying distributions, $10,058.
Limitations: Giving limited to residents of Miami County, OH.
Application information: Application form required.
Trustee: Paul P. Gutman.
EIN: 316224298
Codes: GTI

44072
Husni Memorial Foundation
c/o Elias A. Husni
P.O. Box 189
Gates Mills, OH 44040-0189

Established in 1998 in OH.
Donor(s): Elias A. Husni.
Financial data (yr. ended 06/30/01): Grants paid, $8,500; assets, $149,245 (M); expenditures, $10,566; qualifying distributions, $6,180.
Limitations: Applications not accepted. Giving primarily in Cleveland, OH.
Application information: Contributes only to pre-selected organizations.
Officer: Elias A. Husni, Mgr.; Jane E. Easly, Mgr.
EIN: 341868501

44073
The Pollock Family Foundation
763 W. Waterloo Rd.
Akron, OH 44314 (330) 753-4545
Contact: Jacob Pollock, Pres.

Established in 1998 in OH.
Donor(s): Jacob Pollock.
Financial data (yr. ended 12/31/01): Grants paid, $8,500; assets, $2,337 (M); gifts received, $8,500; expenditures, $8,500; qualifying distributions, $8,500.
Limitations: Giving primarily in Akron, OH.
Officers and Trustees:* Jacob Pollock,* Pres.; Bruce Pollock,* V.P.; Gertrude Pollock, Secy.; Richard D. Pollock, Treas.
EIN: 341880801

44074
W. B. and Mary W. Snow No. 5 Scholarship Fund
c/o FirstMerit Bank, N.A.
121 S. Main St., Ste. 200
Akron, OH 44308-1440
Application address: c/o Phyllis Bernel, Office of Career Education, 65 Steiner Ave., Rm. 210, Akron, OH 44301

Established in 1997 in OH.
Donor(s): W.B. Snow and Mary W. Snow Trust.
Financial data (yr. ended 08/31/00): Grants paid, $8,500; assets, $422,248 (M); expenditures, $14,050; qualifying distributions, $9,550.
Limitations: Giving limited to Akron, OH.
Application information: Application form required.
Trustee: FirstMerit Bank, N.A.
EIN: 311564522

44075
James Albert Gammans Fund
c/o KeyBank, N.A., Trust Div.
800 Superior Ave., 4th Fl.
Cleveland, OH 44114
Contact: Christina Cook, Trust Off., KeyBank, N.A.

Donor(s): James Albert Gammans.‡
Financial data (yr. ended 04/30/01): Grants paid, $8,490; assets, $86,558 (L); expenditures, $10,120; qualifying distributions, $8,414.
Trustee: KeyBank, N.A.

EIN: 016010129

44076
The Martha J. & William A. Apple Foundation
2748 Bahns Dr.
Beavercreek, OH 45434-6606
Contact: Ralph M. Clark, Mgr.

Established in 1982 in OH.
Financial data (yr. ended 09/30/01): Grants paid, $8,461; assets, $1,634 (M); gifts received, $8,291; expenditures, $8,461; qualifying distributions, $8,461.
Limitations: Giving primarily in FL and OH.
Application information: Application form not required.
Officer: Ralph M. Clark, Mgr.
Trustees: Martha J. Apple, William A. Apple.
EIN: 311050168

44077
Jeanne Souers Garcia Scholarship Fund
c/o The Huntington National Bank
P.O. Box 1558
Columbus, OH 43216
Application address: c/o New Philadelphia High School, Guidance Off., New Philadelphia, OH 44663

Established in 1994 in OH.
Financial data (yr. ended 06/30/01): Grants paid, $8,400; assets, $177,687 (M); expenditures, $11,218; qualifying distributions, $8,777.
Limitations: Giving limited to residents of New Philadelphia, OH.
Application information: Application form required.
Advisors: Carol Bichsel, Michael Herchik, Hank Smith.
Trustee: The Huntington National Bank.
EIN: 316496564

44078
Genevieve Dotson Moore Foundation
P.O. Box 448
Aurora, OH 44202-0448 (330) 562-6222

Donor(s): George L. Moore.
Financial data (yr. ended 12/31/01): Grants paid, $8,400; assets, $87,847 (M); expenditures, $20,796; qualifying distributions, $8,400.
Limitations: Giving limited to Aurora, OH.
Application information: Application form not required.
Officer and Trustees:* Craig Moore,* Mgr.; John J. Moore.
EIN: 341318265

44079
The Bay Foundation
23520 Lake Rd.
Bay Village, OH 44140

Financial data (yr. ended 09/30/01): Grants paid, $8,377; assets, $120,686 (M); expenditures, $9,912; qualifying distributions, $8,377.
Officer and Trustees:* Brooks G. Hull,* Pres.; Terry Gimmellie, Jeffrey F. Hull, Norman G. Hull.
EIN: 341853153

44080
Republic Storage Systems Company, Inc., Employees Charitable Fund
c/o Republic Storage Systems Co., Inc.
1038 Belden Ave. N.E.
Canton, OH 44705

Established in 1989 in OH.
Donor(s): Republic Storage Systems Co., Inc.
Financial data (yr. ended 12/31/01): Grants paid, $8,350; assets, $8,352 (M); gifts received, $10,586; expenditures, $8,388; qualifying distributions, $8,350.
Limitations: Applications not accepted. Giving limited to the Canton, OH, area.
Application information: Contributes only to pre-selected organizations.
Officers: R.G. Elder, Pres.; Clark E. Froehlich, V.P.; Charlotte Bartholomew, Secy.
EIN: 341611406
Codes: CS, CD

44081
Hackenberger Family Foundation, Inc.
250 Farrell Rd.
Vandalia, OH 45377-9702

Established in 2000 in OH and DE.
Donor(s): James E. Hackenberger, Lynne E. Hackenberger.
Financial data (yr. ended 12/31/01): Grants paid, $8,300; assets, $238,272 (M); gifts received, $90,000; expenditures, $12,923; qualifying distributions, $8,300.
Limitations: Applications not accepted.
Application information: Contributes only to pre-selected organizations.
Officers and Directors:* James E. Hackenberger,* Pres.; Lynne E. Hackenberger,* Secy.-Treas.
EIN: 582569707

44082
G. Myers Memorial Scholarship Trust
P.O. Box 94651
Cleveland, OH 44101-4651

Financial data (yr. ended 12/31/01): Grants paid, $8,250; assets, $218,371 (M); expenditures, $8,540; qualifying distributions, $8,930.
Limitations: Giving limited to residents of IN.
Application information: Application form required.
Trustee: National City Bank of Indiana.
EIN: 356648858

44083
Katy Danco Foundation, Inc.
5862 Mayfield Rd.
P.O. Box 24219
Mayfield Heights, OH 44124-0268

Established in 1987 in OH.
Donor(s): Leon Danco, Walter T.E. Danco.
Financial data (yr. ended 12/31/01): Grants paid, $8,200; assets, $241,259 (M); gifts received, $1,100; expenditures, $8,645; qualifying distributions, $8,200.
Limitations: Applications not accepted. Giving primarily in OH.
Application information: Contributes only to pre-selected organizations.
Trustees: Helene Danco, Katy Danco, Leon Danco, Walter Ten Eyck Danco, Suzanne Doggett, William Barrows Doggett.
EIN: 341569138

44084
Heartland Foundation of Ohio
133 N. Court St.
Medina, OH 44256-1927
Contact: Gary M. Hetrick, Tr.

Established in 2001 in OH.
Donor(s): Gary M. Hetrick.
Financial data (yr. ended 12/31/01): Grants paid, $8,200; assets, $27,815 (M); gifts received, $43,839; expenditures, $9,945; qualifying distributions, $8,200.
Trustee: Gary M. Hetrick.
EIN: 341937418

44085
Department of Surgery Research & Education Fund of Youngstown, Ohio
540 Parmalee Ave., Ste. 420
Youngstown, OH 44510

Financial data (yr. ended 08/31/01): Grants paid, $8,163; assets, $220,025 (M); gifts received, $7,485; expenditures, $10,838; qualifying distributions, $8,163.
Limitations: Applications not accepted. Giving limited to OH.
Officers: Mounir Awad, M.D., Pres.; Daniel Garritano, M.D., V.P.; Michael Kavic, M.D., Secy.; Nancy L. Gantt, M.D., Treas.
EIN: 341451287

44086
The Ahmed Family Foundation
2327 Beaver Creek
Westlake, OH 44145 (440) 282-3685
Contact: Ismail S. Ahmed, Pres.

Established in 1993 in OH.
Donor(s): Ismail S. Ahmed.
Financial data (yr. ended 12/31/00): Grants paid, $8,150; assets, $33,474 (M); gifts received, $10,500; expenditures, $9,721; qualifying distributions, $8,150.
Application information: Application form not required.
Officers and Trustees:* Ismail S. Ahmed,* Pres. and Treas.; Ahmed S. Ahmed,* V.P.; Miriam Ahmed,* Secy.
EIN: 341757068

44087
Naoma E. Bobbs Trust
c/o Fifth Third Bank
P.O. Box 630858
Cincinnati, OH 45263

Established in 1986 in OH.
Financial data (yr. ended 12/31/01): Grants paid, $8,100; assets, $154,747 (M); expenditures, $9,242; qualifying distributions, $8,100.
Limitations: Applications not accepted. Giving limited to Piqua, OH.
Application information: Contributes only to pre-selected organizations.
Trustee: Fifth Third Bank.
EIN: 316288117

44088
Kelley L. Putman Charitable Trust
c/o National City Bank, Northwest
P.O. Box 94651
Cleveland, OH 44101-4651

Financial data (yr. ended 08/31/02): Grants paid, $8,100; assets, $80,004 (M); expenditures, $10,493; qualifying distributions, $8,100.
Limitations: Applications not accepted. Giving primarily in IA.
Application information: Contributes only to pre-selected organizations.
Trustee: National City Bank.
EIN: 346716883

44089
Tenpenny Charitable Trust
c/o Sherri Tenpenny
7264 River Rd.
Olmsted Falls, OH 44138-1510
(440) 572-1136

Established in 1999 in OH.
Financial data (yr. ended 12/31/00): Grants paid, $8,100; assets, $260,301 (M); expenditures, $8,945; qualifying distributions, $8,100.

Limitations: Applications not accepted. Giving primarily in OH and VA.
Application information: Contributes only to pre-selected organizations.
Director: Sherri Tenpenny.
EIN: 347028466

44090
Elizabeth B. Bush Memorial Scholarship Trust
c/o KeyBank, N.A.
800 Superior Ave., 4th Fl.
Cleveland, OH 44114

Established in 1984 in NY.
Donor(s): Kenneth B. Wolfefor.‡
Financial data (yr. ended 12/31/00): Grants paid, $8,094; assets, $212,665 (M); expenditures, $10,427; qualifying distributions, $8,150.
Limitations: Applications not accepted. Giving limited to residents of Lewis, NY.
Application information: Unsolicited requests for funds not accepted.
Trustee: KeyBank, N.A.
EIN: 146123826

44091
The Martin Foundation
925 Euclid Ave.
Cleveland, OH 44115-1475

Established in 1999 in OH.
Financial data (yr. ended 12/31/01): Grants paid, $8,075; assets, $145,273 (M); expenditures, $8,944; qualifying distributions, $8,075.
Limitations: Applications not accepted. Giving primarily in OH.
Application information: Contributes only to pre-selected organizations.
Trustees: Michael E. Elliott, Charles O'Toole, Robert B. Tomaro.
EIN: 311537504

44092
Wilma S. Bemis Charitable Foundation, Inc.
7999 Mayfield Rd.
Chesterland, OH 44026

Established around 1995.
Donor(s): Wilma S. Bemis.
Financial data (yr. ended 12/31/99): Grants paid, $8,040; assets, $236,822 (M); expenditures, $8,128; qualifying distributions, $8,040.
Limitations: Applications not accepted.
Application information: Contributes only to pre-selected organizations.
Trustees: Wilma S. Bemis, Karen S. Chakford, Bruce G. Van Valkenburgh.
EIN: 341788885

44093
Becker Foundation
5709 Corey Cove
Sylvania, OH 43560-2734

Established in 1996 in OH.
Donor(s): Lewis B. Becker.
Financial data (yr. ended 12/31/01): Grants paid, $8,027; assets, $147,144 (M); expenditures, $8,669; qualifying distributions, $8,027.
Limitations: Giving primarily in CA and OH.
Trustees: Lewis B. Becker, Lillian B. Becker, Robert A. Falk.
EIN: 341787177

44094
Gaylord L. Jackson Scholarship Fund
c/o National City Bank
P.O. Box 94651
Cleveland, OH 44101-4651
Application address: P.O. Box 110, Fort Wayne, IN 46802, tel.: (219) 461-6199
Contact: Michele Delaney, Trust Off., National City Bank

Established in 1992 in IN.
Donor(s): Gaylord L. Jackson.‡
Financial data (yr. ended 11/30/01): Grants paid, $8,024; assets, $169,412 (M); expenditures, $11,209; qualifying distributions, $8,455.
Limitations: Giving limited to residents of Churubusco, IN.
Application information: Application form required.
Trustee: National City Bank.
EIN: 356564249

44095
The Anderson Scholarship Fund
(Formerly Carrie and Frances Anderson Memorial Scholarship Fund)
c/o Jon M. Anderson
41 S. High St., 32nd Fl.
Columbus, OH 43215-6101

Financial data (yr. ended 12/31/01): Grants paid, $8,000; assets, $133,768 (M); expenditures, $8,704; qualifying distributions, $8,182.
Limitations: Giving limited to Carrollton, OH.
Application information: Scholarships applicants recommended by high school principal.
Trustee: Jon M. Anderson.
EIN: 311130710
Codes: GTI

44096
Brecklen Foundation
c/o Donald Croy
1070 Commerce Dr., Ste. 300
Perrysburg, OH 43551
Application address: 2526 Hollydale Ave., Oregon, OH 43616, tel.: (419) 693-2725
Contact: Mark Brecklen, Tr.

Established in 2000 in OH.
Donor(s): Norma R. Brecklen.‡
Financial data (yr. ended 12/31/01): Grants paid, $8,000; assets, $122,474 (M); expenditures, $9,345; qualifying distributions, $8,000.
Limitations: Giving limited to Bowling Green, OH.
Trustees: Mark A. Brecklen, Donald M. Croy.
EIN: 341910770

44097
Jean and Charles Gottfried Scholarship Award
10031 County Hwy. 330
Upper Sandusky, OH 43351

Established in 2000 in OH.
Donor(s): Charles Gottfried, Jean Gottfried.
Financial data (yr. ended 12/31/01): Grants paid, $8,000; assets, $50,996 (M); gifts received, $4,000; expenditures, $8,249; qualifying distributions, $8,000.
Limitations: Giving limited to residents of OH.
Application information: Application form required.
Trustees: Charles Gottfried, Jean Gottfried.
EIN: 341910333

44098
The Kalt Family Foundation
5005 Bradley Rd.
Westlake, OH 44145-5112
Application address: 36700 Sugar Ridge Rd., North Ridgeville, OH 44039, tel.: (440) 327-2102

Financial data (yr. ended 12/31/01): Grants paid, $8,000; assets, $12,437 (M); expenditures, $8,001; qualifying distributions, $8,000.
Limitations: Giving primarily in OH.
Trustees: Timothy J. Conners, Jeanne M. Kalt, Joseph Kalt, Kristine Milkie.
EIN: 341391884

44099
Korzenewski Foundation, Inc.
c/o KeyBank, N.A.
800 Superior Ave., 4th Fl.
Cleveland, OH 44114

Established in 2000 in FL.
Donor(s): Susan Korzenewski.
Financial data (yr. ended 12/31/00): Grants paid, $8,000; assets, $86,480 (M); gifts received, $1,410; expenditures, $10,556; qualifying distributions, $9,962.
Trustee: KeyBank, N.A.
EIN: 650964986

44100
Lone Coyote Foundation
c/o National City Bank of Indiana
P.O. Box 94651
Cleveland, OH 44101-4651
Application address: P.O. Box 110, Fort Wayne, IN 46801, tel.: (219) 461-6199
Contact: Michele Delaney

Established in 1997 in IN.
Donor(s): John Brooks.
Financial data (yr. ended 12/31/00): Grants paid, $8,000; assets, $180,505 (M); gifts received, $25,887; expenditures, $9,583; qualifying distributions, $8,000.
Trustee: National City Bank of Indiana.
EIN: 356640971

44101
Pleasantville High School Student Fund
c/o National City Bank of Pennsylvania
P.O. Box 94651
Cleveland, OH 44101-4651
Application address: c/o National City Bank of Pennsylvania, 127 W. Spring St., Titusville, PA 16354, tel.: (814) 827-5954
Contact: Christopher A. Junker, Pres.

Financial data (yr. ended 12/31/01): Grants paid, $8,000; assets, $140,621 (M); expenditures, $9,351; qualifying distributions, $8,447.
Limitations: Giving limited to residents of PA.
Trustee: National City Bank.
EIN: 256030554

44102
Therese Lange Saenger & Sidney Lange Foundation
c/o Thompson, Hine & Flory
312 Walnut St.
Cincinnati, OH 45202
Contact: Melvin E. Marmer, Secy.

Financial data (yr. ended 04/30/02): Grants paid, $8,000; assets, $408,597 (M); expenditures, $11,406; qualifying distributions, $8,000.
Limitations: Giving primarily in Cincinnati, OH.
Officers and Trustees:* Eugene L. Saenger,* Pres.; Melvin E. Marmer,* Secy.; Eugene L. Saenger, Jr.
EIN: 316029774

44103
Trumbull County Scholarship Foundation
c/o Second National Bank of Warren
108 Main St. S.W.
Warren, OH 44481
Application address: 155 S. Park Ave., Warren, OH 44481, tel.: (330) 394-3773
Contact: Michael Craig, Chair.

Established in 1987 in OH.
Financial data (yr. ended 12/31/01): Grants paid, $8,000; assets, $126,270 (M); expenditures, $9,090; qualifying distributions, $8,000.
Limitations: Giving limited to Trumbull County, OH.
Application information: Application form required.
Officer: Michael P. Craig, Chair.
Trustee: Second National Bank of Warren.
EIN: 346545694

44104
Esther Hamilton Fund
(also known as Santa Claus Club Scholarship Fund)
c/o National City Bank
P.O. Box 94651
Cleveland, OH 44101-4651
Application address: c/o Myra Vitto, National City Bank, P.O. Box 450, Youngstown, OH 44503, tel.: (330) 742-4289

Financial data (yr. ended 12/31/01): Grants paid, $7,950; assets, $192,462 (M); expenditures, $11,259; qualifying distributions, $8,191.
Limitations: Giving limited to Mahoning County, OH.
Application information: Applications are available from Mahoning County high schools. Application form required.
Trustee: National City Bank.
EIN: 346575611

44105
Mary E. Powell Trust
c/o Citizens Federal Bldg.
112 N. Main St.
Bellefontaine, OH 43311-2021
Contact: D. Fred Burton, Pres.

Donor(s): Mary E. Powell.‡
Financial data (yr. ended 12/31/01): Grants paid, $7,920; assets, $123,905 (M); expenditures, $11,826; qualifying distributions, $8,853.
Limitations: Giving on a national basis.
Application information: Application form not required.
Officers and Trustees:* D. Fred Burton,* Pres.; Barbara A. Stewart, V.P.; J. MacAlpine Smith,* Secy. and Treas.
EIN: 346532522
Codes: GTI

44106
Elizabeth White Trust
c/o KeyBank, N.A.
800 Superior Ave., 4th Fl.
Cleveland, OH 44114
Application address: c/o KeyBank, N.A., 35 State St., Albany, NY 12207

Established in 1995 in NY.
Financial data (yr. ended 12/31/01): Grants paid, $7,905; assets, $147,874 (M); expenditures, $9,835; qualifying distributions, $7,904.
Limitations: Giving limited to Cooperstown, NY.
Trustee: KeyBank, N.A.
EIN: 146179502
Codes: GTI

44107
The Knight Hauserman Foundation
c/o Jacquita K. Hauserman
29325 Bolingbrook Rd.
Pepper Pike, OH 44124

Established in 1986 in OH.
Financial data (yr. ended 12/31/00): Grants paid, $7,850; assets, $36,152 (M); expenditures, $8,478; qualifying distributions, $7,850.
Limitations: Applications not accepted. Giving limited to Cleveland, OH.
Application information: Contributes only to pre-selected organizations.
Trustees: Jacquita K. Hauserman, Mark K. Hauserman, Tom Turney.
EIN: 341543991

44108
The Shepard Foundation
1900 Richmond Rd., No. 3N
Cleveland, OH 44124

Donor(s): Horace A. Shepard.
Financial data (yr. ended 12/31/00): Grants paid, $7,825; assets, $195,119 (M); expenditures, $9,998; qualifying distributions, $9,808.
Limitations: Applications not accepted.
Application information: Contributes only to pre-selected organizations.
Officers: Horace A. Shepard, Pres.; Jill Vanderwyst, Secy.-Treas.
EIN: 346578158

44109
Schulzinger-Lucas Family Foundation
6760 E. Beechlands Dr.
Cincinnati, OH 45237

Established in 1997 in OH.
Donor(s): Schulzinger-Frankel Family Foundation.
Financial data (yr. ended 12/31/01): Grants paid, $7,822; assets, $215,089 (M); gifts received, $9,382; expenditures, $9,795; qualifying distributions, $7,822.
Officers: Stanley J. Lucas, Pres.; Judith Lucas, Secy.
EIN: 311577902

44110
The Conrad Family Foundation
9 Ashley Ct.
Rocky River, OH 44116
Contact: Edward J. Conrad, Jr., Tr.

Established in 1999 in OH.
Donor(s): Edward J. Conrad, Jr., Joan A. Conrad.
Financial data (yr. ended 12/31/01): Grants paid, $7,810; assets, $1,257 (M); gifts received, $9,000; expenditures, $7,824; qualifying distributions, $7,810.
Trustees: Edward J. Conrad, Jr., Joan A. Conrad.
EIN: 341874633

44111
Victoria S. Roberts Scholarship Fund
c/o National City Bank of Pennsylvania
P.O. Box 94651
Cleveland, OH 44101-4651

Financial data (yr. ended 12/31/99): Grants paid, $7,800; assets, $235,097 (M); expenditures, $10,416; qualifying distributions, $8,921.
Limitations: Giving limited to residents of PA.
Application information: Application form required.
Trustee: National City Bank.
EIN: 256068156

44112
The Steele Foundation
4977 New Carlisle St. Paris Rd.
New Carlisle, OH 45344-9500

Donor(s): Harold E. Steele.
Financial data (yr. ended 12/31/01): Grants paid, $7,800; assets, $170,436 (M); gifts received, $4,300; expenditures, $8,170; qualifying distributions, $7,800.
Limitations: Applications not accepted. Giving primarily in OH.
Application information: Contributes only to pre-selected organizations.
Officers: Thelma M. Streber, V.P.; Esther L. Steele, Secy.-Treas.; Harold E. Steele, Mgr.
EIN: 237204460

44113
Department of Neurological Surgery Research Foundation
c/o Dr. Robert A. Ratcheson
11100 Euclid Ave., 5th Fl.
Cleveland, OH 44106

Established in 1992 in OH.
Donor(s): University Neurosurgeons of Cleveland, Inc.
Financial data (yr. ended 12/31/99): Grants paid, $7,779; assets, $2,202,540 (M); gifts received, $133,772; expenditures, $713,751; qualifying distributions, $707,804.
Limitations: Giving on a national basis.
Officer and Trustees:* Robert A. Ratcheson, M.D.,* Pres.; Alan Cohen, M.D., Russell W. Hardy, Jr., M.D., Warren R. Selman, M.D.
EIN: 341708133

44114
Mill-Rose Foundation, Inc.
c/o Mill-Rose Co.
7995 Tyler Blvd.
Mentor, OH 44060
Contact: Paul M. Miller, Tr.

Established in 1980.
Donor(s): Mill-Rose Co., and its subsidiary.
Financial data (yr. ended 06/30/02): Grants paid, $7,775; assets, $28,481 (M); expenditures, $8,400; qualifying distributions, $7,775.
Limitations: Giving primarily in OH.
Trustees: Lawrence W. Miller, Paul M. Miller, Richard M. Miller.
EIN: 341345012
Codes: CS, CD

44115
The Riley Family Foundation
c/o U.S. Bank
425 Walnut St., 7th Fl.
Cincinnati, OH 45202

Established in 1999 in OH.
Donor(s): Patrick M. Riley.
Financial data (yr. ended 12/31/01): Grants paid, $7,750; assets, $114,594 (M); gifts received, $115,693; expenditures, $11,167; qualifying distributions, $7,750.
Limitations: Applications not accepted.
Application information: Contributes only to pre-selected organizations.
Officers and Trustees:* Patrick M. Riley,* Pres.; Janet L. Houston,* Secy.; James A. McNeal,* Treas.
EIN: 311691433

44116
Goecke Charitable Trust
295 E. Ankenny Mill Rd.
Xenia, OH 45385

Established in 1995 in OH.

Financial data (yr. ended 12/31/99): Grants paid, $7,700; assets, $616,601 (M); gifts received, $79,671; expenditures, $20,200; qualifying distributions, $20,200.
Limitations: Applications not accepted.
Application information: Contributes only to pre-selected organizations.
Trustees: Daleann Goecke, Garay W. Goecke.
EIN: 367081357

44117
Sharp and Mary Proper Scholarship Fund
c/o National City Bank of Pennsylvania
P.O. Box 94651
Cleveland, OH 44101-4651
Application address: c/o Ronald Joyce, Guidance Dir., Titusville Area High School, Guidance Ctr., 302 E. Walnut, Titusville, PA 16354, tel.: (814) 827-9687

Financial data (yr. ended 12/31/99): Grants paid, $7,700; assets, $173,102 (M); expenditures, $8,921; qualifying distributions, $8,193.
Limitations: Giving primarily to residents of Titusville, PA.
Trustee: National City Bank.
EIN: 256167746

44118
J. D. Robertson Foundation
c/o William R. Robertson
13705 Shaker Blvd., Apt. 3A
Cleveland, OH 44120-1507 (216) 921-5882

Donor(s): James D. Robertson,‡ Bruce M. Robertson.‡
Financial data (yr. ended 12/31/01): Grants paid, $7,600; assets, $116,192 (M); expenditures, $7,848; qualifying distributions, $7,600.
Limitations: Giving on a national basis, with emphasis on the Midwest.
Application information: Application form not required.
Officers and Trustees:* William R. Robertson,* Chair. and Treas.; James C. Robertson,* Vice-Chair. and Secy.
EIN: 237006584

44119
Vermilion Foundation Fund
c/o KeyBank, N.A.
P.O. Box 10099
Toledo, OH 43699-0099

Financial data (yr. ended 03/31/02): Grants paid, $7,600; assets, $229,824 (M); expenditures, $10,296; qualifying distributions, $8,778.
Limitations: Applications not accepted. Giving primarily in Vermilion, OH.
Application information: Contributes only to pre-selected organizations.
Trustee: KeyBank, N.A.
EIN: 346504824

44120
Assistance to the Handicapped, Inc.
8537 Careys Run Pond
P.O. Box 578
Portsmouth, OH 45662 (740) 259-6180
Contact: Thomas Roth, Pres.

Financial data (yr. ended 09/30/01): Grants paid, $7,576; assets, $50,945 (M); expenditures, $25,087; qualifying distributions, $7,576.
Limitations: Giving primarily in OH.
Application information: Application form not required.
Officers: Thomas Roth, Pres.; Ellis Greathouse, Secy.
EIN: 310839856

44121
The Robert & Virginia Burkhardt Charitable Foundation
c/o Perry & O'Brien
1406 W. 6th St., Ste. 200
Cleveland, OH 44113-1300

Established in 1994 in OH.
Donor(s): Robert F. Burkhardt.
Financial data (yr. ended 12/31/01): Grants paid, $7,500; assets, $106,635 (M); expenditures, $8,577; qualifying distributions, $7,500.
Limitations: Giving primarily in OH.
Trustees: Debera M. Brockett, Robert F. Burkhardt, Virginia M. Burkhardt.
EIN: 341778899

44122
DOSTSW Foundation, Inc.
P.O. Box 768
Barberton, OH 44203-0768

Established in 1997 in OH.
Donor(s): James P. Kennedy.
Financial data (yr. ended 12/31/01): Grants paid, $7,500; assets, $37,960 (M); gifts received, $4,600; expenditures, $8,196; qualifying distributions, $7,500.
Trustee: James P. Kennedy.
EIN: 341851072

44123
Robert E. Johnston Foundation
c/o Fifth Third Bank
38 Fountain Sq. Plz., Dept. 630858, M/D 1COM31
Cincinnati, OH 45263

Established in 1998 in OH.
Financial data (yr. ended 12/31/01): Grants paid, $7,500; assets, $185,253 (M); expenditures, $9,419; qualifying distributions, $7,500.
Officers: Robert A. Johnston, Pres. and Treas.; Laurie F. Johnston, Secy.
Trustee: Fifth Third Bank.
EIN: 311579143

44124
Elmer & Eliza Werth Foundation, Inc.
742 Hampton Ave.
Toledo, OH 43609-2978

Established in 1990 in OH.
Donor(s): Elmer Werth,‡ Eliza Werth.‡
Financial data (yr. ended 12/31/99): Grants paid, $7,500; assets, $61,497 (L); expenditures, $8,118; qualifying distributions, $7,500.
Application information: Application forms are available at schools in the Tawas, MI, area. Application form required.
Officers: Corey Elson, Pres.; Laurie J. Pangle, Secy.; Lance Elson, Treas.
Trustee: Beverly Pangle.
EIN: 341636550

44125
Wildermuth Family Foundation
1201 Edgecliff Pl., Ste. 1151
Cincinnati, OH 45206-2853
Contact: Robert E. Wildermuth, Pres.

Established in 1999 in OH.
Donor(s): Robert E. Wildermuth.
Financial data (yr. ended 12/31/01): Grants paid, $7,500; assets, $42,852 (M); gifts received, $16,814; expenditures, $7,500; qualifying distributions, $7,500.
Limitations: Giving primarily in Cincinnati, OH.
Officers: Robert E. Wildermuth, Pres.; Robert G. Wildermuth, Secy.; Judith M. Wells, Treas.
EIN: 311617672

44126
Paul and Alma Klinger Scholarship Trust
c/o National City Bank
P.O. Box 94651
Cleveland, OH 44101-4651
Application address: c/o Myra Vitto, National City Bank, P.O. Box 450, Youngstown, OH 44501, tel.: (330) 742-4289

Financial data (yr. ended 12/31/00): Grants paid, $7,442; assets, $151,133 (M); expenditures, $9,738; qualifying distributions, $8,988.
Limitations: Giving primarily in Youngstown, OH.
Application information: Application form required.
Trustee: National City Bank.
EIN: 341902577

44127
Charles A. Witenhafer Scholarship Fund
c/o FirstMerit Bank, N.A.
P.O. Box 725
Medina, OH 44258 (330) 764-7254

Established in 1989 in OH.
Donor(s): Mrs. E. J. Witenhafer.
Financial data (yr. ended 12/31/99): Grants paid, $7,423; assets, $177,351 (M); expenditures, $9,720; qualifying distributions, $8,259.
Limitations: Giving primarily in Medina, OH.
Application information: Application form required.
Advisory Committee: Ray E. Laribee, Mrs. E. J. Witenhafer.
Trustee: FirstMerit Bank, N.A.
EIN: 346909567

44128
Wildermuth Scholarship Trust
P.O. Box 94651
Cleveland, OH 44101-4651

Donor(s): Andra Kay Antonelli.
Financial data (yr. ended 12/31/01): Grants paid, $7,410; assets, $173,060 (M); expenditures, $9,642; qualifying distributions, $8,363.
Limitations: Applications not accepted. Giving limited to residents of Logansport, IN.
Trustee: National City Bank.
EIN: 356433778

44129
The Clutterbuck Family Foundation
10 Kensington Oval
Rocky River, OH 44116

Established in OH in 1998.
Donor(s): Robert T. Clutterbuck, Virginia C. Clutterbuck.
Financial data (yr. ended 12/31/99): Grants paid, $7,400; assets, $153,370 (M); gifts received, $85,100; expenditures, $10,499; qualifying distributions, $7,400.
Limitations: Applications not accepted.
Application information: Contributes only to pre-selected organizations.
Officers: Robert T. Clutterbuck, Pres. and V.P.; Kimberly A. Clutterbuck, V.P.; Virginia C. Clutterbuck, Secy.-Treas.
EIN: 341868708

44130
George E. Morris & Clara F. Morris Scholarship Fund
c/o KeyBank, N.A., Trust Div.
800 Superior Ave., 4th Fl.
Cleveland, OH 44114

Established in 1992 in ME.

Financial data (yr. ended 05/31/01): Grants paid, $7,250; assets, $181,154 (M); expenditures, $9,790; qualifying distributions, $7,250.
Limitations: Applications not accepted.
Trustee: KeyBank, N.A.
EIN: 046714384

44131
The Stellhorn Foundation, Inc.
113 E. Jefferson St.
Sandusky, OH 44870-2706

Financial data (yr. ended 12/31/99): Grants paid, $7,228; assets, $166,023 (M); gifts received, $1,400; expenditures, $7,600; qualifying distributions, $7,328.
Limitations: Applications not accepted. Giving primarily in Columbus, OH.
Application information: Contributes only to pre-selected organizations.
Officers and Trustees:* Theodorte T. Stellhorn III,* Pres.; Marjorie T. Meredith, V.P.; Laura M. Stellhorn,* Secy.; Rebekah Stellhorn Wernsing,* Treas.; Clair Elizabeth Ellinger, Carol R. Gegner, Arthur K. Stellhorn.
EIN: 237066555

44132
Walter Stone Foundation
415 Bond Pl., Apt. 8D
Cincinnati, OH 45206

Donor(s): Walter Stone.
Financial data (yr. ended 12/31/01): Grants paid, $7,193; assets, $87,934 (M); gifts received, $19,921; expenditures, $7,912; qualifying distributions, $7,193.
Limitations: Applications not accepted. Giving primarily in Cincinnati, OH.
Application information: Contributes only to pre-selected organizations.
Trustee: Walter Stone.
EIN: 316090977

44133
The EPIK Foundation, Inc.
c/o U.S. Bank
P.O. Box 1118, ML CN-WN-07IV
Cincinnati, OH 45201-1118

Established in 2000 in OH.
Donor(s): Laurance L. Browning, Jr.
Financial data (yr. ended 12/31/01): Grants paid, $7,161; assets, $415,438 (M); gifts received, $60,267; expenditures, $21,766; qualifying distributions, $7,161.
Officers and Trustees:* Virginia Browning Illick,* Pres.; Joseph E. Illick IV,* V.P.; Janet L. Houston,* Secy.; James A. McNeal,* Treas.
EIN: 311714719

44134
MARSPF Foundation
P.O. Box 593
Hiram, OH 44234

Donor(s): Margaret I. Pejeau.
Financial data (yr. ended 12/31/01): Grants paid, $7,100; assets, $134,578 (M); expenditures, $9,568; qualifying distributions, $7,100.
Limitations: Applications not accepted.
Application information: Contributes only to pre-selected organizations.
Trustees: Amy Lynn Pejeau, Elizabeth Ann Pejeau, Richard A. Pejeau, Susan E. Pejeau.
EIN: 341861913

44135
Pearson Foundation
c/o Fifth Third Bank
38 Fountain Sq. Plz., Trust Tax Dept., MD 1COM31
Cincinnati, OH 45263
Application address: c/o Fifth Third Bank, Trust & Inv. Mgmt. Dept., P.O. Box 719, Evansville, IN 47705, tel.: (812) 456-3215

Financial data (yr. ended 12/31/01): Grants paid, $7,100; assets, $255,123 (M); expenditures, $10,191; qualifying distributions, $7,100.
Limitations: Giving primarily in IN.
Trustee: Fifth Third Bank.
EIN: 356015590

44136
Medal Charitable Trust
3139 Sunset Blvd.
Steubenville, OH 43952

Donor(s): Rogelio Mupas.
Financial data (yr. ended 09/30/01): Grants paid, $7,008; assets, $51,842 (M); gifts received, $5,000; expenditures, $7,910; qualifying distributions, $7,008.
Limitations: Applications not accepted.
Trustee: Rogelio Mupas.
EIN: 311578375

44137
Annie Wallingford Anderson Foundation
c/o U.S. Bank
P.O. Box 1118
Cincinnati, OH 45201

Established in 1998 in OH.
Financial data (yr. ended 12/31/01): Grants paid, $7,000; assets, $56,928 (M); expenditures, $9,303; qualifying distributions, $7,000.
Limitations: Applications not accepted.
Application information: Contributes only to pre-selected organizations.
Officers and Trustees:* Annie Wallingford Anderson,* Pres.; James Wellinghoff,* V.P.; Joseph Krabbe,* Secy.-Treas.; Christine Butress.
EIN: 311608632

44138
Elizabeth Mendenhall Anderson Foundation
c/o U.S. Bank
P.O. Box 1118
Cincinnati, OH 45201

Established in 1998 in OH.
Financial data (yr. ended 12/31/01): Grants paid, $7,000; assets, $80,913 (M); expenditures, $9,448; qualifying distributions, $7,000.
Limitations: Applications not accepted. Giving primarily in OH.
Application information: Contributes only to pre-selected organizations.
Trustees: Annie Anderson, Christine Buttres, Joseph Krabbe, James Wellinghoff.
EIN: 311608634

44139
Blancheola Bontrager Medical Scholarship Trust
c/o Wayne County National Bank
1776 Beall Ave.
Wooster, OH 44691 (330) 264-7111
Contact: Stephen Kitchen, Sr. Trust Off., Wayne County National Bank

Established in 1995 in OH.
Donor(s): Blancheola Bontrager.‡
Financial data (yr. ended 12/31/01): Grants paid, $7,000; assets, $173,093 (M); expenditures, $8,969; qualifying distributions, $7,916.

44139—OHIO

Limitations: Giving limited to residents of Holmes and Wayne counties, OH.
Application information: Application form not required.
Trustee: Stephen Kitchen.
EIN: 347034110
Codes: GTI

44140
Thomas O. Grove Scholarship Fund
c/o KeyBank, N.A., Trust Div.
P.O. Box 10099
Toledo, OH 43699-0099 (419) 259-8655
Contact: Diane Ohns, Trust Admin., KeyBank, N.A.

Established in 1990 in OH.
Donor(s): Thomas O. Grove.‡
Financial data (yr. ended 12/31/01): Grants paid, $7,000; assets, $250,921 (M); expenditures, $9,682; qualifying distributions, $7,790.
Limitations: Giving limited to the Sylvania, OH, area.
Application information: Application form required.
Trustee: KeyBank, N.A.
EIN: 346942668
Codes: GTI

44141
The Paul T. and Aili R. Jeffries Foundation
72 Braintree Ln.
Mentor, OH 44060-6604

Established in 1998 in OH.
Donor(s): Aili R. Jeffries.
Financial data (yr. ended 12/31/01): Grants paid, $7,000; assets, $116,405 (M); expenditures, $8,092; qualifying distributions, $6,960.
Limitations: Applications not accepted.
Application information: Contributes only to pre-selected organizations.
Trustees: Charles E. Cannon, Aili R. Jeffries.
EIN: 341864788

44142
Philippine Kerwer Fund
c/o National City Bank
P.O. Box 94651
Cleveland, OH 44101-4651
Application address: P.O. Box 450, Youngstown, OH., 44501, tel.: (330) 742-4289
Contact: Thomas Orr, Trust Off., National City Bank

Established in 1989 in OH.
Donor(s): Philippine Kerwer.‡
Financial data (yr. ended 12/31/01): Grants paid, $7,000; assets, $133,299 (M); expenditures, $8,404; qualifying distributions, $7,000.
Limitations: Giving limited to Youngstown, OH.
Trustee: National City Bank.
EIN: 346515578

44143
Lake Erie Marine Trades Association Educational Foundation, Inc.
1269 Bassett Rd.
Westlake, OH 44145 (440) 899-5009

Established in 1996 in OH.
Donor(s): Lake Erie Marine Trades Assoc.
Financial data (yr. ended 04/30/02): Grants paid, $7,000; assets, $4,801 (M); gifts received, $7,300; expenditures, $7,000; qualifying distributions, $7,000.
Application information: Application form required.
Trustees: Charles S. Huffman, Jr., Norman Schultz, William G. Shaeffer.
EIN: 341835791

44144
The John D. Proctor Foundation
2016 Midway Dr.
Twinsburg, OH 44087-1960
Contact: John D. Proctor, Pres.

Donor(s): John D. Proctor.
Financial data (yr. ended 09/30/01): Grants paid, $7,000; assets, $65,372 (M); gifts received, $7,000; expenditures, $7,050; qualifying distributions, $7,000.
Limitations: Giving primarily in OH.
Officers: John D. Proctor, Pres.; Margaret Cunningham, V.P.; James Kohler, Secy.; Stanley M. Proctor, Treas.
EIN: 341401428

44145
The Rip Foundation
12700 Lake Ave.
Lakewood, OH 44107

Established in 1997 in OH.
Financial data (yr. ended 12/31/01): Grants paid, $7,000; assets, $133,726 (M); gifts received, $10,696; expenditures, $7,060; qualifying distributions, $7,000.
Limitations: Applications not accepted.
Application information: Contributes only to pre-selected organizations.
Trustee: Robert Manning.
EIN: 311531644

44146
Ralph Winans Memorial Scholarship Fund
c/o Sky Trust, N.A.
P.O. Box 479
Youngstown, OH 44501-0479
Application addresses: c/o Etheleen Hugli, P.O. Box 482, Canfield, OH 44406; c/o Robert Corli, Superintendent, Western Reserve School System, Berlin Center, OH 44401; c/o Myron Young, 6454 S. Salem Rd., Ellsworth, OH 44416

Established in 1989 in OH.
Financial data (yr. ended 12/31/99): Grants paid, $7,000; assets, $172,450 (M); expenditures, $8,545; qualifying distributions, $7,376.
Limitations: Giving limited to OH.
Scholarship Selection Committee: Robert Coril, Myron E. Young.
Trustees: Etheleen Hugli, Sky Trust, N.A.
EIN: 341631397

44147
Hazel Grimm Fund
c/o U.S. Bank
P.O. Box 1118
Cincinnati, OH 45201-1118

Established in 1997 in OH.
Financial data (yr. ended 12/31/01): Grants paid, $6,934; assets, $315,303 (M); expenditures, $10,943; qualifying distributions, $6,934.
Limitations: Applications not accepted.
Application information: Contributes only to pre-selected organizations.
Trustee: U.S. Bank.
EIN: 316563578

44148
Gladys Gough Charitable Trust
c/o FirstMerit Bank, N.A.
121 S. Main St., Ste. 200
Akron, OH 44308-1440

Established in 1998 in OH.
Donor(s): Gladys Gough Trust.
Financial data (yr. ended 12/31/99): Grants paid, $6,923; assets, $201,936 (M); expenditures, $9,772; qualifying distributions, $7,167.

Limitations: Applications not accepted. Giving primarily in Akron, OH.
Application information: Contributes only to pre-selected organizations.
Trustee: FirstMerit Bank, N.A.
EIN: 347072401

44149
Gertrude L. Moore Trust
c/o National City Bank of Pennsylvania
P. O. Box 94651
Cleveland, OH 44101-4651

Financial data (yr. ended 12/31/00): Grants paid, $6,908; assets, $229,904 (M); expenditures, $8,812; qualifying distributions, $7,938.
Limitations: Applications not accepted. Giving primarily in Oil City, PA.
Application information: Contributes only to pre-selected organizations.
Trustee: National City Bank of Pennsylvania.
EIN: 256031194

44150
The Albert W. and Adele Krotzer Scholarship Fund
c/o National City Bank
P.O. Box 94651
Cleveland, OH 44101-4651
Application address: c/o Warren P. Williamson, Jr. School of Business Administration, Youngstown State Univ., Youngstown, OH 44555, tel.: (330) 742-3064

Established in 1987 in OH.
Financial data (yr. ended 12/31/01): Grants paid, $6,900; assets, $145,278 (M); expenditures, $8,403; qualifying distributions, $6,900.
Limitations: Giving limited to Youngstown, OH.
Application information: Application form required.
Trustee: National City Bank.
EIN: 346610983

44151
Jane E. and Thomas R. Armstrong Foundation, Inc.
c/o Robert F. Weber
931 Garnoa Dr.
Cincinnati, OH 45231-3706

Donor(s): Thomas R. Armstrong.
Financial data (yr. ended 12/31/01): Grants paid, $6,700; assets, $223,780 (M); expenditures, $8,745; qualifying distributions, $6,700.
Limitations: Applications not accepted. Giving limited to OH.
Application information: Contributes only to pre-selected organizations.
Trustees: Jane E. Armstrong, Robert F. Weber.
EIN: 237266679

44152
The Suzanne and Al Fleming Family Foundation
2237 5th Ave.
Youngstown, OH 44504

Established in 1994 in OH.
Donor(s): Suzanne M. Fleming, Alfred J. Fleming.
Financial data (yr. ended 11/30/01): Grants paid, $6,680; assets, $61,393 (M); expenditures, $7,132; qualifying distributions, $6,680.
Limitations: Applications not accepted. Giving primarily in Youngstown, OH.
Application information: Contributes only to pre-selected organizations.
Trustees: Alfred J. Fleming, Suzanne M. Fleming.
EIN: 341784419

44153
The Carbonari Family Foundation
c/o Bruce A. Carbonari
30410 Lake Rd.
Bay Village, OH 44140

Donor(s): Bruce A. Carbonari.
Financial data (yr. ended 12/31/01): Grants paid, $6,628; assets, $49,716 (M); expenditures, $6,628; qualifying distributions, $6,628.
Limitations: Applications not accepted.
Application information: Contributes only to pre-selected organizations.
Officers: Bruce A. Carbonari, Pres. and Treas.; Kathryn E. Carbonari, V.P. and Secy.
Director: Albert F. Carbonari.
EIN: 341787787

44154
Bradley Foundation
7050 Lassiter Dr.
Parma, OH 44129-6351

Established in 1985 in OH.
Donor(s): J.F. Bradley, J.F. Bradley, Jr.
Financial data (yr. ended 06/30/02): Grants paid, $6,600; assets, $168,475 (M); expenditures, $6,990; qualifying distributions, $6,600.
Limitations: Applications not accepted. Giving on a national basis.
Application information: Contributes only to pre-selected organizations.
Officers: J.F. Bradley, Jr., Pres. and Treas.; Angela C. Bradley, V.P. and Secy.
Trustee: Michael B. Bradley.
EIN: 341502222

44155
Feltrup Foundation
c/o Fifth Third Bank
1227 Rookwood Dr.
Cincinnati, OH 45208-3350
Contact: Julia M.F. Becker Jackson, Tr.

Established in 1999 in OH.
Financial data (yr. ended 12/31/01): Grants paid, $6,550; assets, $85,404 (M); gifts received, $70; expenditures, $7,912; qualifying distributions, $6,550.
Limitations: Giving primarily in OH.
Trustees: Brian C. Becker, Eric R. Becker, Annamarie Harten, Julia M.F. Becker Jackson, Fifth Third Bank.
EIN: 311684062

44156
The EWR Foundation
2991 Eaton Rd.
Shaker Heights, OH 44122-2515
(216) 752-1411
Contact: Margaret Rose Giltinan, Treas.

Donor(s): Ernest W. Rose.
Financial data (yr. ended 12/31/01): Grants paid, $6,530; assets, $544,172 (M); gifts received, $496,119; expenditures, $10,537; qualifying distributions, $6,530.
Limitations: Giving primarily in Cuyahoga County, OH.
Officers and Trustees:* John A. Giltinan,* Secy.; Margaret Rose Giltinan,* Treas.
EIN: 341756624

44157
Brent Kirk (Yale '76) Memorial Foundation
c/o The Huntington National Bank
P.O. Box 1558, HC1012
Columbus, OH 43216
Application address: P.O. Box 9240, Canton, OH 44711, tel.: (216) 484-4887
Contact: J. Steven Renkert, Tr.

Financial data (yr. ended 06/30/01): Grants paid, $6,529; assets, $91,868 (M); gifts received, $500; expenditures, $7,817; qualifying distributions, $6,809.
Limitations: Giving limited to residents of New Haven, CT.
Application information: Application form not required.
Trustees: Larry Markworth, J. Steven Renkert, The Huntington National Bank.
EIN: 346732841

44158
Gladwood Foundation
c/o National City Bank
P.O. Box 94651
Cleveland, OH 44101-4651

Established in 1999 in PA.
Donor(s): John H. Willock Charitable Lead Trust.
Financial data (yr. ended 12/31/01): Grants paid, $6,500; assets, $147,510 (M); gifts received, $35,000; expenditures, $8,737; qualifying distributions, $6,500.
Limitations: Applications not accepted.
Application information: Contributes only to pre-selected organizations.
Trustee: National City Bank.
EIN: 232997944

44159
Language Abroad Institute
3300 Terminal Tower
Cleveland, OH 44113

Financial data (yr. ended 12/31/01): Grants paid, $6,500; assets, $150,537 (M); expenditures, $7,716; qualifying distributions, $6,500.
Limitations: Applications not accepted. Giving primarily in Moreland Hills, OH.
Application information: Contributes only to a pre-selected organization.
Officers: John M. Stickney, Pres.; Nicholas B. Merkel, V.P.; Thomas M. Stickney, Secy.
EIN: 340923185

44160
MJB Foundation
P.O. Box 369-004
Columbus, OH 43236-9004

Donor(s): Yhezkel Levi, Merom Brachman, Judith Y. Brachman.
Financial data (yr. ended 12/31/01): Grants paid, $6,500; assets, $58,209 (M); gifts received, $5,000; expenditures, $6,496; qualifying distributions, $6,500.
Limitations: Applications not accepted. Giving primarily in OH.
Application information: Contributes only to pre-selected organizations.
Officers: Merom Brachman, Pres.; Lavea Brachman, V.P.; Norma Webb, Secy.; Judith Y. Brachman, Secy.-Treas.
EIN: 311040130

44161
The Nathan Family Foundation
739 Stanbridge Dr.
Kettering, OH 45429

Established in 1993 in OH.
Donor(s): Milton F. Nathan.
Financial data (yr. ended 12/31/01): Grants paid, $6,500; assets, $114,373 (M); gifts received, $5,000; expenditures, $6,521; qualifying distributions, $6,500.
Limitations: Applications not accepted. Giving primarily in Dayton, OH.
Application information: Contributes only to pre-selected organizations.
Trustees: Jeanne Nathan, Jon J. Nathan, Laura R. Nathan, Milton F. Nathan.
EIN: 311392451

44162
The Southard Foundation
10661 Edgewood Dr.
Dublin, OH 43017
Application address: c/o Lawrence L. Fisher, P.O. Box 1008, Columbus, OH 43216, tel.: (614) 464-6283

Donor(s): Robert C. Southard, Dorothy P. Southard.
Financial data (yr. ended 12/31/01): Grants paid, $6,500; assets, $226,766 (M); gifts received, $1,000; expenditures, $6,911; qualifying distributions, $6,500.
Limitations: Giving primarily in Columbus, OH.
Officers: Dorothy P. Southard, Pres.; Robert C. Southard, Secy.; Steven Rowland Southard, Treas.
EIN: 311229974

44163
The Mintz Family Foundation
985 Linwood Pl.
Mansfield, OH 44906 (419) 524-5072
Contact: Florence B. Mintz, Tr.

Donor(s): John A. Mintz.
Financial data (yr. ended 12/31/99): Grants paid, $6,480; assets, $113,880 (M); expenditures, $7,278; qualifying distributions, $7,141; giving activities include $111 for programs.
Limitations: Giving primarily in OH.
Trustees: Florence B. Mintz, Nancy E. Mintz, Richard O. Mintz, Iris M. Ossauon.
EIN: 346530343

44164
The Gershuny Foundation
7710 Shawnee Run Rd.
Cincinnati, OH 45243-3174 (513) 271-7600
Contact: Shirley Gershuny, Tr.

Financial data (yr. ended 11/30/01): Grants paid, $6,474; assets, $145,741 (M); expenditures, $7,394; qualifying distributions, $6,474.
Limitations: Giving primarily in Cincinnati, OH.
Trustee: Shirley Gershuny.
EIN: 316282632

44165
The McCready Family Foundation
670 W. Market St.
Akron, OH 44303
FAX: (330) 762-5855
Contact: Nancy Allshouse, Secy.

Financial data (yr. ended 12/31/01): Grants paid, $6,450; assets, $2,849,735 (M); expenditures, $40,062; qualifying distributions, $8,093.
Limitations: Giving on a national basis, with emphasis on OH.
Application information: Application form required.
Officer: Nancy Allshouse, Secy.
Trustees: Roland H. Bauer, Gail J. McCready, James P. McCready.
EIN: 341812977

44166
The Reichard Family Foundation
(Formerly St. Francis Xavier Foundation)
25109 Detroit Rd., Ste. 300
Westlake, OH 44145

Donor(s): Patricia M. Reichard, William E. Reichard, Michael X. Mooney.
Financial data (yr. ended 12/31/00): Grants paid, $6,450; assets, $15,660 (M); expenditures, $6,746; qualifying distributions, $6,450.
Limitations: Applications not accepted. Giving primarily in OH.
Application information: Contributes only to pre-selected organizations.
Trustees: Michael X. Mooney, Patricia M. Reichard, William E. Reichard.
EIN: 341339537

44167
AOH Foundation for Children
5040 Everett Rd., P.O. Box 825
Bath, OH 44210

Established in 2000 in OH.
Donor(s): Adel Halasa, Ofelia Halasa.
Financial data (yr. ended 07/31/01): Grants paid, $6,400; assets, $75,065 (M); expenditures, $8,445; qualifying distributions, $6,400.
Limitations: Applications not accepted.
Application information: Contributes only to pre-selected organizations.
Officers: Ofelia Halasa, Pres.; Adel Halasa, V.P.; Katrina Halasa, Secy.
Trustees: Marni Halasa, Malu Halasa.
EIN: 341932839

44168
H. Don & Kathryn Gill Charitable Foundation
4121 Bramshaw Rd., N.W.
Canton, OH 44718-2313

Established in 1996 in OH.
Donor(s): Kathryn J. Gill.
Financial data (yr. ended 06/30/01): Grants paid, $6,400; assets, $104,060 (M); expenditures, $6,605; qualifying distributions, $6,400.
Limitations: Applications not accepted.
Application information: Contributes only to pre-selected organizations.
Trustees: Kathryn J. Gill, Michael P. Gill.
EIN: 341844690

44169
Orange Schools Educational Foundation
3200 Chagrin Blvd.
Pepper Pike, OH 44124-5974

Established around 1992.
Financial data (yr. ended 12/31/99): Grants paid, $6,400; assets, $105,464 (M); gifts received, $69,996; expenditures, $17,450; qualifying distributions, $17,450.
Limitations: Applications not accepted.
Application information: Contributes only to pre-selected organizations.
Officers: Keith Belkin, Pres.; Karen Erlenbalit, V.P.; Daniel Lukich, Treas.
EIN: 341690189

44170
Daniel J. Steiner Scholarship Fund
c/o The Huntington National Bank
P.O. Box 1558
Columbus, OH 43216
Application address: c/o Guidance Counselor, New Philadelphia High School, 343 Ray Ave. N.W., New Philadelphia, OH 44663

Established in 1994 in OH.
Financial data (yr. ended 06/30/01): Grants paid, $6,365; assets, $121,952 (M); expenditures, $7,454; qualifying distributions, $6,449.
Limitations: Giving limited to residents of New Philadelphia and Tuscarawas, OH.
Application information: Application form required.
Trustees: Carol Bichsel, Michael Herchik, Paul Sullivan, The Huntington National Bank.
EIN: 316484643

44171
The Keller Family Foundation
c/o Robert B. Keplinger, Jr.
P.O. Box 119
Minerva, OH 44657
Application address: 1880 S. Broadway, Salem, OH 44460
Contact: Gary Keller, Tr.

Established in 1991 in OH.
Donor(s): J. Harrison Keller III, J. Harrison Keller IV.
Financial data (yr. ended 11/30/01): Grants paid, $6,300; assets, $199,996 (M); expenditures, $13,101; qualifying distributions, $6,300.
Trustees: Jay H. Keller IV, Connie Keller Kiplinger.
EIN: 341695454

44172
Soldiers of the Cross, Inc.
4175 N. High St.
Columbus, OH 43214
Application address: 7417 Murrayfield Dr., Worthington, OH 43085
Contact: Warren Willke, Pres.

Financial data (yr. ended 12/31/99): Grants paid, $6,242; assets, $199,738 (M); gifts received, $175; expenditures, $41,274; qualifying distributions, $41,274; giving activities include $4,204 for programs.
Limitations: Giving limited to Columbus, OH.
Officers: Warren Willke, Pres.; Betty Willke, Secy.-Treas.
EIN: 311360110

44173
Dr. D. R. Nugen Scholarship Fund
c/o KeyBank, N.A., Trust Div.
800 Superior Ave., 4th Fl.
Cleveland, OH 44114

Financial data (yr. ended 12/31/00): Grants paid, $6,237; assets, $130,408 (M); expenditures, $8,762; qualifying distributions, $6,846.
Limitations: Applications not accepted. Giving limited to residents of Nooksack, WA.
Application information: Unsolicited requests for funds not accepted.
Trustee: KeyBank, N.A.
EIN: 916028366

44174
Clark Family Charitable Foundation
1 W. 4th St., 24th Fl.
Cincinnati, OH 45202

Established in 1999 in OH.
Financial data (yr. ended 12/31/01): Grants paid, $6,210; assets, $227,103 (M); gifts received, $109,303; expenditures, $9,303; qualifying distributions, $6,086.
Limitations: Applications not accepted.
Application information: Contributes only to pre-selected organizations.
Officers: Brian G. Clark, Pres.; Taylor Clark, V.P.; Barrett Clark, Secy.-Treas.
Trustee: Susan T. Clark.
EIN: 311680960

44175
The Dale W. and Bonita J. Van Voorhis Family Foundation
5684 Pioneer Trail
Hiram, OH 44234

Established in 2000 in OH.
Donor(s): Dale W. Van Voorhis, Bonita J. Van Voorhis.
Financial data (yr. ended 12/31/01): Grants paid, $6,205; assets, $795 (M); gifts received, $5,400; expenditures, $6,605; qualifying distributions, $6,205.
Limitations: Applications not accepted.
Application information: Contributes only to pre-selected organizations.
Trustees: Bonita J. Van Voorhis, Dale W. Van Voorhis.
EIN: 341936389

44176
Nelson & Belva Stallsmith Scholarship Fund
c/o Champaign National Bank and Trust, Trust Dept.
601 Scioto St.
Urbana, OH 43078

Established in 1998 in OH.
Donor(s): Knights of Pythians, Harmony Lodge No. 8.
Financial data (yr. ended 12/31/01): Grants paid, $6,200; assets, $147,027 (M); expenditures, $10,593; qualifying distributions, $6,200.
Limitations: Giving limited to Urbana, OH.
Application information: Application form required.
Trustees: James T. Oliver, Ray Snarr, Champaign National Bank and Trust.
EIN: 341859951

44177
Joe Prest Educational Trust Fund
c/o Michael J. Calabria
421 Market St.
Steubenville, OH 43952

Established in 1993 in OH.
Donor(s): Joseph Prest, Sr.
Financial data (yr. ended 12/31/99): Grants paid, $6,118; assets, $105,250 (M); gifts received, $13,100; expenditures, $6,285; qualifying distributions, $6,127.
Limitations: Giving primarily in Steubenville, OH.
Trustees: Michael J. Calabria, Anthony Guida, Joseph G. Prest, Sr., Darrell Spatafore.
EIN: 341742248

44178
Alice & Charles Schneider Charitable Trust
c/o Charles Schneider
305 Forest Ave.
Wyoming, OH 45215

Donor(s): Charles Schneider, Alice Schneider.
Financial data (yr. ended 11/30/01): Grants paid, $6,075; assets, $8,077 (M); expenditures, $6,320; qualifying distributions, $6,075.
Limitations: Giving primarily in OH.
Trustees: Alice Schneider, Charles Schneider.
EIN: 316542485

44179
Stanley H. Byram Foundation
c/o National City Bank of Indiana
P.O. Box 94651
Cleveland, OH 44101-4651

Financial data (yr. ended 12/31/99): Grants paid, $6,000; assets, $188,520 (M); expenditures, $8,341; qualifying distributions, $6,875.

Limitations: Applications not accepted. Giving primarily in Martinsville, IN.
Trustee: National City Bank of Indiana.
EIN: 356007637

44180
The Cloyes-Myers Foundation
c/o John D. Drinko
3200 National City Ctr.
Cleveland, OH 44114

Established in 1991 in OH.
Donor(s): Cloyes Gear & Products, Inc., Malcolm R. Myers, John D. Drinko.
Financial data (yr. ended 12/31/01): Grants paid, $6,000; assets, $104,081 (M); expenditures, $8,467; qualifying distributions, $7,083.
Limitations: Applications not accepted. Giving limited to OH.
Application information: Contributes only to pre-selected organizations.
Officers and Trustees:* Malcolm R. Myers,* Pres.; M. Trevor Myers,* V.P.; J. Richard Hamilton,* Secy.; John D. Drinko,* Treas.
EIN: 341670463
Codes: CS, CD

44181
Alfred Duff Memorial Fund
P.O. Box 165
Port Clinton, OH 43452-0165 (419) 732-3145
Contact: Judy Paschen, Secy.-Treas.

Financial data (yr. ended 12/31/99): Grants paid, $6,000; assets, $98,721 (M); expenditures, $3,977; qualifying distributions, $6,000; giving activities include $6,000 for loans to individuals.
Limitations: Giving limited to Ottawa County, OH.
Application information: Application form required.
Officer and Trustees:* Judy Paschen,* Secy.-Treas.; Cathy Davenport, Kim Johnson, Debra Lonneman.
EIN: 346555080

44182
Otto A. Fritz & Lucille Wagner Fritz Scholarship Trust Fund
c/o National City Bank
P.O. Box 94651
Cleveland, OH 44101-4651
Application address: Guidance Counselor, c/o Herscher High School, P.O. Box 504, Herscher, IL 60941

Financial data (yr. ended 12/31/99): Grants paid, $6,000; assets, $119,252 (M); expenditures, $7,734; qualifying distributions, $6,922.
Limitations: Giving limited to Herscher, IL.
Application information: Application form required.
Trustee: National City Bank.
EIN: 366949602

44183
Fuller Memorial Trust
c/o KeyBank, N.A., Trust Div.
800 Superior Ave., 4th Fl.
Cleveland, OH 44114
Application address: c/o William Pelletier, Kennebec Savings Bank, P.O. Box 108, Augusta, ME 04330

Financial data (yr. ended 08/31/01): Grants paid, $6,000; assets, $245,030 (M); expenditures, $7,956; qualifying distributions, $6,000.
Limitations: Giving primarily in ME.
Trustee: KeyBank, N.A.
EIN: 016008546

44184
Trusteeship of the May Green Scholarship Fund
4th at Hickory Sts.
Martins Ferry, OH 43935

Financial data (yr. ended 12/31/00): Grants paid, $6,000; assets, $82,131 (M); expenditures, $6,880; qualifying distributions, $6,130.
Limitations: Applications not accepted. Giving limited to Martins Ferry, OH.
Application information: Scholarship recipients are selected from the graduating class of Martins Ferry High School, OH.
Trustees: James W. Everson, Bill N. Lawrence, Daniel Stephens.
EIN: 341537233

44185
Mosbacher 4-H Educational Fund
c/o National City Bank
P.O. Box 94651
Cleveland, OH 44101-4651
Application address: 301 Southwest Adams, Peoria, IL 61602, tel.: (309) 655-5385
Contact: Jo Ann Harlan, Trust Off., National City Bank

Established around 1974 in IL.
Financial data (yr. ended 12/31/99): Grants paid, $6,000; assets, $50,798 (M); gifts received, $1,000; expenditures, $6,694; qualifying distributions, $6,578.
Limitations: Giving limited to residents of McLean County, IL.
Application information: Application form not required.
Officers: Jeannea Shier, Chair.; Esther Brokaw, Vice-Chair.; Jesse Smart, Exec. Secy.; Brian Basting, Treas.
Trustees: Brad Barclay, Michael Graf, Carolyn Hoffbauer, Doug Oehler, Melanie Stephens, Betty Ann Yoder, National City Bank.
EIN: 366449750

44186
Dennis and Peggy Murray Foundation
142 Bayshore Dr.
Sandusky, OH 44870

Established in 1997 in OH.
Donor(s): Margaret A. Murray, Dennis E. Murray.
Financial data (yr. ended 12/31/01): Grants paid, $6,000; assets, $32,762 (M); gifts received, $10,000; expenditures, $6,165; qualifying distributions, $6,000.
Limitations: Applications not accepted.
Application information: Contributes only to pre-selected organizations.
Trustees: Dennis E. Murray, Margaret A. Murray.
EIN: 311534227

44187
Thompson Family Foundation
30195 Chagrin Blvd., Ste. 210
Pepper Pike, OH 44124

Established in 2000 in OH.
Donor(s): W. Hayden Thompson.
Financial data (yr. ended 12/31/01): Grants paid, $6,000; assets, $7,181 (M); gifts received, $10,000; expenditures, $6,384; qualifying distributions, $6,000.
Limitations: Applications not accepted. Giving primarily in CA, GA, and OH.
Application information: Contributes only to pre-selected organizations.
Officers and Trustees:* W. Hayden Thompson,* Pres. and Treas.; William H. Thompson, V.P. and Secy.; John P. Thompson,* V.P.; Martha R. Thompson,* V.P.; Michael C. Thompson,* V.P.; Patricia M. Thompson,* V.P.
EIN: 341913926

44188
Dr. Thomas E. Wilson Memorial Scholarship Fund
108 Main Ave. S.W., Ste. 500
Warren, OH 44481

Established in 1998 in OH.
Donor(s): Katherine P. Wilson.
Financial data (yr. ended 12/31/01): Grants paid, $6,000; assets, $65,697 (M); gifts received, $9,163; expenditures, $15,948; qualifying distributions, $6,000.
Limitations: Applications not accepted. Giving primarily in OH.
Application information: Contributes only to pre-selected organizations.
Trustee: Patrick K. Wilson.
EIN: 341865160

44189
The Stanley L. and Grace A. Woofter Family Foundation
c/o Stanwade
P.O. Box 10
Hartford, OH 44424

Established in 1999 in OH.
Financial data (yr. ended 12/31/01): Grants paid, $6,000; assets, $80,589 (M); gifts received, $40,833; expenditures, $6,083; qualifying distributions, $6,000.
Limitations: Applications not accepted. Giving primarily in OH.
Application information: Contributes only to pre-selected organizations.
Trustees: Dennis S. Woofter, Grace A. Woofter, Timothy K. Woofter.
EIN: 341892083

44190
Kenneth B. Wyman Scholarship Trust
c/o KeyBank, N.A.
800 Superior Ave., 4th Fl.
Cleveland, OH 44114-1306
Application address: P.O. Box 1054, Augusta, ME 04332

Donor(s): Kenneth B. Wyman.‡
Financial data (yr. ended 04/30/00): Grants paid, $6,000; assets, $270,019 (M); expenditures, $9,337; qualifying distributions, $6,000.
Limitations: Giving limited to residents of Northport, ME.
Trustee: KeyBank, N.A.
EIN: 016075670

44191
Virginia Wright Mothers Guild, Inc.
426 E. Clinton St.
Columbus, OH 43202-2741
Contact: Marjorie Courtwright, Treas.

Financial data (yr. ended 06/30/01): Grants paid, $5,960; assets, $51,853 (M); gifts received, $1,838; expenditures, $7,390; qualifying distributions, $7,390.
Limitations: Applications not accepted. Giving limited to residents of the Columbus, OH, area.
Officers: Florence Sanders, Pres.; Majorie Courtwright, Treas.
EIN: 316034381
Codes: GTI

44192
The Debbie L. & Richard L. Westheimer Family Foundation
36 E. 4th St., Ste. 905
Cincinnati, OH 45202 (513) 651-1110
Contact: Debbie L. Westheimer, V.P.

Established in 1998 in OH.
Donor(s): Richard L. Westheimer.
Financial data (yr. ended 07/31/01): Grants paid, $5,836; assets, $135,537 (M); expenditures, $8,402; qualifying distributions, $5,836.
Limitations: Giving primarily in OH.
Officers: Richard L. Westheimer, Pres. and Treas.; Debbie L. Westheimer, V.P. and Secy.
Trustee: Ruth W. Westheimer.
EIN: 311628719

44193
Olszeski Family Foundation
847 W. Maple St.
Hartville, OH 44632-9404

Established in 1999 in OH.
Financial data (yr. ended 12/31/00): Grants paid, $5,750; assets, $2,278 (M); expenditures, $6,035; qualifying distributions, $6,035.
Limitations: Applications not accepted. Giving primarily in OH.
Application information: Contributes only to pre-selected organizations.
Trustees: Joan O. Coblentz, Judy O. Holcomb, Freda Olszeski, Jane O. Tortola.
EIN: 341905464

44194
Jeanann Gray Dunlap Foundation
8050 Hosbrook Rd., Ste. 210
Cincinnati, OH 45236-2907

Established in OH in 1998.
Financial data (yr. ended 12/31/01): Grants paid, $5,625; assets, $2,353 (M); gifts received, $6,000; expenditures, $5,625; qualifying distributions, $5,625.
Trustees: Lewis Gatch, Benjamin H. Gray.
EIN: 311544745

44195
Kademanay Foundation
2492 W. Dublin-Granville Rd.
Columbus, OH 43235-2709
Application address: 5609 Greenmont Pl., Vienna, WV 26105
Contact: Srini Vasan, Pres.

Established in 1995 in OH.
Donor(s): Srini Vasan.
Financial data (yr. ended 12/31/01): Grants paid, $5,600; assets, $0 (M); gifts received, $100,000; expenditures, $6,095; qualifying distributions, $5,600.
Limitations: Giving on an international basis, with emphasis on India.
Application information: Application form required.
Officers: Srini Vasan, Pres. and Treas.; Teresa Valentine, Secy.
Director: Usha Vasan.
EIN: 311448568

44196
S. Quering & G. Newell Memorial Trust
c/o National City Bank of Pennsylvania
P.O. Box 94651
Cleveland, OH 44101-4651

Financial data (yr. ended 12/31/01): Grants paid, $5,587; assets, $190,828 (M); expenditures, $7,465; qualifying distributions, $5,587.
Limitations: Applications not accepted.
Application information: Contributes only to pre-selected organizations.
Trustee: National City Bank.
EIN: 256559299

44197
Harry A. Mock Trust
19 E. High St.
P.O. Box 189
Mount Gilead, OH 43338-0189

Financial data (yr. ended 12/31/00): Grants paid, $5,586; assets, $88,272 (M); expenditures, $7,363; qualifying distributions, $7,363.
Limitations: Applications not accepted. Giving limited to Cardington, OH.
Trustee: Tom C. Elkin.
EIN: 316317496

44198
Katherine Fry Charitable Trust
c/o National City Bank of Pennsylvania
P.O. Box 94651
Cleveland, OH 44101-4651

Financial data (yr. ended 12/31/01): Grants paid, $5,581; assets, $236,059 (M); expenditures, $7,622; qualifying distributions, $6,602.
Limitations: Applications not accepted.
Application information: Contributes only to pre-selected organizations.
Trustee: National City Bank of Pennsylvania.
EIN: 527142891

44199
Maxine Sprague Lahti Foundation for the Performing Arts
c/o National City Bank
P. O. Box 94651
Cleveland, OH 44101-4651
Application address: c/o Gary Murphy, National City Bank, 3331 W. Big Beaver, Ste. 200, Troy, MI 48084, tel.: (248) 458-0331

Established in 1987 in MI.
Financial data (yr. ended 12/31/01): Grants paid, $5,560; assets, $120,181 (M); expenditures, $6,089; qualifying distributions, $5,560.
Limitations: Giving limited to the Monroe, MI, area.
Application information: Application form required.
Trustee: National City Bank.
EIN: 382720188

44200
Schimberg Family Charitable Foundation
130 Linden Dr.
Cincinnati, OH 45215
Contact: Martha Schimberg, Pres.

Established in 1997 in OH.
Donor(s): Martha Schimberg.
Financial data (yr. ended 12/31/01): Grants paid, $5,559; assets, $108,761 (M); expenditures, $5,798; qualifying distributions, $5,559.
Officers: Martha Schimberg, Pres.; Lee Schimberg, V.P.; David Schimberg, Secy.-Treas.
EIN: 311581894

44201
Nicol Charitable Trust
2170 Hanley Rd.
Lucas, OH 44843-9756

Established in 1999 in OH.
Donor(s): Nicol Asset Management.
Financial data (yr. ended 12/31/99): Grants paid, $5,532; assets, $75 (L); gifts received, $6,075; expenditures, $6,000; qualifying distributions, $5,532.
Trustees: David A. Nicol, Ethel I. Nicol.
EIN: 347092087
Codes: CS

44202
Helfrich Family Fund
c/o Mart L. Helfrich, Jr.
1221 Marion Rd.
Bucyrus, OH 44820-3106

Donor(s): Mart L. Helfrich.
Financial data (yr. ended 12/31/01): Grants paid, $5,525; assets, $172,580 (M); expenditures, $5,641; qualifying distributions, $5,525.
Limitations: Applications not accepted. Giving primarily in OH.
Application information: Contributes only to pre-selected organizations.
Trustees: Ann E. Helfrich, Lee E. Helfrich, Mart L. Helfrich, Jessie A. Raynor.
EIN: 346565647

44203
Pokorny Family Foundation
711 Mariner Village
Huron, OH 44839-1035

Established in 2000 in OH.
Donor(s): Donald Pokorny, Ann Pokorny.
Financial data (yr. ended 12/31/01): Grants paid, $5,525; assets, $106,476 (M); gifts received, $80,000; expenditures, $6,087; qualifying distributions, $5,525.
Limitations: Applications not accepted. Giving primarily in OH.
Application information: Contributes only to pre-selected organizations.
Trustees: Ann Pokorny, David Pokorny, Donald Pokorny, Gwenn Pokorny, Jeffrey Pokorny, Terrence Pokorny, Timothy Pokorny.
EIN: 341922347

44204
Coshocton Rotary Foundation, Inc.
P.O. Box 675
Coshocton, OH 43812-0675
Application address: 305 Main St., Coshocton, OH 43812, tel.: (740) 622-6464
Contact: Michael P. McCullough, Tr.

Financial data (yr. ended 06/30/01): Grants paid, $5,500; assets, $535,452 (M); gifts received, $52,035; expenditures, $13,047; qualifying distributions, $5,500.
Limitations: Giving limited to Coshocton, OH.
Trustees: J. Brown, T. Bryan, B. Emmons, T. France, Michael P. McCullough, A. Miller, S. Pyle, Shane Pyle, D. Truett.
EIN: 237258096

44205
The Brian Goldsmith Memorial Scholarship Fund, Inc.
12007 Drake Rd.
North Royalton, OH 44133

Donor(s): John H. Goldsmith.
Financial data (yr. ended 12/31/99): Grants paid, $5,500; assets, $127,302 (M); expenditures, $6,227; qualifying distributions, $5,500.
Limitations: Applications not accepted.
Officer and Trustees: Randy L. Green,* Admin.; John H. Goldsmith, Lawrence G. Kirshbaum.
EIN: 341444960

44206
B. N. MacGregor Foundation
c/o Second National Bank of Warren
108 Main Ave. S.W.
Warren, OH 44481
Contact: W. Hanshaw

Financial data (yr. ended 12/31/01): Grants paid, $5,450; assets, $93,512 (M); expenditures, $6,899; qualifying distributions, $5,450.
Limitations: Giving primarily in Warren, OH.
Trustees: Marilyn Williams, Robert H. Williams, Second National Bank of Warren.
EIN: 346516725

44207
The Epiphany Foundation
169 Bradstreet Rd.
Centerville, OH 45459-4549 (937) 434-0497

Financial data (yr. ended 06/30/02): Grants paid, $5,440; assets, $131,937 (M); gifts received, $1,410; expenditures, $6,850; qualifying distributions, $5,440.
Limitations: Giving primarily in OH.
Trustees: Robert Hadley, Betsy Kitch, Margot Merz, Richard Metzger.
EIN: 311049287

44208
The Strawbridge Family Foundation
2391 Channing Rd.
Cleveland, OH 44118-3741

Established in 1986 in OH.
Donor(s): Marie S. Strawbridge.
Financial data (yr. ended 12/31/01): Grants paid, $5,400; assets, $128,693 (M); expenditures, $6,220; qualifying distributions, $5,400.
Limitations: Giving primarily in FL and OH.
Officers: Leigh Strawbridge, Pres.; Holly Strawbridge, V.P.; Marie S. Strawbridge, V.P.
EIN: 341542318

44209
Siegfried Family Foundation
674 Davidson Dr.
Highland Heights, OH 44143

Established in 2000 in OH.
Donor(s): John P. Siegfried, Susan A. Siegfried.
Financial data (yr. ended 12/31/01): Grants paid, $5,375; assets, $95,996 (M); expenditures, $5,487; qualifying distributions, $5,375.
Limitations: Applications not accepted.
Application information: Contributes only to pre-selected organizations.
Officers and Trustees:* John P. Siegfried,* Pres.; Susan A. Siegfried,* Secy.; Patrick M. Surdy.
EIN: 341936942

44210
Irving C. & Ruth H. Reynolds Foundation
c/o KeyBank, N.A.
P.O. Box 10099
Toledo, OH 43699-0099 (419) 259-8391
Contact: Imogene S. Meyer, Trust Admin., KeyBank, N.A.

Financial data (yr. ended 12/31/01): Grants paid, $5,350; assets, $97,595 (M); expenditures, $5,969; qualifying distributions, $5,350.
Limitations: Giving primarily in Toledo, OH.
Advisory Committee Members: Jack Hadley, Ruth Hadley, Ruth H. Reynolds.
Trustee: KeyBank, N.A.
EIN: 346504815

44211
Albert Schweitzer Society USA, Inc.
265 Kimbary Dr.
Centerville, OH 45458-4143
Application address: P.O. Box 75203, Dayton, OH 45475-2073
Contact: Harold R. Fetter, Secy.-Treas.

Established in 1998 in AL.
Financial data (yr. ended 12/31/00): Grants paid, $5,350; assets, $2,947,549 (M); gifts received, $23,750; expenditures, $28,464; qualifying distributions, $5,350.
Officers: F.A. Bogaerts, C.E.O.; Albert T. Hastings, Pres.; Melvin R. Singleterry, V.P.; Harold R. Fetter, Secy.-Treas.
EIN: 630940073

44212
The Norann Charitable Trust
P.O. Box 39666
Solon, OH 44139

Established in 1994 in OH.
Donor(s): Norbert J. Tobbe, Ann D. Tobbe.
Financial data (yr. ended 12/31/01): Grants paid, $5,325; assets, $132,984 (M); expenditures, $6,498; qualifying distributions, $5,325.
Limitations: Applications not accepted.
Application information: Contributes only to pre-selected organizations.
Trustees: Ann D. Tobbe, Norbert J. Tobbe.
EIN: 341791471

44213
Eugene & Roberta Stoeckly Foundation
c/o James J. Ryan
425 Walnut St., Ste. 1800
Cincinnati, OH 45202

Established in 1997 in OH.
Donor(s): Eugene Stoeckly, Roberta Stoeckly.
Financial data (yr. ended 12/31/01): Grants paid, $5,275; assets, $14,851 (M); expenditures, $5,368; qualifying distributions, $5,275.
Limitations: Applications not accepted.
Application information: Contributes only to pre-selected organizations.
Officers and Trustees:* Eugene E. Stoeckly,* Pres.; Roberta B. Stoeckly,* V.P.; James J. Ryan,* Secy.
EIN: 311522329

44214
The Dorothea and Fletcher Gleason Family Foundation
3230 Fox Hollow Dr.
Pepper Pike, OH 44124
Contact: Fletcher Gleason, Pres.

Established in 1997 in OH.
Donor(s): Fletcher Gleason.
Financial data (yr. ended 12/31/01): Grants paid, $5,250; assets, $92,884 (M); expenditures, $6,315; qualifying distributions, $5,250.
Limitations: Giving primarily in Cleveland, OH.
Officers: Fletcher Gleason, Pres.; Patricia A. Carleton, Secy.; Kristina L. Gleason, Treas.
EIN: 311497527

44215
Huenefeld Memorial Foundation
7 Denny Pl.
Cincinnati, OH 45227
Contact: Robert C. Huenefeld, Tr.

Donor(s): Robert C. Huenefeld.
Financial data (yr. ended 11/30/00): Grants paid, $5,250; assets, $445 (M); gifts received, $5,600; expenditures, $5,310; qualifying distributions, $5,250.

Application information: Grants are generally made to organizations with which the trustees are familiar.
Trustees: Braden R. Huenefeld, Marie Huenefeld, Robert C. Huenefeld.
EIN: 311095082

44216
Charles F. & Mary M. Yeiser Foundation
4001 Carew Twr., 441 Vine St.
Cincinnati, OH 45202

Donor(s): Charles F. Yeiser, Mary M. Yeiser.
Financial data (yr. ended 12/31/99): Grants paid, $5,250; assets, $1,206 (M); gifts received, $5,500; expenditures, $5,263; qualifying distributions, $5,250.
Limitations: Giving primarily in OH.
Officers and Trustee:* Charles F. Yeiser,* Pres.; Eric B. Yeiser, V.P.; Pamela J. Story, Secy.
EIN: 316033638

44217
Northeastern Ohio Tennis Patrons, Inc.
1 Bratenahl Pl., Ste. 310
Bratenahl, OH 44108-1152

Financial data (yr. ended 11/30/01): Grants paid, $5,245; assets, $316,820 (M); gifts received, $52,892; expenditures, $27,470; qualifying distributions, $5,245.
Limitations: Applications not accepted.
Application information: Contributes only to pre-selected organizations.
Officers: Robert S. Malaga, Pres.; Robert C. Bouhall, V.P.; Lawrence M. Wolf, Secy.-Treas.
EIN: 346555866

44218
Beatrice Prior Memorial Scholarship Trust
146 E. Center St.
Marion, OH 43302

Established in 2000 in OH.
Financial data (yr. ended 12/31/01): Grants paid, $5,203; assets, $326,238 (M); expenditures, $7,339; qualifying distributions, $5,203.
Limitations: Giving limited to residents of Marion, OH.
Trustees: John C. Bartram, Michael J. McCreary, Robert H. Thiede.
EIN: 316637737

44219
Helen Vandenbark Scholarship Fund
c/o First Financial Svcs. Group, N.A.
P.O. Box 2307
Zanesville, OH 43702-2307 (740) 455-7060

Financial data (yr. ended 12/31/01): Grants paid, $5,200; assets, $127,928 (M); expenditures, $6,849; qualifying distributions, $5,305.
Limitations: Giving limited to Zanesville, OH.
Application information: Application form required.
Trustee: First Financial Services Group, N.A.
EIN: 316226483
Codes: GTI

44220
The Weisenburger Family Charitable Foundation, Inc.
300 Madison Ave., Ste. 1100
Toledo, OH 43604
Contact: Thomas E. Weisenburger, Tr.

Established in 1996 in OH.
Donor(s): Sandra L. Weisenburger.
Financial data (yr. ended 12/31/01): Grants paid, $5,175; assets, $223,610 (M); expenditures, $5,826; qualifying distributions, $5,175.
Limitations: Giving primarily in OH.

44220—OHIO

Trustees: John B. Kennedy, Sandra L. Weisenburger, Thomas E. Weisenburger.
EIN: 341845109

44221
Crystal Clinic Research & Education Foundation
3975 Embassy Pkwy.
Akron, OH 44333 (330) 668-4045
Contact: Nina M. Njus, M.D., Pres.

Established in 1993.
Donor(s): J. Whit Ewing, M.D., Nina Njus, Ivan A. Gradisar, Jr.
Financial data (yr. ended 12/31/99): Grants paid, $5,168; assets, $201,664 (M); gifts received, $13,868; expenditures, $6,938; qualifying distributions, $6,888; giving activities include $4,900 for programs.
Limitations: Giving primarily in Akron, OH.
Application information: Application form required.
Officers and Trustees:* Nina Njus, M.D.,* Pres.; Raymond W. Acus III,* V.P.; Robert B. Cooper,* Secy.; J. Whit Ewing, M.D., Ivan A. Gradisar, Jr., Michael L. Stark, Mark Wells, M.D., William C. Wojno, M.D.
EIN: 341654150

44222
John C. Brier Trust
c/o National City Bank
P.O. Box 94651
Cleveland, OH 44101-4651

Financial data (yr. ended 12/31/01): Grants paid, $5,166; assets, $193,897 (M); expenditures, $6,617; qualifying distributions, $5,979.
Limitations: Applications not accepted. Giving primarily in MI.
Application information: Contributes only to pre-selected organizations.
Trustee: National City Bank.
EIN: 386345036

44223
Minton Family Foundation, Inc.
P.O. Box 1027
Warren, OH 44482

Established in 1999 in OH.
Financial data (yr. ended 12/31/01): Grants paid, $5,140; assets, $89,576 (M); expenditures, $5,331; qualifying distributions, $5,140.
Trustees: Randie R. Adamson, Patricia Beal, Audrey J. Minton, Dale C. Minton, Pam A. Schofer.
EIN: 341915353

44224
Dallas and Samuel Shy Goodman Educational Trust Fund
c/o National City Bank
P.O. Box 94651
Cleveland, OH 44101-4651
Application address: c/o Edward E. Fink, Superintendent of Butler Area School District, Butler, PA 16001

Established in 1986 in PA.
Financial data (yr. ended 08/31/00): Grants paid, $5,098; assets, $55,963 (M); expenditures, $8,533; qualifying distributions, $5,590.
Limitations: Giving limited to the Butler, PA, area.
Trustee: National City Bank.
EIN: 251552146

44225
Nailprint Ministries, Inc.
4285 Kent Rd.
Stow, OH 44224

Established in 1995 in OH.
Donor(s): David H. Baker.
Financial data (yr. ended 12/31/01): Grants paid, $5,095; assets, $6,854 (M); gifts received, $12,849; expenditures, $6,213; qualifying distributions, $5,095.
Limitations: Applications not accepted.
Application information: Contributes only to pre-selected organizations.
Directors: David H. Baker, Exec. Dir.; Kenneth Baker, Marlene Baker.
EIN: 341737222

44226
Robert E. and Joanne M. Alspaugh Foundation
c/o R. A. Bumblis
1900 E. 9th St., Ste. 3200
Cleveland, OH 44114-3482

Established in 1997 in OH.
Donor(s): Robert E. Alspaugh.
Financial data (yr. ended 12/31/99): Grants paid, $5,000; assets, $90,072 (M); expenditures, $5,683; qualifying distributions, $5,663.
Limitations: Applications not accepted.
Application information: Contributes only to pre-selected organizations.
Officers and Trustees:* Robert E. Alspaugh,* Pres. and Treas.; Joanne M. Alspaugh,* V.P.; Christopher J. Swift,* Secy.
EIN: 341490240

44227
Jewell Baker Foundation, Inc.
719 Cumberland St.
Caldwell, OH 43724
Application address: 41712 State Rte. 821, Caldwell, OH 43724

Established in 1992 in OH.
Financial data (yr. ended 12/31/01): Grants paid, $5,000; assets, $134,429 (M); expenditures, $5,100; qualifying distributions, $5,000.
Limitations: Giving primarily in OH.
Officers and Trustees:* Jewell Baker,* Pres.; Carl L. Baker, Jr.,* Secy.-Treas.; Alan S. Doris.
EIN: 311363067

44228
The Allan and Jennie Rosenthal Berliant Family Foundation
3040 Wold Ave.
Cincinnati, OH 45206
Contact: Jennie Rosenthal Berliant, Pres. and Treas.

Established in 1999 in OH.
Donor(s): Jennie Rosenthal Berliant.
Financial data (yr. ended 12/31/01): Grants paid, $5,000; assets, $103,052 (M); gifts received, $3,740; expenditures, $8,050; qualifying distributions, $5,000.
Officers: Jennie Rosenthal Berliant, Pres. and Treas.; Allan Berliant, V.P. and Secy.
Trustees: Lois Rosenthal, Richard Rosenthal.
EIN: 311675633

44229
The Peter V. Browning Family Foundation
5710 Wooster Pike, Ste. 212
Cincinnati, OH 45227

Established in 1999 in OH.
Donor(s): Ursula Kurman Browning, Peter V. Browning.
Financial data (yr. ended 12/31/01): Grants paid, $5,000; assets, $211,578 (M); gifts received, $130,963; expenditures, $8,037; qualifying distributions, $5,000.
Officers: Ursula K. Browning, Pres.; R. Frederick Keith, Secy.-Treas.
EIN: 311682742

44230
Cleveland National Air Show Charitable Foundation, Inc.
c/o Burke Lakefront Airport
1501 N. Marginal Rd.
Cleveland, OH 44114 (216) 241-5587
Contact: Miria Batig

Established in 1993 in OH.
Donor(s): Cleveland National Air Show, Inc.
Financial data (yr. ended 10/31/01): Grants paid, $5,000; assets, $306,639 (M); gifts received, $25,000; expenditures, $118,140; qualifying distributions, $118,140.
Limitations: Giving primarily in Cleveland, OH.
Application information: Application form required.
Officers: Theodore A. Gullia, Jr., Pres.; Robert D. Shea, V.P.; David R. Tschantz, Secy.; Michael R. Gallagher, Treas.
EIN: 341741796

44231
Defiance Charitable & Educational Foundation
P.O. Box 218, 1400 E. 2nd St.
Defiance, OH 43512 (419) 783-3215
Contact: Chad L. Peter, Treas.

Established in 1985 in OH.
Financial data (yr. ended 07/31/01): Grants paid, $5,000; assets, $112,819 (M); expenditures, $6,716; qualifying distributions, $5,000.
Limitations: Giving primarily in northwest OH.
Officers and Trustees:* P.E. Brose,* Pres.; J.D. Reeves,* V.P.; R.R. Southworth,* Secy.; Chad L. Peter,* Treas.; W.S. Busteed.
EIN: 237042992

44232
Ethnic Voice of America
c/o Irene Kalada-Smirnov
4606 Bruening Dr.
Parma, OH 44134-4640

Established in 1995 in OH.
Financial data (yr. ended 12/31/01): Grants paid, $5,000; assets, $1,432,169 (M); expenditures, $318,030; qualifying distributions, $314,930; giving activities include $291,458 for programs.
Limitations: Applications not accepted.
Application information: Contributes only to pre-selected organizations.
Officers: Irene Kalada-Smirnov, Pres.; Mario Kavic, V.P.; George Smirnov, Treas.
EIN: 341649643

44233
First Federal Foundation
2 N. 2nd St.
Newark, OH 43055

Established in 2000 in OH.
Donor(s): First Federal Savings & Loan Association of Newark.
Financial data (yr. ended 12/31/01): Grants paid, $5,000; assets, $164,626 (M); gifts received, $68,000; expenditures, $6,052; qualifying distributions, $5,000.
Limitations: Applications not accepted.
Application information: Contributes only to pre-selected organizations.
Officers: J. Gilbert Reese, Chair.; Sarah Wallace, Pres.; Paul M. Thompson, V.P. and Secy.; Glen L. Griebel, Treas.
EIN: 311629866

44234
Great American Life Children's Foundation
P.O. Box 5420
Cincinnati, OH 45201-5420
Application address: 250 E. 5th St., Cincinnati, OH 45202, (513) 333-5300
Contact: Marguerite Meyers, Pres.

Established in 1998 in OH.
Donor(s): Million Dollar Round Table Foundation.
Financial data (yr. ended 12/31/01): Grants paid, $5,000; assets, $26,123 (M); gifts received, $27,500; expenditures, $5,044; qualifying distributions, $5,000.
Limitations: Giving primarily in KY.
Officers and Trustees:* Robert A. Adams,* Chair.; Marguerite Meyers,* Pres. and Exec. Dir.; William J. Maney, Treas.; S. Craig Lindner, Mark F. Muething, Jeffrey S. Tate.
EIN: 311610658

44235
Donald L. Guarnieri Foundation
Sky Trust, N.A.
P.O. Box 479, 23 Federal Plz.
Youngstown, OH 44501-0479 (330) 533-3228
Contact: D. Guarnieri, Dir.

Established in 1990 in OH.
Donor(s): Donald L. Guarnieri.
Financial data (yr. ended 12/31/01): Grants paid, $5,000; assets, $69,302 (M); expenditures, $6,395; qualifying distributions, $5,000.
Limitations: Giving limited to the Warren and Trumball County, OH, areas.
Directors: Harold E. Felger, Donald L. Guarnieri, Lewis P. Guarnieri, Sandra A. Guarnieri.
Trustee: Sky Trust, N.A.
EIN: 341665936

44236
Dwight R. & Julia Guthrie Scholarship Fund
c/o National City Bank
P.O. Box 94651
Cleveland, OH 44101-4651

Established in 1999 in PA.
Donor(s): Dwight R. Guthrie.
Financial data (yr. ended 01/31/01): Grants paid, $5,000; assets, $347,245 (M); gifts received, $192,885; expenditures, $7,561; qualifying distributions, $6,086.
Trustee: National City Bank.
EIN: 256638149

44237
H Squared Foundation
15 Baldwin Ln.
Rocky River, OH 44116

Established in 1999 in OH.
Donor(s): Joseph H. Tzeng.
Financial data (yr. ended 12/31/01): Grants paid, $5,000; assets, $2,500 (M); gifts received, $7,500; expenditures, $5,000; qualifying distributions, $5,000.
Limitations: Applications not accepted. Giving primarily in Cleveland, OH.
Application information: Contributes only to pre-selected organizations.
Officer: Joseph H. Tzeng, Pres.
Trustees: James Griswold, Paul J. Schlather.
EIN: 341914017

44238
Jack Hamer Holloway Foundation
P.O. Box 4489
Sidney, OH 45365-4489 (937) 497-7575
Contact: Mark S. Vondenhuevel

Financial data (yr. ended 06/30/01): Grants paid, $5,000; assets, $73,249 (M); expenditures, $5,000; qualifying distributions, $5,000.
Limitations: Giving limited to residents of Logan and Shelby counties, OH.
Application information: Application form required.
Officers: William Harvey, Pres.; Carroll Lewis, Secy.; James Davis, Treas.
EIN: 341283959

44239
A. Gordon & Betty H. Imhoff Scholarship Foundation
4590 Knightsbridge Blvd., Ste. 673
Columbus, OH 43214-4337
Application address: c/o Guidance Dept., Shelby High School, Shelby OH 44875

Established in 1992 in OH.
Donor(s): A. Gordon Imhoff, Betty H. Imhoff.
Financial data (yr. ended 05/31/00): Grants paid, $5,000; assets, $46,707 (M); gifts received, $820; expenditures, $5,767; qualifying distributions, $5,265.
Limitations: Giving limited to Shelby, OH.
Application information: Application form required.
Officers: Betty H. Inhoff, Pres.; Larry E. Green, Secy.
Trustee: Stephanie Hrivnak.
EIN: 311353990

44240
JPW Foundation
c/o Porter, Wright, Morris & Arthur
P.O. Box 1805, 1 S. Main St.
Dayton, OH 45401-1805
Contact: Thomas A. Holton, V.P.

Financial data (yr. ended 12/31/01): Grants paid, $5,000; assets, $170,543 (M); expenditures, $7,453; qualifying distributions, $5,000.
Officers and Trustees:* Marie J. Williams,* Pres.; John P. Williams, Jr.,* V.P. and Secy.; Alexander J. Williams, Jr.,* V.P. and Treas.; Thomas A. Holton,* V.P.; D.D. Dykstra.
EIN: 316027737

44241
The Kauffman Family Foundation, Inc.
1874 St., Rte. 29 E.
Sidney, OH 45365

Established in 1998 in OH.
Financial data (yr. ended 12/31/01): Grants paid, $5,000; assets, $33,161 (M); gifts received, $10,000; expenditures, $6,008; qualifying distributions, $5,000.
Officers and Trustees:* Virginia Maxine Kauffman,* Pres.; Myrna June Kauffman,* 1st V.P.; Almeda Jean Wooddell,* 2nd V.P.; Sandi Jean Freytag, Secy.; Karen Kauffman, Treas.; James Richard Kauffman, Jerry Wayne Kauffman.
EIN: 311621044

44242
Keeler Foundation
1810 Arlingate Ln.
Columbus, OH 43228

Established in 1999 in OH.
Donor(s): J.F. Keeler, Jr., Diane F. Keeler.

Financial data (yr. ended 12/31/01): Grants paid, $5,000; assets, $44,206 (M); expenditures, $6,400; qualifying distributions, $5,000.
Limitations: Applications not accepted.
Application information: Contributes only to pre-selected organizations.
Officers and Trustees:* J.F. Keeler, Jr.,* Pres. and Treas.; Diane F. Keeler,* V.P. and Secy.; Charles J. Keeler.
EIN: 311627668

44243
The Laura Diane Foundation
P.O. Box 7
Huron, OH 44839-0007 (419) 433-5370
Contact: Nicholas J. Hoty, Pres.

Established in 1999 in OH.
Donor(s): Nicholas J. Hoty, Kathleen L. Hoty.
Financial data (yr. ended 12/31/01): Grants paid, $5,000; assets, $12,924 (M); gifts received, $990; expenditures, $6,001; qualifying distributions, $5,000.
Limitations: Giving primarily in OH.
Officers and Trustees:* Nicholas J. Hoty,* Pres.; Betty L. Hart,* Secy.; Kathleen L. Hoty,* Treas.; R. Todd Hart, Edmond A. Hoty, Louise P. Hoty.
EIN: 341904131

44244
The Zachary Kent Lutz Memorial Foundation
P.O. Box 43368
Cincinnati, OH 45243

Established in 1989 in OH.
Donor(s): W. Kent Lutz, Sandra S. Lutz.
Financial data (yr. ended 12/31/00): Grants paid, $5,000; assets, $94,125 (M); expenditures, $5,287; qualifying distributions, $5,000.
Limitations: Applications not accepted. Giving limited to OH.
Application information: Contributes only to pre-selected organizations.
Officers: William Kent Lutz, Pres. and Treas.; Sandra S. Lutz, V.P. and Secy.
EIN: 311250534

44245
Zepha & Otto Manahan Crippled Children's Trust
c/o KeyBank, N.A., Trust Div.
P.O. Box 10099
Toledo, OH 43699-0099
Contact: Diane Ohns, Trust Off., KeyBank, N.A.

Financial data (yr. ended 05/31/01): Grants paid, $5,000; assets, $6,293 (M); expenditures, $6,463; qualifying distributions, $5,840.
Limitations: Giving limited to the Toledo, OH, area.
Trustees: Richard Swartzbaugh, KeyBank, N.A.
EIN: 346818405

44246
The T. Richard and Elizabeth R. Martin Foundation
364 Lake Park Dr.
Bay Village, OH 44140

Established in 2000 in OH.
Donor(s): T. Richard Martin, Elizabeth R. Martin.
Financial data (yr. ended 12/31/01): Grants paid, $5,000; assets, $70,305 (M); expenditures, $5,080; qualifying distributions, $5,000.
Limitations: Applications not accepted.
Application information: Contributes only to pre-selected organizations.
Trustees: Elizabeth R. Martin, T. Richard Martin.
EIN: 347128310

44247
Dr. William R. Miller Foundation
1788 Old US Rt. 52., Box 232
Moscow, OH 45153
Contact: William R. Miller, M.D., Tr.

Established in 1999 in OH.
Donor(s): William R. Miller, M.D.
Financial data (yr. ended 12/31/01): Grants paid, $5,000; assets, $71,397 (M); expenditures, $6,165; qualifying distributions, $5,000.
Limitations: Giving limited to Clermont County, OH.
Application information: Application form required.
Trustees: Leon H. Loewenstine II, Joan M. Kaes Miller, William R. Miller, M.D.
EIN: 311657916

44248
The Nehring Family Foundation
c/o Floyd Trouten, Hobe & Lucas
5005 Rockside Rd., Ste. 430
Independence, OH 44131
Application address: 3652 Pearl Rd., Medina, OH 44256
Contact: Elizabeth Nehring, Pres., or Hildegard Nehring, V.P.

Established in 1996 in OH.
Donor(s): Elizabeth Nehring, Hildegard Nehring.
Financial data (yr. ended 12/31/01): Grants paid, $5,000; assets, $45,675 (M); expenditures, $8,431; qualifying distributions, $5,000.
Limitations: Giving primarily in OH.
Application information: Application form not required.
Officers: Elizabeth Nehring, Pres.; Hildegard Nehring, V.P.; Linda M. Rich, Secy.; Floyd A. Trouten III, Treas.
EIN: 341838148

44249
Nick and Terry's Foundation
5180 Greenwich Rd.
Seville, OH 44273

Established in 2001 in OH.
Donor(s): Ohio Wholesale, Inc.
Financial data (yr. ended 12/31/01): Grants paid, $5,000; assets, $40,244 (M); gifts received, $46,000; expenditures, $5,756; qualifying distributions, $5,000.
Limitations: Giving primarily in Akron, OH.
Officers: Mark N. Harbarger, C.E.O.; Jeffrey Konce, Pres.; Terry E. Harbarger, Secy.-Treas.
Trustees: Bob Carlisle, Jim Eckelberry.
EIN: 912139815
Codes: CS

44250
Harry S. Papier Foundation
c/o National City Bank of Indiana, Trust Dept.
P.O. Box 94651
Cleveland, OH 44101-4651   (216) 575-2934

Financial data (yr. ended 08/31/02): Grants paid, $5,000; assets, $128,398 (M); expenditures, $5,735; qualifying distributions, $5,000.
Limitations: Applications not accepted. Giving on a national basis.
Application information: Contributes only to pre-selected organization.
Trustee: National City Bank.
EIN: 237215872

44251
Charles Pehna Scholarship Trust
c/o National City Bank
P.O. Box 94651
Cleveland, OH 44101-4651

Financial data (yr. ended 12/31/01): Grants paid, $5,000; assets, $342,725 (M); gifts received, $3,723; expenditures, $16,020; qualifying distributions, $12,991.
Limitations: Applications not accepted.
Application information: Contributes only to pre-selected organizations.
Trustee: National City Bank.
EIN: 527155874

44252
Personal Physician Care of Ohio, Inc.
2475 E. 22nd St., Ste. 210
Cleveland, OH 44115   (216) 621-1933
FAX: (216) 621-4174; E-mail: ppcomail@aol.com
Contact: Oscar E. Saffold, M.D., Exec. Dir.

Established in 1993 in OH.
Financial data (yr. ended 12/31/01): Grants paid, $5,000; assets, $1,151,313 (M); gifts received, $4,450; expenditures, $139,074; qualifying distributions, $5,000.
Limitations: Giving primarily in the Cleveland, OH, metropolitan area.
Application information: Application form required.
Officers: Giesele R. Greene, M.D., Pres.; Bradley Dennis, M.D., M.S., V.P.; Maposure T. Miller, Secy.; Grant L. Franklin, M.D., Treas.; Oscar E. Saffold, M.D., Exec. Dir.
EIN: 341509482

44253
Kimberly Michelle Pugh Scholarship Fund
c/o National City Bank of Indiana
P.O. Box 94651
Cleveland, OH 44101-4651
Application address: P.O. Box 5031, Indianapolis, IN 46255
Contact: David Houck

Financial data (yr. ended 12/31/99): Grants paid, $5,000; assets, $75,697 (M); gifts received, $700; expenditures, $5,721; qualifying distributions, $5,452.
Limitations: Giving limited to Marion Township, Hendricks County, IN.
Application information: Application form not required.
Trustee: National City Bank.
EIN: 356441787

44254
The Rowland Foundation
41641 N. Ridge Rd., Ste. A
Elyria, OH 44035   (440) 324-9933
Contact: Billy S. Rowland, Pres.

Established in 2000 in OH.
Donor(s): Billy S. Rowland.
Financial data (yr. ended 12/31/00): Grants paid, $5,000; assets, $241,217 (M); gifts received, $255,491; expenditures, $9,624; qualifying distributions, $9,624.
Limitations: Giving primarily in OH.
Officers: Billy S. Rowland, Pres.; Fay R. Rowland, V.P.
Trustees: Carla Park, William M. Rowland, Kittie Taylor.
EIN: 341932579

44255
Sanctity of Life Foundation
(also known as Brinck Family Foundation, Inc.)
5545 Annamarie Ct.
Cincinnati, OH 45247

Established in 2000 in OH.
Donor(s): Joseph A. Brinck II, Cynthia A. Brinck.
Financial data (yr. ended 09/30/01): Grants paid, $5,000; assets, $670 (M); gifts received, $15,000; expenditures, $14,330; qualifying distributions, $14,330.
Limitations: Giving primarily in NY.
Officers: Joseph A. Brinck II, Pres.; Cynthia A. Brinck, Secy.-Treas.
Trustee: Joseph A. Brinck III.
EIN: 311774144

44256
Anna D. Stinson Trust
c/o KeyBank, N.A.
800 Superior Ave., 4th Fl.
Cleveland, OH 44114-1306
Application address: c/o KeyBank, N.A., Ellsworth, ME 04605

Financial data (yr. ended 04/30/00): Grants paid, $5,000; assets, $144,225 (M); expenditures, $8,010; qualifying distributions, $4,859.
Limitations: Giving limited to Ellsworth and Surrey, ME.
Trustee: KeyBank, N.A.
EIN: 016057075

44257
Ronald F. and Brenda B. Walker Foundation
(Formerly Ronald F. Walker Foundation)
c/o Provident Bank Capital Mgmt. Group
P.O. Box 2176, Mail Stop 652 A
Cincinnati, OH 45201

Established in 1997 in OH.
Donor(s): Kenneth P. Fullam, Mrs. Kenneth P. Fullam, Linda A. Norwell, Laura B. Paul, Robert E. Schutter, Jr., Mrs. Robert E. Schutter, Jr.
Financial data (yr. ended 12/31/01): Grants paid, $5,000; assets, $774,499 (M); gifts received, $500; expenditures, $7,661; qualifying distributions, $5,745.
Limitations: Applications not accepted. Giving primarily in Cincinnati, OH.
Application information: Contributes only to pre-selected organizations.
Trustees: Brenda B. Walker, Deborah J. Walker, Lori E. Walker, Ronald F. Walker, Jr.
EIN: 311531604

44258
Hugh C. Wallace Charity Trust
c/o KeyBank, N.A.
800 Superior Ave., 4th Fl.
Cleveland, OH 44114

Financial data (yr. ended 12/31/01): Grants paid, $5,000; assets, $150,809 (M); expenditures, $8,297; qualifying distributions, $5,000.
Limitations: Applications not accepted. Giving primarily in Pierce County, WA.
Application information: Contributes only to pre-selected organizations.
Trustee: KeyBank, N.A.
EIN: 237087719

44259
Anastasia Annette Schneider Trust
c/o KeyBank, N.A.
800 Superior Ave., 4th Fl.
Cleveland, OH 44114-1306
Application address: 286 Water St., Augusta, ME 04330
Contact: Cristina Cook, Trust Off., KeyBank, N.A.

Financial data (yr. ended 04/30/00): Grants paid, $4,986; assets, $164,465 (M); expenditures, $7,996; qualifying distributions, $4,986.
Limitations: Giving limited to ME.
Trustee: KeyBank, N.A.
EIN: 016038182

44260
The John and Roene A. Klusch Foundation
1471 Inwood Dr.
Alliance, OH 44601

Established in 1986 in OH.
Donor(s): John Klusch, Roene A. Klusch.
Financial data (yr. ended 09/30/01): Grants paid, $4,983; assets, $522,638 (M); expenditures, $7,474; qualifying distributions, $4,983.
Limitations: Applications not accepted. Giving primarily in Alliance, OH.
Application information: Contributes only to pre-selected organizations.
Trustees: John Klusch, Roene A. Klusch.
EIN: 341542111

44261
Halpin Charitable Trust
3400 Sidney Freyburg Rd.
Sidney, OH 45365

Established in 1997 in OH.
Financial data (yr. ended 12/31/01): Grants paid, $4,973; assets, $713,499 (M); gifts received, $241,677; expenditures, $5,036; qualifying distributions, $4,973.
Limitations: Applications not accepted. Giving primarily in OH.
Application information: Contributes only to pre-selected organizations.
Trustees: Christopher Halpin, Ruth Halpin.
EIN: 311556520

44262
Kile Family Foundation
P.O. Box 182108
Columbus, OH 43218

Donor(s): Phyllis A. Wilson.
Financial data (yr. ended 12/31/01): Grants paid, $4,972; assets, $0 (M); expenditures, $6,100; qualifying distributions, $4,972.
Limitations: Applications not accepted. Giving primarily in OH.
Application information: Contributes only to pre-selected organizations.
Directors: Paul R. Anderson, Heather R. Kile, Bryce C. Wilson, Phyllis A. Wilson.
EIN: 311472747

44263
Edith Williams Small Trust
c/o KeyBank, N.A.
800 Superior Ave., 4th Fl.
Cleveland, OH 44114-1306
Application address: c/o Guidance Office, Mount View High School, Thorndike, ME 04986

Financial data (yr. ended 06/30/01): Grants paid, $4,940; assets, $106,461 (M); expenditures, $6,959; qualifying distributions, $4,851.
Limitations: Giving primarily to residents of Freedom, ME.
Trustee: KeyBank, N.A.

EIN: 016030004

44264
Bramson Foundation
29425 Chagrin Blvd., Ste. 203302
Beachwood, OH 44122-4639

Donor(s): Adelyn Bramson, Jay H. Bramson.
Financial data (yr. ended 12/31/01): Grants paid, $4,910; assets, $9,755 (M); expenditures, $5,451; qualifying distributions, $4,910.
Limitations: Applications not accepted. Giving primarily in New York, NY, and Cleveland, OH.
Application information: Contributes only to pre-selected organizations.
Officers and Trustee:* Jay H. Bramson, Pres.; Adeline Bramson,* Exec. Dir.
EIN: 346597406

44265
Carroll Charities, Inc.
196 Wayne Ave. N.W.
Carrollton, OH 44615 (330) 627-7404
Contact: Brenda L. Stine, Pres.

Financial data (yr. ended 12/31/00): Grants paid, $4,900; assets, $120,931 (M); gifts received, $20,000; expenditures, $5,020; qualifying distributions, $4,955.
Limitations: Giving primarily in OH.
Officers and Trustees:* Brenda L. Stine,* Pres.; W. Scott Stine,* Secy.; David Stine.
EIN: 341810715

44266
Donald L. Kaufman Foundation
2825 Round Hill Dr.
Akron, OH 44313

Established in 1994 in OH.
Donor(s): Donald L. Kaufman.
Financial data (yr. ended 12/31/01): Grants paid, $4,850; assets, $76,134 (M); gifts received, $38,558; expenditures, $6,806; qualifying distributions, $4,850.
Limitations: Applications not accepted.
Application information: Contributes only to pre-selected organizations.
Officers: Donald L. Kaufman, Pres.; Estelle F. Kaufman, V.P.; Craig I. Kaufman, Secy.-Treas.
EIN: 341810865

44267
Alexander Charitable Trust
1505 Chapman Dr.
Akron, OH 44305-1320

Donor(s): Thomas W. Alexander.
Financial data (yr. ended 12/31/00): Grants paid, $4,805; assets, $35,091 (L); gifts received, $31,600; expenditures, $15,964; qualifying distributions, $4,805.
Limitations: Applications not accepted.
Application information: Contributes only to pre-selected organizations.
Trustee: Thomas W. Alexander.
EIN: 341848085

44268
Jacob Scholarship Trust
c/o David Bagley
204 Archer Dr.
Antwerp, OH 45813 (419) 258-5421
Contact: Trustees

Established in 1986 in OH.
Financial data (yr. ended 12/31/99): Grants paid, $4,800; assets, $103,772 (M); expenditures, $5,884; qualifying distributions, $4,776.
Limitations: Giving primarily in Antwerp, OH.
Trustees: Daniel W. Schutt, William Shugars, J. Ray Treece.

EIN: 341605660

44269
Dr. Robert L. & Marian W. Manns Charitable Trust
6576 Danforth Cir. N.W.
Canton, OH 44718-1547

Established in 1986 in OH.
Donor(s): Robert L. Manns, Marian W. Manns.
Financial data (yr. ended 12/31/01): Grants paid, $4,800; assets, $14,355 (M); gifts received, $66; expenditures, $5,481; qualifying distributions, $4,800.
Limitations: Applications not accepted. Giving primarily in Canton, OH.
Application information: Contributes only to pre-selected organizations.
Trustees: Marian W. Manns, Robert L. Manns.
EIN: 346868417

44270
Pierce B. Atwood Scholarship Fund
c/o National City Bank of Kentucky
P.O. Box 94651
Cleveland, OH 44101-4651
Application address: c/o Louisville Male High School Scholarship Committee, 4409 Preston Hwy., Louisville, KY 40213-2033, tel.: (502) 485-8292

Financial data (yr. ended 12/31/01): Grants paid, $4,750; assets, $159,253 (M); expenditures, $5,042; qualifying distributions, $4,823.
Limitations: Giving limited to residents of Louisville, KY.
Application information: Application form required.
Trustee: National City Bank, Kentucky.
EIN: 616022274

44271
Thomas F. Coakley Foundation
22249 Parnell Rd.
Shaker Heights, OH 44122

Established in 1994 in OH.
Financial data (yr. ended 12/31/01): Grants paid, $4,750; assets, $52,960 (M); expenditures, $4,802; qualifying distributions, $4,750.
Limitations: Applications not accepted. Giving primarily in Cleveland, OH.
Application information: Contributes only to pre-selected organizations.
Officers: Thomas F. Coakley, Jr., Pres.; Lawrence Bell, Secy.; John C. Phillips, Treas.
EIN: 341767459

44272
J. Cromer Mashburn Family Foundation
7 Noel Ln.
Cincinnati, OH 45243

Financial data (yr. ended 11/30/01): Grants paid, $4,750; assets, $147,671 (M); expenditures, $6,751; qualifying distributions, $4,750.
Limitations: Applications not accepted. Giving primarily in Cincinnati, OH.
Application information: Contributes only to pre-selected organizations.
Officers: Patricia Zesch, Pres.; Bonnie R. Mashburn, V.P.; J. Cromer Mashburn, Secy.-Treas.
EIN: 316041836

44273
The Dennis and Sara Trachsel Foundation
2034 Matheny Ave.
Marion, OH 43302 (740) 382-1771
Contact: Sam Sparling, Secy.-Treas.

Established in 1997.
Donor(s): Dennis L. Trachsel.

44273—OHIO

Financial data (yr. ended 12/31/00): Grants paid, $4,719; assets, $598,957 (M); gifts received, $400,783; expenditures, $15,734; qualifying distributions, $8,100.
Limitations: Giving primarily in OH.
Application information: Application form required.
Officers and Trustees:* Dennis L. Trachsel,* Pres.; James Waddell,* V.P.; Sam Sparling,* Secy.-Treas.; F. Riley Hall.
EIN: 311472824

44274
The McKarns Family Foundation
29950 Campbell Rd.
Hanoverton, OH 44423

Established in 1990 in OH.
Donor(s): William T. McKarns, Pauline M. McKarns.
Financial data (yr. ended 12/31/01): Grants paid, $4,710; assets, $37,132 (M); expenditures, $5,162; qualifying distributions, $4,710.
Limitations: Applications not accepted. Giving primarily in Hanoverton, OH.
Application information: Contributes only to pre-selected organizations.
Trustees: Pauline M. McKarns, William T. McKarns.
EIN: 341664641

44275
Crowe Family Foundation
30951 Ainsworth Dr.
Pepper Pike, OH 44124

Donor(s): Mary Lind Crowe, Joseph Crowe.
Financial data (yr. ended 12/31/01): Grants paid, $4,700; assets, $110,052 (M); gifts received, $24,820; expenditures, $7,073; qualifying distributions, $4,700.
Limitations: Applications not accepted.
Application information: Contributes only to pre-selected organizations.
Trustees: Joseph Crowe, Kevin M. Crowe, Mary Lind Crowe.
EIN: 341788531

44276
Charles R. Jelm Charitable Foundation, Inc.
c/o Robert J. Cicek
857 Hardwood Ct.
Gates Mills, OH 44040

Established in 1990 in FL.
Donor(s): Charles R. Jelm Trust.
Financial data (yr. ended 01/31/02): Grants paid, $4,654; assets, $2,023,358 (M); gifts received, $2,000,000; expenditures, $12,422; qualifying distributions, $4,654.
Limitations: Applications not accepted.
Application information: Contributes only to pre-selected organizations.
Directors: Robert J. Clark, Camilla Glenn, Barbara A. Jelm, Charles L. Jelm, Cheryl A. Jelm.
EIN: 650122428

44277
Lake County Foundation
P.O. Box 2093
Painesville, OH 44077-3467 (440) 352-5920
Contact: George B. Milbourn, Treas.

Financial data (yr. ended 12/31/01): Grants paid, $4,650; assets, $77,233 (M); expenditures, $4,795.
Limitations: Giving limited to Lake County, OH.
Application information: Application form not required.
Officers: Arthur Sidley, Pres.; John J. Hurley, Jr., Secy.; George Milbourn, Treas.
EIN: 346536532

Codes: CM

44278
Weichert-Kranbuhl Family Foundation
9425 Holly Hill
Cincinnati, OH 45243

Established in OH in 1998.
Donor(s): Kathryn A.W. Kranbuhl.
Financial data (yr. ended 12/31/01): Grants paid, $4,616; assets, $144,614 (M); gifts received, $48,564; expenditures, $11,739; qualifying distributions, $4,616.
Limitations: Applications not accepted. Giving primarily in Cincinnati, OH.
Application information: Contributes only to pre-selected organizations.
Officers: Kathryn A.W. Kranbuhl, Pres.; Kathryn H. Kranbuhl, Secy.; M. Kipp Kranbuhl, Treas.
EIN: 311625846

44279
Mary Ethel Lafferty Trust
c/o National City Bank of Indiana
P.O. Box 94651
Cleveland, OH 44101-4651
Application address: P.O. Box 110, Fort Wayne, IN 46801, tel.: (219) 461-6199
Contact: Michele Herald, Trust Off., National City Bank of IN

Financial data (yr. ended 09/30/01): Grants paid, $4,600; assets, $76,982 (M); expenditures, $6,618; qualifying distributions, $5,790.
Limitations: Giving limited to residents of Fort Wayne, IN.
Application information: Application form required.
Trustee: National City Bank of Indiana.
EIN: 311064816

44280
David Hamilton Ryerson Memorial Foundation
2379 Stockbridges Rd.
Akron, OH 44313

Established in 1998 in OH.
Donor(s): Steven J. Ryerson.
Financial data (yr. ended 12/31/01): Grants paid, $4,591; assets, $87,698 (M); gifts received, $9,899; expenditures, $6,364; qualifying distributions, $4,591.
Limitations: Applications not accepted.
Application information: Contributes only to pre-selected organizations.
Officers: Peter J. Ryerson, Pres.; Nanette G. Ryerson, V.P.; Steven J. Ryerson, Treas.
EIN: 341886337

44281
Vermillion Family Scholarship Fund, Inc.
790 Belvedere Ave. N.E.
Warren, OH 44483-4228 (330) 372-6081
Contact: Patricia Diloreto, Secy.

Established in 2000 in OH.
Donor(s): Edgar Vermillion.‡
Financial data (yr. ended 12/31/01): Grants paid, $4,570; assets, $93,087 (M); expenditures, $8,790; qualifying distributions, $4,570.
Application information: Application form required.
Officers: Marla Bluedorn, Pres.; Nancy Diloreto, V.P.; Patricia Diloreto, Secy.; John Diloreto, Treas.
EIN: 341906407

44282
Family Charitable Foundation
c/o Michael Carapellotti
P.O. Box 729
Steubenville, OH 43952

Established in 1990 in OH.
Donor(s): Paul R. Carapellotti.
Financial data (yr. ended 06/30/01): Grants paid, $4,500; assets, $119,539 (M); expenditures, $5,640; qualifying distributions, $4,500.
Limitations: Applications not accepted. Giving primarily in Steubenville, OH.
Application information: Contributes only to pre-selected organizations.
Trustees: Albert Carapellotti, Dahlia Carapellotti, Michael Carapellotti, Paul P. Carapellotti, Mary Ann Dimitry.
EIN: 346933776

44283
Lois J. Macaluso Charitable Foundation
National City Bank of Pennsylvania
P.O. Box 94651
Cleveland, OH 44101-4651
Application address: c/o National City Bank of PA, Private Client Group, 66 E. State St., Sharon, PA 16146

Established in 1998 in PA.
Donor(s): Lois Macaluso.
Financial data (yr. ended 12/31/01): Grants paid, $4,500; assets, $91,213 (M); gifts received, $25,675; expenditures, $5,550; qualifying distributions, $4,822.
Limitations: Giving limited to residents of PA.
Application information: Application form required.
Advisory Committee: Jack L. Danielson, Henrietta L. Danielson, Lois Macaluso.
Trustee: National City Bank of Pennsylvania.
EIN: 232923692

44284
Metro-West Kiwanis Charitable Foundation
c/o John D. Barber
24441 Detroit Ave., Ste. 300
Westlake, OH 44145-1543
Application address: c/o Baker & Hostetler, LLP, 200 National City Ctr., 1900 E. 9th St., Cleveland, OH 44114-3485
Contact: Stephen J. Petras, Tr.

Financial data (yr. ended 09/30/99): Grants paid, $4,500; assets, $72,637 (M); gifts received, $441; expenditures, $4,550; qualifying distributions, $4,446.
Limitations: Giving limited to residents of Fairview Park, Rocky River, Bay Village, Westlake and North Olmsted, OH.
Application information: Application form required.
Trustees: John D. Barber, Donald J. Bisesi, Stephen J. Petras.
EIN: 341455806

44285
New Bremen Foundation, Inc.
P.O. Box 97
New Bremen, OH 45869

Financial data (yr. ended 11/30/00): Grants paid, $4,500; assets, $248,928 (M); gifts received, $54,463; expenditures, $7,068.
Limitations: Giving limited to New Bremen, OH.
Officers and Trustees:* James Dicke II,* Pres. and Treas.; Thomas Kuenning,* V.P.; James Dicke III,* Secy.; John Gilberg, Doris Kuenning.
EIN: 341837854
Codes: CM

44286
Leroy W. Russell Scholarship Fund
c/o National City Bank, Northeast
P.O. Box 94651
Cleveland, OH 44101-4651
Application address: c/o Principal, Austintown-Fitch High School, 4560 Falcon Dr., Youngstown, OH 44515, tel.: (330) 797-3900

Financial data (yr. ended 06/30/01): Grants paid, $4,500; assets, $107,895 (M); expenditures, $4,507; qualifying distributions, $4,620.
Limitations: Giving limited to residents of Mahoning County, OH.
Publications: Application guidelines.
Application information: Application form required.
Trustee: National City Bank.
EIN: 346745005

44287
L. & J. R. Senior Family Foundation
c/o U.S. Bank
P.O. Box 1118, M.
Cincinnati, OH 45201

Established in 1997 in OH.
Financial data (yr. ended 04/30/02): Grants paid, $4,500; assets, $88,668 (M); expenditures, $6,732; qualifying distributions, $4,500.
Limitations: Applications not accepted.
Application information: Contributes only to pre-selected organizations.
Trustee: Lillie Senior.
EIN: 311536723

44288
Spero Charitable Foundation
(Formerly Spero-Mendelson Charitable Foundation)
650 N. Meridian Rd.
Youngstown, OH 44509-1245

Donor(s): Leslie W. Spero.
Financial data (yr. ended 05/31/01): Grants paid, $4,485; assets, $288,957 (M); gifts received, $347; expenditures, $5,406; qualifying distributions, $4,851.
Limitations: Applications not accepted. Giving primarily in FL.
Application information: Contributes only to pre-selected organizations.
Trustee: Leslie W. Spero.
EIN: 346565557

44289
Windy City Group, Inc.
7919 New Cumberland Rd.
Mineral City, OH 44656
Contact: Marsha L. Webb, Secy.-Treas.

Established in IL and OH in 1997.
Financial data (yr. ended 12/31/99): Grants paid, $4,477; assets, $30,983 (M); gifts received, $40,665; expenditures, $34,499; qualifying distributions, $4,477.
Officers: Bertha H. Dinsio, Pres.; Patricia A. Lyons, V.P.; Marsha L. Webb, Secy.-Treas.
Directors: Vincent M. Dinsio III, Joyce Smith.
EIN: 364117394

44290
Elvira A. Davis Trust
c/o KeyBank, N.A.
800 Superior Ave., 4th Fl.
Cleveland, OH 44114
Application address: c/o Greg Maynard, KeyBank, N.A., 1 Canal Plz., Portland, ME 04107

Donor(s): Elvira A. Davis.‡
Financial data (yr. ended 12/31/00): Grants paid, $4,455; assets, $83,862 (M); expenditures, $5,505; qualifying distributions, $4,400.
Limitations: Giving limited to residents of Denmark, ME.
Trustee: KeyBank, N.A.
EIN: 016035666

44291
The Kier Foundation
29739 Lafayette Way
Westlake, OH 44145-4422
Contact: Kearney K. Kier, Pres.

Financial data (yr. ended 06/30/02): Grants paid, $4,455; assets, $31,862 (M); expenditures, $5,739; qualifying distributions, $4,455.
Limitations: Giving primarily in OH.
Application information: Application form not required.
Officers: Kearney K. Kier, Pres.; Peggy A. Kier, Secy.
Trustees: Douglas Kier Holter, Douglas E. Kier.
EIN: 341503337

44292
Douglas W. Lincoln Scholarship Fund
c/o KeyBank, N.A., Trust Div.
800 Superior Ave., 4th Fl.
Cleveland, OH 44114
Application address: c/o Guidance Office, Albany High School, Albany, NY 12211

Donor(s): Douglas W. Lincoln.‡
Financial data (yr. ended 02/28/01): Grants paid, $4,450; assets, $88,719 (M); expenditures, $5,539; qualifying distributions, $4,365.
Limitations: Giving limited to residents of Albany, NY.
Application information: Application form required.
Trustee: KeyBank, N.A.
EIN: 146090923

44293
The Marie and David Steiner Perry High School Scholarship Trust
P.O. Box 298
Lima, OH 45802-0298
Application address: c/o Awards Comm., Perry High School, 2770 E. Breese Rd., Lima, OH 45802, tel.: (419) 221-2770

Established in 1994.
Financial data (yr. ended 12/31/00): Grants paid, $4,407; assets, $57,949 (M); expenditures, $5,108; qualifying distributions, $4,407.
Limitations: Giving limited to OH.
Application information: Application form required.
Trustees: Steven Hooker, Robert J. Meredith, Donald J. Witter.
EIN: 341777979

44294
Jessie R. Horton Trust
c/o KeyBank, N.A., Trust Div.
800 Superior Ave., 4th Fl.
Cleveland, OH 44114
Application address: c/o Greg Maynard, KeyBank, N.A., 1 Canal Plz., Portland, ME 04107

Donor(s): Jessie R. Horton.‡
Financial data (yr. ended 12/31/01): Grants paid, $4,400; assets, $87,008 (M); expenditures, $6,351; qualifying distributions, $4,400.
Limitations: Giving limited to residents of Harrison, ME.
Trustee: KeyBank, N.A.
EIN: 016021432

Codes: GTI

44295
Fred Lick Foundation
24803 Detroit Rd.
Westlake, OH 44145
Application address: 3820 Clay Mountain Rd., Medina, OH 44256
Contact: Fred Lick, Jr., Tr.

Funded in 2001 by the CRL Fdn., OH.
Donor(s): CRL Foundation.
Financial data (yr. ended 06/30/02): Grants paid, $4,390; assets, $57,539 (M); expenditures, $4,876; qualifying distributions, $4,390.
Limitations: Giving primarily in OH.
Trustees: Robert Haas, Fred Lick, Jr., Karla Telfer, James Weisbarth.
EIN: 346904042

44296
Davis-Wendell Foundation
(Formerly Marvin C. and Martha J. Miner Charitable Trust)
8318 Sweet Briar Ct.
Liberty Township, OH 45044

Donor(s): Marvin C. Miner, Martha J. Miner.
Financial data (yr. ended 12/31/01): Grants paid, $4,372; assets, $93,820 (M); expenditures, $6,519; qualifying distributions, $4,372.
Limitations: Applications not accepted. Giving primarily in FL.
Application information: Contributes only to pre-selected organizations.
Trustees: Martha J. Davis, Deborah A. Wendell.
EIN: 656012814

44297
Abe Margolis Foundation
5425 Spice Bush
Dayton, OH 45429-1967 (937) 299-4773
Contact: Monique Margolis, Mgr.

Financial data (yr. ended 12/31/01): Grants paid, $4,370; assets, $200,373 (M); expenditures, $5,318; qualifying distributions, $4,370.
Limitations: Giving primarily in OH.
Application information: Application form not required.
Officer: Monique Margolis, Mgr.
EIN: 316068719

44298
Dale & Carolyn Anderson Family Foundation
3179 Meadow Ln. N.E.
Warren, OH 44483 (330) 372-5784
Contact: Dale E. Anderson, Pres.

Donor(s): Dale E. Anderson, Carolyn L. Anderson.
Financial data (yr. ended 12/31/01): Grants paid, $4,350; assets, $23,531 (M); expenditures, $5,472; qualifying distributions, $4,350.
Officer and Directors:* Dale E. Anderson,* Pres.; Carolyn L. Anderson, Julie A. Ask, Andrea J. Donovan.
EIN: 341936789

44299
The DiMarco Foundation
c/o Anthony DiMarco
37490 Hunters Ridge
Solon, OH 44139

Established in 1997 in OH.
Donor(s): Anthony DiMarco.
Financial data (yr. ended 12/31/01): Grants paid, $4,300; assets, $83,137 (M); expenditures, $4,575; qualifying distributions, $4,300.
Limitations: Applications not accepted. Giving primarily in Solon, OH.

44299—OHIO

Application information: Contributes only to pre-selected organizations.
Trustees: Anthony DiMarco, Pauline DiMarco.
EIN: 311526393

44300
Cook Charitable Trust
2866 Scenic Dr.
Marion, OH 43302-8471

Established in 1998 in OH.
Financial data (yr. ended 12/31/00): Grants paid, $4,295; assets, $1,310 (M); gifts received, $5,000; expenditures, $4,295; qualifying distributions, $4,295.
Limitations: Applications not accepted.
Application information: Contributes only to pre-selected organizations.
Trustee: Wesley Cook.
EIN: 367249048

44301
John and Denise York Foundation
P.O. Box 9128
7620 Market St.
Youngstown, OH 44513-9128 (330) 765-2000
Contact: John C. York II, Secy.

Established in 1997 in OH.
Donor(s): John C. York II, Marie Denise DeBartolo York.
Financial data (yr. ended 12/31/01): Grants paid, $4,290; assets, $669,750 (M); gifts received, $550; expenditures, $9,225; qualifying distributions, $4,290.
Limitations: Giving primarily in OH.
Officers: Marie Denise DeBartolo York, Pres.; John C. York II, Secy.
EIN: 311536162

44302
Southern Perry County Academic Endowment Fund, Inc.
North Valley St.
P.O. Box 498
Corning, OH 43730-0498
Contact: Rebecca A. Gill, Treas.

Donor(s): Bruce Hannah.
Financial data (yr. ended 12/31/99): Grants paid, $4,275; assets, $106,827 (M); gifts received, $29,505; expenditures, $4,828; qualifying distributions, $4,828.
Limitations: Giving primarily to residents of Perry County, OH.
Application information: Application form required.
Officers: Jo Ellen Alfman, Pres.; Frances Dunlap, V.P.; Clara H. Reho, Secy.; Rebecca A. Gill, Treas.
EIN: 341585950

44303
The Nicholas M. DeVito Foundation
c/o Nicholas M. DeVito
6559 Wilson Mills Rd., Ste. 106
Cleveland, OH 44143-3433

Established in 1992 in OH.
Donor(s): Nicholas M. DeVito,‡ Kathleen R. DeVito.
Financial data (yr. ended 12/31/99): Grants paid, $4,255; assets, $710 (M); gifts received, $1,075; expenditures, $4,255; qualifying distributions, $4,255.
Limitations: Applications not accepted.
Application information: Contributes only to pre-selected organizations.
Trustee: Kathleen R. DeVito.
EIN: 341726632

44304
Isabel Freer Memorial Scholarship Trust
146 East Center St.
Marion, OH 43302-0003
Contact: John C. Bartram, Tr.

Established in 1987 in OH.
Financial data (yr. ended 12/31/01): Grants paid, $4,236; assets, $113,406 (M); expenditures, $4,957; qualifying distributions, $4,823.
Limitations: Giving limited to residents of Marion, OH.
Trustees: John C. Bartram, Michael J. McCreary, Robert H. Thiede.
EIN: 346866821
Codes: GTI

44305
John and Margaret Costello Scholarship Fund
c/o KeyBank, N.A.
800 Superior Ave., 4th Fl.
Cleveland, OH 44114

Established in 1989 in NY.
Donor(s): John B. Costello.‡
Financial data (yr. ended 12/31/00): Grants paid, $4,200; assets, $79,422 (M); expenditures, $5,248; qualifying distributions, $4,173.
Limitations: Applications not accepted. Giving limited to residents of Marlboro, NY.
Application information: Unsolicited requests for funds not accepted.
Trustee: KeyBank, N.A.
EIN: 146139363

44306
Bratenahl Community Foundation
c/o Sheila Birch
9 Haskell Dr.
Bratenahl, OH 44108

Established in 1971 in OH.
Financial data (yr. ended 06/30/99): Grants paid, $4,091; assets, $30,443 (M); gifts received, $16,433; expenditures, $19,275.
Limitations: Giving limited to Bratenahl, OH.
Officers: George Landis, Pres.; Bourne Dempsey, V.P.; Katherine Bolton, Secy.; Sheila Birch, Treas.
EIN: 237091714
Codes: CM

44307
E. R. Kuck Foundation Trust
c/o The Huntington National Bank
P.O. Box 1558, HC-0534
Columbus, OH 43216

Financial data (yr. ended 12/31/01): Grants paid, $4,080; assets, $193,629 (M); expenditures, $6,839; qualifying distributions, $4,080.
Limitations: Applications not accepted. Giving limited to OH.
Application information: Contributes only to pre-selected organizations.
Trustee: The Huntington National Bank.
EIN: 316059226

44308
Harry Zahars Charitable Trust
c/o FirstMerit Bank, N.A.
105 Court St.
Elyria, OH 44035

Established in 1995 in OH.
Financial data (yr. ended 03/31/00): Grants paid, $4,078; assets, $1,087,823 (M); expenditures, $14,786; qualifying distributions, $6,101.
Limitations: Applications not accepted.
Application information: Contributes only to pre-selected organizations.
Trustee: FirstMerit Bank, N.A.
EIN: 341797032

44309
RWK Foundation
(also known as Robert W. Kirk Foundation)
c/o Alvada Construction, Inc.
1950 Industrial Dr.
Findlay, OH 45840
Contact: Robert W. Kirk, Pres.

Donor(s): Alvada Construction, Inc., members of the Kirk family.
Financial data (yr. ended 12/31/01): Grants paid, $4,060; assets, $19,714 (M); expenditures, $4,357; qualifying distributions, $4,060.
Limitations: Giving primarily in Findlay and Fostoria, OH.
Application information: Application form required.
Officers: Robert W. Kirk, Pres.; James L. Kirk, V.P.; Joseph R. Kirk, V.P; Richard C. Kirk, V.P; William T. Kirk, V.P.; Catherine M. Smith, V.P.
EIN: 341250065
Codes: CS, CD

44310
Floyd Hughes VFW Post 693 Charitable Trust Fund
c/o KeyBank, N.A.
800 Superior Ave., 4th Fl.
Cleveland, OH 44114
Application address: c/o Brian Cerkala, Budget Comm., KeyBank, N.A., P.O. Box 9950, Trust. Dept., Canton, OH 44711, tel.: (330) 497-3600

Established in 1984 in OH.
Financial data (yr. ended 12/31/01): Grants paid, $4,002; assets, $74,796 (M); expenditures, $5,545; qualifying distributions, $4,002.
Limitations: Giving limited to the greater Canton, OH, area.
Application information: Application form required.
Trustee: KeyBank, N.A.
EIN: 346819615

44311
Amelia Benner Foundation, Inc.
213 S. Paint St.
Chillicothe, OH 45601-3828
Application address: 36 N. Walnut St., Chillicothe, OH 45601, tel.: (740) 775-8200
Contact: John Patterson, Pres.

Established in 1991 in OH.
Donor(s): Amelia Benner.
Financial data (yr. ended 02/28/02): Grants paid, $4,000; assets, $333,235 (M); expenditures, $4,730; qualifying distributions, $4,000.
Limitations: Giving limited to Highland, Pike, and Ross counties, OH.
Application information: Application form required.
Officers: John Patterson, Pres.; Kay Rittenhouse, Secy.-Treas.
Trustees: Ralph Reed, Jerry Whited.
EIN: 311324162

44312
The Bien Charitable Trust
5669 Kugler Mill Rd.
Cincinnati, OH 45236-2037

Established in 1998 in OH.
Donor(s): James W. Bien.
Financial data (yr. ended 12/31/99): Grants paid, $4,000; assets, $166,181 (M); gifts received, $36,796; expenditures, $8,496; qualifying distributions, $8,835.
Limitations: Applications not accepted. Giving primarily in OH.

Application information: Contributes only to pre-selected organizations.
Trustee: James W. Bien.
EIN: 311497138

44313
Keith N. Browning Family Foundation
c/o U.S. Bank
425 Walnut St., ML 7126
Cincinnati, OH 45202

Donor(s): Pamela O. Browning.
Financial data (yr. ended 12/31/01): Grants paid, $4,000; assets, $76,135 (M); gifts received, $15,928; expenditures, $5,656; qualifying distributions, $4,000.
Limitations: Applications not accepted.
Application information: Contributes only to pre-selected organizations.
Officers: Pamela O. Browning, Pres.; Peter V. Browning, Secy.; Paul T. Ciolino, Treas.
EIN: 311424006

44314
CSC Industries Foundation
4000 Mahoning Ave. N.W.
Warren, OH 44483-1924 (330) 841-6513
Contact: Tim Calderone

Established in 1987 in OH.
Donor(s): CSC Industries, Inc., Daido Steel Co., Ltd., John G. Roberts, Rosemary A. Roberts, CSC Ltd.
Financial data (yr. ended 12/31/99): Grants paid, $4,000; assets, $100,888 (M); expenditures, $4,876; qualifying distributions, $4,827.
Limitations: Giving limited to Trumbull County, OH.
Application information: Application form required.
Officers and Trustees:* Donald J. Caiazza,* Chair.; James R. Duncan, Jr.,* Pres.; Kirk Davies,* V.P.; Cornel A. Kmentt,* Secy.-Treas.; John M. Popa, Secy.-Treas.; William C. Brenneisen, Terri Gilbert, Eugene Rossi.
Selection Committee: David Allen, Elizabeth Graban, Hon. Thomas L. Old.
EIN: 341562874
Codes: CS, CD

44315
The Desch/Sowar Family Foundation
806 N. Parkview Dr.
Coldwater, OH 45828

Established in 2000 in OH.
Financial data (yr. ended 12/31/01): Grants paid, $4,000; assets, $24,821 (M); gifts received, $15,710; expenditures, $9,678; qualifying distributions, $4,000.
Limitations: Applications not accepted.
Application information: Contributes only to pre-selected organizations.
Officers: Donald P. Desch, Pres.; Mary C. Sowar, V.P.; Kathleen A. Desch, Secy.; James W. Sowar, Treas.
EIN: 341940601

44316
Jennifer Ferchill Foundation, Inc.
1468 W. 9th St., Ste. 135
Cleveland, OH 44113 (216) 566-7676

Established in 1994.
Financial data (yr. ended 12/31/01): Grants paid, $4,000; assets, $33,186 (M); gifts received, $14,531; expenditures, $121,812; qualifying distributions, $3,987.
Limitations: Applications not accepted.
Application information: Contributes only to pre-selected organizations.

Trustee: John Ferchill.
EIN: 341439121

44317
Hilliard Gates Scholarship Foundation
c/o National City Bank of Indiana
P.O. Box 94651
Cleveland, OH 44101-4651 (216) 575-2934
Application address: P.O. Box 110, Fort Wayne, IN 46802, tel.: (219) 461-7115
Contact: Gloria Humphreys

Established in 1986 in IN.
Financial data (yr. ended 07/31/00): Grants paid, $4,000; assets, $69,562 (M); expenditures, $5,275; qualifying distributions, $4,829.
Limitations: Giving limited to the Allen County, IN area.
Application information: Application form required.
Trustee: National City Bank of Indiana.
EIN: 311180053
Codes: GTI

44318
Hendrix & Palaskas Scholarship Trust
c/o National City Bank
P.O. Box 94651
Cleveland, OH 44101-4651

Established in 1993 in OH.
Financial data (yr. ended 07/31/99): Grants paid, $4,000; assets, $31,301 (M); gifts received, $4,818; expenditures, $4,062; qualifying distributions, $4,069.
Limitations: Applications not accepted. Giving limited to residents of OH.
Application information: Contributes only to pre-selected organizations.
Trustee: National City Bank.
EIN: 316427046

44319
Harriett Hess Scholarship Trust
c/o KeyBank, N.A., Trust Div.
800 Superior Ave., 4th Fl.
Cleveland, OH 44114

Donor(s): Harriet Hess.‡
Financial data (yr. ended 12/31/01): Grants paid, $4,000; assets, $86,087 (M); expenditures, $4,654; qualifying distributions, $4,034.
Limitations: Applications not accepted. Giving limited to students in Fairbanks, AK.
Application information: Unsolicited requests for funds not accepted.
Trustee: KeyBank, N.A.
EIN: 926007771

44320
Minabelle Abbott Hutchins Memorial Scholarship Fund
c/o Fifth Third Bank
P.O. Box 630858, Trust Dept. 00858
Cincinnati, OH 45263

Financial data (yr. ended 03/31/00): Grants paid, $4,000; assets, $106,216 (M); expenditures, $4,709; qualifying distributions, $4,336.
Limitations: Giving limited to Piqua, OH.
Trustee: Fifth Third Bank.
EIN: 311038251

44321
The Jairus Foundation
c/o J. Gregory Rosenthal
6936 Shadowcreek Dr.
Maumee, OH 43537

Established in 2000 in OH.
Donor(s): J. Gregory Rosenthal.

Financial data (yr. ended 12/31/01): Grants paid, $4,000; assets, $23,375 (M); gifts received, $10,000; expenditures, $4,559; qualifying distributions, $4,000.
Trustees: J. Gregory Rosenthal, Scott J. Savage.
EIN: 341940058

44322
Arlene Goist Moore Scholarship Fund
c/o Second National Bank of Warren
108 Main St. S.W.
Warren, OH 44481
Contact: Jeff Hatchner, Trust Off., Second National Bank of Warren

Established in 1986 in OH.
Financial data (yr. ended 04/30/00): Grants paid, $4,000; assets, $110,157 (M); expenditures, $5,524; qualifying distributions, $4,733.
Limitations: Giving limited to Southington Township, OH.
Trustee: Second National Bank of Warren.
EIN: 346863075

44323
The Morrill Foundation
c/o National City Bank of Indiana
P.O. Box 94651
Cleveland, OH 44101-4651
Application address: P.O. Box 116, Garrett, IN 46738

Donor(s): Electric Motors and Specialties, Inc.
Financial data (yr. ended 12/31/01): Grants paid, $4,000; assets, $172,987 (M); expenditures, $11,247; qualifying distributions, $10,819; giving activities include $6,000 for loans to individuals.
Limitations: Giving primarily in areas of company operations and in the Garrett, IN, area.
Application information: Application form required.
Officers: Marguerite Smith, Pres.; George Pearson, V.P.
Trustee: National City Bank of Indiana.
EIN: 356040178
Codes: CS, CD

44324
Murphy College Fund Trust
c/o National City Bank of Indiana
P.O. Box 94651
Cleveland, OH 44101-4651
Application address: P.O. Box 110, Fort Wayne, IN 46802, tel.: (219) 461-6218
Contact: Teresa Tracey, Trust Off., National City Bank of Indiana

Donor(s): Samuel C. Murphy.‡
Financial data (yr. ended 12/31/99): Grants paid, $4,000; assets, $68,492 (M); expenditures, $5,354; qualifying distributions, $4,702.
Limitations: Giving limited to Kosciusko County, IN.
Application information: Application form required.
Trustee: National City Bank of Indiana.
EIN: 356018330

44325
The Pohlman Family Charitable Trust
41 S. High St.
Columbus, OH 43215 (614) 227-2141
Contact: James E. Pohlman, Tr.

Established in 1994 in OH.
Donor(s): James E. Pohlman.
Financial data (yr. ended 12/31/01): Grants paid, $4,000; assets, $80,288 (M); expenditures, $5,057; qualifying distributions, $4,000.
Limitations: Giving on a national basis.
Trustees: James E. Pohlman, Patricia Pohlman.

44325—OHIO

EIN: 311422947

44326
Paul W. & Marian G. Seitz Foundation, Inc.
c/o National City Bank of Indiana
P.O. Box 94651
Cleveland, OH 44101-4651
Application address: P.O. Box 110, Fort Wayne, IN, tel.: (219) 426-0555

Donor(s): Paul W. Seitz.
Financial data (yr. ended 12/31/01): Grants paid, $4,000; assets, $152,638 (M); expenditures, $5,125; qualifying distributions, $4,000.
Limitations: Giving primarily in Fort Wayne, IN.
Application information: Application form not required.
Officers: David Peters, Secy.; Paul W. Seitz, Mgr.
Trustee: National City Bank.
EIN: 237067463

44327
Vaughn Family Foundation
c/o FirstMerit Bank, N.A.
121 S. Main St., Ste. 200
Akron, OH 44308 (330) 384-7320

Donor(s): L.A. Vaughn.‡
Financial data (yr. ended 12/31/01): Grants paid, $4,000; assets, $22,088 (M); expenditures, $5,560; qualifying distributions, $4,000.
Limitations: Giving primarily in OH.
Officer: L.A. Vaughn, Mgr.
Trustee: FirstMerit Bank.
EIN: 346598059

44328
Peasley Estate - F. W. Peasley Scholarship Fund
c/o KeyBank, N.A., Trust Div.
800 Superior Ave., 4th Fl.
Cleveland, OH 44114

Donor(s): F.W. Peasley.‡
Financial data (yr. ended 06/30/02): Grants paid, $3,995; assets, $55,799 (M); expenditures, $4,737; qualifying distributions, $3,995.
Limitations: Applications not accepted. Giving limited to residents of Glen, NY.
Application information: Recipients are chosen by a committee.
Trustee: KeyBank, N.A.
EIN: 146082789

44329
Faye L. Smith Trust
c/o FirstMerit Bank, N.A.
121 S. Main St., Ste. 200
Akron, OH 44308
Application address: c/o Jim Sabo, Secy., B.P.O.E. No. 982, Barberton, OH 44203

Financial data (yr. ended 12/31/99): Grants paid, $3,990; assets, $95,856 (M); expenditures, $5,696; qualifying distributions, $4,105.
Limitations: Giving limited to OH.
Trustee: FirstMerit Bank, N.A.
EIN: 346796830

44330
Charles A. & Frances M. Poux Charitable Foundation
c/o National City Bank of Pennsylvania
P. O. Box 94651
Cleveland, OH 44101-4651 (216) 575-2934

Established in 1995.
Financial data (yr. ended 12/31/01): Grants paid, $3,965; assets, $127,352 (M); expenditures, $6,310; qualifying distributions, $3,965.
Limitations: Applications not accepted.
Application information: Contributes only to pre-selected organizations.

Trustee: National City Bank.
EIN: 256491453

44331
Michael and Diane Kennedy Charitable Foundation
21831 Avalon Dr.
Rocky River, OH 44116

Established in 1990 in OH.
Donor(s): Michael Kennedy.
Financial data (yr. ended 12/31/01): Grants paid, $3,955; assets, $22,449 (M); gifts received, $765; expenditures, $4,720; qualifying distributions, $3,955.
Limitations: Applications not accepted. Giving limited to OH.
Application information: Contributes only to pre-selected organizations.
Officers and Trustees:* Michael Kennedy,* Pres.; Diane Kennedy,* Secy.-Treas.; Jerry Kish.
EIN: 341648151

44332
Huron Doctors Foundation, Inc.
c/o Glenn J. Trippe, M.D.
282 Benedict Ave., Ste. B
Norwalk, OH 44857

Established in 1995 in OH.
Financial data (yr. ended 12/31/01): Grants paid, $3,833; assets, $7,234 (M); gifts received, $3,555; expenditures, $3,833; qualifying distributions, $3,833.
Limitations: Applications not accepted.
Application information: Contributes only to pre-selected organizations.
Officers: Almeda J. Trippe, Pres.; Glenn J. Trippe, M.D., Secy.-Treas.
EIN: 341800313

44333
The Ned & Lynn Kendall Foundation
P.O. Box 769
Green, OH 44232-0769

Established in 1995.
Donor(s): Lynn Kendall, Ned G. Kendall, Jr.
Financial data (yr. ended 11/30/01): Grants paid, $3,831; assets, $15,765 (M); gifts received, $3,373; expenditures, $6,860; qualifying distributions, $3,831.
Limitations: Applications not accepted.
Application information: Contributes only to pre-selected organizations.
Trustees: Mary L. Kendall, Ned G. Kendall, Jr.
EIN: 341812195

44334
Hughes Family Foundation
33565 Bainbridge Rd.
Solon, OH 44139

Financial data (yr. ended 12/31/01): Grants paid, $3,800; assets, $57,621 (M); gifts received, $16,000; expenditures, $4,072; qualifying distributions, $3,800.
Limitations: Applications not accepted. Giving primarily in Aurora, OH.
Application information: Contributes only to pre-selected organizations.
Officers and Trustees:* Vickie Helt,* Pres.; Kathleen Hughes,* Secy.-Treas.; Harold Hughes, James Reed.
EIN: 341876519

44335
Schoenberger Trust
12966 County Hwy. 63
Upper Sandusky, OH 43351-9567
Contact: Irene L. Schoenberger, Tr.

Established in 1988 in OH.
Financial data (yr. ended 12/31/99): Grants paid, $3,800; assets, $79,407 (M); expenditures, $4,071; qualifying distributions, $3,931.
Limitations: Giving limited to Wyandot, OH, and its surrounding counties.
Application information: Application form required.
Trustees: Stephen Chenny, Eric Schoenberger, Irene L. Schoenberger, Craig Swinehart.
EIN: 346866430

44336
Sigrist-Wardell Educational Fund
c/o The Huntington National Bank
P.O. Box 1558, HC-0534
Columbus, OH 43216
Application address: c/o Judge, Common Pleas Courts, Tuscarawas County, 101 E. High Ave., New Philadelphia, OH 44663

Financial data (yr. ended 06/30/01): Grants paid, $3,800; assets, $46,645 (M); expenditures, $4,269; qualifying distributions, $3,843.
Limitations: Giving limited to residents of Tuscarawas County, OH.
Application information: Contact courthouse for application. Application form required.
Trustee: The Huntington National Bank.
EIN: 346621348

44337
Joseph and Sarah Denmark Memorial Foundation, Inc.
(Formerly Sarah Denmark Memorial Foundation, Inc.)
P.O. Box 1227
Steubenville, OH 43952-2153
Application address: 6046 Wilshire Blvd., Sarasota, FL 34238, tel.: (941) 921-1666
Contact: Meyer Denmark, Tr.

Donor(s): Meyer Denmark.
Financial data (yr. ended 01/31/02): Grants paid, $3,750; assets, $180,319 (M); expenditures, $4,228; qualifying distributions, $3,750.
Limitations: Giving primarily in Steubenville, OH.
Trustees: Meyer Denmark, Morris Denmark.
EIN: 346561037

44338
Caroline F. Dunton Scholarship Fund
c/o KeyBank, N.A.
800 Superior Ave., 4th Fl.
Cleveland, OH 44114

Financial data (yr. ended 08/31/01): Grants paid, $3,750; assets, $112,572 (M); expenditures, $5,375; qualifying distributions, $3,750.
Limitations: Applications not accepted.
Trustee: KeyBank, N.A.
EIN: 016026835
Codes: GTI

44339
The Kurtz Foundation, Inc.
4700 E. 49th St.
Cleveland, OH 44125-1080

Donor(s): Kurtz Bros., Inc.
Financial data (yr. ended 03/31/01): Grants paid, $3,750; assets, $1,439 (M); expenditures, $4,284; qualifying distributions, $3,750.
Limitations: Applications not accepted. Giving limited to Cleveland, OH.

Application information: Contributes only to pre-selected organizations.
Officers and Trustee:* John T. Kurtz, Pres.; Gregory P. Kurtz, V.P.; Thomas A. Kurtz, Secy.; Lisa M. Kurtz,* Treas.
EIN: 341574370

44340
Helen H. Mackey Educational Awards Foundation
P.O. Box 5756
Cleveland, OH 44101-9957
Application address: c/o Senior Counselor, Bay City Central High School, 1624 Columbus Ave., Bay City, MI 48708, tel.: (989) 893-9541

Donor(s): Helen Mackey.‡
Financial data (yr. ended 12/31/01): Grants paid, $3,750; assets, $124,522 (M); expenditures, $5,330; qualifying distributions, $4,320.
Limitations: Giving limited to residents of Bay City, MI.
Application information: Application form required.
Trustee: National City Bank.
EIN: 386058127
Codes: GTI

44341
Anna L. Smith Charitable Trust
c/o National City Bank of Pennsylvania
P.O. Box 94651
Cleveland, OH 44101-4651

Established in 1998 in PA.
Donor(s): Anna L. Smith.
Financial data (yr. ended 12/31/01): Grants paid, $3,725; assets, $129,614 (M); expenditures, $4,555; qualifying distributions, $3,725.
Limitations: Applications not accepted.
Application information: Contributes only to pre-selected organizations.
Trustee: National City Bank.
EIN: 256581638

44342
The Schulte Private Foundation
1106 Indra Ct.
Cincinnati, OH 45240
Contact: Marcia C. Shulte, Pres.

Established in 1997 in OH.
Donor(s): Marcia C. Schulte.
Financial data (yr. ended 12/31/01): Grants paid, $3,700; assets, $69,514 (M); gifts received, $23,746; expenditures, $4,198; qualifying distributions, $3,700.
Officers and Trustees:* Marcia C. Schulte,* Pres. and Treas.; Gerhard Bernard Schulte III,* V.P.; Ellen M. Urban,* Secy.-Treas.
EIN: 311579165

44343
St. Emma Relief Fund
c/o KeyBank, N.A.
800 Superior Ave., 4th Fl.
Cleveland, OH 44114-2601

Established in 1988 in MA.
Financial data (yr. ended 06/30/99): Grants paid, $3,690; assets, $46,693 (M); expenditures, $4,223; qualifying distributions, $3,666.
Limitations: Applications not accepted. Giving limited to Fort Kent, ME.
Trustee: KeyBank, N.A.
EIN: 510170004

44344
Siemer Foundation
c/o Barbara J. Siemer
2 Bottomley Crescent
New Albany, OH 43054-8909

Established in 1987 in OH.
Donor(s): A.B. Siemer.
Financial data (yr. ended 11/30/01): Grants paid, $3,595; assets, $411,646 (M); expenditures, $3,794; qualifying distributions, $3,595.
Limitations: Applications not accepted. Giving primarily in Columbus, OH.
Application information: Contributes only to pre-selected organizations.
Trustees: Roger D. Bailey, A.B. Siemer, Barbara J. Siemer.
EIN: 311260542

44345
Ronald L. and Cinda S. Roudebush Foundation
7386 Riverpoint Ln.
Cincinnati, OH 45255

Established in 1999 in MI.
Donor(s): Ron Roudebush, Cinda Roudebush.
Financial data (yr. ended 12/31/01): Grants paid, $3,580; assets, $62,585 (M); expenditures, $4,834; qualifying distributions, $3,580.
Limitations: Applications not accepted.
Application information: Contributes only to pre-selected organizations.
Officers and Trustees:* Ronald L. Roudebush,* Pres.; Cinda S. Roudebush,* Secy.-Treas.
EIN: 383492405

44346
The Englefield Foundation
447 James Pkwy.
Heath, OH 43056

Established in 1999 in OH.
Donor(s): F.W. Englefield III.
Financial data (yr. ended 12/31/01): Grants paid, $3,553; assets, $177,471 (M); gifts received, $5,000; expenditures, $9,814; qualifying distributions, $3,553.
Limitations: Applications not accepted.
Application information: Contributes only to pre-selected organizations.
Officers: F.W. Englefield III, Pres.; Janet L. Englefield, V.P.; Cynthia E. Arnold, Secy.-Treas.
EIN: 311657317

44347
A. W. Schubert Foundation
7730 Chumani Ln.
Cincinnati, OH 45243-3205

Donor(s): Ruth M. Schubert.
Financial data (yr. ended 11/30/01): Grants paid, $3,550; assets, $104,355 (M); expenditures, $5,164; qualifying distributions, $3,550.
Limitations: Applications not accepted. Giving primarily in Cincinnati, OH.
Application information: Contributes only to pre-selected organizations.
Officers: Ruth M. Schubert, Pres.; Steve Wilhelm, V.P.; Joyce Wilhelm, Secy.
EIN: 316050409

44348
Clifford W. Pleatman Family Foundation
77 Carpenter Ridge
Blue Ash, OH 45242

Established in 1997 in OH.
Donor(s): Clifford W. Pleatman.
Financial data (yr. ended 06/30/00): Grants paid, $3,545; assets, $113,201 (M); gifts received, $7,825; expenditures, $5,878; qualifying distributions, $4,841.
Limitations: Applications not accepted.
Application information: Contributes only to pre-selected organizations.
Officers and Trustees:* Clifford W. Pleatman,* Pres.; Stephen Pleatman,* V.P.; Robert L. Pleatman,* Secy.
EIN: 317576882

44349
John G. Sprankle Memorial Fund Trust No. 1905
c/o KeyBank, N.A.
800 Superior Ave., 4th Fl.
Cleveland, OH 44114-2601

Financial data (yr. ended 12/31/01): Grants paid, $3,536; assets, $104,177 (M); expenditures, $5,972; qualifying distributions, $3,536.
Limitations: Applications not accepted. Giving primarily in OH.
Application information: Contributes only to pre-selected organizations.
Trustee: KeyBank, N.A.
EIN: 346636139

44350
Russell E. & Barbara O. Browning Family Foundation
c/o U.S. Bank
425 Walnut St., ML 7126
Cincinnati, OH 45202

Established in 1998 in OH.
Donor(s): Russell E. Browning.
Financial data (yr. ended 12/31/01): Grants paid, $3,500; assets, $78,698 (M); gifts received, $23,413; expenditures, $4,755; qualifying distributions, $3,500.
Limitations: Applications not accepted. Giving primarily in IL.
Application information: Contributes only to pre-selected organizations.
Officers and Trustees:* Russell E. Browning,* Pres.; Janet L. Houston,* Secy.; James McNeal,* Treas.
EIN: 311628325

44351
Hazel M. Chaney Scholarship Trust
c/o KeyBank, N.A.
800 Superior Ave., 4th Fl.
Cleveland, OH 44114
Application address: c/o KeyBank, N.A., Augusta, ME 04330
Contact: Christina Cook, Trust Off., KeyBank, N.A.

Financial data (yr. ended 08/31/01): Grants paid, $3,500; assets, $160,429 (M); expenditures, $5,309; qualifying distributions, $3,500.
Limitations: Giving limited to Wilton and Franklin County, ME.
Trustee: KeyBank, N.A.
EIN: 016007065
Codes: GTI

44352
Zela I. Christ Trust
1111 Rush Ave.
Bellefontaine, OH 43311-9488

Financial data (yr. ended 12/31/99): Grants paid, $3,500; assets, $95,113 (M); expenditures, $4,534; qualifying distributions, $4,289.
Limitations: Giving limited to Logan County, OH.
Application information: Application form required.
Trustee: Robert MacDonald, Jr.
EIN: 346816164

44353
The Juliana Foundation
c/o James R. Bright
925 Euclid Ave., Ste. 2000
Cleveland, OH 44115-1496

Established in 2000 in OH.
Donor(s): William C. McCoy.
Financial data (yr. ended 12/31/01): Grants paid, $3,500; assets, $68,654 (M); expenditures, $5,073; qualifying distributions, $3,500.
Limitations: Applications not accepted.
Application information: Contributes only to pre-selected organizations.
Trustees: James R. Bright, William C. McCoy.
EIN: 341925557

44354
John E. & Elizabeth Kurtz Charitable Foundation
c/o National City Bank of Pennsylvania
P.O. Box 94651
Cleveland, OH 44101-4651
Application address: c/o National City Bank of PA, 20 Stanwix St., 16th Fl., Pittsburgh, PA 15222; tel.: (412) 644-8002
Contact: Joanna Mayo

Established in 2000 in PA.
Donor(s): John E. Kurtz.‡
Financial data (yr. ended 04/30/02): Grants paid, $3,500; assets, $909,152 (M); expenditures, $10,814; qualifying distributions, $3,500.
Limitations: Giving primarily in Pittsburgh, PA.
Advisory Committee: Roy Thomas Clark, Kenneth J. Kurtz, Susan C. Mill.
Trustee: National City Bank of Pennsylvania.
EIN: 527100427

44355
Murphy Scholarship Trust
c/o National City Bank
P.O. Box 94651
Cleveland, OH 44101-4651

Financial data (yr. ended 12/31/99): Grants paid, $3,500; assets, $90,982 (M); expenditures, $4,434; qualifying distributions, $4,145.
Limitations: Giving primarily in KY.
Officer: David E. Jones, Pres.
Trustee: National City Bank.
EIN: 616229144

44356
Dr. Edwin Pratt Memorial Fund
(also known as Grace K. Orr-Dr. Edwin Pratt Memorial Fund Foundation)
c/o The Huntington National Bank
P.O. Box 1558, HC1012
Columbus, OH 43216
Application address: Joyce Ritter, Public Relations Dir., c/o Mary Rutan Hospital of Logan County, Inc., 205 Palmer Ave., Bellefontaine, OH 43311

Financial data (yr. ended 06/30/01): Grants paid, $3,488; assets, $109,085 (M); expenditures, $4,788; qualifying distributions, $3,746.
Limitations: Giving limited to Logan County, OH.
Application information: Application form required.
Trustee: The Huntington National Bank.
EIN: 316195814

44357
Heimbinder Family Foundation
c/o William E. Reichard
25109 Detroit Rd., Ste. 300
Westlake, OH 44145

Established in 1989 in OH.
Donor(s): Isaac Heimbinder, Sheila Heimbinder.
Financial data (yr. ended 12/31/00): Grants paid, $3,470; assets, $3,370,268 (M); gifts received, $2,954,845; expenditures, $4,186; qualifying distributions, $3,470.
Limitations: Applications not accepted. Giving primarily in TX.
Application information: Contributes only to pre-selected organizations.
Trustees: Isaac Heimbinder, Sheila Heimbinder, William E. Reichard.
EIN: 346921501

44358
The George B. and Katherine D. Wilkinson Foundation
255 E. 5th St.
Cincinnati, OH 45202

Established in 1999 in OH.
Donor(s): George B. Wilkinson, Katherine D. Wilkinson.
Financial data (yr. ended 12/31/00): Grants paid, $3,455; assets, $7,760 (M); expenditures, $3,745; qualifying distributions, $3,455.
Limitations: Applications not accepted. Giving primarily in Cincinnati, OH.
Application information: Contributes only to pre-selected organizations.
Officers: George B. Wilkinson, Pres.; Katherine D. Wilkinson, V.P. and Treas.; Bonnie G. Camden, Secy.
EIN: 311678457

44359
John A. Beck Memorial Scholarship Fund
c/o National City Bank of Pennsylvania
P.O. Box 94651
Cleveland, OH 44101-4651

Financial data (yr. ended 12/31/01): Grants paid, $3,439; assets, $60,112 (M); expenditures, $5,118; qualifying distributions, $4,189.
Limitations: Applications not accepted. Giving limited to residents of PA.
Application information: Unsolicited requests for funds not accepted.
Trustee: National City Bank of Pennsylvania.
EIN: 256060734

44360
Arthur R. Atwood Scholarship Fund
c/o KeyBank, N.A.
800 Superior Ave., 4th Fl.
Cleveland, OH 44114

Donor(s): Arthur R. Atwood.‡
Financial data (yr. ended 02/28/02): Grants paid, $3,420; assets, $63,918 (M); expenditures, $4,284; qualifying distributions, $3,452.
Limitations: Applications not accepted. Giving limited to residents of the town of Champlain and Clinton County, NY.
Application information: Preference given to male students accepted at Yale University.
Trustee: KeyBank, N.A.
EIN: 146014625
Codes: GTI

44361
Tecca Foundation
12900 Lake Ave., Ste. 1009
Lakewood, OH 44107-1552
Contact: Dorothy D'Amico

Donor(s): Michael Tecca.
Financial data (yr. ended 12/31/01): Grants paid, $3,360; assets, $65,716 (M); expenditures, $6,159; qualifying distributions, $3,360.
Director: Dorothy D'Amico.
EIN: 346537073

44362
Kalhan Foundation
2625 Fairwood Dr.
Pepper Pike, OH 44124

Donor(s): Satish Kalhan, Santosh Kalhan.
Financial data (yr. ended 12/31/01): Grants paid, $3,346; assets, $20,971 (M); gifts received, $4,500; expenditures, $3,346; qualifying distributions, $0.
Trustees: Santosh Kalhan, Satish Kalhan.
EIN: 311550279

44363
Joseph J. & Marie P. Schedel Foundation
1200 Edison Plz.
300 Madison Ave.
Toledo, OH 43604
Contact: Charles E. Brown, Pres.

Established in 1963 in OH.
Donor(s): Joseph J. Schedel,‡ Marie P. Schedel.‡
Financial data (yr. ended 12/31/00): Grants paid, $3,250; assets, $6,642,194 (M); gifts received, $69,309; expenditures, $583,614; qualifying distributions, $519,398; giving activities include $521,343 for programs.
Limitations: Applications not accepted. Giving limited to OH.
Publications: Newsletter.
Application information: Contributes only to pre-selected organizations.
Officers and Trustees:* Charles E. Brown,* Pres.; James V. Shindler, Jr.,* V.P. and Secy.; Donald N. Schade, Treas.; Blair D. Miller, Mark T. Reilly.
Director: Reginald D. Noble.
EIN: 346557721

44364
The Baumgartner Family Foundation
P.O. Box 8326
Toledo, OH 43605-0326

Established in 1999 in OH.
Donor(s): Don J. Baumgartner.
Financial data (yr. ended 12/31/01): Grants paid, $3,245; assets, $59,024 (M); gifts received, $2,500; expenditures, $3,694; qualifying distributions, $3,245.
Limitations: Applications not accepted.
Application information: Contributes only to pre-selected organizations.
Officers: Don J. Baumgartner, Pres.; Douglas Baumgartner, V.P. and Treas.; Molly Baumgartner, Secy.
EIN: 341908139

44365
George L. and Goldie Mae Hall Memorial Scholarship Fund Trust
c/o Third Fifth Bank
38 Fountain Sq. Plz., Trust Tax Dept.
Cincinnati, OH 45263
Application address: c/o Waltonville High School, Waltonville, IL 62894

Established in 1987 in IN.
Financial data (yr. ended 04/30/00): Grants paid, $3,200; assets, $156,666 (M); expenditures, $6,641; qualifying distributions, $5,657.
Limitations: Giving limited to Waltonville, IL.
Application information: Application form required.
Trustee: Fifth Third Bank.
EIN: 356471111

44366
Irving and Andy Pike Scholarship Fund
c/o Thomas H. Palmer
41 W. Broad St.
Newton Falls, OH 44444-1643

Established in 2001 in OH.
Financial data (yr. ended 12/31/01): Grants paid, $3,200; assets, $73,098 (M); expenditures, $3,713; qualifying distributions, $0.
Limitations: Applications not accepted. Giving primarily to residents of OH.
Officers and Trustees:* Betty Force,* Pres.; Thomas H. Palmer,* V.P.; Richard Reeves,* Secy.-Treas.
EIN: 341900305

44367
Ottawa County Community Foundation, Inc.
2933 Coho Dr.
Port Clinton, OH 43452   (419) 294-2232
FAX: (419) 294-2488
Contact: Joy Roth, Pres.

Established in 2000 in OH.
Financial data (yr. ended 12/31/00): Grants paid, $3,188; assets, $104,000 (M); gifts received, $87,725; expenditures, $3,188.
Limitations: Giving limited to Ottawa County, OH, and all of its entities.
Publications: Annual report, informational brochure.
Officers and Trustees:* Joy M. Roth,* Pres.; Derrill A. Hablitzel,* V.P.; Thomas W. Salamone,* Secy.-Treas.; Robert B. Armbruster, John W. Blatt, Earl J. Johnson, David B. Martin, Darrell W. Opfer, L. Jack Schiller.
EIN: 341899124
Codes: CM

44368
Cairo Fire Association, Inc.
101 W. Main St.
Cairo, OH 45820

Financial data (yr. ended 12/31/99): Grants paid, $3,180; assets, $19,123 (M); gifts received, $14,621; expenditures, $27,692; qualifying distributions, $0.
Officers: Wilbur Earl, Secy.; Joan Hefner, Treas.
EIN: 341406412

44369
Marjorie & Russell Bean Memorial Foundation
125 Oakmont Dr.
Dover, OH 44622-3200

Financial data (yr. ended 12/31/01): Grants paid, $3,170; assets, $70,534 (M); expenditures, $3,551; qualifying distributions, $3,170.
Limitations: Applications not accepted.
Trustee: Natalie E. McFarland.
EIN: 341601715

44370
The Michaud Charitable Trust
c/o KeyBank, N.A., Trust Div.
800 Superior Ave., 4th Fl.
Cleveland, OH 44114
Application address: c/o KeyBank, N.A., Trust Svcs., 286 Water St., Augusta, ME 04330

Established in 1989 in ME.
Financial data (yr. ended 10/31/00): Grants paid, $3,150; assets, $66,365 (M); expenditures, $4,191; qualifying distributions, $3,150.
Limitations: Giving limited to ME.
Trustee: KeyBank, N.A.
EIN: 046013647

44371
The Mazie Foundation
P.O. Box 692
Maumee, OH 43537

Established in 1999 in OH.
Donor(s): Marilyn Richard.
Financial data (yr. ended 12/31/01): Grants paid, $3,140; assets, $215,414 (M); gifts received, $82,050; expenditures, $3,823; qualifying distributions, $3,140.
Trustees: Lisa Caswell, Belinda Cytlak, Karen McMahon, Marilyn Richard.
EIN: 341910734

44372
Sparkpeople Service, Inc.
1045 Willow Ave.
Cincinnati, OH 45246

Established in 2000 in OH.
Donor(s): Christopher Downie.
Financial data (yr. ended 12/31/01): Grants paid, $3,140; assets, $1,345,041 (M); expenditures, $53,491; qualifying distributions, $3,140.
Limitations: Applications not accepted.
Application information: Contributes only to pre-selected organizations.
Officer: Christopher Downie, Pres.
Trustees: Mike Kramer, Rachel Von Nida.
EIN: 311742502

44373
Coshocton City Schools Foundation
c/o Michael P. McCullough
305 Main St.
Coshocton, OH 43812-1510
Application address: P.O. Box 1445, Coshocton, OH 43812

Established in 1987 in OH.
Financial data (yr. ended 12/31/99): Grants paid, $3,125; assets, $99,476 (M); gifts received, $6,097; expenditures, $4,758; qualifying distributions, $3,125.
Limitations: Giving limited to Coshocton, OH.
Application information: Application form required.
Officer and Trustees:* Michael McCullough,* Secy.-Treas.; Connie Allen, Robin Coffman, Rodney Dobson, Cathy Hudson, Diane Jones, Barry Lentz, Kent Modlin.
EIN: 311188378

44374
Grossman Charitable Trust
17810 Allien Ave.
Cleveland, OH 44111-4011

Donor(s): Valleyview Management Co.
Financial data (yr. ended 12/31/99): Grants paid, $3,100; assets, $35,231 (L); gifts received, $13,600; expenditures, $3,816; qualifying distributions, $3,100.
Limitations: Applications not accepted.
Application information: Contributes only to pre-selected organizations.
Trustee: Walter S. Grossman.
EIN: 341832031

44375
The Aubrey H. and Joyce M. Milnes Foundation
593 Yarmouth Ln.
Bay Village, OH 44140
Contact: Valerie Durica, V.P.

Financial data (yr. ended 12/31/00): Grants paid, $3,100; assets, $45,900 (M); expenditures, $3,868; qualifying distributions, $3,100.
Limitations: Giving primarily in Cleveland, OH.

Officers and Trustees:* Pamela M. Russell,* Pres.; Valerie J. Durica,* V.P. and Secy.; William R. Durica, Jr.,* V.P.
EIN: 341881469

44376
The Steve Goldman Foundation, Inc.
P.O. Box 1308
Mansfield, OH 44901

Established in 1984 in CT.
Financial data (yr. ended 08/31/02): Grants paid, $3,050; assets, $57,629 (M); gifts received, $3,056; expenditures, $3,688; qualifying distributions, $3,050.
Limitations: Applications not accepted. Giving primarily in OH.
Application information: Contributes only to pre-selected organizations.
Officers: Carol Goldman,* Pres.; C. David Goldman,* Secy.; Benjamin Goldman,* Treas.
EIN: 222558678

44377
Mary Fisher Hancock & W. Wayne Hancock Foundation
7910 Shawnee Run Rd.
Cincinnati, OH 45243

Financial data (yr. ended 12/31/01): Grants paid, $3,050; assets, $60,493 (M); expenditures, $3,139; qualifying distributions, $3,050.
Limitations: Applications not accepted. Giving on a national basis.
Application information: Contributes only to pre-selected organizations.
Trustees: Mary H. Fritzsche, John W. Hancock, William W. Hancock, Jr.
EIN: 346501926

44378
George B. Stewart Family Foundation
900 Adams Crossing, Box 13100
Cincinnati, OH 45202
Contact: George B. Stewart, Pres.

Donor(s): George B. Stewart.
Financial data (yr. ended 07/31/00): Grants paid, $3,038; assets, $95 (M); gifts received, $2,500; expenditures, $3,038; qualifying distributions, $3,038.
Limitations: Giving primarily in OH.
Officers: George B. Stewart, Pres.; Anita R. Stewart, V.P.
EIN: 237121732

44379
Hibbert Fund
4557 River Rd.
Toledo, OH 43614-5537

Established in 1991 in OH.
Financial data (yr. ended 12/31/01): Grants paid, $3,030; assets, $56,739 (M); expenditures, $3,113; qualifying distributions, $3,030.
Limitations: Applications not accepted. Giving primarily in OH.
Application information: Contributes only to pre-selected organizations.
Trustees: Martha Boice, Frederick W. Hibbert, Nancy E. Hibbert.
EIN: 346517843

44380
William J. Ayers Trust
P.O. Box 94651
Cleveland, OH 44101-4651

Financial data (yr. ended 12/31/01): Grants paid, $3,000; assets, $80,082 (M); expenditures, $6,086; qualifying distributions, $3,275.
Limitations: Applications not accepted.

44380—OHIO

Application information: Contributes only to pre-selected organizations.
Trustee: National City Bank.
EIN: 347031435

44381
The Brenner Foundation
925 Euclid Ave., Ste. 1995
Cleveland, OH 44115-1407

Established in 1998 in OH.
Donor(s): R. Chad Brenner.
Financial data (yr. ended 12/31/01): Grants paid, $3,000; assets, $65,980 (M); gifts received, $5,000; expenditures, $3,456; qualifying distributions, $3,000.
Officers: R. Chad Brenner, Pres.; Carol Brenner, Secy.
Trustees: Ronald L. Garman, Michael D. McPhillips.
EIN: 341862879

44382
Brewer & McKay Scholarship Foundation
c/o KeyBank, N.A.
800 Superior Ave., 4th Fl.
Cleveland, OH 44114-2601

Established in 1995 ME.
Financial data (yr. ended 10/31/99): Grants paid, $3,000; assets, $50,426 (M); gifts received, $5,000; expenditures, $3,856; qualifying distributions, $3,000.
Limitations: Applications not accepted.
Application information: Unsolicited requests for funds not accepted.
Trustee: KeyBank, N.A.
EIN: 016135476

44383
Richard and Frances Buchholzer Charitable Foundation
830 Chapel Hill Mall
Akron, OH 44310

Financial data (yr. ended 06/30/01): Grants paid, $3,000; assets, $53,069 (M); gifts received, $5,000; expenditures, $3,745; qualifying distributions, $2,978.
Officers and Trustees:* Richard Buchholzer,* Pres.; Frances Buchholzer,* V.P.; Robert W. Malone,* Secy.; Stanley L. Apple,* Treas.; Roy Ray.
EIN: 341848519

44384
Harold C. & Katrina J. Clark Irrevocable Scholarship Fund
c/o KeyBank, N.A.
800 Superior Ave., 4th Fl.
Cleveland, OH 44114
Application address: c/o Principal, Caribou High School, Caribou, ME 04736

Financial data (yr. ended 05/31/01): Grants paid, $3,000; assets, $113,857 (M); expenditures, $3,058; qualifying distributions, $2,881.
Limitations: Giving limited to residents of Caribou and Aroostook County, ME.
Trustee: KeyBank, N.A.
EIN: 222623144

44385
John L. Cohill Memorial Scholarship Foundation
643 E. Tallmadge Ave.
Akron, OH 44310 (330) 253-9959
Contact: Kenneth Dies, Tr.

Financial data (yr. ended 12/31/99): Grants paid, $3,000; assets, $17,638 (M); gifts received, $2,013; expenditures, $3,520; qualifying distributions, $3,262.

Limitations: Giving limited to residents of Akron, OH.
Trustees: Kenneth Dies, Ron Laubau.
EIN: 341584377

44386
Sherman Fuller Foundation
c/o KeyBank, N.A.
800 Superior Ave., 4th Fl.
Cleveland, OH 44114
Contact: John Mulford, Trust Off., KeyBank, N.A.

Established in 2000 in ME.
Financial data (yr. ended 12/31/01): Grants paid, $3,000; assets, $1 (M); gifts received, $17,082; expenditures, $16,600; qualifying distributions, $3,000.
Trustee: KeyBank, N.A.
EIN: 527077013

44387
Leslie Gerding Foundation, Inc.
8428 Wiese Rd.
Brecksville, OH 44141 (440) 526-7065
Contact: Charles C. Gerding, Pres.

Established in 1994 in OH.
Donor(s): Charles C. Gerding.
Financial data (yr. ended 12/31/01): Grants paid, $3,000; assets, $67,776 (M); gifts received, $200; expenditures, $3,434; qualifying distributions, $3,000.
Officers: Charles C. Gerding, Pres.; Christopher C. Gerding, Secy.-Treas.
EIN: 341725986

44388
GK Foundation
3201 Harvard Ave.
Newburgh Heights, OH 44105-3060
(216) 341-0200
Contact: Henry J. Goodman, Pres.

Established in 1981.
Donor(s): Robert Kichler, Henry J. Goodman, H. Goodman, Inc., Bruce Goodman, David Kuppermann.
Financial data (yr. ended 10/31/01): Grants paid, $3,000; assets, $13,691 (M); expenditures, $3,013; qualifying distributions, $3,000.
Limitations: Giving limited to Cleveland, OH.
Officers and Trustees:* Henry J. Goodman,* Pres.; Bruce Goodman,* V.P. and Secy.; Lois Goodman,* V.P.; Steve Goodman,* Treas.
EIN: 341385716

44389
Ceylon E. Hudson Charitable Trust
c/o Wayne County National Bank
1776 Beall Ave.
Wooster, OH 44691 (330) 264-7111
Contact: Stephen Kitchen, Tr.

Financial data (yr. ended 12/31/01): Grants paid, $3,000; assets, $62,465 (M); expenditures, $4,071; qualifying distributions, $3,000.
Limitations: Giving primarily in Wooster, OH.
Application information: Application form not required.
Trustee: Stephen Kitchen.
EIN: 346704144

44390
Irelan Family Foundation
8032 Wingate Pl.
Delaware, OH 43015

Established in 2000 in OH.
Donor(s): Victor D. Irelan, Julia S. Irelan.
Financial data (yr. ended 12/31/01): Grants paid, $3,000; assets, $43,722 (M); gifts received, $8,741; expenditures, $6,652; qualifying distributions, $3,000.
Limitations: Applications not accepted.
Application information: Contributes only to pre-selected organizations.
Officers: Victor D. Irelan, Pres.; Julia S. Irelan, V.P.; Tanya L. Irelan, Secy.; Victoria I. Howe, Treas.
Directors: Lori B. Irelan, Robert J. Howe, Rosemary Irelan.
Trustees: David C. Irelan, Richard W. Irelan, Thomas W. Irelan.
EIN: 311697340

44391
The Jackson Center American Legion Foundation, Inc.
602 S. Main St.
Jackson Center, OH 45334
Contact: James E. Davis, Treas.

Financial data (yr. ended 12/31/99): Grants paid, $3,000; assets, $86,960 (M); expenditures, $3,275; qualifying distributions, $3,275.
Limitations: Giving primarily in OH.
Application information: Application form required.
Officers and Trustees:* Mick McGowan,* Pres.; Don Holt,* V.P.; Ronald E. Leininger,* Secy.; James E. Davis,* Treas.; David Schumann.
EIN: 341607510

44392
The Jake Foundation, Inc.
c/o Jim Gaal
4975 Hamilton Rd.
Cleveland, OH 44114

Established in 1999 in OH.
Donor(s): Anne M. Burkey.
Financial data (yr. ended 12/31/01): Grants paid, $3,000; assets, $12,368 (M); expenditures, $3,368; qualifying distributions, $3,000.
Limitations: Applications not accepted.
Application information: Contributes only to pre-selected organizations.
Officers and Trustees:* James F. Gaal,* Pres.; Jack Corwin, Secy.; R. Chad Brenner, Anne M. Burkey.
EIN: 341902750

44393
The Claude Walden Johnson Foundation
P.O. Box 1271
Cincinnati, OH 45201-1271

Financial data (yr. ended 12/31/01): Grants paid, $3,000; assets, $7,946 (M); expenditures, $3,103; qualifying distributions, $0.
Limitations: Applications not accepted. Giving primarily in Fort Thomas, KY.
Directors: Nancy J. Baker, Michael T. Gibson, Douglas N. Johnson, Robert G. White.
EIN: 611328608

44394
Marks, Inc.
P.O. Box 24079
Cincinnati, OH 45224

Donor(s): Stanley A. Marks.
Financial data (yr. ended 12/31/01): Grants paid, $3,000; assets, $66,531 (M); expenditures, $3,114; qualifying distributions, $3,000.
Limitations: Applications not accepted. Giving primarily in Fort Lauderdale, FL.
Application information: Contributes only to pre-selected organizations.
Officers and Directors:* Stanley A. Marks,* Pres. and Mgr.; Shelly K. Entner, V.P.; Christopher P. Gates, Secy.-Treas.
EIN: 316026072

44395
Harry R. & Mary I. Maxon Family Foundation
425 Walnut St., Ste. 1800
Cincinnati, OH 45202

Established in 2000 in OH.
Donor(s): Harry R. Maxon III.
Financial data (yr. ended 12/31/01): Grants paid, $3,000; assets, $33,807 (M); gifts received, $24,621; expenditures, $10,405; qualifying distributions, $3,000.
Limitations: Applications not accepted.
Application information: Contributes only to pre-selected organizations.
Officers and Trustees:* Harry R. Maxon IV, Pres.; Mary E. Maxon, Exec. V.P.; Jason Blount,* V.P.; Yasushi J. Tomita,* V.P.; Mary L. Rust,* Secy.; Ashley L. Tomita, Treas.
EIN: 311707787

44396
The Mulligan Charitable Foundation
c/o John D. Drinko
3200 National City Ctr., 1900 E. 9th St.
Cleveland, OH 44114-3485

Donor(s): Edwin F. Mulligan, John D. Drinko.
Financial data (yr. ended 12/31/01): Grants paid, $3,000; assets, $45,124 (M); gifts received, $4,000; expenditures, $4,659; qualifying distributions, $3,000.
Limitations: Applications not accepted. Giving primarily in OH.
Application information: Contributes only to pre-selected organizations.
Officers and Trustees:* Edwin F. Mulligan,* Pres.; Marion Mulligan Sutton,* V.P.; John D. Drinko,* Secy.-Treas.; Willard S. Breon, Jay Deaver Drinko.
EIN: 341739215

44397
Kathleen O'Dell Camp Trust
c/o Fifth Third Bank
38 Fountain Sq. Plz.
Cincinnati, OH 45263
Application addresses: c/o Principal, North Posey High School, Poseyville, IN 47633, c/o Principal, New Harmony High School, New Harmony, IN 47631

Established in 1991 in IN.
Financial data (yr. ended 12/31/00): Grants paid, $3,000; assets, $81,734 (M); expenditures, $4,570; qualifying distributions, $3,380.
Limitations: Giving limited to residents of Poseyville and New Harmony, IN.
Application information: Application form required.
Trustee: Third Fifth Bank.
EIN: 356490127

44398
The David A. and Audrey S. Osborne Foundation
11224 Mayfield Rd.
Chardon, OH 44024
Contact: Audrey S. Osborne, Tr.

Established in 1998 in OH.
Donor(s): David A. Osborne,‡ Audrey S. Osborne.
Financial data (yr. ended 06/30/02): Grants paid, $3,000; assets, $66,292 (M); expenditures, $5,722; qualifying distributions, $3,000.
Trustees: Ann L. Osborne, Audrey S. Osborne.
EIN: 311628054

44399
Scholarship 19
c/o Nilah Ankrom
1021 Salineville Rd. N.E.
Carrollton, OH 44615-9103
Application address: c/o Carrollton High School, Guidance Office, 252 3rd St., Carrollton, OH 44615

Established in 1993 in OH.
Donor(s): Nilah J. Ankrom.
Financial data (yr. ended 12/31/99): Grants paid, $3,000; assets, $59,750 (M); expenditures, $3,200; qualifying distributions, $3,200.
Limitations: Giving limited to residents of Carrollton, OH.
Application information: Application form required.
Officers and Trustees:* Nilah J. Ankrom,* Pres.; Sean Smith,* V.P.; Kathleen A. Stoneman,* Secy.-Treas.
EIN: 341727593

44400
Jack Schriner Family Foundation
c/o Jean E. Schriner
29708 Lincoln Rd.
Bay Village, OH 44140

Established in 1998 in OH.
Donor(s): Jean E. Schriner.
Financial data (yr. ended 12/31/01): Grants paid, $3,000; assets, $64,679 (M); gifts received, $800; expenditures, $4,447; qualifying distributions, $3,000.
Limitations: Applications not accepted.
Application information: Contributes only to pre-selected organizations.
Officers: Jean E. Schriner, Chair. and Pres.; John J. Schriner, Jr., V.P.; Catherine A. Schriner, Treas.
EIN: 341881221

44401
Walter E. Stebbins Memorial Scholarship Fund
c/o Walter E. Stebbins High School
1900 Harshman Rd.
Dayton, OH 45424-5022
Contact: Kevin M. O'Hearn, Chair.

Financial data (yr. ended 12/31/99): Grants paid, $3,000; assets, $102,863 (M); gifts received, $585; expenditures, $3,174; qualifying distributions, $3,108.
Limitations: Giving limited to Dayton, OH.
Application information: Application form required.
Officers: Kevin M. O'Hearn, Chair.; Roberta Clouser, Secy.-Treas.
EIN: 316050267

44402
Dr. William A. Turner, Jr. Memorial Scholarship Foundation
629 Euclid Ave., 12th Fl.
Cleveland, OH 44114
Application address: c/o Gregg Kish, Wayne State Univ., Science Store, Detroit, MI 48202

Established in 1996 in OH.
Donor(s): William A. Turner, Miriam D. Turner, Michael Raggio, David Szlag.
Financial data (yr. ended 12/31/99): Grants paid, $3,000; assets, $33,668 (M); gifts received, $3,456; expenditures, $4,771; qualifying distributions, $2,987.
Limitations: Giving primarily in MI.
Trustees: Miriam D. Turner, Thomas M. Turner, William A. Turner.
EIN: 341818265

44403
The Rick Weaver Memorial Scholarship Trust
c/o National City Bank of Pennsylvania
P.O. Box 94651
Cleveland, OH 44101-4961
Application address: c/o Guidance Counselor, Clarion-Limestone Area High School, R.D. 1, Box 205, Strattanville, PA 16258

Established in 1990 in PA.
Financial data (yr. ended 12/31/01): Grants paid, $3,000; assets, $79,201 (M); expenditures, $4,505; qualifying distributions, $3,750.
Limitations: Giving limited to residents of Clarion, PA.
Application information: Application form required.
Trustee: National City Bank.
EIN: 256334467

44404
The Wheeler Foundation
8507 Tyler Blvd.
Mentor, OH 44060

Established in 1997 in OH.
Donor(s): Betsy J. Wheeler, Thomas E. Wheeler.
Financial data (yr. ended 12/31/01): Grants paid, $3,000; assets, $152,059 (M); expenditures, $3,000; qualifying distributions, $3,000.
Limitations: Applications not accepted.
Application information: Contributes only to pre-selected organizations.
Officers: Thomas E. Wheeler, Pres.; Betsy J. Wheeler, V.P.; Michelle L. Mears, Secy.; Rebecca M. Wheeler, Treas.
EIN: 341852595

44405
Clark W. Wilson Trust
c/o KeyBank, N.A.
800 Superior Ave., 4th Fl.
Cleveland, OH 44114

Financial data (yr. ended 12/31/01): Grants paid, $3,000; assets, $114,190 (M); expenditures, $5,475; qualifying distributions, $3,000.
Limitations: Applications not accepted. Giving limited to Canastota, NY.
Application information: Contributes only to pre-selected organizations.
Trustee: KeyBank, N.A.
EIN: 237327739

44406
Phelps Charitable Trust
1520 Butler Warren Rd.
Lebanon, OH 45036

Financial data (yr. ended 12/31/99): Grants paid, $2,963; assets, $75,476 (M); expenditures, $3,254; qualifying distributions, $3,254.
Director: Janet Phelps.
EIN: 311440860

44407
The Ware Foundation
21853 Lake Rd.
Rocky River, OH 44116-1144

Donor(s): Karl E. Ware, Nancy R. Ware.
Financial data (yr. ended 12/31/01): Grants paid, $2,935; assets, $89,736 (M); expenditures, $3,830; qualifying distributions, $2,935.
Limitations: Applications not accepted. Giving primarily in Cleveland, OH.
Application information: Contributes only to pre-selected organizations.
Trustees: Karl E. Ware, Nancy R. Ware.
EIN: 316317871

44408
Manchester Family Foundation
c/o KeyBank, N.A., Trust Div.
P.O. Box 10099
Toledo, OH 43699-0099
Application address: P.O. Box 345, Wauseon, OH 43567, tel.: (419) 335-6786
Contact: Russell C. Manchester, Tr.

Financial data (yr. ended 12/31/01): Grants paid, $2,920; assets, $85,248 (M); expenditures, $4,267; qualifying distributions, $2,920.
Limitations: Giving primarily in OH.
Trustees: Russell C. Manchester, KeyBank, N.A.
EIN: 346504817

44409
Kondracke Family Foundation
2327 Boston Ave.
Columbus, OH 43209 (614) 253-9057
Contact: David R. Kondracke, Pres.

Established in 1998 in OH.
Donor(s): David R. Kondracke.
Financial data (yr. ended 12/31/01): Grants paid, $2,892; assets, $42,720 (M); gifts received, $19,172; expenditures, $2,892; qualifying distributions, $2,892.
Limitations: Giving primarily in OH.
Officers and Trustees:* David R. Kondracke,* Pres.; Jane W. Kondracke,* Secy.-Treas.; David Chris Kondracke, George Scott Kondracke.
EIN: 311603776

44410
Bessie Gray Trust
c/o National City Bank
P.O. Box 94651
Cleveland, OH 44101-4651

Financial data (yr. ended 12/31/01): Grants paid, $2,868; assets, $63,736 (M); expenditures, $3,659; qualifying distributions, $2,868.
Limitations: Applications not accepted.
Application information: Contributes only to pre-selected organizations.
Trustee: National City Bank.
EIN: 366653570

44411
Wendy Walker Memorial Scholarship Fund
(Formerly T. Urling Walker Trust)
c/o KeyBank, N.A.
800 Superior, 4th Fl.
Cleveland, OH 44114-2601

Financial data (yr. ended 12/31/99): Grants paid, $2,861; assets, $101,565 (M); expenditures, $4,863; qualifying distributions, $2,912.
Limitations: Applications not accepted. Giving limited to Watertown, NY.
Application information: Contributes only to pre-selected organizations.
Trustee: KeyBank, N.A.
EIN: 166204852

44412
Florence D. Atwood Trust for Brooks Scholarship Fund
c/o KeyBank, N.A.
800 Superior Ave., 4th Fl.
Cleveland, OH 44114
Application address: c/o Charles O'Conner, Superintendent of Schools, Chazy, NY 12921

Donor(s): Florence D. Atwood.‡
Financial data (yr. ended 06/30/01): Grants paid, $2,850; assets, $66,906 (M); expenditures, $3,678; qualifying distributions, $2,900.
Limitations: Giving limited to residents of the Chazy, NY, area.
Trustee: KeyBank, N.A.
EIN: 222753510
Codes: GTI

44413
Barrett Foundation
26 College Street
Poland, OH 44514-2015

Established in 1986 in OH.
Financial data (yr. ended 12/31/01): Grants paid, $2,850; assets, $54,789 (M); expenditures, $6,365; qualifying distributions, $2,850.
Limitations: Applications not accepted. Giving primarily in Youngstown, OH.
Application information: Contributes only to pre-selected organizations.
Trustees: LaBelle B. Barrett, Richard M. Barrett, Susan K. Barrett, Becky Jean Olmi.
EIN: 341530658

44414
Gene I. & Elsie Mesh Charitable Foundation
c/o U.S. Bank
P.O. Box 1118
Cincinnati, OH 45201-1118
Application address: 3133 Burnett Ave., Cincinnati, OH 45229
Contact: Gene I. Mesh, Chair.

Financial data (yr. ended 12/31/01): Grants paid, $2,850; assets, $51,951 (M); expenditures, $4,485; qualifying distributions, $2,850.
Officers and Trustees:* Gene I. Mesh,* Chair.; Philip Fogel,* Mgr.; Louis Kreindler,* Mgr.; Elise Mesh,* Mgr.; U.S. Bank.
EIN: 237022089

44415
The Joseph Family Foundation
c/o Geoffrey R. Engel
6800 Eastland Rd.
Middleburg Heights, OH 44130

Established in 1996 in OH.
Donor(s): Louis G. Joseph, Valerie J. Joseph.
Financial data (yr. ended 12/31/01): Grants paid, $2,805; assets, $56,555 (M); expenditures, $3,524; qualifying distributions, $2,805.
Limitations: Applications not accepted. Giving primarily in OH.
Application information: Contributes only to pre-selected organizations.
Officers and Trustees:* Louis G. Joseph,* Pres. and Secy.; Valerie J. Joseph,* V.P.; Geoffrey R. Engel,* Treas.
EIN: 311504058

44416
George M. Gray Foundation
330 E. North St.
Fostoria, OH 44830-2825

Financial data (yr. ended 12/31/01): Grants paid, $2,800; assets, $21,359 (M); expenditures, $2,854; qualifying distributions, $2,800.
Limitations: Giving primarily in OH.
Officers: Robert A. Gray, Pres.; Scott A. Gray, V.P.; Sandra E. Gray, Treas.
Director: George A. Gray.
EIN: 237105142

44417
Freda L. Rumble Family Foundation
c/o National City Bank
P.O. Box 94651
Cleveland, OH 44101-4651
Application address: c/o National City Bank, P.O. Box 450, Youngstown, OH 44501, tel.: (330) 742-4289
Contact: Myra Vitto

Established in 1999 in OH.
Financial data (yr. ended 12/31/01): Grants paid, $2,800; assets, $64,689 (M); expenditures, $4,213; qualifying distributions, $3,710.
Limitations: Giving primarily in Washington, DC.
Application information: Application form not required.
Trustee: National City Bank.
EIN: 912099419

44418
Winslow D. & Eleanor G. Siedel Memorial Scholarship Fund
c/o Fifth Third Bank
38 Fountain Sq. Plz.
Cincinnati, OH 45263

Established in 1988 in OH.
Financial data (yr. ended 12/31/01): Grants paid, $2,800; assets, $48,114 (M); expenditures, $3,297; qualifying distributions, $2,800.
Limitations: Giving primarily in OH.
Trustee: Fifth Third Bank.
EIN: 316310642

44419
Prayer Unlimited International
10723 Greenhaven Pkwy.
Brecksville, OH 44141

Financial data (yr. ended 12/31/00): Grants paid, $2,762; assets, $29,210 (M); expenditures, $6,839; qualifying distributions, $2,762.
Limitations: Applications not accepted.
Application information: Contributes only to pre-selected organizations.
Officer: Ernest Gerzeny, Treas. and Exec. Dir.
EIN: 346556106

44420
James A. D. and Christine P. Geier Family Foundation
5729 Dragon Way, Ste. 3
Cincinnati, OH 45227
Contact: Christine P. Geier, Tr. or James A.D. Geier, Tr.

Established in 1987 in OH.
Donor(s): James A.D. Geier, Christine P. Geier.
Financial data (yr. ended 12/31/00): Grants paid, $2,725; assets, $136,756 (M); gifts received, $1,500; expenditures, $5,534; qualifying distributions, $5,375.
Limitations: Giving primarily in ME and OH.
Trustees: Christine P. Geier, James A.D. Geier.
EIN: 311232293

44421
Geiger Foundation for Cancer Research
3433 Oak Alley Ct., Ste. 503
Toledo, OH 43606

Financial data (yr. ended 12/31/01): Grants paid, $2,700; assets, $14,388 (M); gifts received, $2,285; expenditures, $2,774; qualifying distributions, $2,765.
Trustee: Mary Ellen Geiger.
EIN: 341325354

44422
Roach Family Foundation
1150 S. McCord Rd., Ste. 601
Holland, OH 43528
Application address: 4041 Gulf Shore Blvd., PH6, Naples, FL 33940
Contact: Frank J. Roach, Tr.

Established in 1999 in OH.
Donor(s): Frank J. Roach.
Financial data (yr. ended 06/30/01): Grants paid, $2,700; assets, $95,744 (M); gifts received, $3,987; expenditures, $4,622; qualifying distributions, $3,510.
Limitations: Giving primarily in OH.
Application information: Application form not required.
Trustees: Amy R. McVicker Clark, Frank J. Roach.
EIN: 347108252

44423
Stratis Irrevocable Charitable Trust
8749 Woodwind Ct.
Broadview Heights, OH 44147-2570

Established in 1997 in OH.
Donor(s): Stratis Asset Management Irrevocable Trust.
Financial data (yr. ended 12/31/99): Grants paid, $2,676; assets, $246,598 (M); gifts received, $28,200; expenditures, $3,299; qualifying distributions, $2,806.
Limitations: Applications not accepted.
Application information: Contributes only to pre-selected organizations.
Directors: Lorretta J. Stratis, Mark A. Stratis.
EIN: 341846022

44424
John Allen Higman Trust
c/o National City Bank
P.O. Box 94651
Cleveland, OH 44101-4651

Financial data (yr. ended 12/31/00): Grants paid, $2,642; assets, $52,722 (M); expenditures, $3,896; qualifying distributions, $3,501.
Limitations: Applications not accepted.
Application information: Contributes only to pre-selected organizations.
Trustee: National City Bank.
EIN: 366851665

44425
Nellie F. Bash for Charities
c/o KeyBank, N.A.
P.O. Box 10099
Toledo, OH 43699-0099 (419) 259-8655
Contact: Diane Ohns, V.P., KeyBank, N.A.

Financial data (yr. ended 12/31/01): Grants paid, $2,635; assets, $663,511 (M); expenditures, $7,149; qualifying distributions, $2,635.
Limitations: Giving primarily in Toledo, OH.
Trustee: KeyBank, N.A.
EIN: 346502594

44426
Westheimer Rhodes Family Fund
1908 Dexter Ave.
Cincinnati, OH 45206 (513) 861-4648
Contact: Sallie Westheimer, Tr.

Established in 1998 in OH.
Donor(s): Sallie Westheimer.
Financial data (yr. ended 07/31/01): Grants paid, $2,600; assets, $167,394 (M); expenditures, $2,600; qualifying distributions, $2,600.
Limitations: Giving primarily in Cincinnati, OH.
Trustees: Greg Rhodes, Kara Rhodes, Sallie Westheimer.

EIN: 311628721

44427
Colleen DeCrane Family Foundation
17209 Bradgate Ave.
Cleveland, OH 44111

Established in 2000.
Financial data (yr. ended 12/31/00): Grants paid, $2,596; assets, $4,670 (M); gifts received, $9,145; expenditures, $4,475; qualifying distributions, $4,475.
Officers: Kevin A. DeCrane, Pres.; Kelly A. DeCrane, Secy.
Trustees: Kathleen M. DeCrane, Sean DeCrane.
EIN: 341912789

44428
James C. & Emma K. Hardie Foundation
245 Springdale Ln.
Moreland Hills, OH 44022-1343

Established in 1994 in OH.
Donor(s): James C. Hardie, Emma K. Hardie.
Financial data (yr. ended 12/31/99): Grants paid, $2,555; assets, $7,465 (M); gifts received, $1,796; expenditures, $2,770; qualifying distributions, $2,555.
Limitations: Applications not accepted.
Application information: Contributes only to pre-selected organizations.
Officers: James C. Hardie, Pres.; Emma K. Hardie, V.P. and Secy.
EIN: 341786854

44429
T-A R Huckstep Unitrust
c/o National City Bank of IN
P.O. Box 94651
Cleveland, OH 44101-4651

Established in 2000 in IN.
Financial data (yr. ended 12/31/01): Grants paid, $2,547; assets, $144,062 (M); expenditures, $5,485; qualifying distributions, $5,099.
Limitations: Applications not accepted. Giving primarily in Indianapolis, IN.
Application information: Contributes only to pre-selected organizations.
Trustee: National City Bank of Indiana.
EIN: 356306228

44430
John and Dorothy Masternick Foundation
20 E. Liberty St.
Girard, OH 44420

Established in 1999 in OH.
Financial data (yr. ended 12/31/01): Grants paid, $2,531; assets, $67,754 (M); gifts received, $8,114; expenditures, $2,913; qualifying distributions, $2,531.
Limitations: Applications not accepted.
Application information: Contributes only to pre-selected organizations.
Trustees: Theresa Grimes, Dorothy Masternick, John Masternick, John J. Masternick.
EIN: 311681589

44431
Michael Berner Scholarship Fund
c/o 306 W. Main
306 E. Main St.
Anna, OH 45302-9480

Financial data (yr. ended 12/31/99): Grants paid, $2,500; assets, $25,365 (M); gifts received, $2,500; expenditures, $2,500; qualifying distributions, $2,500.
Limitations: Giving limited to residents of Anna, OH.

Application information: Application form required.
Officers: Paul Berner, Pres.; Tom Finkinbiv, Secy.; Gary Berner, Treas.
EIN: 341412732

44432
Frank L. and Lois H. Conant Scholarship Fund
c/o KeyBank, N.A.
800 Superior Ave., 4th Fl.
Cleveland, OH 44114
Application address: c/o Guidance Counselor, Presque Isle High School, Presque Isle, ME 04769

Established in 1987 in ME.
Financial data (yr. ended 05/31/01): Grants paid, $2,500; assets, $53,315 (M); expenditures, $3,265; qualifying distributions, $2,500.
Limitations: Giving limited to residents of Presque Isle, ME.
Trustee: KeyBank, N.A.
EIN: 222873631

44433
Dearth Will for Scholarship Fund
c/o KeyBank, N.A.
800 Superior Ave., 4th Fl.
Cleveland, OH 44114
Application address: c/o Principal, Franklin High School, 750 E. 4th St., Franklin, OH 45005, tel.: (513) 746-6112

Established in 1986 in OH.
Financial data (yr. ended 08/31/01): Grants paid, $2,500; assets, $19,209 (M); expenditures, $2,655; qualifying distributions, $2,484.
Limitations: Giving limited to residents of Franklin, OH.
Application information: Application form not required.
Trustee: KeyBank, N.A.
EIN: 346572552

44434
Gabriel's Third Order Foundation
7852 Fenway Dr.
New Albany, OH 43054

Established in 2001 in OH.
Donor(s): Gregory A. Thompson, Carol A. Thompson.
Financial data (yr. ended 12/31/01): Grants paid, $2,500; assets, $19,447 (M); gifts received, $50,000; expenditures, $30,328; qualifying distributions, $2,500.
Limitations: Giving primarily in OH.
Officers: Gregory A. Thompson, Pres.; Carol A. Thompson, Secy.; Ellen Smith, Treas.
EIN: 311762887

44435
The George Gousios Foundation
14761 Pearl Rd.
Strongsville, OH 44136

Financial data (yr. ended 12/31/01): Grants paid, $2,500; assets, $7,627 (M); gifts received, $10,500; expenditures, $3,431; qualifying distributions, $2,500.
Trustees: Maria Blinkhorn, Andreas Gousios, Angelo Gousios.
EIN: 311490237

44436
L. Edwin Hoppes and Mary C. Hoppes Foundation
c/o John Kambeitz
1321 Richmoor Rd.
Springfield, OH 45503

Established in 1995 in OH.

44436—OHIO

Donor(s): L. Edwin Hoppes.
Financial data (yr. ended 12/31/01): Grants paid, $2,500; assets, $44,743 (M); expenditures, $2,596; qualifying distributions, $2,474.
Limitations: Applications not accepted.
Application information: Contributes only to pre-selected organizations.
Trustee: L. Edwin Hoppes.
EIN: 311451445

44437
Henry and Lauretta Huth Charitable Foundation
1245 S. Cleveland-Massillon Rd., Ste. B
Akron, OH 44321

Established in 2000 in OH.
Donor(s): Henry Huth.
Financial data (yr. ended 12/31/01): Grants paid, $2,500; assets, $32,962 (M); gifts received, $4,295; expenditures, $2,857; qualifying distributions, $2,500.
Limitations: Applications not accepted.
Application information: Contributes only to pre-selected organizations.
Officers and Trustees:* Richard Huth,* Pres.; Henry Huth,* Secy.-Treas.; Theodore Huth.
EIN: 341928164

44438
Richard T. Naples, Sr. Educational Foundation, Inc.
c/o Richard T. Naples, Sr.
2665 N. Main St.
Hubbard, OH 44425-3247

Established in 1997.
Donor(s): Richard T. Naples, Sr.
Financial data (yr. ended 06/30/01): Grants paid, $2,500; assets, $37,964 (M); gifts received, $37,964; expenditures, $3,929; qualifying distributions, $3,267.
Limitations: Applications not accepted. Giving limited to residents of OH.
Trustees: Richard T. Naples, Sr., Richard T. Naples, Jr., Mike Naples, Natalie Simon.
EIN: 341851988

44439
The Mary Louise Patton Foundation
1533 Lakeshore Dr., Ste. 100
Columbus, OH 43204

Donor(s): John B. Patton.
Financial data (yr. ended 12/31/01): Grants paid, $2,500; assets, $40,696 (M); gifts received, $3,000; expenditures, $3,077; qualifying distributions, $2,500.
Limitations: Applications not accepted. Giving primarily in Columbus, OH, and New York, NY.
Application information: Contributes only to pre-selected organizations.
Officer and Trustees:* John B. Patton,* Pres.; Charles J. Kegler, Richard Heer Oman.
EIN: 311203674

44440
Helen Trimble Trust
c/o National City Bank
P.O. Box 94651
Cleveland, OH 44101-4651

Financial data (yr. ended 08/10/01): Grants paid, $2,500; assets, $105,705 (M); expenditures, $3,480; qualifying distributions, $3,773.
Limitations: Applications not accepted.
Application information: Contributes only to pre-selected organizations.
Trustee: National City Bank.
EIN: 376164954

44441
Kay Kelly Wilhelm Memorial Fund
323 S. Marion St.
Cardington, OH 43315-1024 (419) 864-2781
Contact: Jack F. Wilhelm, Pres.

Financial data (yr. ended 12/31/01): Grants paid, $2,500; assets, $15,392 (M); gifts received, $11,764; expenditures, $2,576; qualifying distributions, $2,576.
Limitations: Giving limited to residents of Cardington, OH.
Application information: Application form required.
Officers: Jack F. Wilhelm, Pres.; Patricia R. Wilhelm, V.P.
EIN: 237100701

44442
J. B. Goldstein Family Fund
c/o National City Bank
P.O. Box 94651
Cleveland, OH 44101-4651
Application address: 20 Stanwix St., Pittsburgh, PA 15222, tel.: (414) 644-8027
Contact: Joyce B. Pilewski, Trust Off., National City Bank

Financial data (yr. ended 12/31/01): Grants paid, $2,443; assets, $47,128 (M); expenditures, $3,026; qualifying distributions, $2,664.
Limitations: Giving limited to Titusville, PA.
Trustee: National City Bank.
EIN: 256127717

44443
Joseph A. Williams Medical Foundation
c/o National City Bank of Pennsylvania
P. O. Box 94651
Cleveland, OH 44101-4651
Application address: 20 Stanwix St., Loc 07-063, Pittsburgh, PA 15222
Contact: William P. Anthony, Trust Off., National City Bank of Pennsylvania

Established in 1977 in PA.
Donor(s): Joseph A. Williams.‡
Financial data (yr. ended 12/31/01): Grants paid, $2,443; assets, $47,128 (M); expenditures, $3,026; qualifying distributions, $2,664.
Limitations: Giving limited to residents of PA.
Trustee: National City Bank.
EIN: 256219504

44444
The Cliff Oberlin Foundation
127 Country Club Rd.
Bryan, OH 43506

Established in 2000 in OH.
Financial data (yr. ended 12/31/01): Grants paid, $2,425; assets, $360 (M); gifts received, $2,706; expenditures, $2,815; qualifying distributions, $2,425.
Limitations: Applications not accepted.
Application information: Contributes only to pre-selected organizations.
Director: Cliff Oberlin.
EIN: 341933134

44445
Betty Wycoff Hartley and Randall D. Hartley Memorial Scholarship Fund
c/o Wayne County National Bank
1776 Beall Ave.
Wooster, OH 44691
Contact: Stephen Kitchen, Tr.

Established in 1999 in OH.
Financial data (yr. ended 12/31/00): Grants paid, $2,400; assets, $254,845 (M); expenditures, $5,015; qualifying distributions, $3,546.
Limitations: Giving limited to residents of Columbus, OH.
Trustee: Stephen Kitchen.
EIN: 341907881

44446
Mary Morrow Educational Trust
c/o National City Bank
P.O. Box 94651
Cleveland, OH 44101-4651
Application address: c/o Nancy Salzer, Washington Community High School, Washington, IL 61571, tel.: (309) 444-3167

Donor(s): Ethel M. Storey.‡
Financial data (yr. ended 06/30/01): Grants paid, $2,400; assets, $45,244 (M); expenditures, $3,760; qualifying distributions, $3,314.
Limitations: Giving limited to residents of Washington, IL.
Application information: Application forms available at Washington Community High School, IL. Application form required.
Trustee: National City Bank.
EIN: 376181820

44447
Pennsylvania Industrial Chemical Corporation-Clairton High School Scholarship Fund
c/o National City Bank of Pennsylvania
P.O. Box 94651
Cleveland, OH 44101-4651
Application address: c/o Richard A. Bertini, Principal, Clarion Senior High School, 5th St., Clarion, PA 15025

Financial data (yr. ended 06/30/00): Grants paid, $2,400; assets, $654,314 (M); expenditures, $5,974; qualifying distributions, $3,861.
Limitations: Giving limited to residents of Clairton, PA.
Application information: Application form not required.
Trustee: National City Bank.
EIN: 256032785
Codes: GTI

44448
The Summit County Society for Crippled Children and Adults Education Fund
c/o FirstMerit Bank, N.A.
121 S. Main St., Ste. 200
Akron, OH 44308

Financial data (yr. ended 12/31/99): Grants paid, $2,400; assets, $52,277 (M); expenditures, $3,924; qualifying distributions, $2,374.
Limitations: Applications not accepted. Giving limited to OH.
Application information: Contributes only to pre-selected organizations.
Trustee: FirstMerit Bank, N.A.
EIN: 346621832

44449
Jack and Esther Goldberg Foundation
25101 Chagrin Blvd., Ste. 300
Beachwood, OH 44122

Established in 1969 in OH.
Donor(s): Allan Goldberg, Jack Goldberg, Larry Goldberg.
Financial data (yr. ended 11/30/01): Grants paid, $2,360; assets, $2,472,859 (M); gifts received, $286,000; expenditures, $17,783; qualifying distributions, $2,360.

Limitations: Applications not accepted. Giving primarily in OH.
Application information: Contributes only to pre-selected organizations.
Officers: Jack Goldberg, Pres.; Esther Goldberg, V.P.; Larry Goldberg, Secy.; Allan Goldberg, Treas.
EIN: 341047759

44450
William A. Reaper Scholarship Fund
c/o KeyBank, N.A.
P.O. Box 10099
Toledo, OH 43699-0099 (419) 259-8655
Contact: Diane Ohns, Trust Off., KeyBank, N.A.

Financial data (yr. ended 12/31/00): Grants paid, $2,350; assets, $48,096 (M); expenditures, $5,543; qualifying distributions, $3,563.
Limitations: Giving limited to Lucas County, OH.
Application information: Application form required.
Trustee: KeyBank, N.A.
Advisor: Gerald Miller.
EIN: 346543794

44451
Board of Trustees of Carleton College
c/o Robert Wingett
P.O. Box 78
Syracuse, OH 45779-0078
Contact: John Lisle

Financial data (yr. ended 12/31/01): Grants paid, $2,300; assets, $46,983 (M); gifts received, $4,739; expenditures, $2,448; qualifying distributions, $2,448.
Limitations: Giving limited to residents of Syracuse, OH.
Application information: Application form required.
Officers: Robert Wingett, Pres.; Carroll Norris, V.P.; Sharon Cottrill, Secy.; Katheryn Crow, Treas.
EIN: 311000137
Codes: GTI

44452
Christian Education Video Library
456 E. Dunedin Rd.
Columbus, OH 43214-3808

Donor(s): Robert C. Haines.
Financial data (yr. ended 12/31/99): Grants paid, $2,300; assets, $50,943 (M); gifts received, $10,095; expenditures, $5,634; qualifying distributions, $2,300; giving activities include $2,300 for programs.
Limitations: Applications not accepted. Giving on a national basis.
Trustees: Michael Fisher, Stephanie Fisher, Geraldine G. Haines, Robert C. Haines, Barbara Starner, David Starner, James Tapia.
EIN: 311072391

44453
Eric B. Yeiser Family Foundation
4001 Carew Twr.
Cincinnati, OH 45202
Contact: Eric B. Yeiser, Tr.

Established in 1999 in OH.
Donor(s): Eric B. Yeiser.
Financial data (yr. ended 12/31/01): Grants paid, $2,300; assets, $1,380,100 (M); gifts received, $291,710; expenditures, $3,471; qualifying distributions, $2,300.
Limitations: Giving limited to the Cincinnati, OH, area.
Trustees: James Brun, Joslin Coonan, Philip Smith, Eric B. Yeiser.
EIN: 311646815

44454
Cornerstone Foundation of Clinton County Ohio
c/o National Bank & Trust Co.
P.O. Box 711
Wilmington, OH 45177 (937) 382-1441

Established in 1998 in OH.
Financial data (yr. ended 08/31/02): Grants paid, $2,250; assets, $235,308 (M); gifts received, $64,589; expenditures, $5,235; qualifying distributions, $2,250.
Limitations: Giving limited to Wilmington, OH.
Trustee: National Bank & Trust Co.
EIN: 311665414

44455
Hermann and Margery Wesche Scholarship Fund
(Formerly Hermann D. Wesche Wildlife Scholarship Fund)
105 W. Main St.
Napoleon, OH 43545-1781
Contact: Michael J. Wesche, Pres.

Financial data (yr. ended 09/30/00): Grants paid, $2,250; assets, $2,543 (M); gifts received, $250; expenditures, $2,250; qualifying distributions, $2,250.
Limitations: Giving limited to Henry County, OH.
Application information: Application form required.
Officer and Trustees:* Michael J. Wesche,* Pres.; Joseph H. Wesche, Thomas A. Wesche.
EIN: 237378122

44456
Bentivegna Charitable Trust
2121 39th St. N.W.
Canton, OH 44709

Established in 1999 in OH.
Financial data (yr. ended 12/31/99): Grants paid, $2,190; assets, $42,262 (L); gifts received, $900; expenditures, $2,252; qualifying distributions, $2,190.
Trustees: Rita K. Bentivegna, Terrence A. Bentivegna.
EIN: 341830940

44457
The Bertram L. and Iris S. Wolstein Foundation
34555 Chagrin Blvd.
Moreland Hills, OH 44022

Established in 1994 in OH.
Donor(s): Bertram L. Wolstein.
Financial data (yr. ended 11/30/00): Grants paid, $2,158; assets, $103 (M); expenditures, $4,879; qualifying distributions, $4,879.
Limitations: Applications not accepted. Giving limited to Cleveland, OH.
Application information: Contributes only to pre-selected organizations.
Officers and Trustees:* Bertram L. Wolstein,* Pres.; Iris S. Wolstein,* V.P.; Albert T. Adams,* Treas.
EIN: 341787262

44458
The Dunnivant Family Private Foundation
457 Whitestone Ct.
Cincinnati, OH 45231-2716

Established in 1997 in OH.
Financial data (yr. ended 12/31/01): Grants paid, $2,100; assets, $25,386 (M); expenditures, $2,371; qualifying distributions, $2,100.
Limitations: Applications not accepted.
Application information: Contributes only to pre-selected organizations.
Officers and Trustees:* Kenneth R. Dunnivant,* Pres.; Bryan P. Dunnivant, V.P.; Barbara D. Dunnivant, Secy.-Treas.
EIN: 311480962

44459
The Britten J. Hess Memorial Scholarship
50 W. County Rd. 16
Tiffin, OH 44883-9259
Application address: 75 S. Sandusky St., Tiffin, OH 44883, tel.: (419) 447-5202
Contact: Ted Rombach

Established in 1996 in OH.
Donor(s): Debra Hess, Joseph A. Hess.
Financial data (yr. ended 12/31/99): Grants paid, $2,100; assets, $36,059 (M); gifts received, $1,250; expenditures, $2,567; qualifying distributions, $4,667.
Limitations: Giving limited to Tiffin, OH.
Application information: Application form required.
Trustees: Debra Hess, Joseph A. Hess.
EIN: 347057163

44460
The Ronald and Marilyn Leach Charitable Foundation
7280 W. Baldwin Reserve Dr.
Middleburg Heights, OH 44130

Established in 1999 in OH.
Donor(s): Ronald Leach, Marilyn Leach.
Financial data (yr. ended 12/31/01): Grants paid, $2,100; assets, $334,703 (M); gifts received, $162,272; expenditures, $2,272; qualifying distributions, $2,100.
Limitations: Applications not accepted.
Application information: Contributes only to pre-selected organizations.
Trustees: Cynthia D. Leach, Marilyn R. Leach, Mark R. Leach, Ronald L. Leach.
EIN: 341897319

44461
Roemisch Research Foundation
c/o Elizabeth Roemisch
2772 River Rd.
Willoughby, OH 44094-9446

Financial data (yr. ended 07/31/01): Grants paid, $2,100; assets, $20,102 (M); gifts received, $2,000; expenditures, $2,538; qualifying distributions, $2,538.
Limitations: Applications not accepted. Giving primarily in OH.
Application information: Contributes only to pre-selected organizations.
Trustees: Paul Blackman, Elizabeth N. Roemisch, Francis G.H. Sherman, William B. Webber.
EIN: 341322032

44462
Supelak Family Foundation
12271 Altis Ct.
Strongsville, OH 44149

Established in 1987 in OH.
Financial data (yr. ended 12/31/01): Grants paid, $2,100; assets, $27,764 (M); expenditures, $2,352; qualifying distributions, $2,100.
Limitations: Applications not accepted. Giving primarily in OH.
Application information: Contributes only to pre-selected organizations.
Trustees: Carolyn Paris, Barbara Supelak, R.J. Supelak.
EIN: 341533335

44463
Mary Jane McGonegal Foundation
925 Euclid Ave., Ste. 1100
Cleveland, OH 44115-1475

Established in 1999 in OH.
Donor(s): Mary Jane McGonegal.
Financial data (yr. ended 12/31/01): Grants paid, $2,063; assets, $55,491 (M); expenditures, $3,169; qualifying distributions, $2,063.
Limitations: Applications not accepted. Giving primarily in New York, NY.
Application information: Contributes only to pre-selected organizations.
Trustees: Barry P. Livingston, David P. Livingston, Robert B. Tomaro.
EIN: 341911199

44464
William P. L. Barrett Foundation, Inc.
c/o J. Brun
1 E. 4th St., Ste. 1400
Cincinnati, OH 45202

Donor(s): Maybelle F. Barrett.
Financial data (yr. ended 12/31/01): Grants paid, $2,000; assets, $61,347 (M); gifts received, $28,104; expenditures, $4,111; qualifying distributions, $2,000.
Limitations: Applications not accepted. Giving primarily in Cincinnati, OH.
Application information: Contributes only to pre-selected organizations.
Directors: John F. Barrett, William P. L. Barrett, James H. Brun.
EIN: 311685428

44465
The Robert Birr Scholarship Foundation, Inc.
c/o Cunningham & Assoc.
250 W. Main St.
Bellevue, OH 44811 (419) 483-5670
Contact: Glenn Cunningham, Treas.

Established in 2000 in OH.
Donor(s): Robert E. Birr.
Financial data (yr. ended 12/31/01): Grants paid, $2,000; assets, $132,470 (M); gifts received, $27,936; expenditures, $3,970; qualifying distributions, $2,000.
Application information: Application form required.
Officers: William E. Clark, Pres.; Roger D. Paul, Secy.; Glenn Cunningham, Treas.
Trustees: Janet Scagnetti, Thomas Smith.
EIN: 341940986

44466
The Courtney & Marguerite Rankin Burton Charitable Trust
127 Public Sq.
3900 Society Ctr.
Cleveland, OH 44114-1216

Established in 1952 in OH.
Financial data (yr. ended 12/31/01): Grants paid, $2,000; assets, $1,168,942 (M); expenditures, $8,655; qualifying distributions, $2,000.
Limitations: Applications not accepted. Giving primarily in OH.
Application information: Contributes only to pre-selected organizations.
Trustees: Malvin E. Bank, Margaret L. Burton.
EIN: 346514772

44467
Daso Family Foundation, Inc.
24391 Westwood Rd.
Westlake, OH 44145-4837

Established in 2000.
Donor(s): Jean M. Daso.
Financial data (yr. ended 12/31/01): Grants paid, $2,000; assets, $22,786 (M); expenditures, $2,000; qualifying distributions, $2,000.
Limitations: Giving primarily in OH.
Officers and Trustees:* Jean M. Daso,* Pres.; Betty J. Anderson,* Secy.; Danna L. Daso.
EIN: 341930984

44468
Christ & Anastasia Eftimoff Scholarship Fund
564 Sturgeon Ave.
Akron, OH 44319 (330) 644-7686
Contact: Michael Hadgis, Tr.

Established in 1981 in Ohio.
Financial data (yr. ended 12/31/99): Grants paid, $2,000; assets, $81,330 (M); expenditures, $2,237; qualifying distributions, $2,000.
Limitations: Giving primarily in MI and OH.
Application information: Application form required.
Trustees: Fr. Don Fruede, Michael Hadgis, Bessie Nicoloff.
EIN: 341341164

44469
Alice L. Graham Vassar College Scholarship Trust
c/o National City Bank
P.O. Box 94651
Cleveland, OH 44101-4651
Application address: Bill Randol, Dir. of Student Services, c/o Canton High School, 1001 N. Main St., Canton, IL 61520, tel.: (309) 647-1820

Financial data (yr. ended 12/31/01): Grants paid, $2,000; assets, $27,727 (M); expenditures, $2,333; qualifying distributions, $2,333.
Limitations: Giving limited to residents of the Canton, IL, area.
Application information: Application form required.
Trustee: National City Bank.
EIN: 376042755

44470
Caroline J. & Alice L. Graham-University of Illinois Scholarship Trust
c/o National City Bank
P.O. Box 94651
Cleveland, OH 44101-4651
Application address: c/o Bill Randol, Dir. of Student Services, Canton High School, 1001 N. Main St., Canton, IL 61520, tel.: (309) 647-1820

Financial data (yr. ended 12/31/01): Grants paid, $2,000; assets, $27,727 (M); expenditures, $2,837; qualifying distributions, $2,333.
Limitations: Giving limited to Urbana, IL.
Application information: Application form required.
Trustee: National City Bank.
EIN: 376042754

44471
Earl and Geraldine Heuer Foundation
792 Elk Ridge
Northwood, OH 43619-2659 (419) 691-2318
Contact: S. Orrick Jennings, Dir.

Established in 2000 in OH.
Donor(s): Geraldine Heuer.
Financial data (yr. ended 12/31/01): Grants paid, $2,000; assets, $52,362 (M); expenditures, $7,989; qualifying distributions, $2,000.
Limitations: Giving primarily in northwestern OH.
Director: S. Orrick Jennings.
Trustee: Geraldine Heuer.
EIN: 341925933

44472
Joseph Jones Scholarship Fund
c/o National City Bank
P.O. Box 94651
Cleveland, OH 44101-4651
Application address: 20 Stanwix St., Pittsburgh, PA 15222
Contact: C.A. Kelsey, Trust Off., National City Bank

Financial data (yr. ended 12/31/01): Grants paid, $2,000; assets, $58,306 (M); expenditures, $2,706; qualifying distributions, $2,290.
Limitations: Giving limited to PA.
Trustee: National City Bank.
EIN: 256021372

44473
Kern Charitable Trust
417 Grants Trail
Dayton, OH 45459

Established in 1997.
Financial data (yr. ended 12/31/99): Grants paid, $2,000; assets, $79,896 (L); gifts received, $38,919; expenditures, $15,715; qualifying distributions, $0.
Trustees: Deanne Bender, Carol G. Kern, Jack Kern.
EIN: 311572638

44474
The MacPherson Charitable Trust
125 Manning Dr.
Berea, OH 44017
Application Address: 1191 8th St. S., Naples, FL 34102
Contact: Kenneth E. MacPherson, Tr.

Established in 1996 in OH.
Donor(s): The MacPherson Asset Mgmt. Trust.
Financial data (yr. ended 12/31/00): Grants paid, $2,000; assets, $767,391 (M); gifts received, $157,452; expenditures, $2,999; qualifying distributions, $2,693.
Limitations: Applications not accepted. Giving primarily in WI.
Application information: Contributes only to pre-selected organizations.
Officer and Trustee:* Kenneth E. MacPherson,* Exec. Dir.
EIN: 656212278

44475
Mayberry Foundation
c/o J. Brun
1 E. 4th St., Ste. 1400
Cincinnati, OH 45202

Established in 2000 in OH.
Donor(s): Henry C. Yeiser.
Financial data (yr. ended 12/31/01): Grants paid, $2,000; assets, $86,476 (M); gifts received, $74,895; expenditures, $2,000; qualifying distributions, $2,000.
Limitations: Applications not accepted.
Application information: Contributes only to pre-selected organizations.
Trustees: James H. Brun, Gary J. Wahoff, Henry C. Yeiser.
EIN: 311712221

44476
Felix and Ann Mischak Scholarship Fund
c/o FirstMerit Bank, N.A.
39 Public Sq.
Medina, OH 44256
Application address: c/o Alliance of Poles of America, 6966 Broadway, Cleveland, OH 44105, tel.: (216) 883-3131

Established in 2000 in OH.
Donor(s): Felix Mischak, Ann Mischak.
Financial data (yr. ended 11/30/01): Grants paid, $2,000; assets, $61,139 (M); gifts received, $60,000; expenditures, $3,426; qualifying distributions, $2,788.
Limitations: Giving primarily to residents of OH.
Application information: Application form required.
Trustees: John Borkowski, Felix Mischak, John Oberholtzer, FirstMerit Bank, N.A.
EIN: 912088450

44477
F. Leonard Murphy Scholarship Fund
1891 N. Devon Rd.
Columbus, OH 43212
Application address: 268 Topton Dr., Vandalia, OH 45377, tel.: (513) 898-2462
Contact: D. Michael Brown, Tr.

Established in 1989 in OH.
Financial data (yr. ended 12/31/01): Grants paid, $2,000; assets, $25,277 (M); gifts received, $1,094; expenditures, $2,085; qualifying distributions, $2,000.
Limitations: Giving limited to residents of OH.
Application information: Applicants must complete an essay. Application form not required.
Trustees: Judith Ann Blommel, D. Michael Brown, William F. Slough.
EIN: 316347704

44478
Norwalk Furniture Scholarship Foundation
c/o Selection Committee
100 Furniture Pkwy.
Norwalk, OH 44857

Established in 1987 in OH.
Donor(s): Norwalk Furniture Corporation.
Financial data (yr. ended 12/31/01): Grants paid, $2,000; assets, $19,335 (M); expenditures, $2,017; qualifying distributions, $1,992.
Limitations: Giving limited to the Norwalk, OH, area.
Application information: Application form required.
Officers and Trustee:* Edward J. Gerken, Jr.,* Pres. and Secy.; James E. Gerken, V.P.; Peg Bergstrom, Treas.
EIN: 341538752
Codes: CS, CD

44479
Jacob K. Painter Scholarship Fund
c/o National City Bank of Pennsylvania
P.O. Box 94651
Cleveland, OH 44101-4651
Application address: c/o Guidance Counselor, Ellwood City High School, Ellwood City, PA 16117

Financial data (yr. ended 12/31/00): Grants paid, $2,000; assets, $44,082 (M); expenditures, $2,847; qualifying distributions, $2,436.
Limitations: Giving limited to Ellwood City, PA.
Application information: Recipients are selected by guidance counselors.
Trustee: National City Bank.
EIN: 256060055

44480
Nunzio Polichene Scholarship Fund
250 S. Chestnut St., Ste. 18
Ravenna, OH 44266
Application address: 152 Fairway Dr., Indianapolis, IN 46260
Contact: Bridget P. Chamness, Tr.

Established in 1998.
Financial data (yr. ended 12/31/00): Grants paid, $2,000; assets, $17,597 (M); gifts received, $7,785; expenditures, $2,000; qualifying distributions, $2,000.
Limitations: Giving limited to Ravenna, OH.
Application information: Application form required.
Trustees: Bridget P. Chamness, Frank J. Cimino, Evelyn A. Polichene.
EIN: 341862015

44481
RGK Foundation
1530 Melrose Cir.
Westlake, OH 44145

Established in 1995 in OH.
Donor(s): Mary Klym.
Financial data (yr. ended 12/31/00): Grants paid, $2,000; assets, $455,750 (M); expenditures, $3,495; qualifying distributions, $2,000.
Limitations: Applications not accepted.
Application information: Contributes only to pre-selected organizations.
Trustees: Gina Klym, Mary Klym, Richard Klym.
EIN: 341805107

44482
The Frances G. Shoolroy Foundation
c/o Robert W. Briggs
P.O. Box 1500
Akron, OH 44309-1500

Established in 1999 in OH.
Financial data (yr. ended 12/31/01): Grants paid, $2,000; assets, $1,176,942 (M); gifts received, $544,666; expenditures, $9,937; qualifying distributions, $2,000.
Limitations: Applications not accepted. Giving primarily in OH.
Application information: Contributes only to pre-selected organizations.
Trustees: Charles A. Briggs, David M. Briggs, Robert W. Briggs.
EIN: 341910725

44483
Gladys Stokesbury Scholarship Fund
c/o National Bank & Trust Co.
P.O. Box 711
Wilmington, OH 45177
Application address: 97 College St., New Vienna, OH 45159
Contact: Larry Redfern

Established in 1999 in OH.
Financial data (yr. ended 03/31/01): Grants paid, $2,000; assets, $85,542 (M); gifts received, $9; expenditures, $3,684; qualifying distributions, $2,000.
Limitations: Giving primarily in OH.
Application information: Application form required.
Trustee: National Bank & Trust Co.
EIN: 311682661

44484
Swan Charitable Foundation
443 Janet Dr.
Canfield, OH 44406-1533

Established in 1993 in OH.
Financial data (yr. ended 05/31/02): Grants paid, $2,000; assets, $308,797 (M); expenditures, $2,240; qualifying distributions, $2,000.
Limitations: Applications not accepted. Giving primarily in OH.
Application information: Contributes only to pre-selected organizations.
Trustees: Robert N. Rumberg, Marilyn Wagmiller, Robert L. Wagmiller, Sr.
EIN: 341757292

44485
Margaret Warnock Foundation
10 Center St.
Chagrin Falls, OH 44022
Contact: Don P. Brown, Dir.

Established around 1991.
Donor(s): Margaret Warnock Trust.
Financial data (yr. ended 12/31/00): Grants paid, $2,000; assets, $66,452 (M); expenditures, $3,640; qualifying distributions, $2,000.
Application information: Application form not required.
Director: Don P. Brown.
EIN: 346931016

44486
Milo S. & Edith A. Holdstein Fund
2623 Courtland Oval
Shaker Heights, OH 44118-4761
(216) 321-5530
Contact: Edith A. Holdstein, Pres.

Financial data (yr. ended 12/31/01): Grants paid, $1,973; assets, $3,920 (M); expenditures, $3,006; qualifying distributions, $1,973.
Limitations: Giving primarily in Cleveland, OH.
Officer: Edith A. Holdstein, Pres. and Treas.
EIN: 346554974

44487
Unicare Family Foundation
1457 E. 40th St.
Cleveland, OH 44103

Established in 1998.
Donor(s): Unicare Corp.
Financial data (yr. ended 12/31/01): Grants paid, $1,961; assets, $2,380 (M); gifts received, $15; expenditures, $1,961; qualifying distributions, $1,961.
Limitations: Giving primarily in areas of company operations.
Application information: Unsolicited request for funds not accepted.
Officers: Michael Baird, Pres.; Glen Lair, Secy.
Trustees: Carol Glaser, Karen Horton.
EIN: 341727367
Codes: CS, CD

44488
David Lazarus Family Foundation
2 Pinehurst Ln.
Cincinnati, OH 45208-3318
Contact: David Lazarus, Pres.

Donor(s): David Lazarus.
Financial data (yr. ended 10/31/01): Grants paid, $1,930; assets, $53,141 (M); expenditures, $2,453; qualifying distributions, $1,930.
Limitations: Giving primarily in OH.
Application information: Application form not required.
Officers: David Lazarus, Pres. and Treas.; Eleanor S. Lazarus, V.P. and Secy.
EIN: 316053367

44489
Valentina A. Prugh Charitable Trust
c/o David C. Prugh
3900 Key Ctr., 127 Public SQ.
Cleveland, OH 44114-1216

Established in 1998 in OH.
Donor(s): Valentina A. Prugh.
Financial data (yr. ended 12/31/01): Grants paid, $1,924; assets, $228,537 (M); expenditures, $2,080; qualifying distributions, $1,924.
Limitations: Applications not accepted. Giving primarily in OH.
Application information: Contributes only to pre-selected organizations.
Trustees: David C. Prugh, Valentina A. Prugh.
EIN: 341868473

44490
The Matthew J. Colombo Memorial Scholarship Fund, Inc.
50 S. Chillicothe Rd.
Aurora, OH 44202-8827

Donor(s): Dominic Colombo, Mary E. Colombo, Scott Smith, Mary Ann Colombo, Mary G. Colombo, Don Colombo, Wendy Hughes.
Financial data (yr. ended 11/30/01): Grants paid, $1,889; assets, $4,143 (M); gifts received, $942; expenditures, $1,892; qualifying distributions, $1,887.
Limitations: Giving limited to residents of Aurora, OH.
Officers: Donald E. Colombo, Pres.; Marcia R. Colombo, Secy.; Mark A. Colombo, Treas.
Trustee: Dennis A. Buss.
EIN: 341586933

44491
The Brinkmann Family Foundation
5406 Ridgevale Ct.
Maineville, OH 45039

Established in OH in 1998.
Donor(s): Thomas F. Brinkmann, Jeannine M. Brinkmann.
Financial data (yr. ended 12/31/00): Grants paid, $1,886; assets, $22,349 (M); expenditures, $2,051; qualifying distributions, $1,884.
Officers: Thomas F. Brinkmann, Pres.; Jeannine M. Brinkmann, V.P.; Melonie A. Brinkmann, Secy.; Thomas J. Brinkmann, Treas.
EIN: 311489442

44492
Jane G. Cunningham Foundation
925 Euclid Ave., Ste. 1100
Cleveland, OH 44115-1475

Donor(s): Jane G. Cunningham.
Financial data (yr. ended 12/31/01): Grants paid, $1,873; assets, $53,130 (M); expenditures, $2,258; qualifying distributions, $1,873.
Limitations: Applications not accepted. Giving primarily in Cleveland, OH.
Application information: Contributes only to pre-selected organizations.
Trustees: Michael E. Elliott, Charles J. O'Toole, Robert B. Tomaro.
EIN: 341818429

44493
Northwest Ohio Diabetic Children's Trust Fund
c/o Sky Bank
P.O. Box 479
Youngstown, OH 44501-0479
Application address: 200 W. Pearl St., Findlay, OH 45840, tel.: (419) 424-0380
Contact: Leroy L. Schroeder, Advisory Comm. Member

Donor(s): Theresa A. Kirk.
Financial data (yr. ended 12/31/01): Grants paid, $1,846; assets, $36,837 (M); expenditures, $2,321; qualifying distributions, $2,039.
Limitations: Giving limited to Findlay, OH.
Application information: Application form not required.
Advisory Committee: Jack Hendershot, Theresa A. Kirk, August Mazza, J. Gregory Rosenthal, Leroy L. Schroeder.
Trustee: Sky Bank.
EIN: 341555429

44494
Baker-Hartsell Endowment Trust
c/o First Financial Svcs. Group
P.O. Box 2307
Zanesville, OH 43702-2307

Established in 1997 in OH.
Financial data (yr. ended 12/31/01): Grants paid, $1,833; assets, $44,800 (M); expenditures, $2,443; qualifying distributions, $1,871.
Limitations: Applications not accepted.
Application information: Contributes only to pre-selected organizations.
Trustee: First National Bank.
EIN: 316051885

44495
Marjorie R. Dunn Trust for Dunn Scholarship Fund
c/o KeyBank, N.A.
800 Superior Ave., 4th Fl.
Cleveland, OH 44114
Application address: c/o Northeastern Clinton Central School District, Champlain, NY 12919

Established in 1986 in NY.
Donor(s): Marjorie R. Dunn.‡
Financial data (yr. ended 06/30/02): Grants paid, $1,800; assets, $42,867 (M); expenditures, $2,272; qualifying distributions, $1,800.
Limitations: Giving limited to the Champlain, NY, area.
Trustee: KeyBank, N.A.
EIN: 146135482

44496
Angela B. Eynon Foundation, Inc.
c/o J. Burn
1 E. 4th St., Ste. 1400
Cincinnati, OH 45202
Application address: 2592 Perkins Ln., Cincinnati, OH 45208, tel.: (513) 321-0600
Contact: Angela B. Eynon, Tr.

Established in 1999 in OH.
Financial data (yr. ended 12/31/01): Grants paid, $1,800; assets, $59,157 (M); gifts received, $28,104; expenditures, $3,911; qualifying distributions, $1,800.
Limitations: Giving primarily in Cincinnati, OH.
Trustees: John F. Barrett, James H. Brun, Angela B. Eynon.
EIN: 311685429

44497
Winifred Sperry Memorial Fund
c/o KeyBank, N.A.
800 Superior Ave., 4th Fl.
Cleveland, OH 44114-2601

Financial data (yr. ended 12/31/01): Grants paid, $1,762; assets, $24,381 (M); expenditures, $2,029; qualifying distributions, $1,762.
Limitations: Applications not accepted. Giving primarily in Malone, NY.
Application information: Contributes only to pre-selected organizations.
Trustee: KeyBank, N.A.
EIN: 146074897

44498
Beam Family Foundation
8300 Stoneybrook Dr.
Chagrin Falls, OH 44023

Established in 1996 in OH.
Financial data (yr. ended 12/31/01): Grants paid, $1,760; assets, $22,422 (M); gifts received, $123; expenditures, $2,021; qualifying distributions, $1,760.
Limitations: Applications not accepted.
Application information: Contributes only to pre-selected organizations.
Officers: Francis H. Beam, Pres.; Judd A. Beam, V.P.; Jennifer Beam-Carroll, Secy.; Virginia J. Beam, Treas.
EIN: 341847364

44499
Presque Isle Rotary Club Scholarship Trust
c/o KeyBank, N.A.
800 Superior Ave., 4th Fl.
Cleveland, OH 44114
Application address: Scholarship Comm., Rotary Club, Presque Isle, ME 04769

Established in 1993 in ME.
Financial data (yr. ended 09/30/01): Grants paid, $1,750; assets, $90,099 (M); gifts received, $28,076; expenditures, $2,550; qualifying distributions, $1,750.
Limitations: Giving limited to residents of ME.
Trustee: KeyBank, N.A.
EIN: 016121371

44500
IPPOTLS Foundation
526 E. Main St.
Logan, OH 43138

Financial data (yr. ended 12/31/00): Grants paid, $1,700; assets, $129,642 (M); gifts received, $47,899; expenditures, $1,700; qualifying distributions, $1,893.
Limitations: Applications not accepted.
Application information: Contributes only to pre-selected organizations.
Director: Luther Brimmer.
EIN: 316536557

44501
Frances Hyde Royall Memorial Trust Fund
c/o KeyBank, N.A.
800 Superior Ave., 4th Fl.
Cleveland, OH 44114-2613

Financial data (yr. ended 08/31/01): Grants paid, $1,699; assets, $57,664 (M); expenditures, $3,268; qualifying distributions, $1,699.
Limitations: Applications not accepted. Giving limited to ME.
Application information: Contributes only to pre-selected organizations.
Trustee: KeyBank, N.A.
EIN: 016007235

44502
Jerry W. Robinson Scholarship Trust/Moeller High School
c/o Fifth Third Bank
38 Fountain Sq. Plz.
Cincinnati, OH 45263

Established in 1994 in OH.
Financial data (yr. ended 09/30/01): Grants paid, $1,694; assets, $184,866 (M); expenditures, $4,468; qualifying distributions, $1,694.
Limitations: Applications not accepted. Giving primarily in Cincinnati, OH.
Application information: Contributes only to pre-selected organizations.
Trustee: Fifth Third Bank.
EIN: 316502888

44503
Haber Charitable Trust
125 Churchill Hubbard Rd.
Youngstown, OH 44505
Application address: 376 Cranberry Run, Youngstown, OH 44512
Contact: Jerold Haber, Tr.

Established in 1988 in OH.
Donor(s): Jerold Haber.
Financial data (yr. ended 12/31/01): Grants paid, $1,646; assets, $31,290 (M); expenditures, $1,950; qualifying distributions, $1,646.
Limitations: Giving primarily in OH.
Trustees: Jerold Haber, Vincetta Haber, J. Newman Levy.
EIN: 316353637
Codes: TN

44504
The 2714 Foundation
46155 Fairmount Blvd.
Hunting Valley, OH 44022

Established in 1988 in OH.
Donor(s): Jon A. Lindseth.
Financial data (yr. ended 11/30/00): Grants paid, $1,631; assets, $15,885 (M); expenditures, $1,631; qualifying distributions, $1,625.
Limitations: Applications not accepted. Giving primarily in Ithaca, NY, and Cleveland, OH.
Application information: Contributes only to pre-selected organizations.
Officers and Trustees:* Jon A. Lindseth,* Pres. and Treas.; Virginia M. Lindseth,* V.P. and Secy.; Joseph D. Sullivan.
EIN: 341601580

44505
C. Francis Barrett Foundation, Inc.
c/o J. Brun
1 E. 4th St., Ste. 1400
Cincinnati, OH 45202

Donor(s): Maybelle F. Barrett.
Financial data (yr. ended 12/31/01): Grants paid, $1,630; assets, $61,702 (M); gifts received, $28,104; expenditures, $3,741; qualifying distributions, $1,630.
Limitations: Applications not accepted. Giving primarily in Cincinnati, OH.
Application information: Contributes only to pre-selected organizations.
Directors: C. Francis Barrett, Elisabeth C. Barrett, Peter S. Barrett.
EIN: 311685422

44506
John F. Barrett Foundation, Inc.
c/o J. Brun
1 E. 4th St., Ste. 1400
Cincinnati, OH 45202

Donor(s): Maybelle F. Barrett.
Financial data (yr. ended 12/31/01): Grants paid, $1,630; assets, $61,720 (M); gifts received, $28,104; expenditures, $3,741; qualifying distributions, $1,630.
Limitations: Applications not accepted. Giving primarily in Cincinnati, OH.
Application information: Contributes only to pre-selected organizations.
Directors: John F. Barrett, Michael Barrett, James H. Brun.
EIN: 311685424

44507
Marian B. Leibold Foundation, Inc.
c/o J. Brun
1 E. 4th St., Ste. 1400
Cincinnati, OH 45202

Donor(s): Maybelle F. Barrett.
Financial data (yr. ended 12/31/01): Grants paid, $1,630; assets, $61,532 (M); gifts received, $28,104; expenditures, $3,741; qualifying distributions, $1,630.
Limitations: Applications not accepted. Giving primarily in MA.
Application information: Contributes only to pre-selected organizations.
Directors: William P. L. Barrett, John L. Leibold, Marian B. Leibold.
EIN: 311685431

44508
Webb Trust Fund
c/o James Masi
250 S. Prospect St.
Ravenna, OH 44266-3041

Financial data (yr. ended 12/31/00): Grants paid, $1,600; assets, $38,875 (M); expenditures, $1,632; qualifying distributions, $1,600.
Limitations: Applications not accepted. Giving limited to Garretsville, OH.
Application information: Contributes only to pre-selected organizations.
Trustee: James Masi.
EIN: 346543237

44509
Henson Charitable Trust
131 Terrace Villa Dr.
Centerville, OH 45459

Established in 1999.
Financial data (yr. ended 12/31/99): Grants paid, $1,550; assets, $7,955 (L); gifts received, $8,000; expenditures, $1,560; qualifying distributions, $0.
Trustee: Charles Henson.
EIN: 311579615

44510
Rose B. and Mrs. Samuel Hessberg Memorial Fund
c/o KeyBank, N.A., Trust Div.
800 Superior Ave., 4th Fl.
Cleveland, OH 44114
Application address: c/o Exec. Dir., Albany Jewish Family Svcs., 930 Madison Ave., Albany, NY 12208

Donor(s): Rose Brilleman Hessberg.‡
Financial data (yr. ended 12/31/00): Grants paid, $1,512; assets, $37,398 (M); expenditures, $2,011; qualifying distributions, $1,537.
Limitations: Giving limited to residents of Albany, NY.
Trustee: KeyBank, N.A.
EIN: 146014883

44511
John H. & Eleonora G. Anning Charitable Trust
900 4th and Vine Twr.
Cincinnati, OH 45202

Established in 1998 in OH.
Donor(s): John Anning.
Financial data (yr. ended 12/31/01): Grants paid, $1,500; assets, $480,848 (M); gifts received, $450,000; expenditures, $1,672; qualifying distributions, $1,672.
Trustee: George Wesley Archiable.
EIN: 311619919

44512
Baxley Family Foundation
877 Rosemarie Cir.
Wadsworth, OH 44281 (330) 335-5665
Contact: William Baxley, Tr.

Established in 1996 in OH.
Donor(s): Norma Jean Baxley, William Baxley.
Financial data (yr. ended 12/31/01): Grants paid, $1,500; assets, $776 (M); gifts received, $1,825; expenditures, $1,808; qualifying distributions, $1,500.
Limitations: Giving primarily in OH.
Trustees: Norma Jean Baxley, William Baxley.
EIN: 311500391

44513
Kevin Allen Campbell Memorial Scholarship Fund
1120 Fagins Run Rd.
New Richmond, OH 45157-9734

Financial data (yr. ended 12/31/99): Grants paid, $1,500; assets, $32,852 (M); gifts received, $1,710; expenditures, $1,564; qualifying distributions, $1,564.
Limitations: Applications not accepted. Giving limited to New Richmond, OH.
Application information: Recipients are selected by a committee from New Richmond High School, OH.
Trustees: Joyce A. Campbell, Ralph E. Campbell.
EIN: 316227516

44514
The Michael P. Cochran Scholarship Fund
475 Buckeye Ln.
Napoleon, OH 43545-2329 (419) 599-1331
Application address: 675 Buckeye Ln, Napoleon, OH 43545-2329
Contact: Philip E. Cochran, Dir.

Financial data (yr. ended 12/31/99): Grants paid, $1,500; assets, $27,865 (M); gifts received, $2,700; expenditures, $1,654; qualifying distributions, $1,652.
Limitations: Giving primarily to residents of Napoleon, OH.
Directors: Barbara J. Cochran, Julia Cochran, Michelle Cochran, Philip E. Cochran.
EIN: 341420452

44515
Monsignor Edward B. Conry Memorial Scholarship Trust
1206 1st National Twr.
Akron, OH 44308

Financial data (yr. ended 12/31/99): Grants paid, $1,500; assets, $19,692 (M); expenditures, $1,534; qualifying distributions, $1,489.
Limitations: Giving limited to residents of the Akron, OH, area.

44515—OHIO

Application information: Application form required.
Trustees: Ann Garbor, Phillip S. Kaufmann, Jean Staudt.
EIN: 346611181

44516
Benjamin A. G. & Harriet S. Williams Fuller Memorial Trust
c/o KeyBank, N.A., Trust Div.
800 Superior Ave., 4th Fl.
Cleveland, OH 44114
Application address: c/o William Pelletier, Kennebec Savings Bank, P.O. Box 108, Augusta, ME 04330

Financial data (yr. ended 08/31/00): Grants paid, $1,500; assets, $93,695 (M); expenditures, $2,697; qualifying distributions, $1,500.
Limitations: Giving primarily in SC.
Trustee: KeyBank, N.A.
EIN: 016008548

44517
Orpha Ann Gatch Foundation
8050 Hosbrook Rd., Ste. 210
Cincinnati, OH 45236

Established in 1998 in OH.
Financial data (yr. ended 12/31/01): Grants paid, $1,500; assets, $4,457 (M); gifts received, $5,000; expenditures, $1,500; qualifying distributions, $1,500.
Limitations: Giving primarily in Milford, OH.
Trustee: Lewis G. Gatch.
EIN: 311544843

44518
GER Neurosurgical Development Fund, Inc.
c/o Edgar J. Rennoe
1468 Briarmeadow Dr.
Columbus, OH 43235 (614) 888-0695

Financial data (yr. ended 12/31/01): Grants paid, $1,500; assets, $20,885 (M); gifts received, $500; expenditures, $2,063; qualifying distributions, $1,500.
Limitations: Giving primarily in Columbus, OH.
Application information: Application form required.
Officers: Edgar J. Renoe, Pres.; K. Michael Taylor, Secy.
EIN: 311029894

44519
Andrew M. Johnston Award Fund
c/o KeyBank, N.A., Trust Div.
800 Superior Ave., 4th Fl.
Cleveland, OH 44114

Donor(s): Andrew M. Johnston.‡
Financial data (yr. ended 12/31/00): Grants paid, $1,500; assets, $21,742 (M); expenditures, $1,723; qualifying distributions, $1,500.
Limitations: Applications not accepted. Giving limited to the Chateaugay, NY, area.
Application information: Unsolicited requests for funds not accepted.
Trustee: KeyBank, N.A.
EIN: 146014915

44520
Lebanon Crippled Children's Fund
347 E. Turtlcreek-Union Rd.
Lebanon, OH 45036
Contact: Jerry Addison

Established in 1999 in OH.
Financial data (yr. ended 12/31/01): Grants paid, $1,500; assets, $41,682 (M); gifts received, $181; expenditures, $1,681; qualifying distributions, $1,500.

Trustee: Jerry Addison.
EIN: 311249449

44521
John & Mary McGinley Educational Fund
c/o National City Bank of Pennsylvania
P. O. Box 94651
Cleveland, OH 44101-4651
Application address: Idaho at Pacific Ave., Natrona Heights, PA 15065
Contact: Peter Mervosh, Guidance Chair, Highlands Senior High School

Financial data (yr. ended 12/31/01): Grants paid, $1,500; assets, $57,883 (M); expenditures, $2,156; qualifying distributions, $1,776.
Limitations: Giving limited to Harrison Township, PA.
Trustee: National City Bank of Pennsylvania.
EIN: 256078802

44522
Perrysburg Kiwanis Memorial
P.O. Box 1111
Perrysburg, OH 43552-1111

Financial data (yr. ended 09/30/01): Grants paid, $1,500; assets, $18,390 (M); gifts received, $30; expenditures, $1,783; qualifying distributions, $1,783.
Limitations: Applications not accepted.
Application information: Contributes only to pre-selected organizations.
Officers: Robert Heslup, Pres.; Kenneth Larson, Secy.; Susan Schiffman, Treas.
EIN: 341663335

44523
Franklin B. Powers Fund
c/o National City Bank
P.O. Box 94651
Cleveland, OH 44101-4651
Application address: c/o National City Bank, 20 Federal Plz. W., Youngstown, OH 44503, tel.: (330) 742-4289
Contact: Myra Vitto, Trust Off., National City Bank

Financial data (yr. ended 12/31/01): Grants paid, $1,500; assets, $19,830 (M); expenditures, $2,274; qualifying distributions, $1,869.
Limitations: Giving limited to residents of Poland, OH.
Application information: Contact Poland Seminary High School for application information.
Trustee: National City Bank.
EIN: 346560989

44524
Nancy Kaighin Van Fossan Family Foundation, Inc.
c/o Second National Bank
108 Main Ave. S.W.
Warren, OH 44482-1058

Established in 1999 in OH.
Donor(s): Nancy K. Van Fossan.
Financial data (yr. ended 12/31/01): Grants paid, $1,500; assets, $28,424 (M); expenditures, $2,369; qualifying distributions, $1,500.
Limitations: Applications not accepted. Giving primarily in Warren, OH.
Application information: Contributes only to pre-selected organizations.
Directors: Sally J. Taylor, Charles F. Van Fossan, Nancy K. Van Fossan, Robert K. Van Fossan.
Trustee: Second National Bank.
EIN: 347104554

44525
The Angels on Track Foundation
12376 Chestnut St. N.W.
Canal Fulton, OH 44614-8630
Tel./FAX: (330) 854-6311; E-mail: info@angelsontrack.org; URL: http://www.angelsontrack.org
Contact: Dennis Moore, Tr.; or Vicky Moore, Tr.

Established in 1997 in OH.
Financial data (yr. ended 12/31/00): Grants paid, $1,489; assets, $5,913,141 (M); gifts received, $650; expenditures, $371,284; qualifying distributions, $299,888; giving activities include $289,773 for programs.
Limitations: Giving limited to OH.
Publications: Informational brochure.
Application information: Application form required.
Trustees: Debra A. Messner, Dennis F. Moore, Vicky L. Moore.
EIN: 311549790

44526
J. Carlyle Luther Trust
c/o National City Bank
P.O. Box 94651
Cleveland, OH 44101-4651

Financial data (yr. ended 12/31/00): Grants paid, $1,475; assets, $73,033 (M); expenditures, $2,642; qualifying distributions, $2,216.
Limitations: Applications not accepted.
Application information: Contributes only to pre-selected organizations.
Trustee: National City Bank.
EIN: 376158843

44527
Charles F. Clark Trust
c/o KeyBank, N.A.
800 Superior Ave., 4th Fl.
Cleveland, OH 44114
Application address: c/o Irwin W. Brodofsky, Dir. of Financial Aid, SUNY Upstate Medical Ctr., Syracuse, NY 13210, tel.: (315) 473-4570

Donor(s): Charles F. Clark.‡
Financial data (yr. ended 12/31/01): Grants paid, $1,454; assets, $32,998 (M); expenditures, $1,766; qualifying distributions, $1,479.
Limitations: Giving limited to NY.
Trustee: KeyBank, N.A.
EIN: 156013058

44528
Landskroner Foundation for Children
55 Public Sq.
Cleveland, OH 44113-1901

Donor(s): Heather Landskroner.
Financial data (yr. ended 12/31/00): Grants paid, $1,450; assets, $709 (M); gifts received, $4,575; expenditures, $3,924; qualifying distributions, $3,924.
Trustees: Heather Landskroner, Jack Landskroner.
EIN: 341898201

44529
National Hummel Foundation & Museum
c/o Robert L. Miller
112 Woodland Dr.
Eaton, OH 45320-9671

Financial data (yr. ended 12/31/01): Grants paid, $1,440; assets, $30,714 (M); gifts received, $616; expenditures, $1,456; qualifying distributions, $1,440.
Limitations: Applications not accepted. Giving primarily in OH.

Trustees: Dean A. Genth, Robert L. Miller, Ruth A. Miller.
EIN: 311068759

44530
Carl N. and Sadie Shaheen Charitable Trust
c/o Carl N. Shaheen
2942 Sussex St. N.W.
Canton, OH 44718

Established in 1990 in OH.
Donor(s): Carl N. Shaheen.
Financial data (yr. ended 12/31/99): Grants paid, $1,426; assets, $0 (M); expenditures, $1,514; qualifying distributions, $1,426.
Limitations: Applications not accepted. Giving primarily in Canton, OH.
Application information: Contributes only to pre-selected organizations.
Trustees: Carl N. Shaheen, Sadie Shaheen.
EIN: 341665365

44531
Feldman Foundation
P.O. Box 30
East Liverpool, OH 43920-5030

Financial data (yr. ended 12/31/01): Grants paid, $1,400; assets, $24,949 (M); expenditures, $1,981; qualifying distributions, $1,400.
Limitations: Applications not accepted.
Application information: Contributes only to pre-selected organizations.
Officers: A. Richard Feldman, Pres. and Treas.; Marvin H. Feldman, V.P. and Secy.
EIN: 340937709

44532
The Hunter Charitable Trust
1452 Stanley Ave. S.E.
Girard, OH 44420

Established in 1999.
Financial data (yr. ended 12/31/99): Grants paid, $1,359; assets, $42,916 (M); gifts received, $44,400; expenditures, $1,484; qualifying distributions, $1,359.
Limitations: Applications not accepted.
Application information: Contributes only to pre-selected organizations.
Trustees: Richard Hunter, Yvonne E. Hunter.
EIN: 364265971

44533
Rodney L. Hudson Appellate Advocacy Award Corporation
1640 Sussex Ct.
Columbus, OH 43220
Application address: c/o David Walker, Dean, Drake Univ. Law School, Des Moines, IA 50311, tel.: (515) 271-2824

Financial data (yr. ended 06/30/99): Grants paid, $1,350; assets, $9,705 (M); gifts received, $600; expenditures, $1,389; qualifying distributions, $1,350.
Limitations: Giving limited to Des Moines, IA.
Officers: Margaret H. Rastetter, Pres.; Richard C. Rastetter, Jr., Secy.-Treas.
EIN: 237312806

44534
Paul Larnard King Award
c/o Second National Bank of Warren
108 Main St. S.W.
Warren, OH 44481
Application address: c/o Dir. of Development/Planned Giving, Hamilton College, College Hill Rd., Clinton, NY 13323

Established in 1985 in OH.

Financial data (yr. ended 04/30/02): Grants paid, $1,313; assets, $30,898 (M); expenditures, $2,693; qualifying distributions, $1,313.
Limitations: Giving primarily in Clinton, NY.
Application information: Application form required.
Trustee: Second National Bank of Warren.
EIN: 346842349

44535
Andover Foundation, Inc
124 S. Main St.
P.O. Box 1270
Andover, OH 44003-1270

Established in 2001 in OH.
Financial data (yr. ended 12/31/01): Grants paid, $1,300; assets, $38,944 (M); gifts received, $8,000; expenditures, $1,620; qualifying distributions, $1,620.
Limitations: Giving primarily in Andover, OH.
Officers: Linn W. Newman, Pres.; Robert F. Muth, V.P.; Richard B. Kobla, Secy.; Richard J. Mole, Treas.
Director: Ruth Mary Service.
EIN: 341731179

44536
Alice L. Graham Women's Scholarship
c/o National City Bank
P.O. Box 94651
Cleveland, OH 44101-4651
Application address: c/o Bill Randol, Dir. of Student Services, Canton High School, 1001 N. Main St., Canton, IL 61520, tel.: (309) 647-1820

Financial data (yr. ended 12/31/01): Grants paid, $1,300; assets, $25,324 (M); expenditures, $2,018; qualifying distributions, $1,633.
Limitations: Giving limited to Canton, IL.
Application information: Application form required.
Trustee: National City Bank.
EIN: 376042753

44537
Agnes Lutz Scholarship Fund
116 E. Wyandot Ave.
Upper Sandusky, OH 43351
Contact: Mary E. Fox, Tr.

Financial data (yr. ended 05/31/99): Grants paid, $1,260; assets, $38,386 (M); expenditures, $1,916; qualifying distributions, $1,152.
Limitations: Giving limited to Mount Blanchard, OH.
Application information: Application form required.
Trustees: Robert E. Bash, Mary E. Fox.
EIN: 346900386

44538
RDN Charitable Trust
1055 Hickory Ridge Ln.
Loveland, OH 45140

Established in 1998 in OH.
Financial data (yr. ended 12/31/00): Grants paid, $1,253; assets, $37,995 (M); gifts received, $1,270; expenditures, $2,249; qualifying distributions, $1,253.
Limitations: Applications not accepted. Giving primarily in Cincinnati, OH.
Application information: Contributes only to pre-selected organizations.
Trustees: Karen L. Nelson, Stephen R. Nelson.
EIN: 367251404

44539
Nan & Thomas L. Conlan, Jr. Foundation
c/o U.S. Bank
P.O. Box 1118
Cincinnati, OH 45201-1118

Established in 1996 in OH.
Donor(s): Star Bank, N.A.
Financial data (yr. ended 12/31/01): Grants paid, $1,250; assets, $26,051 (M); expenditures, $1,361; qualifying distributions, $1,250.
Limitations: Applications not accepted. Giving primarily in Cincinnati, OH.
Application information: Contributes only to pre-selected organizations.
Officers: Ann "Nan" D. Conlan, Pres. and Treas.; Thomas L. Conlan, Jr., V.P. and Secy.
Trustee: U.S. Bank.
EIN: 311487070

44540
Holdfield Communication Foundation
c/o Bryan Bergson
27020 Cedar, Ste. 104-1
Beachwood, OH 44122

Established in 2000 in OH.
Donor(s): Bryan Bergson.
Financial data (yr. ended 12/31/01): Grants paid, $1,250; assets, $12,349 (M); expenditures, $1,250; qualifying distributions, $1,250.
Trustee: Bryan Bergson.
EIN: 341937416

44541
Qua Foundation
3393 Warrensville Center Rd.
Shaker Heights, OH 44122

Donor(s): Constance F. Qua.‡
Financial data (yr. ended 12/31/01): Grants paid, $1,250; assets, $48,849 (M); expenditures, $1,607; qualifying distributions, $1,250.
Limitations: Applications not accepted. Giving primarily in Cleveland, OH.
Application information: Contributes only to pre-selected organizations.
Officers: George F. Qua, Pres.; Thomas G. Williams, Treas.
EIN: 346567502

44542
Melanie Snyder Trust
c/o National City Bank of Pennsylvania
P.O. Box 94651
Cleveland, OH 44101-4651
Application address: c/o Ronald Joyce, Guidance Dir., Titusville Area High School, Guidance Center, 302 E. Walnut, Titusville, PA 16354, tel.: (814) 827-9687

Financial data (yr. ended 12/31/99): Grants paid, $1,250; assets, $41,764 (M); expenditures, $1,389; qualifying distributions, $1,361.
Limitations: Giving primarily to residents of Titusville, PA.
Trustee: National City Bank.
EIN: 256174890

44543
Alpha Enterprise Workshop
262 W. Cedar Ave.
P.O. Box 546
Ravenna, OH 44266

Financial data (yr. ended 12/31/00): Grants paid, $1,234; assets, $301,316 (M); gifts received, $423; expenditures, $184,907; qualifying distributions, $1,234.
Officers: Marie Miller, Pres.; Frank Poze, V.P.; Rachael Ciacco, Secy.-Treas.

44543—OHIO

Trustee: Kathy Corron.
EIN: 340903817

44544
B. E. & Gertrude Spero Foundation
1705 Noble Rd.
East Cleveland, OH 44112 (216) 851-3300
Contact: Manny Spero, Dir.

Financial data (yr. ended 12/31/01): Grants paid, $1,218; assets, $90,497 (M); expenditures, $1,357; qualifying distributions, $1,218.
Limitations: Giving primarily in OH.
Director: Manny Spero.
EIN: 237063681

44545
Oscar Wilkins Scholarship Trust Fund
c/o KeyBank, N.A.
800 Superior Ave., 4th Fl.
Cleveland, OH 44114-1306
Contact: Christina Cook, Trust Off., KeyBank, N.A.

Financial data (yr. ended 04/30/00): Grants paid, $1,206; assets, $32,625 (M); expenditures, $2,802; qualifying distributions, $1,206.
Limitations: Giving limited to Waldo County, ME.
Application information: Application form not required.
Trustee: KeyBank, N.A.
EIN: 016010184

44546
Boh Foundation
6913 Normancrest Ct.
Dayton, OH 45459-3130

Established in 2000 in OH.
Financial data (yr. ended 12/31/00): Grants paid, $1,200; assets, $61,795 (M); gifts received, $70,305; expenditures, $4,421; qualifying distributions, $3,176.
Limitations: Applications not accepted.
Application information: Contributes only to pre-selected organizations.
Trustees: Jim Marten, Doug Miller.
EIN: 311682035

44547
Pete Johns Memorial Fund
c/o George N. Williams
4658 E. 355th St.
Willoughby, OH 44094-4630

Financial data (yr. ended 12/31/00): Grants paid, $1,200; assets, $12,732 (M); expenditures, $1,238; qualifying distributions, $1,200.
Limitations: Applications not accepted. Giving primarily in Cleveland, OH.
Application information: Contributes only to pre-selected organizations.
Trustee: George N. Williams.
EIN: 346572935

44548
Herbst Charitable Trust
3201 Modred Cir. N.W.
Canton, OH 44708-1178

Donor(s): Ron Herbst, Andrea Herbst.
Financial data (yr. ended 12/31/99): Grants paid, $1,186; assets, $93,968 (L); gifts received, $70,000; expenditures, $34,441; qualifying distributions, $1,186.
Trustee: Ronald P. Herbst.
EIN: 347037740

44549
Abb and Christine Hendley Charitable Trust
P.O. Box 3308
Zanesville, OH 43702-3308

Established in 2000 in OH.
Donor(s): Albert H. Hendley.
Financial data (yr. ended 12/31/01): Grants paid, $1,182; assets, $93,563 (M); gifts received, $50,000; expenditures, $1,182; qualifying distributions, $1,182.
Limitations: Applications not accepted.
Application information: Contributes only to pre-selected organizations.
Trustees: Albert H. Hendley, Jr., John N. Hendley, John Nance Hendley, Jr.
EIN: 311726902

44550
The Callahan Memorial Award Commission, Inc.
1422 Euclid Ave., Ste. 662
Cleveland, OH 44115

Financial data (yr. ended 12/31/00): Grants paid, $1,174; assets, $78,834 (M); expenditures, $3,701; qualifying distributions, $1,045.
Limitations: Applications not accepted. Giving limited to residents of OH.
Application information: Awards by nomination only.
Officers: Jack W. Gottschalk, Chair.; James F. Mercer, Vice-Chair.; Robert M. Phelps, Secy.-Treas.
Directors: Joseph P. Crowley, Lloyd J. Hagedorn, Karl W. Lange, Timothy S. Rose, David G. Rummel.
EIN: 311334266

44551
The John William Duff Foundation
2111 Coppersmith Ave.
Dayton, OH 45414

Established in 2000 in OH.
Donor(s): Jerald L. Duff.
Financial data (yr. ended 12/31/01): Grants paid, $1,160; assets, $16,005 (M); gifts received, $1,000; expenditures, $1,160; qualifying distributions, $1,160.
Officers: Linda Duff, Pres.; Marcus Duff, V.P.; Jerald Duff, Secy.-Treas.
EIN: 311739278

44552
Richard T. and Dorothy J. Oberfield Foundation
c/o Richard T. Oberfield
1370 Stratford Woods Dr.
Newark, OH 43055

Established in 2000 in OH.
Donor(s): Richard T. Oberfield.
Financial data (yr. ended 06/30/02): Grants paid, $1,150; assets, $20,431 (M); gifts received, $20,000; expenditures, $1,682; qualifying distributions, $1,150.
Limitations: Applications not accepted.
Application information: Contributes only to pre-selected organizations.
Officers: Richard T. Oberfield, Pres. and Treas.; Dorothy J. Oberfield, V.P.; Ann M. Kennedy, Secy.
EIN: 311725452

44553
Bon Charitable Trust
2126 Old Vienna Dr.
Dayton, OH 45459

Established in 1999 in OH.
Financial data (yr. ended 12/31/99): Grants paid, $1,125; assets, $3,951 (M); gifts received, $5,000; expenditures, $1,135; qualifying distributions, $1,134.

Limitations: Applications not accepted. Giving primarily in MD, NY, OH, and VA.
Application information: Contributes only to pre-selected organizations.
Trustees: Judith D. Bon, Theodore J. Bon.
EIN: 316566177

44554
Loving God "Complete Bible" Christian Ministries
7208 Sycamore Hill Ln.
Cincinnati, OH 45243
Contact: Rev. Joan B. Anderson, Pres.

Established in 1995 in OH.
Donor(s): Rev. Joan B. Anderson.
Financial data (yr. ended 12/31/01): Grants paid, $1,073; assets, $19,534 (M); gifts received, $17,893; expenditures, $20,035; qualifying distributions, $1,073.
Limitations: Giving primarily in Cincinnati, OH.
Officers and Director:* Rev. Joan B. Anderson,* Pres.; Kathleen Peyton, V.P. and Secy.; Jerry W. Anderson, V.P. and Mgr.
EIN: 311259206

44555
O. D. Anderson, Inc. Irrevocable Trust
c/o National City Bank of Pennsylvania
P.O. Box 94651
Cleveland, OH 44101

Established in 2001 in PA.
Financial data (yr. ended 12/31/01): Grants paid, $1,030; assets, $40,827 (M); expenditures, $1,893; qualifying distributions, $1,483.
Limitations: Applications not accepted. Giving primarily in PA.
Trustee: National City Bank of Pennsylvania.
EIN: 256310318

44556
Clifford W. & Beryl H. Moul & West Sand Lake Grange No. 949 Scholarship Fund
c/o KeyBank, N.A., Trust Div.
800 Superior Ave., 4th Fl.
Cleveland, OH 44114 (216) 828-9535
Application address: c/o Chair., Grange Scholarship Comm., Box 315-5, RD No. 6, Troy, NY 12180

Financial data (yr. ended 12/31/00): Grants paid, $1,016; assets, $41,950 (M); expenditures, $1,576; qualifying distributions, $1,041.
Limitations: Giving limited to NY.
Trustee: KeyBank, N.A.
EIN: 146015026

44557
Fogler Charitable Trust
8671 Landsdale Ave., N.W.
North Canton, OH 44720

Donor(s): John A. Fogler, Fogler Asset Management Co.
Financial data (yr. ended 12/31/99): Grants paid, $1,014; assets, $20,901 (L); gifts received, $15,967; expenditures, $1,702; qualifying distributions, $1,014.
Limitations: Applications not accepted.
Application information: Contributes only to pre-selected organizations.
Trustee: John A. Fogler.
EIN: 347031840

44558
Sword Charitable Trust
5700 Fox Hollow Cir.
North Ridgeville, OH 44039-2522

Financial data (yr. ended 12/31/00): Grants paid, $1,010; assets, $0 (L); gifts received, $1,500;

expenditures, $1,428; qualifying distributions, $1,010.
Trustees: Charles H. Sword, Mary Ann Sword.
EIN: 347068035

44559
Raeburn E. Barnes Estate Trust
c/o Eugene P. Elsass
P.O. Box 499
Sidney, OH 45365-0499
Application address: P.O. Box 652, Sidney, OH 45365

Established in 1966.
Financial data (yr. ended 12/31/01): Grants paid, $1,000; assets, $7,119,404 (M); expenditures, $97,652; qualifying distributions, $627,071; giving activities include $628,154 for loans to individuals.
Limitations: Giving limited to Shelby County, OH.
Application information: Application form required.
Trustees: Eugene P. Elsass, V. Paul Gahagan, Clayton L. Kiracofe, Thomas Watkins.
EIN: 346639060
Codes: GTI

44560
Michael R. Barrett Foundation, Inc.
c/o J. Brun
1 E. 4th St., Ste. 1400
Cincinnati, OH 45202 (513) 721-2120
Contact: Michael R. Barrett, Tr.

Established in 1999 in OH.
Financial data (yr. ended 12/31/01): Grants paid, $1,000; assets, $58,634 (M); gifts received, $28,104; expenditures, $3,111; qualifying distributions, $1,000.
Limitations: Giving primarily in OH.
Application information: Application form not required.
Trustees: John F. Barrett, Michael R. Barrett, James H. Brun.
EIN: 311685426

44561
The Beischel Family Private Foundation
5367 Meadow Estates Dr.
Cincinnati, OH 45247

Established in 1998 in OH.
Donor(s): Grace Beischel.
Financial data (yr. ended 12/31/01): Grants paid, $1,000; assets, $16,125 (M); gifts received, $100; expenditures, $1,750; qualifying distributions, $1,000.
Limitations: Applications not accepted. Giving primarily in Cincinnati, OH.
Application information: Contributes only to pre-selected organizations.
Officers and Trustees:* Grace Beischel,* Pres. and Treas.; Timothy E. Beischel,* V.P. and Secy.; Brigid A. Almaguer, Sharon T. Beischel, Maureen A. Giesken, Edith C. John.
EIN: 311579864

44562
Ira Block Foundation, Inc.
c/o Peter Block
4 Filson Pl.
Cincinnati, OH 45202

Established in 2000 in NJ.
Donor(s): Peter Block.
Financial data (yr. ended 12/31/01): Grants paid, $1,000; assets, $134,092 (M); gifts received, $49,698; expenditures, $1,150; qualifying distributions, $1,000.
Limitations: Applications not accepted.

Application information: Contributes only to pre-selected organizations.
Officers and Trustees:* Peter Block,* Pres. and Treas.; Cathy Ellen Kramer,* V.P.; Jennifer Beth Block,* Secy.; Heather Block Reilly.
EIN: 223770758

44563
Donald G. Brown Foundation
P.O. Box 523
Sugarcreek, OH 44681
Application address: c/o Guidance Office, Garaway Local School District, 146 Dover Road, Sugarcreek, OH 44681, tel.: (330) 852-4292

Established in 2001.
Donor(s): Mary M. Brown.
Financial data (yr. ended 12/31/01): Grants paid, $1,000; assets, $50,462 (M); gifts received, $52,199; expenditures, $1,882; qualifying distributions, $1,882.
Limitations: Giving limited to residents of OH.
Trustees: Gregory I. Brown, Mary M. Brown, Jenny B. Miller, Judith B. Yoder.
EIN: 341969599

44564
The Cedarcrest Farms Scholarship
c/o Selection Committee
6486 E. Main St.
Reynoldsburg, OH 43068 (614) 861-3636

Established in 2000.
Financial data (yr. ended 12/31/00): Grants paid, $1,000; assets, $19,759 (M); gifts received, $20,000; expenditures, $1,255; qualifying distributions, $1,150.
Trustees: Neal Smith, Vickie J. White.
EIN: 311729907

44565
Paul A. Corey Scholarship Fund
c/o Michael A. Zappa
6161 Busch Blvd., Ste. 87
Columbus, OH 43229-2548

Donor(s): Ohio Coin Machine Association.
Financial data (yr. ended 12/31/01): Grants paid, $1,000; assets, $4,823 (M); gifts received, $165; expenditures, $1,000; qualifying distributions, $1,000.
Limitations: Applications not accepted. Giving limited to residents of OH.
Application information: Unsolicited requests for funds not accepted.
Officers and Directors:* Michael A. Zappa, Chair.; William Westerhaus,* Pres.; Dean DiCarlo,* V.P.; Ryck E. Zarick, Secy.; Larry A. Van Brackel,* Treas.; Michael Fowler, Gary Goldflies, Dan C. Harder, Rodney Stebelton.
EIN: 311560463

44566
Reuben R. Cowles Jersey Youth Award
6486 E. Main St.
Reynoldsburg, OH 43068

Financial data (yr. ended 12/31/00): Grants paid, $1,000; assets, $27,888 (M); expenditures, $1,196; qualifying distributions, $1,050.
Limitations: Giving limited to residents of FL, GA, NC, SC, TN, and VA.
Trustees: Neal Smith, Vickie J. White.
EIN: 311609764

44567
Molly Ellenberger Memorial Scholarship Fund
c/o David Ellenberger
8009 Walnut St. S.W.
Sherrodsville, OH 44675-9546

Established in 1998 in OH.
Donor(s): David Ellenberger.
Financial data (yr. ended 12/31/00): Grants paid, $1,000; assets, $14,930 (M); gifts received, $8,066; expenditures, $1,000; qualifying distributions, $1,000.
Limitations: Giving primarily to residents of Hartville, OH.
Application information: Application form required.
Directors: Pat Anderson, Jeff Durbin, Dave Ellenberger, Marc Hoffman, Karen Knish, Dave Kocher, Bonnie Parenti, Rick Sampson.
EIN: 311523940

44568
The Joan H. and Ronald G. Fountain Foundation
2908 Paxton Rd.
Shaker Heights, OH 44120-1824

Established in 1986 in OH.
Donor(s): Joan H. Fountain, Ronald G. Fountain.
Financial data (yr. ended 11/30/01): Grants paid, $1,000; assets, $10,801 (M); expenditures, $1,028; qualifying distributions, $1,000.
Limitations: Applications not accepted. Giving primarily in Cleveland, OH.
Application information: Contributes only to pre-selected organizations.
Officers: Ronald G. Fountain, Pres. and Treas.; Joan H. Fountain, V.P.; Henry F. Eaton, Secy.
EIN: 341543641

44569
Carol Dixon Fox/Dover First Scholarship Trust
c/o Thomas W. Fox
232 W. 3rd St., Ste. 309
Dover, OH 44622-2969 (330) 364-6621

Established in 1996.
Donor(s): Carol A. Fox, Thomas W. Fox.
Financial data (yr. ended 12/31/99): Grants paid, $1,000; assets, $10,111 (M); expenditures, $1,018; qualifying distributions, $1,018.
Application information: Application form required.
Trustees: Carol A. Fox, Thomas W. Fox.
EIN: 347059394

44570
The David L. Hayes Family Foundation
5973 Forest Hills
Maumee, OH 43537

Established in 1997 in OH.
Donor(s): David L. Hayes, Patty Hayes.
Financial data (yr. ended 12/31/01): Grants paid, $1,000; assets, $24,183 (M); expenditures, $3,337; qualifying distributions, $1,000.
Trustees: David L. Hayes, Patty Hayes.
EIN: 311531801

44571
Klug Family Foundation
21006 Brantley Rd.
Shaker Heights, OH 44122
Contact: Stephen G. Klug, Tr.

Established in 1997 in OH.
Donor(s): Stephen G. Klug.
Financial data (yr. ended 12/31/01): Grants paid, $1,000; assets, $32,104 (M); expenditures, $1,234; qualifying distributions, $1,000.
Limitations: Applications not accepted. Giving primarily in OH.

44571—OHIO

Application information: Contributes only to pre-selected organizations.
Trustee: Stephen G. Klug.
EIN: 341852847

44572
Kenneth B. Long Scholarship Fund
c/o Richard D. DeLamatre
74 Mill St.
Huron, OH 44839-1792
Application address: c/o Principal, Huron High School, Huron, OH 44839

Financial data (yr. ended 12/31/99): Grants paid, $1,000; assets, $42,188 (M); expenditures, $2,442; qualifying distributions, $2,442.
Limitations: Giving limited to Huron, OH.
Trustee: Richard D. DeLamatre.
EIN: 346714661

44573
Richard M. McClure Memorial Foundation, Inc.
c/o Warren W. Gibson
480 Merriman Rd.
Akron, OH 44303-1542

Established in OH in 1998.
Donor(s): Richard M. McClure.
Financial data (yr. ended 12/31/00): Grants paid, $1,000; assets, $63,586 (M); gifts received, $1,000; expenditures, $1,025; qualifying distributions, $1,000.
Limitations: Applications not accepted.
Application information: Contributes only to pre-selected organizations.
Officers: Richard M. McClure, Pres.; Ann Fleming, V.P.; Robert Heydon, V.P.; Warren W. Gibson, Secy.; Edward H. Swanson, Treas.
EIN: 341850245

44574
Jerome & Marjorie Nelson Foundation
2614 Kent Rd.
Columbus, OH 43221-3228

Donor(s): Marjorie Nelson, Jerome Nelson.
Financial data (yr. ended 11/30/01): Grants paid, $1,000; assets, $53,154 (M); expenditures, $11,687; qualifying distributions, $1,000.
Limitations: Applications not accepted. Giving on a national basis.
Application information: Contributes only to pre-selected organizations.
Directors: Jerome Nelson, Marjorie Nelson.
EIN: 237441829

44575
Nelson Scholarship Trust
c/o National City Bank of Indiana
P.O. Box 94651
Cleveland, OH 44101-4651

Financial data (yr. ended 12/31/01): Grants paid, $1,000; assets, $11,273 (M); expenditures, $1,266; qualifying distributions, $1,139.
Limitations: Applications not accepted. Giving limited to residents of IN.
Trustee: National City Bank of Indiana.
EIN: 356393546

44576
The Reynolds Lajadesh Foundation
20600 Chagrin Blvd., Ste. 600, Tower E.
Shaker Heights, OH 44122

Established in 2000 in OH.
Donor(s): Frederic G. Reynolds.
Financial data (yr. ended 12/31/01): Grants paid, $1,000; assets, $1,180,160 (M); gifts received, $5,000; expenditures, $1,000; qualifying distributions, $1,000.
Limitations: Applications not accepted.

Application information: Contributes only to pre-selected organizations.
Trustees: Fredric G. Reynolds, Lundy E. Reynolds.
EIN: 341953315

44577
Charles A. Semler Memorial Foundation
c/o Constance S. Preston
826 Oakridge St. S.W.
North Canton, OH 44720-3411
Application address: c/o Mark Giffele, Asst. Supt., Business & Finance, Benton Harbor Area Schools, Benton Harbor, MI 49023, tel.: (269) 927-0600

Established in 1990 in OH.
Donor(s): Constance S. Preston.
Financial data (yr. ended 06/30/99): Grants paid, $1,000; assets, $12,436 (M); gifts received, $59; expenditures, $1,059; qualifying distributions, $1,000.
Limitations: Giving limited to Benton Harbor, MI.
Officers: James K. Preston, Secy.-Treas.; Constance S. Preston, Admin.
Trustees: Barbara S. Tenenbaum, Frederick M. Worrell.
EIN: 346937570

44578
Reynaldo C. Soriano, M.D. Memorial Fund
N298 County Rd. 14
Napoleon, OH 43545
Application address: 2135 Old Mill Rd., Toledo, OH 43615, tel. (419) 843-2070
Contact: Michael Soriano, Pres.

Financial data (yr. ended 12/31/01): Grants paid, $1,000; assets, $30,013 (M); expenditures, $1,500; qualifying distributions, $1,500.
Limitations: Giving primarily in OH.
Officers: Michael Soriano, Pres. and Treas.; Fe C. Soriano, V.P.; Lisa Soriano, Secy.
EIN: 341924720

44579
Ida B. Wells Foundation
P.O. Box 14991
Cleveland, OH 44114-0991

Donor(s): Rev. Charles V. Hurst, Maria A. Smith.
Financial data (yr. ended 12/31/00): Grants paid, $1,000; assets, $46,500 (M); gifts received, $5,000; expenditures, $1,512; qualifying distributions, $1,000.
Limitations: Giving primarily in OH.
Officers: Rev. Charles V. Hurst, Pres.; Molly Carreon, Secy.; Gisela Pacheco, Treas.
Trustees: Mark Pestak.
EIN: 341903338

44580
The Milton R. & Beulah M. Young Foundation
P.O. Box 117
Loudonville, OH 44842-0117

Established in 1999 in OH.
Financial data (yr. ended 12/31/01): Grants paid, $1,000; assets, $19,871 (M); expenditures, $1,202; qualifying distributions, $1,000.
Trustees: Bill Heichel, Beulah Young, Milton Young.
EIN: 341908082

44581
E. T. Jeffery Foundation
3415 Roundwood Rd.
Hunting Valley, OH 44022

Financial data (yr. ended 12/31/01): Grants paid, $969; assets, $77,169 (M); gifts received, $2,000; expenditures, $1,298; qualifying distributions, $969.

Limitations: Applications not accepted. Giving primarily in OH.
Application information: Contributes only to pre-selected organizations.
Officers: Helen P. Jeffery, Pres.; E.T. Jeffery, Jr., Treas.
EIN: 346548332

44582
The Robert H. Sweeney Charitable Foundation
c/o Butler Wick Trust Co.
City Centre 1, Ste. 700
Youngstown, OH 44503

Established in 1997 in OH.
Donor(s): Robert H. Sweeney.
Financial data (yr. ended 12/31/01): Grants paid, $955; assets, $29,589 (M); expenditures, $2,905; qualifying distributions, $955.
Limitations: Applications not accepted.
Application information: Contributes only to pre-selected organizations.
Advisory Committee: Beth Anne Sweeney, David H. Sweeney, Douglas V. Sweeney, James R. Sweeney, Linda S. Tsoumas.
Trustee: Butler Wick Trust Co.
EIN: 237878526

44583
Stryker Community Emergency Pantry
c/o William J. Brenner
P.O. Box 411
Stryker, OH 43557-0411

Established in 1986 in OH.
Financial data (yr. ended 12/31/01): Grants paid, $949; assets, $1,156 (M); gifts received, $195; expenditures, $949; qualifying distributions, $949.
Limitations: Applications not accepted. Giving limited to Stryker, OH.
Application information: Contributes only to pre-selected organizations.
Officers: Joan Ruffer, Pres.; Nancy Jaggers, V.P.; Elaine Graber, Treas.
EIN: 311096259

44584
Amber & Babe Animal Foundation
P.O. Box 434
Vermilion, OH 44089

Established in 1998.
Financial data (yr. ended 12/31/99): Grants paid, $942; assets, $1,966 (M); gifts received, $1,400; expenditures, $1,490; qualifying distributions, $1,490; giving activities include $1,490 for programs.
Trustees: Dennis F. Bielak, Albert S. Harsar, Teresa Bielak Patton.
EIN: 341711353

44585
Joseph P. Mull, Jr. & Virginia P. Mull Foundation
c/o Belmont National Bank
100 Plaza Dr., Trust Dept.
St. Clairsville, OH 43950

Established in 1998 in OH.
Donor(s): Virginia P. Mull.
Financial data (yr. ended 12/31/01): Grants paid, $916; assets, $7,573 (M); expenditures, $1,620; qualifying distributions, $916.
Limitations: Applications not accepted.
Trustees: Joseph N. Gompers, Quay Mull II, Belmont National Bank.
EIN: 340840293

44586
J. and V. Mull Foundation
(Formerly Joseph P. & Virginia P. Mull, Jr. Foundation)
100 Plaza Dr., Trust Dept.
St. Clairsville, OH 43950

Established in 1998 in OH.
Financial data (yr. ended 12/31/01): Grants paid, $915; assets, $7,572 (M); expenditures, $1,619; qualifying distributions, $915.
Trustees: Joseph N. Gompers, Quay Mull II, Belmont National Bank.
EIN: 550755202

44587
Miller Foundation
6043 Shadow Lake Dr.
Toledo, OH 43623

Established in 1993 in OH.
Donor(s): Lloyd A. Miller.
Financial data (yr. ended 12/31/01): Grants paid, $900; assets, $234,050 (M); expenditures, $1,104; qualifying distributions, $900.
Limitations: Applications not accepted.
Trustees: Lois Jane Chrobak, Mahlon Lau, Lloyd A. Miller.
EIN: 341724739

44588
Tami Sargi Memorial Scholarship, Inc.
1101 Munroe Falls Rd.
Kent, OH 44240

Established in 1990 in OH.
Financial data (yr. ended 06/30/01): Grants paid, $900; assets, $35,957 (M); expenditures, $1,013; qualifying distributions, $900.
Limitations: Applications not accepted. Giving primarily in OH.
Trustees: James Murphy, Terri S. Sargi, Trisha Sargi.
EIN: 341673563

44589
Chillicothe/Ross Community Foundation, Inc.
213 S. Paint St.
Chillicothe, OH 45601

Established in 1997 in OH.
Financial data (yr. ended 12/31/99): Grants paid, $889; assets, $117,053 (M); gifts received, $76,466; expenditures, $1,011.
Limitations: Giving limited to the greater Chillicothe, OH, area.
Officers: Charles Vandecarr, Pres.; Carl Daughters, V.P.; Timothy Nusbaum, Secy.; Dona Smith, Treas.
EIN: 311480939
Codes: CM

44590
The OB Foundation
P.O. Box 402
Ottawa, OH 45875

Financial data (yr. ended 12/31/01): Grants paid, $888; assets, $8,350 (M); gifts received, $4,976; expenditures, $12,073; qualifying distributions, $888.
Limitations: Applications not accepted.
Application information: Contributes only to pre-selected organizations.
Officers: Helen Meyer, Exec. Secy.; Leon Meyer, Exec. Dir.
EIN: 364265177

44591
Robert W. Boyd Memorial Trust
c/o KeyBank, N.A.
800 Superior Ave., 4th Fl.
Cleveland, OH 44114

Established in 1988 in ME.
Donor(s): Robert W. Boyd.‡
Financial data (yr. ended 08/31/01): Grants paid, $857; assets, $6,354 (M); expenditures, $897; qualifying distributions, $848.
Limitations: Applications not accepted. Giving limited to ME.
Application information: Unsolicited requests for funds not accepted.
Trustee: KeyBank, N.A.
EIN: 016028935

44592
Fred W. Dornow Memorial Scholarship Trust
c/o KeyBank, N.A.
800 Superior Ave., 4th Fl.
Cleveland, OH 44114
Application address: c/o Principal or Guidance Counselor, Wellsville Central High School, Wellsville, NY 14895

Donor(s): Doratha E. Dornow.‡
Financial data (yr. ended 12/31/01): Grants paid, $850; assets, $16,252 (M); expenditures, $1,040; qualifying distributions, $843.
Limitations: Giving limited to male residents of Wellsville, NY.
Trustee: KeyBank, N.A.
EIN: 166133301

44593
Girard School Trust
c/o John Masternick
20 E. Liberty St.
Girard, OH 44420

Established in 1997 in OH.
Financial data (yr. ended 12/31/01): Grants paid, $850; assets, $27,081 (M); gifts received, $5,000; expenditures, $971; qualifying distributions, $850.
Limitations: Applications not accepted.
Application information: Contributes only to pre-selected organizations.
Trustees: Theresa A. Grimes, Dorothy F. Masternick, John Masternick, John J. Masternick.
EIN: 316584705

44594
The Salem Rotary Foundation
P.O. Box 1244
Salem, OH 44460-8244 (330) 332-0042
Contact: George W.S. Hays, Pres.

Established in 1995 in OH.
Donor(s): Rotary Club of Salem, Inc.
Financial data (yr. ended 12/31/00): Grants paid, $840; assets, $42,965 (M); gifts received, $2,949; expenditures, $1,040; qualifying distributions, $999.
Limitations: Giving limited to Salem, OH.
Officers: George W.S. Hays, Pres.; Frank A. Zamarelli, V.P.; Geoffrey S. Goll, Secy.; Raymond G. Isabella, Treas.
Trustee: Frank A. Zamarelli, Jr.
EIN: 341794575

44595
McElheny Family Foundation, Inc.
c/o Barbara A. Holcomb
29198 Snare Rd.
Richwood, OH 43344-9020

Established in 1997 in OH.
Donor(s): John D. McElheny.
Financial data (yr. ended 12/31/99): Grants paid, $839; assets, $72,649 (M); expenditures, $1,043; qualifying distributions, $1,026; giving activities include $1,043 for programs.
Limitations: Giving limited to Richwood, OH.
Application information: Awards are made by teachers of North Union High School.
Officers: Barbara Holcomb, Pres.; Eric Hoffman, Secy.; Nancy Hoffman, Treas.
EIN: 341852375

44596
David L. Oblinger Trust Fund
P.O. Box 131
Germantown, OH 45327 (937) 855-4141
Contact: Nelda Lane, Tr.

Financial data (yr. ended 12/31/01): Grants paid, $825; assets, $23,837 (M); expenditures, $860; qualifying distributions, $825.
Limitations: Giving limited to residents of Germantown, OH.
Application information: Application form not required.
Trustees: Nelda Judy Lane, Kent Southard, Rebecca Wafzig.
EIN: 316134909

44597
Martha Harrison High School Educational Fund
c/o Community First Bank & Trust
P.O. Box 170
Celina, OH 45822 (419) 586-7765
Contact: C. Bryan

Established in 1999 in IN.
Financial data (yr. ended 12/31/99): Grants paid, $804; assets, $35,332 (M); expenditures, $1,960; qualifying distributions, $1,913.
Limitations: Giving limited to Union City, IN.
Trustee: Community First Bank & Trust.
EIN: 347083296

44598
Lucy A. Ash Testamentary Trust
c/o National City Bank
P.O. Box 94651
Cleveland, OH 44101-4651
Application address: c/o Canton High School, 1001 N. Main St., Canton, IL 61520, tel.: (309) 647-1820

Financial data (yr. ended 12/31/00): Grants paid, $800; assets, $15,450 (M); expenditures, $1,176; qualifying distributions, $977.
Limitations: Giving limited to Urbana, IL.
Application information: Application form required.
Trustee: National City Bank.
EIN: 376042752

44599
H. & M.B. Stepping Stone Fund
1159 Haselton Rd.
Cleveland Heights, OH 44121-1539

Financial data (yr. ended 06/30/01): Grants paid, $800; assets, $12,516 (M); expenditures, $837; qualifying distributions, $800.
Limitations: Applications not accepted. Giving primarily in Tiffin, OH.
Application information: Contributes only to pre-selected organizations.
Officers: Margaret M. Boehm, Pres.; Helen B. Utz, Secy.; Donald M. Boehm, Treas.
EIN: 341536173

44600
Wiley H. Slater Scholarship Fund
c/o Sky Bank
P.O. Box 479
Youngstown, OH 44501-0479
Application address: c/o Henry Miller, Dir. of Guidance, Boardman High School, 7777 Glenwood Ave., Youngstown, OH 44512, tel.: (330) 758-7511

Financial data (yr. ended 09/30/01): Grants paid, $800; assets, $19,627 (M); expenditures, $2,397; qualifying distributions, $1,328.
Limitations: Giving limited to Youngstown, OH.
Application information: Application form not required.
Advisory Committee: Louis Rucci.
Trustee: Sky Bank.
EIN: 346754777

44601
Cora A. Wilkins Trust
c/o First National Bank
P.O. Box 2370
Zanesville, OH 43702-2458

Financial data (yr. ended 05/31/99): Grants paid, $800; assets, $57,262 (M); expenditures, $1,655; qualifying distributions, $1,170.
Limitations: Giving limited to residents of Muskingum County, OH.
Application information: Application form required.
Trustee: First National Bank.
EIN: 316146732

44602
The Freytag Family Foundation
601 Warren Dr.
Wapakoneta, OH 45895

Established in 2000 in OH.
Financial data (yr. ended 12/31/01): Grants paid, $780; assets, $1,270 (M); gifts received, $700; expenditures, $580; qualifying distributions, $780.
Limitations: Giving primarily in OH.
Trustees: Gwynne Freytag, Thomas R. Freytag.
EIN: 347125519

44603
Charles A. Dunklee Foundation
P.O. Box 246
Gates Mills, OH 44040-0246 (440) 423-4436
Contact: Charles C. Newcomer, Pres.

Established in 1982 in OH.
Financial data (yr. ended 12/31/00): Grants paid, $750; assets, $15,669 (M); expenditures, $960; qualifying distributions, $960.
Limitations: Giving limited to OH.
Officers and Trustees:* Charles C. Newcomer,* Pres.; Caroline D. Newcomer, V.P.; Caroline G. Barney,* Secy.-Treas.; Henry Fuller Grund, David F. Newcomer.
EIN: 341524445

44604
Ida Barnes Laughlin Charitable Trust
c/o Fifth Third Bank
38 Fountain Sq. Plz.
Cincinnati, OH 45263

Financial data (yr. ended 12/31/01): Grants paid, $750; assets, $40,258 (M); expenditures, $2,413; qualifying distributions, $750.
Limitations: Applications not accepted. Giving limited to Rushville, IN.
Application information: Contributes only to pre-selected organizations.
Trustee: Fifth Third Bank.
EIN: 356310435

44605
The Arev and Draphes Yenlov Foundation
c/o Robert V. Shepard
935 Hampton Ridge Dr.
Akron, OH 44313-5038

Established in 1999 in OH.
Financial data (yr. ended 12/31/01): Grants paid, $750; assets, $13,755 (M); gifts received, $2,824; expenditures, $1,019; qualifying distributions, $750.
Officer: Robert V. Shepard, Pres.
Directors: Donald W. Shepard, Hillary Smith.
EIN: 311509995

44606
Belmont County Sabin Scholarship Fund
P.O. Box 249
St. Clairsville, OH 43950
Contact: Nermin Lavapies, M.D., Secy.

Financial data (yr. ended 12/31/99): Grants paid, $705; assets, $38,574 (M); expenditures, $1,723; qualifying distributions, $705.
Application information: Applicant must be enrolled in a medical program at an approved college or university. Application form required.
Officer: Nermin D. Lavapies, M.D., Secy.
Trustee: Belmont National Bank.
EIN: 346550273

44607
The Hubbard Foundation
612 Clinton St.
P.O. Drawer 100
Defiance, OH 43512
Contact: E. Keith Hubbard, Pres.

Established in 1999 in OH.
Donor(s): E. Keith Hubbard.
Financial data (yr. ended 12/31/01): Grants paid, $700; assets, $23,219 (M); gifts received, $21,500; expenditures, $6,545; qualifying distributions, $700.
Officers and Trustees:* E. Keith Hubbard,* Pres.; Janis L. Hubbard,* Secy.-Treas.; Stephen F. Hubbard, Thomas K. Hubbard, Terry L. Melton.
EIN: 341900157

44608
Jeffrey L. Lazarus, Jr. Family Foundation
2444 Madison Rd., No. 710
Cincinnati, OH 45208

Financial data (yr. ended 11/30/01): Grants paid, $700; assets, $14,839 (M); expenditures, $731; qualifying distributions, $700.
Limitations: Applications not accepted.
Application information: Contributes only to pre-selected organizations.
Officer and Trustee:* Jeffrey L. Lazarus, Jr.,* Pres.
EIN: 316021213

44609
The Putman Foundation
405 Madison Ave.
Toledo, OH 43604

Established in 1998 in OH.
Donor(s): Paul Putman.
Financial data (yr. ended 12/31/01): Grants paid, $700; assets, $21,552 (M); expenditures, $1,826; qualifying distributions, $700.
Limitations: Applications not accepted.
Application information: Contributes only to pre-selected organizations.
Officer and Trustee:* Paul Putman,* Pres.
EIN: 341863487

44610
The Methuen & Gertrude Currie Foundation
4342 Courageous Cir.
Cincinnati, OH 45252
Contact: Charlene Rohrer, Secy.

Established in 1987 in OH.
Donor(s): R. Hector Currie, Constance Currie.
Financial data (yr. ended 12/31/01): Grants paid, $675; assets, $13,218 (M); expenditures, $1,002; qualifying distributions, $675.
Limitations: Giving primarily in OH.
Officers: R. Hector Currie, Pres.; Charlene Rohrer, Secy.
Trustees: Louis Freeman, Todd Williams.
EIN: 311193119

44611
The Blaine Foundation
510 Corporation Alley
Cincinnati, OH 45210-1505 (513) 579-9001
Contact: H. Breneman Blaine, Secy.-Treas.

Established in 1998 in OH.
Donor(s): Charlee B. Blaine.
Financial data (yr. ended 12/31/01): Grants paid, $668; assets, $12,380 (M); expenditures, $668; qualifying distributions, $668.
Limitations: Giving primarily in CA, OR, and OH.
Application information: Application form not required.
Officers and Trustees:* Amrita Skye Blaine,* Pres.; Margaret Andrews Blaine,* V.P.; H. Breneman Blaine,* Secy.-Treas.
EIN: 311596808

44612
Dudek Charitable Trust
2010 Devonshire Dr., N.W.
Canton, OH 44708-2014

Financial data (yr. ended 12/31/99): Grants paid, $625; assets, $63,199 (M); gifts received, $1,000; expenditures, $625; qualifying distributions, $625.
Limitations: Applications not accepted.
Application information: Contributes only to pre-selected organizations.
Director: Larry Dudek.
EIN: 341848083

44613
The Beckenbach Family Foundation
(Formerly Midwest Foundation)
8 Haskell Dr.
Bratenahl, OH 44108-1100

Financial data (yr. ended 01/31/02): Grants paid, $600; assets, $92,406 (M); expenditures, $5,272; qualifying distributions, $600.
Limitations: Applications not accepted. Giving primarily in NY and OH.
Application information: Contributes only to pre-selected organizations.
Trustees: J.B. Beckenbach, K.H. Beckenbach, M.W. Beckenbach, W.C. Beckenbach.
EIN: 346541770

44614
Mary C. Donovan Memorial Scholarship Fund
c/o Kevin D. Donovan
3122 Hanna Ave.
Cincinnati, OH 45211-6913

Established in 1995 in OH.
Financial data (yr. ended 12/31/99): Grants paid, $600; assets, $5,988 (M); gifts received, $825; expenditures, $600; qualifying distributions, $598.
Trustees: Brian S. Donovan, Damian S. Donovan, James R. Donovan, Jr., M.D., Kevin O. Donovan, Hon. Mary E. Donovan.
EIN: 311433135

44615
Olinger Charitable Trust
13001 Sarbaugh St. S.W.
Navarre, OH 44662

Donor(s): Jack T. Olinger, Marjorie Olinger.
Financial data (yr. ended 12/31/99): Grants paid, $577; assets, $14,573 (L); gifts received, $1,500; expenditures, $1,215; qualifying distributions, $577.
Limitations: Applications not accepted.
Application information: Contributes only to pre-selected organizations.
Trustee: Jack T. Olinger.
EIN: 341831717

44616
Soemisch Charitable Trust
682 Greenbriar Cir. N.E.
Massillon, OH 44646

Established in 1998.
Donor(s): Richard A. Soemisch, Soemisch Asset Management.
Financial data (yr. ended 12/31/99): Grants paid, $575; assets, $13,531 (L); gifts received, $626; expenditures, $1,031; qualifying distributions, $575.
Limitations: Applications not accepted.
Application information: Contributes only to pre-selected organizations.
Directors: Richard A. Soemisch, Sandra L. Soemisch.
EIN: 341856915

44617
Sandi Smiley Memorial Fund
c/o National City Bank of Pennsylvania
P.O. Box 94651
Cleveland, OH 44101-4651

Financial data (yr. ended 12/31/01): Grants paid, $550; assets, $19,068 (M); expenditures, $840; qualifying distributions, $675.
Limitations: Applications not accepted. Giving limited to residents of the Fayette County, PA, area.
Application information: Unsolicited requests for funds not accepted.
Trustee: National City Bank.
EIN: 256214150

44618
George & Joan Musekamp Family Foundation
7680 Ridge Rd.
Cincinnati, OH 45237

Established in 1999 in OH.
Donor(s): George H. Musekamp, Joan Musekamp.
Financial data (yr. ended 12/31/01): Grants paid, $540; assets, $97,244 (M); gifts received, $38,125; expenditures, $1,265; qualifying distributions, $540.
Limitations: Applications not accepted.
Application information: Contributes only to pre-selected organizations.
Officers and Trustees:* George H. Musekamp,* Pres. and Treas.; Joan Musekamp,* V.P. and Secy.; Helen J. McNerney, Eric R. Musekamp.
EIN: 311683821

44619
Richardson Charitable Trust
360 Derby Ct.
Lebanon, OH 45036-8515

Financial data (yr. ended 12/31/00): Grants paid, $510; assets, $1,007 (M); expenditures, $510; qualifying distributions, $0.
Limitations: Applications not accepted.
Application information: Contributes only to pre-selected organizations.

Trustee: Barton Richardson.
EIN: 364236456

44620
The Lisa M. Alexander Foundation
c/o Lisa M. Alexander
24 Annandale Dr.
South Russell, OH 44022

Established in 1993 in OH.
Financial data (yr. ended 12/31/00): Grants paid, $500; assets, $6,703 (M); expenditures, $1,114; qualifying distributions, $500.
Limitations: Applications not accepted.
Application information: Contributes only to pre-selected organizations.
Trustees: Lisa M. Alexander, Patrick R. Alexander, Michael G. Healey.
EIN: 341722013

44621
George Brownlee Scholarship Fund
c/o Sky Trust, N.A.
P.O. Box 479
Youngstown, OH 44501-0479
Application address: c/o Larry Saxton, Principal, Boardman High School, 7777 Glenwood Ave., Youngstown, OH 44512

Financial data (yr. ended 12/31/99): Grants paid, $500; assets, $9,923 (M); expenditures, $1,061; qualifying distributions, $758.
Limitations: Giving limited to Boardman, OH.
Advisory Committee: Alan Burns, Jack E. Jones, Elm Miller, Larry Saxton, Richard G. Zellers.
Trustee: Sky Trust, N.A.
EIN: 346786514

44622
C.O.I.C. Foundation
c/o Rev. Edward D. Colley
6752 Stoll Ln.
Cincinnati, OH 45236-4039
Application address: c/o Cincinnati Scholarship Foundation, 203 E. 9th St., Cincinnati, OH 45202

Established in 1993 in OH.
Financial data (yr. ended 12/31/00): Grants paid, $500; assets, $335,552 (M); expenditures, $7,016; qualifying distributions, $500.
Limitations: Giving limited to residents of Hamilton County, OH.
Application information: Application form required.
Officer: Rev. Edward D. Colley, Pres.
Trustees: Doriscine L. Colley, Julian Renfro, Rev. Oliver Williams.
EIN: 310966258

44623
Harry & Estella D. Eno Memorial Fund Trust
c/o KeyBank, N.A., Trust Div.
800 Superior Ave., 4th Fl.
Cleveland, OH 44114

Financial data (yr. ended 12/31/00): Grants paid, $500; assets, $19,043 (M); expenditures, $680; qualifying distributions, $500.
Limitations: Applications not accepted. Giving limited to Baldwinsville, NY.
Application information: Unsolicited requests for funds not accepted.
Trustee: KeyBank, N.A.
EIN: 156013121

44624
Clarence M. and Margaret G. Erickson Foundation
c/o Richard Erickson & Robert Erickson
8074 Eastdale Dr.
Cincinnati, OH 45255

Established in 1997 in OH.
Financial data (yr. ended 12/31/99): Grants paid, $500; assets, $40,532 (M); expenditures, $2,015; qualifying distributions, $606.
Limitations: Applications not accepted.
Application information: Contributes only to pre-selected organizations.
Trustees: Richard Erickson, Robert Erickson.
EIN: 316591088

44625
The Mary Fields Scholarship Association and Fund
29050 W. Brockway Dr.
Westlake, OH 44145-5262

Established in 1999.
Financial data (yr. ended 12/31/99): Grants paid, $500; assets, $826 (M); gifts received, $1,275; expenditures, $500; qualifying distributions, $500.
Officers and Trustees:* Leroy Harris,* Chair.; Arthur Williams, Secy.; Lucinda Tucker, Treas.; Vera Phillips, Caesar Tillman, Eddie B. White, Wiley Williams.
EIN: 630924493

44626
Charles Goldfarb Memorial Scholarship Fund
2401 St. James Pl.
Sandusky, OH 44870-5132

Established in 1995.
Financial data (yr. ended 12/31/01): Grants paid, $500; assets, $0 (M); gifts received, $518; expenditures, $517; qualifying distributions, $500.
Limitations: Applications not accepted. Giving limited to Sandusky, OH.
Application information: Contributes only to pre-selected organizations.
Trustees: Jean Goldfarb, Lewis Goldfarb, Sharon Goldfarb.
EIN: 341807731

44627
Charles M. & Julia C. Harrington Scholarship Fund
c/o KeyBank, N.A., Trust Div.
800 Superior Ave., 4th Fl.
Cleveland, OH 44114
Application address: c/o Harrington Scholarship Comm., KeyBank, N.A., 35 State St., Albany, NY 12207

Donor(s): Charles M. Harrington.‡
Financial data (yr. ended 12/31/01): Grants paid, $500; assets, $120,495 (M); expenditures, $1,704; qualifying distributions, $550.
Limitations: Giving limited to residents of Plattsburgh, NY.
Trustee: KeyBank, N.A.
EIN: 146014863
Codes: GTI

44628
The Klema Foundation Charitable Trust
64 East Russell St.
Columbus, OH 43215-2045
Contact: Connie J. Klema, Tr.

Established in 1999 in OH.
Donor(s): Connie J. Klema.
Financial data (yr. ended 12/31/01): Grants paid, $500; assets, $153,631 (M); gifts received, $800;

expenditures, $1,593; qualifying distributions, $500.
Trustees: Connie J. Klema, Jan L. Maiden.
EIN: 316620877

44629
Landau Foundation
2201 Milton Rd., No. 311
Cleveland, OH 44118
Contact: Fay Bauer Landau, Chair.

Established in 1992 in OH.
Donor(s): Susan Landau Golden, Marcia Landau Elbrand.
Financial data (yr. ended 12/31/01): Grants paid, $500; assets, $2,581 (M); expenditures, $500; qualifying distributions, $500.
Limitations: Giving primarily in northern OH.
Officers and Trustees:* Fay Bauer Landau,* Chair.; Susan Landau Golden,* Pres.; Marcia Landau Elbrand,* V.P.; Joanna S. Golden, Judith L. Golden, David E. Sloane, M.D., Richard L. Sloane.
EIN: 341719049

44630
Roger Parker Long Memorial Trust
581 S. 4th Ave.
Middleport, OH 45760-1201 (740) 992-2158
Application address: c/o Principal, Meigs Local High School, 42091 Pomeroy Pike, Pomeroy, OH 45769

Financial data (yr. ended 12/31/99): Grants paid, $500; assets, $10,205 (M); expenditures, $670; qualifying distributions, $500.
Limitations: Giving limited to Pomeroy, OH.
Trustees: Delores J. Long, Harold Roger Long.
EIN: 311024168

44631
NLK Foundation
1340 Depot St., Ste. 102
Rocky River, OH 44116

Donor(s): Norman Klym, Kirkwood Industries, Inc.
Financial data (yr. ended 12/31/01): Grants paid, $500; assets, $5,651 (M); expenditures, $1,572; qualifying distributions, $500.
Officers: Norman Klym, Pres.; Lesley Klym, Secy.-Treas.
Trustee: Mary Klym.
EIN: 341805110

44632
Albert J. & Eunice M. Ortenzio Family Foundation
c/o Sky Trust, N.A.
P.O. Box 479
Youngstown, OH 44501-0479 (330) 742-7486
Contact: John Zador, Trust Off.

Established in 1998 in OH.
Donor(s): Albert Ortenzio.
Financial data (yr. ended 12/31/01): Grants paid, $500; assets, $20,742 (M); expenditures, $701; qualifying distributions, $650.
Directors: Albert J. Ortenzio, Eunice M. Ortenzio, Joseph V. Ortenzio.
Trustee: Sky Trust, N.A.
EIN: 341868705

44633
Ruth L. Pillsbury Scholarship Fund
c/o KeyBank, N.A.
800 Superior Ave., 4th Fl.
Cleveland, OH 44114
Application address: c/o Guidance Counselor, Pinkerton Academy, Pinkerton St., Derry, OH 03038

Established in 1992 in ME.

Financial data (yr. ended 05/31/02): Grants paid, $500; assets, $35,242 (M); expenditures, $615; qualifying distributions, $500.
Application information: Application form not required.
Trustee: KeyBank, N.A.
EIN: 046714385

44634
Albert B. Ratner Family Foundation
(Formerly Faye & Albert B. Ratner Foundation)
50 Public Sq., Ste. 1600
Cleveland, OH 44113-2295
Contact: Albert B. Ratner, Pres.

Financial data (yr. ended 07/31/01): Grants paid, $500; assets, $6,075 (M); gifts received, $5,000; expenditures, $580; qualifying distributions, $500.
Application information: Application form not required.
Officers and Trustees:* Albert B. Ratner,* Pres.; Charles Ratner,* Secy.-Treas.; Audrey Ratner, Brian Ratner, Tawny Ratner, Deborah Ratner Salzberg, Michael Salzberg.
EIN: 237218805

44635
Chester A. Rich Trust
c/o KeyBank, N.A.
800 Superior Ave., 4th Fl.
Cleveland, OH 44114

Financial data (yr. ended 05/31/00): Grants paid, $500; assets, $24,905 (M); expenditures, $996; qualifying distributions, $500.
Limitations: Applications not accepted. Giving limited to Fort Kent, ME.
Trustee: KeyBank, N.A.
EIN: 016030585

44636
Nick and Frances Roslovic Family Foundation
2767 Bryden Rd.
Bexley, OH 43209

Established in 2000 in OH.
Donor(s): Nick Roslovic, Frances Roslovic.
Financial data (yr. ended 12/31/01): Grants paid, $500; assets, $25,867 (M); expenditures, $2,437; qualifying distributions, $500.
Officers: Frances Roslovic, Mgr.; Nick Roslovic, Mgr.
EIN: 311735971

44637
Robert O. Sheckell Memorial Scholarship Trust
P.O. Box 94651
Cleveland, OH 44101-4651

Financial data (yr. ended 12/31/01): Grants paid, $500; assets, $11,916 (M); expenditures, $738; qualifying distributions, $625.
Limitations: Applications not accepted. Giving limited to residents of IN.
Trustee: National City Bank.
EIN: 356433782

44638
Lance B. Slocomb Charitable Trust
c/o First Financial Svcs. Group, N.A.
P.O. Box 2307
Zanesville, OH 43702-2307 (740) 455-7060

Financial data (yr. ended 12/31/99): Grants paid, $500; assets, $9,093 (M); expenditures, $1,296; qualifying distributions, $803.
Limitations: Giving limited to residents of Muskingum County, OH.
Application information: Application form required.
Trustee: First Financial Services Group, N.A.
EIN: 316018739

44639
Heckie Thompson Athletic Scholarship Fund
P.O. Box 578
Piketon, OH 45661
Application address: 175 Beaver Creek Rd., Piketon, OH 45661
Contact: Vicky Hayslip, Tr.

Financial data (yr. ended 12/31/01): Grants paid, $500; assets, $8,295 (M); expenditures, $506; qualifying distributions, $506.
Limitations: Giving limited to Pike County, OH.
Application information: Application form required.
Trustees: Treva Harmon, Vicky Hayslip, Joe Morrison, Euggle Robertson, Bill Thompson, Dennis Thompson.
EIN: 311056818

44640
Kathryn C. White Memorial Scholarship Fund
c/o Fifth Third Bank
P.O. Box 630858, MD 1COM31
Cincinnati, OH 45263
Application address: c/o Joyce Kittel, Trust Off., 110 N. Main St., Dayton, OH 45402

Financial data (yr. ended 02/28/02): Grants paid, $500; assets, $17,492 (M); expenditures, $499; qualifying distributions, $500.
Limitations: Giving limited to residents of Brown Township, FL.
Trustee: Fifth Third Bank.
EIN: 316138569

44641
Esther Scheel Wilson Memorial Scholarship Fund
9560 Creekside Dr.
Loveland, OH 45140

Established in 1998.
Financial data (yr. ended 12/31/00): Grants paid, $500; assets, $10,012 (L); expenditures, $500; qualifying distributions, $500.
Limitations: Giving limited to residents of Loveland, OH.
Trustee: Bonnie W. Kutschenreuter.
EIN: 311451005

44642
James Bennett Knoop Charitable Foundation
3309 Lansmere Rd.
Shaker Heights, OH 44122

Established in 2001 in OH.
Financial data (yr. ended 12/31/01): Grants paid, $490; assets, $1,563 (M); gifts received, $2,053; expenditures, $490; qualifying distributions, $490.
Trustees: Lisa S. Knoop, Stephen J. Knoop.
EIN: 341959072

44643
Louis & Elizabeth Avallone Trust
c/o KeyBank, N.A.
800 Superior Ave., 4th Fl.
Cleveland, OH 44114

Donor(s): Louis Avallone,‡ Elizabeth Avallone.‡
Financial data (yr. ended 12/31/00): Grants paid, $450; assets, $8,768 (M); expenditures, $541; qualifying distributions, $442.
Limitations: Applications not accepted. Giving limited to Lowville, NY.
Application information: Recipient chosen by committee.
Trustee: KeyBank, N.A.
EIN: 166151662

44644
Everlasting Foundation
8810 Brockman Rd.
New Bremen, OH 45869

Financial data (yr. ended 12/31/99): Grants paid, $412; assets, $520,425 (M); gifts received, $211,747; expenditures, $421; qualifying distributions, $412.
Limitations: Applications not accepted.
Application information: Contributes only to pre-selected organizations.
Directors: Nicholas Evers, Pam Evers.
EIN: 341852235

44645
Angle Charitable Trust
8765 Jane St. N.W.
Massillon, OH 44646-1625

Established in 1998.
Donor(s): Angle Asset Management.
Financial data (yr. ended 12/31/00): Grants paid, $405; assets, $0 (M); gifts received, $3,804; expenditures, $800; qualifying distributions, $405.
Limitations: Applications not accepted.
Application information: Contributes only to pre-selected organizations.
Trustees: Roseanne Angle, Thomas Angle.
EIN: 341856914
Codes: CS, CD

44646
G R A C E Fund, Inc.
P.O. Box 567
Wooster, OH 44691

Established in 1999 in OH.
Financial data (yr. ended 12/31/00): Grants paid, $405; assets, $99,206 (M); gifts received, $28,000; expenditures, $530; qualifying distributions, $405.
Limitations: Applications not accepted.
Application information: Contributes only to pre-selected organizations.
Director: Arthur M. Saunders.
EIN: 341768719

44647
ANTIC, Inc.
(also known as Actors-N-Theatre in Cuyahoga Falls, Inc.)
P.O. Box 635
Cuyahoga Falls, OH 44222-0635

Financial data (yr. ended 12/31/01): Grants paid, $395; assets, $4,523 (M); expenditures, $2,645; qualifying distributions, $395.
Limitations: Applications not accepted.
Officers and Trustees:* Marcy E. Crosswiller,* Pres.; Mary Kay Dante,* V.P.; Linda Giffin,* Secy.; Elizabeth Sherman Hickman, Karen Saverbrey, Ann Marie Trunck.
EIN: 341414855

44648
Kaity Bug
380 N. Main St.
Cedarville, OH 45314

Established in 2001 in OH.
Financial data (yr. ended 12/31/01): Grants paid, $386; assets, $150 (M); gifts received, $1,262; expenditures, $6,886; qualifying distributions, $0.
Director: Keith Noble.
EIN: 311771903

44649
Robert & Fern Foster Trust
c/o KeyBank, N.A., Trust Div.
800 Superior Ave., 4th Fl.
Cleveland, OH 44114

Financial data (yr. ended 12/31/00): Grants paid, $380; assets, $7,160 (M); expenditures, $454; qualifying distributions, $377.
Limitations: Applications not accepted. Giving limited to residents of Lowville, NY.
Application information: Unsolicited requests for funds not accepted.
Trustee: KeyBank, N.A.
EIN: 166250070

44650
Linda B. Lange Trust
c/o KeyBank, N.A., Trust Div.
800 Superior Ave., 4th Fl.
Cleveland, OH 44114
Application address: c/o Principal, Hunter-Tannersville High School, Tannersville, NY 12485

Donor(s): Linda B. Lange.‡
Financial data (yr. ended 12/31/00): Grants paid, $375; assets, $12,398 (M); expenditures, $542; qualifying distributions, $375.
Limitations: Giving limited to residents of the Tannersville, NY, area.
Trustee: KeyBank, N.A.
EIN: 146014939

44651
The Cal Stepan Scholarship Fund Educational Trust
c/o Cal Stepan Vocal Competition, St. Dominic Choirs
3450 Norwood Rd.
Shaker Heights, OH 44122
Contact: Barbara Martin, Secy.-Treas.

Established in 1991 in OH.
Financial data (yr. ended 06/30/99): Grants paid, $375; assets, $25,342 (M); expenditures, $375; qualifying distributions, $375.
Limitations: Giving limited to northeastern OH.
Officers and Trustees:* David T. McNamara,* Pres.; Rita G. Kelly,* V.P.; Barbara J. Martin,* Secy.-Treas.; Rev. Martin J. Amos.
EIN: 341690879

44652
Walter & Audrey Deardoff Memorial Trust Fund
610 N. Main St.
P.O. Box 186
Springboro, OH 45066

Financial data (yr. ended 06/30/02): Grants paid, $372; assets, $750,215 (M); gifts received, $384; expenditures, $85,671; qualifying distributions, $372.
Limitations: Applications not accepted.
Application information: Contributes only to pre-selected organizations.
Trustees: Charles Maloney, James D. Ruppert, Rupert E. Ruppert.
EIN: 311118082

44653
Fred D. Hightower Family Foundation
4140 Market St.
Youngstown, OH 44512-1116

Financial data (yr. ended 12/31/01): Grants paid, $363; assets, $866 (M); expenditures, $363; qualifying distributions, $363.
Officers: Renee Fredericka, Mgr.; Keith Hightower, Mgr.; Kevin Hightower, Mgr.
Trustee: Fred D. Hightower.

EIN: 341755758

44654
Ronald W. Lochtefeld Foundation
149 W. Wayne St.
P.O. Box 83
Chickasaw, OH 45826

Established in 1999 in OH.
Donor(s): Lochtefeld Asset Management Co.
Financial data (yr. ended 12/31/99): Grants paid, $360; assets, $306,093 (M); gifts received, $308,000; expenditures, $2,412; qualifying distributions, $360.
Limitations: Applications not accepted. Giving primarily in OH.
Application information: Contributes only to pre-selected organizations.
Directors: Ronald Lochtefeld, Rosann Lochtefeld.
EIN: 364265186
Codes: CS

44655
Mollie S. Roberts Trust
c/o KeyBank, N.A.
800 Superior Ave., 4th Fl.
Cleveland, OH 44114-2601

Donor(s): Mollie S. Roberts.
Financial data (yr. ended 12/31/99): Grants paid, $355; assets, $14,447 (M); expenditures, $502; qualifying distributions, $356.
Limitations: Applications not accepted. Giving limited to Lowville, NY.
Trustee: KeyBank, N.A.
EIN: 156016723

44656
The Luciano Family Foundation
6385 Evergreen Dr.
Independence, OH 44131

Established in 1996 in OH.
Financial data (yr. ended 12/31/01): Grants paid, $350; assets, $146 (M); expenditures, $550; qualifying distributions, $350.
Limitations: Applications not accepted.
Application information: Contributes only to pre-selected organizations.
Officers: Daniel K. Luciano, Pres.; Lisa K. Luciano, V.P. and Treas.; Delores Kurtz, Secy.
EIN: 341824942

44657
David A. Moritz & Florence F. Moritz Foundation and Charitable Trust
5150 Three Village Dr., No. 2-L
Lyndhurst, OH 44124-3753

Financial data (yr. ended 12/31/01): Grants paid, $311; assets, $18,817 (M); expenditures, $589; qualifying distributions, $311.
Limitations: Applications not accepted. Giving limited to Cleveland, OH.
Application information: Contributes only to pre-selected organizations.
Trustees: Robert Katz, Florence A. Moritz, Kathleen Seitz Watson.
EIN: 346527713

44658
Mary E. Brainard Trust
7849 Valley Villas Dr.
Parma, OH 44130 (440) 845-3672
Contact: Walter A. Savage, Tr., or John M. Coyne, Tr.

Donor(s): Mary E. Brainard.‡
Financial data (yr. ended 12/31/99): Grants paid, $300; assets, $111,306 (M); expenditures, $1,134; qualifying distributions, $884.

44658—OHIO

Limitations: Giving limited to Brooklyn and Parma, OH.
Trustees: John M. Coyne, Walter A. Savage.
EIN: 346538164

44659
Robert McNeil Memorial Award Trust f/b/o Scholarship Awards
(Formerly Claude and Stefka McNeil Trust for Robert B. McNeil Memorial Award)
c/o KeyBank, N.A., Trust Div.
800 Superior Ave., 4th Fl.
Cleveland, OH 44114-2601

Financial data (yr. ended 12/31/00): Grants paid, $300; assets, $7,702 (M); expenditures, $393; qualifying distributions, $300.
Limitations: Applications not accepted. Giving limited to Copenhagen, NY.
Application information: Recipient selected from graduating class of Copenhagen High School, NY.
Trustee: KeyBank, N.A.
EIN: 166200944

44660
James L. Ruter Memorial Scholarship Fund
172 Bares Run Dr.
Loveland, OH 45140-5901

Financial data (yr. ended 12/31/01): Grants paid, $300; assets, $3,691 (M); expenditures, $300; qualifying distributions, $300.
Limitations: Applications not accepted. Giving primarily in OH.
Application information: Unsolicited requests for funds not accepted.
Trustees: Laura Ruter Antrim, Jane Harmon, Linda G. Ruter, Louis Ruter.
EIN: 311156340

44661
Francine P. and Ben H. Schwartz Foundation
c/o U.S. Bank
P.O. Box 1118
Cincinnati, OH 45201-1118

Established in 1997 in OH.
Donor(s): Isaac M. Wise Temple.
Financial data (yr. ended 12/31/01): Grants paid, $300; assets, $83,981 (M); expenditures, $1,143; qualifying distributions, $300.
Limitations: Applications not accepted. Giving primarily in Cincinnati, OH.
Application information: Contributes only to pre-selected organizations.
Trustees: Ben H. Schwartz, Francine P. Schwartz, Jane H. Schwartz, U.S. Bank.
EIN: 311532954

44662
Swayne Charitable Trust
215 Sentry Hill Dr.
Loveland, OH 45140-6659

Established in 1999 in OH.
Financial data (yr. ended 12/31/99): Grants paid, $300; assets, $1,205 (M); gifts received, $1,500; expenditures, $300; qualifying distributions, $300.
Limitations: Applications not accepted.
Application information: Contributes only to pre-selected organizations.
Directors: Charles B. Swayne III, Julianne M. Swayne.
EIN: 367288779

44663
Byron L. Tennant Memorial Fund
c/o William A. Morse
933 High St., Ste. 140
Worthington, OH 43085

Financial data (yr. ended 06/30/99): Grants paid, $300; assets, $1,776 (M); expenditures, $319; qualifying distributions, $319.
Limitations: Applications not accepted. Giving limited to Worthington, OH.
Trustee: William A. Morse.
EIN: 316102008

44664
Dr. Dominic and Helen Bitonte Family Foundation
c/o Sky Trust Co.
P.O. Box 479
Youngstown, OH 44501-0479 (330) 742-7035

Established in 2001 in OH.
Donor(s): Dominic Bitonte, Helen Bitonte.
Financial data (yr. ended 12/31/01): Grants paid, $260; assets, $320,400 (M); gifts received, $46,578; expenditures, $3,215; qualifying distributions, $1,496.
Directors: A. Gary Bitonte, M.D.; David A. Bitonte, M.D.
Trustee: Sky Trust.
EIN: 341947750

44665
Cornelia P. Day Trust for Unatego Central School District
c/o KeyBank, N.A.
800 Superior Ave., 4th Fl.
Cleveland, OH 44114

Donor(s): Cornelia P. Day.‡
Financial data (yr. ended 09/30/01): Grants paid, $260; assets, $4,763 (M); expenditures, $348; qualifying distributions, $282.
Limitations: Applications not accepted. Giving limited to Otego, NY.
Application information: Recipient chosen by faculty.
Trustee: KeyBank, N.A.
EIN: 156021233

44666
Bain Family Foundation
30651 Ainsworth Dr.
Pepper Pike, OH 44124

Established in 1994 in OH.
Donor(s): Lawrence D. Bain.
Financial data (yr. ended 12/31/01): Grants paid, $250; assets, $560 (M); expenditures, $526; qualifying distributions, $250.
Limitations: Applications not accepted.
Application information: Contributes only to pre-selected organizations.
Trustees: Kathy Bain, Lawrence D. Bain, Aaron Danzig.
EIN: 341784303

44667
The Cheeseman Family Foundation, Inc.
300 W. Main St.
Greenville, OH 45331

Established in 2000 in OH.
Donor(s): Doris M. Cheeseman.
Financial data (yr. ended 12/31/01): Grants paid, $250; assets, $4,750 (M); expenditures, $250; qualifying distributions, $250.
Limitations: Giving limited to Mercer County, OH.
Application information: Application form not required.
Trustees: Jill Bowling, John Bowling, Doris M. Cheeseman, John R. Cheeseman.
EIN: 341890064

44668
Eddie M. Cole Foundation
1117 Mackow Dr.
Toledo, OH 43607

Financial data (yr. ended 12/31/01): Grants paid, $250; assets, $6,173 (M); expenditures, $250; qualifying distributions, $250.
Officers: Eddie M. Cole, Pres.; Edrene B. Cole, Secy.-Treas.
Trustees: Edwin L. Cole, Elecia L. Smith.
EIN: 341666480

44669
McDonald Memorial Fund Trust
c/o National City Bank of Indiana
P.O. Box 94651
Cleveland, OH 44101-4651

Application address: c/o Superintendent of the Warsaw Community Schools, 1 Administrative Dr., Warsaw, IN 46580

Established in 1944 in IN.
Donor(s): Angus C. McDonald.‡
Financial data (yr. ended 12/31/01): Grants paid, $250; assets, $2,276,695 (M); expenditures, $52,978; qualifying distributions, $124,403; giving activities include $97,000 for loans to individuals.
Limitations: Giving limited to residents of Kosciusko County, IN.
Publications: Informational brochure.
Application information: Application form required.
Trustee: National City Bank of Indiana.
EIN: 356018326
Codes: GTI

44670
Mason M. Roberts Foundation
c/o National City Bank
P.O. Box 94651
Cleveland, OH 44101-4651
Contact: Margery Roberts Anderson, Trust Off., National City Bank

Financial data (yr. ended 12/31/01): Grants paid, $250; assets, $293,286 (M); expenditures, $10,595; qualifying distributions, $250.
Limitations: Giving primarily in CA.
Application information: Application form not required.
Trustee: National City Bank.
EIN: 316024937

44671
Edward D. & Ione Auer Foundation
c/o National City Bank of Indiana
P.O. Box 94651
Cleveland, OH 44101-4651
Application address: c/o National City Bank of Indiana, P.O. Box 110, Ft. Wayne, IN 46801, tel.: (219) 461-6199
Contact: Michele Delaney

Financial data (yr. ended 02/28/02): Grants paid, $234; assets, $5,060 (M); expenditures, $549; qualifying distributions, $234.
Limitations: Giving limited to Fort Wayne, IN.
Trustees: David Meyer, Gene D. Phillips, National City Bank of Indiana.
EIN: 311097946

OHIO—44686

44672
John T. Hedges & Wife Education Fund
c/o Fifth Third Bank
Dept. 00858
Cincinnati, OH 45263
Application address: c/o Fifth Third Bank of Central Kentucky, N.A., 269 W. Main St., Lexington, KY 40505, tel.: (859) 259-4999

Financial data (yr. ended 12/31/99): Grants paid, $225; assets, $71,572 (M); expenditures, $754; qualifying distributions, $343.
Limitations: Giving limited to Bourbon County, KY.
Application information: Application form required.
Trustee: Fifth Third Bank.
EIN: 616021939

44673
Tiverton Foundation
c/o P. Thomas Austin
2 Bratenahl Pl., No. 13BC
Bratenahl, OH 44108-1172

Established in 1993 in OH.
Financial data (yr. ended 12/31/00): Grants paid, $214; assets, $5,653 (M); gifts received, $1,159; expenditures, $260; qualifying distributions, $232.
Trustees: Ann H. Austin, P. Thomas Austin.
EIN: 341725763

44674
Witt Charitable Trust
4040 Resolute Cir.
Cincinnati, OH 45252

Established in 1998 in OH.
Financial data (yr. ended 12/31/00): Grants paid, $175; assets, $80,493 (M); gifts received, $48,240; expenditures, $287; qualifying distributions, $166.
Limitations: Applications not accepted.
Application information: Contributes only to pre-selected organizations.
Trustee: Ronald M. Witt.
EIN: 367244102

44675
William Furber Bean Trust
c/o KeyBank, N.A.
800 Superior Ave., 4th Fl.
Cleveland, OH 44114

Financial data (yr. ended 04/30/01): Grants paid, $150; assets, $155,744 (M); expenditures, $2,142; qualifying distributions, $150.
Limitations: Applications not accepted. Giving limited to Belfast, ME.
Application information: Contributes only to pre-selected organizations.
Trustee: KeyBank, N.A.
EIN: 016010165

44676
Gladys Wittmeyer Knox Foundation
8050 Hosbrook Rd., Ste. 210
Cincinnati, OH 45236

Established in OH in 1998.
Financial data (yr. ended 12/31/01): Grants paid, $150; assets, $663 (M); expenditures, $150; qualifying distributions, $150.
Trustee: Lewis G. Gatch.
EIN: 311550206

44677
The Margaretta B. Schuck Memorial Fund
c/o Thomas R. Schuck
425 Walnut St.
Cincinnati, OH 45202-3957

Financial data (yr. ended 12/31/01): Grants paid, $146; assets, $3,154 (M); expenditures, $150; qualifying distributions, $146.
Limitations: Giving primarily in Findlay, OH.
Trustees: Robert E. Schuck, Thomas R. Schuck, William B. Schuck.
EIN: 341616087

44678
Alpha Kappa Psi Fraternity-Alumni Chapter Scholarship Fund
(also known as Scholarship Fund-PGH Alumni Chapter 4 of Alpha Kappa Psi)
c/o National City Bank of Pennsylvania
P.O. Box 94651
Cleveland, OH 44101-4651
Application address: c/o Alpha Kappa Psi, Allegheny Bldg., 429 Forbes Ave., Ste. 500, Pittsburgh, PA 15219

Financial data (yr. ended 12/31/01): Grants paid, $127; assets, $7,411 (M); expenditures, $252; qualifying distributions, $127.
Limitations: Giving limited to western PA.
Trustee: National City Bank of Pennsylvania.
EIN: 256019630

44679
Knott Foundation
P.O. Box 599
Lima, OH 45802-0599

Established in 1986 in OH.
Donor(s): Theodore K. Knott.
Financial data (yr. ended 12/31/01): Grants paid, $125; assets, $15,917 (M); gifts received, $3,278; expenditures, $1,906; qualifying distributions, $125.
Limitations: Applications not accepted. Giving limited to Lima, OH.
Application information: Contributes only to pre-selected organizations.
Trustees: Gail Knott, Theodore K. Knott, Donald M. Lansky.
EIN: 341528562

44680
First National Foundation
P.O. Box 35913
Canton, OH 44735-5913

Established in 2000 in AZ and OH.
Donor(s): Richard D. Jones.
Financial data (yr. ended 12/31/00): Grants paid, $100; assets, $18,077 (M); gifts received, $20,000; expenditures, $2,268; qualifying distributions, $1,152.
Limitations: Applications not accepted.
Application information: Contributes only to pre-selected organizations.
Officers: Dane A. Goetz, Pres. and Treas.; Richard D. Jones, V.P. and Secy.
Director: Melinda K. Jones.
EIN: 912007691

44681
Granville Ohio Historical Society
P.O. Box 129
Granville, OH 43023

Financial data (yr. ended 12/31/99): Grants paid, $100; assets, $389,082 (M); gifts received, $3,584; expenditures, $19,829; qualifying distributions, $19,829.
Limitations: Giving limited to Granville, OH.

Application information: Application form not required.
Officers: Margaret Brooks, Pres.; Thomas B. Martin, V.P.; Charles Peterson, Secy.; David B. Neel, Treas.
Directors: Lance Clark, Cynthia Cort, Richard Daly, Florence Hoffman, John D. Kessler, Anthony Lisska, George S. Wales, Clarke Wilhelm.
EIN: 314407102

44682
Michael J. Heiman Foundation
c/o Richard I. Heiman
556 Ludlow Ave.
Cincinnati, OH 45220-1579

Established in 1997 in OH.
Financial data (yr. ended 02/28/02): Grants paid, $100; assets, $4,325 (M); expenditures, $800; qualifying distributions, $100.
Trustees: Judith Heiman McKinney, Laura B. Heiman, Richard I. Heiman.
EIN: 311516713

44683
Ralph R. McVeen Charitable Trust
c/o John D. Kedzior
6055 Rockside Woods Blvd., Ste. 200
Cleveland, OH 44131

Established in 2000 in OH.
Donor(s): Ralph R. McVeen Trust dated 5/26/98.
Financial data (yr. ended 12/31/01): Grants paid, $80; assets, $786,882 (M); gifts received, $486,535; expenditures, $10,950; qualifying distributions, $80.
Limitations: Applications not accepted.
Application information: Contributes only to pre-selected organizations.
Trustee: John D. Kedzior.
EIN: 912061487

44684
Joseph Demsey Foundation Trust
P.O. Box 22256
Cleveland, OH 44122

Established in 1997 in OH.
Donor(s): Joseph Demsey.
Financial data (yr. ended 10/31/00): Grants paid, $50; assets, $217,211 (M); expenditures, $1,251; qualifying distributions, $50.
Limitations: Applications not accepted. Giving primarily in Cleveland, OH.
Application information: Contributes only to pre-selected organizations.
Trustees: John Dempsey, Joseph Dempsey.
EIN: 237429270

44685
The Jack and Nancy Huber Family Foundation, Inc.
1237 Greenery Ln.
Cincinnati, OH 45233

Established in 2000 in OH.
Financial data (yr. ended 12/31/01): Grants paid, $50; assets, $441 (M); expenditures, $50; qualifying distributions, $50.
Officers: John R. Huber, Jr., Chair.; Jennifer T. Somers, Vice-Chair.; Lisa A. Trischler, Secy.-Treas.
EIN: 311728706

44686
Bharat Swa-Mutki Foundation
630 Dirlam Ln.
Mansfield, OH 44904-1744 (419) 756-3400
Contact: Ramesh Bellamkonda, M.D., Pres.

Established in 1989 in OH.
Donor(s): Ramesh Bellamkonda, M.D.

44686—OHIO

Financial data (yr. ended 12/31/01): Grants paid, $40; assets, $371,739 (M); expenditures, $14,080; qualifying distributions, $40.
Limitations: Giving on a national basis.
Application information: Application form not required.
Officers and Trustees:* Ramesh Bellamkonda, M.D.,* Pres. and Treas; Bradley Hostetler,* Secy.; Anand K. Pandurangi.
EIN: 341631731

44687
The Broughton Foundation
c/o George Broughton
3177 Cambridge Rd.
Marietta, OH 45750-1304

Established in 1993 in OH.
Donor(s): Carl L. Broughton.
Financial data (yr. ended 12/31/01): Grants paid, $25; assets, $1,044,767 (M); expenditures, $17,793; qualifying distributions, $10,680.
Limitations: Applications not accepted. Giving primarily in OH.
Application information: Contributes only to pre-selected organizations.
Officers: George William Broughton, Chair.; Rodney M. Collier, Vice-Chair.; Jeannette E. Fox, Secy.
Trustees: Nancy Broughton, Ruth Broughton, Samuel R. Cook, Harry Fleming, M.D., Jim Huggins, Samuel Lipscome, Mary Vituccio, Jeffrey D. Welch.
EIN: 311328628

44688
Alyce J. & Ann J. Metka Charitable Foundation
c/o Citizens National Bank
12 E. Main St.
Norwalk, OH 44857

Established in 2000 in OH.
Financial data (yr. ended 12/31/01): Grants paid, $9; assets, $2,852,104 (M); gifts received, $2,822,981; expenditures, $17,456; qualifying distributions, $9.
Trustees: Ninfa Cayayan, M.D., Brian J. Jereb, Citizens National Bank.
EIN: 912072206

44689
Roy & Fannie Adams Family Foundation
c/o U.S. Bank
P.O. Box 1118, CN-WN-06T
Cincinnati, OH 45201-1118

Established in 1998 in OH.
Financial data (yr. ended 12/31/01): Grants paid, $0; assets, $91,430 (M); expenditures, $2,588; qualifying distributions, $0.
Limitations: Applications not accepted.
Application information: Contributes only to pre-selected organizations.
Officers and Trustees:* Roy Adams,* Pres. and Treas.; Scott I. Adams,* V.P. and Secy.; Jeffrey A. Adams,* V.P.; U.S. Bank.
EIN: 311556743

44690
Aitaneet Foundation
P.O. Box 93234
Cleveland, OH 44101
Contact: Victor Shaia, Tr.

Established in 2000 in OH.
Donor(s): Mary Shaia.
Financial data (yr. ended 12/31/00): Grants paid, $0; assets, $22,836 (M); expenditures, $0; qualifying distributions, $0.
Trustees: Roger R. Abood, George Hamway, Jeanne Maroon, Dominic Najem, Victor Shaia.

EIN: 341928941

44691
The Allanwood Foundation
7 Fox Trace Ln.
Hudson, OH 44236

Established in 1993 in OH.
Donor(s): Donald M. Kurdziel, Leesa Hall Kurdziel.
Financial data (yr. ended 12/31/00): Grants paid, $0; assets, $27,682 (M); gifts received, $2,500; expenditures, $1,585; qualifying distributions, $0.
Limitations: Applications not accepted. Giving primarily in NY and OH.
Application information: Contributes only to pre-selected organizations.
Officers and Trustees:* Donald M. Kurdziel,* Pres. and Treas.; Leesa Hall Kurdziel,* V.P. and Secy.; Daniel G. Berick.
EIN: 341720923

44692
The Allen Family Foundation
2904 River Crest Cir.
Spring Valley, OH 45370

Established in 1999 in OH.
Donor(s): Larry B. Allen.
Financial data (yr. ended 12/31/99): Grants paid, $0; assets, $200,000 (L); gifts received, $200,000; expenditures, $0; qualifying distributions, $0.
Trustees: Larry B. Allen, Linda S. Allen.
EIN: 364336806

44693
Allotta Family Foundation
c/o Keybank, N.A.
P.O. Box 10
Toledo, OH 43699-0099 (419) 259-8655
Contact: Diane Ohns, Trust Off., Keybank, N.A.

Established in 2001 in OH.
Donor(s): Joseph Alotta.
Financial data (yr. ended 12/31/01): Grants paid, $0; assets, $138,214 (M); gifts received, $128,233; expenditures, $1,902; qualifying distributions, $921.
Trustee: Keybank, N.A.
EIN: 341935837

44694
Alpha Rho Foundation
1327 Ironwood Dr.
Columbus, OH 43229

Financial data (yr. ended 12/31/01): Grants paid, $0; assets, $8,942 (M); expenditures, $66; qualifying distributions, $0.
Limitations: Applications not accepted. Giving limited to Memphis, TN.
Application information: Contributes only to pre-selected organizations.
Officer: E.H. Gardner, Jr., Treas.
EIN: 316026534

44695
William L. Anderson Trust
(also known as William Anderson Trust, God's Desire for Mankind, Two Creations-Spiritually and Naturally)
c/o William L. Anderson
1013 Clifton Ave.
Springfield, OH 45505

Financial data (yr. ended 09/30/02): Grants paid, $0; assets, $2 (M); expenditures, $0; qualifying distributions, $0.
Trustee: William L. Anderson.
EIN: 311372256

44696
Father Nick Arioli C.P.P.S. Memorial Scholarship
381 Robbins Ave.
Niles, OH 44446-2407

Established in 2001 in OH.
Donor(s): Our Lady of Mt. Carmel Church.
Financial data (yr. ended 12/31/01): Grants paid, $0; assets, $28,831 (M); gifts received, $29,525; expenditures, $50; qualifying distributions, $0.
Limitations: Applications not accepted.
Application information: Contributes only to pre-selected organizations.
Trustees: Ronald Aulet, James Pipino, John Trimbur.
EIN: 341945223

44697
The Roberta and Roger Arling Foundation
6456 W. Fork Rd.
Cincinnati, OH 45247-5706

Established in 1999 in OH.
Donor(s): Roger R. Arling, Roberta W. Arling.
Financial data (yr. ended 12/31/01): Grants paid, $0; assets, $30,694 (M); expenditures, $3,900; qualifying distributions, $0.
Limitations: Applications not accepted. Giving primarily in OH.
Application information: Contributes only to pre-selected organizations.
Trustees: Roberta W. Arling, Roger R. Arling, Stephen W. Arling.
EIN: 311653037

44698
Marion C. and Walter K. Bailey Foundation
3900 Key Ctr.
127 Public Sq.
Cleveland, OH 44114-1216

Established around 1969 in OH.
Donor(s): Walter K. Bailey.
Financial data (yr. ended 12/31/00): Grants paid, $0; assets, $47,401 (M); expenditures, $1,348; qualifying distributions, $0.
Limitations: Applications not accepted. Giving limited to Cleveland, OH.
Application information: Contributes only to pre-selected organizations.
Officers: Richard C. Bailey, Pres.; Robert A. Bailey, V.P.; David B. Bailey, Secy.-Treas.
EIN: 237058592

44699
The Baker & Hostetler Foundation
c/o Christopher J. Swift
1900 E. 9th St., Ste. 3200
Cleveland, OH 44114-3485

Established in 1999 in OH.
Financial data (yr. ended 12/31/00): Grants paid, $0; assets, $4,000 (M); gifts received, $533; expenditures, $533; qualifying distributions, $533.
Limitations: Applications not accepted.
Application information: Contributes only to pre-selected organizations.
Officers and Trustees:* Gary L. Bryenton,* Pres.; Albert T. Adams,* V.P.; Kenneth F. Snyder,* Secy.-Treas.
EIN: 341908798

44700
Margaret E. Baker Foundation
c/o Huntington Bank
P.O. Box 1558
Columbus, OH 43216

Established in 2001 in OH.
Donor(s): Jessie Foos Baker Foundation.

Financial data (yr. ended 12/31/01): Grants paid, $0; assets, $3,238,840 (M); gifts received, $2,834,683; expenditures, $0; qualifying distributions, $0.
Limitations: Applications not accepted.
Application information: Contributes only to pre-selected organizations.
Trustee: James M. Buskirk.
EIN: 316665597

44701
Balch Family Foundation, Inc.
27007 Wolf Rd.
Bay Village, OH 44140
Contact: John A. Balch, Pres.

Established in 1994 in OH.
Financial data (yr. ended 12/31/99): Grants paid, $0; assets, $143,965 (M); gifts received, $100; expenditures, $126; qualifying distributions, $0.
Limitations: Giving primarily in Oxford, OH.
Application information: Application form not required.
Officers and Trustees:* John A. Balch,* Pres.; Carol A. Balch,* Secy.; Andrew Balch, Charles Balch, Wendy Fortunato.
EIN: 341725013

44702
J. J. Bangert for Pre-Mature Nursery
(Formerly John J. Bangert Charitable Trust)
c/o National City Bank of Pennsylvania
P.O. Box 94651
Cleveland, OH 44101-4651

Financial data (yr. ended 06/30/02): Grants paid, $0; assets, $1,250 (M); expenditures, $1,202; qualifying distributions, $0.
Limitations: Applications not accepted. Giving limited to McKeesport, PA.
Application information: Contributes only to pre-selected organizations.
Trustee: National City Bank of Pennsylvania.
EIN: 256106296

44703
Frank J. and Mary Louise Beshara Family Foundation
4137 Boardman-Canfield Rd.
Canfield, OH 44406

Established in 2001 in OH.
Financial data (yr. ended 12/31/01): Grants paid, $0; assets, $563 (M); gifts received, $1,000; expenditures, $450; qualifying distributions, $225.
Directors: Frank J. Beshara, Helen Beshara, Patrick A. Sebastiano.
Trustee: Sky Trust, N.A.
EIN: 347140002

44704
The Beta Foundation
4040 Embassy Pkwy., Ste. 100
Akron, OH 44333 (330) 668-6500
Contact: Alan J. Tobin

Established in 1999 in OH.
Donor(s): Richard W. Sankey.
Financial data (yr. ended 12/31/01): Grants paid, $0; assets, $1,667 (M); gifts received, $1,000; expenditures, $42; qualifying distributions, $0.
Trustees: Dorothy K. Sankey, James K. Sankey, Richard W. Sankey.
EIN: 341896585

44705
Better Business Bureau of Greater Cleveland Foundation, Inc.
2217 E. 9th St., Ste. 200
Cleveland, OH 44115-1299

Financial data (yr. ended 12/31/01): Grants paid, $0; assets, $9,238 (M); gifts received, $15,892; expenditures, $18,422; qualifying distributions, $0.
Officer: David Weiss, Pres.
EIN: 237107110

44706
Hyman Blaushild Charitable Foundation, Inc.
P.O. Box 1889
Akron, OH 44309

Financial data (yr. ended 12/31/01): Grants paid, $0; assets, $7,313 (M); expenditures, $7; qualifying distributions, $0.
Limitations: Applications not accepted. Giving primarily in OH.
Application information: Contributes only to pre-selected organizations.
Officer: Marc S. Weisman, Mgr.
EIN: 346570318

44707
Brauning-Sammons Trust
c/o First Financial Svcs. Group, N.A.
P.O. Box 2307
Zanesville, OH 43702-2307

Financial data (yr. ended 12/31/99): Grants paid, $0; assets, $73,813 (M); expenditures, $1,003; qualifying distributions, $114.
Limitations: Giving limited to Zanesville, OH.
Application information: Application form required.
Trustee: First Financial Services Group, N.A.
EIN: 316183352

44708
Leo J. and Marian F. Breslin Foundation
c/o James H. Smith
312 Walnut St., Ste. 2300
Cincinnati, OH 45202
Contact: Mary Leocadia Bien, V.P.

Established in 2000 in OH.
Financial data (yr. ended 12/31/01): Grants paid, $0; assets, $204,709 (M); gifts received, $550; expenditures, $923; qualifying distributions, $0.
Limitations: Giving primarily in OH.
Officers and Trustees:* Marian F. Breslin,* Pres.; Mary Leocadia Bien,* V.P.; Daniel L. Breslin,* V.P.; Patrick T. Breslin,* V.P.; Margaret Breslin Muething,* V.P.; Mary Christina Schroeder,* V.P.; Mary Elizabeth Stachura,* V.P.; Kevin J. Breslin,* Secy.-Treas.
EIN: 311702770

44709
Bring Out Your Best, Inc.
P.O. Box 3303
Dublin, OH 43016

Established in 2000 in OH.
Financial data (yr. ended 12/31/00): Grants paid, $0; assets, $51,411 (M); gifts received, $50,000; expenditures, $0; qualifying distributions, $0.
Limitations: Applications not accepted.
Application information: Contributes only to pre-selected organizations.
Officer and Directors:* Dannie Mayes,* Treas.; Lynn Elliot, Robert Parrett.
EIN: 311745325

44710
Richard C. & Rosemary E. Bucher, Sr. Family Foundation
5771 Beechgrove Ln.
Cincinnati, OH 45233

Established in 1997 in OH.
Financial data (yr. ended 12/31/01): Grants paid, $0; assets, $375 (M); expenditures, $298; qualifying distributions, $0.
Limitations: Giving primarily in Louisa, KY, and Cincinnati, OH.
Officer: Richard C. Bucher, Mgr.
EIN: 311532262

44711
Joseph M. Budzar Ministries, Inc.
17835 Lake Rd.
Lakewood, OH 44107-1052
Contact: Joseph Budzar, Dir.

Donor(s): Joseph Budzar.
Financial data (yr. ended 06/30/01): Grants paid, $0; assets, $530 (M); gifts received, $508; expenditures, $7,147; qualifying distributions, $7,147; giving activities include $6,003 for programs.
Director: Joseph Budzar.
EIN: 341758247

44712
Robert Buechner Foundation
105 E. 4th St., Ste. 300
Cincinnati, OH 45202-4057

Established in 1986 in OH.
Donor(s): Robert Buechner.
Financial data (yr. ended 12/31/00): Grants paid, $0; assets, $4,350 (M); expenditures, $55; qualifying distributions, $0.
Limitations: Applications not accepted.
Application information: Contributes only to pre-selected organizations.
Officers: Robert W. Buechner, Pres. and Treas.; Francis X. Marnell, V.P. and Secy.
EIN: 311054410

44713
Ed and Olive Bushby Scholarship Fund
c/o Keybank, N.A.
800 Superior Ave., 4th Fl.
Cleveland, OH 44114

Established in 2001 in OR.
Donor(s): Ed & Olive Bushby Trust.
Financial data (yr. ended 12/31/01): Grants paid, $0; assets, $273,386 (M); gifts received, $294,766; expenditures, $0; qualifying distributions, $0.
Limitations: Applications not accepted.
Application information: Contributes only to pre-selected organizations.
Trustee: KeyBank, N.A.
EIN: 866313757

44714
Cairns Family Foundation
c/o J. Donald Cairns
2000 Huntington Bldg.
Cleveland, OH 44115

Donor(s): J. Donald Cairns, Charles E. Cairns.
Financial data (yr. ended 12/31/01): Grants paid, $0; assets, $7,197 (M); expenditures, $1,443; qualifying distributions, $0.
Limitations: Applications not accepted. Giving primarily in Urbana, IL, and Cleveland, OH.
Application information: Contributes only to pre-selected organizations.
Officers and Trustees:* Charles E. Cairns,* V.P.; J. Donald Cairns,* Secy.-Treas.

EIN: 341421719

44715
J. K. Caldwell Charitable Trust
c/o Bank One Trust Co., N.A.
774 Park Meadow Rd.
Westerville, OH 43081

Established in 1995 in KY.
Donor(s): Jane Caldwell.‡
Financial data (yr. ended 12/31/99): Grants paid, $0; assets, $601,575 (M); expenditures, $10,818; qualifying distributions, $269.
Limitations: Applications not accepted. Giving primarily in Louisville, KY.
Application information: Contributes only to pre-selected organizations.
Trustee: Bank One Trust Co., N.A.
EIN: 610985455

44716
Joel and Joy Campbell Family Foundation
9385 White Rose Ct.
Loveland, OH 45140-7403

Established in 2000 in OH.
Donor(s): Joel B. Campbell, Joy M. Campbell.
Financial data (yr. ended 12/31/00): Grants paid, $0; assets, $528,630 (M); gifts received, $527,158; expenditures, $0; qualifying distributions, $0.
Limitations: Applications not accepted.
Application information: Contributes only to pre-selected organizations.
Officers and Trustees:* Joel B. Campbell III,* Pres.; Mike Canterbury,* V.P.; Joy M. Campbell,* Secy.-Treas.
EIN: 311745762

44717
Cardinal Health Foundation
7000 Cardinal Pl.
Dublin, OH 43017 (614) 757-7481
Contact: Debra Hadley

Established in 2000 in OH.
Donor(s): The Baxter Allegiance Foundation.
Financial data (yr. ended 06/30/01): Grants paid, $0; assets, $20,414,015 (M); gifts received, $20,231,348; expenditures, $0; qualifying distributions, $0.
Application information: Application form not required.
Trustees: Amy B. Haynes, John Jackson, Aneezal Mohamed, Paul S. Williams.
EIN: 311746458
Codes: CS

44718
The Marie S. Carroll Foundation
2986 Harriet Rd.
Silver Lake, OH 44224

Established in 2000 in OH.
Donor(s): Marie S. Carroll.
Financial data (yr. ended 11/30/01): Grants paid, $0; assets, $14,919 (M); gifts received, $11,825; expenditures, $0; qualifying distributions, $0.
Trustees: Marie S. Carroll, Ralph C. Huff.
EIN: 341944957

44719
The Cavalena Foundation
726 Sixteenth St., N.E.
Massillon, OH 44646-4839

Established in 2000 in OH.
Donor(s): Larry L. Cavalena.
Financial data (yr. ended 06/30/01): Grants paid, $0; assets, $1,001 (M); gifts received, $1,000; expenditures, $13; qualifying distributions, $0.
Trustees: Larry L. Cavalena, Ralph C. Huff.

EIN: 341936527

44720
Cefalu Charitable Trust
4930 Leffingwell Rd.
Canfield, OH 44406

Established in 1998 in OH.
Financial data (yr. ended 12/31/99): Grants paid, $0; assets, $4,385 (L); expenditures, $0; qualifying distributions, $0.
Limitations: Applications not accepted.
Application information: Contributes only to pre-selected organizations.
Trustees: Janis Cefalu, Vincenzo Cefalu.
EIN: 316558004

44721
Christian Book Summaries, Inc.
30680 Bainbridge Rd.
Solon, OH 44139-2232

Established in 2001 in OH.
Donor(s): David A. Martin.
Financial data (yr. ended 12/31/01): Grants paid, $0; assets, $1,100 (M); gifts received, $33,759; expenditures, $32,787; qualifying distributions, $32,311; giving activities include $32,311 for programs.
Officer: David A. Martin, Pres.
EIN: 341951615

44722
Ken Cleveland Foundation
c/o FirstMerit Bank, N.A.
P.O. Box 725
Medina, OH 44258
Application address: 105 W. Liberty, Medina, OH 44256
Contact: Robert Bux, Mgr.

Established in 1997 in OH.
Donor(s): Ken Cleveland.
Financial data (yr. ended 12/31/01): Grants paid, $0; assets, $163,814 (M); expenditures, $2,848; qualifying distributions, $0.
Limitations: Giving primarily in OH.
Officers: Robert Bux, Mgr.; Les Fuller, Mgr.; George Matsko, Mgr.
Trustee: FirstMerit Bank, N.A.
EIN: 316567861

44723
Cleveland Indians Charities, Inc.
c/o Jacobs Field
2401 Ontario St.
Cleveland, OH 44115

Established in 1989.
Donor(s): Huntington Banks, McDonald Investments, Inc.
Financial data (yr. ended 12/31/00): Grants paid, $0; assets, $295,734 (M); expenditures, $2,867; qualifying distributions, $0; giving activities include $1,171 for programs.
Limitations: Applications not accepted. Giving limited to Cleveland, OH.
Application information: Contributes only to pre-selected organizations.
Officers and Trustees:* Robert A. DiBiasio,* Pres.; Allen Davis, V.P.; Valerie K. Arcuri, Secy.; Kenneth E. Stefanov,* Treas.; E. Dennis Lehman, Mark Shapiro, Jon Starrett.
EIN: 341618536
Codes: CS, CD

44724
Community Design, Inc.
35 N. College St.
Athens, OH 45701-2529

Financial data (yr. ended 12/31/01): Grants paid, $0; assets, $5,729 (M); expenditures, $17; qualifying distributions, $0.
Limitations: Giving primarily in OH.
Application information: Application form not required.
Officers: Keith Chapman, Chair.; John Valentour, Secy.; Cherie Gall, Treas.
EIN: 310915640

44725
Community Foundation of the Mahoning Valley
P.O. Box 44
Youngstown, OH 44501

Financial data (yr. ended 06/30/00): Grants paid, $0; assets, $42,455 (M); gifts received, $46,236; expenditures, $3,954.
Limitations: Giving limited to Mahoning Valley, OH.
Officers: Franklin S. Bennet, Jr., Chair.; Donald Cagigas, Vice-Chair.; Janice E. Strasfeld, Secy.; Frank Dixon, Treas.
Directors: William J. Bresnahan, Delores J. Crawford, Earnest Perry, John L. Pogue, William R. Powell.
EIN: 341904353
Codes: CM

44726
Consortium for Health Education in Southeastern Ohio
P.O. Box 825
Athens, OH 45701

Financial data (yr. ended 08/31/01): Grants paid, $0; assets, $28,990 (M); expenditures, $700; qualifying distributions, $0.
Limitations: Applications not accepted. Giving primarily in southeastern OH.
Officer: Kay Hughes, Records Mgr.
Director: Margo Marozon.
EIN: 310864288

44727
Kathleen Constantini Charitable Foundation
272 N. Bayshore Dr.
Columbiana, OH 44408

Established in 2000 in OH.
Financial data (yr. ended 12/31/00): Grants paid, $0; assets, $1,035 (M); gifts received, $1,000; expenditures, $0; qualifying distributions, $0.
Trustee: Kathleen M. Constantini.
EIN: 347117779

44728
The Cooperative Service League
85 Waters Way
Hamilton, OH 45013
Contact: Eula Martin

Financial data (yr. ended 05/31/02): Grants paid, $0; assets, $96,190 (M); expenditures, $19,082; qualifying distributions, $0.
Officers: Audria Bibelhausen, Pres.; Roselyn Bucher, Treas.
EIN: 316049770

44729
Evan R. & Barbara P. Corns Foundation
3681 Greenwood Dr.
Pepper Pike, OH 44124

Established in 2001 in OH.
Donor(s): Doris Corns.‡

Financial data (yr. ended 12/31/01): Grants paid, $0; assets, $390,213 (M); gifts received, $425,000; expenditures, $415; qualifying distributions, $0.
Limitations: Applications not accepted.
Application information: Contributes only to pre-selected organizations.
Officer: Barbara P. Corns, Pres.
Directors: Evan R. Corns, Nancy Corns, Andrea Hill, Kathryn Walker.
EIN: 341900160

44730
Albert L. Coughlin, Sr. & Lois J. Coughlin Family Foundation
1756 Strathshire Hall Pl.
Powell, OH 43065

Established in 1999 in OH.
Donor(s): Albert L. Coughlin, Lois J. Coughlin.
Financial data (yr. ended 12/31/01): Grants paid, $0; assets, $40,305 (M); expenditures, $0; qualifying distributions, $0.
Limitations: Applications not accepted.
Application information: Contributes only to pre-selected organizations.
Directors: Albert L. Coughlin, Sr., Lois J. Coughlin.
EIN: 311682639

44731
The Countryside Foundation
5400 Silbury Ln.
Dayton, OH 45429-2052

Established in 2000 in OH.
Donor(s): Thomas Owen Stolz.‡
Financial data (yr. ended 12/31/01): Grants paid, $0; assets, $196,236 (M); expenditures, $0; qualifying distributions, $0.
Trustees: Willis H. Frazee, Jr., Jack Savage.
EIN: 311706397

44732
Creston Historical Society
P.O. Box 1113
Creston, OH 44217
Application address: 176 S. Main St., Creston, OH 44217, tel.: (330) 435-6796
Contact: Kathleen Slater, Secy.

Established in 1990 in OH; funded in 1995.
Financial data (yr. ended 12/31/00): Grants paid, $0; assets, $18,517 (M); expenditures, $1,327; qualifying distributions, $0; giving activities include $1,312 for programs.
Limitations: Giving limited to Creston, OH.
Officers: David E. McIlvaine, Pres.; Kathleen Slater, Secy.; Charles E. Stebbins, Treas.
EIN: 341415308

44733
The Daberko Charitable Foundation
c/o Sterling
3550 Lander Rd.
Pepper Pike, OH 44124

Established in 2001 in OH.
Donor(s): David A. Daberko.
Financial data (yr. ended 12/31/01): Grants paid, $0; assets, $152,604 (M); gifts received, $152,029; expenditures, $0; qualifying distributions, $0.
Limitations: Applications not accepted.
Application information: Contributes only to pre-selected organizations.
Trustees: David A. Daberko, Deborah L. Daberko.
EIN: 020533614

44734
Davis Charitable Trust
2936 Stone Mill Ct.
Beavercreek, OH 45434

Established in 1997 in OH.
Financial data (yr. ended 12/31/99): Grants paid, $0; assets, $143,571 (L); expenditures, $0; qualifying distributions, $0.
Limitations: Applications not accepted.
Application information: Contributes only to pre-selected organizations.
Trustees: Jeffrey W. Davis, Laura K. Davis.
EIN: 316587917

44735
The DeGenhart Paperweight and Glass Museum, Inc.
P.O. Box 186
Cambridge, OH 43725-0186

Financial data (yr. ended 03/31/01): Grants paid, $0; assets, $1,020,384 (M); expenditures, $84,692; qualifying distributions, $35,001; giving activities include $35,297 for programs.
Limitations: Applications not accepted.
Application information: Contributes only to pre-selected organizations.
Officers: James A. Caldwell, Pres.; Mary Jackson, Secy.; George S. Garrett, Treas.
Trustees: Richard Degenhart, Joyce Galieti, Val Galieti, and 10 additional trustees.
EIN: 310957101

44736
Thomas M. DeMange Charitable Trust
6710 Pinewood Pl.
Dayton, OH 45459

Established in 1999 in OH.
Financial data (yr. ended 12/31/99): Grants paid, $0; assets, $1,686 (M); gifts received, $1,686; expenditures, $0; qualifying distributions, $0.
Limitations: Applications not accepted.
Application information: Contributes only to pre-selected organizations.
Trustee: Thomas M. DeMange.
EIN: 311583404

44737
The DVI Foundation
c/o Richard A. Cooper
25 W. Prospect Ave.
Cleveland, OH 44115-1048

Established in OH in 1997.
Donor(s): Michael Knoblauch, Mark A. Hauseman.
Financial data (yr. ended 12/31/00): Grants paid, $0; assets, $13,245 (M); gifts received, $500; expenditures, $2,195; qualifying distributions, $2,195.
Limitations: Applications not accepted.
Officers: Michael Knoblauch, Pres.; Mark A. Hauserman, V.P. and Treas.; Richard A. Cooper, Secy.
EIN: 341852726

44738
The Eagle Foundation
76 Orchard Ln.
P.O. Box 1486
Piqua, OH 45356 (937) 773-5649
Contact: Charles W. Lucas, Tr.

Established in 2000 in OH.
Financial data (yr. ended 12/31/00): Grants paid, $0; assets, $5,017 (M); gifts received, $5,000; expenditures, $0; qualifying distributions, $0.
Trustees: Charles W. Lucas, Joann Lucas.
EIN: 311728896

44739
East Liverpool Historical Society
P.O. Box 476
East Liverpool, OH 43920

Established in 1993.
Financial data (yr. ended 12/31/99): Grants paid, $0; assets, $305,633 (M); gifts received, $17,524; expenditures, $10,268; qualifying distributions, $10,032; giving activities include $10,032 for programs.
Officers: Tim Brookes, Pres.; Joan Witt, V.P.; Linda Doak, Secy.; Dick Thompson, Treas.
Trustees: Don Baxter, Charles Brookes, Esther Lanam, Maria Potts, Glenn Waight.
EIN: 346543384

44740
Elizabeth Foundation
52 E. Gay St.
P.O. Box 100B
Columbus, OH 43216-1008

Established in 2001 in OH.
Donor(s): Marcia Ross Blackburn.
Financial data (yr. ended 12/31/01): Grants paid, $0; assets, $273,088 (M); gifts received, $25,067; expenditures, $0; qualifying distributions, $0.
Limitations: Applications not accepted.
Application information: Contributes only to pre-selected organizations.
Officers and Directors:* Marcia Ross Blackburn,* Pres. and Treas.; Katherine Blackburn Reay,* Secy.; William W. Blackburn II,* Treas.; Elizabeth Louise Blackburn, William Ross Blackburn.
EIN: 311796184

44741
The Energetic Foundation
6727 Eastgate Dr.
Mayfield Heights, OH 44124

Established in 2001 in OH.
Donor(s): Team Energetics, LLC.
Financial data (yr. ended 12/31/01): Grants paid, $0; assets, $3,195 (M); gifts received, $15,000; expenditures, $14,720; qualifying distributions, $0; giving activities include $14,720 for programs.
Director: Robert Kaleal III.
EIN: 341920340

44742
Paul B. Evers Trust
c/o David L. Pendry
133 E. Market St.
Xenia, OH 45385-3110
Application address: c/o Vicki Huff, Xenia High School, 303 Kinsey Rd., Xenia, OH 45385, tel.: (937) 372-6983

Financial data (yr. ended 12/31/01): Grants paid, $0; assets, $250,630 (M); expenditures, $5,647; qualifying distributions, $5,647; giving activities include $13,328 for loans to individuals.
Limitations: Giving limited to residents of Xenia, OH.
Application information: Application form required.
Trustee: David L. Pendry.
EIN: 316120701
Codes: GTI

44743
The Foundation for Appalachian Ohio
36 Public Sq.
P.O. Box 456
Nelsonville, OH 45764 (740) 753-1111
FAX: (740) 753-3333; E-mail:
info@appalachianohio.org; URL: http://
www.appalachianohio.org

Established in 1998 in OH.
Financial data (yr. ended 09/30/99): Grants paid, $0; assets, $96,175 (L); gifts received, $215,110; expenditures, $119,370.
Limitations: Giving limited to the 29 counties of Appalachian OH.
Application information: See foundation Web site for full application guidelines and requirements.
Officers and Board Members:* Roger McCauley, Chair.; Robert E. Evans,* Vice-Chair.; Leslie Lilly, C.E.O. and Pres.; Joy Padgett,* Secy.; Dean Schooler,* Treas.; David Bergholz, Susan Henderson, Marianne Campbell Holzer, John Hoopingarner, Rachel Longaberger, Carla Lowry, Carol Mackey, Barbara Ross-Lee, Victor L. Shaffer, Wayne F. White, David Wilhelm.
EIN: 311620483
Codes: CM

44744
Fowler Center for Wildlife Education, Inc.
10619 Mason Rd.
Berlin Heights, OH 44814

Established in 1999 in GA.
Financial data (yr. ended 12/31/99): Grants paid, $0; assets, $183,040 (M); expenditures, $113; qualifying distributions, $0.
Officers: James Fowler, Chair.; William D. Roose, Vice-Chair.; Sharon Roose, Secy.
Directors: Carey Burnett, Han C. Choi.
EIN: 351631285

44745
Free Hand, Inc.
9325 Progress Pkwy.
Mentor, OH 44060 (440) 639-9100
Contact: Jack Zaback, Pres.

Established in 2001 in OH.
Donor(s): Timothy F. McCarthy, Alice B. McCarthy.
Financial data (yr. ended 12/31/01): Grants paid, $0; assets, $250,000 (M); gifts received, $250,000; expenditures, $0; qualifying distributions, $0.
Officers: Jack Zaback, Pres.; Alice B. McCarthy, V.P.; Fr. Norman Smith, Secy.-Treas.
EIN: 341973248

44746
The Friendship Association of Students and Scholars from Peoples Republic of China at University of Cincinnati, Inc.
1224 East Hoewisher Rd.
Sidney, OH 45365 (937) 498-6922
Contact: Shu An

Established in 1997 in OH.
Financial data (yr. ended 12/31/00): Grants paid, $0; assets, $49,160 (M); expenditures, $844; qualifying distributions, $0.
Limitations: Giving primarily in OH.
Application information: Application form required.
Trustees: Ligun Cao, Xuelong Cao, Honghu Chen, Haiou Yao.
EIN: 311307723

44747
Fritz Foundation
c/o Fifth Third Bank
Trust Tax Dept., MD 1COM31
Cincinnati, OH 45263

Financial data (yr. ended 12/31/01): Grants paid, $0; assets, $60,977 (M); expenditures, $2,209; qualifying distributions, $638.
Limitations: Applications not accepted. Giving primarily in Evansville, IN.
Application information: Contributes only to pre-selected organizations.
Trustee: Civitas Bank.
EIN: 356259155

44748
Gastroenterology Consultants of Greater Cincinnati Education Foundation
10600 Montgomery Rd., Ste. 100
Cincinnati, OH 45242

Established in 2000 in OH.
Financial data (yr. ended 12/31/01): Grants paid, $0; assets, $7,890 (M); gifts received, $7,550; expenditures, $5,663; qualifying distributions, $0.
Limitations: Applications not accepted.
Application information: Contributes only to pre-selected organizations.
Officers: Allan L. Peck, M.D., Pres. and Treas.; Nav K. Grandhi, M.D., V.P. and Secy.; Tario Shakor, M.D., V.P.
EIN: 311709920

44749
The Erwin & Katherine Geis Charitable Foundation
10020 Aurora Hudson Rd.
Streetsboro, OH 44241-1621

Established in 2001 in OH.
Donor(s): Katherine Geis.
Financial data (yr. ended 12/31/01): Grants paid, $0; assets, $50,459 (M); gifts received, $50,091; expenditures, $0; qualifying distributions, $0.
Trustees: Mark Brenneman, Erwin Geis, Katherine Geis, James Mirgliotta.
EIN: 912127296

44750
The David & Anne Genshaft Foundation, Inc.
P.O. Box 24040
Mayfield Heights, OH 44124-0040
Contact: David Genshaft, Pres.

Established in 1988 in OH.
Donor(s): David Genshaft.
Financial data (yr. ended 12/31/01): Grants paid, $0; assets, $182,442 (M); expenditures, $0; qualifying distributions, $0.
Officer: David Genshaft, Pres.
EIN: 341326583

44751
Adolphe & Antoinette Gingras Scholarship Trust
c/o KeyBank, N.A., Trust Div.
800 Superior Ave., 4th Fl.
Cleveland, OH 44114
Application address: c/o Rector, St. Augustine's Church, Augusta, ME 04330

Financial data (yr. ended 04/30/01): Grants paid, $0; assets, $27,725 (M); expenditures, $324; qualifying distributions, $0.
Limitations: Giving limited to Augusta, ME.
Trustee: KeyBank, N.A.
EIN: 016019700

44752
Duke Goldberg Family Foundation
c/o Michael Goldberg
3949 Business Park
Columbus, OH 43204

Donor(s): Michael Goldberg.
Financial data (yr. ended 12/31/01): Grants paid, $0; assets, $2,975 (M); expenditures, $223; qualifying distributions, $0.
Limitations: Applications not accepted. Giving primarily in Columbus, OH.
Application information: Contributes only to pre-selected organizations.
Trustees: Michael Goldberg, Dean Schulman, A.C. Strip.
EIN: 311362373

44753
Frank J. Grabill Trust
Foulke Block, Rm. 2
Chillicothe, OH 45601 (740) 774-6152
Contact: Robert C. Hess, Tr.

Established in 1995 in OH.
Financial data (yr. ended 12/31/00): Grants paid, $0; assets, $40,505 (M); expenditures, $829; qualifying distributions, $0; giving activities include $1,500 for loans to individuals.
Limitations: Giving limited to residents of Ross County, OH.
Application information: Application form required.
Trustees: Joseph C. Bennett, M.D., Robert C. Hess, Bambi Huffman, R.N.
EIN: 316243512

44754
GSS Endowment
132 W. 2nd St., Ste. A
Perrysburg, OH 43551

Established in 2001 in OH.
Donor(s): George S. Stranahan.
Financial data (yr. ended 12/31/01): Grants paid, $0; assets, $1,519,813 (M); gifts received, $1,550,000; expenditures, $15; qualifying distributions, $0.
Limitations: Applications not accepted.
Application information: Contributes only to pre-selected organizations.
Advisory Committee Members: Michael McVoy, George S. Stranahan.
Trustee: Thomas Dykstra.
EIN: 347144648

44755
The George Guckenberger Family Private Foundation
15 W. Central Pkwy.
Cincinnati, OH 45202

Established in 1998 in OH.
Donor(s): George Guckenberger III.
Financial data (yr. ended 12/31/01): Grants paid, $0; assets, $9,074 (M); expenditures, $409; qualifying distributions, $0.
Limitations: Applications not accepted. Giving primarily in OH.
Application information: Contributes only to pre-selected organizations.
Officers and Trustees:* George Guckenberger III,* Pres.; George Guckenberger,* V.P.; Wayne Guckenberger,* Secy.-Treas.
EIN: 311532253

44756
H.O.W. Incorporated
2434 Sylvania Ave.
Toledo, OH 43613-4431

Established in 1995 in OH.
Financial data (yr. ended 12/31/01): Grants paid, $0; assets, $46,673 (M); gifts received, $74,690; expenditures, $59,111; qualifying distributions, $0.
Officers: Tom Sallah, Chair. and Pres.; Jennifer Franco, Vice-Chair.; Michelle Woda, Secy.; Roger Davenport, Treas.
Trustee: Steve Shaw.
EIN: 341634872

44757
Robert C. Hammer Memorial Scholarship Fund
c/o Fifth Third Bank
P.O. Box 630858, Dept. 00858
Cincinnati, OH 45263

Financial data (yr. ended 04/30/02): Grants paid, $0; assets, $12,306 (M); expenditures, $133; qualifying distributions, $0.
Limitations: Giving limited to OH.
Application information: Application form not required.
Trustee: Fifth Third Bank.
EIN: 311004410

44758
Harmony Project
3950 Rose Hill Ave.
Cincinnati, OH 45229
Contact: Judith Harmony, Pres.

Established in 2001 in OH.
Donor(s): Richard Jackson.
Financial data (yr. ended 12/31/01): Grants paid, $0; assets, $721,350 (M); gifts received, $724,500; expenditures, $0; qualifying distributions, $0.
Officers: Judith Harmony, Pres.; Richard L. Jackson, Secy.-Treas.
Director: Walter M. Lovenberg.
EIN: 311811562

44759
The Robert E. and Glenna J. Harmuth Family Foundation, Inc.
301 Windhaven Ct.
Englewood, OH 45322 (937) 836-1296
Contact: Glenna J. Harmuth, Chair.

Established in 2001 in OH.
Donor(s): Glenna J. Harmuth.
Financial data (yr. ended 12/31/01): Grants paid, $0; assets, $102,817 (M); gifts received, $105,000; expenditures, $2,325; qualifying distributions, $0.
Application information: Application form not required.
Officers and Directors:* Glenna J. Harmuth,* Chair. and Pres.; Karen Stevens,* V.P.; Laura Hazen,* Secy.; Louise M. Johnson,* Treas.; Michael R. Goldshot, Darrell L. Murphy.
EIN: 311799578

44760
Hellenic Heritage Foundation
7378 Earlsford Dr.
Dublin, OH 43017

Financial data (yr. ended 12/31/01): Grants paid, $0; assets, $3,318 (M); gifts received, $105; expenditures, $1,145; qualifying distributions, $0.
Limitations: Applications not accepted.
Application information: Contributes only to pre-selected organizations.
Officer: Helen Theodotou, Pres.
EIN: 311319158

44761
Louise McCarren Herring Foundation
c/o Curtis L. Robson
5656 Frantz Rd.
Dublin, OH 43017 (614) 764-1900
Contact: Dennis R. Adams

Established in 1989 in OH.
Financial data (yr. ended 12/31/00): Grants paid, $0; assets, $8,996 (M); expenditures, $1; qualifying distributions, $0.
Limitations: Giving on a national basis.
Application information: Application form required.
Trustees: Jose R. Alonzo, Peter Corrigan, William A. Herring.
EIN: 311277811

44762
Hershey Foundation for the Study of Aging Systems
726 Lafayette Ave.
Cincinnati, OH 45220-1053 (513) 751-2723
Contact: Daniel Hershey, Pres.

Established in 1999 in OH.
Donor(s): Daniel Hershey.
Financial data (yr. ended 12/31/01): Grants paid, $0; assets, $36,623 (M); gifts received, $30,000; expenditures, $12,210; qualifying distributions, $0.
Officers: Daniel Hershey, Pres.; Andrea Hershey, V.P.
Trustee: Michael Hershey.
EIN: 311678917

44763
J. & K. Higgins Charitable Trust
601 Traverse Creek Dr.
Milford, OH 45150

Established in 1996 in OH.
Financial data (yr. ended 12/31/99): Grants paid, $0; assets, $38,406 (L); expenditures, $0; qualifying distributions, $0.
Limitations: Applications not accepted.
Application information: Contributes only to pre-selected organizations.
Trustees: Jerome Higgins, Karen Higgins.
EIN: 316542314

44764
Wilson Hirschfeld Fund
c/o Orley R. Bosworth
21861 Winstead Rd., Rm. 509
Circleville, OH 43113

Financial data (yr. ended 12/31/01): Grants paid, $0; assets, $4,338 (M); gifts received, $4; expenditures, $4; qualifying distributions, $0.
Limitations: Applications not accepted.
Trustees: Orley R. Bosworth, Carla Hirshfeld, Richard Zimmerman.
EIN: 310904717

44765
Hit Two Foundation
c/o Key Bank, N.A.
800 Superior Ave., Ste. 1400
Cleveland, OH 44114

Established in 2001 in OH.
Donor(s): Andrea Thome, James Thome.
Financial data (yr. ended 12/31/01): Grants paid, $0; assets, $100,024 (M); gifts received, $100,000; expenditures, $0; qualifying distributions, $0.
Officers: Brent D. Ballard, Pres.; Marcia Wexberg, Treas.
EIN: 341973213

44766
The Judith and Peter Holmes Family Fund
c/o Vanik & Butscher, LLP
1406 W. 6th St., 3rd Fl.
Cleveland, OH 44113

Established in 1999 in OH.
Donor(s): Judith W. Holmes.
Financial data (yr. ended 12/31/99): Grants paid, $0; assets, $148,280 (M); gifts received, $148,280; expenditures, $0; qualifying distributions, $0.
Limitations: Applications not accepted.
Application information: Contributes only to pre-selected organizations.
Trustees: Douglas Q. Holmes, Judith W. Holmes, Peter A. Holmes.
EIN: 341907675

44767
The John E. Hoopes Foundation for Plastic Surgery, Inc.
11100 Euclid Ave.
Cleveland, OH 44106-5044 (216) 844-4780
Contact: Edward Luce, M.D., Pres.

Established in 1994 in MD.
Donor(s): Ellice McDonald, Rosa McDonald.
Financial data (yr. ended 12/31/01): Grants paid, $0; assets, $22,916 (M); gifts received, $20,119; expenditures, $1,144; qualifying distributions, $0.
Limitations: Giving primarily in Arlington, VA.
Officers: Edward Luce, Pres.; William Crawley, V.P.; William Futurell, Secy.
EIN: 521856283

44768
Howfirma Foundation
1722 Larch Ave., Ste. 225
Cincinnati, OH 45224

Established in 2000 in OH.
Donor(s): Jane M. Thompson.
Financial data (yr. ended 12/31/01): Grants paid, $0; assets, $5,081 (M); expenditures, $125; qualifying distributions, $0.
Trustee: Jane M. Thompson.
EIN: 311733201

44769
HPM Foundation
820 Marion Rd.
Mount Gilead, OH 43338-1095
(419) 946-0222
Contact: W.T. Flickinger, Pres.

Financial data (yr. ended 05/31/00): Grants paid, $0; assets, $101,588 (M); expenditures, $0; qualifying distributions, $0.
Limitations: Giving primarily in Marion and Morrow counties, OH.
Application information: Application form not required.
Officers and Trustees:* W.T. Flickinger,* Pres.; J.I. Griffey,* Secy.; Tim Snyder,* Treas.
EIN: 310951596

44770
Huff Charitable Trust
5245 Oakbrook Dr.
Fairfield, OH 45014

Established in 1996 in OH.
Financial data (yr. ended 12/31/99): Grants paid, $0; assets, $233,382 (L); expenditures, $0; qualifying distributions, $0.
Limitations: Applications not accepted. Giving primarily in OH.
Application information: Contributes only to pre-selected organizations.
Trustees: Gary Hufstetler, Vickie Hufstetler.

EIN: 316536156

44771
Hufstetler Charitable Trust
2734 Ravine Run
Cortland, OH 44410

Established in 1997 in OH.
Financial data (yr. ended 12/31/99): Grants paid, $0; assets, $169,045 (L); expenditures, $0; qualifying distributions, $0.
Limitations: Applications not accepted. Giving limited to Cortland, OH.
Application information: Contributes only to pre-selected organizations.
Trustee: Holly Hufstetler.
EIN: 341836950

44772
Elias & Mae Hummer Trust
c/o National City Bank
P.O. Box 94651
Cleveland, OH 44101-4651
Application address: c/o Kenneth Winger, School Superintendent, Titusville Area Schools, 221 N. Washington St., Titusville, PA 16354, tel.: (814) 827-2715

Financial data (yr. ended 12/31/01): Grants paid, $0; assets, $5,118 (M); expenditures, $168; qualifying distributions, $76.
Limitations: Giving limited to residents of the Titusville, PA, area.
Application information: Application form required.
Trustee: National City Bank.
EIN: 256066158

44773
Minnie H. Hunt Educational Fund
c/o National City Bank
P.O. Box 94651
Cleveland, OH 44101-4651
Application address: P.O. Box 5031, Indianapolis, IN 46255, tel.: (317) 267-7280
Contact: Eric Martz, Trust Off., National City Bank

Financial data (yr. ended 06/30/01): Grants paid, $0; assets, $230,334 (M); expenditures, $1,851; qualifying distributions, $6,378; giving activities include $5,000 for loans to individuals.
Limitations: Giving limited to residents of Madison County, IN.
Application information: Application form required.
Trustee: National City Bank.
EIN: 356337245
Codes: GTI

44774
John Russell Hunt Memorial Fund
1324 Friar Ln.
Columbus, OH 43221 (614) 457-8095
Contact: Denham Pride, Tr.

Established in 1967 in OH.
Financial data (yr. ended 12/31/01): Grants paid, $0; assets, $1,819,110 (M); expenditures, $20,861; qualifying distributions, $318,791; giving activities include $315,300 for loans.
Limitations: Giving limited to OH.
Publications: Financial statement, informational brochure (including application guidelines).
Application information: Request application form. Application form required.
Trustees: Gary D. Mann, Denham Pride, Randall J. Richardson.
EIN: 316059048

44775
Jadetree Foundation
(Formerly Jadetree Foundation Charitable Foundation)
925 Euclid Ave., Ste. 2000
Cleveland, OH 44115-1407 (216) 696-4700
FAX: (216) 696-2706
Contact: Rebecca H. Dent

Established in 1996 in OH.
Financial data (yr. ended 06/30/01): Grants paid, $0; assets, $134,699 (M); gifts received, $89,534; expenditures, $5,271; qualifying distributions, $0.
Application information: Application form not required.
Trustees: David D. Watson, Richard T. Watson.
EIN: 341840630

44776
Glenn O. Jenkins Trust
c/o National City Bank
P.O. Box 84651
Cleveland, OH 44101-4651

Established in 2001 in IN.
Donor(s): Glenn O. Jenkins.‡
Financial data (yr. ended 12/31/01): Grants paid, $0; assets, $284,812 (M); gifts received, $301,528; expenditures, $1,220; qualifying distributions, $735.
Limitations: Applications not accepted.
Application information: Contributes only to pre-selected organizations.
Trustee: National City Bank of Indiana.
EIN: 916532529

44777
Jochum Charitable Foundation, Inc.
c/o David J. Hessler
6055 Rockside Woods Blvd., Ste. 200
Cleveland, OH 44131-2301

Established in 2001 in OH.
Donor(s): Emma E. Jochum.
Financial data (yr. ended 12/31/01): Grants paid, $0; assets, $640,516 (M); gifts received, $630,948; expenditures, $1,719; qualifying distributions, $0.
Officer and Trustees:* David J. Hessler,* Secy.-Treas.; Emil Jochum, Emma E. Jochum.
EIN: 341951170

44778
Alfred W. Johnson Trust
c/o KeyBank, N.A., Trust Div.
800 Superior Ave., 4th Fl.
Cleveland, OH 44114

Donor(s): Alfred W. Johnson.‡
Financial data (yr. ended 04/30/01): Grants paid, $0; assets, $40,819 (M); expenditures, $1,037; qualifying distributions, $0.
Limitations: Giving limited to Belfast, ME.
Trustee: KeyBank, N.A.
EIN: 016010139

44779
D. H. Jones Family Foundation
c/o National City Bank
P.O. Box 94651
Cleveland, OH 44101-4651

Established in 2000 in IN.
Donor(s): Donald C. Jones.
Financial data (yr. ended 12/31/01): Grants paid, $0; assets, $126,291 (M); expenditures, $2,683; qualifying distributions, $0.
Limitations: Applications not accepted.
Application information: Contributes only to pre-selected organizations.
Trustee: National City Bank.

EIN: 347124884

44780
Jovanovic Charitable Trust
4536 High Mill N.W.
Massillon, OH 44647-9375

Established in OH in 1998.
Financial data (yr. ended 12/31/99): Grants paid, $0; assets, $5,068 (L); gifts received, $2,000; expenditures, $123; qualifying distributions, $0.
Limitations: Applications not accepted.
Application information: Contributes only to pre-selected organizations.
Director: Mike Jovanovic.
EIN: 347093053

44781
Doris Orr Kaspar Foundation
36 N. 2nd St.
Newark, OH 43055

Established in 1996 in OH.
Financial data (yr. ended 12/31/01): Grants paid, $0; assets, $605,623 (M); expenditures, $6,443; qualifying distributions, $0.
Limitations: Applications not accepted.
Application information: Contributes only to pre-selected organizations.
Officer: Jim Pyle, Pres.
Trustees: John Hazlett, John Uible.
EIN: 311396517

44782
John H. Kelly Scholarship Foundation
c/o Keybank, N.A.
800 Superior Ave., 4th Fl.
Cleveland, OH 44114

Established in 2000 in AK.
Donor(s): John H. Kelly Trust.
Financial data (yr. ended 12/31/00): Grants paid, $0; assets, $498,976 (M); gifts received, $383,982; expenditures, $6,145; qualifying distributions, $1,715.
Limitations: Applications not accepted.
Application information: Contributes only to pre-selected organizations.
Trustee: Keybank, N.A.
EIN: 527156077

44783
Mary Kelly Scholarship Trust
c/o KeyBank, N.A., Trust Div.
800 Superior Ave., 4th Fl.
Cleveland, OH 44114

Donor(s): Mary H. Kelly.‡
Financial data (yr. ended 12/31/00): Grants paid, $0; assets, $6,454 (M); expenditures, $71; qualifying distributions, $0.
Limitations: Applications not accepted. Giving primarily in Potsdam, NY.
Application information: Contributes only to pre-selected organizations.
Trustee: KeyBank, N.A.
EIN: 166250069

44784
William H. Kilcawley Fund
c/o National City Bank
P.O. Box 450
Youngstown, OH 44501-0450
Contact: James H. Sisek

Established in 1946.
Financial data (yr. ended 12/31/01): Grants paid, $0; assets, $3,837,598 (M); expenditures, $25,832; qualifying distributions, $10,415.
Limitations: Giving primarily in Youngstown, OH.
Application information: Application form not required.

Member: Anne K. Christman.
Trustee: National City Bank.
EIN: 346515643

44785
Urban P. Klingshirn Foundation
c/o KeyBank, N.A.
P.O. Box 10099
Toledo, OH 43699-0099
Contact: Diane Ohns, Trust Off., KeyBank, N.A.

Established in 2001 in OH.
Donor(s): Urban P. Klingshirn.
Financial data (yr. ended 12/31/01): Grants paid, $0; assets, $1,384,451 (M); gifts received, $1,296,213; expenditures, $8,338; qualifying distributions, $2,501.
Trustee: KeyBank, N.A.
EIN: 036076375

44786
The John Lord Knight Foundation
(Formerly William & Elsie Knight Foundation)
c/o KeyBank, N.A.
P.O. Box 10099
Toledo, OH 43699-0099 (419) 259-8372
Contact: Erwin Diener

Established in 1957 in OH.
Financial data (yr. ended 12/31/01): Grants paid, $0; assets, $958,567 (M); expenditures, $5,243; qualifying distributions, $2,743.
Limitations: Giving primarily in FL and Toledo, OH.
Advisors: Paget Farrell, Diana K. Foster, Michael Judge, Donald J. Keune, Beverly L. Knight, John L. Knight, Gerald Miller, R. Gregory Stephens.
Trustee: KeyBank, N.A.
EIN: 346504813

44787
Knight-Baldwin Charitable Fund, Inc.
P.O. Box 36
Clyde, OH 43410

Established in 1997 in OH.
Donor(s): Lois Baldwin.
Financial data (yr. ended 12/31/99): Grants paid, $0; assets, $485,151 (M); expenditures, $168; qualifying distributions, $0; giving activities include $24,000 for programs.
Limitations: Giving primarily in GA and OH.
Trustees: Lois Baldwin, Charles Knight, Christopher Knight.
EIN: 311526677

44788
Suzanne & Robert Laboiteaux Family Foundation
c/o PNC Advisors
P.O. Box 1198
Cincinnati, OH 45201-1198
Application address: 201 E. 5th St., Cincinnati, OH 45201, tel.: (513) 651-8377
Contact: Lee Crooks

Established in 2001 in OH.
Donor(s): Suzanne M. Laboiteaux.
Financial data (yr. ended 12/31/01): Grants paid, $0; assets, $1,138,635 (M); gifts received, $1,063,889; expenditures, $2,551; qualifying distributions, $1,445.
Limitations: Giving primarily in OH.
Officers and Trustees:* Antoinette Laboiteaux,* Pres. and Treas.; Eliza Tobias,* V.P.; Gloria Haffer,* Secy.
EIN: 311346390

44789
Lakewood P.T.A. Scholarship Fund Trust
c/o National City Bank of Indiana
800 Superior Ave., 4th Fl.
Cleveland, OH 44114-4651

Financial data (yr. ended 12/31/99): Grants paid, $0; assets, $7,028 (M); expenditures, $663; qualifying distributions, $548.
Limitations: Giving limited to NY.
Trustee: National City Bank of Indiana.
EIN: 166022729

44790
LaMancusa Charitable Trust
c/o Sherry LaMancusa
1352 Sunset Way Blvd.
Kent, OH 44240

Donor(s): Lamacusa Management Co.
Financial data (yr. ended 12/31/99): Grants paid, $0; assets, $80,119 (M); gifts received, $20,000; expenditures, $6,858; qualifying distributions, $0.
Trustee: Carl Lamanacusa.
EIN: 347043149

44791
Lamb Charitable Trust
32178 S. Roundhead
Solon, OH 44139

Established in 1997.
Financial data (yr. ended 12/31/99): Grants paid, $0; assets, $649 (L); expenditures, $0; qualifying distributions, $0.
Limitations: Applications not accepted.
Application information: Contributes only to pre-selected organizations.
Trustee: William Lamb.
EIN: 347063691

44792
Sally J. Lasser Memorial Scholarship Fund
c/o KeyBank, N.A., Trust Div.
800 Superior Ave., 4th Fl.
Cleveland, OH 44114

Financial data (yr. ended 12/31/01): Grants paid, $0; assets, $10,811 (M); expenditures, $102; qualifying distributions, $0.
Limitations: Applications not accepted.
Application information: Unsolicited requests for funds not accepted.
Trustee: KeyBank, N.A.
EIN: 166109602

44793
Lone Star Foundation
2800 S. Arlington Rd., Ste. 10
Akron, OH 44312
Contact: Ernest J. Aranyosi, Treas.

Financial data (yr. ended 12/31/99): Grants paid, $0; assets, $25,900 (M); expenditures, $1,000; qualifying distributions, $998.
Officers: Albert Ploenes, Pres.; Ernest J. Aranyosi, Treas.
EIN: 237031650

44794
Naece Lukens Charitable Foundation
419 Plum St.
Cincinnati, OH 45202

Established in 1999 in KY.
Financial data (yr. ended 12/31/99): Grants paid, $0; assets, $3,986 (M); gifts received, $3,900; expenditures, $0; qualifying distributions, $0.
Trustees: Robert Ernst, Joseph T. Lukens, John Naece.
EIN: 311642444

44795
John M. Maslowski Scholarship Fund
c/o KeyBank, N.A.
800 Superior Ave., 4th Fl.
Cleveland, OH 44114

Financial data (yr. ended 12/31/01): Grants paid, $0; assets, $61,060 (M); expenditures, $1,022; qualifying distributions, $0.
Limitations: Applications not accepted. Giving limited to Chazy, NY.
Application information: Unsolicited requests for funds not accepted.
Trustee: KeyBank, N.A.
EIN: 146014976
Codes: GTI

44796
Dorothy Massie Scholarship Trust
c/o KeyBank, N.A., Trust Div.
800 Superior Ave., 4th Fl.
Cleveland, OH 44114
Application address: c/o Mt. Baker High School Scholarship Comm., Whatcom County, WA 98244

Financial data (yr. ended 12/31/01): Grants paid, $0; assets, $59,012 (M); expenditures, $1,635; qualifying distributions, $400.
Limitations: Giving limited to residents of WA.
Trustee: KeyBank, N.A.
EIN: 916207211

44797
Thelma Masten Charitable Trust
c/o U.S. Bank
P.O. Box 1118
Cincinnati, OH 45201

Established in 2001 in OH.
Donor(s): Thelma Masten.‡
Financial data (yr. ended 12/31/01): Grants paid, $0; assets, $230,148 (M); gifts received, $206,104; expenditures, $512; qualifying distributions, $0.
Limitations: Applications not accepted.
Application information: Contributes only to pre-selected organizations.
Trustees: Daniel P. Randolph, U.S. Bank.
EIN: 046971363

44798
Sam and Carol McAdow Family Foundation
15 Sprague Rd.
South Charleston, OH 45368
Application address: c/o Beth Sullivan, 4802 Macallan Ct., Dublin, OH 43017, tel.: (614)792-6216

Established in 2001 in OH.
Donor(s): McAdow Investment Group.
Financial data (yr. ended 12/31/01): Grants paid, $0; assets, $210,855 (M); gifts received, $112,147; expenditures, $0; qualifying distributions, $0.
Limitations: Giving primarily in Dublin, OH.
Application information: Application form required.
Officers: Carol B. McAdow, Pres.; John M. McAdow, V.P.; Michael R. McAdow, V.P.; Samuel J. McAdow, V.P.; Elizabeth M. Sullivan, Secy.; Samuel James McAdow, Treas.
EIN: 311779858

44799
J. Allen McClain Trust
133 E. Market St.
Xenia, OH 45385 (937) 372-4919
Contact: David L. Pendry, Tr.

Financial data (yr. ended 12/31/01): Grants paid, $0; assets, $506,117 (L); expenditures, $8,580; qualifying distributions, $8,580; giving activities include $11,000 for loans to individuals.
Limitations: Giving limited to residents of Greene County, OH.
Application information: Application form required.
Trustee: David L. Pendry.
EIN: 316060712
Codes: GTI

44800
Grace McClintock & David Wheeler Education Fund
(Formerly Grace McClintock Education Fund)
c/o National City Bank of Pennsylvania
P.O. Box 94651
Cleveland, OH 44101-4651

Financial data (yr. ended 12/31/01): Grants paid, $0; assets, $91,705 (M); expenditures, $1,474; qualifying distributions, $750.
Limitations: Applications not accepted. Giving limited to students attending Allegheny College, PA.
Trustee: National City Bank of Pennsylvania.
EIN: 256093597

44801
Katherine Milan Fund
c/o KeyBank, N.A., Trust Div.
800 Superior Ave., 4th Fl.
Cleveland, OH 44114
Application address: c/o KeyBank, N.A, P.O. Box 12907, Seattle, WA 98111

Financial data (yr. ended 07/31/02): Grants paid, $0; assets, $209,434 (M); expenditures, $4,438; qualifying distributions, $0.
Limitations: Giving limited to WA.
Trustee: KeyBank, N.A.
EIN: 916057035

44802
Kenneth Alan Miller Charitable Foundation
900 W. S. Boundary, Ste. 8-B
Perrysburg, OH 43551

Donor(s): Kenneth A. Miller.
Financial data (yr. ended 12/31/01): Grants paid, $0; assets, $1,681 (M); gifts received, $2,000; expenditures, $364; qualifying distributions, $0.
Limitations: Applications not accepted.
Trustee: Kenneth A. Miller.
EIN: 341876722

44803
Bill E. Mitchell Foundation
10 W. Locust St.
Newark, OH 43055
Application address: 98 Elmwood Ave., Newark, OH 43055, tel.: (614) 349-7943
Contact: Loren H. Briggs, Pres.

Donor(s): Bill E. Mitchell.
Financial data (yr. ended 12/31/01): Grants paid, $0; assets, $65,544 (M); gifts received, $70,000; expenditures, $2,123; qualifying distributions, $0.
Limitations: Applications not accepted. Giving primarily in Newark, OH.
Application information: Contributes only to pre-selected organizations.
Officers: Loren H. Briggs, Pres.; C. Arthur Morrow, Secy.; Joseph G. Johnston, Treas.

EIN: 311062243

44804
Paul Monea Family Charitable Foundation
4735 Belpar St. N.W.
Canton, OH 44718
Contact: Paul M. Monea, Dir.

Established in 1999 in OH.
Donor(s): Paul M. Monea.
Financial data (yr. ended 12/31/00): Grants paid, $0; assets, $26,133 (M); expenditures, $1,344; qualifying distributions, $0.
Directors: Daniel R. Bohlmann, Paul A. Monea, Paul M. Monea.
EIN: 341901001

44805
J. P. Mooney Foundation
50 Public Sq., Ste. 3500
Cleveland, OH 44113

Established in 2001 in OH.
Donor(s): James P. Mooney.
Financial data (yr. ended 12/31/01): Grants paid, $0; assets, $504,686 (M); gifts received, $504,686; expenditures, $0; qualifying distributions, $0.
Limitations: Applications not accepted.
Application information: Contributes only to pre-selected organizations.
Officers: James P. Mooney, Pres.; Thomas J. Mooney, V.P.; Megan A. Mooney, Secy.-Treas.
EIN: 341957299

44806
Nash Memorial Foundation, Inc.
P.O. Box 2213
Youngstown, OH 44504-0213

Financial data (yr. ended 12/31/01): Grants paid, $0; assets, $147,870 (M); expenditures, $888; qualifying distributions, $0.
Limitations: Applications not accepted. Giving limited to East Palestine, OH.
Application information: Contributes only to pre-selected organizations.
Trustees: Eleanor Allison, David Guy, Andrew Jones, Stewart McCormick.
EIN: 237005670

44807
Martha & Marie Neag Family Foundation
6600 Summit Dr.
Canfield, OH 44406-9510
Application address: 111 Sleepy Hollow Dr., Canfield, OH 44406
Contact: Marie Neags, Dir.

Established in 2000 in OH.
Donor(s): Marie Neags.
Financial data (yr. ended 12/31/01): Grants paid, $0; assets, $236 (M); expenditures, $350; qualifying distributions, $0.
Directors: Marie Neags, Patrick A. Sebastiano, John M. Zador.
Trustee: Sky Trust, N.A.
EIN: 341925340

44808
Newark Health Rotary Foundation, Inc.
c/o Jeffrey M. Priest
P.O. Box 4712
Newark, OH 43058-4712

Established in 1995 in OH.
Financial data (yr. ended 10/31/01): Grants paid, $0; assets, $17,057 (M); gifts received, $5,000; expenditures, $40; qualifying distributions, $0.
Limitations: Giving primarily in Newark, OH.
Officers: Mike Myers, Pres.; Jamie Frush, Secy.; Jeffrey M. Priest, Treas.

EIN: 311445644

44809
Wayne G. & Barbara L. Nordine Foundation
c/o National City Bank of Pennsylvania
P.O. Box 94651
Cleveland, OH 44101-4651
Application address: P.O. Box 758, Jamestown, NY 14702
Contact: Barbara L. Nordine

Financial data (yr. ended 12/31/01): Grants paid, $0; assets, $7,368 (M); expenditures, $917; qualifying distributions, $0.
Limitations: Giving primarily in NY.
Trustee: National City Bank of Pennsylvania.
EIN: 251290213

44810
Northeast Ohio Museum of Military Vehicles, Inc.
c/o Wayne Hlavin
6807 Boneta Rd.
Medina, OH 44256

Financial data (yr. ended 12/31/01): Grants paid, $0; assets, $79,601 (M); expenditures, $4,324; qualifying distributions, $0.
Officers: Wayne A. Hlavin, Pres.; Lorriane G. Hlavin, Secy.
EIN: 341657005

44811
Nowak Family Foundation
2325 Patrick Blvd.
Beavercreek, OH 45431
Contact: John M. Nowak, Pres. and Treas.

Established in 2001 in OH.
Donor(s): John M. Nowak.
Financial data (yr. ended 12/31/01): Grants paid, $0; assets, $100,000 (M); gifts received, $100,000; expenditures, $0; qualifying distributions, $0.
Officers: John M. Nowak, Pres. and Treas.; Maureen K. Nowak, V.P.
EIN: 311813059

44812
The Oatey Foundation
c/o Robert R. Galloway
1900 E. 9th St., Ste. 3200
Cleveland, OH 44114-3485

Established in 2001 in OH.
Donor(s): The Oatey Corp.
Financial data (yr. ended 12/31/01): Grants paid, $0; assets, $500,000 (M); gifts received, $500,000; expenditures, $0; qualifying distributions, $0.
Limitations: Applications not accepted.
Application information: Contributes only to pre-selected organizations.
Officers and Trustees:* William Oatey,* Pres.; Nancy Oatey McMillan,* Secy.; Karen Oatey,* Treas.; Gary Oatey.
EIN: 866314738

44813
Ohio Wetlands Foundation
3675 Africa Rd.
Galena, OH 43021 (740) 548-0484
Contact: James Sutliff, Tr.

Established in 1992 in OH.
Financial data (yr. ended 12/31/01): Grants paid, $0; assets, $1,035,714 (M); expenditures, $9,956; qualifying distributions, $0.
Limitations: Giving limited to OH.
Trustees: Ken Danter, Jim Ernst, Robert Monchein, Darrel Seibert, A. Bailey Stanbery, Randy Strauss, James Sutliff, Fred Tobin.

EIN: 311357624

44814
Robert & Gladys Ortner Family Foundation
425 Walnut St., Ste. 1800
Cincinnati, OH 45202

Established in 1999 in OH.
Donor(s): Robert C. Ortner, Sr.
Financial data (yr. ended 12/31/01): Grants paid, $0; assets, $88,472 (M); gifts received, $30,696; expenditures, $542; qualifying distributions, $0.
Limitations: Applications not accepted.
Application information: Contributes only to pre-selected organizations.
Officers and Trustees:* Robert C. Ortner, Jr.,* Pres.; Ross E. Wales,* Secy.; Steven R. Ortner,* Treas.
EIN: 311651491

44815
The Pacholder Family Foundation
c/o Provident Bank Trust, Capital Mgmt. Group
P.O. Box 2176
Cincinnati, OH 45201
Application address: 8044 Montgomery Rd., Ste. 382, Cincinnati, OH 45236, tel.: (513) 985-3200
Contact: Asher O. Pacholder, Tr.

Established in 1991 in OH.
Donor(s): Asher O. Pacholder.
Financial data (yr. ended 12/31/01): Grants paid, $0; assets, $3,641 (M); expenditures, $944; qualifying distributions, $0.
Limitations: Giving primarily in OH.
Trustees: Mary Ellen Cornelius, Asher O. Pacholder, Sylvia A. Pacholder, Thomas D. Pacholder.
EIN: 311354793

44816
W. Stuver & Nancy C. Parry Family Foundation
3383 E. Glencoe Rd.
Richfield, OH 44286

Established in 2001 in OH.
Donor(s): W. Stuver Parry.
Financial data (yr. ended 12/31/01): Grants paid, $0; assets, $5,000 (M); gifts received, $5,000; expenditures, $2,415; qualifying distributions, $0.
Limitations: Applications not accepted.
Application information: Contributes only to pre-selected organizations.
Trustees: Thomas A. Haught, Nancy C. Parry, W. Stuver Parry.
EIN: 341939730

44817
The Past Presidents Foundation
925 Euclid Ave., Ste. 1100
Cleveland, OH 44115-1475

Established in 2001 in OH.
Financial data (yr. ended 12/31/01): Grants paid, $0; assets, $99,229 (M); gifts received, $92,215; expenditures, $79; qualifying distributions, $0.
Limitations: Applications not accepted.
Application information: Contributes only to pre-selected organizations.
Trustees: Margaret Balzano, Michael E. Elliott, Charles J. O'Toole, Robert B. Tomaro.
EIN: 341963590

44818
Evalena Pletcher Trust
P.O. Box 240
Risingsun, OH 43457-0240

Financial data (yr. ended 12/31/99): Grants paid, $0; assets, $4,232 (M); expenditures, $543; qualifying distributions, $0.
Limitations: Giving limited to Risingsun, OH.

Trustees: Nolan Cline, Donald Keller, Fred Schmidt.
EIN: 346698163

44819
Powers Scholarship Fund
c/o Community First Bank & Trust
P.O. Box 170
Celina, OH 45822 (419) 586-7765
Contact: Collin Bryan, Trust Off., Community First Bank & Trust

Financial data (yr. ended 12/31/00): Grants paid, $0; assets, $1,662 (M); expenditures, $870; qualifying distributions, $865.
Limitations: Giving limited to Union City, IN.
Application information: Applicant must include transcript.
Trustee: Community First Bank & Trust.
EIN: 237160823

44820
Edwin A. Preston Charitable Trust
c/o KeyBank, N.A.
127 Public Sq., 16th Fl.
Cleveland, OH 44114-1306

Established in 1989 in OH.
Donor(s): Edwin A. Preston.‡
Financial data (yr. ended 12/31/01): Grants paid, $0; assets, $681,262 (M); expenditures, $11,839; qualifying distributions, $0.
Limitations: Applications not accepted. Giving limited to OH.
Application information: Contributes only to pre-selected organizations.
Trustee: KeyBank, N.A.
EIN: 346738054

44821
W. M. Price Family Foundation, Inc.
3481 Central Pkwy., Ste. 101
Cincinnati, OH 45223-3398 (513) 872-7500
Contact: Robert F. Uhrig, Secy.

Established in 2000 in OH.
Financial data (yr. ended 05/31/01): Grants paid, $0; assets, $217,316 (M); gifts received, $271,258; expenditures, $14; qualifying distributions, $0.
Officers: Mary Elizabeth Price, Pres.; Robert F. Uhrig, Secy.; William C. Price, Treas.
EIN: 311746549

44822
Psalm One Ministries
(Formerly Corban Foundation)
5709 Wilmington Rd.
Oregonia, OH 45054-9704

Established in 2000 in OH.
Donor(s): Kathleen P. Stolle.
Financial data (yr. ended 12/31/00): Grants paid, $0; assets, $22,072 (M); gifts received, $35,040; expenditures, $14,388; qualifying distributions, $26,801; giving activities include $13,501 for programs.
Limitations: Applications not accepted.
Application information: Contributes only to pre-selected organizations.
Officer and Directors:* Kathleen Porter Stolle,* Secy-Treas.; Dr. Dale W. Russell, Wilberta J. Schorr.
EIN: 311735053

44823
The Reading 1 Foundation
c/o Sally Reddig Schulze
1801 E. 9th St., Ste. 1425
Cleveland, OH 44114

Established in 2000 in OH.
Donor(s): Sally R. Schulze.

Financial data (yr. ended 11/30/01): Grants paid, $0; assets, $227,643 (M); gifts received, $214,481; expenditures, $1,165; qualifying distributions, $0.
Limitations: Applications not accepted.
Application information: Contributes only to pre-selected organizations.
Trustee: Sally Reddig Schulze.
EIN: 347129352

44824
H. G. Richardson Charitable Trust
758 Quailwoods Dr.
Loveland, OH 45140

Established in 1996 in OH.
Donor(s): H.G. Asset Management Co.
Financial data (yr. ended 12/31/00): Grants paid, $0; assets, $0 (M); expenditures, $0; qualifying distributions, $0.
Limitations: Applications not accepted. Giving primarily in Cincinnati, OH.
Application information: Contributes only to pre-selected organizations.
Trustees: Gloria Richardson, Homer Richardson.
EIN: 311466959

44825
Ridgeway Foundation
900 Adams Crossing, Ste. 7200
Cincinnati, OH 45202
Contact: Compton Allyn, Tr.

Established in 2000 in OH.
Donor(s): Compton Allyn.
Financial data (yr. ended 12/31/01): Grants paid, $0; assets, $2,292 (M); expenditures, $2,617; qualifying distributions, $0.
Limitations: Giving primarily in Cincinnati, OH.
Trustees: Compton Allyn, Sarah A. Bahlman, Elizabeth Lowsley-Williams.
EIN: 311712320

44826
J. David and Kathleen A. Roberts Family Foundation
5829 Woodbridge Ln.
West Chester, OH 45069-4519

Established in 2001 in OH.
Donor(s): J. David Roberts, Kathleen A. Roberts.
Financial data (yr. ended 12/31/01): Grants paid, $0; assets, $293,368 (M); gifts received, $290,994; expenditures, $0; qualifying distributions, $0.
Limitations: Applications not accepted.
Application information: Contributes only to pre-selected organizations.
Officers: J. David Roberts, Pres. and Treas.; Kathleen A. Roberts, V.P. and Secy.
EIN: 311808573

44827
Hubert and Oese Robinson Foundation
P.O. Box 134
Granville, OH 43023-0134 (740) 587-0373
Contact: Patricia J. Price, Tr.

Established in 1983 in OH.
Financial data (yr. ended 12/31/99): Grants paid, $0; assets, $1,750,731 (M); expenditures, $105,716; qualifying distributions, $82,687; giving activities include $82,687 for programs.
Limitations: Giving limited to Licking County, OH.
Application information: Application form not required.
Trustees: Patricia J. Price, Richard Price, Nancy E. Wince.
EIN: 311080062

44828
Ralph F. & Bessie E. Rogan Memorial Fund
c/o Fifth Third Bank
38 Fountain Sq. Plz.
Cincinnati, OH 45263

Established in 2000 in OH.
Donor(s): Ralph R. Burchenal, William Burchenal, Jr., Thomas H. Carruthers IV, Beth B. Jones.
Financial data (yr. ended 12/31/01): Grants paid, $0; assets, $103,151 (M); expenditures, $5,218; qualifying distributions, $0.
Limitations: Applications not accepted. Giving primarily in Glendale, OH.
Application information: Contributes only to pre-selected organizations.
Trustees: Ralph R. Burchenal, Thomas H. Carruthers IV, Fifth Third Bank.
EIN: 311724387

44829
Root Education Futures Foundation
1715 Indian Wood Cir., Rm. 200
Maumee, OH 43537

Established in 1999 in OH.
Donor(s): James A. Hauden, Randall C. Root.
Financial data (yr. ended 06/30/01): Grants paid, $0; assets, $83,854 (M); expenditures, $3,349; qualifying distributions, $0.
Limitations: Applications not accepted. Giving primarily in Toledo, OH.
Application information: Contributes only to pre-selected organizations.
Trustees: James A. Hauden, Randall C. Root, Scott J. Savage.
EIN: 341912693

44830
The Roselle Foundation
c/o Fifth Third Bank
38 Fountain Sq. Plz., 1COM31
Cincinnati, OH 45263

Established in 2000 in OH.
Financial data (yr. ended 09/30/01): Grants paid, $0; assets, $20,305 (M); expenditures, $1; qualifying distributions, $0.
Trustees: Louise Roselle, Fifth Third Bank.
EIN: 311752016

44831
The Jon R. & Barbara P. Ruhlman Foundation
c/o John D. Drinko
3200 National City Ctr., 1900 E. 9th St.
Cleveland, OH 44114-3485

Established in 1993 in OH.
Donor(s): Jon R. Ruhlman, John D. Drinko.
Financial data (yr. ended 12/31/01): Grants paid, $0; assets, $98,979 (M); gifts received, $50,000; expenditures, $1,184; qualifying distributions, $0.
Limitations: Applications not accepted. Giving primarily in MA.
Application information: Contributes only to pre-selected organizations.
Officers and Trustees:* Jon R. Ruhlman,* Pres.; Barbara P. Ruhlman,* V.P. and Treas.; J. Richard Hamilton,* Secy.; John D. Drinko, Randall M. Ruhlman, Robert G. Ruhlman.
EIN: 341734147

44832
Sala Family Foundation
c/o Earl V. Sala
3930 Bramford Rd.
Columbus, OH 43220

Financial data (yr. ended 12/31/01): Grants paid, $0; assets, $77,086 (M); expenditures, $3,293; qualifying distributions, $0.

Officers: Earl V. Sala, Pres.; Janet Lynn Glandon, Secy.; Penny S. Rothrock, Treas.
EIN: 311575831

44833
George & Marilyn Scherff Family Foundation
c/o Sterling
3550 Lander Rd.
Pepper Pike, OH 44124

Established in 2000 in OH.
Donor(s): George E. Scherff, Marilyn F. Scherff.
Financial data (yr. ended 12/31/00): Grants paid, $0; assets, $247,300 (M); gifts received, $248,938; expenditures, $0; qualifying distributions, $0.
Limitations: Applications not accepted.
Application information: Contributes only to pre-selected organizations.
Trustees: William F. Bates, George E. Scherff, Marilyn F. Scherff.
EIN: 912125183

44834
The Ellen Schneider Foundation
3889 E. Galbraith Rd.
Cincinnati, OH 45236-1514

Established in 2000 in OH.
Financial data (yr. ended 12/31/00): Grants paid, $0; assets, $2,651 (M); gifts received, $2,671; expenditures, $25; qualifying distributions, $0.
Officers and Trustees:* Ashley Butler, Pres.; Diane Torgerson,* V.P.; Henry W. Schneider, V.P.; Debbie Bisel,* Secy.
EIN: 311696777

44835
Jean C. Schroeder Foundation
6068 Cabot Ct.
Mentor, OH 44060

Established in 2001 in OH.
Financial data (yr. ended 12/31/01): Grants paid, $0; assets, $1,003 (M); gifts received, $1,000; expenditures, $0; qualifying distributions, $0.
Limitations: Applications not accepted.
Application information: Contributes only to pre-selected organizations.
Officer: Jean C. Schroeder, Pres.
EIN: 912144754

44836
Hettie Sherwin Scofield Scholarship Fund
c/o National City Bank of Pennsylvania
P.O. Box 94651
Cleveland, OH 44101-4651
Application address: 801 State St., Erie, PA 16538, tel.: (814) 871-1387
Contact: John W. Frey, Trust Off., National City Bank of Pennsylvania

Financial data (yr. ended 12/31/00): Grants paid, $0; assets, $79,893 (M); expenditures, $2,375; qualifying distributions, $1,500.
Limitations: Giving limited to residents of Warren, PA.
Trustee: National City Bank.
EIN: 256064449

44837
Seeman Charitable Foundation
(Formerly Alvin E. & Margaret Seeman Charitable Foundation)
c/o National City Bank
P.O. Box 94651
Cleveland, OH 44101-4651

Financial data (yr. ended 12/31/01): Grants paid, $0; assets, $106,460 (M); expenditures, $1,478; qualifying distributions, $0.

Limitations: Applications not accepted. Giving primarily in Toledo, OH.
Application information: Contributes only to pre-selected organizations.
Trustee: National City Bank.
EIN: 346556381

44838
The Shadybrook Endowment Fund Trust
c/o KeyBank, N.A.
800 Superior Ave., 4th Fl.
Cleveland, OH 44114

Established in 1987 in OH.
Financial data (yr. ended 12/31/01): Grants paid, $0; assets, $34,496 (M); expenditures, $2,277; qualifying distributions, $925.
Limitations: Applications not accepted.
Application information: Contributes only to pre-selected organizations.
Trustees: Arthur D. Baldwin III, Arthur B. King, KeyBank, N.A.
EIN: 346867024

44839
R. J. Shepler & Danny Warner Memorial Foundation
c/o Roal E. Shepler III
3024 Saddlebrook
Findlay, OH 45840-2983
Application address: c/o Guidance Counselor, Liberty Benton High School, 9190 Co. Rd. 9, Findlay, OH 45840, tel.: (419) 424-5351

Established in 1999 in OH.
Donor(s): Roal E. Shepler III, Danny D. Warner, Jr.
Financial data (yr. ended 12/31/99): Grants paid, $0; assets, $19,272 (M); gifts received, $17,306; expenditures, $0; qualifying distributions, $0.
Application information: Application form required.
Officers: Roal E. Shepler III, Pres.; Danny D. Warner, Jr., Secy.-Treas.
EIN: 341886752

44840
Robert A. and Gloria Sherman Foundation
333 Harmon N.W.
Warren, OH 44481

Established in 1999 in OH.
Donor(s): Robert A. Sherman, Gloria Sherman.
Financial data (yr. ended 12/31/99): Grants paid, $0; assets, $140,174 (M); gifts received, $140,000; expenditures, $0; qualifying distributions, $0.
Trustees: Stacey L. Hotchkiss, Gloria Sherman, Jonathan J. Sherman, Robert A. Sherman.
EIN: 311681919

44841
Shifrin Family Foundation
23240 Chagrin Blvd., Ste. 515
Beachwood, OH 44122-5468
Contact: David Shifrin, Tr.

Established in 1999 in OH.
Financial data (yr. ended 12/31/01): Grants paid, $0; assets, $342,062 (M); gifts received, $84,173; expenditures, $2,348; qualifying distributions, $0.
Trustee: David Shifrin.
EIN: 341895618

44842
George L. Sloan Foundation
c/o Butler Wick Trust Co.
City Centre One, Ste. 700
Youngstown, OH 44503

Established in 2000 in OH.
Donor(s): George Sloan Trust.

Financial data (yr. ended 12/31/00): Grants paid, $0; assets, $135,761 (M); gifts received, $131,602; expenditures, $0; qualifying distributions, $0.
Limitations: Applications not accepted.
Application information: Contributes only to pre-selected organizations.
Trustee: Butler Wick Trust Co.
EIN: 347130472

44843
Sluzewicz Charitable Trust
5907 Gloucester Ct.
Dayton, OH 45440

Established in 1997 in OH.
Donor(s): Sluzewicz Asset Management Co. Trust.
Financial data (yr. ended 12/31/99): Grants paid, $0; assets, $387,784 (M); expenditures, $0; qualifying distributions, $0.
Limitations: Applications not accepted.
Application information: Contributes only to pre-selected organizations.
Trustees: Nancy M. Sluzewicz, Raymond C. Sluzewicz.
EIN: 311485067

44844
Smith Educational Memorial Fund
(also known as Earl E. & Marie M. Smith Educational Memorial Fund)
c/o National City Bank of Indiana
P.O. Box 94651
Cleveland, OH 44101-4651
Application address: c/o Teresa Tracey, National City Bank of Indiana, P.O. Box 110, Fort Wayne, IN 46802, tel.: (219)461-6218

Financial data (yr. ended 12/31/01): Grants paid, $0; assets, $176,040 (M); expenditures, $6,669; qualifying distributions, $8,878; giving activities include $5,000 for loans to individuals.
Application information: Application form required.
Trustee: National City Bank.
EIN: 510174338
Codes: GTI

44845
The Michael and Marjorie Smith Foundation, Inc.
202 Montrose W. Ave., Ste. 160
Copley, OH 44321

Established in 1999 in OH.
Donor(s): Michael Smith, Marjorie Smith.
Financial data (yr. ended 03/31/02): Grants paid, $0; assets, $5,043 (M); expenditures, $120; qualifying distributions, $0.
Directors: Marjorie K. Smith, Michael K. Smith.
EIN: 341874574

44846
The Wilma Smith Foundation
c/o KeyBank, N.A.
127 Public Sq., Ste. 4900
Cleveland, OH 44114-1304

Established in 2000 in OH.
Financial data (yr. ended 12/31/01): Grants paid, $0; assets, $1 (M); gifts received, $1,000; expenditures, $3,235; qualifying distributions, $0.
Officers and Trustees:* Wilma Smith,* Pres.; Thomas M. Gerber,* V.P.; George R. Barry.
EIN: 341908581

44847
Norman W. Smith Revolving Loan Trust
c/o The Huntington National Bank
P.O. Box 1558
Columbus, OH 43216
Application address: Nancy Fincham, Trust Off., c/o The Huntington National Bank, P.O. Box 895, Morgantown, WV 26507

Financial data (yr. ended 11/30/00): Grants paid, $0; assets, $1,050,315 (M); expenditures, $8,513; qualifying distributions, $11,789; giving activities include $47,830 for loans to individuals.
Limitations: Giving limited to residents of Berkeley County, WV.
Trustee: The Huntington National Bank.
EIN: 556084952
Codes: GTI

44848
Melinda F. Smyth Education Fund
c/o KeyBank, N.A.
800 Superior Ave., 4th Fl.
Cleveland, OH 44114-2601

Financial data (yr. ended 12/31/00): Grants paid, $0; assets, $88,463 (M); expenditures, $3,114; qualifying distributions, $800.
Limitations: Applications not accepted. Giving limited to residents of Ashtabula, OH.
Application information: Contributes only to pre-selected organizations.
Trustee: KeyBank, N.A.
EIN: 346968313

44849
Soul Choice International
P.O. Box 750455
Dayton, OH 45475-0455

Established in 2000 in OH.
Donor(s): Mary G. Bentz.
Financial data (yr. ended 06/30/01): Grants paid, $0; assets, $3,410 (M); gifts received, $36,701; expenditures, $33,291; qualifying distributions, $33,291; giving activities include $33,291 for programs.
Trustees: Margaret G. Alfare, Audrey C. Bentz, Mary G. Bentz.
EIN: 311766517

44850
Spring of Life Fund
2952 Dover Rd.
Columbus, OH 43209-3022

Established in 2001 in OH.
Financial data (yr. ended 12/31/01): Grants paid, $0; assets, $26,720 (M); gifts received, $34,000; expenditures, $7,280; qualifying distributions, $7,280.
Officers: Nganga Njoroge, Pres.; Johnny Jackson, V.P.; Jamie Martin, V.P.; Craig Nickelson, V.P.
EIN: 311364989

44851
Stark County Terriers
6544 Paris Ave. N.E.
Louisville, OH 44641
Application address: P.O. Box 214, Louisville, OH 44641, tel.: (330) 875-3381
Contact: Dennis H. Biery, Pres.

Donor(s): Dennis H. Biery.
Financial data (yr. ended 12/31/01): Grants paid, $0; assets, $921 (L); gifts received, $36,325; expenditures, $35,236; qualifying distributions, $0.
Limitations: Giving primarily in OH.

Officers and Trustees:* Dennis H. Biery,* Pres.; Paul Gilhousen,* V.P.; Gregory M. Trbovich,* Secy.-Treas.
EIN: 341881670

44852
Edward R. & Jean Geis Stell Foundation
c/o David Hessler
6055 Rockside Woods Blvd., Ste. 200
Cleveland, OH 44131

Established in 2001 in OH.
Donor(s): Jean Geis Stell.
Financial data (yr. ended 12/31/01): Grants paid, $0; assets, $190,584 (M); gifts received, $230,950; expenditures, $7,640; qualifying distributions, $7,640.
Limitations: Applications not accepted.
Application information: Contributes only to pre-selected organizations.
Officer: Jean G. Stell, Pres.
Directors: David J. Hessler, Anthony Messina.
EIN: 341942391

44853
Charles M. Stern Award Trust
c/o KeyBank, N.A.
800 Superior Ave., 4th Fl.
Cleveland, OH 44114-2601

Financial data (yr. ended 12/31/01): Grants paid, $0; assets, $466 (M); expenditures, $11; qualifying distributions, $0.
Limitations: Applications not accepted. Giving primarily in Albany, NY.
Trustee: KeyBank, N.A.
EIN: 146015068

44854
The Stout-Meyers Foundation
2985 Winthrop Rd.
Shaker Heights, OH 44122

Established in 1998 in OH.
Donor(s): Anne Meyers, Craig Stout.
Financial data (yr. ended 12/31/01): Grants paid, $0; assets, $14,095 (M); expenditures, $83; qualifying distributions, $0.
Limitations: Applications not accepted.
Application information: Contributes only to pre-selected organizations.
Trustee: Anne Meyers.
EIN: 341886780

44855
The Summers Family Foundation
1991 Crocker Rd., Ste. 430
Westlake, OH 44145

Established in 2001.
Donor(s): William B. Summers, Jr.
Financial data (yr. ended 12/31/01): Grants paid, $0; assets, $608,500 (M); gifts received, $582,750; expenditures, $0; qualifying distributions, $0.
Limitations: Applications not accepted.
Application information: Contributes only to pre-selected organizations.
Trustee: William B. Summers, Jr.
EIN: 341973148

44856
The Swager Family Foundation
1041 Fernwood Blvd.
Alliance, OH 44601-3762
Contact: Neal Sangree, Tr.

Established in 2001 in OH.
Donor(s): Lois M. Swager.
Financial data (yr. ended 12/31/01): Grants paid, $0; assets, $40,000 (M); gifts received, $40,000; expenditures, $0; qualifying distributions, $0.

Trustees: Jill Sangree, Marjo Sangree, Neal Sangree, Peter Sangree.
EIN: 341972915

44857
Thompson Center Vocational Rehabilitation Trust
c/o National City Bank, Columbus
P.O. Box 94651
Cleveland, OH 44101-4651
Contact: Linda Gaietto, Dir.

Financial data (yr. ended 12/31/01): Grants paid, $0; assets, $27,267 (M); expenditures, $596; qualifying distributions, $0.
Limitations: Giving primarily in Springfield, OH.
Application information: Application form required.
Director: Linda Gaietto.
Trustee: National City Bank.
EIN: 316064533

44858
H. L. Thompson, Jr. Family Foundation
c/o KeyBank, N.A.
P.O. Box 10099
Toledo, OH 43699-0099

Established in 2000 in OH.
Donor(s): Henry L. Thompson, Jr. Trust.
Financial data (yr. ended 12/31/00): Grants paid, $0; assets, $6,495,399 (M); gifts received, $6,940,507; expenditures, $0; qualifying distributions, $0.
Limitations: Applications not accepted.
Application information: Contributes only to pre-selected organizations.
Trustees: Deborah T. Tenney, H. Lawrence Thompson III, Theresa S. Thompson, Victoria T. Winterer, KeyBank, N.A.
EIN: 341912416

44859
Urban Charitable Trust
3740 Laurel Rd.
Brunswick, OH 44212-3669

Established in 1999 in OH.
Financial data (yr. ended 12/31/99): Grants paid, $0; assets, $8,384 (L); gifts received, $8,505; expenditures, $121; qualifying distributions, $0.
Limitations: Applications not accepted.
Application information: Contributes only to pre-selected organizations.
Trustee: Suzanne M. Urban.
EIN: 911972539

44860
Joan D. Van Slyke Testamentary Trust for S.U.N.Y. at Albany Benevolent Association
c/o KeyBank, N.A.
800 Superior Ave., 4th Fl.
Cleveland, OH 44114
Application address: c/o Office of Financial Aid, SUNY Albany, 1400 Washington Ave., Albany, NY 12222

Financial data (yr. ended 12/31/01): Grants paid, $0; assets, $99,197 (M); expenditures, $1,156; qualifying distributions, $50.
Limitations: Giving limited to Albany, NY.
Trustee: KeyBank, N.A.
EIN: 146015305
Codes: GTI

44861
Carlos E. Wakefield and Beatrice E. Wakefield Scholarship Trust
c/o KeyBank, N.A.
800 Superior Ave., 4th Fl.
Cleveland, OH 44114-1306
Application address: Freda Wortman, Chair., c/o Scholarship Comm., Highland Ave., Dexter, ME 04930

Established in 1987 in ME.
Financial data (yr. ended 08/31/01): Grants paid, $0; assets, $847,541 (M); expenditures, $8,380; qualifying distributions, $0.
Limitations: Giving limited to the residents of Dexter and Ripley, ME.
Application information: Application form required.
Trustee: KeyBank, N.A.
EIN: 222929235
Codes: GTI

44862
John E. Wallis and Elizabeth C. Wallis Foundation
c/o Butler Wick Trust Co.
City Centre One, Ste. 700
Youngstown, OH 44503 (330) 744-4351
Contact: Gilbert Manchester

Established in 1999 in OH.
Financial data (yr. ended 12/31/01): Grants paid, $0; assets, $560,568 (M); expenditures, $6,524; qualifying distributions, $0.
Limitations: Giving primarily in PA.
Trustees: Franklin S. Bennett, Jr., Butler Wick Trust Co.
EIN: 341893721

44863
The Wapakoneta Foundation
c/o Fifth Third Bank
38 Fountain Sq. Plz.
Cincinnati, OH 45263
Contact: Frank Fisher

Established in 2001 in OH.
Donor(s): Joan H. Searby.
Financial data (yr. ended 12/31/01): Grants paid, $0; assets, $225,634 (M); gifts received, $636; expenditures, $5,875; qualifying distributions, $544.
Trustees: Bruce H. Searby, Daniel M. Searby, David P. Searby, Fifth Third Bank.
EIN: 316665203

44864
The Watson Family Foundation
c/o Michael J. O'Brien
1406 W. 6th St.
Cleveland, OH 44113-1300

Established in 2000.
Donor(s): Frederick R. Watson.
Financial data (yr. ended 12/31/00): Grants paid, $0; assets, $100,070 (M); gifts received, $100,070; expenditures, $0; qualifying distributions, $0.
Trustees: Frederick R. Watson, Jason M. Watson, Jessica E. Watson.
EIN: 347129805

44865
Richard T. & Judith B. Watson Foundation
925 Euclid Ave., Ste. 2000
Cleveland, OH 44115-1496

Established in 1999 in OH.
Donor(s): Judith B. Watson, Richard T. Watson.
Financial data (yr. ended 12/31/00): Grants paid, $0; assets, $384,243 (M); gifts received, $125,180; expenditures, $12,478; qualifying distributions, $0.
Limitations: Applications not accepted.
Application information: Contributes only to pre-selected organizations.
Trustees: Judith B. Watson, Richard T. Watson.
EIN: 341448717

44866
The Weitzel Family Foundation
7450 Main St.
P.O. Box 508
Gates Mills, OH 44040-0508

Established in 1997 in OH.
Donor(s): Robert A. Weitzel.
Financial data (yr. ended 12/31/01): Grants paid, $0; assets, $0 (M); expenditures, $2,618; qualifying distributions, $0.
Limitations: Applications not accepted.
Application information: Contributes only to pre-selected organizations.
Trustees: James P. Farmer, Jr., Lynnette R. Stuart, Jeanette R. Weitzel, Robert A. Weitzel, Robert P. Weitzel.
EIN: 311531669

44867
The Werner Family Foundation
350 Riverside Dr.
Rossford, OH 43460-1050

Established in 1997 in OH.
Financial data (yr. ended 12/31/00): Grants paid, $0; assets, $940,768 (M); expenditures, $1,250; qualifying distributions, $0.
Limitations: Applications not accepted. Giving primarily in OH.
Application information: Contributes only to pre-selected organizations.
Trustees: Henry G. Werner, Henry Goth Werner, Marsha L. Werner.
EIN: 311500300

44868
Philip S. Willis Student Loan Trust
c/o KeyBank, N.A., Trust Div.
P.O. Box 10099
Toledo, OH 43699-0099

Established in 1960 in OH.
Donor(s): Philip S. Willis.‡
Financial data (yr. ended 12/31/00): Grants paid, $0; assets, $1,275,557 (M); expenditures, $30,951; qualifying distributions, $47,141; giving activities include $26,623 for loans to individuals.
Limitations: Giving limited to residents of the Toledo, OH, area.
Application information: Unsolicited request for funds not accepted.
Trustees: Dale McCullough, Marie I. McCullough, KeyBank, N.A.
EIN: 346518056
Codes: GTI

44869
WKTL-FM Booster, Inc.
c/o Mary Babnic
823 Pearson Cir.
Boardman, OH 44512

Established in 1996 in OH.
Financial data (yr. ended 12/31/01): Grants paid, $0; assets, $13,156 (M); expenditures, $343; qualifying distributions, $0.
Limitations: Applications not accepted.
Application information: Contributes only to pre-selected organizations.
Officers: Libby Fill, Pres.; John Ross, V.P.; James Kiriazis, Secy.; Mary Babnic, Treas.
EIN: 341668572

44870
G. Howard Wood, M.D. Medical and Nursing Student Loan Trust
Foulke Block, Rm. 2
Chillicothe, OH 45601 (740) 774-6152
Contact: Robert C. Hess, Tr.

Established in 1995 in OH.
Donor(s): Jane P. Wood.
Financial data (yr. ended 12/31/00): Grants paid, $0; assets, $58,432 (M); expenditures, $1,119; qualifying distributions, $3,119; giving activities include $2,000 for loans to individuals.
Limitations: Giving limited to residents of OH.
Application information: Application form required.
Trustees: Joseph C. Bennett, M.D., Robert C. Hess, Bambi Huffman.
EIN: 311446754

44871
Harold W. Wott Scholarship Trust
c/o Richard Nolyet
1201 Garrison St.
Fremont, OH 43420-2850
Application address: c/o EECS Dept., University of Toledo, Toledo, OH 43606
Contact: R.G. Malyet, Scholarship Admin.

Financial data (yr. ended 06/31/01): Grants paid, $0; assets, $0 (M); expenditures, $4,064; qualifying distributions, $4,064.
Limitations: Giving limited to Toledo, OH.
Trustees: Richard Molyet, Steven Root, Robert Toth.
EIN: 341705119

44872
Yohe Charitable Foundation
c/o Fifth Third Bank
30 Fountain Sq. Plz.
Cincinnati, OH 45263

Established in 1999 in IN.
Donor(s): James E. Yohe Trust.
Financial data (yr. ended 12/31/01): Grants paid, $0; assets, $27,962 (M); expenditures, $1,502; qualifying distributions, $0.
Limitations: Applications not accepted.
Application information: Contributes only to pre-selected organizations.
Trustee: Fifth Third Bank.
EIN: 352064858

44873
The Yohe Charitable Trust
c/o Fifth Third Bank
30 Fountain Sq. Plz.
Cincinnati, OH 45263

Established in 1999 in IN.
Donor(s): C.L. Yohe Charitable Leadership Trust.
Financial data (yr. ended 11/30/01): Grants paid, $0; assets, $133,693 (M); gifts received, $142,267; expenditures, $3,486; qualifying distributions, $1,046.
Limitations: Applications not accepted.
Application information: Contributes only to pre-selected organizations.
Trustees: James Yohe, Fifth Third Bank.
EIN: 912101314

44874
The Marie Denise DeBartolo York Foundation
7620 Market St.
Youngstown, OH 44512

Established in 2000 in OH.

Financial data (yr. ended 01/31/01): Grants paid, $0; assets, $3,732 (M); gifts received, $3,800; expenditures, $68; qualifying distributions, $0.
Trustees: John C. York, John E. York, Marie Denise DeBartolo York.
EIN: 341938138

44875
Zimmerman Charitable Trust
4906 White Blossom Blvd.
Mason, OH 45040

Established in OH in 1998.
Financial data (yr. ended 12/31/99): Grants paid, $0; assets, $28,500 (L); gifts received, $2,000; expenditures, $740; qualifying distributions, $0.
Trustees: Curtis Zimmerman, Michelle Zimmerman.
EIN: 311504780

44876
The Bruce J. and Rori H. Zoldan Family Foundation
555 Martin Luther King, Jr. Blvd.
Youngstown, OH 44502
Contact: Peter S. Frank, Tr.

Established in 1999 in OH.
Donor(s): Bruce J. Zoldan, Rori H. Zoldan.
Financial data (yr. ended 12/31/01): Grants paid, $0; assets, $155,376 (M); expenditures, $2,369; qualifying distributions, $0.
Limitations: Giving primarily in Youngstown, OH.
Trustees: Peter S. Frank, William A. Weimer, Bruce J. Zoldan, Rori H. Zoldan.
EIN: 341912737

OKLAHOMA

44877
The William K. Warren Foundation
P.O. Box 470372
Tulsa, OK 74147-0372 (918) 492-8100
Contact: W.R. Lissau, Pres.

Incorporated in 1945 in OK.
Donor(s): William K. Warren,‡ Mrs. William K. Warren.‡
Financial data (yr. ended 12/31/00): Grants paid, $32,173,796; assets, $446,235,531 (M); gifts received, $834,208; expenditures, $36,789,231; qualifying distributions, $32,109,090.
Limitations: Giving primarily in OK.
Application information: Application form not required.
Officers and Directors:* W.K. Warren, Jr.,* Chair.; John-Kelly C. Warren, Vice-Chair.; W.R. Lissau,* Pres.; Stephen K. Warren,* Sr. V.P.; David B. Whitehill,* Secy.; M.A. Buntz, C.F.O. and Treas.; Elizabeth Warren Blankenship, John A. Gaberino, Jr., Dorothy Warren King, J. Frederick McNeer, M.D., Patricia Warren Swindle.
EIN: 730609599
Codes: FD, FM

44878
The J. E. and L. E. Mabee Foundation, Inc.
3000 Mid-Continent Tower
401 S. Boston
Tulsa, OK 74103-4017 (918) 584-4286
Contact: John H. Conway, Jr., Vice-Chair.

Incorporated in 1948 in DE.
Donor(s): J.E. Mabee,‡ L.E. Mabee.‡
Financial data (yr. ended 08/31/02): Grants paid, $28,759,122; assets, $696,114,826 (M); expenditures, $30,920,813; qualifying distributions, $29,221,608.
Limitations: Giving limited to AR, KS, MO, NM, OK, and TX.
Publications: Program policy statement, application guidelines.
Application information: Application form not required.
Officers and Trustees:* Joe Mabee,* Chair.; John H. Conway, Jr.,* Vice-Chair. and Secy.-Treas.; Thomas R. Brett, James L. Houghton, Joseph Guy Mabee, Jr., William J. Teague, Raymond L. Tullius, Jr.
EIN: 736090162
Codes: FD, FM

44879
Oklahoma City Community Foundation, Inc.
P.O. Box 1146
Oklahoma City, OK 73101-1146
(405) 235-5603
Additional address: 1300 N. Broadway Dr., Oklahoma City, OK 73103; FAX: (405) 235-5612; E-mail: n.anthony@occf.org; URL: http://www.occf.org
Contact: Nancy B. Anthony, Exec. Dir.

Incorporated in 1968 in OK.
Financial data (yr. ended 06/30/02): Grants paid, $21,088,534; assets, $363,174,929 (M); gifts received, $16,214,605; expenditures, $23,963,769.
Limitations: Giving primarily in the greater Oklahoma City, OK, area.
Publications: Annual report, newsletter.
Application information: See website for guidelines. Application form required.
Officers and Trustees:* Jeanette L. Gamba,* Pres.; James H. Holloman, Jr.,* V.P.; William O. Johnstone,* Treas.; James Clark, Nancy Coats, James Daniel, Paul W. Dudman, John Green, Kirkland Hall, Judith Love, Anne Hodges Morgan, Ronald J. Norick, Paul B. Odom, Jr., Christian K. Reesee, William Shdeed.
EIN: 237024262
Codes: CM, FD

44880
The Bank of Oklahoma Foundation
P.O. Box 2300
Tulsa, OK 74192 (918) 588-6831
Contact: Becky Frank

Established in 1997 in OK.
Donor(s): Bank of Oklahoma, N.A.
Financial data (yr. ended 12/31/00): Grants paid, $11,819,318; assets, $1,187,969 (M); expenditures, $11,895,103; qualifying distributions, $11,818,883.
Limitations: Giving limited to areas of company operations in AR, NM, OK, and TX.
Trustees: Jim Huntzinger, George B. Kaiser, Stanley A. Lybarger, James A. White.
EIN: 731531887
Codes: CS, FD, CD

44881
The Samuel Roberts Noble Foundation, Inc.
2510 Sam Noble Pkwy.
P.O. Box 2180
Ardmore, OK 73402 (580) 223-5810
URL: http://www.noble.org
Contact: Michael A. Cawley, C.E.O. and Pres.

Trust established in 1945 in OK; incorporated in 1952.
Donor(s): Lloyd Noble.‡
Financial data (yr. ended 10/31/01): Grants paid, $7,996,500; assets, $863,492,527 (M); expenditures, $53,056,818; qualifying distributions, $49,046,914; giving activities include $644,000 for loans and $37,653,241 for programs.
Limitations: Giving primarily in the Southwest, with emphasis on OK.
Publications: Annual report, application guidelines, informational brochure.
Application information: Application form required.
Officers and Trustees:* Michael A. Cawley,* C.E.O. and Pres.; Larry Pulliam, Exec. V.P.; Elizabeth A. Aldridge, Secy.; Ann Noble Brown, D. Randolph Brown, Susan Brown, James C. Day, Vivian N. Dubose, William R. Goddard, Jr., Shelley Dru Mullins, Edward E. Noble, Maria Noble, Nick Noble, Rusty Noble, Marianne Rooney, William G. Thurman.
EIN: 730606209
Codes: FD, FM, GTI

44882
E. L. & Thelma Gaylord Foundation
P.O. Box 25125
Oklahoma City, OK 73125

Established in 1994 in OK.
Donor(s): Edward L. Gaylord, Thelma F. Gaylord.
Financial data (yr. ended 12/31/01): Grants paid, $5,699,000; assets, $43,546,291 (M); gifts received, $30,034,712; expenditures, $5,703,359; qualifying distributions, $6,027,044.
Limitations: Applications not accepted. Giving primarily in OK.
Application information: Contributes only to pre-selected organizations.
Trustees: Edward L. Gaylord.
EIN: 731463569
Codes: FD

44883
The Anne and Henry Zarrow Foundation
401 S. Boston, Ste. 900
Tulsa, OK 74103-4012 (918) 295-8004
E-mail: jgillert@zarrow.com; *URL:* http://www.zarrow.com
Contact: Jeanne Gillert, Grants Mgr.

Established in 1986 in OK.
Donor(s): Henry H. Zarrow.
Financial data (yr. ended 12/31/01): Grants paid, $5,032,288; assets, $89,709,323 (M); expenditures, $5,450,759; qualifying distributions, $5,089,172.
Limitations: Giving primarily in the Tulsa, OK, area.
Publications: Application guidelines.
Application information: Application form not required.
Officers and Directors:* Henry H. Zarrow,* Pres.; Anne S. Zarrow,* V.P.; Julie Cohen, Judith Z. Kishner, Stuart A. Zarrow.
EIN: 731286874
Codes: FD, FM, GTI

44884
Presbyterian Health Foundation
655 Research Pkwy., Ste. 500
Oklahoma City, OK 73104-5023
FAX: (405) 271-2911
Contact: Jean G. Gumerson, C.E.O. and Pres.

Established in 1985 in OK; converted from the proceeds of the sale of Presbyterian Hospital to HCA.
Financial data (yr. ended 09/30/01): Grants paid, $4,942,402; assets, $177,204,262 (M); gifts received, $298,455; expenditures, $7,850,956; qualifying distributions, $25,725,324; giving activities include $20,019,903 for program-related investments.
Limitations: Giving primarily in OK.
Publications: Annual report, informational brochure (including application guidelines).
Application information: Application form required.
Officers and Trustees:* Stanton L. Young,* Chair.; Michael D. Anderson,* Vice-Chair.; Jean G. Gumerson,* C.E.O. and Pres.; Dennis McGrath, V.P.; Fred H. Zahn,* Secy.; William M. Beard,* Treas.; William F. Barnes, M.D., R.B. Carl, M.D., Richard G. Dotter, M.D., Carl Edwards, Nancy Payne Ellis, Robert S. Ellis, M.D., Clyde Ingle, David Parke, M.D., J.V. Smith, Harry B. Tate, M.D., Jerry B. Vannatta, M.D.
EIN: 730709836
Codes: FD

44885
The Helmerich Foundation
1579 E. 21st St.
Tulsa, OK 74114
Contact: Walter H. Helmerich III, Tr.

Established in 1965 in OK.
Donor(s): W.H. Helmerich,‡ Walter H. Helmerich III.
Financial data (yr. ended 09/30/01): Grants paid, $4,535,000; assets, $81,527,787 (M); expenditures, $4,894,065; qualifying distributions, $4,554,658.
Limitations: Giving limited to the Tulsa, OK, area.
Publications: Application guidelines, program policy statement.
Application information: Application form not required.
Trustee: Walter H. Helmerich III.
EIN: 736105607

Codes: FD, FM

44886
Southern Oklahoma Memorial Foundation
P.O. Box 1409
Ardmore, OK 73402-1409 (580) 226-0700
FAX: (580) 226-0223
Contact: John Snodgrass, Pres.

Established in 1950 in OK.
Donor(s): Memorial Hospital of OK, Inc., Citizens of Southern OK.
Financial data (yr. ended 06/30/01): Grants paid, $4,513,345; assets, $98,784,018 (M); expenditures, $5,232,679; qualifying distributions, $4,554,305.
Limitations: Giving limited to within a 50-mile radius of Ardmore, OK.
Application information: Application form required.
Officers and Directors:* John Snodgrass,* Pres.; John Kriet,* V.P.; Ann White,* Secy.; Laura Clay, Bridge Cox, Howard Drew, Bill Goddard, Phil McAnally, Mark Riesen, Keith Troop, M.D.
EIN: 731300662
Codes: FD, FM

44887
Tulsa Community Foundation
7010 S. Yale, Ste. 110
Tulsa, OK 74136 (918) 494-8823
FAX: (918) 494-9826; E-mail: TulsaCF@aol.com
Contact: Phil Lakin, Exec. Dir.

Established in Oklahoma in 1998.
Financial data (yr. ended 06/30/00): Grants paid, $4,134,181; assets, $30,730,214 (M); gifts received, $20,335,163; expenditures, $4,355,704; giving activities include $140,000 for programs.
Limitations: Giving limited to the Tulsa, OK area.
Publications: Financial statement, occasional report, informational brochure (including application guidelines).
Application information: Application form not required.
Trustees: George Kaiser, Chair.; Keith Bailey, Chester Cadleux, Fred Dorwart, Phil Frohilch, Hans Helmerich, and 14 additional trustees.
EIN: 731554474
Codes: CM, FD, FM

44888
H. A. and Mary K. Chapman Charitable Trust
1 Warren Pl., Ste. 1816
6100 S. Yale
Tulsa, OK 74136 (918) 496-7882
Contact: J. Jerry Dickman, Tr. or Donne W. Pitman, Tr.

Trust established in 1976 in OK.
Donor(s): H.A. Chapman.‡
Financial data (yr. ended 12/31/00): Grants paid, $3,577,500; assets, $77,386,283 (M); expenditures, $4,064,562; qualifying distributions, $3,647,370.
Limitations: Giving primarily in Tulsa, OK.
Publications: Application guidelines.
Application information: Application form required.
Trustees: J. Jerry Dickman, Donne W. Pitman.
EIN: 736177739
Codes: FD, FM

44889
Charles and Lynn Schusterman Family Foundation
2 W. 2nd St., 20th Fl.
Tulsa, OK 74103-3101 (918) 591-1090
Mailing address: P.O. Box 51, Tulsa, OK 74101-0051; FAX: (918) 591-1758; E-mail: ahughes@schusterman.org; URL: http://www.schusterman.org
Contact: Sanford R. Cardin, Exec. Dir.

Established in 1987 in OK.
Donor(s): Charles Schusterman,‡ Lynn Schusterman.
Financial data (yr. ended 11/30/00): Grants paid, $3,180,818; assets, $82,116,845 (M); expenditures, $3,367,302; qualifying distributions, $3,306,763.
Limitations: Giving primarily to nonsectarian organizations in OK; giving on a local, national, and international basis for Jewish organizations.
Publications: Application guidelines.
Application information: The foundation does not accept proposals sent by FAX or E-mail. Application form not required.
Officers: Lynn Schusterman, Pres.; Stacy H. Schusterman, V.P. and Treas.; Jerome R. Schusterman, Secy.; Sanford R. Cardin, Exec. Dir.
EIN: 731312965
Codes: FD

44890
Sarkeys Foundation
530 E. Main
Norman, OK 73071 (405) 364-3703
FAX: (405) 364-8191; E-mail: Sarkeys@sarkeys.org; URL: http://www.sarkeys.org
Contact: Susan C. Frantz, Prog. Off.

Established in 1962 in OK.
Donor(s): S.J. Sarkeys.‡
Financial data (yr. ended 11/30/01): Grants paid, $2,876,899; assets, $93,131,312 (M); expenditures, $4,095,945; qualifying distributions, $4,869,997.
Limitations: Giving limited to OK.
Publications: Informational brochure (including application guidelines), annual report.
Application information: Call foundation for guidelines; proposals received by FAX or E-mail not considered. Application form required.
Officers and Trustees:* Richard Bell,* Pres.; Joseph W. Morris,* V.P.; Robert S. Rizley,* Secy.-Treas.; Cheri D. Cartwright, Exec. Dir.; Fred Gipson, Dan Little, Paul F. Sharp, Terry W. West, Lee Anne Wilson.
EIN: 730736496
Codes: FD, FM

44891
The McMahon Foundation
714-716 C Ave.
P.O. Box 2156
Lawton, OK 73502 (580) 335-4622
Contact: James F. Wood, Dir.

Incorporated in 1940 in OK.
Donor(s): Eugene D. McMahon,‡ Louise D. McMahon.‡
Financial data (yr. ended 03/31/01): Grants paid, $2,587,463; assets, $56,760,517 (M); expenditures, $3,068,054; qualifying distributions, $2,674,761.
Limitations: Giving limited to OK, with emphasis on Comanche County.
Application information: Application form not required.
Officers and Trustees:* Charles S. Graybill, M.D.,* Chair.; Manville Redman,* Vice-Chair.; Gale Sadler,* Secy.-Treas.; James F. Wood, Dir.; Kenneth Bridges, Ronald E. Cagle, M.D., Kenneth E. Easton, Orville D. Smith.
EIN: 730664314
Codes: FD

44892
Kirkpatrick Foundation, Inc.
P.O. Box 268822
Oklahoma City, OK 73126-8822
(405) 840-2882
FAX: (405) 840-2946; E-mail: KFI@compuserve.com
Contact: Susan McCalmont, Secy.

Incorporated in 1955 in OK.
Donor(s): Eleanor B. Kirkpatrick,‡ John E. Kirkpatrick, Kirkpatrick Oil Co., Joan E. Kirkpatrick, Kathryn T. Blake.‡
Financial data (yr. ended 12/31/01): Grants paid, $2,452,670; assets, $34,601,964 (M); expenditures, $2,676,647; qualifying distributions, $2,503,287.
Limitations: Giving primarily in Oklahoma City, OK.
Publications: Application guidelines.
Application information: Application form required.
Officers and Directors:* John E. Kirkpatrick, Chair.; Joan E. Kirkpatrick,* Pres.; Christian K. Keesee, 1st V.P.; Anne Hodges Morgan,* 2nd V.P.; Susan McCalmont, Secy.; Mischa Gorkuscha,* Treas.; John L. Belt, Joe Howell, Linda Lambert, George Records.
EIN: 730701736
Codes: FD

44893
ONEOK Foundation, Inc.
P.O. Box 871
Tulsa, OK 74102-0871

Established in 1997 in OK.
Donor(s): ONEOK, Inc.
Financial data (yr. ended 12/31/01): Grants paid, $2,366,966; assets, $6,346,846 (M); expenditures, $2,401,865; qualifying distributions, $2,365,866.
Limitations: Giving primarily in KS and OK.
Officers: David L. Kyle, Chair., C.E.O. and Pres.; John A. Gaberino, Sr. V.P. and Gen. Council; Deborah A. Barnes, V.P. and Secy.; James C. Kneale, V.P., Treas., and C.F.O.
Directors: Eugene N. Dubay, Edmund J. Farrell, John W. Gibson, J.D. Holbird, Christopher R. Skoog.
EIN: 731503823
Codes: CS, FD, CD

44894
McCasland Foundation
McCasland Bldg.
P.O. Box 400
Duncan, OK 73534 (580) 252-5580
Contact: Barbara Braught, Exec. Dir.

Trust established in 1952 in OK.
Donor(s): members of the McCasland family, Mack Oil Co., Jath Oil Co.
Financial data (yr. ended 12/31/00): Grants paid, $2,307,199; assets, $50,758,427 (M); expenditures, $2,850,025; qualifying distributions, $2,295,546.
Limitations: Giving primarily in OK.
Officer and Trustees:* Barbara Braught,* Exec. Dir.; T.H. McCasland, Jr., Mary Frances Michaelis, W.H. Phelps.
EIN: 736096032
Codes: FD, FM

44895
John Steele Zink Foundation
1259 E. 26th St.
Tulsa, OK 74114 (918) 749-8249
Contact: Jacqueline A. Zink, Tr.

Established in 1972.
Donor(s): John Steele Zink,‡ Jacqueline A. Zink.
Financial data (yr. ended 10/31/00): Grants paid, $2,257,382; assets, $49,863,319 (M); expenditures, $2,442,574; qualifying distributions, $2,257,382.
Limitations: Giving primarily in Tulsa, OK.
Application information: Application form not required.
Trustees: Caroline H. Abbott, John E. Barry, Swannie Zink Tarbel, Darton J. Zink, Jacqueline A. Zink, John Smith Zink.
EIN: 237246964
Codes: FD

44896
Betty and George Kaiser Foundation
(Formerly Betty E. and George B. Kaiser Foundation)
c/o Frederic Dorwart
P.O. Box 21468
Tulsa, OK 74121
Additional address: 124 E. 4th St., Tulsa, OK 74103
Contact: Frederic Dorwart

Established in 1990 in OK.
Financial data (yr. ended 12/31/00): Grants paid, $2,224,646; assets, $53,817,087 (M); gifts received, $8,766,864; expenditures, $2,294,972; qualifying distributions, $2,218,068.
Limitations: Applications not accepted. Giving primarily in OK.
Application information: Contributes only to pre-selected organizations. Unsolicited requests for funds not considered.
Trustee: Frederic Dorwart.
EIN: 731363237
Codes: FD

44897
The Maxine and Jack Zarrow Family Foundation
(Formerly The Maxine and Jack Zarrow Foundation)
401 S. Boston, Ste. 900
Tulsa, OK 74103 (918) 295-8004
FAX: (918) 295-8049; E-mail: jgillert@zarrow.com; URL: http://www.zarrow.com
Contact: Jeanne Gillert, Grants Mgr.

Established in 1988 in OK.
Donor(s): Jack C. Zarrow.
Financial data (yr. ended 12/31/01): Grants paid, $1,904,282; assets, $45,794,650 (M); expenditures, $2,143,383; qualifying distributions, $1,978,871.
Limitations: Giving primarily in the Tulsa, OK, area.
Officers: Jack C. Zarrow, Pres.; Maxine Zarrow, V.P.; Scott Zarrow, Secy.; Gail Richards, Treas.
EIN: 316640903
Codes: FD

44898
The William Ben Johnson Foundation
5010 E. 68th St., Ste. 104
Tulsa, OK 74136

Established in 1995 in OK.
Donor(s): William Ben Johnson.
Financial data (yr. ended 09/30/01): Grants paid, $1,770,000; assets, $1,861,337 (M); expenditures, $1,775,619; qualifying distributions, $1,768,718.
Limitations: Applications not accepted. Giving primarily in Tulsa, OK.
Application information: Contributes only to pre-selected organizations.
Officers: William Ben Johnson, Pres.; Gail Latham, Secy.
EIN: 731485714
Codes: FD

44899
Herman G. Kaiser Foundation
1350 S. Boulder, Ste. 400
Tulsa, OK 74119
Contact: Carol Wilson, Admin. Asst.

Established around 1976.
Donor(s): Herman Kaiser.‡
Financial data (yr. ended 06/30/00): Grants paid, $1,600,529; assets, $36,535,989 (M); expenditures, $1,721,052; qualifying distributions, $1,600,557.
Limitations: Applications not accepted. Giving primarily in Tulsa, OK.
Application information: Contributes only to pre-selected organizations.
Trustees: Michael S. Nelson, Pamela B. Nelson, Randolph M. Nelson, Timothy B. Nelson.
EIN: 510173653
Codes: FD

44900
The Williams Companies Foundation, Inc.
P.O. Box 2400, Level 49
Tulsa, OK 74102 (918) 573-2248
URL: http://www.williams.com/community/foundation.jsp
Contact: Sylvia Schmidt

Incorporated in 1974 in OK.
Donor(s): The Williams Cos., Inc.
Financial data (yr. ended 12/31/00): Grants paid, $1,597,926; assets, $16,068,935 (M); gifts received, $2,349; expenditures, $1,621,525; qualifying distributions, $1,597,926.
Limitations: Giving primarily in locations where the Williams Companies, Inc. has a strong business presence, with emphasis on Tulsa, OK.
Application information: Application form not required.
Officers and Directors:* Keith E. Bailey,* Chair.; John C. Bumgarner, Jr.,* Pres.; William Von Glahn,* V.P.; James Herbster, V.P.; Jack D. McCarthy, V.P.; Shawna L. Gehres, Secy.; James Ivey, Treas.
EIN: 237413843
Codes: CS, FD, CD

44901
Kerr-McGee Foundation Corporation
(Formerly Kerr-McGee Corporation Foundation)
Kerr-McGee Ctr.
123 Robert S. Kerr Ave., (MT-803)
Oklahoma City, OK 73102 (405) 270-3924
Contact: Martha Brady, Admin., Public Affairs

Established in 1996 in OK.
Donor(s): Kerr-McGee Corp.
Financial data (yr. ended 12/31/01): Grants paid, $1,528,111; assets, $21,654,715 (M); expenditures, $1,622,387; qualifying distributions, $1,509,048.
Limitations: Giving primarily in areas of company and affiliate operations, with emphasis on OK.
Application information: Application form not required.
Officers and Directors:* Luke R. Corbett,* Chair. and C.E.O.; Robert M. Wohleber, Sr. V.P.; Gregory F. Pilcher, V.P. and Secy.; John M. Rauh, V.P. and Treas.
EIN: 731496403

Codes: CS, FD, CD

44902
Grace & Franklin Bernsen Foundation
15 W. 6th St., No. 1308
Tulsa, OK 74119-5407 (918) 584-4711
FAX: (918) 584-4713; E-mail: gfbernsen@aol.com; URL: http://www.bernsen.org

Established in 1985 in OK.
Donor(s): Grace Bernsen,‡ Franklin Bernsen.‡
Financial data (yr. ended 09/30/01): Grants paid, $1,517,604; assets, $30,863,180 (M); expenditures, $1,881,461; qualifying distributions, $1,694,208.
Limitations: Giving primarily in the Tulsa, OK, area.
Publications: Annual report, informational brochure (including application guidelines), application guidelines.
Application information: Application form not required.
Officers and Trustees:* W. Bland Williamson,* Secy.; Sandra L. Griffin, Admin.; J. Warren Jackman, Donald F. Marlar, Donald E. Pray, John D. Strong, Jr.
EIN: 237009414
Codes: FD

44903
Jess L. and Miriam B. Stevens Foundation
3700 First Place Tower
15 E. 5th St.
Tulsa, OK 74103-4344
Contact: Joseph J. McCain, Jr., Tr.

Established in 1999 in OK.
Financial data (yr. ended 07/31/01): Grants paid, $1,510,000; assets, $15,828,521 (M); gifts received, $1,544,766; expenditures, $1,679,085; qualifying distributions, $1,505,492.
Limitations: Giving primarily in St. Louis, MO, Tulsa, OK, and northeastern OH.
Application information: Application form not required.
Trustee: Joseph J. McCain, Jr.
EIN: 731557364
Codes: FD

44904
Sam Viersen Family Foundation, Inc.
6450 S. Lewis, Ste. 200
Tulsa, OK 74136 (918) 742-1979
Contact: I.R. Robertson, Exec. Dir.

Donor(s): Sam K. Viersen, Jr.‡
Financial data (yr. ended 12/31/01): Grants paid, $1,352,050; assets, $24,645,176 (M); expenditures, $1,725,509; qualifying distributions, $1,466,328.
Limitations: Giving primarily in OK.
Application information: Application form not required.
Officers and Directors:* Maralynn V. Sant,* Pres.; Oraetta Swearingen, Secy.; I.R. Robertson, Exec. Dir.; Robert English, Brian C. Johnson, Jill Johnson, Jennifer Miller, Leo M. Sant, Julie Schenk.
EIN: 731295358
Codes: FD

44905
The David E. and Cassie L. Temple Foundation
P.O. Box 35362
Tulsa, OK 74153-0362 (918) 743-9861
Contact: Dr. C. Wayne Bland, Chair.

Established in 1995 in OK.
Donor(s): Cassie L. Temple,‡ David E. Temple.‡
Financial data (yr. ended 06/30/01): Grants paid, $1,099,600; assets, $20,521,593 (M);

expenditures, $1,443,446; qualifying distributions, $1,182,017.
Limitations: Giving primarily in the Tulsa, OK, metropolitan area.
Application information: Application form not required.
Trustees: C. Wayne Bland, Timothy L. Lyons, Betty L. Stephenson.
EIN: 731452166
Codes: FD

44906
The Oxley Foundation
1437 S. Boulder, Ste. 1475
Tulsa, OK 74119
FAX: (918) 582-9419; E-mail: kprater@oxleyfdn.com
Contact: Kyra Prater, Grants Mgr.

Established in 1986 in OK.
Donor(s): John T. Oxley.‡
Financial data (yr. ended 06/30/01): Grants paid, $998,700; assets, $116,340,575 (M); gifts received, $94,338,250; expenditures, $1,673,993; qualifying distributions, $1,086,327.
Limitations: Applications not accepted. Giving primarily in CO, FL, OH and OK.
Application information: Contributes only to pre-selected organizations.
Trustees: Russell H. Harbaugh, Jr., John C. Oxley, Mary Jane Tritsch.
EIN: 736224031
Codes: FD

44907
The Lyon Foundation
(Formerly E. H. and Melody Lyon Foundation, Inc.)
P.O. Box 546
Bartlesville, OK 74005
Application address: 416 E. 5th St., Bartlesville, OK 74003
Contact: James W. Connor, Pres.

Established in 1975 in OK.
Donor(s): E.H. Lyon,‡ Melody Lyon.‡
Financial data (yr. ended 12/31/01): Grants paid, $939,271; assets, $21,515,219 (M); gifts received, $373,138; expenditures, $1,145,961; qualifying distributions, $1,022,034.
Limitations: Giving limited to the Bartlesville, OK, area.
Publications: Application guidelines.
Application information: Application form required.
Officers and Directors:* James W. Connor,* Pres.; Walter W. Allison,* V.P.; Don Donaldson,* V.P.; Charles W. Selby,* Secy.; John F. Kane,* Treas.
EIN: 237299980
Codes: FD

44908
Oklahoma Gas and Electric Company Foundation, Inc.
P.O. Box 321
Oklahoma City, OK 73101 (405) 253-3000
Contact: Steven E. Moore, Pres.

Incorporated in 1957 in OK.
Donor(s): Oklahoma Gas and Electric Co.
Financial data (yr. ended 12/31/01): Grants paid, $926,521; assets, $1,310,413 (M); gifts received, $1,400,000; expenditures, $933,352; qualifying distributions, $926,521.
Limitations: Giving limited to OK, in areas of company operations.
Application information: Application form not required.

Officers and Directors:* Steven E. Moore,* Pres.; J.R. Hatfield,* V.P.; Al M. Strecker,* V.P.; Irma B. Elliott, Secy.-Treas.
EIN: 736093572
Codes: CS, FD, CD

44909
The Meinders Foundation
4101 Perimeter Center Dr., No. 210
Oklahoma City, OK 73112-5466
(405) 947-2422
Contact: Mo Grotjohn, Exec. Dir.

Established in 1993 in OK.
Donor(s): Herman Meinders.
Financial data (yr. ended 12/31/01): Grants paid, $843,899; assets, $11,981,459 (M); expenditures, $1,868,315; qualifying distributions, $840,683.
Limitations: Giving primarily in OK.
Officers and Trustees:* Herman Meinders,* Pres.; LaDonna Meinders,* V.P.; Robert Meinders,* Secy.; Mo Grotjohn, Treas. and Exec. Dir.; Linda Rice.
EIN: 731438459
Codes: FD

44910
Hille Family Charitable Foundation
P.O. Box 537
Ketchum, OK 74349
Application address: 1561 Oak St., Dallas TX 75208; tel.: (214) 941-2444
Contact: Margaret Yar

Established in 1997 in OK.
Donor(s): Jo Bob Hille, Mary Ann Hille.
Financial data (yr. ended 12/31/01): Grants paid, $842,767; assets, $23,171,877 (M); gifts received, $51,078; expenditures, $936,204; qualifying distributions, $861,960.
Limitations: Giving primarily in the Tulsa, OK area.
Trustees: Jo Bob Hille, Mary Ann Hille.
EIN: 731521975
Codes: FD

44911
The Kerr Foundation, Inc.
c/o Asset Svcs. Company, LLC
5101 N. Classen Blvd., Ste. 600
Oklahoma City, OK 73118-4433
(405) 749-7991
FAX: (405) 749-2877; E-mail: kerr@ionet.net
Contact: Robert S. Kerr, Jr., Chair. and C.E.O.

Incorporated in 1963 in OK, and reincorporated in 1985.
Donor(s): Grayce B. Kerr Flynn.‡
Financial data (yr. ended 12/31/00): Grants paid, $792,059; assets, $30,387,430 (M); expenditures, $2,227,850; qualifying distributions, $1,356,595.
Limitations: Giving primarily in AR, CO, Washington, DC, KS, MO, NM, OK, and TX.
Application information: Application form available on website. Application form required.
Officers and Trustees:* Robert S. Kerr, Jr.,* Chair. and C.E.O.; Lou C. Kerr,* Pres. and Vice-Chair.; Steven S. Kerr, Secy.; Royce M. Hammons,* Treas.; Cody T. Kerr, Sharon L. Kerr, Ray Kline, Laura K. Ogle, Elmer B. Staats.
EIN: 731256122
Codes: FD

44912
The R. A. Young Foundation
6313 Harden Dr.
Oklahoma City, OK 73118-1061
Contact: Raymond A. Young, Pres.

Incorporated in 1953 in OK.
Donor(s): Raymond A. Young, Verna N. Young.

Financial data (yr. ended 11/30/99): Grants paid, $745,301; assets, $6,126,647 (M); expenditures, $775,888; qualifying distributions, $742,143.
Limitations: Giving primarily in Oklahoma City, OK.
Application information: Application form not required.
Officers and Trustees:* Raymond A. Young,* Pres.; Verna N. Young,* Secy.-Treas.
EIN: 736092654
Codes: FD

44913
C. W. Titus Foundation
1801 Philtower Bldg.
Tulsa, OK 74103-4123

Established in 1968 in OK.
Financial data (yr. ended 12/31/01): Grants paid, $708,937; assets, $23,545,710 (M); expenditures, $919,402; qualifying distributions, $11,738,351.‡
Limitations: Giving primarily in MO and OK.
Application information: Application form not required.
Trustee: Timothy T. Reynolds.
EIN: 237016981
Codes: FD

44914
The Oklahoman Foundation
P.O. Box 25125
Oklahoma City, OK 73125

Established in 1990 in OK.
Donor(s): The Oklahoma Publishing Co.
Financial data (yr. ended 12/31/01): Grants paid, $652,100; assets, $18,276,496 (M); gifts received, $200,000; expenditures, $658,907; qualifying distributions, $683,378.
Limitations: Applications not accepted. Giving limited to Oklahoma City, OK.
Application information: Contributes only to pre-selected organizations.
Trustees: Christine Gaylord Everest, Edward K. Gaylord II, Edward L. Gaylord.
EIN: 731363152
Codes: CS, FD, CD

44915
8:32, Inc. Foundation
P.O. Box 271054
Oklahoma City, OK 73137-1054
Contact: Tina Cole

Established in 1984 in OK.
Donor(s): Members of the Humphreys family.
Financial data (yr. ended 12/31/99): Grants paid, $634,836; assets, $2,351,602 (M); gifts received, $493,397; expenditures, $645,884; qualifying distributions, $633,682.
Limitations: Applications not accepted. Giving on a national basis.
Application information: Contributes only to pre-selected organizations.
Officers: Kirk D. Humphreys, Pres.; Kent J. Humphreys, V.P.; Joy Fischer, Secy.
EIN: 731214621
Codes: FD

44916
James E. and Mary M. Barnes Foundation
(Formerly J/MB Foundation)
2660 S. Birmingham Pl.
Tulsa, OK 74114 (918) 496-8650
Contact: James E. Barnes, Tr., or Mary E. Barnes, Tr.

Established in 1997.
Donor(s): James E. Barnes.

44916—OKLAHOMA

Financial data (yr. ended 12/31/01): Grants paid, $603,000; assets, $8,732,802 (M); expenditures, $620,059; qualifying distributions, $612,113.
Trustees: James E. Barnes, Mary E. Barnes, Bank of Oklahoma, N.A.
EIN: 311591203
Codes: FD

44917
Warren Charite
P.O. Box 470372
Tulsa, OK 74147-0372 (918) 492-8100
Contact: W.R. Lissau, V.P.

Established in 1968 in OK.
Donor(s): William K. Warren.
Financial data (yr. ended 11/30/00): Grants paid, $596,466; assets, $7,421,887 (M); expenditures, $631,520; qualifying distributions, $586,666.
Limitations: Giving primarily in Tulsa, OK.
Application information: Application form not required.
Officers and Directors:* W.K. Warren, Jr.,* Pres.; W.R. Lissau,* V.P.; P.K. Griffith, Secy.; M.A. Buntz,* Treas.; J.K.C. Warren.
EIN: 730776064
Codes: FD

44918
The Charles B. Goddard Foundation Trust
P.O. Box 1485
Ardmore, OK 73402 (580) 226-6040
Contact: William R. Goddard, Jr., Tr.

Trust established in 1958 in OK.
Donor(s): Charles B. Goddard.‡
Financial data (yr. ended 06/30/01): Grants paid, $561,510; assets, $12,509,451 (M); expenditures, $585,639; qualifying distributions, $561,510.
Limitations: Giving limited to southern OK and northern TX.
Application information: Application form not required.
Trustees: Garland W. Clay, Jr., Ann G. Corrigan, William R. Goddard, William R. Goddard, Jr., William M. Johns.
EIN: 756005868
Codes: FD

44919
The Merrick Foundation
2932 N.W. 122nd St.
Bradley Sq., Ste. D
Oklahoma City, OK 73120-1955
(405) 755-5571
E-mail: fwmerrick@foundationmanagementinc.com; Toll free tel.: (877) 689-7726; FAX: (405) 755-0938
Contact: Frank W. Merrick, V.P.

Trust established in 1948 in OK; incorporated in 1968.
Donor(s): Mrs. Frank W. Merrick.‡
Financial data (yr. ended 12/31/01): Grants paid, $524,400; assets, $12,281,623 (M); expenditures, $729,101; qualifying distributions, $591,826.
Limitations: Giving primarily in OK, with emphasis on southern OK.
Publications: Informational brochure, annual report.
Application information: Application form required.
Officers and Trustees:* Elizabeth Merrick Coe,* Pres.; Frank W. Merrick,* V.P.; Valda M. Buchanan,* Secy.-Treas.; Robert Bramlett, Michael A. Cawley, Laura Clay, Charles R. Coe, Jr., Ross Coe, Ward I. Coe, Robert B. Merrick, Ward S. Merrick III.
EIN: 736111622

Codes: FD

44920
The Mervin Bovaird Foundation
401 S. Boston Ave., Ste. 3300
Tulsa, OK 74103-4070 (918) 592-3300
Contact: R. Casey Cooper, Pres.

Established in 1955.
Donor(s): Mabel W. Bovaird.‡
Financial data (yr. ended 12/31/01): Grants paid, $523,452; assets, $42,928,145 (M); expenditures, $2,551,003; qualifying distributions, $692,990.
Limitations: Giving limited to the Tulsa, OK, area.
Publications: Program policy statement.
Application information: Scholarship recipients are chosen by Tulsa public high schools and Tulsa Community College based on need and ability to attend Tulsa University. Application form not required.
Officers and Trustees:* R. Casey Cooper,* Pres.; David B. McKinney,* V.P. and Treas.; Wanda W. Brown, Secy.; Tilford H. Eskridge, Lance Stockwell, Thomas H. Trower.
EIN: 736102163
Codes: FD, FM

44921
Synagogue Transformation and Renewal (STAR)
2 W. 2nd St., 20th Fl.
Tulsa, OK 74103

Established in 2000 in IL.
Donor(s): Samuel Bronfman Foundation, Michael Steinhardt, Charles and Lynn Schusterman Family Foundation.
Financial data (yr. ended 12/31/01): Grants paid, $507,803; assets, $12,922,882 (M); gifts received, $1,371,588; expenditures, $1,053,795; qualifying distributions, $1,051,282; giving activities include $162,681 for programs.
Limitations: Applications not accepted. Giving on a national basis.
Application information: Contributes only to pre-selected organizations.
Officers and Directors:* Lynn Schusterman,* Pres.; Natalie Goldfein, Secy.-Treas. and Mgr.; Edgar Bronfman, Sr., Michael Steinhardt.
EIN: 742937021
Codes: FD

44922
Robert Glenn Rapp Foundation
2301 N.W. 39th Expwy., Ste. 300
Oklahoma City, OK 73112 (405) 525-8331
Contact: Trustees

Trust established about 1953 in OK.
Donor(s): Florence B. Clark.‡
Financial data (yr. ended 12/31/01): Grants paid, $491,250; assets, $10,838,664 (M); expenditures, $657,062; qualifying distributions, $526,303.
Limitations: Giving primarily in OK, with emphasis on Oklahoma City.
Publications: Informational brochure (including application guidelines), application guidelines.
Application information: Application form required.
Trustees: Jilene K. Boghetich, Tony Boghetich, Merry L. Knowles, James H. Milligan, Lois Darlene Milligan, Michael J. Milligan.
EIN: 730616840
Codes: FD

44923
Southern Hills Country Club Charitable Foundation, Inc.
P.O. Box 702298
Tulsa, OK 74170-2298

Established in 1996 in OK.

Donor(s): Tour Championship, Inc., The Maxine and Jack Zarrow Family Foundation, U.S. Golf Assoc. Foundation, Inc., World Golf Foundation, The Tulsa Foundation, Meinig Family Foundation.
Financial data (yr. ended 12/31/01): Grants paid, $490,164; assets, $251,307 (M); gifts received, $232,547; expenditures, $497,807; qualifying distributions, $492,154.
Limitations: Applications not accepted. Giving primarily in Tulsa, OK.
Application information: Contributes only to pre-selected organizations.
Officers: Peter Adamson III, Pres.; John B. Johnson, Jr., 1st V.P.; John R. Frame, 2nd V.P.; Jack E. Short, 3rd V.P.; Ed A. Schermerhorn, Secy.; James Bost, Treas.
EIN: 731462475
Codes: FD

44924
The Zarrow Families Foundation
401 S. Boston, Ste. 900
Tulsa, OK 74103-4012 (918) 295-8004
FAX: (918) 295-8049; E-mail: jgillert@zarrow.com; URL: http://www.zarrow.com
Contact: Jeanne Gillert

Established in 1987.
Donor(s): Henry Zarrow, Jack Zarrow.
Financial data (yr. ended 07/31/01): Grants paid, $475,140; assets, $12,083,883 (M); expenditures, $521,760; qualifying distributions, $498,520.
Limitations: Applications not accepted. Giving primarily in the Tulsa, OK, area.
Application information: Contributes only to pre-selected organizations.
Officers and Trustees:* Henry H. Zarrow,* Pres.; Jack Zarrow, Exec. V.P.; Steven B. Cochran, Secy.-Treas.; Judy Z. Kishner, Gail Z. Richards, Scott F. Zarrow, Stuart A. Zarrow.
EIN: 731332141
Codes: FD

44925
Ruth K. Nelson Family Foundation
1350 S. Boulder
Tulsa, OK 74119 (918) 582-8083
Contact: Ruth K. Nelson, Tr.

Established in 1983 in OK.
Donor(s): Michael S. Nelson, Pamela B. Nelson, Randolph M. Nelson, Ruth Kaiser Nelson, Timothy B. Nelson.
Financial data (yr. ended 12/31/00): Grants paid, $469,640; assets, $3,346,119 (M); gifts received, $273,938; expenditures, $499,734; qualifying distributions, $469,640.
Limitations: Giving primarily in Tulsa, OK.
Application information: Generally contributes to organizations already known to trustees. Application form not required.
Trustees: Michael Stewart Nelson, Pamela Blair Nelson, Randolph Miles Nelson, Ruth Kaiser Nelson, Timothy Blake Nelson.
EIN: 731210115
Codes: FD

44926
Tulsa Royalties Company
P.O. Box 2485
Shawnee, OK 74802-2485

Incorporated in 1951 in OK.
Donor(s): William S. Bailey, Jr.‡
Financial data (yr. ended 12/31/01): Grants paid, $457,000; assets, $1,577,998 (M); expenditures, $495,778; qualifying distributions, $457,000.
Limitations: Applications not accepted. Giving limited to Shawnee, OK.

Application information: Contributes only to a pre-selected organization.
Officers and Directors:* J. Robert Riggs, Pres.; John W. Parrish,* V.P. and Treas.; Mark Brister, V.P.; Bill Ford, Secy.; Rev. Roger Ferguson, Calvin Vogt.
EIN: 736101744
Codes: TN

44927
Herman P. and Sophia Taubman Foundation
c/o Bank of Oklahoma, N.A.
P.O. Box 880
Tulsa, OK 74101-0880

Trust established in 1955 in OK.
Donor(s): Herman P. Taubman,‡ Sophia Taubman.‡
Financial data (yr. ended 12/31/01): Grants paid, $427,000; assets, $8,706,220 (M); expenditures, $534,632; qualifying distributions, $422,512.
Limitations: Giving primarily in CA, OK, and TX.
Application information: Application form not required.
Agent: Bank of Oklahoma, N.A.
EIN: 736092820
Codes: FD

44928
The Albert and Hete Barthelmes Foundation, Inc.
1601 Main St., Ste. 100
Tulsa, OK 74119

Established in 1993 in OK.
Donor(s): Albert J. Barthelmes, Hedwig Barthelmes.‡
Financial data (yr. ended 12/31/01): Grants paid, $415,286; assets, $21,305,323 (M); gifts received, $98,697; expenditures, $1,683,146; qualifying distributions, $1,121,432; giving activities include $643,278 for programs.
Limitations: Giving primarily in Tulsa, OK.
Application information: Application form not required.
Officers and Directors:* Theresa M. Collins,* Pres.; Joseph L. Hull III,* V.P. and Secy.
EIN: 731423086
Codes: FD

44929
Clark and Wanda Bass Family Foundation
P.O. Box 948
McAlester, OK 74502-0948
Contact: Wanda Bass, Pres.

Established in 1999 in OK.
Donor(s): First National Bank & Trust Co.
Financial data (yr. ended 12/31/01): Grants paid, $415,200; assets, $723,869 (M); gifts received, $145,000; expenditures, $425,502; qualifying distributions, $425,008.
Limitations: Giving primarily in NM and OK.
Application information: Application form required.
Officer: Wanda Bass,* Pres.
Directors: Boyd C. Bass, Carlton C. Bass, Louise Bass.
EIN: 311645055
Codes: FD

44930
The Gelvin Foundation
(Formerly Lyle M. Gelvin Foundation)
Rte. 1, Box 50-A
Eufaula, OK 74432 (918) 452-3703
FAX: (918) 452-3995; *E-mail:*
lpcstarr@yahoo.com; trd@praywalker.com
Contact: Terry R. Doverspike, Tr., and Therese Starr, Tr.

Established in 1992 in OK.

Donor(s): Lyle M. Gelvin,‡ Lyle Pacific Corp.
Financial data (yr. ended 12/31/01): Grants paid, $411,400; assets, $8,184,999 (M); expenditures, $486,425; qualifying distributions, $416,874.
Limitations: Giving primarily in OK.
Publications: Informational brochure (including application guidelines).
Application information: Application form not required.
Officers and Trustees:* Therese Starr,* Pres. and Treas.; Terry Doverspike,* V.P. and Secy.
EIN: 731419663
Codes: FD

44931
Jean I. Everest Foundation
6301 N. Western Ave., Ste. 240
Oklahoma City, OK 73118-1062
(405) 840-1575
Contact: James H. Everest, Pres.

Donor(s): Jean I. Everest, James H. Everest.
Financial data (yr. ended 09/30/01): Grants paid, $408,000; assets, $3,405,419 (M); expenditures, $418,017; qualifying distributions, $407,095.
Limitations: Giving primarily in Oklahoma City, OK.
Application information: Application form not required.
Officers and Trustees:* James H. Everest,* Pres.; Harvey B. Everest,* V.P.; Janell L. Everest,* Secy.; Jean I. Everest II,* Treas.
EIN: 736106627
Codes: FD

44932
Merkel Family Foundation
2431 E. 61st St., Ste. 602
Tulsa, OK 74136-1235 (918) 644-5222
Contact: John B. Turner, Tr.

Established in 1989.
Financial data (yr. ended 12/31/01): Grants paid, $400,000; assets, $6,713,301 (M); expenditures, $579,649; qualifying distributions, $399,631.
Limitations: Giving on a national basis.
Application information: Application form required.
Trustees: Bryant J. Coffman, Carl E. Fritts, John B. Turner.
EIN: 736248411
Codes: FD

44933
Puterbaugh Foundation
215 E. Choctaw, First National Ctr., Ste. 114
P.O. Box 729
McAlester, OK 74502 (918) 426-1591
FAX: (918) 426-1648
Contact: Norris J. Welker, Managing Tr.

Trust established in 1949 in OK.
Donor(s): Jay Garfield Puterbaugh,‡ Leela Oliver Puterbaugh.‡
Financial data (yr. ended 12/31/01): Grants paid, $394,914; assets, $8,866,936 (M); expenditures, $536,650; qualifying distributions, $461,451; giving activities include $44,281 for programs.
Limitations: Giving primarily in OK.
Publications: Financial statement.
Application information: Budgets are set 1 year in advance of year of payment. Application form not required.
Trustees: Norris J. Welker, Managing Tr.; Frank G. Edwards, Steven W. Taylor.
EIN: 736092193
Codes: FD

44934
Fulton and Susie Collins Foundation
1924 S. Utica, Ste. 800
Tulsa, OK 74104 (918) 748-9860
Contact: Suzanne M. Collins, Tr.

Established in 1987 in OK.
Donor(s): G. Fulton Collins III.
Financial data (yr. ended 12/31/00): Grants paid, $390,966; assets, $8,870,526 (M); gifts received, $500,000; expenditures, $476,620; qualifying distributions, $387,023.
Limitations: Giving primarily in Tulsa, OK.
Application information: Application form not required.
Trustees: G. Fulton Collins III, Suzanne M. Collins.
EIN: 731273053
Codes: FD

44935
Educational Fund for Children of Phillips Petroleum Company Employees
1650 PB
Bartlesville, OK 74004
Scholarship application address: 1646 Phillips Bldg., Bartlesville, OK 74004, tel.: (918) 661-6248
Contact: Ron Stanley, Dir., Educational Funds

Established in 1939 in OK.
Donor(s): Phillips Petroleum Co.
Financial data (yr. ended 08/31/01): Grants paid, $382,061; assets, $0 (M); gifts received, $405,398; expenditures, $385,398; qualifying distributions, $385,398.
Limitations: Applications not accepted. Giving on a national basis.
Application information: Unsolicited requests for funds not accepted.
Officer: R.J. Stanley, Admin.
Selection Committee: J.R. Morris, R.W. Poole, Peggy Smith.
EIN: 736095141
Codes: CS, FD, CD, GTI

44936
Herbert and Roseline Gussman Foundation
15 E. 5th St., Ste. 3200
Tulsa, OK 74103

Established in 1951 in OK.
Donor(s): Herbert Gussman, Roseline Gussman,‡ Barbara Gussman, Ellen Jane Adelson.
Financial data (yr. ended 12/31/00): Grants paid, $369,550; assets, $10,990,972 (M); expenditures, $470,145; qualifying distributions, $369,578.
Limitations: Applications not accepted. Giving primarily in, but not limited to, Tulsa and Oklahoma City, OK, and NY.
Application information: Contributes only to pre-selected organizations.
Trustee: Herbert Gussman.
EIN: 736090063
Codes: FD

44937
Better Days Foundation, Inc.
3030 N.W. Expwy., Ste. 1313
Oklahoma City, OK 73112 (405) 942-5489
FAX: (405) 947-4403; *E-mail:*
dwitter@betterdays.org
Contact: Della Witter, Exec. Dir.

Established in 1994 in DE and CA.
Donor(s): Paul G. Heafy.
Financial data (yr. ended 11/30/01): Grants paid, $356,873; assets, $2,085,328 (M); gifts received, $2,000; expenditures, $450,025; qualifying distributions, $351,598.
Limitations: Giving primarily in Oklahoma City, OK.

Publications: Informational brochure (including application guidelines).
Application information: Application form not required.
Officers: Paul G. Heafy, Pres. and Treas.; Rhonda L. Heafy, V.P. and Secy.
EIN: 731440536
Codes: FD

44938
The George and Jennie Collins Foundation
2627 E. 21st St., Ste. 200
Tulsa, OK 74114-1710 (918) 742-5456
Contact: Roger B. Collins, Chair.

Established in 1943 in OK.
Donor(s): George F. Collins, Jr.,‡ Roger B. Collins, Liberty Glass Co.
Financial data (yr. ended 12/31/01): Grants paid, $351,870; assets, $5,273,647 (M); expenditures, $386,518; qualifying distributions, $349,901.
Limitations: Giving primarily in the Tulsa, OK, area.
Application information: Application form not required.
Trustees: Roger B. Collins, Chair.; Frances R. Collins, Fulton Collins.
EIN: 736093053
Codes: FD

44939
Charles Morton Share Trust
c/o Heritage Trust Co.
1900 N.W. Expwy., 50 Penn Pl., Rm. 225
Oklahoma City, OK 73118
Application addresses: c/o Donald L. Benson, Morford & Benson, P.O. Box 448, Alva, OK 73717; c/o Darrell Kline, Northwest Electric, 508 Flynn St., Alva, OK 73717; c/o J.R. Holder, Holder Drug Co., 513 Barnes, Alva, OK 73717; c/o Johnny C. Jones, Rialto Theatre, 516 Flynn St., Alva, OK 73717; c/o B. Michael Carroll, Heritage Trust Co., 1900 N.W. Expwy., 50 Penn Pl., Oklahoma City, OK 73118
Contact: B. Michael Carroll, Sr. V.P., Heritage Trust Co.

Trust established in 1959 in OK.
Donor(s): Charles Morton Share.‡
Financial data (yr. ended 06/30/01): Grants paid, $350,600; assets, $10,049,899 (M); expenditures, $596,749; qualifying distributions, $362,924.
Limitations: Giving primarily in OK.
Application information: Send copy of application to each trustee. Application form not required.
Trustees: Donald Benson, J.R. Holder, Johnny C. Jones, Darrell Kline, Heritage Trust Co.
EIN: 736090984
Codes: FD

44940
French Family Charitable Foundation
c/o Hal French
3404 E. 2nd St.
Edmond, OK 73034-7211

Established in 1999.
Financial data (yr. ended 12/31/01): Grants paid, $349,507; assets, $1,552,686 (M); expenditures, $350,217; qualifying distributions, $349,507.
Directors: Hal French, Kyle Maxwell.
EIN: 731546685

44941
Willard Johnston Foundation, Inc.
P.O. Box 54390
Oklahoma City, OK 73154-1390
(405) 767-7627
Contact: George J. Records, Mgr.

Established in 1951 in OK.
Financial data (yr. ended 12/31/01): Grants paid, $336,115; assets, $17,976,647 (M); gifts received, $6,222,198; expenditures, $421,348; qualifying distributions, $336,115.
Limitations: Applications not accepted. Giving primarily in Oklahoma City, OK.
Application information: Contributes only to pre-selected organizations. Unsolicited requests for funds not considered.
Manager: George J. Records.
EIN: 736093829
Codes: FD

44942
28:19, Inc.
7300 N. Comanche
Oklahoma City, OK 73132

Established in 1961.
Donor(s): Gene Warr, II Timothy 2:2 Foundation, Security Trust, Gibraltar Trust.
Financial data (yr. ended 11/30/00): Grants paid, $335,889; assets, $6,284,646 (M); gifts received, $807,452; expenditures, $741,388; qualifying distributions, $605,447.
Limitations: Applications not accepted. Giving on a national basis.
Application information: Contributes only to pre-selected organizations. Unsolicited requests not considered.
Officers: Gene Warr, Pres.; John R. Repass, V.P.; Robert Ross, Secy.-Treas.
EIN: 736091732
Codes: FD

44943
Tulsa Christian Foundation, Inc.
P.O. Box 4834
Tulsa, OK 74159-0834
Contact: Ray L. Felts, V.P.

Established in 1990 in OK.
Financial data (yr. ended 12/31/01): Grants paid, $335,625; assets, $3,436,633 (M); expenditures, $356,044; qualifying distributions, $346,684.
Publications: Application guidelines.
Application information: Application form required.
Officers: Bill T. Williamson, Pres.; Ray L. Felts, V.P.
Directors: Bill Bequette, Joe Cannon, Mike Davis, Bill Knowles, Ron Magnusson, Robert Mahaffey, Reece B. Morrel, Roy Riggs.
EIN: 730771408
Codes: FD

44944
Nellie Dobson Trust
c/o Bank of Oklahoma, N.A.
P.O. Box 880
Tulsa, OK 74101-0880
Application address: c/o V.P., Financial Affairs, Northeastern Oklahoma A&M College, Miami, OK 74354

Established in 1968 in OK.
Donor(s): Nellie Dobson.‡
Financial data (yr. ended 01/31/01): Grants paid, $335,014; assets, $9,157,380 (M); expenditures, $478,338; qualifying distributions, $389,202.
Limitations: Giving primarily in OK.
Application information: Application form not required.
Trustee: Bank of Oklahoma, N.A.

EIN: 736131333
Codes: FD, GTI

44945
The McGee Foundation, Inc.
P.O. Box 18127
Oklahoma City, OK 73154
Contact: Marcia Bieber, Pres.

Incorporated in 1963 in OK.
Donor(s): Dean A. McGee.‡
Financial data (yr. ended 06/30/01): Grants paid, $330,000; assets, $7,459,235 (M); expenditures, $344,066; qualifying distributions, $330,975.
Limitations: Giving primarily in CA and OK.
Publications: Application guidelines.
Application information: Application form not required.
Officers and Directors:* Marcia McGee Bieber,* Pres.; Patricia McGee Maino,* V.P.; Charles Bieber, M.D.,* Secy.-Treas.; Jerry Love.
EIN: 736099203
Codes: FD

44946
Broken Arrow Medical Center Foundation
P.O. Box 470372
Tulsa, OK 74147-0372 (918) 492-8100
Contact: W.R. Lissau, Pres.

Established in 1998 in OK.
Financial data (yr. ended 12/31/00): Grants paid, $322,275; assets, $4,815,226 (M); expenditures, $337,774; qualifying distributions, $319,374.
Limitations: Giving primarily in OK.
Application information: Application form not required.
Officers and Directors:* W.R. Lissau,* Pres.; M.O. Brown,* V.P.; D.B. Whitehill,* Secy.; M.A. Buntz,* Treas.; J.H. Beavers, S.I. Graham, B.D. Switzer, W.E. Weeks.
EIN: 731532494
Codes: FD

44947
Pearl M. and Julia J. Harmon Foundation
P.O. Box 52568
Tulsa, OK 74152-0568 (918) 743-6191
URL: http://www.harmonfoundation.com
Contact: George L. Hangs, Jr., Exec. Dir.

Established in 1962 in OK.
Donor(s): Claude C. Harmon,‡ Julia J. Harmon.‡
Financial data (yr. ended 05/31/01): Grants paid, $319,657; assets, $34,459,958 (M); expenditures, $804,057; qualifying distributions, $2,057,521; giving activities include $1,500,415 for program-related investments and $252,635 for programs.
Limitations: Giving limited to AR, KS, NM, OK, and TX, with preference given to northeastern OK.
Publications: Application guidelines.
Application information: All available funds are being directed toward the foundation's operating program; the foundation does not expect to solicit proposals over the next several years. However, applications are being accepted for program-related investment loans. Application form not required.
Officer and Trustees:* George L. Hangs, Jr.,* Exec. Dir.; C.H. Frederick, Jean M. Kuntz, B.L. Lee, C.K. Owens.
EIN: 736095893
Codes: FD

44948
Rosalinn Swinka Charitable Trust
c/o The Trust Co. of Oklahoma
P.O. Box 3627
Tulsa, OK 74101-3627

Established in 1999.
Financial data (yr. ended 12/31/01): Grants paid, $313,846; assets, $3,752,839 (M); expenditures, $346,518; qualifying distributions, $313,447.
Limitations: Applications not accepted. Giving limited to OK.
Application information: Contributes only to pre-selected organizations.
Trustee: The Trust Co. of Oklahoma.
EIN: 736310948
Codes: FD

44949
Irene M. and Julian J. Rothbaum Foundation
P.O. Box 21468
Tulsa, OK 74121-1468

Established in 1994 in OK.
Donor(s): Julian Rothbaum, Irene Rothbaum.
Financial data (yr. ended 12/31/99): Grants paid, $305,750; assets, $608,448 (M); expenditures, $309,283; qualifying distributions, $304,134.
Limitations: Applications not accepted.
Application information: Contributes only to pre-selected organizations.
Trustee: Julian J. Rothbaum.
EIN: 731463214
Codes: FD

44950
Harris Foundation, Inc.
6403 N.W. Grand Blvd., Ste. 207
Oklahoma City, OK 73116 (405) 848-3371
Contact: Jimi Humphreys, Secy.-Treas.

Incorporated in 1938 in OK.
Donor(s): Vernon V. Harris.‡
Financial data (yr. ended 12/31/01): Grants paid, $287,870; assets, $1,310,933 (M); expenditures, $321,091; qualifying distributions, $318,588.
Limitations: Giving limited to OK, with emphasis on Oklahoma City.
Application information: Application form not required.
Officers: William V. Harris, Pres.; Judith Garrett, V.P.; Robert H. Long, V.P.; Jimi Davidson, Secy.-Treas.
EIN: 736093072
Codes: FD

44951
Broadhurst Foundation
401 S. Boston, Ste. 100
Tulsa, OK 74103-4002 (918) 584-0661
Contact: Ann Cassidy Baker, Chair.

Established in 1951 in OK.
Donor(s): William Broadhurst.‡
Financial data (yr. ended 12/31/01): Grants paid, $273,737; assets, $7,380,696 (M); expenditures, $658,830; qualifying distributions, $349,125.
Limitations: Giving primarily in Tulsa, OK.
Application information: Application form not required.
Officers: Ann Cassidy Baker, Chair.; Ernestine B. Howard, Vice-Chair.
Trustees: John Cassidy, Jr., Clint V. Cox, Wishard Lemons.
EIN: 736061115
Codes: FD

44952
Dexter G. Johnson Educational and Benevolent Trust
P.O. Box 1620
Tulsa, OK 74101-0880
Application address: P.O. Box 26663, Oklahoma City, OK 73126-0663
Contact: Betty Crews

Established in 1971 in OK.
Financial data (yr. ended 12/31/00): Grants paid, $263,843; assets, $4,570,804 (M); expenditures, $411,590; qualifying distributions, $220,147.
Limitations: Giving limited to OK.
Trustees: David L. Boren, James E. Halligan, Steve Jennings.
Agent: Bank of Oklahoma, N.A.
EIN: 237389204
Codes: FD, GTI

44953
The Norman Foundation Trust
127 N.W. 10th St.
Oklahoma City, OK 73103

Established in 1994 in OK.
Donor(s): Cecelia A. Norman, John W. Norman.
Financial data (yr. ended 12/31/01): Grants paid, $262,292; assets, $447,434 (M); gifts received, $410,000; expenditures, $263,056; qualifying distributions, $262,984.
Limitations: Applications not accepted. Giving primarily in OK.
Application information: Contributes only to pre-selected organizations.
Trustees: Cecelia A. Norman, John W. Norman.
EIN: 731468224
Codes: FD

44954
Paul L. & Helen I. Sisk Charitable Trust
5319 S. Lewis Ave., Ste. 110
Tulsa, OK 74105-6543
Application address: P.O. Box 700597, Tulsa, OK 74170-0597

Established in 1989 in OK.
Financial data (yr. ended 12/31/00): Grants paid, $260,000; assets, $6,142,539 (M); expenditures, $433,061; qualifying distributions, $320,259.
Limitations: Giving primarily in Tulsa, OK.
Application information: Application form required.
Trustees: Charles W. Harris, Ruth Sowards.
EIN: 736243607
Codes: FD

44955
Buford Family Foundation
3310 S. Birmingham Ave.
Tulsa, OK 74105
FAX: (918) 742-8519; E-mail: viperz@ibm.net
Contact: Martha C. Buford, Pres.

Established in 1997 in OK.
Donor(s): Martha C. Buford.
Financial data (yr. ended 12/31/01): Grants paid, $256,500; assets, $2,722,429 (M); expenditures, $266,263; qualifying distributions, $257,110.
Limitations: Applications not accepted. Giving primarily in KS and OK.
Application information: Contributes only to pre-selected organizations.
Officers and Directors:* Martha C. Buford,* Pres. and Secy.; Josephine B. Siegfried,* V.P. and Treas.; Anne S. Buford, C. Robert Buford, R.C. Buford.
EIN: 731519009
Codes: FD

44956
Vose Foundation, Inc.
(Formerly First National Foundation, Inc.)
9520 N. May Ave., Ste. 310
Oklahoma City, OK 73120 (405) 751-7882
Contact: Charles A. Vose, Jr., Pres.

Incorporated in 1954 in OK.
Financial data (yr. ended 12/31/01): Grants paid, $253,709; assets, $657,676 (M); expenditures, $273,273; qualifying distributions, $256,270.
Limitations: Giving primarily in Oklahoma City, OK.
Publications: Application guidelines.
Officers and Directors:* Charles A. Vose, Jr., Pres.; Gene Furnish,* V.P.; June Stevens, Secy.-Treas.; Barbara W. Vose.
EIN: 736099287
Codes: FD

44957
Sanford P. and Irene F. Burnstein Foundation
P.O. Box 582527
Tulsa, OK 74158 (918) 831-3021
Contact: Sanford P. Burnstein, Tr.

Established in 1989 in OK.
Donor(s): Sanford P. Burnstein.
Financial data (yr. ended 12/31/01): Grants paid, $242,450; assets, $1,793,619 (M); gifts received, $1,000,000; expenditures, $247,024; qualifying distributions, $244,434.
Limitations: Giving primarily in Tulsa, OK.
Application information: Application form not required.
Trustees: Irene F. Burnstein, Sanford P. Burnstein.
EIN: 736247047
Codes: FD2

44958
American Fidelity Corporation Founders Fund, Inc.
2000 N. Classen Blvd.
Oklahoma City, OK 73106
Application address: P.O. Box 25523, Oklahoma City, OK 73125
Contact: Jo Ella Ramsey, Secy.

Established in 1984 in OK.
Donor(s): American Fidelity Assurance Co.
Financial data (yr. ended 12/31/01): Grants paid, $233,977; assets, $4,171,933 (M); expenditures, $238,256; qualifying distributions, $232,482.
Limitations: Giving primarily in OK.
Publications: Application guidelines.
Application information: Application form required.
Officers and Directors:* William M. Cameron,* Pres.; John W. Rex,* Exec V.P. and Treas.; Jo Ella Ramsey,* Secy.; Jo Carol Cameron,* Treas.; Brett Barrowman, Laura Cameron, William E. Durrett.
EIN: 731236059
Codes: CS, FD2, CD

44959
The Joullian Foundation, Inc.
13439 Broadway Ext.
Oklahoma City, OK 73114-2202
Contact: Marion Joullian Story, Pres.

Established in 1994 in OK.
Donor(s): Edward C. Joullian III, Letitia R. Joullian, E. Carey Joullian IV, Marion Story.
Financial data (yr. ended 12/31/00): Grants paid, $225,850; assets, $3,951,336 (M); expenditures, $336,982; qualifying distributions, $250,610.
Limitations: Giving primarily in OK.
Application information: Application form not required.
Officers: Marion J. Story, Pres.; E. Carey Joullian IV, V.P.; Letitia R. Joullian, Secy.

44959—OKLAHOMA

EIN: 731463646
Codes: FD2

44960
Silas Foundation
c/o Arvest Trust Company, N.A.
P.O. Box 2448
Bartlesville, OK 74005 (918) 337-3279
Contact: Scott Thompson

Established in 1993 in OK.
Donor(s): C.J. Silas.
Financial data (yr. ended 12/31/01): Grants paid, $224,500; assets, $4,162,083 (M); expenditures, $232,749; qualifying distributions, $223,425.
Limitations: Giving primarily in OK, with emphasis on Bartlesville.
Application information: Application form not required.
Trustees: C.J. Silas, Theo Silas, Arvest Trust Company, N.A.
EIN: 736260168
Codes: FD2

44961
Stephenson Family Foundation
(Formerly Stephenson Family Charitable Foundation)
110 W. 7th St.
Tulsa, OK 74119

Established in 1997 in OK.
Donor(s): Charles C. Stephenson, Jr., Peggy C. Stephenson.
Financial data (yr. ended 12/31/01): Grants paid, $220,304; assets, $3,021,484 (M); gifts received, $3,050; expenditures, $228,390; qualifying distributions, $218,020.
Limitations: Applications not accepted.
Application information: Contributes only to pre-selected organizations.
Trustees: Charles C. Stephenson, Jr., Peggy C. Stephenson.
EIN: 736301100
Codes: FD2

44962
Joe & Jean Holliman Family Foundation
(Formerly Howard E. Felt Foundation)
10 E. 3rd St., Ste. 400
Tulsa, OK 74103-3660
Contact: Joe M. Holliman, Pres.

Established in 1945 in OK.
Financial data (yr. ended 12/31/01): Grants paid, $219,000; assets, $4,265,533 (M); gifts received, $50,269; expenditures, $223,414; qualifying distributions, $219,000.
Limitations: Applications not accepted. Giving primarily in Tulsa, OK.
Application information: Contributes only to pre-selected organizations.
Officers and Directors:* Joe M. Holliman,* Pres.; Joanna H. Potts,* V.P.; Jean F. Holliman,* Secy.-Treas.; John H. Holliman, Janice H. Stanfield.
EIN: 736092860
Codes: FD2

44963
George Fulton Collins, Jr. Foundation
1924 S. Utica, Ste. 800
Tulsa, OK 74104 (918) 748-9860
Contact: Fulton Collins, Chair.

Established in 1968 in OK.
Financial data (yr. ended 12/31/01): Grants paid, $215,000; assets, $3,846,918 (M); expenditures, $223,094; qualifying distributions, $212,982.
Limitations: Applications not accepted. Giving primarily in Tulsa, OK.
Application information: Contributes only to pre-selected organizations.
Officers: Fulton Collins, Chair.; Suzanne M. Collins, Secy.; Roger B. Collins, Treas.
EIN: 237008179
Codes: FD2

44964
The Lucille and Harrold Peterson Foundation
2200 N.W. 50th, Ste. 280
Oklahoma City, OK 73112

Donor(s): Lucille C. Peterson.
Financial data (yr. ended 11/11/01): Grants paid, $194,000; assets, $3,401,565 (M); expenditures, $270,744; qualifying distributions, $194,000.
Limitations: Applications not accepted.
Application information: Contributes only to pre-selected organizations.
Trustees: Harrold R. Peterson, Lucille C. Peterson.
EIN: 731552150
Codes: FD2

44965
Lorene Cooper Hasbrouck Charitable Trust
c/o Boone, Smith, Davis, Hurst, & Dickman
500 Oneok Plz.
Tulsa, OK 74103 (918) 587-0000
E-mail: wkellough@boonesmith.com
Contact: William C. Kellough, Tr.

Established in 1992 in OK.
Donor(s): Lorene Cooper Hasbrouck.‡
Financial data (yr. ended 04/30/01): Grants paid, $185,170; assets, $3,351,026 (M); expenditures, $232,302; qualifying distributions, $184,323.
Limitations: Giving primarily in Tulsa and northeastern OK.
Application information: Application form not required.
Trustees: William C. Kellough, L.K. Smith.
EIN: 736264438
Codes: FD2

44966
Helmerich Trust
1579 E. 21st St.
Tulsa, OK 74114 (918) 742-5531
Contact: Hans C. Helmerich, Tr.

Established in 1992 in OK.
Donor(s): Walter H. Helmerich III.
Financial data (yr. ended 12/31/01): Grants paid, $183,300; assets, $4,436,750 (M); gifts received, $474,350; expenditures, $197,820; qualifying distributions, $180,869.
Limitations: Giving primarily in Tulsa, OK.
Application information: Application form not required.
Trustees: Dow Z. Helmerich, Hans C. Helmerich, Jonathan D. Helmerich, Matthew G. Helmerich, Walter H. Helmerich IV.
EIN: 731304358
Codes: FD2

44967
Inasmuch Foundation
P.O. Box 2325
Oklahoma City, OK 73101-2325
(405) 235-1356
FAX: (405) 604-0297; *E-mail:* inasmuchfdn@coxinet.net
Contact: Rita L. Holder, Coord.

Established in 1982 in OK.
Donor(s): Edith Gaylord Harper.‡
Financial data (yr. ended 06/30/01): Grants paid, $179,500; assets, $5,708,715 (M); gifts received, $1,020,108; expenditures, $305,304; qualifying distributions, $242,037.
Limitations: Giving primarily in Colorado Springs, CO, and OK.
Publications: Informational brochure (including application guidelines).
Application information: Application form required.
Trustees: David O. Hogan, Andrew W. Roff, J. Hugh Roff, Jr., Patrick T. Rooney, Robert J. Ross, William J. Ross.
Advisory Committee: Christine Gaylord Everest, Cathy O. Robbins, Jeanne H. Smith, Barbara L. Yalich.
EIN: 731167188
Codes: FD2

44968
Montfort Jones and Allie Brown Jones Foundation
P.O. Box 1234
Bristow, OK 74010

Established in 1960 in OK.
Donor(s): Allie B. Jones.‡
Financial data (yr. ended 08/31/01): Grants paid, $177,636; assets, $3,920,798 (M); expenditures, $225,550; qualifying distributions, $200,766.
Limitations: Applications not accepted. Giving limited to organizations that specifically benefit Bristow, OK.
Application information: Contributes only to pre-selected organizations.
Officers: David H. Loeffler, Jr.,* Chair.; Hazel S. Earnhardt,* Secy.
Trustees: Roger Collins, Stan Earnhardt.
EIN: 730721557
Codes: FD2

44969
Ethics & Excellence in Journalism Foundation
P.O. Box 2324
Oklahoma City, OK 73101-2324
(405) 235-1356
FAX: (405) 604-0297; *E-mail:* eejfdn@coxinet.net
Contact: Rita L. Holder, Coord.

Established in 1982.
Donor(s): Edith G. Harper.‡
Financial data (yr. ended 06/30/01): Grants paid, $177,539; assets, $5,767,478 (M); gifts received, $770,107; expenditures, $295,188; qualifying distributions, $231,041.
Limitations: Giving on a national basis, with some emphasis on OK.
Publications: Informational brochure (including application guidelines).
Application information: Application form required.
Directors: David O. Hogan, Andrew W. Roff, J. Hugh Roff, Jr., Patrick T. Rooney, Robert J. Ross, William J. Ross.
Advisory Committee Members: Andrew C. Barth, Janet Cromley, Marian Cromley, Kay Dyer, John T. Greiner, Jr., John A. Rieger, Andrew W. Roff, Patrick T. Rooney, Robert J. Ross.
EIN: 731167175
Codes: FD2

44970
Robert C. and Mary E. Lolmaugh Trust Foundation
(Formerly Lolmaugh Trust Foundation)
P.O. Box 1228
Guymon, OK 73942

Established in 1998 in OK.
Financial data (yr. ended 06/30/01): Grants paid, $177,274; assets, $4,093,855 (M); expenditures, $289,903; qualifying distributions, $173,671.
Limitations: Giving primarily in OK.
Trustee: City National Bank & Trust Co.

EIN: 731516313

44971
Tom S. and Marye Kate Aldridge Charitable & Educational Trust
3035 N.W. 63rd, Ste. 207N
Oklahoma City, OK 73116 (405) 840-9916
E-mail: aldro@accessacg.net; *URL:* http://www.tmkaf.org
Contact: Robert Aldridge, Chair.

Established in 1995 in OK.
Donor(s): Tom S. Aldridge.‡
Financial data (yr. ended 06/30/01): Grants paid, $174,364; assets, $3,695,722 (M); expenditures, $270,891; qualifying distributions, $254,089.
Limitations: Giving primarily in Escambie and Santa Rosa counties, FL, Pottawatomie, Grady, Oklahoma and Cleveland counties, OK, and Hunt, Raines and Brazoria counties, TX.
Publications: Informational brochure (including application guidelines), newsletter.
Application information: Application form not required.
Officers and Directors:* Robert S. Aldridge,* Chair. and Treas.; Laverne R. Aldridge,* Vice-Chair.; Kimberly F. Aldridge, M.L. Aldridge, Barbara Foerster, Parris R. Nicholson, Mickie Beth Smith.
EIN: 731484075
Codes: FD2

44972
Oklahoma Scholarship Fund
3030 N.W. Expressway, Ste. 1313
Oklahoma City, OK 73112-5466
(405) 942-5489
Contact: Karen Horton

Established in 1995 in OK.
Donor(s): CEO America, Better Days Foundation.
Financial data (yr. ended 11/30/01): Grants paid, $172,410; assets, $96 (M); gifts received, $170,700; expenditures, $172,475; qualifying distributions, $172,610.
Limitations: Giving limited to OK.
Application information: Application form required.
Officers: Paul G. Heafy, Co-Chair.; Rhonda L. Heafy, Co-Chair.; Della Witter, Exec. Dir.
EIN: 731484452
Codes: FD2, GTI

44973
The Herman and Mary Wegener Foundation, Inc.
P.O. Box 18335
Oklahoma City, OK 73154-0335
Application address: 6301 N. Western, No. 120, Oklahoma City, OK 73118

Incorporated in 1954 in OK.
Donor(s): Herman H. Wegener.‡
Financial data (yr. ended 12/31/01): Grants paid, $171,000; assets, $2,510,644 (M); expenditures, $231,640; qualifying distributions, $178,988.
Limitations: Giving primarily in Oklahoma City, OK.
Officers and Trustees:* Willis B. Sherin,* Pres.; Lee Holmes,* V.P.; Clenard Wegener,* Treas.; Rosemary Fields, Eugene C. Wegener, Jeff Wegener, Raymond Lee Wegener.
EIN: 736095407
Codes: FD2

44974
Edward D. & Janet K. Robson Foundation
7136 S. Yale, Ste. 208
Tulsa, OK 74136
Contact: Sheila Dirck

Established in 2000 in OK.
Donor(s): Edward D. Robson, Janet K. Robson.
Financial data (yr. ended 12/31/00): Grants paid, $169,488; assets, $20,236 (M); gifts received, $202,294; expenditures, $170,434; qualifying distributions, $170,434.
Limitations: Giving primarily in FL and Nowata, OK.
Trustees: Edward D. Robson, Janet K. Robson.
EIN: 731589395
Codes: FD2

44975
Robert A. Parman Foundation
c/o Bank of Oklahoma, Trust Dept.
P.O. Box 24128
Oklahoma City, OK 73124
Application address: 1419 W. Reno, Oklahoma City, OK 73106, tel.: (405) 236-5561
Contact: John L. Hessel, Tr.

Trust established in 1962 in OK.
Donor(s): Robert A. Parman.‡
Financial data (yr. ended 08/31/01): Grants paid, $158,500; assets, $5,477,535 (M); expenditures, $305,307; qualifying distributions, $181,002.
Limitations: Giving primarily in OK.
Application information: Application form not required.
Trustees: John L. Hessel, J.W. "Buzz" Lanier, Jerry M. Thomason, Bank of Oklahoma, N.A.
EIN: 736098053
Codes: FD2

44976
Commonwealth Foundation
2125 E. 32nd Pl.
Tulsa, OK 74105

Established in 1994 in OK.
Donor(s): Randi Stuart Wightman.
Financial data (yr. ended 12/31/01): Grants paid, $158,000; assets, $2,256,581 (M); expenditures, $175,898; qualifying distributions, $158,000.
Limitations: Applications not accepted. Giving primarily in Tulsa, OK.
Application information: Contributes only to pre-selected organizations.
Trustees: Fred Wightman, Kathleen Wightman, Malcolm Stuart Wightman, Randi Stuart Wightman.
EIN: 731463741
Codes: FD2

44977
Bailey Family Memorial Trust
c/o Bank of Oklahoma, N.A.
P.O. Box 880
Tulsa, OK 74101-0880
Additional application address: c/o William A. Ivy, Dir., Ctr. for Global Studies, College of Arts & Science, Oklahoma State Univ., Stillwater, OK 74078
Contact: Cynthia L. Sutton, Bank of Oklahoma, N.A.

Established in 1982 in OK.
Donor(s): J.B. Bailey,‡ Brewster E. Fitz, Lawrence B. Halka, S.J. Jatras.‡
Financial data (yr. ended 08/31/01): Grants paid, $155,808; assets, $2,219,510 (M); expenditures, $177,988; qualifying distributions, $170,891.
Limitations: Giving limited to OK.
Publications: Application guidelines.

Application information: Recipients are recommended by members of the faculty at Oklahoma State University.
Trustee: Bank of Oklahoma, N.A.
EIN: 736210018
Codes: FD2, GTI

44978
Communities Foundation of Oklahoma
(Formerly Oklahoma Communities Foundation, Inc.)
101 N. Broadway, Ste. 920
Oklahoma City, OK 73102 (405) 218-4080
FAX: (405) 218-4082; *E-mail:* okcomfdn@texhoma.net

Established in 1992 in OK.
Financial data (yr. ended 12/31/99): Grants paid, $155,617; assets, $1,426,201 (L); gifts received, $680,988; expenditures, $230,089.
Limitations: Giving primarily in OK.
Publications: Informational brochure.
Officers: Richard E. Dixon, Chair.; Toby Thompson, Pres.
EIN: 731396320
Codes: CM, FD2

44979
The Cuesta Foundation, Inc.
6120 S. Yale, Ste. 1800
Tulsa, OK 74136 (918) 496-0770
Contact: Donald P. Carpenter, V.P.

Incorporated in 1962 in OK.
Donor(s): Charles W. Oliphant,‡ Allene O. Mayo, Allen G. Oliphant, Jr., Gertrude O. Sundgren, Eric B. Oliphant, Nancy B. Oliphant, Mrs. Charles Oliphant, Gregory W. Oliphant.
Financial data (yr. ended 04/30/01): Grants paid, $151,850; assets, $4,243,228 (M); gifts received, $2,000; expenditures, $180,408; qualifying distributions, $162,806.
Limitations: Giving primarily in OK, with emphasis on Tulsa.
Publications: Annual report, financial statement.
Application information: Application form not required.
Officers and Directors:* Eric B. Oliphant,* Chair. and Pres.; Donald P. Carpenter,* V.P.; Richard E. Wright III,* Secy.; Rex M. Shawger, Treas.; Allene O. Mayo, Arline B. Oliphant, Gertrude O. Sundgren.
EIN: 736091550
Codes: FD2

44980
Roy L. Bliss Family Foundation
2551 E. 26th Pl.
Tulsa, OK 74114
Contact: Roy L. Bliss, Dir.

Established in 1997 in OK.
Donor(s): Roy L. Bliss, Toni L. Bliss.
Financial data (yr. ended 12/31/01): Grants paid, $149,330; assets, $479,633 (M); gifts received, $13,142; expenditures, $225,042; qualifying distributions, $149,330.
Limitations: Giving primarily in OK.
Directors: Mark H. Allen, Roy L. Bliss, Toni L. Bliss.
EIN: 731531425
Codes: FD2

44981
Brown Foundation
1707 Elmhurst
Oklahoma City, OK 73120

Established in 1986.
Donor(s): William C. Brown, Carolyn M. Brown.

44981—OKLAHOMA

Financial data (yr. ended 12/31/01): Grants paid, $147,500; assets, $4,720,859 (M); gifts received, $683,180; expenditures, $147,511; qualifying distributions, $146,231.
Limitations: Applications not accepted. Giving primarily in Oklahoma City, OK.
Application information: Contributes only to pre-selected organizations.
Trustees: Carolyn M. Brown, William C. Brown.
EIN: 736230335
Codes: FD2

44982
Cordelia Lunceford Beatty Trust
Security Bank Bldg., 2nd Fl.
P.O. Box 514
Blackwell, OK 74631-0514 (580) 363-3684
Application address: 105 N. Main St., Blackwell, OK 74631
Contact: James R. Rodgers, Tr.

Established in 1943 in OK.
Financial data (yr. ended 12/31/01): Grants paid, $145,965; assets, $3,072,813 (M); expenditures, $185,200; qualifying distributions, $165,805.
Limitations: Giving limited to Blackwell, OK.
Application information: Application form required for scholarships.
Trustees: James R. Rodgers, William W. Rodgers.
EIN: 736094952
Codes: FD2, GTI

44983
The Thomas E. Naugle Foundation
2739 E. 69th Pl.
Tulsa, OK 74136

Established in 1988 in OK.
Donor(s): Thomas E. Naugle, Barbara A. Naugle.
Financial data (yr. ended 12/31/01): Grants paid, $143,860; assets, $261,713 (M); gifts received, $93,181; expenditures, $144,217; qualifying distributions, $143,563.
Limitations: Applications not accepted. Giving primarily in OK.
Application information: Contributes only to pre-selected organizations.
Trustees: Barbara A. Naugle, Thomas E. Naugle.
EIN: 731313508
Codes: FD2

44984
Florence L. J. and Howard G. Barnett Foundation
2619 E. 37th St.
Tulsa, OK 74105-3507
Contact: Florence L.J. Barnett, Tr.

Established in 1997 in OK.
Donor(s): Florence L.J. Barnett, Howard G. Barnett.
Financial data (yr. ended 12/31/01): Grants paid, $141,000; assets, $8,534,427 (M); gifts received, $2,400; expenditures, $241,492; qualifying distributions, $141,000.
Limitations: Giving primarily in Tulsa, OK.
Application information: Application form not required.
Trustees: Florence L.J. Barnett, Howard G. Barnett.
EIN: 736295453
Codes: FD2

44985
The Cleo L. Craig Foundation
907 E. 35th St.
P.O. Box 1213
Shawnee, OK 74802 (405) 273-6800
Contact: Cleo L. Craig, Jr., Chair.

Established in 1997 in OK.

Financial data (yr. ended 12/31/00): Grants paid, $138,884; assets, $3,380,054 (M); expenditures, $181,052; qualifying distributions, $150,788.
Limitations: Giving primarily in OK.
Application information: Application provided by foundation. Application form required.
Officer: Cleo L. Craig, Jr., Chair.
Trustees: Bryant Craig, Helen Craig, April Craig Stobbe, John C. Stobbe.
EIN: 731519557
Codes: FD2

44986
Mr. & Mrs. Henry W. Browne Foundation
600 N. May Ave.
Oklahoma City, OK 73107

Established in 1989 in OK.
Donor(s): Henry W. Browne, Sr., Henry Browne, Mrs. Henry Browne.
Financial data (yr. ended 12/31/01): Grants paid, $135,500; assets, $1,304,221 (M); expenditures, $138,916; qualifying distributions, $134,990.
Limitations: Applications not accepted. Giving primarily in CA and OK.
Application information: Contributes only to pre-selected organizations.
Trustees: Claudine S. Browne, Henry W. Browne, Sr., Henry W. Browne, Jr., Robert F. Browne, Kelsey Browne Hall.
EIN: 736247173
Codes: FD2

44987
Margaret Vivian Bilby Foundation
3501 N.W. 63rd St., Ste. 206
Oklahoma City, OK 73116 (405) 840-4920
Contact: David R. Brown, Pres.

Established in 1999 in OK.
Donor(s): Samuel Noble Roberts Fund.
Financial data (yr. ended 10/31/01): Grants paid, $130,500; assets, $2,848,347 (M); expenditures, $133,914; qualifying distributions, $130,122.
Limitations: Giving limited to OK.
Application information: Application form required.
Officers and Trustees:* David R. Brown,* Pres.; Ann N. Brown,* V.P.; Marianne B. Rooney,* Secy.; D. Randolph Brown, Jr.,* Treas.; Susan Ruppert.
EIN: 731553170
Codes: FD2

44988
Krueger Charitable Foundation
6929 E. 62nd Pl.
Tulsa, OK 74133

Established in 1994 in OK.
Donor(s): W.C. Krueger, Carol K. Krueger, Alma M. Krueger.
Financial data (yr. ended 10/31/01): Grants paid, $130,117; assets, $2,624,238 (M); gifts received, $775; expenditures, $132,942; qualifying distributions, $128,274.
Limitations: Applications not accepted. Giving primarily in CO, MA, and OK.
Application information: Contributes only to pre-selected organizations.
Trustees: Robert Bernthal, Angie Jackson, Carol K. Krueger, W.C. Krueger, Gary Edward Morris.
EIN: 731459816
Codes: FD2

44989
Bilby Foundation
c/o Mary Jane Noble
333 W. Main St., Ste. 380
Ardmore, OK 73401-6300

Established in 1999 in OK.

Financial data (yr. ended 12/31/01): Grants paid, $128,000; assets, $2,448,473 (M); expenditures, $135,285; qualifying distributions, $128,000.
Limitations: Applications not accepted.
Application information: Contributes only to pre-selected organizations.
Officers and Trustees:* Mary Jane Noble,* Pres.; Shelley Mullins,* V.P.; Nicholas Noble,* Secy.; Russell Noble,* Treas.
EIN: 731554618

44990
Hu & Eva Maud Bartlett Foundation
300 S. Oak
Sapulpa, OK 74066

Established in 1950 in OK.
Financial data (yr. ended 12/31/01): Grants paid, $125,486; assets, $2,181,531 (M); expenditures, $141,334; qualifying distributions, $125,486.
Limitations: Giving primarily in Sapulpa, OK.
Trustees: Barbara Benedict, Cale Sherwood, Jerrold Benedict, Sherry Sherwood.
EIN: 736092249
Codes: FD2

44991
Dave Morgan Foundation
P.O. Box 820
Blackwell, OK 74631
FAX: (580) 363-4042; E-mail: dmfound@KSKC.net
Contact: Bill Seymour, Chair.

Established in 1995 in OK.
Donor(s): Dave Morgan.‡
Financial data (yr. ended 02/28/01): Grants paid, $124,400; assets, $3,839,515 (M); expenditures, $183,870; qualifying distributions, $124,400.
Limitations: Giving primarily in Blackwell and Kay County, OK.
Publications: Annual report.
Application information: Application form required.
Officers and Trustees:* Bill Seymour,* Chair.; Shea Erickson, Exec. Dir.; Bank One Trust Co., N.A.
EIN: 731475560
Codes: FD2

44992
K. S. Adams Foundation
c/o Arvest Trust Company, N.A.
P.O. Box 2248
Bartlesville, OK 74005-2248 (918) 337-3279
Contact: Scott Thompson

Established in 1953 in OK.
Financial data (yr. ended 12/31/01): Grants paid, $122,235; assets, $1,539,744 (M); expenditures, $141,324; qualifying distributions, $140,812.
Limitations: Giving primarily in Bartlesville, OK.
Application information: Application form not required.
Trustee: Arvest Trust Company, N.A.
EIN: 736091602
Codes: FD2

44993
M. D. Jirous Foundation, Inc.
c/o Owen & Thorp, Inc.
50 Penn Pl., Ste. 300
Oklahoma City, OK 73118

Established in 1995 in OK.
Donor(s): M.D. Jirous.
Financial data (yr. ended 12/31/01): Grants paid, $121,935; assets, $2,091,786 (M); gifts received, $365,000; expenditures, $140,847; qualifying distributions, $139,223.

Limitations: Applications not accepted. Giving primarily in OK.
Application information: Contributes only to pre-selected organizations.
Officers and Directors:* M.D. Jirous,* Pres.; Barbara L. Jirous,* V.P.; William E. Owen,* Secy.
EIN: 731483496
Codes: FD2

44994
The Margery Mayo Bird Foundation
2145 E. 29th St.
Tulsa, OK 74114-5421

Established in 1998.
Donor(s): Margery Mayo Bird.
Financial data (yr. ended 12/31/01): Grants paid, $121,800; assets, $996,582 (M); gifts received, $232,882; expenditures, $123,980; qualifying distributions, $121,800.
Limitations: Giving primarily in Tulsa, OK.
Trustee: Margery Mayo Bird.
EIN: 731535370
Codes: FD2

44995
Williams Foundation, Inc.
6301 N. Western, Ste. 200
Oklahoma City, OK 73118 (405) 879-2000
Contact: G. Rainey Williams, Jr., Pres.

Established in 1994 in OK.
Donor(s): Martha V. Williams, Vose Foundation, Inc.
Financial data (yr. ended 12/31/01): Grants paid, $118,998; assets, $1,545,657 (M); gifts received, $439,781; expenditures, $127,499; qualifying distributions, $118,532.
Limitations: Giving primarily in Oklahoma City, OK.
Officers: G. Rainey Williams, Jr., Pres.; Martha V. Williams, V.P.; Lucy A. Brown, Secy.-Treas.
EIN: 731464753
Codes: FD2

44996
Ad Astra Foundation
5653 N. Pennsylvania Ave.
Oklahoma City, OK 73112 (405) 848-2113
Contact: Richard L. Sias, Pres.

Established in 1986 in OK.
Donor(s): Richard L. Sias, Jeannette F. Sias.
Financial data (yr. ended 12/31/99): Grants paid, $118,795; assets, $3,131,078 (M); expenditures, $123,399; qualifying distributions, $118,795.
Limitations: Applications not accepted. Giving limited to Oklahoma City, OK.
Application information: Contributes only to pre-selected organizations.
Officers and Trustees:* Richard L. Sias,* Pres.; Jeannette F. Sias,* V.P.; Alice S. Pippin, Secy.-Treas.
EIN: 731278163
Codes: FD2

44997
The Harry and Ursula Guterman Foundation
5821 S. Indianapolis
Tulsa, OK 74135
Application address: 4150 S. 100th East Ave., Ste. 308, Tulsa, OK 74146, tel.: (918) 665-3535
Contact: Harry Guterman, Tr.

Established in 1992 in OK.
Donor(s): Harry Guterman, Ursula Guterman.
Financial data (yr. ended 05/31/02): Grants paid, $118,441; assets, $1,019,446 (M); gifts received, $25,000; expenditures, $131,577; qualifying distributions, $118,441.
Limitations: Giving primarily in Tulsa, OK.
Trustees: Harry Guterman, Ursula Guterman.

EIN: 731416063

44998
Mary K. Chapman Foundation
1 Warren Pl., Ste. 1816
6100 S. Yale
Tulsa, OK 74136 (918) 496-7882
Contact: J. Jerry Dickman, Tr.; or Donne W. Pitman, Tr.

Established in 1996 in OK.
Donor(s): Mary K. Chapman.
Financial data (yr. ended 12/31/01): Grants paid, $117,500; assets, $3,086,669 (M); gifts received, $597,135; expenditures, $132,953; qualifying distributions, $114,714.
Limitations: Giving primarily in Tulsa and northeastern OK.
Application information: Application form required.
Trustees: J. Jerry Dickman, Donne W. Pitman.
EIN: 731499528
Codes: FD2

44999
Mary K. Ashbrook Foundation for El Reno
P.O. Box 627
El Reno, OK 73036-0627

Established in 1978 in OK.
Donor(s): Mary K. Ashbrook,‡ Senior Citizens Center, El Reno.
Financial data (yr. ended 06/30/01): Grants paid, $116,744; assets, $2,043,513 (M); gifts received, $23,000; expenditures, $153,563; qualifying distributions, $132,178.
Limitations: Giving limited to El Reno, OK.
Publications: Application guidelines.
Application information: Application form required.
Trustees: Betty L. Dittmer, Virginia Sue Douglas, Gayle Meinberg.
EIN: 731049531
Codes: FD2

45000
Hargrove Family Foundation
9933 Hidden Hollow Ln.
Oklahoma City, OK 73151

Established in 2000 in OK.
Donor(s): Kevin Hargrove, Julie Hargrove.
Financial data (yr. ended 12/31/01): Grants paid, $115,000; assets, $77,593 (M); gifts received, $95,000; expenditures, $118,911; qualifying distributions, $115,000.
Limitations: Applications not accepted.
Application information: Contributes only to pre-selected organizations.
Officers: Kevin W. Hargrove, Pres. and Treas.; Julie Hargrove, V.P. and Secy.
EIN: 731601947

45001
W. J. Jones Family Foundation
(Formerly Catherine May Jones Foundation)
2 Leadership Sq.
211 N. Robinson, 14th Fl.
Oklahoma City, OK 73102

Established in 1987 in OK.
Donor(s): W.J. Jones.
Financial data (yr. ended 12/31/01): Grants paid, $115,000; assets, $2,418,860 (M); expenditures, $119,007; qualifying distributions, $119,007.
Limitations: Applications not accepted. Giving primarily in Oklahoma City, OK.
Application information: Contributes only to pre-selected organizations.

Trustees: Jerry Austin, Joan Bake, C. Robert Hendrick, Jack Homra, Randall D. Mock, Jon C. Sawvell, Nancy A. Waller.
EIN: 731314764
Codes: FD2

45002
Crowe & Dunlevy Foundation, Inc.
20 N. Broadway, Ste. 1800
Oklahoma City, OK 73102 (405) 239-6614
Contact: Roger A. Stong, V.P. and Treas.

Established in 1986 in OK.
Financial data (yr. ended 12/31/01): Grants paid, $114,557; assets, $201,913 (M); gifts received, $91,446; expenditures, $118,143; qualifying distributions, $116,617.
Limitations: Giving limited to the metropolitan Oklahoma City, Tulsa, and Norman, OK, areas.
Officers: Michael S. Laird, Pres.; Roger A. Stong, V.P. and Treas.; Gary Betow, V.P.; Brooke S. Murphy, V.P.; Todd P. Taylor, V.P.; Tom Keifer, Secy.
EIN: 731237906
Codes: FD2

45003
McPherson Family Foundation
c/o Frank Alfred McPherson
13024 Burnt Oak Rd.
Oklahoma City, OK 73120

Established in 1997 in OK.
Donor(s): Frank A. McPherson.
Financial data (yr. ended 12/31/01): Grants paid, $113,750; assets, $1,280,958 (M); expenditures, $119,986; qualifying distributions, $113,750.
Limitations: Applications not accepted. Giving primarily in OK.
Application information: Contributes only to pre-selected organizations.
Directors: David M. McPherson, Frank A. McPherson, Kenneth C. McPherson, Mark D. McPherson, Nadine F. McPherson, Rebecca Ann Vestal.
EIN: 731511918
Codes: FD2

45004
Rosalie Murphy Charitable Foundation
P.O. Box 470248
Tulsa, OK 74147-0248

Established in 1993 in OK.
Donor(s): Rosalie Murphy.‡
Financial data (yr. ended 12/31/01): Grants paid, $110,530; assets, $1,737,876 (M); expenditures, $114,766; qualifying distributions, $109,483.
Limitations: Applications not accepted. Giving primarily in Tulsa, OK.
Application information: Contributes only to pre-selected organizations.
Trustees: Frank W. Murphy, Jr., Frank W. Murphy III, Henry G. Will.
EIN: 731352619
Codes: FD2

45005
William S. & Ann Atherton Foundation
1924 S. Utica, Ste. 1018
Tulsa, OK 74104
Contact: Jessica A. Faubert, Pres.

Established in 1997 in OK.
Donor(s): William S. Atherton.
Financial data (yr. ended 12/31/01): Grants paid, $109,667; assets, $2,135,787 (M); expenditures, $143,987; qualifying distributions, $118,875.
Limitations: Giving on a national basis.
Officers: William S. Atherton, Chair.; Jessica Ann Faubert, Pres.; John S. Walker, Secy.; J. Thomas Atherton, Treas.

45005—OKLAHOMA

Directors: Delores Ann Atherton, Michael Dirk Atherton.
EIN: 731520309
Codes: FD2

45006
The Adams Foundation
2708 Jeanne's Trail
Edmond, OK 73003

Established in 1996 in OK.
Donor(s): Debra L. Adams, Patrick L. Adams.
Financial data (yr. ended 12/31/99): Grants paid, $109,637; assets, $608,387 (M); gifts received, $701,000; expenditures, $110,266; qualifying distributions, $109,637.
Limitations: Giving primarily in OK.
Directors: Debra L. Adams, Patrick L. Adams.
EIN: 731508582
Codes: FD2

45007
Charles C. Faranna Scholarship Trust
4008 S. Elm Pl., Ste. F
Broken Arrow, OK 74011
Contact: Mark Harper, Tr.

Established in 1989 in OK.
Donor(s): Charles C. Faranna.
Financial data (yr. ended 06/30/01): Grants paid, $109,588; assets, $4,783,661 (M); expenditures, $142,043; qualifying distributions, $109,588.
Limitations: Giving primarily to residents of Broken Arrow and Norman, OK.
Trustees: Mark Harper, Elizabeth Pullum, Jerry Pullum.
EIN: 736251335
Codes: FD2

45008
Lucile Page Testamentary Trust
P.O. Box 308
Sand Springs, OK 74063

Established around 1983.
Financial data (yr. ended 12/31/01): Grants paid, $108,386; assets, $2,154,321 (M); expenditures, $243,219; qualifying distributions, $108,386.
Limitations: Giving limited to the Sand Springs, OK, area.
Application information: Application form not required.
Trustees: Charles Helm, Melynda Parnell, Lotsee E.L. Spradling.
EIN: 736188163

45009
Glen Carrier Charitable Trust
P.O. Box 340
Beaver, OK 73932

Financial data (yr. ended 12/31/00): Grants paid, $107,500; assets, $1,637,763 (M); expenditures, $110,497; qualifying distributions, $106,256.
Limitations: Giving primarily in OK.
Trustees: Keith Drum, Scott Kinsey.
EIN: 731531180
Codes: FD2

45010
Frank W. Murphy Charitable Foundation
(Formerly Frank W. Pat Murphy Charitable Foundation)
P.O. Box 470248
Tulsa, OK 74147

Financial data (yr. ended 12/31/01): Grants paid, $107,500; assets, $1,733,132 (M); expenditures, $119,131; qualifying distributions, $107,177.
Limitations: Applications not accepted. Giving primarily in OK.

Application information: Contributes only to pre-selected organizations.
Trustees: Peter Adamson III, Patricia Murphy Hudson, Frank W. Murphy, Jr., Henry G. Will.
EIN: 731347181
Codes: FD2

45011
The Craig Foundation
P.O. Box 1616
Chickasha, OK 73023-1616 (405) 224-4402
Contact: Michael Thomas Craig, Chair.

Established in 1997 in OK.
Donor(s): Michael Thomas Craig.
Financial data (yr. ended 12/31/01): Grants paid, $105,330; assets, $3,339,889 (M); expenditures, $182,902; qualifying distributions, $155,948.
Limitations: Giving primarily in OK.
Application information: Application provided by the foundation. Application form required.
Officers: Michael Thomas Craig, Chair.; Debbie Jayne Craig, Treas.
Trustees: Diannah M. Parker, J.E. Parker.
EIN: 311591646
Codes: FD2

45012
Watson Family Foundation
630 N. Western, Ste. 250
Oklahoma City, OK 73118 (405) 232-8066
Contact: H.B. Watson, Jr., Tr.

Established in 1997.
Donor(s): H.B. Watson, Jr.
Financial data (yr. ended 12/31/01): Grants paid, $103,300; assets, $58,216 (M); expenditures, $103,300; qualifying distributions, $103,300.
Limitations: Giving primarily in Oklahoma City, OK.
Application information: Application form required.
Trustee: H.B. Watson, Jr.
EIN: 731512470
Codes: FD2

45013
Clements Foods Foundation
P.O. Box 14538
Oklahoma City, OK 73113-0538
Application address: 6601 N. Harvey, Oklahoma City, OK 73113
Contact: Robert H. Clements, Secy.

Established in 1986 in OK.
Donor(s): Clements Foods Co.
Financial data (yr. ended 02/26/01): Grants paid, $100,980; assets, $1,660,321 (L); gifts received, $20,000; expenditures, $104,686; qualifying distributions, $100,158.
Limitations: Giving primarily in Oklahoma City, OK.
Officers: Richard H. Clements, Pres.; Robert H. Clements, Secy.; Richard L. Clements, Treas.
EIN: 731304657
Codes: CS, FD2, CD

45014
Faye Allene Rife Brown Foundation
323 Eyler Ln.
Stillwater, OK 74074

Established in 2000 in OK.
Financial data (yr. ended 12/31/00): Grants paid, $100,000; assets, $2,793,860 (M); gifts received, $2,787,736; expenditures, $105,991; qualifying distributions, $103,765.
Limitations: Applications not accepted.
Application information: Contributes only to pre-selected organizations.

Officers: Everett E. Berry, Pres.; James Plaxico, Secy.
Directors: Jean C. Berry, Lewis Bryant, Jim C. Leonard.
EIN: 731542636
Codes: FD2

45015
Jerome Westheimer Family Foundation, Inc.
218 Colston Bldg.
Ardmore, OK 73401

Established in 1986 in OK.
Donor(s): Jerome M. Westheimer.
Financial data (yr. ended 12/31/01): Grants paid, $98,000; assets, $1,117,798 (M); expenditures, $103,335; qualifying distributions, $98,000.
Limitations: Applications not accepted. Giving primarily in OK.
Application information: Contributes only to pre-selected organizations.
Trustees: Beverly W. Wellnitz, Jerome M. Westheimer, Jerome M. Westheimer, Jr.
EIN: 731267603
Codes: FD2

45016
Mary Gaylord Foundation
P.O. Box 25125
Oklahoma City, OK 73125

Established in 1997 in OK.
Donor(s): Mary Gaylord McClean.
Financial data (yr. ended 12/31/01): Grants paid, $95,363; assets, $2,296,476 (M); gifts received, $381,000; expenditures, $96,480; qualifying distributions, $96,475.
Limitations: Applications not accepted. Giving primarily in KY and OK.
Application information: Contributes only to pre-selected organizations.
Trustees: Edward L. Gaylord, Mary Gaylord McClean.
EIN: 731519735
Codes: FD2

45017
Dave & Barbara Sylvan Foundation
1 W. 3rd St., Ste. 1200
Tulsa, OK 74103

Donor(s): Dave R. Sylvan.
Financial data (yr. ended 12/31/01): Grants paid, $94,716; assets, $1,789,769 (M); expenditures, $96,694; qualifying distributions, $94,716.
Limitations: Giving primarily in OK.
Directors: Debra Sylvan de Leeow, James Framel, Barbara Sylvan, Dave R. Sylvan.
EIN: 731206320

45018
Eddie Foundation, Inc.
6801 N. Classen Blvd., Ste. A
Oklahoma City, OK 73116
Contact: Clay T. Farha, Pres.

Established in 1952 in OK.
Financial data (yr. ended 11/30/01): Grants paid, $94,270; assets, $1,639,049 (M); expenditures, $100,344; qualifying distributions, $90,602.
Limitations: Giving primarily in Oklahoma City, OK.
Officers and Trustees:* Clay T. Farha,* Pres.; B.D. Eddie Farha,* V.P.; Gloria Eddie Farha,* V.P.; Philip Farha,* V.P.
EIN: 736092240
Codes: FD2

45019
C. L. Richards Foundation
3419 E. 75th Pl.
Tulsa, OK 74136

Established in 1992.
Donor(s): C.L. Richards.
Financial data (yr. ended 05/31/01): Grants paid, $92,987; assets, $1,766,798 (M); expenditures, $108,864; qualifying distributions, $92,742.
Limitations: Applications not accepted. Giving primarily in Tulsa, OK.
Application information: Contributes only to pre-selected organizations.
Trustees: Linda McQuillen Kulp, C.L. Richards, Jr., Edwin T. Richards.
EIN: 731404970
Codes: FD2

45020
Philip Boyle Foundation
c/o Foundation Mgmt., Inc.
2932 N.W. 122nd St., Ste. D
Oklahoma City, OK 73120-1955
(405) 755-5571

Established in 1989 in OK.
Donor(s): Philip Boyle.
Financial data (yr. ended 12/31/01): Grants paid, $86,245; assets, $1,961,035 (M); expenditures, $111,363; qualifying distributions, $98,730.
Limitations: Giving limited to OK.
Application information: Application form not required.
Trustees: Dolores Boyle, Dail Boyle Cobb.
EIN: 731354526
Codes: FD2

45021
Waters Charitable Foundation
6846 S. Trenton Ave.
Tulsa, OK 74136-4106 (918) 254-9295
Contact: Barbara Waters, Tr.

Established in 1988 in OK.
Donor(s): Thomas J. Carson, Mary L. Carson, Feron Waters, Barbara Waters, Judy Gayle Waters.
Financial data (yr. ended 06/30/01): Grants paid, $85,125; assets, $2,760,888 (M); expenditures, $102,330; qualifying distributions, $83,564.
Limitations: Giving primarily in Tulsa, OK.
Trustees: Barbara Waters, Judy Waters.
EIN: 731323325
Codes: FD2

45022
Case and Elfreda Zandbergen Charitable Foundation
c/o Bank of Oklahoma, N.A.
P.O. Box 880
Tulsa, OK 74101-0880
Contact: Elise Anderson, V.P., Bank of Oklahoma, N.A.

Established in 1997 in OK.
Financial data (yr. ended 12/31/01): Grants paid, $84,914; assets, $1,902,541 (M); expenditures, $100,489; qualifying distributions, $87,725.
Limitations: Giving primarily in northeastern OK.
Trustee: Bank of Oklahoma, N.A.
EIN: 736300138
Codes: FD2

45023
The Jay Zee Foundation
P.O. Box 52508
Tulsa, OK 74152

Established in 1996 in OK.
Donor(s): John Smith Zink.
Financial data (yr. ended 12/31/01): Grants paid, $83,605; assets, $1,292,333 (M); expenditures, $100,156; qualifying distributions, $83,605.
Trustee: John Smith Zink.
EIN: 731395242

45024
Gemini Industries, Inc., Foundation
2300 Holloway Dr.
El Reno, OK 73036-5725
Application address: 101 S.W. 22nd., El Reno, OK 73036
Contact: Rick McGee, Tr.

Established in 1995 in OK.
Donor(s): Gemini Industries, Inc.
Financial data (yr. ended 12/31/00): Grants paid, $83,311; assets, $824 (M); gifts received, $87,000; expenditures, $87,319; qualifying distributions, $87,311.
Limitations: Giving primarily in OK.
Trustees: Diane Birdsong, Rick McGee, Joe Morse, Michael S. Smith.
EIN: 736282301
Codes: CS, CD

45025
The Dotson Family Charitable Foundation
1918 E. 30th Pl.
Tulsa, OK 74114-5414
Contact: George S. Dotson, Tr.

Established in 1998 in OK.
Donor(s): George S. Dotson, Phyllis N. Dotson.
Financial data (yr. ended 12/31/01): Grants paid, $83,106; assets, $342,009 (M); expenditures, $85,561; qualifying distributions, $82,552.
Limitations: Giving primarily in KS and OK.
Application information: Application form not required.
Trustees: George S. Dotson, Phyllis N. Dotson.
EIN: 746443176
Codes: FD2

45026
Emitom Watson Foundation, Inc.
3442 E. 61st Pl.
Tulsa, OK 74136-1433
Contact: Burl S. Watson, Pres.

Established in 1955 in NY.
Financial data (yr. ended 12/31/01): Grants paid, $82,100; assets, $1,479,364 (M); expenditures, $84,782; qualifying distributions, $84,259.
Limitations: Applications not accepted. Giving primarily in CO, OK, RI, and TX.
Application information: Contributes only to pre-selected organizations.
Officers and Trustees:* Burl S. Watson,* Pres. and Treas.; Angie D'Albora,* V.P. and Secy.; J. Burl D'Albora, Thomas B. D'Albora, Frances Frey, Richard C. Frey, Emily W. Hillsman, Thomas C. Hillsman, Burl Douglas Watson, Byron S. Watson, Nita Watson.
EIN: 136093902
Codes: FD2

45027
Charles W. & Pauline Flint Foundation
c/o Charles W. Flint
P.O. Box 490
Tulsa, OK 74101-0490

Established in 1961 in OK.
Donor(s): Charles W. Flint, Jr., Susan Flint Seay.
Financial data (yr. ended 12/31/01): Grants paid, $80,500; assets, $1,635,169 (M); gifts received, $39,155; expenditures, $131,683; qualifying distributions, $80,500.
Limitations: Applications not accepted. Giving primarily in OK.
Application information: Contributes only to pre-selected organizations.
Trustees: Robin F. Ballenger, Charles W. Flint III, Susan Flint Seay.
EIN: 736093759
Codes: FD2

45028
The Dill Foundation
505 E. Main St., Ste. A
Jenks, OK 74037

Established in 2000 in OK.
Donor(s): G. Michael Dill, Shelley M. Dill.
Financial data (yr. ended 12/31/00): Grants paid, $80,000; assets, $1,227,323 (M); gifts received, $1,495,500; expenditures, $80,117; qualifying distributions, $80,000.
Limitations: Giving primarily in OK.
Officers: G. Michael Dill, Chair. & Pres.; Shelley M. Dill, Secy.
EIN: 751593019
Codes: FD2

45029
Frontiers of Science Foundation of Oklahoma
P.O. Box 26967
Oklahoma City, OK 73126-0967
(405) 290-5600

Donor(s): Rodman A. Frates, Edward Gaylord.
Financial data (yr. ended 06/30/01): Grants paid, $79,500; assets, $885,148 (M); gifts received, $1,084; expenditures, $80,632; qualifying distributions, $79,548.
Limitations: Giving limited to OK.
Application information: Application form required.
Officers: Rodman A. Frates, Chair.; Robert S. Abernathy, Pres.; James Work, Secy.; Richard H. Godfrey, Jr., Treas.
Director: Richard E. Swan.
EIN: 730642039

45030
The Robert S. and Eloise C. Bowers Foundation
6421 Avondale Dr., Ste. 210
Oklahoma City, OK 73116 (405) 848-1930
Additional tel.: (405) 202-7708
Contact: D. Rex Urice, V.P.

Established in 1999 in OK.
Donor(s): Eloise C. Bowers.
Financial data (yr. ended 06/30/01): Grants paid, $79,308; assets, $3,980,079 (M); expenditures, $229,235; qualifying distributions, $167,277.
Limitations: Giving on a national basis.
Application information: Application form required.
Officers and Trustees:* Eloise Cooper Bowers,* Pres.; D. Rex Urice,* V.P.; Paul W. Dudman,* Secy.; David Rainbolt,* Treas.
EIN: 731577594
Codes: FD2

45031
John and Donnie Brock Foundation
20 E. 5th St., Ste. 1500
Tulsa, OK 74103

Established in 1987 in OK.
Donor(s): John A. Brock, Donnie V. Brock.
Financial data (yr. ended 12/31/01): Grants paid, $79,270; assets, $1,564,393 (M); expenditures, $88,605; qualifying distributions, $79,270.
Limitations: Applications not accepted. Giving primarily in Tulsa, OK.
Application information: Contributes only to pre-selected organizations.
Trustees: Donnie V. Brock, John A. Brock.
EIN: 731309703

45031—OKLAHOMA

Codes: FD2

45032
The Mary K. Sanditen Family Foundation, Inc.
3314 E. 51st St., Ste. 207K
Tulsa, OK 74135

Established in 2000 in OK.
Donor(s): Mary K. Sanditen Revocable Trust, Deborah A. Sanditen Revocable Trust.
Financial data (yr. ended 12/31/01): Grants paid, $78,250; assets, $73,145 (M); gifts received, $60,000; expenditures, $85,300; qualifying distributions, $78,250.
Limitations: Applications not accepted.
Application information: Contributes only to pre-selected organizations.
Directors: Deborah A. Sanditen, Mary K. Sanditen, Steven A. Sanditen.
EIN: 731594094

45033
Katharine and Calvin Gatlin Scholarship Fund
c/o The Trust Co. of Oklahoma
P.O. Box 3627
Tulsa, OK 74101

Established in 1994 in OK.
Financial data (yr. ended 12/31/01): Grants paid, $78,173; assets, $1,247,087 (M); expenditures, $91,141; qualifying distributions, $85,107.
Limitations: Applications not accepted. Giving limited to residents of Vinita, OK.
Application information: Unsolicited requests for funds not accepted.
Trustee: The Trust Co. of Oklahoma.
EIN: 736266862
Codes: FD2

45034
Gable & Gotwals Foundation
(Formerly Gable & Gotwals Mock Schwabe Kible Gaberino Foundation)
c/o Grant Comm.
100 W. 5th St., Ste. 1100
Tulsa, OK 74103-4217
Contact: Richard D. Koljack, Chair.

Established in 1992 in OK.
Donor(s): Gable & Gotwals P.C., Mark H. Allen, John R. Barker, Oliver S. Howard, Joseph W. Morris, M. Benjamin Singletary, James M. Sturdivant.
Financial data (yr. ended 10/31/00): Grants paid, $76,895; assets, $19,661 (M); gifts received, $57,500; expenditures, $76,895; qualifying distributions, $76,895.
Limitations: Giving primarily in the Tulsa, OK, area.
Officer and Directors:* Richard D. Koljack,* Chair.; Vivian C. Hale, David L. Kearney, Jeffrey C. Rambach, Sidney K. Swinson.
EIN: 731413740
Codes: CS, CD

45035
Robinowitz-Brodsky Charitable Foundation
(Formerly Mike & Sharon Robonowitz Family Foundation)
6925 S. Canton St.
Tulsa, OK 74136

Established in 1966 in OK.
Financial data (yr. ended 12/31/00): Grants paid, $76,795; assets, $2,014,239 (M); expenditures, $77,531; qualifying distributions, $77,531.
Limitations: Applications not accepted. Giving primarily in Tulsa, OK.
Application information: Contributes only to pre-selected organizations.
Trustees: A.D. Brodsky, Rosetta Brodsky.

EIN: 736108970
Codes: FD2

45036
Benjamin and Laura Parish Martin Memorial Foundation
P.O. Box 1620
Tulsa, OK 74101-1620
Application address: P.O. Box 677, Muckogee, OK 74402
Contact: Golda S. Martin, Tr.

Established in 1987 in OK.
Financial data (yr. ended 12/31/01): Grants paid, $75,830; assets, $640,727 (M); expenditures, $84,092; qualifying distributions, $75,523.
Limitations: Giving primarily in Muskogee, OK.
Application information: Application form not required.
Trustees: Golda S. Martin, Bank of Oklahoma, N.A.
EIN: 731299645
Codes: FD2

45037
A. E. and Jaunita Richardson Charitable Foundation
P.O. Box 432
Nowata, OK 74048

Financial data (yr. ended 12/31/00): Grants paid, $75,602; assets, $1,953,397 (M); expenditures, $113,386; qualifying distributions, $113,386.
Limitations: Applications not accepted. Giving limited to OK.
Application information: Contributes only to pre-selected organizations.
Trustees: Jessie L. Blackwell, Benjamin C. Killion, B.C. Lee, W.E. Maddux, David L. Pierce, Phyllis Willis.
EIN: 911914497
Codes: FD2

45038
Bartlesville Public School Foundation, Inc.
1100 S. Jennings
Bartlesville, OK 74003
Contact: Lisa Rhodes

Financial data (yr. ended 06/30/01): Grants paid, $75,523; assets, $1,893,394 (M); gifts received, $1,527; expenditures, $79,198; qualifying distributions, $78,802.
Limitations: Giving primarily in Bartlesville, OK.
Application information: Application form required.
Officers: David King, Pres.; Denis Doe, V.P.; Glenn Bonner, Secy.-Treas.
Trustees: Linda Befort, Craig Bradshaw, Dawn Brown, Gene Bryngelson, Lori Collins, and 14 additional trustees.
EIN: 731256865
Codes: FD2

45039
Sol Robinowitz Foundation
7130 S. Lewis, Ste. 910
Tulsa, OK 74136

Established in 1969.
Donor(s): Sol Robinowitz.
Financial data (yr. ended 12/31/01): Grants paid, $75,000; assets, $1,377,286 (M); expenditures, $78,435; qualifying distributions, $74,467.
Limitations: Applications not accepted. Giving primarily in Tulsa, OK.
Application information: Contributes only to pre-selected organizations.
Trustee: Sol Robinowitz.
EIN: 237028047

45040
John E. Rooney Charitable Trust
2400 Mid-Continent Tower
Tulsa, OK 74103

Established in 1986 in OK.
Financial data (yr. ended 12/31/99): Grants paid, $74,363; assets, $110,238 (M); gifts received, $74,000; expenditures, $80,345; qualifying distributions, $75,811.
Limitations: Applications not accepted. Giving primarily in Tulsa, OK.
Application information: Contributes only to pre-selected organizations.
Trustee: John E. Rooney.
EIN: 731290760

45041
Blackwell Oklahoma Community Foundation
P.O. Box 514
Blackwell, OK 74631-0514 (580) 363-3684
Contact: James R. Rodgers, Chair.

Financial data (yr. ended 12/31/01): Grants paid, $73,649; assets, $211,517 (M); gifts received, $10,940; expenditures, $75,128; qualifying distributions, $74,283.
Limitations: Giving limited to western Kay County and eastern Grant County, OK.
Officers: James R. Rodgers, Chair.; Carla Sandy, Secy.; Rich Cantillon, Treas.
Trustees: Dick Bladgen, Richard Fellrath, Claudia Goff, Dennis Hutton, David Pennington, Scott Shepherd, Jim Willis.
EIN: 731388218

45042
Cimarron County Historical Society
P.O. Box 655
Boise City, OK 73933-0655
E-mail: museum@dtsi.net
Contact: Phyllis Randolph

Established in 1989.
Donor(s): Charles French.‡
Financial data (yr. ended 04/30/01): Grants paid, $73,100; assets, $1,742,569 (M); expenditures, $99,696; qualifying distributions, $73,100.
Limitations: Applications not accepted. Giving limited to Cimarron County, OK.
Officers: Bonnie C. Heimann, Pres.; Lois Garner, Secy.; Morris Alexander, Treas.
EIN: 731333427

45043
The King's Foundation
P.O. Box 1421
Newcastle, OK 73065 (405) 387-4169
Contact: Steve R. Bailey, Dir.

Established in 1989 in OK.
Donor(s): Steve R. Bailey.
Financial data (yr. ended 12/31/01): Grants paid, $72,750; assets, $116,930 (M); gifts received, $91,405; expenditures, $73,083; qualifying distributions, $72,750.
Limitations: Giving primarily in OK.
Directors: Billye Bailey, Steve R. Bailey.
EIN: 731353810

45044
Christian Life Foundation
10 E. 3rd St., Ste. 400
Tulsa, OK 74103

Established in 1985 in OK.
Donor(s): Gail R. Runnels.
Financial data (yr. ended 11/30/01): Grants paid, $72,514; assets, $2,359 (M); gifts received, $72,500; expenditures, $72,864; qualifying distributions, $72,514.

Limitations: Applications not accepted. Giving on a national basis.
Application information: Contributes only to pre-selected organizations.
Trustees: Gail R. Runnels, Virginia A. Runnels.
EIN: 731263661

45045
Harry and Louise Brown Foundation
3501 N.W. 63rd, Ste. 206
Oklahoma City, OK 73116-2202
FAX: (405) 840-4925
Contact: David R. Brown, Pres.

Established in 1995 in OK.
Donor(s): David R. Brown.
Financial data (yr. ended 12/31/00): Grants paid, $72,500; assets, $1,913,783 (M); gifts received, $274,048; expenditures, $75,334; qualifying distributions, $70,899.
Publications: Application guidelines, annual report.
Application information: Application form required.
Officer: David R. Brown, Pres.
EIN: 731485811

45046
Laura Fields Trust
P.O. Box 2394
Lawton, OK 73502-2394
Contact: Jay Dee Fountain, Mgr.

Established in 1950 in OK.
Donor(s): Laura Fields.‡
Financial data (yr. ended 06/30/01): Grants paid, $70,740; assets, $1,980,809 (M); gifts received, $69,447; expenditures, $102,822; qualifying distributions, $85,954; giving activities include $38,776 for loans to individuals.
Limitations: Giving primarily in Comanche County, OK.
Publications: Annual report.
Application information: Application form required.
Officer: Jay Dee Fountain.
Trustees: Rev. Wayne Ashlock, George Bridges, Jack Brock, Bryan Cain, Hyman Copeland, Joe Roundtree, Lee Woods.
EIN: 736095854
Codes: GTI

45047
The Avery Family Trust
1259 E. 26th St.
Tulsa, OK 74114
Application address: c/o Tullius Taylor Sartain & Sartain LLP, 2424 E. 21st St., Ste. 200, Tulsa, OK 74114
Contact: Jim Burwell

Established in 1999 in OK.
Donor(s): Jacqueline Avery Zink.
Financial data (yr. ended 12/31/01): Grants paid, $70,084; assets, $1,169,222 (M); gifts received, $50,000; expenditures, $82,107; qualifying distributions, $70,084.
Trustees: Etta May Avery, Millicent A. Ogilvie, Jacqueline Avery Zink.
EIN: 736314003

45048
Ruth Ann Fate and Martin E. Fate, Jr. Foundation
7014 E. 60th St.
Tulsa, OK 74145

Established in 1993 in OK.
Donor(s): Martin E. Fate, Jr., Ruth Ann Fate.

Financial data (yr. ended 12/31/00): Grants paid, $69,690; assets, $531,251 (M); expenditures, $80,588; qualifying distributions, $69,690.
Limitations: Applications not accepted. Giving primarily in OK.
Application information: Contributes only to pre-selected organizations.
Trustees: Mary Ann Fate Davis, Gary Martin Fate, Ruth Ann Fate, Steven Lewis Fate.
EIN: 736271269

45049
Keith E. and Patricia L. Bailey Family Charitable Foundation
4900 1 Williams Ctr.
Tulsa, OK 74172

Established in 1996 in OK.
Donor(s): Keith Bailey.
Financial data (yr. ended 12/31/01): Grants paid, $68,000; assets, $1,057,223 (M); gifts received, $323,085; expenditures, $69,410; qualifying distributions, $68,000.
Limitations: Applications not accepted.
Application information: Contributes only to pre-selected organizations. Unsolicited requests for funds not accepted.
Trustees: Keith E. Bailey, Patricia L. Bailey.
EIN: 736297592

45050
Katherine Q. Sinclair Foundation
1924 S. Utica, Ste. 1212
Tulsa, OK 74104 (918) 743-6487
Contact: Katherine Q. Sinclair, Tr.

Established in 1989 in OK.
Donor(s): Katherine Q. Sinclair.
Financial data (yr. ended 06/30/01): Grants paid, $67,780; assets, $8,189 (M); gifts received, $47,540; expenditures, $69,450; qualifying distributions, $67,100.
Limitations: Giving primarily in Tulsa, OK.
Application information: Application form not required.
Trustee: Katherine Q. Sinclair.
EIN: 731353549

45051
Ruthanna B. Snow Charitable Foundation
320 S. Boston, Ste. 1910
Tulsa, OK 74103

Established in 1999 in OK.
Donor(s): Ruthanna B. Snow.
Financial data (yr. ended 09/30/01): Grants paid, $67,400; assets, $1,188,983 (M); expenditures, $92,465; qualifying distributions, $80,133.
Limitations: Applications not accepted. Giving on a national basis, with some emphasis on OK and TN.
Application information: Contributes only to pre-selected organizations.
Trustees: John D. Harwood, Kenneth B. Harwood, Bill R. Snow, Phillip R. Snow, Ruthanna B. Snow, Anna H. Strong.
EIN: 731572883

45052
Larkin Bailey Foundation
612 S. Denver
Tulsa, OK 74119 (918) 250-9080
FAX: (918) 250-0384
Contact: Roy G. Cartwright or Patsy Cravens, Trustees

Established in 1993 in OK.
Donor(s): Larkin Bailey Trust.
Financial data (yr. ended 12/31/01): Grants paid, $67,351; assets, $6,490,143 (M); expenditures, $240,941; qualifying distributions, $67,351.

Limitations: Giving primarily in Owasso and Tulsa, OK.
Publications: Annual report, corporate giving report.
Application information: Application form required.
Trustees: Roy G. Cartwright, Patsy Cravens, Joseph N. Witt.
EIN: 731258217

45053
Helen W. Holliday Foundation, Inc.
513 S.W. C Ave.
Lawton, OK 73501

Established in 1998 in OK.
Financial data (yr. ended 12/31/01): Grants paid, $66,521; assets, $986,837 (M); expenditures, $88,006; qualifying distributions, $67,261.
Limitations: Applications not accepted. Giving primarily in Lawton, OK.
Application information: Contributes only to pre-selected organizations.
Directors: Nancy L. Lewark, Robert L. Ross.
Trustee: Ralph W. Newcombe.
EIN: 730997009

45054
E. Phil and Roberta Kirschner Foundation
P.O. Box 1866
Muskogee, OK 74402-1866 (918) 682-3151
FAX: (918) 682-8594
Contact: Miriam Freedman, Tr.

Established in 1984 in OK.
Donor(s): E. Phil Kirschner,‡ Roberta L. Kirschner.‡
Financial data (yr. ended 05/31/01): Grants paid, $65,300; assets, $2,124,114 (M); expenditures, $114,806; qualifying distributions, $88,305.
Limitations: Giving primarily in OK.
Publications: Annual report, financial statement, application guidelines.
Application information: Some special consideration given to students of the Jewish faith. Application form not required.
Trustees: Miriam Freedman, Sally Freedman, Sondra Gross, Pauli Loeffler.
EIN: 731164196

45055
The Dolese Foundation
P.O. Box 677
Oklahoma City, OK 73101
Contact: W. Bryan Arnn, Tr.

Established in 1979 in OK.
Donor(s): Roger M. Dolese.
Financial data (yr. ended 03/31/02): Grants paid, $64,195; assets, $504 (M); gifts received, $63,945; expenditures, $64,195; qualifying distributions, $64,195.
Limitations: Giving primarily in Oklahoma City, OK.
Application information: Application form not required.
Trustees: Tony Basolo, Roger M. Dolese, Ed Moler.
EIN: 731074447

45056
Anne S. Woolslayer Foundation
2679 E. 69th St.
Tulsa, OK 74136 (918) 492-5037
Contact: J.R. Woolslayer, Tr.

Established in 1995 in OK.
Financial data (yr. ended 12/31/01): Grants paid, $64,000; assets, $1,066,352 (M); expenditures, $82,096; qualifying distributions, $64,000.
Limitations: Giving primarily in Tulsa, OK.
Application information: Application form not required.

45056—OKLAHOMA

Trustee: J.R. Woolslayer.
EIN: 731466433

45057
Robinson Foundation
1924 S. Utica, Ste. 1004
Tulsa, OK 74114

Established in 1976 in OK.
Donor(s): James A. Robinson.
Financial data (yr. ended 10/31/01): Grants paid, $63,240; assets, $33,063 (M); gifts received, $65,000; expenditures, $63,322; qualifying distributions, $63,248.
Limitations: Giving primarily in Tulsa, OK.
Application information: Application form not required.
Trustee: James A. Robinson.
EIN: 731014526

45058
E. P. and Roberta L. Kirschner Foundation
409 NationsBank Bldg.
Muskogee, OK 74401 (918) 682-3151
FAX: (918) 682-8594
Contact: Miriam Freedman, Chair.

Established in 1979 in OK.
Donor(s): E. Phil Kirschner,‡ Roberta L. Kirschner.‡
Financial data (yr. ended 05/31/01): Grants paid, $62,900; assets, $1,454,120 (M); expenditures, $70,830; qualifying distributions, $67,658.
Limitations: Giving primarily in OK, with emphasis on northeastern OK.
Publications: Annual report, financial statement, application guidelines.
Application information: Application form not required.
Officer and Trustees:* Miriam Freedman,* Chair.; Sondra K. Gross, Susan Kirschner.
EIN: 736191753

45059
Jimmie & Marie Austin Foundation
P.O. Box 1240
Seminole, OK 74818-1420

Established in 1996 in OK.
Donor(s): Jimmie Austin, Lucille Marie Austin.
Financial data (yr. ended 12/31/01): Grants paid, $61,800; assets, $8,052 (M); gifts received, $60,000; expenditures, $62,448; qualifying distributions, $61,800.
Limitations: Applications not accepted. Giving limited to OK.
Application information: Contributes only to pre-selected organizations.
Trustees: Jimmie Austin, Lucille Marie Austin.
EIN: 731436042

45060
Bosa Center Foundation
P.O. Box 967
Pauls Valley, OK 73075-0967

Financial data (yr. ended 12/31/01): Grants paid, $61,405; assets, $1,328,547 (M); gifts received, $5,525; expenditures, $125,063; qualifying distributions, $104,373.
Limitations: Giving limited to Pauls Valley, OK.
Officers: Arlen Willians, Pres.; John Blake, V.P.; Edgar Holliday, Secy.; Pat Ham, Treas.
Directors: Jay Boyles, Mike Day, Jeanie Rickey, Bruce Varner.
EIN: 731380373

45061
Maxwell Family Charitable Foundation
6950 S. Utica Ave.
Tulsa, OK 74136

Established in 2000 in OK.
Donor(s): John H. Maxwell, Mary Sue Maxwell.
Financial data (yr. ended 12/31/01): Grants paid, $60,300; assets, $1,056,338 (M); expenditures, $66,937; qualifying distributions, $60,300.
Trustee: Marvin Morse.
Advisors: John H. Maxwell, Mary Sue Maxwell.
EIN: 731603064

45062
Samuel E. Frierson Trust
c/o Bank of Oklahoma, N.A.
Tulsa, OK 74101-0880

Financial data (yr. ended 12/31/01): Grants paid, $60,000; assets, $1,246,258 (M); expenditures, $116,110; qualifying distributions, $60,000.
Limitations: Applications not accepted. Giving primarily in Oklahoma City, OK.
Application information: Contributes only to pre-selected organizations.
Trustee: Bank of Oklahoma, N.A.
EIN: 736094991

45063
The Sam J. & Nona M. Rhoades Foundation
124 E. 4th St., Ste. 200
Tulsa, OK 74103

Financial data (yr. ended 12/31/01): Grants paid, $59,942; assets, $889,709 (M); expenditures, $75,375; qualifying distributions, $59,942.
Limitations: Applications not accepted.
Application information: Contributes only to pre-selected organizations.
Officer: Frank R. Rhoades, Pres.
EIN: 731560308

45064
Roy L. Evans Trust
c/o Bank of Oklahoma, N.A.
P.O. Box 880
Tulsa, OK 74101-0880

Financial data (yr. ended 12/31/99): Grants paid, $58,708; assets, $442,233 (M); expenditures, $68,395; qualifying distributions, $58,708.
Limitations: Applications not accepted.
Application information: Contributes only to pre-selected organizations.
Trustee: Bank of Oklahoma, N.A.
EIN: 736111565

45065
ACGC Foundation
6655 S. Lewis, Ste. 222
Tulsa, OK 74136 (918) 481-6691
Contact: Stephen E. Jackson, Tr.

Established in 1993 in OK.
Donor(s): American Central Gas Cos., Inc.
Financial data (yr. ended 12/31/01): Grants paid, $58,510; assets, $345 (M); gifts received, $58,760; expenditures, $59,110; qualifying distributions, $58,510.
Limitations: Giving primarily in Tulsa, OK.
Trustees: Stephen J. Heyman, Stephen E. Jackson.
EIN: 731433675
Codes: CS, CD

45066
The Teubner Foundation
P.O. Box 1994
Stillwater, OK 74076-1994

Established in 1998 in OK.
Donor(s): Russell W. Teubner.
Financial data (yr. ended 12/31/00): Grants paid, $57,886; assets, $622,984 (M); expenditures, $73,921; qualifying distributions, $57,886.
Limitations: Applications not accepted.
Application information: Contributes only to pre-selected organizations.
Directors: Julie A. Teubner, Russell W. Teubner.
EIN: 731552711

45067
Dillingham Foundation
P.O. Box 1669
Enid, OK 73702-1669
Application address: c/o Jim Turley, 2402 W. Willow Rd., Enid, OK 73703

Donor(s): Tom B. Dillingham, Dan L. Dillingham.
Financial data (yr. ended 12/31/01): Grants paid, $56,750; assets, $304,074 (M); expenditures, $63,474; qualifying distributions, $56,576.
Limitations: Giving primarily in OK.
Trustees: Leslie D. Ballew, Dan L. Dillingham, Lori Evans, Dana Hutton.
EIN: 736108937

45068
Sneed Foundation, Inc.
427 S. Boston, 309 Philtower
Tulsa, OK 74103

Established in 1982 in OK.
Donor(s): Cornelia L. Sneed.
Financial data (yr. ended 06/30/01): Grants paid, $56,600; assets, $1,064 (M); gifts received, $60,000; expenditures, $60,677; qualifying distributions, $60,677.
Limitations: Applications not accepted. Giving primarily in Oklahoma City, OK.
Application information: Contributes only to pre-selected organizations.
Officers and Directors:* Cornelia L. Sneed,* Chair. and Pres.; Ann S. Schriber,* V.P.; Jane B. Sneed,* V.P; Robert E. Sneed,* V.P.; Mary L. Martin, Secy.; Patti P. Brown, Treas.
EIN: 731168046

45069
The JDM Foundation, Inc.
1300 S. Meridan, Ste. 211
Oklahoma City, OK 73108
Application address: 2601 Meadow View Rd., Edmond, OK 73013, tel.: (405) 943-1411
Contact: Joseph D. McKean, Jr., Pres.

Established in 1997 in OK.
Donor(s): Joseph D. McKean, Jr.
Financial data (yr. ended 12/31/01): Grants paid, $55,000; assets, $10,783 (M); gifts received, $10,000; expenditures, $56,522; qualifying distributions, $55,000.
Limitations: Giving primarily in Tulsa and Edmond, OK.
Officers and Directors:* Joseph D. McKean, Jr.,* Pres.; John Stuemky,* V.P.
EIN: 731526078

45070
James H. & Madalynne Norick Foundation
5400 N. Grand Blvd., Ste. 220
Oklahoma City, OK 73112-5354
(405) 943-7123

Established in 1998 in OK.
Donor(s): James H. Norick, Madalynne Norick.
Financial data (yr. ended 12/31/01): Grants paid, $53,825; assets, $579,822 (M); gifts received, $190,000; expenditures, $62,357; qualifying distributions, $53,825.
Officer: James H. Norick, Chair. and Pres.
Trustee: Vickie Koumaris.
EIN: 731544035

45071
Harold C. Stuart Foundation
(Formerly Harold C. and Joan S. Stuart Foundation)
2431 E. 61st St.
Tulsa, OK 74136-1235
Contact: Harold C. Stuart, Tr.

Established in 1969 in OK.
Donor(s): Harold C. Stuart, Joan S. Stuart.‡
Financial data (yr. ended 12/31/01): Grants paid, $53,800; assets, $6,320,486 (M); gifts received, $972,417; expenditures, $180,774; qualifying distributions, $119,498.
Limitations: Giving primarily in the Tulsa, OK, area.
Application information: Application form not required.
Trustees: Frances Langford Stuart, Harold C. Stuart.
EIN: 237052187

45072
The E. P. Kirschner and Roberta L. Kirschner Trust
409 Boatmen's Bank IV Bldg.
Muskogee, OK 74401 (918) 682-3151
FAX: (918) 682-8594
Contact: Miriam Freedman, Chair.

Established in 1979 in OK.
Donor(s): E. Phil Kirschner,‡ Roberta L. Kirschner.‡
Financial data (yr. ended 05/31/01): Grants paid, $53,667; assets, $1,239,227 (M); expenditures, $64,614; qualifying distributions, $57,880.
Limitations: Giving primarily in OK.
Publications: Annual report, application guidelines, financial statement.
Application information: Applicants must be under 21 years of age and orphaned. Application form not required.
Officer and Trustees:* Miriam Freedman,* Chair.; Sondra K. Gross, Susan Kirschner.
EIN: 736191752

45073
Joseph W. Craft III Foundation
4401 Oak Rd.
Tulsa, OK 74105
Contact: Joseph W. Craft III, Tr.

Established in 1996 in OK.
Donor(s): Joseph W. Craft III.
Financial data (yr. ended 12/31/01): Grants paid, $53,150; assets, $876,592 (M); expenditures, $61,611; qualifying distributions, $53,150.
Limitations: Giving primarily in Tulsa, OK.
Trustee: Joseph W. Craft III.
EIN: 731514539

45074
Russell H. & Frances N. Brown Charitable Trust
P.O. Box 1365
El Reno, OK 73036-1365

Financial data (yr. ended 12/31/00): Grants paid, $53,132; assets, $1,265,585 (M); expenditures, $72,946; qualifying distributions, $53,132.
Limitations: Applications not accepted. Giving limited to OK.
Application information: Contributes only to pre-selected organizations.
Trustee: Joe L. Holman.
EIN: 736298972

45075
Evergreen Foundation
15 E. 5th St., Ste. 3200
Tulsa, OK 74103

Established in 1998 in OK.
Donor(s): Barbara G. Heyman, Stephen J. Heyman.
Financial data (yr. ended 12/31/01): Grants paid, $53,010; assets, $12,752 (M); gifts received, $60,850; expenditures, $53,010; qualifying distributions, $53,010.
Limitations: Applications not accepted. Giving primarily in OK.
Application information: Contributes only to pre-selected organizations.
Officers: Barbara G. Heyman, Pres.; Stephen J. Heyman, V.P.
EIN: 731535560

45076
Boulton Foundation
1700 N.E. 66th St.
Oklahoma City, OK 73111

Established in 1997 in OK.
Donor(s): John William Boulton, Jr.
Financial data (yr. ended 12/31/01): Grants paid, $52,430; assets, $809,477 (M); expenditures, $56,957; qualifying distributions, $52,430.
Limitations: Applications not accepted. Giving primarily in Oklahoma City, OK.
Application information: Contributes only to pre-selected organizations.
Trustees: Evelyn F. Boulton, John William Boulton, Jr.
EIN: 731486770

45077
Carson Foundation
821 S. Linwood Ave.
Cushing, OK 74023

Established in 1997 in OK.
Donor(s): Doug Carson.
Financial data (yr. ended 12/31/01): Grants paid, $51,652; assets, $329,819 (M); gifts received, $101,250; expenditures, $67,412; qualifying distributions, $51,652.
Limitations: Applications not accepted.
Application information: Contributes only to pre-selected organizations.
Officers: Doug Carson, Chair.; Jayn Carson, Secy.
EIN: 731508384

45078
Crawley Family Foundation
105 N. Hudson, Ste. 800
Oklahoma City, OK 73102-4803

Donor(s): James B. Crawley.
Financial data (yr. ended 12/31/01): Grants paid, $51,500; assets, $760,033 (M); gifts received, $362,642; expenditures, $52,070; qualifying distributions, $51,500.
Limitations: Applications not accepted. Giving limited to Norman, OK.
Application information: Contributes only to pre-selected organizations.
Officers: James B. Crawley, Pres.; Mary W. Crawley, Secy.; Sara B. Crawley, Treas.
Trustee: Linda S. Crawley.
EIN: 731463271

45079
Clara McGowen Memorial Trust
c/o First National Bank & Trust Co.
P.O. Box 69
Ardmore, OK 73402

Established in 1994 in OK.
Donor(s): Clara McGowen.‡
Financial data (yr. ended 12/31/01): Grants paid, $50,142; assets, $851,690 (M); expenditures, $75,305; qualifying distributions, $50,142.
Limitations: Applications not accepted. Giving primarily in Ardmore, OK.
Application information: Contributes only to pre-selected organizations.
Trustees: Rudy Jack Ellis, First National Bank & Trust Co.
EIN: 736280877

45080
Stanton L. Young Foundation, Inc.
P.O. Box 1466
Oklahoma City, OK 73101
Contact: Stanton L. Young, Pres.

Established in 1960 in OK.
Donor(s): Stanton L. Young.
Financial data (yr. ended 12/31/01): Grants paid, $50,010; assets, $589,086 (M); expenditures, $86,756; qualifying distributions, $50,010.
Limitations: Giving primarily in OK.
Officers: Barbara Young, Chair.; Stanton L. Young, Pres.; Shirley Schritter, Secy.
EIN: 730742287

45081
The Cole Family Foundation
2150 S. Norfolk Terrace
Tulsa, OK 74114

Established in 1999 in OK.
Donor(s): Charles M. Cole III, Marjean F. Cole.
Financial data (yr. ended 12/31/01): Grants paid, $50,000; assets, $198,497 (M); gifts received, $25; expenditures, $53,237; qualifying distributions, $50,000.
Limitations: Applications not accepted.
Application information: Contributes only to pre-selected organizations.
Trustees: Charles M. Cole III, Marjean F. Cole.
EIN: 731577358

45082
Sid and Jane Willis Foundation, Inc.
P.O. Box 618
Madill, OK 73446-0618

Financial data (yr. ended 06/30/01): Grants paid, $49,600; assets, $824,995 (M); expenditures, $50,950; qualifying distributions, $49,123.
Limitations: Applications not accepted. Giving primarily in OK.
Application information: Contributes only to pre-selected organizations.
Directors: John Crooch, David Dunn, Dan Little, W.Y. Spence.
EIN: 731435564

45083
Morris & Libby Singer Foundation, Inc.
6305 Waterford Blvd., Ste. 450
Oklahoma City, OK 73118
Contact: Barbara Starz

Established in 1957.
Donor(s): Joseph B. Singer.
Financial data (yr. ended 08/31/01): Grants paid, $47,972; assets, $955,010 (M); expenditures, $50,815; qualifying distributions, $47,972.
Limitations: Giving primarily in Tulsa, OK.
Officers: Ann Gordon Singer, Pres.; Andrea S. Pollack, V.P.; Martha D. Sundby, Secy.-Treas.
EIN: 736096321

45084
The Barbara & James M. Sturdivant Charitable Trust
100 W. 5th St., Ste. 100
Tulsa, OK 74103-4219

Established in 1997 in OK.
Donor(s): Barbara Sturdivant, James Sturdivant.
Financial data (yr. ended 12/31/01): Grants paid, $47,425; assets, $257,707 (M); gifts received,

45084—OKLAHOMA

$17,757; expenditures, $48,425; qualifying distributions, $47,425.
Directors: Barbara Sturdivant, James Sturdivant.
EIN: 736301068

45085
The Seven S Foundation
P.O. Box 720420
Norman, OK 73070-0420

Established in 1998 in OK.
Donor(s): Domer Scaramucci, Jr., Janis D. Scaramucci.
Financial data (yr. ended 12/31/00): Grants paid, $47,000; assets, $50,667 (M); expenditures, $47,038; qualifying distributions, $46,991.
Limitations: Applications not accepted. Giving primarily in New York, NY.
Application information: Contributes only to pre-selected organizations.
Trustees: Domer Scaramucci, Jr., Janis D. Scaramucci.
EIN: 311629818

45086
The Simmons Charitable Foundation of Oklahoma
500 W. Main, Ste. 200
P.O. Box 307
Oklahoma City, OK 73101-0307

Established in 1993 in OK.
Donor(s): Marjorie Simmons Gray.
Financial data (yr. ended 12/31/00): Grants paid, $46,700; assets, $1,061,789 (M); gifts received, $50,000; expenditures, $48,126; qualifying distributions, $46,700.
Limitations: Applications not accepted. Giving primarily in OK.
Application information: Contributes only to pre-selected organizations.
Officers: Michael A. Scears, Pres. and Treas.; Paul A. Cox, V.P.; Marcia Burrows, Secy.
Directors: Ann Simmons Alspaugh, Holly C. Farabee.
EIN: 731436667

45087
Doug Tewell Foundation
c/o Darrel W. James
P.O. Box 30595
Edmond, OK 73003-0010

Established in 2000 in OK.
Donor(s): Douglas F. Tewell.
Financial data (yr. ended 12/31/01): Grants paid, $45,325; assets, $59,871 (M); gifts received, $54,175; expenditures, $45,360; qualifying distributions, $45,325.
Limitations: Applications not accepted.
Application information: Contributes only to pre-selected organizations.
Trustees: Douglas F. Tewell, Pamela J. Tewell.
EIN: 731602984

45088
Julia Fredin Frasier Foundation
c/o Thomas Dee Frasier
1700 Southwest Blvd.
Tulsa, OK 74107-1713
Contact: Steven R. Hickman, Tr.

Donor(s): Thomas Dee Frasier.
Financial data (yr. ended 12/31/99): Grants paid, $43,967; assets, $370,910 (L); gifts received, $500; expenditures, $132; qualifying distributions, $43,967.
Limitations: Giving limited to Tulsa, OK.
Trustees: Thomas Dee Frasier, Steven R. Hickman.
EIN: 731537946

45089
Nelle and Milt Thompson Foundation
P.O. Drawer 1770
Cushing, OK 74023-1770

Established in 1988 in OK.
Donor(s): Nelle J. Thompson.
Financial data (yr. ended 12/31/99): Grants paid, $43,766; assets, $1,238,012 (M); expenditures, $59,714; qualifying distributions, $56,655.
Limitations: Giving limited to Cushing, OK.
Trustees: Charles E. Phelps, Jr., Kelly Phelps, Margaret Phelps, Sherrie Plunkett.
EIN: 736242219

45090
Texas County Memorial Foundation, Inc.
P.O. Box 1228
Guymon, OK 73942

Established in 1985 in TX.
Donor(s): Robert & Mary Lolmaugh Trust Foundation.
Financial data (yr. ended 06/30/02): Grants paid, $43,733; assets, $809,462 (M); expenditures, $59,781; qualifying distributions, $43,733.
Limitations: Applications not accepted. Giving limited to Texas County, OK.
Application information: Contributes only to pre-selected organizations.
Officers and Directors:* Jimmy R. Webster,* Pres.; Jim Fletcher,* V.P.; Wanda L. Shields,* Secy.; Nancy Childress,* Treas.; David Long, Larry L. Field, and 14 additional directors.
EIN: 730722424

45091
Grace Living Centers Foundation, Inc.
709 Fox Tail Dr.
Edmond, OK 73034

Established in 2000 in OK.
Donor(s): K. Don Greiner, Shellie Greiner.
Financial data (yr. ended 12/31/01): Grants paid, $43,686; assets, $780,143 (M); gifts received, $958,000; expenditures, $45,285; qualifying distributions, $43,686.
Limitations: Applications not accepted.
Application information: Contributes only to pre-selected organizations.
Directors: K. Don Greiner, Shellie Greiner.
EIN: 731596382

45092
J. Lyndall McCrory, Robert Fulton McCrory and Montie Ray McCrory Foundation
303 E St., N.W.
Ardmore, OK 73401
Contact: J. Larry Wilkes, Dir.

Established in 1993.
Donor(s): J. Lyndall McCrory.
Financial data (yr. ended 12/31/01): Grants paid, $43,509; assets, $9,088,704 (M); gifts received, $6,405,980; expenditures, $131,738; qualifying distributions, $43,509.
Limitations: Applications not accepted. Giving primarily in Ardmore, OK.
Application information: Contributes only to pre-selected organizations.
Trustees: Mary Strawn, J. Larry Wilkes.
EIN: 731439304

45093
McKinney & Stringer Foundation
(Formerly The McKinney, Stringer & Webster Foundation)
101 N. Robinson, Ste. 1300
Oklahoma City, OK 73102 (405) 239-6444
Contact: N. Martin Stringer, Tr.

Established in 1991 in OK.
Donor(s): Kenneth N. McKinney, N. Martin Stringer, Rick R. Moore.
Financial data (yr. ended 12/31/01): Grants paid, $42,000; assets, $3,542 (M); gifts received, $45,150; expenditures, $42,057; qualifying distributions, $42,057.
Limitations: Giving primarily in Oklahoma City, OK.
Application information: Application form not required.
Trustees: Kenneth N. McKinney, Rick R. Moore, N. Martin Stringer.
EIN: 736261629

45094
Anna Collins Franklin Foundation
P.O. Box 144
Ardmore, OK 73401
Application address: Rte. 3, Box 174, Ardmore, OK 73401
Contact: Glenn Hendrix, Tr.

Established in 1990 in OK.
Donor(s): Wenzella W. Ripley.‡
Financial data (yr. ended 12/31/01): Grants paid, $41,750; assets, $1,917,428 (M); expenditures, $76,805; qualifying distributions, $62,737.
Limitations: Giving limited to Carter County, OK.
Trustees: Glenn Hendrix, Mark Hendrix.
EIN: 731361437
Codes: GTI

45095
Patti Johnson Wilson Foundation
c/o The Trust Co. of Oklahoma
1924 S. Utica Ave., Ste. 500
Tulsa, OK 74104-6540 (918) 745-2400
Contact: Paul Kallenberger, Tr.

Established in 1973.
Financial data (yr. ended 08/31/01): Grants paid, $41,750; assets, $945,409 (M); expenditures, $52,154; qualifying distributions, $46,982.
Limitations: Giving primarily to individuals in AR, KS, and OK.
Publications: Application guidelines.
Application information: Contact Financial Aid Office. Application form required.
Trustees: Kathleen L. Childs, Barbara Ann Glass, Frank X. Henke III, Paul Kallenberger, Mary Ann Meckfessel, James M. Sturdivant, The Trust Co. of Oklahoma.
EIN: 736156280
Codes: GTI

45096
The Michael Patrick Carmack Foundation
4125 Arrowhead N.E.
Piedmont, OK 73078

Donor(s): Arkla, Inc.
Financial data (yr. ended 12/31/99): Grants paid, $41,629; assets, $23,292 (M); gifts received, $11,913; expenditures, $41,629; qualifying distributions, $41,629.
Limitations: Applications not accepted. Giving primarily in CO and OK.
Application information: Contributes only to pre-selected organizations.
Directors: Patrick S.J. Carmack, Chair.; Mary Lee Carmack.
EIN: 731205888

OKLAHOMA—45110

45097
Carson Foundation
710 S. Adams
Sapulpa, OK 74066
Contact: Edward A. Carson, Tr.

Established in 1998 in OK.
Donor(s): Edward Carson.
Financial data (yr. ended 12/31/01): Grants paid, $41,150; assets, $738,775 (M); expenditures, $47,191; qualifying distributions, $41,150.
Limitations: Applications not accepted. Giving primarily in OK.
Application information: Contributes only to pre-selected organizations.
Trustee: Edward A. Carson.
EIN: 731531905

45098
Clifford L. Knight Foundation
c/o Clifford L. Knight
P.O. Box 95459
Oklahoma City, OK 73143

Established in 1990 in OK.
Donor(s): Clifford L. Knight.
Financial data (yr. ended 12/31/01): Grants paid, $41,100; assets, $230,363 (M); gifts received, $70,940; expenditures, $41,219; qualifying distributions, $41,100.
Limitations: Applications not accepted. Giving primarily in Oklahoma City, OK.
Application information: Contributes only to pre-selected organizations.
Trustees: Clifford L. Knight, Sybil C. Knight.
EIN: 731371834

45099
The Demaris C. and Lyle W. Turner, Jr. Charitable Foundation
6528 D1 E. 101st St., PBM 367
Tulsa, OK 74133-6700

Established in 1998 in OK.
Donor(s): Lyle W. Turner, Jr.
Financial data (yr. ended 12/31/01): Grants paid, $40,700; assets, $113,541 (M); gifts received, $51,180; expenditures, $41,872; qualifying distributions, $40,700.
Limitations: Applications not accepted. Giving primarily in Tulsa, OK.
Application information: Contributes only to pre-selected organizations.
Trustees: Demaris C. Turner, Lyle W. Turner, Jr.
EIN: 736311703

45100
The Dan & Gloria Schusterman Foundation
2121 S. Columbia, Ste. 650
Tulsa, OK 74114

Established in 1996 in OK.
Donor(s): Dan Schusterman, Gloria Schusterman.
Financial data (yr. ended 12/31/01): Grants paid, $40,200; assets, $940,789 (M); expenditures, $57,345; qualifying distributions, $39,709.
Limitations: Applications not accepted. Giving primarily in West Palm Beach, FL.
Application information: Contributes only to pre-selected organizations.
Trustees: Dan Schusterman, Gloria Schusterman.
EIN: 731495727

45101
Ralph and Frances McGill Foundation
c/o The Trust Co. of Oklahoma
P.O. Box 3348
Tulsa, OK 74101-3348

Established in 2000 in OK.
Financial data (yr. ended 12/31/01): Grants paid, $40,000; assets, $8,272,868 (M); gifts received, $8,546,940; expenditures, $45,264; qualifying distributions, $40,000.
Trustee: The Trust Co. of Oklahoma.
EIN: 731590898

45102
The Scroggins Foundation
2833 Hickory Creek Rd.
Muskogee, OK 74403-2333
Application address: 100 Rodman Circle, Muskogee, OK 74403, tel.: (918) 687-4326
Contact: Joe Lightle, Pres.

Financial data (yr. ended 12/31/01): Grants paid, $40,000; assets, $667,253 (M); expenditures, $41,794; qualifying distributions, $40,000.
Limitations: Giving primarily in Muskogee and Tulsa, OK.
Officers: Joe Lightle, Pres.; Barbara Anderson, Secy.-Treas.
EIN: 723719129

45103
Frank & Patricia McDonald Charitable Foundation
5105 E. 80th St.
Tulsa, OK 74136

Established in 2000 in OK.
Financial data (yr. ended 12/31/01): Grants paid, $39,950; assets, $211,471 (M); gifts received, $70; expenditures, $41,813; qualifying distributions, $39,950.
Limitations: Giving primarily in Tulsa, OK.
Trustees: Frank C. McDonald, Patricia C. McDonald.
EIN: 731577052

45104
H. H. Champlin Foundation
P.O. Box 1066
Enid, OK 73702-1066 (580) 233-1155
Contact: H.H. Champlin, Tr.

Financial data (yr. ended 12/31/01): Grants paid, $39,333; assets, $734,772 (M); expenditures, $46,806; qualifying distributions, $39,333.
Limitations: Giving limited to OK.
Trustees: H.H. Champlin, Hiram H. Champlin, H.C. Oven, H.C. Oven, Jr.
EIN: 735682900

45105
Macklanburg-Hulsey Foundation, Inc.
P.O. Box 25188
Oklahoma City, OK 73125-0188
(405) 528-4411
Contact: Mike Samis, Dir.

Financial data (yr. ended 06/30/01): Grants paid, $39,300; assets, $483,318 (M); expenditures, $40,894; qualifying distributions, $39,300.
Limitations: Giving primarily in Oklahoma City, OK.
Officers: Louanne Ellis, Pres.; Karen Samis, V.P.; David Kilburn, Secy.-Treas.
Director: Mike Samis.
EIN: 736094975

45106
The HCL Charitable Trust
7906 S. Darlington Ave.
Tulsa, OK 74136-8451 (918) 586-8165
Contact: Harold J. Colvin, Tr.

Donor(s): Harold J. Colvin.
Financial data (yr. ended 12/31/01): Grants paid, $37,975; assets, $86,198 (M); gifts received, $21,200; expenditures, $38,366; qualifying distributions, $37,975.

Limitations: Giving primarily in OK and WV.
Application information: Application form not required.
Trustees: Harold J. Colvin, Lisa D. Colvin, M. Carol Colvin.
EIN: 731334146

45107
The Elliott and Hannah Davis Family Foundation, Inc.
320 S. Boston, Ste. 1000
Tulsa, OK 74103-3703

Established in 1996 in OK.
Donor(s): Elliott Davis,‡ Hannah Davis.
Financial data (yr. ended 12/31/01): Grants paid, $37,600; assets, $1 (M); expenditures, $42,584; qualifying distributions, $37,600.
Limitations: Applications not accepted. Giving primarily in OK and TX.
Application information: Contributes only to pre-selected organizations.
Officers: Barry M. Davis, V.P.; Hannah Davis, V.P.; Lee H. Davis, V.P.; Mark S. Davis, V.P.; Timothy S. Davis, V.P.
EIN: 731497875

45108
Red Man Charitable Trust
8023 E. 63rd Pl., Ste. 800
Tulsa, OK 74133
Contact: Betty J. Ketchum, Tr.

Established in 1984.
Donor(s): Red Man Pipe & Supply Co., Betty J. Ketchum, Lewis B. Ketchum, Robert W. Keener.
Financial data (yr. ended 01/31/02): Grants paid, $37,600; assets, $106,804 (M); gifts received, $44,000; expenditures, $37,600; qualifying distributions, $37,600.
Limitations: Giving primarily in Tulsa, OK.
Trustee: Betty J. Ketchum.
EIN: 736217632
Codes: CS, CD

45109
Cecil and Virgie Burton Foundation
2021 S. Lewis, Ste. 260
Tulsa, OK 74104 (918) 745-0415
Contact: Tammie L. Maloney, Tr.

Established in 1993 in OK.
Financial data (yr. ended 06/30/01): Grants paid, $37,500; assets, $596,436 (M); expenditures, $38,495; qualifying distributions, $38,002.
Limitations: Giving primarily in KS, and Tulsa, OK.
Trustees: Virgie Burton, Jean Ann Fausser, Tammie L. Maloney.
EIN: 731438062

45110
Kathleen Patton Westby Foundation
4815 S. Harvard, Ste. 395
Tulsa, OK 74135
Contact: John Trygve Westby, Tr.

Established in 1989 in OK.
Donor(s): Kathleen Patton Westby.
Financial data (yr. ended 06/30/01): Grants paid, $36,950; assets, $1,903,762 (M); gifts received, $518,538; expenditures, $56,674; qualifying distributions, $45,950.
Limitations: Giving primarily in Tulsa, OK.
Trustees: Gerald H. Westby, John Trygve Westby, Kathleen H. Westby.
EIN: 731354412

45111
O. K. Detrick Foundation, Inc.
1622 Hampden Rd.
Bartlesville, OK 74006 (918) 333-1884
Contact: C.Q. Cherry, Pres.

Financial data (yr. ended 12/31/01): Grants paid, $36,000; assets, $70,777 (M); gifts received, $405; expenditures, $40,751; qualifying distributions, $36,000.
Limitations: Giving primarily in OK.
Officer and Directors:* C.Q. Cherry,* Pres.; Gail Beals, Laurie Claus, Mary N. Hamilton, Dorothy Kendall, Mary K. Munson.
EIN: 730782662

45112
Jenkin Lloyd Jones Foundation
6683 S. Jamestown Pl.
Tulsa, OK 74136

Established in 1995 in OK.
Donor(s): Jenkin Lloyd Jones.
Financial data (yr. ended 12/31/01): Grants paid, $36,000; assets, $668,850 (M); expenditures, $41,830; qualifying distributions, $36,000.
Limitations: Applications not accepted. Giving primarily in MN, NY, and OK.
Application information: Contributes only to pre-selected organizations.
Trustees: Ana Maria Heinzelman Lloyd Jones, Jenkin Lloyd Jones.
EIN: 731475137

45113
Lee M. Lobeck Marks Foundation
c/o R. Blake Atkins
427 S. Boston
Tulsa, OK 74103

Donor(s): Lee M. Lobeck.
Financial data (yr. ended 12/31/01): Grants paid, $36,000; assets, $486,556 (M); expenditures, $40,327; qualifying distributions, $36,000.
Limitations: Applications not accepted. Giving primarily in Tulsa, OK.
Application information: Contributes only to pre-selected organizations.
Trustees: R. Blake Atkins, Lee M. Lobeck.
EIN: 736297659

45114
All Souls' Angelican Foundation
6909 N.W. Grand Blvd.
Oklahoma City, OK 73116-5001

Financial data (yr. ended 12/31/01): Grants paid, $35,800; assets, $143,456 (M); gifts received, $110,500; expenditures, $38,172; qualifying distributions, $35,800.
Limitations: Applications not accepted. Giving limited to Oklahoma City, OK.
Application information: Contributes only to pre-selected organizations.
Officers: James B. Kite, Jr., Pres.; Mrs. James B. Kite, Jr., Secy.; Jean Hartsuck, Treas.
Directors: Fr. Patrick E. Bright, Robert H. Gilliland, Jr., Frank Hill, Dwight Journey, John McCaleb, Fr. Dale Pettey, Dee A. Replogle, Jr., Jean S. Whiteneck, J.H. Wilson, Jr.
EIN: 731444363

45115
The Anait Foundation
P.O. Box 1495
Bartlesville, OK 74005-1495 (918) 331-9331
Contact: Anait Stephens, Tr.

Donor(s): Anait Stephens.
Financial data (yr. ended 08/31/01): Grants paid, $35,002; assets, $711,415 (M); gifts received, $50,000; expenditures, $38,617; qualifying distributions, $35,002.
Limitations: Giving primarily in Santa Barbara, CA.
Application information: Application form not required.
Trustees: Kyra Gebhardt, Ralph L. Stephens.
EIN: 731104114

45116
Sullivan Charitable Trust
2118 E. 29th St.
Tulsa, OK 74114-5422
Contact: Robert J. Sullivan, Jr., Tr.

Donor(s): Robert J. Sullivan, Jr.
Financial data (yr. ended 04/30/02): Grants paid, $34,900; assets, $550,746 (M); expenditures, $36,579; qualifying distributions, $34,900.
Limitations: Giving primarily in South Bend, IN, and Tulsa, OK.
Trustees: Anthony J. Lauinger, William L. Schloss III, Martin F. Sullivan, Robert J. Sullivan, Jr.
EIN: 237369119

45117
Jearl Smart Foundation, Inc.
P.O. Box 1513
Wewoka, OK 74884
Contact: James R. Smart

Established in 1995 in OK.
Donor(s): James R. Smart, John Smart, Jo Smart.
Financial data (yr. ended 12/31/01): Grants paid, $34,753; assets, $701,125 (M); expenditures, $36,037; qualifying distributions, $34,753.
Limitations: Giving primarily in Wewoka, OK.
Trustees: Richard Pralle, Rob L. Pyron, Jearl Seikel, Jim Smart, Jo Smart, John Smart, Julie Tibbs.
EIN: 731493842

45118
Williams Natural Gas Company Educational Foundation
(Formerly Northwest Central Pipeline Educational Foundation)
c/o Janice Taylor
P.O. Box 2400
Tulsa, OK 74101-2400
Contact: John E. Butler, Treas.

Donor(s): Williams Natural Gas Co., Williams Gas Pipelines Central, Inc.
Financial data (yr. ended 12/31/00): Grants paid, $34,500; assets, $49,777 (M); expenditures, $34,567; qualifying distributions, $34,506.
Limitations: Giving primarily in areas of company operations.
Application information: Applicants must also submit academic standing and ACT or SAT scores. Application form required.
Officers and Directors:* Karen S. Dean,* Pres.; James L. Dancer,* V.P.; John H. Cary,* Secy.; John E. Butler,* Treas.; Lester E. Ritter.
EIN: 731195917
Codes: CS, TN

45119
Aaron & Gertrude Karchmer Memorial Foundation
P.O. Box 436
Oklahoma City, OK 73101
Application address: 120 E. Sheridan, Oklahoma City, OK 73104, tel.: (405) 236-2210
Contact: Don A. Karchmer, Pres.

Established in 1994 in OK.
Donor(s): Don A. Karchmer.
Financial data (yr. ended 12/31/00): Grants paid, $34,106; assets, $264,263 (M); expenditures, $34,865; qualifying distributions, $34,106.
Limitations: Giving primarily in Oklahoma City, OK.
Officers: Don A. Karchmer, Pres. and Treas.; Laura Cooke, Secy.
EIN: 731463604

45120
Tate Foundation
P.O. Box 4529
Tulsa, OK 74159-0529

Established in 1994 in OK.
Donor(s): Joseph N. Tate, Priscilla C. Tate.
Financial data (yr. ended 12/31/01): Grants paid, $33,333; assets, $243,451 (M); gifts received, $10,564; expenditures, $35,295; qualifying distributions, $33,333.
Limitations: Applications not accepted. Giving primarily to residents in Tulsa, OK.
Application information: Contributes only to pre-selected organizations.
Trustees: Joseph N. Tate, Priscilla C. Tate.
EIN: 731456321

45121
Madalynne L. Peel Foundation
116 S. Main
Newkirk, OK 74647-4512 (580) 362-2368
Contact: Jack De McCarty, V.P.

Established in 1997.
Donor(s): Madalynne L. Peel.
Financial data (yr. ended 09/30/01): Grants paid, $33,000; assets, $1,427,936 (M); gifts received, $600,000; expenditures, $37,333; qualifying distributions, $35,500.
Limitations: Giving primarily in OK.
Officers: Jack De McCarty, Pres.; Thomas M. Rigdon, Secy.-Treas.
Directors: Marybeth Glass, Philip A. Ross, Betty J. Scott.
EIN: 731526716

45122
Glenn W. Peel Foundation
116 S. Main St.
Newkirk, OK 74647-4512 (580) 362-2368
Contact: Jack De McCarty, Pres.

Established in 1978 in OK.
Donor(s): Glenn W. Peel.‡
Financial data (yr. ended 09/30/01): Grants paid, $32,985; assets, $4,206,103 (M); expenditures, $43,458; qualifying distributions, $35,985.
Limitations: Giving primarily in OK.
Publications: Application guidelines.
Application information: Application form not required.
Officers: Jack De McCarty, Pres.; Thomas M. Rigden, Secy.-Treas.
Directors: Marybeth Glass, David Ross, Philip A. Ross, Betty J. Scott.
EIN: 731057392

45123
Aaron M. Weitzenhoffer Foundation
20 N. Broadway, Ste. 1800
Oklahoma City, OK 73102

Financial data (yr. ended 05/31/02): Grants paid, $32,921; assets, $630,158 (M); expenditures, $36,565; qualifying distributions, $32,921.
Limitations: Applications not accepted. Giving primarily in Oklahoma City, OK.
Application information: Contributes only to pre-selected organizations.
Trustees: Leroy Rowland, Aaron Max Weitzenhoffer.
EIN: 736092543

45124
Huffman Trust
1810 Philtower Bldg.
Tulsa, OK 74103

Established in 2000 in OK.
Financial data (yr. ended 12/31/00): Grants paid, $32,250; assets, $1,228,419 (M); expenditures, $37,886; qualifying distributions, $37,580.
Limitations: Applications not accepted. Giving primarily in Tulsa, OK.
Application information: Contributes only to pre-selected organizations.
Trustee: Lucien Rouse.
EIN: 736317789

45125
The Darden Family Charitable Foundation
9 E. 4th St., Ste. 800
Tulsa, OK 74103-5114

Established in 1997 in OK.
Donor(s): Larry B. Darden.
Financial data (yr. ended 12/31/01): Grants paid, $31,600; assets, $555,089 (M); gifts received, $500; expenditures, $32,626; qualifying distributions, $31,600.
Limitations: Applications not accepted. Giving primarily in Tulsa, OK and TX.
Application information: Contributes only to pre-selected organizations.
Trustees: Doris J. Darden, Larry B. Darden.
EIN: 731533372

45126
National Association of Insurance Women (International) Education Foundation
(also known as NAIW (International))
1847 E. 15th St.
Tulsa, OK 74104-4610
Application address: P.O. Box 4410, Tulsa, OK 74159, tel.: (800) 766-6249
Contact: Jennifer Warren

Established in 1993 in OK.
Financial data (yr. ended 06/30/01): Grants paid, $31,400; assets, $617,018 (M); gifts received, $153,522; expenditures, $147,363; qualifying distributions, $31,400.
Limitations: Giving on a national basis.
Application information: Application form required.
Officers: Shirley A. Timmons, Chair.; Nancy Noe-Nichols, Pres.; Jeanine R. Kingeter, Secy.
Directors: Bertina Floyd, Sarah Kelly, George A. White, David B. Wiley, Christine L. Lewis, Kim J. O'Conor, Thomas E. Smith, Aleta Stephens.
EIN: 731429257
Codes: TN, GTI

45127
Harold & Hazel Hathcoat Charitable Trust
P.O. Box 286
Nowata, OK 74048

Established in 1997 in OK.
Donor(s): Harold D. Hathcoat.
Financial data (yr. ended 12/31/99): Grants paid, $31,193; assets, $318,110 (M); expenditures, $38,396; qualifying distributions, $31,193; giving activities include $7,203 for programs.
Limitations: Applications not accepted. Giving limited to Nowata County, OK.
Application information: Contributes only to pre-selected organizations.
Officer: Willis K. Johnson, Mgr.
Trustees: Francis Eugene Fry, Roger E. Hathcoat, Dale Turney.
EIN: 736300010

45128
Historical Preservation, Inc.
P.O. Box 1046
Oklahoma City, OK 73101-1046
Contact: John McBryde, Treas.

Established in 1971 in OK.
Donor(s): Carolyn Skelly Burford, Mrs. Hugh M. Johnson.‡
Financial data (yr. ended 12/31/00): Grants paid, $30,681; assets, $2,621,042 (M); expenditures, $62,401; qualifying distributions, $42,782.
Limitations: Giving limited to the Heritage Hills Historical Preservation District in Oklahoma City, OK, and surrounding urban areas.
Application information: Application form not required.
Officers: John Hefner, Pres.; Linda Adams, 1st V.P.; Jeff Erwin, 2nd V.P.; Miles Tolbert, Secy.; John McBryde, Treas.
EIN: 237023817

45129
The Herbster Family Foundation
1427 S. Owasso Ave.
Tulsa, OK 74120

Established in 1997 in OK.
Donor(s): James R. Herbster.
Financial data (yr. ended 12/31/99): Grants paid, $30,667; assets, $464,564 (M); gifts received, $35,711; expenditures, $39,747; qualifying distributions, $30,667.
Limitations: Applications not accepted.
Application information: Contributes only to pre-selected organizations.
Trustees: James R. Herbster, Chair.; Barry F. Herbster, Brad J. Herbster, Stacey L. Herbster.
EIN: 731514860

45130
RGF Family Fund
525 S. Main Pk., Centre Bldg., Ste. 100
Tulsa, OK 74103-4523

Donor(s): Nancy Feldman, Bruce K. Goodman, Joan C. Rosenberg.
Financial data (yr. ended 12/31/01): Grants paid, $30,300; assets, $321,243 (M); expenditures, $39,783; qualifying distributions, $30,300.
Limitations: Applications not accepted. Giving primarily in IL.
Application information: Contributes only to pre-selected organizations.
Officers and Directors:* Nancy Feldman,* Pres.; Raymond Feldman,* V.P.; Richard Feldman,* Secy.-Treas.; John Feldman.
EIN: 366085190

45131
G. L. Brennan Foundation, Inc.
2204 E. 25th Pl.
Tulsa, OK 74114

Financial data (yr. ended 12/31/01): Grants paid, $30,070; assets, $223,622 (M); expenditures, $31,615; qualifying distributions, $30,070.
Limitations: Applications not accepted. Giving primarily in Tulsa, OK.
Application information: Contributes only to pre-selected organizations.
Trustees: J.W. Brownlee, John Brennan Brownlee.
EIN: 736094443

45132
William H. & Martha E. Atkinson Foundation
P.O. Box 20510
Oklahoma City, OK 73156-0510

Financial data (yr. ended 06/30/01): Grants paid, $30,000; assets, $271,466 (M); expenditures, $31,333; qualifying distributions, $9,100.
Limitations: Applications not accepted. Giving limited to Oklahoma City, OK.
Application information: Contributes only to pre-selected organizations.
Officers: Margaret E. DeBee, Pres.; Mary F. Lucado, V.P. and Secy.; James Vallion, V.P.; John DeBee, Treas.
EIN: 237418113

45133
C. Richard Ford Foundation
P.O. Box 21208
Oklahoma City, OK 73156-1208
(405) 755-8218
Contact: Shirley A. Ford, Tr.

Established in 1989 in OK; funded in 1990.
Donor(s): C. Richard Ford, Shirley A. Ford.
Financial data (yr. ended 12/31/01): Grants paid, $30,000; assets, $60,174 (M); gifts received, $20,000; expenditures, $30,958; qualifying distributions, $30,000.
Limitations: Giving primarily in Oklahoma City, OK.
Trustee: Shirley A. Ford.
EIN: 731351737

45134
Tommie Lee Hulme Foundation, Inc.
c/o Heritage Trust Co.
1900 N.W. Expwy., Ste. R225
Oklahoma City, OK 73118

Donor(s): C.A. Hulme.
Financial data (yr. ended 09/30/01): Grants paid, $30,000; assets, $318,743 (M); gifts received, $60; expenditures, $37,574; qualifying distributions, $29,901.
Limitations: Applications not accepted. Giving primarily in Yukon, OK.
Application information: Contributes only to pre-selected organizations.
Officer: June Powell, Pres. and Treas.
Director: Trevor Powell.
Trustee: Heritage Trust Co.
EIN: 237248893

45135
Oklahoma Allergy Clinic Foundation, Inc.
P.O. Box 26827
Oklahoma City, OK 73126-0827
Contact: Warren V. Filley, Pres.

Donor(s): Charles D. Haunschild, Lyle W. Burroughs, James H. Wells, John R. Bozalis, Warren V. Filley, James R. Claflin.
Financial data (yr. ended 05/31/02): Grants paid, $29,985; assets, $59,218 (M); gifts received, $33,708; expenditures, $29,985; qualifying distributions, $29,985.
Limitations: Giving primarily in the Oklahoma City, OK, area.
Officers and Directors:* Warren V. Filley,* Pres.; John R. Bozalis,* V.P.; James R. Claflin,* V.P.; G. Keith Montgomery, Secy.; Patricia Overhulser,* Treas.; Robert S. Ellis, Charles D. Haunschild.
EIN: 736109394

45136
Paul D. Austin Family Foundation
P.O. Box 1240
Seminole, OK 74818-1240

Established in 1991 in OK.
Donor(s): Paul D. Austin, Opal Jane Austin.
Financial data (yr. ended 12/31/01): Grants paid, $29,910; assets, $101,003 (M); expenditures, $30,909; qualifying distributions, $29,910.
Limitations: Applications not accepted. Giving primarily in Norman, OK.
Application information: Contributes only to pre-selected organizations.
Trustees: Opal Jane Austin, Paul D. Austin.
EIN: 731392558

45137
Hedwig Drummer Trust
P.O. Box 1066
Bartlesville, OK 74005-1066 (918) 336-4132
Contact: Jesse J. Worten III, Tr.

Established in 1992 in OK.
Donor(s): Hedwig Drummer.‡
Financial data (yr. ended 08/31/01): Grants paid, $29,827; assets, $26,924 (M); expenditures, $32,341; qualifying distributions, $29,816.
Limitations: Giving limited to Bartlesville, OK, area.
Application information: Application form not required.
Trustee: Jesse J. Worten III.
EIN: 736264229

45138
Will Foundation
P.O. Box 1447
Shawnee, OK 74802-1447

Established in 1989 in OK.
Donor(s): Robert L. Pourchot.
Financial data (yr. ended 12/31/01): Grants paid, $29,600; assets, $263,478 (M); gifts received, $56,000; expenditures, $30,635; qualifying distributions, $29,600.
Limitations: Applications not accepted.
Application information: Contributes only to pre-selected organizations.
Trustees: Donald W. Orr, Robert L. Pourchot.
EIN: 731340405

45139
Carudo/Ford Foundation
P.O. Box 14550
Oklahoma City, OK 73113 (405) 840-0547
Contact: William Doug Ford, Pres.

Established in 1985 in OK.
Donor(s): William Doug Ford.
Financial data (yr. ended 12/31/01): Grants paid, $29,425; assets, $137,247 (M); expenditures, $29,687; qualifying distributions, $29,425.
Limitations: Giving primarily in OK.
Officers and Directors:* William Doug Ford,* Pres.; Tom R. Gray III,* V.P.; Wanda Manek,* Secy.
EIN: 731240437

45140
Valentine Charitable Trust
c/o R. Cole
6100 N. Grand Blvd.
Oklahoma City, OK 73118-1030

Established in 1996 in OK.
Donor(s): Laura D. Valentine Trust.
Financial data (yr. ended 12/31/01): Grants paid, $29,200; assets, $800,474 (M); expenditures, $47,994; qualifying distributions, $29,200.
Limitations: Applications not accepted. Giving primarily in Oklahoma City, OK.
Application information: Contributes only to pre-selected organizations.
Trustee: Roger Cole.
EIN: 736292034

45141
The Filstrup Foundation
6159 E. New Haven
Tulsa, OK 74136
Contact: Elaine H. Filstrup, Chair.

Established in 1999 in OK.
Financial data (yr. ended 12/31/00): Grants paid, $29,166; assets, $1,072,322 (M); gifts received, $1,001,413; expenditures, $30,323; qualifying distributions, $29,019.
Limitations: Giving primarily in OK and PA.
Application information: Application form not required.
Officers: Elaine H. Filstrup, Chair.; Scott H. Filstrup, Secy.-Treas.
Board Member: Alvin W. Filstrup.
EIN: 731576282

45142
McAnaw Family Foundation
1900 Glynnwood Dr.
Bartlesville, OK 74006 (918) 333-5700
Contact: Ernestine A. McAnaw, Dir.

Established in 1993 in OK.
Donor(s): Ernestine A. McAnaw.
Financial data (yr. ended 12/31/01): Grants paid, $29,100; assets, $312,310 (M); expenditures, $30,937; qualifying distributions, $29,100.
Limitations: Giving primarily in Bartlesville, OK.
Directors: Anne E. Marshall, Ernestine A. McAnaw, John J. McAnaw III, Michael N. McAnaw.
EIN: 731427545

45143
Frank Family Foundation
9 E. 4th St., Ste. 702
Tulsa, OK 74103-5113

Established in 1996 in OK.
Donor(s): Irvin E. Frank.
Financial data (yr. ended 06/30/02): Grants paid, $29,000; assets, $503,982 (M); expenditures, $32,217; qualifying distributions, $29,000.
Limitations: Applications not accepted.
Application information: Contributes only to pre-selected organizations.
Officers: Irvin E. Frank, Chair.; Sharna Frank, V.P.; Coleman Robinson, V.P.; May Sheehan, Secy.-Treas.
EIN: 731503704

45144
Loris and Pauline Keen Charitable Trust
P.O. Box 404
Blackwell, OK 74631-0404 (580) 363-2659
Contact: Daniel C. McClung, Tr.

Financial data (yr. ended 12/31/01): Grants paid, $28,581; assets, $783,037 (M); expenditures, $43,340; qualifying distributions, $39,303.
Limitations: Giving limited to OK.
Application information: Application form required.
Trustees: Daniel C. McClung, Walter Shafer.
EIN: 736252829
Codes: GTI

45145
Walters Public Education Foundation
418 S. Broadway
Walters, OK 73572-2099
Contact: Michael C. Flanagan, Pres.

Financial data (yr. ended 12/31/99): Grants paid, $28,008; assets, $183,431 (M); gifts received, $21,799; expenditures, $28,175; qualifying distributions, $27,928.
Limitations: Giving limited to Walters, OK.
Officers: Michael C. Flanagan, Pres.; Jeff Simpson, Secy.; Danny Marlett, Treas.
Directors: Merrill Dilke, Bill Freeman, Lois Marie Kinney, Jimmy W. Rinder, David Schumpert, Harold Taylor.
EIN: 731264832

45146
Livermore Foundation
777 N.W. Grand Blvd., Ste. 512
Oklahoma City, OK 73118 (405) 843-4637
Contact: Edward K. Livermore, Sr., Pres.

Donor(s): Edward K. Livermore, Sr.
Financial data (yr. ended 12/31/01): Grants paid, $28,005; assets, $537,714 (M); gifts received, $4,500; expenditures, $29,034; qualifying distributions, $28,005.
Limitations: Giving primarily in OK.
Application information: Application form not required.
Officers: Edward K. Livermore, Sr., Pres.; Melba H. Livermore, Secy.-Treas.
EIN: 731554174

45147
Welch Family Foundation
1207 E. 21st St.
Tulsa, OK 74114 (918) 584-7474
Contact: William J. Welch, Pres.

Established in 1997 in OK.
Donor(s): William J. Welch.
Financial data (yr. ended 12/31/01): Grants paid, $28,000; assets, $654,854 (M); gifts received, $577; expenditures, $31,397; qualifying distributions, $28,000.
Application information: Application form not required.
Officers and Directors:* William J. Welch,* Pres.; Peggy L. Welch,* V.P. and Secy.; Gary M. Fleener,* V.P.; Douglas S. Welch, Jennifer V. Welch.
EIN: 731502461

45148
W. R. and M. A. Gordon Foundation
1512 Autumn Rd.
Ponca City, OK 74604
Contact: William R. Gordon, Pres.

Established in 1997.
Donor(s): William R. Gordon.
Financial data (yr. ended 12/31/01): Grants paid, $27,750; assets, $244,626 (M); expenditures, $30,082; qualifying distributions, $27,750.
Application information: Application form not required.
Officers and Directors:* William R. Gordon,* Pres.; Gregory Alan Gordon,* V.P.; Mary A. Gordon,* Secy.; Paula Sue Matson, Kathaleen Marie Mertz, Denise Ann Williams.
EIN: 731508101

45149
Julius & Mildred Sanditen Foundation, Inc.
4424 Oak Rd.
Tulsa, OK 74105 (918) 747-4549
Contact: Mildred Sanditen, Pres.

Donor(s): Mildred Sanditen.

Financial data (yr. ended 12/31/99): Grants paid, $27,683; assets, $214,657 (M); gifts received, $50,050; expenditures, $31,575; qualifying distributions, $27,683.
Limitations: Giving primarily in Tulsa, OK.
Officers and Directors:* Mildred Sanditen,* Pres.; Sama Hoffman,* V.P. and Secy.; Deana Maloney,* V.P. and Treas.; Michael Cohen.
EIN: 731353533

45150
Ed and Carol Abel Foundation
1 Leadership Sq.
211 N. Robinson, Ste. 600
Oklahoma City, OK 73102-7107

Established in 1980 in OK.
Donor(s): Carol C. Abel, Edwin D. Abel.
Financial data (yr. ended 12/31/01): Grants paid, $26,800; assets, $5,103 (M); gifts received, $30,953; expenditures, $27,503; qualifying distributions, $26,800.
Limitations: Applications not accepted. Giving primarily in CO, MO, and OK.
Application information: Contributes only to pre-selected organizations.
Trustees: Carol C. Abel, Edwin D. Abel.
EIN: 736250868

45151
Allan Neustadt Charitable Trust
900 S. Rockford Rd.
Ardmore, OK 73401
Application address: P.O. Box 788, Ardmore, OK 73402, tel.: (580) 223-1005
Contact: Allan Neustadt, Tr.

Established in 1997 in OK.
Donor(s): Neustadt Charitable Foundation, Allan Neustadt.
Financial data (yr. ended 12/31/01): Grants paid, $26,495; assets, $566,732 (M); expenditures, $30,862; qualifying distributions, $26,495.
Limitations: Giving primarily in Ardmore, OK.
Trustees: Julie Ashcraft, Allan Neustadt, Marilyn Neustadt.
EIN: 736300551

45152
Ruth & Allen Mayo Charitable Foundation
427 S. Boston, Ste. 306
Tulsa, OK 74103

Established in 1999 in OK.
Donor(s): CMM Charitable Lead Trust I, CMM Charitable Lead Trust II.
Financial data (yr. ended 03/31/02): Grants paid, $25,700; assets, $2,837,764 (M); gifts received, $944,180; expenditures, $101,544; qualifying distributions, $25,700.
Limitations: Applications not accepted. Giving primarily in Tulsa, OK.
Application information: Contributes only to pre-selected organizations.
Trustees: Cathryn Mayo Moore, James D. Moore.
EIN: 736315876

45153
Robinet-Smith Foundation, Inc.
6300 Oaktree Cir.
Edmond, OK 73003-2510
Contact: William and Lois Smith

Donor(s): William H. Smith, Lois Smith.
Financial data (yr. ended 12/31/01): Grants paid, $25,600; assets, $356,693 (M); expenditures, $25,750; qualifying distributions, $25,600.
Limitations: Giving primarily in OK.
Officers: Lois M. Smith, Pres.; William H. Smith, Secy.
Directors: Mark Smith, Michael Smith.

EIN: 731237838

45154
Joel and Carol Jankowsky Foundation
P.O. Box 21468
Tulsa, OK 74121-1468

Established in 1994 in OK and VA.
Financial data (yr. ended 12/31/00): Grants paid, $25,500; assets, $586,299 (M); gifts received, $15,000; expenditures, $27,090; qualifying distributions, $26,694.
Limitations: Applications not accepted.
Application information: Contributes only to pre-selected organizations.
Trustees: Carol Jankowsky, Joel Jankowsky.
EIN: 731463418

45155
Bonnie O' Connor Minshall Foundation, Inc.
320 S. Boston, Ste. 825
Tulsa, OK 74103 (918) 599-0045
Contact: Richard E. Minshall, Pres. or Melissa M. Minshall, V.P.

Established in 1999 in OK.
Financial data (yr. ended 12/31/01): Grants paid, $24,650; assets, $150,091 (M); gifts received, $3,270; expenditures, $29,832; qualifying distributions, $24,650.
Officers: Richard E. Minshall, Pres.; Melissa M. Minshall, V.P. and Secy.
EIN: 731560891

45156
The New Directions Foundation
7010 S. Yale, Ste. 121
Tulsa, OK 74136

Established in 1998 in OK.
Donor(s): Laurie Dobbs.
Financial data (yr. ended 12/31/00): Grants paid, $24,077; assets, $596,722 (M); expenditures, $88,281; qualifying distributions, $24,077.
Limitations: Applications not accepted.
Application information: Contributes only to pre-selected organizations.
Director: Ann Weatherly.
EIN: 731547230

45157
Gallery Foundation, Inc.
4223 S.E. Adams Rd.
Bartlesville, OK 74006
Contact: Dan L. Gallery, Pres.

Donor(s): Elmer L. Gallery.
Financial data (yr. ended 12/31/00): Grants paid, $24,000; assets, $0 (M); expenditures, $24,792; qualifying distributions, $24,792.
Limitations: Giving primarily in OK.
Officers: Dan L. Gallery, Pres.; Carl R. Webb, V.P.
EIN: 730768141

45158
Evelyn R. Daly Foundation, Inc.
P.O. Box 647
Drumright, OK 74030-0647

Financial data (yr. ended 12/31/01): Grants paid, $23,871; assets, $334,907 (M); expenditures, $25,231; qualifying distributions, $23,871.
Limitations: Applications not accepted.
Application information: Contributes only to pre-selected organizations.
Trustees: C.E. Stephenson, C.D. Watson, Jr., Doyle Watson.
EIN: 731323754

45159
Sarah Association, Inc.
8121 National Ave., Ste. 402
Midwest City, OK 73110

Established around 1993.
Donor(s): Zaheer U. Baber.
Financial data (yr. ended 12/31/01): Grants paid, $23,650; assets, $19,570 (M); gifts received, $40,000; expenditures, $24,202; qualifying distributions, $23,650.
Trustee: Zaheer U. Baber.
EIN: 731326783

45160
Renee F. Neuwald Foundation
1350 S. Boulder Ave., Ste. 400
Tulsa, OK 74119-3213 (918) 582-8083
Contact: Ruth K. Nelson, Tr.

Established in 2000 in OK.
Donor(s): Renee F. Neuwald.‡
Financial data (yr. ended 12/31/01): Grants paid, $23,000; assets, $495,628 (M); expenditures, $30,393; qualifying distributions, $23,000.
Application information: Application form not required.
Trustees: George Kaiser, Ruth Nelson.
EIN: 731585360

45161
Frank Parks Foundation, Inc.
P.O. Box 245
Hooker, OK 73945-0245 (580) 652-2454
Contact: Verle Martens, Pres.

Established in 1977 in OK.
Financial data (yr. ended 12/31/01): Grants paid, $23,000; assets, $559,099 (M); expenditures, $53,111; qualifying distributions, $23,000.
Limitations: Giving primarily in Hooker, OK.
Application information: Application form not required.
Officer and Trustees:* Verle Martens,* Pres.; James P. Flanagan, Ralph Flesher, Gwen Hanson.
EIN: 731019708

45162
Millard & Peggy Sanders Foundation
c/0 Peggy Ford Sanders
1501 Duffner Dr.
Oklahoma City, OK 73118-1015

Established in 1989 in OK.
Donor(s): Millard W. Sanders, Peggy Ford Sanders.
Financial data (yr. ended 12/31/99): Grants paid, $22,861; assets, $41,188 (M); gifts received, $50,000; expenditures, $22,870; qualifying distributions, $22,849.
Limitations: Applications not accepted. Giving primarily in Oklahoma City, OK.
Application information: Contributes only to pre-selected organizations.
Trustee: Peggy Ford Sanders.
EIN: 736246996

45163
Miller-Myers-Rothbaum Foundation, Inc.
P.O. Box 21468
Tulsa, OK 74121-1468

Financial data (yr. ended 06/30/01): Grants paid, $22,772; assets, $217,626 (M); expenditures, $27,619; qualifying distributions, $22,772.
Limitations: Applications not accepted. Giving primarily in Tulsa, OK.
Application information: Contributes only to pre-selected organizations.
Officers and Directors:* Julian J. Rothbaum,* Chair.; Herbert J. Miller,* Pres.; Lori Anne Chozen,* Secy.; Brenda Miller Magoon.

45163—OKLAHOMA

EIN: 730794078

45164
Oklahoma County Medical Society Community Foundation
601 N.W. Grand Blvd., Ste. B
Oklahoma City, OK 73118-6074
(405) 843-5619
Contact: V. Ramgopal, M.D., Pres.

Financial data (yr. ended 12/31/01): Grants paid, $22,655; assets, $96,896 (M); gifts received, $23,930; expenditures, $29,457; qualifying distributions, $22,596.
Limitations: Giving primarily in Oklahoma City, OK.
Application information: Application form not required.
Officers: Mukash T. Parekh, M.D., Pres.; Hon. John Amick, V.P.; Shirley Downey, Secy.
Director: Vadakepat Ramgopal.
EIN: 730746253

45165
Wiesner Family Foundation
(Formerly C. R. Anthony Foundation, Inc.)
6349 Harden Dr.
Oklahoma City, OK 73118
Contact: John J. Wiesner, Dir.

Established around 1968.
Donor(s): John J. Wiesner.
Financial data (yr. ended 11/30/01): Grants paid, $22,500; assets, $47,066 (M); expenditures, $22,521; qualifying distributions, $22,475.
Limitations: Giving primarily in Oklahoma City, OK.
Application information: Application form required.
Directors: N. Martin Stringer, Georgiana J. Wiesner, John J. Wiesner, Susan E. Wiesner.
EIN: 736113781

45166
The Robert S. and Helen Grey Trippet Foundation
20 E. 5th St., Ste. 300
Tulsa, OK 74103 (918) 587-3194
Contact: Robert S. Trippet, Pres.

Established in 1991 in OK.
Donor(s): Helen Grey Trippet, Robert S. Trippet.
Financial data (yr. ended 07/31/01): Grants paid, $21,901; assets, $599,353 (M); expenditures, $22,393; qualifying distributions, $21,901.
Limitations: Giving primarily in Tulsa, OK.
Application information: Application form not required.
Officers: Robert S. Trippet, Pres.; J.W. Moore, Jr., V.P.; Helen Grey Trippet, V.P.; Aileen S. Bell, Secy.
EIN: 731390841

45167
New Day Foundation, Inc.
2020 W. Detroit
Broken Arrow, OK 74012

Established in 1996 in OK.
Donor(s): Compservices, Inc.
Financial data (yr. ended 12/31/01): Grants paid, $21,562; assets, $140,865 (M); expenditures, $21,826; qualifying distributions, $21,562.
Officer: Nita Feeley, Pres.
EIN: 731486736

45168
Morris E. & Ethel Carlton Wheeler Scholarship Fund
c/o The Trust Co. of Oklahoma
P.O. Box 3627
Tulsa, OK 74101

Established in 1999 in OK.
Financial data (yr. ended 12/31/01): Grants paid, $21,547; assets, $687,329 (M); expenditures, $28,992; qualifying distributions, $21,547.
Limitations: Applications not accepted. Giving primarily in Pawhuska, OK.
Application information: Contributes only to pre-selected organizations.
Trustee: The Trust Co. of Oklahoma.
EIN: 736252523

45169
Porter Watchorn Foundation, Inc.
6001 N. Brookline, Ste. 1112
Oklahoma City, OK 73112 (405) 840-8444
Contact: John P. Porter, Pres.

Financial data (yr. ended 12/31/00): Grants paid, $21,500; assets, $392,251 (M); expenditures, $26,416; qualifying distributions, $21,500.
Limitations: Giving primarily in Shawnee, OK.
Officers: John P. Porter, Pres.; Ross U. Porter, Jr., V.P.; Jane Lake Porter, Secy.-Treas.
EIN: 730784147

45170
Mock Foundation
1433 Glenbrook Dr.
Oklahoma City, OK 73118

Donor(s): Randall D. Mock, Sally Mock.
Financial data (yr. ended 12/31/01): Grants paid, $20,649; assets, $145,344 (M); gifts received, $50,000; expenditures, $20,890; qualifying distributions, $20,890.
Limitations: Applications not accepted. Giving primarily in OK.
Application information: Contributes only to pre-selected organizations.
Trustees: Randall D. Mock, Sally Mock.
EIN: 736230333

45171
T-F Foundation
3314 E. 51st St., Ste. 206H
Tulsa, OK 74135-3527 (918) 743-7966
Contact: Irving S. Fenster, Tr.

Established in 1990 in OK.
Donor(s): Irene Fenster.
Financial data (yr. ended 12/31/01): Grants paid, $20,243; assets, $187,723 (M); gifts received, $2,358; expenditures, $20,868; qualifying distributions, $20,243.
Limitations: Giving primarily in Tulsa, OK.
Trustee: Irving S. Fenster.
EIN: 731374411

45172
Joseph's Storehouse
5413 East 105th Place
Tulsa, OK 74137 (918) 748-5208
Contact: Doug Fears, Tr., or Jill Fears, Tr.

Established in 2000 in OK.
Donor(s): Doug Fears.
Financial data (yr. ended 12/31/01): Grants paid, $20,005; assets, $144,461 (M); gifts received, $2,655; expenditures, $23,457; qualifying distributions, $20,005.
Limitations: Giving on a national basis, with strong emphasis on OK.
Application information: Application form not required.

Trustees: Doug Fears, Jill Fears, Eve O'Kelley.
EIN: 731228863

45173
W. P. Bill Atkinson Foundation, Inc.
107 Mid America Blvd.
Midwest City, OK 73110-5391
Contact: Jack Wilson, Secy.

Donor(s): W.P. Bill Atkinson.
Financial data (yr. ended 10/31/01): Grants paid, $20,000; assets, $341,070 (M); expenditures, $57,111; qualifying distributions, $20,000.
Limitations: Giving primarily in Midwest City, OK.
Application information: Application form required.
Officers and Trustees:* Eugenia Davis,* V.P.; Jack Wilson,* Secy.
EIN: 736096686

45174
Rainbolt Family Foundation
P.O. Box 26788
Oklahoma City, OK 73126

Donor(s): H.E. Rainbolt, Mrs. H.E. Rainbolt.
Financial data (yr. ended 12/31/01): Grants paid, $20,000; assets, $171,800 (M); gifts received, $3,007; expenditures, $22,495; qualifying distributions, $20,000.
Limitations: Applications not accepted.
Application information: Contributes only to pre-selected organizations.
Officers and Directors:* H.E. Rainbolt,* Pres.; Jeannine T. Rainbolt,* Secy.; David E. Rainbolt,* Treas.; Leslie Jeannine Rainbolt.
EIN: 731531898

45175
Scaramucci Foundation
c/o John Philip Scaramucci
P.O. Box 890720
Oklahoma City, OK 73189-0720

Established in 1999 in OK.
Donor(s): John Philip Scaramucci.
Financial data (yr. ended 12/31/01): Grants paid, $20,000; assets, $188,278 (M); expenditures, $20,050; qualifying distributions, $20,000.
Limitations: Applications not accepted.
Application information: Contributes only to pre-selected organizations.
Trustees: Tohnva Scaramucci Ables, John Philip Scaramucci, Avis Scaramucci, Philip Wade Scaramucci.
EIN: 731559543

45176
Ross Family Foundation
735 First National Ctr. W.
Oklahoma City, OK 73102

Established in 1998 in OK.
Donor(s): Mary L. Ross, William J. Ross.
Financial data (yr. ended 12/31/01): Grants paid, $19,625; assets, $48,649 (M); expenditures, $19,972; qualifying distributions, $19,625.
Trustees: Mary Lillian Ross, Molly K. Ross, Robert J. Ross, William J. Ross, Rebecca Ross Roten.
EIN: 731552681

45177
The Foundation for Visions
2601 N.W. Expwy., Ste. 612E
Oklahoma City, OK 73112
Contact: Donna Kay Harrison, Pres., or Stanley T. Harrison, Secy.-Treas.

Established in 1993 in OK.
Donor(s): Donna Kay Harrison, Stanley T. Harrison.

Financial data (yr. ended 12/31/99): Grants paid, $19,414; assets, $331,560 (M); gifts received, $46,400; expenditures, $21,092; qualifying distributions, $19,414.
Officers and Directors:* Donna Kay Harrison,* Pres.; Stanley T. Harrison,* Secy.-Treas.
EIN: 731412490

45178
Saied Family Foundation
3259 S. Yale Ave.
Tulsa, OK 74135

Established in 1996 in OK.
Donor(s): James G. Saied.
Financial data (yr. ended 12/31/01): Grants paid, $19,390; assets, $347,398 (M); expenditures, $28,372; qualifying distributions, $19,390.
Limitations: Applications not accepted.
Application information: Contributes only to pre-selected organizations.
Directors: Delia Ann Saied Pierson, Helen Louella Saied, James G. Saied, James Robert Saied.
EIN: 731508538

45179
The Weston Charitable Trust
1305 Charleston Ave.
Fort Gibson, OK 74434-8960

Donor(s): Paul H. Weston, Sherry C. Weston.
Financial data (yr. ended 12/31/99): Grants paid, $18,853; assets, $81,348 (L); gifts received, $42,604; expenditures, $20,112; qualifying distributions, $18,853.
Limitations: Applications not accepted.
Application information: Contributes only to pre-selected organizations.
Trustees: Paul H. Weston, Sherry C. Weston.
EIN: 347057935

45180
Everett S. Williams Foundation
c/o Everett S. Williams
P.O. Box 50068
Tulsa, OK 74150-0068

Established in 1991 in OK.
Donor(s): Everett S. Williams.
Financial data (yr. ended 12/31/01): Grants paid, $18,550; assets, $38,559 (M); expenditures, $18,880; qualifying distributions, $18,550.
Limitations: Applications not accepted. Giving primarily in Tulsa, OK.
Application information: Contributes only to pre-selected organizations.
Trustees: S.S. Brassfield, Everett S. Williams, Gail R. Williams.
EIN: 731375893

45181
Bartlesville Area Educational Foundation, Inc.
c/o Arvest Trust Co., N.A.
P.O. Box 2248
Bartlesville, OK 74005-2248

Financial data (yr. ended 12/31/01): Grants paid, $18,000; assets, $170,773 (M); expenditures, $20,221; qualifying distributions, $17,933.
Limitations: Giving limited to Bartlesville, OK.
Trustee: Arvest Trust Company, N.A.
EIN: 237117644
Codes: GTI

45182
Newman Family Foundation
9 E. 4th St., Ste. 702
Tulsa, OK 74106-5113

Established in 1997 in OK.
Donor(s): Donald H. Newman.
Financial data (yr. ended 06/30/02): Grants paid, $18,000; assets, $427,727 (M); gifts received, $6,500; expenditures, $21,551; qualifying distributions, $18,000.
Limitations: Applications not accepted.
Application information: Contributes only to pre-selected organizations.
Officer: Rita E. Newman, Chair.
Trustee: Martin L. J. Newman.
EIN: 731526531

45183
The Stanfield Foundation
4907 Westview
Tulsa, OK 74131-4735

Established in 1992 in OK.
Donor(s): Leslie H. Stanfield, Suzanne H. Stanfield.
Financial data (yr. ended 12/31/00): Grants paid, $17,600; assets, $376,061 (M); expenditures, $27,190; qualifying distributions, $17,600.
Limitations: Applications not accepted. Giving limited to OK.
Application information: Contributes only to pre-selected organizations.
Officers and Directors:* Suzanne S. Lynskey, Chair. and Treas.; Gary L. Stanfield,* Secy.; Amanda S. Stanfield, Brian K. Stanfield.
EIN: 731412624

45184
The Swab Foundation
2222 E. 30th Pl.
Tulsa, OK 74114 (918) 747-4163
Contact: Nancy Swab Vaughn, Tr.

Financial data (yr. ended 05/31/01): Grants paid, $17,550; assets, $292,046 (M); expenditures, $18,666; qualifying distributions, $17,550.
Limitations: Giving primarily in Tulsa, OK.
Trustees: Robert J. Swab, T. Brett Swab, T. Gregg Swab, Nancy Swab Vaughn.
EIN: 731029798

45185
The Forbes Foundation
P.O. Box 843
Tulsa, OK 74101-0843

Established in 1999 in OH.
Financial data (yr. ended 12/31/01): Grants paid, $17,100; assets, $506,903 (M); expenditures, $27,746; qualifying distributions, $17,100.
Limitations: Applications not accepted. Giving primarily in Tulsa, OK.
Application information: Contributes only to pre-selected organizations.
Trustees: William D. Andres, Elizabeth A. Forbes.
EIN: 311581540

45186
Dunitz Family Charitable Foundation
4722 S. Yorktown Pl.
Tulsa, OK 74105

Established in 1997 in OK.
Donor(s): Norman L. Dunitz, Annette Dunitz.
Financial data (yr. ended 12/31/01): Grants paid, $17,085; assets, $145,478 (M); gifts received, $22,000; expenditures, $18,930; qualifying distributions, $17,085.
Limitations: Applications not accepted.
Application information: Contributes only to pre-selected organizations.
Trustees: Elise Dunitz Brennan, Annette Dunitz, Norman L. Dunitz, Scott J. Dunitz.
EIN: 731519626

45187
The Quiet Foundation
2530 E. 71st St., Ste. H
Tulsa, OK 74136-5577

Donor(s): Quendrid W. Veatch.
Financial data (yr. ended 10/31/01): Grants paid, $16,650; assets, $296,229 (M); gifts received, $3,000; expenditures, $18,400; qualifying distributions, $16,650.
Limitations: Applications not accepted. Giving primarily in Tulsa, OK.
Application information: Contributes only to pre-selected organizations.
Trustees: William A. Martin, Quendrid W. Veatch, Ralph W. Veatch, Jr.
EIN: 731081940

45188
The Stringer Family Foundation
101 N. Robinson, Ste. 1300
Oklahoma City, OK 73102-5506

Established in 1998 in OK.
Donor(s): N. Martin Stringer.
Financial data (yr. ended 12/31/01): Grants paid, $16,500; assets, $87,622 (M); expenditures, $16,600; qualifying distributions, $16,500.
Limitations: Applications not accepted. Giving primarily in OK.
Application information: Contributes only to pre-selected organizations.
Trustees: N. Martin Stringer, Theresa Stringer.
EIN: 731554149

45189
Foundation Education, Inc.
903 S. Main
Stillwater, OK 74074-4635

Donor(s): Harry Wyatt.
Financial data (yr. ended 12/31/01): Grants paid, $16,250; assets, $1 (M); gifts received, $16,200; expenditures, $161,245; qualifying distributions, $16,250.
Officers: Donald L. Pogue, Pres.; Debra A. Pogue, Secy.-Treas.
EIN: 731381758

45190
Talley Foundation
9400 Broadway Ext., Ste. 130
Oklahoma City, OK 73114-7401
(405) 848-8444
Contact: William W. Talley II, Tr.

Established in 1987 in OK.
Donor(s): William W. Talley II.
Financial data (yr. ended 12/31/00): Grants paid, $16,225; assets, $415 (M); expenditures, $16,225; qualifying distributions, $16,225.
Limitations: Giving primarily in Oklahoma City, OK.
Application information: Application form not required.
Trustees: Sandra S. Talley, William W. Talley II.
EIN: 736238374

45191
Logan Wright Foundation
3801 N.W. 63rd St., Bldg. 3, Ste. 260
Oklahoma City, OK 73116-1930
Application address: 2701 60th Ave. N.W., Norman, OK 73069, FAX: (405) 329-8411;
E-mail: twright@starnet.com
Contact: Brooks Wright, Mgr.

Incorporated about 1975 in OK.
Donor(s): Logan Wright,‡ Brooks Wright.
Financial data (yr. ended 11/30/00): Grants paid, $15,952; assets, $1,005,705 (M); gifts received,

45191—OKLAHOMA

$9,381; expenditures, $104,279; qualifying distributions, $27,272.
Limitations: Giving primarily in OK.
Publications: Financial statement.
Officer: Brooks Wright, Pres.
Directors: Jaye May, Rob May, Blaine Wright, Kelly Wright, Logan Wright, Patricia "Trish" Wright.
EIN: 730979754

45192
J. A. LaFortune Foundation
427 S. Boston Ave., Ste. 2104
Tulsa, OK 74103-4132

Established in 1945 in OK.
Donor(s): Robert J. LaFortune, J.A. LaFortune, Jr., Mary Ann L. Wilcox.
Financial data (yr. ended 12/31/01): Grants paid, $15,250; assets, $345,929 (M); expenditures, $19,109; qualifying distributions, $15,250.
Limitations: Applications not accepted. Giving primarily in Tulsa, OK.
Application information: Contributes only to pre-selected organizations.
Officers: Robert J. LaFortune, Pres.; J.A. LaFortune, Jr., V.P.; Mary Ann L. Wilcox, Secy.-Treas.
EIN: 736092073

45193
Campbell-Lepley/Hunt Foundation, Inc.
(Formerly Campbell Foundation, Inc.)
P.O. Box 701051
Tulsa, OK 74170

Trust established in 1964 in OK.
Donor(s): Max W. Campbell.‡
Financial data (yr. ended 12/31/01): Grants paid, $15,225; assets, $3,612,810 (M); expenditures, $114,076; qualifying distributions, $15,225.
Limitations: Applications not accepted. Giving primarily in Tulsa, OK.
Application information: Contributes only to pre-selected organizations.
Officers: Joan Lepley Hunt, C.E.O. and Chair.; Robert G. Hunt, V.P. and Secy.-Treas.
Director: Charles T. Bennett.
EIN: 736111626

45194
Jurgensmeyer Family Foundation
c/o Virgil Jurgensmeyer
1920 7th Ave., N.E.
Miami, OK 74354-4957

Established in 1996 in OK; funded in 1997.
Donor(s): Virgil Jurgensmeyer.
Financial data (yr. ended 12/31/01): Grants paid, $15,010; assets, $5,797 (M); gifts received, $16,438; expenditures, $15,022; qualifying distributions, $15,010.
Trustees: Margie M. Jurgensmeyer, Virgil Jurgensmeyer.
EIN: 746445490

45195
The Huffman Scholarship Foundation
P.O. Box 1328
Sapulpa, OK 74067

Established in 2000 in OK.
Donor(s): Ronald E. Huffman.
Financial data (yr. ended 12/31/01): Grants paid, $14,366; assets, $1 (M); gifts received, $16,222; expenditures, $16,222; qualifying distributions, $14,366.
Limitations: Applications not accepted.
Application information: Contributes only to pre-selected organizations.
Trustees: Paul H. Burgess, Ronald E. Huffman.
EIN: 316644239

45196
Gregory F. Walton Foundation
6 Rolling Oaks
Enid, OK 73703

Established in 1997 in OK.
Donor(s): Gregory F. Walton.
Financial data (yr. ended 12/31/00): Grants paid, $14,228; assets, $1 (M); expenditures, $14,228; qualifying distributions, $14,228.
Trustees: Beverly Walton, Grant F. Walton, Gregory F. Walton.
EIN: 731353977

45197
Jerome B. Miller Family Foundation
5818 N.W. 50th St.
Oklahoma City, OK 73122 (405) 495-5602
Contact: Jerome B. Miller, Pres.

Established in 1993 in OK.
Donor(s): Jerome B. Miller.
Financial data (yr. ended 12/31/01): Grants paid, $14,045; assets, $558,918 (M); gifts received, $384,893; expenditures, $15,619; qualifying distributions, $14,045.
Officers and Directors:* Jerome B. Miller,* Pres.; Margaret J. Miller,* V.P.; Juli P. Robinson.
EIN: 731438698

45198
Students Aiding Students Foundation
P.O. Box 954
McAlester, OK 74502-0954
Application address: Box 1067, McAlester, OK 74502, tel.: (918) 423-2265
Contact: John Freeman, Dir.

Financial data (yr. ended 12/31/01): Grants paid, $14,000; assets, $70,735 (M); expenditures, $14,235; qualifying distributions, $14,000.
Limitations: Giving limited to residents of OK.
Officer and Directors:* Joe Brown,* Chair.; Lucille Croniger, John Freeman, Donald R. Hackler.
EIN: 731386892

45199
Way Foundation
510 Pat Way Dr.
Fairview, OK 73737-2704
Contact: Howard W. Way, III, Tr.

Donor(s): Howard W. Way III.
Financial data (yr. ended 12/31/00): Grants paid, $14,000; assets, $88,269 (M); expenditures, $14,528; qualifying distributions, $13,915.
Application information: Application form required.
Trustees: Claud E. Reese, Dan Scott, Howard W. Way III.
EIN: 731553537

45200
Cleary Foundation
2601 N.W. Expwy., Ste. 801W
Oklahoma City, OK 73112-7221

Established in 1989 in OK.
Donor(s): Helen P. Cleary, William B. Cleary.
Financial data (yr. ended 12/31/01): Grants paid, $13,500; assets, $32,820 (M); gifts received, $282; expenditures, $15,612; qualifying distributions, $13,500.
Limitations: Applications not accepted. Giving primarily in Oklahoma City, OK.
Application information: Contributes only to pre-selected organizations.
Officers and Trustees:* William B. Cleary,* Chair.; Helen P. Cleary,* Secy.
EIN: 736248743

45201
Laurence S. Youngblood Foundation, Inc.
P.O. Box 552
Oklahoma City, OK 73101-0552

Donor(s): L. Youngblood.
Financial data (yr. ended 12/31/01): Grants paid, $13,350; assets, $274,631 (M); gifts received, $17,500; expenditures, $13,545; qualifying distributions, $13,350.
Limitations: Applications not accepted. Giving primarily in Oklahoma City, OK.
Application information: Contributes only to pre-selected organizations.
Officers and Trustees:* L. Youngblood,* Pres. and Treas.; John H. Miller,* Secy.; Carl A. Robinson.
EIN: 730767862

45202
The Feen Foundation
P.O. Box 521000
Tulsa, OK 74152-1000
Contact: Alan Feen, Tr.

Established in 1986 in OK.
Donor(s): Alan Feen.
Financial data (yr. ended 06/30/02): Grants paid, $12,945; assets, $250,820 (M); expenditures, $14,567; qualifying distributions, $12,945.
Limitations: Giving primarily in OK.
Trustee: Alan Feen.
EIN: 731285430

45203
Atkinson Family Foundation, Inc.
715 Midcontinent Bldg.
401 S. Boston
Tulsa, OK 74103-4040
Contact: Thomas M. Atkinson, Pres.

Established in 2000 in OK.
Donor(s): Thomas M. Atkinson, Joan B. Atkinson.
Financial data (yr. ended 12/31/01): Grants paid, $12,800; assets, $215,624 (M); expenditures, $13,440; qualifying distributions, $12,800.
Limitations: Giving primarily in Tulsa, OK.
Officers: Thomas M. Atkinson, Pres.; Joan B. Atkinson, V.P. and Secy.; Jill S. Fryer, Treas.
EIN: 731576901

45204
The David W. and Patricia L. Bowman Family Charitable Foundation
3104 S. Columbia Cir.
Tulsa, OK 74105
Contact: David W. Bowman, Tr.

Established in 1999 in OK.
Donor(s): David Bowman, Patricia Bowman.
Financial data (yr. ended 12/31/01): Grants paid, $12,631; assets, $7,390 (M); expenditures, $13,881; qualifying distributions, $12,631.
Trustees: David W. Bowman, Patricia L. Bowman.
EIN: 731570989

45205
The C. & G. Emanuel Charitable Foundation
c/o Pamela B. Tiernan
5503 E. 107th Pl.
Tulsa, OK 74137

Established in 1997.
Donor(s): Hugh A. Barker, Janet M. Barker.
Financial data (yr. ended 12/31/01): Grants paid, $12,600; assets, $246,232 (M); gifts received, $100; expenditures, $12,757; qualifying distributions, $12,600.
Limitations: Applications not accepted.
Application information: Contributes only to pre-selected organizations.
Trustee: Pamela B. Tiernan.

EIN: 736291924

45206
Foundation for Improved Police Protection, Inc.
1211 N. Shartel, Rm. 202
Oklahoma City, OK 73103-2496
Contact: Lloyd A. Owens, Pres.

Established in 1976.
Donor(s): R. Milton Laird, Carlene U. Laird.
Financial data (yr. ended 03/31/02): Grants paid, $12,593; assets, $267,824 (M); gifts received, $16,278; expenditures, $17,175; qualifying distributions, $12,593.
Limitations: Giving limited to the Oklahoma City, OK, area.
Application information: Application form not required.
Officers and Trustees:* Lloyd A. Owens,* Pres. and Treas.; Paul B. Strasbaugh,* V.P. and Secy.; O'Tar T. Norwood.
EIN: 730995747

45207
Sean David Conover Charitable Scholarship Foundation
c/o Neal and Mitsuye Conover
21120 N. 4020 Rd.
Bartlesville, OK 74006-0716
Application address: P.O. Box 3010, Rte. 2, Bartlesville, OK 74006, tel.: (918) 336-4560

Donor(s): Mitsuye Conover, Neal Conover.
Financial data (yr. ended 12/31/01): Grants paid, $12,500; assets, $222,204 (M); gifts received, $620; expenditures, $13,614; qualifying distributions, $13,053.
Limitations: Giving primarily in OK.
Application information: Application form not required.
Trustees: Mitsuye Conover, Neal Conover.
EIN: 731519182

45208
May Thompson Henry Trust
(Formerly Thompson Henry Trust)
c/o Central National Bank & Trust Co. of Enid
P.O. Box 3448
Enid, OK 73702-3448 (580) 213-1613
Contact: Karen Holland, Trust Off., Central National Bank & Trust Co. of Enid

Established in 1986 in OK.
Donor(s): May Thompson Henry.‡
Financial data (yr. ended 12/31/00): Grants paid, $12,500; assets, $347,389 (M); expenditures, $17,450; qualifying distributions, $12,500.
Limitations: Giving primarily in OK.
Application information: Application form required.
Selection Committee: Donald O. Boynton, Karen Holland, David Russell.
Trustee: Central National Bank & Trust Co. of Enid.
EIN: 731308178

45209
Sandago Preston Family Foundation, Inc.
2252 E. 30th St.
Tulsa, OK 74114-5428
Contact: Robert M. Preston, Pres.

Established in 1999 in OK.
Donor(s): Robert M. Preston.
Financial data (yr. ended 12/31/01): Grants paid, $12,450; assets, $61,364 (M); expenditures, $12,932; qualifying distributions, $12,450.
Limitations: Giving primarily in OK.
Officers: Robert M. Preston, Pres.; Sandra Preston, V.P.
EIN: 731552427

45210
Central Catholic Trust
1548 S.W. 25th St.
Oklahoma City, OK 73108-7812
Application address: 401 S.W. 63rd St., Oklahoma City, OK 73139-7040, tel.: (405) 632-3855
Contact: Henry E. Holder, Tr.

Financial data (yr. ended 12/31/01): Grants paid, $11,200; assets, $622,855 (M); expenditures, $31,732; qualifying distributions, $11,200.
Limitations: Giving limited to the greater metropolitan Oklahoma City, OK, area.
Trustees: Clair F. Brunette, Henry E. Holder.
EIN: 736258860

45211
The Hugon Family Foundation
P.O. Box 400
Duncan, OK 73534
Application address: 101 S. 15th St., Duncan, OK 73533, tel.: (580) 252-0711
Contact: John C. Hugon, Tr.

Established in 1998 in OK.
Donor(s): John C. Hugon, Marilyn M. Hugon.
Financial data (yr. ended 05/31/01): Grants paid, $11,000; assets, $191,967 (M); expenditures, $11,387; qualifying distributions, $10,965.
Limitations: Giving primarily in OK.
Trustees: John C. Hugon, Marilyn M. Hugon.
EIN: 731544752

45212
The John L. Wieczorek Foundation
15 E. 5th St., Ste. 2100
Tulsa, OK 74103

Established in 1997 in OK.
Donor(s): John L. Wieczorek.
Financial data (yr. ended 12/31/00): Grants paid, $11,000; assets, $244,933 (M); gifts received, $11,000; expenditures, $11,000; qualifying distributions, $11,000.
Limitations: Giving primarily in Tulsa, OK.
Trustee: John L. Wieczorek.
EIN: 731518384

45213
The Oven Fund
P.O. Box 52950
Tulsa, OK 74152 (918) 592-0305
Contact: Herbert C. Oven, Tr.

Financial data (yr. ended 06/30/02): Grants paid, $10,615; assets, $115,837 (M); expenditures, $10,822; qualifying distributions, $10,615.
Limitations: Giving primarily in Tulsa, OK.
Application information: Application form not required.
Trustees: Herbert C. Oven, Herbert C. Oven, Jr.
EIN: 736111241

45214
Shriner-Smith Scholarship Trust
c/o John D. Montgomery
101 E. Dogwood
Hobart, OK 73651 (580) 726-3867

Established in 1995.
Financial data (yr. ended 06/30/00): Grants paid, $10,500; assets, $445,075 (M); expenditures, $14,067; qualifying distributions, $0.
Limitations: Giving limited to residents of Hobart, OK.
Trustees: Carolyn Montgomery, John D. Montgomery.
EIN: 736285291

45215
Chris and Kimiko Carey Foundation
c/o J. Christopher Carey, M.D.
5709 Normandy Terr.
Oklahoma City, OK 73142

Established in 2001 in OK.
Donor(s): J. Christopher Carey, Kimiko Carey.
Financial data (yr. ended 12/31/01): Grants paid, $10,370; assets, $648 (M); gifts received, $9,810; expenditures, $10,470; qualifying distributions, $10,370.
Trustees: J. Christopher Carey, M.D., Kimiko Carey.
EIN: 731617468

45216
Single Parent Assistance Fund, Inc.
c/o Thomas L. Kivisto
7702 E. 91st St., Ste. 205
Tulsa, OK 74133 (918) 488-0999
Contact: Sharon Pens

Donor(s): Thomas Kivisto.
Financial data (yr. ended 12/31/01): Grants paid, $10,330; assets, $1,417 (M); gifts received, $7,550; expenditures, $10,553; qualifying distributions, $10,553.
Officer: Thomas Kivisto, Pres.; Julie L. Kivisto, Secy.
EIN: 731531820

45217
The Sylvanus G. Felix Foundation
P.O. Box 12056
Oklahoma City, OK 73157

Incorporated in 1952 in OK.
Donor(s): Sylvanus G. Felix.‡
Financial data (yr. ended 10/31/01): Grants paid, $10,048; assets, $320,002 (M); expenditures, $21,185; qualifying distributions, $10,048.
Limitations: Applications not accepted. Giving primarily in FL and OK.
Application information: Contributes only to pre-selected organizations.
Officers: Charles S. Felix, Pres.; Barbara Felix Combes, V.P.
EIN: 736099600

45218
Richard James Family Foundation
P.O. Box 705
Stroud, OK 74079

Established in 2000 in OK.
Donor(s): Richard James.
Financial data (yr. ended 12/31/01): Grants paid, $10,025; assets, $469,570 (M); expenditures, $11,813; qualifying distributions, $10,025.
Limitations: Applications not accepted. Giving primarily in Stroud, OK.
Application information: Contributes only to pre-selected organizations.
Trustees: Mary Lynn Hill, Randa Lea Hohweiler, Patsy James, Richard James, Steven T. James, June Ann Jones.
EIN: 731589377

45219
Cunningham Family Foundation
12436 St. Andrews Dr.
Oklahoma City, OK 73120-8601

Established in 2001 in OK.
Donor(s): Charles L. Cunningham, Karen S. Cunningham.
Financial data (yr. ended 12/31/01): Grants paid, $10,000; assets, $108,625 (M); gifts received, $114,522; expenditures, $10,525; qualifying distributions, $114,522.
Limitations: Applications not accepted.

45219—OKLAHOMA

Application information: Contributes only to pre-selected organizations.
Officers: Charles L. Cunningham, Pres.; Karen S. Cunningham, Secy.-Treas.
EIN: 731620729

45220
The McGowan Family Foundation
4700 Hardy Springs Rd.
McAlester, OK 74502

Established in 2001 in OK.
Donor(s): Michael N. McGowan.
Financial data (yr. ended 12/31/01): Grants paid, $10,000; assets, $190,100 (M); gifts received, $200,000; expenditures, $10,000; qualifying distributions, $10,000.
Limitations: Applications not accepted.
Application information: Contributes only to pre-selected organizations.
Officers: Michael N. McGowan, Pres. and Treas.; Mary Nancy McGowan, V.P.; Michelle McGowan Tompkins, Secy.
EIN: 731624393

45221
Sri Venkateswara Temple
1617 Queenstown Rd.
Nichols Hills, OK 73116

Donor(s): Ravi Malpani, M.D.
Financial data (yr. ended 12/31/01): Grants paid, $9,945; assets, $77,533 (M); expenditures, $10,176; qualifying distributions, $9,945.
Limitations: Applications not accepted.
Application information: Contributes only to pre-selected organizations.
Officers: Ravi K. Malpani, M.D., Pres.; Vijaya Malpani, Secy.
Trustee: D. Narayana.
EIN: 731356366

45222
Class of 1940, Inc.
P.O. Box 402
Bristow, OK 74010-0402
Application address: c/o Principal, Bristow High School, Bristow, OK 74010

Financial data (yr. ended 12/31/99): Grants paid, $9,750; assets, $290,347 (M); gifts received, $15,000; expenditures, $9,960; qualifying distributions, $9,688.
Limitations: Giving primarily to residents of Bristow, OK.
Officers: Robert Chadderdon, Chair.; Francis Hayhurst, Pres.; Albert C. Kelly, V.P.
EIN: 731338004

45223
Helen Muxlow Driskell Scholarship Trust Fund
P.O. Box 26883
Oklahoma City, OK 73126
Application address: c/o Guthrie High School, 200 Crooks Dr., Guthrie, OK 73044
Contact: Terrianne Lowe, Senior Counselor

Established in 1999 in OK.
Financial data (yr. ended 12/31/00): Grants paid, $9,600; assets, $385,788 (M); expenditures, $18,168; qualifying distributions, $18,094.
Application information: Application form required.
Trustee: Bancfirst.
EIN: 736226426

45224
United Methodist Church of Dewey
c/o Arvest Trust Co.
P.O. Box 2248
Bartlesville, OK 74005

Established in 1995.
Donor(s): Mildred Read Adams.‡
Financial data (yr. ended 12/31/99): Grants paid, $9,544; assets, $252,621 (M); expenditures, $12,338; qualifying distributions, $9,389.
Limitations: Applications not accepted. Giving limited to Dewey, OK.
Application information: Contributes only to a pre-selected organization.
Trustee: Arvest Trust Company, N.A.
EIN: 736281950

45225
Williams Family Foundation
2600 Stone Hill Dr.
Lawton, OK 73505

Established in 1990 in OK.
Donor(s): Cheryn Williams, C. Victor Williams, M.D.
Financial data (yr. ended 12/31/01): Grants paid, $9,506; assets, $164,384 (M); expenditures, $11,106; qualifying distributions, $9,506.
Limitations: Applications not accepted. Giving primarily in Norman, OK.
Application information: Contributes only to pre-selected organizations.
Trustees: Charles E. Wade, Jr., Cheryn Williams.
EIN: 731376102

45226
Shah Family Foundation, Inc.
4800 W. Covell Rd.
Edmond, OK 73003 (405) 340-7853
Contact: Mahendra S. Shah, Pres. and Treas.

Established in 1999 in OK.
Donor(s): Mahendra S. Shah, M.D., Purnima M. Shah, M.D.
Financial data (yr. ended 12/31/01): Grants paid, $9,362; assets, $125,157 (M); expenditures, $9,362; qualifying distributions, $9,362.
Limitations: Giving on a national basis.
Officers: Mahendra S. Shah, M.D., Pres. and Treas.; Purnima M. Shah, M.D., V.P. and Secy.
EIN: 731577896

45227
Madge May Vincent Charitable Testamentary Trust
c/o BancTrust
P.O. Box 26883
Oklahoma City, OK 73126-0883

Established in 2000 in OK.
Financial data (yr. ended 12/31/00): Grants paid, $9,273; assets, $245,108 (M); expenditures, $11,810; qualifying distributions, $9,273.
Limitations: Applications not accepted. Giving primarily in Oklahoma City, OK.
Application information: Contributes only to pre-selected organizations.
Trustee: BancTrust.
EIN: 736178781

45228
Patterson Family Foundation
P.O. Box 1262
Wewoka, OK 74884

Established in 1999 in OK.
Donor(s): Kathryn Patterson.
Financial data (yr. ended 12/31/01): Grants paid, $9,000; assets, $158,093 (M); expenditures, $9,774; qualifying distributions, $9,000.

Limitations: Applications not accepted.
Application information: Contributes only to pre-selected organizations.
Officers and Trustees: Robert S. Patterson,* Chair.; Paige Sheffield,* Secy.
EIN: 736318573

45229
H. Sam and Mildred Bunnie Aubrey Foundation
c/o H. Sam Aubrey
P.O. Box 470370
Tulsa, OK 74147

Established in 1995 in OK.
Donor(s): H. Sam Aubrey, Mildred Bunnie Aubrey.
Financial data (yr. ended 12/31/01): Grants paid, $8,995; assets, $263,431 (M); gifts received, $12,000; expenditures, $10,000; qualifying distributions, $8,995.
Limitations: Applications not accepted. Giving primarily in Tulsa, OK.
Application information: Contributes only to pre-selected organizations.
Trustees: H. Sam Aubrey, Mildred Bunnie Aubrey.
EIN: 731457736

45230
S. J. McCroskey Foundation
c/o Bank of Oklahoma, N.A.
P.O. Box 880
Tulsa, OK 74101-0880

Established in 1986 in OK.
Financial data (yr. ended 08/31/01): Grants paid, $8,718; assets, $0 (M); expenditures, $16,121; qualifying distributions, $8,718.
Limitations: Applications not accepted. Giving primarily in SD, Memphis, TN, and Amarillo, TX.
Application information: Contributes only to pre-selected organizations.
Trustee: Bank of Oklahoma, N.A.
EIN: 736232955

45231
Funk Educational Foundation
P.O. Box 179
Piedmont, OK 73078
Application address: 414 Piedmont Rd. N., Piedmont, OK 73078
Contact: Julie A. Funk, Secy.

Established in 1995 in OK.
Donor(s): Robert A. Funk.
Financial data (yr. ended 12/31/00): Grants paid, $8,583; assets, $3,302 (M); gifts received, $19,000; expenditures, $18,147; qualifying distributions, $8,583.
Limitations: Giving limited to residents of Piedmont, OK.
Application information: Applicant must include G.P.A. and ACT scores. Application form required.
Officers: Robert A. Funk, Pres.; Nedra R. Funk, V.P.; Julie A. Funk, Secy. and Exec. Dir.; Robert A. Funk, Jr., Treas.
EIN: 731488498

45232
Ressa Foundation
1856 E. 15th St.
Tulsa, OK 74104
Contact: H.T. Sears, Jr., Tr.

Established in 2000 in OK.
Donor(s): H.T. Sears, Jr.
Financial data (yr. ended 12/31/01): Grants paid, $8,350; assets, $240,686 (M); gifts received, $20,000; expenditures, $10,788; qualifying distributions, $8,350.
Application information: Application form not required.
Trustee: H.T. Sears, Jr.

EIN: 731602154

45233
Robert Cummins Family Foundation, Inc.
1420 W. Chestnut Ave.
Enid, OK 73703-4307 (580) 233-6000
Contact: Ray Feightner, Jr., Secy.

Established in 1996 in OK.
Donor(s): The Cummins Construction Co., Inc., Robert L. Cummins, Robert L. Cummins, Jr.
Financial data (yr. ended 11/30/01): Grants paid, $8,250; assets, $155,862 (M); expenditures, $9,512; qualifying distributions, $8,250.
Limitations: Giving primarily in Enid, OK.
Application information: Application form not required.
Officers: Robert L. Cummins, Pres.; Ray Feightner, Jr., Secy.
Director: Vernon P. Shockley.
EIN: 731486208
Codes: CS, CD

45234
Musical Research Society Endowment Fund, Inc.
(Formerly Musical Research Society Endowment Foundation, Inc.)
804 S.E. Castle Rd.
Bartlesville, OK 74006-9023
Application address: c/o Diana Farris, P.O. Box 2105, Bartlesville, OK 74005, tel.: (918) 333-6719

Financial data (yr. ended 06/30/01): Grants paid, $8,205; assets, $212,914 (M); gifts received, $1,230; expenditures, $11,345; qualifying distributions, $8,096.
Limitations: Giving primarily to residents of Bartlesville, OK.
Application information: Application form required.
Officers: David Kazmierzak, Pres.; Lauren Green, Secy.; Marilyn Cramer, Treas.
EIN: 731282613
Codes: GTI

45235
The Benham Foundation
14500 N. Hiwassee Rd.
Jones, OK 73049

Established in 2000 in OK.
Donor(s): Webster L. Benham, Linda L. Benham.
Financial data (yr. ended 12/31/01): Grants paid, $8,000; assets, $159,674 (M); expenditures, $9,989; qualifying distributions, $8,000.
Limitations: Applications not accepted.
Application information: Contributes only to pre-selected organizations.
Officers and Directors:* Webster L. Benham,* Pres. and Treas.; Linda L. Benham,* V.P.; Jennifer L. Kalkbrenner,* Secy.
EIN: 731601025

45236
Linehan Family Foundation
7103 Nichols Rd.
Oklahoma City, OK 73120

Established in 2000 in OK.
Donor(s): John C. Linehan, Caroline S. Linehan.
Financial data (yr. ended 12/31/01): Grants paid, $8,000; assets, $175,621 (M); gifts received, $3,000; expenditures, $11,139; qualifying distributions, $8,000.
Limitations: Applications not accepted.
Application information: Contributes only to pre-selected organizations.

Officers: John C. Linehan, Pres.; Mark D. Linehan, V.P.; Patrick D. Linehan, V.P.; Mary C. Roy, V.P.; Caroline S. Linehan, Secy.-Treas.
EIN: 731602044

45237
Bruce Z. and Phyllis J. Raines Family Foundation
P.O. Box 471764
Tulsa, OK 74147

Established in 1999 in OK.
Donor(s): Phyllis J. Raines.
Financial data (yr. ended 12/31/01): Grants paid, $8,000; assets, $193,160 (M); gifts received, $80,000; expenditures, $11,361; qualifying distributions, $8,000.
Limitations: Giving primarily in OK.
Trustees: Bryan Kelly Raines, Deanna Lynn Raines, Michael Alan Raines, Phyllis J. Raines.
EIN: 731580265

45238
The George L. & Mary B. Stidham Foundation
300 W. Gentry
Checotah, OK 74426

Established in 1999 in OK.
Financial data (yr. ended 12/31/01): Grants paid, $7,700; assets, $173,890 (M); gifts received, $110,000; expenditures, $9,398; qualifying distributions, $7,700.
Limitations: Applications not accepted.
Application information: Contributes only to pre-selected organizations.
Trustees: Susan S. Brandon, Mary Katherine Jennings, George L. Stidham.
EIN: 731571108

45239
Noble B. Magness Charitable Trust
c/o Richard B. Winters
P.O. Box 689
Poteau, OK 74953
Application address: P.O. Box 1115, Poteau, OK 74953, tel.: (918) 647-8696
Contact: Larry B. Lucas, Tr.

Financial data (yr. ended 12/31/01): Grants paid, $7,295; assets, $469,784 (M); expenditures, $8,548; qualifying distributions, $7,295.
Limitations: Giving limited to LeFlore County, OK.
Trustees: Michael D. Lee, Larry B. Lucas, Richard B. Winters.
EIN: 731303695

45240
Marvin Nelson & Lillian Rose Hammer Benevolent Fund
c/o Ray Allen Clark, Jr.
P.O. Box 635
Pryor, OK 74362

Financial data (yr. ended 12/31/01): Grants paid, $7,175; assets, $101 (M); gifts received, $6,129; expenditures, $7,346; qualifying distributions, $7,175.
Limitations: Applications not accepted.
Trustees: Ray Allen Clark, Jr., William Curtis Kolb, Patrick Stanley Robison, R. David Schumaker.
EIN: 736256389

45241
Seidle Foundation
c/o Neal T. Seidle
7617 S. Quebec Pl.
Tulsa, OK 74136

Established in 1994.
Donor(s): Neal T. Seidle.
Financial data (yr. ended 03/31/02): Grants paid, $6,890; assets, $119,743 (M); expenditures, $6,960; qualifying distributions, $6,890.

Limitations: Applications not accepted.
Application information: Contributes only to pre-selected organizations.
Trustees: Hazel Seidle, Neal T. Seidle.
EIN: 731457019

45242
The R. H. Wilkin Charitable Trust
P.O. Box 76561
Oklahoma City, OK 73147 (405) 722-9393
Application address: P.O. Box 23374, Oklahoma City, OK 73123
Contact: Paul A. Porter, Tr.

Financial data (yr. ended 12/31/99): Grants paid, $6,602; assets, $199,628 (M); expenditures, $14,955; qualifying distributions, $9,962.
Limitations: Giving limited to Oklahoma County, OK.
Trustees: Larry Pittman, Paul A. Porter.
EIN: 736157614

45243
Hazel Rose Family Charitable Foundation
817 W. Utica
Broken Arrow, OK 74011
Application address: 8017 W. Utica, Broken Arrow, OK 74013
Contact: Diane L. Karnuth, Pres.

Established in 1997 in OK.
Donor(s): Nadine N. Holloway.
Financial data (yr. ended 12/31/01): Grants paid, $6,600; assets, $161,441 (M); gifts received, $9,805; expenditures, $8,756; qualifying distributions, $6,600.
Limitations: Giving primarily in OK.
Officers: Diane Love Karnuth, Pres.; Glenda L. Durano, Secy.-Treas.
EIN: 731519254

45244
Wyatt F. & Mattie M. Jeltz Scholarship Foundation
3017 Martin Luther King
P.O. Box 36575
Oklahoma City, OK 73136-6575

Donor(s): Wyatt F. Jeltz,‡ Mattie M. Jeltz.‡
Financial data (yr. ended 12/31/01): Grants paid, $6,540; assets, $291,607 (M); expenditures, $11,606; qualifying distributions, $11,483.
Limitations: Giving limited to OK.
Publications: Informational brochure (including application guidelines).
Application information: Application form required.
Trustees: James L. Mosley, Chair.; Kenneth Arinwine, Lettie R. Hunter.
EIN: 730994084

45245
O. R., Jr. and Thelma Nunley Foundation
HCR 65, Box 376
Pryor, OK 74361

Donor(s): O.R. Nunley, Jr., Thelma Nunley.
Financial data (yr. ended 09/30/01): Grants paid, $6,524; assets, $72,266 (M); expenditures, $6,524; qualifying distributions, $6,524.
Limitations: Applications not accepted.
Application information: Contributes only to pre-selected organizations.
Directors: Jonathan Nunley, O.R. Nunley, Jr., Thelma Nunley.
EIN: 731507737

45246
Tom and Brenda McDaniel Charitable Foundation
P.O. Box 60909
Oklahoma City, OK 73146-0909

Established in 2000 in OK.
Donor(s): Tom J. McDaniel.
Financial data (yr. ended 12/31/01): Grants paid, $6,500; assets, $267,319 (M); gifts received, $274,922; expenditures, $11,918; qualifying distributions, $6,500.
Limitations: Applications not accepted. Giving primarily in Oklahoma City, OK.
Application information: Contributes only to pre-selected organizations.
Officers: Tom J. McDaniel, Chair.; Brenda S. McDaniel, Pres.; Patrick Lance McDaniel, V.P.; Mark Bockelman McDaniel, Secy.; John Randall McDaniel, Treas.
EIN: 731594053

45247
Moyne G. Phillips Scholarship Trust
c/o Arvest Trust Co.
P.O. Box 2248
Bartlesville, OK 74005-2248

Established in 2000 in OK.
Donor(s): Moyne G. Phillips.‡
Financial data (yr. ended 12/31/01): Grants paid, $6,400; assets, $133,222 (M); expenditures, $7,905; qualifying distributions, $6,287.
Limitations: Applications not accepted. Giving primarily in OK.
Application information: Contributes only to pre-selected organizations.
Trustee: Arvest Trust Company, N.A.
EIN: 716182632

45248
The Frank Sides, Jr. and Edna K. Sides Charitable Trust
P.O. Box 337
Sayre, OK 73662
Contact: J. Robert W. Lakey, Tr.

Established in 1993 in OK.
Financial data (yr. ended 12/31/01): Grants paid, $6,385; assets, $204,975 (M); expenditures, $9,698; qualifying distributions, $6,385.
Trustee: J. Robert W. Lakey.
EIN: 736270987

45249
The Tullos Foundation
2470 Liberty Tower
Oklahoma City, OK 73102

Established in 1995 in OK.
Donor(s): Hugh S. Tullos, Robbie H. Tullos.
Financial data (yr. ended 12/31/01): Grants paid, $6,350; assets, $122,038 (M); expenditures, $6,881; qualifying distributions, $6,350.
Application information: Application form required.
Officers: Hugh S. Tullos, Pres.; Mathew Hahn, V.P. and Treas.; Robbie H. Tullos, Secy.
Directors: Edward Schwartz, Paul Tullos.
EIN: 731486784

45250
Harry & Sarah Kirschner Memorial Trust
c/o Miriam Freedman
P.O. Box 1866
Muskogee, OK 74402-1866

Established in 1985 in OK.
Donor(s): Edward Philip Kirschner.‡
Financial data (yr. ended 05/31/02): Grants paid, $6,324; assets, $141,013 (M); expenditures, $6,943; qualifying distributions, $6,601.
Limitations: Applications not accepted. Giving primarily in the New York, NY, area and OK.
Publications: Annual report.
Application information: Contributes only to pre-selected organizations.
Trustees: Miriam Freedman, Raymond Freedman, Sondra Gross, Pauli Loeffler.
EIN: 731164199

45251
Robert Kane High School Scholarship Memorial Trust
c/o Arvest Trust Co., N.A.
P.O. Box 2248
Bartlesville, OK 74005-2248

Financial data (yr. ended 12/31/99): Grants paid, $6,300; assets, $137,071 (M); expenditures, $6,898; qualifying distributions, $6,057.
Limitations: Giving limited to Bartlesville, OK.
Application information: Applicant must supply scholastic and financial information.
Trustee: Arvest Trust Company, N.A.
EIN: 736091639

45252
Moore Family Foundation
13801 Plantation Way
Edmond, OK 73013

Established in 1999 in OK.
Financial data (yr. ended 12/31/00): Grants paid, $6,066; assets, $16,747 (M); gifts received, $22,000; expenditures, $6,566; qualifying distributions, $6,066.
Limitations: Applications not accepted.
Application information: Contributes only to pre-selected organizations.
Officers: Mark A. Moore, Chair.; Pattye L. Moore, Secy.
EIN: 736316133

45253
Lucy Estes Memorial Trust
P.O. Box 389
Blackwell, OK 74631-0389
Application address: 107 W. Blackwell Ave., Blackwell, OK 74631, tel.: (580) 363-4300
Contact: Jonathan C. Ihrig, Tr.

Established in 1986 in OK.
Financial data (yr. ended 12/31/01): Grants paid, $6,000; assets, $156,393 (M); expenditures, $8,946; qualifying distributions, $6,000.
Limitations: Giving on a national basis, with emphasis on the Midwest.
Trustee: Jonathan C. Ihrig.
EIN: 736234810

45254
OWMA Scholarship Fund
(Formerly OATCD Scholarship Fund)
P.O. Box 722220
Norman, OK 73070
Contact: Sandy Ruble, Exec. Dir.

Established in 1989.
Financial data (yr. ended 12/31/01): Grants paid, $6,000; assets, $15,864 (M); gifts received, $4,944; expenditures, $7,094; qualifying distributions, $7,094.
Limitations: Giving limited to residents of OK.
Application information: Application form required.
Officers: Michael Crouch, Chairs.; Dick Dunham, Pres.; Mark Sullivan, V.P.; G.L. McEntire, Treas.; Sandra Ruble, Exec. Dir.
EIN: 731351421

45255
Harold A. White & Edna L. White Foundation
P.O. Box 880
Tulsa, OK 74101

Established in 2000.
Financial data (yr. ended 12/31/01): Grants paid, $6,000; assets, $140,936 (M); expenditures, $9,512; qualifying distributions, $6,000.
Limitations: Giving primarily in OK.
Directors: Edna L. White, Harold A. White.
EIN: 731582836

45256
Paul S. & Conna D. Woolsey Foundation
1600 E. 19th St., Ste. 403
Edmond, OK 73013

Established in 1992 in OK.
Donor(s): Conna D. Woolsey, Paul S. Woolsey.
Financial data (yr. ended 12/31/01): Grants paid, $6,000; assets, $15,131 (M); gifts received, $6,184; expenditures, $8,195; qualifying distributions, $6,000.
Limitations: Applications not accepted. Giving limited to OK.
Application information: Contributes only to pre-selected organizations.
Officers: Paul S. Woolsey, Pres.; Conna D. Woolsey, V.P. and Secy.
EIN: 731399372

45257
Criswell Foundation
c/o Donald E. Criswell
P.O. Box 770484
Oklahoma City, OK 73177-0484

Established in 1995 in OK.
Donor(s): Donald E. Criswell.
Financial data (yr. ended 12/31/01): Grants paid, $5,850; assets, $118,930 (M); gifts received, $5; expenditures, $5,856; qualifying distributions, $5,850.
Limitations: Applications not accepted. Giving limited to Oklahoma City, OK.
Application information: Contributes only to pre-selected organizations.
Trustees: Donald E. Criswell, Donald E. Criswell, Jr.
EIN: 731485820

45258
Robert G. & Norma Jean Chadderdon Foundation
2601 Northwest Expwy.
600 Oil Ctr., E.
Oklahoma City, OK 73112

Established in 1980 in TX and OK.
Donor(s): Robert G. Chadderdon, Norma Jean Chadderdon.
Financial data (yr. ended 11/30/01): Grants paid, $5,400; assets, $5,772 (M); expenditures, $6,200; qualifying distributions, $5,400.
Limitations: Applications not accepted. Giving primarily in Bristow, OK.
Application information: Contributes only to pre-selected organizations.
Trustees: Norma Jean Chadderdon, Robert G. Chadderdon, John J. King.
EIN: 742168410

45259
Hojel Schumacher Foundation
c/o Phyllis S. Hojel
5810 E. Skelly Dr., Ste. 1000
Tulsa, OK 74135

Established in 1990 in OK.
Donor(s): Phyllis S. Hojel.

Financial data (yr. ended 12/31/01): Grants paid, $5,375; assets, $89,793 (M); expenditures, $10,486; qualifying distributions, $5,375.
Limitations: Applications not accepted.
Application information: Contributes only to pre-selected organizations.
Trustees: Phyllis S. Hojel, Albert Schumacher.
EIN: 731373992

45260
M. Youngblood Foundation
c/o Donald & Sherry Youngblood
HCR 62, Box 62
Jay, OK 74346-9309

Established in 2001 in OK.
Donor(s): Donald E. Youngblood, Sherry A. Youngblood.
Financial data (yr. ended 12/31/01): Grants paid, $5,250; assets, $89,189 (M); gifts received, $100,000; expenditures, $6,238; qualifying distributions, $5,250.
Trustees: Donald E. Youngblood, Sherry A. Youngblood.
EIN: 731604531

45261
Roba Lee Thompson Ministries, Inc.
c/o RLT Ministries
4530 S. Sheridan Rd., Ste. 205
Tulsa, OK 74145
Application address: 5549 S. Lewis Ave., Tulsa, OK 74105-7104

Established in 1994 in OK.
Financial data (yr. ended 12/31/00): Grants paid, $5,242; assets, $2,175,563 (M); expenditures, $413,428; qualifying distributions, $46,733; giving activities include $46,733 for programs.
Limitations: Giving primarily in Tulsa, OK.
Officers: Stephen P. Gray, Chair.; Roger G. King, Secy.-Treas.; William G. Elliott, Exec. Dir.
EIN: 731454551

45262
The H. G. Ash Foundation
2758 E. 44th Place
Tulsa, OK 74105

Established in 2001.
Donor(s): Henry G. Ash.
Financial data (yr. ended 12/31/01): Grants paid, $5,000; assets, $45,833 (M); gifts received, $50,000; expenditures, $5,000; qualifying distributions, $5,000.
Limitations: Giving primarily in Tulsa, OK.
Officer and Trustee:* Suzanne A. Kurtz,* Mgr.
EIN: 731614119

45263
Bhatia Foundation
c/o Surindar K. Bhatia
608 N.W. 9th, Ste. 4000
Oklahoma City, OK 73102-1058

Established in 1992 in OK.
Donor(s): Surindar K. Bhatia.
Financial data (yr. ended 07/31/01): Grants paid, $5,000; assets, $13,526 (M); gifts received, $16,000; expenditures, $5,279; qualifying distributions, $5,279.
Limitations: Applications not accepted.
Application information: Contributes only to pre-selected organizations.
Trustees: Mira Bhatia, Surindar K. Bhatia.
EIN: 731411518

45264
Harlan and Virginia Krumme Charitable Trust
3119 S. Columbia Cir.
Tulsa, OK 74105

Established in 2000 in OK.
Financial data (yr. ended 12/31/01): Grants paid, $5,000; assets, $162,154 (M); gifts received, $94,667; expenditures, $5,000; qualifying distributions, $5,000.
Limitations: Applications not accepted.
Application information: Contributes only to pre-selected organizations.
Trustees: Jill K. Burns, Diane K. Cox, Virginia Krumme.
EIN: 731604802

45265
Norman Community Foundation
115 E. Gray St.
Norman, OK 73069-7203

Financial data (yr. ended 06/30/01): Grants paid, $5,000; assets, $609,920 (M); gifts received, $379,183; expenditures, $120,467; giving activities include $102,791 for programs.
Limitations: Giving limited to Norman, OK.
Officers and Directors:* Lewis Beckett, Pres.; Ben Benedum,* V.P.; Joe Sparks,* Secy.; Dianne Bauman,* Treas.; Charles Suggs, Exec. Dir.; Doris Bratton, Ron Burton, Julie Wohlgemuth Cohen, Richard Craig, Nick Hathaway, Barbara Henderson, Lynne Miller, Andy Paden, Don Sickles, Lee Symcox.
EIN: 731478591
Codes: CM

45266
The Susan Flint Seay Charitable Foundation
P.O. Box 490
Tulsa, OK 74101-0490

Established in 1988 in OK.
Financial data (yr. ended 12/31/01): Grants paid, $4,625; assets, $94,315 (M); expenditures, $5,051; qualifying distributions, $4,625.
Limitations: Applications not accepted. Giving primarily in Tulsa, OK.
Application information: Contributes only to pre-selected organizations.
Trustee: Susan Flint Seay.
EIN: 731311956

45267
The Geary Foundation, Inc.
P.O. Box 97
Geary, OK 73040
Application address: Main & Broadway, Geary, OK 73040
Contact: Betty Duncan, Secy.-Treas.

Financial data (yr. ended 12/31/01): Grants paid, $4,585; assets, $101,618 (M); expenditures, $4,947; qualifying distributions, $4,821.
Officers: Rev. Clifford Koehn, Pres.; Allan Long, V.P.; Betty Duncan, Secy.-Treas.
Director: Joan Hiler.
EIN: 731419674

45268
Abby Tarr & Glenn C. Shaw Foundation
141 E. Broadway
Drumright, OK 74030
Application address: P.O. Box 647, Drumright, OK, 74030, tel.: (918) 352-2567
Contact: Doyle Watson, Dir.

Financial data (yr. ended 12/31/01): Grants paid, $4,540; assets, $812,137 (M); expenditures, $18,202; qualifying distributions, $4,540.
Limitations: Giving primarily in Drumright, OK.
Directors: Ruby Hood, Charles Watson, Doyle Watson, William K. Watson.
EIN: 510141334

45269
The Sigmon Foundation, Inc.
4220 Brookline Pl.
Norman, OK 73072

Established in 2000 in OK.
Donor(s): Michael W. Sigmon.
Financial data (yr. ended 12/31/01): Grants paid, $4,500; assets, $155,171 (M); gifts received, $70,500; expenditures, $6,934; qualifying distributions, $4,500.
Application information: Application form not required.
Officers and Directors:* Michael W. Sigmon,* Chair.; Jane Sigmon,* Pres.; John Sigmon,* V.P. and Secy.; Stephen E. Sigmon,* V.P.
EIN: 731592997

45270
The Dickman Foundation
c/o J. Scott Dickman
15 E. 5th St., Ste. 2100
Tulsa, OK 74103

Established in 1997 in OK.
Donor(s): J. Scott Dickman.
Financial data (yr. ended 12/31/00): Grants paid, $4,400; assets, $42,904 (M); gifts received, $5,250; expenditures, $4,400; qualifying distributions, $4,400.
Limitations: Giving primarily in Tulsa, OK.
Trustees: J. Jerry Dickman, J. Scott Dickman, Martha Dickman, Patricia Dickman.
EIN: 731518382

45271
American Medical Foundation
5009 N. Penn, Ste. 113
Oklahoma City, OK 73112   (405) 840-9330
Contact: John J. Griffin, Pres.

Financial data (yr. ended 06/30/02): Grants paid, $4,250; assets, $138,946 (M); expenditures, $5,449; qualifying distributions, $4,250.
Limitations: Giving primarily in Oklahoma City, OK.
Officers and Trustees:* John J. Griffin,* Pres.; Brian C. Griffin,* V.P.; John J. Griffin, Jr.,* V.P.
EIN: 736104267

45272
Jose R. & Laura B. Medina Foundation
2202 E. 30th Pl.
Tulsa, OK 74114-5431

Financial data (yr. ended 11/30/99): Grants paid, $4,250; assets, $119,706 (M); expenditures, $6,113; qualifying distributions, $4,250.
Limitations: Applications not accepted. Giving primarily in OK.
Application information: Contributes only to pre-selected organizations.
Directors: Patricia Medina Collins, Jose R. Medina, Laura B. Medina, Steven E. Medina.
EIN: 731507745

45273
Brockhaus Foundation
c/o Rosemary Brockhaus
4501 W. Robinson
Norman, OK 73072

Established in 1997 in OK.
Donor(s): Rosemary Brockhaus.
Financial data (yr. ended 12/31/01): Grants paid, $4,115; assets, $35,142 (M); expenditures, $4,480; qualifying distributions, $4,115.
Limitations: Applications not accepted.

45273—OKLAHOMA

Application information: Contributes only to pre-selected organizations.
Trustees: Rosemary Brockhaus, Edna L. Carson.
EIN: 731527522

45274
Walter E. Atkinson and Jane A. Baucum Foundation
(Formerly Walter E. Atkinson Foundation)
P.O. Box 20510
Oklahoma City, OK 73156-0510

Established in 1983 in OK.
Financial data (yr. ended 12/31/01): Grants paid, $4,100; assets, $1 (M); gifts received, $25,000; expenditures, $4,124; qualifying distributions, $4,100.
Limitations: Applications not accepted. Giving primarily in TX.
Application information: Contributes only to pre-selected organizations.
Officers: Jane A. Baucum, Pres.; David W. Baucum, V.P.; Cindy L. Berry, Secy.-Treas.
EIN: 736100011

45275
George H. Odell Anthropology Scholarship Foundation
524 S. Allegheny
Tulsa, OK 74112

Established in 1998 in OK.
Donor(s): George H. Odell.
Financial data (yr. ended 12/31/01): Grants paid, $4,000; assets, $89,968 (M); expenditures, $4,549; qualifying distributions, $4,000.
Trustee: Donald Henry.
EIN: 731541135

45276
Parson's Hartshorne High School Senior Scholarship, Inc.
909 Lehigh Ave.
Hartshorne, OK 74547-3631

Financial data (yr. ended 12/31/00): Grants paid, $4,000; assets, $0 (M); gifts received, $2,500; expenditures, $153; qualifying distributions, $0.
Limitations: Applications not accepted. Giving primarily in OK.
Trustees: Robert Burnett, Rhonda McCullar, Jane L. Sherrill, Luke Workman.
EIN: 731166024

45277
Bear Baseball Foundation, Inc.
7912 E. 31st Ct., No. 220
Tulsa, OK 74145-1334 (918) 664-9544
Contact: James F. Schallner, Jr., Dir.

Established in 1994 in OK.
Financial data (yr. ended 12/31/01): Grants paid, $3,800; assets, $73,722 (M); expenditures, $3,980; qualifying distributions, $3,800.
Application information: Application form not required.
Directors: James R. Davis, Jr., Jerry W. Mosley, James F. Schallner, Jr.
EIN: 731458154

45278
Patricia Hampton Roloff Foundation
6351 E. Forrest Hills Rd.
Guthrie, OK 73044-9073

Established in 1999 in OK.
Donor(s): Patty Hampton Roloff.
Financial data (yr. ended 12/31/01): Grants paid, $3,705; assets, $18,749 (M); gifts received, $3,521; expenditures, $4,226; qualifying distributions, $3,705.
Trustee: Patty Hampton Roloff.

EIN: 736316292

45279
Caskey Hurt Foundation
3318 Stoneybrook Rd.
Oklahoma City, OK 73120

Established in 1997 in OK.
Donor(s): Joseph K. Caskey, Sara H. Caskey.
Financial data (yr. ended 12/31/01): Grants paid, $3,675; assets, $80,207 (M); expenditures, $3,675; qualifying distributions, $3,675.
Limitations: Applications not accepted. Giving primarily in Oklahoma City, OK.
Application information: Contributes only to pre-selected organizations.
Trustees: Joseph K. Caskey, Sara H. Caskey.
EIN: 736304483

45280
Hope Foundation
2003 W. Ute St.
Tulsa, OK 74127

Donor(s): John P. Taddiken, Mary B. Taddiken.
Financial data (yr. ended 12/31/01): Grants paid, $3,600; assets, $172,465 (M); expenditures, $3,710; qualifying distributions, $3,543.
Limitations: Applications not accepted.
Application information: Contributes only to pre-selected organizations.
Trustees: John P. Taddiken, Mary V. Takkiken.
EIN: 731455787

45281
Geffen Family Charitable Foundation
2645 Terwilleger Blvd.
Tulsa, OK 74114-4105

Established in 1997 in OK.
Donor(s): Theodore M. Geffen.
Financial data (yr. ended 12/31/01): Grants paid, $3,500; assets, $852 (M); gifts received, $3,500; expenditures, $3,500; qualifying distributions, $3,500.
Trustees: Howard Joseph Geffen, William A. Geffen, Rita Maureen McCullough.
EIN: 731520376

45282
Merle and Richardine Holton Foundation
402 E. Jackson
Hugo, OK 74743 (580) 326-6427
Contact: Bob Rabon, Pres.

Established in 1990 in OK; funded in 1991.
Donor(s): Merle Holton.
Financial data (yr. ended 12/31/99): Grants paid, $3,500; assets, $110,024 (M); expenditures, $4,656; qualifying distributions, $4,250.
Limitations: Giving primarily to residents of Hugo, OK.
Application information: Application form required.
Officer and Director:* Bob Rabon,* Pres.
EIN: 731373753

45283
David and Lezlie Hudiburg Family Foundation
1903 Bedford Dr.
Oklahoma City, OK 73116

Established in 1999 in OK.
Donor(s): David Hudiburg, Lezlie Hudiburg.
Financial data (yr. ended 12/31/01): Grants paid, $3,500; assets, $169,343 (M); gifts received, $88,150; expenditures, $4,755; qualifying distributions, $3,500.
Limitations: Applications not accepted.
Application information: Contributes only to pre-selected organizations.
Trustees: David Hudiburg, Lezlie Hudiburg.

EIN: 731573960

45284
Calhoon Foundation
206 East 7th St.
Beaver, OK 73932

Established in 2000 in OK.
Donor(s): Edward L. Calhoon.
Financial data (yr. ended 12/31/01): Grants paid, $3,400; assets, $143,664 (M); gifts received, $20,000; expenditures, $7,921; qualifying distributions, $3,400.
Limitations: Applications not accepted. Giving primarily in OK.
Application information: Contributes only to pre-selected organizations.
Officers: Lane Calhoon Dolly, Pres.; Edward L. Calhoon, V.P.; Felice Calhoon, Secy.-Treas.
EIN: 731577481

45285
Fishback Family Foundation
3424 Lytal Terr.
Edmond, OK 73013

Established in 1999 in OK.
Donor(s): Joseph William Fishback II, Carolyn J. Fishback.
Financial data (yr. ended 12/31/01): Grants paid, $3,400; assets, $175,924 (M); gifts received, $60,000; expenditures, $3,900; qualifying distributions, $3,400.
Directors: Joseph William Fishback II, Carolyn J. Fishback, Tamara Kay Fishback.
EIN: 731577430

45286
Peyton Family Foundation
440 N.W. 15th St.
Oklahoma City, OK 73103 (405) 235-7966
Contact: Sandra J. Peyton, Tr.

Donor(s): Marvin Peyton, Sandra J. Peyton.
Financial data (yr. ended 12/31/01): Grants paid, $3,285; assets, $51,729 (M); expenditures, $4,102; qualifying distributions, $3,285.
Limitations: Giving primarily in OK.
Trustees: Marvin Peyton, Sandra J. Peyton.
EIN: 731524864

45287
Warren B. Hudson Scholarship Trust
c/o D.C. Anderson
21101 E. 101st St.
Broken Arrow, OK 74014-3602
Application address: c/o Counselor's Office, 1901 N. Albany, Broken Arrow, OK 74012

Financial data (yr. ended 12/31/01): Grants paid, $3,250; assets, $54,163 (M); expenditures, $3,558; qualifying distributions, $3,558.
Limitations: Giving limited to Broken Arrow, OK.
Application information: Application form required.
Trustees: D.C. Anderson, Bill Lemon, Kyle Woods.
EIN: 736151686

45288
Todd Family Charitable Foundation
4360 S. Victor Ave.
Tulsa, OK 74105
Contact: Marilyn Conner, Tr.

Established in 2000 in OK.
Financial data (yr. ended 12/31/01): Grants paid, $3,210; assets, $148,220 (M); gifts received, $91,858; expenditures, $11,696; qualifying distributions, $3,210.
Application information: Application form not required.

Trustees: Marilyn Todd Conner, E. Claude Todd, Thomas C. Todd.
EIN: 736323617

45289
Comanche Public School Foundation
P.O. Box 118
Comanche, OK 73529

Financial data (yr. ended 12/31/01): Grants paid, $3,180; assets, $10,593 (M); gifts received, $2,660; expenditures, $3,250; qualifying distributions, $3,180.
Limitations: Applications not accepted. Giving primarily in Comanche, OK.
Application information: Contributes only to pre-selected organizations.
Officers and Trustees:* Mark Myers,* Pres.; Mario Pineda,* V.P.; Cherri Bennett,* Secy.; Jana Hamm,* Treas.; Lynn Barber, Billy Bennett, Mary Branch, Greg Clinkenbeard, Dee Watson.
EIN: 731366099

45290
Doris, Harriet & Otto Cox Foundation
c/o First National Bank & Trust Co.
P.O. Box 432
Nowata, OK 74048-0432

Established in 1985 in OK.
Financial data (yr. ended 08/31/01): Grants paid, $3,121; assets, $54,916 (M); gifts received, $200; expenditures, $4,787; qualifying distributions, $3,121.
Limitations: Applications not accepted. Giving primarily in Nowata and Stillwater, OK.
Application information: Contributes only to pre-selected organizations.
Trustee: First National Bank & Trust Co.
EIN: 731253049

45291
Freese Foundation
4510 E. 31st St., Ste. 100
Tulsa, OK 74135 (918) 749-9331
Contact: John M. Freese, Sr., Tr.

Financial data (yr. ended 11/30/01): Grants paid, $3,008; assets, $52,849 (M); expenditures, $4,160; qualifying distributions, $3,008.
Limitations: Giving primarily in OK.
Trustees: John M. Freese, Sr., Patricia Freese.
EIN: 736106792

45292
The Hesed Foundation
2121 S. Columbia Ave., Ste. 650
Tulsa, OK 74114-3503

Established in 2000 in OK.
Donor(s): Dan Schusterman, Gloria Schusterman, Dale H. Schusterman, Blanca E. Schusterman.
Financial data (yr. ended 12/31/01): Grants paid, $3,000; assets, $1,251,860 (M); gifts received, $75,183; expenditures, $18,746; qualifying distributions, $3,000.
Limitations: Applications not accepted.
Application information: Contributes only to pre-selected organizations.
Trustees: Dan Schusterman, Gloria Schusterman.
EIN: 731602143

45293
Marsh Foundation
1637 S. Boston
Tulsa, OK 74119

Donor(s): Philip W. Marsh.
Financial data (yr. ended 12/31/00): Grants paid, $3,000; assets, $0 (M); gifts received, $3,500; expenditures, $3,410; qualifying distributions, $3,000.
Limitations: Applications not accepted. Giving primarily in OK and TX.
Application information: Contributes only to pre-selected organizations.
Directors: James W. Linn, William D. Lohrey, William V. Trollinger.
EIN: 731291683

45294
Tulsa Charitable Foundation
1919 S. Wheeling, Ste. 606
Tulsa, OK 74104-5635

Established in 1986 in OK.
Donor(s): Frank N. Fore, M.D., Robert C. Blankenship, M.D.
Financial data (yr. ended 12/31/01): Grants paid, $3,000; assets, $154,016 (M); expenditures, $3,529; qualifying distributions, $3,000.
Directors: Robert C. Blankenship, M.D., W. Kirk Clausing, Frank N. Fore, M.D.
EIN: 731305754

45295
Jack Little Foundation for Aid to the Deaf
P.O. Box 618
Madill, OK 73446 (580) 795-3397
Contact: Oteka D. Little, Tr.

Financial data (yr. ended 01/31/02): Grants paid, $2,800; assets, $92,776 (M); expenditures, $3,631; qualifying distributions, $2,738.
Limitations: Giving primarily in Madill, OK.
Trustee: Don Little.
EIN: 730768139

45296
Richardson Scholarship Trust
c/o BancFirst - Trust Dept.
P.O. Box 1468
Duncan, OK 73534-1468
Application address: c/o Scholarship Selection Comm., Duncan High School, P.O. Box 1548, Duncan, OK 73534-1548

Financial data (yr. ended 10/31/01): Grants paid, $2,800; assets, $42,000 (M); expenditures, $3,338; qualifying distributions, $3,311.
Limitations: Giving limited to residents of Stephens County, OK.
Application information: Application form required.
Trustee: BancFirst.
EIN: 731194321

45297
The Treacy Foundation
(Formerly The Treacy Foundation, Inc.)
2963 E. 75th St.
Tulsa, OK 74136
Contact: Francesca Treacy, Vice-Chair.

Established in 1989 in OK.
Donor(s): James B. Treacy.‡
Financial data (yr. ended 12/31/01): Grants paid, $2,675; assets, $287,963 (M); expenditures, $4,444; qualifying distributions, $2,675.
Limitations: Giving primarily in Tulsa, OK.
Application information: Application form not required.
Officer: Francesca N. Treacy, Vice-Chair.
EIN: 731333867

45298
The Honaker Foundation, Inc.
7783 E. 540 Rd.
Claremore, OK 74017-2335
Contact: Jack D. Honaker, M.D., Pres.

Established in 1992 in OK.
Donor(s): Jack D. Honaker, Frances G. Honaker.
Financial data (yr. ended 12/31/99): Grants paid, $2,600; assets, $1,374 (M); gifts received, $2,000; expenditures, $2,600; qualifying distributions, $2,600.
Limitations: Giving limited to OK.
Application information: Application form required.
Officers: Jack D. Honaker, M.D., Pres.; Frances G. Honaker, Secy.-Treas.
EIN: 731401956

45299
Esther's Child Foundation
2525 Arbor Chase
Edmond, OK 73013
Contact: Deborah L. Andrade, Tr.

Established in 2000 in OK.
Donor(s): Deborah L. Andrade, Stephen A. Andrade.
Financial data (yr. ended 12/31/01): Grants paid, $2,500; assets, $20,905 (M); gifts received, $14,500; expenditures, $2,500; qualifying distributions, $2,500.
Application information: Application form not required.
Trustees: Deborah L. Andrade, Stephen A. Andrade.
EIN: 731597521

45300
The Randall L. Sullivan Foundation
15 E. 5th St., Ste. 2100
Tulsa, OK 74103

Established in 1997.
Donor(s): Randall L. Sullivan.
Financial data (yr. ended 12/31/00): Grants paid, $2,500; assets, $122,477 (M); gifts received, $2,500; expenditures, $3,839; qualifying distributions, $2,500.
Limitations: Giving primarily in Tulsa, OK.
Trustee: Randall L. Sullivan.
EIN: 731518383

45301
Oklahoma City Mavericks-Suns Youth Sports Foundation
2301 W. I-44 Service Rd., Ste. 310
Oklahoma City, OK 73112

Financial data (yr. ended 12/31/01): Grants paid, $2,460; assets, $3,174 (M); gifts received, $2,575; expenditures, $2,478; qualifying distributions, $2,460.
Limitations: Giving primarily in Oklahoma City, OK.
Trustees: T. Philip Kierl, Jr., Walter W. White.
EIN: 736302782

45302
Blake Duncan Memorial Trust
1310 N.W. Lawton Ave.
Lawton, OK 73507

Financial data (yr. ended 06/30/01): Grants paid, $2,000; assets, $47,393 (M); gifts received, $71; expenditures, $2,071; qualifying distributions, $2,071.
Limitations: Applications not accepted. Giving limited to Lawton, OK.
Application information: Unsolicited requests for funds not accepted.
Officer: L.W. Duncan, Mgr.
Trustee: D. Michael Duncan.
EIN: 237134986

45303
David and Lisa Holden Foundation
4146 S. Birmingham Pl.
Tulsa, OK 74105-4352

Established in 1990 in OK.
Donor(s): David W. Holden, Lisa M. Holden.
Financial data (yr. ended 12/31/00): Grants paid, $2,000; assets, $2,512 (M); expenditures, $2,000; qualifying distributions, $1,999.
Limitations: Applications not accepted. Giving primarily in Tulsa, OK.
Application information: Contributes only to pre-selected organizations.
Trustees: David W. Holden, Lisa M. Holden.
EIN: 731365278

45304
Perry Family Foundation
2016 Worthington Ln.
Edmond, OK 73013

Established in 2001 in OK.
Donor(s): Mark Moore, Pattye Moore.
Financial data (yr. ended 12/31/01): Grants paid, $2,000; assets, $1,687 (M); gifts received, $4,650; expenditures, $3,000; qualifying distributions, $3,000.
Trustees: Janet A. Perry, Michael A. Perry.
EIN: 731609751

45305
Edgar and Ira Sanditen Foundation
3314 E. 51st St., Ste. 207K
Tulsa, OK 74135 (918) 742-2417
Contact: Edgar R. Sanditen, Pres.

Incorporated in 1943 in OK.
Donor(s): Otasco, Inc., Edgar R. Sanditen.
Financial data (yr. ended 12/31/01): Grants paid, $2,000; assets, $4,924 (M); expenditures, $2,445; qualifying distributions, $2,000.
Limitations: Giving primarily in the Tulsa, OK, area.
Officers: Edgar R. Sanditen, Pres.; Michael J. Sanditen, V.P.; Steven A. Sanditen, V.P.; Thomas A. Mann, Secy.-Treas.
EIN: 736092466

45306
Arthur D. Scroggs Scholarship Foundation, Inc.
c/o BancTrust
P.O. Box 26883
Oklahoma City, OK 73126-0883

Financial data (yr. ended 12/31/01): Grants paid, $2,000; assets, $41,585 (M); expenditures, $2,672; qualifying distributions, $1,983.
Limitations: Giving limited to residents of OK.
Application information: Application form required.
Trustees: Patrick Evans, BancTrust.
EIN: 736092082

45307
Schmoldt Foundation For Education
3305 Woodland Rd.
Bartlesville, OK 74006-4523 (918) 333-0647
Contact: Hans Schmoldt, Pres.

Established in 1999 in OK.
Financial data (yr. ended 12/31/01): Grants paid, $1,800; assets, $20,855 (M); expenditures, $2,262; qualifying distributions, $1,800.
Limitations: Giving primarily in TX.
Officers: Hans Edward Schmoldt, Pres.; Jimmie Lynn Schmoldt, V.P.; Gretchen Alice Schmoldt Wettlin, Secy.; Hans Karl Schmoldt, Treas.
EIN: 731552717

45308
Compassionate Care Fund
c/o St. Francis Hospital
6161 S. Yale
Tulsa, OK 74136 (918) 494-1585

Established in 1996 in OK.
Donor(s): T.J. Brickner, Jr., M.D., R.G. Ellis, M.D., Sung Ae Lee, M.D., St. Francis Hospital.
Financial data (yr. ended 12/31/99): Grants paid, $1,776; assets, $6,288 (M); gifts received, $500; expenditures, $1,801; qualifying distributions, $1,775.
Application information: Application form required.
Trustee: T.J. Brickner, Jr., M.D.
EIN: 736292807

45309
Pulliam Family Charitable Trust
220 S.E. 24th St.
Norman, OK 73071-4123

Established in 1994 in OK.
Financial data (yr. ended 12/31/01): Grants paid, $1,720; assets, $118,983 (M); gifts received, $5,197; expenditures, $1,850; qualifying distributions, $1,720.
Trustees: A. Kay Pulliam, J. Gordan Pulliam.
EIN: 736278245

45310
Croy Foundation
1516 W. Elk
Duncan, OK 73533

Established in 1997 in OK.
Financial data (yr. ended 12/31/01): Grants paid, $1,700; assets, $32,839 (M); gifts received, $700; expenditures, $2,138; qualifying distributions, $1,700.
Application information: Application form not required.
Officer: D.E. Croy, Pres.
EIN: 731486052

45311
The Burbridge Foundation
3701 N.W. 42nd St.
Oklahoma City, OK 73112-2508

Established in 1959 in OK.
Financial data (yr. ended 07/31/99): Grants paid, $1,605; assets, $5,652,971 (M); gifts received, $2,977; expenditures, $447,073; qualifying distributions, $244,382; giving activities include $200,809 for programs.
Application information: Application form required.
Officers and Directors:* Bobbie Burbridge Lane,* Pres.; Dianne Beffort,* V.P.; Dorothy Anderson, Robin Jones.
EIN: 756028012

45312
Bagwell Foundation
2122 E. 59th Pl.
Tulsa, OK 74105-7010

Established in 1990 in OK.
Donor(s): Richard F. Bagwell.
Financial data (yr. ended 12/31/00): Grants paid, $1,501; assets, $422,472 (M); gifts received, $5,000; expenditures, $9,572; qualifying distributions, $1,501.
Limitations: Applications not accepted. Giving primarily in Clarksville, AR.
Application information: Contributes only to pre-selected organizations.
Officers and Trustees:* Richard F. Bagwell,* Chair.; Katherine S. Bagwell,* Secy.-Treas.; Richard S. Bagwell, Barbee V. Vickburg, Susan B. Watkins.
EIN: 731371605

45313
William S. Allen Scholarship Fund
P.O. Box 230
Sapulpa, OK 74067-0230

Donor(s): Yvonne Allen, Catherine Reed, Sam Allen.
Financial data (yr. ended 12/31/99): Grants paid, $1,500; assets, $6,855 (M); gifts received, $2,400; expenditures, $1,509; qualifying distributions, $1,500.
Limitations: Giving limited to residents of Sapulpa, OK.
Officers: Yvonnie S. Allen, Chair.; Sam T. Allen III, Secy.
Directors: Sam T. Allen IV, Diane Kennedy.
EIN: 731433434

45314
The Boudreau Foundation
427 S. Boston, Ste. 1311
Tulsa, OK 74103 (918) 592-3476
Contact: A.F. Boudreau, Jr., Tr.

Financial data (yr. ended 12/31/01): Grants paid, $1,500; assets, $253,524 (M); gifts received, $1,932; expenditures, $2,140; qualifying distributions, $1,962.
Limitations: Applications not accepted. Giving primarily in Tulsa, OK.
Officer: James H. Lepley, Mgr.
Trustee: Alfred F. Boudreau, Jr.
EIN: 736120548

45315
Drummond Family Foundation
P.O. Box 597
Madill, OK 73446-0597 (580) 795-3758
Contact: Tia Juana Drummond, Tr.

Financial data (yr. ended 06/30/01): Grants paid, $1,500; assets, $66,843 (M); expenditures, $2,000; qualifying distributions, $1,492.
Limitations: Giving primarily in Madill, OK.
Application information: Application form not required.
Trustees: Herschel Beard, Tia Juana Drummond, Jim Ewing, Joe Potter, Tina E. Williams.
EIN: 731029919

45316
Gordona Duca Foundation Trust
(Formerly Gordona Duca Foundation)
c/o Gordona Duca Heiliger
10426 S. Kingston Ave.
Tulsa, OK 74137

Established around 1994.
Donor(s): Gordona Duca-Heiliger.
Financial data (yr. ended 12/31/00): Grants paid, $1,500; assets, $4,583 (M); gifts received, $1,000; expenditures, $1,515; qualifying distributions, $1,500.
Limitations: Applications not accepted. Giving primarily in OK.
Application information: Contributes only to pre-selected organizations.
Trustee: Gordona Duca-Heiliger.
EIN: 736275374

45317
Spencer Barnett Man Memorial Foundation
3517 Quail Creek Rd.
Oklahoma City, OK 73120
Contact: Michael B. Man, Pres.

Established in 1994 in OK.

Financial data (yr. ended 12/31/01): Grants paid, $1,500; assets, $796 (M); gifts received, $1,000; expenditures, $1,500; qualifying distributions, $0.
Limitations: Giving primarily in FL.
Officers: Michael B. Man, Pres.; Carol J. Man, V.P.
EIN: 731448646

45318
Nicholas & Renee Preftakes Foundation
825 N. Broadway Ave., Ste. 300
Oklahoma City, OK 73102

Established in 2001 in OK.
Donor(s): Precor Realty Advisors, Inc.
Financial data (yr. ended 12/31/01): Grants paid, $1,500; assets, $3,477 (M); gifts received, $5,000; expenditures, $1,523; qualifying distributions, $1,500.
Limitations: Applications not accepted.
Application information: Contributes only to pre-selected organizations.
Officers: Renee L.F. Preftakes, Pres.; Nicholas J. Preftakes, V.P.; Patricia Manning, Secy.; Greg Palmer, Treas.
EIN: 731619904

45319
Covington-Douglas Scholarship Foundation
c/o Central National Bank & Trust Co. of Enid
P.O. Box 3448
Enid, OK 73702-3448
Contact: Stella Knowles, Trust Off., Central National Bank & Trust Co. of Enid

Financial data (yr. ended 12/31/01): Grants paid, $1,350; assets, $672,366 (M); expenditures, $3,235; qualifying distributions, $2,289.
Limitations: Giving limited to Covington, OK.
Selection Committee: Cindy Black, Jessee James, Bill Seitter, Karen Holland.
Trustee: Central National Bank & Trust Co. of Enid.
EIN: 237426494

45320
Spence Family Memorial Trust
P.O. Box 100
Sayre, OK 73662
Contact: Leon Willsie, Tr.

Financial data (yr. ended 12/31/00): Grants paid, $1,200; assets, $51,574 (M); expenditures, $3,845; qualifying distributions, $3,845.
Limitations: Giving limited to residents of Beckham County and the portion of Roger Mills County south of the Washita River, OK.
Application information: Application form required.
Trustee: Leon Willsie.
EIN: 731357758

45321
Hedlund Parent Teachers Association, Inc.
c/o Hazel M. Shannon
1211 W. Gore Blvd.
Lawton, OK 73501

Financial data (yr. ended 12/31/01): Grants paid, $1,177; assets, $15,770 (M); expenditures, $1,188; qualifying distributions, $1,177.
Limitations: Applications not accepted. Giving limited to Lawton, OK.
Officers: John N. Fleur, Pres.; Hazel M. Shannon, Secy.-Treas.
EIN: 736130125

45322
Universal Church of God
1366 E. 52 N.
Tulsa, OK 74126-2821

Established in 1986 in OK.
Donor(s): Rebeccah Ann Doty, Charles R. Doty.

Financial data (yr. ended 12/31/01): Grants paid, $1,140; assets, $0 (M); expenditures, $1,368; qualifying distributions, $1,312.
Limitations: Applications not accepted. Giving primarily in Tulsa, OK.
Application information: Unsolicited requests for funds not accepted.
Officer: Charles Doty, Pres.
EIN: 731280015

45323
Stanley and Jerry Lee Foundation
1024 N.W. 71st St.
Oklahoma City, OK 73116 (405) 840-5454
Contact: M. Stanley Lee, Chair.

Established in 2000 in OK.
Donor(s): M. Stanley Lee.
Financial data (yr. ended 12/31/01): Grants paid, $1,130; assets, $114,071 (M); expenditures, $1,280; qualifying distributions, $1,130.
Officers and Directors:* M. Stanley Lee,* Chair.; S. Whitfield Lee,* Pres.; Geraldine C. Lee,* Secy.; Claudia L. Foster, Larry K. Lee, Richard C. Lee.
EIN: 731602299

45324
Thurman Magbee Foundation
3013 N.W. 59th St.
Oklahoma City, OK 73116

Financial data (yr. ended 07/31/01): Grants paid, $1,080; assets, $3,631 (M); expenditures, $1,731; qualifying distributions, $1,080.
Limitations: Applications not accepted. Giving primarily in OK.
Application information: Contributes only to pre-selected organizations.
Officers: Thurman Magbee, Pres.; Betty Magbee, Secy.
Director: Susan Magbee Hall.
EIN: 736119725

45325
The Business and Professional Women's Club of Marlow, OK of The National Federation of Business & Professional Women's Clubs, Inc. Trust
P.O. Box 193
Marlow, OK 73055 (580) 658-2718
Application address: 510 W. Main, Marlow, OK 73055
Contact: Jerry Couch

Financial data (yr. ended 12/31/00): Grants paid, $1,035; assets, $22,292 (M); expenditures, $1,042; qualifying distributions, $1,042.
Limitations: Giving limited to residents of Marlow, OK.
Trustee: D.B. Green.
EIN: 731550018

45326
The Peter Kong-Ming and Mary L. New Student Award Trust
c/o Society for Applied Anthropology
P.O. Box 24803
Oklahoma City, OK 73124 (405) 843-5113

Financial data (yr. ended 12/31/01): Grants paid, $1,000; assets, $75,409 (M); gifts received, $600; expenditures, $5,221; qualifying distributions, $5,202.
Application information: Applicant must submit a paper not exceeding 45 pages, based on research not previously published.
Trustees: Joseph Kaufert, J. Thomas May, John Young.
EIN: 736257539

45327
Milligan/LeBard Foundation, Inc.
2301 N.W. 39th Expwy., Ste. 300
Oklahoma City, OK 73112 (405) 525-8331
Contact: Michael J. Milligan, V.P.

Established in 1986 in OK.
Financial data (yr. ended 12/31/01): Grants paid, $1,000; assets, $14,531 (M); gifts received, $39; expenditures, $1,011; qualifying distributions, $1,000.
Limitations: Giving primarily in Oklahoma City, OK.
Officers and Trustees:* Lois D. Milligan,* Pres.; Michael J. Milligan,* V.P.; Margie S. John,* Secy.; Jilene K. Boghetich,* Treas.; Merry L. Knowles, James H. Milligan, Patricia A. Milligan.
EIN: 731292504

45328
The Moriarity Family Scholarship Trust
2203 Iowa
Norman, OK 73069-6520 (405) 325-5809
Contact: Shane Moriarity, Tr.

Established in 1984 in OK.
Donor(s): Shane Moriarity.
Financial data (yr. ended 12/31/99): Grants paid, $1,000; assets, $8,064 (M); expenditures, $1,012; qualifying distributions, $1,008.
Limitations: Giving limited to Gilbert, MN.
Application information: Application form required.
Trustees: Shane Moriarity, David Mowrey, Eugene Powers.
EIN: 736217241

45329
The Nix Foundation
129 E. Shore Dr.
Arcadia, OK 73007 (405) 396-3033
Contact: James W. Nix III, Pres.

Established in 2000 in OK.
Donor(s): James W. Nix, Mildred Nix.
Financial data (yr. ended 12/31/01): Grants paid, $1,000; assets, $182,194 (M); expenditures, $1,669; qualifying distributions, $1,000.
Application information: Application form not required.
Officers: James W. Nix III, Pres.; Patsiann Smith, Secy.-Treas.
Directors: James W. Nix, Mildred L. Nix.
EIN: 731602013

45330
Robert L. Parker Foundation
c/o Robert L. Parker
8 E. 3rd St.
Tulsa, OK 74103

Donor(s): Robert L. Parker.
Financial data (yr. ended 12/31/01): Grants paid, $1,000; assets, $728 (M); gifts received, $1,000; expenditures, $1,108; qualifying distributions, $1,000.
Limitations: Giving primarily in Tulsa, OK.
Officers: Robert L. Parker, Pres.; Robert L. Parker, Jr., V.P.; John T. Bishop III, Secy.-Treas.
EIN: 731404400

45331
Sewell Family Foundation
1720 Cheyney Ct.
Norman, OK 73071

Established in 2001 in OK.
Financial data (yr. ended 12/31/01): Grants paid, $1,000; assets, $18,991 (M); expenditures, $1,080; qualifying distributions, $1,000.

Officers: Marjorie A. Sewell, Pres.; Betty R. Benedict, V.P. and Secy.; Bert W. Sewell, Treas.
Directors: Gary M. Benedict, Evelyn Sewell.
EIN: 731601030

45332
K. L. Smith Scholarship Foundation, Inc.
Drawer B
Healdton, OK 73438
Application address: P.O. Box 235, Healdton, OK 73436, tel.: (580) 229-1776
Contact: David Smith, Mgr.

Financial data (yr. ended 09/30/99): Grants paid, $1,000; assets, $18,701 (L); gifts received, $5,088; expenditures, $1,000; qualifying distributions, $8,000.
Limitations: Giving limited to residents of OK.
Application information: Application form required.
Officers and Directors:* Brenda Darling, Pres.; Sheri Blevins, V.P.; Kristi Aycox, Secy.-Treas.; David Smith,* Mgr.; John Harris, Bob Miller, Robert Peterson, Oweeta Smith.
EIN: 731528923

45333
The Wells Family Charitable Trust
2201 E. 27th St.
Tulsa, OK 74114

Established in 1999 in OK.
Donor(s): Carolyn Wells Billings.
Financial data (yr. ended 12/31/00): Grants paid, $1,000; assets, $274,601 (M); gifts received, $75,000; expenditures, $2,293; qualifying distributions, $936.
Limitations: Applications not accepted.
Application information: Contributes only to pre-selected organizations.
Trustees: Ellen Ledvina Garland, Patricia Ledvina Himes.
EIN: 731575685

45334
Jack Yoakum Memorial FFA Scholarship, Inc.
215 W. Main
Chouteau, OK 74337
Contact: Randy Deason, Dir.

Established in 1998 in OK.
Financial data (yr. ended 12/31/00): Grants paid, $1,000; assets, $21,078 (M); expenditures, $1,590; qualifying distributions, $1,000.
Limitations: Giving limited to residents of Chouteau, OK.
Application information: Application form required.
Directors: Carla Christine Brown, Patricia Lynn Davis, Randy Deason.
EIN: 731553117

45335
Wood Science Scholarship Fund
323C W. Lafayette Ave.
Checotah, OK 74426-3815
Application address: c/o Counselor, Checotah High School, 320 W. Jefferson, Checotah, OK 74426, tel.: (918) 473-2239

Financial data (yr. ended 12/31/01): Grants paid, $900; assets, $11,104 (M); expenditures, $900; qualifying distributions, $900.
Limitations: Giving primarily in OK.
Application information: Application form not required.
Trustees: Judy Mann, George Park, Lonnie Robison, Logan Sharpe.
EIN: 731342579

45336
Milton Smith Ministries, Inc.
P.O. Box 54700
Tulsa, OK 74155-0700

Established around 1995.
Financial data (yr. ended 12/31/01): Grants paid, $827; assets, $1,475 (M); gifts received, $6,041; expenditures, $8,038; qualifying distributions, $827.
Officers: Milton Smith, Pres.; Sheila Smith, Treas.
EIN: 750324024

45337
Vaughn Brock Foundation
20 E. 5th St., Ste. 1500
Tulsa, OK 74103

Established around 1988.
Donor(s): J. Vaughn Brock.
Financial data (yr. ended 12/31/01): Grants paid, $800; assets, $0 (M); expenditures, $1,493; qualifying distributions, $800.
Limitations: Applications not accepted.
Application information: Contributes only to pre-selected organizations.
Officer: J. Vaughn Brock, Pres.
EIN: 731293701

45338
Mary Clarke Miley Foundation, Inc.
629 24rh Ave., S.W.
Norman, OK 73069
Contact: Stephen W. Bonner, Pres.

Established in 2000 in OK.
Donor(s): Mary Clarke Miley.
Financial data (yr. ended 12/31/00): Grants paid, $800; assets, $56,342 (M); gifts received, $62,333; expenditures, $800; qualifying distributions, $800.
Limitations: Giving primarily in OK.
Officers and Directors:* Stephen W. Bonner,* Pres.; Mary S. Bonner,* Secy.; Mary Clarke Miley.
EIN: 731575511

45339
John Hessel Foundation
P.O. Box 2017
Oklahoma City, OK 73101

Established in 1999.
Donor(s): John L. Hessel, Maxine D. Hessel, H & D Properties, LP.
Financial data (yr. ended 12/31/01): Grants paid, $649; assets, $97,113 (M); expenditures, $649; qualifying distributions, $649.
Limitations: Applications not accepted. Giving primarily in OK.
Application information: Contributes only to pre-selected organizations.
Trustees: John L. Hessel, Maxine D. Hessel.
EIN: 311629729

45340
The John F. Y. and Elizabeth Lorene Stambaugh Foundation
9 E. 4th St., Ste. 700
Tulsa, OK 74103

Established in 1999 in OK.
Donor(s): John F.Y. Stambaugh.
Financial data (yr. ended 12/31/01): Grants paid, $625; assets, $18,431 (M); expenditures, $1,119; qualifying distributions, $625.
Limitations: Giving primarily in OK.
Officers and Trustees:* John F.Y. Stambaugh,* Pres. and Treas.; Elizabeth L. Stambaugh,* V.P. and Secy.; John F.Y. Stambaugh, Jr.
EIN: 731566556

45341
MLE Endowment Foundation
2628 N.W. 68th St.
Oklahoma City, OK 73116

Established in 1996.
Financial data (yr. ended 12/31/99): Grants paid, $595; assets, $768 (M); gifts received, $1,230; expenditures, $1,054; qualifying distributions, $1,054.
Limitations: Applications not accepted. Giving primarily in OK.
Application information: Contributes only to pre-selected organizations.
Trustee: Stephanie Emrick.
EIN: 731477976

45342
Tulsa Skating Foundation, Inc.
c/o Briscoe, Burke & Grigsby, LLP
4120 E. 51st St., Ste. 100
Tulsa, OK 74135-3633
Application address: 5376 E. 27th St., Tulsa, OK 74114, tel.: (918) 744-6838
Contact: Ankie Buitink, Pres.

Financial data (yr. ended 04/30/02): Grants paid, $500; assets, $11,492 (M); expenditures, $540; qualifying distributions, $500.
Officers: Ankie Buitink, Pres.; Liz Kiper, V.P.; Jennifer O'Leary, Secy.-Treas.
Directors: Betty Grabel, Jean Grossheart, Jean Paul.
EIN: 731352277

45343
Kate Frank Manor Religious & Charitable Association, Inc.
201 S. 33rd St.
Muskogee, OK 74401-5035
Contact: James W. Farley, Pres.

Financial data (yr. ended 06/30/01): Grants paid, $400; assets, $0 (M); expenditures, $6,074; qualifying distributions, $6,074.
Limitations: Giving primarily in OK.
Application information: Application form not required.
Officers: James Farley, Pres.; Martha Hagaman, V.P.; Eula Crosbie, Secy.; George Dixon, Treas.
EIN: 731072789

45344
Kate Family Foundation
5801 N.W. 56th St.
Oklahoma City, OK 73122-6216

Established in 2000 in OK.
Donor(s): Frederick H. Kate, Lois M. Kate.
Financial data (yr. ended 12/31/01): Grants paid, $315; assets, $72,450 (M); gifts received, $32,916; expenditures, $2,763; qualifying distributions, $315.
Limitations: Applications not accepted.
Application information: Contributes only to pre-selected organizations.
Trustees: Frederick H. Kate, Lois M. Kate.
EIN: 736322336

45345
Benedict Family Foundation
300 S. Oak St.
Sapulpa, OK 74066-4348

Established in 1996.
Donor(s): David L. Benedict, Barbara B. Benedict.
Financial data (yr. ended 06/30/00): Grants paid, $200; assets, $0 (M); expenditures, $215; qualifying distributions, $200.

Directors: Barbara Benedict, David Benedict, Holly Benedict, M.D., Jerrold L. Benedict, M.D., Lisa D. Butler.
EIN: 731508269

45346
Eshelman Ministries, Inc.
P.O. Box 2073
Sapulpa, OK 74067
Contact: Georgia Eshelman, Pres.

Established in 1989 in OK.
Financial data (yr. ended 12/31/99): Grants paid, $187; assets, $20 (M); gifts received, $1,828; expenditures, $1,807; qualifying distributions, $1,807; giving activities include $1,807 for programs.
Officers and Director:* Georgia Eshelman,* Pres.; Virginia Niles, V.P.; Rona Wheeler, Secy.-Treas.
EIN: 731333192

45347
Consumer Life and Health Association, Inc.
(Formerly CHCA, Inc.)
P.O. Box 25523
Oklahoma City, OK 73125-0523

Financial data (yr. ended 12/31/00): Grants paid, $75; assets, $396 (M); expenditures, $104; qualifying distributions, $75.
Limitations: Giving primarily in OK.
Officers: Thomas O. Francis, Pres.; Stephen P. Garrett, Sr. V.P. and Secy.; Peter C. Weaver, Sr. V.P. and Treas.
EIN: 731490455

45348
The Anderson Family Charitable Foundation
1030 E. 18th St.
Tulsa, OK 74120-7407

Established in 1998 in OK.
Financial data (yr. ended 12/31/00): Grants paid, $1; assets, $9 (M); expenditures, $1; qualifying distributions, $1.
Officer: Sidney L. Anderson, Mgr.
EIN: 731551890

45349
The Adelson Family Foundation
15 E. 5th St., Ste. 3200
Tulsa, OK 74103

Established in 1996 in OK.
Donor(s): Ellen G. Adelson.
Financial data (yr. ended 12/31/01): Grants paid, $0; assets, $70,493 (M); expenditures, $9; qualifying distributions, $0.
Limitations: Applications not accepted.
Application information: Contributes only to pre-selected organizations.
Trustees: David M. Adelson, Ellen G. Adelson, James F. Adelson, Robert S. Adelson, Thomas A. Adelson.
EIN: 731491884

45350
The Ardeneum of Oklahoma Charitable and Educational Foundation, Inc.
P.O. Box 3250
McAlester, OK 74502
Contact: Sabra Tate, Pres.

Established in 2000 in OK.
Donor(s): Allece Garrard.‡
Financial data (yr. ended 12/31/01): Grants paid, $0; assets, $4,019,395 (M); gifts received, $45; expenditures, $208,336; qualifying distributions, $0.
Limitations: Applications not accepted.
Application information: Unsolicited requests for funds not accepted.

Officers: Sabra Tate, Pres.; Carrie Jane Loftis, V.P.
Directors: June Boyd, Ed Harrington, John Shuller.
EIN: 731577200

45351
The Asbjornson Foundation
8917 S. Sandusky
Tulsa, OK 74137
Contact: Norman H. Asbjornson, Tr.

Established in 1999 in OK.
Donor(s): Norman H. Asbjornson.
Financial data (yr. ended 12/31/01): Grants paid, $0; assets, $196,675 (M); expenditures, $573; qualifying distributions, $0.
Trustee: Norman H. Asbjornson.
EIN: 731582633

45352
Asoka Foundation, Inc.
3333 S. Council Rd.
Oklahoma City, OK 73179-4410

Established in 1982.
Financial data (yr. ended 12/31/01): Grants paid, $0; assets, $106,167 (M); gifts received, $13,000; expenditures, $14,636; qualifying distributions, $14,457; giving activities include $14,457 for programs.
Limitations: Giving primarily in IL and NY.
Officers: Harry McMullan, Pres.; Mary Talley, Secy.
EIN: 731137948

45353
Athletes First Foundation II
100 W. Main St., Ste. 287
Oklahoma City, OK 73102

Established in 1999.
Financial data (yr. ended 12/31/99): Grants paid, $0; assets, $345 (M); gifts received, $20,936; expenditures, $20,631; qualifying distributions, $0; giving activities include $20,631 for programs.
Limitations: Applications not accepted.
Application information: Contributes only to pre-selected organizations.
Officer: Gary Vick, Exec. Dir.
Director: J. Calvin Johnson.
EIN: 731563590

45354
The Donald B. and Ellen C. Atkins Foundation
1406 Terrace Dr.
Tulsa, OK 74104

Established in 2001 in OK.
Financial data (yr. ended 12/31/01): Grants paid, $0; assets, $1,029 (M); gifts received, $1,000; expenditures, $0; qualifying distributions, $0.
Trustees: Donald B. Atkins, Ellen C. Atkins.
EIN: 731603888

45355
The Barnabas Group Foundation
11011 Hefner Pointe Dr.
Oklahoma City, OK 73120

Established in 2000 in OK.
Financial data (yr. ended 12/31/00): Grants paid, $0; assets, $3,267 (M); gifts received, $40,565; expenditures, $38,541; qualifying distributions, $38,541; giving activities include $38,541 for programs.
Limitations: Applications not accepted. Giving primarily in OK.
Application information: Contributes only to pre-selected organizations.
Board Members: C. Wesley Lane II, Lori Hansen Lane, M.D., Susan McCalmont.
EIN: 731578669

45356
John Harvey Bass Nursing Trust
(also known as John Harvey Bass Nursing Scholarship Fund)
c/o Arvest Trust Co., N.A.
P.O. Box 900
Norman, OK 73070-0610
Application address: c/o Arvest Trust Company, N.A., 200 E. Main St., Norman, OK 73069, tel.: (405) 321-7170
Contact: El Juana Pollock, Trust Off., Arvest Trust Company, N.A.

Financial data (yr. ended 12/31/01): Grants paid, $0; assets, $5,515 (M); expenditures, $863; qualifying distributions, $0.
Limitations: Giving limited to OK.
Trustee: Arvest Trust Company, N.A.
EIN: 736114311

45357
The Beauty for Ashes Foundation
3501 N.W. 63rd, Ste. 403
Oklahoma City, OK 73116

Established in 1994.
Financial data (yr. ended 12/31/01): Grants paid, $0; assets, $86,621 (M); gifts received, $8,300; expenditures, $8,082; qualifying distributions, $0.
Limitations: Applications not accepted.
Application information: Contributes only to pre-selected organizations.
Directors: Steve R. Bailey, Robert S. Gary.
EIN: 731460981

45358
Louis and Mary Noreitha Bellinghausen Foundation
2301 W. I-44 Service Rd., Ste. 300
Oklahoma City, OK 73112
Contact: T. Philip Kierl, Jr., Tr.

Donor(s): Louis J. Bellinghausen.
Financial data (yr. ended 12/31/01): Grants paid, $0; assets, $31,682 (M); expenditures, $364; qualifying distributions, $0.
Limitations: Giving limited to OK.
Trustees: Louis Bellinghausen, T. Philip Kierl, Jr.
EIN: 731531973

45359
Burton Foundation, Inc.
2932 N.W., 122 Bradley Sq., Ste. D
Oklahoma City, OK 73120

Established in 2001 in FL.
Donor(s): Barry A. Gray.
Financial data (yr. ended 12/31/01): Grants paid, $0; assets, $501,487 (M); gifts received, $504,500; expenditures, $5,842; qualifying distributions, $0.
Limitations: Applications not accepted.
Application information: Contributes only to pre-selected organizations.
Directors: Barry A. Gray, David A. Gray, Gretchen S. Gray, Joseph M. Gray, Robert C. Gray, Elizabeth D. Wall.
EIN: 731584983

45360
The C.E.L. Foundation
1514 Crestwood Dr.
Wagoner, OK 74467 (918) 488-1010

Established in 1989 in OK.
Donor(s): Charles E. Lusk.
Financial data (yr. ended 12/31/99): Grants paid, $0; assets, $7,544 (M); expenditures, $0; qualifying distributions, $0.
Limitations: Applications not accepted. Giving primarily in OK.

45360—OKLAHOMA

Trustees: Charles E. Lusk, Leslie I. Lusk.
EIN: 731342309

45361
Conklin Family Foundation
P.O. Box 609
Stigler, OK 74462

Established in 2001 in OK.
Donor(s): Thomas H. Conklin, Jr., Florence Jean Concklin.
Financial data (yr. ended 12/31/01): Grants paid, $0; assets, $451,538 (M); gifts received, $441,396; expenditures, $3,789; qualifying distributions, $3,789.
Limitations: Applications not accepted.
Application information: Contributes only to pre-selected organizations.
Officers: Thomas H. Conklin, Jr., Pres.; Florence Jean Conklin, Secy.-Treas.
Directors: Kelly Lynn Conklin, Tara Ann Conklin, Thomas Harold Conklin, III.
EIN: 731608278

45362
Consumers Health Care Association, Inc.
2000 Classen Ctr.
Oklahoma City, OK 73106

Established in 1991 in ND and OK.
Financial data (yr. ended 04/30/01): Grants paid, $0; assets, $845 (M); expenditures, $462; qualifying distributions, $541.
Limitations: Giving primarily in Oklahoma City, OK.
Application information: Application form required.
Officers: Thomas O. Francis, Pres.; Stephen P. Garrett, Secy.; Peter C. Weaver, Treas.
EIN: 450372092

45363
Cyert Family Foundation, Inc.
P.O. Box 1648
Tahlequah, OK 74465

Established in 1998 in PA.
Financial data (yr. ended 12/31/01): Grants paid, $0; assets, $3,080 (M); expenditures, $0; qualifying distributions, $0.
Limitations: Applications not accepted. Giving primarily in Pittsburgh, PA.
Application information: Contributes only to pre-selected organizations.
Trustees: Lynn A. Cyert, Martha S. Cyert, Lucinda C. Steffes.
EIN: 232872274

45364
Delta Dental Plan of Oklahoma Charitable Foundation
P. O. Box 54709
Oklahoma City, OK 73154-1709

Financial data (yr. ended 12/31/99): Grants paid, $0; assets, $9,447 (M); gifts received, $50,000; expenditures, $50,181; qualifying distributions, $50,181.
Limitations: Applications not accepted.
Application information: Contributes only to pre-selected organizations.
Officers: Jim Hampton, Chair.; Homer Hilst, Chair.
Trustees: Bob Berry, S. Chris Clark, G.A. Gillenwater, John Gladden, Gary Hawkins, Tad Mabry.
EIN: 731547145

45365
Eagles Wings Foundation
1437 S. Boulder Ave., Ste. 800
Tulsa, OK 74119

Established in 2001 in OK.
Donor(s): Suzanne Taylor.
Financial data (yr. ended 12/31/01): Grants paid, $0; assets, $629,763 (M); gifts received, $590,682; expenditures, $0; qualifying distributions, $0.
Limitations: Applications not accepted.
Application information: Contributes only to pre-selected organizations.
Officers and Trustees:* Suzanne Taylor,* Pres. and Treas.; Edward Taylor,* Secy.; Rhonda Lawes.
EIN: 731624028

45366
Elrod Family Foundation
c/o Hubert K. Elrod
P.O. Box 292
Guymon, OK 73942

Established in 2001 in OK.
Financial data (yr. ended 12/31/01): Grants paid, $0; assets, $50,216 (M); gifts received, $50,000; expenditures, $0; qualifying distributions, $0.
Officer: D.K. Knusz, Secy.-Treas.
Directors: Jerry D. Balentine, Hubert K. Elrod.
EIN: 731614680

45367
Frates Foundation, Inc.
2642 E. 21st St.
Tulsa, OK 74114

Financial data (yr. ended 11/30/01): Grants paid, $0; assets, $153,204 (M); expenditures, $280; qualifying distributions, $0.
Limitations: Applications not accepted. Giving primarily in Tulsa, OK.
Application information: Contributes only to pre-selected organizations.
Officer: J. Anthony Frates, Pres.
EIN: 346554838

45368
Frontline Productions, Inc.
P.O. Box 341
Tulsa, OK 74170

Financial data (yr. ended 12/31/00): Grants paid, $0; assets, $56,334 (L); gifts received, $28,865; expenditures, $28,880; qualifying distributions, $28,880; giving activities include $28,880 for programs.
Officer: Mike Farell, Pres.
EIN: 731398068

45369
The Pat and Kathryn Gallagher Foundation
2519 E. 21st St.
Tulsa, OK 74114-1746

Established in 1998 in OK.
Donor(s): John P. Gallagher, Katherine F. Gallagher.
Financial data (yr. ended 12/31/01): Grants paid, $0; assets, $1 (M); gifts received, $175; expenditures, $175; qualifying distributions, $0.
Trustees: John P. Gallagher, Alan B. Ross.
EIN: 731551330

45370
Goldie Gibson Scholarship Fund
1601 S.E. Harned Dr.
Bartlesville, OK 74006-5704 (918) 333-5268
Contact: Ruth Andrews, Secy.-Treas.

Financial data (yr. ended 02/28/01): Grants paid, $0; assets, $550,435 (M); expenditures, $3,032; qualifying distributions, $16,910; giving activities include $17,000 for loans to individuals.
Limitations: Giving primarily in OK.
Application information: Application form required.
Officers: Woodrow Staats, Chair.; Ruth Andrews, Secy.-Treas.
Director: Susan Dick.
EIN: 736183311
Codes: GTI

45371
Rick and Jean Gillis Foundation
Rte. 1, Box 244
Bristow, OK 74010

Established in 1998.
Donor(s): Rick Gillis, Jean Gillis.
Financial data (yr. ended 12/31/99): Grants paid, $0; assets, $24,636 (M); expenditures, $0; qualifying distributions, $0.
Officer: Rickey D. Gillis, Pres.
EIN: 730126338

45372
The Harold D. and Hazel H. Hathcoat Educational Trust
P.O. Box 286
Nowata, OK 74048

Established in 1997 in OK.
Donor(s): Harold D. Hathcoat.
Financial data (yr. ended 12/31/00): Grants paid, $0; assets, $455,228 (M); expenditures, $7,367; qualifying distributions, $26,765; giving activities include $26,765 for loans to individuals.
Officer and Trustees:* Roger E. Hathcoat,* Mgr.; Francis Eugene Fry, Frank Hufford, Dale Turney.
EIN: 736300011

45373
Flo & Gordon Holland Family Foundation
P.O. Box 1364
Ponca City, OK 74602

Established in 1999 in OK.
Donor(s): Florence Holland.
Financial data (yr. ended 09/30/00): Grants paid, $0; assets, $161,526 (M); gifts received, $19,495; expenditures, $0; qualifying distributions, $0.
Limitations: Applications not accepted.
Application information: Contributes only to pre-selected organizations.
Officers: Florence Holland, Pres. and Secy.; Gordon Holland, V.P. and Treas.
EIN: 731576866

45374
O. H. and Hattie Mae Lachenmeyer Development Trust
P.O. Box 234
Owasso, OK 74055

Established in 1982.
Financial data (yr. ended 06/30/99): Grants paid, $0; assets, $1,488,479 (M); gifts received, $4,807; expenditures, $67,515; qualifying distributions, $50,926; giving activities include $48,845 for programs.
Limitations: Giving limited to Cushing, OK.
Trustees: Glenna Anderson, Marion Cubbage.
Director: Robert L. Smith.
EIN: 731118154

45375
Lester Family Foundation
13525 Green Cedar Ln.
Oklahoma City, OK 73131

Established in 2001.
Donor(s): J. Mark Lester, Carol A. Lester.

Financial data (yr. ended 12/31/01): Grants paid, $0; assets, $9,500 (M); gifts received, $10,000; expenditures, $500; qualifying distributions, $0.
Trustee: J. Mark Lester.
EIN: 731622433

45376
Lewis Foundation
6532 Tower Ln.
Claremore, OK 74017-4373

Financial data (yr. ended 12/31/01): Grants paid, $0; assets, $117,260 (M); expenditures, $436; qualifying distributions, $0.
Limitations: Applications not accepted. Giving primarily in Tulsa, OK.
Application information: Contributes only to pre-selected organizations.
Trustees: Nancy C. Lewis, Scott C. Lewis, Blair Lewis Williams.
EIN: 736111802

45377
The Nickols Miers Lundy Cancer Research Fund
100 W. 5th St., Ste. 1100
Tulsa, OK 74103-4217
Contact: Sheppard F. Miers, Jr., Tr.

Established in 1998 in OK.
Financial data (yr. ended 12/31/01): Grants paid, $0; assets, $614 (M); gifts received, $500; expenditures, $500; qualifying distributions, $0.
Trustees: Allison Geary, Meredith Miers, Sheppard F. Miers, Jr.
EIN: 731553766

45378
The Maguire Foundation
P.O. Box 14801
Oklahoma City, OK 73113

Established in 1986 in OK.
Donor(s): Joan S. Maguire, Malcolm J. Maguire.
Financial data (yr. ended 12/31/01): Grants paid, $0; assets, $887 (M); gifts received, $650; expenditures, $661; qualifying distributions, $0.
Limitations: Applications not accepted. Giving primarily in Oklahoma City, OK.
Application information: Contributes only to pre-selected organizations.
Trustees: Joan S. Maguire, Malcolm J. Maguire.
EIN: 736229607

45379
Lee C. Moore Charitable Foundation
(Formerly Lee C. Moore Corporation Charity)
c/o Integra Trust Co., N.A.
2679 E. 69th St., Tr. Tax Div.
Tulsa, OK 74136-4343 (918) 492-5037
Contact: J.R. Woolslayer, Tr.

Financial data (yr. ended 03/31/02): Grants paid, $0; assets, $20,712 (M); expenditures, $350; qualifying distributions, $0.
Limitations: Giving primarily in OK.
Application information: Application form not required.
Trustee: J.R. Woolslayer.
EIN: 256019578

45380
Clara Noe Charitable Foundation
P.O. Box 369
Chouteau, OK 74337-0446 (918) 585-2133
Contact: Patricia J. Bates, Tr.

Established in 1989 in OK.

Donor(s): Patricia J. Bates, Robert J. Tutty.
Financial data (yr. ended 06/30/02): Grants paid, $0; assets, $34,873 (M); gifts received, $100; expenditures, $352; qualifying distributions, $0.
Limitations: Giving primarily in OK.
Trustees: Patricia J. Bates, Lyman Carter, Jr., Robert J. Tutty, Joann L. Unruh.
EIN: 731346290

45381
Oklahoma Trial Lawyers Foundation, Inc.
2624 E. 21st St., Ste. 1
Tulsa, OK 74114-1708

Established in 1989 in OK.
Donor(s): Glenn R. Beustring.
Financial data (yr. ended 12/31/01): Grants paid, $0; assets, $50,139 (M); expenditures, $752; qualifying distributions, $0.
Limitations: Applications not accepted. Giving limited to OK.
Application information: Contributes only to pre-selected organizations.
Officers: Glenn R. Beustring, Pres.; Cameron Spradling, V.P.; W.C. Sellers, Secy.-Treas.
EIN: 731332446

45382
Penner Foundation
3336 Rock Hollow Rd.
Oklahoma City, OK 73120-1930

Established in 2001 in OK.
Donor(s): Frederic J. Penner, Jennifer F. Penner.
Financial data (yr. ended 12/31/01): Grants paid, $0; assets, $50,531 (M); gifts received, $50,500; expenditures, $0; qualifying distributions, $0.
Limitations: Applications not accepted.
Application information: Contributes only to pre-selected organizations.
Trustees: Frederic J. Penner, Jennifer F. Penner.
EIN: 736331817

45383
Linda Mitchell Price Charitable Foundation, Inc.
2136 E. 26th Pl.
Tulsa, OK 74114
Contact: William Stuart Price, Pres.

Established in 1990.
Donor(s): William Stuart Price.
Financial data (yr. ended 12/31/00): Grants paid, $0; assets, $130,469 (M); expenditures, $0; qualifying distributions, $0.
Limitations: Giving primarily in Tulsa, OK.
Officer and Director:* William Stuart Price,* Pres.
EIN: 731373368

45384
Sonar Foundation, Inc.
7110 S. Mingo, Ste. 107
Tulsa, OK 74133

Financial data (yr. ended 12/31/99): Grants paid, $0; assets, $1,675 (M); gifts received, $2,727; expenditures, $3,182; qualifying distributions, $0.
Officers: Thomas Elliott, Pres.; A.H. Kahn, V.P.; Rich DiGregorio, Secy.
EIN: 731569265

45385
A. R. & Marylouise Tandy Foundation
10 E. 3rd St., Ste. 400
Tulsa, OK 74103-3616

Established in 1985 in OK.
Donor(s): Marylouise Tandy Cowan.

Financial data (yr. ended 12/31/01): Grants paid, $0; assets, $2,067,506 (M); expenditures, $6,038; qualifying distributions, $0.
Limitations: Applications not accepted. Giving primarily in ME.
Application information: Contributes only to pre-selected organizations.
Trustees: Marylouise Tandy Cowan, Joe M. Holliman.
EIN: 731254985

45386
Treeman Family Foundation, Inc.
P.O. Box 1300
Salina, OK 74365

Established in 2001 in OK.
Donor(s): Jeff Treeman.‡
Financial data (yr. ended 12/31/01): Grants paid, $0; assets, $217,306 (M); gifts received, $238,992; expenditures, $0; qualifying distributions, $0.
Limitations: Applications not accepted.
Application information: Contributes only to pre-selected organizations.
Director: Chris Treeman.
EIN: 731589305

45387
Edward and Karen Wachtmeister Foundation
2519 E. 21st St.
Tulsa, OK 74114-1746

Established in 1994.
Donor(s): Edward Wachtmeister, Karen Weichtmeister.
Financial data (yr. ended 12/31/01): Grants paid, $0; assets, $1 (M); expenditures, $0; qualifying distributions, $0.
Limitations: Giving primarily in Salisbury, CT.
Trustees: Mark Riley, Alan B. Ross, Edward C.A. Wachtmeister.
EIN: 731447855

45388
Jon R. Winthrow Charitable Foundation
P.O. Box 1239
Oklahoma City, OK 73101

Established in 2001 in OK.
Donor(s): Jon R. Withrow.
Financial data (yr. ended 12/31/01): Grants paid, $0; assets, $9,978 (M); gifts received, $10,000; expenditures, $23; qualifying distributions, $0.
Limitations: Applications not accepted.
Application information: Contributes only to pre-selected organizations.
Officers and Trustees:* Jon R. Withrow, Chair. and Pres.; Charles M. McFarland,* Secy.-Treas.
EIN: 736330107

45389
Woodson Family Foundation
R.R. 3, Box 23E
Ardmore, OK 73401-9513

Established in 2001 in OK.
Donor(s): James C. Woodson, Connie L. Woodson.
Financial data (yr. ended 12/31/01): Grants paid, $0; assets, $3,445 (M); gifts received, $5,000; expenditures, $1,577; qualifying distributions, $0.
Limitations: Applications not accepted.
Application information: Contributes only to pre-selected organizations.
Trustees: Connie L. Woodson, James C. Woodson.
EIN: 731615556

45390
Young Family Foundation
24481 S. Manard Rd.
Fort Gibson, OK 74434-6386
Application address: c/o Joseph P. Rigali, G.W. & Wade, Inc., 62 Walnut St., Wellesley, MA 02481-2109

Established in 2000 in MA.
Donor(s): Tina B. Young, E. Ryker Young.
Financial data (yr. ended 11/30/01): Grants paid, $0; assets, $6,603,815 (M); expenditures, $139,783; qualifying distributions, $0.

Trustees: E. Ryker Young, Tina B. Young.
EIN: 043525914

45391
Zion's Gate Ministries
9205 Nawassa
Midwest City, OK 73130

Financial data (yr. ended 12/31/99): Grants paid, $0; assets, $9,074 (L); gifts received, $69,355; expenditures, $73,538; qualifying distributions, $72,780; giving activities include $68,939 for programs.

Officers: Gary C. Bachman, Pres.; Connie Bachman, V.P.
EIN: 731123544

OREGON—45399

OREGON

45392
The Oregon Community Foundation
1221 S.W. Yamhill, No. 100
Portland, OR 97205 (503) 227-6846
FAX: (503) 274-7771; E-mail: info@ocf1.org;
URL: http://www.ocf1.org
Contact: Gregory A. Chaille, Pres.

Established in 1973 in OR.
Financial data (yr. ended 12/31/00): Grants paid, $36,406,143; assets, $471,989,656 (M); gifts received, $81,322,109; expenditures, $42,458,819.
Limitations: Giving limited to OR.
Publications: Annual report, newsletter, program policy statement, application guidelines, occasional report, informational brochure.
Application information: Applications sent by FAX are not accepted. Application form required.
Officers and Directors:* William Thorndike, Jr.,* Chair.; Benjamin Whiteley,* Vice-Chair.; Gregory A. Chaille, Pres.; Kathleen Cornett, V.P., Progs.; Brenda VanKanegan, V.P., Finance and Admin.; David Westcott, V.P., Dev.; Mary K. Mark,* Secy.; James A. Meyer, Treas.; George Bell, Duncan Campbell, Steve Corey, Scott Gibson, Lyn Hennion, Eric B. Lindauer, Linda Moore, Gretchen Pierce, Janet Webster, Mary D. Wilcox.
Investment Managers: Columbia Management, Putnam Investments, Inc., Miller Andersen Sherrerel.
EIN: 237315673
Codes: CM, FD, FM, GTI

45393
Intel Foundation
c/o Prog. Off.
5200 N.E. Elam Young Pkwy., AG6-601
Hillsboro, OR 97124-6497
FAX: (503) 456-1539; E-mail:
intel.foundation@intel.com; URL: http://www.intel.com/education/sections/corporate3/index.htm

Established in 1988 in OR.
Donor(s): Intel Corp.
Financial data (yr. ended 12/31/01): Grants paid, $27,850,584; assets, $58,286,500 (M); gifts received, $7,800; expenditures, $27,850,584; qualifying distributions, $27,811,119.
Limitations: Applications not accepted. Giving primarily in major operating areas in Phoenix, AZ, Santa Clara, San Diego and Folsom, CA, Colorado Springs, CO, Albuquerque, NM, Hudson, MA, Portland, OR, Austin, TX, Riverton, UT, and Dupont, WA.
Publications: Annual report.
Officers and Directors:* Craig Barrett,* Chair.; Wendy Hawkens,* Pres.; Patty Murray,* Secy.; Leslie Culbertson,* Treas.; Carlene Ellis.
EIN: 943092928
Codes: CS, FD, CD, FM, GTI

45394
Meyer Memorial Trust
(Formerly Fred Meyer Charitable Trust)
1515 S.W. 5th Ave., Ste. 500
Portland, OR 97201 (503) 228-5512
E-mail: mmt@mmt.org; URL: http://www.mmt.org
Contact: Doug Stamm, Exec. Dir.

Trust established by will in 1978; obtained IRS status in 1982 in OR.
Donor(s): Fred G. Meyer.‡
Financial data (yr. ended 03/31/02): Grants paid, $22,130,646; assets, $475,766,000 (M); expenditures, $26,970,827; qualifying distributions, $21,718,146.
Limitations: Giving primarily in OR and Clark County, WA.
Publications: Annual report, application guidelines.
Application information: Special guidelines for Small Grants Program and Support for Teacher Initiatives Program. Application guidelines and cover sheet available on the internet. Application form required.
Officers and Trustees:* Debbie F. Craig,* Chair.; Wayne G. Pierson, C.F.O. and Treas.; Doug Stamm, Exec. Dir.; John Emrick, Orcilla Z. Forbes, Warne Nunn, Gerry Pratt.
EIN: 930806316
Codes: FD, FM

45395
The Ford Family Foundation
1600 N.W. Stewart Pkwy.
Roseburg, OR 97470 (541) 957-5574
FAX: (541) 957-5720; URL: http://www.tfff.org
Contact: Norman J. Smith, Pres.

Incorporated in 1957 in OR.
Donor(s): Kenneth W. Ford,‡ Hallie E. Ford.
Financial data (yr. ended 03/31/01): Grants paid, $15,319,855; assets, $483,138,339 (M); gifts received, $5,251,710; expenditures, $19,882,998; qualifying distributions, $18,617,819.
Limitations: Giving primarily in rural OR, with special interest in Douglas and Coos counties and in Siskiyou County, CA.
Publications: Annual report, informational brochure (including application guidelines).
Application information: Accepts unsolicited requests three times per year. Application form required.
Officers and Directors:* Ronald C. Parker,* Chair.; Norman J. Smith, Pres.; Allyn C. Ford,* Secy.-Treas.; Gerald E. Bruce, Joseph P. Kearns, Sally M. McCracken, Carmen R. Phillips, Charles U. Walker.
EIN: 936026156
Codes: FD, FM, GTI

45396
The Collins Foundation
1618 S.W. 1st Ave., Ste. 505
Portland, OR 97201-5708 (503) 227-7171
FAX: (503) 295-3794; URL: http://www.collinsfoundation.org
Contact: Jerry E. Hudson, Exec. V.P.

Incorporated in 1947 in OR.
Donor(s): Members of the Collins family.
Financial data (yr. ended 12/31/00): Grants paid, $7,996,859; assets, $180,072,848 (M); expenditures, $8,870,164; qualifying distributions, $8,269,042.
Limitations: Giving limited to OR, with emphasis on Portland.
Publications: Annual report (including application guidelines), informational brochure.
Application information: Application form not required.
Officers and Trustees:* Maribeth W. Collins,* Pres.; Jerry E. Hudson, Exec. V.P.; Ralph Bolliger,* V.P.; Truman W. Collins, Jr.,* V.P.; Cherida C. Smith,* V.P.; Cynthia G. Addams, Secy. and Prog. Dir.; Timothy R. Bishop, Treas.
EIN: 936021893
Codes: FD, FM

45397
The Jeld-Wen Foundation
(Formerly Jeld-Wen, Wenco Foundation)
P.O. Box 1329
Klamath Falls, OR 97601 (541) 882-3451
Contact: Carol Chestnut

Established in 1969.
Donor(s): Jeld-Wen, Inc., Jeld-Wen Fiber Products, Inc. of Iowa, Jeld-Wen Co. of Arizona, Wenco, Inc. of North Carolina, Wenco, Inc. of Ohio, and other Jeld-Wen, Inc. companies.
Financial data (yr. ended 12/31/00): Grants paid, $5,575,784; assets, $45,115,030 (M); gifts received, $1,000,000; expenditures, $5,781,741; qualifying distributions, $5,542,361.
Limitations: Giving primarily in areas of company operations in AZ, FL, IA, KY, NC, OH, OR, SD, and WA for projects serving communities in which company plants exist; projects in adjacent communities may be accepted if sufficient numbers of employees reside in the area and would benefit.
Publications: Program policy statement, application guidelines.
Application information: Application form required.
Officer and Trustees:* R.C. Wendt,* Secy.; W.B. Early, Nancy Wendt, R.L. Wendt, L.V. Wetter.
EIN: 936054272
Codes: CS, FD, CD, FM

45398
Lora L. & Martin N. Kelley Family Foundation Trust
P.O. Box 23503
Eugene, OR 97402

Established in 1990 in OR.
Donor(s): Martin N. Kelley, Lora L. Kelley.
Financial data (yr. ended 12/31/01): Grants paid, $4,927,610; assets, $20,315,786 (M); expenditures, $5,152,835; qualifying distributions, $4,977,265.
Limitations: Applications not accepted. Giving primarily in MT and OR.
Application information: Contributes only to pre-selected organizations.
Officers and Trustees:* Bruce R. Kelley,* Vice-Chair.; Craig C. Kelley,* Secy.; Karen D. Kelley, Kent R. Kelley, Mark Kelley, Martin N. Kelley, Stephen S. Kelley.
EIN: 476174269
Codes: FD

45399
Knight Foundation
1 Bowerman Dr.
Beaverton, OR 97005 (503) 671-3500

Established in 1997 in OR.
Donor(s): Philip H. Knight.
Financial data (yr. ended 12/31/00): Grants paid, $3,000,000; assets, $57,507,732 (M); gifts received, $3,000,000; expenditures, $3,017,099; qualifying distributions, $2,997,684.
Limitations: Applications not accepted.
Application information: Contributes only to pre-selected organizations.
Officers and Directors:* Philip H. Knight, Pres. and Treas.; Brian G. Booth,* V.P. and Secy.; Penelope P. Knight,* V.P.
EIN: 911791788
Codes: FD

45400
NIKE Foundation
(Formerly NIKE P.L.A.Y. Foundation)
c/o NIKE, Inc.
1 Bowerman Dr.
Beaverton, OR 97005-6453 (503) 671-6453
URL: http://www.nikebiz.com
Contact: Maria Eitel, Pres.

Established in 1994 in OR.
Donor(s): NIKE, Inc., Michael Jordan.
Financial data (yr. ended 05/31/02): Grants paid, $2,336,000; assets, $1,075,306 (M); gifts received, $2,915,595; expenditures, $2,391,024; qualifying distributions, $2,391,024.
Limitations: Giving primarily in areas of company operations, including Beaverton, Portland, and Wilsonville, OR, and Memphis, TN, and cities where Niketown retail centers are located.
Publications: Application guidelines.
Application information: See foundation website for complete application guidelines. Application form not required.
Officers: Maria Eitel, Pres.; Marcia Stewart, Treas.
Directors: Charlie Denson, Philip Knight, Mark Parker, Kirk Stewart, Lindsay D. Stewart.
EIN: 931159948
Codes: CS, FD, CD

45401
PacifiCorp Foundation for Learning
(Formerly PacifiCorp Foundation)
825 N.E. Multnomah St., Ste. 2000
Portland, OR 97232 (503) 813-7257
FAX: (503) 813-7249; E-mail: pacificorpfoundation@pacificorp.com; URL: http://www.pacificorpfoundation.org
Contact: Isaac Regenstreif, Exec. Dir.

Established in 1988 in OR.
Donor(s): PacifiCorp.
Financial data (yr. ended 03/31/02): Grants paid, $2,274,322; assets, $35,500,000 (M); expenditures, $2,782,903; qualifying distributions, $2,274,322.
Limitations: Giving primarily in major operating areas in the Northwest, where PacifiCorp has operations, business interests, employees or customers; emphasis on northern CA, ID, OR, UT, WA, and WY.
Publications: Informational brochure (including application guidelines).
Application information: Application form required.
Officers and Directors:* Michael J. Pittman,* Chair.; Pamela Bradford, Secy.; Bruce Williams, Treas.; Isaac Regenstreif II, Exec. Dir.; Barry Cunningham, Donald Furman, Jack Kelly, William Landels, Amanda Nelson, Richard Walje.
EIN: 943089826
Codes: CS, FD, CD, FM

45402
Juan Young Trust
Western Division
P.O. Box 91452
Portland, OR 97291 (503) 735-9831
Additional address: Eastern Division: Scott G. Klusmann, 2020 S.W. 8th Ave., PMB252, West Linn, OR 97068, tel: (503) 702-7080, FAX: (503) 650-0259, E-mail: edjyz@ipns.com; Contact E-mail: juanyoungtrust@msn.com; URL: http://www.gosw.org/juanyoungtrust
Contact: Antoinette K. Arenz, Tr. and Scott C. Klusmann, Tr.

Established in 1996 in OR under the will of Juan Young; funded in 1999.
Donor(s): Juan Young.‡

Financial data (yr. ended 12/31/01): Grants paid, $2,200,626; assets, $25,400,846 (M); expenditures, $2,634,498; qualifying distributions, $2,470,466.
Limitations: Giving limited to OR, with emphasis on the greater Portland area.
Publications: Informational brochure (including application guidelines), grants list, application guidelines.
Application information: See foundation's Web site for additional information. Application form required.
Trustees: Antoinette K. Arenz, Scott G. Klusmann.
EIN: 931245000
Codes: FD

45403
Chiles Foundation
111 S.W. 5th Ave., Ste. 4050
Portland, OR 97204-3643 (503) 222-2143
E-mail: cf@uswest.net

Incorporated in 1949 in OR.
Donor(s): Eva Chiles Meyer,‡ Earle A. Chiles,‡ Virginia H. Chiles.‡
Financial data (yr. ended 12/31/01): Grants paid, $1,784,150; assets, $19,325,175 (M); expenditures, $2,634,020; qualifying distributions, $2,215,897.
Application information: Call foundation for application deadlines. Application form required.
Officer and Trustees:* Earle M. Chiles,* Pres.; Michael Arthur, Pedro Garcia.
EIN: 936031125
Codes: FD, FM

45404
Clark Foundation
P.O. Box 25373
Portland, OR 97298 (503) 223-5290
Contact: Mary Clark, Pres. and Treas.

Established in 1968 in OR.
Donor(s): Maurie D. Clark.‡
Financial data (yr. ended 12/31/00): Grants paid, $1,725,145; assets, $30,100 (M); gifts received, $1,795,000; expenditures, $1,807,663; qualifying distributions, $1,808,621.
Limitations: Giving primarily in the Portland, OR, area.
Publications: Grants list.
Application information: Application form not required.
Officers and Directors:* Mary H. Clark,* Pres. and Treas.; Patrick E. Becker,* Secy.; Candace Clark Beber, Richard M. Clark, Steven A. Nicholes.
EIN: 237423789
Codes: FD

45405
Phillip S. Miller Charitable Trust
c/o U.S. Bank
P.O. Box 3168 Tax Svcs.
Portland, OR 97208-3168
Contact: Deborah J. Smith

Established in 1995 in CO.
Donor(s): Phillip S. Miller.‡
Financial data (yr. ended 12/31/00): Grants paid, $1,678,282; assets, $38,534,492 (L); expenditures, $1,874,705; qualifying distributions, $1,664,094.
Limitations: Applications not accepted. Giving limited to CO.
Application information: Contributes only to pre-selected organizations. Unsolicited requests not considered.
Trustee: U.S. Bank.
EIN: 846290472
Codes: FD

45406
B. P., Lester and Regina John Foundation
(Formerly B. P. John Foundation)
1000 S.W. Vista Ave., Ste. 116
Portland, OR 97205
FAX: (503) 223-9920
Contact: Patricia J. Abraham, Pres.

Established in 1971.
Donor(s): Lester M. John,‡ Regina M. John.
Financial data (yr. ended 12/31/00): Grants paid, $1,322,350; assets, $21,743,639 (M); gifts received, $808,261; expenditures, $1,379,399; qualifying distributions, $1,296,256.
Limitations: Applications not accepted. Giving primarily in Portland, OR.
Application information: Contributes only to pre-selected organizations.
Officers and Trustees:* Patricia J. Abraham,* Pres.; Mary Amstad, Secy.; Philip T. Abraham, Regina M. John.
EIN: 237110263
Codes: FD

45407
Leo Adler Community Trust
(Formerly Leo Adler Trust)
c/o U.S. Bank
P.O. Box 3168
Portland, OR 97208-3168
Contact: Marlyn Norquist, Trust Off., U.S. Bank

Established in 1993 in OR.
Donor(s): Leo Adler.‡
Financial data (yr. ended 12/31/01): Grants paid, $1,315,801; assets, $25,592,850 (M); gifts received, $150; expenditures, $1,722,862; qualifying distributions, $1,391,383.
Limitations: Giving limited to North Powder School District or a school district of Baker County, OR (for scholarships); grants for organizations primarily in Baker County, OR.
Publications: Informational brochure.
Application information: Application forms can be obtained at the counseling offices of eligible high schools or at U.S. Bank, Baker City Branch, between Jan. 1 and Mar. 30. Application form required.
Trustee: U.S. Bank.
EIN: 936289087
Codes: FD, GTI

45408
The Honzel Family Foundation
12929 S.W. Forest Meadows Way
Lake Oswego, OR 97034-1593

Established in 1996 in OR.
Donor(s): Andrew J. Honzel.
Financial data (yr. ended 12/31/00): Grants paid, $1,311,500; assets, $27,932,171 (M); expenditures, $1,562,489; qualifying distributions, $1,283,084.
Limitations: Applications not accepted. Giving on a national basis.
Application information: Contributes only to pre-selected organizations.
Trustees: Andrew J. Honzel, Beverly J. Honzel.
EIN: 931223928
Codes: FD

45409
The Clemens Foundation
P.O. Box 427
Philomath, OR 97370
Contact: Kelly Howard, Exec. Dir.

Incorporated in 1959 in OR.
Donor(s): Rex Clemens,‡ Ethel M. Clemens,‡ Rex Veneer Co.

Financial data (yr. ended 12/31/00): Grants paid, $1,266,786; assets, $32,472,416 (M); expenditures, $1,363,393; qualifying distributions, $1,314,726.
Limitations: Applications not accepted. Giving limited to residents of Philomath, Eddyville, Crane, and Alsea, OR.
Officers and Trustees:* David Lowther,* Pres.; Steven Lowther, V.P.; Ron Edwards,* Secy.; Fred Lowther,* Treas.; Kelly D. Howard,* Exec. Dir.; Elwood Berklund, Wayne L. Howard, Thad Springer.
EIN: 936023941
Codes: FD, GTI

45410
Rose E. Tucker Charitable Trust
900 S.W. 5th Ave., 24th Fl.
Portland, OR 97204 (503) 224-3380
Contact: Thomas B. Stoel, Tr., or Milo E. Ormseth, Tr.

Trust established in 1976 in OR.
Donor(s): Rose E. Tucker,‡ Max and Rose Tucker Foundation.
Financial data (yr. ended 06/30/01): Grants paid, $1,240,750; assets, $23,122,810 (M); expenditures, $1,444,367; qualifying distributions, $1,307,368.
Limitations: Giving limited to organizations and projects in OR, with emphasis on the metropolitan Portland area.
Publications: Annual report (including application guidelines), grants list, application guidelines.
Application information: Organizations may only apply once within a 12 month period. Application form not required.
Trustees: Milo E. Ormseth, Thomas B. Stoel, U.S. Bank, N.A.
EIN: 936119091
Codes: FD

45411
PGE-Enron Foundation
(Formerly PGE Foundation)
121 S.W. Salmon St.
Portland, OR 97204-2901
URL: http://www.pge-enronfoundation.org
Contact: Kathy Koonts, Contribs. Coord.

Established in 1994 in OR.
Donor(s): Portland General Electric Co.
Financial data (yr. ended 12/31/00): Grants paid, $1,239,891; assets, $22,992,328 (M); expenditures, $1,635,003; qualifying distributions, $1,563,655.
Limitations: Giving primarily in OR.
Officers and Directors:* Gwyneth Gamble-Booth,* Chair.; Carol Dillin, Pres.; Rosalie Duron,* Secy.; Mary Turina,* Treas.; David K. Carboneau, Peggy Y. Fowler, Jerry E. Hudson, Fred D. Miller, Randolf L. Miller, Cindy K. Olson.
EIN: 931138806
Codes: CS, FD, CD

45412
The Lazar Foundation
715 S.W. Morrison St., No. 901
Portland, OR 97204 (503) 225-0265
FAX: (503) 225-9620; E-mail: info@lazarfoundation.org; URL: http://www.lazarfoundation.org
Contact: Irene Vlach

Incorporated in 1956 in DE.
Donor(s): Jack Lazar,‡ Helen B. Lazar.‡
Financial data (yr. ended 12/31/00): Grants paid, $980,269; assets, $19,955,173 (M); gifts received, $1,583,866; expenditures, $2,114,016; qualifying distributions, $980,269.

Limitations: Giving primarily in AK, ID, MT, OR, and WA in the U.S., and British Columbia in Canada.
Publications: Grants list, application guidelines.
Application information: Application form required.
Officers and Trustees:* William B. Lazar,* Pres. and Treas.; Jeanne L. Morency,* Secy.; Anne Lazar, Michael Morency.
EIN: 136088182
Codes: FD

45413
The Autzen Foundation
P.O. Box 3709
Portland, OR 97208 (503) 226-6051
Contact: Robin Stewart, Admin.

Incorporated in 1951 in OR.
Donor(s): Thomas J. Autzen.‡
Financial data (yr. ended 12/31/01): Grants paid, $933,857; assets, $18,114,100 (M); expenditures, $1,019,188; qualifying distributions, $968,633.
Limitations: Giving primarily in OR, with some emphasis on Portland. Giving limited to the Pacific Northwest region.
Application information: Application form not required.
Officers and Directors:* Henry C. Houser,* Pres.; Christina Grady,* Secy.; Thomas J. Autzen, Gregory Houser, Robert W. Patton III, Wendy Ulman.
EIN: 936021333
Codes: FD

45414
Braemar Charitable Trust
P.O. Box 25442
Portland, OR 97225
Application address: Dick Lanthrum, c/o Trust Mgmt. Svcs., P.O. Box 1990, Waldport, OR 97394; URL: http://www.trustmanagementservices.net
Contact: Martha B. Cox, Tr.

Established in 1993 in OR.
Donor(s): Hobart M. Bird, Marion A. Bird.
Financial data (yr. ended 09/30/01): Grants paid, $860,444; assets, $15,462,143 (M); gifts received, $1,276,728; expenditures, $1,061,406; qualifying distributions, $929,916.
Limitations: Giving limited to OR.
Application information: Application form required.
Trustees: Hobart M. Bird, Marian A. Bird, Martha B. Cox, Melanie A. Dawson.
EIN: 936272124
Codes: FD

45415
Walters Family Foundation
c/o BKR Fordham, Goodfellow, LLP
233 S.E. 2nd Ave.
Hillsboro, OR 97123
Contact: Clifford Walters, Dir.

Established in 2000 in OR.
Donor(s): Glenn Walters, Viola Walters.
Financial data (yr. ended 09/30/01): Grants paid, $850,761; assets, $4,405,440 (M); gifts received, $636,890; expenditures, $936,835; qualifying distributions, $848,942.
Limitations: Giving primarily in the metropolitan Portland, OR, area with emphasis on the Hillsboro area.
Directors: Lester Fordham, Jr., James Thompson, Clifford Walters, Glenn Walters, Viola Walters.
EIN: 931280994
Codes: FD

45416
The Carpenter Foundation
711 E. Main St., Ste. 10
Medford, OR 97504 (541) 772-5851
Additional tel.: (541) 772-5732; FAX: (541) 773-3970; E-mail: carpfdn@internetcds.com
Contact: Polly Williams, Prog. Off., or Jane Carpenter, Pres.

Incorporated in 1957 in OR.
Donor(s): Helen Bundy Carpenter,‡ Alfred S.V. Carpenter.‡
Financial data (yr. ended 06/30/02): Grants paid, $834,795; assets, $16,148,812 (M); gifts received, $1,000; expenditures, $969,320; qualifying distributions, $834,795.
Limitations: Giving limited to Jackson and Josephine counties, OR.
Publications: Annual report (including application guidelines), financial statement, grants list, informational brochure (including application guidelines).
Application information: Application form not required.
Officers and Trustees:* Jane H. Carpenter,* Pres.; Emily C. Mostue,* V.P.; Karen C. Allan,* Secy.; Dunbar Carpenter,* Treas.; A. Brian Mostue.
Public Trustees: Susan Cohen, Mary Ellen Fleeger, Burke Raymond, Dan Thorndyke, Polly Williams, Prog. Off.
EIN: 930491360
Codes: FD

45417
Maybelle Clark Macdonald Fund
5200 S.W. Macadam Ave., Ste. 470
Portland, OR 97201 (503) 291-9575

Established about 1970.
Donor(s): Maybelle Clark Macdonald.
Financial data (yr. ended 06/30/01): Grants paid, $820,296; assets, $125,581,289 (M); gifts received, $118,550,375; expenditures, $839,026; qualifying distributions, $828,433.
Limitations: Applications not accepted. Giving primarily in OR.
Application information: Contributes only to pre-selected organizations.
Officers and Directors:* Maybelle Clark Macdonald,* Chair.; Clark C. Munro, Sr.,* Pres.; Christian A. Folkestad,* Secy.-Treas.; Gary R. Branden, Gene D'Autremont, Monique M. McCleary, Conrad L. Moore, Clark C. Munro, Jr., Warner R. Munro.
EIN: 237108002
Codes: FD

45418
Fohs Foundation
P.O. Box 1001
Roseburg, OR 97470
Contact: Rose Mary Cooper, Secy.-Treas.

Trust established in 1937 in NY.
Donor(s): F. Julius Fohs,‡ Cora B. Fohs.‡
Financial data (yr. ended 12/31/01): Grants paid, $817,430; assets, $15,778,195 (M); expenditures, $926,305; qualifying distributions, $825,687.
Limitations: Giving primarily in OR; some giving also in Israel.
Application information: Application form not required.
Officers: Frances F. Sohn, Chair.; Fred Sohn, Vice-Chair.; Rose Mary Cooper, Secy.-Treas.
Trustees: Edward F. Sohn, Howard F. Sohn, Mark F. Sohn, Richard F. Sohn, Ruth Sohn.
EIN: 746003165
Codes: FD

45419
The Faith Foundation, Inc.
2746 Front St., N.E.
Salem, OR 97303
Contact: Daniel L. Kerr, Secy.-Treas.

Established in 1993 in OR.
Financial data (yr. ended 12/31/01): Grants paid, $813,500; assets, $16,594,885 (M); gifts received, $2,200,250; expenditures, $834,736; qualifying distributions, $1,805,855; giving activities include $984,685 for loans.
Limitations: Giving primarily in OR.
Application information: Application form not required.
Officers and Directors:* Richard G. Faith,* Pres.; Jodie Ross, V.P.; Jennifer Rowland,* V.P.; Daniel L. Kerr,* Secy.-Treas.
EIN: 931115227
Codes: FD

45420
Cottage Grove Community Foundation
P.O. Box 1326
Cottage Grove, OR 97424

Financial data (yr. ended 06/30/00): Grants paid, $810,000; assets, $47,827 (M); gifts received, $890,767; expenditures, $856,810.
Limitations: Giving limited to the Cottage Grove, OR, area.
Officers: Sherry Duerst-Higgins, Pres.; Bud Stewart, Secy.
Directors: Lila Creager, David Gant, Rudy Haskell, Roger Russell, Darrel Williams, Gary Williams, Casey Woodward, Ralph Zeller.
EIN: 943138507
Codes: CM, FD

45421
The Jackson Foundation
c/o U.S. Bank, Trust Group
P.O. Box 3168
Portland, OR 97208 (503) 275-6564
Contact: Robert H. Depew, V.P., U.S. Bank

Trust established in 1960 in OR; Philip Ludwell Jackson Charitable and Residual Trusts were merged into The Jackson Foundation in 1981.
Donor(s): Maria C. Jackson.‡
Financial data (yr. ended 06/30/01): Grants paid, $793,460; assets, $16,116,768 (M); expenditures, $1,003,649; qualifying distributions, $909,455.
Limitations: Giving limited to OR.
Publications: Annual report.
Application information: Application form required.
Trustees: Milo E. Ormseth, Julie Vigeland, U.S. Bank.
EIN: 936020752
Codes: FD

45422
Chambers Family Foundation
2295 Coburg Rd., Ste. 304
Eugene, OR 97401 (541) 484-2419
FAX: (541) 342-2695
Contact: Carolyn Chambers, Tr.

Established in 1999 in OR.
Donor(s): Carolyn S. Chambers.
Financial data (yr. ended 12/31/01): Grants paid, $769,700; assets, $18,303,035 (M); gifts received, $4,200,000; expenditures, $901,265; qualifying distributions, $799,210.
Limitations: Giving primarily in Lane, Benton and Deschutes counties, OR.
Publications: Informational brochure (including application guidelines).
Application information: Application form required.
Trustees: Carolyn S. Chambers, Elizabeth Chambers, Silva Sullivan.
EIN: 931266648
Codes: FD

45423
Harold & Arlene Schnitzer CARE Foundation
c/o Theodore P. Malaska
P.O. Box 2708
Portland, OR 97208-2708 (503) 973-0286
Contact: Barbara Hall, Admin.

Established in 1994 in OR.
Donor(s): Harold J. Schnitzer, Arlene Schnitzer.
Financial data (yr. ended 12/31/00): Grants paid, $762,050; assets, $67,094,952 (M); gifts received, $1,010; expenditures, $3,248,224; qualifying distributions, $1,167,150; giving activities include $289,732 for programs.
Limitations: Giving primarily in OR and southwest WA.
Publications: Application guidelines.
Application information: Application form not required.
Officers and Directors:* Harold J. Schnitzer,* Pres.; Thomas E. Eyer,* Sr. V.P.; Barbara Hall, V.P.; Theodore P. Malaska, V.P.; Arlene Schnitzer,* Secy.-Treas.; Jordan D. Schnitzer.
EIN: 931159884
Codes: FD

45424
Tektronix Foundation
P.O. Box 5000, M.S. 55-715
Beaverton, OR 97077
Contact: Lisa Aubin

Incorporated in 1952 in OR.
Donor(s): Tektronix, Inc.
Financial data (yr. ended 12/31/01): Grants paid, $748,617; assets, $2,323,523 (M); gifts received, $1,100,000; expenditures, $1,334,709; qualifying distributions, $748,729.
Limitations: Applications not accepted. Giving primarily in OR.
Application information: Unsolicited requests for funds not accepted.
Officers and Trustees:* James F. Dalton,* Chair.; Rich McBee, V.P., Worldwide Sales and Marketing; Barbara Gaffney, V.P., Human Resources.
EIN: 936021540
Codes: CS, FD, CD, GTI

45425
Donald E. Tykeson Foundation
P.O. Box 70006
Eugene, OR 97401

Established in 1995 in OR.
Financial data (yr. ended 12/31/01): Grants paid, $649,604; assets, $13,557,715 (M); expenditures, $785,611; qualifying distributions, $706,363.
Limitations: Applications not accepted. Giving primarily in OR.
Application information: Contributes only to pre-selected organizations.
Officers and Directors:* Donald E. Tykeson,* Pres.; Amy C. Tykeson,* V.P.; Thomas H. Palmer,* Treas.
EIN: 931192478
Codes: FD

45426
Hedinger Family Foundation
1750 N.W. Front Ave., Ste. 106
Portland, OR 97209

Established in 1998 in OR.
Donor(s): American Industries, Inc.
Financial data (yr. ended 12/31/01): Grants paid, $641,028; assets, $129,052 (M); gifts received, $425,000; expenditures, $646,694; qualifying distributions, $641,442.
Limitations: Applications not accepted. Giving primarily in OR.
Application information: Contributes only to pre-selected organizations.
Directors: Hillary H. Clausen, Barkley H. Hedinger, Blake H. Hedinger, Howard H. Hedinger, Juanita Wyndham.
EIN: 931255431
Codes: CS, FD, CD

45427
Wheeler Foundation
1211 S.W. 5th Ave., Ste. 2906
Portland, OR 97204-1911 (503) 228-0261
Contact: Samuel C. Wheeler, Pres.

Established in 1965 in OR.
Donor(s): Coleman H. Wheeler,‡ Coleman H. Wheeler, Jr.,‡ Cornelia T. Wheeler.‡
Financial data (yr. ended 12/31/01): Grants paid, $610,500; assets, $15,484,567 (M); expenditures, $625,656; qualifying distributions, $624,846.
Limitations: Giving primarily in OR.
Application information: Application form not required.
Officers and Directors:* Samuel C. Wheeler,* Pres.; Charles B. Wheeler,* V.P.; John C. Wheeler,* V.P.; Edward T. Wheeler,* Secy.; Thomas K. Wheeler,* Treas.
EIN: 930553801
Codes: FD

45428
Pamplin Foundation
805 S.W. Broadway, Ste. 2400
Portland, OR 97205

Established in 1959.
Donor(s): Robert B. Pamplin, Katherine R. Pamplin.
Financial data (yr. ended 12/31/01): Grants paid, $578,455; assets, $73,009,529 (M); gifts received, $3,504,820; expenditures, $3,775,124; qualifying distributions, $4,570,117; giving activities include $4,570,117 for programs.
Limitations: Giving primarily in Portland, OR.
Officers and Directors:* Robert B. Pamplin, Chair.; Robert B. Pamplin, Jr.,* Secy.; Katherine R. Pamplin.
EIN: 936031259
Codes: FD

45429
Glen Boyd Charitable Foundation
2445 N.W. Westover Rd., Ste. 504
Portland, OR 97210
Contact: W. Glen Boyd, Tr.

Established in 2000 in OR.
Donor(s): W. Glen Boyd.
Financial data (yr. ended 12/31/01): Grants paid, $566,550; assets, $11,173,681 (M); expenditures, $591,671; qualifying distributions, $554,588.
Trustee: W. Glen Boyd.
EIN: 931306727
Codes: FD

45430
Parks Foundation
(Formerly Psychological Research Foundation)
P.O. Box 5669
Beaverton, OR 97006-0669

Established in 1977 as the Psychological Research Foundation.
Donor(s): Loren E. Parks.

Financial data (yr. ended 11/30/01): Grants paid, $546,744; assets, $4,558,200 (M); expenditures, $636,182; qualifying distributions, $602,967.
Limitations: Applications not accepted. Giving limited to Portland, OR.
Application information: Contributes only to pre-selected organizations.
Officers: Loren E. Parks, Pres.; Claudene Gilmore, Secy.
Directors: Gary L. Parks, Ray C. Parks.
EIN: 930729614
Codes: FD

45431
The Samuel S. Johnson Foundation
P.O. Box 356
Redmond, OR 97756-0079 (541) 548-8104
FAX: (541) 548-2014; E-mail: ssjohnson@empnet.com
Contact: Elizabeth Hill Johnson, Pres.

Incorporated in 1948 in CA.
Donor(s): Samuel S. Johnson,‡ Elizabeth Hill Johnson, Robert W. Hill.‡
Financial data (yr. ended 05/31/02): Grants paid, $536,570; assets, $9,657,735 (M); gifts received, $42,175; expenditures, $596,463; qualifying distributions, $536,570; giving activities include $11,500 for loans to individuals.
Limitations: Giving primarily in OR.
Publications: Application guidelines.
Application information: Application form required.
Officers and Directors:* Elizabeth Hill Johnson,* Pres.; Elizabeth K. Johnson-Helm,* V.P. and Secy.; Mary A. Krenowicz, Exec. Secy.-Treas.; Patricia C. Johnson,* C.F.O.; Karen K. Creason, John C. Helm.
EIN: 946062478
Codes: FD, GTI

45432
Lampstand Foundation
(Formerly Agnes Klingensmith Charitable Foundation)
18160 Cottonwood Rd., No. 244
Sunriver, OR 97707
E-mail: dtimwinn@xc.org
Contact: David (Tim) Winn, Tr.

Established in 1990 in WA.
Donor(s): Harry E. Klingensmith.‡
Financial data (yr. ended 12/31/00): Grants paid, $532,024; assets, $4,946,280 (M); gifts received, $288,410; expenditures, $621,287; qualifying distributions, $590,610.
Limitations: Giving on a national basis.
Publications: Application guidelines.
Application information: Application form not required.
Trustees: David A. Winn, Kay Winn.
EIN: 911503479
Codes: FD, GTI

45433
Wessinger Foundation
121 S.W. Salmon, Ste. 1100
Portland, OR 97204 (503) 274-4051

Established in 1979.
Donor(s): Paul Wessinger Trust.
Financial data (yr. ended 09/30/01): Grants paid, $525,500; assets, $7,223,522 (M); expenditures, $570,924; qualifying distributions, $542,778.
Limitations: Giving limited to the Pacific Northwest, with emphasis on the Tri-County, OR, area.
Officers: William W. Wessinger, Pres.; Robert Geddes, Secy.

Directors: Gainor W. Artz, Anna Boggess, E. Charles Wessinger, Henry W. Wessinger, Joseph M. Wessinger, Kathryn W. Withers, Julie Vigeland.
EIN: 930754224
Codes: FD

45434
The Campbell Foundation
260 S.W. Birdshill Loop
Portland, OR 97219 (503) 281-6631
Contact: Mary Kalafatis

Established in 1993 in OR.
Donor(s): J. Duncan Campbell, Jr., Cynthia A. Campbell, Birdshill, Inc., United Asset Mgmt.
Financial data (yr. ended 12/31/00): Grants paid, $524,825; assets, $14,231,522 (M); gifts received, $2,500,000; expenditures, $648,301; qualifying distributions, $521,838.
Limitations: Giving primarily in Portland, OR.
Publications: Financial statement.
Directors: Cynthia A. Campbell, J. Duncan Campbell, Jr., John S. Gilleland.
EIN: 931133917
Codes: FD

45435
The Herbert A. Templeton Foundation
1717 S.W. Park Ave.
Portland, OR 97201 (503) 223-0036
Contact: Ruth B. Richmond, Pres.

Incorporated in 1955 in OR.
Donor(s): Herbert A. Templeton,‡ and other members of the Templeton family.
Financial data (yr. ended 12/31/01): Grants paid, $521,350; assets, $15,469,460 (M); expenditures, $708,906; qualifying distributions, $582,222.
Limitations: Giving limited to OR.
Publications: Program policy statement, application guidelines.
Application information: Application form not required.
Officers and Trustees:* Ruth B. Richmond,* Pres.; Jane T. Bryson,* V.P.; Terrence R. Pancoast,* Secy.-Treas.; Linda McKinley Girard, Henry R. Richmond, Loren L. Wyss.
EIN: 930505586
Codes: FD

45436
J.F.R. Foundation
P.O. Box 1350
Portland, OR 97207

Established in 1993 in OR.
Donor(s): James F. Rippey.
Financial data (yr. ended 12/31/01): Grants paid, $491,000; assets, $7,481,313 (M); gifts received, $739,627; expenditures, $524,719; qualifying distributions, $501,309.
Limitations: Applications not accepted. Giving primarily in OR, with emphasis on Portland.
Application information: Contributes only to pre-selected organizations.
Directors: Jan Demick, Robin R. Holcomb, Jack McCurchie, James F. Rippey, Jeffrey L. Rippey, Shirley K. Rippey, Timothy M. Rippey.
EIN: 943192331
Codes: FD

45437
Collins-McDonald Trust Fund
1618 S.W. 1st Ave., Ste. 300
Portland, OR 97201-5706
Application address: 620 N. 1st St., Lakeview, OR 97630, tel.: (541) 947-2196
Contact: James C. Lynch, Tr.

Incorporated in 1940 in OR.

Financial data (yr. ended 12/31/01): Grants paid, $490,686; assets, $8,933,798 (M); expenditures, $500,613; qualifying distributions, $490,141.
Limitations: Giving limited to Lake County, OR.
Application information: Application form required for scholarships.
Trustees: Timothy R. Bishop, Paul Harlan, James E. Lynch.
EIN: 936021894
Codes: FD, GTI

45438
Charles M. Bair Family Trust
c/o U.S. Bank, Tax Dept.
P.O. Box 3168
Portland, OR 97208-3168
Application address: c/o U.S. Bank, 303 N. Broadway, P.O. Box 20678, Billings, MT 59115

Established in 1993 in MT.
Donor(s): Alberta M. Bair.‡
Financial data (yr. ended 04/30/01): Grants paid, $476,133; assets, $51,905,874 (M); gifts received, $1,100,097; expenditures, $847,758; qualifying distributions, $748,085.
Limitations: Giving primarily in MT, with emphasis on Yellowstone, Meagher and Wheatland counties.
Application information: Application form required.
Officer and Directors:* Lee B. Rostad,* Vice-Chair.; Brent Cromley, Douglas A. Jenkins.
Trustee: U.S. Bank.
EIN: 816075761
Codes: FD

45439
The Swigert Foundation
c/o Robyn Brewer
P.O. Box 3121
Portland, OR 97208 (503) 225-2935
Contact: Robyn E. Beadnell

Established in 1990 in OR.
Donor(s): Ernest C. Swigert, Henry T. Swigert.
Financial data (yr. ended 12/31/01): Grants paid, $457,500; assets, $9,265,675 (M); expenditures, $534,474; qualifying distributions, $457,500.
Limitations: Giving primarily in OR.
Application information: Application form required.
Officer and Directors:* Ernest C. Swigert,* Pres.; George C. Spencer, Henry T. Swigert, Elizabeth K. Warren, Wendy Warren.
EIN: 943122667
Codes: FD

45440
Anna K. Ackerman Trust
c/o U.S. Bank
P.O. Box 3168, Trust Tax Svcs.
Portland, OR 97208

Established in 1963.
Financial data (yr. ended 12/31/01): Grants paid, $454,977; assets, $8,197,260 (M); expenditures, $509,533; qualifying distributions, $463,440.
Limitations: Giving limited to CO, with emphasis on Colorado Springs.
Application information: Application form not required.
Trustee: U.S. Bank.
EIN: 846032046
Codes: FD

45441
The Jordan & Mina Schnitzer Foundation
1121 S.W. Salmon St.
Portland, OR 97205

Established in 1997 in CA and OR.

45441—OREGON

Financial data (yr. ended 06/30/00): Grants paid, $421,666; assets, $20,513,592 (M); expenditures, $1,916,673; qualifying distributions, $1,673,975; giving activities include $1,123,349 for programs.
Limitations: Applications not accepted. Giving primarily in Portland, OR; some giving also in CA and NY.
Application information: Contributes only to pre-selected organizations.
Officers: Jordan D. Schnitzer, Pres. and Secy.-Treas.; Arlene Schnitzer, V.P.; Harold J. Schnitzer, V.P.; Mina M. Schnitzer, V.P.
EIN: 931236637
Codes: FD

45442
Thomason Foundation
1 S.W. Columbia St., Ste. 1110
Portland, OR 97258-2012
Contact: Scott Thomason, Pres.

Established in 1998 in OR.
Donor(s): Scott L. Thomason.
Financial data (yr. ended 12/31/99): Grants paid, $401,647; assets, $1,429,838 (M); gifts received, $500,000; expenditures, $413,449; qualifying distributions, $401,351.
Limitations: Giving primarily in OR.
Officer and Directors:* Scott L. Thomason,* Pres. and Treas.; Deborah J. Autzen, Roderick A. Liviesay.
EIN: 931253882
Codes: FD

45443
William H. Bauman & Mary L. Bauman Foundation
6950 S.W. Hampton St., Ste. 221
Portland, OR 97223-8331

Established in 1991 in OR.
Donor(s): William H. Bauman.‡
Financial data (yr. ended 12/31/01): Grants paid, $401,502; assets, $8,258,078 (M); expenditures, $441,302; qualifying distributions, $409,120.
Limitations: Applications not accepted. Giving primarily in Portland, OR.
Application information: Contributes only to pre-selected organizations.
Trustees: Clarence Knoepfle, Mary Bauman Mirhady, William Vermillion.
Manager: Paul Schwimdt.
EIN: 936234071
Codes: FD

45444
The Fred Meyer Foundation
(Formerly Fred Meyer/Smith Foundation)
3800 S.E. 22nd Ave.
Portland, OR 97202 (503) 797-5605
Additional tel.: (800) 858-9202, ext. 5605;
E-mail: foundation@fredmeyer.com; URL: http://www.fredmeyer.com/corpnewsinfo_charitablegiving_art4_foundation.htm
Contact: Mary M. Loftin, V.P., Community Rels.

Established in 1997 in OR.
Donor(s): Fred Meyer Stores, Inc., Ronald W. Burkle.
Financial data (yr. ended 02/03/02): Grants paid, $380,000; assets, $1,700,000 (M); gifts received, $609,991; expenditures, $473,737; qualifying distributions, $416,331.
Limitations: Giving limited to areas of company operations in AK, ID, OR, UT, and WA.
Publications: Grants list, informational brochure (including application guidelines).

Application information: Applications will be sent to those programs which fit the criteria and budget. Application form required.
Officers and Directors:* Sam Duncan,* Chair. and Pres.; Warren Bryant,* V.P.; Lynn Marmer, Secy.; David Deatherage,* Treas.; Ross Thomas.
EIN: 931231880
Codes: CS, FD, CD

45445
The Coffman Family Foundation
4902 McLoughlin Dr.
Central Point, OR 97502

Established in 1993 in CA.
Donor(s): Ronnie D. Coffman, Adelia A. Coffman.
Financial data (yr. ended 12/31/01): Grants paid, $361,745; assets, $3,173,788 (M); gifts received, $230; expenditures, $375,693; qualifying distributions, $363,371.
Limitations: Applications not accepted.
Application information: Contributes only to pre-selected organizations.
Officers and Directors:* Ronnie D. Coffman,* Pres.; Adelia A. Coffman,* Secy.-Treas.
EIN: 330592687
Codes: FD

45446
Harry A. Merlo Foundation, Inc.
2250 N.E. 25th St.
Hillsboro, OR 97124
Contact: Gary R. Maffei, V.P.

Established in 1988 in OR.
Financial data (yr. ended 12/31/01): Grants paid, $361,439; assets, $4,884,221 (M); gifts received, $280; expenditures, $475,654; qualifying distributions, $468,728.
Limitations: Applications not accepted. Giving primarily in Portland, OR.
Officers and Directors:* Harry A. Merlo, Sr.,* Pres.; Gary R. Maffei,* V.P.; Harry A. Merlo, Jr.
EIN: 943086742
Codes: FD

45447
Poznanski Foundation
7700 Arbor Lake Ct.
Wilsonville, OR 97070
Contact: Robert Poznanski, Pres.

Established in 1992 in OR.
Donor(s): Robert Poznanski.
Financial data (yr. ended 12/31/00): Grants paid, $359,120; assets, $7,063,822 (M); gifts received, $250,000; expenditures, $388,173; qualifying distributions, $356,147.
Limitations: Giving primarily in OR, with some giving in CA.
Application information: Application form not required.
Officers: Robert Poznanski, Pres.; Dorothy Poznanski, Secy.
Directors: Roberta Keller, Linda Merrihew, Suanne Ramar.
EIN: 943157812
Codes: FD

45448
A. J. Frank Family Foundation
P.O. Drawer 79
Mill City, OR 97360
Contact: Douglas Highberger

Incorporated in 1959 in OR.
Donor(s): A.J. Frank, L.D. Frank, Frank Lumber Co., Inc., Frank Timber Products, Inc., and members of the Frank family.
Financial data (yr. ended 09/30/01): Grants paid, $347,408; assets, $7,794,099 (M); gifts received,

$20,000; expenditures, $390,113; qualifying distributions, $347,408.
Limitations: Giving primarily in OR.
Application information: Application form not required.
Directors: C.M. Carey, D.D. Frank, J.T. Frank.
EIN: 930523395
Codes: FD

45449
Merle S. & Emma J. West Scholarship Fund
c/o U.S. Bank
P.O. Box 3168
Portland, OR 97208
Scholarship application address: West Scholarship Comm., 3720 S. 6th St., Klamath Falls, OR 97603, tel.: (503) 883-3857
Contact: Marilyn Norquist

Established around 1984.
Financial data (yr. ended 12/31/01): Grants paid, $328,419; assets, $4,082,547 (M); expenditures, $403,907; qualifying distributions, $340,010.
Limitations: Giving limited to residents of Klamath County, OR.
Application information: Application form required.
Trustee: U.S. Bank.
EIN: 936160221
Codes: FD, GTI

45450
Foreign Mission Foundation
10875 S.W. 89th St.
Tigard, OR 97223-8323

Established around 1982.
Donor(s): Eugene L. Davis, Miriam Larson.
Financial data (yr. ended 02/28/01): Grants paid, $326,869; assets, $6,850,153 (M); gifts received, $128,242; expenditures, $617,967; qualifying distributions, $373,492.
Limitations: Applications not accepted. Giving primarily in India.
Application information: Contributes only to pre-selected organizations.
Officers and Directors:* Eugene L. Davis,* Pres.; Vivian Davis,* Secy.; George Hughes, Robert Waymire.
EIN: 930763215
Codes: FD

45451
Collins Medical Trust
1618 S.W. 1st Ave., Ste. 300
Portland, OR 97201 (503) 227-1219
FAX: (503) 227-5349
Contact: Nancy L. Helseth, Admin.

Established in 1956 in OR.
Donor(s): Truman W. Collins.‡
Financial data (yr. ended 09/30/01): Grants paid, $325,600; assets, $6,559,797 (M); expenditures, $327,559; qualifying distributions, $323,219.
Limitations: Giving limited to OR.
Publications: Application guidelines.
Application information: Application form not required.
Officers: Timothy R. Bishop, Treas.; Nancy L. Helseth, Admin.
Trustees: Maribeth W. Collins, Truman W. Collins, Jr., Joseph F. Paquet, M.D., James R. Patterson, M.D.
EIN: 936021895
Codes: FD

45452
WF Foundation
c/o K. Evans
280 Court St. N.E., Ste. 1
Salem, OR 97301-3443

Donor(s): Chris G. Wolcott, Guy R. Wolcott.
Financial data (yr. ended 08/31/01): Grants paid, $317,600; assets, $533,193 (M); gifts received, $521,000; expenditures, $326,484; qualifying distributions, $326,453.
Limitations: Applications not accepted. Giving primarily in MT, OR and TX.
Application information: Contributes only to pre-selected organizations.
Officers: Guy R. Wolcott, Pres.; Chris G. Wolcott, Secy.
Director: Guy R. Wolcott II.
EIN: 931291150
Codes: FD

45453
The St. Laurent Family Foundation
c/o South Valley Bank & Trust
P.O. Box 1784
Medford, OR 97501-0140

Established in 1994 in OR.
Donor(s): Eleanor St. Laurent, Georges C. St. Laurent, Jr.
Financial data (yr. ended 12/31/01): Grants paid, $307,237; assets, $2,224,918 (M); expenditures, $335,079; qualifying distributions, $308,041.
Limitations: Applications not accepted. Giving primarily in CT, NY, and OR.
Application information: Contributes only to pre-selected organizations.
Trustees: Eleanor St. Laurent, Georges C. St. Laurent, Jr., South Valley Bank & Trust.
EIN: 936289177
Codes: FD

45454
The Larson Legacy
14404 S.E. Krause Ln.
Portland, OR 97236-6534 (503) 222-1305
FAX: (503) 658-5273
Contact: Leland E.G. Larson, Pres.

Established in 1997 in OR.
Donor(s): Leland E.G. Larson, Kathleen C. Larson.
Financial data (yr. ended 12/31/01): Grants paid, $306,339; assets, $4,093,441 (M); gifts received, $700,000; expenditures, $426,493; qualifying distributions, $305,394.
Limitations: Giving primarily in the Northwest.
Publications: Application guidelines, multi-year report.
Application information: Application form not required.
Officers: Leland E.G. Larson, Pres.; Kristen C. Larson, V.P.; Kathleen C. Larson, Secy.-Treas.
EIN: 911859861
Codes: FD

45455
C. Giles Hunt Charitable Trust
c/o Wells Fargo Bank Northwest, N.A.
P.O. Box 609
Eugene, OR 97440-0609
Contact: C.Q. Dukehart, V.P. and Trust Off., Wells Fargo Bank Northwest, N.A.

Trust established in 1974 in OR.
Donor(s): C. Giles Hunt.‡
Financial data (yr. ended 12/31/01): Grants paid, $305,934; assets, $6,372,935 (M); expenditures, $363,182; qualifying distributions, $319,198.
Limitations: Giving primarily in Douglas County, OR.
Publications: Application guidelines.

Application information: Application form required.
Trustee: Wells Fargo Bank Northwest, N.A.
EIN: 237428278
Codes: FD

45456
The Woodard Family Foundation
40 S. 6th
Cottage Grove, OR 97424 (541) 942-4113
E-mail: wff@uci.net
Contact: Tod C. Woodard, V.P.

Incorporated in 1952 in OR.
Donor(s): Walter A. Woodard, Carlton Woodard.
Financial data (yr. ended 06/30/01): Grants paid, $298,280; assets, $6,137,156 (M); expenditures, $426,837; qualifying distributions, $382,642.
Limitations: Giving limited to local organizations in the greater Cottage Grove/Eugene, OR, area.
Publications: Application guidelines.
Application information: Application form required.
Officers and Directors:* Carlton Woodard,* Pres.; Tod C. Woodard,* V.P. and Secy.
EIN: 936026550
Codes: FD

45457
James & Jane Kreitzberg Foundation
1415 Beaumont Dr., N.W.
Salem, OR 97304
Contact: James S. Kreitzberg, Pres.

Established in 1996 in OR.
Donor(s): James S. Kreitzberg, Jane K. Kreitzberg.
Financial data (yr. ended 12/31/01): Grants paid, $280,000; assets, $1,792,239 (M); expenditures, $282,944; qualifying distributions, $279,544.
Limitations: Applications not accepted. Giving primarily in OR.
Application information: Contributes only to pre-selected organizations.
Officers: James S. Kreitzberg, Pres.; John S. Kreitzberg, V.P.; Jane K. Kreitzberg, Secy.
Directors: Cynthia A. Doran, Anthony R. Kreitzberg, Frederick W. Kreitzberg, Jeffrey P. Kreitzberg, Susan C. Kreitzberg.
EIN: 931227643
Codes: FD

45458
Parks Education Foundation
P.O. Box 5669
Aloha, OR 97006

Established in 1998 in OR.
Financial data (yr. ended 07/31/01): Grants paid, $278,000; assets, $5,143,163 (M); expenditures, $286,009; qualifying distributions, $274,788.
Limitations: Applications not accepted. Giving primarily in Washington, DC and OR.
Application information: Contributes only to pre-selected organizations.
Officers: Loren Parks, Pres.; Steven L. Wallace, Secy.-Treas.
Director: Gary L. Parks.
EIN: 931150509
Codes: FD

45459
Nancy J. Wendt Foundation
826 Loma Linda Dr.
Klamath Falls, OR 97601-2360

Established in 1999 in OR.
Financial data (yr. ended 12/31/00): Grants paid, $277,885; assets, $225,248 (M); expenditures, $292,048; qualifying distributions, $179,611.
Limitations: Applications not accepted. Giving primarily in Klamath Falls and Portland, OR.

Application information: Contributes only to pre-selected organizations.
Officers: Nancy J. Wendt, Pres.; Richard Wendt, V.P.; Roderick Wendt, Secy.-Treas.
EIN: 931256104
Codes: FD

45460
Pamplin Christian Foundation
805 S.W. Broadway, Ste. 2400
Portland, OR 97205-3341

Established in 1996 in OR.
Donor(s): Katherine R. Pamplin, Robert B. Pamplin.
Financial data (yr. ended 12/31/01): Grants paid, $275,450; assets, $1,008,577 (M); expenditures, $277,622; qualifying distributions, $274,618.
Limitations: Applications not accepted. Giving primarily in MS and OR.
Application information: Contributes only to pre-selected organizations.
Trustee: Robert B. Pamplin.
EIN: 931188785
Codes: FD

45461
The E. L. & B. G. Lightfoot Foundation
c/o U.S. Bank
P.O. Box 3168, Trust Tax
Portland, OR 97208-3168
Application address: P.O. Box 886, Meridian, ID 83642
Contact: Michael W. Sullivan

Established in 1992 in ID.
Donor(s): Elma Lightfoot Newgen.
Financial data (yr. ended 02/28/01): Grants paid, $271,747; assets, $2,858,643 (M); expenditures, $291,190; qualifying distributions, $271,783.
Limitations: Giving limited to southern ID and eastern OR.
Application information: Application form required.
Charitable Committee: Elma Lightfoot Newgen, Chair.; Maureen L. Howe, Kathleen D. Mayhew, Sydney L. Mitchell.
Trustee: U.S. Bank.
EIN: 820454166
Codes: FD, GTI

45462
James E. & Lila G. Miller Charitable Trust
1805 N.W. Glisan St.
Portland, OR 97209-2010 (503) 295-0580
Contact: Ted M. Miller

Established in 1985 in OR.
Donor(s): James E. Miller, Lila G. Miller.
Financial data (yr. ended 05/31/01): Grants paid, $268,500; assets, $5,583,929 (M); expenditures, $323,747; qualifying distributions, $265,232.
Limitations: Giving limited to OR and the portion of southwestern WA that is included in the Portland, OR, metropolitan area.
Trustees: James E. Miller, Lila G. Miller.
EIN: 936174460
Codes: FD

45463
The I.F.C. Foundation
P.O. Box 1350
Portland, OR 97207-1350

Established in 1992 in OR.
Donor(s): J. Jerry Inskeep, Jr.
Financial data (yr. ended 12/31/01): Grants paid, $264,866; assets, $5,683,075 (M); expenditures, $283,010; qualifying distributions, $265,366.
Limitations: Giving primarily in OR.

45463—OREGON

Officers: J. Jerry Inskeep, Jr., Pres.; M. Jacqueline Inskeep, V.P.; John J. Inskeep III, Secy.-Treas.
Directors: Martha Inskeep Brandt, Jill Inskeep, Sarah Inskeep-Meling.
EIN: 931098708
Codes: FD

45464
Anne And Eli Shapira Charitable Foundation
2434 NW Pinnacle Dr.
Portland, OR 97229-8020

Established in 2000 in OR.
Donor(s): Elijahu Shapira.
Financial data (yr. ended 12/31/01): Grants paid, $237,360; assets, $6,320,306 (M); expenditures, $247,017; qualifying distributions, $237,360.
Trustees: Anne L. Shapira, Elijahu Shapira.
EIN: 931306729

45465
Otterdale Memorial Scholarship
c/o U.S. Bank
P.O. Box 3168
Portland, OR 97208
Application address: c/o U.S. Bank, Trust Dept., P.O. Box 1107, Medford, OR 97501
Contact: Michael S. Harris, V.P.

Established in 1996 in OR.
Donor(s): Myrta E. Otterdale.‡
Financial data (yr. ended 06/30/01): Grants paid, $229,500; assets, $1,759,350 (M); expenditures, $244,939; qualifying distributions, $230,024.
Limitations: Giving limited to residents of OR, with emphasis on Jackson County.
Application information: Application form required.
Trustee: U.S. Bank.
EIN: 936299754
Codes: FD2

45466
W. J. Gallagher Foundation
c/o U.S. Bank
P.O. Box 3168, Trust Tax Dept.
Portland, OR 97208-3168
Application address: P.O. Box 4787, Missoula, MT 59806, tel.: (406) 523-2378
Contact: Steven Polhemus, Trust Off., U.S. Bank

Established in 1960 in MT.
Donor(s): W.J. Gallagher.
Financial data (yr. ended 12/31/01): Grants paid, $225,000; assets, $80,030 (M); expenditures, $243,904; qualifying distributions, $226,889.
Limitations: Giving primarily in Missoula, MT.
Trustee: U.S. Bank.
Selection Committee: Gary Gallagher.
EIN: 816010064
Codes: FD2

45467
Mentor Graphics Foundation
8005 S.W. Boeckman Rd.
Wilsonville, OR 97070 (503) 685-7000
Contact: Marti Brown, V.P.

Established in 1985 in OR.
Donor(s): Mentor Graphics Corp.
Financial data (yr. ended 12/31/00): Grants paid, $220,560; assets, $97,197 (M); gifts received, $22,000; expenditures, $221,507; qualifying distributions, $220,561.
Limitations: Giving primarily in areas where the company has major operations.
Officers and Directors:* Marti Brown,* V.P.; Margaret Browning,* V.P.; Merideth Perrill,* V.P.; Ry Schwark,* V.P.
EIN: 930870309
Codes: CS, FD2, CD

45468
The Earl Family Foundation
6595 Butte Falls Hwy.
Eagle Point, OR 97524 (541) 826-9447
FAX: (541) 826-9792
Contact: Richard A. Earl, Pres.

Established in 1998 in OR.
Donor(s): Richard A. Earl.
Financial data (yr. ended 06/30/02): Grants paid, $219,912; assets, $156,890 (M); expenditures, $221,282; qualifying distributions, $230,002.
Limitations: Giving limited to the Butte Falls-Prospect region of OR.
Application information: Application form required.
Officers: Richard A. Earl, Pres.; Wendy L. Earl, Secy.
Directors: Christopher A. Earl, Terrill L. Earl.
EIN: 931246684
Codes: FD2

45469
The Wyss Foundation
620 S.W. 5th Ave., Ste. 1010
Portland, OR 97204
Contact: Loren L. Wyss, Pres.

Established in 1989 in OR.
Donor(s): Judith Wyss, Loren L. Wyss.
Financial data (yr. ended 04/30/01): Grants paid, $210,150; assets, $4,078,681 (M); expenditures, $218,430; qualifying distributions, $216,581.
Limitations: Giving primarily in the Portland, OR, area.
Publications: Grants list, informational brochure.
Application information: Application form not required.
Officers and Directors:* Loren L. Wyss,* Pres. and Treas.; Judith Wyss,* V.P. and Secy.; James Damis, Edmund Wyss, Emily Wyss, Isabel Wyss, Jennifer Wyss-Jones.
EIN: 931010019
Codes: FD2

45470
Dale Krueger Scholarship
c/o U.S. Bank
P.O. Box 3168, Trust Tax Svcs.
Portland, OR 97208-3168 (503) 275-5929
Contact: Marlyn Norquist

Established in 1999 in OR.
Donor(s): Dale W. Krueger.‡
Financial data (yr. ended 07/31/01): Grants paid, $208,728; assets, $9,113,166 (M); expenditures, $470,028; qualifying distributions, $208,728.
Limitations: Giving primarily in AZ and CA.
Application information: Application form required.
Trustee: U.S. Bank.
EIN: 936331222

45471
Arthur E. & Faye G. Munson Charitable Trust
P.O. Box 3168, Trust Tax Services
Portland, OR 97208

Established in 1999 in WA.
Financial data (yr. ended 12/31/01): Grants paid, $208,106; assets, $2,128,083 (M); expenditures, $221,387; qualifying distributions, $207,874.
Limitations: Applications not accepted. Giving primarily in Seattle, WA.
Application information: Contributes only to pre-selected organizations.
Trustee: U.S. Bank, N.A.
EIN: 916483037
Codes: FD2

45472
Paul F. Wenner Charitable Foundation Trust
1237 S.E. 36th Ave.
Portland, OR 97214 (503) 235-8193
Contact: Giovanni Rosati

Established in 1994 in OR.
Donor(s): Paul F. Wenner.
Financial data (yr. ended 12/31/01): Grants paid, $206,050; assets, $431,603 (M); expenditures, $222,441; qualifying distributions, $205,705.
Limitations: Applications not accepted. Giving primarily in OR.
Application information: Contributes only to pre-selected organizations.
Trustee: Paul F. Wenner.
EIN: 936289211
Codes: FD2

45473
The Renaissance Foundation
(Formerly The Levin Family Foundation)
P.O. Box 80516
Portland, OR 97280

Established in 2000 in OR.
Donor(s): Irving J. Levin.
Financial data (yr. ended 06/30/02): Grants paid, $204,800; assets, $9,791,205 (M); gifts received, $685,900; expenditures, $474,049; qualifying distributions, $204,800.
Limitations: Applications not accepted.
Application information: Contributes only to pre-selected organizations.
Trustees: Stephanie J. Fowler, Irving J. Levin.
EIN: 931306116

45474
B. Grant Foundation
P.O. Box 82878
Portland, OR 97282 (503) 522-9103
FAX: (503) 552-9101
Contact: Lauren K. Forman, Exec. Dir.

Established in 1998 in OR.
Donor(s): Ronald McDonald Children's Charities, B. Grant, Inc.
Financial data (yr. ended 12/31/00): Grants paid, $192,094; assets, $83,234 (M); gifts received, $343,359; expenditures, $284,320; qualifying distributions, $192,063.
Limitations: Giving primarily in Portland, OR.
Publications: Grants list, informational brochure (including application guidelines).
Application information: Application form not required.
Officers and Directors:* Brian W. Grant,* Pres.; Gina R. Grant,* Secy.-Treas.; Lauren K. Forman, Exec. Dir.
EIN: 931239276
Codes: FD2

45475
Paul R. and Anna Lee White Family Charitable Foundation
c/o U.S. Bank, Tax Svcs. Dept.
P.O. Box 3168
Portland, OR 97208-3168
FAX: (503) 275-6746
Contact: J.T. Garcia

Established in 1985 in CO.
Financial data (yr. ended 12/31/01): Grants paid, $186,000; assets, $4,498,203 (M); gifts received, $1,150,000; expenditures, $218,824; qualifying distributions, $190,455.
Limitations: Applications not accepted. Giving primarily in CO and Sheridan, WY.
Application information: Contributes only to pre-selected organizations; unsolicited requests for funds not accepted.

Trustees: Lela Green, Dorothy Oliveira, George J. Robinson, U.S. Bank.
EIN: 846191934
Codes: FD2

45476
Helping Hand of Oregon
165 N. Lotus Beach Dr.
Portland, OR 97217-8021
Contact: William K. Blount, Pres.

Established in 1997 in OR.
Donor(s): William Kay Blount.
Financial data (yr. ended 12/31/01): Grants paid, $183,250; assets, $4,355,500 (M); expenditures, $189,178; qualifying distributions, $187,321.
Limitations: Giving primarily in OR.
Officers: William K. Blount, Pres.; Brian M. Blount, Secy.; Kevin Blount, Treas.
Directors: Nancy J. Blount, Susan B. McNeil.
EIN: 911812237
Codes: FD2

45477
Lamb Foundation
(Formerly OCRI Foundation)
P.O. Box 1705
Lake Oswego, OR 97035-0575
(503) 635-8010
FAX: (503) 635-6544; *E-mail:* lambfnd@teleport.com
Contact: Sarah Malarkey, Admin.

Established in 1971 in OR.
Donor(s): Members of the Lamb family.
Financial data (yr. ended 12/31/01): Grants paid, $180,110; assets, $5,618,838 (M); expenditures, $259,671; qualifying distributions, $201,670.
Limitations: Giving limited to OR and WA.
Publications: Informational brochure (including application guidelines).
Application information: Letters of inquiry required. Unsolicited proposals not considered. Application form not required.
Officers and Directors:* Carl Lamb,* Chair.; Peter Lamb,* Vice-Chair.; Frank G. Lamb,* Secy.; Maryann Lamb,* Treas.; Anita Lamb Bailey, Ben Bailey, Barbara Lamb, Greg Lamb, Helen Lamb, Paula L. Lamb.
EIN: 237120564
Codes: FD2

45478
The Holzman Foundation, Inc.
3724 S.W. 50th Ave.
Portland, OR 97221 (503) 292-5093
Contact: Renee Holzman, Pres.

Established in 1990 in OR.
Donor(s): Irwin B. Holzman, Renee R. Holzman, Reliable Credit Assn.
Financial data (yr. ended 12/31/01): Grants paid, $178,020; assets, $4,047,864 (M); expenditures, $185,071; qualifying distributions, $178,020.
Limitations: Giving primarily in Portland, OR.
Publications: Application guidelines.
Application information: Application form required.
Officers and Directors:* Renee R. Holzman,* Pres.; Irwin B. Holzman,* Secy.-Treas.; Jay L. Holzman, Lawrence J. Holzman, Lee M. Holzman, Rebecca Holzman, Sherri Holzman.
EIN: 931041588
Codes: FD2

45479
H. W. Irwin & D. I. Irwin Foundation
c/o U.S. Bank
P.O. Box 3168
Portland, OR 97208-3168 (503) 275-4879
Contact: Kristen Hinds

Established in 1991 in OR.
Donor(s): Dorise Carlyon Hinton-Irwin.
Financial data (yr. ended 06/30/01): Grants paid, $176,700; assets, $2,967,074 (M); expenditures, $220,636; qualifying distributions, $180,438.
Limitations: Giving primarily in Portland, OR.
Application information: Grant requests will be considered biannually. Application form required.
Officers: Joan I. Green, Pres.; Kelsey Green Grout, Secy.; Eric H.I. Hoffman, Treas.
Directors: Alan Green, Jr., Jean I. Hoffman, Sally H. Miller.
Agent: U.S. Bank.
EIN: 931067941
Codes: FD2

45480
Jed and Celia Meese Foundation
88 Granite St.
Ashland, OR 97520-2711

Established in 1988.
Donor(s): Celia A. Meese, Jed D. Meese.
Financial data (yr. ended 12/31/01): Grants paid, $170,317; assets, $1,143,253 (M); gifts received, $93,641; expenditures, $183,320; qualifying distributions, $170,317.
Limitations: Applications not accepted. Giving primarily in OR.
Application information: Contributes only to pre-selected organizations.
Trustees: Celia A. Meese, Jed D. Meese.
EIN: 880233962
Codes: FD2

45481
McKay Family Foundation
P.O. Box 70313
Eugene, OR 97401-0117 (541) 686-5963
E-mail: mckayfamfound@juno.com; *URL:* http://www.oakwaycenter.com/mckayfamily
Contact: C.B. Kilen, Tr.

Established in 1986 in OR.
Donor(s): Miles E. McKay,‡ Eleanor P. McKay.‡
Financial data (yr. ended 12/31/01): Grants paid, $169,820; assets, $3,742,403 (M); expenditures, $176,785; qualifying distributions, $173,010.
Limitations: Giving limited to OR charities serving Lane County.
Application information: Application form required.
Trustees: Philip F. Baird, Jr., C. Bruce Kilen, Tracie McKay Shojai, Kelly L. Thakkar, Dale Williams.
EIN: 930935036
Codes: FD2

45482
H. G. Hillis Charitable Trust
c/o U.S. Bank, Trust Tax Svcs.
P.O. Box 3168
Portland, OR 97208

Established in 1999 in OR.
Financial data (yr. ended 07/31/01): Grants paid, $169,520; assets, $1,522,748 (M); expenditures, $209,175; qualifying distributions, $174,437.
Limitations: Applications not accepted.
Application information: Contributes only to pre-selected organizations.
Trustee: David Seulean.
Agent: U.S. Bank.
EIN: 936333754
Codes: FD2

45483
Vera L. Smith Charitable Foundation
2165 S.W. Main St.
Portland, OR 97205

Established in 1992 in OR.
Donor(s): Vera L. Smith.‡
Financial data (yr. ended 06/30/01): Grants paid, $167,500; assets, $3,145,997 (M); expenditures, $240,084; qualifying distributions, $202,478.
Limitations: Applications not accepted. Giving primarily in Portland, OR.
Application information: Contributes only to pre-selected organizations.
Officers: Lynn D. Simpson, Pres.; Lisa A. Joerin, V.P.; Edward L. Joy, Secy.-Treas.
EIN: 931095010
Codes: FD2

45484
Joe & Frances Naumes Family Foundation, Inc.
P.O. Box 996
Medford, OR 97501

Established in 1994 in OR.
Donor(s): Frances A. Naumes,‡ Michael D. Naumes.
Financial data (yr. ended 12/31/00): Grants paid, $166,650; assets, $2,358,432 (M); expenditures, $189,712; qualifying distributions, $165,191.
Limitations: Applications not accepted. Giving primarily in OR, with emphasis on Medford.
Application information: Contributes only to pre-selected organizations.
Directors: Michael D. Naumes, Susan F. Naumes.
EIN: 931138741
Codes: FD2

45485
Hitchman Foundation, Inc.
1011 Commercial St. N.E., Ste. 120
Salem, OR 97301-1085
Contact: Kent Aldrich, Pres.

Established in 1969.
Financial data (yr. ended 12/31/01): Grants paid, $166,300; assets, $2,913,844 (M); expenditures, $238,926; qualifying distributions, $164,806.
Limitations: Giving primarily in the greater Salem, OR, area.
Application information: Application form required.
Officers: Kent Aldrich, Pres.; Donovan Jaeger, V.P.; Pamela Scott, Secy.
EIN: 930572469
Codes: FD2

45486
E. V. Giustina Foundation
c/o Rohn Roberts
800 Willamette St., Ste. 800
Eugene, OR 97401

Established in 1997 in OR.
Donor(s): Ehrman V. Giustina, Marion Lee Giustina.
Financial data (yr. ended 12/31/01): Grants paid, $166,100; assets, $3,250,335 (M); expenditures, $188,283; qualifying distributions, $166,100.
Limitations: Applications not accepted. Giving primarily in OR.
Application information: Contributes only to pre-selected organizations.
Trustees: E. Danell Giustina, Ehrman V. Giustina, Marion Lee Giustina, Thomas Anthony Giustina.
EIN: 911776086
Codes: FD2

45487
Frank and Margaret Bitar Foundation
9828 E. Burnside, Ste. 200
Portland, OR 97216-2330

Financial data (yr. ended 12/31/01): Grants paid, $163,300; assets, $1,016,146 (M); expenditures, $204,840; qualifying distributions, $163,300.
Limitations: Applications not accepted.
Application information: Contributes only to pre-selected organizations.
Officers: William F. Bitar, Pres.; Mary Bitar Korek, V.P.; Jeanette Bitar Lucas, Secy.
EIN: 911847903
Codes: FD2

45488
Life Connection Foundation
1500 Valley River Dr., Ste. 250
Eugene, OR 97401

Donor(s): John W. Crowder.
Financial data (yr. ended 12/31/00): Grants paid, $162,000; assets, $2,488,704 (M); expenditures, $173,171; qualifying distributions, $2,732,535.
Limitations: Applications not accepted.
Application information: Contributes only to pre-selected organizations.
Officers: John W. Crowder, Pres.; Jean Paul Dusseault, V.P.; Kenneth Harvey, Secy.; Dennis L. Solin, Treas.
EIN: 931238529
Codes: FD2

45489
J. Frank Schmidt Family Charitable Foundation
P.O. Box 189
Boring, OR 97009 (503) 663-4128
FAX: (503) 663-7629
Contact: Jan Barkley, Tr.

Established in 1986 in OR.
Donor(s): Evelyn Schmidt, J. Frank Schmidt, Jr.
Financial data (yr. ended 09/30/00): Grants paid, $161,121; assets, $3,022,044 (M); gifts received, $100,000; expenditures, $174,117; qualifying distributions, $170,990.
Application information: Telephone proposals will not be accepted or considered. Application form required.
Trustees: Jan Schmidt Barkley, J. Frank Schmidt, Jr., J. Frank Schmidt III, Jean Schmidt Webster.
EIN: 943030041
Codes: FD2

45490
Portland Women's Union
2121 S.W. Broadway, Ste. 350
Portland, OR 97201
Application address: P.O. Box 1033, Portland, OR 97202
Contact: Nancy Graham, Pres.

Established in 1983 in OR.
Financial data (yr. ended 04/30/01): Grants paid, $154,298; assets, $3,213,254 (M); expenditures, $193,031; qualifying distributions, $154,784.
Limitations: Giving limited to the Tri-County area of Multnomah, including Clackamas and Washington counties, OR.
Publications: Application guidelines.
Application information: Application form required.
Officers: Nancy Graham, Pres.; Linda Girard, 1st V.P.; Jeannette Pippin, Corr. Secy.; Patty Brandt, Treas.
Selection Committee: Sharon Grover, Chair., Selection Comm.
Directors: Linda Goebel, Claudia Gray, Catherine Hingas, and 6 additional directors.
EIN: 930386905

Codes: FD2

45491
The Brix Foundation
14020 S.E. Johnson Rd., Ste. 201
Milwaukie, OR 97267

Established in 1998 in OR.
Donor(s): Peter J. Brix, Noydena L. Brix.
Financial data (yr. ended 12/31/01): Grants paid, $151,000; assets, $8,936 (M); gifts received, $10,000; expenditures, $151,682; qualifying distributions, $151,000.
Limitations: Applications not accepted. Giving primarily in Portland, OR.
Application information: Contributes only to pre-selected organizations.
Directors: Noydena L. Brix, Peter J. Brix, Sarah B. Tennant.
EIN: 931243005
Codes: FD2

45492
The Stimson-Miller Foundation
520 S.W. Yamhill, Ste. 700
Portland, OR 97204 (503) 222-1676
Contact: Ronald L. Mundt, Pres.

Established in 1999 in OR.
Financial data (yr. ended 12/31/01): Grants paid, $150,300; assets, $3,874,577 (M); expenditures, $155,563; qualifying distributions, $160,201.
Limitations: Giving primarily in northwest CA, northern ID, western MT, Portland and northwest OR, and eastern WA.
Publications: Informational brochure (including application guidelines).
Application information: Application form required.
Officers and Directors:* Ronald L. Mundt,* Pres.; George C. Spencer,* Secy.; Sallie Dutton, A. Jane Graham, Mark Graham, Joanne M. Lilley, Sarah Miller Meigs.
EIN: 931280388
Codes: FD2

45493
Klamath Medical Service Bureau Foundation
P.O. Box 8191
Klamath Falls, OR 97602 (541) 884-5535
Contact: Tim Bailey, Pres.

Established in 1994 in OR.
Financial data (yr. ended 12/31/00): Grants paid, $149,300; assets, $3,782,575 (M); expenditures, $214,699; qualifying distributions, $161,212.
Limitations: Giving primarily in Klamath Falls, OR.
Application information: Application form required.
Officers and Directors:* Robert W. Graham, M.D., Chair.; Don Crane, Vice-Chair.; Timothy A. Bailey, Pres.; James D. Bocchi,* Secy.-Treas.; Blake Beruen, M.D., Gil Hannigan.
EIN: 931123593
Codes: FD2

45494
Bob Richardson Memorial Trust
c/o U.S. Bank, N.A
P.O. Box 3168
Portland, OR 97208-3168
Scholarship application address: c/o Richardson Scholarship Committee, Toledo High School, 1800 N.E. Sturdevant Rd., Toledo, OR 97391, tel.: (503) 336-5104

Established in 1989 in OR.
Financial data (yr. ended 06/30/01): Grants paid, $149,146; assets, $3,302,040 (M); expenditures, $209,858; qualifying distributions, $157,535.

Limitations: Giving limited to residents of Toledo and Lincoln County, OR.
Trustee: U.S. Bank, N.A.
EIN: 943101770
Codes: FD2, GTI

45495
Benton County Foundation
P.O. Box 911
Corvallis, OR 97339 (541) 753-1603
Contact: Glenn Plemmons, Pres.

Established in 1953 in OR.
Financial data (yr. ended 12/31/00): Grants paid, $147,282; assets, $4,531,256 (M); gifts received, $367,823; expenditures, $171,801.
Limitations: Giving limited to Benton County, OR.
Publications: Newsletter, informational brochure, application guidelines.
Application information: Application form required.
Officers and Directors:* Glenn Plemmons,* Pres.; Susan Schmidt,* Secy.; Ray Stephenson,* Treas.; Joe Kantor,* Grants Chair.; Donna Allen, Scott Fewel, Mal Miner, Jack Stowaser, Ed Woodcock.
EIN: 936022916
Codes: CM, FD2

45496
N. B. Giustina Foundation
P.O. Box 989
Eugene, OR 97440-0989
Contact: N.B. Giustina, Pres.

Established in 1994 in OR.
Donor(s): Natale B. Giustina.
Financial data (yr. ended 09/30/01): Grants paid, $145,000; assets, $3,380,572 (M); expenditures, $183,410; qualifying distributions, $143,603.
Limitations: Applications not accepted. Giving primarily in OR.
Application information: Contributes only to pre-selected organizations.
Officers: N.B. Giustina, Pres.; Natalie Giustina Newlove, V.P.; L.M. Giustina, Secy.-Treas.
EIN: 931139522
Codes: FD2

45497
The Emily Kate Foundation
19480 S.W. 97th Ave.
Tualatin, OR 97062

Donor(s): Charles Eggert, Louanna Eggert.
Financial data (yr. ended 06/30/01): Grants paid, $142,274; assets, $69,244 (M); gifts received, $57,074; expenditures, $144,162; qualifying distributions, $144,162.
Limitations: Applications not accepted. Giving primarily in Portland, OR.
Application information: Contributes only to pre-selected organizations.
Officers: Louanna Eggert, Pres.; Charles Eggert, Secy.
Director: Christopher Eggert.
EIN: 931236578
Codes: FD2

45498
Douglas Community Foundation, Inc.
P.O. Box 2310
Roseburg, OR 97470-5528 (541) 672-4203
Contact: Jack E. Snodgrass

Established in 1956.
Financial data (yr. ended 06/30/01): Grants paid, $139,701; assets, $2,468,166 (M); expenditures, $183,054; qualifying distributions, $152,023.
Limitations: Giving limited to Douglas County, OR.

Application information: Application form required.
Officers and Directors:* Donna Watkins,* Pres.; James S. Edwards, Jr.,* V.P.; John H. Pardon,* Secy.-Treas.; Donald Clithero, John Evans, Milt Herbert, Scott E. Woodruff.
EIN: 930363195
Codes: FD2

45499
The E. C. Brown Foundation
Otis Elevator Bldg.
230 N.W. 10th Ave.
Portland, OR 97209

Established in 1939 in OR; the foundation receives its funding from the trust.
Donor(s): Ellis C. Brown, M.D.‡
Financial data (yr. ended 12/31/01): Grants paid, $138,000; assets, $3,746,784 (M); gifts received, $150,000; expenditures, $252,423; qualifying distributions, $195,956.
Limitations: Applications not accepted.
Publications: Annual report.
Application information: Grants not ordinarily made, except in support of foundation-initiated projects.
Director: John A. Bruce.
EIN: 930491026
Codes: FD2

45500
Abracadabra Foundation
10730 N.W. McDaniel Rd.
Portland, OR 97229
Contact: Steven J. Sharp, Pres.

Established in 1997 in OR.
Donor(s): Steven J. Sharp.
Financial data (yr. ended 06/30/01): Grants paid, $135,900; assets, $3,175,553 (M); expenditures, $145,031; qualifying distributions, $135,900.
Limitations: Giving primarily in OR.
Officer: Steven J. Sharp, Pres. and Secy.-Treas.
Directors: Leo Craft, Patricia Sharp.
EIN: 931246872
Codes: FD2

45501
Mancini Charitable Foundation
3345 N.W. Franklin Ct.
Portland, OR 97210

Donor(s): Anne Mancini.
Financial data (yr. ended 12/31/01): Grants paid, $134,600; assets, $1,153,588 (M); gifts received, $80; expenditures, $147,426; qualifying distributions, $140,560.
Limitations: Applications not accepted. Giving primarily in NY and OR.
Application information: Contributes only to pre-selected organizations.
Trustees: Donald Bilgor, Anne Mancini, Joseph Mancini, M.D., Julie Mancini.
EIN: 237044487
Codes: FD2

45502
Immagia Foundation, Inc.
663 N.W. Jackson Ave.
Corvallis, OR 97330
Application address: 306 N.W. 32nd St., Corvallis, OR 97330
Contact: Paul Ahrens, Pres.

Established in 1995 in OR.
Donor(s): Paul Ahrens.
Financial data (yr. ended 12/31/99): Grants paid, $130,960; assets, $66,273 (M); gifts received, $50,000; expenditures, $164,758; qualifying distributions, $130,936.

Limitations: Giving primarily in OR.
Officers: Paul Ahrens, Pres. and Treas.; Lill Ahrens, Secy.
Director: Billie H. Ahrens.
EIN: 931188930
Codes: FD2

45503
The Bridges Foundation
P.O. Box 613
Turner, OR 97392
Contact: Kathy Bridges, Exec. Dir.

Established in 1987 in CA.
Donor(s): John F. Bridges, Nancy Bridges.
Financial data (yr. ended 12/31/00): Grants paid, $130,000; assets, $1,854,073 (M); gifts received, $200,000; expenditures, $189,616; qualifying distributions, $131,591.
Limitations: Giving primarily in NY and OR.
Officer: Kathy Bridges, Exec. Dir.
Trustees: John F. Bridges, Nancy W.A. Bridges, David W. Thompson.
EIN: 680152512

45504
Archie C. & Gertrude C. Cammack Trust
c/o U.S. Bank, Trust Tax Svcs.
P.O. Box 3168
Portland, OR 97208-3168
Application address: c/o the Medical Research Foundation of Oregon, P.O. Box 458, Portland, OR 97207, tel.: (503) 297-1348

Established in 1971.
Financial data (yr. ended 06/30/01): Grants paid, $130,000; assets, $2,036,396 (M); expenditures, $156,951; qualifying distributions, $131,580.
Limitations: Giving limited to OR.
Application information: Completion of standard medical protocol required.
Trustee: U.S. Bank.
EIN: 936053590
Codes: FD2

45505
Carl and Camilla Rietman Charitable Foundation
P.O. Box D
Lakeside, OR 97449 (541) 396-2169
Scholarship address: P.O. Box 99, Coquille, OR 97423
Contact: Alfred C. Walsh, Jr., Tr.

Established in 1996 in OR.
Donor(s): Albert Hadley.
Financial data (yr. ended 09/30/01): Grants paid, $130,000; assets, $2,216,789 (M); expenditures, $162,912; qualifying distributions, $140,959.
Limitations: Giving limited to graduates of Coquille High School, OR.
Application information: Application form required.
Trustees: John S. Burles, Michael Coen, Alfred C. Walsh, Jr.
EIN: 931221623
Codes: FD2

45506
Louisiana-Pacific Foundation
805 S.W. Broadway
Portland, OR 97205 (503) 221-0800
Additional tel.: (503) 821-5287 (for scholarship information)
Contact: Mary Jo Kaufman

Established in 1973 in OR.
Donor(s): Louisiana-Pacific Corp.
Financial data (yr. ended 12/31/01): Grants paid, $128,250; assets, $37,243 (M); gifts received, $150,000; expenditures, $146,466; qualifying distributions, $146,466.
Limitations: Giving primarily in areas of plant locations.
Publications: Application guidelines.
Application information: Application form required for scholarships only.
Officers and Trustees:* Mark A. Suwyn,* Chair. and Pres.; Mary Cohn,* V.P.; Anton C. Kirchof,* Secy.; William L. Hebert,* Treas.
EIN: 237268660
Codes: CS, FD2, CD

45507
Harry W. & Louis L. Vicksman Charitable Trust
c/o U.S. Bank
P.O. Box 3168
Portland, OR 97208-3168
Application address: c/o U.S. Bank, P.O. Box 5168TA, Denver, CO 80217
Contact: Leonard Campbell, Tr.

Established in 1995 in CO.
Donor(s): Harry W. Vicksman.
Financial data (yr. ended 12/31/00): Grants paid, $125,500; assets, $3,503,370 (M); gifts received, $17,434; expenditures, $163,030; qualifying distributions, $128,101.
Limitations: Giving primarily in CO.
Trustees: Leonard Campbell, U.S. Bank.
EIN: 846281031
Codes: FD2

45508
Bernard Daly Educational Fund
P.O. Box 351
Lakeview, OR 97630-0123 (541) 947-2196
Contact: James C. Lynch, Secy.-Treas.

Established in 1922 in OR.
Donor(s): Bernard Daly,‡ Jess and Alta Roberts Trust.
Financial data (yr. ended 05/31/01): Grants paid, $122,200; assets, $4,400,932 (M); gifts received, $1,150,125; expenditures, $153,076; qualifying distributions, $136,138.
Limitations: Giving primarily in Lake County, OR.
Publications: Application guidelines.
Application information: Application form required.
Officers: Carter E. Fetsch, Chair.; Ann Tracy, Vice-Chair.; James C. Lynch, Secy.-Treas.
Directors: Alan Parks, Jack Pendleton.
EIN: 936025466
Codes: FD2, GTI

45509
M. Lowell Edwards Foundation
9705 S.W. Arborcrest Way
Portland, OR 97225

Established in 2000 in OR.
Donor(s): Margaret Watt Edwards.‡
Financial data (yr. ended 12/31/00): Grants paid, $121,000; assets, $2,092,920 (M); gifts received, $2,042,532; expenditures, $126,129; qualifying distributions, $126,129.
Limitations: Applications not accepted. Giving primarily in Portland, OR.
Application information: Contributes only to pre-selected organizations.
Trustees: Craig Allen, Teresa Edwards Allen, Bruce David Edwards, Cynthia Edwards, Leslie Ann Edwards, Miles J. Edwards, Miles R. Edwards, Nancy E. Edwards, David Schwendeman, Karen Young.
EIN: 931283900
Codes: FD2

45510
Charla Richards-Kreitzberg Charitable Foundation
c/o Karen J. Lord
835 Saginaw St. S.
Salem, OR 97302-4121 (503) 391-1814

Financial data (yr. ended 12/31/00): Grants paid, $116,613; assets, $2,307,409 (M); gifts received, $2,393,601; expenditures, $132,401; qualifying distributions, $116,613.
Limitations: Giving primarily in OR.
Officers: Bonnie Heitsch, Pres.; Karen J. Lord, V.P.; Meredith Russell, Secy.; Britta Franz, Treas.
Directors: Jane Edwards, Mary Ann Kaestner, Susann Kaltwasser, Teya Penniman.
EIN: 931255604
Codes: FD2

45511
Schnitzer/Novack Foundation
P.O. Box 10047
Portland, OR 97296-0047
Application address: 3200 N.W. Yeon Ave., Portland, OR 97210, tel.: (503) 224-9900
Contact: Deborah S. Novack, Tr.

Established in 1996.
Financial data (yr. ended 12/31/01): Grants paid, $116,000; assets, $1,860,477 (M); gifts received, $240,233; expenditures, $125,181; qualifying distributions, $116,251.
Limitations: Applications not accepted. Giving limited to the Pacific Northwest with an emphasis on the Portland, OR, area.
Trustees: Deborah S. Novack, Kenneth M. Novack, Gilbert Schnitzer, Thelma Schnitzer.
EIN: 931220522
Codes: FD2

45512
Sharkey Family Charitable Foundation
650 Forest St.
Ashland, OR 97520

Established in 1994 in OR.
Financial data (yr. ended 12/31/01): Grants paid, $116,000; assets, $2,267,146 (M); gifts received, $997,298; expenditures, $131,271; qualifying distributions, $115,740.
Limitations: Applications not accepted.
Application information: Contributes only to pre-selected organizations.
Officers: Albert Sharkey, Pres.; Patricia Sharkey Wolfe, V.P. and Secy.
Directors: Linda Dunhill, Joseph J. Hanna, Steven Sharkey, Carl Wolfe.
EIN: 931161303
Codes: FD2

45513
The Shrigley Family Foundation
5550 S.W. Macadam, Ste. 310
Portland, OR 97201

Established in 1999 in CA.
Donor(s): David A. Shrigley, Anita R. Shrigley.
Financial data (yr. ended 12/31/00): Grants paid, $115,000; assets, $766,576 (M); gifts received, $300; expenditures, $120,674; qualifying distributions, $107,698.
Limitations: Applications not accepted. Giving primarily in CA.
Application information: Contributes only to pre-selected organizations.
Officers: David A. Shrigley, Chair.; Anita R. Shrigley, Secy.
EIN: 912011269

45514
Laura D. Wanser Foundation, Inc.
P.O. Box 1629
Lake Oswego, OR 97035-0829
(503) 635-8844
Contact: Edna May, Pres.

Established in 1992 in OR.
Donor(s): Laura Wanser.
Financial data (yr. ended 06/30/01): Grants paid, $114,000; assets, $2,108,356 (M); expenditures, $153,174; qualifying distributions, $113,774.
Limitations: Giving primarily in OR.
Application information: Application form not required.
Officer: Edna May, Pres.
Directors: Richard Deich, Roger May.
EIN: 931088293
Codes: FD2

45515
Phileo Foundation
220 N.W. 2nd Ave., Ste. 1000
Portland, OR 97209-3953
Application address: P.O. Box 8783, Portland, OR 97207-8783
Contact: James Crabbe, Pres., or Michael Crabbe, Secy.

Established in 1999 in OR.
Donor(s): James E. Crabbe.
Financial data (yr. ended 12/31/01): Grants paid, $112,450; assets, $4,645,907 (M); expenditures, $239,137; qualifying distributions, $112,450.
Limitations: Giving limited to the Portland, OR, area.
Publications: Multi-year report, annual report (including application guidelines).
Application information: Unsolicited requests for funds not considered. Application form required.
Officers: James E. Crabbe, Pres.; Michael D. Crabbe, Secy.; James E. Crabbe, Jr., Treas.
EIN: 931283076
Codes: FD2

45516
Anna May Family Foundation
2592 E. Barnett Rd.
Medford, OR 97504
Application address: 345 Scenic Dr., Ashland, OR 97520
Contact: Sabra Hoffman, Secy.

Established in 1999 in OR.
Donor(s): Anna L. May.
Financial data (yr. ended 12/31/01): Grants paid, $111,295; assets, $3,400,916 (M); gifts received, $65,342; expenditures, $196,366; qualifying distributions, $111,295.
Limitations: Giving primarily in Medford, OR.
Officers: Stephen G. Jamieson, Pres.; Tom Bolton, V.P.; Sabra Hoffman, Secy.; Ronald H. Holzkamp, Treas.
EIN: 931269424

45517
Bill and Tom Triplett Charitable
c/o William A. Triplett
1600 Pacwest Ctr., 1211 S.W. 5th Ave.
Portland, OR 97204
Application address: c/o Thomas M. Triplett, 1211 S.W. 5th Ave., Ste. 1600, Portland, OR 97204-3716, tel.: (503) 786-2901

Established in 1999 in OR.
Financial data (yr. ended 12/31/00): Grants paid, $111,235; assets, $228,303 (M); gifts received, $1,000,100; expenditures, $111,306; qualifying distributions, $111,235.
Limitations: Giving on a national basis.
Directors: Leslie East, Thomas M. Triplett.

EIN: 911818752
Codes: FD2

45518
Gladys E. Knowles Charitable Memorial Trust
c/o U.S. Bancorp, Tax Svcs.
P.O. Box 31683
Portland, OR 97208-3168
Contact: Helen M. Hancock, V.P. and Trust Off.

Established in 1983 in MT.
Financial data (yr. ended 12/31/01): Grants paid, $107,873; assets, $2,829,237 (M); expenditures, $149,158; qualifying distributions, $110,591.
Limitations: Applications not accepted. Giving primarily in MT.
Application information: Contributes only to pre-selected organizations; unsolicited requests for funds not accepted.
Trustee: U.S. Bank, N.A.
EIN: 810423029
Codes: FD2

45519
Charles O. & Hazel E. Cline Memorial Scholarship Fund
c/o KeyBank, N.A.
P.O. Box 272
Portland, OR 97204

Established in 1981 in OR.
Financial data (yr. ended 03/31/01): Grants paid, $106,800; assets, $1,346,696 (M); expenditures, $130,116; qualifying distributions, $108,511.
Limitations: Giving limited to Crook and Linn counties, OR.
Application information: Applications available through local high school principals and counselors. Application form required.
Trustees: Chal Letourneau, KeyBank, N.A.
EIN: 930931552
Codes: FD2, GTI

45520
Joann Hamilton Memorial Fund
c/o U.S. Bank
P.O. Box 3168
Portland, OR 97208-3168
Application address: c/o U.S. Bank, Trust Dept., P.O. Box 14444, Salem, OR 97309

Established in 1991 in OR.
Donor(s): Wallace L. Hamilton.
Financial data (yr. ended 06/30/01): Grants paid, $106,601; assets, $1,738,151 (M); expenditures, $138,035; qualifying distributions, $109,131.
Limitations: Giving limited to residents of Lincoln County, OR, with emphasis on Newport, OR.
Application information: Application form required.
Trustee: U.S. Bank.
EIN: 936249490
Codes: FD2, GTI

45521
Dussin Family Charitable Trust
0715 S.W. Bancroft St.
Portland, OR 97201-4273 (503) 225-0433
Contact: Guss Dussin, Tr.

Established in 1997 in OR.
Donor(s): Guss Dussin.
Financial data (yr. ended 12/31/99): Grants paid, $105,700; assets, $2,023,966 (M); expenditures, $122,143; qualifying distributions, $120,537.
Limitations: Giving primarily in Portland, OR.
Application information: Application form required.
Officer and Trustees:* Guss Dussin,* Mgr.; Alexandra Cook, Chris Dussin, Sally Dussin.
EIN: 911812614

Codes: FD2

45522
Arthur R. Dubs Foundation
1133 S. Riverside, Ste. 1
Medford, OR 97501 (541) 779-0990
Contact: Arn S. Wihtol, Secy.

Established in 1997 in OR.
Donor(s): Arthur R. Dubs.
Financial data (yr. ended 12/31/01): Grants paid, $104,665; assets, $2,248,817 (M); gifts received, $21,600; expenditures, $106,831; qualifying distributions, $103,796.
Limitations: Giving primarily in OR.
Officers: Arthur R. Dubs, Pres.; Arn S. Wihtol, Secy.
Director: Barbara J. Brown.
EIN: 931192741
Codes: FD2

45523
R. H. Parker/United Foundation
P.O. Box 4487
515 E. Burnside
Portland, OR 97208
Contact: R.H. Parker, Pres.

Established in 1994 in OR.
Financial data (yr. ended 12/31/01): Grants paid, $104,653; assets, $2,013,183 (M); gifts received, $125,000; expenditures, $109,529; qualifying distributions, $108,300.
Limitations: Giving primarily in the Pacific Northwest, with emphasis on OR and WA.
Officers and Directors:* R.H. Parker, Pres.; Deanna L. Vander Kooy,* Secy.; Marcus W. Holling, Richard H. Parker, Jr.
EIN: 931155287
Codes: FD2

45524
Friesen Lumber Co. Foundation, Inc.
P.O. Box 479
St. Helens, OR 97051

Established in 1990 in OR.
Donor(s): Friesen Lumber Co.
Financial data (yr. ended 02/28/01): Grants paid, $104,075; assets, $1,144,187 (M); gifts received, $100,000; expenditures, $108,203; qualifying distributions, $104,308.
Limitations: Applications not accepted. Giving primarily in CA, ID, and OR.
Application information: Contributes only to pre-selected organizations.
Officers and Directors:* Aaron Wilson,* Pres.; David Williamson, Treas.; Harlan Friesen, Jon Friesen.
EIN: 931024760
Codes: CS, FD2, CD

45525
Jane Buttrey Memorial Trust
c/o U.S. Bank
P.O. Box 3168
Portland, OR 97208-3168
Contact: Maureen Guerechit

Established in 1986 in MT.
Financial data (yr. ended 06/30/01): Grants paid, $100,000; assets, $1,562,772 (M); expenditures, $110,114; qualifying distributions, $100,775.
Limitations: Applications not accepted. Giving limited to MT and Austin, TX.
Application information: Unsolicited requests for funds not accepted.
Trustee: U.S. Bank.
EIN: 816014941
Codes: FD2, GTI

45526
Dhanakosha Foundation
c/o Reid, Hanna, & Co., LLP
1101 Siskiyou Blvd.
Ashland, OR 97520-2238

Established in 1998 in OR.
Financial data (yr. ended 12/31/00): Grants paid, $100,000; assets, $536,453 (M); gifts received, $69,469; expenditures, $108,672; qualifying distributions, $100,000.
Limitations: Applications not accepted.
Application information: Contributes only to pre-selected organizations.
Directors: Scott Globus, Mary M.G. Hohenberg, Edmund A. Nix, Jr.
EIN: 931258595
Codes: FD2

45527
The Coit Family Foundation
11025 S.W. Tryon Ave.
Portland, OR 97219-7829

Established in 1997 in OR.
Donor(s): Barbara E. Coit.
Financial data (yr. ended 12/31/01): Grants paid, $96,700; assets, $1,623,930 (M); gifts received, $56,440; expenditures, $100,892; qualifying distributions, $97,281.
Limitations: Applications not accepted. Giving primarily in Portland, OR.
Application information: Contributes only to pre-selected organizations.
Officers: Barbara E. Coit, Pres.; Ann Coit Goss, V.P.; Susan Coit, Secy.; William E. Coit, Treas.
EIN: 911806333
Codes: FD2

45528
Joseph P. Tennant Charitable Fund
P.O. Box 1658
Portland, OR 97207

Donor(s): Joseph P. Tennant.
Financial data (yr. ended 12/31/01): Grants paid, $96,341; assets, $1,074,149 (M); gifts received, $1,947; expenditures, $101,263; qualifying distributions, $96,341.
Limitations: Applications not accepted. Giving primarily in Portland, OR.
Application information: Contributes only to pre-selected organizations.
Directors: Nora Brady, Joseph P. Tennant, Sarah Tennant.
EIN: 931155757
Codes: FD2

45529
Edgar L. Boone Foundation
c/o U.S. Bank
P.O. Box 3168
Portland, OR 97208

Established in 1983 in WA.
Financial data (yr. ended 12/31/01): Grants paid, $96,334; assets, $9,256,906 (M); expenditures, $104,763; qualifying distributions, $97,378.
Limitations: Applications not accepted. Giving limited to WA.
Application information: Contributes only to pre-selected organizations.
Trustee: U.S. Bank.
EIN: 916021758
Codes: FD2

45530
Kinsman Foundation
P.O. Box 67139
Portland, OR 97268-0139
FAX: (503) 659-5244
Contact: Keith Kinsman, V.P.

Established in 1983 in OR.
Donor(s): Elizabeth T. Kinsman,‡ John W. Kinsman.‡
Financial data (yr. ended 12/31/01): Grants paid, $95,000; assets, $23,821,128 (M); gifts received, $20,122,989; expenditures, $211,480; qualifying distributions, $157,127.
Limitations: Giving primarily in OR and southwest WA.
Publications: Annual report (including application guidelines).
Application information: Application form required.
Officer and Directors:* Keith J. Kinsman,* V.P. and Secy.; Mary Kinsman.
EIN: 930861885
Codes: FD2

45531
Pacific Northwest Foundation
(Formerly Cook Family Trust, Inc.)
7619 S.W. 26th Ave.
Portland, OR 97219-2538 (503) 977-3226
FAX: (503) 244-9946; *E-mail:*
asalanti@attbi.com or frank-cook@attbi.com;
URL: http://www.pnf.org
Contact: Anna M. Salanti, Pres.

Established in 1988 in OR as partial successor to the Cook Brothers Educational Fund.
Donor(s): Howard F. Cook.‡
Financial data (yr. ended 12/31/01): Grants paid, $94,625; assets, $3,314,133 (M); expenditures, $227,323; qualifying distributions, $213,509.
Limitations: Applications not accepted. Giving on a national basis.
Publications: Annual report, financial statement.
Application information: Contributes only to pre-selected organizations. Unsolicited requests for funds not considered.
Officers: Anna M. Salanti, Pres.; Franklin C. Cook, V.P. and Secy.-Treas.; Kathleen M. Cook, V.P.
Board Members: Adria Dodici, Tim Mulvihill.
EIN: 770177829
Codes: FD2

45532
Steven McGeady Foundation
c/o Stephen Leasia
01339 S.W. Radcliffe
Portland, OR 97219-4802

Established in 1997 in OR.
Donor(s): Steven McGeady.
Financial data (yr. ended 12/31/01): Grants paid, $93,880; assets, $1,166,867 (M); expenditures, $109,761; qualifying distributions, $94,865.
Limitations: Applications not accepted. Giving primarily in Portland, OR.
Application information: Contributes only to pre-selected organizations.
Directors: Stephen Leasia, Glen McGeady, Linda P. Taylor.
EIN: 911803102
Codes: FD2

45533
McGraw Family Foundation, Inc.
707 S.W. Washington St., No. 934
Portland, OR 97205
Contact: Nancie S. McGraw, Pres.

Established in 1986 in OR.

45533—OREGON

Donor(s): Donald H. McGraw, Nancie S. McGraw.
Financial data (yr. ended 09/30/01): Grants paid, $92,500; assets, $1,834,384 (M); expenditures, $111,331; qualifying distributions, $90,951.
Limitations: Giving limited to Portland, OR.
Officers: Nancie S. McGraw, Pres. and Treas.; Mary M. Richenstein, V.P. and Secy.
EIN: 930934831
Codes: FD2

45534
L. S. (Sam) Shoen Foundation
c/o U.S. Bank
P.O. Box 3168, Trust Tax Services
Portland, OR 97208
Application information: 1253 Umatilla St., Port Townsend, WA 98368
Contact: Samuel W. Shoen, Tr.

Established in 2000 in WA.
Donor(s): Katabasis International.
Financial data (yr. ended 12/31/01): Grants paid, $92,500; assets, $1,291,334 (M); expenditures, $99,866; qualifying distributions, $93,999.
Limitations: Giving primarily in MA and WA.
Trustees: Samuel W. Shoen, U.S. Bank.
EIN: 916508655
Codes: FD2

45535
D. E. and Jane Clark Foundation, Ltd.
c/o U.S. Bank
P.O. Box 3168
Portland, OR 97208

Established in 1997 in OR.
Financial data (yr. ended 12/31/01): Grants paid, $91,000; assets, $1,500,706 (M); expenditures, $118,416; qualifying distributions, $93,683.
Limitations: Giving primarily in OR.
Application information: Application form required.
Trustees: Nikki Hat, David Lindley, Gene Rose, U.S. Bank.
EIN: 930935220
Codes: FD2

45536
VC Fund
6149 S.W. Shattuck Rd.
Portland, OR 97221-1044
Contact: Virginia Mae Cadonau, Tr.

Established in 1994 in OR.
Donor(s): Alpenrose Dairy, Inc.
Financial data (yr. ended 12/31/01): Grants paid, $91,000; assets, $1,547,398 (M); expenditures, $103,496; qualifying distributions, $90,072.
Limitations: Giving primarily in OR.
Application information: Application form not required.
Trustees: Anita J. Cadonau, Carl H. Cadonau, Sr., Carl H. Cadonau, Jr., Randall E. Cadonau, Virginia Mae Cadonau, Barbara Cadonau Samsel.
EIN: 943189006
Codes: FD2

45537
The Robert Brady Trust
c/o U.S. Bank, Trust Dept.
P.O. Box 3168
Portland, OR 97208-3168 (503) 225-4817
Contact: Janis Tucker

Incorporated in 1938 in OR.
Financial data (yr. ended 06/30/01): Grants paid, $90,760; assets, $1,456,993 (M); expenditures, $109,720; qualifying distributions, $91,386.
Limitations: Giving primarily in OR.
Publications: Annual report.

Trustee: U.S. Bank.
EIN: 936019516
Codes: FD2

45538
The Elizabeth Church Clarke Testamentary Trust/Fund Foundation
c/o U.S. Bank
P.O. Box 3168
Portland, OR 97208-3168
Application address: 709 S.W. 15th Ave., Portland, OR 97205, tel.: (503) 228-9405
Contact: G.L. Selmyhr, Exec. Secy.

Established in 1961 in OR; incorporated in 1964.
Donor(s): Elizabeth Church Clark.‡
Financial data (yr. ended 12/31/01): Grants paid, $90,633; assets, $1,980,660 (M); expenditures, $130,119; qualifying distributions, $109,772.
Limitations: Giving limited to OR.
Trustee: U.S. Bank.
EIN: 936024205
Codes: FD2, GTI

45539
J & S Foundation
0333 S.W. Flower St.
Portland, OR 97201
Contact: James A. Thompsen

Donor(s): Joan C. Wilcox, Stephen S. Wilcox, Jr.
Financial data (yr. ended 12/31/01): Grants paid, $89,360; assets, $1,139,207 (M); gifts received, $55,000; expenditures, $89,777; qualifying distributions, $89,360.
Directors: Susan Boaglio, Joan C. Wilcox, Stephen S. Wilcox.
EIN: 930775960
Codes: FD2

45540
Four Way Community Foundation
P.O. Box 652
Grants Pass, OR 97528-0056
Contact: Phil Hart, Exec. Dir.

Established in 1975 in OR.
Financial data (yr. ended 06/30/02): Grants paid, $89,000; assets, $2,200,000 (M); gifts received, $450,000; expenditures, $150,000.
Limitations: Giving limited to Josephine and Western Jackson counties, OR.
Publications: Informational brochure (including application guidelines), application guidelines.
Application information: Application form required.
Officers: Ken Behymer, Pres.; Bob Brownell, V.P.; Ben Freudenberg, Co-Secy.; Kathy Krauss, Co-Secy.; Giff Gates, Treas.
Directors: Ann Bower, Walter Cauble, Sue Cohen, James Dole, Bill Hamilton, Jeri Holt, Steve Welch.
EIN: 510173092
Codes: CM, FD2

45541
Burlingham Trust, Inc.
970 Downs St. S.
Salem, OR 97302
Contact: C. Ronald Peters, Secy.-Treas.

Financial data (yr. ended 12/31/00): Grants paid, $88,927; assets, $2,322,895 (M); expenditures, $165,300; qualifying distributions, $88,927.
Limitations: Giving limited to OR.
Officers and Directors:* Loren Flomer,* Pres.; Tom DeArmond,* V.P.; C. Ronald Peters,* Secy.-Treas.
EIN: 936237912
Codes: FD2

45542
Equinox Foundation
23985 Vaughn Rd.
Veneta, OR 97487-9435
Contact: Victoria Wilson-Charles, Tr.

Established in 1999 in OR.
Financial data (yr. ended 12/31/00): Grants paid, $88,000; assets, $341,416 (M); gifts received, $80,322; expenditures, $90,530; qualifying distributions, $88,000.
Limitations: Applications not accepted. Giving primarily in OR.
Application information: Unsolicited requests for funds not accepted.
Trustees: Jeffrey Wilson-Charles, Victoria Wilson-Charles.
EIN: 931273462
Codes: FD2

45543
Nicoli Foundation
19600 S.W. Circle Rd.
Tualatin, OR 97062 (503) 692-6080
Contact: David P. Nicoli, Pres.

Established in 1995 in OR.
Donor(s): David P. Nicoli.
Financial data (yr. ended 08/31/01): Grants paid, $87,230; assets, $26,926 (M); gifts received, $26,376; expenditures, $117,184; qualifying distributions, $87,230.
Limitations: Giving limited to Tigard and the greater Washington County, OR areas.
Application information: Application form not required.
Directors: David P. Nicoli, James R. Nicoli, Dan Terry.
EIN: 931191224

45544
Harry & Dorothy Murphy Foundation
8835 S.W. Canyon Ln., Ste. 210
Portland, OR 97225 (503) 203-1580
Contact: Edward N. Murphy, Pres.

Established around 1980.
Financial data (yr. ended 01/31/02): Grants paid, $86,647; assets, $855,174 (M); expenditures, $128,458; qualifying distributions, $86,647.
Limitations: Giving primarily in Portland, OR.
Officers: Edward N. Murphy, Pres.; Bryan Murphy, Secy.
EIN: 936022752
Codes: FD2

45545
Dean W. and Julia R. Croft Foundation
4981 Mulholland Dr.
Lake Oswego, OR 97035

Established in 1997 in OR.
Donor(s): Dean W. Croft.
Financial data (yr. ended 12/31/00): Grants paid, $85,000; assets, $418,080 (M); expenditures, $86,588; qualifying distributions, $84,757.
Limitations: Applications not accepted. Giving primarily in OR.
Application information: Contributes only to pre-selected organizations.
Officers: Dean W. Croft, Pres.; Julia R. Croft, Secy.
EIN: 931228842
Codes: FD2

45546
Bechen Family Foundation
15350 S.W. Sequoia, Ste. 300
Portland, OR 97224
Contact: Peter F. Bechen, Dir.

Established in 1997 in OR.

Donor(s): Peter F. Bechen.
Financial data (yr. ended 12/31/00): Grants paid, $83,950; assets, $2,959,537 (M); expenditures, $89,924; qualifying distributions, $82,895.
Limitations: Applications not accepted. Giving primarily in CA and OR.
Application information: Contributes only to pre-selected organizations.
Directors: Jane G. Bechen, Peter F. Bechen, Sarah G. Bechen.
EIN: 911811266

45547
Beattie Charitable Trust
(Formerly Byron J. & Suzanne M. Beattie Charitable Trust)
c/o U.S. Bank
P.O. Box 3168
Portland, OR 97208-3168

Established in 1982 in OR.
Financial data (yr. ended 06/30/01): Grants paid, $83,669; assets, $1,854,383 (M); expenditures, $101,893; qualifying distributions, $86,101.
Limitations: Applications not accepted. Giving primarily in Portland, OR.
Application information: Contributes only to pre-selected organizations.
Trustee: U.S. Bank.
EIN: 936151155
Codes: FD2

45548
St. Martin de Porres Trust
1100 S.W. 6th Ave., Ste. 1504
Portland, OR 97204-3705 (503) 248-9535
FAX: (503) 248-9538
Contact: Eugene E. Feltz, Tr.

Established in 1963 in OR.
Donor(s): Fr. Hugh Gearin.‡
Financial data (yr. ended 12/31/01): Grants paid, $82,650; assets, $1,708,543 (M); expenditures, $87,942; qualifying distributions, $83,519.
Limitations: Giving primarily in OR.
Application information: Application form not required.
Trustees: Harold D. Christianson, Eugene E. Feltz.
EIN: 936031814
Codes: FD2

45549
Robert & Clara Swanson Charitable Trust
c/o U.S. Bank
P.O. Box 3168
Portland, OR 97208

Established in 1991 in ID.
Financial data (yr. ended 08/31/01): Grants paid, $82,381; assets, $1,578,479 (M); gifts received, $1,137,119; expenditures, $97,155; qualifying distributions, $86,192.
Limitations: Applications not accepted.
Application information: Contributes only to pre-selected organizations.
Trustee: U.S. Bank.
EIN: 826072827
Codes: FD2

45550
Ralph & Adolph Jacobs Foundation
1211 S.W. 6th Ave.
Portland, OR 97204
Contact: P. Stuart Rosenfeld, Tr.

Established in OR.
Donor(s): Members of the Jacobs family.‡
Financial data (yr. ended 09/30/01): Grants paid, $82,000; assets, $1,042,425 (M); expenditures, $86,746; qualifying distributions, $82,580.

Limitations: Giving primarily in the tri-county area, with an emphasis on Oregon City, OR.
Officers: William W. Rosenfeld, Pres.; Charles A. Adams, V.P.; William W. Wessinger, Secy.-Treas.
Trustees: Leslie R. Labbe, P. Stuart Rosenfeld.
EIN: 936021910
Codes: FD2

45551
Haugland Foundation
2233 Lasater Blvd.
Eugene, OR 97405-1759 (541) 343-6713
Contact: Richard P. Haugland, Pres.

Established in 1996.
Financial data (yr. ended 09/30/01): Grants paid, $80,900; assets, $2,232,845 (M); gifts received, $1,500,000; expenditures, $108,164; qualifying distributions, $80,900.
Limitations: Giving primarily in OR.
Officers: Richard P. Haugland, Pres.; Rosaria P. Haugland, V.P.; Alexander D. Haugland, Secy.-Treas.
EIN: 931220478
Codes: FD2

45552
Harold & Margaret Taylor Foundation
16396 S.E. 232nd Dr.
Boring, OR 97009
Contact: William H. Taylor, Pres.

Established in 1998 in OR.
Donor(s): Harold Taylor,‡ Margaret Taylor.
Financial data (yr. ended 05/31/01): Grants paid, $80,100; assets, $1,757,923 (M); gifts received, $150,000; expenditures, $101,534; qualifying distributions, $79,742.
Limitations: Applications not accepted. Giving primarily in OR.
Application information: Unsolicited requests for funds not accepted.
Officers: William H. Taylor, Pres.; Margaret Taylor, Secy.-Treas.
EIN: 931247948
Codes: FD2

45553
Helen John Foundation
16727 N.W. Norwalk Dr.
Beaverton, OR 97006

Established in 1971 in OR.
Financial data (yr. ended 12/31/01): Grants paid, $77,595; assets, $1,195,376 (M); expenditures, $88,507; qualifying distributions, $77,595.
Limitations: Applications not accepted. Giving primarily in OR and WA.
Application information: Contributes only to pre-selected organizations.
Officers and Directors:* James G. Condon,* Pres.; Edwin G. Condon,* V.P.; Elizabeth C. Twilegar, Secy.-Treas.; Mary Butler, Kenneth J. Condon.
EIN: 237109040
Codes: FD2

45554
Gordon Elwood Foundation
P.O. Box 4189
Medford, OR 97501 (541) 282-0643
FAX: (541) 282-0644; E-mail: gef@internetcds.com
Contact: Kathy Bryon, Exec. Dir.

Established in 1999 in OR.
Donor(s): Gordon L. Elwood.‡
Financial data (yr. ended 06/30/01): Grants paid, $75,822; assets, $7,660,409 (M); expenditures, $163,648; qualifying distributions, $120,360.

Limitations: Giving limited to Curry, Jackson, Josephine, and Klamath counties, OR.
Publications: Application guidelines.
Application information: Application form required.
Officers: Mike Heverly, Pres.; John A. Duke, V.P.; Janet J. Murphy, Secy.; Burke Raymond, Treas.
EIN: 931267972
Codes: FD2

45555
Ericksen Foundation
c/o Wayne R. Ericksen
1113 S.W. Myrtle Dr.
Portland, OR 97201-2270

Established in 1994 in OR.
Donor(s): Wayne R. Ericksen, Sandra F. Ericksen.
Financial data (yr. ended 12/31/01): Grants paid, $74,886; assets, $1,265,277 (M); expenditures, $93,160; qualifying distributions, $76,882.
Limitations: Applications not accepted.
Application information: Contributes only to pre-selected organizations.
Directors: Suzanne E. Destephano, Robert W. Ericksen, Sandra F. Ericksen, Wayne R. Ericksen, Joseph J. Hannah, Jr.
EIN: 931147933

45556
Iseli Foundation
14917 S.E. 142nd Ave.
Clackamas, OR 97015-7374 (503) 558-0268
Contact: Andre W. Iseli, Pres.

Financial data (yr. ended 12/31/01): Grants paid, $74,800; assets, $1,932,024 (M); gifts received, $5,000; expenditures, $81,160; qualifying distributions, $78,712.
Officer: Andre W. Iseli, Pres.
Directors: Tracy Swift, Scherran Way.
EIN: 952560782

45557
Decker-Fields Foundation
7585 State St. S.E.
Salem, OR 97301

Donor(s): Dale D. Decker, David K. Fields.
Financial data (yr. ended 12/31/01): Grants paid, $74,290; assets, $195,641 (M); gifts received, $60,937; expenditures, $75,312; qualifying distributions, $75,312.
Limitations: Applications not accepted. Giving on a national basis.
Application information: Contributes only to pre-selected organizations.
Officers: David K. Fields, Pres.; Park S. Kriner, V.P.; Dale D. Decker, Secy.
Directors: M. Allene Decker, Myrtle E. Decker, Louise E. Fields, Betty L. Kriner.
EIN: 930571251

45558
Crane Creek Foundation
c/o James W. Ratzlaff
391 Stillwater Rd.
Roseburg, OR 97470

Established in 1994 in OR.
Donor(s): James W. Ratzlaff.
Financial data (yr. ended 12/31/00): Grants paid, $73,150; assets, $378,288 (M); expenditures, $75,131; qualifying distributions, $73,141.
Limitations: Applications not accepted.
Application information: Contributes only to pre-selected organizations.
Officers: James W. Ratzlaff, Pres.; Jane P. Ratzlaff, Secy.
Directors: James W. Ratzlaff, Jr., Susan E. Ratzlaff.
EIN: 931157940

45559
The Singer Foundation
457 Spyglass Dr.
Eugene, OR 97401-2091

Established in 1986 in OR.
Financial data (yr. ended 10/31/01): Grants paid, $72,925; assets, $1,919,087 (M); gifts received, $52,867; expenditures, $80,442; qualifying distributions, $72,925.
Limitations: Applications not accepted.
Officers: Kenneth M. Singer, Pres.; Georgianne T. Singer, Secy.
Director: Roberta L. Singer.
EIN: 943027910

45560
Johnson Family Foundation
650 N.E. Holladay, Ste. 1400
Portland, OR 97232
Contact: David J. Johnson, Pres.

Established in 1997 in OR.
Donor(s): David J. Johnson.
Financial data (yr. ended 12/31/01): Grants paid, $72,430; assets, $1,917,688 (M); expenditures, $107,574; qualifying distributions, $72,321.
Limitations: Giving primarily in OR.
Officers: David J. Johnson, Pres. and Secy.-Treas.; Eileen E. Johnson, V.P.
Director: Myrtle A. Johnson.
EIN: 936310704

45561
Evans-Kelly Family Foundation
c/o Moss Adams, LLP
8705 S.W. Nimbus Ave., Ste. 115
Beaverton, OR 97008-7159

Established in 1999 in WA.
Donor(s): Mary Jacaleen Evans, Danny L. Evans.
Financial data (yr. ended 12/31/00): Grants paid, $71,980; assets, $819,469 (M); expenditures, $100,355; qualifying distributions, $76,254.
Limitations: Giving primarily in OR.
Directors: Danny L. Evans, Ean W. Evans, Hayden B. Evans, Mary Jacaleen Evans, Mason M. Evans.
EIN: 931269604

45562
The Walker Family Foundation
13101 S.E. 84th Ave. B
Clackamas, OR 97015-9733 (503) 653-7791
Contact: Wendell O. Walker, Tr.

Established in 1997 in OR.
Donor(s): Wendell O. Walker, Barbara F. Walker.
Financial data (yr. ended 12/31/01): Grants paid, $71,500; assets, $1,456,927 (M); gifts received, $6,463; expenditures, $83,265; qualifying distributions, $71,500.
Limitations: Giving primarily in OR.
Officers: Wendell O. Walker, Pres.; Barbara F. Walker, V.P.; Ian Walker, Secy.
EIN: 911796945

45563
Harley and Mertie Stevens Memorial Fund
c/o U.S. Bank
P.O. Box 3168
Portland, OR 97208-3168
Application address: c/o Oregon State Scholarship Commission, 1500 Valley River Dr., No. 100, Eugene, OR 97401
Contact: Marlyn Norquist, V.P., U.S. Bank

Established in 1969 in OR.
Financial data (yr. ended 06/30/01): Grants paid, $71,263; assets, $1,444,389 (M); expenditures, $101,105; qualifying distributions, $80,495.
Limitations: Giving only to high school graduates of Clackamas County, OR.
Application information: Application forms available from local area high schools, college financial aid offices, or trustee bank and OSSC. Application form required.
Trustee: U.S. Bank.
EIN: 936053655
Codes: GTI

45564
Harold and Arlene Schnitzer Foundation
P.O. Box 2708
Portland, OR 97208
Contact: Barbara Hall, Admin.

Established in 1996 in OR as successor to the Harold and Arlene Schnitzer Family Foundation.
Donor(s): Harold J. Schnitzer, Arlene Schnitzer.
Financial data (yr. ended 12/31/01): Grants paid, $71,100; assets, $2,347,446 (M); expenditures, $86,324; qualifying distributions, $74,930.
Limitations: Giving primarily in Portland, OR.
Publications: Grants list, application guidelines.
Application information: Unsolicited requests for funds not accepted. Application form not required.
Officers and Directors:* Harold J. Schnitzer, Chair. and Pres.; Thomas E. Eyer, V.P.; Barbara Hall, V.P.; Theodore P. Malaska, V.P.; Arlene Schnitzer,* Secy.-Treas.; Jordan D. Schnitzer.
EIN: 931141738

45565
Leslie G. Ehmann Trust
c/o U.S. Bank
P.O. Box 3168
Portland, OR 97208-3168 (503) 275-5929
Contact: C. Gordon Childs, Tr.

Established in 1985 in OR.
Donor(s): Leslie G. Ehmann.‡
Financial data (yr. ended 06/30/01): Grants paid, $71,000; assets, $1,577,450 (M); expenditures, $92,416; qualifying distributions, $73,999.
Limitations: Giving primarily in OR.
Application information: Application form not required.
Trustees: C. Gordon Childs, U.S. Bank.
EIN: 936176402

45566
Lorenz Family Foundation
521 S.W. Clay
Portland, OR 97201 (503) 222-1161
Contact: Daniel Lorenz, Tr.

Established in 1998 in OR.
Financial data (yr. ended 12/31/01): Grants paid, $70,000; assets, $365,122 (M); gifts received, $156,488; expenditures, $71,731; qualifying distributions, $70,000.
Limitations: Giving on a national and international basis.
Application information: Application form required.
Officer: Jonathan Lorenz, Chair.
Trustees: Karen Bethke, Andrew Lorenz, Daniel Lorenz, James Lorenz.
EIN: 931246599

45567
Merle and Ellen Morgan Gift Fund
28450 S.W. Herd Ln.
Hillsboro, OR 97123

Established in 1980.
Donor(s): David L. Morgan, Steven J. Morgan.
Financial data (yr. ended 10/31/01): Grants paid, $70,000; assets, $1,512,945 (M); expenditures, $74,572; qualifying distributions, $70,000.
Limitations: Applications not accepted. Giving primarily in Nyack, NY, Portland, OR, and Philadelphia, PA.
Application information: Contributes only to pre-selected organizations.
Officers: David L. Morgan, Pres.; Steven J. Morgan, Secy.
EIN: 930771815

45568
Maree Noble/Elizabeth Stumpf Memorial Foundation
8375 Steel Bridge Rd.
Sheridan, OR 97378

Established in 1990.
Donor(s): Richard P. Noble Charitable Remainder Annuity Trust.
Financial data (yr. ended 12/31/01): Grants paid, $69,821; assets, $1,164,149 (M); expenditures, $88,369; qualifying distributions, $88,369.
Limitations: Applications not accepted. Giving primarily in OR.
Application information: Contributes only to pre-selected organizations.
Officer: Richard P. Noble, Pres.
EIN: 943129626

45569
King Family Foundation
3025 N.W. Monte Vista Terr.
Portland, OR 97210

Established in 1998 in OR.
Donor(s): Garr M. King, Mary J. King.
Financial data (yr. ended 12/31/01): Grants paid, $69,325; assets, $853,446 (M); expenditures, $77,354; qualifying distributions, $69,325.
Limitations: Applications not accepted.
Application information: Contributes only to pre-selected organizations.
Officers and Directors:* Garr M. King,* Pres.; Mary J. King,* Secy.; Margaret A. Conant, James P. King, John T. King, Matthew J. King, Michael B. King, Mary E. Powell.
EIN: 931256996

45570
Walter L. J. Davies Memorial Scholarship
c/o U.S. Bank
P.O. Box 3168
Portland, OR 97208-3168
Application address: c/o State Scholarship Commission, 1445 Williamette St., Eugene, OR 97401

Financial data (yr. ended 06/30/01): Grants paid, $69,202; assets, $1,220,416 (M); expenditures, $90,226; qualifying distributions, $76,170.
Limitations: Giving limited to OR.
Application information: Application available at State Scholarship Commission. Application form required.
Trustee: U.S. Bank.
EIN: 936163624
Codes: GTI

45571
Halton Foundation
P.O. Box 3377
Portland, OR 97208 (503) 288-6411
Contact: Susan H. Findlay, Mgr.

Established in 1965 in OR.
Donor(s): The Halton Co.
Financial data (yr. ended 08/31/01): Grants paid, $68,363; assets, $1,361,406 (M); gifts received, $43,875; expenditures, $68,762; qualifying distributions, $67,839.
Limitations: Giving limited to areas of company operations in OR and WA.

Application information: Application form required.
Officer: Susan H. Findlay, Mgr.
Trustees: Kathryn Findlay, E.H. Halton, Jr., Sarah C. Harlan.
EIN: 936036295
Codes: CS, CD, GTI

45572
Crane Family Foundation
c/o Pacwest Ctr., Ste.1100
1211 S.W. 5th Ave.
Portland, OR 97204-3737 (503) 241-0570
Contact: Lawrence Evans, Pres.

Established in 1998 in OR.
Donor(s): Elizabeth Spangler.
Financial data (yr. ended 12/31/01): Grants paid, $68,220; assets, $1,582,504 (M); gifts received, $23,308; expenditures, $100,122; qualifying distributions, $91,049.
Limitations: Giving primarily in OR.
Officers: Lawrence Evans, Pres.; Benjamin M. Crane, V.P.; Timothy M. Crane, Secy.; Douglas A. Crane, Exec. Dir.
EIN: 931241577

45573
John Lamar Cooper Scholarship Loan Fund
c/o U.S. Bank, Trust Tax Svcs.
P.O. Box 3168
Portland, OR 97208-3168
Application address: c/o Oregon State Scholarship Commission, 1500 Valley River Dr., No. 100, Eugene, OR 97401
Contact: Marlyn Norquist, V.P.

Established in 1983.
Financial data (yr. ended 06/30/01): Grants paid, $67,410; assets, $1,034,011 (M); expenditures, $92,281; qualifying distributions, $78,859.
Limitations: Giving limited to Hood River County, OR.
Publications: Informational brochure (including application guidelines).
Application information: Applications available at any U.S. National Bank of Oregon branch, high school guidance counselor's office, or college financial aid office located in OR. Application form required.
Trustee: U.S. Bank.
EIN: 936155856
Codes: GTI

45574
The Morris Family Foundation
8785 Blackwell Rd.
Central Point, OR 97502 (541) 664-2847
Contact: Earl W. Morris, Pres.

Established in 1998 in OR.
Donor(s): Earl W. Morris.
Financial data (yr. ended 12/31/01): Grants paid, $67,361; assets, $859,052 (M); expenditures, $78,531; qualifying distributions, $67,361.
Limitations: Giving limited to residents of Jackson County, OR.
Officers: Earl W. Morris, Pres. and Secy.-Treas.; Bill Montague, V.P.
Trustees: Eric Lieder, Gary Rosenberger.
EIN: 931230039

45575
J. B. Steinbach Scholarship Fund
(Formerly Steinbach Foundation)
c/o U.S. Bank
P.O. Box 3168
Portland, OR 97208-3168

Established in 1961 in OR.
Financial data (yr. ended 06/30/01): Grants paid, $67,183; assets, $1,438,770 (M); expenditures, $92,647; qualifying distributions, $75,206.
Limitations: Giving primarily in OR.
Application information: Application forms available from local area high schools, college financial aid offices, or trustee bank. Application form required.
Trustee: U.S. Bank.
EIN: 936020885
Codes: GTI

45576
Karl Kramer Foundation
1154 Andrews Rd.
Lake Oswego, OR 97034-1718
(503) 635-2618

Established in 1990 in OR.
Donor(s): Ralph Bliquez, Karen Bliquez.
Financial data (yr. ended 12/31/01): Grants paid, $66,906; assets, $731,940 (M); gifts received, $5,239; expenditures, $73,324; qualifying distributions, $66,906.
Limitations: Applications not accepted. Giving primarily in Portland, OR.
Application information: Contributes only to pre-selected organizations.
Directors: Pat Becker, Karen Bliquez, Ralph Bliquez.
EIN: 931045076

45577
E. E. Wilson Scholarship Fund Foundation
c/o U.S. Bank
P.O. Box 3168
Portland, OR 97208
Contact: Marlyn Norquist, V.P., U.S. Bank

Established in 1962.
Financial data (yr. ended 06/30/01): Grants paid, $66,800; assets, $1,044,140 (M); expenditures, $79,748; qualifying distributions, $68,247.
Limitations: Giving limited to Benton County, OR.
Application information: Application form required.
Trustee: U.S. Bank.
EIN: 936022322
Codes: GTI

45578
Ann and Bill Swindells Charitable Trust
3800 Wells Fargo Ctr.
Portland, OR 97201

Established in 1998 in OR.
Donor(s): Ann Swindells, William Swindells.
Financial data (yr. ended 12/31/01): Grants paid, $66,000; assets, $1,808,166 (M); expenditures, $69,743; qualifying distributions, $66,000.
Limitations: Applications not accepted. Giving primarily in Portland, OR.
Application information: Contributes only to pre-selected organizations.
Trustees: Leslie Ann Ballinger, Ann Swindells, Charles Swindells, William Swindells, William R. Swindells.
EIN: 931246433

45579
Roberts Brothers Foundation
P.O. Box 6409
Portland, OR 97228

Established in 1987 in OR.
Donor(s): Aileen Roberts, Richard H. Roberts.
Financial data (yr. ended 12/31/01): Grants paid, $65,750; assets, $1,737,583 (M); expenditures, $69,958; qualifying distributions, $65,750.
Limitations: Giving primarily in Santa Barbara, CA, and Portland, OR.
Officers and Directors:* Richard H. Roberts,* Pres.; Frank H. Spears,* Secy.; Aileen Roberts.
EIN: 237023105

45580
Olga V. Alexandria Trust
c/o U.S. Bank
P.O. Box 3168
Portland, OR 97208
Application address: c/o Univ. of Utah, Financial Aid & Scholarships, University & 200 S., Salt Lake City, UT 84112
Contact: Carl Buck, Fin. Aid Off.

Financial data (yr. ended 05/31/01): Grants paid, $65,700; assets, $878,870 (M); expenditures, $77,252; qualifying distributions, $67,702.
Limitations: Giving limited to Salt Lake City, UT.
Application information: Application form available from University of Utah. Application form required.
Trustee: U.S. Bank.
EIN: 942936907
Codes: GTI

45581
Logsdon Charitable Foundation
180 N.W., 2nd St.
Prineville, OR 97754 (541) 447-6565
Contact: Leslie A. Sundet, Dir.

Established in 1998 in OR.
Financial data (yr. ended 04/30/02): Grants paid, $65,000; assets, $1,449,585 (M); expenditures, $70,066; qualifying distributions, $65,000.
Limitations: Giving primarily in Crook, Deschutes and Jefferson counties, OR.
Directors: Gary J. Bodie, Hans Christianson, Glenda Logsdon, Leslie A. Sundet.
EIN: 931244750

45582
Jenkins Student Aid Fund
c/o U.S. Bank
P.O. Box 3168
Portland, OR 97208-3168 (503) 275-4456
Application address: 1500 Valley River Dr., Ste. 100, Eugene, OR 97401, tel.: (800)452-8807

Established in 1960 in OR.
Donor(s): Hopkin Jenkins.‡
Financial data (yr. ended 06/30/01): Grants paid, $63,451; assets, $1,364,354 (M); expenditures, $103,159; qualifying distributions, $85,358.
Limitations: Giving limited to residents of ID, OR, and WA.
Publications: Program policy statement, application guidelines.
Application information: Application form required.
Trustee: U.S. Bank.
EIN: 936020672
Codes: GTI

45583
Share-It-Now Foundation
P.O. Box 5407
Eugene, OR 97405
Contact: Martha B. Russell, Tr.

Established in 1986 in OR.
Donor(s): Martha B. Russell.
Financial data (yr. ended 12/31/01): Grants paid, $63,190; assets, $805,235 (M); expenditures, $66,391; qualifying distributions, $62,629.
Limitations: Applications not accepted. Giving primarily in CA, NY, and OR.
Application information: Unsolicited requests for funds not accepted. Very limited budget precludes any large donations; grants usually given only once per year.

45583—OREGON

Trustees: Martha B. Russell, Corr. Tr.; Becky Liebman, Darrell Moss.
EIN: 930920814

45584
The Adams Foundation
17675 S.W. Farmington Rd., No. 470
Aloha, OR 97007-3216

Established in 1964 in OR.
Donor(s): Charles A. Adams, Peter F. Adams, Sandra A. Beebe.
Financial data (yr. ended 11/30/01): Grants paid, $63,075; assets, $828,995 (M); expenditures, $71,550; qualifying distributions, $63,075.
Limitations: Applications not accepted. Giving primarily in OR.
Application information: Contributes only to pre-selected organizations.
Directors: Charles A. Adams, Peter F. Adams, Sandra A. Beebe.
EIN: 936037058

45585
The Celebration Foundation
3234 N.E. 62nd Ave.
Portland, OR 97213 (503) 493-9770
Contact: Alan Toribio, Secy.-Treas.

Established in 2000 in OR.
Donor(s): Lysbeth A. Toribio.
Financial data (yr. ended 06/30/01): Grants paid, $62,200; assets, $47,398 (M); gifts received, $99,391; expenditures, $64,430; qualifying distributions, $64,251.
Limitations: Giving primarily in OR.
Application information: Application form required.
Officers and Directors:* Lysbeth A. Toribio,* Pres.; Alan Toribio,* Secy.-Treas.; Monica Schreiber, Edward Toribio.
EIN: 931312787

45586
Early Family Foundation
4310 S.W. Fairview Circus
Portland, OR 97221-2714
Contact: William B. Early, Pres.

Established in 1990 in OR.
Donor(s): William B. Early, Karen L. Early.
Financial data (yr. ended 12/31/01): Grants paid, $60,775; assets, $208,033 (M); gifts received, $52,000; expenditures, $66,326; qualifying distributions, $60,775.
Limitations: Applications not accepted. Giving limited to OR.
Application information: Unsolicited requests for funds not accepted.
Officers: William B. Early, Pres.; Karen L. Early, V.P.; Donald R. Crane, Secy.
EIN: 931043518

45587
Rene Bloch Foundation
c/o U.S. Bank
P.O. Box 3168
Portland, OR 97208-3168 (503) 275-6564
Contact: Marlyn Norquist, V.P.

Established in 1998 in OR.
Donor(s): Rene Bloch.‡
Financial data (yr. ended 12/31/01): Grants paid, $60,000; assets, $1,058,898 (M); expenditures, $69,587; qualifying distributions, $61,338.
Limitations: Giving on a national basis.
Application information: Applications are granted only to those organizations whose proposal has been approved. Application form required.
Trustee: U.S. Bank.
EIN: 916448421

45588
The Corvallis Clinic Foundation, Inc.
c/o Admin.
444 N.W. Elks Dr.
Corvallis, OR 97330-3744
Contact: Judy Corwin, Exec. Secy.

Donor(s): Corvallis Clinic, P.C., David Cutsforth, M.D.
Financial data (yr. ended 12/31/00): Grants paid, $60,000; assets, $200,684 (M); gifts received, $41,452; expenditures, $73,639; qualifying distributions, $64,764; giving activities include $4,873 for programs.
Limitations: Giving limited to the Mid-Willamette Valley area, including Linn and Benton counties, OR.
Trustees: David Cutsforth, M.D., John Erkkila, M.D., John Irving, David Kliewer, M.D., James Nusrala, Wes Price.
EIN: 936021898
Codes: CS, CD

45589
The Gary and Wanda Walsh Private Foundation
61712 Brokentop Dr.
Bend, OR 97702 (541) 389-8092
Contact: Gary L. Walsh, Pres.

Established in 1997 in OR.
Financial data (yr. ended 12/31/00): Grants paid, $60,000; assets, $1,610,064 (M); expenditures, $79,734; qualifying distributions, $60,000.
Limitations: Giving primarily in CA, OR and WA.
Application information: Application form required.
Officers: Gary L. Walsh, Pres.; Wanda F. Walsh, Secy.
EIN: 943288395

45590
George & Edna McDowell Charitable Trust
c/o Wells Fargo Bank Northwest, N.A., Trust Tax Dept.
P.O. Box 2971, MAC 6245-011
Portland, OR 97208 (503) 399-3595

Established in 1995 in OR.
Financial data (yr. ended 12/31/00): Grants paid, $59,652; assets, $1,681,939 (M); expenditures, $82,870; qualifying distributions, $65,768.
Limitations: Applications not accepted. Giving primarily in OR.
Application information: Contributes only to pre-selected organizations.
Trustee: Wells Fargo Bank Northwest, N.A.
EIN: 936288862

45591
Stewart Sullivan Scholarship Trust
c/o U.S. Bank
P.O. Box 3168
Portland, OR 97208

Established in 1999 in OR.
Donor(s): Stewart Sullivan.‡
Financial data (yr. ended 12/31/01): Grants paid, $59,334; assets, $1,060,791 (M); expenditures, $77,115; qualifying distributions, $59,334.
Limitations: Giving limited to Baker County, OR.
Trustee: U.S. Bank.
EIN: 931257512

45592
MacWilliams Family Foundation
20145 S.W. Nancy Ln.
Aloha, OR 97007

Established in 1997 in OR.
Donor(s): Peter MacWilliams, Sharon MacWilliams.

Financial data (yr. ended 12/31/01): Grants paid, $58,650; assets, $969,245 (M); expenditures, $76,853; qualifying distributions, $58,650.
Limitations: Applications not accepted. Giving primarily in OR.
Application information: Contributes only to pre-selected organizations.
Directors: Peter MacWilliams, Rebekah MacWilliams, Sharon MacWilliams.
EIN: 911810520

45593
Freres Foundation
c/o Freres Lumber Co., Inc.
P.O. Box 276
Lyons, OR 97358

Donor(s): Freres Lumber Co., Inc.
Financial data (yr. ended 09/30/01): Grants paid, $58,300; assets, $1,543,582 (M); gifts received, $50,000; expenditures, $58,558; qualifying distributions, $58,300.
Limitations: Applications not accepted. Giving primarily in OR.
Application information: Contributes only to pre-selected organizations.
Officers: Robert T. Freres, Pres.; Robert T. Freres, Jr., V.P.; Theodore F. Freres, V.P.; William M. Smith, Secy.
EIN: 936027213
Codes: CS, CD

45594
A. B. McGuire Trust
c/o George Luoma
P.O. Box 1608
Roseburg, OR 97470

Established in 1985 in OR.
Financial data (yr. ended 09/30/99): Grants paid, $57,703; assets, $2,567,023 (L); expenditures, $78,969; qualifying distributions, $57,703.
Limitations: Applications not accepted. Giving primarily in OR.
Application information: Contributes only to pre-selected organizations.
Trustees: George Luoma, Wanda McGuire.
EIN: 936184488

45595
William C. McCormick Foundation
5550 S.W. Macadam, Ste. 310
Portland, OR 97201-3770

Established in 1994 in OR.
Donor(s): William C. McCormick.
Financial data (yr. ended 12/31/01): Grants paid, $57,500; assets, $741,527 (M); gifts received, $86,400; expenditures, $77,575; qualifying distributions, $57,500.
Limitations: Giving primarily in OR.
Officer: William C. McCormick, Pres. and Secy.-Treas.
Directors: Dirk Edwards, John H. Rosenfeld.
EIN: 931159949

45596
Walter E. Lundquist Scholarship Testamentary Trust
c/o Wells Fargo Bank Northwest, N.A., Trust Tax Dept.
P.O. BOX 2971
Portland, OR 97208
Application address: c/o Walter E. Lundquist Scholarship Comm., Kalama School District, No. 402, P.O. Box 1097, Kalama, WA 98625

Financial data (yr. ended 03/31/01): Grants paid, $56,545; assets, $848,594 (M); expenditures, $71,650; qualifying distributions, $60,754.
Limitations: Giving limited to Kalama, WA.

Application information: Application form not required.
Trustee: Wells Fargo Bank Northwest, N.A.
EIN: 936145913
Codes: GTI

45597
Lilley Family Foundation
520 S.W. Yamhill, Roof Garden, Ste. 8
Portland, OR 97204
Contact: Joanne Lilley, Dir.

Established in 1997 in OR.
Donor(s): Joanne M. Lilley.
Financial data (yr. ended 12/31/01): Grants paid, $56,500; assets, $1,010,897 (M); expenditures, $65,381; qualifying distributions, $56,500.
Limitations: Applications not accepted. Giving primarily in OR.
Application information: Contributes only to pre-selected organizations.
Directors: Sylvia Page Evans, Charles S. Lilley, Douglas F. Lilley, Elizabeth Jane Lilley, Joanne M. Lilley.
EIN: 931233959

45598
Lineburger Foundation of Oregon
4048 S.W. Greenleaf Dr.
Portland, OR 97221-3223

Established in 1997 in OR.
Donor(s): Elisabeth L. Lyon.
Financial data (yr. ended 12/31/01): Grants paid, $56,000; assets, $1,130,376 (M); expenditures, $77,045; qualifying distributions, $56,000.
Limitations: Applications not accepted. Giving primarily in Portland, OR.
Application information: Contributes only to pre-selected organizations.
Officers: Elisabeth L. Lyon, Pres.; Peter B. Lyon, V.P.
Directors: Candace Harvey-Smith, Barbara S. Heffernan.
EIN: 931183224

45599
The Franklin and Dorothy Piacentini Charitable Trust
1034 S.W. Myrtle Dr.
Portland, OR 97201

Established in 1994 in OR.
Donor(s): Franklin D. Piacentini, Dorothy Piacentini.
Financial data (yr. ended 12/31/01): Grants paid, $55,360; assets, $969,217 (M); expenditures, $65,582; qualifying distributions, $55,360.
Limitations: Applications not accepted. Giving primarily in Portland, OR.
Application information: Contributes only to pre-selected organizations.
Trustees: Angela Jean Kilman, Dorothy Piacentini, Franklin D. Piacentini.
EIN: 931246381

45600
Fulton Foundation
1944 Heitzman Way
Eugene, OR 97402
Contact: D. Fulton, Pres.

Established around 1989 in CA.
Donor(s): Robert E. Fulton, Sulie A. Fulton.
Financial data (yr. ended 12/31/01): Grants paid, $55,000; assets, $635,135 (M); gifts received, $500; expenditures, $56,283; qualifying distributions, $55,000.
Limitations: Giving limited to CA.
Application information: Application form required.

Officers: Daniel Fulton, Pres.; Joy Fulton, Secy.; Robert E Fulton, Jr., Treas.
EIN: 330382611

45601
Tarbell Family Foundation
c/o Maginnis & Carey LLP
220 N.W. 2nd Ave., Ste. 1000
Portland, OR 97209-3953
Contact: Harry Tarbell, Tr.

Established in 1993 in OR.
Donor(s): Harry Tarbell, Mary Priscilla Tarbell.
Financial data (yr. ended 12/31/00): Grants paid, $54,000; assets, $825,357 (M); gifts received, $100,000; expenditures, $61,470; qualifying distributions, $54,000.
Limitations: Giving primarily in CA.
Trustees: Peter Buffington, Gary Leiser, Patty Leiser, Beverly Tarbell, Darcy Tarbell, Hank Tarbell, Harry Tarbell, Jim Tarbell, Judy Tarbell.
EIN: 931104762

45602
Pioneer Trust Bank, N.A. Foundation
c/o Pioneer Trust Bank, N.A.
P.O. Box 2305
Salem, OR 97308-2305 (503) 363-3136

Established in 1984 in OR.
Donor(s): Pioneer Trust Bank, N.A.
Financial data (yr. ended 12/31/01): Grants paid, $53,500; assets, $942,762 (M); expenditures, $54,990; qualifying distributions, $53,162.
Limitations: Giving primarily in Salem, OR.
Publications: Application guidelines.
Application information: Application form not required.
Trustee: Pioneer Trust Bank, N.A.
EIN: 930881673
Codes: CS, CD

45603
Merrill Family Foundation, Inc.
17980 S.W. Kemmer Rd.
Beaverton, OR 97007 (503) 591-5256
Contact: Charles W. Merrill, Pres.

Established in 1995 in OR.
Donor(s): Lenore Merrill, Charles Merrill,‡ Kay Merrill.
Financial data (yr. ended 12/31/99): Grants paid, $53,360; assets, $2,584,064 (M); gifts received, $435,440; expenditures, $62,722; qualifying distributions, $53,360.
Limitations: Giving primarily in OR.
Officers: Charles Merrill, Pres.; Kay Merrill, Secy.-Treas.
Director: Anthony C. Merrill, Lisa K. Sickler.
EIN: 931191941

45604
Women's Care Foundation
c/o U.S. Bank
P.O. Box 3168
Portland, OR 97208-3168

Financial data (yr. ended 12/31/01): Grants paid, $53,080; assets, $945,725 (M); gifts received, $1,725; expenditures, $66,279; qualifying distributions, $53,080.
Limitations: Giving primarily in the metropolitan Portland, OR, area.
Application information: Application form required.
Officer: Austin Moller-Bauch, Pres.
Trustee: U.S. Bank.
EIN: 930386973

45605
The David and Loa Mason Charitable Trust
(also known as Mason Trust)
c/o U.S. Bank
P.O. Box 3168
Portland, OR 97208-3168 (503) 275-4855

Established in 1965 in OR.
Donor(s): David Mason, Loa Mason.
Financial data (yr. ended 06/30/02): Grants paid, $51,634; assets, $940,748 (M); expenditures, $59,707; qualifying distributions, $51,634.
Limitations: Giving primarily in Portland, OR.
Application information: Application form not required.
Trustee: U.S. Bank.
EIN: 510171871

45606
Weiss Education Foundation
(also known as Weiss Scientific Foundation)
c/o Admissions Comm.
14380 N.W. Science Park Dr.
Portland, OR 97229-5419
Contact: Robert Jarrett, Dir., Finance

Established in 1984 in OR.
Donor(s): Weiss Scientific Glass Blowing Co., TOSOH Quartz, Inc.
Financial data (yr. ended 12/31/01): Grants paid, $51,433; assets, $306,867 (M); gifts received, $120,000; expenditures, $54,888; qualifying distributions, $51,511.
Limitations: Giving primarily in areas of company operations in CA, OR, and TX.
Application information: Student must maintain a 3.0 GPA; parents must be employed with the company for at least 4 years. Application form required.
Trustees: Lou Myatt, Gunther Weiss, Jeff Wessel.
EIN: 930879802
Codes: CS, CD, GTI

45607
The Wintercross Foundation, Inc.
15000 Davis Ln.
Lake Oswego, OR 97035

Established in 1998 in OR.
Donor(s): Barry C. Barham.‡
Financial data (yr. ended 02/28/01): Grants paid, $51,250; assets, $2,154,481 (M); expenditures, $63,490; qualifying distributions, $63,387.
Limitations: Applications not accepted. Giving primarily in OR.
Application information: Contributes only to pre-selected organizations.
Officer: Ann Ellis, Pres.
Directors: David McNutt, Juan Sforza, Marcella Emma Sforza, Milton R. Smith.
EIN: 931241433

45608
The Gary M. Anderson Children's Foundation
1300 S.W. 5th Ave., Ste. 2300
Portland, OR 97201 (503) 241-2300
Contact: D. Charles Mauritz, Secy.-Treas.

Established in 1996 in OR.
Financial data (yr. ended 06/30/01): Grants paid, $50,988; assets, $599,663 (M); expenditures, $58,166; qualifying distributions, $50,353.
Application information: Application form required.
Officers: Gail C. Lyon, Pres.; Chris Mullman, V.P.; Herb C. Sundby, V.P.; D. Charles Mauritz, Secy.-Treas.
EIN: 931158219

45609
Bratzel-Kremen Foundation
c/o West Coast Trust
P.O. Box 1012
Salem, OR 97308

Established in 1998 in OR.
Donor(s): Hattie Bratzel-Kremen Trust.
Financial data (yr. ended 03/31/02): Grants paid, $50,000; assets, $1,360,013 (M); expenditures, $75,809; qualifying distributions, $50,000.
Limitations: Applications not accepted. Giving primarily in OR.
Application information: Contributes only to pre-selected organizations.
Trustee: West Coast Trust.
EIN: 916435915

45610
Francis Cheney Family Foundation
26051 S.W. Baker Rd.
Sherwood, OR 97140
Contact: Bonnie Wheeler

Established in 1999 in OR.
Financial data (yr. ended 12/31/00): Grants paid, $50,000; assets, $943,092 (M); expenditures, $58,194; qualifying distributions, $50,590.
Limitations: Giving limited to OR.
Trustee: U.S. Bank, N.A.
EIN: 936331202

45611
William R. & Marjory G. Varitz Foundation
2165 S.W. Main St.
Portland, OR 97205

Established in 1992 in OR.
Donor(s): William R. Varitz, Marjory G. Varitz.
Financial data (yr. ended 06/30/01): Grants paid, $49,550; assets, $70,481 (M); expenditures, $51,550; qualifying distributions, $51,522.
Limitations: Applications not accepted. Giving primarily in Portland, OR.
Application information: Contributes only to pre-selected organizations.
Officers: William R. Varitz, Pres.; Marjory G. Varitz, Secy.-Treas.
Director: Lynn D. Simpson.
EIN: 931095466

45612
Charles E. Davis Educational Foundation
c/o Wells Fargo Bank Northwest, N.A.
P.O. Box 2971
Portland, OR 97208-3927
Application address: c/o Sherman County Scholarship Assoc., P.O. Box 0444, Moro, OR 97039-0444

Established in 1984 in OR.
Financial data (yr. ended 07/31/01): Grants paid, $49,174; assets, $894,700 (M); expenditures, $63,821; qualifying distributions, $53,367.
Limitations: Giving limited to Sherman County, OR.
Application information: Application form required.
Trustee: Wells Fargo Bank Northwest, N.A.
EIN: 936170500
Codes: GTI

45613
Margaret Watt Edwards Foundation
c/o Bronwen Edwards-Denney
3309 S.W. Stonebrook Dr.
Portland, OR 97201

Established in 2000 in OR.
Donor(s): Margaret W. Edwards.
Financial data (yr. ended 12/31/01): Grants paid, $48,123; assets, $1,954,516 (M); expenditures, $82,568; qualifying distributions, $48,123.
Limitations: Applications not accepted. Giving primarily in Portland, OR.
Application information: Contributes only to pre-selected organizations.
Trustees: Cameron Shand Denney, Colin Beveridge Denney, Bronwen Edwards-Denney.
EIN: 931284549

45614
Anne A. Berni Foundation
c/o U.S. Bank
P.O. Box 3168
Portland, OR 97208
Application address: c/o Mary C. Becker, Pres., 1117 S.W. Mitchell Ln., Portland, OR 97201
Contact: Marlyn Norquist

Established in 1994 in OR.
Financial data (yr. ended 06/30/02): Grants paid, $47,600; assets, $861,727 (M); expenditures, $52,786; qualifying distributions, $47,600.
Limitations: Giving limited to the Pacific Northwest.
Officers: Mary C. Becker, Pres.; Scott Becker, V.P.; Judith Anderson, Secy.
Trustee: U.S. Bank.
EIN: 931150372

45615
Second Dorothy F. Martin Charitable Foundation
c/o U.S. Bank
P.O. Box 3168
Portland, OR 97208
Application address: c/o U.S. Bank, P.O. Box 3058, Salt Lake City, UT 84110-3058, tel.: (801) 534-6085

Established in 1985 in UT.
Financial data (yr. ended 11/30/01): Grants paid, $46,700; assets, $861,135 (M); expenditures, $58,968; qualifying distributions, $46,700.
Limitations: Giving primarily in Salt Lake City, UT.
Trustee: U.S. Bank.
EIN: 876197628

45616
The Alpaca Research Foundation
33888 S.E. Peoria Rd.
Corvallis, OR 97333-2318

Financial data (yr. ended 12/31/01): Grants paid, $46,649; assets, $319,408 (M); gifts received, $23,215; expenditures, $57,383; qualifying distributions, $55,549.
Limitations: Applications not accepted. Giving primarily in CO.
Application information: Contributes only to pre-selected organizations.
Officers: Karen Baum, Pres.; Allan Dewald, M.D., V.P.; Nancy Irlbeck, Ph.D., Secy.; Patrick Long, Treas.
EIN: 810519605

45617
Marilyn Moyer Charitable Trust
805 S.W. Broadway, Ste. 2020
Portland, OR 97205 (503) 241-1111
Contact: Thomas Paul Moyer, Tr.

Established in 1991 in WA.
Donor(s): Thomas Paul Moyer.
Financial data (yr. ended 07/31/00): Grants paid, $46,083; assets, $1,367,389 (M); expenditures, $70,377; qualifying distributions, $53,687.
Limitations: Giving limited to legal residents of Clark County, WA and OR.
Application information: Applicant must be a legal resident for the past 18 months in Clark County, WA or OR. Application form required.
Officer and Trustees:* Kimberly Moyer Kassab,* Exec. Secy.; Thomas Paul Moyer, Thomas Peter Moyer, Timothy P. Moyer, Colleen Moyer Thrift.
EIN: 936238025
Codes: GTI

45618
Briggs Loosley Foundation
1940 N.W. Excello
Roseburg, OR 97470

Established in 2000 in OR.
Donor(s): Stephen Loosley, Rachelle Briggs-Loosley.
Financial data (yr. ended 12/31/01): Grants paid, $45,750; assets, $1,834,748 (M); expenditures, $65,992; qualifying distributions, $45,750.
Limitations: Applications not accepted.
Application information: Contributes only to pre-selected organizations.
Trustees: Rachelle Briggs-Loosley, Katherine Loosley, Stephen Loosley.
EIN: 931307508

45619
Larson Family Foundation
c/o Charles F. Larson
P.O. Box 10667
Eugene, OR 97440-2667

Established in 1996 in OR.
Donor(s): Charles F. Larson.
Financial data (yr. ended 12/31/01): Grants paid, $45,200; assets, $900,063 (M); expenditures, $57,832; qualifying distributions, $45,200.
Limitations: Applications not accepted.
Application information: Contributes only to pre-selected organizations.
Directors: Charles F. Larson, Charles F. Larson, Jr., Deborah L. Larson.
EIN: 931200088

45620
Hiram V. Rice Charitable Trust
c/o U.S. Bank, Trust Tax Svcs.
P.O. Box 3168
Portland, OR 97208

Financial data (yr. ended 01/31/02): Grants paid, $45,000; assets, $812,935 (M); expenditures, $57,526; qualifying distributions, $46,873.
Limitations: Applications not accepted. Giving limited to ID and OR.
Application information: Contributes only to pre-selected organizations.
Trustee: U.S. Bank.
EIN: 826038772

45621
Curt & Margaret Uschmann Memorial Scholarship Fund
1211 S.W. Fifth Ave.
Portland, OR 97204
Application address: c/o Principal or Counselor, Lebanon Union High School, 1700 S. 5th St., Lebanon, OR 97355

Financial data (yr. ended 03/31/02): Grants paid, $45,000; assets, $747,796 (M); expenditures, $62,832; qualifying distributions, $46,185.
Limitations: Giving limited to Lebanon, OR.
Application information: Unsolicited requests for funds not considered or acknowledged. Application form required.
Trustee: KeyBank, N.A.
EIN: 936146393
Codes: GTI

45622
Max & Cardella Stanger Foundation
c/o U.S. Bank
P.O. Box 3168
Portland, OR 97208-3168

Established in 1997 in UT.
Donor(s): T.M. Max & Cardella Stanger Trust.
Financial data (yr. ended 06/30/01): Grants paid, $44,119; assets, $793,515 (M); expenditures, $52,490; qualifying distributions, $44,934.
Limitations: Applications not accepted.
Application information: Contributes only to pre-selected organizations.
Trustee: U.S. Bank.
EIN: 876237968

45623
Bloomfield Family Foundation
c/o U.S. Bank
P.O. Box 3168, Trust Tax Svcs.
Portland, OR 97208
Contact: Maryln Norquist

Established in 2000 in OR.
Donor(s): Marge Bloomfield.
Financial data (yr. ended 12/31/01): Grants paid, $44,000; assets, $932,570 (M); gifts received, $25,172; expenditures, $79,643; qualifying distributions, $44,000.
Trustee: U.S. Bank.
EIN: 931307278

45624
Martha K. Hall Educational Trust
c/o U.S. Bank, Trust Dept.
P.O. Box 3168
Portland, OR 97208-3168
Application address: c/o U.S. Bank of Washington, P.O. Box 3588 (WSA 680), Spokane, WA 9920

Financial data (yr. ended 09/30/99): Grants paid, $43,400; assets, $858,512 (M); expenditures, $58,056; qualifying distributions, $43,229.
Limitations: Giving limited to residents of Lincoln County, WA.
Application information: Application form required.
Trustee: U.S. Bank of Washington, N.A.
EIN: 916173039
Codes: GTI

45625
Mario & Alma Pastega Family Foundation
2636 N.E. Belvue
Corvallis, OR 97339
Contact: Mario Pastega, Pres.

Established in 1997 in OR.
Donor(s): Mario Pastega, Pastega Charitable Lead Trust.
Financial data (yr. ended 12/31/01): Grants paid, $43,128; assets, $1,075,821 (M); gifts received, $286,862; expenditures, $61,068; qualifying distributions, $43,128.
Officers: Mario Pastega, Pres.; Gary Pastega, Secy.
Directors: Lisa Pastega Altig, Alma Pastega, Bianca Pastega, Dennis Pastega, Kenneth Pastega.
EIN: 931232789

45626
The Friends of Paul Bunyan Foundation
1127 25th St., S.E.
Salem, OR 97309 (503) 364-1330
Application address: P.O. Box 12339, Salem, OR 97309-0339; URL: http://www.oregonloggers.org
Contact: H. Mike Miller, Exec. Dir.

Established in 1997 in OR.

Financial data (yr. ended 06/30/02): Grants paid, $43,000; assets, $644,134 (M); expenditures, $66,281; qualifying distributions, $43,000.
Limitations: Giving primarily in OR.
Publications: Annual report.
Application information: Application form required.
Officers and Board Members:* Hap Huffman,* Pres.; Tom Hirons,* V.P.; Bob Kintigh,* Treas.; H. Mike Miller,* Exec. Dir.; Gary Betts, Jackie Lang, Doug Littlejohn, Bill Lulay, Alex Paul, Marvin Rowley.
EIN: 911830032

45627
Arthur and Doreen Parrett Scholarship Trust Fund
(also known as Parrett Scholarship Fund)
c/o U.S. Bank, Trust Div.
P.O. Box 3169
Portland, OR 97205-0742
Application address: P.O. Box 720, Seattle, WA 88111-0720
Contact: Paul Schneider, Trust Off., U.S. Bank

Financial data (yr. ended 11/30/01): Grants paid, $43,000; assets, $496,665 (M); expenditures, $54,830; qualifying distributions, $48,261.
Limitations: Giving limited to residents of WA.
Application information: Application form required.
Trustee: U.S. Bank.
EIN: 916228230
Codes: GTI

45628
John and Linda Shelk Foundation, Inc.
P.O. Box 26
Powell Butte, OR 97753

Donor(s): John Shelk, Linda S. Shelk.
Financial data (yr. ended 12/31/01): Grants paid, $42,700; assets, $1,277,229 (M); gifts received, $81,949; expenditures, $44,133; qualifying distributions, $42,700.
Limitations: Applications not accepted.
Application information: Contributes only to pre-selected organizations.
Officers: Linda S. Shelk, Pres.; John Shelk, Secy.-Treas.
Director: David A. Kekel.
EIN: 931156903

45629
Kohnstamm Family Foundation
8705 S.W. Nimbus Ave., Ste. 115
Beaverton, OR 97008-7159
Contact: Molly Kohnstamm, V.P.

Established in 1994 in OR.
Donor(s): Molly D. Kohnstamm, Richard L. Kohnstamm.
Financial data (yr. ended 12/31/01): Grants paid, $42,465; assets, $890,564 (M); gifts received, $24,000; expenditures, $47,805; qualifying distributions, $42,465.
Limitations: Applications not accepted. Giving primarily in Portland, OR.
Application information: Contributes only to pre-selected organizations.
Officers and Director:* Richard L. Kohnstamm,* Pres.; Molly D. Kohnstamm,* V.P.; Kevin R. Kohnstamm,* Secy.-Treas.
EIN: 931160719

45630
John & Mary Mock Perpetual Memorial Scholarship Fund
c/o Union Bank of California, N.A.
P.O. Box 2742
Portland, OR 97208-2742
Application address: c/o Principal, Roosevelt High School, Portland, OR 97208

Financial data (yr. ended 12/31/01): Grants paid, $42,191; assets, $1,060,958 (M); expenditures, $53,123; qualifying distributions, $45,933.
Limitations: Giving limited to Portland, OR.
Application information: Scholarship is paid directly to the individual recipient's educational institution. Application form required.
Trustee: Union Bank of California, N.A.
EIN: 930727584
Codes: GTI

45631
Quest Charitable Trust
11040 S.W. Barbur Blvd., Ste. 101
Portland, OR 97219

Established in 1993 in OR.
Donor(s): Barry J. Butcher.
Financial data (yr. ended 03/31/01): Grants paid, $41,387; assets, $34,427 (M); gifts received, $41,859; expenditures, $43,882; qualifying distributions, $41,387.
Limitations: Applications not accepted. Giving primarily in South India, Israel and Romania.
Application information: Contributes only to pre-selected organizations.
Trustee: Barry J. Butcher.
EIN: 943196272

45632
Albert L. & Ivy B. Thomas Educational Fund
c/o U.S. Bank
P.O. Box 3168
Portland, OR 97208-3168
Application address: 1530 Monmouth St., Independence, OR 97351, tel.: (503) 838-0480

Established in 1987 in OR.
Financial data (yr. ended 12/31/00): Grants paid, $41,034; assets, $1,622,441 (M); expenditures, $71,681; qualifying distributions, $46,702.
Limitations: Giving on a national basis.
Application information: Application form required.
Trustees: Chester Scott, U.S. Bank.
EIN: 936196091
Codes: GTI

45633
The Glennco Foundation
2626 Swan Lake Rd.
Klamath Falls, OR 97603

Established in 1996 in OR.
Financial data (yr. ended 12/31/01): Grants paid, $41,000; assets, $1,117,909 (M); gifts received, $5; expenditures, $44,443; qualifying distributions, $41,000.
Limitations: Applications not accepted. Giving primarily in CA and OR.
Application information: Contributes only to pre-selected organizations.
Officers: Glenn J. Lorenz, Pres.; Glenn T. Lorenz, V.P.; Richard Fairclo, Secy.-Treas.
EIN: 931221596

45634
The Kate Fansler Foundation, Inc.
c/o E. Heilbrun
86437 Greenbriar Dr.
Eugene, OR 97402
Application address: 151 Central Park West, New York, NY 10023, tel.: (212) 501-8157
Contact: Carolyn G. Heilbrun, Dir.

Established in 1997 in NY.
Donor(s): Carolyn G. Heilbrun.
Financial data (yr. ended 05/31/01): Grants paid, $40,683; assets, $0 (M); gifts received, $37,718; expenditures, $41,457; qualifying distributions, $40,683.
Limitations: Giving primarily to residents of NY.
Application information: Application form not required.
Officers: Carolyn Heilburn, Co-Chair.; Judith Resnik, Co-Chair.; Emily Heilbrun, Secy.-Treas.
Directors: Joan Ferrrante, Margaret Heilbrum, Robert Heilbrun, Susan Heath.
EIN: 133979080

45635
Gill Family Foundation
01740 S.W. Military Rd.
Portland, OR 97219

Established in 2000 in OR.
Donor(s): Mary Kay Gill, Frank C. Gill.
Financial data (yr. ended 12/31/01): Grants paid, $40,500; assets, $1,594,721 (M); expenditures, $84,614; qualifying distributions, $40,500.
Limitations: Applications not accepted.
Application information: Contributes only to pre-selected organizations.
Officers: Mary Kay Gill, Pres. and Secy.; Frank C. Gill, V.P. and Treas.
Director: Perry V. Olson.
EIN: 931307026

45636
Donovan Family Foundation
c/o Stephen M. Donovan
10553 S.W. Mount Adams Dr.
Beaverton, OR 97007

Established in 2000 in OR.
Donor(s): Stephen M. Donovan, Retina R. Donovan.
Financial data (yr. ended 09/30/01): Grants paid, $40,007; assets, $54,728 (M); gifts received, $94,500; expenditures, $40,126; qualifying distributions, $40,007.
Limitations: Applications not accepted. Giving primarily in Portland, OR.
Application information: Contributes only to pre-selected organizations.
Officers: Retina R. Donovan, Pres.; Stephen M. Donovan, Secy.
Director: Vye Blanchard.
EIN: 931308702

45637
The Equity Group Foundation
7125 S.W. Hampton St.
Portland, OR 97223
URL: http://www.equitygroup.com/company/foundation.php

Established in 2000 in OR.
Donor(s): RE/MAX Equity Group, Inc.
Financial data (yr. ended 12/31/01): Grants paid, $40,000; assets, $11,883 (M); gifts received, $31,653; expenditures, $40,050; qualifying distributions, $40,000.
Limitations: Applications not accepted.
Application information: Contributes only to pre-selected organizations.
Directors: Karin J. Atkins, Kurt H. Dalbey, S. Joan Hamrick.
EIN: 931293204
Codes: CS

45638
Flowerree Foundation
805 S.W. Broadway, Ste. 2290
Portland, OR 97205
Contact: Robert E. Flowerree, Pres.

Established in 1961.
Donor(s): Robert E. Flowerree, Elaine D. Flowerree.
Financial data (yr. ended 12/31/01): Grants paid, $40,000; assets, $1,456,607 (M); gifts received, $130,650; expenditures, $51,626; qualifying distributions, $40,000.
Limitations: Applications not accepted. Giving primarily in OR; giving also in CA and New Orleans, LA.
Application information: Contributes only to pre-selected organizations.
Officers: Robert E. Flowerree, Pres.; Elaine D. Flowerree, V.P.; David Munro, Secy.
EIN: 936034207

45639
Robert L. Ragel Scholarship Fund
1211 S.W. 5th Ave., Ste. 1800
Portland, OR 97204-3795
Contact: Nikki C. Hatton

Established in 1998 in OR.
Donor(s): Robert L. Ragel.
Financial data (yr. ended 12/31/00): Grants paid, $40,000; assets, $802,101 (M); gifts received, $255,938; expenditures, $43,702; qualifying distributions, $43,702.
Limitations: Giving primarily in OR.
Application information: Application form available from Tigard High School guidance counselors. Application form required.
Officers and Directors:* Marian L. Ragel,* Co-Pres.; Robert L. Ragel,* Co-Pres.; Tracy L. Pritulsky, Julie K. Ragel Winn.
EIN: 931254085

45640
The Hubert & Ludmila Schlesinger Foundation
400 Yamhill Plz.
815 S.W. 2nd Ave., Ste. 400
Portland, OR 97204 (503) 221-1188
Contact: Andrew H. Josephson, Tr.

Established in 1986 in OR.
Financial data (yr. ended 12/31/01): Grants paid, $40,000; assets, $1,370,116 (M); expenditures, $77,368; qualifying distributions, $65,046.
Limitations: Giving limited to OR.
Officer and Trustees:* Andrew H. Josephson,* C.E.O. and Mgr.; Susan Josephson, William Uhle.
EIN: 930900123

45641
Rogue Wave Foundation
815 N. W. 9th St., Ste. No. L145
Corvallis, OR 97330

Donor(s): Thomas Keffer.
Financial data (yr. ended 06/30/99): Grants paid, $39,900; assets, $4,649 (M); gifts received, $33,588; expenditures, $39,910; qualifying distributions, $39,910.
Application information: Application form required.
Officers: Sherri Thorn, Pres.; Thomas Keffer, V.P.; Greg Koerper, Secy.; Greg Bumgardner, Treas.
Director: Steve Hansen.
EIN: 931192469

45642
King Charitable Foundation
720 Kenola Ct.
Lake Oswego, OR 97034
Contact: John G. King, Pres.

Established in 1999 in OR.
Donor(s): John G. King, Jane E. King.
Financial data (yr. ended 12/31/01): Grants paid, $39,000; assets, $931,124 (M); gifts received, $231,115; expenditures, $41,603; qualifying distributions, $39,000.
Limitations: Giving on a national basis.
Officers: John G. King, Pres.; Jane E. King, Treas.
Directors: Sara J. King, Jennifer K. Molyneaux.
EIN: 931266813

45643
The Tennant Foundation
(Formerly John J. Tennant Foundation)
P.O. Box 1658
Portland, OR 97207-1658

Established in 1967 in OR.
Donor(s): John J. Tennant.
Financial data (yr. ended 12/31/01): Grants paid, $38,498; assets, $449,101 (M); gifts received, $25,038; expenditures, $39,215; qualifying distributions, $38,498.
Limitations: Applications not accepted. Giving primarily in Portland, OR.
Application information: Contributes only to pre-selected organizations.
Trustees: John J. Tennant, Jr., Joseph P. Tennant.
EIN: 936042963

45644
Noble B. Goettel Charitable Foundation
c/o U.S. Bank
P.O. Box 3168
Portland, OR 97208-3168
Contact: Marilyn Norquist, V.P., U.S. Bank

Established in 1987 in OR.
Financial data (yr. ended 06/30/01): Grants paid, $37,979; assets, $851,478 (M); expenditures, $46,009; qualifying distributions, $37,979.
Limitations: Giving limited to the Douglas County, OR, area.
Application information: Application form required.
Trustee: U.S. Bank.
EIN: 936195656

45645
The Dudley Foundation
(Formerly The Chris Dudley Foundation)
515 N.W. Saltzman Rd., Ste. 789
Portland, OR 97229-6098 (503) 626-4007
Contact: Debbie Wakem, Exec. Dir.

Established in 1994 in CA.
Donor(s): Chris Dudley.
Financial data (yr. ended 09/30/01): Grants paid, $37,856; assets, $815,113 (M); gifts received, $39,625; expenditures, $170,798; qualifying distributions, $137,208; giving activities include $137,208 for programs.
Limitations: Giving on a national basis.
Officer: Chris Dudley, Pres.
Directors: Debbie Wakem, Exec. Dir.; Dan Fegan, Mike Flannery.
EIN: 330634099

45646
Wentworth Foundation
107 S.E. Grand Ave.
Portland, OR 97214

Established in 1997.

Financial data (yr. ended 12/31/01): Grants paid, $37,260; assets, $1,067,091 (M); expenditures, $46,028; qualifying distributions, $37,260.
Limitations: Applications not accepted. Giving primarily in Portland, OR.
Application information: Contributes only to pre-selected organizations.
Officers: Gregory T. Wentworth, Pres.; Scott Wentworth, V.P.; Maurice R. Williams, Secy.; Robert C. Wentworth, Treas.
EIN: 936024043

45647
Constructive Management Foundation
P.O. Box 19299
Portland, OR 97280-0299

Established in 1989 in RI.
Financial data (yr. ended 12/31/01): Grants paid, $36,490; assets, $540,006 (M); expenditures, $47,384; qualifying distributions, $43,792.
Limitations: Applications not accepted. Giving on a national basis, with some emphasis on OR and the Pacific Northwest.
Application information: Contributes only to pre-selected organizations.
Officers and Directors:* Paul R. Farago,* Pres.; Gregory L. Powell,* Secy.; Peter A. Farago.
EIN: 050438672

45648
George Rossman Fund for Pacific University
c/o U.S. Bank
P.O. Box 3168
Portland, OR 97208-3168
Application address: c/o Robert L. Macy, Dir. of Financial Aid, Pacific University, Forest Grove, OR 97116

Donor(s): George Rossman.
Financial data (yr. ended 12/31/00): Grants paid, $35,700; assets, $708,597 (M); expenditures, $42,560; qualifying distributions, $36,633.
Limitations: Giving limited to OR.
Application information: The president of Pacific University has sole discretion in selecting the individual recipients.
Trustee: U.S. Bank.
EIN: 936051550
Codes: GTI

45649
Bill and Jackie Clark Memorial Foundation
P.O. Box 2087
Newport, OR 97365-2087
Contact: Laurie Ellen Clark, Pres.

Established in 1965.
Financial data (yr. ended 11/30/01): Grants paid, $35,500; assets, $0 (M); expenditures, $37,261; qualifying distributions, $35,500.
Limitations: Giving primarily in San Diego, CA.
Officers and Directors:* Laurie Ellen Clark,* Pres. and Treas.; Kurt L. Kicklighter,* Secy.; Ferdinand Fletcher, Serena Pearson.
EIN: 956056000

45650
Thomas S. Colvin Scholarship Trust
c/o South Valley Bank & Trust
P.O. Box 1784
Medford, OR 97501
Application address: c/o Ruthann Brown, Clatskanie High School, P.O. Box 68, Clatskanie, OR 97016

Established in 1993 in OR.
Donor(s): Martha Colvin Trust.
Financial data (yr. ended 12/31/00): Grants paid, $35,340; assets, $542,463 (M); expenditures, $44,826; qualifying distributions, $39,339.

Limitations: Giving limited to residents of the Clatskanie, OR, area.
Application information: Application form required.
Trustee: South Valley Bank & Trust.
EIN: 936267268
Codes: GTI

45651
Ralph D. and Bunny Schlesinger Foundation
(Formerly The Ralph D. Schlesinger Foundation)
610 S.W. Alder St., Ste. 1221
Portland, OR 97205 (503) 223-4128
Contact: Bernice W. Schlesinger, Pres.

Established in 1981.
Donor(s): Bernice W. Schlesinger, Ralph D. Schlesinger.‡
Financial data (yr. ended 06/30/01): Grants paid, $35,215; assets, $788,502 (M); expenditures, $50,103; qualifying distributions, $34,720.
Officer: Bernice W. Schlesinger, Pres.
Directors: Kevin W. Keithley, Stanley M. Samuels, Mark R. Schlesinger, Paul R. Schlesinger.
EIN: 930818169

45652
Western Lane Community Foundation
(Formerly Western Lane County Foundation)
1525 W. 12th St., Ste. 18
P.O. Box 1589
Florence, OR 97439
Tel. and FAX: (541) 997-1274; E-mail: wlcf@oregonfast.net; URL: http://www.wlcfonline.com
Contact: Annie Schmidt, Exec. Dir.

Established in 1974.
Financial data (yr. ended 12/31/00): Grants paid, $35,018; assets, $1,587,968 (M); gifts received, $86,472; expenditures, $74,881.
Limitations: Giving limited to western Lane County, OR, defined as the Mapleton and Siuslaw school districts.
Publications: Annual report, application guidelines, program policy statement, newsletter, informational brochure.
Application information: Application form required.
Officers: Andy Baber, Pres.; Arlis Ulman, Secy.; Kathy West, Treas.; Annie Schmidt, Exec. Dir.
Board Members: Ron Boehi, Dave Dahlberg, Stuart Johnston, Bob Read, Jon Taylor.
EIN: 237438503
Codes: CM

45653
Leotta Gordon Foundation
333 S.W. Taylor St.
Portland, OR 97204-2496 (503) 223-5181
Contact: Neale E. Creamer

Established in 1987 in OR.
Financial data (yr. ended 12/31/01): Grants paid, $35,000; assets, $677,931 (M); expenditures, $44,406; qualifying distributions, $36,843.
Limitations: Giving primarily in Portland, OR.
Application information: Application form not required.
Trustees: James Crumpacker, Paul R. Duden.
EIN: 943064791

45654
Allied Christian Foundation, Inc.
c/o James A. Peterson
0333 S.W. Flower St.
Portland, OR 97201
Application address: Riverpoint 1, Ste. 300, 1201 N.W. Wall St., Bend, OR 97701

Established in 1967 in OR.

Financial data (yr. ended 12/31/01): Grants paid, $34,950; assets, $521,874 (M); expenditures, $59,901; qualifying distributions, $34,950.
Limitations: Giving primarily in OR.
Officers and Directors:* Catherine C. Hoover, Pres.; Roberta Muggerud,* V.P.; Charlie Culver, Secy.; James A. Thompsen,* Treas.; Mary Jane Culver, John Ehrlich, Kathleen Ehrlich.
EIN: 936039838

45655
Bismarck H. Turner Scholarship Trust
c/o U.S. Bank
P.O. Box 3168
Portland, OR 97208-3168
Application address: c/o Helene Paroif, Educational Svc. District No. 101, W. 1025 Indiana Ave., Spokane, WA 99205

Financial data (yr. ended 03/31/02): Grants paid, $34,811; assets, $19,902 (M); expenditures, $42,099; qualifying distributions, $35,830.
Limitations: Giving limited to Bonner and Kootenai counties, ID, and Pend Oreille, ID counties and Spokane, WA.
Application information: Application form required.
Selection Committee: Warren Bakes, Mitch Denning, Edward Humble, Robert Jones, Frances A. Olson, Brian L. Talbot, Superintendent, Post Falls School District, No. 273.
Trustee: U.S. Bank.
EIN: 916254764
Codes: GTI

45656
Howard Cross Foundation, Inc.
22225 Bear Creek Rd.
Bend, OR 97701

Established in 2000 in OR.
Donor(s): Howard Cross.‡
Financial data (yr. ended 05/31/02): Grants paid, $34,150; assets, $1 (M); expenditures, $66,470; qualifying distributions, $34,150.
Limitations: Giving primarily in OR.
Officer: Les Hamilton, Mgr.
Directors: Cindy Hamilton, Debi Hurley.
EIN: 931143002

45657
Rod and Carol Wendt Foundation
2120 Fairmont St.
Klamath Falls, OR 97601-1536

Established in 1998 in OR.
Donor(s): Roderick Wendt, Carol M. Wendt.
Financial data (yr. ended 12/31/01): Grants paid, $34,000; assets, $541,839 (M); expenditures, $35,470; qualifying distributions, $34,000.
Limitations: Applications not accepted.
Application information: Contributes only to pre-selected organizations.
Officers: Roderick Wendt, Pres.; Carol m. Wendt, Secy.
Director: Andrea Wendt.
EIN: 931258619

45658
The Trent and Kaye Young Foundation
1759 Sunburst Terrace N.W.
Salem, OR 97304

Donor(s): Trenton Young.
Financial data (yr. ended 12/31/01): Grants paid, $32,997; assets, $51,244 (M); gifts received, $22,373; expenditures, $33,623; qualifying distributions, $32,997.
Limitations: Applications not accepted.
Application information: Contributes only to pre-selected organizations.

45658—OREGON

Directors: Kaye E. Young, Louise R. Young, Trenton R. Young.
EIN: 931258340

45659
Roland E. Howard & Elizabeth C. Howard Charitable Trust
c/o U.S. Bank
P.O. Box 3168
Portland, OR 97208-3168

Established in 1999.
Donor(s): Roland E. Howard.‡
Financial data (yr. ended 06/30/01): Grants paid, $32,836; assets, $921,112 (M); expenditures, $42,917; qualifying distributions, $32,836.
Limitations: Applications not accepted.
Application information: Contributes only to pre-selected organizations.
Trustee: U.S. Bank.
EIN: 936324967

45660
Arthur M. James Family Foundation
319 S.W. Washington, Ste. 614
Portland, OR 97204

Established in 1998 in OR.
Donor(s): Arthur M. James.
Financial data (yr. ended 12/31/01): Grants paid, $32,725; assets, $683,194 (M); expenditures, $37,701; qualifying distributions, $32,725.
Limitations: Applications not accepted.
Application information: Contributes only to pre-selected organizations. Unsolicited requests for funds not accepted.
Officers: Arthur M. James, Pres.; Christopher James, Secy.
Directors: Andrew James, Sally James Apfel.
EIN: 931258611

45661
Walter C. and Marie C. Schmidt Foundation
c/o U.S. Bank, Trust Tax
P.O. Box 3168
Portland, OR 97208-3168 (503) 275-4887
Contact: Matthew Rast, Trust Admin., U.S. Bank

Established in 1992 in OR.
Financial data (yr. ended 06/30/00): Grants paid, $32,576; assets, $902,660 (M); expenditures, $45,038; qualifying distributions, $37,103.
Limitations: Giving limited to residents of OR.
Application information: Application form required.
Trustee: U.S. Bank.
EIN: 936267092
Codes: GTI

45662
Help for the Poor
18701 S. Sprague Rd.
Oregon City, OR 97045

Financial data (yr. ended 12/31/00): Grants paid, $31,959; assets, $122 (L); gifts received, $32,450; expenditures, $32,528; qualifying distributions, $0.
Officers: Timotei Paul, Pres.; Elisabeth Florean, Secy.-Treas.
Board Member: Dumitru Paul.
EIN: 943228229

45663
Sophia Byers McComas Foundation
c/o U.S. Bank, Trust Dept.
P.O. Box 3168
Portland, OR 97208-3168 (503) 275-6564

Established in 1943 in OR.
Financial data (yr. ended 06/30/00): Grants paid, $31,750; assets, $2,503,089 (M); expenditures, $53,033; qualifying distributions, $42,407.
Limitations: Giving limited to OR.
Application information: Applicants recommended by church groups, social service agencies, or similar groups.
Trustee: U.S. Bank.
EIN: 936019602
Codes: GTI

45664
Clarke Family Foundation
c/o BKR Fordham, Goodfellow, LLP
233 S.E. 2nd Ave.
Hillsboro, OR 97123 (503) 648-6651

Established in 2001 in OR.
Donor(s): Thomas E. Clarke, Julia A. Clarke.
Financial data (yr. ended 12/31/01): Grants paid, $31,505; assets, $496,184 (M); gifts received, $357,795; expenditures, $42,132; qualifying distributions, $31,505.
Officers: Thomas E. Clarke, Pres.; Courtney Clarke, Secy.; Julia A. Clarke, Treas.
EIN: 931314716

45665
John W. McKee Educational Trust
c/o U.S. Bank
P.O. Box 3168, Trust Tax No. 50255290
Portland, OR 97208-3168 (503) 275-4327
Application address: c/o O'Toole Law Firm, Attn: McKee, 209 N. Main, Plentywood, MT 59254, tel.: (406) 765-1630

Established in 1970.
Financial data (yr. ended 12/31/01): Grants paid, $31,500; assets, $545,832 (M); expenditures, $39,642; qualifying distributions, $33,096.
Limitations: Giving limited to residents of Sheridan, Roosevelt, and Daniels counties, MT.
Application information: Application form required.
Trustee: U.S. Bank.
EIN: 237058723
Codes: GTI

45666
Homer I. & Persephone B. Watts Memorial Trust
c/o U.S. Bank
P.O. Box 3168
Portland, OR 97208-3168
Application address: c/o Donald Duncan, Athena, OR 97813, tel.: (503) 566-3773

Financial data (yr. ended 06/30/02): Grants paid, $31,330; assets, $695,802 (M); expenditures, $38,092; qualifying distributions, $31,330.
Limitations: Giving limited to Umatilla County, OR.
Application information: Request application information.
Trustee: U.S. Bank.
EIN: 936082689

45667
Marvin O. Palmer Trust
c/o U.S. Bank
P.O. Box 3168
Portland, OR 97208-3168
Application address: c/o Park High School Principal, Park High School, 102 Vista View Dr., Livingston, MT 59407, tel.: (408) 222-0448

Established in 1995 in MT.
Donor(s): Marvin O. Palmer.‡
Financial data (yr. ended 12/31/01): Grants paid, $31,037; assets, $708,605 (M); expenditures, $38,606; qualifying distributions, $32,334.
Limitations: Giving limited to residents of Livingston, MT.
Application information: Application form required.
Trustee: U.S. Bank.
EIN: 816079218

45668
Isis Foundation
12230 N.W. Sunningdale Dr.
Portland, OR 97229-4746

Established in 1999 in OR.
Financial data (yr. ended 12/31/01): Grants paid, $30,450; assets, $663,131 (M); gifts received, $295,313; expenditures, $42,082; qualifying distributions, $30,450.
Limitations: Applications not accepted. Giving primarily in OR.
Application information: Contributes only to pre-selected organizations.
Officers and Directors:* Marcia Ann Petty,* Pres.; Walter Gorman,* Secy.; Joseph J. Hanna, Jr.
EIN: 931276817

45669
Maria C. Jackson-Gen. George A. White Student Aid for Children of War Veterans Foundation
c/o U.S. Bank
P.O. Box 3168
Portland, OR 97208-3168 (503) 275-4456
Application address: c/o U.S. Bank of Oregon, Trust Student Aid, Portland, OR 97208-3168

Financial data (yr. ended 06/30/00): Grants paid, $30,184; assets, $1,016,859 (M); expenditures, $43,818; qualifying distributions, $34,735.
Limitations: Giving limited to OR.
Application information: Contact high school guidance counselor, college financial aid office, or local U.S. Bank Branch to obtain application. Personal interview required. Application form required.
Trustee: U.S. Bank.
EIN: 936020316
Codes: GTI

45670
Sehar Saleha Ahmad & Abrahim Ekramullah Zafar Foundation
2820 N.W. Circle A Dr.
Portland, OR 97229

Established in 1999 in OR.
Donor(s): Aftab Ahmad, Rehana Ahmad.
Financial data (yr. ended 12/31/01): Grants paid, $30,000; assets, $441,062 (M); gifts received, $15,000; expenditures, $33,090; qualifying distributions, $30,000.
Limitations: Applications not accepted. Giving primarily in Ashland and Portland, OR; some giving in Washington, DC.
Application information: Contributes only to pre-selected organizations.
Officers: Aftab Ahmad, Chair.; Ayesha Ahmad, Secy.
Director: Rehana Ahmad.
EIN: 931267289

45671
David B. Johnson Family Foundation
3401 S.W. Stonebroook
Portland, OR 97201

Established in 1999 in OR.
Donor(s): David B. Johnson, Karen S. Johnson.
Financial data (yr. ended 12/31/01): Grants paid, $29,600; assets, $1,018,788 (M); gifts received, $460,800; expenditures, $46,017; qualifying distributions, $29,600.

Limitations: Applications not accepted. Giving primarily in Portland, OR.
Application information: Contributes only to pre-selected organizations.
Trustees: David B. Johnson, Karen S. Johnson.
EIN: 931280694

45672
Snow Foundation
13855 S.W. Alpine View
Tigard, OR 97224-1790

Established in 1992 in OR.
Donor(s): E. Ned Snow, Carolyn J. Snow.
Financial data (yr. ended 12/31/01): Grants paid, $29,000; assets, $270,383 (M); gifts received, $21,162; expenditures, $29,791; qualifying distributions, $29,000.
Limitations: Applications not accepted. Giving primarily in OR.
Application information: Contributes only to pre-selected organizations.
Officers: E. Ned Snow, Pres.; Carolyn J. Snow, Secy.-Treas.
Directors: John Bayless, Roberta Hutton.
EIN: 931093986

45673
Bertha P. Singer Student Nurses Fund
c/o U.S. Bank
P.O. Box 3168
Portland, OR 97208
Application address: c/o Oregon Student Assistance Commission, 1500 Valley Dr., Ste. 100, Eugene, OR 97401

Financial data (yr. ended 06/30/01): Grants paid, $28,850; assets, $561,935 (M); expenditures, $40,638; qualifying distributions, $32,409.
Limitations: Giving limited to OR.
Application information: Contact financial aid office of local high schools in OR or Oregon Student Assistance Commission for application. Application form required.
Trustee: U.S. Bank.
EIN: 510181219
Codes: GTI

45674
Tim and Mary Boyle Charitable Trust
c/o Tim Boyle
P.O. Box 8307
Portland, OR 97207-8307

Established in 2000 in OR.
Donor(s): Tim Boyle.
Financial data (yr. ended 12/31/01): Grants paid, $28,500; assets, $1,191,163 (M); gifts received, $524,734; expenditures, $45,586; qualifying distributions, $17,549.
Limitations: Applications not accepted.
Application information: Contributes only to pre-selected organizations.
Trustees: Joseph Boyle, Mary Boyle, Tim Boyle.
EIN: 931305219

45675
Frank McCleary Medical Scholarship Fund of the Mary Ball Chapter for the Daughters of the American Revolution
c/o U.S. Bank
P.O. Box 3168
Portland, OR 97208-3168
Application address: 8419 45th St. West, University Place, WA 98466-2317, tel.: (253) 565-3661
Contact: Lt. Hilda L. Walker, Pres.

Donor(s): Frank McCleary.‡

Financial data (yr. ended 12/31/01): Grants paid, $28,500; assets, $530,531 (M); expenditures, $36,724; qualifying distributions, $29,225.
Limitations: Giving primarily in Seattle, WA.
Application information: Application form required.
Officers: Lt. Hilda L. Walker, Pres.; Mrs. James M. Thrasher, V.P.; Mrs. Larry B. Marlott, Secy.; Mrs. Rodney A. Grulke, Treas.
EIN: 510158972
Codes: GTI

45676
The W. E. Stevenson Foundation
919 S.W. Taylor St., Ste. 300
Portland, OR 97205-2523

Established in 1992 in OR.
Donor(s): Wallace E. Stevenson.
Financial data (yr. ended 09/30/01): Grants paid, $28,500; assets, $310,958 (M); expenditures, $34,015; qualifying distributions, $28,500.
Limitations: Applications not accepted. Giving primarily in Portland, OR.
Application information: Contributes only to pre-selected organizations.
Directors: Warren H. Bean, Katherine F. Stevenson.
EIN: 931098127

45677
Ochoco Charitable Fund
(Formerly Ochoco Scholarship Fund)
P.O. Box 668
Prineville, OR 97754
Application address: c/o Crook County High School, 1100 S.E. Lynn Blvd., Prineville, OR 97754, tel.: (541) 416-6900
Contact: Vivian Stock, Tr.

Donor(s): Ochoco Lumber Co., Malheur Lumber Co.
Financial data (yr. ended 12/31/01): Grants paid, $28,450; assets, $485,473 (M); gifts received, $21,519; expenditures, $30,681; qualifying distributions, $30,683.
Limitations: Giving limited to residents of the Prineville, OR, area.
Application information: Application form required.
Officer and Trustees:* Stuart J. Shelk, Jr.,* Pres.; Steve Markell, Vivian Stock.
EIN: 936024014
Codes: CS, CD, GTI

45678
The John & Olive Adams Philanthropic Trust
c/o U.S. Bank
P.O. Box 3168
Portland, OR 97208

Established in 1993 in ID.
Financial data (yr. ended 10/31/01): Grants paid, $28,378; assets, $493,913 (M); expenditures, $36,256; qualifying distributions, $30,135.
Limitations: Applications not accepted. Giving primarily in ID.
Application information: Contributes only to pre-selected organizations.
Trustee: U.S. Bank.
EIN: 826078010

45679
North Star Foundation
4115 N.E. 19th Ave.
Portland, OR 97211

Established in 1997 in OR.
Donor(s): Stanley R. Amy, Christy L. Eugenis.

Financial data (yr. ended 06/30/01): Grants paid, $28,050; assets, $636,330 (M); expenditures, $39,297; qualifying distributions, $28,050.
Limitations: Applications not accepted.
Application information: Contributes only to pre-selected organizations.
Officers: Stanley R. Amy, Pres. and Treas.; Christy L. Eugenis, Secy.
EIN: 931248016

45680
Fischer Family Foundation
c/o W.W. Kirtley
101 S.W. Main, Ste. 1800
Portland, OR 97204-3226 (503) 225-0777
Contact: Alexandra Fischer Morse, Pres.

Established in 1991 in OR.
Donor(s): Ruth Dodd Fischer.
Financial data (yr. ended 12/31/01): Grants paid, $28,000; assets, $582,473 (M); expenditures, $32,713; qualifying distributions, $28,000.
Limitations: Giving primarily in OR and WA.
Officers: Alexandra Fischer Morse, Pres.; Elizabeth Fischer Morse, Secy.; Dodd Fischer, Treas.
EIN: 911544328

45681
Robert W. Cooke Educational Fund
c/o Wells Fargo Bank Northwest, N.A.
P.O. Box 2971
Portland, OR 97208
Application address: c/o J.F. and R.W. Cooke Educational Fund Comm., Att; Secy., Scholarship Comm., Condon, OR 97823

Financial data (yr. ended 05/31/01): Grants paid, $27,917; assets, $626,942 (M); gifts received, $185; expenditures, $40,361; qualifying distributions, $33,381.
Limitations: Giving limited to residents of Gilliam County, OR.
Application information: Application form required.
Trustee: Wells Fargo Bank Northwest, N.A.
EIN: 936017308
Codes: GTI

45682
The Silvey Family Foundation
P.O. Box 205
Tualatin, OR 97062-0205

Established in 1995 in OR.
Donor(s): David H. Silvey, Krista L. Silvey.
Financial data (yr. ended 06/30/01): Grants paid, $27,365; assets, $748,759 (M); gifts received, $122,988; expenditures, $31,281; qualifying distributions, $27,365.
Limitations: Applications not accepted.
Application information: Contributes only to pre-selected organizations.
Officers: Krista L. Silvey, Pres.; Nelson Rutherford, V.P.; David H. Silvey, Secy.-Treas.
EIN: 931191997

45683
Boller-Thomas Foundation of Oregon
c/o U.S. Bank
P.O. Box 3168, Tr. Tax Svcs.
Portland, OR 97208-3168
Application address: c/o Paul DeVore, the Boller-Thomas Foundation of Oregon, 4 Essex Ct., Lake Oswego, OR 97034

Established in 1995 in OR.
Financial data (yr. ended 12/31/01): Grants paid, $27,000; assets, $424,816 (M); expenditures, $32,447; qualifying distributions, $27,000.
Limitations: Giving primarily in Portland, OR.

Application information: Application form not required.
Trustee: U.S. Bank.
EIN: 931162268

45684
Schilling Family Foundation
c/o U.S. Bank
P.O. Box 3168
Portland, OR 97208
Application address: c/o Scholarship Selection Comm., Butte High School, Butte, MT 59701

Established in 1990 in MT.
Donor(s): Raymond Schilling.‡
Financial data (yr. ended 03/31/00): Grants paid, $27,000; assets, $565,325 (M); expenditures, $39,179; qualifying distributions, $32,269.
Limitations: Giving primarily in MT.
Application information: Applicants must request forms from Butte High School. Application form required.
Trustee: U.S. Bank.
EIN: 816067894
Codes: GTI

45685
Louis G. & Elizabeth L. Clarke Endowment Fund
c/o U.S. Bank
P.O. Box 3168
Portland, OR 97208
Application address: c/o Scottish Rite Temple, 709 S.W. 15th Ave., Portland, OR 97205, tel.: (503) 228-9405
Contact: Walter L. Peters, Exec. Secy., Scottish Rite Temple

Established in 1960 in OR.
Financial data (yr. ended 12/31/00): Grants paid, $26,975; assets, $1,808,597 (M); expenditures, $36,508; qualifying distributions, $27,814.
Limitations: Giving limited to the Portland, OR, metropolitan area, including Clackamas, Multnomah, and Washington counties.
Trustee: U.S. Bank.
EIN: 936020655

45686
Henry S. Pernot Scholarship Fund
c/o U.S. Bank
P.O. Box 3168
Portland, OR 97208

Donor(s): Dorothy Pernot.‡
Financial data (yr. ended 06/30/01): Grants paid, $26,500; assets, $423,476 (M); expenditures, $32,742; qualifying distributions, $27,662.
Limitations: Applications not accepted. Giving limited to OR.
Application information: Recipients selected by the dean of Oregon Health Sciences University.
Trustee: U.S. Bank.
EIN: 237385854
Codes: GTI

45687
Peter H. Michaelson Foundation
2865 N.W. Shenandoah
Portland, OR 97210
Contact: Peter H. Michaelson, Pres.

Established in 1988 in NY.
Donor(s): Peter H. Michaelson.
Financial data (yr. ended 12/31/01): Grants paid, $26,150; assets, $388,316 (M); gifts received, $125,000; expenditures, $26,475; qualifying distributions, $26,150.
Limitations: Giving primarily in HI and OR.
Application information: Application form not required.
Officer: Peter H. Michaelson, Pres.

EIN: 133503389

45688
The Starseed Foundation
P.O. Box 1001
Sandy, OR 97055 (503) 668-9692
Contact: Ken Edwards, Dir.

Established in 1998 in OR.
Donor(s): Ken Edwards.
Financial data (yr. ended 12/31/01): Grants paid, $26,052; assets, $365,621 (M); gifts received, $60,439; expenditures, $28,861; qualifying distributions, $26,052.
Limitations: Giving limited to Sandy, OR.
Directors: Bob Backstrom, Ken Edwards, Christopher Weekly.
EIN: 931243038

45689
William S. Walton Charitable Trust
c/o U.S. Bank
P.O. Box 3168
Portland, OR 97208-3168

Trust established in 1958 in OR.
Donor(s): William S. Walton.‡
Financial data (yr. ended 05/31/02): Grants paid, $25,980; assets, $469,948 (M); expenditures, $30,658; qualifying distributions, $25,980.
Limitations: Giving limited to the Salem, OR, area.
Application information: Application form not required.
Trustee: U.S. Bank.
EIN: 930432836

45690
Pendleton Community Memorial Health Corporation
P.O. Box 786
Pendleton, OR 97801
Contact: Dan Ceniga, Pres.

Established in 1989 in OR.
Financial data (yr. ended 12/31/01): Grants paid, $25,594; assets, $739,733 (M); expenditures, $30,024; qualifying distributions, $25,594.
Limitations: Giving primarily in the Pendleton, OR, area.
Application information: Application form required.
Officers: Dan Ceniga, Pres.; Gary Jellum, V.P.; Annette Skinner, Secy.-Treas.
Directors: Steven Bjerke, Paulette Deihl, Rose Anna King, Laurine Kites, Richard Koch, Donald F. New, Douglas Olsen, Norman Vorcick.
EIN: 930477693

45691
Wintz Family Foundation
10610 S.W. Inverness Ct.
Portland, OR 97219
Application address: 1509 S.W. Sunset, No. 2C, Portland, OR 97201, tel.: (503) 244-6902
Contact: Anita W. Beck, Pres.

Established in 1995 in OR.
Donor(s): Helen J. Wintz.
Financial data (yr. ended 06/30/01): Grants paid, $25,463; assets, $479,439 (M); expenditures, $27,251; qualifying distributions, $25,463.
Limitations: Giving primarily in Portland, OR.
Application information: Application form required.
Officers: Anita W. Beck, Pres.; Nancy W. Decherd, Secy.-Treas.
Directors: Alan R. Beck, Jon B. Decherd, Helen J. Wintz.
EIN: 931191743

45692
Abe & Rose Wittels Family Trust
c/o US Bank, N.A.
P.O. Box 3168
Portland, OR 97208-3168

Established in 1997 in CO.
Donor(s): Abe Wittels.
Financial data (yr. ended 12/31/01): Grants paid, $25,186; assets, $613,410 (M); expenditures, $35,678; qualifying distributions, $25,186.
Limitations: Applications not accepted.
Application information: Contributes only to a pre-selected organization.
Trustee: U.S. Bank, N.A.
EIN: 846259388

45693
Franks Foundation Fund
c/o U.S. Bank
P.O. Box 3168
Portland, OR 97208-3168 (503) 275-5929
Scholarship application address: c/o Oregon State Scholarship Commission, 1500 Valley River Dr., Ste. 100, Eugene, OR 97401-2148
Contact: Marlyn J. Norquist, Loan Off., U.S. Bank

Financial data (yr. ended 06/30/01): Grants paid, $25,114; assets, $519,889 (M); expenditures, $35,942; qualifying distributions, $29,457.
Limitations: Giving limited to OR residents: first priority given to those from Deschutes, Crook, or Jefferson counties; second priority given to those from Harney, Lake, Grant, or Klamath counties.
Application information: Application form required.
Trustee: U.S. Bank, N.A.
EIN: 930666994
Codes: GTI

45694
Thelma L. Golding Foundation
1 S.W. Columbia St., Ste. 1620
Portland, OR 97258-2017

Financial data (yr. ended 10/31/00): Grants paid, $25,077; assets, $983,211 (M); expenditures, $44,015; qualifying distributions, $28,275.
Limitations: Applications not accepted. Giving primarily in OR.
Application information: Contributes only to pre-selected organizations.
Trustee: Roscoe C. Nelson, Jr.
EIN: 311603830

45695
Bob Fessler Family Foundation
11796 Monitor McKee Rd., N.E.
Woodburn, OR 97071 (503) 634-2237

Established in 1998 in OR.
Financial data (yr. ended 12/31/01): Grants paid, $25,000; assets, $499,909 (M); gifts received, $20,000; expenditures, $34,452; qualifying distributions, $25,000.
Officers: Robert Fessler, Pres.; Thomas Fessler, V.P.; Martha Fessler, Secy.; Sandra Traeger, Treas.
Directors: Jodi Arritola, Richard Fessler, Karen Jaeger.
EIN: 931258437

45696
The Newcomb Foundation
111 S.W. 5th Ave., Ste. 4040
Portland, OR 97204 (503) 228-8446
Contact: Verne W. Newcomb, Pres.

Donor(s): Verne W. Newcomb.
Financial data (yr. ended 11/30/01): Grants paid, $25,000; assets, $444,654 (M); expenditures, $25,000; qualifying distributions, $25,000.

Limitations: Giving primarily in OR.
Officer: Verne W. Newcomb, Pres.
EIN: 931160967

45697
Vojdani-Trim Family Foundation
4465 S.W. Greenleaf Dr.
Portland, OR 97221

Established in 2000 in OR.
Donor(s): Leslie Trim, Iraj Vojdani.
Financial data (yr. ended 12/31/01): Grants paid, $25,000; assets, $551,361 (M); gifts received, $217,226; expenditures, $29,574; qualifying distributions, $25,000.
Limitations: Applications not accepted.
Application information: Contributes only to pre-selected organizations.
Officers and Directors:* Leslie Trim,* Pres.; Brendan McDonnell,* Secy.; Iraj Vojdani,* Treas.
EIN: 931302981

45698
Janet Spencer Weekes Foundation
1211 S.W. 5th Ave., Ste. 1800
Portland, OR 97204-3718

Established in 1998 in OR.
Financial data (yr. ended 12/31/01): Grants paid, $25,000; assets, $78,269 (M); gifts received, $300; expenditures, $25,090; qualifying distributions, $25,090.
Limitations: Applications not accepted.
Application information: Contributes only to pre-selected organizations.
Officers and Directors:* John M. Weekes,* Pres.; Nikki C. Hatton,* Secy.; David A. Bledsoe, David P. Marshall, Richard Withycombe.
EIN: 931254665

45699
Eugene C. Skourtes Foundation
14025 S.W., Farmington Rd., Ste. 300
Beaverton, OR 97005

Established in 1998 in OR.
Donor(s): Eugene C. Skourtes, Bonnie K. Skourtes.
Financial data (yr. ended 12/31/00): Grants paid, $24,946; assets, $534,029 (M); expenditures, $30,222; qualifying distributions, $24,946.
Limitations: Applications not accepted.
Application information: Contributes only to pre-selected organizations.
Directors: Bonnie K. Skourtes, Eugene C. Skourtes, John Skourtes.
EIN: 931258710

45700
Marshall Christenson Foundation
44490 S.E. Phelps Rd.
Sandy, OR 97055

Donor(s): Jim Cozzetto, Clarence E. Stumpf, Jr.
Financial data (yr. ended 07/31/02): Grants paid, $24,643; assets, $38,431 (M); gifts received, $63,240; expenditures, $47,288; qualifying distributions, $24,643.
Limitations: Giving limited for the benefit of Kazakhstan organizations.
Officers: Jim Cozzetto, Pres.; Marshall Christensen, Secy.-Treas.
Directors: Craig Byrd, John Maring, Clarence E. Stumpf, Jr., Joe F. Yonek.
EIN: 931230131

45701
Richard I. Swenson Trust
c/o West Coast Trust
P.O. Box 1012
Salem, OR 97308-1012

Established in 1997 in OR.
Financial data (yr. ended 12/31/01): Grants paid, $24,592; assets, $683,352 (M); expenditures, $37,118; qualifying distributions, $24,592.
Limitations: Applications not accepted.
Application information: Contributes only to pre-selected organizations.
Trustee: West Coast Trust.
EIN: 936169792

45702
Eton Lane Foundation
P.O. Box 14746
Portland, OR 97293-0746

Established in 1998 in OR.
Donor(s): Frances E. Keller, William M. Keller.
Financial data (yr. ended 05/31/01): Grants paid, $24,190; assets, $147,067 (M); gifts received, $66,288; expenditures, $24,503; qualifying distributions, $24,190.
Limitations: Applications not accepted.
Application information: Contributes only to pre-selected organizations.
Officer and Directors:* William M. Keller,* Pres.; Frances E. Keller, Paul D. Keller.
EIN: 931246688

45703
Mount Angel Community Foundation
P.O. Box 1054
Mount Angel, OR 97362-1054

Financial data (yr. ended 12/31/00): Grants paid, $24,000; assets, $493,186 (M); gifts received, $221,951; expenditures, $25,608; giving activities include $685 for programs.
Limitations: Giving limited to Mount Angel, OR.
Officers: Robert McDonald, Pres.; Jim Hall, Secy.-Treas.
Directors: Bob Fessler, Ron Hammer, Dick Rawie.
EIN: 931205915
Codes: CM

45704
JLR Foundation
4114 N.E. Wistaria Dr.
Portland, OR 97212-2964

Donor(s): Judith L. Rice.
Financial data (yr. ended 12/31/01): Grants paid, $23,709; assets, $549,726 (M); expenditures, $29,399; qualifying distributions, $23,709.
Limitations: Applications not accepted. Giving primarily in OR.
Application information: Contributes only to pre-selected organizations.
Officers: Judith L. Rice, Pres.; Bob Bouneff, Secy.
Directors: Roger Breezley, Denise Mueller.
EIN: 931236069

45705
Winnowski Family Charitable Foundation
11333 S.W. Northgate
Portland, OR 97219

Donor(s): Thaddeus R. Winnowski, Sheila M. Winnowski.
Financial data (yr. ended 12/31/00): Grants paid, $23,611; assets, $230,154 (M); gifts received, $106,400; expenditures, $25,575; qualifying distributions, $23,611.
Limitations: Applications not accepted.
Application information: Contributes only to pre-selected organizations.
Officers: Thaddeus R. Winnowski, Pres.; Sheila M. Winowski, Secy.
Director: Paul T. Winnowski.
EIN: 911822239

45706
Verne Catt McDowell Corporation
P.O. Box 1336
Albany, OR 97321-0440
Contact: Emily Killin, Mgr.

Established in 1968 in OR.
Donor(s): I.A. McDowell.‡
Financial data (yr. ended 12/31/01): Grants paid, $23,509; assets, $358,297 (M); expenditures, $28,974; qualifying distributions, $24,665.
Limitations: Giving primarily in OR.
Application information: Interview required. Application form required.
Officers: Neil Reynolds, Pres.; Emily Killin, Mgr.
Directors: Eldon Chowning, Ray Lindley, Sharron Kay Womack.
EIN: 936022991
Codes: GTI

45707
Agape Foundation, Inc.
1 Skyline Dr., Ste. 3614
Medford, OR 97504-2506
Contact: John R. Dellenback, Pres.

Donor(s): John R. Dellenback.
Financial data (yr. ended 03/31/01): Grants paid, $23,495; assets, $179,953 (M); expenditures, $24,895; qualifying distributions, $23,466.
Limitations: Giving primarily in WA.
Application information: Application form required.
Officers and Directors:* John R. Dellenback,* Pres.; Mary Jane Dellenback,* Secy.-Treas.; Barbara Dellenback, Colleen Evans, Kent Hotaling.
EIN: 930797968

45708
Silverton High School Scholarship Fund, Inc.
125 Cherry St.
Silverton, OR 97381-1053

Established in 1997 in OR.
Financial data (yr. ended 12/31/01): Grants paid, $23,200; assets, $515,013 (M); expenditures, $32,909; qualifying distributions, $23,200.
Officers: Mason Branstetter, Pres.; Craig Roessler, V.P.; Quintin Estell, Secy.; Tom Lynch, Treas.
Directors: Bud Logan, Lorelle Stonex.
EIN: 943164866

45709
Jack S. Higgins Memorial Educational Trust
c/o Union Bank of California, N.A.
P.O. Box 2742
Portland, OR 97208 2742

Financial data (yr. ended 12/31/01): Grants paid, $23,178; assets, $792,248 (M); expenditures, $34,670; qualifying distributions, $23,178.
Limitations: Applications not accepted. Giving limited to Portland, OR.
Application information: Contributes only to a pre-selected organization.
Trustee: Union Bank of California, N.A.
EIN: 936033472

45710
Ben Selling Scholarship Loan Fund
c/o Wells Fargo Bank Northwest, N.A., Trust Tax Dept.
P.O. Box 2971
Portland, OR 97208

Financial data (yr. ended 09/30/01): Grants paid, $22,835; assets, $821,723 (M); expenditures, $35,512; qualifying distributions, $40,750.
Limitations: Giving limited to residents of OR.
Application information: Application form required.

45710—OREGON

Trustee: Wells Fargo Bank Northwest, N.A.
EIN: 936017158
Codes: GTI

45711
Holland Family Foundation
3925 S.W. Humphrey Blvd.
Portland, OR 97221-3235 (503) 223-7374
Contact: James L. Holland, Pres.

Donor(s): James L. Holland.
Financial data (yr. ended 04/30/02): Grants paid, $22,505; assets, $270,350 (M); expenditures, $24,027; qualifying distributions, $22,505.
Limitations: Giving primarily in OR.
Officers: James L. Holland, Pres. and Treas.; Janet M. Hollan, V.P.; Anne F. Puntenney, Secy.
EIN: 936023621

45712
The Roberts Foundation
P.O. Box 954
Canby, OR 97013-0954 (503) 651-3268
Contact: Sandra Ricksger, Tr.

Financial data (yr. ended 12/31/01): Grants paid, $22,305; assets, $328,784 (M); expenditures, $23,629; qualifying distributions, $22,305.
Trustees: Sandra Ricksger, Rohn Roberts.
EIN: 943063700

45713
Newburn Family Foundation
50 Hwy. 99
Eugene, OR 97402
Application Address: P.O. Box 2803, Eugene, OR 97402
Contact: Robert L. Newburn, Tr.

Established in 1998 in OR.
Donor(s): Robert L. Newburn.
Financial data (yr. ended 09/30/01): Grants paid, $22,200; assets, $434,734 (M); gifts received, $22,200; expenditures, $22,264; qualifying distributions, $22,200.
Limitations: Applications not accepted.
Application information: Contributes only to pre-selected organizations.
Trustees: Allen E. Gardner, Alan P. Houck, F.F. Montgomery, Janice E. Newburn, Robert L. Newburn.
EIN: 916458791

45714
Edna Graves Memorial Trust
c/o U.S. Bank
P.O. Box 3168
Portland, OR 97208-3168

Established in 1998 in MT.
Financial data (yr. ended 02/28/02): Grants paid, $22,000; assets, $409,746 (M); expenditures, $26,524; qualifying distributions, $22,000.
Limitations: Applications not accepted.
Application information: Contributes only to pre-selected organizations.
Trustee: U.S. Bank.
EIN: 816085956

45715
Norton L. & Barbara B. Peck Family Foundation
15580 N.W. St. Andrews Dr.
Portland, OR 97229
Contact: Norton L. Peck, Pres.

Established in 1998 in OR.
Donor(s): Barbara B. Peck, Norton L. Peck.
Financial data (yr. ended 12/31/01): Grants paid, $22,000; assets, $494,894 (M); gifts received, $57,000; expenditures, $28,983; qualifying distributions, $22,000.
Limitations: Giving primarily in OR.

Application information: Application form required.
Officers: Norton L. Peck, Pres.; Roger L. Peck, V.P.; Susan B. Hall, Secy.; Donald E. Peck, Treas.
Directors: Richard A. Hall, Terry A. Mitchell.
EIN: 931247276

45716
Frank L. Touvelle Trust
c/o Wells Fargo Bank Northwest, N.A.
P.O. Box 2971
Portland, OR 97208

Financial data (yr. ended 12/31/01): Grants paid, $21,850; assets, $670,569 (M); expenditures, $34,840; qualifying distributions, $25,319.
Limitations: Applications not accepted. Giving primarily in OR.
Trustee: Wells Fargo Bank Northwest, N.A.
EIN: 936018391
Codes: GTI

45717
G. Russell Morgan Scholarship Fund
c/o U.S. Bank
P.O. Box 3168
Portland, OR 97208 (503) 275-4887
Contact: Marlyn Norquist, Fdn. Team

Established in 1992 in OR.
Financial data (yr. ended 06/30/01): Grants paid, $21,824; assets, $401,789 (M); expenditures, $30,653; qualifying distributions, $24,432.
Limitations: Giving limited to residents of Hillsboro, OR.
Application information: Application form required.
Trustee: U.S. Bank.
EIN: 936262437
Codes: GTI

45718
Adtex Scholarship Fund
c/o U.S. Bank
P.O. Box 3168
Portland, OR 97208-3168
Application address: c/o R.C. Johanson, 13187 N.W. Dumar St., Portland, OR 97229

Established in 1991 in OR.
Financial data (yr. ended 09/30/01): Grants paid, $21,722; assets, $112,627 (M); expenditures, $25,707; qualifying distributions, $22,947.
Limitations: Giving limited to OR.
Application information: Application form required.
Trustee: U.S. Bank.
EIN: 943153861
Codes: GTI

45719
John & Jean Loosley Charitable Foundation
c/o John M. Loosley
239 Maplewood Ln.
Roseburg, OR 97470

Established in 1993 in OR.
Donor(s): M. John Loosley, S. Jean Loosley.
Financial data (yr. ended 03/31/02): Grants paid, $21,600; assets, $379,995 (M); gifts received, $11,143; expenditures, $21,675; qualifying distributions, $21,600.
Limitations: Applications not accepted. Giving primarily in OR.
Application information: Contributes only to pre-selected organizations.
Trustees: M. John Loosley, S. Jean Loosley, Stephen J. Loosley, Judith L. Sweeney.
EIN: 936279827

45720
Con Amor Foundation
17350 Wall St.
Lake Oswego, OR 97034 (503) 636-6483

Established in 2000 in OR.
Donor(s): Bruce H. Miller.
Financial data (yr. ended 12/31/00): Grants paid, $21,300; assets, $295,713 (M); gifts received, $326,813; expenditures, $21,300; qualifying distributions, $21,300.
Application information: Application form required.
Officers and Directors:* Bruce H. Miller,* Pres.; Patricia A. Dilworth,* Secy.-Treas.; Scott S. Miller.
EIN: 931299163

45721
Erickson Family Foundation
4900 S.W. Griffith Dr., Ste. 133
Beaverton, OR 97005
Contact: Betty J. Oliver, Pres.

Established in 1997 in OR.
Financial data (yr. ended 12/31/01): Grants paid, $21,000; assets, $299,400 (M); expenditures, $25,480; qualifying distributions, $21,000.
Officers: Betty J. Oliver, Pres.; Sheree L. Stassi, V.P.; Jacqueline E. Thomas, V.P.
EIN: 931230250

45722
Cora Rust Owen Memorial Trust
c/o U.S. Bank
P.O. Box 3168
Portland, OR 97208

Established in 1986 in MT.
Financial data (yr. ended 04/30/02): Grants paid, $20,951; assets, $582,382 (M); expenditures, $29,689; qualifying distributions, $20,951.
Limitations: Applications not accepted. Giving primarily in MN and WI.
Application information: Contributes only to pre-selected organizations.
Trustee: U.S. Bank.
EIN: 816057848

45723
Snow Family Foundation
P.O. Box 423
Astoria, OR 97103

Established in 1998.
Donor(s): Harold A. Snow, Jeanyse R. Snow, Harold H. Snow, Helen A. Snow.
Financial data (yr. ended 12/31/01): Grants paid, $20,080; assets, $626,551 (M); expenditures, $29,870; qualifying distributions, $20,080.
Limitations: Applications not accepted.
Application information: Contributes only to pre-selected organizations.
Officers: Harold A. Snow, Pres.; Harold H. Snow, V.P.; Jeanyse R. Snow, Secy.; Helen A. Snow, Treas.
Directors: Jeremy A. Snow, Randall W. Snow.
EIN: 931246600

45724
Jane Nugent Cochems Trust
c/o U.S. Bank
P.O. Box 3168
Portland, OR 97208
Application address: c/o Pres., Colorado State Medical Society, 5575 DTC Pkwy., Ste. 240, Englewood, CO 80111

Financial data (yr. ended 12/31/99): Grants paid, $20,000; assets, $403,786 (M); expenditures, $24,658; qualifying distributions, $20,131.
Limitations: Giving limited to CO.

Application information: Write for application information.
Trustee: U.S. Bank.
EIN: 846018185

45725
Weston Family Foundation
21354 S. Springwater Rd.
Estacada, OR 97023
Application address: 13328 S.E. Jordan Ct., Clackamas, OR 97015, tel.: (503) 665-2166
Contact: Jeni M. Weston, Treas.

Established in 2000 in OR.
Donor(s): James M. Weston.
Financial data (yr. ended 12/31/01): Grants paid, $20,000; assets, $522,023 (M); gifts received, $220,000; expenditures, $20,433; qualifying distributions, $20,000.
Officers: James M. Weston, Pres.; Jay B. Weston, V.P.; Jan M. Weston, 2nd V.P.; Sharon L. Weston, Secy.; Jeni M. Weston, Treas.
Director: Norman L. Lindstedt.
EIN: 931304439

45726
Lockard Family Foundation
c/o Wesley Lockard
869 Goldenrod
Reedsport, OR 97467

Donor(s): Wesley Lockard.
Financial data (yr. ended 09/30/02): Grants paid, $19,950; assets, $347,725 (M); expenditures, $19,950; qualifying distributions, $19,950.
Officer: Wesley Lockard, Pres.
EIN: 931300861

45727
Monroe Area Foundation
P.O. Box 3
Monroe, OR 97456-0003 (541) 847-5547
Contact: Randall Crowson, Pres.

Established in 1993 in OR.
Financial data (yr. ended 12/31/01): Grants paid, $19,902; assets, $291,184 (M); expenditures, $20,298; qualifying distributions, $19,902.
Limitations: Giving limited to the greater Monroe, OR, area.
Officers: Randall Crowson, Chair.; Colin Crocker, Vice-Chair.; Jolynn Stroda, Secy.-Treas.
Directors: Sue Joyner, Mike Kinkaid.
EIN: 931001600

45728
Wilson-Dean Family Foundation
126 N.E. Loop Rd.
Myrtle Creek, OR 97457
Contact: Cheryl Dean

Established in 1998 in OR.
Donor(s): Cheryl Dean.
Financial data (yr. ended 06/30/02): Grants paid, $19,840; assets, $318,018 (M); expenditures, $24,623; qualifying distributions, $19,840.
Application information: Application form not required.
Director: Dean Management Co., Inc.
EIN: 931236922

45729
Wilson-Atkinson Family Foundation
275 Weaver Rd.
Myrtle Creek, OR 97457

Established in 1998 in OR.
Donor(s): Bonnie Atkinson.
Financial data (yr. ended 12/31/01): Grants paid, $19,831; assets, $301,314 (M); expenditures, $24,948; qualifying distributions, $19,831.
Director: Atkinson Management Co., Inc.

EIN: 931236631

45730
George & Laura Kreitzberg Foundation
2365 Crestmont Cir. S.
Salem, OR 97302

Established in 1998 in OR.
Donor(s): George F. Kreitzberg, Laura A. Kreitzberg.
Financial data (yr. ended 12/31/01): Grants paid, $19,500; assets, $321,700 (M); expenditures, $20,489; qualifying distributions, $19,500.
Limitations: Applications not accepted.
Application information: Contributes only to pre-selected organizations.
Officers: George F. Kreitzberg, Pres.; Mari L. Bailey, Secy.-Treas.
Director: Laura A. Kreitzberg.
EIN: 931248893

45731
Suhr Family Memorial Scholarship Foundation
c/o U.S. Bank
P.O. Box 3168
Portland, OR 97208-3168

Established in 1998 in MT.
Financial data (yr. ended 04/30/02): Grants paid, $18,998; assets, $339,001 (M); expenditures, $23,311; qualifying distributions, $18,998.
Trustee: U.S. Bank, N.A.
EIN: 810515266

45732
Myra Camille Holland Foundation
2961 S.W. Turner Rd.
West Linn, OR 97068

Established in 2000 in OR.
Donor(s): Nicole Pierce-Rhoads, Geoff Rhoads.
Financial data (yr. ended 06/30/01): Grants paid, $18,899; assets, $270,732 (M); gifts received, $152,433; expenditures, $26,257; qualifying distributions, $24,515.
Limitations: Applications not accepted. Giving primarily in OR.
Application information: Contributes only to pre-selected organizations.
Trustees: Nicole Pierce-Rhoads, Geoff Rhoads.
EIN: 931308422

45733
Madison/Elks Benevolent Trust
c/o U.S. Bank
P.O. Box 3168
Portland, OR 97208
Application address: c/o Salem Elks Lodge No. 336, Grants Chair., 680 State St., Salem, OR 97301

Established in 1999 in OR.
Donor(s): Donald J. Madison.‡
Financial data (yr. ended 06/30/02): Grants paid, $18,850; assets, $438,853 (M); expenditures, $24,386; qualifying distributions, $18,850.
Limitations: Giving primarily in OR.
Trustee: U.S. Bank.
EIN: 936329343

45734
Kiwanis Foundation of West Valley
c/o Don Smith
P.O. Box 1144
Willamina, OR 97396-1144 (503) 876-4557

Established in 1997 in OR.
Financial data (yr. ended 12/31/01): Grants paid, $18,849; assets, $261,581 (M); gifts received, $28,059; expenditures, $23,531; qualifying distributions, $18,849.
Limitations: Giving primarily in Willamina, OR.

Application information: Application form required.
Officers: Ted Mayfield, Pres.; Ruth Marsh, Secy.; Don Smith, Treas.
Directors: Gary Brooks, Twila Hill, Gerald McCray, Norma Sampson, Aileen Schnitzler.
EIN: 931211628

45735
Ralph H. Foss Memorial Trust
c/o U.S. Bank
P.O. Box 3168
Portland, OR 97208
Application address: P.O. Box 30678, Billings, MT 30678, tel.: (406) 657-8139
Contact: Lynn Caraveau, Trust Off., U.S. Bank

Financial data (yr. ended 12/31/01): Grants paid, $18,759; assets, $296,309 (M); expenditures, $25,849; qualifying distributions, $20,259.
Limitations: Giving limited to residents of Dawson and Richland counties, MT.
Application information: Application form required.
Trustee: U.S. Bank.
EIN: 816048184
Codes: GTI

45736
Schilling Family Scholarship Fund
c/o U.S. Bank
P.O. Box 3168
Portland, OR 97208-3168

Established in MT.
Financial data (yr. ended 03/31/99): Grants paid, $18,000; assets, $3,275,196 (M); expenditures, $28,193; qualifying distributions, $22,463.
Limitations: Giving primarily in Butte and Missoula, MT.
Application information: Application form required.
Trustee: U.S. Bank.
EIN: 816067849

45737
Children's Research Foundation
11040 S.W. Barbur Blvd.
Portland, OR 97219

Established in 1993.
Financial data (yr. ended 11/30/01): Grants paid, $17,987; assets, $22,048 (M); gifts received, $3,255; expenditures, $19,111; qualifying distributions, $19,104.
Limitations: Applications not accepted. Giving primarily in OR.
Application information: Contributes only to pre-selected organizations.
Trustees: Craig Smith, Marilyn Smith.
EIN: 936275042

45738
James Weir Memorial Fund-Bigelow District
P.O. Box 325
Wasco, OR 97065-0325 (541) 442-5086
Contact: Trena Gray

Financial data (yr. ended 06/30/01): Grants paid, $17,851; assets, $497,230 (M); expenditures, $39,450; qualifying distributions, $24,789.
Limitations: Giving limited to residents of Sherman County, OR.
Application information: Application form required.
Chairman and Trustee: Kevin McCullough, Chair.; Myron Swigart.
EIN: 936041768
Codes: GTI

45739
The Craig D. Wiesberg & Calvin P. Ranney Children's Foundation
21555 S.W. Hells Canyon Rd.
Sherwood, OR 97140-8500
Contact: Steven E. Wiesberg, Dir.

Established in 1997 in OR.
Financial data (yr. ended 12/31/99): Grants paid, $17,687; assets, $18,679 (M); gifts received, $36,058; expenditures, $33,575; qualifying distributions, $17,687.
Limitations: Giving primarily in OR.
Directors: Darin D. Honn, Steven W. Wiesberg, David Zimmell, Bruce L. Zumwalt.
EIN: 931228840

45740
The Manley Foundation
P.O. Box 25121
Eugene, OR 97402 (541) 465-1071
Contact: Michael K. Roth, Pres.

Donor(s): John Tresemer, Alan Tresemer.
Financial data (yr. ended 12/31/01): Grants paid, $17,617; assets, $150,977 (M); gifts received, $11,000; expenditures, $22,250; qualifying distributions, $17,617.
Limitations: Giving on an international basis with emphasis in San Isidro Del General, Costa Rica; giving also in Everett, MA and Memphis, TN.
Officers and Directors:* Michael K. Roth,* Pres.; Roxann Spavak-Moody, Secy.; Glenn Carpenter, Alan Tresemer.
EIN: 931013005

45741
Ruth Mishler Memorial Trust
639 W. Main
P.O. Box 37
Sheridan, OR 97378-0037 (503) 843-3888
Contact: Naomi Kelley, Dir.

Established in 1995.
Financial data (yr. ended 12/31/99): Grants paid, $17,500; assets, $314,910 (M); expenditures, $19,226; qualifying distributions, $17,500.
Limitations: Giving limited to residents of Sheridan/Willamina, OR.
Application information: Applicants must be residents of Sheridan/Willamina, OR for a minimum of one year or a local graduate with need. Application form required.
Directors: Nancy Curtiss, Naomi Kelley, Harley Mishler.
EIN: 943234766

45742
Pacific N.W. Kiwanis Foundation
P.O. Box 747
Beaverton, OR 97005
Contact: Jim McAllister, Treas.

Financial data (yr. ended 09/30/00): Grants paid, $17,500; assets, $491,003 (M); gifts received, $22,765; expenditures, $27,103; qualifying distributions, $17,500.
Application information: Application form required.
Officers: Jerry Noah, Pres.; Russ Hobbs, V.P.; Henry Stevens, Secy.; Jim McAllister, Treas.
Directors: Dick Cassutt, Evelyn Chapman, Chuck Clutts, Dennis Coleman, Bob Collison, Jack Delf, Helen J. Elsmore, Joseph O. Epler, Gene Favell, John Frucci, Don Hallauer, Erling Larsen, Don Miles, Howard Montoure, Dick Peterson, Dick Rust.
EIN: 930900103

45743
The Harold and Jessie Hudson Scholarship Trust
c/o US Bancorp
P.O. Box 3168
Portland, OR 97208-3168

Established in 1998 in ID.
Financial data (yr. ended 12/31/01): Grants paid, $17,437; assets, $511,883 (M); expenditures, $24,542; qualifying distributions, $20,137.
Limitations: Applications not accepted. Giving primarily in Bozeman, MT.
Application information: Contributes only to pre-selected organizations.
Trustee: U.S. Bank, N.A.
EIN: 826052413

45744
Albert D. Woodmansee Trust
c/o Pioneer Trust Bank, N.A.
P.O. Box 2305
Salem, OR 97308

Financial data (yr. ended 11/30/01): Grants paid, $17,104; assets, $395,611 (M); expenditures, $24,188; qualifying distributions, $17,104.
Limitations: Applications not accepted. Giving limited to Salem, OR.
Application information: Contributes only to pre-selected organizations.
Trustee: Pioneer Trust Bank, N.A.
EIN: 936191755

45745
Oral L. & Helen Bell Educational
c/o Oral L. Bell
2439 Bell Ct.
Medford, OR 97504

Established in 1995 in OR.
Donor(s): Oral L. Bell.
Financial data (yr. ended 12/31/01): Grants paid, $17,000; assets, $247,673 (M); gifts received, $5,000; expenditures, $24,022; qualifying distributions, $17,000.
Limitations: Applications not accepted.
Application information: Contributes only to pre-selected organizations.
Officers: Helen Bell, Pres. and Treas.; Oral L. Bell, Pres. and Treas.; Dudley Bell, V.P.; Loretta Dalton, Secy. and Mgr.
Director: Laura Tharp.
EIN: 931166353

45746
Holce Logging Company Scholarship Fund, Inc.
P.O. Box 127
Vernonia, OR 97064-0127
Application address: c/o Guidance Counselor, Vernonia High School, 399 Bridge St., Vernonia, OR 97064

Established in 1983 in OR.
Donor(s): Vernonia Federal Credit Union.
Financial data (yr. ended 04/30/01): Grants paid, $16,884; assets, $266,235 (M); gifts received, $12,000; expenditures, $16,975; qualifying distributions, $16,884.
Limitations: Giving limited to Vernonia, OR.
Application information: Recipient selected by Vernonia High School Guidance Counselor.
Officers and Directors:* Evelyn L. Holce,* Pres.; Bonnie J. Holce,* V.P.; Randall E. Holce,* Secy.-Treas.
EIN: 930845692
Codes: CS, CD, GTI

45747
Simon Benson Fund, Inc.
6441 S.W. Canyon Ct., Ste. 10
Portland, OR 97221

Financial data (yr. ended 12/31/99): Grants paid, $16,500; assets, $209,396 (M); expenditures, $17,513; qualifying distributions, $16,606.
Limitations: Applications not accepted. Giving limited to residents of Portland, OR.
Application information: Scholarship recipients are selected by faculty committee of Benson High School.
Officers: Astrid C. Unander, Pres.; G.T. Benson, V.P.; Ted R. Gamble, Jr., V.P.; Sigfrid B. Unander, Jr., Secy.-Treas.
EIN: 936041516

45748
Baker Family Foundation
3500 Chad Dr.
Eugene, OR 97408 (541) 485-1234
Contact: Bridget Baker, Pres.

Established in 1999 in OR.
Donor(s): Guard Publishing Company.
Financial data (yr. ended 12/31/01): Grants paid, $16,133; assets, $443,869 (M); gifts received, $250; expenditures, $16,987; qualifying distributions, $16,133.
Officers: Bridget Baker Kincaid, Pres.; Ann Baker Mack, V.P.; Scott M. Diehl, V.P.; Susan Diamond, Secy.-Treas.
Directors: Alton F. Baker III, Alton F. Baker, Jr., Edwin M. Baker, Herbert C. Baker, Richard A. Baker, Jr., R. Fletcher Little.
EIN: 931265230
Codes: CS

45749
Commandment Keepers Society, Inc.
50621 Hebo Rd.
Grand Ronde, OR 97347-9503

Financial data (yr. ended 04/30/02): Grants paid, $16,000; assets, $113,537 (M); expenditures, $17,771; qualifying distributions, $16,000.
Limitations: Applications not accepted. Giving primarily in Dunlap, TN.
Application information: Contributes only to pre-selected organizations.
Officers and Directors:* Daniel A. Butler,* Pres.; Sean Carney,* V.P.; Ellen Butler,* Secy.-Treas.; Lucy Fuller.
EIN: 953392440

45750
Fred A. Rosenkrans Trust
c/o Wells Fargo Bank Northwest, N.A.
P.O. Box 2971
Portland, OR 97208
Contact: Charles K. Woodcock, Trust Off., Wells Fargo Bank Northwest, N.A.

Established in 1997 in OR.
Financial data (yr. ended 12/31/01): Grants paid, $16,000; assets, $878,094 (M); expenditures, $26,724; qualifying distributions, $4,351.
Limitations: Applications not accepted. Giving limited to OR.
Application information: Contributes only to pre-selected organizations.
Trustee: Wells Fargo Bank Northwest, N.A.
EIN: 936017353

45751
Chaney Family Charitable Foundation
729 N.E. 194th
Portland, OR 97230

Established in 1999 in OR.

Donor(s): John Chaney, Patricia Chaney.
Financial data (yr. ended 12/31/01): Grants paid, $15,650; assets, $345,639 (M); expenditures, $16,579; qualifying distributions, $15,650.
Limitations: Applications not accepted.
Application information: Contributes only to pre-selected organizations.
Officers and Directors:* John Chaney,* Pres.; Patricia Chaney,* Secy.; Amy Chaney, Brian Chaney, Joshua Chaney.
EIN: 931283075

45752
James Weir Memorial Fund-Emigrant District
c/o Frank Zaniker
P.O. Box 46, Emigrant Dist.
Wasco, OR 97065-0046 (541) 442-5086

Financial data (yr. ended 06/30/99): Grants paid, $15,577; assets, $308,724 (M); expenditures, $23,391; qualifying distributions, $17,580.
Limitations: Giving limited to residents of Sherman County, OR.
Officer: Frank Zaniker, Chair.
Trustee: Deanna Zaniker.
EIN: 936080553
Codes: GTI

45753
Durant Family Trust
P.O. Box 99
Dundee, OR 97115

Established in 1997 in OR.
Donor(s): Kenneth Durant, Katherine Durant.
Financial data (yr. ended 03/31/01): Grants paid, $15,425; assets, $253,455 (M); expenditures, $18,345; qualifying distributions, $15,425.
Limitations: Applications not accepted. Giving primarily in OR.
Application information: Contributes only to pre-selected organizations.
Trustees: Katherine Durant, Kenneth Durant.
EIN: 936311186

45754
Mills Family Foundation
16238 S.W. Burntwood Way
Beaverton, OR 97007-5031 (503) 649-7644
Contact: Milford M. Mills, Pres.

Established in 1997 in OR.
Donor(s): Eileen J. Mills, Milford M. Mills.
Financial data (yr. ended 04/30/02): Grants paid, $15,058; assets, $290,295 (M); expenditures, $15,252; qualifying distributions, $15,058.
Officers: Milford M. Mills, Pres.; John J. Mills, V.P.; Eileen J. Mills, Secy.; Scott S. Mills, Treas.
EIN: 911819132

45755
Lytle Scholarship Trust
(Formerly Carl H. Lytle Scholarship Trust)
c/o US Bank, N.A.
P.O. Box 3168
Portland, OR 97208-3168
Application address: c/o Scholarship Counselor, Univ. of Denver, 2199 S. Univ. Blvd., Denver, CO 80208

Financial data (yr. ended 08/31/01): Grants paid, $14,500; assets, $320,942 (M); expenditures, $20,640; qualifying distributions, $16,940.
Limitations: Giving limited to residents of CO.
Application information: Application form required.
Trustee: US Bank, N.A.
EIN: 846195232
Codes: GTI

45756
The Dorothy and Robert Ryan Charitable Foundation
715 S.W. Morrison St., No. 1000
Portland, OR 97205-3122

Established in 1997 in OR.
Donor(s): Dorothy J. Ryan, Robert Ryan.
Financial data (yr. ended 12/31/99): Grants paid, $14,365; assets, $1,177 (L); gifts received, $17,302; expenditures, $17,231; qualifying distributions, $14,365.
Officers: Dorothy J. Ryan, Pres.; Robert Ryan, Secy.; James S. Borquist, C.F.O.
EIN: 911837467

45757
The Youth Talent Foundation
P.O. Box 10346
Eugene, OR 97440-2346

Donor(s): Gordon W. Tripp.
Financial data (yr. ended 07/31/01): Grants paid, $14,102; assets, $708 (M); gifts received, $16,000; expenditures, $18,233; qualifying distributions, $18,233.
Limitations: Giving primarily in Lane County, OR area.
Officers and Directors:* Richard Long,* Pres.; John Sihler,* Secy.; George M. Riihimaki,* Treas.; Cindi Bartels, Royce Lewis.
EIN: 931126686
Codes: GTI

45758
Hirning Woods Humane Society
4035 S.W. Halycon
Tualatin, OR 97062

Donor(s): Marcia Tharnish.
Financial data (yr. ended 12/31/01): Grants paid, $13,988; assets, $1,118 (M); gifts received, $14,800; expenditures, $14,161; qualifying distributions, $13,988.
Limitations: Applications not accepted.
Officers: Marcia Tharnish, Pres.; Albert Tharnish, Secy.-Treas.
Director: Kathy Kavanaugh.
EIN: 481019386

45759
Portland Valley Acacia Fund, Inc.
(Formerly Scottish Rite Oregon Consistory Almoner Fund, Inc.)
709 S.W. 15th Ave.
Portland, OR 97205-1995 (503) 226-7827
Contact: Allen Kirk, Secy.-Treas.

Financial data (yr. ended 09/30/01): Grants paid, $13,475; assets, $453,526 (M); expenditures, $20,536; qualifying distributions, $16,857.
Limitations: Giving limited to OR.
Officers: Hugh W. Taylor, Chair.; Duane W. Hugulet, Vice-Chairman; Allen A. Kirk, Secy.; W. John Rall, Treas.
Directors: Richard Klockman, L.E. Schiler.
EIN: 237154746
Codes: GTI

45760
Wallace A. Schindel Charitable Trust
c/o U.S. Bank
P.O. Box 3168
Portland, OR 97208
Application address: P.O. Box 7928, Boise, ID 83707

Financial data (yr. ended 12/31/99): Grants paid, $13,400; assets, $419,442 (M); expenditures, $19,415; qualifying distributions, $14,199.
Limitations: Giving primarily in Boise, ID.

Grant Committee: Edward D. Ahrens, L. Kim McDonald.
Trustee: U.S. Bank.
EIN: 826054822

45761
Criswell Scholarship Fund
c/o U.S. Bank
P.O. Box 3168
Portland, OR 97208-3168
Application address: c/o St. Luke's Episcopal Church, 224 N.W., D St., Grants Pass, OR 97526
Contact: Clare Winkle

Financial data (yr. ended 06/30/01): Grants paid, $13,250; assets, $259,026 (M); expenditures, $17,259; qualifying distributions, $14,390.
Limitations: Giving limited to OR.
Application information: Application form required.
Trustee: U.S. Bank.
EIN: 936020612
Codes: GTI

45762
Dawson Foundation
111 S.W. 5th Ave., Ste. 1620
Portland, OR 97204
Application address: 1317 Stonehaven Dr., West Linn, OR 97068
Contact: Edwin J. Kawasaki, Dir.

Established in 1999 in OR.
Financial data (yr. ended 12/31/01): Grants paid, $13,120; assets, $205,954 (M); expenditures, $17,799; qualifying distributions, $13,120.
Limitations: Giving primarily in OR.
Officers: Brandon M. Dawson, Pres.; Cynthia L. Dawson Austin, Secy.
Directors: Cary B. Dawson, Joseph Hanna, Edwin J. Kawasaki.
EIN: 931274668

45763
One Ummah Foundation in Memory of Mustafa Saeed Rahman
7 Walking Woods Dr.
Lake Oswego, OR 97035

Established in 1999 in OR.
Donor(s): Mohammad S. Rahman.
Financial data (yr. ended 12/31/99): Grants paid, $13,000; assets, $250,997 (M); gifts received, $264,000; expenditures, $13,003; qualifying distributions, $13,000.
Limitations: Applications not accepted. Giving primarily in MO.
Application information: Contributes only to pre-selected organizations.
Officers: Mohammed S. Rahman, Pres.; Tasneem Rahman, V.P. and Secy.
EIN: 931281392

45764
Skelligs, Inc.
5241 S.W. Humphrey Blvd.
Portland, OR 97221

Established in 1998 in OR.
Financial data (yr. ended 12/31/00): Grants paid, $12,850; assets, $142,299 (M); expenditures, $13,730; qualifying distributions, $12,850.
Directors: Alexander Glass, Nancy Glass, Nicole T. Glass, Stephen S. Hayes, Adrienne K. Roe.
EIN: 931250187

45765—OREGON

45765
Ruby M. Edwards Foundation, Inc.
821 E. Jackson St.
Medford, OR 97504
Contact: David P. Hyatt, Treas.

Donor(s): Ruby M. Edwards.
Financial data (yr. ended 12/31/01): Grants paid, $12,546; assets, $180,317 (M); expenditures, $16,059; qualifying distributions, $12,546.
Limitations: Giving primarily in OR.
Officers: Ruby M. Edwards, Pres.; Cecil Bailey, V.P.; Val A. Bubb, Treas.
EIN: 931075961

45766
Pauline and Edna Hellstern Foundation
c/o U.S. Bank, Trust Dept.
P.O. Box 3168
Portland, OR 97208
Application address: c/o Pueblo Centennial High School, 2525 Montview Dr., Pueblo, CO 81008

Established in 1988 in CO.
Financial data (yr. ended 02/28/02): Grants paid, $12,500; assets, $286,096 (M); expenditures, $16,093; qualifying distributions, $12,975.
Limitations: Giving limited to Pueblo County, CO.
Officers: Joyce Bales, Anne K. Burmont, David B. Shaw.
Trustee: U.S. Bank.
EIN: 742536168
Codes: GTI

45767
Angie's Foundation, Inc.
24000 S.W. Stafford Rd.
Tualatin, OR 97062

Established in 1997 in OR.
Donor(s): Angela J. Fogg.
Financial data (yr. ended 06/30/01): Grants paid, $12,370; assets, $70,564 (M); expenditures, $12,491; qualifying distributions, $12,312.
Limitations: Applications not accepted.
Application information: Contributes only to pre-selected organizations.
Officer: Angela J. Fogg, Pres.
Directors: Terri L. Kessler, Annette R. Miller, Kristen S. Ogard.
EIN: 931234185

45768
REAACH Ministries, Inc.
84305 Derbyshire Ln.
Eugene, OR 97405-9433

Donor(s): Gerald W. Derby.
Financial data (yr. ended 12/31/01): Grants paid, $12,160; assets, $6,682 (M); gifts received, $18,900; expenditures, $18,390; qualifying distributions, $12,160.
Limitations: Applications not accepted. Giving limited to the U.S., Mexico, the Philippines, Romania, the Ukraine, and Moscow, Russia.
Officers: Jeff Tomlin, Pres.; Marlene McAdams, V.P.; Gerald W. Derby, Secy.; Mark Derby, Treas.
EIN: 930949770

45769
Warren H. Bishop Memorial Scholarship Fund
(also known as Priscilla Hill-Warren Bishop Scholarship Fund)
c/o U.S. Bank
P.O. Box 3168
Portland, OR 97208-3168
Application address: c/o Scholarship Fund Comm., 70 Jackson County Medical Society, Rogue Valley Medical Arts Bldg., 691 Murphy Rd., Ste. 216, Medford, OR 97501

Donor(s): Priscilla Hill.‡
Financial data (yr. ended 06/30/01): Grants paid, $12,000; assets, $98,369 (M); expenditures, $15,755; qualifying distributions, $12,955.
Limitations: Giving limited to Jackson, Josephine, and Klamath counties, OR.
Application information: Write for application information.
Trustee: U.S. Bank.
EIN: 936153739
Codes: GTI

45770
Thomas R. Dargan Minority Scholarship Fund
(Formerly KATU Thomas R. Dargan Minority Scholarship Fund)
c/o KATU Human Resources
P.O. Box 2
Portland, OR 97207-0002
Contact: Rhonda Shelby, Pres.

Established in 1989 in OR.
Donor(s): Fisher Broadcasting Inc.
Financial data (yr. ended 03/31/01): Grants paid, $12,000; assets, $196,664 (M); expenditures, $12,000; qualifying distributions, $11,975.
Limitations: Giving limited to OR and WA.
Publications: Informational brochure (including application guidelines).
Application information: Applicants must be declared majors in communications or broadcasting at a four-year curriculum university and attending a school in WA or OR or be a resident of WA or OR attending an out-of-state university. Application form required.
Officers and Trustees:* Rhonda Shelby,* Pres.; Melinda Davis,* Secy.; Richard Dargan,* Treas.; Jim Boyer, Margaret Carter, Peggy Costa, Mark Hass, John Holley, Dan Luna, Pat Scott.
EIN: 943101223
Codes: CS, CD

45771
Guidance Foundation
c/o Davis Wright Tremaine
1300 S.W. Fifth Ave., Ste. 2300
Portland, OR 97201

Established in 1999 in OR.
Donor(s): Henry Fang.
Financial data (yr. ended 12/31/01): Grants paid, $12,000; assets, $593,865 (M); expenditures, $15,500; qualifying distributions, $12,000.
Limitations: Applications not accepted.
Application information: Contributes only to pre-selected organizations.
Officers: Henry Fang, Pres.; Ta-Yun Fang, V.P.
Directors: Gene Fang, Wei Fang.
EIN: 931258857

45772
John & Judith Kenagy Foundation
1889 Hawthorne
Reedsport, OR 97467
Contact: John Kenagy, Pres.

Established in 2000 in OR.
Donor(s): John Kenagy.

Financial data (yr. ended 06/30/02): Grants paid, $12,000; assets, $1 (M); expenditures, $12,000; qualifying distributions, $12,000.
Application information: Application form not required.
Officer: John Kenagy, Pres.
EIN: 931300847

45773
Dorothy Pearce Charitable Trust
c/o Pioneer Trust Bank, N.A.
P.O. Box 2305
Salem, OR 97308

Financial data (yr. ended 12/31/01): Grants paid, $12,000; assets, $268,804 (M); expenditures, $17,668; qualifying distributions, $12,000.
Limitations: Applications not accepted. Giving primarily in OR.
Application information: Contributes only to pre-selected organizations.
Trustee: Pioneer Trust Bank, N.A.
EIN: 936024156

45774
Pendleton Prints, Inc.
P.O. Box 91
Pendleton, OR 97801-0091

Donor(s): Steven L. Neal, M.D.
Financial data (yr. ended 12/31/01): Grants paid, $12,000; assets, $208,403 (M); expenditures, $19,739; qualifying distributions, $12,000.
Limitations: Applications not accepted.
Application information: Contributes only to pre-selected organizations.
Officers and Directors:* Dan Leonard,* Chair.; Steven L. Neal, M.D.,* Pres.; Suzan C. Neal,* Secy.
EIN: 930993572

45775
The Woodmansee Scholarship Fund
c/o Pioneer Trust Bank, N.A.
P.O. Box 2305
Salem, OR 97308

Established in 1987 in OR.
Financial data (yr. ended 05/31/01): Grants paid, $11,645; assets, $157,264 (M); expenditures, $14,423; qualifying distributions, $11,547.
Limitations: Giving limited to residents of OR.
Trustee: Pioneer Trust Bank, N.A.
EIN: 936195941
Codes: GTI

45776
The Robert & Kathleen Stafford Foundation
21650 N.E. Blue Lake Rd.
Interlachen, OR 97024

Established in 1998 in OR.
Donor(s): Kathleen Stafford, Robert Stafford.
Financial data (yr. ended 12/31/01): Grants paid, $11,630; assets, $26,143 (M); gifts received, $135; expenditures, $12,103; qualifying distributions, $11,630.
Limitations: Applications not accepted.
Application information: Contributes only to pre-selected organizations.
Directors: Barbara Landers, Kathleen Stafford, Robert Stafford.
EIN: 931258610

45777
Dura & Mary Hopkins Family Trust
P.O. Box 3168, Trust Tax Services
Portland, OR 97208

Established in 2000 in OR.
Financial data (yr. ended 12/31/01): Grants paid, $11,523; assets, $158,300 (M); expenditures, $13,827; qualifying distributions, $11,523.

Limitations: Applications not accepted. Giving primarily in ID.
Application information: Contributes only to pre-selected organizations.
Trustee: U.S. Bank, N.A.
EIN: 846315609

45778
W. C. & Pearl Campbell Scholarship Fund for Linfield College Students
c/o U.S. Bank
P.O. Box 3168
Portland, OR 97208-3168

Financial data (yr. ended 06/30/01): Grants paid, $11,500; assets, $225,053 (M); expenditures, $15,919; qualifying distributions, $13,335.
Limitations: Giving limited to McMinnville, OR.
Application information: Application form required.
Trustee: U.S. Bank.
EIN: 936021036
Codes: GTI

45779
Danicas Foundation, Inc.
3250 S.W. Doschdale Dr.
Portland, OR 97239-1158 (503) 246-2886
Contact: Daniel E. Casey, M.D., Dir.

Financial data (yr. ended 12/31/01): Grants paid, $11,200; assets, $494,561 (M); gifts received, $39,760; expenditures, $25,312; qualifying distributions, $23,069; giving activities include $12,028 for programs.
Director: Daniel E. Casey, M.D.
EIN: 930875917

45780
Elmer Bankus Memorial Scholarship Fund
4815 S.W. Patton Rd.
Portland, OR 97221 (503) 297-1610
Contact: Carol Wittenbrock, Tr.

Financial data (yr. ended 06/30/01): Grants paid, $11,045; assets, $155,272 (M); expenditures, $17,508; qualifying distributions, $10,961.
Limitations: Giving limited to Brookings, OR.
Application information: Application form required.
Trustee: Carol Wittenbrock.
EIN: 237432831
Codes: GTI

45781
Bright Seed Foundation, Inc.
1619 Bay View Ln.
Lake Oswego, OR 97034

Established in 2000 in OR.
Donor(s): Craig D. Pfeiffer.
Financial data (yr. ended 12/31/01): Grants paid, $11,000; assets, $38,524 (M); gifts received, $29,855; expenditures, $11,190; qualifying distributions, $11,000.
Limitations: Giving primarily in Portland, OR.
Officers: Craig D. Pfeiffer, Pres.; Cissy H. Pfeiffer, Secy.
Director: John Warton.
EIN: 931301123

45782
Pacific Hospital Association Charitable Foundation, Inc.
c/o Greg McCumsey
250 Country Club Rd.
Eugene, OR 97401 (541) 686-1242
FAX: (541) 683-8328; *E-mail:* mikes@pac-source.com
Contact: Mike Sowinski

Established in 1992 in OR.
Donor(s): Pacific Hospital Assn.
Financial data (yr. ended 06/30/00): Grants paid, $11,000; assets, $554,254 (M); gifts received, $200,000; expenditures, $14,922; qualifying distributions, $13,408.
Limitations: Giving limited to residents of Lane County, OR.
Publications: Annual report, financial statement.
Application information: Application available upon request. Application form required.
Officers and Directors:* Greg McCumsey,* Pres.; Clark Compton,* V.P.; Larry Guistina,* Secy.-Treas.; Mary McCauley Burrows.
EIN: 931100080
Codes: GTI

45783
C.H.R. Foundation, Inc.
c/o U.S. Bank
P.O. Box 3168, Tr. Tax Svcs.
Portland, OR 97208

Financial data (yr. ended 12/31/01): Grants paid, $10,920; assets, $398,133 (M); expenditures, $26,301; qualifying distributions, $10,920.
Limitations: Applications not accepted. Giving primarily in OR and UT.
Application information: Contributes only to pre-selected organizations.
Officers: Rex A. Rice, Pres.; Edward Floyd, V.P.; Beverly A. Rice, Secy.-Treas.
Director: George G. Wells.
Trustee: U.S. Bank.
EIN: 930429008

45784
Peterson Foundation
1300 S.W. 6th Ave., Ste. 300
Portland, OR 97201-3461

Established in 2000 in OR.
Donor(s): Craig B. Peterson, Ruth A. Peterson.
Financial data (yr. ended 12/31/01): Grants paid, $10,718; assets, $366,897 (M); expenditures, $13,023; qualifying distributions, $10,718.
Limitations: Applications not accepted.
Application information: Contributes only to pre-selected organizations.
Officers: Craig B. Peterson, Pres.; Ruth A. Peterson, Secy.-Treas.
Director: Joseph J. Hanna, Jr.
EIN: 931279543

45785
Pacific Rivers Charitable Trust
1672 S.W. Willamette Falls Dr.
West Linn, OR 97068

Donor(s): Randal S. Sebastian.
Financial data (yr. ended 08/31/01): Grants paid, $10,600; assets, $145,983 (M); expenditures, $10,931; qualifying distributions, $10,600.
Limitations: Applications not accepted.
Application information: Contributes only to pre-selected organizations.
Trustees: Randal S. Sebastian, Sandra Sebastian.
EIN: 936275017

45786
Frank Leaphart Charitable Trust
c/o Western Bank, Trust Dept.
P.O. Box 1784
Medford, OR 97501

Financial data (yr. ended 12/31/01): Grants paid, $10,452; assets, $248,584 (M); expenditures, $14,821; qualifying distributions, $10,452.
Limitations: Applications not accepted.
Application information: Contributes only to pre-selected organizations.
Trustee: Western Bank.
EIN: 930863016

45787
The Adler Fund
c/o McDonald, Jacobs, et al.
621 S.W. Morrison St., Ste. 600
Portland, OR 97205

Donor(s): Carol Adler, Annie Bellman.
Financial data (yr. ended 06/30/02): Grants paid, $10,450; assets, $215,559 (M); gifts received, $240; expenditures, $14,175; qualifying distributions, $10,450.
Limitations: Applications not accepted. Giving primarily in San Francisco, CA, and Portland, OR.
Application information: Contributes only to pre-selected organizations.
Officer: Carol Adler, Pres.
EIN: 132989407

45788
Zehntbauer Foundation
P.O. Box 3001
Portland, OR 97208-3001

Financial data (yr. ended 08/31/01): Grants paid, $10,400; assets, $199,481 (M); expenditures, $10,659; qualifying distributions, $10,400.
Limitations: Applications not accepted. Giving primarily in OR.
Application information: Contributes only to pre-selected organizations.
Officers: Steve Fritz, Pres.; Jan Ronzheimer, Secy.; Lee Thorkildson, Treas.
EIN: 936021870

45789
Journal Publishing Company Employees Welfare Fund, Inc.
c/o U.S. Bank
P.O. Box 3168
Portland, OR 97208-3168

Donor(s): The Jackson Foundation.
Financial data (yr. ended 06/30/01): Grants paid, $10,200; assets, $550 (M); gifts received, $10,200; expenditures, $11,719; qualifying distributions, $10,710.
Limitations: Applications not accepted.
Trustee: U.S. Bank.
EIN: 237066006
Codes: GTI

45790
Bruggere Family Foundation
c/o Wells Fargo
1300 S.W. 5th Ave.
Portland, OR 97208
Contact: Thomas Bruggere, Tr.

Established in 2000 in OR.
Donor(s): Thomas E. Bruggere, Kelley C. Bruggere.
Financial data (yr. ended 12/31/01): Grants paid, $10,000; assets, $459,834 (M); expenditures, $25,703; qualifying distributions, $10,000.
Trustees: Kelley C. Bruggere, Thomas E. Bruggere.
EIN: 931307769

45791
Louis & Ruth Romoff Charitable Foundation
c/o Neale Creamer
333 S.W. Taylor St.
Portland, OR 97204-2496

Established in 1997 in OR.
Donor(s): Ruth Romoff.
Financial data (yr. ended 12/31/01): Grants paid, $10,000; assets, $70,597 (M); expenditures, $11,684; qualifying distributions, $10,000.
Limitations: Giving primarily in Los Angeles, CA.
Application information: Application form required.

45791—OREGON

Officers: Ruth Romoff, Pres.; Neale E. Creamer, Secy.-Treas.
EIN: 911748402

45792
Nadie E. Strayer Scholarship Fund
2495 Resort St.
Baker City, OR 97814
Application address: 1995 3rd St., Baker City, OR 97814, tel.: (541) 523-2162
Contact: Ruth Whitnah, Tr.

Established around 1994.
Financial data (yr. ended 12/31/01): Grants paid, $10,000; assets, $72,209 (M); expenditures, $10,060; qualifying distributions, $9,937.
Limitations: Giving limited to residents of the Baker County, OR, area.
Application information: Application form required.
Trustees: Howard D. Britton, Carl R. Kostol, Ruth Whitnah.
EIN: 931137546

45793
BCT Foundation
c/o Elizabeth C. Brunette
49557 Cabbage School Rd.
Pendleton, OR 97801

Established in 1997 in OR.
Donor(s): Elizabeth C. Brunette.
Financial data (yr. ended 12/31/01): Grants paid, $9,775; assets, $63,735 (M); expenditures, $10,118; qualifying distributions, $9,775.
Limitations: Applications not accepted.
Application information: Contributes only to pre-selected organizations.
Officer: Elizabeth C. Brunette, Pres. and Secy.-Treas.
Directors: Andrew T. Brunette, David P. Brunette, Mary F. Brunette.
EIN: 911805895

45794
Charles E. Elliot Trust
c/o U.S. Bank
P.O. Box 3168
Portland, OR 97208-3168 (503) 275-6564

Financial data (yr. ended 06/30/01): Grants paid, $9,500; assets, $155,362 (M); expenditures, $13,243; qualifying distributions, $10,386.
Limitations: Applications not accepted. Giving limited to residents of Umatilla County, OR.
Application information: Recipients recommended by Umatilla County Health Dept. and school districts.
Trustee: U.S. Bank.
EIN: 936021442

45795
Red and Gena Leonard Foundation
P.O. Box 1024
Hermiston, OR 97838

Financial data (yr. ended 06/30/01): Grants paid, $9,333; assets, $480,799 (M); gifts received, $175,000; expenditures, $19,707; qualifying distributions, $19,707.
Limitations: Giving limited to Gilliam, Grant, Morrow, Umatilla, and Wheeler counties, OR.
Officers: Glenn S. Chowing, Pres.; Gena Leonard, V.P.
Directors: Mac Campbell, Ron Daniels, Nellie Madison, Larry Mills.
EIN: 931232272

45796
Tyler Foundation
1950 3rd St.
Baker City, OR 97814-3314
Application address: P.O. Box 965, Baker City, OR 97814-0965, tel.: (541) 523-4442
Contact: Alan J. Schmeits, Tr.

Established in 1988 in OR.
Financial data (yr. ended 08/31/01): Grants paid, $9,331; assets, $305,426 (M); expenditures, $11,648; qualifying distributions, $9,331.
Limitations: Giving limited to Baker County, OR.
Trustee: Alan J. Schmeits.
EIN: 930959028

45797
Lesh Manpower Memorial Trust
22235 Butteville Rd., N.E.
Aurora, OR 97002

Established in 1998 in OR.
Donor(s): Linda Hammersley, William Hammersley.
Financial data (yr. ended 12/31/01): Grants paid, $9,015; assets, $197,283 (M); gifts received, $30,000; expenditures, $12,708; qualifying distributions, $9,015.
Limitations: Applications not accepted.
Application information: Contributes only to pre-selected organizations.
Trustees: Linda Hammersley, William Hammersley.
EIN: 931258849

45798
Professional Engineers of Oregon Educational Foundation
530 N. Col. River Hwy., Ste. C
St. Helens, OR 97051

Financial data (yr. ended 12/31/01): Grants paid, $9,000; assets, $112,325 (M); gifts received, $2,792; expenditures, $13,052; qualifying distributions, $9,000.
Limitations: Giving limited to OR.
Application information: Application form required.
Officers: Tai Funatake, Pres.; Arthur Armstrong, V.P.; Mike Walker, Secy.
Director: Steve Hawk.
EIN: 930666849

45799
Phillip W. Woolwine Trust
c/o U.S. Bank
P.O. Box 3168
Portland, OR 97208

Financial data (yr. ended 10/31/01): Grants paid, $8,708; assets, $167,098 (M); expenditures, $12,110; qualifying distributions, $8,708.
Limitations: Applications not accepted. Giving primarily in Boise, ID.
Application information: Contributes only to pre-selected organizations.
Trustee: U.S. Bank.
EIN: 237343137

45800
Michael J. Tennant Charitable Fund
516 S.W. 13th St.
Bend, OR 97702-3112

Established in 1998 OR.
Donor(s): Michael J. Tennant.
Financial data (yr. ended 12/31/01): Grants paid, $8,600; assets, $42,604 (M); expenditures, $10,553; qualifying distributions, $8,600.
Limitations: Applications not accepted.

Application information: Contributes only to pre-selected organizations.
Officer: Michael J. Tennant, Pres.
Directors: Wesley B. Price III, Adele Tennant, Ron L. White.
EIN: 931246876

45801
Gerald N. Banta Residual Trust
c/o U.S. Bank
P.O. Box 3168
Portland, OR 97208-3168

Established in 1997 in ID.
Financial data (yr. ended 12/31/01): Grants paid, $8,536; assets, $255,223 (M); expenditures, $15,470; qualifying distributions, $9,282.
Limitations: Applications not accepted.
Application information: Contributes only to pre-selected organizations.
Trustee: U.S. Bank.
EIN: 826069475

45802
The Souther Foundation
1130 S.W. Morrison St., No. 200
Portland, OR 97205-2241 (503) 224-4051
Contact: John B. Souther, Pres.

Financial data (yr. ended 12/31/99): Grants paid, $8,532; assets, $131,693 (M); expenditures, $9,235; qualifying distributions, $8,565.
Limitations: Giving primarily in OR and WA.
Application information: Application form required.
Officers and Trustees:* John B. Souther,* Pres.; David W. Souther,* V.P.; Margaret A. Paulbach,* Secy.
EIN: 916048710

45803
June Sou-Keng Q. Shi Memorial Fund
c/o Nai Chow Shi
4417 N.E. 70th Ave.
Portland, OR 97218

Donor(s): Charles Nai-Chow Shi.
Financial data (yr. ended 12/31/01): Grants paid, $8,500; assets, $184,940 (M); gifts received, $1,000; expenditures, $8,832; qualifying distributions, $8,500.
Limitations: Applications not accepted. Giving primarily in Concord, CA.
Application information: Contributes only to pre-selected organizations.
Officers: Charles Nai-Chow Shi, Pres.; Michael P.W. Khaw, V.P.; Patrick P.T. Khaw, Secy.-Treas.
EIN: 931128191

45804
Faith Charitable Foundation, Inc.
c/o Erik Szeto
4130 Southeast Div.
Portland, OR 97202-1647

Established in 1996 in OR.
Financial data (yr. ended 12/31/00): Grants paid, $8,400; assets, $97,966 (M); expenditures, $10,245; qualifying distributions, $8,332.
Officers: Erik K. Szeto, Pres.; Ida Tso, Secy.; Albert Wong, Treas.
EIN: 931195878

45805
Fred & Marie Barnard Scholarship Fund
c/o U.S. Bank
P.O. Box 3168
Portland, OR 97208
Application address: P.O. Box 5000, Great Falls, MT 59403, tel.: (406) 455-1072
Contact: Deborah Schroedel, Admin.

Financial data (yr. ended 05/31/01): Grants paid, $8,100; assets, $147,015 (M); expenditures, $11,445; qualifying distributions, $9,837.
Limitations: Giving limited to residents of Great Falls, MT.
Application information: Application form required.
Trustee: U.S. Bank.
EIN: 816045912

45806
Beatrice Allinger Foundation
P.O. Box 645
Gold Beach, OR 97444

Established in 1999 in OR.
Donor(s): Beatrice Allinger.‡
Financial data (yr. ended 12/31/01): Grants paid, $8,000; assets, $220,003 (M); gifts received, $228,282; expenditures, $8,310; qualifying distributions, $8,155.
Directors: Daniel M. Crofoot, Jessica J. Crofoot, A. Lavina Donaldson.
EIN: 860861949

45807
Daura Foundation
c/o Thomas W. Mapp
1760 Walnut St.
Eugene, OR 97403-2064

Established in 2000 in WA.
Donor(s): Martha R. Daura.
Financial data (yr. ended 12/31/00): Grants paid, $8,000; assets, $4,856 (M); gifts received, $15,000; expenditures, $11,342; qualifying distributions, $8,000.
Limitations: Applications not accepted.
Application information: Contributes only to pre-selected organizations.
Trustees: Martha R. Daura, Paul W. Mapp, Thomas W. Mapp.
EIN: 936329831

45808
Freidberg Family Foundation
c/o Moss Adams, LLP
8705 S.W. Nimbus Ave., Ste. 115
Beaverton, OR 97008

Established in 1999 in OR.
Donor(s): Stanton L. Freidberg, Colleen Freidberg.
Financial data (yr. ended 12/31/01): Grants paid, $8,000; assets, $136,855 (M); gifts received, $1,116; expenditures, $9,478; qualifying distributions, $8,000.
Limitations: Applications not accepted.
Application information: Contributes only to pre-selected organizations.
Officers and Directors: Stanton L. Freidberg,* Pres.; Colleen Freidberg,* Secy.; Mark S. Freidberg,* Treas.; Jill I. Freidberg, Susanne E. Freidberg.
EIN: 931283109

45809
The Harold Glock Memorial Trust
5643 N.W. 204th Pl.
Portland, OR 97229-7118

Established in 2001 in TX.

Financial data (yr. ended 12/31/01): Grants paid, $8,000; assets, $494,871 (M); expenditures, $8,000; qualifying distributions, $8,000.
Limitations: Applications not accepted. Giving primarily in Guthrie, OK.
Application information: Contributes only to pre-selected organizations.
Trustees: Richard Gerlach, Robert L. Gerlach.
EIN: 936343536

45810
Litster Scholarship Trust
c/o U.S. Bank
P.O. Box 3168
Portland, OR 97208-3168
Application address: c/o Crater High School, 4410 Rogue Valley Blvd., Central Point, OR 97502, tel.: (541) 664-6611, ext. 220

Financial data (yr. ended 03/31/02): Grants paid, $8,000; assets, $173,557 (M); expenditures, $10,569; qualifying distributions, $8,000.
Limitations: Giving primarily in Central Point, OR.
Application information: Application form required.
Trustee: U.S. Bank.
EIN: 936030423

45811
Harold & Wilma Haller Foundation Trust
c/o U.S. Bank
P.O. Box 3168
Portland, OR 97208-3168

Established in 1995 in OR.
Financial data (yr. ended 06/30/02): Grants paid, $7,750; assets, $204,449 (M); expenditures, $11,922; qualifying distributions, $7,750.
Limitations: Giving primarily in OR.
Application information: Application form required.
Trustee: U.S. Bank.
EIN: 936301165

45812
T & J Meyer Family Foundation
c/o Edwards & Meyers, LLP
5550 S.W. Macadam, Ste. 310
Portland, OR 97201

Donor(s): Jane Meyer, Timothy J. Meyer.
Financial data (yr. ended 12/31/01): Grants paid, $7,700; assets, $192,963 (M); gifts received, $50,000; expenditures, $11,926; qualifying distributions, $7,700.
Limitations: Applications not accepted. Giving primarily in OR.
Application information: Contributes only to pre-selected organizations.
Officers: Timothy J. Meyer, Pres.; Jane Meyer, Secy.
EIN: 931234568

45813
Beatrice Johnson Irrevocable Charitable Trust
c/o U.S. Bank
P.O. Box 3168
Portland, OR 97208-3168
Application address: David C. Ackley, c/o Principal, Priest River Lamanna High School, P.O. Box 1300, Priest River, ID 83856

Established in 1992 in ID.
Donor(s): Glenard Johnson.
Financial data (yr. ended 10/31/01): Grants paid, $7,667; assets, $155,312 (M); expenditures, $12,195; qualifying distributions, $11,385.
Limitations: Giving limited to residents of the Priest River, ID, area.
Application information: Application form required.
Trustee: U.S. Bank.
EIN: 826075423

45814
Flora Von der Ahe School Trust
c/o U.S. Bank
P.O. Box 3168
Portland, OR 97208-3168

Financial data (yr. ended 06/30/99): Grants paid, $7,615; assets, $371,674 (M); expenditures, $14,340; qualifying distributions, $8,926.
Limitations: Giving limited to Umatilla County, OR.
Application information: Application form required.
Trustee: U.S. Bank.
EIN: 936066821
Codes: GTI

45815
John and Alice Dillard Memorial Trust
P.O. Box 100
Nehalem, OR 97131-0100 (503) 368-3120
Contact: Nancy Dillard, Secy.

Established in 1998 in OR.
Financial data (yr. ended 12/31/00): Grants paid, $7,500; assets, $61,766 (M); gifts received, $29,245; expenditures, $7,683; qualifying distributions, $7,500.
Officers: Robert Hollis, Chair.; Gayle Stephens, Vice-Chair.; Nancy Dillard, Secy.
EIN: 936319500

45816
Algonac Foundation
707 Benjamin Ct.
Ashland, OR 97520 (541) 488-4154
Contact: J.L. Auchincloss

Established in 1998 in OR.
Donor(s): James L. Auchincloss.
Financial data (yr. ended 12/31/01): Grants paid, $7,360; assets, $209,446 (M); gifts received, $101,834; expenditures, $12,586; qualifying distributions, $7,360.
Officer: James L. Auchincloss, Pres.
Directors: David Baker, Anthony Juliano, Joyce Baker Phillips.
EIN: 931258506

45817
Oregonians for Environmental Rights
17575 Jordan Rd.
Sisters, OR 97759

Donor(s): William H. Boyer.
Financial data (yr. ended 12/31/01): Grants paid, $7,308; assets, $3,738 (M); gifts received, $7,000; expenditures, $12,454; qualifying distributions, $12,454.
Limitations: Applications not accepted. Giving primarily in OR.
Application information: Contributes only to pre-selected organizations.
Directors: William H. Boyer, Robert Collin, Jerome Garger, Shannon Wilson.
EIN: 931138369

45818
Mackworth-Mendoza Foundation
701 Terrace Dr.
Lake Oswego, OR 97034

Established in 2000 in OR.
Donor(s): Hugh F. Mackworth, Josie G. Mendoza.
Financial data (yr. ended 12/31/01): Grants paid, $7,081; assets, $559,105 (M); expenditures, $12,811; qualifying distributions, $7,081.
Officers and Directors:* Hugh F. Mackworth,* Pres.; Josie G. Mendoza,* Secy.; Donald L. Krahmer, Jr.

45818—OREGON

EIN: 931296528

45819
Layton, Edith Roehlk & Donna Belle Mann Charitable Trust
P.O. Box 399
Pendleton, OR 97801
Contact: Michael J. Kilkenny, Tr.

Established in 1999 in OR.
Financial data (yr. ended 12/31/01): Grants paid, $7,000; assets, $324,132 (M); expenditures, $22,177; qualifying distributions, $7,000.
Trustee: Michael J. Kilkenny.
EIN: 931274667

45820
Viola Spicer Memorial Scholarship Foundation
873 S.W. Sitka Dr.
McMinnville, OR 97128 (503) 434-9712
Contact: Kenneth Spicer

Financial data (yr. ended 12/31/01): Grants paid, $7,000; assets, $159,345 (M); expenditures, $8,349; qualifying distributions, $7,000.
Officers and Directors:* Kenneth G. Spicer,* Pres.; Cindy Blum, V.P.; David Spicer, V.P.; Dorothy Spicer, Secy.
EIN: 841246174

45821
Gerald N. Banta Fish & Game Trust
c/o U.S. Bank
P.O. Box 3168
Portland, OR 97208-3168 (503) 275-4327

Established in 1997 in ID.
Financial data (yr. ended 12/31/01): Grants paid, $6,834; assets, $199,472 (M); expenditures, $14,423; qualifying distributions, $7,561.
Limitations: Applications not accepted.
Application information: Contributes only to pre-selected organizations.
Trustee: U.S. Bank.
EIN: 826071653

45822
Hazel D. Isbell Charitable Trust
c/o U.S. Bank
P.O. Box 3168, Tr.Tax Svcs.
Portland, OR 97208
Application address: c/o Collegiate Chapter Pres., Delta Delta Delta Sorority, 1987 University St., Eugene, OR 97401

Established in 1986 in OR.
Financial data (yr. ended 06/30/01): Grants paid, $6,780; assets, $80,952 (M); expenditures, $8,221; qualifying distributions, $7,469.
Limitations: Giving limited to residents of OR.
Trustee: U.S. Bank.
EIN: 936193677

45823
Miles Wendell Moore and Geraldine Moore Scholarship Fund
c/p South Valley Bank & Trust
P.O. Box 5210
Klamath Falls, OR 97601-0206

Established in 1995 in OR.
Donor(s): Miles W. Moore, Geraldine Moore.
Financial data (yr. ended 05/31/02): Grants paid, $6,750; assets, $174,408 (M); expenditures, $10,019; qualifying distributions, $8,050.
Limitations: Applications not accepted. Giving primarily in OR.
Application information: Contributes only to pre-selected organizations.
Trustee: South Valley Bank & Trust.
EIN: 931192772

45824
Borgen Family Trust
11040 S.W. Barbur Blvd.
Portland, OR 97219

Established in 1999 in OR.
Donor(s): Arlen Borgen.
Financial data (yr. ended 08/31/00): Grants paid, $6,714; assets, $19,148 (M); gifts received, $24,944; expenditures, $9,871; qualifying distributions, $9,871.
Limitations: Applications not accepted. Giving primarily in OR.
Application information: Contributes only to pre-selected organizations.
Trustees: Arlen Borgen, Heather Borgen, Heidi Borgen.
EIN: 936333221

45825
The Mary Angiola Foundation
2065 N.W. Twilight Dr.
Bend, OR 97701

Established in 1999 in CA.
Donor(s): Henry P. Angiola.
Financial data (yr. ended 12/31/01): Grants paid, $6,700; assets, $124,353 (M); expenditures, $8,373; qualifying distributions, $6,700.
Limitations: Applications not accepted. Giving on a national basis.
Application information: Contributes only to pre-selected organizations.
Officers: Yvonne C. Angiola, Pres.; Gina M. Angiola, Secy.; Dean Angiola, C.F.O.
EIN: 954742537

45826
The Vance Foundation
6400 N. Interstate Ave.
Portland, OR 97217

Established in 2000 in OR.
Donor(s): James Vance.
Financial data (yr. ended 12/31/01): Grants paid, $6,500; assets, $321,614 (M); gifts received, $225,000; expenditures, $6,500; qualifying distributions, $6,500.
Limitations: Applications not accepted.
Application information: Contributes only to pre-selected organizations.
Trustees: James Vance, Rollin Vance.
EIN: 931249351

45827
Ward Rhoden Athletic Scholarship Fund
715 W. 3rd St.
Prineville, OR 97754-0460 (541) 477-1097
Contact: Kathy Rhoden Overall, Tr.

Financial data (yr. ended 12/31/99): Grants paid, $6,400; assets, $104,648 (M); expenditures, $6,564; qualifying distributions, $6,564.
Limitations: Giving limited to Prineville, OR.
Trustees: Kathy Rhoden Overall, Grant Patterson, Jack Rhoden, John Rhoden, Ron Rhoden.
EIN: 237067165

45828
The Jeff Pearson Memorial Scholarship Fund
c/o U.S. Bank
P.O. Box 3168
Portland, OR 97208
Application addresses: c/o South High School, 1801 Hollywood Dr., Pueblo, CO 81005; c/o Pueblo Community College, 900 W. Orman Ave., Pueblo, CO 81004-1499

Established in 1985 in CO.

Financial data (yr. ended 04/30/02): Grants paid, $6,382; assets, $63,371 (M); expenditures, $10,476; qualifying distributions, $6,382.
Limitations: Giving limited to residents of Pueblo, CO.
Application information: Application form required.
Officer and Trustees:* Anne K. Burmont,* Mgr.; Phyllis Shumard, James Wessley Principal,* U.S. Bank.
EIN: 742425238

45829
Footprints Foundation, Inc.
c/o Debra Child
01515 S.W. Radcliffe Ct.
Portland, OR 97201

Established in 1994 in MD.
Donor(s): Debra Feiner Child.
Financial data (yr. ended 09/30/01): Grants paid, $6,371; assets, $82,807 (M); expenditures, $9,597; qualifying distributions, $8,418.
Limitations: Applications not accepted.
Application information: Contributes only to pre-selected organizations.
Directors: Debra Child, Albert Feiner.
EIN: 521867219

45830
The Hollione Foundation
P.O. Box 862
Corvallis, OR 97339

Established in 2000 in OR.
Donor(s): Debra Hollenback.
Financial data (yr. ended 12/31/01): Grants paid, $6,350; assets, $466,010 (M); gifts received, $62,249; expenditures, $12,400; qualifying distributions, $6,350.
Limitations: Applications not accepted. Giving primarily in OR.
Application information: Contributes only to pre-selected organizations.
Officers and Directors:* Debra Hollenback,* Pres.; Beth Buglione,* Secy.; Jeannine Murrell.
EIN: 931300630

45831
Day Management Educational Foundation
P.O. Box 189
Estacada, OR 97023

Established in 1996 in OR.
Financial data (yr. ended 12/31/99): Grants paid, $6,334; assets, $137,733 (M); gifts received, $50,000; expenditures, $6,835; qualifying distributions, $6,810.
Application information: Application form required.
Trustees: Donna Desanno, Matt Enser, Jim Randall, Diane Reynolds, Frank Vanderbilt.
EIN: 931188551

45832
Cedarvall Foundation
937 D Street
Springfield, OR 97477 (541) 726-5671
Contact: Don E. Nickell, Tr.

Financial data (yr. ended 12/31/00): Grants paid, $6,300; assets, $78,517 (M); expenditures, $65,809; qualifying distributions, $6,300.
Limitations: Giving limited to Loma Lida, CA, OR, and College Place, WA.
Trustee: Don Nickell.
EIN: 930861408

45833
Max London Foundation
6809 S.W. Raleighwood Way
Portland, OR 97225-1924

Financial data (yr. ended 12/31/01): Grants paid, $6,200; assets, $120,403 (M); gifts received, $2,200; expenditures, $6,638; qualifying distributions, $6,200.
Limitations: Applications not accepted.
Application information: Contributes only to pre-selected organizations.
Officer and Trustees:* Barbara F. London,* Secy.; Marla London, Ralph L. London, Judith L. Rothbaum.
EIN: 256028559

45834
Ausplund Tooze Family Foundation
5500 S.W. Hewett Blvd.
Portland, OR 97221-2239 (503) 292-1886
Contact: Mary Ausplund Tooze, Pres.

Established in 1999 in OR.
Donor(s): Mary Ausplund Tooze.
Financial data (yr. ended 12/31/01): Grants paid, $6,000; assets, $113,849 (M); expenditures, $6,766; qualifying distributions, $6,000.
Application information: Application form not required.
Officers: Mary Ausplund Tooze, Pres.; Kristen Kern, Secy.
Director: Michael Kern.
EIN: 931271976

45835
Marlene K. Sapinsley Private Foundation
2746 Kincaid St.
Eugene, OR 97405-4154

Established in 1999 in OR.
Financial data (yr. ended 12/31/01): Grants paid, $6,000; assets, $215,931 (M); expenditures, $8,639; qualifying distributions, $6,000.
Limitations: Applications not accepted.
Application information: Contributes only to pre-selected organizations.
Officers: Marlene K. Sapinsley, Pres. and Treas.; Beth Bloch, Secy.
Directors: Lisi McCarthy, Ed Sapinsley.
EIN: 931277040

45836
Mark and Karen Wendt Foundation
3102 Front St.
Klamath Falls, OR 97601

Established in 1999 in OR.
Financial data (yr. ended 12/31/01): Grants paid, $6,000; assets, $187,770 (M); expenditures, $7,166; qualifying distributions, $6,000.
Limitations: Applications not accepted. Giving primarily in Klamath Falls, OR.
Application information: Contributes only to pre-selected organizations.
Officers: Mark Wendt, Pres.; Karen Lynch Wendt, Secy.-Treas.
EIN: 931260293

45837
Donna & Gregory Russell Foundation
7730 S.W. Cedar
Portland, OR 97225

Established in 1997 in OR.
Donor(s): Donna Russell, Greg Russell.
Financial data (yr. ended 12/31/00): Grants paid, $5,605; assets, $0 (M); gifts received, $4,500; expenditures, $7,792; qualifying distributions, $5,603.
Limitations: Applications not accepted.

Application information: Contributes only to pre-selected organizations.
Officers and Directors:* Donna Russell,* Pres.; Gregory Russell,* Secy.
EIN: 931234791

45838
Walter Bailey Foundation
3325 Dry Hollow Ln.
The Dalles, OR 97058

Donor(s): Robert L. R. Bailey, Barbara S. Bailey.
Financial data (yr. ended 12/31/01): Grants paid, $5,589; assets, $144,710 (M); expenditures, $6,339; qualifying distributions, $5,589.
Officers: Brenda Thomas, Pres.; Barbara S. Bailey, V.P.; Robert L. R. Bailey, V.P.; Bridget Bailey Nisley, Secy.-Treas.
EIN: 931246931

45839
The Campbell-Wallace Foundation
27411 S.W. Campbell Ln.
West Linn, OR 97068

Established in 1997 in OR.
Financial data (yr. ended 12/31/01): Grants paid, $5,500; assets, $134,507 (M); expenditures, $6,271; qualifying distributions, $5,500.
Limitations: Applications not accepted. Giving primarily in OR.
Application information: Contributes only to pre-selected organizations.
Officers and Directors:* W. Leigh Campbell,* Pres.; Wiley Leigh Campbell, Jr., V.P.; Ceille W. Campbell,* Secy.
EIN: 911796288

45840
Dwyer Charitable Trust
822 N.W. Murray Blvd., Ste. 216
Portland, OR 97229 (503) 292-9686
Contact: Claire M. Doherty, Tr.

Established in 2001 in OR.
Donor(s): Rosemary D. Frey.‡
Financial data (yr. ended 12/31/01): Grants paid, $5,500; assets, $384,344 (M); gifts received, $198,159; expenditures, $8,092; qualifying distributions, $6,371.
Limitations: Giving on a national basis.
Trustees: Claire M. Doherty, Natt A. McDougall.
EIN: 931301831

45841
Osozaki Foundation
2023 N.W. Lovejoy St.
Portland, OR 97209
Contact: Bradley A. Zenger, Pres.

Established in 2000 in OR.
Donor(s): Bradley A. Zenger.
Financial data (yr. ended 12/31/01): Grants paid, $5,500; assets, $220,763 (M); expenditures, $12,939; qualifying distributions, $5,500.
Application information: Application form required.
Officers and Directors: Bradley A. Zenger,* Pres.; Brenda Melum,* Secy.; David Reichle,* Treas.
EIN: 931306217

45842
Kreinberg Foundation
3145 N.E. 20th Ave.
Portland, OR 97212 (503) 273-2700
Contact: Robert L. Kreinberg, Secy. or Penelope P. Kreinberg, Pres.

Established in 1997 in OR.
Financial data (yr. ended 12/31/01): Grants paid, $5,264; assets, $63,077 (M); expenditures, $7,027; qualifying distributions, $5,264.

Officers: Penelope P. Kreinberg, Pres.; Robert L. Kreinberg, Secy.
Directors: Joshua A. Kreinberg, Patricia D. Kreinberg, Sarah L. Kreinberg.
EIN: 911796733

45843
Geraldine Bagley Foundation Trust
P.O. Box 22000
Florence, OR 97439

Financial data (yr. ended 12/31/01): Grants paid, $5,000; assets, $486,029 (M); expenditures, $13,532; qualifying distributions, $4,862.
Trustees: Lydia Brackney, Thomas K. Grove, Robert King.
EIN: 936311484

45844
Best Student Loan Fund
(Formerly Woodie L. & Mabel Best Student Loan Fund)
c/o U.S. Bank
P.O. Box 3168
Portland, OR 97208-3168
Application address: c/o Oregon State Scholarship Commission, 1500 Valley River Dr., Ste. 100, Eugene, OR 97401-2146, tel.: (800) 452-8807

Financial data (yr. ended 06/30/01): Grants paid, $5,000; assets, $94,995 (M); expenditures, $7,084; qualifying distributions, $6,041.
Limitations: Giving limited to Harney County, OR.
Publications: Application guidelines.
Application information: Application form required.
Trustee: U.S. Bank.
EIN: 510161411

45845
Geraldine C. Heiserman Trust f/b/o Yuma High School
c/o U.S. Bank
P.O. Box 3168, Tr. Tax Svcs.
Portland, OR 97208-3168
Application address: c/o Principal, Yuma High School, 10th & Albany, Yuma, CO 80759, tel.: (970) 848-5488

Financial data (yr. ended 12/31/01): Grants paid, $5,000; assets, $117,057 (M); expenditures, $6,824; qualifying distributions, $5,643.
Limitations: Giving limited to Yuma, CO.
Trustee: U.S. Bank.
EIN: 846092596

45846
Kind Heart Free Spirit Foundation
c/o U.S. Bank
P.O. Box 3168, Trust Tax Svcs.
Portland, OR 97208
Application address: c/o Wesley J. Hickey, P.O. Box 508, Vancouver, WA 98666

Established in 2000 in WA.
Financial data (yr. ended 12/31/01): Grants paid, $5,000; assets, $482,876 (M); gifts received, $200,000; expenditures, $8,401; qualifying distributions, $5,840.
Limitations: Giving primarily in Vancouver, WA.
Agent: U.S. Bank.
EIN: 912047248

45847
Medical and Educational Relief International Association, Inc.
P.O. Box 1108
Scappoose, OR 97056

Donor(s): Stephen Scheer, Jodeanne Bellant, M.D.

45847—OREGON

Financial data (yr. ended 12/31/01): Grants paid, $5,000; assets, $99,937 (M); gifts received, $4,500; expenditures, $5,032; qualifying distributions, $5,000.
Limitations: Applications not accepted. Giving on an international basis.
Application information: Contributes only to pre-selected organizations.
Officers: Stephen Scheer, Pres.; Jeannine Brooks, V.P.; Jodeanne Bellant, M.D., Secy.-Treas.
EIN: 930846770

45848
Mike and Pam Wendt Foundation
2120 Fairmont
Klamath Falls, OR 97601

Established in 1998 in OR.
Donor(s): Richard Wendt, Nancy Wendt.
Financial data (yr. ended 12/31/01): Grants paid, $5,000; assets, $232,888 (M); expenditures, $5,486; qualifying distributions, $5,000.
Officers: Pam Wendt, Pres.; Jamie Wendt, V.P.; Mike Wendt, Secy.-Treas.
EIN: 931273203

45849
Willamette Dental Foundation
14025 S.W. Farmington Rd., Ste. 300
Beaverton, OR 97005

Established in 1999 in OR.
Donor(s): Eugene C. Skourtes, Bonnie K. Skourtes.
Financial data (yr. ended 07/31/01): Grants paid, $5,000; assets, $290,027 (M); expenditures, $9,216; qualifying distributions, $5,000.
Limitations: Applications not accepted.
Application information: Contributes only to pre-selected organizations.
Officers and Directors:* Eugene C. Skourtes,* Pres.; Wee Yuen Chin, Secy.; Frank Rosumny, Sharon Turner.
EIN: 931283766

45850
Eastern Oregon College Foundation Trust
c/o US Bank, N.A.
P.O Box 3168, Trust Tax Svcs.
Portland, OR 97208
Application address: 8th & K, La Grande, OR 97850-2866, tel.: (503)963-2171

Financial data (yr. ended 12/31/01): Grants paid, $4,950; assets, $88,613 (M); expenditures, $6,128; qualifying distributions, $4,950.
Trustee: US Bank, N.A.
EIN: 936071374

45851
Pets & People
P.O. Box 1019
Coos Bay, OR 97420 (541) 756-4151

Financial data (yr. ended 12/31/99): Grants paid, $4,825; assets, $94,636 (M); gifts received, $553; expenditures, $5,440; qualifying distributions, $5,366.
Limitations: Giving limited to residents of OR.
Application information: Application form required.
Officers: Janet Huggins, Pres.; Marjorie Russell, V.P.; Stephanie Thomas, Secy.; Glenora Parker, Treas.
EIN: 931095382

45852
Tyler R. Black Foundation Trust
c/o Judith A. Black
2425 N.E. 155th Pl.
Portland, OR 97230-8216
Application address: c/o Carl Solomon, Grant High School, 2245 N.E. 36th Ave., Portland, OR 97212-5299

Financial data (yr. ended 12/31/01): Grants paid, $4,800; assets, $59,178 (M); expenditures, $5,519; qualifying distributions, $4,779.
Limitations: Giving limited to residents of Portland, OR.
Application information: Application form required.
Trustees: Joyce Harris, Tina Mattern, John Zehrung.
EIN: 936209734

45853
Southeast Asia Scholarship Fund
12491 N.W. Woodland Ct.
Portland, OR 97229-8309 (503) 690-0704
Contact: Tran Thong, Dir.

Donor(s): Tran Thong, Thuy Thi-Bich Nguyen.
Financial data (yr. ended 12/31/01): Grants paid, $4,725; assets, $4,792 (M); gifts received, $5,100; expenditures, $4,768; qualifying distributions, $4,725.
Limitations: Giving limited to residents of Vietnam.
Application information: Application form required.
Directors: Thuy Thi-Bich Nguyen, Tran Thong.
EIN: 931128353

45854
Asa & Adrienne Arnsberg Family Foundation
c/o Joseph Hanna
1300 S.W. 6th Ave., Ste. 300
Portland, OR 97201
Contact: Asa Arnsberg, Dir.

Established in 1998 in OR.
Donor(s): Asa Arnsberg.
Financial data (yr. ended 12/31/01): Grants paid, $4,625; assets, $71,159 (M); expenditures, $7,650; qualifying distributions, $4,625.
Director: Asa Arnsberg.
EIN: 931233333

45855
Bio-Dynamics Foundation
3265 Chambers St.
Eugene, OR 97405
Contact: Barry T. Bates, Pres.

Financial data (yr. ended 09/30/01): Grants paid, $4,500; assets, $66,963 (M); gifts received, $1,500; expenditures, $4,623; qualifying distributions, $4,500.
Limitations: Giving primarily in Eugene, OR.
Officers: Barry T. Bates, Pres.; Janet S. Dufele, Secy.
Director: John Mercer.
EIN: 930863999

45856
Sally Marlin & R. M. Fox Scholarship Fund
(also known as Molalla Scholarship Foundation)
1395 Liberty St., Ste. 200
Salem, OR 97302

Financial data (yr. ended 12/31/99): Grants paid, $4,500; assets, $88,082 (M); expenditures, $7,626; qualifying distributions, $4,500.
Limitations: Giving limited to residents of Molalla, OR.
Application information: Application form required.
Trustee: Marvis R. Mackey.

EIN: 936228665

45857
LaCrosse Family Foundation, Inc.
18550 N.E. Riverside Pkwy.
Portland, OR 97230

Donor(s): LaCrosse Footwear, Inc.
Financial data (yr. ended 12/31/01): Grants paid, $4,500; assets, $2,350 (L); gifts received, $7,750; expenditures, $4,500; qualifying distributions, $4,500.
Limitations: Giving primarily in WI.
Application information: Application form required.
Officers and Directors:* George W. Schneider,* Chair.; Joseph P. Schneider,* Pres.; David P. Carlson, V.P. and Secy.; Kenneth F. Ducke, Treas.; Craig L. Leipold, Richard A. Rosenthal, Frank J. Uhler, Jr., John D. Whitcombe.
EIN: 391659966
Codes: CS, CD

45858
Minnie K. Willens Trust
c/o U.S. Bank
P.O. Box 3168
Portland, OR 97208-3068
Application addresses: c/o Principal, West High School, 951 Elati St., Denver, CO 80204, or c/o Principal, Beth Jacob High School, 5100 W. 14th Ave., Denver, CO 80204

Financial data (yr. ended 12/31/01): Grants paid, $4,158; assets, $76,494 (M); expenditures, $6,373; qualifying distributions, $4,871.
Limitations: Giving limited to residents of Denver, CO.
Trustee: U.S. Bank.
EIN: 846018683

45859
RRB Foundation
P.O. Box 333
North Plains, OR 97133
Contact: Caroline E. Goodall, Pres.

Established in 1997 in OR.
Donor(s): Caroline E. Goodall.
Financial data (yr. ended 12/31/01): Grants paid, $4,150; assets, $69,916 (M); expenditures, $4,949; qualifying distributions, $4,150.
Limitations: Giving primarily in MA and Portland, OR.
Application information: Application form not required.
Officers: Caroline E. Goodall, Pres.; Maia Goodall, Secy.; Duncan Goodall, Treas.
EIN: 911778815

45860
Dan Davis Foundation
4370 N.E. Halsey St.
Portland, OR 97213-1566
Contact: Andrew J. Davis, Pres.

Financial data (yr. ended 12/31/01): Grants paid, $4,137; assets, $28,672 (M); expenditures, $5,218; qualifying distributions, $1,037.
Limitations: Giving limited to Portland, OR.
Officers: Andrew J. Davis, Pres.; Daniel S. Davis, V.P.
EIN: 237009411

45861
The Bean Foundation
205 S.E. 5th St.
Madras, OR 97741-1632 (541) 475-2272
Contact: Don Reeder

Financial data (yr. ended 12/31/01): Grants paid, $4,100; assets, $483,198 (M); expenditures, $18,462; qualifying distributions, $4,100.
Limitations: Giving limited to Jefferson County, OR.
Officers and Directors:* Sumner C. Rodriguez,* Chair.; George Nielson,* V.P.; Carol Peterson,* Secy.; Diane Ramsey,* Treas.; Lou Bean.
EIN: 930788470

45862
Lucille McD. Logan Charitable Trust
c/o U.S. Bank
P.O. Box 3168
Portland, OR 97208-3168

Established in 1985 in MT.
Financial data (yr. ended 12/31/01): Grants paid, $3,849; assets, $99,544 (M); expenditures, $6,051; qualifying distributions, $3,849.
Limitations: Applications not accepted. Giving limited to MT.
Application information: Contributes only to pre-selected organizations.
Trustee: U.S. Bank.
EIN: 816057428

45863
Zeeb Family Foundation
280 Court St., N.E., No. 2
Salem, OR 97301-3443
Contact: Rodney C. Zeeb, Tr.

Established in 1994 in OR.
Donor(s): Rodney C. Zeeb.
Financial data (yr. ended 12/31/01): Grants paid, $3,750; assets, $7,814 (M); gifts received, $1,000; expenditures, $4,467; qualifying distributions, $3,750.
Limitations: Giving on a national basis.
Trustee: Rodney C. Zeeb.
EIN: 931150492

45864
Magic Bar "J" Charitable Trust
1600 Old Hwy. 99
Grants Pass, OR 97526

Established in 2001 in OR.
Donor(s): Spring Creek Holding Co.
Financial data (yr. ended 12/31/01): Grants paid, $3,568; assets, $3,218 (M); gifts received, $8,500; expenditures, $5,282; qualifying distributions, $5,282.
Trustee: Terrance B. Johnson.
EIN: 936347356

45865
Sorensen Student Scholarship Fund
c/o U.S. Bank
P.O. Box 3168
Portland, OR 97208-3168

Financial data (yr. ended 06/30/02): Grants paid, $3,500; assets, $68,828 (M); expenditures, $6,755; qualifying distributions, $3,500.
Limitations: Giving primarily to residents of OR.
Trustee: U.S. Bank.
EIN: 936101030

45866
Carl & Mabel Schafer Scholarship Fund
c/o U.S. Bank
P.O. Box 3168
Portland, OR 97208-3168

Financial data (yr. ended 05/31/02): Grants paid, $3,495; assets, $62,420 (M); expenditures, $6,778; qualifying distributions, $3,495.
Limitations: Giving limited to the Montesano, WA, area.
Application information: Contact high school guidance counselor for application. Application form required.
Trustee: U.S. Bank.
EIN: 916023084

45867
Walter W. Wadsworth Trust
c/o Union Bank of California, N.A.
P.O. Box 2742
Portland, OR 97208-2742

Financial data (yr. ended 12/31/99): Grants paid, $3,325; assets, $277,111 (M); expenditures, $9,379; qualifying distributions, $5,621.
Limitations: Applications not accepted. Giving primarily in OR.
Application information: Contributes only to pre-selected organizations.
Trustee: Union Bank of California, N.A.
EIN: 936038851

45868
Albina Rotary Club Foundation
4636 N. Willaims Ave.
Portland, OR 97217-2838
Contact: Gary Price, Treas.

Established in 1998 in OR.
Financial data (yr. ended 06/30/99): Grants paid, $3,300; assets, $73,225 (M); gifts received, $38,074; expenditures, $13,884; qualifying distributions, $13,840; giving activities include $3,877 for programs.
Limitations: Giving primarily in OR.
Officers: Marleah Llewellyn, Pres.; Keith Raines, Secy.; Gary Price, Treas.
EIN: 930883836

45869
Powell Foundation, Inc.
1100 S.W. 6th Ave., Ste. 1200
Portland, OR 97204-1079 (503) 226-1371
Contact: Philip N. Jones

Established in 1989 in OR.
Donor(s): Michael M. Powell.
Financial data (yr. ended 12/31/01): Grants paid, $3,150; assets, $59,265 (M); expenditures, $3,421; qualifying distributions, $3,150.
Limitations: Giving primarily in Portland, OR.
Application information: Application form not required.
Officers and Directors:* Alice K. Powell,* Pres.; Michael M. Powell,* Secy.; Catherine Gaetjens.
EIN: 930986542

45870
Ed & Eda Ross Scholarship Trust
c/o Wells Fargo Bank Northwest, N.A.
P.O. Box 2971
Portland, OR 97208
Application address: c/o Principal, Astoria Senior High School, 1001 W. Marine Dr., Astoria, OR 97103

Financial data (yr. ended 12/31/01): Grants paid, $3,033; assets, $141,229 (M); expenditures, $8,194; qualifying distributions, $5,067.
Limitations: Giving limited to the Astoria, OR, area.
Application information: Application form required.
Trustee: Wells Fargo Bank Northwest, N.A.
EIN: 936017659
Codes: GTI

45871
The Edna English Charitable Foundation
2323 Fairmont Blvd.
Eugene, OR 97403-1784

Financial data (yr. ended 12/31/01): Grants paid, $3,000; assets, $3,170 (M); gifts received, $3,000; expenditures, $3,000; qualifying distributions, $3,000.
Trustees: Melvin C. Aikens, George F. Wingard.
EIN: 930864462

45872
Envirosafe Services of Idaho, Inc. Charitable Trust
(also known as Envirosafe Charitable Trust)
c/o U.S. Bank
P.O. Box 3168
Portland, OR 97208
Application address: P.O. Box 7928, Boise, ID 83707, tel.: (208) 383-7200
Contact: Terry Teglia, Trust Off., U.S. Bank

Established in 1988 in ID.
Donor(s): Envirosafe Services of Idaho, Inc.
Financial data (yr. ended 02/28/02): Grants paid, $3,000; assets, $55,120 (M); expenditures, $8,208; qualifying distributions, $4,031.
Limitations: Giving limited to Owyhee County, ID.
Publications: Occasional report, application guidelines.
Application information: Application form required.
Trustee: U.S. Bank.
EIN: 826067761
Codes: CS, CD, GTI

45873
Clara Hanley Scholarship Fund
c/o U.S. Bank
P.O. Box 3168
Portland, OR 97208-3168
Application address: c/o Burns High School, 1100 Oregon Ave., Burns, OR 97720
Contact: Charles Vawter, Superintendent

Financial data (yr. ended 06/30/99): Grants paid, $3,000; assets, $90,314 (M); expenditures, $8,274; qualifying distributions, $3,687.
Limitations: Giving limited to OR.
Application information: Application form not required.
Trustee: U.S. Bank.
EIN: 936020151

45874
James E. Itel Educational Trust
c/o Gene C. Jerome
22499 S.W. Munger Ln.
Sherwood, OR 97140-8700 (503) 628-1331
Contact: Edna Itel

Financial data (yr. ended 06/30/00): Grants paid, $3,000; assets, $47,484 (M); expenditures, $3,989; qualifying distributions, $3,680.
Limitations: Giving limited to Sherwood, OR.
Application information: Application form required.
Trustees: Dorothy Adelman, Don Itel, Thomas McCarthy.
EIN: 930728419

45875
Kingzett Family Foundation
1225 Pacific Terr.
Klamath Falls, OR 97601

Established in 1997 in OR.
Donor(s): O.E. Kingzett.
Financial data (yr. ended 12/31/00): Grants paid, $3,000; assets, $6,009 (M); gifts received, $945; expenditures, $3,029; qualifying distributions, $3,000.
Limitations: Applications not accepted. Giving primarily in Eugene, OR.
Application information: Contributes only to pre-selected organizations.
Officers: O.E. Kingzett, Pres.; Edward Kingzett, V.P.; Robert Kingzett, Secy.-Treas.
EIN: 911800131

45876
The Horstkotte Family Charitable Foundation
0333 S.W. Flower St.
Portland, OR 97201 (503) 244-1333
Contact: John Horstkotte, Tr.

Established in 1999 in OR.
Donor(s): Fred Horstkotte, Joan Horstkotte.
Financial data (yr. ended 12/31/01): Grants paid, $2,890; assets, $52,320 (M); expenditures, $2,973; qualifying distributions, $2,871.
Trustees: David Horstkotte, Fred Horstkotte, Joan Horstkotte, Joyce Horstkotte.
EIN: 931279875

45877
John Papazian Education Trust
(Formerly John Papazian Educational Assistance Trust Fund)
c/o U.S. Bank
P.O. Box 3168
Portland, OR 97208-3168

Financial data (yr. ended 09/30/01): Grants paid, $2,868; assets, $40,214 (M); expenditures, $4,182; qualifying distributions, $2,868.
Limitations: Giving limited to Glasgow, MT.
Application information: Contact counselors at Valley County High School for application information.
Trustee: U.S. Bank.
EIN: 810289626

45878
Elizabeth & Bernie Baer Educational Fund
c/o U.S. Bank
P.O. Box 3168
Portland, OR 97208-3168
Contact: Marilyn Nordquist

Established in 1985 in OR.
Financial data (yr. ended 06/30/99): Grants paid, $2,580; assets, $94,247 (M); expenditures, $4,253; qualifying distributions, $3,088.
Limitations: Giving limited to Baker County, OR.
Application information: Application form required.
Trustee: U.S. Bank.
EIN: 936162145

45879
Dorothy Schupp Scholarship Trust
2949 Onyx St.
Klamath Falls, OR 97603-7262
(541) 884-5554
Contact: Kenneth H. Landrum, Chair.

Established in 1995.
Financial data (yr. ended 12/31/99): Grants paid, $2,542; assets, $23,947 (M); expenditures, $2,826; qualifying distributions, $4,535.

Application information: Application form not required.
Officers: Kenneth H. Landrum, Chair.; Paul E. Landrum, Vice-Chair.
EIN: 931178922

45880
Public Health Microbiology Charitable Trust
1863 N.W. Lester Ave.
Corvallis, OR 97330-9133 (541) 737-0123
Contact: Thaddeus Midura, Chief, Dept of Microbiolgy

Established in 1995 in CA and OR.
Donor(s): Eleanor Gay Ford.‡
Financial data (yr. ended 12/31/99): Grants paid, $2,504; assets, $73,829 (M); gifts received, $1,600; expenditures, $4,076; qualifying distributions, $2,504.
Limitations: Giving limited to residents of CA.
Application information: Application form required.
Trustee: William R. Ford.
EIN: 943216399

45881
Eugene/Springfield/Bethel Education Association
450 Country Club Rd., Ste. 170
Eugene, OR 97401 (541) 687-9165
Contact: Janice Eberly, Pres.

Financial data (yr. ended 10/31/01): Grants paid, $2,500; assets, $11,058 (M); gifts received, $3,334; expenditures, $2,578; qualifying distributions, $2,578.
Limitations: Giving primarily in OR.
Application information: Application form not required.
Officers: Janice Eberly, Pres.; Micki Waters, Treas.
Board Member: Jeannine Mainville.
EIN: 930873078

45882
Wayne Rinne Memorial Trust
P.O. Box 1030
Astoria, OR 97103
Application address: 1801 S. Franklin St., Seaside, OR 97138
Contact: Ed Rippett

Financial data (yr. ended 12/31/99): Grants paid, $2,500; assets, $102,139 (M); expenditures, $2,564; qualifying distributions, $5,064.
Application information: Application form required.
Trustee: Blair J. Henningsgaard.
EIN: 936267824

45883
Walker L. Bean Foundation
1211 S.W. 5th Ave., Ste. 2130
Portland, OR 97204-3721

Established in 1997 in OR.
Financial data (yr. ended 12/31/01): Grants paid, $2,437; assets, $274,814 (M); gifts received, $14,095; expenditures, $13,936; qualifying distributions, $2,437.
Limitations: Applications not accepted.
Application information: Contributes only to pre-selected organizations.
Officers: Warren H. Bean, Pres.; Bernice Bean, Secy.; Robert Zagunis, Treas.
EIN: 931233641

45884
Sidney and Alyne Schlesinger Charitable Foundation
P.O. Box 231269
Tigard, OR 97281-1269 (503) 968-6500
Contact: S. Miles Schlesinger, Secy.-Treas.

Established in 1986 in OR.
Financial data (yr. ended 09/30/01): Grants paid, $2,425; assets, $31,370 (M); gifts received, $1,680; expenditures, $2,486; qualifying distributions, $2,425.
Application information: Application form not required.
Officers and Directors:* Alyne Schlesinger,* Pres.; Lynne S. Blank,* V.P.; S. Miles Schlesinger,* Secy.-Treas.
EIN: 930902987

45885
Robert & Jane Caufield Fund
215 Bellevue
Oregon City, OR 97045-3064

Financial data (yr. ended 12/31/99): Grants paid, $2,400; assets, $30,522 (M); gifts received, $134; expenditures, $2,570; qualifying distributions, $2,504.
Limitations: Applications not accepted. Giving limited to Clackamas County, OR.
Officers: J. Thomas Staab, Pres.; Greg Frazier, Secy.; Vernon G. Delap, Treas.
EIN: 936017105

45886
W. L. Shattuck Foundation
c/o U.S. Bank
P.O. Box 3168
Portland, OR 97208
Application address: P.O. Box 51448, Idaho Falls, ID 83405
Contact: Mary Lynn, Boardman

Financial data (yr. ended 12/31/00): Grants paid, $2,329; assets, $93,445 (M); expenditures, $4,900; qualifying distributions, $2,938; giving activities include $2,329 for loans to individuals.
Limitations: Giving limited to residents of School Districts 91 and 93 in ID.
Trustee: U.S. Bank.
EIN: 237124383
Codes: GTI

45887
The Faith and Works Foundation
c/o Debra Moore Kummer
33848 Berg Rd.
Warren, OR 97053-9644

Established in 1999 in OR.
Financial data (yr. ended 12/31/01): Grants paid, $2,010; assets, $44,138 (M); expenditures, $2,041; qualifying distributions, $2,009.
Application information: Application form not required.
Directors: Debra Moore Kummer, Emma J. Kummer, Kathryn Parvin.
EIN: 931282627

45888
Baron Foundation
805 S.W. Broadway, Ste. 1900
Portland, OR 97205-3359 (503) 417-2141
Contact: Dave Roy

Established in 1999 in OR.
Donor(s): Charles Burgess.
Financial data (yr. ended 11/30/01): Grants paid, $2,000; assets, $63,397 (M); gifts received, $10,375; expenditures, $6,025; qualifying distributions, $6,025.

Directors: Bernice Burgess, Dick Burgess, Sandy Burgess.
EIN: 931286906

45889
W. C. & Pearl Campbell Scholarship Fund for Other Than Linfield College
c/o U.S. Bank
P.O. Box 3168
Portland, OR 97208-3168

Financial data (yr. ended 06/30/01): Grants paid, $2,000; assets, $87,365 (M); expenditures, $4,180; qualifying distributions, $2,000.
Limitations: Giving limited to OR.
Application information: Application form required.
Trustee: U.S. Bank.
EIN: 936021037

45890
Cascade Heritage Foundation
P.O. Box 1030
Bend, OR 97709

Donor(s): Allan Bruckner.
Financial data (yr. ended 12/31/01): Grants paid, $2,000; assets, $29,463 (M); expenditures, $2,020; qualifying distributions, $2,000.
Officers: Allan D. Bruckner, Pres.; Kit Carmiencke, V.P.; Mark Stanard, Secy.-Treas.
EIN: 911803767

45891
Neal Family Charitable Trust
7035 S.W. Palmer Way
Beaverton, OR 97007

Established in 1997 in OR.
Donor(s): Carolyn M. Neal, John C. Neal.
Financial data (yr. ended 12/31/01): Grants paid, $2,000; assets, $5,059 (M); expenditures, $2,000; qualifying distributions, $2,000.
Limitations: Applications not accepted.
Application information: Contributes only to pre-selected organizations.
Trustees: Carolyn M. Neal, John M. Neal.
EIN: 931238168

45892
Ponderosa Foundation
P.O. Box 1247
Redmond, OR 97756-0109

Financial data (yr. ended 01/31/01): Grants paid, $2,000; assets, $41,196 (M); expenditures, $2,000; qualifying distributions, $2,000.
Limitations: Giving primarily in OR.
Officers: Kieran P. Madden, Pres.; Marvin E. Horn, V.P.; Ed A. Sturza, Secy.-Treas.
Director: James H. Elliott.
EIN: 930724109

45893
Franklin Conklin Foundation
6015 N.W. Rosewood Dr.
Corvallis, OR 97330

Established in 1997 in OR.
Financial data (yr. ended 12/31/01): Grants paid, $1,978; assets, $24,239 (M); gifts received, $33; expenditures, $3,672; qualifying distributions, $1,978.
Limitations: Applications not accepted. Giving primarily in CA, OR and WY.
Application information: Contributes only to pre-selected organizations.
Officers: Harold H. Demarest, Jr., Pres. and Secy.; Franklin Conklin Demarest, V.P.; Anne Demarest Taft, Treas.
EIN: 911844877

45894
Norem-Sorensen Charitable Trust
90 Cedar St.
La Grande, OR 97850

Established in 1990 in OR.
Donor(s): Jon Norem, Kim Sorenson.
Financial data (yr. ended 12/31/01): Grants paid, $1,945; assets, $27,934 (M); gifts received, $6,012; expenditures, $1,952; qualifying distributions, $1,945.
Limitations: Applications not accepted.
Application information: Contributes only to pre-selected organizations.
Trustees: Jon Norem, Kim Sorensen.
EIN: 936239565

45895
Orgone Biophysical Research Laboratory, Inc.
c/o James Demeo, Jr.
P.O. Box 1148
Ashland, OR 97520

Financial data (yr. ended 12/31/99): Grants paid, $1,880; assets, $276,753 (M); gifts received, $124,243; expenditures, $45,229; qualifying distributions, $45,229; giving activities include $45,229 for programs.
Limitations: Applications not accepted.
Application information: Contributes only to pre-selected organizations.
Officer and Directors:* James Demeo, Jr.,* Pres.; Terry Cimino-Demeo, Theirie Cook, Robert Nunley.
EIN: 480867570

45896
William Annen Family Foundation
P.O. Box 437
Mount Angel, OR 97362-0437
(503) 845-6882
Contact: Gerald Lauzon, Dir.

Established in 1999 in OR.
Donor(s): Elaine Annen.
Financial data (yr. ended 07/31/01): Grants paid, $1,750; assets, $65,601 (M); gifts received, $23,729; expenditures, $1,798; qualifying distributions, $1,750.
Directors: James Hall, Gerald Lauzon, Dean Westbrook.
EIN: 931281073

45897
Jack Holt Family Foundation
c/o Heidi U. Holt
21440 Morrill Rd.
Bend, OR 97701

Established in 1998.
Financial data (yr. ended 12/31/01): Grants paid, $1,750; assets, $926 (M); gifts received, $2,000; expenditures, $1,951; qualifying distributions, $1,750.
Limitations: Giving primarily in OR.
Trustees: Jack N. Holt, Heidi U. Holt, Oliver N. Holt, Timothy H. Holt.
EIN: 931191742

45898
Willamette Trust
c/o Pioneer Trust Bank, N.A.
P.O. Box 2305
Salem, OR 97308

Financial data (yr. ended 12/31/01): Grants paid, $1,686; assets, $20,271 (M); expenditures, $2,443; qualifying distributions, $1,686.
Limitations: Applications not accepted. Giving limited to OR.
Application information: Contributes only to pre-selected organizations.
Trustee: Pioneer Trust Bank, N.A.
EIN: 936018564

45899
Boyer Foundation
17575 Jordan Rd.
Sisters, OR 97759

Established in 1998 in OR.
Donor(s): William H. Boyer.
Financial data (yr. ended 12/31/01): Grants paid, $1,630; assets, $408,240 (M); gifts received, $118,893; expenditures, $9,842; qualifying distributions, $1,630.
Limitations: Applications not accepted. Giving primarily in OR.
Application information: Contributes only to pre-selected organizations.
Directors: David Boyer, Jeffrey Boyer, William H. Boyer.
EIN: 931253884

45900
Anderson Family Foundation
14657 S.W. Teal Blvd., PMB No.336
Beaverton, OR 97007-8499

Established in 2000 in OR.
Financial data (yr. ended 12/31/00): Grants paid, $1,500; assets, $77 (M); gifts received, $5,310; expenditures, $5,233; qualifying distributions, $5,233.
Trustees: Gordon Bruce Anderson, John Dexter Anderson, Peter Alfred Anderson, Judith Anderson Murphy, Cameron Anderson Petering.
EIN: 931275399

45901
Bankoff/Blanchet Family Foundation
28465 Sutherlin Ln.
Eugene, OR 97405

Established in 1997 in OR.
Donor(s): Mel Bankoff, Martha Blanchet.
Financial data (yr. ended 12/31/01): Grants paid, $1,500; assets, $98,879 (M); expenditures, $2,497; qualifying distributions, $1,500.
Limitations: Applications not accepted.
Application information: Contributes only to pre-selected organizations.
Officers: Mel C. Bankoff, Pres.; Martha E. Blanchet, Secy.-Treas.
Directors: Patrick Fagan, Joan Saires, Sarah Westervelt.
EIN: 911788238

45902
Adam A. Clark Family Memorial Fund
P.O. Box 1527
Redmond, OR 97756-0501 (541) 923-3940
Additional application addresses: c/o West Linn High School, P.O. Box 92, West Linn, OR 97068, or c/o Wilsonville High School, Wilsonville, OR 97670
Contact: Larry L. Clark, Pres.

Established in 1994.
Donor(s): Larry L. Clark, Karen R. Clark.
Financial data (yr. ended 06/30/00): Grants paid, $1,500; assets, $35,115 (M); expenditures, $1,500; qualifying distributions, $1,500.
Limitations: Giving limited to residents of West Linn and Wilsonville, OR.
Application information: Application form required.
Officers: Larry L. Clark, Pres.; Karen R. Clark, V.P.
Director: Derrick D. Clark.
EIN: 931164769

45903
The Omega Trust
424 Logan Cut Dr.
Cave Junction, OR 97523

Established in 2001.
Financial data (yr. ended 12/31/01): Grants paid, $1,403; assets, $251 (M); gifts received, $14,310; expenditures, $12,684; qualifying distributions, $1,403.
Limitations: Applications not accepted.
Application information: Contributes only to pre-selected organizations.
Trustees: Kandace A. McClure, Roan A. McClure.
EIN: 936321816

45904
Kerry Foundation
c/o John G. Robatcek
445 Sunset Beach Rd.
Klamath Falls, OR 97601

Financial data (yr. ended 12/31/01): Grants paid, $1,250; assets, $18,652 (M); gifts received, $2,095; expenditures, $1,280; qualifying distributions, $1,250.
Limitations: Applications not accepted. Giving limited to Klamath Falls, OR.
Application information: Contributes only to pre-selected organizations.
Directors: John G. Robatcek, Chair.; Delores I. Gilcrist, Jacqueline J. Metler.
EIN: 942722106

45905
Public Trust Foundation
1045 Brockwood Ave.
McMinnville, OR 97128-6905

Donor(s): Richard F. McGinty, Kathy Belcher.
Financial data (yr. ended 12/31/01): Grants paid, $1,249; assets, $8,816 (M); expenditures, $1,394; qualifying distributions, $1,249.
Officers and Directors:* Richard F. McGinty,* Pres.; Kathy Belcher,* Secy.; Patrick W. McGinty, Treas.
EIN: 931102178

45906
Edwin C. Goodenough Scholarship Trust
(Formerly Edwin C. Goodenough Scholarship Fund)
c/o Pioneer Trust Bank, N.A.
P.O. Box 2305
Salem, OR 97308-2305
Application address: c/o Scholarship Comm., 109 Commercial St. N.E., Salem, OR 97308, tel.: (503) 363-3136

Financial data (yr. ended 06/30/01): Grants paid, $1,189; assets, $161,546 (M); expenditures, $18,272; qualifying distributions, $15,813.
Limitations: Giving limited to Salem, OR.
Trustee: Pioneer Trust Bank, N.A.
EIN: 936119287
Codes: GTI

45907
Republic Fidelity Foundation
14 Icarus Loop
Lake Oswego, OR 97035

Established in 1998 in OR.
Donor(s): Norman Butcher, Beverly Butcher.
Financial data (yr. ended 12/31/01): Grants paid, $1,150; assets, $8,363 (M); gifts received, $1,430; expenditures, $1,168; qualifying distributions, $1,150.
Limitations: Applications not accepted.
Application information: Contributes only to pre-selected organizations.

Trustees: Beverly Butcher, Norman W. Butcher, Sharon Dunn.
EIN: 911796142

45908
Langell Valley Conservation Grant Fund, Inc.
c/o Bonanza High School
P.O. Box 128
Bonanza, OR 97623 (541) 545-6581
Contact: Carolyn Clarke, Dir.

Financial data (yr. ended 12/31/00): Grants paid, $1,000; assets, $14,486 (M); expenditures, $1,673; qualifying distributions, $1,000.
Limitations: Giving limited to the Bonanza, OR, area.
Application information: Applications available at Bonanza High School. Application form required.
Officer and Directors:* Louis Randall,* Pres.; Mel Brooks, Carolyn Clarke, Sandra Peat, Walt Smith, Gary Williams.
EIN: 237424709

45909
Jerry Lillie Scholarship Fund
c/o Elizabeth Lillie
17055 S.E. Oatfield Rd.
Milwaukie, OR 97267-6302
Application address: c/o Sue Johnson, Milwaukie High School, 11300 S.E. 23rd Ave., Milwaukie, OR 97222, tel.: (503) 653-3754

Donor(s): Jay C. Lillie, Ida Mae Lillie.
Financial data (yr. ended 12/31/99): Grants paid, $1,000; assets, $14,862 (L); gifts received, $57; expenditures, $1,068; qualifying distributions, $1,005.
Limitations: Giving limited to residents of Milwaukie, OR.
Application information: Application form required.
Officers: Bernice M. Evans, Admin.; Geraldine Hoyt, Admin.; Elizabeth R. Lillie, Admin.; Ida Mae Lillie, Admin.; Jay C. Lillie, Admin.; Frances A. Whitehill, Admin.
EIN: 931080807

45910
Assessment Training Institute Foundation, Inc.
c/o Richard Stiggins, President
50 SW Second Ave., Ste. No. 300
Portland, OR 97204

Established in 1996 in OR.
Donor(s): Nancy Bridgeford, Richard Stiggins.
Financial data (yr. ended 09/30/01): Grants paid, $874; assets, $26,579 (M); gifts received, $15,000; expenditures, $31,356; qualifying distributions, $874.
Limitations: Giving primarily in OR.
Application information: Application form required.
Officers: Richard Stiggins, Pres.; Nancy Bridgeford, V.P.
Board Members: Tanis Knight, Tim Welch.
EIN: 931228928

45911
End Time Fellowship, Inc.
1209 Valley View Rd.
Ashland, OR 97520

Financial data (yr. ended 12/31/01): Grants paid, $830; assets, $23,288 (M); expenditures, $1,894; qualifying distributions, $830.
Limitations: Applications not accepted.
Application information: Contributes only to pre-selected organizations.
Officer: Gloria Aker, Pres.
EIN: 930576772

45912
Lura Helen Olson Trust
c/o Wells Fargo Bank Northwest, N.A.
P.O. Box 2971
Portland, OR 97208-2971

Financial data (yr. ended 12/31/01): Grants paid, $800; assets, $42,983 (M); expenditures, $3,692; qualifying distributions, $2,505.
Limitations: Applications not accepted. Giving limited to McNary, OR.
Application information: Recipients chosen by Principal and Vice Principal of McCary High School.
Trustee: Wells Fargo Bank Northwest, N.A.
EIN: 936070503

45913
The Rainbow Foundation
P.O. Box 50207
Eugene, OR 97405

Established in 1999 in OR.
Donor(s): John Voorhees.
Financial data (yr. ended 12/31/01): Grants paid, $800; assets, $1 (M); gifts received, $5,000; expenditures, $1,170; qualifying distributions, $800.
Limitations: Applications not accepted.
Application information: Contributes only to pre-selected organizations.
Officers: John Voorhees, Pres.; Robert McLain, Secy.; Lee Davis, Treas.
EIN: 931253880

45914
The Walker Study Center, Inc.
P. O. Box 139
Shady Cove, OR 97539

Established in 1997 in OR.
Financial data (yr. ended 09/30/01): Grants paid, $600; assets, $1,057,012 (M); gifts received, $27,605; expenditures, $50,235; qualifying distributions, $600.
Officers: Ron Boehm, Pres.; Charlotte Boehm, V.P.; Molly Kerr, Secy.
EIN: 943141709

45915
People for People Foundation
11040 S.W. Barbur Blvd.
Portland, OR 97219

Established in 1997 in OR.
Financial data (yr. ended 07/31/01): Grants paid, $566; assets, $210 (M); gifts received, $625; expenditures, $2,352; qualifying distributions, $566.
Trustees: Kare Miller, Scott Miller.
EIN: 931229977

45916
Obie Family Foundation
1300 S.W. 6th Ave., Ste. 300
Portland, OR 97201

Established in 2000 in OR.
Donor(s): Brian B. Obie, Karen L. Obie.
Financial data (yr. ended 12/31/01): Grants paid, $519; assets, $276,459 (M); gifts received, $5,000; expenditures, $3,541; qualifying distributions, $519.
Limitations: Applications not accepted.
Application information: Contributes only to pre-selected organizations.
Officers: Brian B. Obie, Pres.; Karen L. Obie, Secy.
Directors: Brian P. Hagen, Joseph J. Hanna, Jr., Christine L. Obie, Douglas D. Obie.
EIN: 931308694

45917
The Hulbert Foundation
c/o Edwards & Meyers, LLP
5550 S.W. Macadam St., Ste. 310
Portland, OR 97201

Established in 1999 in OR.
Financial data (yr. ended 12/31/01): Grants paid, $500; assets, $8,139 (M); expenditures, $1,600; qualifying distributions, $500.
Limitations: Applications not accepted.
Application information: Contributes only to pre-selected organizations.
Directors: Katherine McDonald, Mary H. Naab, Elden Saathoff.
EIN: 931273032

45918
Chris Barnes Memorial Scholarship Fund
1948 Lindgren Ln.
North Bend, OR 97459-9232
Contact: Jackie L. Shaw, Tr.

Financial data (yr. ended 12/31/00): Grants paid, $100; assets, $10,935 (M); expenditures, $100; qualifying distributions, $0.
Limitations: Giving primarily in North Bend, OR.
Trustee: Jackie L. Shaw.
EIN: 931263327

45919
The Half Baked Trust
P.O. Box 910
Halfway, OR 97834-0910 (541) 742-4115
Contact: Anthony E. Sowers, Tr., or Patricia J. Sowers, Tr.

Financial data (yr. ended 04/30/02): Grants paid, $50; assets, $1 (M); expenditures, $50; qualifying distributions, $50.
Trustees: Anthony E. Sowers, Patricia J. Sowers.
EIN: 930862635

45920
Albany Public Library Foundation
c/o Gary Holliday, Fin. City of Albany
P.O. Box 490
Albany, OR 97321-0144

Donor(s): Doris Scharpf.
Financial data (yr. ended 06/30/01): Grants paid, $0; assets, $814,816 (M); gifts received, $132,319; expenditures, $11,843; qualifying distributions, $0.
Limitations: Applications not accepted.
Application information: Contributes only to pre-selected organizations.
Officers: Bob Reid, Pres.; Margaret Pestalozzi, V.P.; Jane Marshall, Secy.; Rodney Tripp, Treas.
EIN: 931085864

45921
American International Sonus Hearing Foundation
1300 S.W. 6th Ave., Ste. 300
Portland, OR 97201

Established in 1999 in OR.
Financial data (yr. ended 12/31/01): Grants paid, $0; assets, $9,561 (M); gifts received, $6,994; expenditures, $3,138; qualifying distributions, $0.
Limitations: Applications not accepted.
Application information: Contributes only to pre-selected organizations.
Officers and Directors:* Brandon Dawson,* Pres.; Brian Thompson, Secy.; Edwin Kawasaki, J.J. Hanna.
EIN: 931281742

45922
Anne Benson Scholarship Trust Fund
c/o U.S. Bank, Trust Tax
P.O. Box 3168
Portland, OR 97208

Established in 1999 in MT.
Financial data (yr. ended 04/30/00): Grants paid, $0; assets, $344,723 (M); gifts received, $335,878; expenditures, $10,900; qualifying distributions, $9,156.
Limitations: Giving primarily in OR.
Application information: Application form required.
Trustee: U.S. Bank.
EIN: 816087202

45923
The Boyd Family Foundation
P.O. Box 14947
Portland, OR 97293

Established in 2000 in OR.
Donor(s): Boyd Coffee Co.
Financial data (yr. ended 12/31/01): Grants paid, $0; assets, $190,354 (M); gifts received, $120,000; expenditures, $4,273; qualifying distributions, $22.
Limitations: Applications not accepted.
Application information: Contributes only to pre-selected organizations.
Officers: Chris Boyd, Pres.; Matthew Boyd, V.P.; Sean Kiffe, Secy.; Michael Boyd, Treas.
Directors: Brenda Boyd, David Boyd, Julia Boyd, Richard Boyd, Stephen Boyd, John Dutt, Katy Dutt, Mary Ellen Kiffe.
EIN: 931294466
Codes: CS, CD

45924
The Campbell Institute
44 N.E. Morris
Portland, OR 97212

Established in 1997 in OR.
Financial data (yr. ended 12/31/01): Grants paid, $0; assets, $282,609 (M); gifts received, $75,000; expenditures, $37,672; qualifying distributions, $22,359.
Limitations: Applications not accepted.
Application information: Contributes only to pre-selected organizations.
Officer: J. Duncan Campbell, Chair.
Directors: Cynthia Campbell, John S. Gilleland.
EIN: 931095351

45925
Saidie Orr Dunbar Nursing Education Fund
c/o American Lung Assn. of Oregon
7420 S.W. Bridgeport Rd., Ste. 200
Portland, OR 97224-7790 (800) 586-4872
Application address: c/o American Lung Assn. of Oregon, 9320 S.W. Barbur Blvd., Ste. 140, Portland, OR 97219, tel.: (503) 246-1997, ext. 20

Established in 1956 in OR.
Financial data (yr. ended 12/31/01): Grants paid, $0; assets, $74,130 (M); gifts received, $30; expenditures, $1,396; qualifying distributions, $1,396.
Limitations: Giving limited to OR.
Publications: Application guidelines.
Application information: Interviews required of finalists. Application form required.
Trustee: Elizabeth Henderson.
EIN: 936017534

45926
Hermoyn Eckroth Charitable Trust
P.O. Box 3168, Trust Tax Services
Portland, OR 97208
Application address: c/o U.S. Bank Trust, N.A., P.O. Box, Billings, MT 59115
Contact: Helen Hancock

Established in 2000 in MT.
Financial data (yr. ended 12/31/01): Grants paid, $0; assets, $615,452 (M); gifts received, $3,950; expenditures, $12,903; qualifying distributions, $0.
Limitations: Giving primarily in Yellowstone County, MT.
Trustee: U.S. Bank, N.A.
EIN: 810527650

45927
Paul Emerick Vocational Education Foundation
c/o AGC
9450 S.W. Commerce Cir., No. 200
Wilsonville, OR 97070-9626 (503) 682-3363
Contact: James McKune, Pres.

Established in 1996 in OR.
Financial data (yr. ended 12/31/01): Grants paid, $0; assets, $17,890 (M); expenditures, $587; qualifying distributions, $0.
Officer: James McKune, Pres.
EIN: 931109781

45928
Matthew S. Essieh and Family Foundation
13564 S.W. Brim Pl.
Tigard, OR 97223

Established in 2000 in OR.
Donor(s): Matthew S. Essieh.
Financial data (yr. ended 12/31/00): Grants paid, $0; assets, $6,891 (M); gifts received, $10,000; expenditures, $0; qualifying distributions, $0.
Officer: Matthew S. Essieh, Exec. Dir.
EIN: 931282998

45929
Forest Research Trust
1300 N.E. 16th St., Ste. 1202
Portland, OR 97232

Established in 1999 in OR.
Donor(s): Clarence W. Richen.
Financial data (yr. ended 12/31/99): Grants paid, $0; assets, $15,000 (M); gifts received, $19,761; expenditures, $3,305; qualifying distributions, $2,805.
Trustee: Clarence W. Richen.
EIN: 931279112

45930
Fournier Family Foundation
104 Garibaldi St.
Lake Oswego, OR 97035

Established in 2000 in OR.
Donor(s): Bruce R. Fournier.
Financial data (yr. ended 06/30/01): Grants paid, $0; assets, $739,431 (M); gifts received, $712,626; expenditures, $4,104; qualifying distributions, $0.
Officers: Bruce R. Fournier, Pres.; Joanne E. Fournier, V.P.
Director: Viola R. Fournier.
EIN: 931307301

IN THIS SECTION, WITHIN EACH STATE, FOUNDATIONS ARE LISTED IN DESCENDING ORDER BY TOTAL GRANTS PAID

45931
Frisbie Scholarship Trust
c/o US Bank, N.A.
P.O. Box 3168
Portland, OR 97208-3168 (503) 275-5929
Contact: Marlyn Norquist, Tr. Off.

Established in 2000 in OR.
Donor(s): Alvina D. Frisbie.‡
Financial data (yr. ended 06/30/01): Grants paid, $0; assets, $556,150 (M); gifts received, $564,835; expenditures, $3,228; qualifying distributions, $707.
Limitations: Giving limited to WA.
Application information: Application form required.
Trustee: US Bank, N.A.
EIN: 936341760

45932
Gallagher Western Montanan Charitable Foundation
c/o U.S. Bank
P.O. Box 3168
Portland, OR 97208
Application address: c/o U.S. Bank, 209 E. Spruce St., Missoula, MT 59802-4501
Contact: Rosemary Gallagher

Established in 2001 in MT.
Donor(s): W.J. & Rosemary Gallagher Foundation.
Financial data (yr. ended 12/31/01): Grants paid, $0; assets, $3,225,031 (M); gifts received, $2,996,125; expenditures, $3,972; qualifying distributions, $337.
Application information: Application form required.
Trustee: U.S. Bank.
EIN: 912138399

45933
Hayes Family Foundation
P.O. Box 399
Newberg, OR 97132

Established in 2001 in OR.
Donor(s): Delbert J. Hayes, Sandra L. Hayes.
Financial data (yr. ended 12/31/01): Grants paid, $0; assets, $574,194 (M); gifts received, $583,650; expenditures, $0; qualifying distributions, $0.
Limitations: Applications not accepted.
Application information: Contributes only to pre-selected organizations.
Trustees: Delbert J. Hayes, Sandra L. Hayes, Nancy J. Henderson.
EIN: 931330414

45934
Inspiration Incorporated
10172 S.E. 99th Dr.
Portland, OR 97266-7227

Donor(s): Herbert E. Richards.
Financial data (yr. ended 04/30/01): Grants paid, $0; assets, $11,688 (M); expenditures, $3,113; qualifying distributions, $2,792; giving activities include $1,407 for programs.
Limitations: Applications not accepted.
Application information: Contributes only to pre-selected organizations.
Officers: Herbert E. Richards, Pres.; Lois M. Richards, V.P.
EIN: 820251753

45935
Philip D. Jackson Foundation
c/o Ted Jackson
14215 N.W. Melody Ln.
Portland, OR 97229

Established in 2001.
Financial data (yr. ended 12/31/01): Grants paid, $0; assets, $100 (M); gifts received, $100; expenditures, $0; qualifying distributions, $0.
Directors: Jimmie Jackson, Philip Jackson, Ted Jackson.
EIN: 911279688

45936
The Jarvey-McCord Foundation
7212 S. Seven Oaks Ln.
Canby, OR 97013

Established in 1998 in OR.
Financial data (yr. ended 12/31/01): Grants paid, $0; assets, $106,032 (M); expenditures, $2,956; qualifying distributions, $0.
Limitations: Applications not accepted. Giving on a national basis, with emphasis on OR.
Application information: Contributes only to pre-selected organizations.
Officer: Shawn Jarvey, Mgr.
EIN: 931234370

45937
Jubitz Family Foundation
4380 S.W. Macadam Ave., Ste. 210
Portland, OR 97201 (503) 274-6255

Established in 2001 in OR.
Donor(s): Jubitz Corporation, Jubitz Investments, LP, Saybrook, LP.
Financial data (yr. ended 12/31/01): Grants paid, $0; assets, $7,271,122 (M); gifts received, $7,250,000; expenditures, $10,405; qualifying distributions, $9,409.
Limitations: Giving limited to OR.
Officers: M. Albin Jubitz, Jr., Pres.; Elizabeth Jubitz Sayler, V.P.; Katherine H. Jubitz, Secy.; Sarah C. Jubitz, Treas.
EIN: 931324016
Codes: CS

45938
The Frederick D. & Gail Y. Jubitz Foundation
33 N.E. Middlefield Rd.
Portland, OR 97211
Application address: c/o BKR Fordham Goodfellow, LLP, 233 S.E. 2nd Ave., Hillsboro, OR 97123, tel.: (503) 648-6651

Established in 2001 in OR.
Donor(s): Fred Jubitz, Gail Jubitz.
Financial data (yr. ended 12/31/01): Grants paid, $0; assets, $2,018,368 (M); gifts received, $2,000,000; expenditures, $5,621; qualifying distributions, $0.
Officers: Fred Jubitz, Gail Jubitz.
EIN: 931326797

45939
London Floyd Family Foundation
P.O. Box 3339
Sunriver, OR 97707 (541) 593-3199
Contact: Barry J. London, Pres.

Established in 2000 in OR.
Donor(s): Barry J. London, Nancy C. Floyd.
Financial data (yr. ended 12/31/00): Grants paid, $0; assets, $156,110 (M); gifts received, $217,500; expenditures, $6,285; qualifying distributions, $0.
Officers and Directors:* Barry J. London,* Pres.; Mary Martin,* Secy.; Nancy C. Floyd,* Treas.
EIN: 931300797

45940
Arnold Marks Family Charitable Trust
1211 S.W. 5th Ave, Ste. 1800
Portland, OR 97204-3713

Established in 1999 in OR.
Donor(s): Arnold Marks.‡
Financial data (yr. ended 12/31/01): Grants paid, $0; assets, $504,345 (M); expenditures, $36,462; qualifying distributions, $0.
Limitations: Applications not accepted.
Application information: Contributes only to pre-selected organizations.
Trustee: James A. Larpenteur.
EIN: 931272247

45941
Wanda McGuire Trust for Charitable Purposes
P.O. Box 1608
Roseburg, OR 97470

Established in 1998 in OR.
Donor(s): A.B. Mcguire,‡ Wanda Mcguire.‡
Financial data (yr. ended 02/28/99): Grants paid, $0; assets, $1,455,944 (M); gifts received, $1,251,139; expenditures, $2,000; qualifying distributions, $0.
Trustee: George Luoma.
EIN: 931235521

45942
The Morgan Family Foundation
121 S.W. Salmon St.
Portland, OR 97204
Contact: Ellison C. Morgan, Tr.

Established in 1993 in OR.
Donor(s): Ellison C. Morgan.
Financial data (yr. ended 06/30/01): Grants paid, $0; assets, $3,928 (M); expenditures, $812; qualifying distributions, $0.
Limitations: Giving primarily in OR.
Trustees: Ellison C. Morgan, Ellison Christopher Morgan, Erin Lee Morgan.
EIN: 936271849

45943
Norpac Foundation
333 S.W. Taylor St.
Portland, OR 97204-2496
Application address: P.O. Box 458, Stayton, OR 97383, tel.: (503) 769-2101
Contact: Ron Fritz

Established in 1998 in OR.
Financial data (yr. ended 12/31/01): Grants paid, $0; assets, $2,562 (M); expenditures, $0; qualifying distributions, $0.
Officers and Directors:* Mark Dickman,* Pres.; Jack Sebastian, Secy.; Jerry Ditchen, Robert Fessler, Mary Pearmine.
EIN: 931243657

45944
Portland Crime Stoppers
1111 S.W. 2nd Ave.
Portland, OR 97204 (503) 796-3400
Contact: Henry Groepper, Dir.

Established in 1985 in OR.
Financial data (yr. ended 12/31/00): Grants paid, $0; assets, $72,273 (M); gifts received, $80,763; expenditures, $67,220; qualifying distributions, $0.
Limitations: Giving limited to Portland, OR.
Directors: Leif Anderson, Harry Braunstein, Harry Christensen, Karen B. Dunn, Ron Dyches, Sr., Henry Groepper, Charles C. Hindman, Leland "Bud" S. Lewis, Leonard Rotolo, Jim Street, Roger Williams, and 10 additional directors.
EIN: 930816587

Codes: TN

45945
Quantum Charitable Trust
11040 S.W. Barbur Blvd.
Portland, OR 97219-8610

Established in 1994 in OR.
Donor(s): Bruce Williams, Joan Williams.
Financial data (yr. ended 08/31/01): Grants paid, $0; assets, $60,662 (M); expenditures, $1,511; qualifying distributions, $0.
Limitations: Applications not accepted. Giving primarily in OR.
Application information: Contributes only to pre-selected organizations.
Trustees: Bruce Williams, Joan Williams.
EIN: 936289245

45946
The Quest Community Foundation
One S.W. Columbia
Portland, OR 97258-2017

Established in 1997 in OR.
Financial data (yr. ended 12/31/01): Grants paid, $0; assets, $7,425 (M); expenditures, $128; qualifying distributions, $0.
Officers: Monte L. Johnson, Pres.; Cameron M. Johnson, V.P.; Kevin M. Johnson, Secy.
EIN: 911762149

45947
The Rhines Foundation
01605 S.W. Comus St.
Portland, OR 97219

Established in 2001.
Donor(s): Walden C. Rhines.
Financial data (yr. ended 12/31/01): Grants paid, $0; assets, $502,125 (M); gifts received, $502,125; expenditures, $0; qualifying distributions, $0.
Trustee: Walden C. Rhines.
EIN: 931331653

45948
Roots for Success Charitable Foundation
P.O. Box 1928
Bend, OR 97707

Established in 2000 in CA.
Financial data (yr. ended 06/30/01): Grants paid, $0; assets, $473,928 (M); gifts received, $509,785; expenditures, $11,641; qualifying distributions, $11,641.
Officers: Kathy H. Shaker, Pres.; Christopher J. Shaker, Secy.
EIN: 770553725

45949
Rowlett Family Foundation
16799 Hwy. 66
Ashland, OR 97520

Established in 2000 in OR.
Financial data (yr. ended 12/31/00): Grants paid, $0; assets, $0 (M); gifts received, $1,122; expenditures, $1,122; qualifying distributions, $1,122.
Officers and Directors:* Donald E. Rowlett,* Pres.; Jean Rowlett,* V.P.; Jeanne Randall.
EIN: 931255443

45950
RSVP Foundation of Douglas County
P.O. Box 102
Roseburg, OR 97470-0016

Established in 1997 in OR.
Financial data (yr. ended 12/31/99): Grants paid, $0; assets, $11,800 (M); gifts received, $2,500; expenditures, $5,923; qualifying distributions, $5,828; giving activities include $5,577 for programs.
Officers: Ray Lampson, Pres.; David Cloud, V.P.; Buddy E. Smith, Secy.-Treas.
EIN: 943119916

45951
Skaggs Charitable Mission
c/o F. Gilbert Fritzler
1727 N.E. 13th Ave., Ste. 201
Portland, OR 97212

Established in 1991 in OR.
Financial data (yr. ended 09/30/01): Grants paid, $0; assets, $25,864 (M); expenditures, $101,218; qualifying distributions, $0.
Limitations: Applications not accepted.
Application information: Contributes only to pre-selected organizations.
Officers: Wilbur B. Skaggs, Pres.; Sharon Skaggs, V.P.; Evelyn Skaggs, Secy.; F. Gilbert Fritzler, Treas.
EIN: 931067006

45952
James H. Stanard Foundation Trust
c/o U.S. Bank N.A.
P.O. Box 3168
Portland, OR 97208-3168
Application Address: 9354 N.W. Westside Rd., McMinnville, OR 97218
Contact: Rowena M. Steward

Established in 1998 in OR.
Donor(s): Rowena M. Stanard.
Financial data (yr. ended 12/31/01): Grants paid, $0; assets, $743,175 (M); expenditures, $7,293; qualifying distributions, $0.
Limitations: Giving primarily in OH.
Trustee: U.S. Bank, N.A.
EIN: 931248405

45953
Joseph B. Vandervelden Foundation
5100 S.W. Macadam, Ste. 400
Portland, OR 97201

Donor(s): Joy Vandervelden.
Financial data (yr. ended 06/30/01): Grants paid, $0; assets, $312,862 (M); gifts received, $51,450; expenditures, $6,852; qualifying distributions, $0.
Limitations: Applications not accepted.
Application information: Contributes only to pre-selected organizations.
Officers: Earl Vandehey, Chair.; Florence Sheelar, Vice-Chair.; John Larson, Secy.; Joy Vandervelden, Treas.
EIN: 931180188

45954
Robet R. Vickers Charitable Trust
c/o Donald E. Tykeson
P.O. Box 70006
Eugene, OR 97401-0101

Established in 1997 in OR.
Financial data (yr. ended 12/31/01): Grants paid, $0; assets, $447,969 (M); expenditures, $1,513; qualifying distributions, $0.
Limitations: Applications not accepted. Giving primarily in Eugene, OR.
Application information: Contributes only to pre-selected organizations.
Officer: Thomas H. Palmer, Treas.
Trustee: Donald E. Tykeson.
EIN: 931232478

45955
The Wilshire-Essex Foundation
245 S.W. Lincoln St., No. 2212
Portland, OR 97201
Contact: Robert S. Sznewajs

Established in 1997 in OR.
Donor(s): Robert D. Sznewajs.
Financial data (yr. ended 12/31/01): Grants paid, $0; assets, $201,959 (M); gifts received, $1,300; expenditures, $1,385; qualifying distributions, $0.
Officer: Robert D. Sznewajs, Mgr.
Director: Franciene R. Sznewajs.
EIN: 911810973

PENNSYLVANIA

45956
The Annenberg Foundation
St. Davids Ctr.
150 Radnor-Chester Rd., Ste. A-200
St. Davids, PA 19087 (610) 341-9066
E-mail: info@whannenberg.org; URL: http://www.whannenberg.org
Contact: Dr. Gail C. Levin, Exec. Dir.

Established in 1989 in PA.
Donor(s): Hon. Walter H. Annenberg.‡
Financial data (yr. ended 06/30/02): Grants paid, $355,021,336; assets, $2,354,837,085 (M); expenditures, $343,203,846; qualifying distributions, $357,921,582.
Publications: Application guidelines.
Application information: Contact foundation for deadlines and board meetings. Application form not required.
Officers and Trustees:* Leonore A. Annenberg,* Chair. and Pres.; Wallis Annenberg, V.P.; Gail C. Levin, Secy. and Exec. Dir.; Lauren Bon, Charles Weingarten, Gregory Weingarten.
EIN: 236257083
Codes: FD, FM

45957
The Pew Charitable Trusts
1 Commerce Sq.
2005 Market St., Ste. 1700
Philadelphia, PA 19103-7077 (215) 575-9050
FAX: (215) 575-4939; *E-mail:* info@pewtrusts.com; URL: http://www.pewtrusts.com
Contact: Rebecca W. Rimel, C.E.O. and Pres.

Pew Memorial Trust, J.N. Pew, Jr. Charitable Trust, J. Howard Pew Freedom Trust, Mabel Pew Myrin Trust, Medical Trust, Knollbrook Trust, and Mary Anderson Trust established in 1948, 1956, 1957, 1957, 1979, 1965, and 1957 respectively.
Donor(s): Mary Ethel Pew,‡ Mabel Pew Myrin,‡ J. Howard Pew,‡ Joseph N. Pew, Jr.‡
Financial data (yr. ended 12/31/01): Grants paid, $192,291,755; assets, $4,338,580,605 (M); expenditures, $232,220,254; qualifying distributions, $218,451,788.
Limitations: Giving on a national basis, with a special commitment to the Philadelphia, PA, region.
Publications: Grants list, occasional report, application guidelines.
Application information: Contact foundation for brochure on specific guidelines and limitations in each program area or visit the trusts' Web site; applicants should not send full proposals unless requested by trustee representatives. Application form required.
Officer and Board Members:* Rebecca W. Rimel,* C.E.O. and Pres.; Susan W. Catherwood, Robert H. Campbell, Thomas W. Langfitt, M.D.; Arthur E. Pew III, J. Howard Pew II, J.N. Pew III, Joseph N. Pew IV, M.D., Mary Catherine Pew, M.D., R. Anderson Pew, Richard F. Pew, Robert G. Williams.
Trustee: The Glenmede Trust Co.
Codes: FD, FM

45958
The William Penn Foundation
2 Logan Sq., 11th Fl.
100 N. 18th St.
Philadelphia, PA 19103-2757 (215) 988-1830
FAX: (215) 988-1823; *E-mail:* moreinfo@wpennfdn.org; URL: http://www.wpennfdn.org
Contact: Janet F. Haas, M.D., Pres.

Incorporated in 1945 in DE.
Donor(s): Otto Haas,‡ Phoebe W. Haas,‡ Otto Haas & Phoebe W. Haas Charitable Trusts.
Financial data (yr. ended 12/31/01): Grants paid, $65,181,777; assets, $1,047,720,982 (M); gifts received, $17,260,000; expenditures, $69,715,551; qualifying distributions, $65,181,777.
Limitations: Giving limited to Camden, NJ and Philadelphia, Bucks, Chester, Delaware, and Montgomery counties, PA; environmental giving in northern DE, small portion of northeastern MD, southern NJ, and larger area of southeastern PA; no national or international giving (except at foundation's initiative).
Publications: Annual report, application guidelines, informational brochure (including application guidelines), occasional report.
Application information: Accepts Delaware Valley Grantmakers and National Network of Grantmakers (NNG) application form; optional proposal outline available on foundation's Web site. Application form not required.
Officers and Directors:* David W. Haas,* Chair.; Frederick R. Haas,* Vice-Chair. and Secy.; Kathryn J. Engebretson, Ph.D.,* Pres.; Louis J. Mayer, V.P., Finance and Admin. and Treas.; Louise M. Foster, Cont.; Carol R. Collier, Joseph A. Dworetzky, Nancy B. Haas, Robert E. Hanrahan, Jr., Ernest E. Jones, Thomas M. McKenna, John P. Mulroney, Terrie S. Rouse, Gary Walker, Lise Yasui.
EIN: 231503488
Codes: FD, FM

45959
Richard King Mellon Foundation
1 Mellon Bank Ctr.
500 Grant St., 41st Fl., Ste. 4106
Pittsburgh, PA 15219-2502 (412) 392-2800
FAX: (412) 392-2837; URL: http://fdncenter.org/grantmaker/rkmellon
Contact: Michael Watson, V.P.

Trust established in 1947 in PA; incorporated in 1971 in PA.
Donor(s): Richard K. Mellon.‡
Financial data (yr. ended 12/31/01): Grants paid, $58,608,007; assets, $1,661,919,000 (M); expenditures, $80,154,095; qualifying distributions, $72,334,260; giving activities include $11,785,543 for program-related investments.
Limitations: Giving primarily in Pittsburgh and southwestern PA, except for nationwide conservation programs. No grants outside the U.S.
Publications: Annual report (including application guidelines), informational brochure.
Application information: Application form required.
Officers and Trustees:* Richard P. Mellon,* Chair.; Seward Prosser Mellon,* Pres.; Arthur D. Miltenberger, V.P.; Michael Watson,* V.P. and Dir.; Scott Izzo, Secy. and Assoc. Dir.; Robert B. Burr, Jr.,* Treas.; John J. Turcik, Cont.; Lawrence S. Busch.
EIN: 251127705
Codes: FD, FM

45960
Howard Heinz Endowment
30 Dominion Tower
625 Liberty Ave.
Pittsburgh, PA 15222-3115 (412) 281-5777
E-mail: info@heinz.org; *FAX:* (412) 281-5788; URL: http://www.heinz.org
Contact: Maxwell King, Exec. Dir.

Trust established in 1941 in PA.
Donor(s): Howard Heinz,‡ Elizabeth Rust Heinz.‡
Financial data (yr. ended 12/31/01): Grants paid, $41,130,518; assets, $907,657,792 (M); expenditures, $50,406,643; qualifying distributions, $45,082,486.
Limitations: Giving limited to activities which directly benefit the citizens of PA, with emphasis on Pittsburgh and southwestern PA.
Publications: Annual report, application guidelines, program policy statement, newsletter, occasional report.
Application information: Application form not required.
Officers: J.E. Kime, C.F.O.; Ann C. Plunkett, Cont.; Maxwell King, Exec. Dir.
Directors: Teresa F. Heinz, Chair.; Carol R. Brown, Frank V. Cahouet, H. John Heinz IV, Howard M. Love, Shirley Malcom, William H. Rea, Barbara Robinson, Frederick W. Thieman, Mallory Walker.
EIN: 251721100
Codes: FD, FM

45961
McCune Foundation
750 6 PPG Pl.
Pittsburgh, PA 15222 (412) 644-8779
FAX: (412) 644-8059; *E-mail:* info@mccune.org; URL: http://www.mccune.org
Contact: Henry S. Beukema, Exec. Dir.

Established in 1979 in PA.
Donor(s): Charles L. McCune.‡
Financial data (yr. ended 09/30/02): Grants paid, $25,375,494; assets, $497,804,987 (M); expenditures, $25,588,279; qualifying distributions, $25,375,494; giving activities include $1,389,267 for program-related investments.
Limitations: Giving primarily in southwestern PA, with emphasis on the Pittsburgh area.
Publications: Annual report (including application guidelines), application guidelines.
Application information: Applicants are encouraged to wait at least 3 years after receiving a grant before reapplying. Application form required.
Officers: Henry S. Beukema, Exec. Dir.; Martha J. Perry, Assoc. Exec. Dir.
Distribution Committee: James M. Edwards, Chair.; Richard D. Edwards, Chair. Emeritus; Michael M. Edwards, John R. McCune VI.
Trustee: National City Bank of Pennsylvania.
EIN: 256210269
Codes: FD, FM

45962
The Pittsburgh Foundation
1 PPG Pl., 30th Fl.
Pittsburgh, PA 15222-5401 (412) 391-5122
FAX: (421) 391-7259; *E-mail:* email@pghfdn.org; URL: http://www.pittsburghfoundation.org
Contact: Dr. William E. Trueheart, C.E.O. and Pres.

Established in 1945 in PA by bank resolution and declaration of trust.
Donor(s): 919 historical donors, 421 current donors.

Financial data (yr. ended 12/31/01): Grants paid, $24,226,829; assets, $519,616,368 (M); gifts received, $26,058,964; expenditures, $34,780,448.
Limitations: Giving from unrestricted funds limited to Pittsburgh and Allegheny County, PA.
Publications: Annual report, application guidelines, newsletter, informational brochure.
Application information: The foundation accepts the Common Grant Application, but encourages applicants to send a letter of inquiry first. Application form required.
Officers and Directors:* James S. Broadhurst,* Chair; Frieda G. Shapira,* Vice-Chair. Emerita; Dr. William E. Trueheart, C.E.O. and Pres.; Thomas S. Hay, V.P., Finance; Gerri Kay, V.P., Prog. and Policy; Alvin Rogal,* Secy.; Aaron A. Walton,* Treas.; Robert P. Bozzone, Joanne E. Burley, Joseph L. Calihan, Estelle F. Comay, William J. Copeland, Dir. Emeritus; Douglas D. Danforth, George A. Davidson, Jr., Linda A. Dickerson, Robert Dickey III, Dir. Emeritus; Arthur J. Edmunds, Sherin H. Knowles, Mary Lou McLaughlin, Samuel Y. Stroh, Nancy D. Washington, Dorothy R. Williams, Dir. Emerita.
Trustee Banks: Mellon Bank, N.A., National City Bank of Pennsylvania, PNC Bank, N.A.
EIN: 250965466
Codes: CM, FD, FM, GTI

45963
Oberkotter Foundation
1600 Market St., Ste. 3600
Philadelphia, PA 19103-7286 (215) 751-2601
FAX: (215) 751-2678; E-mail: RSTRAUS@Schnader.com
Contact: George H. Nofer, J.D., Exec. Dir.

Established in 1985 in PA.
Donor(s): Paul Oberkotter.‡
Financial data (yr. ended 11/30/00): Grants paid, $21,334,724; assets, $195,278,685 (M); gifts received, $31,505,476; expenditures, $25,805,581; qualifying distributions, $25,097,298; giving activities include $2,780,056 for programs.
Application information: Grants usually made on the initiative of the trustees. Telephone inquiries not accepted. Application form not required.
Officer and Trustees:* George H. Nofer, J.D.,* Exec. Dir.; Bruce A. Rosenfield, Assoc. Exec. Dir.; Mildred Oberkotter.
EIN: 232686151
Codes: FD, FM

45964
Alcoa Foundation
Alcoa Corporate Ctr.
201 Isabella St.
Pittsburgh, PA 15212-5858 (412) 553-2348
E-mail: Alcoa.Foundation@alcoa.com; URL: http://www.alcoa.com/global/en/community/foundation.asp

Trust established in 1952 in PA; incorporated in 1964.
Donor(s): Aluminum Co. of America, Alcoa, Inc.
Financial data (yr. ended 12/31/01): Grants paid, $21,326,190; assets, $409,678,168 (M); gifts received, $500,000; expenditures, $23,784,151; qualifying distributions, $22,677,170.
Limitations: Giving primarily in areas of company operations, national and international; emphasis on local communities: Davenport, IA, Evansville, IN, Massena, NY, Cleveland, OH, Pittsburgh, PA, Knoxville, TN, and Rockdale, TX.
Publications: Annual report (including application guidelines), informational brochure (including application guidelines).

Application information: Application form not required.
Officers and Directors:* Kathleen W. Buechel,* Pres. and Treas.; Grace A. Smith, Secy.; Ricardo E. Belda, Earnest J. Edwards, Barbara S. Jeremiah, Richard B. Kelson, William E. Leahey, Jr., Renata de Camargo Nasicmento, G. John Pizzey, Robert F. Slagle.
Corporate Trustee: Mellon Bank, N.A.
EIN: 251128857
Codes: CS, FD, CD, FM, GTI

45965
John Templeton Foundation
P.O. Box 8322
Radnor, PA 19087-8322
FAX: (610) 687-8961; URL: http://www.templeton.org
Contact: Grants Admin.

Established in 1988 in TN.
Donor(s): John Marks Templeton.
Financial data (yr. ended 12/31/00): Grants paid, $20,863,922; assets, $298,126,612 (M); gifts received, $2,775,911; expenditures $28,130,755; qualifying distributions, $26,640,682; giving activities include $2,572,121 for programs.
Limitations: Giving on a national and international basis.
Publications: Annual report, financial statement, newsletter, informational brochure, application guidelines.
Application information: Application form not required.
Officers and Trustees:* Sir John Marks Templeton,* Chair.; John Marks Templeton, Jr.,* Pres.; Charles Harper, Sr. V.P. and Exec. Dir.; Frances Schapperle, V.P.; Harvey Maxwell Templeton III, Secy.; Ann Templeton Cameron,* Treas.; John Barrow, Paul Davies, Heather E. Dill, George H. Gallup, Jr., Robert L. Hermann, David Myers, Glenn R. Mosley, William E. Simon, F. Russell Stannard, Anne D. Zimmerman.
EIN: 621322826
Codes: FD, FM, GTI

45966
The Philadelphia Foundation
1234 Market St., Ste. 1800
Philadelphia, PA 19107-3794 (215) 563-6417
FAX: (215) 563-6882; URL: http://www.philafound.org
Contact: R. Andrew Swinney, Pres.

Established in 1918 in PA by bank resolution.
Donor(s): 400 different funds.
Financial data (yr. ended 12/31/01): Grants paid, $19,134,323; assets, $195,134,002 (M); gifts received, $7,559,111; expenditures, $23,333,415.
Limitations: Giving limited to Bucks, Chester, Delaware, Montgomery, and Philadelphia counties in southeastern PA, except for designated funds.
Publications: Annual report, application guidelines, informational brochure (including application guidelines), newsletter.
Application information: Accepts Delaware Valley Grantmakers Common Grant Application when accompanied by required foundation forms; grant applications sent by FAX or E-mail will not be considered. Applicants are strongly encouraged to contact foundation for a copy of the application guidelines and submission deadlines. Application form required.
Officers and Managers:* H. Craig Lewis,* Chair.; Ignatius C. Wang,* Vice-Chair.; R. Andrew Swinney, Pres.; Lynette E. Campbell, V.P., Progs.; Jeff Perkins, V.P., Finance and Admin.; Herman Mattleman,* Treas.; Lawrence J. Beaser, Ellen P. Foster, Eric Fraint, Elizabeth T. Frank, Oliver St.C.

Franklin, Gene Locks, James E. Nevels, Stanley A. Simpkins, Judith A.W. Thomas, Laura Luna Trujillo, Cuyler H. Walker, Andrew N. Yao.
Trustees: The Bryn Mawr Trust Co., First National Bank & Trust Co., First Union National Bank, The Glenmede Trust Co., Mellon P.S.F.S., Pitcairn Trust Co., PNC Bank, N.A., Wilmington Trust of Pennsylvania.
EIN: 231581832
Codes: CM, FD, FM

45967
Vira I. Heinz Endowment
30 Dominion Tower
625 Liberty Ave.
Pittsburgh, PA 15222-3115 (412) 281-5777
FAX: (412) 281-5788; E-mail: info@heinz.org; URL: http://www.heinz.org
Contact: Maxwell King, Exec. Dir.

Trust established in 1983 in PA; incorporated in 1995.
Donor(s): Vira I. Heinz.‡
Financial data (yr. ended 12/31/01): Grants paid, $18,506,696; assets, $468,932,556 (M); expenditures, $23,703,192; qualifying distributions, $20,669,709.
Limitations: Giving primarily directed to Pittsburgh and southwestern PA, although in certain cases support may be considered on a national or international basis.
Publications: Annual report, application guidelines, program policy statement, newsletter, occasional report.
Application information: Application form not required.
Officers and Directors:* James M. Walton,* Chair.; Jack E. Kime, C.F.O.; Ann C. Plunkett, Cont.; Maxwell King, Exec. Dir.; J. Carter Brown, Andre T. Heinz, Teresa F. Heinz, Wendy MacKenzie, William H. Rea, Barbara K. Robinson, Konrad M. Weis, S. Donald Wiley.
EIN: 251762825
Codes: FD, FM

45968
Sarah Scaife Foundation, Inc.
1 Oxford Ctr.
301 Grant St., Ste. 3900
Pittsburgh, PA 15219-6401 (412) 392-2900
URL: http://www.scaife.com
Contact: Michael W. Gleba, Exec. V.P.

Trust established in 1941; incorporated in 1959 in PA; present name adopted in 1974.
Donor(s): Sarah Mellon Scaife.‡
Financial data (yr. ended 12/31/01): Grants paid, $18,331,500; assets, $323,029,669 (M); expenditures, $20,837,839; qualifying distributions, $19,520,180.
Publications: Annual report (including application guidelines).
Application information: Application form not required.
Officers and Trustees:* Richard M. Scaife, Chair.; Michael W. Gleba, Exec. V.P.; Barbara L. Slaney, V.P. and Treas.; R. Daniel McMichael, Secy.; T. Westray Battle III, William J. Bennett, T. Kenneth Cribb, Jr., Edwin J. Feulner, Jr., Allan H. Meltzer, Ph.D., Roger W. Robinsin, Jr., James M. Walton, Arthur P. Ziegler, Jr.
EIN: 251113452
Codes: FD, FM

45969
Claude Worthington Benedum Foundation
1400 Benedum-Trees Bldg.
223 4th Ave.
Pittsburgh, PA 15222 (412) 288-0360
URL: http://www.fdncenter.org/grantmaker/benedum
Contact: William P. Getty, Pres.

Incorporated in 1944 in PA.
Donor(s): Michael Late Benedum,‡ Sarah N. Benedum.‡
Financial data (yr. ended 12/31/01): Grants paid, $14,433,564; assets, $324,700,000 (M); expenditures, $18,419,419; qualifying distributions, $16,149,256; giving activities include $250,000 for program-related investments.
Limitations: Giving limited to southwestern PA and WV.
Publications: Annual report, application guidelines, informational brochure (including application guidelines).
Application information: Proposals sent by FAX or E-mail are not considered. Application form not required.
Officers and Trustees:* Paul G. Benedum, Jr.,* Chair.; William P. Getty,* Pres.; Dwight M. Keating, V.P. and Treas.; Beverly Railey Walter, V.P., Progs.; Rose A. McKee, Secy. and Dir., Admin.; Ralph J. Bean, Jr., G. Nicholas Beckwith, Gaston Caperton, Paul R. Jenkins, G. Randolph Worls.
EIN: 251086799
Codes: FD, FM

45970
Connelly Foundation
1 Tower Bridge, Ste. 1450
West Conshohocken, PA 19428
(610) 834-3222
FAX: (610) 834-0866; *E-mail:* info@connellyfdn.org; *URL:* http://www.connellyfdn.org
Contact: Victoria K. Flaville, V.P., Admin.

Incorporated in 1955 in PA.
Donor(s): John F. Connelly,‡ Josephine C. Connelly.‡
Financial data (yr. ended 12/31/01): Grants paid, $12,033,760; assets, $234,882,190 (M); expenditures, $14,154,400; qualifying distributions, $13,490,000.
Limitations: Giving primarily in the Philadelphia, PA, and Delaware Valley areas.
Publications: Application guidelines.
Application information: Application form not required.
Officers and Trustees:* Josephine C. Mandeville,* Chair, Pres., and C.E.O.; Lewis W. Bluemle, Jr.,* Sr. V.P.; Emily C. Riley,* Exec. V.P., Progs.; Victoria K. Flaville, V.P., Admin. and Secy.; Lawrence T. Mangan, V.P., Finance and Treas.; William J. Avery, Andrew J. Bozzelli, Ira Brind, Christine C. Connelly, Daniele Connelly, Thomas S. Connelly, Kurt R. Crowley, Eleanor L. Davis, Philippe Delouvrier, Thomas F. Donovan, Chester C. Hilinski, Emeritus; Barbara W. Riley, Thomas A. Riley, Andrew P. Willis.
EIN: 236296825
Codes: FD, FM

45971
Grable Foundation
650 Smithfield St., Ste. 240
Pittsburgh, PA 15222 (412) 471-4550
FAX: (412) 471-2267; *E-mail:* grable@grablefdn.org; *URL:* http://www.grablefdn.org
Contact: Susan H. Brownlee, Exec. Dir.

Established in 1976 in PA.
Donor(s): Minnie K. Grable.‡
Financial data (yr. ended 12/31/00): Grants paid, $11,724,033; assets, $261,864,424 (M); expenditures, $14,261,591; qualifying distributions, $12,549,670.
Limitations: Giving primarily in southwestern PA.
Publications: Annual report, grants list.
Application information: Accepts common grants application. Application form not required.
Officers and Trustees:* Charles R. Burke, Sr.,* Chair.; Jan Nicholson,* Pres.; Charles R. Burke, Jr.,* V.P.; Barbara N. McFadyen,* V.P.; Patricia Grable Burke,* Secy.; Steven E. Burke,* Treas.; Susan H. Brownlee, Exec. Dir.; Marion Grable Nicholson, William B. Nicholson.
EIN: 251309888
Codes: FD, FM

45972
The PNC Foundation
(Formerly PNC Bank Foundation)
c/o PNC Financial Services Group, Inc.
2 PNC Plz., 25th Fl., 620 Liberty Ave.
Pittsburgh, PA 15222 (412) 762-7076
Contact: Mia Hallett Bernard, Mgr.

Established in 1970 in PA.
Donor(s): PNC Bank, N.A.
Financial data (yr. ended 12/31/01): Grants paid, $11,579,055; assets, $745,925 (M); expenditures, $11,968,545; qualifying distributions, $11,738,337.
Limitations: Giving primarily in headquarters and company locations: DE, IN, KY, NJ, OH, and PA.
Publications: Annual report (including application guidelines).
Application information: The foundation grants interviews with applicants upon request. Application form not required.
Trustee: PNC Bank, N.A.
EIN: 251202255
Codes: CS, FD, CD, FM

45973
E. Rhodes & Leona B. Carpenter Foundation
c/o Joseph A. O'Connor, Jr., Morgan, Lewis & Bockius
1701 Market St.
Philadelphia, PA 19103 (215) 963-5212
Application address: P.O. Box 58880, Philadelphia, PA 19102-8880

Established in 1975 in VA.
Donor(s): E. Rhodes Carpenter,‡ Leona B. Carpenter.‡
Financial data (yr. ended 12/31/00): Grants paid, $10,626,224; assets, $237,865,221 (M); expenditures, $12,867,419; qualifying distributions, $10,703,186.
Limitations: Giving primarily in areas east of the Mississippi River.
Officers and Directors:* Ann B. Day,* Pres.; Paul B. Day, Jr.,* V.P. and Secy.-Treas.; M.H. Reinhart.
EIN: 510155772
Codes: FD, FM

45974
Eden Hall Foundation
600 Grant St., Ste. 3232
Pittsburgh, PA 15219 (412) 642-6697
Contact: Sylvia Fields, Prog. Dir.

Established in 1984 in PA.
Donor(s): Eden Hall Farm.
Financial data (yr. ended 12/31/01): Grants paid, $9,659,150; assets, $168,592,653 (M); expenditures, $10,109,333; qualifying distributions, $9,932,602.
Limitations: Giving limited to southwestern PA.
Publications: Application guidelines.
Application information: Interviews or visitation may be necessary for additional information. Application form not required.
Officers and Directors:* George C. Greer,* Chair.; Debora Foster, Secy.; John M. Mazur, Treas.; E.H. Shifler.
EIN: 251384468
Codes: FD, FM

45975
Independence Foundation
200 S. Broad St., Ste. 1101
Philadelphia, PA 19102 (215) 985-4009
FAX: (215) 985-3989
Contact: Susan E. Sherman, C.E.O. and Pres.

Established in 1932 as International Cancer Research Foundation; incorporated as Donner Foundation in 1945 in DE; divided in 1961 into Independence Foundation and a newly formed William H. Donner Foundation.
Donor(s): William H. Donner.‡
Financial data (yr. ended 12/31/01): Grants paid, $8,973,778; assets, $131,761,086 (M); expenditures, $11,719,549; qualifying distributions, $10,181,821.
Limitations: Giving primarily in Philadelphia, PA, and Bucks, Chester, Delaware, and Montgomery counties.
Publications: Annual report, application guidelines.
Application information: Call foundation for category packet. Exhibit material, if sent, should be in single form. Receipt of proposals is acknowledged. Should the original prove to be within the scope of the foundation's interests, interviews with the board may be arranged prior to final determination. Application form required.
Officers and Directors:* Phyllis W. Beck,* Chair.; Susan E. Sherman,* C.E.O. and Pres.; Eugene C. Fish,* V.P.; Theodore K. Warner, Jr.,* Secy.-Treas.; Andre Dennis, Andrea Mengel.
EIN: 231352110
Codes: FD, FM

45976
John R. McCune Charitable Trust
6 PPG Pl., Ste. 750
Pittsburgh, PA 15222 (412) 644-7796
FAX: (412) 644-8059
Contact: James M. Edwards, Exec. Dir.

Established in 1972 in PA.
Donor(s): John R. McCune IV.‡
Financial data (yr. ended 11/30/00): Grants paid, $8,563,359; assets, $180,910,159 (M); expenditures, $9,145,288; qualifying distributions, $8,729,030.
Limitations: Giving primarily in southwestern PA.
Publications: Application guidelines.
Application information: Unsolicited proposals usually not accepted. Application form not required.
Officers and Dispensing Committee:* David L. Edwards,* Chair.; James M. Edwards,* Exec. Dir.; Janet McCune Edwards Anti, Molly McCune

Cathey, John H. Edwards, Michael M. Edwards, Carrie McCune Katigan, Laurie M. Lewis, Sarah McCune Losinger, John R. McCune VI.
Trustee: National City Bank of Pennsylvania.
EIN: 256160722
Codes: FD, FM

45977
W. W. Smith Charitable Trust
200 Four Falls Corporate Center, Ste. 300
West Conshohocken, PA 19428 (610) 397-1844
FAX: (610) 397-1680
Contact: Frances R. Pemberton, Trust Admin.

Trust established in 1976 in PA.
Donor(s): William Wikoff Smith.‡
Financial data (yr. ended 06/30/01): Grants paid, $7,606,465; assets, $159,631,581 (M); expenditures, $8,007,869; qualifying distributions, $7,651,692.
Limitations: Giving primarily in the Delaware Valley, including Philadelphia, PA, and its six neighboring counties; grants to colleges by invitation only.
Publications: Biennial report (including application guidelines).
Application information: College financial aid programs by invitation only; applications for medical research grants must be submitted in quadruplicate; application forms required for medical research only; accepts Delaware Valley Grantmakers Common Grant Application and Common Report Form.
Trustees: Mary L. Smith, First Union National Bank.
EIN: 236648841
Codes: FD, FM

45978
United States Steel Foundation, Inc.
(Formerly USX Foundation, Inc.)
600 Grant St., Rm. 685
Pittsburgh, PA 15219-4776 (412) 433-5237
FAX: (412) 433-6847; URL: http://www.ussteel.com/corp/ussfoundation/ussfound.htm
Contact: Craig D. Mallick, Genl. Mgr.

Incorporated in 1953 in DE.
Donor(s): United States Steel Corp., and certain subsidiaries.
Financial data (yr. ended 11/30/00): Grants paid, $6,977,577; assets, $7,060,934 (M); gifts received, $6,612,341; expenditures, $7,171,636; qualifying distributions, $7,167,192.
Limitations: Giving primarily in areas of company operations in the U.S., including AK, AL, CO, IL, IN, LA, MI, MN, OH, OK, western PA, and TX.
Publications: Annual report (including application guidelines), application guidelines.
Application information: Grantmakers of Western PA Common Grant Application Format accepted. Application form not required.
Officers and Trustees:* Thomas J. Usher,* Chair.; Marilyn A. Harris,* Pres.; Edward F. Guna, V.P. and Treas.; Larry G. Schultz, V.P. and Compt.; Gary A. Glynn, V.P., Investments; Dan D. Sandman,* Secy. and Genl. Counsel; Robert M. Hernandez,* C.F.O.; Craig D. Mallick, Genl. Mgr.; Gary Walsh, Tax Counsel; Jerry Howard, John T. Mills.
EIN: 136093185
Codes: CS, FD, CD, FM

45979
Brickman Foundation
1 Pitcairn Pl., Ste. 3000
Jenkintown, PA 19046

Established in 1994 in PA.
Donor(s): Sally Brickman, Theodore Brickman, Julie B. Carr, Susan B. McGrath, Scott W. Brickman, Steven G. Brickman.
Financial data (yr. ended 12/31/00): Grants paid, $6,878,701; assets, $5,284,419 (M); expenditures, $6,915,142; qualifying distributions, $6,855,588.
Limitations: Applications not accepted.
Application information: Contributes only to pre-selected organizations.
Trustees: Sally Brickman, Scott W. Brickman, Steven G. Brickman, Theodore Brickman, Julie B. Carr, Susan B. McGrath, Pitcairn Trust Co.
EIN: 237790986
Codes: FD, FM

45980
The Arcadia Foundation
105 E. Logan St.
Norristown, PA 19401-3058 (610) 275-8460
FAX: (610) 275-8460
Contact: Marilyn Lee Steinbright, Pres.

Incorporated in 1964 in PA.
Donor(s): Edith C. Steinbright,‡ Marilyn Lee Steinbright.
Financial data (yr. ended 09/30/02): Grants paid, $6,604,366; assets, $41,027,438 (M); expenditures, $6,879,872; qualifying distributions, $6,573,110.
Limitations: Giving limited to eastern PA organizations whose addresses have zip codes of 18000 - 19000.
Publications: Annual report, application guidelines.
Application information: Application form not required.
Officers and Directors:* Marilyn Lee Steinbright,* Pres.; Tanya Hashorva,* V.P.; David P. Sandler,* Secy.; Harvey S.S. Miller,* Treas.; Edward L. Jones, Jr., Kathleen Shellington.
EIN: 236399772
Codes: FD, FM

45981
CIGNA Foundation
1 Liberty Pl.
1650 Market St.
Philadelphia, PA 19192
Application address for the greater Hartford, CT, area: Arnold W. Wright, Dir., Civic Affairs, CIGNA Foundation., S-320, Hartford, CT 06152-5001; URL: http://www.cigna.com/general/working/atcigna/caring.html
Contact: Arnold W. Wright, Jr., Exec. Dir.

Incorporated in 1962 in PA.
Donor(s): CIGNA Corp.
Financial data (yr. ended 12/31/00): Grants paid, $6,592,067; assets, $1,121,024 (M); gifts received, $6,445,287; expenditures, $5,920,775; qualifying distributions, $5,783,452.
Limitations: Giving primarily in Hartford, CT, Philadelphia, PA, and to selected national organizations.
Publications: Annual report, grants list, corporate giving report (including application guidelines).
Application information: In the greater Hartford, CT, area, direct requests go to Bloomfield office; other requests go to Philadelphia, PA, office. Application form not required.
Officers: Mike A. Fernandez, Pres.; David B. Gerges, V.P. and Treas.; Arnold W. Wright, Jr., V.P. and Exec. Dir.; Carol J. Ward, Secy.
Directors: Judith E. Soltz,* Chair.; H. Edward Hanway, Donald M. Levinson.
EIN: 236261726
Codes: CS, FD, CD, FM

45982
The Helen F. Whitaker Fund
4718 Old Gettysburg Rd., Ste. 209
Mechanicsburg, PA 17055-8411
(717) 763-1600
Contact: Miles J. Gibbons, Jr., Exec. Dir.

Established in 1983.
Donor(s): Helen F. Whitaker.‡
Financial data (yr. ended 07/31/02): Grants paid, $6,494,650; assets, $20,771,480 (M); expenditures, $6,985,312; qualifying distributions, $6,494,650.
Limitations: Giving on a national basis, additional regional programs for the Naples, FL, area and the Harrisburg and Philadelphia, PA, areas.
Publications: Informational brochure (including application guidelines), application guidelines.
Application information: The foundation has begun phasing out its grant programs to coincide with its planned closing in 2006. The foundation will continue to fund existing multiyear awards, but will begin to phase out the awarding of new grants. Applicants to Regional Program should request guidelines from foundation. Application form not required.
Officer and Committee Members:* Miles J. Gibbons, Jr.,* Exec. Dir.; Carmelita Biggie, Ruth W. Holmes.
EIN: 222459399
Codes: FD

45983
H. J. Heinz Company Foundation
P.O. Box 57
Pittsburgh, PA 15230-0057 (412) 456-5773
FAX: (412) 456-7859; E-mail: heinz.foundation@hjheinz.com
Contact: Tammy B. Aupperle, Prog. Dir.

Trust established in 1951 in PA.
Donor(s): H.J. Heinz Co.
Financial data (yr. ended 12/31/00): Grants paid, $6,494,241; assets, $753,778 (M); gifts received, $6,000,000; expenditures, $6,500,494; qualifying distributions, $6,494,922.
Limitations: Giving primarily in areas of company operations, with special focus on southwestern PA.
Publications: Application guidelines.
Application information: The foundation does not acknowledge receipt of proposals; interviews are granted at the applicant foundation's discretion. Application form not required.
Officer and Trustees:* John Runkle,* Chair.; Karyll A. Davis, D. Edward I. Smyth, Laura Stein.
EIN: 256018924
Codes: CS, FD, CD, FM

45984
The Hillman Foundation, Inc.
2000 Grant Bldg.
Pittsburgh, PA 15219 (412) 338-3466
FAX: (412) 338-3463; E-mail: foundation@hillmanfo.com
Contact: Ronald W. Wertz, Pres.

Incorporated in 1951 in DE.
Donor(s): John Hartwell Hillman, Jr.,‡ J.H. Hillman & Sons Co., Hillman Land Co., and family-owned corporations.
Financial data (yr. ended 12/31/01): Grants paid, $6,462,400; assets, $133,410,036 (M); expenditures, $7,178,551; qualifying distributions, $7,026,163.

45984—PENNSYLVANIA

Limitations: Giving primarily in Pittsburgh and southwestern PA.
Publications: Annual report (including application guidelines).
Application information: Common Grant Application approved by foundation members of Grantmakers of Western PA accepted. Application form required.
Officers and Directors:* Henry L. Hillman,* Chair.; Ronald W. Wertz, Pres.; C.G. Grefenstette,* V.P.; H. Vaughan Blaxter III,* Secy.; Lawrence M. Wagner,* Treas.; Elsie H. Hillman.
EIN: 256011462
Codes: FD, FM

45985
The 1994 Charles B. Degenstein Foundation
c/o Mellon Bank, N.A.
P.O. Box 7236, AIM 193-0224
Philadelphia, PA 19101-7236
Application address: 43 S. 5th St., Sunbury, PA 17801-2896
Contact: Appelbaum & Appelbaum

Established in 1996 in PA.
Financial data (yr. ended 06/30/01): Grants paid, $6,370,352; assets, $102,870,466 (M); gifts received, $13,137,204; expenditures, $6,853,502; qualifying distributions, $6,509,879.
Limitations: Giving within a 75-mile radius of Sunbury, PA.
Application information: Application form required.
Trustees: Sidney Apfelbaum, Mellon Bank, N.A.
EIN: 237792979
Codes: FD, FM

45986
The Jewish Healthcare Foundation of Pittsburgh
Centre City Tower, Ste. 2330
650 Smithfield St.
Pittsburgh, PA 15222 (412) 594-2550
FAX: (412) 232-6240; E-mail: info@jhf.org; URL: http://www.jhf.org
Contact: Karen Wolk Feinstein, Ph.D., Pres.

Established in 1990 in PA; converted as a result of Montefiore Hospital's merger with Presbyterian University Hospital.
Donor(s): Presbyterian University Health Systems, Inc.
Financial data (yr. ended 12/31/00): Grants paid, $6,165,478; assets, $133,500,000 (M); gifts received, $1,868,964; expenditures, $7,100,000; qualifying distributions, $7,100,000.
Limitations: Giving limited to western PA.
Publications: Annual report, application guidelines, newsletter, occasional report, program policy statement.
Application information: Application form not required.
Officers and Trustees:* Farrell Rubenstein,* Chair.; Robert A. Paul,* Vice-Chair.; Karen Wolk Feinstein, Ph.D.,* Pres.; Eileen Lane,* Secy.; Charles Cohen,* Treas.; and 55 additional trustees.
EIN: 251624347
Codes: FD, FM

45987
The Erie Community Foundation
127 W. 6th St.
Erie, PA 16501-1001 (814) 454-0843
FAX: (814) 456-4965; E-mail: ecf@team.org;
URL: http://www.cferie.org
Contact: Michael L. Batchelor, Pres.

Established in 1935 in PA as Erie Endowment Foundation; renamed in 1970.
Financial data (yr. ended 12/31/00): Grants paid, $6,100,000; assets, $102,000,000 (M); gifts received, $7,500,000; expenditures, $6,700,000.
Limitations: Giving limited to Erie County, PA.
Publications: Annual report, newsletter, informational brochure (including application guidelines).
Application information: Application form required.
Officers and Trustees:* Ray L. McGarvey,* Chair.; Michael L. Batchelor,* Pres.; M. Peter SciBetta, V.P.; James D. McDonald, Jr.,* Secy.; Edward P. Junker III,* Treas.; Joan F. Bert, Sr. Joan Chittister, O.S.B.; Thomas L. Doolin, William Hilbert, Sr.
Trustee Banks: Advest, Inc., Integra Financial Corp., Mellon Bank, N.A., Merrill Lynch Trust Co., PNC Bank, N.A.
EIN: 256032032
Codes: CM, FD

45988
R. P. Simmons Family Foundation
Birchmere, Quaker Hollow Rd.
Sewickley, PA 15143

Established in 1987 in PA.
Donor(s): Richard P. Simmons.
Financial data (yr. ended 12/31/01): Grants paid, $5,798,581; assets, $5,272,340 (M); gifts received, $7,717; expenditures, $5,877,284; qualifying distributions, $5,764,548.
Limitations: Applications not accepted. Giving primarily in PA, with emphasis on Pittsburgh.
Application information: Contributes only to pre-selected organizations.
Trustee: Richard P. Simmons.
EIN: 256277068
Codes: FD

45989
The Warren V. Musser Foundation
435 Devon Park Dr., No. 800
Wayne, PA 19087 (610) 293-0600
Contact: Diane Swiggard

Established in 1980 in PA.
Donor(s): Claire V. Sams, Warren V. Musser.
Financial data (yr. ended 11/30/00): Grants paid, $5,678,795; assets, $7,988,689 (M); gifts received, $23,146,186; expenditures, $7,576,667; qualifying distributions, $5,678,795.
Limitations: Giving primarily in Philadelphia, PA.
Officers and Director:* Warren V. Musser,* Pres.; Robert E. Keith, V.P.; James A. Ounsworth, Secy.; Carl Sempier.
EIN: 232162497
Codes: FD, FM

45990
Janet A. Hooker Charitable Trust
c/o Hawthorn, A PNC Advisors Co.
1600 Market st., 29th fl.
Philadelphia, PA 19103

Trust established in 1952 in NY.
Donor(s): Janet A. Neff Hooker.
Financial data (yr. ended 12/31/00): Grants paid, $5,455,500; assets, $4,639,358 (M); expenditures, $5,501,605; qualifying distributions, $5,473,722.
Limitations: Applications not accepted. Giving primarily in CA, FL, and NY.
Application information: Contributes only to pre-selected organizations. Unsolicited requests for funds not considered.
EIN: 236286762
Codes: FD, FM

45991
The Sidney Kimmel Foundation
c/o R. Jaffe
1600 Market St.
Philadelphia, PA 19103-7286 (215) 751-2500
URL: http://www.kimmel.org

Established in 1992 in PA.
Donor(s): Sidney Kimmel.
Financial data (yr. ended 07/31/00): Grants paid, $5,134,100; assets, $23,273,641 (M); gifts received, $3,897,325; expenditures, $6,217,097; qualifying distributions, $5,640,654.
Application information: See foundation Web site for application guidelines and requirements; application cover page can be downloaded from Web site.
Directors: Richard Butera, Gary Cohen, Richard Jaffe, Sidney Kimmel.
EIN: 232698492
Codes: FD, FM

45992
PPG Industries Foundation
1 PPG Pl.
Pittsburgh, PA 15272 (412) 434-2453
Contact: Sue Sloan, Sr. Prog. Off.

Incorporated in 1951 in PA.
Donor(s): PPG Industries, Inc.
Financial data (yr. ended 12/31/01): Grants paid, $4,915,874; assets, $22,975,397 (M); gifts received, $5,186,912; expenditures, $5,207,579; qualifying distributions, $5,125,584.
Limitations: Giving primarily in areas of company operations, with emphasis on the Pittsburgh, PA, region.
Publications: Annual report (including application guidelines), informational brochure.
Application information: Grant decisions made by the screening committee and the board of directors. Application form not required.
Officers and Directors:* Raymond W. LeBoeuf,* Chair. and C.E.O.; Charles E. Bunch, Exec. V.P.; James C. Diggs, Sr. V.P.; William H. Hernandez,* Sr. V.P.; Jeffrey R. Gilbert, Exec. Dir.
EIN: 256037790
Codes: CS, FD, CD, FM

45993
Heinz Family Foundation
3200 CNG Tower
625 Liberty Ave.
Pittsburgh, PA 15222 (412) 497-5775
FAX: (412) 497-5790
Contact: Jeffrey R. Lewis, C.O.O.

Established in 1984 in PA; incorporated in 1992.
Financial data (yr. ended 12/31/01): Grants paid, $4,772,442; assets, $69,000,000 (M); gifts received, $7,063,955; expenditures, $8,564,000; qualifying distributions, $4,772,442.
Limitations: Applications not accepted. Giving only in the U.S.
Application information: Contributes only to pre-selected organizations; unsolicited applications not considered.
Officers and Directors:* Teresa Heinz,* Chair. and C.E.O.; Jeffrey R. Lewis, C.O.O. and Exec. Dir.; Wendy Mackenzie, Secy.; S. Donald Wiley, Treas.; Jack E. Kime, C.F.O.; John R. Taylor, C.I.O.; Andre Heinz.
EIN: 251689382
Codes: FD, FM, GTI

45994
The Buhl Foundation
650 Smithfield St., Ste. 2300
Pittsburgh, PA 15222   (412) 566-2711
Contact: Dr. Doreen E. Boyce, Pres.

Established as a trust in 1927 in PA; reincorporated in 1992.
Donor(s): Henry Buhl, Jr.,‡ Henry C. Frick.‡
Financial data (yr. ended 06/30/01): Grants paid, $4,396,118; assets, $80,664,699 (M); gifts received, $100; expenditures, $4,928,477; qualifying distributions, $4,682,030.
Limitations: Giving primarily in southwestern PA, with emphasis on the Pittsburgh area.
Publications: Annual report, informational brochure (including application guidelines).
Application information: Submit final proposal upon invitation only. Application form not required.
Officers and Directors:* Francis B. Nimick, Jr.,* Chair.; Helen S. Faison,* Vice-Chair.; William H. Rea,* Vice-Chair.; Jean A. Robinson,* Vice-Chair.; Albert C. Van Dusen,* Vice-Chair.; Doreen E. Boyce, Pres.; Marsha Zahumensky, Secy.-Treas.
EIN: 250378910
Codes: FD, FM

45995
First Union Regional Foundation
(Formerly CoreStates Foundation)
Widener Bldg., PA 4360
1339 Chestnut St.
Philadelphia, PA 19107   (267) 321-7661
Additional address: P.O. Box 7618, Philadelphia, PA 19101-7618; FAX: (267) 321-7656
Contact: Denise McGregor Armbrister, Exec. Dir.

Established in 1985.
Donor(s): CoreStates Financial Corp, First Union Corp., Wachovia Corp.
Financial data (yr. ended 12/31/01): Grants paid, $4,383,000; assets, $87,823,863 (M); expenditures, $4,650,028; qualifying distributions, $4,487,276.
Limitations: Giving primarily in the DE, NJ, and eastern PA tri-state area.
Publications: Grants list, informational brochure.
Application information: Grant application is by invitation only. A preliminary proposal, as outlined in brochure, is accepted at all times. Application form not required.
Officers and Directors:* Stephanie W. Naidoff, Chair.; Robert L. Reid,* Pres.; Judith N. Allison,* V.P.; Reginald Davis, V.P.; Denise McGregor Armbrister,* Secy.-Treas. and Exec. Dir.; Robert S. Appleby, Lillian Escobar Haskins, Eleanor V. Horne, Carlton E. Hughes, Ernest E. Jones, George V. Lynett, Marlin Miller, Jr., David Newell, Malcolmn M. Pryor, Peter S. Strawbridge, Judith M. von Seldeneck, John D. Wallace.
EIN: 222625990
Codes: CS, FD, CD, FM

45996
The Lenfest Foundation, Inc.
5 Tower Bridge
300 Barr Harbor Dr., Ste. 450
West Conshohocken, PA 19428
(610) 828-4510
FAX: (610) 828-0390; E-mail: lenfestfoundation.org; URL: http://www.lenfestfoundation.org
Contact: Bruce Melgary, Exec. Dir.

Established in 1999 in PA.
Donor(s): H.F. Lenfest, Mrs. H.F. Lenfest.
Financial data (yr. ended 06/30/02): Grants paid, $4,330,000; assets, $152,083,436 (M); expenditures, $11,082,186; qualifying distributions, $4,787,107.
Limitations: Giving primarily in northern DE, southern NJ, and southeastern and south central PA.
Publications: Application guidelines, informational brochure (including application guidelines).
Application information: Application guidelines available on website.
Officers and Trustees:* H.F. Lenfest,* Chair.; Marguerite Lenfest,* Pres.; Bruce Melgary, Exec. Dir.; Albert Bellas, T. Douglas Hale, John Strassburger.
EIN: 233031350
Codes: FD

45997
Scaife Charitable Foundation
(Formerly David N. Scaife Charitable Foundation)
5840 Ellsworth Ave., Ste. 200
Pittsburgh, PA 15232   (412) 362-6000
FAX: 412 362-6600
Contact: J. Nicholas Beldecos, Exec. Dir.

Established in 2000 in PA.
Financial data (yr. ended 12/31/01): Grants paid, $4,319,431; assets, $93,167,985 (M); expenditures, $5,315,101; qualifying distributions, $5,803,512.
Limitations: Giving primarily in southwestern PA.
Application information: Accepts the Common Grant Application Format of Grantmakers of Western Pennsylvania. Application form not required.
Officers and Trustees:* David N. Scaife,* Chair.; Sanford B. Ferguson,* Vice-Chair.; Sara D. Scaife,* Secy.; Edward J. Goncz,* Treas.; J. Nicholas Beldecos, Exec. Dir.; Donald A. Collins, Frances G. Scaife, Joseph C. Walton.
EIN: 251847237
Codes: FD

45998
Mellon Financial Corporation Foundation
(Formerly Mellon Bank Foundation)
1 Mellon Ctr., Ste. 1830
Pittsburgh, PA 15258-0001   (412) 234-2732
Contact: James P. McDonald, Pres.

Established in 1974 in PA.
Donor(s): Mellon Bank Corp., Mellon Financial Corp.
Financial data (yr. ended 12/31/00): Grants paid, $4,300,349; assets, $65,116,758 (M); gifts received, $40,655; expenditures, $4,456,349; qualifying distributions, $4,300,349.
Limitations: Giving primarily in Boston, MA, and Philadelphia and Pittsburgh, PA.
Publications: Corporate giving report (including application guidelines).
Application information: Application form not required.
Officers and Trustees:* Rose M. Cotton,* Chair.; James P. McDonald,* Pres.; Steven G. Elliott,* Treas.; Paul S. Beideman, Michael E. Bleier, Walter R. Day III, Jeffrey L. Leininger, Martin G. McGuinn, James P. Palermo, Lisa B. Peters.
EIN: 237423500
Codes: CS, FD, CD

45999
Philadelphia Health Care Trust
(Formerly Graduate Health System, Inc.)
2129 Chestnut St.
Philadelphia, PA 19103

Financial data (yr. ended 06/30/00): Grants paid, $4,300,000; assets, $118,175,954 (M); expenditures, $8,825,654; qualifying distributions, $4,348,446.
Limitations: Applications not accepted. Giving primarily in PA.
Application information: Contributes only to pre-selected organizations.
Officer and Directors:* Bernard J. Korman,* Chair.; Peter D. Carlino, Harold Cramer, Russell Kunkel, Janice L. Richter.
EIN: 231985544
Codes: FD

46000
Harry C. Trexler Trust
33 S. 7th St., Ste. 205
Allentown, PA 18101   (610) 434-9645
FAX: (610) 437-5721
Contact: Thomas H. Christman, Exec. Dir.

Trust established in 1934 in PA.
Donor(s): Harry C. Trexler,‡ Mary M. Trexler.‡
Financial data (yr. ended 03/31/00): Grants paid, $4,288,375; assets, $137,993,764 (M); expenditures, $5,150,451; qualifying distributions, $4,507,439.
Limitations: Giving limited to Lehigh County, PA.
Publications: Occasional report, application guidelines.
Application information: Application form not required.
Officer: Thomas H. Christman, Exec. Dir.
Trustees: Dexter F. Baker, Daniel G. Gambet, Malcolm J. Gross, Carl J.W. Hessinger, Kathryn Stephanoff.
EIN: 231162215
Codes: FD, FM

46001
Hansjoerg Wyss AO Medical Foundation
c/o Joseph M. Fisher
1690 Russell Rd.
Paoli, PA 19301

Established in 1999 in PA.
Donor(s): Hansjoerg Wyss.
Financial data (yr. ended 12/31/00): Grants paid, $4,132,010; assets, $29,078,518 (M); expenditures, $4,382,171; qualifying distributions, $4,119,200.
Limitations: Applications not accepted. Giving on a national basis.
Application information: Contributes only to pre-selected organizations.
Officers: Hansjoerg Wyss, Chair.; Joseph Fisher, Secy.
EIN: 233012622
Codes: FD, FM

46002
Bayer Foundation
(Formerly Miles Inc. Foundation)
100 Bayer Rd.
Pittsburgh, PA 15205-9741   (412) 777-2000
URL: http://www.bayerus.com/search/index.html
Contact: Rebecca Lucore, Exec. Dir.

Established in 1985 in PA.
Donor(s): Bayer Corp.
Financial data (yr. ended 12/31/01): Grants paid, $4,127,006; assets, $48,563,325 (M); gifts received, $1,437,053; expenditures, $4,127,006; qualifying distributions, $4,127,006.
Limitations: Giving primarily in communities where Bayer operations are located.
Publications: Application guidelines.
Application information: Application form required.
Officers and Directors:* Joseph A. Akers, Pres.; Margo L. Barnes, V.P.; Thomas E. Kerr, Secy.; Jon

R. Wyne, Treas.; Rebecca Lucore, Exec. Dir.; Nicholas T. Cullen, Jr., Helge H. Wehmeier.
EIN: 251508079
Codes: CS, FD, CD, FM

46003
The Henry L. Hillman Foundation
2000 Grant Bldg.
Pittsburgh, PA 15219 (412) 338-3466
FAX: (412) 338-3463; E-mail: foundation@hillmanfo.com
Contact: Ronald W. Wertz, Secy. and Exec. Dir.

Established in 1964 in PA.
Donor(s): Henry L. Hillman.
Financial data (yr. ended 12/31/00): Grants paid, $4,098,150; assets, $89,438,347 (M); gifts received, $9,875,773; expenditures, $4,454,600; qualifying distributions, $4,133,302.
Limitations: Giving primarily in Pittsburgh and southwestern PA.
Publications: Application guidelines.
Application information: Application form not required.
Officers and Directors:* Henry L. Hillman,* Pres.; Ronald W. Wertz,* Secy. and Exec. Dir.; Lawrence M. Wagner, Treas.; H. Vaughan Blaxter III.
EIN: 256065959
Codes: FD, FM

46004
Dominion Foundation
(Formerly Consolidated Natural Gas Company Foundation)
c/o CNG Tower
625 Liberty Ave., 22nd Fl.
Pittsburgh, PA 15222-3199 (412) 690-1376
FAX: (412) 690-7608; URL: http://www.dom.com/about/community/foundation/index.jsp
Contact: James C. Mesloh, Exec. Dir.

Established about 1985 in PA.
Donor(s): Consolidated Natural Gas Co., Dominion Resources, Inc.
Financial data (yr. ended 12/31/00): Grants paid, $4,084,563; assets, $8,048,954 (M); expenditures, $4,213,054; qualifying distributions, $4,184,874.
Limitations: Giving primarily in LA, NC, NY, OH, PA, VA, WV, and areas where the company has business interests.
Publications: Informational brochure (including application guidelines).
Application information: Application form not required.
Officers and Directors:* W.C. Hau, Jr.,* Pres.; M.N. Grier,* V.P.; J.C. Mesloh,* Exec. Dir.; T.F. Farrell, E.S. Teig Hardy, H.D. Riley, P.E. Riley, Jr., E.M. Roacn, Jr.
Trustee: Mellon Bank, N.A.
EIN: 136077762
Codes: CS, FD, CD, FM

46005
Samuel M. Soref & Helene K. Soref Foundation
c/o First Union National Bank
123 S. Broad St., PA1308
Philadelphia, PA 19109-1199

Established in 1983 in FL.
Financial data (yr. ended 12/31/00): Grants paid, $3,857,300; assets, $43,124,999 (M); expenditures, $4,093,283; qualifying distributions, $3,811,535.
Limitations: Applications not accepted. Giving on a national basis.
Application information: Contributes only to pre-selected organizations.
Trustees: Benjamin F. Breslauer, Stephen K. Breslauer, First Union National Bank.

EIN: 592246963
Codes: FD

46006
Roy A. Hunt Foundation
1 Bigelow Sq., Ste. 630
Pittsburgh, PA 15219-3030 (412) 281-8734
FAX: (412) 255-0522; E-mail: info@rahuntfdn.org; URL: http://www.rahuntfdn.org
Contact: Torrence M. Hunt, Jr., Pres.

Established in 1966 in PA.
Donor(s): Roy A. Hunt.‡
Financial data (yr. ended 05/31/02): Grants paid, $3,790,039; assets, $81,535,907 (M); expenditures, $4,306,484; qualifying distributions, $4,200,769.
Limitations: Giving primarily in the Boston, MA, and Pittsburgh, PA, areas.
Application information: See Web site for application information. Application form required.
Officer and Trustees:* Torrence M. Hunt, Jr., Pres.; Helen Hunt Bouscaren, Susan Hunt Hollingsworth, A. James Hunt, Andrew McQ. Hunt, Caroline H. Hunt, Cathryn J. Hunt, Christopher M. Hunt, Daniel K. Hunt, John B. Hunt, Richard M. Hunt, Roy A. Hunt III, Torrence M. Hunt, Sr., William E. Hunt, Marion M. Hunt-Badiner, Rachel Hunt Knowles, Joan F. Scott.
EIN: 256105162
Codes: FD, FM

46007
The Wolf Creek Charitable Foundation
c/o PNC Bank, N.A., Tax Dept.
1600 Market St., 29th Fl.
Philadelphia, PA 19103-7240

Established in 1995 in WY.
Donor(s): A.W. Berry Charitable Remainder Unitrust.
Financial data (yr. ended 12/31/01): Grants paid, $3,788,950; assets, $78,365,726 (M); expenditures, $4,152,595; qualifying distributions, $3,791,074.
Limitations: Applications not accepted.
Application information: Contributes only to pre-selected organizations.
Trustee: Robert Berry.
Agent: PNC Bank, N.A.
EIN: 830310959
Codes: FD

46008
Katherine Mabis McKenna Foundation, Inc.
P.O. Box 186
Latrobe, PA 15650 (724) 537-6900
Contact: Linda McKenna Boxx, Chair.

Incorporated in 1969 in PA.
Donor(s): Katherine M. McKenna.‡
Financial data (yr. ended 12/31/00): Grants paid, $3,717,750; assets, $85,335,916 (M); expenditures, $4,227,822; qualifying distributions, $3,894,751.
Limitations: Giving primarily in Westmoreland County, PA.
Publications: Program policy statement.
Application information: Application form not required.
Officers and Directors:* Linda McKenna Boxx,* Chair.; Wilma F. McKenna,* Vice-Chair.; Zan McKenna Rich,* Secy.; T. William Boxx, Treas.
Trustee: Mellon Bank, N.A.
EIN: 237042752
Codes: FD, FM

46009
Edith L. Trees Charitable Trust
c/o PNC Bank, N.A., MS: P3-POLV-27-1
1 Oliver Plz., 210 6th Ave.
Pittsburgh, PA 15222-2602 (412) 762-3808
Contact: James M. Ferguson III, Trust Off., PNC Bank, N.A.

Established around 1976.
Donor(s): Edith L. Trees Trust.
Financial data (yr. ended 12/31/01): Grants paid, $3,594,470; assets, $68,220,691 (M); gifts received, $2,136,268; expenditures, $3,828,515; qualifying distributions, $3,544,762.
Limitations: Giving primarily in PA.
Trustees: J. Murray Egan, PNC Bank, N.A.
EIN: 256026443
Codes: FD, FM

46010
The Eberly Foundation
2 W. Main St., Ste. 600
Uniontown, PA 15401-3448 (724) 438-3789
FAX: (724) 438-3856
Contact: Robert E. Eberly, Pres.

Established in 1963 in PA.
Financial data (yr. ended 12/31/01): Grants paid, $3,494,803; assets, $17,694,731 (M); expenditures, $3,910,707; qualifying distributions, $3,815,803.
Limitations: Giving primarily in OK, PA, and WV.
Publications: Annual report.
Application information: Application form not required.
Officers: Robert E. Eberly, Pres. and Treas.; Patricia H. Miller, V.P. and Secy.
Trustees: Carolyn E. Blaney, Ruth Ann Carter, Carolyn Jill Drost, Paul O. Eberly, Robert E. Eberly, Jr.
EIN: 237070246
Codes: FD, FM

46011
The Mary Hillman Jennings Foundation
625 Stanwix St., Ste. 2203
Pittsburgh, PA 15222 (412) 434-5606
FAX: (412) 434-5907
Contact: Paul Euwer, Jr., Exec. Dir.

Incorporated in 1968 in PA.
Donor(s): Mary Hillman Jennings.‡
Financial data (yr. ended 12/31/00): Grants paid, $3,408,000; assets, $49,843,763 (M); expenditures, $4,338,621; qualifying distributions, $3,633,374.
Limitations: Giving primarily in the Pittsburgh, PA, area.
Application information: Application form not required.
Officers and Directors:* Evan D. Jennings II,* Pres.; Andrew L. Weil,* Secy.; Irving A. Wechsler,* Treas.; Paul Euwer, Jr.,* Exec. Dir.; Christina Jennings, Cynthia B. Jennings.
EIN: 237002091
Codes: FD

46012
The Benjamin and Mary Siddons Measey Foundation
225 N. Olive St.
P.O. Box 258
Media, PA 19063 (610) 566-5800
Contact: James C. Brennan, Mgr.

Trust established in 1958 in PA.
Donor(s): William Maul Measey.‡
Financial data (yr. ended 12/31/01): Grants paid, $3,014,891; assets, $55,598,194 (M); expenditures, $3,319,546; qualifying distributions, $3,065,078.

Limitations: Giving limited to Philadelphia, PA.
Publications: Informational brochure.
Application information: Accepts applications only for medical libraries. Scholarship applications should be made to the dean of the particular medical school. Application form not required.
Officer: Matthew S. Donaldson, Jr., Secy.
Board of Managers: Brooke Roberts, M.D., Chair.; Clyde F. Barker, M.D.; Marshall E. Blume, Ph.D.; James C. Brennan, Truman G. Schnabel, M.D.
EIN: 236298781
Codes: FD, FM

46013
Oxford Foundation, Inc.
125D Lancaster Ave.
Strasburg, PA 17579   (717) 687-9335
FAX: (717) 687-9336; E-mail: pcalhoun@oxfordfoundation.org; URL: http://www.oxfordfoundation.org
Contact: Philip L. Calhoun, Exec. Dir.

Incorporated in 1947 in DE.
Donor(s): John H. Ware III,‡ Marian S. Ware.
Financial data (yr. ended 12/31/01): Grants paid, $3,010,843; assets, $62,681,937 (M); expenditures, $3,480,265; qualifying distributions, $3,149,573.
Limitations: Giving primarily in Lanaster and Chester counties, PA.
Publications: Occasional report, application guidelines.
Application information: See foundation Web site for application details. Application form not required.
Officers and Trustees:* Paul W. Ware,* Chair. and Pres.; John H. Ware IV,* V.P.; Marilyn W. Lewis,* Secy.; Carol W. Gates,* Treas.; Philip L. Calhoun, Exec. Dir.; Marian S. Ware, Emeritus Tr.
EIN: 236278067
Codes: FD

46014
The RAF Foundation
1 Pitcairn Pl., Ste. 2100
165 Township Line Rd.
Jenkintown, PA 19046-3593
Contact: The Trustees

Established in 1984 in PA.
Donor(s): Robert A. Fox, Bar Plate Mfg., Ferche Millwork, Hardware Supply Co., Vinyl Building Products, Inc.
Financial data (yr. ended 11/30/01): Grants paid, $2,968,612; assets, $6,089,845 (M); gifts received, $893,250; expenditures, $3,031,488; qualifying distributions, $2,965,155.
Limitations: Giving primarily in Philadelphia, PA.
Trustees: Esther G. Fox, Robert A. Fox.
EIN: 232331199
Codes: FD

46015
Claneil Foundation, Inc.
630 W. Germantown Pike, Ste. 400
Plymouth Meeting, PA 19462-1059
Contact: Cathy M. Weiss, Exec. Dir.

Incorporated in 1968 in DE.
Donor(s): Henry S. McNeil,‡ Claneil Enterprises, Inc.
Financial data (yr. ended 12/31/01): Grants paid, $2,948,246; assets, $51,200,000 (M); gifts received, $13,100,000; expenditures, $3,030,570; qualifying distributions, $2,260,679.
Limitations: Giving primarily in southeastern PA.
Publications: Informational brochure (including application guidelines).

Application information: Applications accepted between Jan. 1 and Feb. 15 and July 1 and Aug. 15; grant requests over $10,000 by invitation only. Application form required.
Officers and Directors:* Henry A. Jordan,* Chair.; Marjorie M. Findlay, V.P.; Langhorne B. Smith,* Treas.; Cathy M. Weiss, Exec. Dir.; Geoffrey T. Freeman, Jennifer McNeil, Robert D. McNeil, Gretchen Menzies.
EIN: 236445450
Codes: FD

46016
Safeguard Scientifics Foundation
800 The Safeguard Bldg.
435 Devon Park Dr.
Wayne, PA 19087-1945
Contact: Dorie Culp, V.P., Human Resources

Established in 1989 in PA.
Donor(s): Safeguard Scientifics, Inc.
Financial data (yr. ended 12/31/00): Grants paid, $2,929,806; assets, $59,661 (M); gifts received, $2,546,000; expenditures, $2,931,906; qualifying distributions, $2,929,806.
Limitations: Applications not accepted. Giving primarily in Philadelphia, PA.
Application information: Contributes only to pre-selected organizations.
Officers and Directors:* Warren V. Musser,* Pres.; Joe De Santo, V.P.; Harry Wallaesa,* V.P.; Jim Ounsworth, Secy.; Gerald Blitstein, Treas.
EIN: 232571278
Codes: CS, FD, CD

46017
GlaxoSmithKline Foundation
(Formerly SmithKline Beecham Foundation)
1 Franklin Plz.
P.O. Box 7929
Philadelphia, PA 19101   (215) 751-7024
Additional tel.: (215) 751-5171; FAX: (215) 751-7655
Contact: Jean Glenn, Dir.

Foundation established in 1967 in DE.
Donor(s): SmithKline Beecham Corp.
Financial data (yr. ended 12/31/00): Grants paid, $2,785,297; assets, $3,401,675 (M); gifts received, $3,598,448; expenditures, $3,593,751; qualifying distributions, $2,680,242.
Limitations: Applications not accepted. Giving primarily in Philadelphia, PA.
Application information: Unsolicited request for funds not accepted or acknowledged. The scholarship program has been terminated. The foundation only distributes matching gifts.
Officers: Robert Carr, Pres.
EIN: 232120418
Codes: CS, FD, CD

46018
The Vanguard Group Foundation
100 Vanguard Blvd.
Malvern, PA 19355
Application address: c/o Tami F. Wise, P.O. Box 2600 (V36), Valley Forge, PA 19482, tel.: (610) 669-1000
Contact: Tami F. Wise, Dir., Corp. Contribs.

Established in 1992 in PA.
Donor(s): The Vanguard Group, Inc.
Financial data (yr. ended 12/31/00): Grants paid, $2,726,195; assets, $3,846,048 (M); gifts received, $3,007,326; expenditures, $2,736,504; qualifying distributions, $2,733,400.
Limitations: Giving primarily in the greater Philadelphia, PA, metropolitan area.
Application information: Accepts Delaware Valley Grantmakers Common Grant Application and Common Report Form. Application form required.
Officers: John J. Brennan, C.E.O.; James H. Gately, V.P.; F. William McNabb, V.P.; Raymond J. Klapinsky, Secy.; Ralph K. Packard, Treas.
EIN: 232699769
Codes: CS, FD, CD

46019
The Davenport Family Foundation
P.O. Box 178
Pocopson, PA 19366-9998   (610) 527-7347

Established in 1997 in PA.
Donor(s): Peter D. Davenport.
Financial data (yr. ended 12/31/00): Grants paid, $2,600,729; assets, $61,905,075 (M); expenditures, $3,061,925; qualifying distributions, $2,752,403.
Limitations: Applications not accepted. Giving primarily in CT, NY, and PA.
Application information: Contributes only to pre-selected organizations.
Trustees: Sharon A. Byrne, Peter D. Davenport, Sylvia Davenport, William C. Pickett III.
EIN: 237871419
Codes: FD

46020
Giant Eagle Foundation
101 Kappa Dr.
Pittsburgh, PA 15238   (412) 963-6200
Contact: Jody Clark

Established around 1955.
Donor(s): Giant Eagle, Inc.
Financial data (yr. ended 08/31/01): Grants paid, $2,594,573; assets, $18,844,565 (M); gifts received, $3,600,703; expenditures, $2,789,455; qualifying distributions, $2,594,573.
Limitations: Giving primarily in PA, with emphasis on Pittsburgh.
Trustees: Gerald Chait, Edward Moravitz, Donald S. Plung, Charles Porter, David Shapira, Norman Weizenbaum.
EIN: 256033905
Codes: CS, FD, CD, GTI

46021
Marlin Miller, Jr. Family Foundation
211 N. Tulpehocken Rd.
Reading, PA 19601
Contact: Marlin Miller, Jr., Tr.

Established in 1989 in PA.
Donor(s): Marlin Miller, Jr.
Financial data (yr. ended 12/31/00): Grants paid, $2,514,078; assets, $719,289 (M); expenditures, $2,519,495; qualifying distributions, $2,513,333.
Limitations: Giving primarily in NY and PA.
Trustees: Douglas Miller, Eric Miller, James H. Miller, Marlin Miller, Jr., Regina Miller.
EIN: 232591890
Codes: FD

46022
Armstrong Foundation
(Formerly Armstrong World Industries Charitable Foundation)
P.O. Box 3001
Lancaster, PA 17604   (717) 397-0611
Contact: C.L. Collova, Pres.

Established in 1985 in PA.
Donor(s): Armstrong World Industries, Inc.
Financial data (yr. ended 12/31/00): Grants paid, $2,510,441; assets, $6,619,011 (M); expenditures, $2,589,442; qualifying distributions, $2,507,597.
Limitations: Applications not accepted. Giving on a national basis.

Application information: Contributes only to pre-selected organizations. Unsolicited requests for funds not considered or acknowledged.
Officers and Directors:* C.L. Collova,* Pres.; D.L. Boles,* V.P.; R.J. Shannon, Jr.,* V.P.; J.R. Desanto,* Secy.; J.R. Wittenburg, Treas.; C.R. Witmer.
EIN: 232387950
Codes: CS, FD, CD

46023
The McLean Contributionship
945 Haverford Rd.
Bryn Mawr, PA 19010 (610) 527-6330
FAX: (610) 527-9733; URL: http://fdncenter.org/grantmaker/mclean
Contact: Sandra L. McLean, Exec. Dir.

Trust established in 1951 in PA.
Donor(s): William L. McLean, Jr.,‡ Robert McLean,‡ William L. McLean III, William Clarke Mason,‡ William L. McLean IV, Sandra McLean, Lisa McLean, Bulletin Co., Independent Publication, Inc.
Financial data (yr. ended 12/31/00): Grants paid, $2,494,815; assets, $51,258,803 (M); gifts received, $176,282; expenditures, $2,840,867; qualifying distributions, $2,542,960.
Limitations: Giving primarily in the greater metropolitan Philadelphia, PA, area.
Publications: Application guidelines.
Application information: Accepts Delaware Valley Grantmakers Common Grant Application. Application form not required.
Officers and Trustees:* William L. McLean III,* Chair.; William L. McLean IV,* Vice-Chair.; Charles E. Catherwood, Treas.; Sandra L. McLean, Exec. Dir.; Jean Bodine, Joseph K. Gordon, Carolyn Raymond.
Advisory Committee: Leila Gordon Dyer, Hunter R. Gordon.
EIN: 236396940
Codes: FD

46024
Patricia Kind Family Foundation
c/o Glenmede Trust Co.
1650 Market St.
Philadelphia, PA 19103
Application address: 7707 Pine Rd., Wyndmoor, PA 19038; FAX: (215) 233-2569; E-mail: PKFFoundation@comcast.net
Contact: Laura Kind McKenna, Managing Tr.

Established in 1996 in PA.
Donor(s): Hedwig A. van Amerigen,‡ Louis van Amerigen.‡
Financial data (yr. ended 12/31/01): Grants paid, $2,427,600; assets, $29,634,063 (M); expenditures, $2,489,632; qualifying distributions, $3,229,546.
Limitations: Giving primarily in Philadelphia, PA and surrounding counties.
Publications: Annual report (including application guidelines), grants list, informational brochure (including application guidelines).
Trustees: Laura Kind McKenna, Managing Tr.; Christina Kind Baiocchi, Ken Kind, Patricia Kind, Philip Kind, Valerie Kind-Rubin, Andrew Kindfuller.
EIN: 237839035
Codes: FD

46025
Berks County Community Foundation
P.O. Box 212
Reading, PA 19603-0212 (610) 685-2223
FAX: (610) 685-2240; E-mail: info@bccf.org; URL: http://www.bccf.org
Contact: Kevin K. Murphy, Pres.

Established in 1994 in PA.
Financial data (yr. ended 06/30/02): Grants paid, $2,389,165; assets, $26,171,740 (L); gifts received, $5,524,490; expenditures, $3,301,641.
Limitations: Giving limited to Berks County, PA for discretionary funds.
Publications: Annual report, application guidelines, grants list, informational brochure (including application guidelines), financial statement.
Application information: Application form required.
Officers and Directors:* Robert W. Cardy,* Chair.; Samuel A. McCullough, Vice-Chair.; Kevin K. Murphy,* Pres.; J. William Widing,* Secy.; Andrew Maier II, Treas.; Jan Armfield, Thomas A. Beaver, Mary M. Bertolet, G. Walton Cottrell, Denise M. Draeger, P. Michael Ehlerman, Ronald Foy, T. Jerome Holleran, Julia H. Klein, William Moeller, Glenn E. Moyer, Leon S. Myers, Paul R. Roedel, David L. Thun, Ramona Turpin, Harry D. Yoder.
EIN: 232769892
Codes: CM, FD

46026
Samuel S. Fels Fund
1616 Walnut St., Ste. 800
Philadelphia, PA 19103-5313 (215) 731-9455
FAX: (215) 731-9457; E-mail: samfels.org; URL: http://www.samfels.org
Contact: Helen Cunningham, Exec. Dir.

Incorporated in 1935 in PA.
Donor(s): Samuel S. Fels.‡
Financial data (yr. ended 12/31/01): Grants paid, $2,368,036; assets, $49,017,145 (M); expenditures, $2,756,689; qualifying distributions, $2,673,957.
Limitations: Giving limited to the City of Philadelphia, PA.
Publications: Annual report (including application guidelines), application guidelines.
Application information: Applicant must request guidelines before submitting proposals; the fund accepts Delaware Valley Grantmakers Common Grant Application and Common Report Form. Application form required.
Officers and Directors:* Ida K. Chen, Pres.; Sandra Featherman,* V.P.; Helen Cunningham,* Secy. and Exec. Dir.; David H. Wice,* Treas.; Iso Briselli, Bro. Daniel Burke, F.S.C., Christine James, David C. Melnicoff, Emmanuel Ortiz.
EIN: 231365325
Codes: FD

46027
The Greater Harrisburg Foundation
200 N. 3rd St., 8th Fl.
P.O. Box 678
Harrisburg, PA 17108-0678 (717) 236-5040
FAX: (717) 231-4463; E-mail: info@ght.org; URL: http://www.ghf.org
Contact: Janice R. Black, C.E.O. and Pres.

Established in 1920 in PA; assets first acquired in 1940; grants first made in the mid-1940's.
Financial data (yr. ended 12/31/01): Grants paid, $2,338,397; assets, $23,361,136 (M); gifts received, $6,534,828; expenditures, $5,591,919.
Limitations: Giving primarily in PA, with emphasis on Dauphin, Cumberland, Franklin, Perry, and Lebanon counties.
Publications: Annual report (including application guidelines), informational brochure (including application guidelines), application guidelines, newsletter, financial statement, grants list, program policy statement.
Application information: Call program officer for current application guidelines. Application form available on website. Application form required.
Officers and Distribution Committee:* William Lehr, Jr.,* Chair.; Janice R. Black, C.E.O. and Pres.; Dorothea Aronson, Raymond L. Gover, Leonardo Herrado, Linda Hicks, Joan R. Holman, Ellen Brody Hughes, Harold McInnes, James Mead, John Oyler, Velma Redmond, David Schankweiler, Hasu P. Shah, Kathleen Smarilli, Jonathan Vipond, Mary Webber, Robert Zvillinger.
Trustee Banks: Allfirst, Citizens Bank of Southern Pennsylvania, Farmers & Merchants Trust Co., Farmers Trust of Carlisle, Financial Trust Services, First National Bank & Trust of Waynesboro, First National Bank of Greencastle, First Union National Bank, Fulton Bank, GHF, Inc., Hershey Trust Co., The Juniata Valley Bank, M & T Bank, Mellon Bank, Commonwealth Region, PNC Bank, N.A., Pennsylvania State Bank, Sentry Trust Co., Valley Bank and Trust Co.
EIN: 010564355
Codes: CM, FD

46028
Barra Foundation, Inc.
8200 Flourtown Ave., Ste. 12
Wyndmoor, PA 19038-7976 (215) 233-5115
FAX: (215) 836-1033; E-mail: william.harral@verizon.net
Contact: William Harrall, III, Pres.

Incorporated in 1963 in DE.
Donor(s): Robert L. McNeil, Jr.
Financial data (yr. ended 12/31/01): Grants paid, $2,294,353; assets, $50,692,059 (M); expenditures, $2,687,630; qualifying distributions, $2,489,133.
Limitations: Giving primarily in the Philadelphia, PA, area.
Publications: Program policy statement.
Application information: Application form required.
Officers and Directors:* Robert L. McNeil, Jr.,* Chair. and Treas.; William Harrall III, Pres.; Herman R. Hutchinson,* V.P.; Frank R. Donahue, Jr.,* Secy.; Harry E. Cerino, Robert P. Hauptfuhrer, Victoria M. LeVine, Joanna M. Lewis, Collin F. McNeil, Robert L. McNeil III, Seymour S. Preston III, Lowell S. Thomas, Jr.
EIN: 236277885
Codes: FD, FM

46029
Wyss Foundation
c/o Joseph Fisher
1690 Russell Rd.
Paoli, PA 19301
Application address: 21 Ladera Rd., Santa Fe, NM 87505, tel.: (505) 466-4616
Contact: Geoff Webb, Exec. Dir.

Established in 1999 in PA.
Donor(s): Hansjoerg Wyss.
Financial data (yr. ended 12/31/00): Grants paid, $2,225,732; assets, $46,340,891 (M); expenditures, $2,720,383; qualifying distributions, $2,397,026.
Limitations: Giving primarily from the Rocky Mountains to the West Coast, and AK. Large funding in AZ, Washington, DC, and PA; giving also in CA, CO, NM, NY, OR and UT.
Officers: Hansjoerg Wyss, Chair.; Joseph Fisher, Secy.; Geoff Webb, Exec. Dir.
EIN: 231823874

Codes: FD

46030
The Presser Foundation
385 Lancaster Ave., No. 205
Haverford, PA 19041 (610) 658-9030
Contact: Edith A. Reinhardt, Pres.

Founded in 1916; incorporated in 1939 in PA.
Donor(s): Theodore Presser.‡
Financial data (yr. ended 06/30/01): Grants paid, $2,180,348; assets, $58,243,872 (M); gifts received, $1,203,569; expenditures, $2,625,335; qualifying distributions, $2,481,803; giving activities include $122,158 for program-related investments.
Application information: Application forms available for financial aid to needy music teachers and for scholarships. Application form required.
Officers and Trustees:* Edith A. Reinhardt,* Pres.; Thomas M. Hyndman, Jr.,* V.P.; Bruce Montgomery,* Secy.; William M. Davison IV,* Treas.; Leon Bates, David Boe, Robert Capanna, Anthony P. Checchia, Robert W. Denious, Herbert P. Evert, Martin A. Hechscher, Helen Laird, Wendell Pritchett, Michael Stairs, Henderson Supplee III, Radclyffe F. Thompson, Vera Wilson.
EIN: 232164013
Codes: FD, GTI

46031
Massey Charitable Trust
P.O. Box 1178
Coraopolis, PA 15108 (412) 262-5992
Contact: Walter J. Carroll, Managing Trustee

Established in 1968.
Donor(s): H.B. Massey,‡ Doris J. Massey.‡
Financial data (yr. ended 12/31/00): Grants paid, $2,141,531; assets, $41,671,434 (M); expenditures, $2,298,608; qualifying distributions, $2,191,033.
Limitations: Giving primarily in Pittsburgh and western PA.
Application information: Application form not required.
Officer and Trustees:* Walter J. Carroll,* Managing Tr.; Daniel B. Carroll, Robert C. Connolly, Robert M. Entwisle, Joe B. Massey.
EIN: 237007897
Codes: FD

46032
The Hamilton Family Foundation
200 Eagle Rd., Ste. 316
Wayne, PA 19087 (610) 975-0517
FAX: (610) 293-0967
Contact: Cynthia Smith, Admin.

Established in 1992 in PA.
Donor(s): Dorrance H. Hamilton.
Financial data (yr. ended 12/31/01): Grants paid, $2,121,077; assets, $43,305,076 (M); expenditures, $2,370,045; qualifying distributions, $2,116,322.
Limitations: Giving primarily in Philadelphia, PA and surrounding counties.
Publications: Application guidelines.
Application information: Proposals accepted only once during a 12-month period. Application form required.
Officer and Directors:* Dorrance H. Hamilton,* Pres.; Barbara R. Cobb, Margaret H. Duprey, Nathaniel P. Hamilton, S. Matthews V. Hamilton, Jr., Francis J. Mirabello.
EIN: 232684976
Codes: FD

46033
The Carthage Foundation
1 Oxford Ctr.
301 Grant St., Ste. 3900
Pittsburgh, PA 15219-6401 (412) 392-2900
URL: http://www.scaife.com
Contact: Micahel W. Gleba, Treas.

Incorporated in 1964 in PA.
Donor(s): Richard M. Scaife.
Financial data (yr. ended 12/31/01): Grants paid, $2,115,000; assets, $23,705,949 (M); gifts received, $3,499,415; expenditures, $3,853,679; qualifying distributions, $2,115,000.
Publications: Annual report.
Application information: The foundation does not issue a separate program policy statement or grant application guidelines. The foundation acknowledges receipt of proposals. Application form not required.
Officers and Trustees:* Richard M. Scaife,* Chair.; R. Daniel McMichael,* Secy.; Michael W. Gleba,* Treas.; Alexis J. Konkol, W. McCook Miller, Jr., Roger W. Robinson, Jr.
EIN: 256067979
Codes: FD

46034
The Graham Foundation
P.O. Box 1104
York, PA 17405-1104 (717) 849-4001
Contact: William H. Kerlin, Jr., Tr.

Established in 1986 in PA.
Donor(s): Graham Engineering Corp., Graham Capital Corp., Donald C. Graham.
Financial data (yr. ended 06/30/01): Grants paid, $2,102,810; assets, $25,317,099 (M); gifts received, $30,000; expenditures, $2,177,081; qualifying distributions, $2,089,717.
Limitations: Giving primarily in York, PA.
Application information: Application form not required.
Trustees: Donald C. Graham, William H. Kerlin, Jr.
EIN: 236805421
Codes: CS, FD, CD

46035
Sedwick Foundation
c/o Kirby J. Campbell, Tr.
1 Armstrong Pl.
Butler, PA 16001

Established in 1986 in PA.
Donor(s): Armstrong Utilities, Inc., Jay L. Sedwick, Linda Sedwick, Armstrong Communications, Inc., Armstrong Telephone Co. of West Virginia, Armstrong Telephone Co. of Maryland.
Financial data (yr. ended 06/30/00): Grants paid, $2,068,000; assets, $10,964,507 (M); gifts received, $585,420; expenditures, $2,236,545; qualifying distributions, $2,056,897.
Limitations: Applications not accepted. Giving primarily in Butler, PA.
Application information: Contributes only to pre-selected organizations.
Trustees: Kirby J. Campbell, Jay L. Sedwick, William C. Stewart.
EIN: 256284774
Codes: CS, FD, CD

46036
The Huston Foundation
2 Tower Bridge, Ste. 190
1 Fayette St.
Conshohocken, PA 19428-2064
(610) 832-4949
Additional tel.: (610) 832-4954; *FAX:* (610) 832-4949; *E-mail:* hustonfndn@aol.com
Contact: Susan B. Heilman, Exec. Asst.

Incorporated in 1957 in PA.
Donor(s): Charles L. Huston, Jr.,‡ Ruth Huston.‡
Financial data (yr. ended 12/31/00): Grants paid, $2,059,741; assets, $41,303,651 (M); expenditures, $2,899,856; qualifying distributions, $2,530,025.
Limitations: Giving primarily in southeastern PA.
Publications: Application guidelines, annual report, informational brochure (including application guidelines).
Application information: Accepts Delaware Valley Grantmakers Common Grant Application and Common Report Form. Application form required.
Officers: Nancy G. Huston, Pres.; Nancy Huston Hansen, V.P., Evangelical Rels.; Charles L. Huston III, V.P., Community Rels. and Dir., Opers.; Elinor Huston Lashley, V.P., Arts and Cultural Rels.; Rebecca L. Huston, Secy.; Charles L. Huston IV, Treas.
EIN: 236284125
Codes: FD

46037
Raymond & Ruth Perelman Education Foundation
225 City Line Ave., Ste. 14
Bala Cynwyd, PA 19004

Established in 1995.
Financial data (yr. ended 04/30/00): Grants paid, $2,056,200; assets, $52,209,245 (M); gifts received, $548,899; expenditures, $3,173,895; qualifying distributions, $1,997,444.
Limitations: Giving primarily in PA.
Trustees: Raymond G. Perelman, Ruth Perelman.
EIN: 232819735
Codes: FD

46038
McDonald's Kid's Charities
401 City Ave., Ste. 800
Bala Cynwyd, PA 19004 (610) 668-6700

Donor(s): McDonald's Corp., Formax, Inc., Keystone Foods Corp., McClement Sales, Mead Containers, Simkins Industries, Inc., Union Camp Corp., Weyerhaeuser Paper Co., E.I. du Pont de Nemours and Co.
Financial data (yr. ended 07/31/99): Grants paid, $2,052,261; assets, $4,207,305 (M); gifts received, $118,888; expenditures, $7,168,303; qualifying distributions, $2,051,665; giving activities include $7,168,303 for programs.
Limitations: Applications not accepted. Giving primarily in IL, with emphasis on Oak Brook, and PA.
Application information: Contributes only to pre-selected organizations.
Officers and Directors:* Herbert Lotman,* Pres.; Frank Quinn,* V.P.; Stanley Fronczkowski,* Secy.-Treas.; Betsy Rawls, Exec. Dir.; Chris Gabriel.
EIN: 232148498
Codes: CS, FD, CD

46039
The Stewart Huston Charitable Trust
50 S. 1st Ave., 2nd Fl.
Coatesville, PA 19320 (610) 384-2666
FAX: (610) 384-3396; E-mail:
admin@stewarthuston.org
Contact: Scott G. Huston, Exec. Dir.

Established in 1989 in PA.
Donor(s): Stewart Huston.‡
Financial data (yr. ended 12/31/00): Grants paid, $1,989,454; assets, $24,087,618 (M); expenditures, $2,522,853; qualifying distributions, $2,288,928.
Limitations: Giving primarily in the Savannah, GA, area and Coatesville and Chester County, PA.
Publications: Application guidelines, annual report, informational brochure.
Application information: Application form required.
Officer and Trustees:* Scott G. Huston,* Exec. Dir.; Samuel A. Cann, Charles L. Huston III, Louis N. Seltzer.
EIN: 232612599
Codes: FD

46040
R. K. Mellon Family Foundation
P.O. Box 690
Ligonier, PA 15658-0690 (724) 238-5269
Contact: Michael Watson, Dir.

Incorporated in PA in 1978 through consolidation of Landfall, Loyalhanna, Rachelwood, and Cassandra Mellon Henderson foundations.
Donor(s): Seward Prosser Mellon, Richard P. Mellon, Constance B. Mellon,‡ Cassandra M. Milbury.
Financial data (yr. ended 12/31/01): Grants paid, $1,944,550; assets, $39,571,913 (M); expenditures, $2,265,909; qualifying distributions, $2,136,624.
Limitations: Giving primarily in western PA.
Publications: Informational brochure (including application guidelines).
Application information: Application form required.
Officers and Trustees:* Richard P. Mellon,* Chair.; Scott D. Izzo, Secy.; Robert B. Burr, Jr.,* Treas.; John Turcik, Cont.; Michael Watson, Dir.; W. Russell G. Byers, Jr., Catharine M. Cathey, Richard A. Mellon, Seward Prosser Mellon.
EIN: 251356145
Codes: FD

46041
Richardson Family Foundation, Inc.
Washington Trust Bldg., Rm. 418
Washington, PA 15301
Application address: P.O. Box 690338, Vero Beach, FL 32969-0338
Contact: Tomas Rene Perez, Exec. Dir.

Established in 1963 in PA.
Donor(s): Danforth K. Richardson, Marjorie H. Richardson.
Financial data (yr. ended 12/31/00): Grants paid, $1,904,125; assets, $1,502,068 (M); gifts received, $1,851,279; expenditures, $1,980,727; qualifying distributions, $1,903,000.
Limitations: Giving primarily in FL.
Application information: Application form required.
Officers: Danforth K. Richardson, Pres.; Nancy R. Luther, V.P.; Sandra R. Kahle, Secy.; Susan R. Hopkins, Treas.; Tomas Rene Perez, Exec. Dir.; Gary M. Rust, Dir. of Finance.
EIN: 591027379
Codes: FD

46042
Rossin Foundation
(Formerly Dynamet Foundation)
400 Southpointe Blvd., Ste. 220
Canonsburg, PA 15317
Contact: Viola G. Taboni, Treas.

Established in 1989 in PA.
Donor(s): Dynamet Inc., Peter C. Rossin, Ada E. Rossin.
Financial data (yr. ended 12/31/00): Grants paid, $1,896,470; assets, $21,166,973 (M); expenditures, $2,028,765; qualifying distributions, $1,879,536.
Limitations: Giving primarily in PA, with some emphasis on Pittsburgh and Washington.
Officers and Trustees:* Peter C. Rossin,* Chair.; Peter N. Stephans,* Pres.; J. Robert Van Kirk,* Secy.; Viola G. Taboni,* Treas.; Ada E. Rossin, Joan R. Stephans.
EIN: 256327217
Codes: CS, FD, CD

46043
Laurel Foundation
2 Gateway Ctr., Ste. 1800
Pittsburgh, PA 15222 (412) 765-2400
FAX: (412) 765-2407
Contact: D. Panazzi, V.P.

Incorporated in 1951 in PA.
Donor(s): C. May.
Financial data (yr. ended 12/31/00): Grants paid, $1,895,045; assets, $42,948,724 (M); gifts received, $2,510,750; expenditures, $2,316,640; qualifying distributions, $1,972,404.
Limitations: Giving primarily in southwestern PA.
Publications: Annual report (including application guidelines).
Application information: Common Grant Application form accepted but not required.
Officers and Trustees:* C. May,* Chair.; R. Meyer,* Pres.; D. Panazzi, V.P. and Secy.; T. Inglis, V.P. and Treas.; N. Fales, C. Scaife, T. Schmidt.
EIN: 256008073
Codes: FD

46044
John G. Rangos Charitable Foundation
1500 Ardmore Blvd., Ste. 407
Pittsburgh, PA 15221
URL: http://www.rangosfoundation.org
Contact: Nancy Barnhart

Established in 1987 in PA.
Donor(s): John G. Rangos, Sr.
Financial data (yr. ended 11/30/99): Grants paid, $1,867,850; assets, $11,964,051 (M); expenditures, $2,147,790; qualifying distributions, $1,867,850.
Limitations: Giving primarily in western PA.
Trustees: Alexander Rangos, Jenica Rangos, Jill Rangos, John G. Rangos, Sr., John G. Rangos, Jr.
EIN: 251599198
Codes: FD

46045
The Century Fund Trust
462 Walnut St., Ste. 202
Allentown, PA 18102-5497 (610) 434-4000
Contact: Lisa M. Curran

Established in 1985 in PA.
Financial data (yr. ended 12/31/01): Grants paid, $1,816,030; assets, $32,832,400 (M); gifts received, $4,447; expenditures, $2,025,991; qualifying distributions, $1,806,884.
Limitations: Giving primarily in the greater Lehigh Valley, PA, area.
Publications: Application guidelines.
Application information: Application form not required.
Officers and Trustees:* Alice A. Miller,* Pres.; Rev. Grant E. Harrity,* Secy.; Richard J. Hummel,* Treas.; David K. Bausch, John H. Leh II.
EIN: 226404912
Codes: FD

46046
Charles E. Ellis Grant and Scholarship Fund
c/o PNC Bank, N.A.
1600 Market St. Tax Dept., 4th Fl.
Philadelphia, PA 19103-7240 (215) 585-5597
Application address: c/o White-Williams Scholars, 21st St. & the Pkwy, 1001 Admin. Bldg., Philadelphia, PA 19107

Established in 1981 in PA.
Donor(s): Charles E. Ellis.‡
Financial data (yr. ended 06/30/01): Grants paid, $1,815,869; assets, $40,380,930 (M); expenditures, $1,991,228; qualifying distributions, $1,908,524.
Limitations: Giving limited to Philadelphia County, PA.
Publications: Application guidelines, informational brochure, program policy statement.
Application information: Funds paid directly to the educational institution the individual attends. Application form required.
Trustee: PNC Bank, N.A.
EIN: 236725618
Codes: FD, GTI

46047
Williamsport-Lycoming Foundation
(Formerly Williamsport Foundation)
220 W. 4th St., Ste. C, 3rd Fl.
Williamsport, PA 17701-6102 (570) 321-1500
FAX: (570) 321-6434; E-mail:
wlf@wlfoundation.org; URL: http://www.wlfoundation.org
Contact: Kimberley Pittman-Schulz, Pres.

Established in 1916 in PA by bank resolution.
Financial data (yr. ended 12/31/01): Grants paid, $1,785,232; assets, $46,193,175 (M); gifts received, $704,694; expenditures, $2,468,408; giving activities include $20,000 for loans.
Limitations: Giving primarily to organizations serving Lycoming County, PA.
Publications: Annual report, informational brochure, financial statement, program policy statement, application guidelines.
Application information: Application form required.
Officers and Directors:* Ann M. Alsted,* Chair.; Daniel G. Fultz, Vice-Chair.; Kimberley Pittman-Schulz,* Pres.; Robert More, Thomas C. Raup, John C. Schultz, Carol Sides, John Young.
EIN: 246013117
Codes: CM, FD

46048
John M. Hopwood Charitable Trust
c/o PNC Bank, N.A.
2 PNC Plz., 25th Fl., 620 Liberty Ave.
Pittsburgh, PA 15222-2719 (412) 762-7076
Contact: Mia Hallet Bernard

Trust established about 1948 in PA.
Donor(s): John M. Hopwood,‡ Mary S. Hopwood,‡ William T. Hopwood, Danforth K. Richardsion, Marge Richardson.
Financial data (yr. ended 12/31/01): Grants paid, $1,667,284; assets, $27,340,796 (M); expenditures, $1,926,686; qualifying distributions, $1,774,590.
Limitations: Giving primarily in western PA.
Publications: Application guidelines.

Application information: Application form not required.
Trustees: William T. Hopwood, PNC Bank, N.A.
EIN: 256022634
Codes: FD

46049
Strauss Foundation
c/o First Union National Bank
123 S. Broad St., 16th Fl.
Philadelphia, PA 19109 (215) 670-4226
Contact: Reginald Middleton, V.P., First Union National Bank

Trust established in 1951 in PA.
Donor(s): Maurice L. Strauss.
Financial data (yr. ended 12/31/00): Grants paid, $1,607,325; assets, $29,226,273 (M); expenditures, $1,821,742; qualifying distributions, $1,629,101.
Limitations: Giving primarily in PA and for organizations in Israel.
Application information: Unsolicited applications are not encouraged.
Trustees: Henry A. Gladstone, Scott Rosen Isdaner, Sandra S. Krause, Benjamin Strauss, Robert Perry Strauss.
Corporate Trustee: First Union National Bank.
EIN: 236219939
Codes: FD

46050
Bethlehem Steel Foundation
Martin Tower
1170 8th Ave., Rm. 1711
Bethlehem, PA 18016-7699 (610) 694-6940
FAX: (610) 694-1509; *E-mail:* Kostecky@bethsteel.com
Contact: James F. Kostecky, Exec. Dir.

Established in 1993 in PA.
Donor(s): Bethlehem Steel Corp.
Financial data (yr. ended 12/31/00): Grants paid, $1,580,013; assets, $238,957 (M); gifts received, $1,584,555; expenditures, $1,584,555; qualifying distributions, $1,584,414.
Limitations: Giving primarily in areas of company operations.
Publications: Annual report, application guidelines.
Application information: Application form not required.
Officers and Directors:* D.R. Dunham,* Chair.; Stephen G. Donches,* Pres.; A.E. Moffitt, Jr.,* V.P.; C.W. Campbell, Jr., Secy.; G.L. Millenbruch, Treas.; L.A. Arnett,* Cont.; James F. Kostecky, Exec. Dir.; Frank L. Fisher, Admin.; V.R. Reiner.
EIN: 232709041
Codes: CS, FD, CD

46051
Farber Family Foundation
1845 Walnut St.
Philadelphia, PA 19103-4708

Incorporated in 1992 in FL.
Donor(s): Jack Farber.
Financial data (yr. ended 12/31/01): Grants paid, $1,576,950; assets, $7,687,960 (M); expenditures, $1,599,153; qualifying distributions, $1,577,284.
Limitations: Applications not accepted. Giving primarily in PA.
Application information: Contributes only to pre-selected organizations.
Officers and Directors:* Jack Farber,* Pres.; Vivian Farber,* V.P.; David M. Farber,* V.P.; Ellen B. Kurtzman,* V.P.
EIN: 650336266
Codes: FD

46052
Orris C. Hirtzel and Beatrice Dewey Hirtzel Memorial Foundation
(Formerly Elec Material Hirtzel Memorial Foundation)
c/o Mellon Bank, N.A.
P.O. Box 185
Pittsburgh, PA 15230 (412) 234-0023
Contact: Laurie Montz

Established in 1956 in PA.
Donor(s): Orris C. Hirtzel, Beatrice Dewey Hirtzel.
Financial data (yr. ended 12/31/00): Grants paid, $1,572,074; assets, $25,322,284 (M); expenditures, $1,740,058; qualifying distributions, $1,621,226.
Limitations: Giving primarily in the Town of Ripley in Chautauqua County, NY and the City of North East in Erie County, PA.
Application information: Application form required.
Trustees: James S. Bryan, Robert E. Galbraith, James L. Johnson, Douglas P. Moorhead, Mellon Bank, N.A.
EIN: 256018933
Codes: FD, GTI

46053
Raymond & Ruth Perelman Judaica Foundation
225 City Line Ave., Ste. 14
Bala Cynwyd, PA 19004

Established in 1995.
Financial data (yr. ended 04/30/00): Grants paid, $1,556,980; assets, $36,066,807 (M); gifts received, $548,898; expenditures, $3,441,602; qualifying distributions, $1,501,345.
Limitations: Applications not accepted. Giving primarily in PA.
Application information: Contributes only to pre-selected organizations.
Trustees: Raymond G. Perelman, Ruth Perelman.
EIN: 232820841
Codes: FD

46054
Donahue Family Foundation, Inc.
1001 Liberty Ave., Ste. 850
Pittsburgh, PA 15222 (412) 471-9047
E-mail: bdonahue@thebeechwood.com
Contact: William Donahue, Pres.

Established around 1990.
Donor(s): John F. Donahue, Rhodora J. Donahue.
Financial data (yr. ended 12/31/01): Grants paid, $1,521,766; assets, $2,022,547 (M); expenditures, $1,577,355; qualifying distributions, $1,504,619.
Limitations: Giving primarily in Pittsburgh, PA.
Application information: Unsolicited requests for funds not considered. Application form not required.
Officers and Directors:* William J. Donahue,* Pres.; Daniel McGrogan,* Secy.-Treas.; Rhodora D. Barton, John F. Donahue, Rhodora J. Donahue, Alfonso D'Orazio, Katherine Freyuogel, Bishop Donald W. Wuerl.
EIN: 251619351
Codes: FD

46055
William G. Rohrer Charitable Foundation
c/o PNC Bank, N.A.
1600 Market St., 4th Fl.
Philadelphia, PA 19103-7240
Application address: c/o PNC Bank, N.A., Rt. 38 at Eastgate Dr., Moorestown, NJ 08057, tel.: (856) 755-5735
Contact: John C. Watson, V.P., PNC Bank, N.A.

Established in 1990 in NJ.
Financial data (yr. ended 12/31/99): Grants paid, $1,501,000; assets, $39,959,236 (M); gifts received, $2,000,000; expenditures, $1,855,654; qualifying distributions, $1,549,633.
Limitations: Giving primarily in NJ.
Trustees: Thomas N. Bantivoglio, Daniel J. Ragone, Linda Rohrer, PNC Bank, N.A.
EIN: 226455062
Codes: FD

46056
The Fourjay Foundation
2300 Computer Ave., Bldg. G, Ste. 1
Willow Grove, PA 19090
E-mail: info@fourjay.org; *URL:* http://www.fourjay.org
Contact: Ann Bucci, Grants Coord.

Established in 1988 in PA.
Donor(s): Eugene W. Jackson,‡ Springhouse Realty Co.
Financial data (yr. ended 12/31/01): Grants paid, $1,471,590; assets, $20,863,597 (M); expenditures, $1,716,391; qualifying distributions, $1,464,324.
Limitations: Giving limited to Philadelphia, Bucks, and Montgomery counties, PA.
Publications: Application guidelines.
Application information: Telephone calls not accepted; submit 1 complete proposal and 7 copies of cover proposal letter; only 1 application per organization accepted per year; Grant requests lacking appropriate financial information will not be accepted. All requests for foundation guidelines should be submitted in writing on the grant-seeking organization's letterhead, with the appropriate return mailing and contact information provided. Application form not required.
Directors: G.W. Jackson, Exec. Dir.; Marie L. Jackson, Thomas Lynch, D. O'Connell, Jean Robinson.
Trustees: Geoffrey W. Jackson, Marie L. Jackson, Susan J. Tressider.
EIN: 232537126
Codes: FD

46057
James Hale Steinman Foundation
8 W. King St.
P.O. Box 128
Lancaster, PA 17608-0128 (717) 291-8608
E-mail: mknopp@lnpnews.com
Contact: Mary E. Knopp

Trust established in 1952 in PA.
Donor(s): James Hale Steinman,‡ Louise Steinman von Hess,‡ Lancaster Newspapers, Inc., and others.
Financial data (yr. ended 12/31/01): Grants paid, $1,455,374; assets, $27,083,446 (M); gifts received, $1,000,000; expenditures, $1,576,091; qualifying distributions, $1,432,958.
Limitations: Giving primarily in Lancaster, PA.
Application information: Application form available for employee-related scholarships.
Officers: Caroline S. Nunan, Chair.; Beverly R. Steinman, Vice-Chair.; Dennis A. Getz, Secy.; Willis W. Shenk, Treas.
EIN: 236266377
Codes: FD, GTI

46058
Mary J. Donnelly Foundation
650 Smithfield St., Ste. 1810
Pittsburgh, PA 15222-3924 (412) 471-5828
Contact: Thomas J. Donnelly, Tr.

Trust established in 1951 in PA.
Donor(s): Mary J. Donnelly.‡

46058—PENNSYLVANIA

Financial data (yr. ended 06/30/01): Grants paid, $1,454,500; assets, $5,604,872 (M); gifts received, $3,353,040; expenditures, $1,501,608; qualifying distributions, $1,462,914.
Limitations: Giving primarily in PA.
Application information: Application form not required.
Trustees: Elizabeth A. Donnelly, Thomas J. Donnelly, Fred N. Egler, Ruth D. Egler, C. Holmes Wolfe.
EIN: 256037469
Codes: FD

46059
Allegheny Foundation
301 Grant St., Ste. 3900
Pittsburgh, PA 15219-6401   (412) 392-2900
URL: http://www.scaife.com
Contact: Exec. Dir.

Incorporated in 1953 in PA.
Donor(s): Richard M. Scaife.
Financial data (yr. ended 12/31/01): Grants paid, $1,449,000; assets, $40,260,487 (M); expenditures, $1,784,492; qualifying distributions, $1,672,763.
Limitations: Giving primarily in western PA, with emphasis on Pittsburgh.
Application information: Application form not required.
Officers and Trustees:* Richard M. Scaife,* Chair.; Joanne B. Beyer,* Pres.; Ralph H. Goettler, Doris O'Donnell, Margaret R. Scaife, Nathan J. Stark, George Weymouth, Arthur P. Ziegler, Jr.
EIN: 256012303
Codes: FD

46060
The John H. Foster Foundation
c/o Foster Mgmt. Co., Inc.
1018 W. 9th Ave.
King of Prussia, PA 19406

Established in 1984.
Donor(s): John H. Foster.
Financial data (yr. ended 12/31/00): Grants paid, $1,441,000; assets, $8,749,092 (M); expenditures, $1,861,529; qualifying distributions, $1,432,398.
Limitations: Applications not accepted. Giving primarily in CT and NY.
Application information: Contributes only to pre-selected organizations.
Officers and Directors:* John H. Foster,* Pres.; Nathan Hale,* Secy.; Stephen C. Curley,* Treas.
EIN: 133249353
Codes: FD

46061
The Eustace Foundation
c/o Cabrini Asset Mgmt., Inc.
700 S. Henderson Rd., No. 202
King of Prussia, PA 19406

Established in 1985 in PA.
Donor(s): J. Eustace Wolfington.
Financial data (yr. ended 09/30/01): Grants paid, $1,436,350; assets, $20,106,487 (M); expenditures, $1,683,530; qualifying distributions, $1,436,350.
Limitations: Applications not accepted. Giving primarily in PA; some funding nationally.
Application information: Contributes only to pre-selected organizations.
Trustee: J. Eustace Wolfington.
EIN: 222664349
Codes: FD

46062
Grace S. & W. Linton Nelson Foundation
W. Valley Business Ctr.
940 W. Valley Rd., Ste. 1601
Wayne, PA 19087   (610) 975-9169
Contact: Fred C. Aldridge, Jr., Esq., Pres.

Established in 1984 in PA.
Donor(s): W. Linton Nelson,‡ William P. Brady, Delaware Management Co.
Financial data (yr. ended 12/31/00): Grants paid, $1,435,055; assets, $28,057,800 (M); expenditures, $1,613,167; qualifying distributions, $1,536,794.
Limitations: Giving primarily in Philadelphia, PA, and the surrounding counties.
Application information: Application form not required.
Officers and Directors:* Fred C. Aldridge, Jr.,* Pres. and Treas.; James P. Schellenger,* V.P. and Secy.; William P. Brady,* V.P.
EIN: 222583922
Codes: FD

46063
John Frederick Steinman Foundation
P.O. Box 128
Lancaster, PA 17608-0128   (717) 291-8608
Additional address: 8 W. King St., Lancaster, PA 17603; E-mail: mknopp@lnpnews.com
Contact: Mary E. Knopp

Trust established in 1952 in PA.
Donor(s): John Frederick Steinman,‡ Shirley W. Steinman,‡ Lancaster Newspapers, Inc., and others.
Financial data (yr. ended 12/31/00): Grants paid, $1,429,549; assets, $30,964,523 (M); expenditures, $1,592,554; qualifying distributions, $1,429,549.
Limitations: Giving primarily in PA, with emphasis on the Lancaster area.
Application information: Application for fellowship program available upon request. Application form not required.
Officers and Trustees:* Pamela M. Thye,* Chair.; Dennis A. Getz,* Secy.; Willis W. Shenk, Treas.; John M. Buckwalter, Jack S. Gerhart, Henry Pildner, Jr.
EIN: 236266378
Codes: FD, GTI

46064
Charles M. Morris Charitable Trust
c/o National City Bank of Pennsylvania
20 Stanwix St., LOC 25-162
Pittsburgh, PA 15222
E-mail: joanna.mayo@nationcity.com; URL: http://www.morrisfoundation.org
Contact: Joanna M. Mayo, V.P., National City Bank of Pennsylvania

Established in 1988 in PA.
Donor(s): Charles M. Morris.‡
Financial data (yr. ended 12/31/01): Grants paid, $1,412,854; assets, $33,935,480 (M); expenditures, $1,614,373; qualifying distributions, $1,516,528.
Limitations: Giving primarily in Allegheny County and western PA.
Publications: Grants list, informational brochure, application guidelines, multi-year report.
Application information: Application form required.
Trustee: National City Bank of Pennsylvania.
EIN: 256312920
Codes: FD

46065
Richard C. von Hess Foundation
c/o The Glenmede Trust Co.
1650 Market St., Ste. 1200
Philadelphia, PA 19103-7391   (215) 419-6000

Established in 1989 in PA.
Donor(s): Richard C. von Hess.
Financial data (yr. ended 12/31/01): Grants paid, $1,398,260; assets, $29,764,014 (M); gifts received, $880,558; expenditures, $1,641,346; qualifying distributions, $1,500,935.
Limitations: Applications not accepted. Giving primarily in PA.
Application information: Contributes only to pre-selected organizations.
Trustees: Thomas Hills Cook, Anne Genter, Warren A. Reintzel.
EIN: 236962077
Codes: FD

46066
James B. Davidson Foundation
P.O. Box 185
Pittsburgh, PA 15230-9897
Application address: c/o Mellon Bank, N.A., 1735 Market St., Philadelphia, PA 19101, tel.: (215) 553-3208
Contact: Pat Kling

Established in 1997 in PA.
Financial data (yr. ended 12/31/01): Grants paid, $1,395,000; assets, $28,092 (M); expenditures, $1,425,169; qualifying distributions, $1,395,784.
Limitations: Giving primarily in the Philadelphia, PA area.
Trustee: Mellon Bank, N.A.
EIN: 256443887
Codes: FD

46067
Maplewood Foundation
c/o PNC Advisors Charitable Trust Committee
620 Liberty Ave., 25th Fl.
Pittsburgh, PA 15222-2705
Contact: Mia Hallett Bernard

Established in 1995 in PA.
Financial data (yr. ended 06/30/01): Grants paid, $1,389,975; assets, $22,312,779 (M); expenditures, $1,479,426; qualifying distributions, $1,389,404.
Limitations: Applications not accepted. Giving primarily in Pittsburgh, PA.
Application information: Contributes only to pre-selected organizations.
Trustees: G. William Bissell, PNC Advisors Charitable Trust COmmittee.
EIN: 256502637
Codes: FD

46068
The Wyomissing Foundation, Inc.
12 Commerce Dr.
Wyomissing, PA 19610
FAX: (610) 372-7626; E-mail: wfbbec@nnl.com
Contact: Paul R. Roedel, Pres.

Incorporated in 1929 in DE.
Donor(s): Ferdinand Thun,‡ and family.
Financial data (yr. ended 12/31/01): Grants paid, $1,385,676; assets, $33,641,811 (M); expenditures, $3,381,543; qualifying distributions, $1,439,755.
Limitations: Giving primarily in Berks County, PA, and contiguous counties; limited support also in the mid-Atlantic area.
Publications: Program policy statement, application guidelines.
Application information: Application form not required.

Officers and Trustees:* Paul R. Roedel,* Pres.; Hildegard Ryals,* V.P.; Ned E. Diefenderfer, Secy.; Thomas A. Beaver,* Treas.; Robert W. Cardy, Toni Lake, Samuel McCollough, Steffan Plehn, David Thun, Michael Thun.
EIN: 231980570
Codes: FD

46069
Beneficia Foundation
1 Pitcairn Pl., Ste. 3000
Jenkintown, PA 19046-3593
Contact: Chair., Arts Comm.; or Chair., Environmental Comm.

Incorporated in 1953 in PA.
Donor(s): members of the Theodor Pitcairn Family.
Financial data (yr. ended 04/30/00): Grants paid, $1,377,000; assets, $18,197,264 (M); expenditures, $1,599,443; qualifying distributions, $1,383,560.
Publications: Informational brochure (including application guidelines).
Application information: Small, innovative projects with limited alternative sources of funding are favored. Application form not required.
Officers and Directors:* Laren Pitcairn,* Pres. and Arts Comm. Chair.; John D. Mitchell,* V.P. and Environmental Comm. Chair.; Feodor U. Pitcairn,* Exec. Secy.; Mark J. Pennink,* Treas.; Deana P. Duncan, Sharon Forsyth, Miriam P. Mitchell, Eshowe P. Pennink, Kirstin O. Pitcairn, Mary Eleanor Pitcairn, Heather D. Reynolds.
EIN: 246015630
Codes: FD

46070
The Snider Foundation
First Union Ctr.
Philadelphia, PA 19148

Established in 1977 in PA.
Donor(s): Edward M. Snider.
Financial data (yr. ended 04/30/00): Grants paid, $1,364,350; assets, $13,236,055 (M); gifts received, $4,787,500; expenditures, $1,389,652; qualifying distributions, $1,364,350.
Limitations: Applications not accepted. Giving primarily in CA and Philadelphia, PA.
Application information: Contributes only to pre-selected organizations.
Officers: Edward M. Snider, Pres.; Sanford Lipstein, Secy.-Treas.
Trustee: Fred A. Shabel.
EIN: 232047668
Codes: FD

46071
The 1957 Charity Trust
c/o Mellon Bank, N.A.
P.O. Box 7236
Philadelphia, PA 19101-7236

Trust established in 1957 in PA.
Donor(s): Elizabeth R. Moran.
Financial data (yr. ended 06/30/01): Grants paid, $1,325,562; assets, $2,193 (M); expenditures, $1,691,440; qualifying distributions, $1,531,011.
Limitations: Applications not accepted. Giving primarily in the five-county region in southeastern PA.
Application information: Contributes only to pre-selected organizations.
Trustee: Mellon Bank, N.A.
EIN: 236227603
Codes: FD

46072
Josiah W. and Bessie H. Kline Foundation, Inc.
515 S. 29th St.
Harrisburg, PA 17104 (717) 561-4373
Contact: John A. Obrock, Acct.

Incorporated in 1952 in DE.
Donor(s): Josiah W. Kline,‡ Bessie H. Kline.‡
Financial data (yr. ended 12/31/00): Grants paid, $1,287,628; assets, $25,251,893 (M); expenditures, $1,364,800; qualifying distributions, $1,272,759.
Limitations: Giving primarily in south central PA.
Publications: Program policy statement, application guidelines.
Application information: Application form required.
Officers and Directors:* Robert F. Nation,* Pres.; William J. King,* Treas.; Derek C. Hathoway, James A. Marley, Samuel D. Ross, John A. Russel, David A. Smith.
EIN: 236245783
Codes: FD

46073
Theodora B. Betz Foundation
c/o George Nofer
1600 Market St., Ste. 3600
Philadelphia, PA 19103-7213
Application address: c/o Henry Kwiecinski, 1617 John F. Kennedy Blvd., Ste. 1610, Philadelphia, PA, 19103

Established in 1989 in PA.
Financial data (yr. ended 04/30/01): Grants paid, $1,279,615; assets, $14,029,867 (M); expenditures, $1,417,004; qualifying distributions, $1,318,859.
Limitations: Giving primarily in CA.
Application information: Application form not required.
Trustees: Henry Kwiecinski, George Nofer.
EIN: 236965187
Codes: FD

46074
The Grundy Foundation
680 Radcliffe St.
P.O. Box 701
Bristol, PA 19007 (215) 788-5460
Contact: Roland H. Johnson, Exec. Dir.

Trust established in 1961 in PA.
Donor(s): Joseph R. Grundy.‡
Financial data (yr. ended 12/31/01): Grants paid, $1,275,915; assets, $54,730,917 (M); expenditures, $3,052,760; qualifying distributions, $2,793,966; giving activities include $1,086,139 for programs.
Limitations: Giving limited to Bucks County, PA.
Publications: Informational brochure (including application guidelines), application guidelines.
Application information: Accepts Delaware Valley Grantmakers Common Application Form. Application form not required.
Officers and Trustees:* Frederick J.M. LaValley,* Chair.; James M. Gassaway, Vice-Chair.; Roland H. Johnson, Secy. and Exec. Dir.; Leonard N. Snyder, First Union National Bank.
EIN: 231609243
Codes: FD

46075
Maple Hill Foundation
115 Maple Hill Rd.
Gladwyne, PA 19035
Contact: Ella Warren Miller, Chair.

Established in 1986 in PA.
Donor(s): Paul F. Miller, Jr., Ella Warren Miller.
Financial data (yr. ended 07/31/01): Grants paid, $1,275,100; assets, $7,591,198 (M); expenditures, $1,301,692; qualifying distributions, $1,269,479.
Limitations: Applications not accepted. Giving primarily in Palo Alto CA, MA, NH, and Philadelphia, PA.
Application information: Unsolicited requests for funds not accepted.
Officers and Directors:* Ella Warren Miller,* Chair.; Ella Warren Merrill,* Pres.; Katharine S. Miller,* V.P. and Secy.; Paul F. Miller III,* V.P. and Treas.; Paul F. Miller, Jr.
EIN: 222751182
Codes: FD

46076
Bozzone Family Foundation
311 Hillcrest Dr.
Lower Burrell, PA 15068-6701

Established in 1986 in PA.
Donor(s): Robert P. Bozzone.
Financial data (yr. ended 12/31/01): Grants paid, $1,272,253; assets, $11,544,088 (M); expenditures, $1,324,895; qualifying distributions, $1,276,153.
Limitations: Applications not accepted. Giving primarily in PA.
Application information: Contributes only to pre-selected organizations.
Trustee: Robert P. Bozzone.
EIN: 256277066
Codes: FD

46077
Pine Tree Foundation
120 Righters Mill Rd.
Gladwyne, PA 19035 (610) 649-4601
Contact: A. Morris Williams, Jr., Chair. and Ruth W. Williams, Pres.

Established in 1986 in PA.
Donor(s): A. Morris Williams, Jr., Ruth W. Williams.
Financial data (yr. ended 07/31/01): Grants paid, $1,255,000; assets, $26,060,615 (M); gifts received, $640,400; expenditures, $1,349,581; qualifying distributions, $1,255,000.
Limitations: Giving primarily in GA and PA.
Officers and Directors:* A. Morris Williams, Jr.,* Chair. and Treas.; Ruth W. Williams,* Pres. and Secy.; Susan W. Beltz, Joanne W. Markman.
EIN: 222751187
Codes: FD

46078
Sovereign Bank Foundation
c/o Sovereign Bank
1130 Berkshire Blvd.
Wyomissing, PA 19610 (610) 320-8504
Application address: c/o Joseph E. Schupp, Sovereign Bank, Gateway Bldg., 201 Penn St., Reading, PA 19601, tel.: (610) 988-2001; Additional tel.: (610) 208-8454; E-mail: g-white@sovereignbank.com
Contact: Gail Dawson-White, Secy.-Treas.

Established in 1989 in PA.
Donor(s): Sovereign Bank.
Financial data (yr. ended 12/31/01): Grants paid, $1,250,266; assets, $0 (M); gifts received, $1,250,804; expenditures, $1,250,804; qualifying distributions, $1,250,804.
Limitations: Giving limited to areas of bank service in New Castle County, DE; Bergen, Essex, Middlesex, Monmouth, Morris, Ocean, Somerset, Sussex, and Union counties, NJ; and Berks, Bucks, Chester, Lancaster, Lehigh, Mercer, Montgomery, Northhampton, Philadelphia, and Union counties, PA.

46078—PENNSYLVANIA

Publications: Annual report, application guidelines.
Application information: Do not submit videos; do not use folders or plastic covers. Application form required.
Officers: Lawrence M. Thompson, Jr., Pres.; John V. Killen, V.P.; David A. Silverman, Secy.; Richard Kosak, Treas.; Joseph E. Schupp, Mgr.
Directors: Michael Ehlerman, John Fry, Stewart B. Kean, Richard E. Mohn, George Reinhard, Elizabeth B. Rothermel, Jay S. Sidhu.
EIN: 232548113
Codes: CS, FD, CD

46079
Philip M. McKenna Foundation, Inc.
P.O. Box 186
Latrobe, PA 15650 (724) 537-6900
Contact: T. William Boxx, Chair.

Incorporated in 1967 in PA.
Donor(s): Philip M. McKenna.‡
Financial data (yr. ended 12/31/00): Grants paid, $1,234,495; assets, $19,682,099 (M); gifts received, $325,000; expenditures, $1,432,023; qualifying distributions, $1,383,394.
Limitations: Giving primarily in the Latrobe, PA, area for community and civic programs; grants to PA and national organizations for public policy research, economic education and public affairs.
Publications: Grants list, program policy statement.
Application information: Application form not required.
Officers and Directors:* T. William Boxx,* Chair.; Charles R. Kesler,* Vice-Chair.; Norbert J. Pail,* Secy.; Jonathan C. Hall, Zan M. Rich.
Trustee Bank: Mellon Bank, N.A.
EIN: 256082635
Codes: FD

46080
York Foundation
20 W. Market St.
York, PA 17401-1203 (717) 848-3733
FAX: (717) 854-7231; E-mail: info@yorkfoundation.org; URL: http://www.yorkfoundation.org

Established in 1961 in PA.
Financial data (yr. ended 12/31/01): Grants paid, $1,226,987; assets, $25,529,464 (M); gifts received, $4,565,708; expenditures, $1,531,529.
Limitations: Giving primarily in York County, PA.
Publications: Annual report, informational brochure, application guidelines, newsletter.
Application information: Guidelines available on website. Application form required.
Officers and Directors:* Thomas C. Norris,* Pres.; Cornelia W. Wolf,* V.P.; John J. Shorb,* Secy.; Stephen H. Klunk,* Treas.; Richard H. Brown, Exec. Dir.; and 27 additional directors.
EIN: 236299868
Codes: CM, FD

46081
Henry Janssen Foundation, Inc.
2650 Westview Dr.
Wyomissing, PA 19610

Incorporated in 1931 in DE.
Donor(s): Members of the Janssen family, Helen Wetzel.
Financial data (yr. ended 12/31/01): Grants paid, $1,219,000; assets, $21,453,802 (M); expenditures, $1,356,238; qualifying distributions, $1,232,506.
Limitations: Applications not accepted. Giving primarily in PA, particularly Reading and Berks County.

Application information: Contributes only to pre-selected organizations.
Officers and Trustees:* Elroy P. Master,* Pres.; John W. Bowman, Jr., V.P.; Elizabeth B. Rothermel, Secy.; Elsa M. Hoppman,* Treas.
EIN: 231476340
Codes: FD

46082
Chester County Community Foundation
The Lincoln Bldg.
28 W. Market St.
West Chester, PA 19382 (610) 696-8211
FAX: (610) 696-8213; E-mail: Miker@chescosf.org; URL: http://www.chescocf.org
Contact: H. McPherson, V.P..

Established in 1994 in PA.
Financial data (yr. ended 06/30/00): Grants paid, $1,218,110; assets, $8,424,303 (L); gifts received, $4,113,783; expenditures, $2,110,152.
Limitations: Giving primarily in Chester County, PA.
Publications: Annual report, financial statement, newsletter, informational brochure, application guidelines.
Application information: Guidelines available on Web site.
Officers and Directors:* John A. Featherman III,* Chair.; Michael J. Rawl,* Pres.; and 14 additional directors.
EIN: 232773822
Codes: CM, FD

46083
Louis & Bessie Stein Foundation
1845 Walnut St., Ste. 1620
Philadelphia, PA 19103
Contact: Marilyn Bellet, Pres.

Established in 1953 in NJ.
Donor(s): Louis Stein,‡ Walter Leventhal, Stanley Merves, Stein, Stein & Engel.
Financial data (yr. ended 12/31/00): Grants paid, $1,199,817; assets, $22,752,064 (M); gifts received, $1,591,374; expenditures, $1,460,158; qualifying distributions, $1,289,725.
Limitations: Applications not accepted. Giving primarily in FL, NY, and PA.
Application information: Contributes only to pre-selected organizations.
Officers: Marilyn Bellet, Pres. and Treas.; Ruth Leventhal Nathanson, V.P. and Secy.; Audrey Merves, V.P.
EIN: 236395253
Codes: FD

46084
The Dorothy A. Metcalf Charitable Foundation
c/o PNC Bank, N.A.
1600 Market St.
Philadelphia, PA 19103-7240

Established in 1997 in MD.
Donor(s): Dorothy A. Metcalf.
Financial data (yr. ended 12/31/00): Grants paid, $1,194,000; assets, $196,274 (M); gifts received, $1,341,491; expenditures, $1,796,530; qualifying distributions, $1,193,764.
Limitations: Applications not accepted. Giving on a national basis.
Application information: Contributes only to pre-selected organizations.
Trustees: Dorothy A. Metcalf, Robert A. Metcalf, John E. Mullikin.
Agent: PNC Bank, N.A.
EIN: 522053820
Codes: FD

46085
Cornerstone Foundation
(Formerly GCP Foundation)
P.O. Box 487
Elverson, PA 19520

Established in 1989 in PA; fully funded in 1990.
Financial data (yr. ended 12/31/00): Grants paid, $1,182,120; assets, $19,605,844 (M); expenditures, $1,369,199; qualifying distributions, $1,184,111.
Limitations: Applications not accepted. Giving on a national basis.
Application information: Contributes only to pre-selected organizations.
Officers: Edward H. Cone, Pres. and Treas.; Robert L. Cone, V.P. and Secy.
Director: Derial H. Sanders.
EIN: 232593411
Codes: FD

46086
The Community Foundation for the Alleghenies
(Formerly The Community Foundation of Greater Johnstown)
216 Franklin St., Ste. 606
Johnstown, PA 15901-1911 (814) 536-7741
FAX: (814) 536-5859; E-mail: cfalleghenies@charter.net; URL: http://www.CFAlleghenies.org
Contact: Michael E. Kane, Exec. Dir.

Established in 1990 in PA.
Financial data (yr. ended 06/30/01): Grants paid, $1,179,225; assets, $16,357,483; gifts received, $1,297,774; expenditures, $1,723,966.
Limitations: Giving primarily in Bedford, Cambria, Indiana and Somerset counties, PA.
Publications: Annual report, grants list, newsletter, informational brochure.
Application information: Application form required.
Officer: Michael E. Kane, Exec. Dir.
EIN: 251637373
Codes: CM, FD

46087
Staunton Farm Foundation
Center City Tower, Ste. 210
650 Smithfield St.
Pittsburgh, PA 15222 (412) 281-8020
FAX: (412) 232-3115; E-mail: info@stauntonfarm.org; URL: http://www.stauntonfarm.org
Contact: Joni Schwager, Exec. Dir.

Incorporated in 1937 in PA.
Donor(s): Mathilda Staunton Craig McCready.‡
Financial data (yr. ended 12/31/00): Grants paid, $1,171,699; assets, $47,197,631 (M); expenditures, $1,532,738; qualifying distributions, $1,354,941.
Limitations: Giving limited to a ten-county area in southwestern PA: Allegheny, Armstrong, Beaver, Butler, Fayette, Greene, Indiana, Lawrence, Washington, and Westmoreland counties.
Publications: Informational brochure (including application guidelines), grants list.
Application information: Application form required.
Officers and Directors:* Andrea Q. Griffiths,* Pres.; Lee C. Lundback, V.P.; Albert B. Craig III,* Secy.; Barbara K. Robinson,* Treas.; Ann Austin, Sallie Davis, Joseph D. Dury, Jr., John W. Eichleay, Jr., Richard Frederick III, Philip Gulley, Elizabeth G. Hahl, Andrea Mahone, Richard W. Reed, Jr., Judith K. Sherry.
Manager: Mellon Bank, N.A.
EIN: 250965573
Codes: FD

46088
The Sylvan Foundation
c/o The Main Line Tr. Co.
20 N. Waterloo Rd.
Devon, PA 19333-1458 (610) 975-9700

Established in 1997 in PA.
Donor(s): Betty U. Musser.
Financial data (yr. ended 04/30/01): Grants paid, $1,155,000; assets, $5,321,168 (M); expenditures, $1,225,860; qualifying distributions, $1,152,792.
Limitations: Applications not accepted. Giving primarily in PA.
Application information: Contributes only to pre-selected organizations.
Trustees: Francis R. Grebe, Betty U. Musser.
EIN: 232908169
Codes: FD

46089
Harsco Corporation Fund
c/o Harsco Corp.
P.O. Box 8888
Camp Hill, PA 17001-8888 (717) 763-7064
Contact: Robert G. Yocum, Chair.; or Patty A. Rummel, Admin. Asst. (Scholarship Prog.)

Trust established in 1956 in PA.
Donor(s): Harsco Corp.
Financial data (yr. ended 12/31/00): Grants paid, $1,153,080; assets, $8,775,067 (M); expenditures, $1,265,776; qualifying distributions, $1,145,855.
Limitations: Giving primarily in areas of company operations.
Publications: Program policy statement.
Application information: Application form required for employee-related scholarships, which are administered by the National Merit Scholarship Corp.
Officers and Trustees:* Robert G. Yocum,* Chair.; Salvatore D. Fazzolari,* Secy.-Treas.; P.C. Coppock, D.C. Hathaway.
EIN: 236278376
Codes: CS, FD, CD

46090
Tyco Electronics Foundation
(Formerly AMP Foundation)
c/o Tyco Electronics Corp.
P.O. Box 3608 (M.S. 140-10)
Harrisburg, PA 17105-3608 (717) 592-4869
FAX: (717) 592-4022; E-mail: mjrakocz@tycoelectronics.com; URL: http://www.tycoelectronics.com/about/foundation
Contact: Mary J. Rakoczy

Established in 1977 in PA.
Donor(s): AMP Inc., Tyco Electronics Corp.
Financial data (yr. ended 12/31/01): Grants paid, $1,150,937; assets, $18,490,755 (M); expenditures, $1,335,854; qualifying distributions, $1,150,937.
Limitations: Giving in geographic areas where Tyco Electronics has a major presence; these areas include Harrisburg and central PA, Menlo Park and northern CA, the Carolinas, Detroit, MI, Boston, MA, and Austin, Dallas, and Houston, TX.
Publications: Application guidelines.
Application information: Majority of grants are budgeted in first quarter of the year. Application form required.
Trustee: Allfirst.
EIN: 232022928
Codes: CS, FD, CD

46091
Allegheny Technologies Charitable Trust
(Formerly Allegheny Teledyne Incorporated Charitable Trust)
1000 Six PPG Pl.
Pittsburgh, PA 15222-5479 (412) 394-2800
Contact: Jon D. Walton, Tr.

Established in 1997 in PA.
Donor(s): Allegheny Teledyne Inc., Allegheny Technologies Inc.
Financial data (yr. ended 12/31/01): Grants paid, $1,130,217; assets, $1,899,316 (M); expenditures, $1,144,594; qualifying distributions, $1,130,217.
Limitations: Giving primarily in PA.
Application information: Grants are to public charities only. Application form not required.
Trustees: J. Murdy, Jon D. Walton.
EIN: 237873055
Codes: CS, FD, CD

46092
Edwin Hall 2nd Charitable Trust
c/o Alexander & Pelli
1 Penn Ctr. Plz., Ste. 1100
Philadelphia, PA 19103 (215) 564-6400

Established in 1996 in PA.
Financial data (yr. ended 12/31/01): Grants paid, $1,110,544; assets, $16,113,669 (M); expenditures, $1,209,987; qualifying distributions, $1,157,759.
Limitations: Applications not accepted. Giving limited to PA.
Application information: Contributes only to pre-selected organizations.
Trustees: Robert E.J. Curran, Richard B. Goldbeck, William T. Luskus.
EIN: 237892195
Codes: FD

46093
The James & Agnes Kim Foundation, Inc.
c/o Siana Carr & O'Connor, LLP
1500 E. Lancaster Ave.
Paoli, PA 19301

Established in 1997 in PA.
Donor(s): James J. Kim.
Financial data (yr. ended 12/31/01): Grants paid, $1,102,728; assets, $17,610,408 (M); gifts received, $14,377,008; expenditures, $1,127,406; qualifying distributions, $1,102,531.
Limitations: Applications not accepted. Giving primarily in PA.
Application information: Contributes only to pre-selected organizations.
Officers: Agnes C. Kim, Pres.; Susan Y. Kim, Secy.; James J. Kim, Treas.
EIN: 232899799
Codes: FD

46094
Maxwell Strawbridge Foundation
(Formerly Maxwell Strawbridge Charitable Trust)
c/o Wolf, Block, Schorr & Solis-Cohen
1650 Arch St., 22nd Fl.
Philadelphia, PA 19103

Established in 1992 in PA.
Donor(s): Ethel Guy.‡
Financial data (yr. ended 12/31/01): Grants paid, $1,096,475; assets, $7,324,364 (M); expenditures, $1,119,470; qualifying distributions, $1,099,444.
Limitations: Applications not accepted. Giving primarily in Philadelphia, PA, some funding nationally.
Application information: Contributes only to pre-selected organizations.
Trustees: Edward M. Glickman, Charles G. Kopp.
EIN: 232703172

Codes: FD

46095
AMETEK Foundation, Inc.
37 N. Valley Rd., Bldg. 4
P.O. Box 1764
Paoli, PA 19301-0801 (610) 647-2121
Contact: Kathryn E. Londra

Incorporated in 1960 in NY.
Donor(s): AMETEK, Inc.
Financial data (yr. ended 12/31/01): Grants paid, $1,087,655; assets, $7,623,478 (M); expenditures, $799,359; qualifying distributions, $1,080,802.
Limitations: Giving on a national basis.
Application information: Application form not required.
Officers and Directors:* Frank S. Hermance,* Chair. and Pres.; Elizabeth R. Varet,* V.P.; Kathryn E. Londra, Secy. and Treas.; Lewis Cole, Helmut N. Friedlaender.
EIN: 136095939
Codes: CS, FD, CD

46096
Hilda M. Willis Foundation
3 Mellon Bank Ctr., Rm. 4000
Pittsburgh, PA 15259 (412) 234-1634
Contact: Annette Calgaro, V.P., Mellon Bank, N.A.

Established in 1981 in PA; initial endowment in fiscal 1992.
Donor(s): Hilda M. Willis.‡
Financial data (yr. ended 06/30/01): Grants paid, $1,078,264; assets, $13,544,203 (M); gifts received, $149,598; expenditures, $1,219,271; qualifying distributions, $1,083,686.
Limitations: Giving limited to southwestern PA.
Publications: Application guidelines, grants list.
Trustees: Robert Lovett, Alexander M. Minno, Mellon Bank, N.A.
EIN: 256371417
Codes: FD

46097
The William & Jemima Brossman Charitable Foundation
c/o The Ephrata National Bank
31 E. Main St., P.O. Box 457
Ephrata, PA 17522 (717) 733-6576
Contact: Carl L. Brubaker, V.P. and Trust Off., The Ephrata National Bank

Established in 1986 in PA.
Donor(s): Bertha Brossman Blair.‡
Financial data (yr. ended 10/31/01): Grants paid, $1,048,820; assets, $20,852,111 (M); expenditures, $1,097,748; qualifying distributions, $1,049,968.
Limitations: Giving primarily in south central PA.
Application information: Application form not required.
Trustee: The Ephrata National Bank.
EIN: 236087844
Codes: FD

46098
Thomas and Sandra Usher Charitable Foundation
840 12th St.
Oakmont, PA 15139

Established in 1999 in PA.
Financial data (yr. ended 12/31/01): Grants paid, $1,040,800; assets, $60,822 (M); gifts received, $869,025; expenditures, $1,044,051; qualifying distributions, $1,042,915.
Limitations: Applications not accepted.
Application information: Contributes only to pre-selected organizations.

Trustees: Sandra J. Usher, Thomas J. Usher.
EIN: 256681379
Codes: FD

46099
The Anne L. and George H. Clapp Charitable and Educational Trust
(Formerly G. H. Clapp Charitable and Educational Trust)
c/o Mellon Bank, N.A.
3 Mellon Bank Ctr., Rm. 4000
Pittsburgh, PA 15259 (412) 234-1634
Contact: Annette Calgaro, V.P., Mellon Bank, N.A.

Established in 1949.
Donor(s): George H. Clapp.‡
Financial data (yr. ended 09/30/01): Grants paid, $1,025,500; assets, $20,036,379 (M); expenditures, $1,221,932; qualifying distributions, $1,090,249.
Limitations: Giving limited to southwestern PA.
Application information: Application form not required.
Trustee: Mellon Bank, N.A.
EIN: 256018976
Codes: FD

46100
Dolfinger-McMahon Foundation
c/o Duane, Morris & Heckscher
1 Liberty Pl.
Philadelphia, PA 19103-7396 (215) 979-1768
Contact: Marlene Valcich, Exec. Secy.

Trust established in 1957 in PA, and originally comprised of four separate trusts: T/W of Henry Dolfinger as modified by will of Mary McMahon; 1935 D/T of Henry Dolfinger as modified by will of Caroline D. McMahon; Residuary T/W of Caroline D. McMahon; Dolfinger-McMahon Trust for Greater Philadelphia. In 1986 the 1935 D/T of H. Dolfinger was merged with the residuary T/W of C. McMahon.
Donor(s): Caroline D. McMahon,‡ Mary M. McMahon.‡
Financial data (yr. ended 09/30/01): Grants paid, $1,024,700; assets, $16,906,743 (M); expenditures, $1,140,311; qualifying distributions, $1,011,759.
Limitations: Giving limited to the greater Philadelphia, PA, area.
Publications: Annual report (including application guidelines), application guidelines.
Application information: See guidelines for format required for requests. Application form not required.
Officer: Marlene Valcich, Exec. Secy.
Trustees: David E. Loder, Roland Morris.
EIN: 236207346
Codes: FD

46101
Samuel P. Mandell Foundation
1735 Market St., Ste. 3410
Philadelphia, PA 19103-7501 (215) 979-3410
Contact: Seymour Mandell, Tr.

Trust established in 1955 in PA.
Donor(s): Samuel P. Mandell,‡ Ida S. Mandell.‡
Financial data (yr. ended 12/31/01): Grants paid, $1,023,548; assets, $17,212,965 (M); expenditures, $1,209,497; qualifying distributions, $1,102,599.
Limitations: Giving primarily in PA.
Application information: Application form not required.
Trustees: Harold Cramer, Gerald Mandell, M.D., Judith Mandell, Morton Mandell, M.D., Ronald Mandell, Seymour Mandell.
EIN: 236274709
Codes: FD

46102
Fleming Foundation
7661 Beryl Rd.
Zionsville, PA 18092

Established in 1990 in PA.
Donor(s): Richard Fleming.
Financial data (yr. ended 12/31/01): Grants paid, $1,023,055; assets, $7,329,967 (M); expenditures, $1,047,452; qualifying distributions, $1,044,578.
Limitations: Applications not accepted. Giving limited to Allentown, PA.
Application information: Contributes only to pre-selected organizations.
Trustees: Kathleen Arnold, Richard Fleming, Roberta Fleming.
EIN: 232585510
Codes: FD

46103
Ralph & Suzanne Roberts Foundation
c/o Comcast Corp.
1500 Market St., 35th Fl.
Philadelphia, PA 19102-4735

Established in 1963.
Donor(s): Ralph J. Roberts, Suzanne F. Roberts.
Financial data (yr. ended 11/30/00): Grants paid, $1,018,349; assets, $20,391,968 (M); expenditures, $1,141,467; qualifying distributions, $989,650.
Limitations: Applications not accepted. Giving primarily in PA.
Application information: Grants initiated by trustees.
Trustees: Ralph J. Roberts, Suzanne F. Roberts.
EIN: 237015984
Codes: FD

46104
Firstfruits Foundation
P.O. Box 239
Elverson, PA 19520-0239

Established in 1995 in PA.
Donor(s): Robert L. Cone, Dawn M. Cone.
Financial data (yr. ended 12/31/00): Grants paid, $1,007,500; assets, $14,506,787 (M); expenditures, $1,140,120; qualifying distributions, $1,199,998; giving activities include $200,000 for program-related investments.
Limitations: Applications not accepted. Giving on a national basis.
Application information: Contributes only to pre-selected organizations.
Officers: Robert L. Cone, Pres. and Treas.; Edward H. Cone, V.P. and Secy.
Director: Derial H. Sanders.
EIN: 232808624
Codes: FD

46105
Gerald E. McGinnis Charitable Foundation
3585 Hills Church Rd.
Export, PA 15632

Established in 1991 in PA.
Donor(s): Gerald E. McGinnis.
Financial data (yr. ended 12/31/01): Grants paid, $1,004,753; assets, $3,077,544 (M); expenditures, $1,020,089; qualifying distributions, $989,508.
Limitations: Applications not accepted. Giving primarily in PA.
Application information: Contributes only to pre-selected organizations.
Trustee: Gerald E. McGinnis.
EIN: 251671236
Codes: FD

46106
The Eugene Garfield Foundation
c/o Glenmede Trust Co.
1650 Market St.
Philadelphia, PA 19103
Application address: 24 N. Merion Ave., Bryn Mawr, PA 19010-1905
Contact: Catheryne Stout, V.P.

Established in 1988 in PA.
Donor(s): Eugene Garfield, Catheryne Stout.
Financial data (yr. ended 11/30/01): Grants paid, $1,003,900; assets, $7,463,145 (M); gifts received, $80,000; expenditures, $1,029,198; qualifying distributions, $1,005,022.
Limitations: Giving primarily in NY and PA.
Officers and Directors:* Eugene Garfield,* Chair., Pres. and Treas.; Catheryne Stout, V.P. and Secy.; Robert S. Bramson.
EIN: 232553258
Codes: FD

46107
Natalie A. Leaf Charitable Trust
c/o The Williamson Free School of Mechanical Trades
106 S. New Middleton Rd.
Media, PA 19063-5299 (610) 565-1095
Contact: Gregory L. Lindemuth

Established in 1990 in PA.
Financial data (yr. ended 09/30/00): Grants paid, $1,002,245; assets, $0 (M); expenditures, $1,017,024; qualifying distributions, $1,009,164.
Limitations: Giving limited to PA.
Application information: Application form required.
Trustees: Mitchell G. Crane, PNC Bank, N.A., The Williamson Free School of Mechanical Trades.
EIN: 237648236
Codes: FD, GTI

46108
William B. Dietrich Foundation, Inc.
P.O. Box 58177
Philadelphia, PA 19102-8177 (215) 979-1919
Contact: William B. Dietrich, Pres.

Incorporated in 1936 in DE.
Donor(s): Henry D. Dietrich,‡ Daniel W. Dietrich Foundation, Inc., Dietrich American Foundation.
Financial data (yr. ended 12/31/01): Grants paid, $988,700; assets, $17,349,999 (M); expenditures, $1,128,082; qualifying distributions, $983,514.
Limitations: Giving primarily in PA.
Application information: Application form not required.
Officers: William B. Dietrich, Pres.; Frank G. Cooper, Secy.
EIN: 231515616
Codes: FD

46109
Stackpole-Hall Foundation
44 S. Saint Marys St.
St. Marys, PA 15857-1667 (814) 834-1845
FAX: (814) 834-1869; E-mail: s-hf@ncentral.com
Contact: William C. Conrad, Exec. Secy.

Trust established in 1951 in PA.
Donor(s): Lyle G. Hall, Sr.,‡ J. Hall Stackpole,‡ Harrison C. Stackpole, Lyle G. Hall, Jr., Adelaide Stackpole.‡
Financial data (yr. ended 12/31/01): Grants paid, $980,963; assets, $24,595,464 (M); expenditures, $1,286,101; qualifying distributions, $1,175,802.
Limitations: Giving primarily in Elk County, PA.
Publications: Annual report (including application guidelines).
Application information: Application form not required.

Trustees: Lyle G. Hall, Jr., Chair.; Douglas R. Dobson, Vice-Chair.; William C. Conrad, Secy.; Helen Hall Drew, Megan Hall, J.M. Hamlin Johnson, Alexander Sheble-Hall, R. Dauer Stackpole, Sara-Jane Stackpole, Laurey Stackpole Turner.
Board Members: Heather Conrad, Jeff Drew, Laurey Nixon, Charlotte Hall Perkins.
EIN: 256006650
Codes: FD

46110
Elizabeth R. England Trust
c/o Mellon Bank, N.A.
P.O. Box 7236, AIM 193-0224
Philadelphia, PA 19101-7236

Established in 1987 in PA.
Financial data (yr. ended 06/30/01): Grants paid, $973,098; assets, $22,337,409 (M); expenditures, $1,061,549; qualifying distributions, $946,762.
Limitations: Applications not accepted. Giving limited to residents of Philadelphia, PA.
Application information: Students are selected by the trustee.
Trustee: Mellon Bank, N.A.
EIN: 236606334
Codes: FD, GTI

46111
Forney Family Foundation, Inc.
P.O. Box 549
Unionville, PA 19375-0549

Established in 1997 in DE.
Donor(s): Robert C. Forney.
Financial data (yr. ended 12/31/01): Grants paid, $959,030; assets, $2,941,432 (M); gifts received, $650,000; expenditures, $960,147; qualifying distributions, $957,764.
Limitations: Applications not accepted. Giving on a national basis.
Application information: Contributes only to pre-selected organizations.
Officers: Robert C. Forney, Pres. and Treas.; Marilyn G. Forney, V.P. and Secy.
Trustees: Barbara D. Forney, Gerald G. Forney.
EIN: 237079172
Codes: FD

46112
Buncher Family Foundation
5600 Forward Ave.
Pittsburgh, PA 15217 (412) 422-9900
Contact: Bernita Buncher, Exec. V.P.

Established in 1974 in PA.
Donor(s): Jack G. Buncher, The Buncher Co., Buncher Mgmt. Agency, Buncher Rail Car Svc. Co.
Financial data (yr. ended 11/30/01): Grants paid, $954,672; assets, $10,473,768 (M); gifts received, $1,650,000; expenditures, $974,084; qualifying distributions, $972,514.
Limitations: Giving primarily in PA, with emphasis on Pittsburgh.
Officers and Directors:* Jack G. Buncher,* Chair., C.E.O., and Pres.; Bernita Buncher,* Exec. V.P. and Secy.-Treas.; Thomas J. Balestrieri,* V.P.; Herbert S. Green,* V.P.; H. William Doring, Ruth H. Neff.
EIN: 237366998
Codes: FD

46113
Raymond & Ruth Perelman Community Foundation
225 City Line Ave., Ste. 14
Bala Cynwyd, PA 19004

Established in 1995.
Financial data (yr. ended 04/30/01): Grants paid, $954,500; assets, $23,536,399 (M); gifts received, $1,187,906; expenditures, $1,118,733; qualifying distributions, $878,275.
Limitations: Applications not accepted. Giving primarily in FL and PA.
Application information: Contributes only to pre-selected organizations.
Trustees: Raymond G. Perelman, Ruth Perelman.
EIN: 232820843
Codes: FD

46114
Mine Safety Appliances Company Charitable Foundation
c/o Mine Safety Appliances Co.
PNC Bank, N.A., No. 56222-0
Pittsburgh, PA 15222-2705 (412) 967-3000
Application address: P.O. Box 426, Pittsburgh, PA 15230
Contact: James E. Herald, Secy., Mine Safety Appliances Co.

Established in 1991 in PA as successor to the Mine Safety Appliances Company Charitable Trust.
Donor(s): Mine Safety Appliances Co.
Financial data (yr. ended 12/31/01): Grants paid, $950,850; assets, $2,496,598 (M); gifts received, $500,000; expenditures, $977,064; qualifying distributions, $950,834.
Limitations: Giving primarily in Pittsburgh, PA.
Application information: Application form not required.
Trustee: PNC Bank, N.A.
EIN: 256023104
Codes: CS, FD, CD

46115
Bristol Fund, Inc.
P.O. Box 206
Carversville, PA 18913
Contact: Michael W. Bristol, Treas.

Established in 1962 in NY.
Donor(s): Brian T. Bristol, Pamela W. Bristol, Edith W. Bristol, Michael W. Bristol.
Financial data (yr. ended 12/31/01): Grants paid, $950,425; assets, $1,561,719 (M); gifts received, $436,653; expenditures, $952,962; qualifying distributions, $948,416.
Limitations: Applications not accepted.
Application information: Contributes only to pre-selected organizations in which board members have an active interest. Unsolicited requests not considered or acknowledged.
Officers: Pamela W. Bristol, Pres.; Susannah B. Bristol, V.P.; James D. Bristol, Secy.; Michael W. Bristol, Treas.
EIN: 237209712
Codes: FD

46116
Widener Memorial Foundation in Aid of Handicapped Children
665 Thomas Rd.
P.O. Box 178
Lafayette Hill, PA 19444-0178 (215) 836-7500
Contact: F. Eugene Dixon, Jr., Pres.

Incorporated in 1912 in PA.
Donor(s): Peter A.B. Widener.‡
Financial data (yr. ended 12/31/01): Grants paid, $943,340; assets, $7,445,585 (M); gifts received, $593,382; expenditures, $964,328; qualifying distributions, $944,719.
Limitations: Giving limited to Delaware Valley, PA, for projects relating to orthopedically handicapped children.
Application information: Application form not required.
Officers and Trustees:* F. Eugene Dixon, Jr.,* Pres.; Peter M. Mattoon,* V.P.; Edith Robb Dixon,* Secy.-Treas.; Bruce L. Castor, Michael Clancy, M.D., Mark S. DePillisi.
EIN: 236267223
Codes: FD

46117
Ethel Sergeant Clark Smith Memorial Fund
c/o First Union National Bank
123 S. Broad St., PA 1279
Philadelphia, PA 19109 (215) 985-3920
FAX: (215) 985-3922
Contact: Camie Morrison, V.P., First Union National Bank

Trust established in 1977 in PA.
Donor(s): Ethel Sergeant Clark Smith.‡
Financial data (yr. ended 05/31/01): Grants paid, $938,299; assets, $17,532,231 (M); expenditures, $1,068,287; qualifying distributions, $950,674.
Limitations: Giving limited to Delaware County, PA, or organizations benefiting county residents.
Publications: Application guidelines, financial statement, informational brochure (including application guidelines), program policy statement.
Application information: Personal visits prior to proposal submission discouraged; accepts Delaware Valley Grantmakers Common Grant Application and Common Report Form. Application form required.
Trustee: First Union National Bank.
EIN: 236648857
Codes: FD

46118
Bitz Foundation
c/o Francois Bitz
1640 Pleasant Hill Rd.
Baden, PA 15005-2518

Established in 1997 in PA.
Donor(s): Francois Bitz.
Financial data (yr. ended 12/31/00): Grants paid, $936,524; assets, $10,694,682 (M); gifts received, $345,750; expenditures, $1,377,485; qualifying distributions, $926,178.
Limitations: Applications not accepted. Giving primarily in Pittsburgh, PA.
Application information: Contributes only to pre-selected organizations.
Officers: Francois Bitz, Pres.; Graziella Pruiti, Secy.
EIN: 232901971
Codes: FD

46119
A. J. & Sigismunda Palumbo Charitable Trust
c/o Smithfield Trust Co.
20 Stanwix St., Ste. 650
Pittsburgh, PA 15222-4801 (412) 261-0779
Contact: Robert R. Kopf, Jr., C.E.O., Smithfield Trust Co.

Established in 1974.
Donor(s): A.J. Palumbo.
Financial data (yr. ended 03/31/01): Grants paid, $934,000; assets, $17,372,207 (M); gifts received, $1,360,000; expenditures, $1,065,818; qualifying distributions, $953,896.
Limitations: Giving primarily in western PA.
Application information: Application form required.
Trustees: E. Rolland Dickson, Paul B. Greiner, F.W. Knisley, John W. Kowach, Donald W. Meredith, A.J. Palumbo, Janet F. Palumbo, P.J. Palumbo, Richard L. White, PNC Bank, N.A.
EIN: 256168159
Codes: FD

46120
Federation Foundation of Greater Philadelphia
2100 Arch St.
Philadelphia, PA 19103
Contact: Richard N. Nassau, Exec. Secy.

Established in 1971 in PA.
Financial data (yr. ended 11/30/01): Grants paid, $924,159; assets, $7,262,909 (M); gifts received, $270,600; expenditures, $992,088; qualifying distributions, $926,659.
Limitations: Applications not accepted. Giving on a national basis.
Application information: Grantees are pre-selected by individual donors of the foundation; unsolicited requests for funds not considered.
Officers: Ralph Snyder, Pres.; Susan Freedman, V.P.; Howard Glassman, V.P.; Richard Nassau, Exec. Secy.; Hortense Kaiserman, Secy.; Clifford Schlesinger, Treas.
Directors: Larry Chane, Gary Kleiman, Stuart Silver.
EIN: 237083735
Codes: FD

46121
The Scholler Foundation
1100 One Penn Ctr.
Philadelphia, PA 19103 (215) 568-7500
Contact: E. Brooks Keffer, Jr., Pres.

Trust established in 1939 in PA.
Donor(s): F.C. Scholler.‡
Financial data (yr. ended 12/31/01): Grants paid, $915,911; assets, $15,099,564 (M); expenditures, $1,024,126; qualifying distributions, $955,392.
Limitations: Giving limited to the Delaware Valley, PA, area.
Application information: Application form not required.
Officers and Trustees:* E. Brooks Keffer, Jr.,* Pres.; Edwin C. Dreby III,* Secy.; Lawrence R. Brown, Jr.
EIN: 236245158
Codes: FD

46122
The Brook J. Lenfest Foundation, Inc.
5 Tower Bridge, Ste. 450
300 Barr Harbor Dr.
West Conshohocken, PA 19428
(610) 828-4510
FAX: (610) 828-0390; E-mail: lenfestfoundation.org; URL: http://www.brookjlenfestfoundation.org
Contact: Bruce Melgary, Exec. Dir.

Established in 1999 in PA.
Donor(s): Brook J. Lenfest.
Financial data (yr. ended 06/30/02): Grants paid, $910,691; assets, $31,701,443 (M); gifts received, $24,964,964; expenditures, $3,455,114; qualifying distributions, $808,897.
Limitations: Giving primarily in northern DE, southern NJ, southeastern and south central urban areas of PA, with an emphasis on Philadelphia, PA.
Publications: Application guidelines.
Application information: Guidelines on Web site. Application form not required.
Officers and Directors:* Brook J. Lenfest,* Pres.; Dawn Lenfest,* Secy.; Marguerite Lenfest,* Treas.
Board Members: Bruse Melgany, Exec. Dir.; Grahame Richards, Prog. Dir.
EIN: 233031338
Codes: FD

46123
The Birmingham Foundation
c/o Roesch-Taylor Bldg., N409
2100 Jane St.
Pittsburgh, PA 15203 (412) 481-2777
FAX: (412) 481-2727; E-mail: birmfound@usaor.net; URL: http://www.birminghamfoundation.org
Contact: Mary Phan-Gruber, Exec. Dir.

Established in 1996 in PA; converted with assets from the sale of The South Side Hospital.
Financial data (yr. ended 06/30/02): Grants paid, $901,200; assets, $19,076,724 (M); expenditures, $1,407,544; qualifying distributions, $901,200.
Limitations: Giving limited to the south Pittsburgh, PA, area served by the following zip codes: 15203 (South Side), 15210 (Mt. Oliver and Hilltop), and 15211 (Mt. Washington), including in particular the neighborhoods of Allentown, Arlington, Arlington Heights, Beltzhoover, Bon Air, Carrick, Duquesne Heights, Knoxville, Mt. Oliver, Washington, St. Clair Village, and the South Side Flats and Slopes.
Publications: Biennial report, application guidelines, grants list, newsletter.
Application information: Details available on foundation Web site. The foundation suggests use of the Common Grant Application Format developed by Grantmakers of Western PA; see URL: http://www.gwpa.org for copies. Application form required.
Officers and Directors:* Daniel A. Goetz,* Chair.; Floyd R. Ganassi,* Vice-Chair.; Mihai Marcu,* Vice-Chair.; Judith M. Davenport, Secy.; H. Don Gordon, Treas.; Mark S. Bibro, Louise R. Brown, Hugo Churchill, Cyril Esser, Jane H. Roesch, Hon. William T. Simmons, Eileen O. Smith, Duane Swager II, Terrence L. Wirginis.
EIN: 250965572
Codes: FD

46124
Glencairn Foundation
1 Pitcairn Pl., Ste. 3000
Jenkintown, PA 19046-3593
FAX: (215) 881-6092

Incorporated in 1950 in PA.
Donor(s): Raymond Pitcairn,‡ and members of the Pitcairn family.
Financial data (yr. ended 12/31/01): Grants paid, $898,776; assets, $15,523,715 (M); expenditures, $987,691; qualifying distributions, $922,246.
Limitations: Applications not accepted. Giving primarily in Bryn Athyn, PA.
Application information: Contributes only to pre-selected organizations.
Officers and Directors:* Laird Pitcairn,* Pres.; Lynn Genzlinger, V.P.; Kenneth Schauder,* Secy.-Treas.; Emily Bau-Madsen, Nathaniel Brock, Brandon Junge, Kim Junge, Alan King, Brant Pitcairn.
EIN: 231429828
Codes: FD

46125
McFeely-Rogers Foundation
1110 Ligonier St., Ste. 300
P.O. Box 110
Latrobe, PA 15650-0110 (724) 537-5588
FAX: (724) 537-5589
Contact: James R. Okonak, Exec. Dir.

Incorporated in 1953 in PA.
Donor(s): James H. Rogers,‡ Nancy K. McFeely,‡ Nancy M. Rogers,‡ Fred M. Rogers.
Financial data (yr. ended 12/31/01): Grants paid, $894,245; assets, $20,910,497 (M); expenditures, $1,263,268; qualifying distributions, $1,062,900.
Limitations: Giving primarily in the Latrobe, PA, area, with some giving in Pittsburgh.
Publications: Program policy statement, application guidelines.
Application information: Application form not required.
Officers and Trustees:* Fred M. Rogers,* C.E.O.; Nancy R. Crozier,* Pres.; James R. Okonak,* Secy. and Exec. Dir.; Catherine G. Keefe,* Treas.; William P. Barker, Daniel G. Crozier, Jr., James Brooks Crozier, Douglas R. Nowicki, James B. Rogers, John F. Rogers.
EIN: 251120947
Codes: FD

46126
Shenango Valley Foundation
41 Chestnut St.
Sharon, PA 16146 (724) 981-5882
FAX: (724) 981-5480; E-mail: svf@bronze.svol.net
Contact: Larry Haynes, Exec. Dir.

Established in 1981.
Donor(s): Paul O'Brien, Tina O'Brien.
Financial data (yr. ended 12/31/01): Grants paid, $890,682; assets, $14,112,679 (M); gifts received, $512,949; expenditures, $1,511,002; giving activities include $1,399,436 for loans to individuals.
Limitations: Giving limited to the Shenango Valley area, including Trumbull and Mahoning counties, OH, and Mercer and Lawrence counties, PA.
Publications: Annual report, informational brochure, application guidelines.
Application information: Application form required.
Officers and Trustees:* James A. O'Brien,* Pres.; Robert C. Jazwinski, Exec. V.P.; Karen Winner Hale,* V.P.; Ronald R. Anderson,* Secy.; James E. Feeney,* Treas.; Larry Haynes, Exec. Dir.; Carol Gamble, Mel Grata, Lynda Holm, Paul E. O'Brien, Albert R. Puntureri, William J. Strimbu, Kenneth Turcic, James T. Weller, Sr., James E. Winner, Jr.
EIN: 251407396
Codes: CM, FD, GTI

46127
Norton Company Foundation
P.O. Box 860
Valley Forge, PA 19482
Application address: 1 New Bond St., P.O. Box 15008, Worcester, MA 01615, tel.: (508) 795-5000
Contact: Judith D. Cutts

Trust established in 1953 in MA; incorporated in 1975.
Donor(s): Norton Co.
Financial data (yr. ended 12/31/01): Grants paid, $889,754; assets, $0 (M); gifts received, $889,754; expenditures, $889,754; qualifying distributions, $889,754.
Limitations: Giving primarily in areas of company operations.
Publications: Application guidelines.
Application information: Application form required.
Officers and Directors:* Jean-Francois Phelizon,* Pres.; Dorothy C. Wackerman,* V.P. and Secy.; D. Chris Altmansberger,* V.P.; George B. Amoss, V.P.; Dennis J. Baker,* V.P.; David Boivin,* V.P.; F. Lee Faust,* V.P.; James E. Hilyard,* V.P.; Mark E. Mathisen,* V.P.; Mark J. Scott,* V.P.; James F. Harkins, Jr., Treas.; Robert C. Ayotte.
EIN: 237423043
Codes: CS, FD, CD

46128
Colcom Foundation
2 Gateway Ctr., Ste. 1800
Pittsburgh, PA 15222-1402
Contact: D. Panazzi, Prog. Off.

Established in 1996 in PA.
Donor(s): C. May.
Financial data (yr. ended 12/31/00): Grants paid, $882,000; assets, $25,013,090 (M); gifts received, $2,510,750; expenditures, $1,101,674; qualifying distributions, $895,400.
Officers and Directors:* C. May,* Chair.; R. Meyer,* Pres.; D. Panazzi, Secy.; T. Inglis, Treas.; E. Saxman.
EIN: 311479839
Codes: FD

46129
James M. and Margaret V. Stine Foundation
c/o Robert J. Weinberg
3000 Two Logan Sq.
Philadelphia, PA 19103-2799

Established in 1996 in PA.
Donor(s): James M. Stine, Margaret V. Stine.
Financial data (yr. ended 12/31/01): Grants paid, $871,900; assets, $22,780,654 (M); expenditures, $1,079,036; qualifying distributions, $877,296.
Limitations: Applications not accepted. Giving primarily in MD and PA.
Application information: Contributes only to pre-selected organizations.
Officers and Directors:* Margaret V. Stine,* Pres. and Treas.; Sarah Igler,* V.P.; Martha Lee Boyd,* Secy.; David J. Stine, Robert J. Weinberg.
EIN: 232834787
Codes: FD

46130
Paul E. Kelly Foundation
(Formerly Superior-Pacific Fund)
109 Forrest Ave.
Narberth, PA 19072-2212
FAX: (610) 664-9892
Contact: Paul E. Kelly, Jr., Pres.

Trust established in 1952 in PA.
Donor(s): Superior Tube Co., Pacific Tube Co., Cawsl Enterprises, Inc.
Financial data (yr. ended 12/31/01): Grants paid, $856,850; assets, $20,946,931 (M); expenditures, $1,082,662; qualifying distributions, $938,356.
Limitations: Giving primarily in the Philadelphia, PA, area.
Application information: Application form not required.
Officers and Directors:* Paul E. Kelly, Jr.,* Pres.; Janet F. Kelly,* V.P.; Christine K. Kieman,* V.P.; Judith Shea,* V.P.
EIN: 236298237
Codes: FD, GTI

46131
Colonial Oaks Foundation
850 N. Wyomissing Blvd., Ste. 200
Wyomissing, PA 19610
Application address: P.O. Box 5936, Wyomissing, PA, 19610-5936; FAX: (610) 988-2416
Contact: Christine M. Auman, Exec Dir.; or Kristin E. McGlinn, Exec. Dir.

Established in 1992 in PA.
Donor(s): Terrence J. McGlinn, Sr.
Financial data (yr. ended 09/30/01): Grants paid, $832,180; assets, $17,111,441 (M); expenditures, $895,033; qualifying distributions, $836,450.
Limitations: Giving primarily in Berks County, PA.
Officers and Directors:* Terrence J. McGlinn, Sr.,* Chair. and Pres.; Christine M. Auman,* Secy. and Co-Exec. Dir.; Margaret M. Shields,* Treas.; Kristin E. McGlinn, Co-Exec. Dir.; Barbara T. McGlinn, John F. McGlinn II, Terrence J. McGlinn, Jr.
EIN: 232705277
Codes: FD

46132
Snee-Reinhardt Charitable Foundation
River Park Commons Two
2425 Sidney St.
Pittsburgh, PA 15203 (412) 390-2690
Contact: Joan E. Szymanski, Fdn. Mgr.

Established in 1987 in PA.
Donor(s): Katherine E. Snee.‡
Financial data (yr. ended 12/31/01): Grants paid, $831,298; assets, $21,761,406 (M); gifts received, $11,381,781; expenditures, $1,060,119; qualifying distributions, $843,964.
Limitations: Giving primarily in northern MD, PA (especially the southwestern region) and northeast WV.
Publications: Application guidelines, informational brochure (including application guidelines), grants list, annual report.
Application information: Application form required.
Directors: Paul A. Heasley, Chair.; Virginia M. Davis, Christina R. Heasley, Karen L. Heasley, Richard T. Vail.
Trustee: PNC Bank, N.A.
EIN: 256292908
Codes: FD

46133
Meyer and Stephanie Eglin Foundation
Eglin Sq. Garage
15th & Samson St.
Philadelphia, PA 19102 (215) 564-4242
Contact: Stephanie Eglin, Pres.

Established in 1996 in PA.
Donor(s): Stephanie Eglin.
Financial data (yr. ended 12/31/01): Grants paid, $825,000; assets, $2,383,857 (M); expenditures, $841,443; qualifying distributions, $835,469.
Limitations: Giving primarily in Philadelphia, PA.
Officers: Stephanie Eglin, Pres.; Loretta Zeiger, Secy.
EIN: 232832453
Codes: FD

46134
The Crels Foundation
5917 Main St.
East Petersburg, PA 17520 (717) 581-8130
Contact: Kenneth N. Burkholder, Chair.

Trust established in 1953 in PA.
Donor(s): Edwin B. Nolt.‡
Financial data (yr. ended 12/31/01): Grants paid, $820,000; assets, $17,051 (M); expenditures, $900,869; qualifying distributions, $872,448.
Limitations: Giving primarily in the Lancaster County, PA, area.
Application information: Applications not encouraged. Application form not required.
Officers and Trustees:* Kenneth N. Burkholder,* Chair.; Eugene N. Burkholder, Vice-Chair.; Clarence J. Nelson,* Secy.; J. Michael Burkholder, Leon Ray Burkholder.
EIN: 236243577
Codes: FD

46135
Addison H. Gibson Foundation
1 PPG Pl., Ste. 2230
Pittsburgh, PA 15222-5401 (412) 261-1611
FAX: (412) 261-5733; E-mail: rwallace@gibson-fnd.org (for medical assistance), ldunbar@gibson-fnd.org (for student loans); URL: http://www.gibson-fnd.org
Contact: Rebecca Wallace, Dir., or Lynn S. Dunbar, Asst. Dir.

Foundation established in 1937 in PA.
Donor(s): Addison H. Gibson.‡
Financial data (yr. ended 12/31/01): Grants paid, $818,447; assets, $29,326,754 (M); gifts received, $10,226; expenditures, $1,281,622; qualifying distributions, $2,028,250; giving activities include $901,645 for loans to individuals.
Limitations: Giving limited to residents of western PA.
Application information: Guidelines available on website. Medical grants are paid to the health care provider treating the approved individual applicant, never directly to the individual. No grants for existing medical bills. Application form required.
Officer: Rebecca Wallace, Exec. Dir.
Trustees: Douglas E. Gilbert, Timothy M. Slavish, National City Bank of Pennsylvania.
EIN: 250965379
Codes: FD, GTI

46136
Dr. & Mrs. Arthur William Phillips Charitable Trust
229 Elm St.
P.O. Box 316
Oil City, PA 16301-0316 (814) 676-2736
Contact: William J. McFate, Tr.

Trust established in 1978 in PA.
Donor(s): Arthur William Phillips.‡
Financial data (yr. ended 09/30/01): Grants paid, $813,816; assets, $14,387,421 (M); expenditures, $950,839; qualifying distributions, $836,724.
Limitations: Giving primarily in northwestern PA.
Application information: Application form not required.
Trustees: Hon. William E. Breene, Edith Gilmore Letcher, William J. McFate.
EIN: 256201015
Codes: FD

46137
Boyer Foundation
(also known as Daniel B. & Blanche R. Boyer Foundation)
c/o Investors Trust Co.
2201 Ridgewood Rd., No. 180
Wyomissing, PA 19610-1190
Contact: Jeannette Madaya

Financial data (yr. ended 12/31/99): Grants paid, $792,382; assets, $0 (M); expenditures, $800,351; qualifying distributions, $791,518.
Limitations: Giving limited to Boyertown, PA.
Trustees: Daniel B. Boyer III, Daniel Gerhart, Pastor John Pearson.
EIN: 236259256
Codes: FD

46138
The Rockwell Foundation
c/o PNC Bank, N.A., MS: P2-PTPP-25-1
2 PNC Plz., 620 Liberty Ave.
Pittsburgh, PA 15222-2719 (412) 762-5182
Contact: Bea Lynch, Asst. V.P.

Trust established in 1956 in PA.
Donor(s): Willard F. Rockwell,‡ and family.

46138—PENNSYLVANIA

Financial data (yr. ended 12/31/01): Grants paid, $781,900; assets, $13,708,329 (M); expenditures, $849,708; qualifying distributions, $788,178.
Limitations: Giving primarily in PA.
Application information: Application form not required.
Officer and Trustees:* H. Campbell Stuckeman,* Secy.; George Peter Rockwell, Russell A. Rockwell, PNC Bank, N.A.
EIN: 256035975
Codes: FD

46139
Sherrerd Foundation
(Formerly Muirfield Foundation)
1 Tower Bridge
West Conshohocken, PA 19428
Contact: John J.F. Sherrerd, Pres.

Established in 1986 in PA.
Donor(s): John J.F. Sherrerd, Kathleen C. Sherrerd.
Financial data (yr. ended 07/31/01): Grants paid, $780,124; assets, $16,699,340 (M); gifts received, $199,605; expenditures, $818,825; qualifying distributions, $764,130.
Limitations: Applications not accepted. Giving primarily in PA, with some emphasis on Philadelphia and Bryn Mawr.
Application information: The foundation makes grants only to institutions and organizations with whom the officers have direct relationships. Unsolicited requests for funds not considered.
Officer and Directors:* John J.F. Sherrerd,* Pres.; Kathleen C. Sherrerd.
EIN: 222751186
Codes: FD

46140
Sordoni Foundation, Inc.
45 Owen St.
Forty Fort, PA 18704-4305 (570) 287-3161
FAX: (570) 288-3663
Contact: William B. Sordoni, Secy.-Treas., or Andrew J. Sordoni III, Pres.

Incorporated in 1946 in PA.
Donor(s): Andrew J. Sordoni, Sr.,‡ Andrew J. Sordoni, Jr.,‡ Andrew J. Sordoni III, Mrs. Andrew J. Sordoni, Sr.,‡ Mrs. Andrew J. Sordoni, Jr.,‡ Mrs. Andrew J. Sordoni III, Helen Mary Sekera, William B. Sordoni, Margaret F. Sordoni.
Financial data (yr. ended 12/31/01): Grants paid, $774,205; assets, $13,007,949 (M); gifts received, $100; expenditures, $833,092; qualifying distributions, $775,320.
Limitations: Giving primarily in northeastern PA.
Application information: The foundation has discontinued the scholarships to individuals program. No new grants will be awarded. Application form not required.
Officers and Directors:* Andrew J. Sordoni III,* Pres.; William B. Sordoni, Secy.-Treas.; Richard Allan, A. William Kelly, John J. Menapace, Patrick Solano, Margaret F. Sordoni, Susan F. Sordoni.
EIN: 246017505
Codes: FD

46141
Shaffer Family Charitable Trust
3548 Bingen Rd.
Bethlehem, PA 18015 (610) 867-7568
Contact: David N. Shaffer, Tr.

Established in 1987 in PA.
Donor(s): David Shaffer, Susan Shaffer, Jack M. Shaffer,‡ Cecile Shaffer, Rose Shaffer.
Financial data (yr. ended 12/31/01): Grants paid, $770,025; assets, $12,737,146 (M); gifts received, $1,160,747; expenditures, $865,511; qualifying distributions, $772,132.

Limitations: Giving primarily in Lehigh Valley, PA.
Application information: Application form not required.
Trustees: Cecile Shaffer, David Shaffer, Rose Shaffer, Susan Shaffer.
EIN: 232502319
Codes: FD

46142
Michael Cardone Foundation
5501 Whitaker Ave.
Philadelphia, PA 19124-1799
Application address: c/o Cardone Industries, 5670 Rising Sun Ave., Philadelphia, PA 19120
Contact: Pastor Oliver

Established in 1977.
Donor(s): Michael Cardone, Sr., M. Cardone Industries, Inc.
Financial data (yr. ended 12/31/00): Grants paid, $765,750; assets, $4,915,356 (M); expenditures, $795,335; qualifying distributions, $765,750.
Limitations: Giving on a national basis, with some emphasis on NJ and PA.
Application information: Application form required.
Officers: Jacqueline Cardone, Chair.; Joseph Beretta, Sr., Exec. Dir.
Trustees: Michael Cardone, Jr., Abraham Oliver, Mark Spuler.
EIN: 236652761
Codes: FD

46143
William V. and Catherine A. McKinney Charitable Foundation
c/o National City Bank of Pennsylvania
National City Ctr. (25-154), 20 Stanwix St.
Pittsburgh, PA 15222-4802 (412) 644-8332
Contact: William M. Schmidt, V.P., National City Bank of Pennsylvania

Established in 1990 in PA.
Donor(s): Catherine A. McKinney.‡
Financial data (yr. ended 03/31/02): Grants paid, $765,000; assets, $13,560,256 (M); expenditures, $851,262; qualifying distributions, $805,689.
Limitations: Giving limited to western PA.
Application information: Use Grantmakers of Western Pennsylvania Common Grant Application. Application form required.
Trustee: National City Bank of Pennsylvania.
EIN: 251641619
Codes: FD

46144
The Neubauer Foundation
210 Rittenhouse Sq. W., Ste. 3106
Philadelphia, PA 19103 (215) 238-3880
Contact: Joseph Neubauer, Tr.

Established in 1998 in PA.
Donor(s): Joseph Neubauer.
Financial data (yr. ended 11/30/01): Grants paid, $764,230; assets, $33,262,128 (M); gifts received, $3,969,229; expenditures, $764,452; qualifying distributions, $764,351.
Limitations: Giving primarily in NY and PA.
Trustees: Melissa Neubauer Anderson, Joseph Neubauer, Lawrence Neubauer.
EIN: 256627704
Codes: FD

46145
Margaret Dorrance Strawbridge Foundation of Pennsylvania I, Inc.
4000 Bell Atlantic Twr.
1717 Arch St.
Philadelphia, PA 19103-2793

Established in 1985 in PA.

Donor(s): Margaret Dorrance Strawbridge Foundation, George Strawbridge, Jr.
Financial data (yr. ended 12/31/01): Grants paid, $757,500; assets, $11,395,121 (M); gifts received, $325,000; expenditures, $889,583; qualifying distributions, $757,500.
Limitations: Applications not accepted. Giving on a national basis.
Application information: Contributes only to pre-selected organizations.
Officers: George Strawbridge, Jr., Pres. and Secy.; Nina S. Strawbridge, V.P.
EIN: 232373081
Codes: FD

46146
The Lancaster County Foundation
P.O. Box 1745
Lancaster, PA 17608-1745 (717) 397-1629
FAX: (717) 397-6877; *E-mail:* jimsabino@lancastercountyfoundation.org; *URL:* http://www.lancastercountyfoundation.org
Contact: Deborah B. Schattgen

Established in 1924 in PA.
Donor(s): Martin M. Harnish.‡
Financial data (yr. ended 04/30/01): Grants paid, $750,000; assets, $34,628,700 (M); expenditures, $817,970.
Limitations: Giving limited to Lancaster County, PA.
Publications: Annual report, application guidelines, newsletter.
Application information: Application form required.
Governing Committee: Rev. John R. Baldwin, Chair.; Rev. David Gockley, Vice-Chair.; Deborah B. Schattgen, Exec. Dir.; Carol Falk, William D. Fisher, S. Dale High, Dawn K. Johnston, Roger Moyer, Bruce P. Ryder, Jeff Sidebottom.
EIN: 236419120
Codes: CM, FD

46147
The Philip Chosky Charitable & Educational Foundation
610 Ellsworth Pl.
Pittsburgh, PA 15232

Established in 1998 in PA.
Donor(s): Philip Chosky, Electronic Institutes, Inc., Electronic Institutes Foundation.
Financial data (yr. ended 12/31/00): Grants paid, $745,142; assets, $9,902,808 (M); gifts received, $648,655; expenditures, $1,000,180; qualifying distributions, $768,879.
Limitations: Applications not accepted. Giving primarily in Pittsburgh, PA.
Application information: Contributes only to pre-selected organizations.
Officer: Philip Chosky, Exec. Dir.
Directors: Stanley Barg, Charles Kirshner, Michael O'Malley.
EIN: 232932969
Codes: FD

46148
Elizabeth S. Hooper Foundation
P.O. Box 7453
St. Davids, PA 19087

Established in 1967.
Donor(s): Thomas Hooper, Adrian S. Hooper, Bruce H. Hooper, Ralph W. Hooper, Interstate Marine Transport Co., Interstate Towing Co., Interstate Ocean Transport Co., and members of the Hooper family.
Financial data (yr. ended 06/30/01): Grants paid, $728,000; assets, $2,558,468 (M); gifts received,

$144,668; expenditures, $752,107; qualifying distributions, $728,000.
Limitations: Applications not accepted. Giving on a national basis, with emphasis on Washington, DC, MD, and PA.
Application information: Contributes only to pre-selected organizations.
Officers: Adrian S. Hooper, Pres.; Thomas Hooper, V.P.; Bruce H. Hooper, Secy.; Ralph W. Hooper, Treas.
EIN: 236434997
Codes: FD

46149
J. S. Herr Foundation
P.O. Box 300
Nottingham, PA 19362
Contact: James S. Herr, Pres.

Established in 1990 in PA.
Donor(s): Herr Foods, Inc.
Financial data (yr. ended 12/31/01): Grants paid, $723,000; assets, $2,450,801 (M); gifts received, $208,105; expenditures, $723,942; qualifying distributions, $723,942.
Limitations: Applications not accepted.
Application information: Unsolicited requests for funds not accepted.
Officers and Trustees:* James S. Herr,* Pres.; Miriam Herr,* Secy.; Gene Herr,* Treas.; June Gunden, Edwin Herr, James M. Herr, Martha Thomas.
EIN: 232531170
Codes: FD

46150
George H. and Margaret McClintic Love Foundation
c/o Mellon Bank, N.A.
1 Mellon Bank Ctr., Rm. 3845
Pittsburgh, PA 15258-0001

Trust established in 1952 in PA.
Donor(s): George H. Love, Margaret McClintic Love, Howard M. Love.
Financial data (yr. ended 12/31/01): Grants paid, $712,500; assets, $6,186,986 (M); gifts received, $52,558; expenditures, $764,540; qualifying distributions, $710,143.
Limitations: Giving primarily in PA and on the East Coast.
Officer: Howard M. Love, Dir. of Distribs.
Trustee: Mellon Bank, N.A.
EIN: 256018655
Codes: FD

46151
United Service Foundation, Inc.
P.O. Box 36
New Holland, PA 17557
Contact: Dale M. Weaver, Pres.

Established in 1969 in PA.
Donor(s): Janet Newswanger, Larry Newswanger, Dale M. Weaver, Edith M. Weaver, Irene M. Weaver, Victor F. Weaver,‡ Dawn Isley, Gregory Newswanger, Kendall Newswanger, Randall Newswanger.
Financial data (yr. ended 12/31/01): Grants paid, $710,625; assets, $10,793,221 (M); expenditures, $797,703; qualifying distributions, $707,906.
Limitations: Applications not accepted. Giving limited to CA, IL, IN, MD, and PA.
Application information: Contributes only to pre-selected organizations.
Officers: Dale M. Weaver, Pres.; Larry W. Newswanger, Secy.; Janet Newswanger, Treas.
EIN: 237038781
Codes: FD

46152
Glen and Diane Meakem Foundation, Inc.
703 Cochran St.
Sewickley, PA 15143-1622

Established in 2000 in PA.
Donor(s): Glen T. Meakem, Diane B. Meakem.
Financial data (yr. ended 12/31/01): Grants paid, $710,284; assets, $1,894,917 (M); gifts received, $704,800; expenditures, $723,867; qualifying distributions, $695,987.
Limitations: Applications not accepted. Giving primarily in PA.
Application information: Contributes only to pre-selected organizations.
Officers: Glen T. Meakem, Pres.; Diane B. Meakem, V.P.; Raymond P. Parker, Secy.-Treas.
EIN: 251877307
Codes: FD

46153
The Hamer Foundation
2470 Fox Hill Rd.
State College, PA 16803 (814) 355-8004
Contact: Donald W. Hamer, Tr.

Established in 1989 in PA.
Donor(s): Donald W. Hamer.
Financial data (yr. ended 12/31/01): Grants paid, $705,000; assets, $4,903,128 (M); gifts received, $750,000; expenditures, $722,155; qualifying distributions, $704,155.
Limitations: Giving primarily in Centre County, PA.
Application information: Application form not required.
Trustees: Donald W. Hamer, Diane M. Kerly, Edward Matosziuk.
EIN: 251610780
Codes: FD

46154
100 Acre Wood Foundation Trust
c/o Fox Rothchild O'Brien & Frankel, LLP
P.O. Box 1589
Doylestown, PA 18901-0700

Established in 2000 in PA.
Donor(s): Kenneth F. Brown, Pamela H. Brown.
Financial data (yr. ended 04/30/02): Grants paid, $700,000; assets, $1,454,459 (M); gifts received, $1,000,740; expenditures, $702,761; qualifying distributions, $700,000.
Limitations: Applications not accepted. Giving primarily in Quakertown, PA.
Application information: Contributes only to pre-selected organizations.
Trustees: Kenneth F. Brown, Pamela H. Brown, Shawn Brown.
EIN: 256714457
Codes: FD

46155
The Juliet L. Hillman Simonds Foundation, Inc.
2000 Grant Bldg.
Pittsburgh, PA 15219 (412) 338-3466
FAX: (412) 338-3463; E-mail: foundation@hillmanfo.com
Contact: Ronald W. Wertz, Secy. and Exec. Dir.

Established in 1986 in PA.
Donor(s): Juliet Lea Hillman Simonds, Henry Lea Hillman Charitable Lead Trust.
Financial data (yr. ended 12/31/01): Grants paid, $692,750; assets, $10,130,739 (M); expenditures, $744,812; qualifying distributions, $703,791.
Limitations: Giving primarily in Pittsburgh, PA.
Publications: Application guidelines.
Application information: Application form not required.
Officers and Directors:* Juliet Lea Hillman Simonds,* Pres.; Lawrence M. Wagner,* V.P.; Ronald W. Wertz,* Secy. and Exec. Dir.; Maurice J. White,* Treas.
EIN: 251536654
Codes: FD

46156
John Nesbit Rees and Sarah Henne Rees Charitable Foundation
314 S. Franklin St., Ste. B
P.O. Box 325
Titusville, PA 16354-0325 (814) 827-1844
FAX: (814) 827-6620; E-mail: jnrshrees@stargate.net
Contact: Richard W. Roeder, Tr.

Established in 1989 in PA.
Donor(s): John Nesbit Rees,‡ Sarah Henne Rees.‡
Financial data (yr. ended 12/31/01): Grants paid, $676,813; assets, $13,476,966 (M); expenditures, $760,928; qualifying distributions, $699,463.
Limitations: Giving primarily in the Titusville, PA, area, including parts of Forest, Crawford, Venango, and Warren counties.
Publications: Annual report, application guidelines.
Application information: Application form not required.
Trustees: Richard W. Roeder, Barbara L. Smith.
EIN: 256264847
Codes: FD

46157
The Hedgebrook Foundation
1 Logan Sq.
18th and Cherry Sts.
Philadelphia, PA 19103-6996

Established in 1991 in PA.
Donor(s): Michael A. Wall.
Financial data (yr. ended 03/31/01): Grants paid, $674,595; assets, $2,524,632 (M); gifts received, $2,433,750; expenditures, $727,056; qualifying distributions, $696,428.
Limitations: Applications not accepted. Giving primarily in PA.
Application information: Contributes only to pre-selected organizations.
Trustee: Michael A. Wall.
EIN: 236964253
Codes: FD

46158
The Donald B. and Dorothy L. Stabler Foundation
c/o Allfirst
213 Market St.
Harrisburg, PA 17101
Contact: William J. King, Chair.

Established in 1966 in PA.
Donor(s): Donald B. Stabler, Dorothy L. Stabler, Stabler Cos., Inc., Work Area Protection Corp., Eastern Industries, Inc., Protection Svc., Inc., Stabler Devel. Co.
Financial data (yr. ended 12/31/01): Grants paid, $673,000; assets, $14,739,655 (M); gifts received, $102,085; expenditures, $764,292; qualifying distributions, $673,000.
Limitations: Giving primarily in PA, with some emphasis on Harrisburg.
Application information: Application form not required.
Officers: William J. King,* Chair.; Frank A. Sinon,* Secy.
Directors: Cyril C. Dunmire, Jr., David H. Schaper, Dorothy L. Stabler, Richard A. Zimmerman.
EIN: 236422944
Codes: FD

46159—PENNSYLVANIA

46159
Kevy K. & Hortense M. Kaiserman Foundation
201 S. 18th St., Ste. 300
Philadelphia, PA 19103-5921 (215) 546-2665
Contact: Ronald L. Kaiserman, Tr.

Established in 1980 in PA.
Donor(s): Kaiserman Enterprises, LP.
Financial data (yr. ended 06/30/01): Grants paid, $671,600; assets, $3,936,129 (M); gifts received, $659,775; expenditures, $680,444; qualifying distributions, $669,642.
Limitations: Applications not accepted. Giving primarily in Philadelphia, PA.
Application information: Usually funds same organizations.
Trustees: Hortense M. Kaiserman, Kenneth S. Kaiserman, Ronald L. Kaiserman, Constance K. Robinson.
EIN: 232299921
Codes: FD

46160
Arete Foundation
1845 Walnut St., 10th Fl.
Philadelphia, PA 19103
Contact: Sue Ann Taylor, Exec. Dir.

Established in 1986 in PA.
Financial data (yr. ended 11/30/01): Grants paid, $669,155; assets, $5,663,804 (M); gifts received, $81,924; expenditures, $690,047; qualifying distributions, $669,155.
Limitations: Giving primarily in Philadelphia, PA.
Application information: Application form not required.
Officer: Sue Ann Taylor, Exec. Dir.
Trustees: Betsy Z. Cohen, Edward E. Cohen.
EIN: 236779271
Codes: FD

46161
Dexter F. and Dorothy H. Baker Foundation
c/o Air Products & Chemicals, Inc.
7201 Hamilton Blvd.
Allentown, PA 18195-1526

Established in 1986 in PA.
Donor(s): Dexter F. Baker, Dorothy H. Baker.
Financial data (yr. ended 12/31/01): Grants paid, $668,086; assets, $15,248,521 (M); gifts received, $1,251,032; expenditures, $742,501; qualifying distributions, $705,858.
Limitations: Giving primarily in Collier County, FL, Lehigh, and Northampton counties, PA, and Hilton Head, SC.
Publications: Application guidelines.
Application information: Application form required.
Officers and Trustees:* Dexter F. Baker,* Chair.; Ellen Baker Baltz,* Exec. Dir.; Carolyn Baker, Dorothy H. Baker, Leslie Baker Boris, Susan B. Royal, Mellon Bank, N.A.
EIN: 232453230
Codes: FD

46162
Snyder Charitable Foundation
P.O. Box 1022
Kittanning, PA 16201-5022

Established in 1987 in PA.
Donor(s): Allegheny Mineral Corp., Armstrong Cement & Supply Corp., Snyder Brothers, Inc.
Financial data (yr. ended 12/31/00): Grants paid, $666,415; assets, $644,244 (M); gifts received, $550,000; expenditures, $666,614; qualifying distributions, $666,112.
Limitations: Applications not accepted. Giving primarily in PA.
Application information: Contributes only to pre-selected organizations.
Trustees: Charles H. Snyder, Jr., David E. Snyder, Elmer A. Snyder.
EIN: 251551808
Codes: FD

46163
G. B. Stuart Charitable Foundation
3 S. Hanover St.
Carlisle, PA 17013 (717) 243-3737
Contact: Karen E. Faircloth, Secy.-Treas.

Established in 1977.
Donor(s): George B. Stuart.‡
Financial data (yr. ended 12/31/01): Grants paid, $658,500; assets, $16,527,488 (M); expenditures, $762,190; qualifying distributions, $720,680.
Limitations: Giving limited to Cumberland County, PA, with emphasis on Carlisle.
Officers and Directors:* Barbara E. Falconer,* Pres.; Victoria J. Macauley,* V.P.; Karen E. Faircloth,* Secy.-Treas.; Alison J. Brockmeyer, Keith D. Falconer.
Trustees: M & T Bank, Mellon Bank, N.A.
EIN: 232042245
Codes: FD

46164
The Medleycott Family Foundation
1120 Bristol Rd.
Churchville, PA 18966

Established in 1991.
Donor(s): Clyde Medleycott, Alice E. Medleycott, Superpac, Inc.
Financial data (yr. ended 12/31/01): Grants paid, $657,000; assets, $798,896 (M); gifts received, $872,666; expenditures, $658,212; qualifying distributions, $657,997.
Limitations: Applications not accepted. Giving primarily in PA.
Application information: Contributes only to pre-selected organizations.
Trustees: Leon W. Marchetti, Alice E. Medleycott, Mary E. Medleycott.
EIN: 237683693
Codes: FD

46165
The William Talbott Hillman Foundation, Inc.
2000 Grant Bldg.
Pittsburgh, PA 15219 (412) 338-3466
FAX: (412) 338-3463; E-mail: foundation@hillmanfo.com
Contact: Ronald W. Wertz, Secy. and Exec. Dir.

Established in 1986 in PA.
Donor(s): William Talbott Hillman, Henry Lea Hillman Charitable Lead Trust.
Financial data (yr. ended 12/31/01): Grants paid, $650,050; assets, $10,346,419 (M); expenditures, $705,121; qualifying distributions, $661,054.
Limitations: Giving primarily in New York, NY and Pittsburgh, PA.
Publications: Application guidelines.
Application information: Application form not required.
Officers and Directors:* William Talbott Hillman,* Pres.; Lawrence M. Wagner,* V.P.; Ronald W. Wertz,* Secy. and Exec. Dir.; Maurice J. White,* Treas.
EIN: 251536657
Codes: FD

46166
USA Waste/Chambers Development Foundation for Pittsburgh Charities
c/o PNC Advisors
620 Liberty Ave., P2-PTPP-10-2
Pittsburgh, PA 15222-2705
Application address: c/o Nancy Barnhart, 1500 Ardmore Blvd., Ste. 407, Pittsburgh, PA 15221, tel.: (412) 871-6118

Established in 1995 in PA.
Donor(s): USA Waste Services, Inc., Waste Management, Inc.
Financial data (yr. ended 06/30/00): Grants paid, $650,000; assets, $1,294,633 (M); expenditures, $662,941; qualifying distributions, $649,155.
Limitations: Giving primarily in Pittsburgh, PA.
Trustees: John G. Rangos, Sr., PNC Bank, N.A.
EIN: 256500262
Codes: CS, TN

46167
Jerry Lee Foundation
c/o WBEB FM Radio, Inc.
10 Presidential Blvd.
Bala Cynwyd, PA 19004 (610) 667-8400
E-mail: jerryl@101-FM.com
Contact: Gloria Dreon, Admin.

Established in 1996 in PA.
Donor(s): David Kurtz, Gerald Lee.
Financial data (yr. ended 12/31/01): Grants paid, $644,000; assets, $245,918 (M); gifts received, $807,000; expenditures, $753,155; qualifying distributions, $748,925.
Limitations: Applications not accepted.
Application information: Contributes only to pre-selected organizations.
Directors: David Kurtz, Gerald Lee.
EIN: 232867684
Codes: FD

46168
The Pennsylvania Fund
100 Four Falls Corp. Ctr., Ste. 205
West Conshohocken, PA 19428
(610) 397-0880
Contact: Peter C. Morse, Tr.

Donor(s): Martha F. Morse, Peter C. Morse.
Financial data (yr. ended 06/30/01): Grants paid, $640,250; assets, $2,037,539 (M); expenditures, $656,807; qualifying distributions, $640,250.
Limitations: Giving primarily in PA.
Application information: Generally contributes to pre-selected organizations.
Trustees: Martha F. Morse, Peter C. Morse.
EIN: 232222176
Codes: FD

46169
CMS Endowment Foundation
1926 Arch St.
Philadelphia, PA 19103

Established in 1995 in PA.
Donor(s): Paul Silberberg, Mark Solomon, Kevin Satterthwaite, Rosemary Cataldi, Joseph Lutes, Richard Mitchell, Daniel Melrod, Joseph Melrod, Robert Spivak, William Landman, Brind Lindsay, David Spungen, Ingrid Welch, Morey Goldberg, Michael Sanyour, Russel Holt, Patty Young, Peter Miller, Jeff Rotter, Parkway Corp.
Financial data (yr. ended 09/30/01): Grants paid, $638,206; assets, $388,560 (M); gifts received, $392,686; expenditures, $640,730; qualifying distributions, $638,206.
Limitations: Applications not accepted. Giving primarily in NJ, New York, NY, and PA, with emphasis on Philadelphia.

Application information: Unsolicited requests for funds not accepted.
Trustees: Paul Silberberg, Mark Solomon.
EIN: 237819212
Codes: FD

46170
Asplundh Foundation
708 Blair Mill Rd.
Willow Grove, PA 19090
Contact: Christopher B. Asplundh, Pres.

Incorporated in 1953 in PA.
Donor(s): Carl Hj. Asplundh,‡ Lester Asplundh.‡
Financial data (yr. ended 12/31/01): Grants paid, $636,000; assets, $14,005,679 (M); gifts received, $100,000; expenditures, $648,958; qualifying distributions, $648,958.
Limitations: Applications not accepted. Giving primarily in PA.
Application information: Contributes only to pre-selected organizations.
Officers and Directors:* Christopher B. Asplundh,* Pres.; Barr E. Asplundh,* V.P.; E. Boyd Asplundh,* Secy.-Treas.; Brent D. Asplundh, Carl Hj. Asplundh, Jr., Carl Hj. Asplundh III, Gregg G. Asplundh, Paul S. Asplundh, Robert H. Asplundh, Scott M. Asplundh, Steven G. Asplundh, Stewart L. Asplundh, George E. Graham, Jr., James E. Graham.
EIN: 236297246
Codes: FD

46171
Harriett Ames Charitable Trust
c/o Hawthorn, PNC Advisors
1600 Market St., 19th Fl.
Philadelphia, PA 19103 (610) 341-9270
Contact: L. Dianne Lomonaco, Trust Admin.

Trust established in 1952 in NY.
Donor(s): Harriett Ames.‡
Financial data (yr. ended 12/31/00): Grants paid, $635,120; assets, $9,184,466 (M); expenditures, $689,049; qualifying distributions, $664,772.
Limitations: Applications not accepted. Giving primarily in the metropolitan New York, NY, area.
Application information: Contributes only to pre-selected organizations. Unsolicited requests for funds not considered.
Trustee: Steven Ames.
EIN: 236286757
Codes: FD

46172
Sybiel B. Berkman Foundation
200 Gateway Twrs.
Pittsburgh, PA 15222

Established in 1965.
Donor(s): Myles P. Berkman, Jack N. Berkman.‡
Financial data (yr. ended 12/31/01): Grants paid, $622,100; assets, $12,325,252 (M); expenditures, $688,103; qualifying distributions, $617,364.
Limitations: Applications not accepted. Giving primarily in FL, and New York, NY.
Application information: Contributes only to pre-selected organizations.
Officers: Myles P. Berkman, Pres. and Treas.; Stephen S. Berkman, Secy.
Trustee: Monroe E. Berkman.
EIN: 346566801
Codes: FD

46173
Lilliput Foundation
P.O. Box 70
Lederach, PA 19450
Contact: Drew Lewis, Pres.

Established in 1985 in PA.
Donor(s): Drew Lewis, Marilyn S. Lewis.
Financial data (yr. ended 12/31/00): Grants paid, $620,727; assets, $1,877,531 (M); gifts received, $700,531; expenditures, $644,351; qualifying distributions, $619,823.
Limitations: Giving primarily in Montgomery County, PA.
Application information: Application form not required.
Officers and Trustees:* Drew Lewis,* Pres. and Treas.; Marilyn S. Lewis,* V.P. and Secy.; Andrew L. Lewis IV, Russell S. Lewis.
EIN: 232385383
Codes: FD

46174
CMS Foundation
1926 Arch St.
Philadelphia, PA 19103-1484

Established in 1996 in PA.
Donor(s): Morey Goldberg, Harry Kammerer, Paul Silberberg, Mark I. Solomon, Patty Young, Joe Lutes, Peter Miller.
Financial data (yr. ended 12/31/01): Grants paid, $619,134; assets, $461,223 (M); gifts received, $254,133; expenditures, $676,281; qualifying distributions, $619,149.
Limitations: Applications not accepted. Giving primarily in NY and PA, with emphasis on Philadelphia.
Application information: Contributes only to pre-selected organizations.
Trustees: Paul Silberberg, Mark I. Solomon.
EIN: 237819211
Codes: FD

46175
Helen D. Groome Beatty Trust
c/o Mellon Bank, N.A.
P.O. Box 7236, AIM No. 193-0224
Philadelphia, PA 19101-7236

Trust established in 1951 in PA.
Donor(s): Helen D. Groome Beatty.‡
Financial data (yr. ended 09/30/01): Grants paid, $616,212; assets, $11,567,200 (M); expenditures, $669,929; qualifying distributions, $627,207.
Limitations: Applications not accepted. Giving limited to the 5-county Philadelphia, PA, area.
Application information: Contributes only to pre-selected organizations.
Trustee: Mellon Bank, N.A.
EIN: 236224798
Codes: FD

46176
The Rorer Foundation, Inc.
761 Newtown Rd.
Villanova, PA 19085
FAX: (610) 688-2291
Contact: Gerald B. Rorer, Pres.

Established in 1963.
Donor(s): Edward C. Rorer, Gerald B. Rorer, Herbert T. Rorer.
Financial data (yr. ended 11/30/01): Grants paid, $615,004; assets, $10,716,882 (M); expenditures, $647,753; qualifying distributions, $612,193.
Limitations: Applications not accepted. Giving primarily in New Haven, CT, and the Philadelphia, PA, area.
Application information: Contributes only to pre-selected organizations. Unsolicited requests for funds not accepted.
Officers: Gerald B. Rorer, Pres.; Edward C. Rorer, V.P.; Herbert T. Rorer, Secy.-Treas.
EIN: 516017981
Codes: FD

46177
Rena Rowan Foundation
c/o Hanna, McGlone & Co.
919 Conestoga Rd., Bldg. 1, Ste. 300
Bryn Mawr, PA 19010

Established in 1994 in PA.
Financial data (yr. ended 12/31/00): Grants paid, $609,000; assets, $1,313,910 (M); gifts received, $2,098; expenditures, $653,546; qualifying distributions, $607,196.
Limitations: Applications not accepted. Giving primarily in PA.
Application information: Contributes only to pre-selected organizations.
Officer: Rena Rowan, Pres.
EIN: 232745464
Codes: FD

46178
Glenn and Ruth Mengle Foundation
c/o First Commonwealth Trust Co.
P.O. Box 1046
DuBois, PA 15801
Contact: D. Edward Chaplin, V.P., First Commonwealth Trust Co.

Trust established in 1956 in PA.
Donor(s): Glenn A. Mengle,‡ Ruth E. Mengle Blake.‡
Financial data (yr. ended 12/31/00): Grants paid, $605,094; assets, $14,155,592 (M); expenditures, $771,340; qualifying distributions, $605,094.
Limitations: Giving limited to the Brockway, DuBois, and Erie, PA, areas.
Trustees: DeVere L. Sheesley, First Commonwealth Trust Co.
EIN: 256067616
Codes: FD

46179
The Hallowell Foundation
c/o First Union National Bank
P.O. Box 7558, PA 4394
Philadelphia, PA 19101-7558
Contact: Lynn Ann Leonard, V.P., First Union National Bank

Trust established in 1956 in PA.
Donor(s): Members of the Hallowell family.
Financial data (yr. ended 12/31/01): Grants paid, $600,000; assets, $10,997,045 (M); expenditures, $668,840; qualifying distributions, $609,894.
Limitations: Applications not accepted. Giving primarily in PA.
Application information: Contributes only to pre-selected organizations.
Trustees: Dorothy W. Hallowell, Howard T. Hallowell III, Merritt W. Hallowell, Anne H. Miller.
EIN: 236234545
Codes: FD

46180
Charles S. & Mary Coen Family Foundation
1100 W. Chestnut St.
Washington, PA 15301
Application address: P.O. Box 34, Washington, PA 15301, tel.: (724) 223-5500
Contact: Mona L. Thompson, Tr.

Established in 1959 in PA.
Donor(s): C.S. Coen,‡ Mary Coen,‡ Charles R. Coen, C.S. Coen Land Co.
Financial data (yr. ended 02/28/01): Grants paid, $598,090; assets, $7,889,299 (M); gifts received, $76,000; expenditures, $612,532; qualifying distributions, $599,331.
Limitations: Giving primarily in PA.
Application information: Application form not required.

46180—PENNSYLVANIA

Trustees: Mona Thompson, Lawrence A. Withum, Jr.
EIN: 256033877
Codes: FD

46181
S. Wilson & Grace M. Pollock Foundation
c/o Allfirst, Trust Div.
21 E. Market St., M/C 402-130
York, PA 17401-1500
Application address: P.O. Box 11963, Harrisburg, PA 17108-1963
Contact: Heath Allen

Established in 1997 in PA.
Donor(s): Grace Pollock, S. Wilson Pollock.
Financial data (yr. ended 04/30/01): Grants paid, $596,284; assets, $10,741,185 (M); expenditures, $665,486; qualifying distributions, $577,919.
Limitations: Giving primarily in PA.
Director: Heath Allen.
Trustee: Allfirst.
EIN: 237889770
Codes: FD

46182
National Organization for Hearing Research Foundation
851 Duportail Rd., Ste. 200
Chesterbrook, PA 19087 (610) 664-3135
Application address: 225 Haverford Ave., No.1, Narbeth, PA 19072
Contact: Geraldine Dietz Fox, Pres.

Established in 1988 in PA.
Donor(s): Geraldine Dietz Fox, Richard J. Fox.
Financial data (yr. ended 12/31/01): Grants paid, $591,247; assets, $1,699,444 (M); gifts received, $1,130,151; expenditures, $721,513; qualifying distributions, $706,362.
Limitations: Giving on a national and international basis.
Publications: Annual report, occasional report, informational brochure, application guidelines.
Application information: Application form required.
Officers: Geraldine Dietz Fox, Pres.; Richard J. Fox, Secy.-Treas.
EIN: 232528578
Codes: FD

46183
The Thomas Phillips and Jane Moore Johnson Foundation
605 Oliver Bldg.
535 Smithfield St.
Pittsburgh, PA 15222 (412) 261-9008
Contact: Thomas Phillips Johnson

Established in 1990 in PA.
Donor(s): Thomas Phillips Johnson.
Financial data (yr. ended 12/31/01): Grants paid, $585,900; assets, $51,438,098 (M); gifts received, $48,808,751; expenditures, $643,166; qualifying distributions, $586,005.
Limitations: Giving on a national basis.
Officer and Trustees:* Thomas Phillips Johnson,* Chair.; William L. Casey, Winifred J. Clive, James M. Johnson, Jesse D. Johnson, Thomas Phillips Johnson, Jr.
EIN: 256357015
Codes: FD

46184
The Bruce E. and Robbi S. Toll Foundation
(Formerly The Bruce E. Toll Foundation)
3103 Philmont Ave.
Huntingdon Valley, PA 19006

Established in 1991 in PA.
Donor(s): Bruce E. Toll.

Financial data (yr. ended 01/31/02): Grants paid, $584,177; assets, $13,060,701 (M); gifts received, $6,725,000; expenditures, $609,946; qualifying distributions, $575,280.
Limitations: Applications not accepted. Giving primarily in PA.
Application information: Contributes only to pre-selected organizations.
Officer and Director:* Bruce E. Toll,* Pres., Treas., and Exec. Dir.
EIN: 232667935
Codes: FD

46185
Emma Clyde Hodge Memorial Fund
c/o PNC Bank, N.A., MS: P2-PTPP-25-1
2 PNC Plz., 620 Liberty Ave.
Pittsburgh, PA 15222-2719
Contact: Beatrice A. Lynch

Established in 1990 in PA.
Donor(s): Edwin Hodge, Jr.‡
Financial data (yr. ended 06/30/01): Grants paid, $583,125; assets, $9,856,186 (M); expenditures, $609,787; qualifying distributions, $571,168.
Limitations: Applications not accepted. Giving primarily in PA.
Application information: Unsolicited requests for funds are not accepted.
Trustee: PNC Bank, N.A.
EIN: 256227653
Codes: FD

46186
PTS Foundation
c/o Parkland Mgmt. Co.
580 W. Germantown Pike, Ste. 202
Plymouth Meeting, PA 19462 (216) 479-2200
Tel. for scholarship information: (615) 292-4379
Contact: Thomas H. Oden

Established in 1998 in PA as a follow-up to the Lois U. Horvitz Foundation.
Donor(s): Lois U. Horvitz Foundation.
Financial data (yr. ended 12/31/01): Grants paid, $580,445; assets, $8,795,042 (M); expenditures, $586,808; qualifying distributions, $586,058.
Application information: Application form required.
Officers and Directors:* Pam H. Schneider,* Chair.; Milton S. Schneider,* Pres. and Secy.-Treas.; Thomas H. Oden, Treas.
EIN: 232930670
Codes: FD

46187
St. Mary's Catholic Foundation
1935 State St.
St. Marys, PA 15857 (814) 781-4222
FAX: (814) 781-4223
Contact: Richard J. Reuscher, Secy.-Treas.

Incorporated in 1960 in PA.
Donor(s): Benedict R. Reuscher,‡ Alfred A. Gleixner,‡ Richard J. Reuscher, R.B. Reuscher, E.H. Gleixner, William E. Reuscher, C.J. Kogovsek, E B & Assocs., William P. Gies,‡ Edward J. Crowe,‡ Raymond R. Hoffman.‡
Financial data (yr. ended 11/30/01): Grants paid, $578,425; assets, $9,115,000 (M); expenditures, $1,224,229; qualifying distributions, $1,224,229.
Limitations: Applications not accepted. Giving primarily in Erie Diocese, PA, with emphasis on the St. Marys area and Elk County.
Application information: Contributes only to pre-selected organizations.
Officers and Trustees:* Bishop Donald Troutman,* Chair.; E.H. Gleixner,* Pres.; R.B. Reuscher,* V.P.; Richard J. Reuscher,* Secy.-Treas.; C.J. Kogovsek.

EIN: 256036961
Codes: FD

46188
Knox Family Foundation
2113 Delancey St.
Philadelphia, PA 19103
Contact: Eleanor G. Nalle, Pres. and Treas.

Incorporated in 1961 in NY.
Donor(s): Eleanor E. Knox,‡ Knox Gelatine, Inc.
Financial data (yr. ended 12/31/01): Grants paid, $578,000; assets, $9,062,848 (M); expenditures, $659,663; qualifying distributions, $574,973.
Limitations: Applications not accepted. Giving on a national basis.
Application information: Contributes only to pre-selected organizations. Unsolicited requests for funds not accepted.
Officers and Directors:* Eleanor G. Nalle,* Pres. and Treas.; John K. Graham,* V.P. and Secy.; Rose Ann Armstrong,* V.P.; Roseann K. Beaudoin,* V.P.; Rosemary Birchard,* V.P.; Amy B. Bjerkelund,* V.P.; Peter Foe,* V.P.; Richard W. Hallock,* V.P.
EIN: 146017797
Codes: FD

46189
Joseph and Marie Field Foundation
c/o E.R. Boynton
2600 One Commerce Sq.
Philadelphia, PA 19103

Established in 1999 in PA.
Donor(s): Joseph M. Field, Marie H. Field.
Financial data (yr. ended 07/31/01): Grants paid, $575,000; assets, $12,825,223 (M); gifts received, $1,931,750; expenditures, $645,020; qualifying distributions, $539,108.
Limitations: Applications not accepted. Giving primarily in Philadelphia, PA.
Application information: Contributes only to pre-selected organizations.
Officers and Directors:* Joseph M. Field,* Pres. and Treas.; Marie H. Field,* V.P.; S. Gordon Elkins,* Secy.
EIN: 233009586
Codes: FD

46190
The Arnold D. and Winifred M. Palmer Foundation
P.O. Box 52
Youngstown, PA 15696-0052

Established in 1997 in PA.
Donor(s): Arnold D. Palmer.
Financial data (yr. ended 12/31/01): Grants paid, $570,500; assets, $1,297,168 (M); gifts received, $1,605,000; expenditures, $572,476; qualifying distributions, $572,005.
Limitations: Applications not accepted. Giving primarily in PA.
Application information: Contributes only to pre-selected organizations.
Officer: Arnold D. Palmer, Pres.
Directors: Margaret A. Palmer, Amy L. Saunders.
EIN: 311536438
Codes: FD

46191
The Waldorf Educational Foundation
c/o The Glenmede Trust Co.
1650 Market St., Ste. 1200
Philadelphia, PA 19103-7391 (215) 419-6000
Contact: Stephen R. Starr

Established in 1951 in PA.
Financial data (yr. ended 12/31/01): Grants paid, $568,000; assets, $10,811,583 (M); expenditures, $601,728; qualifying distributions, $588,004.

Limitations: Giving on a national basis.
Publications: Application guidelines, informational brochure.
Application information: Application form not required.
Trustees: Erika V. Aston, Samuel W. Morris, Karin Myrin, The Glenmede Trust Co.
EIN: 236254206
Codes: FD

46192
Community Involvement Foundation
139 Freeport Rd., Ste. 100
Pittsburgh, PA 15215-2943
Contact: Christopher Smith, Exec. Dir.

Established in 1993 in PA.
Donor(s): Bruce Weiner.
Financial data (yr. ended 11/30/01): Grants paid, $562,846; assets, $3,327,723 (M); gifts received, $732,117; expenditures, $946,967; qualifying distributions, $929,190.
Limitations: Applications not accepted. Giving primarily in PA.
Publications: Newsletter.
Application information: Contributes only to pre-selected organizations.
Officers: Susan Weiner, Pres.; Christopher Smith, Exec. Dir.
EIN: 251724052
Codes: FD

46193
ATOFINA Chemicals Foundation
(Formerly Elf Atochem North America Foundation)
2000 Market St.
Philadelphia, PA 19103-3222 (215) 419-7000
Contact: George Hagar, Exec. Secy.

Trust established in 1957 in PA.
Donor(s): Elf Atochem North America, Inc., ATOFINA Chemicals, Inc.
Financial data (yr. ended 12/31/01): Grants paid, $562,036; assets, $42,753 (M); gifts received, $600,000; expenditures, $567,636; qualifying distributions, $562,036.
Limitations: Giving primarily in areas of company operations, with some emphasis on the Philadelphia, PA, area.
Application information: Application form not required.
Trustees: Francis Lauchert, Jr., Peter J. McCarthy, Robert F. Pelliciari, Jean-Pierre Seeuws.
EIN: 236256818
Codes: CS, FD, CD, GTI

46194
Robert E. and Elouise R. Eberly Foundation
2 W. Main St., Ste. 600
Uniontown, PA 15401-3448 (724) 438-3789
Contact: Robert E. Eberly, Pres.

Established in 1993 in PA.
Donor(s): Robert E. Eberly.
Financial data (yr. ended 12/31/01): Grants paid, $560,582; assets, $1,156,404 (M); gifts received, $100,000; expenditures, $590,818; qualifying distributions, $563,909.
Limitations: Giving primarily in PA.
Publications: Annual report.
Officers and Directors:* Robert E. Eberly,* Pres.; Elouise R. Eberly,* Secy.-Treas.; Paul O. Eberly.
EIN: 251723010
Codes: FD

46195
Kinsley Family Foundation
R.R. 1, Box 131 AA
Seven Valleys, PA 17360 (717) 741-8407
Contact: Anne W. Kinsley, V.P.

Established in 1997 in PA.
Donor(s): Robert A. Kinsley, Anne W. Kinsley, Kinsley Construction, Inc.
Financial data (yr. ended 12/31/01): Grants paid, $559,933; assets, $4,475,929 (M); gifts received, $209,999; expenditures, $602,743; qualifying distributions, $558,537.
Limitations: Giving primarily in PA.
Officers: Robert A. Kinsley, Pres.; Anne W. Kinsley, V.P.; Timothy J. Kinsley, Secy.; Christopher A. Kinsley, Treas.
EIN: 232870170
Codes: FD

46196
The Albert M. Greenfield Foundation
P.O. Box 30267
Philadelphia, PA 19103 (215) 333-8949
Contact: Priscilla M. Luce, Chair.

Incorporated in 1953 in PA.
Donor(s): Albert M. Greenfield.‡
Financial data (yr. ended 08/31/01): Grants paid, $556,918; assets, $9,924,198 (M); expenditures, $1,383,201; qualifying distributions, $556,918.
Limitations: Giving primarily in the Philadelphia, PA, area.
Application information: Application form not required.
Officers and Trustees:* Priscilla M. Luce,* Chair.; Deborah G. DeLauro,* Secy.; Juliet G. Six,* Treas.; Albert M. Greenfield III, Bruce H. Greenfield, Bernard M. Guth, Janet H. Guth, Derek G. Howard, Sarah E. Mark.
EIN: 236050816
Codes: FD

46197
Marcus Family Foundation
c/o Stephen Marcus
915 Exeter Crest
Villanova, PA 19085 (610) 519-1123

Registered in 1994 in PA.
Donor(s): Stephen Marcus.
Financial data (yr. ended 09/30/01): Grants paid, $556,634; assets, $5,090,817 (M); expenditures, $711,656; qualifying distributions, $553,984.
Limitations: Giving primarily in southern FL, and Philadelphia, PA.
Application information: Application form not required.
Officers and Directors:* Stephen Marcus,* Pres.; Jonathan H. Newman,* V.P.; Nancy Marcus Newman,* V.P.; Julie Marcus Paul,* V.P.; Russell D. Paul,* V.P.; Lois S. Marcus,* Secy.-Treas.
EIN: 232769110
Codes: FD

46198
Bannerot-Lappe Foundation
c/o Mellon Bank, N.A.
P.O. Box 185
Pittsburgh, PA 15230-9897 (412) 234-0023
Contact: Laurie A. Moritz, Mellon Bank., N.A.

Established in 1994 in PA.
Donor(s): Joane Lappe Bowman.‡
Financial data (yr. ended 05/31/01): Grants paid, $555,000; assets, $7,347,092 (M); expenditures, $661,959; qualifying distributions, $575,380.
Limitations: Giving primarily in NY.
Application information: Application form required.
Trustees: G. Donald Gerlach, Mellon Bank, N.A.
EIN: 256440597

46199
The Arronson Foundation
1 S. Broad St., Ste. 2100
Philadelphia, PA 19107 (215) 238-1700
Additional tel.: (215) 238-1968
Contact: Joseph C. Kohn, Pres. and Secy.

Established in 1957 in DE.
Donor(s): Gertrude Arronson.‡
Financial data (yr. ended 10/31/01): Grants paid, $554,585; assets, $5,694,064 (M); expenditures, $632,019; qualifying distributions, $564,373.
Limitations: Giving primarily in Philadelphia, PA.
Application information: Application form required.
Officers and Trustees:* Joseph C. Kohn,* Pres. and Secy.; Ellen Kohn, V.P. and Treas.; Amy D. Goldberg, V.P.; Edith Kohn,* V.P.
EIN: 236259604
Codes: FD

46200
Samuel and Rebecca Kardon Foundation
c/o LAW
16 Sentry Park W., Ste. 310
Blue Bell, PA 19422-2240
Contact: David Kittner, Pres.

Trust established in 1952 in PA.
Donor(s): Emanuel S. Kardon, American Bag & Paper Corp.
Financial data (yr. ended 12/31/00): Grants paid, $551,430; assets, $9,020,471 (M); expenditures, $633,128; qualifying distributions, $548,681.
Limitations: Giving primarily in PA.
Officer and Trustee:* David Kittner,* Pres.
EIN: 236278123
Codes: FD

46201
Columbia Healthcare Foundation, Inc.
15 N. 3rd St.
Columbia, PA 17512 (717) 684-2077
Contact: C. Edwin Swisher III, Treas.

Established in 1999 in PA.
Financial data (yr. ended 06/30/01): Grants paid, $550,000; assets, $2,424,376 (M); expenditures, $566,063; qualifying distributions, $564,043.
Limitations: Giving limited to the Lancaster County, PA, area.
Officers: Paul H. Dellinger, Chair.; Robert C. Spangler, Pres.; Jacques M. Geisenberger, Jr., Secy.; C. Edwin Swisher III, Treas.
Trustees: Carol Bitts, Philip H. Glatfelter II, John M. Jensen, William R. Korman, John E. Kraft, Michael L. Miller, Donald Nikolaus, Donald L. Smith, Rev. John F. Smith.
EIN: 220485650
Codes: FD

46202
Margaret Briggs Foundation
c/o PNC Bank, N.A.
P.O. Box 937
Scranton, PA 18501

Established in 1969 in PA.
Donor(s): Margaret Briggs.‡
Financial data (yr. ended 12/31/01): Grants paid, $542,141; assets, $11,346,019 (M); expenditures, $619,615; qualifying distributions, $573,043.
Limitations: Giving limited to the greater Scranton/Lackawanna County, PA, area.
Publications: Application guidelines.
Application information: Application form required.

46202—PENNSYLVANIA

Officers and Directors:* Matthew D. Mackie, Jr.,* Pres.; William J. Calpin,* Secy.; Thomas G. Gallagher, Joseph Kreder.
Trustee: PNC Bank, N.A.
EIN: 232719328
Codes: FD

46203
Lalitta Nash McKaig Foundation
c/o PNC Bank, N.A.
620 Liberty Ave., P2-PTPP-1
Pittsburgh, PA 15222-2705 (412) 762-5182
Cumberland office address: P.O. Box 1360, Cumberland, MD 21502, tel.: (301) 777-1533
Contact: Beatrice A. Lynch

Established in 1973 in PA.
Financial data (yr. ended 09/30/01): Grants paid, $538,965; assets, $11,563,297 (M); expenditures, $625,303; qualifying distributions, $545,160.
Limitations: Giving limited to residents who graduated from high schools in Allegany and Garrett counties, MD, Bedford and Somerset counties, PA; and Mineral and Hampshire counties, WV.
Publications: Application guidelines.
Application information: Application forms can be obtained from high school guidance offices in the Cumberland, MD, area, financial aid offices of Frostburg State College and Allegany Community College, the foundation's office in Cumberland, MD, or PNC Bank, N.A. Application form required.
Manager: Geppart McMullen, Paye and Getty.
Trustee: PNC Bank, N.A.
EIN: 256071908
Codes: FD, GTI

46204
Susquehanna Pfaltzgraff Foundation
P.O. Box 2026
York, PA 17405
Application address: c/o John L. Finlayson, V.P., Susquehanna Pfaltzgraff Co., 140 E. Market St., York, PA 17401, tel.: (717) 848-5500

Established in 1966 in PA.
Donor(s): Susquehanna Pfaltzgraff Co., Susquehanna Radio Corp., The Pfaltzgraff Co., Susquehanna Cable Co., and affiliates.
Financial data (yr. ended 12/31/01): Grants paid, $535,068; assets, $1,551,138 (M); gifts received, $400,000; expenditures, $535,630; qualifying distributions, $534,254.
Limitations: Giving primarily in the York, PA, area.
Application information: Application form not required.
Officers and Directors:* Louis J. Appell, Jr.,* Pres. and Treas.; George N. Appell,* V.P.; Helen A. Norton,* V.P.; William H. Simpson, Secy.
EIN: 236420008
Codes: CS, FD, CD

46205
Eden Charitable Foundation
Strafford Bldg. 2
200 Eagle Rd., Ste. 204
Wayne, PA 19087

Established in 1993 in PA.
Donor(s): Franklin C. Eden Revocable Trust.
Financial data (yr. ended 12/31/01): Grants paid, $533,150; assets, $10,175,975 (M); expenditures, $761,904; qualifying distributions, $645,481.
Limitations: Applications not accepted. Giving limited to PA.
Application information: Contributes only to pre-selected organizations.
Officer: John M. Kapp, Pres. and Treas.
Trustees: Earl M. Eden, Donald E. Parlee.

EIN: 232706163
Codes: FD

46206
Saint-Gobain Corporation Foundation
(Formerly CertainTeed Corporation Foundation)
750 Swedesford Rd.
Valley Forge, PA 19482-0101 (610) 341-7000
Application address: P.O. Box 860, Valley Forge, PA 19482-0101
Contact: Dorothy C. Wackerman, V.P. and Secy.

Established in 1955 in PA.
Donor(s): CertainTeed Corp.
Financial data (yr. ended 12/31/01): Grants paid, $532,380; assets, $32,875 (M); gifts received, $426,300; expenditures, $532,380; qualifying distributions, $532,380.
Limitations: Giving primarily in communities where the company is headquartered or has operations.
Application information: Application form required.
Officers and Directors:* Jean-Francois Phelizon,* Pres.; Dorothy C. Wackerman,* V.P. and Secy.; George B. Amoss,* V.P., Finance; Sam Ansley,* V.P.; David Boivin,* V.P.; Bruce H. Cowgill, V.P.; F. Lee Faust, V.P.; Mark Scott,* V.P.; Stephen A. Stockman,* V.P.; Gerald Walsh,* V.P.; Daniel Wiechec,* V.P.; James F. Harkins, Jr., Treas.
EIN: 236242991
Codes: CS, FD, CD

46207
Posner Foundation of Pittsburgh
500 Greentree Commons
381 Mansfield Ave., Ste. 500
Pittsburgh, PA 15220
Contact: Henry Posner, Jr., Tr.

Established about 1965 in PA.
Donor(s): Henry Posner, Jr., James T. Posner.
Financial data (yr. ended 12/31/01): Grants paid, $530,174; assets, $16,146,624 (M); gifts received, $250,000; expenditures, $610,008; qualifying distributions, $530,174.
Limitations: Giving primarily in Pittsburgh, PA.
Trustees: Helen M. Posner, Henry Posner, Jr., Henry Posner III, James T. Posner.
EIN: 256055022
Codes: FD

46208
Michele and Agnese Cestone Foundation, Inc.
Two PNC Plz., 25th Fl.
620 Liberty Ave.
Pittsburgh, PA 15222 (412) 762-3502
FAX: (412) 762-5439; *E-mail:* bruce.bickel@pncadvisors.com
Contact: Bruce Bickel

Established in 1990 in NJ.
Donor(s): Eclesia J. Cestone, Ralph M. Cestone, The Remvac Group, Inc., The Marvec Corp., Macvest Group, Inc., Maria A. Cestone, Vincent R. Cestone, Michele J. Cestone.
Financial data (yr. ended 12/31/01): Grants paid, $529,630; assets, $12,564,769 (M); expenditures, $597,646; qualifying distributions, $529,630.
Limitations: Giving in the U.S., with some emphasis in NJ and NY.
Officers and Trustees:* Michele J. Cestone,* Pres. and Secy.; Vincent Cestone II,* V.P.; William M. Otterbein,* Treas.; Michael Krick.
EIN: 521720903
Codes: FD

46209
The Byers' Foundation
P.O. Box 158
Chalfont, PA 18914-0158
Contact: Joyce F. Byers, Secy.-Treas.

Established in 1986 in PA.
Donor(s): Byers Choice, Ltd.
Financial data (yr. ended 12/31/01): Grants paid, $529,500; assets, $2,830,903 (M); gifts received, $300,000; expenditures, $542,318; qualifying distributions, $529,500.
Limitations: Giving primarily in southeastern PA, with emphasis on the Doylestown and Philadelphia areas, and to charities with which donor employees are directly involved.
Application information: Accepts Delaware Valley Grantmakers Common Grant Application and Common Report Form. Application form not required.
Officers and Trustees:* Robert L. Byers,* Pres.; Robert Leslie Byers, Exec. V.P.; Jeffrey D. Byers,* V.P.; Joyce F. Byers,* Secy.-Treas.
EIN: 232406657
Codes: CS, FD, CD

46210
Caroline Alexander Buck Foundation
1600 Market St., Ste. 3600
Philadelphia, PA 19103 (215) 751-2080
Contact: Bruce A. Rosenfield, Dir.

Established in 1960.
Donor(s): Caroline A. Churchman.‡
Financial data (yr. ended 12/31/01): Grants paid, $520,750; assets, $11,227,255 (M); expenditures, $585,198; qualifying distributions, $537,207.
Limitations: Giving primarily in PA, with emphasis on the greater metropolitan Philadelphia area.
Application information: Application guidelines are available upon request. Application form required.
Directors: John Alexander Churchman, Lee Stirling Churchman, Leidy McIlvaine Churchman, W. Morgan Churchman III, George Connell, Gordon L. Keen, Jr., Bruce A. Rosenfield, Binney H.C. Wietlisbach.
EIN: 236257115
Codes: FD

46211
Salvitti Family Foundation
c/o Reed, Smith, Shaw & McClay
435 6th Ave.
Pittsburgh, PA 15219

Established around 1995.
Financial data (yr. ended 12/31/00): Grants paid, $520,000; assets, $7,031,294 (M); expenditures, $587,587; qualifying distributions, $509,766.
Limitations: Applications not accepted. Giving primarily in Washington, PA.
Application information: Contributes only to pre-selected organizations.
Officers: E. Ronald Salvitti, M.D., Pres.; Constance A. Salvitti, V.P.; Mary Moss, Secy.; Raymond J. Popeck, Treas.
EIN: 251755617
Codes: FD

46212
Edna G. Kynett Memorial Foundation, Inc.
P.O. Box 8228
Philadelphia, PA 19101-8228 (610) 828-8145
Contact: Judith L. Bardes, Mgr.

Incorporated in 1954 in DE.
Donor(s): Harold H. Kynett.‡
Financial data (yr. ended 12/31/01): Grants paid, $517,400; assets, $9,440,184 (M); expenditures, $604,085; qualifying distributions, $537,661.

Limitations: Giving primarily in the greater Philadelphia, PA, area.
Publications: Informational brochure (including application guidelines).
Application information: Application form required.
Officers and Directors:* Norman B. Makous, M.D.,* Pres.; John U. Doherty, M.D., V.P.; Susan C. Day, M.D.,* Secy.; Michael A. Walsh,* Treas.; Oliver Bullock, Elmer H. Funk, Jr., M.D., Ann L. O'Sullivan, M.S.N., Ph.D., Donald F. Schwartz, M.D., Suzanne Vander Veer, Thomas M. Vernon, M.D., Peggy Walsh, D. Stratton Woodruff, Jr., M.D.
EIN: 236296592
Codes: FD

46213
Connemara Fund
c/o The Glenmede Trust Co., 1 Liberty Pl.
1650 Market St., Ste. 1200
Philadelphia, PA 19103-7391
Contact: Herrick Jackson, Tr.

Established in 1968 in NC.
Donor(s): Mary R. Jackson.‡
Financial data (yr. ended 06/30/01): Grants paid, $517,000; assets, $8,789,366 (M); expenditures, $579,942; qualifying distributions, $527,110.
Limitations: Giving primarily in New England.
Trustees: Herrick Jackson, Polly B. Jackson, Alison J. Van Dyk.
EIN: 566096063
Codes: FD

46214
Louis N. Cassett Foundation
1 Penn Ctr., Ste. 1220
Philadelphia, PA 19103-1834
Contact: Malcolm B. Jacobson, Tr.

Trust established in 1946 in PA.
Donor(s): Louis N. Cassett.‡
Financial data (yr. ended 12/31/01): Grants paid, $515,360; assets, $10,500,910 (M); expenditures, $601,117; qualifying distributions, $524,631.
Limitations: Giving primarily in Philadelphia, PA, funding also in FL, and New York, NY.
Application information: Application form not required.
Trustees: William D. Elias, Carol Gerstley, Malcolm B. Jacobson.
EIN: 236274038
Codes: FD

46215
The Albert Trust
c/o Asher & Co., Ltd., Attn.: M. Janowski
1845 Walnut St., 13th Fl.
Philadelphia, PA 19103

Established in 1992 in PA.
Donor(s): Richard A. Greenawalt, Margaret A. Greenawalt.
Financial data (yr. ended 12/31/01): Grants paid, $515,261; assets, $2,540,524 (M); expenditures, $529,354; qualifying distributions, $513,522.
Limitations: Applications not accepted. Giving primarily in Philadelphia, PA.
Application information: Contributes only to pre-selected organizations.
Trustees: Margaret A. Greenawalt, Richard A. Greenawalt.
EIN: 237709316
Codes: FD

46216
The John C. & Chara C. Haas Charitable Trust
c/o Herr, Potts & Herr
175 Strafford Ave., Ste. 314
Wayne, PA 19087-2502

Established in 1989 in PA.
Donor(s): John C. Haas, Chara C. Haas.
Financial data (yr. ended 06/30/01): Grants paid, $514,000; assets, $12,163,915 (M); gifts received, $3,000,000; expenditures, $580,954; qualifying distributions, $526,857.
Limitations: Applications not accepted. Giving primarily in PA.
Application information: Contributes only to pre-selected organizations.
Trustees: Chara C. Haas, John C. Haas, Philip C. Herr II.
EIN: 232587109
Codes: FD

46217
The Dietrich Foundation, Inc.
P.O. Box 649
Gladwyne, PA 19035-0649 (215) 988-0778
Contact: Daniel W. Dietrich II, Pres.

Incorporated in 1953 in DE.
Donor(s): Members of the Dietrich family, Dietrich American Foundation.
Financial data (yr. ended 12/31/00): Grants paid, $512,290; assets, $10,424,273 (M); expenditures, $582,179; qualifying distributions, $502,049.
Limitations: Giving primarily in PA.
Application information: Application form not required.
Officers and Directors:* Daniel W. Dietrich II,* Pres. and Treas.; Joseph G.J. Connolly,* Secy.
EIN: 236255134
Codes: FD

46218
The Angela Foundation
160-A Rte. 41
P.O. Box 529
Gap, PA 17527
Contact: Sam Beiler, Pres.

Established in 1998 in PA.
Donor(s): Anne Beiler, Jonas Beiler.
Financial data (yr. ended 12/31/00): Grants paid, $511,121; assets, $794,704 (M); gifts received, $722,170; expenditures, $517,531; qualifying distributions, $512,845.
Limitations: Giving primarily in the Lancaster County, PA, area.
Application information: Application form not required.
Officers and Board Members:* Jonas Beiler,* Chair.; Samuel Beiler,* Pres.; Doris Swaim,* Secy.; Ronald Risser,* Treas.
EIN: 232985480
Codes: FD

46219
The Richard J. Fox Foundation
955 Chesterbrook Blvd., Ste. 125
Wayne, PA 19087

Established in 1983 in PA.
Donor(s): Richard J. Fox.
Financial data (yr. ended 12/31/01): Grants paid, $510,722; assets, $1,662,222 (M); expenditures, $516,086; qualifying distributions, $511,280.
Limitations: Applications not accepted. Giving primarily in PA.
Application information: Contributes only to pre-selected organizations.
Officer: Richard J. Fox, Pres.
Trustee: Harry D. Fox.
EIN: 232267786
Codes: FD

46220
The Zisman Family Foundation
c/o Robert J. Weinberg
3000 2 Logan Sq.
Philadelphia, PA 19103-2799

Established in 2000 in PA.
Donor(s): Michael D. Zisman.
Financial data (yr. ended 12/31/00): Grants paid, $503,500; assets, $1,760,856 (M); gifts received, $2,530,486; expenditures, $507,495; qualifying distributions, $503,928.
Limitations: Applications not accepted. Giving primarily in New York, NY and Philadelphia, PA.
Application information: Contributes only to pre-selected organizations.
Officers and Directors:* Linda J. Gamble,* Pres. and Secy.; Michael D. Zisman,* V.P. and Treas.
EIN: 233033239
Codes: FD

46221
Federated Investors Foundation, Inc.
Federated Investors Twr.
Pittsburgh, PA 15222-3779

Established in 1997.
Donor(s): Federated Investors, Inc.
Financial data (yr. ended 04/30/01): Grants paid, $500,350; assets, $1,689,790 (M); gifts received, $275,000; expenditures, $502,539; qualifying distributions, $500,350.
Limitations: Applications not accepted. Giving primarily in PA.
Application information: Contributes only to pre-selected organizations.
Officers and Directors:* J. Christopher Donahue,* Pres.; John W. McGonigle, Secy.; Thomas R. Donahue, Treas.; John F. Donahue, Thomas J. Donnelly.
EIN: 232913182
Codes: CS, FD, CD

46222
The Lester and Liesel Baker Foundation
4625 Larchwood Ave.
Philadelphia, PA 19143
Contact: Mrs. L. Baker

Established in 2001 in PA.
Financial data (yr. ended 12/31/01): Grants paid, $500,000; assets, $5,214 (L); gifts received, $505,000; expenditures, $500,000; qualifying distributions, $500,000.
Limitations: Applications not accepted.
Application information: Unsolicited requests for funds not accepted.
Trustee: Liesel Baker.
EIN: 256726162
Codes: FD

46223
The Paul H. O'Neill Charitable Foundation
3 Von Lent Pl.
Pittsburgh, PA 15232-1444

Established in 1991 in PA.
Financial data (yr. ended 12/31/00): Grants paid, $494,700; assets, $1,649,719 (M); gifts received, $3,508; expenditures, $498,963; qualifying distributions, $488,208.
Limitations: Giving primarily in southwestern PA.
Publications: Application guidelines.
Officer: Paul H. O'Neill, Chair.
Director: Nancy J. O'Neill.
EIN: 256378671
Codes: FD

46224
H. G. and A. G. Keasbey Memorial Fund
1701 Market St.
Philadelphia, PA 19103-2921
Contact: Geraldine J. Swindells

Financial data (yr. ended 12/31/01): Grants paid, $490,192; assets, $7,578,411 (M); expenditures, $557,932; qualifying distributions, $515,896.
Limitations: Applications not accepted.
Application information: Unsolicited requests for funds not accepted.
Trustees: Philip J. Greven, Jr., Angus M. Russell, First Union National Bank.
EIN: 236447014
Codes: FD, GTI

46225
Lehigh Valley Community Foundation
(Formerly Bethlehem Area Foundation)
961 Marcon Blvd., Ste. 300
Allentown, PA 18109 (610) 266-4284
FAX: (610) 266-4285; E-mail: lvcf@lehighvalleyfoundation.org; URL: http://www.lehighvalleyfoundation.org
Contact: Carol Dean Henn, Exec. Dir.

Established in 1967 in PA.
Financial data (yr. ended 06/30/01): Grants paid, $488,755; assets, $8,822,998 (M); gifts received, $542,169; expenditures, $803,310.
Limitations: Giving limited to Lehigh, Monroe and Northampton counties, PA.
Publications: Annual report (including application guidelines), grants list, application guidelines, program policy statement, informational brochure (including application guidelines), newsletter.
Application information: Capital funding: must submit invoice copies when requesting release of funds. Site visits will be made; mid-year and final reports required. Application form required.
Officers and Board of Governors:* Robert H. Littner,* Chair.; Patrick Connell,* Vice-Chair.; Carol Dean Henn, Secy. and Exec. Dir.; J. Marshall Wolff,* Treas.; Joseph Boligitz, Llyena Boylan, Walter W. Buckley, Jr., Lee A. Butz, Rev. Douglas Caldwell, Alvina L. Campbell, Maxwell E. Davison, Lesley H. Fallon, Robert Finn, Marlene O. Fowler, Fr. Daniel Gambert, Kostas Kalogeropoulos, Frederick Kutteroff, Cynthia A. Lambert, Richard G. Lang, Michael Lieberman, Stephen Link, Robert Margolis, Jack H. McNairy, Charles M. Meredith III, William K. Murphy, Elizabeth M. Roberts, Robert D. Romeril, Barbara Rothkopf, Barbara Tallman, Ferdinand Thun, John H. Updegrove, M.D.
Investment Management: Dean McDermott & Co., First Union National Bank, Fleet National Bank, Legg Mason, Mellon Bank, N.A., Merrill Lynch.
EIN: 231686634
Codes: CM, FD

46226
T. James Kavanagh Foundation
P.O. Box 609
Broomall, PA 19008 (610) 356-0743
FAX: (610) 356-4606
Contact: Thomas E. Kavanagh, Tr.

Established in 1968 in PA.
Donor(s): T. James Kavanagh.‡
Financial data (yr. ended 12/31/01): Grants paid, $487,702; assets, $14,261,509 (M); expenditures, $624,421; qualifying distributions, $555,092.
Limitations: Giving strictly limited to the U.S., with emphasis on southern NJ and PA.
Publications: Grants list, application guidelines.
Application information: Application guidelines available from the foundation. Application form required.
Trustees: Louis J. Esposito, Thomas E. Kavanagh.
EIN: 236442981
Codes: FD

46227
The Peterson Foundation
c/o John Iskrant
1600 Market St., Ste. 3600
Philadelphia, PA 19103
Application address: 8128 Regents Ct., University Park, FL 34201, tel.: (941) 355-0000
Contact: J. Robert Peterson, Tr.

Established in 1986 in PA.
Donor(s): Lee M. Peterson, J. Robert Peterson.
Financial data (yr. ended 11/30/01): Grants paid, $486,536; assets, $164,194 (M); gifts received, $594,093; expenditures, $566,958; qualifying distributions, $541,063.
Limitations: Giving primarily in FL and NY.
Application information: Application form not required.
Trustees: David John Peterson, J. Robert Peterson, Jeffrey R. Peterson, Kane Deglin Peterson, Lee M. Peterson, Janice Peterson Radder, Timothy W. Radder.
EIN: 236766019
Codes: FD

46228
The SICO Foundation
15 Mount Joy St.
P.O. Box 127
Mount Joy, PA 17552-0127
E-mail: info@sicofoundation.org
Contact: Darlene F. Halterman, Corp. Secy.

Incorporated in 1941 in DE.
Donor(s): Clarence Schock.‡
Financial data (yr. ended 05/31/01): Grants paid, $485,870; assets, $14,267,627 (M); expenditures, $712,675; qualifying distributions, $609,425.
Limitations: Applications not accepted. Giving primarily in PA.
Publications: Informational brochure.
Application information: Contributes only to pre-selected organizations.
Officers and Board Members:* William H. Duncan,* Pres.; John N. Weidman,* V.P.; Darlene F. Halterman, Secy.; Franklin R. Eichler,* Treas.
Directors: Joseph A. Caputo, Anthony F. Ceddia, Harrison L. Diehl, David F. Eichler, Carl R. Hallgren, Fred S. Engle, Dir. Emeritus; Charles W. Ricedorf, Forrest R. Schaeffer, Helen A. Stine.
EIN: 236298332
Codes: FD

46229
The Wood Foundation of Chambersburg, PA
273 Lincoln Way E.
Chambersburg, PA 17201 (717) 267-3174
Contact: C.O. Wood III, Dir.

Established in 1989 as successor foundation to the Wood Foundation of Chambersburg, PA.
Financial data (yr. ended 12/31/01): Grants paid, $485,170; assets, $9,430,612 (M); expenditures, $622,742; qualifying distributions, $544,177.
Limitations: Giving primarily in Chambersburg and Franklin counties, PA.
Application information: Application form not required.
Directors: Emilie W. Robinson, C.O. Wood III, David S. Wood, Miriam M. Wood.
EIN: 251607838
Codes: FD

46230
The Cooper-Siegel Family Foundation
c/o Mellon Bank, N.A.
P.O. Box 185
Pittsburgh, PA 15230
Contact: Robert Lepre

Established in 1996 in PA.
Donor(s): Eric C. Cooper, Cooper-Siegel Foundation Charitable Lead Trusts.
Financial data (yr. ended 04/30/01): Grants paid, $485,000; assets, $1,154,927 (M); gifts received, $895,862; expenditures, $489,376; qualifying distributions, $486,750.
Limitations: Giving primarily in Pittsburgh, PA.
Application information: Application form required.
Trustees: David Margolis, Mellon Bank, N.A.
EIN: 311537177
Codes: FD

46231
The Reidler Foundation
c/o Fleet National Bank
101 W. Broad St.
Hazleton, PA 18201
Contact: Diana L. James, Secy.-Treas.

Incorporated in 1944 in PA.
Donor(s): John W. Reidler,‡ Verna C. Reidler,‡ Howard D. Fegan, Ann B. Fegan.
Financial data (yr. ended 10/31/01): Grants paid, $485,000; assets, $9,119,636 (M); gifts received, $31,458; expenditures, $520,851; qualifying distributions, $486,992.
Limitations: Giving primarily in the Ashland, Hazleton, and Lehigh Valley, PA, areas.
Officers and Trustees:* Ann B. Fegan,* Pres.; Robert K. Gicking,* V.P.; Diana L. James, Secy.-Treas.; Howard D. Fegan, John H. Fegan, Eugene C. Fish, Carl J. Reidler, Paul G. Reidler.
EIN: 246022888
Codes: FD

46232
The Scranton Area Foundation, Inc.
Bank Towers, Ste. 608
321 Spruce St.
Scranton, PA 18503-1409 (570) 347-6203
FAX: (717) 347-7587; E-mail: safinfo@safdn.org; URL: http://www.safdn.org
Contact: Jeanne A. Bovard, Exec. Dir.

Established in 1954 in PA by resolution and declaration of trust; reorganized in 1998.
Financial data (yr. ended 12/31/01): Grants paid, $484,663; assets, $15,706,067 (M); gifts received, $400,861; expenditures, $776,497.
Limitations: Giving limited to the Scranton and Lackawanna County, PA, area.
Publications: Annual report, informational brochure (including application guidelines), occasional report, newsletter, grants list, application guidelines, informational brochure.
Application information: Application form required.
Officers and Governors:* Dorrance R. Belin,* Chair.; James W. Reid,* Vice.-Chair.; Kathleen Graff,* Treas.; Jeanne A. Bovard, Exec. Dir.; James F. Bell III, Richard S. Bishop, Harmar D. Brereton, M.D., Austin J. Burke, Mary Ellen Coleman, Eugene F. Cosgrove, Sr. Jean Coughlin, I.H.M., Carlene Gallo, Kelly Kane, Robert N. Lettieri, Richard C. Marquardt, Sr., Thomas R. Nealon, Carlon E. Preate, Leitha Reinheimer, Gerald W. Seibert.
Investment Managers: PNC Bank, N.A., Penn Security.
EIN: 232890364
Codes: CM, FD

46233
Tippins Foundation
1090 Freeport Rd.
Pittsburgh, PA 15238 (412) 784-8804
Contact: George R. Knapp, Tr.

Established in 1987 in PA.
Donor(s): TMC Investment Co., Carolyn Tippins, George Tippins, Tippins Incorporated.
Financial data (yr. ended 12/31/00): Grants paid, $484,340; assets, $2,186,730 (M); gifts received, $1,985,229; expenditures, $495,723; qualifying distributions, $484,355.
Limitations: Giving primarily in PA.
Officer and Trustees:* George R. Knapp,* Exec. Dir.; Carolyn H. Tippins, George W. Tippins, John H. Tippins, William H. Tippins.
EIN: 256282382
Codes: CS, FD, CD

46234
The Hall Foundation
P.O. Box 1200
Camp Hill, PA 17001 (717) 761-1057
Contact: Gerald N. Hall, Exec. Dir.

Trust established in 1952 in PA.
Donor(s): John N. Hall, Hall's Motor Transit Co.
Financial data (yr. ended 09/30/01): Grants paid, $483,753; assets, $7,934,946 (M); expenditures, $648,766; qualifying distributions, $538,536.
Limitations: Giving primarily in PA.
Application information: Application form provided for scholarship requests.
Officer and Trustees:* Gerald N. Hall,* Exec. Dir.; Shirley H. Carr, Gerald Hall, Jr., Robert E. Hall, Leroy Zimmerman.
EIN: 236243044
Codes: FD

46235
The Wheeler Family Charitable Foundation
415 N. Center Ave.
Somerset, PA 15501 (814) 445-7188
Contact: Joan M. Wheeler, Mgr.

Established in 1997 in PA.
Donor(s): Harold W. Wheeler, Joan M. Wheeler.
Financial data (yr. ended 12/31/01): Grants paid, $479,000; assets, $1,803,560 (M); gifts received, $60,000; expenditures, $490,654; qualifying distributions, $477,661.
Limitations: Giving primarily in Somerset County, PA.
Application information: Application form not required.
Officers and Directors:* Harold W. Wheeler, Jr.,* Chair.; Joan M. Wheeler,* Mgr.; Barbara Davies, David L. Wheeler, Harold W. Wheeler III, Paul J. Wheeler.
Trustee: Somerset Trust Co.
EIN: 232938580
Codes: FD

46236
Ryan Memorial Foundation
P.O. Box 426
Pittsburgh, PA 15230

Established in 1996 in PA.
Financial data (yr. ended 12/31/01): Grants paid, $476,583; assets, $11,611,364 (M); expenditures, $483,494; qualifying distributions, $479,514.
Limitations: Applications not accepted. Giving primarily in PA.
Application information: Contributes only to pre-selected organizations.
Trustees: Julia Ryan Parker, Daniel H. Ryan, John T. Ryan III, Mary Irene Ryan, Michael Denis Ryan, William F. Ryan, Irene R. Shaw.
EIN: 251781266

Codes: FD

46237
Yetta Deitch Novotny Charitable Trust
2 Penn Ctr. Plz., Ste. 400
Philadelphia, PA 19102 (215) 564-1300

Established in 1990 in PA.
Donor(s): Yetta Deitch Novotny.
Financial data (yr. ended 08/31/01): Grants paid, $469,000; assets, $9,432,861 (M); gifts received, $537,444; expenditures, $484,149; qualifying distributions, $465,877.
Limitations: Applications not accepted. Giving primarily in New York, NY, and PA.
Application information: Unsolicited requests for funds not accepted.
Trustees: Andrew Zolot, Stanley L. Zolot.
EIN: 237642807
Codes: FD

46238
Gilroy & Lillian P. Roberts Charitable Foundation
10 Presidential Blvd., Ste. 250
Bala Cynwyd, PA 19004 (610) 668-1998
Contact: Stanley Merves, Mgr.

Established in 1982 in PA.
Donor(s): Gilroy Roberts,‡ Lillian Roberts.‡
Financial data (yr. ended 06/30/02): Grants paid, $468,835; assets, $9,102,346 (M); expenditures, $468,835; qualifying distributions, $505,663.
Limitations: Giving primarily in Montgomery and Delaware counties, PA.
Application information: Board of grantseeker organization must have 100 percent participation in grantmaking. Application form not required.
Officer and Trustees:* Stanley Merves,* Mgr.; Walter G. Arader, Audrey Merves, Jenifer Merves, John T. Roberts.
EIN: 232219044
Codes: FD

46239
The Samuel Epstein Foundation Trust
c/o National City Bank of Pennsylvania
20 Stanwix St., Ste. 25 162
Pittsburgh, PA 15222-4801

Established in 1988 in PA.
Donor(s): Samuel Epstein.‡
Financial data (yr. ended 12/31/01): Grants paid, $468,675; assets, $6,305,332 (M); expenditures, $506,934; qualifying distributions, $483,220.
Limitations: Applications not accepted. Giving primarily in New York, NY, and PA.
Application information: Unsolicited requests for funds not accepted.
Trustee: National City Bank of Pennsylvania.
EIN: 256311365
Codes: FD, GTI

46240
Binswanger Foundation
2 Logan Sq.
Philadelphia, PA 19103-2759 (215) 448-6000
Contact: John K. Binswanger, Pres.

Established in 1942.
Donor(s): John K. Binswanger, The Binswanger Cos.
Financial data (yr. ended 12/31/00): Grants paid, $468,263; assets, $1,230,006 (M); gifts received, $175,000; expenditures, $500,556; qualifying distributions, $467,849.
Limitations: Giving primarily in Philadelphia, PA.
Application information: Application form not required.
Officers: Frank G. Binswanger, Jr., Chair.; Robert B. Binswanger, Vice-Chair.; John K. Binswanger, Pres.; Frank G. Binswanger III, Secy.; David G. Binswanger, Treas.
EIN: 236296506
Codes: CS, FD, CD

46241
The Hassel Foundation
1608 Walnut St., 19th Fl.
Philadelphia, PA 19103 (215) 893-9300
Contact: Michael H. Krekstein, Tr.

Trust established in 1961 in PA.
Donor(s): Morris Hassel,‡ Calvin Hassel.‡
Financial data (yr. ended 12/31/00): Grants paid, $468,200; assets, $934,228 (M); expenditures, $508,005; qualifying distributions, $477,367.
Limitations: Giving primarily in PA.
Application information: Application form not required.
Trustees: Andrea Cohen, Barbara Cohen, Elizabeth Cohen, Ellen Cohen, Sarle H. Cohen, Andrew Goldberg, Jay L. Goldberg, Maxine Goldberg, Michael Goldberg, David Khoury, Lisa Khoury, Marilyn Khoury, Michael H. Krekstein, Ephrain Royfe, Merle A. Wolfson.
EIN: 236251862
Codes: FD, GTI

46242
The Harry Plankenhorn Foundation, Inc.
c/o New Covenant United Church of Christ
202 E. 3rd St.
Williamsport, PA 17701

Incorporated in 1959 in PA.
Donor(s): Harry Plankenhorn.‡
Financial data (yr. ended 12/31/00): Grants paid, $467,308; assets, $9,387,213 (M); gifts received, $50,100; expenditures, $483,281; qualifying distributions, $458,846.
Limitations: Giving primarily in Lycoming County, PA.
Application information: An application may be made to any officer or director orally or in writing; however, any request for the sum of $5,000 or more, must be made in writing and presented to the Board of Directors at a designated meeting.
Officers and Board Members:* Charles F. Greevy III,* Pres.; Abram M. Snyder,* V.P.; W. Herbert Poff III,* Secy.; Fred A. Foulkrod, Treas.; Rev. Bruce Druckenmiller, Barbara Ertel, Carl O. Heiber, Bob Hively, Robert M. Reeder, Carolyn Seifert, Nancy Stearns, Eleanor W. Whiting.
EIN: 246023579
Codes: FD

46243
Joseph G. Bradley Charitable Foundation
c/o Wolf Block
1650 Arch St., 22nd Fl.
Philadelphia, PA 19103

Established in 1990 in PA.
Financial data (yr. ended 11/30/01): Grants paid, $465,000; assets, $8,189,366 (M); expenditures, $491,196; qualifying distributions, $471,807.
Limitations: Giving primarily in Toledo, OH.
Application information: Application form not required.
Trustee: Andrew R. Nehrbas.
EIN: 237647762
Codes: FD

46244—PENNSYLVANIA

46244
The Thomas H. and Mary Williams Shoemaker Fund
1120 Hagues Mill Rd.
Ambler, PA 19002
Tel./FAX: (215) 542-1340
Contact: Carolyn R. Moon

Trust established in 1953 in PA.
Donor(s): Mary Williams Shoemaker,‡ Thomas H. Shoemaker,‡ Thomas H. and Mary Williams Shoemaker Trust.
Financial data (yr. ended 09/30/01): Grants paid, $464,105; assets, $7,387,687 (M); expenditures, $511,410; qualifying distributions, $489,718.
Limitations: Giving primarily in PA.
Publications: Application guidelines, informational brochure (including application guidelines).
Application information: Application form not required.
Trustee: The Glenmede Trust Co.
EIN: 236209783
Codes: FD

46245
The Diane Lenfest Myer Foundation, Inc.
5 Tower Bridge
300 Barr Harbor Dr., Ste. 450
West Conshohocken, PA 19428
FAX: (610) 828-0390
Contact: Bruce Melgary, Exec. Dir.

Established in 1999 in PA.
Donor(s): Diane Lenfest Myer.
Financial data (yr. ended 06/30/02): Grants paid, $461,500; assets, $55,666,632 (M); expenditures, $495,157; qualifying distributions, $471,470.
Limitations: Applications not accepted. Giving primarily in southeastern PA.
Application information: Contributes only to pre-selected organizations.
Officers and Directors:* Diane Lenfest Myer,* Pres.; Marguerite Lenfest,* Secy.; Bruce Melgary, Exec. Dir.
EIN: 233035225
Codes: FD

46246
Auto Racing Fraternity Foundation of America, Inc.
Long Pond Rd.
Long Pond, PA 18334

Established around 1990.
Financial data (yr. ended 03/31/01): Grants paid, $460,342; assets, $4,028,816 (M); expenditures, $467,528; qualifying distributions, $458,348.
Limitations: Applications not accepted. Giving primarily in NC and PA.
Application information: Contributes only to pre-selected organizations.
Officers: Joseph Mattioli, Pres.; Joseph Mattioli, Jr., V.P.; Rose Mattioli, Secy.-Treas.
EIN: 232136313
Codes: FD

46247
Anne McCormick Trust
c/o Allfirst, Trust Div.
21 E. Market St., M/C 402-130
York, PA 17401-1500
Application address: c/o Allfirst, P.O. Box 2961, Harrisburg, PA 17105
Contact: Larry A. Hartman, Trust Off., Allfirst

Trust established in PA.
Donor(s): Anne McCormick.‡
Financial data (yr. ended 12/31/01): Grants paid, $459,950; assets, $8,405,140 (M); gifts received, $9,025; expenditures, $514,632; qualifying distributions, $456,619.
Limitations: Giving limited to Cumberland, Dauphin, Franklin, and Perry counties, PA.
Trustee: Allfirst.
EIN: 236471389
Codes: FD

46248
Hyman Korman Family Foundation
2 Neshaminy Interplex, Ste. 307
Trevose, PA 19053

Trust established in 1947 in PA.
Donor(s): Members of the Korman family, Hyman Korman, Inc.
Financial data (yr. ended 12/31/01): Grants paid, $458,200; assets, $9,445,635 (M); gifts received, $25,000; expenditures, $567,251; qualifying distributions, $451,609.
Limitations: Applications not accepted. Giving primarily in Philadelphia, PA.
Application information: Contributes only to pre-selected organizations.
Trustees: Berton E. Korman, Leonard I. Korman, Steven H. Korman, I. Barney Moss.
EIN: 236297326
Codes: FD

46249
Cranaleith Foundation, Inc.
c/o N. Allen
1701 Market St.
Philadelphia, PA 19103

Established in 1993 in PA.
Donor(s): Francis H. Trainer, Jr., Jeanne A. Trainer.
Financial data (yr. ended 12/31/01): Grants paid, $456,000; assets, $11,245,187 (M); gifts received, $500,000; expenditures, $512,027; qualifying distributions, $457,691.
Limitations: Applications not accepted. Giving primarily in NY.
Application information: Contributes only to pre-selected organizations.
Officers: Francis H. Trainer, Jr., Pres.; Jeanne A. Trainer, V.P.
EIN: 232726952
Codes: FD

46250
Sylvia Perkin Perpetual Charitable Trust
c/o James Kressler, First Union National Bank
702 Hamilton Mall
Allentown, PA 18101
Application address: c/o Arnold C. Rapaport, P.O. Box 443, Allentown, PA 18105-0443
Contact: Arnold C. Rapoport, Tr.

Established in 1986 in PA.
Donor(s): Sylvia Perkin.‡
Financial data (yr. ended 04/30/01): Grants paid, $455,200; assets, $8,230,405 (M); expenditures, $508,358; qualifying distributions, $457,505.
Limitations: Giving primarily in Allentown, PA.
Application information: Application form not required.
Trustees: James D. Christie, Arnold C. Rapoport, First Union National Bank.
EIN: 236792999
Codes: FD

46251
IGN Foundation
300 Berwyn Pk., Ste. 100
Berwyn, PA 19312
Application address: 300 Berwyn Park, Ste. 100, Berwyn, PA 19312, tel.: (610) 408-8600
Contact: Frank Polizzi, Tr.

Established in 1990 in PA.
Donor(s): Frank Polizzi.
Financial data (yr. ended 06/30/01): Grants paid, $450,767; assets, $6,488,007 (M); expenditures, $498,250; qualifying distributions, $457,010.
Limitations: Giving primarily in IL, MN and PA, with an emphasis on Philadelphia.
Trustee: Frank Polizzi.
EIN: 237653516
Codes: FD

46252
Ira J. Gumberg Family Foundation
c/o David Kasper
1051 Brinton Rd.
Pittsburgh, PA 15221

Established in 1999 in PA.
Donor(s): Ira J. Gumberg.
Financial data (yr. ended 12/31/01): Grants paid, $450,000; assets, $2,518,460 (M); gifts received, $400,000; expenditures, $453,842; qualifying distributions, $450,000.
Limitations: Applications not accepted. Giving primarily in Pittsburgh, PA.
Application information: Contributes only to pre-selected organizations.
Trustee: Ira J. Gumberg.
EIN: 251842389

46253
Fair Oaks Foundation, Inc.
(Formerly AMPCO-Pittsburgh Foundation II, Inc.)
600 Grant St., Ste. 4600
Pittsburgh, PA 15219-2903   (412) 456-4418
Contact: Rose Hoover, Secy.

Established in 1988 in PA.
Donor(s): Pittsburgh Forgings Foundation, AMPCO-Pittsburgh Foundation.
Financial data (yr. ended 12/31/01): Grants paid, $446,590; assets, $5,792,049 (M); expenditures, $459,125; qualifying distributions, $442,656.
Limitations: Giving primarily in NY, PA, and VA.
Application information: Application form not required.
Officers and Trustees:* Louis Berkman,* Chair.; Robert A. Paul,* Pres.; Ernest G. Siddons, V.P.; Rose Hoover, Secy.
EIN: 251576560
Codes: CS, FD, CD

46254
The Alter Family Foundation
c/o Wolf Block Schorr & Solis Cohen
12th Fl., Packard Bldg., 111 S. 15th St.
Philadelphia, PA 19102

Established in 1998 in PA.
Donor(s): Dennis Alter, Gisela Alter, Helen Alter.
Financial data (yr. ended 12/31/99): Grants paid, $446,548; assets, $11,655,805 (M); gifts received, $1,007,345; expenditures, $448,548; qualifying distributions, $446,548.
Limitations: Applications not accepted.
Application information: Contributes only to pre-selected organizations.
Officers and Directors:* Dennis Alter,* Pres. and Treas.; Gisela Alter,* V.P. and Secy.; William A. Rosoff,* V.P.
EIN: 232951283

46255
John Crain Kunkel Foundation
P.O. Box 658
Camp Hill, PA 17001
Contact: N.W. Bergert

Established in 1965 in PA.
Financial data (yr. ended 12/31/01): Grants paid, $444,010; assets, $13,052,337 (M); expenditures, $628,138; qualifying distributions, $517,386.

Limitations: Giving primarily in Harrisburg, PA.
Application information: Application form not required.
Trustees: Nancy W. Bergert, Elizabeth K. Davis, Deborah L. Facini, John C. Kunkel II, Paul A. Kunkel, Jay W. Stark, John K. Stark, William T. Wright II.
EIN: 237026914
Codes: FD

46256
The Roemer Foundation
(Formerly Mary Alice Dorrance Malone Foundation)
c/o B. Rosenfield
1600 Market St., Ste. 3600
Philadelphia, PA 19103-7286
Contact: Mary Alice Dorrance Malone, Dir.

Established in 1996 in PA.
Donor(s): Mary Alice Dorrance Malone.
Financial data (yr. ended 06/30/01): Grants paid, $438,000; assets, $8,140,638 (M); gifts received, $20,000; expenditures, $466,829; qualifying distributions, $444,338.
Limitations: Applications not accepted. Giving primarily in PA.
Application information: Contributes only to pre-selected organizations.
Directors: Mary Alice Dorrance Malone, James L. McCabe.
EIN: 232870277
Codes: FD

46257
The M & S Foundation
5 Radnor Corp. Ctr.
100 Matsonford Rd., Ste. 500
Radnor, PA 19087

Established in 1996 in PA.
Donor(s): Alfred W. Martinelli.
Financial data (yr. ended 12/31/00): Grants paid, $433,010; assets, $1,690,421 (M); gifts received, $1,012,273; expenditures, $463,659; qualifying distributions, $432,144.
Limitations: Applications not accepted. Giving primarily in PA.
Application information: Contributes only to pre-selected organizations.
Directors: A.W. Martinelli, Aline Martinelli, Christine Martinelli, David Martinelli, Bill Shea, Susan Shea.
EIN: 311478148
Codes: FD

46258
The Fine Family Foundation
(Formerly Milton Fine Family Charitable Foundation)
c/o FFC Capital Corp.
Foster Plz. X, 680 Andersen Dr., 4th Fl.
Pittsburgh, PA 15220 (412) 919-3512
Contact: Milton Fine, Pres.

Donor(s): Milton Fine, The Milton Fine Irrevocable Trust of 1998, The Milton Fine Irrevocable Trust of 2000.
Financial data (yr. ended 06/30/01): Grants paid, $432,965; assets, $739,486 (M); gifts received, $413,997; expenditures, $445,769; qualifying distributions, $445,485.
Limitations: Giving primarily in MA and PA.
Application information: Application form not required.
Officer and Directors:* Milton Fine,* Pres. and Secy.-Treas.; David Fine, Sheila Fine, Carolyn Fine Friedman, Sibyl Fine King.
EIN: 256335329
Codes: FD

46259
Allen H. & Selma W. Berkman Charitable Trust
1500 Oliver Bldg.
Pittsburgh, PA 15222 (412) 355-8640
Application address: 5000 5th Ave., Apt. 207, Pittsburgh, PA 15232
Contact: Allen H. Berkman, Tr.

Established in 1972 in PA.
Donor(s): Allen H. Berkman, Selma W. Berkman.‡
Financial data (yr. ended 10/31/01): Grants paid, $425,879; assets, $4,471,628 (M); expenditures, $428,459; qualifying distributions, $428,459.
Limitations: Giving primarily in NY and PA.
Publications: Annual report.
Application information: Application form not required.
Trustees: Barbara B. Ackerman, Allen H. Berkman, James S. Berkman, Richard L. Berkman, Helen B. Habbert, Susan B. Rahm.
EIN: 256144060
Codes: FD

46260
Milton G. Hulme Charitable Foundation
519 Frick Bldg.
Pittsburgh, PA 15219

Established in 1960 in PA.
Donor(s): Jocelyn H. MacConnell, Natalie H. Curry, Holiday H. Shoup, Glover & MacGregor, Inc.
Financial data (yr. ended 12/31/01): Grants paid, $425,000; assets, $9,344,933 (M); expenditures, $470,104; qualifying distributions, $453,264.
Limitations: Giving primarily in Pittsburgh, PA.
Application information: Application form not required.
Trustees: Natalie H. Curry, Aura R. Hulme, Jocelyn H. MacConnell, Holiday H. Shoup.
EIN: 256062896
Codes: FD

46261
Myles D. and J. Faye Sampson Family Foundation
772 Pine Valley Dr.
Pittsburgh, PA 15239

Established in 1993 in PA.
Donor(s): Myles D. Sampson, J. Faye Sampson, Twila Sampson Foundation, Rimdo Properties Inc.
Financial data (yr. ended 12/31/01): Grants paid, $424,150; assets, $492,113 (M); gifts received, $540,000; expenditures, $428,217; qualifying distributions, $424,126.
Limitations: Applications not accepted. Giving limited to PA.
Application information: Contributes only to pre-selected organizations.
Trustees: J. Faye Sampson, Myles D. Sampson.
EIN: 256407379
Codes: FD

46262
James Frances McCandless Trust
c/o PNC Advisors Charitable Trust Comm.
2 PNC Plz., 620 Liberty Ave., 25th Fl.
Pittsburgh, PA 15222-2719 (412) 762-7076
Contact: Mia Hallett Bernard

Financial data (yr. ended 12/31/01): Grants paid, $422,350; assets, $5,568,320 (M); expenditures, $464,223; qualifying distributions, $453,222.
Limitations: Giving primarily in Pittsburgh or Allegheny and Mercer counties, PA.
Application information: Application form required.
Trustee: PNC Bank, N.A.
EIN: 251347840
Codes: FD

46263
Thomas Marshall Foundation
c/o Janet Sharpski
600 Grant St., Ste. 3278
Pittsburgh, PA 15219-2712 (412) 433-7801
E-mail: jsharpski@tmfound.org

Established in 1994 in PA.
Donor(s): Thomas Marshall.
Financial data (yr. ended 12/31/01): Grants paid, $422,150; assets, $9,071,088 (M); expenditures, $537,449; qualifying distributions, $514,925.
Limitations: Giving primarily in PA.
Application information: Application form required.
Trustee: Thomas Marshall.
Directors: Theresa Marshall, Virginia Marshall, Sue Marshall Roberts.
Agent: PNC Bank, N.A.
EIN: 256479933
Codes: FD

46264
Charles Talbot Campbell Foundation
c/o National City Bank of Pennsylvania
National City Ctr. (25-154), 20 Stanwix St.
Pittsburgh, PA 15222-4802 (412) 644-8332
Contact: William M. Schmidt, V.P., National City Bank of Pennsylvania

Trust established in 1975 in PA.
Donor(s): Charles Talbot Campbell.‡
Financial data (yr. ended 01/31/02): Grants paid, $421,000; assets, $8,127,500 (M); expenditures, $468,468; qualifying distributions, $461,690.
Limitations: Giving primarily in western PA.
Application information: Grantmakers of Western Pennsylvania Common Grant Application Form required. Application form required.
Trustee: National City Bank of Pennsylvania.
EIN: 251287221
Codes: FD

46265
Rider-Pool Foundation
1050 S. Cedar Crest Blvd., Ste. 202
Allentown, PA 18103 (610) 770-9346
FAX: (610) 770-9361; *E-mail:* drpool@ptd.net;
URL: http://www.pooltrust.com
Contact: Bridget I. Rassler

Established in 1957 in PA.
Donor(s): Dorothy Rider-Pool.‡
Financial data (yr. ended 12/31/01): Grants paid, $421,000; assets, $9,560,080 (M); expenditures, $500,955; qualifying distributions, $501,677.
Limitations: Giving primarily in the Lehigh Valley, PA, area.
Publications: Biennial report, informational brochure (including application guidelines).
Application information: Application form not required.
Trustees: Edward Donley, Leon C. Holt, Jr., John P. Jones III, PNC Bank, N.A.
EIN: 236207356
Codes: FD

46266
William I. & Patricia S. Snyder Foundation
Grant Bldg., 3rd Fl.
Pittsburgh, PA 15219 (412) 338-1108
Contact: K. Sidney Neuman, Secy.

Established in 1995.
Financial data (yr. ended 08/31/01): Grants paid, $419,833; assets, $2,371,548 (M); expenditures, $471,491; qualifying distributions, $424,319.
Limitations: Giving primarily in PA.
Application information: Application form not required.

46266—PENNSYLVANIA

Officers: William I. Snyder, Pres.; Patricia S. Snyder, V.P.; K. Sidney Neuman, Secy.
EIN: 251773015
Codes: FD

46267
Robert S. Waters Charitable Trust
c/o Mellon Bank, N.A.
3 Mellon Ctr., Rm. 153-4000
Pittsburgh, PA 15259 (412) 234-5784
Contact: Barbara K. Robinson, V.P., Mellon Bank, N.A.

Trust established in 1952 in PA.
Donor(s): Robert S. Waters.‡
Financial data (yr. ended 12/31/01): Grants paid, $418,500; assets, $8,648,971 (M); expenditures, $485,589; qualifying distributions, $439,490.
Limitations: Giving primarily in western PA.
Application information: Application form required.
Trustee: Mellon Bank, N.A.
EIN: 256018986
Codes: FD

46268
K. Paul & Virginia M. Singh Private Foundation, Inc.
c/o Bennet Aaron
3000 2 Logan Sq.
Philadelphia, PA 19103-2799

Established in 1997 in PA.
Donor(s): K. Paul Singh, Virginia M. Singh.
Financial data (yr. ended 12/31/01): Grants paid, $418,448; assets, $30,500 (M); gifts received, $5,918; expenditures, $424,366; qualifying distributions, $418,448.
Limitations: Applications not accepted.
Application information: Contributes only to pre-selected organizations.
Officers and Directors:* K. Paul Singh,* Pres.; Virginia M. Singh,* V.P. and Secy.-Treas.
EIN: 232903940
Codes: FD

46269
The Inverso-Baglivo Foundation
824 Hood Rd.
Swarthmore, PA 19081-2814 (610) 544-5960
Contact: Anthony W. Inverso, V.P. and Secy.

Established in 1994 in DE and PA.
Donor(s): Rina A. Sukartawidjaja.
Financial data (yr. ended 12/31/99): Grants paid, $407,763; assets, $95,176 (M); gifts received, $718,056; expenditures, $787,709; qualifying distributions, $697,382.
Limitations: Giving on an international basis.
Officers and Directors:* Daniel A. Inverso,* Chair. and Pres.; Anthony W. Inverso,* V.P. and Secy.-Treas.; Carmella Adams, Daniel Baglivo, Jessie B. Barbuto, Angelo J. Inverso, Gloria C. Melloni, Antoinette Sgro.
EIN: 232775468
Codes: FD

46270
John C. Williams Charitable Trust
c/o PNC Advisors Charitable Trust Comm.
2 PNC Plz., 620 Liberty Ave., 25th Fl.
Pittsburgh, PA 15222-2719 (412) 762-7076
Contact: Mia Hallett Bernard

Trust established in 1936 in PA.
Donor(s): John C. Williams.‡
Financial data (yr. ended 12/31/01): Grants paid, $407,561; assets, $7,405,098 (M); expenditures, $475,426; qualifying distributions, $449,379.
Limitations: Giving limited to Steubenville, OH, and Weirton, WV.

Publications: Application guidelines.
Application information: Application form required.
Trustee: PNC Bank, N.A.
EIN: 256024153
Codes: FD

46271
The Harold Katz Family Foundation
c/o G. Daniel Jones
283 2nd St. Pike, Ste. 150
Southampton, PA 18966 (215) 364-0400
Contact: Harold Katz, Pres.

Established in 1986 in PA.
Donor(s): Harold Katz.
Financial data (yr. ended 12/31/01): Grants paid, $406,584; assets, $13,553 (M); gifts received, $404,649; expenditures, $407,805; qualifying distributions, $406,564.
Limitations: Giving primarily in Kansas City, MO and PA.
Officer: Harold Katz, Pres.
Directors: David Katz, Diane Katz, Marlene Katz, Peggy Katz.
EIN: 232439844
Codes: FD

46272
The Bennet and Jeanne Tanenbaum Family Foundation
4 Tower Bridge
200 Barr Harbor Dr., Ste. 400
West Conshohocken, PA 19428-2978

Donor(s): Myles H. Tanenbaum, Steven R. Tanenbaum.
Financial data (yr. ended 12/31/01): Grants paid, $405,000; assets, $205,725 (M); expenditures, $418,320; qualifying distributions, $404,738.
Limitations: Applications not accepted. Giving primarily in CA and PA.
Application information: Contributes only to pre-selected organizations.
Officer: Myles H. Tanenbaum, Chair.
Trustee: Steven R. Tanenbaum.
EIN: 256636141
Codes: FD

46273
J. & L. Schoonmaker - Sewickley Valley Hospital Trust
c/o Mellon Bank, N.A.
3 Mellon Bank Ctr., Rm. 4000
Pittsburgh, PA 15259-0001 (412) 234-0023
Contact: Laurie A. Moritz

Established around 1981.
Financial data (yr. ended 09/30/01): Grants paid, $402,500; assets, $7,804,093 (M); expenditures, $440,132; qualifying distributions, $404,495.
Limitations: Giving primarily in Pittsburgh, PA.
Application information: Application form required.
Trustee: Mellon Bank, N.A.
EIN: 256016020
Codes: FD

46274
Salt & Light Foundation
P.O. Box 237
Elverson, PA 19520

Established in 1995 in PA.
Donor(s): Robert L. Cone.
Financial data (yr. ended 12/31/00): Grants paid, $402,000; assets, $5,617,780 (M); expenditures, $922,484; qualifying distributions, $855,693; giving activities include $406,977 for programs.
Limitations: Applications not accepted. Giving on a national basis.

Application information: Contributes only to pre-selected organizations.
Officers: Robert L. Cone, Pres. and Treas.; Edward H. Cone, V.P. and Secy.
Director: Derial H. Sanders.
EIN: 232808631
Codes: FD

46275
E. M. Sheary for Charity Trust
c/o Mellon Bank, N.A.
P.O. Box 7236
Philadelphia, PA 19101-7236
Application address: P.O. Box 346, Lewisburg, PA 17837, tel.: (717) 523-1230

Established in 1991 in PA.
Financial data (yr. ended 05/31/01): Grants paid, $397,983; assets, $1,672,338 (M); expenditures, $417,474; qualifying distributions, $398,097.
Limitations: Giving limited to PA.
Application information: Application form required.
Trustee: Mellon Bank, N.A.
EIN: 251695940
Codes: FD

46276
Kennametal Foundation
P.O. Box 231
Latrobe, PA 15650-0231

Established in 1955 in PA.
Donor(s): Kennametal Inc.
Financial data (yr. ended 06/30/01): Grants paid, $397,916; assets, $980,236 (M); gifts received, $300,000; expenditures, $401,237; qualifying distributions, $397,551.
Limitations: Applications not accepted. Giving on a national basis, with emphasis on PA.
Application information: Contributes only to pre-selected organizations.
Officer: Richard P. Gibson, Secy.-Treas.
Trustees: Stanley B. Duzy, Derwin R. Gilbreath, William R. Newlin, Markos I. Tambakeras.
EIN: 256036009
Codes: CS, FD, CD

46277
Earl Knudsen Charitable Foundation
P.O. Box 544
Carnegie, PA 15106-0544 (412) 278-4119
Contact: Judith Morrison

Established about 1975.
Donor(s): Earl Knudsen.‡
Financial data (yr. ended 12/31/01): Grants paid, $397,150; assets, $5,643,049 (M); expenditures, $449,346; qualifying distributions, $409,568.
Limitations: Giving primarily in western PA.
Application information: Application form not required.
Directors: Roy Thomas Clark, Judith Morrison, National City Bank of Pennsylvania.
EIN: 256062530
Codes: FD

46278
Bergstrom Foundation
2 PNC Plz.
620 Liberty Ave., 25th Fl.
Pittsburgh, PA 15222-2719
Contact: Bruce Bickel

Established in 1960 in PA.
Donor(s): Henry A. Bergstrom,‡ Margaret A. Bergstrom.‡
Financial data (yr. ended 12/31/01): Grants paid, $393,000; assets, $7,934,432 (M); expenditures, $504,114; qualifying distributions, $411,589.

Limitations: Applications not accepted. Giving primarily in the Pittsburgh, PA, area.
Application information: Contributes only to pre-selected organizations.
Officers: Henry A. Bergstrom, Jr., Pres.; Robert R. Long, V.P.; Larry E. Phillips, V.P.
EIN: 251112093
Codes: FD

46279
Alex C. Walker Educational and Charitable Foundation
c/o PNC Bank, N.A., 2 PNC Plz.
620 Liberty Ave., 25th Fl., MS: P2-PTPP-25-1
Pittsburgh, PA 15222-2719 (412) 762-3502
Contact: R. Bruce Bickel, Mng. Dir.

Trust established in 1967 in PA.
Donor(s): Alex C. Walker.‡
Financial data (yr. ended 12/31/01): Grants paid, $392,250; assets, $8,454,741 (M); expenditures, $469,939; qualifying distributions, $408,662.
Limitations: Giving on a national basis.
Publications: Program policy statement, application guidelines.
Application information: Application form required.
Trustees: Barrett P. Walker, Thomas Walker, PNC Bank, N.A.
EIN: 256109746
Codes: FD

46280
The Henry Lea Hillman, Jr. Foundation, Inc.
2000 Grant Bldg.
Pittsburgh, PA 15219 (412) 338-3466
FAX: (412) 338-3463; E-mail:
foundation@hillmanfo.com
Contact: Ronald W. Wertz, Secy. and Exec. Dir.

Established in 1986 in PA.
Donor(s): Henry Lea Hillman, Jr., Henry Lea Hillman Charitable Lead Trust.
Financial data (yr. ended 12/31/01): Grants paid, $392,200; assets, $8,249,637 (M); expenditures, $441,854; qualifying distributions, $404,642.
Limitations: Giving primarily in Portland, OR.
Publications: Application guidelines.
Application information: Application form not required.
Officers and Directors:* Henry Lea Hillman, Jr.,* Pres.; Lawrence M. Wagner,* V.P.; Ronald W. Wertz,* Secy. and Exec. Dir.; Maurice J. White,* Treas.
EIN: 251536656
Codes: FD

46281
The R. K. Laros Foundation, Inc.
c/o Nazareth National Bank
76 S. Main St.
Nazareth, PA 18064
Contact: Robert A. Spillman, Secy.

Trust established in 1952 in PA.
Donor(s): Russell K. Laros.‡
Financial data (yr. ended 12/31/01): Grants paid, $389,490; assets, $4,516,889 (M); expenditures, $424,136; qualifying distributions, $400,205.
Limitations: Applications not accepted. Giving primarily in Bethlehem, PA, and surrounding townships.
Application information: Contributes only to pre-selected organizations.
Officers: R.K. Laros, Jr., M.D., Pres.; Robert A. Spillman, Secy.
Trustees: Ronald Donchez, Laurie Gostley Hackett, Russell K. Laros III, Gordon B. Mowrer, Robert H. Young, Jr., Nazareth National Bank.
EIN: 236207353

Codes: FD

46282
The Audrey Hillman Fisher Foundation, Inc.
2000 Grant Bldg.
Pittsburgh, PA 15219 (412) 338-3466
FAX: (412) 338-3463; E-mail:
foundation@hillmanfo.com
Contact: Ronald W. Wertz, Secy. and Exec. Dir.

Established in 1986 in PA.
Donor(s): Audrey Hillman Fisher, Henry Lea Hillman Charitable Lead Trust.
Financial data (yr. ended 12/31/01): Grants paid, $388,820; assets, $7,863,149 (M); expenditures, $436,874; qualifying distributions, $401,397.
Limitations: Giving primarily in central NH and Pittsburgh, PA.
Publications: Application guidelines.
Application information: Application form not required.
Officers and Directors:* Audrey Hillman Fisher,* Pres.; Lawrence M. Wagner,* V.P.; Ronald W. Wertz,* Secy. and Exec. Dir.; Maurice J. White,* Treas.
EIN: 251536655
Codes: FD

46283
The Ralph M. Cestone Foundation, Inc.
2 PNC Plz., 25th Fl.
620 Liberty Ave.
Pittsburgh, PA 15222 (412) 762-3502
FAX: (412) 762-5439; E-mail:
bruce.bickel@pncadvisors.com
Contact: Bruce Bickel

Established in 1997 in NJ.
Donor(s): Maria A. Cestone, Ralph M. Cestone, Vincent R. Cestone, The Marvel Group, The Remvac Group, Inc.
Financial data (yr. ended 12/31/01): Grants paid, $388,188; assets, $7,798,816 (M); expenditures, $442,232; qualifying distributions, $388,188.
Limitations: Giving primarily in NJ, OH, and PA.
Officers and Directors:* Maria A. Cestone,* Pres.; Vincent R. Cestone, Secy.; Michele J. Cestone,* Treas.; William M. Otterbein.
EIN: 226703196
Codes: FD

46284
Charles and Figa Kline Foundation
626 N. Main St.
Allentown, PA 18104-4246
Contact: Fabian I. Fraenkel, Dir.

Incorporated in 1957 in PA.
Donor(s): Charles Kline,‡ Figa Cohen Kline.‡
Financial data (yr. ended 10/31/01): Grants paid, $385,840; assets, $8,462,768 (M); expenditures, $411,060; qualifying distributions, $385,840.
Limitations: Giving primarily in Allentown, PA.
Application information: Application form not required.
Directors: Fabian I. Fraenkel, Stewart Furmansky, Leonard Rapoport.
EIN: 236262315
Codes: FD

46285
Farber Foundation, Inc.
1845 Walnut St., Ste. 800
Philadelphia, PA 19103-4711
Health Professions Scholars Program address: c/o Univ. Office of Financial Aid, College of Health Professions, Thomas Jefferson Univ., 1025 Walnut St., Philadelphia, PA 19107, tel.: (215) 955-2867
Contact: Jacqueline A. Tully, Coord., Scholarship Prog.

Established in 1949.
Donor(s): CSS Industries, Inc.
Financial data (yr. ended 12/31/01): Grants paid, $384,170; assets, $3,151,127 (M); expenditures, $384,446; qualifying distributions, $384,242.
Limitations: Giving primarily in PA, with emphasis on Philadelphia.
Application information: Applications accepted only for scholarships, not for grants made to charitable organizations.
Officers: Jack Farber, Chair.; David J. Erskine, Pres.; Stephen V. Dubin, V.P. and Secy.; Clifford E. Pietrafitta, V.P.
EIN: 236254221
Codes: CS, FD, CD, GTI

46286
Elsie Lee Garthwaite Memorial Foundation
1234 Lancaster Ave.
Bryn Mawr, PA 19010 (610) 527-8101
Application address: P.O. Box 709, Rosemont, PA 19010-0167; FAX: (610) 527-7808
Contact: Thomas Kaneda, Secy.

Established in 1943 in PA.
Donor(s): Albert A. Garthwaite, Jr.‡
Financial data (yr. ended 12/31/01): Grants paid, $383,800; assets, $7,107,415 (M); gifts received, $55,066; expenditures, $460,510; qualifying distributions, $387,400.
Limitations: Giving primarily in Philadelphia, Chester, Montgomery and Delaware counties, PA.
Publications: Application guidelines.
Application information: Does not accept Delaware Valley Grantmakers Common Grant Application and Common Report Form. Grant request cover sheet required. Application form not required.
Officers and Trustees:* Diane Garthwaite,* Pres.; John Acuff,* V.P.; Thomas Kaneda,* Secy.; A. Alexander Ridley,* Treas.; and 5 additional trustees.
EIN: 236290877
Codes: FD

46287
The Donley Foundation
c/o Mellon Bank, N.A.
1735 Market St., P.O. Box 7899
Philadelphia, PA 19101-7899 (215) 553-1204
Application address: c/o Judith Bardes, Grants Coord., P.O. Box 540, Plymouth Meeting, PA 19462, tel.: (610) 828-8145; FAX: (610) 834-8175
Contact: Kathleen Rock, V.P., Mellon Bank, N.A.

Established in 1987 in PA.
Donor(s): Edward J. Donley, Inez C. Donley.
Financial data (yr. ended 06/30/01): Grants paid, $383,700; assets, $15,363,163 (M); expenditures, $437,732; qualifying distributions, $390,652.
Limitations: Giving primarily in northern IL, NH, York County, the greater Lehigh Valley, and south central PA areas; and VT.
Publications: Informational brochure (including application guidelines).

46287—PENNSYLVANIA

Application information: All applications must include proposal cover sheet. Application form required.
Trustees: Edward J. Donley, Inez C. Donley, John W. Donley, Thomas E. Donley, Martha Donley Robb, Ph.D.
EIN: 236859909
Codes: FD

46288
Grass Family Foundation
1000 N. Front St., Ste. 503
Wormleysburg, PA 17043

Established in 1972.
Donor(s): Alex Grass.
Financial data (yr. ended 11/30/01): Grants paid, $382,645; assets, $9,348,437 (M); expenditures, $438,937; qualifying distributions, $387,795.
Limitations: Applications not accepted. Giving primarily in Baltimore, MD, New York, NY, and Harrisburg, PA.
Application information: Contributes only to pre-selected organizations.
Officers and Directors:* Alex Grass,* Chair.; Linda Grass Shapiro,* Secy.; Elizabeth Grass Weese.
EIN: 237218002
Codes: FD

46289
E. R. Crawford Estate Trust Fund "A"
P.O. Box 487
McKeesport, PA 15134-0487 (412) 672-6670
Contact: George F. Young, Jr., Tr.

Trust established in 1936 in PA.
Donor(s): E.R. Crawford.‡
Financial data (yr. ended 12/31/01): Grants paid, $382,430; assets, $7,391,108 (M); expenditures, $439,332; qualifying distributions, $433,132.
Limitations: Giving primarily in PA, with emphasis on Allegheny County.
Application information: Application form required for individuals.
Trustees: William H. Johnson, Edward T. Phillips, George F. Young, Jr.
EIN: 256031554
Codes: FD, GTI

46290
The L. W. Pierce Family Foundation
8 Tower Bridge, Ste. 1040
161 Washington Rd.
Conshohocken, PA 19428
Contact: Leo W. Pierce, Sr., Tr.

Established in 1997 in FL.
Donor(s): Leo W. Pierce, Sr., Marjorie L. Pierce.‡
Financial data (yr. ended 12/31/01): Grants paid, $382,375; assets, $8,922,901 (M); gifts received, $1,098,580; expenditures, $450,439; qualifying distributions, $371,729.
Limitations: Applications not accepted. Giving limited to the Vero Beach, FL and Philadelphia, PA areas.
Application information: Contributes only to pre-selected organizations.
Trustees: Constance Buckley, J. Peter Pierce, Leo W. Pierce, Sr., Leo W. Pierce, Jr., Michael Pierce.
EIN: 597109847
Codes: FD

46291
The Glenn Sample, Jr., M.D. Memorial Fund
c/o PNC Advisors Charitable Trust Comm.
620 Liberty Ave., 25th Fl.
Pittsburgh, PA 15222-2705 (412) 762-7076
Contact: Mia Hallett Bernard

Established in 1999 in PA.
Donor(s): H. Glenn Sample, Jr.‡
Financial data (yr. ended 12/31/01): Grants paid, $381,097; assets, $16,422 (M); gifts received, $6,133; expenditures, $433,061; qualifying distributions, $415,703.
Limitations: Applications not accepted. Giving primarily in PA.
Application information: Contributes only to pre-selected organizations.
Trustee: PNC Bank, N.A.
EIN: 916453143
Codes: FD

46292
Bernard and Annabelle Fishman Family Foundation
The Fairmont, Ste. 409
Bala Cynwyd, PA 19004

Established in 1997 in PA.
Donor(s): Bernard Fishman, Fishman and Tobin, Inc.
Financial data (yr. ended 12/31/01): Grants paid, $379,933; assets, $336,398 (M); gifts received, $200,000; expenditures, $380,141; qualifying distributions, $379,812.
Limitations: Applications not accepted. Giving primarily in PA.
Application information: Contributes only to pre-selected organizations.
Officer: Bernard Fishman, Pres.
EIN: 232921665
Codes: FD

46293
The Honickman Foundation
(Formerly Lynne & Harold Honickman Foundation)
210 W. Rittenhouse Sq., Ste. 3303
Philadelphia, PA 19103
Contact: Lynne Honickman, Tr., or Kathy Ruyak

Established in 1988 in PA.
Donor(s): Lynne Honickman.
Financial data (yr. ended 12/31/01): Grants paid, $379,560; assets, $7,447,324 (M); gifts received, $35,150; expenditures, $457,305; qualifying distributions, $402,801.
Limitations: Applications not accepted. Giving primarily in Philadelphia, PA, and the surrounding 5 counties.
Publications: Grants list.
Application information: Application by invitation only. Unsolicited requests for funds not accepted.
Trustee: Lynne Honickman.
EIN: 232513138
Codes: FD

46294
Drueding Foundation
c/o Mrs. James J. Stokes III
669 Dodds Ln.
Gladwyne, PA 19035

Established in 1986 in PA.
Financial data (yr. ended 06/30/01): Grants paid, $378,000; assets, $7,437,891 (M); expenditures, $406,917; qualifying distributions, $375,213.
Limitations: Applications not accepted. Giving primarily in PA.
Application information: Contributes only to pre-selected organizations.
Officers: Elizabeth Michener, Pres.; Bernard J. Drueding, Jr., V.P.; James Drueding, Secy.; Patricia D. Stokes, Treas.
Trustees: Albert J. Drueding, Jr., Frank J. Drueding, Diana S. Gifford, Diana D. Stewart, Mary Grace Synder.
EIN: 232418214
Codes: FD

46295
The Brossman Family Charitable Trust for Scholarships
c/o The Ephrata National Bank
31 E. Main St., P.O. Box 457
Ephrata, PA 17522
Contact: Carl L. Brubaker, V.P. and Trust Off., The Ephrata National Bank

Established in 1986.
Donor(s): William and Jemima Brossman Charitable Foundation.
Financial data (yr. ended 10/31/00): Grants paid, $377,500; assets, $5,664 (M); gifts received, $396,000; expenditures, $391,270; qualifying distributions, $391,267.
Limitations: Giving limited to residents of the Ephrata, PA, area.
Application information: Student must be a high school graduate and resident of Ephrata area school district, Ephrata, PA, or of a high school served by Denver & Ephrata Telephone & Telegraph Co. Application form required.
Trustee: The Ephrata National Bank.
EIN: 222860047
Codes: FD, GTI

46296
Montgomery County Foundation for Handicapped Children
(also known as Child Development Foundation)
1605 W. Main St.
Norristown, PA 19403 (610) 539-6600
FAX: (610) 539-6033; *E-mail:* childdevelop@earthlink.net; *URL:* http://www.childdevelopmentfoundation.org
Contact: Wendy A. Flango, Mgr.

Established in 1987 in PA.
Financial data (yr. ended 06/30/02): Grants paid, $374,955; assets, $7,458,744 (M); expenditures, $441,751; qualifying distributions, $374,955.
Limitations: Giving limited to Montgomery County, PA.
Publications: Informational brochure (including application guidelines), application guidelines, financial statement.
Application information: Application form required.
Officers and Directors:* James J. Oliver,* Pres.; Raymond L. Butera,* V.P.; Anthony Grasso, Secy.-Treas.; Joanne E. Bryers, Marie B. Constable, Carrie Darden, Francis "Skip" Genuardi, Carole Haas Gravagno, R. Kurtz Holloway, Harry Mirabile.
EIN: 231539361
Codes: FD

46297
Alexander Stewart, M.D. Foundation
c/o Mellon Bank, N.A.
P.O. Box 7236, AIM 193-0224
Philadelphia, PA 19101-7236 (215) 553-8636
Contact: Adelina Martorelli, Trust Off., Mellon Bank, N.A.

Established in 1981 in PA.
Financial data (yr. ended 06/30/01): Grants paid, $374,788; assets, $8,039,095 (M); expenditures, $438,097; qualifying distributions, $387,222.
Limitations: Giving limited to Shippensburg, PA, and vicinity, including Cumberland, Franklin, Fulton, and Perry counties.
Trustee: Mellon Bank, N.A.
EIN: 236732616
Codes: FD

46298
The Frank O. and Clara R. Williams Scholarship Fund
c/o Kosak & Assocs.
P.O. Box 374
Oil City, PA 16301

Established in 1992 in PA.
Financial data (yr. ended 12/31/00): Grants paid, $374,377; assets, $7,574,604 (M); expenditures, $448,188; qualifying distributions, $410,055.
Limitations: Giving limited to residents of Venango County, PA.
Application information: Application form required.
Trustee: National City Bank of Pennsylvania.
EIN: 256031440
Codes: FD, GTI

46299
Hansen Foundation
(Formerly William Stucki Hansen Foundation)
2600 Neville Rd.
Pittsburgh, PA 15225
Contact: William S. Hansen, Pres.

Established in 1984 in PA.
Donor(s): Hansen, Inc.
Financial data (yr. ended 11/30/01): Grants paid, $373,300; assets, $3,684,095 (M); expenditures, $398,989; qualifying distributions, $1,673,300; giving activities include $1,300,000 for loans.
Limitations: Applications not accepted. Giving primarily in western PA.
Application information: Contributes only to pre-selected organizations.
Officers and Directors:* William S. Hansen,* Pres.; William Gregg Hansen,* V.P.; Nancy K. Hansen,* Secy.-Treas.
EIN: 251483674
Codes: FD

46300
McConnell-Willits Charitable Trust
353 W. Lancaster Ave., Ste. 120
Wayne, PA 19087-3907 (610) 687-1600

Donor(s): Christopher F. McConnell, Stacey Willits McConnell.
Financial data (yr. ended 12/31/01): Grants paid, $373,200; assets, $288,308 (M); gifts received, $220,598; expenditures, $377,463; qualifying distributions, $373,200.
Limitations: Giving primarily in NH, NJ, and PA.
Trustees: William McCoy, Merritt N. Willits IV.
EIN: 237867442

46301
The H. O. West Foundation
101 Gordon Dr.
Exton, PA 19341-0645 (610) 594-2900
Contact: George R. Bennyhoff, Chair.; or Maureen Goebel, Admin.

Established in 1972 in PA.
Donor(s): The West Co., Inc., West Pharmaceutical Services, Inc., and members of the West family.
Financial data (yr. ended 12/31/01): Grants paid, $370,247; assets, $478,580 (M); gifts received, $648,518; expenditures, $373,330; qualifying distributions, $373,113.
Limitations: Giving primarily in areas of company operations in FL, NC, NE, and PA.
Publications: Application guidelines.
Application information: Application form not required.
Trustees: George R. Bennyhoff, Chair.; William G. Little, Franklin H. West.
EIN: 237173901
Codes: CS, FD, CD, GTI

46302
The Ross Loan Fund
c/o Allfirst
P.O. Box 459
Chambersburg, PA 17201 (717) 261-2833
Contact: Jacqueline Hill

Financial data (yr. ended 12/31/01): Grants paid, $367,350; assets, $3,346,693 (M); expenditures, $403,657; qualifying distributions, $367,350; giving activities include $367,350 for loans to individuals.
Limitations: Giving limited to Chambersburg, PA.
Application information: Application form required.
Trustee: Allfirst.
EIN: 236262609
Codes: FD, GTI

46303
The Clareth Fund: The Philadelphia Association of Zeta Psi Fraternity
c/o Duanne, Morris & Heckscher, LLP
1 Liberty Pl.
Philadelphia, PA 19103-7396
Application address: 2400 Market St., Philadelphia, PA 19103
Contact: David L. Sims, Pres.

Financial data (yr. ended 12/31/00): Grants paid, $364,990; assets, $6,441,294 (M); expenditures, $394,232; qualifying distributions, $361,238.
Limitations: Giving limited to PA.
Application information: Application form not required.
Officers and Directors:* David L. Sims,* Pres.; Peter B. Pakradooni, V.P.; Gregory E. McElroy,* Secy.; James P. Bodine, Treas.; Peter F. Arfaa, McBee Butcher, Marc C. Ganzi, Charles L. Ingersoll II, Roger Jones, Eric Lombardini, Christopher Rice, Michael A. Walsh.
EIN: 232092500
Codes: FD, GTI

46304
Raymond Klein Charitable Foundation
1700 Market St., Ste. 2600
Philadelphia, PA 19103
Contact: Stephen B. Klein, Pres.

Established in 1988 in PA.
Donor(s): Raymond Klein.
Financial data (yr. ended 10/31/01): Grants paid, $364,950; assets, $5,851,447 (M); expenditures, $384,670; qualifying distributions, $361,630.
Limitations: Giving primarily in Philadelphia, PA.
Application information: Application form not required.
Officer and Trustees:* Stephen B. Klein,* Pres.; Miriam K. Klein.
EIN: 232535513
Codes: FD

46305
The Lasko Family Foundation
820 Lincoln Ave.
West Chester, PA 19380

Established in 1984 in PA.
Donor(s): Oscar Lasko, Lasko Metal Products, Inc.
Financial data (yr. ended 06/30/01): Grants paid, $363,850; assets, $5,127,008 (M); gifts received, $400,000; expenditures, $393,010; qualifying distributions, $361,626.
Limitations: Giving primarily in PA.
Officer: Bernard Eizen, Pres.
Directors: Maury Huberman, Vivian Lasko.
EIN: 232307053
Codes: FD

46306
Nathan Speare Foundation
22 W. 2nd St.
Media, PA 19063 (610) 566-8000
Contact: Robert Speare, Tr.

Established in 1952.
Donor(s): Reba Speare Solis.‡
Financial data (yr. ended 12/31/00): Grants paid, $363,520; assets, $5,603,760 (M); expenditures, $531,929; qualifying distributions, $482,577.
Limitations: Giving primarily in PA.
Application information: Accepts Delaware Valley Grantmakers Common Grant Application and Common Report Form. Application form not required.
Trustees: Bertram Speare, Jon Speare, Robert Speare.
EIN: 236245505
Codes: FD

46307
Myer and Rosaline Feinstein Foundation
1009 Delene Rd.
Rydal, PA 19046
Contact: Peggy F. Freedman, Pres.

Trust established in 1945 in PA; incorporated in 1960 in DE.
Donor(s): Myer Feinstein,‡ Rosaline B. Feinstein,‡ and others.
Financial data (yr. ended 12/31/01): Grants paid, $360,300; assets, $1,462,795 (M); expenditures, $434,541; qualifying distributions, $403,929.
Limitations: Applications not accepted. Giving primarily in PA and Israel.
Application information: Contributes only to pre-selected organizations.
Officers and Directors:* Peggy F. Freedman,* Pres.; Myra Freedman, V.P.; Saul J. Freedman, Secy.-Treas.; Andrew Freedman, Paul Freedman.
EIN: 236235232
Codes: FD

46308
Gold Family Foundation
c/o Claire Gold
252 Ironwood Cir.
Elkins Park, PA 19027

Established in 1986 in PA.
Donor(s): Aaron Gold,‡ Claire Gold.
Financial data (yr. ended 11/30/01): Grants paid, $360,101; assets, $1,153,330 (M); expenditures, $384,049; qualifying distributions, $365,969.
Limitations: Applications not accepted. Giving primarily in PA.
Application information: Contributes only to pre-selected organizations.
Trustee: R. Michael Gold.
Directors: Claire Gold, Joshua Gold, Julie Gold-Goldenberg.
EIN: 222783283
Codes: FD

46309
The Vernon and Doris Bishop Foundation
1616 Fieldcrest Rd.
Lebanon, PA 17042
Contact: Vernon Bishop, Tr.

Established in 1957 in PA.
Financial data (yr. ended 12/31/01): Grants paid, $359,840; assets, $4,420,649 (M); expenditures, $397,500; qualifying distributions, $361,330.
Limitations: Applications not accepted. Giving primarily in Lebanon County, PA.
Application information: Unsolicited requests for fund not accepted.
Trustee: Vernon Bishop.
EIN: 236255835

46309—PENNSYLVANIA

Codes: FD

46310
The Walter L. Schautz Foundation
150 E. Grove St.
Scranton, PA 18510
Contact: Madalene L. Schautz, Pres., and Walter L. Schautz, Jr., Treas.

Incorporated in 1948 in PA.
Donor(s): Walter L. Schautz, Madalene L. Schautz, Grove Silk Co.
Financial data (yr. ended 01/31/01): Grants paid, $355,023; assets, $7,503,736 (M); expenditures, $373,347; qualifying distributions, $356,623.
Limitations: Giving primarily in PA.
Officers: Madalene L. Schautz, Pres.; Nancy Miles, Secy.; Walter L. Schautz, Jr., Treas.
Trustees: John Cherb, James Reid.
EIN: 246018362
Codes: FD

46311
Joseph Skilling Foundation
c/o First Union National Bank, Charitable Svcs. Group
123 S. Broad St., 16th Fl.
Philadelphia, PA 19109 (215) 670-4226
Contact: Reginald Middleton, V.P., First Union National Bank

Financial data (yr. ended 12/31/01): Grants paid, $354,250; assets, $6,629,226 (M); expenditures, $473,170; qualifying distributions, $373,958.
Limitations: Giving limited to Philadelphia, PA.
Trustees: Mary Louise Mann, Christina McKinley, William W. Spalding, First Union National Bank.
EIN: 236419739
Codes: FD

46312
John H. Sykes Charitable Foundation, Inc.
Broad and Walnut Sts., Ste. PA1308
Philadelphia, PA 19109
Contact: Susan Sykes, Pres.

Established in 1997 in FL.
Donor(s): John H. Sykes, Susan Sykes.
Financial data (yr. ended 08/31/01): Grants paid, $353,589; assets, $6,283,561 (M); expenditures, $380,145; qualifying distributions, $352,237.
Limitations: Applications not accepted. Giving primarily in FL.
Application information: Contributes only to pre-selected organizations.
Officers and Directors:* Susan Sykes,* Pres.; Barbara Murphy, Secy.; Samantha Warren,* Treas.; Karen Taylor, Barbara Wilcox.
Agent: First Union National Bank.
EIN: 656218520
Codes: FD

46313
Ethel D. Colket Foundation
c/o PNC Bank, N.A.
1600 Market St., 29th Fl.
Philadelphia, PA 19103 (215) 585-5680
Contact: Robert N. Tropp, V.P., PNC Bank, N.A.

Established in 1964 in PA.
Financial data (yr. ended 08/31/01): Grants paid, $351,676; assets, $5,795,497 (M); expenditures, $374,721; qualifying distributions, $349,998.
Limitations: Giving primarily in the Delaware Valley, PA, area.
Application information: Application form not required.
Trustees: Bryan Colket, Ruth Colket, Tristram Colket, Jr., Carolyn Colket Cullen, PNC Bank, N.A.
EIN: 236292917
Codes: FD

46314
Lita Annenberg Hazen Charitable Trust
c/o PNC Advisors
1600 Market St., 29th Fl.
Philadelphia, PA 19103-7240
Contact: L. Dianne Lomonaco, Trust Admin.

Trust established in 1952 in NY.
Donor(s): Lita A. Hazen.‡
Financial data (yr. ended 12/31/00): Grants paid, $350,000; assets, $3,083,431 (M); expenditures, $367,640; qualifying distributions, $348,744.
Limitations: Applications not accepted. Giving primarily in New York, NY.
Application information: Contributes only to pre-selected organizations.
Trustee: Cynthia H. Polsky.
EIN: 236286759
Codes: FD

46315
The Auldridge Fund
1225 Farview Rd.
Villanova, PA 19085-2037

Established in 1998 in PA.
Donor(s): Roy S. Neff, Rosalind S. Neff.
Financial data (yr. ended 12/31/00): Grants paid, $348,000; assets, $1,532,238 (M); gifts received, $549,923; expenditures, $350,370; qualifying distributions, $342,878.
Limitations: Applications not accepted.
Application information: Contributes only to pre-selected organizations.
Officers and Directors:* Roy S. Neff,* Pres.; Rosalind S. Neff,* Secy.
EIN: 232900851
Codes: FD

46316
P. M. Moore Foundation
1531 2nd St.
P.O. Box 416
Beaver, PA 15009-0416 (724) 774-4997
Contact: Dana L. Duff, Treas.

Incorporated in 1958 in PA.
Donor(s): Paul M. Moore.‡
Financial data (yr. ended 12/31/01): Grants paid, $344,500; assets, $6,365,806 (M); expenditures, $349,600; qualifying distributions, $344,500.
Limitations: Giving primarily in Beaver County, PA.
Application information: Application form not required.
Officers: James S. Ruffner, Pres.; Ruth Ann Duff, Secy.; Dana Duff, Treas.
Trustee: Paul W. Duff.
EIN: 256066268
Codes: FD

46317
The M. S. Grumbacher Foundation
2801 E. Market St.
P.O. Box 2821
York, PA 17402 (717) 757-2606
Contact: M.S. Grumbacher

Established around 1992.
Donor(s): M.S. Grumbacher.
Financial data (yr. ended 08/31/01): Grants paid, $341,650; assets, $7,130,846 (M); expenditures, $395,032; qualifying distributions, $362,957.
Limitations: Giving limited to PA, with emphasis on the York area.
Directors: Richard Grumbacher, D.J. Kaufman, J. Schultz, J. Schvartzer.
EIN: 232697348
Codes: FD

46318
The Psalm 103 Foundation
601 Pembroke Rd.
Bryn Mawr, PA 19010

Established in 1987.
Donor(s): John M. Templeton, Jr.
Financial data (yr. ended 09/30/01): Grants paid, $338,401; assets, $3,670,376 (M); gifts received, $252,233; expenditures, $347,523; qualifying distributions, $344,659.
Limitations: Applications not accepted. Giving primarily in MD and PA.
Application information: Contributes only to pre-selected organizations.
Officers: John M. Templeton, Jr., Pres. and Treas.; Josephine J. Templeton, V.P. and Secy.
EIN: 232500843
Codes: FD

46319
The Kairos Trust
c/o Duane, Morris & Heckscher
1 Liberty Pl.
Philadelphia, PA 19103-7396

Established in 1993 in PA.
Donor(s): Alice Anne Miller.
Financial data (yr. ended 12/31/01): Grants paid, $336,200; assets, $12,550 (M); gifts received, $300,491; expenditures, $341,871; qualifying distributions, $335,655.
Limitations: Applications not accepted. Giving primarily in PA.
Application information: Contributes only to pre-selected organizations.
Trustee: Alice Anne Miller.
EIN: 237743234
Codes: FD

46320
Sonia Raiziss Giop Charitable Foundation
c/o Mellon Bank, N.A.
P.O. Box 7236, AIM 193-0224
Philadelphia, PA 19101-7236

Established in 1994 in PA.
Donor(s): Sonia Giop,‡ Ines Giop Crut.
Financial data (yr. ended 12/31/00): Grants paid, $336,000; assets, $5,769,079 (M); gifts received, $215,135; expenditures, $360,934; qualifying distributions, $335,788.
Limitations: Applications not accepted. Giving primarily in NY and PA.
Application information: Contributes only to pre-selected organizations.
Trustees: Antoinette Denisof, Alfredo DePalchi, Mellon Bank, N.A.
EIN: 256453053
Codes: FD

46321
Violette De Mazia Trust
c/o PNC Bank, N.A.
1600 Market St., Tax Dept.
Philadelphia, PA 19103-7240
Application address: c/o Sharon Hicks, GSB Bldg., Ste. 310, Bala Cynwyd, PA 19004, tel.: (610) 688-1833

Established in 1990.
Financial data (yr. ended 06/30/01): Grants paid, $335,431; assets, $12,195,522 (M); expenditures, $629,035; qualifying distributions, $611,777.
Limitations: Giving primarily in PA.
Application information: Application form required.
Trustees: Ernest Pick, Marcelle Pick, Esther Van Sant, PNC Bank, N.A.
EIN: 236954824
Codes: FD

46322
The Barrack Foundation
930 Rock Creek Rd.
Bryn Mawr, PA 19010
Application address: 3300 2 Commerce Sq., 2001 Market St., Philadelphia, PA 19103, tel.: (215) 963-0600
Contact: Leonard Barrack, Mgr.

Established in 1978.
Donor(s): Leonard Barrack.
Financial data (yr. ended 11/30/01): Grants paid, $335,046; assets, $527,842 (M); expenditures, $337,650; qualifying distributions, $335,772.
Limitations: Giving primarily in PA.
Application information: Application form not required.
Manager: Leonard Barrack.
EIN: 232084461
Codes: FD

46323
The C. K. Williams Foundation
c/o Mellon Bank, N.A.
P.O. Box 185
Pittsburgh, PA 15230

Established in 1963 in PA.
Financial data (yr. ended 12/31/01): Grants paid, $334,616; assets, $15,181,365 (M); expenditures, $418,358; qualifying distributions, $334,616.
Limitations: Applications not accepted. Giving primarily in PA.
Application information: Contributes only to pre-selected organizations.
Directors: Joan W. Rhome, Charles K. Williams, Josephine C. Williams.
EIN: 236292772
Codes: FD

46324
Kal & Lucille Rudman Foundation
c/o Asher & Company, Ltd.
1845 Walnut St., 13th Fl.
Philadelphia, PA 19103

Established in 1996 in NJ.
Donor(s): Kal Rudman, Lucille Rudman.
Financial data (yr. ended 12/31/01): Grants paid, $332,308; assets, $6,645,984 (M); gifts received, $170,600; expenditures, $365,581; qualifying distributions, $324,341.
Limitations: Applications not accepted. Giving primarily in Philadelphia, PA.
Application information: Unsolicited requests for funds not accepted.
Trustees: Lucille Rudman, Solomon Rudman.
EIN: 233237107
Codes: FD

46325
The West Family Foundation
12 Greenbriar Ln.
Paoli, PA 19301-1908

Established in 1996 in PA.
Donor(s): Alfred P. West, Jr.
Financial data (yr. ended 06/30/01): Grants paid, $332,212; assets, $19,302,601 (M); gifts received, $1,179,063; expenditures, $338,977; qualifying distributions, $331,854.
Limitations: Applications not accepted. Giving primarily in PA.
Application information: Contributes only to pre-selected organizations.
Officers and Directors:* Alfred P. West, Jr.,* Pres.; Angela Paige West,* Secy.-Treas.; A. Palmer West, Alfred Paul West III, Loralee West.
EIN: 232870271
Codes: FD

46326
DeFrees Family Foundation, Inc.
419 3rd Ave.
P.O. Box 708
Warren, PA 16365 (814) 723-8150
FAX: (814) 723-8400; *E-mail:* acc@alleghenycoupling.com
Contact: Harold A. Johnson, Pres.

Established in 1978 in PA.
Donor(s): Joseph H. DeFrees,‡ members of the DeFrees family.‡
Financial data (yr. ended 12/31/00): Grants paid, $328,909; assets, $10,316,399 (M); expenditures, $363,839; qualifying distributions, $328,909.
Limitations: Giving primarily in the Warren, PA, area.
Publications: Application guidelines.
Application information: Application form not required.
Officers and Directors:* Harold A. Johnson,* Pres. and Treas.; David E. Martin,* V.P. and Secy.; Mary Garvey, William M. Hill, Jr., Susan Merritt.
EIN: 251320042
Codes: FD

46327
Ferguson Foundation, Inc.
c/o Frederick Farber
110 Regent Ct., Ste. 202
State College, PA 16801

Established in 1994 in PA.
Donor(s): Wallace C. Snipes, Roberta Snipes.
Financial data (yr. ended 12/31/01): Grants paid, $328,000; assets, $1,955,919 (M); expenditures, $353,991; qualifying distributions, $324,739.
Limitations: Applications not accepted. Giving limited to PA.
Application information: Contributes only to pre-selected organizations.
Officers and Directors:* Wallace C. Snipes,* Pres.; Frederick Farber,* Secy.-Treas.; Roberta Snipes.
EIN: 251728428
Codes: FD

46328
Harvey Goodstein Charitable Trust
c/o Sandra Goodstein-Hirsch
Executive Plz., Ste. 323
Fort Washington, PA 19034

Established in 1999 in PA.
Financial data (yr. ended 12/31/01): Grants paid, $327,250; assets, $8,918,119 (M); expenditures, $840,114; qualifying distributions, $341,448.
Limitations: Applications not accepted. Giving primarily in Devon and Philadelphia, PA.
Application information: Contributes only to pre-selected organizations.
Trustee: Sandra Goodstein-Hirsch.
EIN: 237992456
Codes: FD

46329
Karen & Herbert Lotman Foundation
1 Liberty Pl., 32nd Fl.
Philadelphia, PA 19103
Application address: 401 City Ave., Ste. 800, Bala Cynwyd, PA 19004, tel.: (610) 668-6700
Contact: Herbert Lotman, V.P.

Established in 1982 in PA.
Donor(s): Shelly Lotman Fisher, Herbert Lotman, Jeffrey Lotman, Karen Lotman, Keystone Foods Corp.
Financial data (yr. ended 11/30/01): Grants paid, $327,000; assets, $3,467,454 (M); gifts received, $1,000; expenditures, $328,421; qualifying distributions, $325,726.
Limitations: Giving primarily in PA; some giving also in Canada.
Officers: Karen Lotman, Pres.; Herbert Lotman, V.P.; Shelly Lotman Fisher, Secy.; Jeffrey Lotman, Treas.
EIN: 222429821
Codes: FD

46330
The Price Foundation
P.O. Box 369
Indianola, PA 15051-0369
Contact: Douglas Schofield, Tr.

Established in 1993.
Donor(s): Wendell Price.
Financial data (yr. ended 12/31/00): Grants paid, $325,280; assets, $5,311,998 (M); expenditures, $350,139; qualifying distributions, $348,256.
Limitations: Applications not accepted. Giving on a national basis.
Application information: Contributes only to pre-selected organizations.
Trustees: Wendell Price, Douglas Schofield.
EIN: 251701024
Codes: FD

46331
Julius H. Caplan Charity Foundation
401 City Ave., Ste. 200
Bala Cynwyd, PA 19004-1117
Contact: Eli Caplan, Dir.

Incorporated in 1944 in NY.
Donor(s): Hyman S. Caplan,‡ Keystone Weaving Mills, Inc.
Financial data (yr. ended 12/31/00): Grants paid, $325,141; assets, $7,802,002 (M); expenditures, $461,696; qualifying distributions, $381,208.
Limitations: Giving primarily in PA, with emphasis on Lebanon and Philadelphia.
Application information: Application form not required.
Directors: Eli Caplan, Helen Caplan, Perry Caplan.
EIN: 136067379
Codes: FD

46332
Centre County Community Foundation, Inc.
2013 Sandy Dr.
P.O. Box 824
State College, PA 16804-0824 (814) 237-6229
FAX: (814) 237-2624; *E-mail:* info@centrecountycf.org; *URL:* http://www.centrecountycf.org

Established in 1981 in PA.
Financial data (yr. ended 12/31/00): Grants paid, $321,901; assets, $8,968,647 (M); gifts received, $2,609,025; expenditures, $506,046.
Limitations: Giving limited to Centre County, PA.
Application information: See foundation Web site for guidelines and downloadable application forms. Application form required.
Officers and Directors:* Martha L. Starling,* Chair.; Richard L. Kalin,* 1st Vice-Chair.; Jeffrey M. Bower,* 2nd Vice-Chair.; Frances E. Mason,* Secy.; Robert McNichol,* Treas.; Milton J. Bergstein, Richard L. Campbell, Charles J. Curley, Edward A. Friedman, Stanley L. Goldman, Henry B. Haitz III, Donald W. Hamer, Gerald C. Hartman, Bruce Heim, Lou Heldman, William D. Karch, Norman K. Lathbury, Eileen W. Leibowtiz, Robert N. Levy, John P. Mandryk, William H. Martin, James M. Rayback, Charles W. Rohrbeck, Helen Dix Steward, Eloise Dunn Stuhr, Dolares Taricani.
EIN: 251782197
Codes: CM, FD

46333
IKON Office Solutions Foundation, Inc.
(Formerly Alco Standard Foundation)
P.O. Box 834
Valley Forge, PA 19482-0834

Established in 1974 in PA.
Donor(s): IKON Office Solutions, Inc.
Financial data (yr. ended 12/31/01): Grants paid, $321,715; assets, $3,758,248 (M); expenditures, $324,402; qualifying distributions, $321,715.
Limitations: Applications not accepted. Giving primarily in areas of company operations.
Application information: Contributes only to pre-selected organizations.
Officers and Directors: William Urkiel,* Pres.; J.F. Quinn,* V.P. and Treas.; Don Liu,* Secy.
EIN: 237378726
Codes: CS, FD, CD

46334
The Churchill Foundation
435 Devon Park Dr., Ste. 300
Wayne, PA 19087-1935 (610) 964-7860
Contact: Winston J. Churchill, Jr., Chair.

Established in 1997 in PA.
Donor(s): Winston J. Churchill, Jr.
Financial data (yr. ended 04/30/01): Grants paid, $321,485; assets, $2,782,428 (M); gifts received, $2,734,199; expenditures, $322,793; qualifying distributions, $321,384.
Limitations: Giving primarily in Washington, DC and Philadelphia, PA.
Application information: Application form required.
Officer: Winston J. Churchill, Jr., Chair.
Director: Barbara G. Churchill.
EIN: 232904826
Codes: FD

46335
Society for Analytical Chemists of Pittsburgh
300 Penn Ctr. Blvd., Ste. 332
Pittsburgh, PA 15235-5503
Tel.: (412) 825-3220 ext. 208; FAX: (412) 825-3224; E-mail: sacpinfo@pitton.org; URL: http://www.sacp.org
Contact: John E. Graham, Chair.

Established in 1971.
Financial data (yr. ended 06/30/01): Grants paid, $319,059; assets, $112,903 (M); gifts received, $464,357; expenditures, $466,540; qualifying distributions, $319,059.
Limitations: Giving primarily in the Pittsburgh, PA, area.
Publications: Informational brochure.
Application information: Application form required.
Officers: John E. Graham, Chair.; Kevin J. McKaveney, Chair.-Elect.; Susan Zawacky, Secy.; Jane Chan, Treas.
EIN: 256072976
Codes: FD, GTI

46336
Brooks Foundation
c/o PNC Bank, N.A., MS P2 PTPP-26-3
2 PNC Plz., 620 Liberty Ave.
Pittsburgh, PA 15222-2705 (412) 762-3390
Contact: John Culbertson, V.P., PNC Bank, N.A.

Financial data (yr. ended 12/31/01): Grants paid, $317,826; assets, $4,893,730 (M); expenditures, $339,077; qualifying distributions, $321,076.
Limitations: Giving primarily in Pittsburgh, PA.
Trustee: PNC Bank, N.A.
EIN: 256026627
Codes: FD

46337
Charles H. Hoch Foundation
c/o The Trust Company of Lehigh Valley
1620 Pond Rd.
Allentown, PA 18104
Application address: 1825 Lehigh Pkwy., N., Allentown, PA 18103
Contact: Richard J. Hummel, Pres.

Established in 1956.
Financial data (yr. ended 12/31/01): Grants paid, $315,500; assets, $6,261,629 (M); expenditures, $360,528; qualifying distributions, $330,110.
Limitations: Giving primarily in Allentown, PA.
Officers and Directors:* Richard J. Hummel,* Pres. and Treas.; James L. Weierbach,* Secy.; William Daniels, Alfred E. DeMott, Carol Feller.
EIN: 236265016
Codes: FD

46338
Polly A. Levee Charitable Trust A - Krancer Trust
c/o PNC Advisors
1600 Market St., 29th Fl.
Philadelphia, PA 19103

Established in 1993 in PA as partial successor to Polly Annenberg Levee Charitable Trust.
Donor(s): Polly Annenberg Levee.‡
Financial data (yr. ended 12/31/01): Grants paid, $315,000; assets, $5,357,003 (M); expenditures, $337,263; qualifying distributions, $313,015.
Limitations: Applications not accepted. Giving primarily in Philadelphia, PA.
Application information: Contributes only to pre-selected organizations. Unsolicited requests for funds not considered.
Trustees: William J. Henrich, PNC Bank, N.A.
EIN: 232735661
Codes: FD

46339
Tecovas Foundation
c/o Glenmede Trust Co.
1650 Market St., Ste. 1200
Philadelphia, PA 19103

Established in 1999 in TX.
Donor(s): Caroline Bush Emeny.
Financial data (yr. ended 12/31/01): Grants paid, $315,000; assets, $8,649,869 (M); gifts received, $1,486,891; expenditures, $381,883; qualifying distributions, $314,863.
Limitations: Applications not accepted. Giving primarily in Amarillo, TX.
Application information: Contributes only to pre-selected organizations.
Officers and Directors:* Mary T. Emeny,* Chair.; Caroline E. Taylor,* Vice-Chair.; Ann Hodges, Secy.; Alicia E. Ingalls,* Secy.; Janet W. Havener, Treas.; Alexander S. Taylor, Mary Wagley.
EIN: 752829989
Codes: FD

46340
The 25th Century Foundation
c/o Ballard, Spahr, et al
1500 Market St., 1st Fl.
Philadelphia, PA 19103-7559

Established in 2000 in PA.
Financial data (yr. ended 03/31/02): Grants paid, $315,000; assets, $3,915,460 (M); expenditures, $372,958; qualifying distributions, $315,000.
Limitations: Applications not accepted.
Application information: Contributes only to pre-selected organizations.
Officers and Directors:* J. Mahlon Buck, Jr.,* Chair.; Caroline Buck Rogers,* Pres.; James Buck III,* V.P.; Marilyn C. Sanborne,* Secy.; Elia Buck, Elinor Buck, Joseph W. Rogers, Jr., First Union National Bank.
EIN: 311738216

46341
The Drumcliff Foundation
1021 W. Hortter St.
Philadelphia, PA 19119 (215) 849-9080
Contact: Ellen Schurdak, Dir.

Established in 1988 in PA.
Financial data (yr. ended 12/31/01): Grants paid, $311,500; assets, $2,696,658 (L); gifts received, $1,000,000; expenditures, $325,610; qualifying distributions, $311,500.
Limitations: Giving primarily in Philadelphia, PA.
Application information: Applications are received on a rolling basis starting in Jan. Application form not required.
Trustee: Daniel F. Gordon.
Director: Ellen Schurdak.
EIN: 236957302
Codes: FD

46342
Lutron Foundation
c/o Joel Spira
1506 Pleasant View Rd.
Coopersburg, PA 18036

Established around 1985.
Donor(s): Joel Spira.
Financial data (yr. ended 12/31/99): Grants paid, $310,256; assets, $2,015,842 (M); gifts received, $700,000; expenditures, $310,306; qualifying distributions, $310,256.
Limitations: Applications not accepted. Giving primarily in PA.
Application information: Contributes only to pre-selected organizations.
Trustees: Joel Spira, Ruth Spira.
EIN: 232322928
Codes: FD

46343
Robert C. Hoffman Charitable Endowment Trust
c/o PNC Advisors
1600 Market St., Tax Dept.
Philadelphia, PA 19103-7240
Application address: P.O. Box 3547, Gettysburg, PA 17325; Tel./FAX: (717) 338-0344
Contact: Barbara B. Ernico, Consultant to the Advisory Committee

Established in 1999 in PA.
Donor(s): Robert C. Hoffman.‡
Financial data (yr. ended 07/31/01): Grants paid, $309,014; assets, $6,923,847 (M); gifts received, $287,545; expenditures, $366,169; qualifying distributions, $330,180.
Limitations: Giving limited to Adams County, PA.
Application information: Considers up to 4 applications per organization each year, application may be re-typed, but should be no longer than 3-pages, 12-point type, single-spaced, on letter-size paper. Application form required.
Advisory Committee: David Brown, David K. Heiges, John R. White.
Trustee: PNC Bank, N.A.
EIN: 256658643
Codes: FD

46344
The Calihan Foundation
600 Grant St., Ste. 4606
Pittsburgh, PA 15219-2702
Contact: Victoria L. Pacoe, Secy.

Established in 1987 in PA.

Donor(s): Joseph L. Calihan, Martin J. Calihan, Katherine R. Calihan, Mary M. Calihan, Brenda S. Calihan, Bradford Capital Funds.
Financial data (yr. ended 12/31/01): Grants paid, $308,305; assets, $763,725 (M); gifts received, $179,518; expenditures, $311,284; qualifying distributions, $308,720.
Limitations: Giving primarily in Pittsburgh, PA.
Officers: Joseph L. Calihan, Pres.; Victoria L. Pacoe, Secy.; David H. Kropp, Treas.
EIN: 251560562
Codes: FD

46345
Airie Knipel, Harry V. and J. William Warehime Foundation
c/o Bergdoll & Co.
137 W. Market St.
York, PA 17401

Established in 1996 in PA.
Donor(s): J. William Warehime.
Financial data (yr. ended 12/31/99): Grants paid, $306,095; assets, $332,628 (M); gifts received, $110,000; expenditures, $308,103; qualifying distributions, $306,095.
Limitations: Applications not accepted. Giving primarily in Hanover, PA.
Application information: Contributes only to pre-selected organizations.
Officers and Directors:* J. William Warehime,* Pres.; Edward L. Geesaman,* V.P.; Linda A. Loer,* Secy.
EIN: 311481509

46346
The Phyllis & Norman Lipsett Foundation
c/o Bennett Aaron, Pepper Hamilton & Sheetz
3000 Two Logan Sq., 18th & Arch Sts.
Philadelphia, PA 19103-2799
Application address: 1800 Linglestown Rd., Ste. 100, Harrisburg, PA 17110
Contact: Norman B. Lipsett, Pres.

Established in 1981 in PA.
Donor(s): Julie S. Lipsett, Norman B. Lipsett, Phyllis Lipsett, Jane Javitch.
Financial data (yr. ended 08/31/01): Grants paid, $305,159; assets, $2,492,201 (M); gifts received, $399,839; expenditures, $322,893; qualifying distributions, $302,113.
Limitations: Giving primarily in PA.
Application information: Application form not required.
Officers: Norman B. Lipsett, Pres.; Phyllis Lipsett, V.P.; Bennett Aaron, Secy.-Treas.
EIN: 232185093
Codes: FD

46347
The Kent Foundation
404 E. Lancaster Ave.
Wayne, PA 19087

Established in 1998 in PA.
Donor(s): Lawrence J. Kent, Mary A. Kent.
Financial data (yr. ended 12/31/99): Grants paid, $304,500; assets, $2,147,874 (M); gifts received, $817,388; expenditures, $309,589; qualifying distributions, $304,500.
Limitations: Applications not accepted. Giving primarily in PA.
Application information: Contributes only to pre-selected organizations.
Officers: Lawrence J. Kent, Pres.; Mary A. Kent, V.P.; Lawrence A. Palmer, Secy.
EIN: 510382152
Codes: FD

46348
Klorfine Foundation
P.O. Box 128
Gladwyne, PA 19035
Contact: Leonard Klorfine, or Norma Klorfine, Trustees

Established in 1993 in PA.
Donor(s): Leonard Klorfine, Norma E. Klorfine.
Financial data (yr. ended 11/30/01): Grants paid, $302,650; assets, $10,018,176 (M); gifts received, $3,023,044; expenditures, $332,847; qualifying distributions, $298,373.
Limitations: Giving primarily in Philadelphia, PA; some giving also in Washington, DC.
Application information: Application form not required.
Trustees: Leonard Klorfine, Norma E. Klorfine.
EIN: 227743385
Codes: FD

46349
The Charles B. Degenstein Foundation
c/o Mellon Bank, N.A.
P.O. Box 7236, AIM 193-0224
Philadelphia, PA 19101-7236
Application address: 4350 5th St., Sunbury, PA 17801, tel.: (570) 286-1582
Contact: Sidney Apfelbaum

Established in 1989.
Donor(s): Charles Degenstein.‡
Financial data (yr. ended 09/30/01): Grants paid, $301,713; assets, $2,578,408 (M); gifts received, $2,000; expenditures, $323,199; qualifying distributions, $307,876.
Limitations: Giving within a 75-mile radius of Sunbury, PA.
Publications: Informational brochure (including application guidelines).
Application information: Giving for 501(c)(3) organizations. Application form required.
Trustee: Mellon Bank, N.A.
EIN: 236971532
Codes: FD

46350
Whalley Charitable Trust
1210 Graham Ave.
Windber, PA 15963 (814) 467-4000
Contact: David Klementik, Tr.

Established in 1961 in PA.
Donor(s): John J. Whalley, John Whalley, Jr., Mary Whalley.
Financial data (yr. ended 12/31/01): Grants paid, $301,064; assets, $4,843,837 (M); expenditures, $350,494; qualifying distributions, $314,516.
Limitations: Giving primarily in PA, with emphasis on Windber and Johnstown.
Application information: Application form not required.
Trustee: David Klementik.
EIN: 237128436
Codes: FD

46351
The Millstein Charitable Foundation
P.O. Box K
Youngwood, PA 15697
Contact: David Millstein, Exec. Secy., or Jack Millstein, Tr.

Established in 1964.
Donor(s): Jack H. Millstein, Sr.,‡ Mrs. Jack H. Millstein, Sr.‡
Financial data (yr. ended 09/30/01): Grants paid, $300,153; assets, $6,220,470 (M); expenditures, $350,198; qualifying distributions, $295,973.
Limitations: Giving primarily in western PA.
Application information: Requests are reviewed as they are received. Application form not required.
Officer and Trustees:* David J. Millstein,* Exec. Secy.; Jack H. Millstein, Jr.
EIN: 256064981
Codes: FD

46352
The Cochran Family Foundation
c/o Glenmede Trust Co.
1650 Market St., Ste. 1200
Philadelphia, PA 19103

Established in 1998 in DE.
Donor(s): John R. Cochran III.
Financial data (yr. ended 12/31/01): Grants paid, $300,000; assets, $1,130,942 (M); expenditures, $315,202; qualifying distributions, $303,089.
Limitations: Applications not accepted. Giving primarily in Baltimore, MD.
Application information: Contributes only to pre-selected organizations.
Officers: John R. Cochran III, Pres.; Patricia A. Cochran, V.P.
EIN: 522084405
Codes: FD

46353
Myrtle V. C. Huplits & Woodman E. Huplits Foundation Trust
2 Davis Dr.
Washington Crossing, PA 18977
Contact: Arnold M. Peskin, Tr.

Established in 1990.
Financial data (yr. ended 12/31/00): Grants paid, $300,000; assets, $7,219,994 (M); gifts received, $25,000; expenditures, $371,485; qualifying distributions, $344,734.
Limitations: Applications not accepted. Giving primarily in PA.
Application information: Contributes only to pre-selected organizations.
Trustees: Arnold M. Peskin, Marni L. Peskin, Todd E. Peskin.
EIN: 237451411
Codes: FD

46354
Saltsgiver Family Foundation
694 Ganderback Rd.
Hughesville, PA 17737

Established in 1995 in PA.
Donor(s): Thomas M. Saltsgiver.
Financial data (yr. ended 12/31/01): Grants paid, $300,000; assets, $5,727,993 (M); gifts received, $998,514; expenditures, $304,150; qualifying distributions, $300,000.
Limitations: Applications not accepted. Giving on a national basis, with emphasis on PA and VA.
Application information: Contributes only to pre-selected organizations.
Officers: Thomas M. Saltsgiver, Pres.; Joann Saltsgiver, Secy.-Treas.
EIN: 232803397
Codes: FD

46355
The Covenant Foundation
723 Clovelly Ln.
Devon, PA 19333

Established in 1990 in PA.
Donor(s): Dorothy H. Schneider.
Financial data (yr. ended 12/31/01): Grants paid, $299,870; assets, $2,727,422 (M); gifts received, $299,830; expenditures, $307,551; qualifying distributions, $298,486.

46355—PENNSYLVANIA

Limitations: Applications not accepted. Giving primarily in PA.
Application information: Contributes only to pre-selected organizations.
Trustees: Arnold Schneider, Jr., Dorothy H. Schneider.
EIN: 237451873
Codes: FD

46356
Alexander C. & Tillie S. Speyer Foundation
1202 Benedum Trees Bldg.
Pittsburgh, PA 15222-1783
Contact: Fdn. Mgr.

Established in 1962 in PA.
Donor(s): members of the Speyer family.
Financial data (yr. ended 12/31/00): Grants paid, $299,356; assets, $7,097,195 (M); expenditures, $416,885; qualifying distributions, $299,356.
Limitations: Giving primarily in Pittsburgh, PA.
Application information: Application form not required.
Trustees: A. C. Speyer, Jr., Darthea Speyer.
EIN: 256051650
Codes: FD

46357
Ross J. Born Family Charitable Trust
3571 Catherine Ave.
Allentown, PA 18103
Contact: Ross J. Born, Tr.

Established in 1991 in PA.
Donor(s): Ross J. Born.
Financial data (yr. ended 12/31/01): Grants paid, $298,753; assets, $4,099,008 (M); gifts received, $259,100; expenditures, $355,900; qualifying distributions, $299,261.
Limitations: Giving primarily in the Lehigh Valley, PA, area.
Application information: Application form not required.
Trustees: Amy R. Born, Lisa M. Born, Ross J. Born, Wendy G. Born.
EIN: 237653033
Codes: FD

46358
The J.D.B. Fund
404 S. Swedesford Rd.
P.O. Box 157
Gwynedd, PA 19436-0157 (215) 699-2233
Contact: Paul J. Corr, Mgr.

Established in 1966 in PA.
Donor(s): John Drew Betz,‡ Claire S. Betz.
Financial data (yr. ended 12/31/01): Grants paid, $298,455; assets, $2,986,290 (M); gifts received, $18,756; expenditures, $298,455; qualifying distributions, $297,115.
Limitations: Applications not accepted. Giving primarily in Montgomery County, PA.
Application information: Contributes only to pre-selected organizations.
Officer: Paul J. Corr, Mgr.
Trustee: Claire S. Betz.
EIN: 236418867
Codes: FD

46359
Anna M. Vincent Trust
c/o Mellon Bank, N.A.
P.O. Box 7236, AIM No. 193-0224
Philadelphia, PA 19101-7336
Contact: Ann Beatty

Trust established in 1967 in PA.
Donor(s): Anna M. Vincent.‡

Financial data (yr. ended 06/30/01): Grants paid, $297,000; assets, $8,528,270 (M); expenditures, $395,023; qualifying distributions, $363,096.
Limitations: Giving limited to residents of the Delaware Valley, PA, area.
Publications: Application guidelines.
Application information: Application forms available at high schools. Application form required.
Trustees: Robert J. Whiteman, Mellon Bank, N.A.
EIN: 236422666
Codes: FD, GTI

46360
Alvin S. Engle Foundation
c/o Charles A. Engle
P.O. Box 500
Mount Joy, PA 17552-0500

Established in 1993 in PA.
Donor(s): C.A. Engle, Pauline H. Engle, Audrey E. Rutt, Dennis L. Engle, Engle Printing & Publishing Co., Inc.
Financial data (yr. ended 12/31/01): Grants paid, $296,905; assets, $78,495 (M); gifts received, $157,000; expenditures, $297,151; qualifying distributions, $297,151.
Limitations: Applications not accepted. Giving primarily in PA.
Application information: Contributes only to pre-selected organizations.
Officers: C.A. Engle, Pres.; Dennis L. Engle, V.P.; Pauline H. Engle, V.P.; Audrey E. Rutt, Secy.-Treas.
EIN: 232747886
Codes: FD

46361
First Federal Charitable Foundation
12 E. Broad St.
Hazleton, PA 18201-6591 (570) 459-3797
E-mail: ffedfoundation@1stfederalbank.com;
URL: http://www.1stfederalcharitable.com
Contact: Megan Kennedy, Secy.-Treas.

Established in 1998 in PA.
Donor(s): Northeast Pennsylvania Financial Corp.
Financial data (yr. ended 09/30/01): Grants paid, $294,950; assets, $6,329,088 (M); expenditures, $400,967; qualifying distributions, $294,950.
Limitations: Giving limited to headquarters city and major operating areas in northeast and central PA.
Publications: Informational brochure.
Application information: Application form required.
Officers: Thomas Kennedy, Chair.; E. Lee Beard, Pres.; Megan Kennedy, Secy.-Treas.
Directors: Martin Cohn, Anthony Cusatis, John Raynock, John Sink.
EIN: 061512796
Codes: CS, FD, CD

46362
Neubauer Family Foundation
210 Rittenhouse Sq. W., Ste. 3106
Philadelphia, PA 19103 (215) 238-3880
Contact: Joseph Neubauer, Tr.

Established in 1994 in PA.
Donor(s): Joseph Neubauer.
Financial data (yr. ended 11/30/99): Grants paid, $293,895; assets, $13,563,897 (M); gifts received, $2,456,700; expenditures, $293,895; qualifying distributions, $293,895.
Limitations: Giving on a national basis.
Trustees: Melissa Anderson, Joseph Neubauer, Lawrence Neubauer.
EIN: 237748551
Codes: FD

46363
Ruth A. Hill Trust
c/o Mellon Bank, N.A.
P.O. Box 185
Pittsburgh, PA 15230
Application address: 1128 State St., Erie, PA 16522-0001
Contact: James E. Baker, Trust Off., Mellon Bank, N.A.

Financial data (yr. ended 12/31/00): Grants paid, $293,249; assets, $7,523,081 (M); expenditures, $324,503; qualifying distributions, $290,761.
Limitations: Giving limited to residents of PA.
Application information: Application form required for scholarships. Application form required.
Trustee: Mellon Bank, N.A.
EIN: 256031644
Codes: FD, GTI

46364
The Douty Foundation
(also known as The Alfred and Mary Douty Foundation)
c/o PNC Bank, N.A.
1600 Market St.
Philadelphia, PA 19103
FAX: (610) 834-8175
Contact: Judith L. Bardes, Exec. Dir.

Established in 1968 in PA.
Donor(s): Alfred Douty,‡ Mary M. Douty.‡
Financial data (yr. ended 12/31/01): Grants paid, $292,950; assets, $6,585,650 (M); expenditures, $424,660; qualifying distributions, $331,361.
Limitations: Giving primarily in the greater Philadelphia, PA, area, with emphasis on Montgomery and Philadelphia counties.
Publications: Annual report (including application guidelines).
Application information: Submit 1 application per 12 month period, except under special circumstances; organizations with budgets greater than $2 million are discouraged from applying; accepts Delaware Valley Grantmakers Common Grant Application and Common Report Form with cover sheet. Application form required.
Officer and Trustees:* Judith L. Bardes,* Exec. Dir.; Richard G. Alexander, Lynette E. Campbell, Carrolle Perry Devonish, Norma Elias, Thomas B. Harvey, Nancy J. Kirby.
EIN: 236463709
Codes: FD

46365
Copernicus Society of America
P.O. Box 385
Fort Washington, PA 19034

Established in 1972 in PA.
Donor(s): Edward J. Piszek, Sr., James A. Michener.‡
Financial data (yr. ended 06/30/01): Grants paid, $292,672; assets, $5,712,561 (M); gifts received, $200; expenditures, $459,608; qualifying distributions, $325,946.
Limitations: Applications not accepted. Giving primarily in PA; support also to an affiliated foundation in Poland.
Application information: Contributes only to pre-selected organizations.
Officers: Edward J. Piszek, Sr., Chair.; Helen P. Nelson, Pres.; Francis Keenan, V.P.; Edward J. Piszek, Jr., V.P.; George W. Piszek, V.P.; William P. Piszek, V.P.; Ann L. Reitenbaugh, V.P.; P. Erik Nelson, Exec. Dir.
EIN: 237184731
Codes: FD

46366
G. Whitney Snyder Charitable Fund
610 Smithfield St., Ste. 404
Pittsburgh, PA 15222 (412) 471-1331
Contact: Charles E. Ellison, Secy.

Established in 1990 in PA as partial successor to The W. P. Snyder Charitable Fund.
Financial data (yr. ended 12/31/01): Grants paid, $290,500; assets, $6,121,482 (M); expenditures, $353,666; qualifying distributions, $318,924.
Limitations: Giving primarily in PA.
Application information: Application form not required.
Officer: Charles E. Ellison, Secy.
Trustees: Jean Snyder Armstrong, Linda Snyder Hayes, Carolyn Snyder Miltenberger, G. Whitney Snyder, Jr.
EIN: 251611761
Codes: FD

46367
The York Federal Savings and Loan Foundation, Inc.
101 S. George St.
P.O. Box 15068
York, PA 17405-7068 (717) 846-8777
E-mail: rpullo@yorkfed.com
Contact: Robert W. Pullo, Chair.

Established in 1980 in PA.
Donor(s): York Federal Savings and Loan Assn., Waypoint Bank.
Financial data (yr. ended 06/30/01): Grants paid, $289,840; assets, $299,715 (M); gifts received, $336,900; expenditures, $292,381; qualifying distributions, $292,311.
Limitations: Giving primarily in York, PA.
Application information: Application form required.
Officers and Trustees:* Robert W. Pullo,* Chair. and C.E.O.; Robert A. Angelo, Secy.; James H. Moss, Treas.; Cynthia A. Dotzel, Robert W. Erdos, Randall A. Gross, Paul T. Mills, Byron M. Ream, Carolyn E. Steinhauser, Thomas W. Wolf, and 5 additional trustees.
EIN: 232111139
Codes: CS, FD, CD

46368
Foster Charitable Trust
681 Andersen Dr., Ste. 300
Pittsburgh, PA 15220-2747
Contact: Bernard S. Mars, Tr.

Established in 1962 in PA.
Donor(s): Foster Industries, Inc., Foster Investment Co.
Financial data (yr. ended 12/31/01): Grants paid, $288,320; assets, $4,277,899 (M); expenditures, $308,356; qualifying distributions, $288,320.
Limitations: Giving primarily in Pittsburgh, PA.
Application information: Application form not required.
Trustees: Penny F. Alpern, James R. Foster, Lee B. Foster II, Bernard S. Mars, Peter F. Mars, Kim Petracca.
EIN: 256064791
Codes: FD

46369
Ovid D. Robinson Charitable Trust
c/o PNC Bank, N.A., MS: P2-PTPP-25-1
2 PNC Plz., 620 Liberty Ave.
Pittsburgh, PA 15222-2719 (412) 762-7076
Application address: 1 PNC Plz., 249 5th Ave., 29th Fl., Pittsburgh, PA 15222
Contact: Mia Hallett Bernard, PNC Financial Svcs. Grp.

Donor(s): Ovid D. Robinson, Jr.
Financial data (yr. ended 12/31/01): Grants paid, $287,662; assets, $34,890 (M); expenditures, $345,893; qualifying distributions, $315,603.
Limitations: Giving primarily in the Pittsburgh, PA, area.
Application information: Application form not required.
Trustee: PNC Bank, N.A.
EIN: 256023648
Codes: FD

46370
William J. McMannis and A. Haskell McMannis Educational Trust Fund
c/o PNC Bank, N.A.
P.O. Box 8480
Erie, PA 16553 (814) 871-9597

Established in 1974.
Donor(s): Haskell McMannis.‡
Financial data (yr. ended 08/31/01): Grants paid, $286,167; assets, $5,392,272 (M); expenditures, $358,009; qualifying distributions, $319,452.
Limitations: Giving limited to U.S. citizens.
Publications: Informational brochure (including application guidelines).
Application information: Applications must be submitted through qualified schools; applications directly from individual students not considered. Application form required.
Trustees: Fred B. Sieber, PNC Bank, N.A.
EIN: 256191302
Codes: FD, GTI

46371
Morris H. and Gertrude M. Harris Foundation
c/o National City Bank of Pennsylvania
20 Stanwix St., LOC 25-162
Pittsburgh, PA 15222
Application address: c/o Lisa Wick, Office of Fin. Aid, Univ. of Pittsburgh School of Medicine, Pittsburgh, PA 15213
Contact: Joanna M. Mayo, V.P., National City Bank of Pennsylvania

Established in 1994 in PA.
Donor(s): Blanche H. Abrams.‡
Financial data (yr. ended 10/31/01): Grants paid, $285,134; assets, $4,367,812 (M); expenditures, $326,172; qualifying distributions, $306,220.
Limitations: Giving limited to Jewish medical students residing in Pittsburgh, PA.
Publications: Informational brochure (including application guidelines).
Application information: Application form required.
Trustees: Richard S. Crone, National City Bank of Pennsylvania.
EIN: 256508058
Codes: FD

46372
The Michael and Frances Cardone Foundation
c/o Dechert
1717 Arch St., BAT
Philadelphia, PA 19103-2793
Application address: P.O. Box 349, Cheltenham, PA 19012
Contact: Michael Cardone, Jr., Tr.

Established in 1999 in PA.
Donor(s): Michael Cardone.‡
Financial data (yr. ended 12/31/99): Grants paid, $285,099; assets, $0 (M); gifts received, $273,396; expenditures, $285,873; qualifying distributions, $285,099.
Limitations: Giving primarily in PA.
Application information: Application form not required.
Trustees: Philip Buongiorno, Michael Cardone, Jr., Michael Cardone III, Eric Tarno, Roger Tarno, Thomas Trask.
EIN: 256628127
Codes: FD

46373
Solomon & Sylvia Mendel Charitable Trust
c/o PNC Bank, N.A.
620 Liberty Ave., MS: P2-PTPP-33-3
Pittsburgh, PA 15222-2719 (412) 762-2826
Contact: Gary C. Goodlin

Established in 1986 in PA.
Financial data (yr. ended 07/31/01): Grants paid, $285,000; assets, $5,013,559 (M); expenditures, $301,056; qualifying distributions, $287,673.
Limitations: Giving primarily in Pittsburgh, PA.
Application information: Application form not required.
Trustees: Hon. J. Quint Salmon, PNC Bank, N.A.
EIN: 256271818
Codes: FD

46374
Valentine Foundation
300 Quarry Ln.
Haverford, PA 19041-1723 (610) 642-4887
URL: http://www.valentinefoundation.org
Contact: Alexandra Frazier, Dir.

Established in 1985 in PA.
Donor(s): Phoebe V. Valentine.
Financial data (yr. ended 11/30/01): Grants paid, $283,700; assets, $2,773,336 (M); gifts received, $162,364; expenditures, $337,451; qualifying distributions, $281,423.
Limitations: Giving primarily in the Philadelphia, PA, area.
Publications: Biennial report, application guidelines.
Application information: Application form not required.
Trustees: Lisa Gilden, Cynthia Jetter, Mary McTernan, M. Ann Ricksicker, Daphne Rowe, Frances Vilella-Velez.
EIN: 236806061
Codes: FD

46375
The Cove Charitable Trust
c/o Mellon Bank
P.O. Bank 185
Pittsburgh, PA 15230-9897
Application address: Ms. Emma Green, c/o Boston Safe Deposit & Trust Co., 1 Boston Pl., Boston, MA 02108, tel.: (617) 722-7341

Established in 1964 in MA.
Donor(s): Aileen Kelly Pratt,‡ Edwin H.B. Pratt.‡
Financial data (yr. ended 12/31/01): Grants paid, $283,500; assets, $4,896,375 (M); expenditures, $306,308; qualifying distributions, $287,845.
Limitations: Giving primarily in MA.
Trustee: Boston Safe Deposit & Trust Co.
EIN: 046118955
Codes: FD

46376
Teleflex Foundation
630 W. Germantown Pike, Ste. 461
Plymouth Meeting, PA 19462 (610) 834-6364
Contact: Thelma A. Fretz, V.P.

Established in 1980 in PA.
Donor(s): Teleflex Inc.
Financial data (yr. ended 12/31/01): Grants paid, $281,929; assets, $3,909,362 (M); gifts received, $480,000; expenditures, $304,812; qualifying distributions, $304,812.
Publications: Application guidelines.

46376—PENNSYLVANIA

Application information: Application form required.
Officers: Lennox K. Black, Pres.; Thelma A. Fretz, V.P.; John H. Remer, Treas.
Directors: Christopher Black, Thomas Byrne, M.C. Chisholm, Janine Dusossoit, Diane Fukuda, William Haussmann, Stephen Holland, Anita Piacentino, Palmer Retzlaff.
EIN: 232104782
Codes: CS, FD, CD

46377
The Britton Family Foundation
100 State St., Ste. 700
Erie, PA 16507-1459 (814) 870-7600
Contact: John E. Britton, Pres.

Established in 1989 in PA.
Donor(s): John E. Britton.
Financial data (yr. ended 12/31/01): Grants paid, $279,100; assets, $3,470,238 (M); expenditures, $287,725; qualifying distributions, $277,171.
Limitations: Giving strictly limited to Erie, PA.
Application information: Application form not required.
Officers and Directors:* John E. Britton,* Pres.; Suzanne E. Britton,* V.P. and Secy.; John W. Britton,* V.P. and Treas.
EIN: 251618532
Codes: FD

46378
Hoxie Harrison Smith Foundation
(Formerly The Smith Foundation)
350 Pond View
Devon, PA 19333-1732 (610) 688-0143
Contact: Bruce M. Brown, Secy.-Treas.

Incorporated in 1920 in PA.
Donor(s): W. Hinckle Smith,‡ H. Harrison Smith.‡
Financial data (yr. ended 12/31/01): Grants paid, $279,000; assets, $8,933,300 (M); expenditures, $345,440; qualifying distributions, $290,377.
Limitations: Giving limited to southeastern PA, including Bucks, Chester, Delaware, Montgomery, and Philadelphia counties.
Publications: Annual report.
Application information: Application form not required.
Officers and Directors:* Howard W. Busch,* Pres.; Charles P. Barber, V.P.; Robert L. Strayer,* V.P.; Bruce M. Brown,* Secy.-Treas.; Joseph H. Barber, Philip C. Burnham, Lee E. Daney, William W. Heilig, Mark T. Ledger, Jack T. Tomarchio.
Trustee: The Vanguard Group.
EIN: 236238148
Codes: FD

46379
The Rankin Family Foundation
501 Schoolhouse Rd.
Telford, PA 18969
Contact: Alexander Rankin V, Pres.

Established in 1997 in PA.
Donor(s): Alexander Rankin V.
Financial data (yr. ended 12/31/01): Grants paid, $278,250; assets, $781,618 (M); gifts received, $279,550; expenditures, $279,550; qualifying distributions, $277,448.
Limitations: Applications not accepted. Giving primarily in PA.
Officers: Alexander Rankin V, Pres.; Joanne S. Rankin, Secy.-Treas.
EIN: 232867283
Codes: FD

46380
Schuylkill Area Community Foundation
(Formerly Ashland Trusts)
101 N. Centre St., 2nd Fl., Ste. A
Pottsville, PA 17901 (570) 624-1580
FAX: (570) 624-1581
Contact: Therese "Terry" Sadusky, Exec. Dir.

Established in 1967 in PA.
Financial data (yr. ended 04/30/00): Grants paid, $278,176; assets, $4,700,731 (M); gifts received, $974,578; expenditures, $340,715.
Limitations: Applications not accepted. Giving primarily in the Schuylkill County, PA, area; some programs extend to neighboring counties.
Application information: Scholarships paid to educational institutions for named individuals.
Officer and Board Member:* Harry Strouse,* Secy.
EIN: 236422789
Codes: CM, FD, GTI

46381
The W. Dale Brougher Foundation, Inc.
1200 Country Club Rd.
York, PA 17403

Established in 1986 in MD.
Donor(s): W. Dale Brougher.
Financial data (yr. ended 12/31/01): Grants paid, $276,945; assets, $5,098,956 (M); gifts received, $250,000; expenditures, $304,868; qualifying distributions, $276,945.
Limitations: Applications not accepted. Giving primarily in York, PA.
Application information: Contributes only to pre-selected organizations.
Officers: W. Dale Brougher, Pres. and Treas.; Nancy Brougher, V.P. and Secy.
EIN: 521499358
Codes: FD

46382
Leo Niessen, Jr. Charitable Trust
c/o First Union National Bank
Broad & Walnut Sts., PA1308
Philadelphia, PA 19109 (215) 670-4226
Additional tel.: (215) 670-4231
Contact: Eugene Williams, Trust Off., First Union National Bank

Established in 1994 in PA.
Donor(s): Leo Niessen, Jr.‡
Financial data (yr. ended 06/30/01): Grants paid, $276,500; assets, $4,307,750 (M); expenditures, $328,415; qualifying distributions, $274,996.
Limitations: Giving primarily in PA.
Application information: Application form not required.
Trustee: First Union National Bank.
EIN: 237723097
Codes: FD

46383
Vicary Foundation, Inc.
3919 State St.
Erie, PA 16508 (814) 868-9347
FAX: (814) 868-0574; *E-mail:* vicary525@aol.com
Contact: Thomas C. Vicary, Pres.

Established in 1958 in PA.
Donor(s): Arthur C. Vicary,‡ Mary W. Vicary.‡
Financial data (yr. ended 12/31/01): Grants paid, $273,000; assets, $1,904,000 (M); expenditures, $275,000; qualifying distributions, $273,000.
Limitations: Giving primarily in Erie, PA.
Application information: Application form not required.
Officers and Trustees:* Thomas C. Vicary,* Pres.; Cheryl G. Vicary,* Secy.-Treas.; Arthur Curtze, Charles A. Curtze, Louise Curtze.

EIN: 256035971
Codes: FD

46384
York Container Foundation
138 Mt. Zion Rd.
P.O. Box 3008
York, PA 17402-0008
Contact: Dennis E. Willman, Secy.

Established in 1983 in PA.
Financial data (yr. ended 12/31/01): Grants paid, $272,835; assets, $396,220 (M); gifts received, $75,000; expenditures, $273,151; qualifying distributions, $272,751.
Limitations: Applications not accepted. Giving primarily in PA, with emphasis on York.
Application information: Contributes only to pre-selected organizations.
Officers: Dennis E. Willman, Secy.; Charles S. Wolf, Jr., Treas.
Director: Constance L. Wolf.
EIN: 222473590
Codes: FD

46385
Mitrani Family Foundation, Inc.
c/o Norman Belmonte
550 E. 5th St., P.O. Box 568
Bloomsburg, PA 17815

Incorporated in 1959 in NY.
Donor(s): Members of the Mitrani family, Milco Industries, Inc., and others.
Financial data (yr. ended 12/31/01): Grants paid, $272,682; assets, $3,336,001 (M); expenditures, $353,777; qualifying distributions, $337,303.
Limitations: Applications not accepted. Giving primarily in NY and PA; some giving also in Israel.
Application information: Unsolicited requests for funds are not accepted.
Officers: Norman Belmonte, Pres.; Leonard Comerchero, V.P.
EIN: 246018102
Codes: FD, GTI

46386
Acorn Alcinda Foundation, Inc.
c/o Kit C. Kennedy
RR4 Box 710
Mifflintown, PA 17059

Established in 1984 in VA.
Donor(s): Robert J. Kennedy.‡
Financial data (yr. ended 05/31/01): Grants paid, $272,000; assets, $5,675,777 (M); expenditures, $310,945; qualifying distributions, $276,489.
Limitations: Applications not accepted. Giving primarily on the East Coast, with some emphasis on CT and PA.
Application information: Contributes only to pre-selected organizations.
Officers and Directors:* Kit C. Kennedy,* V.P. and Secy.; Jan B. Kennedy,* V.P.
EIN: 541303250
Codes: FD

46387
The Warwick Foundation
1 Liberty Pl.
1650 Market St., Ste. 1200
Philadelphia, PA 19103-7391 (215) 419-6154
Contact: Stephen Starr

Established in 1961 in PA.
Donor(s): Helen H. Gemmill,‡ Kenneth Gemmill.‡
Financial data (yr. ended 12/31/01): Grants paid, $271,000; assets, $30,163,721 (M); expenditures, $645,186; qualifying distributions, $584,583.
Limitations: Giving primarily in the Bucks County and Delaware Valley, PA, areas.

Application information: Application form not required.
Trustees: Elizabeth H. Gemmill, Helen J. Gemmill, Lisa M. Gemmill, Kenneth Norris.
EIN: 236230662
Codes: FD

46388
Jerlyn Foundation
1170 Cedar Hill Dr.
Reading, PA 19605
Contact: T. Jerome Holleran, Pres.

Established in 1992 in PA.
Donor(s): T. Jerome Holleran, Carolyn R. Holleran.
Financial data (yr. ended 12/31/00): Grants paid, $270,451; assets, $2,355,543 (M); expenditures, $288,140; qualifying distributions, $270,451.
Limitations: Applications not accepted. Giving primarily in Berks County, PA.
Application information: Unsolicited requests for funds not accepted.
Officers: T. Jerome Holleran, Pres.; Carolyn R. Holleran, Secy.-Treas.
EIN: 232699256
Codes: FD

46389
The Thomson Family Foundation
54 S. Whitehorse Rd.
Phoenixville, PA 19460-2561

Established in 1999 in PA.
Donor(s): Joe M. Thomson.
Financial data (yr. ended 12/31/01): Grants paid, $269,650; assets, $107,074 (M); expenditures, $270,906; qualifying distributions, $269,650.
Limitations: Applications not accepted.
Application information: Contributes only to pre-selected organizations.
Trustees: Joann M. Thomson, Joe M. Thomson.
EIN: 066480460
Codes: FD

46390
Donald & Sylvia Robinson Family Foundation
6507 Wilkins Ave.
Pittsburgh, PA 15217 (412) 661-1200
FAX: (412) 661-4645
Contact: Donald M. Robinson, Pres.

Established in 1970.
Financial data (yr. ended 10/31/01): Grants paid, $267,885; assets, $3,464,316 (M); expenditures, $273,184; qualifying distributions, $269,197.
Limitations: Giving on a national basis.
Application information: Application form not required.
Officers and Trustees:* Donald M. Robinson,* Pres.; Sylvia Robinson,* V.P.; Carol L. Robinson, Stephen G. Robinson.
EIN: 237062017
Codes: FD

46391
Dollar Bank Foundation
c/o Dollar Bank, Public Affairs Dept.
3 Gateway Ctr., 8 N.
Pittsburgh, PA 15222

Established in 1998 in PA.
Donor(s): Dollar Bank, FSB.
Financial data (yr. ended 11/30/01): Grants paid, $267,500; assets, $3,178,048 (M); expenditures, $269,627; qualifying distributions, $265,277.
Limitations: Giving limited to the geographic boundaries served by Dollar Bank and its subsidiaries.
Application information: Contact foundation for giving guidelines.

Officers: Thomas A. Korbus, Pres.; James Carroll, V.P.; Robert Messner, Secy.; James Jurcic, Treas.
EIN: 251822243
Codes: CS, FD, CD

46392
The Calvin K. Kazanjian Economics Foundation, Inc.
P.O. Box 300
Dallas, PA 18612-0300 (570) 675-7074
FAX: (570) 675-8436; *E-mail:* director@kazanjian.org; *URL:* http://www.kazanjian.org
Contact: Dr. Michael A. MacDowell, Managing Dir.

Incorporated in 1947 in CT.
Donor(s): Calvin K. Kazanjian.‡
Financial data (yr. ended 12/31/01): Grants paid, $266,610; assets, $5,643,321 (M); expenditures, $366,798; qualifying distributions, $338,700.
Limitations: Giving on a national basis.
Publications: Informational brochure, application guidelines.
Application information: Application form not required.
Officers and Trustees:* Lloyd W. Elston,* Pres. and Treas.; Richard L. Elston,* V.P.; Joseph L. Kinsella,* Secy.; Michael A. MacDowell,* Managing Dir.; John Clizbe, Lynn E. Elston, George Hartmann, Worth Loomis, Markie Mueller, John Sumansky.
EIN: 060665174
Codes: FD

46393
Adam and Maria Sarah Seybert Institution for Poor Boys and Girls
(also known as Seybert Institution)
P.O. Box 8228
Philadelphia, PA 19101-8228 (610) 828-8145
FAX: (610) 834-8175
Contact: Judith L. Bardes, Exec. Dir.

Incorporated in 1914 in PA.
Donor(s): Henry Seybert.‡
Financial data (yr. ended 12/31/01): Grants paid, $265,500; assets, $700,307 (M); expenditures, $350,047; qualifying distributions, $299,019.
Limitations: Giving limited to Philadelphia, PA.
Publications: Annual report (including application guidelines).
Application information: Applicants limited to 1 request per calendar year; accepts Delaware Valley Grantmakers Common Grant Application and Common Report Form; submit one original and 9 copies of proposal together with a cover sheet provided by the institution; no more than 3 items of support material. Application form required.
Officers and Trustees:* William C. Bullitt,* Pres. and Treas.; Susan C. Day, M.D.,* V.P.; Graham S. Finney, Rev. David I. Hagan, Luis A. Hernandez, Dee Hillas, Sara Moran, Linda Rich, Lucy Wolf Tuton, Ph.D.
EIN: 236260105
Codes: FD

46394
Christopher Ludwick Foundation
(Formerly The Ludwick Institute)
c/o Athenaeum of Philadelphia
219 S. 6th St.
Philadelphia, PA 19106-3794 (215) 925-2688
FAX: (215) 925-3755; *URL:* http://www.philaathenaeum.org/how4.html
Contact: Roger W. Moss, Secy.

Established in 1799 in PA.
Donor(s): Christopher Ludwick.‡

Financial data (yr. ended 04/30/02): Grants paid, $265,000; assets, $4,884,000 (M); expenditures, $270,000; qualifying distributions, $265,000.
Limitations: Giving limited to the City of Philadelphia, PA.
Publications: Application guidelines.
Application information: Application guidelines available on website. Application form required.
Officers: Hugh A.A. Sargent, Pres.; William M. Davison IV, V.P. and Treas.; Susan Catherwood, V.P.; Roger W. Moss, Secy.; and 9 directors and trustees.
EIN: 236256408
Codes: FD

46395
William R. & Lucilla S. Jackson Charitable Trust
c/o Mellon Bank, N.A.
3 Mellon Bank Ctr., Rm. 4000
Pittsburgh, PA 15259 (412) 234-1634
Contact: Annette Calagaro, V.P., Mellon Bank, N.A.

Established in 1950 in PA.
Financial data (yr. ended 12/31/01): Grants paid, $263,200; assets, $1,440,421 (M); gifts received, $186,450; expenditures, $264,560; qualifying distributions, $263,200.
Limitations: Applications not accepted. Giving primarily in PA.
Application information: Unsolicited requests for funds not accepted.
Trustee: Mellon Bank, N.A.
EIN: 256018923
Codes: FD

46396
Charles L. Cost Foundation
2400 Ardmore Blvd.
Pittsburgh, PA 15221

Established in 1988 in PA.
Donor(s): Charles L. Cost.
Financial data (yr. ended 12/31/00): Grants paid, $262,800; assets, $1,855 (M); gifts received, $262,800; expenditures, $263,733; qualifying distributions, $263,733.
Limitations: Applications not accepted. Giving primarily in Pittsburgh, PA.
Application information: Contributes only to pre-selected organizations.
Officer: Charles L. Cost, Pres.
EIN: 251588998
Codes: FD

46397
W. I. Patterson Charitable Fund
407 Oliver Bldg.
Pittsburgh, PA 15222 (412) 281-5580
Contact: Robert B. Shust, Tr.

Trust established in 1955 in PA.
Donor(s): W.I. Patterson.‡
Financial data (yr. ended 07/31/01): Grants paid, $261,772; assets, $5,252,992 (M); expenditures, $322,442; qualifying distributions, $292,840.
Limitations: Giving primarily in Allegheny County, PA.
Application information: Application form not required.
Trustees: Martin L. Moore, Jr., Robert B. Shust, Robert B. Wolf.
EIN: 256028639
Codes: FD

46398
Arlene H. Smith Charitable Foundation
100 State St., Ste. 700
Erie, PA 16507-1459
Application address: c/o McInnes Steel Co., 441 E. Main St., Corry, PA 16407-0901
Contact: Timothy M. Hunter, Treas.

Established in 1982 in PA.
Donor(s): Arlene H. Smith.‡
Financial data (yr. ended 12/31/01): Grants paid, $260,736; assets, $4,537,087 (M); expenditures, $293,323; qualifying distributions, $260,736.
Limitations: Giving limited to the Corry, PA, area.
Application information: Application form required.
Officers and Directors:* Stephen J. Mahoney,* Pres.; Frank K. Smith,* V.P.; James D. Cullen,* Secy.; Timothy M. Hunter, Treas.; John E. Britton.
EIN: 251515142
Codes: FD

46399
Richard H. Donnell Foundation
P.O. Box 1340
McMurray, PA 15317
FAX: (724) 746-2309
Contact: Richard H. Donnell, Pres.

Established in 1997 in PA.
Donor(s): Richard H. Donnell, Christopher M. Donnell, Marni C. Donnell, David Kresh, Mrs. D. Kresh.
Financial data (yr. ended 12/31/01): Grants paid, $260,000; assets, $1,131,436 (M); gifts received, $3,000; expenditures, $262,864; qualifying distributions, $259,313.
Limitations: Giving primarily in Washington County, PA.
Publications: Annual report, informational brochure.
Application information: Application form required.
Officers and Directors:* Richard H. Donnell,* Pres. and Treas.; Shana M. Donnell,* V.P. and Secy.; Cathi E. Kresh,* Dir. of Opers.; Christopher M. Donnell, Edwin E. Edwards III.
EIN: 232900282
Codes: FD

46400
Baronner-Chatfield Foundation
3117 Washington Pike
Bridgeville, PA 15017-1496
Contact: Susan H. Earley

Established in 1991 in PA.
Donor(s): Glen Chatfield, Elizabeth Chatfield.
Financial data (yr. ended 12/31/01): Grants paid, $258,085; assets, $1,015,416 (M); expenditures, $272,657; qualifying distributions, $258,097.
Limitations: Giving primarily in PA.
Application information: Application form not required.
Officers: Glen Chatfield, Pres.; Elizabeth Chatfield, Secy.-Treas.
EIN: 521739290
Codes: FD

46401
Julius and Ray Charlestein Foundation, Inc.
c/o Premier Dental Products Co.
3600 Horizon Dr.
King of Prussia, PA 19406 (610) 239-6000
Contact: Ellyn Phillips, Exec. Dir.

Established in 1963.
Donor(s): Morton L. Charlestein, Premier Dental Products Co., Premier Medical Co.
Financial data (yr. ended 06/30/01): Grants paid, $257,954; assets, $1,842,919 (M); gifts received, $23,867; expenditures, $312,339; qualifying distributions, $256,364.
Limitations: Giving primarily in the Philadelphia, PA, area.
Application information: Application form not required.
Officers: Morton Charlestein, Pres.; Gary Charlestein, Secy.-Treas.; Ellyn Phillips, Exec. Dir.
EIN: 232310090
Codes: CS, FD, CD

46402
Ray S. Shoemaker Trust for Shoemaker Scholarship Fund
c/o Mellon Bank, N.A.
P.O. Box 1010, Rm. 181-0310
Harrisburg, PA 17108
Scholarship application address: c/o Dir. of Admissions, Harrisburg Area Community College, Cameron St., Harrisburg, PA 17108, tel.: (717) 780-2400

Donor(s): Ray S. Shoemaker.
Financial data (yr. ended 09/30/01): Grants paid, $255,402; assets, $5,835,413 (M); expenditures, $313,228; qualifying distributions, $265,402.
Limitations: Giving limited to residents of the greater Harrisburg, PA, area.
Application information: Application form required.
Trustee: Mellon Bank, N.A.
EIN: 236237250
Codes: FD, GTI

46403
The Bruno & Lena DeGol Foundation
3229 Pleasant Valley Blvd.
Altoona, PA 16602
Contact: Bruno DeGol, Pres.

Established in 1994 in PA.
Donor(s): Bruno DeGol, Lena DeGol.
Financial data (yr. ended 12/31/01): Grants paid, $254,732; assets, $2,037,539 (M); gifts received, $500,191; expenditures, $260,364; qualifying distributions, $255,614.
Limitations: Applications not accepted. Giving primarily in PA.
Application information: Contributes only to pre-selected organizations.
Officers: Bruno DeGol, Pres.; Donald DeGol, V.P.; Dennis DeGol, Secy.; Joseph T. Adams, Treas.
Directors: Gloria DeGol Burbon, Bruno DeGol, Jr., David DeGol, Lena DeGol.
EIN: 251753903
Codes: FD

46404
The Wolf Foundation
P.O. Box 1267
York, PA 17405 (717) 852-4800
Contact: William B. Zimmerman, Chair.

Established in 1969 in PA.
Donor(s): Wolf Distributing, Inc., The Lumber Yard.
Financial data (yr. ended 12/31/00): Grants paid, $254,719; assets, $439,657 (M); gifts received, $17,952; expenditures, $292,054; qualifying distributions, $255,366.
Limitations: Giving primarily in York, PA.
Application information: Application form not required.
Officers: William B. Zimmerman, Chair.; Thomas W. Wolf, Pres.; George Hodges, Secy.-Treas.
EIN: 237028494
Codes: CS, FD, CD

46405
Arthur L. and Lea R. Powell Foundation
c/o David R. Glyn
1650 Arch St., 22nd Fl.
Philadelphia, PA 19103-2097

Established in 1988 in PA.
Donor(s): Arthur Powell, Lea Powell.
Financial data (yr. ended 02/28/01): Grants paid, $252,715; assets, $1,644,181 (M); gifts received, $187,500; expenditures, $263,385; qualifying distributions, $254,285.
Limitations: Applications not accepted. Giving primarily in PA.
Application information: Contributes only to pre-selected organizations.
Officers: Arthur L. Powell, Pres.; Lea R. Powell, V.P.; David J. Kaufman, Secy.
EIN: 232769441
Codes: FD

46406
Copperweld Foundation
4 Gateway Ctr., 22nd Fl., Ste. 2200
Pittsburgh, PA 15222-1211 (412) 263-3200
Contact: Douglas E. Young, Tr.

Established in 1941 in PA.
Donor(s): Copperweld Corp.
Financial data (yr. ended 06/30/01): Grants paid, $252,440; assets, $1,408,612 (M); expenditures, $252,609; qualifying distributions, $251,294.
Limitations: Giving primarily in southwestern PA.
Publications: Application guidelines.
Application information: Application form not required.
Trustees: Eugene R. Pocci, John D. Turner, Douglas E. Young.
EIN: 256035603
Codes: CS, FD, CD

46407
The Robert and Jane Toll Foundation
3103 Philmont Ave.
Huntingdon Valley, PA 19006

Established in 1991 in PA.
Donor(s): Robert I. Toll, Sylvia S. Toll.
Financial data (yr. ended 12/31/01): Grants paid, $251,708; assets, $11,003,299 (M); gifts received, $6,725,000; expenditures, $288,960; qualifying distributions, $251,784.
Limitations: Applications not accepted. Giving primarily in PA.
Application information: Contributes only to pre-selected organizations.
Officer and Director:* Robert I. Toll,* Pres., Treas., and Exec. Dir.
EIN: 232654322
Codes: FD

46408
The Quaker Chemical Foundation
Elm & Lee Sts.
Conshohocken, PA 19428 (610) 832-4127
Contact: Kathleen Lasota

Established in 1959 in PA.
Donor(s): Quaker Chemical Corp.
Financial data (yr. ended 06/30/01): Grants paid, $250,748; assets, $477,145 (M); gifts received, $83,000; expenditures, $276,377; qualifying distributions, $275,825.
Limitations: Giving primarily in areas of company operations, including CA, MI, and PA.
Publications: Application guidelines.
Application information: Application form not required.
Officer and Trustees:* Karl H. Spaeth,* Chair.; Katherine N. Coughenour, Edwin J. Delattre, Alan G. Keyser, J. Everett Wick, Jane Williams.

EIN: 236245803
Codes: CS, FD, CD, GTI

46409
Alderbaugh Foundation
c/o Burton & Browse
444 S. State St.
Newtown, PA 18940 (215) 968-4224
Contact: Clarence E. Denoon, Jr.

Established in 1982.
Donor(s): Clarence E. Denoon, Jr.
Financial data (yr. ended 12/31/01): Grants paid, $250,000; assets, $4,524,890 (M); expenditures, $254,839; qualifying distributions, $250,000.
Limitations: Giving primarily in PA and VA.
Trustees: Ashby Denoon, David Denoon.
EIN: 232173929
Codes: FD

46410
Archer Foundation
208 W. Front St.
Media, PA 19063 (610) 891-2871
Contact: George W. Moffitt, Jr., Pres.

Donor(s): George W. Moffitt, Jr.
Financial data (yr. ended 12/31/00): Grants paid, $250,000; assets, $1,699,405 (M); gifts received, $17,525; expenditures, $253,965; qualifying distributions, $251,548.
Limitations: Giving primarily in PA.
Application information: Application form not required.
Officers: George W. Moffitt, Jr., Pres.; H. Eugene Vickers, Secy.; Robert F. Dolan, Treas.
EIN: 236442014
Codes: FD

46411
The Craig-Dalsimer Fund
c/o Wolf Block
1650 Arch St., 22nd Fl.
Philadelphia, PA 19103

Established in 1987 in PA.
Donor(s): Janet Craig Dalsimer.‡
Financial data (yr. ended 02/28/01): Grants paid, $250,000; assets, $3,617,571 (M); expenditures, $275,653; qualifying distributions, $259,080.
Limitations: Giving primarily in Philadelphia, PA.
Application information: Application form not required.
Officers: Anna-Marie Chirco, Chair.; Lida Freeman, Vice-Chair.; David Kaufman, Secy.-Treas.
EIN: 232714023
Codes: FD

46412
Kendryx Foundation, Inc.
c/o F.C. Revitt, C.P.A.
P.O. Box 779
Marshalls Creek, PA 18335-0779

Established in 1999 in NJ.
Donor(s): John B. Kennedy, Patricia Kennedy.
Financial data (yr. ended 12/31/00): Grants paid, $250,000; assets, $1,788,073 (M); expenditures, $309,745; qualifying distributions, $251,977.
Limitations: Applications not accepted. Giving primarily in NY and PA.
Application information: Contributes only to pre-selected organizations.
Officers: John B. Kennedy, Pres.; Patricia Kennedy, V.P.; Kevin Kennedy, Secy.; Sean Kennedy, Treas.
EIN: 223687305

46413
McFadden Foundation, Inc.
P.O. Box 480
Paoli, PA 19301

Established in 1998 in VA.
Financial data (yr. ended 12/31/00): Grants paid, $250,000; assets, $467,839 (M); expenditures, $251,371; qualifying distributions, $250,000.
Limitations: Applications not accepted.
Application information: Contributes only to pre-selected organizations.
Officers: Charles McFadden, Pres.; Mary McFadden, Secy.
EIN: 541918876
Codes: FD

46414
Reese Foundation
c/o Fulton Financial Advisors, N.A.
P.O. Box 3215
Lancaster, PA 17604
Application address: Vincent J. Lattanzio, c/o Fulton Financial Advisors, N.A., P.O. Box 7989, Lancaster, PA 17604, tel.: (717) 291-2523

Established in 1996 in PA.
Financial data (yr. ended 05/31/00): Grants paid, $250,000; assets, $4,883,855 (M); expenditures, $289,157; qualifying distributions, $250,012.
Limitations: Giving primarily in PA.
Trustee: Fulton Financial Advisors, N.A.
EIN: 232349281
Codes: FD

46415
David Berger Foundation
1515 Market St., Ste. 1700
Philadelphia, PA 19102-1964
Application address: 1622 Locust St., Philadelphia, PA 19103, tel.: (215) 875-3000
Contact: David Berger, Pres.

Established in 1965 in PA.
Donor(s): David Berger.
Financial data (yr. ended 12/31/00): Grants paid, $248,615; assets, $2,058,301 (M); gifts received, $500,000; expenditures, $254,163; qualifying distributions, $248,615.
Limitations: Giving primarily in Palm Beach, FL, and Philadelphia, PA.
Officer: David Berger, Pres.
EIN: 236424659
Codes: FD

46416
T. Wistar Brown Trust
(also known as T. Wistar Brown Teacher's Fund)
c/o PNC Bank, N.A.
1600 Market St.
Philadelphia, PA 19103-7240

Established in 1916 in PA.
Financial data (yr. ended 09/30/01): Grants paid, $247,615; assets, $1,885,832 (M); expenditures, $269,192; qualifying distributions, $252,650.
Application information: Application form required.
Officer and Trustees:* Kay M. Edstend,* Exec. Dir.; Eleanor M. Elkinton, William D. Ravdin, PNC Bank, N.A.
EIN: 236200741
Codes: FD, GTI

46417
The Luzerne Foundation
613 Baltimore Dr.
Wilkes-Barre, PA 18702 (570) 822-5420
FAX: (570) 208-9145; *E-mail:* Luzernefdn@aol.com; *URL:* http://www2.epix.net/~luzerne
Contact: Daylene Burnside, Exec. Dir.

Established in 1994 in PA.
Financial data (yr. ended 12/31/00): Grants paid, $247,426; assets, $4,774,851 (M); gifts received, $462,689; expenditures, $394,014.
Limitations: Giving limited to the Luzerne County, PA, area.
Publications: Application guidelines, informational brochure (including application guidelines), newsletter, program policy statement, annual report, financial statement, grants list.
Application information: Application form required.
Officer: Daylene Burnside, Exec. Dir.
EIN: 232765498
Codes: CM

46418
Polly A. Levee Charitable Trust B - Levee Trust
c/o PNC Advisors
1600 Market St., 29th Fl.
Philadelphia, PA 19103

Established in 1993 in PA as partial successor to Polly Annenberg Levee Charitable Trust.
Donor(s): Polly Annenberg Levee.‡
Financial data (yr. ended 12/31/01): Grants paid, $247,000; assets, $4,424,901 (M); expenditures, $267,355; qualifying distributions, $248,519.
Limitations: Applications not accepted. Giving primarily in New York, NY.
Application information: Contributes only to pre-selected organizations. Unsolicited requests for funds not considered.
Trustees: William J. Henrich, Jr., PNC Bank, N.A.
EIN: 232735662
Codes: FD

46419
The Solomon and Sylvia Bronstein Foundation
c/o Bernard Glassman
1 Logan Sq.
Philadelphia, PA 19103-6998

Established in 1985 in PA.
Donor(s): Solomon Bronstein.‡
Financial data (yr. ended 06/30/01): Grants paid, $246,500; assets, $8,346,919 (M); expenditures, $436,700; qualifying distributions, $279,639.
Limitations: Applications not accepted. Giving primarily in New York, NY, and Philadelphia, PA.
Application information: Contributes only to pre-selected organizations.
Trustees: Gerald Broker, Marvin Comisky, Rabbi Gerald I. Wolpe.
EIN: 222656339
Codes: FD

46420
J. George Schmid, Jr. Memorial Fund
21 E. Market St., M/C 402-130
York, PA 17401-1500

Established in 2000 in PA.
Financial data (yr. ended 12/31/00): Grants paid, $246,260; assets, $3,291,208 (M); gifts received, $2,346,947; expenditures, $270,609; qualifying distributions, $246,260.
Limitations: Applications not accepted. Giving primarily in PA.
Application information: Contributes only to pre-selected organizations.
Trustee: Allfirst.

EIN: 237984603
Codes: FD2

46421
S & T Bancorp Charitable Foundation
c/o S&T Bank, Trust Dept.
P.O. Box 220
Indiana, PA 15701
Application address: P.O. Box 190, Indiana, PA 15701, tel.: (724) 465-1443
Contact: James C. Miller, Pres.

Established in 1993 in PA.
Donor(s): S & T Bancorp, Inc., S & T Bank.
Financial data (yr. ended 12/31/00): Grants paid, $246,250; assets, $552,080 (M); gifts received, $72,900; expenditures, $295,391; qualifying distributions, $293,679.
Limitations: Giving limited to areas of company operations in PA.
Officers: James C. Miller, Pres.; Edward C. Hauck, V.P.; H. William Klumpp, Treas.
Trustee: S & T Bank.
EIN: 251716950
Codes: CS, FD2, CD

46422
The Brun Family Foundation, Inc.
360 Penn Rd.
Wynnewood, PA 19096

Established in 2001 in PA.
Donor(s): Leslie A. Brun, Marcie S. Kennedy.
Financial data (yr. ended 12/31/01): Grants paid, $246,058; assets, $8,337 (M); gifts received, $254,722; expenditures, $246,058; qualifying distributions, $246,056.
Limitations: Applications not accepted. Giving primarily in NY.
Application information: Contributes only to pre-selected organizations.
Officers and Directors:* Marcie S. Kennedy,* Pres.; Leslie A. Brun,* V.P.
EIN: 233048202

46423
Enlightenment Foundation
(Formerly Inner Harmony Foundation)
c/o Robert J. Ciaruffoli
46 Public Sq., Ste. 400
Wilkes-Barre, PA 18701

Established in 1999 in PA.
Financial data (yr. ended 03/31/01): Grants paid, $245,000; assets, $1,485 (M); gifts received, $245,000; expenditures, $245,015; qualifying distributions, $245,000.
Limitations: Applications not accepted.
Application information: Contributes only to pre-selected organizations.
Officers and Trustee:* Peter Amato, Pres. and Secy.; Robert J. Ciaruffoli,* Treas.
EIN: 233007456
Codes: FD2

46424
The Eastwood Family Foundation
c/o James W. Eastwood
705 Sturbridge Dr.
Bryn Mawr, PA 19010-2082

Established in 1998 in PA.
Donor(s): James W. Eastwood, Linda D. Eastwood.
Financial data (yr. ended 12/31/01): Grants paid, $244,715; assets, $225,296 (M); gifts received, $250,359; expenditures, $245,367; qualifying distributions, $244,700.
Limitations: Applications not accepted. Giving primarily in NJ, NY, and PA.
Application information: Contributes only to pre-selected organizations.

Officers: James W. Eastwood, Pres.; Linda D. Eastwood, Secy.
EIN: 311587433
Codes: FD2

46425
Stockton Rush Bartol Foundation
The Belgravia, Ste. 301
1811 Chestnut St.
Philadelphia, PA 19103 (215) 557-7225
FAX: (215) 557-7316; E-mail: info@bartol.org;
URL: http://www.bartol.org
Contact: Beth Feldman Brandt, Exec. Dir.

Established in 1984 in PA.
Donor(s): George E. Bartol III,‡ Mary F. Bartol, Maise Rush Wolfszon.
Financial data (yr. ended 09/30/01): Grants paid, $243,000; assets, $5,805,190 (M); gifts received, $30,000; expenditures, $407,551; qualifying distributions, $366,316.
Limitations: Giving limited to Philadelphia, PA.
Publications: Grants list, application guidelines.
Application information: Applicants must re-apply annually. Application form required.
Officers and Trustees:* Lise Yasui,* Chair.; Jo-Anna Moore, Vice-Chair.; Valerie Clayton,* Secy.; Margaret Sager, Treas.; Beth Feldman Brandt, Exec. Dir.; Abigail Adams, Joan Myers Brown, Dana B. Hall, Roko Kawa, Blair Bartol MacInnes, Cheryl McClenney-Brooker, June W. O'Neill, Susan Terrell Saunders.
EIN: 232318470
Codes: FD2, GTI

46426
Amaranth Foundation
c/o Duane, Morris & Heckscher, LLP
1 Liberty Pl.
Philadelphia, PA 19103-7396

Established in 1993 in PA.
Donor(s): Joan M. Moran.
Financial data (yr. ended 12/31/01): Grants paid, $242,045; assets, $42,272 (M); gifts received, $207,727; expenditures, $252,633; qualifying distributions, $243,420.
Limitations: Applications not accepted. Giving primarily in PA, with emphasis on Allentown.
Application information: Contributes only to pre-selected organizations.
Trustee: Joan M. Moran.
EIN: 237743235
Codes: FD2

46427
Peter F. McManus Charitable Trust
1 Montgomery Plz., Ste. 902
P.O. Box 751
Norristown, PA 19404 (610) 279-3370
Contact: Katharine G. Lidz, Tr.

Established in 2000 in PA.
Financial data (yr. ended 12/31/01): Grants paid, $241,124; assets, $3,613,338 (M); expenditures, $285,712; qualifying distributions, $253,351.
Limitations: Giving on a national basis.
Application information: Application form not required.
Trustee: Katharine G. Lidz.
EIN: 256666319
Codes: FD2

46428
The Helen R. Buck Foundation
c/o The Glenmede Trust Co.
1650 Market St., Ste. 1200
Philadelphia, PA 19103-7391
Contact: Warren Reintzel

Established in 1992 in PA.

Donor(s): Helen R. Buck.‡
Financial data (yr. ended 12/31/01): Grants paid, $240,000; assets, $4,077,011 (M); expenditures, $254,209; qualifying distributions, $245,703.
Limitations: Giving on a national basis.
Application information: Application form not required.
Trustees: Martha B. Bartlett, C. Austin Buck II, Nancy B. Pyne, The Glenmede Trust Co.
EIN: 237693437
Codes: FD2

46429
Maurice A. Neinken Scholarship Grant & Loan Foundation
(Formerly Maurice A. Neinken Scholarship Grant)
P.O. Box 193
164 Sussex at Lion's Gate
Souderton, PA 18964
Contact: C.W. Apple, Chair.

Established in 1994.
Donor(s): Maurice A. Neinken.‡
Financial data (yr. ended 12/31/01): Grants paid, $240,000; assets, $3,030,925 (M); gifts received, $40,000; expenditures, $257,662; qualifying distributions, $232,896.
Limitations: Giving primarily in the Perkasie, Quakertown and Souderton, PA, areas.
Application information: Application form required.
Application Committee: Charles W. Apple, Chair.; J. Lawrence Grim, Jr., Colleen Hamilton, James Underkoffler, Karen Underkoffler.
Trustee: First Union National Bank.
EIN: 237760341
Codes: FD2, GTI

46430
Philo and Sarah Blaisdell Foundation
410 Seneca Bldg.
Bradford, PA 16701 (814) 362-6340
Scholarship application address: c/o Office of Financial Aid, Univ. of Pittsburgh at Bradford, Bradford, PA 16701, tel.: (814) 362-3801
Contact: Howard Fesenmyer, Exec. Secy.

Established in 1950 in PA.
Donor(s): George G. Blaisdell, Zippo Manufacturing Co.
Financial data (yr. ended 12/31/01): Grants paid, $239,971; assets, $4,324,196 (M); gifts received, $1,100; expenditures, $314,767; qualifying distributions, $253,871.
Limitations: Giving primarily in McKean County, PA.
Officer: Howard Fesenmyer, Exec. Secy.
Trustees: Sarah B. Dorn, Richard McDowell, Harriet B. Wick.
EIN: 256035748
Codes: FD2, GTI

46431
HFO Foundation
1600 Market St., Ste. 3600
Philadelphia, PA 19103 (215) 751-2080

Established in 1989 in PA.
Financial data (yr. ended 11/30/01): Grants paid, $239,500; assets, $55 (M); gifts received, $190,557; expenditures, $245,664; qualifying distributions, $241,210.
Limitations: Applications not accepted. Giving primarily in NJ.
Application information: Contributes only to pre-selected organizations.
Trustees: Debra Abdo, Wendy Gronda, Elaine Harmon, John J. Harmon.
EIN: 236870251

PENNSYLVANIA—46441

Codes: FD2

46432
Franklin H. & Ruth L. Wells Foundation
4718 Old Gettysburg Rd., Ste. 209
Mechanicsburg, PA 17055-8411
(717) 763-1157
Contact: Miles J. Gibbons, Jr., Exec. Dir.

Established in 1983 in PA.
Donor(s): Ruth L. Wells Annuity Trust, Frank Wells Marital Trust.
Financial data (yr. ended 05/31/02): Grants paid, $238,550; assets, $5,543,352 (M); expenditures, $297,649; qualifying distributions, $276,539.
Limitations: Giving primarily in Dauphin, Cumberland, and Perry counties, PA.
Application information: Application form not required.
Officer and Committee Members:* Miles J. Gibbons, Jr.,* Exec. Dir.; William Cramer, Julie Thomas.
EIN: 222541749
Codes: FD2

46433
Harry Katz Memorial Fund
c/o First Union National Bank
123 S. Broad St., PA 1279
Philadelphia, PA 19109 (215) 670-4227
Contact: Reginald Middleton, V.P., First Union National Bank

Established in 1955 in NJ.
Financial data (yr. ended 12/31/01): Grants paid, $238,344; assets, $3,022,197 (M); expenditures, $262,851; qualifying distributions, $235,919.
Limitations: Giving primarily in Atlantic County, NJ.
Application information: Application form not required.
Trustees: Florence K. Bernstein, First Union National Bank.
EIN: 510171174
Codes: FD2

46434
The Leeway Foundation
123 S. Broad St., Ste. 2040
Philadelphia, PA 19109 (215) 545-4078
FAX: (215) 545-4021; E-mail: info@leeway.org;
URL: http://www.leeway.org
Contact: Sara Becker, Pres.

Established in 1993.
Donor(s): Helen Berman Alter, Linda L. Alter.
Financial data (yr. ended 12/31/01): Grants paid, $237,089; assets, $10,398,034 (M); gifts received, $26,390; expenditures, $525,421; qualifying distributions, $514,201.
Limitations: Giving primarily to residents in the Philadelphia, PA, area.
Publications: Annual report, multi-year report, grants list, informational brochure (including application guidelines), application guidelines.
Application information: Grant proposals from organizations by invitation only. Complete guidelines available on website. Application form required.
Officers and Directors:* Sara Becker,* Pres.; Barbara J. Silzle,* Exec. Dir.; Suzanne M. Cunningham, Charlene S. Longnecker, Virginia P. Sikes.
EIN: 232727140
Codes: FD2, GTI

46435
Horace B. Packer Foundation
P.O. Box 732
Wellsboro, PA 16901 (570) 724-1800
Contact: E.H. Owlett, V.P.

Incorporated in 1951 in PA.
Donor(s): Horace B. Packer.‡
Financial data (yr. ended 12/31/01): Grants paid, $236,977; assets, $4,539,992 (M); expenditures, $303,551; qualifying distributions, $263,734.
Limitations: Giving limited to the Tioga County, PA, area.
Application information: Application form required.
Officers: Carl E. Carson, Pres.; Edward H. Owlett, V.P.; Hon. Robert M. Kemp, Secy.; David Kupinsky, Treas.
Directors: R. James Dunham, Rev. Gregory P. Hinton, Rhonda Litchfield.
Trustees: Harold Hershberger, M & T Bank.
EIN: 236390932
Codes: FD2

46436
Malcolm W. & Anna G. Myers Scholarship Fund
c/o First Union National Bank
12 E. Market St.
York, PA 17401-1206
Application address: 600 Penn St., P.O. Box 1102, Reading, PA 19603, tel.: (610) 655-3135
Contact: Pamela Nothstein, V.P.

Established in 1997 in PA.
Financial data (yr. ended 12/31/00): Grants paid, $236,818; assets, $3,609,093 (M); expenditures, $239,494; qualifying distributions, $237,399.
Limitations: Giving primarily in PA.
Trustee: First Union National Bank.
EIN: 237879656
Codes: FD2

46437
Joel and Elaine Gershman Foundation
(Formerly Joel Gershman Foundation)
1027 Pheasant Rd.
Rydal, PA 19046-1817
Contact: Joel Gershman, Pres.

Established in 1984.
Donor(s): Joel Gershman.
Financial data (yr. ended 11/30/01): Grants paid, $236,700; assets, $3,871,462 (M); gifts received, $468,878; expenditures, $241,521; qualifying distributions, $235,077.
Limitations: Applications not accepted. Giving primarily in Philadelphia, PA.
Application information: Unsolicited requests for funds not accepted.
Officer: Joel Gershman, Pres.
Trustees: Elaine Levitt Gershman, Bill Levitt, David Levitt.
EIN: 222529629
Codes: FD2

46438
Allen Hilles Fund
P.O. Box 540
Plymouth Meeting, PA 19462 (610) 828-8145
FAX: (610) 834-8175; URL: http://www.dvg.org/Hilles/index.html
Contact: Judith L. Bardes, Mgr.

Established in 1983 in PA.
Donor(s): Edith Hilles Dewees.‡
Financial data (yr. ended 12/31/01): Grants paid, $236,250; assets, $5,328,287 (M); expenditures, $319,020; qualifying distributions, $272,966.
Limitations: Giving primarily in Philadelphia, PA.
Publications: Annual report (including application guidelines).

Application information: Applicants limited to 1 request per calendar year; accepts Delaware Valley Grantmakers Common Grant Application and Common Report Form (with foundation's cover sheet). Preference is given to organizations with operating budgets of less than $2 million. Application form required.
Officer: Judith L. Bardes, Mgr.
Directors: Edward D. Dewees, Robert L. Dewees, Jr., Steve Honeyman, Stephanie D. Judson.
EIN: 516154986
Codes: FD2

46439
Edwill B. Miller Trust
c/o Allfirst, Trust Div.
21 E. Market St.
York, PA 17401 (717) 852-3068
Contact: Arlene C. LaPore, V.P. and Trust Off., Allfirst

Established in 1977 in PA.
Donor(s): Edwill B. Miller.‡
Financial data (yr. ended 03/31/01): Grants paid, $235,053; assets, $3,561,456 (M); expenditures, $257,533; qualifying distributions, $247,843.
Limitations: Giving primarily in central PA.
Trustee: Allfirst.
EIN: 236657558
Codes: FD2

46440
Holt Family Foundation
3003 Parkway Blvd.
Allentown, PA 18104-5384
Application address: 1611 Pond Rd., Ste. 300, Allentown, PA 18104-2256
Contact: Leon C. Holt, Jr., Tr.

Established in 1987 in PA.
Donor(s): Leon C. Holt, Jr.
Financial data (yr. ended 12/31/01): Grants paid, $234,500; assets, $4,726,431 (M); expenditures, $297,051; qualifying distributions, $254,158.
Limitations: Giving primarily in Allentown and Lehigh County, PA.
Publications: Application guidelines.
Application information: Application form not required.
Officer and Trustees:* Leon C. Holt, Jr.,* Mgr.; June W. Holt, Richard W. Holt, Deborah Holt Weil.
EIN: 236906143
Codes: FD2

46441
Union Benevolent Association
117 S. 17th St., Ste. 2300
Philadelphia, PA 19103-5022 (215) 568-2225
FAX: (215) 563-2204
Contact: Joanne R. Denworth, Pres.

Founded in 1831 in PA.
Financial data (yr. ended 12/31/01): Grants paid, $233,800; assets, $4,337,965 (M); gifts received, $3,021; expenditures, $263,656; qualifying distributions, $239,081.
Limitations: Giving limited to Philadelphia, PA.
Publications: Annual report (including application guidelines).
Application information: Application form not required.
Officers and Board Members:* Joanne R. Denworth,* Pres.; Roberta Griffin Torian, V.P.; Craig E.F. Alston, Secy.; Lloyd M. Coates, Jr., Treas.; Lorene E. Cary, Graham S. Finney, William J. Lee, Phyllis Martino, Theodore T. Newbold, Jose A. Rivera-Urrutia, Nettie W. Taylor.
Trustee: Mellon Bank, N.A.
EIN: 231360861

Codes: FD2

46442
G. C. Murphy Company Foundation
211 Oberdick Dr.
Mc Keesport, PA 15135 (412) 751-6649
Contact: Edwin W. Davis, Secy.

Incorporated in 1952 in PA.
Donor(s): G.C. Murphy Co.
Financial data (yr. ended 12/31/01): Grants paid, $233,000; assets, $4,325,107 (M); expenditures, $279,206; qualifying distributions, $236,450.
Limitations: Giving primarily in southeastern Allegheny County, PA.
Application information: Application form not required.
Officers and Directors:* Robert T. Messner,* Pres.; T.F. Hudak,* V.P. and Treas.; Charles W. Breckenridge,* V.P.; Alice J. Hajduk, V.P.; C.A. McElhinny,* V.P.; Edwin W. Davis,* Secy.
EIN: 256028651
Codes: FD2, CD

46443
William B. Butz Memorial Fund
(Formerly William & Alice Butz Memorial Fund)
220 Long Ln.
Oley, PA 19547
Contact: Ilse Morning

Established in 1954 in PA.
Donor(s): William B. Butz.‡
Financial data (yr. ended 12/31/01): Grants paid, $230,000; assets, $4,131,836 (M); expenditures, $327,604; qualifying distributions, $276,469.
Limitations: Applications not accepted. Giving on a national basis.
Application information: Contributes only to pre-selected organizations. Unsolicited requests for funds not considered.
Trustees: Ingrid Morning, Ober Morning II, Scott R. Stoneback.
EIN: 236259515
Codes: FD2

46444
The Eugene Feiner Foundation
c/o Bennett L. Aaron
3000 2 Logan Sq.
Philadelphia, PA 19103-2799

Established in 1994 in PA.
Donor(s): Eugene Feiner.
Financial data (yr. ended 12/31/01): Grants paid, $230,000; assets, $122,651 (M); gifts received, $233,000; expenditures, $231,188; qualifying distributions, $231,035.
Limitations: Applications not accepted. Giving primarily in NY and PA.
Application information: Contributes only to pre-selected organizations.
Officers and Directors:* Eugene Feiner,* Pres.; Bennett L. Aaron,* Secy.-Treas.; Martin A. Coopersmith, Authur D. Kabelow.
EIN: 232775300
Codes: FD2

46445
Jeffrey P. Orleans Charitable Foundation
1 Greenwood Sq.
3333 Street Rd., Ste. 101
Bensalem, PA 19020-2022

Donor(s): Jeffrey P. Orleans.
Financial data (yr. ended 12/31/01): Grants paid, $229,798; assets, $72,342 (M); gifts received, $227,649; expenditures, $231,954; qualifying distributions, $230,830.
Limitations: Applications not accepted.

Application information: Contributes only to pre-selected organizations.
Trustee: Jeffrey P. Orleans.
EIN: 232870134
Codes: FD2

46446
W. H. and Althea F. Remmel Foundation
c/o PNC Advisors, Charitable Trust Comm.
2 PNC Plz., 620 Liberty Ave., 25th Fl.
Pittsburgh, PA 15222-2719 (412) 762-7076
Contact: Mia Hallett Bernard

Established in 1951 in PA.
Donor(s): William H. Remmel,‡ Althea F. Remmel.‡
Financial data (yr. ended 12/31/01): Grants paid, $228,765; assets, $3,806,071 (M); expenditures, $268,897; qualifying distributions, $232,128.
Limitations: Giving primarily in Pittsburgh, PA.
Publications: Informational brochure, application guidelines.
Application information: Application form required.
Trustee: PNC Bank, N.A.
EIN: 237009732
Codes: FD2

46447
The Rolander Family Foundation
Farmhill Rd.
Sewickley, PA 15143
FAX: (412) 741-0407; E-mail: Rolander99@aol.com
Contact: C. Arthur Rolander, Jr., Pres.

Established in 2000 in PA.
Financial data (yr. ended 12/31/01): Grants paid, $228,396; assets, $5,647,720 (M); expenditures, $243,091; qualifying distributions, $323,814.
Limitations: Giving on a national basis.
Officers: C. Arthur Rolander, Jr., Pres.; Stephen B. Rolander, V.P.
Directors: Nancy R. Leroy, C. Arthur Rolander III, Mildred D. Rolander.
EIN: 912080946
Codes: FD2

46448
M. Patton Trust for Charities
c/o Mellon Bank, N.A.
3 Mellon Bank Ctr., Rm. 4000
Pittsburgh, PA 15259 (412) 234-1634
Contact: Annette Calgaro, V.P.

Established in 1976 in PA.
Donor(s): Margaret Patton.‡
Financial data (yr. ended 12/31/00): Grants paid, $228,000; assets, $4,129,383 (M); gifts received, $1,540; expenditures, $263,973; qualifying distributions, $232,557.
Limitations: Applications not accepted. Giving primarily in Armstrong County, PA.
Application information: Unsolicited requests for funds are not accepted.
Trustees: John W. Rohrer III, Mellon Bank, N.A.
EIN: 256170579
Codes: FD2

46449
The Polk Foundation, Inc.
2000 Grant Bldg.
Pittsburgh, PA 15219 (412) 338-3466
FAX: (412) 338-3463; E-mail: foundation@hillmanfo.com
Contact: Ronald W. Wertz, Secy. and Exec. Dir.

Incorporated in 1957 in PA.
Donor(s): Patricia Hillman Miller.‡

Financial data (yr. ended 12/31/01): Grants paid, $227,500; assets, $4,838,833 (M); expenditures, $249,249; qualifying distributions, $233,851.
Limitations: Giving limited to Pittsburgh, PA.
Application information: Application form not required.
Officers and Directors:* Henry L. Hillman,* Pres.; C.G. Grefenstette,* V.P.; Ronald W. Wertz,* Secy. and Exec. Dir.; Lawrence M. Wagner, Treas.; Patricia M. Duggan.
EIN: 251113733
Codes: FD2

46450
The Female Association of Philadelphia
c/o PNC Bank, N.A.
1600 Market St., 8th Fl.
Philadelphia, PA 19103-7240 (610) 525-6234

Established in 1810 in PA.
Financial data (yr. ended 09/30/01): Grants paid, $226,600; assets, $3,657,252 (M); expenditures, $255,384; qualifying distributions, $227,855.
Limitations: Applications not accepted. Giving limited to residents of the Philadelphia, PA, area.
Officers and Trustees:* Mrs. Robert B. Hobbs, Jr.,* Pres.; Mrs. William H. Rorer III,* V.P.; Mrs. Morris A. Stout III, Secy.; Mrs. Rodney D. Day III,* Treas.; and 19 additional trustees.
Agent: PNC Bank, N.A.
EIN: 236214961
Codes: FD2, GTI

46451
Harry E. and Florence W. Snayberger Memorial Foundation
(Formerly Snayberger Memorial Foundation)
c/o M&T Bank
1 S. Centre St.
Pottsville, PA 17901

Established in 1976 in PA.
Donor(s): Harry E. Snayberger.‡
Financial data (yr. ended 03/31/01): Grants paid, $225,017; assets, $4,585,173 (M); expenditures, $273,432; qualifying distributions, $225,017.
Limitations: Giving limited to residents of Schuylkill County, PA.
Application information: Scholarship applicants must be 25 years old or younger at high school graduation. Application form required.
Trustee: M & T Bank.
EIN: 232056361
Codes: FD2, GTI

46452
Geraldine Dietz Fox Foundation
(Formerly The GDF Foundation)
955 Chesterbrook Blvd., Ste. 125
Wayne, PA 19087

Established in 1988 in PA.
Donor(s): Geraldine Dietz Fox.
Financial data (yr. ended 12/31/01): Grants paid, $225,000; assets, $1,116,246 (M); expenditures, $229,000; qualifying distributions, $225,003.
Limitations: Applications not accepted.
Application information: Contributes only to pre-selected organizations.
Trustees: Geraldine Dietz Fox, Richard J. Fox.
EIN: 232542904
Codes: FD2

46453
Soffer Foundation
400 Penn Ctr. Blvd., Ste. 211
Pittsburgh, PA 15235

Established in 1984 in PA.
Donor(s): Joseph Soffer.

Financial data (yr. ended 12/31/00): Grants paid, $224,872; assets, $5,997,880 (M); expenditures, $286,783; qualifying distributions, $224,872.
Limitations: Applications not accepted. Giving primarily in Pittsburgh, PA.
Application information: Contributes only to pre-selected organizations.
Directors: Joseph Soffer, Violet Soffer.
EIN: 251455764
Codes: FD2

46454
Live Oak Foundation
c/o Robert Gallagher, First Union National Bank
P.O. Box 7558, PA 4394
Philadelphia, PA 19101-7558

Established in 1966 in PA.
Donor(s): Charlotte C. Weber.
Financial data (yr. ended 08/31/01): Grants paid, $224,741; assets, $1,250,610 (M); gifts received, $11,500; expenditures, $124,965; qualifying distributions, $223,850.
Limitations: Giving on a national basis.
Application information: Application form not required.
Trustees: Charlotte C. Weber, First Union National Bank.
EIN: 236424637
Codes: FD2

46455
Geraldine M. Murray Foundation
5020 Ritter Rd., Ste. 211
Mechanicsburg, PA 17055
Contact: Jane E. Murray, Tr.

Financial data (yr. ended 06/30/01): Grants paid, $224,281; assets, $169,708 (M); gifts received, $120,000; expenditures, $226,300; qualifying distributions, $224,336.
Limitations: Giving primarily in PA.
Trustees: Jane E. Murray, Patricia L. Murray.
EIN: 251637471
Codes: FD2

46456
AO North America, Inc.
P.O. Box 308
Devon, PA 19333-0308 (610) 251-9007
FAX: (610) 251-9059
Contact: James E. Gerry, Treas.

Established in 1992 in PA.
Donor(s): AO/ASIF Foundation.
Financial data (yr. ended 06/30/01): Grants paid, $223,999; assets, $1,400,438 (M); gifts received, $12,751,155; expenditures, $996,412; qualifying distributions, $990,961.
Limitations: Giving on a national and international basis.
Application information: Grants rarely exceed $5,000 for research projects. Maximum funding for visiting professor program: $3,000 per professor from North America, $6,000 per professor from abroad. Application form required.
Officers: Eric Johnson, Pres.; Larry Bone, V.P.; James E. Gerry, Treas.
EIN: 232701788
Codes: FD2

46457
Richard L. & Lois S. Werner Family Foundation
561 Richmond Dr.
Sharon, PA 16146 (724) 981-1251
Contact: Richard L. Werner, Tr.

Established in 1997 in PA.
Donor(s): Lois S. Werner, Richard L. Werner.

Financial data (yr. ended 12/31/00): Grants paid, $223,165; assets, $3,221,573 (M); expenditures, $250,645; qualifying distributions, $223,390.
Limitations: Giving on a national basis.
Trustees: Elise W. Frost, Bruce D. Werner, Lois S. Werner, Mindy H. Werner, Richard L. Werner.
EIN: 237911213
Codes: FD2

46458
The Alan B. Miller Family Foundation
57 Crosby Brown Rd.
Gladwyne, PA 19035-1512
Contact: Alan B. Miller, Pres. and Treas.

Established in 1998 in PA.
Donor(s): Alan B. Miller.
Financial data (yr. ended 01/31/01): Grants paid, $223,000; assets, $6,885,533 (M); gifts received, $2,010,938; expenditures, $224,060; qualifying distributions, $223,000.
Limitations: Giving primarily in VA, PA, and SC.
Application information: Application form not required.
Officers and Directors:* Alan B. Miller,* Pres. and Treas.; Jill S. Miller,* Secy.; Abby D. Miller, Marc D. Miller, Marni E. Miller.
EIN: 232899896
Codes: FD2

46459
The Margaret M. Hitchcock Foundation
c/o Mellon Bank, N.A.
P.O. Box 185
Pittsburgh, PA 15230-0185 (412) 234-5892
Application address: 3 Mellon Bank Ctr., Ste. 3901, Pittsburgh, PA 15219
Contact: Len Richards, V.P., Mellon Bank, N.A.

Trust established in 1961 in PA.
Donor(s): Margaret Mellon Hitchcock.
Financial data (yr. ended 12/31/00): Grants paid, $222,700; assets, $4,189,771 (M); expenditures, $236,640; qualifying distributions, $223,364.
Limitations: Giving on a national basis.
Application information: Call foundation for guidelines and deadlines. Application form required.
Trustees: Peggy M. Hitchcock, Thomas Hitchcock III, William M. Hitchcock, Alexander M. Laughlin, William J. Simpson, Louise H. Stephaich, Mellon Bank, N.A.
EIN: 256018992
Codes: FD2

46460
Patchwork Charitable Foundation
c/o Mellon Bank N.A.
P.O. Box 7236, AIM No. 193-0224
Philadelphia, PA 19101-7236

Established in 1999 in PA.
Financial data (yr. ended 12/31/01): Grants paid, $222,500; assets, $1,715,084 (M); gifts received, $210,000; expenditures, $268,959; qualifying distributions, $222,500.
Limitations: Applications not accepted.
Application information: Contributes only to pre-selected organizations.
Trustee: Mellon Bank, N.A.
EIN: 233023071

46461
The Harry Stern Family Foundation
The Colonade, Ste. 1-124
100 Old York Rd.
Jenkintown, PA 19046
FAX: (215) 886-4013
Contact: Jerome Stern, Treas.

Established in 1985 in PA.

Donor(s): Members of the Stern family.
Financial data (yr. ended 12/31/01): Grants paid, $222,094; assets, $3,364,490 (M); expenditures, $457,116; qualifying distributions, $320,718.
Limitations: Giving primarily in the New York, NY, and greater Philadelphia, PA, areas.
Application information: Unsolicited requests for funds are not accepted.
Officers and Directors:* Harry Stern, Pres.; Zelda Stern,* Secy.; Jerome Stern,* Treas.; Rebecca Stern Herschkopf, Sheva Stern Mann, Sareva Stern Naor, Amram Stern.
EIN: 236806751
Codes: FD2

46462
Virginia A. McKee Poor Fund
c/o PNC Advisors, Trust Comm.
2 PNC Plz., 620 Liberty Ave., 25th Fl.
Pittsburgh, PA 15222 (412) 762-7076
Contact: Mia Hallett Bernard

Trust established in 1929 in PA.
Donor(s): Virginia A. McKee.‡
Financial data (yr. ended 09/30/01): Grants paid, $220,940; assets, $3,363,179 (M); expenditures, $241,276; qualifying distributions, $216,694.
Limitations: Giving limited to Pittsburgh, PA.
Publications: Informational brochure, application guidelines.
Application information: Application form required.
Trustee: PNC Bank, N.A.
EIN: 256023292
Codes: FD2

46463
W. P. Snyder III Charitable Fund
610 Smithfield St., Ste. 404
Pittsburgh, PA 15222 (412) 471-1331
Contact: Charles E. Ellison, Secy.

Established in 1990 in PA as partial successor to The W. P. Snyder Charitable Fund.
Donor(s): William P. Snyder III.
Financial data (yr. ended 12/31/01): Grants paid, $220,200; assets, $5,355,818 (M); expenditures, $319,159; qualifying distributions, $248,229.
Limitations: Giving primarily in Pittsburgh, PA.
Application information: Application form not required.
Officer: Charles E. Ellison, Secy.
Trustees: J. Brandon Snyder, W.P. Snyder III, W.P. Snyder V.
EIN: 251611760
Codes: FD2

46464
Elaine and Vincent Bell Foundation
7007 Lafayette Ave.
Fort Washington, PA 19034
E-mail: EVBellFoundation@aol.com
Contact: Meg Bell Knysh, Exec. Dir.

Established in 1985 in PA.
Financial data (yr. ended 12/31/01): Grants paid, $219,235; assets, $2,086,586 (M); gifts received, $100; expenditures, $259,424; qualifying distributions, $228,206.
Limitations: Applications not accepted. Giving primarily in AK and PA.
Publications: Informational brochure.
Application information: Contributes only to pre-selected organizations. Unsolicited requests for funds not accepted.
Officers and Trustees:* Vincent G. Bell, Jr.,* Pres.; Meg Bell Knysh,* Exec. Dir.; Elaine V. Bell, Scott Bell, Amy Bell Brody.
EIN: 232384942
Codes: FD2

46465
Women's Aid of Penn Central School
(Formerly Women's Aid Scholarship)
c/o First Union National Bank
123 S. Broad St., PA1279
Philadelphia, PA 19109 (215) 209-5054
Application address: c/o Conrail Inc., 6 Penn Ctr., Rm. 1010, Philadelphia, PA 19102

Established in 1957.
Donor(s): Conrail Inc.
Financial data (yr. ended 12/31/01): Grants paid, $218,119; assets, $2,880,458 (M); expenditures, $268,162; qualifying distributions, $221,121.
Trustee: First Union National Bank.
EIN: 236232572
Codes: CS, FD2, CD, GTI

46466
Bacchieri Foundation
10 Evans Dr.
Landenberg, PA 19350

Established in 2000 in PA.
Donor(s): Gregg Bacchieri, Stacey Bacchieri.
Financial data (yr. ended 12/31/01): Grants paid, $217,250; assets, $2,353,825 (M); gifts received, $1,000,302; expenditures, $244,084; qualifying distributions, $217,250.
Limitations: Applications not accepted.
Application information: Contributes only to pre-selected organizations.
Trustees: Gregg Bacchieri, Stacey Bacchieri.
EIN: 256746273

46467
The Morris & Evelyn Sidewater Foundation, Inc.
c/o RP Mgmt.
1 Wynnewood Rd.
Wynnewood, PA 19096

Established in 1989 in PA.
Financial data (yr. ended 12/31/01): Grants paid, $216,769; assets, $4,594,595 (M); expenditures, $239,398; qualifying distributions, $220,695.
Limitations: Applications not accepted. Giving primarily in NY and PA.
Application information: Contributes only to pre-selected organizations.
Officers: Morris Sidewater, Pres.; Steven J. Sidewater, V.P. and Secy.; Samuel Sidewater, V.P. and Treas.
EIN: 232573603
Codes: FD2

46468
Peter P. III-Dendroica Blanchard Foundation Trust
(Formerly The Dendroica Foundation)
c/o Mellon Bank, N.A.
P.O. Box 185
Pittsburgh, PA 15230-9897
Application address: c/o 3 Mellon Bank Ctr., Pittsburgh, PA 15259; tel.: (412) 234-5892
Contact: Leonard Richards

Established in 1997 in PA.
Financial data (yr. ended 12/31/99): Grants paid, $216,100; assets, $5,639,972 (M); expenditures, $251,669; qualifying distributions, $216,100.
Limitations: Giving primarily in VA.
Trustee: Mellon Bank, N.A.
EIN: 237912826

46469
Spang and Company Charitable Trust
P.O. Box 11422
Pittsburgh, PA 15238 (412) 963-9363
Contact: K.R. McKnight

Established in 1972 in PA.
Donor(s): Spang and Co., Magnetics, Inc., F.E. Rath Trust.
Financial data (yr. ended 12/31/01): Grants paid, $215,250; assets, $9,857,009 (M); gifts received, $2,703; expenditures, $253,074; qualifying distributions, $215,250.
Limitations: Giving primarily in the Butler, PA, area.
Application information: Application form not required.
Trustees: R.K. Brown, D.F. Rath, Frank E. Rath, Jr., Robert A. Rath, Jr.
EIN: 256020192
Codes: CS, FD2, CD

46470
Glendorn Foundation
78 Main St.
Bradford, PA 16701 (814) 368-7171
Contact: William F. Higie, Managing Dir.

Established in 1953 in TX.
Donor(s): Ruth H. Dorn,‡ Forest Oil Corp.
Financial data (yr. ended 12/31/01): Grants paid, $214,500; assets, $3,407,529 (M); gifts received, $100; expenditures, $250,461; qualifying distributions, $213,499.
Limitations: Applications not accepted. Giving on a national basis.
Publications: Financial statement.
Application information: Funds currently committed. Only trustee-originated requests considered.
Officer and Trustees:* William F. Higie,* Managing Dir.; Clayton D. Coburn, David F. Dorn, John C. Dorn, Dale Bird Grubb, Jeffrey W. Miller, Carolynn D. Warner, Leslie D. Young.
EIN: 251024349
Codes: FD2

46471
John A. Gizzio, Sr. Charitable Foundation
1155 Phoenixville Pike, Ste. 109
West Chester, PA 19380

Established in 1997 in PA.
Donor(s): American Computer Estimating, Inc.
Financial data (yr. ended 06/30/01): Grants paid, $213,802; assets, $95,509 (M); gifts received, $213,958; expenditures, $215,790; qualifying distributions, $213,771.
Directors: John Gizzio, Sr., John Gizzio, Jr., Joseph P. Gizzio, Joyce Gizzio, Janet Peterkin.
EIN: 232900098
Codes: FD2

46472
The Richard B. Worley and Leslie A. Miller Charitable Trust
c/o MAS
One Tower Bridge
West Conshohocken, PA 19428
(610) 940-5111
Contact: Richard B. Worley, Tr. and Leslie A. Miller, Tr.

Established in 1996 in PA.
Donor(s): Richard B. Worley.
Financial data (yr. ended 09/30/00): Grants paid, $213,380; assets, $5,111,239 (M); expenditures, $246,448; qualifying distributions, $213,380.
Limitations: Giving primarily in PA.
Application information: Application form not required.
Trustees: Leslie A. Miller, Richard B. Worley.
EIN: 237862650
Codes: FD2

46473
The Mary Jane & Joseph P. Platt, Jr. Family Foundation, Inc.
224 Thorn St.
Sewickley, PA 15143

Established in 1998 in PA.
Donor(s): Mary Jane Platt, Joseph P. Platt.
Financial data (yr. ended 12/31/99): Grants paid, $212,750; assets, $3,452,368 (M); gifts received, $2,033,087; expenditures, $218,274; qualifying distributions, $212,750.
Limitations: Applications not accepted.
Application information: Contributes only to pre-selected organizations.
Officer: Mary Jane Platt, Pres.
EIN: 251815288

46474
Jacques Weber Foundation, Inc.
c/o Scholarship Comm.
P.O. Box 420
Bloomsburg, PA 17815
Contact: Sandra Grasley, Asst. Secy.

Established in 1948.
Financial data (yr. ended 09/30/02): Grants paid, $212,253; assets, $2,738,228 (M); gifts received, $1,730; expenditures, $212,253; qualifying distributions, $212,253.
Limitations: Applications not accepted. Giving primarily in Monroe, NC, Bloomsburg, PA and Clemson, SC.
Application information: Unsolicited requests for funds not accepted.
Officers and Trustees:* James P. Marion III,* Pres. and Secy.; Robert McCoy,* V.P.; Michael Spruyt,* Treas.; Fred F. Evans, Sandra Grasley, Joan McCarty, William Parker.
EIN: 136101161
Codes: FD2, GTI

46475
The Javitch Foundation
c/o Jane Scaccetti
1845 Walnut St., Ste. 1400
Philadelphia, PA 19103

Incorporated in 1981 in PA.
Donor(s): Lee H. Javitch.
Financial data (yr. ended 08/31/01): Grants paid, $211,959; assets, $1,740,574 (M); gifts received, $398,975; expenditures, $255,315; qualifying distributions, $210,924.
Limitations: Applications not accepted. Giving primarily in NY and PA.
Application information: Contributes only to pre-selected organizations.
Officers: Lee H. Javitch, Pres.; Rona Javitch, V.P.; Jonathan Javitch, Secy.-Treas.
EIN: 232185146
Codes: FD2

46476
The Lassin Family Foundation
P.O. Box 427
425 Stump Rd.
Montgomeryville, PA 18936
Contact: Ronald P. Lassin, Tr.

Established in 1977 in PA.
Donor(s): Ronald P. Lassin.
Financial data (yr. ended 11/30/01): Grants paid, $211,747; assets, $699,796 (M); expenditures, $211,762; qualifying distributions, $211,747.
Limitations: Applications not accepted. Giving primarily in Philadelphia, PA.
Application information: Contributes only to pre-selected organizations.
Trustees: Harriet J. Lassin, Ronald P. Lassin.
EIN: 232070532

Codes: FD2

46477
The Ortenzio Family Foundation
4718 Old Gettysburg Rd., Ste. 405
Mechanicsburg, PA 17055 (717) 972-1305
Contact: Robert A. Ortenzio, Tr.

Established in 1986 in PA.
Donor(s): Rocco A. Ortenzio.
Financial data (yr. ended 12/31/01): Grants paid, $209,775; assets, $3,791,648 (M); gifts received, $39,970; expenditures, $259,296; qualifying distributions, $212,253.
Limitations: Giving primarily in PA.
Trustees: John M. Ortenzio, Martin J. Ortenzio, Robert A. Ortenzio, Rocco A. Ortenzio.
EIN: 236805409
Codes: FD2

46478
The Van Name Charitable Trust
c/o The Glenmede Trust Co.
1650 Market St., Ste. 1200
Philadelphia, PA 19103-7391 (215) 419-6000
Contact: John Amalfitano, Tr. Off.

Established in 1989 in NJ.
Donor(s): David E. Van Name.‡
Financial data (yr. ended 12/31/01): Grants paid, $208,333; assets, $37,814 (M); expenditures, $209,167; qualifying distributions, $206,676.
Limitations: Giving primarily in NJ.
Application information: Application form not required.
Trustee: The Glenmede Trust Co.
EIN: 226485771
Codes: FD2

46479
The Crossroads Foundation
2901 Webster Ave.
Pittsburgh, PA 15219-4297

Established in 1985 in PA.
Donor(s): Ann C. Ryan, Edward M. Ryan, Kevin Hayes, Vincent & Margaret Showalter, James P. McQuade, The Brighter Days Foundation, Snee Reinhardt Foundation, Clapp Charitable Trust, McKinney Charitable Foundation, McFeely-Rogers Fund, John McCune Trust, The Pittsburgh Foundation, PNC, Extra Mile Educational Fund, Allegheny Foundation, Calahan Foundation, Pierce Family Foundation, Paul G. Benedum, Jr. Foundation, Diocese of Pittsburgh, Bayer Foundation.
Financial data (yr. ended 06/30/01): Grants paid, $208,081; assets, $266,343 (M); gifts received, $431,352; expenditures, $377,504; qualifying distributions, $310,295.
Limitations: Giving primarily in Pittsburgh, PA.
Officers: Susie Gillespie, Pres.; Dean Calland, V.P.; Carol Boyle, Secy.; Matthew Stalder, Treas.
EIN: 251513510
Codes: FD2

46480
Josephine Jessar and Morris Tulin Foundation
c/o Isdaner & Co.
3 Bala Plz., Ste. 501W
Bala Cynwyd, PA 19004-3484

Financial data (yr. ended 11/30/01): Grants paid, $207,500; assets, $1,036,348 (M); expenditures, $214,608; qualifying distributions, $208,477.
Limitations: Applications not accepted. Giving primarily in MA and NY.
Application information: Contributes only to pre-selected organizations.
Trustee: Stanley B. Tulin.
EIN: 236838442

Codes: FD2

46481
Vesuvius Foundation
(Formerly Vesuvius Crucible Company Charitable Foundation)
c/o PNC Bank, N.A., MS: P2 PTPP-25-1
2 PNC Plz., 620 Liberty Ave.
Pittsburgh, PA 15222-2719 (412) 762-5182
Contact: Bea Lynch, Asst. V.P.

Established in 1966 in PA.
Financial data (yr. ended 12/31/01): Grants paid, $207,000; assets, $3,514,670 (M); expenditures, $215,005; qualifying distributions, $207,831.
Limitations: Giving primarily in Pittsburgh, PA.
Application information: Application form not required.
Trustee: PNC Bank, N.A.
EIN: 256076182
Codes: FD2

46482
Gray Charitable Trust
c/o Duane Morris, LLP
1 Libert Pl.
Philadelphia, PA 19103

Established in 1998 in PA.
Donor(s): Kenneth B. Gray, Jr.
Financial data (yr. ended 12/31/01): Grants paid, $206,742; assets, $8,688,956 (M); gifts received, $3,120,000; expenditures, $261,936; qualifying distributions, $206,742.
Limitations: Applications not accepted.
Application information: Contributes only to pre-selected organizations.
Trustees: Samuel M. Gawthrop, Doreen H. Gray, Kenneth B. Gray, Jr., Kimberly H. Gray, Meredith L. Gray.
EIN: 237987964
Codes: FD2

46483
Sokolski Family Foundation
204 Pamela Dr.
Warren, PA 16365

Established in 1998 in PA.
Donor(s): Robert D. Sokolski.
Financial data (yr. ended 12/31/01): Grants paid, $206,400; assets, $912,541 (M); gifts received, $250,000; expenditures, $206,721; qualifying distributions, $206,400.
Trustee: Robert D. Sokolski.
EIN: 256612279

46484
Charity Randall Foundation
127 Anderson St., Ste. 127
Pittsburgh, PA 15212
Application address: 71 Progress Ave., Cranberry Township, PA 16066, tel.: (724) 776-7000
Contact: Robert P. Randall, Pres.

Established in 1978.
Donor(s): Earl R. Randall, Three Rivers Aluminum Co.
Financial data (yr. ended 06/30/01): Grants paid, $205,750; assets, $4,643,698 (M); gifts received, $201,100; expenditures, $235,488; qualifying distributions, $200,158.
Limitations: Giving primarily in Pittsburgh, PA.
Application information: Application form required.
Officers: Robert P. Randall, Pres.; Robin S. Randall, Secy.; Brett R. Randall, Treas.
EIN: 251329778
Codes: FD2

46485
Christine and Lawrence Smith Charitable Trust
1415 Kriebel Mill Rd.
Collegeville, PA 19426

Established in 1999 in PA.
Donor(s): Lawrence S. Smith, Christine J. Smith.
Financial data (yr. ended 12/31/00): Grants paid, $205,273; assets, $1,357,512 (M); gifts received, $382,480; expenditures, $230,797; qualifying distributions, $202,044.
Limitations: Applications not accepted. Giving primarily in PA.
Application information: Contributes only to pre-selected organizations.
Trustees: Christine J. Smith, Lawrence S. Smith.
EIN: 256632482
Codes: FD2

46486
Mudge Foundation
c/o PNC Bank N.A., Trust Dept.
2 PNC Plz., 33rd Fl.
Pittsburgh, PA 15222-2719 (412) 762-4133
Contact: M. Bradley Dean, V.P.

Established in 1955 in PA.
Financial data (yr. ended 12/31/00): Grants paid, $205,220; assets, $4,457,455 (M); expenditures, $260,685; qualifying distributions, $206,473.
Limitations: Giving primarily in ME, PA, and TX.
Application information: Application form not required.
Trustee: PNC Bank, N.A.
EIN: 256023150
Codes: FD2

46487
Rita M. McGinley Foundation
U.S. Steel Tower
600 Grant St., Ste. 4400
Pittsburgh, PA 15219
Contact: John R. McGinley, Jr., Tr.

Established in 1988 in PA.
Donor(s): Rita M. McGinley.
Financial data (yr. ended 12/31/01): Grants paid, $205,000; assets, $61,385 (M); gifts received, $218,317; expenditures, $208,442; qualifying distributions, $205,000.
Limitations: Giving primarily in Pittsburgh, PA.
Application information: Application form not required.
Trustee: John R. McGinley, Jr.
EIN: 251593336
Codes: FD2

46488
The McCance Foundation
1531 Walnut St.
Philadelphia, PA 19102-3098
Contact: Keith S. Jennings, Tr.

Established in 1994 in MA.
Financial data (yr. ended 12/31/01): Grants paid, $204,500; assets, $7,775,823 (M); expenditures, $238,873; qualifying distributions, $204,750.
Limitations: Giving primarily in MA.
Application information: Application form not required.
Trustees: Keith S. Jennings, Allison J. McCance, Henry F. McCance.
EIN: 046772532
Codes: FD2

46489
The Lebovitz Fund
3050 Tremont St.
Allentown, PA 18104
Contact: Herbert C. Lebovitz, Pres.

Established in 1944 in PA.
Donor(s): Beth Ann Segal Trust.
Financial data (yr. ended 07/31/01): Grants paid, $204,400; assets, $4,026,204 (M); gifts received, $70,000; expenditures, $207,222; qualifying distributions, $201,755.
Limitations: Giving primarily in CT, Minneapolis, MN, New York, NY, and eastern PA.
Application information: Application form not required.
Officers and Directors:* Herbert C. Lebovitz,* Pres. and Treas.; Beth Ann Segal,* V.P. and Secy.; Jonathan Javitch, James Lebovitz.
EIN: 236270079
Codes: FD2

46490
William Goldman Foundation
42 S. 15th St.
Philadelphia, PA 19102 (215) 568-0411
Contact: William R. Goldman, Chair.

Established in 1952 in PA.
Donor(s): William Goldman,‡ Helen L. Goldman.‡
Financial data (yr. ended 12/31/01): Grants paid, $203,060; assets, $3,673,992 (M); expenditures, $241,646; qualifying distributions, $174,589.
Limitations: Giving primarily in the metropolitan Philadelphia, PA, area.
Publications: Application guidelines.
Application information: Application form required for scholarships. Application form not required.
Officers and Trustees:* William R. Goldman,* Chair.; Randolph Louis Goldman,* Vice-Chair.; Barbara G. Susman,* Secy.; Lowell H. Dubrow, Anne B. Goldman, Jeffrey L. Susman, Ronald M. Wiener.
EIN: 236266261
Codes: FD2, GTI

46491
American Eagle Outfitters Foundation
150 Thorn Hill Dr.
Warrendale, PA 15086

Established in 1999 in PA.
Financial data (yr. ended 12/31/99): Grants paid, $202,776; assets, $168,168 (M); gifts received, $377,187; expenditures, $209,019; qualifying distributions, $209,019.
Limitations: Applications not accepted. Giving primarily in MA and PA.
Application information: Contributes only to pre-selected organizations.
Officer: Susan Miller, Chair.
Board Members: George Kolber, Michael Leedy, Laura Weil.
EIN: 251827476
Codes: FD2

46492
The Shirley R. Kaplan Charitable Fund
c/o LAW
16 Sentry Park W., Ste. 310
Blue Bell, PA 19422-2240

Established in 1992 in PA.
Financial data (yr. ended 12/31/00): Grants paid, $202,025; assets, $324,212 (M); gifts received, $103,582; expenditures, $204,051; qualifying distributions, $200,844.
Limitations: Applications not accepted. Giving primarily in NY and PA.

Application information: Contributes only to pre-selected organizations.
Trustees: Elizabeth A. Davis, Seymour Kaplan.
EIN: 232712805
Codes: FD2

46493
The Raymond and Elizabeth Bloch Foundation
830 Frick Bldg.
Pittsburgh, PA 15219
Contact: Bernard L. Bloch, C.E.O. and Pres.

Established in 1989 in PA.
Donor(s): Raymond Bloch.‡
Financial data (yr. ended 12/31/01): Grants paid, $202,000; assets, $3,731,934 (M); expenditures, $282,034; qualifying distributions, $216,132.
Limitations: Giving primarily in PA.
Application information: Application form not required.
Officer: Bernard L. Bloch, C.E.O. and Pres.
EIN: 251561204
Codes: FD2

46494
The Wilson Fund
c/o The Glenmede Trust Co.
1650 Market St., Ste. 1200
Philadelphia, PA 19103-7391
Application address: c/o The Glenmede Trust Co. of New Jersey, 16 Chambers St., Princeton, NJ 08542-3708, tel.: (215) 419-6000
Contact: Megan E. Thomas, Trust Off., The Glenmede Trust Co.

Established in 1995 in NJ.
Donor(s): Donald M. Wilson, Susan N. Wilson.
Financial data (yr. ended 12/31/01): Grants paid, $201,550; assets, $1,943,414 (M); expenditures, $218,181; qualifying distributions, $206,481.
Limitations: Giving in the U.S., with emphasis on NJ and NY.
Trustees: Donald M. Wilson, Susan N. Wilson, The Glenmede Trust Co.
EIN: 226649468
Codes: FD2

46495
Margaret Ogilvie McCormick Charitable Trust
c/o Allfirst, Trust Div.
21 E. Market St., M/C 402-130
York, PA 17401-1500
Application address: c/o Allfirst, P.O. Box 2961, Harrisburg, PA, 17105
Contact: Larry A. Hartman

Established in 1991 in PA.
Financial data (yr. ended 12/31/01): Grants paid, $201,220; assets, $3,629,599 (M); expenditures, $227,838; qualifying distributions, $199,588.
Limitations: Giving limited to the Harrisburg, PA, area.
Trustee: Allfirst.
EIN: 236216167
Codes: FD2

46496
The Ball Family Foundation
(Formerly Russell C. Ball Foundation)
c/o American Manufacturing Corp.
555 Croton Rd., Ste. 300
King of Prussia, PA 19406 (610) 962-3770
Contact: Russell C. Ball, III, Pres.

Donor(s): Philadelphia Gear Corp., American Manufacturing Corp.
Financial data (yr. ended 12/31/00): Grants paid, $200,950; assets, $678,890 (M); expenditures, $201,959; qualifying distributions, $201,053.
Limitations: Giving primarily in PA.

Officers and Directors:* Russell C. Ball III,* Pres. and Treas.; Andrew L. Ball,* V.P.; Gregory J. Kelemen,* Secy.; Robert H. Strouse.
EIN: 516017780
Codes: CS, FD2, CD

46497
Turner Family Foundation
9 Horseshoe Ln.
Paoli, PA 19301-1909

Established in 1994 in PA.
Donor(s): Robert E. Turner, Jr., Carolyn Turner.
Financial data (yr. ended 12/31/99): Grants paid, $200,290; assets, $4,708,687 (M); gifts received, $978,622; expenditures, $206,838; qualifying distributions, $186,701.
Limitations: Applications not accepted.
Application information: Contributes only to pre-selected organizations.
Officers: Robert E. Turner, Jr., Pres.; Carolyn W. Turner, Treas.
EIN: 232792012
Codes: FD2

46498
Fisher Family Foundation
2180 Hornig Rd.
Philadelphia, PA 19116

Established in 1983.
Donor(s): Murray Fisher, Steven Fisher, Ricki Fisher, Carol Rosenthal, Pei Genesis, Mildred Fisher.
Financial data (yr. ended 12/31/01): Grants paid, $200,272; assets, $789,928 (M); gifts received, $64,805; expenditures, $237,433; qualifying distributions, $200,272.
Limitations: Applications not accepted. Giving primarily in PA.
Application information: Contributes only to pre-selected organizations.
Trustees: Mildred Fisher, Murray Fisher, Steven Fisher, Carol Rosenthal.
EIN: 222473752
Codes: FD2

46499
Sansom-Eligator Foundation
105 Fairway Ln.
Pittsburgh, PA 15238

Established in 1996 in PA.
Donor(s): Robert D. Sansom.
Financial data (yr. ended 12/31/00): Grants paid, $200,000; assets, $9,314,695 (M); gifts received, $993,713; expenditures, $292,605; qualifying distributions, $200,000.
Limitations: Giving primarily in Pittsburgh, PA.
Officers: Robert D. Sansom, Pres.; Edith L. Eligator, Treas.
Director: John R. Washlick.
EIN: 232870275
Codes: FD2

46500
Schlarbaum Family Foundation
266 Hothorpe Ln.
Villanova, PA 19085-1116
Contact: Gary G. Schlarbaum, Pres.

Established in 1999 in PA.
Donor(s): Gary G. Schlarbaum.
Financial data (yr. ended 12/31/01): Grants paid, $200,000; assets, $2,654,969 (M); gifts received, $453,750; expenditures, $241,011; qualifying distributions, $196,220.
Limitations: Applications not accepted.
Application information: Contributes only to pre-selected organizations.

Officers: Gary G. Schlarbaum, Pres.; Ruth Anne Schlarbaum, Secy.-Treas.
Directors: Mark R. Schlarbaum, Melinda Schlarbaum.
EIN: 232996673
Codes: FD2

46501
William L. & Margaret L. Benz Foundation
c/o Mellon Bank, N.A.
3 Mellon Bank Ctr., Rm. 4000
Pittsburgh, PA 15259-0001 (412) 234-0023
Contact: Laurie A. Moritz, Asst. V.P., Mellon Bank, N.A.

Established in 1987 in PA.
Donor(s): Margaret L. Benz.‡
Financial data (yr. ended 05/31/01): Grants paid, $199,900; assets, $4,403,593 (M); expenditures, $237,675; qualifying distributions, $215,915.
Limitations: Giving limited to residents of Blairsville, PA for scholarships.
Application information: Request application information from Blairsville, PA, High School. Requests for grants to organizations are not accepted. Application form required.
Trustee: Mellon Bank, N.A.
EIN: 256276186
Codes: FD2, GTI

46502
Howard E. & Nell E. Miller Charitable Foundation
c/o PNC Advisors Trust Comm.
2 PNC Plz., 25th Fl., 620 Liberty Ave.
Pittsburgh, PA 15222-2719 (412) 762-7076
Application address: c/o Thomas M. Mulroy, 1106 Frick Bldg., Pittsburgh, PA 15219; FAX: (412) 705-1043
Contact: Mia Hallett Bernard

Established in 1988 in PA.
Donor(s): Nellie E. Miller.‡
Financial data (yr. ended 05/31/02): Grants paid, $198,000; assets, $7,159,038 (M); expenditures, $235,679; qualifying distributions, $217,014.
Limitations: Giving primarily in Pittsburgh, PA.
Application information: Application form required.
Trustees: Thomas M. Mulroy, John Pillar, PNC Bank, N.A.
EIN: 256305933
Codes: FD2

46503
Alcoa-Alumax Foundation, Inc.
(Formerly Alumax Foundation, Inc.)
201 Isabella St., Ste. 4J06
Pittsburgh, PA 15212-5858 (412) 553-2779
Contact: Kathleen W. Buechel, Pres.

Established in 1996.
Donor(s): Alumax Inc.
Financial data (yr. ended 12/31/01): Grants paid, $197,257; assets, $3,383,804 (M); expenditures, $266,518; qualifying distributions, $219,368.
Limitations: Giving on a national basis.
Application information: Earth sciences scholarship application limited to children of Alumax Inc. employees. Application form required.
Officers: Kathleen W. Buechel, Pres.; Grace A. Smith, Secy.
Director: Robert F. Slagle.
EIN: 582166783
Codes: CS, FD2, CD

46504
Fred G. Smith Golden Rule Trust Fund
c/o Integra Bank
3rd and Oak Sts.
Mount Carmel, PA 17851
Contact: Ruth Skonecki, Trust Off., Union National Bank

Financial data (yr. ended 12/31/00): Grants paid, $195,550; assets, $3,684,638 (M); expenditures, $214,467; qualifying distributions, $193,215.
Limitations: Giving primarily in PA.
Application information: Trade school applications must be filed before end of school year. Application form required.
Trustee: Union National Bank.
EIN: 232394466
Codes: FD2

46505
The Jane & Martin Schwartz Family Foundation
c/o John D. Iskrant
1600 Market St., Ste. 3600
Philadelphia, PA 19103
Application address: 60 Orchard Farm Rd., Port Washington, NY 11050
Contact: Martin Schwartz, Tr. or Jane Schwartz, Tr.

Established in 1988 in PA.
Donor(s): Martin Schwartz, Jane Schwartz.‡
Financial data (yr. ended 11/30/01): Grants paid, $195,145; assets, $336,580 (M); gifts received, $472,992; expenditures, $209,463; qualifying distributions, $197,455.
Limitations: Giving primarily in NY.
Trustees: Jane Schwartz, Martin Schwartz.
EIN: 236913820
Codes: FD2

46506
The Aileen K. and Brian L. Roberts Foundation
c/o Comcast Corp.
1500 Market St., 35th Fl.
Philadelphia, PA 19102

Established in 1994 in PA.
Donor(s): Brian L. Roberts.
Financial data (yr. ended 12/31/00): Grants paid, $194,574; assets, $1,737,751 (M); expenditures, $202,156; qualifying distributions, $192,785.
Limitations: Applications not accepted. Giving primarily in Philadelphia, PA.
Application information: Contributes only to pre-selected organizations.
Officers: Aileen K. Roberts, Pres.; Brian L. Roberts, V.P.
EIN: 232787654
Codes: FD2

46507
The Tobin Family Foundation
(Formerly Sylvan M. & Frances E. Tobin Foundation)
101 Cheswold Ln., Unit 5D
Haverford, PA 19041-1801

Established in 1966 in PA.
Donor(s): Sylvan M. Tobin.
Financial data (yr. ended 12/31/01): Grants paid, $194,500; assets, $306,941 (M); gifts received, $89,000; expenditures, $198,738; qualifying distributions, $193,402.
Limitations: Giving primarily in Philadelphia, PA.
Officer: Frances E. Tobin, Secy.
Trustee: Sylvan M. Tobin.
EIN: 236420013
Codes: FD2

46508
Halpern Foundation
810 Penn Ave.
Pittsburgh, PA 15222

Established in 1952 in PA.
Donor(s): Members of the Halpern family.
Financial data (yr. ended 12/31/01): Grants paid, $193,635; assets, $3,538,653 (M); gifts received, $8,000; expenditures, $257,165; qualifying distributions, $192,131.
Limitations: Applications not accepted. Giving primarily in Pittsburgh, PA.
Application information: Unsolicited requests for funds not accepted.
Trustees: Bernard M. Halpern, Irving J. Halpern, Richard I. Halpern, Stephen F. Halpern.
EIN: 256060720
Codes: FD2

46509
Ewing Cole Cherry Charitable Foundation
100 N. 6th St.
Philadelphia, PA 19106

Established in 1992 in PA.
Donor(s): Ewing Cole Cherry.
Financial data (yr. ended 11/30/01): Grants paid, $193,500; assets, $110,342 (M); gifts received, $139,500; expenditures, $193,500; qualifying distributions, $193,500.
Limitations: Applications not accepted. Giving primarily in PA.
Application information: Contributes only to pre-selected organizations.
Officers: J. Andrew Jarvis, Chair.; James A. Wilson, Pres.; Pradeep R. Patel, Sr. V.P.; Joseph T. Kelly, Treas.
EIN: 232706727
Codes: FD2

46510
Ward Foundation
P.O. Box 1553
Altoona, PA 16603

Financial data (yr. ended 09/30/01): Grants paid, $193,350; assets, $748,914 (M); gifts received, $1,294; expenditures, $196,895; qualifying distributions, $78,648.
Limitations: Applications not accepted. Giving limited to PA.
Application information: Contributes only to pre-selected organizations.
Directors: G. William Ward, Michael E. Ward.
EIN: 256059159
Codes: FD2

46511
Willary Foundation
c/o PNC Bank, N.A.
P.O. Box 937
Scranton, PA 18501-0937 (570) 961-6952
FAX: (570) 961-6913; E-mail: info@willary.org; URL: http://www.willary.org
Contact: M. Linda Donovan, Admin. Dir.

Established in 1968 in PA.
Donor(s): William W. Scranton, Mary L. Scranton.
Financial data (yr. ended 12/31/01): Grants paid, $192,590; assets, $5,402,280 (M); expenditures, $237,585; qualifying distributions, $211,581.
Limitations: Giving primarily in northeastern PA.
Publications: Application guidelines.
Application information: Application form required.
Trustees: Susan Scranton Dawson, Joseph C. Scranton, Mary L. Scranton, Peter K. Scranton, William W. Scranton, William W. Scranton III, PNC Bank, N.A.
EIN: 237014785

46511—PENNSYLVANIA

Codes: FD2

46512
Richard & Annetta Good Foundation
275 Edgemere Dr.
Lancaster, PA 17601
Contact: Richard W. Good, Pres.

Established in 1996 in PA.
Donor(s): Annetta B. Good, Richard W. Good.
Financial data (yr. ended 12/31/01): Grants paid, $192,562; assets, $801,895 (M); gifts received, $102,000; expenditures, $213,045; qualifying distributions, $192,562.
Limitations: Giving primarily in PA.
Application information: Application form not required.
Officers: Richard W. Good, Pres. and Treas.; Annetta B. Good, Secy.
EIN: 232869865
Codes: FD2

46513
Reschini Foundation
922 Philadelphia St.
Indiana, PA 15701

Established in 1999 in PA.
Donor(s): Roger J. Reschini, Reschini Agency, Inc.
Financial data (yr. ended 12/31/01): Grants paid, $192,524; assets, $2,967 (M); gifts received, $195,973; expenditures, $193,006; qualifying distributions, $192,524.
Limitations: Applications not accepted. Giving primarily in PA.
Application information: Unsolicited requests for funds not accepted.
Officers: Michael I. Supinka, Pres.; Thomas Zaucha, V.P.; Barbara Ender, Secy.-Treas.
EIN: 251830308
Codes: FD2

46514
Julius L. and Libbie B. Steinsapir Family Foundation
904 Allegheny Bldg.
Pittsburgh, PA 15219 (412) 261-1505
Contact: Albert C. Shapira, Tr.

Established in 1969 in PA.
Donor(s): I.H. Steinsapir,‡ Standard Emblem Jewelers.
Financial data (yr. ended 01/31/01): Grants paid, $192,225; assets, $3,352,360 (M); expenditures, $256,663; qualifying distributions, $208,550.
Limitations: Giving primarily in PA.
Application information: Application form not required.
Trustees: Samuel Horovitz, Martin A. Mallit, Albert C. Shapira.
EIN: 256104248
Codes: FD2

46515
Roger K. Todd Trust
c/o M&T Bank
101 W. 3rd St., Trust Tax Dept.
Williamsport, PA 17701

Established in 1998 in PA.
Financial data (yr. ended 12/31/99): Grants paid, $191,776; assets, $5,358,658 (M); gifts received, $587,610; expenditures, $286,009; qualifying distributions, $191,776.
Limitations: Applications not accepted. Giving primarily in Carlisle, PA.
Application information: Contributes only to pre-selected organizations.
Trustee: M & T Bank.
EIN: 236684303
Codes: FD2

46516
Health Alliance Charitable Foundation
(Formerly Hospital Association Trust)
4750 Lindle Rd.
Harrisburg, PA 17111 (717) 564-9200
Contact: Michael A. Suchanick, Secy.-Treas.

Donor(s): PHICO Group, Inc.
Financial data (yr. ended 12/31/00): Grants paid, $191,755; assets, $1,943,325 (M); expenditures, $219,688; qualifying distributions, $219,390.
Limitations: Giving limited to Pittsburgh, PA.
Application information: Application form required.
Officers: Msgr. Andrew J. McGowan, Chair.; Carolyn F. Scanlan, Vice-Chair.; Michael A. Suchanick, Secy.-Treas. and Exec. Dir.
Directors: William A. Alexander, Clifford L. Jones, Rodrigue Mortel, M.D., JoAnn K. Mower, Robert F. Nation, H. Sheldon Parker, Jr., Linda M. Rhodes, Ed.D.
EIN: 251642600
Codes: FD2

46517
Rudolf Steiner Charitable Trust
101 Forge Mountain Dr., P.O. Box 472
Valley Forge, PA 19481 (610) 783-7293
Contact: Erika V. Asten, Ph.D., Tr.

Established about 1955.
Donor(s): Dietreich Asten,‡ Karneol Verein.
Financial data (yr. ended 12/31/01): Grants paid, $191,000; assets, $3,013,766 (M); expenditures, $196,351; qualifying distributions, $194,833.
Limitations: Giving primarily in CA, MI, and PA.
Application information: Application form not required.
Trustees: Erika V. Asten, Ph.D., Gerald T. Chapman, Janet Crossen, Stephen Usher, Ph.D.
EIN: 236298220
Codes: FD2

46518
Caroline J. S. Sanders Charitable Trust No. II
c/o First Union National Bank
123 S. Broad St., 16th Fl.
Philadelphia, PA 19109
Contact: Reginald Middleton, V.P., First Union National Bank

Established in 1990 in PA.
Donor(s): Caroline J.S. Sanders Trust.
Financial data (yr. ended 09/30/01): Grants paid, $190,500; assets, $4,019,699 (M); expenditures, $233,092; qualifying distributions, $189,906.
Limitations: Giving primarily in Philadelphia, PA.
Trustees: Thomas A. Brown, First Union National Bank.
EIN: 232676889
Codes: FD2

46519
John Lazarich Foundation
520 Eagleview Blvd.
Exton, PA 19341 (610) 458-0570
Contact: William Kroneberg III, Tr.; or Julie I. Blank, Tr.

Donor(s): William Kronenberg III.
Financial data (yr. ended 11/30/01): Grants paid, $189,500; assets, $5,116,809 (M); gifts received, $1,011,209; expenditures, $238,882; qualifying distributions, $191,225.
Limitations: Giving primarily in PA.
Trustees: Julie I. Kronenberg, William Kronenberg III.
EIN: 237918137
Codes: FD2

46520
Marilyn and J. Robert Birnhak Foundation
c/o J. Robert Birnhak
P.O. Box 2300
Fort Washington, PA 19034-2300

Established in 1986 in PA.
Donor(s): J. Robert Birnhak, Marilyn J. Birnhak.
Financial data (yr. ended 06/30/02): Grants paid, $189,200; assets, $485,698 (M); gifts received, $405,000; expenditures, $191,360; qualifying distributions, $189,200.
Limitations: Applications not accepted. Giving primarily in Philadelphia, PA.
Application information: Contributes only to pre-selected organizations.
Trustees: J. Robert Birnhak, Marilyn J. Birnhak.
EIN: 222779210
Codes: FD2

46521
Salvaggio Family Foundation
c/o Anthony J. Salvaggio
1390 Ridgeview Dr., Ste. 300
Allentown, PA 18104

Established in 1998 in PA.
Donor(s): Norene L. Salvaggio, Anthony Salvaggio.
Financial data (yr. ended 12/31/00): Grants paid, $188,780; assets, $5,541,182 (M); gifts received, $335,594; expenditures, $192,153; qualifying distributions, $187,218.
Limitations: Applications not accepted. Giving primarily in PA.
Application information: Contributes only to pre-selected organizations.
Trustees: Christy A. Salvaggio, Norene L. Salvaggio, Suzie A. Salvaggio, Thomas A. Salvaggio.
EIN: 256614812
Codes: FD2

46522
Zella J. Gahagen Charitable Foundation
c/o Mellon Bank, N.A.
1 Mellon Bank Ctr., Rm. 3825
Pittsburgh, PA 15259 (412) 234-1634
Contact: Annette Calgaro, V.P., Mellon Bank, N.A.

Established around 1981.
Donor(s): Zella Gahagen.‡
Financial data (yr. ended 12/31/01): Grants paid, $188,053; assets, $6,940,436 (M); expenditures, $188,699; qualifying distributions, $188,259.
Limitations: Applications not accepted.
Application information: Contributes only to pre-selected organizations. Unsolicited requests for funds not accepted.
Trustee: Mellon Bank, N.A.
EIN: 256219884
Codes: FD2

46523
T. Vogeley Memorial Trust
c/o Mellon Bank, N.A.
P.O. Box 185
Pittsburgh, PA 15230-9897 (412) 234-0023
Application address: 165 New Castle Rd., Butler, PA 16001
Contact: Scholarship Committee

Financial data (yr. ended 09/30/01): Grants paid, $187,712; assets, $3,332,479 (M); expenditures, $222,178; qualifying distributions, $191,534.
Limitations: Giving limited to Butler, PA.
Application information: Contact a guidance counselor at Butler High School for application information. Application form required.
Trustee: Mellon Bank, N.A.

EIN: 256235851
Codes: FD2, GTI

46524
C & E Foundation
P.O. Box 20467
Lehigh Valley, PA 18002-0467
Application address: 806 Rugby Rd., Phillipsburg, NJ 08865
Contact: Frank W. Stull, Tr.

Established in 1997 in PA.
Financial data (yr. ended 12/31/01): Grants paid, $187,500; assets, $4,939,386 (M); expenditures, $237,235; qualifying distributions, $237,235.
Limitations: Giving on a national basis.
Officers and Trustees:* Russell Singer,* Chair.; James R. Singer,* Secy.; Norman A. Peil, Jr.,* Treas.; Hazel Singer, Frank W. Stull.
EIN: 232929096
Codes: FD2

46525
Alexander B. Gilfillian Trust
c/o National City Bank of Pennsylvania
20 Stanwix St., National City Ctr.
Pittsburgh, PA 15222-4802
Contact: William M. Schmidt, V.P.

Established in 1997 in PA.
Donor(s): Alexander B. Gilfillian.‡
Financial data (yr. ended 12/31/01): Grants paid, $187,172; assets, $3,098,260 (M); expenditures, $215,676; qualifying distributions, $198,427.
Limitations: Applications not accepted. Giving limited to western PA.
Application information: Contributes only to pre-selected organizations.
Trustee: National City Bank of Pennsylvania.
EIN: 237895267
Codes: FD2

46526
PMC Foundation
(Formerly PMA Foundation)
225 State St.
Harrisburg, PA 17101-1135

Established in 1981 in PA.
Donor(s): PMA Industries, Inc.
Financial data (yr. ended 12/31/00): Grants paid, $187,164; assets, $38,680 (M); gifts received, $150,000; expenditures, $191,076; qualifying distributions, $191,076.
Limitations: Applications not accepted. Giving primarily in PA.
Application information: Contributes only to pre-selected organizations.
Trustees: Frederick W. Anton III, Francis W. McDonnell.
EIN: 232159233
Codes: CS, FD2, CD

46527
Paul Hyland Harris Trust
c/o National City Bank of Pennsylvania
801 State St.
Erie, PA 16538-0001 (814) 871-1279
FAX: (814) 454-7831; E-mail: Christopher.junker@nationalcity.com
Contact: Christopher A. Junker, V.P., National City Bank of Pennsylvania

Established in 1949 in PA.
Financial data (yr. ended 12/31/00): Grants paid, $186,644; assets, $4,117,116 (M); expenditures, $198,475; qualifying distributions, $190,959.
Limitations: Giving limited to students residing in Crawford, Venango, and Warren counties, PA.
Application information: Application form required.

Trustee: National City Bank of Pennsylvania.
EIN: 256013264
Codes: FD2

46528
Arnold & Bette Hoffman Family Foundation
1464 Hunter Rd.
Rydal, PA 19046-4755

Established in 1985 in PA.
Donor(s): Arnold S. Hoffman, Bette Hoffman.
Financial data (yr. ended 07/31/01): Grants paid, $185,294; assets, $308,261 (M); gifts received, $189,875; expenditures, $186,694; qualifying distributions, $184,994.
Limitations: Applications not accepted. Giving primarily in PA.
Application information: Contributes only to pre-selected organizations.
Trustees: Louis W. Fryman, Arnold S. Hoffman, Bette Hoffman.
EIN: 222702299
Codes: FD2

46529
Rose Gross Charitable Foundation
3600 Conshohocken Ave.
Philadelphia, PA 19131
Application address: 1500 Walnut St., Ste. 904, Philadelphia, PA 19102-3523, tel.: (215) 985-1200
Contact: Paul L. Feldman

Donor(s): Leon S. Gross.
Financial data (yr. ended 12/31/99): Grants paid, $184,375; assets, $612,500 (M); expenditures, $184,375; qualifying distributions, $184,375.
Trustees: Leon S. Gross, Lawrence M. Miller.
EIN: 237894843
Codes: FD2

46530
The Ciarco Family Foundation
c/o Glenmede Trust Co.
1650 Market St., Ste. 1200
Philadelphia, PA 19103

Established in 1997 in NJ.
Donor(s): Kathleen Ciarco, Philip J. Ciarco III.
Financial data (yr. ended 12/31/01): Grants paid, $184,205; assets, $1,000,488 (M); expenditures, $189,046; qualifying distributions, $181,200.
Limitations: Giving primarily in NJ.
Application information: Application form not required.
Trustees: Kathleen Ciarco, Philip J. Ciarco III, Philip J. Ciarco IV, Shauna Ciarco DeMarco.
EIN: 237870370
Codes: FD2

46531
Mary Sachs Trust
c/o Wachovia Bank
12 E. Market St.
York, PA 17401
Contact: Brenton Hake, V.P.

Established in 1999.
Financial data (yr. ended 12/31/01): Grants paid, $183,900; assets, $3,320,691 (M); expenditures, $212,901; qualifying distributions, $185,991.
Limitations: Applications not accepted. Giving primarily in PA.
Application information: Contributes only to pre-selected organizations.
Trustees: Thomas Wood, First Union National Bank.
EIN: 236239669
Codes: FD2

46532
The Ross Family Foundation
5 Overlook Rd.
Clarks Green, PA 18411 (570) 587-1365
Contact: Adrian E. Ross, Pres.

Established in 1954 in PA.
Donor(s): Adrian E. Ross, Daniel R. Ross, James A. Ross,‡ James A. Ross.
Financial data (yr. ended 12/31/01): Grants paid, $183,450; assets, $3,658,653 (M); gifts received, $27,623; expenditures, $202,715; qualifying distributions, $189,345.
Limitations: Giving primarily in the Scranton, PA, area.
Officers and Trustees:* Adrian E. Ross,* Pres.; James A. Ross,* V.P.; Daniel R. Ross,* Secy.-Treas.
EIN: 246017499
Codes: FD2

46533
John E. duPont Foundation
13 Paoli Ct.
Paoli, PA 19301 (610) 296-9900
Contact: Taras M. Wochok, Treas.

Established in 1988 in PA.
Donor(s): John E. duPont.
Financial data (yr. ended 12/31/99): Grants paid, $182,500; assets, $274,502 (M); gifts received, $150,467; expenditures, $183,328; qualifying distributions, $182,500.
Officers: John E. duPont, Pres.; Taras M. Wochok,* Treas.
EIN: 232499540
Codes: FD2

46534
The Todi Foundation
424 Gwynedd Valley Dr.
Gwynedd Valley, PA 19437
Contact: Nand K. Todi, Pres.

Established in 1993.
Donor(s): Nand Todi.
Financial data (yr. ended 09/30/01): Grants paid, $182,000; assets, $1,975,228 (M); gifts received, $554,826; expenditures, $217,518; qualifying distributions, $182,000.
Limitations: Giving primarily in PA.
Application information: Application form required.
Officer: Nand K. Todi, Pres.
EIN: 232744913
Codes: FD2

46535
Betts Foundation
1800 Pennsylvania Ave. W.
Warren, PA 16365-1932 (814) 723-1250
Application address: P.O. Box 88, Warren, PA 16365
Contact: Richard T. Betts, Tr.

Established in 1957 in PA.
Donor(s): Betts Industries, Inc.
Financial data (yr. ended 12/31/01): Grants paid, $181,281; assets, $3,120,062 (M); gifts received, $25,000; expenditures, $214,375; qualifying distributions, $180,650.
Limitations: Giving primarily in Warren County, PA.
Application information: Contact school for scholarship information.
Trustees: C.R. Betts, R.E. Betts, R.T. Betts, M.D. Hedges.
EIN: 256035169
Codes: CS, FD2, CD

46536
Ford E. & Harriet R. Curtis Foundation
c/o PNC Bank, N.A.
620 Liberty Ave., MS: P2-PTPP-25-1
Pittsburgh, PA 15222
Contact: John Culbertson, Tr. Off., PNC Bank, N.A.

Established in 1966.
Financial data (yr. ended 12/31/01): Grants paid, $181,000; assets, $435,610 (M); expenditures, $183,522; qualifying distributions, $180,878.
Limitations: Applications not accepted. Giving on a national basis.
Application information: Contributes only to pre-selected organizations.
Trustee: PNC Bank, N.A.
EIN: 256076910
Codes: FD2

46537
E. G. & Klara M. Smith Foundation
3333 Penn Ave.
West Lawn, PA 19609

Established in 1987 in PA.
Donor(s): E.G. Smith, Inc., Klara M. Smith, Terre Hill Concrete.
Financial data (yr. ended 12/31/01): Grants paid, $180,792; assets, $585,080 (M); gifts received, $297,378; expenditures, $181,822; qualifying distributions, $181,822.
Limitations: Applications not accepted. Giving limited to PA.
Application information: Contributes only to pre-selected organizations.
Officers: Klara M. Smith, Chair.; Janis L. Weller, Pres.; John Glass, V.P.; E.G. Smith, Secy.-Treas.
EIN: 232494804
Codes: FD2

46538
The James B. and Eileen Ryan Family Foundation, Inc.
122 Center St., Ste. 2
St. Marys, PA 15827

Established in 1999 in PA.
Donor(s): James Ryan, Eileen Ryan.
Financial data (yr. ended 12/31/00): Grants paid, $180,429; assets, $103,491 (M); gifts received, $254,212; expenditures, $192,636; qualifying distributions, $187,169.
Limitations: Giving primarily in Elk County, PA.
Trustees: Eileen Ryan, James Ryan.
EIN: 251839459
Codes: FD2

46539
Paul G. Benedum, Jr. Foundation
1500 Benedum Trees Bldg.
Pittsburgh, PA 15222-1794
Contact: Paul G. Benedum, Jr., Chair.

Established in 1997 in PA.
Donor(s): Paul G. Benedum, Jr.
Financial data (yr. ended 12/31/01): Grants paid, $180,000; assets, $3,161,831 (M); expenditures, $235,957; qualifying distributions, $187,080.
Limitations: Giving primarily in Pittsburgh, PA.
Application information: Application form not required.
Officers and Directors:* Paul G. Benedum, Jr.,* Chair.; Henry A. Bergstrom, Jr., V.P.; Thomas L. Myron, Jr.,* Secy.-Treas.; Richard F. Bumer, C.I.O.
Trustees: John C. Harmon, Michael S. Higgins, John McClay, Edwin F. Scheetz, Jr.
EIN: 232887993
Codes: FD2

46540
Wurster Family Foundation
940 Haverford Rd., Ste. 103
Bryn Mawr, PA 19010

Established in 1997 in PA.
Donor(s): William H. Wurster.
Financial data (yr. ended 12/31/01): Grants paid, $180,000; assets, $2,548,492 (M); expenditures, $230,477; qualifying distributions, $181,906.
Limitations: Applications not accepted.
Application information: Contributes only to pre-selected organizations.
Officers and Trustees:* William H. Wurster,* Pres.; Janine Wurster Putnam,* V.P.; William Glendon Wurster,* V.P.; Donna Ellis, Secy.; Anthony Melvin, Treas.; Jeanne D. Wurster.
EIN: 237880440
Codes: FD2

46541
The Kiefer Charitable Foundation
c/o Mellon Bank, N.A.
1735 Market St., 193-0429
Philadelphia, PA 19103
Contact: Theresa J. Zaccagni

Established in 1992 in PA.
Donor(s): Jacob W. Kiefer.
Financial data (yr. ended 12/31/01): Grants paid, $179,893; assets, $1,548,095 (M); gifts received, $5,732; expenditures, $185,800; qualifying distributions, $181,859.
Limitations: Giving primarily in Savannah, GA.
Trustees: Jacob W. Kiefer, Mellon Bank, N.A.
EIN: 256398522
Codes: FD2

46542
The Max Delfiner Memorial Foundation
c/o Greene Tweed & Co.
P.O. Box 305
Kulpsville, PA 19443-0305

Established in 1989 in PA.
Donor(s): Charlotte Sperber, Greene Tweed & Co.
Financial data (yr. ended 12/31/01): Grants paid, $178,450; assets, $1,513,035 (M); expenditures, $180,924; qualifying distributions, $177,448.
Limitations: Applications not accepted. Giving primarily in New York, NY.
Application information: Contributes only to pre-selected organizations.
Trustee: Charlotte Sperber.
EIN: 236956480
Codes: FD2

46543
Butz Foundation
P.O. Box 509
Allentown, PA 18105

Established in 1997 in PA.
Donor(s): Lee A. Butz, Dolores A. Butz.
Financial data (yr. ended 06/30/01): Grants paid, $178,000; assets, $857,710 (M); gifts received, $318,550; expenditures, $179,250; qualifying distributions, $177,662.
Limitations: Applications not accepted. Giving primarily in PA.
Application information: Contributes only to pre-selected organizations.
Officers: Lee A. Butz, C.E.O. and V.P.; Greg L. Butz, Pres.; Eric R. Butz, V.P.; Shari Butz McKeever, V.P.; Dolores A. Butz, Secy.
EIN: 232940646
Codes: FD2

46544
Posel Foundation
212 Walnut St.
Philadelphia, PA 19106

Established in 1989 in PA.
Donor(s): Ramon L. Posel, Sidney L. Posel.
Financial data (yr. ended 08/31/01): Grants paid, $177,324; assets, $3,228,277 (M); gifts received, $736,860; expenditures, $190,145; qualifying distributions, $177,324.
Limitations: Applications not accepted. Giving primarily in Philadelphia, PA.
Application information: Contributes only to pre-selected organizations.
Directors: Ramon L. Posel, Sidney L. Posel.
EIN: 232581520
Codes: FD2

46545
James T. Hambay Foundation
Allfirst
21 E. Market St., M/C402-130
York, PA 17401-1500 (717) 652-7911
Application address: P.O. Box 2961, Harrisburg, PA 17105
Contact: Joe Macri, Trust Off., Allfirst

Established in 1941 in PA.
Donor(s): J.T. Hambay.‡
Financial data (yr. ended 12/31/00): Grants paid, $177,313; assets, $3,425,572 (M); expenditures, $205,119; qualifying distributions, $167,647.
Limitations: Giving limited to Harrisburg, PA, and vicinity.
Application information: Application form required.
Trustees: Worthington C. Flowers, Allfirst.
EIN: 236243877
Codes: FD2, GTI

46546
Martin D. Cohen Family Foundation
(Formerly J & J Charitable Foundation)
2940 William Penn Hwy.
Easton, PA 18045
Contact: Martin D. Cohen, Pres.

Established in 1984 in PA.
Donor(s): Martin D. Cohen.
Financial data (yr. ended 12/31/00): Grants paid, $176,104; assets, $1,817,656 (M); gifts received, $175,395; expenditures, $194,408; qualifying distributions, $185,383.
Limitations: Giving primarily in PA.
Application information: Application form required.
Officers: Martin D. Cohen, Pres.; Edward Rubin, V.P.
EIN: 232294358
Codes: FD2, GTI

46547
Leon Falk Family Trust
3315 Grant Bldg.
Pittsburgh, PA 15219 (412) 261-5533
Contact: Sigo Falk, Chair.

Trust established in 1952 in PA.
Donor(s): Leon Falk, Jr.,‡ Marjorie L. Falk.‡
Financial data (yr. ended 12/31/01): Grants paid, $175,200; assets, $3,849,748 (M); gifts received, $3,745; expenditures, $187,524; qualifying distributions, $182,201.
Limitations: Applications not accepted. Giving primarily in Allegheny County, PA.
Application information: The grants program is limited to requests for proposals initiated by the trust. Unsolicited requests for funds not accepted.
Trustees: Sigo Falk, Chair.; Andrew D. Falk, Margaret F. Steckel.

EIN: 256065756
Codes: FD2

46548
The Tioga Foundation
2450 Wheatsheaf Ln.
Philadelphia, PA 19137

Established in 1987 in PA.
Donor(s): Eleanor Keiser, Morton Keiser.
Financial data (yr. ended 12/31/01): Grants paid, $175,115; assets, $1,139,208 (M); gifts received, $160,000; expenditures, $175,244; qualifying distributions, $175,115.
Limitations: Applications not accepted. Giving primarily in Philadelphia, PA.
Application information: Contributes only to pre-selected organizations.
Directors: Andrew Keiser, Bennett Keiser, David Keiser, Eleanor Keiser, Morton Keiser.
EIN: 222809250
Codes: FD2

46549
The Graham Foundation
271 S. Pine St.
Hazleton, PA 18201
Contact: Evelyn Dennis, Pres.

Established in 1987 in PA.
Donor(s): Seymour C. Graham, Evelyn Dennis.
Financial data (yr. ended 12/31/01): Grants paid, $175,000; assets, $4,862 (M); gifts received, $170,000; expenditures, $176,111; qualifying distributions, $175,548.
Limitations: Giving primarily in Hazelton, PA.
Application information: Application form not required.
Officers and Directors:* Evelyn Dennis,* Pres.; Russell Graham,* V.P.; Evelyn R. Dennis,* Secy.; Martha D. Cohn, Bradley Graham.
EIN: 232505366
Codes: FD2

46550
Ruth Danley & William Enoch Moore Fund
c/o PNC Advisors
620 Liberty Ave., P2-PTPP-10-2
Pittsburgh, PA 15272-2705 (412) 762-3502
FAX: (412) 762-5439; *E-mail:* bruce.bickel@pncadvisors.com
Contact: Bruce Bickel, Mng. Dir.

Established in 1992 in PA.
Donor(s): Grace Danley Moore.
Financial data (yr. ended 12/31/01): Grants paid, $175,000; assets, $7,265,700 (M); gifts received, $1,647,016; expenditures, $257,457; qualifying distributions, $196,949.
Limitations: Applications not accepted.
Application information: Contributes only to pre-selected organizations.
Trustee: PNC Bank, N.A.
EIN: 256399593

46551
The Peirce Family Foundation, Inc.
707 Grant St., Ste. 2500
Pittsburgh, PA 15219-1919 (412) 281-7229
Contact: Robert N. Peirce, Jr., Pres.

Established in 1997 in PA.
Donor(s): Robert N. Peirce, Jr., Joan Peirce.
Financial data (yr. ended 12/31/01): Grants paid, $173,484; assets, $3,426,249 (M); gifts received, $910,787; expenditures, $226,835; qualifying distributions, $173,484.
Limitations: Giving primarily in PA.
Officers: Robert N. Peirce, Jr., Pres.; Joan Peirce, Secy.
EIN: 232903074

Codes: FD2

46552
The Hilda and Preston Davis Foundation
c/o John Iskrant
1600 Market St., Ste. 3600
Philadelphia, PA 19103
Application address: 35 Mason St., Greenwich, CT 06830, tel.: (203) 629-8320
Contact: Geoffrey M. Parkinson, Dir.

Established in 1998 in PA.
Donor(s): Hilda J. Davis.
Financial data (yr. ended 12/31/01): Grants paid, $173,198; assets, $5,525,860 (M); gifts received, $1,500,010; expenditures, $294,780; qualifying distributions, $224,802.
Limitations: Giving on a national basis, with some emphasis in CT.
Trustees: Hilda J. Davis, John D. Iskrant, Geoffrey M. Parkinson.
EIN: 237966458
Codes: FD2

46553
H & H Charitable Trust, Inc.
300 E. Lancaster Ave., Ste. 104
Wynnewood, PA 19096-1915

Donor(s): Harriett B. Kravitz.
Financial data (yr. ended 12/31/01): Grants paid, $172,851; assets, $3,040,578 (M); expenditures, $174,101; qualifying distributions, $172,851.
Limitations: Applications not accepted. Giving primarily in NY and Philadelphia, PA.
Application information: Contributes only to pre-selected organizations.
Trustee: Harriett B. Kravitz.
EIN: 222924281
Codes: FD2

46554
Jacob R. Hershey Trust for Charities
c/o Fulton Financial Advisors, N.A.
P.O. Box 3215
Lancaster, PA 17604

Established in 1999 in PA.
Donor(s): Jacob R. Hershey.‡
Financial data (yr. ended 11/30/01): Grants paid, $172,295; assets, $2,468,556 (M); expenditures, $194,283; qualifying distributions, $171,453.
Limitations: Applications not accepted. Giving primarily in Lancaster, PA.
Application information: Contributes only to pre-selected organizations.
Trustee: Fulton Financial Advisors, N.A.
EIN: 256684496
Codes: FD2

46555
John Family Foundation
R.R. 1, Box 452
Winfield, PA 17889-9661

Established in 1991 in PA.
Donor(s): Paul R. John, Mildred D. John.
Financial data (yr. ended 12/31/01): Grants paid, $171,500; assets, $3,574,583 (M); gifts received, $296,325; expenditures, $186,806; qualifying distributions, $169,366.
Limitations: Giving primarily in PA.
Officers: Paul R. John, Pres.; Mildred D. John, V.P.
Director: Robert L. Shangraw.
EIN: 232616038
Codes: FD2

46556
C. John & Josephine Muller Foundation, Inc.
2800 Grant Ave.
Philadelphia, PA 19114

Established in 1984 in PA.
Donor(s): C. John Muller, Josephine Muller,‡ Clement & Muller, Inc.
Financial data (yr. ended 12/31/00): Grants paid, $171,000; assets, $910,531 (M); expenditures, $173,960; qualifying distributions, $171,000.
Limitations: Applications not accepted. Giving primarily in PA, with emphasis on the Philadelphia area.
Application information: Contributes only to pre-selected organizations.
Directors: Barbara Ailtmar, C. John Muller, Sandra Muller.
EIN: 232324413
Codes: FD2

46557
Hannah S. and Samuel A. Cohn Memorial Foundation
2 E. Broad St.
Hazleton, PA 18201

Established in 1987 in PA.
Donor(s): Thomas J. Pritzker.
Financial data (yr. ended 03/31/01): Grants paid, $170,676; assets, $4,035,228 (M); gifts received, $7,300; expenditures, $208,916; qualifying distributions, $172,476.
Limitations: Applications not accepted. Giving primarily in PA.
Application information: Contributes only to pre-selected organizations.
Officers: Gerald L. Cohn, Pres.; Martin D. Cohn, Secy.
EIN: 232500519
Codes: FD2

46558
The Thomas P. Waters Foundation
c/o John Iskrant
1600 Market St., Ste. 3600
Philadelphia, PA 19103

Financial data (yr. ended 08/31/01): Grants paid, $170,300; assets, $3,108,229 (M); expenditures, $216,071; qualifying distributions, $184,429.
Limitations: Applications not accepted. Giving on a national basis.
Application information: Contributes only to pre-selected organizations.
Trustees: John D. Iskrant, Damon Waters, James A. Waters, Kenneth M. Waters, Patrick Waters, Robert T. Waters.
EIN: 237836361
Codes: FD2

46559
The Charles H. Taylor Family Foundation
c/o Mellon Bank, N.A.
P.O. Box 185
Pittsburgh, PA 15230-9897
Application address: c/o Boston Safe Deposit & Trust, 1 Boston Pl., Boston, MA 02108, tel.: (617) 722-7316
Contact: Richard Towle, Jr.

Established in 1994 in MA.
Financial data (yr. ended 12/31/01): Grants paid, $170,107; assets, $3,072,585 (M); expenditures, $183,495; qualifying distributions, $174,072.
Limitations: Giving primarily in MA and Manchaca, TX.
Trustees: Rosamond Taylor Dye, Charles B. Taylor, Jr., Dorothy A. Taylor, Pamela Taylor Wetzels, Walter Wetzels, Boston Safe Deposit & Trust Co.
EIN: 043254676

46559—PENNSYLVANIA

Codes: FD2

46560
M. Verna Butterer Educational Trust
P.O. Box 273
Fountainville, PA 18923 (215) 249-0503
Contact: Elissa J. Kirkegard, Admin.

Established in 1996 in PA.
Donor(s): M. Verna Butterer.‡
Financial data (yr. ended 01/31/02): Grants paid, $169,941; assets, $4,355,827 (M); expenditures, $207,716; qualifying distributions, $203,378.
Limitations: Giving limited to Bucks County, PA.
Application information: Application forms available through public high school guidance departments in Bucks County, PA. Application form required.
Trustee: Carol A. Baumhauer, Elizabeth Boudreau, Robert W. Butterer.
EIN: 237751390
Codes: FD2, GTI

46561
The Rocco and Barbara Martino Foundation, Inc.
c/o Rocco L. Martino
512 Watch Hill Rd.
Villanova, PA 19085

Established in 1996 in PA.
Donor(s): Barbara I. Martino, Rocco L. Martino.
Financial data (yr. ended 12/31/01): Grants paid, $169,225; assets, $3,433,911 (M); expenditures, $245,294; qualifying distributions, $163,790.
Limitations: Applications not accepted. Giving primarily in PA.
Application information: Contributes only to pre-selected organizations.
Officers and Directors:* Rocco L. Martino,* Pres.; Barbara I. Martino,* V.P.; John F. Martino,* V.P.; Joseph A. Martino, V.P.; Paul G. Martino, V.P.; Peter D. Martino, V.P.; Fr. Milton E. Jordan.
EIN: 232834739
Codes: FD2

46562
Hankin Foundation
(Formerly Bernard & Henrietta Hankin Foundation)
707 Eagleview Blvd.
P.O. Box 562
Exton, PA 19341
Contact: Robin S. Mukalian

Established in 1984 in PA.
Donor(s): Bernard Hankin.
Financial data (yr. ended 11/30/01): Grants paid, $169,000; assets, $450,967 (M); expenditures, $482,000; qualifying distributions, $164,580.
Limitations: Giving primarily in PA.
Application information: Application form required.
Officers: Robert S. Hankin, Pres.; Henrietta Hankin, Secy.-Treas.
EIN: 251479501
Codes: FD2

46563
Jane B. Barsumian Memorial Fund
c/o First Union National Bank
600 Penn St., P.O. Box 1102
Reading, PA 19603-1102

Established in 1997 in PA.
Financial data (yr. ended 12/31/00): Grants paid, $167,400; assets, $3,943,280 (M); expenditures, $199,664; qualifying distributions, $164,544.
Limitations: Applications not accepted. Giving limited to the greater Lancaster, PA, area.

Application information: Contributes only to pre-selected organizations.
Trustee: First Union National Bank.
EIN: 236492481
Codes: FD2

46564
Leslie E. Morgan Charitable Trust
c/o PNC Bank, N.A.
P.O. Box 937
Scranton, PA 18501

Established in 1985 in PA.
Financial data (yr. ended 12/31/00): Grants paid, $167,354; assets, $5,315,793 (M); expenditures, $198,740; qualifying distributions, $183,202.
Limitations: Applications not accepted. Giving primarily in PA.
Application information: Contributes only to pre-selected organizations.
Trustee: PNC Bank, N.A.
EIN: 237816593
Codes: FD2

46565
Jonathan E. Rhoads Trust
131 W. Walnut Ln.
Philadelphia, PA 19144-2611 (610) 395-8000
Contact: Edward O.F. Rhoads, Secy.-Treas.

Established in 1963 in PA.
Donor(s): Jonathan E. Rhoads, Sr., Philip G. Rhoads, Jonathan E. Rhoads, Jr., George G. Rhoads, Teresa F. Rhoads.‡
Financial data (yr. ended 12/31/01): Grants paid, $167,300; assets, $2,503,196 (M); gifts received, $20,382; expenditures, $171,967; qualifying distributions, $166,483.
Limitations: Giving primarily in PA, with emphasis on Philadelphia.
Application information: Application form not required.
Officers and Trustees:* Jonathan E. Rhoads, Sr.,* Chair.; Edward O.F. Rhoads,* Secy.-Treas.
EIN: 236385682
Codes: FD2

46566
Nelson Family Foundation
c/o John Iskrant
1600 Market St., Ste. 3600
Philadelphia, PA 19103
Application address: 9 Misty Ridge Manor, Atlanta, GA 30327, tel.: (404) 256-9114
Contact: Kent C. Nelson, Tr.

Established in 2000 in PA.
Donor(s): Kent C. Nelson.
Financial data (yr. ended 02/28/02): Grants paid, $166,563; assets, $948,938 (M); expenditures, $196,063; qualifying distributions, $166,563.
Application information: Application form not required.
Trustees: Kent C. Nelson, Ann Starr.
EIN: 233064865

46567
Clarence J. Venne Foundation
645 White Ash Dr.
Langhorne, PA 19047-8026

Established in 2000 in PA.
Donor(s): Clarence J. Venne.
Financial data (yr. ended 12/31/00): Grants paid, $166,300; assets, $768,996 (M); gifts received, $937,060; expenditures, $177,064; qualifying distributions, $176,414.
Officers: Clarence J. Venne, Pres.; Anne Venne, V.P. and Treas.; Ronald Bluestein, V.P.; Margaret Wallick, Secy.
EIN: 233040515

Codes: FD2

46568
Pittsburgh Child Guidance Foundation
425 6th Ave., Ste. 2460
Pittsburgh, PA 15219-1851 (412) 434-1665
FAX: (412) 434-0406; *E-mail:* pcgf@smartbuilding.org; *URL:* http://trfn.clpgh.org/pcgf
Contact: Claire A. Walker, Ph.D., Exec. Dir.

Established in 1982 in PA.
Financial data (yr. ended 12/31/01): Grants paid, $166,267; assets, $5,851,065 (M); expenditures, $278,827; qualifying distributions, $287,172.
Limitations: Giving limited to Allegheny County, PA.
Publications: Informational brochure (including application guidelines).
Application information: Applicants should contact the foundation prior to submitting a proposal. Application form required.
Officers and Trustees:* Jeffrey A. Wlahofsky,* Pres.; W. Thomas McGough, Jr.,* V.P.; Nancy D. Washington, Ph.D.,* Secy.; Thelma Lovette Morris,* Treas.; Rev. Carmen A. D'Amico, Judith M. Davenport, D.M.D., Jesse Fife, Jr., David B. Hartmann, M.D., Claudia L. Hussein, Steven W. Jewell, M.D., Kelly J. Kelleher, M.D., Evelyn L. Murrin, Lloyd F. Stamy, Jr., Karen VanderVen, Ph.D.
EIN: 250965465
Codes: FD2

46569
Castelli Charitable Trust
c/o PNC Bank, N.A., MS: P2-PTPP-25-1
2 PNC Plz., 620 Liberty Ave., 10th Fl.
Pittsburgh, PA 15222-2719
Scholarship application address: 35 W. Pittsburgh, Rear, Greensburg, PA 15601, tel.: (412) 837-1910
Contact: Gregory T. Nichols, Exec. Dir., Charitable Scholarship Fund

Established in 1984 in PA.
Financial data (yr. ended 06/30/01): Grants paid, $166,000; assets, $2,192,304 (M); expenditures, $197,779; qualifying distributions, $182,991.
Limitations: Giving limited to residents of Westmoreland County, PA.
Application information: Application form available from high school guidance counselors. Application form required.
Trustee: PNC Bank, N.A.
EIN: 256242226
Codes: FD2, GTI

46570
Alexis Rosenberg Foundation
P.O. Box 540
Plymouth Meeting, PA 19462 (610) 828-8145
FAX: (610) 834-8175
Contact: Judith L. Bardes, Mgr.

Established in 1983 in PA.
Donor(s): Alexis Rosenberg.‡
Financial data (yr. ended 06/30/01): Grants paid, $166,000; assets, $3,673,633 (M); expenditures, $232,990; qualifying distributions, $174,370.
Limitations: Giving primarily in the greater metropolitan Philadelphia, PA, area.
Publications: Informational brochure (including application guidelines).
Application information: No more than 1 application will be considered in any 12-month period except under special circumstances. Application form required.
Trustees: William Epstein, William S. Greenfield, M.D., Charles Kahn, Jr., Mellon Bank, N.A.
EIN: 232222722

Codes: FD2

46571
North Penn Charitable Foundation
562 Constitution Rd.
Lansdale, PA 19446-4164

Donor(s): Garfield Edmonds, Lorraine Edmonds.
Financial data (yr. ended 11/30/00): Grants paid, $165,185; assets, $612,681 (M); gifts received, $25,000; expenditures, $165,629; qualifying distributions, $165,185.
Limitations: Applications not accepted. Giving primarily in NY and PA.
Application information: Contributes only to pre-selected organizations.
Trustees: Garfield Edmonds, Lorraine Edmonds.
EIN: 236802678
Codes: FD2

46572
The Julian A. and Lois G. Brodsky Foundation
c/o Center Square E.
1500 Market St., 35th Fl.
Philadelphia, PA 19102
Contact: Julian A. Brodsky, Dir.

Established in 1994 in PA.
Donor(s): Julian A. Brodsky.
Financial data (yr. ended 12/31/00): Grants paid, $165,148; assets, $2,822,393 (M); expenditures, $179,686; qualifying distributions, $163,461.
Limitations: Giving primarily in Philadelphia, PA.
Directors: Debra G. Brodsky, Ellen G. Brodsky, Julian A. Brodsky, Laura G. Brodsky, Lois G. Brodsky.
EIN: 232785280
Codes: FD2

46573
W.L.G. Charitable Foundation
c/o PNC Bank, N.A.
1600 Market St.
Philadelphia, PA 19103 (215) 563-6417
Application address: c/o Ynette Campbell, The Philadelphia Foundation, 1234 Market St., Ste. 1800, Philadelphia, PA 19107-3794
Contact: Margaret A. West

Established in 1990 in PA.
Financial data (yr. ended 04/30/01): Grants paid, $164,369; assets, $3,344,309 (M); expenditures, $194,778; qualifying distributions, $162,500.
Limitations: Giving primarily in New York, NY and Philadelphia, PA.
Application information: Most income goes to the Philadelphia Foundation. Income is distributed through the W.L.G. Endowment Fund. Application form not required.
Trustee: PNC Bank, N.A.
EIN: 237649667
Codes: FD2

46574
Keystone Savings Foundation
c/o Keystone Savings Bank
P.O. Box 25012
Lehigh Valley, PA 18002-5012 (610) 861-5000
Contact: Nancy A. Billiard, Secy.-Treas.

Established in 1987 in PA.
Donor(s): Keystone Savings Bank.
Financial data (yr. ended 12/31/01): Grants paid, $164,024; assets, $1,018,635 (M); expenditures, $164,086; qualifying distributions, $163,587.
Limitations: Giving limited to areas of company operations in Lehigh Valley, PA.
Publications: Annual report, application guidelines.
Application information: Application form required.

Officers: Robert S. Pharo, Pres.; Wallace M. Long, V.P.; Frederick E. Kutteroff, Secy.-Treas.
EIN: 232407218
Codes: CS, FD2, CD

46575
Harold and Renee Berger Foundation
1703 Rittenhouse Sq.
Philadelphia, PA 19103 (215) 875-3000
Contact: Harold Berger, Pres.

Established in 1986 in PA.
Donor(s): Harold Berger.
Financial data (yr. ended 12/31/00): Grants paid, $163,095; assets, $823,388 (M); expenditures, $163,662; qualifying distributions, $163,095.
Limitations: Giving primarily in Philadelphia, PA.
Officers: Harold Berger, Pres.; Renee Berger, V.P.
EIN: 232439490
Codes: FD2

46576
Harold & Elaine Friedland Family Foundation
c/o Kofsky & Co.
1001 City Ave., Ste. W8513
Wynnewood, PA 19096
Application address: c/o P. Kofsky, 121 S. Broad St., Ste. 400, Philadelphia, PA 19107, tel.: (215) 893-9041

Established in 1997 in PA.
Financial data (yr. ended 12/31/01): Grants paid, $162,935; assets, $3,174,081 (M); expenditures, $189,449; qualifying distributions, $172,935.
Limitations: Giving primarily in Philadelphia, PA.
Trustees: Elaine Friedland, Harold Friedland.
EIN: 232841007
Codes: FD2

46577
Matthew T. Mellon Foundation
c/o Mellon Bank, N.A.
P.O. Box 185
Pittsburgh, PA 15230-9897
Application address: 3 Mellon Bank Ctr., Pittsburgh, PA 15259, tel.: (412) 234-5892
Contact: Leonard B. Richards

Established in 1946 in PA.
Donor(s): Matthew T. Mellon.‡
Financial data (yr. ended 12/31/99): Grants paid, $161,000; assets, $4,188,099 (M); expenditures, $177,942; qualifying distributions, $159,363.
Limitations: Giving primarily in New York, NY.
Application information: Contact foundation for application information.
Trustee: Mellon Bank, N.A.
EIN: 251286841
Codes: FD2

46578
The Mary B. & Alvin P. Gutman Fund
c/o CMS Cos.
1926 Arch St.
Philadelphia, PA 19103-1484
Contact: Alvin P. Gutman, Chair.

Established around 1961.
Donor(s): Alvin P. Gutman.
Financial data (yr. ended 11/30/01): Grants paid, $160,204; assets, $1,344,110 (M); gifts received, $267,584; expenditures, $178,868; qualifying distributions, $160,204.
Limitations: Giving primarily in Philadelphia, PA.
Application information: Application form not required.
Officers and Trustees:* Alvin P. Gutman,* Chair.; Mary B. Gutman,* Secy.; Helen J. Gutman,* Treas.; James C. Gutman.
EIN: 236391200
Codes: FD2

46579
PKG Foundation
c/o Elizabeth Kapnek Grenald
653 Hidden Pond Ln.
Huntingdon Valley, PA 19006-7724

Established in 1999 in PA.
Donor(s): Elizabeth Kapnek Grenald.
Financial data (yr. ended 11/30/00): Grants paid, $160,086; assets, $3,278,355 (M); gifts received, $3,114,578; expenditures, $182,879; qualifying distributions, $160,086.
Limitations: Giving primarily in PA.
Application information: Application form required.
Officers: Elizabeth Kapnek Grenald, Pres.; Theodore Kapnek III, V.P.; Linda Kapnek Brown, Secy.-Treas.
EIN: 233019837
Codes: FD2

46580
The Armstrong Foundation
(Formerly John C. and Eve S. Bogle Foundation)
2 Penn Center Plz., Ste. 400
Philadelphia, PA 19102

Established in 1993 in PA.
Donor(s): John C. Bogle.
Financial data (yr. ended 12/31/01): Grants paid, $160,000; assets, $4,466,590 (M); expenditures, $163,662; qualifying distributions, $160,197.
Limitations: Applications not accepted. Giving primarily in CT, MA and PA.
Application information: Contributes only to pre-selected organizations.
Trustees: Eve S. Bogle, John C. Bogle.
EIN: 232642354
Codes: FD2

46581
Boiron Research Foundation, Inc.
c/o Thierry Boiron
6 Campus Blvd.
Newtown Square, PA 19073

Established in 1987 in MD.
Donor(s): Boiron-Borneman Company.
Financial data (yr. ended 12/31/01): Grants paid, $159,294; assets, $105,280 (M); gifts received, $168,231; expenditures, $173,003; qualifying distributions, $218,032.
Limitations: Giving on a national basis.
Application information: Unsolicited requests for funds not accepted.
Officers: Thierry Boiron, Pres. and Secy.-Treas.; Christian Boiron, Pres.; Jacky Abecassis, V.P.; Theirry Montfort, V.P.
Board Memeber: Philippe Belon.
EIN: 521268329
Codes: CS, FD2, CD, GTI

46582
The Mary E. Groff Surgical and Medical Research and Education Charitable Trust
c/o Cole Vastine
20 N. Waterloo Rd.
Devon, PA 19333

Established in 1999 in PA.
Donor(s): Mary E. Groff.‡
Financial data (yr. ended 12/31/00): Grants paid, $158,477; assets, $5,804,115 (M); gifts received, $275,957; expenditures, $261,403; qualifying distributions, $179,956.
Limitations: Applications not accepted. Giving primarily in PA.
Application information: Contributes only to pre-selected organizations.
Officer and Trustees:* Manucher Fellahnejad,* Mgr.; Anne M. Cusack, Herbert Wallace.

46582—PENNSYLVANIA

EIN: 232725113
Codes: FD2

46583
The Wilbur Ball Foundation
c/o Herr, Potts and Herr
175 Strafford Ave., Ste. 314
Wayne, PA 19087-2502
Contact: J. Lawrence Wilson, Tr.

Established in 1998 in PA.
Donor(s): J. Lawrence Wilson, Barbara B. Wilson.
Financial data (yr. ended 12/31/01): Grants paid, $158,000; assets, $1,178,098 (M); expenditures, $161,853; qualifying distributions, $158,540.
Limitations: Applications not accepted.
Application information: Contributes only to pre-selected organizations.
Trustees: Alexander E. Wilson, Barbara B. Wilson, J. Lawrence Wilson, Lawrence B. Wilson.
EIN: 237965324
Codes: FD2

46584
Joseph T. & Helen M. Simpson Foundation
21 E. Market St., M/C 402-130
York, PA 17401-1500
Application address: P.O. Box 1103, Harrisburg, PA 17108
Contact: Jerry T. Simpson

Established in 1954 in PA.
Financial data (yr. ended 12/31/00): Grants paid, $157,825; assets, $3,082,078 (M); expenditures, $185,352; qualifying distributions, $151,554.
Limitations: Giving primarily in Harrisburg, PA.
Application information: Application form not required.
Trustees: Helen M. Simpson, Hilary M. Simpson, Hugh J.T. Simpson, Allfirst.
EIN: 236242538
Codes: FD2

46585
The Anna F. Doell Memorial Trust Fund
c/o Allfirst
21 E. Market St., M/C 402-130
York, PA 17401-1500

Financial data (yr. ended 12/31/01): Grants paid, $157,059; assets, $3,910,642 (M); gifts received, $116,951; expenditures, $198,451; qualifying distributions, $156,043.
Limitations: Applications not accepted. Giving primarily in PA.
Application information: Contributes only to pre-selected organizations.
Trustees: Walter C. Flatt, Jr., Allfirst.
EIN: 256536714
Codes: FD2

46586
Lydia Fisher Warner Memorial Trust
c/o First Union National Bank
Broad and Walnut Sts.
Philadelphia, PA 19109
Contact: Vicki Hills

Donor(s): Lydia Fisher Warner.‡
Financial data (yr. ended 12/31/01): Grants paid, $156,505; assets, $2,172,595 (M); expenditures, $161,411; qualifying distributions, $157,530.
Limitations: Giving primarily in Philadelphia, PA.
Trustee: First Union National Bank.
EIN: 236219706
Codes: FD2

46587
Ashland Foundation
645 Willow Valley Sq., Ste. J-305
Lancaster, PA 17602-4872
Contact: Paul G. Reidler, V.P.

Established in 1949.
Financial data (yr. ended 10/31/01): Grants paid, $156,180; assets, $2,974,040 (M); expenditures, $184,989; qualifying distributions, $184,163.
Limitations: Giving primarily in Lancaster and Schulkill counties, PA.
Application information: Application form not required.
Officers: Carl J. Reidler, Pres.; Paul G. Reidler, V.P. and Admin.; Helen Reidler, Secy.; Diane K. Reidler, Treas.
EIN: 236245778
Codes: FD2

46588
Reuben & Mollie Gordon Foundation
121 S. Broad St., 4th Fl.
Philadelphia, PA 19107 (215) 893-9040
Contact: C. Kofsky, Tr.

Established in 1960 in PA.
Donor(s): Reuben Gordon.‡
Financial data (yr. ended 12/31/00): Grants paid, $156,000; assets, $2,515,281 (M); expenditures, $159,056; qualifying distributions, $156,256.
Limitations: Giving primarily in PA.
Trustees: Judith J. Jamison, Charles Kofsky, Fred Lieberman, Harry Lieberman.
EIN: 236251826
Codes: FD2

46589
Judith & David Wachs Family Foundation, Inc.
215 W. Church Rd., Ste. 108
King of Prussia, PA 19406 (610) 277-1200
Contact: Rachel A. Wachs, Secy.

Established in 1985 in PA.
Donor(s): Second Chance Fund, David Wachs.
Financial data (yr. ended 09/30/01): Grants paid, $155,301; assets, $1,166,774 (M); gifts received, $1,212,500; expenditures, $164,664; qualifying distributions, $155,301.
Limitations: Applications not accepted. Giving primarily in PA.
Application information: Contributes only to pre-selected organizations.
Officers: David Wachs, Pres.; Judith Wachs, V.P. and Treas.; Martin Wachs, V.P.; Michael Wachs, V.P.; Philip Wachs, V.P.; Rachel A. Wachs, Secy.
EIN: 222682604
Codes: FD2

46590
The Emporium Foundation, Inc.
2 E. 4th St.
Emporium, PA 15834-1443 (814) 486-3333
Contact: L. William Smith, Treas.

Incorporated in 1929 in PA.
Financial data (yr. ended 12/31/00): Grants paid, $155,244; assets, $4,846,835 (M); expenditures, $190,287; qualifying distributions, $168,839.
Limitations: Giving limited to Cameron County, PA.
Application information: Application form not required.
Officers: James B. Miller, Pres.; Edward B. Lundberg, V.P.; Edwin W. Tompkins III, Secy.; L. William Smith, Treas.
EIN: 250995760
Codes: FD2

46591
The Morris Charitable Trust
440 Parkview Dr.
Wynnewood, PA 19096-1640
Contact: Michael J. Morris, Tr.

Established in 1988 in PA.
Donor(s): Michael J. Morris.
Financial data (yr. ended 12/31/01): Grants paid, $154,995; assets, $1,753,714 (M); expenditures, $157,755; qualifying distributions, $154,995.
Limitations: Giving primarily in Philadelphia, PA.
Application information: Application form not required.
Trustees: Michael J. Morris, Rose M. Morris.
EIN: 222798233
Codes: FD2

46592
Wolf Family Foundation
(Formerly John M. Wolf Charitable Trust)
c/o John M. Wolf, Sr.
125 McFann Rd.
Valencia, PA 16059

Established in 1968.
Financial data (yr. ended 12/31/99): Grants paid, $154,668; assets, $0 (M); expenditures, $160,860; qualifying distributions, $154,668.
Limitations: Applications not accepted. Giving primarily in Pittsburgh, PA.
Officer: John M. Wolf, Sr., Mgr.
Board Members: James Henry Wolf, John M. Wolf, Jr.
EIN: 256106150
Codes: TN

46593
Stanley Benzel Charitable Foundation
(also known as Rose Garden Foundation)
1514 Hanover Ave.
Allentown, PA 18103

Established in 1984 in PA.
Donor(s): Stanley Benzel.
Financial data (yr. ended 12/31/00): Grants paid, $154,378; assets, $326,502 (M); gifts received, $223,627; expenditures, $155,457; qualifying distributions, $154,238.
Limitations: Applications not accepted. Giving primarily in NY.
Application information: Contributes only to pre-selected organizations.
Officer: Stanley Benzel, Pres.
EIN: 222776754
Codes: FD2

46594
Schwab-Spector-Rainess Foundation
P.O. Box 5967
Harrisburg, PA 17110-0967 (717) 255-7803
Contact: Morris Schwab, Tr.

Established about 1965 in PA.
Donor(s): Morris Schwab, D & H Distributing Co.
Financial data (yr. ended 12/31/01): Grants paid, $154,176; assets, $3,686,264 (M); gifts received, $35,321; expenditures, $177,553; qualifying distributions, $163,104.
Limitations: Giving primarily in Baltimore, MD, New York, NY and Harrisburg, PA.
Trustees: Israel Schwab, Morris Schwab.
EIN: 236401901
Codes: FD2

46595
The Stuckey Family Foundation
P.O. Box 65
Hollidaysburg, PA 16648

Established in 1989 in PA.

Donor(s): John W. Stuckey, Barbara A. Stuckey.
Financial data (yr. ended 12/31/00): Grants paid, $153,750; assets, $2,320,737 (M); gifts received, $84,713; expenditures, $172,651; qualifying distributions, $151,143.
Limitations: Applications not accepted. Giving primarily in PA.
Application information: Contributes only to pre-selected organizations.
Officers: John W. Stuckey, Pres.; Barbara A. Stuckey, Secy.; Jennifer Davis, Treas.
EIN: 251611905
Codes: FD2

46596
The Houghton-Carpenter Foundation
P.O. Box 930
Valley Forge, PA 19482-0930 (610) 666-4049
Contact: W.F. MacDonald, Jr., Tr.

Established in 1951 in PA.
Donor(s): Aaron E. Carpenter,‡ Edythe A. Carpenter,‡ E.F. Houghton & Co.
Financial data (yr. ended 06/30/01): Grants paid, $153,634; assets, $3,473,902 (M); expenditures, $168,303; qualifying distributions, $153,634.
Limitations: Giving primarily in PA.
Application information: Application form not required.
Trustees: Stephen B. Harris, Joseph P. Kromdyk, William F. MacDonald, Jr.
EIN: 236230874
Codes: FD2

46597
Up East, Inc.
P.O. Box 155
Chadds Ford, PA 19317
Contact: Andrew Wyeth, Tr.

Established in 1995 in DE, PA and ME.
Donor(s): Andrew N. Wyeth, Betsy James Wyeth.
Financial data (yr. ended 06/30/01): Grants paid, $153,385; assets, $12,270,516 (M); expenditures, $539,431; qualifying distributions, $795,342.
Limitations: Giving primarily in ME.
Application information: Application form not required.
Officers: Betsy James Wyeth, Pres.; Gail A. Graham, Secy.-Treas.
Trustees: William Prickett, J. Robinson West, Prof. John Wilmerding, Andrew N. Wyeth, James Browning Wyeth, Nicholas Wyeth.
EIN: 510367586
Codes: FD2

46598
Fund for Education
25 E. Athens Ave.
Ardmore, PA 19003

Established around 1986 in PA.
Financial data (yr. ended 12/31/00): Grants paid, $153,350; assets, $3,378,662 (M); gifts received, $9,000; expenditures, $160,415; qualifying distributions, $153,350.
Limitations: Applications not accepted. Giving limited to MA and PA.
Application information: Contributes only to pre-selected organizations.
Officer: Paul M. Prusky, Mgr.
Trustee: Susan M. Prusky.
EIN: 236849172
Codes: FD2

46599
The Charles F. Peters Foundation
c/o National City Bank of Pennsylvania
20 Stanwix St., Loc. 25-162
Pittsburgh, PA 15222 (412) 644-8002
Contact: Joanna M. Mayo, V.P., National City Bank of Pennsylvania

Established in 1965 in PA.
Donor(s): Charles F. Peters.‡
Financial data (yr. ended 12/31/01): Grants paid, $153,000; assets, $3,362,679 (M); expenditures, $186,591; qualifying distributions, $167,759.
Limitations: Giving limited to the McKeesport, PA, area.
Administrators: William H. Balter, Herman A. Haase, Robert A. Stone.
Trustee: National City Bank of Pennsylvania.
EIN: 256070765
Codes: FD2

46600
The Stewart Foundation
P.O. Box 902
York, PA 17405

Established in 1986 in PA.
Donor(s): York Building Products, Inc., Stewart & March, Inc.
Financial data (yr. ended 12/31/99): Grants paid, $152,830; assets, $707,657 (M); gifts received, $132,500; expenditures, $153,151; qualifying distributions, $152,830.
Limitations: Applications not accepted. Giving primarily in York, PA.
Application information: Contributes only to pre-selected organizations.
Officers: Gary A. Stewart, Pres.; Karyl L. Gilbert, Secy.-Treas.; Robert Stewart, Jr., Treas.
Directors: Terrence Stewart, Dale C. Voorheis.
EIN: 222762903
Codes: FD2

46601
Lois Lehrman Grass Foundation
(Formerly Lois F. Grass Foundation)
P.O. Box 593
Harrisburg, PA 17108-0593
Contact: Lois Lehrman Grass, Chair.

Established in 1972 in PA.
Donor(s): Lois Lehrman Grass, Jody Grass, Linda Grass Shapiro.
Financial data (yr. ended 11/30/01): Grants paid, $152,348; assets, $3,786,977 (M); gifts received, $2,499; expenditures, $171,669; qualifying distributions, $152,348.
Limitations: Giving primarily in Harrisburg, PA.
Application information: Application form not required.
Officer: Lois Lehrman Grass, Chair.
Directors: Linda Grass Shapiro, Elizabeth Grass Weese.
EIN: 237218005
Codes: FD2

46602
H. M. Bitner Charitable Trust
c/o Mellon Bank, N.A.
3 Mellon Bank Ctr., Rm. 4000
Pittsburgh, PA 15259-0001 (412) 234-1634
Contact: Annette Calgaro, V.P., Mellon Bank, N.A.

Established in 1955 in PA.
Donor(s): H.M. Bitner,‡ Evelyn H. Bitner.
Financial data (yr. ended 12/31/00): Grants paid, $151,650; assets, $2,552,975 (M); expenditures, $194,669; qualifying distributions, $166,428.
Limitations: Giving primarily in San Francisco, CA, Chicago, IL and Pittsburgh, PA.
Application information: Only approved applicants will be notified. Application form not required.
Trustees: John H. Bitner, Kerry Bitner, Evelyn Bitner Pearson, Priscilla Pearson, Mellon Bank, N.A.
EIN: 256018931
Codes: FD2

46603
Mark & Kimberley Miller Charitable Foundation
99 Little John Dr.
McMurray, PA 15317

Established in 1999 in PA.
Financial data (yr. ended 12/31/01): Grants paid, $151,650; assets, $4,025,671 (M); expenditures, $157,428; qualifying distributions, $157,428.
Limitations: Giving primarily in PA.
Trustees: Kimberley Miller, Mark Miller.
EIN: 256585614
Codes: FD2

46604
The Hellendall Family Foundation
8119 Heacock Ln.
Wyncote, PA 19095-1818

Established in 1994 in PA.
Donor(s): Walter Hellendall.
Financial data (yr. ended 12/31/01): Grants paid, $151,475; assets, $209,260 (M); gifts received, $104,930; expenditures, $152,576; qualifying distributions, $151,288.
Limitations: Applications not accepted. Giving primarily in PA.
Application information: Contributes only to pre-selected organizations.
Trustees: Gretel Hellendall, Kenneth C. Hellendall, Ronald D. Hellendall, Walter Hellendall.
EIN: 232798144
Codes: FD2

46605
Negley Flinn Charitable Foundation
c/o PNC Advisors
620 Liberty Ave., P2-PTPP-10-2
Pittsburgh, PA 15222-2705 (412) 762-3502
FAX: 9412) 762-5439; *E-mail:* bruce.bickel@pncadvisors.com
Contact: bruce Bickel

Established in 2000 in PA.
Donor(s): Negley Flinn.
Financial data (yr. ended 06/30/02): Grants paid, $150,000; assets, $4,869,697 (M); expenditures, $208,700; qualifying distributions, $150,000.
Trustee: PNC Bank, N.A.
EIN: 256755515

46606
Maurice D. Kent and Family Foundation
404 E. Lancaster Ave.
Wayne, PA 19087

Established in 2000 in PA.
Donor(s): Maurice D. Kent.
Financial data (yr. ended 09/30/01): Grants paid, $150,000; assets, $54,531 (M); gifts received, $522,750; expenditures, $150,000; qualifying distributions, $150,000.
Limitations: Applications not accepted. Giving primarily in FL and PA.
Application information: Contributes only to pre-selected organizations.
Officers: Maurice D. Kent, Pres.; Lawrence A. Palmer, Secy.; Dorothy M. Kent, Treas.
EIN: 233056928
Codes: FD2

46607
Ernest and Mae Sanctis Foundation
2442 N. Meadowcroft Ave.
Pittsburgh, PA 15216 (412) 343-6479
Contact: Julius Sanctis, Exec. Dir.

Financial data (yr. ended 06/30/01): Grants paid, $150,000; assets, $2,183,097 (M); expenditures, $144,483; qualifying distributions, $119,160.
Limitations: Giving limited to Pittsburgh, PA.
Application information: Application form not required.
Directors: Julius A. Sanctis, Exec. Dir.; Harvey A. Miller, Jr., Stuart H. Perilman.
EIN: 251512455
Codes: FD2

46608
Jeffrey Jay Weinberg Memorial Foundation
490 Norristown Rd., Ste. 250
Blue Bell, PA 19422

Established in 1998 in PA.
Donor(s): Ronald McDonald House Charities of the Philadelphia Region, Inc., McDonald's LPGA Championship, The Karen and Herbert Lotman Foundation, Keystone Foods Corp.
Financial data (yr. ended 12/31/00): Grants paid, $150,000; assets, $83,400 (M); gifts received, $199,024; expenditures, $151,920; qualifying distributions, $151,834.
Limitations: Applications not accepted. Giving primarily in Philadelphia, PA.
Application information: Contributes only to pre-selected organizations.
Officers: Michael Anton, Pres.; John F. Earle, V.P.; Lonnie A. Coombs, Secy.-Treas.
Directors: John Durante, Charles Ehlers, Bill Roberson, Robert Traa, Marlene Weinburg.
EIN: 232939976

46609
Robert B. Conner Foundation
c/o Mauch Chunk Trust Co.
1111 North St.
Jim Thorpe, PA 18229 (570) 325-2721
Contact: Linda L. Snyder, Trust Off., Mauch Chunk Trust Co.

Donor(s): Robert B. Conner.‡
Financial data (yr. ended 12/31/01): Grants paid, $149,799; assets, $3,096,006 (M); expenditures, $184,012; qualifying distributions, $156,415.
Limitations: Giving limited to Jim Thorpe, PA.
Application information: Application form required.
Trustee: Mauch Chunk Trust Co.
EIN: 246024098
Codes: FD2

46610
N. W. Ayer Foundation, Inc.
c/o M. Garber, Duane Morris & Heckscher
1 Liberty Pl., 43rd Fl.
Philadelphia, PA 19103-7396 (215) 752-0421
Contact: John D. Carlucci, Treas.

Donor(s): N.W. Ayer & Son, Inc.
Financial data (yr. ended 12/31/01): Grants paid, $149,500; assets, $609,499 (M); expenditures, $188,490; qualifying distributions, $188,490.
Limitations: Applications not accepted. Giving on a national basis.
Application information: The foundation will no longer make new grants; old commitments will be honored.
Officers and Directors:* Marc R. Garber,* Secy.; John D. Carlucci,* Treas.; Lennox A. Purcell.
EIN: 236296499
Codes: CS, TN, CD, GTI

46611
The Levan Family Foundation
1094 Baltimore Pike
Gettysburg, PA 17325
Contact: David M. Levan, Chair. and Pres.

Established in 1997 in PA.
Donor(s): David M. Levan.
Financial data (yr. ended 12/31/01): Grants paid, $149,500; assets, $1,384,602 (M); gifts received, $1,750; expenditures, $157,283; qualifying distributions, $151,463.
Limitations: Giving primarily in PA.
Application information: Application form required.
Officers and Directors:* David M. Levan, Chair. and Pres.; Todd M. Levan,* V.P.; Jennifer S. Levan,* Secy.-Treas.; Burton K. Stein.
EIN: 232899050
Codes: FD2

46612
Mary and Emmanuel Rosenfeld Foundation
c/o First Union National Bank
Broad & Walnut Sts.
Philadelphia, PA 19109 (215) 670-4226
Contact: Reginald Middleton

Established around 1977.
Financial data (yr. ended 12/31/01): Grants paid, $149,500; assets, $6,839,593 (M); expenditures, $163,876; qualifying distributions, $150,250.
Limitations: Giving primarily in FL and PA.
Application information: Unsolicited requests not encouraged.
Trustees: Lester Rosenfeld, Robert Rosenfeld, Rita E. Stein, First Union National Bank.
EIN: 236220061
Codes: FD2

46613
Corson Foundation
P.O. Box 710
Plymouth Meeting, PA 19462
Contact: John E.F. Corson, Tr.

Established around 1957.
Financial data (yr. ended 12/31/00): Grants paid, $149,280; assets, $2,978,481 (M); expenditures, $170,811; qualifying distributions, $148,399.
Limitations: Giving primarily in PA.
Application information: Application form required.
Trustees: John E.F. Corson, Harry F. Murphy, Carol Posse.
EIN: 236390878
Codes: FD2

46614
Frank Thomson Scholarship Trust
c/o First Union National Bank
Broad & Walnut Sts.
Philadelphia, PA 19109 (215) 670-4226
Contact: Judy Prendergast

Established in 1907 in PA.
Financial data (yr. ended 12/31/01): Grants paid, $149,260; assets, $2,880,240 (M); expenditures, $162,505; qualifying distributions, $152,134.
Application information: Scholarships limited to prospective college freshmen; students already in college are ineligible. Application form required.
Trustee: First Union National Bank.
EIN: 236217801
Codes: FD2, GTI

46615
The Bon-Ton Foundation
2801 E. Market St.
York, PA 17402 (717) 751-3247
Application address: P.O. Box 2821, York, PA 17405
Contact: Christine De Julis, Fdn. Admin.

Established in 1991 in PA.
Donor(s): The Bon-Ton Stores, Inc.
Financial data (yr. ended 01/31/01): Grants paid, $148,663; assets, $259,452 (M); gifts received, $116,850; expenditures, $158,517; qualifying distributions, $157,789.
Limitations: Giving primarily in PA.
Publications: Informational brochure.
Application information: Application form required.
Officers and Directors:* Ryan J. Sattler,* Pres.; Melinda A. Shue, Secy.-Treas.; Ken Heitz, Mary Kerr, Joseph L. Leahy, Jim Volk, Susan M. Wolfe.
EIN: 232656774
Codes: CS, FD2, CD

46616
Louis and Hilda Silverstein Foundation
c/o PNC Bank, N.A.
1600 Market St., 4th Fl.
Philadelphia, PA 19103-7240

Established in 1976 in PA.
Donor(s): Louis J. Silverstein.‡
Financial data (yr. ended 01/31/02): Grants paid, $148,500; assets, $403,136 (M); expenditures, $149,300; qualifying distributions, $148,344.
Limitations: Applications not accepted. Giving primarily in PA.
Application information: Contributes only to pre-selected organizations.
Trustees: Irene C. Beer, Charles Kofsky, Bernice Lewis, Rebecca C. Waldman, PNC Bank, N.A.
EIN: 236620071
Codes: FD2

46617
The Campbell-Oxholm Foundation
622 S. Bowman Ave.
Merion Station, PA 19066-1421
E-mail: campbelloxholm@comcast.net
Contact: Kimberly C. Oxholm, Managing Tr.

Established in 1995 in PA.
Donor(s): Alan K. Campbell.‡
Financial data (yr. ended 12/31/01): Grants paid, $148,000; assets, $2,544,527 (M); expenditures, $175,199; qualifying distributions, $147,475.
Limitations: Giving primarily in OR and southeastern PA.
Officers: C. Duncan Campbell, Pres.; Janet L. Campbell, V.P.; Carl Oxholm III, Secy.; Kimberly C. Oxholm, Treas.
EIN: 232790496
Codes: FD2

46618
The High Foundation
P.O. Box 10008
Lancaster, PA 17605-0008
Contact: Sadie H. High, Chair.

Established in 1980 in PA.
Financial data (yr. ended 08/31/01): Grants paid, $147,000; assets, $3,964,761 (M); gifts received, $50,000; expenditures, $189,734; qualifying distributions, $147,000.
Limitations: Giving primarily in south central PA, including Lancaster County.
Publications: Application guidelines, program policy statement.
Application information: Application form required.

Officers and Trustees:* Sadie H. High,* Chair.; Robin D. Stauffer, Secy.; Richard L. High,* Treas.; and 6 additional trustees.
EIN: 232149972
Codes: FD2, GTI

46619
Samuel L. Abrams Foundation
c/o Mellon Bank, N.A.
P.O. Box 7236, AIM 193-0224
Philadelphia, PA 19101-7236
URL: http://www.slabramsfoundation.org
Student loan application address: 2301 N. 3rd St., Harrisburg, PA 17110, tel.: (717) 234-4344
Contact: Richard E. Abrams, Pres.

Established in 1992.
Donor(s): Beryl Abrams, Richard E. Abrams.
Financial data (yr. ended 12/31/01): Grants paid, $146,500; assets, $2,525,523 (M); gifts received, $1,200; expenditures, $169,731; qualifying distributions, $145,116.
Limitations: Giving limited to the greater Harrisburg, PA, area.
Application information: Application form required.
Officers: Richard E. Abrams, Pres.; Ruth A. Gonzalez, Secy.; James R. Reeser, Treas.
Trustee: Mellon Bank, N.A.
EIN: 236408237
Codes: FD2, GTI

46620
Maslow Family Foundation, Inc.
P.O. Box 174, Huntsville Rd.
Dallas, PA 18612 (570) 674-6532
Application address: 147 Hayfield Rd., Shavertown, PA 18708-9748
Contact: Marilyn J. O'Boyle, Exec. Dir.

Established in 1994 in PA.
Donor(s): Richard Maslow.
Financial data (yr. ended 12/31/01): Grants paid, $146,000; assets, $4,364,484 (M); gifts received, $1,020,704; expenditures, $189,286; qualifying distributions, $147,031.
Limitations: Giving primarily in the greater Wyoming Valley area, in Luzerne County, PA.
Application information: Application form not required.
Officers and Trustees:* Richard Maslow,* Pres.; Douglas Maslow,* V.P.; Jennifer Maslow Holtzman,* Secy.; Melanie Maslow Lumia,* Treas.; Marilyn J. O'Boyle, Exec. Dir.; Allison Maslow, Leslie Maslow, Hillary Maslow Naud, Eugene Roth.
EIN: 232791676
Codes: FD2

46621
Charles O. Wood III & Miriam M. Wood Foundation
273 Lincoln Way E.
Chambersburg, PA 17201

Established in 1987 in PA.
Donor(s): Charles O. Wood III, Miriam M. Wood.
Financial data (yr. ended 12/31/00): Grants paid, $145,256; assets, $1,672,426 (M); expenditures, $155,329; qualifying distributions, $145,287.
Limitations: Applications not accepted. Giving on a national basis.
Application information: Contributes only to pre-selected organizations.
Trustees: Charles O. Wood III, Miriam M. Wood.
EIN: 251568770
Codes: FD2

46622
The Pincus Charitable Fund
Independence Mall E.
Philadelphia, PA 19106

Established in 1986 in PA.
Donor(s): David Pincus, Pincus Brothers, Inc.
Financial data (yr. ended 11/30/00): Grants paid, $145,150; assets, $38,425 (M); gifts received, $96,925; expenditures, $146,685; qualifying distributions, $146,339.
Limitations: Applications not accepted. Giving primarily in NY and PA.
Application information: Contributes only to pre-selected organizations.
Officers: David Pincus, Pres.; Gerry Pincus, Secy.; Bruce Fishberg, Treas.
Directors: Alvin Dorsky, Andrew Epstein, Daniel J. Kachelein, Nathan Pincus, Wendy Pincus.
EIN: 222781261
Codes: FD2

46623
Zeldin Family Foundation
325-41 Chestnut St.
Constitution Pl., Ste. 1320
Philadelphia, PA 19106
Contact: Claudia Zeldin, Tr.

Established in 1986 in PA.
Donor(s): Martin Zeldin.
Financial data (yr. ended 11/30/01): Grants paid, $145,009; assets, $2,716,780 (M); expenditures, $147,705; qualifying distributions, $144,205.
Application information: Limit request to 10 pages. Application form not required.
Trustees: Claudia Zeldin, Jessica Zeldin, Martin Zeldin, Stefanie Zeldin, Sybille Zeldin.
EIN: 236861835
Codes: FD2

46624
The Knoll Charitable Foundation
1235 Water St.
East Greenville, PA 18041-2202
Scholarship application address: c/o Knoll Educational Scholarship Program, Citizens' Scholarship Foundation of America, P.O. Box 297, St. Peter, MN 56082, tel.: (507) 931-1682

Established in 1999 in PA.
Donor(s): Knoll, Inc.
Financial data (yr. ended 12/31/00): Grants paid, $145,000; assets, $3,507,811 (M); gifts received, $446,366; expenditures, $169,760; qualifying distributions, $153,280.
Limitations: Giving primarily in MI and PA.
Officers: Barry L. McCabe, V.P. and Treas.; Kathleen Bradley, V.P.; Patrick Milberger, Secy.
EIN: 232939762
Codes: CS, FD2, CD

46625
The Rosenlund Family Foundation
P.O. Box 297
Haverford, PA 19041
Contact: Hope Rosenlund, Managing Tr.

Established in 1962 in PA.
Donor(s): Arthur O. Rosenlund.‡
Financial data (yr. ended 06/30/02): Grants paid, $145,000; assets, $2,779,621 (M); expenditures, $157,657; qualifying distributions, $147,804.
Limitations: Giving primarily in Philadelphia, PA.
Application information: Application form not required.
Trustees: Hope Rosenlund, Managing Tr.; April Rosenlund Ford, Alarik A. Rosenlund, Arthur O. Rosenlund, Jr., David E. Rosenlund, Mary L. Rosenlund, Stephanie Rosenlund Shim, Kristin Turrill.

EIN: 236243642
Codes: FD2

46626
The Foster Foundation, Inc.
c/o Richard Foster
P.O. Box 390
Newtown, PA 18940

Established in 1995 in PA.
Donor(s): Richard L. Foster.
Financial data (yr. ended 11/30/01): Grants paid, $144,092; assets, $65,261 (M); gifts received, $150,000; expenditures, $145,341; qualifying distributions, $144,092.
Limitations: Applications not accepted.
Application information: Contributes only to pre-selected organizations.
Officers: Richard L. Foster, Pres. and Treas.; Marilyn E. Foster, V.P. and Secy.
EIN: 232807767
Codes: FD2

46627
Western Association of Ladies for the Relief and Employment of the Poor
c/o First Union National Bank
Broad and Walnut Sts.
Philadelphia, PA 19109
Application address: 240 Chatham Way, West Chester, PA 19380
Contact: Marlane Bohon, Exec. Secy.

Established in 1847 in PA.
Financial data (yr. ended 12/31/00): Grants paid, $143,942; assets, $3,428,827 (M); gifts received, $5,300; expenditures, $181,669; qualifying distributions, $150,945.
Limitations: Giving limited to Philadelphia County, PA.
Application information: Application must be submitted through a social service organization. Application form not required.
Officer and Directors:* Marlane Bohon,* Exec. Secy.; Kurt R. Anderson, Jean P. Barr, Luis Cortes, Anne B. Hagele, Rev. Deborah A. McKinley, Judith Prendergast, Abby Ryan.
EIN: 231353393
Codes: FD2, GTI

46628
Black Family Foundation
400 French St.
Erie, PA 16507-1568
Contact: Samuel P. Black III, Pres.

Established in 1993 in PA.
Financial data (yr. ended 12/31/01): Grants paid, $143,575; assets, $1,413,842 (M); gifts received, $90,000; expenditures, $146,337; qualifying distributions, $143,074.
Limitations: Giving limited to Erie, PA.
Officers: Samuel P. Black III, Pres.; James Cullen, Secy.-Treas.
EIN: 251705824
Codes: FD2

46629
Irvin & Marion-Louise Saltzman Family Foundation, Inc.
c/o Jami Saltzman-Levy
420 S. York Rd.
Hatboro, PA 19040

Established in 1995 in PA.
Donor(s): Irvin Saltzman.
Financial data (yr. ended 11/30/01): Grants paid, $143,520; assets, $647,097 (M); gifts received, $114,382; expenditures, $165,108; qualifying distributions, $143,520.

46629—PENNSYLVANIA

Limitations: Applications not accepted. Giving primarily in PA.
Application information: Contributes only to pre-selected organizations.
Officers: Irvin Saltzman, Pres.; Jami Saltzman-Levy, Secy.-Treas.
EIN: 232827744
Codes: FD2

46630
Venango Area Community Foundation
P.O. Box 374
213 Seneca St.
Oil City, PA 16301 (814) 677-8687
Application address: National Transit Bldg., Rm. 27C, Oil City, PA 16301; E-mail: gloryvacf@usachoice.net
Contact: Stephen P. Kosak, Exec. Dir.

Community foundation incorporated in 1975 in PA.
Financial data (yr. ended 08/31/00): Grants paid, $142,970; assets, $2,975,849 (M); gifts received, $793,000; expenditures, $361,089.
Limitations: Giving limited to Venango County, PA.
Publications: Annual report, application guidelines.
Application information: Application form required.
Officers and Trustees:* Diane Hasek,* Pres.; William Bowen,* V.P.; Denise Parisi,* Secy.; Charles Stubler,* Treas.; Stephen P. Kosak, Exec. Dir.; Vicky DePiore, Brandon Hammond, Glory Johnson, Beth McFadden, Robert McFate, Donald Pfohl, Loretta Strawbridge, Ted Welch.
EIN: 251292553
Codes: CM, FD2

46631
Ochiltree Foundation
c/o Jim Zern, Mellon Bank, N.A.
1 Mellon Ctr., Rm. 3711
Pittsburgh, PA 15230

Established in 1997 in PA.
Financial data (yr. ended 12/31/00): Grants paid, $142,000; assets, $1,177,716 (M); expenditures, $157,523; qualifying distributions, $146,691.
Limitations: Giving on a national basis.
Application information: Application form required.
Trustee: Mellon Bank, N.A.
EIN: 237883781
Codes: FD2

46632
John F. Connelly Scholarship Fund
c/o Crown Cork & Seal Co., Inc., Human Resources Dept.
1 Crown Way, Tax Dept.
Philadelphia, PA 19154-4599
Contact: Gary Burgess

Established in 1991 in PA.
Donor(s): The Conelly Foundation.
Financial data (yr. ended 12/31/99): Grants paid, $141,947; assets, $4,095,906 (M); gifts received, $49,644; expenditures, $149,329; qualifying distributions, $141,306.
Limitations: Giving on a national and international basis.
Application information: Application form required.
Officers and Trustees:* William J. Avery,* Pres.; Richard L. Krzyzanowski,* V.P. and Secy.; Alan W. Rutherford, V.P., Fin.; Craig R.L. Calle, Treas.; Michael J. McKenna, Emily C. Riley.
EIN: 232667541
Codes: FD2, GTI

46633
The Martin Foundation
c/o MME, Inc.
3993 Huntingdon Pike
Huntingdon Valley, PA 19006-1927
Contact: Jovina Armento

Established in 1981 in PA.
Donor(s): Alfred S. Martin.
Financial data (yr. ended 03/31/02): Grants paid, $141,700; assets, $2,829,890 (M); expenditures, $191,377; qualifying distributions, $152,271.
Limitations: Giving primarily in ME and PA.
Application information: Application form not required.
Trustees: George J. Hartnett, Alfred S. Martin, Mary M. Martin, Zachary S. Martin, W. James Quigley.
EIN: 232182719
Codes: FD2

46634
Fingold-Rodef Shalom & Duquesne Law Scholarship
c/o PNC Advisors
2 PNC Plz., 620 Liberty Ave.
Pittsburgh, PA 15222-2705

Established in 1999 in PA.
Financial data (yr. ended 06/30/01): Grants paid, $141,026; assets, $2,207,793 (M); expenditures, $164,066; qualifying distributions, $141,026.
Limitations: Applications not accepted.
Application information: Contributes only to pre-selected organizations.
Trustee: PNC Bank, N.A.
EIN: 256636735
Codes: FD2

46635
Benjamin & Fredora K. Wolf Memorial Foundation
Park Towne Pl. N. Bldg. 1205
Parkway at 22nd St.
Philadelphia, PA 19103
Contact: David A. Horowitz, Mgr.

Incorporated in 1955 in PA.
Donor(s): Fredora K. Wolf.‡
Financial data (yr. ended 05/31/00): Grants paid, $141,000; assets, $3,188,696 (M); expenditures, $150,172; qualifying distributions, $145,963.
Limitations: Giving limited to Philadelphia, PA, area residents.
Application information: Application form required.
Officers and Trustees:* Mary Wolf Hurtig,* Pres.; Flora Barth Wolf,* V.P.; Jean Gray,* Secy.; John Tuton, Treas.; David A. Horowitz, Mgr.; Richard I. Abrahams, Virginia Wolf Briscoe, PNC Bank, N.A.
EIN: 236207344
Codes: FD2, GTI

46636
The William M. King Charitable Foundation
4110 Apalogen Rd.
Philadelphia, PA 19144 (215) 844-3500
Contact: William M. King, Pres.

Established in 1996 in PA.
Donor(s): William M. King.
Financial data (yr. ended 12/31/00): Grants paid, $140,850; assets, $508,524 (M); gifts received, $10,000; expenditures, $40,850; qualifying distributions, $140,850.
Limitations: Giving primarily in PA.
Application information: Application form not required.
Officer: William M. King, Pres.
EIN: 237788220
Codes: FD2

46637
Kohn Foundation
1 S. Broad St., Ste. 2100
Philadelphia, PA 19107-2924 (215) 238-1700
Contact: Joseph C. Kohn, V.P.

Established in 1965 in PA.
Donor(s): Harold E. Kohn.
Financial data (yr. ended 12/31/01): Grants paid, $140,795; assets, $1,721,601 (M); gifts received, $100,000; expenditures, $159,538; qualifying distributions, $140,795.
Limitations: Giving primarily in Philadelphia, PA; some giving in Israel.
Application information: Application form not required.
Officers and Directors:* Edith Kohn,* Pres.; Joseph C. Kohn,* V.P. and Secy.; Ellen E. Goddard,* Treas.; Amy K. Goldberg.
EIN: 236398546

46638
Sylk Charitable Trust
c/o Leonard A. Sylk
350 N. Highland Ave.
Merion Station, PA 19066

Established in 1995 in PA.
Donor(s): Leonard A. Sylk, Barbara A. Sylk.
Financial data (yr. ended 12/31/01): Grants paid, $140,334; assets, $827,222 (M); gifts received, $71,000; expenditures, $140,379; qualifying distributions, $140,379.
Limitations: Applications not accepted. Giving limited to the Philadelphia, PA metro area.
Application information: Contributes only to pre-selected organizations.
Trustees: Barbara A. Sylk, Leonard A. Sylk.
EIN: 237809130
Codes: FD2

46639
Margaret G. Jacobs Charitable Trust
c/o Brown Brothers Harriman Trust Co.
1531 Walnut St.
Philadelphia, PA 19102-8910
Contact: William R. Levy, Tr.

Established in 1992 in PA.
Donor(s): Margaret G. Jacobs.‡
Financial data (yr. ended 06/30/01): Grants paid, $139,050; assets, $2,703,443 (M); expenditures, $156,894; qualifying distributions, $146,370.
Limitations: Giving limited to PA.
Application information: Application form not required.
Trustees: Philip Brown, William R. Levy.
EIN: 232743317
Codes: FD2

46640
Kozloff Family Charitable Trust
1150 Bern Rd.
Wyomissing, PA 19610
Contact: Paul J. Kozloff, Dir.

Established in 1991 in PA.
Donor(s): Paul J. Kozloff, Northeastern Distributing Co.
Financial data (yr. ended 12/31/00): Grants paid, $138,613; assets, $1,726,343 (M); gifts received, $20,000; expenditures, $147,630; qualifying distributions, $136,443.
Limitations: Giving primarily in PA.
Directors: Allen Kozloff, Paul J. Kozloff, Lauren Kozloff Sinrod.
EIN: 237680042
Codes: FD2

46641
The Mars Family Charitable Foundation
(Formerly The Barbara and Bernard Mars Charitable Foundation)
681 Andersen Dr., 3rd Fl.
Pittsburgh, PA 15220-2747

Established in 1998 in PA.
Financial data (yr. ended 12/31/01): Grants paid, $137,586; assets, $800,819 (M); expenditures, $140,402; qualifying distributions, $137,586.
Limitations: Applications not accepted.
Application information: Contributes only to pre-selected organizations.
Trustees: Andrew F. Mars, Barbara F. Mars, Bernard S. Mars, David M. Mars, Peter F. Mars, Sally Mars.
EIN: 256585615

46642
Vernon C. Neal and Alvina B. Neal Fund
653 Arden Rd.
Washington, PA 15301-8632
Contact: Margaret L. Johnston, Secy.

Established in 1987 in PA.
Donor(s): Jennie G. Johnston.‡
Financial data (yr. ended 12/31/00): Grants paid, $137,500; assets, $2,594,294 (M); expenditures, $181,941; qualifying distributions, $147,426.
Limitations: Applications not accepted. Giving primarily in PA.
Application information: Contributes only to pre-selected organizations.
Officer and Trustees:* Margaret L. Johnston,* Secy.; Frank L. Corsetti, Rosemary L. Corsetti.
EIN: 251608371
Codes: FD2

46643
Freedom Forge Corporation Foundation
(Formerly American Welding & Manufacturing Company Foundation)
c/o Kish Bank Asset Mgmt.
1 Gateway Dr.
Reedsville, PA 17084
Application address: 500 N. Walnut St., Burnham, PA 17009, tel.: (717) 248-4911

Established about 1956 in OH.
Donor(s): Freedom Forge Corp.
Financial data (yr. ended 12/31/00): Grants paid, $137,237; assets, $1,464,289 (M); expenditures, $147,975; qualifying distributions, $135,933.
Limitations: Giving primarily in OH.
Application information: Application form not required.
Trustee: Kish Bank Asset Mgmt.
EIN: 346516721
Codes: CS, FD2, CD

46644
The Robert J. Kahn Testamentary Foundation
c/o M. Blackman
1900 Market St., Ste. 700
Philadelphia, PA 19103

Established in 1999 in PA.
Financial data (yr. ended 12/31/00): Grants paid, $137,000; assets, $12,955,629 (M); gifts received, $78,630; expenditures, $238,602; qualifying distributions, $133,567.
Limitations: Applications not accepted. Giving primarily in New York, NY and Philadelphia, PA.
Application information: Contributes only to pre-selected organizations.
Trustee: Murray I. Blackman.
EIN: 256667083
Codes: FD2

46645
Fortinsky Charitable Foundation, Inc.
315 Simpson St.
Swoyersville, PA 18704 (570) 288-3666
Contact: Robert Fortinsky, Pres.

Established in 1985 in PA.
Donor(s): Robert Fortinsky, Wyoming Weavers.
Financial data (yr. ended 12/31/01): Grants paid, $136,923; assets, $753,936 (M); gifts received, $102,000; expenditures, $137,976; qualifying distributions, $136,654.
Limitations: Applications not accepted. Giving limited to PA.
Application information: Contributes only to pre-selected organizations.
Officers and Directors:* Robert Fortinsky,* Pres. and Treas.; Jill F. Schwartz,* Secy.
EIN: 232338218
Codes: FD2

46646
Howell A. & Ann M. Breedlove Charitable Foundation
2015 Blairmont Dr.
Pittsburgh, PA 15241-2202

Established in 1991 in PA.
Donor(s): Howell A. Breedlove, Ann M. Breedlove.
Financial data (yr. ended 12/31/01): Grants paid, $136,772; assets, $2,241,684 (L); gifts received, $191,000; expenditures, $186,759; qualifying distributions, $135,920.
Limitations: Applications not accepted. Giving limited to PA.
Application information: Contributes only to pre-selected organizations.
Trustees: Alan Merkle Breedlove, Ann M. Breedlove, Howell A. Breedlove, John Adams Breedlove, Mark Howell Breedlove, William Parker Breedlove, Ann Marie Garbin.
EIN: 251661386
Codes: FD2

46647
Will R. Beitel Children's Community Foundation
P.O. Box 292
Nazareth, PA 18064-0292 (610) 861-8929
Contact: Thomas C. Kelchner, Secy.

Established in 1919 in PA.
Financial data (yr. ended 09/30/01): Grants paid, $136,025; assets, $1,633,594 (M); expenditures, $202,797; qualifying distributions, $136,025.
Limitations: Giving primarily in Northampton County, PA.
Application information: Acknowledgement of receipt of grant and certified use of monies required. Application form not required.
Officers and Directors:* Robert C. Hoch,* Pres.; John M. Dusinski,* V.P.; Thomas C. Kelchner, Secy.; Grant W. Walizer,* Treas.; Stephen Bajan, Elwood G. Buss, Sr., Phillip E. Moll II, Charles J. Peischl.
EIN: 240800920
Codes: FD2

46648
Sarah and Tena Goldstein Memorial Scholarship
c/o Jewish Family and Children's Svcs.
5743 Bartlett St.
Pittsburgh, PA 15217 (412) 422-7200
Additional tel.: (412) 422-5627 (application form requests)

Established in 1987 in PA.
Financial data (yr. ended 12/31/01): Grants paid, $135,986; assets, $2,990,844 (M); expenditures, $156,476; qualifying distributions, $155,986.
Limitations: Giving limited to Allegheny, Beaver, Butler, Clarion, Crawford, Erie, Lawrence, Mercer, Venango, Washington, and Westmoreland counties, PA, with preference given to Titusville, PA, area residents.
Application information: Application form required.
Trustee: Jewish Family and Children's Services.
EIN: 251229795
Codes: FD2, GTI

46649
Amelia Miles Foundation
c/o PNC Advisors, Trust Comm.
2 PNC Plz., 620 Liberty Ave., 25th Fl.
Pittsburgh, PA 15222 (412) 762-7076
Contact: Mia Hallett Bernard

Financial data (yr. ended 12/31/01): Grants paid, $135,618; assets, $2,291,105 (M); expenditures, $166,028; qualifying distributions, $137,791.
Limitations: Giving primarily in PA.
Trustee: PNC Bank, N.A.
EIN: 256092021
Codes: FD2

46650
The Stanley and Lois Elkman Foundation
c/o Bennett L. Aaron, Pepper, Hamilton, & Scheetz
3000 2 Logan Sq.
Philadelphia, PA 19103-2799

Established in 1992 in FL.
Donor(s): Stanley Elkman.
Financial data (yr. ended 12/31/00): Grants paid, $135,350; assets, $2,199 (M); gifts received, $117,938; expenditures, $137,229; qualifying distributions, $135,891.
Limitations: Applications not accepted. Giving primarily in FL, NY and PA.
Application information: Contributes only to pre-selected organizations.
Officers and Directors:* Stanley Elkman,* Pres.; Lois D. Elkman,* V.P.; Carol A. Schwartz,* Secy.; Stuart M. Elkman,* Treas.
EIN: 650372014
Codes: FD2

46651
Bob Hoffman Foundation
c/o Fulton Financial Advisors
P.O. Box 3215
Lancaster, PA 17604-3215
Contact: John B. Terpak, Jr., Tr.

Established about 1964 in PA.
Donor(s): York Barbell Co., Inc., and related companies.
Financial data (yr. ended 03/31/02): Grants paid, $135,283; assets, $1,768,394 (M); gifts received, $25,305; expenditures, $165,166; qualifying distributions, $134,801.
Limitations: Giving primarily in York County, PA.
Publications: Application guidelines.
Application information: Application form required.
Trustees: David J. Fortney, Alda M. Ketterman, George E. MacDonald, Paul Strombaugh, John B. Terpak, Jr.
EIN: 236298674
Codes: CS, FD2, CD

46652
Rotko Family Foundation
1600 Market St., Ste. 3600
Philadelphia, PA 19103 (215) 751-2338
Contact: John D. Iskrant

Established in 1982 in PA.

46652—PENNSYLVANIA

Financial data (yr. ended 12/31/00): Grants paid, $134,500; assets, $1,228,957 (M); expenditures, $154,710; qualifying distributions, $144,289.
Limitations: Giving primarily in PA, with emphasis on Philadelphia.
Application information: Application form not required.
Trustees: Lionel Felzer, Bessie Rotko, Michael J. Rotko, Judith Shipon.
EIN: 232200115
Codes: FD2

46653
Horsehead Community Development Fund, Inc.
P.O. Box 351
Palmerton, PA 18071-0351 (610) 826-2239
Additional tel.: (610) 826-4377
Contact: Charles H. Campton, Exec. Consultant

Established in 1989 in PA.
Donor(s): Horsehead Resource Development Co., Inc.
Financial data (yr. ended 12/31/01): Grants paid, $134,376; assets, $168,594 (M); gifts received, $118,982; expenditures, $136,036; qualifying distributions, $134,891.
Limitations: Giving limited to the Palmerton, PA, area.
Publications: Annual report (including application guidelines), informational brochure (including application guidelines), grants list, occasional report, program policy statement, financial statement.
Application information: Grants must be used in same year awarded. Application form required.
Officers and Directors:* William Bechdolt,* Chair.; Joseph Bechtel,* Vice-Chair.; Richard Hager,* Secy.; Michael Harleman,* Treas.; Charles H. Campton, Exec. Consultant; Joseph Bechtel, Mary Elizabeth Cyr, Michael R. Harleman.
EIN: 232588172
Codes: CS, FD2, CD

46654
Borowsky Family Foundation
220 Society Hill Towers, Ste. 31B
Philadelphia, PA 19106

Established in 1999 in PA.
Donor(s): Irvin J. Borowsky.
Financial data (yr. ended 12/31/00): Grants paid, $134,320; assets, $2,042,143 (M); gifts received, $565,625; expenditures, $143,419; qualifying distributions, $138,437.
Limitations: Giving primarily in PA.
Officers: Irvin J. Borowsky, Pres.; Gwen Borowsky Camp, Secy.; Ned Borowsky, Treas.
EIN: 232949444
Codes: FD2

46655
Charles F. Borgel Trust for Charities
c/o Mellon Bank, N.A.
P.O. Box 7236, AIM 193-0224
Philadelphia, PA 19101-7236

Established in 1996 in PA.
Financial data (yr. ended 04/30/01): Grants paid, $134,277; assets, $2,155,860 (M); expenditures, $154,508; qualifying distributions, $132,399.
Limitations: Applications not accepted. Giving primarily in PA.
Application information: Contributes only to pre-selected organizations.
Trustee: Mellon Bank, N.A.
EIN: 237837203

46656
Washington Federal Charitable Foundation
190 N. Main St.
Washington, PA 15301
Contact: Richard L. White, Dir.

Established in 1991 in PA.
Donor(s): Washington Federal Savings Bank.
Financial data (yr. ended 06/30/01): Grants paid, $134,000; assets, $503,737 (M); gifts received, $100,000; expenditures, $137,128; qualifying distributions, $135,158.
Limitations: Giving limited to southwestern PA, with emphasis on Washington County.
Publications: Financial statement, informational brochure, application guidelines.
Application information: Application form required.
Officers: William M. Campbell, Chair.; Mary Lyn Drewitz, Secy.; William B. Sharp, Treas.
Directors: David R. Andrews, Martin P. Beichner, Jr., James H. Boylan, Joseph M. Jefferson, D. Jackson Milhollan, Thomas R. Milhollan, James R. Proudfit, Telford W. Thomas, Louis E. Waller, Richard L. White.
EIN: 256395164
Codes: CS, FD2, CD

46657
Esther Gowen Hood Trust
c/o Mellon Bank, N.A.
P.O. Box 7236
Philadelphia, PA 19101-7236 (215) 553-3208
Contact: Patricia Kling

Established in 1927 in PA.
Financial data (yr. ended 09/30/01): Grants paid, $133,100; assets, $2,490,004 (M); gifts received, $2,500; expenditures, $142,959; qualifying distributions, $133,691.
Limitations: Giving limited to the Philadelphia, PA, area.
Trustee: Mellon Bank, N.A.
EIN: 236223619
Codes: FD2

46658
The Bergman Foundation
67-69 Public Sq., Ste. 801
Wilkes-Barre, PA 18701-2505
Contact: J. Bergman, Jr., Tr.

Established in 1950 in PA.
Donor(s): Justin Bergman, Jr.
Financial data (yr. ended 09/30/01): Grants paid, $133,084; assets, $3,589,134 (M); expenditures, $143,035; qualifying distributions, $134,484.
Limitations: Applications not accepted. Giving primarily in the Wilkes-Barre, PA, area.
Application information: Contributes only to pre-selected organizations.
Trustees: Cordelia Bergman, Justin Bergman, Jr., Forence Shubilla.
EIN: 246014771
Codes: FD2

46659
The W. B. McCardell Family Foundation
165 Township Line Rd., Ste. 3000
Jenkintown, PA 19046
Application address: 2025 Taylor Rd., Auburn Hills, MI 48326, tel.: (248) 371-9700
Contact: Bradley W. McCardell, Pres.

Established in 1994 in MI.
Donor(s): Willard B. McCardell, Jr.
Financial data (yr. ended 12/31/00): Grants paid, $133,000; assets, $1,508,289 (M); gifts received, $900,000; expenditures, $150,883; qualifying distributions, $135,281.
Limitations: Giving primarily in MI.
Application information: Accepts CMF Common Grant Application Form. Application form required.
Officers: Willard B. McCardell, Jr., Chair.; Sheran M. McCardell, Vice-Chair.; Bradley W. McCardell, Pres.; Michael D. Mulcahy, Secy.; Tracy L. McCardell, Treas.
Trustees: Scott I. Andrews, Tina M. Andrews, Ann-Marie McCardell, Kenneth W. McCardell, Steven R. McCardell.
EIN: 383211106
Codes: FD2

46660
Woodmere Foundation
c/o Robert B. Knutson
300 6th Ave.
Pittsburgh, PA 15222-2511 (412) 562-0900
Contact: Kathy Villalpando, Educ. Mgmt. Corp.

Established in 1993 in PA.
Donor(s): Robert B. Knutson.
Financial data (yr. ended 12/31/99): Grants paid, $132,879; assets, $1,623,763 (M); gifts received, $289,664; expenditures, $145,710; qualifying distributions, $128,836.
Limitations: Giving primarily in PA.
Officer: Robert B. Knutson, Pres.
EIN: 251705913
Codes: FD2

46661
Adams Foundation, Inc.
1000 RIDC Plz.
Pittsburgh, PA 15238
Contact: Shelley M. Taylor, Pres.

Incorporated in 1955 in PA.
Donor(s): Rolland L. Adams,‡ Abarta, Inc.
Financial data (yr. ended 12/31/01): Grants paid, $132,500; assets, $690,992 (M); expenditures, $50,000; expenditures, $142,422; qualifying distributions, $132,411.
Limitations: Giving primarily in PA.
Application information: Application form not required.
Officers and Directors:* Shelley M. Taylor,* Pres.; Mary R. Hudson,* Secy.; James A. Taylor,* Treas.; Nancy A. Taylor.
EIN: 240866511
Codes: FD2

46662
The Newell Devalpine Foundation
c/o Bernard Eizen
2001 Market St., Ste. 3410
Philadelphia, PA 19103-7391

Established in 1995 in CT.
Financial data (yr. ended 12/31/01): Grants paid, $132,350; assets, $3,613,360 (M); expenditures, $171,754; qualifying distributions, $132,440.
Limitations: Applications not accepted. Giving limited to PA.
Application information: Contributes only to pre-selected organizations.
Trustees: Bernard Eizen, The Glenmede Trust Co.
EIN: 237821726
Codes: FD2

46663
Martha Lloyd Services, Inc.
190 W. Main St.
Troy, PA 16947-1131 (570) 297-2185
E-mail: bfranciscus@marthalloyd.org
Contact: Barry N. Franciscus, Cont.

Established in 1996 in PA.
Financial data (yr. ended 06/30/01): Grants paid, $132,194; assets, $1,058,677 (M); gifts received,

$241,111; expenditures, $152,540; qualifying distributions, $152,540.
Limitations: Applications not accepted.
Publications: Annual report.
Application information: Contributes only to pre-selected organizations.
Officers: Lee Cummings, Chair.; Douglas Ulkins, Vice-Chair.; Richard Macintire, Pres.
EIN: 251789856
Codes: FD2

46664
Alpin J. and Alpin W. Cameron Memorial Fund
c/o Ehmann, Van Denbergh & Trainor
2 Penn Ctr. Plz., Ste. 725
Philadelphia, PA 19102
FAX: (215) 851-9820
Contact: F.A. Van Denbergh, Esq.

Trust established in 1957 in PA.
Donor(s): Alpin W. Cameron,‡ Alpin J. Cameron.‡
Financial data (yr. ended 09/30/01): Grants paid, $132,000; assets, $4,370,337 (M); expenditures, $219,603; qualifying distributions, $134,260.
Limitations: Giving primarily in the Philadelphia, PA, area.
Application information: Application form not required.
Trustee: PNC Bank, N.A.
Board Members: Jonathan H. Sprogell, Frederick A. Van Denbergh, Jr., Margaret Anne Van Denbergh, Ross Van Denbergh.
EIN: 236213225
Codes: FD2

46665
The Harvey & Barbara Kroiz Family Foundation
c/o Harvey Kroiz
815 Roscommon Rd.
Bryn Mawr, PA 19010

Established in 1997 in PA.
Financial data (yr. ended 03/31/01): Grants paid, $132,000; assets, $676,558 (M); expenditures, $135,660; qualifying distributions, $132,000.
Limitations: Applications not accepted. Giving primarily in PA.
Application information: Contributes only to pre-selected organizations.
Trustees: Barbara Kroiz, Harvey Kroiz, Karen Kroiz, Michelle Kroiz, Nicole Kroiz.
EIN: 237883529
Codes: FD2

46666
Donald P. Jones Foundation
P.O. Box 58910
Philadelphia, PA 19102-8910
Contact: Arthur W. Jones, Tr.

Established in 1953 in PA.
Donor(s): Donald P. Jones.‡
Financial data (yr. ended 12/31/01): Grants paid, $131,600; assets, $1,839,275 (M); expenditures, $149,839; qualifying distributions, $133,368.
Limitations: Giving primarily in Delaware County, PA.
Application information: Application form not required.
Trustees: Elizabeth J. Gilson, Arthur W. Jones, Lawrence T. Jones.
EIN: 236259820
Codes: FD2

46667
Fred J. Jaindl Foundation
c/o PNC Bank, N.A.
1660 Valley Center Pkwy., Ste. 100
Bethlehem, PA 18017
Application address: 3150 Coffetown Rd., Orefield, PA 18069, tel.: (610) 395-3333
Contact: David Jaindl, Tr.

Established in 1988 in PA.
Financial data (yr. ended 12/31/01): Grants paid, $131,483; assets, $2,736,419 (M); expenditures, $141,285; qualifying distributions, $132,613.
Limitations: Giving primarily in Lehigh Valley, PA.
Application information: Application form not required.
Trustees: David Jaindl, Mark Jaindl, PNC Bank, N.A.
EIN: 232495124
Codes: FD2

46668
R. M. Hoffman Family Memorial Trust
c/o PNC Advisors
1600 Market St., Tax Department
Philadelphia, PA 19103-7240

Financial data (yr. ended 12/31/00): Grants paid, $131,179; assets, $5,329,733 (M); expenditures, $170,064; qualifying distributions, $137,179.
Limitations: Applications not accepted. Giving primarily in PA.
Application information: Contributes only to pre-selected organizations.
Trustee: PNC Bank, N.A.
EIN: 256500388
Codes: FD2

46669
Langworthy Foundation
c/o PNC Advisors
1600 Market St., 4th Fl.
Philadelphia, PA 19103-7240
Application address: 18 W. 11th St., New York, NY 10011
Contact: N.S. Langworthy, Chair.

Established in 1956.
Financial data (yr. ended 12/31/01): Grants paid, $130,950; assets, $1,858,535 (M); expenditures, $150,183; qualifying distributions, $131,950.
Committee Members: N.S. Langworthy, Chair.; K.C. Langworthy, W.B. Langworthy.
Trustee: PNC Bank, N.A.
EIN: 236207359
Codes: FD2

46670
Clarence S. & Margaret F. Fugh Foundation
c/o National City Bank of Pennsylvania
20 Stanwix St., No. 25-162
Pittsburgh, PA 15222
Contact: Joanna M. Mayo, V.P., National City Bank of Pennsylvania

Established in 1964 in PA.
Donor(s): Margaret F. Fugh,‡ Clarence S. Fugh.‡
Financial data (yr. ended 06/30/01): Grants paid, $130,760; assets, $3,517,771 (M); expenditures, $165,803; qualifying distributions, $148,236.
Limitations: Giving primarily in Etna and Shaler, PA.
Application information: Initial approach is through National City Bank of PA. Application form not required.
Trustees: Lee A. Donaldson, Jr., National City Bank of Pennsylvania.
EIN: 256062524
Codes: FD2

46671
Bartlett Foundation
c/o First Union National Bank
P.O. Box 7558, Tax Dept.
Philadelphia, PA 19101-7558
Application address: 60 Penn St., P.O. Box 1102, Reading, PA 19603-1102
Contact: Andrew C. Melzer, V.P.

Financial data (yr. ended 12/31/01): Grants paid, $130,600; assets, $2,209,893 (M); expenditures, $142,858; qualifying distributions, $130,118.
Limitations: Giving primarily in PA.
Trustee: First Union National Bank.
EIN: 236567275
Codes: FD2

46672
The Loualan Foundation
c/o R. Vine, Morgan, Lewis & Bockius, LLP
1701 Market St.
Philadelphia, PA 19103-2921

Established in 1986 in PA.
Donor(s): Alan L. Reed.
Financial data (yr. ended 11/30/01): Grants paid, $130,500; assets, $1,236,907 (M); gifts received, $240,940; expenditures, $132,313; qualifying distributions, $132,313.
Limitations: Applications not accepted. Giving primarily in PA.
Application information: Contributes only to pre-selected organizations.
Officers: Alan L. Reed, Pres. and Treas.; Louise H. Reed, V.P. and Secy.
EIN: 222779310
Codes: FD2

46673
The Maguire Foundation
8405 Flowertown Rd.
Wyndmoor, PA 19038

Established in 2000 in PA.
Donor(s): James J. Maguire.
Financial data (yr. ended 09/30/01): Grants paid, $130,182; assets, $8,833,201 (M); gifts received, $6,928,749; expenditures, $133,010; qualifying distributions, $130,182.
Limitations: Applications not accepted. Giving primarily in Philadelphia, PA.
Application information: Contributes only to pre-selected organizations.
Officers and Directors:* James J. Maguire,* Pres.; Frances M. Maguire,* Secy.-Treas.
EIN: 233057805
Codes: FD2

46674
Gwilym T. Williams Scholarship Fund
c/o PNC Advisors
P.O. Box 937
Scranton, PA 18501-0937 (717) 961-7431

Established in 1963 in PA.
Donor(s): Gwilym T. Williams.‡
Financial data (yr. ended 12/31/01): Grants paid, $129,907; assets, $987,305 (M); expenditures, $138,366; qualifying distributions, $132,724; giving activities include $130,524 for programs.
Limitations: Giving limited to PA.
Application information: Application form required.
Trustee: PNC Advisors.
EIN: 236420348
Codes: FD2, GTI

46675

The Edward & Marthann Samek Foundation
509 St. Davids Ave.
St. Davids, PA 19087

Established in 1999 in PA.
Donor(s): Edward Samek, Marthann Samek.
Financial data (yr. ended 12/31/01): Grants paid, $129,450; assets, $1,232,475 (M); expenditures, $145,983; qualifying distributions, $129,054.
Limitations: Applications not accepted.
Application information: Contributes only to pre-selected organizations.
Officers: Edward L. Samek, Pres. and Treas.; Marthann L. Samek, Exec. V.P. and Secy.; Anne S. Hopkins, V.P.; Christopher Hopkins, V.P.; Elizabeth Samek, V.P.; Margaret Samek-Smith, V.P.; Herman-Jan Smith, V.P.
EIN: 223694197
Codes: FD2

46676

Kennedy T. Friend Education Fund
c/o PNC Advisors, 1703406, P2-PTPP-10-2
620 Liberty Ave.
Pittsburgh, PA 15222-2705 (412) 762-3390
Contact: John Culbertson, Trust Off., PNC Bank, N.A.

Donor(s): Kennedy T. Friend.‡
Financial data (yr. ended 12/31/01): Grants paid, $129,031; assets, $6,427,878 (M); expenditures, $147,469; qualifying distributions, $129,448.
Limitations: Applications not accepted. Giving limited to residents of Allegheny County, PA.
Trustees: James Darby, PNC Bank, N.A., Allegheny County Bar Assn., Pres. Yale Club of Pittsburgh.
EIN: 256026198
Codes: FD2, GTI

46677

The Earl W. & Ina G. Tabor Foundation
P.O. Box 878
Wellsboro, PA 16901-0878 (570) 723-1470
Additional number: (570) 723-1490
Contact: Thomas M. Owlett, Tr.

Established in 1998 in PA.
Donor(s): Ina G. Tabor.‡
Financial data (yr. ended 12/31/01): Grants paid, $128,950; assets, $3,061,868 (M); expenditures, $168,563; qualifying distributions, $145,507.
Limitations: Giving limited to Tioga County, PA.
Application information: Application form required.
Trustees: Elinor Kantz, Richard H. Learn, Thomas M. Owlett.
EIN: 251815106
Codes: FD2

46678

Clinton County Community Foundation
P.O. Box 652
Lock Haven, PA 17745-0652 (570) 748-2481
FAX: (570) 748-7368; *E-mail:*
Lhlaw@LuggLaw.com
Contact: Robert H. Lugg, Chair.

Established in 1968 in PA.
Financial data (yr. ended 12/31/01): Grants paid, $128,611; assets, $3,743,445 (M); gifts received, $306,500; expenditures, $134,228.
Limitations: Giving limited to Clinton County, PA.
Publications: Financial statement.
Application information: Application form required.
Officers and Trustees:* Robert H. Lugg,* Chair.; William Marino,* Vice-Chair.; John Helbley,* Secy.; John P. Brandt, Jocelyn Hartley, John Lipez, Darlene Weaver.
EIN: 256093782
Codes: CM, FD2

46679

Cahouet Family Foundation
c/o Mellon Private Asset Management
3 Mellon Bank Center, Ste. 4000
Pittsburgh, PA 15219

Established in 2000 in PA.
Financial data (yr. ended 12/31/01): Grants paid, $128,000; assets, $1,448,225 (M); expenditures, $136,077; qualifying distributions, $128,000.
Limitations: Applications not accepted.
Application information: Contributes only to pre-selected organizations.
Trustees: Ann Cahouet, Frank Cahouet.
EIN: 256761976

46680

The Martin & Florence Hafter Family Foundation
751 Lantern Ln.
Penllyn, PA 19422-1611 (215) 923-6050
Contact: Martin Hafter, Tr.

Established in 1989 in PA.
Donor(s): Martin Hafter.
Financial data (yr. ended 12/31/01): Grants paid, $126,826; assets, $771,129 (M); gifts received, $198,188; expenditures, $127,414; qualifying distributions, $126,826.
Limitations: Giving primarily in PA.
Trustees: Florence Hafter, Martin Hafter, Robert Hafter.
EIN: 232548688
Codes: FD2

46681

Clemens Foundation
P.O. Box 1555
Kulpsville, PA 19443-1555
Contact: Jack Clemens, Treas.

Established in 1966 in PA.
Donor(s): Clemens Markets, Inc., Abram S. Clemens, James C. Clemens,‡ Lillian H. Clemens.
Financial data (yr. ended 09/30/01): Grants paid, $126,290; assets, $782,578 (M); gifts received, $95,598; expenditures, $133,024; qualifying distributions, $126,290.
Limitations: Giving primarily in PA.
Application information: Application form required.
Officers and Trustees:* Abram S. Clemens,* Pres.; Cheryl Mehl,* V.P.; Janice C. Tyson,* Secy.; Jack Clemens,* Treas.; Lillian H. Clemens, Jill Clemens Kulp, Jules Pearlstine, R. Carl Rhoads, Marilyn Clemens Rohrbach.
EIN: 231675035
Codes: CS, FD2, CD

46682

The Creative Financial Group, Ltd. Charitable Foundation
16 Campus Blvd., Ste. 200
Newtown Square, PA 19073 (610) 325-6100
Contact: Gary E. Daniels, Pres.

Established in 1993 in PA.
Donor(s): Creative Financial Group, CFPO, Inc.
Financial data (yr. ended 12/31/00): Grants paid, $126,218; assets, $9,590 (M); gifts received, $134,995; expenditures, $127,200; qualifying distributions, $126,212.
Limitations: Giving primarily in PA.
Officers: Gary E. Daniels, Pres.; Joseph V. Naselii, Secy.-Treas.
Trustees: Claire Daniels, Diana Naselli.
EIN: 232705803
Codes: CS, FD2, CD

46683

Florence M. Stout Trust
c/o Allfirst
21 E. Market St.
York, PA 17401-1500

Donor(s): Florence M. Stout.‡
Financial data (yr. ended 12/31/00): Grants paid, $126,051; assets, $1,631,685 (M); expenditures, $135,876; qualifying distributions, $123,257.
Limitations: Applications not accepted. Giving primarily in KS.
Application information: Contributes only to pre-selected organizations.
Trustee: Allfirst.
EIN: 256438364
Codes: FD2

46684

Waldman Family Charitable Trust
900 Fairfield Ave.
Easton, PA 18042-1328

Established in 1986 in PA.
Donor(s): Herman B. Waldman.
Financial data (yr. ended 12/31/01): Grants paid, $126,000; assets, $2,218,144 (M); gifts received, $13,319; expenditures, $136,302; qualifying distributions, $125,332.
Limitations: Applications not accepted. Giving primarily in PA.
Application information: Contributes only to pre-selected organizations.
Officers: Bruce Waldman, Mgr.; Herman B. Waldman, Mgr.; Mark Waldman, Mgr.
EIN: 236869549
Codes: FD2

46685

Agnes M. Swanson Trust
c/o PNC Advisors
P.O. Box 8480
Erie, PA 16553

Financial data (yr. ended 12/31/00): Grants paid, $125,668; assets, $2,255,696 (M); expenditures, $141,459; qualifying distributions, $122,962.
Limitations: Applications not accepted. Giving primarily in PA.
Application information: Contributes only to pre-selected organizations.
Trustee: PNC Bank, N.A.
EIN: 256163835
Codes: FD2

46686

George & Miriam Martin Foundation
1818 Market St., 35th Fl.
Philadelphia, PA 19103 (215) 587-8400
Contact: George Martin, Tr.

Established in 1996 in PA.
Donor(s): George Martin.
Financial data (yr. ended 12/31/01): Grants paid, $124,800; assets, $2,405,792 (M); gifts received, $445,000; expenditures, $126,710; qualifying distributions, $124,800.
Limitations: Giving primarily in southeast PA.
Application information: Application form not required.
Trustees: Glenn Emery, George Martin, M. Christine Martin, Rebecca Martin, Regis McCann, Carol Martin Strange, H. Lawrence Strange.
EIN: 232828201
Codes: FD2

46687
Charles F. & Anna E. Frey Foundation
259 Willow Valley Dr.
Lancaster, PA 17602
Contact: Charles F. Frey, Pres.

Established in 1991 in PA.
Donor(s): Charles F. Frey.
Financial data (yr. ended 12/31/01): Grants paid, $124,758; assets, $456,031 (M); gifts received, $400,000; expenditures, $124,927; qualifying distributions, $124,900.
Limitations: Giving primarily in PA.
Officer: Charles F. Frey, Pres.
EIN: 232189219
Codes: FD2

46688
Stephen G. Calvert Memorial Merit Scholarship Foundation
c/o 5 Tower Bridge
300 Barr Harbor Dr., Ste. 600
West Conshohocken, PA 19428-2998
Contact: Geraldine Livingston

Established in 1996 in PA.
Donor(s): Keystone Foods Corp.
Financial data (yr. ended 10/31/01): Grants paid, $124,750; assets, $41,395 (M); gifts received, $138,265; expenditures, $143,122; qualifying distributions, $124,750.
Limitations: Giving primarily in areas of company operations.
Application information: Restricted to dependents of Keystone Foods Corp. employees. Application form required.
Officers: Jeffrey Lotman, Pres.; Shelly Lotman Fisher, Secy.; Karen Lotman, Treas.
Director: Herbert Lotman.
EIN: 232816413
Codes: CS, FD2, CD

46689
The Shane Charitable Foundation
c/o Leonard P. Nalencz
1 Logan Sq.
Philadelphia, PA 19103
Application address: c/o William Shane, 1133 Winding Dr., Cherry Hill, NJ 08003-2730

Established in 1997 in NJ.
Donor(s): Eastbridge Corporation.
Financial data (yr. ended 06/30/01): Grants paid, $124,694; assets, $666,190 (M); expenditures, $141,751; qualifying distributions, $124,694.
Limitations: Giving primarily in NY.
Trustees: Gail M. Shane, William R. Shane.
EIN: 226742414
Codes: FD2

46690
The Mukaiyama-Rice Foundation
c/o Lance Eastman
P.O. Box 547
Bradford, PA 16701-0547

Established in 1998 in PA.
Donor(s): KOA Speer Electronics.
Financial data (yr. ended 12/31/00): Grants paid, $124,008; assets, $3,505,846 (M); gifts received, $133,542; expenditures, $320,307; qualifying distributions, $143,040.
Limitations: Applications not accepted. Giving primarily in Bradford, PA.
Application information: Contributes only to pre-selected organizations.
Officers and Directors:* Lance E. Eastman,* Pres.; Lester Rice,* V.P. and Secy.; Howard L. Fesenmyer, Timothy D. Rice.
EIN: 232949160
Codes: FD2

46691
Holstrom-Kineke Foundation
(Formerly The Holstrom Family Foundation)
20 E. Court St., P.O. Box 1310
Doylestown, PA 18901   (215) 340-1850
Contact: Mary Beth Kineke, Pres.

Established in 1984 in NY.
Donor(s): Carleton A. Holstrom.
Financial data (yr. ended 11/30/01): Grants paid, $124,000; assets, $167,586 (M); gifts received, $100,130; expenditures, $125,204; qualifying distributions, $124,209.
Limitations: Applications not accepted. Giving primarily in NJ and PA.
Application information: Contributes only to pre-selected organizations.
Officers and Directors:* Mary Beth Kineke,* Pres.; Carleton A. Holstrom,* Secy.-Treas; Christina L. Holstrom, Margaret Kineke, Martha Taylor.
EIN: 222611162
Codes: FD2

46692
Triple H Foundation
619 E. 28th Division Highway
Lititz, PA 17543

Established in 1997 in PA.
Donor(s): Esbenshades Greenhouses, Inc.
Financial data (yr. ended 11/30/01): Grants paid, $123,200; assets, $303,606 (M); gifts received, $240,000; expenditures, $126,831; qualifying distributions, $123,119.
Limitations: Applications not accepted. Giving primarily in PA.
Application information: Contributes only to pre-selected organizations.
Officers: Lamar R. Esbenshade, Pres.; Nancy Jane Esbenshade, Secy.
EIN: 232986164
Codes: FD2

46693
The Chappell Culpeper Family Foundation
P.O. Box 7516
St. Davids, PA 19087

Established in 2000 in PA.
Donor(s): John F. Chappell.
Financial data (yr. ended 12/31/01): Grants paid, $123,000; assets, $968,932 (M); gifts received, $174,300; expenditures, $125,662; qualifying distributions, $123,000.
Trustees: Carmen C. Chappell, John F. Chappell.
EIN: 256727111

46694
JGA Foundation
1500 Market St., 38th Fl.
Philadelphia, PA 19102   (215) 972-7828
Contact: Richard T. Frazier

Established in 1984 in PA.
Donor(s): John C. Merritt.
Financial data (yr. ended 10/31/01): Grants paid, $123,000; assets, $2,325,262 (M); gifts received, $150,000; expenditures, $129,094; qualifying distributions, $123,871.
Limitations: Giving on a national basis.
Application information: Application form not required.
Trustee: John R. Dougherty.
EIN: 232326454
Codes: FD2

46695
Sandy and Arnold Rifkin Charitable Foundation
190 Lathrop St.
Kingston, PA 18704

Established in 1987 in PA.
Donor(s): Arnold Rifkin, Harriet Rifkin, Damon Corp., Sandy Rifkin.
Financial data (yr. ended 12/31/01): Grants paid, $122,840; assets, $602,425 (M); expenditures, $123,134; qualifying distributions, $122,840.
Limitations: Applications not accepted. Giving limited to Wilkes-Barre, PA.
Application information: Contributes only to pre-selected organizations.
Trustees: Allan M. Kluger, Joseph Kluger.
EIN: 236869676
Codes: FD2

46696
The Leo Yochum Family Foundation
2024 Blairmont Dr.
Pittsburgh, PA 15241

Established in 1987 in PA.
Donor(s): Leo Yochum.
Financial data (yr. ended 12/31/00): Grants paid, $122,799; assets, $146,312 (M); gifts received, $86,831; expenditures, $126,135; qualifying distributions, $122,799.
Limitations: Applications not accepted. Giving primarily in PA.
Application information: Contributes only to pre-selected organizations.
Officers: Leo Yochum, Chair. and Pres.; Mary Jane Yochum, V.P.
EIN: 251551381
Codes: FD2

46697
The Forst Foundation
c/o A. Loscalzo
101 West Ave.
Jenkintown, PA 19046

Established in 1991 in PA.
Donor(s): Edward S. Forst, Thomas Forst.
Financial data (yr. ended 12/31/01): Grants paid, $122,625; assets, $784,582 (M); gifts received, $69,900; expenditures, $125,634; qualifying distributions, $125,555.
Limitations: Applications not accepted.
Application information: Contributes only to pre-selected organizations.
Trustees: Thomas Forst, Mariellen Forst Paulus.
EIN: 237685957
Codes: FD2

46698
The Ralph T. & Esther L. Warburton Foundation
c/o Mellon Bank, N.A.
P.O. Box 185
Pittsburgh, PA 15230-9897

Established around 1966.
Financial data (yr. ended 12/31/01): Grants paid, $122,500; assets, $2,637,588 (M); expenditures, $160,883; qualifying distributions, $118,147.
Limitations: Applications not accepted. Giving primarily in Stark County, OH.
Application information: Contributes only to pre-selected organizations.
Trustee: Mellon Bank, N.A.
EIN: 346574882
Codes: FD2

46699
Buckingham Mountain Foundation
3400 Spruce St.
Philadelphia, PA 19104-4283 (215) 662-2024
FAX: (215) 349-5849; E-mail: muldoon@mail.med.upenn.edu
Contact: Jonathan E. Rhoads, Sr., Pres.

Established in 1952 in PA.
Donor(s): I.S. Ravdin,‡ E.G. Ravdin,‡ Julian Johnson,‡ Mary B. Johnson, Jonathan E. Rhoads, Jr., Teresa Rhoads,‡ Jonathan E. Rhoads, Sr., George Rhoads, Frances Rhoads.
Financial data (yr. ended 12/31/00): Grants paid, $121,500; assets, $3,026,335 (M); gifts received, $69,743; expenditures, $125,715; qualifying distributions, $121,026.
Limitations: Giving on a national basis, with emphasis on PA.
Application information: Unsolicited applications for funds not encouraged. Application form not required.
Officers: Jonathan E. Rhoads, Sr., Pres.; Mary B. Johnson, V.P.; Jonathan E. Rhoads, Jr., Secy.-Treas.
Directors: George Rhoads, Katharine E.G. Rhoads.
EIN: 236254714
Codes: FD2

46700
Gatter Foundation
c/o L. Gene Gatter
2300 Computer Ave., Ste. H-42
Willow Grove, PA 19090 (215) 839-0100

Donor(s): L. Gene Gatter, Joseph Formica.‡
Financial data (yr. ended 12/31/00): Grants paid, $121,236; assets, $261,227 (M); gifts received, $106,887; expenditures, $121,450; qualifying distributions, $121,236.
Limitations: Applications not accepted. Giving primarily in NJ and PA.
Application information: Contributes only to pre-selected organizations.
Officers and Trustees:* L. Gene Gatter,* Chair.; Joseph Livezey,* Secy.-Treas.
EIN: 236243026
Codes: FD2

46701
A. H. and Helen L. Weiss Foundation
c/o Cozen & O'Connor
200 Four Falls Corp. Ctr., Ste. 400
West Conshohocken, PA 19428-2958
(610) 941-2349
Contact: Burton K. Stein

Established about 1956.
Financial data (yr. ended 09/30/01): Grants paid, $121,090; assets, $342,118 (M); expenditures, $141,093; qualifying distributions, $121,090.
Limitations: Giving primarily in Philadelphia, PA.
Application information: Application form not required.
Trustees: Stephen A. Cozen, Linda Saltz, Helen L. Weiss.
EIN: 236298302
Codes: FD2

46702
Dentsply International Foundation
c/o Tax Dept.
570 W. College Ave.
York, PA 17405

Established in 1955 in PA.
Donor(s): Dentsply International Inc.
Financial data (yr. ended 12/31/01): Grants paid, $120,710; assets, $75,616 (M); gifts received, $160,000; expenditures, $167,380; qualifying distributions, $120,710.
Limitations: Giving primarily in DE and PA.

Application information: Application form not required.
Officer: Brian M. Addison, Secy.
Trustees: William R. Jellison, John C. Miles II.
EIN: 236297307
Codes: CS, FD2, CD

46703
Pfundt Foundation
3111 Old Lincoln Hwy.
Trevose, PA 19053-4931
Contact: Lauren P. Meyer, Dir.

Established in 1967 in PA.
Donor(s): General Machine Products Co., Inc., G. Nelson Pfundt.
Financial data (yr. ended 09/30/01): Grants paid, $120,683; assets, $2,453,719 (M); gifts received, $56,491; expenditures, $123,862; qualifying distributions, $118,457.
Limitations: Giving on a national basis, with emphasis on PA.
Publications: Application guidelines.
Application information: Application form not required.
Officer and Directors:* G. Nelson Pfundt,* Mgr.; Lauren P. Meyer, William N. Pfundt.
EIN: 236442007
Codes: FD2

46704
Samuels Family Foundation
(Formerly A. Samuels Foundation)
2121 S. 12th St.
Allentown, PA 18103 (610) 797-6000
Contact: Abram Samuels, Pres.

Established in 1959.
Financial data (yr. ended 09/30/01): Grants paid, $120,391; assets, $1,802,873 (M); expenditures, $134,659; qualifying distributions, $120,230.
Limitations: Giving primarily in PA.
Application information: Application form not required.
Officers: Abram Samuels, Pres.; John A. Samuels, V.P.; Harriet Samuels, Secy.
EIN: 236259595
Codes: FD2

46705
Meshewa Farm Foundation
c/o Mellon Bank, N.A.
P.O. Box 7236
Philadelphia, PA 19101-7236

Established in 1993 in OH.
Donor(s): Mary C. LeBlond.
Financial data (yr. ended 12/31/00): Grants paid, $120,000; assets, $1,747,038 (M); gifts received, $177,691; expenditures, $131,456; qualifying distributions, $118,954.
Limitations: Applications not accepted.
Application information: Contributes only to pre-selected organizations.
Trustees: Francis R. Grebe, Mary Elizabeth Mitsui, Mellon Bank, N.A.
EIN: 237748707
Codes: FD2

46706
Nimick Forbesway Foundation
(Formerly Forbesway Foundation)
1 Oxford Ctr., 20th Fl.
Pittsburgh, PA 15219 (412) 562-8879
Contact: Jack J. Kessler, Secy.-Treas.

Established in 1989 in PA.
Donor(s): Thomas H. Nimick, Jr.
Financial data (yr. ended 06/30/01): Grants paid, $120,000; assets, $1,937,379 (M); expenditures, $131,653; qualifying distributions, $117,280.

Limitations: Giving primarily in Pittsburgh, PA.
Officers and Directors:* Thomas H. Nimick, Jr.,* Pres.; Theresa L. Nimick,* V.P.; Jack J. Kessler,* Secy.-Treas.; Victoria Nimick Enright.
EIN: 251597437
Codes: FD2

46707
Henry P. and Mary B. Stager Memorial Nursing Scholarship
c/o Fulton Financial Advisors, N.A.
P.O. Box 3215
Lancaster, PA 17604-3215
Application address: 143 E. Lemon St., Lancaster, PA 17602

Established in 1995.
Financial data (yr. ended 10/31/01): Grants paid, $120,000; assets, $1,795,536 (M); expenditures, $142,563; qualifying distributions, $119,640.
Limitations: Giving primarily in PA.
Application information: Application form required.
Trustee: Fulton Financial Advisors, N.A.
EIN: 232821372
Codes: FD2, GTI

46708
Ethel Vincent Charitable Trust
c/o PNC Bank, N.A., MS: P2-PTPP-25-1
2 PNC Plaza, 25th Fl., 620 Liberty Ave.
Pittsburgh, PA 15222-2719 (412) 762-3502
Application address: c/o Joseph M. Wymard, 220 Grant St., Pittsburgh, PA 15219; FAX: (412) 705-1043; E-mail: bruce.bickel@pncbank.com
Contact: R. Bruce Bickel, Mng. Dir., PNC Bank, N.A.

Established in 1996.
Financial data (yr. ended 09/30/01): Grants paid, $120,000; assets, $2,095,686 (M); expenditures, $140,128; qualifying distributions, $122,360.
Limitations: Giving on a national basis.
Trustees: Joseph M. Wymard, PNC Bank, N.A.
EIN: 237886897
Codes: FD2

46709
Morris Waber Fund
c/o Wolf Block
1650 Arch St., 22nd Fl.
Philadelphia, PA 19103

Established in 1963 in PA.
Donor(s): Morris Waber.‡
Financial data (yr. ended 12/31/01): Grants paid, $119,500; assets, $945,933 (M); expenditures, $124,111; qualifying distributions, $121,021.
Limitations: Applications not accepted. Giving primarily in New York, NY, and Philadelphia, PA.
Application information: Contributes only to pre-selected organizations.
Officer: Harry Waber, Mgr.
Trustees: Tanya Corbin, Irwin Jacobs.
EIN: 236281585
Codes: FD2

46710
The Harriette Steele Tabas and Charles L. Tabas Foundation
(Formerly Charles L. Tabas Foundation)
c/o Leslee S. Tabas
737 Montgomery Ave.
Narberth, PA 19072
Contact: Gerald Levinson, Exec. Dir.

Established in 1984 in PA.
Donor(s): Charles L. Tabas Memorial Lead Trust.
Financial data (yr. ended 03/31/02): Grants paid, $119,400; assets, $4,848,361 (M); expenditures, $135,743; qualifying distributions, $119,400.

Limitations: Giving primarily in Philadelphia, PA.
Application information: Application form not required.
Officers: Harriette S. Tabas, Pres.; Nancy C. Fleming, V.P.; Andrew R. Tabas, V.P.; Richard S. Tabas, Secy.; Gerald Levinson, Exec. Dir.
EIN: 222630429
Codes: FD2

46711
Middlemas Petska Foundation, Inc.
270 Walker Dr.
P.O. Box 259
State College, PA 16804

Established in 2000 in PA.
Donor(s): George M. Middlemas.
Financial data (yr. ended 12/31/01): Grants paid, $118,549; assets, $104,179 (M); expenditures, $180,564; qualifying distributions, $118,549.
Limitations: Applications not accepted.
Application information: Contributes only to pre-selected organizations.
Officers and Directors:* George M. Middlemas,* Pres.; Sherry L. Petska,* Secy.-Treas.; John Attard, Leonard Batterson.
EIN: 251872995

46712
The Clayman Family Foundation
101 W. City Line Ave.
Bala Cynwyd, PA 19004
Contact: Bradford Clayman

Established in 1997 in PA.
Financial data (yr. ended 12/31/00): Grants paid, $117,955; assets, $2,288,347 (M); expenditures, $135,116; qualifying distributions, $117,955.
Limitations: Giving on a national basis.
Officers and Directors:* Morton Clayman,* Pres.; Deborah Clayman,* Secy.-Treas.; Roberta Clayman.
EIN: 232893816
Codes: FD2

46713
Tanker Family Charitable Foundation
336 Sinker Rd.
Wyncote, PA 19095-1116 (215) 572-6267
Contact: Paul A. Tanker, Tr.

Established in 1996 in PA.
Donor(s): Paul A. Tanker.
Financial data (yr. ended 12/31/01): Grants paid, $117,865; assets, $311,208 (M); expenditures, $124,233; qualifying distributions, $117,865.
Application information: Application form not required.
Trustees: Joanne G. Tanker, Mary S. Tanker, Paul A. Tanker.
EIN: 232868987

46714
Hughes Foundation, Inc.
P.O. Box 149
Stroudsburg, PA 18360-0149 (717) 393-1226
Contact: R. Clinton Hughes, Jr., Pres.

Established in 1959 in PA.
Donor(s): Russell C. Hughes Trust.
Financial data (yr. ended 04/30/02): Grants paid, $117,300; assets, $2,435,213 (M); gifts received, $135,000; expenditures, $123,396; qualifying distributions, $117,315.
Limitations: Giving only in the Stroudsburg and Monroe County, PA, area.
Application information: Application form not required.
Officers and Directors:* R. Clinton Hughes, Jr.,* Pres.; R. Dale Hughes,* V.P.; Kevin Hughes,*

Secy.; Terri Cramer,* Treas.; Bernard Billick, Bryan E. Hughes, Raymond Price III.
EIN: 236298104
Codes: FD2

46715
The Colonna Family Foundation
790 Holiday Dr.
Pittsburgh, PA 15220
Contact: Robert J. Colonna, Pres.

Established in 1984.
Donor(s): Robert J. Colonna.
Financial data (yr. ended 09/30/01): Grants paid, $117,068; assets, $1,372,626 (M); expenditures, $137,950; qualifying distributions, $116,938.
Limitations: Giving primarily in Pittsburgh, PA.
Application information: Application form not required.
Officers and Directors:* Robert J. Colonna,* Pres.; Richard C. Colonna, V.P. and Secy.; Audrey N. Ballintine,* Treas.
EIN: 251481851
Codes: FD2

46716
The Gelb Foundation
111 Pellar Ave.
Scranton, PA 18505
Contact: Beverly Klein, Secy.-Treas.

Established in 1948.
Donor(s): Mae S. Gelb, Sondra Myers, Beverly Klein.
Financial data (yr. ended 12/31/00): Grants paid, $116,855; assets, $1,291,129 (L); expenditures, $121,712; qualifying distributions, $120,363.
Limitations: Giving on a national basis, with some emphasis on PA.
Officers: Mae S. Gelb, Pres.; Sondra Myers, V.P.; Beverly Klein, Secy.-Treas.
EIN: 246018072
Codes: FD2

46717
The Lida Foundation
504 W. Mermaid Ln.
Philadelphia, PA 19118
Contact: Linda S. Glickstein, Tr.

Established in 1993 in PA.
Financial data (yr. ended 12/31/01): Grants paid, $116,390; assets, $2,377,196 (M); expenditures, $127,179; qualifying distributions, $115,914.
Limitations: Giving primarily in PA.
Trustees: David L. Glickstein, Linda S. Glickstein.
EIN: 232706456
Codes: FD2

46718
Charles G. Berwind Foundation
3000 Centre Sq. W.
1500 Market St.
Philadelphia, PA 19102
Contact: Jessica M. Berwind

Established in 1974.
Donor(s): David Michael Berwind.
Financial data (yr. ended 09/30/01): Grants paid, $116,388; assets, $2,425,384 (M); expenditures, $146,677; qualifying distributions, $134,227.
Limitations: Applications not accepted.
Application information: Unsolicited requests for funds not considered.
Selection Committee: Walter G. Arader, Erika Behrend, Sandra Berwind.
EIN: 237382896
Codes: FD2, GTI

46719
Seymour & Doris Greenberg Foundation
8470 Limekiln Pike
Wyncote, PA 19095

Established in 1995.
Donor(s): Seymour Greenberg, Doris Greenberg.
Financial data (yr. ended 12/31/01): Grants paid, $116,135; assets, $352,262 (M); gifts received, $210,000; expenditures, $118,699; qualifying distributions, $116,135.
Limitations: Applications not accepted. Giving on a national basis.
Application information: Contributes only to pre-selected organizations.
Trustees: Doris Greenberg, Seymour Greenberg.
EIN: 232820633

46720
Jewish Family Assistance Fund
5743 Bartlett St.
Pittsburgh, PA 15217
Contact: Sam Steinberg, Treas.

Established around 1987.
Donor(s): Herman Lipsitz, Mrs. Herman Lipsitz, Jewish Healthcare Foundation.
Financial data (yr. ended 12/31/01): Grants paid, $115,977; assets, $132,035 (M); gifts received, $103,151; expenditures, $121,659; qualifying distributions, $121,659.
Limitations: Giving limited to residents in Pittsburgh, PA.
Officers: James E. Reich, Pres.; Sam Steinberg, Treas.
EIN: 251512726
Codes: FD2, GTI

46721
The Pencoyd Foundation
234 Pembroke Ave.
Wayne, PA 19087-4837 (610) 971-2663
Application address: 687 W. Lancaster Ave., Wayne, PA 19087; E-mail: pencoydlp@aol.com
Contact: Howard R. Morgan, Tr.

Established in 1998 in PA.
Donor(s): Evora K. Morgan.‡
Financial data (yr. ended 03/31/01): Grants paid, $115,750; assets, $1,059,246 (M); expenditures, $119,871; qualifying distributions, $114,727.
Limitations: Giving primarily in the Philadelphia, PA, area, and VA.
Application information: Application form not required.
Trustees: Anna E. Morgan, Carl G. Morgan, Elizabeth T. Morgan, Howard R. Morgan, H. Randall Morgan, Jr.
EIN: 256613197
Codes: FD2

46722
The Jay and Terry Snider Foundation
(Formerly SFW Foundation)
200 W. Montgomery Ave.
Ardmore, PA 19003

Established in 1995 in PA.
Donor(s): Jay Snider.
Financial data (yr. ended 12/31/00): Grants paid, $114,725; assets, $852,708 (M); expenditures, $115,984; qualifying distributions, $114,725.
Limitations: Applications not accepted. Giving primarily in PA.
Application information: Contributes only to pre-selected organizations.
Officers and Directors:* Jay Snider, Pres. and Treas.; Terry Snider, Secy.
EIN: 232815880
Codes: FD2

46723
Edward J. Kavanagh Foundation
1340 Yahres Rd.
Sharon, PA 16146 (724) 347-5215

Established around 1969 in PA.
Financial data (yr. ended 07/31/01): Grants paid, $114,500; assets, $2,030,397 (M); expenditures, $119,974; qualifying distributions, $112,777.
Limitations: Giving primarily in Mercer County, PA.
Officers: Kevin E. Kavanagh, Pres.; Eileen Buchanan, V.P.; Katherine Hammer, V.P.; Thomas E. Kavanagh, V.P.; Joan K. Feeney, Secy.-Treas.
EIN: 237023865
Codes: FD2

46724
Gibbel Foundation, Inc.
2 N. Broad St.
Lititz, PA 17543-1005 (717) 626-4751
Contact: Henry H. Gibbel, Pres.

Established in 1965 in PA.
Donor(s): James C. Gibbel, Henry H. Gibbel, John R. Gibbel.
Financial data (yr. ended 12/31/01): Grants paid, $114,454; assets, $1,658,755 (M); gifts received, $40,665; expenditures, $124,308; qualifying distributions, $114,348.
Limitations: Giving primarily in PA.
Officers: Henry H. Gibbel, Pres. and Treas.; James C. Gibbel, V.P.; John R. Gibbel, Secy.
EIN: 236402619
Codes: FD2

46725
The Dietrich W. Botstiber Foundation
933 Rocklyn Rd.
Springfield, PA 19064 (610) 566-3330
Contact: Robert Boylan, Mgr.

Established in 1995 in PA.
Donor(s): Dietrich W. Botstiber.
Financial data (yr. ended 08/31/01): Grants paid, $114,356; assets, $3,034,794 (M); expenditures, $212,843; qualifying distributions, $151,454.
Limitations: Giving on a national basis.
Publications: Annual report (including application guidelines).
Officer and Trustees:* Robert Boylan,* Mgr.; Dietrich W. Botstiber, Dorothy Boylan.
EIN: 237807828
Codes: FD2

46726
Leslie Family Foundation
c/o PNC Advisors
P.O. Box 8480
Erie, PA 16553

Established in 1994 in PA.
Donor(s): Donald S. Leslie, Jr., Mrs. Donald S. Leslie.
Financial data (yr. ended 12/31/01): Grants paid, $113,800; assets, $485,091 (M); gifts received, $19,879; expenditures, $115,864; qualifying distributions, $113,830.
Limitations: Applications not accepted.
Application information: Contributes only to pre-selected organizations.
Officers and Directors:* Donald S. Leslie, Jr.,* Pres.; Miriam Leslie,* Pres.
Trustee: PNC Bank, N.A.
EIN: 311484689
Codes: FD2

46727
McCole Foundation
(Formerly Cornelius J. McCole and Arline Sweeny McCole Foundation)
190 Lathrop St.
Kingston, PA 18704-5318 (570) 283-2727
Contact: William R. Lazor, Treas.

Established in 1986 in PA.
Donor(s): John A. McCole.‡
Financial data (yr. ended 12/31/00): Grants paid, $113,453; assets, $1,588,420 (M); gifts received, $33,398; expenditures, $134,875; qualifying distributions, $113,453.
Limitations: Giving primarily in PA.
Officers: Cornelius E. McCole, Chair. and V.P.; Constance K. McCole, Pres.; Allan M. Kluger, Secy.; William R. Lazor, Treas.
EIN: 232439590
Codes: FD2

46728
Frank and Edna Walker Residuary Trust
21 E. Market St., MC 402-130
York, PA 17401-1500

Established in 1995.
Financial data (yr. ended 12/31/01): Grants paid, $112,615; assets, $2,134,826 (M); expenditures, $126,214; qualifying distributions, $111,902.
Limitations: Applications not accepted. Giving primarily in PA.
Application information: Contributes only to pre-selected organizations.
Trustee: Allfirst.
EIN: 256187787
Codes: FD2

46729
The Gordon Foundation
700 Fifth Ave.
Pittsburgh, PA 15219 (412) 765-0505
Contact: Ira H. Gordon, Tr.

Financial data (yr. ended 12/31/00): Grants paid, $112,385; assets, $338,377 (M); expenditures, $113,748; qualifying distributions, $112,102.
Limitations: Giving primarily in Pittsburgh, PA.
Trustees: Ira H. Gordon, Peter I. Gordon.
EIN: 256036563
Codes: FD2

46730
O'Grady Family Foundation
1160 Norsam Rd.
Gladwyne, PA 19035

Donor(s): Jeremiah P. O'Grady.
Financial data (yr. ended 12/31/00): Grants paid, $112,250; assets, $527,814 (M); expenditures, $117,562; qualifying distributions, $113,722.
Limitations: Applications not accepted. Giving on a national basis, with some emphasis on PA.
Application information: Contributes only to pre-selected organizations.
Trustees: Jeremiah P. O'Grady, Kathleen A. O'Grady.
EIN: 237770587
Codes: FD2

46731
The J & L Specialty Steel Charitable Foundation
(Formerly J & L Specialty Products Charitable Foundation)
1 PPG Pl.
P.O. Box 3373
Pittsburgh, PA 15230-3373 (412) 338-1732
Contact: James Leonard, Dir., Public Affairs

Established in 1988 in PA.
Donor(s): J & L Specialty Steel, Inc.
Financial data (yr. ended 12/31/01): Grants paid, $111,914; assets, $1,965,348 (M); gifts received, $2,250; expenditures, $115,701; qualifying distributions, $115,701.
Limitations: Applications not accepted. Giving primarily in Louisville and Canton, OH, and Pittsburgh and Beaver County, PA.
Application information: Contributes only to pre-selected organizations.
Officers: Jacques Chabanier, Chair. and Admin.; Darryl K. Fox, Admin.
Trustee Bank: Mellon Bank, N.A.
EIN: 256311251
Codes: CS, FD2, CD

46732
The George T. Handyside Memorial Scholarship Foundation
1019 Rte. 519
Eighty Four, PA 15330-2813 (724) 228-8820
Contact: Daniel Wallach

Established in 1992 in PA.
Donor(s): Joseph A. Hardy III.
Financial data (yr. ended 12/31/01): Grants paid, $111,000; assets, $1,749,354 (M); expenditures, $131,713; qualifying distributions, $18,595.
Limitations: Giving primarily to residents in those areas served by 84 Lumber Co. operations.
Application information: Applications are available at 84 Lumber Co. corporate office. Application form required.
Officers: Joseph A. Hardy III, Pres. and Treas.; Margaret A. Hardy-Magerko, Secy.
EIN: 251667394
Codes: FD2, GTI

46733
H.A./M.K. Wagner Family Foundation
1306 Prospect Ave.
Bethlehem, PA 18018

Established in 1997 in PA.
Donor(s): Harold A. Wagner.
Financial data (yr. ended 12/31/99): Grants paid, $110,363; assets, $715,794 (M); expenditures, $110,373; qualifying distributions, $109,232.
Trustees: Sandra Boyce, Harold A. Wagner, Harold E. Wagner, Kristi Wagner, Marcia K. Wagner, Tracey Wagner.
EIN: 237886100
Codes: FD2

46734
Ruth H. Jackson Charitable Trust
c/o Pitt-Des Moines, Inc.
3400 Grand Ave.
Pittsburgh, PA 15225-1582
Contact: W.R. Jackson, Sr., Tr.

Established in 1951.
Financial data (yr. ended 12/31/01): Grants paid, $110,250; assets, $2,758,582 (M); expenditures, $112,297; qualifying distributions, $110,250.
Limitations: Giving primarily in PA.
Trustees: W.R. Jackson, Polly J. Townsend.
EIN: 256065763
Codes: FD2

46735
Wolstenholme Charitable Foundation
631 Catherine St.
Warminster, PA 18974-2801

Established in 1998 in DE and PA.
Donor(s): Eugene B. Wolstenholme, Jean M. Wolstenholme.
Financial data (yr. ended 06/30/01): Grants paid, $110,100; assets, $1,318,453 (M); gifts received, $596,196; expenditures, $123,542; qualifying distributions, $109,898.

Officers: Jean Wolstenholme, Secy.; Eugene Wolstenholme, Mgr.
EIN: 232937483
Codes: FD2

46736
The Emergency Aid of Pennsylvania Foundation, Inc.
221 Conestoga Rd., Ste. 300
Wayne, PA 19087 (610) 225-0944
FAX: (610) 225-0945; E-mail: eapa@erols.com
Contact: Joanne Platt, Office Mgr.

Established in 1914 in PA.
Financial data (yr. ended 06/30/01): Grants paid, $110,066; assets, $3,031,182 (M); gifts received, $31,900; expenditures, $170,574; qualifying distributions, $143,896.
Limitations: Giving limited to the five counties in the immediate Philadelphia, PA, area.
Publications: Annual report, newsletter, informational brochure.
Application information: Accepts Delaware Valley Grantmakers Common Grant Application; scholarship application mailed to eligible students. No other applications from individuals considered. Application form required.
Officers and Directors:* Michele Howard,* Chair.; Alice Dagit, Vice-Chair.; Ann Bridge, Secy.; Najiye Lynch,* Treas.; and 15 additional directors.
Distribution Committee: Judy Huttaker, and 10 additional members.
Trustee: The Pennsylvania Trust Company.
EIN: 232321913
Codes: FD2, GTI

46737
The Ressler Family Foundation
1124 Berwind Rd.
Wynnewood, PA 19096-2320

Established in 1994 in PA.
Donor(s): Emerich Ressler, Edith S. Ressler.
Financial data (yr. ended 12/31/00): Grants paid, $110,000; assets, $1,516,680 (M); gifts received, $134,438; expenditures, $110,000; qualifying distributions, $110,000.
Limitations: Applications not accepted. Giving primarily in NY.
Application information: Contributes only to pre-selected organizations.
Officers and Directors:* Emerich Ressler,* Pres.; Edith Ressler,* Secy.-Treas.; David Israeli, Katherine Israeli, Lisa G. Israeli.
EIN: 232797835
Codes: FD2

46738
Ray Tyo-St. Ferdinand College Scholarship Foundation
(Formerly George L. Leech-King St. Ferdinand III College Scholarship Foundation)
c/o Allfirst
21 E. Market St., M/C 402-130
York, PA 17401-1500
Application address: c/o Msgr. Edward Quinlan, P.O. Box 3553, Harrisburg, PA 17105-3553, tel.: (717) 657-4804

Established in 1967.
Financial data (yr. ended 12/31/00): Grants paid, $109,650; assets, $2,520,515 (M); expenditures, $141,420; qualifying distributions, $109,650.
Limitations: Applications not accepted. Giving limited to residents of the Harrisburg, PA, area.
Application information: Applications only available through principal or guidance counselor.
Trustee: Allfirst.
EIN: 236508132
Codes: FD2, GTI

46739
The Ryan Family Foundation
2875 Country Club Rd.
Allentown, PA 18103
Contact: Frank Ryan, Tr.

Established in 1997 in PA.
Donor(s): Frank Ryan.
Financial data (yr. ended 12/31/01): Grants paid, $109,250; assets, $1,516,579 (M); expenditures, $139,940; qualifying distributions, $109,250.
Limitations: Applications not accepted. Giving primarily in PA.
Application information: Contributes only to pre-selected organizations.
Directors and Trustee:* Carolyn Healey, Frank Ryan, Jane Ryan.
EIN: 232901049
Codes: FD2

46740
The Hollinger Foundation
755 White Oak Rd.
Denver, PA 17517

Established in 2000 in PA.
Donor(s): David Hollinger, Deborah Hollinger.
Financial data (yr. ended 12/31/01): Grants paid, $108,885; assets, $24,836 (M); gifts received, $170,617; expenditures, $164,988; qualifying distributions, $164,363.
Limitations: Applications not accepted. Giving primarily in PA.
Application information: Contributes only to pre-selected organizations.
Officers: David L. Hollinger, Pres.; Deborah J. Hollinger, Secy.
EIN: 233025306

46741
The Roy F. Johns, Jr. Family Foundation
200 Marshall Dr.
Coraopolis, PA 15108 (412) 264-8383
Contact: Roy F. Johns, Jr., Dir.

Established in 1993.
Donor(s): Roy F. Johns, Jr.
Financial data (yr. ended 12/31/01): Grants paid, $108,400; assets, $1,797,187 (M); expenditures, $184,530; qualifying distributions, $109,475.
Limitations: Giving primarily in western PA.
Application information: Application form not required.
Officer and Directors:* Roy F. Johns, Jr.,* Mgr.; Barbara Johns.
EIN: 256426447
Codes: FD2

46742
Alfred & Constance Wolf Aviation Fund
c/o Wolf, Block, Schorr & Solis-Cohen
1650 Arch St., 22nd Fl.
Philadelphia, PA 19103-2097
FAX: (603) 806-7937; E-mail: mail@wolf-aviation.org; URL: http://www.wolf-aviation.org

Established in 1985.
Financial data (yr. ended 04/30/01): Grants paid, $108,000; assets, $2,109,029 (M); expenditures, $125,983; qualifying distributions, $113,563.
Limitations: Giving on a national basis.
Application information: Application form not required.
Trustees: Leonard J. Cooper, Albert Wolf.
EIN: 232494508
Codes: FD2, GTI

46743
Henry C. Miller Foundation
1640 Freeport Rd.
P.O. Box 528
North East, PA 16428

Established in 1991 in PA.
Financial data (yr. ended 12/31/01): Grants paid, $107,750; assets, $2,605,681 (M); expenditures, $131,951; qualifying distributions, $123,838.
Limitations: Applications not accepted. Giving primarily in PA.
Application information: Contributes only to pre-selected organizations.
Trustees: Michele D. Giesen, H. Daniel Hill III, Christopher R. Miller, H. Wayne Miller, Janet L. Miller, Robert S. Miller, Richard S. Steele.
Agents: Fleet National Bank, Mellon Private Asset Management.
EIN: 251649974
Codes: FD2

46744
The Carl J. and Margot A. Johnson Foundation
1211 Minnesota Ave.
Natrona Heights, PA 15065

Established in 1991 in PA.
Donor(s): Carl J. Johnson, Margot A. Johnson.
Financial data (yr. ended 12/31/01): Grants paid, $107,688; assets, $2,469,069 (M); gifts received, $137,925; expenditures, $111,665; qualifying distributions, $107,688.
Limitations: Applications not accepted. Giving primarily in PA.
Application information: Contributes only to pre-selected organizations.
Trustees: Carl J. Johnson, Margot A. Johnson.
EIN: 251675809

46745
Hayes Foundation
321 Pennwood Ave.
Pittsburgh, PA 15221

Established in 1966 in PA.
Donor(s): Richard Bachelder, C.N. Hayes, Jr., Nellie I. Hayes, Robert D. Hayes.
Financial data (yr. ended 12/31/01): Grants paid, $107,500; assets, $2,076,217 (M); gifts received, $7,900; expenditures, $111,346; qualifying distributions, $107,500.
Limitations: Applications not accepted. Giving primarily in PA.
Application information: Contributes only to pre-selected organizations.
Trustees: Sallie H. Brinkhoff, Nellie I. Hayes, Robert D. Hayes.
EIN: 256079804
Codes: FD2

46746
Coleman Foundation
c/o Pitcairn Trust Co.
165 Township Line Rd., Ste. 3000
Jenkintown, PA 19046 (215) 881-6147
Contact: Paul Irwin

Established in 1935 in PA.
Financial data (yr. ended 12/31/00): Grants paid, $106,000; assets, $1,726,916 (M); expenditures, $107,321; qualifying distributions, $105,888.
Limitations: Giving primarily in PA.
Application information: Application form not required.
Trustees: Agnes Coleman, William S. Coleman, Parke H. Hess, Pitcairn Trust Co.
EIN: 236214964
Codes: FD2

46747—PENNSYLVANIA

46747
Eye & Ear Hospital of Pittsburgh, Pennsylvania Medical Staff Education Fund
8 Elmcrest Rd.
Oakmont, PA 15139

Established in 1989 in PA.
Financial data (yr. ended 06/30/01): Grants paid, $106,000; assets, $2,083,820 (M); gifts received, $2,500; expenditures, $138,027; qualifying distributions, $106,000.
Limitations: Applications not accepted. Giving limited to Pittsburgh, PA.
Officers: Dick Katzin, M.D., Pres.; Albert Biglan, M.D., V.P. and Secy.-Treas.
Directors: David Ebling, M.D., Donald B. Kamerer, M.D., George Schein, M.D., Marshall Stafford, M.D., Edmond C. Watters, M.D.
EIN: 251402374
Codes: FD2

46748
The James W. and Carol A. Hovey Foundation
955 Chesterbrook Blvd., Ste. 125
Chesterbrook, PA 19087

Established in 1988 in PA.
Donor(s): James W. Hovey, Carol A. Hovey.
Financial data (yr. ended 12/31/01): Grants paid, $106,000; assets, $664,818 (M); gifts received, $347,858; expenditures, $107,572; qualifying distributions, $106,000.
Limitations: Applications not accepted. Giving primarily in Philadelphia, PA.
Application information: Contributes only to pre-selected organizations.
Trustees: Carol A. Hovey, James W. Hovey.
EIN: 232544450

46749
Tasty Baking Foundation
2801 Hunting Park Ave.
Philadelphia, PA 19129-1392 (215) 221-8519
Contact: P. Curcio

Established in 1955 in PA.
Donor(s): Tasty Baking Co.
Financial data (yr. ended 12/31/01): Grants paid, $105,575; assets, $450,901 (M); gifts received, $80,000; expenditures, $105,984; qualifying distributions, $105,575.
Limitations: Giving limited to the greater Philadelphia, PA, area.
Application information: Application form required.
Officers and Trustees:* Philip J. Baur, Jr.,* Chair.; John M. Pettine,* Secy.-Treas.; Nelson G. Harris, Carl S. Watts.
EIN: 236271018
Codes: CS, FD2, CD

46750
Andrew R. & Dorothy L. Cochrane Foundation
P.O. Box 366
Eagles Mere, PA 17731-0366
Contact: Eleanor C. Clark, Tr.

Established about 1968.
Donor(s): Andrew R. Cochrane.‡
Financial data (yr. ended 12/31/01): Grants paid, $105,470; assets, $2,227,605 (M); gifts received, $537,614; expenditures, $115,699; qualifying distributions, $115,699.
Limitations: Giving primarily in Pittsburgh, PA.
Application information: Application form not required.
Trustees: Eleanor Cochrane Clark, Dorothy Cochrane, Christine Cochrane Yukevich.
EIN: 256093648
Codes: FD2

46751
Frances C. Sharp Charitable Foundation
c/o First Union National Bank, PA 6497
600 Penn St., P.O. Box 1102
Reading, PA 19603-1102
Contact: Hans F. Hass

Established in 1993 in PA.
Donor(s): Frances C. Sharp.‡
Financial data (yr. ended 06/30/01): Grants paid, $105,007; assets, $4,154,670 (M); expenditures, $130,183; qualifying distributions, $105,757.
Limitations: Applications not accepted. Giving primarily in PA.
Application information: Contributes only to pre-selected organizations.
Trustee: First Union National Bank.
EIN: 237758537
Codes: FD2

46752
Key Foundation
345 Quarry Rd.
Wellsville, PA 17365
Application address: P.O. Box 798, Camp Hill, PA 17001-0798
Contact: Joelle Margolis, Secy.

Established in 1997 in PA.
Donor(s): Joelle Margolis, Martin Margolis.
Financial data (yr. ended 12/31/00): Grants paid, $105,000; assets, $1,957,419 (M); expenditures, $106,433; qualifying distributions, $104,117.
Limitations: Giving primarily in NY and PA.
Application information: Application form not required.
Officers: Martin Margolis, Pres.; Joelle Margolis, Secy.
EIN: 232894154
Codes: FD2

46753
Leon Lowengard Scholarship Fund
c/o Mellon Bank, N.A.
P.O. Box 1010, 2 N. 2nd St., 12th Fl.
Philadelphia, PA 19101-7236
Application address: c/o Harrisburg Area Community College, Admissions Office, Cameron St., Harrisburg, PA 17108, tel.: (717) 780-2400

Established in 1937 in PA.
Financial data (yr. ended 09/30/01): Grants paid, $104,931; assets, $3,335,092 (M); expenditures, $141,729; qualifying distributions, $114,931.
Limitations: Giving limited to residents of the greater Harrisburg, PA, area.
Application information: Must be a Jewish graduate from a greater Harrisburg, PA, area high school. Application form required.
Trustee: Mellon Bank, N.A.
EIN: 236236909
Codes: FD2, GTI

46754
Jacquelin Foundation
451 Atkinson Ln.
Langhorne, PA 19047
Contact: Gary Coombs, Secy.

Established in 1960.
Financial data (yr. ended 05/31/01): Grants paid, $104,905; assets, $107,594 (M); expenditures, $111,612; qualifying distributions, $104,905.
Limitations: Giving primarily in Princeton, NJ, and Philadelphia, PA.
Officers: Margaret C. Burt, Pres.; Christopher C. Burt, V.P.; Gary Coombs, Secy.; Nathaniel Burt, Treas.
EIN: 226071849
Codes: FD2

46755
Conston Foundation
41 Conshohocken State Rd., Ste. 612
Bala Cynwyd, PA 19004
Contact: Charles S. Conston, Tr.

Established in 1959 in PA.
Donor(s): Conston, Inc.
Financial data (yr. ended 12/31/01): Grants paid, $104,600; assets, $2,024,838 (M); expenditures, $132,211; qualifying distributions, $110,490.
Limitations: Giving primarily in Philadelphia, PA.
Trustee: Charles S. Conston.
EIN: 236297587
Codes: CS, FD2, CD

46756
Isadore & Anna Oritsky Foundation
30 Devon Dr.
Reading, PA 19606

Established in 1967 in PA.
Donor(s): H. Oritsky, Inc.
Financial data (yr. ended 12/31/99): Grants paid, $104,515; assets, $1,239,153 (M); expenditures, $107,022; qualifying distributions, $104,046.
Limitations: Applications not accepted. Giving primarily in PA.
Application information: Contributes only to pre-selected organizations.
Officer: Herbert Oritsky, Mgr.
EIN: 236419027
Codes: FD2

46757
Memorial Hospital of Bedford County Foundation
R.D. No. 1, Box 80
Everett, PA 15537 (814) 623-3545
Contact: Sherry Obert

Established in 1997 in PA.
Financial data (yr. ended 06/30/01): Grants paid, $104,381; assets, $6,567,994 (M); gifts received, $25,828; expenditures, $168,031; qualifying distributions, $117,758.
Limitations: Giving limited to residents of Bedford County, PA.
Application information: Application form required.
Officers: John R. Blackburn, Jr., Chair.; Clyde Morris, Co-Chair.; James C. Vreeland, Pres.; Tom Bailey, Treas.
Directors: David Baer, M.D., Henry Beamer, Elliott Bilofsky, Sam Bohn, Rev. Ed Datesman, B. Frank Dunkle, Mark Finder, M.D., Dick Hess, John Holbert, Raymond Jackson, M.D., Mabel Jordan, Ray Koontz, Harry Latshaw, Patricia Morgart, Pat Mueller, William Newman, M.D., William Obert, Joel Pyle, Daniel L. Ritchey, Pat Shuster, Robert Sweet, Anna Swindell, Donn Whetstone.
EIN: 232938090
Codes: FD2, GTI

46758
William and Nina Albert Foundation
210 W. Rittenhouse Sq., Ste. 2807
Philadelphia, PA 19103

Established in 1986 in PA.
Donor(s): William Albert.
Financial data (yr. ended 12/31/01): Grants paid, $103,826; assets, $80,114 (M); gifts received, $107,000; expenditures, $104,006; qualifying distributions, $103,593.
Limitations: Applications not accepted. Giving primarily in Philadelphia, PA.
Application information: Contributes only to pre-selected organizations.
Trustees: Nina Albert, William Albert.

EIN: 222766314
Codes: FD2

46759
David A. Glosser Foundation
72 Messenger St.
Johnstown, PA 15902 (814) 535-7521
Contact: Robert Krantzler, Pres.

Incorporated in 1962 in PA.
Donor(s): David A. Glosser.‡
Financial data (yr. ended 06/30/01): Grants paid, $103,800; assets, $3,068,271 (M); expenditures, $179,698; qualifying distributions, $103,800.
Limitations: Giving primarily in Johnstown, PA.
Officers: Robert Krantzler, Pres.; Lester Goldstein, V.P.; Robert Lux, Secy.-Treas.
Director: Robert Horowitz.
EIN: 256066913
Codes: FD2

46760
Driscoll Family Foundation
615 Saint Andrews Rd.
Philadelphia, PA 19118 (610) 668-0950
Contact: Edward C. Driscoll, Asst. Treas.

Established in 1997 in PA.
Donor(s): Edward C. Driscoll.
Financial data (yr. ended 12/31/00): Grants paid, $103,600; assets, $491,523 (M); gifts received, $40,000; expenditures, $110,201; qualifying distributions, $103,221.
Officers: David B. Driscoll, Pres.; Edward C. Driscoll, Jr., Secy.-Treas.
EIN: 232897985
Codes: FD2

46761
The Peter S. Mozino Foundation
5100 State Rd., Ste. E-500
Drexel Hill, PA 19026

Established in 1990 in PA.
Financial data (yr. ended 12/31/01): Grants paid, $103,500; assets, $1,790,510 (M); expenditures, $148,672; qualifying distributions, $105,331.
Limitations: Applications not accepted. Giving primarily in Philadelphia, PA.
Application information: Contributes only to pre-selected organizations.
Trustees: Catherine Mozino, H. David Seegul.
EIN: 237642668
Codes: FD2

46762
The Ruth B. & Mervyn M. Golder Foundation
1001 Hunters Ln.
Wynnewood, PA 19096-4016

Established in 1986 in PA.
Donor(s): Ruth B. Golder, Mervyn M. Golder.
Financial data (yr. ended 06/30/01): Grants paid, $103,463; assets, $88,382 (M); gifts received, $140,000; expenditures, $104,745; qualifying distributions, $103,446.
Limitations: Applications not accepted. Giving in the U.S., with emphasis on FL and PA.
Application information: Contributes only to pre-selected organizations.
Trustees: Mervyn M. Golder, Ruth B. Golder.
EIN: 236861840
Codes: FD2

46763
The Magee Foundation
20 W. Main St.
Bloomsburg, PA 17815-1598
Contact: Drue A. Magee, Tr.

Established in 1964 in PA.
Financial data (yr. ended 10/31/01): Grants paid, $103,160; assets, $1,962,811 (M); expenditures, $122,519; qualifying distributions, $105,846.
Limitations: Applications not accepted. Giving primarily in Bloomsburg, PA.
Application information: Contributes only to pre-selected organizations.
Trustees: Joanne M. Katerman, Audrey R. Magee, Drue A. Magee, James A. Magee, Barbara Paule.
EIN: 236398294
Codes: FD2

46764
MKM Foundation
c/o The Glenmede Trust Co.
1650 Market St., Ste. 1200
Philadelphia, PA 19103-7391 (215) 419-6000

Established in 1998 in NJ.
Donor(s): James E. O'Donnell.
Financial data (yr. ended 12/31/01): Grants paid, $103,000; assets, $2,103,952 (M); expenditures, $116,112; qualifying distributions, $103,672.
Limitations: Applications not accepted. Giving primarily in NJ and PA.
Application information: Contributes only to pre-selected organizations.
Trustees: Elizabeth O'Donnell, James E. O'Donnell, Marie O'Donnell.
EIN: 237966478
Codes: FD2

46765
The HBE Foundation
c/o Beucler, Kelly & Irwin Ltd.
125 Strafford Ave., Ste. 116
Wayne, PA 19087 (610) 688-0143
Application address: 350 Pond View, Devon, PA 19333-1732
Contact: Bruce Maitland Brown, Tr.

Established in 1988 in PA.
Donor(s): Bruce Maitland Brown.
Financial data (yr. ended 06/30/02): Grants paid, $102,830; assets, $1,318,206 (M); gifts received, $50,433; expenditures, $114,218; qualifying distributions, $106,059.
Limitations: Giving primarily in southeastern PA.
Publications: Multi-year report (including application guidelines).
Application information: Unsolicited proposals not acknowledged unless trustee is interested. Application form not required.
Trustee: Bruce Maitland Brown.
EIN: 236910944
Codes: FD2

46766
Oppenheim Foundation
718 Taylor Ave.
Scranton, PA 18510
Contact: Jane Oppenheim, Pres.

Established in 1992.
Financial data (yr. ended 12/31/01): Grants paid, $101,925; assets, $1,689,553 (M); expenditures, $121,997; qualifying distributions, $101,295.
Limitations: Applications not accepted. Giving primarily in Lackawanna County, PA, with emphasis on Scranton.
Officers: Jane Oppenheim, Pres. and Treas.; Susan Dimond, Secy.
EIN: 236296919
Codes: FD2

46767
Michael A. Bruder Foundation
600 Reed Rd.
P.O. Box 600
Broomall, PA 19008-0600

Trust established in 1956 in PA.
Donor(s): M.A. Bruder & Sons, Inc., and others.
Financial data (yr. ended 12/31/01): Grants paid, $101,550; assets, $406,166 (M); expenditures, $110,189; qualifying distributions, $101,495.
Limitations: Applications not accepted. Giving primarily in areas of company operations.
Application information: Contributes only to pre-selected organizations.
Trustees: Thomas A. Bruder, Jr., William R. Sasso, Dave Winters.
EIN: 236298481
Codes: CS, FD2, CD, GTI

46768
H. A. & M. K. Wagner Family Foundation
1306 Prospect Ave.
Bethlehem, PA 18018

Established in 1997 in PA.
Donor(s): Harold A. Wagner.
Financial data (yr. ended 12/31/00): Grants paid, $101,500; assets, $777,626 (M); gifts received, $1,160; expenditures, $106,480; qualifying distributions, $100,470.
Limitations: Giving primarily in Bethlehem, PA.
Trustees: Sandra Boyce, Harold E. Wagner, Kristi Wagner, Tracey Wagner.
EIN: 227886100
Codes: FD2

46769
Lintner Scholarship Trust
c/o PNC Bank, N.A.
620 Liberty Ave., P2-PTPP-10-2, 10th Fl.
Pittsburgh, PA 15222-2705
Application address: 195 N. Walnut St., Blairsville, PA 15717

Established in 1993 in PA.
Financial data (yr. ended 03/31/01): Grants paid, $101,450; assets, $2,075,542 (M); expenditures, $103,526; qualifying distributions, $101,450.
Limitations: Giving limited to residents of the greater Indiana County, PA, area.
Application information: Application form not required.
Trustee: PNC Bank, N.A.
EIN: 256406800
Codes: FD2, GTI

46770
Robertshaw Charitable Foundation
116 N. Main St.
Greensburg, PA 15601 (724) 832-7576
FAX: (724) 834-5044; *E-mail:* robertshaw@wpa.net
Contact: Jane A. Himes

Established in 1989 in PA.
Donor(s): Anne B. Robertshaw, John A. Robertshaw, Jr.
Financial data (yr. ended 06/30/01): Grants paid, $101,146; assets, $1,506,276 (M); expenditures, $124,246; qualifying distributions, $119,450.
Limitations: Giving primarily in Greensburg and central Westmoreland County, PA.
Publications: Program policy statement, application guidelines.
Application information: Application form not required.
Officer and Directors:* John A. Robertshaw, Jr.,* Chair.; Natalie R. Kelley, Lisa Robertshaw Moeller, Anne B. Robertshaw, John A. Robertshaw III, Marc B. Robertshaw.

46770—PENNSYLVANIA

EIN: 251622184
Codes: FD2

46771
The Mann Family Foundation
c/o Arthur K. Mann, Donsco Inc.
P.O. Box 2001
Wrightsville, PA 17368

Established in 1992 in PA.
Donor(s): Marianne E. Mann.‡
Financial data (yr. ended 12/31/00): Grants paid, $101,000; assets, $557,338 (M); expenditures, $103,282; qualifying distributions, $101,959.
Limitations: Applications not accepted. Giving primarily in Lancaster, PA.
Application information: Contributes only to pre-selected organizations.
Officers and Directors:* Arthur K. Mann,* Pres.; Arthur K. Mann, Jr.,* V.P.
EIN: 232683304
Codes: FD2

46772
T. L. Rhoads Foundation
(Formerly Leidy-Rhoads Foundation Trust)
c/o Mellon Bank, N.A.
P.O. Box 7899
Philadelphia, PA 19101-7236 (215) 553-2584
Application address: c/o Jean Butt, Boyertown Area School District, 911 Montgomery Ave., Boyertown, PA 19512, tel.: (610) 367-6031

Established in 1930.
Financial data (yr. ended 12/31/00): Grants paid, $101,000; assets, $1,805,897 (M); expenditures, $109,056; qualifying distributions, $99,448.
Limitations: Giving limited to residents of Boyertown, PA.
Application information: Applicants must be residents of Boyertown, PA. Application form required.
Trustee: Mellon Bank, N.A.
EIN: 236227398
Codes: FD2, GTI

46773
Joseph Z. & Agnes F. Dickson Trust for Dickson Prizes
c/o Mellon Bank, N.A.
P.O. Box 185
Pittsburgh, PA 15230-9897
Contact: Laurie Moritz

Financial data (yr. ended 09/30/01): Grants paid, $100,200; assets, $2,214,640 (M); expenditures, $107,961; qualifying distributions, $102,468.
Limitations: Applications not accepted. Giving on a national basis.
Application information: Awards are limited to research purposes only; not for students. Awards determined solely by University of Pittsburgh School of Medicine and Carnegie Mellon University.
Trustee: Mellon Bank, N.A.
EIN: 256088346
Codes: FD2

46774
Camp Council, Inc.
c/o Herbert Sachs
961 Frog Hollow Terr.
Rydal, PA 19046-2402

Established in 1995 in PA.
Financial data (yr. ended 12/31/01): Grants paid, $100,000; assets, $1,085,150 (M); expenditures, $107,525; qualifying distributions, $99,418.
Limitations: Applications not accepted. Giving primarily in PA.
Application information: Contributes only to pre-selected organizations.
Officers: Judy Kramer, Pres.; Tracy Kauffman-Wood, Secy.; Herbert Sachs, Treas.
EIN: 236000790
Codes: FD2

46775
Winifred Johnson Clive Foundation
605 Oliver Bldg.
Pittsburgh, PA 15222 (412) 355-6416
Contact: Thomas P. Johnson, Secy.

Established in 1986 in FL.
Donor(s): Winifred Johnson Clive, Margaret P. Johnson, Thomas P. Johnson, Winifred J. Sharp.
Financial data (yr. ended 11/30/01): Grants paid, $100,000; assets, $360,115 (M); expenditures, $102,831; qualifying distributions, $99,978.
Limitations: Giving primarily in FL.
Officers and Trustees:* Grace J. Perkins,* Chair.; Thomas P. Johnson,* Secy.; Stephanie J. Kewlich, Winifred J. Sharp.
EIN: 256277031
Codes: FD2

46776
Melvin & Melva Herrin Charitable Foundation
1156 Mill Road Cir.
Rydal, PA 19046

Established in 1998 in PA.
Donor(s): Melvin B. Herrin, Melva Herrin.
Financial data (yr. ended 12/31/01): Grants paid, $100,000; assets, $201,172 (M); gifts received, $121,443; expenditures, $102,171; qualifying distributions, $101,300.
Limitations: Applications not accepted. Giving primarily in Philadelphia, PA.
Application information: Contributes only to pre-selected organizations.
Trustees: Melvin B. Herrin, Melva Herrin.
EIN: 232954135
Codes: FD2

46777
Burrell L. & Frances Craver Northam Scholarship Foundation
c/o PNC Advisors, Tr.
1600 Market St., Tax Dept.
Philadelphia, PA 19103-7240

Established in 2000 in NJ.
Donor(s): Frances Craver Northam Trust.
Financial data (yr. ended 05/31/00): Grants paid, $100,000; assets, $1,092,730 (M); gifts received, $951,353; expenditures, $109,023; qualifying distributions, $100,000.
Limitations: Applications not accepted. Giving primarily in Brooklyn, NY.
Application information: Contributes only to pre-selected organizations.
Trustee: PNC Bank, N.A.
EIN: 912161953
Codes: FD2

46778
The Solms Family Foundation
c/o Joan Nelson
237 Chestnut St.
Philadelphia, PA 19106

Established in 2000 in PA.
Donor(s): David H. Solms.‡
Financial data (yr. ended 12/31/01): Grants paid, $100,000; assets, $72,046 (M); gifts received, $118,936; expenditures, $101,665; qualifying distributions, $100,000.
Limitations: Applications not accepted.
Application information: Contributes only to pre-selected organizations.
Officers and Directors:* Kenneth A. Solms,* Pres.; Stephen E. Solms,* Secy.-Treas.
EIN: 232969496

46779
Bright & Christella Erichson Charitable Trust
1735 Market St., Ste. 3800
Philadelphia, PA 19103-7598
Contact: Harvey N. Shapiro, Tr.

Established in 1980 in PA.
Financial data (yr. ended 10/31/01): Grants paid, $99,879; assets, $1,888,608 (M); expenditures, $110,121; qualifying distributions, $108,321.
Limitations: Applications not accepted. Giving limited to Philadelphia, PA.
Application information: Contributes only to pre-selected organizations.
Trustees: Rev. Gonzalo Correa Santa Cruz, Harvey N. Shapiro.
EIN: 236697739
Codes: FD2

46780
The Jim and Lorraine Mann Foundation
1285 Drummers Ln.
Wayne, PA 19087 (610) 341-8704
Contact: James L. Mann, Tr.

Established in 1998 in PA.
Donor(s): James L. Mann.
Financial data (yr. ended 12/31/01): Grants paid, $99,867; assets, $1,513,663 (M); expenditures, $105,835; qualifying distributions, $99,867.
Trustee: James L. Mann.
EIN: 237978501
Codes: FD2

46781
Rittenhouse Foundation
225 S. 15th St.
Philadelphia, PA 19102 (215) 735-3863
Contact: Judith Francis, V.P.

Incorporated in 1952 in PA.
Donor(s): Philip Klein.‡
Financial data (yr. ended 12/31/01): Grants paid, $99,725; assets, $2,098,331 (M); expenditures, $198,498; qualifying distributions, $137,208.
Limitations: Giving primarily in the Philadelphia, PA, area.
Publications: Annual report (including application guidelines).
Application information: Application form not required.
Officers and Directors:* Joshua Klein,* Pres.; Esther Klein,* Exec. V.P.; Judith Francis,* V.P.; Michael Temin, Secy.
EIN: 236005622
Codes: FD2

46782
Blair County Community Endowment
(Formerly Greater Altoona Blair County Community Endowment)
1216 11th Ave., Ste. 310
Altoona, PA 16601 (814) 944-6102
Contact: Jodi Cessna, Exec. Dir.

Established in 1995 in PA.
Financial data (yr. ended 12/31/01): Grants paid, $99,435; assets, $2,012,622 (M); gifts received, $942,860; expenditures, $145,647.
Limitations: Giving limited to Blair County, PA.
Publications: Newsletter, informational brochure, application guidelines.
Officers and Directors:* Gerald Wolf,* Chair.; Allan G. Hancock,* Pres.; Ann Benzel,* V.P.; Nancy Devorris,* V.P.; Len Whiting,* Secy.; John Kazmaier,* Treas.; Jodi Cessna, Exec. Dir.
EIN: 251761379

Codes: CM, FD2

46783
The Patsy & Rose H. Billera Foundation
P.O. Box 788
Allentown, PA 18105-0788
Contact: Joseph J. Billera, Pres.

Established in 1982 in PA.
Donor(s): Joseph P. Billera.
Financial data (yr. ended 12/31/01): Grants paid, $99,315; assets, $617,344 (M); expenditures, $99,666; qualifying distributions, $98,691.
Limitations: Applications not accepted. Giving primarily in PA.
Publications: Annual report.
Application information: Contributes only to pre-selected organizations.
Officers: Joseph P. Billera, Pres.; Howard A. Wiener, Secy.; Patsy Billera, Mgr.
EIN: 232184588
Codes: FD2

46784
Common Sense for Drug Policy Foundation
1377-C Spencer Ave.
Lancaster, PA 17603

Established in 1999 in PA.
Financial data (yr. ended 12/31/01): Grants paid, $99,189; assets, $216,599 (M); gifts received, $490,105; expenditures, $499,023; qualifying distributions, $99,189.
Limitations: Applications not accepted.
Application information: Contributes only to pre-selected organizations.
Officers and Trustees:* Robert E. Field,* Chair. and Treas.; Kevin Zeese,* Pres.; Melvin R. Allen,* Secy.
EIN: 232792942

46785
Lebovitz Foundation
2018 Monongahela Ave.
Pittsburgh, PA 15218-2510 (412) 351-4422
Contact: Stephen H. Lebovitz, V.P.

Established in 1966 in PA.
Financial data (yr. ended 12/31/01): Grants paid, $99,126; assets, $946,336 (M); gifts received, $61,539; expenditures, $245,322; qualifying distributions, $146,196.
Limitations: Giving primarily in Miami, FL, and Pittsburgh, PA.
Officers: R.A. Lebovitz, Pres.; C.N. Lebovitz, V.P.; S.H. Lebovitz, V.P.; C.R. Lebovitz, Secy.; R.D. Lebovitz, Treas.
EIN: 237007749
Codes: FD2

46786
Miller-Plummer Foundation
7036 Sheaff Ln.
Fort Washington, PA 19034 (215) 646-1300
Contact: J. Randall Plummer, Pres.

Established around 1989.
Donor(s): Harvey S. Shipley Miller, Marion Boulton Strand.
Financial data (yr. ended 04/30/01): Grants paid, $99,000; assets, $84,221 (M); gifts received, $40,525; expenditures, $99,551; qualifying distributions, $99,551.
Limitations: Giving primarily in Philadelphia, PA.
Officers: J. Randall Plummer, Pres.; Harvey S. Shipley Miller, Secy.-Treas.
EIN: 232373703
Codes: FD2

46787
Whitcomb Charitable Foundation
P.O. Box 369
Indianola, PA 15051-0369
Contact: Douglas F. Schofield, Tr.

Established in 1986 in PA.
Donor(s): James S. Whitcomb, Jr.
Financial data (yr. ended 11/30/01): Grants paid, $99,000; assets, $1,663,295 (M); expenditures, $99,743; qualifying distributions, $98,785.
Limitations: Giving primarily in Pittsburgh, PA.
Officers and Trustees:* James S. Whitcomb, Jr.,* Chair.; Dorothy J. Whitcomb,* Secy.; Lisa Capra, Pamela W. Larson, Douglas F. Schofield.
EIN: 251552861
Codes: FD2

46788
Willow Grove Foundation
Welsh and Norristown Rds.
P.O. Box 3030
Maple Glen, PA 19002-8030
Application address: 2440 Oaks Cir., Huntingdon Valley, PA 19006
Contact: C. Harold Schuler, Jr., Exec. Dir.

Established in 1998 in PA.
Donor(s): Willow Grove Bank.
Financial data (yr. ended 06/30/01): Grants paid, $98,850; assets, $939,457 (M); gifts received, $82,866; expenditures, $128,325; qualifying distributions, $127,147.
Limitations: Giving primarily in PA.
Application information: Application form required.
Officers and Directors:* Charles F. Kremp III, Chair.; William B. Weihenmayer, Vice-Chair.; Frederick A. Marcell, Jr.,* Secy.-Treas.; C. Harold Schuler, Jr., Exec. Dir.; Robert Abel, Donald L. Clark, Shirley M. Dennis, Stewart J. Greenleaf.
EIN: 233002286
Codes: FD2

46789
Laurel Charitable Trust
c/o Duane, Morris & Heckscher
4200 1 Liberty Pl.
Philadelphia, PA 19103-7396

Established in 1990 in PA.
Donor(s): Ann R. Baruch.
Financial data (yr. ended 12/31/00): Grants paid, $98,773; assets, $171,365 (M); expenditures, $103,279; qualifying distributions, $98,513.
Limitations: Applications not accepted. Giving primarily in PA.
Application information: Contributes only to pre-selected organizations.
Trustee: Ann R. Baruch.
EIN: 237453139
Codes: FD2

46790
The Wenger Foundation, Inc.
P.O. Box 409
Myerstown, PA 17067-0409

Established in 1995 in PA.
Donor(s): Durchvalley Food Distributors, Inc.
Financial data (yr. ended 12/31/01): Grants paid, $98,600; assets, $38,459 (M); gifts received, $87,155; expenditures, $133,244; qualifying distributions, $98,600.
Officers and Directors:* Rose Walmer, Pres.; Robin Wenger,* Secy.; Nancy L. Layser, Treas.; Carl I. Wenger, Margaret Wenger, and 3 additional directors.
EIN: 251779023
Codes: FD2

46791
Herbert M. Rehmeyer Trust
c/o The York Bank & Trust Co.
21 E. Market St.
York, PA 17401 (717) 846-9800
Application address: 35 S. Duke St., York, PA 17401
Contact: Henry B. Leader, Tr.

Established in 1981 in PA.
Donor(s): Herbert M. Rehmeyer.‡
Financial data (yr. ended 04/30/01): Grants paid, $98,500; assets, $1,110,306 (M); expenditures, $117,512; qualifying distributions, $106,501.
Limitations: Giving primarily in York County, PA.
Application information: Application form required.
Trustees: Henry B. Leader, The York Bank & Trust Co.
EIN: 236708035
Codes: FD2

46792
Debemac Foundation
c/o Drinker, Biddle & Reath
1 Logan Sq., 18th & Cherry Sts.
Philadelphia, PA 19103-6996

Established in 1958 in PA.
Donor(s): Lewis H. Van Dusen, Jr., Maria P.W. Van Dusen, Marian A. Boyer.
Financial data (yr. ended 09/30/01): Grants paid, $98,499; assets, $138,014 (M); expenditures, $108,067; qualifying distributions, $106,221.
Limitations: Applications not accepted. Giving primarily in PA.
Application information: Contributes only to pre-selected organizations.
Trustees: William C. Bullitt, Nora E. Pomerantz, Lewis H. Van Dusen, Jr.
EIN: 236222789
Codes: FD2

46793
Levitties Foundation
280 Brookway Rd.
Merion Station, PA 19066-1528

Established in 1953 in PA.
Donor(s): Samuel W. Levitties.
Financial data (yr. ended 12/31/01): Grants paid, $97,707; assets, $1,659,765 (M); expenditures, $105,904; qualifying distributions, $97,707.
Limitations: Applications not accepted. Giving primarily in PA, with emphasis on Philadelphia.
Application information: Contributes only to pre-selected organizations.
Officer: Marvin B. Levitties, Mgr.
EIN: 236200022
Codes: FD2

46794
Edward B. Brunswick Foundation
c/o Sol Sardinsky & Co.
10 Penn Ctr., Ste. 617
Philadelphia, PA 19103-0000

Established in 1986 in DE.
Financial data (yr. ended 09/30/01): Grants paid, $97,693; assets, $108,909 (M); expenditures, $105,614; qualifying distributions, $97,393.
Limitations: Applications not accepted. Giving primarily in ME and NY.
Application information: Contributes only to pre-selected organizations.
Officers and Directors:* Edward B. Brunswick,* Pres.; Beth Brunswick,* Treas.; Joseph Sedlack.
EIN: 133401549
Codes: FD2

46795
Regina B. & Walter E. Thompson Charitable Trust
c/o Mellon Bank, N.A.
P.O. Box 7236, AIM 193-0224
Philadelphia, PA 19101-7236

Established in 1994 in PA.
Financial data (yr. ended 12/31/00): Grants paid, $97,550; assets, $1,667,863 (M); expenditures, $120,301; qualifying distributions, $103,572.
Limitations: Applications not accepted. Giving primarily in PA.
Trustee: Mellon Bank, N.A.
EIN: 256377634

46796
The Shane Foundation
21 College Ave.
Swarthmore, PA 19081

Established in 1998 in PA.
Donor(s): J. Lawrence Shane.
Financial data (yr. ended 12/31/01): Grants paid, $97,415; assets, $228,448 (M); expenditures, $97,644; qualifying distributions, $97,366.
Limitations: Applications not accepted. Giving primarily in PA.
Application information: Contributes only to pre-selected organizations.
Officers: J. Lawrence Shane, Pres. and Treas.; Martha P. Shane, Secy.
EIN: 232967286
Codes: FD2

46797
Sidney R. Rosenau Foundation
c/o Francis X. Connell
1100 Shadeland Ave.
Drexel Hill, PA 19026-1915
Application address: P.O. Box 5667, Snowmass Village, CO 81615
Contact: Gary Rosenau, Mgr.

Established about 1941 in PA.
Financial data (yr. ended 12/31/00): Grants paid, $97,350; assets, $687,000 (M); expenditures, $106,536; qualifying distributions, $101,943.
Limitations: Giving primarily in CO, MA, NY, and PA.
Officer: Gary Rosenau, Mgr.
EIN: 236259121
Codes: FD2

46798
George J. and Mary T. D'Angelo Foundation
3232 Westwood Estates Dr.
Erie, PA 16505
Application address: 100 S. Ashle Dr., Ste. 200, Tampa, FL 33602
Contact: Gina D'Angelo, Tr.

Established in 1991 in PA.
Donor(s): George J. D'Angelo.
Financial data (yr. ended 12/31/00): Grants paid, $97,250; assets, $368,995 (M); gifts received, $160,000; expenditures, $139,931; qualifying distributions, $106,857.
Limitations: Giving primarily in northwest PA.
Application information: Application form not required.
Trustees: George J. D'Angelo II, Gina D'Angelo, Josephine D'Angelo, Mary T. D'Angelo.
EIN: 251661862
Codes: FD2

46799
The David M. and Marjorie D. Rosenberg Foundation
893 Parkes Run Ln.
Villanova, PA 19085 (610) 458-1090
Contact: David M. Rosenberg, Tr., or Marjorie D. Rosenberg, Tr.

Established in 1993.
Donor(s): David M. Rosenberg, Marjorie D. Rosenberg.
Financial data (yr. ended 12/31/01): Grants paid, $97,215; assets, $2,414,072 (M); gifts received, $80,000; expenditures, $98,670; qualifying distributions, $98,530.
Limitations: Giving primarily in PA.
Trustees: David M. Rosenberg, Marjorie D. Rosenberg.
EIN: 237715847
Codes: FD2

46800
Broughton Foundation
P.O. Box 397
Drexel Hill, PA 19026 (610) 284-9944
Contact: Douglas E. Cook, Tr.

Established in 1994 in PA.
Donor(s): Minewa B. Stanford.
Financial data (yr. ended 12/31/01): Grants paid, $97,000; assets, $2,310,642 (M); expenditures, $118,313; qualifying distributions, $97,000.
Limitations: Giving limited to PA.
Trustees: Delbert E. Broughton, Jr., Douglas E. Cook, Frank C. Wilhelm, Jr.
EIN: 232792113
Codes: FD2

46801
The Rosewater Fund
8207 Cedar Rd.
Elkins Park, PA 19027-2113

Donor(s): Edward Rosewater, Madeline Rosewater.
Financial data (yr. ended 05/31/02): Grants paid, $96,770; assets, $2,316,862 (M); expenditures, $111,491; qualifying distributions, $96,770.
Limitations: Applications not accepted. Giving primarily in PA.
Application information: Contributes only to pre-selected organizations.
Officers: Edward Rosewater, Chair.; Ann Rosewater, Secy.; Lewis Rosewater, Treas.
EIN: 236261858
Codes: FD2

46802
The Caritas Foundation
700 Hobbs Rd.
Wayne, PA 19087

Established in 1984 in PA.
Donor(s): Dominic P. Toscani, Sr.
Financial data (yr. ended 09/30/01): Grants paid, $96,300; assets, $1,906,039 (M); gifts received, $58,797; expenditures, $153,813; qualifying distributions, $124,464.
Limitations: Applications not accepted. Giving primarily in NY and PA.
Application information: Contributes only to pre-selected organizations.
Trustees: Patrice A. McGinley, Dominic P. Toscani, Jr., Gerard M. Toscani, Lisa M. Toscani.
EIN: 236802982
Codes: FD2

46803
The Harry and Julia Abrahamson Fund
186 Springlawn Rd.
Glen Mills, PA 19342

Established in 1993 in PA.
Donor(s): Harry Abrahamson.
Financial data (yr. ended 06/30/01): Grants paid, $96,000; assets, $1,397,154 (M); gifts received, $548,741; expenditures, $98,749; qualifying distributions, $95,359.
Limitations: Applications not accepted. Giving primarily in New York, NY.
Application information: Contributes only to pre-selected organizations.
Trustees: Marjorie Barnard, Anne Tyler Modarressi, Adaline Satterthwaite.
EIN: 232747364
Codes: FD2

46804
The Elizabeth M. Gitt Foundation
120 Eichelberger St.
P.O. Box 693
Hanover, PA 17331-2229

Established in 1995.
Donor(s): Elizabeth M. Gitt.‡
Financial data (yr. ended 05/31/01): Grants paid, $96,000; assets, $1,817,121 (M); expenditures, $109,348; qualifying distributions, $95,213.
Limitations: Applications not accepted. Giving primarily in Hanover, PA.
Application information: Contributes only to pre-selected organizations.
Officers and Directors:* Susan G. Gordon, Pres.; Cynthia Gitt,* Secy.; Marian G. Rebert, Treas.; Forrest Schaeffer, Carson G. Taylor.
Trustee: M & T Bank.
EIN: 232790834
Codes: FD2

46805
The William G. & M. Virginia Simpson Foundation
208 Spencer Ct.
Moon Township, PA 15108
Contact: William S. Kistler, Pres.

Established in 1984 in PA.
Donor(s): William G. Simpson,‡ Virginia Simpson.‡
Financial data (yr. ended 06/30/01): Grants paid, $96,000; assets, $1,757,130 (M); expenditures, $146,530; qualifying distributions, $95,173.
Limitations: Applications not accepted. Giving limited to western PA.
Application information: Grant decisions made by schools. Please do not write or call foundation for application.
Officers and Trustees:* William S. Kistler,* Pres.; Mark G. Schoeppner,* Secy.
EIN: 251488701
Codes: FD2, GTI

46806
George W. Rentschler Foundation
c/o Obermayer, Rebmann, Maxwell & Hippel
1 Penn Ctr., 19th Fl., 1617 J.F.K. Blvd.
Philadelphia, PA 19103-1895 (215) 665-3144
Contact: Hugh Sutherland, Secy.-Treas.

Established in 1975 in PA.
Financial data (yr. ended 01/31/02): Grants paid, $95,700; assets, $2,199,878 (M); expenditures, $120,919; qualifying distributions, $95,700.
Limitations: Giving primarily in Philadelphia, PA.
Application information: Application form required.
Officers: William O'Neill, Pres.; Samuel Evans III, V.P.; Hugh Sutherland, Secy.-Treas.

EIN: 236627872

46807
The Neducsin Foundation
161 Leverington Ave.
Philadelphia, PA 19127
Contact: Daniel R. Neducsin, Pres.

Established in 1997 in PA.
Donor(s): Daniel R. Neducsin, Luana Neducsin.
Financial data (yr. ended 06/30/02): Grants paid, $95,667; assets, $554,706 (M); expenditures, $117,100; qualifying distributions, $95,667.
Limitations: Giving primarily in PA.
Application information: Application form required.
Officers: Daniel R. Neducsin, Pres.; Luana Neducsin, Secy.
EIN: 232938583
Codes: FD2

46808
Frezel Family Foundation
233 S. 6th St., Ste. 1302
Philadelphia, PA 19106-3755

Established in 2000 in PA.
Donor(s): Jerrold Frezel.
Financial data (yr. ended 12/31/01): Grants paid, $95,600; assets, $1,201,121 (M); expenditures, $105,202; qualifying distributions, $95,424.
Limitations: Applications not accepted. Giving primarily in PA.
Application information: Contributes only to pre-selected organizations.
Officer: Jerrold Frezel, Pres.
EIN: 256693450
Codes: FD2

46809
The Stanley R. Wolfe Foundation
7303 Emlen St.
Philadelphia, PA 19119 (215) 875-3000
Contact: Stanley R. Wolfe, Pres.

Established in 1995 in PA.
Donor(s): Stanley R. Wolfe.
Financial data (yr. ended 12/31/00): Grants paid, $95,443; assets, $494,727 (M); gifts received, $47,525; expenditures, $97,303; qualifying distributions, $95,443.
Limitations: Giving primarily in Philadelphia, PA.
Application information: Application form not required.
Officer: Stanley R. Wolfe, Pres.
EIN: 232829995
Codes: FD2

46810
The Morrison Foundation
c/o Perry E. Morrison
5000 5th Ave., Rm. 309
Pittsburgh, PA 15232-2150

Established in 1991 in PA.
Donor(s): Beatrice E. Morrison, Perry E. Morrison.
Financial data (yr. ended 12/31/00): Grants paid, $95,363; assets, $735,559 (M); gifts received, $7,200; expenditures, $95,836; qualifying distributions, $94,755.
Limitations: Applications not accepted. Giving primarily in NY and Pittsburgh, PA.
Application information: Contributes only to pre-selected organizations.
Trustees: Beatrice E. Morrison, Perry E. Morrison.
EIN: 251671840
Codes: FD2

46811
The Burke Foundation
650 Smithfield St., Ste. 250
Pittsburgh, PA 15222

Established in 1981 in PA.
Financial data (yr. ended 12/31/01): Grants paid, $95,152; assets, $839,336 (M); gifts received, $532,355; expenditures, $102,130; qualifying distributions, $95,152.
Limitations: Giving primarily in Pittsburgh, PA.
Officers: Steven E. Burke, Pres.; Patricia G. Burke, V.P. and Treas.
Trustee: Charles R. Burke.
EIN: 251407410
Codes: FD2

46812
Burke Family Foundation
650 Smithfield St., Ste. 250
Pittsburgh, PA 15222

Established in 1998 in PA.
Donor(s): Charles R. Burke Charitable Trust.
Financial data (yr. ended 12/31/01): Grants paid, $95,151; assets, $840,211 (M); gifts received, $532,355; expenditures, $102,079; qualifying distributions, $95,151.
Limitations: Giving primarily in PA.
Application information: Application form required.
Officers and Trustees:* Charles R. Burke,* Pres.; Patricia G. Burke, V.P. and Treas.; Steven E. Burke.
EIN: 311583757
Codes: FD2

46813
Helen L. Bailey Foundation
c/o Mellon Bank, N.A.
P.O. Box 185
Pittsburgh, PA 15230-9897
Contact: Laurie Moritz, Trust Off., Mellon Bank, N.A.

Established in 1958 in PA; trust instrument amended in 1970.
Donor(s): Helen L. Bailey.‡
Financial data (yr. ended 12/31/01): Grants paid, $95,000; assets, $1,766,548 (M); expenditures, $102,478; qualifying distributions, $96,361.
Limitations: Applications not accepted. Giving primarily in PA.
Application information: Contributes only to pre-selected organizations.
Trustee: Mellon Bank, N.A.
EIN: 256018937
Codes: FD2

46814
Parker Foundation
c/o Jennifer Lyons
1 Mellon Bank Ctr., Rm. 3810
Pittsburgh, PA 15258

Established in 1997 in PA.
Financial data (yr. ended 12/31/01): Grants paid, $95,000; assets, $2,737,362 (M); expenditures, $127,607; qualifying distributions, $107,040.
Limitations: Giving on a national basis.
Trustee: Mellon Bank, N.A.
EIN: 237883782
Codes: FD2

46815
The St. Martha Foundation
c/o Alan Mittelman
1635 Market St., 7th Fl.
Philadelphia, PA 19103

Established in PA in 1998.
Donor(s): Jerry Francesco, Lucille M. Francesco.
Financial data (yr. ended 12/31/01): Grants paid, $95,000; assets, $150,364 (M); gifts received, $200,000; expenditures, $98,450; qualifying distributions, $95,000.
Limitations: Applications not accepted. Giving primarily in PA.
Application information: Contributes only to pre-selected organizations.
Officers: Jerry Francesco, Pres.; Lucille M. Francesco, Treas.
EIN: 232982957
Codes: FD2

46816
Frank J. & Sylvia T. Pasquerilla Foundation
c/o Mark E. & Leah M. Pasquerilla
Pasquerilla Plz.
Johnstown, PA 15901

Established in 2000 in PA.
Donor(s): Sylvia T. Pasquerilla.‡
Financial data (yr. ended 12/31/01): Grants paid, $94,500; assets, $1,519,893 (M); expenditures, $107,390; qualifying distributions, $94,500.
Limitations: Applications not accepted.
Application information: Contributes only to pre-selected organizations.
Trustees: Leah M. Pasquerilla, Mark E. Pasquerilla.
EIN: 256690814

46817
Alex & Leona Robinson Foundation
4 Gateway Ctr., 9th Fl.
Pittsburgh, PA 15222 (412) 281-8771
Contact: Donald Plung, Tr.

Established about 1957 in PA.
Donor(s): Alex Robinson.‡
Financial data (yr. ended 03/31/99): Grants paid, $94,500; assets, $3,009,015 (M); expenditures, $103,034; qualifying distributions, $94,764.
Limitations: Giving primarily in the Pittsburgh, PA, area.
Trustees: Edward Goldberg, Donald Plung, Donald Robinson, Harold Robinson.
EIN: 256033880
Codes: FD2

46818
Lawrence B. Sheppard Foundation, Inc.
c/o Buchen, Wise & Dorr
126 Carlisle St.
Hanover, PA 17331 (717) 637-2160

Incorporated in 1946 in PA.
Donor(s): Lawrence B. Sheppard,‡ Charlotte N. Sheppard.‡
Financial data (yr. ended 11/30/01): Grants paid, $94,500; assets, $1,566,746 (M); expenditures, $113,825; qualifying distributions, $94,500.
Limitations: Giving primarily in the Hanover, PA, area.
Officers: Charlotte S. DeVan, Pres.; W. Todd DeVan, V.P.; Donald W. Dorr, Secy.; Lawrence S. DeVan,* Treas.
EIN: 236251690
Codes: FD2

46819
Adrienne and Milton Porter Charitable Foundation
681 Andersen Dr., 3rd Fl.
Pittsburgh, PA 15220-2747

Established in 1995 in PA.
Donor(s): Milton Porter.‡
Financial data (yr. ended 12/31/00): Grants paid, $94,260; assets, $2,297,390 (M); expenditures, $101,719; qualifying distributions, $89,310.
Limitations: Applications not accepted. Giving primarily in Pittsburgh, PA.

46819—PENNSYLVANIA

Application information: Contributes only to pre-selected organizations.
Trustee: Lee B. Foster II.
EIN: 256500406
Codes: FD2

46820
John K. Henne Charitable Trust
c/o National City Bank of Pennsylvania
248 Seneca St.
Oil City, PA 16301

Established in 1985 in PA.
Financial data (yr. ended 12/31/00): Grants paid, $94,141; assets, $2,271,401 (M); gifts received, $6,367; expenditures, $126,398; qualifying distributions, $99,849.
Limitations: Giving primarily in PA.
Application information: Application form not required.
Trustee: National City Bank of Pennsylvania.
EIN: 256261354
Codes: FD2

46821
William & Dora Horwitz Endowment Fund
c/o Mellon Bank, N.A.
P.O. Box 185
Pittsburgh, PA 15230-0185
Application address: 148 Haverford Dr., Butler, PA 16001, tel.: (724) 287-5166
Contact: Maurice Horwitz, Tr.

Established in 1964 in PA.
Donor(s): Temma Horwitz Memorial Foundation.
Financial data (yr. ended 03/31/01): Grants paid, $94,000; assets, $1,761,101 (M); expenditures, $116,500; qualifying distributions, $94,000.
Limitations: Giving primarily in Butler and Pittsburgh, PA.
Trustees: Maurice Horwitz, Mellon Bank, N.A.
EIN: 251151970
Codes: FD2

46822
Bucks County Foundation
c/o PNC Bank, N.A.
1600 Market St.
Philadelphia, PA 19103-7240

Financial data (yr. ended 12/31/00): Grants paid, $93,440; assets, $2,895,100 (M); expenditures, $107,557.
Limitations: Giving limited to the Bucks County, PA area.
Trustee: PNC Bank, N.A.
EIN: 239031005
Codes: CM, FD2

46823
Nancy and Richard Wolfson Charitable Foundation
560 Leslie Ln.
P.O. Box 685
Blue Bell, PA 19422-0685

Established in 1992 in PA.
Donor(s): Nancy Wolfson, Richard Wolfson.
Financial data (yr. ended 06/30/01): Grants paid, $93,350; assets, $1,224,085 (M); gifts received, $1,632; expenditures, $94,982; qualifying distributions, $93,350.
Limitations: Applications not accepted. Giving primarily in Philadelphia, PA.
Application information: Contributes only to pre-selected organizations.
Trustees: Nancy Wolfson, Richard Wolfson.
EIN: 237716735
Codes: FD2

46824
Alice B. Cooper Trust
123 S. Broad St., 16th Fl.
Philadelphia, PA 19109

Financial data (yr. ended 12/31/01): Grants paid, $93,135; assets, $2,137,926 (M); expenditures, $118,380; qualifying distributions, $93,135.
Limitations: Applications not accepted. Giving primarily in Philadelphia, PA.
Application information: Contributes only to pre-selected organizations.
Trustee: First Union National Bank.
EIN: 236690099
Codes: FD2

46825
NAT HWILC Foundation
c/o Cookson Peirce & Co., Inc.
535 Smithfield St.
Pittsburgh, PA 15222
Contact: Robert A. Walsh, Tr. or Jean Ann Walsh, Tr.

Established in 1987 in PA.
Financial data (yr. ended 12/31/01): Grants paid, $93,022; assets, $1,266,906 (M); expenditures, $105,029; qualifying distributions, $93,022.
Limitations: Giving primarily in the Pittsburgh, PA area.
Trustees: Susan Walsh Lanier, Jean Ann Walsh, Kevin R. Walsh, Rebecca A. Walsh, Robert A. Walsh.
EIN: 222899613

46826
The Winokur Foundation
c/o Barton J. Winokur
4000 Bell Atlantic Tower, 1717 Arch St.
Philadelphia, PA 19103-2793

Established in 1986 in PA.
Donor(s): Barton J. Winokur.
Financial data (yr. ended 07/31/01): Grants paid, $92,813; assets, $416,428 (M); gifts received, $180,188; expenditures, $95,738; qualifying distributions, $92,813.
Limitations: Applications not accepted. Giving primarily in Waltham, MA.
Application information: Contributes only to pre-selected organizations.
Trustee: Barton J. Winokur.
EIN: 236856163
Codes: FD2

46827
Satell Family Foundation
c/o Edward M. Satell
370 Technology Dr.
Malvern, PA 19355

Established in 1995 in PA.
Donor(s): Edward Satell.
Financial data (yr. ended 12/31/00): Grants paid, $92,762; assets, $600,762 (M); gifts received, $200,000; expenditures, $98,109; qualifying distributions, $92,962.
Limitations: Applications not accepted. Giving primarily in PA.
Application information: Contributes only to pre-selected organizations.
Trustee: Edward M. Satell.
EIN: 237769039
Codes: FD2

46828
Grandom Institution
366 Roumfort Rd.
Philadelphia, PA 19119
Contact: John N. Childs, Secy.-Treas.

Incorporated in 1841 in PA.
Donor(s): Hartt Grandom.‡
Financial data (yr. ended 06/30/01): Grants paid, $92,308; assets, $1,707,024 (M); expenditures, $97,583; qualifying distributions, $91,930.
Limitations: Giving limited to the Philadelphia, PA, area.
Publications: Informational brochure.
Application information: Application form not required.
Officers: F. Preston Buckman, Pres.; John N. Childs, Secy.-Treas.; Robert C. Bodine, Mgr.; Mary Buckman, Mgr.; Thomas O. Ely, Mgr.; Carolyn Moon, Mgr.; Robert Neff, Mgr.; Louise Senopoulos, Mgr.; Gerald van Arkel, Mgr.
EIN: 230640770
Codes: FD2

46829
Griffith D. Morgan Memorial Fund
c/o PNC Bank, N.A.
620 Liberty Ave.
Pittsburgh, PA 15222-2705
Application address: c/o Mary L. Ferrara, Guidance Counselor, Armstrong Central Senior High School, Orr Ave., Kittanning, PA 15602, tel.: (412) 543-1591

Financial data (yr. ended 12/31/00): Grants paid, $92,264; assets, $1,925,322 (M); expenditures, $95,250; qualifying distributions, $90,656.
Limitations: Giving limited to residents of the East Brady, PA, area.
Application information: Application form required.
Trustee: PNC Bank, N.A.
EIN: 256066552
Codes: GTI

46830
The Grumbacher Family Foundation
(Formerly The Nancy and Tim Grumbacher Family Foundation)
Packard Bldg., 12th Fl.
15th and Chestnut Sts.
Philadelphia, PA 19102

Established in 1988 in PA.
Financial data (yr. ended 01/30/01): Grants paid, $91,935; assets, $536,250 (M); gifts received, $1,550; expenditures, $97,085; qualifying distributions, $97,085.
Limitations: Applications not accepted. Giving primarily in York, PA.
Application information: Contributes only to pre-selected organizations.
Officers and Directors:* M.T. Grumbacher,* Pres.; D.R. Glyn,* Secy.
EIN: 232524417
Codes: FD2

46831
Sidney J. Stein Foundation
416 E. Church Rd.
King of Prussia, PA 19406-1533

Established in 1980 in PA.
Donor(s): Bertha Stein, Sidney J. Stein, Electro Science Laboratories, Inc.
Financial data (yr. ended 03/31/02): Grants paid, $91,750; assets, $2,168,659 (M); expenditures, $109,123; qualifying distributions, $93,625.
Limitations: Applications not accepted. Giving primarily in PA.

Application information: Contributes only to pre-selected organizations.
Officer and Trustees:* Sidney J. Stein,* Mgr.; Bertha Stein, Michael Alan Stein.
EIN: 222315982
Codes: FD2

46832
The Seven Trees, Inc.
3601 Gettysburg Rd.
Camp Hill, PA 17011-6816 (717) 975-3590
Contact: Ernest S. Burch, Jr., Pres.

Established in 1953 in PA.
Financial data (yr. ended 12/31/01): Grants paid, $91,675; assets, $1,379,689 (M); expenditures, $94,033; qualifying distributions, $91,675.
Limitations: Giving primarily in PA.
Application information: Application form not required.
Officers: Ernest S. Burch, Jr., Pres.; Elsie L. Burch, V.P.; Deanne M. Burch, Secy.-Treas.
EIN: 236245788

46833
Joseph B. and Virginia H. Banks Foundation
403 Coal St.
Wilkes-Barre, PA 18702-6626

Established in 1998 in PA.
Donor(s): Virginia H. Banks.
Financial data (yr. ended 12/31/00): Grants paid, $91,500; assets, $1,135,649 (M); expenditures, $100,696; qualifying distributions, $93,280.
Limitations: Applications not accepted. Giving primarily in PA.
Application information: Contributes only to pre-selected organizations.
Trustee: Virginia H. Banks.
Advisory Board Members: J. Christopher Banks, J. Gregory Banks, Jennifer Banks, Lisa Banks, Margaret L. Banks.
EIN: 232953650
Codes: FD2

46834
The Garbose Family Foundation
c/o William M. & Lynne L. Garbose
P.O. Box 642, 545 Station Ln.
Gwynedd Valley, PA 19437-0642

Established in 1995 in PA.
Donor(s): Lynne Garbose, William Garbose.
Financial data (yr. ended 11/30/00): Grants paid, $90,559; assets, $579,225 (M); gifts received, $167,974; expenditures, $93,572; qualifying distributions, $91,054.
Limitations: Applications not accepted. Giving on a national basis.
Application information: Contributes only to pre-selected organizations.
Trustees: Lynne Garbose, William Garbose.
EIN: 237818372
Codes: FD2

46835
The Aaron Family Foundation
2401 Pennsylvania Ave., Apt. 5824
Philadelphia, PA 19130

Established in 1998 in PA.
Donor(s): Daniel Aaron.
Financial data (yr. ended 12/31/01): Grants paid, $90,559; assets, $1,739,920 (M); expenditures, $97,617; qualifying distributions, $89,555.
Limitations: Applications not accepted. Giving primarily in PA.
Application information: Contributes only to pre-selected organizations.
Trustees: Daniel Aaron, Geraldine Aaron.
EIN: 237996346

Codes: FD2

46836
The TEOC Foundation
(Formerly The Carl & Beth Apter Family Foundation)
c/o Glenmede Trust Co.
1650 Market St., Ste. 1200
Philadelphia, PA 19103 (215) 699-8701
Contact: Carl Apter, Pres.

Established in 1986 in PA.
Donor(s): Molly Apter, Robert F. Apter, Allen Apter, Carl Apter, R.A. Industries, Inc.
Financial data (yr. ended 10/31/01): Grants paid, $90,250; assets, $112,689 (M); expenditures, $92,494; qualifying distributions, $91,000.
Limitations: Giving primarily in PA.
Application information: Application form not required.
Officers and Directors:* Carl Apter,* Pres.; Beth Apter,* Secy.-Treas.
EIN: 236849939
Codes: FD2

46837
Apgar-Black Foundation
42 River Rd.
Point Pleasant, PA 18950
Contact: Allen D. Black, Tr.

Established in 1999.
Donor(s): Allen D. Black.
Financial data (yr. ended 11/30/01): Grants paid, $90,000; assets, $406,706 (M); gifts received, $100,000; expenditures, $101,959; qualifying distributions, $90,000.
Limitations: Giving primarily in Philadelphia, PA.
Trustees: Randy Apgar, Allen D. Black.
EIN: 233024321
Codes: FD2

46838
Marian J. Wettrick Charitable Foundation
c/o CTC Executor
10 N. Main St.
Coudersport, PA 16915 (814) 274-9150
FAX: (814) 274-0401

Established in 1996 in PA.
Financial data (yr. ended 12/31/01): Grants paid, $90,000; assets, $1,683,179 (M); expenditures, $102,503; qualifying distributions, $92,604.
Application information: Application form required.
Trustee: Citizens Trust Co.
EIN: 256545149
Codes: FD2

46839
The Beach Foundation
3 Radnor Corporate Ctr., Ste. 410
Radnor, PA 19087 (610) 225-1100
Contact: Thomas E. Beach, Pres.

Established in 1997 in PA.
Donor(s): Thomas E. Beach.
Financial data (yr. ended 12/31/00): Grants paid, $89,990; assets, $2,261,655 (M); expenditures, $95,207; qualifying distributions, $88,968.
Limitations: Giving on a national basis, with emphasis on CA, MA, NH, and PA.
Officers and Directors:* Thomas E. Beach,* Pres.; Walter T. Beach,* V.P.; Jonathan T. Beach,* Secy.; Theodore T. Beach,* Treas.
EIN: 232897351
Codes: FD2

46840
Sophia K. Reeves Foundation Trust
c/o Mellon Bank, N.A.
P.O. Box 7236
Philadelphia, PA 19101-7236 (215) 553-3208
Contact: Patricia Kling, Trust Off., Mellon Bank, N.A.

Established in 1958.
Financial data (yr. ended 06/30/01): Grants paid, $89,986; assets, $1,604,817 (M); gifts received, $10,775; expenditures, $106,610; qualifying distributions, $93,849.
Limitations: Giving limited to Camden County, and Laurel Springs, NJ, and to the Philadelphia, PA, area.
Application information: Applications available Jan. through Mar. Application form required.
Trustee: Mellon Bank, N.A.
EIN: 236226072
Codes: GTI

46841
Center for Research on Women and Newborn Health Foundation
c/o Dorwart, Andrew & Co.
1685 Crown Ave.
Lancaster, PA 17601-6396
Application address: 1059 Columbia Ave., Lancaster, PA 17603, tel.: (717) 393-1338
Contact: Daniel Kegel, M.D., Treas.

Established in 1994 in PA.
Financial data (yr. ended 08/31/01): Grants paid, $89,231; assets, $933,931 (M); expenditures, $112,035; qualifying distributions, $93,784.
Limitations: Giving primarily in CA and PA.
Application information: Contact foundation for appropriate application forms. Application form required.
Officers: Dianne M. Nast, Pres.; Dale Matt, V.P.; Mark Regan, M.D., Secy.; Daniel Kegel, M.D., Treas.
Directors: William Haggarty, H. Carol Lebischak, M.D.
EIN: 232744470
Codes: GTI

46842
The Herman and Jerry Finkelstein Foundation
c/o Bernard Glassman
1 Logan Sq., 8th Fl.
Philadelphia, PA 19103

Established in 1994 in PA.
Financial data (yr. ended 02/28/01): Grants paid, $89,000; assets, $1,681,729 (M); expenditures, $124,997; qualifying distributions, $88,354.
Limitations: Applications not accepted. Giving primarily in Philadelphia, PA.
Application information: Contributes only to pre-selected organizations.
Trustees: Paul Auerbach, Samuel N. Rabinowitz.
EIN: 237690111
Codes: FD2

46843
Dickert Family Foundation
c/o PNC Advisors
620 Liberty Ave., Ste. 10-2
Pittsburgh, PA 15222-2705
Application address: 2211 Armburst Rd., Greensburg, PA 15601, tel.: (724) 837-6114
Contact: Eugene J. Dickert, Jr., Pres.

Established in 1998 in PA.
Financial data (yr. ended 12/31/00): Grants paid, $88,950; assets, $844,623 (M); expenditures, $99,822; qualifying distributions, $89,187.
Limitations: Giving primarily in PA.

46843—PENNSYLVANIA

Officers and Directors:* Eugene J. Dickert, Jr.,* Pres. and Secy.-Treas.; Lucretta A. Dickert,* V.P.; Stacy A. Dickert Colin, Kimberly L. Dickert, Julie L. Jones.
Trustee: PNC Bank, N.A.
EIN: 251820176
Codes: FD2

46844
Donald M. & Barbara L. Werner Family Foundation
770 Woodlawn Dr.
Hermitage, PA 16148-1577
Contact: Donald M. Werner, Tr.

Established in 1998 in PA.
Donor(s): Barbara L. Werner, Donald M. Werner.
Financial data (yr. ended 12/31/00): Grants paid, $88,438; assets, $175,801 (M); gifts received, $19,889; expenditures, $89,699; qualifying distributions, $87,719.
Application information: Application form not required.
Trustees: Barbara L. Werner, Donald M. Werner.
EIN: 237933631
Codes: FD2

46845
Malfer Foundation
716 W. Mount Airy Ave.
Philadelphia, PA 19119
Contact: Frank E. Reed, Tr.

Established in 1994 in PA.
Donor(s): Ann L. Reed, Frank E. Reed.
Financial data (yr. ended 12/31/01): Grants paid, $88,300; assets, $1,936,523 (M); expenditures, $109,613; qualifying distributions, $96,647.
Limitations: Applications not accepted. Giving primarily in PA.
Application information: Contributes only to pre-selected organizations.
Trustees: Ann L. Reed, Frank E. Reed, Jeffrey L. Reed, Timothy G. Reed, First Union National Bank.
EIN: 232791318
Codes: FD2

46846
The Muriel Fusfeld Foundation
c/o Kathy C. Mandelbaum
1600 Market St., Ste. 3600
Philadelphia, PA 19103   (215) 751-2220

Established in 1995 in NY.
Financial data (yr. ended 12/31/00): Grants paid, $88,000; assets, $1,612,370 (M); expenditures, $99,659; qualifying distributions, $96,943.
Limitations: Applications not accepted. Giving limited to NY.
Application information: Contributes only to pre-selected organizations.
Trustees: Henry Guberman, Caryl P. Rubenfeld.
EIN: 237852070
Codes: FD2

46847
J. Melvin & Beulah M. Isett Community Foundation
c/o Penn Central National Bank, Trust Dept.
431 Penn St.
Huntingdon, PA 16652   (814) 643-5916
Contact: Judith G. Fleming, Sr. Trust Off., Penn Central National Bank

Established in 1999 in PA.
Donor(s): J. Melvin Isett, Beulah M. Isett.‡
Financial data (yr. ended 12/31/01): Grants paid, $87,971; assets, $1,832,167 (M); expenditures, $100,352; qualifying distributions, $99,519.

Limitations: Giving limited to Huntington County, PA.
Application information: Application form not required.
Trustees: Chester P. Isett, J. Melvin Isett, Penn Central National Bank.
EIN: 256684452
Codes: FD2

46848
Otis H. Childs Trust
c/o PNC Advisors, Char. Trust Comm.
620 Liberty Ave., 25th Fl.
Pittsburgh, PA 15222-2705   (412) 762-7076
Application address: 1 PNC Plz., 249 5th Ave., 29th Fl., Pittsburgh, PA 15222
Contact: Mia Hallett Bernard

Financial data (yr. ended 12/31/01): Grants paid, $87,897; assets, $1,380,558 (M); expenditures, $101,038; qualifying distributions, $88,111.
Limitations: Giving primarily in CO and Pittsburgh, PA.
Trustee: PNC Bank, N.A.
EIN: 256024249
Codes: FD2

46849
Hyman Family Foundation
6315 Forbes Ave.
Pittsburgh, PA 15217

Established in 1957 in PA.
Donor(s): Samuel M. Hyman.
Financial data (yr. ended 08/31/01): Grants paid, $87,884; assets, $1,232,308 (M); expenditures, $112,419; qualifying distributions, $86,709.
Limitations: Applications not accepted. Giving primarily in Pittsburgh, PA.
Application information: Contributes only to pre-selected organizations.
Officer: Lois Rubin, Mgr.
Trustees: Saul Elinoff, William Elinoff, Yetta Elinoff.
EIN: 256065761
Codes: FD2

46850
David H. Pleet Foundation
c/o W.B.S.S.C.
1650 Arch St., 22nd Fl.
Philadelphia, PA 19103

Financial data (yr. ended 07/31/02): Grants paid, $87,700; assets, $118,010 (M); expenditures, $92,312; qualifying distributions, $87,700.
Limitations: Giving primarily in Philadelphia, PA.
Application information: Application form not required.
Officers and Directors:* Donald Bean,* Pres.; Oliver Goldman,* Secy.-Treas.
EIN: 236391178
Codes: FD2

46851
A. L. & Jennie L. Luria Foundation
c/o Wolf, Block, Schorr & Solis
1650 Arch St., 22nd Fl.
Philadelphia, PA 19103-2097
Contact: Nelson J. Luria, Treas.

Established in 1952 in PA.
Financial data (yr. ended 12/31/01): Grants paid, $87,500; assets, $1,773,473 (M); expenditures, $95,594; qualifying distributions, $89,025.
Limitations: Applications not accepted. Giving primarily in New York, NY.
Application information: Contributes only to pre-selected organizations.
Officers and Trustees:* Sylvia Ablon,* Chair.; Fanch L. Elkins,* Secy.; Nelson J. Luria,* Treas.; Judith Biel Lipsett.

EIN: 236255232
Codes: FD2

46852
Abraham & Rose Ellis Foundation
c/o The Glenmede Trust Co.
1650 Market St.
Philadelphia, PA 19103-7391

Established in 1952 in PA.
Financial data (yr. ended 12/31/01): Grants paid, $87,490; assets, $1,632,718 (M); gifts received, $100; expenditures, $102,579; qualifying distributions, $90,503.
Limitations: Applications not accepted. Giving primarily in Philadelphia, PA.
Application information: Contributes only to pre-selected organizations.
Officers and Trustees:* Michael D. Ellis, M.D.,* Pres.; Sylvia M. Keller,* V.P.; Anne Lieberman,* Secy.; Carol Ellis, Jeffrey B. Ellis, Robert Ellis, Donald Lieberman.
EIN: 237442471
Codes: FD2

46853
The Coltman Family Foundation, Inc.
P.O. Box 2138
Media, PA 19063
Contact: Charles L. Coltman, III, Pres.

Established in 1998 in PA.
Donor(s): Charles L. Coltman III.
Financial data (yr. ended 01/31/02): Grants paid, $87,150; assets, $3,651,174 (M); expenditures, $107,401; qualifying distributions, $87,150.
Limitations: Applications not accepted. Giving primarily in DE and PA.
Application information: Contributes only to pre-selected organizations.
Officers and Directors:* Charles L. Coltman III,* Pres.; Joann F. Coltman,* V.P.; Clayton F. Coltman,* Secy.; Charles L. Coltman IV,* Treas.
EIN: 232954759
Codes: FD2

46854
Irving & Francine Suknow Foundation
c/o Reading Body Works, Inc.
P.O. Box 650
Shillington, PA 19607
Contact: Irving Suknow and Francine Suknow, Trustees

Established in 1999 in PA.
Donor(s): Francine Suknow, Irving Suknow.
Financial data (yr. ended 12/31/01): Grants paid, $87,150; assets, $1,353,088 (M); gifts received, $127,128; expenditures, $88,634; qualifying distributions, $87,150.
Limitations: Giving primarily in West Palm Beach, FL.
Trustees: Francine Suknow, Irving Suknow.
EIN: 256648797

46855
Hess & Helyn Kline Foundation
c/o Wolf, Block, Schorr & Solis-Cohen
1650 Arch St., 22nd Fl.
Philadelphia, PA 19103

Established around 1954 in PA.
Donor(s): Hess Kline.‡
Financial data (yr. ended 12/31/00): Grants paid, $87,020; assets, $1,594,457 (M); expenditures, $93,010; qualifying distributions, $87,554.
Limitations: Giving primarily in MA and NY.
Application information: Application form not required.
Trustees: Barbara Ann Eldridge, Stephen H. Judson, Denise Jo Levy, Jennifer Mentzer.

EIN: 236243380
Codes: FD2

46856
The Partners Charitable Trust
518 Rodgers Dr.
Pittsburgh, PA 15238

Established in 1995.
Donor(s): John C. Campbell, James L. Campbell.
Financial data (yr. ended 06/30/02): Grants paid, $87,000; assets, $195,587 (M); expenditures, $88,138; qualifying distributions, $87,000.
Limitations: Giving primarily in PA.
Officer: John C. Campbell, Pres.
Trustee: James L. Campbell.
EIN: 256501559

46857
Sterling Financial Foundation
101 N. Pointe Blvd.
Lancaster, PA 17601
Contact: Jennifer Seiger

Established in 1999 in PA.
Financial data (yr. ended 12/31/01): Grants paid, $87,000; assets, $24,090 (M); expenditures, $87,200; qualifying distributions, $87,000.
Limitations: Giving primarily in PA.
Officers: Gregory S. Lefever, Pres.; Teri R. McHale, Secy.; J. Roger Moyer, Jr., Treas.
Directors: Joan R. Henderson, John E. Stefan.
EIN: 232986337
Codes: FD2

46858
The Michael Foundation, Inc.
518 Kimberton Rd., PMB 320
Phoenixville, PA 19460
FAX: (610) 917-0800
Contact: Edward R. Hill, Pres.

Established in 1991 in PA.
Donor(s): Adelaide Hill.‡
Financial data (yr. ended 06/30/02): Grants paid, $86,720; assets, $2,557,393 (M); expenditures, $132,252; qualifying distributions, $86,720.
Limitations: Giving within North America, including Canada and Mexico.
Publications: Informational brochure (including application guidelines).
Application information: Application form not required.
Officers and Directors:* Edward R. Hill,* Pres.; Marsha Hill,* V.P.; Stuart O.R. Mays,* Treas.
EIN: 581992204
Codes: FD2

46859
Evans Foundation
225 N. Olive St.
P.O. Box 258
Media, PA 19063 (610) 566-5800
Contact: Megan E. Zavawski, Secy.-Treas.

Established in 1983 in NY.
Donor(s): Anita Seits.
Financial data (yr. ended 01/31/02): Grants paid, $86,600; assets, $1,997,341 (M); expenditures, $302,955; qualifying distributions, $101,552.
Limitations: Giving primarily in NJ and PA.
Officers: Anita Seits, Pres.; Kevin D. Seits, V.P.; Megan E. Zavawski, Secy.-Treas.
Director: Joy M. Brennan.
EIN: 133178754
Codes: FD2

46860
James H. Matthews & Company Educational and Charitable Trust
2 Northshore Ctr.
Pittsburgh, PA 15212-5851

Established in 1940.
Donor(s): Matthews International Corp.
Financial data (yr. ended 09/30/00): Grants paid, $86,485; assets, $2,258,780 (M); gifts received, $90,000; expenditures, $87,863; qualifying distributions, $86,485.
Limitations: Applications not accepted. Giving primarily in Pittsburgh, PA.
Application information: Contributes only to pre-selected organizations.
Trustees: E.J. Boyle, D.M. Kelly.
EIN: 256028582
Codes: CS, FD2, CD

46861
John C. & Lucine O. B. Marous Charitable Foundation
28 The Trillium
Pittsburgh, PA 15238

Established in 1986 in PA.
Donor(s): John C. Marous, Jr., Lucine O.B. Marous.
Financial data (yr. ended 12/31/01): Grants paid, $86,250; assets, $227,910 (M); gifts received, $101,574; expenditures, $92,750; qualifying distributions, $89,551.
Limitations: Applications not accepted. Giving primarily in PA.
Application information: Contributes only to pre-selected organizations.
Officers: John C. Marous, Jr., Pres.; Lucine O.B. Marous, V.P. and Treas.; Edward J. Greene, Secy.
EIN: 251544612
Codes: FD2

46862
The Edward G. Kucker Charitable Foundation
600 Reed Rd.
Broomall, PA 19008
Contact: Thomas Bruder, Tr.

Established in 1994.
Financial data (yr. ended 12/31/01): Grants paid, $86,100; assets, $317,370 (M); expenditures, $91,979; qualifying distributions, $86,100.
Trustee: Martin L. Longstreth.
EIN: 237772284

46863
E. Roy Knoppel Charitable Trust
121 Putney Ln.
Malvern, PA 19355 (610) 651-0156
Contact: Joseph E. Greene, Jr., Tr.

Established in 1989 in PA.
Financial data (yr. ended 12/31/01): Grants paid, $86,000; assets, $156,558 (M); expenditures, $90,135; qualifying distributions, $86,000.
Limitations: Giving primarily in PA.
Trustee: Joseph E. Greene, Jr.
EIN: 236963605

46864
Patroni Scholastici
c/o James R. Ledwith
400 Berwyn Park
Berwyn, PA 19312-1183
Application address: 307 Lincoln Ave., Highland Park, NJ 08904
Contact: William W. Fortenbaugh, Pres.

Established in 1977 in PA.
Financial data (yr. ended 12/31/01): Grants paid, $86,000; assets, $541,613 (M); expenditures, $88,350; qualifying distributions, $86,833.
Limitations: Giving primarily in NJ, NY, and PA.
Application information: Application form not required.
Officers: William W. Fortenbaugh, Pres.; Samuel B. Fortenbaugh III, Secy.
EIN: 232068469
Codes: FD2

46865
Isadore and Yetta Joshowitz Charitable Foundation
c/o Isadore Joshowitz
46 6th St.
Braddock, PA 15104

Established in 1991 in PA.
Donor(s): Isadore Joshowitz, Yetta Joshowitz.
Financial data (yr. ended 06/30/01): Grants paid, $85,925; assets, $1,597,541 (M); gifts received, $217,697; expenditures, $89,308; qualifying distributions, $85,150.
Limitations: Applications not accepted. Giving on a national basis.
Application information: Contributes only to pre-selected organizations.
Trustees: Isadore Joshowitz, James H. Joshowitz, Steven M. Joshowitz.
EIN: 256381619
Codes: FD2

46866
Baltimore Family Foundation, Inc.
34 S. River St.
Wilkes-Barre, PA 18702-2406

Established in 1984 in PA.
Donor(s): Members of the Baltimore family.
Financial data (yr. ended 11/30/01): Grants paid, $85,900; assets, $995,659 (M); expenditures, $88,114; qualifying distributions, $84,818.
Limitations: Applications not accepted. Giving limited to PA, with emphasis on Wilkes-Barre.
Application information: Contributes only to pre-selected organizations. Unsolicited requests for funds not considered or acknowledged.
Officers and Directors:* David M. Baltimore, Pres.; Muriel Baltimore,* Secy.; Charles Baltimore, Lynn Baltimore, Terry S. Baltimore.
EIN: 232308091
Codes: FD2

46867
Arthur & Estelle Sidewater Foundation
c/o Lafayette Financial Svcs.
215 W. Church Rd., Ste. 108
King of Prussia, PA 19406

Established in 1990 in PA.
Donor(s): Arthur Sidewater.
Financial data (yr. ended 12/31/01): Grants paid, $85,500; assets, $2,835,446 (M); expenditures, $102,410; qualifying distributions, $85,500.
Limitations: Applications not accepted. Giving primarily in PA.
Application information: Contributes only to pre-selected organizations.
Officers: June Wolfson, Pres.; Stephen Wolfson, V.P. and Secy.-Treas.
EIN: 232582882
Codes: FD2

46868—PENNSYLVANIA

46868
Richard C. Marquardt Family Foundation
P.O. Box 26
Waverly, PA 18471-0026 (570) 586-9237
Application address: c/o Richard C. Marquardt, B.D.A. Building, Ste. 102, Abington Executive Pk., Clarks Summit, PA 18411

Established in 1997 in PA.
Donor(s): Richard C. Marquardt.
Financial data (yr. ended 12/31/01): Grants paid, $85,450; assets, $1,737,055 (M); gifts received, $194,382; expenditures, $88,122; qualifying distributions, $84,942.
Limitations: Giving primarily in PA.
Officers: Richard C. Marquardt, Pres. and Treas.; Sarah W. Marquardt, V.P. and Secy.
Director: Jeffrey W. Marquardt.
EIN: 232896467
Codes: FD2

46869
Erlbaum Family Foundation
44 W. Lancaster Ave., Ste. 110
Ardmore, PA 19003
Contact: Gray E. Erlbaum

Established in 1998 in PA.
Donor(s): Philip Youtie, Gary E. Erlbaum.
Financial data (yr. ended 12/31/00): Grants paid, $84,951; assets, $1,200,296 (M); gifts received, $277,288; expenditures, $86,387; qualifying distributions, $81,834.
Limitations: Giving on a national basis.
Officer: Gray E. Erlbum, Pres.
Directors: Daniel Erlbaum, John Erlbaum, Marc Erlbaum, Vicky Erlbaum.
EIN: 232962563
Codes: FD2

46870
Spiegel Charitable Foundation
(Formerly William & Sulamita Spiegel Charitable Foundation)
500 Philip Rd.
Huntingdon Valley, PA 19006

Established in 1991 in PA.
Donor(s): William J. Spiegel, Sulamita Spiegel.
Financial data (yr. ended 12/31/01): Grants paid, $84,912; assets, $102,833 (M); expenditures, $85,256; qualifying distributions, $85,237.
Limitations: Applications not accepted. Giving primarily in Philadelphia, PA.
Application information: Contributes only to pre-selected organizations.
Trustees: Sulamita Spiegel, William J. Spiegel.
EIN: 232649352
Codes: FD2

46871
Flora Lind
c/o Mellon Bank, N.A.
P.O. Box 7236 AIM 193-0224
Philadelphia, PA 19101-7236 (215) 553-0585

Established in 1993 in PA.
Financial data (yr. ended 12/31/00): Grants paid, $84,716; assets, $1,873,842 (M); expenditures, $99,175; qualifying distributions, $85,851.
Limitations: Applications not accepted. Giving primarily in PA and VA.
Application information: Contributes only to pre-selected organizations.
Trustee: Mellon Bank, N.A.
EIN: 237884658
Codes: FD2

46872
Harry A. Lieberman Foundation
101 Cheswold Ln., Apt. 3C
Haverford, PA 19041

Established in 1986 in PA.
Donor(s): Harry A. Lieberman.
Financial data (yr. ended 12/31/01): Grants paid, $84,500; assets, $1,327,224 (M); gifts received, $7,825; expenditures, $89,549; qualifying distributions, $85,263.
Limitations: Applications not accepted. Giving primarily in NY and PA.
Application information: Contributes only to pre-selected organizations.
Trustee: Harry A. Lieberman.
EIN: 232328740
Codes: FD2

46873
Edward G. Mayers Charitable Trust
c/o Mellon Bank, N.A.
P.O. Box 7236
Philadelphia, PA 19101-7236
Contact: Donna Rhoades, Trust Off., Mellon Bank, N.A.

Established in 1994 in PA.
Financial data (yr. ended 07/31/01): Grants paid, $84,291; assets, $1,335,779 (M); expenditures, $98,355; qualifying distributions, $87,496.
Limitations: Giving primarily in Columbus, OH.
Trustee: Mellon Bank, N.A.
EIN: 256441164
Codes: FD2

46874
Isabel M. Spackman Foundation
c/o PNC Advisors
620 Liberty Ave., P2-PTPP-10-2
Pittsburgh, PA 15222-2705

Financial data (yr. ended 12/31/01): Grants paid, $84,019; assets, $1,173,990 (M); expenditures, $94,256; qualifying distributions, $84,193.
Limitations: Giving primarily in PA.
Trustee: PNC Bank, N.A.
EIN: 237226511
Codes: FD2, GTI

46875
The Ehlerman Family Foundation
11 Cardinal Pl.
Wyomissing, PA 19610

Established in 2000 in PA.
Financial data (yr. ended 12/31/01): Grants paid, $84,000; assets, $893,482 (M); gifts received, $63,249; expenditures, $96,359; qualifying distributions, $84,000.
Limitations: Applications not accepted.
Application information: Contributes only to pre-selected organizations.
Officers: P. Michael Ehlerman, Pres.; Judith A. Ehlerman, V.P.; Rosemary E. Kase, Secy.; P. Michael Ehlerman, Jr., Treas.
EIN: 233064362

46876
Minnie Payton Stayman Foundation
P.O. Box 185
Pittsburgh, PA 15230
Application address: c/o Mellon Bank, N.A., Central Trust Div., P.O. Box 19, State College, PA 16804

Established in 1986 in PA.
Financial data (yr. ended 12/31/01): Grants paid, $84,000; assets, $1,159,367 (M); expenditures, $92,461; qualifying distributions, $86,283.

Limitations: Giving limited to residents of Altoona, PA.
Application information: Application form required.
Trustee: Mellon Bank, N.A.
EIN: 236235009
Codes: FD2

46877
Wright-Cook Foundation
c/o The Glenmede Trust Co.
1650 Market St., Ste. 1200
Philadelphia, PA 19103-7391
Contact: Diana Deane

Established in 1990 in PA.
Donor(s): Susanna W. Cook.
Financial data (yr. ended 12/31/00): Grants paid, $84,000; assets, $1,832,013 (M); expenditures, $102,417; qualifying distributions, $89,718.
Application information: Application form not required.
Trustees: John W. Church, Susanna W. Cook, The Glenmede Trust Co.
EIN: 236962132
Codes: FD2

46878
Sgt. Philip German Memorial Foundation
c/o Allfirst
21 E. Market St.
York, PA 17401-1500
Application address: P.O. Box 2961, Harrisburg, PA 17105
Contact: Joe Macri, Trust Off., Allfirst

Established in 1986 in PA.
Financial data (yr. ended 12/31/00): Grants paid, $83,700; assets, $1,838,192 (M); expenditures, $102,515; qualifying distributions, $83,700.
Limitations: Giving limited to PA.
Application information: Application form required.
Trustee: Allfirst.
EIN: 236745697
Codes: FD2, GTI

46879
Vivian O. and Meyer P. Potamkin Foundation
(Formerly Vipa Foundation)
237 S. 18th St., Ste. 20B
Philadelphia, PA 19103 (215) 636-0911
Contact: Vivian O. Potamkin, Tr.

Established around 1982 in PA.
Donor(s): Meyer P. Potamkin, Vivian O. Potamkin.
Financial data (yr. ended 12/31/00): Grants paid, $83,697; assets, $212,637 (M); gifts received, $5,000; expenditures, $84,681; qualifying distributions, $83,505.
Limitations: Giving primarily in Philadelphia, PA.
Trustee: Vivian O. Potamkin.
EIN: 232197860
Codes: FD2

46880
James Sutton Home for Aged & Infirm Men Trust
c/o Robert W. Hall, C.P.A.
1065 Hwy. 315, Ste. 302
Wilkes-Barre, PA 18702-6941

Established in 1917 in PA.
Financial data (yr. ended 06/30/01): Grants paid, $83,640; assets, $2,527,754 (M); expenditures, $146,484; qualifying distributions, $133,068.
Limitations: Giving primarily in Wilkes-Barre, PA.
Application information: Application form required.
Trustees: Paul Adams, James I. Alexander, Richard Hogaboom.

EIN: 240795490

46881
The Shore Fund
c/o Mellon Bank, N.A.
P.O. Box 185
Pittsburgh, PA 15230-0185 (412) 234-0023
Contact: Laurie A. Moritz

Established in 1982.
Donor(s): Benjamin R. Fisher, Fisher Charitable Trusts I and II.
Financial data (yr. ended 12/31/01): Grants paid, $83,500; assets, $4,314,715 (M); gifts received, $1,750; expenditures, $119,377; qualifying distributions, $95,389.
Limitations: Applications not accepted. Giving primarily in Naples, FL, and Pittsburgh, PA.
Application information: Contributes only to pre-selected organizations.
Trustees: Christine F. Allen, Benjamin R. Fisher, Jr., Lillian H. Fisher, Margaret F. McKean, Mellon Bank, N.A.
EIN: 256220659
Codes: FD2

46882
The William E. C. and Mary Dearden Foundation
c/o Hershey Trust Co.
P.O. Box 445
Hershey, PA 17033

Established in 1986 in PA.
Donor(s): William E.C. Dearden, Mary Dearden.
Financial data (yr. ended 12/31/01): Grants paid, $83,000; assets, $358,888 (M); expenditures, $85,995; qualifying distributions, $82,825.
Limitations: Applications not accepted. Giving primarily in CA and PA.
Application information: Contributes only to pre-selected organizations.
Officers: William E.C. Dearden, Chair.; Mary Dearden, Pres.
Trustee: Hershey Trust Co.
EIN: 236814400
Codes: FD2

46883
The Harvey S. Gitlin Family Foundation
270 New Jersey Dr.
Fort Washington, PA 19034

Established in 1999 in PA.
Donor(s): Harvey S. Gitlin.
Financial data (yr. ended 12/31/01): Grants paid, $83,000; assets, $4,061,221 (M); gifts received, $2,000,000; expenditures, $85,515; qualifying distributions, $82,553.
Limitations: Applications not accepted. Giving primarily in PA.
Application information: Contributes only to pre-selected organizations.
Trustee: Harvey S. Gitlin.
EIN: 256645244
Codes: FD2

46884
Founders Memorial Fund of the American Sterilizer Company
2424 W. 23rd St.
Erie, PA 16506
Contact: Patricia Brewer, Tr.

Established in 1938 in PA.
Donor(s): George F. Hall, J. Everett Hall.
Financial data (yr. ended 12/31/01): Grants paid, $82,750; assets, $1,768,697 (M); expenditures, $102,317; qualifying distributions, $88,248.
Limitations: Giving primarily in areas of company operations.
Application information: Application form required.
Trustee: Patricia Brewer.
EIN: 256062068
Codes: CS, FD2, CD, GTI

46885
Russell & Eleanor Horn Foundation
40 S. Richland Ave.
York, PA 17404
Contact: Rosalind H. Kunkel, Pres.

Established in 1985 in PA.
Donor(s): Russell E. Horn, Sr.
Financial data (yr. ended 12/31/01): Grants paid, $82,689; assets, $2,009,203 (M); gifts received, $257,143; expenditures, $97,090; qualifying distributions, $84,217.
Limitations: Giving primarily in York County, PA.
Publications: Application guidelines, financial statement.
Application information: Application form required.
Officers and Directors:* Rosalind H. Kunkel,* Pres.; Russell E. Horn, Sr.,* Secy.; William H. Kiick, Treas.; Carole O. Horn, Ralph E. Horn, Jr., Russell E. Horn III, Rev. Owen Walter.
EIN: 222663207
Codes: FD2

46886
Alton & Mildred Cross Scholarship Fund
3330 Peach St., Ste. 101
Erie, PA 16508
Contact: Eugene Cross, Tr.

Established in 1993 in PA.
Donor(s): Mildred Cross.
Financial data (yr. ended 12/31/01): Grants paid, $82,500; assets, $0 (M); expenditures, $99,763; qualifying distributions, $82,500.
Limitations: Giving limited to residents of Waterford Borough, Waterford Township, Mill Village Borough, and Lebouef Township, PA.
Application information: Application form required.
Trustees: Eugene Cross, Norbert Cross.
EIN: 251709602
Codes: FD2, GTI

46887
Carol E. & Myles P. Berkman Foundation
200 Gateway Ctr.
Pittsburgh, PA 15222

Established in 1994.
Donor(s): Myles P. Berkman, Carol E. Berkman.
Financial data (yr. ended 12/31/00): Grants paid, $82,450; assets, $1,546,068 (M); expenditures, $83,723; qualifying distributions, $82,450.
Limitations: Applications not accepted. Giving primarily in MA and PA.
Application information: Contributes only to pre-selected organizations.
Officers: Myles P. Berkman, Pres. and Secy.; Carol E. Berkman, V.P.; David J. Berkman, V.P; Mara I. Landis, V.P.; Pamela T. Berkman, V.P.; William H. Berkman, V.P.
EIN: 251754310
Codes: FD2

46888
J. J. Medveckis Foundation
c/o Cooke & Bieler, Inc.
1700 Market St., Ste. 3222
Philadelphia, PA 19103-3991

Established in 1986 in PA.
Donor(s): John J. Medveckis.
Financial data (yr. ended 11/30/01): Grants paid, $82,050; assets, $50,249 (M); expenditures, $84,365; qualifying distributions, $82,036.
Limitations: Applications not accepted. Giving primarily in New York, NY and Philadelphia, PA.
Application information: Contributes only to pre-selected organizations.
Trustee: John J. Medveckis.
EIN: 236838439

46889
The Florence Lamme Feicht Boyer Family Foundation
c/o R.M. Daniel
301 Grant St., 20th Fl.
Pittsburgh, PA 15219

Established in 1996 in PA.
Donor(s): Florence F. Boyer.‡
Financial data (yr. ended 04/30/01): Grants paid, $81,600; assets, $1,749,393 (M); gifts received, $12,869; expenditures, $84,465; qualifying distributions, $82,146.
Limitations: Applications not accepted. Giving primarily in PA.
Application information: Contributes only to pre-selected organizations.
Trustees: Dorothy L. Boyer, John L. Boyer.
EIN: 251801104
Codes: FD2

46890
Gamber Foundation
2220 Dutch Gold Dr.
Lancaster, PA 17601-1997
Contact: William R. Gamber II, Pres.

Established in 1984 in PA.
Donor(s): W. Ralph Gamber, Luella M. Gamber, Dutch Gold Honey, Inc., Gamber Glass Container Co.
Financial data (yr. ended 09/30/01): Grants paid, $81,500; assets, $1,521,634 (M); gifts received, $5,000; expenditures, $86,762; qualifying distributions, $82,250.
Limitations: Giving primarily in Lancaster, PA.
Application information: Application form not required.
Officers: William R. Gamber II, Pres.; Marianne M. Gamber, Secy.; Nancy J. Gamber, Treas.
Directors: Kitty L. Gamber, Luella M. Gamber, Robert D. Garner, Julie A. Good, Michael T. Kane, W. Scott Stoner.
EIN: 232331958
Codes: FD2

46891
The Concord Foundation
c/o Charles Lyons
P.O. Box 1329
Fort Washington, PA 19034
Application address: 919 Stoneybrook Dr., Springfield, PA 19064-3828, tel.: (610) 328-2549
Contact: Richard Castafaro

Established in 1995 in PA.
Donor(s): Albert Berman, Trudy Berman.
Financial data (yr. ended 11/30/01): Grants paid, $81,002; assets, $893,122 (M); gifts received, $19,147; expenditures, $83,498; qualifying distributions, $81,001.
Application information: Application form not required.
Officers: Norman Loev, Pres.; Michael Rogers, Secy.-Treas.
EIN: 232828303
Codes: FD2

46892—PENNSYLVANIA

46892
The Good Friend Foundation
c/o Juliet F. Goodfriend
334 Rosemary Ln.
Penn Valley, PA 19072

Established in 1999 in PA.
Financial data (yr. ended 12/31/01): Grants paid, $81,000; assets, $435,321 (M); expenditures, $87,975; qualifying distributions, $81,000.
Limitations: Applications not accepted.
Application information: Contributes only to pre-selected organizations.
Trustees: Juliet J. Goodfriend, Marc R. Moreau.
EIN: 256658819

46893
The Hess Trust
170 Ridge Ave.
Ephrata, PA 17522 (717) 738-4819
Contact: Kenneth E. Hess, Tr.

Established in 1979.
Donor(s): Claude H. Hess, Kenneth E. Hess.
Financial data (yr. ended 06/30/02): Grants paid, $81,000; assets, $178,917 (M); expenditures, $86,000; qualifying distributions, $81,000.
Limitations: Giving primarily in PA.
Trustees: J. Clair Hess, Kenneth E. Hess.
EIN: 232112168

46894
S. Ira McDowell Foundation
c/o Mellon Bank, N.A.
204 N. George St., Ste. 290
York, PA 17401
Contact: Angela R. Thompson, Trust Off., Mellon Bank, N.A.

Established in 1969.
Donor(s): Ira McDowell.‡
Financial data (yr. ended 12/31/01): Grants paid, $81,000; assets, $479,433 (M); expenditures, $92,166; qualifying distributions, $81,215.
Limitations: Giving primarily in York and York County, PA.
Trustee: Mellon Bank, N.A.
EIN: 236465481
Codes: FD2

46895
Richard A. Zappala Family Foundation
4 Gateway Ctr., Ste. 212
Pittsburgh, PA 15222

Established in 1997 in PA.
Donor(s): Richard A. Zappala, Nancy B. Zappala.
Financial data (yr. ended 12/31/01): Grants paid, $80,933; assets, $1,772,936 (M); expenditures, $110,545; qualifying distributions, $80,933.
Limitations: Applications not accepted. Giving primarily in Pittsburgh, PA.
Application information: Contributes only to pre-selected organizations.
Trustees: Lori Z. Hardiman, Thomas M. Hardiman, Nancy B. Zappala, Richard A. Zappala.
EIN: 237876878
Codes: FD2

46896
Vang Memorial Foundation
P.O. Box 11727
Pittsburgh, PA 15228-0727 (412) 563-0261
Contact: E.J. Hosko, Treas.

Established in 1946.
Financial data (yr. ended 12/31/01): Grants paid, $80,878; assets, $1,567,695 (M); expenditures, $103,480; qualifying distributions, $91,266.
Limitations: Giving limited to areas where George Vang, Inc. and its subsidiaries operate nationwide.

Officers and Trustees:* F.C. Schroeder,* Pres.; Alice M. Meinel,* Secy.; E.J. Hosko,* Treas.; Kevin Gallagher, R.G. Lanz, Patti Tranquilli.
EIN: 256034491
Codes: FD2, GTI

46897
Gates Family Foundation
840 Yorkshire Rd.
Bethlehem, PA 18017-3012

Established in PA in 1998.
Donor(s): Elmer D. Gates, Betty S. Gates.
Financial data (yr. ended 12/31/99): Grants paid, $80,520; assets, $14,569 (M); gifts received, $75,975; expenditures, $81,855; qualifying distributions, $80,520.
Limitations: Applications not accepted.
Trustees: Betty S. Gates, Elmer D. Gates, Jodi A. Key, Patti G. Smith.
EIN: 237962091

46898
Walden Trust
c/o Henry P. Hoffstot, Jr., et al.
5057 5th Ave.
Pittsburgh, PA 15232

Established in 1973 in PA.
Financial data (yr. ended 12/31/00): Grants paid, $80,450; assets, $1,585,250 (M); expenditures, $86,449; qualifying distributions, $83,602.
Limitations: Applications not accepted. Giving primarily in Pittsburgh and southwestern PA.
Application information: Contributes only to pre-selected organizations.
Trustees: Thayer H. Drew, Henry P. Hoffstot, Jr., Henry P. Hoffstot III, Lora H. Jenkins, Lorna K. Tahtinen, Arthur P. Ziegler, Jr.
EIN: 256027635
Codes: FD2

46899
The Francis J. Dixon Foundation
c/o Francis J. Dixon
328 N. 14th St.
Lebanon, PA 17046

Established in 1989 in PA.
Donor(s): Francis J. Dixon, Brandywine Recycles Inc.
Financial data (yr. ended 12/31/01): Grants paid, $80,400; assets, $1,691,881 (M); gifts received, $50,000; expenditures, $143,922; qualifying distributions, $80,400.
Limitations: Applications not accepted. Giving primarily in PA.
Application information: Contributes only to pre-selected organizations.
Officer and Directors:* Francis J. Dixon,* Pres.; Timothy J. Huber, Christine Rathbum, Richard P. Scott, Thomas I. Siegal, JoAnn D. White.
EIN: 251600852
Codes: FD2

46900
The Otto and Gertrude K. Pollak Scholarship Fund
c/o John Iskrant
1600 Market St., Ste. 3600
Philadelphia, PA 19103

Established in 1999 in PA.
Donor(s): Gertrude K. Pollak.‡
Financial data (yr. ended 03/31/01): Grants paid, $80,362; assets, $3,892,760 (M); gifts received, $821,924; expenditures, $99,208; qualifying distributions, $84,457.
Limitations: Applications not accepted. Giving primarily in PA.

Application information: Contributes only to pre-selected organizations.
Trustee: John D. Iskrant.
EIN: 256624630
Codes: FD2

46901
Charles & Betty Degenstein Foundation
400 Market St.
Sunbury, PA 17801

Established in 1977.
Financial data (yr. ended 12/31/01): Grants paid, $80,200; assets, $1,964,757 (M); expenditures, $97,840; qualifying distributions, $97,148.
Limitations: Giving limited to Snyder, Union, and Northumberland counties, PA.
Officer: Kathryn Pakuta, Chair.
Board Members: Rev. Jonathan Albright, Sidney Apfelbaum, Belle Kamsler, Fred Kelley, Jr., Helen Nunn, Carl Rohrbach.
Trustee: First National Trust Bank.
EIN: 236661599
Codes: FD2

46902
Laughlin Memorial, Inc.
202 Orchard Ln., Edgeworth
Sewickley, PA 15143 (412) 741-8889
Contact: Frederick C. Emerick, Jr., Secy.-Treas.

Established about 1927 in PA.
Donor(s): Mary M. Laughlin.‡
Financial data (yr. ended 12/31/01): Grants paid, $80,000; assets, $2,560,310 (M); gifts received, $13,390; expenditures, $139,326; qualifying distributions, $137,378.
Limitations: Giving limited to the Ambridge, PA, area.
Application information: Application form required.
Officers and Trustees:* Alexander M. Laughlin,* Pres.; Frederick C. Emerick, Jr.,* Secy.-Treas.; Carl M. Kerchner, David W. Laughlin, James F. Schell, William J. Simpson, Robert E. Taggart, James P. Wetzel, Jr.
EIN: 251072140
Codes: FD2

46903
The Pelson Foundation
c/o J. Iskrant
1600 Market St., Ste. 3600
Philadelphia, PA 19103
Application address: 9 Woodstone Rd., Chester, NJ 07930-2731, tel.: (561) 747-6886
Contact: Victoria A. Pelson, Tr.

Established in 1997 in PA.
Donor(s): Barbara A. Pelson.
Financial data (yr. ended 12/31/01): Grants paid, $80,000; assets, $234,771 (M); expenditures, $86,348; qualifying distributions, $81,270.
Limitations: Giving primarily in NJ and NY.
Trustees: Barbara A. Pelson, Victor A. Pelson.
EIN: 237880442
Codes: FD2

46904
Martha W. Rogers Charitable Trust
c/o Mellon Bank, N.A.
P.O. Box 185
Pittsburgh, PA 15230-9897
Application address: P.O. Box 7899, Philadelphia, PA 19101
Contact: Pat Kling

Established in 1993 in PA.
Donor(s): Martha W. Rogers.‡

Financial data (yr. ended 12/31/01): Grants paid, $80,000; assets, $1,433,190 (M); expenditures, $86,530; qualifying distributions, $80,260.
Limitations: Giving primarily in Philadelphia, PA.
Trustee: Mellon Bank, N.A.
EIN: 256412239
Codes: FD2

46905
SNAVE Foundation
P.O. Box 179
Gwynedd Valley, PA 19437-0179

Established in 1988 in PA.
Donor(s): J. Morris Evans, Anne T. Evans.
Financial data (yr. ended 12/31/00): Grants paid, $80,000; assets, $2,069,310 (M); gifts received, $181,311; expenditures, $90,456; qualifying distributions, $80,457.
Limitations: Applications not accepted. Giving primarily in PA.
Application information: Contributes only to pre-selected organizations.
Trustees: Anne T. Evans, J. Morris Evans, Joseph M. Evans, Jr., Walter C. Evans, Wendy E. Kravitz.
EIN: 236928009
Codes: FD2

46906
The Frank Strick Foundation, Inc.
765 Moredon Rd.
Meadowbrook, PA 19046 (215) 887-1601
Contact: Edith Sheppard, M.D., Secy.-Treas.

Established in 1987 in PA.
Financial data (yr. ended 12/31/00): Grants paid, $80,000; assets, $20,294,644 (M); expenditures, $95,783; qualifying distributions, $80,000.
Limitations: Giving primarily in New York, NY, and PA.
Officers: Maida Gordon, Chair.; Edith Sheppard, M.D., Secy.-Treas.
Directors: Brad Sheppard, Jr., Jacob Strick, Joseph Strick.
EIN: 232484958
Codes: FD2

46907
Toll Charitable Foundation
c/o Silberman-DiFilippo
150 Monument Rd., Ste. 603
Bala Cynwyd, PA 19004-1725

Established in 1985 in PA.
Financial data (yr. ended 11/30/00): Grants paid, $80,000; assets, $254,558 (M); expenditures, $83,323; qualifying distributions, $80,000.
Limitations: Applications not accepted. Giving primarily in FL and NJ.
Application information: Contributes only to pre-selected organizations.
Trustee: Gilbert Toll.
EIN: 222779206
Codes: FD2

46908
The Robert and Nina McCarthy Foundation
c/o Citizens & Northern Bank, Trust Dept.
90 Main St.
Wellsboro, PA 16901
Application address: 100 Fellows Ave., Wellsboro, PA 16901
Contact: Nina McCarthy, Dir. or Robert McCarthy, Dir.

Established in 1999 in PA.
Donor(s): Robert McCarthy, Nina McCarthy.
Financial data (yr. ended 12/31/00): Grants paid, $79,624; assets, $18,524 (M); gifts received, $9,132; expenditures, $79,663; qualifying distributions, $78,835.

Limitations: Giving primarily in the Tioga and Lycoming, PA, areas.
Application information: Application form required.
Directors: Nina McCarthy, Robert McCarthy.
EIN: 311623543
Codes: FD2

46909
Armstrong-McKay Foundation
1706 Allegheny Towers
625 Stanwix St., Ste. 1706
Pittsburgh, PA 15222

Established in 1994 in PA.
Donor(s): James C. McKay Charitable Remainder Trust.
Financial data (yr. ended 12/31/01): Grants paid, $79,500; assets, $666,743 (M); gifts received, $18,013; expenditures, $93,455; qualifying distributions, $79,354.
Limitations: Applications not accepted. Giving primarily in CA and PA.
Application information: Contributes only to pre-selected organizations.
Trustee: James McKay Armstrong.
EIN: 251754629
Codes: FD2

46910
The Merwin Foundation
Asbury Rd. at W. 23rd St.
Erie, PA 16506

Donor(s): Robert F. Merwin.
Financial data (yr. ended 12/31/00): Grants paid, $79,450; assets, $4,341,649 (M); expenditures, $113,567; qualifying distributions, $79,450.
Limitations: Applications not accepted. Giving primarily in Erie, PA.
Application information: Contributes only to pre-selected organizations.
Officers and Directors:* Richard A. Merwin,* Pres. and Treas.; John E. Britton,* Secy.; James E. Spoden, Jr.
EIN: 256060860
Codes: FD2

46911
Spero Samer Trust
c/o First Commonwealth Trust Co.
111 S. Main St.
Greensburg, PA 15601 (724) 834-6062

Established around 1976.
Financial data (yr. ended 12/31/01): Grants paid, $79,330; assets, $2,186,836 (M); expenditures, $101,729; qualifying distributions, $78,363.
Application information: Application form required.
Trustees: George W. Lamproplos, First Commonwealth Trust Co.
EIN: 256175080
Codes: FD2, GTI

46912
Peter J. Wood Foundation
55 Crosby Brown Rd.
Gladwyne, PA 19035-1512

Established in 1996.
Financial data (yr. ended 10/31/01): Grants paid, $79,050; assets, $215,820 (M); expenditures, $80,672; qualifying distributions, $80,612.
Limitations: Applications not accepted. Giving on a national basis.
Application information: Contributes only to pre-selected organizations.
Officers: Peter J. Wood, Pres.; Michael Krekstein, Secy.
EIN: 232868525

Codes: FD2

46913
Margaret M. Walker Charitable Foundation
1 E. State St.
Sharon, PA 16146

Financial data (yr. ended 12/31/01): Grants paid, $78,950; assets, $158 (M); gifts received, $79,513; expenditures, $81,415; qualifying distributions, $78,930.
Advisors: Richard Epstein, Joe Evans, David Levine.
Trustee: Butler Wick Trust Co.
EIN: 251790413
Codes: FD2

46914
Denenberg Foundation
(Formerly Gertrude Denenberg Charitable Trust)
c/o Adelphia Lamps & Shades Inc.
5000 Paschall Ave.
Philadelphia, PA 19143-5136

Financial data (yr. ended 12/31/01): Grants paid, $78,770; assets, $66,524 (M); expenditures, $82,712; qualifying distributions, $78,770.
Limitations: Applications not accepted. Giving primarily in the Northeast, with emphasis on Philadelphia, PA.
Application information: Contributes only to pre-selected organizations.
Trustees: Alfred Denenberg, Robert Denenberg.
EIN: 236431888

46915
Raymond & Ellen Goldberg Foundation
2701 Red Lion Rd.
Philadelphia, PA 19154

Established in 1986.
Donor(s): Ellen Goldberg, Raymond Goldberg.
Financial data (yr. ended 11/30/01): Grants paid, $78,289; assets, $399,798 (M); expenditures, $79,388; qualifying distributions, $78,154.
Limitations: Applications not accepted. Giving primarily in PA.
Application information: Contributes only to pre-selected organizations.
Trustees: Raymond Goldberg, Rick Goldberg.
EIN: 222787780
Codes: FD2

46916
Nick & Paris N. Panagos Charitable Trust
1012 Wood St.
Bristol, PA 19007-5347
Contact: Arthur Midouhas, Tr.

Established in 1996 in PA.
Financial data (yr. ended 12/31/00): Grants paid, $77,953; assets, $1,308,286 (M); expenditures, $100,859; qualifying distributions, $76,624.
Limitations: Giving primarily in PA.
Application information: Application form not required.
Trustee: Arthur Midouhas.
EIN: 237802567
Codes: FD2

46917
The King Foundation
1180 Long Run Rd., Ste. A
Mc Keesport, PA 15131

Established in 1995 in PA.
Donor(s): King's Country Shoppes, Inc., Hartley C. King.
Financial data (yr. ended 12/31/00): Grants paid, $77,475; assets, $17,643 (M); expenditures, $77,497; qualifying distributions, $77,490.
Officer and Trustee:* Hartley C. King,* Pres.

46917—PENNSYLVANIA

EIN: 251762453
Codes: FD2

46918
Citizens Bank Foundation
P.O. Box 1550
Butler, PA 16003-1550

Established in 1998 in PA.
Donor(s): Citizens National Bank of Evans City, PA.
Financial data (yr. ended 12/31/00): Grants paid, $77,434; assets, $92,200 (M); expenditures, $78,623; qualifying distributions, $77,397.
Limitations: Applications not accepted. Giving limited to Evans City, PA.
Trustee: Citizens National Bank of Evans City, PA.
EIN: 311631195
Codes: CS, FD2, CD

46919
Bernard F. Boyle Memorial Scholarship Fund
c/o Mellon Bank, N.A.
P.O. Box 185
Pittsburgh, PA 15230-9877

Established in 1985 in PA.
Financial data (yr. ended 12/31/01): Grants paid, $77,161; assets, $1,104,264 (M); expenditures, $85,126; qualifying distributions, $77,564.
Limitations: Giving primarily in Nesquehoning, PA.
Application information: Application form required.
Trustee: Mellon Bank, N.A.
EIN: 236790683
Codes: FD2, GTI

46920
Berks Products Foundation
c/o Allfirst
21 E. Market St.
York, PA 17401-1500

Financial data (yr. ended 12/31/00): Grants paid, $77,027; assets, $581,241 (M); expenditures, $87,170; qualifying distributions, $76,512.
Limitations: Applications not accepted. Giving primarily in PA.
Application information: Contributes only to pre-selected organizations.
Trustee: Allfirst.
EIN: 236396201
Codes: FD2

46921
Schwartz Family Charitable Foundation
305 N. Highland Ave.
Merion Station, PA 19066
Contact: Daniel M. Schwartz, Tr.

Established in 2000 in PA.
Financial data (yr. ended 12/31/01): Grants paid, $76,727; assets, $1 (M); gifts received, $49,670; expenditures, $76,768; qualifying distributions, $76,727.
Trustees: Daniel M. Schwartz, Jammie A. Schwartz.
EIN: 256683798
Codes: FD2

46922
J. Clifford & Ruth M. Kopp Charitable Trust
c/o Fulton Financial Advisors, N.A.
P.O. Box 3215
Lancaster, PA 17604-3215

Established in 1997 in PA.
Financial data (yr. ended 10/31/01): Grants paid, $76,523; assets, $2,640,280 (M); expenditures, $96,536; qualifying distributions, $76,523.

Limitations: Applications not accepted. Giving primarily in Lebanon, PA.
Application information: Contributes only to pre-selected organizations.
Trustee: Fulton Financial Advisors, N.A.
EIN: 256569052
Codes: FD2

46923
The J. Robert & Barbara A. Hillier Foundation, Inc.
2846 River Rd.
New Hope, PA 18938

Established in 1999 in PA.
Donor(s): J. Robert Hillier, Barbara A. Hillier.
Financial data (yr. ended 12/31/01): Grants paid, $76,500; assets, $734,047 (M); expenditures, $86,292; qualifying distributions, $76,292.
Limitations: Applications not accepted. Giving primarily in NJ and PA.
Application information: Contributes only to pre-selected organizations.
Officers and Trustees:* J. Robert Hillier,* Pres. and Treas.; Barbara A. Hillier,* V.P. and Secy.; Conrad L. Druker.
EIN: 223695705
Codes: FD2

46924
Landon Family Foundation
c/o Ronald A. Landon
1404 Anvil Ct.
Downingtown, PA 19335-1335

Established in 1997 in PA.
Donor(s): Ronald A. Landon, Joyce S. Landon.
Financial data (yr. ended 12/31/01): Grants paid, $76,260; assets, $432,810 (M); gifts received, $6,500; expenditures, $84,206; qualifying distributions, $76,260.
Limitations: Applications not accepted. Giving primarily in PA.
Application information: Contributes only to pre-selected organizations.
Officers: Ronald A. Landon, Pres. and Mgr.; Joyce S. Landon, V.P. and Treas.
Directors: Joseph McGrath, Katherine McGrath, Harry Norton, Nancy Norton.
EIN: 232868535
Codes: FD2

46925
Packman Family Foundation
214 Sycamore Ave.
Merion Station, PA 19066-1529
(610) 623-2100
Contact: Elias W. Packman, Tr.

Donor(s): Elias W. Packman, Jane Packman.
Financial data (yr. ended 12/31/01): Grants paid, $76,233; assets, $326,980 (M); expenditures, $78,040; qualifying distributions, $78,040.
Limitations: Giving on a national basis.
Trustees: Elias W. Packman, Jane Packman.
EIN: 222781594
Codes: FD2

46926
The Schoffstall Family Foundation, Inc.
1818 Signal Hill Rd.
Mechanicsburg, PA 17055 (717) 728-9090

Established in 1997 in PA.
Donor(s): Martin L. Schoffstall.
Financial data (yr. ended 12/31/00): Grants paid, $76,000; assets, $352,564 (M); gifts received, $100,000; expenditures, $85,379; qualifying distributions, $76,000.
Limitations: Giving primarily in PA.

Directors: Louann Martin, Brenda Pinckney, Martin L. Schoffstall, Marvin L. Schoffstall, Stephen A. Schoffstall.
EIN: 232872636
Codes: FD2

46927
The Stewart Family Foundation
c/o Andrea Hyatt
1600 Market St., Ste. 3600
Philadelphia, PA 19103
Application address: 202 Roanoke St., Cherry Hill, NJ 08003
Contact: George E. Stewart, Tr.

Established in 2000 in NJ.
Donor(s): George E. Stewart.
Financial data (yr. ended 12/31/01): Grants paid, $76,000; assets, $967,953 (M); expenditures, $110,362; qualifying distributions, $76,000.
Limitations: Giving primarily in OH.
Trustees: Joann S. Bissell, David M. Stewart, George E. Stewart, Glenna G. Stewart, Robert E. Stewart, William C. Stewart.
EIN: 233050745

46928
Fred J. Rosenau Foundation
c/o Francis X. Connell
1100 Shadeland Ave.
Drexel Hill, PA 19026-1915
Application address: P.O. Box 5667, Snowmass Village, CO 81615
Contact: Gary Rosenau, Mgr.

Established in 1944.
Financial data (yr. ended 12/31/00): Grants paid, $75,875; assets, $1,500,000 (M); expenditures, $90,818; qualifying distributions, $83,347.
Limitations: Giving primarily in CO and PA.
Officer: Gary Rosenau, Mgr.
Trustee: Donald Bean.
EIN: 236251768
Codes: FD2

46929
Hanover Shoe Farms Foundations, Inc.
Rte. 194 S.
P.O. Box 339
Hanover, PA 17331 (717) 637-8931
Contact: Russell C. Williams, Pres.

Established in 1991 in PA.
Donor(s): Lawrence B. Sheppard Foundation.
Financial data (yr. ended 11/30/01): Grants paid, $75,750; assets, $2,064,931 (M); expenditures, $97,630; qualifying distributions, $75,750.
Limitations: Giving primarily in PA.
Officers: Russell C. Williams, Pres.; James W. Simpson, V.P.; Shawn R. Eisenhauer, Secy.; Shirley J. Kuhn, Treas.
Directors: Patricia Eisenhower, Sharon Young.
EIN: 232647725
Codes: FD2

46930
Children's Home of Harrisburg, Inc.
(also known as Children's Home Foundation)
P.O. Box 11537
Harrisburg, PA 17108-1537 (717) 233-0092
Contact: Sheila M. Ross, Secy.

Established in 1983.
Financial data (yr. ended 11/30/01): Grants paid, $75,000; assets, $1,008,550 (M); expenditures, $88,942; qualifying distributions, $83,034.
Limitations: Giving limited to Cumberland, Dauphin, and Perry counties, PA.
Publications: Application guidelines, program policy statement.

Application information: Application form required.
Officers: Charles Fromer, Pres.; Dean Weidner, V.P.; Sheila M. Ross, Secy.; Joseph A. Macri, Treas.
Directors: Kara Arnold, Joyce Bolden, Catherine Jones, Paul L. Mahoney, Christopher Markley, Cassandra Pepinsky, Alice Ann Schwab.
EIN: 231352079

46931
The Jordon Charitable Foundation
2001 market St.
Two Commerce Sq., Ste. 3410
Philadelphia, PA 19103-7044
Contact: Bernard Eizen

Established in 1999 in DE.
Donor(s): Barbara L. Jordan, John L. Jordan.
Financial data (yr. ended 02/28/01): Grants paid, $75,000; assets, $381,571 (M); expenditures, $83,352; qualifying distributions, $75,020.
Limitations: Applications not accepted. Giving primarily in Morristown, PA.
Application information: Contributes only to pre-selected organizations.
Officers and Directors:* John L. Jordan,* Pres. and Treas.; Barbara L. Jordan,* Secy.; Bernard Eizen.
EIN: 510381471

46932
The Jeffery and Cynthia King Family Foundation
2062 General Alexander Dr.
Malvern, PA 19355

Established in 1999 in PA.
Donor(s): Jeffery L. King, Cynthia M. King.
Financial data (yr. ended 05/31/02): Grants paid, $75,000; assets, $201,841 (M); gifts received, $128,363; expenditures, $75,098; qualifying distributions, $75,000.
Limitations: Applications not accepted.
Application information: Contributes only to pre-selected organizations.
Trustees: Jeffery L. King, Cynthia M. King.
EIN: 256638460

46933
Lloyd Foundation
c/o PNC Advisors, Char. Trust Comm.
620 Liberty Ave., 25th Fl.
Pittsburgh, PA 15222-2705 (412) 762-7076
Contact: Mia Hallett Bernard

Established in 1981 in PA.
Financial data (yr. ended 06/30/01): Grants paid, $75,000; assets, $2,005,985 (M); expenditures, $90,314; qualifying distributions, $76,275.
Limitations: Giving primarily in Pittsburgh, PA.
Trustee: PNC Bank, N.A.
EIN: 256228888
Codes: FD2

46934
Pritchard Foundation
c/o Douglas M. Newton
115 Aarons Ave.
New Britain, PA 18901-5103

Established in 1998 in PA.
Financial data (yr. ended 12/31/00): Grants paid, $75,000; assets, $1,265,284 (M); expenditures, $89,841; qualifying distributions, $75,000.
Limitations: Applications not accepted. Giving primarily in New York, NY.
Application information: Contributes only to pre-selected organizations.
Trustees: Peter L. Buttenwieser, Allen Grossman, Lee P. Klingenstein.
EIN: 237982138

46935
Roth Foundation
500 Horizon Dr., Ste. 503
Chalfont, PA 18914-3962 (215) 947-3750
Application address: 1182 Wrack Rd., Meadowbrook, PA 19046-2544
Contact: Henry Boreen, Tr.

Established in 1953 in PA.
Donor(s): Edythe M. Roth, Abraham Roth.‡
Financial data (yr. ended 10/31/01): Grants paid, $75,000; assets, $356,404 (M); expenditures, $78,037; qualifying distributions, $74,444.
Limitations: Giving primarily in PA.
Application information: Applicants must have completed 1 year in a recognized school of nursing. Scholarship awards are made directly to nursing institution on recipient's behalf. Application form not required.
Trustees: Henry Boreen, Roland P. Ruth, Linda Schwartz.
EIN: 236271428
Codes: GTI

46936
Harrison & Margaret Snyder Charitable Trust
c/o M&T Bank, Trust Dept.
P.O. Box 2007
Altoona, PA 16603-2007
Contact: Marie Boyle, Asst. V.P. and Trust Off.

Established in 1994 in PA.
Donor(s): Margaret Snyder,‡ Harrison Snyder.‡
Financial data (yr. ended 12/31/01): Grants paid, $74,999; assets, $1,418,438 (M); expenditures, $97,228; qualifying distributions, $74,752.
Limitations: Giving limited to Blair County, PA.
Trustees: William R. Collins, Daniel Ratchford, M & T Bank.
EIN: 256436588

46937
Wolf-Kuhn Foundation
129 Summit Dr.
Hollidaysburg, PA 16648 (814) 696-2721
FAX: (814) 696-7510
Contact: Gerald P. Wolf, Chair.

Established in 1957.
Donor(s): George A. Wolf,‡ Herbert T. Wolf, Sr.,‡ Margery Wolf-Kuhn.‡
Financial data (yr. ended 09/30/01): Grants paid, $74,884; assets, $1,564,125 (M); expenditures, $82,466; qualifying distributions, $74,884.
Limitations: Giving primarily in central PA.
Publications: Occasional report.
Application information: Application form required.
Officer and Trustees:* Gerald P. Wolf,* Chair.; Anne S. Borland, Michael Master, Marie Riley, Steven Sloan, Herbert T. Wolf II.
EIN: 256064237

46938
Fire Streak Ministry
c/o Robert G. Watkins
34 Longview Rd.
Coatesville, PA 19320-4312

Established in 1995 in PA.
Donor(s): Robert G. Watkins.
Financial data (yr. ended 12/31/00): Grants paid, $74,550; assets, $103,630 (M); gifts received, $75,650; expenditures, $74,572; qualifying distributions, $74,550.
Limitations: Applications not accepted.
Application information: Contributes only to pre-selected organizations.
Officer: Robert G. Watkins, Pres.
EIN: 232663299

46939
Otto Ruth Varner-Seneca Valley High School Scholarship Fund
c/o Mellon Bank, N.A.
P.O. Box 185
Pittsburgh, PA 15230-9897 (412) 234-0023
Contact: Laurie Moritz, Trust Off., Mellon Bank, N.A.

Financial data (yr. ended 05/31/01): Grants paid, $74,500; assets, $1,493,830 (M); expenditures, $83,671; qualifying distributions, $78,772.
Limitations: Giving limited to residents of PA.
Application information: Contact a guidance counselor at Seneca Valley High School for application information. Application form required.
Trustee: Mellon Bank, N.A.
EIN: 256292867
Codes: GTI

46940
Elmer & Gertrude Kaplin Foundation
226 W. Rittenhouse Sq., Ste. 205
Philadelphia, PA 19103
Contact: Elmer L. Kaplin, Dir.

Established in 1994 in PA.
Donor(s): Elmer L. Kaplin, Gertrude R. Kaplin.
Financial data (yr. ended 12/31/01): Grants paid, $74,275; assets, $1,220,633 (M); expenditures, $78,718; qualifying distributions, $74,275.
Limitations: Giving primarily in PA.
Application information: Application form not required.
Directors: Elmer L. Kaplin, Gertrude R. Kaplin, Marc B. Kaplin, Ned J. Kaplin.
EIN: 232791482

46941
Marci Lynn Bernstein Private Foundation
c/o Longboat Capital
139 Freeport Rd., Ste. 200
Pittsburgh, PA 15215

Established in 1997 in PA.
Donor(s): Thomas Bernstein, Mrs. Thomas Bernstein, Bernstein Family, Ltd.
Financial data (yr. ended 04/30/01): Grants paid, $74,121; assets, $262,805 (M); expenditures, $76,204; qualifying distributions, $74,022.
Limitations: Giving limited to Pittsburgh, PA.
Director: Thomas Bernstein.
EIN: 656235943

46942
Kate M. Kelley Foundation
311 Washington Rd.
Pittsburgh, PA 15216
Contact: Rev. Leo V. Vanyo, Tr.

Established in 1976 in PA.
Donor(s): Edward J. Kelley.‡
Financial data (yr. ended 12/31/01): Grants paid, $74,000; assets, $3,940,379 (M); expenditures, $108,571; qualifying distributions, $88,059.
Limitations: Applications not accepted. Giving primarily in Pittsburgh, PA.
Application information: Contributes only to pre-selected organizations.
Trustees: Rev. Roy G. Getty, Edward C. Ifft, Jr., Rev. Leo Vanyo.
EIN: 256090985

46943
Quaker City Fund
1400 Liberty Ridge Dr., Ste. 103
Wayne, PA 19087-5525

Established in 1976 in DE.

Financial data (yr. ended 12/31/01): Grants paid, $74,000; assets, $1,813,153 (M); expenditures, $83,772; qualifying distributions, $74,000.
Limitations: Applications not accepted. Giving on a national basis, with some emphasis on PA.
Application information: Contributes only to pre-selected organizations.
Officer: Scott F. Schumacker, Pres.
Director: John C. Voss.
EIN: 510200152

46944
The Louis L. Stott Foundation
c/o E.B. Stott
250 Chandler Rd.
Chadds Ford, PA 19317
Contact: Kristine Stott, Tr.

Established in 1968 in PA.
Donor(s): Martha Stott Diener.
Financial data (yr. ended 09/30/01): Grants paid, $74,000; assets, $2,456,079 (M); expenditures, $85,964; qualifying distributions, $74,000.
Limitations: Giving primarily in Vineyard Haven, MA.
Publications: Application guidelines, program policy statement.
Trustees: Benjamin W. Stott, Edward Barrington Stott, Kristine Stott.
EIN: 237009027

46945
Helene and Allen Apter Foundation
7131 Sheaff Ln.
Fort Washington, PA 19034 (215) 699-8701
Contact: Allen Apter, Secy.-Treas.

Established in 1994 in PA.
Donor(s): Allen Apter, Helene Apter.
Financial data (yr. ended 12/31/00): Grants paid, $73,950; assets, $1,122,767 (M); gifts received, $272,493; expenditures, $78,990; qualifying distributions, $73,950.
Limitations: Giving primarily in PA.
Officers and Directors:* Helene Apter,* Pres.; Joshua Apter,* V.P.; Sherri Apter Wexler,* V.P.; Allen Apter, Secy.-Treas.
EIN: 232724364

46946
Krzyzanowski Foundation
1 Crown Way
Philadelphia, PA 19154

Established in 1988 in PA.
Donor(s): Richard L. Krzyzanowski.
Financial data (yr. ended 12/31/01): Grants paid, $73,600; assets, $627,355 (M); expenditures, $83,868; qualifying distributions, $73,508.
Limitations: Applications not accepted. Giving on an international basis.
Application information: Contributes only to pre-selected organizations.
Officer: Richard L. Krzyzanowski, Pres.
EIN: 232501529

46947
Gospa Missions
230 E. Main St.
Evans City, PA 16033 (724) 538-3171
Contact: Thomas Rutkoski, Dir.

Established in 1990 in PA.
Financial data (yr. ended 12/31/00): Grants paid, $73,432; assets, $1,025,273 (M); gifts received, $265,086; expenditures, $339,370; qualifying distributions, $73,432; giving activities include $40,290 for programs.
Directors: Fr. William Kiel, James Paras, Thomas Rutkoski, Patrick Shannon.
EIN: 251630737

46948
Roberta and Ernest Scheller, Jr. Family Foundation
1 S. Church St.
Hazleton, PA 18201

Established in 1995 in PA.
Donor(s): Ernest Scheller, Jr., Roberta Scheller.
Financial data (yr. ended 12/31/00): Grants paid, $73,410; assets, $1,731,510 (M); gifts received, $40,000; expenditures, $110,919; qualifying distributions, $73,410.
Limitations: Applications not accepted. Giving primarily in PA.
Application information: Contributes only to pre-selected organizations.
Officer: Ernest Scheller, Jr., Chair.
Trustees: Lisa Jane Peretz, Roberta Scheller.
EIN: 237828732

46949
Bernard & Audrey Berman Foundation
2830 Gordon St.
Allentown, PA 18104
Contact: Bernard Berman, Pres.

Established in 1960.
Financial data (yr. ended 11/30/01): Grants paid, $73,156; assets, $1,208,300 (M); expenditures, $93,753; qualifying distributions, $76,734.
Limitations: Giving primarily in PA.
Officers: Bernard Berman, Pres.; Ann E. Berman, V.P.; Eileen S. Fischmann, Secy.-Treas.
EIN: 236268670

46950
Henry E. Haller, Jr. Foundation
6507 Wilkins Ave.
Pittsburgh, PA 15217
Contact: Henry E. Haller, Jr., Tr.

Established in 2000 in PA.
Donor(s): Henry E. Haller, Jr.
Financial data (yr. ended 12/31/01): Grants paid, $73,145; assets, $4,730,710 (M); expenditures, $155,950; qualifying distributions, $89,943.
Limitations: Giving primarily in Washington, DC, Pittsburgh, PA, and VA.
Trustees: Henry E. Haller, Jr., Linda L. Boyce Haller, Evans Rose, Jr., Joseph S. Scherle.
EIN: 522250015

46951
Robert H. & Janet S. Fleisher Foundation
c/o Sheldon M. Bonovitz
4200 1 Liberty Pl.
Philadelphia, PA 19103-7396

Financial data (yr. ended 05/31/01): Grants paid, $73,000; assets, $1,224,896 (M); expenditures, $80,426; qualifying distributions, $77,468.
Limitations: Applications not accepted. Giving primarily in PA.
Application information: Contributes only to pre-selected organizations.
Trustees: Jill F. Bonovitz, Janet S. Fleisher, Nancy F. Hellebrand.
EIN: 236758238

46952
Charles K. Williams II Trust
c/o Mellon Bank, N.A.
P.O. Box 7236, AIM NO. 193-0224
Philadelphia, PA 19101-7236
Application address: One Mellon Bank Ctr., Philadelphia, PA 19103, tel.: (215) 553-3038
Contact: Glenn Deibert, Trust Off., Mellon Bank, N.A.

Established in 1985 in PA.
Donor(s): Charles K. William.

Financial data (yr. ended 11/30/01): Grants paid, $72,735; assets, $45,555 (M); gifts received, $98,909; expenditures, $70,944; qualifying distributions, $72,735.
Application information: Application form not required.
Trustee: Mellon Bank, N.A.
EIN: 236758319
Codes: GTI

46953
Kirschner Family Foundation
518 W. Lancaster Ave.
Haverford, PA 19041-0535 (610) 527-4200
Contact: Michael S. Kirschner, Tr.

Established in 1964 in PA.
Donor(s): Greenwood Warehousing II, Michael S. Kirschner, Kirschner Bros. Oil Co., Helen Kirschner, Frederick Kirschner.
Financial data (yr. ended 12/31/01): Grants paid, $72,267; assets, $77,326 (M); gifts received, $29,000; expenditures, $72,402; qualifying distributions, $72,267.
Limitations: Giving primarily in PA.
Trustees: Frederick Kirschner, Michael S. Kirschner.
EIN: 236299767

46954
Gunard Berry Carlson Memorial Foundation, Inc.
P.O. Box 526
Thorndale, PA 19372 (610) 384-2800
Contact: Barbara C. Travaglini, V.P.

Established in 1957 in PA.
Financial data (yr. ended 12/31/00): Grants paid, $72,075; assets, $1,795,614 (M); gifts received, $7,500; expenditures, $75,769; qualifying distributions, $72,075.
Limitations: Giving primarily in PA.
Application information: Application form not required.
Officer: Barbara C. Travaglini, V.P.
Director: Benjamin Bacharach, Rev. Vincent R. Negherbon, A.F. Travaglini.
EIN: 236261693

46955
Reliance Bank Foundation
1119 12th St.
Altoona, PA 16601

Established in 1999 in PA.
Donor(s): Reliance Bank.
Financial data (yr. ended 12/31/01): Grants paid, $72,032; assets, $174,368 (M); gifts received, $135,600; expenditures, $72,230; qualifying distributions, $71,972.
Limitations: Applications not accepted. Giving primarily in PA.
Application information: Contributes only to pre-selected organizations.
Officers and Directors:* Bruce R. Hostler, Chair.; Tim Sissler,* Pres.; John W. Musser, Exec. V.P.; Dennis E. Doll, V.P.; Lisa A. Michelone, V.P.; Susan M. Meier, Secy.; Brian Lemman, Treas.; James B. Plummer, Bernard E. Stapelfeld, David K. Ward.
EIN: 311675396
Codes: CS, CD

46956
William Gerstley II Foundation
1617 J.F.K. Blvd., Ste. 335
Philadelphia, PA 19103-1803 (215) 563-8886
Contact: Carol K. Gerstley, Tr.

Established in 1954 in PA.
Financial data (yr. ended 12/31/00): Grants paid, $72,005; assets, $643,306 (M); expenditures, $82,093; qualifying distributions, $9,079.

Limitations: Giving primarily in PA.
Trustees: Carol K. Gerstley, Leon Sunstein, Jr.
EIN: 236275982

46957
The Blackhorse Foundation, Inc.
454 S. Main St.
Wilkes-Barre, PA 18701-2208

Established in 1993 in PA.
Donor(s): A.L. Simms, Ronald Simms.
Financial data (yr. ended 12/31/01): Grants paid, $72,000; assets, $1,704,252 (M); gifts received, $7,500; expenditures, $73,196; qualifying distributions, $72,000.
Limitations: Applications not accepted. Giving primarily in PA.
Application information: Contributes only to pre-selected organizations.
Officers: A.L. Simms, Pres.; Ronald Simms, V.P.
EIN: 232725907

46958
Murphy Charitable Foundation, Inc.
c/o Glenmede Trust Co.
1650 Market St., Ste. 1200
Philadelphia, PA 19103-7391

Established in 1993 in PA.
Donor(s): William B. Murphy.‡
Financial data (yr. ended 12/31/01): Grants paid, $72,000; assets, $1,372,938 (M); expenditures, $81,898; qualifying distributions, $74,544.
Limitations: Applications not accepted. Giving primarily in CT, ME, and PA.
Application information: Contributes only to pre-selected organizations.
Officers and Directors:* R. Blair Murphy, Pres.; Eleanor K. Richard, Secy.; Ann M. Zabel,* Treas.; Eric S. Murphy, John H. Murphy.
EIN: 232747488

46959
The Cotswold Foundation
2997 Pennview Ave.
Broomall, PA 19008
Application address: 5 Corporate Ctr., Matsonford Rd., Radnor, PA 19087
Contact: I. Wistar Morris, III, Tr.

Established in 1994 in PA.
Donor(s): I. Wistar Morris III.
Financial data (yr. ended 12/31/99): Grants paid, $71,900; assets, $2,236,658 (M); gifts received, $70,598; expenditures, $92,757; qualifying distributions, $74,069.
Limitations: Giving limited to PA.
Trustees: I. Wistar Morris III, Martha Morris.
EIN: 237767257

46960
The Deanne and Arnold Kaplan Foundation
2336 Fox Meadow, Dr.
Allentown, PA 18104

Established in 1998 in MN.
Donor(s): Deanne Kaplan, Arnold Kaplan.
Financial data (yr. ended 12/31/01): Grants paid, $71,890; assets, $1,008,373 (M); gifts received, $92,280; expenditures, $87,860; qualifying distributions, $71,780.
Limitations: Applications not accepted. Giving primarily in MN and PA.
Application information: Contributes only to pre-selected organizations.
Trustees: Arnold H. Kaplan, Deanne Kaplan, Pamela Ryba.
EIN: 232961830

46961
John J. and Marjorie M. Passan Foundation, Inc.
1 Passan Dr.
Wilkes-Barre, PA 18702-7320

Established in 1996 in PA.
Donor(s): John J. Passan.
Financial data (yr. ended 09/30/01): Grants paid, $71,700; assets, $876,100 (M); gifts received, $306,913; expenditures, $81,545; qualifying distributions, $71,700.
Limitations: Applications not accepted. Giving primarily in Wilkes-Barre, PA.
Application information: Contributes only to pre-selected organizations.
Directors: Michael O'Boyle, Ann Passan, John J. Passan.
EIN: 232870593

46962
C.A.R.E.S. Committee
160-A Rte. 41
P.O. Box 529
Gap, PA 17527
Application address: P.O. Box 529, Gap, PA 17527
Contact: Wendy Miller, Chair.

Established in 2000 in PA.
Financial data (yr. ended 12/31/00): Grants paid, $71,594; assets, $3,010 (M); gifts received, $10,680; expenditures, $104,251; qualifying distributions, $104,251.
Officers: Wendy Miller, Co-Chair.; Christopher Martin, Co-Chair.; Beth Monahan, Secy.; Denise Fulmer, Treas.
EIN: 233026106

46963
Blue Mountain Foundation
1015 Penn Ave.
Wyomissing, PA 19610 (610) 376-1595
Contact: Thomas A. Beaver, Secy.-Treas.

Established in 1989 in PA.
Donor(s): Olive D. Overly Cook, Lynda O. Levengood.
Financial data (yr. ended 12/31/01): Grants paid, $71,500; assets, $1,570,278 (M); expenditures, $93,661; qualifying distributions, $71,500.
Limitations: Giving primarily in PA.
Officers: Lynda O. Levengood, Pres.; Anne O. Watts, V.P.; Thomas A. Beaver, Secy.-Treas.
EIN: 232586321

46964
Horst Foundation
c/o Clyde W. Horst
P.O. Box 3330
Lancaster, PA 17604-3330

Established in 2000 in PA.
Donor(s): Clyde W. Horst.
Financial data (yr. ended 12/31/01): Grants paid, $71,500; assets, $326,179 (M); gifts received, $266,479; expenditures, $73,967; qualifying distributions, $71,500.
Limitations: Applications not accepted. Giving on a national basis, with emphasis on PA.
Application information: Contributes only to pre-selected organizations.
Officers and Directors:* Clyde W. Horst,* Pres.; Daniel W. Haines,* V.P.; Randall L. Horst,* Secy.; A. Steven Horst III,* Treas.; Barbara A. Horst.
EIN: 233028700

46965
Harold D. & Eleanor G. Hoopman Charitable Foundation
c/o PNC Bank, N.A.
249 5th Ave., 2nd Fl.
Pittsburgh, PA 15222-2705 (412) 762-2284
Contact: Joanne S. Welsh

Established in 1998 in PA.
Donor(s): Eleanor Hoopman, Harold Hoopman.
Financial data (yr. ended 03/31/01): Grants paid, $71,000; assets, $912,319 (M); expenditures, $73,659; qualifying distributions, $71,000.
Trustee: PNC Bank, N.A.
EIN: 237879528

46966
Larking Hill Foundation
330 Thornbrook Ave.
Rosemont, PA 19010
Contact: Thomas L. Bennett, Tr.

Established in 1998 in PA.
Donor(s): Thomas L. Bennett.
Financial data (yr. ended 05/31/02): Grants paid, $71,000; assets, $1,926,059 (M); gifts received, $245,850; expenditures, $86,070; qualifying distributions, $71,000.
Trustees: Carolyn E. Bennett, Christopher F. Bennett, Geoffrey T. Bennett, Thomas L. Bennett.
EIN: 237978393

46967
Lisa S. Roberts & David Seltzer Charitable Trust
614 S. 8th St., Ste. 306
Philadelphia, PA 19147

Established in 1997 in PA.
Donor(s): Lisa S. Roberts.
Financial data (yr. ended 12/31/00): Grants paid, $71,000; assets, $1,056,295 (M); expenditures, $81,365; qualifying distributions, $71,000.
Limitations: Applications not accepted. Giving primarily in Philadelphia, PA; some giving also in Crested Butte, CO.
Application information: Contributes only to pre-selected organizations.
Trustees: Lisa S. Roberts, David Seltzer.
EIN: 237909451

46968
Barbara R. and Charles Kahn, Jr. Foundation, Inc.
2600 1 Commerce Sq.
Philadelphia, PA 19103

Established in 1997 in PA.
Donor(s): Charles Kahn, Jr., Barbara R. Kahn.
Financial data (yr. ended 06/30/01): Grants paid, $70,600; assets, $881,056 (M); expenditures, $71,081; qualifying distributions, $70,504.
Limitations: Applications not accepted. Giving primarily in Philadelphia, PA.
Application information: Contributes only to pre-selected organizations.
Officers and Directors:* Charles Kahn, Jr.,* Pres.; Barbara R. Kahn, Secy.-Treas.; C. David Goff.
EIN: 232898465

46969
Dorothy Davis Scholarship Fund
c/o PNC Advisors
1600 Market St., 4th Fl.
Philadelphia, PA 19103-7211 (215) 585-3977
Application address: c/o Trust Dept., PNC Bank, N.A., Metro Park Plz., 499 Thornall St., Edison, NJ 08818-0600
Contact: Cheryl Colletti

Established in 1994.
Donor(s): Dorothy B. Davis Trust.

46969—PENNSYLVANIA

Financial data (yr. ended 07/31/01): Grants paid, $70,560; assets, $1,010,939 (M); expenditures, $82,452; qualifying distributions, $71,110.
Limitations: Giving limited to residents of Rumson, NJ.
Application information: Application form required.
Trustee: PNC Bank, N.A.
EIN: 226631276
Codes: GTI

46970
Agnes and Sophie Dallas Irwin Memorial Fund
c/o PNC Advisors
1600 Market St., 4th Fl.
Philadelphia, PA 19103-7240

Established in 1916 in PA.
Financial data (yr. ended 12/31/01): Grants paid, $70,273; assets, $1,173,098 (M); expenditures, $80,523; qualifying distributions, $70,632.
Limitations: Giving primarily in PA.
Trustees: Saranne B. DuBois, Ellen Nalle Hass, Meta L. Neilson, Adele G. Sands, Maraban Sparkman, PNC Bank, N.A.
EIN: 236207350
Codes: GTI

46971
Robert M. & Marion M. Jones Foundation
c/o First Citizens National Bank
15 S. Main St.
Mansfield, PA 16933 (570) 662-0463
Contact: Jean A. Knapp, Trust Off., First Citizens National Bank

Financial data (yr. ended 12/31/00): Grants paid, $70,258; assets, $821,753 (M); gifts received, $4,000; expenditures, $75,793; qualifying distributions, $75,793.
Limitations: Giving primarily in Blossburg, PA.
Directors: Wendy Albur, Mark Dalton, Richard J. Hall, John L. Kaiser, Mary Catherine Phinney, Dorothy Rakoski, Carol J. Tama.
Trustee: First Citizens National Bank.
EIN: 256289194

46972
G. Fred & Sylvia Dibona Family Foundation
1211 Mt. Pleasant Rd.
Villanova, PA 19085
Application address: c/o Drucker & Scaccetti, PC, 1845 Walnut St., 14th Fl., Philadelphia, PA 19103, tel.: (215) 665-3960
Contact: Sylvia Dibona, Secy.-Treas.

Established in 1996 in PA.
Donor(s): Fred G. Dibona, Sylvia M. Dibona.
Financial data (yr. ended 12/31/01): Grants paid, $70,245; assets, $148,712 (M); gifts received, $63,281; expenditures, $70,726; qualifying distributions, $70,245.
Limitations: Giving primarily in PA.
Officers: Fred Dibona, Jr., Pres.; Sylvia M. Dibona, Secy.-Treas.
EIN: 232867497

46973
Valeria E. Hoffert Scholarship Trust
c/o Allfirst, Trust Tax Div.
21 E. Market St., M/C 402130
York, PA 17401-1500

Established in 1994 in PA.
Financial data (yr. ended 12/31/01): Grants paid, $70,140; assets, $1,272,411 (M); expenditures, $82,604; qualifying distributions, $70,140.
Limitations: Applications not accepted. Giving limited to residents of Reading, PA.
Application information: Unsolicited requests for funds not accepted.

Trustee: Allfirst.
EIN: 237763256
Codes: GTI

46974
Doyle S. & Helen Poorman Foundation
c/o Hershy Trust Co.
P.O. Box 445
Hershey, PA 17033

Established in 1999 in PA.
Financial data (yr. ended 12/31/99): Grants paid, $70,018; assets, $1,921,799 (M); gifts received, $1,977,738; expenditures, $108,022; qualifying distributions, $70,018.
Limitations: Applications not accepted.
Application information: Contributes only to pre-selected organizations.
Trustee: Hershey Trust Co.
EIN: 256582756

46975
Charles H. & Annetta R. Masland Foundation
497 Orlando Ave.
State College, PA 16803-3477

Established in 1948.
Financial data (yr. ended 12/31/01): Grants paid, $70,000; assets, $1,249,415 (M); expenditures, $80,626; qualifying distributions, $70,000.
Limitations: Applications not accepted. Giving on a national basis.
Application information: Contributes only to pre-selected organizations.
Officers and Trustees:* David M. McCoy,* Chair.; Peter M. Lavin,* Secy.-Treas.; John D. Bakke, Frank E. Masland III, Walter H. McCoy, Christopher H. Stetser, Virginia Stetser.
EIN: 236296887

46976
Frederick E. G. Valergakis Charitable Trust
c/o Margaret G. Thompson
1600 Market St., Ste. 3600
Philadelphia, PA 19103

Established in 1979 in PA.
Financial data (yr. ended 12/31/01): Grants paid, $70,000; assets, $1,261,783 (M); expenditures, $89,424; qualifying distributions, $72,750.
Limitations: Applications not accepted. Giving primarily in MA and NJ.
Application information: Contributes only to pre-selected organizations.
Trustees: Lillian Borden, George Bordon, Maria Limberakis.
EIN: 232057515

46977
The Motter Foundation
3900 E. Market St.
York, PA 17402-2776

Established in 1961.
Financial data (yr. ended 02/28/02): Grants paid, $69,900; assets, $1,177,084 (M); expenditures, $74,013; qualifying distributions, $69,900.
Limitations: Applications not accepted. Giving primarily in York, PA.
Application information: Contributes only to pre-selected organizations.
Officers and Trustee:* Frank Motter,* Chair.; Edward L. Motter, Secy.
EIN: 236280401

46978
The Skier Foundation
(Formerly Abram M. & Mabel B. Skier Foundation)
209 Main Ave.
Hawley, PA 18428-1327

Donor(s): Members of the Skier family.
Financial data (yr. ended 12/31/01): Grants paid, $69,050; assets, $111,049 (M); gifts received, $62,940; expenditures, $69,050; qualifying distributions, $69,050.
Limitations: Applications not accepted.
Application information: Contributes only to pre-selected organizations.
Trustee: Henry M. Skier.
EIN: 232186639

46979
Caroline D. Bloomer Charitable Trust
c/o PNC Advisors
1600 Market St., 4th Fl.
Philadelphia, PA 19103-7240

Established in 1970.
Financial data (yr. ended 06/30/02): Grants paid, $69,000; assets, $1,266,672 (M); expenditures, $85,476; qualifying distributions, $69,000.
Limitations: Applications not accepted. Giving primarily in PA.
Application information: Contributes only to pre-selected organizations.
Trustees: Eleanor M. Haupt, John A. Keeley, John van Roden, Jr., PNC Bank, N.A.
EIN: 232120151

46980
The Cain Foundation
P.O. Box 205
Bristol, PA 19007-0205

Established in 1987 in PA.
Donor(s): George P. Cain, Mary J. Cain.
Financial data (yr. ended 11/30/01): Grants paid, $69,000; assets, $561,335 (M); gifts received, $100,000; expenditures, $69,385; qualifying distributions, $68,671.
Limitations: Applications not accepted. Giving primarily in PA.
Application information: Contributes only to pre-selected organizations.
Trustees: George P. Cain, Mary J. Cain.
EIN: 232494912

46981
The Khalaf Foundation
122 Aspen Rd.
Punxsutawney, PA 15767

Established in 1995 in PA.
Donor(s): Kamal Khalaf, M.D.
Financial data (yr. ended 12/31/01): Grants paid, $69,000; assets, $103,065 (M); gifts received, $104,000; expenditures, $69,426; qualifying distributions, $69,426.
Limitations: Applications not accepted. Giving primarily in the Middle East for the benefit of Palestinians.
Application information: Contributes only to pre-selected organizations.
Officers: Kamal Khalaf, M.D., Pres. and Secy.; Maysoun Khalaf, V.P.; Aman Khalaf, Treas.
EIN: 251736562

46982
The John K. & Elizabeth W. Knorr Foundation
1650 Market St., Ste. 1200
Philadelphia, PA 19103-7391

Established in 1997 in PA.

Financial data (yr. ended 12/31/01): Grants paid, $69,000; assets, $1,492,539 (M); gifts received, $254,922; expenditures, $75,064; qualifying distributions, $69,000.
Limitations: Applications not accepted.
Application information: Contributes only to pre-selected organizations.
Trustees: Elizabeth W. Knorr, John K. Knorr, Elizabeth K. Payne.
EIN: 237876318

46983
Rae S. Uber Trust
c/o Mellon Bank, N.A.
P.O. Box 7236
Philadelphia, PA 19101-7236 (215) 553-3208
Contact: Patricia Kling, Trust Off., Mellon Bank, N.A.

Established in 1970 in PA.
Financial data (yr. ended 06/30/01): Grants paid, $68,500; assets, $1,215,465 (M); expenditures, $75,084; qualifying distributions, $69,533.
Limitations: Giving primarily in Philadelphia, PA.
Trustee: Mellon Bank, N.A.
EIN: 236578512

46984
The Mitchell and Hilarie Morgan Family Foundation
c/o Bruce A. Rosenfield
1600 Market St., Ste. 3600
Philadelphia, PA 19103-7286

Established in 1999 in PA.
Donor(s): Mitchell L. Morgan, Hilarie L. Morgan.
Financial data (yr. ended 12/31/01): Grants paid, $68,250; assets, $960,558 (M); expenditures, $69,050; qualifying distributions, $68,250.
Limitations: Applications not accepted.
Application information: Contributes only to pre-selected organizations.
Trustees: Hilarie L. Morgan, Mitchell L. Morgan.
EIN: 256683715

46985
Babcock Charitable Trust
2220 Palmer St.
Pittsburgh, PA 15218 (412) 351-3515
Contact: Courtney B. Borntraeger, Tr.

Established in 1957 in PA.
Donor(s): Fred C. Babcock.
Financial data (yr. ended 12/31/01): Grants paid, $68,216; assets, $4,617,877 (M); expenditures, $69,447; qualifying distributions, $68,216.
Limitations: Giving primarily in PA.
Application information: Application form not required.
Trustees: Courtney B. Borntraeger, Richard S. Cuda, Carl P. Stillitano.
EIN: 256035161

46986
Doris Crane Charitable Trust
c/o Mellon Bank, N.A.
P.O. Box 7236
Philadelphia, PA 19101

Established in 1999.
Financial data (yr. ended 04/30/02): Grants paid, $67,864; assets, $1,286,338 (M); expenditures, $77,967; qualifying distributions, $67,864.
Limitations: Applications not accepted. Giving limited to the Wyoming Valley, PA, area.
Application information: Contributes only to pre-selected organizations.
Trustee: Mellon Bank, N.A.
EIN: 256706530

46987
Community Service Society, Inc.
P.O. Box A
Wayne, PA 19087 (610) 313-0910
Contact: Alberta Pew Baker, Pres.

Established about 1963.
Donor(s): Alberta Pew Baker.
Financial data (yr. ended 09/30/01): Grants paid, $67,818; assets, $35 (M); gifts received, $71,621; expenditures, $73,011; qualifying distributions, $67,818.
Limitations: Giving primarily in MD, PA, and VA; some giving in Nova Scotia, Canada.
Application information: Application form not required.
Officers: Alberta Pew Baker, Pres.; David W. Baker, V.P.; Edward M. Watters III, Secy.; Joseph W. Roskos, Treas.
EIN: 237264528

46988
Genuardi Family Foundation
c/o Blue Bell Executive Campus
470 Norristown Rd.
Blue Bell, PA 19422 (610) 834-2030
Contact: Robert C. Fernandez, Exec. Dir.

Established in 2000 in PA.
Donor(s): Anthony D. Genuardi, Charles A. Genuardi, David T. Genuardi, Dominic S. Genuardi, Jr., Francis L. Genuardi, Gasper A. Genuardi, James V. Genuardi, Laurence P. Genuardi, Michael A. Genuardi.
Financial data (yr. ended 01/31/02): Grants paid, $67,500; assets, $18,667,825 (M); gifts received, $12,973,753; expenditures, $307,864; qualifying distributions, $67,500.
Officers and Directors:* James V. Genuardi,* Pres.; Michael A. Genuardi, V.P.; Laurence P. Genuardi,* Secy.; Dominic S. Genuardi, Jr.,* Treas.; Robert C. Fernandez, Exec. Dir.; Anthony D. Genuardi, Charles A. Genuardi, David T. Genuardi, Francis L. Genuardi, Gasper A. Genuardi.
EIN: 233041300

46989
Andrea Cavitolo Foundation
303 W. Lancaster Ave., Ste. 265
Wayne, PA 19087-3318 (215) 656-4301
Contact: Francis Carter

Established in 1995 in PA.
Donor(s): Warren Kantor, ACF Holding Co., Inc.
Financial data (yr. ended 05/31/01): Grants paid, $67,235; assets, $923,156 (M); gifts received, $483,223; expenditures, $82,788; qualifying distributions, $67,768.
Limitations: Giving primarily in PA.
Application information: Application form required.
Officer: Donna Caulfield, Pres.
EIN: 232818544

46990
Dorsett L. & Mary D. Spurgeon Charitable Trust
c/o PNC Bank, N.A.
1600 Market St., 4th Fl.
Philadelphia, PA 19103-7240 (215) 585-5597

Established in 1996 in NJ.
Financial data (yr. ended 12/31/00): Grants paid, $67,219; assets, $1,261,452 (M); expenditures, $72,292; qualifying distributions, $66,685.
Limitations: Applications not accepted. Giving primarily in MA, MO, and NJ.
Application information: Contributes only to pre-selected organizations.
Trustees: Edward D. Spurgeon, PNC Bank, N.A.
EIN: 526761872

46991
John Charles & Kathryn S. Redmond Foundation
P.O. Box 1146
Blue Bell, PA 19422

Established in 1955.
Financial data (yr. ended 12/31/01): Grants paid, $67,200; assets, $1,545,578 (M); expenditures, $85,217; qualifying distributions, $67,200.
Limitations: Applications not accepted. Giving primarily in PA.
Application information: Contributes only to pre-selected organizations; unsolicited requests for funds not considered.
Officers: John C. Redmond III, Pres.; Maree Redmond, V.P.; Barbara Redmond, Secy.; Dorothy Roche, Treas.
EIN: 236279089

46992
The French Benevolent Society of Philadelphia
c/o Clairmong Paciello & Co.
250 Tanglewood Ln.
King of Prussia, PA 19406-2365
Application address: c/o Directors, or Schol. Comm., 1301 Medical Arts Bldg., 1601 Walnut St., Philadelphia, PA 19102, tel.: (215) 563-3276

Established in 1793 in PA.
Donor(s): Stephen Guicud.
Financial data (yr. ended 10/31/01): Grants paid, $66,860; assets, $1,309,443 (M); expenditures, $101,424; qualifying distributions, $86,335.
Publications: Informational brochure (including application guidelines).
Application information: Application form required.
Officers: Pierre Ravacon, Pres.; Yves P. Quintin, V.P.; Mrs. Robert Driscoll, Secy.; John W. Nilon, Jr., Treas.
Directors: Carlos J. Alvare, Robert E. Chatot, Rene Desjardins, Mrs. Robert Haley, Alison Douglas Knox, Catherine Lafarge, Josette Smith.
Trustee: First Union National Bank.
EIN: 231401532
Codes: GTI

46993
Sanford Foundation
1653 Brintons Bridge Rd.
Chadds Ford, PA 19317 (610) 388-2500
Contact: Richard D. Sanford, Tr.

Established in 1989 in PA.
Donor(s): Richard D. Sanford, Sheila Sanford.
Financial data (yr. ended 11/30/01): Grants paid, $66,300; assets, $518,754 (M); gifts received, $14,500; expenditures, $68,312; qualifying distributions, $66,300.
Limitations: Giving primarily in Chester County, PA.
Publications: Informational brochure.
Application information: Application form required.
Trustees: Barry Abelson, Richard D. Sanford, Sheila Sanford.
EIN: 236971120

46994
The John A. & Wilhelmina S. Johnson Foundation, Inc.
5150 Hoffmansille Rd.
Orefield, PA 18069 (610) 395-1823
Contact: John A. Johnson, Jr., Pres.

Established in 1977 in PA.
Financial data (yr. ended 12/31/01): Grants paid, $66,200; assets, $1,485,724 (M); expenditures, $69,187; qualifying distributions, $71,031.
Limitations: Giving primarily in DE and PA.

46994—PENNSYLVANIA

Application information: Application form not required.
Officer and Directors:* John A. Johnson, Jr.,* Pres.; Arthur W. Johnson.
Trustees: Frank P. Johnson, William G. Malkames, Marian G. Wallsten.
EIN: 232010791

46995
The Smukler/Lasch Family Foundation
(Formerly The Mildred and Louis Earle Lascho/Smukler Family Charitable Foundation)
c/o B. Flacker
2000 Market St., 10th Fl.
Philadelphia, PA 19103-3291

Established in 1995 in PA.
Donor(s): Mildred Lasch, Constance Smukler.
Financial data (yr. ended 12/31/01): Grants paid, $65,900; assets, $46,609 (M); expenditures, $65,984; qualifying distributions, $65,900.
Limitations: Applications not accepted. Giving primarily in the Philadelphia, PA, area.
Application information: Contributes only to pre-selected organizations.
Trustees: Mildred Lasch, Constance Smukler.
EIN: 232829857

46996
Charles A. Dailey Foundation
5127 Wolf Run Village Ln.
Erie, PA 16505

Established in 1952.
Donor(s): Charles A. Dailey.
Financial data (yr. ended 11/30/01): Grants paid, $65,700; assets, $1,259,666 (M); expenditures, $70,640; qualifying distributions, $65,700.
Limitations: Applications not accepted. Giving primarily in Erie, PA.
Application information: Contributes only to pre-selected organizations.
Officer and Directors:* Charles A. Dailey,* Pres.; Deborah D. Currie, Ellen G. Dailey, William C. Sennett.
EIN: 256035686

46997
Karl W. & Mary Ann Poorbaugh Foundation
690 Clover Hill Rd.
Somerset, PA 15501

Financial data (yr. ended 12/31/01): Grants paid, $65,600; assets, $1,061,724 (M); expenditures, $68,476; qualifying distributions, $65,600.
Limitations: Applications not accepted.
Application information: Contributes only to pre-selected organizations.
Trustee: Karl W. Poorbaugh.
EIN: 251647906

46998
The Ginsburg Family Foundation
50 Belmont Ave., Ste. 1016
Bala Cynwyd, PA 19004

Financial data (yr. ended 12/31/01): Grants paid, $65,550; assets, $13,644 (M); gifts received, $68,395; expenditures, $65,901; qualifying distributions, $65,550.
Officer and Directors:* Stanley D. Gindburg,* Chair.; Arlene Ginsburg.
EIN: 232980572

46999
Pennsylvania Industrial Chemical Corporation-Chester High School Scholarship Fund
c/o First Union National Bank
P.O. Box 7558, F.C. 1-3-9-20
Philadelphia, PA 19101-7558
Application address: c/o Chester High School, Chester, PA 19013, tel.: (610) 447-3700
Contact: Duretta Carey

Financial data (yr. ended 12/31/99): Grants paid, $65,500; assets, $2,134,263 (M); expenditures, $87,054; qualifying distributions, $72,040.
Limitations: Giving limited to Chester, PA.
Trustee: First Union National Bank.
EIN: 236233922
Codes: GTI

47000
Roland & Doris Sigal Foundation
313 N. Main St.
Allentown, PA 18104 (610) 433-0851
Contact: Roland Sigal, Pres.

Established in 1986 in PA.
Financial data (yr. ended 09/30/01): Grants paid, $65,394; assets, $99,380 (M); gifts received, $111,048; expenditures, $67,162; qualifying distributions, $65,394.
Limitations: Giving primarily in PA.
Application information: Application form not required.
Officers: Roland Sigal, Pres.; Doris Sigal, Secy.-Treas.
EIN: 232433373

47001
Samuel Tabas Family Foundation
915 Montgomery Ave., Ste. 401
Narberth, PA 19072 (610) 664-5100
Contact: Daniel M. Tabas, Tr.

Trust established in 1951 in PA.
Donor(s): Members of the Tabas family.
Financial data (yr. ended 05/31/01): Grants paid, $65,278; assets, $1,456,634 (M); expenditures, $87,496; qualifying distributions, $65,376.
Limitations: Giving primarily in PA.
Officer: Nicholas Randazzo, Mgr.
Trustees: Daniel M. Tabas, Richard S. Tabas.
EIN: 236254348

47002
Elisabeth M. Shiras Charitable Trust
c/o PNC Advisors
620 Liberty Ave., P2-PTPP-10-2
Pittsburgh, PA 15222-2705 (412) 762-5858
Contact: Diane C. Blanton, Trust Off., PNC Advisors

Established in 1990 in PA.
Financial data (yr. ended 05/31/01): Grants paid, $65,185; assets, $1,774,807 (M); expenditures, $78,918; qualifying distributions, $69,181.
Limitations: Giving primarily in Pittsburgh, PA.
Publications: Annual report (including application guidelines).
Trustee: PNC Bank, N.A.
EIN: 256347429

47003
Irving and Edythe Grossman Foundation
c/o Norman Harris
507 Linden St., Ste. 500
Scranton, PA 18503

Established in 1992.
Donor(s): Irving Grossman.‡

Financial data (yr. ended 12/31/01): Grants paid, $65,000; assets, $1,192,954 (M); expenditures, $71,492; qualifying distributions, $64,435.
Limitations: Applications not accepted. Giving limited to PA.
Application information: Contributes only to pre-selected organizations.
Officers: Irving Atlas, Pres.; Jeanne Atlas, V.P. and Treas.
Trustees: Cynthia Atlas Gricus, Judith Atlas Jackson.
EIN: 232574759

47004
GT Foundation
c/o Michael Delfiner
P.O. Box 305
Kulpsville, PA 19443-0305

Established in 1998 in PA.
Financial data (yr. ended 12/31/01): Grants paid, $65,000; assets, $1,931,678 (M); gifts received, $450,000; expenditures, $65,597; qualifying distributions, $65,000.
Limitations: Applications not accepted. Giving primarily in New York, NY.
Application information: Contributes only to pre-selected organizations.
Trustees: Hannah Delfiner, Michael Delfiner, Ruth Delfiner, Joan Stanley, Kenneth Stanley, Nancy Stanley.
EIN: 237927474

47005
The Julius and Katheryn Hommer Foundation
c/o First Union National Bank
645 Hamilton Mall
Allentown, PA 18101

Established in 1996 in PA.
Donor(s): Katheryn M. Hommer.
Financial data (yr. ended 12/31/01): Grants paid, $65,000; assets, $1,865,073 (M); gifts received, $905,172; expenditures, $71,010; qualifying distributions, $65,000.
Trustee: Katheryn M. Hommer.
EIN: 232847257

47006
Mirowski Family Foundation, Inc.
905 Merion Square Rd.
Gladwyne, PA 19035-1509

Established in 1997 in MD.
Donor(s): Anna Mirowski.
Financial data (yr. ended 12/31/00): Grants paid, $65,000; assets, $392,036 (M); gifts received, $174; expenditures, $65,254; qualifying distributions, $65,000.
Limitations: Applications not accepted. Giving primarily in Baltimore, MD.
Application information: Contributes only to pre-selected organizations.
Officers and Trustee:* Anna Mirowski,* Pres.; Ariella Rosengard, M.D., Secy.-Treas.
EIN: 522069951

47007
Rushen Family Foundation
c/o Frank J. Rushen
204 Amy Ct.
Stroudsburg, PA 18360-9166

Established in 2000 in PA.
Donor(s): Frank J. Rushen, Marilyn Rushen.
Financial data (yr. ended 12/31/01): Grants paid, $65,000; assets, $1,167,010 (M); expenditures, $72,250; qualifying distributions, $65,000.
Limitations: Applications not accepted.
Application information: Contributes only to pre-selected organizations.

Trustees: Frank J. Rushen, Marilyn Rushen.
EIN: 912078489

47008
The Dylan Todd Simonds Foundation, Inc.
2000 Grant Bldg.
Pittsburgh, PA 15219 (412) 338-3466
FAX: (412) 338-3463; E-mail:
foundation@hillmanfo.com
Contact: Ronald W. Wertz, Secy.

Established in 1994 in PA.
Donor(s): Henry L. Hillman.
Financial data (yr. ended 12/31/00): Grants paid, $65,000; assets, $1,196,759 (M); expenditures, $81,633; qualifying distributions, $67,459.
Limitations: Giving primarily in Pittsburgh, PA.
Officers and Directors:* Dylan T. Simonds,* Pres.; Lawrence M. Wagner,* V.P.; Ronald W. Wertz,* Secy. and Exec. Dir.; Maurice J. White,* Treas.
EIN: 251752987

47009
Manus A. Langan Trust
c/o PNC Advisors
P.O. Box 937
Scranton, PA 18501-0937
Application address: c/o Laura Kelly Langan Education Fund, Office of Financial Aid, Univ. of Scranton, Scranton, PA 18510

Financial data (yr. ended 12/31/01): Grants paid, $64,850; assets, $1,292,993 (M); expenditures, $74,441; qualifying distributions, $64,850.
Limitations: Giving primarily in PA.
Application information: Application form required.
Trustee: PNC Bank, N.A.
EIN: 236645283

47010
George H. Benford Charities
c/o PNC Bank, N.A.
2 PNC Plz.
Pittsburgh, PA 15222-2719 (412) 762-3706
Contact: Bea Lynch

Financial data (yr. ended 09/30/00): Grants paid, $64,765; assets, $2,301,063 (M); expenditures, $93,754; qualifying distributions, $64,765.
Limitations: Giving limited to PA.
Application information: Contributes to 2 pre-selected organizations. Application form required for scholarships, restricted to graduates of Meyersdale, PA Joint High School.
Trustee: PNC Bank, N.A.
EIN: 256038490
Codes: GTI

47011
Gospel Evangelism Foundation
c/o PNC Bank, N.A.
620 Liberty Ave., P2-PTPP-25-1
Pittsburgh, PA 15222-2705
Contact: R. Bruce Bickel, Managing Dir.

Established in 1999 in PA.
Donor(s): Joseph F. Sprankle III.
Financial data (yr. ended 12/31/01): Grants paid, $64,700; assets, $2,937,981 (M); expenditures, $90,842; qualifying distributions, $64,700.
Limitations: Applications not accepted.
Application information: Contributes only to pre-selected organizations.
Trustees: Joseph F. Sprankle III, PNC Bank, N.A.
EIN: 256639102

47012
The Lilah Hilliard Fisher Foundation, Inc.
2000 Grant Bldg.
Pittsburgh, PA 15219 (412) 338-3466
FAX: (412) 338-3463; E-mail:
foundation@hillmanfo.com
Contact: Ronald W. Wertz, Secy.

Established in 1994 in PA.
Donor(s): Henry L. Hillman.
Financial data (yr. ended 12/31/00): Grants paid, $64,500; assets, $1,192,231 (M); expenditures, $73,374; qualifying distributions, $67,970.
Limitations: Giving primarily in Pittsburgh and southwestern PA.
Officers and Directors:* Lilah H. Fisher,* Pres.; Lawrence M. Wagner,* V.P.; Ronald W. Wertz,* Secy. and Exec. Dir.; Maurice J. White,* Treas.; Audrey H. Fisher.
EIN: 251752994

47013
New Millennium Foundation
(Formerly The Mickey Rubin Foundation)
c/o Ballard, Spahr, Andrews & Ingersoll
1735 Market St., 51st Fl.
Philadelphia, PA 19103-7599

Donor(s): Paul Rosenberg.
Financial data (yr. ended 12/31/01): Grants paid, $64,500; assets, $1,213,835 (M); expenditures, $74,090; qualifying distributions, $63,938.
Limitations: Applications not accepted. Giving primarily in PA.
Application information: Contributes only to pre-selected organizations.
Officer: Paul Rosenberg, Pres. and Secy.-Treas.
EIN: 232903172

47014
The Downs Foundation
c/o The Glenmede Trust Co.
1650 Market St., Ste. 1200
Philadelphia, PA 19103-7391
Application address: c/o George T. Downs III, P.O. Box 475, Willow Grove, PA 19090

Established in 1960 in PA.
Donor(s): George T. Downs.‡
Financial data (yr. ended 12/31/01): Grants paid, $64,000; assets, $1,330,474 (M); expenditures, $70,845; qualifying distributions, $66,326.
Limitations: Giving primarily in the Philadelphia, PA, area.
Application information: Application form not required.
Trustees: Joan Downs Brehm, George T. Downs III.
EIN: 236257328

47015
Shusterman Foundation
c/o Fox, Rothschild, Obrien, & Frankel
2000 Market St., 10th Fl.
Philadelphia, PA 19103-3231 (215) 299-2026
Additional tel.: (215) 299-2150; Additional application address: c/o Robert J. Shusterman, 1608 Walnut St., 18th Fl., Philadelphia, PA 19103, tel.: (215) 772-0200
Contact: Murray H. Shusterman, Mgr.

Established in 1981.
Donor(s): Murray H. Shusterman.
Financial data (yr. ended 06/30/01): Grants paid, $63,792; assets, $1,942,128 (M); expenditures, $70,471; qualifying distributions, $63,792.
Limitations: Giving primarily in the New York, NY, and Philadelphia, PA, areas through local and national organizations.
Application information: Application form not required.

Officer and Directors:* Murray H. Shusterman,* Mgr.; Robert J. Shusterman.
EIN: 232187215

47016
Netzer Charitable Foundation
Box 4336, Corliss Sta.
Pittsburgh, PA 15204-0336
Contact: Leon Netzer, Tr.

Donor(s): Leon L. Netzer.
Financial data (yr. ended 01/31/02): Grants paid, $63,704; assets, $453,483 (M); expenditures, $64,853; qualifying distributions, $63,704.
Limitations: Giving primarily in Pittsburgh, PA.
Trustees: Edith Netzer, Leon L. Netzer, Nancy Netzer, Thomas Netzer.
EIN: 256065741

47017
Bruce D. & Treasure Sachnoff Charitable Family Foundation
1223 Bennington Ave.
Pittsburgh, PA 15217

Established in 1990 in PA.
Donor(s): Bruce D. Sachnoff, Treasure Sachnoff.
Financial data (yr. ended 04/30/02): Grants paid, $63,385; assets, $520,915 (M); gifts received, $3,104; expenditures, $76,287; qualifying distributions, $63,385.
Limitations: Applications not accepted. Giving primarily in PA.
Application information: Contributes only to pre-selected organizations.
Trustees: Donald S. Plung, Bruce D. Sachnoff, Treasure Sachnoff.
EIN: 256346205

47018
The Kiwanis Foundation of Allentown, Pennsylvania, Inc.
P.O. Box 4355
Allentown, PA 18105 (610) 434-5191
Contact: Chair., Svc. Committee

Established in 1952.
Financial data (yr. ended 09/30/01): Grants paid, $63,266; assets, $480,808 (M); gifts received, $1,446; expenditures, $73,391; qualifying distributions, $63,041.
Limitations: Giving limited to the Lehigh Valley, PA, area.
Officers: Tom Harp, Pres.; Enos Martin, V.P.; James Snyder, Secy.; James Fronheiser, Treas.
Trustees: Ann Bieber, John Denuel, Ron Lewis, John Stoffa, Judy M. Wannemacher.
EIN: 236050029

47019
Hyman Family Charitable Foundation
c/o Gazer, Kohn, Maher & Co.
6 Neshaminy Interplex
Trevose, PA 19053
Contact: Valerie A. Hyman, Tr.

Established in 1997 in NJ.
Donor(s): Valerie A. Hyman.
Financial data (yr. ended 12/31/01): Grants paid, $63,060; assets, $998,731 (M); expenditures, $66,427; qualifying distributions, $63,060.
Limitations: Giving primarily in NY.
Trustees: Allen I. Hyman, Valerie A. Hyman.
EIN: 237898544

47020
Summer Lea Hillman Foundation, Inc.
2000 Grant Building
Pittsburgh, PA 15219 (412) 338-3466
FAX: (412) 338-3463; E-mail:
foundation@hillmanfo.com
Contact: Ronald W. Wertz, Secy.

Established in 1998.
Donor(s): Henry L. Hillman.
Financial data (yr. ended 12/31/00): Grants paid, $63,000; assets, $1,169,174 (M); expenditures, $71,547; qualifying distributions, $65,456.
Limitations: Giving primarily in Portland, OR.
Application information: Application form not required.
Officers and Directors:* Henry L. Hillman, Sr.,* Pres.; Lawrence M. Wagner,* V.P.; Ronald W. Wertz,* Secy.; Maurice J. White,* Treas.
EIN: 251824111

47021
R. Dale and Frances M. Hughes Foundation
PNC Bank, N.A.
P.O. Box 937
Scranton, PA 18501

Established in 1997 in PA.
Donor(s): Frances M. Hughes, R. Dale Hughes.
Financial data (yr. ended 12/31/99): Grants paid, $63,000; assets, $1,871,720 (M); expenditures, $82,281; qualifying distributions, $63,370.
Limitations: Applications not accepted.
Application information: Contributes only to pre-selected organizations.
Trustees: Frances M. Hughes, R. Dale Hughes, PNC Bank, N.A.
EIN: 237914215

47022
John Schmidt Foundation
c/o Allfirst, Trust Div.
21 E. Market St.
York, PA 17401
Application address: 511 Shady Dell Rd., York, PA 17403, tel.: (717) 854-6402
Contact: John C. Schmidt, Tr.

Established in 1952 in PA.
Financial data (yr. ended 12/31/01): Grants paid, $63,000; assets, $1,669,441 (M); expenditures, $69,187; qualifying distributions, $63,000.
Limitations: Giving limited to the greater York County, PA, area.
Trustees: D. Duncan Schmidt, Dana E. Schmidt, John C. Schmidt, Allfirst.
EIN: 236298307

47023
Anna Bohorad Foundation Trust
(Formerly Anna C. Bohorad Trust B)
c/o M & T Bank
1 S. Centre St.
Pottsville, PA 17901-3001 (570) 628-9291
Contact: E. Lori Smith, Trust Off., M & T Bank

Donor(s): Anna C. Bohorad Trust C.
Financial data (yr. ended 02/28/01): Grants paid, $62,946; assets, $1,207,804 (M); expenditures, $73,377; qualifying distributions, $62,946.
Limitations: Giving primarily in Pottsville, PA.
Trustees: James Bohorad, Robert C. Bohorad, Robert N. Bohorad, M & T Bank.
EIN: 236627730

47024
Reldon & Hattie Cooper Charitable Foundation
145 State St.
P.O. Box 149
Saxonburg, PA 16056-0149 (724) 352-1511
Contact: Reldon W. Cooper, Chair.

Established in 1985.
Donor(s): Reldon W. Cooper.
Financial data (yr. ended 12/31/01): Grants paid, $62,776; assets, $1,461,494 (M); gifts received, $100,000; expenditures, $64,362; qualifying distributions, $62,776.
Limitations: Giving primarily in PA.
Officers: Reldon W. Cooper, Chair. and Pres.; Linda Knapp, Secy.; Lora Saiber, Treas.
EIN: 251515561

47025
The Symmco Foundation
5 Park St.
Sykesville, PA 15865
Application address: c/o Betty Hoare, Symmco Inc., Sykesville, PA 15865, tel.: (814) 894-2461

Established in 1983 in PA.
Donor(s): Symmco Inc.
Financial data (yr. ended 12/31/01): Grants paid, $62,613; assets, $1,384,769 (M); gifts received, $50,000; expenditures, $72,790; qualifying distributions, $62,613.
Limitations: Giving limited to Jefferson, PA, and neighboring counties.
Application information: Application form not required.
Trustee: John W. Bean.
EIN: 251480507
Codes: CS, CD

47026
The Pilgrim Foundation
540 Pennsylvania Ave., Ste. 318
Fort Washington, PA 19034

Financial data (yr. ended 06/30/01): Grants paid, $62,500; assets, $6,034,884 (M); gifts received, $3,984,818; expenditures, $68,844; qualifying distributions, $62,500.
Officers: Gary L. Pilgrim, Pres.; Suzanne T. Daniel, Secy.
EIN: 232955610

47027
The Krisbergh Family Foundation
1538 Meadowbrook Rd.
Rydal, PA 19046

Established in 1999.
Donor(s): Audrey Krisbergh, Harold Krisbergh.
Financial data (yr. ended 12/31/01): Grants paid, $62,330; assets, $843,451 (M); gifts received, $759,000; expenditures, $62,552; qualifying distributions, $62,330.
Limitations: Applications not accepted.
Application information: Contributes only to pre-selected organizations.
Trustees: Audrey Krisbergh, Deborah Krisbergh, Harold Krisbergh, Jonathan Krisbergh.
EIN: 256679346

47028
The Louise A. Havens Foundation for Diabetes Research and Treatment
100 Four Falls Corporate Ctr., Ste. 202
West Conshohocken, PA 19428

Financial data (yr. ended 12/31/01): Grants paid, $62,300; assets, $636,545 (M); expenditures, $71,529; qualifying distributions, $62,300.
Limitations: Applications not accepted. Giving primarily in Wynnewood, PA.
Application information: Contributes only to pre-selected organizations.
Trustee: Louise A. Havens.
EIN: 256587514

47029
The Gibb Foundation
c/o Wolf Block
1650 Arch St., 22nd Fl.
Philadelphia, PA 19103-2097

Established in 1984.
Financial data (yr. ended 07/31/01): Grants paid, $62,000; assets, $1,095,555 (M); expenditures, $69,483; qualifying distributions, $62,000.
Limitations: Giving primarily in the Northeast, with emphasis on MA, NJ, and PA.
Application information: Application form not required.
Trustees: Robert I. Friedman, Matthew H. Kemens, Edwina A. Robb, F. Richard Robb, Ronald W. Robb.
EIN: 236766810

47030
Superior Group Foundation
3 Radnor Corporate Ctr., Ste. 400
Radnor, PA 19087-8760

Established in 2001 in PA.
Donor(s): Superior Group, Inc.
Financial data (yr. ended 12/31/01): Grants paid, $61,966; assets, $38,034 (M); gifts received, $100,000; expenditures, $61,966; qualifying distributions, $61,966.
Limitations: Applications not accepted.
Application information: Contributes only to pre-selected organizations.
Trustees: Catherine W. Elkins, Mane-Adel Le Menestrel, John A. Sanders, Warren T. Stone, Jr.
EIN: 256798167
Codes: CS

47031
Helen Parkhill Memorial Trust for Crippled Children, the Blind and Incurables
c/o PNC Advisors
620 Liberty Ave., P2-PTPP-10-2
Pittsburgh, PA 15222-2705
Contact: E. Robert Green, Trust Off., PNC Bank, N.A.

Financial data (yr. ended 12/31/01): Grants paid, $61,787; assets, $606,205 (M); expenditures, $71,487; qualifying distributions, $61,787.
Limitations: Giving primarily in southern NJ.
Trustee: PNC Bank, N.A.
EIN: 216011032

47032
John W. Rollison Educational Scholarship Trust
c/o First Union National Bank
123 S. Broad St.
Philadelphia, PA 19109-9989

Established in 1996 in VA.
Financial data (yr. ended 12/31/99): Grants paid, $61,500; assets, $1,429,671 (M); expenditures, $73,709; qualifying distributions, $60,430.
Limitations: Giving limited to residents of Franklin and Southampton counties, VA.
Trustee: First Union National Bank.
EIN: 546485419

47033
Elmer and Annabelle Snyder Foundation
c/o Elmer A. Snyder
P.O. Box 1022
Kittanning, PA 16201-5022

Donor(s): Elmer A. Snyder, Annabelle Snyder.

Financial data (yr. ended 12/31/01): Grants paid, $61,376; assets, $474,502 (M); expenditures, $61,894; qualifying distributions, $61,376.
Limitations: Applications not accepted. Giving primarily in Cowansville, PA.
Application information: Contributes only to pre-selected organizations.
Trustees: David E. Snyder, Mark A. Snyder, Thomas C. Snyder.
EIN: 256479936

47034
Gitlin Family Foundation
270 New Jersey Dr.
Fort Washington, PA 19034

Established in 1986 in PA.
Donor(s): Harvey S. Gitlin.
Financial data (yr. ended 11/30/01): Grants paid, $61,300; assets, $902,705 (M); expenditures, $64,239; qualifying distributions, $61,300.
Limitations: Applications not accepted. Giving primarily in PA.
Application information: Contributes only to pre-selected organizations.
Officer: Harvey S. Gitlin, Mgr.
Trustee: Phyllis S. Gitlin.
EIN: 222770930

47035
The Bobby Higginson Foundation
c/o E.J. Hayes
2000 Market St., 10th Fl.
Philadelphia, PA 19103-3291

Established in 1998 in PA.
Donor(s): Bobby Higginson.
Financial data (yr. ended 12/31/01): Grants paid, $61,000; assets, $2,250 (M); gifts received, $53,500; expenditures, $61,000; qualifying distributions, $61,000.
Limitations: Applications not accepted. Giving primarily in MI.
Application information: Contributes only to pre-selected organizations.
Officers: Bobby Higginson, Pres.; Edward J. Hayes, Secy.
EIN: 232975350

47036
1976 Foundation
200 Eagle Rd., Ste. 308
Wayne, PA 19087 (610) 254-9401
Contact: Nathaniel Peter Hamilton, Secy.

Established in 1976 in PA.
Financial data (yr. ended 12/31/01): Grants paid, $61,000; assets, $913,347 (M); expenditures, $66,559; qualifying distributions, $61,000.
Limitations: Giving primarily in PA.
Officers and Directors:* E. McGregor Strauss,* Pres.; James Sands, Jr.,* V.P.; Nathaniel Peter Hamilton,* Secy.; Pamela M. Hamilton,* Treas.
EIN: 232495676

47037
E. C. Lindsey Charity Fund Trust
c/o Mellon Bank, N.A.
P.O. Box 185, 1 Mellon Bank Ctr.
Pittsburgh, PA 15230-9897
Application address: c/o Marilyn King, Trust Off., Mellon Bank, N.A., 1128 State St., Erie, PA 16152

Established in 1991 in PA.
Financial data (yr. ended 12/31/00): Grants paid, $60,900; assets, $1,085,880 (M); expenditures, $77,348; qualifying distributions, $65,027.
Limitations: Giving primarily in Mercer, PA.
Application information: Application form required.

Trustees: J.G. Johnson, Mellon Bank, N.A.
EIN: 251404227

47038
Ethel Jefferson Scholarship Fund
c/o First National Bank & Trust Co. of Newtown
34 S. State St., P.O. Box 158
Newtown, PA 18940 (215) 968-4872
Contact: Barry L. Pflueger, Jr., V.P., Secy., and Sr. Trust Off., First National Bank

Established in 1994 in PA.
Donor(s): Ethel Jefferson.‡
Financial data (yr. ended 12/31/01): Grants paid, $60,610; assets, $1,358,534 (M); expenditures, $78,720; qualifying distributions, $78,720.
Limitations: Giving limited to residents of Bucks County, PA.
Application information: Obtain application from First National Bank and Trust Co. of Newtown. Application form required.
Trustees: Joseph Colacicco, Richard Danese, Richard Fusco, Barry L. Pflueger, Jr.
EIN: 237749232
Codes: GTI

47039
The Rosehil Foundation
705 Ashurst Rd.
Havertown, PA 19083

Established in 1999 in PA.
Donor(s): Constance P. Buckley, Bruce Buckley.
Financial data (yr. ended 12/31/01): Grants paid, $60,543; assets, $2,313,871 (M); gifts received, $925,000; expenditures, $86,626; qualifying distributions, $60,543.
Limitations: Applications not accepted. Giving primarily in PA.
Application information: Contributes only to pre-selected organizations.
Trustees: Bruce Buckley, Constance P. Buckley.
EIN: 256638432

47040
The Elaine & Bernard P. Beifield Family Foundation
2 Penn Ctr. Plz., Ste. 400
Philadelphia, PA 19102

Established in 1996 in FL & PA.
Donor(s): Bernard P. Beifield, Elaine Beifield.
Financial data (yr. ended 12/31/01): Grants paid, $60,375; assets, $594,834 (M); expenditures, $69,270; qualifying distributions, $60,375.
Limitations: Applications not accepted. Giving primarily in Palm Beach, FL.
Application information: Contributes only to pre-selected organizations.
Trustees: Bernard P. Beifield, Henry M. Kuller, Barry Spevak, Mitchell Warwick.
EIN: 650710824

47041
Susan and Leonard Lodish Charitable Foundation
301 Kent Rd.
Wynnewood, PA 19096

Established in 2000 in PA.
Donor(s): Susan Lodish, Leonard Lodish.
Financial data (yr. ended 12/31/01): Grants paid, $60,223; assets, $61,614 (M); gifts received, $27,331; expenditures, $60,223; qualifying distributions, $60,223.
Limitations: Applications not accepted. Giving primarily in Philadelphia, PA.
Application information: Contributes only to pre-selected organizations.
Officer: Susan Lodish, C.F.O.
EIN: 233025482

47042
Arthur T. Cantwell Charitable Foundation
c/o Citizens Trust Co.
10 N. Main St.
Coudersport, PA 16915 (814) 274-9150
Contact: Trust Off.

Financial data (yr. ended 12/31/01): Grants paid, $60,150; assets, $1,017,401 (M); expenditures, $66,988; qualifying distributions, $60,150.
Limitations: Giving primarily in PA.
Application information: Application form required.
Trustee: Citizens Trust Co.
EIN: 251643251

47043
W. J. Brundred Charitable Fund
c/o Mellon Bank, N.A.
P.O. Box 185
Pittsburgh, PA 15230-9897
Application address: c/o Mellon Bank, N.A., P.O. Box 9, Oil City, PA 16301
Contact: James Baker

Established in 1980.
Financial data (yr. ended 12/31/00): Grants paid, $60,000; assets, $1,351,247 (M); expenditures, $75,078; qualifying distributions, $65,491.
Limitations: Giving limited to residents of Venango County, PA.
Application information: Application form required.
Trustee: Mellon Bank, N.A.
EIN: 256031974
Codes: GTI

47044
Alexander Gushner Family Foundation
1818 Chestnut St.
Philadelphia, PA 19103-4902 (215) 564-9000
Contact: Mark L. Gushner, Tr.

Established in 1965.
Donor(s): Gerald Gushner, Mark L. Gushner.
Financial data (yr. ended 12/31/01): Grants paid, $60,000; assets, $66,912 (M); gifts received, $60,000; expenditures, $60,069; qualifying distributions, $60,035.
Limitations: Giving primarily in Philadelphia, PA.
Trustees: Gerald Gushner, Mark L. Gushner.
EIN: 236393631

47045
Means Charitable Trust
c/o M.A. Gillen, DM&H, LLP
1 Liberty Pl.
Philadelphia, PA 19103
Application address: 1936 William Penn Annex, Philadelphia, PA 19105
Contact: John B. Means, Tr.

Established in 1994 in PA.
Donor(s): Walker Means, Rosetta Means.
Financial data (yr. ended 12/31/01): Grants paid, $60,000; assets, $145,166 (M); expenditures, $65,144; qualifying distributions, $60,000.
Limitations: Giving limited to the Delaware Valley, PA, area.
Application information: Application form not required.
Trustee: John B. Means.
EIN: 237743238

47046
Clarence A. Rowell Trust No. 2
c/o PNC Bank, N.A.
1600 Market St.
Philadelphia, PA 19103

Financial data (yr. ended 01/31/01): Grants paid, $60,000; assets, $1,912,230 (M); expenditures, $65,417; qualifying distributions, $60,455.
Limitations: Applications not accepted. Giving limited to the Germantown section of Philadelphia, PA.
Application information: Contributes only to pre-selected organizations.
Trustees: Eleanor O. Dunning, PNC Bank, N.A.
EIN: 237217984

47047
Ernest Q. Johnson Trust for Charity
c/o Mellon Bank, N.A.
P.O. Box 185
Pittsburgh, PA 15230-9897
Contact: Laurie Moritz

Established in 1970.
Financial data (yr. ended 09/30/01): Grants paid, $59,890; assets, $1,387,161 (M); expenditures, $76,052; qualifying distributions, $59,890.
Limitations: Giving limited to Canonsburg, PA.
Application information: Write for application information. Application form required.
Trustee: Mellon Bank, N.A.
EIN: 256103319

47048
Sickles Charitable Trust
c/o Wolf Block
1650 Arch St., 22nd Fl.
Philadelphia, PA 19103
Contact: Edward Sickles, Tr.

Established in 1972 in PA.
Donor(s): Edward Sickles, Ann G. Sickles.
Financial data (yr. ended 11/30/01): Grants paid, $59,650; assets, $564,384 (M); expenditures, $62,535; qualifying distributions, $59,650.
Limitations: Giving primarily in Philadelphia, PA.
Application information: Application form not required.
Trustees: Ann Sickles, Edward Sickles.
EIN: 237250391

47049
Louis Nayovitz Foundation
Briar House
8302 Old York Rd., No. A33
Elkins Park, PA 19027
Contact: Neysa C. Adams, Tr.

Established in 1980.
Financial data (yr. ended 12/31/01): Grants paid, $59,400; assets, $1,394,812 (M); expenditures, $67,956; qualifying distributions, $59,400.
Limitations: Giving primarily in PA.
Trustees: Judith Adams, Neysa C. Adams, Margaret D. Nayovitz, Ralph S. Snyder.
EIN: 232142539

47050
Ellis A. Gimbel Charitable Trust
1650 Arch St., 22nd Fl.
Philadelphia, PA 19103

Donor(s): Ellis A. Gimbel.‡
Financial data (yr. ended 12/31/99): Grants paid, $59,300; assets, $1,343,239 (M); expenditures, $66,410; qualifying distributions, $60,908.
Limitations: Giving primarily in Hartford, CT and Philadelphia, PA.
Application information: Application form not required.

Trustees: Paul A. Gimbel, Doris A. Simon, Salley G. Taussig.
EIN: 236503956

47051
Jack Arpajian Armenian Educational Foundation, Inc.
P.O. Box 1090
Exton, PA 19341
Contact: Marguerite Parkinson, Pres.

Established in 1996 in PA.
Financial data (yr. ended 12/31/00): Grants paid, $59,167; assets, $1,543,376 (M); expenditures, $92,166; qualifying distributions, $76,659.
Application information: Application form required.
Officers and Directors:* Marguerite Parkinson,* Pres. and Exec. Dir.; Laurel Connelly,* Secy.-Treas.; Kevin Connelly, Joan Gallagher, Dante W. Renzulli, Jr.
EIN: 232761002

47052
Edith Davis Eve Foundation
c/o Mellon Bank, N.A.
P.O. Box 7236
Philadelphia, PA 19101-7236
Application address: c/o Mellon Bank, N.A., Central Trust Div., P.O. Box 19, State College, PA 18604

Financial data (yr. ended 12/31/00): Grants paid, $59,000; assets, $1,139,742 (M); expenditures, $71,250; qualifying distributions, $57,707.
Limitations: Giving primarily in PA.
Application information: Application form not required.
Trustee: Mellon Bank, N.A.
EIN: 236235141

47053
The Matthew Hillman Fisher Foundation, Inc.
2000 Grant Bldg.
Pittsburgh, PA 15219 (412) 338-3466
FAX: (412) 338-3463; E-mail: foundation@hillmanfo.com
Contact: Ronald W. Wertz, Secy.

Established in 1994 in PA.
Donor(s): Henry L. Hillman.
Financial data (yr. ended 12/31/00): Grants paid, $59,000; assets, $1,197,894 (M); expenditures, $67,688; qualifying distributions, $61,463.
Limitations: Giving primarily in New York, NY and Pittsburgh, PA.
Application information: Application form not required.
Officers and Directors:* Matthew H. Fisher,* Pres.; Lawrence M. Wagner,* V.P.; Ronald W. Wertz,* Secy. and Exec. Dir.; Maurice J. White,* Treas.
EIN: 251752985

47054
The Hauber Foundation
1491 Candlewood Dr.
Pittsburgh, PA 15241

Established in 1997 in PA.
Financial data (yr. ended 12/31/01): Grants paid, $58,977; assets, $1,381,051 (M); gifts received, $628,541; expenditures, $72,651; qualifying distributions, $55,689.
Officers: William M. Hauber, Chair.; Gregory A. Harbaugh, Secy.-Treas.
Trustee: Jean D. Hauber.
EIN: 237887198

47055
W. Clark Hagan Trust
c/o PNC Bank, N.A.
620 Liberty Ave.
Pittsburgh, PA 15222-2719 (412) 762-3390
Contact: Bruce Bickel, Mgr., PNC Bank, N.A.

Financial data (yr. ended 12/31/01): Grants paid, $58,771; assets, $892,872 (M); expenditures, $65,540; qualifying distributions, $59,386.
Limitations: Giving primarily in PA.
Trustee: PNC Bank, N.A.
EIN: 256070592

47056
Mellinger Scholarship Fund
(Formerly Gertrude & Clarence Mellinger Scholarship Fund)
c/o The Ephrata National Bank
P.O. Box 457
Ephrata, PA 17522 (717) 733-6576
Contact: Carl Brubaker, Trust Off., The Ephrata National Bank

Established in 1995 in PA.
Donor(s): Clarence Mellinger.‡
Financial data (yr. ended 12/31/00): Grants paid, $58,750; assets, $1,147,450 (M); expenditures, $66,972; qualifying distributions, $65,066.
Limitations: Giving limited to residents of Ephrata, PA.
Application information: Application form required.
Trustee: The Ephrata National Bank.
EIN: 232833247
Codes: GTI

47057
The Rasheed A. Wallace Foundation
c/o Mitchell & Titus, LLP
1 Logan Sq., Ste. 2929
Philadelphia, PA 19103
Application address: 2207 Chestnut St., Philadelphia, PA 19144, tel.: (215) 568-1678
Contact: Jacqueline Wallace, Exec. Dir.

Established in 1998 in PA and OR.
Donor(s): Rasheed A. Wallace.
Financial data (yr. ended 12/31/01): Grants paid, $58,661; assets, $2,432 (M); gifts received, $249,833; expenditures, $269,443; qualifying distributions, $58,661.
Limitations: Giving primarily in Philadelphia, PA.
Officers: Rasheed A. Wallace, Pres.; Tennis Young, Treas.; Jacqueline Wallace, Exec. Dir.
Directors: Malcom Wallace, Muhammed Wallace, Joe Watson.
EIN: 232913768

47058
Ray and Antoinette Westphal Foundation
c/o Stefanie Lucas
1041 Old Cassatt Rd.
Berwyn, PA 19312

Established in 2001 in PA.
Donor(s): Ray Westphal, Antoinette Westphal.
Financial data (yr. ended 12/31/01): Grants paid, $58,500; assets, $91,542 (M); gifts received, $150,000; expenditures, $58,518; qualifying distributions, $58,500.
Limitations: Applications not accepted. Giving primarily in PA.
Application information: Contributes only to pre-selected organizations.
Trustees: Antoinette Westphal, Rainer J. Westphal.
EIN: 256789338

47059
Charles G. Glazer Scholarship Fund
c/o Allfirst
21 E. Market St., M/C 402-130
York, PA 17401-1500
Application address: c/o Guidance Officer,
James Buchanan High School, 4773 Fort
Loudon Rd., Mercersburg, PA 17236, tel.: (717)
328-2146

Financial data (yr. ended 12/31/00): Grants paid,
$58,109; assets, $64,750 (M); gifts received,
$69,203; expenditures, $59,001; qualifying
distributions, $58,032.
Limitations: Giving primarily in PA.
Application information: Application form
required.
Trustee: Allfirst.
EIN: 236485096

47060
Whitaker Fund
1265 Drummers Ln., Ste. 304
Wayne, PA 19087

Established around 1980 in PA.
Financial data (yr. ended 12/31/01): Grants paid,
$58,000; assets, $1,168,889 (M); expenditures,
$69,595; qualifying distributions, $58,000.
Limitations: Applications not accepted. Giving
primarily in GA, NC, PA, and VA.
Application information: Contributes only to
pre-selected organizations.
Officers and Directors:* Floyd L. Firing, Jr.,* Pres.;
Scott F. Schumacker, Secy.-Treas.; Fred C.
Whitaker, Jr.
EIN: 237289515

47061
The Talbott Lea Simonds Foundation, Inc.
2000 Grant Bldg.
Pittsburgh, PA 15219 (412) 338-3466
FAX: (412) 338-3463; *E-mail:*
foundation@hillmanfo.com
Contact: Ronald W. Wertz, Secy.

Established in 1994 in PA.
Donor(s): Henry L. Hillman.
Financial data (yr. ended 12/31/00): Grants paid,
$57,850; assets, $1,198,348 (M); expenditures,
$66,494; qualifying distributions, $61,120.
Limitations: Giving primarily in San Francisco, CA
and Pittsburgh, PA.
Application information: Application form not
required.
Officers and Directors:* Talbott L. Simonds,*
Pres.; Lawrence M. Wagner,* V.P.; Ronald W.
Wertz,* Secy.; Maurice J. White,* Treas.
EIN: 251752984

47062
Wallace P. Hough Charitable Trust
c/o PNC Advisors
620 Liberty Ave., P2-PTPP-10-2
Pittsburgh, PA 15222-2705
Contact: John Hagan, Admin., PNC Advisors

Established in 1993 in PA.
Donor(s): Mary Helen Hough Abbott Irrevocable
Trust.
Financial data (yr. ended 12/31/01): Grants paid,
$57,817; assets, $913,284 (M); expenditures,
$66,065; qualifying distributions, $57,731.
Limitations: Giving limited to western PA.
Trustee: PNC Bank, N.A.
EIN: 256352924

47063
Curtis I. Kossman Charity Foundation
(Formerly Curtis I. & Paul Kossman Charity
Foundation)
c/o Mellon Bank, N.A.
P.O. Box 185
Pittsburgh, PA 15230-9397
Contact: Laurie Moritz, Trust Off., Mellon Bank,
N.A.

Donor(s): Paul Kossman.
Financial data (yr. ended 12/31/01): Grants paid,
$57,600; assets, $1,681,247 (M); expenditures,
$71,747; qualifying distributions, $60,978.
Limitations: Applications not accepted. Giving
primarily in Pittsburgh, PA.
Trustee: Mellon Bank, N.A.
EIN: 256066759

47064
Gerald A. & Mary Alice White Foundation
c/o Gerald A. White
3714 Laurel Ln.
Center Valley, PA 18034

Established in 1997 in PA.
Donor(s): Gerald A. White, Mary Alice White.
Financial data (yr. ended 12/31/01): Grants paid,
$57,500; assets, $424,086 (M); gifts received,
$1,204; expenditures, $58,704; qualifying
distributions, $57,500.
Limitations: Applications not accepted. Giving
primarily in PA.
Application information: Contributes only to
pre-selected organizations.
Trustees: Gerald A. White, Mary Alice White.
EIN: 237877903

47065
J. & R. Doverspike Charitable Foundation
c/o S & T Bank, Trust Dept.
P.O. Box 220
Indiana, PA 15701
Application address: c/o Selection Committee,
P.O. Box 1034, Punxsutawney, PA 15767

Established in 1997 in PA.
Donor(s): James R. Doverspike, Ruby L.
Doverspike.
Financial data (yr. ended 12/31/00): Grants paid,
$57,300; assets, $1,552,360 (M); gifts received,
$1; expenditures, $60,553; qualifying
distributions, $58,176.
Limitations: Giving primarily in PA.
Trustee: S & T Bank.
EIN: 256571881

47066
Charles A. Kahaner Foundation
2200 Walnut St.
Philadelphia, PA 19103-5521

Established in 1952 in PA.
Donor(s): Life & Health Insurance Co. of America.
Financial data (yr. ended 12/31/00): Grants paid,
$57,022; assets, $695,174 (M); gifts received,
$62,920; expenditures, $69,266; qualifying
distributions, $57,022.
Limitations: Applications not accepted. Giving
primarily in Philadelphia, PA.
Application information: Contributes only to
pre-selected organizations.
Trustees: Herbert Brill, Joyce Brill, Susan Kater,
Jonathan S. Miller, and 5 additional trustees.
EIN: 236296585

47067
Brookmead Trust
c/o Wendy Fritz
431 Glyn Wynne Rd.
Haverford, PA 19041-1702

Established in 1994 in PA.
Donor(s): Wendy C. Fritz.
Financial data (yr. ended 12/31/01): Grants paid,
$57,000; assets, $998,065 (M); expenditures,
$63,118; qualifying distributions, $57,000.
Limitations: Applications not accepted.
Application information: Contributes only to
pre-selected organizations.
Trustees: Charles A. Fritz IV, Jennifer C. Fritz,
Wendy C. Fritz.
EIN: 237787805

47068
The Stuckeman Foundation
1330 Old Freeport Rd., Ste. 1A
Pittsburgh, PA 15238
Contact: H. Campbell Stuckeman, Mgr.

Established in 1994 in PA.
Donor(s): H. Campbell Stuckeman.
Financial data (yr. ended 12/31/01): Grants paid,
$57,000; assets, $1,112,689 (M); expenditures,
$59,474; qualifying distributions, $57,000.
Limitations: Applications not accepted. Giving
limited to Pittsburgh, PA.
Application information: Contributes only to
pre-selected organizations. Unsolicited requests
for funds not accepted.
Officer and Directors:* H. Campbell Stuckeman,*
Mgr.; Joyce S. Biffar, Ellen S. Easley, Alan R.
Stuckeman.
EIN: 251757468

47069
Edgar V. Weir Family Foundation, Inc.
345 Brownsdale Rd.
Butler, PA 16002-0425 (724) 586-2631

Donor(s): Edgar V. Weir.
Financial data (yr. ended 12/31/01): Grants paid,
$57,000; assets, $995,788 (M); expenditures,
$60,488; qualifying distributions, $57,000.
Limitations: Giving primarily in Butler, PA.
Application information: Application form
required.
Directors: Mary Ellen Gallagher, Edgar V. Weir, Jr.,
Rebecca Ann Weir.
EIN: 256070443

47070
George L. Laverty Foundation
c/o Allfirst, Trust Tax Div.
P.O. Box 2961
Harrisburg, PA 17105-2961 (717) 255-2174
Contact: Joseph A. Macri, Trust Off., Allfirst

Established in 1980.
Financial data (yr. ended 03/31/02): Grants paid,
$56,856; assets, $1,165,236 (M); expenditures,
$64,465; qualifying distributions, $56,856.
Limitations: Giving primarily in Harrisburg, PA.
Application information: Application form not
required.
Trustee: Allfirst.
EIN: 232102516

47071
Eichleay Foundation
6585 Penn Ave.
Pittsburgh, PA 15206-4491

Established about 1956 in PA.
Financial data (yr. ended 12/31/01): Grants paid,
$56,800; assets, $1,899,552 (M); expenditures,
$58,736; qualifying distributions, $56,800.

47071—PENNSYLVANIA

Limitations: Applications not accepted. Giving primarily in PA.
Application information: Contributes only to pre-selected organizations.
Trustees: George F. Eichleay, John W. Eichleay, Jr.
EIN: 256065754

47072
Cole Foundation
P.O. Box 878
Wellsboro, PA 16901 (570) 723-1451
Contact: Edward H. Owlett, Tr.

Established in 1989 in PA.
Donor(s): Bruce E. Eilenberger, Vicki Eilenberger.
Financial data (yr. ended 12/31/01): Grants paid, $56,700; assets, $2,525,502 (M); expenditures, $73,528; qualifying distributions, $59,487.
Limitations: Giving primarily in Lancaster, PA.
Application information: Application form required.
Trustees: Ami Eilenberger, Bruce E. Eilenberger, Vicki Eilenberger, Edward H. Owlett.
EIN: 256339152

47073
Melvin and Eunice A. Miller Foundation
475 Warick Rd.
Wynnewood, PA 19096 (610) 649-1311
Contact: Eunice A. Miller, Pres.

Established in 1995 in PA.
Donor(s): Melvin N. Miller, Eunice A. Miller.
Financial data (yr. ended 12/31/01): Grants paid, $56,700; assets, $411,192 (M); expenditures, $122,024; qualifying distributions, $91,190.
Limitations: Giving primarily in New York, NY, and Philadelphia, PA.
Application information: Application form required.
Officers: Eunice A. Miller, Pres.; Deborah J. Miller, Secy.; Rachel S. Miller, Treas.
Trustees: Emily N. Miller, Melvin N. Miller.
EIN: 237705908

47074
The Benjamin Shein Foundation for Humanity
c/o M.L. Silow
2000 Market St., 10th Fl.
Philadelphia, PA 19103-3291

Established in 1998 in PA.
Donor(s): Benjamin P. Shein.
Financial data (yr. ended 12/31/01): Grants paid, $56,460; assets, $30,695 (M); gifts received, $45,000; expenditures, $56,560; qualifying distributions, $56,460.
Limitations: Applications not accepted. Giving primarily in PA.
Application information: Contributes only to pre-selected organizations.
Trustee: Benjamin P. Shein.
EIN: 232939286

47075
Ann and Joseph Farda Foundation
c/o Joseph Farda
The Summit, Box 130
Tannersville, PA 18372

Established in 1999 in PA.
Financial data (yr. ended 12/31/01): Grants paid, $56,350; assets, $12,702 (M); expenditures, $56,798; qualifying distributions, $56,350.
Limitations: Applications not accepted. Giving primarily in PA.
Application information: Contributes only to pre-selected organizations.
Directors: Ann Farda, Joseph Farda.
EIN: 232985745

47076
Lieutenant Robert Bolenius Ritchie Memorial Fund
c/o First Union National Bank, PA 6497
600 Penn St., P.O. Box 1102
Reading, PA 19603-1102
Contact: Hans F. Hass

Financial data (yr. ended 12/31/01): Grants paid, $56,167; assets, $937,437 (M); expenditures, $61,308; qualifying distributions, $55,826.
Limitations: Giving limited to Lancaster, PA.
Application information: Applicants must be graduates of Lancaster County, PA public high school and be recommended to the committee by high school guidance counselor. Application form required.
Trustee: First Union National Bank.
EIN: 236718706
Codes: GTI

47077
Progressive Business Publications Charitable Trust
c/o Edward M. Satell
370 Technology Dr.
Malvern, PA 19355

Established in 1996 in PA.
Donor(s): American Future Systems, Inc., Edward M. Satell.
Financial data (yr. ended 12/31/00): Grants paid, $56,100; assets, $490,153 (M); gifts received, $204,744; expenditures, $116,979; qualifying distributions, $92,784; giving activities include $56,979 for programs.
Limitations: Applications not accepted. Giving primarily in Philadelphia, PA.
Application information: Contributes only to pre-selected organizations.
Trustee: Edward M. Satell.
EIN: 237835073
Codes: CS, CD

47078
The Nina Baldwin Fisher Foundation, Inc.
2000 Grant Bldg.
Pittsburgh, PA 15219 (412) 338-3466
FAX: (412) 338-3463; *E-mail:* foundation@hillmanfo.com
Contact: Ronald W. Wertz, Secy.

Established in 1994 in PA.
Donor(s): Henry L. Hillman Trust.
Financial data (yr. ended 12/31/00): Grants paid, $56,000; assets, $1,197,630 (M); expenditures, $64,676; qualifying distributions, $58,466.
Limitations: Giving primarily in Pittsburgh and southwestern PA.
Application information: Application form not required.
Officers and Directors:* Nina Baldwin,* Pres.; Lawrence M. Wagner,* V.P.; Ronald W. Wertz,* Secy. and Exec. Dir.; Maurice J. White,* Treas.; Audrey Hillman Fisher.
EIN: 251752991

47079
Lawrence L. and Julia Z. Hoverter Charitable Foundation
c/o Ronald H. Katzman
Box 1268
Harrisburg, PA 17108-1268

Established in 1998 in PA.
Donor(s): Julia Hoverter, Lawrence Hoverter.
Financial data (yr. ended 12/31/01): Grants paid, $56,000; assets, $4,357,745 (M); gifts received, $3,162,850; expenditures, $68,407; qualifying distributions, $56,000.
Limitations: Applications not accepted.
Application information: Contributes only to pre-selected organizations.
Officers: Lawrence Hoverter, Pres.; Julia Hoverter, V.P.; Ronald M. Katzman, Secy.
Trustees: Joe Ceceri, Amos Miller.
EIN: 232944271

47080
The McCausland Foundation
P.O. Box 6675
Radnor, PA 19087-8675
Contact: Bonnie McCausland, Pres.

Established in 1994 in PA.
Donor(s): Bonnie McCausland.
Financial data (yr. ended 12/31/01): Grants paid, $56,000; assets, $80,693 (M); expenditures, $57,545; qualifying distributions, $56,000.
Limitations: Giving primarily in Philadelphia, PA.
Officers: Bonnie McCausland, Pres.; Peter McCausland, V.P.; Cornelia B. Gross, Secy.-Treas.
Director: Gordon L. Keen, Jr.
EIN: 232776475

47081
Meyers Foundation of Philadelphia
c/o Wolf, Block, Schorr & Solis-Cohen
1650 Arch St., 22nd Fl.
Philadelphia, PA 19102 (215) 977-2387

Financial data (yr. ended 12/31/00): Grants paid, $56,000; assets, $879,126 (M); gifts received, $1,500; expenditures, $64,676; qualifying distributions, $56,000.
Limitations: Giving primarily in Philadelphia, PA.
Application information: Application form not required.
Officers and Trustees:* Helen S. Sax,* Secy.; Peter E. Meyers,* Treas.; Joan Meyers.
EIN: 236243367

47082
George & Rita Patterson Foundation
P.O. Box 6595
Harrisburg, PA 17112

Established in 2000 in PA.
Donor(s): George F. Patterson.
Financial data (yr. ended 12/31/01): Grants paid, $55,985; assets, $5,039,787 (M); expenditures, $88,545; qualifying distributions, $55,985.
Limitations: Applications not accepted.
Application information: Contributes only to pre-selected organizations.
Trustees: M. Geralyn Patterson Hempt, George F. Patterson, George F. Patterson, Jr., Nathaniel J. Patterson III, Rita C. Patterson, M. Sharon Patterson Turner.
EIN: 256719662

47083
Ruby and John H. Updegrove Family Trust
4430 Fairview Dr.
Easton, PA 18045

Established in 1986 in PA.
Donor(s): Ruby H. Updegrove, John H. Updegrove.
Financial data (yr. ended 12/31/01): Grants paid, $55,976; assets, $280,739 (M); gifts received, $519; expenditures, $56,914; qualifying distributions, $55,976.
Limitations: Applications not accepted. Giving primarily in Bethlehem and Easton, PA.
Application information: Contributes only to pre-selected organizations.
Trustees: Andrew Updegrove, John H. Updegrove, Ruby H. Updegrove, Stephen Updegrove.
EIN: 236869477

47084
Cervelli Charitable Trust
c/o Joyce Rehorst
2123 Fox Creek Rd.
Berwyn, PA 19312

Donor(s): Andrew Cervelli.
Financial data (yr. ended 03/31/01): Grants paid, $55,700; assets, $741,786 (M); expenditures, $73,254; qualifying distributions, $55,700.
Limitations: Applications not accepted. Giving primarily in NY and PA.
Application information: Contributes only to pre-selected organizations.
Trustees: Brian Bernhardt, Levia Cervelli, Joyce L. Rehost.
EIN: 232118559

47085
Peggy & Ellis Wachs Family Foundation
237 S. 18th St., Apt. 8B
Philadelphia, PA 19103-6113

Established in 1985 in PA.
Donor(s): Ellis G. Wachs.
Financial data (yr. ended 12/31/01): Grants paid, $55,688; assets, $1,983,515 (M); expenditures, $56,891; qualifying distributions, $54,462.
Limitations: Applications not accepted. Giving primarily in Philadelphia, PA.
Application information: Contributes only to pre-selected organizations.
Trustees: Ellis G. Wachs, Peggy B. Wachs.
EIN: 236802696

47086
Harold C. Gift Scholarship Trust
c/o First Union National Bank
P.O. Box 1102, 600 Penn St.
Reading, PA 19603-1102 (610) 655-3148
Application Address: c/o Guidance Office, Reading, PA H.S., Reading, PA 19603
Contact: Hans F. Hass

Established in 1986 in PA.
Financial data (yr. ended 12/31/01): Grants paid, $55,198; assets, $1,745,328 (M); expenditures, $57,406; qualifying distributions, $55,648.
Limitations: Giving limited to residents of Reading, PA.
Trustee: First Union National Bank.
EIN: 236524243
Codes: GTI

47087
Milton L. and Shirley Rock Foundation
c/o MLR Holdings, LLC
1845 Walnut St., Ste. 900
Philadelphia, PA 19103-4710
Contact: Milton L. Rock, Pres.

Established in 1985 in PA.
Financial data (yr. ended 12/31/01): Grants paid, $55,085; assets, $2,600,756 (M); gifts received, $250,000; expenditures, $62,255; qualifying distributions, $59,202.
Limitations: Applications not accepted. Giving primarily in Philadelphia, PA.
Application information: Contributes only to pre-selected organizations.
Officers and Directors:* Milton L. Rock,* Pres.; Susan Mae Rock,* V.P. and Secy.; Robert H. Rock,* V.P. and Treas.
EIN: 222670382

47088
The Agnew Foundation of New York
2605 Houghton Lean
Macungie, PA 18062-9506
Contact: Arthur H. Rubin, Tr.

Established in 1967.
Financial data (yr. ended 12/31/01): Grants paid, $55,000; assets, $1,082,060 (M); expenditures, $82,825; qualifying distributions, $55,000.
Limitations: Applications not accepted. Giving primarily in FL and NY.
Publications: Annual report.
Application information: Contributes only to pre-selected organizations.
Trustees: Lester I. Brookner, Nathan Ende, Arthur H. Rubin.
EIN: 136277850

47089
The Walter & Alma Bastian Foundation, Inc.
1611 Pond Rd., Ste. 300
Allentown, PA 18104-2256 (610) 391-1800
FAX: (610) 391-1805
Contact: Robert G. Tallman, Pres.

Established in 1956 in MD as the A & B Foundation; name changed in 1975; reincorporated in 1987 in PA.
Donor(s): Alma F. Bastian,‡ Walter Bastian.‡
Financial data (yr. ended 12/31/01): Grants paid, $55,000; assets, $1,063,976 (M); expenditures, $72,089; qualifying distributions, $55,420.
Limitations: Giving limited to Lehigh Valley, PA.
Application information: Application form not required.
Officer and Directors:* Robert G. Tallman,* Pres. and Secy.-Treas.; Ray W. Biondi, John B. Lizak.
EIN: 236278134

47090
Hofmann Family Foundation
c/o Armada Group Ltd.
10040 Timbarra Ct.
Wexford, PA 15090

Established in 2000 in PA.
Donor(s): Armada Group, Ltd.
Financial data (yr. ended 12/31/01): Grants paid, $55,000; assets, $270,208 (M); gifts received, $259,000; expenditures, $55,067; qualifying distributions, $54,738.
Limitations: Applications not accepted. Giving primarily in Pittsburgh, PA.
Application information: Contributes only to pre-selected organizations.
Trustees: Mark C. Hofmann, Robert G. Hofmann.
EIN: 256724068
Codes: CS

47091
T. P. Stathis Foundation
521 Legion Dr.
West Chester, PA 19380

Established in 2000 in PA.
Donor(s): Peter N. Stathis.
Financial data (yr. ended 12/31/01): Grants paid, $55,000; assets, $3,191,399 (M); expenditures, $59,521; qualifying distributions, $55,000.
Limitations: Applications not accepted.
Application information: Contributes only to pre-selected organizations.
Trustee: Peter N. Stathis.
EIN: 256715011

47092
Thayer Corporation
c/o Hemmenway & Reinhardt
4 Park Ave.
Swarthmore, PA 19081
Application address: 10 Brettagne, Arbordeau, Devon, PA 19333, tel.: (610) 725-0473
Contact: Paul E. Macht, Pres.

Established in 1951 in PA.
Financial data (yr. ended 12/31/01): Grants paid, $55,000; assets, $1,418,018 (M); expenditures, $70,996; qualifying distributions, $55,000.
Limitations: Giving primarily in PA.
Application information: Application form not required.
Officers and Directors:* Paul E. Macht, Pres.; Alice T. Macht,* V.P.; Elmer L. Macht,* V.P.; Albert L. Doering III,* Secy.; James T. Macht,* Treas.; Patricia M. Bulat, Thomas F. Bulat, Debra Macht, James T. Macht.
EIN: 236266383

47093
Liss Family Charitable Trust
5698 Rising Sun Ave.
Philadelphia, PA 19120-1624

Established in 1987.
Donor(s): Joseph R. Liss, Betty J. Liss.
Financial data (yr. ended 04/30/02): Grants paid, $54,916; assets, $129,558 (M); expenditures, $64,633; qualifying distributions, $54,916.
Limitations: Applications not accepted. Giving primarily in NY and PA.
Application information: Contributes only to pre-selected organizations.
Trustees: Betty J. Liss, Joseph R. Liss.
EIN: 236868703

47094
The Engle Foundation
241 S. 6th St.
Philadelphia, PA 19106
Contact: Marilyn J. Engle, Tr.

Established in 1986 in PA.
Donor(s): Stanley H. Engle, Marilyn J. Engle.
Financial data (yr. ended 12/31/01): Grants paid, $54,775; assets, $1,108,812 (M); expenditures, $61,487; qualifying distributions, $54,405.
Limitations: Giving primarily in PA.
Application information: Unsolicited requests for funds not accepted.
Trustees: Marilyn J. Engle, Scott Engle, Stanley H. Engle, Kimberley Forbes.
EIN: 232440499

47095
Di Loreto Foundation
P.O. Box 784
Southeastern, PA 19399 (610) 647-1280
Contact: Richard Di Loreto, Pres.

Established around 1958 in PA.
Donor(s): Richard Di Loreto.
Financial data (yr. ended 12/31/01): Grants paid, $54,750; assets, $10,569 (M); gifts received, $60,000; expenditures, $55,389; qualifying distributions, $54,750.
Limitations: Giving on a national basis.
Application information: Application form not required.
Officer: Richard Di Loreto, Pres.
EIN: 116036781

47096
The Brooks Foundation
c/o F.J. Gerhart, Dechert, Price & Rhoads
4000 Bell Atlantic Twr., 1717 Arch St.
Philadelphia, PA 19103-2793

Established in 1986 in PA.
Donor(s): Robert T. Brooks.
Financial data (yr. ended 12/31/01): Grants paid, $54,600; assets, $968,015 (M); expenditures, $57,487; qualifying distributions, $54,600.
Limitations: Applications not accepted. Giving on a national basis.
Application information: Contributes only to pre-selected organizations.
Officers and Trustees:* Robert T. Brooks,* Pres. and Treas.; Rhea A. Brooks,* Secy.
EIN: 232410692

47097
Fountainhead Foundation
1000 RIDC Plz., Ste. 404
Pittsburgh, PA 15238 (412) 963-6226
Contact: Charles W. Bitzer, Pres.

Established in 1989 in PA.
Donor(s): Abarta, Inc.
Financial data (yr. ended 12/31/01): Grants paid, $54,600; assets, $220,832 (M); gifts received, $50,000; expenditures, $54,899; qualifying distributions, $54,600.
Limitations: Giving on a national basis.
Officers and Board Members:* Charles W. Bitzer,* Pres.; Michelle R. Bitzer,* V.P. and Secy.; Astrid S. Bitzer,* Treas.
EIN: 251605441

47098
The Yeehaw Foundation
1512 Colesville Rd.
Bethlehem, PA 18015

Established in 2000 in PA.
Donor(s): Michael J. Gausling, Sharon M. Gausling.
Financial data (yr. ended 12/31/01): Grants paid, $54,550; assets, $810,200 (M); gifts received, $797,630; expenditures, $56,580; qualifying distributions, $54,550.
Limitations: Applications not accepted.
Application information: Contributes only to pre-selected organizations.
Trustees: Michael J. Gausling, Sharon M. Gausling.
EIN: 256703094

47099
Marc and Friends Charitable Trust
4 Station Sq., Ste. 500
Pittsburgh, PA 15219

Financial data (yr. ended 01/31/01): Grants paid, $54,500; assets, $903,345 (M); gifts received, $50,000; expenditures, $55,665; qualifying distributions, $54,500.
Limitations: Applications not accepted. Giving primarily in PA.
Application information: Contributes only to pre-selected organizations.
Officers: Louis J. Cardamone, Chair.; Norbert J. Sieber, Vice-Chair.; Stuart M. Zolot, Secy.-Treas.
EIN: 256070473

47100
Moffat Charitable Trust
c/o PNC Bank, N.A.
P.O. Box 937
Scranton, PA 18501

Established in 1990 in PA.
Donor(s): Robert Y. Moffat, Jr.
Financial data (yr. ended 12/31/01): Grants paid, $54,500; assets, $502,162 (M); expenditures, $59,045; qualifying distributions, $54,500.
Limitations: Giving limited to PA.
Application information: Application form not required.
Trustees: Dorrance R. Belin, Robert Y. Moffat, Jr., PNC Bank, N.A.
EIN: 236967783

47101
The Henry John Simonds Foundation, Inc.
2000 Grant Bldg.
Pittsburgh, PA 15219 (412) 338-3466
FAX: (412) 338-3463; E-mail: foundation@hillmanfo.com
Contact: Ronald W. Wertz, Secy.

Established in 1994 in PA.
Donor(s): Henry L. Hillman.
Financial data (yr. ended 12/31/01): Grants paid, $54,350; assets, $1,058,568 (M); expenditures, $63,889; qualifying distributions, $54,350.
Limitations: Giving primarily in Pittsburgh and southwestern PA.
Application information: Application form not required.
Officers and Directors:* Henry J. Simonds,* Pres.; Lawrence M. Wagner,* V.P.; Ronald W. Wertz,* Secy. and Exec. Dir.; Maurice J. White,* Treas.
EIN: 251752986

47102
H. B. Alexander Foundation, Inc.
3300 N. 3rd St.
Harrisburg, PA 17110
Contact: Marion C. Alexander, Chair.

Established in 1959 in PA.
Donor(s): H.B. Alexander & Son, Inc., Mid-State, Inc.
Financial data (yr. ended 12/31/01): Grants paid, $54,300; assets, $1,082,805 (M); gifts received, $136,473; expenditures, $64,327; qualifying distributions, $54,300.
Limitations: Giving limited to Cumberland and Dauphin counties, PA.
Application information: Gives only to organizations with which members of the Alexander family are involved.
Officers and Directors:* Marion C. Alexander, Chair.; William H. Alexander,* Vice-Chair. and Treas.; Charles W. Alexander,* Secy.; Kathryn M. Alexander, Robert W. Alexander, Elizabeth A. Schluter.
Trustee: Hershey Trust Co.
EIN: 236242501

47103
The Sandra Glaberson Foundation
(Formerly The Sandra Robyn Glaberson Foundation)
1 S. Broad St., Ste. 1630
Philadelphia, PA 19107

Established in 1994 in PA.
Donor(s): Arnold Glaberson, Amy Glaberson.
Financial data (yr. ended 12/31/01): Grants paid, $54,245; assets, $740,741 (M); gifts received, $6,500; expenditures, $57,839; qualifying distributions, $56,427.
Limitations: Applications not accepted.
Application information: Contributes only to pre-selected organizations.
Officer and Director:* Arnold Glaberson,* Pres.
EIN: 232774133

47104
Murray B. Pfeffer Trust f/b/o Unger-Pfeffer Family Foundation
1501 Preble Ave.
Pittsburgh, PA 15233-2248 (412) 322-1363

Donor(s): Freid-El, Inc., Murray Pfeffer, Elvira Pfeffer, Freda Unger.
Financial data (yr. ended 11/30/01): Grants paid, $54,162; assets, $121,743 (M); gifts received, $40,135; expenditures, $54,809; qualifying distributions, $54,162.
Limitations: Giving primarily in the metropolitan New York, NY, area.
Officer and Trustees:* Joel Pfeffer,* Mgr.; Elvira Pfeffer, Murray Pfeffer, Freda Unger.
EIN: 256253815

47105
The Robert C. Daniels Foundation
1650 Market St., 21st Fl.
Philadelphia, PA 19103-7393

Established in 1987 in PA.
Donor(s): Robert C. Daniels.
Financial data (yr. ended 12/31/00): Grants paid, $54,105; assets, $562,894 (M); expenditures, $56,149; qualifying distributions, $54,105.
Limitations: Giving primarily in Philadelphia, PA.
Trustee: Robert C. Daniels.
EIN: 222773507

47106
The J. P. Brenneman & M. H. Brenneman Fund
c/o Mellon Bank, N.A.
P.O. Box 7236
Philadelphia, PA 19101-7236
Application address: c/o Robert O. Beers, Esq., Blakey, Yost, Bupp & Schauman, 17 E. Market St., York, PA 17401

Established in 1996 in PA.
Financial data (yr. ended 12/31/99): Grants paid, $54,100; assets, $1,781,762 (M); expenditures, $63,221; qualifying distributions, $55,003.
Limitations: Giving limited to residents of York County, PA.
Application information: Application form required.
Trustee: Mellon Bank, N.A.
EIN: 237850463
Codes: GTI

47107
C. H. Burgess Charitable Trust
c/o Mellon Bank, N.A.
P.O. Box 7236, AIM No. 193-0224
Philadelphia, PA 19101-7236
Contact: Donna Rhoades

Established in 1997 in PA.
Financial data (yr. ended 07/31/99): Grants paid, $54,000; assets, $1,134,696 (M); expenditures, $66,055; qualifying distributions, $58,493.
Trustee: Mellon Bank, N.A.
EIN: 237899535

47108
Caroline J. S. Sanders Trust
c/o First Union National Bank
123 S. Broad St., 16th Fl.
Philadelphia, PA 19109 (215) 670-4226
Contact: Reginald Middleton, V.P., First Union National Bank

Established in 1984.
Financial data (yr. ended 09/30/00): Grants paid, $54,000; assets, $1,207,214 (M); expenditures, $66,324; qualifying distributions, $56,379.
Limitations: Giving primarily in Philadelphia, PA, and VA.

Trustee: First Union National Bank.
EIN: 236781822

47109
Samuel & Emma Winters Foundation
c/o PNC Advisors
620 Liberty Ave., P2-PTPP-10-2
Pittsburgh, PA 15222-2705 (412) 762-5182
Contact: Bea Lynch, Trust Off., PNC Advisors

Established in 1959.
Financial data (yr. ended 12/31/01): Grants paid, $54,000; assets, $1,309,463 (M); expenditures, $57,145; qualifying distributions, $53,793.
Limitations: Giving primarily in Pittsburgh, PA.
Trustee: PNC Bank, N.A.
EIN: 256024170

47110
Allene S. Trushel Scholarship Trust
c/o Citizens Trust Co.
10 N. Main St.
Coudersport, PA 16915 (814) 274-9150
Application address: c/o Superintendent, Oswayo Valley School District, P.O. Box 610, Shinglehouse, PA 16478, tel.: (814) 697-7175

Established in 1982 in PA.
Donor(s): Willard Trushel,‡ Allene Trushel.
Financial data (yr. ended 12/31/01): Grants paid, $53,946; assets, $831,125 (M); expenditures, $61,011; qualifying distributions, $55,222.
Limitations: Giving limited to the Oswayo Valley School District in Potter County, PA.
Publications: Application guidelines.
Application information: Application form required.
Trustee: Citizens Trust Co.
EIN: 251419907
Codes: GTI

47111
Stern-Wolf Fund
c/o L.H. DuBrow
401 City Ave., Ste. 200
Bala Cynwyd, PA 19004-1117

Donor(s): Fred Wolf, Jr., Margery S. Wolf.
Financial data (yr. ended 09/30/01): Grants paid, $53,892; assets, $30,215 (M); expenditures, $54,076; qualifying distributions, $53,892.
Limitations: Giving primarily in New York, NY, and Philadelphia, PA.
Application information: Application form not required.
Trustees: Fred Wolf III, John S. Wolf, Margery S. Wolf.
EIN: 236243376

47112
Russell L. Hartman Trust
c/o Mellon Bank, N.A.
P.O. Box 7899
Philadelphia, PA 19101-7236
Application address: c/o Boyerstown Area School District, Boyerstown, PA 19101
Contact: Frances T. Smith, Portfolio Off.

Established in 1985 in PA.
Financial data (yr. ended 09/30/01): Grants paid, $53,800; assets, $998,596 (M); expenditures, $64,216; qualifying distributions, $53,800.
Limitations: Giving limited to residents of the Boyertown, PA, area.
Application information: Application form required.
Trustee: Mellon Bank, N.A.
EIN: 236810792
Codes: GTI

47113
Byham Charitable Foundation
c/o Development Dimensions Intl.
1225 Washington Pike
Bridgeville, PA 15017-2838
Contact: Karen Ann Krauss, Mgr.

Established in 1994 in PA.
Donor(s): William C. Byham.
Financial data (yr. ended 12/31/00): Grants paid, $53,740; assets, $896,478 (M); gifts received, $605,000; expenditures, $65,662; qualifying distributions, $56,740.
Limitations: Giving primarily in Pittsburgh, PA.
Officer: Karen Ann Krauss, Mgr.
Directors: Carter W. Byham, Tacy M. Byham Lehman.
Trustees: Carolyn M. Byham, William C. Byham.
EIN: 251739254

47114
Altoona Foundation
c/o Altoona Chamber of Commerce
1212 12th Ave.
Altoona, PA 16601

Financial data (yr. ended 12/31/00): Grants paid, $53,601; assets, $1,197,203 (M); expenditures, $67,227; qualifying distributions, $52,368.
Limitations: Applications not accepted. Giving primarily in Altoona, PA.
Application information: Contributes only to pre-selected organizations.
Officers: Joe Hurd, Secy.; Ray Hess, Treas.
EIN: 256067478

47115
The Frederick & Mildred Maltby Charitable Trust
c/o Stockton, Bates, & Co., LLP
42 South 15th St., Suite 600
Philadelphia, PA 19102

Established in 1993 in PA.
Donor(s): Frederick L. Maltby, Mildred N. Maltby.
Financial data (yr. ended 12/31/01): Grants paid, $53,550; assets, $13,192 (M); gifts received, $45,000; expenditures, $57,336; qualifying distributions, $53,550.
Limitations: Applications not accepted. Giving primarily in PA.
Application information: Contributes only to pre-selected organizations.
Trustees: Frederick L. Maltby, Mildred N. Maltby.
EIN: 237723088

47116
The Eleanor & Howard Morgan Family Foundation
764 Mount Moro Rd.
Villanova, PA 19085

Established in 1996 in PA.
Donor(s): Howard L. Morgan.
Financial data (yr. ended 12/31/01): Grants paid, $53,300; assets, $48,581 (M); expenditures, $55,550; qualifying distributions, $53,300.
Limitations: Applications not accepted.
Application information: Contributes only to pre-selected organizations.
Trustees: Danielle A. Morgan, Eleanor K. Morgan, Elizabeth S. Morgan, Howard L. Morgan, Kimberly Morgan.
EIN: 232868322

47117
Edward J. & Myrna K. Goodman Foundation
930 Meetinghouse Rd.
Rydal, PA 19046-2432
Contact: Myrna K. Goodman, Tr.

Established in 1986 in PA.
Donor(s): Edward J. Goodman, Myrna K. Goodman.
Financial data (yr. ended 10/31/01): Grants paid, $53,283; assets, $977,117 (M); expenditures, $55,716; qualifying distributions, $53,283.
Limitations: Giving primarily in PA.
Director: Myrna K. Goodman.
EIN: 222770994

47118
Keller Charitable Foundation, Inc.
662 Keller's Creamery Rd.
Telford, PA 18969
Contact: Arden L. Keller, Pres.

Established in 1993 in PA.
Donor(s): Arden Keller, Indian Valley Camping Center.
Financial data (yr. ended 12/31/01): Grants paid, $53,000; assets, $452,582 (M); expenditures, $53,513; qualifying distributions, $53,000.
Officers and Directors:* Arden Keller,* Pres.; Shirley G. Keller,* Secy.-Treas.; Claire Keller, Donna Keller.
EIN: 232703552

47119
Spring Garden Soup Society
c/o Douglas E. Cook
P.O. Box 397
Drexel Hill, PA 19026-0397

Established in 1995 in PA.
Financial data (yr. ended 10/31/01): Grants paid, $53,000; assets, $943,566 (M); gifts received, $802; expenditures, $53,736; qualifying distributions, $53,000.
Limitations: Applications not accepted. Giving primarily in PA.
Application information: Contributes only to pre-selected organizations.
Managers: Douglas E. Cook, Kenneth L. Gibb, Frank B. Baldwin III, John Dallas Bowers, Richard K. Brown, C.P. Becker, Robert J. Gill, M.D., Philip H. Peterson, Jr., R. Brooke Porch, Theodore L. Ricker, Jr., William Z. Suplee III, J. Jon Veloski.
EIN: 232838394

47120
Albert E. & Mabel C. Walker Foundation
c/o Mellon Bank
P.O. Box 185
Pittsburgh, PA 15230

Established in 1999 in PA.
Financial data (yr. ended 12/31/01): Grants paid, $53,000; assets, $910,440 (M); expenditures, $67,794; qualifying distributions, $53,000.
Limitations: Applications not accepted.
Application information: Contributes only to pre-selected organizations.
Trustees: Silas R. Mountsier III, Mellon Bank, N.A.
EIN: 256637309

47121
The Vernekoff-Zuritsky Foundation
150 N. Broad St.
Philadelphia, PA 19102-1424 (215) 569-8400

Established in 1986 in PA.
Donor(s): Herman Zuritsky, Lee Zuritsky.
Financial data (yr. ended 12/31/01): Grants paid, $52,350; assets, $898,883 (M); expenditures, $60,760; qualifying distributions, $52,023.

47121—PENNSYLVANIA

Limitations: Applications not accepted. Giving primarily in Philadelphia, PA.
Application information: Contributes only to pre-selected organizations.
Trustees: Etta Winigrad, Joseph Zuritsky.
EIN: 222734623

47122
Henry K. & Evelyn Reitnauer Scholarship Fund
c/o Investors Trust Co.
2201 Ridgewood Rd., No. 180
Wyomissing, PA 19610
Application address: c/o Boyertown Area High School, Guidance Dept., 4th St., Boyertown, PA 19512, tel.: (610) 369-7436

Financial data (yr. ended 12/31/99): Grants paid, $52,235; assets, $1,530,632 (M); expenditures, $52,272; qualifying distributions, $52,277.
Limitations: Giving primarily in PA.
Application information: Application form required.
Trustee: Investors Trust Co.
EIN: 232214468
Codes: GTI

47123
Elias Family Charitable Trust
509 Spring Ave.
Elkins Park, PA 19027
Contact: Gabriel Elias

Established in 1980.
Donor(s): Gabriel Elias.
Financial data (yr. ended 11/30/99): Grants paid, $52,025; assets, $1,178,637 (M); expenditures, $197,436; qualifying distributions, $51,520.
Limitations: Giving primarily in the Delaware Valley, PA, area.
Officer: Alma Elias, Mgr.
EIN: 236749244

47124
Millard Foundation
P.O. Box 8303
Radnor, PA 19087
Application address: c/o Marion M. Thompson, Secy., 44 Pembroke Rd., Mendham, NJ 07945
Contact: John Irwin, Pres.

Established around 1987 in PA.
Financial data (yr. ended 12/31/01): Grants paid, $52,020; assets, $582,932 (M); gifts received, $503,703; expenditures, $53,410; qualifying distributions, $52,020.
Limitations: Giving primarily in PA.
Officers: John N. Irwin, Pres.; Marsha Solmssen, Secy.; Marion M. Thompson, Secy.; Klaus Naude, Treas.
EIN: 232452507
Codes: GTI

47125
The Betty and Leo Balzereit Foundation
c/o The Glenmede Trust Co.
1650 Market St., Ste. 1200
Philadelphia, PA 19103-7391 (215) 419-6000
Contact: Joseph Rink

Established in 1999 in PA.
Financial data (yr. ended 12/31/01): Grants paid, $52,000; assets, $1,035,015 (M); gifts received, $26,000; expenditures, $56,497; qualifying distributions, $54,115.
Trustees: Leo G. Balzereit, George C. Balzereit, Jane B. Gruson, The Glenmede Trust Co.
EIN: 256655172

47126
ECOG Research and Education Foundation, Inc.
c/o Donna Marinucci
2115 S. St., 3rd Fl.
Philadelphia, PA 19146

Established in 1992 in WI.
Financial data (yr. ended 12/31/99): Grants paid, $52,000; assets, $1,595,332 (M); gifts received, $310,203; expenditures, $244,175; qualifying distributions, $250,003.
Limitations: Applications not accepted. Giving primarily in PA and WI.
Application information: Contributes only to pre-selected organizations.
Officers: Robert L. Comis, Pres.; David Harrington, V.P.; Donna Marinucci, Secy.-Treas.; Eleanor McFadden, Exec. Dir.
Directors: Janice Dutcher, Thomas Habermann, David Johnson, John Kirkwood, Patrick Loehrer.
EIN: 391723095

47127
W. F. and L. C. Roemer Charitable Foundation
c/o National City Bank of PA
20 Stanwix St.
Pittsburgh, PA 15222
Contact: William F. Roemer, Distribution Comm. Member

Established in 1999 in PA.
Donor(s): Wiliam F. Roemer, Linda C. Roemer.
Financial data (yr. ended 03/31/02): Grants paid, $52,000; assets, $2,320,392 (M); gifts received, $226,738; expenditures, $62,592; qualifying distributions, $52,000.
Trustee: James L. Schrott.
Distribution Committee Members: Linda C. Roemer, William F. Roemer.
EIN: 256636816

47128
Bruce R. Helwig Reading High School Scholarship Fund
c/o Terry Weiler, Esq.
1136 Penn Ave.
Wyomissing, PA 19610

Established in 1996 in PA.
Financial data (yr. ended 08/31/01): Grants paid, $51,904; assets, $368,361 (M); expenditures, $58,149; qualifying distributions, $51,904.
Limitations: Applications not accepted. Giving limited to Reading, PA residents.
Application information: Recommended by Reading High School staff.
Trustee: Terry Weiler.
EIN: 232843839

47129
Percy Edward Delkard Trust
c/o Allfirst, Trust Tax Div.
21 E. Market St., MC 402-130
York, PA 17401-1500

Financial data (yr. ended 08/31/01): Grants paid, $51,602; assets, $1,009,334 (M); expenditures, $60,027; qualifying distributions, $51,602.
Limitations: Applications not accepted. Giving limited to PA.
Application information: Contributes only to pre-selected organizations.
Trustee: Allfirst.
EIN: 236662736

47130
Jack Kellmer Company Foundation
717 Chestnut St.
Philadelphia, PA 19107-2391
Contact: James Kellmer, Tr.

Established in 1982.
Donor(s): Jack Kellmer Co., Jack Kellmer, Marjorie Kellmer.
Financial data (yr. ended 07/31/01): Grants paid, $51,600; assets, $224,473 (M); gifts received, $6,303; expenditures, $53,760; qualifying distributions, $53,760.
Limitations: Giving primarily in NJ and PA.
Trustees: James Kellmer, Marjorie Kellmer, Diane Young.
EIN: 236701981
Codes: CS, CD

47131
The Pearlman Family Foundation, Inc.
332 5th Ave.
Pittsburgh, PA 15222

Established in 1997 in PA.
Financial data (yr. ended 12/31/01): Grants paid, $51,324; assets, $184,927 (M); expenditures, $51,549; qualifying distributions, $50,965.
Limitations: Applications not accepted.
Application information: Contributes only to pre-selected organizations.
Officers: Doris M. Pearlman, Pres.; Emanuel V. Dinatale, Secy.-Treas.
EIN: 232938419

47132
Farrell Family Charitable Foundation
c/o PNC Advisors
1600 Market St., P2-PTPP-26
Pittsburgh, PA 15222-2705
application address: c/o Farrell & Co., 1200 Reedsdale St., Pittsburgh, PA 15233

Established in 1998 in PA.
Financial data (yr. ended 12/31/01): Grants paid, $51,250; assets, $419,805 (M); expenditures, $56,729; qualifying distributions, $51,680.
Limitations: Giving limited to PA.
Trustee: PNC Bank, N.A.
EIN: 237940677

47133
The Goedeker Foundation
c/o Group Against Intellectual Neglect
P.O. Box 95
Beaver, PA 15009-0095
Contact: David R. Berk

Established in 1996.
Donor(s): Delmar E. Goedeker, Margaret J. Goedeker.
Financial data (yr. ended 12/31/99): Grants paid, $51,100; assets, $820,073 (M); gifts received, $22,757; expenditures, $54,236; qualifying distributions, $49,843.
Application information: Application form required.
Trustees: Delmar E. Goedeker, Margaret J. Goedeker, Michelle M. Reichect, Melanie A. Rubocki, Mary Beth Stuver.
EIN: 256565140

47134
Helen Forde Gander & Mary A. Baldwin Trust
c/o Edward J. Aufman
2200 Georgetown Dr., Ste. 401
Sewickley, PA 15143-8753

Established in 1993 in PA.
Donor(s): Helen Forde Gander Trust.

Financial data (yr. ended 12/31/00): Grants paid, $51,000; assets, $1,117,109 (M); expenditures, $66,919; qualifying distributions, $49,828.
Limitations: Applications not accepted. Giving limited to PA.
Application information: Contributes only to pre-selected organizations.
Trustee: Edward J. Aufman.
EIN: 256405906

47135
The Arthur & Gail Morgenstern Family Foundation
c/o Ronald M. Wiener
1650 Arch St., 22nd Fl.
Philadelphia, PA 19103-2097

Established in 2000 in PA.
Donor(s): Arthur B. Morgenstern.‡
Financial data (yr. ended 12/31/01): Grants paid, $50,866; assets, $505,139 (M); gifts received, $512,185; expenditures, $52,325; qualifying distributions, $50,866.
Limitations: Applications not accepted.
Application information: Contributes only to pre-selected organizations.
Trustees: Rabbi Sholom Kamenetsky, Gail S. Morgenstern.
EIN: 256716020

47136
Margaret Baker Memorial Fund Trust
c/o Mellon Bank, N.A.
P.O. Box 185
Pittsburgh, PA 15230-9897
Application address: c/o L. Darlington Lessig, P.O. Box 663, Phoenixville, PA 19460

Established in 1945 in PA.
Donor(s): Charles J. Baker.‡
Financial data (yr. ended 12/31/01): Grants paid, $50,800; assets, $549,933 (M); gifts received, $24,258; expenditures, $55,526; qualifying distributions, $53,649.
Limitations: Giving limited to the Phoenixville, PA, area.
Application information: Application form not required.
Trustee: Mellon Bank, N.A.
EIN: 236227403
Codes: GTI

47137
Thomas Taylor Poor Fund
c/o PNC Advisors
620 Liberty Ave.
Pittsburgh, PA 15222

Financial data (yr. ended 09/30/01): Grants paid, $50,694; assets, $929,684 (M); expenditures, $60,015; qualifying distributions, $50,694.
Limitations: Applications not accepted. Giving limited to Pottstown, PA.
Application information: Contributes only to pre-selected organizations.
Trustee: PNC Bank, N.A.
EIN: 236249419
Codes: GTI

47138
Orleans Family Charitable Foundation
c/o Jeffrey P. Orleans
3333 Street Rd., Ste. 101
Bensalem, PA 19020-2022

Established in 1997.
Donor(s): Jeffrey P. Orleans, Selma H. Orleans.
Financial data (yr. ended 12/31/01): Grants paid, $50,607; assets, $69,955 (M); expenditures, $51,928; qualifying distributions, $50,607.
Limitations: Applications not accepted.
Application information: Contributes only to pre-selected organizations.
Trustees: Jeffrey P. Orleans, Selma H. Orleans.
EIN: 232868577

47139
Rosenberger Family Charitable Foundation
c/o PNC Advisors
1600 Market St., 4th Fl.
Philadelphia, PA 19103
Application address: c/o Samuel T. Swansen, 640 Sentry Pkwy., Blue Bell, PA 19422-2361

Established in 1990 in PA.
Donor(s): Members of the Rosenberg family.
Financial data (yr. ended 12/31/01): Grants paid, $50,500; assets, $950,475 (M); gifts received, $171,518; expenditures, $56,691; qualifying distributions, $52,045.
Limitations: Giving on a national basis.
Trustees: Rev. Nancy Rosenberger Faus, Cynthia A. Markham, Rev. W. Clemens Rosenberger, PNC Bank, N.A.
EIN: 232583927

47140
George A. Rumsey Foundation
c/o PNC Bank, N.A.
1600 Market St., 8th Fl.
Philadelphia, PA 19103

Financial data (yr. ended 12/31/01): Grants paid, $50,500; assets, $950,475 (M); gifts received, $171,518; expenditures, $56,691; qualifying distributions, $52,045.
Limitations: Giving limited to Ithaca, NY.
Trustees: Rev. Nancy Rosenberger Faus, Cynthia A. Markham, Rev. W. Clemens Rosenberger, PNC Bank, N.A.
EIN: 236480029

47141
Leo and Kathryne E. Friedman Memorial Scholarship Fund
c/o PNC Advisors
P.O. Box 937
Scranton, PA 18501-0937

Established in 1999 in PA.
Financial data (yr. ended 12/31/01): Grants paid, $50,453; assets, $948,509 (M); expenditures, $60,200; qualifying distributions, $50,453.
Limitations: Applications not accepted. Giving primarily in PA.
Application information: Contributes only to pre-selected organizations.
Trustee: PNC Bank, N.A.
EIN: 237904320

47142
The William & Patricia Kassling Family Foundation
540 Squaw Run Rd. E.
Pittsburgh, PA 15238 (412) 963-0421
Contact: William E. Kassling, Dir.

Established in 1996.
Donor(s): William E. Kassling.
Financial data (yr. ended 12/31/00): Grants paid, $50,450; assets, $930,649 (M); expenditures, $56,690; qualifying distributions, $55,600.
Limitations: Applications not accepted.
Application information: Contributes only to pre-selected organizations.
Officers: Patricia J. Kassling, Pres.; William E. Kassling, Secy.-Treas.
EIN: 463664886

47143
William L. & Philip H. Glatfelter Memorial Foundation
c/o PNC Advisors
1600 Market St., 4th Fl.
Philadelphia, PA 19103-7240

Established in 1990 in PA.
Donor(s): Elizabeth G. Rosenmiller.
Financial data (yr. ended 04/30/02): Grants paid, $50,374; assets, $897,318 (M); expenditures, $52,977; qualifying distributions, $50,374.
Limitations: Giving primarily in Gettysburg, PA.
Trustee: PNC Bank, N.A.
EIN: 237649676

47144
Daniel Zaccheus Foundation
c/o PNC Advisors
620 Liberty Ave., P2-PTPP-10-3
Pittsburgh, PA 15222-2705
Application address: c/o PNC Advisors, 2 PNC Plz., 5th Fl., Pittsburgh, PA 15222-2705

Financial data (yr. ended 12/31/01): Grants paid, $50,150; assets, $628,135 (M); expenditures, $52,907; qualifying distributions, $50,179.
Limitations: Giving limited to residents of PA.
Application information: Application form required.
Trustee: PNC Advisors.
EIN: 256065413
Codes: GTI

47145
Robert H. and Mary Gamble Hewitt Memorial Fund
c/o Mark Cohen
1600 Market St., Ste. 3600
Philadelphia, PA 19103
Contact: Elizabeth H. Hewitt, Pres.

Established in 1991 in PA.
Financial data (yr. ended 12/31/00): Grants paid, $50,100; assets, $1,066,507 (M); expenditures, $83,421; qualifying distributions, $54,724.
Limitations: Applications not accepted. Giving on a national basis.
Application information: Contributions only to pre-selected organizations.
Officers: Elizabeth H. Hewitt, Pres. and Treas.; Robert W. Hewitt, V.P.; Ruth Scofield, Secy.
EIN: 232618765

47146
Jeffrey J. and Mary E. Burdge Charitable Trust
c/o Allfirst Trust Co.
213 Market St.
Harrisburg, PA 17101-2141
Application address: c/o Allfirst Trust Co. of Pennsylvania, NA, P.O. Box 2961, Harrisburg, PA 17105-2961
Contact: Sue Mauery

Established in 1999 in PA.
Donor(s): Jeffrey J. Burdge.
Financial data (yr. ended 08/31/01): Grants paid, $50,000; assets, $1,373,885 (M); expenditures, $67,915; qualifying distributions, $51,595.
Limitations: Giving primarily in PA and VA.
Officer and Directors:* Jeremy J. Burdge,* Chair.; Gavin F. Burdge, Randall D. Burdge.
Trustee: Allfirst.
EIN: 256682889

47147
Community Nursing Services in Greensburg, Inc.
P.O. Box 98
Greensburg, PA 15601 (724) 837-6827

Donor(s): William A. Coulter Trust.
Financial data (yr. ended 04/30/01): Grants paid, $50,000; assets, $1,261,238 (M); gifts received, $54,710; expenditures, $63,892; qualifying distributions, $50,000.
Limitations: Giving limited to PA.
Application information: Application form required.
Officers: Edward Benson, Pres.; Ronald Silvis, V.P.; Anita Leonard, Secy.; Mark Zagar, Treas.
EIN: 250967471

47148
The Wilson J. and Karen A. Farmerie Charitable Foundation
20 Stanwix St., Ste. 650
Pittsburgh, PA 15222-4801

Established in 1997 in PA.
Donor(s): Karen A. Farmerie, Wilson J. Farmerie.
Financial data (yr. ended 09/30/01): Grants paid, $50,000; assets, $760,552 (M); expenditures, $63,592; qualifying distributions, $50,000.
Limitations: Applications not accepted. Giving primarily in Pittsburgh, PA.
Application information: Contributes only to pre-selected organizations.
Trustee: Smithfield Trust Co.
EIN: 237931543

47149
The Linda & Irwin Gross Foundation
722 Pine St.
Philadelphia, PA 19106-4005

Established in 1996 in PA.
Donor(s): Irwin Lee Gross, Linda C. Gross.
Financial data (yr. ended 12/31/00): Grants paid, $50,000; assets, $1,490,094 (M); expenditures, $50,030; qualifying distributions, $50,015.
Limitations: Applications not accepted. Giving primarily in Monsey, NY.
Application information: Contributes only to pre-selected organizations.
Officers: Linda C. Gross, Pres.; Irwin Lee Gross, Secy.-Treas.
EIN: 261768490

47150
The Hoss Foundation, Inc.
219 Pittsburgh St.
Uniontown, PA 15401

Donor(s): N. Douglas Hostetler, W. Jeffrey Hostetler.
Financial data (yr. ended 06/30/01): Grants paid, $50,000; assets, $871,556 (M); expenditures, $50,423; qualifying distributions, $50,423.
Application information: Application form not required.
Officers: N. Douglas Hostetler, Pres.; W. Jeffrey Hostetler, Treas.
EIN: 521751819

47151
The Karabots Foundation
P.O. Box 736
Fort Washington, PA 19034

Established in 1999 in PA.
Donor(s): Nicholas Karabots, Athena Karabots.
Financial data (yr. ended 06/30/01): Grants paid, $50,000; assets, $1,038,472 (M); expenditures, $50,427; qualifying distributions, $49,400.
Limitations: Applications not accepted. Giving primarily in Lafayette, PA.
Application information: Contributes only to pre-selected organizations.
Officers: Nicholas Karabots, Pres. and Treas.; Athena Karabots, V.P. and Secy.
EIN: 232939856

47152
The March Foundation
c/o J. Iskrant
1600 Market St.
Philadelphia, PA 19103
Application address: P.O. Box 261936, Plano, TX 75026-1936, tel.: (972) 403-1907
Contact: Kenneth B. Jarvis, Tr.

Established in 1998 in PA.
Donor(s): Kenneth B. Jarvis, Dennis Obregon, Douglas T. Smalls, Kenneth D. Parks.
Financial data (yr. ended 10/31/01): Grants paid, $50,000; assets, $87,168 (M); gifts received, $55,872; expenditures, $51,301; qualifying distributions, $50,000.
Application information: Application form not required.
Officers: Medford Turrentine, Secy.; Norman Charmichael, Treas.
Trustees: James E. Castillo, Jr., Arthur B. Hil, Kenneth B. Jarvis, William H. Lewis, Dennis Obregon, Kenneth D. Parks, James H. Pierce, Douglas T. Smalls, James Winestock.
EIN: 237989378

47153
The Sonnenberg Foundation
591 Frassetto Dr.
Southampton, PA 18966 (215) 864-7879
Contact: Erika Sonnenberg, Tr.

Established in 1994 in PA.
Donor(s): Alan Sonnenberg, Erika Sonnenberg.
Financial data (yr. ended 12/31/00): Grants paid, $50,000; assets, $494 (M); gifts received, $50,000; expenditures, $50,949; qualifying distributions, $50,000.
Limitations: Giving limited to PA.
Trustees: Alan Sonnenberg, Beverly Sonnenberg, Erika Sonnenberg.
EIN: 232792283

47154
Dorothy and Irvin Stein & Katherine and Keith Sachs Charitable Foundation, Inc.
c/o Katherine and Keith Sachs
1035 Washington Ln.
Rydal, PA 19046-1708

Established in 2001 in PA.
Donor(s): Deborah M. Sachs, Katherine Sachs, Keith Sachs.
Financial data (yr. ended 12/31/01): Grants paid, $50,000; assets, $1,141,781 (M); gifts received, $1,223,806; expenditures, $59,204; qualifying distributions, $50,834.
Limitations: Applications not accepted. Giving primarily in Philadelphia, PA.
Application information: Contributes only to pre-selected organizations.
Directors: Deborah M. Sachs, Katherine Sachs, Keith Sachs.
EIN: 582560411

47155
Barbara K. Wright Trust
c/o Susquehanna Trust & Investment Co.
329 Pine St.
Williamsport, PA 17701

Financial data (yr. ended 12/31/01): Grants paid, $50,000; assets, $847,054 (M); expenditures, $55,562; qualifying distributions, $51,833.
Limitations: Applications not accepted. Giving primarily in PA.
Application information: Contributes only to pre-selected organizations.
Trustee: Susquehanna Trust & Investment Co.
EIN: 237668582

47156
Charles Wentz Carter Memorial Foundation
74 Pasture Ln., Apt. 120
Bryn Mawr, PA 19010-1766 (610) 527-3303
Additional tel.: (703) 476-7975
Contact: Mrs. Clarkson Wentz, Pres.

Established in 1962 in PA.
Donor(s): Emmett B. Carter,‡ Mrs. Emmett B. Carter,‡ Charles Wentz Carter.‡
Financial data (yr. ended 12/31/01): Grants paid, $49,950; assets, $965,594 (M); gifts received, $15; expenditures, $53,677; qualifying distributions, $51,728.
Limitations: Giving primarily in PA.
Publications: Application guidelines.
Application information: Application form not required.
Officers and Directors:* Mrs. Clarkson Wentz, Pres.; Charles R. Wentz,* V.P.; Helen W. Panitt,* Secy.; Bess W. Woodworth,* Treas.; Harriet B. Wentz.
EIN: 236395203

47157
The Morganroth-Morrison Foundation
1040 Stony Ln.
Gladwyne, PA 19035
Contact: Joel Morganroth, Dir.

Established in 1980 in PA.
Donor(s): Joel Morganroth, Gail Morrison Morganroth.
Financial data (yr. ended 12/31/01): Grants paid, $49,600; assets, $249,229 (M); expenditures, $50,378; qualifying distributions, $49,600.
Limitations: Applications not accepted. Giving limited to PA and surrounding states.
Application information: Contributes only to pre-selected organizations.
Directors: Gail Morrison Morganroth, Joel Morganroth.
EIN: 232244767

47158
Richard and Mary K. Hosfeld Memorial Trust No. 1
c/o Mellon Bank, N.A.
P.O. Box 7236, Aim 193-0224
Philadelphia, PA 19103-7236
Application address: c/o Mellon Bank, N.A., P.O. Box 40, Shippensburg, PA 17257, tel.: (215) 532-2151

Established in 1991 in PA.
Financial data (yr. ended 04/30/02): Grants paid, $49,500; assets, $990,870 (M); expenditures, $58,429; qualifying distributions, $49,500.
Limitations: Giving limited to Shippensburg, PA.
Application information: Application form required.
Trustee: Mellon Bank, N.A.
EIN: 256377613

47159
Howard & Carole Weinstein Family Foundation
1456 Hampton Rd.
Rydal, PA 19046
Contact: Howard Weinstein, Pres. and Treas.

Established in 1999 in PA.
Donor(s): Howard Weinstein.
Financial data (yr. ended 11/30/01): Grants paid, $49,400; assets, $15,099 (M); expenditures, $50,068; qualifying distributions, $49,400.
Officers: Howard Weinstein, Pres. and Treas.; Carole Weinstein, V.P. and Secy.
EIN: 233022222

47160
Morris and Sophie Kardon Foundation
1201 Chestnut St., Ste. 1002
Philadelphia, PA 19107 (215) 665-9600
Contact: Leroy Kardon, Tr.

Established in 1947 in PA.
Donor(s): Robert Kardon, Members of the Kardon family, Kardon Industries.
Financial data (yr. ended 10/31/00): Grants paid, $49,275; assets, $78,941 (M); gifts received, $12,444; expenditures, $50,035; qualifying distributions, $49,275.
Limitations: Giving primarily in New York, NY, and Philadelphia, PA.
Application information: Application form not required.
Trustees: Lawrence Kardon, Leroy Kardon, Lynda Kardon, Richard Kardon, Robert Kardon.
EIN: 236251913

47161
The Reichlin Family Foundation
41 Conshohocken State Rd., Ste. 604
Bala Cynwyd, PA 19004-2419

Established in 1995.
Donor(s): Robert Reichlin.
Financial data (yr. ended 12/31/01): Grants paid, $49,235; assets, $879,166 (M); gifts received, $1,946; expenditures, $49,424; qualifying distributions, $49,235.
Limitations: Applications not accepted. Giving primarily in PA.
Application information: Contributes only to pre-selected organization.
Officer: Robert Reichlin, Pres.
EIN: 232815231

47162
Ash Family Foundation
c/o Robin B. Matlin
2000 Market St., 10th Fl.
Philadelphia, PA 19103-3291

Established in 1982.
Donor(s): Joseph Ash,‡ Franklin C. Ash, Larry Ash.
Financial data (yr. ended 10/31/01): Grants paid, $49,150; assets, $630,137 (M); gifts received, $5,000; expenditures, $51,135; qualifying distributions, $49,150.
Limitations: Applications not accepted. Giving primarily in Philadelphia, PA.
Application information: Contributes only to pre-selected organizations.
Trustees: Franklin C. Ash, Larry Ash.
EIN: 232225051

47163
Agnes Devlin Memorial Fund
c/o PCFIS
1650 Market St., Ste. 3050
Philadelphia, PA 19103
Contact: Lou Denton, Trust Off.

Financial data (yr. ended 12/31/01): Grants paid, $49,000; assets, $890,605 (M); expenditures, $78,385; qualifying distributions, $49,000.
Limitations: Giving limited to Blue Bell, PA.
Application information: Application form required.
Trustees: A. Louis Denton, Eunice Rubel, Edith Rubin.
EIN: 521932531

47164
Robert E. and Marie Orr Smith Foundation
c/o Glenmede Trust Co.
1650 Market St.
Philadelphia, PA 19103-7391

Established in 1992 in PA.
Donor(s): Robert E. Smith, Marie Orr Smith.
Financial data (yr. ended 11/30/01): Grants paid, $49,000; assets, $278,403 (M); gifts received, $259,486; expenditures, $54,126; qualifying distributions, $49,000.
Limitations: Applications not accepted. Giving primarily in PA.
Application information: Contributes only to pre-selected organizations.
Trustee: Robert E. Smith.
EIN: 237709897

47165
The Stork Charitable Trust
5727 Twin Silo Rd.
Doylestown, PA 18901
Application address: c/o Erica Zoino Curran, 146 Cockle Cove Rd., S. Chatham, MA 02659

Established in 1988 in PA.
Donor(s): Wayne Stork.
Financial data (yr. ended 09/30/01): Grants paid, $49,000; assets, $521,669 (M); expenditures, $50,250; qualifying distributions, $48,743.
Limitations: Giving limited to Brockton, MA.
Application information: Application form required.
Trustee: Wayne Stork.
EIN: 236951762
Codes: GTI

47166
David B. Garver Charity Fund f/b/o Bellefonte Elks Lodge No. 1094
c/o Mellon Bank, N.A.
P.O. Box 7236
Philadelphia, PA 19101-7236
Application address: c/o Bellefonte Elks Lodge No. 1094, 120 High St., Bellefonte, PA 16823

Donor(s): David B. Garver.‡
Financial data (yr. ended 01/31/02): Grants paid, $48,976; assets, $922,576 (M); expenditures, $56,303; qualifying distributions, $48,976.
Limitations: Giving limited to the Bellefonte, PA, area.
Trustee: Mellon Bank, N.A.
EIN: 256212802

47167
Samuel & Barbara Sternberg Charitable Foundation
c/o Stephen Bleyer
401 E. City Ave., Ste. 600
Bala Cynwyd, PA 19004

Donor(s): Barbara Sternberg.‡
Financial data (yr. ended 08/31/01): Grants paid, $48,775; assets, $863,229 (M); expenditures, $51,877; qualifying distributions, $48,192.
Limitations: Applications not accepted. Giving primarily in NY and PA.
Application information: Contributes only to pre-selected organizations.
Trustees: Cora Sternberg, Harvey Sternberg.
EIN: 236765536

47168
The Ideal Foundation
P.O. Box 1006
DuBois, PA 15801-1006 (814) 371-8616
Contact: John W. Bean, Tr.

Established in 1969.
Donor(s): Calvin Z. Bean,‡ Kathryn L. Bean,‡ John W. Bean.
Financial data (yr. ended 06/30/01): Grants paid, $48,729; assets, $1,831,456 (M); expenditures, $837,957; qualifying distributions, $719,395.
Limitations: Giving in the U.S., with emphasis on FL and PA.
Application information: Application form not required.
Trustee: John W. Bean.
EIN: 237046799

47169
Raleigh Carver, Jr. Trust
c/o First Union National Bank
Broad and Walnut Sts.
Philadelphia, PA 19109
Application address: c/o Donald Alexander, Chair., Scholarship Comm., 22 Carter Rd., Elizabeth City, NC 27909

Established in 1986 in NC.
Donor(s): Raleigh Carver, Jr.‡
Financial data (yr. ended 03/31/00): Grants paid, $48,552; assets, $1,343,070 (M); expenditures, $62,700; qualifying distributions, $48,646.
Limitations: Giving primarily in Pasquotank County, NC, but outside the corporate limits of Elizabeth City.
Application information: Application form required.
Trustee: First Union National Bank.
EIN: 566271497

47170
BridgeBuilders Foundation
560 Epsilon Dr. - RIDC Park
Pittsburgh, PA 15238
FAX: (412) 963-0240
Contact: Katie K. Wilson, Exec. Dir.

Established in 1957 in PA.
Donor(s): George E. Klingelhofer II.
Financial data (yr. ended 12/31/01): Grants paid, $48,500; assets, $1,389,076 (M); expenditures, $78,072; qualifying distributions, $48,500.
Limitations: Giving primarily in western PA and the northern Rockies areas.
Publications: Annual report (including application guidelines), grants list, informational brochure.
Application information: Application form not required.
Officer and Trustees:* Katie K. Wilson,* Exec. Dir.; Kristan Klingelhofer, Ned Klingelhofer.
Advisory Committee: Eleanore Childs, George E. Klingelhofer.
EIN: 256074470

47171
The Garrison Family Foundation
220 N. Jackson St., 2nd Floor
Media, PA 19063-2615

Established in 1990 in PA.

47171—PENNSYLVANIA

Donor(s): Walter R. Garrison.
Financial data (yr. ended 12/31/00): Grants paid, $48,500; assets, $706,994 (M); expenditures, $59,487; qualifying distributions, $61,658.
Limitations: Applications not accepted. Giving limited to PA.
Application information: Contributes only to pre-selected organizations.
Trustees: Michael J.J. Campbell, Ann-Michelle Garrison, Bruce Garrison, C. Jeffery Garrison, Heather Garrison, Jayne B. Garrison, Jennifer Garrison, Mark R. Garrison, Susan K. Garrison, Walter R. Garrison, Lawrence T. Phelan, Pamela G. Phelan.
EIN: 237650510

47172
Edward D. and Opal C. Loughney Foundation
P.O. Box 551
Ligonier, PA 15658-0551

Established in 1984.
Donor(s): Edward D. Loughney.
Financial data (yr. ended 11/30/01): Grants paid, $48,500; assets, $364,306 (M); gifts received, $10,014; expenditures, $61,435; qualifying distributions, $48,500.
Limitations: Applications not accepted. Giving primarily in Pittsburgh, PA.
Application information: Contributes only to pre-selected organizations.
Trustee: Edward D. Loughney.
EIN: 251487046

47173
Maria Foundation
c/o PNC Advisors
620 Liberty Ave., P2-PTPP-10-2
Pittsburgh, PA 15222-2719 (412) 762-3502
Contact: Bruce Bickel

Established in 1997 in PA.
Financial data (yr. ended 12/31/01): Grants paid, $48,500; assets, $1,027,090 (M); expenditures, $68,309; qualifying distributions, $49,924.
Trustee: PNC Bank, N.A.
EIN: 237892071

47174
William F. Price Foundation
c/o Michael J. Restrepo
1109 Albright Ave.
Wyomissing, PA 19610
Application address: 2012 Meadow Glen, Wyomissing, PA 19610, tel.: (610) 775-2539
Contact: Patricia A. Restrepo, Tr.

Financial data (yr. ended 11/30/01): Grants paid, $48,320; assets, $265,005 (M); expenditures, $53,150; qualifying distributions, $48,320.
Limitations: Giving primarily in PA.
Application information: Application form not required.
Trustees: William F. Price, Michael J. Restrepo, Patricia A. Restrepo.
EIN: 236243630

47175
Blanchard Family Foundation
P.O. Box N
Kennett Square, PA 19348 (610) 388-2926
Contact: Elwood P. Blanchard, Jr., Board Member

Established in 1999 in DE.
Financial data (yr. ended 07/31/02): Grants paid, $48,000; assets, $1,018,644 (M); expenditures, $48,842; qualifying distributions, $48,000.
Limitations: Giving primarily in DE, MD, NY, and PA.
Application information: Application form not required.

Board Members: Barbara Ann Blanchard, Barbara D. Blanchard, Elwood N. Blanchard, Elwood P. Blanchard, Jr., Marguerite Dunn.
EIN: 233010655

47176
Phillip F. Craft Memorial Foundation
30 Broadleaf Tr.
Malvern, PA 19355
Application address: 1423 Ardleigh Cir., West Chester, PA 19380
Contact: Robert Craft, Tr.

Established in 2001 in PA.
Donor(s): Robert Craft.
Financial data (yr. ended 12/31/01): Grants paid, $48,000; assets, $13,311 (M); gifts received, $65,000; expenditures, $52,147; qualifying distributions, $49,026.
Limitations: Applications not accepted. Giving primarily in PA.
Application information: Contributes only to pre-selected organizations.
Trustees: Cindy Carrow, Robert Craft.
EIN: 233060773

47177
The Mullen Foundation
(Formerly The Mullen Family Foundation)
204 Coventry Ln.
Media, PA 19063 (215) 565-5617
Contact: Joan A. Mullen, Tr.

Established in 1979 in PA.
Donor(s): John J. Mullen, Joan A. Mullen.
Financial data (yr. ended 09/30/01): Grants paid, $48,000; assets, $581,445 (M); expenditures, $48,015; qualifying distributions, $48,000.
Limitations: Giving primarily in the Philadelphia, PA, area.
Trustees: Joan A. Mullen, John J. Mullen.
EIN: 232125388

47178
Howard A. Power Scholarship Fund
c/p PNC Advisors
620 Liberty Ave., P2-PTPP-10-2
Pittsburgh, PA 15222-2705
Application address: c/o School of Medicine, Univ. of Pittsburgh, Scaife Hall, Terrace St., Pittsburgh, PA 15261

Financial data (yr. ended 12/31/00): Grants paid, $48,000; assets, $948,068 (M); expenditures, $51,208; qualifying distributions, $48,005.
Limitations: Giving limited to Pittsburgh, PA.
Publications: Application guidelines.
Application information: Application form required.
Trustee: PNC Bank, N.A.
EIN: 256234582

47179
The Michael L. and Susan K. Wert Foundation
341 Pineville Rd.
Newtown, PA 18940

Donor(s): Michael L. Wert, Susan K. Wert.
Financial data (yr. ended 12/31/01): Grants paid, $48,000; assets, $285,031 (M); expenditures, $49,908; qualifying distributions, $47,871.
Limitations: Applications not accepted.
Application information: Contributes only to pre-selected organizations.
Trustees: Michael L. Wert, Susan K. Wert.
EIN: 232901015

47180
The Glasser Family Foundation, Inc.
(Formerly A. & G. Glasser Foundation, Inc.)
1419 Highview Dr.
Greensburg, PA 15601
Application address: 5742 N.W. 24th Ave., Boca Raton, FL 33496, tel.: (561) 241-5632
Contact: Gloria Glasser, Secy.-Treas.

Established in 1986 in PA.
Donor(s): Abe Glasser, Gloria Glasser.
Financial data (yr. ended 12/31/01): Grants paid, $47,950; assets, $752,158 (M); gifts received, $311,614; expenditures, $52,458; qualifying distributions, $47,950.
Limitations: Giving primarily in PA.
Officers and Directors:* Abe Glasser,* Pres.; Gloria Glasser,* Secy.-Treas.
EIN: 251496445

47181
Magovern Family Foundation
251 Old Mill Rd.
Pittsburgh, PA 15238-1939

Established in 1987 in PA.
Donor(s): George J. Magovern, M.D., Margaret A. Magovern.
Financial data (yr. ended 12/31/01): Grants paid, $47,600; assets, $224,896 (M); expenditures, $48,644; qualifying distributions, $47,600.
Limitations: Applications not accepted. Giving primarily in Pittsburgh, PA.
Application information: Contributes only to pre-selected organizations.
Trustees: George J. Magovern, M.D., Margaret A. Magovern.
EIN: 256282388

47182
Arnold Foundation
c/o Paciotti, C.P.A.
Plaza 315, 1994 Rte. 315
Wilkes-Barre, PA 18702-6943 (717) 823-8855
Contact: Arnold K. Biscontini, Pres.

Donor(s): Arnold K. Biscontini.
Financial data (yr. ended 03/31/01): Grants paid, $47,191; assets, $1,255,035 (M); expenditures, $63,797; qualifying distributions, $48,602.
Limitations: Giving primarily in NC and PA, with emphasis on Luzerne County, PA.
Application information: Application form not required.
Officers: Arnold K. Biscontini, Pres. and Treas.; Cynthia W. Ross, Secy.
EIN: 236417708

47183
The Justin Brooks Fisher Foundation, Inc.
2000 Grant Bldg.
Pittsburgh, PA 15219 (412) 338-3466
FAX: (412) 338-3463; E-mail: foundation@hillmanfo.com
Contact: Ronald W. Wertz, Secy. and Exec. Dir.

Established in 1994 in PA.
Donor(s): Henry L. Hillman.
Financial data (yr. ended 12/31/01): Grants paid, $47,150; assets, $1,049,824 (M); expenditures, $56,311; qualifying distributions, $47,150.
Limitations: Giving primarily in Pittsburgh, PA and the Boulder, CO area.
Application information: Application form not required.
Officers and Directors:* Justin Brooks Fisher,* Pres.; Lawrence M. Wagner,* V.P.; Ronald W. Wertz,* Secy. and Exec. Dir.; Maurice J. White,* Treas.; Audrey H. Fisher.
EIN: 251752992

47184
The Della C. Lerew Trust
(Formerly Russel L. Lerew and Della C. Lerew Memorial Trust)
c/o Allfirst, Trust Tax. Div.
21 E. Market St.
York, PA 17401-1500

Financial data (yr. ended 12/31/01): Grants paid, $47,103; assets, $973,688 (M); gifts received, $128,115; expenditures, $52,136; qualifying distributions, $47,103.
Limitations: Applications not accepted. Giving primarily in PA.
Application information: Contributes only to pre-selected organizations.
Trustee: Allfirst.
EIN: 236986879

47185
The Carl M. Lindberg Family Foundation, Inc.
c/o J.R. Beam
2600 One Commerce Sq.
Philadelphia, PA 19103

Established in 1998 in PA.
Donor(s): Carl M. Lindberg.
Financial data (yr. ended 12/31/01): Grants paid, $47,100; assets, $938,139 (M); expenditures, $50,150; qualifying distributions, $47,100.
Limitations: Applications not accepted.
Application information: Contributes only to pre-selected organizations.
Officer: Carl M. Lindberg, Pres.
EIN: 232966581

47186
Joseph Bonadei Trust
c/o PNC Advisors
P.O. Box 8480
Erie, PA 16501

Established in 1996 in PA.
Financial data (yr. ended 06/30/01): Grants paid, $47,069; assets, $730,487 (M); expenditures, $55,139; qualifying distributions, $47,290.
Limitations: Applications not accepted.
Application information: Contributes only to pre-selected organizations.
Trustee: PNC Bank, N.A.
EIN: 256155137

47187
Richard E. Einstein Surviving Trust
c/o Allfirst, Trust Tax Div.
21 E. Market St.
York, PA 17401-1500
Application address: P.O. Box 2961, Harrisburg, PA 17105
Contact: Joe Macri, Trust Off., Allfirst, Trust Tax Div.

Financial data (yr. ended 12/31/00): Grants paid, $47,000; assets, $957,537 (M); expenditures, $52,874; qualifying distributions, $45,772.
Limitations: Giving limited to Dauphin County and the Harrisburg, PA, area.
Trustee: Allfirst.
EIN: 236508094

47188
Gulack Foundation
5 S. Sunnybrook Rd., Ste. 100
Pottstown, PA 19464 (610) 323-4900
Contact: Byron L. Shoemaker, Treas.

Established in 1967 in PA.
Financial data (yr. ended 12/31/01): Grants paid, $47,000; assets, $885,087 (M); expenditures, $49,957; qualifying distributions, $46,619.
Limitations: Giving primarily in the Perkiomen Valley, PA, area.
Application information: Application form not required.
Officers: Robert Mumbauer, Pres.; Richard Quigley, V.P.; Ronald J. Psaris, Secy.; Byron L. Shoemaker, Treas.
Directors: T. Eddinger, Peter Reigner.
EIN: 236432037

47189
McCormick Family Charitable Trust
P.O. Box 964
958 Netherwood Dr.
Blue Bell, PA 19422 (610) 279-8473
Contact: William J. McCormick, Jr., Tr.

Established in 1992 in PA.
Donor(s): William J. McCormick, Jr.
Financial data (yr. ended 12/31/01): Grants paid, $47,000; assets, $945,088 (M); expenditures, $49,912; qualifying distributions, $47,000.
Limitations: Giving primarily in PA.
Trustee: William J. McCormick, Jr.
EIN: 237688160

47190
Margaret B. Stimmel Trust
c/o Mellon Bank, N.A.
P.O. Box 7236
Philadelphia, PA 19101-7236

Financial data (yr. ended 09/30/00): Grants paid, $47,000; assets, $521,782 (M); expenditures, $54,857; qualifying distributions, $49,155.
Limitations: Applications not accepted. Giving limited to Kutztown, PA.
Application information: Contributes only to pre-selected organizations.
Trustee: Mellon Bank, N.A.
EIN: 236594488

47191
The Tabitha Foundation, Inc.
12 W. Willow Grove Ave.
P.O. Box 128
Philadelphia, PA 19118-3952 (215) 753-9200

Established in 1996 in PA.
Donor(s): Patricia L. Squire, W.F. Hurlburt, Marjorie H. Squire.
Financial data (yr. ended 12/31/01): Grants paid, $47,000; assets, $958,628 (M); gifts received, $225,745; expenditures, $61,734; qualifying distributions, $47,000.
Limitations: Giving primarily in Philadelphia, PA.
Application information: Application form required.
Officers and Director:* Patricia L. Squire,* Pres.; Edith Giese, V.P.; Carol A. Weir, Secy.; Elizabeth J. Walker, Treas.
EIN: 232867456

47192
James Frederick Fox Foundation
1 Pitcairn Pl., Ste. 2100
165 Township Line Rd.
Jenkintown, PA 19046-3593 (215) 572-0738
Contact: Robert A. Fox, Mgr.

Donor(s): Robert A. Fox.
Financial data (yr. ended 12/31/00): Grants paid, $46,850; assets, $902,115 (M); gifts received, $50; expenditures, $52,972; qualifying distributions, $46,530.
Limitations: Giving limited to PA.
Officer and Trustee:* Robert A. Fox,* Mgr.
EIN: 237034155

47193
Light of the World Foundation
P.O. Box 310
Strasburg, PA 17579 (717) 687-4220
Contact: Shirley R. Eshelman, Secy.-Treas.

Established in 1996 in PA.
Donor(s): Glenn M. Eshelman, Shirley R. Eshelman.
Financial data (yr. ended 12/31/01): Grants paid, $46,850; assets, $1,033,201 (M); expenditures, $48,375; qualifying distributions, $46,850.
Limitations: Giving primarily in PA.
Officers and Directors:* Glenn M. Eshelman,* Pres.; Shirley R. Eshelman,* Secy.-Treas.
EIN: 232871256

47194
Roy Pressman Foundation
2401 Pennsylvania Ave., Apt. 9A5
Philadelphia, PA 19130
Contact: Sylvan H. Savadove, Pres.

Established in 1994 in PA.
Financial data (yr. ended 05/31/02): Grants paid, $46,700; assets, $614,229 (M); expenditures, $53,759; qualifying distributions, $46,700.
Limitations: Giving primarily in PA.
Officer and Directors:* Sylvan H. Savadove,* Pres. and Secy.-Treas.; Paul L. Feldman.
EIN: 232690562

47195
The Broadbent Foundation
c/o John H. Broadbent, Jr.
1 Chestnut Hill Dr.
Mohnton, PA 19540

Established in 1992 in PA.
Donor(s): John H. Broadbent, Jr.
Financial data (yr. ended 06/30/00): Grants paid, $46,657; assets, $977,948 (M); expenditures, $53,604; qualifying distributions, $44,666.
Limitations: Giving primarily to residents of Berks County, PA.
Application information: Application form required.
Trustees: John H. Broadbent, Jr., Richard L. Broadbent, Dana L. Bunting.
EIN: 232703271
Codes: GTI

47196
The Jacob Fend Foundation
P.O. Box 98
Johnstown, PA 15907
FAX: (814) 536-2278
Contact: Janet E. Gillen, Secy.-Treas.

Established in 1978 in PA.
Donor(s): Matilda Frend Gageby,‡ Ettie Fend,‡ Jacob Fend Trust.‡
Financial data (yr. ended 12/31/01): Grants paid, $46,642; assets, $0 (M); gifts received, $48,534; expenditures, $49,534; qualifying distributions, $49,535.
Limitations: Giving limited to the greater Johnstown, PA, area.
Application information: Applicant must comply with the foundation's "Rules and Regulations to Determine Eligibility". Application form not required.
Officers and Directors:* John H. Anderson,* Chair.; Carl J. Motter, Jr.,* Vice-Chair.; Janet E. Gillen,* Secy.-Treas.; Martin Goldhaber, Ethel J. Otrosina, Charles S. Price, Gerald W. Swatsworth.
EIN: 251371934

47197
Nancy Shuman Hock Foundation
533 Back Branch Rd.
Bloomsburg, PA 17815
Contact: Nancy Hock, Pres.

Established in 1998 in PA.
Donor(s): Nancy Hock.
Financial data (yr. ended 12/31/01): Grants paid, $46,612; assets, $982,106 (M); expenditures, $52,473; qualifying distributions, $46,612.
Limitations: Giving primarily in PA.
Application information: Application form not required.
Officers: Nancy Hock, Pres.; John H. Shuman, Jr., Secy.-Treas.
EIN: 232903249

47198
Newport Foundation, Inc.
c/o William W. Moyer, III
1119 Ashbourne Rd.
Cheltenham, PA 19012-1108

Established in 1986 in PA.
Donor(s): Jacalyn Moyer, William W. Moyer III, Arthur Sidewater.‡
Financial data (yr. ended 12/31/00): Grants paid, $46,500; assets, $1,603,821 (M); gifts received, $30,174; expenditures, $51,320; qualifying distributions, $46,500.
Limitations: Applications not accepted. Giving primarily in Philadelphia, PA.
Application information: Contributes only to pre-selected organizations.
Officers and Directors:* William W. Moyer III,* Pres.; Jacalyn Moyer,* V.P. and Secy.-Treas.; Daniel J. Paci.
EIN: 222788864

47199
The Walrus Foundation, Inc.
(Formerly Wick-Kearney Foundation, Inc.)
1075 High St.
P.O. Box 363
Bradford, PA 16701 (814) 362-9192
Contact: Susan R. Dennis, Secy.

Established in 1999 in PA.
Financial data (yr. ended 12/31/01): Grants paid, $46,178; assets, $1,071,265 (M); gifts received, $259,748; expenditures, $71,864; qualifying distributions, $46,178.
Limitations: Giving primarily in PA.
Officers: Harriett B. Wick, Pres.; D. Blaise Wick, V.P.; Susan R. Dennis, Secy.; Barbara W. Kearney, Treas.
EIN: 251841169

47200
Calvary Foundation
104 Trenton Cir.
McMurray, PA 15317 (724) 941-1414
Contact: Schuyler L. Brooks, Dir.

Established in 1990 in PA.
Donor(s): Schuyler L. Brooks, Joan G. Brooks.
Financial data (yr. ended 12/31/01): Grants paid, $46,152; assets, $915,220 (M); expenditures, $52,563; qualifying distributions, $46,152.
Limitations: Giving primarily in Pittsburgh, PA.
Application information: Application form not required.
Directors: Joan G. Brooks, Peter S. Brooks, Schuyler L. Brooks, Stephen G. Brooks, Margaret E. Schmitt.
EIN: 251633965

47201
The O'Connor Family Foundation
442 Inverary Rd.
Villanova, PA 19085-1138

Established in 1997 in PA.
Donor(s): Gerald J. O'Connor, Sr.
Financial data (yr. ended 12/31/01): Grants paid, $46,015; assets, $301,819 (M); expenditures, $50,201; qualifying distributions, $46,015.
Limitations: Applications not accepted.
Application information: Contributes only to pre-selected organizations.
Trustees: Gerald J. O'Connor, Sr., Sheila T. O'Connor.
EIN: 237927963

47202
John J. Thomas Foundation
c/o PNC Advisors
620 Liberty Ave., P2-PTPP-10-2
Pittsburgh, PA 15222-2705 (412) 768-8360
Contact: Kara Chickson, Trust Off., PNC Advisors

Established in 1987 in PA.
Donor(s): John J. Thomas.‡
Financial data (yr. ended 09/30/01): Grants paid, $46,001; assets, $589,828 (M); expenditures, $51,956; qualifying distributions, $46,207.
Limitations: Giving limited to residents of McKees Rocks and Pittsburgh, PA.
Trustee: PNC Bank, N.A.
EIN: 251381212
Codes: GTI

47203
The Dicerbo Foundation, Inc.
c/o The PA Trust Co.
5 Radnor Corp. Ctr., Ste. 450
Radnor, PA 19087 (610) 975-4300

Established in 1994 in NY.
Donor(s): Louis P. Dicerbo II.
Financial data (yr. ended 12/31/01): Grants paid, $46,000; assets, $1,161,292 (M); gifts received, $295,400; expenditures, $59,484; qualifying distributions, $46,250.
Limitations: Applications not accepted. Giving primarily in NY.
Application information: Contributes only to pre-selected organizations.
Officers: Louis P. Dicerbo II, Chair.; Eileen Patricia Dicerbo, Vice-Chair.; Joy Bushwell, V.P.; Cheri DiCerbo, V.P.; Cindy Silverstein, V.P.; Nancy Reddan, Secy.
EIN: 113202308

47204
Harris Scholarship Fund
c/o PNC Advisors
1600 Market St., 4th Fl.
Philadelphia, PA 19103

Financial data (yr. ended 12/31/01): Grants paid, $46,000; assets, $645,475 (M); expenditures, $52,576; qualifying distributions, $47,652.
Limitations: Applications not accepted. Giving limited to Salem, NJ.
Application information: Recipients are selected by Scholarship Committee.
Trustee: PNC Bank, N.A.
EIN: 226485592
Codes: GTI

47205
Innisfree Foundation of Bryn Mawr, Pennsylvania
c/o Center Bridge Group, Inc.
234 Mall Blvd., Rm. 105
King of Prussia, PA 19406
Contact: Kate Testorf, CPA

Established in 1989 in PA.
Donor(s): Harold G. Schaeffer.
Financial data (yr. ended 09/30/01): Grants paid, $46,000; assets, $308,785 (M); expenditures, $46,844; qualifying distributions, $46,429.
Limitations: Applications not accepted. Giving primarily in Philadelphia, PA.
Application information: Contributes only to pre-selected organizations.
Trustees: Adele K. Schaeffer, Anthony L. Schaeffer, Harold G. Schaeffer, James R. Schaeffer, Robert D. Schaeffer.
EIN: 232810871

47206
George A. Ohl, Jr. Cancer Foundation
c/o First Union National Bank
123 S. Broad St.
Philadelphia, PA 19109-9989
Application address: c/o First Union National Bank, N.A., 765 Broad St., Newark, NJ 07101

Established around 1949 in NJ.
Donor(s): George A. Ohl, Jr.‡
Financial data (yr. ended 02/28/99): Grants paid, $46,000; assets, $560,928 (M); expenditures, $48,827; qualifying distributions, $46,000.
Limitations: Giving primarily in New Brunswick, NJ.
Trustee: First Union National Bank.
EIN: 226042348

47207
The Spira Family Foundation
1506 Pleasant View Rd.
Coopersburg, PA 18036-9652

Established in 2000 in PA.
Donor(s): Joel Spira, Ruth Spira.
Financial data (yr. ended 12/31/01): Grants paid, $45,805; assets, $894,633 (M); gifts received, $20,000; expenditures, $52,824; qualifying distributions, $45,805.
Limitations: Applications not accepted. Giving primarily in PA.
Application information: Contributes only to pre-selected organizations.
Officers: Joel Spira, Pres. and Treas.; Ruth Spira, V.P. and Secy.
EIN: 233027959

47208
Richard E. Woosnam Charitable Trust
2000 Market St., Ste. 1400
Philadelphia, PA 19103 (215) 564-3960
Contact: Richard E. Woosnam, Tr.

Established in 1986 in PA.
Donor(s): Richard E. Woosnam.
Financial data (yr. ended 12/31/01): Grants paid, $45,705; assets, $1,068,142 (M); expenditures, $49,348; qualifying distributions, $45,705.
Limitations: Giving primarily in IN and PA.
Application information: Application form not required.
Trustee: Richard E. Woosnam.
EIN: 236870650

47209
Norman C. Ray Foundation Trust C
600 Grant St., Ste. 3100
Pittsburgh, PA 15219-2784 (412) 562-8234
Contact: J. Edgar Williams, Tr.

Donor(s): Norman C. Ray.‡
Financial data (yr. ended 01/31/99): Grants paid, $45,598; assets, $1,642,605 (M); expenditures, $49,926; qualifying distributions, $45,598.
Limitations: Giving primarily in Pittsburgh, PA.
Application information: Application form not required.
Trustees: Nathan K. Parker, Jr., J. Edgar Williams.
EIN: 256186356

47210
Allen-Toebe Foundation
19 Forest Rd.
P.O. Box 444
Wayne, PA 19087-0444

Established in 1987 in PA.
Donor(s): John W. Toebe, John M. Toebe.
Financial data (yr. ended 12/31/01): Grants paid, $45,385; assets, $68,469 (M); gifts received, $32,107; expenditures, $46,520; qualifying distributions, $45,385.
Limitations: Applications not accepted. Giving primarily in PA.
Application information: Contributes only to pre-selected organizations.
Trustees: Elizabeth Allen, C. Barry Buckley, John M. Toebe, John W. Toebe, Patricia M. Toebe.
EIN: 236871066

47211
The Peter D. Carlino Family Foundation
1735 Market St.
Philadelphia, PA 19103

Established in 1999 in PA.
Donor(s): Peter D. Carlino.
Financial data (yr. ended 12/31/01): Grants paid, $45,250; assets, $14,578 (M); gifts received, $50,938; expenditures, $45,250; qualifying distributions, $45,250.
Officer: Robert Krause, Pres.
EIN: 233008833

47212
Hafner Charitable Foundation
c/o PNC Advisors
620 Liberty Ave., P2-PTPP-10-2
Pittsburgh, PA 15222 (412) 762-3390
Contact: John Culbertson, Trust Off., PNC Advisors

Financial data (yr. ended 06/30/01): Grants paid, $45,000; assets, $1,077,334 (M); expenditures, $51,919; qualifying distributions, $47,550.
Limitations: Giving limited to PA.
Application information: Application form not required.
Trustees: Richard S. Crone, PNC Bank, N.A.
EIN: 256222970

47213
Lackner Family Foundation
c/o J. Battaglini
337 W. Lancaster Ave.
Wayne, PA 19087

Established in 1999 in PA.
Financial data (yr. ended 08/31/01): Grants paid, $45,000; assets, $2,806 (M); gifts received, $50,000; expenditures, $47,205; qualifying distributions, $45,000.
Limitations: Applications not accepted.
Application information: Contributes only to pre-selected organizations.

Director: David M. Lackner.
EIN: 137153253

47214
Lorenzen Foundation
c/o Douglas F. Schofield
P.O. Box 369
Indianola, PA 15051-0369

Established in 1990 in PA.
Donor(s): Pearl B. Lorenzen.
Financial data (yr. ended 12/31/01): Grants paid, $45,000; assets, $904,748 (M); expenditures, $45,582; qualifying distributions, $45,000.
Limitations: Applications not accepted. Giving primarily in Phoenix, AZ.
Application information: Contributes only to pre-selected organizations.
Trustees: Robert F. Lorenzen, Douglas F. Schofield.
EIN: 251622146

47215
Security Savings Charitable Foundation
P.O. Box 2370
Hazleton, PA 18201
Contact: Peter B. Deisroth, Admin.

Established in 1998 in PA.
Donor(s): Security of Pennsylvania Financial Corp.
Financial data (yr. ended 06/30/02): Grants paid, $44,825; assets, $1,106,405 (M); expenditures, $83,874; qualifying distributions, $44,825.
Limitations: Giving primarily in Hazelton, PA.
Application information: Application form required.
Officers: John J. Raynock, Chair.; David P. Marchetti, Sr., Secy.-Treas.; Peter B. Deisroth, Admin.
Directors: George J. Hayden, Thomas L. Kennedy, Gary F. Lamont.
EIN: 232992148

47216
Howard H. Steel Orthopaedic Foundation
1526 Mt. Pleasant Rd.
Villanova, PA 19085-2113
Application address: c/o Binder & Weiss, P.C., 1880 JFK Blvd., Ste. 1401, Philadelphia, PA 19103
Contact: Howard H. Steel, Secy.

Donor(s): Archie W. Berry, Grace Berry, Howard H. Steel.
Financial data (yr. ended 09/30/01): Grants paid, $44,542; assets, $106,819 (M); gifts received, $50,000; expenditures, $57,292; qualifying distributions, $55,069.
Limitations: Giving on a national basis.
Officers and Directors:* Betty Jo Steel,* Pres.; Howard H. Steel,* Secy.; Townsend Smith,* Treas.; Joseph S. Binder, Brian Carroll, David Clack, Turner C. Smith.
EIN: 232192892

47217
The Millmont Foundation
4237 Middle Rd.
Allison Park, PA 15101
Contact: Carrie M. Stanny, Secy.-Treas.

Established about 1956.
Financial data (yr. ended 07/31/01): Grants paid, $44,537; assets, $877,535 (M); expenditures, $45,326; qualifying distributions, $44,537.
Officers and Directors:* Peter Cholnoky,* Pres.; Carrie M. Stanny,* Secy.-Treas.; Dorothy Cholnoky, Richard M. Montague, Theodore G. Montague, Jr.
EIN: 066051671

47218
Richmond-Pennock Family Scholarship Fund
c/o First Union National Bank
P.O. Box 1102, 600 Penn St.
Reading, PA 19603-1102
Contact: Hans Hass

Financial data (yr. ended 09/30/00): Grants paid, $44,419; assets, $2,287,238 (M); expenditures, $52,044; qualifying distributions, $44,419.
Limitations: Giving limited to Lancaster County, PA.
Application information: Recipients are chosen by the High School Awarding Committee.
Trustee: First Union National Bank.
EIN: 236637016

47219
Koppelman Family Foundation
c/o Robert Friedman
111 S. 15th St., 12th Fl., Packard Bldg.
Philadelphia, PA 19102 (215) 977-2090

Established in 1997 in PA.
Donor(s): Jeanette Koppelman, Joseph Koppelman.
Financial data (yr. ended 12/31/01): Grants paid, $44,274; assets, $1,115,445 (M); expenditures, $45,869; qualifying distributions, $44,274.
Limitations: Applications not accepted. Giving primarily in FL and MA.
Application information: Contributes only to pre-selected organizations.
Directors: Jeanette Koppelman, Stanley Koppelman.
EIN: 232903238

47220
Wendell W. McMillen Foundation
203 Center St.
Sheffield, PA 16347 (814) 968-3241
Contact: Joyce E. Olson, Dir.

Donor(s): Wendall W. McMillen, Irwin Wood Products, Inc., McMillen Lumber Products Corp., McMillen Lumber Co. of Shaffield, Inc.
Financial data (yr. ended 03/31/01): Grants paid, $44,150; assets, $489,830 (M); expenditures, $55,809; qualifying distributions, $44,150.
Limitations: Giving primarily in the Sheffield, PA, area.
Directors: James W. McMillen, Robert W. McMillen, Joyce E. Olson.
EIN: 256060174
Codes: GTI

47221
Lt. Frederick W. Kulicke III Fund
(also known as The Kulicke Fund)
c/o Frederick W. Kulicke, Jr.
537 Rolling Glen Dr.
Horsham, PA 19044

Donor(s): Frederick W. Kulicke, Jr.
Financial data (yr. ended 12/31/00): Grants paid, $44,004; assets, $893,590 (M); expenditures, $46,943; qualifying distributions, $44,004.
Limitations: Applications not accepted. Giving primarily in Philadelphia, PA.
Application information: Contributes only to pre-selected organizations.
Trustees: Harry S. Cherken, Jr., C. Scott Kulicke, Danielle Kulicke, Frederick W. Kulicke, Jr., Allison F. Page.
EIN: 237094864

47222
Martha Mack Lewis Foundation
c/o PNC Advisors
620 Liberty Ave., P2-PTTP-10-2
Pittsburgh, PA 15222-2705 (412) 762-3502
Contact: R. Bruce Bickel

Established in 1998 in PA.
Financial data (yr. ended 12/31/01): Grants paid, $44,000; assets, $1,176,362 (M); expenditures, $53,276; qualifying distributions, $46,418.
Limitations: Giving primarily in Pittsburgh, PA.
Application information: Application form not required.
Trustees: John C. Harmon, PNC Bank, N.A.
EIN: 232936195

47223
Mortel Family Charitable Foundation
1229 Sand Hill Dr.
Hummelstown, PA 17036
Contact: Rodrigue Mortel, Pres.

Established in 1996 in PA.
Donor(s): Rodrigue Mortel.
Financial data (yr. ended 12/31/01): Grants paid, $43,903; assets, $213,626 (M); gifts received, $133,540; expenditures, $61,280; qualifying distributions, $43,903.
Officers: Rodrigue Mortel, Pres.; Cecilia Mortel, Secy.-Treas.
EIN: 232875876

47224
A. Donald & Mary G. Behler Foundation
c/o A. Donald Behler
333 Columbia Ave.
Palmerton, PA 18071

Established in 1997 in PA.
Financial data (yr. ended 12/31/01): Grants paid, $43,875; assets, $897,377 (M); expenditures, $61,209; qualifying distributions, $47,320.
Limitations: Applications not accepted. Giving primarily in PA.
Application information: Contributes only to pre-selected organizations.
Officers and Directors:* A. Donald Behler,* Pres. and Treas.; Mary G. Behler,* Secy.; Judith Ann Bartholomew, Andrew D. Behler, Donna L. Correll.
EIN: 232903583

47225
Joseph Elias Charitable Trust
Epsilon Dr., RIDC Park
P.O. Box 2812
Pittsburgh, PA 15230

Established in 1987 in PA.
Donor(s): Tap South, Inc., Norman Elias.
Financial data (yr. ended 12/31/01): Grants paid, $43,833; assets, $100,171 (M); gifts received, $104,000; expenditures, $43,914; qualifying distributions, $43,833.
Limitations: Applications not accepted. Giving primarily in AL, FL, NY, and PA.
Application information: Contributes only to pre-selected organizations.
Trustees: Norman Elias, Sylvia M. Elias.
EIN: 256284538

47226
Washington County Community Foundation, Inc.
77 S. Main St.
Washington, PA 15301 (724) 222-6330
FAX: (724) 223-8564; *E-mail:* wccf@cobweb.net; *URL:* http://www.wccf.net
Contact: Betsie Trew, Exec. Dir.

Established in 1993 in PA.
Financial data (yr. ended 12/31/01): Grants paid, $43,760; assets, $1,104,294 (M); gifts received, $488,365; expenditures, $148,834.
Limitations: Giving primarily in Washington County, PA.
Publications: Annual report, informational brochure, financial statement, application guidelines, newsletter.
Application information: Application form required.
Officers: Louis E. Waller, Chair.; Charles Keller, Vice-Chair.; Janet Abernathy, Secy.; R. Carlyn Belczyk, Treas.; Betsie Trew, Exec. Dir.
EIN: 251726013
Codes: CM

47227
The Juliet Ashby Hillman Foundation, Inc.
2000 Grant Bldg.
Pittsburgh, PA 15219 (412) 338-3466
FAX: (412) 338-3463; *E-mail:* foundation@hillmanfo.com
Contact: Ronald W. Wertz, Exec. Dir.

Established in 1994 in PA.
Donor(s): Henry L. Hillman.
Financial data (yr. ended 12/31/01): Grants paid, $43,500; assets, $1,053,412 (M); expenditures, $54,048; qualifying distributions, $46,754.
Limitations: Giving primarily in Portland, OR.
Officers and Directors:* Henry L. Hillman, Jr.,* Pres.; Lawrence M. Wagner,* V.P.; Ronald W. Wertz,* Secy. and Exec. Dir.; Maurice J. White,* Treas.
EIN: 251752989

47228
Marilyn K. Kiefer Foundation
c/o The Scottdale Bank & Trust Co.
150 Pittsburgh St.
Scottdale, PA 15683 (724) 887-8330

Established in 1995.
Donor(s): The Scottdale Bank & Trust Co.
Financial data (yr. ended 12/31/01): Grants paid, $43,500; assets, $912,081 (M); gifts received, $60,000; expenditures, $44,230; qualifying distributions, $43,500.
Limitations: Giving primarily in Fayette and Westmoreland counties, PA.
Officers: Marilyn K. Kiefer, Pres.; Donald F. Kiefer, V.P.; Marilyn Andras, Secy.; Lawrence J. Kiefer, Treas.
EIN: 251759914
Codes: CS, CD

47229
Pottstown Mercury Foundation
c/o Scott Armstrong
24 N. Hanover St.
Pottstown, PA 19464

Established around 1969.
Donor(s): Pottstown Mercury, Peerless Publications, Inc.
Financial data (yr. ended 11/30/00): Grants paid, $43,473; assets, $29,431 (M); gifts received, $58,558; expenditures, $45,637; qualifying distributions, $43,473.
Limitations: Applications not accepted. Giving limited to Pottstown, PA.
Application information: Contributes only to pre-selected organizations.
Director: Dennis Pfeiffer.
EIN: 236256419
Codes: CS, CD, GTI

47230
C. B. Hollingsworth Trust
c/o Southwest National Bank
111 S. Main St.
Greensburg, PA 15601

Financial data (yr. ended 12/31/99): Grants paid, $43,400; assets, $1,251,798 (M); expenditures, $56,466; qualifying distributions, $43,400.
Limitations: Applications not accepted. Giving primarily in Greensburg, PA.
Application information: Contributes only to pre-selected organizations.
Trustee: Southwest National Bank.
EIN: 256021413

47231
Corad Foundation
875 Main St.
Pennsburg, PA 18073-1601

Established in 1986.
Donor(s): Clare Moyer.
Financial data (yr. ended 10/31/01): Grants paid, $43,350; assets, $395,246 (M); gifts received, $12,016; expenditures, $43,754; qualifying distributions, $43,350.
Limitations: Applications not accepted. Giving primarily in PA.
Application information: Contributes only to pre-selected organizations.
Trustee: Marvin Torgan.
EIN: 232443194

47232
Daniel M. & Wilma T. Horner Foundation
c/o Allfirst, Trust Div.
21 E. Market St.
York, PA 17401-1500
Application address: P.O. Box 186, Free Union, VA 28940
Contact: Edith Warner, Tr.

Financial data (yr. ended 12/31/01): Grants paid, $43,000; assets, $824,648 (M); expenditures, $48,057; qualifying distributions, $43,000.
Limitations: Giving primarily in PA and VA.
Trustees: Edith Warner, Allfirst.
EIN: 236242523

47233
Melvin H. & Thelma N. Jenkins Scholarship Fund
c/o M&T Bank
1 S. Centre St.
Pottsville, PA 17901 (570) 628-9270
Contact: Ann L. Rich, Trust Off., M & T Bank

Established in 1991 in PA.
Financial data (yr. ended 12/31/01): Grants paid, $43,000; assets, $936,693 (M); expenditures, $59,121; qualifying distributions, $43,000.
Limitations: Giving primarily to residents of PA.
Application information: Applications available at M&T Bank and Minersville Area High School between Oct. 1 and Feb. 15. Application form required.
Trustees: Thomas J. Nickels, M&T Bank.
EIN: 256373763
Codes: GTI

47234
Laurel Foundation
c/o Glenmede Trust Co.
1650 Market St., Ste. 1200
Philadelphia, PA 19103

Established in 1998 in CN.
Donor(s): Sylvia M. Thompson.
Financial data (yr. ended 12/31/01): Grants paid, $43,000; assets, $823,470 (M); expenditures, $53,663; qualifying distributions, $43,000.
Limitations: Applications not accepted.
Application information: Contributes only to pre-selected organizations.
Officers: Jo Anne T. Manofsky, Pres. and Treas.; Sylvia M. Thompson, V.P. and Secy.
EIN: 562091840

47235
The Sycamore Foundation
1650 Market St., Ste. 1200
Philadelphia, PA 19103

Established in 1998 in NC.
Financial data (yr. ended 06/30/02): Grants paid, $43,000; assets, $784,104 (M); expenditures, $50,495; qualifying distributions, $43,000.
Limitations: Applications not accepted.
Application information: Contributes only to pre-selected organizations.
Officer: Jessie T. Derham, Pres. and Secy.-Treas.
EIN: 562091833

47236
The Cora & Saul Kaufmann Memorial Foundation
1521 Morestein Rd.
Frazer, PA 19355-1967 (610) 251-2270
Contact: Gary R. Gross, Tr.

Financial data (yr. ended 12/31/01): Grants paid, $42,822; assets, $312,630 (M); expenditures, $46,847; qualifying distributions, $42,822.
Trustee: Gary R. Gross.
EIN: 526041716

47237
The Christine and John Connolly Foundation
P. O. Box 219
Gwynedd, PA 19436

Established in 1998 in PA.
Financial data (yr. ended 05/31/01): Grants paid, $42,700; assets, $424,486 (M); expenditures, $43,450; qualifying distributions, $42,700.
Limitations: Giving primarily in Philadelphia, PA.
Trustees: Christine A. Connolly, John L. Connolly.
EIN: 237980525

47238
E. Van Horne Educational Fund
c/o Mellon Bank, N.A.
P.O. Box 185
Pittsburgh, PA 15230-9897
Application address: 3 Mellon Bank Ctr., Rm. 4130, Pittsburgh, PA 15259, tel.: (412) 234-0023
Contact: Laurie Moritz, Trust Off., Mellon Bank, N.A.

Established in 1988 in PA.
Donor(s): Estella Van Horne.‡
Financial data (yr. ended 12/31/00): Grants paid, $42,550; assets, $916,021 (M); expenditures, $55,119; qualifying distributions, $47,057.
Limitations: Giving limited to residents of Crawford County, PA.
Application information: Application form required.
Trustee: Mellon Bank, N.A.
EIN: 256220814
Codes: GTI

47239
Donald J. Rosato Charitable Foundation
c/o Donald J. Rosato
176 E. Conestoga Rd.
Devon, PA 19333

Established in 1993 in PA.
Donor(s): Donald J. Rosato, M.D.
Financial data (yr. ended 12/31/01): Grants paid, $42,440; assets, $786,875 (M); expenditures, $50,904; qualifying distributions, $42,440.
Limitations: Applications not accepted.
Application information: Contributes only to pre-selected organizations.
Trustees: Joseph F. Parella, Jr., Donald J. Rosato, M.D., Judith Rosato, Robert Rosato.
EIN: 232746893

47240
The Ira and Myrna Brind Foundation
1926 Arch St.
Philadelphia, PA 19103-1444
Contact: Ira Brind, Tr.

Established in 1998.
Donor(s): Ira Brind, Myrna Brind.
Financial data (yr. ended 12/31/01): Grants paid, $42,105; assets, $514,987 (M); gifts received, $59,453; expenditures, $46,931; qualifying distributions, $42,105.
Limitations: Giving primarily in Philadelphia, PA.
Trustees: David Brind, Ira Brind, Myrna Brind.
EIN: 237978519

47241
ADCO Foundation
c/o American Atlantic Co.
900 E. 8th Ave., Ste. 300
King of Prussia, PA 19406
Contact: Christopher H. Browne, Tr.

Donor(s): American Dredging Co.
Financial data (yr. ended 12/31/01): Grants paid, $42,000; assets, $824,612 (M); expenditures, $51,237; qualifying distributions, $41,365.
Limitations: Giving primarily in NY.
Trustees: Bruce A. Beal, Christopher H. Browne, James M. Clark, Jr.
EIN: 236278135
Codes: CS, CD

47242
The Real Light Foundation
225 Jamestown St.
Philadelphia, PA 19128

Established in 1994 in PA.
Financial data (yr. ended 12/31/01): Grants paid, $42,000; assets, $583,920 (M); expenditures, $43,724; qualifying distributions, $42,000.
Limitations: Applications not accepted. Giving primarily in Philadelphia, PA.
Application information: Contributes only to pre-selected organizations.
Officers: Freeman Zausner, Pres.; James Pyne, V.P.
EIN: 232796251

47243
The Zeelander Foundation
230 Mathers Rd.
Ambler, PA 19002 (215) 643-7197
Contact: Norbert J. Zeelander, V.P.

Established in 1996 in PA.
Donor(s): Norbert J. Zeelander, Susan Zeelander.
Financial data (yr. ended 12/31/01): Grants paid, $41,596; assets, $495,112 (M); expenditures, $53,646; qualifying distributions, $41,596.
Limitations: Giving primarily in PA.
Officers: Susan Zeelander, Pres.; Elliot Zeelander, V.P.; Jeffrey Zeelander, V.P.; Julie Zeelander, V.P.; Norbert J. Zeelander, V.P.
EIN: 232866230

47244
Joseph N. Gorson Foundation
8045 W. Chester Pike
Upper Darby, PA 19082-1317 (610) 853-4800
Contact: Murray S. Gorson, Tr.

Established in 1953.
Financial data (yr. ended 11/30/01): Grants paid, $41,576; assets, $465,563 (M); expenditures, $44,138; qualifying distributions, $41,576.
Limitations: Giving primarily in Philadelphia, PA.
Trustees: Janice W. Gorson, Murray S. Gorson, S. Marshall Gorson.
EIN: 236297463

47245
Tzedakah Foundation
5851 Phillips Ave.
Pittsburgh, PA 15217-2119

Established in 1994 in PA.
Donor(s): Philip J. Samson.
Financial data (yr. ended 12/31/01): Grants paid, $41,565; assets, $559,139 (M); expenditures, $46,899; qualifying distributions, $41,565.
Limitations: Giving primarily in PA.
Trustees: Iris M. Samson, Philip J. Samson.
EIN: 251752556

47246
Swartzlander Charitable Trust
c/o PNC Bank, N.A.
1600 Market St.
Philadelphia, PA 19103

Established in 1986 in PA.
Financial data (yr. ended 12/31/01): Grants paid, $41,381; assets, $1,176,649 (M); expenditures, $51,438; qualifying distributions, $41,381.
Limitations: Applications not accepted. Giving primarily in Doylestown, PA.
Application information: Contributes only to pre-selected organizations.
Trustee: PNC Bank, N.A.
EIN: 232476944

47247
The Alchon Family Foundation
c/o Guy Alchon
7 Hoops Dr.
Landenberg, PA 19350

Established in 1990 in IL.
Donor(s): Bernard F. Alchon.
Financial data (yr. ended 12/31/99): Grants paid, $41,000; assets, $478,112 (M); expenditures, $56,243; qualifying distributions, $41,000.
Limitations: Applications not accepted. Giving primarily in New Orleans, LA.
Application information: Contributes only to pre-selected organizations.
Directors: Bernard Alchon, Mimi Altman, Pam McGinty.
EIN: 363677300

47248
Bethel Park Community Foundation, Inc.
5311 Brightwood Rd.
Bethel Park, PA 15102 (412) 261-3644

Established in 1995.
Financial data (yr. ended 12/31/00): Grants paid, $40,950; assets, $63,563 (M); gifts received, $17,859; expenditures, $46,510.
Limitations: Giving limited to the Bethel Park, PA, area.

47248—PENNSYLVANIA

Officers: Susan J. Hughes, Pres.; James D. Kling, V.P.; Henry J. Szymanski, Secy.; David H. Ross, Treas.
Trustees: David A. Allison, David Amaditz, Diane Doyle, Ronald J. Fees, Robert Fragasso, Fred Green, Jane S. Lupia, Charles Manion, Samuel Moore, David L. Peet, Richard Rose, Lisa P. Sbei, Timothy G. Shack, C. Dean Streator, Richard W. Talarico.
EIN: 251749936
Codes: CM

47249
The Gilbert Foundation
135 S. 19th St., Ste. 503
Philadelphia, PA 19103-4912

Financial data (yr. ended 12/31/01): Grants paid, $40,815; assets, $579,807 (M); expenditures, $41,031; qualifying distributions, $40,815.
Limitations: Giving primarily in PA.
Trustees: Alfred A. Gilbert, Louise Gilbert.
EIN: 232155419

47250
Paul A. Troutman Foundation
c/o Community Banks, N.A.
P.O. Box 350
Millersburg, PA 17061
Application address: 150 Market St., Millersburg, PA 17061, tel.: (717) 692-4781
Contact: Shirley Helwig, Trust Off., Community Banks, N.A.

Financial data (yr. ended 11/30/00): Grants paid, $40,800; assets, $884,138 (M); expenditures, $50,230; qualifying distributions, $44,190.
Limitations: Giving primarily in Millersburg, PA.
Application information: Application form not required.
Trustees: John A. Hayes, Community Bank.
EIN: 232086508

47251
Fern & Gladys Moyer Memorial Trust
c/o SunBank
P.O. Box 57
Selinsgrove, PA 17870-0057
Application address: 43 S. 5th St., Sunbury, PA 17801-2896, tel.: (570) 286-1582

Established in 1992 in PA.
Donor(s): Gladys M. Moyer.
Financial data (yr. ended 12/31/01): Grants paid, $40,765; assets, $1,137,561 (M); expenditures, $57,514; qualifying distributions, $49,943.
Limitations: Giving primarily in Snyder and Northumberland counties, PA.
Application information: Application form required.
Committee Members: Jeffrey Apfelbaum, Sidney Apfelbaum, Jill Fecker, Margaret Keller, Mary Jane Mitterling.
Trustee: SunBank.
EIN: 232689605

47252
The Edwin T. and Cynthia S. Johnson Foundation
c/o Edwin T. Johnson
Spring Lane Farm, 3 Jefferson Ct.
Newtown, PA 18940-2000

Established in 1986 in PA.
Donor(s): Edwin T. Johnson, Cynthia S. Johnson.
Financial data (yr. ended 04/30/02): Grants paid, $40,512; assets, $766,347 (M); expenditures, $47,100; qualifying distributions, $40,512.
Limitations: Applications not accepted. Giving primarily in PA.
Application information: Contributes only to pre-selected organizations.

Trustees: Cynthia S. Johnson, E. Thomas Johnson, Jr., Edwin T. Johnson, Rebecca J. Johnson.
EIN: 222777060

47253
Helen W. Coleman Residuary Trust Foundation
c/o Pitcairn Trust Co.
165 Township Line Rd., Ste. 3000
Jenkintown, PA 19046 (215) 881-6147
Contact: Paul Irwin

Donor(s): Helen W. Coleman.‡
Financial data (yr. ended 12/31/01): Grants paid, $40,500; assets, $1,054,787 (M); expenditures, $43,198; qualifying distributions, $40,750.
Limitations: Giving primarily in PA.
Application information: Application form not required.
Trustees: Agnes Coleman, John M. Coleman, William S. Coleman, Parke H. Hess, Pitcairn Trust Co.
EIN: 236439502

47254
Eberhard L. Faber Foundation
918 Mellon Bank Ctr.
Wilkes-Barre, PA 18701

Financial data (yr. ended 12/31/01): Grants paid, $40,400; assets, $695,438 (M); expenditures, $45,579; qualifying distributions, $40,773.
Limitations: Applications not accepted. Giving primarily in PA.
Application information: Contributes only to pre-selected organizations.
Trustees: Eberhard Faber, Mary Louise Faber, John M. Randolph, Jr.
EIN: 236292125

47255
The Rotenberger Foundation
240 S. 9th St.
Quakertown, PA 18951

Established in 1987 in PA.
Financial data (yr. ended 12/31/01): Grants paid, $40,400; assets, $200,656 (M); expenditures, $46,790; qualifying distributions, $40,022.
Limitations: Applications not accepted. Giving on a national basis, with emphasis on PA.
Application information: Contributes only to pre-selected organizations.
Trustees: Kathy Pickering, Donna Roberts, Nancy Zintak.
EIN: 222846655

47256
Wayne County Community Foundation
c/o W. B. McAllister
214 9th St., Ste. 201
Honesdale, PA 18431 (570) 253-5005
Contact: Warren Schloesser, Pres.

Financial data (yr. ended 06/30/01): Grants paid, $40,318; assets, $1,105,542 (M); gifts received, $69,924; expenditures, $70,248.
Limitations: Giving primarily in Wayne County, PA.
Officers: Warren Schloesser, Pres.; Vicki Lamberton, 1st V.P.; Greg Davis, 2nd V.P.; Rev. William Samford, Secy.; William B. McAllister, Treas.
Directors: Terry Blaum, Robert Chavey, Greg A. Davis, Ruth Frederick, Frances Gruber, Kuni Holbert, Robert Kramer, Tom LaTournas, Paul Meagher, Pat Mohn, P.R. Monaghan, Joseph Murray, Justin O'Donnell, Dan O'Neill, John Weidner, Bill Young, Bob Zabady, and 4 additional directors.
EIN: 232656896
Codes: CM

47257
John and Jacqueline Swartz Foundation
2201 Pennsylvania Ave., Ste. 801
Philadelphia, PA 19130-3524
Contact: Jacqueline Swartz, Tr.

Established in 1986.
Donor(s): John Swartz.
Financial data (yr. ended 12/31/00): Grants paid, $40,287; assets, $1 (M); expenditures, $41,346; qualifying distributions, $41,346.
Limitations: Giving primarily in Philadelphia, PA.
Application information: Application form not required.
Trustees: Edward M. Glickman, Jacqueline Swartz.
EIN: 236500270

47258
Christian Heritage Foundation
300 E. Rock Rd.
Allentown, PA 18103-7519

Donor(s): Richard C. Dean.
Financial data (yr. ended 12/31/00): Grants paid, $40,190; assets, $2,220,568 (M); expenditures, $45,957; qualifying distributions, $40,190.
Limitations: Applications not accepted. Giving primarily in VA.
Application information: Contributes only to pre-selected organizations.
Officers: Wendy D. Shubert, Pres.; Michael A. Kulp, Secy.-Treas.
EIN: 232973157

47259
The Frieder Foundation
Box 352 RD1
Dalton, PA 18414

Established in 2000 in PA.
Donor(s): Leonard P. Frieder.
Financial data (yr. ended 12/31/01): Grants paid, $40,103; assets, $311,789 (M); gifts received, $192,232; expenditures, $41,428; qualifying distributions, $40,103.
Limitations: Applications not accepted. Giving primarily in PA.
Application information: Contributes only to pre-selected organizations.
Trustee: Leonard P. Frieder.
EIN: 256651216

47260
Northeast Harbor Library Trust
1500 E. Lancaster Ave., Ste. 202
Paoli, PA 19301

Financial data (yr. ended 12/31/01): Grants paid, $40,088; assets, $743,058 (M); expenditures, $43,332; qualifying distributions, $40,088.
Limitations: Applications not accepted. Giving primarily in Radnor, PA.
Application information: Contributes only to pre-selected organizations.
Trustees: William Verplank Newlin, Lucy B. Newlin Sellers.
EIN: 236409729

47261
Harry and Esther Brown Charitable Foundation
820 Homestead Rd.
Jenkintown, PA 19046 (215) 887-5300
Contact: Pual Feldman, Tr.

Established in 2001 in PA.
Donor(s): Esther Brown.‡
Financial data (yr. ended 12/31/01): Grants paid, $40,000; assets, $810,446 (M); gifts received, $847,793; expenditures, $40,000; qualifying distributions, $40,000.
Trustees: Paul Feldman, Stephen Feldman.

EIN: 256724854

47262
Aubrey L. Hanford Memorial Fund
825 Norman Dr.
Lebanon, PA 17042
Application address: 1601 Elm St., Lebanon, PA 17042
Contact: A.L. Hanford, Jr., Dir.

Established in 1965.
Donor(s): A.L. Hanford, Jr., A.L. Hanford III, and members of the Hanford family.
Financial data (yr. ended 05/31/02): Grants paid, $40,000; assets, $854,189 (M); expenditures, $54,589; qualifying distributions, $40,000.
Limitations: Giving primarily in Lebanon County, PA.
Application information: Application form not required.
Directors: A.L. Hanford, Jr., A.L. Hanford III.
EIN: 237041851

47263
Kurz Foundation
P.O. Box 1134
Bala Cynwyd, PA 19004-5134 (610) 617-6834
Contact: A.B. Kurz, Pres.

Financial data (yr. ended 12/31/01): Grants paid, $40,000; assets, $367,538 (M); gifts received, $22,540; expenditures, $44,305; qualifying distributions, $40,000.
Application information: Application form not required.
Officers: A.B. Kurz, Pres.; P.W.J. Fisher, V.P.; C. Kurz II, Secy.; J.F. Fricko, Treas.
EIN: 236235374

47264
The Medal of Honor Foundation
c/o Nancy Barnhart
1500 Ardmore Blvd., Ste. 407
Pittsburgh, PA 15221

Established in 1999 in PA.
Donor(s): John G. Rangos Charitable Foundation.
Financial data (yr. ended 12/31/00): Grants paid, $40,000; assets, $133,240 (M); gifts received, $6,500; expenditures, $40,030; qualifying distributions, $40,000.
Officers: John G. Rangos, Jr., Pres.; Ronald E. Ray, V.P.; Peter Clyde Papadakos, Secy.
EIN: 251828488

47265
Raymond-Cryder Foundation
101 S. 3rd. St.
P.O. Box 483
Easton, PA 18044-0483 (610) 253-9111
Contact: Thomas P. Stitt, Sr., Tr.

Established in 1993 in PA.
Donor(s): John D. Raymond.
Financial data (yr. ended 12/31/01): Grants paid, $40,000; assets, $722,199 (M); expenditures, $54,960; qualifying distributions, $40,000.
Application information: Application form required.
Trustees: John D. Raymond, Melinda M. Stitt, Thomas P. Stitt, Sr.
EIN: 232663528

47266
Lloyd J. Schumacker Fund
825 Duportail Rd., Ste. 103
Wayne, PA 19087

Donor(s): Lloyd J. Schumacker.
Financial data (yr. ended 12/31/01): Grants paid, $40,000; assets, $924,421 (M); expenditures, $48,354; qualifying distributions, $40,000.

Limitations: Applications not accepted. Giving primarily in Key Largo, FL.
Application information: Contributes only to pre-selected organizations.
Trustees: Betsy Schumacker, Scott F. Schumacker.
EIN: 236251929

47267
Robert M. Thompson, Jr. Foundation
204 Hawthorne St.
Pittsburgh, PA 15218
FAX: (412) 371-2631
Contact: Robert M. Thompson, Jr., Tr.

Established in 1985 in PA.
Donor(s): Robert M. Thompson, Jr.
Financial data (yr. ended 06/30/00): Grants paid, $40,000; assets, $574,976 (M); expenditures, $40,854; qualifying distributions, $39,767.
Limitations: Giving primarily in southwestern PA.
Trustee: Robert M. Thompson, Jr.
EIN: 251518805

47268
Graham Sefton Baskin & Anna Mae Sweeney Baskin Foundation
131 Cambridge St.
Indiana, PA 15701
Contact: Edward E. Mackey, Tr.

Established in 1996 in PA.
Donor(s): Anna Mae Sweeny Baskin.‡
Financial data (yr. ended 12/31/01): Grants paid, $39,914; assets, $1,080,595 (M); expenditures, $55,023; qualifying distributions, $46,088.
Limitations: Giving primarily in Indiana County, PA.
Application information: Application form required.
Trustees: Loren C. Alico, Cecelia A. Mackey, Edward E. Mackey.
EIN: 251777790
Codes: GTI

47269
Paul & Wendy Rosen Charitable Foundation
1830 Rittenhouse Sq., Ste. 7C
Philadelphia, PA 19103

Established in 1999.
Donor(s): Paul Rosen, Wendy Rosen.
Financial data (yr. ended 12/31/00): Grants paid, $39,766; assets, $389,674 (M); gifts received, $312,942; expenditures, $40,401; qualifying distributions, $39,766.
Limitations: Applications not accepted.
Application information: Contributes only to pre-selected organizations.
Directors: Paul Rosen, Wendy Rosen.
EIN: 233008895

47270
Alan D. & Marsha W. Bramowitz Charitable Trust
5430 Forbes Ave.
Pittsburgh, PA 15217-1106

Donor(s): Alan D. Bramowitz, Marsha W. Bramowitz.
Financial data (yr. ended 12/31/01): Grants paid, $39,678; assets, $374,468 (M); expenditures, $45,561; qualifying distributions, $39,678.
Limitations: Applications not accepted. Giving primarily in MA, NC, and PA.
Application information: Contributes only to pre-selected organizations.
Trustees: Alan D. Bramowitz, Emily A. Bramowitz, Marsha W. Bramowitz, David H. Ehrenworth, L. Stephen Kline.
EIN: 256232163

47271
First Savings Community Foundation
1211 N. 5th St.
P.O. Box 176
Perkasie, PA 18944 (215) 257-5035

Established in 1998.
Donor(s): First Savings Bank of Perkasie.
Financial data (yr. ended 12/31/01): Grants paid, $39,675; assets, $1,352,580 (M); gifts received, $650,000; expenditures, $41,205; qualifying distributions, $39,814.
Limitations: Applications not accepted. Giving limited to Bucks, Bethlehem, Lehigh, and Montgomery counties, PA.
Application information: Contributes only to pre-selected organizations.
Directors: Claude H. Buerhle, Walter Cressman, Edward Gana, Jr., Robert Heacock, John D. Hollenbach, Jefrey Naugle, Bernard Suess, Vernon Wehrung.
EIN: 232984663
Codes: CS

47272
Sylvia M. Harley Nursing Scholarship Fund
c/o Main Street Bank
P.O. Box 1100
Pottsville, PA 17901-7100
Application address: c/o Main Street Bank, 120 S. Centre St., Pottsville, PA 17901, tel.: (570) 628-6640

Financial data (yr. ended 12/31/01): Grants paid, $39,650; assets, $815,742 (M); expenditures, $47,710; qualifying distributions, $39,210.
Limitations: Giving limited to residents of PA.
Application information: Application form required.
Trustee: Main Street Bank.
EIN: 232402538
Codes: GTI

47273
Margaret J. Biddle Charitable Trust
c/o PNC Advisors
620 Liberty Ave.
Pittsburgh, PA 15222-2705 (412) 762-7645
Contact: Susan Blake, Trust Off., PNC Advisors

Financial data (yr. ended 09/30/01): Grants paid, $39,542; assets, $223,131 (M); expenditures, $42,408; qualifying distributions, $39,554.
Limitations: Giving primarily in Pittsburgh, PA.
Trustee: PNC Bank, N.A.
EIN: 256021765

47274
Bethany Foundation
c/o Harold S. Evans
5220 5th Ave., Apt. 3G
Pittsburgh, PA 15232-2123

Established in 1993 in PA.
Donor(s): Harold S. Evans.
Financial data (yr. ended 12/31/01): Grants paid, $39,500; assets, $1,573,062 (M); expenditures, $108,397; qualifying distributions, $39,500.
Limitations: Applications not accepted. Giving primarily in Pittsburgh, PA.
Application information: Contributes only to pre-selected organizations.
Officers and Directors:* Harold S. Evans,* Pres.; Elizabeth W. Evans,* V.P. and Secy.
Trustee: Rev. Drew Morgan.
EIN: 251718608

47275
Northwest Bancorp, Inc. Charitable Foundation
c/o Northwest Bancorp, Inc.
Liberty at 2nd Ave.
Warren, PA 16365 (814) 726-2140
Contact: Vicki Stec, Secy.

Established in 1998 in PA.
Donor(s): Corry Savings Bank, Northwest Bancorp, MHC.
Financial data (yr. ended 06/30/02): Grants paid, $39,425; assets, $1,072,639 (M); gifts received, $250,000; expenditures, $48,668; qualifying distributions, $39,425.
Limitations: Giving primarily in PA.
Application information: Application form required.
Officers: John O. Hanna, Pres.; William J. Wagner, V.P.; Vicki Stec, Secy.; Gregory C. LaRocca, Treas.
EIN: 251819537
Codes: CS, CD

47276
J. A. Van Wynen, Jr. & W. F. Van Wynen Trust A
(also known as The John A. & Winnifred F. Van Wynen Scholarship Fund)
c/o PNC Advisors
1600 Market St.
Philadelphia, PA 19103-7240

Established in 1990 in NJ.
Donor(s): Winnifred F. Van Wynen.‡
Financial data (yr. ended 12/31/01): Grants paid, $39,399; assets, $1,102,986 (M); expenditures, $59,104; qualifying distributions, $39,399.
Limitations: Giving primarily in NJ and NY.
Trustees: Gloria E. Grieco, PNC Bank, N.A.
EIN: 226502704
Codes: GTI

47277
Grace M. Navarra Trust
c/o First Union National Bank
123 S. Broad St., PA1308
Philadelphia, PA 19109

Established in 1995 in FL.
Financial data (yr. ended 12/31/00): Grants paid, $39,321; assets, $725,409 (M); expenditures, $51,853; qualifying distributions, $39,321.
Limitations: Applications not accepted. Giving primarily in Palm Beach, FL.
Application information: Contributes only to pre-selected organizations.
Trustee: First Union National Bank.
EIN: 596976079

47278
Alvin Kacin Family Foundation
1011 Poke Run Church Rd.
Apollo, PA 15613-9625 (724) 733-7717
Contact: Alvin R. Kacin, Tr.

Donor(s): Alvin C. Kacin.
Financial data (yr. ended 12/31/01): Grants paid, $39,250; assets, $105,805 (M); gifts received, $20,000; expenditures, $39,848; qualifying distributions, $39,250.
Limitations: Giving primarily in Plum Borough, PA.
Application information: Application form not required.
Trustees: Alvin C. Kacin, Charmaine Kacin, Timothy Kacin, Todd Kacin.
EIN: 251472340

47279
Allen Family Foundation
c/o First Union National Bank
Broad & Walnut Sts., Ste. PA1308
Philadelphia, PA 19109

Established in 1997 in FL.
Donor(s): Richard E. Allen.
Financial data (yr. ended 12/31/99): Grants paid, $39,200; assets, $985,269 (M); expenditures, $50,945; qualifying distributions, $39,200.
Limitations: Applications not accepted. Giving primarily in Kenton, OH.
Application information: Contributes only to pre-selected organizations.
Officer: Richard E. Allen, Pres.
Directors: Karen Allen, Rex Allen, Richard S. Allen.
Trustee: First Union National Bank.
EIN: 650783002

47280
Catherine V. & Martin Hofmann Foundation
3145 Shillington Rd.
Sinking Spring, PA 19608-1606

Established in 1968 in PA.
Donor(s): Catherine V. Hofmann, Martin W. Hofmann.‡
Financial data (yr. ended 12/31/01): Grants paid, $39,181; assets, $747,667 (M); expenditures, $41,792; qualifying distributions, $39,181.
Limitations: Applications not accepted. Giving primarily in Berks County, PA.
Application information: Contributes only to pre-selected organizations.
Trustee: Bernard Hofmann.
EIN: 236447843

47281
Martin Guitar Charitable Foundation
c/o C. F. Martin & Co., Inc.
510 Sycamore St.
Nazareth, PA 18064

Established in 1996 in PA.
Donor(s): C.F. Martin & Co., Inc., C.F. Martin Guitar Co.
Financial data (yr. ended 12/31/01): Grants paid, $39,000; assets, $1,029,587 (M); gifts received, $200,000; expenditures, $47,997; qualifying distributions, $41,085.
Limitations: Giving primarily in PA.
Officers: Christian F. Martin IV, Pres.; Diane S. Repyneck, V.P.; Sylvia Fehnel, Secy.
EIN: 311483218
Codes: CS, CD

47282
Premo J. Pappafava Foundation
Greensburg-Hempfield Industrial Park
P.O. Box C
Greensburg, PA 15601

Established in 1986 in PA.
Donor(s): Premo J. Pappafava.
Financial data (yr. ended 12/31/01): Grants paid, $39,000; assets, $137,764 (M); expenditures, $39,942; qualifying distributions, $39,000.
Limitations: Applications not accepted. Giving limited to PA.
Application information: Contributes only to pre-selected organizations.
Trustee: Premo J. Pappafava.
EIN: 256277032

47283
Philadelphia Stock Exchange Foundation
c/o Philadelphia Stock Exchange
1900 Market St.
Philadelphia, PA 19103-3527
Contact: Meyer S. Frucher, Chair.

Established in 1982 in PA.
Donor(s): Philadelphia Stock Exchange.
Financial data (yr. ended 12/31/01): Grants paid, $39,000; assets, $1,165,880 (M); expenditures, $42,662; qualifying distributions, $39,061.
Limitations: Applications not accepted. Giving primarily in Philadelphia, PA.
Application information: Contributes only to pre-selected organizations.
Officers: Meyer S. Frucher,* Chair.; John F. Wallace, Vice-Chair.
Trustees: Michael J. Curcio, Lawrence N. Gage, Kevin J. Kennedy, Eleanor W. Myers, Christopher Nagy, Constantie Papadakis, Ph.D., Thomas W. Wynn.
EIN: 222437173
Codes: CS, CD

47284
Carl S. and Wanda M. Weyandt Foundation
c/o Hill, Barth & King, LLC
9500 Brooktree Rd., Ste. 300
Wexford, PA 15090
Application address: c/o Ted Tishman, Leech & Tishman, 2 Chatham Ctr., Ste. 220, Pittsburgh, PA 15219

Established in 1991 in PA.
Donor(s): Wanda M. Weyandt.‡
Financial data (yr. ended 12/31/01): Grants paid, $38,880; assets, $756,932 (M); gifts received, $35,030; expenditures, $41,885; qualifying distributions, $38,880.
Limitations: Giving primarily in Indiana, PA.
Trustees: John T. Edelman, John J. Weyandt, Kathleen Weyandt.
EIN: 251668618

47285
The Saul and Bernardine Kaplan Foundation
101 Rhonda Dr.
Scranton, PA 18505

Established in 2000 in PA.
Donor(s): Saul Kaplan, Bernardine Kaplan.
Financial data (yr. ended 09/30/01): Grants paid, $38,812; assets, $167,023 (M); expenditures, $40,042; qualifying distributions, $38,812.
Limitations: Applications not accepted. Giving primarily in Scranton, PA.
Application information: Contributes only to pre-selected organizations.
Officers: Saul Kaplan, Pres.; Bernardine Kaplan, V.P.
EIN: 232831053

47286
Marks Foundation
c/o James E. Marks
P.O. Box 589, 101 Mill Creek Rd.
Ardmore, PA 19003

Established in 2000 in PA.
Donor(s): James E. Marks, Peggy J. Marks.
Financial data (yr. ended 12/31/01): Grants paid, $38,627; assets, $108,087 (M); expenditures, $40,394; qualifying distributions, $38,627.
Limitations: Applications not accepted. Giving primarily in NY.
Application information: Contributes only to pre-selected organizations.
Trustee: James E. Marks.
EIN: 256632487

47287
The Lassin Philanthropic Foundation
c/o Gary D. Lassin
425 Stump Rd.
Montgomeryville, PA 18936

Established in 1996 in PA.
Donor(s): Gary D. Lassin.
Financial data (yr. ended 11/30/01): Grants paid, $38,450; assets, $843,260 (M); gifts received, $268,495; expenditures, $39,750; qualifying distributions, $38,450.
Limitations: Applications not accepted.
Application information: Contributes only to pre-selected organizations.
Trustees: Gary D. Lassin, Robin Lassin.
EIN: 237862354

47288
John L. and Jeanette Witmer Trust
c/o PNC Advisors
1600 Market St.
Philadelphia, PA 19103-7240

Established in 1995 in PA.
Financial data (yr. ended 09/30/01): Grants paid, $38,406; assets, $833,707 (M); expenditures, $45,445; qualifying distributions, $39,296.
Limitations: Applications not accepted. Giving primarily in PA.
Application information: Contributes only to pre-selected organizations.
Trustee: PNC Bank, N.A.
EIN: 256515276

47289
R. W. & Shirley Rissinger Foundation
900 Manor Dr.
Millersburg, PA 17061 (717) 692-4758
Contact: R.W. Rissinger, Pres.

Established in 1998 in PA.
Donor(s): R.W. Rissinger.
Financial data (yr. ended 07/31/02): Grants paid, $38,391; assets, $119,200 (M); gifts received, $15,429; expenditures, $39,101; qualifying distributions, $38,391.
Limitations: Giving primarily in Millersburg, PA.
Application information: Application form not required.
Officers: R.W. Rissinger, Pres.; Dawn Shrawder, V.P.; Shirley Rissinger, Secy.-Treas.
EIN: 232937516

47290
Samuel H. Newsome Trust
c/o First Union National Bank
P.O. Box 7558
Philadelphia, PA 19101-7558

Financial data (yr. ended 05/31/00): Grants paid, $38,388; assets, $963,482 (M); expenditures, $48,523; qualifying distributions, $37,234.
Trustee: First Union National Bank.
EIN: 236709483

47291
SPS Foundation
c/o SPS Technologies, Inc.
165 Township Line Rd., Ste. 200
Jenkintown, PA 19046-3597
Contact: William Scher, Tr.

Trust established in 1953 in PA.
Donor(s): SPS Technologies, Inc.
Financial data (yr. ended 12/31/01): Grants paid, $38,307; assets, $36,229 (M); expenditures, $38,502; qualifying distributions, $38,307.
Limitations: Giving on a national basis.
Application information: Application form not required.

Trustee: William Scher.
EIN: 236294553
Codes: CS, CD

47292
Stephen I. Richman & Audrey G. Richman Foundation
206 Washington Trust Bldg.
Washington, PA 15301

Established in 1994 in PA.
Donor(s): Ben & Bessie Richman Foundation.
Financial data (yr. ended 05/31/01): Grants paid, $38,250; assets, $504,141 (M); gifts received, $16,677; expenditures, $39,537; qualifying distributions, $38,250.
Limitations: Applications not accepted. Giving primarily in PA.
Application information: Contributes only to pre-selected organizations.
Trustees: Audrey G. Richman, Stephen I. Richman.
EIN: 251738946

47293
Benevolent Association of Pottsville
1632 Lightfoot Dr.
Auburn, PA 17922
Contact: Marian A. Yanaitis

Financial data (yr. ended 12/31/01): Grants paid, $38,214; assets, $788,389 (M); gifts received, $12,415; expenditures, $52,485; qualifying distributions, $38,214.
Limitations: Giving limited to Schuylkill County, PA.
Application information: Application form required.
Officers: William C. Schuettler, Pres.; Frances Weiss, V.P.; Robert Yanaitis, Treas.
EIN: 236279703

47294
Nicholas G. Nicholas Foundation
(Formerly Nicholas G. & Annette M. Nicholas Foundation)
127 Timber Ct.
127 Anderson St., Ste. 127
Pittsburgh, PA 15212-5801
Application address: 23 Market Pl., Pittsburgh, PA 15222, tel.: (412) 471-2208
Contact: Nicholas G. Nicholas, Pres.

Established in 1990 in PA.
Donor(s): Nicholas G. Nicholas, Annette M. Nicholas.
Financial data (yr. ended 12/31/00): Grants paid, $38,200; assets, $365,026 (M); gifts received, $1,140; expenditures, $38,512; qualifying distributions, $37,971.
Limitations: Giving primarily in PA.
Application information: Application form required.
Officers and Directors:* Nicholas G. Nicholas,* Pres.; Robert G. Panagulias,* V.P. and Secy.
EIN: 251646744

47295
Donald W. Bumgarner Foundation
c/o First Union National Bank
Broad & Walnut Sts.
Philadelphia, PA 19109-1199

Established in 1995 in NC.
Financial data (yr. ended 12/31/99): Grants paid, $38,165; assets, $1,259,796 (M); expenditures, $51,860; qualifying distributions, $38,253.
Limitations: Applications not accepted.
Application information: Contributes only to pre-selected organizations.
Trustee: First Union National Bank.
EIN: 566446949

47296
Conarro Family Foundation
105 East St.
Warren, PA 16365

Established in 1998 in PA.
Donor(s): Harry W. Conarro.
Financial data (yr. ended 12/31/01): Grants paid, $38,100; assets, $687,432 (M); gifts received, $180,000; expenditures, $38,624; qualifying distributions, $38,100.
Trustee: Harry W. Conarro.
EIN: 256612120

47297
Robert A. dePalma Family Charitable Foundation
(Formerly Robert A. and MaryAnn A. dePalma Charitable Foundation)
70 Woodland Dr.
Pittsburgh, PA 15228-1758
Contact: MaryAnn dePalma Burnett, Tr.

Established in 1986 in PA.
Donor(s): MaryAnn dePalma Burnett, Robert A. dePalma.‡
Financial data (yr. ended 12/31/01): Grants paid, $38,100; assets, $239,238 (M); expenditures, $42,892; qualifying distributions, $38,100.
Limitations: Giving primarily in Pittsburgh, PA.
Trustees: MaryAnn dePalma Burnett, Robert M. dePalma, Diane D. Lange.
EIN: 251546487

47298
The Bernard G. Segal Foundation
1600 Market St., Ste. 3600
Philadelphia, PA 19103

Established in 1955.
Donor(s): Geraldine R. Segal.
Financial data (yr. ended 06/30/02): Grants paid, $38,000; assets, $940,081 (M); gifts received, $99,946; expenditures, $50,047; qualifying distributions, $38,000.
Limitations: Applications not accepted. Giving primarily in CA, NJ, and PA.
Application information: Contributes only to pre-selected organizations.
Trustees: Marc Cohen, Thomas P. Glassmoyer, Bruce A. Rosenfield, Geraldine R. Segal.
EIN: 236232487

47299
Joseph J. Anselmo, Sr. Charitable Trust
c/o Northumberland National Bank
245 Front St.
Northumberland, PA 17857 (570) 473-3531
Contact: Stephen A. Hafer, Trust Off., Northumberland National Bank

Established in 1998 in PA.
Financial data (yr. ended 12/31/01): Grants paid, $37,891; assets, $734,847 (M); expenditures, $41,426; qualifying distributions, $37,891.
Limitations: Giving primarily in Northumberland and Point Township, PA.
Trustee: Northumberland National Bank.
EIN: 237898558

47300
Society of the Friendly Sons of St. Patrick for the Relief of Emigrants from Ireland
P.O. Box 969
Dublin, PA 18917-0969
Contact: Thomas J. Lynch, Dir.

Established around 1954.
Financial data (yr. ended 06/30/01): Grants paid, $37,703; assets, $796,020 (M); expenditures, $89,206; qualifying distributions, $37,703.

47300—PENNSYLVANIA

Limitations: Giving on an international and national basis primarily in the Delaware Valley and the metropolitan Philadelphia, PA area; some giving also in Ireland.
Application information: Application form required.
Officers: Thomas P. O'Malley, Pres.; J. Thomas Showler, V.P.; Timothy P. Dunigan, Jr., Secy.; Thomas O. Peterman, Treas.
Directors: Thomas J. Coyne, Jr., John F. Donovan, George J. Flannery, Jr., John E. Kane, John F. Kull, Jr., Edward P. Last, Thomas J. Lynch.
EIN: 231445675

47301
Evelev Family Foundation
18 Bridge 4 Ln.
Pipersville, PA 18947 (215) 563-2889
Contact: Leonard Evelev, Dir.

Established in 1999 in PA.
Donor(s): Leonard Evelev, Helen Evelev.
Financial data (yr. ended 12/31/01): Grants paid, $37,671; assets, $226,694 (M); gifts received, $129,897; expenditures, $39,083; qualifying distributions, $37,671.
Directors: Helen Evelev, Leonard Evelev.
EIN: 256678456

47302
Jerrehian Foundation
257 E. Lancaster Ave.
Wynnewood, PA 19096-1932 (610) 896-8802
Contact: Aram K. Jerrehian, Tr.

Financial data (yr. ended 12/31/01): Grants paid, $37,605; assets, $989,625 (M); expenditures, $43,513; qualifying distributions, $37,605.
Limitations: Giving primarily in PA.
Application information: Application form not required.
Trustee: Aram K. Jerrehian.
EIN: 236261005

47303
The Aspire Foundation
1 Oxford Ctr., Ste. 3300
Pittsburgh, PA 15219
Contact: David, Borroni

Established in 1995.
Donor(s): Equitable Resources, Inc., Energy Technology Corp.
Financial data (yr. ended 12/31/01): Grants paid, $37,500; assets, $198,352 (M); expenditures, $43,827; qualifying distributions, $43,136.
Limitations: Giving limited to residents of PA.
Application information: Application form required.
Officers and Directors:* Judy Coughlin, Pres.; Jennifer Eckles,* Secy.; Carol B. Gras, Treas.; Clifford W. Baker, Babatunde O. Fapohunda, Harley Hudson.
EIN: 251759917
Codes: GTI

47304
Arthur Judson Foundation, Inc.
111 N. 6th St.
P.O. Box 679
Reading, PA 19603-0679 (610) 478-2080
Contact: J. William Widing III, Secy.

Established in 1972 in NY.
Donor(s): Arthur Judson.‡
Financial data (yr. ended 05/31/02): Grants paid, $37,500; assets, $1,057,321 (M); expenditures, $64,044; qualifying distributions, $37,500.
Limitations: Giving primarily in NJ, NY, and PA.
Publications: Application guidelines.

Application information: Application form required.
Officers and Directors:* Henrietta Judson,* Pres.; J. William Widing III,* Secy.; Alex L. Rosenthal,* Treas.; Arthur Judson III, Bright Miller Judson, Frances J. Kennedy, James Kennedy, Helen J. Widing.
EIN: 237411037

47305
The Kanter Foundation
P.O. Box 445, 436 Stump Rd.
Montgomeryville, PA 18936

Established in 1999 in PA.
Financial data (yr. ended 12/31/01): Grants paid, $37,500; assets, $49,888 (M); gifts received, $50,000; expenditures, $37,515; qualifying distributions, $37,500.
Limitations: Applications not accepted.
Application information: Contributes only to pre-selected organizations.
Officers: Allen L. Kanter, Pres.; Valentina Kanter, Treas.
EIN: 232972888

47306
Wasserman Family Foundation
191 Presidential Blvd.
Bala Cynwyd, PA 19004

Established in 1999 in PA.
Donor(s): Leonard Wasserman.
Financial data (yr. ended 12/31/01): Grants paid, $37,455; assets, $142,011 (M); gifts received, $10,558; expenditures, $38,201; qualifying distributions, $37,455.
Limitations: Applications not accepted.
Application information: Contributes only to pre-selected organizations.
Trustees: Dorothy Wasserman, Leonard Wasserman.
EIN: 311681321

47307
The Shabel Foundation
c/o Glenmede Trust Co.
1650 Market St., Ste. 1200
Philadelphia, PA 19103-7391
Application address: 210 W. Rittenhouse Sq., Ste. 1606, Philadelphia, PA 19103
Contact: Fred A. Shabel, Dir.

Established in 2000 in PA.
Donor(s): Fred A. Shabel.
Financial data (yr. ended 12/31/01): Grants paid, $37,261; assets, $87,024 (M); gifts received, $67,433; expenditures, $38,912; qualifying distributions, $37,261.
Limitations: Giving primarily in Philadelphia, PA.
Application information: Application form not required.
Directors: Sanford Lipstein, Fred A. Shabel.
EIN: 233054313

47308
Leon M. Seidel Trust
c/o First Union National Bank
Broad & Walnut Sts.
Philadelphia, PA 19109-1199

Financial data (yr. ended 04/30/99): Grants paid, $37,234; assets, $906,110 (M); expenditures, $48,654; qualifying distributions, $36,998.
Limitations: Applications not accepted. Giving limited to Bordentown, NJ.
Trustee: First Union National Bank.
EIN: 226104262

47309
Paul L. Newman Foundation
(Formerly Paul L. and Marcia S. Newman Foundation)
117 Raynham Rd.
Merion Station, PA 19066

Established in 1990 in OH.
Donor(s): Paul L. Newman.
Financial data (yr. ended 12/31/01): Grants paid, $37,229; assets, $536,643 (M); expenditures, $40,776; qualifying distributions, $37,193.
Limitations: Applications not accepted. Giving primarily in NY, OH, and PA.
Application information: Contributes only to pre-selected organizations.
Officer: Paul L. Newman, Pres.
Trustee: Nancy Helwig.
EIN: 311287223

47310
American Food Service Charitable Trust
400 Drew Ct.
King of Prussia, PA 19406 (610) 933-9792
Contact: Richard S. Downs, Tr.

Established in 1998 in PA.
Donor(s): American Foodservice Corp.
Financial data (yr. ended 12/31/01): Grants paid, $37,180; assets, $15,133 (M); gifts received, $30,000; expenditures, $37,210; qualifying distributions, $37,207.
Limitations: Giving primarily in eastern PA and mid-TX.
Trustees: Ronald G. Allen, Richard S. Downs.
EIN: 237933778

47311
Bernice & Jerry G. Rubenstein Foundation
223 Glenmoor Rd.
Gladwyne, PA 19035-1501
Contact: Bernice G. Rubenstein, Tr. or Jerry G. Rubenstein, Tr.

Donor(s): Jerry G. Rubenstein, Bernice G. Rubenstein.
Financial data (yr. ended 12/31/01): Grants paid, $37,155; assets, $380,729 (M); expenditures, $38,583; qualifying distributions, $37,155.
Limitations: Giving primarily in Philadelphia, PA.
Application information: Application form not required.
Trustees: Laura M. Barzilai, Bernice G. Rubenstein, Daniel A. Rubenstein, Jerry G. Rubenstein, Karen B. Rubenstein.
EIN: 232045912

47312
William Bass Charitable Foundation
c/o Burton K. Stein
The Atrium, 1900 Market St., 3rd Fl.
Philadelphia, PA 19103-2598

Established in 1984 in PA.
Donor(s): Rosalind Bass.
Financial data (yr. ended 12/31/01): Grants paid, $37,000; assets, $491,065 (M); gifts received, $1,000; expenditures, $43,874; qualifying distributions, $37,000.
Limitations: Applications not accepted.
Application information: Contributes only to pre-selected organizations.
Officers: Rosalind B. Bass, Pres.; Robert S. Bass, V.P.; Jerome Bass, M.D., Secy.
EIN: 232339056

47313
Raymond J. Harris Educational Trust
c/o Mellon Bank, N.A.
P.O. Box 7236
Philadelphia, PA 19101-7236

Financial data (yr. ended 09/30/01): Grants paid, $37,000; assets, $104,884 (M); expenditures, $40,108; qualifying distributions, $36,765.
Limitations: Giving primarily in the Philadelphia, PA, area.
Application information: Application form required.
Trustee: Mellon Bank, N.A.
EIN: 236224306
Codes: GTI

47314
Shafer Family Charitable Trust
c/o Nazareth National Bank
76 S. Main St.
Nazareth, PA 18064
Contact: Sally Jablonski, Trust Off., Nazareth National Bank

Established in 1989.
Donor(s): Lester Shafer.
Financial data (yr. ended 12/31/01): Grants paid, $37,000; assets, $1,484,298 (M); expenditures, $42,814; qualifying distributions, $37,000.
Limitations: Giving primarily in PA.
Trustee: Nazareth National Bank.
EIN: 236952392

47315
Samuel Rosenblum Foundation
1361 Drayton Ln.
Wynnewood, PA 19096-3313

Financial data (yr. ended 12/31/01): Grants paid, $36,985; assets, $488,338 (M); expenditures, $38,877; qualifying distributions, $36,985.
Limitations: Applications not accepted. Giving primarily in Philadelphia, PA.
Application information: Contributes only to pre-selected organizations.
Officers: David Rosenblum, Pres.; Donald Jay Wolfe, V.P.; Zena Rosenblum Wolfe, Secy.
EIN: 236295709

47316
Save the Species Foundation
112 Mineford Rd.
Bala Cynwyd, PA 19004
Contact: Eric Raymond, Pres.

Established in 1996 in NY.
Donor(s): Eric Raymond.
Financial data (yr. ended 12/31/01): Grants paid, $36,833; assets, $245,415 (M); expenditures, $38,083; qualifying distributions, $34,770.
Limitations: Giving on a national basis.
Officer: Eric Raymond, Pres.
EIN: 232967731

47317
Abram and D. Walter Cohen Foundation
(Formerly Abram Cohen Foundation)
210 W. Rittenhouse Sq., Ste. 2905
Philadelphia, PA 19103-5726 (215) 732-4541
Contact: Abram Cohen, Pres.

Donor(s): Abram Cohen.
Financial data (yr. ended 12/31/01): Grants paid, $36,754; assets, $680,570 (M); gifts received, $21,000; expenditures, $39,893; qualifying distributions, $36,754.
Limitations: Giving primarily in Philadelphia, PA.
Trustee: D. Walter Cohen.
EIN: 236413811

47318
The Roman-Mason Foundation
c/o Summit Bank, Trust Dept.
100 Brodhead Rd., Newpointe Ctr.
Bethlehem, PA 18017 (610) 865-8440
Contact: William Evans, Trust Off., Summit Bank

Financial data (yr. ended 01/31/01): Grants paid, $36,600; assets, $525,016 (M); expenditures, $41,847; qualifying distributions, $36,631.
Limitations: Giving primarily in Hazleton, PA.
Trustees: Charles J. Mason, Summit Bank.
EIN: 236298763

47319
Herbert & Eloise Hirsh Elish Charitable Foundation
108 Woodland Rd.
Pittsburgh, PA 15232
Contact: Herbert Elish, Tr. or Eloise Elish, Tr.

Established in 1996 in PA.
Donor(s): Herbert Elish, Eloise Elish.
Financial data (yr. ended 11/30/01): Grants paid, $36,550; assets, $58,527 (M); gifts received, $11,676; expenditures, $38,724; qualifying distributions, $36,550.
Limitations: Giving primarily in Montgomery, AL and Pittsburgh, PA.
Trustees: Eloise Elish, Herbert Elish.
EIN: 251779189

47320
Quail Hill Foundation
128 Beaver Creek Ct.
Sewickley, PA 15143
Contact: Stuart L. Bell, Secy.

Established in 1989 in PA.
Donor(s): Robert B. Knutson, Carolyn M. Knutson.
Financial data (yr. ended 12/31/01): Grants paid, $36,430; assets, $232,184 (M); expenditures, $47,574; qualifying distributions, $36,430.
Limitations: Giving on a national basis.
Officers: Carolyn M. Knutson, Chair. and Pres.; Sarah G. Flanagan, V.P.; Anne K. Hargrave, V.P.; Stuart L. Bell, Secy.; Todd M. Knutson, Treas.
EIN: 251616338

47321
Kramer Family Fund, Inc.
c/o Trimfit, Inc.
1900 Frost Rd.
Bristol, PA 19007-1519 (800) 347-7697
Application address: c/o Robert Kramer, 9 Park Ln., Rancho Mirage, CA 99270-2588
Contact: Arnold A. Kramer, Tr.

Established about 1953.
Financial data (yr. ended 09/30/01): Grants paid, $36,379; assets, $159,040 (M); expenditures, $38,665; qualifying distributions, $36,379.
Limitations: Giving primarily in NY and PA.
Trustees: Arnold A. Kramer, Martin B. Kramer, Robert Kramer.
EIN: 136117359

47322
The Richard and Bernice Bogash Family Foundation
101 Cheswold Ln., Ste. 4F
Haverford, PA 19041
Contact: Bernice Bogash, Tr.

Established in 1998 in PA.
Donor(s): Bernice Bogash.
Financial data (yr. ended 10/31/01): Grants paid, $36,350; assets, $48,078 (M); gifts received, $31,566; expenditures, $36,500; qualifying distributions, $36,113.
Trustee: Bernice Bogash.
EIN: 237996185

47323
Alexander & Jane Boyd Foundation
c/o Allfirst, Trust Tax Div.
21 E. Market St.
York, PA 17401-1500
Application address: P.O. Box 2961, Harrisburg, PA 17105-2961, tel.: (717) 255-2174
Contact: Joe Macri, Trust Off., Allfirst

Donor(s): Alexander Boyd, Paul Mahoney.
Financial data (yr. ended 12/31/01): Grants paid, $36,000; assets, $600,411 (M); expenditures, $40,366; qualifying distributions, $36,000.
Limitations: Giving primarily in Dauphin County, PA, with emphasis on Lower Paxton, Susquehanna, and Swatara.
Trustee: Allfirst.
EIN: 232251378

47324
Vance C. McCormick Trust
c/o Allfirst, Trust Div.
21 E. Market St.
York, PA 17401-1500
Contact: Larry A. Hartman, Trust Off., Allfirst

Financial data (yr. ended 12/31/00): Grants paid, $36,000; assets, $653,735 (M); expenditures, $42,091; qualifying distributions, $33,367.
Limitations: Giving limited to the Harrisburg, PA, area.
Trustee: Allfirst.
EIN: 236508188

47325
The Martin and Sylvia Kreithen Foundation
900 Roscommon Rd.
Bryn Mawr, PA 19010 (610) 527-5278
Contact: Martin Kreithen, Pres.

Established in 2000 in PA.
Donor(s): Martin Kreithen, Sylvia Kreithen.
Financial data (yr. ended 12/31/01): Grants paid, $35,900; assets, $144,402 (M); expenditures, $36,873; qualifying distributions, $35,900.
Officers: Martin Kreithen, Pres.; Sylvia Kreithen, Secy.
EIN: 233035305

47326
CMS Realize Your Dream Foundation
c/o Bernard E. Stoecklein, Jr.
235 Alpha Dr., Ste. 300
Pittsburgh, PA 15238 (412) 967-6200

Established in 1997 in PA.
Donor(s): Bernard E. Stoecklein, Jr.
Financial data (yr. ended 12/31/99): Grants paid, $35,725; assets, $886,581 (M); gifts received, $20,200; expenditures, $63,043; qualifying distributions, $35,391.
Limitations: Giving limited to the City of Pittsburgh, PA, and surrounding areas as far east as Lower Burrell, west to Sewickley, north to Butler, and south to the Allegheny and Ohio rivers.
Application information: Application form required.
Scholarship Committee: Ronald Bowes, Sr. Clarice Carlson, Linda W. Ebel, and 4 additional members.
Trustee: Bernard E. Stoecklein, Jr.
EIN: 232884514
Codes: GTI

47327
The Craig Foundation
P.O. Box 817
Spring House, PA 19477

Established in 1998 in PA.

47327—PENNSYLVANIA

Donor(s): Christian Community Foundation, Miriam McKenna.
Financial data (yr. ended 12/31/01): Grants paid, $35,675; assets, $589,331 (M); gifts received, $45,000; expenditures, $41,730; qualifying distributions, $35,675.
Limitations: Applications not accepted.
Application information: Contributes only to pre-selected organizations.
Officer: Barbara Osinski, Pres.
EIN: 232984311

47328
The Riggs-Conrad Trust Fund
c/o Fulton Financial Advisors, N.A.
P.O. Box 3215
Lancaster, PA 17604-3215
Application address: c/o Hagerstown Community College, Student Financial Aid Office, 11400 Robinwood Dr., Hagerstown, MD 21740

Established in 1997 in MD.
Financial data (yr. ended 11/30/01): Grants paid, $35,620; assets, $423,271 (M); gifts received, $8,857; expenditures, $42,061; qualifying distributions, $35,478.
Limitations: Giving primarily in Hagerstown, MD.
Application information: Contact Hagerstown Community College for application. Application form required.
Trustees: Charles W. Riggs, Fulton Financial Advisors, N.A.
EIN: 522057152

47329
Clarence E. and Marie Warren Dickey Foundation
c/o Sharkey, Piccirillo, LLP
P.O. Box 1084
DuBois, PA 15801
Application address: 332 Joy Ln., West Chester, PA 19380, tel.: (610) 696-5924
Contact: David W. Dickey, Tr.

Established around 1987 in PA.
Donor(s): David W. Dickey.
Financial data (yr. ended 12/31/01): Grants paid, $35,500; assets, $561,498 (M); gifts received, $1,040; expenditures, $37,258; qualifying distributions, $35,500.
Limitations: Giving on a national basis, with emphasis on PA.
Trustees: Ann G. Dickey, David W. Dickey.
EIN: 251563520

47330
Gooding Group Foundation
345 S. Reading Rd.
Ephrata, PA 17522
Contact: John S. Gooding, Pres.

Established in 1988 in PA.
Donor(s): GSM Industrial, Inc.
Financial data (yr. ended 12/31/01): Grants paid, $35,195; assets, $355,124 (M); gifts received, $46,150; expenditures, $62,793; qualifying distributions, $35,195.
Limitations: Giving primarily in PA.
Officers: John S. Gooding, Pres.; James K. Towers III, V.P.; Robert E. Burkholder, Secy.-Treas.
EIN: 232516754
Codes: CS, CD

47331
Pharo Foundation, Inc.
298 Keystone Dr.
Bethlehem, PA 18017-9464
Contact: John W. Pharo, Mgr.

Financial data (yr. ended 12/31/00): Grants paid, $35,183; assets, $854,023 (M); expenditures, $36,125; qualifying distributions, $34,902.
Limitations: Giving primarily in Bethlehem, PA.
Officers: Donald N. Pharo, Mgr.; John W. Pharo, Mgr.; Robert S. Pharo, Mgr.
EIN: 237376724

47332
W. J. Francis Memorial Scholarship Fund
c/o First Union National Bank
Broad and Walnut Sts., PA1308
Philadelphia, PA 19109
Application address: c/o Mars Hill College, Endowment Dept., Mars Hill, NC 28754-0370

Financial data (yr. ended 12/31/99): Grants paid, $35,171; assets, $1,049 (M); expenditures, $38,254; qualifying distributions, $35,171.
Limitations: Giving limited to Haywood County, NC.
Application information: Application form required.
Trustee: First Union National Bank.
EIN: 566049216

47333
Seymore & Helen Ann Rubin Foundation
c/o Steven J. Kobasa
42 S. 15th St.
Philadelphia, PA 19102 (215) 241-7500

Established in 1989 in PA.
Donor(s): Seymore Rubin, Mark Rubin.
Financial data (yr. ended 12/31/00): Grants paid, $35,166; assets, $535,258 (M); expenditures, $36,017; qualifying distributions, $34,959.
Limitations: Giving primarily in Merion Station and Philadelphia, PA.
Officers: Seymore Rubin, Pres.; Mark Rubin, V.P.; Karen Spewak, Secy.; Helen Ann Rubin, Treas.
EIN: 232586851

47334
Mary Jane Weir Kerr Trust
c/o Mellon Bank, N.A.
P.O. Box 185
Pittsburgh, PA 15230-9897

Donor(s): Mary Jane Weir Kerr.‡
Financial data (yr. ended 12/31/99): Grants paid, $35,150; assets, $927,814 (M); expenditures, $46,459; qualifying distributions, $37,980.
Limitations: Applications not accepted. Giving primarily in PA.
Application information: Contributes only to pre-selected organizations.
Trustee: Mellon Bank, N.A.
EIN: 256031833

47335
Northeast High School Alumni Foundation
c/o Northeast High School
Cottman & Algon Aves.
Philadelphia, PA 19111 (215) 728-5018
Contact: B.K. Barton, Principal

Financial data (yr. ended 06/30/01): Grants paid, $35,139; assets, $698,615 (M); gifts received, $45,681; expenditures, $37,428; qualifying distributions, $35,139.
Limitations: Giving limited to residents of Philadelphia, PA.
Officer and Trustees:* George E. Nelson, Jr.,* Chair.; M. Mark Mendel, Robert Rovner, Anthony D. Stagliano, Millard Wilkinson, Jr., John R. Winter, Myron Zonies.
EIN: 236463349
Codes: GTI

47336
Brumby-Leonard Family Foundation
c/o First Union National Bank
P.O. Box 7558
Philadelphia, PA 19109

Established in 1998 in GA.
Financial data (yr. ended 12/31/99): Grants paid, $35,000; assets, $981,517 (M); expenditures, $47,937; qualifying distributions, $35,660.
Officers: Spain B. Gregory, Chair.; Elisabeth Dobbs Leonard, Secy.
Trustees: Anna P. Brumby, Lee D. Brumby, Martha E. Brumby, Otis A. Brumby III, Earl T. Leonard III, First Union National Bank.
EIN: 582389703

47337
The Joseph and Carolyn DeMarco Foundation, Inc.
2600 One Commerce Sq.
Philadelphia, PA 19103

Established in 1998 in PA.
Donor(s): Joseph A. DeMarco.
Financial data (yr. ended 12/31/01): Grants paid, $35,000; assets, $707,404 (M); expenditures, $45,706; qualifying distributions, $35,000.
Limitations: Applications not accepted. Giving primarily in Philadelphia, PA, area.
Application information: Contributes only to pre-selected organizations.
Officers: Joseph A. DeMarco, Pres.; Carolyn DeMarco, Secy.; Jeffrey J. Idler, Treas.
EIN: 232956437

47338
Thomas & Carolyn Langfitt Family Foundation
c/o Glenmede Trust Co.
1650 Market St., Ste. 1200
Philadelphia, PA 19103-7391

Established in 2001 in PA.
Donor(s): Thomas W. Langfitt, Carolyn Payne Langfitt.
Financial data (yr. ended 12/31/01): Grants paid, $35,000; assets, $1,046,458 (M); gifts received, $1,090,001; expenditures, $68,260; qualifying distributions, $44,255.
Limitations: Applications not accepted.
Application information: Contributes only to pre-selected organizations.
Trustees: Carolyn Payne Langfitt, David D. Langfitt, Frank D. Langfitt, John T. Langfitt, Thomas W. Langfitt.
EIN: 256757723

47339
Perlow Family Foundation
Forster Plz. X
680 Andersen Dr.
Pittsburgh, PA 15220
Contact: Rodney W. Fink, Secy.-Treas.

Established in 1997 in PA.
Donor(s): Charles S. Perlow.
Financial data (yr. ended 12/31/01): Grants paid, $35,000; assets, $872,898 (M); gifts received, $600,500; expenditures, $45,008; qualifying distributions, $35,000.
Limitations: Giving limited to Pittsburgh, PA.
Officers and Directors:* Ellen P. Kessler,* V.P.; Charles S. Perlow,* V.P.; Lori Perlow,* V.P.; Rodney W. Fink, Secy.-Treas.
EIN: 232894160

47340
Three Rivers Community Foundation
100 N. Braddock Ave., Ste. 302
Pittsburgh, PA 15208-2509 (412) 243-9250
FAX: (412) 243-0504; E-mail:
threeriverscommfund@juno.com; URL: http://
trfn.clpgh.org/trcf
Contact: Marianne Perry, Office Admin.

Established in 1989.
Financial data (yr. ended 06/30/00): Grants paid, $35,000; assets, $169,000 (M); expenditures, $48,275.
Limitations: Giving limited to southwestern PA.
Publications: Grants list, newsletter, occasional report, informational brochure, application guidelines, financial statement.
Application information: Application form required.
Officers and Directors:* Carrie Leana,* Pres.; Pat Murphy,* V.P.; Rhonda Goldblatt,* Secy.; Mary Reynolds,* Treas.
EIN: 251615511
Codes: CM

47341
J. R. & D. Warfel Foundation
P.O. Box 4488
Lancaster, PA 17604-4488 (717) 393-8103
Contact: J. Richard Warfel, C.E.O., or Doreen Warfel, Secy.

Established in 1994 in PA.
Donor(s): J. Richard Warfel.
Financial data (yr. ended 12/31/01): Grants paid, $34,845; assets, $896,061 (M); gifts received, $49,963; expenditures, $44,900; qualifying distributions, $34,845.
Limitations: Giving primarily in PA.
Officers and Directors:* J. Richard Warfel,* C.E.O.; Doreen Warfel,* Secy.; Derrick M. Warfel,* Treas.; John S. Ross, Jr.
EIN: 232788089

47342
Sidney H. & Mary L. Gray Family Scholarship Fund
(Formerly Sidney H. & Mary L. Langille Gray Family Scholarship Fund Trust)
c/o PNC Advisors
1600 Market St., 4th Fl., Tax Dept.
Philadelphia, PA 19103-7240
Application address: c/o PNC Advisors, Trust Dept., 125 High St., Boston, MA 02110-2713, tel.: (800) 842-6512

Financial data (yr. ended 05/31/01): Grants paid, $34,800; assets, $507,902 (M); expenditures, $40,111; qualifying distributions, $34,484.
Limitations: Giving primarily to residents of MA.
Application information: Write for application. Application form required.
Trustee: PNC Bank, N.A.
EIN: 046314384

47343
Goldsmith-Weiss Foundation
c/o Bruce A. Rosenfield
1600 Market St., Ste. 3600
Philadelphia, PA 19103-7286

Established in 1998 in PA.
Donor(s): Olga G. Weiss.
Financial data (yr. ended 12/31/01): Grants paid, $34,719; assets, $700,308 (M); expenditures, $37,195; qualifying distributions, $34,719.
Trustee: Arlin M. Adams.
EIN: 237913889

47344
Eugene Dozzi Charitable Foundation
2000 Lincoln Rd.
Pittsburgh, PA 15235-1129

Established in 1969.
Donor(s): Domenic P. Dozzi, Peter C. Dozzi, Dwight E. Kuhn, Petrina A. Lloyd, Thomas J. Murphy.
Financial data (yr. ended 04/30/00): Grants paid, $34,685; assets, $1,640,936 (M); gifts received, $284,500; expenditures, $44,877; qualifying distributions, $34,685.
Limitations: Applications not accepted. Giving primarily in Pittsburgh, PA.
Application information: Contributes only to pre-selected organizations.
Officer and Trustees:* Petrina A. Lloyd,* Mgr.; Domenic P. Dozzi, Peter C. Dozzi, Dwight E. Kuhn, Thomas J. Murphy.
EIN: 237023479

47345
Henry E. and Laurana S. Fish Foundation
2802 Zuck Road
Erie, PA 16506-3155
Application address: 3535 Hershey Rd., Erie, PA 16506
Contact: Henry E. Fish, Tr.

Established in 1987.
Donor(s): Henry E. Fish, Laurana S. Fish.
Financial data (yr. ended 12/31/01): Grants paid, $34,685; assets, $674,581 (M); expenditures, $49,674; qualifying distributions, $34,685.
Limitations: Giving primarily in PA.
Application information: Application form not required.
Trustees: Henry E. Fish, Laurana S. Fish.
EIN: 251567601

47346
Fischer Memorial Burial Park
c/o Alan Mandeloff
1420 Walnut St., Ste. 200
Philadelphia, PA 19102

Financial data (yr. ended 12/31/99): Grants paid, $34,675; assets, $339,385 (M); gifts received, $4,545; expenditures, $58,795; qualifying distributions, $45,353; giving activities include $45,619 for programs.
Limitations: Applications not accepted. Giving limited to PA.
Application information: Contributes only to pre-selected organizations.
Director: Anthony Fischer.
EIN: 236263254

47347
Harry K. Constandy, Vaseleke H. Constandy, and C. Harry Constandy Memorial Trust
c/o Dave Hunter
Koppers Building 5th Floor
Pittsburgh, PA 15219

Established in 1993 in PA.
Donor(s): Vaseleke H. Constandy.‡
Financial data (yr. ended 12/31/01): Grants paid, $34,637; assets, $708,375 (M); expenditures, $44,520; qualifying distributions, $34,637.
Limitations: Applications not accepted. Giving primarily in PA.
Application information: Contributes only to pre-selected organizations.
Trustee: David W. Hunter.
EIN: 256397698

47348
The Dorothy B. and S. Lawrence Koplovitz Foundation
c/o PNC Advisors
1600 Market St., 4th Fl.
Philadelphia, PA 19103-7240

Established in 1999 in PA.
Donor(s): S. Lawrence Koplovitz.‡
Financial data (yr. ended 09/30/01): Grants paid, $34,617; assets, $581,126 (M); expenditures, $47,500; qualifying distributions, $40,488.
Limitations: Applications not accepted. Giving primarily in MO and PA.
Application information: Contributes only to pre-selected organizations.
Trustees: David Bronstein, PNC Bank, N.A.
EIN: 256658644

47349
The Quinn Family Foundation
4 E. Mercer Ave.
Havertown, PA 19083

Established in 2000 in PA.
Donor(s): Daniel Quinn, Sr.
Financial data (yr. ended 12/31/01): Grants paid, $34,400; assets, $270,593 (M); gifts received, $29,530; expenditures, $38,702; qualifying distributions, $34,400.
Trustee: Daniel J. Quinn.
EIN: 256703112

47350
Walker Foundation Trust
c/o Clearfield Bank & Trust Co.
P.O. Box 171
Clearfield, PA 16830-0171

Established in 1984 in PA.
Donor(s): Charles Alan Walker, Anne W. Macko, Ray S. Walker.
Financial data (yr. ended 06/30/02): Grants paid, $34,400; assets, $375,787 (M); gifts received, $20,000; expenditures, $39,682; qualifying distributions, $34,400.
Limitations: Applications not accepted. Giving limited to the Clearfield County, PA, area.
Application information: Contributes only to pre-selected organizations.
Officer: Gloria Thoman, Secy.
Trustees: Susan W. Kriner, Anne W. Macko, William R. Owens, Charles Alan Walker, Louise S. Walker, Ray S. Walker, Clearfield Bank & Trust Co.
EIN: 256253677

47351
The William K. Nitterhouse Charitable Foundation
P.O. Box N
Chambersburg, PA 17201-0813

Established in 1987 in PA.
Donor(s): William K. Nitterhouse.
Financial data (yr. ended 06/30/01): Grants paid, $34,352; assets, $507,998 (M); gifts received, $32,200; expenditures, $34,669; qualifying distributions, $34,214.
Limitations: Applications not accepted. Giving primarily in Chambersburg, PA.
Application information: Contributes only to pre-selected organizations.
Trustees: Karen N. Diller, Diane R. Nitterhouse, William K. Nitterhouse.
EIN: 232493715

47352
Margaret Evans Tuten Foundation
128 Ashwood Rd.
Villanova, PA 19085-1502

Established in 1996 in PA.
Donor(s): Margaret Evans Tuten.
Financial data (yr. ended 12/31/01): Grants paid, $34,330; assets, $619,715 (M); expenditures, $35,615; qualifying distributions, $34,330.
Limitations: Applications not accepted.
Application information: Contributes only to pre-selected organizations.
Trustees: John C. Tuten, Jr., Margaret Evans Tuten.
EIN: 237856551

47353
Clair H. Kinney Scholarship and Library Science Reference Fund
(Formerly Clair Kinney Trust)
c/o First Columbia Bank & Trust Co.
11 W. Main St.
Bloomsburg, PA 17815-1702 (570) 387-4609
Contact: John Thompson, V.P. and Trust Off., First Columbia Bank & Trust Co.

Financial data (yr. ended 12/31/01): Grants paid, $34,303; assets, $204,632 (M); gifts received, $24,513; expenditures, $36,662; qualifying distributions, $34,204.
Limitations: Giving limited to residents of Columbia and Montour counties, PA.
Application information: Application form required.
Trustee: First Columbia Bank & Trust Co.
EIN: 236664657
Codes: GTI

47354
The Manuel & Beatrice Sloane Foundation
1001 City Ave., Ste. 1106
Wynnewood, PA 19096-3902

Established in 1995 in PA.
Donor(s): Beatrice Sloane, Manuel Sloane.
Financial data (yr. ended 11/30/01): Grants paid, $34,300; assets, $582,374 (M); expenditures, $37,373; qualifying distributions, $34,300.
Limitations: Applications not accepted. Giving primarily in NY and PA.
Application information: Contributes only to pre-selected organizations.
Trustees: Beatrice Sloane, Manuel Sloane.
EIN: 237818373

47355
The Powder Mill Foundation
c/o Louis J. Appel, Jr.
140 E. Market St.
York, PA 17401 (717) 848-5500
Contact: John L. Finlayson, Tr.

Established in 1993 in PA.
Donor(s): Louis J. Appel, Jr.
Financial data (yr. ended 12/31/01): Grants paid, $34,271; assets, $1,048,799 (M); gifts received, $527; expenditures, $38,597; qualifying distributions, $34,271.
Limitations: Giving limited to York, PA.
Trustees: Josephine S. Appell, Louis J. Appell, Jr., John L. Finlayson.
EIN: 237751589

47356
Jones/Lippincott Family Foundation
c/o N. Allen
1701 Market St.
Philadelphia, PA 19103

Established in 1999 in PA.
Donor(s): Elizabeth Hanger Lippincott.
Financial data (yr. ended 12/31/01): Grants paid, $34,250; assets, $1,086,093 (M); expenditures, $54,345; qualifying distributions, $35,375.
Limitations: Applications not accepted.
Application information: Contributes only to pre-selected organizations.
Trustees: Elizabeth L. Edie, Hadley Jones Ferguson, Roger Livingston Jones, Edith Bolling Jones, Elizabeth Hanger Lippincott.
EIN: 256678655

47357
William G. Davis Charitable Trust
c/o PNC Advisors
620 Liberty Ave., P2-PTPP-10-2
Pittsburgh, PA 15222-2705
Application address: c/o David L. Wylie, Secy., Doric Lodge No. 630, 409 Chestnut Rd., Sewickley, PA 15143

Financial data (yr. ended 12/31/01): Grants paid, $34,004; assets, $655,181 (M); expenditures, $37,153; qualifying distributions, $33,995.
Limitations: Giving limited to residents of the Sewickley, PA, area.
Application information: Application form required for scholarships.
Trustee: PNC Bank, N.A.
EIN: 251289600
Codes: GTI

47358
Fetterolf Family Foundation
Glen Mitchell Rd.
Sewickley, PA 15143

Established in 1990 in PA.
Donor(s): C. Frederick Fetterolf.
Financial data (yr. ended 12/31/01): Grants paid, $34,000; assets, $690,831 (M); gifts received, $32,500; expenditures, $38,656; qualifying distributions, $34,000.
Limitations: Applications not accepted.
Application information: Contributes only to pre-selected organizations.
Officers: C. Frederick Fetterolf, Pres.; Frances S. Fetterolf, V.P.; Regan J. Fetterolf, Secy.; Scott F. Fetterolf, Treas.
EIN: 251630949

47359
Jerome P. & Flora P. Heilweil Foundation
524 N. Providence Rd.
Media, PA 19063 (610) 565-3930
Contact: Jerome P. Heilweil, Mgr.

Established in 1986 in PA.
Donor(s): Jerome P. Heilweil.
Financial data (yr. ended 11/30/01): Grants paid, $33,874; assets, $619,265 (M); expenditures, $35,890; qualifying distributions, $33,874.
Limitations: Giving primarily in FL and PA.
Officer: Jerome P. Heilweil, Mgr.
EIN: 232438595

47360
Spellissy Foundation
c/o Arthur E. Spellisy & Assocs.
308 W. Lancaster Ave.
Wayne, PA 19087-3905
Application address: P.O. Box 659, Rockport, ME 04856, tel.: (206) 236-0775
Contact: Amy S. Campbell, Tr.

Financial data (yr. ended 12/31/01): Grants paid, $33,800; assets, $582,774 (M); expenditures, $38,699; qualifying distributions, $33,800.
Limitations: Giving primarily in ME.
Application information: Application form not required.
Trustees: Amy S. Campbell, Arthur E. Spellissy, Jr., Donald W. Weaver.
EIN: 236414775

47361
Thomas Memorial Foundation
c/o PNC Advisors
1600 Market St.
Philadelphia, PA 19103-7240
Application address: 1523 Saddle Woode Dr., Ft. Myers, FL 33919, tel.: (941) 489-3264
Contact: Susan T. Mahan, Secy.

Established in 1989 in FL and DE, as successor to Honey Locust Foundation; funded in 1990.
Financial data (yr. ended 06/30/01): Grants paid, $33,600; assets, $814,034 (M); expenditures, $70,438; qualifying distributions, $59,893.
Limitations: Giving on a national basis, with some emphasis on the South.
Officers and Directors:* Elwood Hamilton,* Pres.; Lee T. Hamilton,* V.P.; Susan T. Mahan,* Secy.; Allen S. Hamilton,* Treas.; Catherine H. Adams, Jane H. Goss, Charles M. Hamilton, Robert Mahan, Susan H. Schexnaildre.
EIN: 581909736

47362
Patricia & Stephen Segal Family Foundation
c/o Wolf, Block, Schorr & Sollis, Cohen
1650 Arch St., 22nd Fl.
Philadelphia, PA 19103

Established in 1997 in PA.
Donor(s): Patricia Segal, Stephen P. Segal.
Financial data (yr. ended 12/31/01): Grants paid, $33,500; assets, $181,727 (M); gifts received, $79,480; expenditures, $37,379; qualifying distributions, $33,500.
Trustees: Patricia Segal, Stephen P. Segal.
EIN: 237880724

47363
Shickman Family Foundation
c/o S. Sardinsky
10 Penn Ctr., Ste. 617
Philadelphia, PA 19103

Established in 1997 in PA.
Donor(s): Herman Shickman, Lila Shickman.

Financial data (yr. ended 12/31/01): Grants paid, $33,500; assets, $357,751 (M); gifts received, $99,997; expenditures, $39,070; qualifying distributions, $33,500.
Limitations: Applications not accepted.
Application information: Contributes only to pre-selected organizations.
Officers: Lila Shickman, Pres. and Treas.; Herman Shickman, V.P. and Secy.
EIN: 232902143

47364
The Schiel Family Foundation
P.O. Box 916
Bryn Mawr, PA 19010

Established in 1999 in PA.
Financial data (yr. ended 04/30/02): Grants paid, $33,360; assets, $610,794 (M); expenditures, $36,521; qualifying distributions, $33,360.
Limitations: Applications not accepted.
Application information: Contributes only to pre-selected organizations.
Officers: George L. Schiel, Pres.; Jane B. Schiel, V.P.; Mary Jane Kirkpatrick, Secy.; Arthur L. Schiel, Treas.
EIN: 233022575

47365
The ACE INA Foundation
(Formerly ACE USA Foundation)
2 Liberty Pl.
1601 Chestnut St., Ste. TL31
Philadelphia, PA 19101 (215) 640-1000
Contact: Eden Kratchman, Exec. Dir.

Established in 1998 in DE.
Donor(s): ACE USA Inc.
Financial data (yr. ended 12/31/00): Grants paid, $33,333; assets, $21,289 (M); expenditures, $36,458; qualifying distributions, $33,333.
Limitations: Giving primarily in areas of company operations.
Officers: Peter O'Connor, Chair.; Eden Kratchman, Exec. Dir.
Trustees: Dominic Frederico, Robert Jefferson, Jerome Jurschak, Dennis Reding, B. Kingsley Schubert.
EIN: 582430571
Codes: CS, CD

47366
Howard A. and Martha R. Wolf Fund
c/o PNC Advisors
620 Liberty Ave., P2-PTPP-10-2
Pittsburgh, PA 15222-2705
Application address: 1650 Arch St., Philadelphia, PA 19103-2097, tel.: (215) 977-2106
Contact: David R. Glyn, Tr.

Financial data (yr. ended 12/31/01): Grants paid, $33,300; assets, $625,293 (M); expenditures, $42,282; qualifying distributions, $36,458.
Limitations: Giving primarily in MA and PA.
Trustees: Pauline Wolf Frankel, David R. Glyn, Albert E. Wolf, Anne A. Wolf, Stephanie G. Wolf.
EIN: 236207349

47367
Charlotte L. Rohrbach Trust
c/o Allfirst, Trust Co.
21 E. Market St., M/C 402-130
York, PA 17401-1500

Established in 2000 in PA.
Financial data (yr. ended 12/31/01): Grants paid, $33,254; assets, $586,830 (M); expenditures, $45,303; qualifying distributions, $33,254.
Limitations: Applications not accepted. Giving primarily in PA.

Application information: Contributes only to pre-selected organizations.
Trustee: Allfirst.
EIN: 256423660

47368
Annette Evans Trust f/b/o Annette Evans Foundation for Arts & Humanities
c/o PNC Advisors
P.O. Box 937
Scranton, PA 18501-0937
Application address: c/o Advisory Committee, Wilkes University, Box 11, Wilkes-Barre, PA 18702

Donor(s): Annette Evans.‡
Financial data (yr. ended 09/30/01): Grants paid, $33,000; assets, $500,660 (M); expenditures, $36,913; qualifying distributions, $34,590.
Limitations: Giving primarily in Wilkes-Barre, PA.
Trustees: Christopher Breiseth, Alfred Groh, Ruth Schooley, PNC Bank, N.A.
EIN: 236498179

47369
John B. Gates Memorial Scholarship Fund
P.O. Box 846
Clearfield, PA 16830

Established in 1993 in PA.
Donor(s): Mary Helen Gates.
Financial data (yr. ended 06/30/01): Grants paid, $33,000; assets, $267,976 (L); expenditures, $33,754; qualifying distributions, $33,674.
Limitations: Applications not accepted. Giving limited to residents of Curwensville, PA.
Application information: Unsolicited request for funds not accepted.
Trustees: Andrew P. Gates, James K. Gates II, Susan Gates Seaman.
EIN: 251721073

47370
Betty Bergson Kook Memorial Foundation
c/o Jack Yampolsky
1420 Walnut St., Ste. 200
Philadelphia, PA 19102

Financial data (yr. ended 12/31/01): Grants paid, $33,000; assets, $654,473 (M); expenditures, $36,391; qualifying distributions, $33,000.
Limitations: Applications not accepted. Giving on an international basis.
Application information: Contributes only to pre-selected organizations.
Trustees: Astra Bergson-Kook, Peter Bergson-Kook, Rebecca Bergson-Kook, Nili Kook, Jack Yampolsky, Phillip Yampolsky.
EIN: 237000127

47371
The Harper W. Spong Family Scholarship Foundation
(also known as Spong Family Foundation)
c/o Allfirst, Trust Div.
21 E. Market St.
York, PA 17401-1500
Application address: P.O. Box 2961, Harrisburg, PA 17105
Contact: Larry A. Hartman, Trust Off., Allfirst

Donor(s): Marion M. Spong.
Financial data (yr. ended 12/31/01): Grants paid, $33,000; assets, $95,398 (M); expenditures, $37,953; qualifying distributions, $33,000.
Limitations: Giving primarily in PA.
Application information: Application form required.
Trustee: Allfirst.
EIN: 232247380
Codes: GTI

47372
Flora Paxton Hickman Foundation
c/o Mellon Bank, N.A.
P.O. Box 185
Pittsburgh, PA 15230-9897
Contact: Michael Knies, Trust Off., Mellon Bank, N.A.

Established around 1974.
Financial data (yr. ended 12/31/01): Grants paid, $32,792; assets, $847,362 (M); expenditures, $47,274; qualifying distributions, $35,984.
Limitations: Giving primarily in IL, NY, and VA.
Application information: Contact foundation for application information. Application form required.
Trustee: Mellon Bank, N.A.
EIN: 256159785

47373
Fisher Hess Foundation, Inc.
3003 N. Mercer St. Ext.
New Castle, PA 16105-1626 (724) 658-3335
Contact: Marianne Hess, Pres.; or Marshall Hess, V.P.

Donor(s): Marianne Hess.
Financial data (yr. ended 12/31/01): Grants paid, $32,600; assets, $151,178 (M); expenditures, $33,062; qualifying distributions, $32,600.
Limitations: Giving primarily in New Castle, PA.
Officers: Marianne Hess, Pres.; Marshall Hess, V.P.
EIN: 251267981

47374
The Smith Foundation
c/o Stock and Leader
35 S. Duke St.
York, PA 17405-5167 (717) 846-9800
Contact: W. Bruce Wallace

Established in 1993 in PA.
Donor(s): Donald M. Smith.
Financial data (yr. ended 12/31/01): Grants paid, $32,525; assets, $1,294,092 (M); gifts received, $830; expenditures, $71,827; qualifying distributions, $32,525.
Limitations: Giving limited to the Borough of Columbia, Borough of Wrightsville, and the Eastern York County School District, PA.
Directors: Arthur K. Mann, Mary Elizabeth Mann, Julianne S. McNamara.
EIN: 232633100

47375
Lawrence A. Appley Foundation, Inc.
c/o Hershey Trust Co.
P.O. Box 445
Hershey, PA 17033-0445 (717) 520-1105

Donor(s): Lawrence A. Appley.
Financial data (yr. ended 12/31/01): Grants paid, $32,500; assets, $897,106 (M); gifts received, $894,683; expenditures, $38,823; qualifying distributions, $32,500.
Limitations: Giving primarily in central NY and Columbia, KY.
Application information: Application form not required.
Officer: Ronald Glosser, Pres.
Trustee: Katherine Appley.
EIN: 136119187

47376
Floyd & Arlene Zimmerman Charitable Trust
P.O. Box 1102
Reading, PA 19602

Established in 1996 in PA.
Donor(s): Floyd R. Zimmerman.

47376—PENNSYLVANIA

Financial data (yr. ended 05/31/00): Grants paid, $32,500; assets, $577,626 (M); expenditures, $39,259; qualifying distributions, $32,500.
Limitations: Applications not accepted.
Application information: Contributes only to pre-selected organizations.
Trustees: Peggy L. Strack, Floyd R. Zimmerman, Lynn Zimmerman, First Union National Bank.
EIN: 237848279

47377
Berks County Tuberculosis Society
P.O. Box 1561
Reading, PA 19603
Application address: 542 Elm St., Reading, PA 19601, tel.: (610) 374-4951
Contact: William Alexander, Pres.

Financial data (yr. ended 12/31/01): Grants paid, $32,398; assets, $43,068 (M); gifts received, $43,908; expenditures, $34,600; qualifying distributions, $32,398.
Application information: Application form not required.
Officers: William Alexander, Pres.; Jerome A. LaManna, V.P.; Arline Cocroft, Secy.
EIN: 231409703

47378
John Boyer First Troop
(Formerly John Boyer First Troop Philadelphia City Cavalry Memorial Fund)
c/o Mellon Bank, N.A.
P.O. Box 7236
Philadelphia, PA 19101-7236

Financial data (yr. ended 06/30/01): Grants paid, $32,171; assets, $1,632,788 (M); expenditures, $55,206; qualifying distributions, $45,613.
Limitations: Applications not accepted. Giving primarily in Philadelphia, PA.
Application information: Recipients are chosen by First City Troop members.
Officer: John J. Gallagher, Mgr.
Trustee: Mellon Bank, N.A.
EIN: 236227636
Codes: GTI

47379
The Hinmam Family Foundation
c/o John Iskrant
1600 Market St., Ste. 3600
Philadelphia, PA 19103
Application address: 3560 Creekview Dr., Bonita Springs, FL 34134-2624, tel.: (941) 498-2931
Contact: Larry J. Hinman, Tr.

Established in 1997 in PA.
Donor(s): Larry J. Hinman.
Financial data (yr. ended 12/31/01): Grants paid, $32,000; assets, $130,127 (M); gifts received, $103,180; expenditures, $32,010; qualifying distributions, $32,000.
Trustees: Susan E. Argenziano, Beverly J. Hinman, Larry J. Hinman.
EIN: 237845383

47380
Vernon S. Lehr Scholarship Fund
c/o Sterling Financial Trust
25 Carlisle St.
Hanover, PA 17331-9934

Established in 2001 in PA.
Donor(s): Vernon Lehr.
Financial data (yr. ended 12/31/01): Grants paid, $32,000; assets, $37,585 (M); gifts received, $70,000; expenditures, $33,926; qualifying distributions, $33,243.
Trustee: John A. Donnelly.

EIN: 251872650

47381
George B. Heidmann, Jr. Foundation
P.O. Box 185
Jenkintown, PA 19046 (215) 886-4300
Contact: Barbara R. Heidmann, Tr.

Financial data (yr. ended 12/31/01): Grants paid, $31,925; assets, $359,144 (M); expenditures, $36,371; qualifying distributions, $31,925.
Limitations: Giving limited to the Philadelphia, PA, area, and surrounding counties.
Trustees: Barbara R. Heidmann, Ruth E. Heidmann.
EIN: 232191012

47382
D. & C.N. Trust
334 Grays Ln.
Haverford, PA 19041-1907

Financial data (yr. ended 12/31/01): Grants paid, $31,825; assets, $961,319 (M); expenditures, $32,123; qualifying distributions, $31,397.
Limitations: Applications not accepted. Giving primarily in PA.
Application information: Contributes only to pre-selected organizations.
Trustees: Charles P. Neidig, Dorothy A. Neidig.
EIN: 236427949

47383
Muse Foundation
c/o Albert Muse
200 9 Parkway Ctr.
Pittsburgh, PA 15220-3616

Donor(s): Albert C. Muse.
Financial data (yr. ended 12/31/01): Grants paid, $31,800; assets, $695,721 (M); expenditures, $79,753; qualifying distributions, $31,800.
Limitations: Applications not accepted. Giving primarily in Pittsburgh, PA.
Application information: Contributes only to pre-selected organizations.
Trustees: Albert C. Muse, Charles H. Muse, Jr.
EIN: 256042685

47384
Daniel M. Tabas Family Foundation
915 Montgomery Ave., Rm. 401
Narberth, PA 19072-2012 (610) 664-5100
Contact: Daniel M. Tabas, Tr.

Established in 1988 in PA.
Donor(s): Daniel M. Tabas.
Financial data (yr. ended 12/31/00): Grants paid, $31,720; assets, $4,230,852 (M); gifts received, $1,144,129; expenditures, $73,281; qualifying distributions, $31,853.
Limitations: Giving primarily in PA.
Officer: Nicholas Randazzo, Mgr.
Trustees: James J. McSwiggan, Jr., Murray Stempel III, Daniel M. Tabas, Evelyn R. Tabas, Lee E. Tabas, Robert R. Tabas, Susan Tabas Tepper, Jo Ann Tabas Wurzak.
EIN: 236934594

47385
John A. Apple Foundation
c/o Butter Krust Baking Co.
249 N. 11th St.
Sunbury, PA 17801

Established around 1963 in PA.
Donor(s): Jane C. Apple.
Financial data (yr. ended 07/31/01): Grants paid, $31,650; assets, $153,417 (M); expenditures, $37,504; qualifying distributions, $31,408.
Limitations: Applications not accepted. Giving primarily in PA.

Application information: Contributes only to pre-selected organizations.
Trustees: James G. Apple, John B. Apple, Joan Zimmerman.
EIN: 246014089

47386
William B. and Edith Crane Memorial Scholarship Fund
P.O. Box 7236
Philadelphia, PA 19103-7236

Established in 1999 in PA.
Financial data (yr. ended 12/31/01): Grants paid, $31,584; assets, $1,294,645 (M); gifts received, $147,065; expenditures, $50,368; qualifying distributions, $31,584.
Officer: Martina Edwards, V.P.
EIN: 256680661

47387
Benjamin & Lillie E. Apple Foundation
c/o Butter Crust Baking Co.
249 N. 11th St.
Sunbury, PA 17801

Financial data (yr. ended 07/31/01): Grants paid, $31,500; assets, $422,050 (M); expenditures, $40,650; qualifying distributions, $31,267.
Limitations: Applications not accepted. Giving limited to PA.
Application information: Contributes only to pre-selected organizations.
Trustees: James G. Apple, John B. Apple, Joan A. Zimmerman.
EIN: 246014088

47388
Samuel Sidewater Foundation
1600 Market St., Ste. 3600
Philadelphia, PA 19103

Established in 1991 in FL.
Donor(s): Samuel Sidewater.
Financial data (yr. ended 11/30/01): Grants paid, $31,466; assets, $280,148 (M); expenditures, $34,695; qualifying distributions, $31,466.
Limitations: Applications not accepted. Giving primarily in Philadelphia, PA.
Application information: Contributes only to pre-selected organizations.
Trustee: Samuel Sidewater.
EIN: 232673126

47389
Karr Foundation, Inc.
5 Cambridge Ln.
Newtown, PA 18940 (215) 504-9720
FAX: (215) 504-9721; *E-mail:* quakergroup@aol.com
Contact: Thelma V. Karr, Pres.

Financial data (yr. ended 12/31/01): Grants paid, $31,350; assets, $215,967 (M); gifts received, $90,000; expenditures, $32,714; qualifying distributions, $31,350.
Limitations: Giving limited to NJ and PA.
Application information: Application form not required.
Officer: Thelma Karr, Pres.
EIN: 237011973

47390
Nadon Trust
(Formerly Hargraves Charitable Company Trust)
c/o PNC Advisors
620 Liberty Ave., P2-PTPP-10-2
Pittsburgh, PA 15222-2705 (412) 768-9186
Contact: Brenda Harris, Trust Off., PNC Advisors

Established in 1985 in DE.

Financial data (yr. ended 08/31/01): Grants paid, $31,250; assets, $623,327 (M); expenditures, $36,090; qualifying distributions, $30,670.
Limitations: Giving primarily in NH and NY.
Application information: Application form not required.
Trustee: PNC Bank, N.A.
EIN: 516158604

47391
C. S. Yoo Educational Foundation, Inc.
4035 Ludwick St.
Pittsburgh, PA 15217

Established in 1999 in PA.
Donor(s): Sung Wha Oh.
Financial data (yr. ended 12/31/01): Grants paid, $31,106; assets, $3,937 (M); gifts received, $26,077; expenditures, $31,752; qualifying distributions, $31,106.
Limitations: Applications not accepted.
Application information: Contributes only to pre-selected organizations.
Officer: Sung Wha Oh, Pres.
Director: Shirley S. Yoo.
EIN: 251845176

47392
The Nestor Charitable Foundation
c/o Reiff & Nestor Co.
Reiff & West Sts.
Lykens, PA 17048
Application address: P.O. Box 147, Lykens, PA 17048, tel.: (717) 453-7113
Contact: Donald E. Nestor, Pres.

Established in 1952.
Donor(s): Reiff & Nestor Co.
Financial data (yr. ended 06/30/01): Grants paid, $31,064; assets, $590,770 (M); expenditures, $33,426; qualifying distributions, $33,093.
Limitations: Giving primarily in the Lykens, PA, area.
Officers: Donald E. Nestor, Pres.; Robin M. Nestor, Secy.
EIN: 236255983
Codes: CS, CD

47393
Damico Family Foundation
1588 Fairfield Rd.
Gettysburg, PA 17325

Established in 1999 in PA.
Donor(s): Paul Damico.
Financial data (yr. ended 03/31/02): Grants paid, $31,050; assets, $14,614 (M); gifts received, $13,800; expenditures, $31,602; qualifying distributions, $31,050.
Limitations: Applications not accepted. Giving primarily in Rockville, MD.
Application information: Contributes only to pre-selected organizations.
Officer: Paul Damico, Pres.
EIN: 233025052

47394
Fort Pitt Society
c/o Sally Malstrom
5700 5th Ave., Apt. 1-C
Pittsburgh, PA 15232-2726

Established in 1987 in PA.
Financial data (yr. ended 04/30/99): Grants paid, $31,000; assets, $1,374,019 (M); expenditures, $65,110; qualifying distributions, $62,729; giving activities include $32,382 for programs.
Limitations: Applications not accepted. Giving primarily in Pittsburgh, PA and Tamassee, SC.
Application information: Contributes only to pre-selected organizations.

Officers: Marilyn G. Shimp, Pres.; Catherine Schaughency, V.P.; Elizabeth Ruh, Secy.; Sarah Kelly Malstrom, Treas.
EIN: 250965320

47395
Oliver Reeder Herman Memorial Trust
c/o Edward J. Conover
10790 Rose Valley Rd.
Trout Run, PA 17771

Established in 1997.
Donor(s): Oliver Reeder Herman.
Financial data (yr. ended 04/30/01): Grants paid, $31,000; assets, $312,439 (M); expenditures, $26,184; qualifying distributions, $30,987.
Limitations: Applications not accepted. Giving primarily in PA.
Application information: Contributes only to pre-selected organizations.
Trustee: Edward J. Conover.
EIN: 237899364

47396
Charles S. Swope Memorial Scholarship Trust
c/o First National Bank of Chester County
P.O. Box 3105
West Chester, PA 19381
Application address: c/o Swope Scholarship Comm., Financial Aid Office, West Chester University, E.O. Bull Ctr., Rm. 138, West Chester, PA 19383, tel.: (610) 692-1400

Donor(s): Charles E. Swope.
Financial data (yr. ended 12/31/01): Grants paid, $31,000; assets, $435,172 (M); gifts received, $5,475; expenditures, $51,328; qualifying distributions, $44,295; giving activities include $5,058 for programs.
Limitations: Giving limited to the West Chester, PA, area.
Application information: Application form required.
Officers and Trustees:* Charles E. Swope,* Pres.; Richard M. Swope,* V.P.; Maryann L. Himes, Exec. Dir.; First National Bank of Chester County, and 19 additional trustees.
EIN: 236390730
Codes: GTI

47397
Aimee Y. Decker Charitable Trust
c/o Fulton Financial Advisors, N.A.
P.O. Box 3215
Lancaster, PA 17604

Established in 1995 in PA.
Donor(s): Aimee Y. Decker.‡
Financial data (yr. ended 05/31/02): Grants paid, $30,945; assets, $853,535 (M); expenditures, $43,958; qualifying distributions, $30,945.
Limitations: Applications not accepted. Giving limited to Millersville, PA.
Application information: Contributes only to pre-selected organizations.
Trustee: Fulton Financial Advisors, N.A.
EIN: 237819484

47398
Kiwanis Foundation of Easton, Pennsylvania, Inc.
728 Coleman St.
Easton, PA 18042-1406
Application address: 3780 Southwood Dr., Easton, PA 18045, tel.: (610) 253-8575
Contact: Roger J. Conners II, V.P.

Financial data (yr. ended 02/28/02): Grants paid, $30,928; assets, $182,479 (M); gifts received, $16,127; expenditures, $31,042; qualifying distributions, $30,928.

Limitations: Giving limited to Easton and the Lehigh Valley, PA, area.
Officers: Rev. Charles L. Bomboy, Pres.; Roger J. Connors II, V.P.; Fred C. Finken, Jr., Secy.-Treas.; Victor F. Dennis, Recording Secy.
Directors: Thomas F. Barton III, Cyrus S. Fleck, Paula Leffel, Thomas Malerba, Elaine Rutherford, Clarence Snyder, Gary D. Tempest.
EIN: 236299967

47399
Carl & Nellie Naugle Foundation, Inc.
c/o Allfirst, Trust Div.
21 E. Market St.
York, PA 17401-1500
Application address: c/o Alan B. Rhinehart, Trust Off., Allfirst, P.O. Box 459, Chambersburg, PA 17201-0459, tel.: (717) 261-2822

Donor(s): Nellie I. Nangle.
Financial data (yr. ended 12/31/01): Grants paid, $30,800; assets, $572,164 (M); gifts received, $9,300; expenditures, $37,973; qualifying distributions, $30,800.
Limitations: Giving primarily in the Shippensburg, PA, area.
Trustee: Allfirst.
EIN: 236266566

47400
Segel Foundation
(Formerly Franklin Foundation)
c/o Stanley Merves
10 Presidential Blvd., Ste. 250
Bala Cynwyd, PA 19004 (610) 668-1998
Contact: Stanley Merves, Tr.

Established in 1969.
Financial data (yr. ended 12/31/01): Grants paid, $30,750; assets, $1,212,236 (M); gifts received, $12,000; expenditures, $86,420; qualifying distributions, $30,750.
Limitations: Giving primarily in PA.
Officer: Rickey Bogdanoff, Mgr.
Trustees: Stanley Merves, Doris Segel, Joseph M. Segel.
EIN: 237014746

47401
The Henzel Family Foundation
431 Montgomery Ave.
Merion, PA 19066
Contact: Marc Henzel, Tr.

Established in 2000 in PA.
Donor(s): Marc S. Henzel, Cindy F. Henzel.
Financial data (yr. ended 12/31/01): Grants paid, $30,742; assets, $41,937 (M); gifts received, $8,900; expenditures, $31,717; qualifying distributions, $30,742.
Limitations: Giving primarily in NY and PA.
Trustees: Cindy F. Henzel, Marc S. Henzel.
EIN: 256723310

47402
Gustave G. and Valla Amsterdam Foundation
135 S. 19th St., 2nd Fl.
Philadelphia, PA 19103
Contact: Barb Deaner, Mgr.

Established in 2001 in PA.
Donor(s): Valla Amsterdam.
Financial data (yr. ended 12/31/01): Grants paid, $30,700; assets, $11,524 (M); gifts received, $46,000; expenditures, $34,663; qualifying distributions, $31,355.
Officers: Valla Amsterdam, Pres.; Jonathan Amsterdam, Secy.; Adam Amsterdam, Treas.; Barb Deaner, Mgr.
EIN: 233077771

47403
Frank & Marie Hamilton Charitable Trust
1 Liberty Pl.
1650 Market St., Ste. 3100
Philadelphia, PA 19103-7392 (215) 587-0818
E-mail: jkaplan@albk.com
Contact: Jerome Kaplan, Tr.

Established in 1991 in PA.
Donor(s): Marie Hamilton.
Financial data (yr. ended 12/31/01): Grants paid, $30,690; assets, $744,946 (M); expenditures, $42,090; qualifying distributions, $30,690.
Limitations: Giving primarily in PA.
Application information: Application form not required.
Trustee: Jerome Kaplan.
EIN: 237667824

47404
Walter J. Lindquist Foundation
(Formerly Walter J. Lindquist Discretionary Charitable Trust)
c/o First National Trust Co.
1 FNB Blvd.
Hermitage, PA 16148-3363

Established in 1997 in PA.
Donor(s): Walter J. Lindquist.‡
Financial data (yr. ended 12/31/01): Grants paid, $30,500; assets, $369,463 (M); expenditures, $37,407; qualifying distributions, $30,500.
Limitations: Applications not accepted.
Application information: Contributes only to pre-selected organizations.
Trustees: Evelyn L. Bolton, William J. McFate, First National Trust Co.
EIN: 237950549

47405
The Beaver County Foundation
P.O. Box 569
Beaver, PA 15009 (724) 728-1331
FAX: (724) 847-5017; *URL:* http://www.beavercounty.com/Service/bcfoundationintro.asp
Contact: Jean Macaluso, Secy.

Established in 1992 in PA.
Financial data (yr. ended 12/31/00): Grants paid, $30,300; assets, $871,671 (M); gifts received, $161,176; expenditures, $104,674.
Limitations: Giving limited to Beaver County, PA; support for pharmacological research or addiction interdiction given nationwide.
Publications: Newsletter, informational brochure, application guidelines.
Application information: Application form required.
Officers: Charles N. O'Data, Pres.; Jean Macaluso, Secy.; Joseph N. Tosh III, Treas.; Robert A. Smith, Exec. Dir.
Directors: Irving Bennett, W. Scott Bliss, Vince Dioguardi, Sally Erath, Del Goedeker, David J. Kuder, Celeste LaBate, Claire Mervis, Beverly O'Leary, Robert A. Rimbey, Ruth Ann Duff, Michael I. Roman, John F. Salopek, Phyllis Snedden, Paul R. Vochko, James Wetzel, Thomas P. Woolaway.
EIN: 251660309
Codes: CM

47406
Wechsler Research Foundation
220 Meyran Ave.
Pittsburgh, PA 15213-3311 (412) 681-3300
Contact: Richard L. Wechsler, Mgr.

Donor(s): Richard L. Wechsler.
Financial data (yr. ended 12/31/00): Grants paid, $30,261; assets, $556,186 (M); expenditures, $34,047; qualifying distributions, $30,261.
Limitations: Giving primarily in PA.
Officer: Richard L. Wechsler, Mgr.
EIN: 256038039

47407
The Clair E. Stuck and Flora E. Stuck Foundation, Inc.
7956 U.S. Hwy. 522 S.
McVeytown, PA 17051 (717) 248-8245
Contact: Gloria J. Shank, Pres.

Established in 1993 in PA.
Donor(s): Flora E. Stuck.
Financial data (yr. ended 12/31/01): Grants paid, $30,230; assets, $177,608 (M); gifts received, $376; expenditures, $31,730; qualifying distributions, $31,265.
Limitations: Giving limited to residents of Juniata and Mifflin counties, PA.
Application information: Application form not required.
Officers: Gloria J. Shank, Pres. and Treas.; Nevin L. Shank, V.P. and Secy.
Trustees: Stephen P. Dalton, Flora E. Stuck.
EIN: 251709803
Codes: GTI

47408
Richard L. Yuengling, Jr. Charitable Foundation
110 N. 2nd St.
Pottsville, PA 17901
Contact: William L. Jones III, Tr.

Established in 1994 in PA.
Donor(s): Richard L. Yuengling, Jr.
Financial data (yr. ended 12/31/01): Grants paid, $30,200; assets, $688,906 (M); expenditures, $38,757; qualifying distributions, $30,200.
Limitations: Giving primarily in Schuylkill County, PA.
Trustee: William L. Jones III.
EIN: 232790830

47409
Harry C. Winslow Foundation
c/o PNC Advisors
P.O. Box 8480
Erie, PA 16553
Application address: c/o PNC Advisors, 940 Park Ave., Meadville, PA 16335

Donor(s): Harry C. Winslow.‡
Financial data (yr. ended 12/31/01): Grants paid, $30,051; assets, $695,943 (M); expenditures, $34,708; qualifying distributions, $30,516.
Limitations: Giving primarily in Meadville, PA.
Application information: Application form required.
Trustee: PNC Bank, N.A.
EIN: 256184815

47410
The Edwin J. and Barbara R. Berkowitz Family Foundation
506 Oak Terr.
Merion Station, PA 19066 (610) 664-8335
Contact: Edwin J. Berkowitz, Tr.

Established in 1998.
Donor(s): Edwin J. Berkowitz.
Financial data (yr. ended 12/31/01): Grants paid, $30,000; assets, $185,168 (M); gifts received, $156,585; expenditures, $31,266; qualifying distributions, $29,999.
Limitations: Giving on a national basis.
Trustees: Alan Berkowitz, Arthur M. Berkowitz, Barbara R. Berkowitz, Daniel M. Berkowitz, Edwin J. Berkowitz, Pnina B. Siegler.
EIN: 237978506

47411
The Catherwood Foundation
P.O. Box 80
Bryn Mawr, PA 19010-0080 (610) 525-3720
Contact: Cummins Catherwood, Jr., Pres.

Established in 1948 in PA.
Donor(s): Cummins Catherwood,‡ Cummins Catherwood, Jr.
Financial data (yr. ended 12/31/01): Grants paid, $30,000; assets, $348,891 (M); expenditures, $37,015; qualifying distributions, $30,000.
Limitations: Giving primarily in the metropolitan Philadelphia, PA, area.
Officers: Cummins Catherwood, Jr., Pres.; W. Perry Gresh, V.P.; Tucker C. Gresh, Secy.-Treas.
EIN: 236235334

47412
Christ the Divine Teachers Catholic Academy Trust
(also known as Christ the Divine Teacher Trust)
c/o Douglas Schofield
P.O. Box 369
Indianola, PA 15051-0369

Established in 2000 in PA.
Financial data (yr. ended 12/31/01): Grants paid, $30,000; assets, $161,104 (M); expenditures, $30,015; qualifying distributions, $30,000.
Limitations: Applications not accepted.
Application information: Contributes only to pre-selected organizations.
Trustee: Douglas F. Schofield.
EIN: 251861938

47413
Mary Clark League Trust
(also known as Clark-AFF League Memorial Fund)
c/o Mellon Bank, N.A.
P.O. Box 7236
Philadelphia, PA 19101-7236

Donor(s): Mary Clark.‡
Financial data (yr. ended 06/30/01): Grants paid, $30,000; assets, $548,645 (M); expenditures, $30,707; qualifying distributions, $29,462.
Limitations: Giving limited to Philadelphia, PA.
Application information: Application forms available from the financial aid offices of local medical schools in Philadelphia, PA. Application form required.
Trustee: Mellon Bank, N.A.
EIN: 236225542
Codes: GTI

47414
Commonwealth National Foundation
c/o Brett Rhode
250 Babylon Rd.
Horsham, PA 19044

Established in 1999 in PA.
Financial data (yr. ended 12/31/01): Grants paid, $30,000; assets, $133,971 (M); gifts received, $45,380; expenditures, $88,351; qualifying distributions, $30,000.
Limitations: Applications not accepted. Giving primarily in PA.
Application information: Contributes only to pre-selected organizations.
Officers and Directors:* George McLaughlin,* Pres.; James Goldstein,* V.P.; Terrance Turnolo,* Secy.; Brett J. Rhode,* Treas.; Matthew Bellis, David Craig, Debbie Craig, David Katz, Joel Sackarowitz, Richard Stulson, William Turner, Robert J. Twomey.
EIN: 233015337

47415
The Elder Foundation
c/o Somerset Trust Co.
151 W. Main St., Box 777
Somerset, PA 15501-5624

Established in 1993 in PA.
Donor(s): Paul G. Elder.
Financial data (yr. ended 12/31/01): Grants paid, $30,000; assets, $554,980 (M); expenditures, $33,715; qualifying distributions, $30,000.
Limitations: Applications not accepted.
Application information: Contributes only to pre-selected organizations.
Trustees: Georgiann Petrilla, Somerset Trust Co.
EIN: 237749572

47416
Gailliot Family Foundation
5734 W. Woodland Rd.
Pittsburgh, PA 15232

Established in 1994 in PA.
Donor(s): Henry J. Gailliot, Mary Louise Gailliot.
Financial data (yr. ended 12/31/01): Grants paid, $30,000; assets, $638,640 (M); expenditures, $34,181; qualifying distributions, $29,646.
Limitations: Applications not accepted.
Application information: Contributes only to pre-selected organizations.
Trustees: Anne L. Gailliot, Charles H. Gailliot, Henry J. Gailliot, Mary Louise Gailliot.
EIN: 251754605

47417
Victoria Greenberg Trust
c/o Mellon Bank, N.A.
P.O. Box 7236
Philadelphia, PA 19101-7236
Application address: c/o Mellon Bank, N.A., 1735 Market St., 3rd Fl., Philadelphia, PA 19103
Contact: Patricia Kling, Trust Off., Mellon Bank, N.A.

Financial data (yr. ended 09/30/01): Grants paid, $30,000; assets, $509,407 (M); expenditures, $34,921; qualifying distributions, $31,859.
Limitations: Giving primarily in Philadelphia, PA.
Trustee: Mellon Bank, N.A.
EIN: 236676705

47418
The Ithan Foundation, Inc.
2600 One Commerce Sq.
Philadelphia, PA 19103

Established in 1997 in PA.
Donor(s): Ethyl S. Levenson.
Financial data (yr. ended 12/31/01): Grants paid, $30,000; assets, $591,989 (M); expenditures, $32,239; qualifying distributions, $30,000.
Limitations: Applications not accepted.
Application information: Contributes only to pre-selected organizations.
Officers: George R. Atterbury, Pres. and Treas.; Moira Atterbury, V.P.; Susannah A. Garder, Secy.
EIN: 232896573

47419
The J. S. Mack Foundation
c/o Board of Trustees
P.O. Box 34
Indiana, PA 15701 (724) 463-7300

Trust established in 1935 in PA.
Financial data (yr. ended 12/31/01): Grants paid, $30,000; assets, $2,722,422 (M); gifts received, $234,680; expenditures, $397,975; qualifying distributions, $30,000.
Limitations: Giving primarily in Indiana, PA.

Officers and Trustees:* L. Blaine Grube,* Pres.; Joseph N. Mack,* Secy.; Jonathan B. Mack, L. Merle Rife, Pete Stewart.
EIN: 256002036

47420
Richard J. Madden Foundation
11 The Trillium
Pittsburgh, PA 15238-1929 (724) 453-6150
Contact: Richard J. Madden, Pres.

Established in 2001 in PA.
Donor(s): Richard J. Madden.
Financial data (yr. ended 12/31/01): Grants paid, $30,000; assets, $301,065 (M); gifts received, $331,000; expenditures, $30,000; qualifying distributions, $30,000.
Officer and Director:* Richard J. Madden,* Pres. and Secy.-Treas.
EIN: 251883459

47421
Jack B. Piatt Foundation
400 Southpointe Blvd., Ste. 400
Canonsburg, PA 15317 (724) 743-3400
Contact: Jack B. Piatt, Tr.

Established in 1967.
Donor(s): Millcraft Products, Millcraft Industries, Inc.
Financial data (yr. ended 10/31/01): Grants paid, $30,000; assets, $24 (M); gifts received, $30,400; expenditures, $30,452; qualifying distributions, $30,000.
Limitations: Giving primarily in PA.
Trustee: Jack B. Piatt.
EIN: 237079264
Codes: CS, CD

47422
The Rappolt Charitable Foundation
c/o William C. Rappolt
1156 Eleni Ln.
West Chester, PA 19382

Established in 1998 in PA.
Financial data (yr. ended 12/31/01): Grants paid, $30,000; assets, $374,937 (M); expenditures, $34,111; qualifying distributions, $32,000.
Limitations: Applications not accepted.
Application information: Contributes only to pre-selected organizations.
Trustees: Pamela H. Rappolt, William C. Rappolt.
EIN: 251823899

47423
The Dale L. Reese Foundation
801 Yale Ave., Ste. 309
Swarthmore, PA 19081 (610) 328-5400
Contact: Dale L. Reese, Tr.

Established in 2000 in PA.
Donor(s): Dale L. Reese.
Financial data (yr. ended 06/30/02): Grants paid, $30,000; assets, $624,235 (M); expenditures, $30,693; qualifying distributions, $30,000.
Trustee: Dale L. Reese.
EIN: 256741622

47424
C. J. & J. A. Schlemmer Family Foundation
c/o T.J. Cook, Jr.
4021 W. 12th St.
Erie, PA 16505

Established in 2000 in PA.
Donor(s): Carl J. Schlemmer, Joan A. Schlemmer.
Financial data (yr. ended 06/30/02): Grants paid, $30,000; assets, $335,997 (M); gifts received, $290,946; expenditures, $32,693; qualifying distributions, $30,000.

Limitations: Applications not accepted. Giving primarily in IL, IN, and MO.
Application information: Contributes only to pre-selected organizations.
Officers and Directors:* Carl J. Schlemmer,* Pres.; Joan A. Schlemmer,* V.P.; Carla Schlemmer Stillman,* V.P.; William A. Stillman,* V.P.
EIN: 251873214

47425
William K. Stewart, Sr. Foundation
428 Inveraray Rd.
Villanova, PA 19085-1138

Donor(s): William K. Stewart, Sr.
Financial data (yr. ended 12/31/01): Grants paid, $30,000; assets, $467,258 (M); expenditures, $32,468; qualifying distributions, $29,907.
Limitations: Applications not accepted. Giving primarily in FL and PA.
Application information: Contributes only to pre-selected organizations.
Officers: William K. Stewart, Sr., Pres.; William K. Stewart, Jr., Secy.; Mary Harmer, Treas.
EIN: 232441723

47426
The Walton Family Foundation
c/o Mellon Bank, N.A.
P.O. Box 185
Pittsburgh, PA 15230-9897
Application address: c/o Len Richards, 3 Mellon Bank Ctr., Upper Lobby, Pittsburgh, PA 15258
Contact: Len Richards

Established in 1996 in PA.
Donor(s): Rachel Mellon Walton.
Financial data (yr. ended 12/31/01): Grants paid, $30,000; assets, $460,349 (M); expenditures, $35,316; qualifying distributions, $30,000.
Limitations: Giving primarily in Pittsburgh, PA.
Trustees: James N. Walton, John F. Walton, Rachel Mellon Walton, Farley Walton Whetzel, Mellon Bank, N.A.
EIN: 256568399

47427
Henkels Foundation
985 Jolly Rd.
Blue Bell, PA 19422-0900

Established in 1956 in DE and PA.
Donor(s): Henkels & McCoy, Inc., Paul M. Henkels.
Financial data (yr. ended 12/31/01): Grants paid, $29,550; assets, $43,244 (M); gifts received, $27,500; expenditures, $29,848; qualifying distributions, $29,810.
Limitations: Applications not accepted. Giving on a national basis, with some emphasis on PA.
Application information: Contributes only to pre-selected organizations.
Officers: Paul M. Henkels, Pres.; Barbara B. Henkels, Secy.-Treas.
Directors: Christopher B. Henkels, Paul M. Henkels, Jr.
EIN: 236235239
Codes: CS, CD

47428
Richard L. & Marion K. Pearsall Family Foundation, Inc.
Highland Acres, R.R. 4
Dallas, PA 18612

Established in 1998 in PA.
Financial data (yr. ended 12/31/01): Grants paid, $29,500; assets, $763,300 (M); expenditures, $37,255; qualifying distributions, $30,200.
Limitations: Applications not accepted.

47428—PENNSYLVANIA

Application information: Contributes only to pre-selected organizations.
Officers: Richard L. Pearsall, Pres.; Marion K. Pearsall, Secy.-Treas.
EIN: 232954560

47429
Stephen S. and Dolores R. Smith Foundation
c/o John L. Kreischer
200 Gibralter Rd.
Horsham, PA 19044

Established in 1999 in PA.
Donor(s): Stephen S. Smith.
Financial data (yr. ended 12/31/00): Grants paid, $29,500; assets, $854,319 (M); expenditures, $29,500; qualifying distributions, $22,037.
Limitations: Applications not accepted.
Application information: Contributes only to pre-selected organizations.
Officers: Stephen S. Smith, Pres.; Dolores R. Smith, Secy.-Treas.
EIN: 233019893

47430
William G. Rohrer, Jr. Educational Foundation
c/o PNC Advisors
1600 Market St.
Philadelphia, PA 19103-7240
Application address: c/o PNC Advisors, Rte. 38 at Eastgate Dr., Morristown, NJ 08057, tel.: (856) 755-5735
Contact: John C. Watson, V.P., PNC Advisors

Financial data (yr. ended 12/31/01): Grants paid, $29,400; assets, $791,351 (M); expenditures, $54,567; qualifying distributions, $29,400.
Limitations: Giving primarily to residents of NJ.
Application information: Application form required.
Trustees: Linda Rohrer, PNC Bank, N.A.
EIN: 226070758
Codes: GTI

47431
Stephanie J. Boyd Charitable Trust
c/o Mellon Bank, N.A.
P.O. Box 7899
Philadelphia, PA 19101-7236

Established in 1997 in PA.
Financial data (yr. ended 12/31/99): Grants paid, $29,390; assets, $347,785 (M); expenditures, $38,312; qualifying distributions, $29,768.
Limitations: Applications not accepted. Giving limited to Elkins Park, PA.
Application information: Contributes only to a pre-selected organization.
Trustee: Mellon Bank, N.A.
EIN: 256445445

47432
Herman and Helen Lipsitz Charitable Trust
1100 5th Ave.
Pittsburgh, PA 15219 (412) 281-4777

Established around 1972.
Donor(s): Herman Lipsitz, Helen Lipsitz.
Financial data (yr. ended 11/30/99): Grants paid, $29,390; assets, $1,804,552 (M); gifts received, $222,732; expenditures, $29,390; qualifying distributions, $28,990.
Application information: Application form not required.
Trustees: Helen Lipsitz, Herman Lipsitz.
EIN: 256134327

47433
The Stuart and Jill Siegel Charitable Trust
166 Tinari Ln.
Richboro, PA 18954 (215) 785-0900
Contact: Stuart Siegel, Tr.

Established in 1995 in NY.
Donor(s): Stuart Siegel.
Financial data (yr. ended 12/31/00): Grants paid, $29,365; assets, $622,914 (M); expenditures, $30,315; qualifying distributions, $29,365.
Application information: Application form not required.
Trustees: Jill Siegel, Stuart Siegel.
EIN: 113297021

47434
The Lemole Family Charitable Trust
(Formerly The Building Bridges Foundation)
2771 Philmont Ave.
Huntingdon Valley, PA 19006

Established in 1996 in PA.
Donor(s): Emily Jane A. Lemole, Gerald M. Lemole.
Financial data (yr. ended 10/31/01): Grants paid, $29,350; assets, $3,187 (M); expenditures, $29,365; qualifying distributions, $29,350.
Limitations: Applications not accepted. Giving primarily in PA.
Application information: Contributes only to pre-selected organizations.
Trustees: Emily Jane A. Lemole, Gerald M. Lemole.
EIN: 232887165

47435
The Robert J. & Jean C. Kahn Charitable Foundation
c/o M. Blackman
1900 Market St., Ste. 700
Philadelphia, PA 19103

Established in 1994 in PA.
Donor(s): Robert J. Kahn, Jean C. Kahn.
Financial data (yr. ended 12/31/00): Grants paid, $29,300; assets, $506,654 (M); expenditures, $53,480; qualifying distributions, $29,300.
Limitations: Applications not accepted.
Application information: Contributes only to pre-selected organizations.
Trustee: Robert J. Kahn.
EIN: 237787340

47436
Lil-Maur Foundation
c/o Philip Weiner and Co., Ltd.
14 N. Mercer St., Ste. 662
New Castle, PA 16101-3762
Application address: 116 Valhalla Dr., New Castle, PA 16105, tel.: (724) 654-4155
Contact: Maureen Flaherty Flannery, Pres.

Financial data (yr. ended 09/30/01): Grants paid, $29,300; assets, $506,463 (M); expenditures, $34,893; qualifying distributions, $32,851.
Limitations: Giving limited to New Castle, PA.
Officers: Maureen Flaherty Flannery, Pres.; Harry A. Flannery, Secy.
EIN: 256066104

47437
Pirret Foundation
c/o Dilworth, Paxson, LLP
1739 Market St., Ste. 3200
Philadelphia, PA 19103

Established in 1994.
Donor(s): Joseph B. Pirret.‡
Financial data (yr. ended 12/31/01): Grants paid, $29,259; assets, $671,031 (M); expenditures, $31,103; qualifying distributions, $29,259.

Limitations: Applications not accepted. Giving primarily in NJ and NY.
Application information: Contributes only to pre-selected organizations.
Trustee: Milagros M. Pirret.
EIN: 223351348

47438
Faith Foundation
c/o Richard S. Griffith
458 Pike Rd.
Huntingdon Valley, PA 19006

Established in 1994 in PA.
Donor(s): Griffith, Inc., Richard S. Griffith, Helga L. Griffith, Scott M. Griffith, Brett R. Griffith.
Financial data (yr. ended 09/30/01): Grants paid, $29,080; assets, $421,080 (M); gifts received, $228,874; expenditures, $31,337; qualifying distributions, $30,361.
Limitations: Applications not accepted. Giving primarily in areas of company operations in PA and NJ.
Application information: Contributes only to pre-selected organizations.
Trustees: Barbara L. Baldwin, Brett R. Griffith, Helga L. Griffith, Richard S. Griffith, Richard S. Griffith, Jr., Scott M. Griffith.
EIN: 237794551
Codes: CS, CD

47439
Gertrude English Trust
c/o Allfirst, Trust Tax Div.
21 E. Market St., M/C 402-130
York, PA 17401-1500

Established in 2000 in PA.
Financial data (yr. ended 12/31/00): Grants paid, $29,054; assets, $599,490 (M); expenditures, $32,173; qualifying distributions, $29,054.
Limitations: Applications not accepted. Giving primarily in PA.
Application information: Contributes only to pre-selected organizations.
Trustee: Allfirst.
EIN: 256324558

47440
Coslett Foundation
27 Wallingford Ave.
Wallingford, PA 19086 (610) 566-8071
Contact: Edward W. Coslett, Jr., Tr.

Financial data (yr. ended 12/31/01): Grants paid, $29,000; assets, $678,268 (M); expenditures, $30,554; qualifying distributions, $29,000.
Limitations: Giving primarily in PA.
Trustees: Edward W. Coslett, Jr., Edward W. Coslett III, Harry W. Coslett.
EIN: 236231832

47441
Myer H. Goldman Foundation
c/o Schachtel, Gerstley, Levin & Koplin
1600 Market St., Ste. 3450
Philadelphia, PA 19103-7275

Donor(s): Charles Goldman.‡
Financial data (yr. ended 12/31/99): Grants paid, $29,000; assets, $642,933 (M); expenditures, $41,081; qualifying distributions, $34,838.
Limitations: Applications not accepted. Giving limited to PA.
Application information: Contributes only to pre-selected organizations.
Directors: Charles G. Blumstein, Michael D. Fishbein, Charlotte W. Levin.
EIN: 237243855

47442
B. Clair & Louise P. & Louise W. Jones Charitable Trust
P.O. Box 878
Wellsboro, PA 16901 (570) 723-1451
Contact: Edward H. Owlett, Tr.

Established in 1998 in PA.
Financial data (yr. ended 12/31/01): Grants paid, $29,000; assets, $842,251 (M); expenditures, $39,361; qualifying distributions, $29,000.
Limitations: Giving primarily in FL and PA.
Application information: Application form required.
Trustees: Edward H. Owlett, Louise W. Jones, Thomas M. Owlett.
EIN: 237960049

47443
Harold & Shirley Robinson Foundation
4 Gateway Ctr., 9th Fl.
Pittsburgh, PA 15222 (412) 281-8771

Financial data (yr. ended 09/30/01): Grants paid, $29,000; assets, $665,036 (M); expenditures, $30,968; qualifying distributions, $29,000.
Limitations: Applications not accepted. Giving primarily in Pittsburgh, PA.
Application information: Contributes only to pre-selected organizations.
Trustees: Edward Goldberg, Donald S. Plung, Harold Robinson, Shirley Robinson.
EIN: 256112618

47444
Grove City Foundation
209 W. Pine St.
Grove City, PA 16127 (724) 458-9550
Contact: Timothy Bonner, Secy.

Established in 1948 in PA.
Financial data (yr. ended 12/31/99): Grants paid, $28,985; assets, $1,051,401 (M); gifts received, $45,554; expenditures, $42,550; qualifying distributions, $30,217.
Limitations: Giving primarily in the Grove City, PA, area.
Officers: Ernest D. May, Chair.; Timothy Bonner, Secy.; Norman S. Crill, Joy R. Gallagher, Delores Rodgers, Richard Stevenson.
Directors: Norman S. Crill, Joy R. Gallagher, Dolores Rodgers, Richard Stevenson.
EIN: 256065759

47445
The Max L. & Charlotte G. Bluestone Charitable Trust
220 N. Dithridge St., Apt. 1100
Pittsburgh, PA 15213
Application address: c/o I.J. Rudoy, 436 7th Ave., Koppers Bldg., Pittsburgh, PA 15219

Donor(s): Max L. Bluestone, Charlotte Bluestone.
Financial data (yr. ended 11/30/01): Grants paid, $28,890; assets, $560,771 (M); gifts received, $6,635; expenditures, $31,418; qualifying distributions, $28,890.
Limitations: Giving primarily in Pittsburgh, PA.
Application information: Application form not required.
Trustees: Burton Bluestone, Charlotte Bluestone, Joan Bluestone, Max L. Bluestone, Stuart M. Bluestone.
EIN: 251430964

47446
The William R. and Esther Richmond Foundation
c/o PNC Advisors
1600 Market St.
Philadelphia, PA 19103-7240

Established in 1997 in PA.
Donor(s): William Robert Richmond.
Financial data (yr. ended 11/30/01): Grants paid, $28,872; assets, $626,495 (M); expenditures, $36,841; qualifying distributions, $29,300.
Limitations: Applications not accepted. Giving limited to NY and PA.
Application information: Contributes only to pre-selected organizations.
Trustee: PNC Bank, N.A.
EIN: 237918063

47447
Maxine P. & Martin Epstein Family Foundation
c/o First Union National Bank
P.O. Box 7558
Philadelphia, PA 19101-7558

Established in 1987 in PA.
Financial data (yr. ended 12/31/99): Grants paid, $28,700; assets, $689,851 (M); expenditures, $36,803; qualifying distributions, $28,700.
Limitations: Applications not accepted. Giving primarily in southern NJ and PA.
Application information: Contributes only to pre-selected organizations.
Trustee: First Union National Bank.
EIN: 222815417

47448
The Bruce Family Foundation, Inc.
930 Cass St.
New Castle, PA 16101

Established in 1997 in PA.
Donor(s): M. Joyce Bruce, Robert J. Bruce.
Financial data (yr. ended 12/31/00): Grants paid, $28,670; assets, $1,520,397 (M); gifts received, $160,901; expenditures, $30,491; qualifying distributions, $28,670.
Limitations: Applications not accepted. Giving primarily in PA.
Application information: Contributes only to pre-selected organizations.
Officers: Robert J. Bruce, Pres.; M. Joyce Bruce, Secy.-Treas.
EIN: 232892817

47449
Schiowitz Family Foundation, Inc.
1 George Ave.
Wilkes-Barre, PA 18705

Established in 1992 in PA.
Donor(s): Members of the Schiowitz family.
Financial data (yr. ended 12/31/01): Grants paid, $28,619; assets, $628,503 (M); expenditures, $29,634; qualifying distributions, $28,619.
Limitations: Applications not accepted.
Application information: Contributes only to pre-selected organizations.
Officers: Nathan Schiowitz, Pres.; Albert Schiowitz, V.P.; Morton Schiowitz, Secy.
EIN: 232672420

47450
Harry Cook Foundation
Noble Plz., Ste. 1
Jenkintown, PA 19046
Contact: Seymour Saslow, Treas.

Established in 1969.
Donor(s): Herbert Cook.
Financial data (yr. ended 11/30/01): Grants paid, $28,525; assets, $640,673 (M); expenditures, $29,472; qualifying distributions, $29,115.
Limitations: Applications not accepted. Giving primarily in Philadelphia, PA.
Application information: Contributes only to pre-selected organizations.
Officers: Herbert Cook, Pres.; Seymour Saslow, Treas.
Trustees: Eve L. Cook, Harry L. Cook, Robert M. Cook, Susan B. Gevurtz.
EIN: 236439332

47451
Leo & Kathryne E. Friedman Memorial Charitable Trust
c/o PNC Advisors
P.O. Box 937
Scranton, PA 18501-0937

Established in 1999 in PA.
Financial data (yr. ended 12/31/01): Grants paid, $28,512; assets, $570,785 (M); expenditures, $35,852; qualifying distributions, $31,476.
Limitations: Applications not accepted.
Application information: Contributes only to pre-selected organizations.
Trustee: PNC Bank, N.A.
EIN: 237904319

47452
Lloyd S. Jackson Charitable Trust
c/o Banknorth Investment Management Group, N.A.
24 S. 3rd St.
Oxford, PA 19363

Established in 1990 in PA.
Financial data (yr. ended 12/31/01): Grants paid, $28,500; assets, $696,789 (M); expenditures, $33,970; qualifying distributions, $28,500.
Limitations: Applications not accepted. Giving on a national basis.
Application information: Contributes only to pre-selected organizations.
Trustee: Banknorth Investment Management Group, N.A.
EIN: 236981019

47453
George W. Karr, Jr. and Barbara M. Karr Foundation
61 Gessner Rd.
Kintnersville, PA 18930
Contact: George W. Karr, Jr., Pres.

Established in 1986 in PA.
Donor(s): George W. Karr, Jr.
Financial data (yr. ended 08/31/01): Grants paid, $28,500; assets, $387,027 (M); expenditures, $31,611; qualifying distributions, $28,500.
Limitations: Giving primarily in Philadelphia, PA.
Officer and Director:* George W. Karr, Jr.,* Pres.
EIN: 222773554

47454
Raub Foundation
c/o Hess & Hess, C.P.A.
901 Rohrerstown Rd.
Lancaster, PA 17601-1938
Contact: Stuart H. Raub, Tr.

Donor(s): Stuart H. Raub.
Financial data (yr. ended 12/31/01): Grants paid, $28,500; assets, $487,689 (M); gifts received, $1,750; expenditures, $35,971; qualifying distributions, $28,500.
Limitations: Giving primarily in Lancaster, PA.
Trustees: Marie T. Raub, Stuart H. Raub.
EIN: 222743870

47455
The Marsha and Richard Rothman Family Foundation
925 Chestnut St.
Philadelphia, PA 19107-4216

Established in 2000 in PA.
Donor(s): Richard Rothman, Mrs. Richard Rothman.
Financial data (yr. ended 12/31/01): Grants paid, $28,366; assets, $51,792 (M); gifts received, $30,000; expenditures, $29,416; qualifying distributions, $28,366.
Officer: Richard Rothman, Pres.
EIN: 256683779

47456
The Susan & Ivan Popkin Foundation
8317 Fairview Rd.
Elkins Park, PA 19027

Established in 1996 in PA.
Donor(s): Ruth S. Alexander.
Financial data (yr. ended 12/31/01): Grants paid, $28,300; assets, $9,988 (M); expenditures, $28,300; qualifying distributions, $28,300.
Limitations: Applications not accepted. Giving primarily in Philadelphia, PA.
Application information: Contributes only to pre-selected organizations.
Officers: Susan Popkin, Pres.; Ivan Popkin, Secy.-Treas.
EIN: 232824452

47457
The Sparr Foundation
P.O. Box 6007
Wyomissing, PA 19610
Contact: John R. Allen, Tr. or Jeff Howell, Tr.

Established in 1985 in PA.
Financial data (yr. ended 06/30/01): Grants paid, $28,300; assets, $294,904 (M); expenditures, $31,427; qualifying distributions, $28,455.
Limitations: Giving primarily in AR and PA.
Officers: Joseph Bolognese, Chair.; Tom Fowler, Secy.; John A. Wiest, Treas.
Trustees: John R. Allen, Jeff Howell.
EIN: 222512696

47458
South Butler County School District Foundation
P.O. Box 657, Knoch Rd.
Saxonburg, PA 16056
Application address: c/o Counseling Center, Knoch Senior High School, P.O. Box 628, Saxonburg, PA 16056

Donor(s): Hattie Cooper, Reldon Cooper.
Financial data (yr. ended 06/30/01): Grants paid, $28,200; assets, $1,691,904 (M); gifts received, $14,001; expenditures, $73,646; qualifying distributions, $99,800.
Limitations: Giving limited to residents of South Butler County, PA.
Officers: Regis Schiebel, Pres.; Violet Galey, V.P.; Mary Clare Habenicht, Secy.; Kathryn Helfer, Treas.
Directors: Scott Briggs, David Howard, Linda Knapp, T. Leslie.
EIN: 251735818
Codes: GTI

47459
Lawrence H. and Elizabeth S. Dunlap Foundation
237 W. Chestnut St.
Lancaster, PA 17603
Contact: Hallowell Dunlap, Pres.

Established in 1998 in PA.
Financial data (yr. ended 12/31/01): Grants paid, $28,024; assets, $509,839 (M); expenditures, $35,170; qualifying distributions, $28,190.
Limitations: Giving limited to Kandiyohi County, MN, and Lancaster County, PA.
Application information: Application form required.
Officers and Directors:* Hallowell Dunlap,* Pres.; Mary Frances Dunlap Lindstrom,* V.P. and Secy.-Treas.
EIN: 232964287

47460
R & M Barker Foundation 2
c/o Mellon Bank
P.O. Box 185
Pittsburgh, PA 15230-9897
Application address: c/o Laurie Moritz, 3 Mellon Bank Ctr., Pittsburgh, PA 15230

Financial data (yr. ended 12/31/01): Grants paid, $28,000; assets, $416,573 (M); gifts received, $471,961; expenditures, $43,174; qualifying distributions, $26,689.
Limitations: Giving primarily in MA and IL.
Trustee: Mellon Bank, N.A.
EIN: 256755710

47461
Robert F. Long Foundation
300 Belvedere St.
Carlisle, PA 17013

Established around 1986.
Financial data (yr. ended 12/31/01): Grants paid, $28,000; assets, $213,305 (M); expenditures, $31,052; qualifying distributions, $27,787.
Limitations: Applications not accepted. Giving primarily in PA.
Application information: Contributes only to pre-selected organizations.
Trustees: Benjamin James, Katherine Long, Robert F. Long.
EIN: 222719260

47462
Robert L. Morelli Foundation
535 Smithfield St., Ste. 1300
Pittsburgh, PA 15222

Donor(s): Robert L. Morelli.
Financial data (yr. ended 10/31/01): Grants paid, $27,900; assets, $451,370 (M); expenditures, $32,235; qualifying distributions, $27,900.
Limitations: Applications not accepted. Giving primarily in Beaver Falls, PA.
Application information: Contributes only to pre-selected organizations.
Trustees: Eleanor T. Morelli, Norma Jean Morelli, Robert L. Morelli.
EIN: 237319091

47463
Elmer E. Naugle Foundation
c/o Allfirst, Trust Div.
21 E. Market St.
York, PA 17401-1500
Application address: c/o Alan Rhinehart, Trust Off., Allfirst, P.O. Box 459, Chambersburg, PA 17201

Donor(s): Elmer E. Naugle.
Financial data (yr. ended 07/31/01): Grants paid, $27,900; assets, $516,427 (M); expenditures, $33,200; qualifying distributions, $27,900.
Limitations: Giving limited to the Shippensburg, PA, area.
Trustee: Allfirst.
EIN: 236853070

47464
Charlotte Cushman Foundation
P.O. Box 40037
Philadelphia, PA 19106 (215) 735-4676
Contact: Donna Thomas, Pres.

Financial data (yr. ended 08/31/01): Grants paid, $27,850; assets, $1,124,292 (M); expenditures, $107,539; qualifying distributions, $36,666.
Limitations: Giving primarily in Philadelphia, PA.
Application information: Application form required.
Officers: Donna Thomas, Pres.; Audrey Walters, 1st V.P.; Margaret Chimples, 2nd V.P.; Virgina Maloney, 3rd V.P.; Cirel Magen, Secy.; Lois Flook, Treas.
Trustees: Betty Burke, Anne Elder, Ann Kalbach, Annette Linck, Carol Peterson Nitzberg, Norma Pomerantz, Jeanne P. Wrobleski.
EIN: 231280780

47465
Lillian J. Williams Charitable Trust
c/o Mellon Bank
P.O. Box 185
Pittsburgh, PA 15230-9897

Established in 2001 in PA.
Donor(s): L.J. Williams.
Financial data (yr. ended 12/31/01): Grants paid, $27,713; assets, $528,664 (M); gifts received, $614,100; expenditures, $33,227; qualifying distributions, $29,879.
Limitations: Applications not accepted.
Application information: Contributes only to pre-selected organizations.
Trustee: Mellon Bank, N.A.
EIN: 256595045

47466
Sidney & Lillian Klemow Foundation, Inc.
7 W. Aspen St.
Hazleton, PA 18201
Contact: Sidney Klemow, Pres.

Established in 1985 in NY.
Donor(s): Lillian Klemow, Sidney Klemow.
Financial data (yr. ended 12/31/01): Grants paid, $27,661; assets, $488,265 (M); expenditures, $29,689; qualifying distributions, $27,661.
Limitations: Giving primarily in PA.
Application information: Application form not required.
Officer: Sidney Klemow, Pres.
EIN: 112729095

47467
Harry A. Laudermilch Scholarship Fund
c/o Fulton Financial Advisors, N.A.
P.O. Box 3215
Lancaster, PA 17604-3215
Application address: c/o Lebanon School District, Guidance Dept., 100 S. 8th St., Lebanon, PA 17042

Financial data (yr. ended 09/30/01): Grants paid, $27,527; assets, $450,650 (M); expenditures, $39,213; qualifying distributions, $26,530.
Limitations: Giving limited to residents of Lebanon, PA.
Application information: Application form required.
Trustee: Fulton Financial Advisors, N.A.
EIN: 231989571
Codes: GTI

47468
Russell Charitable Foundation
3100 Dominion Tower
625 Liberty Ave.
Pittsburgh, PA 15222 (412) 562-0148
Contact: C. Andrew Russell, Mgr.

Established in 1999 in PA.
Donor(s): C. Andrew Russell.
Financial data (yr. ended 12/31/00): Grants paid, $27,475; assets, $58,245 (M); expenditures, $27,475; qualifying distributions, $27,475.
Limitations: Giving primarily in Pittsburgh, PA.
Officer and Trustees:* C. Andrew Russell,* Mgr.; Andrew K. Russell, Amy R. Zemper.
EIN: 256619892

47469
The Kopelman Foundation
333 Lancaster Ave., Ste. 177
Wynnewood, PA 19096

Established in 2001 in PA.
Donor(s): Joshua Kopelman, Rena Kopelman.
Financial data (yr. ended 12/31/01): Grants paid, $27,430; assets, $531,196 (M); gifts received, $567; expenditures, $37,492; qualifying distributions, $27,430.
Limitations: Applications not accepted.
Application information: Contributes only to pre-selected organizations.
Trustees: Joshua Kopelman, Rena Kopelman.
EIN: 233096766

47470
Edith Demain Trust
c/o Allfirst, Trust Tax Div.
21 E. Market St., M/C 402-130
York, PA 17401-1500

Established in 2000 in PA.
Financial data (yr. ended 12/31/00): Grants paid, $27,367; assets, $567,221 (M); expenditures, $31,016; qualifying distributions, $27,367.
Limitations: Applications not accepted. Giving primarily in Harrisburg, PA.
Application information: Contributes only to pre-selected organizations.
Trustee: Allfirst.
EIN: 256448960

47471
The Williams Family Foundation
646 Clovelly Ln.
Devon, PA 19333

Established in 1989 in PA.
Donor(s): William L. Williams, Dorothy L. Williams.
Financial data (yr. ended 06/30/02): Grants paid, $27,319; assets, $162,267 (M); gifts received, $60,273; expenditures, $28,412; qualifying distributions, $27,319.
Limitations: Applications not accepted. Giving primarily in PA.
Application information: Contributes only to pre-selected organizations.
Trustees: Dorothy L. Williams, William L. Williams.
EIN: 236978816

47472
The Gail & Michael Rosenberg Foundation
229 Barker Rd.
Wyncote, PA 19095

Established in 1996 in PA.
Donor(s): Florane Sloane.‡
Financial data (yr. ended 12/31/00): Grants paid, $27,264; assets, $146,092 (M); expenditures, $28,496; qualifying distributions, $27,264.
Limitations: Applications not accepted.
Application information: Contributes only to pre-selected organizations.
Trustees: Gail Rosenberg, Michael Rosenberg.
EIN: 232753387

47473
Giving Productively, Inc.
c/o Radnor Financial Advisors, Inc.
485 Devon Park Dr., Ste. 119
Wayne, PA 19087-1807

Established in 1997 in PA.
Donor(s): C. Ian Sym-Smith.
Financial data (yr. ended 12/31/00): Grants paid, $27,220; assets, $703,141 (M); expenditures, $30,452; qualifying distributions, $25,747.
Limitations: Applications not accepted. Giving primarily in Philadelphia, PA.
Application information: Contributes only to pre-selected organizations.
Officer and Directors:* C. Ian Sym Smith,* Pres. and Secy.-Treas.; Alexandra Smith, Andrea Claudia Sym-Smith, Andrew James Sym-Smith, David Bruce Sym-Smith.
EIN: 232931801

47474
The Ingerman Family Foundation
(Formerly Ingerman-Ginsberg Israeli Fellowship Foundation)
c/o Ira Ingerman
1320 Centennial Rd.
Narberth, PA 19072

Established in 1983 in PA.
Donor(s): Ira Ingerman, Stanley Ginsburg.
Financial data (yr. ended 11/30/01): Grants paid, $27,104; assets, $11,460 (M); gifts received, $2,350; expenditures, $28,370; qualifying distributions, $27,104.
Limitations: Applications not accepted. Giving primarily in PA.
Application information: Contributes only to pre-selected organizations.
Officer: Ira Ingerman, Chair.
Director: Eileen Ingerman.
EIN: 232278199

47475
Charles A. & Leona K. Gruber Foundation
c/o First Union National Bank
640 Hamilton St.
Allentown, PA 18101 (610) 439-4686
Contact: James Kressler, Pres.

Financial data (yr. ended 03/31/02): Grants paid, $27,000; assets, $516,291 (M); expenditures, $34,632; qualifying distributions, $27,000.
Limitations: Giving limited to residents of Northampton and Lehigh counties, PA.
Officers: James Kressler, Pres.; Andrew C. Melzer, Secy.-Treas.
Directors: Kindra Brown, Robin Crawford, John Labukas.
EIN: 232003708

47476
The Levit Family Foundation
3440 Lehigh St.
Allentown, PA 18103
Additional address: c/o F.R. Grebe, Main Line Trust Co., 111 Waynewood Ave., Wayne, PA 19087

Established in 1994 in PA.
Donor(s): Irving Levit.
Financial data (yr. ended 06/30/02): Grants paid, $27,000; assets, $210,999 (M); gifts received, $4,688; expenditures, $28,718; qualifying distributions, $27,000.
Limitations: Applications not accepted. Giving primarily in Lehigh Valley, PA.
Application information: Contributes only to pre-selected organizations.
Officers: Irving Levit, Pres. and Treas.; Judith M. Levit, V.P. and Secy.
EIN: 232792552

47477
The Bernard W. & Bernadette Herbst Loeb Charitable Foundation
c/o Murray Y. Alderfer
935 S. Trooper Rd.
Norristown, PA 19403-2312

Established in 1991 in PA.
Donor(s): Bernadette H. Loeb, Bernard W. Loeb.
Financial data (yr. ended 12/31/01): Grants paid, $27,000; assets, $548,378 (M); gifts received, $100; expenditures, $28,792; qualifying distributions, $27,000.
Limitations: Applications not accepted. Giving primarily in Berwyn and Norristown, PA.
Application information: Contributes only to pre-selected organizations.
Officers: Bernard W. Loeb,* Pres.; Robert Gangier,* Secy.; Murray Y. Alderfer,* Treas.
EIN: 232641004

47478
Evelyn Keen Livingood Trust
c/o Allfirst, Trust Tax Div.
21 E. Market St., M/C 402-130
York, PA 17401-1500

Established in 2000 in PA.
Financial data (yr. ended 12/31/01): Grants paid, $26,938; assets, $833,754 (M); expenditures, $48,495; qualifying distributions, $26,938.
Limitations: Applications not accepted. Giving primarily in PA.
Application information: Contributes only to pre-selected organizations.
Trustee: Allfirst.
EIN: 236633304

47479
Florence Y. Flach Music Appreciation Fund
c/o First Union National Bank
Broad and Walnut Sts.
Philadelphia, PA 19109
Application address: c/o James Kressler, First Union National Bank, 702 Hamilton Mall, Allentown, PA 18101

Established in 1992 in PA.
Financial data (yr. ended 05/31/99): Grants paid, $26,800; assets, $428,802 (M); expenditures, $30,031; qualifying distributions, $26,440.
Limitations: Giving primarily in Allentown, PA.
Application information: Application form required.
Trustees: Karl Y. Donecker, First Union National Bank.
EIN: 237711957

47480
Ruth Keith Scholarship Fund
c/o The First National Bank & Trust Co. of Newtown, Trust Dept.
34 S. State St.
Newtown, PA 18940 (215) 968-4872

Financial data (yr. ended 12/31/01): Grants paid, $26,728; assets, $673,432 (M); expenditures, $33,625; qualifying distributions, $33,625.
Limitations: Giving primarily in Bucks County, PA.
Application information: Application form required.

47480—PENNSYLVANIA

Trustees: Joseph Colacicco, Wayne Cordes, Richard Fusco, Barry L. Pflueger, Jr., Sidney T. Yates.
EIN: 236503403
Codes: GTI

47481
Foreman Fleisher Trust
(also known as Foreman Fleisher Trust No. 2)
c/o PNC Advisors
620 Liberty Ave., P2-PTPP-10-2
Pittsburgh, PA 15222-2705
Application address: c/o The Federation of Jewish Agencies of Greater Philadelphia, 2100 Arch St., Philadelphia, PA 19103-1300
Contact: Richard Nassau

Financial data (yr. ended 09/30/01): Grants paid, $26,600; assets, $728,956 (M); expenditures, $28,220; qualifying distributions, $26,600.
Limitations: Giving primarily in PA.
Trustee: PNC Bank, N.A.
EIN: 236201637
Codes: GTI

47482
Jane Patterson Endowment Fund
213 Fairhill Rd.
Hatfield, PA 19440-1141

Established in 1997.
Financial data (yr. ended 12/31/00): Grants paid, $26,550; assets, $476,077 (M); expenditures, $27,150; qualifying distributions, $26,550.
Limitations: Giving primarily in NJ.
Trustee: Donald C. Patterson III.
EIN: 226720021

47483
James K. Adams & Arlene L. Adams Foundation
624 N. Front St.
Wormleysburg, PA 17043   (717) 236-9318
Contact: David H. Radcliff, Tr.

Donor(s): James K. Adams, Arlene L. Adams.
Financial data (yr. ended 12/31/00): Grants paid, $26,500; assets, $291,050 (M); gifts received, $48,000; expenditures, $28,049; qualifying distributions, $26,500; giving activities include $26,500 for loans to individuals.
Limitations: Giving primarily in eastern Cumberland County, PA.
Trustees: James K. Adams II, David H. Radcliff.
EIN: 251665127

47484
William H. & Karen A. Tippins Foundation
112 Fairway Dr.
Pittsburgh, PA 15238-2218

Established in 1995 in PA.
Donor(s): William H. Tippins, Karen A. Tippins.
Financial data (yr. ended 12/31/01): Grants paid, $26,500; assets, $62,723 (M); expenditures, $27,364; qualifying distributions, $26,486.
Limitations: Applications not accepted. Giving primarily in Pittsburgh, PA.
Application information: Contributes only to pre-selected organizations.
Trustees: Karen A. Tippins, William H. Tippins.
EIN: 256507667

47485
Zalman & Evelyn Shapiro Charitable Trust
1045 Lyndhurst Dr.
Pittsburgh, PA 15206-4535
Contact: Zalman Shapiro, Dir. or Evelyn Shapiro, Dir.

Established in 1969 in PA.
Donor(s): Zalman Shapiro, Evelyn Shapiro.

Financial data (yr. ended 12/31/01): Grants paid, $26,495; assets, $85,106 (M); expenditures, $27,609; qualifying distributions, $26,495.
Limitations: Giving primarily in New York, NY and Pittsburgh, PA.
Directors: Evelyn Shapiro, Zalman Shapiro.
EIN: 237011257

47486
R. J. Conrad Charitable Foundation
106 S. Main St., Ste. 808
Butler, PA 16001
Contact: Jeffrey M. Thompson, Tr.

Donor(s): Robert J. Conrad.
Financial data (yr. ended 12/31/99): Grants paid, $26,430; assets, $449,855 (M); gifts received, $335,498; expenditures, $37,473; qualifying distributions, $26,430.
Limitations: Giving primarily in PA.
Application information: Application form not required.
Trustees: Robert J. Conrad, Chair.; David J. Caruso, Jeffrey M. Thompson.
EIN: 237863991

47487
The Markow-Totevy Foundation, Inc.
c/o PNC Advisors
1600 Market St., 4th Fl.
Philadelphia, PA 19103-7240

Established in 1998 in NJ.
Donor(s): George Markow-Totevy.
Financial data (yr. ended 06/30/01): Grants paid, $26,300; assets, $486,525 (M); gifts received, $19,757; expenditures, $27,499; qualifying distributions, $26,266.
Limitations: Applications not accepted. Giving primarily in Boston, MA and New York, NY.
Trustees: Jean-Paul Blachier, Jean-Louis Deville, James B. Foley, George Markow-Totevy, David Rawson, PNC Bank, N.A.
EIN: 223586455

47488
Lamm Family Foundation
c/o BDO Seidman, LLP
1601 Market St.
Philadelphia, PA 19103-2337

Established in 1992 in PA.
Donor(s): Harvey Lamm, Sandra Lamm.
Financial data (yr. ended 12/31/01): Grants paid, $26,230; assets, $79,361 (M); expenditures, $26,376; qualifying distributions, $26,230.
Limitations: Applications not accepted. Giving primarily in New York, NY, and Philadelphia, PA.
Application information: Contributes only to pre-selected organizations.
Directors: Harvey Lamm, Sandra Lamm.
EIN: 232699481

47489
Albert B. Millett Memorial Fund
c/o Mellon Bank, N.A.
P.O. Box 7236, 193-0224
Philadelphia, PA 19101-7236   (215) 553-3208
Contact: Patricia Kling, Asst. V.P., Mellon Bank, N.A.

Established around 1976 in PA.
Financial data (yr. ended 06/30/01): Grants paid, $26,225; assets, $2,024,715 (M); gifts received, $20,000; expenditures, $28,418; qualifying distributions, $26,968.
Limitations: Giving limited to NJ, NY, and PA.
Trustee: Mellon Bank, N.A.
EIN: 236225988

47490
Maier Family Foundation
c/o Wilhelm Maier
6100 W. Ridge Rd.
Erie, PA 16506-1098   (814) 838-6664
Contact: Peggy J. Maier, Tr.

Established in 1993 in PA.
Donor(s): Peggy J. Maier, Wilhelm Maier.
Financial data (yr. ended 12/31/01): Grants paid, $26,200; assets, $1,123,222 (M); expenditures, $37,766; qualifying distributions, $26,542.
Limitations: Giving limited to Erie, PA.
Trustees: Mark W. Maier, Peggy J. Maier, Wilhelm Maier, Daniel L.R. Miller, Stephen E. Morse, Hunter Pugh, Alan F. Woolslare.
EIN: 256397893

47491
Joella P. Bane Trust
c/o PNC Advisors
620 Liberty Ave., P2-PTPP-10-2
Pittsburgh, PA 15222-2705   (412) 762-7645
Contact: Susan Blake, Trust Off., PNC Advisors

Financial data (yr. ended 06/30/01): Grants paid, $26,180; assets, $458,964 (M); expenditures, $29,862; qualifying distributions, $26,263.
Limitations: Giving primarily in PA.
Trustee: PNC Bank, N.A.
EIN: 256229084

47492
Eberhardt I for Scholarship Fund
(also known as Melville A. Eberhardt Trust I for Scholarship Fund)
c/o Mellon Bank, N.A.
P.O. Box 185
Pittsburgh, PA 15230-9897
Application address: Laurie Moritz, Trust Off., Mellon Bank, N.A, 1 Mellon Bank Ctr., Pittsburgh, PA 15258

Financial data (yr. ended 02/28/00): Grants paid, $26,000; assets, $465,898 (M); expenditures, $33,273; qualifying distributions, $26,000.
Limitations: Giving limited to PA.
Application information: Application form required.
Trustee: Mellon Bank, N.A.
EIN: 256129741
Codes: GTI

47493
Irvin E. Herr Foundation
c/o Allfirst, Trust Div.
21 E. Market St.
York, PA 17401-1500
Application address: P.O. Box 2961, Harrisburg, PA 17105-2961
Contact: Joe A. Macri, Trust Admin., Allfirst

Financial data (yr. ended 12/31/01): Grants paid, $26,000; assets, $514,470 (M); expenditures, $29,388; qualifying distributions, $25,485.
Limitations: Giving limited to Cumberland, Dauphin, Northumberland, and Perry counties, PA.
Application information: Application form not required.
Trustee: Allfirst.
EIN: 222550087
Codes: GTI

47494
Agnes Douglas Kuentzel Foundation
c/o Agnes Douglas Kuentzel
1113 Nissley Rd.
Lancaster, PA 17601

Established in 1997 in PA.

Donor(s): Agnes D. Kuentzel.
Financial data (yr. ended 12/31/01): Grants paid, $26,000; assets, $292,243 (M); expenditures, $31,026; qualifying distributions, $26,000.
Limitations: Applications not accepted.
Application information: Contributes only to pre-selected organizations.
Trustee: Agnes D. Kuentzel.
EIN: 232895347

47495
A. Marlyn Moyer, Jr. Scholarship Foundation
409 Hood Blvd.
Fairless Hills, PA 19030 (215) 943-7400
Contact: Susan M. Harkins, Recording Secy.

Financial data (yr. ended 12/31/01): Grants paid, $26,000; assets, $655,655 (M); expenditures, $32,322; qualifying distributions, $27,207.
Limitations: Giving limited to residents of Bucks County, PA.
Application information: Application forms available from guidance counselors in Bucks County high schools or from the Bucks County Chamber of Commerce. Application form required.
Officers and Directors:* Hon. Edward G. Biester, Jr.,* Pres.; Sidney T. Yates,* V.P.; John E. Knoell,* Secy.; Susan M. Harkins,* Recording Secy. and Treas.; Sr. Clare Carty, Virginia Dare, Dirk Dunlap, Frank Fabian, Peter J. Farmer, William A. Morrill, Jacqueline Rattigan, Charles Rollins, Clark L. Shuster, Rosemarie Vassaluzzo.
EIN: 232037282
Codes: GTI

47496
Tribune-Review Charities
503 Martindale St., 3rd Fl.
Pittsburgh, PA 15212
Contact: Raymond A. Hartung, Jr., Treas.

Established in 2000 in PA.
Donor(s): Tribune-Review Publishing Co.
Financial data (yr. ended 12/31/01): Grants paid, $26,000; assets, $49,221 (M); gifts received, $25,000; expenditures, $26,002; qualifying distributions, $25,999.
Application information: Application form not required.
Officers: Edward Harrel, Pres.; H. Yale Gutnick, V.P. and Secy.; Kraig Cawley, V.P.; Raymond A. Hartung, Treas.
Director: Janet Corrinne.
EIN: 251848276
Codes: CS

47497
The Peter Martino Foundation, Inc.
c/o J.C. Hook
2600 One Commerce Sq.
Philadelphia, PA 19103

Established in 1999 in PA.
Donor(s): Peter Martino.
Financial data (yr. ended 12/31/01): Grants paid, $25,900; assets, $602,728 (M); expenditures, $47,330; qualifying distributions, $25,900.
Limitations: Applications not accepted.
Application information: Contributes only to pre-selected organizations.
Officer: Peter Martino, Pres. and Secy.-Treas.
EIN: 233032423

47498
Gicking Family Foundation Trust
Roughshod Farm
39 Mountain Rd.
Sugarloaf, PA 18249
Application address: 130 Walnut St., Sugar Loaf, PA 18249
Contact: Jeffrey S. Gicking, Secy.

Established in 1990 in PA.
Donor(s): Robert K. Gicking, Linda M. Gicking.
Financial data (yr. ended 12/31/00): Grants paid, $25,750; assets, $343,858 (M); expenditures, $27,247; qualifying distributions, $26,650.
Limitations: Giving primarily in PA.
Application information: Application form not required.
Officers: Robert K. Gicking, Chair.; Linda M. Gicking, Vice-Chair.; Jeffrey S. Gicking, Secy.; John M. Gicking, Treas.
EIN: 236995405

47499
Harry T. Stoddart Trust
c/o Mellon Bank, N.A.
P.O. Box 7236
Philadelphia, PA 19101-7236

Donor(s): Harry T. Stoddart.‡
Financial data (yr. ended 09/30/00): Grants paid, $25,750; assets, $1,320,575 (M); expenditures, $32,524; qualifying distributions, $26,228.
Limitations: Applications not accepted. Giving limited to Philadelphia, PA.
Application information: Contributes to 4 pre-selected organizations. Also awards educational scholarships.
Trustee: Mellon Bank, N.A.
EIN: 236224343
Codes: GTI

47500
Haley Foundation
P.O. Box 205
New Hope, PA 18938 (215) 753-3446
Contact: Jeanne Marie Gilbert

Established in 1996.
Donor(s): Robert D. Huxley, Sally Huxley.
Financial data (yr. ended 12/31/01): Grants paid, $25,650; assets, $536,941 (M); gifts received, $50,138; expenditures, $27,510; qualifying distributions, $26,378.
Officer and Trustees:* Robert D. Huxley,* Exec. Dir.; Sally Huxley.
EIN: 232869076

47501
The Geraldine Diehl Wilson Charitable Foundation of Delanco, New Jersey
1900 Market St., Ste. 706
Philadelphia, PA 19103-3514
Contact: Benham Fuhrman, Pres.

Established in 1995 in PA.
Donor(s): Geraldine Diehl Wilson.
Financial data (yr. ended 12/31/01): Grants paid, $25,580; assets, $125,498 (M); gifts received, $25,000; expenditures, $27,344; qualifying distributions, $25,580.
Limitations: Giving primarily in southern NJ.
Officers and Trustees:* Benham Fuhrman,* Pres. and Treas.; Susan F. Holin,* V.P. and Secy.; Donald Beckman, Steven F. Fuhrman, Joseph H. Miller, Geraldine Diehl Wilson.
EIN: 232829467

47502
Raymond B. Carey Foundation, Inc.
c/o Jerry B. McQueen
561 Main St.
Bethlehem, PA 18018

Established in 1987 in PA.
Donor(s): Raymond B. Carey, Jr.
Financial data (yr. ended 12/31/01): Grants paid, $25,525; assets, $109,465 (M); expenditures, $36,186; qualifying distributions, $25,525.
Limitations: Applications not accepted. Giving primarily in NY.
Officers: Raymond B. Carey, Jr., Pres.; Michael Carey, Clerk; Jerry B. McQueen, Treas.
Directors: Lisa Carey, Sheila Carey.
EIN: 222859837

47503
The Sergio Vincent and Penelope Pattrill Proserpi Foundation, Inc.
1906 Philadelphia Ave.
Reading, PA 19607

Established in 1997 in PA.
Donor(s): Sergio V. Proserpi.
Financial data (yr. ended 12/31/01): Grants paid, $25,392; assets, $49,367 (M); expenditures, $28,625; qualifying distributions, $25,392.
Limitations: Applications not accepted. Giving primarily in NY and PA.
Application information: Contributes only to pre-selected organizations.
Officers: Sergio V. Proserpi, Pres.; Penelope Pattrill Proserpi, Secy.-Treas.
EIN: 237849593

47504
Anthony F. Bauer Foundation
c/o First Union National Bank
Broad & Walnuts Sts.
Philadelphia, PA 19109-9989
Application address: c/o First Union National Bank, 10 State House Sq., 2nd Fl., Hartford, CT 06103

Established in 1991 in CT.
Financial data (yr. ended 01/31/00): Grants paid, $25,345; assets, $402,155 (M); expenditures, $29,985; qualifying distributions, $24,953.
Limitations: Giving limited to CT.
Trustee: First Union National Bank.
EIN: 066361528

47505
The G. Leonard Fogelsonger Foundation
c/o Orrstown Bank, Trust Dept.
P.O. Box 250
Shippensburg, PA 17257 (717) 530-2405
Contact: Phyllis Nye, Trust Off., Orrstown Bank

Financial data (yr. ended 05/31/02): Grants paid, $25,250; assets, $270,112 (M); expenditures, $27,523; qualifying distributions, $25,250.
Limitations: Giving primarily in Shippensburg, PA.
Trustee: Orrstown Bank.
Distribution Committee Members: Peggy Boinis, Forest Myers, Kenneth Shoemaker.
EIN: 222599260

47506
Dorothy M. Froelich Charitable Trust
8041 Brittany Pl.
Pittsburgh, PA 15237-6302

Established in 1995 in PA.
Donor(s): Dorothy M. Froelich.‡
Financial data (yr. ended 06/30/01): Grants paid, $25,250; assets, $515,551 (M); expenditures, $27,510; qualifying distributions, $25,250.
Limitations: Giving primarily in Pittsburgh, PA.

47506—PENNSYLVANIA

Trustee: Ross F. Dacal.
EIN: 256507209

47507
Nancy Wagman Foundation
2508 Grant Rd.
Broomall, PA 19008

Established in 1993 in PA.
Financial data (yr. ended 11/30/01): Grants paid, $25,200; assets, $346,800 (M); expenditures, $31,442; qualifying distributions, $25,200.
Limitations: Giving primarily in PA.
Application information: Application form not required.
Officer: Howard Wagman, Chair.
Trustees: Lowell H. Dubrow, James Wagman, Joel Wagman, Mary Wagman, Nela Wagman, Rita Wagman.
EIN: 232709851

47508
The Baxter Foundation
P.O. Box 8186
Radnor, PA 19087

Established in 1998 in PA.
Donor(s): Thomas G. Baxter.
Financial data (yr. ended 12/31/01): Grants paid, $25,185; assets, $762,413 (M); expenditures, $25,250; qualifying distributions, $25,185.
Limitations: Applications not accepted.
Application information: Contributes only to pre-selected organizations.
Trustee: Thomas G. Baxter.
EIN: 256603101

47509
Lauren Albert Foundation
c/o Todd Albert, Rothman Inst.
925 Chestnut St., 5th Fl.
Philadelphia, PA 19107-4216

Established in 1999 in PA.
Donor(s): Todd J. Albert, M.D.
Financial data (yr. ended 12/31/01): Grants paid, $25,000; assets, $40,555 (M); gifts received, $100; expenditures, $25,022; qualifying distributions, $25,000.
Limitations: Applications not accepted. Giving primarily in Philadelphia, PA.
Application information: Contributes only to pre-selected organizations.
Officers: Todd J. Albert, M.D., Pres.; Richard H. Rothman, M.D., V.P. and Secy.; Jonathan Albert, V.P.
EIN: 233000980

47510
Robert Bard Foundation
c/o Mellon Bank, N.A., 3rd Fl.
P.O. Box 7899
Philadelphia, PA 19101-7899 (215) 553-2596
FAX: (215) 553-4542
Contact: Frances T. Smith, Portfolio Off., Mellon Bank

Established in 1988 in PA.
Donor(s): Agnes Cook Bard.‡
Financial data (yr. ended 06/30/01): Grants paid, $25,000; assets, $4,313,448 (M); expenditures, $76,677; qualifying distributions, $35,267.
Limitations: Giving primarily in Royersford and the greater Montgomery County, PA, area.
Application information: Application form not required.
Trustees: Norman E. Donoghue II, Mellon Bank, N.A.
EIN: 236806099

47511
Fine Foundation, Inc.
(Formerly G.E.T. Foundation, Inc.)
c/o SEI Investments
1 Freedom Valley Dr.
Oaks, PA 19456
Contact: R. Menkiewicz

Established in 1984 in DE.
Financial data (yr. ended 12/31/01): Grants paid, $25,000; assets, $1,106,141 (M); expenditures, $33,906; qualifying distributions, $25,000.
Limitations: Giving primarily in DE.
Trustees: SEI Investments, PNC Bank, Delaware.
EIN: 510280052

47512
Frank O. Genuardi Family Foundation
1906 Brandon Rd.
Norristown, PA 19403

Established in 1995.
Donor(s): Francis L. Genuardi, Frank O. Genuardi.
Financial data (yr. ended 09/30/01): Grants paid, $25,000; assets, $449,548 (M); expenditures, $32,080; qualifying distributions, $25,000.
Limitations: Applications not accepted. Giving primarily in PA; some giving also in Italy.
Application information: Contributes only to pre-selected organizations.
Officers: Laurence P. Genuardi, Pres.; Frank O. Genuardi, V.P.; Francis L. Genuardi, Secy.-Treas.
EIN: 232828488

47513
Edith Fitton Herrin Trust
c/o Mellon Bank, N.A.
P.O. Box 7236
Philadelphia, PA 19101-7236

Financial data (yr. ended 06/30/01): Grants paid, $25,000; assets, $600,393 (M); expenditures, $32,644; qualifying distributions, $27,149.
Limitations: Giving limited to PA.
Application information: Application forms are available through Financial Aid offices of local medical schools. Application form required.
Trustee: Mellon Bank, N.A.
EIN: 236500294
Codes: GTI

47514
Gladys M. Hess Memorial Scholarship Fund
1240 Lawyers Bldg.
Pittsburgh, PA 15219
Application address: c/o Daniel A. Angeloni, 11 Ideal Ave., R.D. No. 2, Cheswick, PA 15024
Contact: David P. Siegel, Tr.

Established in 1993 in PA.
Financial data (yr. ended 12/31/01): Grants paid, $25,000; assets, $341,869 (M); expenditures, $28,530; qualifying distributions, $25,000.
Limitations: Giving limited to Allegheny County, PA.
Trustees: Daniel A. Angeloni, David P. Siegel.
EIN: 256400630

47515
Lloyd E. Mitchell Foundation
c/o First Union National Bank
Broad & Walnuts Sts.
Philadelphia, PA 19109
Application address: c/o Vicki Novak, First Union National Bank, P.O. Box 17034, Baltimore, MD 21203, tel.: (410) 332-5242

Financial data (yr. ended 12/31/99): Grants paid, $25,000; assets, $539,610 (M); expenditures, $31,006; qualifying distributions, $25,000.
Limitations: Giving primarily in Baltimore, MD.

Application information: Application form not required.
Trustee: First Union National Bank.
EIN: 526033555

47516
The Philadelphia Award
c/o PNC Advisors
1600 Market St.
Philadelphia, PA 19103-7240
Application address: c/o WHYY Inc., Independence Mall W., 150 N. 6th St., Philadelphia, PA 19106
Contact: William J. Marrazzo, Tr.

Established in 1921.
Financial data (yr. ended 12/31/01): Grants paid, $25,000; assets, $2,035,017 (M); expenditures, $125,481; qualifying distributions, $109,137.
Limitations: Giving limited to residents of the Philadelphia, PA, area.
Application information: Nominations are solicited by advertisement.
Trustees: Denise McGregor Armbrister, Edward G. Boehne, Paul C. Brucker, William J. Marrazzo, PNC Bank, N.A., and 12 additional trustees.
EIN: 236414396
Codes: GTI

47517
Robert W. Riordan Charitable Trust
c/o Smithfield Trust Co.
20 Stanwix St., Ste. 650
Pittsburgh, PA 15222-4801

Established in 1997 in PA.
Donor(s): Robert W. Riordan.
Financial data (yr. ended 09/30/01): Grants paid, $25,000; assets, $215,445 (M); expenditures, $32,744; qualifying distributions, $25,000.
Limitations: Applications not accepted.
Application information: Contributes only to pre-selected organizations.
Trustee: Smithfield Trust Co.
EIN: 237913373

47518
The Sauer Family Foundation
c/o Harry J. Sauer
1079 Victor Ln.
Bryn Mawr, PA 19010

Financial data (yr. ended 12/31/01): Grants paid, $25,000; assets, $73,367 (M); gifts received, $239; expenditures, $25,048; qualifying distributions, $25,000.
Officer: Harry J. Sauer, Pres.
EIN: 232963352

47519
Martha F. Wells Family Foundation
100 Four Falls Corporate Ctr., Ste. 202
West Conshohocken, PA 19428

Established in 2000.
Donor(s): Martha F. Wells.
Financial data (yr. ended 12/31/00): Grants paid, $25,000; assets, $1,073,971 (M); gifts received, $1,000,000; expenditures, $28,789; qualifying distributions, $28,687.
Limitations: Applications not accepted. Giving primarily in Lake Forest, CA.
Application information: Contributes only to pre-selected organizations.
Officers and Directors:* Martha F. Wells,* Pres.; David P. Wells,* Secy.; Daniel D. Wells,* Treas.
EIN: 233052776

47520
Stratton Foundation
525 Skippack Pike
Blue Bell, PA 19422-2148
Contact: James W. Stratton, Pres.

Established in 1988 in PA.
Donor(s): James W. Stratton.
Financial data (yr. ended 12/31/01): Grants paid, $24,950; assets, $604,706 (M); gifts received, $116,945; expenditures, $26,536; qualifying distributions, $24,950.
Limitations: Giving primarily in PA.
Application information: Application form not required.
Officers: James W. Stratton, Pres.; Arlene E. Stratton, Secy.-Treas.
EIN: 232508658

47521
The Regina Pearl Foundation
560 Bryn Mawr Ave.
Bryn Mawr, PA 19010

Established in 1994 in PA.
Donor(s): Michael S. Haber, Lois S. Haber.
Financial data (yr. ended 11/30/01): Grants paid, $24,859; assets, $20,371 (M); gifts received, $45,801; expenditures, $24,977; qualifying distributions, $24,859.
Limitations: Applications not accepted.
Application information: Contributes only to pre-selected organizations.
Directors: Lois S. Haber, Michael S. Haber.
EIN: 237787120

47522
Florence E. Sinclair Memorial Fund
c/o First Union National Bank, Trust Tax
123 S. Broad St.
Philadelphia, PA 19109-9989
Application address: 200 E. Broward Blvd., Fort Lauderdale, FL 33301
Contact: Thomas Long, Trust Off., First Union National Bank

Financial data (yr. ended 03/31/00): Grants paid, $24,766; assets, $711,106 (M); expenditures, $31,669; qualifying distributions, $24,766.
Limitations: Giving primarily in FL.
Application information: Application form not required.
Trustee: First Union National Bank.
EIN: 596177808

47523
James L. Carino Family Foundation
300 N. 5th St.
Indiana, PA 15701
Contact: James L. Carino, Tr.

Established in 2000 in PA.
Donor(s): James L. Carino.
Financial data (yr. ended 12/31/01): Grants paid, $24,750; assets, $140,143 (M); gifts received, $50,000; expenditures, $24,762; qualifying distributions, $24,750.
Trustee: James L. Carino.
EIN: 251877039

47524
The Lieber Foundation
1 Oxford Ctr., 40th Fl.
Pittsburgh, PA 15219-6498 (412) 392-2000
Contact: Jerome B. Lieber, Chair.

Donor(s): Members of the Lieber family.
Financial data (yr. ended 11/30/01): Grants paid, $24,730; assets, $225,669 (M); expenditures, $27,147; qualifying distributions, $24,730.
Limitations: Giving limited to Pittsburgh, PA.

Trustees: Jerome B. Lieber, Chair.; Ruth Lieber, Julian Ruslander.
EIN: 237000487

47525
Albert A. Alley Family Foundation
1510 Cornwall Rd.
Lebanon, PA 17042

Established in 1986 in PA.
Donor(s): Albert A. Alley, M.D.
Financial data (yr. ended 12/31/01): Grants paid, $24,485; assets, $249 (M); gifts received, $24,700; expenditures, $24,974; qualifying distributions, $24,485.
Limitations: Applications not accepted. Giving limited to PA.
Application information: Contributes only to pre-selected organizations.
Trustees: Albert A. Alley, M.D., Richard Alley, M.D.
EIN: 236862791

47526
Bucks-Montgomery Home Builders Charitable Foundation
721 Dresher Rd., Ste. 1200
Horsham, PA 19044

Established in 1993 in PA.
Donor(s): Westrum Development.
Financial data (yr. ended 12/31/99): Grants paid, $24,366; assets, $118,576 (M); gifts received, $31,432; expenditures, $38,832; qualifying distributions, $34,990.
Limitations: Applications not accepted.
Officers: George Parry, Pres.; Duane L. Searles, Exec. V.P.; Brad Elliot, V.P.; Tony Chieffo, Sr., Assoc. V.P.; Joy Thomas, Secy.; Jim Moultan, Treas.
EIN: 232669947

47527
Delligatti Charitable Foundation, Inc.
147 Delta Dr.
Pittsburgh, PA 15238-2805
Contact: James A. Delligatti, Pres.

Established in 1986 in PA.
Financial data (yr. ended 12/31/01): Grants paid, $24,250; assets, $316,981 (M); expenditures, $27,058; qualifying distributions, $24,250.
Limitations: Giving primarily in PA.
Officer and Director:* James A. Delligatti,* Pres.
EIN: 256289193

47528
E. E. Murry Family Foundation
1899 Lititz Pike
Lancaster, PA 17601-6518
Contact: J.B. Ford

Established in 1986 in PA.
Financial data (yr. ended 12/31/01): Grants paid, $24,250; assets, $4,459,912 (M); gifts received, $147,176; expenditures, $46,879; qualifying distributions, $46,879.
Limitations: Giving primarily in Hot Springs, AR and Lancaster County, PA.
Application information: Application form not required.
Trustees: Emanuel E. Murry, William E. Murry.
EIN: 231948416

47529
Plotkin-Katz Foundation
59 Glenview Rd.
Glen Mills, PA 19342-1115
Contact: Stephen Plotkin, Tr. or Marcia Plotkin, Tr.

Donor(s): Marcia Plotkin, Stephen Plotkin.

Financial data (yr. ended 12/31/01): Grants paid, $24,236; assets, $303,668 (M); expenditures, $25,486; qualifying distributions, $24,236.
Trustees: Marcia Plotkin, Stephen Plotkin.
EIN: 237866034

47530
Robert T. & Beatrice V. Bowman Scholarship Fund
c/o Allfirst, Trust Tax Dept.
21 E. Market St., M/C 402-130
York, PA 17401-1500
Application address: c/o Guidance Office, South Western High School, 200 Bowman Rd., Hanover, PA 17331

Financial data (yr. ended 12/31/00): Grants paid, $24,000; assets, $769,923 (M); expenditures, $27,795; qualifying distributions, $24,000.
Limitations: Giving limited to residents of Penn, Manheim, or West Manheim townships, PA.
Trustee: Allfirst.
EIN: 237684863

47531
Harold Newlin Hill Foundation
c/o Mellon Bank, N.A.
P.O. Box 7236
Philadelphia, PA 19101-7236

Financial data (yr. ended 06/30/01): Grants paid, $24,000; assets, $426,887 (M); expenditures, $29,947; qualifying distributions, $25,776.
Limitations: Applications not accepted. Giving on a national basis.
Application information: Unsolicited requests for funds not accepted.
Trustee: Mellon Bank, N.A.
EIN: 236228294
Codes: GTI

47532
Kirkwood Charitable Trust
(Formerly Edgewater Corporation Charitable Trust)
c/o Resource Conservancy, Inc.
3 Gateway Ctr., Ste. 290
Pittsburgh, PA 15222-2602 (412) 471-9117
Contact: Kathy Shotwell

Donor(s): Edgewater Corp.
Financial data (yr. ended 12/31/01): Grants paid, $24,000; assets, $421,664 (M); expenditures, $61,765; qualifying distributions, $24,000.
Limitations: Giving primarily in areas of company operations in PA.
Trustee: John B. Kirkwood.
EIN: 256022200
Codes: CS, CD

47533
Litvin, Bumberg, Matusow, & Young Lawyers Concerned for Kids
c/o M.L. Silow
2000 Market St., 10th Fl.
Philadelphia, PA 19103-3291

Established in 1999 in PA.
Financial data (yr. ended 12/31/01): Grants paid, $24,000; assets, $2,752 (M); gifts received, $26,000; expenditures, $24,127; qualifying distributions, $24,000.
Limitations: Applications not accepted. Giving primarily in Philadelphia, PA.
Application information: Contributes only to pre-selected organizations.
Directors: Theodore J. Caldwell, Jr., Frederic S. Eisenberg, Rosalind T. Kaplan, S. Gerald Litvin, Donald E. Matusow, Gerald A. McHugh, Michael J. Panichelli.
EIN: 311629205

47534
St. Francis Educational Endowment Fund
212 S. Front St.
Clearfield, PA 16830-2218
Contact: Rev. Dennis C. Hadberg, Dir.

Financial data (yr. ended 12/31/01): Grants paid, $24,000; assets, $422,760 (M); gifts received, $18,453; expenditures, $27,652; qualifying distributions, $24,000.
Limitations: Giving limited to Clearfield, PA.
Application information: Application form required.
Directors: James P. Moore.
Trustee: Susan Bracco, Timothy B. Fannin, Fr. Dennis C. Hodberg, Scott Nutt, William Schriner.
EIN: 251422246

47535
Stafford Family Foundation
c/o First Union National Bank
Broad and Walnut Sts., Ste. PA1308
Philadelphia, PA 19109

Established in 1997 in FL.
Donor(s): Ardietta Stafford, John Stafford.
Financial data (yr. ended 12/31/99): Grants paid, $24,000; assets, $588,357 (M); expenditures, $26,814; qualifying distributions, $24,000.
Limitations: Applications not accepted.
Application information: Contributes only to pre-selected organizations.
Directors: Ardietta F. Stafford, John M. Stafford, John M. Stafford, Jr., Michael A. Stafford.
Trustee: First Union National Bank.
EIN: 593484911

47536
The Peter & Betsy Longstreth Foundation, Inc.
301 W. Gravers Ln.
Philadelphia, PA 19118

Financial data (yr. ended 12/31/01): Grants paid, $23,950; assets, $464,627 (M); gifts received, $123,113; expenditures, $24,507; qualifying distributions, $23,950.
Limitations: Applications not accepted.
Application information: Contributes only to pre-selected organizations.
Directors: Elizabeth Longstreth, Peter Longstreth.
EIN: 232974092

47537
The Angelo Brothers Company Founders Scholarship Foundation
c/o Barton Pasternak
12401 McNulty Rd.
Philadelphia, PA 19154-3297 (215) 671-2000

Donor(s): Seagull Lighting, Jih Kuang Electric, Viva (HK) Co., Ltd., Mospen Products.
Financial data (yr. ended 12/31/00): Grants paid, $23,750; assets, $413,493 (M); gifts received, $10,140; expenditures, $24,108; qualifying distributions, $23,453.
Limitations: Giving limited to PA.
Application information: Application form required.
Trustees: John Angelo, Raymond Angelo, Stanley Angelo, Barton Pasternak.
EIN: 232825756
Codes: GTI

47538
William G. Gale Foundation
688 Center Rd.
Pittsburgh, PA 15239 (412) 793-4388
Contact: Paul J. O'Block, Tr.

Established in 1996 in PA.

Financial data (yr. ended 12/31/00): Grants paid, $23,685; assets, $15,632 (M); expenditures, $26,685; qualifying distributions, $23,519.
Limitations: Giving limited to residents of Export, PA.
Application information: Applicant must include high school transcript and letters of recommendation.
Trustees: William Jelochen, Paul J. O'Block.
EIN: 251701420
Codes: GTI

47539
Meyerson Family Foundation
2016 Spruce St.
Philadelphia, PA 19103-6524 (215) 732-6116
Contact: Martin Meyerson, Dir. or Margy E. Meyerson, Dir.

Established in 1993.
Donor(s): Martin Meyerson, Margy Ellin Meyerson.
Financial data (yr. ended 11/30/01): Grants paid, $23,550; assets, $522,599 (M); expenditures, $28,160; qualifying distributions, $23,550.
Limitations: Giving primarily in NY and PA.
Trustees: Margy Ellin Meyerson, Martin Meyerson.
EIN: 237743081

47540
Carlson Cultural Trust
901 Rohrerstown Rd.
Lancaster, PA 17601

Established in 1994 in PA.
Donor(s): Lois Carlson.
Financial data (yr. ended 12/31/01): Grants paid, $23,508; assets, $732,323 (M); expenditures, $30,086; qualifying distributions, $23,508.
Limitations: Applications not accepted. Giving primarily in PA.
Application information: Contributes only to pre-selected organizations.
Trustees: Judith A. Bergdoll, Richard Humphreys, John W. Roberts, Stephen Roka.
EIN: 237752835

47541
Silver Levine Charitable Trust
1844 Meadowbrook Ln.
P.O. Box 1
Abington, PA 19001 (215) 884-8093
Contact: Evelyn Silver, Tr. or Harry Silver, Tr.

Donor(s): Evelyn Silver, Harry Silver.
Financial data (yr. ended 12/31/01): Grants paid, $23,499; assets, $283,433 (M); gifts received, $35,044; expenditures, $24,227; qualifying distributions, $23,499.
Limitations: Giving primarily in PA.
Trustees: Evelyn Silver, Harry Silver.
EIN: 232188614

47542
Abram M. Snyder Foundation, Inc.
3791 Lycoming Creek Rd.
Cogan Station, PA 17728-9802

Donor(s): Abram M. Snyder.
Financial data (yr. ended 12/31/01): Grants paid, $23,468; assets, $1 (M); expenditures, $25,769; qualifying distributions, $23,468.
Limitations: Giving primarily in PA.
Officers: Abram M. Snyder, Pres.; Lucinda Snyder, V.P. and Secy.; Carl Snyder, V.P. and Treas.; Dorothy Snyder, V.P.
EIN: 232746308

47543
Bonnie and Bruce Feinberg Family Foundation
1307 Wrenfield Way
Villanova, PA 19085 (610) 896-6321
Contact: Bruce Feinberg, Tr.

Established in 1999 in PA.
Donor(s): Bruce Feinberg, Bonnie Feinberg.
Financial data (yr. ended 09/30/01): Grants paid, $23,335; assets, $49,908 (M); gifts received, $55,582; expenditures, $26,913; qualifying distributions, $23,335.
Limitations: Giving primarily in Philadelphia, PA.
Trustees: Bonnie Feinberg, Brad Feinberg, Brian Feinberg, Bruce Feinberg, Beth Feinberg Rosenstein.
EIN: 256657258

47544
The Merz Family Foundation
c/o Jill R. Fowler
1 Logan Sq., Ste. 555
Philadelphia, PA 19103-6996

Established in 1999 in PA.
Donor(s): J. Fred Merz, Jr.
Financial data (yr. ended 12/31/01): Grants paid, $23,200; assets, $267,622 (M); expenditures, $24,786; qualifying distributions, $23,200.
Limitations: Applications not accepted. Giving primarily in Blacksburg, VA; some giving also in MN, PA, and TX.
Application information: Contributes only to pre-selected organizations.
Trustee: J. Fred Merz, Jr.
EIN: 233023616

47545
Paul & Dorothy Reitz Charitable Trust
20 Stanwix St., Ste. 650
Pittsburgh, PA 15222-4801

Financial data (yr. ended 12/31/01): Grants paid, $23,200; assets, $516,715 (M); expenditures, $28,003; qualifying distributions, $23,200.
Limitations: Applications not accepted. Giving primarily in DuBois, PA.
Application information: Contributes only to pre-selected organizations.
Trustee: Smithfield Trust Co.
EIN: 256480905

47546
The Chris Blazakis Foundation
650 Palmer Ln.
Yardley, PA 19067

Established in 1994.
Donor(s): Chris J. Blazakis.
Financial data (yr. ended 09/30/01): Grants paid, $23,100; assets, $169,556 (M); gifts received, $30,000; expenditures, $24,930; qualifying distributions, $23,752.
Limitations: Applications not accepted. Giving primarily in MA.
Application information: Contributes only to pre-selected organizations.
Trustees: Chris Blazakis, Hresanthe Calogredes, Rev. James Calogredes, Georgia Presti.
EIN: 232792334

47547
Sparky and Anne Herman Trust
c/o First Union National Bank
123 S. Broad St., Ste. PA 1308
Philadelphia, PA 19109-1199

Financial data (yr. ended 12/31/00): Grants paid, $23,092; assets, $744,634 (M); expenditures, $34,311; qualifying distributions, $23,092.
Limitations: Applications not accepted.

Application information: Contributes only to pre-selected organizations.
Trustee: First Union National Bank.
EIN: 596977873

47548
Anton Charitable Trust
c/o DM & H
One Liberty Pl.
Philadelphia, PA 19103-7396

Established in 1998 in PA.
Donor(s): Frederick W. Anton III.
Financial data (yr. ended 10/31/01): Grants paid, $23,000; assets, $414,190 (M); gifts received, $163,150; expenditures, $24,825; qualifying distributions, $23,000.
Limitations: Applications not accepted. Giving primarily in Philadelphia, PA.
Application information: Contributes only to pre-selected organizations.
Trustee: Frederick W. Anton III.
EIN: 237987969

47549
Bentley Foundation
1595 Paoli Pike
West Chester, PA 19380-6167 (610) 436-5500
Contact: Thomas G.M. Bentley, Tr.

Established in 1994 in PA.
Donor(s): Thomas G.M. Bentley.
Financial data (yr. ended 12/31/01): Grants paid, $23,000; assets, $1 (M); gifts received, $20,500; expenditures, $23,605; qualifying distributions, $23,000.
Limitations: Giving primarily in PA.
Trustees: Thomas G.M. Bentley, Mitchell Reddy.
EIN: 232792411

47550
Robert H. & Beverly U. Fowler Foundation Trust
c/o Mellon Bank, N.A.
P.O. Box 7236, AIM No. 193-0224
Philadelphia, PA 19101-7236

Established in PA in 1998.
Donor(s): Robert H. Fowler, Beverly U. Fowler.
Financial data (yr. ended 12/31/01): Grants paid, $23,000; assets, $455,034 (M); expenditures, $29,307; qualifying distributions, $23,000.
Limitations: Applications not accepted.
Trustee: Mellon Bank, N.A.
EIN: 256578901

47551
The Strine Foundation
c/o John A. Gilles, Jr.
630 Fairview Rd., Ste. 205
Swarthmore, PA 19081-2336

Donor(s): Walter M. Strine, Sr.
Financial data (yr. ended 11/30/01): Grants paid, $23,000; assets, $1 (M); gifts received, $50,000; expenditures, $23,083; qualifying distributions, $23,000.
Limitations: Giving limited to PA.
Application information: Application form not required.
Officers: Walter M. Strine, Sr., Chair.; William B. Strine, Vice-Chair.; Walter M. Strine, Jr., Secy.
EIN: 232140514

47552
Blanche and Dewayne Wivagg Charitable Foundation
c/o PNC Advisors
620 Liberty Ave., P2-PTPP-10-2
Pittsburgh, PA 15222-2705
Contact: Susan Blake, Trust Off., PNC Advisors

Established in 1999 in PA.
Donor(s): Blanche Wivagg, Dewayne Wivagg.
Financial data (yr. ended 12/31/01): Grants paid, $23,000; assets, $393,191 (M); expenditures, $24,552; qualifying distributions, $22,888.
Limitations: Giving primarily in McKeesport, PA.
Trustee: PNC Bank, N.A.
EIN: 237933106

47553
Carl C. Yount Charitable Trust
c/o PNC Advisors
620 Liberty Ave., P2-PTPP-10-2
Pittsburgh, PA 15222
Application addresses: c/o Chatham College, Woodland Rd., Pittsburgh, PA 15232, tel.: (412) 441-8200; c/o University of Pittsburgh, P.O. Box 7436, Pittsburgh, PA 15213, tel.: (412) 624-4571

Financial data (yr. ended 12/31/01): Grants paid, $22,900; assets, $237,918 (M); expenditures, $25,954; qualifying distributions, $22,950.
Limitations: Giving limited to Pittsburgh, PA.
Trustee: PNC Bank, N.A.
EIN: 256085369

47554
Roger C. Gibson Family Foundation
1304 Regency Dr.
Pittsburgh, PA 15237 (412) 369-9925
Contact: Roger G. Gibson, Tr.

Established in 1993 in PA.
Financial data (yr. ended 12/31/00): Grants paid, $22,876; assets, $40,807 (M); gifts received, $14,530; expenditures, $24,433; qualifying distributions, $22,876.
Limitations: Giving primarily in Pittsburgh, PA.
Trustee: Roger C. Gibson.
EIN: 256297679

47555
Alice Livingston Trout Family Memorial Fund
c/o Fulton Financial Advisors, N.A.
P.O. Box 3215
Lancaster, PA 17604-3215
Contact: Vincent Lattanzio, Trust Off., Fulton Financial Advisors, N.A.

Established in 1992 in PA.
Donor(s): Frank B. Trout.‡
Financial data (yr. ended 02/28/01): Grants paid, $22,826; assets, $451,270 (M); expenditures, $28,214; qualifying distributions, $22,091.
Limitations: Giving primarily in eastern PA.
Trustees: John S. May, Fulton Financial Advisors, N.A.
EIN: 237660671
Codes: GTI

47556
Rachel H. Miller Trust
c/o Allfirst, Trust Div.
21 E. Market St.
York, PA 17401-1500
Contact: Arlene C. LaPore, V.P. and Trust Off., Allfirst

Financial data (yr. ended 06/30/01): Grants paid, $22,775; assets, $905,723 (M); expenditures, $28,744; qualifying distributions, $27,049.
Limitations: Giving primarily in central PA.
Trustee: Allfirst.
EIN: 236642645

47557
John Calvin Noyes Scholarship Fund
c/o Mellon Bank
P.O. Box 185
Pittsburgh, PA 15230-9897

Established in 1998 in MA.

Financial data (yr. ended 12/31/01): Grants paid, $22,750; assets, $893,400 (M); gifts received, $1,000; expenditures, $33,446; qualifying distributions, $26,179.
Limitations: Giving limited to the Newburyport, MA, area.
Application information: Recipients are chosen by the Newburyport School Committee. Application form required.
Trustees: Boston Safe Deposit & Trust Co., First & Ocean National Bank.
EIN: 046040470
Codes: GTI

47558
Franklin County Chapter N.S.D.A.R.
171 N. Coldbrook Ave.
Chambersburg, PA 17201
Application address: c/o Mrs. John Stumbaugh, 10 Downing Ct., Chambersburg, PA 17201, tel.: (717) 263-1238

Established in 1999 in PA.
Financial data (yr. ended 12/31/99): Grants paid, $22,717; assets, $635,663 (M); expenditures, $34,932; qualifying distributions, $31,495.
Limitations: Giving primarily in Franklin and Fulton counties, PA.
Application information: Application forms for scholarship funds distributed to guidance departments of high schools in Franklin and Fulton counties.
Officer: Mrs. Alfred M. Strang, Treas.
EIN: 256057241

47559
Masel Family Charitable Trust
P.O. Box 513
Huntingdon Valley, PA 19006
Contact: Edythe Masel, Tr.; or Theresa Masel-Auerbach, Tr.

Established in 1990 in PA.
Donor(s): Theresa Masel-Auerbach, Edythe Masel.
Financial data (yr. ended 12/31/01): Grants paid, $22,652; assets, $197,667 (M); gifts received, $15,000; expenditures, $23,183; qualifying distributions, $22,652.
Limitations: Giving on a national basis, with emphasis on PA.
Application information: Application form not required.
Trustees: Edythe Masel, Theresa Masel-Auerbach.
EIN: 237452541

47560
Simpson Family Foundation
102 Buckingham Rd.
Pittsburgh, PA 15215

Established in 2001 in PA.
Financial data (yr. ended 12/31/01): Grants paid, $22,525; assets, $564,112 (M); gifts received, $568,306; expenditures, $31,905; qualifying distributions, $22,525.
Limitations: Giving primarily in Pittsburgh, PA.
Trustee: William Simpson.
EIN: 256742398

47561
The William and Kathleen Brady Foundation, Inc.
2600 1 Commerce Sq.
Philadelphia, PA 19103-7098
Application address: 1680 Hunters Cir., West Chester, PA 19380; Tel.: (610) 644-2272
Contact: William P. Brady, Treas.

Established in 1997 in PA.
Donor(s): Kathleen G. Brady.

47561—PENNSYLVANIA

Financial data (yr. ended 12/31/01): Grants paid, $22,500; assets, $363,227 (M); gifts received, $10,000; expenditures, $29,497; qualifying distributions, $22,500.
Application information: Application form required.
Officers: Kathleen G. Brady, Pres.; William P. Brady, Secy.-Treas.
EIN: 232938437

47562
G. Scott & Bessie K. Guyer Foundation
c/o SunBank
P.O. Box 57
Selinsgrove, PA 17870
Application address: 43 S. 5th St., Sunbury, PA 17801, tel.: (570) 286-1582

Established in 1975 in PA.
Financial data (yr. ended 12/31/01): Grants paid, $22,500; assets, $835,319 (M); expenditures, $38,960; qualifying distributions, $31,685.
Limitations: Giving limited to organizations within a ten-mile radius of Shamokin Dam, Snyder County, PA.
Application information: Application form required.
Committee Members: Sidney Apfelbaum, Margaret Chubb, Donald Micozzi, Lavina Truslow, Ann L. Winegartener, Martha Zellers.
Trustee: SunBank.
EIN: 237413781

47563
Klein Schricker Charitable Foundation
318 Thornbrook Ave.
Rosemont, PA 19010-1637

Established in 2001 in PA.
Donor(s): Jonathan H. Klein, Sara Klein.
Financial data (yr. ended 12/31/01): Grants paid, $22,500; assets, $61,340 (M); gifts received, $86,759; expenditures, $22,551; qualifying distributions, $22,500.
Limitations: Applications not accepted. Giving primarily in Washington, DC and PA.
Application information: Contributes only to pre-selected organizations.
Directors: Jonathan H. Klein, Sara Klein.
EIN: 256748019

47564
Louis G. and Karen A. Pavoni Foundation
958 Catfish Ln.
Pottstown, PA 19464

Established in 1986 in PA.
Donor(s): Karen A. Pavoni, Louis G. Pavoni.
Financial data (yr. ended 12/31/01): Grants paid, $22,436; assets, $164,320 (M); gifts received, $30,000; expenditures, $24,273; qualifying distributions, $24,273.
Limitations: Applications not accepted. Giving primarily in PA.
Application information: Contributes only to pre-selected organizations.
Trustee: Karen A. Pavoni.
EIN: 232432421

47565
Burket-Plack Foundation, Inc.
c/o Glenmede Trust Co.
1650 Market St., Ste. 1200
Philadelphia, PA 19103-7391
Application address: 134 Fitzwater St., Philadelphia, PA 19147
Contact: Carmen W. Burket, Chair.

Established in 1993 in PA.
Donor(s): Carmen W. Burket.

Financial data (yr. ended 12/31/01): Grants paid, $22,400; assets, $611,706 (M); expenditures, $31,645; qualifying distributions, $22,400.
Limitations: Giving primarily in Philadelphia, PA.
Application information: Application form not required.
Officer: Carmen W. Burket, Chair. and Secy.-Treas.
EIN: 232735643

47566
The Thomas P. & Marian G. Wolf Trust
c/o Thomas P. Wolf
33 Spring Trail
Fairfield, PA 17320

Donor(s): Thomas P. Wolf.
Financial data (yr. ended 04/30/02): Grants paid, $22,290; assets, $64,181 (M); gifts received, $15,680; expenditures, $23,759; qualifying distributions, $22,290.
Limitations: Applications not accepted. Giving primarily in the Northeast, with emphasis on MD, NY, and PA.
Application information: Contributes only to pre-selected organizations.
Trustees: Martin L. Edelman, Thomas P. Wolf.
EIN: 136208693

47567
Lamco Foundation
c/o M&T Bank
101 W. 3rd St., Trust Tax Dept.
Williamsport, PA 17701
Application address: c/o Lamco Communications, Inc., 460 Market St., Ste. 310, Williamsport, PA 17701
Contact: Andrew Stabler, Jr., Advisory Comm.

Donor(s): Lamco Communications, Inc.
Financial data (yr. ended 12/31/01): Grants paid, $22,133; assets, $487,119 (M); gifts received, $15,000; expenditures, $29,990; qualifying distributions, $21,901.
Limitations: Giving primarily in Williamsport, PA.
Advisory Committee Members: Howard Lamade, J. Robert Lamade, James S. Lamade, Andrew Stabler, Jr.
Trustee: M&T Bank.
EIN: 246012727
Codes: CS, CD

47568
Herbert J. and Geneva S. Hull Scholarship Fund, Inc.
c/o Rev. Elbridge Holland
85 Laurel Ln., P.O. Box 863
Greentown, PA 18426-0863
Contact: John Frank, Treas.

Established in 1993 in NJ.
Donor(s): Geneva S. Hull.‡
Financial data (yr. ended 12/31/01): Grants paid, $22,125; assets, $385,595 (M); expenditures, $26,053; qualifying distributions, $22,125.
Limitations: Giving primarily in NJ.
Application information: Application form required.
Officer and Directors:* John Frank,* Treas.; William T. Archer, Rev. Elbridge Hull, Elizabeth Hontz, Hon. Frederic Webber.
EIN: 223173661
Codes: GTI

47569
The Lipstein Family Foundation
417 Conestoga Rd.
Malvern, PA 19355

Established in 1999 in PA.
Donor(s): Sanford Lipstein.

Financial data (yr. ended 12/31/01): Grants paid, $22,100; assets, $934,826 (M); gifts received, $351,594; expenditures, $23,336; qualifying distributions, $22,100.
Limitations: Applications not accepted.
Application information: Contributes only to pre-selected organizations.
Officers: Sanford Lipstein, Pres.; Gail M. Lipstein, Secy.
EIN: 233008418

47570
William and L. R. Gale Community Foundation
c/o Citizens & Northern Bank
P.O. Box 58
Wellsboro, PA 16901

Financial data (yr. ended 12/31/01): Grants paid, $22,000; assets, $93,305 (M); expenditures, $25,241; qualifying distributions, $21,566.
Limitations: Applications not accepted.
Application information: Contributes only to pre-selected organizations.
Committee: Michael E. Callahan, Deborah J. Long, Henry W. Lush.
Trustee: Citizens & Northern Bank.
EIN: 236925368

47571
Hilliard A. Hasenkamp Trust
21 E. Market St., M/C 402-130
York, PA 17401-1500

Established in 1999 in PA.
Financial data (yr. ended 12/31/01): Grants paid, $22,000; assets, $385,335 (M); expenditures, $26,123; qualifying distributions, $22,000.
Limitations: Giving on a national basis.
Application information: Application form not required.
Trustee: Allfirst.
Committee Member: Donn L. Snyder.
EIN: 256582125

47572
Betty Jane & Marc H. Hollender Foundation
1845 Walnut St., Ste. 1300
Philadelphia, PA 19103

Donor(s): Betty Jane Hollender.
Financial data (yr. ended 12/31/01): Grants paid, $22,000; assets, $315,077 (M); expenditures, $22,042; qualifying distributions, $21,729.
Limitations: Applications not accepted. Giving primarily in New York, NY.
Application information: Contributes only to pre-selected organizations.
Officer: Lisa A. Paparone, Mgr.
Trustee: Betty Jane Hollender.
EIN: 236462595

47573
Henry M. and Beatrice B. Miller Foundation
4708 Galen Rd.
Harrisburg, PA 17110-3236
Application address: 2284 Maple Hill Rd., Shaftsbury, VT 05262, tel.: (802) 375-6773
Contact: Linda Miller, Dir.

Financial data (yr. ended 12/31/01): Grants paid, $22,000; assets, $214,408 (M); expenditures, $24,317; qualifying distributions, $22,000.
Limitations: Giving primarily in the Boston, MA, area; some giving also in New York, NY, Harrisburg and Philadelphia, PA, and VT.
Application information: Application form not required.
Officer: Beatrice Miller, Pres.
Director: Linda Miller.
EIN: 236282470

47574
John Schwab Foundation
c/o Emporium Trust Co.
P.O. Box 57
Selinsgrove, PA 17870
Application address: 2 E. 4th St., Emporium, PA 15834

Financial data (yr. ended 12/31/01): Grants paid, $22,000; assets, $540,002 (M); expenditures, $28,053; qualifying distributions, $24,451.
Application information: Application form required.
Trustees: Charles Borchetta, Rev. Brent Davidson, SunBank.
EIN: 256029493
Codes: GTI

47575
Onyshko Foundation
3620 Fleming Ave.
Pittsburgh, PA 15212

Established in 2000 in PA.
Donor(s): William Onyshko.
Financial data (yr. ended 12/31/01): Grants paid, $21,890; assets, $22,633 (M); gifts received, $30,000; expenditures, $22,522; qualifying distributions, $21,890.
Limitations: Giving primarily in PA.
Officer: William Onyshko, Pres.
EIN: 256724618

47576
Paul M. Smucker Family Foundation
2727 Old Philadelphia Pike
Bird In Hand, PA 17505-9707

Donor(s): Smucker Mgmt. Corp.
Financial data (yr. ended 08/31/02): Grants paid, $21,877; assets, $12,458 (M); gifts received, $15,000; expenditures, $22,402; qualifying distributions, $21,877.
Limitations: Applications not accepted. Giving primarily in PA.
Application information: Contributes only to pre-selected organizations.
Trustees: Jerald L. Smucker, John E. Smucker II, Paul M. Smucker.
EIN: 232267540

47577
The Dina and Jerry Wind Foundation
c/o Yoram & Vardina Wind
1041 Waverly Rd.
Gladwyne, PA 19035

Established in 1993 in PA.
Donor(s): Yoram J. Wind.
Financial data (yr. ended 12/31/01): Grants paid, $21,875; assets, $1,094,661 (M); expenditures, $25,873; qualifying distributions, $21,875.
Limitations: Applications not accepted. Giving primarily in PA.
Application information: Contributes only to pre-selected organizations.
Directors: Vardina Wind, Yoram J. Wind.
EIN: 232745202

47578
Gurrentz Family Charitable Foundation
c/o Morton E. Gurrentz
2020 Ardmore Blvd., Ste. 250
Pittsburgh, PA 15221

Established in 1996 in PA.
Donor(s): Morton E. Gurrentz.
Financial data (yr. ended 12/31/01): Grants paid, $21,824; assets, $129,255 (M); expenditures, $21,841; qualifying distributions, $21,824.
Limitations: Applications not accepted. Giving primarily in PA.
Application information: Contributes only to pre-selected organizations.
Officer: Morton E. Gurrentz, Pres. and Secy.-Treas.
Directors: Patrick H. Gurrentz, Rodger B. Gurrentz, Thomas L. Gurrentz.
EIN: 251790376

47579
Juliano Family Foundation
755 Chestnut Rd.
Sewickley, PA 15143

Established in 1999 in PA.
Donor(s): Mark Juliano, Lisa Juliano.
Financial data (yr. ended 04/30/02): Grants paid, $21,740; assets, $470,979 (M); expenditures, $24,240; qualifying distributions, $21,740.
Limitations: Applications not accepted.
Application information: Contributes only to pre-selected organizations.
Directors: Lisa Juliano, Mark Juliano.
EIN: 522170559

47580
Mayer A. Green Allergy Foundation
120 Woodshire Dr.
Pittsburgh, PA 15215-1714 (412) 471-3818

Financial data (yr. ended 12/31/01): Grants paid, $21,600; assets, $336,029 (M); gifts received, $50; expenditures, $27,048; qualifying distributions, $21,600.
Limitations: Giving primarily in Pittsburgh, PA.
Application information: Application form not required.
Officers: Richard L. Green, Pres.; Dana S. Green, Secy.; Paul K. Rudoy, Treas.
EIN: 237068003

47581
The Dubrow Foundation
c/o W. Ellman
3237 Bristol Rd., Ste. 204
Bensalem, PA 19020
Application address: P.O. Box 314, Moorestown, NJ 08057-0314, tel.: (856) 234-0111
Contact: Walter Dubrow, Tr.

Donor(s): Walter Dubrow.
Financial data (yr. ended 12/31/01): Grants paid, $21,396; assets, $118,119 (M); gifts received, $19,200; expenditures, $21,509; qualifying distributions, $21,460.
Limitations: Giving primarily in NJ and PA.
Trustees: Walter Dubrow, Walter Ellman.
EIN: 236393596

47582
The Evergreen Foundation
250 Beechwood Dr.
Rosemont, PA 19010

Established in 1988 in PA.
Donor(s): Viki Laura List.
Financial data (yr. ended 12/31/01): Grants paid, $21,345; assets, $324,399 (M); expenditures, $24,408; qualifying distributions, $21,345.
Limitations: Applications not accepted. Giving primarily in PA.
Application information: Contributes only to pre-selected organizations.
Trustee: Viki Laura List.
EIN: 236919877

47583
The Miles Family Foundation
310 Alpha Dr.
Pittsburgh, PA 15238

Established in 1995 in PA.
Donor(s): Richard C. Miles, Virginia E. Miles.
Financial data (yr. ended 12/31/01): Grants paid, $21,307; assets, $132,334 (M); gifts received, $13,850; expenditures, $21,502; qualifying distributions, $21,307.
Limitations: Applications not accepted. Giving on a national basis.
Application information: Contributes only to pre-selected organizations.
Trustees: Kathleen Miles Limauro, Jerome A. Miles, Joseph A. Miles, Richard C. Miles, Richard P. Miles, Virginia E. Miles.
EIN: 256507666

47584
The Fischer Foundation
1735 Market St., 10th Fl.
Philadelphia, PA 19103-7505 (215) 988-0700
Contact: Bruce Fischer, Pres.

Donor(s): Bruce Fischer, Nedra Fischer.
Financial data (yr. ended 12/31/01): Grants paid, $21,285; assets, $187,709 (M); expenditures, $27,224; qualifying distributions, $21,285.
Limitations: Giving primarily in PA.
Officer: Bruce Fischer, Pres.
Trustees: Marc Fischer, Nedra Fischer, Stephanie Fischer, Margelle Liss.
EIN: 226104376

47585
Reinecke Family Charitable Foundation
c/o PNC Advisors
620 Liberty Ave., P2-PTPP-10-2
Pittsburgh, PA 15222-2705
Application address: c/o Farrell & Co., 1200 Reedsdale St., Pittsburgh, PA 15233

Established in 1998 in PA.
Donor(s): Farrell & Co.
Financial data (yr. ended 12/31/01): Grants paid, $21,250; assets, $451,575 (M); expenditures, $26,775; qualifying distributions, $21,737.
Limitations: Giving primarily in Pittsburgh, PA.
Trustee: PNC Bank, N.A.
EIN: 232937856
Codes: CS

47586
Freeport Brick Company Charitable Trust
P.O. Box F
Freeport, PA 16229-0306
Contact: Francis H. Lauge, III, Secy.

Established in 1964 in PA.
Donor(s): Freeport Brick Co.
Financial data (yr. ended 12/31/01): Grants paid, $21,200; assets, $730,221 (M); expenditures, $21,600; qualifying distributions, $21,200.
Limitations: Giving primarily in Freeport and Kittanning, PA; giving also to local chapters of national charities.
Application information: Application form not required.
Officers: Donald P. Thiry, Chair.; J.C. Overholt, Vice-Chair.; F.H. Lauge III, Secy.; J. Terry Medovitch, Treas.
EIN: 256074334
Codes: CS, CD

47587
York County Medical Society Educational Trust
c/o Allfirst, Trust Div.
21 E. Market St.
York, PA 17401-1500
Application address: c/o York Hospital, 1001 S. George St., York, PA 17405, tel.: (717) 843-6744
Contact: Rhonda S. Renninger, Exec. Dir.

Donor(s): York County Medical Soc.
Financial data (yr. ended 12/31/01): Grants paid, $21,200; assets, $352,921 (M); expenditures, $22,152; qualifying distributions, $22,143.
Limitations: Giving limited to York County, PA.
Application information: Applicant must supply transcript.
Scholarship Committee Member: Rhonda S. Renninger, Exec. Dir.
Trustee: Allfirst.
EIN: 236284266
Codes: GTI

47588
The Merle E. & Olive Lee Gilliand Foundation
c/o PNC Advisors
620 Liberty Ave., P2-PTPP-10-2
Pittsburgh, PA 15222-2705 (412) 762-3808
Contact: James M. Ferguson

Established in 2001 in PA.
Donor(s): Olive Lee Gilliand.
Financial data (yr. ended 06/30/02): Grants paid, $21,133; assets, $854,071 (M); expenditures, $40,495; qualifying distributions, $21,133.
Limitations: Giving primarily in Pittsburgh, PA.
Trustee: PNC Bank, N.A.
EIN: 256755561

47589
Katharine Masland Lavin Foundation
497 Orlando Ave.
State College, PA 16803-3477

Financial data (yr. ended 12/31/00): Grants paid, $21,000; assets, $348,560 (M); expenditures, $22,696; qualifying distributions, $21,000.
Limitations: Applications not accepted. Giving primarily in PA.
Application information: Contributes only to pre-selected organizations.
Trustees: Cynthia L. Hurley, Michael B. Hurley, Peter M. Lavin, Ruth Ann Lavin.
EIN: 256296612

47590
Robert D. & Margaret W. Quin Foundation
c/o Summit Bank
2 E. Broad St.
Hazleton, PA 18201

Donor(s): Robert D. Quin Insurance Trust.
Financial data (yr. ended 12/31/01): Grants paid, $20,945; assets, $866 (M); gifts received, $14,489; expenditures, $25,337; qualifying distributions, $25,377.
Limitations: Giving limited to within a 10-mile radius of Hazleton, PA.
Application information: Application form required.
Officers: Eugene F. Gallagher, Pres.; Thelma Yuhas, Secy.; Mary Ann Zubris, Treas.
Directors: Jane Bartol, Rev. Thomas Cvammen, Donna Grobelny, Lori Roth, Beth M. Turnbach.
EIN: 222439876
Codes: GTI

47591
The Paul and Pearl Fertell Foundation
c/o Paul Fertell
1459 Yellow Springs Rd.
Chester Springs, PA 19425-1506

Established in 1998 in PA.
Donor(s): Paul Fertell.
Financial data (yr. ended 12/31/01): Grants paid, $20,934; assets, $14,080 (M); gifts received, $20,000; expenditures, $24,487; qualifying distributions, $20,934.
Officer: Paul Fertell, Pres.
Director: Lynn Field.
EIN: 232968588

47592
The John M. Feeney Foundation
872 Canterbury Ln.
Pittsburgh, PA 15232-2105

Financial data (yr. ended 11/30/01): Grants paid, $20,825; assets, $67,749 (M); gifts received, $1,000; expenditures, $23,295; qualifying distributions, $20,825.
Limitations: Applications not accepted. Giving limited to Pittsburgh, PA.
Application information: Contributes only to pre-selected organizations.
Officer and Directors:* John M. Feeney,* Pres. and Secy.-Treas.; Erin Feeney, Patrick Feeney, Terrance Feeney.
EIN: 251416510

47593
Sheerr Foundation
c/o Bruce Rosenfeild
1600 Market St., Ste. 3600
Philadelphia, PA 19103

Financial data (yr. ended 12/31/01): Grants paid, $20,810; assets, $331,091 (M); expenditures, $22,466; qualifying distributions, $21,078.
Limitations: Applications not accepted. Giving primarily in the Northeast.
Application information: Contributes only to pre-selected organizations.
Trustees: Constance Kittner, Betsey Sheerr, Lillian Sheerr, Richard C. Sheerr.
EIN: 236298319

47594
Alvin & Shirley Weinberg Foundation
c/o Gordon Scherer
436 7th Ave., Ste. 600
Pittsburgh, PA 15219 (412) 391-2920
Contact: Shirley Weinberg, Tr.

Established in 1981 in PA.
Donor(s): Alvin Weinberg, Shirley Weinberg.
Financial data (yr. ended 11/30/01): Grants paid, $20,726; assets, $489,898 (M); expenditures, $20,726; qualifying distributions, $20,726.
Limitations: Giving primarily in Pittsburgh, PA.
Application information: Application form not required.
Trustees: Lisa Antin, Jeffrey Weinberg, Shirley Weinberg.
EIN: 251415942

47595
Jacob Reist Hershey Trust
c/o Farmers First Bank
P.O. Box 1000, 24 N. Cedar St.
Lititz, PA 17543-7000

Established in 1995 in PA.
Donor(s): Jacob Reist Hershey.
Financial data (yr. ended 12/31/01): Grants paid, $20,653; assets, $422,635 (M); expenditures, $25,027; qualifying distributions, $21,648.
Limitations: Applications not accepted. Giving primarily in Elm, PA.
Application information: Contributes only to pre-selected organizations.
Trustee: Farmers First Bank.
EIN: 237800721

47596
The Mabel Zimmerman and Adelia Klinger Scholarship Fund
(Formerly The Mabel and Adelia Zimmerman Foundation)
c/o Fulton Financial Advisors, N.A.
P.O. Box 3215
Lancaster, PA 17604-3215
Application address: c/o Fulton Financial Advisors, N.A., 555 Willow St., Lebanon, PA 17042

Established in 1986 in PA.
Donor(s): Adelia Klinger,‡ Mabel Zimmerman.‡
Financial data (yr. ended 07/31/01): Grants paid, $20,633; assets, $1,207,542 (M); expenditures, $68,210; qualifying distributions, $20,883.
Limitations: Giving limited to Pine Grove, PA.
Application information: Applicant must include statement of financial need. Application form required.
Advisory Committee: Debra Ernst, Frederick Fisher, Ron Hill, Myra Huber, Joanne M. Snyder-Hoffman.
Trustee: Fulton Financial Advisors, N.A.
EIN: 236887468
Codes: GTI

47597
Genevieve B. & James L. McCain, Sr. Foundation
c/o PNC Advisors
620 Liberty Ave., P2-PTPP-10-2
Pittsburgh, PA 15222-2705
Application address: c/o Michael O'Donnell, Trust Off., Trust Div., 2 PNC Plz., 32nd Fl., Pittsburgh, PA 15222-2705, tel.: (412) 762-3617

Established in 1986 in PA.
Donor(s): Genevieve H. McCain, John McCain, Jr.
Financial data (yr. ended 09/30/01): Grants paid, $20,600; assets, $406,589 (M); gifts received, $1,340; expenditures, $30,154; qualifying distributions, $20,954.
Limitations: Giving on a national basis, with emphasis on PA.
Trustees: Genevieve H. McCain, John L. McCain, Jr., PNC Bank, N.A.
EIN: 251557328

47598
Maurice Falk Medical Fund
3315 Grant Bldg.
Pittsburgh, PA 15219-2395 (412) 261-2485
FAX: (412) 471-7739
Contact: Kerry J. O'Donnell, Pres.

Incorporated in 1960 in PA.
Donor(s): Maurice and Laura Falk Foundation.
Financial data (yr. ended 08/31/01): Grants paid, $20,578; assets, $17,559,288 (M); gifts received, $37,663; expenditures, $202,064; qualifying distributions, $707,039; giving activities include $26,476 for programs.
Limitations: Applications not accepted. Giving primarily in NY and PA, with emphasis on the Pittsburgh, PA, area.
Publications: Occasional report.
Application information: Unsolicited requests for funds not accepted.
Officers and Trustees:* Sigo Falk,* Chair.; Kerry J. O'Donnell, Pres.; Estelle Comay,* Secy.-Treas.; Bertram S. Brown, M.D., Michelle R. Cooper, Eric W. Springer.

EIN: 251099658

47599
Harold Baxter Foundation, Inc.
P.O. Box 916
Bryn Mawr, PA 19010-0912

Financial data (yr. ended 12/31/01): Grants paid, $20,550; assets, $5,159 (M); expenditures, $27,400; qualifying distributions, $20,550.
Limitations: Applications not accepted. Giving on a national basis, with emphasis on FL and PA.
Application information: Contributes only to pre-selected organizations.
Officers: Samuel B. Wheeler, Pres.; Henry F. Michell, V.P.; Elizabeth Baxter Michell, Secy.; Martha D. Baxter, Treas.
EIN: 231628244

47600
The Jack M. Brown Foundation
732 S. Front St.
Philadelphia, PA 19147
Application address: c/o Penn Warehousing & Distribution Co., 2147 S. Delaware Ave., Philadelphia, PA 19148, tel.: (215) 218-3000
Contact: Jack M. Brown, Sr., Pres.

Donor(s): Jack M. Brown, Sr.
Financial data (yr. ended 12/31/00): Grants paid, $20,550; assets, $195,486 (M); expenditures, $23,849; qualifying distributions, $20,550.
Limitations: Giving limited to PA.
Officer: Jack M. Brown, Sr., Pres.
EIN: 236088706

47601
La Mel Garden Foundation
c/o First Union National Bank
P.O. Box 7558
Philadelphia, PA 19101-7558
Application address: c/o First Union National Bank, 4259 Swamp Rd., Doylestown, PA 18901, tel.: (215) 340-4789

Financial data (yr. ended 12/31/99): Grants paid, $20,500; assets, $513,934 (M); expenditures, $26,241; qualifying distributions, $20,500.
Limitations: Giving limited to Perkasie, PA.
Trustees: Russell Hollenbach, William E. Keim, First Union National Bank.
EIN: 236277099

47602
Mary Margaret Nestor Foundation
c/o Reiff & Nestor Co.
Reiff & West Sts.
Lykens, PA 17048
Application address: P.O. Box 147, Lykens, PA 17048-0147, tel.: (717) 453-7113
Contact: Donald E. Nestor, Pres.

Established in 1953.
Donor(s): Reiff & Nestor Co.
Financial data (yr. ended 06/30/01): Grants paid, $20,500; assets, $134,717 (M); gifts received, $3,700; expenditures, $22,686; qualifying distributions, $20,447.
Limitations: Giving limited to residents of Dauphin County, PA.
Officers: Donald E. Nestor, Pres. and Treas.; Robin M. Nestor, Secy.
EIN: 236277570
Codes: GTI

47603
Professional Underwriters Foundation
151 S. Warner Rd., Ste. 100
Wayne, PA 19087-2198 (610) 995-2222

Established in 1993 in PA.
Donor(s): Michael P. Miles.
Financial data (yr. ended 12/31/01): Grants paid, $20,500; assets, $29,430 (M); expenditures, $20,560; qualifying distributions, $20,500.
Limitations: Applications not accepted. Giving primarily in PA.
Application information: Contributes only to pre-selected organizations.
Trustees: Robert B. Hill, Michael P. Miles, S. Alan Pcsolvar.
EIN: 232746886

47604
Michael Bill Avner Memorial Foundation
c/o Citron & Alex PC
429 Forbes Ave., Ste. 1700
Pittsburgh, PA 15219
Application address: 1700 Allegheny Bldg., Pittsburgh, PA 15219, tel.: 412-765-2720
Contact: Howard M. Alex, Esq., Tr.

Donor(s): Louis L. Avner.
Financial data (yr. ended 12/31/01): Grants paid, $20,350; assets, $352,687 (M); expenditures, $22,580; qualifying distributions, $20,350.
Limitations: Giving primarily in PA.
Application information: Application form required.
Trustees: Howard M. Alex, Helen Avner, Louis L. Avner, Constance Buchannon, Robin A. Urbach.
EIN: 256074647

47605
The Schusler Foundation
P.O. Box 935
Paoli, PA 19301-0935 (610) 296-3012
Contact: David W. Schusler, Tr.

Established in 1997.
Donor(s): David W. Schusler.
Financial data (yr. ended 12/31/01): Grants paid, $20,250; assets, $183,896 (M); expenditures, $21,120; qualifying distributions, $20,250.
Limitations: Giving primarily in PA.
Application information: Application form not required.
Trustees: David W. Schusler, Linda K. Schusler.
EIN: 232191242

47606
Sukonik Foundation
621 E. Germantown Pike, Ste. 100
Norristown, PA 19401-2454

Established in 1986 in PA.
Donor(s): Harold Sukonik.
Financial data (yr. ended 09/30/01): Grants paid, $20,250; assets, $366,767 (M); gifts received, $150,000; expenditures, $21,613; qualifying distributions, $20,250.
Limitations: Applications not accepted. Giving primarily in PA.
Application information: Contributes only to pre-selected organizations.
Officers: Harold Sukonik, Pres.; Neil Sukonik, Secy.; Jonathan Sukonik, Treas.
EIN: 232439850

47607
Industrial Scientific Foundation
(Formerly Industrial Scientific/McElhattan Foundation)
c/o James P. Hart
1001 Oakdale Rd.
Oakdale, PA 15071-1500

Established in 1994 in PA.
Donor(s): Kenton E. McElhattan, Kent D. McElhattan.
Financial data (yr. ended 06/30/01): Grants paid, $20,200; assets, $440,828 (M); gifts received, $20,000; expenditures, $22,200; qualifying distributions, $19,893.
Limitations: Applications not accepted.
Application information: Contributes only to pre-selected organizations.
Officers and Directors:* Kent D. McElhattan,* Pres.; Kenton E. McElhattan,* Secy.; James P. Hart, Treas.; Elaine L. Bonoma, Charles C. Cohen.
EIN: 251756557

47608
Allergy & Asthma Foundation of Lancaster County, Pennsylvania
P.O. Box 6265
Lancaster, PA 17607

Established in 1991 in PA.
Financial data (yr. ended 12/31/01): Grants paid, $20,000; assets, $350,104 (M); gifts received, $1,623; expenditures, $24,701; qualifying distributions, $20,000.
Limitations: Applications not accepted. Giving limited to PA.
Application information: Contributes only to pre-selected organizations.
Officers: Doris Lockey Geier, Pres.; Stephen D. Lockey III, M.D., V.P.; James E. Lockey, M.D., Secy.; Susan L. Hawkins, Treas.
Directors: Paul L. Geier, Sarah R. Landis, Anna F. Lockey, Brian Lockey, Catherine A. Lockey, Elizabeth J. Lockey, Richard F. Lockey, M.D., Napoleon Monroe.
EIN: 236424184

47609
The Michelle H. & David Bader Family Foundation
165 Geigel Hill Rd.
P.O. Box 242
Erwinna, PA 18920-0242

Financial data (yr. ended 06/30/01): Grants paid, $20,000; assets, $61,852 (M); gifts received, $14,417; expenditures, $20,082; qualifying distributions, $20,000.
Trustees: David Bader, Michelle Henkin Bader.
EIN: 311496075

47610
Mildred R. Davis Charitable Foundation
c/o PNC Advisors
1600 Market St., 4th Fl.
Philadelphia, PA 19103

Established in 1994 in NJ.
Financial data (yr. ended 06/30/01): Grants paid, $20,000; assets, $545,785 (M); expenditures, $24,888; qualifying distributions, $20,440.
Limitations: Applications not accepted. Giving primarily in NJ.
Application information: Contributes only to pre-selected organizations.
Trustee: PNC Bank, N.A.
EIN: 226631262

47611
Delaware Valley Senior Citizens Scholarship Trust
115 Connard Dr.
Easton, PA 18042
Application address: c/o Delaware Valley Regional High School, 19 Senator Stout Rd., Frenchtown, NJ 08825-3721
Contact: Louis DiLullo, Tr.

Established in 1992 in NJ.
Donor(s): Graver F. Tarpenning.‡
Financial data (yr. ended 12/31/01): Grants paid, $20,000; assets, $337,259 (L); expenditures, $21,575; qualifying distributions, $19,826.
Limitations: Giving limited to residents of NJ.

47611—PENNSYLVANIA

Application information: Application form required.
Trustee: Louis DiLullo.
EIN: 226555205
Codes: GTI

47612
Heinz Institute of Nutritional Sciences, Inc.
c/o Lori Varady
600 Grant St., 60th Fl.
Pittsburgh, PA 15219

Established in 1994 in PA and DE.
Donor(s): H.J. Heinz Foundation.
Financial data (yr. ended 06/30/00): Grants paid, $20,000; assets, $88,226 (M); gifts received, $150,000; expenditures, $127,093; qualifying distributions, $85,542; giving activities include $57,000 for programs.
Limitations: Applications not accepted.
Application information: Contributes only to pre-selected organizations.
Officers: D.L. Yeung, Ph.D., Pres.; Helen Guthrie, Ph.D., V.P.; Lori J. Varady, Secy.-Treas.
Trustees: G. Harvey Anderson, Ph.D., William J. Klish, Alessandro Micardi, Ph.D., Leilo G. Parducci.
EIN: 251712251

47613
J. Leon Lockard Charitable Trust
c/o PNC Advisors
1600 Market St., 4th Fl.
Philadelphia, PA 19103-7240
Contact: Brooke Cheston

Established in 1994 in PA.
Financial data (yr. ended 12/31/01): Grants paid, $20,000; assets, $640,541 (M); expenditures, $23,207; qualifying distributions, $20,625.
Limitations: Giving primarily in Philadelphia, PA.
Trustee: PNC Bank, N.A.
EIN: 236836910

47614
Andrew C. Long Foundation
c/o Community Bank, N.A.
P.O. Box 350
Millersburg, PA 17061-1330 (717) 692-4781

Established in 1987 in PA.
Donor(s): Andrew C. Long.
Financial data (yr. ended 12/31/01): Grants paid, $20,000; assets, $189,655 (M); expenditures, $21,584; qualifying distributions, $20,000.
Limitations: Applications not accepted. Giving primarily in Shamokin, PA.
Application information: Contributes only to pre-selected organizations.
Trustees: John Woytowisz, Community Bank.
EIN: 222807255

47615
Frank S. Lucente Foundation
c/o Somerset Trust Co.
P.O. Box 777
Somerset, PA 15501

Established in 1997 in PA.
Donor(s): Frank S. Lucente.
Financial data (yr. ended 12/31/01): Grants paid, $20,000; assets, $332,446 (M); expenditures, $22,635; qualifying distributions, $20,000.
Limitations: Applications not accepted.
Application information: Contributes only to pre-selected organizations.
Trustees: Frank S. Lucente, Somerset Trust Co.
EIN: 237949281

47616
The Meadowbrook Charitable Foundation
c/o Glenmede Trust Co.
1650 Market St., Ste. 1200
Philadelphia, PA 19103-7391
Application address: 584 Waterloo Rd., Devon, PA 19333
Contact: J. Jay Rhoads, Tr.

Established in 2000 in PA.
Donor(s): J. Jay Rhoads, Michael D. Rhoads.
Financial data (yr. ended 12/31/01): Grants paid, $20,000; assets, $902,089 (M); expenditures, $38,055; qualifying distributions, $20,000.
Application information: Application form not required.
Trustees: J. Jay Rhoads, Michael D. Rhoads.
EIN: 256742338

47617
The Orlando Foundation
c/o Frank P. Orlando
1 S. Church St.
Hazleton, PA 18201-6204

Established in 1997 in PA.
Financial data (yr. ended 12/31/01): Grants paid, $20,000; assets, $53,130 (M); expenditures, $20,608; qualifying distributions, $19,993.
Limitations: Applications not accepted. Giving primarily in Freeland, PA.
Application information: Contributes only to pre-selected organizations.
Trustees: Anthony W. Orlando, Frank P. Orlando, Sandra J. Orlando.
EIN: 232928154

47618
Penseco Foundation
150 N. Washington Ave.
Scranton, PA 18503

Established in 2000.
Donor(s): Penn Security Bank and Trust Co.
Financial data (yr. ended 12/31/01): Grants paid, $20,000; assets, $100,000 (M); gifts received, $120,000; expenditures, $20,000; qualifying distributions, $20,000.
Limitations: Applications not accepted. Giving primarily in Scranton, PA.
Application information: Contributes only to pre-selected organizations.
Trustees: Richard E. Grimm, Otto P. Robinson, Jr., Patrick Scanlon.
EIN: 251886434
Codes: CS

47619
The Louise von Hess Foundation for Medical Education
123 N. Prince St.
Lancaster, PA 17603

Classified as a private operating foundation in 1980; reclassified as an independent foundation in 2000.
Financial data (yr. ended 12/31/00): Grants paid, $20,000; assets, $1,355,190 (M); expenditures, $86,008; qualifying distributions, $55,046.
Limitations: Giving primarily in PA.
Officers and Trustees:* Donald H. Nikolaus,* Secy.-Treas.; John H. Esbenshade, Jr., M.D., Exec. Dir.; Thomas H. Bamford, Richard Kneedler, Roland A. Loeb, M.D., Wilson D. McElhinny, Samuel A. Rice, M.D., David E. Wiley, D.O.
EIN: 232116999

47620
Wolf Foundation for Education Trust
c/o The Ephrata National Bank
31 E. Main St.
Ephrata, PA 17522-0457 (717) 733-4181
Contact: Carl Brubaker, Trust Off., The Ephrata National Bank

Donor(s): Alfred Wolf.‡
Financial data (yr. ended 12/31/01): Grants paid, $20,000; assets, $440,408 (M); expenditures, $23,762; qualifying distributions, $20,608.
Limitations: Giving limited to Ephrata, PA.
Application information: Application form required.
Trustee: The Ephrata National Bank.
EIN: 236750958
Codes: GTI

47621
The Woodstock Foundation
1650 Arch St., 22nd Fl.
Philadelphia, PA 19103

Donor(s): Craig Stein, Lynda Barness.
Financial data (yr. ended 11/30/01): Grants paid, $20,000; assets, $5,592 (M); expenditures, $21,344; qualifying distributions, $20,000.
Limitations: Applications not accepted. Giving primarily in MA and PA.
Application information: Contributes only to pre-selected organizations.
Officer: Craig Stein, Pres.
EIN: 232121983

47622
The Idyll Development Foundation, Inc.
P.O. Box 405
Media, PA 19063 (610) 565-5242
Contact: Harold E. Taussig, Pres.

Established in 1993 in PA.
Donor(s): Harold E. Taussig.
Financial data (yr. ended 12/31/01): Grants paid, $19,985; assets, $2,162,324 (M); gifts received, $629,264; expenditures, $32,119; qualifying distributions, $19,985.
Officers: Harold E. Taussig, Pres.; Norma Taussig, V.P.
EIN: 232703497

47623
Al Paul Lefton Company Foundation
100 Independence Mall W.
Philadelphia, PA 19106 (215) 351-4242
Contact: Al Paul Lefton, Jr., Tr.

Donor(s): Al Paul Lefton Co., Inc.
Financial data (yr. ended 12/31/01): Grants paid, $19,970; assets, $41,728 (M); gifts received, $20,000; expenditures, $20,037; qualifying distributions, $20,037.
Limitations: Giving primarily in Philadelphia, PA.
Trustees: Al Paul Lefton, Jr., Raymond D. Scanlon.
EIN: 236298693
Codes: CS, CD

47624
Kaji Charitable Trust
c/o Vikram H. Kaji
1900 Yardley Rd.
Yardley, PA 19067-3207

Donor(s): Vikram H. Kaji.
Financial data (yr. ended 12/31/99): Grants paid, $19,947; assets, $32,693 (M); gifts received, $33,000; expenditures, $19,947; qualifying distributions, $19,947.
Limitations: Applications not accepted.
Application information: Contributes only to pre-selected organizations.

Trustees: Andrea L. Kaji, Vikram H. Kaji.
EIN: 222193591

47625
The Otto Company
110 Spruce Ln.
Ambler, PA 19002

Donor(s): David Mallery.
Financial data (yr. ended 12/31/00): Grants paid, $19,943; assets, $380,490 (M); expenditures, $24,286; qualifying distributions, $24,100.
Limitations: Applications not accepted. Giving primarily in Philadelphia, PA.
Application information: Unsolicited requests for funds not accepted.
Officers: David Mallery, Pres.; Judith P. Mallery, V.P.
EIN: 236296932

47626
Frances Jean Addams Charitable Trust
518 Edann Rd.
Glenside, PA 19038-1405 (215) 886-1940
Contact: J. Howard Brosius, Mgr.

Established in 1993 in PA.
Financial data (yr. ended 12/31/99): Grants paid, $19,906; assets, $52,025 (M); expenditures, $22,763; qualifying distributions, $19,906.
Limitations: Giving primarily in Philadelphia, PA.
Officer and Trustee:* J. Howard Brosius,* Mgr.
EIN: 237721716

47627
Boscov-Berk-Tek, Inc., Scholarship Fund
c/o Nexans, Inc., Kevin St. Cyr
132 White Oak Rd.
New Holland, PA 17557-9722
(717) 354-6200
Contact: Harold L. Styer, Tr.

Established in 1994 in PA.
Donor(s): Berk-Tek, Inc.
Financial data (yr. ended 12/31/01): Grants paid, $19,870; assets, $284,533 (M); expenditures, $19,870; qualifying distributions, $19,870.
Limitations: Giving limited to residents of PA.
Application information: Application form required.
Trustee: Kevin St. Cyr.
EIN: 237763668
Codes: CS, CD

47628
Mary L. C. Biddle Foundation
c/o PNC Advisors
620 Liberty Ave., P2-PTPP-10-2
Pittsburgh, PA 15222-2705 (800) 762-2272
FAX: (800) 339-8404; E-mail: pncadvisors@pncadvisors.com
Contact: Dawn Thomas

Financial data (yr. ended 12/31/01): Grants paid, $19,800; assets, $355,377 (M); expenditures, $24,017; qualifying distributions, $20,387.
Limitations: Giving limited to Philadelphia, PA.
Trustee: PNC Bank, N.A.
EIN: 236205851
Codes: GTI

47629
The Robert J. and Susan K. Weis Foundation
1347 Squirrel Hill Ave.
Pittsburgh, PA 15217

Donor(s): Robert J. Weis, Susan K. Weis.
Financial data (yr. ended 09/30/01): Grants paid, $19,800; assets, $444,470 (M); expenditures, $20,417; qualifying distributions, $19,800.
Limitations: Applications not accepted. Giving limited to Pittsburgh, PA.

Application information: Contributes only to pre-selected organizations.
Officers: Robert J. Weis, Pres.; Susan K. Weis, V.P.
EIN: 251538895

47630
Rosenberg Charitable Foundation
7 Viewmont Estates
Scranton, PA 18508

Established in 2000 in PA.
Donor(s): Paul Rosenberg, Margery Rosenberg.
Financial data (yr. ended 01/31/02): Grants paid, $19,757; assets, $154,547 (M); gifts received, $68,721; expenditures, $21,173; qualifying distributions, $19,757.
Limitations: Applications not accepted.
Application information: Contributes only to pre-selected organizations.
Officers: Paul Rosenberg, Pres.; Margery Rosenberg, Secy.
EIN: 233074423

47631
Franklin C. Snyder/Longue Vue Club Employee Scholarship Foundation
400 Longue Vue Dr.
Verona, PA 15147-1799 (412) 793-2375
Contact: Kenneth R. Pizzica, V.P.

Established in 1993 in PA.
Donor(s): Patricia G. Snyder.
Financial data (yr. ended 12/31/01): Grants paid, $19,750; assets, $132,972 (M); expenditures, $24,832; qualifying distributions, $19,750.
Limitations: Giving limited to residents of PA.
Application information: Application form required.
Officers and Directors:* Patricia G. Snyder,* Pres. and Secy.; Kenneth R. Pizzica,* V.P. and Treas.; David McSorley, Joseph Pesavento, Edward Schmidt, Joseph Sepesy, Lex Winans.
EIN: 251715070
Codes: GTI

47632
Wagner Family Charitable Trust
c/o PNC Advisors
620 Liberty Ave., P2-PTPP-10-2
Pittsburgh, PA 15222-2705
Application address: c/o Robert K. Wagner, Koppers Industries, Inc., 2915 Koppers Bldg., Pittsburgh, PA 15219, tel.: (412) 227-2398

Established in 2000 in PA.
Donor(s): Robert K. Wagner, Elinor R. Wagner.
Financial data (yr. ended 12/31/01): Grants paid, $19,600; assets, $844,336 (M); gifts received, $507,208; expenditures, $22,511; qualifying distributions, $19,558.
Limitations: Giving primarily in Pittsburgh, PA.
Trustee: PNC Bank, N.A.
EIN: 256735042

47633
The Ralph E. Cades Family Foundation
191 Presidential Blvd., Ste. 924
Bala Cynwyd, PA 19004-1238
Contact: Stewart R. Cades, Treas.

Financial data (yr. ended 11/30/01): Grants paid, $19,520; assets, $145,685 (M); gifts received, $21,400; expenditures, $23,679; qualifying distributions, $19,520.
Limitations: Giving primarily in Philadelphia, PA.
Application information: Application form not required.
Officers: Lillian G. Cades, Pres. and Secy.; Stewart R. Cades, Treas. and Mgr.
EIN: 232164662

47634
American Institute of Economics
P.O. Box 216
New Wilmington, PA 16142

Financial data (yr. ended 06/30/01): Grants paid, $19,500; assets, $483,281 (M); expenditures, $35,588; qualifying distributions, $20,533.
Limitations: Applications not accepted. Giving limited to Pittsburgh, PA.
Application information: Contributes only to pre-selected organizations.
Officer: William McKee, Pres.
EIN: 256001201

47635
Butwel Family Foundation
1536 Blueberry Ct.
Jamison, PA 18929
Contact: Nancy Devlin, Admin.

Established in 1994.
Donor(s): Henry E. Butwel, Catherine M. Butwel.
Financial data (yr. ended 12/31/01): Grants paid, $19,500; assets, $249,473 (M); expenditures, $22,353; qualifying distributions, $22,340.
Limitations: Giving primarily in PA.
Officers: Susan A. Goetter, Secy.; Nancy Devlin, Admin.
Trustees: Catherine M. Butwel, Henry E. Butwel.
EIN: 237770589

47636
Gilmore-Hoerner Endowment
c/o Rosie Coldsmith, F & M Trust
P.O Box 6010
Chambersburg, PA 17201

Financial data (yr. ended 12/31/01): Grants paid, $19,500; assets, $515,293 (M); expenditures, $25,560; qualifying distributions, $19,500.
Limitations: Applications not accepted. Giving limited to the Chambersburg, PA area.
Application information: Contributes only to pre-selected organizations.
Officers: George Glenn, Pres.; Frank Rhodes, Treas.
Directors: Joan Applegate, Ruth Harrison, Lisbeth Luka.
EIN: 256084059

47637
J. Fithian Tatem Scholarship Fund
c/o PNC Advisors
1600 Market St.
Philadelphia, PA 19103-2740

Financial data (yr. ended 12/31/01): Grants paid, $19,500; assets, $203,818 (M); expenditures, $22,253; qualifying distributions, $19,500.
Limitations: Giving limited to residents of Haddonfield, NJ.
Trustee: PNC Bank, N.A.
EIN: 226109433

47638
Sley Foundation
c/o Wolf Block
1650 Arch St., 22nd Fl.
Philadelphia, PA 19103

Established in 1953 in PA.
Financial data (yr. ended 12/31/01): Grants paid, $19,400; assets, $31,680 (M); expenditures, $21,321; qualifying distributions, $19,400.
Limitations: Giving primarily in Philadelphia, PA.
Application information: Application form not required.
Trustee: Edward M. Glickman.
EIN: 236298329

47639
Djerassi Foundation
(Formerly Djerassi Cancer Research Foundation)
1820 Rittenhouse Sq., Ste. 14A
Philadelphia, PA 19103-3484

Established in 1982 in PA.
Donor(s): Isaac Djerassi, M.D., Nira Djerassi.
Financial data (yr. ended 06/30/01): Grants paid, $19,390; assets, $904,072 (M); expenditures, $26,852; qualifying distributions, $22,176.
Limitations: Applications not accepted. Giving primarily in Philadelphia, PA.
Application information: Contributes only to pre-selected organizations.
Trustee: Isaac Djerassi, M.D.
EIN: 232224978

47640
Kane Community Development Foundation, Inc.
c/o Harlcolm Bard, C.P.A.
38 Fraley St.
Kane, PA 16735

Established in 1995 in PA.
Financial data (yr. ended 12/31/01): Grants paid, $19,347; assets, $391,404 (M); expenditures, $21,369; qualifying distributions, $19,347.
Limitations: Giving primarily in Kane, PA.
Officers: Edgar James, Pres.; Tim Mague, V.P.; Michael Baker, Secy.; Halcolm Bard, Treas.
Directors: Kenneth Carlson, Robert Hathorn, Don Payne.
EIN: 251324911

47641
Will S. & Anna S. Fox Foundation
P.O. Box 1280
Pottsville, PA 17901-7280

Financial data (yr. ended 10/31/01): Grants paid, $19,239; assets, $463,597 (M); gifts received, $7,463; expenditures, $25,269; qualifying distributions, $21,388.
Limitations: Applications not accepted. Giving primarily in PA.
Application information: Contributes only to pre-selected organizations.
Officers: Alvin B. Marshall, Pres.; Robert N. Bohorad, V.P.; Fred J. Boote, Secy.; Margaret A. Daniels, Treas.
EIN: 236395250

47642
The McFarland Family Charitable Foundation
255 W. Tulpehocken St.
Philadelphia, PA 19144

Established in 1999 in PA.
Donor(s): Paul P. McFarland, Sheila E. McFarland.
Financial data (yr. ended 12/31/01): Grants paid, $19,200; assets, $65,149 (M); gifts received, $72,994; expenditures, $19,200; qualifying distributions, $19,200.
Limitations: Applications not accepted. Giving primarily in FL, NJ and PA.
Application information: Contributes only to pre-selected organizations.
Directors: Maureen M. McFarland, Paul P. McFarland, Peter McFarland, Philip E. McFarland, Sheila E. McFarland.
EIN: 233015971

47643
Port Family Foundation
c/o Neil M. Port
1600 Market St., Ste. 3600
Philadelphia, PA 19103-7240 (215) 751-2080

Established in 1994 in PA.
Donor(s): Marilyn J. Port, Neil M. Port.
Financial data (yr. ended 12/31/01): Grants paid, $19,150; assets, $380,965 (M); expenditures, $20,202; qualifying distributions, $19,150.
Limitations: Applications not accepted.
Application information: Contributes only to pre-selected organizations.
Trustees: Lawrence Port, Marilyn J. Port, Neil M. Port, Douglas Simon, Susan Port Simon, Lisa D. Port White, Malcolm White.
EIN: 232777280

47644
Ella B. Chase Memorial Fund
c/o PNC Advisors
620 Liberty Ave., P2-PTPP-10-2
Pittsburgh, PA 15222-2705
Application address: c/o Pastor, Collingswood Presbyterian Church, Fern and Maple Aves., Collingswood, NJ 08108

Financial data (yr. ended 12/31/01): Grants paid, $19,117; assets, $283,219 (M); expenditures, $22,225; qualifying distributions, $19,022.
Limitations: Giving limited to Collingswood, NJ.
Trustee: PNC Bank, N.A.
EIN: 222470581

47645
Sedlacek Family Foundation, Inc.
c/o John J. Sedlacek
17 Painters Ln.
Wayne, PA 19087

Established in 1990 in PA.
Donor(s): John J. Sedlacek.
Financial data (yr. ended 12/31/01): Grants paid, $19,110; assets, $300,183 (M); expenditures, $19,863; qualifying distributions, $19,110.
Limitations: Applications not accepted. Giving primarily in PA.
Application information: Contributes only to pre-selected organizations.
Officers: John J. Sedlacek, Pres. and Treas.; Vivian Sedlacek, V.P.
EIN: 232615234

47646
Raymond R. Start Trust
c/o Mellon Bank, N.A.
P.O. Box 7236
Philadelphia, PA 19101-7236

Financial data (yr. ended 09/30/01): Grants paid, $19,095; assets, $859,845 (M); expenditures, $33,287; qualifying distributions, $19,095.
Limitations: Giving limited to Philadelphia, PA.
Trustees: Michael J. Cantwell, Jr., Mellon Bank, N.A.
EIN: 236634349

47647
Hilda Feibus Foundation
c/o Shirley Feibus Alperin
35 Oakford Glen
Clarks Summit, PA 18411-8984
(570) 586-3968

Donor(s): David Feibus, Steven Feibus.
Financial data (yr. ended 12/31/01): Grants paid, $19,000; assets, $297,408 (M); expenditures, $26,689; qualifying distributions, $26,307.
Limitations: Giving primarily in NJ and PA.
Officer and Directors:* Shirley Feibus Alperin,* Pres. and Secy.-Treas.; Belle Estroff, Rabbi David Geffen.
EIN: 237029768

47648
Hannah L. Hamlin Memorial Fund, Inc.
333 W. Main St.
Smethport, PA 16749-0367

Established in 1943 in PA.
Donor(s): Robert A. Digel.
Financial data (yr. ended 12/31/01): Grants paid, $19,000; assets, $364,750 (M); expenditures, $22,000; qualifying distributions, $19,000.
Limitations: Applications not accepted. Giving primarily in PA.
Application information: Contributes only to pre-selected organizations.
Officer: Robert A. Digel, Jr., Pres.
Director: Martin Digel.
EIN: 256001645

47649
Eugene R. Kotur Foundation
c/o PNC Advisors
1600 Market St., 4th Fl.
Philadelphia, PA 19103-7240
Application address: c/o Ukranian Fraternal Asson., 440 Wyoming Ave., Scranton, PA 18503-1290, tel.: (717) 342-0937

Established in 1997 in PA.
Financial data (yr. ended 12/31/01): Grants paid, $19,000; assets, $352,840 (M); expenditures, $25,290; qualifying distributions, $20,575.
Application information: Application form required.
Trustee: PNC Bank, N.A.
EIN: 256394138

47650
Wright Family Charitable Foundation
115 Mayer St.
Reading, PA 19606

Established in 1998 in PA.
Financial data (yr. ended 12/31/01): Grants paid, $19,000; assets, $48,755 (M); gifts received, $30,265; expenditures, $19,155; qualifying distributions, $19,000.
Limitations: Applications not accepted.
Application information: Contributes only to pre-selected organizations.
Trustees: Catherine D. Wright, Robert T. Wright.
EIN: 232967798

47651
Mary E. Cromwell Scholarship Fund
c/o First Union National Bank
Broad and Walnut Sts., PA1308
Philadelphia, PA 19109

Established around 1995.
Financial data (yr. ended 12/31/99): Grants paid, $18,950; assets, $493,760 (M); expenditures, $22,279; qualifying distributions, $16,615.
Limitations: Applications not accepted. Giving primarily in Towson, MD.
Application information: Contributes only to pre-selected organizations.
Trustee: First Union National Bank.
EIN: 526224609

47652
St. Benedict's Charitable Society
1663 Bristol Pike
Bensalem, PA 19020-5702 (215) 244-9900
Contact: Margaret Kuehmstedt, Treas.

Financial data (yr. ended 12/31/01): Grants paid, $18,900; assets, $458,801 (M); gifts received, $1,500; expenditures, $21,226; qualifying distributions, $21,226.
Limitations: Giving on a national basis.

Officers: Sr. Monica Loughlin, Pres.; Roger A. Johnsen, V.P.; Sr. Beatrice Jeffries, Secy.; Margaret Kuehmstedt, Treas.
EIN: 236256990

47653
The Sam & Charles Foundation
c/o Erskine, Wolfson & Gibbon
2010 Chancellor St.
Philadelphia, PA 19103

Established in 1997 in PA.
Donor(s): Alissa U'Prichard, David U'Prichard.
Financial data (yr. ended 12/31/01): Grants paid, $18,875; assets, $175,617 (M); gifts received, $32,937; expenditures, $21,233; qualifying distributions, $18,875.
Trustees: Alissa U'Prichard, David U'Prichard.
EIN: 237919005

47654
The Leonard and Beverly Bloch Foundation
321 S. Carlisle St.
Allentown, PA 18103-2721 (610) 432-9808
Application address: 3346 Trexler Blvd., Allentown, PA 18104, tel.: (610) 432-9808
Contact: Leonard Bloch, Tr.

Donor(s): Leonard Bloch, Beverly Bloch.
Financial data (yr. ended 12/31/01): Grants paid, $18,840; assets, $271,433 (M); expenditures, $19,507; qualifying distributions, $18,840.
Application information: Application form not required.
Trustees: Beverly Bloch, Leonard Bloch.
EIN: 236779289

47655
Frank Molle Foundation
704 Haywood Dr.
Exton, PA 19341-1136 (610) 458-1090
Contact: Frank A. Piliero, Tr. and Sandra L. Piliero, Tr.

Established in 1998 in PA.
Donor(s): Frank A. Piliero.
Financial data (yr. ended 12/31/01): Grants paid, $18,825; assets, $121,265 (M); gifts received, $5,000; expenditures, $18,985; qualifying distributions, $18,825.
Limitations: Giving primarily in PA.
Trustees: Frank A. Piliero, Sandra L. Piliero.
EIN: 232941216

47656
Brooks Family Foundation
3465 Treeline Dr.
Murrysville, PA 15668

Established in 1995 in PA.
Donor(s): Robert J. Brooks.
Financial data (yr. ended 12/31/01): Grants paid, $18,750; assets, $991,969 (M); gifts received, $900; expenditures, $18,819; qualifying distributions, $18,712.
Limitations: Applications not accepted. Giving primarily in PA.
Application information: Contributes only to pre-selected organizations.
Directors: Robert J. Brooks, Susan C. Brooks.
EIN: 251774477

47657
William A. March Education Fund
c/o PNC Advisors
1600 Market St., 4th Fl.
Philadelphia, PA 19103-7240

Financial data (yr. ended 12/31/01): Grants paid, $18,750; assets, $962,733 (M); expenditures, $23,417; qualifying distributions, $33,862; giving activities include $18,750 for loans to individuals.

Limitations: Giving primarily in PA.
Application information: Application form required.
Trustee: PNC Bank, N.A.
EIN: 236295283
Codes: GTI

47658
Mamie B. Bush Trust
c/o Allfirst, Trust Tax Div.
21 E. Market St., M/C 402-130
York, PA 17401-1205

Financial data (yr. ended 12/31/01): Grants paid, $18,713; assets, $367,528 (M); expenditures, $23,117; qualifying distributions, $18,713.
Limitations: Applications not accepted. Giving primarily in IL and PA.
Application information: Contributes only to pre-selected organizations.
Trustee: Allfirst.
EIN: 256197546

47659
Denenberg Charitable Trust
616 Addison St.
Philadelphia, PA 19147-1413

Established in 2000 in PA.
Donor(s): Alfred Denenberg, Susan Denenberg.
Financial data (yr. ended 12/31/01): Grants paid, $18,590; assets, $177,343 (M); gifts received, $64,220; expenditures, $18,608; qualifying distributions, $18,590.
Limitations: Applications not accepted. Giving primarily in Washington, DC and Philadelphia, PA.
Application information: Contributes only to pre-selected organizations.
Officers: Alfred Denenberg, Pres.; Susan Denenberg, Secy.-Treas.
EIN: 233038348

47660
The Ferst Foundation
120 Tall Trees Dr.
Bala Cynwyd, PA 19004
Contact: Barton E. Ferst, Tr.

Donor(s): Barton E. Ferst, Robert L. Ferst, Stanley D. Ferst, Bess K. Staren.‡
Financial data (yr. ended 12/31/01): Grants paid, $18,550; assets, $192,945 (M); expenditures, $18,982; qualifying distributions, $18,550.
Limitations: Giving primarily in Philadelphia, PA.
Application information: Application form not required.
Trustees: Barton E. Ferst, Richard J. Ferst, Robert L. Ferst, Stanley D. Ferst, Walter B. Ferst, Carol Baer Mott, Susan F. Shapiro.
EIN: 236297112

47661
The Mayer Family Foundation
P.O. Box 717
Ambler, PA 19002-0717

Donor(s): Lester R. Mayer, Lester R. Mayer, Jr., Lester R. Mayer III, Thomas N. Mayer.
Financial data (yr. ended 12/31/01): Grants paid, $18,540; assets, $276,142 (M); gifts received, $22,206; expenditures, $18,786; qualifying distributions, $18,540.
Limitations: Giving primarily in Philadelphia, PA.
Application information: Application form not required.
Trustee: Lester R. Mayer, Jr.
EIN: 232407011

47662
The Harry A. Fields Foundation
P.O. Box 566
Media, PA 19063-0566

Established in 1997 in OH and PA.
Financial data (yr. ended 08/31/99): Grants paid, $18,500; assets, $594,044 (M); expenditures, $58,291; qualifying distributions, $29,819.
Limitations: Applications not accepted.
Officers: Richard A. Fields, Pres. and Treas.; John B. Crain, V.P.; Terry D. Crain, Secy.
Trustee: Louise M. Fields.
EIN: 340892632

47663
Ben Jerome Charitable Testamentary Trust
654 Wolf Ave.
Easton, PA 18042 (610) 250-6585
Contact: Gary S. Figore, Tr.

Established in 1999 in PA.
Donor(s): Ben Jerome.‡
Financial data (yr. ended 12/31/01): Grants paid, $18,500; assets, $1,271,617 (M); expenditures, $57,969; qualifying distributions, $18,500.
Limitations: Giving primarily in PA.
Application information: Application form required.
Trustee: Gary S. Figore.
EIN: 237984640

47664
The Sloane Family Foundation
527 N. Easton Rd.
Glenside, PA 19038-5097

Established in 1986 in PA.
Financial data (yr. ended 12/31/00): Grants paid, $18,500; assets, $154,399 (M); expenditures, $21,803; qualifying distributions, $18,500.
Limitations: Applications not accepted. Giving primarily in PA.
Application information: Contributes only to pre-selected organizations.
Trustee: Robert Sloane.
EIN: 222779195

47665
Marcella Green Scholarship Trust
c/o PNC Advisors
620 Liberty Ave., P2-PTPP-10-2
Pittsburgh, PA 15222-2705

Financial data (yr. ended 12/31/01): Grants paid, $18,373; assets, $329,079 (M); expenditures, $21,632; qualifying distributions, $18,221.
Limitations: Applications not accepted. Giving limited to residents of Ocean and Monmouth counties, NJ.
Application information: Unsolicited requests for funds not accepted.
Trustee: PNC Bank, N.A.
EIN: 226475773
Codes: GTI

47666
Harold & Nancy Kaplan Foundation
102 Windmere Cir.
Dalton, PA 18414

Established in 1995 in PA.
Donor(s): Harold Kaplan, Nancy Kaplan.
Financial data (yr. ended 09/30/01): Grants paid, $18,287; assets, $242,643 (M); expenditures, $22,238; qualifying distributions, $18,287.
Limitations: Applications not accepted. Giving primarily in Scranton, PA.
Application information: Contributes only to pre-selected organizations.
Directors: Harold Kaplan, Nancy Kaplan.

47666—PENNSYLVANIA

EIN: 232831054

47667
Paddington Foundation
125 1st Ave.
Pittsburgh, PA 15222-1590 (412) 391-8510
Contact: Philip E. Beard, Tr.

Established in 2000 in PA.
Donor(s): Philip E. Beard, Melinda B. Beard.
Financial data (yr. ended 12/31/01): Grants paid, $18,250; assets, $101,678 (M); gifts received, $32,500; expenditures, $22,192; qualifying distributions, $18,250.
Trustees: Melinda B. Beard, N. Beaumont Beard, Philip E. Beard.
EIN: 256742854

47668
Property Management, Inc. Charitable Foundation
c/o Property Management, Inc.
P.O. Box 622
Lemoyne, PA 17043

Established in 1994 in PA.
Donor(s): Property Management, Inc., Rhodes Development Group, Inc.
Financial data (yr. ended 12/31/01): Grants paid, $18,250; assets, $210,972 (M); gifts received, $25,000; expenditures, $19,955; qualifying distributions, $18,189.
Application information: Application form required.
Officers: John H. Rhodes, Pres.; Lawrence M. Means, V.P.; Dianne L. Fairall, Secy.; Jeffrey D. Billman, Treas.; Bonnie F. Rhodes, Exec. Dir.
Directors: David E. Dyson, Gail R. Siegel, Thomas R. Wenger.
EIN: 251721134
Codes: CS, CD

47669
Michael J. Mooney Charitable Trust
201 Bowman St.
Wilkes-Barre, PA 18702-5404

Established in 1997 in PA.
Donor(s): Michael J. Mooney.‡
Financial data (yr. ended 12/31/99): Grants paid, $18,174; assets, $305,337 (M); expenditures, $23,311; qualifying distributions, $18,174.
Limitations: Applications not accepted. Giving primarily in Reno, NV.
Application information: Contributes only to pre-selected organizations.
Trustee: Joseph T. Coyne.
EIN: 237875628

47670
Mr. & Mrs. J. C. "Buddy" Hawkins Memorial Fund
c/o First Union National Bank
Broad & Walnut Sts.
Philadelphia, PA 19109

Established in 1995 in VA.
Donor(s): J.C. "Buddy" Hawkins.‡
Financial data (yr. ended 12/31/99): Grants paid, $18,141; assets, $476,512 (M); expenditures, $22,188; qualifying distributions, $18,141.
Limitations: Applications not accepted. Giving primarily in VA.
Application information: Contributes only to pre-selected organizations.
Trustee: First Union National Bank.
EIN: 541764100

47671
Margaret L. Henry Children's Home, Inc.
c/o Anna Mary Mooney
301 Shaw St.
New Castle, PA 16101
Application address: R.D. 4, Box 319, New Castle, PA 16101-9668, tel.: (724) 658-3535
Contact: Jean Reynolds, Secy.

Financial data (yr. ended 03/31/02): Grants paid, $18,061; assets, $300,881 (M); gifts received, $5,000; expenditures, $21,146; qualifying distributions, $18,061.
Limitations: Giving limited to Lawrence County, PA.
Application information: Application form not required.
Officers: Richard Flannery, Pres.; Patti Chambers, V.P.; Debra Mcelwain, Secy.; Anna Mary Mooney, Treas.
EIN: 256065991

47672
Wachs-Weingarten Charitable Trust
c/o M. Wachs Weingarten & B. Weingarten
211 Glenn Rd.
Ardmore, PA 19003

Established in PA in 1997.
Donor(s): Bryan Weingarten, Marjorie Wachs.
Financial data (yr. ended 10/31/01): Grants paid, $18,034; assets, $238,021 (M); expenditures, $20,657; qualifying distributions, $18,034.
Application information: Application form not required.
Trustees: Bryan Weingarten, Marjorie Wachs Weingarten.
EIN: 237922107

47673
The Edward and Gwendolyn Asplundh Family Foundation
2000 Market St., 10th Fl.
Philadelphia, PA 19103-3291
Contact: Martin G. Heckler

Established in 1998 in PA.
Donor(s): Edward Asplundh, Gwendolyn Asplundh.
Financial data (yr. ended 12/31/01): Grants paid, $18,000; assets, $205,534 (M); expenditures, $19,226; qualifying distributions, $18,000.
Limitations: Giving on a national basis, primarily in the eastern U.S.
Application information: Application form not required.
Officers: Edward Asplundh, Pres.; Gwendolyn Asplundh, Secy.-Treas.
EIN: 237921981

47674
The Brown-Daub Foundation
c/o William Daub
819 Nazareth Pike
Nazareth, PA 18064

Donor(s): L. Anderson Daub, William Daub.
Financial data (yr. ended 12/31/01): Grants paid, $18,000; assets, $422,215 (M); gifts received, $55,000; expenditures, $18,345; qualifying distributions, $18,007.
Limitations: Applications not accepted.
Application information: Contributes only to pre-selected organizations.
Officers and Directors:* L. Anderson Daub,* Pres.; William John Daub III,* Secy.
EIN: 232900410

47675
Matt Stager Memorial Scholarship Fund
1900 Arch St.
Philadelphia, PA 19103-1404

Financial data (yr. ended 12/31/01): Grants paid, $18,000; assets, $132,751 (M); gifts received, $15,500; expenditures, $23,436; qualifying distributions, $18,000.
Director: Kenneth R. Hulton.
EIN: 311480297

47676
P. A. Staples Testamentary Trust
c/o Hershey Trust Co.
P.O. Box 445
Hershey, PA 17033-0455 (717) 520-1130
Contact: Raymond T. Cameron, V.P., Hershey Trust Co.

Financial data (yr. ended 12/31/01): Grants paid, $17,850; assets, $244,805 (M); expenditures, $21,050; qualifying distributions, $17,850.
Limitations: Giving primarily in Hershey, PA.
Trustee: Hershey Trust Co.
EIN: 236242753

47677
Ronald R. and Linda S. Perin Trust
818 Grand Central Rd.
Pen Argyl, PA 18072
Application address: c/o Parkhill Reality, P.O. Box 7, Pen Argyl, PA 18072, tel.: (610) 863-7070
Contact: Ronald Perin, Tr. or Linda Perin, Tr.

Established in 1997 in PA.
Donor(s): Linda S. Perin, Ronald R. Perin.
Financial data (yr. ended 12/31/01): Grants paid, $17,800; assets, $309,680 (M); expenditures, $17,827; qualifying distributions, $17,800.
Limitations: Giving limited to the greater Lehigh Valley, PA, area.
Trustees: Linda S. Perin, Ronald R. Perin.
EIN: 237895570

47678
Bradburd Family Foundation
1879 Hemlock Cir.
Abington, PA 19001-4706 (215) 542-5070
Contact: Arnold W. Bradburd, Tr.

Established in 1999 in PA.
Donor(s): Arnold W. Bradburd, Julia A. Bradburd.
Financial data (yr. ended 05/31/02): Grants paid, $17,750; assets, $10,129 (M); gifts received, $10,000; expenditures, $18,828; qualifying distributions, $18,823.
Trustees: Arnold W. Bradburd, Julia A. Bradburd.
EIN: 237978514

47679
Richard & Patricia Penske Foundation
3910 Adler Pl.
P.O. Box 25007
Lehigh Valley, PA 18002-5007

Established in 1996 in PA.
Financial data (yr. ended 12/31/01): Grants paid, $17,750; assets, $51,406 (M); expenditures, $17,930; qualifying distributions, $17,750.
Limitations: Applications not accepted. Giving primarily in PA.
Application information: Contributes only to pre-selected organizations.
Officers: Richard H. Penske, Pres.; Patricia L. Penske, V.P.; Victoria L. Penske-Aitchison, Secy.; Crislyn A. Penske, Treas.
EIN: 232858131

47680
David Downs Higbee Trust
c/o PNC Advisors
1600 Market St., 4th Fl.
Philadelphia, PA 19103

Donor(s): David Downs Higbee.‡
Financial data (yr. ended 12/31/01): Grants paid, $17,712; assets, $444,807 (M); expenditures, $23,440; qualifying distributions, $18,337.
Limitations: Applications not accepted. Giving limited to residents of Audubon, NJ.
Application information: Unsolicited requests for funds not accepted.
Trustees: Richard Serfling, William J. Westphal, PNC Bank, N.A.
EIN: 226375372
Codes: GTI

47681
Pierre Koncurat Foundation Charitable Trust
411 Waterloo Rd.
Devon, PA 19333

Established in 1986 in PA.
Donor(s): Pierre J. Koncurat.
Financial data (yr. ended 12/31/01): Grants paid, $17,662; assets, $283,488 (M); gifts received, $28,292; expenditures, $17,813; qualifying distributions, $17,662.
Limitations: Applications not accepted.
Application information: Contributes only to a pre-selected organization.
Trustees: Pierre J. Koncurat.
EIN: 222783294

47682
Albert T. Hess Foundation, Inc.
P.O. Box 127
Quincy, PA 17247
Contact: Donald L. Walters, Secy.-Treas.

Established in 1953.
Donor(s): Hess Manufacturing Co., Inc.
Financial data (yr. ended 09/30/01): Grants paid, $17,600; assets, $275,934 (M); expenditures, $19,704; qualifying distributions, $17,600.
Limitations: Giving primarily in Franklin County, PA.
Officers: Richard L. Bakner, Pres.; Donald L. Walters, Secy.-Treas.
Directors: Ruth Grundy, A. Tracey Hess-King.
EIN: 236272406

47683
Elise Galman Dee Foundation
c/o The Galman Group
P.O. Box 646
Jenkintown, PA 19046

Established in 1997 in PA.
Donor(s): Arnold Galman, Robert Dee.
Financial data (yr. ended 11/30/01): Grants paid, $17,500; assets, $186,127 (M); expenditures, $21,468; qualifying distributions, $17,500.
Limitations: Applications not accepted. Giving primarily in PA.
Application information: Contributes only to pre-selected organizations.
Officers: Arnold Galman, Pres.; Robert J. Dee, V.P.
EIN: 232938431

47684
Bruce R. Snyder & Madelyn G. Snyder Foundation
710 Wise Ave.
Red Lion, PA 17356-2515 (717) 244-7653
Contact: B. Robert Snyder, Pres.

Established in 1992 in PA.
Donor(s): B. Robert Snyder, William Snyder.
Financial data (yr. ended 09/30/01): Grants paid, $17,500; assets, $434,262 (M); gifts received, $105,000; expenditures, $17,951; qualifying distributions, $17,500.
Limitations: Giving on a national basis.
Application information: Application form not required.
Officers: B. Robert Snyder, Pres.; William Snyder,* V.P.
Directors: Carolyn Kline, Joann Seidenstricker.
EIN: 232706874

47685
W. C. and Stella B. Hennessee Foundation, Inc.
c/o First Union National Bank
Broad and Walnuts Sts., Ste. PA1308
Philadelphia, PA 19109-1199

Established in 1986 in NC.
Financial data (yr. ended 02/28/00): Grants paid, $17,400; assets, $982,795 (M); expenditures, $29,041; qualifying distributions, $17,955.
Limitations: Applications not accepted. Giving primarily in Sylva, NC.
Application information: Contributes only to pre-selected organizations.
Trustees: Isaac Coe, Jeff Covington, Jack Hennessee, First Union National Bank.
EIN: 561503261

47686
The Alice, Debra, & Donna Powell Trust Foundation
c/o GM Hatfield
2000 Market St., 10th Fl.
Philadelphia, PA 19103-3201

Established in 1994 in PA.
Donor(s): Alice Powell.
Financial data (yr. ended 12/31/01): Grants paid, $17,400; assets, $301,762 (M); expenditures, $19,831; qualifying distributions, $17,400.
Limitations: Applications not accepted.
Application information: Contributes only to pre-selected organizations.
Trustees: Donna Abel, Alice Powell, Debra Powell.
EIN: 232762647

47687
J. Howard Kenworthy Trust
c/o Mellon Bank, N.A.
P.O. Box 7236
Philadelphia, PA 19101-7236
Application address: c/o Mellon Bank Center, Philadelphia, PA 19103, tel.: (215) 553-3038
Contact: Glem Deibert

Financial data (yr. ended 12/31/00): Grants paid, $17,345; assets, $554,666 (M); expenditures, $25,821; qualifying distributions, $18,066.
Trustee: Mellon Bank, N.A.
EIN: 236599429

47688
Lillian and Robert Brent Fund
1543 Ulser Ct.
West Chester, PA 19380-6838

Established in 1993 in PA.
Donor(s): Robert Brent, Lillian Brent.
Financial data (yr. ended 12/31/01): Grants paid, $17,318; assets, $419,390 (M); gifts received, $88,807; expenditures, $19,210; qualifying distributions, $17,318.
Limitations: Applications not accepted.
Officers: Robert Brent, C.E.O.; Lillian Brent, Treas.
EIN: 232735247

47689
Lucie F. Hollingsworth Trust
c/o First Commonwealth Trust Co.
111 S. Main St.
Greensburg, PA 15601

Financial data (yr. ended 12/31/01): Grants paid, $17,240; assets, $340,501 (M); expenditures, $21,362; qualifying distributions, $17,240.
Limitations: Applications not accepted. Giving limited to Greensburg, PA.
Application information: Contributes only to pre-selected organizations.
Trustee: First Commonwealth Trust Co.
EIN: 256021447

47690
Calvin Z. Bean Community Service Fund
c/o John M. Read Temple Assn.
P.O. Box 213
Reynoldsville, PA 15851-0213

Established in 1990 in PA.
Financial data (yr. ended 06/30/02): Grants paid, $17,200; assets, $389,101 (M); gifts received, $20,894; expenditures, $19,673; qualifying distributions, $17,200.
Limitations: Applications not accepted. Giving primarily in Reynoldsville, PA.
Application information: Contributes only to pre-selected organizations.
Officers: Robert L. Vizza, Pres.-Treas.; Bradley Wells, V.P.; Frank B. Bussard, Secy.
EIN: 256341398

47691
Franklin W. & Helen S. Bowen Charitable Trust
1127 Arrowood Dr.
Pittsburgh, PA 15243-1801

Donor(s): Franklin W. Bowen.
Financial data (yr. ended 12/31/00): Grants paid, $17,164; assets, $251,283 (M); gifts received, $16,578; expenditures, $18,817; qualifying distributions, $17,060.
Limitations: Applications not accepted. Giving primarily in PA.
Application information: Unsolicited requests for funds not accepted.
EIN: 256091907
Codes: GTI

47692
Robert Hunter Swindell Charitable Trust
831 Academy Pl.
Pittsburgh, PA 15243-2003
Contact: Phyllis S. Swindell, Tr.

Donor(s): Phyllis S. Swindell.
Financial data (yr. ended 12/31/01): Grants paid, $17,100; assets, $307,275 (M); expenditures, $18,127; qualifying distributions, $17,100.
Limitations: Giving primarily in Pittsburgh, PA.
Application information: Application form required.
Trustee: Phyllis S. Swindell.
EIN: 237188657

47693
Lebanon Mutual Foundation
137 W. Penn Ave.
Cleona, PA 17042 (717) 272-6655
Application address: P.O. Box 2005, Cleona, PA 17042
Contact: Rollin Rissinger, Jr., Dir.

Donor(s): Lebanon Mutual Insurance Co.
Financial data (yr. ended 12/31/01): Grants paid, $17,025; assets, $335,996 (M); gifts received, $25,000; expenditures, $18,189; qualifying distributions, $16,827.

47693—PENNSYLVANIA

Limitations: Giving limited to the Lebanon, PA, area.
Officers and Directors:* Rollin Rissinger, Jr.,* Pres.; Darwin Glick,* V.P.; Keith A. Ulsh, Secy.-Treas.; Milton Garrison, Mark J. Keyser, S. Bruce Kurtz, Joseph Lauck, Warren Lewis, William Schadler.
EIN: 222521649
Codes: CS, CD

47694
American Legion Charles F. Moran Trust
(also known as American Legion Charles F. Moran Post No. 475, Scholarship Trust and Baseball Trust)
c/o First Financial Bank
100 E. Lancaster Ave.
Downingtown, PA 19335

Financial data (yr. ended 12/31/01): Grants paid, $17,000; assets, $169,412 (M); expenditures, $19,023; qualifying distributions, $16,909.
Limitations: Giving limited to residents of Downington, PA.
Application information: Application form required.
Trustee: First Financial Bank.
EIN: 237718697
Codes: GTI

47695
R & M Barker Foundation 1
c/o Mellon Bank
P.O. Box 185
Pittsburgh, PA 15230-9897
Application address: c/o Laurie Moritz, 3 Mellon Bank Ctr., Pittsburgh, PA 15230

Financial data (yr. ended 12/31/01): Grants paid, $17,000; assets, $427,576 (M); expenditures, $32,170; qualifying distributions, $15,649.
Trustee: Mellon Bank, N.A.
EIN: 256761841

47696
The Lewis Bokser Trust
c/o The Pennsylvania Trust Co.
5 Radnor, Ste. 450
Radnor, PA 19087

Established in 1998 in PA.
Donor(s): Lewis Bokser Crut.
Financial data (yr. ended 12/31/01): Grants paid, $17,000; assets, $295,006 (M); expenditures, $22,204; qualifying distributions, $16,959.
Limitations: Applications not accepted.
Application information: Contributes only to pre-selected organizations.
Trustee: The Pennsylvania Trust Co.
EIN: 236974871

47697
Richard E. Fox Charitable Foundation
370 Leonard Ave.
Washington, PA 15301

Established in 1999 in PA.
Financial data (yr. ended 12/31/01): Grants paid, $17,000; assets, $317,002 (M); gifts received, $333,333; expenditures, $17,331; qualifying distributions, $17,000.
Trustees: Leonard Boss, Joseph Kolter, Michael Pivarnik, Doris J. Regotti.
EIN: 256657059

47698
John J. McCormick Foundation
P.O. Box 176
Erie, PA 16512

Financial data (yr. ended 12/31/01): Grants paid, $17,000; assets, $65,680 (M); expenditures, $17,594; qualifying distributions, $17,000.
Limitations: Applications not accepted. Giving primarily in Erie, PA.
Application information: Contributes only to pre-selected organizations.
Officers: Richard T. McCormick, Pres.; Mary Therese Riley, Secy.; John J. McCormick, Jr., Mgr.
EIN: 256071598

47699
Don McLean Foundation, Inc.
c/o The Pavilion Shubert
261 Old York Rd., Ste. 720
Jenkintown, PA 19046

Donor(s): Don McLean.
Financial data (yr. ended 06/30/02): Grants paid, $17,000; assets, $115,150 (M); expenditures, $17,219; qualifying distributions, $17,000.
Limitations: Applications not accepted.
Application information: Contributes only to pre-selected organizations.
Officer: Don McLean, Pres.
EIN: 133307700

47700
Sickler Foundation
1368 Patrick Henry Dr.
Phoenixville, PA 19460

Established in 1997 in PA.
Donor(s): Doris E. Sickler, John J. Sickler.
Financial data (yr. ended 12/31/00): Grants paid, $17,000; assets, $364,192 (M); gifts received, $401; expenditures, $17,435; qualifying distributions, $17,000.
Limitations: Applications not accepted. Giving primarily in PA.
Application information: Contributes only to pre-selected organizations.
Officers and Directors:* John J. Sickler,* Pres.; Doris E. Sickler,* Secy.-Treas.; Beth A. Sickler, Donna M. Sickler, John J. Sickler, Jr.
EIN: 232926508

47701
Panizza Family Foundation
921 Briarwood Cir.
West Chester, PA 19380
Contact: John Panizza, Treas.

Established in 1998.
Financial data (yr. ended 12/31/99): Grants paid, $16,997; assets, $199,835 (M); expenditures, $21,179; qualifying distributions, $16,997.
Limitations: Giving limited to residents of PA.
Officers and Directors:* Edward M. Panizza,* Pres.; Paul A. Panizza,* V.P.; John Panizza, Treas.
EIN: 232986055

47702
PNC Corporation
1518 Willowbrook Ln.
Villanova, PA 19085
Contact: Priscilla Cohn Ferrater-Mora, Pres.

Financial data (yr. ended 12/31/01): Grants paid, $16,986; assets, $66,539 (M); expenditures, $22,702; qualifying distributions, $16,986.
Limitations: Giving primarily in OH.
Application information: Application form not required.
Officer: Priscilla N. Cohn, Pres.
EIN: 232274586

47703
Max & Bella Black Foundation
c/o Allia & Assocs.
3257 Disston St.
Philadelphia, PA 19149-2821
Application address: 595 Commercial St., Provincetown, MA 02657, tel.: (508) 487-2096
Contact: Honey Black Kay, Mgr.

Financial data (yr. ended 11/30/00): Grants paid, $16,935; assets, $701,717 (M); expenditures, $32,723; qualifying distributions, $21,783.
Limitations: Giving primarily in Cambridge, MA, and Philadelphia, PA.
Officer and Trustees:* Honey Black Kay,* Mgr.; Carole Cohn, David Kay.
EIN: 237037812

47704
Doris S. Casper Foundation
(Formerly Lee A. Casper Foundation)
c/o Society Hill Towers
200 Locust St., Apt. 17-A-H
Philadelphia, PA 19106

Established in 1986 in PA.
Donor(s): Lee A. Casper, Doris S. Casper.
Financial data (yr. ended 09/30/00): Grants paid, $16,905; assets, $6,989 (M); gifts received, $18,000; expenditures, $18,121; qualifying distributions, $18,120.
Limitations: Applications not accepted. Giving primarily in PA.
Application information: Contributes only to pre-selected organizations.
Officers: Doris S. Casper, Pres. and Treas.; Stanley J. Casper, Secy.
EIN: 232756872

47705
The John Cannon Charitable Foundation
c/o Glenmede Trust Co.
1650 Market St., Ste. 1200
Philadelphia, PA 19103-7391

Established in 1995 in PA.
Donor(s): Kathryn Lee Cannon-Courant.
Financial data (yr. ended 12/31/01): Grants paid, $16,800; assets, $65,846 (M); expenditures, $18,155; qualifying distributions, $16,800.
Limitations: Applications not accepted. Giving primarily in CT, NC, and PA.
Application information: Contributes only to pre-selected organizations.
Trustee: Kathryn Lee Cannon-Courant.
EIN: 237824942

47706
Smith Family Foundation
1419 Highland Ave.
Downingtown, PA 19335-3926

Established in 1999 in PA.
Financial data (yr. ended 09/30/01): Grants paid, $16,800; assets, $459,770 (M); expenditures, $25,099; qualifying distributions, $25,099.
Limitations: Giving primarily in PA.
Officers: Frederick J. Smith, Pres.; Mary Ellen Smith, V.P. and Treas.
EIN: 233018741

47707
Kathryn Schiffner Music Fund
c/o Allfirst, Trust Div.
21 E. Market St., M/C 402-130
York, PA 17401-1500
Application address: c/o Reading Musical Foundation, 147 N. 5th St., Reasing, PA 19601

Established in 2000 in PA.

Financial data (yr. ended 12/31/00): Grants paid, $16,784; assets, $190,285 (M); expenditures, $21,784; qualifying distributions, $16,784.
Limitations: Giving primarily in Reading, PA.
Trustee: Allfirst.
EIN: 256641692

47708
Helen M. Schiffner Scholarship Fund
c/o Allfirst, Trust Div.
21 E. Market St., M/C 402-130
York, PA 17401-1500

Established in 2000 in PA.
Financial data (yr. ended 12/31/00): Grants paid, $16,784; assets, $190,308 (M); expenditures, $21,790; qualifying distributions, $16,784.
Trustee: Allfirst.
EIN: 256641691

47709
Kapoor Foundation, Inc.
795 W. Macada Rd.
Bethlehem, PA 18017 (610) 868-9305
Contact: Gopal K. Kapoor, Pres.

Donor(s): Gopal K. Kapoor.
Financial data (yr. ended 12/31/01): Grants paid, $16,774; assets, $126,747 (M); expenditures, $16,774; qualifying distributions, $16,774.
Limitations: Giving on a national and international basis.
Officers: Gopal K. Kapoor, Pres.; Preeta Kapoor, V.P.; Nimita Kapoor Atiyeh, Treas.
Director: Rajil Kapoor.
EIN: 232960127

47710
Milton & Ronnie Sheftel Foundation, Inc.
c/o Ken Ciliberti
2121 31st St., S.W.
Allentown, PA 18103

Established in 1997 in FL.
Financial data (yr. ended 12/31/00): Grants paid, $16,758; assets, $19,286 (M); gifts received, $20,000; expenditures, $16,819; qualifying distributions, $16,758.
Limitations: Applications not accepted. Giving primarily in PA.
Application information: Contributes only to pre-selected organizations.
Officers and Directors:* Milton S. Sheftel,* Pres. and Treas.; Ronnie L. Sheftel,* Secy.; Mark H. Scoblionko.
EIN: 650790710

47711
Ruby Marsh Eldred Scholarship Trust
c/o PNC Advisors
620 Liberty Ave., P2-PTPP-10-2
Pittsburgh, PA 15222-2705
Application address: 941 Federal Ct., Old Post Off. Bldg., Meadville, PA 16334
Contact: Mary Ann Kirkpatrick

Financial data (yr. ended 06/30/01): Grants paid, $16,700; assets, $315,062 (M); expenditures, $17,172; qualifying distributions, $16,252.
Limitations: Giving limited to residents of Meadville, PA, area.
Application information: Application form not required.
Trustee: PNC Bank, N.A.
EIN: 256114997
Codes: GTI

47712
Mortimer S. and Vera M. Schiff Foundation
(Formerly Lawrence & Mortimer S. Schiff Foundation)
590 California Rd.
Quakertown, PA 18951-2487
Contact: Richard J. Schiff, Secy.

Donor(s): Richard J. Schiff, Vera M. Schiff.
Financial data (yr. ended 12/31/01): Grants paid, $16,698; assets, $216,501 (M); gifts received, $4,135; expenditures, $18,360; qualifying distributions, $16,698.
Limitations: Giving primarily in PA.
Application information: Application form not required.
Officers and Directors:* Vera M. Schiff,* Pres. and Treas.; Richard J. Schiff,* Secy.
EIN: 222450589

47713
The Marian & Eva Rokacz Family Foundation
c/o Lawrence S. Chane
1 Logan Sq.
Philadelphia, PA 19103-6998

Established in 1986 in PA.
Donor(s): Eva Rokacz.
Financial data (yr. ended 11/30/01): Grants paid, $16,545; assets, $76,871 (M); gifts received, $9,000; expenditures, $16,616; qualifying distributions, $16,545.
Limitations: Applications not accepted. Giving primarily in the metropolitan New York, NY, area.
Application information: Contributes only to pre-selected organizations.
Trustees: Eva Rokacz, John Rokacz, Joseph Rokacz.
EIN: 236887255

47714
The Brian H. and Elizabeth Hartzell Dovey Family Foundation
704 Plymouth Rd.
Gwynedd Valley, PA 19437

Donor(s): Brian H. Dovey.
Financial data (yr. ended 12/31/01): Grants paid, $16,500; assets, $568,339 (M); expenditures, $26,943; qualifying distributions, $16,500.
Limitations: Applications not accepted.
Application information: Contributes only to pre-selected organizations.
Trustees: Kimberly Dovey Culligan, Patrick Culligan, Brian H. Dovey, Christine Hartzell Dovey, Elizabeth Hartzell Dovey, Edward F. Stack, Laurel Dovey Stack.
EIN: 237927419

47715
Ganassi Foundation
c/o Reed, Smith, Shaw & McClay
P.O. Box 2009
Pittsburgh, PA 15230

Established in 1988.
Donor(s): Floyd R. Ganassi.
Financial data (yr. ended 11/30/01): Grants paid, $16,500; assets, $325,194 (M); expenditures, $16,982; qualifying distributions, $16,500.
Limitations: Applications not accepted. Giving primarily in Pittsburgh, PA.
Application information: Contributes only to pre-selected organizations.
Trustees: Annette D. Ganassi, Floyd R. Ganassi, Edward W. Seifert.
EIN: 251591687

47716
William F. McCann Trust
c/o Mellon Bank, N.A.
P.O. Box 7236
Philadelphia, PA 19101-7236

Financial data (yr. ended 09/30/01): Grants paid, $16,500; assets, $272,927 (M); expenditures, $20,568; qualifying distributions, $18,075.
Limitations: Applications not accepted. Giving primarily in PA.
Application information: Contributes only to pre-selected organizations.
Trustee: Mellon Bank, N.A.
EIN: 236225244

47717
Polish American Board of Education of Berks County, PA
44 N. 6th St.
Reading, PA 19603
Application address: 311 Mifflin Blvd., Shillington, PA 19607, tel.: (610) 777-2770
Contact: Eleanor Parker, Treas.

Financial data (yr. ended 12/31/01): Grants paid, $16,500; assets, $217,278 (M); gifts received, $13,655; expenditures, $16,958; qualifying distributions, $16,683.
Limitations: Giving limited to residents of Berks County, PA.
Officers: Maryann Zerkowski, Pres.; Helen Nowotarski, V.P.; Catherine A. Konik, Secy.; Eleanor Parker, Treas.
EIN: 232061281
Codes: GTI

47718
Fred and Janet Brubaker Foundation
c/o Somerset Trust Co.
P.O. Box 777
Somerset, PA 15501-0777

Established in 1992 in PA.
Donor(s): I. Fred Brubaker, Janet H. Brubaker.
Financial data (yr. ended 12/31/01): Grants paid, $16,400; assets, $334,488 (M); expenditures, $18,737; qualifying distributions, $16,400.
Limitations: Applications not accepted. Giving primarily in PA.
Application information: Contributes only to pre-selected organizations.
Trustees: I. Fred Brubaker, Janet M. Brubaker, Somerset Trust Co.
EIN: 256401741

47719
Berkheimer Foundation
1883 Jury Rd.
Pen Argyl, PA 18072

Established in 1989 in PA.
Donor(s): H.A. Berkheimer, Inc.
Financial data (yr. ended 12/31/01): Grants paid, $16,350; assets, $145,059 (M); gifts received, $10,000; expenditures, $18,005; qualifying distributions, $16,350.
Limitations: Applications not accepted. Giving primarily in PA.
Application information: Contributes only to pre-selected organizations.
Officers and Directors:* John D. Berkheimer,* Pres.; Henry U. Sandt,* Secy.-Treas.; William Carson, Dennis J. Harris, Robert Pharo.
EIN: 232582881
Codes: CS, CD

47720
The Michael Foundation
c/o Myra Johns
P.O. Box 11
Bryn Athyn, PA 19009-0011

Established in 2001 in PA.
Financial data (yr. ended 12/31/01): Grants paid, $16,234; assets, $8,727 (M); gifts received, $11,195; expenditures, $21,137; qualifying distributions, $21,137.
Limitations: Applications not accepted. Giving primarily in PA.
Application information: Contributes only to pre-selected organizations.
Officers and Directors:* Myra Johns Asplundh,* Pres. and Treas.; Boyd Asplundh,* V.P. and Secy.
EIN: 233052808

47721
Josiah Sleeper & Lottie S. Hill Fund
c/o PNC Advisors
1600 Market St.
Philadelphia, PA 19103-7240
Application address: c/o "The Fund," Taylor Hospital, Ridley Park, PA 19078

Financial data (yr. ended 03/31/01): Grants paid, $16,215; assets, $919,578 (M); expenditures, $23,176; qualifying distributions, $19,189.
Limitations: Giving primarily in PA.
Application information: Application form required.
Trustees: Barbara J. Andrew, Glenn Hirsch, Donald L. Laughlin, John C. McMeekin, William Michael Tomlinson, PNC Bank, N.A.
EIN: 232120878
Codes: GTI

47722
Lena Hoffmaster Trust
21 E. Market St., M/C 402-130
York, PA 17401-1500

Established in 2000 in PA.
Financial data (yr. ended 12/31/01): Grants paid, $16,185; assets, $300,026 (M); expenditures, $19,449; qualifying distributions, $16,185.
Limitations: Applications not accepted. Giving primarily in PA.
Application information: Contributes only to pre-selected organizations.
Trustee: Allfirst.
EIN: 236877116

47723
Edward F. McGinley III Foundation
741 Newtown Rd.
Villanova, PA 19085-1027

Financial data (yr. ended 12/31/00): Grants paid, $16,060; assets, $321,943 (M); expenditures, $18,450; qualifying distributions, $16,060.
Limitations: Applications not accepted. Giving primarily in PA.
Application information: Contributes only to pre-selected organizations.
Trustee: Edward F. McGinley III.
EIN: 231984830

47724
Wilmer R. and Evelyn M. Schultz Family Foundation
1540 Chestnut St.
P.O. Box 449
Emmaus, PA 18049

Established in 1998 in PA.
Financial data (yr. ended 12/31/01): Grants paid, $16,050; assets, $682,734 (M); gifts received, $373,411; expenditures, $16,669; qualifying distributions, $16,050.
Officer: Wilmer R. Schultz, Pres.
EIN: 232902342

47725
The Suzanne H. Arnold Foundation
c/o M. Thompson
1600 Market St., Ste. 3600
Philadelphia, PA 19103
Application address: 136 Woodside Ct., Annville, PA 17003
Contact: Suzanne H. Arnold, Tr.

Established in 1997 in PA.
Donor(s): Suzanne H. Arnold.
Financial data (yr. ended 10/31/01): Grants paid, $16,000; assets, $446,121 (M); gifts received, $235,795; expenditures, $19,164; qualifying distributions, $16,000.
Limitations: Giving primarily in PA and WV.
Application information: Application form not required.
Trustees: Cynthia Arnold, Hillary K. Arnold, Jeffery E. Arnold, Suzanne H. Arnold, Thomas Peter Arnold, G. Daniel Massad.
EIN: 237913891

47726
Anthony P. Baratta Foundation
2661 Huntingdon Pike
Huntingdon Valley, PA 19006-5109

Established in 1998 in PA.
Donor(s): Anthony P. Baratta.
Financial data (yr. ended 12/31/01): Grants paid, $16,000; assets, $257,754 (M); gifts received, $100,000; expenditures, $16,262; qualifying distributions, $16,000.
Officers: Anthony P. Baratta, Pres. and Treas.; Helen Pusicz, V.P. and Secy.
EIN: 232985316

47727
Elizabeth B. Demarest Trust
c/o Mellon Bank, N.A.
P.O. Box 185
Pittsburgh, PA 15230-9897 (412) 234-0023
Contact: Laurie Moritz, Trust Off., Mellon Bank, N.A.

Donor(s): Elizabeth B. Demarest.‡
Financial data (yr. ended 12/31/01): Grants paid, $16,000; assets, $342,459 (M); expenditures, $17,105; qualifying distributions, $16,290.
Application information: Application form required.
Trustee: Mellon Bank, N.A.
EIN: 256108821
Codes: GTI

47728
The Judith and Marc Felgoise Charitable Foundation
120 Belle Cir.
Blue Bell, PA 19422
Contact: Marc Felgoise, Tr.

Established in 1997 in PA.
Donor(s): Judith Felgoise, Marc Felgoise.
Financial data (yr. ended 12/31/01): Grants paid, $16,000; assets, $265,303 (M); gifts received, $1,553; expenditures, $17,015; qualifying distributions, $16,149.
Limitations: Giving limited to Blue Bell, PA.
Trustees: Judith Felgoise, Marc Felgoise.
EIN: 237857249

47729
Annette and Ira W. Fine Family Foundation, Inc.
c/o Glenmede Trust Co.
1650 Market St., Ste. 1200
Philadelphia, PA 19103

Established in 1998 in NJ.
Donor(s): Annette Fine.
Financial data (yr. ended 12/31/01): Grants paid, $16,000; assets, $281,280 (M); expenditures, $18,629; qualifying distributions, $16,588.
Limitations: Applications not accepted.
Application information: Contributes only to pre-selected organizations.
Officer: Annette Fine, Secy.-Treas.
Trustees: Barbara Fine Eisenberg, Ellen Fine, Moira Fine Tenzer.
EIN: 226768245

47730
Sproul Foundation
1760 Bristol Rd., Box 160
Warrington, PA 18976

Financial data (yr. ended 10/31/01): Grants paid, $16,000; assets, $289,266 (M); expenditures, $17,543; qualifying distributions, $16,000.
Limitations: Applications not accepted. Giving primarily in PA.
Application information: Contributes only to pre-selected organizations.
Trustees: Stephen B. Harris, John Jeffords, Kathleen Jeffords.
EIN: 222725129

47731
Muriel Dauer Stackpole Foundation
c/o County National Bank, Trust Dept.
P.O. Box 1992
St. Marys, PA 15857

Established in 1993 in PA.
Donor(s): Members of the Stackpole family.
Financial data (yr. ended 10/31/01): Grants paid, $16,000; assets, $266,529 (M); expenditures, $18,569; qualifying distributions, $16,000.
Limitations: Giving primarily in St. Marys, PA.
Trustee: County National Bank.
EIN: 251723753

47732
Walter J. Wolf Trust
c/o PNC Advisors
620 Liberty Ave., P2-PTPP-10-2
Pittsburgh, PA 15222-2705

Financial data (yr. ended 12/31/01): Grants paid, $16,000; assets, $323,588 (M); expenditures, $19,018; qualifying distributions, $16,449.
Limitations: Giving limited to Potts Grove, PA.
Application information: Application form required.
Trustee: PNC Bank, N.A.
EIN: 236429959
Codes: GTI

47733
The Greater Pottstown Foundation
P.O. Box 696
Pottstown, PA 19464-0696
Application address: P.O. Box 85, Pottstown, PA 19464
Contact: Harold H. Prince, Secy.

Donor(s): Shandy Hill.‡
Financial data (yr. ended 12/31/99): Grants paid, $15,900; assets, $2,071,807 (M); expenditures, $60,705; qualifying distributions, $44,158.
Limitations: Giving primarily in Pottstown, PA.
Application information: Application form required.

Officers: Paul Prince, Pres.; Harold H. Prince, Secy.
Trustees: Patricia Crossen, Anthony Giamo.
EIN: 232568998

47734
Bray Family Foundation
c/o Robert & Susan Bray
2826 Mount Carmel Ave.
Glenside, PA 19038 (215) 885-9900

Established in 1994 in PA.
Donor(s): Susan H. Bray, M.D., Robert J. Bray.
Financial data (yr. ended 11/30/01): Grants paid, $15,850; assets, $530,032 (M); expenditures, $34,092; qualifying distributions, $28,431.
Limitations: Giving primarily in PA.
Application information: Application form not required.
Officers: Susan H. Bray, M.D., Pres.; Robert J. Bray, V.P. and Secy.; Molly E. O'Neill, Treas.
Directors: Brian J. Bray, Joanne M. Kyle, Anne S. Muir, Janice C. Muir.
EIN: 232791988

47735
Clyde L. and Mary C. Shaull Education Foundation
c/o PNC Advisors
1600 Market St.
Philadelphia, PA 19103-7240
Application address: P.O. Box 308, Camp Hill, PA 17001
Contact: James Best, Trust Off., PNC Advisors

Established in 1970.
Donor(s): Clyde L. Shaull,‡ Mary C. Shaull.‡
Financial data (yr. ended 12/31/00): Grants paid, $15,750; assets, $673,283 (M); expenditures, $21,458; qualifying distributions, $15,750.
Limitations: Giving limited to residents of Mechanicsburg, PA.
Application information: Application forms are available from Mechanicsburg High School. Application form required.
Trustees: Douglas R. Bleggi, Charles E. Shields III, Thomas Wetzel, PNC Bank, N.A.
EIN: 237101845
Codes: GTI

47736
Ellis Eye Foundation
(Formerly Morris Ellis Foundation)
109 Clwyd Rd.
Bala Cynwyd, PA 19004-2302

Donor(s): Gilda Ellis, Richard Ellis.
Financial data (yr. ended 12/31/01): Grants paid, $15,691; assets, $3,088 (M); gifts received, $18,908; expenditures, $15,973; qualifying distributions, $15,691.
Limitations: Applications not accepted. Giving primarily in PA.
Application information: Contributes only to pre-selected organizations.
Officers: Richard Ellis, Pres.; Aaron Ellis, V.P.; Gilda Ellis, Secy.-Treas.
EIN: 236291178

47737
Anna M. Rohrer Trust
c/o Allfirst, Trust Co.
21 E. Market St.
York, PA 17401-1500

Financial data (yr. ended 10/31/01): Grants paid, $15,661; assets, $472,970 (M); expenditures, $19,419; qualifying distributions, $19,419.
Limitations: Applications not accepted. Giving primarily in Tampa, FL and PA.

Application information: Contributes only to pre-selected organizations.
Trustee: Allfirst.
EIN: 236845426

47738
The Sue Perel Rosefsky Foundation
2 Thatcher Ct.
Haverford, PA 19041

Established in 1993 in PA.
Financial data (yr. ended 12/31/01): Grants paid, $15,650; assets, $232,126 (M); expenditures, $17,882; qualifying distributions, $15,650.
Limitations: Applications not accepted.
Application information: Contributes only to pre-selected organizations.
Officers and Directors:* Sue Perel Rosefsky,* Pres. and Treas.; Robert L. Gorman,* Secy.
EIN: 232675269

47739
Sunil & Nita Wadhwani Family Foundation
930 Osage Rd.
Pittsburgh, PA 15243 (412) 276-6394
Contact: Sunil Wadhwani, Pres.

Established in 2000 in PA.
Donor(s): Sunil Wadhwani, Nita Wadhwani.
Financial data (yr. ended 12/31/01): Grants paid, $15,590; assets, $127,114 (M); expenditures, $15,590; qualifying distributions, $15,590.
Officers and Directors:* Sunil Wadhwani,* Pres. and Treas.; Nita Wadhwani,* Secy.
EIN: 251873137

47740
Nina & Philip Friedman Memorial Scholarship Fund
c/o Allfirst, Trust Div.
21 E. Market St.
York, PA 17401-1500
Application address: c/o Financial Aid Office, York College, Country Club Rd., York, PA 17403, tel.: (717) 846-7788

Financial data (yr. ended 08/31/01): Grants paid, $15,587; assets, $1,218,490 (M); expenditures, $26,826; qualifying distributions, $26,564.
Limitations: Giving limited to Tampa, FL and York, PA.
Application information: Application form required.
Trustees: Leon I. Butler, Allfirst.
Scholarship Committee: Pastor, St. Paul's Lutheran Church, Rabbi, Temple Beth Israel, Pres., York College.
EIN: 236677121

47741
Schaefer Foundation, Inc.
161 Hardt Hill Rd.
Bechtelsville, PA 19505-9302

Financial data (yr. ended 12/31/01): Grants paid, $15,580; assets, $337,356 (M); expenditures, $16,470; qualifying distributions, $15,580.
Limitations: Applications not accepted.
Application information: Contributes only to pre-selected organizations.
Officers: J.B. Schaefer, Jr., Pres.; William C. Schaefer, Secy.-Treas.
Trustees: Mrs. Robert Hamlin, Sue M. Larson, Herbert S. Meeker, Margaret T. Schaefer, Terry A. Thompson.
EIN: 226042871

47742
C. Arthur and Elizabeth Hammers Charitable Trust
c/o First Union National Bank
Broad and Walnut Sts., PA1308
Philadelphia, PA 19109

Established in 1997 in PA.
Financial data (yr. ended 01/31/00): Grants paid, $15,569; assets, $263,179 (M); expenditures, $17,856; qualifying distributions, $15,637.
Limitations: Giving limited to residents of Lehighton, PA.
Trustee: First Union National Bank.
EIN: 237840919

47743
Ralph C. & Dorothy C. Reese Foundation
c/o Hershey Trust Co.
P.O. Box 445
Hershey, PA 17033

Established in 1997 in PA.
Donor(s): Dorothy C. Reese, Ralph C. Reese.
Financial data (yr. ended 12/31/01): Grants paid, $15,550; assets, $172,001 (M); expenditures, $17,639; qualifying distributions, $15,550.
Limitations: Applications not accepted.
Application information: Contributes only to pre-selected organizations.
Officers and Trustees:* Ralph C. Reese,* Chair.; Patricia R. Foltz,* Secy.; Dorothy C. Reese, Hershey Trust Co.
EIN: 237931814

47744
McAlaine Family Foundation
401 Gatcombe Ln.
Bryn Mawr, PA 19010 (610) 527-0489
Contact: Anne S. McAlaine, Secy.-Treas.

Established in 1998 in PA.
Donor(s): Anne S. McAlaine, Robert M. McAlaine.
Financial data (yr. ended 12/31/01): Grants paid, $15,500; assets, $219,732 (M); expenditures, $17,469; qualifying distributions, $15,500.
Limitations: Giving on a national basis, with some emphasis on PA.
Officers: Robert M. McAlaine, Pres.; Anne S. McAlaine, Secy.-Treas.
Trustees: Daniel R. McAlaine, Katherine E. McAlaine, Margaret M. McAlaine, Thomas S. McAlaine.
EIN: 232985960

47745
Jeffrey P. McKee Foundation
2032 B Arch St.
Philadelphia, PA 19103-1447 (215) 416-0741
Contact: Jeffrey P. McKee, Tr.

Financial data (yr. ended 12/31/00): Grants paid, $15,500; assets, $310,771 (M); gifts received, $15,000; expenditures, $16,534; qualifying distributions, $15,500.
Limitations: Giving primarily in NH and PA.
Trustees: Jeffrey P. McKee, Pierce McKee.
EIN: 232484718

47746
The Kleinert's, Inc. Scholarship Fund
(Formerly Victor J. Montemayor Scholarship Fund)
c/o Kleinert's, Inc., H.R. Dept.
120 W. Germantown Pike, Ste. 100
Plymouth Meeting, PA 19462 (610) 828-7261

Established in 1987 in PA.
Donor(s): Kleinert's, Inc.
Financial data (yr. ended 12/31/01): Grants paid, $15,464; assets, $3,829 (M); gifts received,

47746—PENNSYLVANIA

$15,000; expenditures, $15,513; qualifying distributions, $15,514.
Limitations: Giving primarily in areas of company operations and its subsidiaries.
Application information: Unsolicited requests for funds not accepted.
Directors: Jack Brier, Joseph J. Connors, E. Gerald Riesenbach.
EIN: 222787097
Codes: CS, CD, GTI

47747
The Ira Schwartz Foundation
c/o Sardinsky, Braunstein & Co.
10 Penn Ctr., No. 617
Philadelphia, PA 19103

Established in 1994 in PA.
Donor(s): Ira Schwartz.
Financial data (yr. ended 06/30/02): Grants paid, $15,428; assets, $74,590 (M); gifts received, $2,500; expenditures, $16,795; qualifying distributions, $15,428.
Limitations: Applications not accepted. Giving primarily in Philadelphia, PA.
Application information: Contributes only to pre-selected organizations.
Trustees: John Kehner, Sol Sardinsky, Ira Schwartz.
EIN: 232787036

47748
The Matzkin Foundation
230 Maple Hill Rd.
Gladwyne, PA 19035

Donor(s): Stanley Matzkin.
Financial data (yr. ended 12/31/01): Grants paid, $15,388; assets, $124,896 (M); expenditures, $16,485; qualifying distributions, $15,388.
Limitations: Applications not accepted. Giving primarily in Philadelphia, PA.
Application information: Contributes only to pre-selected organizations.
Trustee: Stanley Matzkin.
EIN: 222659502

47749
Arthur B. and Marion V. Myers Cancer Research Fund Trust
c/o Allfirst, Trust Div.
21 E. Market St., M/C 402-130
York, PA 17401-1500

Established in 2000 in PA.
Financial data (yr. ended 12/31/01): Grants paid, $15,361; assets, $373,958 (M); expenditures, $26,927; qualifying distributions, $15,361.
Limitations: Applications not accepted. Giving primarily in Washington, DC.
Application information: Contributes only to pre-selected organizations.
Trustee: Allfirst.
EIN: 256480501

47750
Ralph B. Hull Charitable Trust
c/o Fulton Financial Advisors, N.A.
P.O. Box 3215
Lancaster, PA 17604-3215

Established in 1996 in PA.
Financial data (yr. ended 12/31/01): Grants paid, $15,290; assets, $381,701 (M); expenditures, $17,518; qualifying distributions, $15,290.
Limitations: Applications not accepted.
Application information: Contributes only to pre-selected organizations.
Trustee: Fulton Financial Advisors, N.A.
EIN: 232851302

47751
Clarence Mensching Trust
c/o First Union National Bank
Broad & Walnut Sts., Ste PA1308
Philadelphia, PA 19109

Established in 1997 in FL.
Financial data (yr. ended 12/31/99): Grants paid, $15,269; assets, $550,720 (M); expenditures, $24,922; qualifying distributions, $15,357.
Limitations: Applications not accepted.
Application information: Contributes only to pre-selected organizations.
Trustee: First Union National Bank.
EIN: 656147542

47752
Sonny Hill Foundation
429 S. 50th St.
Philadelphia, PA 19143 (215) 474-2801
Contact: William R. Hill, Chair.

Donor(s): William R. Hill.
Financial data (yr. ended 12/31/00): Grants paid, $15,250; assets, $38,550 (M); gifts received, $53,500; expenditures, $26,374; qualifying distributions, $15,250.
Publications: Application guidelines.
Application information: Application form and interviews required for scholarships.
Officers and Directors:* William R. Hill,* Chair.; K. Brent Hill, Pres.; Michael C. Richman,* Secy.-Treas.; Linda A. Hill, Secy.; Dr. Billy Floyd, Herm Rogul, Tyrone Shields.
EIN: 232397219

47753
James K. Boyer Family Foundation
2201 Ridgewood Rd., No. 180
Wyomissing, PA 19610

Donor(s): Nancy Lang Boyer.
Financial data (yr. ended 12/31/01): Grants paid, $15,200; assets, $445,260 (M); expenditures, $22,679; qualifying distributions, $15,200.
Limitations: Applications not accepted.
Application information: Contributes only to pre-selected organizations.
Officers: Nancy Lang Boyer, Pres.; Walter Lang Boyer, Secy.; James K. Boyer, Jr., Treas.
Directors: Mary Ann Boyer, Patricia Lang Boyer.
EIN: 237788030

47754
Fair Oaks Charitable Trust
5433 Kipling Rd.
Pittsburgh, PA 15217 (412) 521-2951
Contact: John F. Kraft, III, Dir.

Donor(s): F. Gordon Kraft, John F. Kraft III.
Financial data (yr. ended 12/31/01): Grants paid, $15,200; assets, $40,528 (M); gifts received, $2,168; expenditures, $15,449; qualifying distributions, $15,200.
Limitations: Giving primarily in Pittsburgh, PA.
Application information: Application form not required.
Directors: F. Gordon Kraft, John F. Kraft III.
EIN: 237081299

47755
R. R. Wright Educational Fund
c/o Mellon Bank, N.A.
P.O. Box 185
Pittsburgh, PA 15230-9897 (412) 234-5524
Contact: Donna Bricker, Trust. Off., Mellon Bank, N.A.

Established in 1925 in PA.
Financial data (yr. ended 04/30/02): Grants paid, $15,200; assets, $341,701 (M); expenditures, $18,268; qualifying distributions, $18,172.
Limitations: Giving limited to Mercer, PA.
Application information: Application form required.
Trustee: Mellon Bank, N.A.
EIN: 236785914
Codes: GTI

47756
The Lee F. & Phoebe A. Driscoll Family Foundation
720 Swedesford Rd.
Ambler, PA 19002
Contact: Lee F.Driscoll, Pres. and Phoebe A. Driscoll, V.P.

Established in 1998 in PA.
Donor(s): Lee F. Driscoll, Phoebe A. Driscoll.
Financial data (yr. ended 06/30/01): Grants paid, $15,192; assets, $431,889 (M); expenditures, $16,750; qualifying distributions, $16,292.
Limitations: Giving primarily in PA, with emphasis on the Philadelphia area.
Officers: Lee F. Driscoll, Pres. and Treas.; Phoebe A. Driscoll, V.P. and Secy.
EIN: 232982380

47757
The Murray and Marjorie Sachs Foundation
1344 Squirrel Hill Ave.
Pittsburgh, PA 15217-1150 (412) 621-1200

Established in 1986 in PA.
Donor(s): Murray Sachs.
Financial data (yr. ended 11/30/01): Grants paid, $15,165; assets, $83,281 (M); expenditures, $18,644; qualifying distributions, $15,165.
Limitations: Giving primarily in Pittsburgh, PA.
Trustees: Carol C. Mullaugh, Marjorie Sachs, Murray Sachs.
EIN: 251550424

47758
Horowitz Family Foundation
c/o RAF Industries, Inc.
165 Township Line Rd., Ste. 2100
Jenkintown, PA 19046

Established in 2000 in PA.
Donor(s): Richard M. Horowitz.
Financial data (yr. ended 12/31/01): Grants paid, $15,100; assets, $6,230 (M); expenditures, $16,380; qualifying distributions, $15,100.
Limitations: Applications not accepted. Giving primarily in PA.
Application information: Contributes only to pre-selected organizations.
Officers and Directors:* Richard M. Horowitz,* Pres. and Secy.; Ruth M. Horowitz,* V.P. and Treas.
EIN: 233036053

47759
Isaly Co., Inc. Charitable Trust
(Formerly Isaly Dairy Charitable Trust)
c/o PNC Advisors
620 Liberty Ave, M.S. P2-PTPP-26-3
Pittsburgh, PA 15222-2719
Application address: c/o Isaly Klondike Co., H. William Isaly, 5400 118th Ave. N., Clearwater, FL 33520, tel.: (813) 576-8424

Donor(s): Isaly Klondike Co., Isaly Co., Inc.
Financial data (yr. ended 12/31/01): Grants paid, $15,100; assets, $263,757 (M); expenditures, $17,208; qualifying distributions, $15,132.
Limitations: Giving primarily in FL.
Application information: Unsolicited requests for funds not accepted.
Trustee: PNC Bank, N.A.

EIN: 256024887
Codes: CS, CD

47760
The Steinour Family Foundation
1735 Market St., 8th Fl.
Philadelphia, PA 19103

Established in 2000 in RI.
Donor(s): Stephen D. Steinour.
Financial data (yr. ended 12/31/01): Grants paid, $15,098; assets, $295,799 (M); expenditures, $15,142; qualifying distributions, $15,098.
Trustee: Stephen D. Steinour.
EIN: 056125430

47761
Amshel Charitable Foundation
220 Conover Rd.
Pittsburgh, PA 15208-2604

Established in 1999 in PA.
Donor(s): Albert L. Amshel, MD.
Financial data (yr. ended 11/30/01): Grants paid, $15,000; assets, $320,258 (M); expenditures, $15,065; qualifying distributions, $15,000.
Limitations: Applications not accepted. Giving primarily in Pittsburgh, PA.
Application information: Contributes only to pre-selected organizations.
Trustees: Albert L. Amshel, MD, Bruce B. Amshel, Gail B. Amshel.
EIN: 256684453

47762
Dorotha A. Anderson Charitable Foundation
c/o Doug Anderson
1 Anderson Plz.
Greenville, PA 16125

Established in 1996 in PA.
Financial data (yr. ended 12/31/01): Grants paid, $15,000; assets, $341,453 (M); gifts received, $108,770; expenditures, $16,205; qualifying distributions, $15,000.
Limitations: Giving primarily in PA.
Trustees: Douglas Anderson, Lyle Anderson, Karen Jones, Sue Ann Nicklin.
EIN: 237885028

47763
Gibbs Foundation
(Formerly J. H. Gibbs Foundation)
c/o First Union National Bank
Broad and Walnut Sts., Ste. PA1308
Philadelphia, PA 19109

Established in 1991 in VA.
Donor(s): Jack Gibbs.‡
Financial data (yr. ended 12/31/99): Grants paid, $15,000; assets, $430,720 (M); expenditures, $24,680; qualifying distributions, $15,000.
Limitations: Applications not accepted. Giving for scholarships limited to Wise County, VA; giving for organizations limited to Appalachia and the Big Stone Gap, VA, area.
Trustees: Faith Cox, First Union National Bank.
EIN: 546317007

47764
James and Marilyn A. Gilmore Foundation
1331 Inverness Ave.
Pittsburgh, PA 15217-1755

Established in 2000 in PA.
Donor(s): James Gilmore.‡
Financial data (yr. ended 12/31/01): Grants paid, $15,000; assets, $6,060,089 (M); gifts received, $6,274,980; expenditures, $68,390; qualifying distributions, $14,623.
Limitations: Applications not accepted.

Application information: Contributes only to pre-selected organizations.
Trustees: Janet W. Danforth, Marilyn A. Gilmore, David M. Walradt.
EIN: 256699697

47765
Greenhill Research Foundation
c/o Brian Price & Assoc.
140 E. Butler Ave.
Chalfont, PA 18914

Financial data (yr. ended 03/31/02): Grants paid, $15,000; assets, $268,628 (M); expenditures, $17,898; qualifying distributions, $15,000.
Limitations: Applications not accepted. Giving primarily in NY and PA.
Application information: Contributes only to pre-selected organizations.
Officers: Carl B. Hess, Pres.; John D. Hess, Treas.
EIN: 366056619

47766
Keystone CDC, Inc.
1 Keystone Plz.
Front & Market Sts.
Harrisburg, PA 17105-3660

Established in 1989 in PA.
Financial data (yr. ended 12/31/99): Grants paid, $15,000; assets, $313,269 (M); expenditures, $15,270; qualifying distributions, $14,866.
Limitations: Applications not accepted. Giving primarily in PA.
Application information: Contributes only to pre-selected organizations.
Officers: Donald L. Williams, Pres.; Joseph A. Grosso, V.P.; Timothy A. Hoy, Secy.; Donald F. Holt, Treas.
Directors: Carl L. Campbell, Ben G. Rooke, William J. Rossman.
EIN: 251575749

47767
The Herbert M. and Naomi R. Leavitt Family Charitable Trust
c/o Nancy R. Matus
425 Dogwood Terr.
Easton, PA 18040

Established in 1997 in PA.
Donor(s): Herbert M. Leavitt, Naomi R. Leavitt.
Financial data (yr. ended 12/31/01): Grants paid, $15,000; assets, $356,539 (M); expenditures, $22,928; qualifying distributions, $15,000.
Limitations: Applications not accepted. Giving primarily in PA.
Application information: Contributes only to pre-selected organizations.
Trustees: Herbert M. Leavitt, Naomi R. Leavitt, Nancy R. Matus.
EIN: 237891877

47768
Mulhearn-Von Schack Family Foundation, Inc.
c/o Robert Beilstein
1424 Frick Building
Pittsburgh, PA 15219
Contact: Mary Mulhearn-Von Schack, Pres.

Established in 1999 in PA.
Donor(s): Wesley W. Von Schack.
Financial data (yr. ended 12/31/00): Grants paid, $15,000; assets, $259,898 (M); gifts received, $5,000; expenditures, $16,467; qualifying distributions, $15,000.
Officers: Mary Mulhearn-Von Schack, Pres.; Wesley W. Von Schack, Secy.-Treas.
EIN: 251848203

47769
PARTS Scholarship Foundation
(Formerly Pennsylvania Auto & Truck Salvage Association Scholarship Foundation)
1106 Carlisle Rd.
Camp Hill, PA 17011
Application address: c/o Harrisburg Area Community College, Office of Financial Aid, 1 HACC Dr., Harrisburg, PA 17110, tel.: (717) 780-2300

Established in 1990 in PA.
Donor(s): Pennsylvania Automotive Recycling Trade Society.
Financial data (yr. ended 09/30/01): Grants paid, $15,000; assets, $73,083 (M); gifts received, $2,300; expenditures, $31,327; qualifying distributions, $15,000.
Limitations: Giving limited to residents of PA.
Application information: Application form required.
Officers and Directors:* Michael Angelo,* Chair.; Jeff A. McNelly,* Admin.; Charles Bauer.
EIN: 232361314
Codes: GTI

47770
Jeffrey Perkins Charitable Foundation
c/o Robert Y. Kopf
20 Stanwix St., Ste. 650
Pittsburgh, PA 15222-4801

Established in 1996 in PA.
Donor(s): Buchanan Ingersoll.
Financial data (yr. ended 12/31/01): Grants paid, $15,000; assets, $19,650 (M); expenditures, $15,006; qualifying distributions, $15,000.
Limitations: Applications not accepted.
Application information: Contributes only to pre-selected organizations.
Trustee: Robert Y. Kopf, Jr.
EIN: 251778198

47771
Joseph B. Scheller and Rita P. Scheller Foundation
1 S. Church St.
Hazleton, PA 18201-6200

Established in 1995 in PA.
Donor(s): Joseph B. Scheller.
Financial data (yr. ended 12/31/00): Grants paid, $15,000; assets, $2,447,237 (M); gifts received, $1,510,464; expenditures, $24,688; qualifying distributions, $15,000.
Limitations: Applications not accepted.
Application information: Contributes only to pre-selected organizations.
Officer: Joseph B. Scheller, Chair.
Trustees: Susan Scheller Arsht, Nancy Scheller Hays, Michael H. Scheller, Rita P. Scheller.
EIN: 237824343

47772
Three Trees Foundation
c/o Stuart D. Teacher
1220 Warwick Furnace Rd.
Glenmoore, PA 19343-2617

Established in 1999 in PA.
Donor(s): Stuart D. Teacher.
Financial data (yr. ended 12/31/01): Grants paid, $15,000; assets, $1,169 (M); gifts received, $15,000; expenditures, $15,000; qualifying distributions, $15,000.
Limitations: Applications not accepted.
Application information: Contributes only to pre-selected organizations.
Officer and Trustees:* Stuart D. Teacher,* Mgr.; Janet M. Bukovinsky, Matthew Teacher.
EIN: 256614426

47773
William C. Troutman and Dorothy T. Troutman Foundation, Inc.
640 State St.
Millersburg, PA 17061   (717) 896-3903
Contact: David A. Troutman, Dir.

Established in 1996 in PA.
Donor(s): Dorothy T. Troutman, William C. Troutman.‡
Financial data (yr. ended 07/31/01): Grants paid, $15,000; assets, $261,905 (M); expenditures, $17,451; qualifying distributions, $15,000.
Limitations: Giving primarily in northern Dauphin County and the western portion of Schuykill County, PA.
Directors: Steven Shade, David A. Troutman, Dorothy T. Troutman.
EIN: 251777792

47774
The Wilding Family Foundation
14 Callery Way
Malvern, PA 19355

Established in 2000 in PA.
Donor(s): Peter Wilding, Audrey Wilding.
Financial data (yr. ended 06/30/01): Grants paid, $15,000; assets, $714,702 (M); gifts received, $2,475; expenditures, $48,395; qualifying distributions, $42,972.
Limitations: Applications not accepted.
Application information: Contributes only to pre-selected organizations.
Trustees: Audrey Wilding, Elisabeth Wilding, Matthew R. Wilding, Peter Wilding, Stuart P. Wilding.
EIN: 233047746

47775
Wyncote Foundation, Inc.
c/o Kersky & Co.
121 S. Broad St.
Philadelphia, PA 19107

Established in 1992 in FL.
Financial data (yr. ended 12/31/00): Grants paid, $15,000; assets, $181,611 (M); expenditures, $16,341; qualifying distributions, $15,000.
Limitations: Giving on a national basis.
Trustees: Charles Kofsky, Mitchell Miller, Carol Russo.
EIN: 650087209

47776
Camp Foundation
c/o Law Co.
16 Sentry Park W., Ste. 310
Blue Bell, PA 19422
Application address: 1611 Gerson Dr., Narbeth, PA 19072
Contact: David I. Camp, Tr.

Financial data (yr. ended 12/31/00): Grants paid, $14,752; assets, $97,678 (M); expenditures, $16,833; qualifying distributions, $14,678.
Limitations: Giving primarily in Philadelphia, PA.
Application information: Application form not required.
Trustees: David I. Camp, Jonathan C. Camp.
EIN: 236478899

47777
Emil H. & Rose A. Beck Nursing School Charitable Trust
c/o First Union National Bank
123 S. Broad St.
Philadelphia, PA 19109

Established in 1992 in FL.

Financial data (yr. ended 12/31/99): Grants paid, $14,665; assets, $452,132 (M); expenditures, $20,109; qualifying distributions, $14,665.
Limitations: Giving primarily in FL.
Application information: Application form not required.
Trustee: First Union National Bank.
EIN: 596987541

47778
Edwin M. Gilberg Family Foundation
1122 Gainsboro Rd., Ste. 3200
Bala Cynwyd, PA 19004
Contact: Edwin M. Gilberg, Tr.

Established in 1996 in PA.
Donor(s): Edwin M. Gilberg.
Financial data (yr. ended 12/31/99): Grants paid, $14,626; assets, $707,712 (M); gifts received, $70,312; expenditures, $16,613; qualifying distributions, $14,626.
Trustee: Edwin M. Gilberg.
EIN: 232868994

47779
Nixon Memorial Education Fund
c/o PNC Advisors
620 Liberty Ave., P2-PTPP-10-2
Pittsburgh, PA 15222-2705   (412) 762-7645
Contact: Susan Blake, V.P., PNC Bank, N.A.

Financial data (yr. ended 12/31/00): Grants paid, $14,552; assets, $258,609 (M); expenditures, $15,301; qualifying distributions, $14,567.
Limitations: Giving limited to residents of Penn Township and Butler County, PA.
Application information: Application form required.
Trustees: William D. Sutton, PNC Bank, N.A.
EIN: 256072006

47780
Michael Dunitz Crisis Foundation, Inc.
c/o Loretta M. Bausher
127 Main St.
Stouchsburg, PA 19567

Financial data (yr. ended 06/30/02): Grants paid, $14,500; assets, $441,965 (M); gifts received, $15; expenditures, $35,883; qualifying distributions, $14,500.
Limitations: Applications not accepted. Giving primarily in MD and PA.
Application information: Contributes only to pre-selected organizations.
Officers: Roberta Dunitz, Pres.; Jan Dunitz, V.P.; Debra Greenblatt, Treas.
EIN: 232195430

47781
Mary J. Heerdt Charitable Trust
600 Lindley Rd.
Glenside, PA 19038

Donor(s): Robert J. Heerdt.
Financial data (yr. ended 02/28/02): Grants paid, $14,500; assets, $224,223 (M); gifts received, $5,576; expenditures, $15,747; qualifying distributions, $14,500.
Limitations: Applications not accepted. Giving primarily in PA.
Application information: Contributes only to pre-selected organizations.
Trustees: Robert J. Heerdt, Charlotte J. Homan, Catherine J. Struck.
EIN: 237798748

47782
The November Fund
c/o Mark S. Dichter
1017 Clinton St.
Philadelphia, PA 19107

Established in 1999 in PA.
Donor(s): Mark S. Dichter, Tobey Gordon Dichter.
Financial data (yr. ended 10/31/01): Grants paid, $14,500; assets, $307,304 (M); expenditures, $29,192; qualifying distributions, $14,500.
Limitations: Applications not accepted. Giving primarily in Philadelphia, PA.
Application information: Contributes only to pre-selected organizations.
Directors: Mark S. Dichter, Tobey Gordon Dichter.
EIN: 912072454

47783
Orange Foundation, Inc.
20 N. York Rd.
P.O. Box 175
Hatboro, PA 19040-0175

Financial data (yr. ended 06/30/02): Grants paid, $14,500; assets, $454,964 (M); gifts received, $1,125; expenditures, $19,270; qualifying distributions, $14,500.
Limitations: Applications not accepted. Giving primarily in PA.
Application information: Contributes only to pre-selected organizations.
Officers and Directors:* Howard M. Gaul,* Pres.; Frederick E. Stewart,* V.P.; Walter C. Wilson,* Secy.; William E. Orr,* Treas.; Harold Alexander, Rev. Gregory F. Dimick, Meta S. Gaul, Darlene Guest, Kevin Heckman, James Huey, Edith Mackey, Grace Peterson, Charles Romanowitz, George W. Taylor, Jr., Sallie C. Wilson.
EIN: 231261147

47784
Harry Leon Lobsenz Foundation, Inc.
218 Kent Rd.
Wyncote, PA 19095-1815

Financial data (yr. ended 11/30/01): Grants paid, $14,478; assets, $235,644 (M); expenditures, $15,937; qualifying distributions, $14,389.
Limitations: Applications not accepted. Giving primarily in Philadelphia, PA.
Application information: Contributes only to pre-selected organizations.
Officers and Directors:* Roger E. Copland,* Pres. and Treas.; Alan L. Copland,* V.P. and Secy.; Debbie Copland,* V.P.
EIN: 136113561

47785
Florence & Julian Rappaport Scholarship Trust
c/o Allfirst, Trust Div.
21 E. Market St., M/C 402-130
York, PA 17401
Application address: c/o Principal, York Catholic High School, 601 E. Springettsbury Ave., York, PA 17403-2896, tel.: (717) 846-8871

Established in 1998 in PA.
Donor(s): Florence R. Rappaport.‡
Financial data (yr. ended 05/31/02): Grants paid, $14,350; assets, $267,196 (M); expenditures, $17,704; qualifying distributions, $14,350.
Limitations: Giving limited to residents of York, PA.
Selection Committe: John Kennedy, Bishop of Diocese of Harrisburg, Principal of York Catholic High School.
Trustee: Allfirst.
EIN: 256574160

47786
Mandeville Foundation
P.O. Box A
Wayne, PA 19087
Contact: Joseph W. Roskos & Co.

Established in 1999 in PA.
Donor(s): Josephine Mandeville.
Financial data (yr. ended 11/30/01): Grants paid, $14,300; assets, $264,269 (M); expenditures, $16,304; qualifying distributions, $14,300.
Trustees: Caroline M. Crowley, Josephine Mandeville, Peter O. Mandeville.
EIN: 256595897

47787
Charles Levy Foundation
1 Alton Rd.
Yardley, PA 19067-3030
Contact: James A. Levy, Tr.

Financial data (yr. ended 12/31/01): Grants paid, $14,290; assets, $331,947 (M); expenditures, $17,574; qualifying distributions, $14,290.
Limitations: Giving primarily in NJ and NY.
Trustees: Elinor Levy, James A. Levy, Paul G. Levy.
EIN: 226076221

47788
BJNB Foundation, Inc.
1265 S. Avignon Dr.
Gladwyne, PA 19035-1042 (610) 520-1844
Contact: Barry D. Bergman, Secy.-Treas.

Established in 1996 in PA.
Donor(s): Barry D. Bergman, Jacqueline L. Bergman.
Financial data (yr. ended 12/31/01): Grants paid, $14,250; assets, $213,779 (M); gifts received, $20,792; expenditures, $19,329; qualifying distributions, $14,250.
Application information: Application form not required.
Officers: Jacqueline L. Bergman, Pres.; Barry D. Bergman, Secy.-Treas.
EIN: 232865970

47789
Beatrice L. Compton Memorial Fund
110 Central Square Dr.
Beaver Falls, PA 15010

Financial data (yr. ended 12/31/01): Grants paid, $14,100; assets, $464,307 (M); expenditures, $20,668; qualifying distributions, $14,100.
Trustee: Richard Rocereto.
EIN: 251676211

47790
The Chakrabarti Foundation
c/o Srimata Chakrabarti
P.O. Box 98
Stockertown, PA 18083
Tel.: (610) 759-3690, ext. 20

Established in 1996 in PA.
Donor(s): Paritosh Chakrabarti, Srimata Chakrabarti.
Financial data (yr. ended 12/31/00): Grants paid, $14,075; assets, $2,161 (M); expenditures, $14,603; qualifying distributions, $14,075.
Application information: Application form required.
Officers and Trustees:* Srimata Chakrabarti,* Pres.; Paritosh Chakrabarti,* V.P. and Secy.; Debtosh Chakrabarti, Raj Chakrabarti.
EIN: 251735900

47791
Pacifico Family Foundation
6701 Essington Ave.
Philadelphia, PA 19153
Contact: Kerry T. Pacifico, Dir.

Established in 1988 in PA.
Donor(s): Pacifico Airport Valet Partnership, Joseph Pacifico.
Financial data (yr. ended 12/31/01): Grants paid, $14,060; assets, $212,610 (M); expenditures, $14,850; qualifying distributions, $14,060.
Limitations: Giving primarily in Philadelphia, PA.
Directors: Joseph R. Pacifico, Kerry T. Pacifico.
EIN: 222782890

47792
Jewell D. Rodgers Foundation
700 Beatty Rd., Ste. 350
Monroeville, PA 15146

Established in 1999 in PA.
Donor(s): Jewell D. Rodgers.
Financial data (yr. ended 12/31/01): Grants paid, $14,031; assets, $269,069 (M); expenditures, $14,827; qualifying distributions, $14,031.
Limitations: Applications not accepted. Giving primarily in Pittsburgh, PA.
Application information: Contributes only to pre-selected organizations.
Trustees: Jewell D. Rodgers, Richard C. Walker.
EIN: 251840974

47793
The Richard F. Baruch Private Foundation, Inc.
25 North Buck Ln.
Haverford, PA 19041

Established in 1997 in PA.
Donor(s): Richard F. Baruch.
Financial data (yr. ended 12/31/01): Grants paid, $14,000; assets, $303,147 (M); gifts received, $770; expenditures, $14,770; qualifying distributions, $14,239.
Limitations: Applications not accepted.
Application information: Contributes only to pre-selected organizations.
Officers and Directors:* Richard F. Baruch,* Pres. and Secy.-Treas.; David G. Baruch,* V.P.; Mary C. Baruch,* V.P.; Richard F. Baruch, Jr.,* V.P.; Rodney Day,* V.P.
EIN: 232903488

47794
B. E. Block 4 Memorial Children's Fund
c/o PNC Advisors
620 Liberty Ave., P2-PTPP-10-2
Pittsburgh, PA 15222

Financial data (yr. ended 09/30/01): Grants paid, $14,000; assets, $222,499 (M); expenditures, $15,973; qualifying distributions, $14,000.
Limitations: Giving limited to the Norristown, PA, area.
Trustee: PNC Bank, N.A.
EIN: 236202581

47795
The Anne L. & Robert K. Bowman Family Foundation
436 Ringneck Ln.
Lancaster, PA 17601-2856

Established in 1997 in PA.
Donor(s): Anne L. Bowman, Robert K. Bowman.
Financial data (yr. ended 12/31/01): Grants paid, $14,000; assets, $315,161 (M); gifts received, $22,000; expenditures, $14,951; qualifying distributions, $14,000.
Limitations: Applications not accepted. Giving primarily in PA.
Application information: Contributes only to pre-selected organizations.
Officers: Robert K. Bowman, Chair.; Anne L. Bowman, Secy.
Trustees: Mark W. Bowman, Susan E. Bowman.
EIN: 237850323

47796
Fulton Bank Scholarship Foundation
c/o Fulton Financial Advisors, N.A.
P.O. Box 3215
Lancaster, PA 17604-3215
Application address: c/o Human Resources Dept., P.O. Box 4887, Lancaster, PA 17604

Donor(s): Fulton Financial Corporation.
Financial data (yr. ended 12/31/01): Grants paid, $14,000; assets, $83 (M); gifts received, $14,000; expenditures, $14,000; qualifying distributions, $14,000.
Limitations: Giving primarily in areas of company operations and its affiliate companies.
Application information: Application form required.
Trustee: Fulton Financial Advisors, N.A.
EIN: 236769593
Codes: CS, CD, GTI

47797
John C. McClure Continuing Education Scholarship
c/o First Union National Bank
123 S. Broad St., PA 1308
Philadelphia, PA 19109
Application address: c/o Louella Glessner, First Union National Bank, P.O. Box 26311, Richmond, VA 23260

Established in 1996 in VA.
Financial data (yr. ended 12/31/99): Grants paid, $14,000; assets, $1,194,846 (M); expenditures, $30,697; qualifying distributions, $14,000.
Limitations: Giving limited to high school graduates of VA.
Application information: Application form required.
Trustee: First Union National Bank.
EIN: 541819359

47798
The MorningStar Foundation
19 Short Rd.
Doylestown, PA 18901-3212 (215) 348-5063
Contact: Katherine N. Murphy, Pres.

Established in 1996 in PA.
Donor(s): Joseph A. Murphy.
Financial data (yr. ended 12/31/01): Grants paid, $14,000; assets, $221,082 (M); expenditures, $16,182; qualifying distributions, $14,000.
Officers and Trustees:* Katherine N. Murphy,* Pres. and Treas.; Martha J. Murphy,* V.P.; Joseph A. Murphy.
EIN: 232855899

47799
XX Gulf Oil Corporation Foundation
c/o Mellon Bank, N.A.
P.O. Box 185
Pittsburgh, PA 15230-9897
Application address: 3 Mellon Bank Ctr., Pittsburgh PA 15259, tel.: (412) 234-0023
Contact: Laurie Moritz, Trust Off., Mellon Bank

Established in 1959 in PA; trust instrument amended in 1970 and 1985.
Financial data (yr. ended 12/31/01): Grants paid, $14,000; assets, $263,511 (M); expenditures, $16,290; qualifying distributions, $14,000.
Limitations: Giving primarily in TX.

Trustees: L.I. Beebe, P.S. Hobin, M.C. Lardge, Anna A. Perez, J.W. Rhodes, Jr., D.P. Smay, A.G. Weaver, Mellon Bank, N.A.
EIN: 256018988

47800
Pepper Hollow Fund
c/o Benjamin Alexander
1779 Oak Hill Dr.
Huntingdon Valley, PA 19006

Donor(s): Frederick J. Rosenau Foundation, Benjamin Alexander.
Financial data (yr. ended 11/30/00): Grants paid, $13,925; assets, $107,108 (M); gifts received, $10,000; expenditures, $15,533; qualifying distributions, $13,925.
Limitations: Applications not accepted. Giving primarily in DE, ME, NY, and PA.
Application information: Contributes only to pre-selected organizations.
Trustee: Benjamin Alexander.
EIN: 236411419

47801
Seltzer Family Foundation, Inc.
1019 Morris Ave.
Bryn Mawr, PA 19010

Established in 1995 in PA.
Donor(s): Louis Seltzer, Stefanie Seltzer.
Financial data (yr. ended 12/31/00): Grants paid, $13,921; assets, $868,940 (M); expenditures, $39,492; qualifying distributions, $13,921.
Limitations: Giving primarily in NY and PA.
Officers: Stefanie Seltzer, Pres.; Stephen Zlotowski, V.P.; David Zlotowski, Secy.; Louis Seltzer, Treas.
Trustee: Debra Seltzer.
EIN: 232829071

47802
John Dotson, M.D. Fund
c/o PNC Advisors
620 Liberty Ave., P2-PTPP-10-2
Pittsburgh, PA 15222-2705
Contact: Judy Rice, Trust Off., PNC Advisors

Financial data (yr. ended 12/31/01): Grants paid, $13,870; assets, $235,779 (M); expenditures, $16,669; qualifying distributions, $13,759.
Limitations: Giving limited to residents of Closter, NJ.
Application information: Application form required.
Trustee: PNC Bank, N.A.
EIN: 226040599
Codes: GTI

47803
Edgar P. Kable Foundation
c/o First Union National Bank
P.O. Box 7558
Philadelphia, PA 19101-7558

Financial data (yr. ended 12/31/99): Grants paid, $13,869; assets, $309,743 (M); expenditures, $14,952; qualifying distributions, $13,869.
Limitations: Applications not accepted. Giving primarily in York, PA.
Application information: Contributes only to pre-selected organizations.
Trustee: First Union National Bank.
EIN: 236240611

47804
Harold & Jean Greenspan Family Trust
c/o R. B. Matlin
2000 Market St., 10th Fl.
Philadelphia, PA 19103-3291

Established in 1999 in PA.
Donor(s): Harold Greenspan.‡
Financial data (yr. ended 12/31/01): Grants paid, $13,765; assets, $186,159 (M); expenditures, $14,465; qualifying distributions, $13,765.
Limitations: Applications not accepted. Giving primarily in PA.
Application information: Contributes only to pre-selected organizations.
Trustees: Claire G. Akselrad, Jerald B. Greenspan.
EIN: 526951350

47805
The Inerfeld Family Foundation
1735 Market St., 38th Fl.
Philadelphia, PA 19103-7598

Established in 2000 in PA.
Donor(s): Ivan Inerfeld, Linda Inerfeld.
Financial data (yr. ended 12/31/01): Grants paid, $13,760; assets, $108,518 (M); gifts received, $98,072; expenditures, $13,820; qualifying distributions, $13,760.
Limitations: Applications not accepted. Giving primarily in New York, NY and Philadelphia, PA.
Application information: Contributes only to pre-selected organizations.
Trustees: Ivan Inerfeld, Linda Inerfeld.
EIN: 311729485

47806
The Lois Kaplan Charitable Foundation for the Prevention of Child Abuse
1910 Cochran Rd., Ste. 333
Pittsburgh, PA 15220

Established in 1997 in PA.
Donor(s): Ivan Kaplan.
Financial data (yr. ended 12/31/00): Grants paid, $13,750; assets, $39,595 (M); gifts received, $11,000; expenditures, $14,181; qualifying distributions, $13,727.
Limitations: Applications not accepted. Giving primarily in Pittsburgh, PA.
Application information: Contributes only to pre-selected organizations.
Trustees: Robert Glimcher, Ivan Kaplan, Jason Sambreny.
EIN: 256535974

47807
Solis-Cohen, Spigel Family Fund
Packard Bldg., 12th Fl.
Philadelphia, PA 19102

Donor(s): Helen Spigel Sax, D. Hays Solis-Cohen, Jr., Erna Solis-Cohen,‡ Hays Solis-Cohen.‡
Financial data (yr. ended 12/31/00): Grants paid, $13,725; assets, $628,172 (M); gifts received, $2,000; expenditures, $18,357; qualifying distributions, $15,982.
Limitations: Giving primarily in Philadelphia, PA.
Application information: Application form not required.
Trustees: Helen Spigel Sax, David H. Solis-Cohen III, Virginia Solis-Cohen, James H. Spigel.
EIN: 236243375

47808
The Binnion Foundation
c/o Stanley P. Halbert, C.P.A.
121 S. Broad St.
Philadelphia, PA 19107

Donor(s): Robert C. Binnion.
Financial data (yr. ended 11/30/01): Grants paid, $13,705; assets, $209,376 (M); gifts received, $2,000; expenditures, $13,833; qualifying distributions, $13,663.
Limitations: Applications not accepted. Giving on a national basis, with emphasis on FL.
Application information: Contributes only to pre-selected organizations.
Trustees: Janie Binnion, Robert C. Binnion.
EIN: 236765534

47809
Chester County Housing Development Corp.
311 E. Bernard St.
West Chester, PA 19382-3113

Financial data (yr. ended 12/31/00): Grants paid, $13,666; assets, $60,340 (M); gifts received, $10,000; expenditures, $447,408; qualifying distributions, $13,666; giving activities include $84,224 for programs.
Limitations: Applications not accepted. Giving primarily in West Chester, PA.
Officer: Julie A. Barr, Chair.
EIN: 232330706

47810
Les Oiseaux Foundation
323 Llandrillo Rd.
Bala Cynwyd, PA 19004

Established in 1999 in PA.
Donor(s): Kenneth B. Dunn.
Financial data (yr. ended 12/31/01): Grants paid, $13,650; assets, $4,061,231 (M); expenditures, $32,057; qualifying distributions, $13,650.
Limitations: Applications not accepted. Giving primarily in PA.
Application information: Contributes only to pre-selected organizations.
Trustees: Amy Dunn, Brett Dunn, Kenneth B. Dunn, Pamela R. Dunn, Chester Spatt.
EIN: 256642155

47811
Mary Ann Irvin Scholarship Foundation
c/o S&T Bank, Trust Dept.
P.O. Box 220
Indiana, PA 15701-0220
Application address: c/o Emily Cassidy, Punxsutawney High School, Punxsutawney, PA 15767, tel.: (724) 456-1443

Incorporated in 1966 in PA.
Financial data (yr. ended 12/31/00): Grants paid, $13,600; assets, $412,813 (M); expenditures, $18,378; qualifying distributions, $13,600.
Limitations: Giving limited to the Punxsutawney, PA, area.
Application information: Application form required.
Officers: Thomas Frantz, Pres.; Rev. Shuey, Secy.; William Cooper, Treas.
Trustee: S & T Bank.
EIN: 256079669
Codes: GTI

47812
Miller Family Foundation
5921 Atkinson Rd.
New Hope, PA 18938 (215) 826-2811
Contact: Lawrence Miller

Established in 1998 in PA.
Donor(s): Lawrence Miller, Dolores Miller.
Financial data (yr. ended 12/31/01): Grants paid, $13,600; assets, $27,134 (M); gifts received, $1,702; expenditures, $15,555; qualifying distributions, $13,508.
Application information: Application form not required.
Trustees: Dolores Miller, Lawrence Miller.
EIN: 237986423

47813
Arthur L. & Geraldine C. Schneeberg Foundation
7900 Old York Rd., Ste. 712A
Elkins Park, PA 19027

Financial data (yr. ended 12/31/01): Grants paid, $13,575; assets, $81,760 (M); expenditures, $14,225; qualifying distributions, $13,575.
Directors: Arthur L. Schneeberg, Geraldine C. Schneeberg.
EIN: 232866495

47814
Kranzdorf Family Foundation
340 Sprague Rd.
Narberth, PA 19072 (610) 825-7100
Contact: Norman Kranzdorf, Tr.

Established in 2001 in PA.
Donor(s): Norman M. Kranzdorf, Hermina Kranzdorf.
Financial data (yr. ended 12/31/01): Grants paid, $13,555; assets, $28,409 (M); gifts received, $42,000; expenditures, $13,591; qualifying distributions, $13,579.
Limitations: Giving primarily in PA.
Trustees: Betty Kranzdorf, Hermina Kranzdorf, Michael Kranzdorf, Norman M. Kranzdorf.
EIN: 311806522

47815
Free Quaker Society
c/o Radclyffe Thomson
1509 Montgomery
Bryn Mawr, PA 19010
Application address: 2642 Butler Pike, Plymouth Meeting, PA 19462, tel.: (610) 828-5680
Contact: Elkins Wetherill, Jr., Clerk

Financial data (yr. ended 12/31/01): Grants paid, $13,500; assets, $227,202 (M); gifts received, $200; expenditures, $22,279; qualifying distributions, $13,500.
Limitations: Giving primarily in PA.
Application information: Application form not required.
Officers: Elkins Wetherill, Jr., Clerk; Radclyffe F. Thompson, Treas.
Trustees: Mrs. John H. Hallock, George Stout Hundt, Lester Thomas Hundt, Jr., Mrs. Clarence J. Lewis, Jr., Christopher W. Parker, Mrs. William Henry Parker, Mrs. Lawrence L. Stevens, Jr., Mrs. Wirt L. Thompson, Elkins Wetherill, and 4 additional directors.
EIN: 237336758

47816
Anne McCormick Charitable Trust
c/o Allfirst, Trust Div.
21 E. Market St.
York, PA 17401-1500

Financial data (yr. ended 12/31/00): Grants paid, $13,500; assets, $245,791 (M); expenditures, $16,883; qualifying distributions, $12,930.
Limitations: Giving limited to Dauphin, Cumberland, and Perry counties, PA.
Trustee: Allfirst.
EIN: 236508184

47817
Mark H. Wholey Family Foundation
816 Woodland Ave.
Oakmont, PA 15139

Established in 2000 in PA.
Donor(s): Mark H. Wholey.
Financial data (yr. ended 12/31/01): Grants paid, $13,490; assets, $494,420 (M); gifts received, $288,452; expenditures, $13,765; qualifying distributions, $13,490.
Limitations: Applications not accepted. Giving primarily in PA.
Application information: Contributes only to pre-selected organizations.
Trustee: Mark H. Wholey.
EIN: 316654511

47818
Progress Foundation
4 Sentry Pkwy, Ste. 200
Blue Bell, PA 19422

Financial data (yr. ended 12/31/99): Grants paid, $13,475; assets, $122,918 (M); gifts received, $57,713; expenditures, $39,996; qualifying distributions, $37,129; giving activities include $9,450 for programs.
Limitations: Applications not accepted. Giving primarily in PA.
Application information: Contributes only to pre-selected organizations.
Officers: George E. Gunning, Jr., Pres.; W. Kirk Wycoff, Exec. V.P.; Georgann McKenna, V.P.; Eric Morgan, Treas.
Directors: Timothy Casey, Joseph DiMino, Fran Fusco, John Ondik, Thomas Speers.
EIN: 232421995

47819
Mario and Sara Rafalin Foundation
606 Ballytore Rd.
Wynnewood, PA 19096-2210

Donor(s): Mario Rafalin.
Financial data (yr. ended 11/30/01): Grants paid, $13,450; assets, $179,525 (M); gifts received, $11,163; expenditures, $13,810; qualifying distributions, $13,450.
Limitations: Applications not accepted. Giving primarily in PA.
Application information: Contributes only to pre-selected organizations.
Officer: Mario Rafalin, Pres.
EIN: 232489543

47820
The Patricia and Lionel Savadove Fund, Inc.
6 Old Mill Ln.
New Hope, PA 18938

Established in 1987 in PA.
Donor(s): Lionel Savadove.
Financial data (yr. ended 12/31/00): Grants paid, $13,400; assets, $101,006 (M); expenditures, $13,950; qualifying distributions, $13,400.
Limitations: Applications not accepted. Giving primarily in Philadelphia, PA.
Application information: Contributes only to pre-selected organizations.
Officers: Lionel Savadove, Pres.; Patricia Savadove, V.P. and Secy.-Treas.
Directors: Lane J. Savadove, Lorin M. Savadove.
EIN: 232442430

47821
Timothy J. McCormick Foundation, Inc.
413 Seminole Dr.
Erie, PA 16505

Donor(s): Timothy J. McCormick, Ann S. McCormick.
Financial data (yr. ended 11/30/01): Grants paid, $13,396; assets, $88,830 (M); expenditures, $13,546; qualifying distributions, $13,396.
Limitations: Applications not accepted. Giving primarily in Erie, PA.
Application information: Contributes only to pre-selected organizations.
Officers: Timothy J. McCormick, Pres.; Kathleen M. Kiebansky, V.P.; Ann S. McCormick, V.P.; Timothy J. McCormick, Jr., V.P.
EIN: 251290613

47822
Candace Sneberger Charitable Trust
2374 Fairway Rd.
Huntingdon Valley, PA 19006

Established in 1999 in PA.
Donor(s): Candace L. Sneberger.
Financial data (yr. ended 06/30/01): Grants paid, $13,230; assets, $351,445 (M); expenditures, $21,769; qualifying distributions, $13,230.
Limitations: Applications not accepted.
Application information: Contributes only to pre-selected organizations.
Trustees: Candace L. Sneberger, Daniel F. Sneberger.
EIN: 251850010

47823
Longvue Foundation
c/o Ronald E. Long
Scaife Rd.
Sewickley, PA 15143

Established in 1997 in PA.
Donor(s): Ronald E. Long.
Financial data (yr. ended 12/31/01): Grants paid, $13,200; assets, $45,498 (M); gifts received, $11,485; expenditures, $14,240; qualifying distributions, $13,200.
Limitations: Applications not accepted. Giving primarily in PA.
Application information: Contributes only to pre-selected organizations.
Trustees: Mary Owen Long, Ronald E. Long.
EIN: 237920494

47824
Sports Medicine Foundation, Inc.
1779 5th Ave.
York, PA 17403 (717) 846-7846
Contact: Dean Nachtigall, Pres.

Established around 1993.
Donor(s): Dean Nachtigall, D.O.
Financial data (yr. ended 06/30/00): Grants paid, $13,111; assets, $3,712 (M); gifts received, $14,415; expenditures, $13,129; qualifying distributions, $13,109.
Limitations: Giving limited to residents of PA.
Application information: Application form required.
Officer: Dean Nachtigall, Pres.
EIN: 232663406
Codes: GTI

47825
RISA Charitable Trust
(Formerly Kearsarge Institute)
R.R. 1, Box 172A
Union Dale, PA 18470-0288
Contact: O. Sam Folin, Pres.

Financial data (yr. ended 06/30/01): Grants paid, $13,058; assets, $41,087 (M); gifts received, $52,155; expenditures, $17,227; qualifying distributions, $16,890.
Limitations: Giving in the U.S. and South Africa.
Officer: O. Sam Folin, Pres.
Trustees: Myriah Conroy, Bob Schminkey.
EIN: 232699699

47826
Spring Hill Foundation
P.O. Box 55
Sterling, PA 18463-0055

Financial data (yr. ended 03/31/02): Grants paid, $13,050; assets, $319,759 (M); gifts received, $19,068; expenditures, $16,846; qualifying distributions, $13,050.
Limitations: Applications not accepted. Giving primarily in Danville, PA.
Application information: Contributes only to pre-selected organizations.
Officer: Michael Caputo, Pres. and Mgr.
EIN: 232217537

47827
Berdan Support Fund
2 Cedarwood Ln.
Mendenhall, PA 19357-0812 (610) 388-1667
Contact: John D. Sheridan, Pres.

Donor(s): John Sheridan, Annamae Sheridan.
Financial data (yr. ended 12/31/99): Grants paid, $13,000; assets, $325,264 (M); gifts received, $30,500; expenditures, $14,811; qualifying distributions, $13,000.
Officers: John D. Sheridan, Pres.; Annamae Sheridan, Secy.-Treas.
Director: Daniel P. Dougherty.
EIN: 232746616

47828
Monsignor John J. Bonner Foundation
301 N. Broad St.
Philadelphia, PA 19107-1011

Financial data (yr. ended 12/31/01): Grants paid, $13,000; assets, $214,894 (M); expenditures, $13,859; qualifying distributions, $13,000.
Limitations: Applications not accepted. Giving limited to Philadelphia, PA.
Application information: Contributes only to pre-selected organizations.
Trustees: Joseph R. Hindman, John March.
EIN: 236257249

47829
T. Manning Curtis Athletic Scholarship Fund
c/o PNC Advisors
P.O. Box 937
Scranton, PA 18501
Application address: c/o Superintendent, Stroudsburg Area School District, 123 Linden St., Stroudsburg, PA 18360, tel.: (717) 421-1990

Financial data (yr. ended 12/31/01): Grants paid, $13,000; assets, $267,863 (M); expenditures, $13,849; qualifying distributions, $13,492.
Limitations: Giving limited to residents of Stroudsburg, PA.
Application information: Application form required.
Scholarship Committee: Alfred Arena, Terry Fouts, William Stoudt, Andrew Weingartner.
Trustee: PNC Bank, N.A.
EIN: 236979929
Codes: GTI

47830
The Doran Family Foundation
27 Druim Moir Ln.
Philadelphia, PA 19118

Financial data (yr. ended 12/31/01): Grants paid, $13,000; assets, $312,304 (M); gifts received, $179,880; expenditures, $13,562; qualifying distributions, $13,000.
Limitations: Applications not accepted. Giving primarily in PA.
Application information: Contributes only to pre-selected organizations.
Officer and Directors:* William M. Doran,* Pres. and Treas.; Heather D. Stauffer, Leigh N. Doran, Melissa Doran-Rayer, Susan L. Doran.
EIN: 233064436

47831
Maxine Patman Charitable Trust
820 Pine Hill Rd.
King of Prussia, PA 19406

Established in PA in 1998.
Financial data (yr. ended 12/31/01): Grants paid, $13,000; assets, $408,856 (M); expenditures, $14,612; qualifying distributions, $13,000.
Limitations: Giving primarily in New York, NY and Philadelphia, PA.
Trustees: Wayne Hardee, Wilhelmina Hardee.
EIN: 311578453

47832
Malcolm A. Schweiker, Jr. Memorial Foundation
c/o PNC Advisors
1600 Market St.
Philadelphia, PA 19103-7240

Financial data (yr. ended 12/31/01): Grants paid, $13,000; assets, $807,322 (M); expenditures, $14,717; qualifying distributions, $13,440.
Limitations: Giving limited to the Lansdale, PA, area.
Trustee: PNC Bank, N.A.
EIN: 236207352

47833
Jane & Dan Gray Charitable Trust
c/o PNC Advisors
620 Liberty Ave., P2-PTPP-10-2
Pittsburgh, PA 15222-2705 (412) 768-3352
Contact: Amy L. Phillips, Trust Off., PNC Advisors

Financial data (yr. ended 12/31/01): Grants paid, $12,965; assets, $199,912 (M); expenditures, $14,720; qualifying distributions, $13,393.
Limitations: Giving primarily in the Pittsburgh, PA, area.
Trustee: PNC Bank, N.A.
EIN: 256065758

47834
The Norman & Nancy Norris Private Foundation
P.O. Box 29
Birchrunville, PA 19421

Donor(s): Norman Norris, Nancy L. Norris.
Financial data (yr. ended 12/31/01): Grants paid, $12,956; assets, $199,635 (M); expenditures, $14,561; qualifying distributions, $12,956.
Limitations: Applications not accepted. Giving primarily in PA.
Application information: Contributes only to pre-selected organizations.
Trustees: Nancy Norris, Norman L. Norris.
EIN: 232707519

47835
Heritage Helping Hand
c/o Summit Bank
100 Brodhead Rd.
Bethlehem, PA 18017

Established in 1983 in PA.
Donor(s): Carl J. Reidler.
Financial data (yr. ended 12/31/01): Grants paid, $12,850; assets, $200,707 (M); gifts received, $5,000; expenditures, $13,847; qualifying distributions, $12,850.
Limitations: Applications not accepted. Giving limited to PA.
Application information: Contributes only to pre-selected organizations.
Officer: Carl J. Reidler, Mgr.
Trustee: Summit Bank.
EIN: 222456684

47836
Chowdary Family Foundation
4115 Pheasant Ct.
Allentown, PA 18103
Contact: Raj P. Chowdary, Tr.

Established in 1992 in PA.
Donor(s): Raj P. Chowdary.
Financial data (yr. ended 12/31/01): Grants paid, $12,770; assets, $231,897 (M); gifts received, $34,641; expenditures, $13,536; qualifying distributions, $12,770.
Trustees: Jhansi L. Chowdary, Raj P. Chowdary.
EIN: 237716358

47837
The Rose and Bernard Strauss Foundation, Inc.
c/o Ellis Coffee Co.
2835 Bridge St.
Philadelphia, PA 19137-1809

Established in 1993 in PA.
Donor(s): Bernard Strauss, Rose Strauss.
Financial data (yr. ended 12/31/01): Grants paid, $12,761; assets, $279,879 (M); gifts received, $164; expenditures, $13,675; qualifying distributions, $12,761.
Limitations: Applications not accepted. Giving primarily in PA.
Application information: Contributes only to pre-selected organizations.
Officer and Director:* Rose Strauss,* Pres. and Secy.
EIN: 232742581

47838
World Health Foundation
1704 Pittsburgh St.
Cheswick, PA 15024

Donor(s): Sukhdev S. Grover, M.D.
Financial data (yr. ended 09/30/01): Grants paid, $12,754; assets, $123,757 (M); gifts received, $550; expenditures, $14,113; qualifying distributions, $12,754.
Limitations: Applications not accepted. Giving on an international basis, with some emphasis on India.
Application information: Contributes only to pre-selected organizations.
Officers: Sukhdev S. Grover, M.D., Pres. and Treas.; Jasbir Makar, Secy.
Directors: Joseph Garuccio, Anand Sharma, Joan Singh, Daniel Splain.
EIN: 251347717

47839
Ulderico & Anna C. Milani Charitable Foundation
c/o Crescent Iron Works
4901 Grays Ave.
Philadelphia, PA 19143-5810

Financial data (yr. ended 12/31/01): Grants paid, $12,750; assets, $114,562 (M); gifts received, $50,000; expenditures, $13,738; qualifying distributions, $12,750.
Trustees: Gemma Fitzpatrick, Albert M. Milani, Anna C. Milani, Joseph W. Milani.
EIN: 237948901

47840
Leo M. and Jeremy A. Rosenau Foundation
(Formerly Jeremy A. Rosenau Foundation)
1764 Oak Hill Dr.
Huntingdon Valley, PA 19006

Donor(s): Jeremy A. Rosenau, Lois G. Rosenau.
Financial data (yr. ended 05/31/02): Grants paid, $12,750; assets, $127,122 (M); gifts received, $4,008; expenditures, $13,361; qualifying distributions, $12,750.
Limitations: Applications not accepted. Giving primarily in Philadelphia, PA.
Application information: Contributes only to pre-selected organizations.
Trustees: Jeremy A. Rosenau, Lois G. Rosenau.
EIN: 236298132

47841
The Ann and Murray Spain Foundation
1429 Garrison Dr.
Ambler, PA 19002

Established in 2000 in PA.
Donor(s): Murray Spain.
Financial data (yr. ended 12/31/01): Grants paid, $12,750; assets, $3,357,741 (M); gifts received, $1,385,626; expenditures, $28,529; qualifying distributions, $12,750.
Trustees: Ann Spain, Murray Spain.
EIN: 256728781

47842
Alan R. Warehime Charitable Trust
c/o Allfirst, Trust Div.
21 E. Market St.
York, PA 17401-1500

Financial data (yr. ended 12/31/00): Grants paid, $12,742; assets, $193,945 (M); expenditures, $14,758; qualifying distributions, $12,415.
Limitations: Applications not accepted. Giving primarily in PA.
Application information: Contributes only to pre-selected organizations.
Trustee: Allfirst.
EIN: 236811123

47843
The Krishnarpan Foundation
966 Hunt Dr.
Yardley, PA 19067-4244

Established around 1995.
Donor(s): Mukund Sheth, Prahma Sheth.
Financial data (yr. ended 12/31/01): Grants paid, $12,672; assets, $1 (M); gifts received, $15,000; expenditures, $13,051; qualifying distributions, $12,672.
Limitations: Applications not accepted.
Application information: Contributes only to pre-selected organizations.
Directors: Navnit D. Patel, Harish Shah, Mukuns Sheth, Pratima Sheth.
EIN: 232629257

47844
The Naomi and Ira Sved Charitable Foundation
314 Sycamore ave.
Merion Station, PA 19066

Established in 1999 in PA.
Donor(s): Naomi Sved, Ira Sved.
Financial data (yr. ended 06/30/01): Grants paid, $12,600; assets, $81,275 (M); gifts received, $100,000; expenditures, $14,566; qualifying distributions, $12,600.
Limitations: Applications not accepted.
Application information: Contributes only to pre-selected organizations.
Trustees: Ira Sved, Naomi Sved.

EIN: 256669426

47845
Stephen Watchorn Foundation, Inc.
100 Pine St.
P.O. Box 1166
Harrisburg, PA 17108-1166

Financial data (yr. ended 08/31/01): Grants paid, $12,600; assets, $410,232 (M); expenditures, $32,015; qualifying distributions, $12,600.
Limitations: Applications not accepted.
Application information: Contributes only to pre-selected organizations.
Officers and Directors:* Robert Watchorn III,* Pres.; Barbara Watchorn Fiddler,* V.P. and Treas.; Kathryn Watchorn Hearn,* V.P.; W. Jeffery Jamouneau, Secy.
EIN: 237037270

47846
Jennie Perelman Foundation, Inc.
225 City Line Ave., Ste. 14
Bala Cynwyd, PA 19004

Established in 1985 in PA.
Donor(s): General Refractories Co.
Financial data (yr. ended 02/28/01): Grants paid, $12,587; assets, $5,016,009 (M); expenditures, $16,587; qualifying distributions, $12,587.
Limitations: Applications not accepted.
Application information: Contributes only to pre-selected organizations.
Trustees: Raymond G. Perelman, Ruth Perelman.
EIN: 236251650

47847
ERI Educational Foundation
c/o Equitable Resources, Inc.
1 Oxford Ctr., Ste. 3300
Pittsburgh, PA 15219
Contact: Stephanie Macus

Established in 1996.
Donor(s): Equitable Resources, Inc.
Financial data (yr. ended 12/31/01): Grants paid, $12,500; assets, $2,179 (M); gifts received, $10,000; expenditures, $12,501; qualifying distributions, $12,500.
Limitations: Giving primarily in areas of company operations.
Application information: Application form required.
Officers: Murry Gerber, Pres. and C.E.O.; Gregory Spencer, Sr. V.P. and C.A.O.; David Porges, Sr. V.P. and C.F.O.; Johanna O'Loughlin, V.P.
EIN: 251789716
Codes: CS, CD, GTI

47848
Chuck Foley Memorial Foundation
121 Normandy Ct.
Presto, PA 15142-1003 (412) 278-0948
Contact: Patricia A. Foley, Secy.-Treas.

Established in 2000 in PA.
Financial data (yr. ended 12/31/01): Grants paid, $12,500; assets, $19,504 (M); gifts received, $755; expenditures, $33,480; qualifying distributions, $12,500.
Limitations: Giving primarily in PA.
Officers: Timothy P. Foley, Pres.; Charles F. Foley, V.P.; Patricia A. Foley, Secy.-Treas.
EIN: 311717135

47849
The O'Neill Foundation
930 Stoke Rd.
Villanova, PA 19085

Established in 1996 in PA.

Financial data (yr. ended 12/31/99): Grants paid, $12,500; assets, $124,260 (M); gifts received, $87,344; expenditures, $14,410; qualifying distributions, $12,500.
Application information: Application form not required.
Officers: Miriam O'Neill, Pres.; J. Brian O'Neill, Secy.-Treas.
Director: Michael P. Haney.
EIN: 311496748

47850
Whipple Sunbury Foundation
c/o Susquechanna Trust & Investment Co.
400 Market St.
Sunbury, PA 17801-2336

Financial data (yr. ended 12/31/01): Grants paid, $12,500; assets, $345,302 (M); expenditures, $15,507; qualifying distributions, $12,500.
Limitations: Giving limited to the Sunbury, PA, area.
Application information: Application form not required.
Trustee: Susquehanna Trust & Investment Co.
EIN: 236528682

47851
Anne J. Yellott Charitable Foundation
c/o PNC Advisors
1600 Market St.
Philadelphia, PA 19103

Donor(s): Anne J. Yellott.
Financial data (yr. ended 12/31/01): Grants paid, $12,500; assets, $212,615 (M); expenditures, $17,117; qualifying distributions, $12,567.
Limitations: Applications not accepted. Giving primarily in Harrisburg, PA.
Application information: Contributes only to pre-selected organizations.
Trustees: Henry W. Rhoads, PNC Bank, N.A.
EIN: 237705674

47852
Zausmer Foundation
c/o Bruce A. Rosenfield
1600 Market St., Ste. 3600
Philadelphia, PA 19103

Established in 2000 in PA.
Financial data (yr. ended 12/31/01): Grants paid, $12,500; assets, $1,590,780 (M); gifts received, $49,789; expenditures, $31,123; qualifying distributions, $12,500.
Limitations: Applications not accepted.
Application information: Contributes only to pre-selected organizations.
Trustee: Bruce A. Rosenfield.
EIN: 256688717

47853
George D. & Dorothy S. Bowers Memorial Trust Fund
21 E. Market St., M/C 402-130
York, PA 17401-1500

Established in 2000 in PA.
Donor(s): Dorothy S. Bowers.‡
Financial data (yr. ended 01/31/02): Grants paid, $12,493; assets, $193,252 (M); expenditures, $14,116; qualifying distributions, $12,493.
Limitations: Applications not accepted. Giving primarily in PA.
Application information: Contributes only to pre-selected organizations.
Trustee: Allfirst.
EIN: 256702275

47854
Esther B. Herman Charitable Trust
21 E. Market St.
York, PA 17401-1500

Financial data (yr. ended 12/31/01): Grants paid, $12,396; assets, $428,341 (M); expenditures, $18,962; qualifying distributions, $12,396.
Limitations: Applications not accepted. Giving primarily in York, PA.
Application information: Contributes only to pre-selected organizations.
Trustee: Allfirst.
EIN: 237752348

47855
John A. Robbins Foundation
555 E. City Line Ave., Ste. 1130
Bala Cynwyd, PA 19004-1101

Established in 1987 in PA.
Financial data (yr. ended 12/31/01): Grants paid, $12,343; assets, $52,836 (M); gifts received, $50; expenditures, $13,541; qualifying distributions, $12,343.
Limitations: Applications not accepted. Giving primarily in PA.
Application information: Contributes only to pre-selected organizations.
Officer: Ann Cimini, Mgr.
Trustee: Faith Robbins.
EIN: 222840041

47856
R. & R. Mellinger Medical Research Memorial Fund
c/o Fulton Financial Advisors, N.A.
P.O. Box 3215
Lancaster, PA 17604-3215
Contact: Vincent Lattanzio, Trust Off., Fulton Financial Advisors, N.A.

Established in 1995 in PA.
Financial data (yr. ended 02/28/01): Grants paid, $12,330; assets, $287,666 (M); expenditures, $15,884; qualifying distributions, $12,354.
Limitations: Giving limited to PA.
Trustees: John S. May, Fulton Financial Advisors, N.A.
EIN: 232823954
Codes: GTI

47857
PNC Memorial Foundation
c/o PNC Advisors
620 Liberty Ave., P2-PTPP-10-2
Pittsburgh, PA 15222-2705
Contact: R. Bruce Bickel, Sr. V.P. and Trust Off., PNC Bank, N.A.

Established in 1994 in PA.
Donor(s): PNC Bank, N.A.
Financial data (yr. ended 12/31/01): Grants paid, $12,300; assets, $207,480 (M); expenditures, $13,524; qualifying distributions, $12,250.
Limitations: Giving primarily in areas of company operations.
Application information: Application form required.
Trustee: PNC Bank, N.A.
EIN: 256487950
Codes: CS, CD

47858
Constance H. Smith Trust
c/o Allfirst, Trust Div.
21 E. Market St., M/C 402-130
York, PA 17401-1500

Established in 2000 in PA.
Financial data (yr. ended 12/31/01): Grants paid, $12,288; assets, $207,913 (M); expenditures, $14,614; qualifying distributions, $12,288.
Limitations: Applications not accepted. Giving primarily in PA.
Application information: Contributes only to pre-selected organizations.
Trustee: Allfirst.
EIN: 256582124

47859
Ballard Angels, Inc.
2600 1 Commerce Sq.
Philadelphia, PA 19103

Donor(s): James B. Ballard, Nancy Ballard.
Financial data (yr. ended 12/31/01): Grants paid, $12,255; assets, $85,836 (M); expenditures, $16,003; qualifying distributions, $12,255.
Limitations: Applications not accepted. Giving primarily in PA.
Application information: Contributes only to pre-selected organizations.
Officers and Directors:* James B. Ballard,* Pres.; Wendy S. Kilburn,* V.P.; Belinda L. Klovekorn,* V.P.; Nancy Ballard,* Secy.-Treas.
EIN: 232940033

47860
Delaware County Medical Society Public Health Fund, Inc.
P.O. Box 449
Wayne, PA 19087 (610) 687-7906
Contact: John Rosecky, Pres.

Financial data (yr. ended 12/31/00): Grants paid, $12,250; assets, $553,942 (M); expenditures, $12,776; qualifying distributions, $12,250.
Limitations: Giving limited to Delaware County, PA.
Officers: Robert F. Plotkin, Chair.; John Rosecky, Pres.; David M. Smilk, Secy.
Trustees: Graham D. Andrews, Kenneth Kirkpatrick, David McKeighan, Richard C. Nelson, Deana Smith, Rehya P. Yagnik, M.D.
EIN: 236436066

47861
Jerome Foundation
654 Wolf Ave.
Easton, PA 18042
Contact: Gary S. Figore, Tr.

Donor(s): Benny J. Jerome.
Financial data (yr. ended 12/31/01): Grants paid, $12,200; assets, $910,435 (M); expenditures, $50,236; qualifying distributions, $12,200.
Limitations: Giving primarily in PA.
Application information: Application form required.
Trustees: Gary S. Figore, R. Jerry Little.
EIN: 256066649

47862
J. H. Levit Foundation
1218 Chestnut St., No. 802
Philadelphia, PA 19107-4825
Contact: Henri Levit, Dir.; or Joseph Levit, Dir.

Established in 1986 in PA.
Financial data (yr. ended 12/31/01): Grants paid, $12,187; assets, $147,473 (M); expenditures, $12,454; qualifying distributions, $12,187.
Limitations: Giving primarily in Philadelphia, PA.
Trustees: Henri Levit, Joseph Levit.
EIN: 237408956

47863
The Papernick Family Foundation
c/o Alan & Judith R. Papernick
146 N. Bellefield Ave., No. 1201
Pittsburgh, PA 15213

Established in 1993 in PA.
Donor(s): Alan Papernick, Judith R. Papernick.
Financial data (yr. ended 11/30/01): Grants paid, $12,187; assets, $55,738 (M); expenditures, $12,971; qualifying distributions, $12,187.
Limitations: Applications not accepted. Giving primarily in Pittsburgh, PA.
Application information: Contributes only to pre-selected organizations.
Trustees: Amy B. Glick, Lisa G. Glick, Alan Papernick, Judith R. Papernick, Stephen M. Papernick.
EIN: 237750564

47864
Paul Kostkan Foundation, Inc.
53 E. State St.
Albion, PA 16401 (814) 756-4138
Contact: Edward J. Kempf, Jr., Secy.-Treas.

Established in 1988 in PA.
Financial data (yr. ended 12/31/01): Grants paid, $12,186; assets, $245,314 (M); expenditures, $12,811; qualifying distributions, $12,186.
Limitations: Giving limited to Albion, Conneaut, Cranesville, and Elk Creek, PA.
Application information: Application form required.
Officers: James F. Mikovich, Pres.; William B. Tucker, V.P.; Edward J. Kempf, Jr., Secy.-Treas.
EIN: 251564430

47865
Caplan Family Charitable Trust
c/o James Caplan
P.O. Box 14
Bryn Mawr, PA 19010 (610) 472-9740

Established in 1994 in PA.
Donor(s): James Caplan.
Financial data (yr. ended 12/31/01): Grants paid, $12,175; assets, $206,344 (M); expenditures, $12,175; qualifying distributions, $12,175.
Limitations: Giving primarily in Washington, DC, and PA.
Application information: Application form not required.
Trustee: James Caplan.
EIN: 237749795

47866
Anne Nash-Davis, Frank and Mary Irrevocable Trust
c/o Rev. Timothy G. Hall
75 Prospect St.
Nanticoke, PA 18634

Established in 1999 in PA.
Financial data (yr. ended 12/31/99): Grants paid, $12,123; assets, $226,372 (M); gifts received, $184,872; expenditures, $12,123; qualifying distributions, $12,123.
Limitations: Applications not accepted. Giving primarily in Nanticoke, PA.
Application information: Contributes only to pre-selected organizations.
Trustee: Rev. Timothy G. Hall.
EIN: 256645542

47867
Richard and Dana Green Philanthropic Foundation
120 Woodshire Rd.
Pittsburgh, PA 15215-1714
Contact: Richard L. Green, Tr.

Established in 2000 in PA.
Donor(s): Mayer A. Green Allergy Foundation.
Financial data (yr. ended 04/30/02): Grants paid, $12,112; assets, $308,128 (M); gifts received, $200; expenditures, $15,222; qualifying distributions, $12,112.
Limitations: Giving primarily in Pittsburgh, PA.
Application information: Application form not required.
Trustees: Dana S. Green, Jessica L. Green, Jonathon M. Green, Richard L. Green, Todd D. Green.
EIN: 311714818

47868
Lillian & Edward Meyers Family Foundation
c/o Lapensohn & Assoc., C.P.A.
P.O. Box 2234
Bala Cynwyd, PA 19004-6234

Established in 1997 in PA.
Donor(s): Lillian Meyers.
Financial data (yr. ended 10/31/99): Grants paid, $12,105; assets, $14,785 (M); gifts received, $20,000; expenditures, $12,271; qualifying distributions, $12,271.
Trustee: Lillian Meyers.
EIN: 237918138

47869
The Donald C. Patterson III Endowment Fund
213 Fairhill Rd.
Hatfield, PA 19440-1141
Application address: 31 Mill Pond Rd., New Providence, NJ 07974
Contact: Donald C. Patterson III

Established in 1997.
Donor(s): Donald C. Patterson III.
Financial data (yr. ended 12/31/99): Grants paid, $12,100; assets, $201,401 (M); expenditures, $13,006; qualifying distributions, $12,100.
Limitations: Giving primarily in NJ and PA.
Trustee: Donald C. Patterson III.
EIN: 223616194

47870
Darlington Charitable Trust
c/o PNC Advisors
620 Liberty Ave., P2-PTPP-10-2
Pittsburgh, PA 15272-2705 (412) 762-3390
Contact: John Culbertson, Trust Off., PNC Bank, N.A.

Established in 1986 in PA.
Financial data (yr. ended 06/30/02): Grants paid, $12,091; assets, $187,000 (M); expenditures, $12,217; qualifying distributions, $12,091.
Limitations: Giving limited to the Boston, MA, area.
Application information: Application form required.
Trustee: PNC Bank, N.A.
EIN: 256255624

47871
The Kaplan Foundation, Inc.
c/o Michael B. Solomon
919 Conestoga Rd., Ste. 200
Bryn Mawr, PA 19010

Established in 1996 in NJ.
Financial data (yr. ended 06/30/01): Grants paid, $12,067; assets, $218,880 (M); gifts received, $602; expenditures, $14,444; qualifying distributions, $12,067.
Trustees: Sharon Berman, Annette Kaplan, Dean Kaplan, Rita Kaplan.
EIN: 223471257

47872
Jeanette M. & Joseph F. Brenner Foundation
217 Butler St.
Kingston, PA 18704

Financial data (yr. ended 12/31/01): Grants paid, $12,017; assets, $254,798 (M); expenditures, $20,901; qualifying distributions, $12,017.
Limitations: Applications not accepted. Giving primarily in PA.
Application information: Contributes only to pre-selected organizations.
Officers: Joseph M. Nelson, Pres.; Sue R. Viener, V.P.; Joseph Nelson, Secy.-Treas.
Directors: Louise Nelson, George Viener.
EIN: 236282254

47873
The Golden Age Foundation
3000 Valley Forge Cir., Ste. 109
King of Prussia, PA 19406
Application address: 1 Crows Nest Cir., West Chester, PA 19382, tel.: (610) 783-7750
Contact: Erich Radtke, Tr.

Established in 2000 in PA.
Donor(s): Laura B. Toy.
Financial data (yr. ended 12/31/01): Grants paid, $12,000; assets, $297,273 (M); gifts received, $151,171; expenditures, $80,880; qualifying distributions, $12,000.
Application information: Application form not required.
Trustees: Phillip J. Cannella III, Erich Radtke.
EIN: 256731051

47874
Walter P. Harris Foundation
934 Charter Cir.
Elkins Park, PA 19027
Application address: 216 David Dr., Havertown, PA, tel.:(215) 545-5001
Contact: Walter P. Harris, Jr., Pres.

Donor(s): Walter P. Harris, Jr.
Financial data (yr. ended 09/30/01): Grants paid, $12,000; assets, $60,606 (M); expenditures, $13,591; qualifying distributions, $12,000.
Limitations: Giving primarily in Wynnewood, PA.
Officer: Walter P. Harris, Jr., Pres.
EIN: 541344783

47875
Jeds Foundation
981 Idlewild Rd.
Gladwyne, PA 19035-1437

Established in 2000 in PA.
Donor(s): Steven B. Katznelson.
Financial data (yr. ended 12/31/01): Grants paid, $12,000; assets, $173,218 (M); expenditures, $14,943; qualifying distributions, $12,000.
Limitations: Applications not accepted. Giving primarily in Philadelphia, PA.
Application information: Contributes only to pre-selected organizations.
Trustees: Steven B. Katznelson, Laurie L. MacKimmie.
EIN: 256696272

47876
A. Karnavas Foundation
127 Timber Ct.
127 Anderson St.
Pittsburgh, PA 15212
Application address: 240 Merchant St., Ambridge, PA 15003, tel.: (724) 266-4060
Contact: Jack A. Karnavas, V.P.

Donor(s): Sophie Karnavas.
Financial data (yr. ended 06/30/01): Grants paid, $12,000; assets, $294,088 (M); expenditures, $12,583; qualifying distributions, $12,000.
Limitations: Giving primarily in PA.
Application information: Proposal required for research grants. Application form required.
Officers and Directors:* George Karnavas,* Pres.; Jack A. Karnavas,* V.P.; Robert G. Panagulias.
EIN: 251197658

47877
The Colin U. Miller & Mary May Miller Charitable Trust for the Advancement of Education
c/o U.S. Bancorp Trust Co.
P.O. Box 520
Johnstown, PA 15907-0520
Contact: Carol Stern, Trust Off., U.S. Bancorp Trust Co.

Financial data (yr. ended 12/31/99): Grants paid, $12,000; assets, $278,298 (M); expenditures, $16,639; qualifying distributions, $12,000.
Application information: Application form required.
Trustees: Margaret O'Malley, U.S. Bancorp Trust Co.
EIN: 256303529

47878
Vincent A. Pronio Charitable Trust
c/o Hershey Trust Co.
100 Mansion Rd. E.
Hershey, PA 17033

Established in 1997 in PA.
Donor(s): Vincent A. Pronio.
Financial data (yr. ended 12/31/01): Grants paid, $12,000; assets, $214,534 (M); expenditures, $14,435; qualifying distributions, $12,000.
Limitations: Applications not accepted.
Application information: Contributes only to pre-selected organizations.
Advisory Committee: Victoria Pronio, Vincent A. Pronio.
Trustee: Hershey Trust Co.
EIN: 237880699

47879
James M. Schoonmaker II Foundation
c/o PNC Advisors
1600 Market St.
Philadelphia, PA 19103-7240
Application address: c/o Jennifer Stuve, PNC Bank, N.A., 3003 Tamiami Trail N., Ste. 100, Naples, FL 34103

Donor(s): James M. Schoonmaker II.
Financial data (yr. ended 12/31/01): Grants paid, $12,000; assets, $382,603 (M); expenditures, $15,281; qualifying distributions, $12,440.
Limitations: Giving primarily in FL.
Trustees: Charles A. Cook, James M. Schoonmaker II, Patrice H. Schoonmaker, PNC Bank, N.A.
EIN: 596964359

47880
Girling Foundation
c/o David Glyn
1650 Arch St., 22nd Fl.
Philadelphia, PA 19103-2097

Established in 1999 in PA.
Donor(s): Robert T. Girling.
Financial data (yr. ended 12/31/01): Grants paid, $11,900; assets, $467,699 (M); gifts received, $177,875; expenditures, $13,495; qualifying distributions, $11,900.
Limitations: Giving primarily in Allentown, PA.
Officers: Robert T. Girling, Pres.; John Girling, V.P.; Louise Girling, V.P.; Robert M. Segal, V.P.
EIN: 232994852

47881
Thelma K. Klugh Trust
c/o PNC Advisors
620 Liberty Ave., P2-PTTP-10-2
Pittsburgh, PA 15222-2705

Established in 1999 in PA.
Financial data (yr. ended 12/31/01): Grants paid, $11,888; assets, $198,331 (M); expenditures, $14,338; qualifying distributions, $11,888.
Limitations: Applications not accepted. Giving primarily in PA.
Application information: Contributes only to pre-selected organizations.
Trustee: PNC Bank, N.A.
EIN: 236745350

47882
The Ritter Foundation
P.O. Box 1577
Harrisburg, PA 17105-1577
Application address: 1511 N. Cameron St., Harrisburg, PA 17105, tel.: (717) 234-3061
Contact: William Brightbill, Pres.

Financial data (yr. ended 12/31/00): Grants paid, $11,870; assets, $4,117 (M); expenditures, $51,065; qualifying distributions, $11,870.
Limitations: Giving limited to PA.
Officers: William Brightbill, Pres. and Treas.; Steve Daniels, V.P. and Secy.
EIN: 236290484

47883
Michael Singer Foundation
1117 Spruce St.
Philadelphia, PA 19107 (215) 925-8597
Additional tel.: (215) 925-8683
Contact: Michael Singer, Pres.

Established in 1988 in PA.
Donor(s): Michael Singer.
Financial data (yr. ended 08/31/01): Grants paid, $11,744; assets, $5,177 (M); gifts received, $7,500; expenditures, $11,745; qualifying distributions, $11,744.
Limitations: Giving on a national basis.
Officers: Michael Singer, Pres.; David Singer, V.P. and Secy.; Eli Gabay, Treas.
EIN: 232559062

47884
Leonard & Ruth Levine Temple Skin Research Fund
c/o Ruth H. Levine
P.O. Box 389
Norristown, PA 19404-0389 (610) 272-3650
Contact: Patrick J. Broderick, Mgr.

Donor(s): Ruth Levine.
Financial data (yr. ended 12/31/01): Grants paid, $11,686; assets, $135,043 (M); gifts received, $1,634; expenditures, $13,867; qualifying distributions, $11,686.

Limitations: Giving primarily in PA.
Officer: Patrick J. Broderick, Mgr.
Trustees: Bruce Genter, M.D., Richard Genter, Evelyn Horenstein-Brown, Ph.D., Eugene T. Van Scott, M.D.
EIN: 236865790

47885
Alexander and Cassia Rau Trust
c/o Allfirst, Trust Div.
21 E. Market St., M/C 402-130
York, PA 17401-1500
Application address: c/o Pres., St. Mark's Lutheran Church Council, 700 E. Market St., York, PA 17403

Financial data (yr. ended 12/31/01): Grants paid, $11,670; assets, $282,985 (M); expenditures, $15,195; qualifying distributions, $11,670; giving activities include $11,670 for loans to individuals.
Limitations: Giving primarily in York, PA.
Application information: Application form required.
Trustee: Allfirst.
EIN: 236417951
Codes: GTI

47886
Green Clover Foundation
c/o Hoffman Industries
3145 Shillington Rd.
Sinking Spring, PA 19608-1606

Financial data (yr. ended 12/31/01): Grants paid, $11,581; assets, $215,688 (M); expenditures, $11,828; qualifying distributions, $11,581.
Limitations: Applications not accepted. Giving primarily in PA.
Application information: Contributes only to pre-selected organizations.
Officer: Richard Schreck, Pres. and Treas.
EIN: 236264992

47887
Edith L. Reynolds Trust
c/o Mellon Bank, N.A.
P.O. Box 185
Pittsburgh, PA 15230-9897

Established in 1965 in PA.
Financial data (yr. ended 12/31/01): Grants paid, $11,574; assets, $458,023 (M); expenditures, $16,633; qualifying distributions, $13,920.
Limitations: Applications not accepted. Giving primarily in Wilkes-Barre, PA.
Application information: Contributes only to pre-selected organizations.
Trustee: Mellon Bank, N.A.
EIN: 236409220

47888
T. S. Fitch Memorial Scholarship Fund
c/o Mellon Bank, N.A.
P.O. Box 185
Pittsburgh, PA 15230-9897 (412) 234-0023
Application address: 3 Mellon Bank Ctr., Pittsburgh, PA 15259
Contact: Laurie Moritz, Trust Off., Mellon Bank, N.A.

Established in 1990 in PA.
Financial data (yr. ended 12/31/99): Grants paid, $11,486; assets, $287,216 (M); gifts received, $390; expenditures, $16,109; qualifying distributions, $12,702.
Limitations: Giving limited to residents of PA.
Trustee: Mellon Bank, N.A.
EIN: 256123538

47889
Newman Family Charitable Foundation
1120 Ginkgo Ln.
Gladwyne, PA 19035
Contact: Julius Newman, Tr.

Established in 2000 in PA.
Donor(s): Julius Newman, Sandra Schultz Newman.
Financial data (yr. ended 12/31/01): Grants paid, $11,451; assets, $141,638 (M); expenditures, $12,218; qualifying distributions, $11,451.
Limitations: Giving primarily in Villanova, PA.
Trustees: Julius Newman, Sandra Schultz Newman.
EIN: 233045779

47890
The James and Arlene Ginsberg Foundation
1496 Hampton Rd.
Rydal, PA 19046-1211
Contact: James J. Ginsberg, Tr.

Donor(s): James J. Ginsberg.
Financial data (yr. ended 12/31/01): Grants paid, $11,405; assets, $37,990 (M); gifts received, $24,230; expenditures, $12,422; qualifying distributions, $11,405.
Limitations: Giving primarily in PA.
Trustees: Arlene Ginsberg, James J. Ginsberg, Morris A. Wilensky.
EIN: 236697761

47891
Charles Kerr Foundation
127 N. Main St.
New Hope, PA 18938

Established in 1996 in PA.
Donor(s): Charles Kerr, Doro Kerr.
Financial data (yr. ended 09/30/01): Grants paid, $11,400; assets, $81,673 (M); gifts received, $28,288; expenditures, $11,969; qualifying distributions, $11,356.
Limitations: Applications not accepted. Giving primarily in NJ and PA.
Application information: Contributes only to pre-selected organizations.
Officers: Charles Kerr, Pres.; David P. Sandler, V.P.; Doro Kerr, Secy.-Treas.
EIN: 232901887

47892
Howard J. & George R. Lamade Foundation
c/o M&T Bank
101 W. 3rd St., Trust Tax Dept.
Williamsport, PA 17701
Application address: Andrew Stabler, c/o Lamco Communications, 460 Market St., Ste. 310, Williamsport, PA 17701
Contact: Andrew W. Stabler, Jr., Advisory Comm. Member

Financial data (yr. ended 12/31/01): Grants paid, $11,400; assets, $370,998 (M); expenditures, $19,723; qualifying distributions, $11,400.
Limitations: Giving limited to Williamsport, PA.
Advisory Committee: Howard Lamade, J. Robert Lamade, James S. Lamade, Andrew W. Stabler, Jr.
Trustee: M&T Bank.
EIN: 246012802

47893
Molly Gingold Trust
(also known as Dr. Ralph B. Little Fund)
21 E. Market St.
York, PA 17401-1500

Established in 2000 in PA.

Financial data (yr. ended 08/31/01): Grants paid, $11,398; assets, $151,804 (M); expenditures, $15,306; qualifying distributions, $11,398.
Limitations: Applications not accepted. Giving primarily in PA.
Application information: Contributes only to pre-selected organizations.
Trustee: Allfirst.
EIN: 236767559

47894
M. L. and J. H. Longstreth Foundation
8502 Ellisten Dr.
Wyndmoor, PA 19038
Contact: Ronald J. Altieri, Pres.

Established in 1987 in PA.
Financial data (yr. ended 12/31/01): Grants paid, $11,350; assets, $188,094 (M); expenditures, $12,318; qualifying distributions, $11,350.
Limitations: Giving primarily in Philadelphia, PA.
Officers: Ronald J. Altieri, Pres.; Suzanne E. Altieri, V.P.; Elizabeth A. Morris, Secy.; Dorothy L. Hunshaw, Treas.
Director: Suzanne S. Mayes.
EIN: 222804880

47895
Cherry Lane Foundation
711 Sarah St.
Stroudsburg, PA 18360-2121

Established in 1990 in PA.
Financial data (yr. ended 05/31/01): Grants paid, $11,300; assets, $321,682 (M); expenditures, $12,406; qualifying distributions, $11,300.
Limitations: Applications not accepted. Giving limited to PA.
Application information: Contributes only to pre-selected organizations.
Officers: Ronald E. Vican, Chair. and Pres.; Timothy J. McManus, Vice-Chair. and V.P.; Jeffrey L. Wright, Secy.-Treas.
EIN: 232616927

47896
Descendants of the Signers of the Declaration of Independence
P.O. Box 305
Toughkenamon, PA 19374

Financial data (yr. ended 04/30/99): Grants paid, $11,200; assets, $406,491 (M); gifts received, $34,603; expenditures, $34,268; qualifying distributions, $11,200.
Limitations: Applications not accepted.
Officers: Philip Schuyler Pyre, Pres.; Edward Ridley Finch, Jr., V.P.; John Dendridge Nelson, Secy.; William Ward IV, Treas.
EIN: 236397427

47897
Jule C. Modlin, Jr. Scholarship Fund
c/o First Union National Bank
125 S. Broad St., Ste. PA1308
Philadelphia, PA 19109-9989
Application address: c/o First Union National Bank of Virginia, CMG-VA5262, Norfolk, VA 23501
Contact: R.H. Marriott, III, Trust Off.

Established in 1989 in NC.
Financial data (yr. ended 01/31/00): Grants paid, $11,187; assets, $245,578 (M); expenditures, $13,779; qualifying distributions, $11,148.
Limitations: Giving limited to Pasquotank County, NC.
Trustee: First Union National Bank.
EIN: 566312873

47898
Stanley E. and Dorothy Y. Abelson Charitable Foundation
233 S. 6th St., Ste. 2304P
Philadelphia, PA 19106 (215) 574-9595
Contact: Stanley E. Abelson, Tr.

Donor(s): Stanley E. Abelson.
Financial data (yr. ended 12/31/01): Grants paid, $11,120; assets, $17,491 (M); gifts received, $9,568; expenditures, $11,122; qualifying distributions, $11,120.
Limitations: Giving primarily in Philadelphia, PA.
Application information: Application form not required.
Trustees: Dorothy Y. Abelson, Stanley E. Abelson.
EIN: 236764142

47899
Donald L. & Bernice Durgin Flegal Charitable Foundation
c/o Woodlands Bank
2450 E. Third St.
Williamsport, PA 17701

Established in 1998 in PA.
Financial data (yr. ended 12/31/01): Grants paid, $11,098; assets, $270,569 (M); expenditures, $14,638; qualifying distributions, $14,638.
Limitations: Applications not accepted.
Application information: Contributes only to pre-selected organizations.
Trustees: James L. Green, Woodlands Bank.
EIN: 311578320

47900
Gabriele Family Foundation
62 Bridle Way
Newtown Square, PA 19073

Donor(s): Alfonse Gabriele, Barbara Gabriele.
Financial data (yr. ended 12/31/01): Grants paid, $11,000; assets, $188,072 (M); gifts received, $2,500; expenditures, $16,981; qualifying distributions, $11,000.
Limitations: Applications not accepted.
Application information: Contributes only to pre-selected organizations.
Trustees: Alfonse Gabriele, Barbara Gabriele.
EIN: 232870613

47901
Wilbur K. Jones Foundation
c/o Allfirst, Trust Tax Div.
21 E. Market St., M/C 402-130
York, PA 17401-1500
Application address: 213 Market St., Harrisburg, PA 17105
Contact: Joseph A. Macri, Trust Off., Allfirst

Financial data (yr. ended 12/31/01): Grants paid, $11,000; assets, $521,636 (M); expenditures, $14,490; qualifying distributions, $11,000.
Limitations: Giving primarily in FL.
Trustee: Allfirst.
EIN: 236291359

47902
Markel Corporation Memorial Scholarship Fund, Inc.
P.O. Box 752
Norristown, PA 19404

Established in 2000 in PA.
Financial data (yr. ended 12/31/00): Grants paid, $11,000; assets, $552 (M); gifts received, $6,000; expenditures, $11,032; qualifying distributions, $11,000.
Limitations: Applications not accepted. Giving primarily in Norristown, PA.

Officers: Warren G. Mang, C.E.O.; James A. Hoban, Secy.-Treas.
Board Members: Janice T. Mang, Cynthia Reynolds.
EIN: 232836753

47903
Eleanor & Rudolph Nelson Charitable Trust
c/o Mellon Bank, N.A.
P.O. Box 185
Pittsburgh, PA 15230-9897
Application address: 1128 State St., Erie, PA 16152
Contact: Marilyn King, Trust Off., Mellon Bank, N.A.

Financial data (yr. ended 12/31/99): Grants paid, $11,000; assets, $313,516 (M); expenditures, $15,955; qualifying distributions, $12,680.
Limitations: Giving limited to Oil City, PA.
Trustee: Mellon Bank, N.A.
EIN: 256128716

47904
Henrik & Emile Ovesen Foundation
c/o Mellon Bank, N.A.
P.O. Box 185
Pittsburgh, PA 15230-9897 (412) 234-0023
Contact: Laurie Moritz, Trust Off., Mellon Bank, N.A.

Financial data (yr. ended 12/31/01): Grants paid, $11,000; assets, $331,521 (M); expenditures, $13,065; qualifying distributions, $11,000.
Application information: Application form required.
Trustee: Mellon Bank, N.A.
EIN: 256018903

47905
Philippian Foundation, Inc.
1323 Horsham Rd.
Ambler, PA 19002-1002

Donor(s): Philip J. Baur, Jr.
Financial data (yr. ended 03/31/02): Grants paid, $11,000; assets, $271,755 (M); expenditures, $13,180; qualifying distributions, $11,000.
Limitations: Applications not accepted. Giving primarily in Dresher, PA.
Application information: Contributes only to pre-selected organizations.
Officers and Trustees:* Philip J. Baur, Jr.,* Pres.; Barbara Baur,* V.P.; William S. Pilling III, Secy.; Ruth Schutz,* Treas.
EIN: 236296979

47906
Spolan Family Foundation
2007 Delancey Place
Philadelphia, PA 19103-6509

Established in 1998 in PA.
Donor(s): Harmon S. Spolan, Betty Spolan.
Financial data (yr. ended 12/31/01): Grants paid, $11,000; assets, $53,821 (M); expenditures, $11,500; qualifying distributions, $11,000.
Limitations: Applications not accepted. Giving primarily in New York, NY and Philadelphia, PA.
Application information: Contributes only to pre-selected organizations.
Directors: Betty Spolan, Harmon S. Spolan, Michael Spolan, Suzanne Spolan.
EIN: 232962337

47907
G. R. and Grace M. Sponaugle Charitable Foundation
4391 Chambers Hill Rd.
Harrisburg, PA 17111
Application address: 2491 Schoolhouse Rd., Middletown, PA 17057
Contact: Maxine A. Haynes, Pres.

Established in 2000 in PA.
Donor(s): G.R. Sponaugle & Sons, Inc.
Financial data (yr. ended 12/31/01): Grants paid, $11,000; assets, $148,661 (M); gifts received, $71,000; expenditures, $15,761; qualifying distributions, $11,000.
Application information: Application form required.
Officers: Maxine A. Haynes, Pres.; Thomas S. Palanica, V.P.; Diane W. Bekelja, Secy.; Shelva J. Hendricks, Treas.; Duane E. Snell, Treas.
EIN: 251877748

47908
John Tyndale Scholarship Fund
(also known as John Tyndale Testamentary Trust)
c/o Mellon Bank, N.A.
P.O. Box 7236
Philadelphia, PA 19101-7236

Financial data (yr. ended 09/30/01): Grants paid, $11,000; assets, $249,207 (M); expenditures, $11,479; qualifying distributions, $10,905.
Limitations: Applications not accepted. Giving limited to Philadelphia, PA.
Trustee: Mellon Bank, N.A.
EIN: 236223859

47909
Wishing Star Foundation
1006 Apache Trail
Mechanicsburg, PA 17055

Established in 1999 in PA.
Donor(s): Steve D. Shadowen, Dawn S. Sunday.
Financial data (yr. ended 12/31/01): Grants paid, $11,000; assets, $40,331 (M); gifts received, $500; expenditures, $11,540; qualifying distributions, $11,000.
Limitations: Applications not accepted.
Application information: Contributes only to pre-selected organizations.
Trustees: Steve D. Shadowen, Dawn S. Sunday.
EIN: 256683240

47910
Drumheller-Swank, Keyser & Bargo Poor Fund
c/o First National Trust Bank
400 Market St.
Sunbury, PA 17801

Financial data (yr. ended 12/31/01): Grants paid, $10,833; assets, $188,916 (M); expenditures, $12,512; qualifying distributions, $12,375.
Limitations: Giving limited to the Sunbury, PA, area.
Application information: Application form not required.
Trustee: First National Trust Bank.
EIN: 246016944

47911
Sharon H. Limaye Foundation
10 Andover Rd.
Haverford, PA 19041-1003 (610) 658-2989
Contact: Dilip R. Limaye, Tr.

Established in 1993 in PA.
Donor(s): Dilip R. Limaye, Ryan D. Limaye.
Financial data (yr. ended 12/31/01): Grants paid, $10,776; assets, $217,499 (M); gifts received, $40,848; expenditures, $12,168; qualifying distributions, $10,776.
Trustees: Dilip R. Limaye, Kris N. Limaye, Ryan D. Limaye.
EIN: 232738735

47912
William & Marion French Scholarship Fund
c/o Fulton Financial Advisors, N.A.
P.O. Box 3215
Lancaster, PA 17604-3215

Established in 1997 in PA.
Donor(s): Marion French.‡
Financial data (yr. ended 05/31/02): Grants paid, $10,634; assets, $383,079 (M); expenditures, $16,215; qualifying distributions, $10,634.
Limitations: Applications not accepted. Giving primarily in Lancaster, PA.
Application information: Contributes only to pre-selected organizations.
Trustee: Fulton Financial Advisors, N.A.
EIN: 311604263

47913
Elizabeth Boone Vastine & Katherine Vastine Bernheimer Memorial Fund
c/o Fulton Financial Advisors, N.A.
P.O. Box 3215
Lancaster, PA 17604-3215
Application address: c/o Carl Marrara, Guidance Counselor, Danville Senior High School, Northumberland Rd., Danville, PA 17821, tel.: (570) 275-4113

Financial data (yr. ended 12/31/00): Grants paid, $10,629; assets, $282,545 (M); expenditures, $14,469; qualifying distributions, $10,629.
Limitations: Giving primarily in Danville, PA.
Application information: Giving restricted to graduates of Montour County high schools. Application form required.
Trustee: Fulton Financial Advisors, N.A.
EIN: 232120313
Codes: GTI

47914
Nobadeer Foundation, Inc.
c/o Thomas McKean Thomas
3450 Church School Rd.
Doylestown, PA 18901

Established in 1996 in PA.
Donor(s): Thomas Travel Services.
Financial data (yr. ended 12/31/01): Grants paid, $10,600; assets, $148,706 (M); expenditures, $11,868; qualifying distributions, $10,600.
Limitations: Applications not accepted. Giving primarily in PA.
Application information: Contributes only to pre-selected organizations.
Officers: Thomas McKean Thomas, Pres.; Rebecca R. Thomas, Secy.; Patricia R. Thomas, Treas.
EIN: 232870056

47915
Kermit and Annette Berman Charitable Foundation
421 N. 7th St., Ste. 700
Philadelphia, PA 19123

Established in 1999 in PA.
Financial data (yr. ended 12/31/01): Grants paid, $10,500; assets, $51,019 (M); gifts received, $2,017; expenditures, $10,842; qualifying distributions, $10,500.
Limitations: Applications not accepted. Giving primarily in Philadelphia, PA.
Application information: Contributes only to pre-selected organizations.
Trustee: Myron J. Berman.
EIN: 256648479

47916
Rev. William J. Fitzpatrick Memorial Scholarship Fund
c/o Allfirst, Trust Tax Div.
21 E. Market St.
York, PA 17401 (717) 852-3051
Application address: c/o Principal, York Catholic High School, 601 Springettsbury Ave., York, PA 17403

Donor(s): Edward J. Brady.
Financial data (yr. ended 12/31/01): Grants paid, $10,500; assets, $287,452 (M); expenditures, $13,474; qualifying distributions, $13,474.
Limitations: Giving limited to residents of York, PA.
Application information: Applications handled by York Catholic High School, PA. Application form required.
Trustee: Allfirst.
EIN: 236692323
Codes: GTI

47917
The Leslie and Barbara Kaplan Family Foundation
215 Mcclenahan Mill Rd.
Wynnewood, PA 19096
Contact: Leslie Kaplan, Tr.

Established in 1999 in PA.
Donor(s): Barbara Kaplan, Leslie Kaplan.
Financial data (yr. ended 12/31/01): Grants paid, $10,500; assets, $38,013 (M); expenditures, $10,620; qualifying distributions, $10,500.
Limitations: Giving primarily in PA.
Trustees: Barbara Kaplan, Douglas Kaplan, Emily Kaplan, Leslie Kaplan.
EIN: 256638444

47918
The Marc David Foundation
180 New Britain Blvd.
Chalfont, PA 18914
Application address: P.O. Box 336, Ambler, PA 19002
Contact: Marc Berman, Tr.

Established in 1999 in PA.
Donor(s): Marc H. Berman.
Financial data (yr. ended 12/31/00): Grants paid, $10,500; assets, $224,347 (M); expenditures, $10,653; qualifying distributions, $10,500.
Application information: Application form required.
Trustees: Marc H. Berman, David I. Cohen.
EIN: 256627678

47919
John R. Miller Nursing Scholarship
c/o Main St. Bank
P.O. Box 1100
Pottsville, PA 17901

Established in 2000 in PA.
Donor(s): John R. Miller.‡
Financial data (yr. ended 12/31/00): Grants paid, $10,500; assets, $313,201 (M); gifts received, $6,808; expenditures, $17,817; qualifying distributions, $10,500.
Limitations: Giving primarily in PA.
Trustee: Main Street Bank.
EIN: 237985997

47920
Thomas J. & Ruth S. Miles Memorial Fund
c/o Allfirst, Trust Div.
21 E. Market St., M/C 402-130
York, PA 17401-1500

Established in 2000 in PA.
Donor(s): Thomas Miles.‡
Financial data (yr. ended 04/30/02): Grants paid, $10,430; assets, $418,473 (M); expenditures, $15,877; qualifying distributions, $10,430.
Limitations: Applications not accepted. Giving primarily in PA.
Application information: Contributes only to pre-selected organizations.
Trustee: Allfirst.
EIN: 233051596

47921
Elias & Blanche Jones Memorial Trust
c/o PNC Advisors
P.O. Box 8480
Erie, PA 16553

Established in 1998 in PA.
Financial data (yr. ended 12/31/01): Grants paid, $10,401; assets, $166,914 (M); expenditures, $11,961; qualifying distributions, $10,407.
Limitations: Applications not accepted. Giving primarily in Corry, PA.
Application information: Contributes only to pre-selected organizations.
Trustee: PNC Bank, N.A.
EIN: 256487552

47922
Helen M. Cramer Foundation
c/o First Union National Bank
Broad & Walnut St., Ste. PA1308
Philadelphia, PA 19109
Application address: c/o Financial Assistance Comm., Francis Marion Univ., P.O. Box 100547, Florence, SC 29501-0547

Established in 1991 in SC.
Donor(s): Helen M. Cramer.
Financial data (yr. ended 12/31/99): Grants paid, $10,380; assets, $86,777 (M); expenditures, $11,905; qualifying distributions, $10,380.
Limitations: Giving limited to Florence, SC.
Application information: Application form required.
Trustee: First Union National Bank.
EIN: 586252407

47923
H. Kay Jarvis and Kenneth B. Jarvis Foundation
c/o John Iskrant
1600 Market St., Ste. 3600
Philadelphia, PA 19103
Application address: 3400 Rambling Way, Plano, TX 75093-7601, tel.: (972) 403-1907
Contact: Kenneth B. Jarvis, Tr.

Established in 2000 in PA.
Donor(s): Kenneth B. Jarvis.
Financial data (yr. ended 12/31/01): Grants paid, $10,375; assets, $357,185 (M); gifts received, $359,902; expenditures, $11,378; qualifying distributions, $10,375.
Limitations: Giving primarily in Philadelphia, PA and Dallas, TX.
Application information: Application form not required.
Trustees: H. Kay Jarvis, Kenneth B. Jarvis, Kenneth B. Jarvis II, Michele W. Jarvis.
EIN: 233050754

47924
Marsha Kay Mase Foundation
c/o First Citizens National Bank
15 S. Main St.
Mansfield, PA 16933-1590 (570) 662-0463
Contact: Sara J. Roupp, Trust Off., First Citizens National Bank

Financial data (yr. ended 12/31/01): Grants paid, $10,375; assets, $172,779 (M); expenditures, $11,851; qualifying distributions, $10,375.
Limitations: Giving limited to Tioga County, PA.
Trustees: Elaine Hickey, Richard D. Mase, Sylvia B. Mase, John E. Novak, Joanne Ogden, Rudolph J. van der Hiel, First Citizens National Bank.
EIN: 222482780

47925
Guinn & Phyllis Unger Foundation
c/o PNC Advisors
1600 Market St.
Philadelphia, PA 19103-7240

Financial data (yr. ended 12/31/01): Grants paid, $10,371; assets, $196,014 (M); gifts received, $1,495; expenditures, $12,393; qualifying distributions, $10,371.
Limitations: Applications not accepted. Giving primarily in PA.
Application information: Contributes only to pre-selected organizations.
Trustee: PNC Bank, N.A.
EIN: 237699788

47926
Maurice Harlimg Charitable Trust
Broad & Walnut Sts.
Philadelphia, PA 19109

Financial data (yr. ended 12/31/99): Grants paid, $10,361; assets, $357,519 (M); expenditures, $14,710; qualifying distributions, $10,361.
Limitations: Applications not accepted. Giving limited to Pensacola, FL.
Application information: Contributes only to pre-selected organizations.
Trustee: First Union National Bank.
EIN: 656255785

47927
Arnold Schlossberg Charitable Trust
c/o First Union National Bank
123 S. Broad St.
Philadelphia, PA 19109-9989

Established in 1992 in VA.
Donor(s): Arnold Schlossberg.
Financial data (yr. ended 12/31/99): Grants paid, $10,320; assets, $411,724 (M); expenditures, $14,230; qualifying distributions, $10,320.
Limitations: Applications not accepted. Giving primarily in the metropolitan New York, NY, area, and Roanoke, VA.
Application information: Contributes only to pre-selected organizations.
Trustee: First Union National Bank.
EIN: 546325254

47928
Mary Lindsay Endowment Fund
c/o First National Bank & Trust Co.
34 S. State St.
Newtown, PA 18940

Established in 2000 in PA.
Financial data (yr. ended 12/31/01): Grants paid, $10,310; assets, $401,443 (M); expenditures, $16,223; qualifying distributions, $10,310.
Officer: Clifford C. David, Jr., Cont.
EIN: 311485283

47929
Horsham Lions Foundation
c/o Thomas Burgess
708 Canterbury Ln.
Horsham, PA 19044

Established in 1998 in PA.
Financial data (yr. ended 12/31/01): Grants paid, $10,200; assets, $1 (M); gifts received, $17,100; expenditures, $10,284; qualifying distributions, $10,200.
Limitations: Applications not accepted.
Application information: Contributes only to pre-selected organizations.
Officers and Directors:* James R. Faber,* Pres.; Thomas H. Burgess,* Secy.-Treas.; Salvatore Calise,* V.P.; John R. Bill, Theodore L. Truver.
EIN: 232826356

47930
The Lotsch-Zelman Foundation, Inc.
(Formerly Dr. Joseph M. Lotsch Foundation, Inc.)
c/o C.D.L. Levin, PC
314 Countryview Dr.
Bryn Mawr, PA 19010-2035

Financial data (yr. ended 06/30/02): Grants paid, $10,200; assets, $334,009 (M); expenditures, $27,499; qualifying distributions, $10,200.
Limitations: Applications not accepted. Giving primarily in PA and ME.
Application information: Contributes only to pre-selected organizations.
Officers: Betty Zelman, Pres.; Doris E. Lotsch, V.P.; Victor Zelman, V.P.; Charles F. Lotsch, Treas.
EIN: 136104669

47931
Takashi & Yuriko Moriuchi Charitable Foundation
c/o Glenmede Trust Co.
1650 Market St., Ste. 1200
Philadelphia, PA 19103 (215) 419-6000
Contact: Takashi Moriuchi, Tr.

Established in 1989 in NJ.
Donor(s): Takashi Moriuchi, Yuriko Moriuchi.
Financial data (yr. ended 12/31/01): Grants paid, $10,200; assets, $163,728 (M); expenditures, $12,795; qualifying distributions, $10,200.
Trustees: Norman D. Col, Takashi Moriuchi, Yuriko Moriuchi.
EIN: 226471255

47932
Paul E. & Shirley U. Lehman Family Foundation
5800 Cumberland Hwy.
Chambersburg, PA 17201-7307
Contact: Paul E. Lehman, Pres.

Donor(s): PELCO Inc.
Financial data (yr. ended 12/31/01): Grants paid, $10,170; assets, $20,789 (M); gifts received, $5,710; expenditures, $10,350; qualifying distributions, $10,161.
Officers: Paul E. Lehman, Pres. and Treas.; Shirley U. Lehman, Secy.
EIN: 251830429
Codes: CS, CD

47933
David Dinnocenti Memorial Foundation
c/o PNC Advisors
620 Liberty Ave., P2-PTPP-10-2
Pittsburgh, PA 15222-2705
Application address: c/o Richard G. Roesler, Twin County Construction Co., 324 Limerick Center Rd., Pottstown, PA 19464

Established in 1989 in NJ.

47933—PENNSYLVANIA

Donor(s): Eugene Dinnocenti, Anthony Dinnocenti, Ronald Dinnocenti.
Financial data (yr. ended 02/28/02): Grants paid, $10,100; assets, $221,177 (M); expenditures, $12,600; qualifying distributions, $10,100.
Limitations: Giving primarily in PA.
Application information: Application form not required.
Trustee: PNC Bank, N.A.
EIN: 232576371

47934
The Richard and Jacquelyn Kurtz Foundation
380 Keller Rd.
Berwyn, PA 19312

Established in 1994 in PA.
Financial data (yr. ended 12/31/01): Grants paid, $10,100; assets, $100,666 (M); expenditures, $11,786; qualifying distributions, $10,100.
Limitations: Applications not accepted.
Application information: Contributes only to pre-selected organizations.
Trustees: Jacquelyn Kurtz, Richard Kurtz.
EIN: 232791486

47935
The Dietrich Foundation
c/o William S. Dietrich II
500 Grant St., Ste. 2226
Pittsburgh, PA 15219

Established in 1995 in PA.
Donor(s): William S. Dietrich II.
Financial data (yr. ended 11/30/01): Grants paid, $10,090; assets, $171,891 (M); expenditures, $10,090; qualifying distributions, $10,090.
Limitations: Applications not accepted. Giving primarily in Pittsburgh, PA.
Application information: Contributes only to pre-selected organizations.
Trustee: William S. Dietrich II.
EIN: 256537645

47936
Paul Lynch Foundation
P.O. Box 1446
New Castle, PA 16103
Application address: 201 N. Mercer St., New Castle, PA 16101, tel.: (724) 654-1116
Contact: Paul Lynch, Tr.

Established in 1998.
Donor(s): Paul Lynch.
Financial data (yr. ended 12/31/00): Grants paid, $10,075; assets, $308,729 (M); gifts received, $37,401; expenditures, $20,323; qualifying distributions, $15,392.
Trustee: Paul Lynch.
EIN: 256583550

47937
The Joan and Bernard Spain Foundation
233 S. 6th St.
Philadelphia, PA 19106-3749

Established in 2000 in PA.
Donor(s): Bernard Spain.
Financial data (yr. ended 12/31/01): Grants paid, $10,055; assets, $2,146,286 (M); gifts received, $458,672; expenditures, $22,010; qualifying distributions, $10,055.
Trustees: Bernard Spain, Joan Spain.
EIN: 256728780

47938
AFR Foundation, Inc.
c/o Saul Ewing
2 N. 2nd St., 7th Fl.
Harrisburg, PA 17101-1619

Established in 1993 in PA.

Donor(s): Anne F. Ruggaber.
Financial data (yr. ended 12/31/01): Grants paid, $10,000; assets, $366,535 (M); expenditures, $10,172; qualifying distributions, $10,000.
Limitations: Applications not accepted. Giving primarily in PA.
Application information: Contributes only to pre-selected organizations.
Officers and Directors:* Anne F. Ruggaber,* Chair. and Pres.; Mark R. Parthemer,* Secy.; Donn L. Snyder,* Treas.
EIN: 251710230

47939
Helen Brice Scholarship Fund
c/o Mellon Bank, N.A.
P.O. Box 185
Pittsburgh, PA 15230-0185
Application address: c/o Three Mellon Bank Ctr., Pittsburgh, PA 15230, tel.: (412) 234-0023
Contact: Laurie Moritz, Trust Off., Mellon Bank, N.A.

Donor(s): Helen Brice.‡
Financial data (yr. ended 12/31/01): Grants paid, $10,000; assets, $243,420 (M); expenditures, $13,197; qualifying distributions, $10,831.
Limitations: Giving limited to Uniontown, PA.
Application information: Application form required.
Trustee: Mellon Bank, N.A.
EIN: 256119807
Codes: GTI

47940
Class of 1931 Lower Moreland H.S. Scholarship Fund
c/o First National Bank & Trust Co. of Newton
34 S. State St.
Newtown, PA 18940

Financial data (yr. ended 12/31/01): Grants paid, $10,000; assets, $333,532 (M); expenditures, $28,102; qualifying distributions, $28,102.
Selection Committee: Laura Blanche, Julien Dreenen, Janet Dunn, JoAnn Fricker, Jeanette Hausman, Mark Mayson, Frank McKee, Diane Miller, William Pezza, Karen Steely, Anthony Tamaccio, Joseph Wosley.
EIN: 256714460

47941
G. Kenneth Crawford and Margaret B. Crawford Memorial Scholarship Fund
c/o U.S. Bancorp Trust Co.
P.O. Box 520
Johnstown, PA 15907-0520
Application address: c/o Deborah Madden, Thomas Jefferson High School, P.O. Box 18019, Pleasant Hills, Pittsburgh, PA 15236-0019

Established in 1995 in PA.
Financial data (yr. ended 12/31/01): Grants paid, $10,000; assets, $314,999 (M); expenditures, $14,758; qualifying distributions, $10,000.
Application information: Application form required.
Trustee: U.S. Bancorp Trust Co.
EIN: 251738804
Codes: GTI

47942
The Culbertson Family Charitable Foundation
c/o The Glenmede Trust Co.
1650 Market St., Ste. 1200
Philadelphia, PA 19103-7391 (215) 419-6000
Contact: Melinda Rath, Trust Off., The Glenmede Trust Co.

Established in 1997 in NJ.

Donor(s): John N. Culbertson, Jr., Donna Culbertson.
Financial data (yr. ended 12/31/01): Grants paid, $10,000; assets, $80,654 (M); expenditures, $10,898; qualifying distributions, $10,000.
Trustees: Donna Culbertson, John N. Culbertson, Jr., The Glenmede Trust Co.
EIN: 226749888

47943
De La Torre Foundation
c/o Edward De La Torre
300 Alpha Drive
Pittsburgh, PA 15238 (412) 599-1111

Established in 1995 in PA.
Donor(s): Paul De La Torre, Jill De La Torre, Manuel De La Torre, Nellie De La Torre, Edward De La Torre, Mary De La Torre.
Financial data (yr. ended 12/31/01): Grants paid, $10,000; assets, $184,256 (M); gifts received, $19,200; expenditures, $13,233; qualifying distributions, $10,000.
Limitations: Applications not accepted.
Application information: Contributes only to pre-selected organizations.
Trustees: Edward De La Torre, Manuel De La Torre, Nellie De La Torre, Paul De La Torre.
EIN: 251766039

47944
Fasnacht Family Foundation
359 E. Granada Ave.
Hershey, PA 17033-1346
Contact: Allen R. Fasnacht, Secy.-Treas.

Established in 1999 in PA.
Donor(s): Allen R. Fasnacht, Don E. Fasnacht.
Financial data (yr. ended 12/31/01): Grants paid, $10,000; assets, $330,648 (M); gifts received, $50,250; expenditures, $16,776; qualifying distributions, $10,000.
Application information: Application form not required.
Officers: Don E. Fasnacht, Pres.; Allen R. Fasnacht, Secy.-Treas.
EIN: 251849488

47945
Leonard C. Grasso Charitable Foundation
204 S. 1st St.
West Newton, PA 15089
Application address: P.O. Box 426, Monroeville, PA 15146
Contact: Alice E. Grasso, Pres.

Established in 1995 in PA.
Donor(s): Alice E. Grasso.
Financial data (yr. ended 12/31/01): Grants paid, $10,000; assets, $168,957 (M); gifts received, $15,000; expenditures, $12,370; qualifying distributions, $10,000.
Officers: Alice E. Grasso, Pres.; Kimberly J. Gallagher, V.P.; Kemper Arnold, Secy.-Treas.
EIN: 251778803

47946
Jacobus-Iacobucci Foundation
450 Pinkerton Rd.
Mount Joy, PA 17552

Established in 1998 in PA.
Financial data (yr. ended 12/31/00): Grants paid, $10,000; assets, $185,869 (M); expenditures, $12,594; qualifying distributions, $10,000.
Limitations: Applications not accepted.
Application information: Contributes only to pre-selected organizations.
Trustees: Barbara Carr, Aldo F.P. Jacobus, Thomas C. Mayer.
EIN: 232878087

47947
The Charles and Miriam Kanev Foundation
210 W. Rittenhouse Sq., Ste. 2603
Philadelphia, PA 19103 (215) 545-4800

Established in 1993 in PA.
Donor(s): Charles Kanev, Miriam Kanev.
Financial data (yr. ended 06/30/01): Grants paid, $10,000; assets, $132,813 (M); expenditures, $11,282; qualifying distributions, $10,000.
Limitations: Applications not accepted.
Application information: Contributes only to pre-selected organizations.
Trustees: Charles Kanev, Miriam Kanev.
EIN: 237750570

47948
The Harold and Berta Keen Family Scholarship Foundation
1951 Harrisburg Pike
Carlisle, PA 17013 (717) 243-6622
Contact: Harold Keen, Pres.

Donor(s): Keen Transport, Inc.
Financial data (yr. ended 12/31/01): Grants paid, $10,000; assets, $3,647 (M); gifts received, $10,000; expenditures, $10,000; qualifying distributions, $9,999.
Limitations: Giving primarily in central PA.
Application information: Application form required.
Officers and Directors:* Harold M. Keen,* Pres.; William R. Keen,* V.P.; Elizabeth A. Keen, Secy.; Jesse H. Keen,* Treas.; Berta H. Keen.
EIN: 251843433
Codes: CS

47949
La Salle University Alumni Association
c/o La Salle University
1900 West Olney Ave.
Philadelphia, PA 19141

Financial data (yr. ended 06/30/01): Grants paid, $10,000; assets, $128,974 (M); gifts received, $7,620; expenditures, $29,047; qualifying distributions, $10,722.
Limitations: Giving primarily in Philadelphia, PA.
Officers: Gerard J. Binder, Pres.; John F. Carabelle, V.P.; Kenneth G. Hager, Secy.; William W. Matthews III, Treas.
EIN: 237179225

47950
The Joseph & Bessie Levine Fund
4737 St. Rd.
Trevose, PA 19053
Contact: Joseph H. Levine, Tr.

Established in 1995 in PA.
Financial data (yr. ended 12/31/01): Grants paid, $10,000; assets, $38,136 (M); gifts received, $10,000; expenditures, $13,847; qualifying distributions, $10,000.
Limitations: Giving primarily in Philadelphia, PA.
Trustee: Joseph H. Levine.
EIN: 236296625

47951
Montefiore History Fund
6425 Beacon St.
Pittsburgh, PA 15217

Established in 1997 in PA.
Financial data (yr. ended 12/31/00): Grants paid, $10,000; assets, $664 (M); expenditures, $17,191; qualifying distributions, $9,993.
Limitations: Applications not accepted. Giving primarily in PA.
Application information: Contributes only to pre-selected organizations.

Director: Samuel P. Granowitz.
EIN: 251637685

47952
Ray and Lynn Wood Neag Charitable Foundation
1216 Old Mill Rd.
Wyomissing, PA 19610

Established in 1992 in PA.
Donor(s): Raymond Neag, Lynn J. Neag.
Financial data (yr. ended 06/30/02): Grants paid, $10,000; assets, $550,078 (M); expenditures, $16,663; qualifying distributions, $10,000.
Limitations: Applications not accepted. Giving primarily in Berks County, PA.
Application information: Contributes only to pre-selected organizations.
Trustees: Harriet H. Lawson, Raymond Neag, Nancy Neag Satalino.
EIN: 232712023

47953
Maria Grazia Panaro Foundation
c/o Michael J. Saile
405 Executive Dr.
Langhorne, PA 19047

Financial data (yr. ended 04/30/01): Grants paid, $10,000; assets, $181,437 (M); gifts received, $28,281; expenditures, $13,187; qualifying distributions, $10,000.
Directors: Anthony J. Panaro, Eva Panaro, Lenora Panaro, Vincent R. Panaro, Michael J. Saile.
EIN: 237813766

47954
Pennsylvania Metalcasting Environmental Research Foundation
1 Plymouth Meeting, Ste. 412
Plymouth Meeting, PA 19462 (610) 825-5126
Contact: Christopher G. Moyer, V.P.

Financial data (yr. ended 12/31/01): Grants paid, $10,000; assets, $6,622 (M); gifts received, $5,000; expenditures, $19,336; qualifying distributions, $10,000.
Officers: Steven S. Wolfberg, Pres.; Christopher G. Moyer, V.P.; Bruce M. Eckert, Secy.-Treas.
EIN: 232673129

47955
Lynn W. & Timothy W. Peters Foundation
1314 Deer Ln.
Lancaster, PA 17601

Established in 1999.
Donor(s): Lynn W. Peters, Timothy W. Peters.
Financial data (yr. ended 12/31/00): Grants paid, $10,000; assets, $146,705 (M); gifts received, $80,248; expenditures, $10,100; qualifying distributions, $10,000.
Limitations: Applications not accepted.
Application information: Contributes only to pre-selected organizations.
Directors: Lynn W. Peters, Megan L. Peters, Timothy W. Peters, Timothy W. Peters, Jr.
EIN: 233024753

47956
Philadelphia Community Foundation, Inc.
c/o Mellon Bank Ctr.
1735 Market St., Ste. 3200
Philadelphia, PA 19103

Financial data (yr. ended 12/31/01): Grants paid, $10,000; assets, $77,686 (M); expenditures, $10,978; qualifying distributions, $10,000.
Limitations: Applications not accepted. Giving limited to the Philadelphia, PA, area.
Application information: Contributes only to pre-selected organizations.

Officers: Harry A. Kalish, Pres.; Barbara Curtis, Secy.
EIN: 236243763
Codes: TN

47957
Progressive Business Publications Foundation
370 Technology Dr.
Malvern, PA 19355-0719

Established in 2000 in PA.
Donor(s): American Future Systems, Inc.
Financial data (yr. ended 12/31/01): Grants paid, $10,000; assets, $0 (M); gifts received, $10,000; expenditures, $10,000; qualifying distributions, $10,000.
Limitations: Applications not accepted. Giving primarily in Malvern, PA.
Trustees: Marc S. Maser, Edward J. Satell.
EIN: 256665358
Codes: CS

47958
The Samuel and Irene Saligman Charitable Fund
261 Old York Rd., Ste. 613
Jenkintown, PA 19046-3706 (215) 886-7260
Contact: Irene Saligman, Tr.

Established in 1995 in PA.
Donor(s): Samuel Saligman.‡
Financial data (yr. ended 12/31/01): Grants paid, $10,000; assets, $147,675 (M); expenditures, $12,267; qualifying distributions, $10,000.
Trustees: Herschel Cravitz, Herbert Kurtz, Irene Saligman.
EIN: 232810084

47959
The Schwab Foundation
407 Atwater Rd.
Broomall, PA 19008-2006

Financial data (yr. ended 12/31/01): Grants paid, $10,000; assets, $180,342 (M); gifts received, $12,000; expenditures, $10,144; qualifying distributions, $10,000.
Limitations: Applications not accepted.
Application information: Contributes only to pre-selected organizations.
Officers: Carl W. Schwab, Pres.; Robert J. Schwab, V.P.; Julius C. Schwab, Secy.-Treas.
EIN: 232789934

47960
Sithong Bounsawat Foundation
P.O. Box 182
Media, PA 19063

Donor(s): Terry Kline.
Financial data (yr. ended 08/31/99): Grants paid, $10,000; assets, $18,559 (M); gifts received, $6,815; expenditures, $10,100; qualifying distributions, $10,000.
Limitations: Applications not accepted. Giving primarily in Philadelphia, PA.
Application information: Contributes only to pre-selected organizations.
Trustees: Robert T. Boylan, Terry Kline, Leslie F. Kurtas.
EIN: 232861903

47961
The Sulivan Foundation
c/o PNC Advisors
P.O. Box 937
Scranton, PA 18501

Established in 2001 in PA.
Donor(s): Robert J. Sullivan, Patricia P. Sullivan.
Financial data (yr. ended 12/31/01): Grants paid, $10,000; assets, $489,602 (M); gifts received,

47961—PENNSYLVANIA

$500,011; expenditures, $10,409; qualifying distributions, $10,205.
Limitations: Applications not accepted.
Application information: Contributes only to pre-selected organizations.
Trustees: Patricia P. Sullivan, Robert J. Sullivan, PNC Bank, N.A.
EIN: 256780226

47962
The Richard and Johnette Venne Foundation
1664 Powderhorn Dr.
Newtown, PA 18940
Contact: Richard A. Venne, V.P.

Established in 2000 in PA.
Donor(s): Richard A. Venne.
Financial data (yr. ended 12/31/01): Grants paid, $10,000; assets, $180,057 (M); expenditures, $10,000; qualifying distributions, $9,975.
Officers and Directors:* Johnette Venne,* Pres.; Richard A. Venne,* V.P.; John G. Venne,* Secy.; Jillian R. Venne,* Treas.; Richard A. Venne, Jr.
EIN: 233063796

47963
Dorothy Hill Memorial Grants
c/o Mellon Bank, N.A.
P.O. Box 7236, AIM No. 193-0224
Philadelphia, PA 19101-7236
Application address: c/o First United Methodist Church, 61 E. High St., Carlisle, PA 17103

Financial data (yr. ended 06/30/99): Grants paid, $9,920; assets, $255,438 (M); expenditures, $15,879; qualifying distributions, $9,676.
Limitations: Giving limited to residents of Carlisle, PA.
Application information: Application form not required.
Trustee: Mellon Bank, N.A.
EIN: 236762599

47964
Sturges Foundation
500 Thompson Ave.
McKees Rocks, PA 15136-3828

Financial data (yr. ended 12/31/01): Grants paid, $9,900; assets, $145,864 (M); expenditures, $10,068; qualifying distributions, $9,900.
Limitations: Applications not accepted. Giving primarily in Pittsburgh, PA.
Application information: Contributes only to pre-selected organizations.
Trustees: Mary Lee Clark, Ralph R. Sands, Thomas B. Sturges III.
EIN: 256036983

47965
RMS Technologies, Inc. Foundation
c/o Angela Huggins
1900 Rittenhouse Sq., Ste. 6B
Philadelphia, PA 19103
Application address: 5 Eves Dr., Marlton, NJ 08053

Established in 1993 in NJ.
Donor(s): RMS Technologies, Inc., Angela M. Huggins.
Financial data (yr. ended 12/31/01): Grants paid, $9,812; assets, $297 (M); gifts received, $9,812; expenditures, $10,280; qualifying distributions, $10,280.
Limitations: Giving primarily in NJ.
Application information: Application form required.
Officers and Directors:* Angela M. Huggins, Chair., Pres., and Treas.; Gail A. Huggins,* Secy.; V. Thomas Fooks, Sheryl E. Huggins.
EIN: 223259828

Codes: CS, CD

47966
Bar-Nir Bergreen Foundation
896 Brushtown Rd.
P.O. Box 488
Gwynedd Valley, PA 19437

Established in 1999 in PA.
Donor(s): Zahava Bar-Nir, Zvi Bergreen.
Financial data (yr. ended 12/31/01): Grants paid, $9,784; assets, $227,747 (M); expenditures, $9,804; qualifying distributions, $9,741.
Limitations: Applications not accepted. Giving primarily in PA.
Application information: Contributes only to pre-selected organizations.
Officers and Directors:* Zahava Bar-Nir,* Pres.; Karen Bar-Nir,* Secy.; Anat B. Dubin,* Treas.; Zvi Bergreen.
EIN: 233024104

47967
Katselas Family Foundation
5221 Fifth Ave.
Pittsburgh, PA 15232 (412) 681-7242
Contact: Tasso G. Katselas, Tr.

Established in 1995 in PA.
Donor(s): Tasso G. Katselas.
Financial data (yr. ended 12/31/01): Grants paid, $9,750; assets, $297,599 (M); expenditures, $10,246; qualifying distributions, $9,750.
Trustees: Dana Katselos, Jane Katselas, Lisa Katselas, Tasso G. Katselas.
EIN: 251777845

47968
Pennsylvania Knitted Outerwear Foundation
c/o First Union National Bank
123 S. Broad St.
Philadelphia, PA 19109-9989 (215) 731-9982
Application address: c/o Lois Reed, Unite ILGWU Scholarship Fund, 35 S. 4th St., Philadelphia, PA 19106

Donor(s): The Pennsylvania Knitted Outerwear Manufacturing Association.
Financial data (yr. ended 11/30/01): Grants paid, $9,750; assets, $34,423 (M); expenditures, $9,750; qualifying distributions, $9,750.
Limitations: Giving primarily in PA.
Officers and Trustees:* Nat Neuman,* Chair.; Harry Neuman,* Secy.; Edwin B. Shils.
EIN: 236296951

47969
Kathleen A. Smith Scholarship Fund
c/o First Union National Bank
123 S. Broad St.
Philadelphia, PA 19109-9989
Application address: c/o Warren Regional H.S. Faculty Scholarship Comm., Warren, NJ 07059, tel.: (908) 647-4800

Established in 1994 in NJ.
Donor(s): Kathleen Smith.‡
Financial data (yr. ended 08/31/99): Grants paid, $9,725; assets, $330,007 (M); expenditures, $12,342; qualifying distributions, $9,804.
Limitations: Giving limited to residents of Warren, NJ.
Trustee: First Union National Bank.
EIN: 237773022

47970
Brudnock Memorial Scholarship Fund
c/o Punxsutawney Area High School
600 N. Findley St.
Punxsutawney, PA 15767

Established in 1999.

Financial data (yr. ended 12/31/01): Grants paid, $9,720; assets, $398,547 (M); expenditures, $12,696; qualifying distributions, $9,720.
Trustees: Emily Cassidy, Ronald J. Ploucha, Alan G. Towns.
EIN: 251821313

47971
Spatt Family Charitable Foundation
1714 Beechwood Blvd.
Pittsburgh, PA 15217-1714

Financial data (yr. ended 12/31/00): Grants paid, $9,687; assets, $179,096 (M); expenditures, $11,490; qualifying distributions, $9,122.
Trustees: Chester S. Spatt, Ellen Gordon Spatt.
EIN: 232903992

47972
Edwill B. & Rachel H. Miller Trust
c/o Allfirst, Trust Div.
21 E. Market St.
York, PA 17401-1500
Contact: Arlene C. La Pore, V.P. and Trust Off., Allfirst

Financial data (yr. ended 12/31/01): Grants paid, $9,641; assets, $185,942 (M); expenditures, $11,621; qualifying distributions, $9,641.
Limitations: Giving primarily in central PA.
Trustee: Allfirst.
EIN: 236542778

47973
Paul L. Smith Charitable Foundation Trust
c/o Allfirst, Trust Div.
21 E. Market St.
York, PA 17401-1500

Donor(s): Paul L. Smith.
Financial data (yr. ended 11/30/01): Grants paid, $9,628; assets, $218,503 (M); expenditures, $10,582; qualifying distributions, $10,405.
Limitations: Applications not accepted. Giving limited to PA.
Application information: Contributes only to pre-selected organizations.
Trustees: Paul L. Smith, Allfirst.
EIN: 236807863

47974
Marshall Ruscetti Foundation
23 Bristol Ln.
New Castle, PA 16105 (724) 652-1236
Contact: Marshall Ruscetti, Pres.

Financial data (yr. ended 12/31/01): Grants paid, $9,625; assets, $84,343 (M); gifts received, $11,400; expenditures, $9,649; qualifying distributions, $9,625.
Limitations: Giving primarily in PA.
Officers: Marshall Ruscetti, Pres.; Frank D. Ruscetti, Secy.
EIN: 251425887

47975
Schramm Foundation
800 E. Virginia Ave.
West Chester, PA 19380 (610) 696-2500

Financial data (yr. ended 12/31/01): Grants paid, $9,600; assets, $127,497 (M); expenditures, $10,125; qualifying distributions, $9,987.
Limitations: Applications not accepted. Giving primarily to residents of West Chester, PA.
Application information: Unsolicited requests for funds not accepted.
Officers and Directors:* Leslie B. Schramm,* Pres.; Richard E. Schramm,* V.P.; Florence J. Schramm,* Secy.; John A. Bellis, Jr., Austin M. Lee, Cecilia C. Schramm.
EIN: 236291235

Codes: GTI

47976
Guard Foundation
c/o Judd Shoval
24 S. River St.
Wilkes-Barre, PA 18703

Established in 1999 in PA.
Donor(s): The Guard Group.
Financial data (yr. ended 12/31/01): Grants paid, $9,550; assets, $537,885 (M); gifts received, $200,000; expenditures, $10,504; qualifying distributions, $9,550.
Limitations: Applications not accepted.
Application information: Contributes only to pre-selected organizations.
Officers: Y. Judd Shoval, Pres. and Secy.; Susan W. Shoval, Treas.
EIN: 233013490

47977
John G. & Julia Geiling Charitable Trust
c/o Mellon Bank, N.A.
P.O. Box 7236, AIM No. 193-0224
Philadelphia, PA 19101-7236

Established in 1999 in PA.
Financial data (yr. ended 02/28/02): Grants paid, $9,424; assets, $208,641 (M); expenditures, $11,892; qualifying distributions, $9,424.
Limitations: Applications not accepted.
Application information: Contributes only to pre-selected organizations.
Trustee: Mellon Bank, N.A.
EIN: 256706541

47978
Robert M. Currens & Grace A. Currens Trust
c/o Allfirst, Trust Tax Div.
21 E. Market St.
York, PA 17401-1500
Application address: P.O. Box 459, Chambersburg, PA 17201, tel.: (717) 263-2822
Contact: Alan B. Rhinehart, Trust Off., Allfirst, Trust Tax Div.

Financial data (yr. ended 12/31/01): Grants paid, $9,400; assets, $154,786 (M); expenditures, $11,525; qualifying distributions, $9,400.
Limitations: Giving primarily in the Shippensburg, PA, area.
Trustee: Allfirst.
EIN: 236266569

47979
The Robert & Ardath Rodale Family Foundation
2098 S. Cedar Crest Blvd.
Allentown, PA 18103-9627
Application address: c/o Heather Stonebeck, 2168 S. Cedar Crest Blvd., Allentown, PA 18103

Established in 1997 in PA.
Financial data (yr. ended 12/31/01): Grants paid, $9,380; assets, $256,554 (M); expenditures, $9,597; qualifying distributions, $9,380.
Limitations: Giving primarily in PA; some giving also in Canada.
Officers: Ardath H. Rodale, Pres.; Heidi Rodale, V.P.; Anthony Rodale, Secy.
EIN: 232715042

47980
Wendell P. Hampson Trust
c/o First Union National Bank
Broad & Walnut Sts., Ste. PA1308
Philadelphia, PA 19109

Established in 1997 in FL.
Financial data (yr. ended 12/31/99): Grants paid, $9,316; assets, $330,521 (M); expenditures, $13,198; qualifying distributions, $9,316.
Limitations: Applications not accepted. Giving primarily in St. Augustine, FL.
Application information: Contributes only to pre-selected organizations.
Trustee: First Union National Bank.
EIN: 596740065

47981
Mirabile Foundation, Inc.
190 W. Germantown Pike, Ste. 150
Norristown, PA 19401

Established in 1986 in PA.
Financial data (yr. ended 12/31/01): Grants paid, $9,300; assets, $137,292 (M); expenditures, $10,194; qualifying distributions, $9,300.
Limitations: Applications not accepted. Giving limited to Norristown and the five-county Philadelphia, PA, area.
Application information: Contributes only to pre-selected organizations.
Officers: Joseph Mirabile, Jr., Pres.; Paul Mirabile, V.P.; Harry Mirabile, Secy.-Treas.
EIN: 232441598

47982
Hyman and Lillyann Parker Foundation
801 Pasadena Dr.
Erie, PA 16505

Donor(s): Lillyann G. Parker.
Financial data (yr. ended 12/31/01): Grants paid, $9,200; assets, $168,942 (M); expenditures, $10,574; qualifying distributions, $9,200.
Limitations: Applications not accepted. Giving primarily in Pittsburgh, PA.
Application information: Contributes only to pre-selected organizations.
Trustee: David S. Parker.
EIN: 251663354

47983
The Waz Family Foundation
c/o Joseph W. Waz, Jr.
46 Summit St.
Philadelphia, PA 19118-2833

Established in 2000 in PA.
Donor(s): Joe W. Waz, Jr.
Financial data (yr. ended 11/30/01): Grants paid, $9,200; assets, $160,758 (M); gifts received, $188,710; expenditures, $14,301; qualifying distributions, $12,021.
Limitations: Applications not accepted. Giving primarily in Philadelphia, PA.
Application information: Contributes only to pre-selected organizations.
Officers and Directors:* Joe W. Waz, Jr.,* Pres.; Martha Stookey,* Secy.-Treas.
EIN: 233063821

47984
Kelly Family Charitable Foundation
c/o Thomas J. Minarcik
150 E. 8th St.
Erie, PA 16501

Established in 1998 in PA.
Donor(s): Kelly Revocable Trust.
Financial data (yr. ended 12/31/01): Grants paid, $9,175; assets, $307,882 (M); expenditures, $10,445; qualifying distributions, $9,175.
Trustee: Elizabeth K. Kelly.
EIN: 251810962

47985
Philip & Muriel Berman Foundation
1150 S. Cedar Crest Blvd., Ste. 203
Allentown, PA 18103-7900

Donor(s): Philip I. Berman,‡ Muriel M. Berman.
Financial data (yr. ended 05/31/02): Grants paid, $9,150; assets, $224,608 (M); expenditures, $35,022; qualifying distributions, $9,150.
Limitations: Applications not accepted. Giving limited to PA.
Application information: Contributes only to pre-selected organizations.
Officers: Nancy Berman Bloch, Pres.; Muriel M. Berman, V.P. and Treas.
EIN: 236270983

47986
AAA Scholarship Fund of the Lehigh Valley Motor Club
1020 Hamilton St.
Allentown, PA 18101-1085 (610) 434-5141
Contact: John H. Kern, Treas.

Established in 1985 in PA.
Donor(s): AAA Lehigh Valley.
Financial data (yr. ended 12/31/01): Grants paid, $9,000; assets, $161,175 (M); expenditures, $9,000; qualifying distributions, $9,000.
Limitations: Giving limited to AAA Lehigh Valley territory in PA.
Application information: Application form required.
Officers: Charles Meredith, Chair.; Steven Wojnarowicz, Pres.; G. Patrick Frank, Secy.; John H. Kern, Treas.
EIN: 232325177
Codes: GTI

47987
May Wilson Adams Charitable Foundation
c/o Mellon Bank, N.A.
P.O. Box 7236, AIM 193-0224
Philadelphia, PA 19101-7236

Established in 1997 in PA.
Financial data (yr. ended 02/28/02): Grants paid, $9,000; assets, $155,458 (M); expenditures, $11,682; qualifying distributions, $9,000.
Limitations: Applications not accepted.
Application information: Contributes only to pre-selected organizations.
Trustees: Rev. Alan R. Wilson, Karen L. Wilson, Mellon Bank, N.A.
EIN: 237878702

47988
J. B. Finley Charitable Trust
c/o PNC Advisors
620 Liberty Ave., 2 PNC Plz.
Pittsburgh, PA 15222-2719 (412) 762-7076
Contact: Mia Hallett Bernard

Trust established in 1919 in PA.
Donor(s): J.B. Finley.‡
Financial data (yr. ended 09/30/01): Grants paid, $9,000; assets, $3,491,032 (M); expenditures, $37,079; qualifying distributions, $11,620.
Limitations: Giving primarily in PA.
Publications: Informational brochure, application guidelines.
Trustee: PNC Bank, N.A.
EIN: 256024443

47989
GVM Charitable Foundation
220 S. Washington St.
Titusville, PA 16354

Established in 1999 in PA; funded in 2000.
Donor(s): Grand Valley Manufacturing Co.
Financial data (yr. ended 12/31/01): Grants paid, $9,000; assets, $55 (M); gifts received, $4,653; expenditures, $9,925; qualifying distributions, $9,900.
Application information: Unsolicited requests for funds not accepted.

47989—PENNSYLVANIA

Trustee: H. Richard Ewing.
EIN: 251847356
Codes: CS, CD

47990
Painfree - International Foundation
30 Admore Ave.
Ardmore, PA 19003-9998

Established in 2001 in PA.
Financial data (yr. ended 12/31/01): Grants paid, $9,000; assets, $2,806 (M); gifts received, $15,488; expenditures, $12,682; qualifying distributions, $1,404.
Limitations: Giving primarily in Philadelphia, PA.
Officers: Jerome M. Zaslow, Pres.; Darlene Andrews, V.P.
EIN: 233048672

47991
C. P. Scoboria, Jr. Athletic Scholarship Foundation
423 Eisenbrown St.
Reading, PA 19605-2402

Established in 1992 in PA.
Donor(s): Raymond Scoboria.
Financial data (yr. ended 12/31/01): Grants paid, $9,000; assets, $9,992 (M); gifts received, $9,121; expenditures, $9,355; qualifying distributions, $9,000.
Limitations: Giving limited to Kintnersville, PA.
Trustees: Lynn Greening, Clarence P. Scoboria III, Raymond Scoboria.
EIN: 232703449

47992
Daniel C. & Thirza J. Tanney Foundation
3268 Clive Ave.
Bensalem, PA 19020 (215) 994-1067
Contact: Michael Tanney, Dir.

Established in 1999 in PA.
Donor(s): Thirza Tanney,‡ Michael Tanney, Edward Snitzer.
Financial data (yr. ended 12/31/01): Grants paid, $9,000; assets, $271,508 (M); expenditures, $12,802; qualifying distributions, $9,000.
Directors: Joanne Brown, Jeanne Hughes, Theresa Murray, Kathleen Tanney, Mary Tanney, Michael Tanney.
EIN: 256627223

47993
Edward I. Siegal Private Foundation
c/o Martha Siegal
2200 Park Towne Pl., S-911
Philadelphia, PA 19130

Established in 1989 in PA.
Financial data (yr. ended 12/31/00): Grants paid, $8,992; assets, $10,245 (M); gifts received, $10,000; expenditures, $9,824; qualifying distributions, $8,992.
Limitations: Applications not accepted. Giving limited to the Philadelphia, PA, area.
Application information: Contributes only to pre-selected organizations.
Officer and Trustees:* Martha Siegal,* Pres.; Elkan J. Siegal, Ira H. Siegal, Izette Siegal Stern.
EIN: 232535375

47994
Perilstein Foundation
1001 City Ave., Ste. 1107WA
Wynnewood, PA 19096
Contact: Betty P. Krestal, Tr.

Financial data (yr. ended 10/31/01): Grants paid, $8,985; assets, $159,901 (M); expenditures, $10,195; qualifying distributions, $8,985.
Limitations: Giving primarily in Philadelphia, PA.

Trustees: Charlotte Kirshner, Betty P. Krestal, William Perilstein.
EIN: 236276160

47995
Guy K. & Virginia K. Ludwig Trust
c/o Allfirst, Trust Tax Div.
21 E. Market St.
York, PA 17401-1500

Financial data (yr. ended 12/31/01): Grants paid, $8,870; assets, $302,420 (M); expenditures, $15,595; qualifying distributions, $8,870.
Limitations: Applications not accepted.
Application information: Contributes only to pre-selected organizations.
Trustee: Allfirst.
EIN: 236708044

47996
Donegal School District Education Foundation
c/o John Rios
366 S. Market Ave.
Mount Joy, PA 17552

Financial data (yr. ended 06/30/00): Grants paid, $8,817; assets, $115,251 (M); gifts received, $7,567; expenditures, $18,570; qualifying distributions, $8,817.
Limitations: Applications not accepted. Giving limited to Donegal, PA.
Officers: John Rios, Pres.; Glenn Hess, V.P.; Tracy Shank, Secy.; Deborah Owens, Treas.
EIN: 232679755

47997
Bloom Staloff Foundation
c/o James J. Bloom
2000 Market St. 18th Fl.
Philadelphia, PA 19103

Established in 1997 in PA.
Donor(s): James Bloom, Arnold Staloff.
Financial data (yr. ended 10/31/01): Grants paid, $8,800; assets, $37,903 (M); gifts received, $20,000; expenditures, $8,826; qualifying distributions, $8,800.
Limitations: Applications not accepted.
Directors: James J. Bloom, Arnold Staloff.
EIN: 232934148

47998
Harvey F. and Raymond F. Hoffman Trust
c/o PNC Advisors
620 Liberty Ave., P2-PTPP-10-2
Pittsburgh, PA 15222

Established in 1998 in PA.
Financial data (yr. ended 12/31/01): Grants paid, $8,800; assets, $155,013 (M); expenditures, $11,255; qualifying distributions, $8,800.
Trustee: PNC Bank, N.A.
EIN: 236619830

47999
The Lehr Foundation
1637 Paper Mill Rd.
Meadowbrook, PA 19046-1016

Established in 2000 in PA.
Financial data (yr. ended 12/31/01): Grants paid, $8,800; assets, $49,087 (M); gifts received, $48,840; expenditures, $9,408; qualifying distributions, $8,800.
Limitations: Applications not accepted.
Application information: Contributes only to pre-selected organizations.
Trustees: Ellyn Lehr, Seth Lehr.
EIN: 256684176

48000
Adams County Foundation
101 W. Middle St.
Gettysburg, PA 17325-2109

Financial data (yr. ended 03/31/00): Grants paid, $8,786; assets, $380,146 (M); gifts received, $9,088; expenditures, $21,110.
Limitations: Giving limited to Adams County, PA.
Officer: Bradley R. Hoch, M.D., Chair.
Directors: E.C. Grim, Ronald Hankey, John W. Phillips, Charles Ritter, B.C. Robbins, C.K. Roulette, Richard E. Selby, Sally Shultz.
EIN: 225144001
Codes: CM

48001
Roland and Sara K. Davis Memorial Trust
c/o Allfirst, Trust Tax Div.
21 E. Market St.
York, PA 17401-1500

Established in 2001 in PA.
Financial data (yr. ended 08/31/01): Grants paid, $8,710; assets, $372,900 (M); expenditures, $10,456; qualifying distributions, $10,465.
Limitations: Applications not accepted. Giving primarily in Lebanon, PA.
Application information: Contributes only to pre-selected organizations.
Trustee: Allfirst.
EIN: 236522683

48002
The Lake Foundation Charitable Trust
P.O. Box 331
Lake Ariel, PA 18436-0331

Established in 1986 in PA.
Donor(s): Douglas M. Holcomb, Madge M. Holcomb.
Financial data (yr. ended 12/31/01): Grants paid, $8,700; assets, $156,142 (M); expenditures, $9,335; qualifying distributions, $8,700.
Limitations: Applications not accepted. Giving primarily in PA.
Application information: Contributes only to pre-selected organizations.
Trustees: Douglas M. Holcomb, Madge M. Holcomb.
EIN: 222816562

48003
The Marjorie C. Greenberger Charitable Trust
1232 Murdoch Rd.
Pittsburgh, PA 15217

Established in 1996 in PA.
Donor(s): Marjorie C. Greenberger.
Financial data (yr. ended 12/31/01): Grants paid, $8,658; assets, $113,865 (M); expenditures, $13,078; qualifying distributions, $8,658.
Limitations: Applications not accepted.
Application information: Contributes only to pre-selected organizations.
Trustee: Marjorie C. Greenberger.
EIN: 237866153

48004
Bruce & Adele Greenfield Foundation
1845 Walnut St., Ste. 800
Philadelphia, PA 19103 (215) 569-9900
Contact: Bruce H. Greenfield, Tr.

Donor(s): Bruce H. Greenfield, Adele G. Greenfield.
Financial data (yr. ended 12/31/01): Grants paid, $8,650; assets, $224,480 (M); expenditures, $8,861; qualifying distributions, $8,650.
Application information: Application form not required.

Trustees: Gustave G. Amsterdam, Adele G. Greenfield, Bruce H. Greenfield.
EIN: 236296554

48005
Fayette S. Olmstead Foundation
c/o PNC Advisors
620 Liberty Ave., P2-PTPP-10-2
Pittsburgh, PA 15222-2705 (412) 762-3390
Contact: John Culbertson, V.P. and Trust Off., PNC Advisors

Established in 1950 in PA.
Donor(s): Fayette S. Olmsted.
Financial data (yr. ended 09/30/01): Grants paid, $8,625; assets, $130,943 (M); expenditures, $10,639; qualifying distributions, $8,496.
Limitations: Applications not accepted. Giving limited to PA.
Application information: Contributes only to pre-selected organizations.
Trustee: PNC Bank, N.A.
EIN: 256043515

48006
Daniel D. Solomon Foundation
451 Copper Beach Cir.
Elkins Park, PA 19027
Contact: Sandra Axelrod, Tr.

Financial data (yr. ended 08/31/01): Grants paid, $8,620; assets, $101,571 (M); expenditures, $9,537; qualifying distributions, $8,620.
Limitations: Giving primarily in PA.
Trustees: Sandra Axelrod, Ethel Muskat, Howard Solomon, Sophia Solomon.
EIN: 236429186

48007
Grig Fund
c/o Wolf Block
1650 Arch St., 22nd Fl.
Philadelphia, PA 19103

Financial data (yr. ended 12/31/01): Grants paid, $8,602; assets, $171,315 (M); expenditures, $10,346; qualifying distributions, $9,327.
Limitations: Giving primarily in FL and PA.
Application information: Application form not required.
Officer: Milton H. Snellenburg, Sr., Chair.
Trustees: Leonard J. Cooper, Milton H. Snellenburg, Jr., Roger G. Snellenburg.
EIN: 236243362

48008
Arthur B. and Marion V. Myers Trust - Religious Trust
c/o Allfirst, Trust Div.
21 E. Market St., M/C 402-130
York, PA 17401-1500

Established in 2000 in PA.
Financial data (yr. ended 12/31/01): Grants paid, $8,521; assets, $172,903 (M); expenditures, $17,013; qualifying distributions, $8,521.
Limitations: Applications not accepted. Giving primarily in Harrisburg, PA.
Application information: Contributes only to pre-selected organizations.
Trustee: Allfirst.
EIN: 256480500

48009
Paul B. Entrekin Foundation Trust
c/o Mellon Bank, N.A.
P.O. Box 7236
Philadelphia, PA 19101-7236
Application address: c/o Pat Kline, 1 Mellon Bank Ctr., Philadelphia, PA 19101, tel.: (215) 553-3208

Financial data (yr. ended 12/31/01): Grants paid, $8,500; assets, $166,071 (M); expenditures, $10,736; qualifying distributions, $8,500.
Limitations: Giving limited to Sarasota, FL.
Trustee: Mellon Bank, N.A.
EIN: 236228008

48010
J.A. Foundation
1 Amato Dr.
Moosic, PA 18507

Established in 1997 in PA.
Financial data (yr. ended 12/31/01): Grants paid, $8,500; assets, $464,718 (M); gifts received, $49,729; expenditures, $13,256; qualifying distributions, $10,059.
Limitations: Applications not accepted.
Application information: Contributes only to pre-selected organizations.
Officers: Joseph Amato, Pres. and Treas.; Robert T. Kelly, Jr., Secy.
EIN: 232883862

48011
Millbach Foundation, Inc.
Charming Forge
P.O. Box 63
Womelsdorf, PA 19567

Established in 2000 in PA.
Donor(s): Earle H. Henderson.
Financial data (yr. ended 12/31/00): Grants paid, $8,500; assets, $289,098 (M); gifts received, $289,098; expenditures, $21,722; qualifying distributions, $17,785.
Limitations: Giving primarily in Womelsdorf, PA.
Officers: Mark H. Henderson, Pres.; Lon L. Hunt, V.P.; Earle H. Henderson, Secy.-Treas.
Directors: Jeffrey C. Firestone, Barry Stover, Laurence F. Ward, A. Mark Winter.
EIN: 233025476

48012
Helen N. Ross Charitable Trust
c/o Mellon Bank, N.A.
P.O. Box 185, 1 Mellon Bank Ctr.
Pittsburgh, PA 15230-9897

Established in 1991 in PA.
Donor(s): Helen N. Ross.‡
Financial data (yr. ended 12/31/99): Grants paid, $8,500; assets, $247,921 (M); expenditures, $12,427; qualifying distributions, $9,830.
Limitations: Applications not accepted. Giving limited to PA.
Application information: Contributes only to pre-selected organizations.
Trustee: Mellon Bank, N.A.
EIN: 256378894

48013
Twila Sampson Family Foundation
100 Sandune Dr.
Pittsburgh, PA 15239
Contact: Benard Sampson, Tr.

Established in 1983.
Donor(s): Toro Development Co., Myles D. Sampson.

Financial data (yr. ended 12/31/01): Grants paid, $8,500; assets, $39,179 (M); expenditures, $9,586; qualifying distributions, $8,500.
Limitations: Applications not accepted. Giving primarily in Pittsburgh, PA.
Application information: Contributes only to pre-selected organizations.
Trustees: Benard Sampson, Myles D. Sampson.
EIN: 251437507

48014
Helen B. Shartzer Scholarship Fund
c/o PNC Advisors
620 Liberty Ave., P2-PTPP-10-2
Pittsburgh, PA 15222-2705
Application address: c/o Scholarship Comm., Norristown Area High School, Norristown, PA 19401

Financial data (yr. ended 12/31/01): Grants paid, $8,500; assets, $155,271 (M); expenditures, $10,216; qualifying distributions, $8,561.
Limitations: Giving limited to residents of Norristown, PA.
Trustee: PNC Bank, N.A.
EIN: 236398364
Codes: GTI

48015
Elsie L. Plank Trust f/b/o C. Plank Scholarship Trust
c/o Mellon Bank, N.A.
P.O. Box 7236
Philadelphia, PA 19101-7236
Application address: c/o Peg Watson, 1735 Market St., 3rd Fl., Philadelphia, PA 19013

Financial data (yr. ended 12/31/99): Grants paid, $8,493; assets, $153,147 (M); expenditures, $11,728; qualifying distributions, $8,323.
Limitations: Giving limited to residents of PA.
Application information: Application form required.
Trustee: Mellon Bank, N.A.
EIN: 236241620

48016
Janice Dana Spear Scholarship Foundation
c/o First Union National Bank
123 S. Broad St., PA1308
Philadelphia, PA 19109-1199

Financial data (yr. ended 04/30/00): Grants paid, $8,490; assets, $198,497 (M); expenditures, $10,358; qualifying distributions, $8,490.
Limitations: Applications not accepted. Giving limited to New York, NY.
Application information: Contributes only to a pre-selected organization.
Trustee: First Union National Bank.
EIN: 226377147

48017
Wojdak Foundation
(Formerly Joseph M. Haskell Foundation)
c/o Haskell of Pittsburgh, Inc.
231 Haskell Ln.
Verona, PA 15147-3999 (412) 828-6000
Contact: Chris Thurston, Tr.

Financial data (yr. ended 03/31/00): Grants paid, $8,485; assets, $41,911 (M); expenditures, $9,356; qualifying distributions, $8,485.
Limitations: Giving limited to PA.
Application information: Application form required.
Trustees: Chris Thurston, Joseph Wojdak.
EIN: 256065760

48018
South Village Community Development Corp.
c/o Charles J. Hardy
135 S. 19th St., Ste. 400
Philadelphia, PA 19103

Financial data (yr. ended 12/31/00): Grants paid, $8,460; assets, $18 (M); gifts received, $9,000; expenditures, $9,168; qualifying distributions, $8,460.
Limitations: Applications not accepted. Giving primarily in Philadelphia, PA.
Application information: Contributes only to pre-selected organizations.
Directors: Edward Bell, Rev. William Green, Oscar Hankinson, Alan Hunter, Bernard Smith.
EIN: 232822048

48019
Kentucky School Reform Corporation
c/o Mandelbaum, Esquire, Schnader, et. al.
1600 Market St., Ste. 3600
Philadelphia, PA 19103-7286

Established in 1995 in KY.
Donor(s): Ashland, Inc., Humana Foundation, UPS Foundation, Prichard Committee for Academic Excellence, Ashland Foundation, Bank One Service Corp.
Financial data (yr. ended 12/31/99): Grants paid, $8,395; assets, $1,586,172 (M); gifts received, $1,217,823; expenditures, $565,618; qualifying distributions, $564,921; giving activities include $146,200 for programs.
Limitations: Applications not accepted.
Application information: Contributes only to pre-selected organizations.
Officers and Directors:* David Jones,* Pres.; James Kelly,* V.P.; Doug Kuelpman,* Secy.-Treas.; Dan Lacy.
EIN: 611208482

48020
TWM Foundation
1589 Oakleaf Ln.
Pittsburgh, PA 15237

Established in 2000 in PA.
Financial data (yr. ended 06/30/01): Grants paid, $8,375; assets, $40,397 (M); expenditures, $10,625; qualifying distributions, $8,375.
Limitations: Applications not accepted.
Application information: Contributes only to pre-selected organizations.
Directors: Anna M. Hosack, Leslie M. Hosack.
EIN: 251867443

48021
Perelman Foundation
26 E. Washington St.
New Castle, PA 16101-3810

Financial data (yr. ended 04/30/02): Grants paid, $8,360; assets, $121,074 (M); gifts received, $6,000; expenditures, $9,613; qualifying distributions, $8,360.
Limitations: Applications not accepted. Giving primarily in New Castle, PA.
Officers: Dale Perelman, Pres.; Lawrence Perelman, V.P. and Secy.-Treas.
Director: Mark Perelman.
EIN: 256041019

48022
The James C. and Margaret W. Pontious Foundation, Inc.
105 Bella Vista Dr.
Murrysville, PA 15668 (412) 825-1114
Contact: James C. Pontious

Established in 1996 in PA.
Donor(s): Karlanco.
Financial data (yr. ended 12/31/01): Grants paid, $8,320; assets, $155,068 (M); expenditures, $10,613; qualifying distributions, $8,320.
Directors: James C. Pontious, Jr., Karen D. Pontious, Margaret W. Pontious, Deborah J. Sloat.
EIN: 232870268

48023
Bennington Foundation, Inc.
c/o Kenneth M. Wasserman
P.O. Box 2256
Pittsburgh, PA 15230-2256

Financial data (yr. ended 09/30/01): Grants paid, $8,311; assets, $261,998 (M); expenditures, $29,371; qualifying distributions, $8,311.
Limitations: Applications not accepted. Giving on a national basis, with emphasis on FL.
Application information: Contributes only to pre-selected organizations.
Officers: Richard P. Shapera, Pres.; Marilyn Shapera, Secy.-Treas.
Directors: Gerald Levine, Todd Levitt.
EIN: 251335649

48024
James Armstrong, Jr. and Rachel Armstrong Trust
c/o First Commonwealth Trust Co.
111 S. Main St.
Greensburg, PA 15601 (724) 832-6061

Donor(s): James Armstrong, Jr.,‡ Rachel Armstrong.‡
Financial data (yr. ended 12/31/01): Grants paid, $8,300; assets, $148,595 (M); expenditures, $10,286; qualifying distributions, $8,263.
Limitations: Giving limited to Greensburg, PA.
Application information: Application form not required.
Trustee: First Commonwealth Trust Co.
EIN: 256021415

48025
The Stancato Family Foundation
c/o LDP, Inc.
P.O. Box 0
Hazleton, PA 18201

Established in 1994 in PA.
Donor(s): Frank P. Stancato.‡
Financial data (yr. ended 08/31/00): Grants paid, $8,250; assets, $160,828 (M); expenditures, $10,661; qualifying distributions, $8,250.
Limitations: Applications not accepted. Giving primarily in West Hazleton, PA.
Application information: Contributes only to pre-selected organizations.
Directors: Judith Matriccino, Frank Stancato, Jr., Nancy A. Stancato.
EIN: 237741420

48026
Arthur B. and Marion V. Myers Trust f/b/o Dr. Ajani's Research Fund
c/o Allfirst, Trust Div.
21 E. Market St., M/C 402-130
York, PA 17401-1500

Established in 2000 in PA.
Financial data (yr. ended 12/31/01): Grants paid, $8,215; assets, $149,910 (M); expenditures, $14,073; qualifying distributions, $8,215.
Limitations: Applications not accepted.
Application information: Contributes only to pre-selected organizations.
Trustee: Allfirst.
EIN: 256480499

48027
Lewis & Mary Matilda Howard Memorial Trust
21 E. Market St., M/C 402-130
York, PA 17401-1500

Established in 2000 in PA.
Financial data (yr. ended 12/31/01): Grants paid, $8,186; assets, $138,482 (M); expenditures, $10,727; qualifying distributions, $8,186.
Limitations: Applications not accepted.
Application information: Contributes only to pre-selected organizations.
Trustee: Allfirst.
EIN: 256429229

48028
Gary Rosenau Foundation
c/o Fran Connell
1100 Shade Land Ave.
Drexel Hill, PA 19026-1915

Financial data (yr. ended 12/31/01): Grants paid, $8,175; assets, $18,149 (M); gifts received, $10,000; expenditures, $9,137; qualifying distributions, $8,175.
Limitations: Applications not accepted.
Application information: Contributes only to pre-selected organizations.
Officer and Trustee:* Gary Rosenau,* Mgr.
EIN: 236251892

48029
The Warrell Corporation
(Formerly The Pennsylvania Dutch Company Foundation)
366 Belvedere St.
Carlisle, PA 17013

Established in 1976.
Donor(s): Pennsylvania Dutch Co., Inc., Jonas E. Warrell, The Warrell Corporation.
Financial data (yr. ended 10/31/01): Grants paid, $8,150; assets, $1,327 (M); gifts received, $9,000; expenditures, $8,968; qualifying distributions, $8,150.
Limitations: Applications not accepted. Giving primarily in PA.
Application information: Contributes only to pre-selected organizations.
Officer: Lincoln A. Warrell, Mgr.
EIN: 232022526
Codes: CS, CD

48030
Matilda P. Herbst Trust
21 E. Market St., M/C 402-130
York, PA 17401-1500

Established in 2000 in PA.
Financial data (yr. ended 12/31/00): Grants paid, $8,141; assets, $323,348 (M); expenditures, $10,374; qualifying distributions, $8,141.
Limitations: Applications not accepted. Giving primarily in PA.
Application information: Contributes only to pre-selected organizations.
Trustee: Allfirst.
EIN: 236694431

48031
Jacob Aronson Charitable Trust
c/o PNC Advisors
620 Liberty Ave., P2-PTPP-10-2
Pittsburgh, PA 15222-2705
Application address: c/o United Jewish Federation, 224 McKee Pl., Pittsburgh, PA 15213

Financial data (yr. ended 12/31/00): Grants paid, $8,050; assets, $160,909 (M); expenditures, $8,938; qualifying distributions, $8,080.
Limitations: Giving limited to residents of PA.

Trustee: PNC Bank, N.A.
EIN: 256215150

48032
Howard J. and Emily J. Bromberg Family Foundation
232 Sheryl Ln.
Pittsburgh, PA 15221

Established in 1998 in PA.
Donor(s): Howard J. Bromberg, Emily J. Bromberg.
Financial data (yr. ended 12/31/00): Grants paid, $8,050; assets, $209,633 (M); expenditures, $11,109; qualifying distributions, $8,050.
Limitations: Giving primarily in PA.
Directors: Emily J. Bromberg, Howard J. Bromberg.
EIN: 237957240

48033
Shelton H. Short, Jr. Trust
c/o First Union National Bank
123 S. Broad St.
Philadelphia, PA 19109-9989

Financial data (yr. ended 12/31/99): Grants paid, $8,050; assets, $1,479,474 (M); expenditures, $14,364; qualifying distributions, $8,050.
Trustee: First Union National Bank.
EIN: 546140127

48034
The Jim Conner Foundation
1030 State St.
Erie, PA 16501
Contact: William B. Conner, Pres.

Donor(s): Robinson-Conner, Inc.
Financial data (yr. ended 06/30/99): Grants paid, $8,025; assets, $253,416 (M); expenditures, $9,566; qualifying distributions, $9,566.
Limitations: Giving limited to Erie, PA.
Application information: Applications are presented by McDowell High School. Application form not required.
Officers: William B. Conner, Pres.; Barbara W. Conner, Secy.-Treas.
Trustee: Daniel Miller.
EIN: 251320114

48035
Sweetgum Foundation, Inc.
2203 Almanack Ct.
Pittsburgh, PA 15237 (412) 630-8060
Application address: 100 Saybrook Harbor, Bradford Woods, PA 15015, tel.: (724) 935-0692
Contact: Carolyn S. Johnson, Pres.

Established in 1998 in PA.
Donor(s): Carolyn S. Johnson.
Financial data (yr. ended 12/31/01): Grants paid, $8,025; assets, $179,460 (M); expenditures, $9,993; qualifying distributions, $7,711.
Limitations: Giving primarily in Pittsburgh, PA.
Officer and Directors:* Carolyn S. Johnson,* Pres. and Secy.-Treas.; Leah G. Ross, Thad Spreg.
EIN: 251813172

48036
William & Frances Aloe Charitable Foundation
200 Neville Rd.
Neville Island, PA 15225
Contact: Daniel Aloe, Dir.

Established in 1986 in PA.
Donor(s): Andrew Aloe, Daniel Aloe, Frances Aloe, Joseph Aloe.
Financial data (yr. ended 12/31/01): Grants paid, $8,000; assets, $336,887 (M); expenditures, $9,347; qualifying distributions, $8,000.
Application information: Application form not required.

Officers: Frances Aloe, Pres.; Andrew Aloe, Secy.-Treas.
Directors: Daniel Aloe, David Aloe, Joseph Aloe, Mark Aloe, Kathryn Aloe Cashman.
EIN: 251540814

48037
The Robert T. Hanley Foundation, Inc.
c/o Robert T. Hanley
100 Stover Park Rd.
Pipersville, PA 18947

Established in 1998 in PA.
Donor(s): Robert T. Hanley.
Financial data (yr. ended 11/30/01): Grants paid, $8,000; assets, $440,977 (M); gifts received, $296,312; expenditures, $10,972; qualifying distributions, $8,000.
Limitations: Applications not accepted.
Application information: Contributes only to pre-selected organizations.
Officers and Directors:* Robert T. Hanley,* Pres.; Kevin M. Hanley,* V.P.; Catherine A. Comerford,* Secy.; Mary E. Gleason,* Treas.
EIN: 232985597

48038
J.D. Charitable Trust
c/o PNC Advisors
620 Liberty Ave., P2-PTPP-10-2
Pittsburgh, PA 15222-2705
Application address: c/o W. David Kerr, 13 Deer Path, P.O. Box 225, Farmington, PA 15437

Financial data (yr. ended 09/30/01): Grants paid, $8,000; assets, $326,872 (M); expenditures, $11,276; qualifying distributions, $8,595.
Limitations: Giving primarily in Uniontown, PA.
Application information: Application form not required.
Trustee: PNC Bank, N.A.
EIN: 256026556

48039
Hoffman Mills Scholarship Fund, Inc.
35 Springhouse Rd.
P.O. Box 330
Shippensburg, PA 17257-0330
Application address: Ralma Fry, Lloyd Heller or Thomas Moriarty, c/o Hoffman Mills, Inc., 120 N. Seneca St., Shippensburg, PA 17257

Established in 1998 in PA.
Donor(s): A. Heuberger, Interior by Priscilla, J. Don Frail.
Financial data (yr. ended 12/31/01): Grants paid, $8,000; assets, $42,901 (M); gifts received, $10,582; expenditures, $8,100; qualifying distributions, $8,000.
Limitations: Giving primarily in Shippenburg, PA.
Application information: Application form required.
Officers: Jerry Rohr, Pres.; David Rohr, V.P.; Linda Reed, Secy.; Joseph Leone, Treas.
Directors: Donald Frail, Peter Lahnovych, Louis Massar.
EIN: 251808499
Codes: CS

48040
Julia Moran Trust
c/o Fulton Financial Advisors, N.A.
P.O. Box 3215
Lancaster, PA 17604-3215
Application address: Edward Moore, c/o Temple Univ., 3223 N. Broad St., Philadelphia, PA 19140

Financial data (yr. ended 12/31/00): Grants paid, $8,000; assets, $543,003 (M); expenditures, $13,941; qualifying distributions, $8,007.

Limitations: Giving primarily in PA.
Application information: Application form required.
Trustee: Fulton Financial Advisors, N.A.
EIN: 236642828
Codes: GTI

48041
Smith Memorial Scholarship Fund
(Formerly Patrick M. and Janet T. Smith Scholarship Fund)
c/o Patrick M. Smith, Jr.
5760 Michael Dr.
Bensalem, PA 19020

Established in 1994 in PA.
Donor(s): Patrick M. Smith, Anthony Smith, Teresa M. Ball, Michael Smith.
Financial data (yr. ended 06/30/01): Grants paid, $8,000; assets, $56,671 (M); gifts received, $20,030; expenditures, $18,410; qualifying distributions, $18,378.
Limitations: Applications not accepted. Giving primarily in Philadelphia, PA.
Officers: Patrick M. Smith, Jr., Pres.; Anthony Smith, V.P.; Michael Smith, Secy.; Teresa M. Smith-Ball, Treas.
Directors: Julia Barnle, Martin Kahnmanian, Donna Mannucci, D. Stephen Sharp, Martin Walsh.
EIN: 232791619

48042
Wesel Foundation
1141 N. Washington Ave.
Scranton, PA 18509-2719

Financial data (yr. ended 12/31/01): Grants paid, $7,900; assets, $170,833 (M); expenditures, $8,029; qualifying distributions, $7,900.
Limitations: Applications not accepted. Giving primarily in PA.
Application information: Contributes only to pre-selected organizations.
Officers: John R. Thomas, Pres.; William I. Pentecost, Secy.; Russell A. Cammer, Treas.
EIN: 236413635

48043
N. Robert Moore Charitable Scholarship Trust
c/o S & T Bank
P.O. Box 247
DuBois, PA 15801-0247
Contact: Dorothy Mattern

Established in 1996 in PA.
Financial data (yr. ended 12/31/00): Grants paid, $7,875; assets, $233,580 (M); expenditures, $10,177; qualifying distributions, $8,215.
Limitations: Giving limited to the DuBois, PA, area.
Application information: Application form required.
Trustee: S & T Bank.
EIN: 251802886

48044
Adrian M. and Doris K. Pearsall Family Foundation, Inc.
1950 Englewood Ave.
Forty Fort, PA 18704

Established in 1998 in PA.
Donor(s): Adrian M. Pearsall, Doris K. Pearsall.
Financial data (yr. ended 12/31/01): Grants paid, $7,755; assets, $787,235 (M); expenditures, $14,898; qualifying distributions, $7,755.
Limitations: Applications not accepted. Giving primarily in PA.
Application information: Contributes only to pre-selected organizations.

Officers: Adrian M. Pearsall, Pres.; Doris K. Pearsall, V.P.; Kenneth Krogulski, Secy.-Treas.
EIN: 232963241

48045
Redner Foundation
3 Quarry Rd.
Reading, PA 19605

Established in 1989 in PA.
Donor(s): Redner's Markets, Inc., Gordon B. Hoch, members of the Redner family.
Financial data (yr. ended 12/31/00): Grants paid, $7,750; assets, $5,063 (M); gifts received, $6,000; expenditures, $7,750; qualifying distributions, $8,275.
Limitations: Applications not accepted. Giving limited to PA, with emphasis on Reading.
Application information: Contributes only to pre-selected organizations.
Officer: Roger Pasquale, Mgr.
Trustees: Gordon B. Hoch, Chere R. Kelly, Earl W. Redner, Gary W. Redner, Mary G. Redner, Richard E. Redner, Kevin J. Snyder.
EIN: 232527369
Codes: CS, CD

48046
Milewski Family Scholarship Fund
(Formerly P. Milewski Scholarship Fund)
c/o Mellon Bank, N.A.
P.O. Box 7236
Philadelphia, PA 19101-7236

Established in 1995 in PA.
Donor(s): Paulibe R. Milewski.
Financial data (yr. ended 01/31/02): Grants paid, $7,701; assets, $154,121 (M); expenditures, $9,542; qualifying distributions, $7,701.
Limitations: Applications not accepted. Giving limited to Wilkes-Barre, PA.
Application information: Contributes only to pre-selected organizations.
Trustee: Mellon Bank, N.A.
EIN: 256490164

48047
George & Rosalia Lesnick Fund
21 S. 12th St., Ste. 401
Philadelphia, PA 19107 (215) 564-2466
Contact: George M. Farion, Tr.

Financial data (yr. ended 12/31/01): Grants paid, $7,700; assets, $164,085 (M); expenditures, $9,216; qualifying distributions, $7,700.
Trustees: Natalka Danylenko, George M. Farion, Dmytro Tkachuk.
EIN: 236673331

48048
T. R. Paul Charitable Trust
800 Martha St.
Munhall, PA 15120

Financial data (yr. ended 12/31/01): Grants paid, $7,620; assets, $155,352 (M); expenditures, $9,365; qualifying distributions, $7,620.
Limitations: Applications not accepted. Giving primarily in Pittsburgh, PA.
Application information: Contributes only to pre-selected organizations.
Trustees: Theodore H. Paul, Ellen B. Winston.
EIN: 251451235

48049
Vincent E. and Louise K. Huether Charitable Trust
Broad and Walnut St., Ste. PA1308
Philadelphia, PA 19109

Financial data (yr. ended 03/31/00): Grants paid, $7,609; assets, $200,000 (M); gifts received, $200,000; expenditures, $9,578; qualifying distributions, $7,609.
Limitations: Applications not accepted.
Application information: Contributes only to pre-selected organizations.
Trustee: First Union National Bank.
EIN: 256626970

48050
Gottlieb Family Foundation
1434 County Line Rd.
Huntingdon Valley, PA 19006 (215) 322-1800
Contact: Samuel Gottlieb, Tr.

Established in 1986 in PA.
Donor(s): Samuel Gottlieb, Bernard Gottlieb.
Financial data (yr. ended 11/30/01): Grants paid, $7,600; assets, $227,576 (M); gifts received, $3,000; expenditures, $8,157; qualifying distributions, $7,600.
Limitations: Giving primarily in PA.
Application information: Individuals should submit a brief resume of academic qualifications for research grant. Application form not required.
Trustees: Bernard Gottlieb, Samuel Gottlieb.
EIN: 236870692

48051
Nellie E. Leighow Scholarship Fund
c/o Northumberland National Bank
245 Front St.
Northumberland, PA 17857
Contact: Stephen A. Hafer, Trust Off., Northumberland National Bank

Established in 1992.
Financial data (yr. ended 12/31/00): Grants paid, $7,600; assets, $143,469 (M); expenditures, $8,555; qualifying distributions, $7,556.
Limitations: Giving primarily in PA.
Application information: Application form not required.
Trustee: Northumberland National Bank.
EIN: 237692684
Codes: GTI

48052
Mattleman Family Foundation
2226 Land Title Bldg.
Philadelphia, PA 19110

Established in 1996 in PA.
Donor(s): Herman Mattleman.
Financial data (yr. ended 11/30/01): Grants paid, $7,600; assets, $90,868 (M); expenditures, $7,672; qualifying distributions, $7,600.
Limitations: Applications not accepted.
Application information: Contributes only to pre-selected organizations.
Officer and Trustee:* Herman Mattleman,* Pres.
EIN: 232871138

48053
Montgomery County Medical Society Foundation
1529 Dekalb St.
Norristown, PA 19401-3498 (610) 277-3690
Contact: Frank J. Tornetta, Co-Chair.

Financial data (yr. ended 12/31/01): Grants paid, $7,600; assets, $130,832 (M); expenditures, $9,048; qualifying distributions, $7,600.
Limitations: Giving limited to Montgomery County, PA.
Officers: H. Tom Tamaki, Co-Chair.; Frank J. Tornetta, Co-Chair.
EIN: 236291381

48054
The Auman Family Foundation
1968 Meadow Ln.
Wyomissing, PA 19610

Established in 1997 in PA.
Donor(s): Theodore C. Auman III.
Financial data (yr. ended 06/30/02): Grants paid, $7,500; assets, $45,442 (M); expenditures, $10,600; qualifying distributions, $7,500.
Limitations: Applications not accepted. Giving primarily in PA.
Application information: Contributes only to pre-selected organizations.
Trustee: Theodore C. Auman III.
EIN: 232927126

48055
Bloomsburg Area Community Foundation
Town Hall
301 E. Main St.
Bloomsburg, PA 17815

Financial data (yr. ended 12/31/00): Grants paid, $7,500; assets, $266,626 (M); gifts received, $500; expenditures, $11,023.
Limitations: Applications not accepted. Giving primarily in Bloomsburg, PA.
Application information: Contributes only to pre-selected organizations.
Officers: Elwood Harding, Jr., Pres.; Paul E. Reichart, V.P.; Linda Bailey, Secy.; John Thompson, Treas.
Directors: Ed Edwards, Donna Kreisher, Mary Lenzini-Howe, Rev. Marjorie Mewaul, Isabell Tarr.
EIN: 232843673
Codes: CM

48056
Lamb Foundation
c/o J. Iskrant
1600 Market St., Ste. 3600
Philadelphia, PA 19103-4247
Application address: 2408 Vintage Hill Dr., Durham, NC 27712, tel.: (919) 477-5480
Contact: George C. Lamb, Jr., Tr.

Established in 1985 in PA.
Donor(s): George C. Lamb, Jr.
Financial data (yr. ended 11/30/01): Grants paid, $7,500; assets, $165,597 (M); expenditures, $12,872; qualifying distributions, $10,500.
Limitations: Giving primarily in Dallas, TX.
Application information: Application form not required.
Trustees: Elizabeth B. Lamb, George C. Lamb, Jr., George C. Lamb III, Margaret Lamb, Melissa M. Lamb, William R. Lamb, Carl W. Solly, Claire S.L. Solly.
EIN: 222768469

48057
The Light Charitable Trust
615 Creek Ln.
Flourtown, PA 19031

Donor(s): Mun R. Chung, Byung T. Hwang, Chang K. Suh, Yong S. Kim, Yoo Sup Choi.
Financial data (yr. ended 12/31/01): Grants paid, $7,500; assets, $92,430 (M); gifts received, $10,800; expenditures, $7,808; qualifying distributions, $7,500.
Limitations: Applications not accepted.
Application information: Contributes only to pre-selected organizations.
Officers: Mun R. Chung, Pres.; Byung Tak Hwang, Secy.; Eun Ja Chung, Treas.
EIN: 232522063

48058
Frank L. Marcon Foundation
c/o First Union National Bank
P.O. Box 7558
Philadelphia, PA 19101-7558

Financial data (yr. ended 12/31/99): Grants paid, $7,500; assets, $87,883 (M); expenditures, $9,085; qualifying distributions, $7,500.
Limitations: Applications not accepted. Giving primarily in Center Valley, PA.
Application information: Contributes only to pre-selected organizations.
Trustee: First Union National Bank.
EIN: 236296888

48059
The Winokur Family Foundation
40 Trent Rd.
Wynnewood, PA 19096-3707 (610) 642-1794
Contact: Irving Winokur, Pres.

Established in 2000 in PA.
Donor(s): Irving Winokur, Helen Winokur.
Financial data (yr. ended 12/31/01): Grants paid, $7,487; assets, $146,434 (M); gifts received, $37,500; expenditures, $9,718; qualifying distributions, $7,487.
Limitations: Giving primarily in NY and PA.
Officers: Irving Winokur, Pres.; Helen Winokur, Secy.-Treas.
EIN: 232802717

48060
Howard J. & Ruth H. Sheen Scholarship Fund
c/o PNC Advisors
P.O. Box 8480
Erie, PA 16553
Application address: c/o Michael L. Stahlman, Principal, Corry Area High School, 534 E. Pleasant St., Corry, PA 16407

Financial data (yr. ended 12/31/01): Grants paid, $7,474; assets, $151,960 (M); expenditures, $7,768; qualifying distributions, $7,474.
Limitations: Giving limited to residents of Corry, PA.
Application information: Application form required.
Trustee: PNC Bank, N.A.
EIN: 256257707
Codes: GTI

48061
Ned & Marcia Kaplin Foundation
70 Portland Rd.
West Conshohocken, PA 19428

Established in 2000 in PA.
Donor(s): Marcia Kaplin, Ned Kaplin.
Financial data (yr. ended 12/31/01): Grants paid, $7,400; assets, $91,854 (M); expenditures, $7,581; qualifying distributions, $7,400.
Limitations: Giving primarily in Philadelphia, PA.
Director: Ned Kaplin.
EIN: 256677269

48062
Alfred O. Breinig Foundation
c/o First Union National Bank
Broad & Walnut Sts., Ste. 1308
Philadelphia, PA 19109
Application address: c/o Alfred O. Breinig, 801 Duchess Condo, 220 S. Collier Blvd., Narcotela, FL 33155

Established in 1956 in PA.
Donor(s): Alfred O. Breinig.
Financial data (yr. ended 12/31/99): Grants paid, $7,325; assets, $200,689 (M); expenditures, $8,767; qualifying distributions, $7,404.

Limitations: Giving primarily in FL and PA.
Application information: Application form not required.
Trustee: First Union National Bank.
EIN: 236228065

48063
Lulu A. Pool Trust
c/o First Commonwealth Trust Co.
111 S. Main St.
Greensburg, PA 15601 (724) 834-2310

Financial data (yr. ended 12/31/01): Grants paid, $7,255; assets, $168,127 (M); expenditures, $9,467; qualifying distributions, $7,186.
Limitations: Giving limited to central Westmoreland County, PA.
Trustee: First Commonwealth Trust Co.
EIN: 256185275

48064
Dolly & George Martz Scholarship Fund
c/o Fulton Financial Advisors, N.A.
P.O. Box 3215
Lancaster, PA 17604-3215
Application address: Harry Heath, Trust Off., c/o Fulton Financial Advisors, N.A., P.O. Box 4887, Lancaster, PA 17604

Established in 1989 in PA.
Financial data (yr. ended 12/31/00): Grants paid, $7,250; assets, $132,587 (M); expenditures, $9,777; qualifying distributions, $7,142.
Limitations: Giving primarily to residents of PA.
Application information: Application form required.
Trustee: Fulton Financial Advisors, N.A.
EIN: 236696968

48065
The Tillow Fund
763 Merchant St.
Ambridge, PA 15003
Application address: 120 W. 74th St., Ste. 3R, New York, NY 10023, tel.: (212) 874-8560
Contact: Walter Tillow, Tr.

Financial data (yr. ended 12/31/01): Grants paid, $7,250; assets, $174,770 (M); expenditures, $8,572; qualifying distributions, $7,250.
Limitations: Giving primarily in NJ, NY, and PA.
Officers and Trustees:* Madeline Arnstein,* Admin.; Walter Tillow,* Admin.
EIN: 251412363

48066
The Matthews Fund
33 Wistar Rd.
Paoli, PA 19301

Established in 1992 in PA.
Donor(s): James G. Matthews.
Financial data (yr. ended 12/31/01): Grants paid, $7,221; assets, $80,030 (M); expenditures, $9,115; qualifying distributions, $7,221.
Limitations: Applications not accepted. Giving primarily in PA.
Application information: Contributes only to pre-selected organizations.
Trustees: F. Claire Hughes, Jr., Josephine R. Matthews.
EIN: 226551198

48067
Richard P. Kahn Foundation
1515 Locust St., Ste. 301
Philadelphia, PA 19102 (215) 546-1500
Contact: Richard P. Kahn, Pres.

Established in 1996 in PA.
Donor(s): Richard P. Kahn.

Financial data (yr. ended 11/30/01): Grants paid, $7,200; assets, $112,809 (M); expenditures, $7,558; qualifying distributions, $7,509.
Limitations: Giving primarily in FL and PA.
Officer and Directors:* Richard P. Kahn,* Pres. and Treas.; Charles Kahn, Jr., Todd C. Vanett.
EIN: 232440216

48068
The Judy & Frank Campbell Foundation, Inc.
c/o Siana Carr & O'Connor, LLP
1500 E. Lancaster Ave.
Paoli, PA 19301

Established in 1997 in PA.
Donor(s): Frank J. Campbell III.
Financial data (yr. ended 12/31/01): Grants paid, $7,175; assets, $90,403 (M); expenditures, $8,889; qualifying distributions, $7,918.
Limitations: Applications not accepted.
Application information: Contributes only to pre-selected organizations.
Officers: Frank J. Campbell III, Pres.; Judith W. Campbell, Secy.-Treas.
EIN: 232941026

48069
David and Emily Adler Foundation
c/o David Adler
First and Miles Sts.
Old Forge, PA 18518

Established in 1999 in PA.
Donor(s): David H. Adler, Emily Adler.
Financial data (yr. ended 11/30/01): Grants paid, $7,100; assets, $81,162 (M); gifts received, $20,000; expenditures, $7,827; qualifying distributions, $7,100.
Limitations: Applications not accepted.
Application information: Contributes only to pre-selected organizations.
Trustees: David H. Adler, Emily Adler, Jonathan Adler, Candance Adler, Robert Adler, Earl Helbing.
EIN: 236682643

48070
The RG Charitable Foundation
258 W. Market St.
P.O. Box 2824
York, PA 17405

Established in 1989 in PA.
Donor(s): RG Industries, Inc., Die-A-Matic, Inc.
Financial data (yr. ended 01/31/02): Grants paid, $7,050; assets, $77 (M); gifts received, $5,500; expenditures, $7,722; qualifying distributions, $7,722.
Limitations: Applications not accepted. Giving primarily in York, PA.
Application information: Contributes only to pre-selected organizations.
Trustees: Randall A. Gross, Gregory Plitt.
EIN: 232589813
Codes: CS, CD

48071
Bucks County Medical Society Foundation
c/o PNC Advisors
620 Liberty Ave., P2-PTPP-10-2
Pittsburgh, PA 15222-2705

Established in 1991 in PA.
Financial data (yr. ended 12/31/01): Grants paid, $7,030; assets, $182,504 (M); expenditures, $8,356; qualifying distributions, $7,030.
Limitations: Applications not accepted. Giving primarily in PA.
Application information: Contributes only to pre-selected organizations.
Trustee: PNC Bank, N.A.
EIN: 236563688

48072—PENNSYLVANIA

48072
The Irene and Kenneth Campbell Foundation
1419 Lanes End
Villanova, PA 19085

Established in 1999 in PA.
Donor(s): Irene A. Campbell, Kenneth D. Campbell.
Financial data (yr. ended 12/31/01): Grants paid, $7,000; assets, $49,819 (M); gifts received, $27,000; expenditures, $10,420; qualifying distributions, $7,000.
Limitations: Applications not accepted. Giving on a national and international basis.
Application information: Contributes only to pre-selected organizations.
Officers: Kenneth D. Campbell, Pres. and Secy.; Irene A. Campbell, V.P. and Treas.
EIN: 232984301

48073
The Commons Family Charitable Trust
c/o Previte J. Dennis
109 Bigler Ave.
Spangler, PA 15775

Established around 1995.
Financial data (yr. ended 12/31/01): Grants paid, $7,000; assets, $143,024 (M); expenditures, $10,389; qualifying distributions, $7,000.
Limitations: Applications not accepted.
Application information: Contributes only to pre-selected organizations.
Trustees: Fred J. Gibbons, Wendale H. Routch, Mark E. Thomas, Promistar Trust Co.
EIN: 256448419

48074
Nathan and Harry Daly Scholarship Fund
c/o Mellon Bank, N.A.
P.O. Box 185
Pittsburgh, PA 15230-9897
Application address: 3 Mellon Bank Ctr., Pittsburgh, PA 15259
Contact: Laurie Moritz, Trust Off., Mellon Bank, N.A.

Financial data (yr. ended 12/31/99): Grants paid, $7,000; assets, $163,617 (M); expenditures, $9,631; qualifying distributions, $7,786.
Limitations: Giving limited to residents of Butler County, PA.
Application information: Application form required.
Trustee: Mellon Bank, N.A.
EIN: 256082584

48075
Wrenn Dietzel Charitable Foundation
c/o PNC Advisors
620 Liberty Ave., P2-PTPP-10-2
Pittsburgh, PA 15222-2705

Established in 2000 in PA.
Donor(s): Kathryn Wrenn Trust.
Financial data (yr. ended 12/31/01): Grants paid, $7,000; assets, $1,677,925 (M); gifts received, $962,884; expenditures, $8,567; qualifying distributions, $6,861.
Limitations: Applications not accepted. Giving primarily in Pittsburgh, PA.
Application information: Contributes only to pre-selected organizations.
Trustee: PNC Bank, N.A.
EIN: 256730328

48076
Marie Ambrose Levitz Scholarship Fund
c/o Fulton Financial Advisors, N.A.
P.O. Box 3215
Lancaster, PA 17604-3215
Application address: Scholarship Selection Comm., c/o Fulton Financial Advisors, N.A., P.O. Box 448, Lebanon, PA 17042-0448

Established in 1999 in PA.
Donor(s): Marie A. Levitz.
Financial data (yr. ended 08/31/01): Grants paid, $7,000; assets, $101,798 (M); expenditures, $8,857; qualifying distributions, $6,907.
Limitations: Giving limted to residents of Lebanon County, PA.
Application information: Application form required.
Trustee: Fulton Financial Advisors, N.A.
EIN: 256681537

48077
B. B. McGinnis Scholarship Fund
601 Grant St., Ste. 350
Pittsburgh, PA 15219-4478   (412) 281-2738
Contact: Raymond W. Cromer, Tr.

Financial data (yr. ended 12/31/00): Grants paid, $7,000; assets, $59,959 (M); expenditures, $11,728; qualifying distributions, $10,626.
Limitations: Giving limited to Allegheny County, PA.
Application information: Application form required.
Trustee: Raymond W. Cromer.
EIN: 237272629

48078
The Wice Foundation
1901 Walnut St., Apt. 1201
Philadelphia, PA 19103

Established in 1996 in PA.
Donor(s): Betsy W. Wice, David H. Wice.
Financial data (yr. ended 12/31/01): Grants paid, $7,000; assets, $119,413 (M); expenditures, $7,927; qualifying distributions, $7,000.
Limitations: Applications not accepted.
Application information: Contributes only to pre-selected organizations.
Officers: Betsy W. Wice, Pres. and Secy.; David H. Wice, V.P. and Treas.
EIN: 232867659

48079
The Lambert Foundation, Inc.
1027 Valley Forge Rd., Ste. 357
Devon, PA 19333-1105   (610) 293-9283
Contact: David B. Lambert, Pres.

Established in 1993.
Donor(s): David B. Lambert.
Financial data (yr. ended 12/31/01): Grants paid, $6,974; assets, $213,721 (M); gifts received, $37,170; expenditures, $7,064; qualifying distributions, $6,974.
Limitations: Giving primarily in Philadelphia, PA.
Officer: David B. Lambert, Pres.
EIN: 232742907

48080
H. A. William Trust for Battenberg
c/o PNC Advisors
620 Liberty Ave., P2-PTPP-10-2
Pittsburgh, PA 15222-2705
Application address: c/o Alexander J. Chelik, Secondary Principal, Lakeland High School, RD No. 1, Jermyn, PA 18433

Donor(s): H.A. Willman.‡

Financial data (yr. ended 12/31/01): Grants paid, $6,967; assets, $66,934 (M); expenditures, $8,664; qualifying distributions, $7,353.
Limitations: Giving limited to residents of Jermyn, PA.
Trustee: PNC Bank, N.A.
EIN: 246021745

48081
H. Clark Witman Trust
21 E. Market St., M/C 402-130
York, PA 17401-1500

Established in 2000 in PA.
Financial data (yr. ended 12/31/01): Grants paid, $6,960; assets, $143,231 (M); expenditures, $10,967; qualifying distributions, $6,960.
Limitations: Applications not accepted. Giving primarily in Reading, PA.
Application information: Contributes only to pre-selected organizations.
Trustee: Allfirst.
EIN: 236633341

48082
John W. Jenks Memorial Foundation
c/o David A. Smith, C.P.A.
327 N. Main St.
Punxsutawney, PA 15767-1234
Application address: North Jefferson St., Punxsutawney, PA 15767
Contact: Richard W. Fait, Tr.

Donor(s): Katherine L. Rodgers.‡
Financial data (yr. ended 12/31/00): Grants paid, $6,950; assets, $179,741 (M); expenditures, $7,100; qualifying distributions, $6,950.
Limitations: Giving primarily in Punxsutawney, PA.
Application information: Application form required.
Trustees: Robert Barrett, Ted E. Bish, Richard W. Fait, John Hunger, Paul B. Johnston, David A. Smith, Edwin L. Snyder.
EIN: 256065932

48083
Norman Raab Foundation
P.O. Box 657
Holicong, PA 18928-0657
Contact: Stephen Raab, Tr.

Donor(s): Norman Raab, Stephen Raab, Whitney Raab.
Financial data (yr. ended 09/30/01): Grants paid, $6,945; assets, $145,835 (M); expenditures, $6,982; qualifying distributions, $6,945.
Limitations: Giving primarily in FL, MD, and PA.
Trustees: Norman Raab, Stephen Raab, Whitney Raab.
EIN: 237006390

48084
G. D. & Mary J. Krumrine Foundation
c/o Omega Bank, N.A.
P.O. Box 298
State College, PA 16804-0298

Financial data (yr. ended 12/31/01): Grants paid, $6,861; assets, $187,980 (M); expenditures, $9,218; qualifying distributions, $6,861.
Limitations: Giving primarily in PA.
Application information: Application form not required.
Trustees: Anne Krumrine, Mary Louise Krumrine, Omega Bank, N.A.
EIN: 246019043

48085
Frances M. Sayers Trust f/b/o William Sayers Memorial Fund
c/o PNC Advisors
620 Liberty Ave., P2-PTPP-10-2
Pittsburgh, PA 15222-2705 (412) 768-9833
Contact: Christine Seidling, Trust Off., PNC Advisors

Financial data (yr. ended 09/30/01): Grants paid, $6,800; assets, $112,506 (M); expenditures, $9,289; qualifying distributions, $7,386.
Limitations: Giving primarily in the Cincinnati, OH, area.
Trustee: PNC Bank, N.A.
EIN: 316018064

48086
D. Lyda Rouzer Foundation
P.O. Box 299
Biglerville, PA 17307
Application address: 322 Gettys St., Gettysburg, PA 17325, tel.: (717) 334-1932
Contact: Richard E. Shaffer, Tr.

Financial data (yr. ended 12/31/99): Grants paid, $6,780; assets, $200,810 (M); expenditures, $15,948; qualifying distributions, $21,300; giving activities include $14,016 for programs.
Limitations: Giving primarily in PA.
Application information: Application form not required.
Trustees: Robert Hartz, Richard E. Shaffer.
EIN: 236396185

48087
The Roger C. Panella Family Charitable Foundation
118 Glover Rd.
New Castle, PA 16105

Established in 1997 in PA.
Donor(s): Roger C. Panella.
Financial data (yr. ended 12/31/01): Grants paid, $6,761; assets, $115,967 (M); expenditures, $6,938; qualifying distributions, $6,761.
Limitations: Applications not accepted.
Application information: Contributes only to pre-selected organizations.
Trustees: Roger C. Panella, Sandra Lou Panella.
EIN: 232881667

48088
Holtz Charitable Foundation
2200 Georgetown Dr., Ste. 401
Sewickley, PA 15143

Established in 1998.
Donor(s): Albert M. Holtz.
Financial data (yr. ended 12/31/01): Grants paid, $6,755; assets, $104,262 (M); expenditures, $6,871; qualifying distributions, $6,755.
Limitations: Applications not accepted.
Application information: Contributes only to pre-selected organizations.
Officer: Edward J. Aufman, Mgr.
Trustees: Albert M. Holtz, Mildred B. Holtz.
EIN: 256577991

48089
W. Marshall Hughes, Jr. Scholarship Foundation
1631 Farr Rd.
Wyomissing, PA 19610
Application address: 122 W. Lancaster Ave., Shillington, PA 19607
Contact: W. Marshall Hughes, Jr., Tr.

Established in 1988 in PA.
Financial data (yr. ended 12/31/01): Grants paid, $6,750; assets, $264,212 (M); expenditures, $12,410; qualifying distributions, $6,750.

Limitations: Giving limited to Berks County, PA.
Application information: Interview and audition required. Application form required.
Trustees: Thomas K. Williams, C. Thomas Work.
EIN: 236934996
Codes: GTI

48090
Reidbord Foundation
5000 Baum Blvd.
Pittsburgh, PA 15213-1849 (412) 687-3000
Contact: Murray S. Reidbord, Dir.

Financial data (yr. ended 12/31/01): Grants paid, $6,700; assets, $137,545 (M); expenditures, $7,603; qualifying distributions, $6,700.
Limitations: Giving primarily in Pittsburgh, PA.
Application information: Application form not required.
Director: Murray S. Reidbord.
EIN: 256079442

48091
Taylor Family Foundation
132 Ivy Ln.
P.O. Box 62407
King of Prussia, PA 19406-0389

Established in 1997 in PA.
Donor(s): Kenneth R. Taylor, Arthur S. Taylor.
Financial data (yr. ended 12/31/01): Grants paid, $6,700; assets, $41,456 (M); expenditures, $7,879; qualifying distributions, $6,700.
Limitations: Applications not accepted.
Application information: Contributes only to pre-selected organizations.
Trustees: Susan E. Bell, Arthur S. Taylor, Cathy I. Taylor.
EIN: 237875149

48092
The Smithfield Township College Assistance Fund
(Formerly Jessie B. Kautz Trust)
c/o Mellon Bank, N.A.
P.O. Box 185
Pittsburgh, PA 15230
Application address: c/o Stephen Carey, United Penn Bank, Trust Div., 8 W. Market St., Wilkes-Barre, PA 18711, tel.: (717) 424-7180

Donor(s): Jessie B. Kautz.‡
Financial data (yr. ended 12/31/01): Grants paid, $6,693; assets, $194,493 (M); expenditures, $9,190; qualifying distributions, $7,406.
Limitations: Giving limited to PA.
Application information: Application form not required.
Trustee: Mellon Bank, N.A.
EIN: 236720230
Codes: GTI

48093
William A. Whittaker Scholarship Trust
c/o M&T Bank
101 W. 3rd St.
Williamsport, PA 17701
Application address: c/o Sharon Fasenmyer or Dean Wilt, 1415 6th Ave., Altoona, PA 16602

Established in 1997 in PA.
Financial data (yr. ended 12/31/99): Grants paid, $6,692; assets, $266,841 (M); expenditures, $10,504; qualifying distributions, $12,365.
Limitations: Giving limited to residents of PA.
Trustee: M&T Bank.
EIN: 237892041

48094
Joseph Y. Moses Foundation, Inc.
2016 W. State St.
New Castle, PA 16101
Contact: James Moses, Pres.

Financial data (yr. ended 12/31/00): Grants paid, $6,675; assets, $123,974 (M); expenditures, $6,902; qualifying distributions, $6,675.
Limitations: Giving primarily in PA.
Application information: Application form not required.
Officers: James Moses, Pres.; Edward Moses, Sr., Secy.; Donald Moses, Treas.
EIN: 251341833

48095
The Richless Foundation
305 Timber Ct.
Pittsburgh, PA 15238
Contact: Connie I. Richless Tr., or Lloyd K. Richless, M.D., Tr., Tr.

Financial data (yr. ended 12/31/01): Grants paid, $6,600; assets, $42,442 (M); gifts received, $3,000; expenditures, $7,782; qualifying distributions, $6,600.
Limitations: Giving limited to PA.
Trustees: Connie L. Richless, Lloyd K. Richless, M.D.
EIN: 251540217

48096
Seligsohn Foundation
1221 Centennial Rd.
Narberth, PA 19072 (610) 664-0151
Contact: Sherwin Seligsohn, Tr.

Donor(s): Sherwin Seligsohn.
Financial data (yr. ended 11/30/00): Grants paid, $6,600; assets, $528,148 (M); expenditures, $18,384; qualifying distributions, $6,600.
Trustee: Sherwin Seligsohn.
EIN: 232267682

48097
Community Scholarship Fund
c/o First Union National Bank
Broad and Walnut Sts., PA1308
Philadelphia, PA 19109
Application address: c/o First Union National Bank of North Carolina, 101 13th St., Columbus, GA 31993

Financial data (yr. ended 12/31/99): Grants paid, $6,567; assets, $219,555 (M); expenditures, $7,807; qualifying distributions, $6,567.
Limitations: Giving limited to Columbus, GA.
Application information: Application form not required.
Trustee: First Union National Bank.
EIN: 586066397

48098
Marie H. Holland Charitable Foundation
c/o Thomas M. Holland
1522 Locust St., Grace Hall
Philadelphia, PA 19102

Established in 2000 in PA.
Donor(s): Thomas M. Holland.
Financial data (yr. ended 12/31/01): Grants paid, $6,500; assets, $29,539 (M); gifts received, $7,938; expenditures, $6,600; qualifying distributions, $6,496.
Limitations: Applications not accepted. Giving primarily in DE.
Application information: Contributes only to pre-selected organizations.
Director: Thomas M. Holland.
EIN: 233055443

48099
Kirkwood Foundation
c/o M. Roy Jackson
546 Street Rd.
West Grove, PA 19390-9005

Financial data (yr. ended 12/31/01): Grants paid, $6,500; assets, $112,628 (M); expenditures, $6,640; qualifying distributions, $6,500.
Limitations: Applications not accepted. Giving primarily in PA.
Application information: Contributes only to pre-selected organizations.
Trustee: M. Roy Jackson.
EIN: 237003365

48100
The Max and Tillie Rosenn Foundation, Inc.
177 James St.
Kingston, PA 18704 (570) 826-6424

Established in 1993 in PA.
Donor(s): Tillie Rosenn,‡ Max Rosenn.
Financial data (yr. ended 12/31/01): Grants paid, $6,500; assets, $215,406 (M); expenditures, $7,341; qualifying distributions, $6,500.
Limitations: Applications not accepted. Giving primarily in Wilkes-Barre, PA.
Application information: Contributes only to pre-selected organizations.
Officers: Max Rosenn, Pres.; Harold Rosenn, V.P.
Trustees: Daniel W. Rosenn, Eva Rosenn, Keith S. Rosenn.
EIN: 232724911

48101
Buzzy Wittmer Scholarship Fund
c/o Fulton Financial Advisors, N.A.
P.O. Box 3215
Lancaster, PA 17604-3215
Application address: c/o Atlee Kepler, 101 Oak Hill Ave., Hagerstown, MD 21742

Financial data (yr. ended 12/31/00): Grants paid, $6,500; assets, $186,282 (M); gifts received, $51,036; expenditures, $8,052; qualifying distributions, $6,714.
Limitations: Giving limited to Washington County, MD.
Application information: Application form required.
Trustee: Fulton Financial Advisors, N.A.
EIN: 521084293

48102
Leon Miller Child Trust
c/o Sovereign Bank
120 S. Centre St.
Pottsville, PA 17901

Financial data (yr. ended 12/31/01): Grants paid, $6,492; assets, $106,928 (M); expenditures, $10,434; qualifying distributions, $6,492.
Limitations: Applications not accepted.
Application information: Contributes only to pre-selected organizations.
Trustee: Sovereign Bank.
EIN: 236232259

48103
The Yampolsky Foundation
1420 Walnut St., Ste. 200
Philadelphia, PA 19102

Established in 1998 in PA.
Donor(s): Jack Yampolsky.
Financial data (yr. ended 12/31/01): Grants paid, $6,485; assets, $138,609 (M); gifts received, $12,000; expenditures, $6,639; qualifying distributions, $6,485.
Limitations: Applications not accepted.

Application information: Contributes only to pre-selected organizations.
Directors: Jack Yampolsky, Judith Yampolsky, Michael Yampolsky, Philip Yampolsky, Robert Yampolsky.
EIN: 232985647

48104
Robert R. Mumma Trust Share No. 2
21 E. Market St., M/C 402-130
York, PA 17401-1500

Established in 2000 in PA.
Financial data (yr. ended 12/31/00): Grants paid, $6,460; assets, $207,428 (M); expenditures, $7,450; qualifying distributions, $7,450.
Limitations: Applications not accepted. Giving primarily in PA.
Application information: Contributes only to pre-selected organizations.
Trustee: Allfirst.
EIN: 256572058

48105
Comisky Family Foundation Trust
1109 Orleans Rd.
Cheltenham, PA 19012

Established in 1994 in PA.
Donor(s): Marvin Comisky, Goldye Comisky.
Financial data (yr. ended 12/31/01): Grants paid, $6,450; assets, $23,013 (M); expenditures, $6,450; qualifying distributions, $6,450.
Limitations: Applications not accepted. Giving primarily in PA.
Application information: Contributes only to pre-selected organizations.
Trustees: Goldye Comisky, Marvin Comisky.
EIN: 237747091

48106
Rabbis Fund of Philadelphia
c/o Wolf Block
1650 Arch St., 22nd Fl.
Philadelphia, PA 19103

Financial data (yr. ended 08/31/02): Grants paid, $6,430; assets, $118,784 (M); gifts received, $2,087; expenditures, $10,290; qualifying distributions, $6,430.
Limitations: Giving primarily in Philadelphia, PA.
Application information: Application form not required.
Officer and Directors:* Rabbi Robert Layman,* Secy.; Alvin Dorsky, Jay L. Goldberg, Rabbi Sanford Hahn, David Pincus, Elizabeth Pincus.
EIN: 232260986

48107
The Serenbetz Charitable Foundation, Inc.
P.O. Box 1127
Newtown, PA 18940-8062

Established in 1997 in PA.
Donor(s): Robert Serenbetz.
Financial data (yr. ended 12/31/01): Grants paid, $6,422; assets, $5,863 (M); gifts received, $7,764; expenditures, $6,665; qualifying distributions, $6,422.
Officer and Directors:* Robert Serenbetz,* Pres.; Gregg Serenbetz, Karen Serenbetz, Kathryn Serenbetz, Todd Serenbetz.
EIN: 232893297

48108
Eichelsbacher Family Trust
c/o PNC Advisors
620 Liberty Ave., P2-PTPP-10-2
Pittsburgh, PA 15222-2705

Financial data (yr. ended 06/30/01): Grants paid, $6,411; assets, $309,873 (M); expenditures, $6,456; qualifying distributions, $6,411.
Limitations: Applications not accepted. Giving primarily in Pittsburgh, PA.
Application information: Contributes only to pre-selected organizations.
Trustee: PNC Bank, N.A.
EIN: 237902868

48109
Starck Foundation
246 Rock School Rd.
Burgettstown, PA 15021-2340
Application address: 9002 St. Andrews Dr., Seminole, FL 33543
Contact: M.J. Starck

Financial data (yr. ended 12/31/01): Grants paid, $6,400; assets, $223,045 (M); gifts received, $4,228; expenditures, $6,629; qualifying distributions, $6,400.
Limitations: Giving primarily in PA and WV.
Trustee: Robert J. Starck.
EIN: 556036990

48110
Charles C. Williams Scholarship Foundation
(Formerly Charles Williams Trust)
1400 2 Penn Ctr. Plz.
1500 John F. Kennedy Blvd.
Philadelphia, PA 19102
Contact: Harry J.J. Bellwoar, III, Tr.

Donor(s): Charles C. Williams.‡
Financial data (yr. ended 09/30/01): Grants paid, $6,400; assets, $118,173 (M); expenditures, $10,256; qualifying distributions, $6,380.
Limitations: Giving limited to Philadelphia and Delaware counties, PA.
Trustee: Harry J.J. Bellwoar III.
EIN: 236709734

48111
Betty R. Morrison Trust
c/o First Columbia Bank & Trust Co.
11 W. Main St.
Bloomsburg, PA 17815

Financial data (yr. ended 12/31/01): Grants paid, $6,372; assets, $177,795 (M); expenditures, $8,517; qualifying distributions, $6,372.
Limitations: Applications not accepted. Giving limited to PA.
Application information: Contributes only to pre-selected organizations.
Trustees: John Barton, Richard Morrison, First Columbia Bank & Trust Co.
EIN: 237700530

48112
The Lois and Morton Victor Foundation
1650 Arch St., 22nd Fl.
Philadelphia, PA 19103

Established in 2000 in PA.
Donor(s): Lois Victor.
Financial data (yr. ended 09/30/01): Grants paid, $6,370; assets, $829,288 (M); gifts received, $901,590; expenditures, $8,574; qualifying distributions, $8,574.
Limitations: Applications not accepted. Giving primarily in FL and NY.
Application information: Contributes only to pre-selected organizations.

PENNSYLVANIA—48126

Officers and Director:* Lois Victor,* Pres. and Treas.; Morton Victor, Secy.
EIN: 233058320

48113
Myers Foundation
P.O. Box 931
Warren, PA 16365-0931
Application address: 1401 Lexington Ave., Warren, PA 16365-2849, tel.: (814) 726-2470
Contact: Steven A. Rothenberg, Tr.

Established in 1950.
Financial data (yr. ended 10/31/00): Grants paid, $6,350; assets, $119,809 (M); expenditures, $6,697; qualifying distributions, $6,350.
Limitations: Giving primarily in Warren, PA.
Trustees: Sharon D. Myers, Sandra M. Rothenberg, Steven A. Rothenberg.
EIN: 256067046

48114
Stark Family Foundation
5023 Frew St., Apt. 1A
Pittsburgh, PA 15213-3829 (412) 521-6653
Contact: Sidney Stark, Jr., Dir.

Financial data (yr. ended 12/31/01): Grants paid, $6,350; assets, $20,970 (M); expenditures, $6,766; qualifying distributions, $6,350.
Limitations: Giving on a national basis.
Application information: Application form not required.
Director: Sidney Stark, Jr.
EIN: 256037922

48115
John H. Harris Foundation
c/o A.F. McGervey & Williams Co.
2445 Old Greentree Rd.
Carnegie, PA 15106-3842 (412) 276-5443
Contact: Geneva H. Hahn, Tr.

Financial data (yr. ended 12/31/01): Grants paid, $6,330; assets, $46,361 (M); expenditures, $8,702; qualifying distributions, $6,330.
Limitations: Giving primarily in NJ, NY, OH, and Pittsburgh, PA.
Trustees: Cynthia C. Hahn, Geneva H. Hahn, Joel P. Hahn.
EIN: 256064257

48116
Louis Trauger Foundation for Charities
c/o Mellon Bank, N.A.
P.O. Box 185
Pittsburgh, PA 15230-9897
Contact: Laurie Moritz, Asst. V.P., Mellon Bank, N.A.

Donor(s): Lewis Trauger.
Financial data (yr. ended 12/31/01): Grants paid, $6,323; assets, $119,288 (M); expenditures, $7,655; qualifying distributions, $6,755.
Application information: Application form not required.
Trustee: Mellon Bank, N.A.
EIN: 256018879

48117
Sol & Naomi Berman Charitable Foundation
952 Briar Ln.
Pottstown, PA 19464 (610) 970-2233

Donor(s): Sol Berman, Naomi Berman.
Financial data (yr. ended 12/31/99): Grants paid, $6,271; assets, $223,686 (M); expenditures, $7,379; qualifying distributions, $6,585.
Limitations: Applications not accepted. Giving primarily in FL and PA.
Application information: Contributes only to pre-selected organizations.

Officers: Sol Berman, Pres.; Naomi Berman, V.P.
EIN: 236289693

48118
Ellen R. Schlecht Trust
c/o Allfirst, Trust Div.
21 E. Market St., M/C 402-130
York, PA 17401-1500

Established in 2000 in PA.
Financial data (yr. ended 12/31/01): Grants paid, $6,261; assets, $121,581 (M); expenditures, $9,637; qualifying distributions, $6,261.
Limitations: Applications not accepted. Giving primarily in PA.
Application information: Contributes only to pre-selected organizations.
Trustee: Allfirst.
EIN: 236680680

48119
The Meade Foundation
374 Cir. of Progress
Pottstown, PA 19464-3810 (610) 970-2800
Contact: James F. Meade, Secy.-Treas.

Established in 1988 in PA.
Donor(s): Columbia Boiler Co. of Pottstown.
Financial data (yr. ended 06/30/02): Grants paid, $6,250; assets, $108,476 (M); expenditures, $6,832; qualifying distributions, $6,250.
Limitations: Giving primarily in PA.
Officers: John J. Meade, Jr., Pres.; Thomas A. Meade, Sr., V.P.; James F. Meade, Secy.-Treas.
EIN: 232484734

48120
To Every Creature, Inc.
167 Richdale Dr.
Lower Burrell, PA 15068

Donor(s): Lawrence Jay Pavlocs.
Financial data (yr. ended 12/31/00): Grants paid, $6,200; assets, $115,487 (M); gifts received, $112,075; expenditures, $6,216; qualifying distributions, $6,200.
Limitations: Applications not accepted. Giving on a national basis.
Application information: Contributes only to pre-selected organizations.
Officers: David J. Pala, Pres.; Donald C. Fisher, Secy.-Treas.
Directors: Michael B. Fisher, Robert E. Whitaker, Jr.
EIN: 251552336

48121
The Thomas E. Weintraub Foundation
2695 Philmont Ave.
Huntingdon Valley, PA 19006-5301
(215) 938-7540

Established in 1985.
Donor(s): Thomas E. Weintraub.
Financial data (yr. ended 06/30/00): Grants paid, $6,132; assets, $266,274 (M); gifts received, $50,000; expenditures, $6,802; qualifying distributions, $6,132.
Limitations: Giving limited to PA.
Trustees: Thomas E. Weintraub, Thomas E. Weintraub, Jr.
EIN: 226404320

48122
Robert R. Mumma Trust Share No. 4
21 E. Market St., M/C 402-130
York, PA 17401-1500

Established in 2000 in PA.
Financial data (yr. ended 12/31/00): Grants paid, $6,117; assets, $207,056 (M); expenditures, $7,108; qualifying distributions, $7,108.

Limitations: Applications not accepted. Giving primarily in Mechanicsburg, PA.
Application information: Contributes only to pre-selected organizations.
Trustee: Allfirst.
EIN: 256572060

48123
Robert F. Burgin, Sr. Education Trust
c/o First Union National Bank
Broad and Walnut Sts.
Philadelphia, PA 19109
Application address: c/o Randolph County Hospital Authority, 109 Randolf St., Cuthbert, GA 31740

Donor(s): Burgin Land Limited.
Financial data (yr. ended 12/31/99): Grants paid, $6,106; assets, $186,463 (M); gifts received, $250; expenditures, $8,227; qualifying distributions, $6,106.
Limitations: Giving primarily in Cuthbert and Randolph County, GA.
Trustee: First Union National Bank.
EIN: 582065623

48124
George S. Arnold Educational Trust
c/o First Union National Bank
Broad and Walnut Sts.
Philadelphia, PA 19109
Application address: c/o Romney Rotary Club, Romney, WV 26757

Financial data (yr. ended 12/31/99): Grants paid, $6,000; assets, $298,234 (M); expenditures, $10,096; qualifying distributions, $6,079.
Limitations: Giving limited to residents of Hampshire County, WV.
Application information: Application form not required.
Trustee: First Union National Bank.
EIN: 546191759

48125
Catawissa Lumber & Specialty Co., Inc. College Educational Fund
c/o First Columbia Bank & Trust Co.
11 W. Main St.
Bloomsburg, PA 17815
Contact: Janice Dreese, Trust Off., Fist Columbia Bank & Trust Co.

Donor(s): Catawissa Lumber & Specialty Co., Inc.
Financial data (yr. ended 12/31/01): Grants paid, $6,000; assets, $147,552 (M); gifts received, $5,810; expenditures, $9,950; qualifying distributions, $6,000.
Limitations: Giving primarily in the Catawissa, PA, area.
Application information: Application form required.
Trustee: First Columbia Bank & Trust Co.
EIN: 237676581
Codes: CS, CD, GTI

48126
The Eagles Mere Foundation
Box 402
Eagles Mere, PA 17731
Application address: 698 Strafford Cir. Strafford, PA 19087
Contact: William O. Albertini, Pres.

Established in 1986 in PA.
Donor(s): Frederick A. Godley, John C. Lundy.
Financial data (yr. ended 12/31/01): Grants paid, $6,000; assets, $156,024 (M); gifts received, $9,575; expenditures, $8,125; qualifying distributions, $6,000.

IN THIS SECTION, WITHIN EACH STATE, FOUNDATIONS ARE LISTED IN DESCENDING ORDER BY TOTAL GRANTS PAID

Limitations: Giving limited to Sullivan County, PA, with emphasis on the Eagles Mere area.
Officers and Trustees:* William O. Albertini,* Pres.; Martha Detwiler,* Secy.; John C. Lundy, Treas.; Rita Brownback, Carter R. Buller, Willis S. DeLaCour, William Gruver.
EIN: 236805376

48127
Eleanor Bell Elliott Friedberg Memorial Art Scholarship Foundation
4240 Greensburg Pike
Pittsburgh, PA 15221-4297 (412) 351-5800
Contact: Robin F. Quimette, Tr.

Established in 1997 in PA.
Financial data (yr. ended 05/31/00): Grants paid, $6,000; assets, $64,807 (M); gifts received, $18,430; expenditures, $12,594; qualifying distributions, $11,910.
Limitations: Giving limited to Pittsburgh, PA.
Trustees: Stanford Friedberg, Stephen M. Friedberg, Robin Ouimette.
EIN: 237894931

48128
Merle E. Gilliland Scholarship Fund
c/o PNC Advisors
620 Liberty Ave., P2- PTPP-10-2
Pittsburgh, PA 15222-2705 (412) 762-3808
Contact: Jay Ferguson, V.P., PNC Advisors

Established in 1985 in PA.
Financial data (yr. ended 06/30/02): Grants paid, $6,000; assets, $116,197 (M); expenditures, $6,842; qualifying distributions, $6,000.
Limitations: Giving primarily in Pittsburgh, PA.
Application information: Application form required.
Trustee: PNC Bank, N.A.
EIN: 256255425

48129
The Gray Bradley Hayman Foundation II
310 Old Lancaster Rd.
Devon, PA 19333

Established in 1998 in PA.
Donor(s): Harry G. Hayman III.
Financial data (yr. ended 12/31/00): Grants paid, $6,000; assets, $241,493 (M); gifts received, $3,000; expenditures, $6,010; qualifying distributions, $6,000.
Limitations: Applications not accepted.
Application information: Contributes only to pre-selected organizations.
Trustee: Harry G. Hayman III.
EIN: 237927519

48130
Kil Chung-Hee Fellowship Fund, Inc.
7818 Oak Lane Rd.
Cheltenham, PA 19012-1015
Contact: Sangduk Kim, Dir.

Donor(s): Sangduk Kim.
Financial data (yr. ended 12/31/01): Grants paid, $6,000; assets, $132,617 (M); gifts received, $10,000; expenditures, $7,268; qualifying distributions, $7,268.
Application information: Applicants must submit a resume of academic qualifications. For research grants, applicant must submit an outline of the proposed investigation. Application form not required.
Directors: Yong H. Chun, Sangduk Kim.
EIN: 232199550

48131
Kenneth Kratz Family Charitable Foundation
95 N. Main St., Ste. B
Sellersville, PA 18960-2377

Established in 1999 in PA.
Donor(s): Kenneth K. Kratz.
Financial data (yr. ended 12/31/01): Grants paid, $6,000; assets, $1 (M); gifts received, $35,000; expenditures, $6,010; qualifying distributions, $6,000.
Trustee: Kenneth K. Kratz.
EIN: 256667064

48132
Winfield Scott Lane Scholarship Fund
c/o First Commonwealth Trust Co.
111 S. Main St.
Greensburg, PA 15601 (724) 832-6061

Financial data (yr. ended 12/31/01): Grants paid, $6,000; assets, $121,635 (M); gifts received, $6,000; expenditures, $7,695; qualifying distributions, $5,959; giving activities include $6,000 for loans to individuals.
Limitations: Giving limited to residents of Westmoreland County, PA.
Trustee: First Commonwealth Trust Co.
EIN: 256052312

48133
The Lenise-Allou Foundation
c/o John Iskrant
1600 Market St., Ste. 3600
Philadelphia, PA 19103
Application address: 2412 Pate's Creek, Williamsburg, VA 23185, tel.: (757) 253-1457
Contact: Leopold A. Schmidt, Tr.

Established in 2000 in PA.
Donor(s): Leopold A. Schmidt.
Financial data (yr. ended 12/31/01): Grants paid, $6,000; assets, $1,351,466 (M); expenditures, $11,058; qualifying distributions, $6,000.
Trustees: Karen E. Monahan, Timothy G. Monahan, Carol L. Schmidt, Douglas S. Schmidt, Leopold A. Schmidt.
EIN: 233047923

48134
Red Lion Foundation
7026 Sheaff Ln.
Fort Washington, PA 19034

Established in 1999 in PA.
Donor(s): Michael R. Sharp.
Financial data (yr. ended 12/31/01): Grants paid, $6,000; assets, $82,708 (M); gifts received, $25,590; expenditures, $7,273; qualifying distributions, $6,000.
Limitations: Applications not accepted.
Application information: Contributes only to pre-selected organizations.
Trustees: Michael R. Sharp, Pamela L. Sharp.
EIN: 233024001

48135
Stephen A. and Nina B. Schafer Foundation
826 N. Muhlenberg St.
Allentown, PA 18104-3940

Established in 1984 in PA.
Financial data (yr. ended 07/31/01): Grants paid, $6,000; assets, $186,191 (L); expenditures, $8,571; qualifying distributions, $6,000.
Limitations: Applications not accepted. Giving on a national basis, with emphasis on CT, New York, NY, NH, PA, and St. Thomas, VI.
Application information: Contributes only to pre-selected organizations.
Officer: Nina B. Schafer, Secy.

EIN: 222630838

48136
Sharp Foundation
67 Foxcroft Ln.
Phoenixville, PA 19460
Contact: Richard A. Ebert

Financial data (yr. ended 03/31/02): Grants paid, $6,000; assets, $92,850 (M); gifts received, $1,000; expenditures, $6,969; qualifying distributions, $6,000.
Application information: Application form not required.
Trustees: Patricia Sharp, William L. Sharp, Jr.
EIN: 232013450

48137
Elmer A. Snyder & Anna Belle C. Snyder Scholarship Fund
P.O. Box 1022
Kittanning, PA 16201-1901 (724) 548-8101
Contact: Oliver Schaub, Tr.

Established around 1995.
Donor(s): Elmer Snyder, Annabelle Snyder.
Financial data (yr. ended 12/31/99): Grants paid, $6,000; assets, $123,655 (M); gifts received, $100; expenditures, $6,118; qualifying distributions, $5,938.
Limitations: Giving limited to residents of Armstrong County, PA.
Application information: Application form required.
Trustees: Glenn George, Oliver Schaub, David E. Snyder.
EIN: 256373182

48138
St. Andrew's Educational Trust
P.O. Box 167
Waynesboro, PA 17268

Donor(s): Lillian White.‡
Financial data (yr. ended 06/30/01): Grants paid, $5,995; assets, $130,377 (M); gifts received, $2,935; expenditures, $6,407; qualifying distributions, $5,721.
Limitations: Applications not accepted. Giving limited to Hagerstown, MD and Waynesboro, PA.
Application information: Contributes only to 7 pre-selected organizations.
Trustees: Joseph E. Bowling, James Caron, Joseph L. Doyle, Bernard J. McGarity.
EIN: 237092791

48139
W. G. Fronheiser Trust
c/o First Union National Bank
Broad and Walnut Sts.
Philadelphia, PA 19109-1199
Contact: Katherine Bonner

Financial data (yr. ended 04/30/00): Grants paid, $5,970; assets, $199,111 (M); expenditures, $7,244; qualifying distributions, $5,970.
Limitations: Giving limited to Pottstown, PA.
Application information: Application form not required.
Trustee: First Union National Bank.
EIN: 236265130

48140
Gertrude S. Lane Foundation
c/o Omega Group
937 Haverford Rd.
Bryn Mawr, PA 19010
Contact: Renee M. Love, Tr.

Established in 1999 in PA.
Donor(s): Renee M. Love, John Barry Love.

Financial data (yr. ended 12/31/01): Grants paid, $5,958; assets, $133,428 (M); gifts received, $4,105; expenditures, $5,958; qualifying distributions, $5,958.
Trustees: John Breen, John Barry Love, Renee M. Love, Sean Patrick Mellody, Steven Piltch, Rebecca M. Wiggins, Stacey E. Yarnall.
EIN: 256681642

48141
Teck Fund
c/o F. Peter Kohler
314 Avon Rd.
Bryn Mawr, PA 19010-3654 (610) 527-1761

Donor(s): F. Peter Kohler.
Financial data (yr. ended 12/31/01): Grants paid, $5,930; assets, $63,992 (M); expenditures, $6,399; qualifying distributions, $5,930.
Limitations: Applications not accepted. Giving primarily in Philadelphia, PA.
Application information: Contributes only to pre-selected organizations.
Trustee: F. Peter Kohler.
EIN: 236411414

48142
Cable Family Charitable Foundation
c/o Herbert Cable
3001 W. Carson St.
Pittsburgh, PA 15204-1826

Established in 1999 in PA.
Financial data (yr. ended 06/30/02): Grants paid, $5,900; assets, $180,357 (M); expenditures, $6,053; qualifying distributions, $5,900.
Limitations: Applications not accepted. Giving primarily in AZ and PA.
Application information: Contributes only to pre-selected organizations.
Trustee: Herbert E. Cable, Jr.
EIN: 256680570

48143
Walter T. & Bessie H. Cooper Charitable Trust
c/o Allfirst, Trust Tax Div.
21 E. Market St.
York, PA 17401-1500

Established in 1993 in PA.
Donor(s): Bessie H. Cooper.
Financial data (yr. ended 06/30/01): Grants paid, $5,878; assets, $107,585 (M); expenditures, $8,020; qualifying distributions, $7,424.
Limitations: Applications not accepted. Giving primarily in PA.
Application information: Contributes only to pre-selected organizations.
Trustee: Allfirst.
EIN: 256429227

48144
John G. & Julia Geiling Memorial Fund
c/o Mellon Bank, N.A.
P.O. Box 7236, AIM No. 193-0224
Philadelphia, PA 19101-7236

Financial data (yr. ended 02/28/02): Grants paid, $5,868; assets, $248,898 (M); expenditures, $9,222; qualifying distributions, $5,868.
Limitations: Applications not accepted.
Application information: Contributes only to pre-selected organizations.
Trustee: Mellon Bank, N.A.
EIN: 256706540

48145
John W. & Shirley E. Richman Foundation
P.O. Box 232
Washington, PA 15301-0232

Established in 1994 in PA.

Financial data (yr. ended 09/30/01): Grants paid, $5,864; assets, $303,811 (M); expenditures, $11,066; qualifying distributions, $5,864.
Limitations: Giving primarily in PA.
Trustees: John W. Richman, Shirley E. Richman.
EIN: 251753663

48146
Pauline-Morton Foundation
38 Balmoral Dr.
Chadds Ford, PA 19317

Financial data (yr. ended 12/31/01): Grants paid, $5,850; assets, $93,549 (M); expenditures, $8,619; qualifying distributions, $5,850.
Limitations: Applications not accepted. Giving primarily in DE.
Application information: Contributes only to pre-selected organizations.
Officers and Directors:* Margot S. Taylor,* Pres.; Eugene S. Taylor,* V.P.; Carol S. Taylor,* Secy.; E. Shaw Taylor, Jr.,* Treas.
EIN: 446010847

48147
Leo Rosner Trust f/b/o Charities
(also known as Leo Rosner, L. & A. Charitable Trust)
c/o First Union National Bank
123 S. Broad St.
Philadelphia, PA 19109-9989

Financial data (yr. ended 11/30/99): Grants paid, $5,801; assets, $135,258 (M); expenditures, $7,055; qualifying distributions, $6,147.
Limitations: Applications not accepted. Giving primarily in New York, NY.
Application information: Contributes only to pre-selected organizations.
Trustees: Mildred R. Caplow, Stacy Caplow, Anna H. Rosner, June Rosner, First Union National Bank.
EIN: 226335512

48148
The Kennedy Idea Foundation
503 Chestnut Ln.
Wayne, PA 19087

Established in 1999 in PA.
Donor(s): Edward A. Kennedy.
Financial data (yr. ended 12/31/01): Grants paid, $5,750; assets, $42,831 (M); gifts received, $20,000; expenditures, $9,138; qualifying distributions, $5,750.
Limitations: Giving primarily in PA.
Officers: Edward A. Kennedy, Pres.; Dr. Eileen Kennedy-Moore, V.P.; Kenneth M. Kennedy, V.P.; Sheila Kennedy Hickey, Secy.
EIN: 364314816

48149
Harry A. Robinson Foundation
c/o Len Moskoff
44 Greenfield Ave., Ardmore Plz.
Ardmore, PA 19003

Financial data (yr. ended 09/30/99): Grants paid, $5,750; assets, $94,533 (M); expenditures, $6,987; qualifying distributions, $5,750.
Limitations: Applications not accepted. Giving primarily in Philadelphia, PA.
Application information: Contributes only to pre-selected organizations.
Trustees: Fred Robinson, Herman Robinson.
EIN: 236243440

48150
Frank & Julian Lehman Educational Foundation Trust
c/o Fulton Financial Advisors, N.A.
P.O. Box 3215
Lancaster, PA 17604-3215
Application address: c/o Advisory Comm., St. Luke's Episcopal Church, 22 S. 6th St., Lebanon, PA 17042

Financial data (yr. ended 12/31/01): Grants paid, $5,725; assets, $94,378 (M); expenditures, $7,383; qualifying distributions, $5,696.
Limitations: Giving limited to residents of Lebanon, PA.
Application information: Application form required.
Trustee: Fulton Financial Advisors, N.A.
EIN: 236487849

48151
I.A. Construction Foundation
c/o Robert Field
P.O. Box 8
Concordville, PA 19331
Contact: James Kutys, Secy.

Financial data (yr. ended 12/31/01): Grants paid, $5,714; assets, $55,496 (M); expenditures, $5,764; qualifying distributions, $5,714.
Limitations: Giving primarily in MA and PA.
Application information: Application form not required.
Officers: Robert Field, Pres.; Eric Sussman, V.P. and Treas.; James Kutys, Secy.
EIN: 222454957

48152
Hannah & Marvin Kamin Family Foundation
1018 Wilkins Heights Rd.
Pittsburgh, PA 15217
Contact: Hannah Kamin, Tr.

Established in 2000 in PA.
Donor(s): Hannah Kamin, Marvin Kamin.
Financial data (yr. ended 12/31/01): Grants paid, $5,675; assets, $302,925 (M); expenditures, $6,377; qualifying distributions, $5,675.
Application information: Application form not required.
Trustees: Hannah Kamin, Marvin Kamin.
EIN: 256537557

48153
Rosario Foundation
100 Broadway Ave.
Carnegie, PA 15106-2421
FAX: (412) 276-6215
Contact: Susan M. Latella, Mgr.

Established in 1986 in PA.
Donor(s): Ronald V. Pellegrini, M.D., Ross F. DiMarco, Jr., M.D., Mercy Hospital of Pittsburgh.
Financial data (yr. ended 12/31/01): Grants paid, $5,610; assets, $45,785 (M); expenditures, $5,741; qualifying distributions, $5,610.
Limitations: Applications not accepted. Giving limited to OH, PA, and WV.
Officer: Susan M. Latella, Mgr.
Directors: Seth Bekoe, M.D., Ross F. DiMarco, Jr., M.D., Kathleen J. Grant, M.D., Ronald V. Pellegrini, M.D.
EIN: 251519395

48154
R. C. Hughes Spelling Bee Fund
c/o Mellon Bank, N.A.
P.O. Box 7236
Philadelphia, PA 19101-7236

Financial data (yr. ended 04/30/99): Grants paid, $5,600; assets, $126,453 (M); expenditures, $7,993; qualifying distributions, $7,323.
Limitations: Applications not accepted. Giving limited to residents of Stroudsburg, PA.
Application information: Contributes only to pre-selected organizations.
Trustee: Mellon Bank, N.A.
EIN: 236665023

48155
The Mildred R. Landis Foundation
339 E. Jamestown Rd.
Greenville, PA 16125-9294

Donor(s): Mildred R. Landis.
Financial data (yr. ended 10/31/01): Grants paid, $5,600; assets, $37,150 (M); gifts received, $11,000; expenditures, $6,450; qualifying distributions, $5,600.
Limitations: Applications not accepted.
Application information: Contributes only to pre-selected organizations.
Officers: Mildred R. Landis, Pres.; Dianne H. Lee, V.P.; J. Randy Smith, V.P.; Jeffrey C. Weiss, V.P.
EIN: 760322039

48156
The O'Donnell Family Foundation
2 Kinder Rd.
Conshohocken, PA 19428

Established in 2000 in PA.
Donor(s): William O'Donnell, Theresa O'Donnell.
Financial data (yr. ended 03/31/02): Grants paid, $5,600; assets, $198,648 (M); gifts received, $100,000; expenditures, $8,033; qualifying distributions, $5,600.
Officers: William O'Donnell, Pres.; Theresa O'Donnell, Secy.-Treas.
EIN: 256734187

48157
F. Odom Trust f/b/o First United Methodist Church
c/o First Union National Bank
123 S. Broad St.
Philadelphia, PA 19109-9989
Application address: c/o First United Methodist Church, P.O. Box 926, Newton, NC 28658

Financial data (yr. ended 04/30/99): Grants paid, $5,600; assets, $126,453 (M); expenditures, $7,993; qualifying distributions, $7,323.
Limitations: Giving primarily in NC.
Trustee: First Union National Bank.
EIN: 566191761

48158
The Evelyn W. Bushwick Family Charitable Trust
1535 Wyndham Dr., S.
York, PA 17403

Established in 1999 in MD.
Donor(s): Evelyn W. Bushwick.
Financial data (yr. ended 11/30/01): Grants paid, $5,515; assets, $98,569 (M); expenditures, $10,333; qualifying distributions, $5,515.
Limitations: Applications not accepted.
Application information: Contributes only to pre-selected organizations.
Trustees: Brian Bushwick, Bruce Bushwick, Nancy B. Bushwick-Malloy.
EIN: 526994552

48159
The Cherry Foundation
P.O. Box 408
Wynnewood, PA 19096-0408

Financial data (yr. ended 12/31/01): Grants paid, $5,500; assets, $108,681 (M); gifts received, $1,250; expenditures, $6,469; qualifying distributions, $5,500.
Limitations: Giving primarily in Philadelphia, PA.
Trustees: Mary Cherry, Robert Cherry, Andrew Greenberg, Carole Phillips.
EIN: 232014500

48160
Crawford Heritage Foundation
363 Chestnut St.
Meadville, PA 16335 (814) 336-5206
Application address: 180 Mercer St., Meadville, PA 16335; URL: http://www.sideroads.com/grassroots/chf.html
Contact: Lisa Youngs

Established in 1997 in PA.
Financial data (yr. ended 12/31/01): Grants paid, $5,500; assets, $1,156,635 (M); gifts received, $10,000; expenditures, $5,500.
Limitations: Giving limited to Crawford County, PA.
Publications: Annual report, informational brochure.
Application information: Application guidelines available on Web site. Application form required.
Officers: Lisa Pepicell-Youngs, Pres.; Paul Huber, 1st V.P.; Christine Lang, 2nd V.P.; Mary Alice Kirkpatrick, 3rd V.P.; Kenneth Montag, Recording Secy.; John Hodges, Treas.
Directors: Rev. Susan Buell, Harold Coleman, Rev. Barry Cressman, Dwight Haas, Christopher Junker, Milosh Mamula, Melissa Mencotti, John Nesbitt, Rev. William Smith, Mark Strausbaugh, Earl Yingling.
EIN: 251813245
Codes: CM

48161
The Terry and Eileen Glenn Family Foundation
c/o B. Rosenfield
1600 Market St., Ste. 3600
Philadelphia, PA 19103

Established in 2000 in PA.
Financial data (yr. ended 12/31/01): Grants paid, $5,500; assets, $965,882 (M); gifts received, $659,924; expenditures, $19,637; qualifying distributions, $5,500.
Limitations: Applications not accepted.
Application information: Contributes only to pre-selected organizations.
Trustees: Eileen Glenn, Terry K. Glenn.
EIN: 233034255

48162
Isenberg/Sarkisian Foundation
c/o Frank G. Cooper, Duane, Morris & Heckscher
1 Liberty Pl.
Philadelphia, PA 19103-7396

Established in 1987 in PA.
Donor(s): Judith E. Isenberg Sarkisian.
Financial data (yr. ended 11/30/01): Grants paid, $5,500; assets, $114,015 (M); expenditures, $6,701; qualifying distributions, $5,422.
Limitations: Applications not accepted. Giving primarily in PA.
Application information: Contributes only to pre-selected organizations.
Trustee: Judith E. Isenberg Sarkisian.
EIN: 236868742

48163
Annabelle M. Manbeck Trust
c/o Fulton Financial Advisors, N.A.
P.O. Box 3215
Lancaster, PA 17604-3215

Established in 1993 in PA.
Donor(s): Annabelle M. Manbeck Trust.
Financial data (yr. ended 12/31/01): Grants paid, $5,500; assets, $62,529 (M); expenditures, $5,958; qualifying distributions, $5,500.
Limitations: Giving limited to residents of Lancaster, PA.
Trustee: Fulton Financial Advisors, N.A.
EIN: 237651313

48164
Bruce L. Rothrock Charitable Foundation
Rte. 22 & 15th St.
Allentown, PA 18104

Donor(s): Bruce L. Rothrock, Sr.
Financial data (yr. ended 11/30/01): Grants paid, $5,500; assets, $130,882 (M); expenditures, $7,400; qualifying distributions, $5,500.
Limitations: Applications not accepted. Giving limited to PA.
Application information: Contributes only to pre-selected organizations.
Officers and Directors:* Bruce L. Rothrock, Sr.,* Pres.; Bruce L. Rothrock, Jr.,* V.P.; Debra A. Rothrock,* Treas.; David Rothrock.
EIN: 232441688

48165
The Margaret Wright Steele and Franklin A. Steele Foundation
c/o Gazer, Kohn & Maher
6 Neshaminy, Ste. 213
Trevose, PA 19053
Contact: Thomas J. Maher

Established in 1999 in PA.
Donor(s): Margaret Wright Steele, Franklin A. Steele.
Financial data (yr. ended 12/31/01): Grants paid, $5,500; assets, $52,526 (M); expenditures, $5,636; qualifying distributions, $5,500.
Limitations: Giving primarily in NJ, NY, and Philadelphia, PA.
Trustees: Mark S. Blaskey, Franklin A. Steele, Margaret Wright Steele.
EIN: 232986360

48166
Dorothy R. Young Trust
c/o PNC Advisors
620 Liberty Ave., P2-PTPP-10-2
Pittsburgh, PA 15222-2705

Financial data (yr. ended 04/30/02): Grants paid, $5,500; assets, $115,172 (M); expenditures, $7,831; qualifying distributions, $5,500.
Limitations: Applications not accepted. Giving limited to NJ.
Application information: Unsolicited requests for funds not accepted.
Trustee: PNC Bank, N.A.
EIN: 226647704

48167
Doctor A. C. & S. A. Shoemaker Trust
c/o Mellon Bank, N.A.
P.O. Box 7236
Philadelphia, PA 19101-7236

Established in 1995 in PA.
Financial data (yr. ended 06/30/02): Grants paid, $5,496; assets, $73,433 (M); expenditures, $7,079; qualifying distributions, $5,496.

Limitations: Applications not accepted. Giving primarily in West Pittston, PA.
Application information: Contributes only to pre-selected organizations.
Trustee: Mellon Bank, N.A.
EIN: 237813132

48168
Jacob Justice Free Medical Dispensary
P.O. Box 416
Mount Pleasant, PA 15666
Application address: c/o William George, 775 W. Vine St., Mount Pleasant, PA 15666, tel.: (724) 547-2447

Financial data (yr. ended 12/31/01): Grants paid, $5,470; assets, $78,142 (M); expenditures, $7,158; qualifying distributions, $5,470.
Limitations: Giving limited to a three-mile radius of Mount Pleasant, PA.
Application information: Application form required.
Officers: Robert Copeland, Pres.; Thomas Milliron, V.P.; Claudia W. Stahl, Secy.; William George, Treas.; Waide Miller, Eugene Saloom, Bonnie Wilson.
EIN: 251038795

48169
Samuel and Eva Kress Scholarship Fund
c/o PNC Advisors
620 Liberty Ave., P2-PTTP-10-2
Pittsburgh, PA 15222-2705

Financial data (yr. ended 01/31/02): Grants paid, $5,457; assets, $296,305 (M); expenditures, $8,910; qualifying distributions, $5,457.
Limitations: Applications not accepted. Giving limited to NJ.
Application information: Contributes only to pre-selected organizations.
Trustee: PNC Bank, N.A.
EIN: 236723474

48170
The Levine Foundation
c/o Alpern Rosenthal & Co.
332 5th Ave., Ste. 400
Pittsburgh, PA 15222

Donor(s): Ruth F. Levine.
Financial data (yr. ended 12/31/01): Grants paid, $5,450; assets, $65,200 (M); gifts received, $975; expenditures, $6,575; qualifying distributions, $5,450.
Limitations: Applications not accepted. Giving primarily in Minneapolis, MN.
Application information: Contributes only to pre-selected organizations.
Trustees: Ruth F. Levine, Samuel C. Levine.
EIN: 256411767

48171
North Central Pennsylvania Golf Association Scholarship Trust
c/o First Union National Bank
P.O. Box 57
Selinsgrove, PA 17870
Application address: P.O. Box S, Hummels Wharf, PA 17831

Established in 1992 in PA.
Financial data (yr. ended 12/31/99): Grants paid, $5,400; assets, $94,481 (M); gifts received, $106; expenditures, $6,575; qualifying distributions, $6,083.
Limitations: Giving limited to residents of PA.
Trustees: Edward G. Mikalik, Jr., Jeffrey S. Ranck, Gene Stock, First Union National Bank.
EIN: 232500516

48172
Stillinger Charitable Trust
c/o First Union National Bank
Broad and Walnut Sts., PA 1308
Philadelphia, PA 19109
Application address: c/o Stephen Mills, P.O. Box 9333, Bradenton, FL 34206

Financial data (yr. ended 04/30/00): Grants paid, $5,400; assets, $404,242 (M); expenditures, $11,512; qualifying distributions, $5,479.
Limitations: Giving primarily in Manatee County, FL.
Trustee: First Union National Bank.
EIN: 596734229

48173
Thomas E. & Marcia W. Philips Family Foundation
4737 Rock Ledge Dr.
Harrisburg, PA 17110-3255

Established in 1990 in PA.
Donor(s): Thomas E. Philips, Marcia W. Philips.
Financial data (yr. ended 12/31/01): Grants paid, $5,346; assets, $322,454 (M); expenditures, $5,576; qualifying distributions, $5,346.
Limitations: Applications not accepted. Giving limited to Harrisburg, PA.
Application information: Contributes only to pre-selected organizations.
Trustees: Marcia W. Philips, Thomas E. Philips.
EIN: 236982149

48174
William Bache Memorial Fund
c/o Citizens & Northern Bank, Tr. Dept.
P.O. Box 58
Wellsboro, PA 16901-0058
Contact: Robert C. Bair, M.D., Chair., Screening Comm.

Financial data (yr. ended 12/31/01): Grants paid, $5,306; assets, $90,668 (M); expenditures, $6,410; qualifying distributions, $5,269.
Limitations: Giving limited to Wellsboro, PA.
Directors: J. Robert Bower, Chair.; Robert C. Bair, Carl E. Carson, R. James Dunham, Warren Goodrich, Edmund Osgood, Beth Owlett, Edward H. Owlett, George C. Williams.
EIN: 236449711

48175
Philadelphia Soup House
c/o Grandom Institute
366 Roumfort Rd.
Philadelphia, PA 19119 (215) 248-1465
Contact: Jack Childs

Financial data (yr. ended 06/30/02): Grants paid, $5,300; assets, $90,388 (M); expenditures, $5,506; qualifying distributions, $5,300.
Limitations: Giving primarily in PA.
Application information: Application form not required.
Officers: F. Preston Buckman, Pres.; John N. Childs, Jr., Secy.-Treas.; Robert C. Bodine, Mgr.; Mary L. Buckman, Mgr.; Thomas O. Ely, Mgr.; Carolyn Moon, Mgr.; Robert Neff, Mgr.; Louise W. Senopoulos, Mgr.; Gery van Arkel, Mgr.
EIN: 231574319

48176
Robert R. Mumma Trust Share No. 3
21 E. Market St., M/C 402-130
York, PA 17401-1500

Established in 2000 in PA.
Financial data (yr. ended 12/31/00): Grants paid, $5,296; assets, $207,088 (M); expenditures, $6,286; qualifying distributions, $6,286.

Limitations: Applications not accepted. Giving primarily in Harrisburg, PA.
Application information: Contributes only to pre-selected organizations.
Trustee: Allfirst.
EIN: 256572059

48177
Applebaum Family Foundation
c/o Louis Applebaum
29 Bluebonnet Rd.
Langhorne, PA 19047

Donor(s): Louis Applebaum, Arlene Applebaum.
Financial data (yr. ended 12/31/01): Grants paid, $5,245; assets, $25,642 (M); gifts received, $13,500; expenditures, $5,245; qualifying distributions, $5,245.
Limitations: Applications not accepted. Giving primarily in Philadelphia, PA.
Application information: Contributes only to pre-selected organizations.
Trustees: Arlene Applebaum, Louis Applebaum.
EIN: 222774244

48178
The Clayton Foundation, Inc.
1631 Stony Rd.
Warminster, PA 18974-1041

Established in 1987 in PA.
Donor(s): EFE Laboratories, Inc.
Financial data (yr. ended 12/31/01): Grants paid, $5,243; assets, $27,657 (M); expenditures, $5,499; qualifying distributions, $5,243.
Limitations: Applications not accepted. Giving primarily in PA.
Application information: Contributes only to pre-selected organizations.
Officer: Peter Clayton, Pres.
EIN: 232481304

48179
Charles R. Grissinger Fund
c/o PNC Advisors
620 Liberty Ave., P2-PTPP-10-2
Pittsburgh, PA 15222-2705
Application address: c/o John A. Lander, Pres., Girard College, Corinthian & Girard Aves., Philadelphia, PA 19121

Established in 1982 in PA.
Financial data (yr. ended 09/30/01): Grants paid, $5,241; assets, $104,115 (M); expenditures, $6,282; qualifying distributions, $5,406.
Limitations: Giving limited to residents of PA.
Application information: Applicants must be enrolled at Girard College. Application form required.
Trustee: PNC Bank, N.A.
EIN: 256234976

48180
C. E. Gibbs Memorial Fund Trust
c/o The Honesdale National Bank
733 Main St.
Honesdale, PA 18431
Contact: Mary McElroy, Trust Off., The Honesdale National Bank

Financial data (yr. ended 12/31/00): Grants paid, $5,155; assets, $335,872 (M); expenditures, $8,651; qualifying distributions, $5,155.
Limitations: Giving limited to Wayne County, PA.
Trustee: The Honesdale National Bank.
EIN: 236496941
Codes: GTI

48181—PENNSYLVANIA

48181
Dorothy Nash Trust
c/o First Union National Bank
Broad & Walnut Sts.
Philadelphia, PA 19109

Established in 1997 in FL.
Financial data (yr. ended 12/31/99): Grants paid, $5,126; assets, $184,431 (M); expenditures, $9,244; qualifying distributions, $5,214.
Limitations: Applications not accepted.
Application information: Contributes only to pre-selected organizations.
Trustee: First Union National Bank.
EIN: 596787523

48182
Morris Wheeler Foundation
8315 Saint Martins Ln.
Philadelphia, PA 19118

Financial data (yr. ended 12/31/01): Grants paid, $5,125; assets, $96,252 (M); expenditures, $5,840; qualifying distributions, $5,125.
Limitations: Applications not accepted. Giving primarily in PA.
Application information: Contributes only to pre-selected organizations.
Trustees: B.L. Castor, C.M. Turman III, M.C. Turman.
EIN: 236392152

48183
Gaines Family Foundation
c/o Lewis H. Gaines
1441 N. 40th St.
Allentown, PA 18104-2127

Established in 1999.
Donor(s): Lewis Gaines, Roberta Gaines.
Financial data (yr. ended 12/31/01): Grants paid, $5,100; assets, $69,849 (M); gifts received, $35,623; expenditures, $5,529; qualifying distributions, $5,100.
Limitations: Applications not accepted.
Application information: Contributes only to pre-selected organizations.
Officers: Lewis Gaines, Pres.; Roberta Gaines, V.P.; Sheryl Bartos, Secy.; Brian Gaines, Treas.
EIN: 233010707

48184
Piasecki Foundation
2 Bala Plz., No. 525
Bala Cynwyd, PA 19004-1501 (610) 667-3240
Contact: Arthur J. Kania, Mgr.

Financial data (yr. ended 12/31/01): Grants paid, $5,100; assets, $592,005 (M); expenditures, $5,420; qualifying distributions, $5,100.
Limitations: Giving on a national basis.
Application information: Application form not required.
Officer: Arthur J. Kania, Mgr.
EIN: 237006412

48185
Russell Educational Foundation
c/o PNC Advisors
620 Liberty Ave., P2-PTPP-10-2
Pittsburgh, PA 15222-2750

Donor(s): Russel Standard Corp., Russell Industries, Inc.
Financial data (yr. ended 12/31/01): Grants paid, $5,092; assets, $1,072 (M); gifts received, $2,000; expenditures, $5,345; qualifying distributions, $5,101.
Limitations: Applications not accepted. Giving limited to areas of company operations.
Application information: Unsolicited requests for funds not accepted, only employees of Russell Industries, Inc.
Trustee: PNC Bank, N.A.
EIN: 256025677
Codes: CS, CD, GTI

48186
Irvin Green Family Foundation
c/o Voynew, Bayard & Co.
1530 Chestnut St., Ste. 200
Philadelphia, PA 19102

Established in 1985 in PA.
Financial data (yr. ended 09/30/01): Grants paid, $5,075; assets, $120,623 (M); expenditures, $8,038; qualifying distributions, $5,075.
Limitations: Applications not accepted. Giving primarily in PA.
Application information: Contributes only to pre-selected organizations.
Director: Irvin Green.
EIN: 222769584

48187
Rudnitsky Family Charitable Foundation
108 Susquehanna Ave.
Selinsgrove, PA 17870-1142

Established in 2000 in PA.
Donor(s): Marvin J. Rudnitsky, Carolyn W. Rudnitsky.
Financial data (yr. ended 12/31/01): Grants paid, $5,070; assets, $79,055 (M); gifts received, $4,910; expenditures, $6,632; qualifying distributions, $5,070.
Limitations: Applications not accepted.
Application information: Contributes only to pre-selected organizations.
Officers: Carolyn W. Rudnitsky, Pres. and Treas.; Marvin J. Rudnitsky, V.P. and Secy.
EIN: 233065358

48188
Louise and Perry J. Dick Foundation
c/o Trumbull Corp.
P.O. Box 98100
Pittsburgh, PA 15227

Established in 1992 in PA.
Donor(s): Trumbull Corp., P.J. Dick Contracting Co.
Financial data (yr. ended 12/31/01): Grants paid, $5,058; assets, $65,128 (M); expenditures, $5,901; qualifying distributions, $5,058.
Limitations: Giving primarily in PA.
Officers and Directors:* Stephen M. Clark,* V.P.; William C. McClure,* Secy.; Jane Hecht, Mgr.; Diane Rowe, Mgr.
EIN: 251605354

48189
Dennis & Rose Heindl Family Foundation
P.O. Box 146
Ridgway, PA 15853-1209 (814) 375-0938
Contact: Dennis D. Heindl, Tr.

Established in 1990 in PA.
Donor(s): Dennis D. Heindl.
Financial data (yr. ended 12/31/01): Grants paid, $5,025; assets, $7,519 (M); gifts received, $5,100; expenditures, $5,229; qualifying distributions, $5,025.
Limitations: Giving primarily in Ridgway, PA.
Trustee: Dennis D. Heindl.
EIN: 526468833

48190
HSC-One Foundation, Inc.
P.O. Box 6058
Harrisburg, PA 17112

Established in 2000 in PA and VA.
Donor(s): Martin Schoffstall.
Financial data (yr. ended 12/31/01): Grants paid, $5,020; assets, $87,972 (M); expenditures, $12,583; qualifying distributions, $5,020.
Directors: Martin L. Schoffstall, Marvin L. Schoffstall, Kim Lee White.
EIN: 251862323

48191
Andrea Mills Barbieri Foundation
c/o Alexis Barbieri
501 W. Mermaid Ln.
Philadelphia, PA 19118-4205

Financial data (yr. ended 12/31/01): Grants paid, $5,005; assets, $128,232 (M); expenditures, $5,673; qualifying distributions, $5,005.
Limitations: Applications not accepted. Giving limited to PA.
Application information: Contributes only to pre-selected organizations.
Trustees: Alexis L. Barbieri, Christina J. Barbieri, M.M. Nuss.
EIN: 236299918

48192
The Aim-One Foundation, Inc.
P.O. Box 6059
Harrisburg, PA 17112

Established in 2000 in PA and VA.
Donor(s): Martin Schoffstall.
Financial data (yr. ended 12/31/01): Grants paid, $5,000; assets, $87,667 (M); gifts received, $800; expenditures, $12,916; qualifying distributions, $5,000.
Directors: Martin L. Schoffstall, Marvin L. Schoffstall, Kim Lee White.
EIN: 251862238

48193
Clarke Family Foundation
629 Academy Ave.
Sewickley, PA 15143

Established in 2000 in PA.
Donor(s): Edwin V. Clarke, Jr., Kathryn Donegan Clarke, Judith Clarke Walter, Edwin V. Clarke III, Kathryn D. Clarke.
Financial data (yr. ended 12/31/01): Grants paid, $5,000; assets, $770,993 (M); gifts received, $5,234; expenditures, $12,605; qualifying distributions, $5,000.
Limitations: Applications not accepted.
Application information: Contributes only to pre-selected organizations.
Officers: Edwin V. Clarke, Jr., Pres.; Edwin V. Clarke III, V.P.; Kathryn Donegan Clarke, Exec. V.P.; Kathryn D. Clarke, Secy.; Judith Clarke Walter, Treas.
EIN: 251875223

48194
Edward A. & Sherley F. Craig Charitable Foundation
c/o Charles J. Queenan, Jr.
535 Smithfield St.
Pittsburgh, PA 15222

Established in 1996 in PA.
Donor(s): Kirkpatrick & Lockhart, LLP, The Hillman Co., Mary M. Spaulding.
Financial data (yr. ended 12/31/01): Grants paid, $5,000; assets, $58,018 (M); expenditures, $5,160; qualifying distributions, $5,000.

Limitations: Applications not accepted. Giving primarily in Pittsburgh, PA.
Application information: Contributes only to pre-selected organizations.
Trustees: Karen A. Craig, Sherley F. Craig, Cynthia Craig-Johnson, Lucy C. Szklinski.
EIN: 256515546

48195
Sybil H. Erickson Charitable Foundation
c/o Eckersley and Ostrowski LLP
434 Lackawanna Ave., Ste. 300
Scranton, PA 18503
Contact: c/o Sybil Erickson, Pres.

Established in 2001 in FL.
Donor(s): Sybil H. Erickson.
Financial data (yr. ended 12/31/01): Grants paid, $5,000; assets, $480 (M); gifts received, $5,500; expenditures, $5,020; qualifying distributions, $5,020.
Officers: Sybil H. Erickson, Pres.; Robert N. Eckersley, Secy.
EIN: 656271668

48196
The Evergreen Foundation
549 Carlisle St.
Hanover, PA 17331-2162

Financial data (yr. ended 12/31/01): Grants paid, $5,000; assets, $471,485 (M); gifts received, $337,765; expenditures, $6,055; qualifying distributions, $5,764.
Trustees: Warren F. Miller, Jr., Warren F. Miller III.
EIN: 256581573

48197
The Fenstermacher Foundation
c/o R.T. Fenstermacher
1901 Howard Ave.
Pottsville, PA 17901

Financial data (yr. ended 10/31/01): Grants paid, $5,000; assets, $102,639 (M); expenditures, $5,028; qualifying distributions, $5,028.
Limitations: Applications not accepted. Giving limited to PA.
Trustees: R.T. Fenstermacher, T.F. Fenstermacher, Patricia May.
EIN: 236278702

48198
Foundation for Urban Research, Inc.
910 Hill House
201 W. Evergreen Ave.
Philadelphia, PA 19118
Contact: Paul S. Weinberg, Pres.

Donor(s): Paul S. Weinberg.
Financial data (yr. ended 04/30/02): Grants paid, $5,000; assets, $85,927 (M); gifts received, $2,804; expenditures, $6,421; qualifying distributions, $5,000.
Limitations: Giving primarily in NM.
Officers: Paul S. Weinberg, Pres.; Pennie Peck, V.P. and Secy.; Bruce Weinberg, V.P.
EIN: 516016043

48199
The Matthew C. Greenburg Trust
401 City Ave.
Bala Cynwyd, PA 19004
Contact: Mark S. Greenburg, Tr.

Financial data (yr. ended 12/31/00): Grants paid, $5,000; assets, $6,858 (M); gifts received, $700; expenditures, $5,000; qualifying distributions, $5,000.
Limitations: Giving primarily in PA.
Trustees: Julie Greenburg, Mark S. Greenburg, Sheldon Greenburg, Jon B. Morris.

EIN: 237648466

48200
The Dorothy S. Groff Scholarship Fund
P.O. Box 47, E. Main St.
Morgantown, PA 19543-0047

Established in 1997 in PA.
Financial data (yr. ended 12/31/99): Grants paid, $5,000; assets, $62,834 (M); expenditures, $5,050; qualifying distributions, $4,956.
Limitations: Giving limited to residents of PA.
Trustees: Dorothy S. Groff, Terry Weiler.
EIN: 232905717

48201
The Barry J. and Marlene M. Halbritter Foundation
(also known as The Halbritter Foundation)
Rd. No. 2, Box 582
Altoona, PA 16601-9349

Established in 1995 in PA.
Financial data (yr. ended 12/31/00): Grants paid, $5,000; assets, $40,480 (M); expenditures, $5,000; qualifying distributions, $5,000.
Limitations: Applications not accepted. Giving primarily in Martinsburg, PA.
Application information: Contributes only to pre-selected organizations.
Trustees: Barry Halbritter, Marlene Halbritter.
EIN: 251788472

48202
Jay F. Keefer Scholarship Trust
c/o Susquehanna Trust & Investment Co.
329 Pine St.
Williamsport, PA 17701

Financial data (yr. ended 12/31/01): Grants paid, $5,000; assets, $60,345 (M); gifts received, $434; expenditures, $5,050; qualifying distributions, $4,975.
Limitations: Giving limited to residents of PA.
Trustee: Susquehanna Trust & Investment Co.
EIN: 236760450

48203
Edward & Kathleen Kelly Family Foundation
249 Sugartown Rd.
Devon, PA 19333
Contact: Edward Kelly, Dir., or Kathlee Kelly, Dir.

Established in 2000 in PA.
Donor(s): Edward Kelly.
Financial data (yr. ended 12/31/01): Grants paid, $5,000; assets, $185,269 (M); gifts received, $79,705; expenditures, $5,483; qualifying distributions, $5,000.
Directors: Edward Kelly, Kathleen Kelly.
EIN: 256638459

48204
The John Kelly Foundation
c/o Kreischer, Miller & Co.
200 Gibraltar Rd.
Horsham, PA 19044
Application address: 28 S. Waterloo Rd., P.O. Box 125, Devon, PA 19333

Established in 1985 in PA.
Financial data (yr. ended 12/31/01): Grants paid, $5,000; assets, $98,125 (M); expenditures, $5,061; qualifying distributions, $5,000.
Limitations: Giving limited to the greater Philadelphia, PA, area.
Application information: Application form not required.
Trustee: John Kelly.
EIN: 232332513

48205
The Vivian Simkins Lasko Foundation
101 Clarke St.
West Chester, PA 19380-2324

Established in 1986 in PA.
Financial data (yr. ended 11/30/01): Grants paid, $5,000; assets, $19,504 (M); expenditures, $5,000; qualifying distributions, $5,000.
Limitations: Applications not accepted. Giving primarily in Philadelphia, PA.
Application information: Contributes only to pre-selected organizations.
Trustee: Vivian Lasko.
EIN: 236779299

48206
Lehigh Valley Memorial Workers Scholarship Fund
c/o M. Wallery
2779 Hill Dr.
Bath, PA 18014-9145
Application address: P.O. Box 20226, Lehigh Valley, PA 18002-0226

Established in 1990 in PA.
Financial data (yr. ended 12/31/99): Grants paid, $5,000; assets, $138,252 (M); gifts received, $760; expenditures, $7,783; qualifying distributions, $5,000.
Limitations: Giving limited to residents of Lehigh Valley, PA.
Application information: Application form required.
Officers and Committee Members:* Pete DePietro,* Co-Chair.; Dawn D'Andria,* Co-Chair.; Ron Achey, Arthur Barwick, Neil Brown, Dominick Buscemi, Wendy Derr, John W. Halasovski, James Hunt, Sheryl Hunt, Ben Marcune, Ron Rejician, Paul V.D. Smith, Ann Marie Snowden, Dennis W. Thomma, Michael Wallery, John Werkheiser.
EIN: 232649768

48207
Louden Family Foundation
544 Marion Ave., Ste. 3
Norristown, PA 19403

Established in 1999 in PA.
Donor(s): Barbara Louden.
Financial data (yr. ended 09/30/01): Grants paid, $5,000; assets, $45,923 (M); expenditures, $6,200; qualifying distributions, $5,000.
Limitations: Applications not accepted.
Application information: Contributes only to pre-selected organizations.
Officers and Trustees:* Michael W. Louden, C.E.O.; Barbara Louden, Chair.; Richard O. Louden,* Secy.; Rebecca Louden Hicklin, George W. Louden.
EIN: 233021523

48208
The Stephen E. & Louise Anne E. Luongo Family Foundation
(Formerly Luongo Family Foundation)
1 Logan Sq.
Philadelphia, PA 19103-6998

Established in 1996 in PA.
Financial data (yr. ended 11/30/01): Grants paid, $5,000; assets, $13,476 (M); gifts received, $200; expenditures, $5,174; qualifying distributions, $5,000.
Limitations: Applications not accepted.
Application information: Contributes only to pre-selected organizations.
Trustees: Louise Anne E. Luongo, Stephen E. Luongo.
EIN: 237862345

48209
The Henry A. and Mary J. MacDonald Foundation
100 State St., Ste. 700
Erie, PA 16507-1498
Contact: James D. Cullen, Pres.

Established in 1998 in PA.
Donor(s): Mary J. MacDonald.‡
Financial data (yr. ended 12/31/01): Grants paid, $5,000; assets, $81,980 (M); expenditures, $7,522; qualifying distributions, $5,000.
Application information: Application form required.
Officers and Directors:* James D. Cullen,* Pres.; Shaun B. Adrian,* V.P. and Treas.; John A. Lauer,* Secy.
EIN: 251640459

48210
Morris Perelman Foundation
2113 E. Rush St.
Philadelphia, PA 19134-3910 (215) 739-5718
Contact: Bernard Gerhardt, Tr.

Established in 1988 in PA.
Financial data (yr. ended 12/31/01): Grants paid, $5,000; assets, $1,212 (M); gifts received, $5,000; expenditures, $5,165; qualifying distributions, $5,140.
Limitations: Giving primarily in Philadelphia, PA.
Trustee: Bernard Gerhardt.
EIN: 232542735

48211
Alfred H. & Ada O. Repp Scholarship Fund
(Formerly Alfred H. Repp Trust)
c/o Mellon Bank, N.A.
P.O. Box 7236
Philadelphia, PA 19101-7236

Financial data (yr. ended 12/31/99): Grants paid, $5,000; assets, $118,994 (M); expenditures, $6,015; qualifying distributions, $5,112.
Limitations: Applications not accepted. Giving limited to residents of Monroe County, PA.
Application information: Recipients are recommended by high school principal.
Trustee: Mellon Bank, N.A.
EIN: 236648386

48212
Sally Love Saunders Poetry & Arts Foundation
639 Timber Ln.
Devon, PA 19333-1247 (610) 688-0721
Contact: Marion Arnold, Exec. Dir.

Established in 1993 in PA.
Donor(s): Sally Love Saunders.
Financial data (yr. ended 12/31/01): Grants paid, $5,000; assets, $112,639 (M); expenditures, $5,543; qualifying distributions, $5,000.
Officers: Sally Love Saunders, Chair.; Robert Arnold, Secy.-Treas.; Marion Arnold, Exec. Dir.
EIN: 232724613

48213
Donald J. Seebold Scholarship Fund
c/o Fulton Financial Advisors, N.A.
P.O. Box 3215
Lancaster, PA 17604-3215
Application address: c/o Guidance Counselor, Danville Senior High School, Northumberland Rd., Danville, PA 17821, tel.: (570) 275-4113

Financial data (yr. ended 12/31/00): Grants paid, $5,000; assets, $105,728 (M); expenditures, $6,698; qualifying distributions, $5,000.
Limitations: Giving primarily in Danville, PA.
Application information: Application form required.
Trustee: Fulton Financial Advisors, N.A.
EIN: 232643229

48214
Dr. James W. Sinden Scholarship Fund
c/o Banknorth Investment Management Group, N.A.
24 S. 3rd St.
Oxford, PA 19363-0500
Application address: c/o Sara Manning, American Mushroom Inst., 1284 Gap-Newport Pike, Ste. 2, Avondale, PA 19311, tel.: (610) 268-7483

Financial data (yr. ended 12/31/00): Grants paid, $5,000; assets, $114,338 (M); expenditures, $6,239; qualifying distributions, $4,982.
Limitations: Applications not accepted. Giving limited to PA.
Trustee: Banknorth Investment Management Group, N.A.
EIN: 232170419

48215
The W. Keith & Katherine W. Smith Foundation
116 Riding Trail Ln.
Pittsburgh, PA 15215
Contact: W. Keith Smith, Tr.

Established in 2000 in PA.
Donor(s): W. Keith Smith.
Financial data (yr. ended 12/31/01): Grants paid, $5,000; assets, $58,416 (M); expenditures, $5,000; qualifying distributions, $5,000.
Limitations: Giving primarily in PA.
Application information: Application form not required.
Trustees: Kelly Kurschner, Katherine W. Smith, W. Keith Smith.
EIN: 311720606

48216
Dup Thouron Charitable Foundation
c/o Glenmede Trust Co.
1650 Market St., Ste. 1200
Philadelphia, PA 19103-7391
Application address: P.O. Box 249, Nottingham, PA 19362
Contact: John Julius Thouron, Tr.

Established in 2000 in PA.
Donor(s): John R.H. Thouron.
Financial data (yr. ended 12/31/01): Grants paid, $5,000; assets, $539,128 (M); gifts received, $250,000; expenditures, $14,577; qualifying distributions, $5,000.
Application information: Application form not required.
Trustees: Rachel Thouron Nicoll, John Julius Thouron, John R.H. Thouron, John Rupert Thouron.
EIN: 516514644

48217
Wallace/Ferree Memorial Foundation
(Formerly Clifford B. Ferree Menorial Foundation)
243 Twin Hills Dr.
Pittsburgh, PA 15216

Financial data (yr. ended 12/31/00): Grants paid, $5,000; assets, $78,671 (M); expenditures, $6,087; qualifying distributions, $4,936.
Limitations: Applications not accepted. Giving primarily in Pittsburgh, PA.
Application information: Contributes only to pre-selected organizations.
Officer: Jane C. Wallace, Pres.
EIN: 237046794

48218
Cora M. Weeber Irrevocable Trust
c/o Fulton Financial Advisors, N.A.
P.O. Box 3215
Lancaster, PA 17604
Application address: c/o J.E. Zimmerman, Pastor, 3550 N. Progress Ave., Harrisburg, PA 17110

Established in 1987 in PA.
Donor(s): Paxton United Methodist Church.
Financial data (yr. ended 10/31/01): Grants paid, $5,000; assets, $83,631 (M); expenditures, $7,076; qualifying distributions, $4,922.
Limitations: Giving primarily in Harrisburg, PA.
Trustee: Fulton Financial Advisors, N.A.
EIN: 236902747

48219
Wright-Hayre Foundation
3900 Ford Rd.
Philadelphia, PA 19131

Established in 1999 in PA.
Financial data (yr. ended 12/31/01): Grants paid, $5,000; assets, $557,489 (M); expenditures, $40,253; qualifying distributions, $5,000.
Trustee: Sylvia Hayre.
EIN: 232980038

48220
L. R. Smith Trust for Various Charities
c/o Mellon Bank, N.A.
P.O. Box 185
Pittsburgh, PA 15230

Established in 1998 in PA.
Financial data (yr. ended 12/31/01): Grants paid, $4,936; assets, $105,067 (M); expenditures, $6,366; qualifying distributions, $4,936.
Limitations: Applications not accepted. Giving limited to FL and Emlenton and Pittsburgh, PA.
Application information: Contributes only to pre-selected organizations.
Trustee: Mellon Bank, N.A.
EIN: 256222838

48221
Petok Charitable Foundation
2200 Georgetown Dr., Ste. 401
Sewickley, PA 15143

Established in PA in 1997.
Donor(s): Samuel Petok.
Financial data (yr. ended 12/31/01): Grants paid, $4,920; assets, $61,462 (M); expenditures, $5,678; qualifying distributions, $4,920.
Limitations: Giving primarily in NJ.
Officers and Directors:* Samuel Petok,* Chair.; Fayne Petok, Secy.; Edward J. Aufman.
EIN: 237890011

48222
Ora and Joseph Mendels Family Foundation
737 Canterbury Ln.
Villanova, PA 19085-2065 (610) 520-2557
Contact: Joseph Mendels, Pres.

Established in 2000 in PA.
Donor(s): Joseph Mendels.
Financial data (yr. ended 12/31/00): Grants paid, $4,909; assets, $66,952 (M); gifts received, $42,977; expenditures, $5,057; qualifying distributions, $5,029.
Limitations: Giving primarily in CA, NY, and PA.
Application information: Application form not required.
Officers and Directors:* Joseph Mendels,* Pres. and Treas.; Ora Mendels,* Secy.; Charles Mendels, David Ralph Mendels, Gilla Mendels Robbins.
EIN: 233016652

48223
Clarence and Miriam Rosenberger Scholarship Fund
c/o First Union National Bank
P.O. Box 7558
Philadelphia, PA 19101-7558
Application address: c/o First Union National Bank, 4259 Swamp Rd., Ste. 310, Doylestown, PA 18901

Established in 1990 in PA.
Financial data (yr. ended 06/30/99): Grants paid, $4,900; assets, $80,769 (M); expenditures, $6,411; qualifying distributions, $5,834.
Limitations: Giving limited to residents of PA.
Application information: Application form required.
Officers: Donald B. Smith, Jr., Chair.; Marie Miller, Vice-Chair.; William H. Kantner, Secy.
Trustee: First Union National Bank.
EIN: 232663304

48224
Tracy-Sandford Foundation
c/o Lucinda S. Mezey
731 Spruce St.
Philadelphia, PA 19106 (215) 592-8398

Financial data (yr. ended 12/31/01): Grants paid, $4,900; assets, $86,820 (M); gifts received, $6,200; expenditures, $6,016; qualifying distributions, $4,900.
Limitations: Applications not accepted. Giving on a national basis, primarily in the eastern U.S.
Application information: Contributes only to pre-selected organizations.
Officers and Directors:* Barbara T. Sandford,* Pres.; Joseph Sandford,* V.P.; Priscilla Sandford,* Secy.; Lucinda S. Mezey,* Treas.; Catherine S. Morgan, Sarah Sandford-Miller, Tracy S. Whitehead.
EIN: 511161498

48225
Woodruff Family Services Foundation
2820 Washington Rd.
McMurray, PA 15317

Established in 1998 in PA.
Donor(s): Richard C. Beinhauer.
Financial data (yr. ended 06/30/01): Grants paid, $4,900; assets, $92,354 (M); expenditures, $7,140; qualifying distributions, $5,628.
Limitations: Applications not accepted.
Application information: Contributes only to pre-selected organizations.
Officers and Director:* Richard C. Beinhauer,* Pres.; Regina M. Beinhauer, Secy.-Treas.
EIN: 251824279

48226
E. A. Zacks Charitable Foundation, Inc.
4910 Sunnydale Blvd.
Erie, PA 16509-2337

Financial data (yr. ended 12/31/01): Grants paid, $4,886; assets, $62 (M); gifts received, $4,500; expenditures, $5,186; qualifying distributions, $4,886.
Limitations: Applications not accepted.
Officers: Edward A. Zacks, Pres.; Ruth H. Zacks, Mgr.
EIN: 256089949

48227
The Gelbach Foundation
6029 Joshua Rd.
Fort Washington, PA 19034

Established in 1986 in PA.
Donor(s): Myron S. Gelbach.
Financial data (yr. ended 12/31/01): Grants paid, $4,805; assets, $87,520 (M); expenditures, $5,252; qualifying distributions, $4,805.
Limitations: Applications not accepted.
Application information: Contributes only to pre-selected organizations.
Officers: Myron S. Gelbach, Pres.; Loretta M. Gelbach, V.P.
Director: Thomas M. Gelbach.
EIN: 236836651

48228
John A. Lathwood Education Trust
c/o PNC Advisors
620 Liberty Ave., P2-PTPP-10-2
Pittsburgh, PA 15222-2705
Application address: c/o Dean and Chapter of the Cathedral, Trinity Protestant Episcopal Cathedral Church, 6th Ave., Pittsburgh, PA 15222

Financial data (yr. ended 12/31/01): Grants paid, $4,800; assets, $852,660 (M); expenditures, $6,354; qualifying distributions, $4,885.
Limitations: Giving limited to Pittsburgh, PA.
Application information: Application form not required.
Trustee: PNC Bank, N.A.
EIN: 256077125

48229
Judith Peale Strattan Memorial Educational Trust
c/o County National Bank, Trust Dept.
P.O. Box 42
Clearfield, PA 16830

Financial data (yr. ended 11/30/01): Grants paid, $4,768; assets, $102,074 (M); expenditures, $6,999; qualifying distributions, $4,768.
Limitations: Applications not accepted. Giving primarily in Clearfield, PA.
Application information: Contributes only to pre-selected organizations.
Trustee: County National Bank.
EIN: 256494298

48230
McCleary Family Foundation
19 W. King St.
Chambersburg, PA 17201

Established in 1999 in PA.
Financial data (yr. ended 12/31/01): Grants paid, $4,750; assets, $134,641 (M); gifts received, $50,000; expenditures, $6,437; qualifying distributions, $4,750.
Limitations: Applications not accepted.
Application information: Contributes only to pre-selected organizations.
Trustees: H. Huber McCleary, Michael McCleary, Michelle McCleary, Sandra R. McCleary.
EIN: 256612433

48231
Thomas P. Rogers Trust for C. H. Rogers Memorial Fund
c/o Mellon Bank, N.A.
P.O. Box 185
Pittsburgh, PA 15230-9897

Established in 1992 in PA.
Donor(s): Thomas P. Rogers.‡
Financial data (yr. ended 12/31/01): Grants paid, $4,750; assets, $119,598 (M); expenditures, $5,722; qualifying distributions, $5,058.
Limitations: Applications not accepted. Giving limited to residents of East Stroudsburg, PA.
Application information: Unsolicited requests for funds not accepted.
Trustee: Mellon Bank, N.A.
EIN: 232171552

48232
M. I. Ali Foundation, Inc.
50 Valhalla Dr.
New Castle, PA 16105

Established in 1997 in PA.
Financial data (yr. ended 12/31/00): Grants paid, $4,700; assets, $182,425 (M); gifts received, $29,114; expenditures, $5,929; qualifying distributions, $4,700.
Limitations: Giving primarily in PA.
Officers and Directors:* Mohammad I. Arif,* Pres.; Mohammad Arif Ali,* Secy.-Treas.
EIN: 232909032

48233
Nathan and May B. Teitelman Charitable Foundation
c/o Plymoth Corporate Ctr.
625 Ridge Pike, Ste. C-101
Conshohocken, PA 19428

Financial data (yr. ended 12/31/01): Grants paid, $4,700; assets, $68,090 (M); expenditures, $4,857; qualifying distributions, $4,700.
Limitations: Applications not accepted. Giving primarily in PA.
Application information: Contributes only to pre-selected organizations.
Trustees: Gilbert E. Teitelman, Louis E. Teitelman.
EIN: 232222165

48234
Green Family Foundation, Inc.
319 Merchant St.
Ambridge, PA 15003-2523
Contact: Samuel J. Green, Pres.

Financial data (yr. ended 12/31/00): Grants paid, $4,693; assets, $15,948 (M); gifts received, $500; expenditures, $4,983; qualifying distributions, $4,983.
Limitations: Giving primarily in PA.
Officer: Samuel J. Green, Pres.
EIN: 251578168

48235
The Tessler Family Foundation
41 Conshohocken St. Rd.
Bala Cynwyd, PA 19004

Established in 1997 in PA.
Donor(s): Mildred Tessler.
Financial data (yr. ended 12/31/01): Grants paid, $4,600; assets, $51,207 (M); gifts received, $20,000; expenditures, $4,756; qualifying distributions, $4,600.
Limitations: Applications not accepted.
Application information: Contributes only to pre-selected organizations.
Officers: Mildred Tessler, Pres.; A. Robert Tessler, V.P.; Dennis J. Tessler, V.P.; Cindy R. Auslander, Secy.-Treas.
EIN: 232939764

48236
John D. Bare Memorial Scholarship
c/o Allfirst, Trust Tax Div.
21 E. Market St.
York, PA 17401-1500
Application address: c/o Allfirst, Trust Dept., 13 Baltimore St., Hanover, PA 17335, tel.: (717) 630-4544

Financial data (yr. ended 12/31/00): Grants paid, $4,500; assets, $116,230 (M); expenditures, $5,871; qualifying distributions, $4,500.
Limitations: Giving limited to residents of PA.
Trustee: Allfirst.
EIN: 236858178

48237
The Sam L. and Judy Barker 1999 Charitable Trust
c/o Glenmede Trust Company of N.J.
1650 Market St., Ste. 1200
Philadelphia, PA 19103-7391
Application address: 16 Chambers St.,
Princeton, NJ 08542-3708, tel.: (215) 419-6000
Contact: Megan Thomas, Trust Off., Glenmede Trust Co. of N.J.

Established in 1999 in NJ.
Donor(s): Sam L. Barker, Judy Barker.
Financial data (yr. ended 12/31/01): Grants paid, $4,500; assets, $200,551 (M); expenditures, $6,867; qualifying distributions, $4,500.
Limitations: Giving primarily in VA.
Trustees: Edward F. Barker, Judy A. Barker, Sam L. Barker, Karen Barker Workman, The Glenmede Trust Co.
EIN: 226810579

48238
M. Catherine Murphy Memorial Fund
c/o First Columbia Bank & Trust Co.
11 W. Main St.
Bloomsburg, PA 17815-1702 (570) 387-4609
Contact: John Thompson, Sr. V.P. & Trust Off., First Columbia Bank & Trust Co.

Donor(s): M. Catherine Murphy.
Financial data (yr. ended 12/31/01): Grants paid, $4,498; assets, $409,802 (M); expenditures, $10,764; qualifying distributions, $4,498; giving activities include $4,498 for loans to individuals.
Limitations: Giving limited to residents of Catawissa, PA.
Application information: Application form required.
Trustee: First Columbia Bank & Trust Co.
EIN: 236648433
Codes: GTI

48239
Teresa Youtz Arnold Memorial Scholarship Fund
c/o Fulton Financial Advisors, N.A.
P.O. Box 3215
Lancaster, PA 17604-3215
Application address: c/o Guidance Office, Lebanon Catholic High School, 1400 Chestnut St., Lebanon, PA 17042-4590, tel.: (717) 273-3731

Established in 1991 in PA.
Financial data (yr. ended 12/31/01): Grants paid, $4,476; assets, $60,063 (M); expenditures, $5,686; qualifying distributions, $4,476.
Limitations: Giving limited to residents of Lebanon, PA.
Application information: Application form required.
Trustee: Fulton Financial Advisors, N.A.
EIN: 256363468
Codes: GTI

48240
June C. Hutton Trust
21 E. Market St., M/C 402-130
York, PA 17401-1500

Established in 2000 in PA.
Financial data (yr. ended 12/31/01): Grants paid, $4,472; assets, $153,681 (M); expenditures, $7,995; qualifying distributions, $4,472.
Limitations: Applications not accepted. Giving primarily in PA.
Application information: Contributes only to pre-selected organizations.
Trustee: Allfirst.
EIN: 256582106

48241
Stewart Carter Swartz Trust
21 E. Market St.
York, PA 17401-1500

Established in 2000 in PA.
Financial data (yr. ended 11/30/01): Grants paid, $4,472; assets, $156,831 (M); expenditures, $7,247; qualifying distributions, $7,247.
Limitations: Applications not accepted. Giving primarily in PA.
Application information: Contributes only to pre-selected organizations.
Trustee: Allfirst.
EIN: 236646426

48242
E. & E. Hertzler Foundation, Inc.
2402 Main St.
Narvon, PA 17555

Donor(s): Elmer K. Hertzler.
Financial data (yr. ended 12/31/01): Grants paid, $4,450; assets, $72,805 (M); expenditures, $5,395; qualifying distributions, $4,450.
Officers: Elmer K. Hertzler, Pres. and Treas.; Esther M. Hertzler, V.P. and Secy.
EIN: 232828180

48243
Robert & Sheila Chamovitz Family Charitable Trust
564 Forbes Ave., Manor Bldg., No. 803
Pittsburgh, PA 15219-2903 (412) 391-2920
Application address: c/o Gerald I. Rosenfeld, P.C., Manor Bldg., Suite 803, Pittsburg, PA 15219, tel.: (412) 261-2959
Contact: Shelia Chamovitz, Tr.

Donor(s): Robert Chamovitz.
Financial data (yr. ended 11/30/01): Grants paid, $4,416; assets, $60,197 (M); expenditures, $4,493; qualifying distributions, $4,416.
Limitations: Giving primarily in Pittsburgh, PA.
Application information: Application form not required.
Trustees: David Chamovitz, Sheila Chamovitz.
EIN: 251409268

48244
Adam Reineman Charitable Trust
c/o PNC Advisors
620 Liberty Ave., P2-PTPP-10-2
Pittsburgh, PA 15222-2705 (412) 762-3637

Donor(s): Adam Reineman.‡
Financial data (yr. ended 09/30/01): Grants paid, $4,407; assets, $84,831 (M); expenditures, $5,814; qualifying distributions, $4,430.
Limitations: Giving primarily in PA.
Application information: Application form required.
Trustee: PNC Bank, N.A.
EIN: 256023582

48245
Lefco Foundation
c/o Herman Lefco
100 Breyer Dr., Rm. 4B
Elkins Park, PA 19027

Financial data (yr. ended 12/31/01): Grants paid, $4,400; assets, $98,420 (M); expenditures, $4,446; qualifying distributions, $4,400.
Limitations: Applications not accepted. Giving primarily in PA.
Application information: Contributes only to pre-selected organizations.
Trustees: Arthur W. Lefco, Deborah Lefco, Herman Lefco.
EIN: 236296622

48246
The Christopher B. Asplundh Foundation
708 Blair Mill Rd.
Willow Grove, PA 19090 (215) 784-4200
Contact: Christopher B. Asplundh, Tr.

Established in 1986 in PA.
Financial data (yr. ended 12/31/01): Grants paid, $4,340; assets, $75,240 (M); expenditures, $4,491; qualifying distributions, $4,491.
Limitations: Giving primarily in PA.
Trustee: Christopher B. Asplundh.
EIN: 222781600

48247
Moyer-Longacre Scholarship Fund
c/o Fulton Financial Advisors, N.A.
P.O. Box 3215
Lancaster, PA 17604-3215

Financial data (yr. ended 06/30/01): Grants paid, $4,300; assets, $51,042 (M); expenditures, $5,019; qualifying distributions, $4,248.
Limitations: Giving limited to the Lebanon, PA, area.
Application information: Unsolicited request for funds accepted, recipients selection based on academic merit.
Trustee: Fulton Financial Advisors, N.A.
EIN: 236522613

48248
Prostejovsky Charitable Trust
c/o Portage National Bank, Trust Dept.
737 Main St.
Portage, PA 15946

Established in 1997.
Donor(s): Richard Prostejovsky, Theresa Prostejovsky.
Financial data (yr. ended 12/31/01): Grants paid, $4,290; assets, $75,449 (M); expenditures, $5,574; qualifying distributions, $4,290.
Limitations: Applications not accepted.
Officers: Richard Prostejovsky, Mgr.; Theresa Prostejovsky, Mgr.
EIN: 237869816

48249
Kauffman Anspach Trust
c/o Allfirst, Trust Tax Div.
21 E. Market St.
York, PA 17401

Financial data (yr. ended 06/30/01): Grants paid, $4,280; assets, $83,227 (M); expenditures, $5,306; qualifying distributions, $4,280.
Limitations: Applications not accepted. Giving primarily in PA.
Application information: Contributes only to pre-selected organizations.
Trustee: Allfirst.
EIN: 236744419

48250
The Barbara Silver Levin Foundation, Inc.
510 Walnut St., Ste. 500
Philadelphia, PA 19106-3697
Application Address: 162 Gramercy Rd., Bala Cynwyd, PA 19004, tel.: (215) 592-1500
Contact: Arnold Levin, C.E.O.

Established in 1998 in PA.
Donor(s): Arnold Levin.
Financial data (yr. ended 12/31/01): Grants paid, $4,250; assets, $114,876 (M); gifts received, $60,175; expenditures, $4,271; qualifying distributions, $4,250.
Limitations: Giving primarily in PA.
Officers and Trustees:* Arnold Levin,* C.E.O.; Daniel Levin,* Secy.-Treas.

EIN: 232984801

48251
The Carol & George Weinbaum Family Foundation
6532 N. 12th St.
Philadelphia, PA 19126

Established in 1999 in PA.
Financial data (yr. ended 12/31/01): Grants paid, $4,250; assets, $59,766 (M); expenditures, $4,714; qualifying distributions, $4,250.
Limitations: Applications not accepted.
Application information: Contributes only to pre-selected organizations.
Trustees: Carol Weinbaum, Cindy Merle Weinbaum, Elliot Weinbaum, Eve Weinbaum, George Weinbaum, Laura Ilene Weinbaum.
EIN: 256657252

48252
Warrell Family Historical Foundation
c/o Financial Trust Co.
P.O. Box 3068
Williamsport, PA 17701

Financial data (yr. ended 12/31/99): Grants paid, $4,223; assets, $120,608 (M); expenditures, $5,064; qualifying distributions, $4,223.
Limitations: Applications not accepted.
Application information: Contributes only to a pre-selected organization.
Trustee: Financial Trust Co.
EIN: 232022530

48253
Berman Charitable Foundation
3277 W. Ridge Pike
P.O. Box 957, Ste. A101
Pottstown, PA 19464

Financial data (yr. ended 03/31/02): Grants paid, $4,200; assets, $386,753 (M); expenditures, $8,017; qualifying distributions, $4,200.
Limitations: Applications not accepted. Giving primarily in Pottstown, Allentown, and Philadelphia, PA.
Application information: Contributes only to pre-selected organizations.
Officers: Jay S. Berman, Pres.; Jennifer B. Scotese, V.P. and Treas.; Susan C Berman, Secy.
EIN: 236239058

48254
Dorothy Cook Fund
c/o PNC Advisors
620 Liberty Ave., P2-PTPP-10-2
Pittsburgh, PA 15222-2705

Established in 1997 in NJ.
Donor(s): Dorothy C. Cook.‡
Financial data (yr. ended 12/31/01): Grants paid, $4,200; assets, $96,215 (M); expenditures, $6,254; qualifying distributions, $4,200.
Limitations: Applications not accepted. Giving primarily in Millington, NJ.
Application information: Contributes only to pre-selected organizations.
Trustees: John H. Priestman, PNC Bank, N.A.
EIN: 237868423

48255
Nathan Charitable Foundation
2 Penn Blvd., Ste. 103
Philadelphia, PA 19144 (215) 842-0406
Contact: Meera V. Nathan, M.D., Tr.

Established in 1997.
Financial data (yr. ended 06/30/01): Grants paid, $4,200; assets, $179,746 (M); gifts received, $25,000; expenditures, $4,934; qualifying distributions, $4,098.
Limitations: Giving primarily in Portland, OR.
Trustees: Leslie Molnar, Meera V. Nathan, M.D.
EIN: 237821437

48256
Claribel E. Dutcher Trust f/b/o Dean Dutcher Memorial Music
c/o Allfirst, Trust Tax Div.
21 E. Market St
York, PA 17401-1500

Established in 2000 in PA.
Financial data (yr. ended 12/31/01): Grants paid, $4,192; assets, $48,331 (M); expenditures, $5,818; qualifying distributions, $5,491.
Limitations: Giving limited to residents of PA.
Trustee: Allfirst.
EIN: 256362181

48257
FGB Foundation
81 Winged Foot Dr.
Reading, PA 19607

Donor(s): Fred G. Bollman.
Financial data (yr. ended 01/31/02): Grants paid, $4,179; assets, $6,771 (M); expenditures, $4,182; qualifying distributions, $4,179.
Limitations: Applications not accepted. Giving on a national basis.
Application information: Contributes only to pre-selected organizations.
Trustees: Jeffrey Rickenbach, Nancy B. White.
EIN: 232281487

48258
The Haney Foundation
P.O. Box 1429
New Castle, PA 16103

Financial data (yr. ended 09/30/01): Grants paid, $4,175; assets, $169,902 (M); expenditures, $5,374; qualifying distributions, $4,175.
Limitations: Applications not accepted. Giving primarily in New Castle, PA.
Application information: Contributes only to pre-selected organizations.
Officer: Sidney M. Shenkan, Pres. and Treas.
EIN: 256066918

48259
Womans Club of Warren Educational Scholarship & Historical Preservation Group
c/o E. Jones
310 Market St.
Warren, PA 16365 (814) 723-9007
Application address: 2 Briggs Dr., Warren, PA 16365
Contact: Mary Jane Kemp

Established in 1997 in PA.
Donor(s): DeFries Foundation, Marian Wendell, Margaret Putnam.
Financial data (yr. ended 12/31/99): Grants paid, $4,169; assets, $43,033 (M); gifts received, $12,790; expenditures, $4,169; qualifying distributions, $4,169.
Limitations: Giving limited to the Warren, PA, area.
Application information: Application form required.
Officers: Jane C. Betts, Pres.; Sharon Drennen, V.P.; Susan J. Merritt, Corr. Secy.; Cathy Zawacki, Rec. Secy.; Elizabeth Jones, Treas.
EIN: 251713814

48260
Erie Sand Charitable Foundation
P.O. Box 179
Erie, PA 16512-0179 (814) 453-6721
Contact: Sidney E. Smith, Jr., Pres.

Established in 1985 in PA.
Donor(s): Erie Sand & Gravel Co., Inc.
Financial data (yr. ended 12/31/01): Grants paid, $4,164; assets, $80,668 (M); gifts received, $82; expenditures, $4,275; qualifying distributions, $4,275.
Limitations: Giving primarily in Erie, PA.
Application information: Application form required for employees; no specific form required for non-employees.
Officer: Sidney E. Smith, Jr., Pres.
EIN: 251517616
Codes: CS, CD

48261
Job Mann Trust No. 2
c/o PNC Advisors
620 Liberty Ave., P2-PTPP-10-2
Pittsburgh, PA 15222
Application address: c/o PNC Bank, N.A., Resource Connect, 620 Liberty Ave., 5th Fl., Pittsburgh, PA 15222

Financial data (yr. ended 09/30/01): Grants paid, $4,135; assets, $232,039 (M); expenditures, $5,482; qualifying distributions, $4,135.
Limitations: Giving limited to male residents of Bedford County, PA.
Trustee: PNC Bank, N.A.
EIN: 236201775

48262
Joseph G. Olszewski Scholarship Fund
925 French St.
Erie, PA 16501-1254
Contact: Louis A. Colussi, Tr.

Financial data (yr. ended 12/31/99): Grants paid, $4,100; assets, $228,228 (M); expenditures, $9,098; qualifying distributions, $9,098.
Limitations: Giving limited to residents of Erie County, PA.
Application information: Application form required.
Trustee: Louis A. Colussi.
EIN: 251376193

48263
Orlando & Jennie Barbetti Scholarship Fund
1421 E. Drinker St.
Dunmore, PA 18512

Established in 2000 in PA.
Donor(s): Michael A. Barbetti, Kronick, Kalada, Berdy & Co.
Financial data (yr. ended 03/31/01): Grants paid, $4,000; assets, $120,230 (M); gifts received, $124,001; expenditures, $4,072; qualifying distributions, $4,000.
Limitations: Applications not accepted. Giving primarily in Old Forge, PA.
Officers: Joseph J. Giombetti, Chair.; James Pocius, Vice-Chair.; Donna M. Barbetti, Secy.; W. Boyd Hughes, Treas.
Board Members: Angelo Cinti, Joseph Solfanelli, Jerry Weinberger.
EIN: 311709836

48264
Callahan McKenna Educational Foundation
31 S. Eagle Rd., Ste. 202
Havertown, PA 19083 (610) 853-1402

Established in 1999 in PA.
Donor(s): Michael J. Callahan, Mary E. McKenna.

48264—PENNSYLVANIA

Financial data (yr. ended 11/30/01): Grants paid, $4,000; assets, $49,029 (M); expenditures, $4,125; qualifying distributions, $4,000.
Limitations: Giving primarily in Philadelphia and Delaware County, PA.
Application information: Application form required.
Officers: Michael J. Callahan, Pres.; Mary E. McKenna, V.P.
Directors: John Caffenty, Mimi McKenna, Deborah Young.
EIN: 233025047

48265
Ray T. Charley Family Fund
c/o Steven J. Lynch
5440 Centre Ave., 2nd Fl.
Pittsburgh, PA 15232

Established in 1990 in PA.
Donor(s): Ray T. Charley.
Financial data (yr. ended 11/30/01): Grants paid, $4,000; assets, $40,569 (M); expenditures, $4,080; qualifying distributions, $4,000.
Limitations: Applications not accepted. Giving limited to PA.
Application information: Contributes only to pre-selected organizations.
Officers and Trustee:* Ray T. Charley,* Pres.; Stephen J. Lynch, Secy.
EIN: 251646082

48266
Christian Orthodox Monastery Preservation Foundation
1248 Old Meadow Rd.
Pittsburgh, PA 15241

Established in 2000 in PA.
Donor(s): Michael T. Pappas.
Financial data (yr. ended 12/31/01): Grants paid, $4,000; assets, $80,851 (M); gifts received, $8,540; expenditures, $6,063; qualifying distributions, $4,000.
Limitations: Applications not accepted.
Application information: Contributes only to pre-selected organizations.
Trustee: Michael T. Pappas.
EIN: 256742860

48267
Cole Family Scholarship Fund
c/o Fulton Financial Advisors, N.A.
P.O. Box 3215
Lancaster, PA 17604-3215
Application address: c/o Carl Marrara, Guidance Counselor, Danville Senior High School, Northumberland Rd., Danville, PA 17821, tel.: (717) 275-4113

Established in 1990 in PA.
Financial data (yr. ended 12/31/00): Grants paid, $4,000; assets, $80,878 (M); expenditures, $5,705; qualifying distributions, $4,000.
Limitations: Giving primarily in PA.
Application information: Application form required.
Trustee: Fulton financial Advisors, N.A.
EIN: 236997878

48268
The DNJ Friendship Foundation
960 S. Wisteria Dr.
Malvern, PA 19355-2336
Contact: David M. Milberg, Tr.

Established in 2000 in PA.
Donor(s): David M. Milberg.
Financial data (yr. ended 12/31/01): Grants paid, $4,000; assets, $106,212 (M); gifts received, $40,000; expenditures, $4,016; qualifying distributions, $4,000.
Limitations: Giving primarily in Philadelphia, PA.
Trustee: David M. Milberg.
EIN: 256678476

48269
The Roscoe A. Faust and William C. Heller Family Trust
c/o Fulton Financial Advisors, N.A.
P.O. Box 3215
Lancaster, PA 17604-3215
Application address: c/o Carl Marrara, Guidance Counselor, Danville Senior High School, Northumberland Rd., Danville, PA 17821, tel.: (570) 275-4113

Established in 1995 in PA.
Donor(s): Emma A. Heller, Emerson L. Faust.
Financial data (yr. ended 12/31/00): Grants paid, $4,000; assets, $107,290 (M); expenditures, $5,885; qualifying distributions, $3,910.
Limitations: Giving primarily in PA.
Application information: Application form required.
Trustee: Fulton Financial Advisors, N.A.
EIN: 237828105

48270
David and Edith E. Hill Scholarship Fund
c/o PNC Advisors
620 Liberty Ave., P2-PTPP-10-2
Pittsburgh, PA 15222-2705 (412) 762-9018
Application address: c/o PNC Advisors, 620 Liberty Ave., 8th Fl., Pittsburgh, PA 15222-2705
Contact: Amy Phillips

Donor(s): Edith E. Hill.
Financial data (yr. ended 12/31/01): Grants paid, $4,000; assets, $133,995 (M); expenditures, $5,846; qualifying distributions, $4,517.
Limitations: Giving limited to residents of PA.
Trustee: PNC Bank, N.A.
EIN: 236940311

48271
Kessler Fund Trust
c/o Wolf, Block, Schorr & Solis-Cohen
1650 Arch St., 22nd Fl.
Philadelphia, PA 19103-2097

Established in 1996 in PA.
Financial data (yr. ended 05/31/99): Grants paid, $4,000; assets, $961,364 (M); expenditures, $8,012; qualifying distributions, $4,636.
Limitations: Giving primarily in Philadelphia, PA.
Application information: Application form not required.
Trustee: Michael Dean.
EIN: 237839028

48272
The William F. Martin Charitable Foundation
200 Tower Rd.
Villanova, PA 19085-1214 (610) 525-4066
Contact: William F. Martin, Tr.

Established in 1997 in PA.
Donor(s): William F. Martin.
Financial data (yr. ended 11/30/01): Grants paid, $4,000; assets, $38,193 (M); expenditures, $4,770; qualifying distributions, $4,000.
Limitations: Giving primarily in PA.
Trustee: William F. Martin.
EIN: 237941420

48273
Morris & Dorothy Rubinoff Foundation
1418 Bywood Ave.
Upper Darby, PA 19082

Financial data (yr. ended 12/31/01): Grants paid, $4,000; assets, $228,764 (M); expenditures, $5,149; qualifying distributions, $5,149.
Limitations: Applications not accepted. Giving primarily in PA.
Application information: Contributes only to pre-selected organizations.
Officers: Morris Rubinoff, Chair. and Treas.; Dorothy Rubinoff, Secy.
Trustee: Avrun Rivel.
EIN: 232042415

48274
Joseph T. Urban and Margaret L. Minder Urban Scholarship Fund
c/o Anthony J. Urban
35 S. Main St.
Mahanoy City, PA 17948

Financial data (yr. ended 12/31/00): Grants paid, $4,000; assets, $104,383 (M); expenditures, $4,481; qualifying distributions, $4,000.
Limitations: Applications not accepted. Giving limited to residents of Mahanoy City, PA.
Application information: Unsolicited requests for funds not accepted.
Trustee: Anthony J. Urban.
EIN: 237658598

48275
Sarah Yarborough Charitable Trust
c/o John S. Coates
414 Audorra Glen Ct.
Lafayette Hill, PA 19444-2524

Financial data (yr. ended 12/31/00): Grants paid, $4,000; assets, $17,807 (M); gifts received, $336; expenditures, $4,000; qualifying distributions, $4,000.
Limitations: Applications not accepted. Giving limited to Federal Way, WA.
Director: Laura Yarborough.
Trustees: John S. Coates, Thomas S. Yarborough.
EIN: 916351176

48276
McCrudden Family Foundation, Inc.
c/o Robert Fernandez
470 Norristown Rd., Ste. 300
Blue Bell, PA 19422

Established in 2000.
Donor(s): James McCrudden.
Financial data (yr. ended 11/30/01): Grants paid, $3,944; assets, $22,483 (M); expenditures, $4,144; qualifying distributions, $3,944.
Limitations: Applications not accepted.
Application information: Contributes only to pre-selected organizations.
Officer: James McCrudden,* Pres.
EIN: 233023539

48277
The Hoechst Foundation
340 Barren Rd.
Media, PA 19063

Established in 1986 in PA.
Donor(s): Christian M. Hoechst.
Financial data (yr. ended 12/31/01): Grants paid, $3,930; assets, $67,412 (M); expenditures, $5,424; qualifying distributions, $5,230.
Limitations: Applications not accepted. Giving primarily in PA.
Application information: Contributes only to pre-selected organizations.

Trustees: Christian M. Hoechst, Jeanne C. Hoechst.
EIN: 236856183

48278
Helen R. Ahl Scholarship Fund
(also known as P. Vaughn Ahl Trust)
c/o Allfirst, Trust Tax Div.
21 E. Market St.
York, PA 17401-1500
Application addresses: c/o Allfirst, Financial Services, 2 W. Hign St., Carlisle, PA 17013; or c/o Carlisle High School, 624 W. Penn St., Carlisle, PA 17013

Financial data (yr. ended 12/31/01): Grants paid, $3,922; assets, $118,290 (M); expenditures, $5,533; qualifying distributions, $5,424.
Limitations: Giving limited to Carlisle, PA.
Application information: Application form not required.
Trustee: Allfirst.
EIN: 236626688

48279
Paul E. Kanjorski Foundation
(Formerly Congressman Paul E. Kanjorski Foundation)
126 S. Franklin St.
Wilkes-Barre, PA 18701

Financial data (yr. ended 12/31/99): Grants paid, $3,900; assets, $3,296 (M); expenditures, $4,516; qualifying distributions, $4,015.
Limitations: Applications not accepted. Giving limited to residents of the 11th Congressional District in PA.
Officers and Trustee: A. Peter Kanjorski, Pres.; Nancy T. Kanjorski, V.P.; Nancy M. Kanjorski, Secy./Treas.; Mellon Bank, N.A.
EIN: 236910719

48280
Elizabeth Louise Glasgow Foundation
914 Saint James St.
Pittsburgh, PA 15232-2115

Financial data (yr. ended 12/31/01): Grants paid, $3,800; assets, $71,372 (M); expenditures, $4,430; qualifying distributions, $3,800.
Limitations: Applications not accepted. Giving primarily in PA.
Application information: Contributes only to pre-selected organizations.
Trustees: David Glasgow, Joseph Glasgow.
EIN: 237282968

48281
Fred M. Klaus and Harold L. Murphy Foundation
c/o First Union National Bank
Broad & Walnut Sts.
Philadelphia, PA 19109

Established in 1990 in FL.
Donor(s): Fred M. Klaus, Harold L. Murphy.
Financial data (yr. ended 04/30/00): Grants paid, $3,754; assets, $1,413,108 (M); expenditures, $13,933; qualifying distributions, $3,754.
Limitations: Applications not accepted.
Application information: Contributes only to pre-selected organizations.
Trustees: Harold L. Murphy, James E. Stewart, First Union National Bank.
EIN: 656049287

48282
Yentis Foundation
7300 City Line Ave.
Philadelphia, PA 19151 (215) 878-7300
Contact: George R. Goldstone, Tr.

Financial data (yr. ended 08/31/02): Grants paid, $3,751; assets, $1,174 (M); gifts received, $1,460; expenditures, $3,854; qualifying distributions, $3,751.
Limitations: Giving primarily in Philadelphia, PA.
Application information: Application form not required.
Trustees: Louis J. Carter, George R. Goldstone.
EIN: 236441451

48283
Oblender Foundation
c/o Fulton Financial Advisors, N.A.
P.O. Box 3215
Lancaster, PA 17604-3215

Financial data (yr. ended 05/31/02): Grants paid, $3,750; assets, $40,825 (M); expenditures, $4,624; qualifying distributions, $3,750.
Limitations: Applications not accepted. Giving primarily in Lancaster, PA.
Application information: Contributes only to pre-selected organizations.
Trustee: Fulton Financial Advisors, N.A.
EIN: 236273752

48284
Henry M. Barnhart Trust
c/o Allfirst, Trust Tax Div.
21 E. Market St., M/C 402-130
York, PA 17401-1500

Established in 2000 in PA.
Financial data (yr. ended 12/31/00): Grants paid, $3,745; assets, $135,162 (M); expenditures, $8,617; qualifying distributions, $5,174.
Limitations: Applications not accepted. Giving primarily in PA.
Application information: Contributes only to pre-selected organizations.
Trustee: Allfirst.
EIN: 256480476

48285
The Reinhardt Foundation
P.O. Box 577
Manchester, PA 17345-0577
Application address: 2971 Elkridge Ln., York, PA 17404
Contact: Faye E. Reinhardt, Pres.

Donor(s): Faye E. Reinhardt, Richard L. Reinhardt.
Financial data (yr. ended 02/28/00): Grants paid, $3,700; assets, $134,804 (M); gifts received, $6,000; expenditures, $4,918; qualifying distributions, $3,734.
Limitations: Giving primarily in PA.
Application information: Application form required.
Officers: Faye E. Reinhardt, Pres.; Richard L. Reinhardt, V.P.; Joyce B. Mummert, Secy.; Gerald Rogers, Treas.
EIN: 232279192

48286
John C. Jordan Trust
c/o The York Bank & Trust Co.
21 E. Market St.
York, PA 17401-1205

Established in 1984 in PA.
Financial data (yr. ended 12/31/01): Grants paid, $3,661; assets, $174,492 (M); expenditures, $6,155; qualifying distributions, $3,661.
Limitations: Applications not accepted. Giving primarily in PA.
Application information: Contributes only to pre-selected organizations.
Trustee: The York Bank & Trust Co.
EIN: 236285886

48287
The Gupta Foundation
150 W. Queen Ln.
Philadelphia, PA 19144-6273

Established in 1998 in PA.
Financial data (yr. ended 12/31/01): Grants paid, $3,623; assets, $4,037 (M); gifts received, $733; expenditures, $4,211; qualifying distributions, $3,623.
Limitations: Applications not accepted. Giving primarily in India.
Application information: Contributes only to pre-selected organizations.
Officer: Margot Gupta, Secy.
Director: Chandrakant Gupta.
EIN: 232984211

48288
Sam Damico Foundation
c/o Rome, Comisky, McCauley
4 Penn Ctr.
Philadelphia, PA 19103
Application address: 31 Andrian Rd., Glen Mills, PA 19342
Contact: Sam Damico, Pres.

Financial data (yr. ended 06/30/00): Grants paid, $3,600; assets, $73,644 (M); expenditures, $4,302; qualifying distributions, $4,205.
Limitations: Giving primarily in PA and NY.
Officers: Sam Damico, Pres.; Nancy Damico, V.P.
EIN: 236901457

48289
Bachove Family Fund
123 S. Broad St., 25th Fl.
Philadelphia, PA 19109 (215) 772-7302
Contact: Mervin J. Hartman, Tr.

Financial data (yr. ended 09/30/01): Grants paid, $3,500; assets, $4,172 (M); expenditures, $3,500; qualifying distributions, $3,499.
Limitations: Giving primarily in New York, NY, and the Philadelphia, PA, area.
Application information: Application form not required.
Trustee: Mervin J. Hartman.
EIN: 232225694

48290
The Susan M. Huffman Foundation
P.O. Box 193
Wayne, PA 19087

Established in 1997 in PA.
Donor(s): Kenneth J. Huffman.
Financial data (yr. ended 12/31/01): Grants paid, $3,500; assets, $98,476 (M); expenditures, $3,822; qualifying distributions, $3,500.
Limitations: Applications not accepted. Giving primarily in PA.
Application information: Contributes only to pre-selected organizations.
Officers: Kenneth J. Huffman, Pres.; Laura Huffman, Secy.; Jay Huffman, Treas.
EIN: 232904595

48291
H. E. and Dorothy Rairigh Family Foundation
P.O. Box 73, Rte. 286
Hillsdale, PA 15746

Established in 1999 in PA.
Donor(s): Dorothy R. Rairigh.

48291—PENNSYLVANIA

Financial data (yr. ended 12/31/01): Grants paid, $3,500; assets, $77,981 (M); expenditures, $7,508; qualifying distributions, $3,500.
Limitations: Giving primarily in PA.
Trustees: Dorothy R. Rairigh, R. Wayne Rairigh.
EIN: 251812817

48292
Radnor Children's Foundation Trust
c/o Catharine Brennan
303 W. Lancaster Ave., Box 130
Wayne, PA 19087 (610) 648-4228
Contact: Jo Ann Jenkins, Dir.

Established in 1996 in PA.
Donor(s): John Brennan, George Jenkins.
Financial data (yr. ended 12/31/01): Grants paid, $3,463; assets, $5,793 (M); gifts received, $2,000; expenditures, $4,296; qualifying distributions, $3,935.
Limitations: Giving limited to residents of Radnor, PA.
Application information: Application form required.
Directors: Catharine Brennan, Jo Ann Jenkins, Cynthia B. Ritz.
EIN: 237847893

48293
Eli-Sar Graf Foundation
c/o Mellon Bank, N.A.
P.O. Box 185
Pittsburgh, PA 15230
Contact: Jennifer Lyons

Established in 1998 in PA.
Donor(s): Elizabeth Graf.
Financial data (yr. ended 12/31/99): Grants paid, $3,425; assets, $107,021 (M); expenditures, $5,569; qualifying distributions, $4,194.
Limitations: Giving primarily in PA.
Application information: Application form required.
Trustee: Mellon Bank, N.A.
EIN: 257926270

48294
The Selwyn A. Horvitz Foundation
(also known as The Horvitz, Fisher, Miller & Sedlack Foundation)
2500 One Liberty Pl.
Philadelphia, PA 19103 (215) 851-8194
Contact: Selwyn A. Horvitz, Tr.

Established in 1986 in PA.
Financial data (yr. ended 01/31/00): Grants paid, $3,409; assets, $18,656 (M); expenditures, $4,109; qualifying distributions, $3,409.
Limitations: Giving primarily in Philadelphia, PA.
Trustee: Selwyn A. Horvitz.
EIN: 232415323

48295
Deutsch Family Foundation
111 Wyndwood Rd.
Dalton, PA 18414-9546

Established in 1986 in PA.
Donor(s): Ignatz Deutsch, Henri Deutsch.
Financial data (yr. ended 10/31/01): Grants paid, $3,347; assets, $344,841 (M); gifts received, $1,000; expenditures, $4,515; qualifying distributions, $3,347.
Limitations: Applications not accepted. Giving primarily in PA.
Application information: Contributes only to pre-selected organizations.
Officers: Ignatz Deutsch, Pres. and Secy.-Treas.; Henri Deutsch, V.P.
EIN: 222783304

48296
The Besson Foundation
c/o James R. Ledwith
3000 Two Logan Sq.
Philadelphia, PA 19103-2799

Established in 1997 in PA.
Donor(s): Michel L. Besson, Marie-Jose Besson.
Financial data (yr. ended 12/31/01): Grants paid, $3,300; assets, $81,152 (M); expenditures, $3,386; qualifying distributions, $3,300.
Limitations: Applications not accepted.
Application information: Contributes only to pre-selected organizations.
Officers and Directors:* Michel L. Besson,* Pres.; Marie-Jose Beson,* Exec. V.P. and Secy.; Frederique Besson,* V.P.; Pascal Besson,* V.P.; Thomas Besson,* V.P.; John D. Funk, Treas.
EIN: 232939551

48297
Burrell Township Scholarship Fund
c/o PNC Advisors
620 Liberty Ave., P2-PTPP-10_2
Pittsburgh, PA 15222-2705
Contact: Susan Ambrosini, Trust Off., PNC Advisors

Financial data (yr. ended 12/31/00): Grants paid, $3,300; assets, $94,827 (M); expenditures, $3,930; qualifying distributions, $3,301.
Limitations: Giving limited to residents of Burrell Township and Armstrong County, PA.
Application information: Application form required.
Trustee: PNC Bank, N.A.
EIN: 256126287

48298
Nestler Scholarship Foundation
c/o First Union National Bank
14 Main St.
Souderton, PA 18964-0197
Application address: P.O. Box 147, 5th & Walnut Sts., Green Ln., PA 18054, tel.: (215) 234-8354
Contact: Paul R. Nestler, Jr., Trust Off., First Union National Bank

Financial data (yr. ended 07/31/00): Grants paid, $3,300; assets, $28,653 (M); expenditures, $1,885; qualifying distributions, $3,359.
Limitations: Giving limited to PA.
Application information: Application form required.
Trustee: First Union National Bank.
EIN: 236410916

48299
The Abigail L. Longenecker Memorial Foundation
1019 Hunt Club Ln.
Lancaster, PA 17601

Financial data (yr. ended 12/31/01): Grants paid, $3,290; assets, $43,897 (M); gifts received, $11,857; expenditures, $3,949; qualifying distributions, $3,290.
Limitations: Applications not accepted.
Application information: Contributes only to pre-selected organizations.
Officers: Thomas C. Longenecker, Pres.; Jan D. Longenecker, V.P.; Shannon Cortese, Secy.; Jill D. Smith, Treas.
Board Member: Corby Rambler.
EIN: 232952312

48300
Pearl M. Bricker Trust
c/o John M. Eakin
Market Sq. Bldg.
Mechanicsburg, PA 17055

Established in 1987 in PA.
Financial data (yr. ended 07/31/99): Grants paid, $3,250; assets, $5,650 (M); expenditures, $3,669; qualifying distributions, $3,248.
Limitations: Applications not accepted. Giving primarily in PA.
Application information: Contributes only to pre-selected organizations.
Trustee: John M. Eakin.
EIN: 232518367

48301
Beatrice and Francis Thompson Scholarship Trust
c/o Alan A. Sanders
1650 Market St., Ste. 3100
Philadelphia, PA 19103
Application address: 233 S. 6th St., Apt. 1609, Philadelphia, PA 19106, tel.: (215) 925-8362
Contact: Alan A. Sanders, Tr.

Established in 1990 in PA.
Financial data (yr. ended 12/31/01): Grants paid, $3,250; assets, $73,765 (M); expenditures, $4,621; qualifying distributions, $3,250.
Limitations: Giving primarily in Philadelphia, PA.
Trustees: Diann Duffy, Alan A. Sanders.
EIN: 236971811

48302
Preston F. Amspacher Scholarship Trust
c/o Allfirst, Trust Tax Div.
21 E. Market St., M/C 402-130
York, PA 17401-1500

Financial data (yr. ended 12/31/01): Grants paid, $3,238; assets, $62,398 (M); expenditures, $4,721; qualifying distributions, $3,238.
Limitations: Applications not accepted. Giving primarily in PA.
Application information: Contributes only to pre-selected organizations.
Trustee: Allfirst.
EIN: 237705562

48303
Ralph Larosh Church Flower Fund
c/o First Union National Bank
P.O. Box 7558
Philadelphia, PA 19101-7558

Established in 1993 in PA.
Financial data (yr. ended 08/31/00): Grants paid, $3,233; assets, $65,473 (M); expenditures, $4,707; qualifying distributions, $4,459.
Limitations: Applications not accepted. Giving primarily in PA.
Application information: Contributes only to pre-selected organizations.
Trustee: First Union National Bank.
EIN: 236681112

48304
Adelaide Cole Bellows Scholarship Trust
c/o First National Bank of Chester County
P.O. Box 3105, FMS
West Chester, PA 19381-3105
Application address: Principal, Henderson Senior High School, Adams St., West Chester, PA 19380-4493, tel.: (610) 436-7220

Financial data (yr. ended 12/31/01): Grants paid, $3,228; assets, $34,371 (M); expenditures, $3,302; qualifying distributions, $3,228.

Limitations: Giving limited to the West Chester, PA, area.
Application information: Application form required.
Trustee: Charles E. Swope.
Scholarship Committe: Principal, West Chester East High School, Principal, Henderson High School, Superintendent, West Chester Area School District.
EIN: 236253506

48305
The Ruth & Earl Scott Charitable Trust
982 Frazier Rd.
Rydal, PA 19046-2408

Established around 1992.
Donor(s): Ruth R. Scott.
Financial data (yr. ended 12/31/01): Grants paid, $3,200; assets, $982,691 (M); expenditures, $9,727; qualifying distributions, $3,200.
Limitations: Applications not accepted.
Application information: Contributes only to pre-selected organizations.
Officer: Ruth R. Scott, Pres.
EIN: 232629692

48306
Schoeneck Area Civic Association
305 Gockley Rd.
Stevens, PA 17578

Financial data (yr. ended 02/28/02): Grants paid, $3,162; assets, $215,536 (M); expenditures, $3,833; qualifying distributions, $3,162.
Limitations: Applications not accepted. Giving limited to the Schoeneck, PA, area.
Application information: Contributes only to pre-selected organizations.
Officers: Forrest C. Wealand, Pres.; Richard L. Sensenig, V.P.; Sally Wealand, Secy.; Gladys Eberly, Treas.
EIN: 237243666

48307
Bill & Rita Hoffman Family Charitable Trust
c/o Horovitz, Rudoy & Roteman
428 Forbes Ave., 900 Lawyers Bldg.
Pittsburgh, PA 15219
Contact: Rita Hoffman, Tr.

Financial data (yr. ended 05/31/01): Grants paid, $3,118; assets, $19,401 (M); expenditures, $3,137; qualifying distributions, $3,118.
Limitations: Giving primarily in Pittsburgh, PA.
Application information: Application form not required.
Trustees: Morris Goldberg, Rita Hoffman, Samuel Horovitz.
EIN: 251437432

48308
McBrier Foundation, Inc.
6721 Brier Hill Rd.
Fairview, PA 16415

Donor(s): James R. McBrier.
Financial data (yr. ended 12/31/01): Grants paid, $3,100; assets, $19,261 (M); expenditures, $3,100; qualifying distributions, $3,100.
Limitations: Applications not accepted. Giving primarily in Erie, PA.
Application information: Contributes only to pre-selected organizations.
Officer: Blossom P. McBrier, Pres.
EIN: 251113448

48309
Helen S. Macklin Charitable Trust
c/o Mellon Bank
P.O. Box 185
Pittsburgh, PA 15230

Financial data (yr. ended 10/31/01): Grants paid, $3,072; assets, $95,370 (M); expenditures, $4,492; qualifying distributions, $3,072.
Limitations: Applications not accepted. Giving primarily in PA.
Application information: Contributes only to pre-selected organizations.
Trustee: Mellon Bank, N.A.
EIN: 256190655

48310
William Mong Memorial Foundation
c/o Mellon Bank, N.A.
P.O. Box 185
Pittsburgh, PA 15230-9897
Application address: 1128 State St., Erie, PA 16152
Contact: Marilyn King, Trust Off., Mellon Bank, N.A.

Donor(s): Anna B. Mong.‡
Financial data (yr. ended 12/31/00): Grants paid, $3,056; assets, $115,757 (M); expenditures, $5,173; qualifying distributions, $3,626.
Limitations: Giving limited to residents of northwestern PA.
Application information: Applicants must be under the age of 30 and suffering from respiratory diseases. Application form required.
Trustee: Mellon Bank, N.A.
EIN: 256034070

48311
Levan Memorial Scholarship Trust
c/o Allfirst, Trust Tax Div.
21 E. Market St.
York, PA 17401-1500
Application address: c/o Auxiliary of the Washington County Medical Society, Washington County Hospital, Hagerstown, MD 21740

Financial data (yr. ended 12/31/00): Grants paid, $3,010; assets, $40,979 (M); expenditures, $3,403; qualifying distributions, $2,973.
Limitations: Giving limited to MD.
Trustee: Allfirst.
EIN: 236643620

48312
The Berger Family Foundation
2701 E. Luzerne St.
Philadelphia, PA 19137 (215) 743-7315

Established in 1987 in PA.
Financial data (yr. ended 11/30/01): Grants paid, $3,000; assets, $66,477 (M); expenditures, $5,804; qualifying distributions, $3,125.
Limitations: Applications not accepted. Giving primarily in Philadelphia, PA.
Application information: Contributes only to pre-selected organizations.
Trustees: Barbara L. Aronson, Doris S. Berger, Max M. Berger, Robert L. Berger, Steven A. Berger.
EIN: 232500631

48313
The Berman Scholarship Fund
c/o Mathias J. Barton
3400 E. Walnut St.
Colmar, PA 18915
Contact: Scholarship Comm.

Established in 1999 in PA.
Donor(s): Richard N. Berman, Steven L. Berman.

Financial data (yr. ended 12/31/01): Grants paid, $3,000; assets, $40,641 (M); expenditures, $3,342; qualifying distributions, $3,000.
Application information: Application form required.
Trustees: Richard N. Berman, Steven L. Berman.
EIN: 256677260

48314
Castle Foundation
c/o E.C. Dearden
774 Mount Moro Rd.
Villanova, PA 19085

Established in 2000 in PA.
Donor(s): Joseph L. Pyle, Edward C. Dearden.
Financial data (yr. ended 12/31/01): Grants paid, $3,000; assets, $42,042 (M); gifts received, $17,706; expenditures, $3,707; qualifying distributions, $3,000.
Limitations: Applications not accepted.
Application information: Contributes only to pre-selected organizations.
Directors: Charles L. Bryan, Edward C. Dearden, Frederick A. Tucker, Jr.
EIN: 256693748

48315
Castle Foundation Trust
c/o Edward C. Dearden
774 Mount Moro Rd.
Villanova, PA 19085-2007

Donor(s): Edward C. Dearden, Townsend T. Mink, William R. Hudson.
Financial data (yr. ended 12/31/01): Grants paid, $3,000; assets, $42,042 (M); gifts received, $17,706; expenditures, $3,707; qualifying distributions, $3,707.
Limitations: Applications not accepted. Giving primarily in PA.
Application information: Contributes only to pre-selected organizations.
Directors: Charles L. Bryan, Edward C. Dearden, Frederick A. Tucker, Jr.
EIN: 236693748

48316
Joseph P. Chiaradio Memorial Scholarship Foundation
c/o PNC Advisors
1600 Market St., 4th Fl.
Philadelphia, PA 19103

Established in 1999 in NJ.
Donor(s): Joesph P. Chiaradio.‡
Financial data (yr. ended 06/30/01): Grants paid, $3,000; assets, $93,778 (M); expenditures, $12,093; qualifying distributions, $10,829.
Limitations: Applications not accepted. Giving primarily in NY and PA.
Application information: Contributes only to pre-selected organizations.
Trustee: PNC Bank, N.A.
EIN: 256658703

48317
Eleanor G. Cornmesser Scholarship Trust
c/o M&T Bank
101 W. 3rd St.
Williamsport, PA 17701-2301
Contact: Marie Boyle

Established in 1990 in PA.
Financial data (yr. ended 09/30/01): Grants paid, $3,000; assets, $46,784 (M); expenditures, $4,061; qualifying distributions, $2,978.
Limitations: Giving limited to residents of PA.
Trustee: M & T Bank.
EIN: 256301105

48318
The Curry Foundation, Inc.
1055 W. Strasburg Rd.
West Chester, PA 19382-1967

Established in 1994.
Donor(s): James Curry, Bernadette Curry.
Financial data (yr. ended 12/31/00): Grants paid, $3,000; assets, $8,221 (M); gifts received, $5,000; expenditures, $3,760; qualifying distributions, $3,000.
Limitations: Applications not accepted.
Application information: Contributes only to pre-selected organizations.
Officers: James Curry, Pres.; Bernadette Curry, Exec. Dir.
EIN: 232767070

48319
The Patrick J. Gallagher Memorial Foundation, Inc.
710 W. Baltmore Pike
P.O. Box 790
Kennett Square, PA 19348

Established in 1994 in PA.
Financial data (yr. ended 02/28/02): Grants paid, $3,000; assets, $321 (M); gifts received, $3,000; expenditures, $3,000; qualifying distributions, $3,000.
Limitations: Applications not accepted. Giving limited to residents of Kennett, PA.
Application information: Contributes only to pre-selected organizations.
Officer: Thomas P. Gallagher, Pres.
EIN: 232791573

48320
Golden Scholarship Trust
21 E. Market St., M/C 402-130
York, PA 17401-1500
Application address: c/o Hanover High School, Guidance Office, 401 Moul Ave., Hanover, PA 17331

Established in 2000 in PA.
Financial data (yr. ended 12/31/00): Grants paid, $3,000; assets, $98,900 (M); gifts received, $7,884; expenditures, $3,000; qualifying distributions, $3,000.
Limitations: Giving primarily in PA.
Application information: Application form not required.
Trustee: Allfirst.
EIN: 236919224

48321
Brett A. Hardt Memorial Foundation
1632 Rte. 8
Glenshaw, PA 15116
Application address: 1405 Burchfield Rd., Allison Park, PA 15101, tel.: (412) 487-2400
Contact: Clifford D. Hardt, Dir.

Financial data (yr. ended 06/30/01): Grants paid, $3,000; assets, $34,454 (M); gifts received, $2,200; expenditures, $3,097; qualifying distributions, $2,980.
Limitations: Giving primarily in PA.
Officer and Directors:* Terri L. Hardt,* Secy.; Clifford D. Hardt, Paulina B. Hardt.
EIN: 251534091

48322
Hoehn Scholarship Fund f/b/o St. Vincent's Seminary
c/o PNC Advisors
620 Liberty Ave., P2-PTPP-10-2
Pittsburgh, PA 15222-2705
Application address: c/o Rev. Thomas Aklin, O.S.B., St. Vincents Seminary, 300 Frazer Rd., Latrobe, PA 15650

Established in 1994 in PA.
Financial data (yr. ended 12/31/01): Grants paid, $3,000; assets, $50,653 (M); expenditures, $4,207; qualifying distributions, $3,000.
Limitations: Giving limited to Latrobe, PA.
Trustee: PNC Bank, N.A.
EIN: 256437542

48323
Joseph Fred Ihle Estate Trust
1101 Market St., Ste. 2820
Philadelphia, PA 19107
Contact: George A. Butler, Jr., Tr.

Financial data (yr. ended 12/31/01): Grants paid, $3,000; assets, $33,231 (M); expenditures, $4,749; qualifying distributions, $2,979.
Limitations: Giving primarily in Philadelphia, PA.
Trustee: George A. Butler, Jr.
EIN: 236641524

48324
Enola M. Lewis Trust for Musicians
c/o Mellon Bank, N.A.
P.O. Box 185
Pittsburgh, PA 15230
Contact: Laurie Moritz, Trust Off., Mellon Bank, N.A.

Donor(s): Enola M. Lewis.‡
Financial data (yr. ended 09/30/01): Grants paid, $3,000; assets, $169,050 (M); expenditures, $3,561; qualifying distributions, $3,013.
Limitations: Giving primarily in the Pittsburgh, PA, area.
Application information: Application form required.
Trustee: Mellon Bank, N.A.
EIN: 256018822

48325
Liberty Chevrolet-Cadillac, Inc. Education Trust
420 Central Rd.
Bloomsburg, PA 17815-3121 (570) 784-2720
Contact: Don P. Bridenstine, Tr.

Established in 1992 in PA.
Donor(s): Liberty Chevrolet-Cadillac, Inc.
Financial data (yr. ended 12/31/01): Grants paid, $3,000; assets, $58,708 (M); expenditures, $3,416; qualifying distributions, $3,000.
Limitations: Giving limited to residents of the Bloomsburg, PA, area.
Application information: Application form required.
Trustees: Don P. Bridenstine, Alex J. Dubil, Alvin J. Luschas.
EIN: 236905772
Codes: CS, CD

48326
Howard Mayberry Memorial Scholarship Trust of Cameron County, Pennsylvania
P.O. Box 108
Emporium, PA 15834-0108
Application address: c/o Bucktail Bank & Trust, Trust Dept., 1004 W. 5th St., Emporium, PA 15834, tel.: (814) 486-3333

Financial data (yr. ended 12/31/99): Grants paid, $3,000; assets, $40,619 (M); expenditures, $3,501; qualifying distributions, $3,431.
Limitations: Giving limited to Cameron County, PA.
Application information: Application form required.
Officers: Judd A. Schager, Pres.; Donna Holly, Secy.-Treas.
EIN: 237007741

48327
Charles A. McCloskey Memorial Scholarship Fund
c/o Austin Area School District
P.O. Box 7
Austin, PA 16720
Application address: c/o Rev. Charles E. Gummo, Austin United Methodist Church, Costello Ave., Austin, PA 16720

Established in 1990 in PA.
Donor(s): Charles A. McCloskey.‡
Financial data (yr. ended 06/30/01): Grants paid, $3,000; assets, $106,344 (M); expenditures, $3,623; qualifying distributions, $3,000.
Limitations: Giving limited to the Austin, PA, area.
Application information: Application form required.
Officer: Christine Mohr, Mgr.
EIN: 256355191
Codes: GTI

48328
Jacques H. Mitrani Foundation
R.R. 3, Box 3028, Rm. 9607
Berwick, PA 18603-9401
Contact: Selma Mitrani, Tr.

Established in 1969.
Donor(s): Selma Mitrani.
Financial data (yr. ended 07/31/01): Grants paid, $3,000; assets, $368,696 (L); expenditures, $6,118; qualifying distributions, $3,000.
Limitations: Applications not accepted. Giving limited to Columbia County, PA.
Application information: Contributes only to pre-selected organizations.
Trustees: Leonard Comerchero, Selma Mitrani, Ralph Reissman.
EIN: 237103779
Codes: GTI

48329
Mike Mussina Foundation
426 Broad St.
Montoursville, PA 17754

Established in 2000 in PA.
Donor(s): Michael Mussina.
Financial data (yr. ended 12/31/01): Grants paid, $3,000; assets, $10,257 (M); expenditures, $6,149; qualifying distributions, $3,000.
Limitations: Applications not accepted. Giving primarily in Williamsport, PA.
Application information: Contributes only to pre-selected organizations.
Officers: Mike Mussina, Pres.; Jana Mussina, Secy.; Mark Mussina, Treas.
EIN: 233022314

48330
David Nimick Family Foundation
P.O. Box 597
Sewickley, PA 15143-0597

Established in 1997 in PA.
Donor(s): David Nimick, June Nimick.
Financial data (yr. ended 12/31/01): Grants paid, $3,000; assets, $84,986 (M); gifts received, $26,630; expenditures, $3,053; qualifying distributions, $3,000.
Limitations: Applications not accepted.
Application information: Contributes only to pre-selected organizations.
Trustees: David Nimick, June Nimick.
EIN: 232882735

48331
Petsonk Foundation
c/o Edward M. Petsonk
1272 Buckeye Rd.
Mount Morris, PA 15349

Established in 1989 in PA.
Financial data (yr. ended 12/31/01): Grants paid, $3,000; assets, $55,935 (M); expenditures, $3,584; qualifying distributions, $2,973.
Limitations: Applications not accepted. Giving primarily in FL and MA.
Application information: Contributes only to pre-selected organizations.
Trustees: Carol A. Petsonk, Edward L. Petsonk, Edward M. Petsonk.
EIN: 256317250

48332
Lee Scott Rubin Memorial Fund
c/o PNC Advisors
620 Liberty Ave., P2-PTPP-10-2
Pittsburgh, PA 15222-2705

Financial data (yr. ended 12/31/01): Grants paid, $3,000; assets, $69,602 (M); gifts received, $1,290; expenditures, $4,004; qualifying distributions, $3,012.
Limitations: Giving limited to the Lower Merion region of PA.
Trustee: PNC Bank, N.A.
EIN: 232103657

48333
Schwartz Mack Foundation
(Formerly Harry and Helen Mack Foundation)
300 Gerard Bldg.
434 Lackawanna Ave., Ste. 300
Scranton, PA 18503
Contact: Esther K. Schwartz, Pres.

Established in 1990 in PA.
Donor(s): Helen Mack, Esther K. Schwartz.
Financial data (yr. ended 12/31/01): Grants paid, $3,000; assets, $21,468 (M); gifts received, $10,000; expenditures, $3,981; qualifying distributions, $3,981.
Limitations: Giving primarily in Scranton, PA.
Officers: Esther K. Schwartz, Pres.; Robert N. Eckersley, Secy.
EIN: 232625170

48334
Jack M. Shaffer Charitable Trust
c/o Just Born, Inc.
1300 Stefko Blvd.
Bethlehem, PA 18016
Contact: Dave Moyer, Tr.

Established in 1999 in PA.
Financial data (yr. ended 12/31/01): Grants paid, $3,000; assets, $11,784 (M); gifts received, $5,326; expenditures, $3,231; qualifying distributions, $3,000.

Trustee: Dave Moyer.
EIN: 256644748

48335
James T. Williams Scholarship Fund
c/o Trustees
360 Holiday Ln.
Lewistown, PA 17044

Established in 1992 in PA.
Financial data (yr. ended 12/31/99): Grants paid, $3,000; assets, $6,921 (M); gifts received, $4,645; expenditures, $3,250; qualifying distributions, $2,995.
Limitations: Giving limited to residents of Lewistown, PA.
Application information: Application form required.
Officers and Trustees:* Tona H. Williams,* Chair.; Tona Y. Williams,* Secy.; Richard A. Williams.
EIN: 256402620

48336
Frances M. Zaberer Foundation
HC 1, Box 1070
Blakeslee, PA 18610-9416
Application address: c/o Linda De Santis, Cape Atlantic Community College, Mays Landing, NJ, 08330, tel.: (609) 343-5129

Established in 1988.
Financial data (yr. ended 03/31/01): Grants paid, $3,000; assets, $3,000 (M); expenditures, $3,000; qualifying distributions, $3,000.
Limitations: Giving limited to NJ.
Application information: Application form required.
Officer: Charles E. Holliday, Mgr.
Trustees: Edward Olwell, Jon Edwin Zaberer.
EIN: 222597593

48337
The Hilbush Foundation
(Formerly Hilbush Foundation Charitable Trust)
c/o C. Rockafellow
1408 Favonius Way
West Chester, PA 19382

Established in 1997 in PA.
Financial data (yr. ended 12/31/01): Grants paid, $2,925; assets, $36,838 (M); expenditures, $7,812; qualifying distributions, $2,925.
Officer: Carol A. Rockafellow, Mgr.
EIN: 237890392

48338
Joyce and Bryce Douglas Foundation
1694 Pughtown Rd.
P.O. Box 672
Kimberton, PA 19442-0672

Established in 1986 in PA.
Donor(s): Bryce Douglas.
Financial data (yr. ended 12/31/99): Grants paid, $2,910; assets, $44,512 (M); expenditures, $2,995; qualifying distributions, $2,995.
Limitations: Applications not accepted. Giving on a national basis, with some emphasis on PA.
Application information: Contributes only to pre-selected organizations.
Trustee: Bryce Douglas.
EIN: 222778760

48339
The Fay Gurrentz Charitable Foundation
c/o Carolyn T. Olbum
1118 S. Braddock Ave.
Pittsburgh, PA 15218

Established in 1996 in PA.
Donor(s): Fay Gurrentz.

Financial data (yr. ended 12/31/01): Grants paid, $2,850; assets, $53,192 (M); expenditures, $3,908; qualifying distributions, $2,850.
Limitations: Applications not accepted. Giving primarily in CO, Washington, DC and Pittsburgh, PA.
Application information: Contributes only to pre-selected organizations.
Officer: Carolyn T. Olbum, Pres. and Secy.-Treas.
Directors: David-Aaron Olbum, Jennifer R.T. Olbum, Jon H. Olbum.
EIN: 251790377

48340
Leonard R. Yoder Boston University Scholarship Trust Fund
c/o Allfirst, Trust Div.
21 E. Market St.
York, PA 17401-1500
Application address: c/o Allfirst, Trust Div., 3507 Derry St., Harrisburg, PA 17111

Financial data (yr. ended 12/31/00): Grants paid, $2,850; assets, $177,829 (M); expenditures, $6,818; qualifying distributions, $2,850.
Limitations: Giving limited to residents of Berks County, PA.
Application information: Personal interview required. Application form required.
Trustee: Allfirst.
EIN: 236844448

48341
The W. B. and Ruth J. Brandenbaugh Foundation
231 Valley Rd.
Lebanon, PA 17042-8930
Application address: 231 Valley Rd., Lebanon, PA 17042
Contact: Daniel W. Hottenstein, M.D., Tr.

Established in 1994.
Financial data (yr. ended 12/31/01): Grants paid, $2,826; assets, $289,730 (M); gifts received, $350; expenditures, $2,973; qualifying distributions, $2,826.
Trustees: Daniel W. Hottenstein, M.D., Thomas B. Hottenstein.
EIN: 256408650

48342
Dex Family Foundation
3890 Larkspur Dr.
Allentown, PA 18103

Established in 1999 in PA.
Financial data (yr. ended 12/31/01): Grants paid, $2,800; assets, $46,958 (M); expenditures, $3,661; qualifying distributions, $2,766.
Limitations: Applications not accepted.
Application information: Contributes only to pre-selected organizations.
Directors: Daniel D. Dex, Ruth R. Dex, Walter J. Dex, Walter J. Dex, Jr., Laura L. Dex Wallace.
EIN: 232960258

48343
Edward J. Filippone, M.D. Foundation
2228 S. Broad St.
Philadelphia, PA 19145 (215) 467-8955
Contact: Edward J. Filippone, M.D., Tr.

Donor(s): Edward J. Filippone, M.D.
Financial data (yr. ended 12/31/01): Grants paid, $2,797; assets, $16,652 (M); gifts received, $3,058; expenditures, $3,987; qualifying distributions, $2,797.
Application information: Application form not required.
Trustees: Edward J. Filippone, M.D., Mark E. Kogan.

48343—PENNSYLVANIA

EIN: 232660453

48344
Shoval Foundation
24 S. River St.
Wilkes-Barre, PA 18702

Established in 1999 in PA.
Donor(s): Jeffrey Weiss.
Financial data (yr. ended 12/31/01): Grants paid, $2,780; assets, $184,790 (M); gifts received, $352,246; expenditures, $4,957; qualifying distributions, $2,780.
Limitations: Applications not accepted.
Application information: Contributes only to pre-selected organizations.
Officers: Y. Judd Shoval, Pres.; Susan W. Shoval, Treas.
EIN: 233024646

48345
Jack Ehrlich Foundation
231 Brydon Rd.
Wynnewood, PA 19096-3306

Financial data (yr. ended 12/31/01): Grants paid, $2,750; assets, $62,851 (M); expenditures, $3,486; qualifying distributions, $2,750.
Limitations: Applications not accepted. Giving primarily in PA.
Application information: Contributes only to pre-selected organizations.
Officers: Virginia Ehrlich Kendall, Pres.; Rosalie Johanna Gelb, V.P.; Sanford B. Gelb, Secy.; Benjamin Kendall, M.D., Treas.
EIN: 236297314

48346
Marschall-Ferguson Charitable Foundation
c/o PNC Advisors
620 Liberty Ave., P2-PTPP-10-2
Pittsburgh, PA 15222-2705 (412) 762-3808
Application address: c/o PNC Bank, N.A., Trust Div., 1 Oliver Plz., 29th Fl., Pittsburgh, PA 15265
Contact: James M. Ferguson III, Tr.

Established in 1986 in PA.
Financial data (yr. ended 06/30/01): Grants paid, $2,750; assets, $276 (M); gifts received, $750; expenditures, $2,788; qualifying distributions, $2,750.
Limitations: Giving on a national basis.
Trustees: James M. Ferguson III, PNC Bank, N.A.
EIN: 251557329

48347
Morris Witmer Metzger Scholarship Fund
c/o Allfirst, Trust Div.
21 E. Market St.
York, PA 17401-1500
Application address: c/o Superintendent of Hempfield School Dist., Scholarship Fund Comm., 200 Stanley Ave., Landisville, PA 17358, tel.: (717) 898-5500

Established in 1986 in PA.
Financial data (yr. ended 01/31/01): Grants paid, $2,750; assets, $106,708 (M); expenditures, $4,144; qualifying distributions, $3,912.
Limitations: Giving limited to the Landisville, PA, area.
Trustee: Allfirst.
Scholarship Committee Member: David T. Mountz.
EIN: 236853061

48348
Valeria Walton Woods Scholarship Fund Trust
c/o Fulton Financial Advisors, N.A.
P.O. Box 3215
Lancaster, PA 17604-3215
Application address: c/o Guidance Counselor, Danville Senior High School, Northumberland Rd., Danville, PA 17821, tel.: (570) 275-4113

Established in 1960 in PA.
Financial data (yr. ended 12/31/01): Grants paid, $2,750; assets, $64,918 (M); expenditures, $4,398; qualifying distributions, $2,750.
Limitations: Giving limited to the Danville, PA, area.
Application information: Application form required.
Trustee: Fulton Financial Advisors, N.A.
EIN: 246015619
Codes: GTI

48349
The Bogutz Foundation
c/o Christie, Pabarue, Mortensen, Young
1880 John F. Kennedy Blvd., 10th Fl.
Philadelphia, PA 19103-7424
Contact: Jerome E. Bogutz, Pres.

Donor(s): Jerome E. Bogutz, Helen R. Bogutz.
Financial data (yr. ended 09/30/01): Grants paid, $2,720; assets, $60,227 (M); expenditures, $3,822; qualifying distributions, $2,720.
Limitations: Giving primarily in Philadelphia and Villanova, PA.
Officers: Jerome E. Bogutz, Pres.; Helen R. Bogutz, V.P.
EIN: 222434113

48350
The Sidney A. and Margaret C. Inman Foundation
c/o PNC Advisors
620 Liberty Ave., P2-PTPP-10-2
Pittsburgh, PA 15222-2705

Established in 1998 in MA.
Financial data (yr. ended 12/31/01): Grants paid, $2,705; assets, $99,538 (M); expenditures, $4,530; qualifying distributions, $2,705.
Limitations: Applications not accepted.
Application information: Contributes only to pre-selected organizations.
Trustee: PNC Bank, N.A.
EIN: 256636985

48351
Colen Family Fund
4940 Ellsworth Ave.
Pittsburgh, PA 15213

Financial data (yr. ended 07/31/01): Grants paid, $2,675; assets, $111 (M); gifts received, $3,500; expenditures, $4,071; qualifying distributions, $3,975.
Limitations: Giving primarily in PA.
Application information: Application form not required.
Officers: Frederick H. Colen, Chair. and Treas.; Nancy C. Dykhouse, Vice-Chair. and Secy.
EIN: 256065027

48352
Floyd & Mary Jane Meisenhelter Trust
c/o Allfirst, Trust Div.
21 E. Market St., M/C 402-130
York, PA 17401-1500

Established in 2000 in PA.
Donor(s): Floyd Meisenhelter.
Financial data (yr. ended 12/31/01): Grants paid, $2,655; assets, $103,008 (M); gifts received, $6,098; expenditures, $5,560; qualifying distributions, $2,655.
Limitations: Applications not accepted. Giving primarily in Red Lion, PA.
Application information: Contributes only to pre-selected organizations.
Trustee: Allfirst.
EIN: 256523502

48353
Barbara Stannard Residuary Trust
c/o PNC Advisors
620 Liberty Ave., P2-PTPP-10-2
Pittsburgh, PA 15222-2705
Application address: c/o Louise R. Brennen, Superintendent of Pittsburgh Public Schools, 341 S. Bellefield Ave., Pittsburgh, PA 15213, tel.: (412) 622-3700

Financial data (yr. ended 12/31/00): Grants paid, $2,650; assets, $56,509 (M); expenditures, $3,179; qualifying distributions, $2,661.
Limitations: Giving limited to residents of the Pittsburgh, PA, area.
Application information: Application form required.
Trustee: PNC Bank, N.A.
EIN: 256025018

48354
Epic Metals Corporation Charitable Foundation
11 Talbot Ave.
Rankin, PA 15104

Established in 1999 in PA.
Financial data (yr. ended 12/31/01): Grants paid, $2,630; assets, $173,548 (M); gifts received, $140,000; expenditures, $2,659; qualifying distributions, $2,630.
Limitations: Applications not accepted. Giving primarily in PA.
Application information: Contributes only to pre-selected organizations.
Officers and Directors:* David F. Landis,* Pres.; Laurence R. Landis,* Secy.-Treas.
EIN: 251831496

48355
Eileen M. Heck Foundation
c/o Accupac, Inc.
P.O. Box 250
Southampton, PA 18966

Established in 1994 in PA.
Donor(s): Accupac, Inc.
Financial data (yr. ended 12/31/01): Grants paid, $2,600; assets, $477,870 (M); expenditures, $7,029; qualifying distributions, $3,033.
Limitations: Applications not accepted. Giving primarily in PA.
Application information: Contributes only to pre-selected organizations.
Trustees: Kimberly Cilio, Eileen Heck Slawek, Kellyann Heck.
EIN: 237788354
Codes: CS, CD

48356
Howard and Terri Abrams Foundation
c/o Norman Finkel
12002 Panrail Pl.
Philadelphia, PA 19116

Established in 1986 in PA.
Financial data (yr. ended 12/31/01): Grants paid, $2,593; assets, $88,114 (M); expenditures, $3,479; qualifying distributions, $2,593.
Limitations: Applications not accepted. Giving primarily in Philadelphia, PA.
Application information: Contributes only to pre-selected organizations.

Trustees: Norman Finkel, Susan Katz.
EIN: 232432973

48357
Benevento & Mayo Foundation
46 Public Sq., Ste. 500
Wilkes-Barre, PA 18701

Established in 1997 in PA.
Donor(s): Benevento & Mayo Partners.
Financial data (yr. ended 12/31/01): Grants paid, $2,500; assets, $625,703 (M); gifts received, $2,500; expenditures, $3,704; qualifying distributions, $2,750.
Limitations: Applications not accepted. Giving primarily in PA.
Application information: Contributes only to pre-selected organizations.
Trustees: Brian J. Parente, Charles E. Parente, Charles E. Parente, Jr., John Parente, Marla Parente Sgarlat, Mary M. Parente.
EIN: 237880441
Codes: CS, CD

48358
The Berky Benevolent Foundation Trust
c/o Paul W. Putney
1717 Arch St.
Philadelphia, PA 19103-2793

Donor(s): H. Charles Berky, Jr.
Financial data (yr. ended 06/30/01): Grants paid, $2,500; assets, $41,596 (M); expenditures, $5,962; qualifying distributions, $3,627.
Limitations: Applications not accepted.
Application information: Contributes only to pre-selected organizations.
Trustees: Bradford S. Berky, Dolores Berky, Elli Berky, H. Charles Berky, Jr., Howard C. Berky, Sharon Berky Riggenbach.
EIN: 232154128

48359
Mark Engel-Jack Seibel Memorial Music Scholarship Fund
P.O. Box 175
Washington, PA 15301-0175
Application address: c/o Trinity High School, Park Ave., Washington, PA 15301, tel.: (724) 225-5380
Contact: William Galvin, Band Dir.

Chartered in 1968 in PA.
Financial data (yr. ended 06/30/00): Grants paid, $2,500; assets, $44,702 (M); gifts received, $114; expenditures, $2,585; qualifying distributions, $46,565; giving activities include $43,969 for loans.
Limitations: Giving limited to residents of Washington County, PA.
Application information: Application form required.
Officers: Thomas H. Diehl, Pres.; Joyce Camlin, Secy.; William A. Rehmon, Treas.; Rick Dorazio, Financial Secy.
EIN: 237052480

48360
The Jones Family Foundation
c/o Monaghan Transportation
106 Carpenter St.
Blossburg, PA 16912
Application address: 805 Tanager Dr., Bluefield, VA 24605
Contact: Robert M. Jones, Jr., Tr.

Established in 1998 in PA.
Donor(s): Marion M. Jones.
Financial data (yr. ended 12/31/01): Grants paid, $2,500; assets, $319,071 (M); gifts received, $54,468; expenditures, $6,051; qualifying distributions, $2,500.
Limitations: Giving primarily in Bluefield, VA.
Trustees: Robert M. Jones, Jr., Carol J. Tama.
EIN: 066466491

48361
Satyaram Health Clinic, Inc.
1707 Scott Dr.
P.O. Box 1625
Newtown, PA 18940

Donor(s): Murty Vepuri.
Financial data (yr. ended 12/31/01): Grants paid, $2,500; assets, $13,252 (M); expenditures, $2,946; qualifying distributions, $2,500.
Limitations: Applications not accepted. Giving on an international basis, primarily in India.
Application information: Contributes only to pre-selected organizations.
Officer: Murty Vepuri, Pres.
EIN: 222943918

48362
John K. Young Scholarship Fund
c/o Masonic Temple
1 N. Broad St.
Philadelphia, PA 19107-2598

Financial data (yr. ended 07/31/01): Grants paid, $2,500; assets, $47,494 (M); expenditures, $4,337; qualifying distributions, $2,500.
Trustee: Charles E. Rusk.
EIN: 232602645

48363
Phillip K. Dupre Family Foundation
c/o PNC Advisors
620 Liberty Ave., P2-PTPP-10-2
Pittsburgh, PA 15222-2705
Application address: Seven Springs, Champion, PA 15622
Contact: Lois Dupre Shuster, Mgr.

Established in 1997 in PA.
Financial data (yr. ended 12/31/01): Grants paid, $2,450; assets, $210,119 (M); gifts received, $250; expenditures, $7,054; qualifying distributions, $2,450.
Limitations: Giving primarily in PA.
Trustee: PNC Bank, N.A.
EIN: 237895524

48364
Edward S. Spangler Memorial Trust
c/o Fulton Financial Advisors, N.A.
P.O. Box 3215
Lancaster, PA 17604-3215

Financial data (yr. ended 12/31/01): Grants paid, $2,443; assets, $74,180 (M); expenditures, $5,423; qualifying distributions, $2,443.
Limitations: Applications not accepted. Giving limited to York, PA.
Application information: Contributes only to pre-selected organizations.
Trustee: Fulton Financial Advisors, N.A.
EIN: 236840055

48365
Catherine C. Peterson Trust
226 California Dr.
Erie, PA 16505

Financial data (yr. ended 12/31/01): Grants paid, $2,411; assets, $39,798 (M); expenditures, $2,459; qualifying distributions, $2,411.
Limitations: Applications not accepted. Giving primarily in the Erie, PA, area.
Application information: Contributes only to pre-selected organizations.
Trustees: Rev. James W. Peterson, Paul W. Peterson, Thomas L. Peterson.
EIN: 256087710

48366
Charles H. Clark Foundation
Farmers Trust Bldg.
1 W. High St., Ste. 206
Carlisle, PA 17013

Financial data (yr. ended 12/31/01): Grants paid, $2,400; assets, $201,759 (M); expenditures, $4,739; qualifying distributions, $2,400.
Limitations: Applications not accepted. Giving primarily in Carlisle, PA.
Application information: Contributes only to pre-selected organizations.
Officers: Robert W. Chilton, Pres.; Virginia C. Chilton, V.P.; Evelyn C. Craig, V.P.; Mary C. McKnight, V.P.; Jeff Boswell, Secy.; John H. McKnight, Treas.
EIN: 236243797

48367
Royston Foundation, Inc.
570 Colebrook Rd.
Exton, PA 19341 (610) 363-6242
Contact: Patricia Royston, V.P.

Financial data (yr. ended 02/28/02): Grants paid, $2,390; assets, $33,803 (M); expenditures, $3,168; qualifying distributions, $2,390.
Limitations: Giving primarily in PA.
Officers: Toby L. Royston, Pres. and Treas.; Patricia Royston, V.P.; Herbert S. Riband, Jr., Secy.
EIN: 231668997

48368
Thomas Roy Jones and Lura Jones Foundation, Inc.
c/o PNC Advisors
1600 Market St., 4th Fl.
Philadelphia, PA 19103-7240
Contact: Maria Tormey

Established in 1986 in NJ.
Donor(s): Lura M.F. Jones.‡
Financial data (yr. ended 12/31/01): Grants paid, $2,337; assets, $55,855 (M); expenditures, $3,355; qualifying distributions, $2,943.
Limitations: Giving primarily in Monterey, CA.
Application information: Application form not required.
Trustees: Robert B. Buell, Robert Jones, Julia Martin.
EIN: 222762191

48369
Sara C. Felding Memorial Charitable Trust
(Formerly Sara Felding Memorial Foundation)
c/o Mellon Bank, N.A.
P.O. Box 185
Pittsburgh, PA 15230

Financial data (yr. ended 12/31/01): Grants paid, $2,316; assets, $80,848 (M); expenditures, $3,218; qualifying distributions, $2,677.
Limitations: Giving limited to PA.
Application information: Application form required.
Trustee: Mellon Bank, N.A.
EIN: 246013216

48370
Thomas L. Kelly, Jr. Foundation
c/o James A. Ross
1 Old Windmill Rd.
Clarks Summit, PA 18411

Established in 1985 in PA.
Donor(s): Thomas L. Kelly.

48370—PENNSYLVANIA

Financial data (yr. ended 06/30/01): Grants paid, $2,300; assets, $84,070 (M); expenditures, $2,610; qualifying distributions, $2,300.
Limitations: Applications not accepted. Giving primarily in Darien and Fairfield, CT.
Application information: Contributes only to pre-selected organizations.
Officers: Thomas L. Kelly, Pres.; James A. Ross, Secy.-Treas.
EIN: 232327601

48371
Joseph Wacker Family Scholarship Fund
c/o Fulton Financial Advisors, N.A.
P.O. Box 3215
Lancaster, PA 17604-3215
Application address: c/o Lancaster Catholic High School, Business Off., 650 Juliette Ave., Lancaster, PA 17602

Financial data (yr. ended 12/31/00): Grants paid, $2,300; assets, $20,580 (M); expenditures, $2,696; qualifying distributions, $2,290.
Limitations: Giving limited to residents of Lancaster, PA.
Trustee: Fulton Financial Advisors, N.A.
EIN: 236439757

48372
Charles R. & Elizabeth J. M. Wagner Charitable Scholarship Trust
c/o Fulton Financial Advisors, N.A.
P.O. Box 3215
Lancaster, PA 17604-3215
Application address: c/o St. Johns Lutheran Church, 200 S. Broad St., Nazareth, PA 18064, tel.: (610) 759-3090

Established in 1996 in PA.
Donor(s): Charles Wagner, Elizabeth J.M. Wagner.
Financial data (yr. ended 11/30/01): Grants paid, $2,300; assets, $41,353 (M); expenditures, $3,068; qualifying distributions, $2,299.
Limitations: Giving limited to residents of Nazareth, PA.
Application information: Application form required.
Trustee: Fulton Financial Advisors, N.A.
EIN: 237873158

48373
James E. Henretta Trust A
c/o Mellon Bank N.A.
P.O. Box 185, 1 Mellon Bank Ctr.
Pittsburgh, PA 15230-9897

Established in 1961 in PA.
Financial data (yr. ended 12/31/99): Grants paid, $2,290; assets, $80,460 (M); expenditures, $2,673; qualifying distributions, $2,379.
Limitations: Applications not accepted. Giving limited to Linesville and Harmonsburg, PA.
Application information: Contributes only to pre-selected organizations.
Trustee: Mellon Bank, N.A.
EIN: 256034035

48374
Mende Foundation, Inc.
85 Hidden Woods Ln.
Warminster, PA 18974-4383

Established in 1987 in PA.
Financial data (yr. ended 12/31/01): Grants paid, $2,280; assets, $38,903 (M); expenditures, $3,299; qualifying distributions, $2,280.
Limitations: Applications not accepted. Giving primarily in PA.
Application information: Contributes only to pre-selected organizations.
Officer: Harry Mende, Pres.
EIN: 232481303

48375
From Greg Fund
241 S. 7th St.
Philadelphia, PA 19106-4135 (215) 625-2991

Established in 1986 in PA.
Donor(s): Nicholas J. Nastasi.
Financial data (yr. ended 12/31/01): Grants paid, $2,275; assets, $2,490 (M); expenditures, $2,275; qualifying distributions, $2,275.
Limitations: Applications not accepted. Giving primarily in the Philadelphia, PA, area.
Application information: Contributes only to pre-selected organizations.
Trustee: Nicholas J. Nastasi.
EIN: 232440310

48376
The Frangakis Family Charitable Foundation
68 Oak Tree Ct.
West Middlesex, PA 16159

Established in 1999 in PA.
Financial data (yr. ended 12/31/01): Grants paid, $2,250; assets, $1,415 (M); gifts received, $2,000; expenditures, $2,250; qualifying distributions, $2,250.
Trustees: F. John Frangakis, Joyce Frangakis.
EIN: 251849784

48377
Matthew P. Klinger Memorial Trust
c/o Don W. Klinger
P.O. Box 342
Millersburg, PA 17061

Financial data (yr. ended 12/31/01): Grants paid, $2,250; assets, $42,055 (M); gifts received, $270; expenditures, $2,250; qualifying distributions, $2,250.
Limitations: Applications not accepted.
Application information: Contributes only to pre-selected organizations.
Trustee: Don W. Klinger.
EIN: 237685418

48378
Klionsky Foundation
5867 Wilkins Ave.
Pittsburgh, PA 15217-1256

Established in 1999 in PA.
Financial data (yr. ended 12/31/01): Grants paid, $2,250; assets, $60,956 (M); gifts received, $24,000; expenditures, $3,479; qualifying distributions, $2,250.
Trustees: Bernard Klionsky, Esther W. Klionsky.
EIN: 256614875

48379
Lucy A. Valero Memorial Scholarship Fund
c/o Mellon Bank, N.A.
P.O. Box 7236, Aim No. 193-0224
Philadelphia, PA 19101-7236
Application address: c/o Pennsylvania State Education Assn., 400 N. 3rd St., Harrisburg, PA 17108

Donor(s): David E. Helfman, Pennsylvania State Education Assn.
Financial data (yr. ended 08/31/01): Grants paid, $2,220; assets, $62,050 (M); gifts received, $20,921; expenditures, $3,148; qualifying distributions, $2,220.
Limitations: Giving limited to residents of PA.
Application information: Application form required.
Trustee: Mellon Bank, N.A.
EIN: 232225710

48380
Thomas H. Gough Memorial Fund
c/o PNC Advisors
620 Liberty Ave., P2-PTPP-10-2
Pittsburgh, PA 15222-2705
Application address: c/o Principal, Highlands Senior High School, Idaho at Pacific Ave., Natrona Heights, PA 15065, tel.: (724) 226-1000

Established in 1987 in PA.
Financial data (yr. ended 12/31/01): Grants paid, $2,200; assets, $38,070 (M); expenditures, $2,638; qualifying distributions, $2,195.
Limitations: Giving limited to the Natrona Heights, PA, area.
Application information: Application form not required.
Trustee: PNC Bank, N.A.
EIN: 256022448

48381
American Legion Baseball Trust
c/o First Financial Bank
100 E. Lancaster
Downingtown, PA 19335

Financial data (yr. ended 12/31/01): Grants paid, $2,197; assets, $93,771 (M); expenditures, $3,293; qualifying distributions, $2,197.
Limitations: Applications not accepted. Giving primarily in Downingtown, PA.
Application information: Contributes only to pre-selected organizations.
Trustees: First Financial Bank.
EIN: 236438643

48382
Albert E. Deckter Foundation
57 Roberts Rd.
Newtown Square, PA 19073
Contact: Albert Deckter, Dir.

Financial data (yr. ended 12/31/01): Grants paid, $2,152; assets, $7,979 (M); expenditures, $2,439; qualifying distributions, $2,152.
Limitations: Giving primarily in Philadelphia, PA.
Director: Albert Deckter.
EIN: 222776111

48383
Morris L. & Lois G. Forer Foundation
2401 Pennsylvania Ave., 10A2
Philadelphia, PA 19130

Financial data (yr. ended 09/30/01): Grants paid, $2,150; assets, $30,617 (M); expenditures, $4,465; qualifying distributions, $2,150.
Limitations: Giving primarily in Philadelphia, PA.
Application information: Application form not required.
Officer: John L. Forer, Chair.
EIN: 236264346

48384
Dr. Stanley J. Wilcox Charitable Foundation
17 W. Miner St.
West Chester, PA 19381 (610) 840-0239
Contact: Joseph A. Bellinghieri

Established in 2000 in PA.
Donor(s): Stanley J. Wilcox.
Financial data (yr. ended 12/31/01): Grants paid, $2,100; assets, $38,443 (M); gifts received, $1,805; expenditures, $3,847; qualifying distributions, $2,100.
Limitations: Giving primarily in PA.
Trustee: Stanley J. Wilcox.
EIN: 233045739

48385
Lippert Scholarship Trust
c/o David Homish
P.O. Box 85
Factoryville, PA 18419-0085

Financial data (yr. ended 06/30/01): Grants paid, $2,063; assets, $40,896 (M); expenditures, $2,498; qualifying distributions, $2,045.
Limitations: Giving limited to residents of the Dalton, PA, area.
Application information: Students chosen by secret ballot by teachers in school district.
Trustees: Nancy Brown, Sandra Burnell, Ellen Frank, Bonnie Gregory, Michael J. Healey, George Hyduchak, Jacque Petherick.
EIN: 232383577

48386
The Love Foundation
102 E. Main St.
Schuylkill Haven, PA 17972-1606

Financial data (yr. ended 06/30/02): Grants paid, $2,050; assets, $5,578 (M); gifts received, $165; expenditures, $2,066; qualifying distributions, $2,050.
Limitations: Applications not accepted.
Application information: Contributes only to pre-selected organizations.
Officers: Mary C. Dinger, Pres.; Robert F. Dinger, Secy.
EIN: 232307131

48387
Protestant Orphan's Relief Fund-Jacoby
c/o PNC Advisors
620 Liberty Ave., P2-PTPP-10-2
Pittsburgh, PA 15222-2705
Contact: Roberta McCann, Trust Off., PNC Advisors

Donor(s): George T. Jacoby.‡
Financial data (yr. ended 12/31/01): Grants paid, $2,017; assets, $129,262 (M); expenditures, $3,884; qualifying distributions, $2,236.
Limitations: Giving limited to Allegheny County, PA.
Trustee: PNC Bank, N.A.
EIN: 256024241

48388
The August Foundation
(also known as Steven P. August Scholarship)
206 Clay Ave.
Jeannette, PA 15644
Application address: 928 Zimmerman St., Jeanette, PA 15644
Contact: Margaret Lock, Chair.

Established in 1984 in PA.
Donor(s): Steve August.
Financial data (yr. ended 12/31/99): Grants paid, $2,000; assets, $31,749 (M); gifts received, $1,000; expenditures, $2,212; qualifying distributions, $1,973.
Limitations: Giving limited to the Jeannette, PA, area.
Application information: Application form required.
Officers and Directors:* Margaret Lock,* Chair. and Pres.; Steve August,* V.P.; Anthony D. DeNunzio,* Secy.; Charles A. Deluzio,* Treas.
EIN: 251480998

48389
James Alan Auld Foundation
4499 Mount Royal Blvd.
Allison Park, PA 15101
Contact: John H. Auld II, Trustee

Financial data (yr. ended 12/31/01): Grants paid, $2,000; assets, $36,007 (M); expenditures, $2,087; qualifying distributions, $2,074.
Trustees: John H. Auld II, Robert F. Auld, Karen H. Clark.
EIN: 251463364

48390
Deutsch Family Memorial Scholarship Fund f/b/o Danville Area High School
c/o Fulton Financial Advisors, N.A.
P.O. Box 3215
Lancaster, PA 17604-3215
Application address: c/o Carl Marrara, Guidance Counselor, c/o Danville Senior High School, Northumberland Rd., Danville, PA 17821, tel.: (570) 275-4113

Financial data (yr. ended 12/31/00): Grants paid, $2,000; assets, $35,091 (M); expenditures, $2,824; qualifying distributions, $1,986.
Limitations: Giving limited to the Danville, PA, area.
Application information: Application form required.
Trustee: Fulton Financial Advisors, N.A.
EIN: 236701362

48391
R. Douglas Fixter Memorial Trust
646 Malin Rd.
Newtown Square, PA 19073-2613
Application address: 3090 Sever Lakes West, West End, NC 27376
Contact: Marjorie Fixter, Tr.

Financial data (yr. ended 12/31/01): Grants paid, $2,000; assets, $33,029 (M); expenditures, $2,143; qualifying distributions, $2,143.
Limitations: Giving primarily in PA.
Application information: Application form not required.
Trustees: Clifford B. Allen, Elizabeth F. Bosek, Marjorie Fixter, Jere A. Young.
EIN: 232274109

48392
Jane Forsyth Garrity Scholarship Trust
RD 1, Box 108A
Pleasant Mount, PA 18453-9731
(570) 448-9036
Contact: William B. Quaglio, Tr.

Established in 1991 in NJ.
Donor(s): Thomas J. Garrity.
Financial data (yr. ended 12/31/99): Grants paid, $2,000; assets, $38,753 (M); expenditures, $2,030; qualifying distributions, $1,993.
Limitations: Giving limited to NJ.
Application information: Application form required.
Trustee: William B. Quaglio.
Directors: Gregory G. Quaglio, James J. Quaglio, Jean M. Quaglio, Kathleen G. Quaglio, Laura Quaglio.
EIN: 223109734

48393
Manuel Gordon Foundation
c/o Pitcairn Trust Co.
1 Pitcairn Pl., Ste. 3000
Jenkintown, PA 19046
Contact: Myrna G. Snider, Pres.

Established in 1987 in PA.
Donor(s): Myrna G. Snider.
Financial data (yr. ended 12/31/00): Grants paid, $2,000; assets, $172,456 (M); expenditures, $2,146; qualifying distributions, $2,000.
Limitations: Giving primarily in PA.
Application information: Application form not required.
Officers: Myrna G. Snider, Pres. and Treas.; Lindy Snider, V.P.; Tina Snider, V.P.
EIN: 232448329

48394
Frank Greenberg Foundation
c/o Mark Stutman
2001 Market St., Ste. 3100
Philadelphia, PA 19103-7044

Established in 1986 in PA.
Financial data (yr. ended 03/31/02): Grants paid, $2,000; assets, $6,122 (M); expenditures, $2,035; qualifying distributions, $2,000.
Limitations: Applications not accepted. Giving limited to PA.
Application information: Contributes only to pre-selected organizations.
Trustees: Irving Chasen, Sanford Lipstein, Mark Stutman.
EIN: 232406488

48395
Lancaster Medical Society Foundation
c/o John Garofola
137 E. Walnut St.
Lancaster, PA 17602

Established in 1991 in PA.
Financial data (yr. ended 09/30/01): Grants paid, $2,000; assets, $54,389 (M); gifts received, $5,360; expenditures, $2,075; qualifying distributions, $2,000.
Limitations: Applications not accepted. Giving primarily in PA.
Application information: Unsolicited requests for funds not accepted.
Directors: Victor E. Augusta, M.D., John Garofola, M.D., John Gastablo, M.D., Jeffrey Kirchner, Joseph Knepper, M.D., James Saxon, David Wiley.
EIN: 232633979

48396
Mangold Family Foundation
4900 Cole Rd.
Murrysville, PA 15668-9406

Established in 1998 in PA.
Financial data (yr. ended 12/31/00): Grants paid, $2,000; assets, $439 (M); gifts received, $2,000; expenditures, $2,000; qualifying distributions, $2,000.
Limitations: Giving primarily in Westmoreland County, PA.
Officers: Jay R. Mangold, Pres.; Carol W. Mangold, Secy.-Treas.
EIN: 251819908

48397
The Marino Foundation
5330 N. Sydenham St.
Philadelphia, PA 19141 (215) 329-6485
Contact: Stephen A. Marino, Tr.

Established in 1990 in NJ.
Donor(s): Stephen A. Marino Trust.‡
Financial data (yr. ended 12/31/01): Grants paid, $2,000; assets, $2,571 (M); gifts received, $3,000; expenditures, $2,410; qualifying distributions, $2,000.
Limitations: Giving limited to Philadelphia, PA.
Trustee: Stephen A. Marino.
EIN: 226499509

48398
The McMaster Foundation
490 E. North Ave., Ste. 500
Pittsburgh, PA 15212-4740

Established in 1992.
Donor(s): James H. McMaster, Judith L. McMaster.
Financial data (yr. ended 12/31/01): Grants paid, $2,000; assets, $29,211 (M); gifts received, $6,000; expenditures, $2,876; qualifying distributions, $2,000.
Limitations: Applications not accepted. Giving primarily in Pittsburgh, PA.
Application information: Contributes only to pre-selected organizations.
Trustees: James H. McMaster, Judith L. McMaster.
EIN: 256401534

48399
The Stella E. Metzger Scholarship Fund
c/o Allfirst, Trust Div.
21 E. Market St.
York, PA 17401-1500
Application address: c/o Superintendent, Lebanon School District, Scholarship Fund Comm., 1000 S. 8th St., Lebanon, PA 17042, tel.: (717) 273-9391

Established in 1986 in PA.
Financial data (yr. ended 01/31/02): Grants paid, $2,000; assets, $97,824 (M); expenditures, $3,242; qualifying distributions, $3,040.
Limitations: Giving limited to Lebanon, PA.
Trustee: Allfirst.
Scholarship Committee Members: David T. Mountz, Superintendent, Lebanon High School, Principal, Lebanon High School.
EIN: 236853062
Codes: GTI

48400
Arthur & Phyllis Nemroff Family Foundation
25 Washington Ln., Apt. 823
Wyncote, PA 19095-1408
Contact: Arthur Nemroff, Mgr.

Financial data (yr. ended 12/31/01): Grants paid, $2,000; assets, $1,191 (M); gifts received, $2,200; expenditures, $2,209; qualifying distributions, $2,000.
Limitations: Giving primarily in PA.
Officer and Trustees:* Arthur Nemroff,* Mgr.; Phyllis Nemroff.
EIN: 222631179

48401
Panagulias Family Foundation
127 Anderson St., Ste. 127
Pittsburgh, PA 15212-5803 (412) 321-9433
Contact: Robert G. Panagulias, Pres.

Established in 1999 in PA.
Financial data (yr. ended 11/30/01): Grants paid, $2,000; assets, $67,910 (M); gifts received, $12,811; expenditures, $3,557; qualifying distributions, $2,000.
Limitations: Giving primarily in Ithaca, NY and Pittsburgh, PA.
Officers: Robert G. Panagulias, Pres.; Lillian B. Panagulias, V.P.; Constantine J. Panagulias, Treas.
EIN: 251851261

48402
Daryl and Lois Paules Foundation
3986 Bowser Rd.
New Freedom, PA 17349

Established in 2000 in PA.
Donor(s): Daryl Paules, Lois Paules.
Financial data (yr. ended 12/31/01): Grants paid, $2,000; assets, $17,904 (M); gifts received, $15,500; expenditures, $2,292; qualifying distributions, $2,000.
Limitations: Applications not accepted. Giving primarily in Randallstown, MD.
Application information: Contributes only to pre-selected organizations.
Trustees: Daryl Paules, Lois Paules.
EIN: 256666134

48403
The Mike Schmidt Foundation
610 Old York Rd., Ste. 230
Jenkintown, PA 19046-2837

Financial data (yr. ended 03/31/02): Grants paid, $2,000; assets, $1 (M); expenditures, $2,982; qualifying distributions, $2,000.
Limitations: Applications not accepted. Giving primarily in FL.
Application information: Contributes only to pre-selected organizations.
Officers and Directors:* Michael J. Schmidt,* Pres.; Arthur Rosenberg,* V.P.; Donna Schmidt,* V.P.; Paul Shapiro,* V.P.
EIN: 232198787

48404
Ruth H. Schumm and Darline R. Hammer Foundation
c/o Darline R. Hammer
1001 E. Oregon Rd.
Lititz, PA 17543

Established in 2000 in PA.
Donor(s): Darline R. Hammer.
Financial data (yr. ended 12/31/01): Grants paid, $2,000; assets, $30,925 (M); expenditures, $3,137; qualifying distributions, $2,000.
Limitations: Giving on a national basis.
Officer and Trustees:* Darline R. Hammer,* Pres. and Secy.; Robert E. Kauffman.
EIN: 233028166

48405
Seiple Family Foundation
245 Front St.
Northumberland, PA 17857
Application address: c/o Deb Reid, 159 S. 2nd St., Sunbury, PA 17801

Established in 2001 in PA.
Donor(s): Rachel D. Seiple.
Financial data (yr. ended 12/31/01): Grants paid, $2,000; assets, $1,958,921 (M); gifts received, $2,000,000; expenditures, $3,881; qualifying distributions, $2,000.
Limitations: Giving primarily in IN.
Trustees: Penn Seiple, Stan Seiple, Northumberland National Bank.
EIN: 256788065

48406
The Robert J. "Tag" Welker Memorial Scholarship Trust
39 N. Maple St.
Mount Carmel, PA 17851 (570) 339-1937
Contact: Robert W. Welker, Tr.

Financial data (yr. ended 12/31/01): Grants paid, $2,000; assets, $16,793 (M); expenditures, $2,000; qualifying distributions, $2,000.
Limitations: Giving limited to residents of Mount Carmel, PA.
Trustees: Catherine Besser, Catherine L. Welker, Robert W. Welker.
EIN: 237685759

48407
Louis Wolf Foundation
8 Pen-Y-Bryn Dr.
Scranton, PA 18505
Application address: Monroe and Gibson Sts., Scranton, PA 18510, tel.: (570) 342-0350
Contact: Michael Mardo, Exec. Dir.

Financial data (yr. ended 07/31/01): Grants paid, $2,000; assets, $38,057 (M); gifts received, $565; expenditures, $2,351; qualifying distributions, $2,351.
Limitations: Giving primarily in Scranton, PA.
Officers: Jerome Klein, Pres.; Michael Mardo, Exec. Dir.
EIN: 237167018

48408
Catherine Graves Advanced Educational Fund
c/o PNC Advisors
620 Liberty Ave., P2-PTPP-10-3
Pittsburgh, PA 15222-2705
Application address: c/o Robert Morris College, Student Fin. Aid Office, Coraopolis, PA 15108

Financial data (yr. ended 12/31/01): Grants paid, $1,992; assets, $28,839 (M); expenditures, $2,377; qualifying distributions, $1,983.
Limitations: Giving limited to Coraopolis, PA.
Trustee: PNC Bank, N.A.
EIN: 256022456

48409
Clint Reichert Memorial Trust
c/o Allfirst, Trust Div.
21 E. Market St.
York, PA 17401-1500
Application address: c/o Raymond J. Kline, Jr., Penn Township Lions Club, 1140 Hoff Rd., Hanover, PA 17331

Financial data (yr. ended 12/31/01): Grants paid, $1,907; assets, $20,007 (M); expenditures, $2,434; qualifying distributions, $1,907.
Limitations: Giving limited to PA.
Application information: Unsolicited request for funds not accepted (except of pre-selected organization affiliation).
Trustee: Allfirst.
EIN: 232249583

48410
Fallat Family Charitable Foundation
901 Hartge Rd.
New Kensington, PA 15068-8732

Donor(s): Thomas E. Fallat.
Financial data (yr. ended 12/31/01): Grants paid, $1,900; assets, $57,462 (M); expenditures, $7,140; qualifying distributions, $1,900.
Limitations: Applications not accepted.
Application information: Contributes only to pre-selected organizations.
Officers and Directors:* Thomas E. Fallat,* Chair. and Mgr.; Charles E. Weston,* Mgr.; Anna Marie Wigley, John T. Fallat, Opal A. Fallat, Stephanie D. Verona.
EIN: 237896622

48411
RSN Foundation
c/o Ronald J. Naples
Elm & Lee Sts.
Conshohocken, PA 19428

Established in 1987 in PA.
Financial data (yr. ended 12/31/99): Grants paid, $1,825; assets, $127,261 (M); expenditures, $2,268; qualifying distributions, $1,825.
Limitations: Giving primarily in Philadelphia, PA.
Trustees: Ronald J. Naples, Suzanne Naples.

EIN: 236805422

48412
The Fred J. & Florence J. Eckel Memorial Foundation
2209 Mount Carmel Ave.
Glenside, PA 19038-4709

Financial data (yr. ended 12/31/01): Grants paid, $1,800; assets, $43,991 (M); expenditures, $1,800; qualifying distributions, $1,800.
Limitations: Applications not accepted. Giving primarily in NC, SC, and PA.
Application information: Contributes only to pre-selected organizations.
Trustees: Edith M. DiStefano, Bruce J. Eckel, Elaine M. Eckel, Fred M. Eckel, Paul B. Eckel, Philip J. Eckel, Timothy B. Eckel.
EIN: 232181308

48413
Edward W. Helfrick Senior Citizens Trust
c/o First Susquehanna Bank & Trust
400 Market St.
Sunbury, PA 17801-2336

Financial data (yr. ended 12/31/01): Grants paid, $1,800; assets, $17,372 (M); expenditures, $2,464; qualifying distributions, $2,450.
Limitations: Giving limited to residents of the 107th Legislative District in PA.
Application information: Application form required.
Trustee: First Susquehanna Bank & Trust.
Committee Members: Jacob P. Betz, Rev. Philip Burger, Mana Scicchitano.
EIN: 232018916

48414
Little League Baseball Summer Camp
c/o M&T Bank
101 W. 3rd St.
Williamsport, PA 17701

Financial data (yr. ended 06/30/00): Grants paid, $1,770; assets, $8,336 (M); expenditures, $1,926; qualifying distributions, $1,765.
Limitations: Giving primarily in PA.
Trustee: M&T Bank.
EIN: 236924066

48415
Bryant Family Foundation
4232 Kota Ave.
Harrisburg, PA 17110-9596

Donor(s): Albert I. Bryant.
Financial data (yr. ended 09/30/01): Grants paid, $1,750; assets, $48,771 (M); gifts received, $1,000; expenditures, $2,208; qualifying distributions, $1,750.
Limitations: Applications not accepted. Giving primarily in Harrisburg, PA.
Application information: Contributes only to pre-selected organizations.
Officer: Albert I. Bryant, Mgr.
EIN: 232189610

48416
Eckman Family Foundation
850 MacArthur Dr.
Pittsburgh, PA 15228-1787

Established in 1992 in PA.
Financial data (yr. ended 12/31/01): Grants paid, $1,736; assets, $19,036 (M); gifts received, $3,770; expenditures, $1,756; qualifying distributions, $1,736.
Limitations: Applications not accepted. Giving limited to Pittsburg, PA.
Application information: Contributes only to pre-selected organizations.

Trustees: Alexander L. Eckman, Alexander P. Eckman, Mary S. Eckman.
EIN: 251694300

48417
Marie A. Heintzelman Memorial Music Award Fund
c/o First Union National Bank
P.O. Box 7558
Philadelphia, PA 19101-7558

Financial data (yr. ended 12/31/99): Grants paid, $1,720; assets, $12,546 (M); expenditures, $2,251; qualifying distributions, $1,805.
Limitations: Applications not accepted. Giving primarily in Reading, PA.
Trustee: First Union National Bank.
EIN: 236426282

48418
Kaplan Family Charitable Trust
1 Liberty Pl.
1650 Market St., Ste. 3100
Philadelphia, PA 19103-7392 (215) 587-0818
Contact: Jerome Kaplan, Tr.

Established in 1992 in PA.
Donor(s): Jerome Kaplan, Edith Kaplan.
Financial data (yr. ended 12/31/01): Grants paid, $1,707; assets, $91,530 (M); expenditures, $1,852; qualifying distributions, $1,707.
Limitations: Giving primarily in PA.
Application information: Application form not required.
Trustee: Jerome Kaplan.
EIN: 237667825

48419
Raymond J. Coleman Scholarship Fund
c/o Fulton Financial Advisors, N.A.
P.O. Box 3215
Lancaster, PA 17604-3215
Application address: c/o Miriam Wilson, Lebanon School District, 1000 S. 8th St., Lebanon, PA 17042, tel.: (717) 273-9391

Financial data (yr. ended 11/30/01): Grants paid, $1,700; assets, $36,429 (M); expenditures, $2,674; qualifying distributions, $1,700.
Limitations: Giving limited to residents of Lebanon, PA.
Application information: Application form required.
Trustee: Fulton Financial Advisors, N.A.
EIN: 251782441

48420
A. & L. Lynn Charity Trust
c/o Mellon Bank, N.A.
P.O. Box 185
Pittsburgh, PA 15230-9897
Contact: Donna Bricker, Trust Off., Mellon Bank, N.A.

Financial data (yr. ended 12/31/01): Grants paid, $1,664; assets, $26,254 (M); expenditures, $1,771; qualifying distributions, $1,664.
Limitations: Giving primarily in Franklin, PA.
Trustee: Mellon Bank, N.A.
EIN: 256122173

48421
Michele Thinnes Memorial Scholarship Fund
c/o John H. Thinnes, Sr.
2235 Hedgewood Rd.
Hatfield, PA 19440-2151

Established in 1997 in PA.
Financial data (yr. ended 12/31/01): Grants paid, $1,535; assets, $634 (M); expenditures, $1,580; qualifying distributions, $1,535.
Director: John H. Thinnes, Sr.

EIN: 232863444

48422
Ray S. & Lizzie S. Bicksler & Anna B. Greiner Memorial Scholarship Fund
c/o Fulton Financial Advisors, N.A.
P.O. Box 3215
Lancaster, PA 17604-3215
Application address: c/o The Daniel Weaver Co., Scholarship Comm., P.O. Box 525, Lebanon, PA 17042, tel.: (717) 274-6100

Financial data (yr. ended 08/31/01): Grants paid, $1,500; assets, $25,220 (M); expenditures, $2,587; qualifying distributions, $1,482.
Limitations: Giving limited to residents of Lebanon, PA.
Application information: Application form required.
Trustee: Fulton Financial Advisors, N.A.
EIN: 232141591

48423
Cheng Lee Educational Foundation
1637 Blackburn Heights Dr.
Sewickley, PA 15143-8627

Established in 1991 in PA.
Donor(s): Chung-Pin Cheng, Kwan Il Lee.
Financial data (yr. ended 12/31/01): Grants paid, $1,500; assets, $24,162 (M); expenditures, $2,000; qualifying distributions, $1,500.
Limitations: Applications not accepted. Giving primarily in PA.
Application information: Contributes only to pre-selected organizations.
Officers and Directors:* Kwan Il Lee,* Pres.; Chung-Pin Cheng,* Secy.-Treas.
EIN: 251654880

48424
The William Greenfield and Joan Rockower Greenfield Foundation
915 Montgomery Ave., Ste. 304
Narberth, PA 19072

Established in 1991 in PA.
Donor(s): William Greenfield, Joan Rockower Greenfield.
Financial data (yr. ended 12/31/01): Grants paid, $1,500; assets, $64,680 (M); expenditures, $1,817; qualifying distributions, $1,500.
Limitations: Applications not accepted. Giving primarily in Philadelphia, PA.
Application information: Contributes only to pre-selected organizations.
Officers: Ora Pierce, Pres.; Margaretta Baker, V.P.; Kathy Babcock, Secy.; John Alexander, Treas.
Directors: Kimberly Andrews, Elizabeth Barnet-Williams, Patrick Dean, Dorothy McCabe.
EIN: 232665810

48425
Hoehn Scholarship Fund f/b/o Elk County Christian High School
c/o PNC Advisors
620 Liberty Ave., P2-PTPP-10-2
Pittsburgh, PA 15222-2705
Application address: c/o John Kowach, Headmaster, Elk County Christian High School, 600 Maurus St., St. Mary, PA 15857

Established in 1994 in PA.
Donor(s): Dorothy Hoehn Trust.
Financial data (yr. ended 12/31/01): Grants paid, $1,500; assets, $31,096 (M); expenditures, $2,599; qualifying distributions, $1,548.
Limitations: Giving limited to residents of Elk County, PA.
Application information: Application form not required.

48425—PENNSYLVANIA

Trustee: PNC Bank, N.A.
EIN: 256437543

48426
Magaro Foundation
Rd. No. 1, Box 175-C
Newport, PA 17074

Established in 2000 in PA.
Donor(s): Betty Magaro, James E. Magaro.
Financial data (yr. ended 12/31/01): Grants paid, $1,500; assets, $132,262 (M); gifts received, $1,488; expenditures, $2,988; qualifying distributions, $1,500.
Limitations: Applications not accepted.
Application information: Contributes only to pre-selected organizations.
Officers: James E. Magaro, Pres.; Betty Magaro, V.P.
EIN: 256729469

48427
E. Charles Makdad Memorial Fund
P.O. Box 831
Altoona, PA 16603-0831

Established in 1996.
Financial data (yr. ended 12/31/01): Grants paid, $1,500; assets, $34,616 (M); expenditures, $1,829; qualifying distributions, $1,500.
Limitations: Applications not accepted.
Application information: Contributes only to pre-selected organizations.
Trustee: John C. Makdad.
EIN: 256169220

48428
Everett I. & Louise A. Mundy Charitable Foundation
c/o Glenmede Trust Co.
1650 Market St., Ste. 1200
Philadelphia, PA 19103-7391

Established in 2000 in PA.
Donor(s): Everett I. Mundy.
Financial data (yr. ended 12/31/01): Grants paid, $1,500; assets, $37,311 (M); expenditures, $2,012; qualifying distributions, $1,500.
Limitations: Applications not accepted.
Application information: Contributes only to pre-selected organizations.
Trustees: James L. Green, Everett I. Mundy, Louise A. Mundy, The Glenmede Trust Co.
EIN: 256700898

48429
Novak Family Foundation
2400 S. Weccacoe Ave.
Philadelphia, PA 19148
Contact: Everett Novak, Tr.

Established in 1986 in PA.
Financial data (yr. ended 11/30/01): Grants paid, $1,500; assets, $25,005 (M); expenditures, $1,861; qualifying distributions, $1,500.
Limitations: Giving primarily in the Philadelphia, PA, area.
Application information: Generally contributes to pre-selected organizations, but unsolicited applications are reviewed by the trustees.
Trustees: Ann Marie Novak, Everett Novak.
EIN: 222774823

48430
The Bonnie Rome Memorial Foundation
c/o L.R. Fogg
1735 Market St., 38th Fl.
Philadelphia, PA 19103-7501

Established in 1987 in PA.
Donor(s): Joel E. Rome.

Financial data (yr. ended 12/31/01): Grants paid, $1,500; assets, $48,138 (M); gifts received, $63; expenditures, $1,563; qualifying distributions, $1,500.
Limitations: Applications not accepted. Giving primarily in Philadelphia, PA.
Application information: Contributes only to pre-selected organizations.
Trustees: Joel E. Rome, Jonathan Rome, Allan B. Schneirov.
EIN: 222776756

48431
Kerri A. Welc Memorial Scholarship Foundation
51 Vine St.
Mount Pleasant, PA 15666 (724) 547-6149
Contact: Robert W. Welc, Tr.

Established in 1994 in PA.
Donor(s): Robert W. Welc, Mary Ann Welc.
Financial data (yr. ended 05/31/01): Grants paid, $1,500; assets, $37,822 (M); gifts received, $5,117; expenditures, $1,958; qualifying distributions, $1,958.
Limitations: Giving limited to residents of Mount Pleasant, PA.
Application information: Application form required.
Trustees: Mary Ann Welc, Robert W. Welc.
EIN: 251735519

48432
The Yates Family Foundation
c/o James R. Yates
P.O. Box 269, Rd. 2
Tyrone, PA 16686

Established in 2000 in PA.
Donor(s): James R. Yates.
Financial data (yr. ended 09/30/01): Grants paid, $1,450; assets, $1,880 (M); gifts received, $8,600; expenditures, $6,720; qualifying distributions, $1,450.
Limitations: Applications not accepted.
Application information: Contributes only to pre-selected organizations.
Trustee: James R. Yates.
EIN: 256759005

48433
Hope Lubin Byer Foundation
c/o Isdaner & Co.
3 Bala Plz., Ste. 501 W.
Bala Cynwyd, PA 19004

Established in 1995 in PA.
Donor(s): Hope Lubin Byer.
Financial data (yr. ended 06/30/02): Grants paid, $1,400; assets, $112,615 (M); expenditures, $2,832; qualifying distributions, $1,400.
Limitations: Applications not accepted. Giving primarily in NY.
Application information: Contributes only to pre-selected organizations.
Trustee: Hope Lubin Byer.
EIN: 232828436

48434
Catherine Graves Wheeling, West Virginia Fund
c/o PNC Advisors
620 Liberty Ave., P2-PTPP-10-2
Pittsburgh, PA 15222-2705
Application address: c/o Bethany College, Bethany, WV 26032

Financial data (yr. ended 12/31/01): Grants paid, $1,342; assets, $17,978 (M); expenditures, $1,597; qualifying distributions, $1,336.
Limitations: Giving limited to residents of Wheeling, WV.

Application information: Application form not required.
Trustee: PNC Bank, N.A.
EIN: 256022457

48435
Cecil and Czerna Cohen Foundation
160 Woodland Rd.
Greensburg, PA 15601

Financial data (yr. ended 09/30/01): Grants paid, $1,317; assets, $24,031 (M); expenditures, $1,641; qualifying distributions, $1,317.
Limitations: Applications not accepted.
Officers: Marvin Adelson, Pres.; Stephen Tannenbaum, Secy.-Treas.
Trustee: Cecil Cohen.
EIN: 237055621

48436
Michael T. & Ellen M. McDonnell Family Foundation
40 W. Eagle Rd.
Havertown, PA 19083-1425

Established in 1999 in PA.
Financial data (yr. ended 12/31/00): Grants paid, $1,315; assets, $67,427 (M); expenditures, $1,315; qualifying distributions, $1,315.
Limitations: Giving primarily in Immaculata, PA.
Trustees: Ellen M. McDonnell, Michael T. McDonnell.
EIN: 256594310

48437
Neal J. Katila Scholarship Fund
1247 Forsythe Dr.
Fort Washington, PA 19034

Established in 1988 in OH.
Donor(s): C.M. Katila.
Financial data (yr. ended 12/31/01): Grants paid, $1,300; assets, $31,451 (M); gifts received, $2,240; expenditures, $1,390; qualifying distributions, $1,300.
Limitations: Applications not accepted. Giving primarily in OH.
Trustees: James M. Gillette, Carl M. Katila, Jr., Clemens Urbanski.
EIN: 311224618

48438
Bernard & Rachel Latterman Family Foundation
3 Shadyside Ln.
Pittsburgh, PA 15232

Donor(s): Rachel Latterman.
Financial data (yr. ended 11/30/01): Grants paid, $1,300; assets, $24,195 (M); gifts received, $123; expenditures, $1,340; qualifying distributions, $1,300.
Limitations: Applications not accepted. Giving primarily in Pittsburgh, PA.
Application information: Contributes only to pre-selected organizations.
Trustees: Jay Latterman, Rachel Latterman.
EIN: 251389649

48439
Wilhelmina Mayerle Schwaiger Memorial Fund
c/o PNC Advisors
620 Liberty Ave., P2-PTPP-10-2
Pittsburgh, PA 15222-2705

Financial data (yr. ended 12/31/01): Grants paid, $1,300; assets, $66,547 (M); expenditures, $2,227; qualifying distributions, $1,300.
Limitations: Applications not accepted. Giving limited to Philadelphia, PA.
Application information: Unsolicited requests for funds not accepted.
Trustee: PNC Bank, N.A.

EIN: 236598382

48440
Sunbury Kiwanis Foundation
P.O. Box 711
Sunbury, PA 17801
Application address: R.D. 2, Box 452, Sunbury, PA 17801, tel.: (570) 286-7733
Contact: William K. Greis, Treas.

Financial data (yr. ended 09/30/01): Grants paid, $1,275; assets, $35,061 (M); expenditures, $1,587; qualifying distributions, $1,275.
Limitations: Giving limited to the Sunbury, PA, area.
Officers and Directors:* David S. Campbell,* Chair.; William K. Greis,* Treas.; Roy Glick, J. Thomas Harris.
EIN: 236403895

48441
Anastasia Foundation
3701 Windridge Dr.
Doylestown, PA 18901
Contact: Georgia Presti, Tr.

Established in 1996.
Donor(s): Georgia Presti.
Financial data (yr. ended 08/31/02): Grants paid, $1,265; assets, $0 (M); expenditures, $18,369; qualifying distributions, $1,265.
Limitations: Giving primarily in NJ and PA.
Trustees: Georgia Presti, Bruce Robinson, Linay Robinson.
EIN: 232868550

48442
PFC Bank Charitable Foundation
(Formerly New Bethlehem Bank)
363 Broad St.
New Bethlehem, PA 16242

Donor(s): New Bethlehem Bank.
Financial data (yr. ended 12/31/01): Grants paid, $1,225; assets, $1,078 (M); expenditures, $1,233; qualifying distributions, $1,225.
Limitations: Applications not accepted. Giving limited to Clarion County, PA.
Application information: Contributes only to pre-selected organizations.
Trustees: Darl Hetrick, R.B. Robertson.
EIN: 256383224
Codes: CS

48443
Minnie Diebler Trust
c/o Melon Bank, N.A.
P.O. Box 7236, AIM No. 193-0224
Philadelphia, PA 19101-7236

Established in 1994 in PA.
Financial data (yr. ended 09/30/00): Grants paid, $1,220; assets, $61,953 (M); expenditures, $2,166; qualifying distributions, $1,227.
Trustee: Mellon Bank, N.A.
EIN: 256264622

48444
Churchill Foundation
c/o Douglas F. Schofield
Box 369
Indianola, PA 15051-0369

Established in 1992 in PA.
Donor(s): Edward S. Churchill, Jr.
Financial data (yr. ended 12/31/01): Grants paid, $1,200; assets, $17,303 (M); expenditures, $1,200; qualifying distributions, $1,200.
Limitations: Applications not accepted. Giving primarily in PA.
Application information: Contributes only to pre-selected organizations.

Trustees: Edward S. Churchill, Jr., Joanne Churchill, Douglas F. Schofield.
EIN: 251671629

48445
Richard E. and Louise K. Jordan Foundation
c/o Henry W. Rhoads
2001 State Rd.
Camp Hill, PA 17011-5927

Established in 1997.
Donor(s): Richard E. Jordan II, Louise K. Jordan.
Financial data (yr. ended 12/31/01): Grants paid, $1,200; assets, $371,948 (M); expenditures, $6,257; qualifying distributions, $1,200.
Limitations: Applications not accepted.
Application information: Contributes only to pre-selected organizations.
Officers and Directors:* Richard E. Jordan II,* Pres. and Treas.; Louise K. Jordan,* V.P.; Barbara J. Schenck,* V.P.; Sharon N. Jordan,* Secy.; Richard E. Jordan III, Clark B. Schenck III, Robert C. Sherwood.
EIN: 311559400

48446
The Anne R. Monroe Foundation
1500 Oliver Bldg.
Pittsburgh, PA 15222-2312 (412) 355-6552
Contact: J. Michael Ewing, Tr.

Established in 1994 in PA.
Donor(s): James Monroe.
Financial data (yr. ended 09/30/01): Grants paid, $1,200; assets, $25,970 (M); gifts received, $1,425; expenditures, $9,726; qualifying distributions, $1,200.
Limitations: Giving primarily in Pittsburgh, PA.
Application information: Application form required.
Trustees: J. Michael Ewing, James R. Monroe, James C. Natale.
EIN: 251751863

48447
Leona S. Wellinger Charitable Trust
c/o Aligned Partners Trust Co.
707 Grant St.
Pittsburgh, PA 15219-1908
Contact: John P. Shaffey

Established in 2000 in PA.
Financial data (yr. ended 12/31/01): Grants paid, $1,200; assets, $87,335 (M); gifts received, $52,710; expenditures, $2,380; qualifying distributions, $1,188.
Trustee: Aligned Partners Trust Co.
EIN: 256706258

48448
Jake Czekaj Memorial Environmental Foundation
117 Bridgeport St.
Mount Pleasant, PA 15666-2033
(724) 547-3359
Contact: Esther L. Czekaj

Established in 1994 in PA.
Financial data (yr. ended 12/31/01): Grants paid, $1,180; assets, $6,662 (M); gifts received, $741; expenditures, $1,687; qualifying distributions, $1,686.
Limitations: Giving primarily in PA.
Officers: Theodore William Czekaj, Pres.; Corrinna Louise Czekaj, V.P.; Brenda Lee Czekaj, Secy.; Esther Louise Czekaj, Treas.
EIN: 251715899

48449
Charles E. Duffield Trust
c/o Allfirst, Trust Tax Div.
21 E. Market St., M/C 402-130
York, PA 17401-1500

Established in 2000 in PA.
Financial data (yr. ended 12/31/00): Grants paid, $1,168; assets, $49,008 (M); expenditures, $1,570; qualifying distributions, $1,168.
Limitations: Applications not accepted. Giving primarily in PA.
Application information: Contributes only to pre-selected organizations.
Trustee: Allfirst.
EIN: 256205349

48450
S. L. & Mollie Weiner Family Foundation
c/o Airway Industries, Inc.
Airway Park
Ellwood City, PA 16117
Contact: Cathy White, Scholarship Prog. Off.

Donor(s): Betty Weiner Shuman.
Financial data (yr. ended 08/31/01): Grants paid, $1,138; assets, $53,238 (M); expenditures, $3,106; qualifying distributions, $1,138.
Limitations: Giving primarily in PA.
Application information: Application form required for scholarships.
Trustees: Betty Weiner Shuman, Jay Weiner.
EIN: 256033908

48451
The Laurwood Foundation
c/o Michael & Margaret Ambrose
925 Greenwood Ave.
Wyncote, PA 19095

Established in 2000 in PA.
Donor(s): Michael Ambrose, Margaret Ambrose.
Financial data (yr. ended 12/31/01): Grants paid, $1,100; assets, $21,226 (M); expenditures, $1,238; qualifying distributions, $1,100.
Limitations: Giving primarily in PA.
Directors: Margaret Ambrose, Michael Ambrose.
EIN: 256638441

48452
The June Medovitch Memorial Scholarship Fund
c/o J. Terry Medovitch
407 Edgewood Dr.
Sarver, PA 16055

Established in 1994 in PA.
Donor(s): J. Terry Medovitch.
Financial data (yr. ended 12/31/99): Grants paid, $1,067; assets, $16,695 (M); gifts received, $100; expenditures, $1,205; qualifying distributions, $1,056.
Limitations: Applications not accepted.
Trustee: J. Terry Medovitch.
EIN: 251711084

48453
Mary A. Malone Trust
c/o M&T Bank
1 S. Centre St.
Pottsville, PA 17901-3001 (570) 628-9291
Contact: E. Lori Smith, V.P. & Trust Off., M&T Bank

Financial data (yr. ended 12/31/99): Grants paid, $1,032; assets, $131,194 (M); expenditures, $3,192; qualifying distributions, $1,032.
Limitations: Giving primarily in Washington, DC, FL, and PA.
Trustee: M&T Bank.
EIN: 236514591

48454
The Miramare Foundation
c/o Jack J. Kessler
1 Oxford Ctr., 20th Fl.
Pittsburgh, PA 15219

Established in 1994 in MA.
Donor(s): Richard M. Hunt, Priscilla S. Hunt.
Financial data (yr. ended 05/31/01): Grants paid, $1,009; assets, $22,380 (M); expenditures, $1,155; qualifying distributions, $1,009.
Limitations: Applications not accepted. Giving primarily in Dorchester, MA.
Application information: Contributes only to pre-selected organizations.
Trustees: Priscilla S. Hunt, Richard M. Hunt.
EIN: 256447779

48455
BNG Foundation
91 Cardinal Rd.
Reading, PA 19610
Contact: Bruce Bengtson, Tr.

Established in 2000 in PA.
Donor(s): Bruce Bengtson.
Financial data (yr. ended 12/31/01): Grants paid, $1,000; assets, $33,779 (M); gifts received, $10,000; expenditures, $1,500; qualifying distributions, $1,000.
Trustees: Bruce Bengtson, Ruth A. Bengtson.
EIN: 233008332

48456
Israel I. & Birdye E. Brody Foundation
c/o S&T Bank, Trust Dept.
P.O. Box 220
Indiana, PA 15701-0220
Application address: 6153 Terramere Cir., Boynton Beach, FL 33437, tel.: (724) 465-1443
Contact: Robert Brody, Pres.

Financial data (yr. ended 12/31/01): Grants paid, $1,000; assets, $80,296 (M); expenditures, $3,166; qualifying distributions, $1,000.
Limitations: Giving primarily in Indiana County, PA.
Officer: Robert Brody, Pres.
Trustee: S & T Bank.
EIN: 256064603

48457
Dean R. Carl Memorial Scholarship Fund
1600 W. Lynn St.
Coal Township, PA 17866

Donor(s): Lois Carl, Richard Carl.
Financial data (yr. ended 12/31/01): Grants paid, $1,000; assets, $15,489 (M); expenditures, $1,000; qualifying distributions, $1,536.
Limitations: Applications not accepted.
Application information: Unsolicited requests for funds not accepted.
Trustees: Lois Carl, Richard Carl.
EIN: 232827992

48458
Carosella Family Foundation
c/o F. Mirabello
1701 Market St.
Philadelphia, PA 19103

Established in 1998 in FL.
Donor(s): Vincent F. Carosella.
Financial data (yr. ended 12/31/01): Grants paid, $1,000; assets, $49,353 (M); gifts received, $1,781; expenditures, $2,211; qualifying distributions, $1,000.
Limitations: Applications not accepted.
Application information: Contributes only to pre-selected organizations.

Trustee: Joan R. Carosella.
EIN: 237976456

48459
Brother Victor Cipriani Educational Foundation
222 Salem Dr.
Pittsburgh, PA 15241

Financial data (yr. ended 12/31/01): Grants paid, $1,000; assets, $20,999 (M); gifts received, $2,000; expenditures, $1,000; qualifying distributions, $1,000.
Trustees: Evo Cipriani, Louise Cipriani.
EIN: 311628617

48460
Horace N. Clark Educational Fund
c/o PNC Advisors
620 Liberty Ave., PT-PTPP-10-2
Pittsburgh, PA 15222-2705

Financial data (yr. ended 12/31/00): Grants paid, $1,000; assets, $47,108 (M); expenditures, $1,840; qualifying distributions, $1,000.
Limitations: Giving limited to PA.
Trustees: Jessie P. Clark, PNC Bank, N.A.
EIN: 236250821

48461
The Danner Foundation Trust
c/o Allfirst, Trust Tax Div.
21 Market St.
York, PA 17401
Application address: c/o Allfirst, Trust Tax Div., 13 Baltimore St., Hanover, PA 17331

Financial data (yr. ended 12/31/00): Grants paid, $1,000; assets, $52,348 (M); expenditures, $1,707; qualifying distributions, $1,000.
Limitations: Giving limited to PA.
Application information: Application form required.
Trustee: Allfirst.
EIN: 222827320

48462
Mark A. Defibaugh Memorial Scholarship Trust
c/o Allfirst, Trust Tax Div.
21 E. Market St., M/C 402-130
York, PA 17401-1500
Application address: c/o Principal of Southwestern High School, 225 Bowman Rd., Hanover, PA 17331

Established in 2000 in PA.
Financial data (yr. ended 12/31/00): Grants paid, $1,000; assets, $16,051 (M); expenditures, $1,000; qualifying distributions, $1,000.
Limitations: Applications not accepted. Giving primarily in PA.
Trustee: Allfirst.
EIN: 236953047

48463
Charles and Anne S. Genuardi Family Foundation
c/o Josephine McCabe
307 Thomas Dr.
King of Prussia, PA 19406-2325
(610) 279-2480

Established in 1999 in PA.
Donor(s): Charles Genuardi, Anne S. Genuardi.
Financial data (yr. ended 12/31/00): Grants paid, $1,000; assets, $157,618 (M); gifts received, $18,150; expenditures, $3,118; qualifying distributions, $1,000.
Application information: Application form not required.
Officers: Gasper A. Genuardi, Pres.; Charles A. Genuardi, V.P.; Antoinette G. Deever, Secy.; Josephine G. McCabe, Treas.

Director: Paula G. Molnar.
EIN: 232984191

48464
William A. and Loene M. Gettig Foundation
P.O. Box 85
Spring Mills, PA 16875

Donor(s): Loene M. Gettig, William A. Gettig.
Financial data (yr. ended 12/31/99): Grants paid, $1,000; assets, $28,951 (M); expenditures, $1,062; qualifying distributions, $1,034.
Limitations: Applications not accepted. Giving limited to Angola, IN.
Application information: Contributes only to pre-selected organizations.
Trustees: Loene M. Gettig, William A. Gettig.
EIN: 251620358

48465
Harvey and Rosalie Goldberg Private Foundation
106 Hampton Ln.
Blue Bell, PA 19422

Established in 2000 in PA.
Donor(s): Harvey Goldberg, Rosalie Goldberg.
Financial data (yr. ended 11/30/01): Grants paid, $1,000; assets, $967,469 (M); gifts received, $1,251,141; expenditures, $3,360; qualifying distributions, $1,500.
Limitations: Applications not accepted. Giving primarily in Philadelphia, PA.
Application information: Contributes only to pre-selected organizations.
Trustees: Brett Goldberg, Brian Goldberg, Harvey Goldberg, Randi Goldberg, Rosalie Goldberg.
EIN: 256728817

48466
Michael A. Greene Foundation
1985 Bridgetown Pike
Feasterville Trevose, PA 19053-2302

Established in 1995 in PA.
Financial data (yr. ended 12/31/01): Grants paid, $1,000; assets, $16,142 (M); expenditures, $1,000; qualifying distributions, $1,000.
Trustee: Michael A. Greene.
EIN: 232779497

48467
Theodore D. & Elizabeth A. Hadley Fund
c/o Hadley Comm.
P.O. Box 370
Kennett Square, PA 19348-0370

Financial data (yr. ended 08/31/00): Grants paid, $1,000; assets, $19,952 (M); gifts received, $40,584; expenditures, $35,335; qualifying distributions, $35,335; giving activities include $29,899 for programs.
Limitations: Giving primarily in PA.
Officers: Wally Maw, Chair.; Gloria Collins, Vice-Chair.; Carol Love, Secy.; Robert McKinstry, Treas.
EIN: 236274664

48468
Howard Hanna Foundation
119 Gamma Drive
Pittsburgh, PA 15238

Established in 1998 in PA.
Financial data (yr. ended 12/31/00): Grants paid, $1,000; assets, $202,324 (M); gifts received, $100,000; expenditures, $1,000; qualifying distributions, $1,000.
Limitations: Applications not accepted.
Application information: Contributes only to pre-selected organizations.
Officer: Howard W. Hanna, Pres.

EIN: 311621640

48469
Hanover Area Historical Society Scholarship Award Trust
21 E. Market St.
York, PA 17401-1500

Established in 2000 in PA.
Financial data (yr. ended 12/31/01): Grants paid, $1,000; assets, $22,252 (M); expenditures, $1,410; qualifying distributions, $1,150.
Limitations: Giving primarily in PA.
Trustee: Allfirst.
EIN: 236959885

48470
Charles A. & Elizabeth Guy Holmes Foundation
c/o Mellon Bank, N.A.
P.O. Box 7236
Philadelphia, PA 19101-7236
Application address: c/o Mellon Bank, N.A., P.O. Box 1010, Harrisburg, PA 17108, tel.: (717) 780-3018

Established in 1987 in PA.
Financial data (yr. ended 05/31/02): Grants paid, $1,000; assets, $464,458 (M); expenditures, $8,176; qualifying distributions, $1,000.
Limitations: Giving primarily in PA.
Trustee: Mellon Bank, N.A.
EIN: 236807649

48471
The David Thomas Lightner Foundation
1210-G Hampton Hill Ct.
Harrisburg, PA 17111

Established in 2000.
Donor(s): Linda D. Lightner.
Financial data (yr. ended 12/31/01): Grants paid, $1,000; assets, $23,151 (M); expenditures, $1,000; qualifying distributions, $1,000.
Limitations: Applications not accepted.
Application information: Contributes only to pre-selected organizations.
Trustees: Linda D. Lightner, Patricia Lightner.
EIN: 311759521

48472
Locks Family Foundation
(Formerly The Marion Locks Foundation)
600 Washington Sq. S.
Philadelphia, PA 19106 (215) 629-1000
Contact: Gene Locks, Pres.

Donor(s): Gene Locks.
Financial data (yr. ended 06/30/01): Grants paid, $1,000; assets, $9,396,484 (M); gifts received, $1,000,000; expenditures, $1,482; qualifying distributions, $648,500; giving activities include $647,500 for program-related investments.
Limitations: Giving primarily in PA, with emphasis on Philadelphia.
Application information: Application form not required.
Officers: Gene Locks, Pres.; Sueyun Locks, Secy.-Treas.
EIN: 222709744

48473
Maria Dickerson Logan Trust
c/o Mellon Bank, N.A.
P.O. Box 7236
Philadelphia, PA 19101-7236 (215) 553-3208
Contact: Patricia Kling, Trust Off., Mellon Bank, N.A

Donor(s): Maria D. Logan.‡
Financial data (yr. ended 06/30/99): Grants paid, $1,000; assets, $627,217 (M); gifts received, $2,000; expenditures, $3,626; qualifying distributions, $1,343.
Limitations: Giving limited to Germantown, PA.
Trustee: Mellon Bank, N.A.
EIN: 236225776

48474
The Madia Family Foundation
503 Salem Heights Dr.
Gibsonia, PA 15044
Contact: Frank Madia, Tr.

Established in 1996 in PA.
Donor(s): Frank Madia, Jean Madia.
Financial data (yr. ended 12/31/01): Grants paid, $1,000; assets, $413,959 (M); gifts received, $404,250; expenditures, $2,030; qualifying distributions, $1,000.
Limitations: Giving limited to PA.
Trustees: Frank Madia, Jean Madia.
EIN: 311490172

48475
Chrissie B. Mayr Educational Trust Fund
c/o First Union National Bank
P.O. Box 7558
Philadelphia, PA 19101-7558

Financial data (yr. ended 08/31/99): Grants paid, $1,000; assets, $36,053 (M); expenditures, $1,887; qualifying distributions, $1,443.
Limitations: Applications not accepted. Giving limited to Montoursville, PA.
Directors: David P. Black, Richard A. Gray.
Trustee: First Union National Bank.
EIN: 236448408

48476
The Annette Miele Memorial Scholarship Fund
214 E. Washington St.
Mount Pleasant, PA 15666 (724) 547-5661
Contact: Vincent Miele, Tr.

Established in 1992 in PA.
Donor(s): Vincent Miele, Ann Miele.
Financial data (yr. ended 08/31/99): Grants paid, $1,000; assets, $39,484 (M); gifts received, $940; expenditures, $1,000; qualifying distributions, $1,000.
Limitations: Giving limited to residents of Mount Pleasant, PA.
Application information: Application form required.
Trustee: Vincent Miele.
EIN: 251690908

48477
Omeed Nooreyazdan Memorial Scholarship
c/o The Ephrata National Bank
P.O. Box 457, 31 E. Main St.
Ephrata, PA 17522-0457 (717) 733-6576
Contact: Carl L. Brubaker, Trust Off., The Ephrata National Bank

Established in 1998 in PA.
Financial data (yr. ended 12/31/00): Grants paid, $1,000; assets, $48,249 (M); gifts received, $88; expenditures, $2,763; qualifying distributions, $2,203.
Limitations: Giving limited to PA.
Application information: Application form required.
Trustee: The Ephrata National Bank.
EIN: 232990891

48478
O'Donnell Family Foundation
P.O. Box 153
Lakewood, PA 18439

Established in 2001 in PA.
Donor(s): Justin C. O'Donnell.
Financial data (yr. ended 12/31/01): Grants paid, $1,000; assets, $99,424 (M); gifts received, $45,750; expenditures, $1,000; qualifying distributions, $1,000.
Limitations: Applications not accepted.
Application information: Contributes only to pre-selected organizations.
Trustees: Justin C. O'Donnell, Marilyn M. O'Donnell.
EIN: 256788408

48479
Joseph T. Quinn Memorial Football Scholarship Fund
200 S. Providence Rd.
Wallingford, PA 19086-6334

Established in 1989.
Financial data (yr. ended 12/31/01): Grants paid, $1,000; assets, $1,427 (M); expenditures, $1,002; qualifying distributions, $1,002.
Limitations: Applications not accepted. Giving limited to residents of the Wallingford, PA, area.
Officer: Dorothy C. Katauskas.
EIN: 230954438

48480
R. W. Reed Charitable Foundation
900 5th Ave., Ste. 500
Pittsburgh, PA 15219

Established in 1984 in PA.
Donor(s): Robert W. Reed.
Financial data (yr. ended 12/31/00): Grants paid, $1,000; assets, $46,138 (M); expenditures, $1,000; qualifying distributions, $1,000.
Limitations: Applications not accepted. Giving primarily in Pittsburgh, PA.
Application information: Contributes only to pre-selected organizations.
Trustees: Richard W. Reed, Richard W. Reed, Jr., Frank E. Sparr.
EIN: 251469969

48481
Research Fund for Cystic Fibrosis, Inc.
42 Llanberris Rd.
Bala Cynwyd, PA 19004-2403

Financial data (yr. ended 06/30/00): Grants paid, $1,000; assets, $645,579 (M); gifts received, $1,825; expenditures, $25,558; qualifying distributions, $1,000.
Limitations: Applications not accepted. Giving primarily in Philadelphia, PA.
Application information: Contributes only to pre-selected organizations.
Officers: Douglas S. Holsclaw, Jr., M.D., Pres.; Stephanie Brown, Secy.
EIN: 232186239

48482
Joseph T. Rickards Memorial Scholarship
255 Fox Rd.
Media, PA 19063 (610) 521-4654
Application address: 617 Saude Ave., Essington, PA 19029
Contact: Anne M. Rickards, Pres.

Established in 1998 in PA.
Donor(s): Thomas F. O'Brien, Anne C. O'Brien.
Financial data (yr. ended 12/31/99): Grants paid, $1,000; assets, $10,326 (M); gifts received, $83; expenditures, $1,018; qualifying distributions, $1,018.
Limitations: Giving primarily in Prospect Park, PA.
Application information: Application form not required.
Officers: Anne M. Rickards, Pres.; Anne C. O'Brien, V.P.; Thomas F. O'Brien, Secy.-Treas.
Director: Jeffrey J. Rickards.

48482—PENNSYLVANIA

EIN: 232939449

48483
The Schoch Foundation
c/o Lawrence A. Isdaner
3 Bala Plz., Ste. 501 W.
Bala Cynwyd, PA 19004-3484
Application address: 641 Black Rock Rd., Bryn Mawr, PA 19010
Contact: Elizabeth Bowden, Tr.

Established in 1987 in PA.
Donor(s): Elizabeth Schoch-Bowden.
Financial data (yr. ended 08/31/01): Grants paid, $1,000; assets, $93,795 (M); expenditures, $1,968; qualifying distributions, $1,460.
Limitations: Giving primarily in Philadelphia, PA.
Application information: Application form not required.
Trustee: Elizabeth Bowden.
EIN: 232506027

48484
Silberman-Weinberger Family Foundation
838 Braddock Ave.
Braddock, PA 15104-1715

Established in 1997 in PA.
Financial data (yr. ended 09/30/01): Grants paid, $1,000; assets, $1,749 (M); expenditures, $1,000; qualifying distributions, $1,000.
Trustees: David Silberman, Lisa Wyner Silberman, Mark Silberman.
EIN: 232930313

48485
Donald M. Simmons Family Foundation
807 W. Lockhart St.
Sayre, PA 18840-1332

Donor(s): Donald M. Simmons, Sr.
Financial data (yr. ended 12/31/99): Grants paid, $1,000; assets, $25,087 (M); expenditures, $1,172; qualifying distributions, $1,000.
Limitations: Applications not accepted. Giving primarily in NY and PA.
Application information: Contributes only to pre-selected organizations.
Trustees: Jay L. Jackler, Richard S. Scolaro.
EIN: 222503586

48486
Jim Smith Memorial Fund
182 Strawberry Cir.
Langhorne, PA 19047-1272

Established in 1986 in PA.
Financial data (yr. ended 12/31/01): Grants paid, $1,000; assets, $25,181 (M); gifts received, $250; expenditures, $1,446; qualifying distributions, $1,000.
Limitations: Applications not accepted. Giving limited to residents of Langhorne, PA.
Application information: Recipient is selected by school officials.
Trustees: Kathleen Dillon, Siobhan Dillon, Elaine E. Smith, Marie Wrigley.
EIN: 232338697

48487
The Sokol Family Foundation
1312 Wrenfield Way
Villanova, PA 19085

Established in 1995 in OH.
Donor(s): David M. Sokol.
Financial data (yr. ended 12/31/00): Grants paid, $1,000; assets, $16,984 (M); expenditures, $1,080; qualifying distributions, $1,000.
Limitations: Applications not accepted. Giving primarily in Kent, OH.

Application information: Contributes only to pre-selected organizations.
Officers: David M. Sokol, Pres.; Christine A. Sokol, V.P.; Alexander A. Sokol, Secy.; Joel M. Sokol, Treas.
EIN: 341798696

48488
George Thompson, Jr. Foundation
c/o George Thompson, Jr.
P.O. Box 945
Glenside, PA 19038-0945 (215) 247-4643

Financial data (yr. ended 12/31/99): Grants paid, $1,000; assets, $0 (M); gifts received, $1,000; expenditures, $1,000; qualifying distributions, $1,000.
Limitations: Applications not accepted.
Application information: Contributes only to pre-selected organizations.
Officer: George Thompson, Jr., Exec. Dir.
EIN: 510277636

48489
Valley Grove School District Scholarship Fund
429 Wiley Ave.
Franklin, PA 16323-2834 (814) 432-4919

Financial data (yr. ended 06/30/01): Grants paid, $1,000; assets, $17,349 (M); expenditures, $1,000; qualifying distributions, $1,009.
Application information: Application form required.
Officer and Directors:* Thomas C. Brink,* Secy.; Raymond J. Brown, Jr., Michael Stahlman.
EIN: 251660820

48490
Window Cleaning & Building Service Foundation
104 W. North Ave.
Pittsburgh, PA 15212

Financial data (yr. ended 11/30/01): Grants paid, $1,000; assets, $1,101,978 (M); gifts received, $53,000; expenditures, $9,868; qualifying distributions, $1,000.
Limitations: Giving primarily in PA.
Officers: Steve R. Gaber, Mgr.; Steve R. Gaber, Jr., Mgr.
EIN: 256033918

48491
Judith M. Maggiaro Memorial Scholarship Trust
c/o Allfirst, Trust Tax. Div.
21 E. Market St.
York, PA 17401-1500

Financial data (yr. ended 12/31/00): Grants paid, $951; assets, $18,994 (M); expenditures, $1,032; qualifying distributions, $941.
Limitations: Giving limited to PA.
Application information: Application form required.
Trustee: Allfirst.
EIN: 236654895

48492
Jeanne Zweig Charitable Foundation
2320 Faunce St.
Philadelphia, PA 19152-4112
Contact: Jeanne Zweig, Pres.

Established in 1999 in PA.
Donor(s): Jeanne Zweig.
Financial data (yr. ended 10/31/01): Grants paid, $947; assets, $26,753 (M); gifts received, $9,469; expenditures, $965; qualifying distributions, $925.
Limitations: Giving primarily in Philadelphia, PA.
Officer: Jeanne Zweig, Pres. and Secy.-Treas.
EIN: 233024313

48493
M. L. Musselman Trust f/b/o M. L. Ranck Award
c/o Allfirst, Trust Div.
21 E. Market St., M/C 402-130
York, PA 17401-1500
Application address: c/o Faculty of Millersville State College, Development Office, P.O. Box 1002, Millersville, PA 17551

Established in 2000 in PA.
Financial data (yr. ended 12/31/00): Grants paid, $934; assets, $43,187 (M); expenditures, $1,320; qualifying distributions, $1,320.
Application information: Application form required.
Trustee: Allfirst.
EIN: 236632342

48494
Esther Wachs Book & Leslie Book Family Foundation
c/o Esther Wachs Book & Leslie Book
217 E. Laurier Pl.
Bryn Mawr, PA 19010

Established in 2000 in PA.
Donor(s): Esther Wachs Book, Leslie Book.
Financial data (yr. ended 11/30/01): Grants paid, $900; assets, $160,406 (M); gifts received, $8,675; expenditures, $14,206; qualifying distributions, $900.
Limitations: Applications not accepted.
Application information: Contributes only to pre-selected organizations.
Trustees: Esther Wachs Book, Leslie Book.
EIN: 223693688

48495
W. W. Keen & Madeleine A. K. Butcher Family Foundation
500 Telner St.
Philadelphia, PA 19118

Financial data (yr. ended 12/31/01): Grants paid, $900; assets, $139,357 (M); expenditures, $2,175; qualifying distributions, $900.
Limitations: Applications not accepted. Giving primarily in Philadelphia, PA.
Application information: Contributes only to pre-selected organizations.
Director: W.W. Keen Butcher.
EIN: 237061681

48496
The Goldberg Family Fund
(Formerly The Maxine S. Goldberg Family Fund)
22 W. Levering Mill Rd.
Bala Cynwyd, PA 19004

Established in 1987 in PA.
Donor(s): Maxine S. Goldberg.
Financial data (yr. ended 11/30/01): Grants paid, $900; assets, $14,009 (M); expenditures, $900; qualifying distributions, $900.
Limitations: Applications not accepted. Giving primarily in PA.
Application information: Contributes only to pre-selected organizations.
Officers: Maxine S. Goldberg, Pres.; Jay L. Goldberg, V.P.
EIN: 232493545

48497
Margaret B. Stimmel Trust for Dr. & Mrs. George Stimmel Scholarship Fund
c/o Mellon Bank, N.A.
P.O. Box 7236
Philadelphia, PA 19101-7236

Financial data (yr. ended 06/30/99): Grants paid, $900; assets, $29,528 (M); expenditures, $1,119; qualifying distributions, $942.
Limitations: Applications not accepted. Giving limited to the Souderton, PA, area.
Trustee: Mellon Bank, N.A.
EIN: 236578513

48498
Frank S. Labar Memorial Fund
1735 Mareket St.
Philadelphia, PA 19101-7236

Financial data (yr. ended 12/31/01): Grants paid, $851; assets, $17,835 (M); expenditures, $1,036; qualifying distributions, $908.
Limitations: Applications not accepted. Giving limited to the greater Stroudsburg, PA, area.
Application information: Contributes only to pre-selected organizations.
Trustee: Mellon Bank, N.A.
EIN: 236513387

48499
Asbury Trust
c/o Carol L. Thomas
3235 Glengreen Dr.
Lancaster, PA 17601-1338

Established in 1995 in PA.
Financial data (yr. ended 12/31/01): Grants paid, $834; assets, $67,948 (M); expenditures, $1,096; qualifying distributions, $834.
Limitations: Applications not accepted. Giving primarily in PA.
Application information: Contributes only to pre-selected organizations.
Trustee: Carol L. Thomas.
EIN: 237648415

48500
Francine and Richard Bank Foundation
1247 Dundee Dr.
Dresher, PA 19025-1617

Established in 1985 in PA.
Financial data (yr. ended 11/30/01): Grants paid, $815; assets, $12,869 (M); expenditures, $815; qualifying distributions, $815.
Limitations: Giving primarily in PA.
Trustees: Ari Bank, Cory Bank, Francine Bank, Richard Bank.
EIN: 232374806

48501
Goodall Rubber Company Charitable & Welfare Foundation
c/o Goodall Rubber Co.
790 Birney Hwy., Ste. 100
Aston, PA 19014
Contact: Robert M. Bissinger

Donor(s): Goodall Rubber Co., Inc.
Financial data (yr. ended 12/31/01): Grants paid, $800; assets, $5,612 (M); expenditures, $801; qualifying distributions, $800.
Limitations: Giving primarily in PA.
Officer: Robert M. Bissinger, Secy.-Treas.
Trustee: Terry Taylor.
EIN: 216015777
Codes: CS, CD

48502
Northeast High School 131st Graduating Class
1601 Kenmare Dr.
Dresher, PA 19025-1223

Financial data (yr. ended 06/30/02): Grants paid, $800; assets, $17,794 (M); expenditures, $851; qualifying distributions, $800.
Limitations: Giving primarily in Philadelphia, PA.
Application information: Application form not required.
Officers: Leonard Malamud, Pres.; Mark Sailor, Treas.
EIN: 232013241

48503
Gail L. Usner Memorial Scholarship
c/o Fulton Financial Advisors, N.A.
P.O. Box 3215
Lancaster, PA 17604-3215
Application address: c/o Ephrata High School, Guidance Dept., 803 Oak Blvd., Ephrata, PA 17522

Donor(s): James A. Althouse.
Financial data (yr. ended 09/30/01): Grants paid, $795; assets, $29,504 (M); expenditures, $1,528; qualifying distributions, $795.
Limitations: Giving limited to residents of Ephrata, PA.
Application information: Application form required.
Trustee: Fulton Financial Advisors, N.A.
EIN: 237902656

48504
The Melchiorre Family Charitable Foundation, Inc.
2229 S. Juniper St.
Philadelphia, PA 19148

Established in 2000 in PA.
Financial data (yr. ended 12/31/01): Grants paid, $761; assets, $17,827 (M); expenditures, $861; qualifying distributions, $761.
Limitations: Applications not accepted. Giving primarily in Philadelphia, PA.
Application information: Contributes only to pre-selected organizations.
Officers: Elaine Melchiorre, Pres.; Sandra Caraffa, V.P.; Deborah Peacock, V.P.; Paul L. Melchiorre, Secy.-Treas.
EIN: 233040306

48505
The Riebman Family Fund
1170 St. Andrews Rd.
Bryn Mawr, PA 19010-1951

Established in 1995 in PA.
Donor(s): Leon Riebman, Claire E. Riebman.
Financial data (yr. ended 04/30/02): Grants paid, $760; assets, $1,488 (M); expenditures, $1,607; qualifying distributions, $760.
Limitations: Applications not accepted. Giving primarily in the Philadelphia, PA, area.
Application information: Contributes only to pre-selected organizations.
Officers: Leon Riebman, Pres.; Claire E. Riebman, V.P.; Barbara Riebman, Secy.-Treas.
EIN: 237806313

48506
Revington Arthur Foundation, Inc.
809 Cornwall Rd.
State College, PA 16803

Established in 1989 in CT.
Financial data (yr. ended 07/31/01): Grants paid, $750; assets, $192,909 (M); gifts received, $3,600; expenditures, $19,711; qualifying distributions, $16,518; giving activities include $16,692 for programs.
Limitations: Applications not accepted.
Application information: Contributes only to pre-selected organizations.
Officers and Directors:* Sandra Byham, Pres. and Treas.; Edward E. Byham,* V.P.; Francene A. Dale,* V.P.; Kevin B. Dale,* Secy.; Kathryn J. McMasters.
EIN: 222840443

48507
Borough and Township Police Association
6510 Brownsville Rd.
Pittsburgh, PA 15236-1513
Application address: 5241 Brightwood Rd., Ste. 1, Bethel Park, PA 15102, tel.: (412) 334-5039
Contact: Kirke McClain, Treas.

Financial data (yr. ended 12/31/99): Grants paid, $750; assets, $66,181 (M); gifts received, $59,024; expenditures, $74,097; qualifying distributions, $66,462.
Limitations: Giving primarily in PA.
Application information: Application form required.
Officers: James Wabby, Pres.; Bernie Tomayko, V.P.; Richard Danko, Secy.; Kirke McClain, Treas.
EIN: 251630543

48508
Central and Southern African Legal Assistance Foundation
c/o Rhoads & Sinon, LLP
1 S. Market Sq., 12th Fl.
Harrisburg, PA 17101

Financial data (yr. ended 12/31/01): Grants paid, $750; assets, $0 (M); gifts received, $750; expenditures, $750; qualifying distributions, $750.
Limitations: Applications not accepted. Giving primarily in Zimbabwe.
Application information: Contributes only to pre-selected organizations.
Officers and Board Members:* Henry W. Rhoads,* Pres.; William Berkley,* V.P.; Trevor Harris,* Secy.-Treas.; Daryl R. Buffenstein, David Coltart, Clifford L. Klein.
EIN: 251647703

48509
William Lyster May Foundation
217 E. Washington St.
West Chester, PA 19380
Contact: Richard K. May, Tr.

Established in 1997 in PA.
Financial data (yr. ended 12/31/01): Grants paid, $750; assets, $15,139 (M); gifts received, $850; expenditures, $755; qualifying distributions, $750.
Trustee: Richard K. May.
EIN: 237862364

48510
Benjamin G. McFate Memorial Scholarship Fund
c/o Mellon Bank, N.A.
P.O. Box 185
Pittsburgh, PA 15230-9897
Application address: P.O. Box 300, Erie, PA 16152, tel.: (814) 453-7320
Contact: James Baker, Trust Off., Mellon Bank, N.A.

Established in 1983 in PA.
Financial data (yr. ended 02/28/00): Grants paid, $750; assets, $33,167 (M); expenditures, $1,329; qualifying distributions, $958.
Limitations: Giving limited to the Oil City, PA, area.

48510—PENNSYLVANIA

Application information: Application form required.
Trustee: Mellon Bank, N.A.
EIN: 251431929

48511
James D. & Sheryl Samter Family Foundation
1 Caras Ct.
Fort Washington, PA 19034

Financial data (yr. ended 11/30/01): Grants paid, $750; assets, $11,458 (M); expenditures, $754; qualifying distributions, $750.
Trustees: Barry Jacobson, Stacey Jacobson, James D. Samter, Scott A. Samter, Sheryl Samter, Susan Samter.
EIN: 237927430

48512
Herbert Rieders Foundation for the Recovery of Objects Judaica
P.O. Box 215
Williamsport, PA 17703-0215

Financial data (yr. ended 12/31/01): Grants paid, $725; assets, $11,448 (M); gifts received, $13,000; expenditures, $2,755; qualifying distributions, $725.
Officers: Clifford A. Rieders, Pres.; Sylvia Rieders, V.P.; Susan Hope Kahn, Secy.; Cyrus Kahn, Treas.
EIN: 232651994

48513
Clark Foundation, Inc.
601 Rouse Ave.
Youngsville, PA 16371-1603 (814) 563-4601
Contact: David G. Clark, Secy.-Treas.

Financial data (yr. ended 06/30/02): Grants paid, $700; assets, $28,496 (M); gifts received, $24,400; expenditures, $701; qualifying distributions, $700.
Limitations: Giving primarily in PA.
Officers: Robert J. Clark, Pres.; Nancy Church, V.P.; Judy Clark, V.P.; David G. Clark, Secy.-Treas.
EIN: 251411319

48514
The Alan Jay Davis Memorial Trust
429 Forbes Ave., Ste. 1000
Pittsburgh, PA 15219 (412) 391-2226
Contact: Howard D. Davis, Tr.

Established in 1992 in PA.
Financial data (yr. ended 12/31/01): Grants paid, $700; assets, $21,000 (M); gifts received, $263; expenditures, $713; qualifying distributions, $700.
Limitations: Giving primarily in PA.
Trustee: Howard D. Davis.
EIN: 256388764

48515
Schulman Foundation, Inc.
c/o George Feldman
8300 Great Springs Rd.
Bryn Mawr, PA 19010-1720

Financial data (yr. ended 02/28/01): Grants paid, $700; assets, $152,669 (M); expenditures, $1,765; qualifying distributions, $700.
Limitations: Applications not accepted. Giving primarily in Boston, MA, and Philadelphia, PA.
Application information: Contributes only to pre-selected organizations.
Officers: George J. Feldman, Jr., Pres.; Margot Feldman, Treas.
EIN: 136085817

48516
Rev. Joseph J. Ostheimer Memorial Scholarship Fund
c/o James Veghte
31 E. Centre St.
Shenandoah, PA 17976

Donor(s): Marie Ostheimer.
Financial data (yr. ended 12/31/01): Grants paid, $687; assets, $17,111 (M); expenditures, $1,363; qualifying distributions, $687.
Limitations: Giving limited to residents of Coplay and Mahanoy City, PA.
Trustee: Patricia A. Jackson.
EIN: 236855992

48517
Abraham & Hinda Ehrlich Charitable Trust
c/o Brodsky Berk
1653 The Fairway, Ste. 214
Jenkintown, PA 19046

Financial data (yr. ended 12/31/01): Grants paid, $650; assets, $2,808 (M); expenditures, $671; qualifying distributions, $650.
Limitations: Applications not accepted. Giving on a national basis.
Application information: Contributes only to pre-selected organizations.
Trustees: Gertrude Adler, Maxwell H. Rasman.
EIN: 236422845

48518
Kahn Foundation
c/o Jonns
765 Bethlehem Pike
Montgomeryville, PA 18936-9602
Contact: Harry C. Kahn, II, Pres.

Donor(s): Harry C. Kahn II.
Financial data (yr. ended 07/31/02): Grants paid, $650; assets, $2,359 (M); gifts received, $2,000; expenditures, $930; qualifying distributions, $650.
Officers: Harry C. Kahn II, Mgr.; Joan P. Kahn, Mgr.
EIN: 236243794

48519
J. Jerome & Clara G. Katz Scholarship Fund
c/o First Union National Bank
P.O. Box 7558
Philadelphia, PA 19101-7558

Financial data (yr. ended 12/31/99): Grants paid, $610; assets, $20,471 (M); expenditures, $1,250; qualifying distributions, $610.
Limitations: Applications not accepted. Giving primarily in Philadelphia, PA.
Application information: Contributes only to pre-selected organizations.
Trustee: First Union National Bank.
EIN: 236397541

48520
E. Clive Anderson Foundation
8012 Seminole St.
Philadelphia, PA 19118

Financial data (yr. ended 12/31/01): Grants paid, $600; assets, $8,671 (M); expenditures, $612; qualifying distributions, $600.
Limitations: Giving primarily in CT.
Officers: E. Clive Anderson, Pres.; Beatrice R. Cromwell, Secy.
EIN: 222789550

48521
Leidy Oak Foundation
250 Cherry Ln.
Souderton, PA 18964-1903

Established in 2000 in PA.
Donor(s): Terrance K. Leidy.
Financial data (yr. ended 12/31/01): Grants paid, $600; assets, $10,069 (M); expenditures, $600; qualifying distributions, $600.
Limitations: Applications not accepted.
Application information: Contributes only to pre-selected organizations.
Officers: Terrance K. Leidy, Pres.; Darlene K. Leidy, Secy.-Treas.
EIN: 233044885

48522
Betty Byfield Paul Foundation
140 Guernsey Rd.
Swarthmore, PA 19081-1209

Established in 2000 in PA.
Donor(s): Norman Paul.
Financial data (yr. ended 12/31/01): Grants paid, $600; assets, $202,328 (M); expenditures, $5,554; qualifying distributions, $600.
Limitations: Applications not accepted.
Application information: Contributes only to pre-selected organizations.
Officers: Norman Paul, Pres.; Marilyn Paul, V.P.; David Paul, Secy.-Treas.
EIN: 233063865

48523
Tom L. Waring Trust Fund
c/o Fulton Financial Advisors, N.A.
P.O. Box 3215
Lancaster, PA 17604-3215

Established in 1993 in PA.
Financial data (yr. ended 12/31/00): Grants paid, $600; assets, $10,549 (M); expenditures, $785; qualifying distributions, $602.
Limitations: Giving limited to residents of Stroudsburg, PA.
Trustee: Fulton Financial Advisors, N.A.
EIN: 236254477

48524
The Boyd Foundation
1243 1/2 Country Club Rd.
Monongahela, PA 15063

Established in 1988 in PA.
Donor(s): David R. Boyd, Rosa B. Snyder-Boyd.
Financial data (yr. ended 12/31/01): Grants paid, $590; assets, $11,035 (M); expenditures, $629; qualifying distributions, $590.
Limitations: Applications not accepted. Giving primarily in PA.
Application information: Contributes only to pre-selected organizations.
Director: David R. Boyd.
EIN: 251591723

48525
Bedford Elks Youth and Trust Fund
937 S. Richard St.
Bedford, PA 15522
Application address: c/o Bedford Elks Trustees, R.R. 6, Box 480, Bedford, IL 15522, tel.: (814) 623-9714

Financial data (yr. ended 12/31/01): Grants paid, $579; assets, $12,633 (M); gifts received, $125; expenditures, $579; qualifying distributions, $0.
Limitations: Giving limited to Bedford, Fulton, Huntington, Blair, Cambria, and Somerset counties, PA.
Application information: Application form required.
Trustees: Thomas Hagen, William Leibfreid, Tom Oster, Fred Shoemaker, William Wise.
EIN: 251526163

48526
Roll Foundation
c/o William J. Roll
227 Wild Cherry Ln.
Northumberland, PA 17857-9681

Donor(s): William Roll, Ann Roll.
Financial data (yr. ended 09/30/02): Grants paid, $577; assets, $31,612 (M); gifts received, $41,056; expenditures, $583; qualifying distributions, $577.
Limitations: Giving primarily in PA.
Officers: William J. Roll, Pres.; Ann M. Roll, V.P.
Directors: Elizabeth A. Roll, Kathleen J. Roll.
EIN: 233016370

48527
The Rose Rosen and Harry Rosen Foundation
5327 Darlington Rd.
Pittsburgh, PA 15217-1551
Application address: 2347 Beechwood Blvd., Pittsburgh, PA 15217
Contact: Roberta A. Recht, Tr.

Donor(s): Harry Rosen.
Financial data (yr. ended 12/31/01): Grants paid, $570; assets, $21,438 (M); expenditures, $996; qualifying distributions, $570.
Limitations: Giving primarily in PA.
Application information: Application form not required.
Trustees: Roberta A. Recht, Elayne Rosen, Harry Rosen.
EIN: 256063051

48528
The LaMotte Family Foundation
P.O. Box 1009
Paoli, PA 19301

Established in 1999 in ME and PA.
Financial data (yr. ended 12/31/01): Grants paid, $560; assets, $12,863 (M); expenditures, $898; qualifying distributions, $560.
Limitations: Applications not accepted. Giving primarily in Paoli, PA.
Application information: Contributes only to pre-selected organizations.
Trustees: Ferdinand LaMotte IV, Nicholas H. LaMotte, Danielle Lamotte London.
EIN: 232612699

48529
The Tom and Judy Leidy Foundation
316 Leidy Rd.
Souderton, PA 18964-1903

Established in 2000 in PA.
Donor(s): Thomas K. Leidy.
Financial data (yr. ended 12/31/01): Grants paid, $520; assets, $9,828 (M); expenditures, $556; qualifying distributions, $520.
Limitations: Applications not accepted.
Application information: Contributes only to pre-selected organizations.
Officers: Thomas K. Leidy, Pres.; Judith Ann Leidy, Secy.-Treas.
EIN: 233028371

48530
The DiMarco Family Foundation, Inc.
63 Yale Dr.
Richboro, PA 18954-1255

Established in 1990 in PA.
Donor(s): Albert J. DiMarco.
Financial data (yr. ended 09/30/01): Grants paid, $518; assets, $183,062 (M); expenditures, $20,942; qualifying distributions, $518.
Limitations: Giving primarily in PA.
Officers: Albert J. DiMarco, Pres.; Michael N. Prosini, Secy.-Treas.
EIN: 232626830

48531
The Jay R. Baer Fund
1650 Arch St., 22nd Fl.
Philadelphia, PA 19103-2003

Established around 1988.
Financial data (yr. ended 06/30/01): Grants paid, $500; assets, $21,864 (M); expenditures, $520; qualifying distributions, $500.
Limitations: Applications not accepted.
Application information: Contributes only to pre-selected organizations.
Officer: Carol Baer Mott, Pres.
Directors: Rob T. Blacksberg, Donald Joseph.
EIN: 232500840

48532
Michael S. Bianco Memorial Scholarship Fund
505 E. Curtin St.
Bellefonte, PA 16823
Contact: Frank Bianco, Tr.

Financial data (yr. ended 08/31/00): Grants paid, $500; assets, $5,789 (M); expenditures, $500; qualifying distributions, $500.
Limitations: Giving limited to residents of Cold Spring Harbor, NY.
Application information: Application form required.
Trustees: Frank Bianco, Marie Bianco.
EIN: 112784152

48533
The Gluck Family Charitable Foundation
5622 Aylesboro Ave.
Pittsburgh, PA 15217-1402
Contact: Dolores K. Gluck, Tr.

Established in 2000 in PA.
Donor(s): Dolores K. Gluck.
Financial data (yr. ended 12/31/01): Grants paid, $500; assets, $120,858 (M); expenditures, $500; qualifying distributions, $500.
Application information: Application form not required.
Trustee: Dolores K. Gluck.
EIN: 256731075

48534
John M. and Gertrude E. Petersen Foundation
124 Voyageur Dr.
Erie, PA 16505-5435

Established in 2000 in PA.
Financial data (yr. ended 12/31/01): Grants paid, $500; assets, $3,251,839 (M); gifts received, $2,019,689; expenditures, $2,305; qualifying distributions, $500.
Officers: John M. Petersen, Pres.; Gertrude E. Petersen, V.P.
EIN: 251859031

48535
Harry, Gladys & Rosana Wassall Charitable Foundation, Inc.
c/o J. Yampolsky
1420 Walnut St., Ste. 200
Philadelphia, PA 19102-4002

Established in 2001 in FL.
Donor(s): Rosana Wassall.
Financial data (yr. ended 12/31/01): Grants paid, $500; assets, $24,513 (M); gifts received, $25,000; expenditures, $500; qualifying distributions, $500.
Limitations: Applications not accepted. Giving primarily in Phoenix, AZ.
Application information: Contributes only to pre-selected organizations.
Officers and Directors:* Rosana Wassall,* Pres.; Matias D. Pittaluga,* V.P.; Jack Yampolsky,* Secy.-Treas.
EIN: 912164480

48536
Alice K. Wolf Memorial Scholarship Trust
c/o PNC Advisors
620 Liberty Ave., P2-PTPP-10-2
Pittsburgh, PA 15222-2705
Application address: c/o Warren E. Elliot, Millville Senior High School, Millville, NJ 08322

Financial data (yr. ended 12/31/01): Grants paid, $500; assets, $57,381 (M); expenditures, $1,303; qualifying distributions, $590.
Limitations: Giving limited to residents of Millville, NJ.
Application information: Recipients are selected by a committee chosen by the principal at Millville High School.
Trustee: PNC Bank, N.A.
EIN: 226071088

48537
Lillian Wurzel Memorial Foundation
329 Sinkler Rd.
Wyncote, PA 19095
Contact: Roy C. Malis, Tr.

Financial data (yr. ended 10/31/01): Grants paid, $500; assets, $2,924 (M); expenditures, $779; qualifying distributions, $500.
Limitations: Giving primarily in PA.
Trustee: Roy C. Malis.
EIN: 236265700

48538
Scott Archer Wychgel Memorial Scholarship Trust
3407 Eaton Ct.
Chester Springs, PA 19425-8749

Established in 1997 in PA.
Financial data (yr. ended 12/31/01): Grants paid, $500; assets, $10,222 (M); gifts received, $565; expenditures, $500; qualifying distributions, $500.
Limitations: Applications not accepted.
Application information: Unsolicited requests for funds not accepted.
Trustee: Steven Forgione.
EIN: 237707447

48539
Clair Cornelius/Clay Township Award to the Southern Huntingdon County Schools
c/o First Commonwealth Trust Co.
501 Penn St.
Huntingdon, PA 16652

Financial data (yr. ended 12/31/99): Grants paid, $490; assets, $16,977 (M); expenditures, $752; qualifying distributions, $490.
Limitations: Applications not accepted. Giving limited to Huntingdon County, PA.
Application information: Recipients selected by faculty of the Southern Huntingdon County High School, PA.
Trustee: First Commonwealth Trust Co.
EIN: 256211208

48540
William E. Keller Charitable Foundation
344 Campbell Rd.
York, PA 17402-8695

Established in 1992 in PA.
Financial data (yr. ended 12/31/01): Grants paid, $470; assets, $16,931 (M); gifts received, $725;

48540—PENNSYLVANIA

expenditures, $1,292; qualifying distributions, $470.
Limitations: Applications not accepted. Giving primarily in PA.
Application information: Contributes only to pre-selected organizations.
Trustees: Lisa C. Keller, Kathy M. Ranzinger, Robert Rembisz.
EIN: 256391757

48541
A. H. Burchfield Family Foundation
5 Indian Hill Rd.
Pittsburgh, PA 15238

Established in 2000 in PA.
Donor(s): Albert H. Burchfield III.
Financial data (yr. ended 12/31/01): Grants paid, $446; assets, $302,759 (M); gifts received, $50,025; expenditures, $976; qualifying distributions, $446.
Limitations: Applications not accepted.
Application information: Contributes only to pre-selected organizations.
Officers: Albert H. Burchfield III, Pres.; Janice L. Burchfield, Secy.-Treas.
Directors: Albert H. Burchfield IV, Steven M. Burchfield.
EIN: 251876112

48542
The Thoma Family Foundation
1481 E. Bristol Rd.
Churchville, PA 18966

Established in 1998 in PA.
Donor(s): Ronald R. Thoma.
Financial data (yr. ended 12/31/01): Grants paid, $420; assets, $7,942 (M); gifts received, $131; expenditures, $420; qualifying distributions, $420.
Limitations: Applications not accepted.
Application information: Contributes only to pre-selected organizations.
Directors: Mary L. Thoma, Ronald R. Thoma.
Trustee: Mary Ellen Bradley.
EIN: 232733656

48543
Margaret Butcher Foundation
c/o PNC Advisors
1600 Market St., 4th Fl.
Philadelphia, PA 19103

Established in 1996 in PA.
Financial data (yr. ended 06/30/01): Grants paid, $400; assets, $5,217 (M); expenditures, $419; qualifying distributions, $400.
Limitations: Giving primarily in PA.
Trustee: PNC Bank, N.A.
EIN: 237850671

48544
John H. Hartman Trust
c/o Mellon Bank, N.A.
P.O. Box 7236
Philadelphia, PA 19101-7236

Established in 1985 in PA.
Financial data (yr. ended 06/30/01): Grants paid, $400; assets, $7,730 (M); expenditures, $406; qualifying distributions, $404.
Limitations: Applications not accepted. Giving limited to PA.
Trustee: Mellon Bank, N.A.
EIN: 236225844

48545
David H. Goodman Foundation
c/o Nancy P. Freedman
3000 Two Logan Sq., 18th and Arch St.
Philadelphia, PA 19103-2799

Established in 1986 in PA.
Donor(s): David H. Goodman.
Financial data (yr. ended 11/30/01): Grants paid, $375; assets, $844,727 (M); gifts received, $74,240; expenditures, $2,434; qualifying distributions, $840,207.
Limitations: Applications not accepted. Giving primarily in PA.
Application information: Contributes only to pre-selected organizations.
Directors: David H. Goodman, Robert Goodman.
EIN: 231895503

48546
Luther V. Hendricks Memorial Fund
c/o G. Carnes
212 Hendricks Hall
Edinboro, PA 16444
Contact: Richard Gromen, Dir.

Financial data (yr. ended 10/31/01): Grants paid, $330; assets, $7,035 (M); expenditures, $337; qualifying distributions, $325.
Limitations: Giving limited to Edinboro, PA.
Application information: Application form not required.
Directors: Gerald Carnes, Richard Gromen, Harvey Heath, Greg Lessig, Andrew Rosnak.
EIN: 237212857

48547
Pauline S. Wright Trust f/b/o Garden Spot High School
21 E. Market St., MC 402-130
York, PA 17401-1500
Application address: 669 E. Main St., P.O. Box 609, New Holland, PA 17557

Financial data (yr. ended 12/31/00): Grants paid, $328; assets, $14,751 (M); expenditures, $478; qualifying distributions, $478.
Limitations: Giving limited to New Holland, PA.
Trustee: Allfirst.
EIN: 256349919

48548
Thomas F. Becker Memorial Scholarship Fund
c/o Heritage National Bank
P.O. Box 1100
Pottsville, PA 17901

Established in 1973 in PA.
Financial data (yr. ended 12/31/99): Grants paid, $300; assets, $10,269 (M); expenditures, $544; qualifying distributions, $538.
Limitations: Applications not accepted. Giving limited to the greater Shenandoah, PA, area.
Trustee: Heritage National Bank.
EIN: 237398931

48549
Bringing the Outside World Inside Foundation
755 Bryn Mawr Ave.
Bryn Mawr, PA 19010

Financial data (yr. ended 12/31/01): Grants paid, $300; assets, $50 (M); gifts received, $500; expenditures, $647; qualifying distributions, $300.
Limitations: Applications not accepted.
Application information: Contributes only to pre-selected organizations.
Officer: Lee M. Rosenbluth, Pres.
EIN: 232877393

48550
William C. Green Charitable Foundation Trust
12300 Perry Hwy., Ste. 303
Wexford, PA 15090

Established in 1988 in PA.
Donor(s): William C. Green, Palmer Donavin Manufacturing Co., Robert J. Woodward, Jr., Robert W. Woodward, Sr.‡
Financial data (yr. ended 12/31/01): Grants paid, $300; assets, $27,068 (M); expenditures, $773; qualifying distributions, $750.
Limitations: Giving limited to PA.
Application information: Application form required.
Officers: Robert J. Woodward, Jr., Chair.; Ronald E. Calhoun, Secy.; Robyn M. Pollina, Treas.
EIN: 256315004

48551
McGinley Family Foundation
P.O. Box 312
Bala Cynwyd, PA 19004-0312

Established in 1998 in PA.
Donor(s): Joseph P. McGinley.
Financial data (yr. ended 12/31/00): Grants paid, $300; assets, $1,017 (M); gifts received, $2,200; expenditures, $1,394; qualifying distributions, $300.
Limitations: Applications not accepted.
Application information: Contributes only to pre-selected organizations.
Officers and Directors:* Sharon McGinley,* Pres.; Kathleen M. Toner, Secy.-Treas.; Lisa McGinley, Robert J. McGinley.
EIN: 232979036

48552
Sweet Charity, Inc.
c/o John R. Patterson, Jr.
1209 Villanova Ave.
Folsom, PA 19033-1032

Established in 1994 in PA.
Financial data (yr. ended 12/31/01): Grants paid, $300; assets, $0 (M); gifts received, $556; expenditures, $556; qualifying distributions, $300.
Director: John R. Patterson, Jr.
EIN: 232733126

48553
The Yoskin Family Foundation
1606 Pine St., 2nd Fl.
Philadelphia, PA 19103

Established in 1997 in PA.
Donor(s): Jon W. Yoskin II.
Financial data (yr. ended 12/31/01): Grants paid, $300; assets, $3,566 (M); gifts received, $2,500; expenditures, $488; qualifying distributions, $300.
Limitations: Applications not accepted.
Application information: Contributes only to pre-selected organizations.
Officer: Jon W. Yoskin II, Pres. and Secy.-Treas.
EIN: 232858780

48554
Florence March Fund
105 S. 12th St.
Philadelphia, PA 19107-4809 (215) 625-9070

Financial data (yr. ended 12/31/00): Grants paid, $278; assets, $1 (M); expenditures, $768; qualifying distributions, $278.
Limitations: Applications not accepted. Giving limited to Philadelphia, PA.
Application information: Contributes only to pre-selected organizations.
Trustees: Samuel Rappaport, Betty Robinson.
EIN: 232097620

48555
J. Alexander & Reba C. Kline Foundation
1219 N. Woodbine Ave.
Narberth, PA 19072
Contact: Stuart W. Kline, Tr.

Financial data (yr. ended 12/31/01): Grants paid, $275; assets, $234 (M); gifts received, $400; expenditures, $335; qualifying distributions, $275.
Limitations: Giving primarily in Philadelphia, PA.
Application information: Application form not required.
Trustee: Stuart W. Kline.
EIN: 236299529

48556
Lambert-Tyson Foundation, Inc.
1336 Faxon Cir.
Williamsport, PA 17701 (570) 326-9471

Established in 1988 in PA.
Donor(s): Michael Tyson.
Financial data (yr. ended 12/31/01): Grants paid, $250; assets, $26,261 (M); expenditures, $268; qualifying distributions, $250.
Limitations: Applications not accepted. Giving limited to PA.
Application information: Contributes only to pre-selected organizations.
Officers: Michael Tyson, Pres.; Marie M. Tyson, Secy.; Robert G. Bowers, Treas.
Directors: Toby M. Hagmaier, Carol A. Henninger, Peter A. Zollers.
EIN: 232499587

48557
The Lancaster Alliance
44 N. Queen St.
Lancaster, PA 17603

Established in 1993.
Financial data (yr. ended 12/31/01): Grants paid, $250; assets, $432,548 (M); gifts received, $821,119; expenditures, $579,863; qualifying distributions, $250.
Limitations: Applications not accepted. Giving primarily in Lancaster, PA.
Application information: Contributes only to pre-selected organizations.
Officer and Directors:* Jack Howell,* Exec. V.P.; John M. Buckwalter, Gar W. Davidson, Lawrence A. Downing, Rufus A. Fulton, Jr., S. Dale High, David R. Keller, W. Kirk Liddell, Christian E. McMurtrie, Albert Morrison III, Robert R. Stoyko, Michael Winn, and 7 additional directors.
EIN: 232728559

48558
Jerome W. & Lois Rosenberg Family Foundation
233 S. 6th St., Ste. 2001
Philadelphia, PA 19106-3755 (215) 925-8214
Contact: Jerome and Lois Rosenberg, Trustees

Established in 1999 in PA.
Donor(s): Lois Rosenberg.
Financial data (yr. ended 12/31/01): Grants paid, $250; assets, $5,878 (M); gifts received, $800; expenditures, $361; qualifying distributions, $250.
Trustees: Jerome W. Rosenberg, Lois Rosenberg.
EIN: 232983809

48559
David Rubinow Roth Foundation
436 Jefferson Ave.
Scranton, PA 18510-2413

Financial data (yr. ended 05/31/02): Grants paid, $250; assets, $1,701 (M); gifts received, $25; expenditures, $250; qualifying distributions, $250.
Officers: Michael H. Roth, Pres.; James D. Roth, Secy.
EIN: 232486863

48560
The Weiler Family Foundation, Inc.
1 Wildwood Dr.
Cresco, PA 18326

Established in 1998 in PA.
Donor(s): Karl M. Weiler, Ann Weiler.
Financial data (yr. ended 12/31/01): Grants paid, $250; assets, $448,325 (M); gifts received, $35,000; expenditures, $1,267; qualifying distributions, $250.
Limitations: Applications not accepted.
Application information: Contributes only to pre-selected organizations.
Officer: Karl M. Weiler, Pres.
Director: Christopher Weiler.
EIN: 232962255

48561
The Adolph and Rose Levis Family Foundation
c/o J.K. Thomas
1735 Market St.
Philadelphia, PA 19103-7899

Established in 1993.
Donor(s): Adolph Levis.‡
Financial data (yr. ended 11/30/00): Grants paid, $210; assets, $715 (M); expenditures, $210; qualifying distributions, $210.
Limitations: Applications not accepted.
Application information: Contributes only to pre-selected organizations.
Trustee: Judy Lewis Markhoff.
EIN: 236670893

48562
John R. Post Charitable Foundation
1133 Reading Blvd.
Wyomissing, PA 19610

Financial data (yr. ended 12/31/01): Grants paid, $200; assets, $937 (M); gifts received, $200; expenditures, $260; qualifying distributions, $200.
Limitations: Applications not accepted.
Trustees: John R. Post, Maryanne H. Post.
EIN: 237866158

48563
R. A. Graciano Family Foundation
209 Sigma Dr.
Pittsburgh, PA 15238-2826

Established in 1998 in PA.
Financial data (yr. ended 12/31/01): Grants paid, $150; assets, $2,762 (M); gifts received, $550; expenditures, $422; qualifying distributions, $150.
Officers: Richard A. Graciano, Pres.; Jeffrey J. Graciano, Secy.-Treas.
EIN: 232919763

48564
Nirmal Foundation
1711 La Costa Ct.
Pittsburgh, PA 15237

Established in 1998.
Financial data (yr. ended 12/31/99): Grants paid, $150; assets, $4,976 (L); expenditures, $175; qualifying distributions, $150.
Officers: Om Sharma, Chair.; Alka Kaushik, Pres.; Van Dana Sharma, Secy.
EIN: 251715130

48565
Austin Foundation
c/o Robert Austin
660 Willow Valley Sq., M403
Lancaster, PA 17602

Established in 1987 in NJ.
Donor(s): Robert M. Austin.
Financial data (yr. ended 12/31/01): Grants paid, $122; assets, $73,075 (M); gifts received, $15,484; expenditures, $5,822; qualifying distributions, $122.
Limitations: Applications not accepted. Giving on a national basis.
Application information: Contributes only to pre-selected organizations.
Trustees: Claudia R. Austin, Robert G. Austin, Robert M. Austin.
EIN: 222773164

48566
H. Mary Sprangler Trust
(Formerly H. Mary Spangler Scholarship Trust)
c/o Allfirst, Trust Div.
21 E. Market St., M/C 402-130
York, PA 17401-1500
Application address: c/o Elizabethtown College, Financial Aid Off., 1 Alpha Dr., Elizabethtown, PA 11022

Financial data (yr. ended 12/31/00): Grants paid, $115; assets, $2,805 (M); expenditures, $140; qualifying distributions, $134.
Limitations: Giving limited to residents of PA.
Trustee: Allfirst.
EIN: 236262616

48567
Bliley Electric Foundation
c/o Bliley Electric Co.
P.O. Box 3428
Erie, PA 16508
Contact: James Hymes

Donor(s): Bliley Electric Co.
Financial data (yr. ended 06/30/00): Grants paid, $108; assets, $0 (M); expenditures, $185; qualifying distributions, $185.
Limitations: Giving limited to areas of company operations in Erie, PA.
Application information: Application form not required.
Officers and Directors:* Roger W. Richards,* Pres.; James H. Hynes,* Secy.-Treas.; David A. Christopher.
EIN: 256038018
Codes: CS, CD

48568
The Haffner-Trinkle Foundation
c/o Julia Haffner
1814 Ruth St.
Allentown, PA 18104

Established in 2000 in PA.
Financial data (yr. ended 12/31/01): Grants paid, $100; assets, $815 (M); gifts received, $922; expenditures, $630; qualifying distributions, $100.
Trustees: Alfred G. Haddad II, Julia W. Haffner, Erich R. Trinkle.
EIN: 256685211

48569
Jane Hutchinson Foundation
c/o PNC Advisors
620 Liberty Ave., P2-PTPP-10-2
Pittsburgh, PA 15222-2705

Financial data (yr. ended 12/31/01): Grants paid, $98; assets, $10,791 (M); expenditures, $208; qualifying distributions, $98.
Limitations: Giving limited to Philadelphia, PA.
Trustee: PNC Bank, N.A.
EIN: 236205969

48570
Glassman Family Foundation
637 Clay Ave.
Scranton, PA 18510

Established in 1986 in PA.
Donor(s): Lee Glassman, Marion Glassman, and members of the Glassman family.
Financial data (yr. ended 11/30/01): Grants paid, $58; assets, $595 (M); expenditures, $108; qualifying distributions, $58.
Limitations: Applications not accepted. Giving primarily in Washington, DC, and Scranton, PA; some giving also in Israel.
Application information: Contributes only to pre-selected organizations.
Officers: Lee Glassman, Pres.; Marion Glassman, Secy.-Treas.
EIN: 232492151

48571
Zeve Family Foundation, Inc.
430 Devonshire St.
Pittsburgh, PA 15213 (412) 683-8288

Established in 1999 in PA.
Donor(s): Harvey L. Zeve, Florence Zeve.
Financial data (yr. ended 12/31/00): Grants paid, $50; assets, $139,966 (M); gifts received, $128,073; expenditures, $4,339; qualifying distributions, $4,323.
Officers and Trustees:* Harvey L. Zeve,* Pres.; Florence Zeve,* Secy.
EIN: 251842951

48572
The Charming Forge Foundation, Inc.
P.O. Box 63
Womelsdorf, PA 19567

Established in 1999 in PA.
Donor(s): Earle H. Henderson.
Financial data (yr. ended 12/31/00): Grants paid, $39; assets, $64,858 (M); gifts received, $69,556; expenditures, $5,047; qualifying distributions, $39.
Officers: Earle H. Henderson, Pres.; Yvonne Henderson, V.P.; Mark H. Henderson, Secy.; Lori L. Hunt, Treas.
Directors: Gary Baer, William Coleman, Terrence E. Connor, David B. Emich, CDR, Jeffrey C. Firestone, Patricia Herr, Elizabeth H. Meyer, Susan Poskitt, Barry Stover, Laurence F. Ward, A. Mark Winter.
EIN: 232870185

48573
Washburn Family Foundation
49 Rickert Dr.
Yardley, PA 19067

Established in 2000 in PA.
Donor(s): Barbara R. Washburn.
Financial data (yr. ended 12/31/01): Grants paid, $25; assets, $44,140 (M); gifts received, $11,659; expenditures, $3,473; qualifying distributions, $25.
Limitations: Applications not accepted.
Application information: Contributes only to pre-selected organizations.
Officers: Barbara R. Washburn, Pres.; Mark D. Washburn, V.P.; Diana J. Slaymaker, Secy.; Elizabeth W. Pesce, Treas.
EIN: 233059858

48574
Anthony F. and Dena Marie Berenato Charitable Trust
P.O. Box 178
Springfield, PA 19064-0178 (717) 791-1681
Application address: P.O. Box 197, Palmer, PR 00721, tel.: (787) 791-1681
Contact: Anthony F. Berenato, Tr.

Donor(s): Anthony F. Berenato.
Financial data (yr. ended 03/31/99): Grants paid, $15; assets, $2,708 (M); expenditures, $110; qualifying distributions, $110.
Limitations: Giving primarily in PA.
Trustees: Anthony F. Berenato, Dena Marie Berenato.
EIN: 237001108

48575
Affirm Foundation
c/o James M. and Carol H. Vanartsdalen
1936 Paul Ave.
Bethlehem, PA 18018

Established in 2001 in PA.
Donor(s): James M. Vanartsdalen, Carol H. Vanartsdalen.
Financial data (yr. ended 12/31/01): Grants paid, $0; assets, $500,000 (M); gifts received, $500,000; expenditures, $0; qualifying distributions, $0.
Limitations: Applications not accepted.
Application information: Contributes only to pre-selected organizations.
Trustees: Carol H. Vanartsdalen, James M. Vanartsdalen.
EIN: 256780233

48576
Alpha Upsilon Scholarship Foundation
1500 Oliver Bldg.
Pittsburgh, PA 15222
Contact: Robert D. Yeager, Mgr.

Financial data (yr. ended 09/30/01): Grants paid, $0; assets, $29,236 (M); expenditures, $6; qualifying distributions, $0.
Limitations: Giving limited to Pittsburgh, PA.
Officer: Robert D. Yeager, Mgr.
EIN: 256056369

48577
American Hellenic Information and Communications Group, Inc.
c/o Nancy Barnhart
1500 Ardmore Blvd., Ste. 407
Pittsburgh, PA 15221 (412) 871-6120

Established in 1998 in PA.
Donor(s): John Rangos Charitable Foundation.
Financial data (yr. ended 12/31/00): Grants paid, $0; assets, $12,740 (M); expenditures, $15,719; qualifying distributions, $15,719; giving activities include $15,719 for programs.
Officers: John G. Rangos, Sr., Pres.; Andrew A. Athens, V.P.; Nicholas P. Papadakos, Treas.
EIN: 251813405

48578
Ampersand Foundation
c/o Dale R. Smith, Jr.
1260 Wyndham Dr.
York, PA 17403-4445

Established in 2001 in PA.
Donor(s): Dale Smith, Elizabeth Smith.
Financial data (yr. ended 12/31/01): Grants paid, $0; assets, $20,192 (M); gifts received, $20,000; expenditures, $0; qualifying distributions, $0.
Limitations: Applications not accepted.

Application information: Contributes only to pre-selected organizations.
Officer: Dale R. Smith, Jr., Pres.
EIN: 233048908

48579
Annenberg Foundation Trust at Sunnylands
150 Radnor-Chester Rd., Ste. A-200
St. Davids, PA 19087

Established in 2001 in PA.
Donor(s): The Annenberg Foundation.
Financial data (yr. ended 06/30/01): Grants paid, $0; assets, $250,000,000 (M); gifts received, $250,000,000; expenditures, $0; qualifying distributions, $0.
Limitations: Applications not accepted.
Application information: Contributes only to pre-selected organizations.
Trustee: Leonore Annenberg.
EIN: 256774871

48580
Mary Barker Trust for R. & M. Barker Foundation I
c/o Mellon Bank, N.A.
P.O. Box 185
Pittsburgh, PA 15230

Established in 2000 in PA.
Donor(s): Mary H. Barker.
Financial data (yr. ended 12/31/00): Grants paid, $0; assets, $496,800 (M); gifts received, $158,628; expenditures, $0; qualifying distributions, $0.
Limitations: Applications not accepted.
Application information: Contributes only to pre-selected organizations.
Trustee: Mellon Bank, N.A.
EIN: 256718442

48581
Mary Barker Trust for R. & M. Barker Foundation II
c/o Mellon Bank, N.A.
P.O. Box 185
Pittsburgh, PA 15230

Established in 2000 in PA.
Donor(s): Mary H. Barker.
Financial data (yr. ended 12/31/00): Grants paid, $0; assets, $496,800 (M); gifts received, $175,933; expenditures, $0; qualifying distributions, $0.
Limitations: Applications not accepted.
Application information: Contributes only to pre-selected organizations.
Trustee: Mellon Bank, N.A.
EIN: 256718443

48582
Chuck Barris Foundation
c/o Chartwell Investment Partners
1235 Westlakes Dr.
Berwyn, PA 19312-2401
Application address: 177 S. Rodeo Dr., Beverly Hills, CA 90213
Contact: Charles H. Barris, Pres.

Established in 1984 in CA.
Donor(s): Charles H. Barris.
Financial data (yr. ended 09/30/01): Grants paid, $0; assets, $0 (M); expenditures, $2,000; qualifying distributions, $0.
Limitations: Giving primarily in New York, NY.
Director: Charles H. Barris.
EIN: 953954357

48583
Baxter Family Foundation
1054 S. Leopard Rd.
Berwyn, PA 19312 (610) 578-1200
Contact: Harold J. Baxter, Pres. and Christine E. Baxter, V.P.

Established in 2000 in PA.
Donor(s): Harold J. Baxter.
Financial data (yr. ended 12/31/01): Grants paid, $0; assets, $3,538,604 (M); gifts received, $39,467; expenditures, $39,467; qualifying distributions, $0.
Officers: Harold J. Baxter, Pres.; Christine E. Baxter, V.P.
EIN: 311739566

48584
Fred and Bryna Berman Family Foundation, Inc.
P.O. Box 326
Gwynedd Valley, PA 19437

Established in 2001 in PA.
Donor(s): Fred Berman, Bryna Berman.
Financial data (yr. ended 12/31/01): Grants paid, $0; assets, $497,307 (M); gifts received, $502,884; expenditures, $0; qualifying distributions, $0.
Trustees: Fred Berman, Ilene Berman.
EIN: 260001020

48585
Steven and Ilene Berman Family Foundation, Inc.
P.O. Box 554
Gwynedd Valley, PA 19437-0554

Established in 2001 in PA.
Donor(s): Steven Berman, Ilene Berman.
Financial data (yr. ended 12/31/01): Grants paid, $0; assets, $198,056 (M); gifts received, $200,787; expenditures, $0; qualifying distributions, $0.
Trustees: Ilene Berman, Steven Berman.
EIN: 260005599

48586
Frank Bernstein Memorial Scholarship Fund
P.O. Box 1589
Doylestown, PA 18901
Application address: c/o Principal, Freehold Twp. High School, Freehold, NJ 07728

Donor(s): Robert J. Bernstein.
Financial data (yr. ended 09/30/00): Grants paid, $0; assets, $47,956 (M); expenditures, $0; qualifying distributions, $0.
Limitations: Giving limited to Freehold, NJ.
Trustee: Robert J. Bernstein.
EIN: 236765598

48587
L. L. & Elizabeth C. Biddle Charitable Foundation
P.O. Box 643, R.R. 4
Ligonier, PA 15658 (724) 238-9641
Contact: Livingston L. Biddle, Tr.

Established in 2000 in PA.
Donor(s): Livingston L. Biddle, Elizabeth C. Biddle.
Financial data (yr. ended 12/31/01): Grants paid, $0; assets, $80,136 (M); expenditures, $2,832; qualifying distributions, $0.
Trustees: Elizabeth C. Biddle, Livingston L. Biddle.
EIN: 256747444

48588
Max E. & Martha E. Bingaman Charitable Foundation
c/o SunBank
216 S. Market St.
Selinsgrove, PA 17870-1814
Application address: P.O. Box 247, Kreamer, PA 17833, tel.: (570) 374-4252

Established in 1996 in PA.
Donor(s): Max E. Bingaman.
Financial data (yr. ended 12/31/01): Grants paid, $0; assets, $221,913 (M); gifts received, $48,000; expenditures, $36,939; qualifying distributions, $2,446.
Limitations: Giving primarily in PA.
Trustees: Clair R. Berge, William R. Hartman, Scott H. Shaffer, Rev. John Thornbury, SunBank.
EIN: 232590474

48589
Boni's Angel Foundation, Inc.
6013 Split Log Dr.
Pipersville, PA 18947

Established in 1998 in PA.
Donor(s): Boni E. Wheaton.
Financial data (yr. ended 12/31/01): Grants paid, $0; assets, $51,215 (M); expenditures, $570; qualifying distributions, $0.
Limitations: Applications not accepted.
Application information: Contributes only to pre-selected organizations.
Officers: Boni E. Wheaton, Pres.; Carolyn S. Glazier, Secy.; Carole M. Allsop, Treas.
EIN: 232941393

48590
Samuel B. Brodsky Foundation
6812 Verbena Ave.
Philadelphia, PA 19126
Contact: Harry Brodsky, Tr.

Financial data (yr. ended 08/31/99): Grants paid, $0; assets, $13,328 (M); expenditures, $181; qualifying distributions, $181.
Limitations: Giving primarily in Philadelphia, PA.
Application information: Application form not required.
Trustee: Harry Brodsky.
EIN: 237240907

48591
Jeffrey and Tracy Brown Foundation, Inc.
c/o Barry H. Frank
1600 Market St., Ste. 3600
Philadelphia, PA 19103
Application address: 14 Dressage Ct., Cherry Hill, NJ 08003
Contact: Jeffrey Brown, Tr.

Established in 2001 in NJ.
Donor(s): Jeffrey Brown, Tracy Brown.
Financial data (yr. ended 12/31/01): Grants paid, $0; assets, $240,229 (M); gifts received, $240,000; expenditures, $0; qualifying distributions, $0.
Trustees: Jeffrey Brown, Tracy Brown, Barry H. Frank.
EIN: 223843780

48592
Sidney and Sandy Brown Foundation, Inc.
c/o Barry H. Frank
1600 Market St., Ste. 3600
Philadelphia, PA 19103
Application address: 24 Holly Oak Dr., Voorhees, NJ 08043
Contact: Sidney Brown, Tr.

Established in 2001 in NJ.
Donor(s): Sidney Brown, Sandy Brown.
Financial data (yr. ended 12/31/01): Grants paid, $0; assets, $240,229 (M); gifts received, $240,000; expenditures, $0; qualifying distributions, $0.
Trustees: Sandy Brown, Sidney Brown, Barry H. Frank.
EIN: 223843782

48593
Buck Foundation, Inc.
1433 Fawcett Ave.
White Oak, PA 15131
Application address: c/o David Stash, McKeesport High School, 1960 Eden Park Blvd., McKeesport, PA 15132, tel.: (412) 664-3650

Established in 2000 in PA.
Donor(s): Rudolph L. Buck, M.D.
Financial data (yr. ended 12/31/00): Grants paid, $0; assets, $109,987 (M); gifts received, $109,632; expenditures, $0; qualifying distributions, $0.
Limitations: Giving limited to residents of McKeesport, PA, area.
Application information: Application form required.
Officer: Rudolph L. Buck, M.D., Pres.
EIN: 251874132

48594
Bucktrout Braithwaite Memorial Foundation
c/o Bruce Cleveland
P.O. Box 271
State College, PA 16804-0271

Established around 1992.
Financial data (yr. ended 10/31/01): Grants paid, $0; assets, $18,245 (M); expenditures, $1,579; qualifying distributions, $0.
Limitations: Applications not accepted.
Application information: Contributes only to pre-selected organizations.
Officers: Bruce Cleveland, Pres.; Louise M. Crispin, 1st V.P.; Penny Haughwout, Secy.; Elizabeth L. Stone, Treas.
EIN: 541586102

48595
The Carefree Foundation
c/o E. Scott Urdang
630 W. Germantown Pike, Ste. 321
Plymouth Meeting, PA 19462

Established in 2000 in PA.
Donor(s): E. Scott Urdang, Marilyn Urdang.
Financial data (yr. ended 12/31/00): Grants paid, $0; assets, $140,000 (M); gifts received, $140,000; expenditures, $0; qualifying distributions, $0.
Limitations: Applications not accepted.
Application information: Contributes only to pre-selected organizations.
Trustees: Emily R. Christensen, Jamie R. Christensen, E. Scott Urdang, Jennifer G. Urdang, Marilyn Urdang, Melissa J. Urdang.
EIN: 256741662

48596
Caye Foundation, Inc.
305 Academy St.
Boalsburg, PA 16827 (814) 466-7075
Contact: Virginia Hubbs, Pres.

Financial data (yr. ended 09/30/01): Grants paid, $0; assets, $51,053 (M); expenditures, $310; qualifying distributions, $218.
Limitations: Giving primarily in CA.
Officers: Virginia Hubbs, Pres.; Elizabeth McIntyre, Secy.-Treas.
EIN: 136132638

48597
The Center for Sexuality & Religion
987 Old Eagle School Rd.
Wayne, PA 19087
Contact: Charles Cesaretti, Exec. Dir.

Financial data (yr. ended 12/31/01): Grants paid, $0; assets, $589,210 (M); gifts received, $61,503; expenditures, $157,948; qualifying distributions, $0.
Officers and Directors:* Harold I. Lief, M.D.,* Chair.; J. Lee Westrate,* Secy.-Treas.; Rev. Charles A. Cesaretti,* Exec. Dir.
EIN: 232616566

48598
Charles J. Ciarrocchi Foundation, Inc.
c/o Charles J. Ciarrocchi, Jr.
P.O. Box 340
Avondale, PA 19311-0340

Established in 2000 in PA.
Financial data (yr. ended 12/31/01): Grants paid, $0; assets, $22,921 (M); gifts received, $100; expenditures, $265; qualifying distributions, $0.
Limitations: Applications not accepted.
Application information: Contributes only to pre-selected organizations.
Directors: Charles J. Ciarrocchi, Jr., James J. Ciarrocchi, Mary B. Ciarrocchi, Patricia A. Ciarrocchi.
EIN: 510395250

48599
Clinical Nutrition Foundation
c/o The Glenmede Trust Co.
1650 Market St.
Philadelphia, PA 19103 (215) 419-6000
Contact: Estelle R. Soppe, Dir.

Established in 1988 in PA.
Donor(s): Estelle R. Soppe.
Financial data (yr. ended 12/31/01): Grants paid, $0; assets, $20,512 (M); gifts received, $2,160; expenditures, $28,944; qualifying distributions, $0.
Limitations: Giving primarily in Philadelphia, PA.
Application information: Application form not required.
Directors: George T. Atwood, John J. Lombard, Jr., James L. Mullen, M.D., William H. Pope, Jr., Estelle R. Soppe, Steven B. Soppe.
EIN: 232507225

48600
Irvin and Lois E. Cohen Foundation
1505 Lorraine Rd.
Reading, PA 19604-1863

Donor(s): Irvin Cohen, Lois Cohen.
Financial data (yr. ended 12/31/01): Grants paid, $0; assets, $39,113 (M); expenditures, $565; qualifying distributions, $0.
Trustees: Irvin Cohen, Lois Cohen.
EIN: 222781597

48601
Cole Foundation for Renewing the Culture
2959 Buck Rd.
P.O. Box 722
Bryn Athyn, PA 19009-0722
Application address: P.O. Box 248, Bryn Athyn, PA 19009, tel. (215) 938-2615
Contact: Brand E. Odhner, Chair.

Established in 2001 in PA.
Donor(s): Charis P. Cole.
Financial data (yr. ended 12/31/01): Grants paid, $0; assets, $527,963 (M); gifts received, $500,513; expenditures, $6,256; qualifying distributions, $6,256.

Officers and Trustees:* Brand E. Odhner,* Chair.; Dan A. Synnestvedt,* Vice-Chair.; Donald C. Fitzpatrick, Exec. Dir.
EIN: 256789806

48602
Columbus Quincentennial Foundation
c/o Guy A. Sileo
8-D W. Brookhaven Rd.
Brookhaven, PA 19015

Established in 1992 in PA.
Financial data (yr. ended 12/31/00): Grants paid, $0; assets, $13,186 (M); expenditures, $631; qualifying distributions, $0.
Limitations: Applications not accepted.
Application information: Contributes only to pre-selected organizations.
Officers: Robert N. Speare, Pres.; Guy A. Sileo, Treas.
EIN: 232678811

48603
Milton Keen Cornell Charitable Foundation
North Shore Rd.
Pocono Lake Preserve, PA 18348
Contact: Milton Keen Cornell, Pres.

Donor(s): Milton Keen Cornell.
Financial data (yr. ended 12/31/01): Grants paid, $0; assets, $67,779 (M); expenditures, $0; qualifying distributions, $0.
Limitations: Giving primarily in Kingston, PA.
Application information: Application form not required.
Officer: Milton Keen Cornell, Pres. and Secy.-Treas.
EIN: 232639915

48604
Crystal Channel Foundation, Inc.
800 Hillsdale Rd.
West Chester, PA 19382

Established in 1986 in NY.
Donor(s): M. Christine Jurzykowski.
Financial data (yr. ended 12/31/00): Grants paid, $0; assets, $982 (M); gifts received, $1,000; expenditures, $152; qualifying distributions, $0.
Limitations: Giving on a national basis.
Application information: Application form not required.
Officers: M. Christine Jurzykowski, Pres.; James R. Jackson, Secy.-Treas.; Mary E. Radford, Admin.
Directors: Carol Burland, Shirlee Ann Stokes.
EIN: 133384064

48605
David Family Charitable Foundation
123 Bridle Ln.
Lower Gwynedd, PA 19002-2046

Established in 1998.
Financial data (yr. ended 12/31/01): Grants paid, $0; assets, $814 (M); expenditures, $303; qualifying distributions, $0.
Limitations: Giving primarily in FL.
Trustees: Clifford C. David, Ethel B. David.
EIN: 237922429

48606
The Diana Family Foundation
995 Marshall Dr.
Pottstown, PA 19465 (610) 326-6351
Contact: Stephen Diana, Tr.

Established in 2000 in PA.
Donor(s): Guy D. Diana.
Financial data (yr. ended 12/31/00): Grants paid, $0; assets, $551,624 (M); gifts received, $557,180; expenditures, $5,556; qualifying distributions, $0.

Officer: Guy D. Diana, Mgr.
Trustees: Laura Braaksma, David Diana, John Diana, Stephen Diana.
EIN: 061603589

48607
Dietz & Watson Foundation
c/o Glenmede Trust Co.
1650 Market St., Ste. 1200
Philadelphia, PA 19103-7391

Established in 2001 in PA.
Donor(s): Dietz & Watson, Inc.
Financial data (yr. ended 12/31/01): Grants paid, $0; assets, $500,000 (M); gifts received, $500,000; expenditures, $0; qualifying distributions, $0.
Limitations: Applications not accepted.
Application information: Contributes only to pre-selected organizations.
Officers and Trustees:* Cynthia Eni Yingling,* Pres.; Ruth Eni,* Secy.-Treas.; Christopher W. Eni, Louis J. Eni, Jr.
EIN: 233028685
Codes: CS

48608
Jeffrey A. Donald Memorial Scholarship Trust
63 Grove Rd.
Mercer, PA 16137 (724) 662-5070
Contact: Martha Donald, Dir.

Established in 1987 in PA.
Financial data (yr. ended 12/31/01): Grants paid, $0; assets, $10,552 (M); expenditures, $0; qualifying distributions, $0.
Limitations: Giving limited to the Mercer, PA, area.
Directors: George Donald, Martha Donald.
EIN: 251546541

48609
The Michael J. Donnelly Foundation
c/o Eckert, Seamans, et al.
USX Tower, 600 Grant St., 44th Fl.
Pittsburgh, PA 15219
Contact: Raymond C. Vogliano

Established in 2000 in PA.
Donor(s): Michael J. Donnelly.
Financial data (yr. ended 12/31/00): Grants paid, $0; assets, $27,583 (M); gifts received, $32,320; expenditures, $4,987; qualifying distributions, $0.
Limitations: Giving limited to residents of Mount Lebanon, PA.
Application information: Application form required.
Officer and Directors:* Michael J. Donnelly,* Pres. and Secy.-Treas.; Mary Louise Ford, Stephen L. Kline.
EIN: 912056090

48610
Dreibelbis Farm Historical Society, Inc.
c/o Mark J. Dreibelbis
53 Fox Rd.
Hamburg, PA 19526

Established in 1998 in PA.
Donor(s): G. Parker Dreibelbis.
Financial data (yr. ended 12/31/01): Grants paid, $0; assets, $78,043 (M); gifts received, $9,539; expenditures, $450; qualifying distributions, $0.
Officers: Mark J. Dreibelbis, Pres.; Norman E. Dresher, Secy.; Lewis Freeman III, Treas.
EIN: 232986673

PENNSYLVANIA—48623

48611
Mignon W. Dubbs Fellowship Fund
c/o First Union National Bank
P.O. Box 7558
Philadelphia, PA 19101-7558

Established in 1993 in PA.
Financial data (yr. ended 11/30/99): Grants paid, $0; assets, $2,260,585 (M); expenditures, $14,299; qualifying distributions, $1,967.
Limitations: Applications not accepted.
Application information: Contributes only to pre-selected organizations.
Trustee: First Union National Bank.
EIN: 237789064

48612
William Eckstein Trust Nurses Relief Fund
c/o First Union National Bank
Broad and Walnut Sts.
Philadelphia, PA 19109

Financial data (yr. ended 05/31/99): Grants paid, $0; assets, $6,586 (M); expenditures, $789; qualifying distributions, $11.
Trustee: First Union National Bank.
EIN: 236217289

48613
Educational Trust Fund in Memory of J. Lupton Simpson and Marion Porter Simpson
(also known as Simpson Education Trust)
c/o First Union National Bank
Broad and Walnut Sts.
Philadelphia, PA 19109

Established in 1987 in VA.
Financial data (yr. ended 12/31/99): Grants paid, $0; assets, $21,632 (M); expenditures, $989; qualifying distributions, $0.
Limitations: Applications not accepted. Giving limited to Loudoun County, VA.
Trustees: First Union National Bank.
EIN: 546251486

48614
Eichelberger Family Foundation
c/o Lloyd R. Eichelberger
4 Barlow Cir.
Dillsburg, PA 17019-1624

Established in 1998 in PA.
Donor(s): Lloyd R. Eichelberger.
Financial data (yr. ended 12/31/01): Grants paid, $0; assets, $4,109 (M); expenditures, $1,016; qualifying distributions, $0.
Limitations: Applications not accepted.
Application information: Contributes only to pre-selected organizations.
Officers: Lloyd R. Eichelberger, Pres.; Barbara A. Eichelberger, V.P.
Director: William P. Eichelberger II.
EIN: 251822452

48615
1144 Om Foundation
c/o Holiday Inn
183 & Exit 18A
New Cumberland, PA 17070

Established in 1995 in PA.
Donor(s): 544 Assocs., 644 Assocs., 344 Assocs., 244 Assocs., MEPS Assocs.
Financial data (yr. ended 06/30/01): Grants paid, $0; assets, $59,925 (M); gifts received, $1,500; expenditures, $250; qualifying distributions, $0.
Limitations: Applications not accepted.
Application information: Contributes only to pre-selected organizations.
Officers: Hasu P. Shah, Pres.; Kiran Patel, Treas.

Directors: Rajendra Ghandi, Bharat Mehta, Kanti D. Patel.
EIN: 251772101

48616
Elk County Community Foundation
111 Erie Ave.
St. Marys, PA 15857
E-mail: eccf@penn.com
Contact: Martha A. Engel, Exec. Dir.

Established in 2000.
Financial data (yr. ended 12/31/00): Grants paid, $0; assets, $119,484 (M); gifts received, $158,264; expenditures, $40,382.
Limitations: Giving primarily in Elk County, PA.
Publications: Informational brochure.
Application information: Application form required.
Officer: Martha A. Engel, Exec. Dir.
Directors: Paul Brazinski, Jr., William Conrad, Charles Constable, Douglas Dobson, J.M. Hamlin Johnson, Judy Manno-Stager, Richard Masson, Jake Meyer, Lou Radkowski, Dan Straub, Bea Terbovich, Larry Thorwart, Larry Whiteman.
EIN: 251859637
Codes: CM

48617
Epsilon Alumni Group
800 Belvedere St.
Carlisle, PA 17013
Contact: Earl M. Barnhart, Secy.-Treas.

Established in 1995 in PA.
Financial data (yr. ended 06/30/01): Grants paid, $0; assets, $139,743 (M); expenditures, $1,903; qualifying distributions, $1,705.
Application information: Application form required.
Officers: Jack Howell, Pres.; James G. Bowers, V.P.; Earl M. Barnhart, Secy.-Treas.; Dale O. Hartzell, Secy.-Treas.
EIN: 232824344

48618
D. A. & J. A. Evans Memorial Foundation
c/o Ellwood Group, Inc.
Commercial Ave., P.O. Box 31
Ellwood City, PA 16117

Incorporated in 1953 in PA.
Donor(s): Members of the Evans family.
Financial data (yr. ended 12/31/01): Grants paid, $0; assets, $2,085 (M); expenditures, $0; qualifying distributions, $0.
Limitations: Applications not accepted. Giving primarily in the Ellwood City, PA, area.
Application information: Unsolicited requests for funds not accepted.
Directors: David Barensfeld, Robert Barensfeld.
EIN: 256032325
Codes: GTI

48619
The Fallen Angels Foundation, Inc.
6 Edgewood Rd.
Yardley, PA 19067

Established in 2001.
Donor(s): Barry S. Gluck, Joan T. Gluck.
Financial data (yr. ended 12/31/01): Grants paid, $0; assets, $101,039 (M); gifts received, $104,000; expenditures, $2,645; qualifying distributions, $0.
Officers: Barry S. Gluck, Pres.; Joan T. Gluck, V.P.; Kenneth W. Van Leeuwen, Secy.
EIN: 223830268

48620
A. T. Fallquist Memorial Scholarship Fund
P.O. Box 520
Johnstown, PA 15907-0520
Application address: c/o Mon Valley Education Consortium, 336 Shaw Ave., McKeesport, PA 15132-2917

Established in 2001 in PA.
Donor(s): Alice Gumbert.‡
Financial data (yr. ended 12/31/01): Grants paid, $0; assets, $299,501 (M); gifts received, $300,001; expenditures, $500; qualifying distributions, $0.
Limitations: Giving limited to residents of McKeesport, PA.
Application information: Application form required.
Trustee: Ameriserve Trust & Financial Services Co.
EIN: 251893905

48621
Family Preserve Foundation, Inc.
721 Glengarry Rd.
Philadelphia, PA 19118-4110
Contact: Elizabeth Gubb Dolan, Pres.

Established in 1999 in PA.
Financial data (yr. ended 12/31/01): Grants paid, $0; assets, $1 (M); expenditures, $52; qualifying distributions, $0.
Officers and Trustees:* Elizabeth G. Dolan,* Pres.; Helen Lydia Clay,* V.P.; Christine P. Scarlett,* V.P.; Sherryn E. Stauffer,* Secy.; Thomas Dolan IV,* Treas.; John W. Claghorn III, John F. Meigs.
EIN: 233006161

48622
Donald & Linda Fetterolf Foundation
627 New Centerville Rd.
Somerset, PA 15501-8639

Established in 2001 in PA.
Donor(s): Donald L. Fetterolf, Linda K. Fetterolf.
Financial data (yr. ended 12/31/01): Grants paid, $0; assets, $77,514 (M); gifts received, $81,685; expenditures, $4,171; qualifying distributions, $0.
Officers and Directors:* Donald L. Fetterolf,* Pres.; Linda K. Fetterolf,* V.P. and Secy.; Brian S. Fetterolf, Michael L. Fetterolf.
EIN: 251893642

48623
The FIDELIO Foundation
2826 Mt. Carmel Ave.
Glenside, PA 19038

Established in 2001 in PA.
Donor(s): FIDELIO Insurance, Inc., Dental Delivery, Inc.
Financial data (yr. ended 12/31/01): Grants paid, $0; assets, $60,000 (M); gifts received, $60,000; expenditures, $500; qualifying distributions, $500.
Limitations: Applications not accepted.
Application information: Contributes only to pre-selected organizations.
Trustee: Mario V. Mele.
EIN: 036074145
Codes: CS

48624
First Union Regional Community Development Corporation, Inc.
(Formerly CoreStates Community Development Corporation, Inc.)
1339 Chestnut St., 13th Fl., PA 4360
Philadelphia, PA 19107 (267) 321-7661
FAX: (267) 321-7656
Contact: Kimberly Allen

Established in 1998 in PA.
Donor(s): CoreStates Financial Corp.
Financial data (yr. ended 12/31/00): Grants paid, $0; assets, $6,245,390 (M); expenditures, $26,250; qualifying distributions, $42,500; giving activities include $42,500 for loans.
Limitations: Giving primarily in DE, NJ, and the eastern half of PA.
Application information: Application form not required.
Officer and Board Members:* Denise McGregor,* Exec. Dir.; Judith Allison, Robert S. Appleby, Reginald Davis, Lillian Escobar Haskins, Eleanor Horne, Carlton Huhges, Ernest Jones, George Lynett, Marlin Miller, Jr., Stephanie W. Naidoff, David Newell, Malcolm Pryor, Robert L. Reid, Peter Strawbridge.
EIN: 232735410
Codes: CS, CD

48625
FJN Charitable Foundation
c/o Francis L. Genuardi
470 Norristown Rd., Ste. 300
Blue Bell, PA 19422

Established in 2001 in PA.
Donor(s): Francis L. Genuardi.
Financial data (yr. ended 12/31/01): Grants paid, $0; assets, $1,955,448 (M); gifts received, $1,955,000; expenditures, $0; qualifying distributions, $0.
Trustee: Francis L. Genuardi.
EIN: 233100839

48626
Clark Flegal Educational Trust
c/o County National Bank, Trust Dept.
P.O. Box 42
Clearfield, PA 16830-0042 (814) 765-1683

Financial data (yr. ended 10/31/01): Grants paid, $0; assets, $332,790 (M); expenditures, $5,169; qualifying distributions, $5,412; giving activities include $5,000 for loans to individuals.
Limitations: Giving primarily in Clearfield, PA.
Application information: Application form not required.
Trustee: County National Bank.
EIN: 256030462
Codes: GTI

48627
The Myrtle Forsha Memorial Trust
c/o PNC Advisors
620 Liberty Ave., P2-PTPP-10-2
Pittsburgh, PA 15222-2705 (412) 762-4971
Contact: Elizabeth Gay, Trust Off., PNC Bank, N.A.

Established in 2000 in PA.
Donor(s): Myrtle Forsha Trust.
Financial data (yr. ended 09/30/01): Grants paid, $0; assets, $1,933,915 (M); gifts received, $2,445,618; expenditures, $925; qualifying distributions, $0.
Limitations: Giving on a national basis.
Trustee: PNC Bank, N.A.
EIN: 256742914

48628
The Mark Foster Family Foundation
1 Pitcairn Pl., Ste. 3000
Jenkintown, PA 19046
Application address: 60 Rutledge Rd., Scarsdale, NY 10583
Contact: Mark Foster, Pres.

Donor(s): Mark Foster.
Financial data (yr. ended 12/31/00): Grants paid, $0; assets, $2,815 (M); expenditures, $34; qualifying distributions, $0.
Application information: Application form not required.
Officers: Mark Foster, Pres.; Sylvia Foster, V.P. and Treas.; Lawrence J. Rothenberg, Secy.
EIN: 134028930

48629
Foundation for Performing Arts Education, Inc.
c/o John T. Rago
51 Dinsmore Ave.
Pittsburgh, PA 15205-3110

Established in 1998 in NY.
Financial data (yr. ended 12/31/99): Grants paid, $0; assets, $29,119 (M); expenditures, $960; qualifying distributions, $960.
Limitations: Applications not accepted.
Application information: Contributes only to pre-selected organizations.
Trustee: John T. Rago.
EIN: 133558140

48630
Foundation for Research in Pediatric Colitis
133 Heather Rd.
Bala Cynwyd, PA 19004

Established in 1997 in PA.
Financial data (yr. ended 12/31/01): Grants paid, $0; assets, $246,041 (M); gifts received, $270; expenditures, $2,133; qualifying distributions, $0.
Limitations: Applications not accepted. Giving primarily in New York, NY.
Application information: Contributes only to pre-selected organizations.
Officers: Judith Berman, Pres.; Randi Berman, Secy.-Treas.
Trustee: Gerald Berman.
EIN: 236430335

48631
Harriet G. Fredericks Foundation
c/o First Union National Bank
P.O. Box 7558, Ste. PA1308
Philadelphia, PA 19101-7558

Established in 1998 in PA.
Financial data (yr. ended 12/31/99): Grants paid, $0; assets, $1,474,829 (M); expenditures, $18,996; qualifying distributions, $9,273.
Limitations: Applications not accepted.
Application information: Contributes only to pre-selected organizations.
Trustees: Harris Verner, First Union National Bank.
EIN: 237957478

48632
Fulton Family Foundation
550 Randolph Dr.
Lititz, PA 17543 (717) 560-4908
Contact: Mary Fulton Gingrich, Pres.

Established in 2001 in PA.
Donor(s): Rufus A. Fulton, Jr.
Financial data (yr. ended 12/31/01): Grants paid, $0; assets, $204,997 (M); gifts received, $71,765; expenditures, $0; qualifying distributions, $0.
Officers: Mary Fulton Gingrich, Pres.; Julie B. Fulton, Secy.; Ann M. Fulton, Treas.

EIN: 233100987

48633
Helen Gallagher Charitable Trust
c/o PNC Advisors
P.O. Box 937
Scranton, PA 18501

Established in 2001 in PA.
Donor(s): Helen Gallagher.‡
Financial data (yr. ended 12/31/01): Grants paid, $0; assets, $545,684 (M); gifts received, $546,517; expenditures, $2,668; qualifying distributions, $1,334.
Limitations: Applications not accepted.
Application information: Contributes only to pre-selected organizations.
Trustee: PNC Bank, N.A.
EIN: 256800846

48634
William F. & Lynn D. Gauss Foundation
c/o PNC Advisors
620 Liberty Ave., P2-PTPP-10-2
Pittsburgh, PA 15222-2705 (412) 762-3189
Contact: W. Brewster Cockrell

Established in 2001 in PA.
Donor(s): William F. Gauss.
Financial data (yr. ended 12/31/01): Grants paid, $0; assets, $3,748,091 (M); gifts received, $3,797,118; expenditures, $18,352; qualifying distributions, $0.
Application information: Application form not required.
Trustees: R. Michael, Daniel, Mary S. Kroll, PNC Bank, N.A.
EIN: 256784891

48635
Edward Gelb and Florence Gelb Fund
c/o Mellon Bank, N.A.
P.O. Box 185
Pittsburgh, PA 15230-9897

Established in 2001 in PA.
Financial data (yr. ended 12/31/01): Grants paid, $0; assets, $51,469 (M); gifts received, $50,000; expenditures, $1,042; qualifying distributions, $0.
Limitations: Applications not accepted.
Application information: Contributes only to pre-selected organizations.
Trustee: Mellon Bank, N.A.
EIN: 256764376

48636
Glazer Family Foundation
2213 Delancey St.
Philadelphia, PA 19103-6501

Established in 2000 in PA.
Donor(s): Herman Glazer.
Financial data (yr. ended 12/31/00): Grants paid, $0; assets, $956,887 (M); gifts received, $1,008,155; expenditures, $0; qualifying distributions, $0.
Limitations: Applications not accepted.
Application information: Contributes only to pre-selected organizations.
Trustees: Bernard Brewstein, Herman Glazer, Richard Glazer.
EIN: 256743950

48637
Global Industrial Technologies Foundation
600 Grant St., Ste. 5100
Pittsburgh, PA 15219
Contact: Ken Stackawitz, Pres.

Established in 1996 in TX.
Donor(s): Global Industrial Technologies, Inc.

Financial data (yr. ended 10/31/01): Grants paid, $0; assets, $1,071,820 (M); expenditures, $5,158; qualifying distributions, $0.
Limitations: Giving primarily in TX.
Application information: Application form required.
Officers and Directors:* Ken Stackawitz, Jr.,* Pres.; Francis R. Doyle, Jr.,* Treas.
EIN: 752699251
Codes: CS, CD

48638
Global Source Net, Inc.
(Formerly Central Asian Foundation, Inc.)
c/o Achenbach
405 Chocolate Ave.
Hershey, PA 17033

Established around 1991.
Financial data (yr. ended 12/31/99): Grants paid, $0; assets, $740 (M); expenditures, $75; qualifying distributions, $75.
Limitations: Giving primarily in London, England.
Officers: Michael Stroope, Pres.; Lewis I. Meyers, Jr., V.P.; Kenneth Shirley, Secy.-Treas.
EIN: 232583719

48639
The Lloyd V. Guild Charitable Foundation
337 Thomas Rd.
McMurray, PA 15317

Established in 2001 in PA.
Donor(s): Lloyd V. Guild, SKC Inc.
Financial data (yr. ended 12/31/01): Grants paid, $0; assets, $265,654 (M); gifts received, $265,500; expenditures, $592; qualifying distributions, $592.
Limitations: Applications not accepted.
Application information: Contributes only to pre-selected organizations.
Trustees: Daniel L. Guild, Richard L. Guild, Linda Guild Lawler.
EIN: 256794527

48640
The George J. and Kathleen M. Hall Foundation, Inc.
1724 Clocktower Dr.
West Chester, PA 19380 (610) 429-5840
Contact: George J. Hall, Dir.

Established in 2001 in PA.
Donor(s): George J. Hall.
Financial data (yr. ended 12/31/01): Grants paid, $0; assets, $5,000 (M); gifts received, $5,000; expenditures, $0; qualifying distributions, $0.
Directors: George J. Hall, Kathleen M. Hall.
EIN: 260008305

48641
The Hallinan Foundation
17 W. Miner St.
West Chester, PA 19381

Established in 1999 in PA.
Financial data (yr. ended 12/31/01): Grants paid, $0; assets, $750 (M); gifts received, $750; expenditures, $750; qualifying distributions, $0.
Trustees: Cecilia M. Hallinan, Francis S. Hallinan, John J. Hallinan.
EIN: 233003482

48642
Lester A. Hamburg Foundation
c/o Farrell, Rubenstein, Deloitte & Touche
2330 One PPG Pl.
Pittsburgh, PA 15222-5401

Established in 1986 in PA.
Financial data (yr. ended 12/31/01): Grants paid, $0; assets, $32,031 (M); expenditures, $451; qualifying distributions, $0.
Limitations: Applications not accepted. Giving primarily in Pittsburgh, PA.
Application information: Contributes only to pre-selected organizations.
Trustee: Farrell Rubenstein.
EIN: 251528514

48643
Margaret I. Handy Foundation for Children
c/o PNC Advisors
620 Liberty Ave., P2-PTPP-10-2
Pittsburgh, PA 15222-2705

Financial data (yr. ended 12/31/01): Grants paid, $0; assets, $271,584 (M); expenditures, $3,025; qualifying distributions, $0.
Limitations: Giving limited to DE.
Application information: Application form not required.
Trustee: PNC Bank, N.A.
EIN: 516010467

48644
Harbaugh/Thomas Foundation
4 S. Main St.
Biglerville, PA 17307

Established in 1998 in PA.
Donor(s): Marion Harbaugh, Jean Thomas.
Financial data (yr. ended 04/30/01): Grants paid, $0; assets, $231,640 (M); gifts received, $55,000; expenditures, $4,807; qualifying distributions, $4,807; giving activities include $4,807 for programs.
Officers: Marion T. Harbaugh, Pres.; Jean E. Thomas, V.P. and Secy.; John Fenwick Shugrue, Treas.
EIN: 232961961

48645
Ann L. Harrison Foundation
(Formerly H & H Foundation)
P.O. Box 1166
Harrisburg, PA 17108

Donor(s): C. Scott Harrison, M.D.
Financial data (yr. ended 12/31/00): Grants paid, $0; assets, $1,076 (M); gifts received, $376; expenditures, $376; qualifying distributions, $0.
Trustees: C. Scott Harrison, M.D., Sarah L. Harrison, Michael Smith.
EIN: 222680032

48646
Isabel V. Heckert Memorial Fund
(Formerly Oscar H. Heckert Scholarship Fund)
c/o The York Bank & Trust Co.
21 E. Market St.
York, PA 17401-1500 (717) 852-3077

Financial data (yr. ended 09/30/01): Grants paid, $0; assets, $86,270 (M); expenditures, $1,680; qualifying distributions, $0.
Limitations: Giving limited to residents of York, PA.
Application information: Application form required.
Trustee: The York Bank & Trust Co.
EIN: 236285852

48647
Joseph A. & Clara S. Heim Foundation
c/o First Union National Bank
P.O. Box 7558
Philadelphia, PA 19101-7558

Established in 1990 in PA.
Financial data (yr. ended 12/31/01): Grants paid, $0; assets, $635,668 (M); gifts received, $2,333; expenditures, $5,769; qualifying distributions, $0.
Limitations: Applications not accepted. Giving limited to PA.
Application information: Contributes only to pre-selected organizations.
Trustees: Richard W. DeWald, Maryanne W. Freeman, Constance Metherell, First Union National Bank.
EIN: 232528851

48648
Helene Foundation, Inc.
c/o First Union National Bank
Broad & Walnut Sts.
Philadelphia, PA 19109
Application address: 455 E. 86th St., No. 33A, New York, NY 10028, tel.: (212) 876-3340
Contact: Wagner P. Thielens, Jr., Pres.

Financial data (yr. ended 12/31/99): Grants paid, $0; assets, $1,692,599 (M); expenditures, $19,193; qualifying distributions, $79.
Limitations: Giving primarily in New York, NY.
Application information: Application form not required.
Officers: Wagner P. Thielens, Jr., Pres. and Treas.; John L. Grover, Sr. V.P.; James C.P. Berry, Secy.
Agent: First Union National Bank.
EIN: 136161748

48649
Florence Heppe Memorial Fund
c/o Mellon Bank, N.A.
P.O. Box 7236, AIM 193-0224
Philadelphia, PA 19101-7236

Financial data (yr. ended 06/30/02): Grants paid, $0; assets, $979,972 (M); expenditures, $2,235; qualifying distributions, $0.
Limitations: Applications not accepted. Giving primarily in Philadelphia, PA.
Application information: Contributes only to pre-selected organizations.
Trustee: Mellon Bank, N.A.
EIN: 236227223

48650
Herring Gut Learning Center
(Formerly Marshall Point Educational Foundation)
355 Fairville Rd.
Chadds Ford, PA 19317

Established in 1999 in PA.
Financial data (yr. ended 12/31/00): Grants paid, $0; assets, $444,323 (M); gifts received, $165,333; expenditures, $75,384; qualifying distributions, $0.
Trustee: P.M. Wyeth.
EIN: 233007187

48651
The Herriott-Granger Foundation, Inc.
c/o J. Christopher Nurney, Ltd.
70 W. Oakland Ave.
Doylestown, PA 18901

Donor(s): H.T. Herriott.
Financial data (yr. ended 08/31/00): Grants paid, $0; assets, $163,643 (L); expenditures, $8,508; qualifying distributions, $8,508.
Limitations: Giving primarily in Venice, FL.
Trustees: B. Anderson, Rev. W. Culton, J.C. Nurney, Tom Roberts, R. Scheetz, Jr.
EIN: 232778244
Codes: GTI

48652
Highbourne Foundation
105 Leader Heights Rd., Ste. 140
York, PA 17403

Established in 2000 in PA.

48652—PENNSYLVANIA

Financial data (yr. ended 12/31/01): Grants paid, $0; assets, $348 (M); expenditures, $52; qualifying distributions, $0.
Officers and Directors:* John R. Behrmann, Chair.; Nancy P. Behrmann,* Pres.; Nancy Lorraine Littlefield,* V.P. and Exec. Dir.; Marie E. Behrmann,* Secy.; John Scott Behrmann, Kent V. Littlefield.
EIN: 233053226

48653
Highmark Foundation
120 5th Ave., Ste. 922
Pittsburgh, PA 15222

Established in 2000 in PA.
Donor(s): Highmark, Inc.
Financial data (yr. ended 12/31/00): Grants paid, $0; assets, $8,076,289 (M); gifts received, $8,000,000; expenditures, $132,785; qualifying distributions, $0.
Officers and Directors:* George F. Grode,* Chair.; Doris Carson Williams, Vice-Chair.; Aaron A. Walton, Pres.; Elaine B. Krasik, Secy.; Thomas J. Rohner, Jr., M.D., Secy.; Melissa M. Anderson, Treas.; Deborrah Beck, Scott Becker.
EIN: 251876666

48654
The Hoffman Foundation, Inc.
c/o Aufman Associates, Inc.
2200 Georgetown Dr., Ste. 401
Sewickley, PA 15143

Established in 2000 in PA.
Donor(s): Ronald R. Hoffman.
Financial data (yr. ended 12/31/01): Grants paid, $0; assets, $110,482 (M); expenditures, $628; qualifying distributions, $0.
Limitations: Applications not accepted.
Application information: Contributes only to pre-selected organizations.
Officers and Directors:* Ronald R. Hoffman,* Pres.; Linda W. Hoffman,* Secy.-Treas.; Edward J. Aufman, Mgr.
EIN: 251855299

48655
Esther Gowen Hood Music Fund
c/o Mellon Bank, N.A.
P.O. Box 7236
Philadelphia, PA 19101-7236 (215) 553-3208
Contact: Patricia Kling, Trust Off., Mellon Bank, N.A.

Financial data (yr. ended 09/30/01): Grants paid, $0; assets, $243,369 (M); expenditures, $999; qualifying distributions, $156.
Limitations: Giving limited to the Philadelphia, PA, area.
Trustee: Mellon Bank, N.A.
EIN: 236223620
Codes: GTI

48656
George W. & Anne A. Hoover Scholarship Loan Fund
c/o SunBank
P.O. Box 57
Selinsgrove, PA 17870 (570) 374-4252

Financial data (yr. ended 07/31/01): Grants paid, $0; assets, $782,606 (M); expenditures, $4,264; qualifying distributions, $43,496.
Limitations: Giving limited to Snyder County, PA.
Application information: Application form required.
Trustee: SunBank.
EIN: 232078823

48657
Abram and Marian R. Horst Foundation
2060 Waterford Dr.
Lancaster, PA 17601

Financial data (yr. ended 12/31/01): Grants paid, $0; assets, $93,786 (M); gifts received, $50,000; expenditures, $13,096; qualifying distributions, $13,055.
Limitations: Applications not accepted. Giving primarily in PA.
Application information: Contributes only to pre-selected organizations.
Officers: Marian R. Horst, Pres.; William R. Horst, Secy.; Robert L. Horst, Treas.
Directors: Barbara J. Hess, Judi E. Martin, Marilou Horst Schaffer.
EIN: 232968157

48658
Hospital Service Association of Northeastern Pennsylvania Foundation
19 N. Main St.
Wilkes-Barre, PA 18711 (570) 200-6302
URL: http://www.bcnepa.com/charitable.htm
Contact: Lisa Baker, Exec. Dir.

Established in 2001 in PA.
Donor(s): Blue Cross of Northeastern Pennsylvania.
Financial data (yr. ended 12/31/01): Grants paid, $0; assets, $7,534,859 (M); gifts received, $7,489,784; expenditures, $0; qualifying distributions, $0.
Limitations: Giving limited to the 13-county area of northeastern PA: Bradford, Carbon, Clinton, Lackawanna, Luzerne, Lycoming, Monroe, Pike, Sullivan, Susquehanna, Tioga, Wayne, and Wyoming.
Application information: Application form can be downloaded from foundation Web site. Application form required.
Officers: Denise S. Cesare, Pres.; Edwin R. Goodlander, Secy.; J. Kenneth Suchoski, Treas.
Directors: Alan S. Hollander, M. Martin DePorres McHale, John J. Menapace, John P. Moses.
EIN: 233101673
Codes: CS

48659
Hutchinson Family Foundation
610 Sentry Pkwy., No. 220
Blue Bell, PA 19422

Established in 2001.
Financial data (yr. ended 12/31/01): Grants paid, $0; assets, $1,007 (M); gifts received, $1,000; expenditures, $0; qualifying distributions, $0.
Trustees: Mary Ellen Hutchinson, Robert M. Hutchinson, Jr., William M. Hutchinson.
EIN: 256774580

48660
Alan and Sondra Isen Foundation
110 Fairview Rd.
Narberth, PA 19072-1331

Established in 2001 in PA.
Financial data (yr. ended 12/31/01): Grants paid, $0; assets, $51,533 (M); gifts received, $1,900; expenditures, $0; qualifying distributions, $0.
Limitations: Applications not accepted.
Application information: Contributes only to pre-selected organizations.
Trustees: Alan Isen, Sondra Isen.
EIN: 233100237

48661
Harold Isen Foundation
c/o John R. Latourette, Jr.
3200 Mellon Bank Ctr., 1735 Market St.
Philadelphia, PA 19103

Established in 2001 in PA.
Financial data (yr. ended 12/31/01): Grants paid, $0; assets, $24,590 (M); gifts received, $950; expenditures, $0; qualifying distributions, $0.
Limitations: Applications not accepted.
Application information: Contributes only to pre-selected organizations.
Officers and Directors:* Harold Isen,* Pres. and Treas.; Robert Isen,* V.P. and Secy.
EIN: 233094317

48662
The Jake Foundation
311 Edgehill Rd.
Wayne, PA 19087

Established in 1999 in PA.
Donor(s): Leo W. Pierce, Jr., Bruce Buckley.
Financial data (yr. ended 12/31/99): Grants paid, $0; assets, $336,793 (M); gifts received, $287,275; expenditures, $150; qualifying distributions, $0.
Limitations: Applications not accepted.
Application information: Contributes only to pre-selected organizations.
Trustees: Bruce Buckley, Leo W. Pierce, Jr.
EIN: 256638422

48663
The Robert Junge Trust
4000 Bell Atlantic Tower
1717 Arch St.
Philadelphia, PA 19103-2793

Established in 1969 in PA.
Financial data (yr. ended 12/31/01): Grants paid, $0; assets, $1,228,544 (M); expenditures, $21,434; qualifying distributions, $0.
Limitations: Applications not accepted. Giving primarily in PA.
Application information: Contributes only to pre-selected organizations.
Trustees: Kent Junge, Robert S. Junge, Lawson M. Smith, and 8 additional trustees.
EIN: 236482504

48664
William J. and Dora J. Kalnoski Memorial Scholarship Fund
c/o First Columbia Bank & Trust Co.
11 W. Main St.
Bloomsburg, PA 17815 (570) 784-1660
Contact: John Thompson

Established in 2001 in PA.
Donor(s): Dora J. Kalnoski.‡
Financial data (yr. ended 12/31/01): Grants paid, $0; assets, $1,104,893 (M); gifts received, $1,151,129; expenditures, $7,089; qualifying distributions, $0.
Limitations: Giving limited to residents of Columbia and Schuylkill counties, PA.
Application information: Application form required.
Trustee: First Columbia Bank & Trust Co.
EIN: 251882103

48665
The Katherinealexandra Charitable Foundation
c/o Michael Kalogris
P.O. Box 431
Devault, PA 19432

Established in 2001 in PA.
Donor(s): Michael E. Kalogris.

Financial data (yr. ended 12/31/01): Grants paid, $0; assets, $1,467,500 (M); gifts received, $1,647,750; expenditures, $0; qualifying distributions, $0.
Trustees: Alexandra Kalogris, Elisabeth Kalogris, Katherine Kalogris, Michael E. Kalogris.
EIN: 256799731

48666
Kidsbank.com Foundation
1130 Berkshire Blvd.
Wyomissing, PA 19610
Application address: c/o Sovereign Bank, 36 Washington St., Toms River, NJ 08753, tel.: (732) 914-5043
Contact: Marshall J. Kern, Pres.

Established in 1999 in PA.
Donor(s): Sovereign Bank Foundation.
Financial data (yr. ended 12/31/01): Grants paid, $0; assets, $154 (M); expenditures, $0; qualifying distributions, $0.
Limitations: Giving primarily in NJ.
Officers: Marshall Kern, Pres.; Susan Roselli, Secy.; Yvonne Daley, Treas.
Directors: Lou Adickes, Jeff Bonnell, Mary Beth Ciccone, Michael Poll, Harvey Klein, Jamie Lykes, Christine Mitchell, Virginia Reilly, Alise Ruder.
EIN: 232957596

48667
David L. Kirtland and Marijo M. Kirtland Foundation
305 E. Drinker St.
Dunmore, PA 18512

Established in 1997 in PA.
Donor(s): David L. Kirtland, Marijo M. Kirtland.
Financial data (yr. ended 12/31/01): Grants paid, $0; assets, $52,515 (M); expenditures, $395; qualifying distributions, $0.
Trustee: Nicholas D. Tellie.
EIN: 237661166

48668
Kiwanis Club of Erie Foundation
P.O. Box 3715
Erie, PA 16508-0715
Contact: Joseph E. Kline, Secy.

Donor(s): Kiwanis Club of Erie.
Financial data (yr. ended 12/31/01): Grants paid, $0; assets, $22,736 (M); expenditures, $0; qualifying distributions, $0.
Limitations: Giving primarily in Erie, PA.
Officers and Directors:* Robert Haibach,* Pres.; Marilee Evans,* 1st V.P.; Frank Burns,* 2nd V.P.; Susan Musolff,* Secy.; John Tullio,* Treas.; Rose Hanks, Arthur Krause, William Liebel, Joe Murphy, Cathy Szymanski, Adam Trott, Merle Wood, Maryann Yochim.
EIN: 251631552

48669
The Kopen Foundation, Inc.
285 E. Center St.
Shavertown, PA 18708

Established in 1999 in PA.
Donor(s): Dan F. Kopen, Kathleen Kopen.
Financial data (yr. ended 12/31/01): Grants paid, $0; assets, $867 (M); gifts received, $500; expenditures, $200; qualifying distributions, $0.
Limitations: Applications not accepted.
Application information: Contributes only to pre-selected organizations.
Officers: Dan F. Kopen, Pres.; Kathleen Kopen, Secy.-Treas.
EIN: 233013143

48670
The Lally Foundation
911 Ligonier St., Ste. 102
Latrobe, PA 15650
Contact: Patrick T. Lally, M.D., Tr.

Financial data (yr. ended 12/31/01): Grants paid, $0; assets, $21,211 (M); expenditures, $175; qualifying distributions, $0.
Application information: Application form required.
Trustees: John M. Lally, Patrick T. Lally, Valerie M. Lally.
EIN: 256277039

48671
Benjamin Garver Lamme Fund
(Formerly Benjamin Garver Lamme Scholarship Fund)
c/o Provost, Carnegie Mellon University
500 Warner Hall, 5000 Forbes Ave.
Pittsburgh, PA 15213 (412) 642-5130
Contact: Cheryl Kubelick

Financial data (yr. ended 12/31/00): Grants paid, $0; assets, $1,205,180 (M); expenditures, $12,991; qualifying distributions, $10,257.
Limitations: Giving on a national basis.
Application information: Scholarships to employees of CBS Corp. and its subsidiaries.
Officer: V.J. Carpenter, Secy.
EIN: 256030362
Codes: GTI

48672
Maurice and Sara Land Foundation
10447 Drummond Rd.
Philadelphia, PA 19154
Application address: 2600 One Commerce Sq., Philadelphia, PA 19103-7098
Contact: C. Clark Hodgson, Jr., Secy.

Established in 1987.
Donor(s): Wissahickon Spring Water, Inc., Sara Land.
Financial data (yr. ended 12/31/01): Grants paid, $0; assets, $31,685 (M); expenditures, $5; qualifying distributions, $0.
Limitations: Giving primarily in Philadelphia, PA.
Officers: James J. Land, Pres.; C. Clark Hodgson, Jr., Secy.; John O. Heck, Treas.
EIN: 232491242
Codes: CS, CD

48673
Jules Laurent - Paulette Leroy Laurent Scholarship Trust
c/o First Commonwealth Trust Co.
P.O. Box 760, 111 S. Main St.
Greensburg, PA 15601 (724) 832-6127

Financial data (yr. ended 05/31/99): Grants paid, $0; assets, $214,067 (M); expenditures, $2,484; qualifying distributions, $0.
Limitations: Giving limited to residents of Cheswick, PA.
Trustee: First Commonwealth Trust Co.
EIN: 256233126

48674
Margery P. and B. Herbert Lee Foundation
P.O. Box 568
Bryn Mawr, PA 19010

Established in 1987 in PA.
Donor(s): B. Herbert Lee.
Financial data (yr. ended 09/30/01): Grants paid, $0; assets, $77,601 (M); expenditures, $149; qualifying distributions, $0.
Limitations: Applications not accepted. Giving limited to PA.

Application information: Contributes only to pre-selected organizations.
Officers and Trustees:* B. Herbert Lee,* Pres.; Margery P. Lee,* Secy.-Treas.; Edward G. Kaier.
EIN: 232484359

48675
William H. & Patti A. Lehr Foundation
734 Paxinosa Ave.
Easton, PA 18042

Established in 2001 in PA.
Donor(s): William Lehr, Patti Lehr.
Financial data (yr. ended 12/31/01): Grants paid, $0; assets, $250,010 (M); gifts received, $250,000; expenditures, $0; qualifying distributions, $0.
Trustees: Patti Lehr, William Lehr.
EIN: 256780232

48676
The H. Chase Lenfest Foundation, Inc.
1332 Enterprise Dr.
West Chester, PA 19380

Established in 1999 in PA.
Financial data (yr. ended 06/30/01): Grants paid, $0; assets, $803 (M); expenditures, $1,586; qualifying distributions, $0.
Limitations: Applications not accepted.
Application information: Contributes only to pre-selected organizations.
Directors: H. Chase Lenfest, Marguerite Lenfest.
EIN: 233031335

48677
Arnold I. & Adelyne Roth Levine Foundation
326 3rd Ave., 4th Fl.
Pittsburgh, PA 15222

Donor(s): Arnold I. Levine, Adelyne Roth Levine.‡
Financial data (yr. ended 01/31/02): Grants paid, $0; assets, $8,798 (M); expenditures, $0; qualifying distributions, $0.
Limitations: Applications not accepted. Giving primarily in New York, NY, and Pittsburgh, PA.
Application information: Contributes only to pre-selected organizations.
Trustees: Arnold I. Levine, Michael Levine, Thomas M. Levine.
EIN: 237001360

48678
Leon Levy Foundation
c/o Alex Satinsky
2000 Market St., 10th Fl.
Philadelphia, PA 19103-3291

Trust established in 1952 in PA.
Donor(s): Leon P. Levy, Robert P. Levy.
Financial data (yr. ended 11/30/01): Grants paid, $0; assets, $131 (M); expenditures, $1,505; qualifying distributions, $0.
Limitations: Applications not accepted. Giving primarily in PA.
Application information: Contributes only to pre-selected organizations.
Trustees: Robert P. Levy, Alex Satinsky.
EIN: 236245802

48679
Lindisfarne Foundation
8871 Norwood Ave.
Philadelphia, PA 19118

Established in 2000 in PA.
Financial data (yr. ended 12/31/01): Grants paid, $0; assets, $1 (M); expenditures, $0; qualifying distributions, $0.
Officers and Directors:* Robert P. Olson,* Pres. and Treas.; Elizabeth Q. Olson,* V.P. and Secy.; Katherine Q. Olson,* V.P.

48679—PENNSYLVANIA

EIN: 233028100

48680
Glenn R. Logan Scholarship Trust Fund
c/o First National Bank of Slippery Rock
234 S. Main St.
Slippery Rock, PA 16057
Application address: c/o Dale Lumley, Principal, Butler Area Senior High School, 120 Campus Ln., Butler, PA 16001

Established in 2001 in ME.
Donor(s): Glenn R. Logan.‡
Financial data (yr. ended 02/28/02): Grants paid, $0; assets, $201,138 (M); gifts received, $200,000; expenditures, $0; qualifying distributions, $0.
Limitations: Giving limited to Butler, PA.
Application information: Application form required.
Scholarship Committee Members: Dale Lumley, Robert R. Heaton, C. Timothy Shaffer.
Trustee: First National Bank.
EIN: 016191572

48681
McCallen Medical Center Foundation
367 S. Gulph Rd.
P.O. Box 61558
King of Prussia, PA 19406-0958
Application address: c/o Selection Comm., 301 W. Expwy. 83, McAllen, TX 78503, tel.: (973) 632-4000

Established in 1994 in TX.
Financial data (yr. ended 12/31/01): Grants paid, $0; assets, $1,020,852 (M); expenditures, $10,334; qualifying distributions, $0.
Limitations: Giving limited to residents of Hildalgo County, TX.
Officers and Trustees:* Alan B. Miller, Pres.; Steve Filton, V.P.; Bruce R. Gilbert,* Secy.; Kirk Gorman, Treas.; John Mims, John Shrouck.
EIN: 232749074

48682
McCarl Foundation
1413 9th Ave.
Beaver Falls, PA 15010

Established in 1997 in PA.
Donor(s): Foster McCarl, Jr.
Financial data (yr. ended 12/31/00): Grants paid, $0; assets, $108,940 (M); gifts received, $3,500; expenditures, $5,054; qualifying distributions, $0.
Limitations: Applications not accepted.
Application information: Contributes only to pre-selected organizations.
Officer and Directors:* Foster McCarl, Jr.,* Mgr.; Murial P. McCarl, James W. Ummer.
EIN: 232902138

48683
Elinor Jones McConnell Trust Fund
315 5th St.
Trafford, PA 15085

Established in 2000 in PA.
Financial data (yr. ended 12/31/01): Grants paid, $0; assets, $2,821,394 (M); expenditures, $270; qualifying distributions, $0.
Trustee: William M. McKay.
EIN: 256747287

48684
The Laddie and Linda Montague Foundation
c/o Asher & Co., Ltd.
1845 Walnut St.
Philadelphia, PA 19103-4755

Established in 2000 in PA.
Donor(s): H. Laddie Montague, Jr., Linda P. Montague.
Financial data (yr. ended 12/31/00): Grants paid, $0; assets, $532,341 (M); gifts received, $414,546; expenditures, $0; qualifying distributions, $0.
Limitations: Applications not accepted.
Application information: Contributes only to pre-selected organizations.
Trustees: H. Laddie Montague, Jr., Linda P. Montague.
EIN: 256734545

48685
Mourning Dove Foundation
470 Morristown Rd., Ste. 300
Blue Bell, PA 19422 (610) 834-8100
Contact: Charles A. Genuardi, Pres.

Established in 2001 in PA.
Donor(s): Charles A. Genuardi.
Financial data (yr. ended 12/31/01): Grants paid, $0; assets, $1,500,000 (M); gifts received, $1,500,000; expenditures, $0; qualifying distributions, $0.
Officers and Directors:* Charles A. Genuardi,* Pres.; Patricia T. Genuardi,* V.P.; Joy P. Genuardi,* Secy.; Charles G. Genuardi,* Treas.; Catherine Ann Genuardi Ciocca, Damian G. Genuardi.
EIN: 233102205

48686
My Giants, Inc.
1939 Waverly St.
Philadelphia, PA 19146
Application address: 1900 Market St., Philadelphia, PA 19103
Contact: Susan Ciallella, Dir.

Established in 1999 in PA.
Donor(s): Babette Josephs.
Financial data (yr. ended 12/31/01): Grants paid, $0; assets, $49,517 (M); expenditures, $1,846; qualifying distributions, $0.
Limitations: Giving primarily in Philadelphia, PA.
Officers: Babette Josephs, Pres.; Jach E. Hunter, Jr., Treas.
Directors: Susan Ciallella, Elizabeth Master, Lee Newberg.
EIN: 233005112

48687
F. Gregg Ney Scholarship Charitable Foundation
c/o First National Trust Co.
1 First National Bank Blvd.
Hermitage, PA 16148-3363

Established in 1999 in PA.
Financial data (yr. ended 12/31/99): Grants paid, $0; assets, $63,058 (M); gifts received, $63,482; expenditures, $52; qualifying distributions, $26.
Limitations: Applications not accepted.
Application information: Contributes only to pre-selected organizations.
Trustee: First National Trust Co.
EIN: 251850862

48688
The Niedbala Family Foundation
4093 Maulfair Dr.
Allentown, PA 18104

Established in 2001 in PA.
Donor(s): Raymond S. Niedbala, Linda-Lee Niedbala.
Financial data (yr. ended 12/31/01): Grants paid, $0; assets, $641,520 (M); gifts received, $651,024; expenditures, $0; qualifying distributions, $0.
Limitations: Applications not accepted.

Application information: Contributes only to pre-selected organizations.
Trustees: Linda-Lee Niedbala, Raymond S. Niedbala.
EIN: 256785415

48689
Ralph L. Noble Scholarship Fund
c/o Allfirst, Trust Div.
21 E. Market St.
York, PA 17401-1500
Application address: c/o Penn Township P.T.A., Southwestern School District, 225 Bowman Rd., Hanover, PA 17331

Financial data (yr. ended 12/31/00): Grants paid, $0; assets, $13,547 (M); expenditures, $20; qualifying distributions, $0.
Limitations: Giving limited to residents of Shippensburg, PA.
Application information: Application form required.
Trustee: Allfirst.
EIN: 236429668

48690
North & Schanz Charitable Foundation, Inc.
1525 Oregon Pike, Ste. 702
Lancaster, PA 17601-4374
URL: http://www.northschanz.com/charity.htm
Contact: Virginia Badger, Dir.

Established in 2001 in PA.
Donor(s): North & Schanz Consulting Group, Inc., Roger S. North, Laura L. Shanz.
Financial data (yr. ended 12/31/01): Grants paid, $0; assets, $16,515 (M); gifts received, $22,740; expenditures, $15,615; qualifying distributions, $0.
Limitations: Giving primarily in central PA.
Directors: Virginia Badger, Michael Brickley, Ronald Ford, Dottie Martin, Roger S. North, Laura L. Schanz, Scott R. Scheffey.
EIN: 233091818
Codes: CS

48691
The Arlene R. Olson Charitable Foundation
c/o J. Iskrant
1600 Market St., Ste. 3600
Philadelphia, PA 19103
Application address: c/o Arlene R. Olson, 742 Cherry Cir., Wynnewood, PA 19096-1233, tel. (610) 649-7868

Established in 2001 in PA.
Donor(s): Sidney Olson Trust, Miriam K. Olson Trust.
Financial data (yr. ended 12/31/01): Grants paid, $0; assets, $980,721 (M); gifts received, $1,000,000; expenditures, $9,011; qualifying distributions, $4,417.
Trustee: Arlene S. Olson.
EIN: 233066380

48692
Thomas & Mary Paterson Charitable Foundation
c/o S & T Bank, Trust Dept.
P.O. Box 220
Indiana, PA 15701
Application address: 1011 Lentz Rd., Latrobe, PA 15650, tel.: (724) 465-1443
Contact: Andrew Paterson, Pres.

Established in 2000 in PA.
Financial data (yr. ended 12/31/01): Grants paid, $0; assets, $3,145 (M); gifts received, $650; expenditures, $452; qualifying distributions, $0.
Application information: Application form not required.

Officers: Andrew Paterson, Pres.; Alexander Paterson, V.P.; Joseph Paterson, Secy.-Treas.
Trustee: S & T Bank.
EIN: 251855312

48693
The Paulits Foundation, Inc.
998 Old Eagle School Rd., Ste. 1215
Wayne, PA 19087

Established in 1999.
Donor(s): John Hines, R. David Sadoo.
Financial data (yr. ended 12/31/99): Grants paid, $0; assets, $818,026 (M); gifts received, $653,010; expenditures, $0; qualifying distributions, $0.
Officers: James H. Paulits, Pres.; R. David Sadoo, Secy.; John Hines, Treas.
EIN: 233015108

48694
The Eric & Virginia Pearson Foundation
701 W. Gravers Ln.
Philadelphia, PA 19118-4140

Established in 1985 in PA.
Donor(s): Eric G. Pearson, Virginia R. Pearson.
Financial data (yr. ended 12/31/00): Grants paid, $0; assets, $397 (M); expenditures, $82; qualifying distributions, $0.
Limitations: Giving primarily in NJ and PA.
Officers and Directors:* Eric G. Pearson,* Pres.; Virginia R. Pearson,* Secy.-Treas.
EIN: 232411337

48695
Pennsylvania Dental Foundation
P.O. Box 3341
Harrisburg, PA 17105 (717) 234-5941
Contact: Jim Steeley

Donor(s): Pennsylvania Dental Assn.
Financial data (yr. ended 08/31/01): Grants paid, $0; assets, $55,293 (M); gifts received, $12,145; expenditures, $1,895; qualifying distributions, $900.
Limitations: Giving limited to PA.
Application information: Application form required.
Officers and Trustees:* William G. Glecos,* Pres.; Joseph A. Donato,* Secy.; Joel A. Casar, Michael Cerveris, Brian D. Christian, Thomas E. Cressley, Saul N. Miller, Stephen T. Radack III, Ronald C. Szish, Charles R. Weber, William P. Yeomans.
EIN: 236407862

48696
Pennsylvania Environmental Defense Foundation
P.O. Box 371
Camp Hill, PA 17001-0371
Application address: 32 Wistar Rd., Paoli, PA 19301
Contact: Charles Marshall, Chair.

Financial data (yr. ended 05/31/99): Grants paid, $0; assets, $288,360 (M); gifts received, $47,956; expenditures, $182,040; qualifying distributions, $182,040; giving activities include $171,428 for programs.
Limitations: Giving limited to PA.
Officers: Charles Marshall, Chair.; Frederick Johnson, Vice-Chair.; Letitia Ryan, Vice-Chair.; Averill Shepps, Treas.
EIN: 232425827

48697
Pennsylvania Farmers Association Legal Fund
(also known as P.F.A. Legal Fund)
510 S. 31st St.
Camp Hill, PA 17011
Application address: c/o Board of Directors, PFA Legal Fund, P.O. Box 8736, Camp Hill, PA 17011

Established in 1986 in PA.
Financial data (yr. ended 12/31/01): Grants paid, $0; assets, $11,121 (M); gifts received, $1,330; expenditures, $470; qualifying distributions, $0.
Limitations: Applications not accepted. Giving limited to PA.
Officer: Kent D. Shelhamer, Chair.
Directors: William Goodwin, Geary Huntsburger, Roxy Levan, Ralph McGregor, Sandra Merwarth, John F. Peters, Harold Shaulis, Robert Stoch, C. James Yeatman, John Zerbie.
EIN: 251524460

48698
Pennsylvania Public Education Foundation
774 Limekiln Rd.
New Cumberland, PA 17070-2398

Financial data (yr. ended 06/30/01): Grants paid, $0; assets, $25,410 (M); gifts received, $6,148; expenditures, $50,900; qualifying distributions, $30,402; giving activities include $30,402 for programs.
Officers: Barbara L. Bolas, Pres.; Alex Matthews, V.P.; Joseph V. Oravitz, Secy.
EIN: 222837815

48699
Ida G. & Roosevelt Peterson Scholarship Fund
c/o R.B. Matlin
2000 Market St., 10th Fl.
Philadelphia, PA 19103-3291

Established in 2000 in PA.
Donor(s): Ida G. Peterson.
Financial data (yr. ended 12/31/01): Grants paid, $0; assets, $372,276 (M); gifts received, $375,000; expenditures, $0; qualifying distributions, $0.
Limitations: Giving limited to Atlanta, GA.
Trustee: Howard B. Zavodnick.
EIN: 256714458

48700
Wendy & Derek Pew Foundation, Inc.
1732 Pine St.
Philadelphia, PA 19103

Established in 2001 in PA.
Donor(s): Wendy Pew, Derek Pew.
Financial data (yr. ended 12/31/01): Grants paid, $0; assets, $738,882 (M); gifts received, $749,881; expenditures, $0; qualifying distributions, $0.
Limitations: Applications not accepted.
Application information: Contributes only to pre-selected organizations.
Officers and Trustees:* Wendy Pew,* Pres. and Treas.; Derek Pew,* Secy.
EIN: 010566881

48701
Philadelphia Bar Association International Human Rights Fund
1101 Market St., 11th Fl.
Philadelphia, PA 19107 (215) 238-6300

Financial data (yr. ended 12/31/01): Grants paid, $0; assets, $3,178 (M); expenditures, $67; qualifying distributions, $0.
Directors: Irv Ackelsberg, Donna E. Baker, Karl Baker, Lawrence Jay Beaser, and 20 additional directors.
EIN: 220968283
Codes: TN

48702
Philadelphia Men's and Boys' Apparel Association Endowed Scholarship Aid Fund
133 Heather Rd., No. 202
Bala Cynwyd, PA 19004

Financial data (yr. ended 12/31/01): Grants paid, $0; assets, $81,739 (M); expenditures, $863; qualifying distributions, $0.
Limitations: Giving limited to Philadelphia, PA.
Application information: Application form required.
Officer: Marc Kantor,* Chair.
Directors: Bennett Oltman, Steven Saft.
EIN: 232104421

48703
Phillips Family Foundation
c/o Bruce A. Rosenfield
1600 Market St., Ste. 3600
Philadelphia, PA 19103-7286

Established in 2000 in PA.
Donor(s): Thomas G. Phillips III.
Financial data (yr. ended 12/31/01): Grants paid, $0; assets, $1,110,489 (M); gifts received, $128,370; expenditures, $24,414; qualifying distributions, $0.
Limitations: Applications not accepted.
Application information: Contributes only to pre-selected organizations.
Trustees: Elizabeth A. Davies, David S. Phillips, Peter H. Phillips, Thomas G. Phillips III, Virginia A. Phillips.
EIN: 256716692

48704
The Pillmore Family Foundation
186 Ash Way
Doylestown, PA 18901

Established in 2000 in PA.
Donor(s): Eric Pillmore.
Financial data (yr. ended 12/31/00): Grants paid, $0; assets, $234,412 (M); gifts received, $232,650; expenditures, $0; qualifying distributions, $0.
Officer: Eric Pillmore, C.E.O. and Pres.
EIN: 233064365

48705
Piper Foundation, Inc.
222 1/2 E. Main St.
P.O. Box 227
Lock Haven, PA 17745
Contact: William T. Piper, Jr., Pres.

Established around 1957.
Donor(s): Piper Aircraft.
Financial data (yr. ended 12/31/01): Grants paid, $0; assets, $1,288,042 (M); expenditures, $10,514; qualifying distributions, $2,425.
Limitations: Applications not accepted. Giving primarily in PA; scholarship fund limited to Keystone Central School District.
Publications: Annual report.
Application information: Contributes only to pre-selected organizations. Scholarship recipients chosen by high school administrators.
Officers and Directors:* William T. Piper, Jr.,* Pres. and Treas.; Patricia Piper-Smyer,* V.P.; John R. Piper,* Secy.
EIN: 240863140
Codes: GTI

48706
Queequeeg Foundation Trust
428 Blvd. of the Allies
Pittsburgh, PA 15219   (412) 471-0677
Contact: Edwin I. Grinberg, Tr.

Established in 1994 in PA.
Donor(s): Ralph H. Reese, Diane I. Samuels.
Financial data (yr. ended 12/31/01): Grants paid, $0; assets, $344,995 (M); expenditures, $2,168; qualifying distributions, $0.
Limitations: Giving primarily in Pittsburgh, PA.
Application information: Application form not required.
Trustees: Edwin I. Grinberg, Ralph H. Reese, Diane I. Samuels.
EIN: 256429739

48707
Redzinak Family Foundation
1 FNB Blvd.
Hermitage, PA 16148-3363

Established in 2001 in PA.
Donor(s): Helen Redzinak.‡
Financial data (yr. ended 12/31/01): Grants paid, $0; assets, $1,047,796 (M); gifts received, $1,034,248; expenditures, $2,668; qualifying distributions, $1,196.
Limitations: Applications not accepted.
Application information: Contributes only to pre-selected organizations.
Trustee: First National Trust Co.
EIN: 256809508

48708
The Respiratory Distress Syndrome Foundation
P.O. Box 723
Montgomeryville, PA 18936
Application address: 24 Wilson Ave., Chalfont, PA 18914
Contact: F.X. Cannon, Chair.

Established in 1990.
Financial data (yr. ended 07/31/00): Grants paid, $0; assets, $2,943 (M); gifts received, $1,766; expenditures, $1,083; qualifying distributions, $0.
Limitations: Giving on a national basis.
Officers: F.X. Cannon, Chair.; E.F. Hansen, Jr., Vice-Chair.; R.T. Hansen, Pres.
EIN: 232526029
Codes: GTI

48709
The Rooney Foundation
c/o David R. Berk
1 Oxford Ctr., 40th Fl.
Pittsburgh, PA 15219-6498
Contact: Daniel M. Rooney, Tr.

Established in 1995.
Donor(s): The Arthur J. Rooney Charitable Trust.
Financial data (yr. ended 12/31/01): Grants paid, $0; assets, $295,329 (M); gifts received, $329; expenditures, $2,822; qualifying distributions, $0.
Trustees: Arthur J. Rooney, Jr., Daniel M. Rooney, Patrick J. Rooney.
EIN: 256500407

48710
Sanders Foundation
c/o Filip S. Sanders
219 Chrislena Ln.
West Chester, PA 19380

Established in 2000 in PA.
Donor(s): Filip S. Sanders.
Financial data (yr. ended 10/31/01): Grants paid, $0; assets, $411,084 (M); gifts received, $419,838; expenditures, $4,917; qualifying distributions, $0.
Limitations: Applications not accepted.
Application information: Contributes only to pre-selected organizations.
Trustees: Paula D. Kales, Elkan D. Sanders, Filip S. Sanders, Hans G. Sanders, Josephine E. Sanders-Levie.
EIN: 316653312

48711
Rose & Joseph H. Schimmel Foundation
3233 Hunting Park Ave.
Philadelphia, PA 19129

Financial data (yr. ended 02/28/02): Grants paid, $0; assets, $3,894 (M); expenditures, $0; qualifying distributions, $0.
Limitations: Giving primarily in Philadelphia, PA.
Trustees: Marvin Schimmel, Paul B. Schimmel.
EIN: 236294543

48712
Science Research Foundation for the New Church
c/o High, Swartz, Roberts & Seidel, LLP
40 E. Airy St.
Norristown, PA 19401

Established in 1989.
Financial data (yr. ended 12/31/01): Grants paid, $0; assets, $101,998 (M); expenditures, $5,600; qualifying distributions, $0.
Limitations: Applications not accepted. Giving limited to Bryn Athyn, PA.
Application information: Contributes only to a pre-selected organization.
Trustees: Hugh R. Brown, Janina Cole Brown, Anna Boyesen Cole, G. Owen Cole, Karen P. Cole, Kendra S. Cole, Janice Cole King, Steven King, Glynn Cole Schauder, Kenneth Schauder.
EIN: 236898636

48713
Security on Campus, Inc.
601 Henderson Rd., No. 205
King of Prussia, PA 19406
Contact: Constance Clery, Secy.

Donor(s): Constance Clery, Howard Clery.
Financial data (yr. ended 12/31/99): Grants paid, $0; assets, $80,516 (L); gifts received, $274,914; expenditures, $200,299; qualifying distributions, $198,402.
Application information: Application form not required.
Officers: Benjamin Clery, Pres.; S. Daniel Carter, V.P.; Constance Clery, Secy.; Howard Clery III, Treas.
EIN: 232485759

48714
Maurice Seltzer Publishing Trust
c/o First Union National Bank
P.O. Box 7558
Philadelphia, PA 19101

Established in 1994.
Financial data (yr. ended 09/30/00): Grants paid, $0; assets, $235,777 (M); expenditures, $5,266; qualifying distributions, $5,266.
Limitations: Applications not accepted.
Application information: Contributes only to pre-selected organizations.
Trustee: First Union National Bank.
EIN: 237787911

48715
D. D. Sharma Eye Foundation
3253-C Old Frankstown Rd.
Pittsburgh, PA 15239-2910   (724) 733-2627
Contact: Jashwant Sharma, M.D., Tr.

Established in 1990 in PA.
Financial data (yr. ended 03/31/00): Grants paid, $0; assets, $89,411 (M); gifts received, $84,233; expenditures, $74,985; qualifying distributions, $67,267.
Application information: Application form not required.
Trustee: Jashwant Sharma, M.D.
EIN: 251387674

48716
Joan M. & David S. Shrager Foundation
c/o David Shrager
100 Breyer Dr., Ste. 4H
Elkins Park, PA 19027
Contact: David S. Shrager, Tr.

Established in 2000 in PA.
Donor(s): David S. Shrager, Joan M. Shrager.
Financial data (yr. ended 11/30/01): Grants paid, $0; assets, $481,061 (M); gifts received, $499,363; expenditures, $430; qualifying distributions, $0.
Application information: Application form not required.
Trustee: David S. Shrager.
EIN: 233064289

48717
Herman Shuster Memorial Trust
c/o Bernard Glassman
1 Logan Sq.
Philadelphia, PA 19103-6998

Established in 1987 in PA.
Financial data (yr. ended 02/28/02): Grants paid, $0; assets, $2,171,353 (M); expenditures, $10,988; qualifying distributions, $0.
Limitations: Applications not accepted. Giving limited to Israel.
Application information: Contributes only to pre-selected organizations.
Trustees: Warren Rubin, Walter Shuster.
EIN: 236875505

48718
Louis E. Silvi Foundation
1600 University Dr.
State College, PA 16801

Established in 2000 in PA.
Donor(s): Louis E. Silvi.
Financial data (yr. ended 12/31/01): Grants paid, $0; assets, $1,442 (M); expenditures, $500; qualifying distributions, $0.
Limitations: Applications not accepted.
Application information: Contributes only to pre-selected organizations.
Officers and Directors:* Louis E. Silvi,* Pres. and Secy.-Treas.; Thomas J. Taricani,* V.P.; Edward R. Book, James J. Raytek.
EIN: 251865517

48719
B. K. Simon Education Foundation
c/o Mellon Bank, N.A.
P.O. Box 185
Pittsburgh, PA 15230
Application address: 3 Mellon Bank Center, Pittsburgh, PA 15259, tel.: (412) 234-1584
Contact: Daniel Pfaff

Established in 2000 in PA.
Donor(s): B. Kenneth Simmon.
Financial data (yr. ended 12/31/00): Grants paid, $0; assets, $1,822,805 (M); gifts received, $2,016,869; expenditures, $1,573; qualifying distributions, $629.
Application information: Application form not required.
Trustee: Mellon Bank, N.A.
EIN: 251880653

48720
The Richard and Carolyn Sloane Family Foundation
124 Righters Mill Rd.
Gladwyne, PA 19035

Established in 1999 in PA.
Donor(s): Richard Sloane, Carolyn Sloane.
Financial data (yr. ended 12/31/00): Grants paid, $0; assets, $49,822 (M); gifts received, $767; expenditures, $767; qualifying distributions, $0.
Limitations: Applications not accepted.
Application information: Contributes only to pre-selected organizations.
Trustees: A. Richard Sloane, Carolyn J. Sloane, Jill K. Sloane.
EIN: 256614388

48721
Herchel Smith Charitable Foundation
c/o R. Vine
1701 Market St.
Philadelphia, PA 19103-2921

Donor(s): Herchel Smith.
Financial data (yr. ended 12/31/00): Grants paid, $0; assets, $177,066 (M); expenditures, $7,419; qualifying distributions, $0.
Limitations: Applications not accepted.
Application information: Contributes only to pre-selected organizations.
Trustees: John J. Lombard, Jr., Thomas A. Masterson, Herchel Smith.
EIN: 256408917

48722
Mary R. Smith Testamentary Trust
c/o Adams County National Bank
P.O. Box 4566
Gettysburg, PA 17325

Established in 2001 in PA.
Donor(s): Mary R. Smith Trust.‡
Financial data (yr. ended 12/31/01): Grants paid, $0; assets, $32,009 (M); expenditures, $50; qualifying distributions, $0.
Trustee: Adams County National Bank.
EIN: 306001604

48723
The Stadtlanders Foundation
c/o Stadtlanders Drug Co., Inc.
600 Penn Center Blvd.
Pittsburgh, PA 15235
Contact: Allan C. Silber, Pres.

Established in 1993 in PA.
Donor(s): Stadtlanders Drug Co., Inc.
Financial data (yr. ended 12/31/99): Grants paid, $0; assets, $46,295 (M); expenditures, $1,501; qualifying distributions, $0.
Officers and Directors:* Alan C. Silber,* Pres.; Morris Perlis,* V.P.
EIN: 251716700
Codes: CS, CD

48724
Staiman Brothers Charitable Trust
(Formerly Marvin H. Staiman-Staiman Brothers Charitable Trust)
c/o Woodlands Bank
2450 E. 3rd St.
Williamsport, PA 17701 (570) 246-8468

Donor(s): Staiman Bros.
Financial data (yr. ended 12/31/01): Grants paid, $0; assets, $16,132 (M); expenditures, $557; qualifying distributions, $0.
Limitations: Giving limited to Williamsport, PA.
Trustees: Jeffrey W. Staiman, Marvin H. Staiman, Woodlands Bank.
EIN: 236610250

48725
The Star Foundation
1775 Arden Ln.
Bethlehem, PA 18015

Established in 2001 in PA.
Donor(s): John Stella, Aurelia Stella.
Financial data (yr. ended 12/31/01): Grants paid, $0; assets, $801,390 (M); gifts received, $800,625; expenditures, $0; qualifying distributions, $0.
Trustees: Jennifer Indresano, Elisabeth Moughty, Aurelia Stella, John A. Stella, John C. Stella, Krista Stella, Matthew Stella.
EIN: 256761169

48726
Emily O'Neill Sullivan Foundation
c/o Edwin S. Heins, Jr.
1329 Beaumont Dr.
Gladwyne, PA 19035 (610) 642-0123
Contact: Philip A. Sullivan, Tr.

Established in 1995.
Financial data (yr. ended 12/31/01): Grants paid, $0; assets, $113,833 (M); expenditures, $1,554; qualifying distributions, $0.
Application information: Application form not required.
Trustees: Paula S. Snyder, Philip A. Sullivan, Stephen J. Sullivan.
EIN: 232808366

48727
The Klare S. Sunderland Foundation
4444 Carlisle Pike
Camp Hill, PA 17011

Established in 1993 in PA.
Donor(s): Klare S. Sunderland.
Financial data (yr. ended 09/30/00): Grants paid, $0; assets, $192,989 (M); expenditures, $1,298; qualifying distributions, $0.
Limitations: Applications not accepted. Giving primarily in PA.
Application information: Contributes only to pre-selected organizations.
Officers: Klare S. Sunderland, Pres.; Daniel Sunderland, Secy.-Treas.
Director: R. Stephen Shibla.
EIN: 251723087

48728
M. J. Surgala Trust
1210 Wilkins Rd.
Erie, PA 16505 (814) 838-4921
Contact: Mary Lincoln, Exec. Dir.

Established in 2001 in NY.
Donor(s): M.J. Surgala.‡
Financial data (yr. ended 12/31/01): Grants paid, $0; assets, $15,025,378 (M); gifts received, $14,200,000; expenditures, $0; qualifying distributions, $0.
Officer and Trustee:* Mary Lincoln,* Exec. Dir.
EIN: 116556638

48729
Templeton Foundation, Inc.
5 Radnor Corp. Ctr.
100 Matsonford Rd., Ste. 120
Radnor, PA 19087

Established in 1953 in NJ.
Donor(s): John Templeton.
Financial data (yr. ended 12/31/99): Grants paid, $0; assets, $5,162,688 (M); gifts received, $971,536; expenditures, $881,481; qualifying distributions, $745,311; giving activities include $745,673 for programs.
Limitations: Applications not accepted.
Application information: Contributes only to pre-selected organizations.
Officers and Trustees:* Sir John Templeton, Chair.; John M. Templeton, Pres.; Joanna Hill, V.P. and Dir. of Publications; Pamela Lairdierson, Secy.; Ann Cameron,* Treas.; Wendy Brooks, Christopher Templeton, Harvey Templeton, Anne Zimmerman.
EIN: 226035108

48730
John J. & Josephine Thomas Charitable Foundation
c/o John P. Moses
120 S. Franklin St.
Wilkes-Barre, PA 18701

Established in 2001 in PA.
Donor(s): Josephine Thomas.‡
Financial data (yr. ended 12/31/01): Grants paid, $0; assets, $598,031 (M); gifts received, $597,380; expenditures, $3,046; qualifying distributions, $0.
Limitations: Applications not accepted.
Application information: Contributes only to pre-selected organizations.
Trustees: John P. Moses, Hon. John J. Thomas.
EIN: 256800841

48731
Paul Thompson III Charitable Foundation
c/o Paul Thomson III
667 Dodds Ln.
Gladwyne, PA 19035-1514

Established in 1993 in PA.
Donor(s): Paul Thompson III, Judith Ann Thompson.
Financial data (yr. ended 06/30/00): Grants paid, $0; assets, $201,018 (M); gifts received, $101,360; expenditures, $1,175; qualifying distributions, $0.
Limitations: Applications not accepted. Giving primarily in Philadelphia, PA.
Application information: Contributes only to pre-selected organizations.
Trustees: Leonard C. Green, Judith Ann Thompson, Paul Thompson III.
EIN: 232719735

48732
The Evelyn Toll Family Foundation
c/o PNC Advisors
1600 Market St.
Philadelphia, PA 19103-7240

Established in 1997 in PA.
Donor(s): Evelyn Toll.
Financial data (yr. ended 06/30/01): Grants paid, $0; assets, $1,080,702 (M); expenditures, $6,541; qualifying distributions, $0.
Limitations: Applications not accepted.
Application information: Contributes only to pre-selected organizations.
Officers and Directors:* Evelyn Toll,* Pres.; Barbara E. Toll,* V.P.; Richard D. Toll,* V.P.; Richard J. Braemer,* Secy.-Treas.
Trustee: PNC Bank, N.A.
EIN: 232896797

48733
Tree of Concern International Foundation, Inc.
3600 Conshohocken Ave.
Philadelphia, PA 19131

Established in 1995 in PA.
Financial data (yr. ended 12/31/00): Grants paid, $0; assets, $387 (M); gifts received, $3,205; expenditures, $3,075; qualifying distributions, $0.

48733—PENNSYLVANIA

Limitations: Applications not accepted. Giving primarily in PA.
Application information: Contributes only to pre-selected organizations.
Officers and Director:* James R. Burnett, Co-Chair.; Raymond V. Lawrence, Co-Chair.; Jennifer Coleman Pugh,* Co-Chair.; Agnes Ogletree, Chair., Marketing; Edward Melvin, Chair., Nomination; Raymond T. Jones, Chair., Media Relations; Mark S. Cohen, Corp. Secy. and Legal Counsel; Lorna Gossett, Recording Secy.
EIN: 232039182

48734
The Trellis Fund
718 Bigelow Corporate Ctr.
Pittsburgh, PA 15219-3030

Established in 2000 in PA.
Donor(s): J. Donahue, R. Donahue, K. Freyvogel, T. Freyvogel.
Financial data (yr. ended 12/31/00): Grants paid, $0; assets, $47,465 (M); gifts received, $47,465; expenditures, $0; qualifying distributions, $0.
Limitations: Applications not accepted.
Application information: Contributes only to pre-selected organizations.
Officers: Ronald M. Petnuch, Pres.; Susan D. Petnuch, V.P.; Megan E. Donley, Secy.-Treas.
EIN: 251874424

48735
Van Aken Family Foundation
c/o Pitcairn Trust Co.
165 Township Line Rd., Ste. 3000
Jenkintown, PA 19046
Application address: 46 Bowman's Dr. W., New Hope, PA 18938, tel.: (215) 862-3775
Contact: Dale Van Aken, Tr.

Established in 1999 in PA.
Donor(s): Dale Van Aken.
Financial data (yr. ended 12/31/01): Grants paid, $0; assets, $321,886 (M); expenditures, $1; qualifying distributions, $0.
Trustees: Dale Van Aken, Deborah Van Aken, Pitcairn Trust Co.
EIN: 137210757

48736
Philip Wachs & Juliet Spitzer Foundation
464 Conshohocken State Rd.
Bala Cynwyd, PA 19004

Established in 1992 in PA.
Donor(s): Philip Wachs, Juliet Spitzer.
Financial data (yr. ended 12/31/01): Grants paid, $0; assets, $2,904 (M); expenditures, $150; qualifying distributions, $0.
Limitations: Applications not accepted. Giving primarily in New York, NY, and PA.
Application information: Contributes only to pre-selected organizations.
Trustees: Juliet Spitzer, Philip Wachs.

EIN: 237709345

48737
The Sara & Warren Welch Foundation
P.O. Box 125
Newville, PA 17241-0125

Financial data (yr. ended 04/30/01): Grants paid, $0; assets, $255,625 (M); expenditures, $7,235; qualifying distributions, $52,102; giving activities include $46,406 for loans to individuals.
Limitations: Giving limited to the Newville, PA, area.
Application information: Application form required.
Officers: Markwood C. Reid, Pres.; John W. Grane, V.P.; A.B. McCarter, Secy.; Frank C. Eggar, Treas.
Directors: Stephen F. Ginter, Dolores Lezzer.
EIN: 232130843
Codes: GTI

48738
John G. Williams Scholarship Foundation
3425 Simpson Ferry Rd.
Camp Hill, PA 17011-6405 (717) 763-1333
Contact: Connie E. Williams Jack, Exec. Dir.

Established in 1993 in PA.
Donor(s): John G. Williams.
Financial data (yr. ended 03/31/01): Grants paid, $0; assets, $641,095 (M); expenditures, $560; qualifying distributions, $452,328; giving activities include $451,768 for loans to individuals.
Limitations: Giving primarily in PA.
Officer: Connie E. Williams Jack, Exec. Dir.
EIN: 232329462

48739
Winner Family Foundation
32 W. State St.
Sharon, PA 16146 (724) 981-1152
Contact: James E. Winner, Jr., Pres.

Established in 1998 in PA.
Donor(s): Donna C. Winner, James E. Winner.
Financial data (yr. ended 12/31/00): Grants paid, $0; assets, $266,265 (M); gifts received, $102,500; expenditures, $101,870; qualifying distributions, $0.
Officers and Directors:* James E. Winner, Jr.,* Pres.; Donna C. Winner,* Secy.-Treas.
EIN: 251783656

48740
The Joan M. Wismer Foundation
c/o John Iskrant
1600 Market St., Ste. 3600
Philadelphia, PA 19103
Application address: c/o Joan M. Wismer, 12400 Magnolia Blvd., North Hollywood, CA 91607, tel. (818) 763-4686

Established in 2001 in PA.

Donor(s): Joan M. Wismer.
Financial data (yr. ended 12/31/01): Grants paid, $0; assets, $276,910 (M); gifts received, $245,200; expenditures, $361; qualifying distributions, $0.
Trustees: N. Jack Dilday, John D. Iskrant, Joan M. Wismer.
EIN: 233089181

48741
The Marvin and Dee Woodall Foundation
775 Pebble Hill Rd.
Doylestown, PA 18901
Contact: Marvin L. Woodall, Dir.

Established in 2001.
Financial data (yr. ended 12/31/01): Grants paid, $0; assets, $959,500 (M); gifts received, $573,000; expenditures, $0; qualifying distributions, $0.
Directors: Amy Carroll, Dee Ann Woodall, Mark E. Woodall, Marvin L. Woodall.
EIN: 233097172

48742
Young People's Church of the Air, Inc.
P.O. Box 3003
Blue Bell, PA 19422

Established in 1987 in PA.
Financial data (yr. ended 10/31/01): Grants paid, $0; assets, $82,381 (M); gifts received, $384; expenditures, $1,216; qualifying distributions, $0.
Limitations: Applications not accepted. Giving primarily in New York, NY.
Application information: Contributes only to pre-selected organizations.
Officers: Donald B. Crawford, Pres.; Donald B. Crawford, Jr., V.P.; Dean A. Crawford, Secy.-Treas.
EIN: 231484204

48743
Young Scholars Foundation, Inc.
202 Park West Dr.
Pittsburgh, PA 15275

Established in 2001 in PA.
Donor(s): Maronda Homes, Inc., Maronda Inc.
Financial data (yr. ended 12/23/01): Grants paid, $0; assets, $222,300 (M); gifts received, $222,222; expenditures, $25; qualifying distributions, $0.
Limitations: Applications not accepted.
Application information: Contributes only to pre-selected organizations.
Officers and Directors:* Ronald W. Wolf,* Pres.; William J. Wolf,* C.F.O.
EIN: 311797213

PUERTO RICO

48744
Puerto Rico Community Foundation
P.O. Box 70362
San Juan, PR 00936-8362 (787) 721-1037
FAX: (787) 721-1673; *E-mail:* fcpr@fcpr.org
Contact: Juan J. Reyes, Admin.

Incorporated in 1984 in PR; began operations in 1985.
Financial data (yr. ended 12/31/01): Grants paid, $1,367,348; assets, $21,095,627 (M); gifts received, $1,358,583; expenditures, $2,959,198; giving activities include $884,458 for programs.
Limitations: Giving limited to PR.
Publications: Annual report, newsletter, informational brochure (including application guidelines), financial statement, program policy statement, application guidelines.
Application information: Application form required.
Officers and Directors:* Antonio Escudero Viera,* Chair.; Mabel Burckhart,* V.P.; William Lockwood, Secy.; Alina Herrera, Treas.; and 11 additional directors.
EIN: 660413230
Codes: CM, FD

48745
FNZ Foundation, Inc.
Box 3425
Carolina, PR 00984
FAX: (787) 762-2115; *E-mail:* RonadK@prtc.net
Contact: James D. Klau, Pres.

Established in 1996 in DE.
Financial data (yr. ended 12/31/01): Grants paid, $624,787; assets, $11,266,312 (M); expenditures, $743,132; qualifying distributions, $624,787.
Limitations: Giving on a national basis.
Officer: James D. Klau, Pres.
Member: Susan L. Klau.
EIN: 660535017
Codes: FD

48746
Harvey Foundation, Inc.
First Federal Bldg.
1519 Ponce de Leon Ave., Ste. 507
San Juan, PR 00909 (787) 725-1814
Contact: Charles M. Hitt, Treas.

Incorporated in 1963 in PR.
Financial data (yr. ended 12/31/01): Grants paid, $89,500; assets, $2,042,979 (M); expenditures, $103,454; qualifying distributions, $97,525.
Limitations: Giving primarily in PR.
Application information: Application form not required.
Officers: Vincent A. Mabert, Pres.; Alfonso Miranda Cardenas, Secy.; Charles M. Hitt, Treas.
Trustees: Jose Miranda Daleccio, Marilyn von Hillerbant.
EIN: 660271454
Codes: FD2, GTI

RHODE ISLAND

48747
The Champlin Foundations
300 Centerville Rd, Ste. 300S
Warwick, RI 02886-0226 (401) 736-0370
FAX: (401) 736-7248; E-mail: champlinfdns@worldnet.att.net; URL: http://www.fdncenter.org/grantmaker/champlin
Contact: David A. King, Exec. Dir.

Trusts established in 1932, 1947, and 1975 in DE.
Donor(s): George S. Champlin,‡ Florence C. Hamilton,‡ Hope C. Neaves.‡
Financial data (yr. ended 12/31/01): Grants paid, $20,742,979; assets, $432,556,992 (M); expenditures, $22,860,722; qualifying distributions, $21,513,443.
Limitations: Giving primarily in RI.
Publications: Program policy statement, application guidelines, annual report, grants list.
Application information: No grants are awarded on a continuing basis, but applicants may qualify annually. Application form not required.
Distribution Committee: David A. King, Exec. Dir.; John Gorham, Louis R. Hampton, Earl W. Harrington, Jr., Robert W. Kenyon, Norma B. LaFreniere, Keith H. Lang, John W. Linnell.
Trustee: PNC Bank, N.A.
Codes: FD, FM

48748
The Rhode Island Foundation
1 Union Sta.
Providence, RI 02903 (401) 274-4564
FAX: (401) 331-8085; URL: http://www.rifoundation.org
Contact: Karen Voci, Sr. V.P., Prog.

Incorporated in 1916 in RI (includes The Rhode Island Community Foundation in 1984).
Financial data (yr. ended 12/31/01): Grants paid, $19,486,289; assets, $366,346,451 (M); gifts received, $16,087,287; expenditures, $24,430,836.
Limitations: Giving limited to RI.
Publications: Annual report (including application guidelines), program policy statement, application guidelines, newsletter, informational brochure, occasional report.
Application information: Organizations are invited to submit a full application after letter of intent is received. For scholarship information from the designated and donor-advised funds contact the foundation. Application form not required.
Officers: Ronald V. Gallo, C.E.O. and Pres.; Carol Golden, Sr. V.P., Devel.; Karen Voci, Sr. V.P., Prog.; Michael Jenkinson, V.P., Finance and Admin.; Jennifer Reid, Cont.
Board of Directors: Pablo Rodriguez, Chair.; Elizabeth Z. Chace, Peter Damon, George Graboys, Carol Grant, Margaret Goddard Leeson, Florence K. Murray, Ruth Simmons, Walter R. Stone, John W. Wall.
EIN: 050208270
Codes: CM, FD, FM, GTI

48749
The Melville Charitable Trust
P.O. Box 6767
Providence, RI 02940-6767

Established in 1987 in NY.
Donor(s): Dorothy Melville.‡
Financial data (yr. ended 12/31/00): Grants paid, $4,954,288; assets, $90,107,113 (M); expenditures, $6,126,020; qualifying distributions, $5,593,382.
Limitations: Applications not accepted. Giving primarily in CT.
Application information: Contributes only to pre-selected organizations.
Trustee: Fleet National Bank.
Distribution Committee: John R. Gibb, Alan Melville, Frank Melville, Stephen Melville.
EIN: 133415258
Codes: FD, FM

48750
The Textron Charitable Trust
P.O. Box 1861
Providence, RI 02901 (401) 457-2430
Scholarship application addresses: Jeffrey Little, National Merit Scholarship Corp., 1 Rotary Ctr., Ste. 200, 1560 Sherman Ave., Evanston, IL 60201, James Mahoney, College Scholarship Svc., CN 6730, Princeton, NJ 08541, Herbert J. D'Arcy, Jr., Exec. Dir. of Financial Aid, Providence College, Providence, RI 02918, Joe Marina, Dean of School of Continuing Education, Providence College, Providence, RI, 02918
Contact: Elizabeth W. Monahan, Contribs. Coord.

Trust established in 1953 in VT.
Donor(s): Textron Inc.
Financial data (yr. ended 12/31/00): Grants paid, $3,577,311; assets, $16,151,845 (M); gifts received, $9,130,440; expenditures, $3,645,863; qualifying distributions, $3,568,324.
Limitations: Giving primarily in areas of company operations nationwide.
Publications: Application guidelines.
Application information: Application form not required.
Contributions Committee: Raymond W. Caine, Jr., Chair.; Elizabeth W. Monahan, Contribs. Coord.
Trustee: Fleet National Bank.
EIN: 256115832
Codes: CS, FD, CD, FM

48751
van Beuren Charitable Foundation, Inc.
P.O. Box 4098
Middletown, RI 02842 (401) 846-8167
FAX: (401) 849-6859; E-mail: vBCFnd@aol.com; URL: http://www.vBCF.net
Contact: Barbara van Beuren, Exec. Dir.

Established in 1986 in RI.
Donor(s): Members of the van Beuren family.
Financial data (yr. ended 12/31/01): Grants paid, $3,191,464; assets, $51,286,298 (M); expenditures, $3,632,381; qualifying distributions, $3,259,175.
Limitations: Giving primarily in Newport County, RI.
Publications: Annual report (including application guidelines), grants list.
Application information: Call or write for complete guidelines. Application form required.
Officers and Directors:* John A. van Beuren,* Chair. and Treas.; Barbara van Beuren,* Pres. and Exec. Dir.; Hope Hill van Beuren,* V.P.; Leonard Boehner, Secy.; Andrea van Beuren, Archbold D. van Beuren.
EIN: 222773769
Codes: FD

48752
Dorot Foundation
439 Benefit St.
Providence, RI 02903 (401) 351-8866
E-mail: info@dorot.org; URL: http://www.dorot.org
Contact: Ernest S. Frerichs, Exec. Dir.

Incorporated in 1958 in NY as Joy and Samuel Ungerleider Foundation.
Donor(s): Joy G. Ungerleider-Mayerson,‡ D.S. and R.H. Gottesman Foundation.
Financial data (yr. ended 03/31/01): Grants paid, $2,877,927; assets, $49,662,944 (M); gifts received, $2,683,031; expenditures, $4,299,352; qualifying distributions, $3,780,929.
Limitations: Applications not accepted. Giving primarily in the U.S.; some giving also in Israel.
Application information: Contributes only to pre-selected organizations. Does not accept unsolicited requests for funds.
Officers and Directors:* Jeane Ungerleider,* Pres.; Steven Ungerleider,* V.P.; Steven Baum, Secy. and Treas.; Ernest S. Frerichs, Exec. Dir.
EIN: 136116927
Codes: FD, FM, GTI

48753
Citizens Charitable Foundation
c/o Citizens Bank of Rhode Island
870 Westminster St.
Providence, RI 02903 (401) 456-7285
Application Address: 1 Citizens Plz., Providence, RI 02903; FAX: (401) 456-7366
Contact: D. Faye Sanders, Tr.

Established in 1967 in RI.
Donor(s): Citizens Savings Bank, Citizens Trust Co., Citizens Bank of Rhode Island.
Financial data (yr. ended 12/31/01): Grants paid, $2,749,785; assets, $10,650,030 (M); gifts received, $526,135; expenditures, $2,816,513; qualifying distributions, $2,780,376.
Limitations: Giving limited to RI.
Application information: Employee-related scholarships are administered directly by the schools receiving funds from the foundation. Application form not required.
Trustees: Lawrence K. Fish, Mark J. Formica, D. Faye Sanders, Citizens Bank of Rhode Island.
EIN: 056022653
Codes: CS, FD, CD

48754
The Hassenfeld Foundation
1011 Newport Ave.
Pawtucket, RI 02861

Established in 1944 in RI.
Donor(s): Hasbro, Inc., Stephen Hassenfeld Charitable Lead Trust, and members of the Hassenfeld family.
Financial data (yr. ended 12/31/00): Grants paid, $2,184,311; assets, $15,002,312 (M); gifts received, $1,817,267; expenditures, $2,270,613; qualifying distributions, $2,196,311.
Limitations: Applications not accepted.
Application information: Contributes only to pre-selected organizations.
Officers and Director:* Sylvia K. Hassenfeld,* Pres.; Alan G. Hassenfeld, V.P. and Treas.; Ellen Block, Secy.
EIN: 056015373
Codes: FD, FM

48755
The Thomas J. Watson Foundation
293 S. Main St.
Providence, RI 02903-2910 (401) 274-1952
FAX: (401) 274-1954; *URL:* http://www.watsonfellowship.org
Contact: Dr. Tori Haring-Smith, Exec. Dir.

Trust established in 1961 in NY.
Donor(s): Jeannette K. Watson,‡ Arthur K. Watson,‡ Thomas J. Watson, Jr.,‡ Mrs. John N. Irwin II,‡ Helen W. Buckner.‡
Financial data (yr. ended 05/31/99): Grants paid, $1,996,692; assets, $71,086,222 (M); expenditures, $2,941,660; qualifying distributions, $2,441,568.
Publications: Informational brochure.
Application information: Applicants for fellowships must be nominated by a participating private college or university and must be a graduating senior; other grants are initiated by the foundation; independent applications not accepted. Application form required.
Officers and Advisory Committee:* Tori Haring-Smith, Exec. Dir.; David McKinney,* Exec. Secy.; Elizabeth Buckner, Walker G. Buckner, Jr., John N. Irwin III, Daniel L. Mosley, Thomas J. Watson III.
Trustee: J.P. Morgan & Co. Incorporated.
EIN: 136038151
Codes: FD, GTI

48756
McAdams Charitable Foundation
320 S. Main St.
Providence, RI 02903

Established in 1992 in RI.
Donor(s): Norman Estes McCulloch, Jr., Microfibres, Inc.
Financial data (yr. ended 12/31/99): Grants paid, $1,778,633; assets, $25,124,768 (M); gifts received, $250,000; expenditures, $2,015,068; qualifying distributions, $1,898,165.
Limitations: Applications not accepted. Giving primarily in RI.
Application information: Contributes only to pre-selected organizations.
Officers and Trustees:* Norman Estes McCulloch, Jr.,* Pres. and Treas.; Dorothy R. McCulloch,* V.P.; Robert S. Davis, Richard Ramsden.
EIN: 050468638
Codes: FD

48757
The Frank Loomis Palmer Fund
c/o Fleet Private Clients Group
P.O. Box 6767
Providence, RI 02940-6767
Application address: 777 Main St., Hartford, CT 06115, tel.: (860) 986-7696
Contact: Marjorie Alexandre Davis

Trust established in 1936 in CT.
Donor(s): Virginia Palmer.‡
Financial data (yr. ended 07/31/01): Grants paid, $1,647,315; assets, $37,157,503 (M); expenditures, $1,900,351; qualifying distributions, $1,759,364.
Limitations: Giving limited to New London, CT.
Publications: Informational brochure (including application guidelines).
Application information: Application form required.
Trustee: Fleet National Bank.
EIN: 066026043
Codes: FD

48758
The Feinstein Foundation, Inc.
41 Alhambra Cir.
Cranston, RI 02905
Contact: Alan Shawn Feinstein, Pres.

Established in 1991 in RI.
Donor(s): Alan Shawn Feinstein.
Financial data (yr. ended 12/31/00): Grants paid, $1,509,816; assets, $36,256,264 (M); gifts received, $135,741; expenditures, $1,952,211; qualifying distributions, $1,910,738.
Limitations: Applications not accepted.
Application information: Contributes only to pre-selected organizations.
Officer and Directors:* Alan Shawn Feinstein,* Pres.; J. Troy Earhart, Beverly S. Vale, Edward Walton.
EIN: 223142312
Codes: FD

48759
Iorio Family Foundation
c/o Fleet Private Clients Group
P.O. Box 6767
Providence, RI 02940-6767

Established in 1993 in MA.
Financial data (yr. ended 10/31/01): Grants paid, $1,450,000; assets, $3,306,830 (M); expenditures, $1,467,162; qualifying distributions, $1,460,574.
Limitations: Applications not accepted. Giving primarily in MA.
Application information: Contributes only to pre-selected organizations.
Trustee: Fleet National Bank.
EIN: 046745180
Codes: FD

48760
Hasbro Charitable Trust, Inc.
(Formerly Hasbro Industries Charitable Trust, Inc.)
c/o Hasbro, Inc.
1027 Newport Ave.
Pawtucket, RI 02862 (401) 727-5429
URL: http://www.hasbro.org
Contact: Karen Davis, Dir.

Established in 1984 in RI.
Donor(s): Hasbro, Inc.
Financial data (yr. ended 12/31/01): Grants paid, $1,371,085; assets, $1,365,927 (M); gifts received, $1,150,200; expenditures, $1,092,517; qualifying distributions, $1,398,793.
Limitations: Giving primarily in Vernon Hills, IL, Springfield, MA, RI, Seattle, WA, and areas of major company operations.
Publications: Application guidelines, corporate giving report, informational brochure.
Application information: Application form required.
Officers: Alan G. Hassenfeld, Pres.; Richard B. Holt, Sr. V.P. and Cont.; Alfred J. Verrecchia, C.O.O.
Director: Karen Davis.
EIN: 222538470
Codes: CS, FD, CD

48761
FM Global Foundation
(Formerly Allendale Insurance Foundation)
1301 Atwood Ave.
P.O. Box 7500
Johnston, RI 02919
Contact: Gail Russell

Established in 1986 in RI.
Donor(s): Allendale Mutual Insurance Co.
Financial data (yr. ended 12/31/01): Grants paid, $1,369,058; assets, $2,744,522 (M); gifts received, $3,003,000; expenditures, $1,455,731; qualifying distributions, $1,339,404.
Limitations: Applications not accepted. Giving on a national basis.
Publications: Financial statement.
Application information: Contributes only to pre-selected organizations.
Officers: Shivan S. Subramaniam, Chair., C.E.O. and Pres.; William A. Mekrut, Treas.
Directors: Norman D. Baker, Jr., John M. Lemieux, Nelson G. Wester.
Trustee: Investors Bank and Trust.
EIN: 222773230
Codes: CS, FD, CD

48762
Shriners of Rhode Island Charities Trust
(Formerly Palestine Temple Charities Trust)
1 Rhodes Pl.
Cranston, RI 02905 (401) 737-7100
Contact: A. Sheffield Reynolds, Treas.

Established in 1993 in RI.
Donor(s): Abbey Francis Lawton, Hodges-Lawton Charities.
Financial data (yr. ended 12/31/01): Grants paid, $1,197,510; assets, $22,550,137 (M); gifts received, $137,124; expenditures, $1,356,147; qualifying distributions, $1,196,329.
Limitations: Giving primarily in RI.
Officer: A. Sheffield Reynolds, Treas.
Trustees: Morphis A. Jamiel, George Nelson, John Takian, Jr.
EIN: 223191072
Codes: FD, GTI

48763
Vera J. Clark Irrevocable Trust
P.O. Box 6767
Providence, RI 02940-6767

Financial data (yr. ended 12/31/01): Grants paid, $1,086,199; assets, $4,833,372 (M); expenditures, $1,127,116; qualifying distributions, $1,109,990.
Limitations: Giving primarily in NY and RI.
Trustee: Fleet National Bank.
EIN: 056126789
Codes: FD

48764
Bonnie and Donald Dwares Charitable Foundation
750 School St.
Pawtucket, RI 02860

Established in 1998 in RI.
Financial data (yr. ended 06/30/01): Grants paid, $1,000,000; assets, $249,075 (M); gifts received, $1,166,515; expenditures, $1,000,000; qualifying distributions, $999,213.
Limitations: Applications not accepted. Giving primarily in Boston, MA.
Application information: Contributes only to pre-selected organizations.
Trustees: Bonnie Dwares, David Dwares, Donald Dwares.
EIN: 050507748
Codes: FD

48765
Elizabeth Peters Binney Charitable Trust
c/o Fleet Private Clients Group
P.O. Box 6767
Providence, RI 02940-6767

Established in 1961 in MA.
Financial data (yr. ended 05/31/01): Grants paid, $999,972; assets, $21,493,386 (M); expenditures, $1,148,324; qualifying distributions, $1,069,712.
Limitations: Applications not accepted. Giving primarily in OR.

48765—RHODE ISLAND

Application information: Contributes only to pre-selected organizations.
Trustee: Fleet National Bank.
EIN: 046020266
Codes: FD

48766
Russell Grinnell Memorial Trust
c/o Fleet National Bank
P.O. Box 6767
Providence, RI 02940-6767

Established in 1998 in RI.
Financial data (yr. ended 12/31/01): Grants paid, $792,099; assets, $17,640,955 (M); expenditures, $898,491; qualifying distributions, $855,960.
Limitations: Applications not accepted.
Application information: Contributes only to pre-selected organizations.
Trustee: Fleet National Bank.
EIN: 311603440
Codes: FD

48767
The Carter Family Charitable Trust
P.O. Box 41119
Providence, RI 02940-1119
Contact: John S. Carter, and Letitia Carter, Trustees

Established in 1991 in RI.
Donor(s): Letitia M. Carter, John S. Carter, Jr.
Financial data (yr. ended 06/30/01): Grants paid, $790,009; assets, $10,952,212 (M); gifts received, $9,419,212; expenditures, $822,858; qualifying distributions, $790,009.
Limitations: Giving primarily in RI.
Trustees: John S. Carter, Jr., Letitia M. Carter.
EIN: 056093256
Codes: FD

48768
Amica Companies Foundation
100 Amica Way
Lincoln, RI 02865 (800) 652-6422
Contact: Mary Q. Williamson, V.P.

Established in 1997 in RI.
Donor(s): Amica Mutual Insurance Co.
Financial data (yr. ended 12/31/01): Grants paid, $786,371; assets, $12,826,816 (M); expenditures, $831,851; qualifying distributions, $777,184.
Limitations: Giving on a national basis.
Publications: Financial statement, grants list.
Application information: Application form not required.
Officers and Directors:* Thomas A. Taylor,* Pres.; Peter F. Goldbecker, Secy.; Robert A. DiMuccio, Treas.; Jeffrey P. Aiken, Patricia W. Chadwick, Andrew M. Erickson, Robert R. Faulkner, Peter B. Freeman, Barry G. Hittner, Ronald K. Machtley, Lowell C. Smith, Cheryl W. Snead, Henry S. Woodbridge, Jr.
EIN: 050493445
Codes: CS, FD, CD

48769
The Chace Fund, Inc.
1 Providence Washington Plz.
Providence, RI 02903
Contact: Malcolm G. Chace, Pres.

Established in 1947 in RI.
Donor(s): Malcolm G. Chace III, Arnold B. Chace, Berkshire Hathaway, Inc., Kathleen Osborne,‡ Beatrice O. Chace.‡
Financial data (yr. ended 12/31/01): Grants paid, $768,176; assets, $5,681,358 (M); gifts received, $93,049; expenditures, $807,623; qualifying distributions, $768,176.
Limitations: Giving primarily in MA, NY, and RI.

Officers and Directors:* Malcolm G. Chace,* Pres.; Arnold B. Chace, Jr.,* V.P.; Thomas E. Gardiner, Secy.-Treas.; Malcolm G. Chace, Jr.
EIN: 056008849
Codes: FD

48770
Marion Gardner Jackson Charitable Trust
c/o Fleet Private Clients Group
P.O. Box 6767
Providence, RI 02940-6767
Application address: c/o Fleet National Bank, 100 Federal St., Boston, MA 02110
Contact: Nathaniel Murphy

Established in 1968.
Financial data (yr. ended 12/31/01): Grants paid, $688,684; assets, $11,735,466 (M); expenditures, $759,906; qualifying distributions, $731,840.
Limitations: Giving primarily in Adams County, IL.
Application information: Application form not required.
Trustee: Fleet National Bank.
EIN: 046010559
Codes: FD

48771
CVS Charitable Trust, Inc.
(Formerly CVS Corporation Foundation)
1 CVS Dr.
Woonsocket, RI 02895

Established in 1992 in MA and DE.
Donor(s): Melville Corp., CVS Corp.
Financial data (yr. ended 09/30/01): Grants paid, $610,470; assets, $48,685,112 (M); gifts received, $48,810,769; expenditures, $610,470; qualifying distributions, $606,646.
Limitations: Giving limited to areas of company operations.
Application information: Application form required.
Officers and Directors:* David B. Rickard,* Pres.; Michael K. Golub, V.P.; John R. Kramer,* V.P.; Rosemary Mead, V.P.; Zenon P. Lankowsky, Secy.; Larry D. Solberg, Treas.; Thomas M. Ryan.
EIN: 223206973
Codes: CS, FD, CD, GTI

48772
Frank R. Peters Trust
c/o Fleet National Bank
P.O. Box 6767
Providence, RI 02940-6767
Application address: c/o Fleet National Bank, Charitable Trust Group, P.O. Box 1890, 01-05-04, Boston, MA 02105
Contact: Sharon M. Driscoll, Comm. Secy.

Established in 1935 in MA.
Financial data (yr. ended 12/31/01): Grants paid, $605,000; assets, $9,918,114 (M); expenditures, $699,425; qualifying distributions, $635,088.
Limitations: Giving limited to the greater Boston, MA, area.
Application information: Application form not required.
Trustee: Fleet National Bank.
EIN: 046012009
Codes: FD

48773
Bafflin Foundation
1500 Fleet Ctr.
Providence, RI 02903-2319
Contact: Paul A. Silver, Secy.

Established in 1990 in RI.
Donor(s): Lois Orswell.
Financial data (yr. ended 12/31/01): Grants paid, $580,000; assets, $20,808,981 (M); gifts received,

$537,499; expenditures, $773,191; qualifying distributions, $617,232.
Application information: Application form not required.
Officers and Directors:* Paul A. Silver,* Secy.; Michael M. Edwards,* Treas.
EIN: 050454795
Codes: FD

48774
The Harold Brooks Foundation
c/o Fleet Private Clients Group
P.O. Box 6767
Providence, RI 02940-6767
Application address: c/o Emma Greene, 100 Federal St., Boston, MA 02110; tel.: (617) 434-0329

Established in 1984.
Donor(s): Harold Brooks.‡
Financial data (yr. ended 12/31/01): Grants paid, $575,975; assets, $10,436,645 (M); expenditures, $678,470; qualifying distributions, $657,319.
Limitations: Giving limited to MA, with emphasis on the South Shore area.
Publications: Application guidelines.
Application information: Application form not required.
Trustees: Arthur R. Connelly, Rev. M. James Workman, Fleet National Bank.
EIN: 046043983
Codes: FD

48775
Charles E. & Caroline J. Adams Trust
(Formerly Frank W. and Carl S. Adams Memorial Fund)
c/o Fleet Private Clients Group
P.O. Box 6767
Providence, RI 02940-6767
Application address: c/o Fleet National Bank, attn.: Charitable Trust Svcs., 100 Federal St., Boston, MA 02110

Established in 1955 in MA.
Donor(s): Charles E. Adams,‡ Caroline J. Adams.‡
Financial data (yr. ended 05/31/01): Grants paid, $550,511; assets, $15,683,700 (M); expenditures, $815,954; qualifying distributions, $699,422.
Limitations: Giving primarily in Boston, MA.
Trustee: Fleet National Bank.
EIN: 046011995
Codes: FD

48776
Jacob F. & Wilma S. Schoellkopf Fund
c/o Fleet Private Clients Group
P.O. Box 6767
Providence, RI 02940-6767

Financial data (yr. ended 09/30/01): Grants paid, $525,000; assets, $14,408,432 (M); expenditures, $554,571; qualifying distributions, $525,000.
Limitations: Applications not accepted. Giving in the U.S. and Germany.
Application information: Contributes only to pre-selected organizations.
Trustee: Fleet National Bank.
EIN: 046008242
Codes: FD

48777
The Alperin/Hirsch Family Foundation
(Formerly The Alperin Foundation)
327 Pine St.
Pawtucket, RI 02860 (401) 725-3880
Contact: Melvin Alperin, Tr.

Established in 1956 in RI.
Donor(s): Members of the Alperin family.

Financial data (yr. ended 04/30/01): Grants paid, $524,668; assets, $6,817,775 (M); expenditures, $504,282; qualifying distributions, $519,008.
Limitations: Giving primarily in MA, NY, and RI.
Trustees: Barry Alperin, Melvin Alperin, David Hirsch, Hope L. Hirsch.
EIN: 056008387
Codes: FD

48778
Roosa Family Foundation Trust
P.O. Box 6767
Providence, RI 02940-6767
Application address: 65 LaSalle Rd., West Hartford, CT 06017, tel.: (860) 586-7257
Contact: Cathy Iacovazzi

Established in 1994 in CT.
Financial data (yr. ended 12/31/01): Grants paid, $521,929; assets, $8,319,019 (M); expenditures, $603,140; qualifying distributions, $570,564.
Limitations: Giving primarily in CT and RI.
Trustee: Fleet National Bank.
EIN: 223295175
Codes: FD

48779
TriMix Foundation
5784 Post Rd., Ste. 5
Warwick, RI 02818-2139 (401) 885-4680
Contact: Lynn C. Zarrella

Established in 1997 in RI.
Donor(s): David P. Mixer, Gail S. Mixer.
Financial data (yr. ended 12/31/01): Grants paid, $479,430; assets, $4,273,645 (M); expenditures, $543,743; qualifying distributions, $541,433.
Limitations: Giving primarily in MA and RI.
Application information: Application form not required.
Officers: Gail S. Mixer, Pres.; Matthew A. Thibault, Secy.; Arthur X. Duffy, Treas.
Trustees: Deborah Kazlauskas, Brian Mixer, David P. Mixer.
EIN: 050494244
Codes: FD

48780
Nan and Matilda Heydt Fund
c/o Fleet Private Clients Group
P.O. Box 6767
Providence, RI 02940-6767
Application address: c/o Fleet National Bank, One Monarch Pl., Springfield, MA 01101
Contact: Thea Katsounakis

Established in 1966 in MA.
Donor(s): Matilda L. Heydt.‡
Financial data (yr. ended 12/31/01): Grants paid, $477,283; assets, $5,973,467 (M); expenditures, $528,237; qualifying distributions, $508,975.
Limitations: Giving limited to Hampden and Hampshire counties, MA.
Publications: Informational brochure (including application guidelines).
Application information: Application form required.
Trustee: Fleet National Bank.
EIN: 046136421
Codes: FD

48781
The Papitto Foundation
50 Kennedy Plz., Ste. 1250
Providence, RI 02903-2360

Established in 1986 in RI; absorbed the Ralph R. Papitto Foundation and the Nortek Foundation in 1990.
Donor(s): Ralph R. Papitto, Nortek, Inc., Carl H. Rosati, Jr.

Financial data (yr. ended 12/31/01): Grants paid, $474,474; assets, $5,298,943 (M); expenditures, $504,434; qualifying distributions, $473,834.
Limitations: Applications not accepted. Giving primarily in RI, with emphasis on Providence.
Application information: Contributes only to pre-selected organizations.
Officers and Directors:* Ralph R. Papitto, Pres. and Treas.; David Papitto,* V.P.; Virginia P. Johnson, Secy.; Barbara A. Papitto.
Trustees: Andrea Crump, Aurelia J. Papitto.
EIN: 050426569
Codes: FD

48782
Earle P. Charlton, Jr. Discretionary Charitable Trust
(Formerly Earle P. Charlton, Jr. Charitable Trust)
c/o Fleet National Bank
P.O. Box 6767
Providence, RI 02940-6767
Application address: 100 Federal St., Boston, MA 02110, tel.: (617) 434-0330
Contact: Nathaniel Murphy

Trust established in 1973 in MA.
Donor(s): Earle P. Charlton, Jr.‡
Financial data (yr. ended 12/31/01): Grants paid, $442,480; assets, $8,591,373 (M); expenditures, $513,494; qualifying distributions, $472,054.
Limitations: Giving primarily in Boston and Fall River, MA.
Trustees: E.P. Charlton II, Alfred W. Fuller, Fleet National Bank.
EIN: 046334412
Codes: FD

48783
Henry C. Lord Scholarship Fund Trust
c/o Citizens Bank
870 Westminster St.
Providence, RI 02903
Application address: c/o Citizens Bank New Hampshire, 875 Elm St., NE4-06 Manchester, NH 03101, tel.: (603) 634-7749
Contact: Verna Pare, V.P. and Trust Off.

Trust established in 1978 in NH.
Donor(s): Henry C. Lord.‡
Financial data (yr. ended 06/30/01): Grants paid, $442,394; assets, $13,131,452 (M); expenditures, $600,389; qualifying distributions, $494,376.
Limitations: Giving limited to NH residents.
Application information: Application form required.
Trustee: Citizens Bank New Hampshire.
EIN: 026051741
Codes: FD, GTI

48784
George Dudley Seymour Trust
c/o Fleet Private Client's Group
P.O. Box 6767
Providence, RI 02940-6767
Application address: c/o Fleet National Bank, 777 Main St., Hartford, CT 06115
Contact: Peter Weston, V.P., Fleet National Bank

Established in 1986 in CT.
Financial data (yr. ended 07/31/01): Grants paid, $440,000; assets, $6,455,802 (M); expenditures, $511,165; qualifying distributions, $471,020.
Limitations: Giving limited to CT.
Trustee: Fleet National Bank.
EIN: 066021772
Codes: FD

48785
The Washington Trust Charitable Foundation
c/o The Washington Trust Co.
23 Broad St.
Westerly, RI 02891
Contact: John C. Warren

Established in 1994 in RI.
Donor(s): The Washington Trust Co.
Financial data (yr. ended 12/31/01): Grants paid, $418,000; assets, $1,152,535 (M); gifts received, $355,780; expenditures, $427,033; qualifying distributions, $416,229.
Limitations: Giving primarily in New England, with emphasis on CT and RI.
Trustee: The Washington Trust Co.
EIN: 050477294
Codes: CS, FD, CD

48786
Warren Alpert Foundation
27 Warren Way
P.O. Box 72743
Providence, RI 02907

Established in 1986 in RI.
Donor(s): Warren Alpert, Warren Equities, Inc.
Financial data (yr. ended 12/31/01): Grants paid, $395,500; assets, $1,023,201 (L); gifts received, $240,000; expenditures, $482,995; qualifying distributions, $482,995.
Limitations: Giving primarily in the Northeast.
Application information: Unsolicited applications from individuals not accepted.
Officers: Warren Alpert, Pres.; Edward M. Cosgrove, V.P.; Herbert Kaplan, V.P.; Jeffrey Walker, Secy.; John Dziedzic, Treas.
EIN: 050426623
Codes: FD, GTI

48787
Mabel A. Horne Fund
c/o Fleet National Bank
P.O. Box 6767
Providence, RI 02940-6767
Application address: c/o Fleet Bank Charitable Trust Comm., Fleet National Bank, P.O. Box 1890, Boston, MA 02105, tel.: (617) 434-3768
Contact: Ms. Sharon M. Driscoll, Committee Secy., Fleet National Bank

Trust established in 1964 in MA.
Donor(s): Mabel A. Horne.‡
Financial data (yr. ended 09/30/01): Grants paid, $394,500; assets, $6,341,745 (M); expenditures, $462,861; qualifying distributions, $412,951.
Limitations: Giving limited to MA, with emphasis on Boston, Cambridge and Somerville.
Publications: Application guidelines.
Application information: Application form required.
Trustee: Fleet National Bank.
EIN: 046089241
Codes: FD

48788
The Elms Foundation
c/o Doris J. Licht
1500 Fleet Ctr.
Providence, RI 02903
Application address: 70 Harwich Rd., Providence, RI 02903
Contact: Stanley Goldstein, Pres.

Established in 1989 in RI.
Donor(s): Stanley P. Goldstein.
Financial data (yr. ended 12/31/01): Grants paid, $393,076; assets, $3,980,965 (M); expenditures, $461,049; qualifying distributions, $403,377.
Limitations: Giving primarily in NY and RI.

48788—RHODE ISLAND

Officers and Directors:* Stanley P. Goldstein,* Pres. and Treas.; Merle F. Goldstein,* Secy.; Eugene S. Goldstein, Larry M. Goldstein, Doris J. Licht.
EIN: 050450051
Codes: FD

48789
Cuno Foundation
c/o Fleet Private Clients Group
P.O. Box 6767
Providence, RI 02940-6767
Application address: c/o Trudy Magnolia, Secy., Fleet National Bank, 18 Devon Ct., Meriden, CT 06450

Established in 1948 in CT.
Donor(s): Frank Davelia.
Financial data (yr. ended 12/31/01): Grants paid, $381,547; assets, $10,191,334 (M); gifts received, $1,002,000; expenditures, $814,755; qualifying distributions, $433,206.
Limitations: Giving primarily to residents of the Meriden, CT, area.
Application information: Application form not required.
Trustee: Fleet National Bank.
EIN: 066033040
Codes: FD, GTI

48790
The Mann Family Foundation
50 Channing Ave.
Providence, RI 02906
Contact: Robert Mann, Pres.

Established in 1996 in RI.
Donor(s): Robert Mann, Leon Mann, Carol Mann.
Financial data (yr. ended 12/31/01): Grants paid, $358,367; assets, $852,914 (M); gifts received, $300,878; expenditures, $369,790; qualifying distributions, $358,287.
Limitations: Applications not accepted. Giving limited to RI.
Application information: Contributes only to pre-selected organizations.
Officers and Trustees:* Robert Mann,* Pres. and Treas.; Leon Mann,* Secy.; Carol Mann.
EIN: 050494136
Codes: FD

48791
The Roy T. Morgan Foundation
c/o Armstrong Gibbons
155 S. Main St.
Providence, RI 02903

Established in 1976 in RI.
Donor(s): Roy T. Morgan.‡
Financial data (yr. ended 03/31/01): Grants paid, $327,800; assets, $4,284,833 (M); expenditures, $382,600; qualifying distributions, $365,347.
Limitations: Applications not accepted. Giving primarily in New England.
Application information: Contributes only to pre-selected organizations.
Trustees: Russell S. Boles, Walter F. Gibbons, Joseph Kinder.
EIN: 050368103
Codes: FD

48792
Catherine McCarthy Memorial Trust Fund
c/o Fleet Private Clients Group
P.O. Box 6767
Providence, RI 02940-6767
Contact: Thomas F. Caffrey, Tr.

Established in 1984 in MA.
Donor(s): John J. McCarthy.‡

Financial data (yr. ended 06/30/01): Grants paid, $316,119; assets, $5,235,249 (M); expenditures, $399,009; qualifying distributions, $367,172.
Limitations: Giving primarily in MA, with emphasis on the greater Lawrence area.
Publications: Application guidelines.
Application information: A personal interview may be requested after the receipt of a written application. Application form not required.
Trustees: Thomas F. Caffrey, Fleet National Bank.
EIN: 222549008
Codes: FD

48793
The Samuel Rapaporte, Jr. Foundation
c/o Rosenstein, Halper & Maselli, LLP
27 Dryden Ln.
Providence, RI 02904-2728

Trust established in 1946 in RI.
Donor(s): Samuel Rapaporte, Jr., Renee Burrows.
Financial data (yr. ended 11/30/01): Grants paid, $307,725; assets, $5,549,720 (M); expenditures, $341,035; qualifying distributions, $320,387.
Limitations: Applications not accepted. Giving primarily in MA and RI.
Application information: Contributes only to pre-selected organizations. Unsolicited requests for funds not accepted.
Trustee: Renee Burrows.
EIN: 056006254
Codes: FD

48794
Marjorie Moore Charitable Foundation Trust
c/o Fleet Private Clients Group
P.O. Box 6767
Providence, RI 02940-6767 (860) 986-7696
Application address: 777 Main St., Hartford, CT 06115, tel.: (860) 986-7696
Contact: Marjorie Davis, Trust Off., Fleet National Bank

Established in 1958 in CT.
Donor(s): Marjorie Moore.‡
Financial data (yr. ended 07/31/02): Grants paid, $307,457; assets, $3,207,245 (M); expenditures, $339,393; qualifying distributions, $327,715.
Limitations: Giving limited to Berlin and Kensington, CT.
Publications: Informational brochure (including application guidelines).
Application information: Application form required.
Trustee: Fleet National Bank.
EIN: 066050196
Codes: FD

48795
The Robertson Foundation
c/o Stephen Hamblett
66 Williams St.
Providence, RI 02906 (401) 277-7965

Established in 1994 in RI.
Donor(s): Stephen Hamblett.
Financial data (yr. ended 12/31/01): Grants paid, $300,065; assets, $3,535,861 (M); expenditures, $338,539; qualifying distributions, $299,554.
Limitations: Giving primarily in Providence, RI.
Officers and Directors:* Stephen Hamblett,* Pres. and Treas.; Jocelin G. Hamblett,* V.P. and Secy.; Paul P. St. Onge.
EIN: 050481538
Codes: FD

48796
Galkin Private Foundation
155 Brookside Ave.
West Warwick, RI 02893

Established in 1996 in RI.
Donor(s): Robert T. Galkin, Warren B. Galkin.
Financial data (yr. ended 12/31/99): Grants paid, $296,780; assets, $709,024 (M); gifts received, $344,971; expenditures, $299,622; qualifying distributions, $294,325.
Limitations: Applications not accepted. Giving primarily in RI.
Application information: Contributes only to pre-selected organizations.
Officers: Robert T. Galkin, Pres.; Steven Rosenbaum, Secy.; Warren B. Galkin, Treas.
EIN: 050494243
Codes: FD

48797
F. B. Hazard General Charity Fund
P.O. Box 6767
Providence, RI 02940-6767
Application address: c/o Augusta Haydock, Fleet National Bank, 100 Federal St., Boston, MA 02110

Financial data (yr. ended 12/31/01): Grants paid, $293,480; assets, $5,426,127 (M); expenditures, $336,542; qualifying distributions, $319,078.
Limitations: Giving primarily in Providence, RI.
Application information: Application form required.
Trustee: Fleet National Bank.
EIN: 056004659
Codes: FD

48798
Alice I. Sullivan Charitable Trust
162 Middle St.
Pawtucket, RI 02860

Established in 1997 in RI.
Financial data (yr. ended 12/31/01): Grants paid, $288,537; assets, $233,335 (M); gifts received, $700; expenditures, $308,723; qualifying distributions, $308,557.
Trustees: John Galvin, Daniel J. Sullivan, Sr., Daniel J. Sullivan, Jr.
EIN: 050494296
Codes: FD

48799
The Joseph S. and Rosalyn K. Sinclair Family Foundation
170 Westminster St.
Providence, RI 02903
FAX: (401) 331-5636
Contact: Gail P. Fraser-Giacchi, Off. Mgr.

Established in 1978.
Donor(s): Joseph S. Sinclair, Rosalyn K. Sinclair.
Financial data (yr. ended 09/30/01): Grants paid, $283,191; assets, $3,764,861 (M); expenditures, $310,913; qualifying distributions, $280,257.
Limitations: Applications not accepted. Giving primarily in New England, with emphasis on MA and RI.
Application information: Contributes only to pre-selected organizations.
Officers: Joseph S. Sinclair, Pres.; Rosalyn K. Sinclair, V.P.; Alan M. Gilstein, Treas.
EIN: 050380039
Codes: FD

48800
Citizens Community Foundation
c/o Citizens Bank of Rhode Island
870 Westminster St.
Providence, RI 02903
Application address: c/o D. Faye Sanders, Citizens Bank of Rhode Island, 1 Citizens Plz., Providence, RI 02903, tel.: (401) 456-7285

Established around 1969.
Donor(s): Citizens Financial Group, Inc.
Financial data (yr. ended 10/31/01): Grants paid, $271,533; assets, $6,310,002 (M); expenditures, $310,963; qualifying distributions, $291,248.
Limitations: Giving limited to RI.
Trustee: Citizens Bank of Rhode Island.
Distribution Committee: Levi Adams, Brian Cavanagh, Karen Jesup, Robert Marsello, Hon. O. Rogeriee Thompson.
EIN: 056035997
Codes: CS, FD, CD

48801
Harry Hartman Trust
c/o Fleet Private Clients Group
P.O. Box 6767
Providence, RI 02940-6767

Financial data (yr. ended 12/31/00): Grants paid, $266,997; assets, $4,734,587 (M); expenditures, $314,222; qualifying distributions, $290,393.
Limitations: Applications not accepted. Giving primarily in NJ; some funding also in FL.
Application information: Contributes only to pre-selected organizations.
Trustee: Fleet National Bank.
EIN: 226302588
Codes: FD

48802
Edward Wagner and George Hosser Scholarship Fund Trust
c/o Citizens Bank
870 Westminster St.
Providence, RI 02903
Application address: c/o Citizens Bank New Hampshire, 875 Elm St. NE4-06, Manchester, NH 03101, tel.: (603) 634-7749
Contact: Verna Pare, V.P. and Trust Off.

Trust established in 1964 in NH.
Donor(s): Ottilie Wagner Hosser.‡
Financial data (yr. ended 06/30/01): Grants paid, $260,803; assets, $6,856,678 (M); expenditures, $320,259; qualifying distributions, $282,229.
Limitations: Giving limited to residents of Manchester, NH.
Application information: Application form required.
Trustee: Citizens Bank New Hampshire.
EIN: 026005491
Codes: FD, GTI

48803
The Koffler Family Foundation
c/o The Koffler Group
1 Providence Washington Plz., 9th Fl.
Providence, RI 02903

Established in 1978 in RI.
Donor(s): The Koffler Corp., Lillian Koffler.
Financial data (yr. ended 07/31/01): Grants paid, $258,823; assets, $5,135,114 (M); expenditures, $306,041; qualifying distributions, $258,823.
Limitations: Applications not accepted. Giving primarily in RI.
Application information: Contributes only to pre-selected organizations.
Trustees: Richard S. Bornstein, Lillian Koffler.
EIN: 050376269
Codes: FD

48804
The Irving and Edyth S. Usen Family Charitable Foundation
c/o Fleet Private Clients Group
P.O. Box 6767
Providence, RI 02940-6767
Application address: c/o Fleet National Bank, 100 Federal St., Boston, MA 02110
Contact: Voralak Suwanvanichk

Established in 1992 in MA.
Financial data (yr. ended 04/30/02): Grants paid, $250,500; assets, $3,993,572 (M); expenditures, $288,920; qualifying distributions, $273,081.
Limitations: Giving primarily in the greater Boston, MA, area.
Trustees: Sumner Bernstein, Richard Usen, Robert Usen.
Agent: Fleet National Bank.
EIN: 046708737
Codes: FD

48805
The Darrell & Susan Ross Charitable Foundation
290 Irving Ave.
Providence, RI 02906
Application address: c/o Stephen J. Carlotti, Hinkley, Allen & Snyder, LLP, 1500 Fleet Center, Providence, RI 02903-2393, tel.: (401) 274-2000

Established in 2000 in RI.
Donor(s): Darrell S. Ross, Susan S. Ross.
Financial data (yr. ended 12/31/01): Grants paid, $250,000; assets, $3,637,597 (M); gifts received, $9,354; expenditures, $262,313; qualifying distributions, $250,000.
Trustees: Darrell S. Ross, Susan S. Ross.
EIN: 056125455

48806
Felicia Fund, Inc.
22 Parsonage St.
Providence, RI 02903 (401) 274-1550
Contact: Pauline C. Metcalf, Pres.

Established in 1985.
Donor(s): Pauline C. Metcalf.
Financial data (yr. ended 11/30/01): Grants paid, $233,400; assets, $5,036,082 (M); gifts received, $300,011; expenditures, $268,904; qualifying distributions, $228,162.
Limitations: Giving primarily in MA, NY, and RI.
Application information: Application form not required.
Officers and Trustees:* Pauline C. Metcalf,* Pres.; Frank Mauran,* Secy.; Paul W. Whyte,* Treas.; Christopher Monkhouse.
EIN: 050420703
Codes: FD2

48807
Arthur E. Thornton Trust
c/o Fleet National Bank
P.O. Box 6767
Providence, RI 02940-6767

Financial data (yr. ended 12/31/01): Grants paid, $232,802; assets, $5,098,505 (M); expenditures, $279,380; qualifying distributions, $259,637.
Limitations: Applications not accepted. Giving primarily in CT.
Application information: Contributes only to pre-selected organizations.
Trustee: Fleet National Bank.
EIN: 066445132
Codes: FD2

48808
L & E Dwinnell Charitable Trust
(Formerly Lane & Elizabeth C. Dwinnell Foundation)
c/o Fleet Investment Svcs.
P.O. Box 6767
Providence, RI 02940-6767

Established in 1997 in NH.
Donor(s): Lane Dwinnell.‡
Financial data (yr. ended 12/31/01): Grants paid, $231,094; assets, $4,368,311 (M); gifts received, $400,000; expenditures, $275,131; qualifying distributions, $257,325.
Limitations: Applications not accepted. Giving primarily in NH.
Application information: Contributes only to pre-selected organizations.
Advisory Committee: Pamela B. Bean, Channing T. Brown, Edwin D. Cushman, Garfield Miller, Benjamin Thompson, Jr.
Trustee: Fleet National Bank.
EIN: 161543787
Codes: FD2

48809
Shaughnessy Charitable Trust
(Formerly John J. and Mary E. Shaughnessy Charitable Trust)
P.O. Box 6767
Providence, RI 02940-6767

Established in 1988 in MA.
Donor(s): Shaughnessy Crane Service, Inc., John J. Shaughnessy, Shaughnessy & Ahearn Co., Mary E. Shaughnessy.
Financial data (yr. ended 08/31/01): Grants paid, $230,000; assets, $2,469,495 (M); gifts received, $50,000; expenditures, $260,142; qualifying distributions, $243,887.
Limitations: Applications not accepted. Giving limited to MA.
Application information: Contributes only to pre-selected organizations.
Trustee: Fleet National Bank.
EIN: 046595469
Codes: CS, FD2, CD

48810
The Cranston Foundation
c/o Cranston Fdn. Trustees
1381 Cranston St.
Cranston, RI 02920-6789 (401) 943-4800

Trust established in 1960 in RI.
Donor(s): Cranston Print Works Co.
Financial data (yr. ended 06/30/01): Grants paid, $220,283; assets, $14,226 (M); gifts received, $230,307; expenditures, $221,361; qualifying distributions, $220,283.
Limitations: Giving primarily in MA, NY, and RI.
Application information: Application form required for scholarships.
Trustees: Brian Adriance, B. Grandison, J. Menzies, G. Nickeson, C. Pietruszka, Frederic L. Rockefeller, George W. Shuster, S. Wollseiffen.
EIN: 056015348
Codes: CS, FD2, CD, GTI

48811
C. Pringle Charitable Foundation
(Formerly Charles G. Pringle Foundation)
c/o Fleet Private Client Group
P.O. Box 6767
Providence, RI 02940-6767
Application address: 11 Lawrence St., 6th Fl., Lawrence, MA 01840-1423
Contact: Patricia Karl, Tr.

Established in 1940 in MA.

48811—RHODE ISLAND

Financial data (yr. ended 10/31/01): Grants paid, $215,955; assets, $3,150,404 (M); gifts received, $676; expenditures, $250,421; qualifying distributions, $237,655.
Limitations: Giving primarily in Lawrence, MA.
Trustees: John F. Burke, Patricia Dowling, Patricia Karl, Robert O'Sullivan, Fleet National Bank.
EIN: 046020426
Codes: FD2, GTI

48812
Marguerite Magraw Trust
c/o Fleet Private Clients Group
P.O. Box 6767
Providence, RI 02940-6767
Scholarship application address: c/o Scholarship Comm., Fleet Private Clients Group, 777 Main St., Hartford, CT 06115
Contact: Peter Wilson

Established in 1975 in CT.
Financial data (yr. ended 06/30/01): Grants paid, $205,600; assets, $1,835,531 (M); expenditures, $227,472; qualifying distributions, $217,874.
Limitations: Giving limited to the Waterbury, CT, area.
Application information: Application form available from scholarship committee. Application form required.
Trustee: Fleet National Bank.
EIN: 066113177
Codes: FD2, GTI

48813
Florence Elliott Seeley Education Foundation
c/o Fleet Private Clients Group
P.O. Box 6767
Providence, RI 02940-6767

Established in 1998 in MA.
Financial data (yr. ended 08/31/01): Grants paid, $200,000; assets, $4,812,329 (M); expenditures, $261,683; qualifying distributions, $235,072.
Limitations: Applications not accepted. Giving primarily in MA.
Application information: Contributes only to pre-selected organizations.
Trustee: Fleet National Bank.
EIN: 043435338
Codes: FD2

48814
The Woodward Fund
c/o Fleet Private Clients Group
P.O. Box 6767
Providence, RI 02940-6767
Contact: S.A. Curtis, Jr.

Established in 1965 in NY.
Donor(s): Florence S. Woodward.
Financial data (yr. ended 11/30/01): Grants paid, $200,000; assets, $3,709,339 (M); expenditures, $204,509; qualifying distributions, $200,689.
Limitations: Applications not accepted. Giving primarily in AZ, CA, and ME.
Application information: Unsolicited requests for funds not accepted.
Trustee: Fleet National Bank.
EIN: 166064221
Codes: FD2

48815
Christine L. Beck Trust
P.O. Box 6767
Providence, RI 02940-6767
Application address: c/o Carol Gray, Fleet National Bank, 100 Federal St., Boston, MA 02110, tel.: (617) 434-3768

Established in 1998 in MA.

Financial data (yr. ended 12/31/01): Grants paid, $196,752; assets, $3,677,451 (M); expenditures, $235,063; qualifying distributions, $208,750.
Limitations: Giving primarily in MA, with emphasis on Clinton.
Trustee: Fleet National Bank.
EIN: 046427501
Codes: FD2

48816
Morey and Helen McCarthy Miller Scholarship Fund
c/o Fleet Private Clients Group
P.O. Box 6767
Providence, RI 02940-6767
Scholarship application address: c/o Beverly Cochran, 56 Valley View Ln., Vernon, CT 06066

Established in 1994 in CT.
Financial data (yr. ended 02/28/02): Grants paid, $192,552; assets, $3,544,015 (M); expenditures, $239,552; qualifying distributions, $213,272.
Limitations: Giving limited to Rockville, CT.
Application information: Application form required.
Trustee: Fleet National Bank.
EIN: 043222995
Codes: FD2, GTI

48817
Ira S. and Anna Galkin Charitable Trust
c/o Rosenstein, Halper & Maselli, LLP
27 Dryden Ln.
Providence, RI 02904 (401) 331-6851
Contact: Arnold T. Galkin, Tr.

Established in 1947 in RI.
Donor(s): Ira S. Galkin.
Financial data (yr. ended 12/31/01): Grants paid, $189,746; assets, $4,425,870 (M); expenditures, $211,117; qualifying distributions, $207,311.
Limitations: Giving primarily in RI.
Trustees: Arnold T. Galkin, Herbert S. Galkin, Irwin S. Galkin.
EIN: 056006231
Codes: FD2

48818
Imogene M. Maybury Trust
c/o Fleet Private Clients Group
P.O. Box 6767
Providence, RI 02940-6767
Application address: c/o Guidance Counselor, Dexter Regional High School, Dexter, ME 04930

Financial data (yr. ended 04/30/02): Grants paid, $189,400; assets, $3,191,101 (M); expenditures, $224,952; qualifying distributions, $210,170.
Limitations: Giving limited to Dexter, ME.
Application information: Contact school for application form. Applicant must include transcript, letters of recommendation, and personal and employment data. Application form required.
Trustee: Fleet National Bank.
EIN: 016023401
Codes: FD2, GTI

48819
John Clarke Trust
c/o Fleet National Bank, Boston, MA
P.O. Box 6767
Providence, RI 02940-6767

Established in 1676 in Rhode Island.
Donor(s): John Clark.‡
Financial data (yr. ended 12/31/01): Grants paid, $187,300; assets, $3,987,760 (M); gifts received, $157; expenditures, $222,232; qualifying distributions, $210,507.
Limitations: Giving primarily in RI.

Application information: Application form not required.
Trustees: William W. Corcoran, Barbara N. Watterson, Fleet National Bank.
EIN: 056006062
Codes: FD2, GTI

48820
Frederick McDonald Trust
c/o Fleet Private Clients Group
P.O. Box 6767
Providence, RI 02940-6767
Application address: 69 State St., Albany, NY 12207, tel.: (518) 447-4231

Established in 1950 in NY.
Donor(s): Frederick McDonald.‡
Financial data (yr. ended 12/31/01): Grants paid, $186,547; assets, $3,261,551 (M); expenditures, $224,876; qualifying distributions, $204,502.
Limitations: Giving limited to Albany, NY.
Application information: Application form required.
Trustee: Fleet National Bank.
EIN: 146014233
Codes: FD2

48821
Hope Foundation
50 S. Main St.
Providence, RI 02903-2919
Contact: Angela B. Fischer, Tr.

Established in 1960 in RI.
Donor(s): Angela B. Fischer, J. Carter Brown, Nicholas Brown.
Financial data (yr. ended 12/31/01): Grants paid, $183,200; assets, $2,067,420 (M); gifts received, $515,387; expenditures, $185,428; qualifying distributions, $180,702.
Limitations: Applications not accepted. Giving limited to MA, Baltimore, MD, RI, and VA.
Application information: Unsolicited requests for funds not accepted.
Trustees: J. Carter Brown, Nicholas Brown, Angela B. Fischer.
EIN: 056006366
Codes: FD2

48822
Donald Salmanson Foundation
155 S. Main St.
Providence, RI 02903-2963

Established in 1984 in RI.
Donor(s): Donald Salmanson.
Financial data (yr. ended 09/30/01): Grants paid, $182,575; assets, $2,961,231 (M); expenditures, $243,663; qualifying distributions, $177,826.
Limitations: Applications not accepted.
Application information: Unsolicited requests for funds not accepted.
Trustees: Charles Salmanson, Donald Salmanson.
EIN: 222571911
Codes: FD2

48823
Dorothy L. Morgan Trust
c/o Fleet Private Clients Group
P.O. Box 6767
Providence, RI 02940-6767

Donor(s): Dorothy L. Morgan.‡
Financial data (yr. ended 01/31/01): Grants paid, $182,262; assets, $4,423,073 (M); expenditures, $208,087; qualifying distributions, $199,048.
Limitations: Applications not accepted. Giving limited to New London, CT.
Application information: Contributes only to a pre-selected organization.
Trustee: Fleet National Bank.

EIN: 066297473
Codes: TN

48824
The Russell A. Boss Family Foundation
c/o Russell A. Boss
40 Peaked Rock Ln.
Narragansett, RI 02882

Established in 1997 in RI.
Donor(s): Russell A. Boss.
Financial data (yr. ended 12/31/01): Grants paid, $175,000; assets, $555,125 (M); expenditures, $183,515; qualifying distributions, $175,000.
Limitations: Applications not accepted.
Trustees: Martha B. Bennett, Marjorie B. Boss, Russell A. Boss, Robin B. Dornan.
EIN: 061483688

48825
Edwin S. Soforenko Foundation
c/o Citizens Bank of Rhode Island, Tax Dept.
1 Citizens Plz., RC0316
Providence, RI 02903
Contact: Scott Scales

Established in 1967 in RI.
Donor(s): Edwin S. Soforenko.‡
Financial data (yr. ended 12/31/01): Grants paid, $171,000; assets, $3,376,187 (M); gifts received, $1,000; expenditures, $212,406; qualifying distributions, $182,472.
Limitations: Giving primarily in Providence, RI.
Application information: Application form not required.
Trustees: Max Kohlenberg, Larry Soforenko, Citizens Bank of Rhode Island.
EIN: 056019803
Codes: FD2

48826
McCarthy Family Foundation
(Formerly McCarthy Foundation Charity Fund)
c/o Fleet Private Clients Group
P.O. Box 6767
Providence, RI 02940-6767
Application address: c/o Fleet National Bank, N.A., MS MADE10005C, 100 Federal St., Boston, MA 02110
Contact: Janice McGunnigle

Established in 1983 in MA.
Financial data (yr. ended 12/31/01): Grants paid, $169,858; assets, $3,821,228 (M); expenditures, $182,619; qualifying distributions, $166,910.
Limitations: Giving primarily in MA, especially residents of the North Shore and Route 128 areas.
Application information: Application form not required.
Trustees: Caroline Lee Herter, Elton McCausland, J. David Moran, Fleet National Bank.
EIN: 046020152
Codes: FD2

48827
Walter J. Kenney Scholarship Fund
c/o Fleet National Bank
P.O. Box 6767
Providence, RI 02940-6767
Application address: c/o Fleet National Bank, 777 Main St., Hartford, CT 06115

Established in 1990 in CT.
Financial data (yr. ended 12/31/01): Grants paid, $165,773; assets, $382,968 (M); expenditures, $198,169; qualifying distributions, $184,905.
Limitations: Giving limited to residents of New Britain, CT.
Application information: Application form required.
Trustee: Fleet National Bank.

EIN: 066111411
Codes: FD2, GTI

48828
Jonathan M. Nelson Family Foundation
c/o Providence Equity Partners, Inc.
50 Kennedy Pl., 9th Fl.
Providence, RI 02903

Established in 1999 in RI.
Donor(s): Jonathan M. Nelson.
Financial data (yr. ended 12/31/01): Grants paid, $164,150; assets, $11,491,397 (M); gifts received, $6,407,160; expenditures, $196,968; qualifying distributions, $164,150.
Limitations: Applications not accepted. Giving primarily in RI.
Application information: Contributes only to pre-selected organizations.
Trustees: David K. Duffell, Jane S. Nelson, Jonathan M. Nelson.
EIN: 050504814
Codes: FD2

48829
The Riesman Foundation of Rhode Island
15 Westminster St., Ste. 806
Providence, RI 02903 (401) 421-2094
Contact: Robert A. Riesman, Tr.

Donor(s): Robert A. Reisman.
Financial data (yr. ended 04/30/01): Grants paid, $162,260; assets, $300,842 (M); gifts received, $231,946; expenditures, $166,942; qualifying distributions, $160,752.
Limitations: Giving limited to RI.
Trustees: Marcia S. Riesman, Robert A. Riesman.
EIN: 056008382
Codes: FD2

48830
Telaka Foundation, Inc.
170 Westminster St.
Providence, RI 02903

Established in 1997 in MA.
Donor(s): Charlotte Metcalf.
Financial data (yr. ended 12/31/01): Grants paid, $159,591; assets, $2,161,339 (M); gifts received, $64; expenditures, $164,246; qualifying distributions, $155,702.
Limitations: Applications not accepted. Giving primarily in New England area, with an emphasis on MA, ME, and RI.
Application information: Contributes only to pre-selected organizations.
Officers: Charlotte Metcalf, Pres.; Alan M. Gilstein, Treas.; Gail Giacchi, Exec. Dir.
Directors: Hannah S. Metcalf, Jesse P. Metcalf, Lucy D. Metcalf.
EIN: 043357529
Codes: FD2

48831
Granoff Family Foundation
170 Westminster St., Ste. 1200
Providence, RI 02903

Established in 1996 in RI.
Donor(s): Leonard Granoff, Paula Granoff, Lloyd W. Granoff, Evan J. Granoff.
Financial data (yr. ended 07/31/01): Grants paid, $158,527; assets, $3,059,959 (M); gifts received, $353,362; expenditures, $164,422; qualifying distributions, $157,103.
Limitations: Applications not accepted. Giving primarily in RI.
Application information: Contributes only to pre-selected organizations.
Trustees: Evan J. Granoff, Leonard Granoff, Lloyd W. Granoff.

EIN: 050493514
Codes: FD2

48832
The Francis H. Curren, Jr. Foundation
75 Pennsylvania Ave.
Warwick, RI 02888

Established in 1997 in RI.
Donor(s): Francis F. Curren, Jr.
Financial data (yr. ended 12/31/01): Grants paid, $157,500; assets, $69,961 (M); gifts received, $174,181; expenditures, $158,765; qualifying distributions, $156,238.
Limitations: Applications not accepted.
Application information: Contributes only to pre-selected organizations.
Trustees: Francis H. Curren, Jr., Francis H. Curren III, Meredith A. Curren.
EIN: 061488311
Codes: FD2

48833
William G. McGuire, Jr. Memorial Fund
c/o Fleet Private Clients Group
P.O. Box 6767
Providence, RI 02940-6767
Application address: c/o Principal, Sanford High School, Sanford, ME 04073

Financial data (yr. ended 08/31/01): Grants paid, $157,500; assets, $3,219,506 (M); expenditures, $244,769; qualifying distributions, $189,031.
Limitations: Giving limited to Sanford, ME.
Trustee: Fleet National Bank.
EIN: 016057090

48834
Mary E. Hodges Fund
c/o Masonic Grand Lodge Charities
222 Taunton Ave.
East Providence, RI 02914-4556
(401) 435-4650
Contact: John M. Faulhaber, Secy.

Established in 1974.
Financial data (yr. ended 10/31/99): Grants paid, $156,000; assets, $4,714,276 (M); expenditures, $205,368; qualifying distributions, $200,508.
Limitations: Giving limited to RI.
Application information: Application form required for scholarships.
Officers: Robert B. Yates, Pres.; John M. Faulhaber, Secy.; Norman Tierney, Jr., Treas.
EIN: 056049444
Codes: FD2, GTI

48835
Miles & Gertrude W. Hanson Foundation
c/o Fleet Private Clients Group
P.O. Box 6767
Providence, RI 02940-6767
Application address: c/o Fleet National Bank, 100 Federal St., 8th Fl., Boston, MA 02110-1898
Contact: Sharon Driscoll

Established in 1996 in MA.
Donor(s): Gertrude W. Hanson.‡
Financial data (yr. ended 12/31/01): Grants paid, $155,000; assets, $2,594,791 (M); expenditures, $180,254; qualifying distributions, $172,788.
Trustee: Fleet National Bank.
EIN: 046814621
Codes: FD2

48836
Ralph & Helen Kelley Foundation
c/o Fleet National Bank
P.O. Box 6767
Providence, RI 02940-6767
Application address: c/o Principal, Gardner High School, Gardner, MA

Established in 1989 in MD.
Financial data (yr. ended 12/31/01): Grants paid, $149,995; assets, $6,063,399 (M); expenditures, $231,278; qualifying distributions, $195,759.
Limitations: Giving limited to students in the Gardner, MA, area.
Application information: Applications available at Fleet National Bank of Massachusetts. Application form required.
Trustees: G. Albert Anderson, John F. Bohman, Fleet National Bank.
EIN: 043042476
Codes: FD2, GTI

48837
Robert B. Cranston/Theophilus T. Pitman Fund
55 Memorial Blvd.
Newport, RI 02840 (401) 847-0217
Application address: c/o Fr. John Edmonds, 18 Market Sq., Newport, RI 02840, tel.: (401) 847-4260
Contact: Vernon A. Harvey, Tr.

Financial data (yr. ended 12/31/01): Grants paid, $147,722; assets, $2,502,052 (M); expenditures, $171,127; qualifying distributions, $159,979.
Limitations: Giving limited to the residents of Newport County, RI.
Application information: Only residents of Newport, RI are eligible.
Trustees: Vernon A. Harvey, Wilbur Nelson, Robert Rick.
EIN: 056008897
Codes: FD2, GTI

48838
Sophia F. Romero Trust
c/o Fleet Private Clients Group
P.O. Box 6767
Providence, RI 02940-6767

Established in 1953 in MA.
Financial data (yr. ended 04/30/02): Grants paid, $145,500; assets, $2,686,605 (M); expenditures, $178,103; qualifying distributions, $160,546.
Limitations: Applications not accepted. Giving limited to MA.
Application information: Contributes only to pre-selected organizations.
Trustee: Fleet National Bank.
EIN: 046029538
Codes: FD2

48839
William J. Munson Fund
P.O. Box 6767
Providence, RI 02940-6767
Application address: 71 Scott Rd., Watertown, CT 06795, tel.: (203) 274-4288
Contact: Alfred Morency, Chair.

Financial data (yr. ended 12/31/01): Grants paid, $143,778; assets, $1,922,800 (M); expenditures, $167,020; qualifying distributions, $157,747.
Limitations: Giving limited to residents of Watertown, CT.
Application information: Unsolicited requests from organizations not considered. Application form required.
Officer and Trustees:* Alfred Morency,* Chair.; William H. Eppehimer, Sherman R. Slavin, Fleet National Bank.
EIN: 066024564

Codes: FD2, GTI

48840
Kenneth K. Mills Trust for First Congregational Church of Washington
P.O. Box 6767
Providence, RI 02940-6767
Application address: c/o Principal, Shepaug Valley Regional High School, Roxbury, CT 06783, tel.: (203) 868-7326

Financial data (yr. ended 12/31/01): Grants paid, $140,379; assets, $2,762,154 (M); expenditures, $164,832; qualifying distributions, $156,501.
Limitations: Giving limited to Washington, CT.
Application information: Applicants for scholarships must be nominated by high school principal. Unsolicited requests for funds not accepted.
Trustee: Fleet National Bank.
EIN: 066119402
Codes: FD2

48841
Fanny H. Ames and Edna L. Holt Trust
P.O. Box 6767
Providence, RI 02940-6767

Established in 2000 in MA.
Financial data (yr. ended 12/31/01): Grants paid, $140,227; assets, $5,568,206 (M); expenditures, $224,935; qualifying distributions, $170,200.
Limitations: Applications not accepted. Giving primarily in South Easton, MA.
Application information: Contributes only to pre-selected organizations.
Trustee: Fleet National Bank.
EIN: 046905273
Codes: FD2

48842
The Herbert E. & Daisy A. Stride Memorial Foundation
c/o Aquidneck Medical Assn.
Memorial Blvd.
Newport, RI 02840-3699 (401) 847-2290
Contact: A.R.G. Wallace, M.D., Dir.

Established in 1959 in RI.
Financial data (yr. ended 12/31/01): Grants paid, $136,057; assets, $2,287,127 (M); expenditures, $157,511; qualifying distributions, $137,630.
Limitations: Giving limited to RI.
Publications: Annual report, application guidelines.
Application information: Application form required.
Directors: W.D. Levin, M.D., C.P. Shoemaker, M.D., A.R.G. Wallace, M.D.
EIN: 237097640
Codes: FD2

48843
Norman & Rosalie Fain Fund Trust
355 Blackstone Blvd.
Providence, RI 02906

Established in 1964 in RI.
Donor(s): Norman M. Fain.
Financial data (yr. ended 12/31/00): Grants paid, $134,575; assets, $6,892,429 (M); expenditures, $169,605; qualifying distributions, $134,575.
Limitations: Applications not accepted. Giving primarily in RI.
Application information: Contributes only to pre-selected organizations.
Trustees: Norman M. Fain, Rosalie B. Fain.
EIN: 056022655
Codes: FD2

48844
The Sophie & Murray Danforth Foundation
22 Parsonage St.
Providence, RI 02903
Contact: Murray S. Danforth III, Treas.

Established in 1996 in RI.
Donor(s): Sophie F. Danforth, Stephanie D. Chafee.
Financial data (yr. ended 12/31/01): Grants paid, $128,500; assets, $2,969,480 (M); gifts received, $420,500; expenditures, $148,484; qualifying distributions, $128,500.
Limitations: Giving primarily in PA.
Application information: Application form not required.
Officers and Directors:* Sophie F. Danforth,* Pres.; Stephanie D. Chafee,* Secy.; Murray S. Danforth III,* Treas.
EIN: 050494224
Codes: FD2

48845
Elva S. Smith Trust
c/o Citizens Bank New Hampshire
870 Westminster St.
Providence, RI 02903
Application address: c/o Martha Washington, Office of the Dean, Univ. of Pittsburgh, School of Library & Information Science, 509 SLIS Bldg., Pittsburgh, PA 15260, tel.: (412) 624-5230
Contact: Herb Nelson, Admin. Off.

Established in 1965 in NH.
Donor(s): Elva S. Smith.‡
Financial data (yr. ended 12/31/01): Grants paid, $124,877; assets, $2,402,068 (M); expenditures, $142,243; qualifying distributions, $129,545.
Limitations: Giving limited to Pittsburgh, PA, and VT.
Trustee: Citizens Bank New Hampshire.
EIN: 026014169
Codes: FD2, GTI

48846
Hugh Gregg Foundation
c/o Fleet Private Clients Group
P.O. Box 6767
Providence, RI 02940
Application address: R.F.D. 5, Gregg Rd., Nashua, NH 03062
Contact: Hugh Gregg, Tr.

Financial data (yr. ended 12/31/01): Grants paid, $124,125; assets, $287,026 (M); expenditures, $128,244; qualifying distributions, $126,680.
Limitations: Giving primarily in NH.
Trustees: Catherine Gregg, Hugh Gregg, Fleet National Bank.
EIN: 026004636
Codes: FD2

48847
Vigneron Memorial Fund
c/o Fleet National Bank
P.O. Box 6767
Providence, RI 02940-6767
Application address: c/o Fleet National Bank, 100 Westminster St., Providence, RI 02903
Contact: Karen Hibbert

Financial data (yr. ended 12/31/01): Grants paid, $121,924; assets, $2,539,880 (M); expenditures, $143,690; qualifying distributions, $135,362.
Limitations: Applications not accepted. Giving limited to RI.
Application information: Contributes only to pre-selected organizations.
Trustee: Fleet National Bank.
EIN: 056005884
Codes: FD2

48848
The Heald Foundation
c/o Fleet Private Clients Group
P.O. Box 6767
Providence, RI 02940-6767
Application address: c/o Carol Lawrence, Fleet National Bank, 446 Main St., Worcester, MA 01608, tel.: (508) 831-2582

Established in 1958.
Financial data (yr. ended 12/31/01): Grants paid, $120,500; assets, $428,141 (M); expenditures, $128,355; qualifying distributions, $126,568.
Limitations: Giving limited to the Worcester, MA, area.
Trustees: Jack Adam, Jr., James N. Heald II, Fleet National Bank.
EIN: 046028076
Codes: FD2

48849
The Doyle Charitable Foundation
c/o Fleet National Bank
P.O. Box 6767
Providence, RI 02940-6767
Application address: c/o Fleet National Bank, 100 Federal St., Boston, MA 02110
Contact: Sharon M. Driscoll, Trust Off., Fleet National Bank

Established in 1957 in MA.
Financial data (yr. ended 12/31/01): Grants paid, $120,000; assets, $3,102,506 (M); expenditures, $149,005; qualifying distributions, $131,497.
Limitations: Giving primarily in the greater Boston, MA, area.
Application information: Only 1 proposal may be submitted per calendar year. Application form not required.
Trustees: Louise I. Doyle, Fleet National Bank.
EIN: 046010367
Codes: FD2

48850
The Charles Salmanson Family Foundation
155 S. Main St.
Providence, RI 02903

Established in 1984 in RI.
Donor(s): Charles Salmanson.
Financial data (yr. ended 09/30/01): Grants paid, $119,868; assets, $1,721,203 (M); expenditures, $132,039; qualifying distributions, $119,868.
Limitations: Applications not accepted. Giving primarily in RI.
Application information: Funding is given at the discretion of the foundation manager. Unsolicited requests for funds not accepted.
Trustees: Charles Salmanson, Donald Salmanson.
EIN: 222571909
Codes: FD2

48851
Bristol Home for Aged Women
c/o Mrs. Frederick Gilbert
1030 Hope St.
Bristol, RI 02809

Established in 1873 in RI.
Financial data (yr. ended 06/30/02): Grants paid, $117,475; assets, $2,149,443 (M); gifts received, $3,507; expenditures, $139,404; qualifying distributions, $125,812.
Limitations: Applications not accepted. Giving limited to Bristol County, RI.
Application information: Contributes only to pre-selected organizations.
Trustees: Jacquin Thomas, Fleet National Bank.
EIN: 050262707
Codes: FD2

48852
Paul O. & Mary Boghossian Foundation
(Formerly Paul O. & Mary Boghossian Memorial Trust)
c/o Fleet National Bank
P.O. Box 6767
Providence, RI 02940-6767
Application address: c/o Charitable Trust Svcs., Attn:Emma Greene, 100 Federal St., Boston, MA 02110, tel.: (617) 434-0329

Established in 1974 in RI.
Donor(s): Paul O. Boghossian, Jr.
Financial data (yr. ended 04/30/02): Grants paid, $114,450; assets, $1,929,033 (M); expenditures, $132,737; qualifying distributions, $126,465.
Limitations: Giving primarily in RI.
Application information: Application form required for scholarships.
Trustees: David M. Boghossian, Paul O. Boghossian III, Fleet National Bank.
EIN: 056051815
Codes: FD2, GTI

48853
The Baxt Fund
25 Channing Ave.
Providence, RI 02906

Established in 1967 in RI.
Donor(s): Victor J. Baxt.
Financial data (yr. ended 12/31/01): Grants paid, $114,250; assets, $900,882 (M); expenditures, $118,302; qualifying distributions, $114,085.
Limitations: Giving limited to RI.
Trustees: Gussie Baxt, Victor J. Baxt.
EIN: 056020675
Codes: FD2

48854
Charles H. Pearson Trust
P.O. Box 6767
Providence, RI 02940-6767

Financial data (yr. ended 09/30/01): Grants paid, $113,500; assets, $3,024,658 (M); expenditures, $173,984; qualifying distributions, $127,802.
Limitations: Applications not accepted. Giving primarily in Boston, MA.
Application information: Contributes only to pre-selected organizations.
Trustee: Fleet National Bank.
EIN: 046009458
Codes: FD2

48855
Alice L. Carlisle Trust for Children of Goshen Trust
c/o Fleet Private Clients Group
P.O. Box 6767
Providence, RI 02940-6767
Application address: c/o Fleet National Bank, P.O. Box 2210, Waterbury, CT 06722-2210
Contact: Peter Weston

Established in 1998 in CT.
Donor(s): Alice L. Carlisle.‡
Financial data (yr. ended 12/31/01): Grants paid, $112,832; assets, $1,801,585 (M); expenditures, $132,658; qualifying distributions, $125,338.
Limitations: Giving limited to residents of Goshen, CT.
Trustee: Fleet National Bank.
EIN: 066115749
Codes: FD2, GTI

48856
Mary Dexter Chafee Fund
81 Henry Case Way
Wakefield, RI 02879
Application address: c/o Nat Murphy, Fleet National Bank, 100 Federal St., Boston, MA 02110
Contact: Mark H. Chafee, Treas.

Established in 1933 in RI.
Financial data (yr. ended 12/31/01): Grants paid, $108,900; assets, $2,445,611 (M); gifts received, $500; expenditures, $137,407; qualifying distributions, $123,144.
Limitations: Giving primarily in RI.
Application information: Application form required.
Officers and Directors:* Alexandra Reynolds, Pres.; Richard S. Chafee,* Secy.; William G. Chafee,* Treas.; Mark H. Chafee, Treas.; Zechariah Chafee.
Agent: Fleet National Bank.
EIN: 056006295
Codes: FD2

48857
The Biokinetix Foundation
146 Beechwood Hill
Exeter, RI 02822

Established in 1997 in RI.
Donor(s): Asa S. Davis III.
Financial data (yr. ended 12/31/01): Grants paid, $108,890; assets, $423,830 (M); expenditures, $109,311; qualifying distributions, $108,687.
Limitations: Applications not accepted.
Application information: Contributes only to pre-selected organizations.
Directors: Asa S. Davis III, Lauren Kelly-Davis.
EIN: 061483507
Codes: FD2

48858
Masonic Grand Lodge Charities of Rhode Island, Inc.
222 Taunton Ave.
East Providence, RI 02914 (401) 435-4650
Contact: John M. Faulhaber, Secy.

Established in 1912.
Financial data (yr. ended 10/31/99): Grants paid, $106,823; assets, $1,079,359 (M); gifts received, $136,360; expenditures, $150,499; qualifying distributions, $129,882.
Limitations: Giving primarily in RI.
Application information: Application form required.
Officers: Robert B. Yates, Pres.; Benjamin A. Phillips, V.P.; John M. Faulhaber, Secy.; Norman D. Tierney, Jr., Treas.
EIN: 056014340
Codes: FD2, GTI

48859
Richard Waterman Trust
c/o Tillinghast, Licht & Semonoff
1 Park Row
Providence, RI 02903
Application address: P.O. Box 5055, Greene, RI 02827
Contact: Rev. Byron O. Waterman, Tr.

Established in 1847 in RI.
Donor(s): Richard Waterman.‡
Financial data (yr. ended 12/31/01): Grants paid, $106,150; assets, $2,897,731 (M); expenditures, $162,606; qualifying distributions, $154,317.
Limitations: Giving primarily in RI.
Application information: Application form not required.

48859—RHODE ISLAND

Officer and Trustees:* Walter D. Waterman III,* Mgr.; Rev. Byron O. Waterman, Wilma S. Waterman.
EIN: 056040728
Codes: FD2, GTI

48860
Thompson Scholarship Fund
c/o William W. Corcoran
P.O. Box 389
Newport, RI 02840
Application address: c/o Guidance Office, Rogers High School, Wickham Rd., Newport, RI 02840, tel.: (401) 849-3585

Financial data (yr. ended 12/31/01): Grants paid, $105,000; assets, $1,970,462 (M); gifts received, $4,445; expenditures, $121,605; qualifying distributions, $103,698.
Limitations: Giving limited to Newport, RI.
Application information: Application form required.
Officers and Trustees:* William W. Corcoran,* Chair.; Nancy E. Allan,* Secy.; Terrance C. Burns, Kathleen McGrath, Miriam E. Smith.
EIN: 056012968
Codes: FD2, GTI

48861
Neal Rantoul Charitable Trust
Fleet Private Clients Group
P.O. Box 6767
Providence, RI 02940-6767
Application address: c/o Fleet National Bank, Charitable Trust Comm., Secy., 100 Federal St., Boston, MA 02110
Contact: Sharon M. Driscoll, Comm. Secy.

Established about 1960 in MA.
Financial data (yr. ended 12/31/01): Grants paid, $100,000; assets, $1,914,138 (M); expenditures, $125,191; qualifying distributions, $107,967.
Limitations: Giving primarily in Beverly and Lynn, MA.
Trustees: Richard K. Thorndike, Fleet National Bank.
EIN: 237426426
Codes: FD2

48862
Ann de Nicola Trust
c/o Citizens Bank
870 Westminster St.
Providence, RI 02903
Contact: Bill Sirak

Established in 1993 in NH.
Financial data (yr. ended 11/30/01): Grants paid, $98,600; assets, $2,130,259 (M); gifts received, $1,000; expenditures, $137,561; qualifying distributions, $116,080.
Limitations: Applications not accepted. Giving primarily in Bedford, Merrimack, and Nashua, NH.
Publications: Program policy statement.
Application information: Contributes only to pre-selected organizations.
Trustees: James Yakovakis, Citizens Bank New Hampshire.
EIN: 222534442
Codes: FD2

48863
Comstock Memorial Scholarship Trust
(Formerly James A. Comstock Memorial Scholarship Trust)
c/o Fleet Private Clients Group
P.O. Box 6767
Providence, RI 02940-6767
Application address: c/o Fleet National Bank, 10 Fountain Plz., Buffalo, NY 14202

Established in 1981 in NY.
Donor(s): James A. Comstock,‡ Louise Comstock.
Financial data (yr. ended 05/31/01): Grants paid, $96,810; assets, $2,548,829 (M); expenditures, $124,507; qualifying distributions, $112,430.
Limitations: Giving primarily in NY.
Application information: Application form required.
Trustee: Fleet National Bank.
EIN: 222327403
Codes: FD2, GTI

48864
Armbrust Foundation
282 Tuckertown Rd.
Wakefield, RI 02879 (401) 783-0735

Established about 1951 in RI.
Donor(s): Donald G. Armbrust, Armbrust Chain Co.
Financial data (yr. ended 12/31/01): Grants paid, $94,130; assets, $1,577,965 (M); expenditures, $110,502; qualifying distributions, $93,099.
Limitations: Applications not accepted. Giving primarily in RI.
Application information: Contributes only to pre-selected organizations.
Trustee: Howard W. Armbrust.
EIN: 056088332
Codes: CS, FD2, CD

48865
Memorial Baptist Church Trust
c/o Fleet Private Clients Group
P.O. Box 6767
Providence, RI 02940-6767

Financial data (yr. ended 12/31/01): Grants paid, $92,629; assets, $1,980,984 (M); expenditures, $99,850; qualifying distributions, $96,615.
Limitations: Applications not accepted. Giving limited to Seekonk, MA.
Application information: Contributes only to pre-selected organizations.
Trustee: Fleet National Bank.
EIN: 056004511
Codes: FD2

48866
The Feibelman Foundation
c/o H. Jack Feibelman
11 Baldwin Orchard Dr.
Cranston, RI 02920

Established in 1998 in RI.
Donor(s): H. Jack Feibelman.
Financial data (yr. ended 12/31/01): Grants paid, $92,493; assets, $1,514,974 (M); gifts received, $360,009; expenditures, $94,469; qualifying distributions, $92,493.
Limitations: Applications not accepted. Giving on a national basis, with emphasis on MA, New York, NY and RI.
Application information: Contributes only to pre-selected organizations.
Trustee: H. Jack Feibelman.
EIN: 050499644
Codes: FD2

48867
The John and Happy White Foundation
c/o Taco, Inc.
1120 Cranston St.
Cranston, RI 02920 (401) 942-8000
Contact: John Ricottilli, Jr., Pres.

Established in 2000 in RI.
Donor(s): Taco, Inc.
Financial data (yr. ended 12/31/00): Grants paid, $92,151; assets, $0 (M); gifts received, $90,000; expenditures, $95,581; qualifying distributions, $95,581.
Limitations: Giving primarily in RI.
Officers: John Ricottilli, Jr., Pres.; John Hazen White, Jr., Secy.; Glenn Graham, Treas.
Board Member: Mary Tefft White.
EIN: 050509502
Codes: FD2

48868
Frank R. Peters Trust
c/o Fleet Private Clients Group
P.O. Box 6767
Providence, RI 02940-6767

Financial data (yr. ended 09/30/01): Grants paid, $92,000; assets, $1,589,043 (M); expenditures, $115,760; qualifying distributions, $101,242.
Limitations: Applications not accepted.
Application information: Contributes only to pre-selected organizations.
Trustee: Fleet National Bank.
EIN: 046012026
Codes: FD2

48869
The Clements Foundation, Inc.
c/o Paula Sager
P.O. Box 41690
Providence, RI 02940

Established in 1997 in CT.
Donor(s): Robert Clements.
Financial data (yr. ended 12/31/01): Grants paid, $91,970; assets, $1,906,025 (M); gifts received, $500,000; expenditures, $120,767; qualifying distributions, $91,782.
Limitations: Applications not accepted. Giving on a national basis, with emphasis on the New England area.
Application information: Contributes only to pre-selected organizations.
Officers: Robert Clements, Pres. and Treas.; Jeffrey D. Clements, Secy.; Paula J. Clements Sager, Exec. Dir.
EIN: 061480882
Codes: FD2

48870
Allen and Katharine Howland Foundation
70 Manning St.
Providence, RI 02906

Established in 2000 in RI.
Financial data (yr. ended 06/30/01): Grants paid, $90,000; assets, $870,789 (M); gifts received, $935,916; expenditures, $93,089; qualifying distributions, $90,000.
Limitations: Applications not accepted. Giving primarily in MA.
Application information: Contributes only to pre-selected organizations.
Trustees: Frances H. Gambell, Janet K. Howland, John H. Howland, Katherine Howland, Peter A. Howland, Mary Loius Kennedy.
EIN: 056124057
Codes: FD2

48871
Paul B. Kazarian Family Charitable Foundation
30 Kennedy Plz., 2nd Fl.
Providence, RI 02903

Established in 1993 in NY.
Donor(s): Paul B. Kazarian, Robert H. Setrakian.
Financial data (yr. ended 12/31/00): Grants paid, $89,900; assets, $2,853,309 (M); gifts received, $500; expenditures, $98,121; qualifying distributions, $89,929.
Limitations: Applications not accepted. Giving primarily in RI.
Application information: Contributes only to pre-selected organizations.
Trustee: Paul B. Kazarian.
EIN: 050474999
Codes: FD2

48872
Helen R. Coe Trust
c/o Fleet Private Clients Group
P.O. Box 6767
Providence, RI 02940-6767
Loan application address: c/o Coe Governing Committee, P.O. Box 185, Center Lovell, ME 04016

Established in 1978 in ME.
Financial data (yr. ended 03/31/02): Grants paid, $89,500; assets, $2,131,592 (M); gifts received, $150; expenditures, $117,175; qualifying distributions, $106,988; giving activities include $72,200 for loans to individuals.
Limitations: Giving limited to ME.
Trustee: Fleet National Bank.
EIN: 010351827
Codes: FD2, GTI

48873
The Sachem Foundation
22 Parsonage St.
Providence, RI 02903
Contact: Esther E.M. Mauran, Pres.

Established in 1997 in RI.
Donor(s): Esther E.M. Mauran.
Financial data (yr. ended 12/31/01): Grants paid, $88,550; assets, $2,333,366 (M); gifts received, $250,001; expenditures, $97,650; qualifying distributions, $88,550.
Limitations: Giving primarily in ME and RI.
Officers and Trustees:* Esther E.M. Mauran,* Pres.; Frank Mauran IV,* Secy.; Paul W. Whyte, Treas.; Pauline C. Metcalf.
EIN: 061483391
Codes: FD2

48874
Frederick C. Tanner Memorial Fund, Inc.
c/o Citizens Bank of RI
1 Citizens Plz.
Providence, RI 02903
Application address: 151 Exchange St., Pawtucket, RI 02862, tel.: (401) 722-6530
Contact: F. Paul Mooney, Jr., Secy.-Treas.

Established in 1952 in RI.
Financial data (yr. ended 03/31/01): Grants paid, $88,300; assets, $2,149,710 (M); expenditures, $113,599; qualifying distributions, $93,500.
Limitations: Giving limited to RI.
Application information: Application form not required.
Officers and Directors:* Jonathan R. Knowles,* Pres.; William F. Lunnie,* V.P.; F. Paul Mooney, Jr.,* Secy.-Treas.; John C. Drew, John Gorham, William H. Heisler III, DeWitte T. Kersh, Jr., Jerry Knowles, Edward J. O'Donnell, Brad Steere.
EIN: 056011617
Codes: FD2

48875
Grace E. Brooks Trust
c/o Fleet Private Clients Group
P.O. Box 6767
Providence, RI 02940-6767
Additional address: c/o Emma Greene, Fleet National Bank, 100 Federal St., Boston, MA 02110

Established in 1999 in MA.
Financial data (yr. ended 12/31/01): Grants paid, $88,000; assets, $2,104,047 (M); expenditures, $122,038; qualifying distributions, $101,159.
Limitations: Giving primarily in MA.
Trustee: Fleet National Bank.
EIN: 046446179

48876
The Bess Eaton Foundation
c/o Blish & Cavanagh
30 Exchange Terr.
Providence, RI 02903

Financial data (yr. ended 08/31/01): Grants paid, $87,712; assets, $32,588 (M); gifts received, $68,600; expenditures, $87,920; qualifying distributions, $87,703.
Limitations: Applications not accepted.
Application information: Contributes only to pre-selected organizations.
Officers: Louis A. Gencarelli, Sr., Chair.; Paul Gencarelli, Vice-Chair.
Distribution Committee Members: Stephen F. Larkin, Charles Renzoni.
Trustee: Scott T. Spear.
EIN: 050492079
Codes: FD2

48877
Henry Herbert Smythe Trust
c/o Fleet Private Client Group
P.O. Box 6767
Providence, RI 02940-6767
Contact: Emma Greene, Acct. Mgr.

Financial data (yr. ended 09/30/01): Grants paid, $87,584; assets, $1,834,659 (M); expenditures, $112,438; qualifying distributions, $91,786.
Limitations: Giving limited to MA.
Application information: Application form not required.
Trustee: Fleet National Bank.
EIN: 046008387
Codes: FD2, GTI

48878
Rhode Island Infantile Paralysis Foundation
607 Namquid Dr.
Warwick, RI 02888
Contact: Mark S. McGovern, Secy.

Donor(s): W.A. Thompson Trust.
Financial data (yr. ended 12/31/01): Grants paid, $87,404; assets, $1,345,413 (M); gifts received, $39,850; expenditures, $113,161; qualifying distributions, $87,404.
Officers: Gerald J. Fogarty, Jr., Pres.; Richard P. Kelaghan, V.P.; Mark S. McGovern, Secy.; Raymond J. Bolster II, Treas.
EIN: 050298523
Codes: FD2

48879
The Barber Family Foundation
c/o Summit South
300 Centerville Rd.
Warwick, RI 02886

Established in 2000 in RI.
Donor(s): Gregory P. Barber.
Financial data (yr. ended 12/31/00): Grants paid, $87,100; assets, $141,197 (M); gifts received, $282,625; expenditures, $87,795; qualifying distributions, $87,100.
Limitations: Applications not accepted. Giving primarily in MA and RI.
Application information: Contributes only to pre-selected organizations.
Trustee: Gregory P. Barber.
EIN: 050511880
Codes: FD2

48880
The Molder Family Foundation
c/o Fleet Private Clients Group
P.O. Box 6767
Providence, RI 02940-6767
Application address: c/o James Dudley, Fleet National Bank, 100 Westminster St., Providence, RI 02903

Established in 1997 in RI.
Financial data (yr. ended 12/31/01): Grants paid, $85,320; assets, $1,531,017 (M); expenditures, $91,831; qualifying distributions, $88,933.
Limitations: Giving on a national basis.
Trustee: Fleet National Bank.
EIN: 056115363
Codes: FD2

48881
Hathaway Memorial Charitable Trust
P.O. Box 6767
Providence, RI 02940-6767
Application address: c/o Fleet National Bank, 100 Federal St., 8th Fl., Boston, MA 02110-1898, tel.: (617) 434-4664
Contact: Augusta Haydock, Chair.

Established in 1988 in MA.
Financial data (yr. ended 07/31/01): Grants paid, $85,141; assets, $2,021,665 (M); expenditures, $102,471; qualifying distributions, $95,473.
Limitations: Giving limited to the Somerset, MA area.
Application information: Application form not required.
Trustee: Fleet National Bank.
EIN: 046599655
Codes: FD2

48882
The Ralph and Clara Shuster Foundation, Inc.
c/o Ralph Shuster Metals, Inc.
909 N. Main St.
Providence, RI 02904   (401) 785-4800
Contact: Mathew Shuster, Dir.

Established in 1959 in RI.
Donor(s): Mathew Shuster, Ralph Shuster, Inc.
Financial data (yr. ended 11/30/01): Grants paid, $85,015; assets, $2,257,626 (M); gifts received, $7,852; expenditures, $99,098; qualifying distributions, $91,568.
Limitations: Applications not accepted. Giving primarily in RI.
Application information: Contributes only to pre-selected organizations.
Directors: Grace Goldberg, Lee Malkin, Mathew Shuster, Adele Zuckerman.
EIN: 221714042
Codes: FD2

48883

Charlotte and Raymond W. Marshall Fund
c/o Fleet Private Clients Group
P.O. Box 6767
Providence, RI 02940-6767
CT tel.: (860) 952-7405

Financial data (yr. ended 12/31/01): Grants paid, $85,000; assets, $1,573,234 (M); gifts received, $31,804; expenditures, $91,422; qualifying distributions, $88,129.
Limitations: Applications not accepted. Giving on a national basis.
Application information: Contributes only to pre-selected organizations.
Trustee: Fleet National Bank.
EIN: 066098256
Codes: FD2

48884

Townsend Aid for the Aged
43 Benedict Ave.
Portsmouth, RI 02871
Application address: c/o Janice Barrows, 12 Madeline Dr., Newport, RI 02840
Contact: Caroline Kaull, Pres.

Established in 1882 in RI.
Financial data (yr. ended 04/30/01): Grants paid, $83,850; assets, $2,900,997 (M); expenditures, $115,471; qualifying distributions, $106,474.
Limitations: Giving limited to residents of Newport, RI.
Application information: Applicants must be residents of Newport, RI. Unsolicited requests for funds not accepted. Application form not required.
Officers: Caroline Kaull, Pres.; Nancy Allen, V.P.; Janice M. Barrows, Treas.
Trustee: Fleet National Bank.
EIN: 056009549
Codes: FD2, GTI

48885

Everett Charitable Trust
c/o Fleet Private Clients Group
P.O. Box 6767
Providence, RI 02940-6767
Application address: William McKee, V.P. c/o Fleet National Bank, 120 Genesee St., Auburn, NY 13201

Established in 1957 in NY.
Donor(s): Fred M. Everett.‡
Financial data (yr. ended 12/31/01): Grants paid, $83,800; assets, $1,914,306 (M); expenditures, $157,487; qualifying distributions, $144,342.
Limitations: Giving limited to Auburn and Cayuga County, NY.
Application information: Application form not required.
Trustee: Fleet National Bank.
EIN: 156018093
Codes: FD2

48886

Stokes Scholarship Trust
c/o Fleet Private Clients Group
P.O. Box 6767
Providence, RI 02940-6767
Contact: Michael Wrenn

Established in 1993 in NH.
Financial data (yr. ended 12/31/01): Grants paid, $83,221; assets, $1,449,411 (M); gifts received, $596; expenditures, $98,874; qualifying distributions, $91,495.
Limitations: Giving limited to residents of Langdon, NH.
Application information: Application form required.
Trustee: Fleet National Bank.

EIN: 026092657
Codes: FD2, GTI

48887

Joseph W. Martin Trust
393 Market St.
Warren, RI 02885 (401) 841-4679
Contact: Douglas M. Domina

Established around 1941 in RI.
Financial data (yr. ended 05/31/01): Grants paid, $82,820; assets, $3,573,091 (M); expenditures, $131,636; qualifying distributions, $117,407.
Limitations: Giving limited to Warren, RI.
Application information: Application form not required.
Trustees: Douglas M. Domina, Ely Barkett, Luis DaSilva.
Agent: Fleet National Bank.
EIN: 056011809
Codes: FD2

48888

C. Alice Rowell Bean Trust
P.O. Box 6767
Providence, RI 02940-6767

Financial data (yr. ended 11/30/01): Grants paid, $82,000; assets, $1,495,740 (M); expenditures, $114,650; qualifying distributions, $105,108.
Limitations: Applications not accepted.
Application information: Contributes only to pre-selected organizations.
Trustees: Michael G. Conway, Ernest Dixon, Fleet National Bank.
EIN: 046014549
Codes: FD2

48889

Virginia A. Bowmaker Scholarship Trust
(Formerly V. A. Bowmaker Scholarship Trust)
c/o Fleet Private Clients Group
P.O. Box 6767
Providence, RI 02940-6767
Application address: c/o Fleet National Bank, 268 Genessee St., Utica, NY 13502

Established in 1990 in NY.
Financial data (yr. ended 12/31/01): Grants paid, $82,000; assets, $1,646,639 (M); expenditures, $108,042; qualifying distributions, $92,942.
Limitations: Giving limited to high school graduates in Utica, NY.
Application information: Application form required.
Trustee: Fleet National Bank.
EIN: 161381376
Codes: GTI

48890

Sundel-Strauss Family Foundation
(Formerly Sundel Family Foundation)
21 Campbell St.
P.O. Box 2370
Pawtucket, RI 02861-0370 (401) 723-2000
Contact: Sylvia Strauss, Dir.

Established in 1969 in RI.
Donor(s): Jacob Sundel,‡ Claire Sundel.‡
Financial data (yr. ended 12/31/00): Grants paid, $81,317; assets, $663,932 (M); gifts received, $50,000; expenditures, $82,961; qualifying distributions, $82,448.
Limitations: Giving primarily in RI.
Application information: Generally contributes to pre-selected organizations but will accept unsolicited requests.
Trustees: Sylvia Sundel Strauss, David Strauss, Debra Strauss-Levine.
EIN: 237011406
Codes: FD2

48891

Mustard Seed Foundation, Inc.
c/o Paster & Harpootian, Ltd.
1 Providence Washington Plz.
Providence, RI 02903 (401) 455-9800

Established in 1984 in RI.
Donor(s): Russell Family Charitable Lead Trust, Tewes Charitable Remainder Trust, Robert Russell II, Carol L. Russell.
Financial data (yr. ended 11/30/01): Grants paid, $80,699; assets, $159,253 (M); expenditures, $87,227; qualifying distributions, $87,227.
Limitations: Giving primarily in MA and RI.
Officers and Trustees:* Rev. Thomas L. Crum,* Pres.; Benjamin G. Paster,* Treas.; Carol L. Russell, Robert J. Russell.
EIN: 222714666
Codes: FD2

48892

B. B. Lederer Sons Foundation
c/o Fleet Private Clients Group
P.O. Box 6767
Providence, RI 02940-6767
Application address: c/o Fleet National Bank, 100 Westminster St., Providence, RI 02903

Established in 1990 in RI.
Financial data (yr. ended 12/31/01): Grants paid, $80,000; assets, $1,293,228 (M); expenditures, $113,118; qualifying distributions, $101,329.
Limitations: Giving primarily in MA and RI.
Trustees: Carol A. Schneider, Gloria A. Sonnabend, Fleet National Bank.
EIN: 056005322
Codes: FD2

48893

Corinne and Victor Rice Foundation
c/o Harmen & Assocs.
P.O. Box 6767
Providence, RI 02940-6767

Established in 1995 in NY.
Donor(s): Victor Rice.
Financial data (yr. ended 12/31/00): Grants paid, $78,675; assets, $1,532,066 (M); expenditures, $103,411; qualifying distributions, $86,651.
Limitations: Applications not accepted. Giving primarily in Buffalo, NY.
Application information: Contributes only to pre-selected organizations.
Directors: Immanuel Kohn, Corinne Rice, Victor A. Rice.
EIN: 161492084
Codes: FD2

48894

The King Family Fund
(Formerly Theophilus King Fund Trust)
c/o Fleet Private Clients Group
P.O. Box 6767
Providence, RI 02940-6767
Application address: c/o Fleet National Bank, Charitable Trusts-Augusta Haydock, 100 Federal St., Boston, MA 02110

Financial data (yr. ended 12/31/01): Grants paid, $78,500; assets, $1,461,812 (M); expenditures, $94,202; qualifying distributions, $86,451.
Limitations: Giving primarily in MA.
Trustees: James D. Asher, Karl L. Briggs, Jr., Forrest R. Cook, Jr., Fleet National Bank.
EIN: 046020918
Codes: FD2

48895
The Robert F. and Linda R. Fischer Family Charitable Foundation
94 Woodbury St.
Providence, RI 02906

Established in 1998 in RI.
Donor(s): Robert F. Fischer, Linda R. Fischer.
Financial data (yr. ended 12/31/00): Grants paid, $78,180; assets, $579,371 (M); expenditures, $80,761; qualifying distributions, $76,971.
Limitations: Applications not accepted. Giving primarily in Providence, RI.
Application information: Contributes only to pre-selected organizations.
Trustees: Linda R. Fischer, Robert F. Fischer.
EIN: 050499464
Codes: FD2

48896
Lochridge-Watkins Charitable Fund
c/o Fleet Private Clients Group
P.O. Box 6767
Providence, RI 02940-6767

Established in 1998 in MA.
Financial data (yr. ended 12/31/01): Grants paid, $78,011; assets, $2,105,353 (M); expenditures, $98,760; qualifying distributions, $90,888.
Limitations: Applications not accepted. Giving primarily in MA.
Application information: Contributes only to pre-selected organizations.
Trustee: Fleet National Bank.
EIN: 043408546
Codes: FD2

48897
Delivery from Heaven Foundation
756 N. Main Rd.
Jamestown, RI 02835 (401) 423-2103
Contact: Michael T. Casey, Pres. or Laurie Casey

Established in 1997 in RI.
Donor(s): Michael T. Casey.
Financial data (yr. ended 12/31/00): Grants paid, $77,570; assets, $176,926 (M); expenditures, $79,120; qualifying distributions, $77,482.
Application information: Application form not required.
Officer: Michael T. Casey, Pres.
EIN: 061484358
Codes: FD2

48898
The Thelma S. Rodbell Charitable Foundation
c/o Paster & Harpootian
1 Providence Washington Plz.
Providence, RI 02903

Financial data (yr. ended 12/31/01): Grants paid, $76,100; assets, $549,507 (M); expenditures, $79,170; qualifying distributions, $76,100.
Limitations: Applications not accepted.
Application information: Contributes only to pre-selected organizations.
Trustees: Benjamin G. Paster, Thelma S. Rodbell.
EIN: 061486581

48899
Van and Joanna Christy Scholarship Fund
c/o Citizens Bank New Hampshire
870 Westminster St.
Providence, RI 02903
Application address: 875 Elm St., Manchester, NH 03101, tel.: (603) 634-7752
Contact: Bill Sirak, Trust Off., Citizens Bank New Hampshire

Established in 1995.
Financial data (yr. ended 08/31/01): Grants paid, $75,500; assets, $1,355,432 (M); expenditures, $97,287; qualifying distributions, $81,806.
Limitations: Giving limited to the Manchester, NH area.
Application information: Application form required.
Trustee: Citizens Bank New Hampshire.
EIN: 020484968
Codes: FD2

48900
Horace A. Kimball and S. Ella Kimball Foundation
c/o The Washington Trust Co.
23 Broad St.
Westerly, RI 02891 (401) 364-3565
FAX: (401) 364-7799; URL: http://www.hkimballfoundation.org
Contact: Thomas F. Black III, Pres.

Incorporated in 1956 in DE.
Donor(s): H. Earle Kimball.‡
Financial data (yr. ended 10/31/01): Grants paid, $75,250; assets, $6,956,701 (M); expenditures, $86,416; qualifying distributions, $77,868.
Limitations: Giving limited to RI, with emphasis on South County.
Application information: Submit application through website only. Application form required.
Officers and Trustees:* Thomas F. Black III,* Pres.; Norman D. Baker, Jr.,* Secy.-Treas.; F. Thomas Lenihan.
EIN: 056006130
Codes: FD2

48901
Charles E. Montague Charitable Trust
c/o Fleet Private Clients Group
P.O. Box 6767
Providence, RI 02940-6767
Application address: c/o Fleet National Bank, 100 Federal St., Boston, MA 02110

Established in MA in 1997.
Financial data (yr. ended 09/30/01): Grants paid, $73,702; assets, $1,563,220 (M); expenditures, $94,154; qualifying distributions, $85,034.
Limitations: Giving limited to residents of Wakefield, MA.
Application information: Application form not required.
Trustee: Fleet National Bank.
EIN: 046047134
Codes: GTI

48902
The Ruth & Samuel Markoff Foundation
123 Dyer St.
Providence, RI 02903

Financial data (yr. ended 12/31/01): Grants paid, $73,550; assets, $1,219,463 (M); expenditures, $103,305; qualifying distributions, $73,550.
Limitations: Applications not accepted. Giving primarily in RI.
Application information: Contributes only to pre-selected organizations.
Trustees: Bernice M. Gourse, Dorothy M. Nelson, Gloria M. Winston.
EIN: 050376170

48903
Frank O'Brion Trust
c/o Fleet Private Clients Group
P.O. Box 6767
Providence, RI 02940-6767
Application address: c/o Anne Zartarian, Office of Fin. Aid., P.O. Box 248, Cortland, NY 13045

Established in 1972 in CT.
Donor(s): Fleet National Bank, CBT Corp.
Financial data (yr. ended 10/31/01): Grants paid, $73,500; assets, $1,516,982 (M); expenditures, $99,502; qualifying distributions, $87,786.
Limitations: Giving primarily in CT.
Application information: Application form required.
Trustee: Fleet National Bank.
EIN: 066154532
Codes: GTI

48904
John J. and Margaret B. Brennan Charitable Trust
c/o Citizens Bank
870 Westminster St.
Providence, RI 02903

Established in 2000 in NH.
Donor(s): John J. Brennan.
Financial data (yr. ended 12/31/01): Grants paid, $72,000; assets, $1,374,298 (M); expenditures, $184,660; qualifying distributions, $118,360.
Limitations: Applications not accepted.
Application information: Contributes only to pre-selected organizations.
Trustee: Citizens Bank New Hampshire.
EIN: 026125090

48905
Mary H. Agostine Trust
c/o Fleet Private Clients Group
P.O. Box 6767
Providence, RI 02940-6767

Established in 1983.
Financial data (yr. ended 12/31/01): Grants paid, $71,623; assets, $1,363,652 (M); expenditures, $126,174; qualifying distributions, $110,023.
Limitations: Applications not accepted. Giving on an international basis, primarily in Italy.
Application information: Contributes only to pre-selected organizations.
Trustee: Fleet National Bank.
EIN: 046489996

48906
John P. & Mable I. Ogsbury Memorial Trust
c/o Fleet Private Clients Group
P.O Box 6767
Providence, RI 02940-6767

Financial data (yr. ended 12/31/00): Grants paid, $71,173; assets, $1,286,742 (M); expenditures, $84,548; qualifying distributions, $78,547.
Limitations: Applications not accepted. Giving primarily in upstate NY.
Application information: Contributes only to pre-selected organizations.
Trustee: Fleet National Bank.
EIN: 146032158

48907
RM2 Foundation
c/o Marc Perlman
180 Shady Cove Rd.
North Kingstown, RI 02852

Established in 1996 in RI.
Financial data (yr. ended 11/30/00): Grants paid, $70,800; assets, $1,153,678 (M); expenditures, $75,981; qualifying distributions, $70,504.
Limitations: Applications not accepted.
Application information: Contributes only to pre-selected organizations.
Trustee: Fleet National Bank.
EIN: 050494286

48908
Isidore and Selma Wise Travel Foundation Trust
c/o Fleet Private Clients Group
P.O. Box 6767
Providence, RI 02940-6767

Financial data (yr. ended 12/31/01): Grants paid, $70,172; assets, $972,091 (M); expenditures, $95,216; qualifying distributions, $85,391.
Limitations: Applications not accepted. Giving primarily in Hartford, CT.
Application information: Recipients are selected by The Board of Education of Hartford, CT.
Trustee: Fleet National Bank.
EIN: 066030200

48909
Richard M. and Sandra D. Oster Charitable Foundation
c/o Stanley Kanter
2300 Hospital Trust Tower
Providence, RI 02903

Financial data (yr. ended 12/31/00): Grants paid, $67,300; assets, $403,447 (M); expenditures, $71,932; qualifying distributions, $66,534.
Limitations: Applications not accepted.
Application information: Contributes only to pre-selected organizations.
Directors: Stanley Kanter, Richard M. Oster, Sandra D. Oster, B. Burton Schneider.
EIN: 223135468

48910
Louis F. Bell Fund
c/o Fleet Private Clients Group
P.O. Box 6767
Providence, RI 02940-6767

Established in 2000 in FL.
Financial data (yr. ended 12/31/01): Grants paid, $66,106; assets, $1,034,550 (M); expenditures, $88,962; qualifying distributions, $78,393.
Limitations: Applications not accepted. Giving primarily in RI.
Application information: Contributes only to pre-selected organizations.
Trustee: Fleet National Bank.
EIN: 056007804

48911
Isaac E. Palmer Fund Trust
c/o Fleet Private Clients Group
P.O. Box 6767
Providence, RI 02940-6767
Contact: Irene Melasky, Trust Off., Fleet National Bank

Financial data (yr. ended 12/31/01): Grants paid, $65,000; assets, $1,570,042 (M); expenditures, $83,373; qualifying distributions, $76,210.
Limitations: Giving limited to residents of Montville, CT.
Application information: Application form required.
Trustee: Fleet National Bank.
EIN: 066026227
Codes: GTI

48912
The Pearle W. & Martin M. Silverstein Foundation
10 Weybosset St.
Providence, RI 02903-1235 (401) 421-8030
Contact: Melvin L. Zurier, Tr.

Established in 1988 in RI.
Donor(s): Pearle N. Silverstein.
Financial data (yr. ended 12/31/99): Grants paid, $64,311; assets, $1,352,017 (M); gifts received, $1,984; expenditures, $81,682; qualifying distributions, $69,138.
Limitations: Giving primarily in Providence, RI.
Trustee: Melvin L. Zurier.
EIN: 050442756

48913
Grace Atkins Charities
c/o Fleet Private Clients Group
P.O. Box 6767
Providence, RI 02940-6767
Application address: c/o Fleet Bank, N.A., 777 Main St., Hartford, CT 06115

Financial data (yr. ended 12/31/01): Grants paid, $63,620; assets, $1,489,112 (M); expenditures, $88,297; qualifying distributions, $76,789.
Limitations: Giving limited to Bristol, CT.
Application information: Scholarship applications obtained from public library or high school guidance department. Application form required.
Trustee: Fleet National Bank.
EIN: 066138990
Codes: GTI

48914
Carroll K. Steele Trust
c/o Fleet Private Clients Group
P.O. Box 6767
Providence, RI 02940-6767

Established in 1996 in MA.
Financial data (yr. ended 12/31/01): Grants paid, $63,192; assets, $1,753,165 (M); expenditures, $83,294; qualifying distributions, $63,192.
Limitations: Applications not accepted. Giving primarily in MA.
Application information: Contributes only to pre-selected organizations.
Trustee: Fleet National Bank.
EIN: 046798723

48915
McMahon Foundation
c/o Richard P. McMahon
P.O. Box 2251
Pawtucket, RI 02861
Application address: 121 Mt. Vernon Blvd., Pawtucket, RI 02861, tel.: (401) 724-8200
Contact: Paul B. McMahon, Tr.

Donor(s): Richard P. McMahon.
Financial data (yr. ended 12/31/01): Grants paid, $63,000; assets, $183,073 (M); expenditures, $63,711; qualifying distributions, $63,000.
Limitations: Giving primarily in RI.
Trustees: Paul B. McMahon, Richard P. McMahon.
EIN: 056008233

48916
Mildred & Charles Page Fund
c/o Fleet Private Clients Group
P.O. Box 6767
Providence, RI 02940-6767

Established in 1998.
Financial data (yr. ended 12/31/01): Grants paid, $62,781; assets, $2,066,572 (M); expenditures, $81,402; qualifying distributions, $74,902.
Limitations: Applications not accepted.
Application information: Contributes only to pre-selected organizations.
Trustee: Fleet National Bank.
EIN: 046479105

48917
Joseph How Charitable Trust
c/o Fleet Private Clients Group
P.O. Box 6767
Providence, RI 02940-6767
Application address: c/o Fleet National Bank, P.O. Box 9791, Portland, ME 04104

Financial data (yr. ended 12/31/01): Grants paid, $62,662; assets, $1,445,600 (M); expenditures, $79,186; qualifying distributions, $71,272.
Limitations: Giving limited to ME.
Trustee: Fleet National Bank.
EIN: 016010195

48918
Peter C. Salerno Trust f/b/o UPCASA Scholarships
c/o Fleet Private Clients Group
P.O. Box 6767
Providence, RI 02940-6767
Application address: c/o Tina Hamilton, 777 Main St., Hartford, CT 06115

Financial data (yr. ended 12/31/01): Grants paid, $61,000; assets, $3,356 (M); expenditures, $62,427; qualifying distributions, $61,992.
Limitations: Giving limited to Northfield, MA.
Application information: Application form not required.
Trustee: Fleet National Bank.
EIN: 066250441
Codes: GTI

48919
The Chase Family Foundation
1 Ann & Hope Way
Cumberland, RI 02864-7502
Contact: Irwin J. Chase, Tr.

Established in 1986 in RI.
Donor(s): Marjorie C. Alpert, Irwin J. Chase, Samuel N. Chase.
Financial data (yr. ended 12/31/01): Grants paid, $60,928; assets, $787,034 (M); expenditures, $68,290; qualifying distributions, $60,928.
Limitations: Applications not accepted. Giving primarily in Providence, RI.
Application information: Unsolicited requests for funds not accepted.
Trustees: Marjorie C. Alpert, Irwin J. Chase, Samuel N. Chase.
EIN: 222743634

48920
Thomas Atkins Memorial Fund Trust
c/o Fleet Private Clients Group
P.O. Box 6767
Providence, RI 02940-6767
CT tel.: (860) 952-7405
Contact: Marjorie Davis, Trust Off., Fleet National Bank

Financial data (yr. ended 12/31/01): Grants paid, $60,390; assets, $1,414,322 (M); expenditures, $77,358; qualifying distributions, $70,730.
Limitations: Giving limited to the Middlesex County, CT, area.
Publications: Application guidelines.
Application information: Application form required.
Trustee: Fleet National Bank.
EIN: 066030489

48921
Kane-Barrengos Foundation
85 Scrabbletown Rd.
North Kingstown, RI 02852
FAX: (401) 294-7699; E-mail:
jcohen@efortress.com
Contact: Diana K. Cohen, Pres.

Financial data (yr. ended 12/31/01): Grants paid, $60,000; assets, $847,813 (M); expenditures, $59,635; qualifying distributions, $60,000.
Limitations: Giving primarily in Providence, RI.
Officers: Diana K. Cohen, Pres.; John B. Barrengos, V.P.
EIN: 237032347

48922
Mallett Charitable Trust
(Formerly The Ethel & Jennie Mallett Charitable Trust)
c/o Fleet Private Clients Group
P.O. Box 6767
Providence, RI 02940-6767
Application address: 211 State St., Bridgeport, CT 06604
Contact: Aram H. Tellalian, Tr.

Established in 1983 in CT.
Financial data (yr. ended 10/31/00): Grants paid, $60,000; assets, $1,974,469 (M); expenditures, $101,532; qualifying distributions, $86,897.
Limitations: Giving primarily in Trumbull, CT.
Trustees: Aram H. Tellalian, Fleet National Bank.
EIN: 066273514

48923
Ellen V. and Robert H. Smith Scholarship Fund
c/o Fleet Private Clients Group
P.O. Box 6767
Providence, RI 02940-6767
Application address: c/o The Smith Scholarship Selection Committee, P.O. Box 2482, East Side Sta., Providence, RI 02906
Contact: Beth Kernan, Trust Admin., Fleet Investment Mgmt.

Established in 1992 in RI.
Financial data (yr. ended 12/31/01): Grants paid, $59,690; assets, $1,729,098 (M); expenditures, $85,311; qualifying distributions, $77,093.
Limitations: Giving limited to residents of South Kingston, RI.
Application information: Write for guidelines and application. Application form required.
Trustee: Fleet National Bank.
EIN: 056069745
Codes: GTI

48924
Victor Hatchwell Trust
c/o Fleet Private Clients Group
P.O. Box 6767
Providence, RI 02940-6767

Established in 1998 in NJ.
Donor(s): Victor Hatchwell.‡
Financial data (yr. ended 09/30/01): Grants paid, $58,283; assets, $1,212,624 (M); gifts received, $6,091; expenditures, $72,110; qualifying distributions, $67,796.
Limitations: Applications not accepted. Giving primarily in Philadelphia, PA.
Application information: Contributes only to pre-selected organizations.
Trustee: Fleet National Bank.
EIN: 066467019

48925
Meriden Record Journal Foundation
c/o Fleet Private Clients Group
P.O. Box 6767
Providence, RI 02940-6767
Application address: 11 Crown St., Meriden, CT 06450
Contact: Elliott White

Established in 1987 in CT.
Donor(s): Record Journal Publishing Co.
Financial data (yr. ended 12/31/01): Grants paid, $58,250; assets, $386,913 (M); gifts received, $2,220; expenditures, $64,767; qualifying distributions, $62,175.
Limitations: Giving primarily in the Meriden, CT, area.
Application information: Application form required.
Trustee: Fleet National Bank.
EIN: 066074903
Codes: CS, CD, GTI

48926
Joan and Leonard Engle Family Foundation
132 Freeman Pkwy.
Providence, RI 02906-4219 (401) 521-1182
Contact: Leonard Engle, Tr.

Established in 1986 in RI.
Donor(s): Joan Engle, Leonard Engle, Judith Engle Clifford, James Engle, Robin Engle, Richard Engle.
Financial data (yr. ended 12/31/01): Grants paid, $58,000; assets, $1,184,739 (M); expenditures, $71,321; qualifying distributions, $58,000.
Limitations: Giving primarily in Providence, RI.
Application information: Application form not required.
Trustees: Judith Engle Clifford, James Engle, Leonard Engle, Richard Engle, Robin Engle.
EIN: 222751779

48927
L. S. Benas Memorial Fund
c/o Fleet Private Clients Group
P.O. Box 6767
Providence, RI 02940-6767
Application address: c/o Fleet Bank, CT EH 40222C, 777 Main St., CT 06115
Contact: Peter Weston, V.P.

Established in 2001 in CT.
Financial data (yr. ended 12/31/01): Grants paid, $57,327; assets, $1,667,807 (M); expenditures, $108,575; qualifying distributions, $103,450.
Limitations: Giving primarily in Litchfield, CT, and contiguous towns.
Application information: Application form not required.
Trustee: Fleet National Bank.
EIN: 061616940

48928
L. & A. Audino Charitable Trust
c/o Fleet Private Clients Group
P.O. Box 6767
Providence, RI 02940-6767

Established in 2001 in RI.
Financial data (yr. ended 12/31/01): Grants paid, $54,655; assets, $598,376 (M); expenditures, $70,400; qualifying distributions, $60,635.
Limitations: Applications not accepted. Giving on a national basis.
Application information: Contributes only to pre-selected organizations.
Trustee: Fleet National Bank.
EIN: 056042077

48929
The Edward F. and Janet E. Ricci Family Charitable Foundation
210 Blackstone Blvd.
Providence, RI 02906 (401) 272-9639
Contact: Edward F. Ricci, Tr.

Established in 1999 in RI.
Donor(s): Edward F. Ricci, Janet E. Ricci.
Financial data (yr. ended 12/31/01): Grants paid, $53,500; assets, $426,965 (M); expenditures, $56,442; qualifying distributions, $53,500.
Limitations: Giving primarily in RI.
Application information: Application form required.
Trustees: Edward F. Ricci, Janet E. Ricci.
EIN: 056120603

48930
Paul and Navyn Salem Charitable Trust
c/o Providence Equity Partners
50 Kennedy Pl., 9th Fl.
Providence, RI 02903

Established in 2000 in RI.
Donor(s): Paul J. Saleni.
Financial data (yr. ended 12/31/01): Grants paid, $53,000; assets, $940,977 (M); gifts received, $501,000; expenditures, $54,200; qualifying distributions, $53,000.
Limitations: Applications not accepted. Giving primarily in RI.
Application information: Contributes only to pre-selected organizations.
Trustee: Paul J. Salem.
EIN: 137196668

48931
Tzapik Bagdasarian Charitable Trust
c/o Fleet Private Clients Group
P.O. Box 6767
Providence, RI 02940-6767

Established in 1987 in MA.
Financial data (yr. ended 12/31/01): Grants paid, $52,856; assets, $1,156,303 (M); gifts received, $8,388; expenditures, $71,520; qualifying distributions, $62,701.
Limitations: Applications not accepted. Giving primarily in New York, NY.
Application information: Contributes only to pre-selected organizations.
Trustee: Fleet National Bank.
EIN: 042768324

48932
W. Gerald Moore Educational Foundation
c/o Fleet Private Clients Group
P.O. Box 6767
Providence, RI 02940-6767
Application address: c/o Fleet National Bank, 100 Federal St., Boston, MA 02110, tel.: (617) 434-4644
Contact: Augusta Haydock, Trust Off., Fleet National Bank

Financial data (yr. ended 12/31/01): Grants paid, $52,849; assets, $1,058,037 (M); expenditures, $64,866; qualifying distributions, $58,839.
Limitations: Giving primarily in MA.
Trustee: Fleet National Bank.
EIN: 046010445

48933
Edward S. Dunton Charitable Remainder Trust
c/o Fleet Private Clients Group
P.O. Box 6767
Providence, RI 02940-6767

Established in 1992 in ME.

48933—RHODE ISLAND

Financial data (yr. ended 12/31/01): Grants paid, $52,300; assets, $1,344,134 (M); expenditures, $74,862; qualifying distributions, $65,983.
Limitations: Applications not accepted. Giving limited to ME.
Application information: Contributes only to pre-selected organizations.
Trustees: Theodore H. Warner, Fleet National Bank.
EIN: 016072876

48934
Nathaniel Wheeler Trust
c/o Fleet Private Clients Group
P.O. Box 6767
Providence, RI 02940-6767
Contact: Vincent J. Hoffman, Tr. Off., Fleet National Bank

Established in 1979 in MA.
Donor(s): Nathaniel Wheeler.‡
Financial data (yr. ended 12/31/01): Grants paid, $52,170; assets, $1,428,469 (M); expenditures, $70,447; qualifying distributions, $61,562.
Limitations: Giving limited to Worcester, MA.
Publications: Application guidelines.
Trustee: Fleet National Bank.
EIN: 046437271

48935
Alexis Bierman Hafken Family Foundation
1500 Fleet Ctr.
Providence, RI 02903-2319
Contact: Paul A. Silver, Tr.

Established in 1997 in RI.
Donor(s): Alexis Bierman Hafken.
Financial data (yr. ended 12/31/01): Grants paid, $51,749; assets, $716,618 (M); expenditures, $59,987; qualifying distributions, $51,749.
Limitations: Giving primarily in RI.
Application information: Application form not required.
Trustees: Alexis Bierman Hafken, Paul A. Silver.
EIN: 061484432

48936
Nicholas J. Caldarone Foundation
c/o Citizens Bank
870 Westminster St.
Providence, RI 02903
Application address: 420 Angell St., Providence, RI 02906
Contact: Irving J. Waldman, Tr.

Established in 1992 in RI.
Financial data (yr. ended 05/31/02): Grants paid, $51,000; assets, $1,170,961 (M); gifts received, $729,436; expenditures, $81,651; qualifying distributions, $51,000.
Trustees: James J. McGaire, Irving J. Waldman, Citizens Bank of Rhode Island.
EIN: 050467833

48937
Florian O. Bartlett Trust
c/o Fleet Private Clients Group
P.O. Box 6767
Providence, RI 02940-6767
Application address: 100 Federal St., Boston, MA 02110

Financial data (yr. ended 09/30/01): Grants paid, $50,000; assets, $869,426 (M); expenditures, $68,471; qualifying distributions, $54,120.
Limitations: Giving primarily in MA.
Trustee: Fleet National Bank.
EIN: 046008674

48938
Trustees of Long Wharf & Public School
31 1/2 Forwell St.
Newport, RI 02840

Chartered in 1795 in RI.
Financial data (yr. ended 12/31/01): Grants paid, $50,000; assets, $894,880 (M); expenditures, $59,901; qualifying distributions, $50,000.
Limitations: Applications not accepted. Giving limited to Newport, RI.
Application information: Scholarship applicants other than Newport students are not considered. For other grants, foundation contributes only to pre-selected organizations.
Officers and Trustees:* William Leys,* Pres.; Charlotte A. Yeomans, Secy.-Treas.; Craig P. Baker, Edward B. Corcoran, Charles E. Gibbons, Leonard J. Panaggio, John F. Smith, and 9 additional trustees.
EIN: 056016284

48939
Marzahl Charitable Trust
c/o Fleet Private Clients Group
P.O. Box 6767
Providence, RI 02940-6767

Established in 2001 in CT.
Donor(s): Anne L. Marzahl Trust.
Financial data (yr. ended 12/31/01): Grants paid, $50,000; assets, $956,850 (M); gifts received, $790,777; expenditures, $61,805; qualifying distributions, $57,822.
Limitations: Applications not accepted. Giving primarily in Waterbury, CT.
Application information: Contributes only to pre-selected organizations.
Trustee: Fleet National Bank.
EIN: 043559568

48940
Thomas F. Gilbane, Jr. Family Foundation
151 Grotto Ave.
Providence, RI 02906-5720 (401) 456-5800
Contact: Thomas F. Gilbane Jr., Dir.

Established in 1987 in RI.
Donor(s): Thomas F. Gilbane, Jr.
Financial data (yr. ended 12/31/01): Grants paid, $49,540; assets, $67,808 (M); gifts received, $49,540; expenditures, $49,604; qualifying distributions, $49,540.
Application information: Application form not required.
Directors: Mary Gilbane, Thomas F. Gilbane, Jr., H. Peter Olsen.
EIN: 050427056

48941
Fradin Family Foundation
c/o Rosenstein Halper & Maselli, LLP
27 Dryden Ln.
Providence, RI 02904

Established in 1994.
Donor(s): Paul M. Fradin.
Financial data (yr. ended 09/30/01): Grants paid, $49,500; assets, $7,150 (M); gifts received, $53,000; expenditures, $49,667; qualifying distributions, $49,500.
Limitations: Applications not accepted. Giving primarily in RI.
Application information: Unsolicited applications not considered.
Officers: Paul M. Fradin, Pres.; Charles S. Fradin, Secy.; Frank G. Halper, Treas.
EIN: 050481553

48942
John A. & Irene Papines Scholarship Trust
c/o Fleet Private Clients Group
P.O. Box 6767
Providence, RI 02940-6767
Application address: c/o Fleet National Bank, 1125 Rte. 22 W., Bridgewater, NJ 08807

Financial data (yr. ended 12/31/00): Grants paid, $49,400; assets, $751,943 (M); expenditures, $56,107; qualifying distributions, $51,594.
Limitations: Giving limited to Atlantic, Cape May, Cumberland, and Ocean counties, NJ.
Application information: Application form required.
Trustee: Fleet National Bank.
EIN: 226321385
Codes: GTI

48943
Diana S. Adelson Trust
c/o Corcoran, Peckham & Hayes
P.O. Box 389
Newport, RI 02840
Application address: 31 America's Cup Ave., Newport, RI 02840, tel.: (401) 847-0872
Contact: Edward B. Corcoran

Established in 1992 in RI.
Donor(s): Diana Adelson.‡
Financial data (yr. ended 12/31/01): Grants paid, $49,000; assets, $700,375 (M); expenditures, $64,341; qualifying distributions, $49,000.
Limitations: Giving limited to RI.
Application information: Application form not required.
Trustees: Edwin S. Gozonsky, Rita Slom, Jeffrey J. Teitz.
EIN: 050466295

48944
The John and Karin McCormick Foundation, Inc.
3 Pawcatuck Ave.
Westerly, RI 02891

Established in 1986.
Donor(s): John McCormick, Karin McCormick.
Financial data (yr. ended 05/31/02): Grants paid, $48,650; assets, $237,299 (M); expenditures, $51,240; qualifying distributions, $48,650.
Limitations: Applications not accepted. Giving primarily in CT and RI.
Application information: Contributes only to pre-selected organizations.
Officers and Directors:* John McCormick,* Pres. and Treas.; Karin McCormick,* Secy.; Robert Lombardo, M.D.
EIN: 050426399

48945
Mabel Glidden Smith Trust
c/o Fleet Private Clients Group
P.O. Box 6767
Providence, RI 02940-6767
Application address: 777 Main St., Hartford, CT 06115
Contact: Marjorie Alexandre Davis, Trust Off., Fleet National Bank

Financial data (yr. ended 12/31/01): Grants paid, $48,543; assets, $1,537,373 (M); expenditures, $65,812; qualifying distributions, $58,411.
Limitations: Giving primarily in New London, CT.
Application information: Application form required.
Trustee: Fleet National Bank.
EIN: 066031161

48946
Edward V. & Larry V. Egavian Foundation
c/o Rosenstein, Halper & Maselli, LLP
27 Dryden Ln.
Providence, RI 02904-2782
Application address: 155 S. Main St., Providence, RI 02903, tel.: (401) 751-7500
Contact: Walter F. Gibbons, Tr.

Financial data (yr. ended 12/31/00): Grants paid, $48,397; assets, $1 (M); expenditures, $55,149; qualifying distributions, $48,397.
Limitations: Giving limited to RI.
Trustees: Walter F. Gibbons, Torkam Manogian.
EIN: 056017874

48947
Eaton & Reed Scholarship Fund Trust
c/o Fleet Private Clients Group
P.O. Box 6767
Providence, RI 02940-6767
Application address: c/o Guidance Office, Manchester High School, 134 Middle Tpke., East Manchester, CT 06040

Established in 1985 in CT.
Financial data (yr. ended 09/30/01): Grants paid, $47,900; assets, $682,396 (M); expenditures, $58,858; qualifying distributions, $54,318.
Limitations: Giving limited to Manchester, CT.
Application information: Application form required.
Trustee: Fleet National Bank.
EIN: 237146710
Codes: GTI

48948
Narragansett Preservation and Improvement Association
c/o Edwards & Angell
1 Financial Plz.
Providence, RI 02903-2499
Contact: Bernard Buonanno, Jr., Pres.

Financial data (yr. ended 12/31/00): Grants paid, $47,215; assets, $786,131 (M); expenditures, $58,750; qualifying distributions, $55,683.
Limitations: Giving limited to the Narragansett, RI, area.
Application information: Application form required.
Officer: Bernard Buonanno, Jr., Pres. and Secy.-Treas.
Directors: Sandra Dennelle, John Hickey, William O'Neill, Joseph Sinclair.
EIN: 056019179

48949
Helen E. Ellis Trust
c/o Fleet Private Clients Group
P.O. Box 6767
Providence, RI 02940-6767
Application address: c/o Carol Gray, 100 Federal St., Boston, MA 02110, tel.: (617) 434-3768

Established in 1988 in MA.
Financial data (yr. ended 12/31/01): Grants paid, $46,690; assets, $974,849 (M); expenditures, $56,868; qualifying distributions, $46,690.
Limitations: Giving primarily in Westport, MA.
Trustee: Fleet National Bank.
EIN: 046015314

48950
The Moore Company Foundation
c/o Alexandra Moore, Barber-Moore Co.
P.O. Box 538
Westerly, RI 02891 (401) 596-2816

Established in 1998.
Donor(s): The Moore Company.
Financial data (yr. ended 12/31/01): Grants paid, $45,650; assets, $785,123 (M); expenditures, $50,891; qualifying distributions, $45,478.
Limitations: Giving limited to NY and RI.
Application information: Unsolicited request for funds not accepted.
Trustees: Alexandra Moore Barber, George W. Markham, Dorothea B. Moore, George C. Moore, Jr., Peter F. Moore.
EIN: 050499128
Codes: CS, CD

48951
Norman J. and Anna B. Gould Scholarship Fund
c/o Fleet Private Clients Group
P.O. Box 6767
Providence, RI 02940-6767
Application address: c/o Dick Landers, Goulds Pumps, Inc., 291 Fall St., Seneca Falls, NY 13148

Established in 1988 in NY.
Financial data (yr. ended 09/30/01): Grants paid, $45,150; assets, $1,095,740 (M); expenditures, $56,883; qualifying distributions, $53,038.
Limitations: Giving limited to residents of Seneca Falls, NY.
Application information: Application form not required.
Trustee: Fleet National Bank.
EIN: 166318641
Codes: GTI

48952
Charles Samdperil Humanitarian Memorial Foundation
P.O. Box 992
Providence, RI 02901

Financial data (yr. ended 12/31/01): Grants paid, $45,106; assets, $945,299 (M); gifts received, $17,600; expenditures, $47,509; qualifying distributions, $45,106.
Limitations: Applications not accepted. Giving primarily in FL and RI.
Application information: Contributes only to pre-selected organizations.
Director: Gabriel Samdperil.
EIN: 050397612

48953
Waldo & Alice Ayer Trust
c/o Citizens Bank New Hampshire
870 Westminster St.
Providence, RI 02903
Application address: c/o Citizens Bank New Hampshire, 875 Elm St., Manchester, NH 03101, tel.: (603) 634-4752
Contact: Bill Sirak

Financial data (yr. ended 09/30/01): Grants paid, $45,084; assets, $821,920 (M); expenditures, $59,054; qualifying distributions, $49,759.
Limitations: Giving limited to NH.
Trustee: Citizens Bank New Hampshire.
EIN: 026059690
Codes: GTI

48954
Aaron Hollander Trust
c/o Fleet Private Clients Group
P.O. Box 6767
Providence, RI 02940-6767

Donor(s): Aaron Hollander.‡
Financial data (yr. ended 12/31/01): Grants paid, $44,575; assets, $1,055,922 (M); expenditures, $59,591; qualifying distributions, $53,217.
Limitations: Applications not accepted. Giving primarily in Hartford, CT.
Application information: Contributes only to pre-selected organizations.
Trustees: Samuel H. Title, Frederic Werner, Fleet National Bank.
EIN: 066028519

48955
Forman Family Charitable Trust
P.O. Box 603328
Providence, RI 02906

Financial data (yr. ended 12/31/01): Grants paid, $44,275; assets, $701,230 (M); expenditures, $44,709; qualifying distributions, $43,857.
Limitations: Giving primarily in RI.
Officer and Trustees:* Roy Forman,* Mgr.; Audrey Robbins, Jill Starr.
EIN: 056069697

48956
Frank S. Parmenter Trust
c/o Fleet Private Clients Group
P.O. Box 6767
Providence, RI 02940-6767
Application address: 75 State St., Boston, MA 02109
Contact: D. Pearce, Trust Admin., Fleet National Bank

Donor(s): Frank S. Parmenter.‡
Financial data (yr. ended 09/30/01): Grants paid, $44,000; assets, $886,086 (M); expenditures, $58,815; qualifying distributions, $51,243.
Limitations: Giving limited to the Athol, MA, area.
Application information: Application form required.
Trustees: R. Rand Haven, Edward J. Herd, Leonard E. King, Robert M. Tyler, Fleet National Bank.
EIN: 046025922

48957
G.P.B. Foundation
99 E. Sakonnet Point Rd.
Little Compton, RI 02837

Established in 1997 in RI.
Donor(s): Greta P. Brown.
Financial data (yr. ended 12/31/01): Grants paid, $43,700; assets, $608,881 (M); expenditures, $47,460; qualifying distributions, $43,700.
Limitations: Applications not accepted. Giving primarily in Little Compton, RI.
Application information: Contributes only to pre-selected organizations.
Officers and Directors:* Greta P. Brown,* Pres. and Treas.; James P. Brown III,* V.P.; Kristin M. Brown,* V.P.; Scott Pearson Brown,* V.P.; Robert Cummings,* Secy.
EIN: 061484294

48958
Margaret & Donald Matheson Scholarship Fund
c/o Fleet Private Clients Group
P.O. Box 6767
Providence, RI 02940-6767
Application address: c/o Winslow High School, Scholarship Comm., 14 Danielson St., Winslow, ME 04901-6895

Established in 1997 in ME.
Financial data (yr. ended 12/31/01): Grants paid, $43,375; assets, $650,609 (M); expenditures, $50,116; qualifying distributions, $47,594.
Limitations: Giving limited to residents of ME.
Trustee: Fleet National Bank.
EIN: 010504173

48959
George B. Corby Memorial Fund
c/o Fleet Private Clients Group
P.O. Box 6767
Providence, RI 02940-6767

Financial data (yr. ended 01/31/02): Grants paid, $43,084; assets, $329,302 (M); expenditures, $51,103; qualifying distributions, $43,084.
Limitations: Applications not accepted. Giving primarily in NY.
Application information: Contributes only to pre-selected organizations.
Trustees: Byron Johnson, Fleet National Bank.
EIN: 166148217

48960
Laura A. Burgess Fund
c/o Fleet Private Clients Group
P.O. Box 6767
Providence, RI 02940-6767
Application address: c/o Emma Greene, Fleet National Bank, 100 Federal St., Boston, MA 02110, tel.: (617) 434-4644

Financial data (yr. ended 12/31/01): Grants paid, $42,689; assets, $1,005,128 (M); expenditures, $57,190; qualifying distributions, $50,870.
Limitations: Giving for the benefit of female residents of RI.
Trustee: Fleet National Bank.
EIN: 056004330
Codes: GTI

48961
Joseph S. Stackpole Trust
c/o Fleet Private Clients Group
P.O. Box 6767
Providence, RI 02940-6767
Contact: Sheila P. Rostow

Financial data (yr. ended 03/31/02): Grants paid, $42,550; assets, $1,022,720 (M); expenditures, $57,277; qualifying distributions, $50,040.
Limitations: Giving primarily in the Hartford, CT, area.
Trustee: Fleet National Bank.
EIN: 066024048

48962
Harry C. & Mary E. Grafton Memorial Fund
(also known as Harry C. Grafton, Jr. Memorial Fund)
c/o Fleet Private Clients Group
P.O. Box 6767
Providence, RI 02940-6767
Applicaton address: c/o John M. Dolan, 28 State St., Boston, MA 02109-1775

Donor(s): Harry C. Grafton, Jr.‡
Financial data (yr. ended 12/31/01): Grants paid, $42,500; assets, $960,401 (M); expenditures, $57,034; qualifying distributions, $50,733.
Limitations: Giving limited to Duxbury, MA.
Trustees: William Boynton, Fleet National Bank.
EIN: 046118945

48963
The Weingeroff Family Foundation
1 Weingeroff Blvd.
Cranston, RI 02910-4019

Established in 1998 in RI.
Donor(s): Frederick Weingeroff.
Financial data (yr. ended 11/30/01): Grants paid, $42,239; assets, $117,276 (M); expenditures, $44,838; qualifying distributions, $42,239.
Limitations: Applications not accepted. Giving limited to Palm Beach, FL, New York, NY, and Providence, RI.
Application information: Contributes only to pre-selected organizations.
Trustees: Frederick Weingeroff, Gregg Weingeroff.
EIN: 056115653

48964
Mary Louise Billings Trust
c/o Citizens Bank
870 Westminster St.
Providence, RI 02903
Contact: Bill Sirak, Trust Off., Citizens Bank

Established in 1974.
Financial data (yr. ended 12/31/01): Grants paid, $42,123; assets, $955,305 (M); expenditures, $53,803; qualifying distributions, $42,123.
Limitations: Giving primarily in NH.
Trustee: Citizens Bank New Hampshire.
EIN: 026021132

48965
The Larry V. and Dorothy T. Egavian Foundation
c/o Ralph M. Kinder
155 S. Main St.
Providence, RI 02903-2963

Established in 2000 in RI.
Donor(s): Dorothy Egavian.
Financial data (yr. ended 12/31/01): Grants paid, $42,000; assets, $958,383 (M); expenditures, $50,784; qualifying distributions, $42,000.
Limitations: Applications not accepted.
Application information: Contributes only to pre-selected organizations.
Officers: Dorothy T. Egavian, Pres.; Ralph M. Kinder, V.P.; Cathy A. Brien, Secy.; James E. Tweedy, Treas.
Directors: James Norberg, Robert Norberg, Susan Stickel, David A. Tweedy.
EIN: 050510792

48966
The DeBlois Foundation
c/o DeBlois Oil Co.
P.O. Box 9471
Providence, RI 02940 (401) 722-8005
Application address: c/o Scholarship Comm., P.O. Box 6027, Providence, RI 02940
Contact: Robert C. DeBlois

Established in 1988 in RI.
Donor(s): DeBlois Oil Co.
Financial data (yr. ended 12/31/01): Grants paid, $41,900; assets, $672,923 (M); expenditures, $46,751; qualifying distributions, $41,900.
Limitations: Giving primarily in RI.
Application information: Application form required.
Trustees: Arthur J. DeBlois III, Robert E. DeBlois.
EIN: 222887276
Codes: CS, CD

48967
Parker-Nelson Foundation
c/o Citizens Bank New Hampshire
870 Westminster St., 2nd Fl.
Providence, RI 02903
Application address: 875 Elm St., Manchester, NH 03101, tel.: (603) 634-7752
Contact: William Sirak, V.P., Citizens Bank New Hampshire

Financial data (yr. ended 09/30/02): Grants paid, $41,131; assets, $605,068 (M); expenditures, $52,294; qualifying distributions, $41,131.
Limitations: Giving primarily in NH.
Publications: Application guidelines.
Trustee: Citizens Bank New Hampshire.
EIN: 026013012

48968
Sarah G. McCarthy Memorial Foundation
c/o Fleet Private Clients Group
P.O. Box 6767
Providence, RI 02940-6767
Application address: 100 Federal St., Boston, MA 02110
Contact: Laura McGregor, V.P., Fleet National Bank

Established in 1948.
Financial data (yr. ended 12/31/01): Grants paid, $41,000; assets, $1,070,048 (M); expenditures, $54,571; qualifying distributions, $49,378.
Limitations: Giving limited to Peabody, MA.
Trustees: Caroline Lee Herter, Elton McCausland, J. David Moran, Fleet National Bank.
EIN: 046020729

48969
Helen U. Kiely Trust
c/o Fleet Private Clients Group
P.O. Box 6767
Providence, RI 02940-6767
Application address: c/o Fleet National Bank, 100 Federal St., Boston, MA 02110

Established in 1984 in MA.
Financial data (yr. ended 12/31/01): Grants paid, $40,450; assets, $1,256,909 (M); expenditures, $65,860; qualifying distributions, $50,587.
Limitations: Giving limited to Northampton, MA.
Application information: Application form required.
Trustees: John F. Foley, Fleet National Bank.
EIN: 046278297
Codes: GTI

48970
Greater Bridgeport Retired Teachers Building Fund
c/o Fleet Private Clients Group
P.O. Box 6767
Providence, RI 02940-6767
Application address: c/o Wanda Dick, 17 Channing Rd., Trumbull, CT 06611

Established in 1988 in CT.
Financial data (yr. ended 06/30/01): Grants paid, $40,262; assets, $1,225,549 (M); expenditures, $50,997; qualifying distributions, $45,967.
Limitations: Giving limited to the greater Bridgeport, CT, area.
Application information: Application form not required.
Officers: Wanda Dick, Pres.; Margaret Bierbaum, V.P.; Rose Pellegrino, 2nd V.P.; Steven Balgach, Secy.; Catherine Bunting, Corresponding Secy.; Ella Rice, Treas.
Trustee: Fleet National Bank.
EIN: 237258527
Codes: GTI

48971
J. Wilfred Anctil Foundation
c/o Citizens Bank
870 Westminster St.
Providence, RI 02903
Application address: c/o Wayne Nelson, P.O. Box 96, Nashua, NH 03061-0096

Established in 1956 in NH.
Financial data (yr. ended 12/31/01): Grants paid, $40,250; assets, $1,312,760 (M); expenditures, $65,848; qualifying distributions, $51,910.
Limitations: Giving limited to the greater Nashua, NH, area.
Application information: Application form required.
Officers: Berard Masse, Chair.; Stanley Stoncius, Pres.; Maurice L. Arel, Secy.-Treas.

Trustee: Citizens Bank.
EIN: 026007760
Codes: GTI

48972
Anna F. Ardenghi Trust for General Charitable Purposes
c/o Fleet Private Clients Group
P.O. Box 6767
Providence, RI 02940-6767
Application address: c/o Barbara Daniels, Fleet National Bank, P.O. Box 2210, Waterbury, CT 06702

Financial data (yr. ended 12/31/01): Grants paid, $40,000; assets, $761,482 (M); expenditures, $49,021; qualifying distributions, $40,000.
Limitations: Giving limited to New Haven, CT.
Trustee: Fleet National Bank.
EIN: 066240247

48973
Almira N. Simons Trust
c/o Fleet Private Clients Group
P.O. Box 6767
Providence, RI 02940-6767
Application address: P.O. Box 1861, Boston, MA 02205-1781
Contact: Augusta K. Haydock, Trust Off., Fleet National Bank

Financial data (yr. ended 09/30/01): Grants paid, $39,401; assets, $932,968 (M); expenditures, $51,182; qualifying distributions, $46,291.
Limitations: Giving limited to residents of Wellesley, MA.
Application information: Application form not required.
Trustee: Fleet National Bank.
EIN: 046008364

48974
Ress Family Foundation
P.O. Box 6485
Providence, RI 02940-6485

Established in 1955 in RI.
Donor(s): Joseph W. Ress, Anne Ress, Betsy Jacobson, Ellen G. Reeves, Joan Ress Reeves.
Financial data (yr. ended 12/31/00): Grants paid, $38,856; assets, $2,115,725 (M); expenditures, $47,676; qualifying distributions, $40,157.
Limitations: Applications not accepted. Giving primarily in RI.
Application information: Contributes only to pre-selected organizations.
Trustees: Ellen G. Reeves, Joan Ress Reeves.
EIN: 056006308

48975
Lucy J. McMurtrie Foundation
c/o Fleet Private Clients Group
P.O. Box 6767
Providence, RI 02940-6767
Application address: c/o Office of the Principal, Roxbury High School, Succasunna, NJ 07876, tel.: (201) 584-1200

Established in 1990 in NJ.
Donor(s): Lucy J. McMurtrie.‡
Financial data (yr. ended 12/31/01): Grants paid, $38,750; assets, $605,988 (M); expenditures, $46,015; qualifying distributions, $43,465.
Limitations: Giving limited to Succasunna, NJ.
Trustees: George W. Johnson, Fleet National Bank.
EIN: 226426610
Codes: GTI

48976
Kilmartin Charitable Corporation
517 Mineral Spring Ave.
Pawtucket, RI 02860-3408 (401) 274-1600
Contact: John J. Kilcoyne, Treas.

Established in 1982 in RI.
Donor(s): International Packaging Corp.
Financial data (yr. ended 12/31/01): Grants paid, $38,600; assets, $876,187 (M); gifts received, $100,000; expenditures, $44,910; qualifying distributions, $39,100.
Limitations: Giving primarily in NY and RI.
Officers: John D. Kilmartin III, Pres.; Paul F. Kilmartin III, Secy.; John J. Kilcoyne, Treas.
EIN: 050398850

48977
O'Farrell Family Foundation, Inc.
76 Taber Ave.
Providence, RI 02906

Established in 2001 in RI.
Donor(s): William J. O'Farrell, Noreen Drexel O'Farrell.
Financial data (yr. ended 12/31/01): Grants paid, $38,535; assets, $39,328 (M); gifts received, $1,772; expenditures, $38,615; qualifying distributions, $38,535.
Limitations: Applications not accepted.
Application information: Contributes only to pre-selected organizations.
Officers: William J. O'Farrell, Pres. and Treas.; Noreen Drexel O'Farrell, V.P. and Secy.
EIN: 050514165

48978
Lillian M. Baker Trust
c/o Fleet Private Clients Group
P.O. Box 6767
Providence, RI 02940-6767
Application address: 100 Federal St., Boston, MA 02110, tel.: (617) 434-5669
Contact: Sharon M. Driscoll, Trust Off., Fleet National Bank

Financial data (yr. ended 12/31/01): Grants paid, $38,500; assets, $769,130 (M); expenditures, $46,293; qualifying distributions, $42,262.
Limitations: Giving primarily in ME.
Trustee: Fleet National Bank.
EIN: 046010588
Codes: GTI

48979
Franklin H. Putnam Trust
c/o Fleet Private Clients Group
P.O. Box 6767
Providence, RI 02940-6767
Application address: 100 Federal St., Boston, MA 02105, tel.: (617) 434-3768
Contact: Carol Gray, Trust Off., Fleet National Bank

Financial data (yr. ended 12/31/01): Grants paid, $38,095; assets, $869,294 (M); expenditures, $53,510; qualifying distributions, $43,481.
Limitations: Giving limited to MA.
Application information: Application form required.
Trustee: Fleet National Bank.
EIN: 046009430
Codes: GTI

48980
Henry E. & Abigail E. Ellsworth Fund
c/o Fleet Private Clients Group
P.O. Box 6767
Providence, RI 02940-6767

Established in 1993 in CT.

Financial data (yr. ended 05/31/02): Grants paid, $38,021; assets, $842,102 (M); expenditures, $49,392; qualifying distributions, $45,575.
Limitations: Applications not accepted. Giving primarily in CT.
Application information: Contributes only to pre-selected organizations.
Trustee: Fleet National Bank.
EIN: 066399085

48981
Marvin and Roberta Holland Family Foundation
4 Woodland Terr.
Providence, RI 02906-5808

Established in 1986 in RI.
Donor(s): Betsy Holland, Bruce Holland, Marvin S. Holland, Roberta Holland, American Chemical Works.
Financial data (yr. ended 12/31/01): Grants paid, $37,855; assets, $63,621 (M); gifts received, $19,000; expenditures, $38,170; qualifying distributions, $37,855.
Limitations: Applications not accepted. Giving primarily in Providence, RI.
Application information: Contributes only to pre-selected organizations.
Trustees: Bruce S. Holland, Marvin S. Holland, Roberta Holland.
EIN: 056080166

48982
The O'Halloran Family Foundation
158 Main St.
Wickford, RI 02852

Established in 2000 in RI.
Donor(s): Alice O'Halloran, Gerard O'Halloran.
Financial data (yr. ended 12/31/01): Grants paid, $37,800; assets, $1,187,570 (M); gifts received, $297,162; expenditures, $37,853; qualifying distributions, $37,800.
Limitations: Applications not accepted.
Application information: Contributes only to pre-selected organizations.
Trustees: Gerard O'Halloran, Mary Ann O'Halloran.
EIN: 050514803

48983
Primate Conservation, Inc.
1411 Shannock Rd.
Charlestown, RI 02813
E-mail: 74227.2342@compuserve.com
Contact: Noel Rowe, Pres.

Established in 1992 in NY.
Donor(s): Noel Rowe.
Financial data (yr. ended 12/31/99): Grants paid, $37,775; assets, $434,141 (M); gifts received, $49,964; expenditures, $45,364; qualifying distributions, $37,775.
Application information: Application form required.
Officer: Noel Rowe, Pres.
EIN: 113152696
Codes: GTI

48984
Walter S. Bartlett Trust Fund
c/o Fleet Private Clients Group
P.O. Box 6767
Providence, RI 02940-6767

Financial data (yr. ended 12/31/01): Grants paid, $37,311; assets, $708,216 (M); expenditures, $45,905; qualifying distributions, $41,522.
Limitations: Applications not accepted. Giving limited to Boston, MA, and Kingston, NH.
Application information: Contributes only to pre-selected organizations.

48984—RHODE ISLAND

Trustee: Fleet National Bank.
EIN: 026007741

48985
The Orr Foundation
c/o Fleet Private Clients Group
P.O. Box 6767
Providence, RI 02940-6767
Application addresses: c/o Guidance Counselor, Newton North High School, 360 Lowell Ave., Newtonville, MA 02660-1831; c/o Guidance Counselor, Newton South High School, 140 Brandeis Rd., Newton Centre, MA 02459-2745

Financial data (yr. ended 12/31/01): Grants paid, $37,200; assets, $829,799 (M); expenditures, $45,084; qualifying distributions, $40,650.
Limitations: Giving limited to residents of Newtonville and Newton Centre, MA.
Application information: Application form required.
Trustee: Fleet National Bank.
EIN: 046034509
Codes: GTI

48986
Darthea Morrow Scholarship Trust
c/o Fleet Private Clients Group
P.O. Box 6767
Providence, RI 02940-6767
Application address: c/o Scholarship Comm., Nauset Regional High School, North Eastham, MA 02651
Contact: Deborah Dillon Pearce

Financial data (yr. ended 12/31/01): Grants paid, $37,000; assets, $1,112,532 (M); expenditures, $48,242; qualifying distributions, $43,641.
Limitations: Giving limited to the North Eastham, MA, area.
Application information: Application form required.
Trustee: Fleet National Bank.
EIN: 042866532
Codes: GTI

48987
Standish Foundation Trust
c/o Fleet Private Clients Group
P.O. Box 6767
Providence, RI 02940-6767
Application address: c/o Fleet National Bank, 69 State St., Albany, NY 12201

Financial data (yr. ended 11/30/01): Grants paid, $37,000; assets, $598,449 (M); expenditures, $44,189; qualifying distributions, $40,735.
Limitations: Giving primarily in Albany, NY.
Trustee: Fleet National Bank.
EIN: 146079338

48988
Cecile Belliveau Charitable Trust
c/o Fleet Private Clients Group
P.O. Box 6767
Providence, RI 02940-6767

Established in 1997 in NY.
Financial data (yr. ended 12/31/01): Grants paid, $36,824; assets, $1,006,740 (M); expenditures, $49,382; qualifying distributions, $43,338.
Limitations: Applications not accepted. Giving primarily in NY.
Application information: Contributes only to pre-selected organizations.
Trustee: Fleet National Bank.
EIN: 050486928

48989
Marion W. Rich Fund
c/o Fleet Private Clients Group
P.O. Box 6767
Providence, RI 02940-6767
Application address: 100 Federal St., Boston, MA 02110, tel.: (614) 434-4644
Contact: Augusta Haydock, Trust Off., Fleet National Bank

Established in 1985 in MA.
Donor(s): Charles J. Rich.‡
Financial data (yr. ended 12/31/01): Grants paid, $36,665; assets, $811,499 (M); expenditures, $44,496; qualifying distributions, $40,107.
Limitations: Giving limited to Norwood, MA.
Trustee: Fleet National Bank.
EIN: 046133986

48990
The Attleboro Foundation
(Formerly U-A Attleboro Foundation)
c/o Fleet Private Clients Group
P.O. Box 6767
Providence, RI 02940-6767

Financial data (yr. ended 12/31/01): Grants paid, $36,414; assets, $814,787 (M); expenditures, $45,527; qualifying distributions, $42,007.
Limitations: Applications not accepted. Giving limited to Attleboro, MA.
Trustee: Fleet National Bank.
EIN: 046007842

48991
Urania C. Sherburne Trust
c/o Fleet Private Clients Group
P.O. Box 6767
Providence, RI 02940-6767
Application address: c/o Fleet National Bank, 100 Federal St. Boston, MA 02110, tel.: (617) 434-4644

Financial data (yr. ended 12/31/01): Grants paid, $35,750; assets, $735,936 (M); expenditures, $48,652; qualifying distributions, $42,732.
Limitations: Giving limited to RI.
Trustees: Richard L. Holmes, Fleet National Bank.
EIN: 056004108

48992
Elizabeth Woodward Means Trust
c/o Fleet Private Clients Group
P.O. Box 6767
Providence, RI 02940-6767
Application address: c/o Fleet National Bank of Maine, Exchange St., Bangor, ME 04401

Financial data (yr. ended 04/30/01): Grants paid, $35,650; assets, $723,080 (M); expenditures, $45,001; qualifying distributions, $41,341.
Limitations: Giving limited to Bangor, ME.
Trustee: Fleet National Bank.
EIN: 016040690

48993
Forsyth Educational Fund
(Formerly Fred Forsyth Educational Trust Fund)
c/o Fleet Private Clients Group
P.O. Box 6767
Providence, RI 02940-6767
Application address: c/o Bucksport High School Guidance Office, Bucksport, ME 04416

Financial data (yr. ended 07/31/01): Grants paid, $35,400; assets, $860,979 (M); expenditures, $44,566; qualifying distributions, $40,896.
Limitations: Giving limited to Bucksport, ME.
Trustee: Fleet National Bank.
EIN: 016059631
Codes: GTI

48994
Providence Female Charitable Society
87 Don Ave.
Rumford, RI 02916
Contact: Mrs. Charles E. Gross, Treas.

Financial data (yr. ended 03/31/01): Grants paid, $35,200; assets, $678,826 (M); expenditures, $39,255; qualifying distributions, $34,088.
Limitations: Giving limited to residents of RI.
Officers: Mrs. William Slater Allen, Secy.; Mrs. Charles E. Gross, Treas.
Directors: Mrs. A. Middletown Gammell, Mrs. Peter Westervelt.
EIN: 056008631
Codes: GTI

48995
Hamilton Fish Webster Medical Fund
c/o Fleet Private Clients Group
P.O. Box 6767
Providence, RI 02940-6767
Application address: 114 Bayview Ave., Portsmouth, RI 02871
Contact: Virginia B. Samson, Chair.

Established in 1939.
Financial data (yr. ended 12/31/01): Grants paid, $34,808; assets, $1,167,438 (M); expenditures, $56,654; qualifying distributions, $49,649.
Limitations: Giving limited to Aquidneck Island, RI.
Application information: Applicants may contact any member of the Board of Directors. Application form required.
Officer and Directors:* Virginia B. Samson,* Chair.; Canon D. Lorne Coyle, Stephanie Fore-Keating, Rev. Everett H. Greene, Raymond Isacco.
Trustee: Fleet National Bank.
EIN: 056007212
Codes: GTI

48996
Meehan Foundation
9 Meeting St.
Providence, RI 02903 (401) 751-1414
Contact: David J. Meehan, Tr.

Financial data (yr. ended 12/31/01): Grants paid, $34,725; assets, $347,736 (M); expenditures, $35,669; qualifying distributions, $34,725.
Limitations: Giving primarily in Providence, RI.
Application information: Application form not required.
Trustee: David J. Meehan.
EIN: 056015366

48997
Relief Association Trust
(Formerly Relief Association, Inc)
c/o Fleet Private Clients Group
P.O. Box 6767
Providence, RI 02940-6767

Donor(s): D & C Ellis, Tuancy-Harris.
Financial data (yr. ended 12/31/01): Grants paid, $33,890; assets, $749,692 (M); gifts received, $3,000; expenditures, $45,850; qualifying distributions, $39,617.
Limitations: Applications not accepted. Giving limited to residents of Nantucket, MA.
Application information: Unsolicited requests for funds not accepted.
Trustee: Fleet National Bank.
EIN: 046066321
Codes: GTI

48998
The Cowan Family Foundation
c/o Vetter & White
20 Washington Pl.
Providence, RI 02903
Contact: Benjamin V. White, III, Tr.

Established in 1999 in MA.
Donor(s): Rory J. Cowan.
Financial data (yr. ended 12/31/01): Grants paid, $33,751; assets, $189,731 (M); expenditures, $36,385; qualifying distributions, $33,751.
Limitations: Giving on a national basis.
Application information: Application form not required.
Trustee: Benjamin V. White III.
EIN: 050508150

48999
Andrew W. Preston Charity Fund
c/o Fleet Private Clients Group
P.O. Box 6767
Providence, RI 02940-6767
Application address: 100 Federal St., Boston, MA 02110
Contact: Augusta K. Haydock, Trust Off., Fleet National Bank

Financial data (yr. ended 09/30/01): Grants paid, $33,750; assets, $719,650 (M); expenditures, $47,891; qualifying distributions, $36,998.
Limitations: Giving primarily in MA.
Trustee: Fleet National Bank.
EIN: 046008332

49000
Janice T. Berry Trust
c/o Citizens Bank
870 Westminster St.
Providence, RI 02903
Application address: c/o Verna Pare, Citizens Bank New Hampshire, 875 Elm St., Manchester, NH 03101, tel.: (603) 634-7749

Established in 1991 in NH.
Financial data (yr. ended 12/31/01): Grants paid, $33,473; assets, $466,184 (M); expenditures, $40,709; qualifying distributions, $36,792.
Limitations: Giving primarily in Manchester, NH.
Application information: Application form required.
Trustee: Citizens Bank New Hampshire.
EIN: 026067436
Codes: GTI

49001
Frank E. Robbins Memorial Scholarship Fund
c/o Fleet Private Clients Group
P.O. Box 6767
Providence, RI 02940-6767
Application address: c/o Augusta Haydock, Fleet National Bank, 100 Federal St., Boston, MA 02110

Donor(s): Edith M. Robbins.
Financial data (yr. ended 12/31/01): Grants paid, $32,393; assets, $912,000 (M); expenditures, $44,226; qualifying distributions, $35,583.
Limitations: Giving limited to Ann Arbor, MI.
Trustee: Fleet National Bank.
EIN: 046072097

49002
Ernest Guertin Trust
c/o Fleet Private Clients Group
P.O. Box 6767
Providence, RI 02940-6767
Application address: c/o Endowment, 650 Elm St., Manchester, NH 03110

Financial data (yr. ended 12/31/01): Grants paid, $32,025; assets, $442,522 (M); expenditures, $38,085; qualifying distributions, $35,476.
Limitations: Giving on a national basis, with emphasis on NH.
Application information: Application form required. Application form required.
Trustee: Fleet National Bank.
EIN: 026075479
Codes: GTI

49003
Fred L. Murray Irrevocable Trust
c/o Fleet Private Clients Group
P.O. Box 6767
Providence, RI 02940-6767

Established in 1999 in ME.
Financial data (yr. ended 12/31/01): Grants paid, $32,000; assets, $1,029,299 (M); expenditures, $46,193; qualifying distributions, $40,185.
Trustee: Fleet National Bank.
EIN: 016154705

49004
Stauble Scholarship Fund
c/o Fleet Private Clients Group
P.O. Box 6767
Providence, RI 02940-6767
Application address: c/o Wilbur C. Stauble Trust Scholarship Program, Citizen's Scholarship Foundation of America, Inc., P.O. Box 297, 1505 Riverview Rd., St. Peter, MN 56082

Financial data (yr. ended 06/30/01): Grants paid, $32,000; assets, $751,541 (M); expenditures, $43,196; qualifying distributions, $38,336.
Application information: Application form required.
Trustee: Fleet National Bank.
EIN: 060993576

49005
Elwin L. Cilley Trust
c/o Citizens Bank New Hampshire
870 Westminster St.
Providence, RI 02903
Application address: 875 Elm St., Manchester, NH 03101, tel.: (603) 664-7742
Contact: Deborah Drumm, Trust Off., Citizens Bank New Hampshire

Established in 1991 in NH.
Financial data (yr. ended 06/30/02): Grants paid, $31,797; assets, $438,893 (M); expenditures, $39,332; qualifying distributions, $35,190.
Limitations: Giving limited to residents of Nottingham, NH.
Trustee: Citizens Bank New Hampshire.
EIN: 026044555
Codes: GTI

49006
Benjamin J. Donnell Trust
c/o Fleet Privates Clients Group
P.O. Box 6767
Providence, RI 02940-6767

Established in 1991 in ME.
Financial data (yr. ended 08/31/01): Grants paid, $30,989; assets, $645,513 (M); expenditures, $39,582; qualifying distributions, $35,921.
Limitations: Applications not accepted. Giving limited to ME.
Application information: Contributes only to pre-selected organizations.
Trustee: Fleet National Bank.
EIN: 016008020

49007
F. Roger Miller Trust
c/o Fleet Private Clients Group
P.O. Box 6767
Providence, RI 02940-6767
Application address: c/o Scholarship Comm., Waldoboro High School, Waldoboro, ME 03908

Established in 1992 in ME.
Financial data (yr. ended 12/31/01): Grants paid, $30,894; assets, $778,830 (M); expenditures, $39,261; qualifying distributions, $36,197.
Limitations: Giving limited to residents of Waldoboro, ME.
Application information: Application form required for scholarship program. Application form required.
Trustee: Fleet National Bank.
EIN: 016048187
Codes: GTI

49008
The James and Marjorie Yashar Charitable Foundation
c/o James J. Yashar, M.D.
1 Randall Sq., Ste. 408
Providence, RI 02904

Established in 1997 in RI.
Donor(s): James J. Yashar, M.D., Marjorie R. Yashar.
Financial data (yr. ended 02/28/02): Grants paid, $30,890; assets, $735,321 (M); gifts received, $55,800; expenditures, $40,351; qualifying distributions, $30,890.
Limitations: Applications not accepted. Giving primarily in Providence, RI.
Application information: Contributes only to pre-selected organizations.
Trustees: James J. Yashar, M.D., Marjorie R. Yashar.
EIN: 061479766

49009
Norris Cotton Trust
c/o Fleet Private Clients Group
P.O. Box 6767
Providence, RI 02940-6767

Established in 1999 in NH.
Financial data (yr. ended 12/31/01): Grants paid, $30,769; assets, $643,487 (M); expenditures, $38,712; qualifying distributions, $30,769.
Trustee: Fleet National Bank.
EIN: 026060522

49010
David N. Lane Fund
(Formerly David Lane Fund for Indegent Women)
c/o Fleet Private Clients Group
P.O. Box 6767
Providence, RI 02940-6767
Application address: c/o Team, Inc., 30 Elizabeth St., Derby, CT 06418-1846

Financial data (yr. ended 12/31/01): Grants paid, $30,600; assets, $1,043,664 (M); expenditures, $43,245; qualifying distributions, $37,116.
Limitations: Giving limited to Ansonia, Derby, and Shelton, CT.
Application information: Request application forms from Team, Inc. or Connecticut Visiting Nurses Assn. Application form required.
Trustee: Fleet National Bank.
EIN: 066038194

49010—RHODE ISLAND

Codes: GTI

49011
Isaac B. Lawton Trust
c/o Fleet Private Clients Group
P.O. Box 6767
Providence, RI 02940-6767

Financial data (yr. ended 12/31/00): Grants paid, $30,536; assets, $1,005,773 (M); expenditures, $38,942; qualifying distributions, $35,811.
Limitations: Applications not accepted. Giving limited to RI.
Application information: Contributes only to pre-selected organizations.
Trustee: Fleet National Bank.
EIN: 056004620

49012
Claiborne & Nuala Pell Fund
112 Bellevue Ave.
Newport, RI 02840 (401) 846-0120

Donor(s): Claiborne Pell.
Financial data (yr. ended 12/31/01): Grants paid, $30,506; assets, $7,617 (M); gifts received, $35,926; expenditures, $31,151; qualifying distributions, $30,954.
Limitations: Giving primarily in RI.
Trustees: Claiborne Pell, Nuala Pell.
EIN: 056016272

49013
Newell C. Mansir Trust
c/o Fleet Private Cliens Group
P.O. Box 6767
Providence, RI 02940-6767
Application address: 127 State St., Springfield, MA 01144, tel.: (413) 721-2295
Contact: Margaret Mallalieu, Trust Off., Fleet National Bank

Donor(s): Newell C. Mansir.‡
Financial data (yr. ended 12/31/01): Grants paid, $30,500; assets, $750,400 (M); expenditures, $41,220; qualifying distributions, $36,790.
Limitations: Giving primarily in western MA.
Application information: Application form required.
Trustee: Fleet National Bank.
EIN: 046035803

49014
Blacher Foundation
P.O. Box 1417
Providence, RI 02901

Financial data (yr. ended 12/31/01): Grants paid, $30,244; assets, $324,551 (M); expenditures, $30,867; qualifying distributions, $30,244.
Limitations: Applications not accepted. Giving primarily in RI.
Application information: Contributes only to pre-selected organizations.
Trustees: John M. Blacher, Stanley P. Blacher.
EIN: 056008350

49015
Bristolite Foundation
c/o Joan D. Martin
324 North Ln.
Bristol, RI 02809-1575

Financial data (yr. ended 12/31/01): Grants paid, $29,869; assets, $465,283 (M); expenditures, $32,433; qualifying distributions, $29,869.
Limitations: Applications not accepted. Giving limited to RI.
Application information: Contributes only to pre-selected organizations.

Officers and Directors:* Joan D. Martin,* Chair. and Secy.; Edward L. Wrobel,* Vice-Chair. and Treas.; Nathan W. Chase, Elaine Shaw.
EIN: 056010418

49016
Brightman Hill Charitable Foundation
651 Main St.
Hope Valley, RI 02832-2409
Contact: W. Edward Wood, Tr.

Established in 1999.
Donor(s): W. Edward Wood.
Financial data (yr. ended 12/31/00): Grants paid, $29,600; assets, $442,033 (M); expenditures, $36,636; qualifying distributions, $29,427.
Limitations: Giving primarily in RI.
Trustees: Linda P. Wood, W. Edward Wood.
EIN: 050508705

49017
Gladys Reynolds Trust
c/o Fleet Private Clients Group
P.O. Box 6767
Providence, RI 02940-6767

Established in 2000 in MA.
Financial data (yr. ended 12/31/01): Grants paid, $29,586; assets, $1,266,606 (M); expenditures, $46,563; qualifying distributions, $37,835.
Limitations: Giving primarily in New Bedford, MA.
Trustee: Fleet National Bank.
EIN: 046307934

49018
Baker-Adams Scholarship Fund
c/o Fleet Private Clients Group
P.O. Box 6767
Providence, RI 02940-6767
Application address: c/o Georgetown School Dept., Office of the Superintendent, 51 North St., Georgetown, MA 01833

Financial data (yr. ended 12/31/01): Grants paid, $29,500; assets, $569,152 (M); expenditures, $36,735; qualifying distributions, $33,721.
Limitations: Giving limited to residents of Georgetown, MA.
Application information: Application form required.
Trustee: Fleet National Bank.
EIN: 316636824

49019
Almond M. Paine Trust
c/o Fleet Private Clients Group
P.O. Box 6767
Providence, RI 02940-6767

Financial data (yr. ended 12/31/00): Grants paid, $29,500; assets, $559,393 (M); expenditures, $32,503; qualifying distributions, $30,040.
Limitations: Applications not accepted. Giving primarily in CT.
Trustee: Fleet National Bank.
EIN: 056006029

49020
Ida S. Barter Trust
c/o Fleet Private Clients Group
P.O. Box 6767
Providence, RI 02940-6767
Application address: P.O. Box 1890, Boston, MA 02105, tel.: (617) 434-3768
Contact: Sharon M. Driscoll, Trust Off., Fleet National Bank

Financial data (yr. ended 09/30/01): Grants paid, $29,000; assets, $1,499,667 (M); expenditures, $49,464; qualifying distributions, $37,632.
Limitations: Giving primarily in the greater Boston, MA, area.

Trustee: Fleet National Bank.
EIN: 046009254

49021
Ottmar Foundation
c/o Fleet Private Clients Group
100 Westminster St., 2nd Fl.
Providence, RI 02903

Financial data (yr. ended 12/31/99): Grants paid, $28,996; assets, $549,818 (M); expenditures, $34,050; qualifying distributions, $29,059.
Limitations: Applications not accepted. Giving on a national basis, with emphasis on the East.
Application information: Contributes only to pre-selected organizations.
Trustees: Barbara R. Ottmar, David J. Ottmar, Peter H. Ottmar, Fleet National Bank.
EIN: 046224794

49022
Bristol Female Charitable Society
42 Sunset Rd.
Bristol, RI 02809

Financial data (yr. ended 09/30/00): Grants paid, $28,490; assets, $543,855 (M); gifts received, $4,366; expenditures, $29,465; qualifying distributions, $28,588.
Limitations: Giving limited to Bristol, RI.
Application information: Recipients are recommended to the board by local church groups. Application form not required.
Officers: Betty Gilbert, Secy.; Sara Woodruff, Treas.
Directors: Patricia Sanford, Betty Vargas.
EIN: 056011787

49023
The 2300 Foundation
c/o Benjamin G. Paster
1 Providence Washington Plz.
Providence, RI 02903-7104

Established in 1995 in RI.
Donor(s): Harry Farrand Jones.‡
Financial data (yr. ended 12/31/01): Grants paid, $28,280; assets, $52,987 (M); expenditures, $30,183; qualifying distributions, $28,280.
Trustees: John Harpootian, Benjamin G. Paster.
EIN: 056106480

49024
The Burton Trust Fund
c/o Fleet Private Clients Group
50 Kennedy Plz.
Providence, RI 02903
Application address: c/o Principal, Norton High School, 66 W. Main St., Norton, MA 02766
Contact: Maureen Charlonne, Trust Admin., Fleet National Bank

Established in 1994 in MA.
Donor(s): Katherine Burton Grantor Trust.
Financial data (yr. ended 07/31/02): Grants paid, $28,000; assets, $598,341 (M); expenditures, $38,005; qualifying distributions, $28,000.
Limitations: Giving limited to residents of Norton, MA.
Trustee: Fleet National Bank.
EIN: 046571320

49025
Gromack Scholarship Fund
c/o Fleet Private Clients Group
P.O. Box 6767
Providence, RI 02940-6767
Contact: Judy Zalansky

Established in 1998 in CT.
Donor(s): Paul Gromack.‡

Financial data (yr. ended 04/30/01): Grants paid, $28,000; assets, $513,082 (M); expenditures, $35,199; qualifying distributions, $32,221.
Application information: Application form required.
Trustee: Fleet National Bank.
EIN: 061514838

49026
The Solstice Trust
c/o Louis G. Murphy, Jr.
1 Turks Head Pl., Ste. 800
Providence, RI 02903

Established in 2000.
Donor(s): Kristin M. Brown.
Financial data (yr. ended 06/30/02): Grants paid, $28,000; assets, $326,043 (M); expenditures, $32,994; qualifying distributions, $28,000.
Limitations: Applications not accepted.
Application information: Contributes only to pre-selected organizations.
Officers and Directors:* Kristin M. Brown,* Pres. and Treas.; Stuart T. Close,* V.P.; Louis G. Murphy, Jr.,* Secy.
EIN: 030367216

49027
Marion Isabelle Coe Fund
c/o Fleet Private Clients group
P.O. Box 6767
Providence, RI 02940-6767
Application address: c/o Fleet National Bank,. 777 Main St., Hartford, CT 06115, tel.: 860-986-6102
Contact: Peter Weston, Trust Off., Fleet National Bank

Financial data (yr. ended 12/31/01): Grants paid, $27,984; assets, $716,435 (M); expenditures, $41,720; qualifying distributions, $34,734.
Limitations: Giving limited to Goshen, Litchfield, Morris, and Warren, CT.
Application information: Application form not required.
Trustee: Fleet National Bank.
EIN: 066040150
Codes: GTI

49028
Everett Trust f/b/o Cayuga County
c/o Fleet Private Clients Group
P.O. Box 6767
Providence, RI 02940-6767
Application address: William McKee, V.P., c/o Fleet National Bank, 1 East Ave., Rochester, NY, tel.: (716) 546-9289

Established in 2001 in NY.
Donor(s): Everett Charitable Trust.
Financial data (yr. ended 12/31/01): Grants paid, $27,934; assets, $640,317 (M); gifts received, $596,914; expenditures, $29,888; qualifying distributions, $29,139.
Limitations: Giving limited to Auburn and Cayuga County, NY.
Trustee: Fleet National Bank.
EIN: 010676696

49029
William F. Starr Fellowship Fund
c/o Fleet Private Clients Group
P.O. Box 6767
Providence, RI 02940-6767

Financial data (yr. ended 06/30/01): Grants paid, $27,742; assets, $829,516 (M); gifts received, $191; expenditures, $35,970; qualifying distributions, $33,090.
Limitations: Applications not accepted. Giving limited to Hartford, CT.

Application information: Recipients are selected based on merit by the board of trustees.
Trustees: Laura D. Allen, Fred A. Hitt, George M. Purtill, Richard C. Robinson, Frederick M. Tobin, Fleet National Bank.
EIN: 066024050
Codes: GTI

49030
Arlene E. Phelps Trust
c/o Fleet Private Clients Group
P.O. Box 6767
Providence, RI 02940-6767

Financial data (yr. ended 12/31/01): Grants paid, $27,475; assets, $685,228 (M); expenditures, $35,601; qualifying distributions, $27,475.
Limitations: Applications not accepted. Giving limited to McConnellsville, NY.
Application information: Contributes only to pre-selected organizations.
Trustee: Fleet National Bank.
EIN: 166237220

49031
Helen F. Wylie Foundation
c/o Fleet Private Clients Group
P.O. Box 6767
Providence, RI 02940-6767
Application address: HC 32 Box 41C, Owls Head, ME 04854
Contact: Marilyn L. Hotch, Tr.

Donor(s): Helen F. Wylie.‡
Financial data (yr. ended 12/31/01): Grants paid, $27,300; assets, $718,463 (M); gifts received, $90; expenditures, $35,869; qualifying distributions, $32,792.
Limitations: Giving limited to residents of Owls Head, ME.
Application information: Application form required.
Trustees: Marilyn L. Hotch, Fleet National Bank.
EIN: 010342663
Codes: GTI

49032
Elizabeth P. Snyder Trust
c/o Fleet Private Clients Group
P.O. Box 6767
Providence, RI 02940-6767
Application address: c/o Dolgeville Central School, Dolgeville, NY 13329

Financial data (yr. ended 12/31/01): Grants paid, $27,200; assets, $605,879 (M); expenditures, $31,743; qualifying distributions, $31,356.
Limitations: Giving limited to the Dolgeville, NY, area.
Trustee: Fleet National Bank.
EIN: 156021382
Codes: GTI

49033
Veturia I. Wiley Trust
c/o Fleet Private Clients Group
P.O. Box 6767
Providence, RI 02940-6767

Established in 1988 in NY.
Financial data (yr. ended 12/31/01): Grants paid, $27,128; assets, $603,235 (M); expenditures, $29,988; qualifying distributions, $27,128.
Limitations: Applications not accepted. Giving primarily in NY.
Application information: Contributes only to pre-selected organizations.
Trustee: Fleet National Bank.
EIN: 166229170

49034
Alfred N. Johnson Memorial Fund Trust
c/o Fleet Private Clients Group
P.O. Box 6767
Providence, RI 02940-6767
Application address: c/o Guidance Secy., Gloversville High School, 199 Lincoln St., Gloversville, NY 12078-1999, tel.: (518) 725-0671

Financial data (yr. ended 01/31/01): Grants paid, $27,100; assets, $637,885 (M); expenditures, $33,648; qualifying distributions, $31,244.
Limitations: Giving primarily in Gloversville, NY.
Application information: Application form required.
Trustee: Fleet National Bank.
EIN: 146099201
Codes: GTI

49035
Keith Henney Trust
c/o Fleet Private Clients Group
P.O. Box 6767
Providence, RI 02940-6767
Application address: P.O. Box 2, Eaton Center, NH 03832
Contact: Leona Hurley

Financial data (yr. ended 12/31/01): Grants paid, $27,065; assets, $619,543 (M); gifts received, $250; expenditures, $35,127; qualifying distributions, $30,382.
Limitations: Giving limited to residents of Eaton, NH.
Application information: Application form required.
Trustee: Fleet National Bank.
EIN: 026065480
Codes: GTI

49036
George Gardner & Fanny Whiting Blanchard Scholarship Fund
c/o Fleet Private Clients Group
P.O. Box 6767
Providence, RI 02940-6767
Application address: c/o Fleet National Bank, P.O. Box 3730, Nashua, NH 03061

Financial data (yr. ended 03/31/01): Grants paid, $27,000; assets, $445,752 (M); expenditures, $29,444; qualifying distributions, $27,799.
Limitations: Giving limited to residents of the Wilton, NH, area.
Application information: Application form required.
Trustee: Fleet National Bank.
EIN: 026004699
Codes: GTI

49037
Countess Frances Thorley Palen-Klar Scholarship Fund
c/o Fleet Private Clients Group
P.O. Box 6767
Providence, RI 02940-6767
Application address: c/o Greenwich Scholarship Assoc., United Way of Greenwich, 1 Lafayette Ct., Greenwich, CT 06830, tel.: Beth Bean, (203) 625-8093; John Whalon, (203) 625-8097; Sharon Vacchiolla, (203) 531-4229
Contact: Marie Hertzig

Financial data (yr. ended 12/31/01): Grants paid, $27,000; assets, $528,599 (M); expenditures, $35,696; qualifying distributions, $31,582.
Limitations: Giving limited to residents of Greenwich, CT.
Application information: Application form required.

49037—RHODE ISLAND

Trustee: Fleet National Bank.
EIN: 066033692
Codes: GTI

49038
Barbara Thorndike Wiggin Fund
c/o Fleet Private Clients Group
P.O. Box 6767
Providence, RI 02940-6767
Application address: c/o Fleet National Bank, P.O. Box 9791, Portland, ME 04104

Donor(s): Leola T. Wiggin.‡
Financial data (yr. ended 12/31/01): Grants paid, $27,000; assets, $645,720 (M); expenditures, $36,979; qualifying distributions, $32,549.
Limitations: Giving limited to residents of Knox County, ME.
Application information: Interviews recommended, where possible.
Trustee: Fleet National Bank.
EIN: 016013826
Codes: GTI

49039
Clinton G. Mills Fund
c/o Fleet Private Clients Group
P.O. Box 6767
Providence, RI 02940-6767
Application address: 75 State St., Boston, MA 02109, tel.: (617) 346-1245
Contact: Kerry Sullivan, Trust Admin., Fleet National Bank

Financial data (yr. ended 12/31/01): Grants paid, $26,990; assets, $630,224 (M); expenditures, $37,629; qualifying distributions, $32,415.
Limitations: Giving limited to graduates of public schools who will be continuing their education at a college in MA.
Application information: Application form not required.
Trustee: Fleet National Bank.
EIN: 046024752
Codes: GTI

49040
Inez Sprague Trust
c/o Fleet Private Clients Group
P.O. Box 6767
Providence, RI 02940-6767
Application address: c/o Fleet National Bank, Attn: Charitable Trust, 100 Federal St., Boston, MA 02110

Financial data (yr. ended 06/30/01): Grants paid, $26,490; assets, $798,729 (M); expenditures, $39,014; qualifying distributions, $33,193.
Limitations: Giving primarily in Washington County, RI, with emphasis on Narragansett.
Application information: Application form not required.
Trustee: Fleet National Bank.
EIN: 056067971
Codes: GTI

49041
Dorothy H. Sears Trust
c/o Fleet Private Clients Group
P.O. Box 6767
Providence, RI 02940-6767
Application address: c/o Scholarship Comm., Plymouth High Schools, 41 Obery St., Plymouth, MA 02360

Established in 1992 in MA.
Donor(s): Dorothy H. Sears.‡
Financial data (yr. ended 04/30/01): Grants paid, $26,457; assets, $846,749 (M); expenditures, $35,758; qualifying distributions, $32,535.
Limitations: Giving limited to MA.
Application information: Application form required.
Trustee: Fleet National Bank.
EIN: 046702776

49042
Godfrey F. Klein Trust
c/o Fleet Private Clients Group
P.O. Box 6767
Providence, RI 02940-6767
Application address: c/o Fleet Investment Svcs., Endowment Dept., 650 Elm St., Manchester, NH 03101

Donor(s): Godfrey F. Klein.‡
Financial data (yr. ended 12/31/01): Grants paid, $26,406; assets, $758,622 (M); expenditures, $35,374; qualifying distributions, $29,368.
Limitations: Giving primarily in Keene, NH, and New York, NY.
Application information: Application form required.
Trustee: Fleet National Bank.
EIN: 026051956

49043
The Phoebe Foundation
c/p Fleet Private Clients Group
P.O. Box 6767
Providence, RI 02940-6767

Established in 1999 in RI.
Financial data (yr. ended 12/31/01): Grants paid, $26,400; assets, $456,972 (M); expenditures, $30,931; qualifying distributions, $29,289.
Limitations: Applications not accepted. Giving primarily in New Haven, CT.
Application information: Contributes only to pre-selected organizations.
Trustee: Fleet National Bank.
EIN: 043488515

49044
Emma F. Makinson Trust
c/o Fleet Private Clients Group
P.O. Box 6767
Providence, RI 02940-6767
Application address: c/o Patricia Lowe, Superintendent of Schools, North Attleboro, MA 02703

Financial data (yr. ended 12/31/01): Grants paid, $26,125; assets, $677,434 (M); expenditures, $37,959; qualifying distributions, $32,954.
Limitations: Giving limited to North Attleboro, MA.
Application information: Application form required.
Trustee: Fleet National Bank.
EIN: 046224805
Codes: GTI

49045
Louis S. Cox Trust
c/o Fleet Private Clients Group
P.O. Box 6767
Providence, RI 02940-6767

Financial data (yr. ended 12/31/01): Grants paid, $26,100; assets, $598,400 (M); expenditures, $32,568; qualifying distributions, $30,379.
Limitations: Applications not accepted. Giving primarily in MA.
Application information: Contributes only to pre-selected organizations.
Trustee: Fleet National Bank.
EIN: 046034986

49046
Newstead Foundation, Inc.
P.O. Box 6444
Providence, RI 02940-6444 (401) 274-4138
Contact: Walter Schwab, Pres.

Donor(s): Walter Schwab.
Financial data (yr. ended 06/30/01): Grants paid, $26,000; assets, $82,260 (M); expenditures, $29,657; qualifying distributions, $26,000.
Limitations: Giving primarily in CT and MA.
Officer: Walter Schwab, Pres.
EIN: 222666821
Codes: GTI

49047
Nathaniel Wheeler Trust
c/o Fleet Private Clients Group
P.O. Box 6767
Providence, RI 02940-6767

Financial data (yr. ended 12/31/01): Grants paid, $26,000; assets, $702,432 (M); expenditures, $37,734; qualifying distributions, $32,485.
Limitations: Applications not accepted. Giving limited to York, ME.
Application information: Contributes only to pre-selected organizations.
Trustee: Fleet National Bank.
EIN: 016064602

49048
Herbert Fales Educational Trust
c/o Fleet Private Clients Group
P.O. Box 6767
Providence, RI 02940-6767
Contact: Andrew Morgens

Financial data (yr. ended 12/31/01): Grants paid, $25,950; assets, $859,109 (M); expenditures, $37,063; qualifying distributions, $32,796.
Limitations: Giving limited to residents within 10 miles of Framingham, MA.
Application information: Application form required.
Trustee: Fleet National Bank.
EIN: 046044998
Codes: GTI

49049
Clinton G. Mills Trust
c/o Fleet Private Clients Group
P.O. Box 6767
Providence, RI 02940-6767
Application address: c/o Fleet National Bank, 75 State St., Boston, MA 02109

Financial data (yr. ended 12/31/01): Grants paid, $25,950; assets, $514,789 (M); expenditures, $32,963; qualifying distributions, $30,095.
Limitations: Giving limited to residents of Lynn and Swampscott, MA.
Application information: Application form required.
Trustee: Fleet National Bank.
EIN: 046111074
Codes: GTI

49050
Frederick Lobel for Charities
c/o Fleet Private Clients Group
P.O. Box 6767
Providence, RI 02940-6767
Application address: 100 Federal St., Boston, MA 02110, tel.: (617) 434-4645
Contact: Susan Forster-Castillo, Trust Off., Fleet National Bank

Financial data (yr. ended 12/31/01): Grants paid, $25,616; assets, $845,254 (M); expenditures, $38,892; qualifying distributions, $32,953.

Limitations: Giving limited to Middleboro, MA.
Trustee: Fleet National Bank.
EIN: 046249689

49051
Horace A. Moses Charitable Trust
c/o Fleet Private Clients Group
P.O. Box 6767
Providence, RI 02940-6767
Application address: c/o Fleet National Bank, 100 Federal St., Boston, MA 02110

Financial data (yr. ended 10/31/01): Grants paid, $25,500; assets, $826,325 (M); expenditures, $46,671; qualifying distributions, $36,900.
Limitations: Giving limited to the Springfield, MA, and Ticonderoga, NY, areas.
Trustee: Fleet National Bank.
EIN: 237342412

49052
I. M. Wardwell Charitable Fund
c/o Fleet Private Clients Group
P.O. Box 6767
Providence, RI 02940-6767

Financial data (yr. ended 12/31/00): Grants paid, $25,404; assets, $597,984 (M); expenditures, $28,566; qualifying distributions, $26,617.
Limitations: Applications not accepted.
Application information: Contributes only to pre-selected organizations.
Trustee: Fleet National Bank.
EIN: 056004615

49053
Benjamin A. Armstrong Trust
c/o Fleet Private Clients Bank
P.O. Box 6767
Providence, RI 02940-6767
Application address: c/o Barbara Daniels, Fleet National Bank, 777 Main St., Hartford, CT 06103

Financial data (yr. ended 12/31/01): Grants paid, $25,063; assets, $478,693 (M); expenditures, $32,974; qualifying distributions, $28,136.
Limitations: Giving primarily in CT.
Trustee: Fleet National Bank.
EIN: 066026283
Codes: GTI

49054
Linford C. & Mildred I. White Foundation
c/o Fleet Private Clients Group
P.O. Box 6767
Providence, RI 02940-6767
Application address: 777 Main St., Hartford, CT 06103
Contact: Barbara Daniels, Trust Off., Fleet National Bank

Established in 1967.
Financial data (yr. ended 12/31/01): Grants paid, $25,063; assets, $478,693 (M); expenditures, $32,974; qualifying distributions, $28,136.
Limitations: Giving limited to the Waterbury, CT, area.
Trustee: Fleet National Bank.
EIN: 066025573

49055
The Narragansett Charitable Foundation, Inc.
165 Pitman St.
Providence, RI 02906
Application address: 35 Barberry Hill, Providence, RI 02906
Contact: Scott B. Laurans, Pres.

Established in 1987.
Donor(s): Scott B. Laurans.

Financial data (yr. ended 12/31/01): Grants paid, $25,000; assets, $2,094 (M); gifts received, $68,690; expenditures, $68,288; qualifying distributions, $25,000.
Limitations: Giving primarily in Boston, MA and Providence, RI.
Officers and Directors:* Scott B. Laurans,* Pres.; Edmund Pacheco,* V.P. and Secy.; Eudine Laurans, Treas.
EIN: 222890950

49056
Scott Family Foundation, Inc.
c/o James E. Ross
1 Financial Plz.
Providence, RI 02903

Established in 1999 in NM.
Financial data (yr. ended 08/31/00): Grants paid, $25,000; assets, $885,840 (M); gifts received, $69,486; expenditures, $39,555; qualifying distributions, $31,334.
Officers: Joel Scott, Pres.; Elizabeth T. Scott, Secy.
Trustees: Thomas I. Allen, Wendy Scott Allen, Natasha Scott, Sean M. Scott, Fleet National Bank.
EIN: 850465381

49057
Edward Syder Trust
c/o Fleet Private Clients Group
P.O. Box 6767
Providence, RI 02940-6767
Application address: c/o Scholarship Comm., P.O. Box 360, Ramsey, NJ 07446, tel.: (201) 607-2314

Donor(s): Edward C. Syder.‡
Financial data (yr. ended 12/31/01): Grants paid, $25,000; assets, $635,240 (M); expenditures, $32,723; qualifying distributions, $30,631.
Limitations: Giving limited to residents of Ramsey, NJ.
Application information: Application form required.
Scholarship Committee: Rev. Robert A. Coleman, Bruce W. De Young, James Scanlon, John Scerbo, Robert A. Scott.
Trustee: Fleet National Bank.
EIN: 226513992
Codes: GTI

49058
William T. Sloper Trust
c/o Fleet Private Clients Group
P.O. Box 6767
Providence, RI 02940-6767
Contact: Marjorie Y. Alexander, Trust Off., Fleet National Bank

Financial data (yr. ended 12/31/01): Grants paid, $24,900; assets, $425,217 (M); expenditures, $30,234; qualifying distributions, $28,159.
Limitations: Giving primarily in New Britain, CT.
Trustee: Fleet National Bank.
EIN: 066024334

49059
Beatrice D. Pierce Trust
c/o Fleet Private Clients Group
P.O. Box 6767
Providence, RI 02940-6767

Financial data (yr. ended 09/30/01): Grants paid, $24,750; assets, $551,616 (M); expenditures, $36,221; qualifying distributions, $28,484.
Limitations: Giving limited to residents of Lebanon, NH.
Trustee: Fleet National Bank.
EIN: 046089261
Codes: GTI

49060
Mildred E. Gates Trust
c/o Fleet Private Clients Group
P.O. Box 6767
Providence, RI 02940-6767
Application address: c/o Gardner High School, 200 Catherine St., Gardner, MA 01440
Contact: Walter Dubzinski, Jr., Principal

Established in 1994 in MA.
Financial data (yr. ended 12/31/01): Grants paid, $24,700; assets, $842,933 (M); expenditures, $36,665; qualifying distributions, $31,713.
Limitations: Giving primarily in MA.
Application information: Application form required.
Trustee: Fleet National Bank.
EIN: 046643614
Codes: GTI

49061
The Robert B. McColl Charitable Trust
c/o Fleet Private Clients Group
P.O. Box 6767
Providence, RI 02940

Financial data (yr. ended 12/31/01): Grants paid, $24,648; assets, $688,871 (M); expenditures, $32,120; qualifying distributions, $24,648.
Limitations: Applications not accepted. Giving on an international basis; giving also in the Schenectady, NY, area.
Application information: Contributes only to pre-selected organizations.
Trustee: Fleet National Bank.
EIN: 146081223

49062
David T. Langrock Foundation
c/o Fleet Private Clients Group
P.O. Box 6767
Providence, RI 02940-6767

Established in 1981.
Donor(s): David T. Langrock.‡
Financial data (yr. ended 11/30/00): Grants paid, $24,500; assets, $313,427 (M); gifts received, $20,416; expenditures, $30,099; qualifying distributions, $27,994.
Limitations: Applications not accepted. Giving limited to CT.
Application information: Contributes only to pre-selected organizations.
Trustee: Fleet National Bank.
EIN: 056039393

49063
The Barker Foundation, Inc.
400 Benefit St.
Providence, RI 02903
Contact: Preston A. Atwood, Pres.

Financial data (yr. ended 12/31/01): Grants paid, $24,000; assets, $795,821 (M); expenditures, $26,162; qualifying distributions, $25,909.
Limitations: Giving limited to Providence, RI.
Application information: Application form not required.
Officers: Joseph W. Riker, Jr., Pres.; Alma J. Fontana, V.P.; David P. Crossley, Secy.; James D. Kilpatrick, Treas.
Trustees: Preston A. Atwood, Samuel C. Coale, Walter B. Cotter, Thomas E. Harrison, Joseph R. Weisberger.
EIN: 056010560

49064
The Greene River Foundation, Inc.
153 Vaughn Ave.
Warwick, RI 02886

Established in 1984 in RI.
Donor(s): John H. Chafee.
Financial data (yr. ended 12/31/01): Grants paid, $23,594; assets, $63,167 (M); expenditures, $25,192; qualifying distributions, $23,588.
Limitations: Applications not accepted. Giving primarily in RI.
Application information: Contributes only to pre-selected organizations.
Officers and Trustees:* Virginia C. Chafee,* Pres. and Secy.-Treas.; Barbara P. Berke, Mgr.; Zechariah Chafee.
EIN: 222585688

49065
Dorothy Cooke Trust
c/o Fleet Private Clients Group
P.O. Box 6767
Providence, RI 02940-6767

Established in 1999 in MA.
Donor(s): Dorothy Cooke Unitrust.
Financial data (yr. ended 12/31/01): Grants paid, $23,130; assets, $358,255 (M); expenditures, $28,350; qualifying distributions, $23,130.
Limitations: Applications not accepted. Giving primarily in VT.
Application information: Contributes only to pre-selected organizations.
Trustee: Fleet National Bank.
EIN: 316628238

49066
Mary S. Bannister Fund
(Formerly Harold P. Bannister Trust)
c/o Fleet Private Clients Group
P.O. Box 6767
Providence, RI 02940-6767

Donor(s): Harold R. Bannister.
Financial data (yr. ended 12/31/01): Grants paid, $23,000; assets, $532,006 (M); expenditures, $30,293; qualifying distributions, $25,636.
Limitations: Applications not accepted. Giving limited to Bristol, RI.
Application information: Contributes only to pre-selected organizations.
Trustees: Fleet National Bank.
EIN: 056105958

49067
William C. and Mabel D. Hunt Memorial Scholarship
c/o Fleet Private Clients Group
P.O. Box 6767
Providence, RI 02940-6767
Application address: c/o Fleet National Bank, 1125 Rte. 22 W., Bridgewater, NJ 08807

Financial data (yr. ended 12/31/01): Grants paid, $23,000; assets, $707,399 (M); expenditures, $32,265; qualifying distributions, $25,612.
Limitations: Giving limited to residents of Cape May County, NJ.
Application information: Application form required.
Trustee: Fleet National Bank.
EIN: 222690724
Codes: GTI

49068
Betsey W. Taber Trust
(Formerly Taber Scholarship Fund)
c/o Fleet Private Clients Group
P.O. Box 6767
Providence, RI 02940
Application address: 100 Federal St., Boston, MA 02110

Established in 1978 in MA.
Financial data (yr. ended 09/30/01): Grants paid, $22,929; assets, $555,353 (M); expenditures, $34,291; qualifying distributions, $26,807.
Limitations: Giving limited to residents of the greater New Bedford, MA, area.
Application information: Application form not required.
Trustee: Fleet National Bank.
EIN: 046418554
Codes: GTI

49069
Nina Paganelli Trust
c/o Fleet Private Clients Group
P.O. Box 6767
Providence, RI 02940-6767
Application address: c/o Principal, Sanford High School, Sanford, ME 04073

Donor(s): Nina Paganelli.‡
Financial data (yr. ended 04/30/02): Grants paid, $22,848; assets, $539,240 (M); expenditures, $29,863; qualifying distributions, $22,848.
Limitations: Giving limited to Sanford, ME.
Application information: Application form not required.
Trustee: Fleet National Bank.
EIN: 223180798

49070
The Robert Cummings Family Foundation
99 E. Sakonnet Point Rd.
Little Compton, RI 02837

Established in 2000.
Donor(s): Robert Cummings.
Financial data (yr. ended 12/31/01): Grants paid, $22,800; assets, $301,953 (M); expenditures, $29,704; qualifying distributions, $22,800.
Limitations: Applications not accepted.
Application information: Contributes only to pre-selected organizations.
Officers and Directors:* Robert Cummings,* Pres. and Treas.; Louis G. Murphy, Jr.,* V.P.; Marilyn L. McCabe,* Secy.
EIN: 050512145

49071
R. Elaine Croston Scholarship Fund
c/o Fleet Private Clients Group
P.O. Box 6767
Providence, RI 02940-6767
Application address: c/o Karen K. Baker, Principal, Haverhill High School, 137 Monument St., Haverhill, MA 01832-2697, tel.: (508) 374-5712

Donor(s): R. Elaine Croston.‡
Financial data (yr. ended 12/31/01): Grants paid, $22,790; assets, $520,142 (M); expenditures, $29,553; qualifying distributions, $26,474.
Limitations: Giving limited to residents of the Haverhill, MA, area.
Application information: Application form required.
Trustee: Fleet National Bank.
EIN: 046079522
Codes: GTI

49072
Catherine & Nicholas R. Mele Memorial Trust
c/o Fleet Private Clients Group
P.O. Box 6767
Providence, RI 02940-6767

Established in 1997 in CT.
Financial data (yr. ended 12/31/01): Grants paid, $22,691; assets, $493,769 (M); expenditures, $33,405; qualifying distributions, $22,691.
Limitations: Applications not accepted. Giving primarily in New York, NY.
Application information: Contributes only to pre-selected organizations.
Trustee: Fleet National Bank.
EIN: 066441768

49073
Susannah Schofield Trust
c/o Citizens Bank New Hampshire
870 Westminster St.
Providence, RI 02903

Financial data (yr. ended 06/30/00): Grants paid, $22,640; assets, $773,819 (M); expenditures, $34,698; qualifying distributions, $27,621.
Limitations: Applications not accepted. Giving primarily in Melvin Village, NH.
Application information: Contributes only to pre-selected organizations.
Trustee: Citizens Bank New Hampshire.
EIN: 026060700

49074
Elmer Smith Scholarship Trust
c/o Fleet Private Clients Group
P.O. Box 6767
Providence, RI 02940-6767

Established in 1999 in NJ.
Financial data (yr. ended 12/31/00): Grants paid, $22,500; assets, $741,193 (M); expenditures, $28,825; qualifying distributions, $25,994.
Limitations: Giving primarily in Cape May, NJ.
Application information: Applications available at Cape May County and Holy Spirit high schools, Cape May, NJ.
Trustee: Fleet National Bank.
EIN: 226213088

49075
Mary E. Brock Trust
c/o Citizens Bank
870 Westminster St.
Providence, RI 02903

Financial data (yr. ended 12/31/00): Grants paid, $22,320; assets, $670,666 (M); expenditures, $31,931; qualifying distributions, $31,931.
Limitations: Applications not accepted. Giving primarily in NH.
Trustee: Citizens Bank New Hampshire.
EIN: 026030934

49076
Malin Family Foundation
26 Bluff Rd.
Barrington, RI 02806 (401) 245-2588
Contact: Herbert Malin, Pres.

Donor(s): Herbert Malin.
Financial data (yr. ended 12/31/01): Grants paid, $22,000; assets, $258,638 (M); gifts received, $25,000; expenditures, $23,013; qualifying distributions, $22,000.
Officer: Herbert Malin, Pres.
EIN: 056096498

49077
Clinton B. Newell Trust
c/o Fleet Private Clients Group
P.O. Box 6767
Providence, RI 02940-6767
Application address: c/o Jerry Goldberg, Scholarship Coord., Peabody Veterans Mem. H.S., Reading Scholarship Fdn., P.O. Box 492, Reading, MA 01867, tel.: (617) 434-3768

Established in 1995.
Financial data (yr. ended 12/31/00): Grants paid, $22,000; assets, $575,614 (M); expenditures, $32,104; qualifying distributions, $28,565.
Limitations: Giving primarily in Reading and Peabody, MA.
Application information: Application form not required.
Trustees: David J. Latham, Fleet National Bank.
EIN: 046493078

49078
Nathan D. Prince Trust No. 2
c/o Fleet Private Clients Group
P.O. Box 6767
Providence, RI 02940-6767
Application address: c/o David Cressy, Killingly High School, 190 Main St., Danielson, CT 06239-2823

Financial data (yr. ended 09/30/01): Grants paid, $22,000; assets, $798,720 (M); expenditures, $33,130; qualifying distributions, $28,276.
Limitations: Giving limited to residents of CT.
Application information: Application form not required.
Trustee: Fleet National Bank.
EIN: 066031329
Codes: GTI

49079
Jennie Smith Education Fund
(Formerly Smith Educational Fund)
c/o Fleet Private Clients Group
P.O. Box 6767
Providence, RI 02940-6767
Application address: c/o Superintendent, South Hadley Schools, Town Hall, South Hadley, MA 01075

Financial data (yr. ended 12/31/01): Grants paid, $21,816; assets, $479,552 (M); expenditures, $25,959; qualifying distributions, $24,515.
Limitations: Giving limited to residents of South Hadley, MA.
Application information: Application form required.
Trustee: Fleet National Bank.
EIN: 046033742
Codes: GTI

49080
Vera Grace Greenlaw Trust
c/o Fleet Private Clients Group
P.O. Box 6767
Providence, RI 02940-6767
Application addresses: c/o Principal, East Belfast High School, Belfast, 04915; c/o Principal, Searsport District High School, 20 Church St., Searsport, ME 04974; c/o Principal, Mountian View High School, Franklyn, ME 04607

Established in 1986 in ME.
Financial data (yr. ended 04/30/02): Grants paid, $21,560; assets, $583,195 (M); expenditures, $29,821; qualifying distributions, $26,427.
Limitations: Giving limited to residents, Waldo County, ME.
Application information: Application form not required.
Trustee: Fleet National Bank.
EIN: 016080221
Codes: GTI

49081
Additon Scholarship Fund
c/o Citizens Bank
870 Westminster St., 2nd Fl.
Providence, RI 02903-4089
Application address: c/o Bill Sirak, 875 Elm St., Manchester, NH 03105, tel.: (603) 634-7752

Donor(s): Mr. Additon.
Financial data (yr. ended 09/30/01): Grants paid, $21,500; assets, $464,582 (M); gifts received, $1,500; expenditures, $30,624; qualifying distributions, $25,580.
Limitations: Giving limited to residents of Manchester, NH.
Application information: Application form required.
Trustee: Citizens Bank New Hampshire.
EIN: 237435466
Codes: GTI

49082
Frances Maude Children's Fund
c/o Fleet Private Clients Group
P.O. Box 6767
Providence, RI 02940-6767
Application address: Lizz Davin, c/o Mulhark Regional High School, Shelburne Falls, MA 01370, tel.: (413) 625-2516

Established in 1993 in RI.
Financial data (yr. ended 08/31/01): Grants paid, $21,500; assets, $623,803 (M); expenditures, $30,975; qualifying distributions, $27,418.
Limitations: Giving limited to residents of Shelburne Falls, MA.
Application information: Applicant must include transcript, a list of references and recommendation from guidance counselor.
Directors: Jacqueline Anderson, James Brandt, Lucille D. Brown, June Dobias Pease, Frances Sessions, Donna Shippee, Lorna T. White.
Trustee: Fleet National Bank.
EIN: 046019146
Codes: GTI

49083
Edward Austin Trust
c/o Fleet Private Clients Group
P.O. Box 6767
Providence, RI 02940-6767
Application address: c/o Fleet National Bank, David Maxwell, 100 Federal St., Boston, MA 02110, tel.: (617) 434-4551

Donor(s): Edward Austin.‡
Financial data (yr. ended 12/31/01): Grants paid, $21,294; assets, $540,134 (M); expenditures, $27,967; qualifying distributions, $25,853.
Limitations: Giving limited to Boston, MA.
Application information: 2 copies of Grant Coversheet must be submitted.
Trustee: Fleet National Bank.
EIN: 046024257

49084
Katherine L. Peck Trust
c/o Fleet Private Clients Group
P.O. Box 6767
Providence, RI 02940-6767
Application address: c/o First Congregational Church Scholarship Comm., 222 W. Main St., Waterbury, CT 06708, tel.: (203) 757-0331

Financial data (yr. ended 12/31/01): Grants paid, $21,000; assets, $429,977 (M); expenditures, $29,618; qualifying distributions, $25,114.
Limitations: Giving limited to the Waterbury, CT, area.
Trustee: Fleet National Bank.
EIN: 066024593
Codes: GTI

49085
Adelaide Dawson Lynch Memorial Trust
c/o Fleet Private Clients Group
P.O. Box 6767
Providence, RI 02940-6767

Established around 1994.
Financial data (yr. ended 12/31/01): Grants paid, $20,993; assets, $419,937 (M); expenditures, $29,345; qualifying distributions, $25,890.
Limitations: Applications not accepted. Giving limited to RI.
Application information: Contributes only to pre-selected organizations.
Trustee: Fleet National Bank.
EIN: 056095568

49086
Howard Kane Foundation
222 Richmond St., Ste. 111
Providence, RI 02903-4225

Financial data (yr. ended 12/31/01): Grants paid, $20,750; assets, $571,986 (M); expenditures, $28,319; qualifying distributions, $20,750.
Limitations: Applications not accepted. Giving primarily in FL.
Application information: Contributes only to pre-selected organizations.
Officers: Scott E. Herman, Pres. and Treas.; Priscilla Kane, V.P.; Carol K. Mathews, Exec. V.P.; Art Mathews, Secy.
EIN: 237032343

49087
Justin McKean Trust
c/o Fleet National Bank
P.O. Box 6767
Providence, RI 02940-6767

Established in 2000 in MA.
Donor(s): Justin McKean Unitrust.
Financial data (yr. ended 12/31/01): Grants paid, $20,639; assets, $553,152 (M); expenditures, $30,226; qualifying distributions, $20,639.
Limitations: Applications not accepted.
Application information: Contributes only to pre-selected organizations.
Trustee: Fleet National Bank.
EIN: 046373485

49088
Florence C. Allen Memorial Scholarship Fund
c/o Fleet Private Clients Group
P.O. Box 6767
Providence, RI 02940-6767
Application addresses: c/o George G. Hamaty, Supt. of Schools, Corning-Painted Post Area School District, 165 Charles St., Painted Post, NY 14870, tel.: (607) 936-3704, or c/o A. Lyman Warner, Supt., Addison Central School District, Coldwell St., Addison, NY 14801, tel.: (607) 359-2243

Established in 1984.
Donor(s): Florence C. Allen.‡
Financial data (yr. ended 09/30/01): Grants paid, $20,500; assets, $60,164 (M); expenditures, $21,545; qualifying distributions, $21,103; giving activities include $20,500 for loans.
Limitations: Giving limited to Addison, Corning, and Painted Post, NY.
Application information: Application form required.
Trustee: Fleet National Bank.

49088—RHODE ISLAND

EIN: 222850271
Codes: GTI

49089
George Norman Albree Trust
c/o Fleet Private Clients Group
P.O. Box 6767
Providence, RI 02940-6767
Contact: David A. Maxwell, Trust Off., Fleet National Bank

Established in 1948 in MA.
Financial data (yr. ended 09/30/01): Grants paid, $20,000; assets, $434,544 (M); expenditures, $30,345; qualifying distributions, $27,516.
Limitations: Giving primarily in MA.
Trustee: Fleet National Bank.
EIN: 046026213

49090
Annie Wentworth Baer Scholarship Fund
c/o Fleet Private Clients Group
P.O. Box 6767
Providence, RI 02940-6767
Application address: 100 Federal St, Boston. MA 02110, tel.: (617) 434-4645
Contact: Susana Forster-Castillo, Trust Admin., Fleet National Bank

Financial data (yr. ended 12/31/01): Grants paid, $20,000; assets, $943,688 (M); expenditures, $35,331; qualifying distributions, $29,661.
Limitations: Giving limited to residents of Rollinsford, NH.
Trustee: Fleet National Bank.
EIN: 046401501

49091
David E. Bryant Trust
c/o Fleet Private Clients Group
P.O. Box 6767
Providence, RI 02940-6767

Established in 1987 in NY.
Financial data (yr. ended 10/31/01): Grants paid, $20,000; assets, $606,587 (M); expenditures, $27,823; qualifying distributions, $24,917.
Limitations: Applications not accepted.
Application information: Contributes only to pre-selected organizations.
Trustee: Fleet National Bank.
EIN: 166304397

49092
The Del Prete Family Foundation
251 Smith St.
Providence, RI 02908 (401) 272-9773
Contact: Daniel B. Del Prete, Tr.

Established in 1999 in RI.
Donor(s): Daniel B. Del Prete.
Financial data (yr. ended 12/31/01): Grants paid, $20,000; assets, $393,973 (M); gifts received, $100,000; expenditures, $20,452; qualifying distributions, $19,861.
Limitations: Giving primarily in RI.
Trustee: Daniel B. Del Prete.
EIN: 050508471

49093
George & Elsie Hodder Classical Music Fund
c/o Fleet Private Client Group
P.O. Box 6767
Providence, RI 02940-6767
Contact: David Maxwell, Trust Off., Fleet National Bank

Established in 1999 in MA.
Donor(s): George & Elsie Hodder Unitrust.
Financial data (yr. ended 12/31/01): Grants paid, $20,000; assets, $532,620 (M); expenditures, $26,229; qualifying distributions, $23,356.

Limitations: Giving limited to Boston, MA.
Application information: Application form required.
Trustee: Fleet National Bank.
EIN: 056120559

49094
Eva March Tappan Trust
c/o Fleet Private Clients Group
P.O. Box 6767
Providence, RI 02940-6767
Application address: 100 Federal St., Boston, MA 02110
Contact: Michelle Neubauer-Pinkett, Trust Off., Fleet National Bank

Financial data (yr. ended 10/31/01): Grants paid, $19,539; assets, $839,046 (M); expenditures, $32,154; qualifying distributions, $26,876.
Limitations: Giving to residents of Worcester, MA.
Directors: Joanne Choystaff, Christopher Shustaek, Lisa Tingue.
Trustee: Fleet National Bank.
EIN: 046023587
Codes: GTI

49095
King Scholarship Fund
(also known as Cora E. King Scholarship Fund)
c/o Fleet Private Clients Group
P.O. Box 6767
Providence, RI 02940-6767
Application address: c/o First Presbyterian Church, 112 South St., Auburn, NY 13021

Financial data (yr. ended 12/31/01): Grants paid, $19,500; assets, $620,898 (M); expenditures, $28,947; qualifying distributions, $24,506.
Limitations: Giving primarily in NY.
Application information: Application form required.
Officers and Directors:* Barbara Estep,* Chair.; Charlotte Pedersen,* Secy.; Mary Jo Bower, Elizabeth Bowman, Arthur P. Pedersen, Martha Russell, James Vargason.
Trustee: Fleet National Bank.
EIN: 222589716
Codes: GTI

49096
The John F. Reed Charitable Trust 1997
P.O. Box 8943
Cranston, RI 02920

Donor(s): John F. Reed.
Financial data (yr. ended 12/31/01): Grants paid, $19,500; assets, $6,794 (M); gifts received, $20,760; expenditures, $22,400; qualifying distributions, $19,500.
Limitations: Applications not accepted.
Application information: Contributes only to pre-selected organizations.
Trustee: V. Duncan Johnson.
EIN: 066451367

49097
William H. Coe Medical & Surgical Fund for Education
c/o Fleet Private Clients Group
P.O. Box 6767
Providence, RI 02940-6767
Application address: c/o Auburn Board of Education, Thornton Ave., Auburn, NY 13021

Financial data (yr. ended 12/31/00): Grants paid, $19,497; assets, $345,572 (M); expenditures, $24,520; qualifying distributions, $22,272.
Limitations: Giving limited to Auburn, NY.
Application information: Application form required.
Trustee: Fleet National Bank.

EIN: 156018065
Codes: GTI

49098
Harold B. Walker Charitable Trust
c/o Fleet Private Clients Group
P.O. Box 6767
Providence, RI 02940-6767
Application address: c/o Carol M. Brewster, Ashland High School, 87 W. Union St., Ashland, MA 01721

Established in 1990 in MA.
Financial data (yr. ended 12/31/01): Grants paid, $19,362; assets, $518,145 (M); expenditures, $29,746; qualifying distributions, $26,806.
Limitations: Giving limited to residents of Ashland, MA.
Application information: Application form required.
Trustee: Fleet National Bank.
EIN: 046633929
Codes: GTI

49099
Helen J. Busiel Trust
c/o Citizens Bank New Hampshire
870 Westminster St.
Providence, RI 02903

Financial data (yr. ended 12/31/01): Grants paid, $19,119; assets, $512,253 (M); expenditures, $26,627; qualifying distributions, $22,491.
Limitations: Applications not accepted. Giving primarily in Laconia, NH.
Application information: Contributes only to pre-selected organizations.
Trustee: Citizens Bank New Hampshire.
EIN: 026004698

49100
Bernard W. McCormick Scholarship Fund Trust
c/o Fleet Private Clients Group
P.O. Box 6767
Providence, RI 02940-6767
Application address: c/o Sister Carolyn Schanz, Principal, Catholic Central High School, 116th St. and 7th Ave., Troy, NY 12182, tel.: (518) 235-7100

Financial data (yr. ended 12/31/00): Grants paid, $19,000; assets, $400,048 (M); expenditures, $23,973; qualifying distributions, $21,562.
Limitations: Giving limited to Troy, NY.
Application information: Application form not required.
Trustee: Fleet National Bank.
EIN: 146089372

49101
Jerrold A. Salmanson Foundation
155 S. Main St.
Providence, RI 02903

Donor(s): Jerrold A. Salmanson.
Financial data (yr. ended 09/30/01): Grants paid, $18,874; assets, $232,223 (M); expenditures, $20,336; qualifying distributions, $18,874.
Limitations: Applications not accepted. Giving primarily in RI.
Application information: Contributes only to pre-selected organizations.
Trustees: Charles Salmanson, Jerrold A. Salmanson.
EIN: 222571912

49102
Thomas & Marguerite Moore Family Foundation
c/o Hinckley, Allen & Snyder
1500 Fleet Ctr.
Providence, RI 02903-2393

Established in 1997.
Donor(s): Marguerite R. Moore, Thomas F. Moore.
Financial data (yr. ended 12/31/01): Grants paid, $18,864; assets, $325,007 (M); expenditures, $21,394; qualifying distributions, $18,864.
Limitations: Applications not accepted.
Application information: Contributes only to pre-selected organizations.
Trustees: Alexander M. Barber, John C. Moore, Marguerite R. Moore, Thomas F. Moore, Jr.
EIN: 061484436

49103
Isabel T. Goss Fund
c/o Fleet Private Clients Group
P.O. Box 6767
Providence, RI 02940-6767

Financial data (yr. ended 12/31/01): Grants paid, $18,627; assets, $603,726 (M); expenditures, $27,125; qualifying distributions, $23,249.
Limitations: Applications not accepted.
Application information: Contributes only to pre-selected organizations.
Trustee: Fleet National Bank.
EIN: 156018109

49104
James J. Garvey Trust
c/o Fleet Private Clients Group
P.O. Box 6767
Providence, RI 02940-6767

Established in 1999 in MA.
Financial data (yr. ended 03/31/02): Grants paid, $18,622; assets, $559,185 (M); expenditures, $29,881; qualifying distributions, $18,622.
Limitations: Applications not accepted. Giving primarily in MA and NY.
Application information: Contributes only to pre-selected organizations.
Trustees: Edward J. Barry, Fleet National Bank.
EIN: 056123647

49105
Kroger-Choi Charitable Foundation
154 Tobie St.
Pawtucket, RI 02861

Established in 1996 in RI.
Donor(s): Edward Choi, Harriet Choi.
Financial data (yr. ended 12/31/01): Grants paid, $18,515; assets, $278,578 (M); expenditures, $21,153; qualifying distributions, $18,515.
Limitations: Applications not accepted.
Application information: Contributes only to pre-selected organizations.
Trustees: Edward Choi, Harriet Choi, Daniel J. Ryan.
EIN: 061474592

49106
Liberty Foundation, Inc.
c/o Fleet Private Clients Group
P.O. Box 6767
Providence, RI 02940-6767
Application address: 1404 Clubhouse Cir., Jupiter, FL 33477

Financial data (yr. ended 11/30/01): Grants paid, $18,500; assets, $421,652 (M); expenditures, $22,808; qualifying distributions, $19,248.
Limitations: Giving primarily in Tampa and West Palm Beach, FL, and CT.

Officers: Ralph P. Hankey, Secy.; Dorothy H. Hartzog, Treas.
Directors: Donald L. Hartzog, Elizabeth W. Hartzog, Thomas C. Hartzog.
Trustee: Fleet National Bank.
EIN: 066053589

49107
Grace Hewett Charitable Trust
c/o Fleet Private Clients Group
P.O. Box 6767
Providence, RI 02940-6767

Financial data (yr. ended 09/30/01): Grants paid, $18,060; assets, $528,831 (M); expenditures, $23,685; qualifying distributions, $21,716.
Limitations: Applications not accepted. Giving primarily in FL, MA, and NY.
Application information: Contributes only to pre-selected organizations.
Trustee: Fleet National Bank.
EIN: 046953955

49108
The Major Jeremiah P. Murphy Scholarship Foundation
c/o Home Loan & Investment Bank
1 Home Loan Plz., Ste. 3
Warwick, RI 02886-1765
Contact: John M. Murphy, Pres.

Established in 1995 in RI.
Donor(s): Home Loan & Investment Bank, John M. Murphy.
Financial data (yr. ended 12/31/99): Grants paid, $18,000; assets, $234,294 (M); gifts received, $2,911; expenditures, $20,432; qualifying distributions, $17,883.
Limitations: Giving primarily in Providence, RI.
Application information: Application form not required.
Officers: John M. Murphy, Pres.; Edwin Furtado, Treas.
Directors: Ann Brown, Col. Bernard E. Gannon, Robert D. Laurie, Anthony Mancuso.
EIN: 050483640
Codes: GTI

49109
Pawtucket Red Sox Charitable Foundation
P.O. Box 2365
Pawtucket, RI 02861

Established in 1997 in RI.
Financial data (yr. ended 12/31/01): Grants paid, $18,000; assets, $101,917 (M); gifts received, $101,795; expenditures, $18,007; qualifying distributions, $18,000.
Limitations: Applications not accepted.
Application information: Contributes only to pre-selected organizations.
Trustees: Kathy Crowley, James F. McAleer, Bernard Mondor, Daniel J. Ryan, Michael Tamburro.
EIN: 061494102

49110
Thomas P. Quinn Scholarship Fund
c/o Fleet Private Clients Group
P.O. Box 6767
Providence, RI 02940-6767

Established in 1988 in CT.
Financial data (yr. ended 12/31/01): Grants paid, $18,000; assets, $401,664 (M); expenditures, $25,341; qualifying distributions, $22,272.
Limitations: Giving limited to residents of New London County, CT.
Application information: Application form required.
Trustee: Fleet National Bank.

EIN: 223003812
Codes: GTI

49111
John A. & Elsa J. DeAngelis Charitable Trust
27 Foundry St.
Central Falls, RI 02863

Financial data (yr. ended 01/31/02): Grants paid, $17,925; assets, $320,733 (M); expenditures, $19,956; qualifying distributions, $17,925.
Limitations: Applications not accepted. Giving primarily in RI.
Application information: Contributes only to pre-selected organizations.
Trustee: Don A. DeAngelis.
EIN: 056019885

49112
Katherine H. Simmons Trust
c/o Fleet Private Clients Group
P.O. Box 6767
Providence, RI 02940-6767
Application address: c/o Parish of St. Bernard's Church, Waterville, NY

Established in 1997 in NY.
Financial data (yr. ended 12/31/01): Grants paid, $17,538; assets, $194,445 (M); expenditures, $20,775; qualifying distributions, $17,538.
Limitations: Giving primarily in Waterville, NY.
Application information: Applicants must be students from the Parish of St. Bernard's Church, Waterville, NY.
Trustee: Fleet National Bank.
EIN: 161541560

49113
Rueben J. and Dorothy S. Cohen Scholarship Trust Fund
c/o Fleet Private Clients Group
P.O. Box 6767
Providence, RI 02940-6767
Application address: 1125 Rte. 22 W., Bridgeport, NJ 00807
Contact: Maggie Willard, Trust Off., Fleet National Bank

Established in 1994.
Donor(s): Dorothy Cohen.‡
Financial data (yr. ended 12/31/00): Grants paid, $17,500; assets, $519,334 (M); expenditures, $21,812; qualifying distributions, $18,845.
Limitations: Giving primarily to residents of Philadelphia, PA.
Application information: Application form required.
Trustee: Fleet National Bank.
EIN: 226618260
Codes: GTI

49114
Melinda W. Tobie Trust
c/o Citizens Bank New Hampshire
870 Westminster St.
Providence, RI 02903
Application address: c/o Citizens Bank New Hampshire, 875 Elm St., Manchester, NH 03105

Donor(s): Melinda W. Tobie.‡
Financial data (yr. ended 12/31/01): Grants paid, $17,300; assets, $303,185 (M); expenditures, $22,546; qualifying distributions, $19,648.
Limitations: Applications not accepted. Giving limited to NH.
Application information: Contributes only to pre-selected organizations.
Trustee: Citizens Bank New Hampshire.
EIN: 026005052

49115—RHODE ISLAND

49115
Birch Memorial Fund Trust
c/o Fleet Private Clients Group
P.O. Box 6767
Providence, RI 02940-6767

Financial data (yr. ended 12/31/01): Grants paid, $17,240; assets, $468,981 (M); expenditures, $22,322; qualifying distributions, $17,240.
Limitations: Applications not accepted. Giving primarily in NY.
Application information: Contributes only to a pre-selected organization.
Trustee: Fleet National Bank.
EIN: 146076795

49116
Mynde & Gary Siperstein Charitable Foundation
130 Joseph Ct.
Warwick, RI 02886 (401) 855-0075
Contact: Gary S. Siperstein, Tr.

Established in 2000 in RI.
Donor(s): Mynde S. Siperstein, Gary S. Siperstein.
Financial data (yr. ended 12/31/01): Grants paid, $17,000; assets, $127,136 (M); gifts received, $10,711; expenditures, $22,162; qualifying distributions, $17,000.
Limitations: Giving primarily in RI.
Trustees: Gary S. Siperstein, Mynde S. Siperstein.
EIN: 050514202

49117
Arthur H. Carr Trust
c/o Edwards & Angell
2800 Financial Plz.
Providence, RI 02903
Application address: P.O. Box 506, Bristol, RI 02809-0506
Contact: Janice Carr Williams, Tr.

Established in 1993 in RI.
Donor(s): Janice Carr Williams, Dudley A. Williams.
Financial data (yr. ended 12/31/01): Grants paid, $16,925; assets, $280,481 (M); expenditures, $19,366; qualifying distributions, $16,812.
Limitations: Giving primarily in Bristol, RI.
Trustees: Dudley A. Williams, Janice Carr Williams.
EIN: 056008412

49118
Mary P. Costa Scholarship Fund Trust
(Formerly John D. Costa Scholarship Fund Trust)
c/o Fleet Private Clients Group
P.O. Box 6767
Providence, RI 02940-6767
Contact: Deborah Dillon Pearce, Trust Admin., Fleet National Bank

Financial data (yr. ended 07/31/01): Grants paid, $16,650; assets, $227,937 (M); expenditures, $20,125; qualifying distributions, $18,451.
Limitations: Giving limited to residents of Plymouth, MA.
Application information: Recipient selected by Plymouth-Carver High School Staff.
Trustee: Fleet National Bank.
EIN: 046144750

49119
The Grace W. Allsop Foundation
49 Roslyn Ave.
Providence, RI 02908 (401) 272-8318
Contact: Brian Larkin, Chair.

Established in 2001 in RI.
Financial data (yr. ended 12/31/01): Grants paid, $16,630; assets, $757,748 (M); expenditures, $52,235; qualifying distributions, $23,293.

Application information: Application form not required.
Officer: Brian Lark, Chair.
EIN: 050513795

49120
Northern Highlands Scholarship Foundation, Inc.
c/o Fleet Private Clients Group
P.O. Box 6767
Providence, RI 02940-6767
Contact: Rona Meyers

Established in 1997 in NJ.
Financial data (yr. ended 12/31/01): Grants paid, $16,000; assets, $289,678 (M); gifts received, $8,196; expenditures, $19,176; qualifying distributions, $16,000.
Limitations: Giving primarily in Allendale, NJ.
Application information: Application form required.
Trustee: Fleet National Bank.
EIN: 226418777

49121
Leroy M. Bickford Trust
c/o Fleet Private Clients Group
P.O. Box 6767
Providence, RI 02940-6767
Application address: P.O. Box 1861, Boston, MA 02205
Contact: Augusta Haydock, Trust Off., Fleet National Bank

Financial data (yr. ended 09/30/01): Grants paid, $15,648; assets, $384,480 (M); expenditures, $22,128; qualifying distributions, $17,567.
Limitations: Giving limited to Newburgh, ME.
Trustee: Fleet National Bank.
EIN: 046008408

49122
Margaret Kennedy Scholarship Trust
c/o Fleet Private Clients Group
P.O. Box 6767
Providence, RI 02940-6767
Application address: c/o Guidance Counselor, Bucksport High School, Bucksport, ME 04416, tel.: (207) 469-7300

Financial data (yr. ended 04/30/02): Grants paid, $15,382; assets, $331,869 (M); expenditures, $20,504; qualifying distributions, $18,331.
Limitations: Giving limited to residents of Bucksport, ME.
Application information: Application form required.
Trustee: Fleet National Bank.
EIN: 016027394

49123
Clarence H. Bellinger Trust
c/o Fleet Private Clients Group
P.O. Box 6767
Providence, RI 02940-6767
Application address: c/o Board of Trustees, Syracuse Univ., Syracuse, NY 13220

Financial data (yr. ended 12/31/00): Grants paid, $15,000; assets, $428,475 (M); expenditures, $21,066; qualifying distributions, $18,908.
Limitations: Giving limited to Chenango and Madison counties, NY.
Trustee: Fleet National Bank.
EIN: 156015051
Codes: GTI

49124
Bertrum D. Blaisdell Trust
c/o Fleet Private Clients Group
P.O. Box 6767
Providence, RI 02940-6767
Application address: 100 Federal St., Boston, MA 02110
Contact: Augusta Haydock, Trust Off., Fleet National Bank

Established in 1995 in MA.
Financial data (yr. ended 12/31/01): Grants paid, $15,000; assets, $410,548 (M); expenditures, $19,666; qualifying distributions, $18,286.
Limitations: Giving limited to MA.
Application information: Grants are determined by Greater Boston Bankers Assn. Directors.
Trustee: Fleet National Bank.
EIN: 911863880

49125
The Callanen Foundation
c/o Fleet Private Clients Group
P.O. Box 6767
Providence, RI 02940-6767

Established in 1998 in CT.
Financial data (yr. ended 08/31/02): Grants paid, $15,000; assets, $332,529 (M); expenditures, $17,603; qualifying distributions, $15,000.
Trustee: Fleet National Bank.
EIN: 061533282

49126
James L. Cassidy Trust
c/o Fleet Private Clients Group
P.O. Box 6767
Providence, RI 02940-6767

Financial data (yr. ended 12/31/01): Grants paid, $15,000; assets, $734,946 (M); expenditures, $39,200; qualifying distributions, $29,815.
Limitations: Applications not accepted. Giving primarily in Greenfield, MA.
Application information: Contributes only to pre-selected organizations.
Trustees: Gregory M. Olchowski, Jane S. Olchowski, Hon. Edward J. Shea, Kathleen M. Shea, Fleet National Bank.
EIN: 046570087

49127
Lida P. Underhill Trust
c/o Fleet Private Clients Group
P.O. Box 6767
Providence, RI 02940-6767

Established in 1998 in ME.
Donor(s): Lida P. Underhill Irrevocable Trust.
Financial data (yr. ended 12/31/01): Grants paid, $15,000; assets, $345,066 (M); expenditures, $20,752; qualifying distributions, $17,936.
Limitations: Applications not accepted. Giving primarily in Monhegan, ME.
Application information: Contributes only to pre-selected organizations.
Trustee: Fleet National Bank.
EIN: 010515885

49128
Rose M. Rondeau Trust
c/o Fleet Private Clients Group
P.O. Box 6767
Providence, RI 02940-6767

Financial data (yr. ended 09/30/01): Grants paid, $14,700; assets, $356,267 (M); expenditures, $22,033; qualifying distributions, $17,219.
Limitations: Applications not accepted. Giving primarily in MA and RI.

Application information: Contributes only to pre-selected organizations.
Trustee: Fleet National Bank.
EIN: 046067105

49129
Robert Pape Charitable Foundation
c/o Fleet Private Clients Group
P.O. Box 6767
Providence, RI 02940-6767
Application address: 1 Post Office Sq., Boston, MA 02109
Contact: James R. Degiacomo, Tr.

Established in 1992 in MA.
Financial data (yr. ended 12/31/01): Grants paid, $14,695; assets, $472,080 (M); expenditures, $23,570; qualifying distributions, $20,081.
Limitations: Giving limited to residents of Cohasset, MA.
Application information: Application form required.
Trustees: James R. Degiacomo, Fleet National Bank.
EIN: 046692518
Codes: GTI

49130
The Olga D. Rasmussen Award
c/o Fleet Private Clients Group
P.O. Box 6767
Providence, RI 02940-6767
Application address: c/o Principal, Mohawk Central School, 28 Grove St., Mohawk, NY 13407

Financial data (yr. ended 04/30/02): Grants paid, $14,285; assets, $314,878 (M); expenditures, $18,326; qualifying distributions, $14,285.
Limitations: Giving limited to Mohawk, NY.
Application information: Application form required.
Trustee: Fleet National Bank.
EIN: 166332307

49131
LeBaron C. Colt Memorial Ambulance Fund, Inc.
c/o Fleet Private Clients Group
P.O. Box 6767
Providence, RI 02940-6767

Donor(s): First Federal Trust.
Financial data (yr. ended 12/31/01): Grants paid, $14,121; assets, $349,914 (M); gifts received, $10,510; expenditures, $18,859; qualifying distributions, $16,577.
Limitations: Applications not accepted. Giving primarily in Bristol, RI.
Application information: Contributes only to pre-selected organizations.
Trustees: Harold R. Bannister, Joseph A. Cavallaro, Victoria Van Voast, Fleet National Bank.
EIN: 050404220

49132
Charles Main 1917 Scholarship Fund
c/o Fleet Private Clients Group
P.O. Box 6767
Providence, RI 02940-6767
Application address: c/o Virginia Keist, Secy. and Trust Off., Auburn Board of Education, Thorton Ave., Auburn, NY 13021

Donor(s): Charles E. Main.‡
Financial data (yr. ended 12/31/01): Grants paid, $13,562; assets, $226,959 (M); expenditures, $16,606; qualifying distributions, $15,290.
Limitations: Giving limited to residents of Auburn, NY.

Application information: Application form required.
Trustee: Fleet National Bank.
EIN: 226407279

49133
Walter W. Farnum Trust
c/o Masonic Grand Lodge Charities, Relief Comm.
222 Taunton Ave.
East Providence, RI 02914-4556
(401) 435-4650

Financial data (yr. ended 10/31/01): Grants paid, $13,500; assets, $420,608 (M); expenditures, $21,105; qualifying distributions, $13,500.
Limitations: Giving limited to RI.
Application information: Application form required.
Officers: Robert B. Yates, Pres.; Benjamin A. Phillips, V.P.; John M. Faulhaber, Secy.; Norman Tierney, Jr., Treas.
EIN: 237352668

49134
Marian Schwartz Family Foundation
100 Baystate Ave.
Warwick, RI 02888-5346 (401) 274-4444
Contact: Jack Pomeranz, Tr.

Established in 1987 in RI.
Financial data (yr. ended 12/31/01): Grants paid, $13,353; assets, $160,386 (M); expenditures, $14,505; qualifying distributions, $13,353.
Limitations: Giving primarily in RI.
Trustees: Jack Pomeranz, Joel Pomeranz, Lynne Pomeranz, Glenn Silverman.
EIN: 056080363

49135
Kostas C. Yerontitis Trust
c/o Fleet Private Client's Group
P.O. Box 6767
Providence, RI 02940-6767

Financial data (yr. ended 12/31/01): Grants paid, $13,339; assets, $309,772 (M); expenditures, $17,287; qualifying distributions, $15,594.
Limitations: Applications not accepted. Giving primarily in Greece.
Application information: Contributes only to pre-selected organizations.
Trustee: Fleet National Bank.
EIN: 046009630

49136
William Hosier Trust
c/o Fleet Private Clients Group
P.O. Box 6767
Providence, RI 02940-6767
Application address: c/o Carol Gray, Fleet National Bank, 100 Federal St., Boston, MA 02110

Established in 1994 in MA.
Financial data (yr. ended 12/31/01): Grants paid, $13,329; assets, $322,768 (M); expenditures, $19,113; qualifying distributions, $16,475.
Limitations: Giving limited to Nantucket, MA.
Trustee: Fleet National Bank.
EIN: 046266114

49137
George Ensworth Memorial Fund Trust
c/o Fleet Private Clients Group
P.O. Box 6767
Providence, RI 02940-6767
Application address: Marjorie Alexandre Davis, c/o Fleet National Bank, 777 Main St., Hartford, CT 08115, tel.: (860) 986-7696

Financial data (yr. ended 05/31/01): Grants paid, $13,300; assets, $810,088 (M); expenditures, $24,940; qualifying distributions, $20,068.
Limitations: Giving primarily in Glastonbury, CT.
Application information: Application form required.
Trustee: Fleet National Bank.
EIN: 066114690

49138
Frank E. Green Trust
c/o Citizens Bank New Hampshire
870 Westminster St., 1st. Fl.
Providence, RI 02903

Financial data (yr. ended 12/31/01): Grants paid, $13,279; assets, $232,382 (M); expenditures, $18,243; qualifying distributions, $13,279.
Limitations: Applications not accepted. Giving limited to NH.
Application information: Contributes only to pre-selected organizations.
Trustee: Citizens Bank New Hampshire.
EIN: 026004488

49139
Mary D. Vitullo Trust
c/o Citizens Bank
870 Westminster St.
Providence, RI 02903

Established in 2001 in RI.
Donor(s): Mary D. Vitullo.‡
Financial data (yr. ended 09/30/02): Grants paid, $13,253; assets, $294,706 (M); expenditures, $23,543; qualifying distributions, $18,140.
Limitations: Applications not accepted.
Application information: Contributes only to pre-selected organizations.
Trustee: Citizens Bank.
EIN: 050519508

49140
Maude E. Arnold Memorial Fund
(Formerly Maude E. Arnold Trust for Memorial Fund)
c/o Fleet Private Clients Group
P.O. Box 6767
Providence, RI 02940-6767
Application address: c/o Scholarship Comm. Chair., First Baptist Church, P.O. Box 121, 2-4 North St., Plymouth, CT 06782, tel.: (860) 283-6181

Financial data (yr. ended 12/31/01): Grants paid, $13,000; assets, $225,453 (M); expenditures, $14,855; qualifying distributions, $13,851.
Limitations: Giving limited to residents of Waterbury, CT.
Application information: Transcript directly from college to church.
Trustee: Fleet National Bank.
EIN: 066140957
Codes: GTI

49141
Grace H. Humphrey Residuary Trust
c/o Fleet Private Clients Group
P.O. Box 6767
Providence, RI 02940-6767

Filing state: RI.

49141—RHODE ISLAND

Financial data (yr. ended 12/31/01): Grants paid, $13,000; assets, $343,666 (M); expenditures, $17,846; qualifying distributions, $16,304.
Limitations: Applications not accepted. Giving limited to the Simsbury, CT, area.
Trustee: Fleet National Bank.
EIN: 066055126
Codes: GTI

49142
Mary G. Croston Trust
c/o Citizens Bank New Hampshire
870 Westminster St., 2nd Fl.
Providence, RI 02903
Application address: c/o Fr. Frederick B. McGowan, St. James Parish, 6 Cottage St., Haver Hill, MA 01830, tel.: (508) 327-8537

Donor(s): Mary G. Croston.‡
Financial data (yr. ended 08/31/01): Grants paid, $12,900; assets, $278,178 (M); expenditures, $18,017; qualifying distributions, $15,217.
Limitations: Giving limited to residents of Haverhill, MA.
Application information: Application form required.
Trustee: Citizens Bank New Hampshire.
EIN: 026027098
Codes: GTI

49143
Mabel W. Mason Trust
c/o Fleet Private Clients Group
P.O. Box 6767
Providence, RI 02940-6767

Financial data (yr. ended 12/31/01): Grants paid, $12,762; assets, $324,087 (M); expenditures, $18,948; qualifying distributions, $12,762.
Limitations: Applications not accepted. Giving primarily in Attleboro, MA.
Application information: Contributes only to pre-selected organizations.
Trustee: Fleet National Bank.
EIN: 046037275

49144
The Oliver Fund
c/o Hinkley, Allen & Snyder
1500 Fleet Center
Providence, RI 02903
Contact: Bentley Tobin, Secy.

Established in 1986 in RI.
Donor(s): Sidney S. Goldstein, Ruth Goldstein.
Financial data (yr. ended 12/31/00): Grants paid, $12,750; assets, $8,351 (M); gifts received, $15,804; expenditures, $14,308; qualifying distributions, $12,750.
Limitations: Giving limited to RI.
Application information: Application form not required.
Officers: Ruth S. Goldstein, Pres.; Bentley Tobin, Secy.
Trustee: Stanley Goldstein.
EIN: 056080079

49145
Zartarian Foundation
5 Chestnut Dr.
East Greenwich, RI 02818-2101
(401) 884-0477
Contact: Patricia Nanian, Tr.

Financial data (yr. ended 12/31/01): Grants paid, $12,250; assets, $564,183 (M); expenditures, $13,261; qualifying distributions, $12,250.
Trustees: Patricia Nanian, Rose Zartarian, Sarkis M. Zartarian, Jr.
EIN: 046116930

49146
Rena Burney Fund
c/o Fleet Private Clients Group
P.O. Box 6767
Providence, RI 02940-6767

Donor(s): Thomas W. Burney.
Financial data (yr. ended 12/31/01): Grants paid, $12,200; assets, $969,092 (M); expenditures, $25,725; qualifying distributions, $12,200.
Limitations: Applications not accepted. Giving primarily in RI.
Application information: Contributes only to pre-selected organizations.
Trustee: Fleet National Bank.
EIN: 056117210

49147
Marion Flagg Trust
c/o Fleet Private Clients Group
P.O. Box 6767
Providence, RI 02940-6767

Established in 1997 in NH.
Financial data (yr. ended 12/31/01): Grants paid, $12,045; assets, $232,832 (M); expenditures, $14,810; qualifying distributions, $12,045.
Limitations: Applications not accepted.
Application information: Contributes only to pre-selected organizations.
Trustee: Fleet National Bank.
EIN: 026037484

49148
The Chandler Foundation
c/o Fleet Clients Group
P.O. Box 6767
Providence, RI 02940-6767
Additional address: c/o Gregory Crete, Fleet National Bank, 1155 Elm St., Nashua, NH 03060-6466

Donor(s): James E. Chandler.
Financial data (yr. ended 12/31/01): Grants paid, $12,037; assets, $235,902 (M); expenditures, $13,667; qualifying distributions, $12,037.
Limitations: Giving primarily in NH.
Trustees: Christine R. Chandler, James E. Chandler, Fleet National Bank.
EIN: 026069770

49149
Watkins Burnham Fund
22 Parsonage St.
Providence, RI 02903

Established in 1997 in RI.
Donor(s): Mrs. Richard I. Burnham.
Financial data (yr. ended 12/31/01): Grants paid, $12,000; assets, $168,348 (M); expenditures, $13,675; qualifying distributions, $12,000.
Officers and Trustees:* Richard I. Burnham,* Pres.; Fanchon M. Burnham,* V.P. and Secy.; Paul W. Whyte,* Treas.; Helen Metcalf Burnham, John Burnham.
EIN: 061483377

49150
B. L. & W. H. Heald Scholarship Trust
c/o Fleet Private Clients Group
P.O. Box 6767
Providence, RI 02940-6767

Established in 1985 in CT.
Financial data (yr. ended 09/30/01): Grants paid, $12,000; assets, $350,152 (M); expenditures, $19,162; qualifying distributions, $16,155.
Limitations: Applications not accepted. Giving limited to residents of CT.
Application information: Unsolicited requests for grants not accepted.

Trustee: Fleet National Bank.
EIN: 066087125
Codes: GTI

49151
John & Helen Nicholson Scholarship Fund
Fleet Private Clients Group
P.O. Box 6767
Providence, RI 02940-6767
Application address: c/o Principal, Newbury High School, 241 High St., Newburyport, MA 01950

Established in 2000 in MA.
Financial data (yr. ended 11/30/01): Grants paid, $12,000; assets, $234,660 (M); gifts received, $267,131; expenditures, $14,817; qualifying distributions, $13,876.
Limitations: Giving limited to residents of Newburyport, MA.
Application information: Application form required.
Trustee: Fleet National Bank.
EIN: 043545128

49152
Drs. Ward & Virginia Oliver Foundation
c/o Fleet Private Clients Group
P.O. Box 6767
Providence, RI 02940-6767

Established in 1997 in NY.
Financial data (yr. ended 12/31/01): Grants paid, $12,000; assets, $255,744 (M); expenditures, $15,314; qualifying distributions, $12,000.
Limitations: Applications not accepted.
Application information: Contributes only to pre-selected organizations.
Trustee: Fleet National Bank.
EIN: 141800379

49153
Frank H. Scheehl Trust
(also known as Emeline H. Scheehl College Scholarship Fund)
c/o Fleet Private Clients Group
P.O. Box 6767
Providence, RI 02940-6767
Application address: C/o Scholarship Committee, Conard High School, 110 Berkshire Rd., West Hartford, CT 06107

Financial data (yr. ended 06/30/01): Grants paid, $12,000; assets, $263,311 (M); expenditures, $15,983; qualifying distributions, $14,257.
Limitations: Giving limited to residents of the West Hartford, CT, area.
Application information: Application form required.
Trustees: Hon. Robert Satter, Fleet National Bank.
EIN: 066177823

49154
The Vera H. and William R. Todd Foundation
c/o Fleet Private Clients Group
P.O. Box 6767
Providence, RI 02940-6767
Contact: Marjorie Alexadre Davis

Financial data (yr. ended 12/31/01): Grants paid, $12,000; assets, $243,958 (M); expenditures, $16,143; qualifying distributions, $14,628.
Limitations: Giving limited to residents of Derby and Shelton, CT.
Application information: Application form not required.
Trustee: Fleet National Bank.
EIN: 066031931
Codes: GTI

49155
Henry Walker Trust for Others
c/o Fleet Private Clients Group
P.O. Box 6767
Providence, RI 02940-6767
Application address: c/o Unitarian Universalist Assoc., 25 Beacon St., Boston, MA 02109

Established in 1989 in MA.
Financial data (yr. ended 12/31/00): Grants paid, $12,000; assets, $364,597 (M); expenditures, $18,613; qualifying distributions, $15,720.
Limitations: Giving limited to Roxbury, MA.
Trustee: Fleet National Bank.
EIN: 046020367

49156
Stanley W. Barrows, Sr. Trust
c/o Fleet Private Clients Group
P.O. Box 6767
Providence, RI 02940-6767

Established in 1989 in ME.
Financial data (yr. ended 06/30/02): Grants paid, $11,739; assets, $290,076 (M); expenditures, $16,159; qualifying distributions, $11,739.
Limitations: Applications not accepted. Giving primarily in ME.
Application information: Contributes only to pre-selected organizations.
Trustee: Fleet National Bank.
EIN: 016099154

49157
Andrew Adams and Alice Adams Trust
c/o Fleet Private Clients Group
P.O. Box 6767
Providence, RI 02940-6767

Established in 1989 in ME.
Financial data (yr. ended 12/31/01): Grants paid, $11,628; assets, $303,667 (M); expenditures, $15,903; qualifying distributions, $14,340.
Limitations: Applications not accepted. Giving primarily in ME.
Application information: Contributes only to pre-selected organizations.
Trustee: Fleet National Bank.
EIN: 016020440

49158
George W. Davenport Charitable Trust
c/o Fleet Private Clients Group
P.O. Box 6767
Providence, RI 02940-6767
Application address: 1 Monarch Pl., Springfield, MA 01101, tel.: (413) 787-8524
Contact: Thea Katsounakis, Trust Admin., Fleet National Bank

Financial data (yr. ended 12/31/01): Grants paid, $11,524; assets, $536,844 (M); expenditures, $22,331; qualifying distributions, $18,164.
Limitations: Giving limited to residents of Bernardston, Greenfield, and Leydon, MA.
Application information: Application form required.
Trustees: Irmarie Jones, Charles Sylvester, Fleet National Bank.
EIN: 046312563
Codes: GTI

49159
Fannie August Charitable Trust
c/o Fleet Private Clients Group
P.O. Box 6767
Providence, RI 02940-6767
Application address: 100 Federal St., Boston, MA 02110
Contact: Carol Gray, Trust Off., Fleet National Bank

Financial data (yr. ended 12/31/01): Grants paid, $11,500; assets, $318,960 (M); expenditures, $14,639; qualifying distributions, $13,107.
Limitations: Giving limited to the metropolitan Boston, MA, area.
Trustee: Fleet National Bank.
EIN: 046027010
Codes: GTI

49160
Miriam Sutro Price Scholarship Fund
c/o Fleet Private Clients Group
P.O. Box 6767
Providence, RI 02940-6767
Application address: c/o Peter Weston, Fleet National Bank, 77 Main St., Hartfourn, CT 06115

Financial data (yr. ended 06/30/01): Grants paid, $11,500; assets, $221,672 (M); expenditures, $14,892; qualifying distributions, $12,941.
Limitations: Giving limited to residents of Bridgewater, Kent, New Milford, Roxbury, Sherman, and Washington, CT.
Application information: Application form required.
Trustee: Fleet National Bank.
EIN: 066076246

49161
Rhode Island Building Industry Scholarship Fund
29 New York Ave.
Cumberland, RI 02864

Established in 1976 in RI.
Financial data (yr. ended 12/31/01): Grants paid, $11,500; assets, $93,354 (M); expenditures, $12,681; qualifying distributions, $11,441.
Limitations: Giving limited to residents of RI.
Officers and Directors:* Stephen Cardi, Jr.,* Chair.; Dan Peloquin, Secy.; Maureen Myette, Treas.; George Geisser, Richard Mayo, Gerold Visconte.
EIN: 050375250
Codes: GTI

49162
Howard & Christine Shifler Memorial Foundation
c/o Fleet Private Clients Group
P.O. Box 6767
Providence, RI 02940-6767

Financial data (yr. ended 12/31/01): Grants paid, $11,500; assets, $258,425 (M); expenditures, $13,832; qualifying distributions, $12,585.
Limitations: Giving limited to residents of Manahawkin, NJ.
Application information: Application form required.
Trustee: Fleet National Bank.
EIN: 226403942
Codes: GTI

49163
Helen W. Moulton Scholarship Fund
(Formerly Harold E. Moulton Scholarship Fund)
c/o Fleet Private Clients Group
P.O. Box 6767
Providence, RI 02940
Application address: 159 E. Main St., Rm 3089, Rochester, NY 14638
Contact: William A. McKee, Trust Off., Fleet National Bank

Financial data (yr. ended 04/30/02): Grants paid, $11,375; assets, $381,008 (M); expenditures, $16,536; qualifying distributions, $14,415.
Limitations: Giving limited to residents of Clarksville, NY.
Application information: Application form required.
Trustee: Fleet National Bank.
EIN: 510197187
Codes: GTI

49164
A. Miles Herrold Scholarship Trust
c/o Fleet Private Clients Group
P.O. Box 6767
Providence, RI 02940-6767

Established in 1999 in MA.
Financial data (yr. ended 12/31/01): Grants paid, $11,207; assets, $313,465 (M); expenditures, $16,099; qualifying distributions, $13,720.
Limitations: Applications not accepted. Giving primarily in MA.
Application information: Contributes only to pre-selected organizations.
Trustee: Fleet National Bank.
EIN: 046502498

49165
Eleanor Hayes Foundation
c/o Fleet Private Clients Group
P.O. Box 6767
Providence, RI 02940-6767
Application address: 121 State St., Springfield, MA 02914, tel.: (413) 787-8524
Contact: Thea Katsounakis, Trust Admin., Fleet National Bank

Financial data (yr. ended 12/31/01): Grants paid, $11,105; assets, $293,357 (M); expenditures, $14,977; qualifying distributions, $13,474.
Limitations: Giving limited to the metropolitan Springfield, MA, area.
Trustee: Fleet National Bank.
EIN: 046055362

49166
The Bancroft Family Foundation
25 Enterprise Ctr.
Middletown, RI 02842-5201

Established in 2000 in RI.
Donor(s): Arthur Bancroft.
Financial data (yr. ended 12/31/01): Grants paid, $11,025; assets, $248,683 (M); gifts received, $104,000; expenditures, $15,940; qualifying distributions, $11,025.
Limitations: Applications not accepted.
Application information: Contributes only to pre-selected organizations.
Officers and Trustees:* Arthur D. Bancroft,* Pres.; Laurie J. Mandly,* V.P. and Secy.-Treas.; Stephen P. Bancroft,* V.P.; Carol A. Verrochi,* V.P.; Diane M. Zuspan,* V.P.; Barry G. Hittner.
EIN: 050509060

49167
Jeremiah Foundation, Inc.
c/o Ralph M. Kinder
155 S. Main St.
Providence, RI 02903

Established in 1992 in RI.
Financial data (yr. ended 12/31/01): Grants paid, $11,000; assets, $5,400 (M); expenditures, $11,829; qualifying distributions, $11,000.
Limitations: Applications not accepted. Giving primarily in FL.
Application information: Contributes only to pre-selected organizations.
Officers: Michael T. Hartney, Pres.; Ralph M. Kinder, Secy.; Robert R. Washburn, Treas.
Director: Sheryl J. Hartney.
EIN: 050462855

49168
Florence J. Tryon Trust
c/o Fleet Private Clients Group
P.O. Box 6767
Providence, RI 02940-6767
Application addresses: c/o Guidance Dept., Westfield Vocational High School, Westfield, MA 01085; c/o Guidance Dept., St. Mary's High School, Westfield, MA 01085

Financial data (yr. ended 10/31/01): Grants paid, $11,000; assets, $399,542 (M); expenditures, $16,975; qualifying distributions, $14,335.
Limitations: Giving limited to Westfield, MA.
Application information: Application form required.
Trustee: Fleet National Bank.
EIN: 046033568
Codes: GTI

49169
The Kristen & John Carter Charitable Trust
977 Waterman Ave.
East Providence, RI 02914 (401) 434-1680
Contact: John S. Carter III, Tr.

Established in 1999 in RI.
Donor(s): John Carter, Kristen Carter.
Financial data (yr. ended 06/30/02): Grants paid, $10,920; assets, $4,101 (M); gifts received, $11,000; expenditures, $14,513; qualifying distributions, $10,920.
Limitations: Giving primarily in RI.
Trustees: John S. Carter III, Kristen Carter.
EIN: 137186559

49170
Frances A. DeBlois Trust
c/o Fleet Private Clients Group
P.O. Box 6767
Providence, RI 02940-6767
Application address: c/o Emma Green, P.O. Box 9477, Boston, MA 02205

Financial data (yr. ended 12/31/01): Grants paid, $10,870; assets, $448,208 (M); expenditures, $18,598; qualifying distributions, $13,246.
Limitations: Giving primarily in RI.
Trustee: Fleet National Bank.
EIN: 056064103

49171
Alice W. Miles HSSF Trust
(Formerly Alice W. Miles Trust High School Scholarship)
c/o Fleet Private Clients Group
P.O. Box 6767
Providence, RI 02940-6767
Application address: c/o Principal, Worcester Public High School, Worcester, MA 01613

Financial data (yr. ended 10/31/01): Grants paid, $10,800; assets, $320,711 (M); expenditures, $15,907; qualifying distributions, $13,291.
Limitations: Giving to residents of Worcester, MA.
Application information: Application form required.
Trustee: Fleet National Bank.
EIN: 046019793
Codes: GTI

49172
John P. Sheehan Scholarship Fund
c/o Fleet Private Clients Group
P.O. Box 6767
Providence, RI 02940-6767
Application address: c/o Fleet National Bank, TSU-268, Genesee St., 2nd Fl., Utica, NY 13502, tel.: (315) 798-2553

Financial data (yr. ended 12/31/00): Grants paid, $10,800; assets, $386,039 (M); expenditures, $17,207; qualifying distributions, $14,835.
Limitations: Giving primarily to residents of Utica, NY.
Application information: Application form required.
Trustee: Fleet National Bank.
EIN: 156014981
Codes: GTI

49173
The William H. Ghiloni Charitable Foundation
c/o Kalander
146 Westminster St.
Providence, RI 02903

Established in 1997 in RI.
Donor(s): William H. Ghiloni.
Financial data (yr. ended 12/31/01): Grants paid, $10,750; assets, $215,466 (M); expenditures, $30,476; qualifying distributions, $10,750.
Limitations: Applications not accepted.
Application information: Contributes only to pre-selected organizations.
Trustees: G. Winona Handford, Jonathan V. Kalander, William R. Kalander, Jr.
EIN: 061473878

49174
Ruth and W. Irving Wolf, Jr. Foundation
30 Argyle Ave., No. 106
Riverside, RI 02915
Contact: David Harris Wolf, Mgr.

Donor(s): Ruth Wolf, W. Irving Wolf, Jr.
Financial data (yr. ended 12/31/01): Grants paid, $10,727; assets, $112,684 (M); expenditures, $11,453; qualifying distributions, $10,727.
Limitations: Giving primarily in Pawtucket and Providence, RI.
Application information: Application form not required.
Officer and Trustees:* David Harris Wolf,* Mgr.; James Scott Wolf, Ruth Wolf, W. Irving Wolf, Jr.
EIN: 056035370

49175
Cranston High School Athletic Scholarship Fund
c/o Leslie Kenney
1000 Jefferson Blvd.
Warwick, RI 02886-2201
Application address: 1052 Park Ave., Cranston, RI 02910, tel.: (401) 461-5056
Contact: Edward L. Rondeau, Secy.

Established in 1990 in RI.
Financial data (yr. ended 12/31/01): Grants paid, $10,600; assets, $138,733 (M); expenditures, $14,704; qualifying distributions, $10,546.
Limitations: Giving limited to residents of Cranston, RI.
Application information: Application form required.
Officers and Directors:* H. William Carpenter,* Pres.; Edward L. Rondeau,* Secy.; Leslie Kenney,* Treas.; John S. Adams, Donald Frederick, Kenneth Hopkins, Edmond J. Lemoi, H. Peter Olsen, Hon. John Orton III, Joseph Ventetuolo.
EIN: 222982274

49176
The Kiwanis Foundation of Pawtucket, Inc.
P.O. Box 3128
Pawtucket, RI 02861 (401) 521-4111
Contact: William O'Connell, Treas.

Financial data (yr. ended 12/31/01): Grants paid, $10,600; assets, $75,002 (M); expenditures, $12,293; qualifying distributions, $10,600.
Limitations: Giving primarily in Pawtucket, RI.
Officers: Thomas Henderson, Pres.; Joseph Worzycha, Secy.; William O'Connell, Treas.
EIN: 050453096

49177
The Schein Family Foundation
125 Hartshorn Rd.
Providence, RI 02906

Established in 2000 in RI.
Donor(s): Harold I. Schein.
Financial data (yr. ended 12/31/01): Grants paid, $10,450; assets, $97,939 (M); expenditures, $15,073; qualifying distributions, $10,450.
Limitations: Applications not accepted.
Application information: Contributes only to pre-selected organizations.
Officers and Directors:* Harold I. Schein,* Pres. and Treas.; Ellen R. Schein,* V.P. and Secy.; Leslie J. Fontaine, Michael L. Schein, Phillip D. Schein.
EIN: 050514737

49178
R. C. Smith Memorial Foundation Trust
c/o Fleet Private Clients Group
P.O. Box 6767
Providence, RI 02940-6767
Application address: 777 Main St., Hartford, CT 06115
Contact: Marjorie Alexandre Davis, Trust Off., Fleet Bank

Financial data (yr. ended 12/31/00): Grants paid, $10,200; assets, $18,880 (M); gifts received, $10,061; expenditures, $11,495; qualifying distributions, $11,024.
Limitations: Giving limited to the New London County, CT, area.
Trustee: Fleet National Bank.
EIN: 066036742

49179
Laura Brooks Harney/P. J. Harney Scholarship Trust
c/o Fleet Private Clients Group
P.O. Box 6767
Providence, RI 02940-6767 (401) 276-7316
Application address: c/o David Clark, Chair., Town of Webb Schools, Crosby Blvd., Old Forge, NY 13420

Financial data (yr. ended 12/31/01): Grants paid, $10,069; assets, $229,984 (M); gifts received, $50; expenditures, $12,702; qualifying distributions, $11,683.
Limitations: Giving limited to Potsdam, NY.
Trustee: Fleet National Bank.
EIN: 166283916

49180
The Egavian Foundation
c/o Ralph M. Kinder
155 S. Main St.
Providence, RI 02903-2963

Established in 1998 in RI.
Donor(s): Seroon Egavian.
Financial data (yr. ended 12/31/01): Grants paid, $10,059; assets, $210,989 (M); expenditures, $12,214; qualifying distributions, $10,059.
Officers: Ralph M. Kinder, Pres.; George N. Najarian, V.P.; Cathy A. Brien, Secy.; Leon Najarian, Treas.
EIN: 050499331

49181
Arlington Catholic High School Scholarship Fund
c/o Fleet Private Clients Group
P.O. Box 6767
Providence, RI 02940-6767
Application address: c/o Carol Gray, Fleet National Bank, 100 Federal St., Boston, MA 02110

Financial data (yr. ended 12/31/01): Grants paid, $10,000; assets, $270,390 (M); expenditures, $15,142; qualifying distributions, $13,054.
Limitations: Giving limited to residents of Arlington, MA.
Application information: Application form not required.
Trustee: Fleet National Bank.
EIN: 046116950
Codes: GTI

49182
The Philip & Bette Ayoub Foundation
P.O. Box 2464
Pawtucket, RI 02861

Established in 1999 in RI.
Donor(s): Philip Ayoub, Bette Ayoub.
Financial data (yr. ended 12/31/00): Grants paid, $10,000; assets, $194,064 (M); gifts received, $98,373; expenditures, $10,819; qualifying distributions, $10,801.
Directors: Bette Ayoub, Philip A. Ayoub, Philip G. Ayoub.
EIN: 050508597

49183
Richard D. Carmel Charitable Remainder Trust
c/o Fleet Private Clients Group
P.O. Box 6767
Providence, RI 02940-6767 (401) 276-7248

Established in 1993 in MA.
Financial data (yr. ended 09/30/01): Grants paid, $10,000; assets, $754,682 (M); expenditures, $38,833; qualifying distributions, $34,237.
Trustee: Fleet National Bank.

EIN: 046741222

49184
Green Scholarship Fund
c/o Fleet Private Clients Group
P.O. Box 6767
Providence, RI 02940-6767

Established in 2001 in NJ.
Donor(s): Robert E. Green.‡
Financial data (yr. ended 12/31/01): Grants paid, $10,000; assets, $118,083 (M); gifts received, $125,000; expenditures, $11,383; qualifying distributions, $10,845.
Limitations: Giving limited to residents of Berkeley, NJ.
Application information: Recipients chosen by school board members. Application form required.
Trustee: Fleet National Bank.
EIN: 527140821

49185
Frances P. Parker Scholarship Fund
c/o Fleet Private Clients Group
P.O. Box 6767
Providence, RI 02940-6767

Financial data (yr. ended 12/31/01): Grants paid, $10,000; assets, $232,640 (M); expenditures, $14,597; qualifying distributions, $10,000.
Limitations: Applications not accepted. Giving limited to West Hartford, CT.
Application information: Contributes only to pre-selected organizations.
Trustee: Fleet National Bank.
EIN: 066286040

49186
The Alan C. Salmanson Foundation
c/o Donald Salmanson
155 S. Main St.
Providence, RI 02903-2963

Established in 1984 in RI.
Donor(s): Alan C. Salmanson.
Financial data (yr. ended 09/30/01): Grants paid, $10,000; assets, $90,362 (M); expenditures, $12,858; qualifying distributions, $10,000.
Limitations: Applications not accepted. Giving primarily in NY.
Application information: Contributes only to pre-selected organizations.
Trustees: Alan C. Salmanson, Donald Salmanson.
EIN: 222571916

49187
Guilford Smith Trust
c/o Fleet Private Clients Group
P.O. Box 6767
Providence, RI 02940-6767

Donor(s): Guilford Smith.‡
Financial data (yr. ended 12/31/00): Grants paid, $10,000; assets, $204,655 (M); expenditures, $13,999; qualifying distributions, $11,910.
Limitations: Applications not accepted. Giving limited to Willimantic, CT.
Application information: Contributes only to pre-selected organizations.
Trustee: Fleet National Bank.
EIN: 066090015

49188
Bernice R. Crocker Charitable Trust
c/o Fleet Private Clients Group
P.O. Box 6767
Providence, RI 02940-6767

Financial data (yr. ended 12/31/01): Grants paid, $9,892; assets, $250,720 (M); expenditures, $14,309; qualifying distributions, $9,892.

Limitations: Applications not accepted. Giving primarily in CT and IL.
Application information: Contributes only to pre-selected organizations.
Trustee: Fleet National Bank.
EIN: 066195853

49189
The Robert J. and Louise P. Miorelli Foundation
c/o Fleet Private Clients Group
P.O. Box 6767
Providence, RI 02940-6767

Established in 1995 in PA.
Donor(s): Robert J. Miorelli, Louise P. Miorelli.
Financial data (yr. ended 12/31/01): Grants paid, $9,885; assets, $109,548 (M); expenditures, $11,145; qualifying distributions, $10,722.
Limitations: Applications not accepted. Giving primarily in Hazleton, PA.
Application information: Contributes only to pre-selected organizations.
Trustees: Louis J. Miorelli, Robert Miorelli, Fleet National Bank.
EIN: 237816449

49190
Rostra Engineered Component Sunshine Fund
(Formerly Century Brass Sunshine Fund)
c/o Fleet Private Clients Group
P.O. Box 6767
Providence, RI 02940-6767

Donor(s): Rostra Precision Controls, Inc.
Financial data (yr. ended 12/31/01): Grants paid, $9,842; assets, $51,594 (M); expenditures, $11,711; qualifying distributions, $11,043.
Limitations: Giving primarily in areas of company operations.
Application information: Application form not required.
Trustee: Fleet National Bank.
EIN: 066219258
Codes: CS, CD, GTI

49191
Wyman Whitney & Della Whitney Fund
c/o Fleet Private Clients Group
P.O. Box 6767
Providence, RI 02940-6767

Financial data (yr. ended 12/31/01): Grants paid, $9,752; assets, $334,543 (M); expenditures, $14,748; qualifying distributions, $9,752.
Limitations: Applications not accepted. Giving primarily in Bar Harbor, ME.
Application information: Contributes only to pre-selected organizations.
Trustee: Fleet National Bank.
EIN: 166374611

49192
Arthur Bolles Trust for Residents of Washington, CT
c/o Fleet Private Clients Group
P.O. Box 6767
Providence, RI 02940-6767
Application address: c/o First Selectman, Town Hall, Washington, CT 06793

Financial data (yr. ended 12/31/01): Grants paid, $9,685; assets, $122,496 (M); expenditures, $11,796; qualifying distributions, $1,060.
Limitations: Giving limited to Washington, CT.
Application information: Application form not required.
Trustee: Fleet National Bank.
EIN: 066040108

49193
Helen L. Blake Trust
c/o Fleet Private Clients Group
P.O. Box 6767
Providence, RI 02940-6767

Donor(s): Helen L. Blake.‡
Financial data (yr. ended 03/31/01): Grants paid, $9,546; assets, $204,672 (M); expenditures, $14,092; qualifying distributions, $11,352.
Limitations: Applications not accepted. Giving limited to Webster, NH.
Application information: Contributes only to a pre-selected organization.
Trustee: Fleet National Bank.
EIN: 066122846

49194
Marie D. Parritt and William G. Parritt Fund
c/o Fleet Private Clients Group
P.O. Box 6767
Providence, RI 02940-6767
Application address: c/o Fleet National Bank, 100 Federal St., Boston, MA 02110, tel.: (617) 434-4645
Contact: Susanna Forster-Castillo, Trust Admin., Fleet National Bank

Financial data (yr. ended 12/31/01): Grants paid, $9,523; assets, $284,390 (M); expenditures, $14,263; qualifying distributions, $14,460.
Limitations: Giving primarily in MA.
Trustee: Fleet National Bank.
EIN: 046020373

49195
George A. Dix Trust
c/o Fleet Private Clients Group
P.O. Box 6767
Providence, RI 02940-6767
Application address: c/o Michael T. Rivard, Dir. of Financial Affairs, Fitchburg State College, 160 Pearl St., Fitchburg, MA 01420-2697

Financial data (yr. ended 12/31/01): Grants paid, $9,508; assets, $481,672 (M); expenditures, $17,710; qualifying distributions, $14,437.
Limitations: Giving limited to residents of Worcester County, MA.
Trustee: Fleet National Bank.
EIN: 046023246

49196
The George Holopigian Memorial Fund
c/o Fleet Private Clients Group
P.O. Box 6767
Providence, RI 02940-6767
Application addresses: c/o Armenian Students' Assn. of America, Inc., P.O. Box 6947, Providence, RI 02904; c/o Armenian General Benevolent Union, 585 Saddle River Rd., Saddlebrook, NJ 07662

Financial data (yr. ended 06/30/01): Grants paid, $9,500; assets, $483,409 (M); expenditures, $16,812; qualifying distributions, $14,446.
Limitations: Giving limited to residents of Providence, RI.
Application information: Application form required.
Trustee: Fleet National Bank.
EIN: 056044531
Codes: GTI

49197
E. B. and C. G. Smith Scholarship
(Formerly Elizabeth B. Smith Trust)
c/o Fleet Private Clients Group
P.O. Box 6767
Providence, RI 02940-6767
Application address: c/o Principal, Westfield High School, Smith Ave., Westfield, MA 01085

Financial data (yr. ended 10/31/01): Grants paid, $9,500; assets, $231,011 (M); expenditures, $14,571; qualifying distributions, $12,677.
Limitations: Giving limited to residents of Westfield, MA, area.
Application information: Contact Westfield High School principal for application information.
Trustee: Fleet National Bank.
EIN: 046033567

49198
Greenwald Family Foundation, Inc.
23 Surrey Rd.
Barrington, RI 02806

Established in 1985 in RI.
Donor(s): Roy F. Greenwald, Carol Greenwald.
Financial data (yr. ended 11/30/01): Grants paid, $9,350; assets, $77,467 (M); gifts received, $27,219; expenditures, $9,422; qualifying distributions, $9,314.
Limitations: Applications not accepted. Giving primarily in Providence, RI.
Application information: Contributes only to pre-selected organizations.
Officers: Roy F. Greenwald, Pres. and Treas.; C. Gail Greenwald, V.P. and Secy.
Director: Sidney F. Greenwald.
EIN: 222667283

49199
Emma Y. Stocker Trust
c/o Fleet Private Clients Group
P.O. Box 6767
Providence, RI 02940-6767
Application address: 29 Buchanan Cir., Lynn, MA 01902
Contact: Lillian Collver

Financial data (yr. ended 12/31/01): Grants paid, $9,300; assets, $218,434 (M); expenditures, $12,775; qualifying distributions, $11,866.
Limitations: Giving limited to residents of Swampscott, MA.
Application information: Application form required.
Trustee: Fleet National Bank.
EIN: 046043607

49200
Lucien L. Audet Trust
c/o Fleet Private Clients Group
P.O. Box 6767
Providence, RI 02940-6767

Financial data (yr. ended 04/30/02): Grants paid, $9,199; assets, $257,339 (M); expenditures, $14,225; qualifying distributions, $11,743.
Limitations: Applications not accepted. Giving primarily in Winslow and Waterville, ME.
Application information: Contributes only to pre-selected organizations.
Trustee: Fleet National Bank.
EIN: 016059798

49201
Streeter Scholarship Fund
c/o Fleet Private Clients Group
P.O. Box 6767
Providence, RI 02940-6767
Application address: c/o Principal, Lyons Central School, 9 Lawrence St., Lyons, NY 14489

Financial data (yr. ended 12/31/00): Grants paid, $9,098; assets, $376,022 (M); expenditures, $14,807; qualifying distributions, $12,106.
Limitations: Giving limited to residents of the Lyons, NY, area.
Application information: Application form required.
Trustee: Fleet National Bank.
EIN: 166053773

49202
The Ayres Foundation
P.O. Box 6767
Providence, RI 02940-6767

Established in 1999 in RI.
Donor(s): Stephen O'Connor, Lucy O'Connor.
Financial data (yr. ended 09/30/01): Grants paid, $9,000; assets, $308,786 (M); expenditures, $10,984; qualifying distributions, $9,652.
Limitations: Giving primarily in RI.
Trustee: Fleet National Bank.
EIN: 056121827

49203
Frank J. Cummings Trust
c/o Fleet Private Clients Group
P.O. Box 6767
Providence, RI 02940-6767
Application address: c/o St. Francis of Assisi Church, Priest In Charge, 160 Main St., Torrington, CT 06790, tel: (860) 482-5571

Financial data (yr. ended 12/31/00): Grants paid, $9,000; assets, $208,639 (M); expenditures, $12,497; qualifying distributions, $11,246.
Limitations: Giving limited to Torrington, CT.
Trustee: Fleet National Bank.
EIN: 066134859

49204
Robert Rimmele Scholarship Fund
c/o Fleet Private Clients Group
P.O. Box 6767
Providence, RI 02940-6767
Application address: c/o Susana Forster-Castillo, Fleet National Bank, 100 Federal St., Boston, MA 02110

Established in 1992 in MA.
Financial data (yr. ended 12/31/01): Grants paid, $9,000; assets, $306,586 (M); expenditures, $14,307; qualifying distributions, $12,137.
Limitations: Giving limited to residents of Needham, MA.
Application information: Application form required.
Trustee: Fleet National Bank.
EIN: 046712607
Codes: GTI

49205
Gregory Kent Hill and Robert Harrison Gregory Memorial Fund
c/o Fleet Private Clients Group
P.O. Box 6767
Providence, RI 02940-6767

Established in 1999 in CT.
Financial data (yr. ended 12/31/01): Grants paid, $8,998; assets, $169,799 (M); expenditures, $12,851; qualifying distributions, $11,571.
Trustee: Fleet National Bank.

EIN: 066241259

49206
Emily Gill Trust f/b/o Chas Abbey Scholarship
c/o Fleet Private Clients Group
P.O. Box 6767
Providence, RI 02940-6767
Application addresses: c/o Chicopee High School, 650 Front St., Chicopee, MA 01013; c/o Chicopee Comprehensive High School, 617 Montogmery St., Chicopee, MA 01020
Financial data (yr. ended 12/31/01): Grants paid, $8,900; assets, $314,845 (M); expenditures, $13,213; qualifying distributions, $11,771.
Limitations: Giving limited to residents of Chicopee, MA.
Trustee: Fleet National Bank.
EIN: 046021060

49207
Edward Thornton Trust
c/o Citizens Bank New Hampshire
870 Westminster St.
Providence, RI 02903
Application address: c/o Robert C. Massie, Chair., Penacook Advisory Comm., Concord Savings Bank, Concord, NH 03301
Financial data (yr. ended 12/31/01): Grants paid, $8,850; assets, $216,689 (M); expenditures, $12,872; qualifying distributions, $8,850.
Limitations: Giving limited to Boscawen and Penacook, NH.
Trustee: Citizens Bank New Hampshire.
EIN: 026004033

49208
Gilbert Family Trust Fund
c/o Fleet Private Clients Group
P.O. Box 6767
Providence, RI 02940-6767
Established in 1999 in NY.
Financial data (yr. ended 06/30/00): Grants paid, $8,764; assets, $330,020 (M); gifts received, $309,893; expenditures, $9,260; qualifying distributions, $9,057.
Limitations: Applications not accepted.
Application information: Contributes only to pre-selected organizations.
Trustee: Fleet National Bank.
EIN: 066480753

49209
Alice Kee Trust
c/o Fleet Private Clients Group
P.O. Box 6767
Providence, RI 02940-6767
Application address: Tina Hamilton, c/o Fleet National Bank, 1 Constitution Plz., Hartford, CT 06115
Established in 1992 in CT.
Donor(s): Alice R. Kee.‡
Financial data (yr. ended 04/30/01): Grants paid, $8,700; assets, $292,009 (M); expenditures, $12,913; qualifying distributions, $11,430.
Limitations: Giving limited to residents of New London and Groton, CT.
Application information: Application form required.
Trustee: Fleet National Bank.
EIN: 066361300

49210
Charles C. Morris Charitable Trust
c/o Fleet Private Clients Group
P.O. Box 6767
Providence, RI 02940-6767
Financial data (yr. ended 04/30/01): Grants paid, $8,616; assets, $226,668 (M); expenditures, $11,866; qualifying distributions, $10,713.
Limitations: Applications not accepted. Giving primarily in Bangor, ME.
Application information: Contributes only to pre-selected organizations.
Trustee: Fleet National Bank.
EIN: 016080946

49211
John C. Babcock Fund
(Formerly Betsey E. Babcock Trust)
c/o Fleet Private Clients Group
P.O. Box 6767
Providence, RI 02940-6767
Application address: c/o Lillian B. Collyer, 29 Buchanan Cir., Lynn, MA 01902
Financial data (yr. ended 12/31/01): Grants paid, $8,500; assets, $250,520 (M); expenditures, $10,694; qualifying distributions, $9,990.
Limitations: Giving limited to the greater Lynn, MA, area, including Swampscott, Nahant, and Saugus.
Application information: Application form required.
Trustee: Fleet National Bank.
EIN: 046043639

49212
Henry E. Ellsworth Scholarship Fund
c/o Fleet Private Clients Group
P.O. Box 6767
Providence, RI 02940-6767
Application address: c/o Scholarship Comm., 34 Farms Village Rd., Simsbury High School, Simsbury, CT 06070
Financial data (yr. ended 12/31/01): Grants paid, $8,500; assets, $97,460 (M); gifts received, $8,183; expenditures, $10,518; qualifying distributions, $9,966.
Limitations: Giving limited to residents of the Simsbury, CT, area.
Application information: Application form required.
Trustee: Fleet National Bank.
EIN: 066032904

49213
Lawrence Foundation
c/o Fleet Private Clients Group
P.O. Box 6767
Providence, RI 02940-6767
Contact: Kerry Sullivan, Trust Admin., Fleet National Bank
Financial data (yr. ended 12/31/01): Grants paid, $8,400; assets, $176,722 (M); expenditures, $11,035; qualifying distributions, $9,871.
Limitations: Giving limited to Brookline, MA.
Officer: Susan T. Farago, V.P.
Director: Richard G. Small.
Trustees: Paul F. Farago, Fleet National Bank.
EIN: 046051721

49214
Harvey H. Moses & Catherine Allis Moses Educational Fund
c/o Fleet Private Clients Group
P.O. Box 6767
Providence, RI 02940-6767
Application address: c/o Guidance Off., Ticonderoga High School, Calkins Place, Ticonderoga, NY 12883, tel.: (518) 585-6661
Contact: Judy Zalansky
Financial data (yr. ended 08/31/00): Grants paid, $8,400; assets, $404,035 (M); expenditures, $13,494; qualifying distributions, $11,815.
Limitations: Giving limited to residents of Ticonderoga, NY.
Application information: Application form required.
Trustee: Fleet National Bank.
EIN: 046487087

49215
John P. and Mable I. Ogsbury Trust
c/o Fleet Private Clients Group
P.O. Box 6767
Providence, RI 02940-6767
Financial data (yr. ended 12/31/01): Grants paid, $8,341; assets, $163,667 (M); expenditures, $9,960; qualifying distributions, $8,341.
Limitations: Applications not accepted. Giving limited to NY.
Application information: Contributes only to pre-selected organizations.
Trustee: Fleet National Bank.
EIN: 146029362

49216
James Edward Kinsley Trust
(Formerly James Edward Kinsley Educational Foundation)
c/o Fleet Private Clients Group
P.O. Box 6767
Providence, RI 02940-6767
Application address: c/o James Kesler, Superintendent, Acton Boxbourough Regional High School, 96 Hayward Rd., Acton, MA 01720
Financial data (yr. ended 05/31/01): Grants paid, $8,330; assets, $335,531 (M); expenditures, $13,708; qualifying distributions, $11,996.
Limitations: Giving limited to residents of Acton, MA.
Application information: Recipients selected by Acton school committee. Application form not required.
Trustee: Fleet National Bank.
EIN: 046342377

49217
Clyde Park Charitable Foundation
(Formerly Clyde Park Trust)
c/o Fleet Private Clients Group
P.O. Box 6767
Providence, RI 02940-6767
Application address: Deborah Dillon Pearce, Trust Admin., c/o Fleet National Bank, 100 Federal St., Boston, MA 02109, tel.: (617) 348-2329
Financial data (yr. ended 05/31/01): Grants paid, $8,328; assets, $222,140 (M); expenditures, $11,758; qualifying distributions, $10,477.
Limitations: Giving limited to Brookline, MA.
Application information: Application form not required.
Trustee: Fleet National Bank.
EIN: 046051719

49218
Lois Lenski Covey Trust
c/o Fleet Private Clients Group
P.O. Box 6767
Providence, RI 02940-6767

Financial data (yr. ended 12/31/01): Grants paid, $8,298; assets, $224,790 (M); expenditures, $12,988; qualifying distributions, $8,298.
Limitations: Applications not accepted. Giving limited to New York, NY, and Philadelphia, PA.
Application information: Contributes only to pre-selected organizations.
Trustee: Fleet National Bank.
EIN: 066026402

49219
Elizabeth S. Carr Trust Fund for Scholarships
(Formerly Roy W. Carr & Elizabeth S. Carr Trust Fund for Scholarships)
c/o Fleet Private Clients Group
P.O. Box 6767
Providence, RI 02940-6767
Application address: c/o Rhode Island College, Dev. Office, 600 Mt. Pleasant Ave., Providence, RI 02908

Financial data (yr. ended 12/31/01): Grants paid, $8,181; assets, $303,899 (M); expenditures, $12,436; qualifying distributions, $10,555.
Limitations: Giving limited to RI.
Trustee: Fleet National Bank.
EIN: 056063899

49220
John B. McLean Scholarship Fund
c/o Fleet Private Clients Group
P.O. Box 6767
Providence, RI 02940-6767
Application address: c/o Guidance Dept., Simsbury High School, 34 Farms Village Rd., Simsbury, CT 06070, tel.: (203) 658-9451

Financial data (yr. ended 12/31/01): Grants paid, $8,180; assets, $211,014 (M); gifts received, $5,491; expenditures, $11,913; qualifying distributions, $10,359.
Limitations: Giving limited to residents of the Simsbury, CT, area.
Application information: Application form required.
Trustee: Fleet National Bank.
EIN: 066032660

49221
The Robert J. Avila Foundation
654 Metacom Ave., Ste. 3
Warren, RI 02885-2316 (401) 245-0250
Contact: Robert J. Avila, Tr.

Established in 1993 in RI.
Donor(s): Robert J. Avila.
Financial data (yr. ended 06/30/02): Grants paid, $8,100; assets, $147,049 (M); expenditures, $9,529; qualifying distributions, $8,100.
Limitations: Giving limited to Bristol County, RI.
Application information: Application form not required.
Trustee: Robert J. Avila.
EIN: 050470783

49222
Lt. Stafford Leighton Brown Memorial Fund
c/o Fleet Private Clients Group
P.O. Box 6767
Providence, RI 02940-6767
Application address: c/o Fleet National Bank, 100 Federal St., Boston, MA 02110, tel.: (617) 434-4644
Contact: Augusta Haydock

Financial data (yr. ended 12/31/01): Grants paid, $8,000; assets, $200,082 (M); expenditures, $11,971; qualifying distributions, $9,639.
Limitations: Giving limited to Newton, MA.
Trustee: Fleet National Bank.
EIN: 237392553

49223
Fundacao Beneficente Faialense, Inc.
P.O. Box 14291
East Providence, RI 02914
Contact: Conselho Supremo

Donor(s): Antonio Andrade.
Financial data (yr. ended 03/31/02): Grants paid, $8,000; assets, $216,460 (M); gifts received, $6,436; expenditures, $8,934; qualifying distributions, $7,953.
Limitations: Giving primarily to residents of Portugal; some giving also to residents of RI and MA.
Officers: Joseph J. Martins, Pres.; Jaime Silva, V.P.; Fatima Correia, Secy.; Manuel Silveira, Treas.
EIN: 042722163
Codes: GTI

49224
Stanley & Sophia Hujsak Scholarship Trust
c/o Fleet Private Clients Group
P.O. Box 6767
Providence, RI 02940-6767

Established in 1988 in NH.
Financial data (yr. ended 05/31/02): Grants paid, $8,000; assets, $230,604 (M); expenditures, $12,700; qualifying distributions, $11,469.
Limitations: Giving limited to Merrimack, NH.
Application information: Recipients are selected by Merrimack School Board.
Trustee: Fleet National Bank.
EIN: 026075219

49225
Lincoln Family Foundation
c/o Fleet Private Clients Group
P.O. Box 6767
Providence, RI 02940-6767
Application address: c/o Fleet National Bank, 75 State St., Boston, MA 02109
Contact: Dana Whiteside, Trust Off., Fleet National Bank

Established in 1997 in MA.
Financial data (yr. ended 12/31/01): Grants paid, $8,000; assets, $300,480 (M); expenditures, $16,235; qualifying distributions, $8,000.
Limitations: Giving primarily in MA.
Trustee: Fleet National Bank.
EIN: 911815643

49226
Oscar R. O'Gorman Scholarship Trust
c/o Fleet Private Clients Group
P.O. Box 6767
Providence, RI 02940-6767
Application address: c/o Augusta Haydock, Fleet National Bank, 100 Federal St., Boston, MA 02110, tel.: (617) 434-4644

Established in 1987 in MA.
Financial data (yr. ended 12/31/01): Grants paid, $8,000; assets, $180,576 (M); expenditures, $10,019; qualifying distributions, $9,307.
Limitations: Giving limited to residents of the Arlington, MA, area.
Application information: Application form not required.
Trustee: Fleet National Bank.
EIN: 046551845

49227
The Pamela A. Riley Somers Foundation
c/o Fleet Private Clients Group
P.O. Box 6767
Providence, RI 02940-6767
Application address: P.O. Box 1861, Boston, MA 02105
Contact: Augusta Haydock, Trust Off., Fleet National Bank

Established in 1997 in MA.
Donor(s): Pamela Riley Somers.
Financial data (yr. ended 12/31/01): Grants paid, $8,000; assets, $218,676 (M); expenditures, $11,512; qualifying distributions, $10,601.
Limitations: Giving primarily in MA, ME, and NH.
Application information: Application form not required.
Trustee: Pamela R. Somers, Fleet National Bank.
EIN: 046855279

49228
Slawsby Charitable Fund
c/o Fleet Private Clients Group
P.O. Box 6767
Providence, RI 02940-6767

Established in 1998 in NH.
Financial data (yr. ended 01/31/02): Grants paid, $7,945; assets, $398,002 (M); expenditures, $15,692; qualifying distributions, $7,945.
Limitations: Applications not accepted. Giving primarily in NH.
Application information: Contributes only to pre-selected organizations.
Trustee: Fleet National Bank.
EIN: 026059149

49229
Stephanie Kamenski Trust
c/o Fleet Private Clients Group
P.O. Box 6767
Providence, RI 02940-6767
Application address: c/o Thomas Gavin, Principal, Berlin High School, 139 Patterson St., Berlin, CT 06037, tel.: (860) 828-6577

Established in 1985 in CT.
Financial data (yr. ended 07/31/00): Grants paid, $7,835; assets, $404,648 (M); expenditures, $15,677; qualifying distributions, $13,053.
Limitations: Giving limited to Berlin and New Britain, CT.
Application information: Applicant must include transcript and parent's 1040 form. Application form required.
Trustee: Fleet National Bank.
EIN: 066288857
Codes: GTI

49230
Josephine Dolliver Fund
c/o Fleet Private Clients Group
P.O. Box 6767
Providence, RI 02940-6767

Financial data (yr. ended 12/31/01): Grants paid, $7,800; assets, $152,396 (M); expenditures, $9,655; qualifying distributions, $8,636.
Limitations: Applications not accepted. Giving limited to residents of Gloucester, MA.

Application information: Recipients are recommended to the Fund.
Trustee: Fleet National Bank.
EIN: 237012035

49231
Adella H. & Alfred T. Giller Charitable Trust
c/o Fleet Private Clients Group
P.O. Box 6767
Providence, RI 02940-6767

Established in 1999 in MA.
Donor(s): Alfred Giller.
Financial data (yr. ended 08/31/02): Grants paid, $7,771; assets, $131,043 (M); expenditures, $8,619; qualifying distributions, $7,771.
Trustee: Fleet National Bank.
EIN: 056121264

49232
Ramsay Foundation
c/o Seekonk Lace Co.
P.O. Box 2366
Pawtucket, RI 02861 (401) 723-1135
Contact: Edward W. Barlow, Tr.

Financial data (yr. ended 12/31/01): Grants paid, $7,765; assets, $7,440 (M); expenditures, $8,589; qualifying distributions, $7,765.
Limitations: Giving primarily in RI.
Application information: Application form not required.
Trustee: Edward W. Barlow.
EIN: 056010509

49233
Margaret W. Leighton Trust
c/o Fleet Private Clients Group
P.O. Box 6767
Providence, RI 02940-6767
Application address: Fleet National Bank, 100 Federal St., Boston, MA 02110
Contact: Deborah Dillon Pearce, Trust Admin., Fleet National Bank

Financial data (yr. ended 12/31/01): Grants paid, $7,680; assets, $243,655 (M); expenditures, $11,413; qualifying distributions, $10,138.
Limitations: Giving limited to residents of Newburyport, MA.
Trustee: Fleet National Bank.
EIN: 046025524

49234
Elliott M. Grover Trust
c/o Fleet Private Clients Group
P.O. Box 6767
Providence, RI 02940-6767
Application address: c/o Fleet National Bank, P.O. Box 4276, Boston, MA 02211

Financial data (yr. ended 09/30/01): Grants paid, $7,582; assets, $260,547 (M); expenditures, $11,429; qualifying distributions, $10,143.
Limitations: Giving limited to Wakefield, MA.
Application information: Application form required.
Trustee: Fleet National Bank.
EIN: 046047110

49235
Sam & Rose Dahdah Memorial Fund
c/o Fleet Private Clients Group
P.O. Box 6767
Providence, RI 02940-6767

Financial data (yr. ended 07/31/02): Grants paid, $7,533; assets, $215,515 (M); expenditures, $12,707; qualifying distributions, $7,533.
Limitations: Applications not accepted. Giving primarily in NY.

Application information: Contributes only to pre-selected organizations.
Trustee: Fleet National Bank.
EIN: 050507030

49236
John A. & Irene Papines Scholarship Trust-Ermoupolis
c/o Fleet Private Clients Group
P.O. Box 6767
Providence, RI 02940-6767
Application address: c/o Fleet Asset Management, Attn: John & Irene Papines Scholarship, NJ EH 47402C, 1125 Rte. 22 W., Bridgewater, NJ 08807

Financial data (yr. ended 12/31/01): Grants paid, $7,500; assets, $248,837 (M); expenditures, $9,628; qualifying distributions, $8,650.
Limitations: Giving limited to residents of Greece.
Application information: Application form required.
Trustee: Fleet National Bank.
EIN: 226321386
Codes: GTI

49237
Leonard Rumpler Foundation
P.O. Box 969
Pawtucket, RI 02862-0969 (401) 722-2989
Contact: Leonard M. Rumpler, Tr.

Financial data (yr. ended 12/31/01): Grants paid, $7,300; assets, $25,148 (M); gifts received, $4,700; expenditures, $7,892; qualifying distributions, $7,300.
Application information: Application form not required.
Trustee: Leonard M. Rumpler.
EIN: 050389549

49238
Bruce H. Mahan Scholarship Fund
c/o Fleet Private Clients Group
P.O. Box 6767
Providence, RI 02940-6767
Application address: c/o William G. Keeley, New Britain National Bank, Trust Div., P.O. Drawer 2230, 51 W. Main St., New Britain, CT 06050

Financial data (yr. ended 09/30/01): Grants paid, $7,200; assets, $175,754 (M); expenditures, $10,769; qualifying distributions, $9,150.
Limitations: Giving limited to residents of Berlin and New Britain, CT.
Application information: Application form required.
Trustee: Fleet National Bank.
EIN: 066256073

49239
Mary P. Sears Trust
c/o Fleet Private Clients Group
P.O. Box 6767
Providence, RI 02940-6767

Financial data (yr. ended 09/30/01): Grants paid, $7,120; assets, $181,885 (M); expenditures, $11,351; qualifying distributions, $9,072.
Limitations: Applications not accepted.
Trustee: Fleet National Bank.
EIN: 046009466

49240
Herbert E. Wadsworth Fund
c/o Fleet Private Clients Group
P.O. Box 6767
Providence, RI 02940-6767

Financial data (yr. ended 11/30/01): Grants paid, $7,013; assets, $294,509 (M); expenditures, $11,930; qualifying distributions, $9,935.
Limitations: Applications not accepted. Giving limited to ME.
Application information: Unsolicited requests for funds not accepted.
Trustee: Fleet National Bank.
EIN: 016017480

49241
Arthur Flynn Educational Trust
c/o Fleet Private Clients Group
P.O. Box 6767
Providence, RI 02940-6767
Contact: Kathleen Callahan, Trust Admin., Fleet National Bank

Established in 1997 in MA.
Financial data (yr. ended 12/31/01): Grants paid, $7,000; assets, $155,767 (M); expenditures, $10,700; qualifying distributions, $9,471.
Limitations: Giving limited to residents of Salem, MA.
Application information: Federal financial aid form is used as application.
Trustee: Fleet National Bank.
EIN: 226373612

49242
C. J. Parker Trust f/b/o Public Music Fund
c/o Fleet Private Clients Group
P.O. Box 6767
Providence, RI 02940-6767
Application address: 777 Main St., Hartford, CT 06115, tel.: (860) 986-7696
Contact: Marjorie Alexandre, Trust Off., Fleet National Bank

Donor(s): C.J. Parker.‡
Financial data (yr. ended 03/31/00): Grants paid, $7,000; assets, $255,209 (M); expenditures, $11,420; qualifying distributions, $9,778.
Limitations: Giving limited to CT.
Trustee: Fleet National Bank.
EIN: 066036450

49243
Arthur D. & Marvis S. Rolland Scholarship Fund
(Formerly A. & M. Rolland Scholarship Fund)
c/o Fleet Private Clients Group
P.O. Box 6767
Providence, RI 02940-6767
Application address: c/o Town Clerk, Worthington, MA 01908, tel.: (413) 238-5877

Established in 1990 in MA.
Financial data (yr. ended 12/31/01): Grants paid, $7,000; assets, $183,232 (M); expenditures, $11,859; qualifying distributions, $10,371.
Limitations: Giving limited to residents of Worthington, MA.
Application information: Application form required.
Trustee: Fleet National Bank.
EIN: 046657747

49244
Byron S. Schuyler Child Educational Fund Trust
c/o Fleet Private Clients Group
P.O. Box 6767
Providence, RI 02940-6767
Application Address: c/o James J. Calnon, V.P., Fleet Investment Svcs., 69 State St., Albany, N.Y. 12207

Financial data (yr. ended 01/31/02): Grants paid, $7,000; assets, $175,865 (M); expenditures, $9,067; qualifying distributions, $8,122.
Limitations: Giving limited to residents of Fulton County, NY.
Application information: Application form required.
Trustee: Fleet National Bank.
EIN: 146083934
Codes: GTI

49245
Ethan Taylor Benevolent Fund
(Formerly Ethan Taylor Trust)
c/o Fleet Private Clients Group
P.O. Box 6767
Providence, RI 02940-6767
Application address: c/o Taylor Benevolent Fund Committee, South Congregational Church, 45 Maple St., Springfield, MA 01105, tel.: (413) 732-0117

Donor(s): Ethan Taylor.‡
Financial data (yr. ended 12/31/01): Grants paid, $7,000; assets, $236,554 (M); expenditures, $10,369; qualifying distributions, $9,275.
Limitations: Giving limited to Hampden County, MA.
Trustee: Fleet National Bank.
EIN: 046019085

49246
Ethel Arnold Wood Scholarship Fund
c/o Fleet Private Clients Group
P.O. Box 6767
Providence, RI 02940-6767
Application addresses: c/o John C. Newburn, Principal, Fairhaven High School, 12 Huttleston Ave., Fairhaven, MA 02719, tel.: (617) 997-2971; c/o Joseph Didato, Guidance Counselor, Martha's Vineyard High School, Oak Bluffs, MA 02557, tel.: (617) 693-1033

Financial data (yr. ended 09/30/01): Grants paid, $6,700; assets, $171,159 (M); expenditures, $11,259; qualifying distributions, $9,718.
Limitations: Giving limited to Fairhaven and Martha's Vineyard, MA.
Application information: Application form required.
Trustee: Fleet National Bank.
EIN: 046332654
Codes: GTI

49247
George Landis Arboretum Trust
c/o Fleet Private Clients Group
P.O. Box 6767
Providence, RI 02940-6767

Established in 1987 in NY.
Financial data (yr. ended 12/31/01): Grants paid, $6,511; assets, $238,702 (M); expenditures, $10,403; qualifying distributions, $6,511.
Limitations: Applications not accepted. Giving primarily in NY.
Application information: Contributes only to pre-selected organizations.
Trustee: Fleet National Bank.
EIN: 146132759

49248
Providence Charitable Fuel Society
P.O. Box 535
Little Compton, RI 02837-0535
(401) 635-8421
Contact: Charles G. Edwards, Dir.

Financial data (yr. ended 12/31/00): Grants paid, $6,500; assets, $167,089 (M); expenditures, $7,265; qualifying distributions, $6,500.
Limitations: Giving limited to the Cranston, Johnston, North Providence, and Providence, RI, areas.
Application information: Application form not required.
Officers: Richard C. Gower, Pres.; F. Richard Dietz, Jr., V.P.; John C. Drew, V.P.; Jonathan R. Knowles, Secy.; Norman D. Baker, Jr., Treas.
Directors: Sidney Clifford, Jr., Charles G. Edwards, Peter Reid, Stephen B. Van Sciver, Robert C. Wood.
EIN: 056012369

49249
The Zenie Foundation
104 Blueberry Ln.
Jamestown, RI 02835
Contact: Francis H. & Dorothy P. Zenie, Trustees

Donor(s): Francis H. Zenie, Dorothy P. Zenie.
Financial data (yr. ended 12/31/01): Grants paid, $6,448; assets, $500,020 (M); expenditures, $7,310; qualifying distributions, $7,310.
Limitations: Giving primarily in MA.
Trustees: Dorothy P. Zenie, Francis H. Zenie.
EIN: 222500224

49250
Mary B. Mannweiler Trust for Emil Mannweiler Scholarship Fund
c/o Fleet Private Clients Group
P.O. Box 6767
Providence, RI 02940-6767
Application address: c/o Principal, Naugatuck High School, Naugatuck, CT 06770, tel.: (203) 720-5400

Financial data (yr. ended 12/31/01): Grants paid, $6,400; assets, $123,615 (M); expenditures, $9,189; qualifying distributions, $8,007.
Limitations: Giving limited to CT.
Trustee: Fleet National Bank.
EIN: 066024961
Codes: GTI

49251
Clement L. Yaeger Trust
(also known as Clement L. Yaeger Scholarship Fund)
c/o Fleet Private Clients Group
P.O. Box 6767
Providence, RI 02940-6767
Application addresses: c/o Theresa Coish, Scholarship Chair., New Bedford Public Library, Library Science, 613 Pleasant St., New Bedford, MA 02740, tel.: (508) 991-6279, c/o Donald Ramsbottom, Dir., UMASS Dartmouth Foundation, Art Dept., North Dartmouth, MA 02747-2300, tel.: (508) 999-8605, c/o Janet Radcliffe, Chair., Music Dept., 45 Bonney St., New Bedford, MA 02740, tel.: (508) 993-6246

Financial data (yr. ended 09/30/01): Grants paid, $6,350; assets, $193,383 (M); expenditures, $9,681; qualifying distributions, $8,876.
Limitations: Giving limited to residents of New Bedford, MA, and its surrounding area.
Application information: Application form required.
Trustee: Fleet National Bank.
EIN: 046049740

49252
Dansville Hospital Trust
c/o Fleet Private Clients Group
P.O. Box 6767
Providence, RI 02940-6767

Financial data (yr. ended 12/31/01): Grants paid, $6,336; assets, $137,277 (M); expenditures, $8,588; qualifying distributions, $7,514.
Limitations: Applications not accepted. Giving limited to Dansville, NY.
Application information: Contributes only to pre-selected organizations.
Trustee: Fleet National Bank.
EIN: 166022898

49253
John C. Burney and Mary A. Burney Charitable Foundation Trust
157 Indian Ave.
Portsmouth, RI 02871-5151

Financial data (yr. ended 12/31/99): Grants paid, $6,225; assets, $103,213 (M); expenditures, $6,225; qualifying distributions, $6,225; giving activities include $2,900 for programs.
Trustees: John C. Burney, Mary A. Burney.
EIN: 222864947

49254
Russell T. & Olive V. Bartlett Trust
c/o Citizens Bank New Hampshire
870 Westminster St., 2nd Fl.
Providence, RI 02903
Application address: c/o Guidance Counselor, Woodsville High School, Woodsville, NH 03785, tel.: (603) 747-2451

Financial data (yr. ended 09/30/01): Grants paid, $6,204; assets, $924,710 (M); expenditures, $25,034; qualifying distributions, $13,537.
Limitations: Giving limited to residents of Bath and Haverhill, NH.
Application information: Application must be made in person with guidance counselor at Woodsville High School.
Trustee: Citizens Bank New Hampshire.
EIN: 026003957
Codes: GTI

49255
Clarence H. Martin Scholarship Fund
(Formerly Martin Charitable Scholarship)
c/o Fleet Private Clients Group
P.O. Box 6767
Providence, RI 02940-6767
Application address: c/o Selection Comm., Martin Charitable Scholarship, Weathersfield School District, Weathersfield, VT 05156
Contact: Michael Wrenn

Financial data (yr. ended 12/31/00): Grants paid, $6,094; assets, $159,698 (M); expenditures, $7,326; qualifying distributions, $6,631.
Limitations: Giving limited to residents of Weathersfield, VT.
Application information: Application form required.
Trustee: Fleet National Bank.
EIN: 026026823

49256
Abrams-Bell Foundation
(Formerly Saul Abrams Foundation)
376 Slater Ave.
Providence, RI 02906 (401) 272-2856
Contact: Bernard Bell, Tr.

Financial data (yr. ended 12/31/01): Grants paid, $6,088; assets, $181,116 (M); expenditures, $7,290; qualifying distributions, $6,088.

Trustee: Bernard Bell.
EIN: 056003415

49257
Robert J. Benham, Jr. Scholarship Fund
c/o Fleet Private Clients Group
P.O. Box 6767
Providence, RI 02940-6767
Application address: c/o Guidance Dept., Shepaug Valley Regional High School, 12 South St., Washington, CT 06793, tel.: (203) 868-7326
Financial data (yr. ended 12/31/00): Grants paid, $6,000; assets, $141,637 (M); expenditures, $8,577; qualifying distributions, $7,346.
Limitations: Giving limited to residents of Washington, CT.
Application information: Application form required.
Trustee: Fleet National Bank.
EIN: 066025588

49258
Helen C. S. Botsford Trust
c/o Fleet Private Clients Group
P.O. Box 6767
Providence, RI 02940-6767
Application address: c/o Mount Greylock Regional School District, Guidance Office, Williamstown, MA 01267
Financial data (yr. ended 03/31/01): Grants paid, $6,000; assets, $211,460 (M); expenditures, $9,427; qualifying distributions, $8,259.
Limitations: Giving limited to residents of Williamstown, MA.
Application information: Application form required.
Trustee: Fleet National Bank.
EIN: 046130605

49259
Gould Scholarship Fund
(Formerly Norman J. and Anna B. Gould Scholarship Fund)
c/o Fleet Private Clients Group
P.O. Box 6767
Providence, RI 02940-6767
Application address: c/o M.J. Catoe, Goulds Pumps, Inc., 240 Fall St., Seneca Falls, NY 13148

Present name adopted in 1988.
Donor(s): Goulds Pumps, Inc.
Financial data (yr. ended 12/31/01): Grants paid, $6,000; assets, $191,060 (M); expenditures, $8,638; qualifying distributions, $7,482.
Limitations: Giving primarily in areas of company operations.
Application information: Application form not required.
Trustee: Fleet National Bank.
EIN: 166051306
Codes: CS, CD

49260
Sasso Scholarship Fund Trust
(Formerly Sasso Consolidation Fund Trust)
c/o Fleet Private Clients Group
P.O. Box 6767
Providence, RI 02940-6767
Application address: c/o Pomfret Board of Education, 20 Pomfret St., Pomfret Ctr., CT 06259
Contact: Thomas N. James

Established in 1987 in CT.
Financial data (yr. ended 12/31/01): Grants paid, $6,000; assets, $167,413 (M); expenditures, $9,365; qualifying distributions, $8,076.

Limitations: Giving limited to residents of the Meriden, CT, area.
Trustee: Fleet National Bank.
EIN: 066131106
Codes: GTI

49261
Joseph E. Duffy Private Foundation
572 Main St.
Warren, RI 02885-4367
Contact: Thomas E. Wright, Tr.

Established around 1992.
Financial data (yr. ended 12/31/01): Grants paid, $5,857; assets, $120,778 (M); expenditures, $10,093; qualifying distributions, $5,857.
Limitations: Giving limited to Cranston, RI.
Application information: Application form not required.
Trustee: Thomas E. Wright.
EIN: 056084904

49262
L. W. Tiffany Trust
c/o Fleet Private Clients Group
P.O. Box 6767
Providence, RI 02940-6767

Financial data (yr. ended 06/30/01): Grants paid, $5,821; assets, $114,847 (M); expenditures, $7,356; qualifying distributions, $6,559.
Limitations: Applications not accepted. Giving limited to CT.
Trustee: Fleet National Bank.
EIN: 066029923

49263
The Medwed Foundation
c/o Fleet Private Clients Group
P.O. Box 6767
Providence, RI 02940-6767
Application address: 1 Merchants Plz., Bangor, ME 04401

Financial data (yr. ended 12/31/01): Grants paid, $5,796; assets, $140,206 (M); expenditures, $7,702; qualifying distributions, $7,027.
Limitations: Giving primarily in ME.
Trustee: Fleet National Bank.
EIN: 016014226

49264
John T. Galligan Scholarship Trust
c/o Fleet Private Clients Group
P.O. Box 6767
Providence, RI 02940-6767
Application address: 50 Kennedy Plz., Providence, RI 02903, tel.: (401) 278-5077
Contact: Dorothy Derick

Established in 2000 in MA.
Financial data (yr. ended 12/31/01): Grants paid, $5,650; assets, $207,883 (M); expenditures, $8,212; qualifying distributions, $7,464.
Limitations: Giving primarily in MA.
Application information: Application form required.
Trustee: Fleet National Bank.
EIN: 046473132

49265
Dr. Aziz & Ulker Alasyali Foundation
c/o Neset Hikmet
P.O. Box 1702
Kingston, RI 02881

Established in 1998 in OH.
Donor(s): Aziz Alasyali.
Financial data (yr. ended 05/31/99): Grants paid, $5,500; assets, $712,823 (M); gifts received, $706,376; expenditures, $33,021; qualifying distributions, $7,866.

Limitations: Applications not accepted. Giving primarily in RI.
Application information: Contributes only to pre-selected organizations.
Trustees: Aziz Alasyali, Neset Hikmet, Andrew Laviano.
EIN: 311598582

49266
B. K. Brennan Scholarship Fund, Inc.
374 Greenwood Ave.
Warwick, RI 02886 (401) 737-1457
Contact: Ralph Knox, Secy.

Financial data (yr. ended 12/31/01): Grants paid, $5,500; assets, $112,294 (M); gifts received, $6,544; expenditures, $6,285; qualifying distributions, $6,285.
Limitations: Giving limited to residents of RI.
Application information: Application form required.
Officers: Robert Hamilton, Pres.; Ralph Knox, Secy.; Ruth Knox, Treas.
EIN: 050519622

49267
Henrietta Dexter Trust
c/o Fleet Private Clients Group
P.O. Box 6767
Providence, RI 02940-6767
Application address: 100 Federal St., Boston, MA 02110, tel.: (617) 434-3768
Contact: Carol Gray, Trust Off., Fleet National Bank

Financial data (yr. ended 12/31/01): Grants paid, $5,500; assets, $157,796 (M); expenditures, $8,020; qualifying distributions, $6,885.
Limitations: Giving limited to residents of Springfield, MA.
Application information: Application form required.
Trustee: Fleet National Bank.
EIN: 046018706

49268
J. M. Linton Trust f/b/o Berkeley Divinity School
c/o Fleet Private Clients Group
P.O. Box 6767
Providence, RI 02940-6767
Application address: c/o Ray Wood, Berkeley Divinity School, 409 Prospect St., New Haven, CT 06510

Financial data (yr. ended 12/31/01): Grants paid, $5,478; assets, $121,599 (M); expenditures, $7,367; qualifying distributions, $6,563.
Limitations: Giving limited to New Haven, CT.
Application information: Applicant must submit budget of expenses and earnings and prove financial need.
Trustee: Fleet National Bank.
EIN: 066071274

49269
Henry C. Badgley Trust
c/o Fleet Private Clients Group
P.O. Box 6767
Providence, RI 02940-6767
Application address: c/o Superintendent, Board of Education, Schoharie Central School, Schoharie, NY 12157

Financial data (yr. ended 11/30/01): Grants paid, $5,470; assets, $64,342 (M); expenditures, $6,428; qualifying distributions, $5,918.
Limitations: Giving limited to Schoharie, NY.
Application information: Application form required.
Trustee: Fleet National Bank.
EIN: 146013917

49270
Hazel Tiedemann Fund
c/o Fleet Private Clients Group
P.O. Box 6767
Providence, RI 02940-6767
Application address: c/o Hoosac Valley High School, Scholarship Program, Adams, MA 01120

Established in 1992 in MA.
Financial data (yr. ended 12/31/01): Grants paid, $5,356; assets, $181,328 (M); expenditures, $8,671; qualifying distributions, $7,325.
Limitations: Giving limited to residents of Adams, MA.
Application information: Application form required.
Trustee: Fleet National Bank.
EIN: 046553899

49271
Robert Frost Teaching Chairs Trust
c/o Fleet Private Clients Group
P.O. Box 6767
Providence, RI 02940-6767
Contact: Thea Katsounakis, Trust Admin., Fleet National Bank

Financial data (yr. ended 06/30/00): Grants paid, $5,293; assets, $103,562 (M); expenditures, $13,458; qualifying distributions, $12,336.
Limitations: Giving limited to Amherst, MA.
Application information: Unsolicited requests for funds not accepted.
Trustee: Fleet National Bank.
EIN: 046027359

49272
Joseph E., Herman & Adele Snyder Memorial Fund
(also known as Joseph E. Snyder Memorial Fund)
c/o Fleet Private Clients Group
P.O. Box 6767
Providence, RI 02940-6767

Financial data (yr. ended 12/31/01): Grants paid, $5,225; assets, $124,706 (M); expenditures, $6,871; qualifying distributions, $6,112.
Trustee: Fleet National Bank.
EIN: 237423794

49273
Doris Magee Scholarship Trust
c/o Fleet Private Clients Group
P.O. Box 6767
Providence, RI 02940-6767
Application address: c/o Guidance Dept., Camden Central High School, 55 Oswego St., Camden, NY 13316

Financial data (yr. ended 01/31/02): Grants paid, $5,200; assets, $186,507 (M); expenditures, $7,863; qualifying distributions, $6,522.
Limitations: Giving limited to the residents of Camden, NY.
Application information: Application form required.
Trustee: Fleet National Bank.
EIN: 166285000

49274
John T. Galligan Tobey Hospital Trust
c/o Fleet Private Clients Group
P.O. Box 6767
Providence, RI 02940-6767

Established in 2000 in MA.
Financial data (yr. ended 12/31/01): Grants paid, $5,138; assets, $164,256 (M); expenditures, $7,828; qualifying distributions, $5,138.
Limitations: Applications not accepted. Giving primarily in MA.

Application information: Contributes only to pre-selected organizations.
Trustee: Fleet National Bank.
EIN: 046473127

49275
Robert Life Trust
c/o Fleet Private Clients Group
P.O. Box 6767
Providence, RI 02940-6767
Application address: 1 Monarch Pl., Springfield, MA 01101
Contact: Anne Chernick, Trust Admin., Fleet National Bank

Financial data (yr. ended 12/31/01): Grants paid, $5,107; assets, $141,138 (M); expenditures, $10,953; qualifying distributions, $5,973.
Limitations: Giving limited to residents of Haydenville, MA.
Trustee: Fleet National Bank.
EIN: 046019151

49276
Mary C. Jolly Charitable Trust
(Formerly Mary C. Jolly Trust)
23 Broad St.
Westerly, RI 02891

Established in 1994 in RI.
Financial data (yr. ended 12/31/01): Grants paid, $5,068; assets, $441,272 (M); gifts received, $184,500; expenditures, $22,643; qualifying distributions, $5,068.
Limitations: Applications not accepted.
Application information: Contributes only to pre-selected organizations.
Trustee: The Washington Trust Co.
EIN: 050481805

49277
The R. Y. Cho Foundation
c/o Marie Langlois, Phoenix Inv.
68 S. Main St.
Providence, RI 02903

Established in 1999 in RI.
Donor(s): Yohan Cho, Rumie Cho.
Financial data (yr. ended 06/30/01): Grants paid, $5,000; assets, $72,503 (M); gifts received, $2,000; expenditures, $11,847; qualifying distributions, $4,980; giving activities include $4,980 for programs.
Limitations: Applications not accepted. Giving primarily in Korea.
Application information: Contributes only to pre-selected organizations.
Trustees: Rumie Cho, Yohan Cho, Marie Langlois.
EIN: 050509649

49278
M. P. Howard Trust
c/o Fleet Private Clients Group
P.O. Box 6767
Providence, RI 02940-6767
Application address: c/o Mortimer P. Howard Schol. Comm., Drury High School, North Adams, MA 02144, tel.: (413) 662-3245

Donor(s): Mortimer P. Howard.‡
Financial data (yr. ended 12/31/01): Grants paid, $5,000; assets, $208,310 (M); expenditures, $8,570; qualifying distributions, $7,125.
Limitations: Giving limited to residents of Drury, MA.
Trustee: Fleet National Bank.
EIN: 046385719

49279
The Norton Family Foundation
c/o Fleet Private Clients Group
P.O. Box 6767
Providence, RI 02940-6767
Application address: c/o Mary Kochek, 1125 Rte. 22 W., Bridgewater, NJ 08807, tel.: (908) 552-8407

Established in 1998 in NJ.
Financial data (yr. ended 12/31/01): Grants paid, $5,000; assets, $53,121 (M); expenditures, $6,578; qualifying distributions, $6,196.
Trustee: Fleet National Bank.
EIN: 226770982

49280
Nicholas Picchione-Dome Foundation
10 New England Way
Warwick, RI 02886
Contact: Nicholas Picchione II, Tr.

Financial data (yr. ended 12/31/01): Grants paid, $5,000; assets, $159,138 (M); expenditures, $6,281; qualifying distributions, $5,000.
Limitations: Giving limited to Providence, RI.
Trustee: Nicholas Picchione II.
EIN: 056035368

49281
Slowinski Estate Fund Trust
c/o Fleet National Bank
P.O. Box 6767
Providence, RI 02940-6767
Application address: c/o Fleet Bank, 777 Main St., Hartford, CT 06115, tel.: (860) 986-7696
Contact: Marjorie A. Davis, Trust Off.

Established in 1988.
Financial data (yr. ended 12/31/01): Grants paid, $5,000; assets, $225,708 (M); expenditures, $9,303; qualifying distributions, $5,000.
Limitations: Giving primarily in New York, NY.
Trustee: Fleet National Bank.
EIN: 066314132

49282
Pauline Smith Memorial Fund
c/o Fleet Private Clients Group
P.O. Box 6767
Providence, RI 02940-6767
Application address: c/o Mt. Greylock Regional School District, Williamstown, MA 02650

Established in 1992 in MA.
Financial data (yr. ended 12/31/01): Grants paid, $5,000; assets, $172,650 (M); expenditures, $7,667; qualifying distributions, $6,578.
Limitations: Giving limited to residents of Williamstown, MA.
Application information: Application form required.
Trustee: Fleet National Bank.
EIN: 046584005

49283
Helen H. Townsend Scholarship Trust
c/o Fleet Private Clients Group
P.O. Box 6767
Providence, RI 02940-6767

Established in 1992 in NY.
Donor(s): Helen H. Townsend.‡
Financial data (yr. ended 08/31/01): Grants paid, $5,000; assets, $82,857 (M); expenditures, $6,613; qualifying distributions, $5,550.
Limitations: Applications not accepted. Giving limited to residents of the Rome, NY, area.
Trustee: Fleet National Bank.
EIN: 223279301

49284
Grace Lazarus Memorial Fund
c/o Fleet Private Clients Group
P.O. Box 6767
Providence, RI 02940-6767

Financial data (yr. ended 12/31/01): Grants paid, $4,903; assets, $87,032 (M); expenditures, $6,316; qualifying distributions, $5,621.
Limitations: Applications not accepted. Giving primarily in NY.
Application information: Contributes only to pre-selected organizations.
Trustee: Fleet National Bank.
EIN: 166218697

49285
Edward Little High School Alumni Association Trust
c/o Fleet Private Clients Group
P.O. Box 6767
Providence, RI 02940-6767
Application address: c/o Edward Little High School, Guidance Office, Auburn, ME 04401

Established in 1988 in ME.
Donor(s): Edward Little High School Alumni Assn.
Financial data (yr. ended 07/31/01): Grants paid, $4,800; assets, $106,896 (M); gifts received, $12,413; expenditures, $5,633; qualifying distributions, $6,308.
Limitations: Giving limited to residents of Auburn, ME.
Trustee: Fleet National Bank.
EIN: 016029596
Codes: GTI

49286
Mary Swart Scholarship Fund
c/o Fleet Private Clients Group
P.O. Box 6767
Providence, RI 02940-6767
Application address: c/o Cindy Leip, 1125 Rt. 22 W., Bridgewater, NJ 08807, tel.: (908) 253-4883

Established in 2000 in PA.
Financial data (yr. ended 12/31/01): Grants paid, $4,800; assets, $72,509 (M); gifts received, $17,037; expenditures, $6,754; qualifying distributions, $6,399.
Limitations: Giving primarily in PA.
Trustee: Fleet National Bank.
EIN: 527137246

49287
James & Phyllis Tracy Scholarship Foundation
c/o Fleet Private Clients Group
P.O. Box 6767
Providence, RI 02940-6767
Application address: 100 Pearl St., Hartford, CT 06103, tel.: (860) 727-6704
Contact: Peter Weston

Financial data (yr. ended 12/31/00): Grants paid, $4,800; assets, $150,194 (M); expenditures, $7,918; qualifying distributions, $6,347.
Limitations: Giving limited to residents of Waterbury, CT.
Application information: Application forms available from guidance counselors of various high schools in Waterbury, CT. Application form required.
Trustee: Fleet National Bank.
EIN: 066025726
Codes: GTI

49288
Max Richter Foundation
c/o Norman Orodenker
1 Park Rd.
Providence, RI 02903-1235

Donor(s): Jacob Neusner.
Financial data (yr. ended 12/31/01): Grants paid, $4,655; assets, $46,965 (M); expenditures, $5,613; qualifying distributions, $4,655.
Limitations: Applications not accepted. Giving on a national basis.
Application information: Contributes only to pre-selected organizations.
Officer: Jacob Neusner, Pres.
EIN: 237040554

49289
Wickersham Fund Trust
c/o Fleet Private Clients Group
P.O. Box 6767
Providence, RI 02940-6767
Application address: c/o Sheilah B. Rostow, Trust Off., Fleet National Bank, 777 Main St., Hartford, CT 06115

Financial data (yr. ended 12/31/01): Grants paid, $4,510; assets, $126,165 (M); expenditures, $7,650; qualifying distributions, $6,756.
Limitations: Giving primarily in the Hartford, CT, area.
Trustee: Fleet National Bank.
EIN: 066066735

49290
Joseph Finberg Educational Fund
c/o Fleet Private Clients Group
P.O. Box 6767
Providence, RI 02940-6767
Application address: 100 Federal St., Boston, MA 02110
Contact: Carol V. Gray, Trust Off.

Financial data (yr. ended 04/30/01): Grants paid, $4,500; assets, $132,319 (M); expenditures, $7,307; qualifying distributions, $6,418.
Limitations: Giving limited to residents of Attleboro, MA.
Trustee: Fleet National Bank.
EIN: 046007843

49291
Donald & Gladys Heath Charitable Memorial Fund
c/o Fleet Private Clients Group
P.O. Box 6767
Providence, RI 02940-6767

Financial data (yr. ended 02/28/02): Grants paid, $4,500; assets, $185,061 (M); expenditures, $6,941; qualifying distributions, $6,011.
Limitations: Giving on a national basis.
Application information: Application form required.
Trustee: Fleet National Bank.
EIN: 166353241

49292
Richard W. Langshaw Scholarship Fund
c/o Fleet Private Clients Group
P.O. Box 6767
Providence, RI 02940-6767
Application address: 50 Kennedy Plz., Providence, RI 02903
Contact: Maureen Charlonne, Trust Admin., Fleet Svcs. Corp.

Financial data (yr. ended 09/30/01): Grants paid, $4,500; assets, $38,142 (M); expenditures, $5,309; qualifying distributions, $4,839.
Limitations: Giving limited to residents of New Bedford, MA.
Application information: Application form required.
Trustee: Fleet National Bank.
EIN: 046049685

49293
Roberts/Purple Scholarship Trust
(Formerly Allan Roberts Scholarship Trust)
c/o Fleet Private Clients Group
P.O. Box 6767
Providence, RI 02940-6767

Financial data (yr. ended 12/31/01): Grants paid, $4,500; assets, $110,181 (M); expenditures, $7,418; qualifying distributions, $6,523.
Limitations: Applications not accepted. Giving limited to residents of East Haddam, CT.
Trustee: Fleet National Bank.
EIN: 066098170

49294
Paul F. Ronci Memorial Scholarship Trust
c/o Joseph Passaretti, C.P.A.
357 Putnam Pike
Smithfield, RI 02917 (401) 231-4022

Established in 1998 in RI.
Donor(s): Frank Ronci, Viola Ronci.
Financial data (yr. ended 12/31/01): Grants paid, $4,500; assets, $106,231 (M); gifts received, $20,000; expenditures, $16,844; qualifying distributions, $13,367.
Trustee: Joseph Passaretti.
EIN: 586368004

49295
Doris and Vivian Horton Scholarship Trust
c/o Fleet Private Clients Group
P.O. Box 6767
Providence, RI 02940-6767
Application address: c/o Atkinson Congregational Church, Scholarship Comm., Main St., Atkinson, NH 03811

Established in 1991 in NH.
Financial data (yr. ended 12/31/00): Grants paid, $4,475; assets, $98,520 (M); expenditures, $5,677; qualifying distributions, $4,940.
Limitations: Giving limited to Atkinson, NH.
Trustee: Fleet National Bank.
EIN: 020444870

49296
J. J. Hurley Fund B.
c/o Fleet Private Clients Group
P.O. Box 6767
Providence, RI 02940-6767
Application address: c/o Fleet National Bank, Old Colony United Way, 1 Federal St., Boston, MA 02110-2012

Financial data (yr. ended 12/31/01): Grants paid, $4,303; assets, $145,005 (M); expenditures, $7,036; qualifying distributions, $6,015.
Limitations: Giving primarily in Brockton, MA.
Trustee: Fleet National Bank.
EIN: 046036309

49297
J. M. Linton Trust f/b/o Marjorie Ann Linton Scholarship Fund
c/o Fleet Private Clients Group
P.O. Box 6767
Providence, RI 02940-6767
Application address: c/o Hartford College for Women, 1265 Asylum Ave., Hartford, CT 06105

Financial data (yr. ended 12/31/01): Grants paid, $4,133; assets, $81,739 (M); expenditures, $5,660; qualifying distributions, $5,207.

49297—RHODE ISLAND

Limitations: Giving limited to Hartford, CT.
Application information: Applicants must submit academic and financial information.
Trustee: Fleet National Bank.
EIN: 066066400

49298
Donald B. Shaw, Jr. Charitable Trust
c/o Fleet Private Clients Group
P.O. Box 6767
Providence, RI 02940-6767

Established in 1992 in NY.
Financial data (yr. ended 12/31/00): Grants paid, $4,068; assets, $81,354 (M); expenditures, $5,231; qualifying distributions, $4,672.
Limitations: Applications not accepted.
Application information: Contributes only to a pre-selected organization.
Trustee: Fleet National Bank.
EIN: 166379012

49299
William E. Brigham Trust
c/o Fleet Private Clients Group
P.O. Box 6767
Providence, RI 02940-6767
Appllication address: c/o Augusta Haydock, 100 Federal St., Boston, MA 02110, tel.: (617) 434-4644

Donor(s): William E. Brigham.‡
Financial data (yr. ended 12/31/01): Grants paid, $4,000; assets, $127,733 (M); expenditures, $6,677; qualifying distributions, $5,874.
Limitations: Giving limited to North Attleboro, MA.
Trustee: Fleet National Bank.
EIN: 046057256

49300
George A. Comstock Scholarship Fund
(Formerly George A. Comstock Trust)
c/o Fleet Private Clients Group
P.O. Box 6767
Providence, RI 02940-6767
Application address: 500 Post Rd. E., Ste. 280, Westport, CT 06880, tel.: (203) 226-9426
Contact: Robert L. Ross, Comm. Chair.

Financial data (yr. ended 12/31/01): Grants paid, $4,000; assets, $82,547 (M); expenditures, $5,740; qualifying distributions, $4,998.
Limitations: Giving limited to CT.
Application information: Application form required.
Trustee: Fleet National Bank.
EIN: 066038152

49301
East Providence Rotary Educational Trust
c/o John L. Garceau
P.O. Box 14303
East Providence, RI 02914

Established in 1990 in RI.
Financial data (yr. ended 06/30/99): Grants paid, $4,000; assets, $57,271 (M); gifts received, $5,000; expenditures, $4,229; qualifying distributions, $4,229.
Limitations: Giving limited to residents of Seekonk, MA, and Providence, RI.
Application information: Application form required.
Trustees: William Allen, John L. Garceau, George J. Geisser III, Robert Pearson, William H. Smith.
EIN: 050451409

49302
John & Mary Finn Memorial Trust
(Formerly William J. Finn Trust)
c/o Fleet Private Clients Group
P.O. Box 6767
Providence, RI 02940-6767
Application address: c/o Finn Scholarship Comm., Kent Center School, Kent, CT 06757, tel.: (203) 927-3537

Financial data (yr. ended 12/31/01): Grants paid, $4,000; assets, $81,866 (M); expenditures, $5,733; qualifying distributions, $4,989.
Limitations: Giving limited to residents of Kent, CT.
Application information: Application form required.
Trustee: Fleet National Bank.
EIN: 066145699

49303
Henry F. Hall Trust
c/o Fleet Private Clients Group
P.O. Box 6767
Providence, RI 02940-6767
Application address: c/o Wanda L. Kleinart, Trust Off., Fleet National Bank, 1 Constitution Plz., Hartford, CT 06115

Financial data (yr. ended 06/30/01): Grants paid, $4,000; assets, $86,534 (M); expenditures, $5,308; qualifying distributions, $4,384.
Limitations: Giving limited to CT.
Application information: Application form required.
Trustee: Fleet National Bank.
EIN: 066117487

49304
D. Maes Trust
c/o Fleet Private Clients Group
P.O. Box 6767
Providence, RI 02940-6767
Application address: c/o Methuen High School Guidance Dept., 1 Ranger Rd., Methuen, MA 01844

Established in 1991 in MA.
Financial data (yr. ended 12/31/01): Grants paid, $4,000; assets, $126,311 (M); expenditures, $8,113; qualifying distributions, $5,478.
Limitations: Giving limited to residents of Methuen, MA.
Application information: Application form required.
Trustee: Fleet National Bank.
EIN: 046660485

49305
Lorena Marhaver Trust
c/o Fleet Private Clients Group
P.O. Box 6767
Providence, RI 02940-6767
Application address: c/o Fleet Trust Co., 268 Genesee St., Utica, NY 13502, tel.: (315) 798-2788

Financial data (yr. ended 12/31/00): Grants paid, $4,000; assets, $184,954 (M); expenditures, $8,433; qualifying distributions, $5,286.
Limitations: Giving limited to Ilion, NY.
Trustee: Fleet National Bank.
EIN: 166199387

49306
Arthur Price Scholarship Trust
c/o Fleet Private Clients Group
P.O. Box 6767
Providence, RI 02940-6767
Application address: c/o Guidance Dept., Valley Regional High School, 256 Kelsey Hill Rd., Deep River, CT 06417-1508

Established in 1998 in CT.
Financial data (yr. ended 12/31/01): Grants paid, $4,000; assets, $1,796 (M); gifts received, $2,311; expenditures, $4,533; qualifying distributions, $4,531.
Limitations: Giving limited to residents of Chester, Deep River, and Essex, CT.
Application information: Application form required.
Trustee: Fleet National Bank.
EIN: 050503629

49307
Senter-Cole Scholarship Fund
c/o Fleet Private Client's Group
P.O. Box 6767
Providence, RI 02940-6767
Application address: c/o Senior High School Principal, Scholarship Committee, Whitesboro Central School, Whitesboro, NY 13492

Financial data (yr. ended 12/31/01): Grants paid, $4,000; assets, $160,145 (M); expenditures, $6,278; qualifying distributions, $5,319.
Limitations: Giving limited to residents of Whitesboro, NY.
Application information: Application form required.
Trustee: Fleet National Bank.
EIN: 166253349

49308
Rufus & Caroline E. Wiles Scholarship Fund
c/o Fleet Private Clients Group
P.O. Box 6767
Providence, RI 02940-6767
Application address: c/o Dorothy S. Robinson, Secy.-Treas., Scholarship Foundation of Fort Plain, 33 Clinton Ave., Fort Plain, NY 13339

Financial data (yr. ended 12/31/01): Grants paid, $3,875; assets, $107,834 (M); expenditures, $6,168; qualifying distributions, $4,728.
Limitations: Giving limited to the Fort Plain, NY, area.
Application information: Application form not required.
Trustee: Fleet National Bank.
EIN: 146014151

49309
William & Gladys Murdock Trust Fund
c/o Fleet Private Clients Group
P.O. Box 6767
Providence, RI 02940-6767
Application address: c/o Pomfret Board of Education, Pomfret Center, CT 06259
Contact: Thomas N. James, Superintendent

Financial data (yr. ended 12/31/00): Grants paid, $3,750; assets, $78,516 (M); expenditures, $5,495; qualifying distributions, $4,819.
Limitations: Giving limited to the Pomfret, CT, area.
Trustee: Fleet National Bank.
EIN: 066160070

49310
The Stephen C. Owen, Sr. Charitable Trust
c/o Armstrong, Gibbons & Gnys, LLP
155 S. Main St.
Providence, RI 02903-2963

Financial data (yr. ended 12/31/01): Grants paid, $3,750; assets, $49,073 (M); expenditures, $4,217; qualifying distributions, $3,750.
Limitations: Applications not accepted.
Application information: Contributes only to pre-selected organizations.
Trustees: Margaret O. Carpenter, Joseph G. Kinder.
EIN: 050393657

49311
Bristol Children's Home
26 Acacia Rd.
Bristol, RI 02809-1330 (401) 253-7079
Contact: Jessie S. Huey, Chair.

Financial data (yr. ended 05/01/99): Grants paid, $3,600; assets, $2,893 (M); gifts received, $2,507; expenditures, $3,673; qualifying distributions, $3,673.
Limitations: Giving limited to Bristol, RI.
Application information: Application form required.
Officers and Directors:* Jessie S. Huey,* Chair. and Treas.; Betty Gilbert,* Secy.; Susan Church, Olive Luther, Virginia Martin, Patricia Sanford, Sally Smith, Carol Wardwell.
EIN: 222670696

49312
The Ogontz Charitable Trust
128 Dorrance St., Ste. 520
Providence, RI 02903

Established in 2000 in RI.
Donor(s): Peter M. Loescher.
Financial data (yr. ended 05/31/02): Grants paid, $3,594; assets, $74,303 (M); expenditures, $3,665; qualifying distributions, $3,594.
Limitations: Applications not accepted.
Application information: Contributes only to pre-selected organizations.
Trustees: Cori W. Loescher, Peter M. Loescher.
EIN: 050512004

49313
Almon B. Cook Scholarship Fund
c/o Fleet Private Clients Group
P.O. Box 6767
Providence, RI 02940-6767
Application address: c/o Sarah Whitaker, Fleet National Bank, 75 State St., Boston, MA 02109

Financial data (yr. ended 10/31/01): Grants paid, $3,500; assets, $137,046 (M); expenditures, $5,632; qualifying distributions, $4,875.
Limitations: Giving limited to residents of Gloucester and Rockport, MA.
Application information: Contact Gloucester High School or Rockport High School for application. Application form required.
Trustees: Robert H. Natti, Fleet National Bank.
EIN: 046038998

49314
Chris W. Cruickshank Scholarship Foundation
c/o Mr. & Mrs. Steven Scales
30 Rockridge Rd.
Westerly, RI 02891 (401) 596-0183
Contact: George Cruickshank, V.P.

Established in 1994 in RI.
Donor(s): George Cruickshank.
Financial data (yr. ended 12/31/01): Grants paid, $3,500; assets, $78,952 (M); gifts received, $4,143; expenditures, $4,562; qualifying distributions, $3,500.
Limitations: Giving limited to residents of Westerly, RI.
Application information: Application form required.
Officers: Laurie A. Scales, Pres.; George Cruickshank, V.P.; Stephen Cruickshank, Secy.; Elizabeth Cruickshank, Treas.
EIN: 050441379

49315
Mary Martin Pettingal Foundation
c/o Ann P. Perlman
121 Hidden Mere Ln.
North Kingstown, RI 02852

Established in 2000 in RI.
Financial data (yr. ended 12/31/01): Grants paid, $3,422; assets, $49,531 (M); gifts received, $60; expenditures, $3,669; qualifying distributions, $3,422.
Limitations: Applications not accepted.
Application information: Contributes only to pre-selected organizations.
Trustee: Ann P. Perlman.
EIN: 050508845

49316
Moosehead Manufacturing Company Trust
c/o Fleet Private Clients Group
P.O. Box 6767
Providence, RI 02940-6767
Application address: c/o Fleet National Bank, P.O. Box 923, Exchange St., Bangor, ME 04401

Established in 1987 in ME.
Donor(s): Moosehead Manufacturing Co.
Financial data (yr. ended 05/31/01): Grants paid, $3,400; assets, $585 (M); gifts received, $1,700; expenditures, $3,500; qualifying distributions, $3,464.
Limitations: Giving limited to Monson, ME.
Trustee: Fleet National Bank.
EIN: 226456641
Codes: CS, CD

49317
Hattie L. Carr Trust
c/o Fleet Private Clients Group
P.O. Box 6767
Providence, RI 02940-6767
Application address: c/o Elizabeth McDonald, Trust Admin., Fleet National Bank, 75 State St., Boston, MA 02109, tel.: (617) 346-2466

Financial data (yr. ended 12/31/01): Grants paid, $3,200; assets, $97,923 (M); expenditures, $5,275; qualifying distributions, $4,460.
Limitations: Giving limited to Brookline, MA.
Trustee: Fleet National Bank.
EIN: 046051688

49318
Marjorie Moore Trust
(Formerly Marjorie Moore Educational Fund)
c/o Fleet Private Clients Group
P.O. Box 6767
Providence, RI 02940-6767

Financial data (yr. ended 07/31/02): Grants paid, $3,150; assets, $133,138 (M); gifts received, $25,000; expenditures, $5,433; qualifying distributions, $3,150.
Limitations: Giving limited to residents of Berlin, CT.
Application information: Application form required.
Trustee: Fleet National Bank.
EIN: 066024229

49319
George Moller Scholarship Fund
c/o Fleet Private Clients Group
P.O. Box 6767
Providence, RI 02940-6767
Application address: Principle c/o Hoboken High School, 9th & Clinton Sts., Hoboken, NJ 07030

Financial data (yr. ended 12/31/01): Grants paid, $3,000; assets, $138,120 (M); expenditures, $4,182; qualifying distributions, $3,582.
Limitations: Giving limited to residents of Hoboken, NJ.
Application information: Application form required.
Trustee: Fleet National Bank.
EIN: 226157430

49320
V. Gerard Ryan Fund
(Formerly V. Gerard Ryan Fund f/b/o Portland High School)
c/o Fleet Private Client's Group
P.O. Box 6767
Providence, RI 02940-6767

Financial data (yr. ended 06/30/01): Grants paid, $3,000; assets, $102,229 (M); expenditures, $4,742; qualifying distributions, $3,685.
Limitations: Giving limited to residents of Portland, CT.
Application information: Recipients are recommended by Portland High School faculty. Application form not required.
Trustees: Allen Cohen, William J. Connell, Susanne Emmons, Fleet National Bank.
EIN: 066214894
Codes: GTI

49321
Arthur Webster Trust
c/o Fleet Private Clients Group
P.O. Box 6767
Providence, RI 02940-6767
Application address: c/o Theodore Rokicke, Superintendent of Schools, or Thomas Galvin, Principal, Berlin High School, 139 Patterson Way, Berlin, CT 06037

Financial data (yr. ended 02/28/02): Grants paid, $3,000; assets, $91,773 (M); expenditures, $5,069; qualifying distributions, $4,542.
Limitations: Giving limited to CT.
Application information: Application form required.
Trustee: Fleet National Bank.
EIN: 066024231

49322
D. V. Burnett Scholarship Fund
c/o Fleet Private Clients Group
P.O. Box 6767
Providence, RI 02940-6767

Financial data (yr. ended 12/31/00): Grants paid, $2,950; assets, $107,705 (M); expenditures, $4,492; qualifying distributions, $3,785.
Limitations: Giving primarily in NY.
Application information: Application form required. Application form required.
Trustee: Fleet National Bank.
EIN: 166238559

49323—RHODE ISLAND

49323
C. J. Parker Trust f/b/o Student Aid Fund
c/o Fleet Private Clients Group
P.O. Box 6767
Providence, RI 02940-6767
Contact: Marjorie Alexandre Davis, Trust Off.

Donor(s): C.J. Parker.‡
Financial data (yr. ended 01/31/00): Grants paid, $2,900; assets, $178,501 (M); expenditures, $7,533; qualifying distributions, $6,190.
Limitations: Giving limited to New Britain, CT.
Application information: Application form not required.
Trustee: Fleet National Bank.
EIN: 066036451

49324
Lieutenant John Cullen Westcott Trust
c/o Fleet Private Clients Group
P.O. Box 6767
Providence, RI 02940-6767
Application address: c/o Trust Dept., Fleet National Bank, 19 Park St., Attleboro, MA 02703

Financial data (yr. ended 05/31/01): Grants paid, $2,900; assets, $103,828 (M); expenditures, $4,184; qualifying distributions, $3,643.
Limitations: Giving limited to residents of North Attleboro, MA.
Application information: Application form not required.
Trustee: Fleet National Bank.
EIN: 046037276

49325
Anna M. Posemann Trust
c/o Fleet Private Clients Group
P.O. Box 6767
Providence, RI 02940-6767

Financial data (yr. ended 06/30/02): Grants paid, $2,800; assets, $113,937 (M); expenditures, $5,814; qualifying distributions, $2,800.
Limitations: Applications not accepted. Giving limited to Providence and Smithfield, RI.
Trustees: Robert O. Tiernan, Fleet National Bank.
EIN: 056061511

49326
Mildred Bassett Chase Memorial Fund
c/o Citizens Bank New Hampshire
870 Westminster St., 1st Fl.
Providence, RI 02903

Financial data (yr. ended 12/31/01): Grants paid, $2,658; assets, $96,221 (M); expenditures, $5,257; qualifying distributions, $3,888.
Limitations: Applications not accepted. Giving limited to NH.
Application information: Contributes only to pre-selected organizations.
Trustee: Citizens Bank New Hampshire.
EIN: 026004050

49327
David & Betsey Kilmartin Charitable Foundation, Inc.
(Formerly Kilmartin Industries Charitable Foundation, Inc.)
247 Farnum Rd.
Chepachet, RI 02814 (401) 949-1166
Contact: David F. Kilmartin, Pres.

Established in 1986 in MA.
Donor(s): Kilmartin Industries, David F. Kilmartin.
Financial data (yr. ended 02/28/02): Grants paid, $2,648; assets, $534,023 (M); gifts received, $11,080; expenditures, $14,573; qualifying distributions, $2,648.
Limitations: Giving primarily in MA and RI.

Officers and Directors:* David F. Kilmartin,* Pres.; Betsey Kilmartin,* Secy.
EIN: 222727613
Codes: CS, CD

49328
Georgiana Richardson Baker Fund
c/o Fleet Private Clients Group
P.O. Box 6767
Providence, RI 02940-6767

Financial data (yr. ended 09/30/01): Grants paid, $2,500; assets, $50,357 (M); expenditures, $4,057; qualifying distributions, $3,682.
Limitations: Giving limited to Uxbridge, MA.
Application information: Application form required.
Trustee: Fleet National Bank.
EIN: 046036987

49329
Alice N. Warren Trust f/b/o Warren Scholarship Fund
c/o Fleet Private Clients Group
P.O. Box 6767
Providence, RI 02940-6767

Financial data (yr. ended 12/31/01): Grants paid, $2,500; assets, $141,877 (M); expenditures, $7,301; qualifying distributions, $4,939.
Limitations: Giving limited to residents of MA.
Trustee: Fleet National Bank.
EIN: 237432471

49330
Earl C. Hughes Scholarship Fund
c/o Fleet Private Clients Group
P.O. Box 6767
Providence, RI 02940-6767

Financial data (yr. ended 12/31/01): Grants paid, $2,481; assets, $104,517 (M); expenditures, $4,472; qualifying distributions, $3,820.
Limitations: Giving limited to Worcester, MA.
Trustee: Fleet National Bank.
EIN: 046028081

49331
Helen Moore Trust f/b/o Ernest A. Moore Scholarship Fund
c/o Fleet Private Clients Group
P.O. Box 6767
Providence, RI 02940-6767
Application address: c/o Deborah Dillon Pearce, Trust Admin. Fleet National Bank, 100 Federal St., Boston, MA 02110

Financial data (yr. ended 04/30/01): Grants paid, $2,400; assets, $119,395 (M); expenditures, $5,060; qualifying distributions, $4,185.
Limitations: Giving limited to residents of MA.
Application information: Application form not required.
Trustee: Fleet National Bank.
EIN: 046194046

49332
Binney Foundation
c/o Fleet Private Clients Group
P.O. Box 6767
Providence, RI 02940-6767
Application address: c/o Tyler & Reynolds, 45 School St., Boston, MA 02108
Contact: H. Burton Powers

Financial data (yr. ended 12/31/01): Grants paid, $2,370; assets, $92,530 (M); expenditures, $5,170; qualifying distributions, $4,338.
Limitations: Giving on a national basis.
Trustee: Fleet National Bank.
EIN: 046020240

49333
Sarah Darrah Trust
c/o Fleet Private Clients Group
P.O. Box 6767
Providence, RI 02940-6767
Application address: c/o Augusta Haydock, Fleet National Bank, 100 Federal St., Boston, MA 02110

Financial data (yr. ended 12/31/01): Grants paid, $2,250; assets, $106,057 (M); expenditures, $4,377; qualifying distributions, $3,381.
Limitations: Giving limited to residents of North Attleboro, MA.
Trustee: Fleet National Bank.
EIN: 046007847

49334
Rose D. Wright Trust
c/o Fleet Private Clients Group
P.O. Box 6767
Providence, RI 02940-6767
Application address: c/o Lamme, Linscott & Flournoy, 22 Elm St., Great Barrington, MA 01230
Contact: Wendy T. Linscott, Trust Off.

Donor(s): R.D. Wright.‡
Financial data (yr. ended 12/31/01): Grants paid, $2,200; assets, $85,681 (M); expenditures, $4,035; qualifying distributions, $3,223.
Limitations: Giving limited to residents of Berkshire County, MA.
Application information: Application form required.
Trustee: Fleet National Bank.
EIN: 046296200

49335
Church of the Reconciliation
c/o Fleet Private Clients Group
P.O. Box 6767
Providence, RI 02940-6767

Established in 1988 in NY.
Financial data (yr. ended 12/31/01): Grants paid, $2,164; assets, $76,311 (M); expenditures, $3,401; qualifying distributions, $2,164.
Limitations: Applications not accepted. Giving limited to Utica, NY.
Application information: Contributes only to a pre-selected organization.
Trustee: Fleet National Bank.
EIN: 156014926

49336
Franklin-Tilton-Northfield School Trust
c/o Citizens Bank New Hampshire
870 Westminster St.
Providence, RI 02903-4024
Application addresses: c/o Winnisquam High School, Tilton, NH 03276, tel.: (603) 286-4531; or c/o Franklin High School, Franklin, NH 03235, tel.: (603) 934-5441

Financial data (yr. ended 12/31/00): Grants paid, $2,150; assets, $96,377 (M); expenditures, $4,514; qualifying distributions, $3,272.
Limitations: Giving primarily in Franklin, Northfield, and Tilton, NH areas.
Trustee: Citizens Bank New Hampshire.
EIN: 026005055

49337
Anna Cramer Scholarship Trust
c/o Fleet Private Clients Group
P.O. Box 6767
Providence, RI 02940-6767

Financial data (yr. ended 12/31/00): Grants paid, $2,075; assets, $68,811 (M); expenditures, $3,611; qualifying distributions, $2,407.
Limitations: Applications not accepted. Giving primarily in FL, NJ, and PA.
Application information: Unsolicited requests for funds not accepted.
Trustee: Fleet National Bank.
EIN: 226252400

49338
Eugene G. Blackford Memorial Scholarship Fund
c/o Fleet Private Clients Group
P.O. Box 6767
Providence, RI 02940-6767

Donor(s): Margaret M. Blackford.‡
Financial data (yr. ended 12/31/00): Grants paid, $2,000; assets, $84,906 (M); expenditures, $3,153; qualifying distributions, $2,747.
Limitations: Giving limited to Fairfield County, CT.
Application information: Application form required.
Trustees: William Blackford, Fleet National Bank.
EIN: 066250201

49339
Robert and Donna Colucci Charitable Foundation
c/o Robert G. Colucci
25 Factory Pond Cir.
Greenville, RI 02828

Established in 1997 in RI.
Donor(s): Robert G. Colucci, Donna M. Colucci.
Financial data (yr. ended 06/30/01): Grants paid, $2,000; assets, $30,195 (M); expenditures, $2,144; qualifying distributions, $2,144.
Limitations: Applications not accepted.
Application information: Contributes only to pre-selected organizations.
Officers and Directors:* Robert G. Colucci,* Pres. and Treas.; Donna Colucci,* V.P.; Edward Colucci,* Secy.
EIN: 050495406

49340
Mary Irene Fay Tuition Fund
c/o Fleet Private Clients Group
P.O. Box 6767
Providence, RI 02940-6767

Established in 1999 in MA.
Financial data (yr. ended 12/31/99): Grants paid, $2,000; assets, $390,314 (M); expenditures, $7,737; qualifying distributions, $5,693.
Limitations: Applications not accepted.
Application information: Contributes only to pre-selected organizations.
Trustee: Fleet National Bank.
EIN: 046020550

49341
Louis B. Fox & Julian Karger Scholarship Fund
(Formerly Louis B. Fox & Julian Karger Trust)
c/o Fleet Private Clients Group
P.O. Box 6767
Providence, RI 02940-6767
Application address: c/o Scholarship Committee, Revere High School, Revere, MA 02151

Financial data (yr. ended 12/31/01): Grants paid, $2,000; assets, $102,548 (M); expenditures, $4,529; qualifying distributions, $3,814.
Limitations: Giving limited to Revere, MA.
Trustee: Fleet National Bank.
EIN: 046334789
Codes: GTI

49342
Francis E. Hart Scholarship Fund
c/o Fleet Private Clients Group
P.O. Box 6767
Providence, RI 02940-6767
Application address: c/o Thea Katsounakis, Fleet National Bank, 1 Monarch Pl., Springfield, MA 01102-0391

Financial data (yr. ended 04/30/01): Grants paid, $2,000; assets, $74,913 (M); gifts received, $1,230; expenditures, $4,128; qualifying distributions, $3,399.
Limitations: Giving limited to Amherst, MA.
Trustee: Fleet National Bank.
EIN: 046335717

49343
The Carol A. Peterson Foundation
28 Bradford Rd.
Cranston, RI 02910

Established in 2000 in RI.
Donor(s): Carol Peterson.
Financial data (yr. ended 12/31/01): Grants paid, $2,000; assets, $106,032 (M); gifts received, $78,497; expenditures, $5,785; qualifying distributions, $2,000.
Limitations: Applications not accepted.
Application information: Contributes only to pre-selected organizations.
Officers: Carol Peterson, Pres.; Edward Pieroni, V.P.; Mary Lou Kennedy, Treas.
EIN: 050514676

49344
Frank Randall Trust
c/o Fleet Private Clients Group
P.O. Box 6767
Providence, RI 02940-6767
Application address: c/o Guidance Counselor, Oliver Ames High School, 100 Lothrop St., North Easton, MA 02356

Established in 1985 in MA.
Financial data (yr. ended 12/31/01): Grants paid, $2,000; assets, $109,358 (M); expenditures, $4,366; qualifying distributions, $3,438.
Limitations: Giving limited to residents of North Easton, MA.
Application information: Application form not required.
Trustee: Fleet National Bank.
EIN: 046063169

49345
V. Gerard Ryan Trust Fund f/b/o Ansonia High School
c/o Fleet Private Clients Group
P.O. Box 6767
Providence, RI 02940-6767

Financial data (yr. ended 06/30/01): Grants paid, $2,000; assets, $79,825 (M); expenditures, $4,553; qualifying distributions, $3,300.
Limitations: Giving primarily in Ansonia, CT.
Application information: Recipients are selected based on recommendation of Ansonia High School faculty committee. Application form not required.
Trustees: Wilheminia Christon, Linda Gentile, William McAllister, Fleet National Bank.
EIN: 066219587

49346
Wright Memorial Scholarship Fund
c/o Fleet Private Clients Group
P.O. Box 6767
Providence, RI 02940-6767
Application address: Emma Greene, 100 Federal St., Boston, MA 02110
Contact: Emma Greene, Trust Off., Fleet National Bank

Established in 1986 in MA.
Financial data (yr. ended 06/30/02): Grants paid, $2,000; assets, $79,619 (M); expenditures, $5,581; qualifying distributions, $2,000.
Limitations: Giving primarily in MA.
Application information: Application form required.
Trustee: Fleet National Bank.
EIN: 046552717

49347
Regina M. Holt Trust for Blind Children
c/o Fleet Private Clients Group
P.O. Box 6767
Providence, RI 02940-6767

Financial data (yr. ended 06/30/01): Grants paid, $1,950; assets, $38,356 (M); expenditures, $2,636; qualifying distributions, $2,210.
Limitations: Applications not accepted. Giving limited to CT.
Application information: Recipients are selected by State of Connecticut case workers.
Trustee: Fleet National Bank.
EIN: 066028532

49348
Marie Ann Federowski Trust
c/o Fleet Private Clients Group
P.O. Box 6767
Providence, RI 02940-6767

Established in 1988 in NY.
Financial data (yr. ended 12/31/01): Grants paid, $1,855; assets, $77,662 (M); expenditures, $2,971; qualifying distributions, $2,518.
Limitations: Applications not accepted. Giving primarily in NY.
Application information: Contributes only to pre-selected organizations.
Trustee: Fleet National Bank.
EIN: 166159240

49349
Francis & Bessie Tarr Memorial Scholarship Trust
c/o Fleet Private Clients Group
P.O. Box 6767
Providence, RI 02940-6767
Application addresses: c/o Dir. of Guidance, Gloucester High School, 32 Leslie O. Johnson Rd., Gloucester, MA 01930-2595; c/o Dir. of Guidance, Rockport High School, 24 Jerdens Ln., Rockport, MA 01966-2198

Financial data (yr. ended 07/31/01): Grants paid, $1,800; assets, $42,602 (M); expenditures, $2,285; qualifying distributions, $2,233.
Limitations: Giving limited to residents of Gloucester and Rockport, MA.
Application information: Application form required.
Trustee: Fleet National Bank.
EIN: 046411191

49350
Sarah S. Vert Student Fund Trust
c/o Fleet Private Clients Group
P.O. Box 6767
Providence, RI 02940-6767
Application address: c/o Arthur P. Momet, Superintendent, Plattsburgh City School District, 106 Oak St., Plattsburgh, NY 12901, tel.: (518) 561-6670

Donor(s): Charles J. Vert.‡
Financial data (yr. ended 12/31/01): Grants paid, $1,800; assets, $46,349 (M); gifts received, $384; expenditures, $2,438; qualifying distributions, $2,095.
Limitations: Giving limited to Clinton County, NY.
Application information: Application form required.
Trustee: Fleet National Bank.
EIN: 146014136

49351
Harry E. Knight Scholarship Fund Trust
c/o Fleet Private Clients Group
P. O. Box 6767
Providence, RI 02940-6767
Application address: Arthur P. Momet, Superintendent of Schools, Plattsburgh City School District, 106 Oak St., Plattsburgh, NY 12901, tel.: (518) 561-6670

Financial data (yr. ended 12/31/01): Grants paid, $1,600; assets, $50,076 (M); expenditures, $2,331; qualifying distributions, $1,600.
Limitations: Giving limited to Plattsburgh, NY.
Application information: Application form required.
Trustee: Fleet National Bank.
EIN: 146014039

49352
Ann H. Vickery Scholarship Fund
c/o Fleet Private Clients Group
P. O. Box 6767
Providence, RI 02940-6767
Application address: c/o Guidance Dir., Valley Regional High School, Deep River, CT 06417

Financial data (yr. ended 09/30/01): Grants paid, $1,600; assets, $41,673 (M); expenditures, $2,824; qualifying distributions, $2,154.
Limitations: Giving limited to the Deep River, CT, area.
Application information: Application form required.
Trustee: Fleet National Bank.
EIN: 066158543

49353
Peter F. Findlay Memorial Fund, Inc.
129 Dendron Rd.
Peace Dale, RI 02879-2500
Application address: c/o Eric Werth Elmer, Principal, South Kingstown High School, Wakefield, RI 02879

Financial data (yr. ended 12/31/99): Grants paid, $1,500; assets, $39,880 (M); gifts received, $1,794; expenditures, $3,948; qualifying distributions, $3,948.
Limitations: Giving limited to South County, RI.
Application information: Application form required.
Officers: Doris W. Findlay, Pres.; Elton Rayack, V.P.; Prentice Stout, Secy.; James F. Findlay, Jr., Treas.
EIN: 222549666

49354
Eliza H. Faunce Trust
(Formerly The Sewall Allen Faunce Fund)
c/o Fleet Private Clients Group
P.O. Box 6767
Providence, RI 02940-6767
Application address: c/o Fleet National Bank, 100 Federal St., Boston, MA 02100

Financial data (yr. ended 10/31/01): Grants paid, $1,400; assets, $88,970 (M); expenditures, $3,274; qualifying distributions, $2,885.
Limitations: Giving limited to residents of Kingston, MA.
Trustee: Fleet National Bank.
EIN: 046038603

49355
Maude M. Howes Memorial Scholarship Fund Trust
c/o Fleet Private Clients Group
P.O. Box 6767
Providence, RI 02940-6767
Application address: 100 Federal St., Boston, MA 02110, tel.: (617) 434-3768
Contact: Carol Gray, Trust Off., Fleet National Bank

Financial data (yr. ended 12/31/01): Grants paid, $1,400; assets, $54,213 (M); expenditures, $2,949; qualifying distributions, $2,598.
Limitations: Giving limited to Quincy, MA.
Application information: Application form required.
Trustee: Fleet National Bank.
EIN: 046020903

49356
Paul E. Scholz Trust
c/o Fleet Private Clients Group
P.O. Box 6767
Providence, RI 02940-6767
Application address: c/o Guidance Dept., Whitman Hanson Regional High School, Franklin St., Whitman, MA 02328

Financial data (yr. ended 05/31/01): Grants paid, $1,300; assets, $40,053 (M); expenditures, $1,487; qualifying distributions, $1,385.
Limitations: Giving limited to Whitman, MA.
Application information: Application form required.
Trustee: Fleet National Bank.
EIN: 046227955

49357
Nice Guy Foundation, Inc.
569 Warwick Ave.
Warwick, RI 02888

Established in 1998.
Donor(s): Michael Degulio.
Financial data (yr. ended 10/31/01): Grants paid, $1,292; assets, $4,165 (M); gifts received, $15,186; expenditures, $12,273; qualifying distributions, $10,705; giving activities include $10,705 for programs.
Limitations: Giving primarily in RI.
Officers: William Cocroft, Pres.; Michael Degiulio, V.P.; Robin Larkin, Secy.; James W. Messere, Treas.
EIN: 050496138

49358
The Anne Walker Scholarship Fund
c/o Fleet Private Clients Group
P.O. Box 6767
Providence, RI 02940-6767
Application address: c/o Scholarship Comm., Dunkirk Public Schools, P.O. Box 1298, W. 6th St., Dunkirk, NY 14048

Established in 1962 in NY.
Donor(s): Anne Walker.‡
Financial data (yr. ended 12/31/01): Grants paid, $1,200; assets, $19,703 (M); expenditures, $1,440; qualifying distributions, $1,356.
Limitations: Giving limited to residents of Dunkirk, NY.
Application information: Application form required.
Trustee: Fleet National Bank.
EIN: 166131793

49359
Mina H. Sprague Trust
(also known as The Hamer Trust)
c/o Fleet Private Clients Group
P.O. Box 6767
Providence, RI 02940-6767
Application address: c/o Principal, Frankfort-Schuyler Central School, Palmer St., Frankfort, NY 14850

Financial data (yr. ended 12/31/00): Grants paid, $1,100; assets, $24,869 (M); expenditures, $1,441; qualifying distributions, $1,314.
Limitations: Giving primarily in NY.
Application information: Application form not required.
Trustee: Fleet National Bank.
EIN: 166172161

49360
Johnson Charitable Fund
c/o Fleet Private Clients Group
P.O. Box 6767
Providence, RI 02940-6767
Application address: c/o Clifton Johnson, Jr., 1434 Memorial Ave., West Springfield, MA 01089

Established in 1994 in RI.
Financial data (yr. ended 12/31/01): Grants paid, $1,075; assets, $102,323 (M); expenditures, $3,262; qualifying distributions, $2,483.
Limitations: Giving primarily in NC.
Application information: Application form not required.
Trustee: Fleet National Bank.
EIN: 046301593

49361
The Foundation for Neurology
c/o J. Donald Easton
7 Seaview Ave.
Jamestown, RI 02835

Established in 1986 in TX.
Financial data (yr. ended 12/31/01): Grants paid, $1,012; assets, $24,864 (M); gifts received,

$34,000; expenditures, $19,294; qualifying distributions, $1,012.
Limitations: Applications not accepted.
Application information: Contributes only to pre-selected organizations.
Officers and Directors:* J. Donald Easton,* Pres.; Leonard D. Hudson,* V.P.; Karen Von Gunten Easton,* Secy.-Treas.; Sydney Louis, Merle A. Sande, David G. Sherman.
EIN: 742406107

49362
August R. and Marie A. Fasolino Memorial Fund
575 Shore Acres Ave.
North Kingstown, RI 02852

Established in 1995 in NJ.
Donor(s): Victor P. Fasolino.
Financial data (yr. ended 12/31/01): Grants paid, $1,000; assets, $23,915 (M); expenditures, $1,085; qualifying distributions, $1,085.
Limitations: Applications not accepted.
Application information: Contributes only to pre-selected organizations.
Officers: Victor P. Fasolino, Pres.; Gabriel Fasolino, Secy.; Mary Lou McGurkin, Treas.
EIN: 223385440

49363
Lena C. Howard Trust
c/o Fleet Private Clients Group
P.O. Box 6767
Providence, RI 02940-6767
Application address: c/o Dir. of Guidance Service, Brockton Public School, 43 Crescent St., Brockton, MA 02403

Financial data (yr. ended 05/31/01): Grants paid, $1,000; assets, $98,656 (M); expenditures, $3,485; qualifying distributions, $2,785.
Limitations: Giving limited to Brockton, MA.
Application information: Application form required.
Trustee: Fleet National Bank.
EIN: 046137069

49364
Leonard J. Sholes Charitable Foundation
310 Norwood Ave.
Cranston, RI 02905-2712
Contact: Leonard J. Sholes, Tr.

Donor(s): Leonard J. Sholes.
Financial data (yr. ended 12/31/01): Grants paid, $960; assets, $23,204 (M); gifts received, $1,500; expenditures, $975; qualifying distributions, $975.
Limitations: Giving primarily in NY and RI.
Trustees: Andrew G. Sholes, David H. Sholes, Leonard J. Sholes, Richard K. Sholes.
EIN: 237089984

49365
St. Anthony Relief Fund
c/o Fleet Private Clients Group
P.O. Box 6767
Providence, RI 02940-6767

Financial data (yr. ended 07/31/01): Grants paid, $950; assets, $26,197 (M); expenditures, $1,575; qualifying distributions, $1,340.
Limitations: Applications not accepted. Giving primarily in ME.
Trustee: Fleet National Bank.
EIN: 016046513

49366
John Walker Bowron Scholarship Fund
c/o Fleet Private Clients Group
P.O. Box 6767
Providence, RI 02940-6767
Application address: c/o Mary Jo VanAcker, Dir. of Guidance, Northeastern Clinton Central School, P.O. Box 339, Rte. 276, Champlain, NY 12919

Financial data (yr. ended 12/31/00): Grants paid, $850; assets, $37,665 (M); expenditures, $1,349; qualifying distributions, $1,157.
Limitations: Giving limited to residents of Rouses Point and Champlain, NY.
Application information: Application form required.
Trustee: Fleet National Bank.
EIN: 146013929

49367
Louis T. Groat Fund
c/o Fleet Private Clients Group
P.O. Box 6767
Providence, RI 02940-6767

Financial data (yr. ended 12/31/01): Grants paid, $722; assets, $12,557 (M); expenditures, $778; qualifying distributions, $752.
Limitations: Giving primarily in NY.
Application information: Application form not required.
Trustee: Fleet National Bank.
EIN: 166184507

49368
Grace L. Carver Scholarship Fund
c/o Fleet Private Clients Group
P.O. Box 6767
Providence, RI 02940-6767
Application address: Headmaster, c/o New Bedford High School, 230 Hathaway Blvd., New Bedford, MA 02740

Established in 1998 in MA.
Financial data (yr. ended 09/30/01): Grants paid, $675; assets, $16,453 (M); expenditures, $987; qualifying distributions, $887.
Limitations: Giving limited to New Bedford, MA.
Application information: Application form required.
Trustee: Fleet National Bank.
EIN: 046184211

49369
Frederic H. Cowan Memorial Fund
c/o Fleet Private Clients Group
P.O. Box 6767
Providence, RI 02940-6767

Financial data (yr. ended 09/30/01): Grants paid, $600; assets, $17,664 (M); expenditures, $1,232; qualifying distributions, $1,060.
Limitations: Applications not accepted. Giving primarily in MA.
Application information: Contributes only to pre-selected organizations.
Trustee: Fleet National Bank.
EIN: 046008062

49370
Benjamin D. Evans Memorial Fund
c/o David F. Evans
P.O. Box 430
Albion, RI 02802

Financial data (yr. ended 12/31/01): Grants paid, $600; assets, $5,434 (M); expenditures, $765; qualifying distributions, $600.
Officers: David F. Evans, Pres.; Thomas S. Evans, V.P. and Treas.; Susan H. Evans, Secy.

EIN: 050497163

49371
Mary E. Austin Scholarship Fund
c/o Fleet Private Clients Group
P.O. Box 6767
Providence, RI 02940-6767
Application address: c/o Headmaster, New Bedford High School, 230 Hathaway Blvd., New Bedford, MA 02740

Financial data (yr. ended 09/30/01): Grants paid, $525; assets, $15,169 (M); expenditures, $740; qualifying distributions, $663.
Limitations: Giving limited to residents of New Bedford, MA.
Application information: Application form required.
Trustee: Fleet National Bank.
EIN: 046049624

49372
Jeannette S. Tuttle Trust
c/o Fleet Private Clients Group
P.O. Box 6767
Providence, RI 02940-6767
Application address: c/o Principal, Naugatuck High School, 543 Rubber Ave., Naugatuck, CT 12030, tel.: (203) 723-0951

Financial data (yr. ended 12/31/00): Grants paid, $525; assets, $12,705 (M); expenditures, $801; qualifying distributions, $755.
Limitations: Giving limited to Naugatuck, CT.
Application information: Application form required.
Trustee: Fleet National Bank.
EIN: 066025600

49373
The Central Falls Scholarship Trust
P.O. Box 215
Central Falls, RI 02863

Donor(s): James A. Briden.
Financial data (yr. ended 12/31/01): Grants paid, $500; assets, $9,993 (M); gifts received, $500; expenditures, $550; qualifying distributions, $550.
Limitations: Applications not accepted. Giving limited to RI.
Application information: Contributes to pre-selected organizations.
Trustee: James A. Briden.
EIN: 056094876

49374
Patrick Mansfield Memorial Scholarship Fund
c/o Gale Hanna
9 Hanna Ln.
North Scituate, RI 02857

Established in 1990.
Donor(s): Gale Hanna.
Financial data (yr. ended 06/30/01): Grants paid, $500; assets, $2,986 (M); gifts received, $291; expenditures, $791; qualifying distributions, $3,484.
Limitations: Applications not accepted. Giving limited to residents of Chepachet, RI.
Application information: Unsolicited requests for funds not accepted.
Trustee: Gale Hanna.
EIN: 050449419

49375
Helen M. Palmer Trust f/b/o Daughters of the American Revolution
c/o Fleet Private Clients Group
P.O. Box 6767
Providence, RI 02940-6767
Application address: P.O. Box 173, South Woodstock, CT 06267
Contact: Mary Brown, Tr.

Financial data (yr. ended 07/31/01): Grants paid, $500; assets, $603,090 (M); expenditures, $15,454; qualifying distributions, $13,117.
Limitations: Giving limited to residents of CT, with preference given first to those residing in the town of Brooklyn, second to those in Windham County.
Application information: Application form required.
Trustees: Mary Brown, Mary Ellen Tomeo, Fleet National Bank.
EIN: 066029229

49376
Bertha Dillon Trust
(Formerly Bertha Dillon Trust for the Frank Lawrence Dillon Fund)
c/o Fleet Private Clients Group
P.O. Box 6767
Providence, RI 02940-6767
Application address: c/o Superintendent of Schools, 24 Converse St., Palmer, MA 01069

Financial data (yr. ended 05/31/01): Grants paid, $485; assets, $23,498 (M); expenditures, $1,115; qualifying distributions, $883.
Limitations: Giving limited to Palmer, MA.
Application information: Application form not required.
Trustee: Fleet National Bank.
EIN: 046290999

49377
Brian J. Pfannebecker Trust
c/o Fleet Private Clients Group
P.O. Box 6767
Providence, RI 02940-6767
Application address: c/o Principal, Dolgeville Central Schools, Dolgeville, NY 13329, tel.: (315) 429-3155

Financial data (yr. ended 12/31/00): Grants paid, $450; assets, $6,762 (M); expenditures, $475; qualifying distributions, $462.
Limitations: Giving limited to residents of Dolgeville, NY.
Trustee: Fleet National Bank.
EIN: 166222026

49378
Edna Emery Lawrence Trust
c/o Fleet Private Clients Group
P.O. Box 6767
Providence, RI 02940-6767
Application address: c/o Guidance Office, Lawrence High School, Fairchild, ME 04937

Financial data (yr. ended 04/30/01): Grants paid, $449; assets, $27,728 (M); expenditures, $1,074; qualifying distributions, $839.
Limitations: Giving limited to residents of Shawmut Village in Fairchild, ME.
Application information: Letter with personal data, employment record, school records and references. Application form not required.
Trustee: Fleet National Bank.
EIN: 016036902

49379
Veturia I. Wiley Trust under paragraph 5
c/o Fleet Private Clients Group
P.O. Box 6767
Providence, RI 02940-6767

Established in 1988 in NY.
Financial data (yr. ended 12/31/01): Grants paid, $341; assets, $5,960 (M); expenditures, $365; qualifying distributions, $341.
Limitations: Applications not accepted. Giving primarily in NY.
Application information: Contributes only to pre-selected organizations.
Trustee: Fleet National Bank.
EIN: 166135692

49380
Raymond T. & Ann T. Mancini Family Foundation
119 Hopkins Hill Rd.
West Greenwich, RI 02817

Established in 2000 in RI.
Donor(s): Raymond T. Mancini.
Financial data (yr. ended 12/31/01): Grants paid, $300; assets, $409,186 (M); expenditures, $450; qualifying distributions, $300.
Limitations: Applications not accepted.
Application information: Contributes only to pre-selected organizations.
Trustees: Ann T. Mancini, Raymond T. Mancini.
EIN: 050514875

49381
Lucy A. Whitaker Trust
c/o Fleet Private Clients Group
P.O. Box 6767
Providence, RI 02940-6767

Financial data (yr. ended 12/31/01): Grants paid, $274; assets, $4,730 (M); expenditures, $291; qualifying distributions, $285.
Limitations: Applications not accepted. Giving primarily in Holland Patent, NY.
Application information: Contributes only to pre-selected organizations.
Trustee: Fleet National Bank.
EIN: 156014941

49382
Hymen & Clara Sitrin KZS Award
c/o Fleet Private Clients Group
P.O. Box 6767
Providence, RI 02940-6767

Established in 1994 in RI.
Financial data (yr. ended 12/31/00): Grants paid, $253; assets, $4,441 (M); expenditures, $274; qualifying distributions, $263.
Limitations: Applications not accepted. Giving on an international basis, with emphasis on Israel.
Trustee: Fleet National Bank.
EIN: 156021392

49383
Winnifred C. Walsh Scholarship Fund
(also known as Winnifred C. Walsh Trust)
c/o Fleet Private Clients Group
P.O. Box 6767
Providence, RI 02940-6767
Application address: Vauntina Franklin, c/o Fleet National Bank, 100 Federal St., Boston, MA 02110, tel.: (617) 434-4627

Donor(s): Winnifred C. Walsh.‡
Financial data (yr. ended 02/28/01): Grants paid, $250; assets, $53,619 (M); expenditures, $415; qualifying distributions, $335.
Limitations: Applications not accepted. Giving limited to residents of the Stoughton, MA, area.
Application information: Recipients are nominated by their respective high schools.
Trustee: Fleet National Bank.
EIN: 046205092

49384
George M. Griffith Memorial Trust
(Formerly Ernest Griffith Memorial Trust)
c/o Fleet Private Clients Group
P.O. Box 6767
Providence, RI 02940-6767

Financial data (yr. ended 12/31/01): Grants paid, $230; assets, $3,579 (M); expenditures, $230; qualifying distributions, $230.
Limitations: Applications not accepted. Giving primarily in NY.
Trustee: Fleet National Bank.
EIN: 166061580

49385
Barbara Ann Waldron Memorial Fund
(also known as R. Waldron Memorial Fund)
c/o Fleet Private Clients Group
P.O. Box 6767
Providence, RI 02940-6767

Financial data (yr. ended 12/31/01): Grants paid, $230; assets, $4,410 (M); expenditures, $250; qualifying distributions, $240.
Limitations: Applications not accepted. Giving limited to Utica, NY.
Trustee: Fleet National Bank.
EIN: 166075554

49386
H. & B. Rosenblum Trust Memorial Fund
c/o Fleet Private Clients Group
P.O. Box 6767
Providence, RI 02940-6767
Application address: c/o Principal, Utica Free Academy, Utica, NY 13501

Financial data (yr. ended 12/31/00): Grants paid, $225; assets, $3,604 (M); expenditures, $263; qualifying distributions, $223.
Limitations: Giving limited to residents of the Utica, NY, area.
Trustee: Fleet National Bank.
EIN: 166184534

49387
P. Joseph Curran Memorial Scholarship Fund
c/o Fleet Private Clients Group
P.O. Box 6767
Providence, RI 02940-6767
Application address: P.O. Box 492, West Springfield, MA 01089

Financial data (yr. ended 12/31/00): Grants paid, $200; assets, $24,764 (M); expenditures, $1,285; qualifying distributions, $892.
Limitations: Giving limited to the residents of Agawam and West Springfield, MA.
Application information: Application form required.
Trustee: Fleet National Bank.
EIN: 237039403

49388
The David Mallery Scholarship Fund
c/o Fleet Private Clients Group
P.O. Box 6767
Providence, RI 02940-6767

Financial data (yr. ended 12/31/00): Grants paid, $200; assets, $3,655 (M); expenditures, $242; qualifying distributions, $227.
Limitations: Applications not accepted. Giving primarily in NY.
Trustee: Fleet National Bank.
EIN: 166138926

49389
William F. Potter Scholarship Fund
c/o Fleet Private Clients Group
P.O. Box 6767
Providence, RI 02940-6767
Application address: c/o Headmaster, New Bedford High School, 230 Hathaway Blvd., New Bedford, MA 02740, tel.: (508) 997-8704
Contact: Judy Zalansky

Financial data (yr. ended 09/30/99): Grants paid, $175; assets, $17,811 (M); expenditures, $699; qualifying distributions, $458.
Limitations: Giving limited to New Bedford, MA.
Application information: Application form required.
Trustee: Fleet National Bank.
EIN: 046312370

49390
Hymen & Clara Sitrin Awards - Utica Free Academy
c/o Fleet Private Clients Group
P.O. Box 6767
Providence, RI 02940-6767

Financial data (yr. ended 12/31/00): Grants paid, $150; assets, $2,638 (M); expenditures, $152; qualifying distributions, $150.
Limitations: Applications not accepted. Giving limited to Utica, NY.
Trustee: Fleet National Bank.
EIN: 156015038

49391
Utica Free Academy Class of 1919 Memorial Prize Fund
c/o Fleet Private Clients Group
P.O. Box 6767
Providence, RI 02940-6767

Financial data (yr. ended 12/31/01): Grants paid, $140; assets, $2,169 (M); expenditures, $146; qualifying distributions, $138.
Limitations: Applications not accepted. Giving limited to Utica, NY.
Application information: Unsolicited requests for funds not accepted.
Trustee: Fleet National Bank.
EIN: 156014949

49392
Beth Ann Bernardi Memorial Fund
c/o Fleet Private Clients Group
P.O. Box 6767
Providence, RI 02940-6767
Established in 1986 in NY.
Financial data (yr. ended 12/31/01): Grants paid, $122; assets, $2,327 (M); expenditures, $122; qualifying distributions, $136.
Limitations: Applications not accepted. Giving primarily in NY.
Application information: Contributes only to pre-selected organizations.
Trustee: Fleet National Bank.
EIN: 166179104

49393
Hymen & Clara Sitrin Awards - Hughes School
c/o Fleet National Bank
P.O. Box 6767
Providence, RI 02940-6767

Financial data (yr. ended 12/31/00): Grants paid, $100; assets, $2,036 (M); expenditures, $100; qualifying distributions, $100.
Limitations: Applications not accepted. Giving limited to residents of Utica, NY.
Application information: Awards to 1st and 2nd ranking graduates at John F. Hughes School.
Trustee: Fleet National Bank.
EIN: 156015043

49394
Eugene Ionta Trust
c/o Fleet Private Clients Group
P.O. Box 6767
Providence, RI 02940-6767

Financial data (yr. ended 12/31/01): Grants paid, $80; assets, $4,380 (M); expenditures, $85; qualifying distributions, $80.
Limitations: Applications not accepted. Giving primarily in NY.
Application information: Contributes only to pre-selected organizations.
Trustee: Fleet National Bank.
EIN: 166172154

49395
Edward S. Babcock Scholarship Fund
c/o Fleet Private Clients Group
P.O. Box 6767
Providence, RI 02940-6767

Financial data (yr. ended 12/31/00): Grants paid, $50; assets, $848 (M); expenditures, $50; qualifying distributions, $50.
Limitations: Applications not accepted. Giving limited to Utica, NY.
Trustee: Fleet National Bank.
EIN: 156014950

49396
Utica Free Academy Spanish Prize Fund
c/o Fleet Private Clients Group
P.O. Box 6767
Providence, RI 02940-6767

Financial data (yr. ended 12/31/00): Grants paid, $30; assets, $405 (M); expenditures, $30; qualifying distributions, $30.
Limitations: Applications not accepted. Giving limited to Utica, NY.
Trustee: Fleet National Bank.
EIN: 156014934

49397
Utica Free Academy Salutatorian Scholarship Fund
c/o Fleet Private Clients Group
P.O. Box 6767
Providence, RI 02940-6767

Financial data (yr. ended 12/31/00): Grants paid, $25; assets, $395 (M); expenditures, $25; qualifying distributions, $25.
Limitations: Applications not accepted. Giving limited to Utica, NY.
Trustee: Fleet National Bank.
EIN: 156014947

49398
Bertha W. Merselis Trust under paragraph 4
c/o Fleet Private Clients Group
P.O. Box 6767
Providence, RI 02940-6767
Donor(s): Bertha W. Merselis.‡
Financial data (yr. ended 12/31/00): Grants paid, $20; assets, $382 (M); expenditures, $20; qualifying distributions, $20.
Limitations: Applications not accepted.
Trustee: Fleet National Bank.
EIN: 166135684

49399
PTA Wetmore Street School Scholarship
c/o Fleet Private Clients Group
P.O. Box 6767
Providence, RI 02940-6767

Financial data (yr. ended 12/31/00): Grants paid, $20; assets, $330 (M); expenditures, $20; qualifying distributions, $20.
Limitations: Applications not accepted. Giving limited to Rochester, NY.
Trustee: Fleet National Bank.
EIN: 166064955

49400
Utica Free Academy Alumni Art Fund
c/o Fleet Private Clients Group
P.O. Box 6767
Providence, RI 02940-6767

Financial data (yr. ended 12/31/00): Grants paid, $20; assets, $388 (M); expenditures, $20; qualifying distributions, $20.
Limitations: Applications not accepted. Giving limited to Utica, NY.
Trustee: Fleet National Bank.
EIN: 156014946

49401
Utica Free Academy Class of 1934 Scholarship Prize Fund for Juniors
c/o Fleet Private Clients Group
P.O. Box 6767
Providence, RI 02940-6767

Financial data (yr. ended 12/31/00): Grants paid, $20; assets, $392 (M); expenditures, $20; qualifying distributions, $20.
Limitations: Applications not accepted. Giving limited to Utica, NY.
Trustee: Fleet National Bank.
EIN: 156014939

49402
Utica Free Academy Public Speaking Fund
c/o Fleet Private Clients Group
P.O.Box 6767
Providence, RI 02940

Financial data (yr. ended 12/31/00): Grants paid, $20; assets, $405 (M); expenditures, $20; qualifying distributions, $20.
Limitations: Applications not accepted. Giving limited to Utica, NY.
Trustee: Fleet National Bank.
EIN: 156014933

49403
Bertha W. Merselis Trust under paragraph 5
c/o Fleet Private Clients Group
P.O. Box 6767
Providence, RI 02940-6767
Donor(s): Bertha W. Merselis.‡
Financial data (yr. ended 12/31/00): Grants paid, $15; assets, $375 (M); expenditures, $15; qualifying distributions, $15.
Limitations: Applications not accepted. Giving primarily in NY.
Trustee: Fleet National Bank.
EIN: 166135685

49404
Mazzini Society of Utica Prize
c/o Fleet Private Clients Group
P.O. Box 6767
Providence, RI 02940-6767

Financial data (yr. ended 12/31/01): Grants paid, $10; assets, $179 (M); expenditures, $10; qualifying distributions, $10.

49404—RHODE ISLAND

Limitations: Applications not accepted. Giving limited to Utica, NY.
Trustee: Fleet National Bank.
EIN: 166072357

49405
Baker Adams Scholarship Fund
c/o Fleet Private Clients Group
P.O. Box 6767
Providence, RI 02940-6767
Application address: c/o Georgetown School Dept., Office of the Superintendent, 51 North St., Georgetown, MA 01833

Established in 2000 in MA.
Donor(s): Baker Adams.
Financial data (yr. ended 12/31/00): Grants paid, $0; assets, $604,041 (M); gifts received, $600,000; expenditures, $4,408; qualifying distributions, $4,261.
Limitations: Giving to residents of Georgetown, MA.
Trustee: Fleet National Bank.
EIN: 046012804

49406
Charles S. Ashley Scholarship Fund
c/o Fleet Private Clients Group
P.O. Box 6767
Providence, RI 02940-6767
Application address: c/o Headmaster, New Bedford High School, 230 Hathaway Rd., New Bedford, MA 02746-1037

Financial data (yr. ended 09/30/01): Grants paid, $0; assets, $24,694 (M); expenditures, $309; qualifying distributions, $213.
Limitations: Giving limited to New Bedford, MA.
Application information: Applicant must submit application form and letter of request. Application form required.
Trustee: Fleet National Bank.
EIN: 046049623

49407
William W. Bird Trust
c/o Fleet Private Clients Group
P.O. Box 6767
Providence, RI 02940-6767
Application address: 75 State Ste., Boston, MA 02109, tel.: (617) 346-2472
Contact: Marijane Tudhy, Trust off., Fleet National Bank

Financial data (yr. ended 12/31/01): Grants paid, $0; assets, $510,821 (M); expenditures, $8,594; qualifying distributions, $4,741.
Limitations: Giving limited to Worcester, MA.
Trustee: Fleet National Bank.
EIN: 046023203

49408
Caroline E. Brayton Trust
c/o Fleet Private Clients Group
P.O. Box 6767
Providence, RI 02940-6767

Financial data (yr. ended 07/31/02): Grants paid, $0; assets, $4,535 (M); expenditures, $259; qualifying distributions, $0.
Limitations: Applications not accepted. Giving limited to Fall River, MA.
Application information: Contributes only to pre-selected organizations.
Trustee: Fleet National Bank.
EIN: 046029315

49409
Cavanagh Family Foundation
c/o Salvadore
50 Kennedy Pl., Ste. 11225822
Providence, RI 02903-2393

Financial data (yr. ended 12/31/01): Grants paid, $0; assets, $106,701 (M); expenditures, $3,815; qualifying distributions, $3,815.
Limitations: Applications not accepted.
Application information: Contributes only to pre-selected organizations.
Officer and Directors:* Helena E. Cavanagh,* Pres. and Treas.; Brian P. Cavanagh, Mark J. Cavanagh, Steven J. Cavanagh.
EIN: 050475194

49410
The Citizens Bank Mid-Atlantic Charitable Foundation
c/o Citizens Bank
870 Westminster St.
Providence, RI 02903
Application address: 1 Citizens Plz., Providence, RI 02903, tel. (401) 456-7689
Contact: Pat Zeller, Trust Off., Citizens Bank

Established in 2001 in PA.
Donor(s): Citizens Financial Group, Inc.
Financial data (yr. ended 03/31/02): Grants paid, $0; assets, $34,948,497 (M); gifts received, $35,000,000; expenditures, $52,235; qualifying distributions, $26,118.
Trustees: Donald Gaiter, Stephen Steinour.
EIN: 256795399
Codes: CS

49411
The Class of 2000, Inc.
c/o Fleet Private Clients Group
P.O. Box 6767
Providence, RI 02940-6767
Application address: 1125 Route 22 W., 3rd Fl., Bridgewater, NJ 08807
Contact: Abby O'Neil, Pres.

Established in 2000 in NJ.
Financial data (yr. ended 05/31/02): Grants paid, $0; assets, $1,215 (M); expenditures, $900; qualifying distributions, $0.
Limitations: Giving limited to NJ.
Officers: Abby O'Neill, Pres.; Janet Calhoun, Secy.; Barbara Bye, Treas.
Director: Joyce Harley.
EIN: 223086525

49412
Copeland Foundation Trust
c/o Fleet Private Clients Group
P.O. Box 6767
Providence, RI 02940-6767
Application address: c/o Admin., Fleet National Bank, 216 State St., Schenectady, NY 13221

Financial data (yr. ended 06/30/01): Grants paid, $0; assets, $101,266 (M); expenditures, $1,501; qualifying distributions, $863.
Limitations: Giving primarily in NY.
Trustee: Fleet National Bank.
EIN: 146014176

49413
Beth Evans Dearborn Memorial Fund
c/o Fleet Private Clients Group
P.O. Box 6767
Providence, RI 02940-6767
Application address: 75 State Street, Boston, MA 02109
Contact: Thea Katsounakis, Trust Admin., Fleet National Bank

Financial data (yr. ended 12/31/01): Grants paid, $0; assets, $30,573 (M); expenditures, $1,415; qualifying distributions, $887.
Limitations: Giving limited to residents of Northampton, MA.
Application information: Selected by Committee of Roman Catholic Pastors of North Hampton, MA. Application form not required.
Trustee: Fleet National Bank.
EIN: 046132498

49414
The Adele R. Decof Foundation
c/o Leonard Decof
21 Marine Ave.
Newport, RI 02840

Established in 2000 in RI.
Financial data (yr. ended 12/31/00): Grants paid, $0; assets, $51,119 (M); gifts received, $50,394; expenditures, $0; qualifying distributions, $0.
Limitations: Applications not accepted.
Application information: Contributes only to pre-selected organizations.
Trustees: Andrea Decof, Leonard Decof, Mark Decof.
EIN: 056124506

49415
Eleanor Dillenbeck Scholarship Trust
c/o Fleet Private Clients Group
P.O. Box 6767
Providence, RI 02940-6767

Established in 2000 in RI.
Donor(s): George E. Dillenbeck.
Financial data (yr. ended 12/31/00): Grants paid, $0; assets, $570,992 (M); gifts received, $488,461; expenditures, $5,249; qualifying distributions, $3,839.
Limitations: Giving limited to Montgomery, NY.
Application information: Application form required.
Trustee: Fleet National Bank.
EIN: 056121934

49416
The Foundation for Newport
320 Thames St., Ste. 276
Newport, RI 02840-6633

Donor(s): Alletta Morris McBean Charitable Trust, Prince Charitable Trust, Van Beuren Charitable Foundation.
Financial data (yr. ended 06/30/01): Grants paid, $0; assets, $230,064 (M); gifts received, $230,456; expenditures, $258,220; qualifying distributions, $0; giving activities include $9,375 for programs.
Limitations: Applications not accepted.
Application information: Contributes only to pre-selected organizations.
Officers: Frank N. Ray, Chair.; Henry P. Bernhard, Pres.; Craig A. Kercheval, Exec. Dir.
Board Members: David J. Aguiar, Hugh D. Auchincloss III, John Bach-Sorenson, Ade Bethune, Ralph E. Carpenter, Jr., Ann Conner, Kathy Irving, David P. Leys, Coles Mallory, L. Michael Rives, Jeffrey L. Staats.
EIN: 223295172

49417
Jack Gleckman Scholarship Fund
c/o Fleet Private Clients Group
P.O. Box 6767
Providence, RI 02940-6767
Application address: c/o Headmaster, New Bedford High School, 230 Hathaway Blvd., New Bedford, MA 02740

Financial data (yr. ended 09/30/01): Grants paid, $0; assets, $9,026 (M); expenditures, $142; qualifying distributions, $105.
Limitations: Giving limited to New Bedford, MA.
Application information: Application form required.
Trustee: Fleet National Bank.
EIN: 046049669

49418
John F. Gracia Scholarship Fund
c/o Fleet Private Clients Group
P.O. Box 6767
Providence, RI 02940-6767
Application address: c/o Theodore Calnan, Headmaster, New Bedford High School, 230 Hathaway Blvd., New Bedford, MA 02740, tel.: (508) 997-8704

Financial data (yr. ended 09/30/99): Grants paid, $0; assets, $12,839 (M); expenditures, $361; qualifying distributions, $183.
Limitations: Giving limited to New Bedford, MA.
Application information: Application form required.
Trustee: Fleet National Bank.
EIN: 046242080

49419
Arden Gustafson Foundation
c/o Fleet Private Clients Group
P.O. Box 6767
Providence, RI 02940-6767

Established in 2000 in MA.
Donor(s): Arden Gustafson.
Financial data (yr. ended 07/31/02): Grants paid, $0; assets, $144,277 (M); expenditures, $2,108; qualifying distributions, $0.
Limitations: Giving primarily in MA.
Trustees: Arden Gustafson, Fleet National Bank.
EIN: 043537063

49420
Higgins Family Foundation
c/o Fleet Private Clients Group
P.O. Box 6767
Providence, RI 02940-6767

Established in 1999 in RI.
Donor(s): Robert J. Higgins.
Financial data (yr. ended 09/30/01): Grants paid, $0; assets, $1,225,346 (M); gifts received, $990,745; expenditures, $23,623; qualifying distributions, $2,365.
Limitations: Applications not accepted.
Application information: Contributes only to pre-selected organizations.
Trustee: Fleet National Bank.
EIN: 056121825

49421
Italo-American Foundation for Medical Education
205 Airport Rd.
Warwick, RI 02889

Established in 1997.
Financial data (yr. ended 12/31/00): Grants paid, $0; assets, $0 (M); expenditures, $1,451; qualifying distributions, $0.

Officers and Directors:* Girard R. Visconti,* Pres.; Victor E. Pricolo,* V.P.; Francis Scola,* Treas.; William Andreoni, Mary Betucio Arnold, Kirby I. Bland, Paul Calabresi, Ronald W. Delsesto, Edward Iannuccili, Dean Donald J. Marsh, Pasquale Ruggieri, Arthur Russo, Luis Sorrentino, Alfred Toseli, Vincent Vacca, Armond Versaci.
EIN: 050455774

49422
Dr. Price Lewis Medical Scholarship Fund
c/o Fleet Private Clients Group
P.O. Box 6767
Providence, RI 02940-6767

Financial data (yr. ended 12/31/00): Grants paid, $0; assets, $25,881 (M); expenditures, $141; qualifying distributions, $32.
Limitations: Applications not accepted. Giving limited to the Holland Patent, NY, area.
Trustee: Fleet National Bank.
EIN: 156015105

49423
Bernard G. & Madeleine J. Mondor Charitable Foundation
c/o Daniel J. Ryan
1 Davol Sq., Ste. 308
Providence, RI 02903

Established in 1998 in RI.
Donor(s): Bernard G. Mondor.
Financial data (yr. ended 12/31/01): Grants paid, $0; assets, $30,060 (M); expenditures, $263; qualifying distributions, $0.
Limitations: Applications not accepted.
Application information: Contributes only to pre-selected organizations.
Officers: Bernard G. Mondor, Pres.; Madeleine J. Mondor, V.P.; Daniel J. Ryan, Secy.-Treas.
EIN: 050495865

49424
National Foundation for Adolescent Drug Education
194 Waterman St.
Providence, RI 02906

Established in 1998.
Financial data (yr. ended 12/31/01): Grants paid, $0; assets, $1,265 (M); gifts received, $3,500; expenditures, $3,571; qualifying distributions, $0.
Officer: Robert Testa, Exec. Dir.
EIN: 050483764

49425
Lucy D. Nisbet Charitable Trust
c/o Fleet Private Clients Group
P.O. Box 6767
Providence, RI 02940-6767

Established in 2001 in VT.
Donor(s): Lucy D. Nisbet.‡
Financial data (yr. ended 01/31/02): Grants paid, $0; assets, $3,162,494 (M); gifts received, $1,753,218; expenditures, $100,055; qualifying distributions, $44,700.
Limitations: Applications not accepted.
Application information: Contributes only to pre-selected organizations.
Trustees: Ward Cleary, Fleet National Bank.
EIN: 066519058

49426
The Regina M. O'Hara Charitable Foundation, Inc.
c/o William F. Paquin
190 Commerce Dr.
Warwick, RI 02886

Established in 1997 in RI.

Donor(s): Regina M. O'Hara.
Financial data (yr. ended 12/31/01): Grants paid, $0; assets, $0 (M); expenditures, $49; qualifying distributions, $0.
Limitations: Applications not accepted.
Application information: Contributes only to pre-selected organizations.
Trustees: Martha M. Capaldi, Randolph K. Dittmar, Rev. Philip T. Morrissey, Regina M. O'Hara.
EIN: 050493657

49427
Lou K. Parker Memorial Fund
c/o Citizens Bank
870 Westminster St.
Providence, RI 02903
Application address: 875 Elm St., Manchester, NH 03101, tel.: (603) 634-7752
Contact: Bill Sirak, Trust Off., Citizens Bank

Financial data (yr. ended 12/31/01): Grants paid, $0; assets, $192,785 (M); expenditures, $3,757; qualifying distributions, $1,818.
Limitations: Giving limited to residents of Manchester and Bedford, NH, areas.
Application information: Application form required.
Trustee: Citizens Bank New Hampshire.
EIN: 026008023
Codes: GTI

49428
Edith L. and H. Danforth Ross Scholarship Fund
c/o Fleet Private Clients Group
P.O. Box 6767
Providence, RI 02940-6767

Financial data (yr. ended 01/31/01): Grants paid, $0; assets, $269,377 (M); gifts received, $18,867; expenditures, $2,536; qualifying distributions, $33,582; giving activities include $31,700 for loans to individuals.
Limitations: Giving limited to Sanford, ME.
Application information: Contact principals of high schools in Sanford, ME. Application form not required.
Trustee: Fleet National Bank.
EIN: 016075602

49429
The Robert & Virginia Siener Family Fund
375 Narrow Ln.
Greene, RI 02827
Application address: c/o Cooley, 50 Esten Ave., Pawtucket, RI 02860, tel.: (401) 721-6200
Contact: P. Robert Siener

Established in 2001 in RI.
Donor(s): Robert Siener, Virginia Siener.
Financial data (yr. ended 12/31/01): Grants paid, $0; assets, $100,000 (M); gifts received, $100,000; expenditures, $0; qualifying distributions, $0.
Trustees: Robert Siener, Virginia Siener.
EIN: 100003741

49430
Mabel Glidden Smith Trust f/b/o Williams School Loan Fund
c/o Fleet Private Clients Group
P.O. Box 6767
Providence, RI 02940-6767
Application address: c/o Marjorie Alexandre Davis, 777 Main St., Hartford, CT 06115

Financial data (yr. ended 12/31/01): Grants paid, $0; assets, $359,421 (M); gifts received, $14,563; expenditures, $6,736; qualifying distributions, $18,378; giving activities include $14,000 for loans to individuals.

Limitations: Giving limited to residents of CT.
Application information: Application form required.
Trustee: Fleet National Bank.
EIN: 066060068
Codes: GTI

49431
Sunningdale Foundation
c/o Peter Olsen
1500 Fleet Ctr.
Providence, RI 02903   (401) 274-2000

Donor(s): Dennis M. Glass.
Financial data (yr. ended 12/31/01): Grants paid, $0; assets, $0 (M); gifts received, $660; expenditures, $660; qualifying distributions, $0.
Limitations: Applications not accepted.
Application information: Contributes only to pre-selected organizations.
Officers and Directors:* Dennis E. Glass,* Pres. and Treas.; Tanya Trinkhaus Glass,* V.P. and Secy.; W. Bruce Glass.
EIN: 050476925

49432
David Lewis Toothaker Charitable Trust
c/o Fleet Private Clients Group
P.O. Box 6767
Providence, RI 02940-6767

Established in 2001 in ME.
Donor(s): David Lewis Toothaker Trust.
Financial data (yr. ended 03/31/02): Grants paid, $0; assets, $710,336 (M); gifts received, $616,841; expenditures, $47,740; qualifying distributions, $5,877.
Limitations: Applications not accepted.
Trustee: Fleet National Bank.
EIN: 016167681

49433
Howard A. and Lillian H. Walsh Trust
c/o Fleet Private Clients Group
P.O. Box 6767
Providence, RI 02940-6767

Established in 2000 in RI.
Financial data (yr. ended 12/31/01): Grants paid, $0; assets, $234,628 (M); expenditures, $5,645; qualifying distributions, $0.
Limitations: Applications not accepted. Giving primarily in MA and RI.
Application information: Contributes only to pre-selected organizations.
Trustee: Fleet National Bank.
EIN: 056107149

49434
Charles F. Williams Trust
c/o Fleet Private Clients Group
P.O. Box 6767
Providence, RI 02940-6767

Established in 1921 in CT.
Financial data (yr. ended 10/31/01): Grants paid, $0; assets, $312,947 (M); expenditures, $6,075; qualifying distributions, $2,640.
Limitations: Applications not accepted. Giving limited to New York, NY.
Application information: Recipients are chosen by the faculty of the Cathedral Choir School.
Trustee: Fleet National Bank.
EIN: 066138018

49435
Frederick H. Williams Trust f/b/o Williams Scholarship
c/o Fleet Private Clients Group
P.O. Box 6767
Providence, RI 02940-6767
Contact: Diane Stables, Trust Off., Fleet National Bank

Financial data (yr. ended 06/30/01): Grants paid, $0; assets, $138,102 (M); expenditures, $3,169; qualifying distributions, $1,590.
Limitations: Giving limited to residents of Granby, CT.
Application information: Applicant must include college expenses, employment records, educational background and amount of income available. Application form not required.
Trustee: Fleet National Bank.
EIN: 066023781

SOUTH CAROLINA

49436
Community Foundation of Greater Greenville, Inc.
27 Cleveland St., Ste. 101
Greenville, SC 29601 (864) 233-5925
FAX: (864) 242-9292; E-mail:
bmorris@cfgg.com; URL: http://www.cfgg.com
Contact: Robert W. Morris, Pres.

Established in 1956 in SC; incorporated in 1970.
Financial data (yr. ended 12/31/00): Grants paid, $9,796,938; assets, $29,067,903 (M); gifts received, $5,912,955; expenditures, $10,655,652.
Limitations: Giving limited to greater Greenville, SC.
Publications: Annual report, application guidelines, program policy statement, newsletter, informational brochure.
Application information: Application form required.
Officers and Directors:* David Massey,* Chair.; Susan Shi, Vice-Chair.; Robert W. Morris, Pres.; Ernest Lathem, Secy.; Charles Whitmire, Jr., Treas.; Tod Hyche, Legal Counsel; and 27 additional directors.
EIN: 576019318
Codes: CM, FD

49437
Drs. Bruce and Lee Foundation
181 E. Evans St.
BTC Box 022
Florence, SC 29506 (843) 664-2870
FAX: (843) 664-2815; E-mail:
blfound@bellsouth.net
Contact: L. Bradley Callicott, Exec. Dir.

Established in 1995 in SC; converted from the sale of the assets of Carolinas Hospital System to Quorum, Inc.
Financial data (yr. ended 12/31/01): Grants paid, $5,114,697; assets, $145,012,031 (M); gifts received, $350; expenditures, $14,299,623; qualifying distributions, $5,433,445.
Limitations: Giving primarily in the Florence, SC, area.
Publications: Annual report (including application guidelines), grants list, occasional report, application guidelines.
Application information: Application form required.
Officer and Trustees:* L. Bradley Callicott,* Exec. Dir.; Gordon Baker, Jr., John L. Bruce, Mark Buyck, Jr., C. Edward Floyd, Thomas C. Griffin, Frank B. Lee, Sr., Haigh Porter, Henry Swink, John M. Thomason, and 3 additional trustees.
EIN: 570902483
Codes: FD

49438
The Spartanburg County Foundation
320 E. Main St., Ste. 3
Spartanburg, SC 29302-1943 (864) 582-0138
FAX: (864) 573-5378; E-mail: info@spcf.org;
URL: http://www.spcf.org
Contact: John H. Dargan, Pres.

Incorporated in 1943 in SC.
Financial data (yr. ended 12/31/01): Grants paid, $4,918,274; assets, $61,266,233 (M); gifts received, $8,887,527; expenditures, $7,423,903.
Limitations: Giving from unrestricted funds limited to the Spartanburg County, SC, area.
Publications: Annual report (including application guidelines), informational brochure, newsletter, biennial report, application guidelines.
Application information: Application form not required.
Officers: Robert H. Chapman, Chair.; John H. Dargan, Pres.; John Harrill, Jr., Secy.; Betty Montgomery, Treas.
Trustees: Sally D. Foster, Donald C. Johnston, Edward P. Perrin, Robert L. Wynn III.
EIN: 570351398
Codes: CM, FD

49439
Inman-Riverdale Foundation
P.O. Box 207
Inman, SC 29349 (864) 472-2121

Incorporated in 1946 in SC.
Donor(s): Inman Mills.
Financial data (yr. ended 11/30/01): Grants paid, $4,906,248; assets, $7,261,070 (M); expenditures, $5,088,506; qualifying distributions, $1,032,280.
Limitations: Giving primarily in Inman and Enoree, SC.
Application information: Application form not required.
Officers and Trustees:* Robert H. Chapman III,* Chair.; Patricia H. Robbins, Secy.; John F. Renfro, Jr.,* Treas.; Norman H. Chapman, James C. Pace, Jr.
EIN: 576019736
Codes: CS, FD, CD, GTI

49440
The Community Foundation Serving Coastal South Carolina
(Formerly Trident Community Foundation)
90 Mary St.
Charleston, SC 29403-6230 (843) 723-3635
FAX: (843) 577-3671; E-mail: info@tcfgives.org;
URL: http://www.tcfgives.org
Contact: Madeleine McGee, Pres.

Incorporated in 1974 in SC.
Financial data (yr. ended 06/30/02): Grants paid, $3,947,445; assets, $88,134,629 (M); gifts received, $7,720,092; expenditures, $5,443,621; giving activities include $143,816 for programs.
Limitations: Giving primarily in Beaufort, Berkeley, Charleston, Colleton, Dorchester, Georgetown, Hampton and Jasper counties, SC.
Publications: Biennial report, newsletter, application guidelines, financial statement, grants list, informational brochure, informational brochure (including application guidelines), occasional report.
Application information: Application form required.
Officers and Directors:* Linda Plunkett,* Chair.; Henry Blackford III, Vice-Chair.; Madeleine McGee, Pres.; Richard Hendry, V.P., Progs.; Brian Hussain, V.P., Finance; George Miller,* Secy.-Treas.; and 22 additional directors.
EIN: 237390313
Codes: CM, FD, GTI

49441
Mary Black Foundation, Inc.
945 E. Main St.
Spartanburg, SC 29302 (864) 573-9500
FAX: (864) 573-5805; E-mail:
info@maryblackfoundation.org; URL: http://www.maryblackfoundation.org
Contact: Philip B. Belcher, Pres.

Established in 1986 in SC; converted from the proceeds from the sale of Mary Black Memorial Hospital in 1996.
Financial data (yr. ended 06/30/02): Grants paid, $3,440,794; assets, $63,409,001 (L); gifts received, $427,183; expenditures, $3,372,675; qualifying distributions, $3,033,400.
Limitations: Giving primarily in Spartanburg County, SC.
Publications: Annual report, informational brochure, application guidelines, newsletter.
Application information: Application form required.
Officers and Trustees:* Sally D. Foster,* Chair.; H. Walter Barre,* Vice Chair.; Philip Belcher,* Pres.; J. Allen Mast, Jr.,* V.P., Progs.; Gaston C. Harris, Jr.,* Treas.; Sheila Breitweiser, Grady S. Brooks, Jr., M.D., R. Ray Dennis, Susan K. Dent, C. Tyrone Gilmore, Sr., M.D., Marianna B. Habisreutinger, June M. Uhler, Marvin C. Woodson, Ph.D.
EIN: 570843135
Codes: FD

49442
Norman J. Arnold Foundation
(Formerly Ben Arnold Memorial Foundation)
P.O. Box 211787
Columbia, SC 29221

Financial data (yr. ended 12/31/00): Grants paid, $2,959,020; assets, $5,141,230 (M); expenditures, $3,034,271; qualifying distributions, $2,962,615.
Limitations: Applications not accepted. Giving primarily in NY and SC.
Application information: Contributes only to pre-selected organizations.
Manager: Norman J. Arnold.
Trustee: John S. Rainey.
EIN: 576029371
Codes: FD

49443
Central Carolina Community Foundation
P.O. Box 11222
Columbia, SC 29211-1222 (803) 254-5601
FAX: (803) 799-6663; E-mail: cccf@cccfsc.org;
URL: http://www.cccfsc.org
Contact: J. Mac Bennett, Exec. Dir.

Incorporated in 1984 in SC.
Financial data (yr. ended 06/30/01): Grants paid, $2,898,906; assets, $39,477,375 (M); gifts received, $4,801,366; expenditures, $3,534,594.
Limitations: Giving limited to Calhoun, Clarendon, Fairfield, Kershaw, Lee, Lexington, Newberry, Orangeburg, Richland, Saluda, and Sumter counties, SC.
Publications: Annual report, informational brochure, application guidelines, newsletter.
Application information: Application form required.
Officers and Directors:* Charles T. Cole, Jr.,* Pres.; Samuel J. Tenenbaum,* V.P.; Peter M. Bristow,* Secy.-Treas.; J. Mac Bennett, Exec. Dir.; and 30 additional directors.
EIN: 570793960
Codes: CM, FD

49444
The Abney Foundation
100 Vine St.
Anderson, SC 29621 (864) 964-9201
FAX: (864) 964-9201; E-mail:
info@abneyfoundation.org; URL: http://www.abneyfoundation.org
Contact: J.R. Fulp, Jr., Chair.

Trust established in 1957 in SC.
Donor(s): John S. Abney,‡ Susie M. Abney.‡
Financial data (yr. ended 12/31/01): Grants paid, $2,474,550; assets, $42,177,438 (M); expenditures, $2,907,658; qualifying distributions, $2,567,985.

49444—SOUTH CAROLINA

Limitations: Giving primarily in SC, with emphasis on the Anderson area.
Publications: Application guidelines.
Application information: Application form not required.
Officers and Trustees:* J.R. Fulp, Jr.,* Chair.; William N. Bobo,* Secy.; D. Wellsman Johnson,* Treas.; Carl T. Edwards, Exec. Dir.; Lebrena F. Campbell, Carlette F. Holmes, Sally A. Rose.
EIN: 576019445
Codes: FD

49445
The Self Family Foundation
(Formerly The Self Foundation)
P.O. Drawer 1017
Greenwood, SC 29648 (864) 941-4011
FAX: (864) 941-4091; E-mail: SelfFound@greenwood.net, fwideman@greenwood.net, mamienic@greenwood.net; URL: http://www.selffoundation.org
Contact: Frank J. Wideman III, Pres.

Incorporated in 1942 in SC.
Donor(s): James C. Self.‡
Financial data (yr. ended 12/31/00): Grants paid, $2,049,578; assets, $53,204,629 (M); expenditures, $2,900,904; qualifying distributions, $2,393,705.
Limitations: Giving limited to SC, with primary emphasis on Greenwood.
Publications: Annual report (including application guidelines).
Application information: Application form not required.
Officers and Trustees:* Virginia S. Brennan,* Chair.; W.M. Self,* Vice-Chair.; Frank J. Wideman III, Pres.; Sally E. Self, M.D.,* Secy.; William B. Allin, Treas.; Bal Ballentine, Sid Johnston, J.C. Self III.
EIN: 570400594
Codes: FD

49446
The Fullerton Foundation, Inc.
515 W. Buford St.
Gaffney, SC 29341
Application address: P.O. Box 2208, Gaffney, SC 29342-2208; E-mail: cjbonner@fullertonfoundation.org
Contact: Walter E. Cavell, Exec. Dir.

Established in 1954 in NY.
Donor(s): Alma H. Fullerton.‡
Financial data (yr. ended 11/30/01): Grants paid, $2,005,000; assets, $43,741,795 (M); expenditures, $2,655,774; qualifying distributions, $2,218,039.
Limitations: Giving primarily in NC and SC.
Publications: Application guidelines.
Officers and Directors:* Wylie L. Hamrick,* Chair.; Charles F. Hamrick II,* Vice-Chair.; Lyman W. Hamrick,* Secy.; W. Carlisle Hamrick,* Treas.; Walter E. Cavell, Exec. Dir.; Helen T. Baden, Catherine H. Beattie, Jean H. Haas, A. Wardlaw Hamrick, Charles F. Hamrick, John M. Hamrick, Volina V. Lyons, Frances R. Ross, Volina C. Valentine, Dir. Emeritus.
EIN: 570847444
Codes: FD

49447
Sonoco Foundation
1 N. 2nd St., M.S. A09
Hartsville, SC 29550
Contact: Joyce Beasley

Established in 1983 in SC.
Donor(s): Sonoco Products Co.
Financial data (yr. ended 12/31/00): Grants paid, $1,844,154; assets, $0 (M); gifts received, $1,835,000; expenditures, $1,844,154; qualifying distributions, $1,844,154.
Limitations: Giving primarily in areas of company operations.
Publications: Application guidelines.
Application information: Application form not required.
Trustees: C.W. Coker, C.J. Hupfer.
EIN: 570752950
Codes: CS, FD, CD

49448
Liberty Corporation Foundation
P.O. Box 502
Greenville, SC 29602 (864) 241-5496
Contact: Sophia G. Vergas, Secy.

Established in 1965 in SC.
Donor(s): The Liberty Corp.
Financial data (yr. ended 08/31/01): Grants paid, $1,725,880; assets, $895,706 (M); gifts received, $2,500,000; expenditures, $1,731,277; qualifying distributions, $1,727,121.
Limitations: Giving primarily in SC.
Application information: Application form not required.
Officers and Directors:* W. Hayne Hipp,* Chair. and Pres.; Mary Anne Bunton, V.P.; Sophia G. Vergas, Secy.; Mark D. Wesson, Treas.; Martha G. Williams.
EIN: 570468195
Codes: CS, FD, CD

49449
Community Foundation of the Lowcountry
(Formerly Hilton Head Island Foundation, Inc.)
4 Northridge Dr., Ste. A
P.O. Box 23019
Hilton Head Island, SC 29925-3019
(843) 681-9100
FAX: (843) 681-9101; E-mail: foundation@cf-lowcountry.org; URL: http://www.cf-lowcountry.org
Contact: Dianne K. Garnett, C.E.O.

Established in 1983 in SC; converted to a community foundation in 1994 from the proceeds of the sale of Hilton Head Hospital to AMI.
Financial data (yr. ended 06/30/02): Grants paid, $1,674,956; assets, $29,227,554 (L); gifts received, $1,102,316; expenditures, $2,457,339.
Limitations: Giving limited to Beauford, Colleton, Hampton and Jasper counties, SC.
Publications: Annual report, newsletter, informational brochure, grants list (including application guidelines).
Application information: Application form required.
Officers and Trustees:* Fran H. Marscher,* Chair.; David W. Ames,* Vice-Chair.; Dianne K. Garnett, C.E.O., Pres. and Secy.; Randy K. Dolyniuk,* Treas.; Kaye Black, Charlie H. Brown, Clifford Bush III, Emory Campbell, James L. Elder, Hector Esquivel, Susan M. Ketchum, Bernard Moscovitz, Dorothy G. Perkins, Julius S. Scott, Jr., Ph.D., G. Thomas Upshaw.
EIN: 570756987
Codes: CM, FD

49450
John I. Smith Charities, Inc.
c/o Bank of America, Trust Dept.
P.O. Box 608
Greenville, SC 29608 (864) 271-5930
Contact: Bill Bridges

Established in 1985 in SC.
Donor(s): John I. Smith.‡
Financial data (yr. ended 07/31/00): Grants paid, $1,655,500; assets, $28,462,151 (M); expenditures, $1,761,484; qualifying distributions, $1,625,277.
Limitations: Giving primarily in SC.
Application information: Application form not required.
Officers: Wilbur Y. Bridges, Pres. and Secy.; W. Thomas Smith, V.P. and Secy.
Director: Jefferson V. Smith III.
Trustee: Bank of America.
EIN: 570806327
Codes: FD

49451
Springs Foundation, Inc.
1826 Second Baxter Crossing
Fort Mill, SC 29708 (803) 548-2002
FAX: (803) 548-1797; Additional address: P.O. Box 460, Lancaster, SC 29721, tel.: (803) 286-2197, FAX: (803) 416-4626
Contact: H.W. Close, Jr., Pres.

Incorporated in 1942 in DE.
Donor(s): Elliott W. Springs,‡ Anne Springs Close, Frances Ley Springs.‡
Financial data (yr. ended 12/31/01): Grants paid, $1,472,090; assets, $35,488,538 (M); expenditures, $2,089,350; qualifying distributions, $1,812,619.
Limitations: Giving limited to Lancaster County and the townships of Fort Mill and Chester, SC.
Publications: Annual report, application guidelines, annual report (including application guidelines).
Application information: Application form required.
Officers and Directors:* Anne Springs Close,* Chair.; H.W. Close, Jr.,* Pres.; William G. Taylor,* Secy.-Treas.; Crandall Close Bowles, James Bradley, Charles A. Bundy, Derick S. Close, Elliott Springs Close, Frances A. Close, Katherine Anne Close, Leroy Springs Close, Pat Close, Dehler Hart, Robert L. Holcombe, Jr.
EIN: 570426344
Codes: FD, GTI

49452
Close Foundation, Inc.
1826 2nd Baxter Crossing
Fort Mill, SC 29708 (803) 548-2002
FAX: (803) 548-1797; Additional address: P.O. Box 460, Lancaster, SC 29721, tel.: (803) 286-2197, FAX: (803) 416-4626
Contact: H.W. Close, Pres.

Incorporated in 1968 in SC as Frances Ley Springs Foundation, Inc.; renamed Close Foundation in 1985.
Donor(s): Anne Springs Close, Frances Ley Springs,‡ Eliotte White Springs,‡ and members of the Springs and Close families.
Financial data (yr. ended 12/31/01): Grants paid, $1,129,274; assets, $14,286,512 (M); gifts received, $1,900; expenditures, $1,304,674; qualifying distributions, $1,231,364.
Limitations: Giving primarily in Lancaster County, Chester Township of Chester County, and Fort Mill Township, SC.
Publications: Annual report (including application guidelines), application guidelines.
Application information: Application form required.
Officers and Directors:* Anne Springs Close,* Chair.; H.W. Close,* Pres.; William G. Taylor,* Secy.-Treas.; Crandall Close Bowles, James Bradley, Charles A. Bundy, Derick S. Close, Elliott Springs Close, Frances A. Close, Katherine Anne Close, Leroy Springs Close, Pat Close, Dehler Hart, Robert L. Holcombe, Jr.

EIN: 237013986
Codes: FD

49453
The Roe Foundation
301 N. Main St., Ste. 1735
Greenville, SC 29601 (864) 242-5007
FAX: (864) 242-5014; E-mail: roefdn@aol.com
Contact: Shirley W. Roe, Chair.

Incorporated in 1968 in SC.
Donor(s): Thomas A. Roe.‡
Financial data (yr. ended 12/31/01): Grants paid, $1,017,093; assets, $30,536,735 (M); gifts received, $5,640,000; expenditures, $1,216,526; qualifying distributions, $1,062,192.
Limitations: Giving on an international basis.
Publications: Program policy statement, application guidelines.
Application information: Application form not required.
Officers and Trustees:* Shirley W. Roe,* Chair. and Treas.; Edwin J. Feulner, Jr.,* Vice-Chair.; Carl O. Helstrom, Byron S. Lamm.
EIN: 237011541
Codes: FD

49454
The Jimmy and Marsha Gibbs Foundation
P.O. Box 1727
Spartanburg, SC 29304

Established in 1989 in SC.
Donor(s): Jimmy I. Gibbs, Marsha H. Gibbs, Gibbs International, Inc.
Financial data (yr. ended 12/31/01): Grants paid, $999,487; assets, $556,732 (M); gifts received, $305,000; expenditures, $1,001,121; qualifying distributions, $999,487.
Limitations: Applications not accepted. Giving primarily in Spartanburg, SC.
Application information: Contributes only to pre-selected organizations.
Director: Marsha H. Gibbs.
EIN: 570892089
Codes: FD

49455
Rose & Walter Montgomery Foundation
P.O. Box 5565
Spartanburg, SC 29304 (864) 585-9213
Application address: P.O. Box 1658, Spartanburg, SC 29304, tel.: (864) 574-0211
Contact: Walter S. Montgomery, Jr., Tr.

Donor(s): Walter S. Montgomery,‡ Rose C. Montgomery Trust A.
Financial data (yr. ended 12/31/00): Grants paid, $977,500; assets, $18,600,037 (M); expenditures, $1,450,768; qualifying distributions, $951,504.
Limitations: Giving primarily in Spartanburg, SC, and Memphis, TN.
Trustees: Rose M. Johnston, Walter S. Montgomery, Jr.
EIN: 570986535
Codes: FD

49456
The Byerly Foundation
P.O. Drawer 1925
Hartsville, SC 29551-1925 (843) 383-2400
FAX: (843) 383-0661; URL: http://www.byerlyfoundation.org
Contact: Richard A. Puffer, Exec. Dir.

Established in 1995 in SC; converted from the sale of local hospital.
Financial data (yr. ended 09/30/01): Grants paid, $896,671; assets, $13,133,867 (M); gifts received, $121,946; expenditures, $1,012,984; qualifying distributions, $944,963.
Limitations: Giving primarily in Hartsville, SC.
Publications: Annual report, informational brochure (including application guidelines).
Application information: Application form not required.
Officers and Trustees:* Harris E. DeLoach, Jr.,* Pres.; Howard W. Tucker, Jr.,* Secy.; Charles J. Hupfer,* Treas.; Richard A. Puffer, Exec. Dir.; Gloria Bell, Lee S. Hicks, Franklin Hines, Edgar H. Lawton, Frank J. Popelars, Leroy Robinson, Paula Terry.
EIN: 570324909
Codes: FD

49457
Wardle Family Foundation
710 Bluefish Rd.
Fripp Island, SC 29920

Established in 1987 in PA.
Donor(s): Robert V. Wardle.
Financial data (yr. ended 12/31/00): Grants paid, $863,100; assets, $17,804,507 (M); expenditures, $885,375; qualifying distributions, $852,885.
Limitations: Applications not accepted. Giving on a national basis.
Application information: Contributes only to pre-selected organizations.
Trustees: Megan K. Neary, Corinne G. Wardle, Douglas G. Wardle, Robert B. Wardle, William G. Wardle.
EIN: 256290322
Codes: FD

49458
The Arkwright Foundation
P.O. Box 1086
Spartanburg, SC 29304 (864) 585-9213
Contact: Jack Hawkins, Secy.-Treas.

Incorporated in 1945 in SC.
Donor(s): members of the M.L. Cates family, and members of the W.S. Montgomery family.
Financial data (yr. ended 12/31/01): Grants paid, $842,945; assets, $13,359,766 (M); expenditures, $932,366; qualifying distributions, $840,352.
Limitations: Giving primarily in SC.
Officers: M.L. Cates, Sr., Chair.; Walter S. Montgomery, Jr., Vice-Chair.; Jack Hawkins, Secy.-Treas.
EIN: 576000066
Codes: FD

49459
Post and Courier Foundation
134 Columbus St.
Charleston, SC 29403-4800
Contact: J. Douglas Donehue, Admin.

Incorporated in 1951 in SC.
Donor(s): Evening Post Publishing Co.
Financial data (yr. ended 12/31/00): Grants paid, $770,644; assets, $8,338,992 (M); gifts received, $534,825; expenditures, $807,685; qualifying distributions, $770,614.
Limitations: Giving primarily in Charleston, SC.
Application information: Application form not required.
Officers: Peter Manigault, Pres.; Ivan V. Anderson, Jr., Exec. V.P.; Pierre Manigault, V.P.; James W. Martin, Treas.; J. Douglas Donehue, Admin.
EIN: 576020356
Codes: CS, FD, CD

49460
Phifer/Johnson Foundation
961 E. Main St.
Spartanburg, SC 29302

Established in 1993 in SC.
Financial data (yr. ended 12/31/01): Grants paid, $719,275; assets, $9,606,081 (M); expenditures, $755,919; qualifying distributions, $719,275.
Limitations: Applications not accepted. Giving on a national basis, primarily in FL, NC, and SC.
Application information: Contributes only to pre-selected organizations.
Directors: George Dean Johnson, Jr., Stewart H. Johnson, Susan P. Johnson.
EIN: 576153679
Codes: FD

49461
Robert S. Campbell Foundation
101 N. Main St.
Greenville, SC 29601

Established in 1995 in SC.
Financial data (yr. ended 12/31/01): Grants paid, $706,667; assets, $13,848,243 (M); expenditures, $998,684; qualifying distributions, $751,902.
Limitations: Applications not accepted. Giving primarily in SC, some funding also in NC.
Application information: Contributes only to pre-selected organizations.
Trustee: William W. Brown.
EIN: 571031564
Codes: FD

49462
Thomas G. Small Foundation
c/o Robert S. Small
555 N. Pleasantburg Dr., Park Central Ste. 309
Greenville, SC 29607-2194

Donor(s): Robert S. Small.
Financial data (yr. ended 12/31/01): Grants paid, $654,339; assets, $1,031,203 (M); expenditures, $670,305; qualifying distributions, $654,228.
Limitations: Applications not accepted. Giving primarily in SC.
Application information: Contributes only to pre-selected organizations.
Trustee: Robert S. Small.
EIN: 576019438
Codes: FD

49463
P. S. Bailey and Ouida C. Bailey Foundation
P.O. Box 494
Clinton, SC 29325

Donor(s): Emily Bailey.
Financial data (yr. ended 12/31/01): Grants paid, $632,958; assets, $14,407,957 (M); gifts received, $30,125; expenditures, $729,355; qualifying distributions, $1,017,826.
Limitations: Applications not accepted. Giving primarily in SC.
Application information: Unsolicited requests for funds not accepted.
Officers and Trustees:* Emily F. Bailey,* Chair.; Ruth F. Nelson,* Secy.; Bishop Alex D. Dixon, Rev. Charles H. Murphy.
EIN: 570813063
Codes: FD

49464
AVX/Kyocera Foundation
801 17th Ave. S., Box 2A
Myrtle Beach, SC 29577

Established in 1996 in SC.
Financial data (yr. ended 03/31/02): Grants paid, $632,390; assets, $6,205,061 (M); gifts received, $4,206,300; expenditures, $643,256; qualifying distributions, $643,197.
Limitations: Applications not accepted. Giving in the U.S., with strong emphasis on SC; giving internationally, primarily in El Salvador, Israel, and Japan.

49464—SOUTH CAROLINA

Application information: Contributes only to pre-selected organizations.
Officers: Benedict P. Rosen, Pres.; C. Marshall Jackson, V.P.; Raymond Spitz, Treas.
EIN: 571057412
Codes: FD

49465
J. M. Smith Foundation
c/o James C. Wilson, Jr.
P.O. Box 1779
Spartanburg, SC 29304-1779

Established in 1996 SC.
Donor(s): JM Smith Corp.
Financial data (yr. ended 02/28/01): Grants paid, $566,054; assets, $280,109 (M); gifts received, $567,670; expenditures, $573,312; qualifying distributions, $565,931.
Limitations: Applications not accepted. Giving primarily in SC.
Application information: Contributes only to pre-selected organizations.
Officers: Kenneth R. Couch, Pres.; A.W. Smith, Secy.; James C. Wilson, Jr., Treas.
Directors: Tammy Devine, Henry D. Smith, Russ Weber.
EIN: 571046595
Codes: CS, FD

49466
Daniel-Mickel Foundation
(Formerly The Daniel Foundation of South Carolina)
P.O. Box 9278
Greenville, SC 29604-9278
Contact: Tamara Scarbrough, Asst. to Secy.

Established in 1978 in SC as partial successor to The Daniel Foundation.
Donor(s): Daniel International Corp., Charles E. Daniel.‡
Financial data (yr. ended 12/31/01): Grants paid, $522,503; assets, $16,166,389 (M); expenditures, $624,928; qualifying distributions, $536,621.
Limitations: Applications not accepted. Giving primarily in SC.
Application information: Contributes only to pre-selected organizations.
Officers and Trustees:* Minor M. Shaw,* Chair.; Minor H. Mickel, Pres.; Buck A. Mickel, V.P.; Charles Mickel, V.P.; Ken Lewis,* Secy.-Treas.
EIN: 570673409
Codes: FD

49467
John T. Stevens Foundation
P.O. Box 158
Kershaw, SC 29067 (803) 475-3655
Contact: Steve G. Williams, Sr., Pres.

Established in 1948 in SC.
Donor(s): John T. Stevens.‡
Financial data (yr. ended 05/31/01): Grants paid, $509,047; assets, $0 (M); expenditures, $439,611; qualifying distributions, $495,697.
Limitations: Giving primarily in Kershaw and Lancaster County, SC.
Application information: Application form not required.
Officers: Steve G. Williams, Sr., Pres.; Douglas Williams, V.P.; Mattie Seegars, Secy.; Steve Williams, Jr., Treas.
Trustees: Joey Munn, Lanny M. Williams.
EIN: 576005554
Codes: FD

49468
The Bailey Foundation
P.O. Box 494
Clinton, SC 29325 (864) 938-2632
FAX: (864) 938-2669
Contact: Thomas E. Sebrell, IV, Admin.

Trust established in 1951 in SC.
Donor(s): M.S. Bailey & Son, Bankers, Clinton Investment Co.
Financial data (yr. ended 08/31/01): Grants paid, $506,555; assets, $5,781,554 (M); gifts received, $54,080; expenditures, $539,946; qualifying distributions, $503,608.
Limitations: Giving limited to Laurens County, SC.
Publications: Annual report, informational brochure (including application guidelines).
Application information: Applications for students available from guidance counselors at Clinton High School and Laurens High School. Application form not required.
Trustee: Carolina First Bank.
Advisory Committee: George H. Cornelson, Chair.; C. Bailey Dixon, Walter S. Montgomery, Sr., Mary V. Suitt, Toccoa W. Switzer, James Von Hollen.
Grants Advisory Committee: Joseph O. Nixon, Chair.; Wanda B. Isaac, Sam Moore, Donny Ross, Donny Wilder.
EIN: 576018387
Codes: FD, GTI

49469
Youths' Friends Association, Inc.
P.O. Box 5387
Hilton Head Island, SC 29938 (843) 671-5060
Contact: Walter J. Graver, Secy.-Treas.

Incorporated in 1950 in NY.
Donor(s): Johan J. Smit,‡ Mrs. Johan J. Smit.‡
Financial data (yr. ended 12/31/01): Grants paid, $498,500; assets, $11,414,800 (M); expenditures, $631,042; qualifying distributions, $556,441.
Limitations: Giving on a national basis.
Publications: Financial statement.
Application information: Application form not required.
Officers and Directors:* Sheila Smit,* Pres.; Stephen C. Smit,* V.P.; Walter J. Graver,* Secy.-Treas.; Barbara Graver, Evan Kirchen, Helen Kirchen, Robert Kirchen, Judith Rist, Lisa Smit, Peta Smit.
EIN: 136097828
Codes: FD

49470
Lipscomb Family Foundation
P.O. Box 61159
Columbia, SC 29260 (803) 256-0609
FAX: (803) 256-6039; *E-mail:* iff@bellsouth.net
Contact: Marshall Foster, Exec. Dir.

Established in 1995 in SC.
Financial data (yr. ended 12/31/01): Grants paid, $481,989; assets, $16,060,714 (M); gifts received, $276,116; expenditures, $690,771; qualifying distributions, $521,204.
Limitations: Giving primarily in the midlands of SC.
Application information: Application form required.
Officers and Trustees:* Guy F. Lipscomb, Jr.,* Pres.; Margaret F. Lipscomb,* V.P.; Marshall L. Foster,* Secy.; Georgia L. Cheek, George C. Fant, Louise L. Howell, Elizabeth L. Tracy.
EIN: 581368915
Codes: FD

49471
The Jerry and Anita Zucker Family Foundation, Inc.
4838 Jenkins Ave.
North Charleston, SC 29406

Established in 1996.
Donor(s): Jerry Zucker.
Financial data (yr. ended 12/31/99): Grants paid, $464,032; assets, $11,103,765 (M); expenditures, $498,698; qualifying distributions, $452,277.
Limitations: Applications not accepted. Giving primarily in SC.
Application information: Contributes only to pre-selected organizations.
Officers: Jerry Zucker, Pres. and Treas.; Jonathan M. Zucker, V.P.; Anita G. Zucker, Secy.
EIN: 571061131
Codes: FD

49472
Security's Lending Hand Foundation
204 E. Main St.
Spartanburg, SC 29306

Established in 1994 in SC.
Donor(s): Security Finance Corp.
Financial data (yr. ended 12/31/00): Grants paid, $440,667; assets, $1,490 (M); gifts received, $124,461; expenditures, $445,478; qualifying distributions, $440,670.
Limitations: Applications not accepted. Giving on a national basis.
Application information: Contributes only to pre-selected organizations.
Officers: Susan A. Bridges, Chair; Clarence H. Edwards, Vice-Chair; A.R. Biggs, C.O.O.; A.G. Williams, Secy.-Treas.
EIN: 571012986
Codes: CS, FD, CD

49473
Callie & John Rainey Foundation
402nd Blvd.
Anderson, SC 29621
Contact: John S. Rainey, Tr.

Established in 1995 in SC.
Financial data (yr. ended 12/31/01): Grants paid, $437,425; assets, $5,487,983 (M); gifts received, $348; expenditures, $582,741; qualifying distributions, $473,494.
Limitations: Giving primarily in SC.
Application information: Application form not required.
Trustees: Mary R. Belser, Nancy R. Crowley, John S. Rainey, Robert M. Rainey.
EIN: 570970656
Codes: FD

49474
Gregg-Graniteville Foundation, Inc.
P.O. Box 418
Graniteville, SC 29829 (803) 663-7552
Contact: Patricia H. Knight, Admin.

Established in 1941 in SC.
Financial data (yr. ended 12/31/01): Grants paid, $390,700; assets, $19,590,273 (M); expenditures, $1,066,397; qualifying distributions, $390,700; giving activities include $58,198 for programs.
Limitations: Giving primarily in Richmond County, GA, and Aiken County, SC.
Publications: Annual report.
Application information: 1 grant application per organization per calendar year accepted. Application form required.
Officers and Directors:* Robert M. Bell,* Pres.; John W. Cunningham,* V.P.; J. Paul Reeves,* V.P.; Patricia H. Knight,* Secy.-Treas. and Admin.; Ira E.

Coward III, Jerry R. Johnson, Joan F. Phibbs, James A. Randall, Robert P. Timmerman.
EIN: 570314400
Codes: FD, GTI

49475
The Fat Cat Foundation
c/o Sellars & Cole, LLC
P.O. Box 11878
Columbia, SC 29211-1878

Established in 1998 in SC.
Donor(s): Harriott H. Faucette.
Financial data (yr. ended 12/31/00): Grants paid, $390,000; assets, $409,924 (M); expenditures, $400,769; qualifying distributions, $388,291.
Limitations: Applications not accepted. Giving primarily in Columbia, SC.
Application information: Contributes only to pre-selected organizations.
Trustees: Mary R. Cantey, Harriott H. Faucette, Martha M. Faucette.
EIN: 582337838
Codes: FD

49476
J. E. Sirrine Textile Foundation, Inc.
P.O. Box 929
Greer, SC 29652
Contact: The Trustees

Financial data (yr. ended 06/30/01): Grants paid, $362,887; assets, $6,825,942 (M); expenditures, $429,285; qualifying distributions, $363,931.
Limitations: Giving limited to Clemson, SC.
Application information: Application form not required.
Trustees: Jack W. Burnett III, Frederick B. Dent, Jr., Lester A. Hudson, Joseph L. Jennings, Jr., George E. Stone, and 16 additional trustees.
EIN: 576025551
Codes: FD

49477
Rowley Foundation, Inc.
P.O. Box 5070
Hilton Head Island, SC 29938
Contact: Brock C. Rowley, Dir.; or Kathleen H. Rowley, Dir.

Established in 1993 in SC.
Donor(s): Brock C. Rowley, Kathleen H. Rowley.
Financial data (yr. ended 12/31/00): Grants paid, $361,374; assets, $1,225,893 (M); gifts received, $2,780; expenditures, $377,784; qualifying distributions, $361,374.
Limitations: Giving primarily in SC, with emphasis on Hilton Head.
Application information: Application form not required.
Directors: Brock C. Rowley, Kathleen H. Rowley.
EIN: 570964774
Codes: FD

49478
The W. Hayne Hipp Foundation
P.O. Box 789
Greenville, SC 29602-0789

Established in 1987 in SC.
Donor(s): W. Hayne Hipp.
Financial data (yr. ended 12/31/00): Grants paid, $357,786; assets, $13,047,879 (M); expenditures, $370,084; qualifying distributions, $361,274.
Limitations: Applications not accepted. Giving limited to SC and VA.
Application information: Contributes only to pre-selected organizations.
Officers: W. Hayne Hipp, Pres.; Martha Williams, Secy.
EIN: 570861526

Codes: FD

49479
The Mungo Foundation
441 Western Ln.
Irmo, SC 29063
Contact: Michael J. Mungo, Tr.

Established in 1987 in SC.
Donor(s): Michael J. Mungo, M. Stewart Mungo.
Financial data (yr. ended 07/31/01): Grants paid, $355,573; assets, $353,086 (M); gifts received, $339,119; expenditures, $358,358; qualifying distributions, $358,358.
Limitations: Giving limited to central SC.
Trustees: Bryan Graham, Michael J. Mungo.
EIN: 570858553
Codes: FD

49480
Hopewell Foundation, Inc.
P.O. Box 470
Rock Hill, SC 29731-6470

Established in 1985 in SC.
Financial data (yr. ended 02/28/02): Grants paid, $352,000; assets, $6,446,791 (M); expenditures, $353,418; qualifying distributions, $347,772.
Limitations: Applications not accepted. Giving primarily in Rock Hill, SC.
Application information: Contributes only to pre-selected organizations.
Officers and Directors:* Frank S. Barnes, Jr.,* Pres.; E.L. Barnes,* Secy.-Treas.; John M. Barnes, L.A. Barnes, Jr., Robert L. Helmly.
EIN: 570792719
Codes: FD

49481
Foothills Community Foundation
P.O. Box 1228
Anderson, SC 29622 (864) 222-9096

Established in 1999 in SC.
Financial data (yr. ended 12/31/01): Grants paid, $330,848; assets, $5,386,639 (M); gifts received, $225,296; expenditures, $470,137.
Limitations: Giving primarily in SC.
Publications: Occasional report.
Officers and Directors:* Cordes Seabrook, Jr.,* Chair.; Tom J. Ervin,* Pres.; Lamar Bailes, James T. Boseman, Marie Collins, Charles Dalton, Fred Foster, Sue Greene, Lee Logan, John A. Miller, Jr., Earle E. Morris, and 7 additional directors.
EIN: 582453349
Codes: CM, FD

49482
Greenleaf Foundation, Inc.
200 Winding Way
Spartanburg, SC 29306-6826 (864) 583-0831
Contact: Kathleen C. Johnson

Established in 1993 in SC.
Donor(s): Greenleaf, Inc.
Financial data (yr. ended 12/31/01): Grants paid, $328,545; assets, $7,792,512 (M); expenditures, $361,467; qualifying distributions, $328,545.
Limitations: Applications not accepted. Giving primarily in FL and SC.
Application information: Unsolicited requests for grants not accepted.
Officers: Robert E. Caldwell, Chair.; Sylvia R. Caldwell, Vice-Chair.
Director: Hugh H. Brantley.
EIN: 570989702
Codes: FD

49483
Campbell Young Leaders, Inc.
101 N. Main St.
Greenville, SC 29601

Established in 1999 in SC.
Donor(s): William W. Brown.
Financial data (yr. ended 12/31/01): Grants paid, $312,648; assets, $865 (M); gifts received, $380,000; expenditures, $384,312; qualifying distributions, $383,732.
Limitations: Applications not accepted. Giving primarily in NC and SC.
Application information: Contributes only to pre-selected organizations.
Trustee: William W. Brown.
EIN: 223670039
Codes: FD

49484
Carolina First Foundation
151 Corley Mill Rd.
Lexington, SC 29072
Contact: Bruce Thomas, Exec. Dir.

Established in 1999 in SC.
Donor(s): Carolina First Bank.
Financial data (yr. ended 12/31/99): Grants paid, $304,255; assets, $12,437,040 (M); gifts received, $23,200; expenditures, $1,604,672; qualifying distributions, $344,013.
Limitations: Giving primarily in areas served by the South Financial Group in SC.
Application information: Use Carolina First Foundation Application Form. Application form required.
Officer: Bruce Thomas, Exec. Dir.
Directors: William Hummers, Mack Whittle.
EIN: 571077098
Codes: CS, FD

49485
D. L. Scurry Foundation
P.O. Box 5026
Columbia, SC 29250 (803) 738-9025
Contact: James F. Burgess, Jr., Tr.

Trust established in 1968 in SC.
Donor(s): D.L. Scurry.‡
Financial data (yr. ended 12/31/01): Grants paid, $293,821; assets, $5,306,318 (M); expenditures, $354,802; qualifying distributions, $293,821.
Limitations: Giving limited to SC.
Application information: Application form not required.
Trustees: James F. Burgess, Jr., Gail Grett.
EIN: 576036622
Codes: FD

49486
The Cline Foundation
c/o N.Q. Cline, Sr.
P.O. Box 3768
Greenville, SC 29608

Established in 1983.
Donor(s): The Cline Company, Inc., N.Q. Cline, Sr.
Financial data (yr. ended 12/31/01): Grants paid, $288,759; assets, $2,240,692 (M); gifts received, $1,016; expenditures, $293,125; qualifying distributions, $287,993.
Limitations: Applications not accepted. Giving primarily in Greenville, SC.
Application information: Contributes only to pre-selected organizations.
Officers: Martha Cline, Pres.; David M. Cline, Secy.
EIN: 570752730
Codes: CS, FD, CD

49487
Nathan and Marlene Addlestone Foundation, Inc.
P.O. Box 979
Charleston, SC 29402

Established in 1979 in SC.
Donor(s): Nathan S. Addlestone, Associated Iron & Metal Co., Inc., Columbia Steel & Metal Co., Inc., Addlestone International Corp.
Financial data (yr. ended 12/31/01): Grants paid, $281,408; assets, $2,094,054 (M); expenditures, $304,566; qualifying distributions, $280,696.
Limitations: Applications not accepted. Giving primarily in Charleston, SC.
Application information: Contributes only to pre-selected organizations.
Officers: Marlene Addlestone, Pres.; Susan Addlestone, V.P.; Edward Kronsberg, Secy.-Treas.
EIN: 570697712
Codes: FD

49488
Alfred Moore Foundation
367 S. Pine St.
Spartanburg, SC 29302-2623 (864) 573-5298
Contact: C.L. Page, Jr, Chair.

Incorporated in 1949 in SC.
Donor(s): the Page Family.
Financial data (yr. ended 12/31/00): Grants paid, $277,067; assets, $4,652,950 (M); expenditures, $330,157; qualifying distributions, $290,851.
Limitations: Giving limited to residents of Spartanburg and Anderson counties, SC.
Application information: Application forms are obtained from and processed through participating high schools; the foundation does not consider unsolicited requests for funds.
Officers: Cary L. Page, Jr., Chair.; Bernelle Demo, Vice-Chair.
Director: Deborah S. Demo.
EIN: 576018424
Codes: FD, GTI

49489
The Philip and Linda LeSourd Lader Foundation
151 Meeting St., Ste. 600
Charleston, SC 29401

Established in 1986 in SC.
Donor(s): Linda Lesourd Lader, Philip Lader.
Financial data (yr. ended 12/31/01): Grants paid, $276,484; assets, $2,999,129 (M); gifts received, $60,580; expenditures, $284,601; qualifying distributions, $275,761.
Limitations: Applications not accepted. Giving on a national and international basis.
Application information: Contributes only to pre-selected organizations.
Officer and Trustees:* Linda Lesourd Lader,* Mgr.; Kenneth D. Fullerton, Marc A. Punterieri.
EIN: 576111836
Codes: FD

49490
Ellison S. & Noel P. McKissick Foundation
(Formerly Alice Manufacturing Company, Inc. Foundation)
P.O. Box 369
Easley, SC 29641-0369

Established in 1983.
Donor(s): Alice Manufacturing Co., Inc.
Financial data (yr. ended 06/30/01): Grants paid, $276,165; assets, $6,896,723 (M); expenditures, $344,797; qualifying distributions, $276,165.
Limitations: Applications not accepted. Giving primarily in SC.
Application information: Contributes only to pre-selected organizations.

Officer: Noel P. McKissick, Secy.
Directors: Elizabeth M. Fauntleroy, Ellison Smyth McKissick, Jr., Caroline M. Reber.
EIN: 570739969
Codes: CS, FD, CD

49491
The Echlin Foundation, Inc.
321 Tom Fripp Rd.
St. Helena Island, SC 29920

Trust established in 1960 in CT.
Donor(s): John E. Echlin, Beryl G. Echlin.
Financial data (yr. ended 11/30/01): Grants paid, $275,500; assets, $4,396,721 (M); expenditures, $277,175; qualifying distributions, $272,882.
Limitations: Applications not accepted. Giving primarily in CT and FL.
Application information: Contributes only to pre-selected organizations.
Trustees: John E. Echlin, Jr., Jane Kammerer.
EIN: 066037282
Codes: FD

49492
Sunshine Foundation, Inc.
872 Chinaberry Rd.
Barnwell, SC 29812
Contact: Nellie Rosier, Admin.

Established in 1997 in SC.
Donor(s): Terry E. Richardson, Jr.
Financial data (yr. ended 12/31/01): Grants paid, $262,593; assets, $3,976,137 (M); expenditures, $301,104; qualifying distributions, $262,593.
Limitations: Applications not accepted.
Application information: Contributes only to pre-selected organizations.
Board Members: Gail Ness Richarson, Julius N. Richardson, Katherine N. Richardson, Matthew T. Richardson, Terry E. Richardson, Jr.
EIN: 571060737
Codes: FD

49493
Schuyler & Yvonne Moore Family Foundation
P.O. Box 2044
West Columbia, SC 29171

Established in 1993.
Donor(s): Schuyler Moore, Yvonne Moore.
Financial data (yr. ended 12/31/00): Grants paid, $259,449; assets, $868,996 (L); expenditures, $267,344; qualifying distributions, $259,449.
Limitations: Applications not accepted. Giving on a national basis.
Application information: Contributes only to pre-selected organizations.
Trustees: Schuyler Moore, Yvonne Moore.
EIN: 943182712
Codes: FD

49494
Spectle Foundation
47 Hamilton's Ferry
Lake Wylie, SC 29710

Established in 1998 in SC.
Donor(s): Thomas G. Carlisle, Elizabeth R. Carlisle.
Financial data (yr. ended 12/31/00): Grants paid, $245,150; assets, $1,694,036 (M); expenditures, $250,060; qualifying distributions, $245,150.
Limitations: Applications not accepted. Giving primarily in SC.
Application information: Contributes only to pre-selected organizations.
Officers: Thomas G. Carlisle, Pres.; Elizabeth R. Carlisle, Secy.
EIN: 562112576
Codes: FD2

49495
Clarence H. and Anna E. Lutz Foundation
1373 West End Rd.
Chester, SC 29706-8030 (803) 581-3743
Contact: Dewey G. Guyton, Pres.

Established in 1996 in NC and SC.
Financial data (yr. ended 02/28/02): Grants paid, $245,000; assets, $5,204,823 (M); expenditures, $291,167; qualifying distributions, $242,053.
Limitations: Giving primarily in Chester County, SC.
Publications: Grants list, program policy statement.
Application information: Application form required.
Officers: Dewey G. Guyton, Pres.; Joan L. Guyton, V.P. and Treas.; Mary S. Jolly, Secy.
EIN: 570940342
Codes: FD2

49496
Piedmont Health Care Foundation, Inc.
P.O. Box 9303
Greenville, SC 29604-9303
Contact: Philip Southerland, Exec. Dir.

Established in 1985 in SC.
Financial data (yr. ended 12/31/00): Grants paid, $239,020; assets, $3,384,791 (M); gifts received, $3,096; expenditures, $333,528; qualifying distributions, $333,528.
Limitations: Giving limited to the Piedmont and Greenville, SC, areas.
Application information: Application form required.
Officer: Phillip Southerland, Exec. Dir.
EIN: 570782523
Codes: FD2

49497
Joanna Foundation
P.O. Box 308
Sullivans Island, SC 29482 (843) 883-9199
Contact: Margaret P. Schachte, Exec. V.P.

Established in 1945 in SC.
Donor(s): Marquette Charitable Organization.
Financial data (yr. ended 12/31/01): Grants paid, $226,000; assets, $4,273,429 (M); expenditures, $346,631; qualifying distributions, $252,069.
Limitations: Giving primarily in Berkeley, Charleston, Dorchester, Laurens and Newberry counties, SC.
Publications: Informational brochure (including application guidelines).
Application information: Application form not required.
Officers and Trustees:* Walter C. Regnery,* Pres.; Margaret P. Schachte,* Exec. V.P.; Charles E. Menefee, Jr.,* Secy.-Treas.; Yonge R. Jones, Eugenie F. Regnery, Patricia Regnery.
EIN: 570314444
Codes: FD2

49498
Bryan Family Foundation, Inc.
c/o William K. Bryan
208 Crescent Ave.
Greenville, SC 29605

Established in 2001 in NC.
Donor(s): William K. Bryan.
Financial data (yr. ended 12/31/01): Grants paid, $224,417; assets, $356,126 (M); gifts received, $520,618; expenditures, $224,457; qualifying distributions, $224,417.
Limitations: Applications not accepted.
Application information: Contributes only to pre-selected organizations.
Officers: William K. Bryan, Sr., Pres.; Frances J. Bryan, Secy.; William K. Bryan, Jr., Treas.

EIN: 571117560

49499
Eugene I. Kane Foundation, Inc.
5 Neptune Ct.
Hilton Head Island, SC 29926

Established in 1998.
Financial data (yr. ended 12/31/00): Grants paid, $223,700; assets, $68,724 (M); gifts received, $218,374; expenditures, $224,711; qualifying distributions, $224,698.
Limitations: Applications not accepted. Giving limited to Washington, DC.
Application information: Contributes only to pre-selected organizations.
Officers: Eugene I. Kane, Pres.; John G. Wharton, Secy.; Gerald K. Lash, Treas.
EIN: 522126118
Codes: FD2

49500
The Four Bees Foundation
c/o Clarence B. Bauknight
P.O. Box 2183
Greenville, SC 29602

Established in 1987 in SC.
Donor(s): Clarence B. Bauknight, Harriet L. Bauknight, Canterbury Antiques.
Financial data (yr. ended 12/31/00): Grants paid, $210,899; assets, $1,236,079 (M); gifts received, $300,000; expenditures, $212,471; qualifying distributions, $210,899.
Limitations: Applications not accepted. Giving primarily in NC and SC.
Application information: Contributes only to pre-selected organizations.
Trustees: Clarence B. Bauknight, Harriet L. Bauknight.
EIN: 570854555
Codes: FD2

49501
The Bannon Foundation
P.O. Box 1057
Greenville, SC 29602

Established in 1987 in SC.
Financial data (yr. ended 12/31/01): Grants paid, $209,000; assets, $3,717,872 (M); expenditures, $279,777; qualifying distributions, $206,699.
Limitations: Applications not accepted. Giving primarily in SC and TX.
Application information: Contributes only to pre-selected organizations.
Trustees: Judy B. Ballew, James G. Bannon, Jr., James G. Bannon III, John R. Thomas.
EIN: 570833931
Codes: FD2

49502
Everett N. McDonnell Foundation
c/o Wallace Evans
16 Starboard Tack Dr.
Salem, SC 29676

Incorporated in 1946 in IL.
Donor(s): Everett N. McDonnell.‡
Financial data (yr. ended 10/31/01): Grants paid, $208,220; assets, $3,861,585 (M); expenditures, $261,920; qualifying distributions, $216,643.
Limitations: Applications not accepted. Giving primarily in GA and IL.
Application information: Contributes only to pre-selected organizations.
Officers and Directors:* Florence L. McDonnell,* Pres. and Treas.; Gwyneth O. Moran,* V.P.; John D. Marshall,* Secy.
EIN: 366109359
Codes: FD2

49503
Schafer Foundation
P.O. Box 1328
Dillon, SC 29536-1328

Established in 1961 in SC.
Donor(s): Palmetto Properties, Inc., S.O.B. Shops, Inc.
Financial data (yr. ended 12/31/01): Grants paid, $205,750; assets, $2,496,554 (M); gifts received, $503,382; expenditures, $208,269; qualifying distributions, $204,284.
Limitations: Applications not accepted. Giving primarily in SC.
Application information: Contributes only to pre-selected organizations.
Officers: Patricia C. Schafer, Pres.; Victor H. Cook, V.P.; Lulu F. Holiday, Treas.
EIN: 576033789
Codes: FD2

49504
E. Erwin Maddrey II & Nancy B. Maddrey Foundation
233 N. Main St.
Hammond Sq., Ste. 200
Greenville, SC 29601

Established in 1989 in SC.
Donor(s): E. Erwin Maddrey II.
Financial data (yr. ended 12/31/01): Grants paid, $200,000; assets, $1,289,719 (M); gifts received, $1,500; expenditures, $201,624; qualifying distributions, $200,398.
Limitations: Applications not accepted. Giving primarily in Davidson, NC.
Application information: Contributes only to pre-selected organizations. Unsolicited requests for funds not accepted.
Officers: E. Erwin Maddrey II, Co-Chair.; Nancy B. Maddrey, Co-Chair.
Trustee: Bank of America.
EIN: 576125748
Codes: FD2

49505
The Lucyle S. Love Foundation
P.O. Box 10045
Greenville, SC 29603

Established in 1989 in SC.
Donor(s): Lucyle S. Love.‡
Financial data (yr. ended 12/31/00): Grants paid, $190,000; assets, $3,533,253 (M); expenditures, $282,960; qualifying distributions, $180,492.
Limitations: Giving primarily in Greenville County, SC.
Trustees: Susan H. Hart, Ben R. Lever, Jr., D.R. McAlister.
EIN: 570902382
Codes: FD2, GTI

49506
C. G. Fuller Foundation
c/o Bank of America
P.O. Box 448
Columbia, SC 29202-0448 (803) 255-7334
Contact: Ross Walters

Established in 1972 in SC.
Donor(s): Cornell G. Fuller.‡
Financial data (yr. ended 12/31/01): Grants paid, $186,000; assets, $3,852,247 (M); expenditures, $226,273; qualifying distributions, $195,016.
Limitations: Giving limited to SC.
Application information: Application form required.
Trustees: Victor B. John, Clinton C. Lemon, Bank of America.
EIN: 576050492
Codes: FD2, GTI

49507
ScanSource Charitable Foundation
6 Logue Ct.
Greenville, SC 29615

Established in 1998 in SC.
Financial data (yr. ended 12/31/00): Grants paid, $178,809; assets, $172,583 (M); gifts received, $260,197; expenditures, $179,632; qualifying distributions, $179,632.
Limitations: Applications not accepted.
Application information: Contributes only to pre-selected organizations.
Officer: Joan Peters, Chair.
Directors: Nicki Breon, Sherry Brian, Kristy Laughter, Joe Leocadio, Cathy Lundeen, Wendi McMinn, Kristin Robinson, Tony Sorrentino, Larry Tallant, Bradley Wright.
EIN: 571002959
Codes: FD2

49508
Fred Collins Foundation
1341 Rutherford Rd.
Greenville, SC 29609-9603

Established in 1986 in SC.
Donor(s): Fred Collins.
Financial data (yr. ended 12/31/00): Grants paid, $170,000; assets, $3,686,365 (M); gifts received, $108,800; expenditures, $194,569; qualifying distributions, $168,350.
Limitations: Applications not accepted. Giving primarily in the Greenville, SC, area.
Application information: Contributes only to pre-selected organizations.
Trustee: Fred Collins.
EIN: 576107255
Codes: FD2

49509
Dick Horne Foundation
P.O. Box 306
Orangeburg, SC 29116
Application address: 1360 Russell St., S.E., Orangeburg, SC 29115, tel.: (803) 534-2096
Contact: Helen Williams

Established in 1966 in SC.
Donor(s): Amelia S. Horne.‡
Financial data (yr. ended 12/31/99): Grants paid, $167,881; assets, $7,680,197 (M); expenditures, $212,169; qualifying distributions, $194,601.
Limitations: Giving primarily in the Orangeburg County, SC, area.
Application information: Application form required.
Trustees: W. Louis Griffin, Buster Smith.
EIN: 237015996
Codes: FD2, GTI

49510
The Esther B. Ferguson Foundation
(Formerly The James L. and Esther B. Ferguson Foundation)
P.O. Box 1457
Charleston, SC 29402-1457
Contact: Esther Ferguson, Tr.

Established in 1986 in NY.
Donor(s): James L. Ferguson.
Financial data (yr. ended 12/31/99): Grants paid, $167,824; assets, $289,162 (M); gifts received, $85,245; expenditures, $171,083; qualifying distributions, $167,500.
Limitations: Giving primarily in Charleston, SC.
Trustees: Esther B. Ferguson, James L. Ferguson.
EIN: 133391662
Codes: FD2

49511
William Barnet III Foundation Trust
(also known as The Barnet Foundation Trust)
507 E. St. Johns St.
Spartanburg, SC 29302

Established in 1986 in SC.
Donor(s): William Barnett & Son, William Barnett II.
Financial data (yr. ended 09/30/01): Grants paid, $156,233; assets, $4,826,594 (M); gifts received, $647,722; expenditures, $179,543; qualifying distributions, $156,233.
Limitations: Applications not accepted. Giving primarily in SC.
Application information: Contributes only to pre-selected organizations.
Trustees: Valerie Barnet, William Barnet III, Vernett Lamp, D. Byrd Miller III.
EIN: 576114255
Codes: FD2

49512
Adrianne B. Reilly Foundation
c/o Putnam Trust Co., Inc.
1 N. Adgers Wharf
Charleston, SC 29401
Application address: 92 Rockwood Ln., Greenwich, CT 06830, tel.: (203) 869-9837
Contact: Adrianne B. Reilly, Tr.

Established in 1990 in CT and SC.
Donor(s): Adrianne B. Reilly.
Financial data (yr. ended 12/31/00): Grants paid, $151,078; assets, $714,310 (M); gifts received, $130,689; expenditures, $155,097; qualifying distributions, $151,078.
Limitations: Giving primarily in CT.
Trustees: Adrianne B. Reilly, John Winthrop.
EIN: 223109258
Codes: FD2

49513
Williams/Brice-Edwards Charitable Trust
110 Mason Croft Dr.
Sumter, SC 29150-4014
Contact: Philip L. Edwards, Tr.

Established in SC.
Donor(s): Philip L. Edwards.
Financial data (yr. ended 12/31/01): Grants paid, $149,780; assets, $2,777,849 (M); gifts received, $308,120; expenditures, $150,366; qualifying distributions, $149,179.
Limitations: Giving primarily in Sumter, SC.
Application information: Application form not required.
Trustees: Philip L. Edwards, Florence M. Ervin, James C. McLeod, Jr.
EIN: 576105891
Codes: FD2

49514
Ralph and Virginia Hendricks Foundation
P.O. Box 278
Simpsonville, SC 29681-0278

Established in 1986 in SC.
Donor(s): Ralph S. Hendricks.
Financial data (yr. ended 12/31/01): Grants paid, $147,000; assets, $3,448,377 (M); expenditures, $238,072; qualifying distributions, $147,180.
Limitations: Applications not accepted. Giving primarily in SC.
Application information: Contributes only to pre-selected organizations.
Trustees: Randy Harling, Ralph S. Hendricks, G. Wilson Jenkins, Richard C. Moore, Marc L. Saunders.
EIN: 570822180
Codes: FD2

49515
Bonner Family Private Foundation, Inc.
130 Deliesseline Rd.
Cayce, SC 29033-4312
Contact: Hazel A. Bonner, Secy.-Treas.

Established in 1987 in SC.
Donor(s): Hazel A. Bonner, T.L. Bonner, Northwoods L.P.
Financial data (yr. ended 12/31/00): Grants paid, $146,000; assets, $3,599,968 (M); gifts received, $200,000; expenditures, $148,237; qualifying distributions, $146,035.
Limitations: Giving primarily in Columbia, SC.
Application information: Application form not required.
Officers: Sheila B. Kolb, Pres.; Hazel A. Bonner, Secy.-Treas.
Trustee: Janice B. Norman.
EIN: 570844469
Codes: FD2

49516
Brown Family Foundation
351 Persimmon Fork Rd.
Blythewood, SC 29016
Contact: Joyce M. Brown, Tr.

Established in 1993.
Donor(s): Joyce M. Brown.
Financial data (yr. ended 12/31/01): Grants paid, $145,000; assets, $1,690,414 (M); gifts received, $422,813; expenditures, $157,500; qualifying distributions, $148,676.
Limitations: Applications not accepted.
Application information: Contributes only to pre-selected organizations.
Trustee: Joyce M. Brown.
EIN: 363924795
Codes: FD2

49517
E. E. Stone IV Foundation
3027 Wade Hampton Blvd., Ste. 2
Taylors, SC 29687

Donor(s): The Stone Foundation.
Financial data (yr. ended 12/31/00): Grants paid, $141,833; assets, $126,485 (M); expenditures, $144,756; qualifying distributions, $142,548.
Limitations: Applications not accepted. Giving primarily in SC.
Application information: Contributes only to pre-selected organizations.
Trustees: Rosalie S. Morris, E. E. Stone IV.
EIN: 576171809
Codes: FD2

49518
Budweiser of Columbia, Anderson and Greenville Foundation, Inc.
(Formerly Budweiser of the Carolinas Foundation, Inc.)
825 Bluff Rd.
Columbia, SC 29202-0684
Application address: P.O. Box 684, Columbia, SC 29202-0684
Contact: R. Roy Pearce, Chair.

Established in 1981.
Donor(s): Budweiser of Columbia, Inc., Budweiser of Anderson, Inc., Budweiser of Greenville, Inc.
Financial data (yr. ended 12/31/00): Grants paid, $140,150; assets, $2,798,417 (M); gifts received, $100,000; expenditures, $216,083; qualifying distributions, $140,150.
Limitations: Giving primarily in Columbia, Greenville, Charleston, and Newberry, SC.
Application information: Application form not required.
Officers: R. Roy Pearce, Chair.; James T. Pearce, Vice-Chair.; Gene E. Williams, Pres.; C. John Wentzell, Secy.-Treas.
EIN: 570734278
Codes: CS, FD2, CD

49519
Milkon Christian Foundation, Inc.
1233 Washington St., Ste. 800
Columbia, SC 29201 (803) 252-4146
FAX: (803) 749-3532
Contact: Pat Cannon, Pres.

Established in 1986.
Donor(s): Harvey J.E. Milkon.‡
Financial data (yr. ended 12/31/01): Grants paid, $136,500; assets, $2,464,971 (M); gifts received, $64,000; expenditures, $212,614; qualifying distributions, $173,796.
Publications: Informational brochure (including application guidelines).
Application information: Proposals will be requested after review of initial letter. No unsolicited proposals accepted.
Officers and Directors:* Annette T. Milkon,* Chair.; Patricia Cannon,* Pres.; Ronald Cannon, V.P.; Richard A. Cannon,* Secy.; Robert Cannon,* Treas.; Karlene Cannon, Peter J. Cannon, Sheri Cannon.
EIN: 592628783
Codes: FD2

49520
The Touch the Ground Foundation
305 Buckland Way
Greenville, SC 29615 (864) 286-0804
Contact: J. Ricky Vaughan, Chair.; or Theda L. Vaughan, Tr.

Established in 2000 in SC.
Donor(s): J. Ricky Vaughan.
Financial data (yr. ended 12/31/01): Grants paid, $132,200; assets, $2,932,932 (M); gifts received, $1,474,037; expenditures, $163,668; qualifying distributions, $163,004.
Limitations: Giving primarily in SC and VA.
Application information: Application form not required.
Officer and Trustees:* J. Ricky Vaughan,* Chair.; Theda L. Vaughan.
EIN: 571112375
Codes: FD2

49521
The Cart Foundation
1741 Hwy. 56
Spartanburg, SC 29302

Established in 1996 in SC.
Financial data (yr. ended 12/31/01): Grants paid, $132,000; assets, $1,969,916 (L); expenditures, $140,157; qualifying distributions, $140,157.
Limitations: Applications not accepted. Giving on a national basis.
Application information: Contributes only to pre-selected organizations.
Officer and Trustees:* Joan M. Cart,* Mgr.; Ben M. Cart, Walter M. Cart, Elizabeth M. White.
EIN: 570987085
Codes: FD2

49522
Black & Phillips Foundation, Inc.
c/o Marianna B. Habisreutinger
408 E. Main St.
Spartanburg, SC 29302

Established in 1991 in SC.
Donor(s): Mary Black Phillips.‡
Financial data (yr. ended 04/30/01): Grants paid, $130,000; assets, $2,166,023 (M); gifts received,

$100,025; expenditures, $148,020; qualifying distributions, $131,192.
Limitations: Applications not accepted. Giving limited to the city and county of Spartanburg, SC.
Application information: Contributes only to pre-selected organizations.
Trustees: Paula B. Baker, Marianna B. Habisreutinger.
EIN: 570928657
Codes: FD2

49523
Betsy M. Campbell Foundation
101 N. Main St.
Greenville, SC 29601

Established in 1997 in SC.
Financial data (yr. ended 12/31/01): Grants paid, $130,000; assets, $8,074,279 (M); expenditures, $339,380; qualifying distributions, $166,374.
Limitations: Applications not accepted. Giving primarily in NC and SC.
Application information: Contributes only to pre-selected organizations.
Trustee: William W. Brown.
EIN: 586346237
Codes: FD2

49524
Baker & Baker Foundation, Inc.
P.O. Box 12397
Columbia, SC 29211

Established in 1982 in SC.
Donor(s): Baker & Baker, Patricia M. Baker, Lee J. Baker, David Baker.
Financial data (yr. ended 12/31/01): Grants paid, $125,950; assets, $185,567 (M); gifts received, $100,000; expenditures, $129,071; qualifying distributions, $125,881.
Limitations: Applications not accepted. Giving primarily in Columbia, SC.
Publications: Annual report.
Application information: Contributes only to pre-selected organizations.
Officers: John Baker, Pres.; Steve Anastasion, V.P.
EIN: 570752311
Codes: CS, FD2, CD

49525
The Summer Foundation
1426 Main St.
Columbia, SC 29201
Contact: Jo Ann Butler, Secy.-Treas.

Established in 1984 in SC.
Donor(s): South Carolina Electric & Gas Co., SCANA Corp.
Financial data (yr. ended 12/31/00): Grants paid, $125,000; assets, $1,491,826 (M); gifts received, $40,000; expenditures, $146,509; qualifying distributions, $123,362.
Limitations: Giving limited to SC.
Officers: William B. Timmerman, Pres.; Neville O. Lorick, V.P.; Jo Ann Butler, Secy.-Treas.
Trustees: Randolph R. Mahan, Kevin B. Marsh.
EIN: 570784136
Codes: CS, FD2, CD

49526
The McNair Law Firm Foundation
P.O. Box 11390
Columbia, SC 29211
Application address: Bank of America Twr., 1301 Gervais St., 17th Fl., Columbia, SC 29201
Contact: O. Wayne Corley, Chair.

Established in 1999 in SC.
Donor(s): O. Wayne Corley, Richard J. Morgan.
Financial data (yr. ended 12/31/01): Grants paid, $124,550; assets, $123,963 (M); gifts received, $218,100; expenditures, $125,060; qualifying distributions, $124,550.
Limitations: Giving primarily in SC.
Officers and Board Members:* O. Wayne Corley,* Chair.; Jonathan H. Nason,* Secy.; Missy Schumpert, Treas.; Erik P. Doerring, Richard J. Morgan, M. William Youngblood.
EIN: 571090042
Codes: FD2

49527
Henry Repokis Foundation
269 Connecticut Ave.
Spartanburg, SC 29302
Contact: Henry Repokis, Tr.

Established in 1966.
Donor(s): Henry A. Repokis.
Financial data (yr. ended 12/31/01): Grants paid, $124,400; assets, $27,882 (M); gifts received, $93,820; expenditures, $130,285; qualifying distributions, $124,400.
Limitations: Applications not accepted. Giving primarily in Spartanburg, SC.
Application information: Contributes only to pre-selected organizations.
Trustees: Henry Repokis, Marion L. Repokis, Mark H. Repokis, Wesley L. Repokis.
EIN: 576024180

49528
The J. Edgar Hoover Foundation
P.O. Box 5914
Hilton Head Island, SC 29938 (843) 671-5020
Application address: 50 Gull Point Rd., Hilton Head Island, SC 29928
Contact: Cartha D. DeLoach, Chair.

Established in 1965 in SC.
Donor(s): William G. Simon, Mrs. William G. Simon, Livvie Andersen,‡ Edward A. Lozick.
Financial data (yr. ended 12/31/01): Grants paid, $121,500; assets, $939,982 (M); gifts received, $73,507; expenditures, $221,338; qualifying distributions, $163,917.
Application information: Application form not required.
Officers and Directors:* Cartha D. DeLoach,* Chair.; William M. Baker,* V.P.; William D. Branon,* V.P.; Joseph F. D'Angelo,* V.P.; Gary L. Penrith,* V.P.; Marion S. Ramey,* V.P.; Richard S. Woods, Secy.-Treas.
EIN: 526060988
Codes: FD2, GTI

49529
Jean and Verne Smith Charitable Trust
113 Peachtree Dr.
Greer, SC 29651
Application address: 119 Peachtree Dr., Greer, SC 29651, tel.: (864) 877-3975
Contact: Carole S. Olmert, Tr.

Established in 1999 in SC.
Financial data (yr. ended 12/31/01): Grants paid, $113,750; assets, $841,013 (M); expenditures, $133,734; qualifying distributions, $113,400.
Application information: Application available upon request. Application form required.
Trustees: Kyle Allen, Carole S. Olmert, Jean M. Smith.
EIN: 586404187
Codes: FD2

49530
The Rushing Foundation
P.O. Box 6648
Greenville, SC 29606

Established in 1994 in SC.
Donor(s): John Carroll Rushing.
Financial data (yr. ended 12/31/01): Grants paid, $113,327; assets, $488,079 (M); gifts received, $94; expenditures, $121,336; qualifying distributions, $113,443.
Limitations: Applications not accepted.
Application information: Contributes only to pre-selected organizations.
Officers: John Carroll Rushing, Pres.; Billie T. Cleveland, Secy.; Richard Grant, Treas.
EIN: 571013202
Codes: FD2

49531
Lucy Hampton Bostick Charitable Trust
c/o H. Simmons Tate, Jr.
P.O. Box 11889
Columbia, SC 29211

Established in 1968 in SC.
Financial data (yr. ended 12/31/00): Grants paid, $113,000; assets, $2,356,935 (M); expenditures, $122,066; qualifying distributions, $111,087.
Limitations: Applications not accepted. Giving primarily in SC.
Application information: Contributes only to pre-selected organizations.
Trustees: A. Mason Gibbes, H. Simmons Tate, Jr., George R.P. Walker.
EIN: 576042059
Codes: FD2

49532
Barbara M. Lindstedt Charitable Trust
1 Meeting St.
Charleston, SC 29401 (843) 577-6457
Contact: Nancy D. Hawk, Dir.

Established in 1990 in SC.
Financial data (yr. ended 12/31/00): Grants paid, $111,404; assets, $1,251,020 (M); expenditures, $137,537; qualifying distributions, $111,404.
Limitations: Giving primarily in SC.
Director: Nancy D. Hawk.
EIN: 576133109
Codes: FD2

49533
County Bank Foundation
P.O. Box 3129
Greenwood, SC 29648
Contact: Denise Lollis, Secy.

Established in 1971 in SC.
Donor(s): The County Bank, R.T. Dunlap, Jr.
Financial data (yr. ended 08/31/01): Grants paid, $110,449; assets, $10,131 (M); gifts received, $120,199; expenditures, $110,449; qualifying distributions, $110,449.
Limitations: Giving primarily in Greenwood, SC.
Application information: Application form required.
Trustee: R.T. Dunlap, Jr.
EIN: 237128545
Codes: CS, FD2, CD

49534
The Arcadia Foundation
c/o Mayfair Mills, Inc.
1885 Hayne St.
Arcadia, SC 29320
Contact: F.B. Dent, Pres.

Established in 1950 in SC.
Financial data (yr. ended 12/31/00): Grants paid, $106,970; assets, $3,065,699 (M); gifts received, $13,731; expenditures, $139,046; qualifying distributions, $106,970.
Limitations: Giving primarily in SC.
Application information: Application form not required.

49534—SOUTH CAROLINA

Officers and Directors:* F.B. Dent,* Pres. and Treas.; F.B. Dent, Jr., V.P. and Treas.; R.F. Bonsal,* V.P.; Cecil Hutcherson, Secy.
EIN: 570298275
Codes: FD2

49535
Dwight and Jessie Holder Foundation
P.O. Box 313
Pickens, SC 29671

Established in 1985.
Donor(s): Dwight A. Holder, Jessie M. Holder.
Financial data (yr. ended 10/31/01): Grants paid, $102,615; assets, $48,046 (M); gifts received, $72,000; expenditures, $106,860; qualifying distributions, $106,110.
Limitations: Applications not accepted. Giving primarily in SC.
Application information: Contributes only to pre-selected organizations.
Officer and Trustees:* P. McCrady Gwinn,* Mgr.; Dwight A. Holder, Jessie M. Holder.
EIN: 586038036
Codes: FD2

49536
Jayvee Foundation
c/o Robert D. Pope
110 Wynwood Ct.
Seneca, SC 29672-7085

Established in 1986 in KY and SC.
Donor(s): Robert D. Pope, Carol C. Pope.
Financial data (yr. ended 12/31/00): Grants paid, $98,675; assets, $1,116,748 (M); gifts received, $275,313; expenditures, $103,469; qualifying distributions, $98,675.
Limitations: Applications not accepted. Giving primarily in Louisville, KY.
Application information: Contributes only to pre-selected organizations.
Directors: Carol C. Pope, Robert D. Pope.
EIN: 363466516
Codes: FD2

49537
Ethel S. Brody Charitable Foundation, Inc.
c/o Ethel S. Brody
19 Quinine Hill
Columbia, SC 29204

Established in 2001 in SC.
Donor(s): Ethel S. Brody.
Financial data (yr. ended 07/31/02): Grants paid, $95,968; assets, $725,885 (M); gifts received, $369,830; expenditures, $99,661; qualifying distributions, $95,968.
Officers: Ethel S. Brody, Chair.; David S. Brody, Vice-Chair.; Leona Sobel, Secy.-Treas.
Directors: Laura C. Brody, Janet B. Rush, Jerel F. Rush.
EIN: 571116814

49538
M. B. Kahn Foundation, Inc.
P.O. Box 1608
Columbia, SC 29202

Established in 1964 in SC.
Donor(s): M.B. Kahn Construction Co., Inc.
Financial data (yr. ended 09/30/01): Grants paid, $95,015; assets, $77,547 (M); gifts received, $113,432; expenditures, $95,630; qualifying distributions, $95,015.
Limitations: Applications not accepted. Giving primarily in SC.
Application information: Contributes only to pre-selected organizations.
Officer and Director:* Alan B. Kahn,* Pres.
EIN: 576024465

Codes: FD2

49539
Hamrick Mills Foundation, Inc.
P.O. Box 48
Gaffney, SC 29342-0048 (864) 489-4731
Contact: Wylie L. Hamrick, Pres.

Established in 1952 in SC.
Donor(s): Hamrick Mills Inc.
Financial data (yr. ended 12/31/00): Grants paid, $94,877; assets, $2,012,662 (M); expenditures, $121,225; qualifying distributions, $92,932.
Limitations: Giving primarily in Cherokee County, SC.
Officers and Directors:* Wylie L. Hamrick,* Pres.; C.F. Hamrick II,* Secy.-Treas.; J.M. Hamrick, L.W. Hamrick, W.C. Hamrick, R.C. Thomson.
EIN: 576024261
Codes: CS, FD2, CD

49540
Wateree Dreams Foundation
273 Blue Heron Dr.
Rock Hill, SC 29732

Established in 1998 in SC.
Donor(s): Richard K. Carlisle, Kay M. Carlisle.
Financial data (yr. ended 12/31/00): Grants paid, $93,500; assets, $1,657,577 (M); expenditures, $98,520; qualifying distributions, $93,500.
Limitations: Applications not accepted. Giving primarily in SC.
Application information: Contributes only to pre-selected organizations.
Officers: Richard K. Carlisle, Pres.; Kay M. Carlisle, Secy.
EIN: 562112579
Codes: FD2

49541
The Stewart Family Foundation
P.O. Box 2266
Beaufort, SC 29901
Contact: Richard H. Stewart, Chair.

Established in 1999 in GA.
Donor(s): Richard H. Stewart, Sharon S. Stewart.
Financial data (yr. ended 12/31/01): Grants paid, $92,000; assets, $1,463,486 (M); gifts received, $500; expenditures, $96,843; qualifying distributions, $91,622.
Limitations: Applications not accepted. Giving primarily in SC.
Application information: Unsolicited requests for funds not accepted.
Officer and Trustees:* Richard H. Stewart,* Chair.; Sharon S. Stewart.
EIN: 586365313
Codes: FD2

49542
Pope-Brown Foundation
P.O. Drawer 7125
Columbia, SC 29202-7125
Contact: Thomas H. Pope III, Tr.

Established in 1997 in SC.
Financial data (yr. ended 12/31/00): Grants paid, $91,000; assets, $2,063,392 (M); expenditures, $110,518; qualifying distributions, $91,000.
Limitations: Giving primarily in SC.
Trustees: Carroll B. Hart, Gary T. Pope, Thomas H. Pope III.
EIN: 576173490
Codes: FD2

49543
Betty and James K. Stone Foundation
P.O. Box 219
Wellford, SC 29385

Established in 1992 in PA.
Donor(s): Betty Stone.‡
Financial data (yr. ended 12/31/01): Grants paid, $90,000; assets, $1,724,197 (M); expenditures, $102,099; qualifying distributions, $93,839.
Limitations: Applications not accepted. Giving primarily in FL, NY, PA, and SC.
Application information: Contributes only to pre-selected organizations.
Trustees: Mary S. Phipps, Jane S. Pratt, George E. Stone.
EIN: 570958629
Codes: FD2

49544
Edward B. Timmons, Jr. Charitable Trust
c/o Bank of America
P.O. Box 448
Columbia, SC 29202-0448 (803) 255-7376
Application address: 101 S. Tryon, Charlotte, NC 28255, tel.: (704) 388-2837

Established in 1991 in SC.
Financial data (yr. ended 08/31/01): Grants paid, $89,412; assets, $2,707,937 (M); gifts received, $32,323; expenditures, $122,799; qualifying distributions, $96,351.
Limitations: Giving limited to the central midland region of SC.
Application information: Contributes mostly to pre-selected organizations.
Trustees: H. Dewain Herring, Jr., Michael W. Lowrance, Bank of America.
EIN: 576137580
Codes: FD2

49545
The Smith Foundation
c/o Eugena S. Potts
515 Wade Hampton Blvd.
Greer, SC 29652-0505 (864) 879-4300
Contact: W. Carl Smith, Tr.

Established in 1995 in SC.
Donor(s): W. Carl Smith.
Financial data (yr. ended 12/31/01): Grants paid, $89,356; assets, $683,250 (M); gifts received, $23,940; expenditures, $91,336; qualifying distributions, $89,356.
Trustees: Eugenia Potts, Mary Smith, W. Carl Smith.
EIN: 576167112

49546
Charitable Contribution Fund, Inc.
2711 Middleburg Dr., Ste. 316
Columbia, SC 29204

Established in 1993 in SC.
Financial data (yr. ended 12/31/01): Grants paid, $85,591; assets, $20,883 (M); gifts received, $75,000; expenditures, $85,621; qualifying distributions, $85,591.
Limitations: Applications not accepted. Giving primarily in Columbia, SC.
Application information: Contributes only to pre-selected organizations.
Officer: W. James Kitchens, Pres.
EIN: 570966202

49547
The Laura E. Dupont Foundation
(Formerly The Echols-Johnston Family Foundation)
P.O. Box 8099
Greenville, SC 29604-8099

Established in 1997 in SC.
Donor(s): Laura E. Dupont.
Financial data (yr. ended 04/30/01): Grants paid, $85,250; assets, $1,495,527 (M); expenditures, $122,659; qualifying distributions, $100,250.
Limitations: Applications not accepted. Giving primarily in SC.
Application information: Contributes only to pre-selected organizations.
Trustees: Laura E. Dupont, Charles P. Johnston, Ellis M. Johnston II, James S. Johnston, Jr.
EIN: 586340729
Codes: FD2

49548
New Hope Foundation
5 Pee Dee Pointe
St. Helena Island, SC 29920

Established in 1997 in SC.
Donor(s): James W. Crook.
Financial data (yr. ended 12/31/99): Grants paid, $84,300; assets, $747,804 (M); expenditures, $85,865; qualifying distributions, $84,300.
Limitations: Applications not accepted.
Application information: Contributes only to pre-selected organizations.
Trustees: Bruce D. Crook, James W. Crook, James W. Crook, Jr., Jamie R. Dent.
EIN: 582366362
Codes: FD2

49549
E. Craig Wall, Sr. Foundation
P.O. Box 260001
Conway, SC 29526-2601

Established in 1970.
Donor(s): E.C. Wall, Sr.,‡ E. Craig Wall, Jr.‡
Financial data (yr. ended 11/30/01): Grants paid, $83,065; assets, $1,039,273 (M); expenditures, $101,603; qualifying distributions, $84,115.
Limitations: Giving primarily in NC and SC.
Application information: Application form not required.
Trustees: Harriet Wall Martin, Nell Wall Otto, Benjamin R. Wall II, E. Craig Wall III, Judith A. Wall, May H. Wall.
EIN: 237095547
Codes: FD2

49550
J. B. Cornelius Foundation
181 Rutledge Rd.
Greenwood, SC 29649 (864) 229-7151
Contact: John L. Sherrill, Secy.-Treas.

Established about 1935 in NC.
Donor(s): J.B. Cornelius.‡
Financial data (yr. ended 04/30/01): Grants paid, $79,500; assets, $1,867,926 (M); expenditures, $96,043; qualifying distributions, $87,771.
Limitations: Giving limited to students attending NC colleges and universities.
Application information: Application form required.
Officers: Mrs. Edwin S. Young, Pres.; John L. Sherrill, Secy.-Treas.
Directors: C. Kermit Sherrill II, Frank C. Sherrill II, John L. Sherrill, Jr., Edwin S. Young, Jr.
EIN: 566060705
Codes: FD2, GTI

49551
Hundred Club of Greater Charleston, Inc.
P.O. Box 875
Ladson, SC 29456-0875

Established in 1997 in SC.
Financial data (yr. ended 12/31/00): Grants paid, $79,462; assets, $8,787 (M); gifts received, $81,431; expenditures, $99,097; qualifying distributions, $101,707.
Limitations: Applications not accepted.
Application information: Contributes only to pre-selected organizations.
Officers: Lee Wilson, Pres.; Lee Waters, V.P.; Clark Hobbie, Treas.
EIN: 570862483

49552
John Winthrop Charitable Trust
c/o Wood, Struthers & Winthrop
1 N. Adgers Wharf
Charleston, SC 29401

Established in 1993 in NY.
Donor(s): John Winthrop, John Winthrop, Jr.
Financial data (yr. ended 06/30/01): Grants paid, $78,467; assets, $1,867,629 (M); expenditures, $95,683; qualifying distributions, $78,467.
Limitations: Applications not accepted. Giving on a national basis.
Application information: Contributes only to pre-selected organizations.
Trustees: John Winthrop, John Winthrop, Jr.
EIN: 132982306
Codes: FD2

49553
Wayland H. Cato, Jr. Foundation, Inc.
5 Exchange St.
Charleston, SC 29401

Established in 1997 in SC.
Donor(s): Wayland H. Cato, Wayland H. Cato, Jr.
Financial data (yr. ended 12/31/00): Grants paid, $77,605; assets, $2,878,767 (M); gifts received, $783,750; expenditures, $78,319; qualifying distributions, $76,835.
Limitations: Applications not accepted. Giving primarily in SC.
Application information: Contributes only to pre-selected organizations.
Officers: Wayland H. Cato, Pres.; Clarice Cato Goodyear, Secy.-Treas.
Directors: Henry P. Cato, John P.D. Cato, Joseph C. Cato, Thomas E. Cato, Wayland H. Cato III, Catherine Cato DeStefano.
EIN: 570988435
Codes: FD2

49554
Siebert Charitable Trust
c/o First Citizens Bank, Trust Dept.
1230 Main St., P.O. Box 29
Columbia, SC 29202
Contact: William K. Brumbach, Jr., Sr. V.P.

Established in 1997 in SC.
Financial data (yr. ended 12/31/01): Grants paid, $75,613; assets, $1,598,460 (M); expenditures, $93,211; qualifying distributions, $81,918.
Limitations: Giving primarily in SC.
Application information: Application form not required.
Trustee: First Citizens Bank.
EIN: 626340467
Codes: FD2

49555
Hebrew Orphan Society of Charleston, SC
(Formerly Hebrew Orphan Society)
P.O. Box 30011
Charleston, SC 29417-0011 (843) 556-6232
FAX: (843) 402-0791; *E-mail:* colonelf@mindspring.com
Contact: Henry H. Freudenberg, Secy.-Treas.

Established in 1801 in SC.
Donor(s): Nathan Miles.‡
Financial data (yr. ended 12/31/01): Grants paid, $74,343; assets, $1,594,917 (M); gifts received, $22,835; expenditures, $100,346; qualifying distributions, $73,891.
Limitations: Giving limited to Metro, Charleston, Dorchester, and Berkeley counties, SC.
Application information: Application form not required.
Officers: Rita L. Banov, Pres.; Hugo M. Spitz, V.P.; Henry Freudenberg, Secy.-Treas.
EIN: 576034375

49556
S. Lewis & Lucia B. Bell Foundation
P.O. Box 832
Chester, SC 29706-0832 (803) 581-9198
Contact: Joseph M. McElwee, Mgr.

Established in 1991 in SC.
Donor(s): Lucia Beason Bell Trust.
Financial data (yr. ended 12/31/01): Grants paid, $74,235; assets, $1,541,531 (M); gifts received, $130,000; expenditures, $96,384; qualifying distributions, $74,235.
Limitations: Giving limited to Chester County, SC.
Trustees: Ladson F. Stringfellow, D.C. Wylie, Jr.
EIN: 570932788

49557
Joseph R. Moss Educational & Charitable Trust
P.O. Box 299
York, SC 29745
Contact: Melvin B. McKeown, Tr.

Established in 1995 in SC.
Financial data (yr. ended 08/31/01): Grants paid, $73,000; assets, $1,466,450 (M); expenditures, $73,977; qualifying distributions, $72,470.
Application information: Request application form. Application form required.
Trustee: Melvin B. McKeown.
EIN: 576162069

49558
Dorothy M. & Clement F. Haynsworth, Jr. Foundation, Inc.
293 E. Bay St.
Charleston, SC 29401

Established in 1991 in SC.
Donor(s): Dorothy M. Haynsworth.
Financial data (yr. ended 12/31/00): Grants paid, $72,665; assets, $253,506 (M); gifts received, $81,376; expenditures, $87,551; qualifying distributions, $72,665.
Limitations: Applications not accepted. Giving primarily in Charleston, SC.
Application information: Contributes only to pre-selected organizations.
Trustee: Nella G. Barley.
EIN: 570927691

49559
Charles E. and Ellen H. Taylor Family Foundation
120 Long Cove Dr.
Hilton Head Island, SC 29928

Established in 1999 in SC.
Donor(s): Charles E. Taylor, Ellen H. Taylor.

49559

Financial data (yr. ended 12/31/01): Grants paid, $71,000; assets, $175,279 (M); expenditures, $73,380; qualifying distributions, $71,000.
Limitations: Applications not accepted. Giving primarily in Hilton Head Island, SC.
Application information: Contributes only to pre-selected organizations.
Directors: Charles E. Taylor, Ellen H. Taylor.
EIN: 571081862

49560
Kinney Foundation
P.O. Box 656
Bennettsville, SC 29512-0656 (843) 479-3815
Application address: 100 Fayetteville Ave., Bennettsville, SC 29512; FAX: (843) 479-7671; E-mail: ekmcniel@marlboroelectric.net
Contact: Elisabeth K. McNiel, Chair.

Established about 1974.
Donor(s): C.A. Kinney Trust, P.M. Kinney Trust, William L. Kinney, Jr.
Financial data (yr. ended 12/31/00): Grants paid, $69,500; assets, $1,512,062 (M); expenditures, $89,063; qualifying distributions, $70,798.
Limitations: Giving primarily in Bennettsville and Marlboro County, SC.
Publications: Application guidelines.
Application information: Application form not required.
Officers and Directors:* Elisabeth K. McNiel,* Chair.; Wade R. Crow,* Secy.; James E. Brogdon, Margaret P. Kinney, William L. Kinney, Jr., Harvey H. McCants, Charles P. Midgley, Hal Trimmier.
Trustee: Wachovia Bank of South Carolina, N.A.
EIN: 576047689

49561
The Arnold Foundation
c/o Bank of America
1901 Main St.
Columbia, SC 29201
Application address: 7 N. Laurens St., Greenville, SC 29601
Contact: William A. Bridges

Established in 1998 in SC.
Financial data (yr. ended 12/31/01): Grants paid, $63,333; assets, $728,420 (M); expenditures, $72,622; qualifying distributions, $65,986.
Limitations: Giving primarily in SC.
Agent: Bank of America.
EIN: 586366924

49562
Earle Foundation
c/o East Broad Trust Co.
245 E. Broad St., Ste. B
Greenville, SC 29601 (864) 271-3422
FAX: (864) 271-8740; E-mail: earle@eastbroadtrustcompany.com
Contact: F. Jordan Earle, V.P.

Established in 1991 in SC; funded in 1992.
Donor(s): Louise M. Earle.‡
Financial data (yr. ended 12/31/01): Grants paid, $62,000; assets, $682,604 (M); expenditures, $64,034; qualifying distributions, $62,000.
Limitations: Giving primarily in the Greenville, SC area.
Publications: Informational brochure, grants list.
Application information: Application form required.
Officer and Trustees:* F. Jordan Earle,* V.P.; O. Perry Earle, Jr., O. Perry Earle III, Louise Earle Oxner.
EIN: 576120078

49563
Robert L. Huffines, Jr. Foundation, Inc.
P.O. Box 875
Walterboro, SC 29488
Contact: Robert L. Huffines III, Secy.

Established in 1961 in NY and VA.
Financial data (yr. ended 12/31/01): Grants paid, $61,653; assets, $1,447,843 (M); expenditures, $65,943; qualifying distributions, $61,653.
Limitations: Applications not accepted. Giving primarily in SC, and Richmond, VA.
Application information: Contributes only to pre-selected organizations.
Officers: Calvert W. Huffines, Pres.; Douglas N. Martin, V.P.; Robert L. Huffines III, Secy.
EIN: 136090862

49564
P.A.C.E. Foundation
533 Water Garden Ct.
Irmo, SC 29063
Contact: Michael D. Blackwell, Tr.

Established in 1990 in SC.
Donor(s): M.D. Blackwell.
Financial data (yr. ended 12/31/01): Grants paid, $60,699; assets, $107,362 (M); gifts received, $34,176; expenditures, $66,416; qualifying distributions, $60,651.
Limitations: Applications not accepted. Giving primarily in Cola, SC.
Application information: Contributes only to pre-selected organizations.
Trustees: D.P. Blackwell, Michael D. Blackwell, Marion H. Davis, R. Moss.
EIN: 570918115

49565
The Tom and Jane Addison Foundation, Inc.
c/o R. Stephen Heckard
P.O. Box 11001
Rock Hill, SC 29731

Established in 1996 in SC.
Financial data (yr. ended 12/31/01): Grants paid, $60,000; assets, $1,201,975 (M); expenditures, $73,213; qualifying distributions, $60,000.
Limitations: Applications not accepted. Giving primarily in SC.
Application information: Contributes only to pre-selected organizations.
Trustees: T.E. Addison, Jr., Murray Addison Handback, Mary Jane Addison Heckard.
EIN: 570977111

49566
The Wallace Foundation
21 Chestnut Ridge Rd.
Greenville, SC 29609 (864) 233-5037
Contact: Frances W. Wallace, Tr.

Established in 1997 in SC.
Financial data (yr. ended 12/31/01): Grants paid, $60,000; assets, $1,489,691 (M); expenditures, $76,219; qualifying distributions, $60,000.
Limitations: Giving primarily in Greenville, SC.
Trustees: Martha W. Pellett, Frances W. Wallace.
EIN: 586343201

49567
Marlboro General Hospital, Inc.
(also known as Marlboro General Hospital Charities)
P.O. Box 33
Bennettsville, SC 29512
Application address: 108 N. Liberty St., Bennettsville, SC 29512
Contact: Charles P. Midgley, Chair.

Established in 1982.

Financial data (yr. ended 09/30/99): Grants paid, $59,926; assets, $1,452,146 (M); gifts received, $102,181; expenditures, $87,663; qualifying distributions, $63,626.
Limitations: Giving primarily in Marlboro County, SC.
Application information: Application form not required.
Officers and Trustees:* Charles P. Midgley,* Chair.; Charles O'Neal,* Vice-Chair.; Tracy Kea, Jr.,* Secy.; W.H. Bellinger, Treas.
EIN: 570750184

49568
S. J. Wall Charitable Trust
P.O. Box 747
Marion, SC 29571-0747

Established in 1989 in SC.
Financial data (yr. ended 12/31/01): Grants paid, $59,674; assets, $70,799 (M); gifts received, $71,000; expenditures, $60,361; qualifying distributions, $59,674.
Limitations: Applications not accepted. Giving primarily in Marion and Mullins, SC.
Application information: Contributes only to pre-selected organizations.
Trustees: Chester A. Duke, J.M. McLendon, W.B. Norton.
EIN: 576023857

49569
Russ & Andrea Gullotti Charitable Foundation
c/o Russ Gullotti
1 Crabtree Ln.
Bluffton, SC 29910

Established in 2000 in MN.
Donor(s): Russ Gullotti.
Financial data (yr. ended 12/31/01): Grants paid, $59,050; assets, $897,868 (M); gifts received, $50,000; expenditures, $72,351; qualifying distributions, $59,050.
Limitations: Applications not accepted.
Application information: Contributes only to pre-selected organizations.
Officers: Russ Gullotti, Pres.; Andrea Gullotti, Secy.-Treas.
EIN: 416481751

49570
The John & Kathleen Rivers Foundation, Inc.
(Formerly John M. Rivers, Jr. Foundation, Inc.)
40 Calhoun St., Ste. 500
Charleston, SC 29401
Application address: P.O. Box 21050, Charleston, SC 29413; FAX: (843) 723-5221
Contact: John M. Rivers, Jr., Pres.

Established in 1995 SC.
Financial data (yr. ended 12/31/01): Grants paid, $58,600; assets, $2,952,688 (M); gifts received, $525; expenditures, $69,236; qualifying distributions, $59,215.
Limitations: Giving primarily in Wallingford, CT, Atlanta, GA, Cashiers and Chapel Hill, NC, and Charleston, SC.
Application information: Application form not required.
Officers and Directors:* John M. Rivers, Jr.,* Pres.; Kathleen H. Rivers,* V.P.; Edward H. Daniell,* Treas.; A. Palmer Elebash, Legrand Elebash, Thomas Waring, J. Rutledge Young, Jr.
EIN: 570907666

49571
Tribble Foundation
P.O. Box 796
Seneca, SC 29679-0796 (864) 882-9440
Application address: P.O. Box 794, Seneca, SC 29678-0794
Contact: Robert N. McLellan, Tr.

Established in 1968.
Financial data (yr. ended 06/30/01): Grants paid, $58,220; assets, $1,071,681 (M); expenditures, $60,344; qualifying distributions, $59,108.
Limitations: Giving limited to Seneca, SC.
Application information: Applications available at guidance office of high school. Application form required.
Trustees: J. Patrick Cromer, Jr., Robert N. McLellan, Betty Nix.
EIN: 237023624

49572
The McCraw Family Foundation
100 Chapman Pl.
Greenville, SC 29605

Established in 2000 in SC.
Donor(s): Leslie G. McCraw, Jr., Mary Earle Brown McCraw.
Financial data (yr. ended 12/31/01): Grants paid, $57,105; assets, $197,527 (M); expenditures, $58,681; qualifying distributions, $57,105.
Limitations: Applications not accepted. Giving primarily in Clemson and Greenville, SC.
Application information: Contributes only to pre-selected organizations.
Trustees: Leslie G. McCraw, Jr., Mary Earle Brown McCraw.
EIN: 571088866

49573
First Citizens Foundation, Inc.
1230 Main St.
Columbia, SC 29201
Contact: Peter Bristow, V.P.

Established in 2000 in SC.
Donor(s): First Citizens Bancorporation of SC.
Financial data (yr. ended 12/31/00): Grants paid, $56,667; assets, $91,254 (M); gifts received, $147,938; expenditures, $56,684; qualifying distributions, $56,667.
Application information: Application form required.
Officers: Jim Apple, Pres.; Peter Bristow, V.P.; E.W. Wells, Secy.; Jay Case, Treas.
EIN: 571108547

49574
Waite C. Hamrick, Jr. Foundation
(Formerly Hamrick Companies Foundation)
P.O. Box 1000
Gaffney, SC 29342-1000

Established in 1961 in SC.
Donor(s): Waite C. Hamrick, Jr.
Financial data (yr. ended 12/31/01): Grants paid, $56,000; assets, $937,237 (M); expenditures, $74,697; qualifying distributions, $56,000.
Limitations: Applications not accepted. Giving limited to SC.
Application information: Contributes only to pre-selected organizations.
Directors: Kay H. Bradley, William R. Bradley, Barbara H. Moorhead, Florence H. Sumner.
EIN: 576021057

49575
Sottile Foundation
P.O. Box 242
Charleston, SC 29402-0242 (843) 722-2615
Contact: Michael Macy, Treas.

Financial data (yr. ended 12/31/01): Grants paid, $53,750; assets, $682,049 (M); expenditures, $54,192; qualifying distributions, $53,750.
Limitations: Giving limited to the Charleston, SC, area.
Officer: Michael Macy, Treas.
Trustees: Joyce L. Darby, Mary Ellen Way.
EIN: 576025623

49576
Helm Foundation
c/o John E. Eisinger
P.O. Box 1769
Pawleys Island, SC 29585 (843) 237-1384
Contact: John R. Helm, Tr.

Donor(s): Harold Helm.‡
Financial data (yr. ended 12/31/00): Grants paid, $53,200; assets, $672,747 (M); gifts received, $899; expenditures, $57,515; qualifying distributions, $55,431.
Limitations: Applications not accepted. Giving primarily in MA and NJ.
Application information: Contributes only to pre-selected organizations.
Trustees: Henry Bessire, John R. Helm, Eleanor Ketcham, John Ketcham, Thomas Troxell.
EIN: 226041312

49577
Nalley Charitable Trust
P.O. Box 1929
Easley, SC 29641

Established in 1980.
Donor(s): George B. Nalley, Jr.
Financial data (yr. ended 11/30/01): Grants paid, $52,253; assets, $1,130,934 (M); gifts received, $2,212; expenditures, $65,459; qualifying distributions, $52,253.
Limitations: Giving primarily in SC.
Trustees: George B. Nalley, Jr., T. Ashton Phillips.
EIN: 570727567

49578
Taylor Foundation of Newberry, Inc.
P.O. Box 399
Newberry, SC 29108
Contact: C. Otis Taylor, Jr., Pres.

Established in 1986 in SC.
Donor(s): C. Otis Taylor, Jr.
Financial data (yr. ended 12/31/01): Grants paid, $50,400; assets, $1,029,838 (M); expenditures, $52,878; qualifying distributions, $50,400.
Limitations: Giving primarily in SC.
Application information: Application form not required.
Officer and Directors:* C. Otis Taylor, Jr.,* Pres.; C. Otis Taylor III, E. Cannon Taylor, Amelia T. Webb.
Trustee: Ann C. Taylor.
EIN: 570809199

49579
Dick Smith Foundation, Inc.
4030 Beltline Blvd.
Columbia, SC 29204-1507
Contact: Richard D. Smith, Pres.

Established in 1988 in SC.
Financial data (yr. ended 06/30/01): Grants paid, $50,375; assets, $484,430 (M); gifts received, $60,000; expenditures, $56,990; qualifying distributions, $50,375.
Limitations: Giving primarily in SC.
Officers: Richard D. Smith, Pres.; Brian K. Smith, V.P.; David W. Smith, V.P.; Wilma W. Smith, Secy.-Treas.
EIN: 570878887

49580
Ethel-Jane Westfeldt Bunting Foundation Trust
c/o W. Thomas Rutledge, Jr.
P.O. Box 22828
Charleston, SC 29413-2828

Established in 1998.
Financial data (yr. ended 12/31/01): Grants paid, $50,250; assets, $967,885 (M); expenditures, $67,566; qualifying distributions, $50,250.
Limitations: Giving primarily in SC.
Trustee: W. Thomas Rutledge, Jr.
EIN: 311486079

49581
McShane Family Foundation, Inc.
c/o Mary Ann Doyle
9 Wedgefield Dr.
Hilton Head Island, SC 29926

Established in 1997 in SC.
Donor(s): Mary Ann Doyle.
Financial data (yr. ended 12/31/01): Grants paid, $50,000; assets, $902,631 (M); expenditures, $53,159; qualifying distributions, $50,000.
Limitations: Applications not accepted.
Application information: Contributes only to pre-selected organizations.
Officers and Directors:* Mary Ann Doyle,* Pres.; Karen Doyle Buterbaugh,* Secy.; Marianne Doyle,* Treas.; John Disbrow, Michael L.M. Jordan.
EIN: 562027936

49582
Llelanie Sutton Orcutt Foundation Trust
c/o Llelanie Orcutt
67 Surfwatch
Kiawah Island, SC 29455

Established in 1997 in SC.
Donor(s): Llelanie S. Orcutt.
Financial data (yr. ended 12/31/99): Grants paid, $50,000; assets, $414,484 (M); expenditures, $50,000; qualifying distributions, $48,684.
Limitations: Applications not accepted. Giving primarily in SC.
Application information: Contributes only to pre-selected organizations.
Trustee: Llelanie S. Orcutt.
EIN: 576163928

49583
The Hunt Foundation, Inc.
1830 N. Main St.
Greenville, SC 29609

Established in 1989 in SC.
Donor(s): Roy F. Hunt, Jr.
Financial data (yr. ended 12/31/01): Grants paid, $49,398; assets, $18,756 (M); gifts received, $155; expenditures, $50,560; qualifying distributions, $49,398.
Limitations: Applications not accepted. Giving primarily in SC.
Application information: Contributes only to pre-selected organizations.
Officer: Roy F. Hunt, Jr., Pres.
Directors: Eva P. Hunt, W. Powers Hunt.
EIN: 570885975

49584
The CMI Foundation
P.O. Drawer 11589
Columbia, SC 29211
Application address: 600 Academy St., Clinton, SC 29325, tel.: (803) 748-1713
Contact: C. Mack Parsons

Established in 1989.
Donor(s): CMI Industries, Inc.
Financial data (yr. ended 12/31/01): Grants paid, $49,150; assets, $32,867 (M); gifts received, $28,255; expenditures, $49,167; qualifying distributions, $49,166.
Application information: Application form required.
Trustee: James A. Ovenden.
EIN: 570857309

49585
The Frank J. and Lucy C. Hartzog Memorial Foundation, Inc.
8354 Reynolds Rd.
Blackville, SC 29817   (803) 266-3925
Contact: Don B. Still, V.P.

Established in 1989 in SC; funded in 1990.
Financial data (yr. ended 12/31/01): Grants paid, $48,249; assets, $938,300 (M); expenditures, $53,486; qualifying distributions, $49,221.
Limitations: Giving primarily in Barnwell County, SC.
Application information: Application form required.
Officers: William R. Delk, Pres. and Treas.; Don B. Still, V.P. and Secy.
Directors: John R. Delk, Howard C. Still.
EIN: 570888865

49586
Julia Porter Scurry Family Foundation
P.O. Box 1547
Greenwood, SC 29648
Contact: Kenneth W. Poston

Established in 1999 in SC.
Donor(s): John C. Scurry.
Financial data (yr. ended 03/31/02): Grants paid, $46,000; assets, $825,340 (M); expenditures, $49,218; qualifying distributions, $46,000.
Officers: John C. Scurry, Chair.; John C. Scurry, Jr., Vice-Chair. and Secy.-Treas.
Trustees: Harriet S. Johnson, Jane S. Kiser, William P. Scurry.
EIN: 562136364

49587
Atlantic Services of Charleston Charitable Trust
c/o Atlantic Charitable
P.O. Box 62948
North Charleston, SC 29419   (843) 566-7670
Contact: David Maybank, Jr., Tr.

Established in 1982.
Donor(s): Atlantic Services Group, Inc., David Maybank, Jr.
Financial data (yr. ended 06/30/01): Grants paid, $45,500; assets, $283,350 (M); gifts received, $24,000; expenditures, $51,392; qualifying distributions, $122,359.
Limitations: Giving primarily in Charleston, SC.
Trustees: David Maybank, Jr., Louise J. Maybank.
EIN: 570741318
Codes: CS, CD

49588
The Capricorn Foundation
c/o L.E. & Jan B. Jones
931 Norris Dr.
Pawleys Island, SC 29585-5173
Contact: L.E. Jones, Pres.

Established in 1995 in SC.
Financial data (yr. ended 12/31/01): Grants paid, $44,051; assets, $192,034 (M); expenditures, $47,258; qualifying distributions, $43,921.
Limitations: Giving primarily in SC.
Application information: Application form required.
Officer: L.E. Jones, Pres.
EIN: 571011351
Codes: GTI

49589
Charleston Scientific & Cultural Educational Fund
P.O. Box 340
Charleston, SC 29402-0340   (843) 722-3366
Contact: Charlton deSaussure, Jr., Secy.-Treas.

Financial data (yr. ended 12/31/01): Grants paid, $43,733; assets, $446,742 (M); expenditures, $63,585; qualifying distributions, $43,733.
Limitations: Giving limited to residents of SC.
Application information: Application form required.
Officer: Charlton deSaussure, Jr., Secy.
Directors: J. Walker Coleman, J. Palmer Gaillard, Jr., Maj. Gen. James A. Grimsley, Jr., Barbara S. Williams.
Trustee: Bank of America.
EIN: 576019987
Codes: GTI

49590
George D. Shore Residual Trust
c/o The National Bank of South Carolina, Trust Dept.
P.O. Box 1798
Sumter, SC 29151

Financial data (yr. ended 12/31/00): Grants paid, $43,370; assets, $628,940 (M); expenditures, $56,373; qualifying distributions, $43,370.
Limitations: Applications not accepted. Giving limited to VA.
Application information: Contributes only to a pre-selected organization.
Trustee: The National Bank of South Carolina.
EIN: 576136896

49591
Francis Nathaniel and Katheryn Padgett Kennedy Foundation
P.O. Box 49
Laurens, SC 29360
Contact: Don Johnson

Established in 1973 in SC.
Donor(s): Katheryn Padgett Kennedy,‡ Francis Nathaniel Kennedy.‡
Financial data (yr. ended 06/30/01): Grants paid, $43,250; assets, $1,388,934 (M); expenditures, $63,216; qualifying distributions, $48,750.
Limitations: Giving limited to residents of Abbeville, Anderson, Cherokee, Greenville, Greenwood, Laurens, McCormick, Oconee, Pickens, Spartanburg, Union, and York counties, SC.
Publications: Informational brochure (including application guidelines).
Application information: Application form required.
Trustees: James E. Bryan, Jr., James P. Faris, Sr., B.T. Kennedy, Jimmy McAdams, L. Leon Patterson, James Yarbrough.
EIN: 237347655
Codes: GTI

49592
H. & N. Morgan Foundation, Inc.
84 Woodvale Ave.
Greenville, SC 29605-1131

Established in 1988 in SC.
Donor(s): C. Heyward Morgan.
Financial data (yr. ended 12/31/01): Grants paid, $43,200; assets, $320,590 (M); expenditures, $44,212; qualifying distributions, $43,200.
Limitations: Applications not accepted.
Application information: Contributes only to pre-selected organizations.
Trustees: C. Heyward Morgan, Nancy P. Morgan, Raymond P. Morgan.
EIN: 570880214

49593
C. W. Anderson Foundation
P.O. Box 765
Clinton, SC 29325-0765
Contact: Collie W. Lehn, Chair.

Established in 1961.
Financial data (yr. ended 07/31/01): Grants paid, $42,234; assets, $1,097,725 (M); expenditures, $51,288; qualifying distributions, $42,234.
Limitations: Giving limited to Laurens County, SC.
Application information: Application form not required.
Officer and Trustees:* Collie W. Lehn,* Chair.; Barbara A. Frady, Norma A. Lehn, Catherine A. Orr, Robert M. Strickland.
EIN: 576018388

49594
Dorothy Hooper Beattie Foundation
c/o Bank of America
P.O. Box 608
Greenville, SC 29602
Contact: Mary W. Green, Trust Off., Bank of America

Financial data (yr. ended 10/30/00): Grants paid, $42,200; assets, $664,696 (M); expenditures, $50,724; qualifying distributions, $44,409.
Limitations: Giving limited to SC.
Selection Committee Members: Wilbur Y. Bridgers, Chair.; Rev. Dannals, Todd Harward.
Trustee: Bank of America.
EIN: 576084747

49595
The Hart-Oeland Foundation Trust
P.O. Box 127
Belton, SC 29627
Contact: Carroll B. Hart, Sr., Tr.

Established in 1999 in SC.
Donor(s): Carroll B. Hart, Sr., Carroll Hart, Jr., Martha O. Hart.
Financial data (yr. ended 12/31/01): Grants paid, $40,000; assets, $692,272 (M); expenditures, $52,473; qualifying distributions, $39,883.
Officer and Trustees:* Carroll B. Hart, Sr.,* Chair.; Carroll B. Hart, Jr., Martha H. Kent.
EIN: 571062433

49596
Vandy Charitable Foundation, Inc.
c/o Lucille V. Pate
P.O. Drawer 458
Georgetown, SC 29442

Established in 1995 in SC.
Financial data (yr. ended 03/31/02): Grants paid, $39,000; assets, $745,666 (M); gifts received, $159,488; expenditures, $45,258; qualifying distributions, $39,000.

Limitations: Applications not accepted.
Application information: Contributes only to pre-selected organizations.
Director: Lucille V. Pate.
EIN: 571029335

49597
The West Foundation, Inc.
P.O. Box 643
Camden, SC 29020-0643 (803) 425-1115
E-mail: westpsi@aol.com
Contact: Lois R. West, Chair.

Established in 1984 in SC.
Financial data (yr. ended 05/31/00): Grants paid, $34,750; assets, $996,262 (M); gifts received, $7,650; expenditures, $88,434; qualifying distributions, $57,969.
Limitations: Giving primarily in SC.
Application information: Application form required.
Officers: Lois R. West, Chair.; Shelton W. Bosley, Secy.-Treas.
Directors: Martha Bee Anderson, Col. Robert E. David, W.M. Grooms, Douglas A. West, J.C. West, Jr., C.H. Whickenburg.
EIN: 237405238

49598
Wherry Family Foundation
(Formerly The Wherry-Miller Foundation)
P.O. Box 5025, Station B
Greenville, SC 29606-5025

Established in 1990 in SC.
Donor(s): Elizabeth Wherry.
Financial data (yr. ended 11/30/01): Grants paid, $34,450; assets, $766,598 (M); gifts received, $20,000; expenditures, $49,836; qualifying distributions, $34,650.
Limitations: Applications not accepted.
Application information: Contributes only to pre-selected organizations.
Trustee: John Knox Wherry.
EIN: 576023443

49599
The George E. Tucker Educational and Charitable Trust
P.O. Box 181
York, SC 29745 (803) 684-4968

Financial data (yr. ended 11/30/01): Grants paid, $34,200; assets, $703,168 (M); expenditures, $36,059; qualifying distributions, $34,200.
Limitations: Giving primarily in the York, SC, area.
Application information: Application form required.
Trustees: John S. Adkins, Melvin B. McKeown, C. Curtis Sigmon.
EIN: 576103971

49600
Encouragement Foundation Trust
c/o Betty Wray Anderson
98 King St.
Charleston, SC 29401

Established in 2000 in LA.
Donor(s): Helen H. Wray Charitable Remainder Trust.
Financial data (yr. ended 12/31/01): Grants paid, $34,000; assets, $159 (M); gifts received, $36,500; expenditures, $36,511; qualifying distributions, $36,400.
Limitations: Applications not accepted. Giving on a national basis, with emphasis on the South.
Application information: Contributes only to pre-selected organizations.
Trustees: Betty Wray Anderson, Brady Anderson.
EIN: 316637537

49601
Tuller Educational Foundation
2700 William H. Tuller Dr.
Columbia, SC 29205 (803) 799-5335
Contact: William H. Tuller, Jr., Mgr.

Donor(s): William H. Tuller, Jr.
Financial data (yr. ended 12/31/99): Grants paid, $33,096; assets, $67,175 (M); expenditures, $33,192; qualifying distributions, $32,976.
Limitations: Giving primarily in Columbia, SC.
Application information: Application form not required.
Officers: W. Dubose Tuller, Mgr.; William H. Tuller, Jr., Mgr.
EIN: 576026832

49602
Robert & Patricia Goodyear Family Foundation
P.O. Box 632
Aiken, SC 29802

Donor(s): Robert M. Goodyear, Patricia S. Goodyear.
Financial data (yr. ended 12/31/01): Grants paid, $33,030; assets, $130,133 (M); gifts received, $6,000; expenditures, $41,548; qualifying distributions, $33,030.
Limitations: Giving primarily in Aiken, SC.
Trustees: Patricia S. Goodyear, Robert M. Goodyear, Robert M. Goodyear, Jr.
EIN: 166468633

49603
The Reese & Sis Hart Foundation
1309 Highmarket St.
Georgetown, SC 29440
Application address: P.O. Box 423, Georgetown, SC 29442
Contact: J.S. Bourne, Dir.

Established in 1999 in SC.
Donor(s): W. Reese Hart.‡
Financial data (yr. ended 12/31/00): Grants paid, $32,350; assets, $478,048 (M); expenditures, $51,537; qualifying distributions, $32,008.
Limitations: Giving primarily in Georgetown, SC.
Application information: Application form required.
Directors: J.S. Bourne, David Tanner, Craig M. Thomas.
EIN: 582435805

49604
The Provence Foundation
214 W. McBee Ave.
P.O. Box 1808
Greenville, SC 29602-1808
Contact: Herbert H. Provence, Jr., Chair.

Established in 1994 in SC.
Donor(s): Gwendolyn F. Provence.
Financial data (yr. ended 11/30/01): Grants paid, $31,650; assets, $138,252 (M); gifts received, $1,000; expenditures, $33,054; qualifying distributions, $31,650.
Application information: Application form required.
Officers and Directors:* Herbert H. Provence, Jr.,* Chair.; H. Hall Provence III,* Pres. and Treas.; Gwendolyn F. Provence,* Secy.; Julia Provence Lane.
EIN: 571012469

49605
Samuel J. Goldfarb Foundation, Inc.
P.O. Box 1130
West Columbia, SC 29171

Established about 1949.
Donor(s): House of Perfection.

Financial data (yr. ended 09/30/01): Grants paid, $31,359; assets, $60,377 (M); gifts received, $50,000; expenditures, $31,612; qualifying distributions, $31,359.
Limitations: Applications not accepted.
Application information: Contributes only to pre-selected organizations.
Officer: David M. Nishtile, Cont.
Director: Gene Goldfarb.
EIN: 136161407

49606
The Cashion Foundation
c/o Marshall Nichols
P.O. Box 266
Fountain Inn, SC 29644-0266

Financial data (yr. ended 12/31/01): Grants paid, $31,321; assets, $53,169 (M); gifts received, $300; expenditures, $33,554; qualifying distributions, $31,321.
Application information: Application form required.
Trustees: Marshall Nichols, J. Samuel Peden, Joane W. Rampey.
EIN: 570958029

49607
The Calhoun Lemon Family Foundation
(Formerly Lemon Family Foundation, Inc.)
P.O. Box 385
Barnwell, SC 29812 (803) 259-3546
Contact: Clinton C. Lemon, Jr.

Financial data (yr. ended 12/31/01): Grants paid, $31,300; assets, $177,868 (M); gifts received, $98,500; expenditures, $40,466; qualifying distributions, $36,982.
Limitations: Giving primarily in Barnwell, SC.
Officers: Clinton C. Lemon, Jr., Pres.; Mary L. Townsend, V.P. and Secy.; Kathryn Lemon Clark, V.P. and Treas.
EIN: 570694098

49608
The Waggoner Family Foundation, Inc.
Rte. 4, Box 1262-B
Manning, SC 29102

Established in 1992 in SC.
Donor(s): William D. Waggoner.
Financial data (yr. ended 03/31/02): Grants paid, $31,000; assets, $477,264 (M); expenditures, $32,790; qualifying distributions, $31,000.
Limitations: Applications not accepted. Giving primarily in SC.
Application information: Contributes only to pre-selected organizations.
Officers and Director:* William D. Waggoner,* Pres.; Richard L. Waggoner, V.P.; Elizabeth W. Holder, Secy.; Judith W. Bourne, Treas.
EIN: 561797439

49609
The Appleby Family Foundation, Inc.
5 Fisher's Alley
Isle of Palms, SC 29451

Established in 1999 in NY.
Donor(s): Michael Appleby.
Financial data (yr. ended 09/30/01): Grants paid, $30,500; assets, $61,298 (M); gifts received, $60,362; expenditures, $30,500; qualifying distributions, $30,500.
Limitations: Applications not accepted. Giving primarily in SC.
Application information: Contributes only to pre-selected organizations.
Directors: Michael Appleby, Cynthia Straney, Diane Straney.
EIN: 134098021

49610
Osbon Family Foundation
4031 Pennington Rd.
Greer, SC 29651

Established in 2000 in SC.
Donor(s): Robert E. Osbon.
Financial data (yr. ended 12/31/00): Grants paid, $30,000; assets, $29,937 (M); gifts received, $60,000; expenditures, $30,072; qualifying distributions, $30,063.
Limitations: Applications not accepted. Giving primarily in MS.
Application information: Contributes only to pre-selected organizations.
Directors: Patricia Z. Osbon, Robert E. Osbon.
EIN: 571110453

49611
Easterby Charitable Foundation
P.O. Box 49
Laurens, SC 29360
Application address: 1004 W. Main St., Laurens, SC 29360
Contact: Harriett E. Faris, Tr.

Financial data (yr. ended 09/30/01): Grants paid, $29,406; assets, $521,192 (M); gifts received, $1,138; expenditures, $36,235; qualifying distributions, $28,513.
Limitations: Giving primarily in Laurens County, SC.
Trustee: Harriett Faris.
EIN: 570639616

49612
Elizabeth Calvin Bonner Foundation
P.O. Box 22828
Charleston, SC 29413-2828
Contact: W. Thomas Rutledge, Jr., Tr.

Established in 2001.
Financial data (yr. ended 12/31/01): Grants paid, $28,500; assets, $970,645 (M); gifts received, $1,022,819; expenditures, $38,725; qualifying distributions, $28,500.
Trustee: W. Thomas Rutledge, Jr.
EIN: 571123927

49613
The Toporek Family Foundation, Inc.
2720 Bayonne St.
Sullivans Island, SC 29482

Financial data (yr. ended 12/31/01): Grants paid, $28,248; assets, $77,667 (M); gifts received, $5,000; expenditures, $28,248; qualifying distributions, $28,248.
Limitations: Applications not accepted.
Application information: Contributes only to pre-selected organizations.
Officer: Edwin S. Toporek.
EIN: 571090356

49614
Glenmore & May Sharp Trust
P.O. Box 998
Sumter, SC 29151
Application address: 211 Wactor St., Sumter, SC 29150
Contact: Glenmore R. Sharp, Tr.

Established in 1997.
Financial data (yr. ended 12/31/01): Grants paid, $28,100; assets, $580,045 (M); expenditures, $29,100; qualifying distributions, $28,100.
Limitations: Giving primarily in SC.
Application information: Letter.
Trustee: Glenmore R. Sharp.
EIN: 586344359

49615
H. M. Shaw, Sr. Trust
c/o Wachovia Bank of North Carolina, N.A.
P.O. Box 494
Clinton, SC 29325-0494
Application address: Merrie Oaks, Clinton, SC 29325
Contact: Ann S. Cornelson, Advisory Comm. Member

Financial data (yr. ended 12/31/01): Grants paid, $28,079; assets, $581,395 (M); expenditures, $32,927; qualifying distributions, $28,079.
Advisory Committee Members: Ann S. Cornelson, George H. Cornelson, Scott Cornelson.
Trustee: Wachovia Bank of North Carolina, N.A.
EIN: 566035982

49616
Harvey I. Yoder Foundation
9496 S. Highway II
Westminster, SC 29693

Established in 1999 in SC.
Financial data (yr. ended 06/30/02): Grants paid, $28,000; assets, $514,282 (M); gifts received, $97,000; expenditures, $29,404; qualifying distributions, $28,000.
Limitations: Applications not accepted.
Application information: Contributes only to pre-selected organizations.
Officer and Directors:* Floyd H. Yoder,* Pres.; Titus Overholt, Joseph H. Yoder.
EIN: 571080071

49617
Joan Sasser Coker and Charles Westfield Coker Charitable Foundation
407 Woodland Dr.
Hartsville, SC 29550-3641

Established in 1998 in SC.
Donor(s): Ellen C. Baldwin, Charles W. Coker, Sr., Charles W. Coker, Jr., Robert Howard Coker, Thomas Lide Coker, Margaret C. Galloway, Carrie C. Haley.
Financial data (yr. ended 12/31/01): Grants paid, $27,880; assets, $533,941 (M); expenditures, $30,182; qualifying distributions, $27,880.
Limitations: Giving primarily in SC.
Trustees: Ellen C. Baldwin, Charles W. Coker, Charles W. Coker, Jr., Robert Howard Coker, Thomas Lide Coker, Margaret C. Galloway, Carrie C. Haley.
EIN: 571067455

49618
The C. Y. Thomason Foundation of Greenwood, South Carolina
c/o The County Bank
P.O. Box 3208
Greenwood, SC 29648-3208 (864) 223-8111
Contact: G. William Thomason, Dir.

Established around 1974.
Financial data (yr. ended 12/31/99): Grants paid, $27,689; assets, $784,858 (M); expenditures, $30,503; qualifying distributions, $27,689.
Limitations: Giving primarily in Greenwood, SC.
Directors: Suzanne T. Roland, G. William Thomason, Richard H. Thomason.
EIN: 237441175

49619
Pellett Foundation
P.O. Box 6266, Sta. B
Greenville, SC 29606-6266

Established around 1966.
Donor(s): John D. Pellett, Jr.
Financial data (yr. ended 03/31/02): Grants paid, $25,500; assets, $719,012 (M); expenditures, $28,888; qualifying distributions, $25,500.
Limitations: Applications not accepted.
Application information: Contributes only to pre-selected organizations.
Officer: John D. Pellett, Jr., Mgr.
EIN: 237011052

49620
The David W. and Susan G. Robinson Foundation
1901 Main St., Ste. 1500
Columbia, SC 29202 (803) 779-8900

Established in 1998 in SC.
Donor(s): Robinson Lead Trust.
Financial data (yr. ended 12/31/01): Grants paid, $25,284; assets, $655,518 (M); gifts received, $197,720; expenditures, $31,999; qualifying distributions, $25,284.
Limitations: Giving primarily in SC.
Directors: David Mason Ellerbe, Frank R. Ellerbe III, Susan W. Ravenel, Heyward G. Robinson.
EIN: 582425864

49621
Prosser Foundation
P.O. Box 1146
Murrells Inlet, SC 29576

Financial data (yr. ended 12/31/01): Grants paid, $25,240; assets, $294,352 (M); gifts received, $1,000; expenditures, $37,418; qualifying distributions, $25,240.
Limitations: Applications not accepted.
Application information: Contributes only to pre-selected organizations.
Officer: Larry N. Prosser, Pres.
EIN: 571012468

49622
Albert Dial Educational Trust
P.O. Box 247
Laurens, SC 29360-0131
Application address: P.O. Box 49, Laurens, SC, 29360, tel.: (864) 984-4551
Contact: David Martin, Tr. Off., Palmetto Bank

Financial data (yr. ended 10/31/01): Grants paid, $25,100; assets, $422,029 (M); gifts received, $1,000; expenditures, $30,035; qualifying distributions, $25,011.
Limitations: Giving limited to residents of Laurens County, SC.
Trustees: Elizabeth D. Boone, Thomas Hardy, Albert D. McAlister, Leon Patterson, R. Bland Roper.
EIN: 237203948
Codes: GTI

49623
The Malloy Foundation
P.O. Drawer 807
Cheraw, SC 29520-0807

Financial data (yr. ended 10/31/01): Grants paid, $24,925; assets, $562,605 (M); expenditures, $25,564; qualifying distributions, $24,925.
Limitations: Applications not accepted. Giving primarily in SC.
Application information: Contributes only to pre-selected organizations.
Officers and Trustees:* Edwin Malloy, Jr.,* Chair.; H. Malloy Evans, Secy.; William Manning Malloy, Treas.; B.E. Coggeshall, Jr., J.G. Owens.
EIN: 576021142

SOUTH CAROLINA—49637

49624
John B. & Louise M. Thomson Family Foundation
3 Planters Pl.
Sheldon, SC 29941-0030

Established in 1986 in NY.
Donor(s): Thomson Industries.
Financial data (yr. ended 11/30/01): Grants paid, $23,955; assets, $25,329 (M); gifts received, $34,875; expenditures, $24,112; qualifying distributions, $24,103.
Limitations: Giving primarily in Nassau County, NY.
Application information: Application form not required.
Trustees: Richard M. Cummins, Dudley G. Thomson, John B. Thomson.
EIN: 112846188

49625
South Carolina Federation of Women's Clubs-Progress Foundation, Inc.
4009 Rockbridge Rd.
Columbia, SC 29206
Contact: Sylvia Ayers, Chair.

Financial data (yr. ended 02/28/02): Grants paid, $22,950; assets, $498,121 (M); gifts received, $1,053; expenditures, $24,857; qualifying distributions, $22,950.
Limitations: Giving limited to SC.
Application information: Application form required.
Officers and Trustees:* Sylvia Ayers,* Chair.; Bobbie Wilhite,* Secy.; Jan Hadwin,* Treas.; Susie Childress, Mary Higgins, Earline Odom, Mary Watts.
EIN: 576019262

49626
The From Him and Through Him Foundation
114 Blackhawk Trail
West Columbia, SC 29169 (803) 939-3373

Established in 1993 in SC.
Donor(s): W. Tobin Cassels III.
Financial data (yr. ended 12/31/01): Grants paid, $22,800; assets, $420,670 (M); expenditures, $25,813; qualifying distributions, $22,800.
Limitations: Applications not accepted. Giving primarily in Columbia, SC.
Application information: Contributes only to pre-selected organizations.
Officers and Directors:* W. Tobin Cassels III,* Pres.; Patricia H. Cassels,* Secy.; W.T. Cassels, Jr.,* Treas.
EIN: 570981565

49627
F. N. Cecchini Foundation
429 Press Lindler Rd.
Columbia, SC 29212-8322

Established in SC in 1998.
Financial data (yr. ended 12/31/99): Grants paid, $22,100; assets, $541,708 (L); expenditures, $31,995; qualifying distributions, $22,100.
Limitations: Applications not accepted. Giving primarily in Orangeburg, SC.
Application information: Contributes only to pre-selected organizations.
Trustees: Dorothy V. Farner, James L. Parnell.
EIN: 582277649

49628
Thomson Foundation
107 Carter Hill Dr.
Anderson, SC 29621-1976

Financial data (yr. ended 12/31/00): Grants paid, $22,080; assets, $388,240 (M); expenditures, $24,220; qualifying distributions, $22,080.
Limitations: Applications not accepted. Giving limited within a 60-mile radius of Greenville, SC.
Application information: Contributes only to pre-selected organizations.
Officers and Trustees:* Janie R. Curtis,* Mgr.; James C. Thomson,* Mgr.; Pauline T. Rice, Eleanor T. Roy.
EIN: 576029007

49629
W. R. & E. H. Floyd Foundation
P.O. Box 1150
Drayton, SC 29333

Established in 2000 in SC.
Donor(s): Elizabeth H. Floyd.
Financial data (yr. ended 10/31/01): Grants paid, $21,800; assets, $330,790 (M); gifts received, $350,000; expenditures, $22,009; qualifying distributions, $22,009.
Limitations: Giving primarily in Spartanburg, SC.
Trustees: A. Gordon Floyd, Angeleita Stevens Floyd, William Russell Floyd, Jr., Suzan Floyd Mabry.
EIN: 571112879

49630
The Sherman Family Charitable Trust
P.O. Box 981
Charleston, SC 29402-0981

Financial data (yr. ended 12/31/01): Grants paid, $21,500; assets, $61,880 (M); expenditures, $21,500; qualifying distributions, $21,500.
Limitations: Applications not accepted. Giving primarily in SC.
Application information: Contributes only to pre-selected organizations.
Trustees: Harold I. Sherman, Howard B. Sherman, Ivan M. Sherman, Mitchell L. Sherman.
EIN: 576100160

49631
The Bates Family Foundation
4371 Charlotte Hwy., Ste. 10
Lake Wylie, SC 29710 (803) 831-0577
Contact: Ann M. Fielding, Secy.

Established around 1993.
Donor(s): Randy J. Bates.
Financial data (yr. ended 12/31/01): Grants paid, $21,000; assets, $289,826 (M); expenditures, $21,431; qualifying distributions, $21,000.
Limitations: Giving primarily in Atlanta, GA, and NC.
Officers and Directors:* Randy J. Bates,* Pres.; Kathy D. Bates,* Secy.; Kenneth E. Hester, Treas.
EIN: 561803229

49632
Margaret H. Harrison Foundation
8 Pelican Watch Ct.
Hilton Head Island, SC 29928 (843) 681-8255
Contact: Margaret H. Harrison, Chair.

Established in 1986 in SC.
Financial data (yr. ended 12/31/01): Grants paid, $21,000; assets, $647,508 (M); expenditures, $32,529; qualifying distributions, $21,000.
Limitations: Giving primarily in Hilton Head Island, SC.
Application information: Application form not required.

Officers and Directors:* Margaret H. Harrison,* Chair.; Arthur Bruce Harrison,* Vice-Chair.; Josephine H. Tobin, Secy.; Richard R. Lazard, Treas.
EIN: 570839086

49633
Alphons and Ruth Vink Foundation, Inc
1083 West End Rd.
Chester, SC 29706

Established in 2001 in NJ.
Financial data (yr. ended 12/31/01): Grants paid, $20,900; assets, $325,837 (M); expenditures, $25,217; qualifying distributions, $21,570.
Limitations: Giving primarily in Canton, OH.
Trustee: Lee Barber.
EIN: 223530774

49634
The Premier Foundation
206 Riverside Ct. A
Greer, SC 29650-4508

Established in 1998 in SC.
Donor(s): Gary Gentry.
Financial data (yr. ended 06/30/01): Grants paid, $20,540; assets, $331,465 (M); gifts received, $1,320; expenditures, $22,875; qualifying distributions, $20,373.
Limitations: Applications not accepted. Giving primarily in MD and SC.
Application information: Contributes only to pre-selected organizations.
Trustees: Debbie Gentry, Gary Gentry.
EIN: 562066166

49635
The Lowndes Foundation, Inc.
P.O. Box 5042
Spartanburg, SC 29304 (864) 583-3635

Established in 1997; funded in 1999.
Financial data (yr. ended 12/31/01): Grants paid, $20,500; assets, $1,964,562 (M); gifts received, $1,608,262; expenditures, $132,945; qualifying distributions, $20,500.
Officers: William Lowndes III, Pres. and Treas.; Henrietta Lowndes, Secy.
EIN: 571027898

49636
Sol and Celia Cohen Endowment Fund
171 Church St., Ste. 360
Charleston, SC 29401-3140

Established in 1991 in SC.
Donor(s): Celia F. Cohen.
Financial data (yr. ended 06/30/02): Grants paid, $20,334; assets, $381,254 (M); expenditures, $21,054; qualifying distributions, $20,334.
Limitations: Applications not accepted. Giving primarily in Charleston, SC.
Application information: Contributes only to pre-selected organizations.
Officers: Celia F. Cohen, Pres.; David L. Cohen, V.P. and Treas.; Linda G. Cohen, Secy.
EIN: 570946147

49637
The Brooks Family Foundation, Inc.
2420 Royal Oak Dr.
Johns Island, SC 29455

Established in 1998 in SC.
Financial data (yr. ended 12/31/01): Grants paid, $20,175; assets, $151,973 (M); gifts received, $25,405; expenditures, $21,076; qualifying distributions, $20,175.
Limitations: Applications not accepted. Giving primarily in Charleston, SC.

49637—SOUTH CAROLINA

Application information: Contributes only to pre-selected organizations.
Officers: John J. Brooks, Pres.; Jane C. Brooks, V.P.; Deborah B. Durden, Secy.-Treas.
Director: John J. Brooks, Jr.
EIN: 562112856

49638
Mary Eldredge Greenwell Family Foundation, Inc.
44 Brams Point Rd.
Hilton Head Island, SC 29926

Established in 2000 in FL.
Donor(s): Mary Greenwell, Jon Greenwell.
Financial data (yr. ended 06/30/02): Grants paid, $20,000; assets, $284 (M); gifts received, $5,000; expenditures, $20,034; qualifying distributions, $20,000.
Limitations: Applications not accepted. Giving primarily in Miami, FL.
Application information: Contributes only to pre-selected organizations.
Officers and Directors:* Mary Greenwell,* Pres.; Jon Greenwell,* Secy.-Treas.; Donald Tescher.
EIN: 311706010

49639
The Marjorie & Langdon Ligon Foundation
c/o Langdon S. Ligon Jr.
1101 Edwards Rd.
Greenville, SC 29615

Established in 2000 in SC.
Donor(s): Ligon Christian Endowment.
Financial data (yr. ended 12/31/01): Grants paid, $20,000; assets, $730,278 (M); gifts received, $831,183; expenditures, $27,220; qualifying distributions, $26,942.
Limitations: Applications not accepted.
Application information: Contributes only to pre-selected organizations.
Officers: Lang Ligon, Pres.; Harrell Ligon, V.P.; George Short, Secy.-Treas.
EIN: 571071472

49640
The Nesbitt Family Foundation, Inc.
13 Angel Wing Dr.
Hilton Head Island, SC 29926

Established in 1996 in SC.
Financial data (yr. ended 12/31/01): Grants paid, $20,000; assets, $187,255 (M); expenditures, $21,760; qualifying distributions, $20,000.
Limitations: Applications not accepted.
Application information: Contributes only to pre-selected organizations.
Officer and Trustees:* George A. Nesbitt,* Pres.; Sherron Nesbitt.
EIN: 571060698

49641
Harriet Jackson Phelps Charitable Trust
P.O. Box 428
Camden, SC 29020-0428
Contact: Austin M. Sheheen, Jr., Tr.

Financial data (yr. ended 12/31/01): Grants paid, $20,000; assets, $511,034 (M); expenditures, $20,332; qualifying distributions, $20,000.
Limitations: Giving primarily in SC.
Trustees: Walter Bull, Caroline Kane Butts, Austin M. Sheheen, Jr., Harriet P. Sobell.
EIN: 570734293

49642
Associated Charities of Kershaw County, Inc.
P.O. Box 862
Camden, SC 29020-0862
Application address: 1112 Roberts St., Camden, SC 29020, tel.: (803) 432-7454
Contact: Jean C. Rowland, Secy.

Financial data (yr. ended 12/31/01): Grants paid, $19,884; assets, $492,120 (M); expenditures, $32,913; qualifying distributions, $19,884.
Limitations: Giving limited to Kershaw County, SC.
Application information: Application form required.
Officers and Directors:* Dean Jordan,* Pres.; R.A. Carswell,* V.P.; Jean C. Rowland,* Secy.; Judy Brock, G.T. Cooper, Jr., John Kirkland, Jack West, Lynn Wooten.
EIN: 570347064

49643
Hipp Brothers Family Foundation
1412 Ashley River Rd.
Charleston, SC 29407

Established in 2000 in SC.
Donor(s): G. Preston Hipp, Charles R. Hipp, Jr.
Financial data (yr. ended 12/31/00): Grants paid, $19,830; assets, $2,948 (M); gifts received, $25,280; expenditures, $19,830; qualifying distributions, $19,830.
Limitations: Applications not accepted. Giving primarily in Charleston and Mount Pleasant, SC.
Application information: Contributes only to pre-selected organizations.
Directors: Charles R. Hipp, Jr., G. Preston Hipp.
EIN: 571111848

49644
Cox Foundation
c/o Cox Wood Preserving Co.
P.O. Box 1124
Orangeburg, SC 29115-1124 (803) 534-7467
Contact: Cathy C. Yeadon, Dir.

Established in 1986 in SC.
Donor(s): Cox Wood Preserving Co.
Financial data (yr. ended 04/30/01): Grants paid, $19,641; assets, $308,848 (M); gifts received, $10,567; expenditures, $19,964; qualifying distributions, $19,410.
Limitations: Giving limited to NC and SC.
Application information: Applicant must submit high school or college transcript, SAT scores, class rank, G.P.A., and two recommendations. Application form required.
Directors: Pat Black, Elizabeth B. Malinder, Carol H. Riley, Cathy C. Yeadon.
EIN: 570823753
Codes: CS, CD, GTI

49645
Sullivan and Taylor Family Foundation
c/o Nancy S. Taylor
30 Middleton Gardens Pl.
Bluffton, SC 29910

Established in 1999 in NV.
Donor(s): J.D. Taylor, Nancy S. Taylor.
Financial data (yr. ended 12/31/01): Grants paid, $19,295; assets, $549,084 (M); gifts received, $250,113; expenditures, $31,647; qualifying distributions, $19,295.
Limitations: Applications not accepted.
Application information: Contributes only to pre-selected organizations.
Trustees: Barbara Ann Becker, Barbara Sullivan, Nancy S. Taylor.
EIN: 880448358

49646
The Genesis Foundation
(Formerly The TM Foundation)
4747 National Dr.
Myrtle Beach, SC 29579-7213 (843) 347-1965
Contact: Joseph L. Anderson, Pres.

Established in 1988 in UT.
Financial data (yr. ended 12/31/01): Grants paid, $19,132; assets, $295,254 (M); expenditures, $24,489; qualifying distributions, $19,019.
Limitations: Giving primarily in IL.
Application information: Application form not required.
Officers: Joseph L. Anderson, Pres.; Mrs. Scott Anderson III, Exec. V.P. & Treas.; Rita McLamb, Secy.
Directors: Mrs. Richard C. Anderson, Terry Booth.
EIN: 742479631

49647
Henry A. Strominger Family Foundation
1426 N. Waccamaw Dr.
Garden City, SC 29576

Established in 1998 in SC.
Donor(s): Henry A. Strohminger.
Financial data (yr. ended 12/31/01): Grants paid, $19,050; assets, $327,716 (M); expenditures, $20,461; qualifying distributions, $19,050.
Officer: Henry A. Strohminger, Chair.
Trustees: Judy Ann Friedberg, Henry A. Strohminger III.
EIN: 571066687

49648
Steffen Brown Foundation
c/o Carolyn B. Griffith
220 Silver Fox Ln.
Columbia, SC 29212 (803) 732-2460
Contact: Steffen A. Brown II, Tr.

Established about 1960.
Financial data (yr. ended 12/31/01): Grants paid, $18,000; assets, $536,171 (M); expenditures, $59,339; qualifying distributions, $18,000.
Limitations: Giving primarily in OH.
Application information: Application form not required.
Trustees: Marianna Brown, Martin K. Brown, Steffen A. Brown II, Carolyn Griffith, Marianna B. Young.
EIN: 316039665

49649
Ruth B. Wood Foundation, Inc.
c/o First Citizens Bank & Trust Co.
P.O. Box 29
Columbia, SC 29202
Application address: 202 Augusta Rd., Clemson, SC 29631
Contact: Robert M. Wood, Pres.

Established in 1994.
Donor(s): Ruth Wood,‡ Mack Wood.
Financial data (yr. ended 12/31/01): Grants paid, $17,900; assets, $741,982 (M); expenditures, $26,598; qualifying distributions, $17,900.
Limitations: Giving primarily in SC.
Officer: Robert M. Wood, Pres.
EIN: 582018115

49650
Magnolia Foundation
c/o Allen Thames
P.O. Box 11767
Columbia, SC 29211

Established in 1998 in SC.
Donor(s): Allen Thames.

Financial data (yr. ended 12/31/01): Grants paid, $17,565; assets, $9,624 (M); expenditures, $18,165; qualifying distributions, $17,565.
Limitations: Applications not accepted.
Application information: Contributes only to pre-selected organizations.
Director: Allen Thames.
EIN: 582357906

49651
The John A. and Betty G. Warren Foundation
P.O. Box 764
Columbia, SC 29218-0764

Established in 1994 in SC.
Donor(s): John A. Warren, Betty G. Warren.
Financial data (yr. ended 12/31/01): Grants paid, $17,165; assets, $165,756 (M); expenditures, $17,311; qualifying distributions, $17,165.
Limitations: Applications not accepted. Giving primarily in SC.
Application information: Contributes only to pre-selected organizations.
Trustees: Betty G. Warren, John A. Warren.
EIN: 571007059

49652
Citizens Building & Loan Charitable Foundation
229 Trade St.
Greer, SC 29651-3427

Established in 1999 in SC.
Financial data (yr. ended 12/31/01): Grants paid, $17,000; assets, $273,038 (M); gifts received, $100,000; expenditures, $17,043; qualifying distributions, $17,000.
Directors: Maurice Belue, Terry Dobson, Laurens I. James, Jr., Ralph Johnson, Robert Lynn, Benjamin Waters.
EIN: 562158345

49653
The George & Patricia DeCoursey Foundation
1015 Wordsworth Dr.
Columbia, SC 29209
Contact: Patricia J. DeCoursey, Pres.

Established in 2000 in SC.
Donor(s): Patricia J. DeCoursey.
Financial data (yr. ended 12/31/01): Grants paid, $17,000; assets, $176,652 (M); gifts received, $100,757; expenditures, $18,447; qualifying distributions, $17,000.
Limitations: Giving primarily in SC.
Officer: Patricia J. DeCoursey, Pres.
Directors: J. Edward Kellett, Nancy Muller.
EIN: 571100672

49654
Burroughs Foundation
P.O. Box 260
Conway, SC 29526-0260

Donor(s): Ruth Gaul, Margaret Holmes, R.V. Bruno, Mrs. R.V. Bruno.
Financial data (yr. ended 11/30/01): Grants paid, $16,600; assets, $311,810 (M); gifts received, $14,800; expenditures, $18,638; qualifying distributions, $16,600.
Limitations: Applications not accepted. Giving primarily in Conway, SC.
Application information: Contributes only to pre-selected organizations.
Trustees: L.V. Bruno, Margaret Holmes, Michael R. McMillan, Tamsley Seaborn, Jean Thompson.
EIN: 570694085

49655
Barbara Judy Thomas Memorial Foundation
2711 Middleburg Dr., Ste. 316
Columbia, SC 29204

Donor(s): Holcombe H. Thomas.
Financial data (yr. ended 12/31/01): Grants paid, $16,546; assets, $272,289 (M); expenditures, $19,096; qualifying distributions, $16,546.
Limitations: Applications not accepted. Giving primarily in SC.
Application information: Contributes only to pre-selected organizations.
Trustees: John C. Judy, Jr., Sara J. Kitchens, Barbara J. Thomas, Carolyn J. Weathers.
EIN: 576037541

49656
John Sam Lay Estate Trust
1108 Roe Ford Rd.
Greenville, SC 29617

Financial data (yr. ended 12/31/99): Grants paid, $16,000; assets, $156,454 (M); expenditures, $17,725; qualifying distributions, $15,924.
Limitations: Applications not accepted.
Application information: Contributes only to pre-selected organizations.
Trustees: Betty Alexander, Bobby Lay, James R. Lay, William E. Lay, N. Gruber Sires.
EIN: 576140757

49657
The Wingate Foundation
P.O. Box 276
Clover, SC 29710
Application address: c/o Principal, Clover High School, Clover, SC 29710

Established in 1979.
Donor(s): Chester A. Wingate.
Financial data (yr. ended 11/30/01): Grants paid, $15,826; assets, $475,759 (M); expenditures, $16,100; qualifying distributions, $15,826.
Limitations: Giving limited to Clover, SC.
Application information: Application form required.
Trustees: Patsy A. Robinson, Chester A. Wingate, Chester A. Wingate, Jr., Stewart A. Wingate.
EIN: 570694433
Codes: GTI

49658
The Dave Cameron Educational Foundation
P.O. Box 181
York, SC 29745-0181 (803) 684-4968

Financial data (yr. ended 03/31/02): Grants paid, $15,000; assets, $313,200 (M); expenditures, $15,167; qualifying distributions, $14,662.
Limitations: Giving limited to the York, SC, area.
Application information: Application form required.
Directors: John S. Adkins, Melvin B. McKeown.
EIN: 237080657
Codes: GTI

49659
Herman N. Hipp First Foundation
P.O. Box 546
Greenville, SC 29602

Established in 1958 in SC.
Financial data (yr. ended 12/31/01): Grants paid, $15,000; assets, $945,473 (M); expenditures, $19,103; qualifying distributions, $15,000.
Limitations: Applications not accepted. Giving primarily in Greenville, SC.
Application information: Contributes only to pre-selected organizations.
Trustee: H. Neel Hipp.
EIN: 576017334

49660
Lando Land Fund
(Formerly Manetta Mills Fund)
c/o Manetta Mills, Inc.
P.O. Box 100
Lando, SC 29724

Donor(s): Manetta Mills, Inc.
Financial data (yr. ended 12/31/01): Grants paid, $15,000; assets, $333,559 (M); expenditures, $15,450; qualifying distributions, $15,000.
Limitations: Giving primarily in NC and SC.
Application information: Unsolicited requests for funds not accepted.
Trustees: J.R. Bolton, H.B. Heath, W.O. Nisbet III.
EIN: 566067781
Codes: CS, CD

49661
C. E. Runion Foundation
P.O. Box 12158
Greenville, SC 29612-0158

Established in 2000 in SC.
Donor(s): C.E. Runion.
Financial data (yr. ended 12/31/01): Grants paid, $15,000; assets, $260,548 (M); gifts received, $45,000; expenditures, $16,259; qualifying distributions, $15,000.
Limitations: Applications not accepted.
Application information: Contributes only to pre-selected organizations.
Trustees: C.E. Runion, Charles E. Runion, Katherine L. Runion, Mildred K. Runion.
EIN: 571112091

49662
The Smith Family Fund
120 Edisto Ave.
Columbia, SC 29205
Contact: Joel A. Smith III, Pres.

Established in 1999 in SC.
Donor(s): Joel A. Smith III.
Financial data (yr. ended 11/30/01): Grants paid, $15,000; assets, $482,263 (M); gifts received, $228,745; expenditures, $24,128; qualifying distributions, $15,000.
Officers and Directors:* Joel A. Smith III,* Chair. and Pres.; Kathryn S. Smith,* Vice-Chair. and V.P.; Mary Lowndes Bryan, Secy.; J. Edgerton Smith, Treas.
Trustee: Bank of America.
EIN: 912056433

49663
The Taylor Family Foundation
1 Atlantic St.
Charleston, SC 29401

Established in 1998 in SC.
Donor(s): George J. Taylor IV.
Financial data (yr. ended 12/31/01): Grants paid, $15,000; assets, $218,657 (M); gifts received, $1,080; expenditures, $17,733; qualifying distributions, $15,000.
Limitations: Applications not accepted. Giving primarily in Charleston, SC.
Application information: Contributes only to pre-selected organizations.
Officers and Directors:* George J. Taylor IV,* Pres. and Treas.; Lucian A. Taylor, V.P. and Secy.; Marilyn B. Taylor, Matthew B. Taylor.
EIN: 582398521

49664—SOUTH CAROLINA

49664
Charleston Union of Kings Daughters
2064 Maybank Hwy.
Charleston, SC 29412
Contact: Alice Lingenfelter, Treas.

Financial data (yr. ended 12/31/00): Grants paid, $14,775; assets, $381,244 (M); expenditures, $27,382; qualifying distributions, $27,382.
Limitations: Giving primarily in Charleston, SC.
Officers: Margaret Atwater, Pres.; Betty Cannon, Corresponding Secy.; Jane Moring, Recording Secy.; Alice Lingenfelter, Treas.
EIN: 570357957

49665
James F. & Nelle E. Burgess Foundation
200 Bromsgrove Dr.
Greenville, SC 29609-1448

Financial data (yr. ended 12/31/01): Grants paid, $13,922; assets, $263,928 (M); expenditures, $20,622; qualifying distributions, $13,922.
Limitations: Applications not accepted. Giving limited to SC.
Application information: Contributes only to pre-selected organizations.
Trustees: Burgess Shucker, Pamela B. Shucker.
EIN: 576023535

49666
Davis Family Foundation, Inc.
P.O. Box 428
Greenwood, SC 29648

Established in 1999 in SC.
Donor(s): Emmett Davis, Jr.
Financial data (yr. ended 12/31/01): Grants paid, $13,700; assets, $444,836 (M); gifts received, $122,960; expenditures, $23,376; qualifying distributions, $13,700.
Officer: Emmett Davis, Jr., Pres.
EIN: 582432024

49667
Independent Insurance Agents of South Carolina Foundation
800 Gracern Rd.
Columbia, SC 29210

Established in 1995 in SC.
Financial data (yr. ended 12/31/01): Grants paid, $13,500; assets, $625,048 (M); gifts received, $7,435; expenditures, $24,698; qualifying distributions, $13,500.
Officers and Trustees:* Rupert M. Stalvey,* Chair.; Lee Brinkley,* V.P.; William M. Thomason,* Secy.-Treas.; Robert C. Heffron, Robert Livingston, T. T. Mappus.
EIN: 570781364

49668
The Terrell Sovey Foundation, Inc.
c/o L. Terrell Sovey, Jr.
367 S. Pine St.
Spartanburg, SC 29302-2623 (864) 573-9802

Established in 1993 in SC.
Donor(s): L. Terrell Sovey, Jr.
Financial data (yr. ended 12/31/01): Grants paid, $13,300; assets, $198,977 (M); expenditures, $18,799; qualifying distributions, $13,300.
Limitations: Applications not accepted. Giving primarily in GA and SC.
Application information: Contributes only to pre-selected organizations.
Trustees: L. Terrell Sovey, Jr., Miriam M. Weaver.
EIN: 570974803

49669
VSP Foundation
228 S. Alabama Ave.
Chesnee, SC 29323

Financial data (yr. ended 12/31/00): Grants paid, $13,019; assets, $69,652 (M); gifts received, $42,568; expenditures, $15,841; qualifying distributions, $13,020.
Limitations: Applications not accepted. Giving primarily in SC.
Application information: Contributes only to pre-selected organizations.
Officers: Terry L. Cash, Chair.; Nancy J. Ogle, Pres.
Board Members: Andy Falatok, Katie Hodge, Marion McMillan, Bill Painter, Norman Pulliam.
EIN: 571067827

49670
John and J. D. Dowdy Foundation, Inc.
310 Springhouse Dr.
Aiken, SC 29803
Contact: Carol Sue Roberts, Pres.

Donor(s): John Dowdy.
Financial data (yr. ended 12/31/01): Grants paid, $13,000; assets, $256,860 (M); expenditures, $13,400; qualifying distributions, $12,840.
Limitations: Giving primarily in TX.
Officers: Carol Sue Roberts, Pres. and Secy.-Treas.; John V. Dowdy, Jr., V.P.
EIN: 751658880

49671
Harold B. Risher Foundation
1010 Arden Way
Spartanburg, SC 29302 (864) 572-9713

Donor(s): Harold B. Risher.
Financial data (yr. ended 12/31/01): Grants paid, $13,000; assets, $235,578 (M); expenditures, $14,130; qualifying distributions, $13,000.
Limitations: Applications not accepted. Giving primarily in SC.
Application information: Contributes only to pre-selected organizations.
Trustees: Harold B. Risher, Margaret M. Risher, Thomas H. Risher.
EIN: 576019801

49672
Edgefield County Foundation
108 1/2 Courthouse Sq.
P.O. Box 388
Edgefield, SC 29824

Established in 1991 in SC.
Donor(s): Bettis C. Rainsford.
Financial data (yr. ended 12/31/00): Grants paid, $12,500; assets, $33,064 (M); expenditures, $27,269; qualifying distributions, $12,500.
Limitations: Applications not accepted. Giving limited to Edgefield, SC.
Application information: Contributes only to pre-selected organizations.
Officer and Trustees:* Bettis C. Rainsford,* Chair.; Joseph F. Anderson, Jr., Butler C. Derrick, Jr., Albert E. Rainsford, Jr., J. Strom Thurmond, Jr.
EIN: 570945737

49673
Beckham Foundation
112 Manly St.
Greenville, SC 29601

Established in 1998 in SC.
Donor(s): Andrew S. Carroll, Charles W. Carroll.
Financial data (yr. ended 06/30/02): Grants paid, $12,000; assets, $47,058 (M); gifts received, $12,000; expenditures, $13,225; qualifying distributions, $12,000.
Limitations: Applications not accepted.
Application information: Contributes only to pre-selected organizations.
Officers and Directors:* Andrew S. Carroll,* Pres.; Charles W. Carroll,* V.P.
EIN: 341880603

49674
The Palmetto Farms Foundation
121 Hathaway Cir.
Greenville, SC 29617-6117

Established in 1998 in SC.
Donor(s): Dixon C. Cunningham, Eudora M. Cunningham.
Financial data (yr. ended 12/31/01): Grants paid, $11,730; assets, $189,233 (M); gifts received, $500; expenditures, $11,914; qualifying distributions, $11,730.
Limitations: Applications not accepted.
Application information: Contributes only to pre-selected organizations.
Trustees: Dixon C. Cunningham, Eudora M. Cunningham.
EIN: 576178213

49675
WPW Foundation
P.O. Box 448
Columbia, SC 29202-0448 (803) 255-7402

Financial data (yr. ended 12/31/99): Grants paid, $11,700; assets, $235,791 (M); expenditures, $18,585; qualifying distributions, $11,700.
Trustee: Bank of America.
EIN: 586338488

49676
First Federal Savings & Loan Association of Cheraw Foundation
P.O. Box 512
Cheraw, SC 29520

Established in 1997 in DE/SC.
Donor(s): Great Pee Dee Bancorp, First Federal Savings & Loan Association.
Financial data (yr. ended 06/30/01): Grants paid, $11,564; assets, $235,948 (M); expenditures, $21,696; qualifying distributions, $12,187.
Limitations: Applications not accepted.
Application information: Contributes only to pre-selected organizations.
Officers: William Rhett Butler, Pres.; Cornelius B. Young, Secy.-Treas.
EIN: 562068430

49677
The Stringer Foundation, Inc.
402 Boulevard
Anderson, SC 29621-4004 (864) 222-0804
FAX: (864) 225-2131; E-mail: Raggedspec@aol.com
Contact: John S. Rainey, Chair.

Established in 1947.
Financial data (yr. ended 12/31/01): Grants paid, $11,526; assets, $2,047,164 (M); expenditures, $74,603; qualifying distributions, $11,526.
Limitations: Giving primarily in SC.
Application information: Application form not required.
Officers and Trustees:* John S. Rainey,* Chair. and Pres.; Nancy Crowley,* V.P.; Mary R. Belser,* Secy.; Robert M. Rainey,* Treas.
EIN: 576022719

49678
The Richard Eric Rosenberg Foundation, Inc.
1873 Farrow Dr.
Rock Hill, SC 29732-7705
Application address: 24 Leonard Ave.,
Cambridge, MA 02139, tel.: (617) 491-3692
Contact: Lawrence G. Rosenberg, Clerk

Established in 1995 in MA.
Donor(s): Bruce Leonard, Carol B. Leonard, Alvan F. Rosenberg, Richard E. Rosenberg,‡ Beverly I. Rosenberg, Lawrence G. Rosenberg, B.W. Rosen, Mrs. B.W. Rosen.
Financial data (yr. ended 04/30/02): Grants paid, $11,000; assets, $199,591 (M); expenditures, $12,869; qualifying distributions, $11,000.
Officers: Jeffrey D. Rosenberg, Pres.; Lawrence G. Rosenberg, Clerk; Carol B. Leonard, Treas.
Directors: Alvan F. Rosenberg, Beverly I. Rosenberg.
EIN: 043321452

49679
G.J.F. Foundation
c/o James W. Foley
P.O. Box 22185
Hilton Head Island, SC 29925

Established in 1986 in SC.
Donor(s): James W. Foley.
Financial data (yr. ended 12/31/01): Grants paid, $10,900; assets, $132,218 (M); gifts received, $52,050; expenditures, $11,689; qualifying distributions, $10,900.
Limitations: Applications not accepted. Giving primarily in NC, TX, and WY.
Application information: Contributes only to pre-selected organizations.
Officers: Gretchen Foley, Mgr.; James W. Foley, Mgr.
EIN: 570835461

49680
GMK Associates Foundation, Inc.
1333 Main St., Ste. 400
Columbia, SC 29201

Financial data (yr. ended 12/31/01): Grants paid, $10,513; assets, $1,401 (M); gifts received, $11,045; expenditures, $10,976; qualifying distributions, $10,513.
Limitations: Giving limited to SC.
Trustees: Robert H. Kennedy, Thomas P. Manahan, Vallentine A. Satko.
EIN: 570805352

49681
Dick Anderson Chapter 75 (1896) United Daughters of the Confederacy Trust
c/o National Bank of South Carolina
P.O. Box 1798
Sumter, SC 29151-1798   (803) 775-1211
Contact: Kathy Ward, Trust Off.

Financial data (yr. ended 12/31/00): Grants paid, $10,318; assets, $333,161 (M); expenditures, $17,662; qualifying distributions, $10,318.
Limitations: Giving limited to the Sumter, SC, area.
Application information: Application form required.
Trustee: National Bank of South Carolina.
EIN: 576108972
Codes: GTI

49682
The Gillespie Foundation, Inc.
839 Duck Hawk Retreat
Charleston, SC 29412-9056   (843) 795-4833
Contact: John M. Gillespie, III, Mgr.

Financial data (yr. ended 02/28/02): Grants paid, $10,152; assets, $182,047 (M); expenditures, $13,752; qualifying distributions, $10,152.
Officer: John M. Gillespie III, Mgr.
EIN: 562019456

49683
Daltondemorest Foundation, Inc.
3643 Pompano Ct.
Johns Island, SC 29455

Established in 2000 in GA.
Donor(s): Rhonda K. Dean.
Financial data (yr. ended 11/30/01): Grants paid, $10,000; assets, $192,870 (M); gifts received, $200,000; expenditures, $10,467; qualifying distributions, $10,000.
Limitations: Applications not accepted.
Application information: Contributes only to pre-selected organizations.
Officers: Rhonda K. Dean, Pres.; Debra L. Dean, Secy.-Treas.
Directors: Elizabeth Attias, Dorothy Leeds.
EIN: 582592530

49684
The WebbCraft Family Foundation, Inc.
938 Simpson Rd.
Belton, SC 29627

Established in 2000 in SC.
Donor(s): Joy Craft Malcolm.
Financial data (yr. ended 12/31/01): Grants paid, $10,000; assets, $1,107,455 (M); gifts received, $1,164,200; expenditures, $105,796; qualifying distributions, $10,000.
Officers: Joy Craft Malcolm, Chair.; Jerry Craft, Exec. Dir.
Directors: Jerri Lynn Craft, Jimmy Craft, Jane Kay, Julie Kay, Mike Pascuzzi, Faye Stalon.
EIN: 571111833

49685
The McAlister Foundation
104 Creek Dr.
Laurens, SC 29360
Contact: Paul W. McAlister, Tr.

Established in 2000 in SC.
Donor(s): Barbara D. McAlister, Paul W. McAlister, Albert D. McAlister.
Financial data (yr. ended 04/30/02): Grants paid, $9,997; assets, $471,412 (M); gifts received, $333,739; expenditures, $14,480; qualifying distributions, $9,962.
Trustees: Albert D. McAlister, Barbara D. McAlister, Donald R. McAlister, Paul W. McAlister, Patricia E. Watts.
EIN: 571112302

49686
William and Margaret S. Hamilton Foundation, Inc.
c/o Cleveland Sanders
732 Columbia Dr.
Myrtle Beach, SC 29577
Application address: 4614 Oleander Dr., Myrtle Beach, SC 29577
Contact: Scott B. Umstead

Established in 1998 in SC.
Financial data (yr. ended 12/31/01): Grants paid, $9,780; assets, $329,653 (M); expenditures, $20,918; qualifying distributions, $9,780.
Directors: Ruby Marshall, Cleveland B. Sanders, Jimmy Watson.
EIN: 582334593

49687
Columbia Garden Club Foundation
P.O. Box 5925
Columbia, SC 29250

Established in 1983 in SC.
Donor(s): Columbia Garden Club.
Financial data (yr. ended 05/31/02): Grants paid, $9,747; assets, $162,351 (M); gifts received, $9,545; expenditures, $11,062; qualifying distributions, $9,747.
Limitations: Applications not accepted. Giving limited to Columbia, SC.
Application information: Contributes only to pre-selected organizations.
Officers: Elizabeth Crew, Chair.; Joann Campbell, Co-Pres.; Jane Suggs, Co-Pres.; Nancy Denkins, Treas.
EIN: 570756773

49688
W. W. Hill Memorial Trust, Inc.
P.O. Box 1588
Sumter, SC 29151

Established in 1995 in SC.
Financial data (yr. ended 03/31/00): Grants paid, $9,000; assets, $168,441 (M); gifts received, $7,000; expenditures, $9,231; qualifying distributions, $9,000.
Trustee: James K. Rogers.
EIN: 570991231

49689
Society of Saint Mary Magdalene, Inc.
P.O. Box 352
Fountain Inn, SC 29644-0352

Established in 1980.
Financial data (yr. ended 12/31/00): Grants paid, $8,718; assets, $20,159 (M); gifts received, $57,698; expenditures, $67,136; qualifying distributions, $8,718; giving activities include $17,099 for programs.
Limitations: Applications not accepted. Giving primarily in SC.
Application information: Contributes only to pre-selected organizations.
Directors: Fr. Thomas Bernard, Fr. Herbert Conner, Fr. Howard Coughlin, Sandra Ferreria, Edmond Filliette.
EIN: 042696334

49690
Michael E. Bambauer Charitable Foundation
30 Marsh Edge Ln.
Kiawah Island, SC 29455-5731
Contact: R.L. Bambauer, Dir.

Donor(s): Robert L. Bambauer.
Financial data (yr. ended 12/31/00): Grants paid, $8,216; assets, $0 (M); gifts received, $7,900; expenditures, $8,216; qualifying distributions, $0.
Directors: Jeanette V. Bambauer, R.L. Bambauer, Timothy Bambauer, Tina J. Bambauer.
EIN: 566240813

49691
Whitfield Family Charitable Trust
6518 C Dorchester Rd.
North Charleston, SC 29418

Financial data (yr. ended 11/30/01): Grants paid, $8,000; assets, $2,931 (M); expenditures, $8,000; qualifying distributions, $8,000.
Limitations: Applications not accepted. Giving limited to Charleston, SC.

49691—SOUTH CAROLINA

Application information: Contributes only to pre-selected organizations.
Officers: William F. Whitfield, Pres.; Shirley D. Whitfield, Secy.
Directors: Timothy W. Whitfield, William F. Whitfield, Jr.
EIN: 576107128

49692
Slocum-Lunz Foundation, Inc.
c/o Richard H. Stoughton
P.O. Box 10968
Charleston, SC 29401 (843) 795-6350
Contact: J. David Whitaker, Tr.

Financial data (yr. ended 12/31/99): Grants paid, $7,838; assets, $823 (M); expenditures, $9,293; qualifying distributions, $7,838.
Limitations: Giving limited to SC.
Application information: Application form required.
Officer and Trustees:* Richard H. Stoughton,* Treas.; Bruce Coull, Robert Johnson, J. David Whitaker, and 5 additional trustees.
EIN: 570371213

49693
Gray Family Foundation, Inc.
c/o James L. Gray
55 N. Calibogue Cay Rd.
Hilton Head Island, SC 29928-2913

Established in 2001 in SC.
Donor(s): James L. Gray, Patricia C. Gray.
Financial data (yr. ended 12/31/01): Grants paid, $7,500; assets, $279,260 (M); gifts received, $284,000; expenditures, $9,760; qualifying distributions, $7,500.
Limitations: Applications not accepted.
Application information: Contributes only to pre-selected organizations.
Directors: Grant S. Bailey, Lesley A. Bailey, James L. Gray, Michael D. Gray, Patricia C. Gray.
EIN: 621839018

49694
Mary Katherine & Thomas J. Longwell Charitable Trust
515 Woodrow St.
Columbia, SC 29205-2318 (803) 771-7245
Contact: Ann L. Furr, Tr.

Established in 1992 in SC.
Financial data (yr. ended 12/31/01): Grants paid, $7,000; assets, $55,136 (M); expenditures, $7,705; qualifying distributions, $7,000.
Limitations: Giving primarily in New York, NY and SC.
Trustees: Ann L. Furr, Mary Katherine Longwell.
EIN: 576142582

49695
Baker Charitable Trust
3526 Boundbrook Ln.
Columbia, SC 29206-3402
Contact: Sam Baker, Tr.

Financial data (yr. ended 12/31/00): Grants paid, $6,246; assets, $163,340 (M); expenditures, $7,072; qualifying distributions, $6,246.
Application information: Application form not required.
Trustee: Samuel Baker.
EIN: 257248956

49696
Cotesworth Family Foundation, Inc.
34 Oyster Reed Dr.
Hilton Head Island, SC 29926 (843) 681-4730
Application address: 72 Brams Point Rd., Hilton Head Island, SC 29926
Contact: Harry A. Cotesworth, Chair.

Established in 1997 in SC.
Donor(s): Harry A. Cotesworth.
Financial data (yr. ended 12/31/01): Grants paid, $6,115; assets, $43,285 (M); expenditures, $6,816; qualifying distributions, $6,115.
Officer and Trustees:* Harry A. Cotesworth,* Chair.; Yolanda L. Cotesworth.
EIN: 562027607

49697
Hope Foundation Trust
3017 Old Williamston Rd.
Anderson, SC 29621 (864) 226-7983
Contact: William R. McCoy, Chair.

Donor(s): William R. McCoy.
Financial data (yr. ended 12/31/99): Grants paid, $6,000; assets, $114,593 (M); expenditures, $6,000; qualifying distributions, $6,000.
Application information: Application form not required.
Officer: William R. McCoy, Chair.
Trustees: Ann S. McCoy, Julie Ann McCoy, Mary Elizabeth McCoy.
EIN: 576155127

49698
Jacobs Family Charitable Foundation Trust
34 Wexford Dr.
Hilton Head Island, SC 29928-3364
Contact: Joseph Charles Jacobs, Tr.

Established in 1999 in SC.
Donor(s): Joseph Charles Jacobs, D. Lucinda Jacobs.
Financial data (yr. ended 08/31/02): Grants paid, $6,000; assets, $255,063 (M); gifts received, $82,859; expenditures, $7,177; qualifying distributions, $6,000.
Trustees: D. Lucinda Jacobs, Joseph Charles Jacobs.
EIN: 527030654

49699
Mary R. Ramseur Charitable Foundation
1207 Rutledge Way
Anderson, SC 29621-4056 (864) 226-5977
Contact: Barbara R. Pickens, Tr.

Established in 1994 in SC.
Financial data (yr. ended 12/31/01): Grants paid, $6,000; assets, $134,403 (M); expenditures, $6,042; qualifying distributions, $6,000.
Trustees: Barbara R. Pickens, Mary R. Ramseur.
EIN: 576158369

49700
D. and M. Howell Foundation
912 Rollingview Ln.
Columbia, SC 29210-4925
Contact: Don N. Howell, Jr., Dir.

Established in 1999 in GA.
Donor(s): Don N. Howell, Jr.
Financial data (yr. ended 12/31/01): Grants paid, $5,600; assets, $98,874 (M); gifts received, $61,467; expenditures, $6,213; qualifying distributions, $5,600.
Directors: Don N. Howell, Jr., Melissa Howell.
EIN: 586396642

49701
John Burdell Hospital Fund for the Alleviation of Suffering Humanity
P.O. Box 296
Camden, SC 29020-0296
Application address: 416 Chestnut St., Camden, SC 29020, tel.: (803) 432-6226
Contact: H. Davis Green, Jr., Tr.

Financial data (yr. ended 05/31/01): Grants paid, $5,500; assets, $0 (M); expenditures, $8,568; qualifying distributions, $6,904.
Trustees: H.D. Green, Jr., Dr. W.F. Summers.
EIN: 570340239

49702
Phillips Foundation
15 Dawson Rd.
Greenville, SC 29609-1309 (864) 246-4637

Donor(s): Gilbert M. Phillips.
Financial data (yr. ended 12/31/01): Grants paid, $5,500; assets, $117,827 (M); expenditures, $5,858; qualifying distributions, $5,500.
Limitations: Applications not accepted. Giving primarily in SC.
Application information: Contributes only to pre-selected organizations.
Trustees: Gilbert M. Phillips, Lilly Phillips.
EIN: 576115760

49703
The McCall Foundation
(Formerly Arthur McCall Charitable Trust)
P.O. Box 607
Greenville, SC 29602-0607

Established in 1986.
Donor(s): Arthur C. McCall.
Financial data (yr. ended 12/31/00): Grants paid, $5,400; assets, $221,445 (M); expenditures, $6,956; qualifying distributions, $5,400.
Limitations: Applications not accepted.
Application information: Contributes only to pre-selected organizations.
Officer: Arthur C. McCall, Mgr.
EIN: 570835071

49704
White Stone Foundation
c/o Kirby G. Kee
P.O. Box 3017
Greenville, SC 29602-3017

Financial data (yr. ended 12/31/99): Grants paid, $5,330; assets, $12,956 (M); gifts received, $3,646; expenditures, $53,747; qualifying distributions, $5,330; giving activities include $48,417 for programs.
Limitations: Applications not accepted.
Application information: Contributes only to pre-selected organizations.
Officers and Directors:* Kirby G. Kee,* Chair. and Pres.; Helen R. Kee,* V.P.; Doris Brackett.
EIN: 570921536

49705
Suzanne F. Anderson Memorial Foundation, Inc.
15 Stonegate Dr.
Hilton Head Island, SC 29928-1980

Donor(s): Martin L. Anderson.
Financial data (yr. ended 12/31/01): Grants paid, $5,300; assets, $100,697 (M); gifts received, $500; expenditures, $6,297; qualifying distributions, $5,300.
Limitations: Applications not accepted.
Application information: Contributes only to pre-selected organizations.
Officers: Ruth Ann Anderson, Pres.; Martin L. Anderson, Secy.-Treas.

Directors: Brian Anderson, Jeff Anderson, Mary Law.
EIN: 581966318

49706
Georgetown County Environmental Protection Society
P.O. Box 1901
Pawleys Island, SC 29585
Application address: P.O. Box 1917, Pawleys Island, SC 29585, tel.: (843) 237-8180
Contact: J. Brooks McIntyre, Pres.

Established in 1996 in SC.
Financial data (yr. ended 12/31/00): Grants paid, $5,000; assets, $154,793 (M); gifts received, $1,000; expenditures, $8,045; qualifying distributions, $5,000.
Limitations: Giving primarily in Georgetown, SC.
Officers: J. Brooks McIntyre, Pres.; Robert J. Moran, Secy.
Director: Ronald K. Lawn.
EIN: 570945690

49707
Christian Youth Education Foundation, Inc.
1 Paradise Point
Lake Wylie, SC 29710-9277

Established in 1995 in NC.
Donor(s): Henry C. Gilewicz, Alicia G. Gilewicz.
Financial data (yr. ended 12/31/00): Grants paid, $4,714; assets, $1,332 (M); gifts received, $4,339; expenditures, $4,714; qualifying distributions, $4,713.
Limitations: Applications not accepted.
Application information: Contributes only to pre-selected organizations.
Directors: Alicia Gilewicz, Henry Gilewicz, Mark Gilewicz.
EIN: 561889743

49708
The Cassels Foundation
P.O. Box 1691
Columbia, SC 29202

Financial data (yr. ended 12/31/01): Grants paid, $4,500; assets, $202,788 (M); expenditures, $6,093; qualifying distributions, $4,500.
Limitations: Applications not accepted.
Application information: Contributes only to pre-selected organizations.
Officers and Directors:* Rosalie O. Cassels,* Pres.; W.T. Cassels, Jr.,* V.P.; Katherine Cassels Wolfe,* V.P.; W.T. Cassels III,* Secy.
EIN: 571029022

49709
Mike Muth Basketball Scholarship Fund
2 Camellia Cir.
Williamston, SC 29697

Financial data (yr. ended 12/31/00): Grants paid, $4,500; assets, $50,555 (M); gifts received, $14,245; expenditures, $4,610; qualifying distributions, $4,500.
Limitations: Giving primarily to residents of SC.
Officers: Marion W. Middleton, Chair.; Dale Bell, Secy.; Dan Collins, Treas.
EIN: 571019671

49710
Family Unity Enterprises, Inc.
105 Stadium View Dr.
Greenville, SC 29609-5113

Donor(s): Timothy G. Corey, Hampton Park Baptist Church.
Financial data (yr. ended 12/31/01): Grants paid, $4,386; assets, $7,041 (M); gifts received, $2,125; expenditures, $4,438; qualifying distributions, $4,386.
Officers: Kenneth Hay, Secy.; Timothy G. Corey, Treas.
Directors: Ken Collier, Walter G. Fremont, Jr.
EIN: 570732142

49711
The Collins Family Foundation, Inc.
302 Raven Rd.
Greenville, SC 29615 (864) 234-7051
Contact: Marshall J. Collins, Jr., V.P.

Established in 2000 in SC.
Donor(s): Marshall J. Collins, Jr., Diane R. Collins.
Financial data (yr. ended 12/31/01): Grants paid, $4,325; assets, $465,337 (M); gifts received, $368,246; expenditures, $6,478; qualifying distributions, $4,325.
Officers and Directors:* Diane R. Collins,* Pres. and Treas.; Marshall J. Collins, Jr.,* V.P. and Secy.; Marshall J. Collins III, Rebecca Collins Kelly, Pam Collins Olafsson.
EIN: 571092285

49712
Virginia-Carolinas Scholarships Foundation
P.O. Box 1268
Greenville, SC 29602-1268
Application address: P.O. Box 6826, Columbia, SC 29260

Established in 1995 in SC.
Financial data (yr. ended 12/31/00): Grants paid, $3,956; assets, $820,876 (M); gifts received, $10,000; expenditures, $15,718; qualifying distributions, $3,956.
Limitations: Applications not accepted.
Application information: Contributes only to pre-selected organizations.
Trustee: Central Carolina Bank.
EIN: 570948342

49713
Fort Mill School District Scholarship Fund Council, Inc.
120 E. Elliott St.
Fort Mill, SC 29715-1848
Application address: c/o Guidance Dept., Fort Mills High School, 225 Munn Rd., Fort Mill, SC 29715

Established in 1995 in SC.
Donor(s): Pinckney Purcell, H.M. McCallum, Phoebe McCallum.
Financial data (yr. ended 12/31/99): Grants paid, $3,900; assets, $60,139 (M); gifts received, $7,039; expenditures, $4,015; qualifying distributions, $3,875.
Limitations: Giving limited to Fort Mill, SC.
Application information: Application form required.
Officers: Tec Dowling, Pres.; Karen D. Puthoff, Secy.-Treas.
EIN: 582129230

49714
James R. Bonds Charitable Trust
c/o Theodore L. Collier
3926 Hilda St.
North Charleston, SC 29418 (843) 554-7801

Established around 1993.
Financial data (yr. ended 12/31/01): Grants paid, $3,852; assets, $168,209 (M); expenditures, $7,783; qualifying distributions, $3,852.
Limitations: Applications not accepted.
Application information: Contributes only to pre-selected organizations.
Trustee: Theodore L. Collier.
EIN: 576150019

49715
The Eloise C. Snyder Foundation
121 Cowdray Park Dr.
Columbia, SC 29223-8127 (803) 788-8396

Established in SC in 1998.
Financial data (yr. ended 12/31/01): Grants paid, $3,500; assets, $57,578 (M); gifts received, $4,747; expenditures, $4,747; qualifying distributions, $3,500.
Trustees: Nancy Mindlick, Eloise C. Snyder, Geneva A. Wilkins.
EIN: 576180092

49716
The Crystal Bradshaw Foundation Charitable Trust
P.O. Box 2044
West Columbia, SC 29171

Financial data (yr. ended 06/30/02): Grants paid, $3,250; assets, $42,924 (M); expenditures, $3,298; qualifying distributions, $3,250.
Limitations: Applications not accepted. Giving primarily in Columbia, SC.
Application information: Contributes only to pre-selected organizations.
Trustees: Michael Bradshaw, Andrea B. Bundrick, Ronald H. Burkett.
EIN: 570856203

49717
Broadus & Evelyn Littlejohn Foundation
P.O. Box 6666
Spartanburg, SC 29304

Financial data (yr. ended 12/31/01): Grants paid, $3,100; assets, $220,536 (M); gifts received, $7,500; expenditures, $16,863; qualifying distributions, $3,100.
Limitations: Giving limited to SC.
Trustees: Anne L. Gowan, Broadus R. Littlejohn, Jr., Broadus R. Littlejohn III.
EIN: 576027579

49718
B. F. Carmichael Scholarship Fund
c/o Latta Rotary Club
111 W. Main St.
Latta, SC 29565-1505

Financial data (yr. ended 06/30/01): Grants paid, $3,000; assets, $36,106 (M); expenditures, $6,222; qualifying distributions, $3,314.
Limitations: Giving limited to Dillon County, SC.
Officers: Roger Dean Richardson, Pres.; Harold J. Kornblut, Treas.
EIN: 237089032

49719
The Concetta Charitable Foundation
501 Turkey Pointe Cir.
Columbia, SC 29223

Established in 1999 in NY.
Financial data (yr. ended 12/31/01): Grants paid, $3,000; assets, $47,838 (M); gifts received, $4,505; expenditures, $6,403; qualifying distributions, $3,000.
Limitations: Applications not accepted.
Application information: Contributes only to pre-selected organizations.
Trustees: Kenneth Farsalas, Laurie Nothnagle, Cheryl Spatorico, Derrick Spatorico, Nancy Spatorico.
EIN: 571076782

49720 — SOUTH CAROLINA

49720
Small Change Foundation
P.O. Drawer 7125
Columbia, SC 29202-7125
Contact: Adele J. Pope, Tr.

Established in 1998 in SC.
Financial data (yr. ended 12/31/01): Grants paid, $3,000; assets, $60,649 (M); gifts received, $3,025; expenditures, $3,023; qualifying distributions, $3,000.
Trustees: Jane J. Eubanks, Adele J. Pope.
EIN: 576178622

49721
The Ceres Foundation, Inc.
40 Calhoun St., 2nd Fl.
Charleston, SC 29401

Established in 1999.
Donor(s): Diane D. Terni.
Financial data (yr. ended 12/31/00): Grants paid, $2,861; assets, $1,615,319 (M); gifts received, $1,083,386; expenditures, $86,824; qualifying distributions, $2,861.
Limitations: Applications not accepted.
Application information: Contributes only to pre-selected organizations.
Officers: Diane D. Terni, Pres.; Stephen L. Gavel, V.P.; Linda G. Webb, Secy.; Frank J. Gavel, Jr., Treas.
EIN: 582479387

49722
John W. Reed Foundation
7 N. Laurens St.
Greenville, SC 29601 (864) 271-5930
Contact: William A. Bridges

Established in 1997 in SC.
Donor(s): John W. Reed.
Financial data (yr. ended 12/31/01): Grants paid, $2,701; assets, $368,994 (M); expenditures, $2,809; qualifying distributions, $2,701.
Officer: Bank of America.
EIN: 586359537

49723
Millie Colvin Scholarship Fund
c/o First National Bank
P.O. Box 38
Holly Hill, SC 29059

Financial data (yr. ended 08/31/99): Grants paid, $2,580; assets, $50,004 (M); expenditures, $3,010; qualifying distributions, $2,551.
Limitations: Applications not accepted. Giving limited to Holly Hill, SC.
Application information: Recipients are determined by class rank.
Trustees: M.C. Colvin, Jr., R.D. Colvin, First National Bank.
EIN: 570760026

49724
The Fred Collins Scholarship Fund, Inc.
1341 Rutherford Rd.
Greenville, SC 29609 (864) 268-1111

Established in 1999 in SC.
Donor(s): Fred J. Collins.
Financial data (yr. ended 12/31/00): Grants paid, $2,500; assets, $60,795 (M); gifts received, $14,000; expenditures, $4,465; qualifying distributions, $2,500.
Application information: Application form required.
Officer and Trustees:* Fred Collins,* Pres.; Cynthia Biggerstaff, Felicia C. Robbins.
EIN: 582448379

49725
John P. and Harriett E. Faris Foundation
c/o Palmetto Bank
P.O. Box 49
Laurens, SC 29360 (864) 984-3098
Application Address: 1004 W. Main St., Laurens SC 29360
Contact: John P. Faris, Tr.

Established in 1997 in SC.
Donor(s): John P. Faris, Harriett E. Faris.
Financial data (yr. ended 09/30/01): Grants paid, $2,407; assets, $45,334 (M); expenditures, $3,570; qualifying distributions, $2,407.
Limitations: Giving primarily in Laurens, SC.
Trustees: Harriett E. Faris, John P. Faris.
EIN: 586355172

49726
Nannie T. Leopard Foreign Mission Trust Fund
c/o Palmetto Bank, Trust Dept.
P.O. Box 49
Laurens, SC 29360-0049

Financial data (yr. ended 06/30/01): Grants paid, $2,207; assets, $57,727 (M); expenditures, $2,499; qualifying distributions, $2,382.
Limitations: Giving primarily in SC.
Trustees: Lee G. Royce, Palmetto Bank.
EIN: 576069941

49727
Sally S. Deveer Memorial Fund, Inc.
c/o Robert Deveer
8 Eastwind
Hilton Head Island, SC 29928-5227

Established in 1994 in NJ.
Donor(s): Michael Lerner.
Financial data (yr. ended 12/31/99): Grants paid, $2,200; assets, $30,124 (M); expenditures, $2,270; qualifying distributions, $2,200.
Limitations: Applications not accepted. Giving limited to residents of Milburn, NJ.
Officers: Robert K. Deveer III, Pres.; James B. Deveer, Secy.
EIN: 223281819

49728
Ennis Educational Trust
P.O. Box 428
Camden, SC 29020-0428
Contact: Austin M. Sheheen, Jr., Tr.

Donor(s): Barney A. Willens.
Financial data (yr. ended 11/30/00): Grants paid, $2,100; assets, $48,125 (M); expenditures, $3,784; qualifying distributions, $2,100.
Limitations: Giving limited to Kershaw County, SC.
Application information: Application form required.
Trustees: Theresa Ennis, Austin M. Sheheen, Jr., Barney A. Willens, Barbara E. Willens.
EIN: 576155975

49729
Graham Memorial Fund
P.O. Box 533
Bennettsville, SC 29512
Application address: 308 W. Main St., Bennettsville, SC 29512
Contact: Doris L. Gentry, Chair.

Financial data (yr. ended 09/30/00): Grants paid, $2,100; assets, $116,796 (M); expenditures, $2,183; qualifying distributions, $2,100.
Limitations: Giving limited to Marlboro County, SC.
Application information: Application form required.

Officer and Trustees:* Doris L. Gentry,* Chair.; Glenn Allen, Tim Barnett, Thomas P. Bostick, Sr., Martin Driggers, and 17 additional trustees.
EIN: 576026184
Codes: GTI

49730
Dr. William R. Holmes, Jr. Scholarship Fund Charitable Trust
P.O. Box 1186
Mount Pleasant, SC 29465
Contact: J. Robert Holmes, Dir.

Established in 1991 in SC.
Donor(s): Sandra Holmes.
Financial data (yr. ended 12/31/01): Grants paid, $2,000; assets, $53,950 (M); gifts received, $5,000; expenditures, $2,458; qualifying distributions, $2,338.
Limitations: Giving primarily in WV.
Application information: Application form required.
Director: J. Robert Holmes.
EIN: 570942186

49731
C. Rivers Stone Foundation
1720 N. Pleasantburg Dr.
Greenville, SC 29609-4022

Donor(s): The Stone Foundation.
Financial data (yr. ended 12/31/01): Grants paid, $1,950; assets, $544,328 (M); gifts received, $25; expenditures, $30,988; qualifying distributions, $1,950.
Limitations: Applications not accepted. Giving primarily in NC and SC.
Application information: Contributes only to pre-selected organizations.
Trustees: Mary Fraser, C. Rivers Stone.
EIN: 576171808

49732
Columbia, SC Section of the American Nuclear Society
1329 Firetower Rd.
Prosperity, SC 29127
Contact: Damon Bryson, Treas.

Established in 1999.
Financial data (yr. ended 12/31/99): Grants paid, $1,750; assets, $36,693 (L); gifts received, $649; expenditures, $5,583; qualifying distributions, $5,308; giving activities include $3,551 for programs.
Officers: Sam Bailey, Chair.; Jeff Bradfute, Vice-Chair.; Ed Pulver, Secy.; Damon Bryson, Treas.
EIN: 570773073

49733
The Lawrence C., Jr. and Mildred B. Davis Foundation
158 St. Andrews Dr.
Spartanburg, SC 29301-6638

Established in 1986 in SC.
Donor(s): Lawrence C. Davis, Mildred B. Davis.
Financial data (yr. ended 06/30/01): Grants paid, $1,100; assets, $30,920 (M); expenditures, $1,682; qualifying distributions, $0.
Limitations: Applications not accepted.
Application information: Contributes only to pre-selected organizations.
Trustees: Lawrence C. Davis, Mildred B. Davis.
EIN: 576111084

49734
Albertine Moore Scholarship Fund
c/o Bank of America
1901 Main St., SC3-240-04-15
Columbia, SC 29201

Financial data (yr. ended 12/31/99): Grants paid, $1,097; assets, $86,400 (M); expenditures, $3,190; qualifying distributions, $1,496.
Limitations: Applications not accepted.
Application information: Contributes only to pre-selected organizations.
Trustee: Bank of America.
EIN: 570918209

49735
Bridgewater Foundation
206 Winding Way
Spartanburg, SC 29306
Contact: Gordon A. Wilhite, Chair.

Financial data (yr. ended 12/31/01): Grants paid, $1,000; assets, $2,040 (M); expenditures, $1,000; qualifying distributions, $1,000.
Officers: Gordon A. Wilhite, Chair.; Mark E. Johnson, Vice-Chair.; Sarah L. Caldwell, Secy.; Robert E. Caldwell, Jr., Treas.
Directors: Hugh H. Brantley, Robert E. Caldwell, Sr., Sylvia R. Caldwell, Kathleen Johnson.
EIN: 582421520

49736
Falk-Griffin Foundation
202 Sea Oats Cir.
Pawleys Island, SC 29585

Established in 2000 in SC.
Donor(s): Carl O. Falk.
Financial data (yr. ended 12/31/01): Grants paid, $1,000; assets, $1,886,982 (M); gifts received, $5,936; expenditures, $79,487; qualifying distributions, $1,000.
Limitations: Applications not accepted.
Application information: Contributes only to pre-selected organizations.
Officers: Carl O. Falk, Pres.; Marcia Falk, V.P. and Secy.; Carla Falk, C.F.O.
EIN: 522255664

49737
Rick Palmer Memorial Scholarship Fund, Inc.
P.O. Box 95
Bamberg, SC 29003-0095
Application address: Guidance Off., c/o Eastern Alamanee High School, Woodlawn Rd., Mebane, NC 27302, tel.: (919) 563-6013

Financial data (yr. ended 12/31/01): Grants paid, $1,000; assets, $8,310 (M); gifts received, $536; expenditures, $1,013; qualifying distributions, $1,000.
Limitations: Giving limited to Mebane, NC.
Application information: Application form required.
Directors: Fred Brady, Norma A. Palmer, Syble Yancey.
EIN: 581492024

49738
Alpha-Omega Foundation
4618 Kilbourne Rd.
Columbia, SC 29206-4537

Financial data (yr. ended 03/31/02): Grants paid, $914; assets, $620 (M); gifts received, $1,174; expenditures, $974; qualifying distributions, $914.
Officer and Directors:* Betty M. Wilds,* Secy.-Treas.; Susan Wilds McArver, James T. Wilds, Jr.
EIN: 570252838

49739
Faithful and True Ministries
c/o Jan Dickson
151 Holly Ridge Ln.
West Columbia, SC 29169

Established in 1998.
Donor(s): James B. Dickson, Jan Dickson.
Financial data (yr. ended 12/31/99): Grants paid, $790; assets, $1,342 (M); gifts received, $45,820; expenditures, $44,499; qualifying distributions, $44,499.
Limitations: Applications not accepted.
Application information: Contributes only to pre-selected organizations.
Officers: Jan Dickson, Pres.; Sheilah Dixon, V.P. and Secy.-Treas.
Director: Carmen Roberson.
EIN: 582315195

49740
Frances & Mason Alexander Foundation
P.O. Box 16594
Greenville, SC 29606

Financial data (yr. ended 12/31/01): Grants paid, $750; assets, $11,144 (M); gifts received, $5,500; expenditures, $769; qualifying distributions, $750.
Limitations: Applications not accepted. Giving primarily in Greenville, SC.
Application information: Contributes only to pre-selected organizations.
Trustees: Frances S. Alexander, Mason G. Alexander.
EIN: 582441736

49741
Genevieve & John Sakas Foundation
201 Chapman Rd.
Greenville, SC 29605

Established in 1986 in SC.
Donor(s): Genevieve L. Sakas, Berkshire Hathaway, Inc.
Financial data (yr. ended 12/31/01): Grants paid, $500; assets, $1,689,991 (M); gifts received, $720; expenditures, $2,350; qualifying distributions, $500.
Limitations: Applications not accepted. Giving primarily in Greenville, SC.
Application information: Contributes only to pre-selected organizations.
Trustees: Genevieve L. Sakas, John J. Sakas.
EIN: 570835677

49742
Rose and Joseph Sokol Charitable Trust
118 Chadwick Dr.
Charleston, SC 29407-7451 (843) 766-4766
Contact: Dorothy S. Kipnis, Tr.

Financial data (yr. ended 12/31/01): Grants paid, $500; assets, $10,000 (M); expenditures, $592; qualifying distributions, $530.
Limitations: Giving limited to SC.
Trustees: Frances S. Halio, Dorothy S. Kipnis, Evelyn S. Needle, Allen Sokol.
EIN: 576097923

49743
Heather Dawn Volk Foundation
c/o Sheila F. Collins
22 Egret Dr.
Beaufort, SC 29902-1903

Established in 1994 in SC and WV.
Financial data (yr. ended 12/31/99): Grants paid, $500; assets, $7,963 (M); gifts received, $1,000; expenditures, $500; qualifying distributions, $500.
Officer: Sheila F. Collins, Pres.
EIN: 570990229

49744
Wateree Floodlands Memorial Forest, Inc.
P.O. Box 129
Camden, SC 29020-0129

Established in 1983.
Donor(s): James L. Guy II.
Financial data (yr. ended 12/31/01): Grants paid, $500; assets, $1,110,773 (M); expenditures, $13,266; qualifying distributions, $500.
Limitations: Applications not accepted. Giving primarily in SC.
Application information: Contributes only to pre-selected organizations.
Officers: James L. Guy II, Pres.; Leslie G. Copland, V.P.; James L. Guy III, Secy.-Treas.
EIN: 570741451

49745
Edwin L. and Jill M. Buker Foundation
106 Tuscany Way
Greer, SC 29650

Established in 2000 in MI.
Financial data (yr. ended 07/31/01): Grants paid, $450; assets, $5,002 (M); expenditures, $621; qualifying distributions, $450.
Limitations: Applications not accepted.
Application information: Contributes only to pre-selected organizations.
Officers: Edwin L. Buker, Pres. and Treas.; Jill M. Buker, V.P. and Secy.
EIN: 383485580

49746
The Evangelical Stewardship Foundation
305 Timber Ridge Dr.
West Columbia, SC 29169-5413

Established in 1995 in SC.
Financial data (yr. ended 12/31/01): Grants paid, $300; assets, $874 (M); gifts received, $400; expenditures, $378; qualifying distributions, $300.
Officer: Margit O. Giles, Mgr.
EIN: 237071432

49747
King Family Charitable Foundation
10 Target Rd.
Hilton Head Island, SC 29928

Established in 1997 in GA.
Donor(s): John Dudley King, Jr.
Financial data (yr. ended 12/31/01): Grants paid, $250; assets, $4,456 (M); expenditures, $250; qualifying distributions, $250.
Limitations: Applications not accepted.
Application information: Contributes only to pre-selected organizations.
Trustees: John Dudley King, Jr., Thad Denton King.
EIN: 586345326

49748
The Cindy Nord Foundation
P.O. Box 989
Blythewood, SC 29016

Established in 2001 in SC.
Donor(s): Cynthia W. Nord.
Financial data (yr. ended 12/31/01): Grants paid, $250; assets, $4,750 (M); gifts received, $5,000; expenditures, $250; qualifying distributions, $250.
Officers and Directors:* Cynthia W. Nord,* Pres.; Bruce B. Nord,* V.P.; Kathleen Nord Peterson,* Secy.; Allyson Wanutke,* Treas.
EIN: 571118065

49749—SOUTH CAROLINA

49749
Harold F. Gallivan, Jr. Family Foundation
P.O. Box 10332
Greenville, SC 29603-0332

Established in 1999 in SC.
Donor(s): Harold F. Gallivan, Jr.
Financial data (yr. ended 12/31/01): Grants paid, $82; assets, $2,187 (M); gifts received, $1,500; expenditures, $1,738; qualifying distributions, $82.
Trustee: Harold F. Gallivan, Jr.
EIN: 571082872

49750
The Walter A. Sigman, Jr. and Ercell J. Sigman Foundation Trust
c/o Walter A. Sigman, Jr.
8637 Palmetto Rd.
Edisto Island, SC 29438

Established in 1993.
Financial data (yr. ended 12/31/01): Grants paid, $50; assets, $822 (M); expenditures, $50; qualifying distributions, $50.
Trustees: Ercell J. Sigman, Walter A. Sigman, Jr.
EIN: 576154727

49751
Anna M. Black Charitable Foundation
408 E. Main St.
Spartanburg, SC 29302-1933

Established in 1995 in SC.
Financial data (yr. ended 12/31/01): Grants paid, $0; assets, $106 (M); gifts received, $350; expenditures, $267; qualifying distributions, $0.
Limitations: Applications not accepted.
Application information: Contributes only to pre-selected organizations.
Officers: Marianna B. Habisreutinger, Pres.; Paula B. Baker, Secy.-Treas.
EIN: 571013959

49752
Frederick W. and Doris E. Bristol Foundation
c/o Michael L.M. Jordan
23-B Shelter Cove Ln., Ste. 400
Hilton Head Island, SC 29928

Established in 1996 in SC.
Financial data (yr. ended 12/31/01): Grants paid, $0; assets, $1,519,028 (M); gifts received, $88,157; expenditures, $20,429; qualifying distributions, $0.
Limitations: Applications not accepted.
Application information: Contributes only to pre-selected organizations.
Officers: Frederick W. Bristol, Jr., Pres.; Linnea Bristol, V.P.; Michael L.M. Jordan, Secy. and Mgr.; Mary B. Davidson, Treas.
EIN: 571052195

49753
Jeff Davis Dill & Earline B. Dill Foundation
c/o Clark Anderson, B.B. & T. Trust Dept.
P.O. Box 408
Greenville, SC 29602-0408

Established in 2000.
Donor(s): Jeff Davis Dill.‡
Financial data (yr. ended 03/31/01): Grants paid, $0; assets, $182,602 (M); gifts received, $200,000; expenditures, $1,692; qualifying distributions, $6,845.
Trustee: B.B. & T.
EIN: 576151295

49754
Fitzhenry Family Foundation
30 Morgans Cove Dr.
Isle of Palms, SC 29451

Established in 2000 in SC.
Donor(s): Oscar C. Fitzhenry, Ruth B. Fitzhenry.
Financial data (yr. ended 06/30/01): Grants paid, $0; assets, $2,000 (M); gifts received, $2,000; expenditures, $0; qualifying distributions, $0.
Trustees: Linda S. Campbell, Charles M. Fitzhenry, Mark B. Fitzhenry, Oscar C. Fitzhenry, Ruth B. Fitzhenry, Sharon L. Fitzhenry.
EIN: 571108261

49755
Marian Leake Harris Foundation
P.O. Box 1405
Greenwood, SC 29648-1405

Established in 1986 in SC.
Financial data (yr. ended 11/30/01): Grants paid, $0; assets, $3,865 (M); expenditures, $0; qualifying distributions, $0.
Limitations: Applications not accepted.
Application information: Contributes only to pre-selected organizations.
Trustees: John B. Harris III, Marian Leake Harris, Jack S. Moorman.
EIN: 570849877

49756
The Jacobs Family Foundation
P.O. Box 1726
Spartanburg, SC 29304 (864) 573-9211

Donor(s): Henry D. Jacobs, Jr.
Financial data (yr. ended 12/31/01): Grants paid, $0; assets, $55,923 (M); gifts received, $1,500; expenditures, $1,469; qualifying distributions, $0.
Limitations: Giving primarily in Spartanburg, SC.
Application information: Application form not required.
Officers and Trustees:* Henry D. Jacobs, Jr.,* Chair.; Brett S. Jacobs,* Secy.; Clay S. Jacobs,* Treas.
EIN: 576154661

49757
Kellett Family Foundation
105 Hummingbird Ridge
Greenville, SC 29605 (864) 271-2651
Scholarship address: 113 Creek's Edge Ct., Greenville, SC 29615
Contact: William W. Kellett, Jr., Chair.

Established in 1999 in SC.
Donor(s): William W. Kellett III.
Financial data (yr. ended 12/31/00): Grants paid, $0; assets, $15,623 (M); gifts received, $3,403; expenditures, $1,155; qualifying distributions, $0.
Limitations: Giving primarily in SC.
Application information: Application form required.
Officers and Directors:* William W. Kellett, Jr.,* Chair.; William W. Kellett III,* Pres.; Lydia Kellett,* Secy.; Michael P. Kellett,* Treas.; Cookie Kellett, Helen P. Kellett, James W. Kellett, Joan Kellett.
EIN: 571088077

49758
Lebanon Relief Fund
P.O. Box 26925
Greenville, SC 29616-1925

Established in 1999 in SC.
Financial data (yr. ended 12/31/99): Grants paid, $0; assets, $1,206 (M); expenditures, $68; qualifying distributions, $68.
Director: Peter J. Ashy.
EIN: 570657244

49759
Longwood Plantation Foundation, Inc.
553 Longwood Ln.
Huger, SC 29450

Established in 2001 in SC.
Financial data (yr. ended 12/31/01): Grants paid, $0; assets, $4,951 (M); gifts received, $8,367; expenditures, $3,416; qualifying distributions, $0.
Officer: Robert H. Lockwood, Mgr.
EIN: 571119217

49760
The McLeigh Foundation
224 Treyburn Cir.
Irmo, SC 29063

Established in 2001 in SC.
Donor(s): Harvey M. Williamson.
Financial data (yr. ended 04/30/02): Grants paid, $0; assets, $123,321 (M); gifts received, $122,112; expenditures, $60; qualifying distributions, $0.
Limitations: Applications not accepted.
Application information: Contributes only to pre-selected organizations.
Director: Harvey N. Williamson, Jr.
EIN: 020538592

49761
The Natrone Means Foundation
P.O. Box 947
Columbia, SC 29202

Established in 2000 in SC.
Donor(s): Natrone Means.
Financial data (yr. ended 12/31/00): Grants paid, $0; assets, $14,262 (M); gifts received, $36,000; expenditures, $49,810; qualifying distributions, $49,810; giving activities include $49,810 for programs.
Limitations: Applications not accepted.
Application information: Contributes only to pre-selected organizations.
Officers: Natrone Means, Pres.; Brantley Evans, V.P.; Joseph R. Lefft, Treas.
EIN: 571087563

49762
The Mission Mercy Foundation
1175 Cook Rd., Ste. 115
Orangeburg, SC 29118 (803) 531-2677
Application address: 1148 Putter Path, Orangeburg, SC 29118
Contact: M. Said Nassri

Established in 1999 in SC.
Donor(s): Mohammad S. Nassri, Rashed Tabba, Nazir Hamoui.
Financial data (yr. ended 12/31/01): Grants paid, $0; assets, $331,503 (M); gifts received, $25,000; expenditures, $0; qualifying distributions, $0.
Officer and Trustees:* Mohammad S. Nassri,* Chair.; Nazir Hamoui, Rashed Tabba.
EIN: 571077772

49763
The Ken O'Connor Foundation, Inc.
17 Fox Chase Rd.
Columbia, SC 29223-3005

Established in 1998 in SC.
Financial data (yr. ended 06/30/99): Grants paid, $0; assets, $1,014 (M); gifts received, $1,006; expenditures, $0; qualifying distributions, $0.
Directors: Drale O'Connor, Kenneth O'Connor.
EIN: 571071381

49764
L. Arthur O'Neill, Jr. Education Fund
P.O. Box 1798
Sumter, SC 29151-1798 (803) 469-6137
Application address: P.O. Box 2091, Sumter, SC 29151
Contact: Vivian Brogdon

Established in 1922.
Financial data (yr. ended 04/30/00): Grants paid, $0; assets, $2,153,639 (M); expenditures, $49,860; qualifying distributions, $221,938; giving activities include $207,150 for loans to individuals.
Limitations: Giving limited to residents of Sumter County, SC.
Application information: Application form required.
Trustees: Isabel Gist, Deborah Nix, Philip G. Palmer, Bobby R. Rabon, Elmore E. Thomas, and 4 additional trustees.
EIN: 237227009
Codes: GTI

49765
Mary Barratt Park Foundation
P.O. Box 31
Greenwood, SC 29647-0001

Established around 1968.
Donor(s): George W. Park Seed Co., Inc.
Financial data (yr. ended 12/31/01): Grants paid, $0; assets, $2 (M); expenditures, $0; qualifying distributions, $0.
Limitations: Applications not accepted. Giving primarily in SC.
Application information: Contributes only to pre-selected organizations.
Officer: Karen P. Jennings, Mgr.
Directors: J. Leonard Park, William John Park.
EIN: 237025200

49766
The W. O. Powers Foundation, Inc.
P.O. Drawer 5839
Florence, SC 29502

Financial data (yr. ended 12/31/01): Grants paid, $0; assets, $1 (M); expenditures, $217; qualifying distributions, $0.

Directors: Ann W. Powers, W.O. Powers, Joe Rogers III.
EIN: 582335552

49767
Rahman Educational Fund, Inc.
115 N. Ridge Ln.
Columbia, SC 29223
Contact: Mujibar Rahman, Pres.

Established in 1998 in SC.
Financial data (yr. ended 12/31/00): Grants paid, $0; assets, $91,740 (M); gifts received, $9,000; expenditures, $0; qualifying distributions, $0.
Officer: Mujibar Rahman, Pres.
Director: Kana Rahman.
EIN: 585216020

49768
The Fred and Jean Reed Foundation
51 Club Forest Dr.
Greenville, SC 29605

Established in 2001 in SC.
Donor(s): Jean C. Reed.
Financial data (yr. ended 12/31/01): Grants paid, $0; assets, $10,017 (M); gifts received, $10,000; expenditures, $0; qualifying distributions, $0.
Limitations: Applications not accepted.
Application information: Contributes only to pre-selected organizations.
Officers: Timothy J. Reed, Pres.; John W. Reed, Secy.; Ben A. Reed, Treas.
Board Members: Frederick E. Reed, Jr., Jean C. Reed.
EIN: 571114395

49769
Peter Donald Schild Memorial Scholarship Fund
c/o Paul Schild
33 Queens Way
Hilton Head Island, SC 29928

Financial data (yr. ended 05/31/02): Grants paid, $0; assets, $20,173 (M); gifts received, $115; expenditures, $148; qualifying distributions, $0.
Limitations: Giving limited to SC.
Application information: Applicant must include academic rank and economic need.
Directors: Mae E. Schild, Paul Schild, Richard L. Schild.
EIN: 112655545

49770
The Mary Peace Sterling Foundation
122 Kellett Park Dr.
Greenville, SC 29607

Established in 2001 in SC.
Donor(s): Mary Peace Sterling.
Financial data (yr. ended 06/30/01): Grants paid, $0; assets, $975,218 (M); gifts received, $1,033,935; expenditures, $20,310; qualifying distributions, $42.
Limitations: Applications not accepted.
Application information: Contributes only to pre-selected organizations.
Trustee: Mary Peace Sterling.
EIN: 571114028

49771
Suitt Foundation
1400 Cleveland St.
P.O. Box 8858
Greenville, SC 29604

Established in 1987 in SC.
Donor(s): Thomas H. Suitt.
Financial data (yr. ended 12/31/01): Grants paid, $0; assets, $92,739 (M); expenditures, $3,288; qualifying distributions, $0.
Limitations: Applications not accepted. Giving primarily in SC.
Application information: Contributes only to pre-selected organizations.
Officers: Thomas H. Suitt, Pres.; H.B. Suitt, Secy.; Thomas H. Suitt, Jr., Treas.
EIN: 570857883

49772
The P. D. Tankersley Foundation
503 N. Main St.
Travelers Rest, SC 29690-1529
Contact: Laurie M. Tankersley

Established in 1993 in SC.
Donor(s): S. Tankersley, B. Tankersley.
Financial data (yr. ended 12/31/01): Grants paid, $0; assets, $31,858 (M); expenditures, $633; qualifying distributions, $0.
Officers: M. Brett Tankersley, Pres.; M. Shay Tankersley, V.P.; Marilyn Tankersley, Treas.
EIN: 570965749

SOUTH DAKOTA

49773
Gerald Rauenhorst Family Foundation
101 S. Phillips Ave. Ste. 102
Sioux Falls, SD 57104-6719
Contact: Margaret Bozesky

Incorporated in 1965 in MN.
Donor(s): Gerald A. Rauenhorst, Henrietta Rauenhorst, Rauenhorst Corp.
Financial data (yr. ended 04/06/01): Grants paid, $30,617,757; assets, $0 (M); expenditures, $45,070; qualifying distributions, $40,118.
Limitations: Applications not accepted. Giving primarily in MN.
Application information: Contributes only to pre-selected organizations.
Officers: Gerald A. Rauenhorst, Pres.; Henrietta Rauenhorst, Exec. V.P.; Keith P. Bednarowski, V.P. and Secy.
EIN: 460454593
Codes: FD

49774
South Dakota Community Foundation
207 E. Capitol
P.O. Box 296
Pierre, SD 57501-0296 (605) 224-1025
Additional tel.: (800) 888-1842; FAX: (605) 224-5364; URL: http://www.sdcommunityfoundation.org
Contact: Bernard W. Christenson, Exec. Dir.

Incorporated in 1987 in SD.
Financial data (yr. ended 12/31/01): Grants paid, $4,373,896; assets, $33,815,629 (M); gifts received, $2,965,535; expenditures, $4,730,607.
Limitations: Giving limited to SD.
Publications: Annual report, newsletter, informational brochure, application guidelines.
Application information: Application form required.
Officers and Directors:* John Lillibridge,* Chair.; Rod Farberg,* Vice-Chair.; Bernard W. Christenson, Exec. Dir.; and 22 additional directors.
EIN: 460398115
Codes: CM, FD

49775
Sioux Falls Area Community Foundation
300 N. Phillips Ave., Ste. 102
Sioux Falls, SD 57104-6035 (605) 336-7055
FAX: (605) 336-0038; E-mail: sbrown@sfacf.org; URL: http://www.sfacf.org
Contact: Sue Brown, C.E.O.

Established in 1976 in SD.
Financial data (yr. ended 06/30/01): Grants paid, $3,321,567; assets, $33,231,051 (M); gifts received, $7,241,487; expenditures, $4,117,394.
Limitations: Giving limited to the Sioux Falls, SD, area.
Publications: Annual report (including application guidelines), application guidelines, informational brochure (including application guidelines), newsletter, grants list, financial statement.
Application information: Scholarship application forms available from high school counseling offices. Application form required.
Officers and Directors:* Tom Everist,* Chair.; Jeff Scherschligt,* Vice-Chair.; Sue Brown, C.E.O and Pres.; Candy Hanson, V.P., Devel.; Mary Lynn Myers,* Secy.; Dan Hylland,* Treas.; Larry Bierman, Jack Carmody, Dick Corcoran, Steve Crim, Caroline Deinema, Steve Garry, Vance Goldammer, Kevin Kirby, Helen Madsen, Paul Schiller, Mary Pat Sweetman, Hugh Venrick.
EIN: 311748533
Codes: CM, FD, GTI

49776
Kind World Foundation
(Formerly Andrea and Norman Waitt, Jr. Foundation)
P.O. Box 980
Dakota Dunes, SD 57049 (605) 232-9139
FAX: (605) 232-3098
Contact: Arlene T. Curry, Exec. Dir.

Established in 1991 in SD.
Donor(s): Norman W. Waitt, Jr.
Financial data (yr. ended 12/31/00): Grants paid, $2,093,624; assets, $32,570,270 (M); gifts received, $4,149,654; expenditures, $2,639,604; qualifying distributions, $2,401,662.
Limitations: Giving primarily in northwest IA, northeast NE, southeast SD, and for national programs and projects.
Publications: Informational brochure (including application guidelines).
Application information: Application form not required.
Officer and Directors:* Arlene T. Curry,* Exec. Dir.; David M. Curry, Matt L. Rix, Norman W. Waitt, Jr.
EIN: 363776553
Codes: FD

49777
Milbank Community Foundation
301 S. Main St.
P.O. Box 446
Milbank, SD 57252 (605) 432-9229
E-mail: mcf@tnics.com; URL: http://www.milbankcf.org
Contact: David Gulck, Exec. Dir.

Established in 1993 in SD.
Financial data (yr. ended 12/31/00): Grants paid, $2,060,530; assets, $8,694,352 (M); gifts received, $1,929,081; expenditures, $2,571,307.
Limitations: Giving primarily in Grant County, SD.
Publications: Annual report, multi-year report, financial statement, occasional report, informational brochure.
Application information: Application form not required.
Officers: Rudy Neif, Pres.; John Hansen, V.P.; Chuck Monson, Secy.; David Gulck, Exec. Dir.
Directors: Russel Fischer, Sylvia Konstant, Kevin Kouba, Mark Leddy, Richard Lentz, Chuck Monson, Bill Schunenman.
EIN: 460427565
Codes: CM, FD

49778
Alpha & Omega Family Foundation
c/o Wells Fargo Bank South Dakota, N.A.
101 S. Phillips Ave., Ste. 102
Sioux Falls, SD 57104 (605) 357-8694

Established in 1994 in SD.
Financial data (yr. ended 12/31/00): Grants paid, $1,480,877; assets, $31,700,041 (M); expenditures, $1,581,536; qualifying distributions, $1,458,419; giving activities include $5,279 for program-related investments.
Limitations: Applications not accepted. Giving primarily in MN.
Application information: Contributes only to pre-selected organizations.
Officers and Directors:* J.R. Mahoney,* Pres. and Treas.; John Agee,* V.P.; A.R. Goldman,* Secy.; John H. Harris.
EIN: 460434399
Codes: FD

49779
Maas Foundation
P.O. Box 7
Watertown, SD 57201

Established in 1986 in SD.
Donor(s): George E. Maas.
Financial data (yr. ended 12/31/01): Grants paid, $1,100,000; assets, $10,105,329 (M); expenditures, $1,394,653; qualifying distributions, $1,099,817.
Limitations: Applications not accepted. Giving primarily in MN.
Application information: Contributes only to pre-selected organizations.
Officer and Trustees:* George E. Maas,* Pres.; Thomas K. Berg, Patricia A. Maas.
EIN: 460393558
Codes: FD

49780
Larson Foundation
2333 Eastbrook Dr.
Brookings, SD 57006-2899
Contact: Maree Larson, Secy.

Established in 1990.
Donor(s): O. Dale Larson.
Financial data (yr. ended 04/30/01): Grants paid, $889,915; assets, $8,918,053 (M); expenditures, $937,347; qualifying distributions, $889,915.
Limitations: Giving primarily in SD, with emphasis on Brookings, and the community of Lake Mills, IA.
Application information: Application form required.
Officers: Patricia M. Larson, Pres.; O. Dale Larson, V.P. and Treas.; Maree Larson, Secy.
EIN: 460412311
Codes: FD

49781
Dakota Charitable Foundation, Inc.
c/o Ray J. Hillenbrand
P.O. Box 8303
Rapid City, SD 57709

Established in 1992 in SD.
Donor(s): Margaret Lally, and members of the Hillenbrand family.
Financial data (yr. ended 12/31/01): Grants paid, $573,000; assets, $31,312,119 (M); gifts received, $27,949,419; expenditures, $684,070; qualifying distributions, $577,660.
Limitations: Applications not accepted. Giving primarily in Rapid City, SD.
Application information: Contributes only to pre-selected organizations.
Directors: Gretchen Hillenbrand, Heidi Hillenbrand, Margaret Hillenbrand, Ray Hillenbrand.
EIN: 460422869
Codes: FD

49782
Marion Bradley Via Memorial Foundation
c/o First Premier Bank, Trust Dept.
601 S. Minnesota Ave.
Sioux Falls, SD 57104-4868

Established in 1991 in VA.
Donor(s): Marion Bradley Via,‡ Edward B. Via.
Financial data (yr. ended 12/31/00): Grants paid, $416,116; assets, $7,168,950 (M); gifts received, $60,000; expenditures, $514,944; qualifying distributions, $410,920.
Limitations: Applications not accepted. Giving primarily in Roanoke, VA.

Application information: Contributes only to pre-selected organizations.
Officer: John G. Rocovich, Jr., Mgr.
Directors: J. Tracy O'Rourke, Frederick P. Stratton, Jr., C.R. Whitney.
Trustee: First Premier Bank.
EIN: 541601560
Codes: FD

49783
John T. Vucurevich Foundation
c/o Wells Fargo Bank South Dakota, N.A.
P.O. Drawer 1040
Rapid City, SD 57709 (605) 343-0820
Application address: P.O. Box 170, Rapid City, SD 57709; E-mail: jtvfnd@qwest.net
Contact: Paul F. Phelan, Secy.

Established in 1985 in SD.
Donor(s): John T. Vucurevich.
Financial data (yr. ended 12/31/01): Grants paid, $351,415; assets, $9,115,516 (M); expenditures, $530,137; qualifying distributions, $450,270; giving activities include $36,608 for programs.
Limitations: Giving primarily in SD.
Application information: Application form required.
Trustee: Wells Fargo Bank South Dakota, N.A.
Advisory Board: Dale Clement, Renee Parker, Alex Vucurevich, Connie Vucurevich, Thomas Vucurevich.
EIN: 460359829
Codes: FD

49784
William Mibra Griffith and Bryne Smith Griffith Foundation, Inc.
P.O. Box 848
Huron, SD 57350

Established in 1991 in SD.
Financial data (yr. ended 12/31/00): Grants paid, $336,000; assets, $7,823,283 (M); expenditures, $389,468; qualifying distributions, $323,011.
Limitations: Applications not accepted. Giving primarily in SD.
Application information: Contributes only to pre-selected organizations.
Directors: William Anderson, Tom Batcheller, Hilton M. Briggs, Paul Christen, Lynn V. Schneider, Alvin A. Schock, Robert T. Wagner.
EIN: 460416533
Codes: FD

49785
Watertown Community Foundation
1200 33rd St., S.E., Ste. 309A
P.O. Box 116
Watertown, SD 57201-0116 (605) 882-3731
FAX: (605) 886-5957; E-mail: foundation@dailypost.com
Contact: Jan DeBerg, Exec. Dir.

Incorporated in 1979 in SD.
Financial data (yr. ended 12/31/01): Grants paid, $252,545; assets, $55,641,197 (M); expenditures, $258,721.
Limitations: Giving limited to the metropolitan Watertown, SD, area.
Publications: Annual report (including application guidelines), informational brochure, newsletter.
Application information: Application form required.
Officers and Directors:* Rick Melmer,* Chair.; John Hopper,* Vice-Chair.; Jan DeBerg, Exec. Dir.; Paul Hinderaker, John Redlinger, Nancy J. Turbak.
EIN: 460350319
Codes: CM, FD

49786
The Hatterscheidt Foundation, Inc.
c/o Wells Fargo Bank, N.A.
P.O. Box 849
Aberdeen, SD 57402-0849 (605) 226-1116
Contact: Kaye L. DeYoung, V.P., Wells Fargo Bank, N.A.

Incorporated in 1947 in DE.
Donor(s): Ruth K. Hatterscheidt,‡ F.W. Hatterscheidt Trusts.
Financial data (yr. ended 12/31/01): Grants paid, $246,710; assets, $5,087,493 (M); expenditures, $281,875; qualifying distributions, $252,193.
Limitations: Giving limited to SD.
Application information: Scholarship applications must go directly through specific SD colleges; applications from organizations or individuals outside of SD are not accepted.
Officer: Kaye L. DeYoung, V.P.
EIN: 466012543
Codes: FD, GTI

49787
James A. Brown Private Foundation
2201 St. Charles Cir.
Sioux Falls, SD 57108

Established in 1987 in NC.
Donor(s): James A. Brown.
Financial data (yr. ended 12/31/01): Grants paid, $234,200; assets, $358,848 (M); gifts received, $20,000; expenditures, $259,821; qualifying distributions, $234,200.
Limitations: Applications not accepted. Giving on a national basis.
Application information: Contributes only to pre-selected organizations.
Trustees: James A. Brown, Lara L. Brown, Mary Beth Brown.
EIN: 566312776

49788
Sheldon F. Reese Foundation
P.O. Box 89704
Sioux Falls, SD 57109-1010 (605) 336-1699
FAX: (605) 361-4040
Contact: John Quello, Pres.

Established about 1980 in SD.
Donor(s): Sheldon F. Reese.‡
Financial data (yr. ended 12/31/01): Grants paid, $192,819; assets, $3,966,965 (M); expenditures, $199,330; qualifying distributions, $194,517.
Limitations: Giving primarily in SD, with strong emphasis on Sioux Falls.
Application information: Application form required.
Officers and Directors:* John Quello, Pres.; Ernest G. Carlson,* V.P.; Virginia Pavelka Luke, Secy.; Vance Goldammer,* Treas.; Curtis L. Hage.
EIN: 460358682
Codes: FD2

49789
Welk Family Foundation
c/o Dacotah Bank
P.O. Box 1210
Aberdeen, SD 57402 (605) 225-5611

Established in 1988 in SD.
Financial data (yr. ended 12/31/00): Grants paid, $182,100; assets, $3,835,808 (M); expenditures, $203,697; qualifying distributions, $180,109.
Limitations: Giving limited to Roberts County, SD.
Application information: Application form required.
Trustee: Dacotah Bank.
Advisory Committee: Kaye Cahill, Lavonne Grimsrud, Harlan Hammer, Guy Mackner, Laurel Pistorius.

EIN: 363579562
Codes: FD2

49790
Elmen Family Foundation
P.O. Box 5103
Sioux Falls, SD 57117-5103
FAX: (605) 338-9511
Contact: Robert C. Elmen, Pres.

Established in 1995 in SD.
Financial data (yr. ended 12/31/01): Grants paid, $151,400; assets, $4,547,539 (M); expenditures, $211,738; qualifying distributions, $163,839.
Limitations: Giving primarily in SD.
Application information: Application form not required.
Officers: Robert C. Elmen, Pres.; James W. Elmen, V.P.; Vance R.C. Goldammer, Secy.; Thomas J. Whalen, Treas.
EIN: 460433641
Codes: FD2

49791
Tom and Danielle Aman Foundation
P.O. Box 38
Aberdeen, SD 57402 (605) 226-0015
Contact: Heidi Kramer, Dir.

Established in 1997 in SD.
Donor(s): Danielle Ross Aman, Thomas E. Aman.
Financial data (yr. ended 12/31/01): Grants paid, $149,618; assets, $2,781,554 (M); expenditures, $287,608; qualifying distributions, $197,632.
Limitations: Giving primarily in Fort Yates, ND and Aberdeen and Mobridge, SD.
Publications: Application guidelines, occasional report, program policy statement.
Application information: Application form not required.
Officers: Danielle Ross Aman, Pres.; Thomas E. Aman, Secy.-Treas.
Director: Heidi Kramer.
EIN: 411876001
Codes: FD2

49792
Gwendolyn L. Stearns Foundation, Inc.
c/o Wells Fargo Bank
P.O. Box 1040
Rapid City, SD 57709

Established in 2001 in SD.
Donor(s): Gwendolyn L. Stearns.‡
Financial data (yr. ended 12/31/01): Grants paid, $144,600; assets, $6,551,015 (M); gifts received, $6,318,729; expenditures, $157,043; qualifying distributions, $145,161.
Limitations: Giving primarily in SD.
Officers and Directors:* Jerald M. Gerdes,* Pres.; Charles J. Ray,* V.P.; Phyllis S. Dixon,* Secy.; C.D. Dunmire,* Treas.; Ed L. Anderson, William Howard, Doris Rudel.
EIN: 311737658

49793
Anza Foundation
514 10th Ave. S.E.
P.O. Box 1445
Watertown, SD 57201 (605) 886-3889
Contact: Michele Roseth, Mgr.

Established in 1995 in SD.
Donor(s): Anza, Inc.
Financial data (yr. ended 12/31/00): Grants paid, $101,000; assets, $39,980 (M); expenditures, $102,059; qualifying distributions, $101,000.
Limitations: Giving limited to areas of company operations in SD.
Officer: Michele Roseth, Mgr.
Directors: Dennis Holien, Greg Kulesa.

49793—SOUTH DAKOTA

EIN: 460438174
Codes: FD2

49794
Jerstad Family Foundation
19 S. Riverview Heights
Sioux Falls, SD 57105
Contact: Sandy Jerstad, Dir.

Established in 1997 in SD.
Donor(s): Mark A. Jerstad.‡
Financial data (yr. ended 12/31/00): Grants paid, $100,000; assets, $2,792,092 (M); gifts received, $64,455; expenditures, $112,389; qualifying distributions, $100,430.
Limitations: Giving primarily in MN and SD.
Application information: Application form not required.
Officers and Directors:* Sandra I. Jerstad,* Pres.; Sarah Jerstad,* Secy.; Michael Jerstad,* Treas.; Rachel Jerstad.
EIN: 911757487
Codes: FD2

49795
Raft Charitable Foundation
c/o Dorsey Whitney Trust Co.
401 E. 8th St., Ste. 319
Sioux Falls, SD 57103

Established in 1999 in MN.
Donor(s): Raft 1999 Charitable Annuity Trust.
Financial data (yr. ended 12/31/01): Grants paid, $100,000; assets, $2,763,829 (M); gifts received, $1,340,962; expenditures, $113,671; qualifying distributions, $98,899.
Limitations: Applications not accepted. Giving primarily in MN; and some giving in Cumberland, WI.
Application information: Contributes only to pre-selected organizations.
Trustees: Gary Johnson, Faye L. Youngren, Thomas R. Youngren.
EIN: 416463940
Codes: FD2

49796
Baron & Emilie Dow Home, Inc.
c/o Wells Fargo Bank South Dakota, N.A.
101 N. Phillips Ave., P.O. Box 5953
Sioux Falls, SD 57117-5953
Application address: c/o Ralph Jenson, 1000 N. Lake, Sioux Falls, SD 57104, tel.: (605) 336-1490

Financial data (yr. ended 12/31/01): Grants paid, $72,000; assets, $1,774,689 (M); expenditures, $84,353; qualifying distributions, $74,011.
Limitations: Giving limited to residents of Sioux Falls, SD.
Trustee: Wells Fargo Capital Mgmt.
EIN: 466018386
Codes: GTI

49797
Paul & Mayme Green Memorial Foundation
Wells Fargo Bank South Dakota, N.A.
P.O. Box 114
Aberdeen, SD 57402-0114 (605) 225-1200
Contact: Carlyle E. Richards, Pres.

Established in 1984 in SD.
Financial data (yr. ended 06/30/01): Grants paid, $71,700; assets, $1,487,666 (M); expenditures, $84,845; qualifying distributions, $77,255.
Limitations: Giving limited to ND and SD.
Application information: Application form not required.
Officers: Carlyle E. Richards, Pres.; Dave Arlt, V.P.; Vi Hormann, Secy.-Treas.

Directors: Dennis Batteen, Bruce Cutler, Ka Squire, Jr., Dan Van Dover.
Trustee: Wells Fargo Bank South Dakota, N.A.
EIN: 460380149

49798
Boehnen Foundation
P.O. Box 66
Mitchell, SD 57301
Contact: L.L. Boehnen, Pres.

Established in 1985.
Donor(s): David Boehnen, Lloyd Boehnen.
Financial data (yr. ended 12/31/01): Grants paid, $65,000; assets, $112,080 (M); expenditures, $65,631; qualifying distributions, $65,000.
Officers: L.L. Boehnen, Pres.; David L. Boehnen, V.P. and Secy.; D.A. Boehnen, V.P. and Treas.
Director: Shari Boehnen.
EIN: 363371953

49799
The Putney Foundation
600 Stevens Port Dr., Ste. 101
Dakota Dunes, SD 57049

Donor(s): Mark W. Putney, Ray A. Putney.
Financial data (yr. ended 12/31/01): Grants paid, $62,446; assets, $175,901 (M); expenditures, $65,015; qualifying distributions, $62,446.
Limitations: Applications not accepted. Giving primarily in IA and MN.
Application information: Contributes only to pre-selected organizations.
Officers: Mark W. Putney, Pres.; William Bradford Putney, V.P.; Kelly Putney, Secy.
EIN: 421286937

49800
Westendorf Family Foundation
600 Stevens Port Dr., Ste. 325
Dakota Dunes, SD 57049-5149

Donor(s): Westendorf Manufacturing Co., Inc.
Financial data (yr. ended 10/31/00): Grants paid, $60,118; assets, $1,086,602 (M); expenditures, $61,512; qualifying distributions, $59,828.
Limitations: Applications not accepted. Giving primarily in Onawa, IA.
Application information: Unsolicited requests for funds not accepted.
Trustee: Neal Westendorf.
EIN: 426373031
Codes: GTI

49801
Walter & Frances Green Charitable Trust
c/o Wells Fargo Bank South Dakota, N.A.
P.O. Box 1040
Rapid City, SD 57709
Application address: c/o Green Scholarship Comm., 320 S. Main, Lead, SD 57754

Established in 1995 in SD.
Donor(s): Walter Green, Frances Green.
Financial data (yr. ended 12/31/00): Grants paid, $60,000; assets, $1,377,446 (M); expenditures, $71,228; qualifying distributions, $60,627.
Limitations: Giving limited to Lead and Deadwood, SD.
Application information: Application form required.
Trustees: Barb Allen, Tom Blair, Donald L. Marchant, Cynthia Trucano, Dennis York, Wells Fargo Bank South Dakota, N.A.
EIN: 466096446
Codes: GTI

49802
Howard Memorial Fund
P.O. Box 114
Aberdeen, SD 57402-0114
Application address: 222 Midwest Capitol Bldg., Aberdeen, SD 57401, tel.: (605) 225-1200
Contact: Carlyle Richards, Secy.-Treas.

Established in 1964 in SD.
Donor(s): Kenneth Vaughn.
Financial data (yr. ended 12/31/01): Grants paid, $54,510; assets, $896,784 (M); expenditures, $61,998; qualifying distributions, $58,178.
Limitations: Giving primarily to residents of Brown County, SD.
Officers and Directors:* Maurice Webb,* Pres.; Charles Ingerson,* V.P.; Carlyle Richards, Secy.-Treas.; Kenneth Vaughn, Kerwin Winkler.
EIN: 466014133
Codes: GTI

49803
John & Sara Griffin Foundation
c/o Wells Fargo Bank South Dakota, N.A.
101 North Phillips Ave.
Sioux Falls, SD 57117-5953
Application addresses: c/o Mark Griffin, 2701 S. Minnesota Ave., Sioux Falls, SD 57105; c/o Sara Griffin, 2615 Ridgeview Way, Sioux Falls, SD 57105

Financial data (yr. ended 11/30/01): Grants paid, $49,406; assets, $192,221 (M); gifts received, $24,398; expenditures, $52,197; qualifying distributions, $49,406.
Limitations: Giving primarily in Sioux Falls, SD.
Application information: Application form not required.
Officers: Sara Griffin, Pres. and Treas.; Mark E. Griffin, V.P.; Scott Cross, Secy.
EIN: 466014528

49804
R. R. R. Elmen Family Foundation
P.O. Box 5103
Sioux Falls, SD 57117-5103
Application address: 1808 S. Kiwanis, Sioux Falls, SD 57105, tel.: (605) 339-2628
Contact: Richard J. Elmen, Pres.

Established in 1999 in SD.
Donor(s): Richard J. Elmen, Connie Renee Elmen Hollan.
Financial data (yr. ended 12/31/01): Grants paid, $45,510; assets, $567,844 (M); expenditures, $51,665; qualifying distributions, $45,510.
Application information: Application form not required.
Officers: Richard J. Elmen, Pres. and Treas.; Connie Renee Elmen Hollan, V.P. and Secy.
EIN: 460451639

49805
KB Charitable Trust
207 Lakeside Ln.
Pierre, SD 57501

Established in 1998 in SD.
Donor(s): K & S Asset Management Co.
Financial data (yr. ended 12/31/00): Grants paid, $42,830; assets, $4,259 (M); gifts received, $31,655; expenditures, $43,481; qualifying distributions, $43,476.
Limitations: Applications not accepted. Giving on a national basis, primarily in the Midwest and Mountain regions of the U.S.
Application information: Contributes only to pre-selected organizations.
Trustee: Kent A. Bowers.
EIN: 460446045

49806
William J. Holland Foundation
509 8th Ave. E.
Sisseton, SD 57262
Contact: Wallace R. Brantseg, Mgr.

Established in 1984 in SD.
Financial data (yr. ended 04/30/02): Grants paid, $42,610; assets, $624,686 (M); expenditures, $53,413; qualifying distributions, $42,610.
Limitations: Giving limited to the Sisseton, SD, area.
Application information: Application form required.
Officer and Trustees:* Wallace R. Brantseg,* Mgr.; Alyce I. Holland, Harold L. Torness.
EIN: 460381838

49807
Grace Lemley Foundation, Inc.
c/o Denise Webster
P.O. Box 3140
Rapid City, SD 57709
Application address: 2630 Jackson Blvd., Ste. 202, Rapid City, SD 57702
Contact: Shane Taylor, Pres.

Established in 2000 in SD.
Donor(s): Margaret Lemley Warren Trust.
Financial data (yr. ended 12/31/01): Grants paid, $35,000; assets, $20,643 (M); gifts received, $31,562; expenditures, $36,733; qualifying distributions, $35,000.
Limitations: Giving limited to Custer, Lawrence, Meade, and Pennington counties, SD.
Officers: Shane Taylor, Pres.; Darlene Anderson, V.P.; Constance Drew, Secy.
EIN: 460452571

49808
Sioux Steel Company Foundation
196 1/2 E. 6th St.
Sioux Falls, SD 57101 (605) 336-1750
Contact: Phillip M. Rysdon, Pres.

Established in 1945 in TN.
Donor(s): Sioux Steel Co.
Financial data (yr. ended 08/31/01): Grants paid, $33,953; assets, $1,418,284 (M); gifts received, $30,872; expenditures, $51,645; qualifying distributions, $42,444.
Limitations: Giving primarily in Sioux Falls, SD.
Officers: Phillip M. Rysdon, Pres. and Treas.; Scott Rysdon, V.P. and Secy.
EIN: 466012618
Codes: CS, CD

49809
Dorothy D. Graham Scholarship Fund
c/o Wells Fargo Bank South Dakota, N.A.
101 N. Phillips Ave.
Sioux Falls, SD 57117-5953 (605) 575-7400
Contact: Jennifer Sheets, Trust Off.

Established in 1995 in SD.
Financial data (yr. ended 12/31/00): Grants paid, $30,000; assets, $403,801 (M); expenditures, $36,305; qualifying distributions, $30,249.
Limitations: Giving primarily in SD.
Application information: Application form required.
Trustee: Wells Fargo Bank South Dakota, N.A.
EIN: 466034811

49810
Rau Family Trust
c/o Dacotah Bank
P.O. Box 1210
Aberdeen, SD 57401 (605) 225-5611
Contact: Tom Appletoft, Trust Off., Dacotah Bank

Established in 1994 in SD.
Financial data (yr. ended 12/31/01): Grants paid, $28,644; assets, $588,153 (M); expenditures, $32,812; qualifying distributions, $28,644.
Limitations: Giving limited to Roberts County, SD.
Application information: Application form required.
Advisory Committee: Harley Deutsch, Neil D. Long, Truman Nelson.
Trustee: Dacotah Bank.
EIN: 460428883

49811
Thelma J. Serr Charitable Trust
P.O. Box 5953
Sioux Falls, SD 57117-5953

Financial data (yr. ended 12/31/01): Grants paid, $28,461; assets, $650,790 (M); expenditures, $32,909; qualifying distributions, $30,123.
Limitations: Applications not accepted. Giving primarily in SD.
Application information: Contributes only to pre-selected organizations.
Trustee: Wells Fargo Bank South Dakota, N.A.
EIN: 466088909

49812
Louie & Frank Kramer Educational Fund
c/o Wells Fargo Bank South Dakota, N.A.
P.O. Box 31
Winner, SD 57580
Application address: c/o Lynnette Kucera, Wells Fargo Bank S.D., N.A., Trust Dept., Winner, SD 57325, tel.: (605) 842-8218

Financial data (yr. ended 12/31/00): Grants paid, $26,800; assets, $276,329 (M); expenditures, $30,052; qualifying distributions, $26,975.
Limitations: Giving limited to Chamberlain, SD.
Application information: Application form required.
Trustee: Wells Fargo Bank South Dakota, N.A.
EIN: 510190074
Codes: GTI

49813
Jiju Charitable Trust
P.O. Box 338
Pierre, SD 57501-0338

Established in 1998 in SD.
Financial data (yr. ended 12/31/00): Grants paid, $25,438; assets, $12,050 (M); gifts received, $32,000; expenditures, $25,444; qualifying distributions, $25,438.
Limitations: Applications not accepted. Giving on a national basis.
Application information: Contributes only to pre-selected organizations.
Trustees: James H. Bowers, Judy L. Bowers.
EIN: 460446005

49814
William & Ruth Cozard Educational Scholarship Trust
c/o Wells Fargo Bank South Dakota, N.A., Trust Dept.
P.O. Box 31
Winner, SD 57580 (605) 842-8218
Contact: Jessica Beavers, Trust Off., Wells Fargo Bank South Dakota, N.A.

Financial data (yr. ended 12/31/00): Grants paid, $24,400; assets, $140,965 (M); expenditures, $28,476; qualifying distributions, $24,748; giving activities include $24,400 for loans to individuals.
Limitations: Giving limited to residents of Chamberlain, SD.
Application information: Application form required.
Trustee: Wells Fargo Bank South Dakota, N.A.
EIN: 466039141
Codes: GTI

49815
The Prostrollo Foundation
P.O. Box 325
Madison, SD 57042

Established in 1997 in SD.
Donor(s): Jerry Prostrollo.
Financial data (yr. ended 03/31/02): Grants paid, $22,821; assets, $1,389 (M); expenditures, $23,352; qualifying distributions, $22,821.
Officers: Jerry Prostrollo, Pres.; Angie Prostrollo, V.P.; Nancy Carlson, Secy.
EIN: 911815645

49816
Yankton Rural Area Health Education Center
1017 W. 5th St.
Yankton, SD 57078

Financial data (yr. ended 09/30/01): Grants paid, $20,000; assets, $412,815 (M); expenditures, $23,034; qualifying distributions, $22,309.
Limitations: Applications not accepted.
Application information: Contributes only to pre-selected organizations.
Officers: Gale Walker, Pres.; Robert Karolevitz, V.P.; Harriet Gobel, Secy.-Treas.
Directors: John Hughes, T. H. Sattler.
EIN: 460354137

49817
Blanche Doolittle Private Foundation
c/o Wells Fargo Bank South Dakota, N.A.
P.O. Box 5953
Sioux Falls, SD 57117-5953
Application address: c/o Jennifer Sheets, Wells Fargo Bank South Dakota, N.A., 101 N. Phillips Ave., Sioux Falls, SD 57104-6714

Established in 1999 in SD.
Financial data (yr. ended 12/31/00): Grants paid, $19,800; assets, $415,017 (M); expenditures, $26,128; qualifying distributions, $20,291.
Limitations: Giving limited to residents of Sioux Falls, SD.
Application information: Application form required.
Trustee: Wells Fargo Bank South Dakota, N.A.
EIN: 466056120

49818
John E. Solem Scholarship Trust
P.O. Box 5186
Sioux Falls, SD 57117-5186
Application addresses: c/o Leonard Bettnemg, Baltic High School, Baltic, SD 57003, tel.: (605) 529-5466; c/o George Henry, Dell Rapids High School, Dell Rapids, SD 57002, tel.: (605) 428-5473; c/o Clarence Kooistra, Garretson High School, Garretson, SD 57030; tel.: (605) 594-3452

Financial data (yr. ended 12/31/00): Grants paid, $17,600; assets, $213,855 (M); expenditures, $21,263; qualifying distributions, $17,502.
Limitations: Giving limited to Baltic, Dell Rapids, and Garretson, SD.
Application information: Application form required.
Trustee: First National Bank of Sioux Falls.
EIN: 466010949
Codes: GTI

49819
A. L. Spilde Scholarship Trust
P.O. Box 409
Milbank, SD 57252-0409
Contact: Michael Misterek, Tr.

Established in 1988 in SD.
Financial data (yr. ended 06/30/01): Grants paid, $16,000; assets, $170,046 (M); expenditures, $16,349; qualifying distributions, $15,697.
Limitations: Giving primarily in MT, NM, and SD.
Application information: Application form required.
Trustees: Michael Misterek, Charles Mykelgard.
EIN: 466080893
Codes: GTI

49820
Eunice T. Reese Charitable Trust
P.O. Box 848
Huron, SD 57350

Established in 1994.
Donor(s): Eunice T. Reese.‡
Financial data (yr. ended 12/31/01): Grants paid, $15,817; assets, $237,397 (M); expenditures, $17,320; qualifying distributions, $15,817.
Trustee: Marquette Bank.
EIN: 466096016

49821
Hansen Family Foundation
301 N. Dakota Ave.
Sioux Falls, SD 57104-6008

Donor(s): Bus Systems, Inc., Lowell C. Hansen II, Lynne Hansen, Jack Rabbit Lines, Inc.
Financial data (yr. ended 06/30/02): Grants paid, $15,745; assets, $13,260 (M); gifts received, $15,000; expenditures, $16,203; qualifying distributions, $15,745.
Limitations: Applications not accepted. Giving primarily in Sioux Falls, SD.
Application information: Contributes only to pre-selected organizations.
Officer: Lowell C. Hansen II, Pres.
EIN: 460377062

49822
Clover Charitable Fund, Inc.
c/o Andrew Hollander
HC 55, Box 180
Sturgis, SD 57785-9195

Established in 1986 in NY.
Donor(s): Anne Bodman.
Financial data (yr. ended 09/30/01): Grants paid, $15,302; assets, $79,167 (M); gifts received, $3,100; expenditures, $15,647; qualifying distributions, $15,302.
Limitations: Giving primarily in SD.
Application information: Application form not required.
Officers: Anne Bodman, Pres.; Andy Hollander, V.P.
Director: Carol Hallock.
EIN: 222780214

49823
A. R. Wood Educational Trust
c/o Wells Fargo Bank South Dakota N.A.
P.O. Box 1040
Sioux Falls, SD 57117-5953 (605) 575-7400

Financial data (yr. ended 12/31/00): Grants paid, $13,750; assets, $215,294 (M); expenditures, $18,785; qualifying distributions, $14,221.
Limitations: Giving limited to Luverne, MN.
Application information: Application form required.
Trustee: Wells Fargo Bank South Dakota, N.A.
EIN: 416023357
Codes: GTI

49824
Tom Callahan Trust
3913 Ridgemoor Dr.
Rapid City, SD 57702

Established in 1995 in SD.
Financial data (yr. ended 12/31/00): Grants paid, $9,667; assets, $153,670 (M); expenditures, $11,480; qualifying distributions, $9,582.
Limitations: Applications not accepted. Giving primarily in Rapid City, SD.
Application information: Contributes only to pre-selected organizations.
Trustee: Shirley Stec.
EIN: 466093025

49825
James E. and Lillian E. Shea Charitable Trust
P.O. Box 1040
Rapid City, SD 57709
Application address: 4 Washington St., Deadwood, SD 57732, tel.: (605) 578-3870 or (605) 578-1928
Contact: Mary Austin Harnish-Kopco, Chair.

Established in 1999.
Financial data (yr. ended 12/31/01): Grants paid, $9,000; assets, $137,874 (M); gifts received, $50,000; expenditures, $11,099; qualifying distributions, $9,000.
Limitations: Giving primarily in Lawrence County, SD.
Officers: Mary Austin Harnish-Kopco, Chair.; Shirley Bergen, Vice-Chair.; Aileen Brunner, Secy.
Board Members: Gina M. Ferris, Larry Shama.
EIN: 466104853

49826
JKB Charitable Trust
117 Riverplace Dr.
Pierre, SD 57501-4600

Established in 1998 in SD.
Financial data (yr. ended 12/31/00): Grants paid, $8,014; assets, $12,220 (M); gifts received, $6,050; expenditures, $8,570; qualifying distributions, $8,484.
Limitations: Applications not accepted. Giving primarily in OR and SD.
Application information: Contributes only to pre-selected organizations.
Trustee: Kurt Bowers.
EIN: 460445967

49827
Soaring Eagle Foundation
932 Enchantment Rd.
Rapid City, SD 57701

Donor(s): Dexter Thiel, Sherry Thiel.
Financial data (yr. ended 12/31/01): Grants paid, $8,000; assets, $157,240 (M); gifts received, $15,000; expenditures, $8,015; qualifying distributions, $8,000.
Limitations: Applications not accepted.
Application information: Contributes only to pre-selected organizations.
Officers: William Newhouse, Pres.; Dexter Thiel, V.P.; Sherry Thiel, Secy.-Treas.
Director: Harry W. Child.
EIN: 810497192

49828
Gramberg-Millner Scholarship Fund
c/o Wells Fargo Bank South Dakota, N.A.
P.O. Box 1040
Rapid City, SD 57709-1040

Financial data (yr. ended 11/30/01): Grants paid, $7,000; assets, $207,937 (M); expenditures, $10,827; qualifying distributions, $9,006.
Limitations: Giving limited to SD.
Application information: Application form required.
Trustee: Wells Fargo Bank South Dakota, N.A.
EIN: 466018116
Codes: GTI

49829
Rew & Edna Walz Scholarship Trust
Wells Fargo South Dakota, N.A.
P.O. Box 1040
Rapid City, SD 57709-1040
Application address: c/o First Presbyterian Church, Rew and Edna Walz Scholarship Comm., 710 Kansas City St., Rapid City, SD 57701

Established in 1994 in SD.
Financial data (yr. ended 12/31/00): Grants paid, $7,000; assets, $191,663 (M); expenditures, $9,221; qualifying distributions, $7,452.
Limitations: Giving limited to residents of SD.
Application information: Application form required.
Directors: Dave Dixon, John Locks, Lisle Owens.
Trustee: Wells Fargo Bank South Dakota, N.A.
EIN: 466093427
Codes: GTI

49830
Lois Weber Charities, Inc.
c/o Joe Giovanetto
P.O. Box 206
Murdo, SD 57559-0206
Application address: P.O. Box 469, Murdo, SD 57559-0469, tel.: (605) 669-2406
Contact: Reverend David Otten, Secy.

Established in 1998 in SD.
Financial data (yr. ended 12/31/00): Grants paid, $6,680; assets, $44,420 (M); gifts received, $33,000; expenditures, $37,514; qualifying distributions, $38,256; giving activities include $30,834 for programs.
Limitations: Giving limited to Murdo, SD.
Application information: Application form required.
Officers: Paul Anderson, Pres.; David Otten, Secy.; Joseph Giovanetto, Treas.
Director: Tim Aoag.
EIN: 411903004

49831
Jessie Bonham Scholarship Trust
c/o Wells Fargo Bank South Dakota, N.A.
P.O. Box 849
Aberdeen, SD 57402-0849   (605) 226-1116

Financial data (yr. ended 02/28/02): Grants paid, $6,402; assets, $174,050 (M); expenditures, $8,465; qualifying distributions, $7,524; giving activities include $3,902 for loans to individuals.
Limitations: Giving limited to the Britton, SD, area.
Application information: Students of Britton Independent School District only need apply. Application form required.
Trustee: Wells Fargo Bank South Dakota, N.A.
EIN: 526171509

49832
Doolittle Memorial Scholarship Trust
c/o Wells Fargo Bank South Dakota, N.A.
204 S. 1st St.
Aberdeen, SD 57401
Application address: c/o Aberdeen Central High School, Aberdeen, SD 57401

Established in 1993 in SD.
Financial data (yr. ended 12/31/01): Grants paid, $6,325; assets, $130,742 (M); expenditures, $8,360; qualifying distributions, $7,098.
Limitations: Giving limited to residents of Aberdeen, SD.
Application information: Application form required.
Trustee: Wells Fargo Bank South Dakota, N.A.
EIN: 466091497

49833
Selom Trust for Helping Needy Exceptional Children of Lincoln County, South Dakota
P.O. Box 38
Canton, SD 57013-0038
Application addresses: 215 W. First, Canton, SD 57013, tel.: (605) 764-5538; 625 E. Maple, Canton, SD 57013, tel.: (605) 987-2447
Contact: Luverne Hammerstrom, Tr., or Carol Crawford, Tr.

Financial data (yr. ended 08/31/01): Grants paid, $6,250; assets, $138,187 (M); expenditures, $8,144; qualifying distributions, $6,250.
Limitations: Giving primarily in SD.
Trustees: Carol Crawford, Luverne Hammerstrom.
EIN: 466016494

49834
Hansen Scholarship Trust
26928 Cliff Ave.
Sioux Falls, SD 57108   (605) 332-9018
Contact: Victor Nield, Pres.

Established in 1994 in SD.
Financial data (yr. ended 12/31/00): Grants paid, $5,600; assets, $43,256 (M); expenditures, $6,013; qualifying distributions, $5,611.
Limitations: Giving limited to residents of Sioux Falls, SD.
Application information: Application form required.
Officer: Victor Nield, Pres.
EIN: 466094569

49835
Earl and Helen Bohlen Family Foundation
P.O. Box 1267
Watertown, SD 57201-6267

Established in 1996 in SD.
Donor(s): Earl Bohlen, Helen Bohlen.
Financial data (yr. ended 12/31/01): Grants paid, $5,500; assets, $120,472 (M); expenditures, $6,771; qualifying distributions, $5,500.
Limitations: Applications not accepted.
Application information: Contributes only to pre-selected organizations.
Officer: Earl Bohlan, Pres.; Helen Bohlen, Secy.-Treas.
Director: Douglas Bohlen.
EIN: 460444386

49836
Arthur C. & Jessie Bonham Educational Loan Fund
c/o Wells Fargo Bank South Dakota, N.A.
P.O. Box 849
Aberdeen, SD 57402-0849   (605) 226-1116

Financial data (yr. ended 02/28/02): Grants paid, $5,250; assets, $290,905 (M); gifts received, $3,903; expenditures, $10,848; qualifying distributions, $8,601.
Limitations: Giving limited to Britton, SD.
Application information: Application form required.
Trustee: Wells Fargo Bank South Dakota, N.A.
EIN: 466020004

49837
Bertha Wieck Charitable Trust Foundation
26928 Cliff Ave.
Sioux Falls, SD 57108

Established in 1995 in SD.
Financial data (yr. ended 12/31/01): Grants paid, $4,200; assets, $61,987 (M); expenditures, $4,812; qualifying distributions, $4,200.
Limitations: Applications not accepted.
Application information: Contributes only to pre-selected organizations.
Officer: Victor Nield, Pres.
EIN: 364115360

49838
Educational Aide Trust
c/o Boys Club of Rapid City
P.O. Box 907
Rapid City, SD 57709
Application address: c/o Exec. Dir., Rapid City Club for Boys, 320 N. 4th St., Rapid City, SD 57701, tel.: (605) 343-3500

Financial data (yr. ended 12/31/01): Grants paid, $3,926; assets, $39,314 (M); expenditures, $3,926; qualifying distributions, $3,926.
Limitations: Giving limited to Rapid City, SD.
Application information: Application form required.
Board Members: Wanda Blair, Bob Johnson, Pete Skovran, Dean Snyder, Connie Vucurevich, Dave Wojtalewicz.
EIN: 237047880

49839
C. C. Lee Memorial Fund, Inc.
c/o Karl O. Lee Co., Inc.
200 S. Harrison St.
Aberdeen, SD 57401-4747

Financial data (yr. ended 09/30/00): Grants paid, $3,750; assets, $52,729 (M); expenditures, $4,319; qualifying distributions, $3,750.
Limitations: Giving limited to Aberdeen, SD.
Officers and Directors:* Krestie W. Utech,* Pres.; Glenn I. Nelson,* Secy.; Karl O. Lee,* Treas.
EIN: 460359219

49840
South Dakota Automobile Dealers Association Education Trust Fund
(also known as SDADA Education Trust Fund)
3801 S. Kiwanis Ave.
Sioux Falls, SD 57105-4233   (605) 336-2616

Established in 1986 in SD.
Donor(s): The South Dakota Automobile Dealers Association, SDADA Group Insurance Trust.
Financial data (yr. ended 06/30/01): Grants paid, $3,600; assets, $173,517 (M); gifts received, $5,740; expenditures, $4,293; qualifying distributions, $3,877.
Limitations: Giving primarily in SD.
Application information: Application form required.
Officers: Tom Mahan, Pres.; John Deniger, V.P.; Jim Wegner, Secy.-Treas.
Directors: John Ehret, Mark McKie.
EIN: 466075676

49841
The Glenn E. & Eleanor E. Ullyot Educational Trust
c/o Farmers & Merchants Bank & Trust
P.O. Box 877
Watertown, SD 57201-0877
Application address: Pius J. Lacher, Superintendent, c/o Clark School District No. 12-2, Clark, SD 57224, tel.: (605) 532-3605

Donor(s): Glenn E. Ullyot.
Financial data (yr. ended 12/31/00): Grants paid, $3,600; assets, $92,655 (M); expenditures, $4,872; qualifying distributions, $3,733.
Limitations: Giving limited to residents of Clark County, SD.
Application information: Application form required.
Trustees: Glenn E. Ullyot, Farmers & Merchants Bank & Trust.
EIN: 460355003

49842
Earl Papke Fund for Needy Children
106 Main Ave.
Lemmon, SD 57638-1222   (605) 374-3388
Contact: David S. Anderson, Treas.

Financial data (yr. ended 12/31/01): Grants paid, $3,449; assets, $61,401 (M); expenditures, $4,068; qualifying distributions, $3,449.
Limitations: Giving limited to residents of Lemmon, SD.
Application information: Application form not required.
Officer: David S. Anderson, Treas.
Trustees: Vernon Evanson, Mark Gannon, Floyd Short, Jr.
EIN: 237173662

49843
Margery L. Orr Memorial Scholarship Fund
1829 Park Ave.
Sturgis, SD 57785
Application address: c/o Counselor, Lead-Deadwood High School, 320 S. Main St., Lead, SD 57754, tel.: (605) 584-3711

Established in 1997 in SD.
Donor(s): Larry L. Orr.
Financial data (yr. ended 12/31/01): Grants paid, $3,200; assets, $38,166 (M); expenditures, $3,290; qualifying distributions, $3,200.
Application information: Application form required.
Officers: Dean E. Orr, Pres.; Dee Ora Lee Keller, V.P.; Larry L. Orr, Exec. Dir.
EIN: 911801994

49844
40 et 8 Nurses Training Foundation of South Dakota
1315 E. Wells Ave.
Pierre, SD 57501 (605) 224-1635
Contact: Gary L. Galinat, Secy.-Treas.

Financial data (yr. ended 12/31/00): Grants paid, $3,000; assets, $52,832 (M); gifts received, $56; expenditures, $263; qualifying distributions, $2,998.
Limitations: Giving limited to SD.
Application information: Application form required.
Officers and Directors:* DeLeano Haupal,* Chair.; Gary L. Galinat, Secy.-Treas.; William Bauer, Gary Huettl, Larry Nupen, Frank O'Berle, Jimmie Rowley, Lyle Waltner.
EIN: 466011903

49845
Seim-Herbert Scholarship Trust
c/o Wells Fargo South Dekota, N.A.
P.O Box 1040
Rapid City, SD 57709-1040

Established in 1993 in SD.
Financial data (yr. ended 12/31/00): Grants paid, $2,000; assets, $56,328 (M); expenditures, $3,981; qualifying distributions, $2,947.
Limitations: Applications not accepted. Giving limited to residents of Lead, SD.
Trustee: Wells Fargo Bank South Dakota, N.A.
EIN: 466074988

49846
Walter J. and Joanne Rouleau Foundation
P.O. Box 3148
Rapid City, SD 57709-3148
Contact: Joanne Rouleau, Dir.

Financial data (yr. ended 09/30/01): Grants paid, $1,900; assets, $85,793 (M); gifts received, $1,900; expenditures, $1,900; qualifying distributions, $1,900.
Limitations: Giving primarily in Rapid City, SD.
Directors: Joanne Rouleau, Walter J. Rouleau.
EIN: 942819034

49847
The VanDemark Foundation
(Formerly VanDemark Educational and Charitable Trust)
321 E. 27th St.
Sioux Falls, SD 57105 (605) 330-0159
Contact: Richard E. VanDemark, Pres.

Established in 1984 in SD.
Donor(s): Robert E. VanDemark, Sr., M.D., Robert E. VanDemark, Jr., M.D., Mrs. Robert E. VanDemark, Sr., Mrs. Robert E. VanDemark, Jr.
Financial data (yr. ended 12/31/01): Grants paid, $1,900; assets, $14,197 (M); gifts received, $12; expenditures, $2,363; qualifying distributions, $1,900.
Limitations: Giving limited to Sioux Falls, SD.
Officer: Richard E. VanDemark, Pres. and Treas.
Directors: Vance R.C. Goldammer, Bertie VanDemark, Marilyn VanDemark, Robert E. VanDemark, Jr., M.D.
EIN: 460382926

49848
Muryl and Lu Myhre Foundation, Inc.
3805 S. Birchwood
Sioux Falls, SD 57103

Established in 2000 in MT.
Financial data (yr. ended 12/31/01): Grants paid, $677; assets, $608,375 (M); gifts received, $65,000; expenditures, $4,229; qualifying distributions, $677.
Limitations: Applications not accepted.
Application information: Contributes only to pre-selected organizations.
Officers and Directors:* Donald S. Hooper,* Pres.; Robert Bronson,* V.P.; P. Daniel Donohue,* Secy.; Gayle M. Hooper, Treas.
EIN: 460459194

49849
Mayclin Family Charitable Trust
R.R. 1, P.O. Box 5
Plankinton, SD 57368
Scholarship address: c/o Ida Hoffman, Plankinton High School, P.O. Box 190, Plankinton, SD 57368, tel.: (605) 942-7743

Established in 1993 in SD.
Donor(s): James Mayclin.
Financial data (yr. ended 08/31/01): Grants paid, $500; assets, $6,713 (M); expenditures, $560; qualifying distributions, $480.
Limitations: Giving limited to residents of Plankinton, SD.
Application information: Application form may be obtained from Plankinton High School. Application form required.
Trustees: Dan K. Mayclin, James H. Mayclin, Mark S. Mayclin, Michael V. Mayclin, Patrick L. Mayclin, Thomas J. Mayclin, Tim Mayclin.
EIN: 460428001

49850
Memorial Scholarship Fund for A-Squad Cheerleaders of 1967-68
c/o Wells Fargo Bank South Dakota, N.A.
P.O. Box 1040
Rapid City, SD 57709-1040
Application address: c/o Asst. Principal, Rapid City Central High School, 433 N. 8th St., Rapid City, SD 57701, tel.: (605) 394-4041

Financial data (yr. ended 12/31/00): Grants paid, $250; assets, $3,910 (M); expenditures, $585; qualifying distributions, $423.
Limitations: Giving primarily in Rapid City, SD.
Publications: Application guidelines.
Trustee: Wells Fargo Bank South Dakota, N.A.
EIN: 466024410

49851
Earl Hamill Memorial 4-H Scholarship Fund
c/o Haakon County Extension Agent
P.O. Box 519
Philip, SD 57567-0519 (605) 859-2840

Financial data (yr. ended 12/31/01): Grants paid, $175; assets, $2,325 (M); expenditures, $175; qualifying distributions, $175.
Limitations: Giving limited to Haakon County, SD.
Application information: Application form required.
Trustees: Russell Hicks, John Kangas, Ralph Matz.
EIN: 237432358

49852
P. J. Barber Family Foundation
3315 Flint Dr.
Rapid City, SD 57702

Established in 1999 in SD.
Financial data (yr. ended 12/31/99): Grants paid, $0; assets, $2,000 (M); gifts received, $2,000; expenditures, $0; qualifying distributions, $0.
Directors: Eric P. Barber, Holly S. Barber, Patricia L. Barber, Paul J. Barber.
EIN: 460454188

49853
Black Hills Corporation Foundation
625 9th St.
P.O. Box 1400
Rapid City, SD 57709-1400
Contact: Barbara Thirstrup

Established in 2001 in SD.
Donor(s): Black Hills Corp.
Financial data (yr. ended 12/31/01): Grants paid, $0; assets, $3,000,000 (M); gifts received, $3,150,000; expenditures, $0; qualifying distributions, $0.
Limitations: Giving limited to SD and WY.
Officers: Barbara Thurstrup, Pres.; James Mattern, V.P.; Kyle White, Secy.; Garner Anderson, Treas.
Directors: David Emery, Everett Hoyt, Danile Longduth.
EIN: 752986866
Codes: CS

49854
Citizen's Equal Rights Foundation
HCR 30, Box 1
Mobridge, SD 57601

Established in 1999.
Financial data (yr. ended 12/31/99): Grants paid, $0; assets, $3,105 (L); gifts received, $8,342; expenditures, $5,237; qualifying distributions, $0; giving activities include $3,878 for programs.
Officers: Scott Kayla Morrison, Pres.; J. Tonny Bowman, V.P.; Darrel Smith, Secy.-Treas.
EIN: 460450222

49855
Dan Dugan Foundation
3015 S. Phillips Ave.
Sioux Falls, SD 57105
Contact: J.P. Everist, Mgr.

Financial data (yr. ended 12/31/01): Grants paid, $0; assets, $149,841 (M); gifts received, $10,000; expenditures, $377; qualifying distributions, $0.
Limitations: Giving primarily in Sioux Falls, SD.
Officers and Directors:* John Everist, Jr.,* Pres.; Nancy Ann Everist,* Secy.-Treas.; J.P. Everist,* Mgr.
EIN: 466010853

49856
Fred & Mary Maas Private Foundation
P.O. Box 205
Gettysburg, SD 57442 (605) 765-2494
Contact: Craig Smith, V.P.

Established in 2000 in SD.
Donor(s): Melvin Maas.
Financial data (yr. ended 12/31/01): Grants paid, $0; assets, $26,089 (M); gifts received, $20,000; expenditures, $13,990; qualifying distributions, $0.
Officers: Melvin Maas, Pres.; Craig Smith, V.P.; Lila Hericks, Secy.
EIN: 460458582

49857
Wolpert Family Foundation
c/o Paul W. Wolpert
612 N. Sioux Point Rd., Ste. 400
Dakota Dunes, SD 57049

Financial data (yr. ended 06/30/01): Grants paid, $0; assets, $5,993 (M); expenditures, $430; qualifying distributions, $165.
Limitations: Applications not accepted.
Application information: Contributes only to pre-selected organizations.
Trustees: Regina M. Ratino, John A. Wolpert, Katherine M. Wolpert, Paul W. Wolpert, M.D.
EIN: 421431227

TENNESSEE

49858
Paul W. Barret, Jr. Charitable Trust
c/o Community Foundation of Greater Memphis
1900 Union Ave.
Memphis, TN 38104-4029 (901) 722-0054
E-mail: mwolowicz@cfgm.org; *URL:* http://www.cfgm.org
Contact: Melissa Wolowicz

Established in 2000 in TN.
Donor(s): Paul W. Barret, Jr.‡
Financial data (yr. ended 12/31/01): Grants paid, $57,500,000; assets, $219,644 (M); gifts received, $57,814,831; expenditures, $57,636,796; qualifying distributions, $57,568,393.
Limitations: Giving primarily in Shelby County, TN.
Trustees: John P. Douglas, Graves C. Leggett.
EIN: 316642475
Codes: FD

49859
Community Foundation of Middle Tennessee, Inc.
(Formerly Nashville Community Foundation, Inc.)
3833 Cleghorn Ave., No. 400
Nashville, TN 37215-2519 (615) 321-4939
Additional tel.: (888) 540-5200; *FAX:* (615) 327-2746; *E-mail:* mail@cfmt.org; *URL:* http://www.cfmt.org
Contact: Ellen Lehman, Pres.

Established in 1991 in TN.
Financial data (yr. ended 12/31/01): Grants paid, $44,152,926; assets, $143,572,951 (M); gifts received, $52,502,405; expenditures, $44,937,179.
Limitations: Giving limited to central TN.
Publications: Annual report, newsletter, informational brochure, application guidelines.
Application information: Application form not required.
Officers and Directors:* Aubrey Harwell, Jr.,* Chair.; Charles Fraizer,* Vice-Chair.; Ellen E. Lehman,* Pres.; Jack Bovender,* Secy.; John Maupin, Jr.,* Treas; and 18 additional directors.
EIN: 621471789
Codes: CM, FD

49860
Community Foundation of Greater Memphis
1900 Union Ave.
Memphis, TN 38104 (901) 728-4600
FAX: (901) 722-0010; *URL:* http://www.cfgm.org
Contact: Gid H. Smith, C.E.O. and Pres.

Established in 1969 in TN; combined operations with The Memphis-Plough Community Foundation in 1989.
Financial data (yr. ended 04/30/02): Grants paid, $34,773,750; assets, $214,378,323 (M); gifts received, $45,941,482; expenditures, $38,760,147.
Limitations: Giving limited to Crittenden County, AR, DeSoto County, MS, and Fayette, Shelby, and Tipton counties, TN.
Publications: Annual report, application guidelines, newsletter, informational brochure.
Application information: Application form required.
Officers and Governors:* Herman Morris, Jr.,* Chair.; Gid H. Smith,* C.E.O. and Pres.; Andrea L. Reynolds, V.P., Donor Rels. and Progs.; Kristin A. Croone,* Secy. and Dir., Planned Giving; Mack E. McCaul, Jr.,* Treas.; and 28 additional governors.
EIN: 581723645
Codes: CM, FD, FM

49861
The Maclellan Foundation, Inc.
Provident Bldg., Ste. 501
Chattanooga, TN 37402 (423) 755-1366
FAX: (423) 755-1640; *URL:* http://www.maclellanfdn.org
Contact: Hugh O. Maclellan, Jr., Pres.

Incorporated in 1945 in DE; reincorporated in TN in 1992.
Donor(s): Robert J. Maclellan,‡ and members of the Maclellan family.
Financial data (yr. ended 12/31/01): Grants paid, $17,796,860; assets, $403,953,114 (M); expenditures, $20,299,571; qualifying distributions, $18,705,860.
Limitations: Giving nationally, with emphasis on the Chattanooga, TN, area; giving internationally in Eastern Europe, Asia, Africa, Latin America, and the Middle East.
Application information: Application form not required.
Officers and Trustees:* Hugh O. Maclellan, Jr.,* Pres.; Charlotte M. Heffner,* V.P.; Thomas H. McCallie III, Secy. and Exec. Dir.; Robert H. Maclellan,* Treas.; Ron Blue, Frank A. Brock, G. Richard Hostetter, Pat MacMillan, Dudley Porter, Jr.
EIN: 626041468
Codes: FD, FM

49862
East Tennessee Foundation
550 W. Main St., Ste. 550
Knoxville, TN 37902 (865) 524-1223
FAX: (865) 637-6039; *E-mail:* etf@etf.org; *URL:* http://www.easttennesseefoundation.org
Contact: Jerry W. Asken, Exec. Dir.

Incorporated in 1958 in TN.
Financial data (yr. ended 12/31/99): Grants paid, $14,034,002; assets, $56,299,574 (M); gifts received, $18,099,547; expenditures, $16,330,046.
Limitations: Giving limited to Knoxville, TN, and its 20 surrounding counties.
Publications: Annual report, newsletter, application guidelines, informational brochure (including application guidelines).
Application information: Application guidelines available upon request. Application form not required.
Officers and Directors:* Joan D. Allen,* Chair.; Lloyd Montgomery III,* Vice-Chair.; Jerry W. Askew,* Pres.; Carolyn Schwenn,* V.P., Fin. and Secy.; Michael Crabtree,* Treas.
EIN: 620807696
Codes: CM, FD

49863
The Frist Foundation
(Formerly The HCA Foundation)
3319 West End Ave., Ste. 900
Nashville, TN 37203-1076 (615) 292-3868
FAX: (615) 292-5843; *E-mail:* askfrist@fristfoundation.org; *URL:* http://www.fristfoundation.org
Contact: Peter F. Bird, Jr., C.E.O. and Pres.

Established in 1982 in TN.
Donor(s): Hospital Corp. of America.
Financial data (yr. ended 12/31/01): Grants paid, $13,363,804; assets, $188,478,270 (M); gifts received, $15,543; expenditures, $14,448,059; qualifying distributions, $14,512,865; giving activities include $600,000 for program-related investments.
Limitations: Giving primarily in Nashville, TN.
Publications: Annual report (including application guidelines), informational brochure (including application guidelines).
Application information: Information brochures available, for Nashville, TN-based organizations only, for Frist Foundation Teacher and Principal Awards Programs, Frist Foundation Achievement Awards for Nonprofit Management, Frist Foundation Internship Program, and Frist Foundation Technology Grants Program. Application form not required.
Officers and Directors:* Thomas F. Frist, Jr.,* Chair.; Peter F. Bird, Jr.,* C.E.O. and Exec. Dir.; Kenneth L. Roberts,* Pres.; Lani Wilkeson, Secy. and Sr. Prog. Off.; Colette R. Easter, Treas.; Jack O. Bovender, Jr., Robert C. Crosby, Helen K. Cummings, Frank F. Drowota III, Patricia C. Frist, Fred Russell, Dir., Emeritus.
EIN: 621134070
Codes: FD, FM

49864
Plough Foundation
6410 Poplar Ave., Ste. 710
Memphis, TN 38119 (901) 761-9180
FAX: (901) 761-6186; *E-mail:* Haynes@plough.org
Contact: Noris R. Haynes, Jr., Exec. Dir.

Trust established in 1972 in TN.
Donor(s): Abe Plough.‡
Financial data (yr. ended 12/31/00): Grants paid, $13,263,520; assets, $216,854,545 (M); gifts received, $56,857; expenditures, $15,671,214; qualifying distributions, $14,060,419.
Limitations: Giving primarily in Shelby County, TN, with an emphasis on Memphis.
Publications: Informational brochure (including application guidelines).
Application information: Application form required.
Officer and Trustees:* Noris R. Haynes, Jr.,* Exec. Dir.; Patricia R. Burnham, Eugene J. Callahan, Larry Papasan, Diane R. Rudner, Jocelyn P. Rudner, James Springfield, Steve Wishnia, National Bank of Commerce.
EIN: 237175983
Codes: FD, FM

49865
Lyndhurst Foundation
517 E. 5th St.
Chattanooga, TN 37403-1826 (423) 756-0767
FAX: (423) 756-0770; *URL:* http://www.lyndhurstfoundation.org
Contact: Jack E. Murrah, Pres.

Incorporated in 1938 in DE.
Donor(s): T. Cartter Lupton,‡ Central Shares Corp.
Financial data (yr. ended 12/31/01): Grants paid, $10,052,081; assets, $157,202,266 (M); expenditures, $11,138,357; qualifying distributions, $10,848,200.
Limitations: Giving limited to the southeastern U.S., with some emphasis on Chattanooga, TN.
Publications: Annual report (including application guidelines).
Application information: Applications or nominations not accepted for Lyndhurst Prizes. Application form not required.
Officers and Trustees:* Allen L. McCallie,* Chair.; Jack E. Murrah,* Pres.; Benic M. Clark III, V.P. and Secy.; Charles B. Chitty, Treas.; Nelson D. Campbell, George R. Fontaine, Margaret L. Gerber, Katherine L. Juett, T. Cartter Lupton II, L. Thomas Montague, Alice L. Smith.
EIN: 626044177

49865—TENNESSEE

Codes: FD, FM, GTI

49866
The Assisi Foundation of Memphis, Inc.
(Formerly Assisi Foundation)
6077 Primacy Pkwy., Ste. 253
Memphis, TN 38119
URL: http://www.assisifoundation.org
Contact: Barry J. Flynn, Exec. Dir.

Established in 1994 in TN; converted from the sale of St. Francis Hospital.
Financial data (yr. ended 02/28/00): Grants paid, $9,214,148; assets, $214,961,325 (M); expenditures, $11,876,394; qualifying distributions, $9,883,265.
Limitations: Giving primarily in Memphis and Shelby County, TN.
Publications: Multi-year report, application guidelines.
Application information: Application form required.
Officers and Directors:* Philip Zanone,* Chair.; C. Thomas Whitman,* Vice-Chair.; Lee J. Chase III,* Secy.; Forest N. Jenkins,* Treas.; Barry J. Flynn, Exec. Dir.; Neal S. Beckford, M.D., Jack A. Beltz, John D. Canale III, Fred L. Davis, Kathy Buckman Davis, Edward Duke, William E. Frulla, Barbara R. Hyde, William I. Loewenberg, John D. Pera, Ph.D., Richard H. Remmert, Deborah O. Schadt, Ph.D., Lynda Mead Shea, Martin F. Thompson, Russel L. Wiener, D.D.S., John L. Zoccola.
EIN: 621558722
Codes: FD, FM

49867
The Community Foundation of Greater Chattanooga, Inc.
1270 Market St.
Chattanooga, TN 37402 (423) 265-0586
FAX: (423) 265-0587; E-mail: pcooper@cfgc.org; URL: http://www.cfgc.org
Contact: Peter T. Cooper, Pres.

Incorporated in 1963 in TN.
Financial data (yr. ended 12/31/01): Grants paid, $8,368,482; assets, $49,705,054 (M); gifts received, $12,147,227; expenditures, $9,092,585.
Limitations: Giving limited to the greater Chattanooga,TN, area.
Publications: Annual report (including application guidelines), informational brochure (including application guidelines), application guidelines, informational brochure.
Application information: The foundation requires a letter of intent 2 months prior to the application deadline; all applicants are by invitation following staff consideration of the letter of intent. Application form required.
Officers and Directors:* Grant Law,* Chair.; Ruth S. Holmberg, Vice-Chair.; Spencer McCallie,* Vice-Chair.; Virginia Anna Sharber,* Vice-Chair.; Peter T. Cooper, Pres.; Jennifer R. Jackson, V.P., Prog.; Marty Robinson, V.P., Donor Relations; Amber L. Tappin, V.P., Finance and Admin.; E. Liston Bishop, Secy.; Nick Decosimo, Treas.; Paul K. Brock, Susan Burkett, Paul Campbell, George Clark III, Ann Coulter, Mike Cranford, Jane Harbaugh, Angela Hayes, Jerry Konahia, Jill Levine, Warren Logan, Kincaid Mills, Tom Montague, Chris Ramsey, Pete Serodino, Edna Varner.
EIN: 626045999
Codes: CM, FD, GTI

49868
Bridgestone/Firestone Trust Fund
(Formerly The Firestone Trust Fund)
50 Century Blvd.
Nashville, TN 37214 (615) 872-1415
FAX: (615) 872-1414; E-mail: bfstrustfund@bfusa.com
Contact: Bernice Csaszar, Admin.

Trust established in 1952 in OH.
Donor(s): Bridgestone/Firestone, Inc.
Financial data (yr. ended 12/31/01): Grants paid, $6,236,614; assets, $38,681,821 (M); expenditures, $7,712,766; qualifying distributions, $6,113,143.
Limitations: Giving primarily in areas of major company operations: AR, CO, CT, FL, IA, IL, IN, KY, LA, MI, NC, OH, OK, PA, SC, TN, TX, and UT.
Publications: Application guidelines.
Application information: Application form not required.
Committee Members: Christine Karbowiak, Chair.; Hal Horton, Gene Stephens, Ronald Tepner.
Trustee: KeyBank, N.A.
EIN: 346505181
Codes: CS, FD, CD, FM

49869
The Longleaf Foundation
(Formerly Hawkins Charitable Foundation)
6410 Poplar Ave., Ste. 900
Memphis, TN 38119-4843 (901) 818-5125
Contact: Joseph L. Ott, Secy.

Established in 1994 in TN.
Donor(s): O. Mason Hawkins.
Financial data (yr. ended 12/31/00): Grants paid, $5,316,750; assets, $15,527,112 (M); gifts received, $4,001,385; expenditures, $5,316,764; qualifying distributions, $5,316,750.
Limitations: Giving primarily in Memphis, TN.
Application information: Application form not required.
Officers and Directors:* Ann B. Hawkins,* Pres.; G. Staley Cates,* V.P.; Joseph L. Ott,* Secy. and Mgr.; O. Mason Hawkins.
EIN: 621586727
Codes: FD, FM

49870
Christy-Houston Foundation, Inc.
1296 Dow St.
Murfreesboro, TN 37129 (615) 898-1140
FAX: (615) 895-9524
Contact: Robert B. Mifflin, Exec. Dir.

Established in 1986 in TN; converted from the sale of Middle Tennessee Medical Center to Mid-State Baptist and Saint Thomas Hospitals.
Financial data (yr. ended 12/31/01): Grants paid, $4,641,636; assets, $80,075,099 (M); gifts received, $25; expenditures, $5,504,540; qualifying distributions, $4,822,233.
Limitations: Giving limited to Rutherford County, TN.
Publications: Grants list, application guidelines.
Application information: Application form not required.
Officers and Directors:* Ed Elam, Chair.; Ed Delbridge, Vice-Chair.; Robert B. Mifflin, Exec. Dir.; Granville S.R. Bouldin, Henry King Butler, Larry N. Haynes, William H. Huddleston, Roger C. Maples, Hubert McCullough, Jr., Matt B. Murfree III.
EIN: 621280998
Codes: FD

49871
Hyde Family Foundations
6075 Poplar Ave., Ste. 335
Memphis, TN 38119 (901) 685-3400
FAX: (901) 683-3147
Contact: Teresa Sloyan, Exec. Dir.

J.R. Hyde Senior Family Foundation and J.R. Hyde III Family Foundation established in TN in 1961 and 1993, respectively.
Donor(s): J.R. Hyde, Sr.,‡ J.R. Hyde III, Barbara R. Hyde.
Financial data (yr. ended 12/31/00): Grants paid, $4,297,642; assets, $96,075,548 (M); gifts received, $28,604,121; expenditures, $5,125,924; qualifying distributions, $4,503,889.
Limitations: Giving primarily in Memphis, TN.
Publications: Application guidelines.
Application information: Application form not required.
Officer: Teresa Sloyan, Exec. Dir.
Codes: FD, GTI

49872
The HCA Foundation
(Formerly Columbia/HCA Healthcare Foundation, Inc.)
1 Park Plz., Building 1-4E
Nashville, TN 37203 (615) 344-2390
FAX: (615) 344-5722; E-mail: Joanne.Pulles@HCAhealthcare.com; URL: http://www.hcacaring.org
Contact: Joanne Pulles, Exec. Dir.

Established in 1992 in KY.
Donor(s): Columbia/HCA Healthcare Corp., HCA-The Healthcare Co., HCA Inc.
Financial data (yr. ended 12/31/01): Grants paid, $4,257,614; assets, $138,729,190 (M); expenditures, $4,387,573; qualifying distributions, $4,399,541.
Limitations: Giving primarily in KY and TN.
Publications: Informational brochure (including application guidelines), corporate giving report.
Application information: Mar. 1-deadline for submitting employee-related scholarship application; Application for funding available online. Application form required.
Officers and Directors:* Thomas F. Frist, Jr., M.D.,* Chair. and C.E.O; Jack O. Bovender,* C.O.O. and Pres.; Phil Patton,* Sr. V.P.; David G. Anderson, V.P. and Treas.; Milton Johnson,* V.P.; Bruce Moore, Jr.,* V.P.; Gary Pack, Secy.; Joanne Pulles, Exec. Dir.; Richard M. Bracken, Kenneth L. Roberts.
EIN: 611230563
Codes: CS, FD, CD

49873
Benwood Foundation, Inc.
SunTrust Bank Bldg.
736 Market St., Ste. 1600
Chattanooga, TN 37402 (423) 267-4311
FAX: (423) 267-9049; E-mail: Benwoodfnd@Benwood.org
Contact: Corinne Allen, Exec. Dir.

Incorporated in 1944 in DE, and 1945 in TN.
Donor(s): George Thomas Hunter.‡
Financial data (yr. ended 12/31/01): Grants paid, $4,256,643; assets, $112,728,675 (M); expenditures, $5,048,578; qualifying distributions, $4,581,836.
Limitations: Giving primarily in the Chattanooga, TN, area.
Publications: Application guidelines.
Application information: Application form required.
Officers and Trustees:* Sebert Brewer, Jr.,* Chair.; E.Y. Chapin III,* Pres.; Robert J. Sudderth, Jr.,* V.P.;

Susan R. Randolph,* Secy.-Treas.; Corinne Allen, Exec. Dir.
EIN: 620476283
Codes: FD, FM

49874
Joe C. Davis Foundation
28 White Bridge Rd., Ste. 210
Nashville, TN 37205
E-mail: bartonshan@aol.com
Contact: Mrs. Anne Fergerson, Admin.

Established in 1976 in TN.
Donor(s): Joe C. Davis.‡
Financial data (yr. ended 09/30/01): Grants paid, $4,217,950; assets, $83,488,046 (M); gifts received, $52,499; expenditures, $5,643,661; qualifying distributions, $4,181,596.
Limitations: Giving primarily in the Nashville, TN, area.
Publications: Application guidelines.
Application information: Send copy of application to Dr. and Mrs. William R. DeLoache, 72 Round Pond Rd., Greenville, SC 29607. Application form not required.
Trustees: Bond Davis DeLoache, William DeLoache, M.D., William R. DeLoache, Jr., Frances D. Ellison.
EIN: 626125481
Codes: FD, FM

49875
Martha and Bronson Ingram Foundation
4400 Harding Rd., 9th Fl.
Nashville, TN 37205
Contact: Martha R. Ingram, Pres.

Established in 1988 in TN.
Donor(s): Martha A. Ingram.
Financial data (yr. ended 12/31/00): Grants paid, $3,944,520; assets, $1,199,346 (M); gifts received, $660,267; expenditures, $3,944,243; qualifying distributions, $3,944,520.
Limitations: Applications not accepted. Giving primarily in TN.
Application information: Unsolicited requests for funds not accepted.
Officers and Trustees:* Martha R. Ingram,* Pres.; John R. Ingram,* V.P.; Orrin H. Ingram,* V.P.; Robin Ingram Patton,* V.P.; David B. Ingram,* Secy.-Treas.
EIN: 626210987
Codes: FD

49876
Jack C. Massey Foundation
(Formerly JCM Foundation)
5123 Virginia Way, Ste. B-22
Brentwood, TN 37027 (615) 377-8595

Reincorporated in 1998.
Financial data (yr. ended 12/31/99): Grants paid, $3,482,239; assets, $42,946,029 (M); gifts received, $1,538,232; expenditures, $4,139,377; qualifying distributions, $3,484,019.
Limitations: Applications not accepted. Giving primarily in FL and TN.
Application information: Contributes only to pre-selected organizations.
Officers and Directors:* Alyne Massey, Co-Chair.; Barbara M. Rogers, Co-Chair.; J. Brad Reed,* Pres.; Clarence Edmonds.
EIN: 621649826
Codes: FD

49877
The Patricia C. & Thomas F. Frist, Jr. Foundation
c/o Thomas F. Frist, Jr.
3319 West End Ave., Ste. 900A
Nashville, TN 37203

Established in 1994 in TN.
Donor(s): Thomas F. Frist, Jr., Patricia C. Frist, Cate Frist.‡
Financial data (yr. ended 12/31/01): Grants paid, $3,435,661; assets, $7,380,504 (M); gifts received, $1,248,949; expenditures, $3,512,152; qualifying distributions, $3,433,703.
Limitations: Applications not accepted. Giving primarily in Nashville, TN.
Application information: Contributes only to pre-selected organizations.
Officers: Patricia C. Frist, Pres.; Thomas F. Frist, Jr., Secy.-Treas.
Directors: Patricia Frist Elcan, Thomas F. Frist III, William R. Frist.
EIN: 621491418
Codes: FD

49878
Hamico, Inc.
1715 W. 38th St.
Chattanooga, TN 37409-1248

Incorporated in 1956 in TN.
Donor(s): Chattem, Inc.
Financial data (yr. ended 12/31/00): Grants paid, $3,369,090; assets, $8,933,495 (M); expenditures, $3,512,435; qualifying distributions, $3,512,435.
Limitations: Applications not accepted. Giving primarily in Chattanooga, TN.
Application information: Contributes only to pre-selected organizations.
Officers and Directors:* Zan Guerry,* Pres.; Robert E. Bosworth,* Secy.; Herbert Barks, Alexis G. Bogo, John P. Guerry.
EIN: 626040782
Codes: FD

49879
Union Planters Community Foundation
c/o Union Planter Bank
P.O. Box 387
Memphis, TN 38147

Established in 1998 in TN.
Donor(s): Union Planters Holding Corporation, Union Planters Corporation.
Financial data (yr. ended 12/31/99): Grants paid, $3,058,295; assets, $4,331,177 (M); gifts received, $1,936,579; expenditures, $3,106,033; qualifying distributions, $3,009,350.
Limitations: Applications not accepted. Giving on a national basis.
Application information: Contributes only to pre-selected organizations.
Officers and Directors:* Jack W. Moore,* Pres.; E. James House,* Secy.; M. Kirk Walters,* Treas.; Brad L. Champlin, Benjamin W. Rawlins.
EIN: 311635388
Codes: CS, FD, CD

49880
The Cal Turner Family Foundation
138 2nd Ave. N., Ste. 200
Nashville, TN 37201 (615) 846-4946
Contact: Jennifer Bruner

Established in 1991 in TN.
Donor(s): Cal Turner, Sr., Gertrude W. Burnett, Cal Turner, Jr.
Financial data (yr. ended 12/31/00): Grants paid, $2,659,092; assets, $53,630,956 (M); gifts received, $4,566,388; expenditures, $2,667,765; qualifying distributions, $2,661,137.
Limitations: Giving primarily in TN.

Application information: Application form required.
Trustee: Cal Turner, Jr.
EIN: 626255589
Codes: FD

49881
The Dorothy Cate & Thomas F. Frist Foundation
(Formerly The Frist Medical Foundation)
102 Woodmont Blvd.
Nashville, TN 37205 (615) 345-0338
FAX: (615) 342-6028
Contact: Bette C. Harrell, Admin.

Established in 1980.
Donor(s): Thomas F. Frist, Sr.,‡ Dorothy Cate Frist.‡
Financial data (yr. ended 11/30/01): Grants paid, $2,500,000; assets, $44,106,959 (M); gifts received, $258,246; expenditures, $2,854,341; qualifying distributions, $2,544,394.
Limitations: Applications not accepted. Giving limited to Nashville, TN.
Application information: Contributes only to pre-selected organizations.
Officers: William H. Frist, Pres.; Mary Louise Frist Barfield, V.P.; Dorothy Frist Boenseh, V.P.; Thomas F. Frist, Jr., V.P.; Robert A. Frist, Secy.
EIN: 621103568
Codes: FD, FM

49882
Ezell Foundation, Inc.
P.O. Box 100957
Nashville, TN 37224
Contact: F. Miles Ezell, Jr., Pres.

Established in 1964.
Donor(s): F. Miles Ezell, Sr.,‡ and members of the Ezell family.
Financial data (yr. ended 06/30/01): Grants paid, $2,464,704; assets, $14,171,052 (M); gifts received, $57,422; expenditures, $2,798,204; qualifying distributions, $2,470,679.
Limitations: Giving primarily in TN.
Application information: Application form not required.
Officers: F. Miles Ezell, Jr., Pres.; Roy C. Ezell, 1st V.P.; David Thomas, 2nd V.P.; Stanley M. Ezell, Secy.; John W. Ezell, Treas.
EIN: 626046865
Codes: FD

49883
The Tucker Foundation
600 Krystal Bldg.
Chattanooga, TN 37402 (423) 756-1202
Contact: M. Hayne Hamilton, Pres.

Established in 1996.
Financial data (yr. ended 12/31/00): Grants paid, $2,046,003; assets, $23,409,551 (M); expenditures, $2,046,815; qualifying distributions, $2,043,876.
Limitations: Giving primarily in Atlanta, GA, and Hamilton and Bradley counties, TN.
Application information: Application form not required.
Officers and Trustees:* M. Hayne Hamilton,* Pres.; Pamela K. Cuzzort,* Secy.-Treas; Lavinia J. Cherry, Andrew G. Cope, S.K. Johnston, Jr.
EIN: 621603398
Codes: FD

49884
The Thompson Charitable Foundation
P.O. Box 10516
Knoxville, TN 37939
Contact: Monica Luke, Fdn. Mgr.

Established in 1987 in TN.

49884—TENNESSEE

Donor(s): B.R. Thompson, Sr.‡
Financial data (yr. ended 06/30/01): Grants paid, $2,039,473; assets, $46,344,119 (M); expenditures, $2,291,922; qualifying distributions, $2,099,276.
Limitations: Giving limited to Bell, Clay, Laurel, and Leslie counties, KY; Anderson, Blount, Knox, and Scott counties, TN; and Buchanan and Tazewell counties, VA.
Officers and Directors:* Merle D. Wolfe,* Pres.; Monica Luke, Mgr.; Carl Ensor, Jr., Greg Erickson, Jesse J. Thompson, Sylvia M. Thompson, Lindsay Young.
EIN: 581754763
Codes: FD

49885
Eastman Chemical Company Foundation, Inc.
100 N. Eastman Rd.
Kingsport, TN 37662 (423) 229-1413
Application address: P.O. Box 511, Kingsport, TN 37662-5075
Contact: Paul Montgomery

Established in 1996 in TN.
Financial data (yr. ended 12/31/01): Grants paid, $2,011,471; assets, $6,311,816 (M); gifts received, $1,000,000; expenditures, $2,021,321; qualifying distributions, $2,010,531.
Limitations: Giving on a national basis.
Officers and Directors:* James P. Rogers,* Pres.; Brian L. Henry, Secy.; Albert J. Wargo, Treas.; Betty W. Devinney, B. Fielding Rolston.
EIN: 621614800
Codes: CS, FD, CD

49886
The Day Foundation
530 Oak Court Dr., Ste. 325
Memphis, TN 38117
Contact: Clarence C. Day, Tr.

Established in 1960 in MS.
Donor(s): Clarence C. Day, Day Cos., Inc.
Financial data (yr. ended 12/31/00): Grants paid, $1,814,618; assets, $29,499,489 (M); expenditures, $2,284,705; qualifying distributions, $1,814,618.
Limitations: Giving primarily in AR, Cuthbert, GA, and the Memphis, TN, area.
Publications: Application guidelines, annual report, informational brochure.
Application information: Write for guidelines. Telephone inquiries are discouraged. Application form not required.
Officers and Trustees:* Clarence C. Day,* Chair.; Gary Ravetto, Exec. Dir.; Steve Miller, Jack Murrah, Herbert Rhea.
EIN: 646025122
Codes: FD

49887
First Tennessee Foundation
(Formerly Tennessee Charitable Foundation)
c/o First Tennessee National Corp.
165 Madison Ave., 8th Fl.
Memphis, TN 38103 (901) 532-4380
Additional tel.: (901) 523-4352; FAX: (901) 523-4354
Contact: Terry Lee

Established in 1993 in TN.
Donor(s): First Tennessee National Corp.
Financial data (yr. ended 12/31/01): Grants paid, $1,731,385; assets, $12,667,276 (M); expenditures, $1,731,385; qualifying distributions, $1,731,385.
Limitations: Giving primarily in TN.
Application information: Application form not required.

Officers: Harry A. Johnson III, Chair.; Gregg I. Lansky, Pres. and Treas.; Clyde A. Billings, Jr., Secy.
EIN: 621533987
Codes: CS, FD, CD

49888
AmSouth/First American Foundation
(Formerly First American Foundation)
315 Deaderick St., 4th Fl.
Nashville, TN 37237-0401 (615) 748-2241

Established in 1994 in TN.
Donor(s): First American National Bank.
Financial data (yr. ended 12/31/00): Grants paid, $1,721,244; assets, $13,368,667 (M); gifts received, $13,880; expenditures, $1,805,766; qualifying distributions, $1,712,364.
Limitations: Applications not accepted. Giving primarily in TN.
Application information: Contributes only to pre-selected organizations.
Officers and Directors:* Beth Monney,* Chair.; DeVan Ard,* Pres.; Pamela Welch, Secy.; Steve Yoder, Treas.; Walter Knestrick, Ted Welch, Jr., Toby Wilt.
EIN: 582071018
Codes: CS, FD, CD

49889
Eagle Foundation, Inc.
P.O. Box 1792
Brentwood, TN 37027

Established in 1987 in TN.
Donor(s): Jamie P. O'Rourke.
Financial data (yr. ended 12/31/00): Grants paid, $1,432,626; assets, $132,003 (M); gifts received, $164,000; expenditures, $1,480,181; qualifying distributions, $1,478,961.
Limitations: Applications not accepted. Giving primarily in TN.
Application information: Contributes only to pre-selected organizations.
Directors: Cydney O'Rourke, Jamie O'Rourke.
EIN: 621299979
Codes: FD

49890
Justin & Valere Blair Potter Foundation
1 Bank of America Plz., Ste. M-7
Nashville, TN 37239-1697 (615) 749-3916
Contact: Patrick Nelson, Trust Off., Bank of America

Established in 1953.
Financial data (yr. ended 12/31/00): Grants paid, $1,408,000; assets, $28,132,213 (M); expenditures, $1,522,990; qualifying distributions, $1,429,925.
Limitations: Giving primarily in Nashville, TN.
Trustees: Albert L. Menefee, Jr., Valere Menefee, Bank of America.
EIN: 626306577
Codes: FD

49891
The Martin Foundation
116 30th Ave., S.
Nashville, TN 37212
Contact: Ellen H. Martin, Exec. Dir.

Established in 1996 in TN.
Donor(s): Charles N. Martin, Jr.
Financial data (yr. ended 12/31/01): Grants paid, $1,400,070; assets, $10,639,324 (M); expenditures, $1,517,271; qualifying distributions, $1,396,762.
Limitations: Applications not accepted. Giving primarily in TN.
Application information: Contributes only to pre-selected organizations.

Officer: Charles N. Martin, Jr., Chair.
Trustees: Jonathan Harwell, Ellen Harrison Martin.
EIN: 621679129
Codes: FD

49892
Belz Foundation
100 Peabody Pl., Ste. 1400
Memphis, TN 38103

Incorporated in 1952 in TN.
Donor(s): Philip Belz,‡ Martin S. Belz, Ronald A. Belz, Jack A. Belz, Andrew Groveman, Jan B. Groveman.
Financial data (yr. ended 12/31/99): Grants paid, $1,207,426; assets, $9,059,729 (M); gifts received, $761,029; expenditures, $1,252,586; qualifying distributions, $1,201,429.
Limitations: Applications not accepted. Giving primarily in Memphis, TN.
Application information: Contributes only to pre-selected organizations.
Officers and Directors:* Jack A. Belz,* Pres.; Martin S. Belz,* V.P.; Jimmie D. Williams, Secy.-Treas.; Ronald A. Belz, Andrew Groveman, Jan B. Groveman, Raymond Shainberg.
EIN: 626046715
Codes: FD

49893
1939 Foundation
900 S. Gay St., Ste. 1600
Knoxville, TN 37902-1857
Contact: Doris Ballew, Secy.

Established in 1983 in TN.
Donor(s): F. Rodney Lawler.
Financial data (yr. ended 11/30/01): Grants paid, $1,153,149; assets, $11,164,021 (M); expenditures, $1,221,909; qualifying distributions, $1,145,805.
Limitations: Giving primarily in TN, with emphasis on Knoxville.
Officers: F. Rodney Lawler, Pres.; Phillip O. Lawson, V.P.; Doris Ballew, Secy.
Directors: Robin L. Gibson, Dell R. Lawler, Jon R. Lawler.
EIN: 621183557
Codes: FD

49894
EBS Foundation
c/o Elizabeth Bullard Stadler, Tr.
2212 Hillsboro Valley Rd.
Brentwood, TN 37027

Established in 1989.
Donor(s): Ella Hayes.
Financial data (yr. ended 12/31/01): Grants paid, $1,124,390; assets, $10,384,083 (M); gifts received, $412,319; expenditures, $1,362,598; qualifying distributions, $1,194,627.
Limitations: Applications not accepted. Giving primarily in TN.
Application information: Contributes only to pre-selected organizations.
Trustee: Elizabeth Bullard Stadler.
EIN: 581797047
Codes: FD

49895
The Bill Gatton Foundation
P.O. Box 1147
Bristol, TN 37621
Application address: 1000 W. State St., Bristol, TN 37620, tel.: (423) 764-5121
Contact: Frank Winston, Tr.

Donor(s): C.M. Gatton, Customer 1 One, Inc.
Financial data (yr. ended 11/30/01): Grants paid, $1,079,550; assets, $20,968,043 (M); gifts

received, $900,750; expenditures, $1,118,919; qualifying distributions, $1,066,673.
Limitations: Giving on a national basis.
Application information: Application form not required.
Trustees: C.M. Gatton, Allan R. Rhodes, Frank Winston.
EIN: 621266284
Codes: FD

49896
Weldon F. Osborne Foundation, Inc.
Krystal Bldg.
1 Union Sq., Ste. 210
Chattanooga, TN 37402-2501 (423) 267-0931
FAX: (423) 267-0931
Contact: Harold S. Wilson, Pres.

Established in 1959.
Donor(s): Osborne Enterprises, Inc., Osborne Building Corp.
Financial data (yr. ended 06/30/01): Grants paid, $1,002,725; assets, $22,644,536 (M); expenditures, $1,526,746; qualifying distributions, $1,079,001.
Limitations: Giving primarily in the Chattanooga and Hamilton County, TN, areas.
Publications: Annual report, application guidelines.
Application information: Application form required.
Officers and Directors:* Harold S. Wilson,* Pres. and Exec. Dir.; C. Duffy Franck, Jr.,* V.P.; Ray C. Marlin,* V.P.; Glenn C. Stophel,* Secy.; Arch Trimble III,* Treas.; Scott Mattice.
EIN: 626026442
Codes: FD

49897
The Chrysalis Foundation
Republic Centre
633 Chestnut St., Rm. 740
Chattanooga, TN 37450 (423) 756-0882
Contact: Mary N. Moore, Pres.

Established in 1992 in TN.
Donor(s): Mary N. Moore.
Financial data (yr. ended 12/31/01): Grants paid, $1,000,554; assets, $10,717,750 (M); expenditures, $1,026,000; qualifying distributions, $995,832.
Officers and Directors:* Mary N. Moore,* Pres. and Treas.; Carl A. Navarre, Jr.,* Secy.; William N. Bailey.
EIN: 621497058
Codes: FD

49898
Orion L. & Emma B. Hurlbut Memorial Fund
701 Market St.
Chattanooga, TN 37402
Application address: c/o Jo Ann Clifford, Chattanooga Tumor Clinic, 975 E. 3rd St., Chattanooga, TN 37403, tel.: (423) 778-7503

Established in 1937 in TN.
Financial data (yr. ended 04/30/01): Grants paid, $892,361; assets, $21,965,249 (M); expenditures, $1,198,526; qualifying distributions, $1,059,191.
Limitations: Giving primarily in Chattanooga, TN.
Application information: Applicants should include physicians' detailed expense voucher.
Directors: Stella Anderson, John F. Boxell, C. Windom Kimsey, M.D.
Trustee: First Tennessee Bank, N.A.
EIN: 626034546
Codes: FD, GTI

49899
The Clayton Family Foundation
5000 Clayton Rd.
Maryville, TN 37802 (865) 380-3212
Contact: Kay M. Clayton, Mgr.

Established in 1991 in TN.
Donor(s): James L. Clayton.
Financial data (yr. ended 12/31/01): Grants paid, $886,251; assets, $23,948,894 (M); gifts received, $1,500,188; expenditures, $886,784; qualifying distributions, $886,251.
Limitations: Giving primarily in areas of company operations, particularly the Knoxville, TN, area, and the east TN area.
Application information: One grant request per calendar year. Application form not required.
Officers and Directors:* James L. Clayton,* Pres.; Karen Clayton Davis,* Secy.; James L. Clayton, Jr., Kevin T. Clayton.
Manager: Kay M. Clayton.
EIN: 581970851
Codes: FD

49900
The Laura Jo Turner Dugas Foundation
c/o H. Calister Turner, Jr.
138 2nd Ave. N., Ste. 200
Nashville, TN 37201

Established in 1996 in TN.
Donor(s): Laura Jo Turner Dugas, Wayne Dugas.
Financial data (yr. ended 12/31/01): Grants paid, $844,600; assets, $596,576 (M); expenditures, $850,926; qualifying distributions, $846,480.
Limitations: Applications not accepted. Giving primarily in FL.
Application information: Contributes only to pre-selected organizations.
Trustee: H. Calister Turner, Jr.
EIN: 621627128
Codes: FD

49901
The Knapp Foundation, Inc.
3173 Kirby Whitten Pkwy., Ste. 105
Bartlett, TN 38134-2823
Contact: Marcia R. Brasel, Chair.

Established in 1999 in TN.
Financial data (yr. ended 12/31/01): Grants paid, $827,105; assets, $10,225,614 (M); gifts received, $10,000; expenditures, $1,186,145; qualifying distributions, $965,201.
Limitations: Giving primarily in Memphis, TN.
Officers: Marcia R. Brasel, Chair.; Sandra J. Taylor, Secy.; Lori Condo, Treas.
Directors: June N. Deutsch, Ellen C. Douglas.
EIN: 621794837
Codes: FD

49902
H. W. Durham Foundation
5050 Poplar Ave., Ste. 2132
Memphis, TN 38157 (901) 683-3583
Contact: Jenks McCrory, Prog. Dir.

Incorporated in 1955 in TN.
Donor(s): H.W. Durham.‡
Financial data (yr. ended 12/31/01): Grants paid, $762,217; assets, $15,135,917 (M); gifts received, $39,090; expenditures, $1,152,362; qualifying distributions, $1,052,164.
Limitations: Giving primarily in Memphis and western TN.
Publications: Application guidelines, informational brochure (including application guidelines).
Application information: Application form required.
Officers and Directors:* Thomas H. Durham, Jr.,* Pres.; Jenks McCrory,* V.P. and Prog. Dir.; Jo Scott,* Secy.; John Coleman,* Treas.; Kaye Brooksbank, Evertt Huffard, Ralph Lawrence, Hugh McHenry, Linda Nichols.
EIN: 620583854
Codes: FD

49903
The Aslan Foundation
P.O. Box 550
Knoxville, TN 37901-0550 (865) 637-1440
FAX: (865) 546-9808
Contact: Robert S. Young III, Pres.

Established in 1995 in TN.
Donor(s): Lindsay Young.
Financial data (yr. ended 12/31/01): Grants paid, $747,000; assets, $14,188,743 (M); expenditures, $858,695; qualifying distributions, $746,817.
Limitations: Giving primarily in east TN.
Application information: Application form required.
Officers and Directors:* Robert S. Young III,* Pres.; Robert S. Young, Jr.,* V.P.; Mark K. Williams,* Secy.; Gregory E. Erickson,* Treas.; Lindsay Y. McDonough, Lindsay Young.
EIN: 621520208
Codes: FD

49904
Wayne G. Basler Charitable Foundation
P.O. Box 2049
Kingsport, TN 37662 (423) 246-4546
Contact: Shari L. Hillman, Mgr.

Established in 1988 in TN.
Financial data (yr. ended 12/31/01): Grants paid, $682,851; assets, $11,019,978 (M); expenditures, $836,328; qualifying distributions, $690,426.
Limitations: Giving primarily in IA and TN.
Officer: Shari L. Hillman, Mgr.
Trustee: Wayne G. Basler.
EIN: 621347054
Codes: FD

49905
Elvis Presley Memorial Foundation, Inc.
3734 Elvis Presley Blvd.
P.O. Box 16508
Memphis, TN 38116-0508

Established in 1986 as a public charity in TN; reclassified as a private foundation by the IRS in 1990.
Financial data (yr. ended 07/31/01): Grants paid, $676,368; assets, $17,922 (M); gifts received, $482,259; expenditures, $677,072; qualifying distributions, $676,368.
Limitations: Applications not accepted. Giving limited to Memphis, TN.
Application information: Contributes only to pre-selected organizations.
Officers and Trustees:* Priscilla B. Presley,* Pres.; Jack R. Soden,* V.P.
EIN: 581632547
Codes: FD

49906
Goodlett Foundation
6055 Primacy Pkwy., Ste. 450
Memphis, TN 38119
Contact: Kathleen S. Williams, Treas.

Established in 1997 in TN.
Donor(s): Robert B. Blow.
Financial data (yr. ended 09/30/01): Grants paid, $652,000; assets, $6,652,515 (M); expenditures, $724,226; qualifying distributions, $652,000.
Limitations: Applications not accepted. Giving primarily in Memphis, TN.

49906—TENNESSEE

Application information: Contributes only to pre-selected organizations.
Officers and Directors:* David A. Dunehew,* Pres.; Patricia A. Alexander,* Secy.; Kathleen S. Williams,* Treas.; Pamela D. Blow, Robert B. Blow, Wallace C. Madewell, Warner B. Rodda.
EIN: 621663934
Codes: FD

49907
The William B. Stokely, Jr. Foundation
620 Campbell Station Rd.
Station W., Ste. 27
Knoxville, TN 37922-1636 (865) 966-4878
Contact: William B. Stokely III, Pres.

Incorporated in 1951 in IN.
Donor(s): William B. Stokely, Jr.‡
Financial data (yr. ended 12/31/01): Grants paid, $648,979; assets, $11,521,865 (M); expenditures, $869,849; qualifying distributions, $684,288.
Limitations: Giving primarily in eastern TN.
Application information: Application form not required.
Officers and Directors:* William B. Stokely III,* Pres.; Kay H. Stokely,* Exec. V.P.; Andrea A. White-Randall, V.P. and Secy.-Treas.; Stacy S. Byerly, Clayton F. Stokely, Shelley K. Stokely, William B. Stokely IV.
EIN: 356016402
Codes: FD

49908
Louise B. Wallace Foundation
4400 Harding Rd., Ste. 310
Nashville, TN 37205-5215

Established in 1989 in TN.
Donor(s): George Newton Bullard Foundation.
Financial data (yr. ended 12/31/01): Grants paid, $613,834; assets, $12,193,534 (M); gifts received, $160,630; expenditures, $736,536; qualifying distributions, $626,771.
Limitations: Applications not accepted. Giving primarily in Nashville, TN.
Application information: Contributes only to pre-selected organizations.
Trustees: Elizabeth W. Caldwell, Elena W. Graves, Anne B. Nesbitt, Elizabeth B. Stadler, J. Bransford Wallace, Jr.
EIN: 581797048
Codes: FD

49909
Cannon Family Foundation
7574 Poplar Ave.
Germantown, TN 38138

Donor(s): Kathryn Gracey Cannon, Robert E. Cannon.
Financial data (yr. ended 12/31/01): Grants paid, $603,500; assets, $118,979 (M); expenditures, $612,097; qualifying distributions, $455,467.
Limitations: Applications not accepted.
Application information: Contributes only to pre-selected organizations.
Officers and Directors:* Robert E. Cannon,* Pres.; Kathryn Gracey Cannon,* V.P.; Henry Patton Doggrell,* Secy.; Richard Prosser Guenther,* Treas.; Robert Howard Cannon, Timothy Hall Cannon.
EIN: 311650513
Codes: FD

49910
The Haslam Family Foundation, Inc.
P.O. Box 10146
Knoxville, TN 37939-0146 (865) 588-7488
Contact: Todd Ellis, Asst. Secy.

Established in 1998 in TN.
Donor(s): James A. Haslam III.
Financial data (yr. ended 12/31/00): Grants paid, $579,100; assets, $11,267,336 (M); expenditures, $635,555; qualifying distributions, $600,444.
Limitations: Giving primarily in eastern TN.
Officers and Directors:* James A. Haslam II,* Pres.; Ann Haslam Bailey,* V.P.; Natalie L. Haslam,* Secy.; Jim R. Shelby,* Treas.; James A. Haslam III, William E. Haslam.
EIN: 621692007
Codes: FD

49911
The Atticus Foundation
(Formerly The Atticus Trust)
c/o SunTrust Banks, Inc.
P.O. Box 305110
Nashville, TN 37230-5110 (615) 748-5813
Contact: Kim Williams

Established in 1986 in TN.
Financial data (yr. ended 12/30/00): Grants paid, $578,833; assets, $13,482,721 (M); gifts received, $1,000,000; expenditures, $637,726; qualifying distributions, $605,139.
Limitations: Giving primarily in TN.
Application information: Application form not required.
Trustees: Doug Brown, Jr., Martin S. Brown, Jr.
Trust Committee Members: Elizabeth M. Brown, Elizabeth M. Brown, Margaret W. Brown, Martin S. Brown, Sr., Susannah L. Brown.
Agent: SunTrust Banks, Inc.
EIN: 581796390
Codes: FD

49912
Washington Foundation
(Formerly Church of Christ Foundation, Inc.)
P.O. Box 159057
Nashville, TN 37215
Contact: Paul A. Hargis

Incorporated in 1946 in TN.
Donor(s): G.L. Comer.
Financial data (yr. ended 12/31/01): Grants paid, $578,600; assets, $11,736,182 (M); expenditures, $684,364; qualifying distributions, $607,102.
Limitations: Giving primarily in Nashville, TN.
Trustees: Howard R. Amacher, Andrew Benedict, William W. Berry, R. Hix Clark, James N. Denton III, Miles Ezell, Jr., Paul A. Hargis, Harold Hazelip, Neal L. Jennings, E.M. Shepherd, Paschal Young.
EIN: 620649477
Codes: FD

49913
Wilson Foundation
1629 Winchester Rd.
Memphis, TN 38116-3519

Established about 1961 in TN.
Financial data (yr. ended 12/31/01): Grants paid, $576,035; assets, $6,283,041 (M); expenditures, $638,389; qualifying distributions, $589,682.
Limitations: Applications not accepted. Giving primarily in Memphis, TN.
Application information: Contributes only to pre-selected organizations.
Officers: Spence Wilson, Pres.; Charles K. Wilson, Jr., V.P.; Robert Wilson, V.P.; R.E. Wallin, Secy.; William Batt, Treas.
Directors: C. Kemmons Wilson, Jr., Kemmons Wilson, Elizabeth Wilson-Moore, Carol Wilson-West.
EIN: 626046687
Codes: FD

49914
The Eden Foundation
202 Hillwood Blvd.
Nashville, TN 37205

Established in 1993 in TN as partial successor to the Werthan Foundation.
Donor(s): Morris Werthan II, Libby Werthan.
Financial data (yr. ended 12/31/01): Grants paid, $563,005; assets, $5,524,994 (M); gifts received, $207,434; expenditures, $632,801; qualifying distributions, $558,377.
Limitations: Applications not accepted. Giving primarily in TN.
Application information: Contributes only to pre-selected organizations.
Trustees: Jeremy Werthan, Libby Werthan, Melissa Werthan, Michael Werthan, Morris Werthan, Nancy Werthan.
EIN: 621543809
Codes: FD

49915
Thomas W. Briggs Foundation, Inc.
845 Crossover Ln., Ste. 138
Memphis, TN 38117
Contact: JoAnne Tilley, Secy. and Exec. Dir.

Established in 1957.
Donor(s): Thomas W. Briggs Residuary Trust.
Financial data (yr. ended 09/30/01): Grants paid, $558,926; assets, $10,837,215 (M); gifts received, $147,134; expenditures, $1,225,153; qualifying distributions, $582,469.
Limitations: Giving limited to Memphis, TN.
Publications: Application guidelines.
Application information: Application form not required.
Officers and Directors:* Harry J. Phillips, Sr.,* Chair.; Spence Wilson, Pres.; Jim Witherington, Jr., V.P.; JoAnne Tilley, Secy. and Exec. Dir.; S. Herbert Rhea,* Treas.; Kathleen Blair, Jim Bland, Jr., Bena Cates, Buzzy Hussey, William T. Morris, Richard Rantzow.
EIN: 626039986
Codes: FD

49916
Caldwell Foundation, Inc.
c/o SunTrust Banks, Inc.
P.O. Box 1638
Chattanooga, TN 37401 (423) 757-3933
FAX: (423) 757-3691; E-mail: Barbara.Marter@SunTrust.com
Contact: Robert H. Caldwell, Pres.

Established about 1960 in TN.
Financial data (yr. ended 12/31/01): Grants paid, $526,944; assets, $7,023,671 (M); expenditures, $580,952; qualifying distributions, $527,989.
Limitations: Giving limited to Chattanooga, TN.
Application information: Application form not required.
Officers and Trustees:* Robert H. Caldwell,* Pres.; L. H. Caldwell, Jr.,* V.P.; Summer Bryan, L.H. Caldwell III, Mark A. Caldwell, Robert H. Caldwell, Jr., Theodore C. Caldwell.
EIN: 620678446
Codes: FD

49917
Margaret F. Shackelford Charitable Trust
c/o NBC, Trust Division
1 Commerce Sq.
Memphis, TN 38150
Application address: 326 S. Goodlet St., Memphis, TN 38117, tel.: (901) 458-6654
Contact: Paul A. Calame, Jr.

Established in 1999 in TN.

Financial data (yr. ended 12/31/00): Grants paid, $525,262; assets, $12,099,337 (M); expenditures, $609,894; qualifying distributions, $517,860.
Limitations: Giving primarily in TN.
Trustee: National Bank of Commerce.
EIN: 626363101
Codes: FD

49918
Raymond Zimmerman Charitable Trust
c/o Ron Mills
111 Westwood Pl.
Brentwood, TN 37027
FAX: (615) 298-2068
Contact: Roger L. Proctor

Established in 1982 in TN.
Donor(s): Raymond Zimmerman.
Financial data (yr. ended 12/31/02): Grants paid, $522,923; assets, $769,475 (M); expenditures, $541,143; qualifying distributions, $526,923.
Limitations: Applications not accepted. Giving limited to Boca Raton, FL and Nashville, TN.
Application information: Contributes only to pre-selected organizations.
Trustees: Ron Mills, Robyn Z. Rubinoff, Fred E. Zimmerman.
EIN: 621327356
Codes: FD

49919
SunTrust Banks of Tennessee Foundation
(Formerly TCH Third National Foundation)
c/o SunTrust Banks Inc., Trust Tax Dept.
P.O. Box 305110
Nashville, TN 37230-5110 (615) 748-5813
Contact: Kim Williams

Established in 1993.
Donor(s): The First National Bank of Florence, SunTrust Banks of Tennessee, Inc.
Financial data (yr. ended 12/31/01): Grants paid, $521,754; assets, $2,202,103 (M); gifts received, $217,655; expenditures, $540,122; qualifying distributions, $529,872.
Limitations: Giving limited to central TN.
Application information: Application form not required.
Trustees: Sam Franklin, SunTrust Banks, Inc.
EIN: 626263340
Codes: CS, FD, CD

49920
Starfish Foundation
(Formerly McInnes Family Foundation)
116 30th Ave. S.
Nashville, TN 37212

Established in 1991 in TN.
Donor(s): William W. McInnes.
Financial data (yr. ended 12/31/01): Grants paid, $513,200; assets, $221,030 (M); gifts received, $135,000; expenditures, $522,366; qualifying distributions, $520,489.
Limitations: Applications not accepted. Giving limited to Nashville, TN.
Application information: Contributes only to pre-selected organizations.
Officers: William W. McInnes, Pres. and Treas.; Marge Crabtree, Secy.
Director: Beverly W. McInnes.
EIN: 621459425
Codes: FD

49921
Louie M. & Betty M. Phillips Foundation
200 42nd Ave. N.
Nashville, TN 37209 (615) 385-5949
FAX: (615) 385-2507; E-mail: louie@phillipsfoundation.org; URL: http://www.phillipsfoundation.org
Contact: Louie Buntin, C.E.O.

Established in 1978 in TN.
Donor(s): Betty M. Phillips,‡ Louie M. Phillips.‡
Financial data (yr. ended 12/31/01): Grants paid, $505,450; assets, $10,150,538 (M); expenditures, $753,967; qualifying distributions, $645,834.
Limitations: Giving limited to Nashville, TN.
Publications: Informational brochure (including application guidelines).
Application information: Application form not required.
Officer and Trustees:* Louie Buntin,* C.E.O.; Trustmark National Bank.
EIN: 581326615
Codes: FD

49922
The Harnisch Family Foundation, Inc.
P.O. Box 50797
Nashville, TN 37205-2867
E-mail: info@thehf.com
Contact: Ruth Ann Harnisch, Pres.

Established in 1998 in DE.
Donor(s): Harnisch Family.
Financial data (yr. ended 05/31/01): Grants paid, $489,090; assets, $2,481,291 (M); gifts received, $11,280; expenditures, $515,022; qualifying distributions, $514,653.
Application information: Application form required.
Officer: Ruth Ann Harnisch, Pres.
EIN: 510381959
Codes: FD

49923
Jane L. Pettway Foundation
c/o First Tennessee Bank, N.A., Trust Div.
800 S. Gay St.
Knoxville, TN 37995-1230 (865) 971-2165

Established in 1999 in TN.
Financial data (yr. ended 08/31/01): Grants paid, $484,122; assets, $8,004,291 (M); gifts received, $419,695; expenditures, $535,541; qualifying distributions, $502,788.
Limitations: Giving primarily in TN.
Application information: Application form required.
Officers: David Lantz, Exec. V.P. and Mgr.; Dean John Ross, Mgr.; Patricia Watson, Mgr.
Trustee: First Tennessee Bank, N.A.
EIN: 626371465
Codes: FD

49924
Joel C. and Bernice W. Gordon Family Foundation
3102 West End Ave., Ste. 650
Nashville, TN 37203-1498
Contact: Joel C. Gordon, Pres.

Established in 1986 in TN.
Donor(s): Joel C. Gordon, Bernice W. Gordon, Sherrie Gordon Eisenman, Robert A. Gordon, Frank E. Gordon, Gail E. Gordon.
Financial data (yr. ended 06/30/01): Grants paid, $483,925; assets, $11,203,036 (M); gifts received, $12,085; expenditures, $529,526; qualifying distributions, $484,609.
Limitations: Applications not accepted. Giving primarily in TN.
Application information: Contributes only to pre-selected organizations.
Officers: Joel C. Gordon, Pres.; Bernice W. Gordon, Secy.
Trustees: Alan J. Eisenman, Sherrie Gordon Eisenman, Frank E. Gordon, Gwen L. Gordon, Julie S. Gordon, Robert A. Gordon, Gail Gordon Jacobs, Jeffrey M. Jacobs.
EIN: 621306906
Codes: FD

49925
Louis R. Draughon Foundation
c/o AmSouth Bank
315 Deaderick St., 4th Fl.
Nashville, TN 37237-0401

Established in 1982 in TN.
Donor(s): Elizabeth F. Draughon.‡
Financial data (yr. ended 12/31/01): Grants paid, $475,500; assets, $6,606,380 (M); gifts received, $45,959; expenditures, $526,931; qualifying distributions, $478,000.
Limitations: Applications not accepted. Giving primarily in TN.
Application information: Contributes only to pre-selected organizations.
Officers and Directors:* Edith Perry,* Pres.; Jim Willhite, V.P.; Robert Neman,* Secy-Treas.; Bob Andrews, Jeanette Dorris, James Walton.
EIN: 621147685
Codes: FD

49926
The Ragsdale Family Foundation
113 Seaboard Ln., Ste. C-200
Franklin, TN 37067

Established in 1991 in TN.
Donor(s): Richard E. Ragsdale.
Financial data (yr. ended 12/31/01): Grants paid, $464,400; assets, $5,337,727 (M); expenditures, $571,908; qualifying distributions, $462,765.
Limitations: Applications not accepted. Giving primarily in Nashville, TN.
Application information: Contributes only to pre-selected organizations.
Officers and Directors:* Richard E. Ragsdale,* Pres.; Anne E. Ragsdale,* Secy.; Bethany R. Corrieri, Brett T. Corrieri, Kevin G. Ragsdale, Richard E. Ragsdale II.
EIN: 621481225
Codes: FD

49927
M. B. Seretean Foundation, Inc.
12424 Creek Hollow Ln.
Soddy Daisy, TN 37379-5902

Established in 1964 in GA.
Donor(s): M.B. Seretean.
Financial data (yr. ended 06/30/01): Grants paid, $461,800; assets, $7,607,777 (L); expenditures, $476,159; qualifying distributions, $450,510.
Limitations: Applications not accepted. Giving primarily in FL, GA, OK, and TN.
Application information: Contributes only to pre-selected organizations.
Officers: M.B. Seretean, Pres. and Treas.; Sue C. Moore, Secy.
EIN: 620725600
Codes: FD

49928
Judy and Noah Liff Foundation
404 James Robertson Pkwy., Ste. 1200
Nashville, TN 37219

Established in 1994 in TN.
Donor(s): Noah Liff.

49928—TENNESSEE

Financial data (yr. ended 08/31/01): Grants paid, $460,188; assets, $3,664,320 (M); gifts received, $1,828,891; expenditures, $498,712; qualifying distributions, $467,259.
Limitations: Applications not accepted. Giving primarily in TN.
Application information: Contributes only to pre-selected organizations.
Trustees: Judy Liff, Noah Liff.
EIN: 621587938
Codes: FD

49929
The Goldsmith Family Foundation, Inc.
(Formerly The Goldsmith Foundation)
1900 Union Ave.
Memphis, TN 38104-4029

Incorporated in 1944 in TN.
Donor(s): Members of the Goldsmith family.
Financial data (yr. ended 12/31/01): Grants paid, $451,840; assets, $8,598,069 (M); expenditures, $512,700; qualifying distributions, $447,581.
Limitations: Giving primarily in TN.
Officers and Trustees:* Harry L. Goldsmith,* Pres.; Elvis G. Goldsmith,* V.P.; Fred Goldsmith III,* V.P.; Melvin Goldsmith, V.P.; Thomas B. Goldsmith, V.P.; Sylvia Goldsmith Marks, V.P.; Larry J. Goldsmith,* Secy.-Treas.; Elias J. Goldsmith, Jr.
EIN: 626039604
Codes: FD

49930
The Tennessee Trust
c/o SunTrust Banks, Inc.
P.O. Box 305110
Nashville, TN 37230-5110 (615) 748-4725
Contact: Elizabeth Mayhall, Tr.

Established in 1991 in TN.
Donor(s): Douglas Henry, Jr.
Financial data (yr. ended 01/31/02): Grants paid, $437,286; assets, $118,411 (M); gifts received, $18,036; expenditures, $445,726; qualifying distributions, $437,286.
Application information: Application form not required.
Officer: Douglas Henry, Jr., Chair.
Trustees: Mary L. Henry, Elizabeth Mayhall, SunTrust Banks, Inc.
EIN: 581951574

49931
The Danner Foundation
2 International Dr., Ste. 510
Nashville, TN 37217-2010 (615) 367-9092
Contact: Raymond L. Danner, Pres.

Established in 1988 in TN.
Donor(s): Raymond L. Danner.
Financial data (yr. ended 12/31/01): Grants paid, $423,924; assets, $7,807,814 (M); expenditures, $549,930; qualifying distributions, $423,924.
Limitations: Giving primarily in TN.
Application information: Application form not required.
Officers and Directors:* Raymond L. Danner,* Pres. and Secy.-Treas.; Judith B. Danner,* V.P.; Gail D. Greil, Donna D. Wilson.
EIN: 581803926
Codes: FD

49932
The Wright-Bentley Foundation
c/o Richard A. Park
1000 Tallan Bldg., 2 Union Sq.
Chattanooga, TN 37402 (423) 757-0208
Contact: Richard A. Park, Treas.

Established in 1994 in TN.
Donor(s): Spencer H. Wright.
Financial data (yr. ended 12/31/01): Grants paid, $420,300; assets, $2,459,160 (M); gifts received, $351,545; expenditures, $437,306; qualifying distributions, $422,438.
Limitations: Giving primarily in Chattanooga, TN.
Application information: Application form not required.
Officers: Spencer H. Wright, Pres.; J. Nelson Irvine, Secy.; Richard A. Park, Treas.
Director: Donna B. Wright.
EIN: 621585737
Codes: FD

49933
Bernal Foundation
P.O. Box 1310
Nashville, TN 37202-1310 (615) 259-9331
Contact: Herbert M. Shayne, Tr.

Established in 1953 in TN.
Donor(s): Albert Werthan, and members of the Werthan family.
Financial data (yr. ended 12/31/01): Grants paid, $412,536; assets, $336,594 (M); gifts received, $867; expenditures, $432,606; qualifying distributions, $423,041.
Limitations: Giving primarily in TN.
Application information: Application form not required.
Officers and Trustees:* Albert Werthan,* Chair.; Bernard Werthan, Jr.,* Secy.; Morris Werthan II,* Treas.; Herbert M. Shayne.
EIN: 626037906
Codes: FD

49934
The Pattee Foundation, Inc.
c/o Dennis McCurry
The Krystal Bldg., Ste. 700
Chattanooga, TN 37402-2581
Contact: Gordon B. Pattee, Pres.

Established in 1989 in TN.
Financial data (yr. ended 06/30/01): Grants paid, $396,500; assets, $7,375,848 (M); expenditures, $591,198; qualifying distributions, $397,983.
Limitations: Giving primarily in CA, Washington, DC, New York, NY, and TN.
Officers and Directors:* Gordon B. Pattee,* Pres.; Anne L. Pattee,* Secy.; Dorothy E. Pattee.
EIN: 621376116
Codes: FD

49935
The Annette and Irwin Eskind Family Foundation
541 Jackson Blvd.
Nashville, TN 37205

Established in 1986 in TN.
Donor(s): Annette Eskind, Irwin Eskind, Jeffrey Eskind, Steven Eskind.
Financial data (yr. ended 06/30/01): Grants paid, $396,205; assets, $9,333,572 (M); expenditures, $406,713; qualifying distributions, $386,706.
Limitations: Applications not accepted. Giving primarily in Nashville, TN; some funding also in Boston, MA.
Application information: Contributes only to pre-selected organizations.
Officers: Irwin Eskind, Pres.; Annette Eskind, Secy.
Directors: Jeffrey Eskind, Steven Eskind.
EIN: 621289997
Codes: FD

49936
The Schadt Foundation, Inc.
555 Perkins Extended, Ste. 416
Memphis, TN 38117

Incorporated in 1958 in TN.
Donor(s): Charles F. Schadt, Sr., Harry E. Schadt, Sr.,‡ Harry E. Schadt, Jr.
Financial data (yr. ended 12/31/01): Grants paid, $395,050; assets, $6,546,969 (M); expenditures, $468,386; qualifying distributions, $391,818.
Limitations: Applications not accepted. Giving limited to Memphis, TN.
Application information: Contributes only to pre-selected organizations.
Officers: Stephen C. Schadt, Sr., Pres.; Lynn Schadt Thomas, Secy.
Directors: Charles F. Schadt, Jr., Harry E. Schadt, Reid Schadt.
EIN: 626040050
Codes: FD

49937
The Jane and Richard Eskind and Family Foundation
104 Lynnwood Blvd.
Nashville, TN 37205-2904

Established in 1986 in TN.
Donor(s): Jane Eskind, Richard Eskind.
Financial data (yr. ended 06/30/01): Grants paid, $386,031; assets, $10,820,905 (M); expenditures, $411,182; qualifying distributions, $389,001.
Limitations: Applications not accepted. Giving primarily in Nashville, TN.
Application information: Contributes only to pre-selected organizations.
Officers: Jane Eskind, Pres.; Richard Eskind, Secy.
Trustees: William H. Eskind, Ellen E. Lehman.
EIN: 621289998
Codes: FD

49938
Conwood Charitable Trust
(Formerly American Snuff Company Charitable Trust)
c/o Union Planters Bank
P.O. Box 387
Memphis, TN 38147
Additional address: 701 Main St., Memphis, TN 38101
Contact: David Simpson, III

Established in 1952 in TN.
Donor(s): American Snuff Company, Conwood Company.
Financial data (yr. ended 12/31/01): Grants paid, $376,040; assets, $6,623,915 (M); expenditures, $417,383; qualifying distributions, $374,055.
Limitations: Giving primarily in the Memphis, TN, area.
Trustees: David L. Simpson III, Union Planters Bank.
EIN: 626036034
Codes: CS, FD, CD

49939
Mary G. K. Fox Foundation
c/o First Tennessee Bank, N.A., Trust Div.
800 S. Gay St.
Knoxville, TN 37995-1230 (865) 971-2076
Contact: Janet Campbell, Trust Off., First Tennessee Bank, N.A.

Established in 1981 in TN.
Financial data (yr. ended 12/31/01): Grants paid, $364,245; assets, $3,480,343 (M); expenditures, $395,321; qualifying distributions, $368,245.
Limitations: Giving limited to Greeneville, TN.
Board Members: Myron Bernard, William G. Brown, Thomas Wright.

Trustee: First Tennessee Bank, N.A.
EIN: 626160483
Codes: FD

49940
The Emily & Robert Beasley Charitable Trust
150 4th Ave., N., Ste. 1500
Nashville, TN 37219-2434

Established around 1984.
Financial data (yr. ended 12/31/01): Grants paid, $362,990; assets, $1,762,040 (M); expenditures, $406,804; qualifying distributions, $362,792.
Limitations: Applications not accepted. Giving primarily in Sparta, TN.
Application information: Contributes only to pre-selected organizations.
Trustees: George Elrod, William Johnson.
Manager: Morgan Keegan Trust Co.
EIN: 581552213
Codes: FD

49941
LifeWorks Foundation
(Formerly George N. Bullard Foundation)
P.O. Box 50276
Nashville, TN 37205 (615) 269-6663
FAX: (615) 269-7496
Contact: George Bullard, Dir.

Established in 1967 in TN; reorganized in 1988 in FL; name change in 1990.
Donor(s): Ella Hayes Trust.
Financial data (yr. ended 12/31/00): Grants paid, $358,975; assets, $9,455,614 (M); gifts received, $368,906; expenditures, $576,392; qualifying distributions, $486,443.
Limitations: Applications not accepted. Giving limited to Nashville, TN.
Application information: Unsolicited applications not considered.
Director: George Bullard.
EIN: 621428468
Codes: FD

49942
The Rust Foundation
c/o Jane C. Rust
373 Old Woodbury Pike
Readyville, TN 37149
Contact: Trustees

Trust established in 1950 in PA.
Donor(s): The Rust family.
Financial data (yr. ended 12/31/01): Grants paid, $357,329; assets, $6,429,988 (M); gifts received, $223; expenditures, $457,226; qualifying distributions, $365,579.
Limitations: Applications not accepted. Giving on a national basis.
Application information: Unsolicited requests for funds not accepted.
Officers: S.M. Rust III, Pres.; Ann S. Gillies, V.P.; Molly Rust Montgomery, Secy.; John M. Rust, Treas.
Trustees: Mary Rust Gillies, Thatcher O. Montgomery, Robert B. Rust, S.M. Rust, Jr., Alice Rust Scheetz.
EIN: 256049037
Codes: FD

49943
The Hermoine and Glen Nelson Foundation
315 Deaderick St., 4th Fl.
Nashville, TN 37237-0401

Established in 1987 in TN.
Donor(s): Hermoine Corlew Adkisson.
Financial data (yr. ended 12/31/01): Grants paid, $355,000; assets, $12,738,223 (M); gifts received, $11,996,929; expenditures, $388,147; qualifying distributions, $355,000.
Limitations: Applications not accepted.
Application information: Contributes only to pre-selected organizations.
Officers and Directors:* Hermoine Corlew Adkisson,* Pres.; Barbara Nelson Lamberson,* V.P. and Secy.; Bob L. Andrews.
EIN: 621317088
Codes: FD

49944
The Robert H. and Monica M. Cole Foundation
c/o Home Federal Bank, Trust Dept.
515 Market St.
Knoxville, TN 37902-2145
Contact: Robert Page

Established in 1976.
Financial data (yr. ended 09/30/01): Grants paid, $346,600; assets, $6,417,451 (M); expenditures, $497,206; qualifying distributions, $348,012.
Limitations: Giving limited to southeast KY, and eastern TN, including Knoxville.
Application information: Application form not required.
Trustees: W.W. Davis, Sr., James R. McKenry, Jr., Monica Cole McKenry, Margaret McKenry-Nash, Sarah C. Page, Home Federal Bank.
EIN: 626137973
Codes: FD

49945
AMJ Foundation
500 Elmington Ave., Ste. 210
Nashville, TN 37205-2520 (615) 259-9331
Contact: Albert Werthan, Tr.

Established in 1993 in TN as partial successor to the Werthan Foundation.
Donor(s): Elizabeth Werthan.
Financial data (yr. ended 12/31/01): Grants paid, $335,490; assets, $3,706,653 (M); gifts received, $335; expenditures, $356,698; qualifying distributions, $351,688.
Limitations: Giving primarily in Davidson County, TN, with emphasis on Nashville.
Application information: Application form not required.
Trustees: Albert Werthan, Elizabeth Werthan, Robert Werthan.
EIN: 621543217
Codes: FD

49946
The Ann and Monroe Carell Foundation
(Formerly The Monroe Carell, Jr. Foundation)
2401 21st Ave. S., Ste. 200
Nashville, TN 37212

Established in 1983 in TN.
Donor(s): Monroe Carell, Jr.
Financial data (yr. ended 12/31/01): Grants paid, $327,656; assets, $4,697,724 (M); expenditures, $344,365; qualifying distributions, $329,131.
Limitations: Applications not accepted. Giving primarily in Nashville, TN.
Application information: Contributes only to pre-selected organizations.
Officers and Directors:* Monroe Carell, Jr.,* Pres.; Ann Scott Carell,* Secy.-Treas.; Kathryn C. Brown, Edith C. Johnson, Julie Carell Stadler.
EIN: 581537831
Codes: FD

49947
The Rose Foundation
6305 Humphrey Blvd., Ste. 110
Memphis, TN 38120-2300

Established in 1990 in TN.
Donor(s): Gayle S. Rose, Michael D. Rose.
Financial data (yr. ended 12/31/00): Grants paid, $326,850; assets, $4,254,728 (M); gifts received, $503,500; expenditures, $368,509; qualifying distributions, $326,850.
Limitations: Applications not accepted. Giving primarily in Memphis, TN.
Application information: Contributes only to pre-selected organizations.
Officers and Directors:* Michael D. Rose,* Pres.; Dale Ericson,* Secy.; Gabrielle E. Rose, Matthew D. Rose.
EIN: 621450062
Codes: FD

49948
B & B Foundation
(Formerly Betty and Bernard Werthan, Jr. Foundation)
P.O. Box 1310
Nashville, TN 37202-1310

Established in 1993 in TN as partial successor to the Werthan Foundation.
Donor(s): Leah Rose Werthan.‡
Financial data (yr. ended 12/31/01): Grants paid, $322,124; assets, $2,795,322 (M); gifts received, $437,062; expenditures, $363,165; qualifying distributions, $319,270.
Limitations: Applications not accepted.
Application information: Contributes only to pre-selected organizations.
Officers: Bernard Werthan, Jr., Pres.; Betty Werthan, Secy.
EIN: 621543218
Codes: FD

49949
Hazel Montague Hutcheson Foundation
c/o SunTrust Banks, Inc.
736 Market St., P.O. Box 1638
Chattanooga, TN 37401 (423) 757-3933
E-mail: barbara.marter@suntrust.com
Contact: Barbara Marter, V.P., SunTrust Banks, Inc.

Established in 1962 in TN.
Donor(s): Hazel G.M. Montague.‡
Financial data (yr. ended 06/30/01): Grants paid, $322,000; assets, $6,010,631 (M); expenditures, $366,190; qualifying distributions, $330,757.
Limitations: Applications not accepted. Giving primarily in TN.
Trustees: John Banks, Theodore M. Hutcheson, Jr., Thomas R. Hutcheson, W. Frank Hutcheson.
EIN: 626045925
Codes: FD

49950
Van Vleet Foundation
850 Ridge Lake Blvd., Ste. 1010
Memphis, TN 38120

Established in 1962 in TN.
Donor(s): Harriet Smith Van Vleet.‡
Financial data (yr. ended 12/31/00): Grants paid, $320,274; assets, $12,770,380 (M); expenditures, $459,918; qualifying distributions, $315,296.
Limitations: Applications not accepted. Giving limited to Memphis, TN.
Application information: Contributes only to pre-selected organizations.
Advisors: B. Snowden Boyle, Jr., Thomas C. Farnsworth, Jr., William L. Richmond.
Trustee: National Bank of Commerce.
EIN: 626034067
Codes: FD

49951
Moses and Leba Lebovitz Charitable Trust
c/o Charles Levine
1000 Riverfront Pkwy.
Chattanooga, TN 37402
Application address: 2030 Hamilton Place Blvd., Chattanooga, TN 37421, tel.: (423) 265-8604
Contact: Charles B. Lebovitz, Tr.

Established in 1991 in TN.
Financial data (yr. ended 12/31/01): Grants paid, $318,050; assets, $5,405,637 (M); gifts received, $5,000; expenditures, $339,769; qualifying distributions, $338,205.
Limitations: Giving limited to Chattanooga, TN.
Trustees: Alan Cates, Charles B. Lebovitz, Charles Levine, Faye L. Peterken.
EIN: 626247365
Codes: FD

49952
The Jeniam Foundation
(also known as The Jeniam Clarkson Foundation)
270 Bremington Pl.
Memphis, TN 38111 (901) 454-7080
Contact: Charlotte G. King, Exec. Dir.

Established in 1992 in TN.
Donor(s): Andrew M. Clarkson, Carole G. Clarkson.
Financial data (yr. ended 12/31/00): Grants paid, $305,308; assets, $7,625,278 (M); gifts received, $181,875; expenditures, $431,277; qualifying distributions, $366,782; giving activities include $13,000 for program-related investments.
Limitations: Giving on a national basis for conservation; in New Canaan, CT, for education and aging; and in Memphis, TN, for the arts.
Publications: Informational brochure (including application guidelines).
Application information: Contact Exec. Dir. for application guidelines. Application form not required.
Officer: Charlotte G. King, Exec. Dir.
Trustees: Andrew M. Clarkson, Carole G. Clarkson, Jennifer M. Clarkson.
EIN: 621516244
Codes: FD

49953
Solomon Family Foundation
4333 Chickering Ln.
Nashville, TN 37215

Established in 1997 in TN.
Donor(s): David L. Solomon, Rita B. Solomon.
Financial data (yr. ended 12/31/00): Grants paid, $299,895; assets, $521,924 (M); expenditures, $302,745; qualifying distributions, $300,178.
Limitations: Applications not accepted. Giving primarily in TN.
Application information: Contributes only to pre-selected organizations.
Trustees: David L. Solomon, Rita B. Solomon.
EIN: 436789183
Codes: FD

49954
The Menke Foundation
1103 Kansas St.
Memphis, TN 38101 (901) 774-8860
Contact: Melinda Menke Burns, Tr.

Established in 1986 in TN.
Financial data (yr. ended 12/31/01): Grants paid, $298,710; assets, $4,547,624 (M); expenditures, $300,790; qualifying distributions, $296,828.
Limitations: Giving primarily in Memphis, TN.
Trustees: Melinda Menke Burns, Stella S. Menke.
EIN: 581708804
Codes: FD

49955
The Mick Foundation
9230 Old Smyrna Rd.
Brentwood, TN 37027-6115 (615) 377-2470
Contact: John Mick, V.P.

Established in 1992 in TN.
Donor(s): Roger E. Mick, Barbara D. Mick.
Financial data (yr. ended 12/31/00): Grants paid, $286,200; assets, $6,027,981 (M); expenditures, $355,345; qualifying distributions, $282,802.
Limitations: Giving limited to TN.
Application information: Application form not required.
Officers and Directors:* Roger E. Mick,* Pres.; Jennifer Mick,* V.P.; John R. Mick,* V.P.; Barbara D. Mick,* Secy.
EIN: 621491417
Codes: FD

49956
Raymond Zimmerman Family Foundation
c/o Jack Byrd
111 Westwood Pl., Ste. 400
Brentwood, TN 37027
FAX: (615) 298-2068
Contact: Roger Proctor

Established in 1982.
Donor(s): Raymond Zimmerman.
Financial data (yr. ended 05/31/02): Grants paid, $275,763; assets, $4,609,052 (M); expenditures, $343,549; qualifying distributions, $285,371.
Limitations: Applications not accepted. Giving primarily in FL and TN.
Application information: Contributes only to pre-selected organizations.
Trustees: Robyn Z. Rubinoff, Fred E. Zimmerman, Raymond Zimmerman.
EIN: 626166380
Codes: FD

49957
The Pfeffer Foundation
836 Treemont Ct.
Nashville, TN 37220

Established in 1997 in TN.
Financial data (yr. ended 12/31/01): Grants paid, $273,097; assets, $276,464 (M); gifts received, $248,121; expenditures, $276,971; qualifying distributions, $273,093.
Limitations: Applications not accepted.
Application information: Contributes only to pre-selected organizations.
Trustee: Pamela K. Pfeffer.
Member: Philip M. Pfeffer.
EIN: 621694538
Codes: FD

49958
The Melkus Family Foundation
102 Woodmont Blvd., Ste. 110
Nashville, TN 37205

Established in 1993 in TN.
Donor(s): Melkus Partners, Ltd.
Financial data (yr. ended 12/31/01): Grants paid, $270,050; assets, $10,864,240 (M); expenditures, $306,931; qualifying distributions, $270,445.
Limitations: Applications not accepted. Giving primarily in Nashville, TN.
Application information: Contributes only to pre-selected organizations.
Officers: Kenneth J. Melkus, Pres.; Barbara L. Melkus, Secy.; Lauren E. Melkus, Treas.
EIN: 621518285
Codes: FD

49959
Webster Foundation
c/o SunTrust Banks, Inc., Trust Dept.
P.O. Box 305110
Nashville, TN 37230-5110 (615) 748-4456
Contact: Leonard Wood, Trust Off., SunTrust Banks, Inc., Nashville, N.A.

Established in 1958.
Financial data (yr. ended 12/31/99): Grants paid, $269,358; assets, $614,891 (M); gifts received, $534,324; expenditures, $272,184; qualifying distributions, $269,358.
Limitations: Giving primarily in TN.
Application information: Application form not required.
Trustees: Frances Earthman, Anthony Johnston, SunTrust Banks, Inc.
EIN: 626032866

49960
Thomas M. Garrott Foundation
c/o National Bank of Commerce, Trust Div.
1 Commerce Sq.
Memphis, TN 38150
Application adress: c/o National Bank of Commerce, Trust Div., 850 Ridgelake Blvd., Ste. 101, Memphis, TN 38120, tel.: (901) 415-6410
Contact: Arthur Oliver

Established in 1995 in TN.
Financial data (yr. ended 12/31/00): Grants paid, $267,000; assets, $5,709,656 (M); expenditures, $285,790; qualifying distributions, $265,244.
Limitations: Giving on a national basis.
Application information: Application form not required.
Trustee: National Bank of Commerce.
EIN: 626289645
Codes: FD

49961
E. R. Behrend Trust Fund
6400 Poplar Ave., 4th Fl.
Memphis, TN 38197
Scholarship application address: 438 Pittsburgh Ave., Erie, PA 16505
Contact: Richard A. Reeves, Chair.

Established in 1946.
Financial data (yr. ended 12/31/01): Grants paid, $265,188; assets, $4,326,118 (M); expenditures, $308,727; qualifying distributions, $264,147.
Application information: Scholarships awarded between Feb. and Apr.
Officers and Trustees:* Richard A. Reeves,* Chair.; James S. Stolley,* Vice-Chair. and Secy.; Donald S. Leslie, Jr., Treas.; J.B. Enders, T.C. Guelcher.
EIN: 256037040
Codes: FD, GTI

49962
Massengill-DeFriece Foundation, Inc.
P.O. Box 966
Bristol, TN 37621-0966
FAX: (423) 989-6509
Contact: C. Thomas Davenport, Jr., Pres.

Incorporated in 1949 in TN.
Donor(s): Frank W. DeFriece,‡ Pauline M. DeFriece,‡ Frank W. DeFriece, Jr., Josephine D. Wilson, The S.E. Massengill Co.
Financial data (yr. ended 12/31/01): Grants paid, $262,190; assets, $3,716,652 (M); expenditures, $339,934; qualifying distributions, $282,102.
Limitations: Giving primarily in the tri-city area including Bristol, TN-VA, and Kingsport and Johnson City, TN.
Application information: Application form not required.

Officers and Directors:* C. Thomas Davenport, Jr.,* Pres.; C. Richard Hagerstrom, Jr.,* Secy.-Treas.; Frank W. DeFriece, Jr., Paul E. DeFriece, Stephen Everhart, Ronan King, Polly D. Wills, Josephine D. Wilson.
EIN: 626044873
Codes: FD

49963
Gene & Florence Monday Foundation, Inc.
612 S. Gay St., Ste. 500
Knoxville, TN 37902
Application address: 1618 Hightop Trail, Knoxville, TN 37923
Contact: Wayne Murdock, Pres.

Established in 1994 in TN.
Financial data (yr. ended 12/31/01): Grants paid, $261,100; assets, $5,236,504 (M); gifts received, $35,500; expenditures, $263,419; qualifying distributions, $260,456.
Application information: Application form required.
Officers and Directors:* Wayne Murdock, Pres.; Frank H. Rothermel,* V.P.; Joan Vestal Ellis-Akard, Secy.; Kenneth W. Holbert, Treas.; Veda Bateman, Ron Cunningham, Katie S. Gryder, James S. Monday, Robert W. Monday, William E. Monday III.
EIN: 621518306
Codes: FD

49964
The Daniel Ashley and Irene Houston Jewell Memorial Foundation
c/o Sun Trust Bank, Chattanooga, N.A.
P.O. Box 1638
Chattanooga, TN 37401-1638 (423) 757-3933
Application address: 115 Old Homestead Dr., Chickamauga, GA 30707, tel.: (404) 624-7636
Contact: Barbara Marter, V.P., Sun Trust Bank, Chattanooga, N.A.

Trust established in 1951 in GA.
Donor(s): The Crystal Springs Textiles Corp.
Financial data (yr. ended 06/30/01): Grants paid, $250,000; assets, $5,151,059 (M); expenditures, $293,550; qualifying distributions, $248,927.
Limitations: Giving limited to the Chickamauga, GA, and Chattanooga, TN, metropolitan areas. Scholarships available only to high school seniors attending Gordon Lee High School located in Chickamauga, GA.
Application information: Application form not required.
Officers and Trustees:* E. Dunbar Jewell, Sr.,* Chair.; D. Ashley Jewell V,* Secy.; George M. McMillan, Jr.,* Treas.; Elizabeth J. Berry, Carol J. Browder, Juanita C. Crowder, E. Dunbar Jewell, Jr., Ellen J. Siegfried, James P. Staub, W. Miller Welborn, Michael S. Wright.
EIN: 586034213
Codes: FD, GTI

49965
Williams Family Charitable Foundation
c/o Joseph P. Williams
705 Westview Ave.
Nashville, TN 37205
Contact: Advisory Comm.

Established in 1992 in AL and TN.
Donor(s): Joseph P. Williams.
Financial data (yr. ended 12/31/01): Grants paid, $249,776; assets, $141,559 (M); gifts received, $100,000; expenditures, $252,157; qualifying distributions, $249,689.
Limitations: Applications not accepted.
Application information: Contributes only to pre-selected organizations.

Trustee: Joseph P. Williams.
Director: Mary H. Williams.
EIN: 621495295
Codes: FD

49966
Shayne Foundation
P.O. Box 305112
Nashville, TN 37230-5112

Established in 1993 in TN as partial successor to the Werthan Foundation.
Donor(s): Herbert M. Shayne, May W. Shayne.
Financial data (yr. ended 12/31/00): Grants paid, $247,650; assets, $3,970,698 (M); gifts received, $295,436; expenditures, $278,521; qualifying distributions, $247,692.
Limitations: Applications not accepted. Giving primarily in TN.
Application information: Contributes only to pre-selected organizations.
Trustees: David Shayne, Elizabeth Shayne, Herbert M. Shayne.
EIN: 621540372
Codes: FD

49967
T & T Family Foundation
P.O. Box 101444
Nashville, TN 37224-1444
Contact: Lester L. Turner, Jr., Tr.

Established in 1998 in TN.
Donor(s): Betty M. Turner.‡
Financial data (yr. ended 12/31/01): Grants paid, $246,110; assets, $10,577,561 (M); expenditures, $705,920; qualifying distributions, $246,110.
Limitations: Giving primarily in Nashville, TN; large funding also in Abilene, TX.
Trustees: Curry Turner Thornton, Lester L. Turner, Jr.
EIN: 626324206
Codes: FD2

49968
L. P. Brown Foundation
119 Racine St.
P.O. Box 11514
Memphis, TN 38111-0514
Contact: L.P. Brown III, Pres.

Established in 1956.
Donor(s): L.P. Brown III.
Financial data (yr. ended 12/31/01): Grants paid, $244,130; assets, $4,923,906 (M); gifts received, $100,065; expenditures, $249,357; qualifying distributions, $244,957.
Limitations: Giving primarily in Memphis, TN.
Application information: Application form not required.
Officers: L.P. Brown III, Pres.; Grady Bryan Morgan, V.P.; Stella A. Lowery, Secy.-Treas.
Directors: Hubert A. McBride, Axson Brown Morgan, Darcia Bryan Morgan, Octavia Evans Morgan.
EIN: 626036338
Codes: FD2

49969
The Jennings & Rebecca Jones Foundation, Inc.
2923 Dilton Mankin Rd.
Murfreesboro, TN 37127

Established in 1987.
Donor(s): Jennings A. Jones.
Financial data (yr. ended 12/31/99): Grants paid, $241,650; assets, $6,216,177 (M); gifts received, $135,000; expenditures, $248,264; qualifying distributions, $236,070.
Limitations: Applications not accepted. Giving primarily in Murfreesboro, TN.

Application information: Contributes only to pre-selected organizations.
Officers: Jennings A. Jones, Pres.; Rebecca R. Jones, V.P.; J. Paul Vaughan, Secy.-Treas.
Directors: Barbara Haskew, Lee Moss.
EIN: 581698633
Codes: FD2

49970
The Chazen Family Foundation
P.O. Box 6308
1810 Chestnut St.
Chattanooga, TN 37401-6308

Financial data (yr. ended 11/30/01): Grants paid, $240,424; assets, $1,969,169 (M); expenditures, $247,688; qualifying distributions, $240,138.
Limitations: Applications not accepted. Giving primarily in NC and TN.
Application information: Contributes only to pre-selected organizations.
Directors: Gary D. Chazen, Robert G. Chazen, Ruth E. Chazen.
EIN: 621722318
Codes: FD2

49971
P. K. Seidman Trust
3173 Kirby Whitten Pkwy., Ste. 105
Bartlett, TN 38134
Contact: Marcia R. Brasel, Tr.

Established around 1986.
Donor(s): Thomas Erler Foundation, Seidman Foundation.
Financial data (yr. ended 12/31/01): Grants paid, $234,327; assets, $3,884,084 (M); expenditures, $300,790; qualifying distributions, $257,223.
Limitations: Giving primarily in TN.
Trustees: Marcia R. Brasel, Lori Condo.
EIN: 626034052
Codes: FD2

49972
Lichterman-Loewenberg Foundation
P.O. Box 6
Memphis, TN 38101
Contact: Fredrika Felt, Pres.

Established in 1945.
Donor(s): Southern Leather Co., and members of the Lichterman and Loewenberg families.
Financial data (yr. ended 12/31/01): Grants paid, $231,576; assets, $4,143,934 (M); gifts received, $142,185; expenditures, $244,737; qualifying distributions, $231,637.
Limitations: Giving primarily in Memphis, TN.
Application information: Application form not required.
Officers: Fredrika Felt, Pres.; William Ira Loewenberg, Secy.; Barry Lichterman, Treas.
EIN: 626048265
Codes: FD2

49973
Andrew Woodfin Miller Foundation
3102 West End Ave., Ste. 650
Nashville, TN 37203

Established in 1989 in TN.
Donor(s): Andrew W. Miller.
Financial data (yr. ended 06/30/01): Grants paid, $224,848; assets, $3,838,055 (M); expenditures, $248,947; qualifying distributions, $244,322.
Limitations: Applications not accepted. Giving primarily in TN.
Application information: Contributes only to pre-selected organizations.
Officers: Andrew W. Miller, Pres.; R.C. Combs, Secy.; D.E. Nauss, Treas.
EIN: 621412881

49973—TENNESSEE

Codes: FD2

49974
Kennedy Foundation, Inc.
P.O. Box 1607
Chattanooga, TN 37401 (423) 756-5537
Contact: James D. Kennedy, Jr., Pres.

Established in 1986 in TN.
Donor(s): James D. Kennedy, Jr.
Financial data (yr. ended 12/31/01): Grants paid, $223,775; assets, $4,779,244 (M); expenditures, $225,812; qualifying distributions, $221,449.
Limitations: Giving primarily in Chattanooga, TN.
Application information: Application form not required.
Officers and Directors:* James D. Kennedy, Jr.,* Pres.; James D. Kennedy III,* Secy.; Jane Green, Molly Kennedy, Elizabeth Spratlin.
EIN: 621296643
Codes: FD2

49975
The Joyce Family Foundation
c/o SunTrust Banks, Inc., Trust Tax Dept.
P.O. Box 305110
Nashville, TN 37230-5110 (615) 748-4725
Contact: Elizabeth Mayhall, Trust Off., SunTrust Banks, Inc.

Established in 1990 in TN.
Donor(s): Kathryn Craig Henry.
Financial data (yr. ended 12/31/99): Grants paid, $223,300; assets, $2,171,848 (M); gifts received, $334,565; expenditures, $254,727; qualifying distributions, $230,036.
Limitations: Giving primarily in AL, SC, and TN.
Application information: Application form not required.
Officer: Margaret Henry Wood, Chair.
Directors: Benjamin F. Byrd, Jr., Douglas Henry, Richard D. Holton, Alexis Jones Joyce.
Trustee: SunTrust Banks, Inc.
EIN: 626225946
Codes: FD2

49976
Irvin and Beverly Small Foundation
c/o Irvin Small
333 Vaughn Rd.
Nashville, TN 37221

Established in 1995 in TN.
Financial data (yr. ended 12/31/01): Grants paid, $223,295; assets, $1,270,198 (M); gifts received, $137,751; expenditures, $244,612; qualifying distributions, $223,161.
Limitations: Applications not accepted.
Application information: Contributes only to pre-selected organizations.
Officers: Irvin Small, Pres.; Beverly Small, Secy.-Treas.
Directors: Linda S. Gluck, Douglas Small.
EIN: 621639814
Codes: FD2

49977
The Cartinhour-Woods Foundation, Inc.
305 Claras Point Rd.
Sewanee, TN 37375-2033 (931) 598-5877
Contact: Marie C. Woods, Pres.

Established in 1961 in DE; reincorporated in 1993 in TN.
Donor(s): W.C. Cartinhour, Sr.‡
Financial data (yr. ended 06/30/01): Grants paid, $218,500; assets, $6,659,039 (M); expenditures, $299,759; qualifying distributions, $230,148.
Limitations: Giving primarily in TN.
Application information: Application form required.
Officers and Trustees:* Marie Cartinhour Woods,* Pres. and Treas.; Kathleen M. Woods,* V.P.; Ellen Woods Polansky,* Secy.; Caroline T. Woods, Margaret C. Woods.
EIN: 621504440
Codes: FD2

49978
Blair J. Wilson Charitable Trust
(Formerly Sunnyside Foundation)
28 White Bridge Rd., Ste. 210
Nashville, TN 37205
Contact: Blair J. Wilson, Mgr.

Established in 1992 in TN.
Donor(s): Blair J. Wilson, Linde B. Wilson.
Financial data (yr. ended 12/31/01): Grants paid, $217,800; assets, $5,517,091 (M); gifts received, $444,947; expenditures, $220,783; qualifying distributions, $216,126.
Officer and Trustee:* Blair J. Wilson,* Mgr.
EIN: 621498117
Codes: FD2

49979
The Jeffrey and Donna Eskind Family Foundation
416 Ellendale
Nashville, TN 37205-3402

Established in 1986 in TN.
Donor(s): Jeffrey Eskind, Donna Eskind.
Financial data (yr. ended 06/30/01): Grants paid, $211,666; assets, $1,404,074 (M); gifts received, $403,239; expenditures, $213,207; qualifying distributions, $212,974.
Limitations: Applications not accepted. Giving primarily in Nashville, TN.
Application information: Contributes only to pre-selected organizations.
Officers: Jeffrey Eskind, Pres.; Donna Eskind, Secy.
EIN: 621306904
Codes: FD2

49980
Stephens Christian Trust
(Formerly Stephens Foundation Trust)
Rte. 5, Pasquo Rd.
Nashville, TN 37221

Established in 1987 in TN.
Donor(s): Juanita W. Stephens,‡ W.E. Stephens, Jr., Billy C. Pentecost, Helen Richardson.
Financial data (yr. ended 07/31/01): Grants paid, $208,701; assets, $3,976,739 (M); gifts received, $12,000; expenditures, $246,668; qualifying distributions, $223,036.
Limitations: Applications not accepted. Giving primarily in TN.
Application information: Contributes only to pre-selected organizations.
Trustees: J. Greg Hardeman, Walter C. Leaver III, Keith Nikolaus, Neika Stephens, W.E. Stephens, Jr., James Vandiver.
EIN: 626201842
Codes: FD2

49981
Speer Charitable Trust
5856 Garden Oak Cove
Memphis, TN 38120

Established in 1987 in TN.
Donor(s): R. Wayne Speer.
Financial data (yr. ended 11/30/01): Grants paid, $205,100; assets, $3,178,510 (M); expenditures, $215,859; qualifying distributions, $202,773.
Limitations: Applications not accepted. Giving primarily in Memphis, TN.
Application information: Contributes only to pre-selected organizations.
Officers and Directors:* R. Wayne Speer,* Pres.; Deborah S. Hopkins, Secy.-Treas.; Herschel L. Feibleman, Cheryl S. Robert.
EIN: 621338941
Codes: FD2

49982
The Ware Family Foundation
5250 Virginia Way
P.O. Box 1869
Brentwood, TN 37024-1869

Established in 2001 in TN.
Donor(s): Scot Ware, Sharon Ware.
Financial data (yr. ended 12/31/01): Grants paid, $200,000; assets, $2,241,279 (M); gifts received, $2,443,973; expenditures, $204,395; qualifying distributions, $203,893.
Limitations: Applications not accepted. Giving primarily in WV.
Application information: Contributes only to pre-selected organizations.
Trustees: Scot Ware, Sharon Ware.
EIN: 621868116

49983
Idalia Roth Charitable Trust
c/o National Bank of Commerce, Trust Div.
1 Commerce Sq.
Memphis, TN 38150
Contact: Sheri Nakhleh, V.P. and Tr. Off., National Bank of Commerce

Established in 1994 in TN.
Financial data (yr. ended 12/31/00): Grants paid, $198,700; assets, $3,922,293 (M); expenditures, $228,837; qualifying distributions, $198,700.
Limitations: Applications not accepted. Giving primarily in Memphis, TN.
Application information: Contributes only to pre-selected organizations.
Trustee: National Bank of Commerce.
EIN: 626285270
Codes: FD2

49984
Sam S. and Rose L. Margolin Charitable Trust
800 Monroe Ave., Ste. 700
Memphis, TN 38103 (901) 685-5799
Application address: 550 S. Yates, Memphis, TN 38120
Contact: Gerry M. Fink, Tr.

Established in 1994.
Financial data (yr. ended 12/31/01): Grants paid, $198,075; assets, $877,949 (M); gifts received, $135,000; expenditures, $199,137; qualifying distributions, $382,150.
Limitations: Giving primarily in Nashville, TN.
Trustees: Gerry M. Fink, David Katz, Sylvia Weissman.
EIN: 626289044
Codes: FD2

49985
C. A. Craig II Family Foundation
1800 Chickering Rd.
Nashville, TN 37215 (615) 661-0748

Established in 1993 in IN.
Donor(s): C.A. Craig II.
Financial data (yr. ended 11/30/01): Grants paid, $196,195; assets, $4,542,219 (M); expenditures, $200,289; qualifying distributions, $193,333.
Limitations: Applications not accepted. Giving primarily in TN.
Application information: Contributes only to pre-selected organizations.
Officers: C.A. Craig II, Chair.; Michel G. Kaplan, Secy.

Trustees: Deborah Ann Craig, Elizabeth Weaver Lane.
EIN: 621550883
Codes: FD2

49986
James Stephen Turner Charitable Foundation
138 2nd Ave. N., Ste. 500
Nashville, TN 37201

Established in 1997 in TN.
Donor(s): James Stephen Turner.
Financial data (yr. ended 12/31/01): Grants paid, $195,500; assets, $1,101,001 (M); gifts received, $104,000; expenditures, $197,807; qualifying distributions, $197,668.
Limitations: Applications not accepted. Giving primarily in TN.
Application information: Contributes only to pre-selected organizations.
Trustees: James Stephen Turner, Sr., James Stephen Turner, Jr., Judith Payne Turner, Laura Turner.
EIN: 621689256
Codes: FD2

49987
The Caudle Rymer Foundation, Inc.
c/o S.B. Rymer, Jr.
28 Stonedge, 100 Scenic Hwy.
Lookout Mountain, TN 37350

Established in 1983.
Donor(s): S.B. Rymer, Jr.
Financial data (yr. ended 12/31/01): Grants paid, $190,000; assets, $3,388,641 (M); gifts received, $157,500; expenditures, $191,695; qualifying distributions, $190,848.
Limitations: Applications not accepted. Giving primarily in Chattanooga, TN.
Application information: Contributes only to pre-selected organizations.
Officers and Directors:* S.B. Rymer, Jr.,* Pres. and Treas.; Anne Caudle Rymer,* V.P. and Secy.; B. Harvey Hill, Jr., Forrester W. Rogers, S. Bradford Rymer III, Elise R. Turner.
EIN: 581514882
Codes: FD2

49988
The Brinkley Foundation
c/o National Bank of Commerce, Trust Div.
1 Commerce Sq.
Memphis, TN 38150 (901) 415-6412
Contact: Virginia Thornton, Trust Off., National Bank of Commerce

Established in 1968 in TN.
Donor(s): Hugh M. Brinkley.‡
Financial data (yr. ended 12/31/00): Grants paid, $183,000; assets, $3,746,962 (M); expenditures, $175,774; qualifying distributions, $182,185.
Limitations: Giving primarily in the Memphis, TN, area.
Application information: Application form not required.
Trustee: National Bank of Commerce.
EIN: 626079631
Codes: FD2

49989
John A. Jordan, Jr. Charitable Trust
c/o SunTrust Banks, Inc., Nashville, Trust Tax Dept.
P.O. Box 305110
Nashville, TN 37230-5110

Established in 1994 in TN.
Financial data (yr. ended 03/31/01): Grants paid, $182,707; assets, $2,821,361 (M); expenditures, $209,102; qualifying distributions, $193,398.
Limitations: Applications not accepted. Giving primarily in TN.
Application information: Contributes only to pre-selected organizations.
Trustee: SunTrust Banks, Inc.
EIN: 582177091
Codes: FD2

49990
The Ronald H. Cordover Family Foundation
2008 Breakers Pt.
Knoxville, TN 37922

Established in 1990 in TN.
Donor(s): Ronald H. Cordover, The Berkline Corp.
Financial data (yr. ended 12/31/01): Grants paid, $182,346; assets, $3,558,086 (M); expenditures, $188,540; qualifying distributions, $185,526.
Limitations: Applications not accepted. Giving on a national basis, with emphasis on NJ and NY.
Application information: Contributes only to pre-selected organizations.
Trustee: Ronald H. Cordover.
EIN: 226498278
Codes: CS, FD2, CD

49991
Douglas and Robbie Odom Foundation, Inc.
(Formerly Douglas G. Odom Foundation)
1201 Neelys Bend Rd.
Madison, TN 37115-5446

Established in 1985 in TN.
Donor(s): Douglas G. Odom, Jr.
Financial data (yr. ended 12/31/01): Grants paid, $181,878; assets, $794,269 (M); expenditures, $187,474; qualifying distributions, $183,007.
Limitations: Applications not accepted. Giving primarily in TN.
Application information: Contributes only to pre-selected organizations.
Directors: Douglas G. Odom, Jr., Larry Douglas Odom, Robbie Hawkins Odom.
EIN: 581660437
Codes: FD2

49992
The Houghland Foundation
P.O. Box 198062
Nashville, TN 37219

Established in 1986 in TN.
Donor(s): Calvin Houghland.
Financial data (yr. ended 06/30/01): Grants paid, $180,800; assets, $3,427,087 (M); expenditures, $187,016; qualifying distributions, $179,333.
Limitations: Giving primarily in Nashville, TN.
Officers and Trustees:* George R. Ragsdale,* Co-Pres.; James W. Webb, Jr.,* Co-Pres.; Davis H. Carr,* Secy.
Committee Member: Calvin Houghland.
EIN: 626199041
Codes: FD2

49993
James H. Prentiss Foundation
5118 Park Ave., Ste. 208
Memphis, TN 38117-5722 (901) 766-1861
Contact: James H. Prentiss, Dir.

Established in 1985 in TN.
Donor(s): James H. Prentiss.
Financial data (yr. ended 12/31/01): Grants paid, $178,808; assets, $203,753 (M); gifts received, $17,406; expenditures, $183,462; qualifying distributions, $180,472.
Limitations: Giving primarily in TN.
Application information: Application form not required.
Officers and Directors:* Raymond M. Shainberg,* Pres.; Carol Wandling,* Secy.-Treas.; Carol Prentiss, James H. Prentiss, James H. Prentiss, Jr.
EIN: 621237684
Codes: FD2

49994
Citizens Bank Tri-Cities Foundation, Ltd.
(Formerly Joe LaPorte, Jr. Foundation, Ltd.)
1 Citizens Plz., Broad St., Ste. 301
Elizabethton, TN 37643 (423) 543-1851
Contact: Sam J. LaPorte, Dir.

Established in 1990 in TN.
Donor(s): Joseph LaPorte, Sam LaPorte, Citizens Bank, GSC, Inc.
Financial data (yr. ended 12/31/00): Grants paid, $177,038; assets, $98,640 (M); gifts received, $170,727; expenditures, $177,847; qualifying distributions, $176,607.
Limitations: Giving limited to the greater Elizabethton, TN, area.
Directors: Christopher LaPorte, Joseph LaPorte III, Sam LaPorte, Stephen LaPorte.
EIN: 581914223
Codes: FD2

49995
Donald J. and Katherine T. Israel Foundation
P.O. Box 2285
Brentwood, TN 37024-2285

Established in 1995 in TN.
Donor(s): Donald J. Israel, Katherine T. Israel.
Financial data (yr. ended 12/31/00): Grants paid, $177,000; assets, $1,748,177 (M); expenditures, $193,669; qualifying distributions, $175,669.
Limitations: Applications not accepted. Giving primarily in St. Louis, MO and Nashville, TN.
Application information: Contributes only to pre-selected organizations.
Officer and Directors:* Donald J. Israel,* Pres.; Charles A. Israel, John K. Israel, Katherine T. Israel.
EIN: 621578562
Codes: FD2

49996
Gordon Street Foundation
1418 Winding Way
Chattanooga, TN 37405

Established in 1957.
Financial data (yr. ended 11/30/01): Grants paid, $175,000; assets, $5,832,832 (M); expenditures, $322,831; qualifying distributions, $282,279.
Limitations: Giving primarily in Chattanooga, TN.
Officers and Trustees:* Gordon P. Street, Jr.,* Pres.; Ruth L. Street,* V.P.; John P. Gaither,* Secy.; Frances Street Smith,* Treas.
EIN: 620634450
Codes: FD2

49997
Robin & Peter Formanek Charitable Trust
530 Oak Court Dr.
Memphis, TN 38117-3724
Contact: Peter R. Formanek, Tr.

Established in 1986 in TN.
Donor(s): Peter R. Formanek.
Financial data (yr. ended 12/31/00): Grants paid, $171,235; assets, $4,492,567 (M); expenditures, $226,697; qualifying distributions, $159,787.
Limitations: Giving primarily in Memphis, TN.
Trustees: Jonathan P. Formanek, Peter R. Formanek, Robin K. Formanek.
EIN: 586203536
Codes: FD2

49998
William P. and Marie R. Lowenstein Foundation
100 N. Main St., Bldg. 3020
Memphis, TN 38103 (901) 525-5744
Contact: Alvin A. Gordon, Dir.

Incorporated about 1959 in TN.
Donor(s): Marie R. Lowenstein.‡
Financial data (yr. ended 12/31/01): Grants paid, $166,040; assets, $2,750,887 (M); expenditures, $235,680; qualifying distributions, $352,139.
Limitations: Giving primarily in New York, NY.
Application information: Application form available upon request. Application form required.
Directors: Alvin A. Gordon, Elaine K. Gordon, Marshall D. Gordon, Robert Gordon, Ed Marlowe.
EIN: 626037976
Codes: FD2

49999
Alvin and Sally Beaman Foundation
105 Westpark Dr., Ste. 400
Brentwood, TN 37027
FAX: (615) 376-3016
Contact: Larry T. Thrailkill, Secy.

Established in 1998 in TN.
Donor(s): Sally M. Beaman.
Financial data (yr. ended 12/31/01): Grants paid, $165,000; assets, $3,444,868 (M); expenditures, $198,284; qualifying distributions, $163,346.
Limitations: Applications not accepted.
Application information: Contributes only to pre-selected organizations.
Officers and Trustees:* Sally M. Beaman,* Pres.; Larry T. Thrailkill,* Secy.; Lee A. Beaman,* Treas.
EIN: 621743008
Codes: FD2

50000
Clifton and Clara Ward Foundation
7 N. Lynncrest Dr.
Chattanooga, TN 37411-1820
Application address: 1000 Tallan Bldg., 2 Union Sq., Chattanooga, TN 37402-2500, tel.: (423) 756-3000
Contact: Glenn C. Stophel, Secy.-Treas.

Established in 1990 in TN.
Financial data (yr. ended 09/30/01): Grants paid, $165,000; assets, $1,941,816 (M); expenditures, $186,109; qualifying distributions, $165,935.
Limitations: Giving primarily in TN.
Officers and Trustees:* Clara T. Ward,* Pres.; Glenn C. Stophel,* Secy.-Treas.; J. Ralph McIntyre, Betty T. Potter, Ray Thompson, Carl K. Ward.
EIN: 581917676
Codes: FD2

50001
Scheidt Family Foundation, Inc.
54 S. White Station Rd.
Memphis, TN 38117
Contact: Helen H. Scheidt, Pres.

Established in 1976 in TN.
Donor(s): Rudi E. Scheidt, Helen H. Scheidt.
Financial data (yr. ended 10/31/01): Grants paid, $164,290; assets, $5,622,735 (M); gifts received, $1,006,937; expenditures, $212,810; qualifying distributions, $164,290.
Limitations: Giving primarily in NY and Memphis, TN.
Officers: Helen H. Scheidt, Pres.; Susan Scheidt Arney, V.P.; Helen Scheidt Gronauer, V.P.; E. Elkan Scheidt, V.P.; Rudi E. Scheidt, Jr., V.P.; Rudi E. Scheidt, Secy.
EIN: 620989531
Codes: FD2

50002
Kathryn Ellis Foundation
1308 Highcrest Dr.
Hixson, TN 37343 (423) 870-1163
Contact: Judy Christian, Secy.

Established in 1991 in IL.
Donor(s): William H. Ellis.
Financial data (yr. ended 12/31/99): Grants paid, $162,474; assets, $14,251 (M); gifts received, $400,512; expenditures, $378,137; qualifying distributions, $329,267.
Limitations: Giving on a national basis.
Application information: Application form not required.
Officers: William H. Ellis, Pres.; Judy Christian, Secy.
Director: Harris P. Byrd.
EIN: 363741896
Codes: FD2

50003
Malcolm Fraser Foundation
3100 Walnut Grove, Ste. 603
Memphis, TN 38111
FAX: (912) 638-1740
Contact: Jane H. Fraser, Pres.

Established in 1992 in TN.
Donor(s): Malcolm Fraser.‡
Financial data (yr. ended 05/31/01): Grants paid, $160,452; assets, $2,770,901 (M); expenditures, $168,356; qualifying distributions, $167,259.
Limitations: Applications not accepted. Giving on a national basis.
Application information: Unsolicited requests for funds not accepted.
Officers and Directors:* Jane Hough Fraser,* Pres.; Joe R.G. Fulcher, V.P. and Treas.; Celia Fraser Gruss,* V.P.; Jean Fraser Gruss,* Secy.
EIN: 582026294
Codes: FD2

50004
Charles H. Boyle Foundation, Inc.
P.O. Box 17800
Memphis, TN 38119-3900

Established in 1972.
Donor(s): J. Bayard Boyle, Jr., Elizabeth R. Boyle, Snowden B. Morgan, Boyle Investment Co.
Financial data (yr. ended 12/31/01): Grants paid, $160,100; assets, $1,323,403 (M); gifts received, $58,415; expenditures, $160,822; qualifying distributions, $160,100.
Limitations: Applications not accepted. Giving primarily in Memphis, TN.
Application information: Contributes only to pre-selected organizations.
Officers and Directors:* J. Bayard Boyle, Jr.,* Pres.; Henry W. Morgan,* V.P.; J. Roy Taylor, Secy.-Treas.; Snowden B. Morgan.
EIN: 237256010
Codes: FD2

50005
Grandview Foundation, Inc.
601 Grandview Ave.
Lookout Mountain, TN 37350-1225
FAX: (423) 821-0769
Contact: Carter Paden, Dir.

Established in 1991 in GA.
Donor(s): Carter N. Paden, Jr., Janet C. Paden.
Financial data (yr. ended 11/30/00): Grants paid, $159,508; assets, $821,357 (M); gifts received, $154,882; expenditures, $163,235; qualifying distributions, $162,863.
Limitations: Applications not accepted. Giving primarily in TN.
Application information: Contributes only to pre-selected organizations.
Officers and Directors:* Carter N. Paden, Jr.,* Pres. and Treas.; Janet C. Paden,* Secy.; Dean P. Gill, Carter N. Paden III, R.M. Paden, Thomas C. Paden.
EIN: 582004351
Codes: FD2

50006
The Sunrise Foundation
P.O. Box 5462
Knoxville, TN 37928-5462
URL: http://www.korrnet.org/sunrise
Contact: Becky K. Johnston, Exec. Dir.

Established in 1998.
Donor(s): Carol Ann Campbell Bolton.
Financial data (yr. ended 12/31/01): Grants paid, $157,535; assets, $2,126,445 (M); expenditures, $264,337; qualifying distributions, $157,535.
Limitations: Applications not accepted. Giving limited to Knox County and the eastern TN area.
Publications: Annual report.
Application information: Unsolicited requests for funds not accepted.
Officers: Carol Ann Campbell Bolton, Pres.; Rebecca K. Johnston, Secy. and Dir., Prog. Svcs.
Directors: Anne M. McKinney, Thomas H. Schumpert.
EIN: 621749028
Codes: FD2

50007
M. Stratton Foster Charitable Foundation
315 Deaderick St., 4th Fl.
Nashville, TN 37237-0401
Contact: Robert Newman

Established in 1986 in TN.
Donor(s): M. Stratton Foster.‡
Financial data (yr. ended 04/30/01): Grants paid, $156,000; assets, $5,244,771 (M); expenditures, $186,506; qualifying distributions, $169,523.
Limitations: Giving primarily in Nashville, TN and surrounding area.
Publications: Informational brochure, application guidelines.
Application information: Funds are virtually fully committed. Application form required.
Trustees: Bob L. Andrews, W. Lipscomb Davis, Jr., Joe Thompson, Jr.
EIN: 626195713
Codes: FD2

50008
Toby S. Wilt Family Foundation
315 Deaderick St., 4th Fl.
Nashville, TN 37237-0401 (615) 736-6679
Contact: Joseph Chickey

Established in 1987 in TN.
Donor(s): Toby S. Wilt.
Financial data (yr. ended 12/31/01): Grants paid, $153,460; assets, $3,043,446 (M); gifts received, $112,200; expenditures, $178,287; qualifying distributions, $154,998.
Limitations: Giving primarily in Nashville, TN; some giving in CA.
Committee Member: Toby S. Wilt.
Trustee: AmSouth Bank.
EIN: 626195897
Codes: FD2

50009
Sells Foundation, Inc.
P.O. Box 480
Johnson City, TN 37605
Scholarship application address: 410 S. Roan St., Johnson City, TN 37601, tel.: (423) 928-7591
Contact: Sam R. Sells, Pres.

Established in 1973 in TN.
Donor(s): Sam R. Sells, Frances Grimes.
Financial data (yr. ended 10/31/01): Grants paid, $153,302; assets, $2,792,177 (M); gifts received, $99,821; expenditures, $157,088; qualifying distributions, $151,241.
Application information: Potential applicants are contacted by the foundation and furnished with forms to complete. Application form required.
Officers and Directors:* Sam R. Sells,* Pres. and Treas.; Ellen W. Sells,* V.P.; Frances Grimes,* Secy.; Harry H. Jones, Jr., Ben W. Konopa, Jr., Ben F. Lyle.
EIN: 237322421
Codes: FD2, GTI

50010
The Drake Foundation
8275 Tournament Dr.
Memphis, TN 38125
Contact: Michael L. Drake, Pres.

Established in 1997 in TN.
Donor(s): Hendrick Manufacturing Co.
Financial data (yr. ended 12/31/01): Grants paid, $152,600; assets, $39,819 (M); gifts received, $162,774; expenditures, $153,331; qualifying distributions, $152,588.
Limitations: Giving primarily in PA and TN.
Officers and Directors:* Michael L. Drake,* Pres.; Pansy L. Drake,* Secy.
EIN: 621684643
Codes: CS, FD2, CD

50011
Charles and Lillian Tibbals Foundation
P.O. Box 8
Huntsville, TN 37756

Established in 2000 in TN.
Financial data (yr. ended 12/31/01): Grants paid, $152,000; assets, $2,708,284 (M); expenditures, $193,337; qualifying distributions, $152,000.
Limitations: Applications not accepted.
Application information: Contributes only to pre-selected organizations.
Officers and Directors:* Howard Tibbals,* Pres.; Don C. Stansberry, Jr.,* Secy.; Don Billingsley, Angelina Bridges, Bruce Coffey, M.D., Guy Shields, Tracey Stansberry, Michael G. Swain.
EIN: 581902588

50012
The Sandra and Bill Johnson Scholarship Fund, Inc.
c/o John T. Bobo
P.O. Box 169
Shelbyville, TN 37162 (931) 684-4611
Contact: Kathy Anderson

Established in 1996 in TN.
Donor(s): William B. Johnson.
Financial data (yr. ended 12/31/01): Grants paid, $151,128; assets, $52,748 (M); gifts received, $105,000; expenditures, $160,596; qualifying distributions, $159,912.
Application information: Application form required.
Officers: John T. Bobo, Pres.; David L. Howard, Secy.-Treas.
Directors: Sandra Johnson, William B. Johnson, R. Randall Rollins, Rev. Charles A. Stanley, Ron Thomas.

EIN: 621622697
Codes: FD2, GTI

50013
Robin & Bill King Family Foundation
3946 Woodlawn Ave.
Nashville, TN 37205

Established in 1997 in TN.
Donor(s): William B. King, Jr.
Financial data (yr. ended 12/31/01): Grants paid, $150,000; assets, $1,220,840 (M); expenditures, $160,582; qualifying distributions, $160,582.
Limitations: Applications not accepted. Giving primarily in TN.
Application information: Contributes only to pre-selected organizations.
Trustee: William B. King, Jr.
EIN: 626328848
Codes: FD2

50014
Agape Love Foundation, Inc.
650 25th St. N.W., Ste. 100
Cleveland, TN 37311 (423) 476-9160
Contact: Kenneth D. Higgins, Mgr.

Established in 1997 in TN.
Financial data (yr. ended 12/31/00): Grants paid, $148,623; assets, $9,005 (M); gifts received, $149,842; expenditures, $151,965; qualifying distributions, $151,965.
Officers: Kenneth D. Higgins, Chief Mgr.; Elizabeth Higgins, Secy.
Board Members: Ronald Hines, Joe Rodgers.
EIN: 621731414
Codes: FD2

50015
The Nehemiah Foundation, Inc.
4564 Peytonsville Rd.
Franklin, TN 37064-7611 (615) 794-7029
Contact: Thomas W. Singleton, Pres.

Established in 1987 in TN.
Financial data (yr. ended 12/31/01): Grants paid, $148,121; assets, $157,830 (M); gifts received, $119,000; expenditures, $148,980; qualifying distributions, $148,070.
Limitations: Applications not accepted. Giving primarily in TN.
Application information: Contributes only to pre-selected organizations.
Officer: Thomas W. Singleton, Pres.
Director: Silvia A. Singleton.
EIN: 621281778
Codes: FD2

50016
Wood Family Foundation, Inc.
c/o 1600 Riverview Tower
900 S. Gay St.
Knoxville, TN 37902

Established in 1994 in TN.
Donor(s): H. Pat Wood, Sr.
Financial data (yr. ended 11/30/01): Grants paid, $146,875; assets, $904,917 (L); expenditures, $148,307; qualifying distributions, $146,875.
Limitations: Applications not accepted. Giving primarily in TN.
Application information: Contributes only to pre-selected organizations.
Officers and Directors:* H. Pat Wood, Sr.,* Pres.; Phillip O. Lawson,* V.P.; Timothy D. Ellis,* Secy.
EIN: 621586595
Codes: FD2

50017
Wayne and Ida Bowman Foundation
1000 Tallan Bldg., 2 Union Sq.
Chattanooga, TN 37402-2500
Application address: 7 W. Lake Dr., St. Simon's Island, GA 31522, tel.: (912) 638-8670
Contact: Donald W. Bowman, Pres.

Established in 1995 in TN.
Financial data (yr. ended 09/30/01): Grants paid, $146,518; assets, $902,827 (M); expenditures, $155,405; qualifying distributions, $152,129.
Limitations: Giving primarily in KY and TN.
Application information: Telephone or write for application instructions.
Officers and Directors:* Donald W. Bowman,* Pres.; Mayre J. Bowman,* V.P.; William H. Bowman, Secy.; David S. Bowman.
EIN: 621600157
Codes: FD2

50018
The Eleanor T. Reynolds Foundation
P.O. Box 156
Bristol, TN 37621-0156
Contact: David S. Haynes, Tr.

Established in 1988 in TN.
Donor(s): Eleanor T. Reynolds.‡
Financial data (yr. ended 12/31/01): Grants paid, $146,100; assets, $1,754,726 (M); expenditures, $181,171; qualifying distributions, $180,587.
Limitations: Applications not accepted.
Application information: Contributes only to pre-selected organizations.
Trustees: Alethia P. Haynes, David Bruce Haynes, David S. Haynes.
EIN: 621342279
Codes: FD2

50019
Reginald Wurzburg Foundation
c/o National Bank of Commerce, Trust Dept.
1 Commerce Sq.
Memphis, TN 38150
Application address: 710 S. 4th St., P.O. Box 710, Memphis, TN 38101-0710
Contact: Minda Wurzburg

Established in 1964 in TN.
Donor(s): Wurzburg Brothers, Inc.
Financial data (yr. ended 12/31/00): Grants paid, $145,750; assets, $2,457,935 (M); gifts received, $37,500; expenditures, $166,704; qualifying distributions, $145,084.
Limitations: Giving primarily in the Memphis, TN, area.
Trustee: National Bank of Commerce.
EIN: 626048546
Codes: FD2

50020
Ayers Foundation
68 W. Main St., 2nd Fl.
Parsons, TN 38363

Established in 1999 in TN.
Donor(s): James W. Ayers, Nancy Sharon Ayers.
Financial data (yr. ended 12/31/01): Grants paid, $141,347; assets, $29,654 (M); gifts received, $231,000; expenditures, $216,903; qualifying distributions, $141,347.
Limitations: Applications not accepted. Giving primarily in TN.
Application information: Contributes only to pre-selected organizations.
Officers: James W. Ayers, Chair.; Bernard Clipper, Jr., Pres.; Clay Petrey, Secy.
Director: Nancy Sharon Ayers.
EIN: 621773033

50021
The Tully-Graves Foundation
4928 William Arnold Rd.
Memphis, TN 38117-4238

Established in 1999 in TN.
Financial data (yr. ended 12/31/00): Grants paid, $137,583; assets, $1,062,390 (M); expenditures, $193,476; qualifying distributions, $173,229.
Limitations: Applications not accepted. Giving primarily in TN.
Application information: Contributes only to pre-selected organizations.
Trustee: Parnell S. Lewis, Jr.
EIN: 626356784
Codes: FD2

50022
B & R Charitable Foundation, Inc.
88 Valley Forge
Nashville, TN 37205 (615) 256-4336
Contact: David D. Dortch, Tr.

Established in 1997 in TN.
Donor(s): David D. Dortch.
Financial data (yr. ended 12/31/01): Grants paid, $137,540; assets, $519,862 (M); expenditures, $140,634; qualifying distributions, $137,228.
Application information: Application form not required.
Trustees: David D. Dortch, Beth Franklin.
EIN: 621664477
Codes: FD2

50023
R. Brad Martin Family Foundation
(Formerly R. Brad & Jean L. Martin Family Foundation)
1025 Cherry Rd.
Memphis, TN 38117

Established in 1994 in TN.
Donor(s): R. Brad Martin.
Financial data (yr. ended 09/30/01): Grants paid, $136,566; assets, $263,990 (M); gifts received, $113,209; expenditures, $140,997; qualifying distributions, $137,423.
Limitations: Applications not accepted.
Application information: Contributes only to pre-selected organizations.
Officers and Directors:* R. Brad Martin,* Pres.; Eric Steven Faires,* V.P. and Secy.; Scott Imorde,* V.P.; C.T. Courtenay,* Treas.; Daniel H.L. Martin.
EIN: 621548977
Codes: FD2

50024
Jack LaMar Family Charitable Foundation
6442 Harrison Pike
Chattanooga, TN 37416-1413
Contact: Jack LaMar, Tr.

Established in 1996 in TN.
Donor(s): Jack LaMar.
Financial data (yr. ended 12/31/01): Grants paid, $136,500; assets, $719,908 (M); gifts received, $15,301; expenditures, $141,521; qualifying distributions, $138,352.
Limitations: Applications not accepted. Giving primarily in TN.
Application information: Contributes only to pre-selected organizations.
Trustee: Jack LaMar.
EIN: 621665660
Codes: FD2

50025
Greater Nashville Regional Community Foundation
211 Commerce St., Ste. 100
Nashville, TN 37201

Financial data (yr. ended 06/30/00): Grants paid, $136,320; assets, $432,561; gifts received, $302,832; expenditures, $367,900; giving activities include $361,900 for programs.
Limitations: Giving primarily in Nashville, TN.
Officers and Directors: Marty Dickens,* Chair.; Cal Turner, Jr.,* Vice-Chair.; Michael W. Rollins,* Pres.; Doyle R. Rippee, Secy.; Jeffrey G. Mefford,* Treas.; Gordon E. Nichols,* Counsel; Thomas F. First, Jr.
EIN: 621413808
Codes: CM, FD2

50026
The Zimmerman Foundation
c/o Byrd, Proctor & Mills, PC
111 Westwood Pl., Ste. 400
Brentwood, TN 37027
Contact: Roger Proctor

Established in 1979.
Donor(s): Jack Byrd Trust, Mary K. Zimmerman.‡
Financial data (yr. ended 11/30/01): Grants paid, $136,000; assets, $1,794,828 (M); expenditures, $183,126; qualifying distributions, $145,727.
Limitations: Applications not accepted. Giving primarily in Atlanta, GA.
Application information: Contributes only to pre-selected organizations.
Officers and Directors:* Raymond Zimmerman,* Pres.; James R. Mills, Secy.; Rabbi Randall Falk, Sue Kresge, Robyn Rubinoff, Fred Zimmerman.
EIN: 621058309
Codes: FD2

50027
In Him Resources Foundation
2800 2nd Ave.
Chattanooga, TN 37407
Contact: Nickey A. Bowman, Pres.

Established in 1992 in TN.
Donor(s): Nabco Electric Company, Inc.
Financial data (yr. ended 12/31/01): Grants paid, $135,000; assets, $148,636 (M); gifts received, $135,000; expenditures, $135,216; qualifying distributions, $135,000.
Limitations: Giving primarily in Chattanooga, TN.
Officers: Nickey A. Bowman, Pres.; Gregory Bowman, V.P.; Wes Bowman, Secy.-Treas.
EIN: 581983451
Codes: FD2

50028
The Life Extension Foundation, Inc.
c/o Dr. H.K. Johnson
1315 Saxon Dr.
Nashville, TN 37215

Established in 1954 in NY.
Financial data (yr. ended 12/31/01): Grants paid, $135,000; assets, $2,230,047 (M); expenditures, $165,862; qualifying distributions, $144,043.
Limitations: Applications not accepted.
Application information: Contributes only to pre-selected organizations.
Officers: H.K. Johnson, Pres.; N.N. Johnson, Secy.-Treas.
Trustees: F. Fraser, M.D. Johnson, T.H. Johnson.
EIN: 136108278
Codes: FD2

50029
The Albert Jay Martin Family Foundation
4260 E. Raines Rd.
Memphis, TN 38118-6977

Established in 1997 in TN.
Donor(s): Albert Jay Martin.
Financial data (yr. ended 11/30/01): Grants paid, $134,120; assets, $978,084 (M); expenditures, $155,084; qualifying distributions, $134,120.
Limitations: Applications not accepted.
Application information: Contributes only to pre-selected organizations.
Board Members: Albert Jay Martin, Charles A. Pinkham, Jr., Henry M. Turley, Jr.
EIN: 626345910
Codes: FD2

50030
Jim Blevins Foundation
P.O. Box 150056
Nashville, TN 37215-0056 (615) 298-5000
Contact: James V. Blevins, Tr.

Established in 1955.
Donor(s): James V. Blevins.
Financial data (yr. ended 10/31/01): Grants paid, $133,886; assets, $2,613,129 (M); expenditures, $135,998; qualifying distributions, $133,913.
Limitations: Applications not accepted. Giving primarily in TN.
Application information: Unsolicited request for funds not accepted.
Trustee: James V. Blevins.
EIN: 626043234
Codes: GTI

50031
Herbert & Gertrude Halverstadt Foundation
3511 Belmont Blvd.
Nashville, TN 37215-1607

Established in 1960 in TN.
Financial data (yr. ended 12/31/01): Grants paid, $133,849; assets, $1,838,023 (M); expenditures, $186,764; qualifying distributions, $127,594.
Limitations: Applications not accepted. Giving primarily in OH and TN.
Application information: Contributes only to pre-selected organizations.
Officer and Directors:* Hugh F. Halverstadt,* Treas.; Albert Halverstadt, David Halverstadt, Peter B. Halverstadt, Linda McDuffie, Constance A. Miller.
EIN: 626073690
Codes: FD2

50032
Robert M. and Lenore W. Carrier Foundation
c/o Union Planters Bank, Trust Dept.
P.O. Box 387
Memphis, TN 38147 (901) 383-6196
Contact: Steve Spencer, Trust Off., Union Planters Bank

Established in 1952.
Financial data (yr. ended 10/31/01): Grants paid, $130,989; assets, $2,211,845 (M); expenditures, $153,044; qualifying distributions, $140,627.
Limitations: Giving limited to residents of MS.
Application information: Send high school transcripts and brief resume of academic qualifications. Application form not required.
Trustee: Union Planters Bank.
EIN: 626035575
Codes: FD2, GTI

TENNESSEE—50044

50033
Ethel Brickey Hicks Charitable Corporation
P.O. Box 1990
Knoxville, TN 37901
Contact: James S. Tipton, Jr., Pres.

Established in 1990.
Financial data (yr. ended 12/31/01): Grants paid, $129,000; assets, $478,361 (M); expenditures, $144,201; qualifying distributions, $128,739.
Application information: Application form required.
Officers: James S. Tipton, Jr., Pres.; Janet Moore, Secy.-Treas.
EIN: 710698966
Codes: FD2, GTI

50034
The David Foundation
605 Granny White Pike
Brentwood, TN 37027 (615) 373-4233
Contact: Stuart Southard, Pres.

Established in 1994 in TN.
Donor(s): Stuart Southard.
Financial data (yr. ended 12/31/01): Grants paid, $128,838; assets, $189,719 (M); expenditures, $129,194; qualifying distributions, $128,838.
Limitations: Giving primarily in TN, with some giving in MS.
Officers: Stuart Southard, Pres.; Anne M. Southard, Secy.
Trustees: S. Jackson Faris, Meredith E. Flautt.
EIN: 621585839
Codes: FD2

50035
Mount Rest Home Foundation
P.O. Box 11327
Knoxville, TN 37939-1327
Contact: Elizabeth Rochelle, Treas.

Established around 1943.
Financial data (yr. ended 09/30/01): Grants paid, $127,050; assets, $2,418,139 (M); gifts received, $7,209; expenditures, $154,080; qualifying distributions, $127,249.
Limitations: Giving limited to Knox County, TX.
Application information: Application form required.
Officers: Joan Schwarzenberg, Pres.; Mary Tod Finch, V.P; Margaret M. Brownlee, Secy.; Marian Hunter, Corr. Secy.; Elizabeth Rochelle, Treas.
Directors: Mary Nell Johnson, Beth Knight, Angy Koella, Peggy Rochelle, Evelyn Seymour, Chalmers Wilson.
Trustee: Mary Anne Beall.
EIN: 620518289
Codes: FD2

50036
The Baulch Family Foundation
c/o SunTrust Banks, Inc., Trust Tax Dept.
P.O. Box 305110
Nashville, TN 37230-5110
Contact: Leonard Wood

Established in 1990 in TN.
Donor(s): Viola S. Baulch Trusts.
Financial data (yr. ended 12/31/01): Grants paid, $126,250; assets, $2,422,056 (M); gifts received, $168,437; expenditures, $138,539; qualifying distributions, $130,830.
Application information: Application form not required.
Trustee: SunTrust Banks, Inc.
EIN: 626233587
Codes: FD2

50037
Fensterwald Foundation
1108 Nichol Ln.
Nashville, TN 37205-4418 (615) 297-1211
Contact: Robert Eisenstein, Pres.

Established in 1960 in DE and TN.
Financial data (yr. ended 12/31/01): Grants paid, $125,400; assets, $2,098,022 (M); expenditures, $130,822; qualifying distributions, $125,400.
Limitations: Giving primarily in Nashville, TN.
Officers and Trustees:* Robert Eisenstein,* Pres.; Daniel B. Eisenstein,* V.P.; Nan E. Speller,* Secy.-Treas.
EIN: 626037726
Codes: FD2

50038
Ware Foundation
231 Ensworth Pl.
Nashville, TN 37205

Established in 2001 in TN.
Financial data (yr. ended 12/31/01): Grants paid, $124,850; assets, $2,243,707 (M); gifts received, $2,444,073; expenditures, $141,272; qualifying distributions, $141,216.
Limitations: Applications not accepted. Giving primarily in TN.
Application information: Contributes only to pre-selected organizations.
Trustees: Brent J. Ware, Judy V. Ware.
EIN: 626382732

50039
George R. Johnson Charitable Trust
c/o First Tennessee Bank
701 Market St.
Chattanooga, TN 37402 (423) 757-4246
Contact: Stella Anderson, Trust Off., First Tennessee

Established in 1999 in TN.
Donor(s): George R. Johnson.‡
Financial data (yr. ended 12/31/00): Grants paid, $123,400; assets, $14,924,745 (M); gifts received, $9,000,000; expenditures, $155,526; qualifying distributions, $123,400.
Limitations: Giving primarily in Catoosa, Dade, Murray and Walker counties, GA, and Bledsoe, Bradley, Grundy, Hamilton, Loudon, Marion, Meigs, Monroe, Polk, Rhea and Sequatchie counties, TN.
Trustees: Janice J. Wilson, Cleveland Bank & Trust Company.
EIN: 626369022
Codes: FD2

50040
Arthur K. and Sylvia S. Lee Scholarship Foundation
P.O. Box 681943
Franklin, TN 37068-1943
Application address: 810 Crescent Centre Dr., Ste. 600, Franklin, TN 37067
Contact: James B. Ford, Secy.-Treas.

Established in 1962 in IL.
Donor(s): M. Mervyn K. Wrench, Chapman and Cutler, United Cities Gas Co.
Financial data (yr. ended 12/31/01): Grants paid, $122,502; assets, $1,474,627 (M); gifts received, $30,000; expenditures, $157,043; qualifying distributions, $122,502.
Limitations: Giving primarily in the southern U.S.
Application information: Priority given to dependents of employees of United Cities Gas Co. Application form required.
Officer: James B. Ford, Secy.-Treas.

Trustees: Adrienne Brandon, Dorothy B. Bryson, Bradford Gioia, Glenn R. King, Malcolm Liles, Mack S. Linebaugh, Jr., Ogden Stokes.
EIN: 366069067
Codes: FD2, GTI

50041
The Rasmussen Foundation
856 Curtiswood Ln.
Nashville, TN 37204

Established in 1999 in TN.
Donor(s): Wallace Rasmussen.
Financial data (yr. ended 12/31/01): Grants paid, $122,500; assets, $450,295 (M); gifts received, $92,028; expenditures, $125,816; qualifying distributions, $121,760.
Limitations: Applications not accepted. Giving primarily in Nashville, TN.
Application information: Contributes only to pre-selected organizations.
Trustees: Ada Almering, Wallace N. Rasmussen, Walter Rasmussen.
EIN: 621786550
Codes: FD2

50042
The Keel Foundation
P.O. Box 1778
Morristown, TN 37816

Established in 1997 in TN.
Financial data (yr. ended 12/31/00): Grants paid, $120,000; assets, $1,963,414 (M); expenditures, $159,496; qualifying distributions, $146,231.
Limitations: Applications not accepted.
Application information: Contributes only to pre-selected organizations.
Officer: L. Kirk Wyss, Pres.
Board Members: Leslie Vittur, Lawrence Eric Wyss.
EIN: 621722004
Codes: FD2

50043
Dorothy Snider Foundation
c/o First Tennessee Bank, N.A.
P.O. Box 84
Memphis, TN 38101-0084
Application address: Clarke Tower, 5100 Poplar Ave., Ste. 2929, Memphis, TN 38137
Contact: Jack Magids

Financial data (yr. ended 01/31/02): Grants paid, $120,000; assets, $2,532,021 (M); gifts received, $1,300; expenditures, $159,449; qualifying distributions, $130,894.
Limitations: Giving limited to AR and western TN.
Trustees: Jack Magids, First Tennessee Bank, N.A.
EIN: 526120444
Codes: FD2

50044
Roy L. White Foundation
c/o David H. Lillard, Jr.
130 N. Court Ave.
Memphis, TN 38103

Established in 1999 in TN.
Financial data (yr. ended 12/31/01): Grants paid, $120,000; assets, $1,479,680 (M); expenditures, $186,873; qualifying distributions, $146,665.
Limitations: Applications not accepted.
Application information: Contributes only to pre-selected organizations.
Officers and Directors:* Roy L. White,* Pres.; Mark A. Medford,* Secy.; Tom Batchelor, David S. Dockery, L.G. Hansen, David H. Lillard, Jr., Harry L. Smith, John Mark White.
EIN: 621804818
Codes: FD2

50045
Hohenberg Charity Trust
54 S. White Station Rd.
Memphis, TN 38117 (901) 682-8371
Contact: Rudi E. Scheidt, Tr.

Established in 1954 in TN.
Donor(s): Hohenberg Bros. Co.
Financial data (yr. ended 12/31/01): Grants paid, $119,800; assets, $2,154,169 (M); expenditures, $136,456; qualifying distributions, $125,568; giving activities include $9,672 for programs.
Limitations: Giving primarily in the Memphis, TN, area.
Application information: Application form not required.
Trustees: Susan Scheidt Arney, Julien J. Hohenberg, Rudi E. Scheidt, Rudi E. Scheidt, Jr., Juliet Hohenberg Wischmeyer.
EIN: 626036168
Codes: FD2

50046
Margolin Brothers Foundation
P.O. Box 18961
Memphis, TN 38181

Established in 1951.
Donor(s): National Insurance Agency, Inc., National Mortgage Co.
Financial data (yr. ended 04/30/01): Grants paid, $118,900; assets, $13,770 (M); expenditures, $119,704; qualifying distributions, $119,704.
Limitations: Applications not accepted. Giving primarily in GA and TN.
Application information: Contributes only to pre-selected organizations.
Officers: Marlin Graber, Pres.; Michael Parker, Secy.
EIN: 626040609
Codes: FD2

50047
The Dixie Group Foundation, Inc.
(Formerly Dixie Yarns Foundation, Inc.)
c/o The Dixie Group, Inc.
P.O. Box 25107
Chattanooga, TN 37422-5107
Contact: Starr T. Klein, Secy.-Treas.

Established in 1944 in DE.
Donor(s): Dixie Yarns, Inc., The Dixie Group, Inc.
Financial data (yr. ended 12/31/01): Grants paid, $116,800; assets, $734,530 (M); gifts received, $50,000; expenditures, $126,491; qualifying distributions, $116,680.
Limitations: Giving primarily in the South in areas of company operations and its subsidiaries, with preference given to GA and TN.
Officers and Trustees:* Daniel K. Frierson,* Pres.; W. Derek Davis,* V.P.; Starr T. Klein, Secy.-Treas.
EIN: 620645090
Codes: CS, FD2, CD

50048
The Sparrow Foundation
101 Winners Cir.
Brentwood, TN 37024-5085

Established in 1992 in TN.
Donor(s): Sparrow Corp.
Financial data (yr. ended 06/30/01): Grants paid, $116,600; assets, $1,442,614 (M); gifts received, $20,000; expenditures, $196,691; qualifying distributions, $144,872.
Limitations: Applications not accepted.
Publications: Informational brochure.
Application information: Contributes only to pre-selected organizations.
Officers and Directors:* Billy Ray Hearn,* Pres.; Rick Horne,* Secy.; Holly Hearn-Whaley, Exec. Dir.; Margaret Becker, Richard Green, Steve Green, Bill Hearn, Vicki Horne.
EIN: 621516024
Codes: CS, FD2, CD

50049
The John and Heidi Hassenfeld Family Foundation
4334 Chickering Ln.
Nashville, TN 37215

Established in 1998 in TN.
Donor(s): John Hassenfeld.
Financial data (yr. ended 12/31/01): Grants paid, $116,190; assets, $161,456 (M); expenditures, $117,507; qualifying distributions, $116,190.
Limitations: Applications not accepted.
Application information: Contributes only to pre-selected organizations.
Trustees: Heidi Hassenfeld, John Hassenfeld.
EIN: 621768433

50050
Wills Foundation
3200 Del Rio Pike
Franklin, TN 37069-8714
Contact: W. Ridley Wills, II, Tr.

Established in 1992 in TN.
Donor(s): Mrs. Jesse Wills,‡ W. Ridley Wills II.
Financial data (yr. ended 12/31/01): Grants paid, $116,000; assets, $4,118,363 (M); gifts received, $2,801,742; expenditures, $118,094; qualifying distributions, $116,000.
Limitations: Giving primarily in Nashville, TN.
Application information: Unsolicited requests for funds not accepted.
Trustees: Irene J. Wills, Morgan J. Wills, Thomas W. Wills, W. Ridley Wills II, W. Ridley Wills III.
EIN: 626245453

50051
Helping Hands Foundation
(Formerly The Blanton Harrell Foundation)
c/o Curtis & Co.
109 Westpark Dr., Ste. 400
Brentwood, TN 37027
Contact: Beverly Bartsch

Established in 1993 in TN.
Donor(s): E. Michael Blanton, Dan E. Harrell.
Financial data (yr. ended 12/31/99): Grants paid, $115,744; assets, $1,231,092 (M); gifts received, $40,584; expenditures, $139,823; qualifying distributions, $138,620.
Limitations: Giving primarily in TN.
Trustees: E. Michael Blanton, Dan E. Harrell.
EIN: 621516791
Codes: FD2

50052
Hudson Family Charitable Foundation
c/o Thomas M. Hudson, Sr.
120 Bonaventure Pl.
Nashville, TN 37205

Established in 1997 in TN.
Financial data (yr. ended 12/31/01): Grants paid, $115,700; assets, $2,632,618 (M); expenditures, $122,252; qualifying distributions, $115,715.
Limitations: Applications not accepted. Giving primarily in Nashville, TN.
Application information: Contributes only to pre-selected organizations.
Trustees: Ellen W. Hudson, Thomas M. Hudson, Jr., Kate H. Ragan.
EIN: 621690861
Codes: FD2

50053
Bala Cares Foundation
211-B E. Court Ave.
Selmer, TN 38375

Established in 1999 in TN.
Donor(s): Lakshmanan Ganapathy.
Financial data (yr. ended 12/31/00): Grants paid, $115,150; assets, $456 (M); gifts received, $115,451; expenditures, $115,670; qualifying distributions, $115,150.
Limitations: Applications not accepted. Giving primarily in India.
Application information: Contributes only to pre-selected organizations.
Officers: Lakshmanan Ganapathy, Pres.; Gail Shultz, Secy.
Director: Amanda Ingle.
EIN: 621763812
Codes: FD2

50054
Bill Latimer Family Foundation Trust
201 W. Main St., Ste. E
Union City, TN 38281
Contact: William H. Latimer, III, Tr.

Established in 1997 in TN.
Donor(s): Bill & Gail Latimer Charitable Trust, William H. Latimer III.
Financial data (yr. ended 12/31/01): Grants paid, $114,318; assets, $8,604,624 (M); gifts received, $417,974; expenditures, $176,186; qualifying distributions, $176,186; giving activities include $45,900 for loans to individuals.
Limitations: Applications not accepted.
Application information: Contributes only to pre-selected organizations.
Trustee: William H. Latimer III.
EIN: 621680941
Codes: FD2

50055
Willard & Frances Hendrix Foundation
c/o SunTrust Banks, Inc.
P.O. Box 305110
Nashville, TN 37230-5110 (615) 748-5519
Contact: Charlotte Csabi

Established in 1981 in TN.
Donor(s): Frances Hendrix.
Financial data (yr. ended 04/30/01): Grants paid, $113,265; assets, $53,828 (M); gifts received, $42,507; expenditures, $115,379; qualifying distributions, $113,797.
Limitations: Giving primarily in Nashville, TN.
Application information: Application form not required.
Trustees: John Anderson, James Gooch, James Hendrix, Richard Holdton, Jane Star, SunTrust Banks, Inc.
EIN: 626158855
Codes: FD2

50056
The Cobble Family Foundation, Inc.
308 McReynolds Rd.
Friendsville, TN 37737-2312 (865) 995-3356
Contact: Bill L. Cobble, Pres.

Established in 1998 in TN.
Financial data (yr. ended 12/31/01): Grants paid, $111,437; assets, $975,312 (M); expenditures, $117,773; qualifying distributions, $110,757.
Limitations: Giving primarily in TN.
Officers: Bill L. Cobble, Pres.; Courtland S. Cobble, V.P.; Cheryl S. Nicholson, V.P.; Laura C. Schield, V.P.; Donna M. Cobble, Secy.
EIN: 621737825
Codes: FD2

50057
The Restoration Foundation
626 Fatherland St.
Nashville, TN 37206

Established in 1999 in TN.
Donor(s): John Elam, Lulu Elam.
Financial data (yr. ended 02/28/01): Grants paid, $111,000; assets, $2,982,827 (M); expenditures, $179,478; qualifying distributions, $111,000.
Limitations: Applications not accepted. Giving primarily in Nashville, TN.
Application information: Contributes only to pre-selected organizations.
Trustees: John Elam, Lulu Elam.
EIN: 626355168
Codes: FD2

50058
The Deupree Family Foundation
c/o National Bank of Commerce, Trust Division
1 Commerce Sq.
Memphis, TN 38150
Application address: c/o National Bank of Commerce, Trust Division, 850 Ridgelake Blvd., Ste. 101, Memphis, TN 38120
Contact: Sheri Nakhleh

Established in 1998 in TN.
Financial data (yr. ended 12/31/00): Grants paid, $110,100; assets, $2,677,305 (M); gifts received, $519,146; expenditures, $134,347; qualifying distributions, $101,291.
Limitations: Giving limited to the Memphis, TN, area.
Trustee: National Bank of Commerce.
EIN: 626334424
Codes: FD2

50059
"Soli Deo Gloria" Foundation
6520 Radcliff Dr.
Nashville, TN 37221
Contact: Philip R. Patton, Pres.

Established in 1992 in TN.
Donor(s): Philip R. Patton, Susan D. Patton.
Financial data (yr. ended 12/31/00): Grants paid, $106,730; assets, $1,068,793 (M); gifts received, $394,599; expenditures, $113,142; qualifying distributions, $106,730.
Limitations: Giving primarily in Nashville, TN.
Application information: Application form not required.
Officers and Directors:* Philip R. Patton,* Pres. and Treas.; Susan D. Patton,* Secy.; Helen K. Cummings.
EIN: 621516325

50060
Aladdin Industries Foundation, Inc.
703 Murfreesboro Rd.
Nashville, TN 37210-4521 (615) 748-3360
Contact: L.B. Jenkins, Secy.-Treas.

Incorporated in 1964 in TN.
Donor(s): Aladdin Industries, Inc., Aladdin Industries, LLC.
Financial data (yr. ended 12/31/01): Grants paid, $106,240; assets, $2,673,678 (M); expenditures, $138,097; qualifying distributions, $103,460.
Limitations: Giving primarily in TN.
Application information: Application form not required.
Officer and Directors:* Lillian B. Jenkins,* Secy.-Treas.; Dave Britt, V.S. Johnson III.
EIN: 620701769
Codes: CS, FD2, CD

50061
Magdovitz Family Foundation
P.O. Box 650
Memphis, TN 38101

Established in 1975 in TN.
Donor(s): Joseph A. Magdovitz, Earl J. Magdovitz.
Financial data (yr. ended 06/30/01): Grants paid, $105,127; assets, $2,121,467 (M); gifts received, $15,200; expenditures, $124,917; qualifying distributions, $122,311.
Limitations: Applications not accepted. Giving limited to the Memphis, TN, area.
Application information: Contributes only to pre-selected organizations.
Officers: Joseph A. Magdovitz, Pres. and Treas.; Earl J. Magdovitz, V.P. and Secy.
EIN: 510164695
Codes: FD2

50062
David T. Vandewater Foundation
425 Jackson Blvd.
Nashville, TN 37205

Established in 1995 in KY and TN.
Donor(s): David T. Vandewater.
Financial data (yr. ended 12/31/00): Grants paid, $104,700; assets, $1,389,706 (M); expenditures, $122,205; qualifying distributions, $104,235.
Limitations: Applications not accepted. Giving primarily in Nashville, TN.
Application information: Contributes only to pre-selected organizations.
Directors: Stephen T. Braun, David T. Vandewater, Phyllis Vandewater.
EIN: 611273415
Codes: FD2

50063
Hawthorn Charitable Foundation
201 4th Ave. N., Ste. 1390
Nashville, TN 37219

Established in 1995 in TN.
Donor(s): W.L. Davis, Jr., Adelaide Shull Davis, Harrison S. Davis.
Financial data (yr. ended 06/30/01): Grants paid, $103,320; assets, $643,082 (M); gifts received, $250,962; expenditures, $107,445; qualifying distributions, $103,320.
Limitations: Applications not accepted. Giving primarily in TN.
Application information: Contributes only to pre-selected organizations.
Trustees: Adelaide Shull Davis, W. Lipscomb Davis, Jr.
EIN: 621624638
Codes: FD2

50064
Birdwell Family Foundation
407 N. Main St.
Carthage, TN 37030
Contact: Walter G. Birdwell Jr., Pres.

Established in 1998 in TN.
Donor(s): Walter G. Birdwell, Jr., Sue Birdwell.
Financial data (yr. ended 12/31/00): Grants paid, $102,270; assets, $53,273 (M); expenditures, $103,236; qualifying distributions, $102,245.
Limitations: Giving primarily in TN.
Officers: Walter G. Birdwell, Jr., Pres.; Helen Birdwell, Secy.-Treas.
Directors: Sue Birdwell, Ann Birdwell Dobson.
EIN: 621697881
Codes: FD2

50065
Bernice H. & Richard Hussey Foundation
P.O. Box 242045
Memphis, TN 38124-2045 (901) 682-6220
Contact: Bernice H. Hussey, Pres.

Established in 1989 in TN.
Donor(s): Bernice H. Hussey, Richard W. Hussey, Jr.
Financial data (yr. ended 12/31/01): Grants paid, $100,659; assets, $19,670 (M); gifts received, $121,000; expenditures, $101,911; qualifying distributions, $100,659.
Limitations: Giving primarily in Memphis, TN.
Officer: Bernice H. Hussey, Pres.
EIN: 621173921
Codes: FD2

50066
Elizabeth Craig Weaver Proctor Charitable Foundation
215 Evelyn Ave.
Nashville, TN 37205

Established in 2000 in TN.
Donor(s): Elizabeth C. Proctor.
Financial data (yr. ended 12/31/01): Grants paid, $100,000; assets, $4,801,796 (M); expenditures, $270,969; qualifying distributions, $100,000.
Limitations: Applications not accepted.
Application information: Contributes only to pre-selected organizations.
Officer: Elizabeth C. Proctor, Chair.
Trustees: C.A. Craig II, Michel G. Kaplan, Elizabeth McAlister, Margaret A. Robinson, William C. Weaver, III.
EIN: 621819464

50067
Kate Collins Roddy and J. P. Roddy, Sr. Foundation, Inc.
(Formerly The Roddy Foundation, Inc.)
6701 Baum Dr., Ste. 250
Knoxville, TN 37919
Application address: 3340 Peachtree Rd., Ste. 1660, Atlanta, GA 30326
Contact: Thomas R. Roddy, Exec. Dir.

Established in 1991 in TN.
Donor(s): J.P. Roddy, Jr.,‡ Roddy Coca-Cola Bottling Co., Inc.
Financial data (yr. ended 12/31/01): Grants paid, $100,000; assets, $1,965,534 (M); expenditures, $118,605; qualifying distributions, $100,000.
Limitations: Giving primarily in eastern TN.
Officers: James P. Roddy III, Pres.; Ellen R. Mitchell, Secy.; Rev. Thomas R. Roddy,* Exec. Dir.
Trustees: William J. Mitchell, Sr., Alexandra W. Roddy, Dorothy M. Roddy.
EIN: 621464394
Codes: FD2

50068
Roshan Institute of Cultural Heritage
c/o SunTrust Banks, Inc.
P.O. Box 305110
Nashville, TN 37230-5110
Contact: Kim Williams

Established in 2000 in TN.
Donor(s): Pierre Omidyar.
Financial data (yr. ended 06/30/01): Grants paid, $100,000; assets, $10,474,433 (M); gifts received, $7,050,000; expenditures, $133,817; qualifying distributions, $116,999.
Application information: Application form not required.
Directors: James Alatis, Elah'e Mir-Djalali Omidyar, Pierre Omidyar.
Trustee: SunTrust Banks, Inc.
EIN: 770560800

50068—TENNESSEE

Codes: FD2

50069
Carl A. & Theresa K. Swafford Foundation, Inc.
2265 Oakleigh Dr.
Murfreesboro, TN 37129
Contact: Carl A. Swafford, Jr., Pres.

Established around 1962 in TN.
Financial data (yr. ended 10/31/01): Grants paid, $99,845; assets, $2,082,707 (M); expenditures, $121,686; qualifying distributions, $105,380.
Limitations: Giving primarily in MD and TN.
Application information: Application form not required.
Officers: Carl A. Swafford, Jr., Pres.; Michael Tomshack, Secy.; Ann Swafford, Treas.
EIN: 626039681
Codes: FD2

50070
The Steven & Laurie Eskind Family Foundation
2322 Golf Club Ln.
Nashville, TN 37215

Donor(s): Steven Eskind, Laurie Eskind.
Financial data (yr. ended 06/30/01): Grants paid, $97,595; assets, $1,329,577 (M); gifts received, $403,239; expenditures, $99,228; qualifying distributions, $98,830.
Limitations: Applications not accepted. Giving primarily in Nashville, TN.
Application information: Contributes only to pre-selected organizations.
Officers: Steven Eskind, Pres.; Laurie Eskind, Secy.
EIN: 621306903
Codes: FD2

50071
Ridgeview Foundation
c/o SunTrust Banks, Inc.
P.O. Box 305110
Nashville, TN 37230-5110 (615) 748-4731
Contact: Richard Gammel, Trust Off., SunTrust Banks, Inc.

Financial data (yr. ended 12/31/00): Grants paid, $96,050; assets, $669,704 (M); expenditures, $109,921; qualifying distributions, $100,343.
Limitations: Giving primarily in Nashville, TN.
Application information: Application form not required.
Trustee: SunTrust Banks, Inc.
EIN: 626077709
Codes: FD2

50072
Purity Foundation, Inc.
P.O. Box 100957
Nashville, TN 37224-0957
Contact: F. Miles Ezell, Jr., V.P.

Established in 1998 in TN.
Financial data (yr. ended 12/31/01): Grants paid, $95,090; assets, $2,103,038 (M); gifts received, $500; expenditures, $109,445; qualifying distributions, $95,812.
Limitations: Giving limited to the Nashville, TN area.
Application information: Application form not required.
Officers: Mark V. Ezell, Pres.; Stanley N. Ezell, V.P. and Secy.; F. Miles Ezell, Jr., V.P. and Treas.; J. William Ezell, V.P.; John R. Robinson, V.P.
EIN: 621749066
Codes: FD2

50073
Peter H. and Mildred F. Brown Foundation
P.O. Box 27
Crump, TN 38327-0027
Application address: P.O. Box 39, Savannah, TN 38372
Contact: Susan Brown, Tr.

Established in 1989 in MS.
Donor(s): Mildred Brown, Susan A. Brown.
Financial data (yr. ended 12/31/01): Grants paid, $95,000; assets, $1,059,194 (M); gifts received, $10,000; expenditures, $95,961; qualifying distributions, $94,334.
Limitations: Giving primarily in TN.
Trustees: Jack L. Adams, Michael N. Brown, Susan A. Brown.
EIN: 640774404
Codes: FD2

50074
Elizabeth Buford Shepherd Scholarship Committee
315 Deaderick St., 4th Fl.
Nashville, TN 37237-0401
Contact: Joseph Chickey

Established in 1956 in TN.
Financial data (yr. ended 12/31/01): Grants paid, $95,000; assets, $1,902,985 (M); expenditures, $120,728; qualifying distributions, $98,968.
Limitations: Giving limited to residents living within a 250-mile radius of Nashville, TN.
Application information: Scholarship payments are made directly to the school on behalf of individual recipients. Application form required.
Scholarship Committee Members: David Mohning, Ann M. Neeley.
EIN: 626047221
Codes: FD2, GTI

50075
Mobile Medical Mission Hospital, Inc.
1919 First Tennessee Plz.
Knoxville, TN 37929
Application address: 1017 W. Choctawhatcee, Niceville, FL 32578
Contact: Samuel O. Massey, Jr., Pres.

Established in 1983 in TN.
Financial data (yr. ended 10/31/01): Grants paid, $92,186; assets, $890,237 (M); gifts received, $9,810; expenditures, $116,959; qualifying distributions, $95,186; giving activities include $27,415 for programs.
Limitations: Giving on a national and international basis.
Application information: Application form not required.
Officers and Directors:* Samuel O. Massey, Jr., M.D.,* Pres.; Jamie Massey,* V.P.; Mrs. Chelye Amis,* Secy.; Rip Prichard, Rev. Charles M. Rice, and 11 additional directors.
EIN: 581348941
Codes: FD2, GTI

50076
North American Royalties, Inc. Foundation
(Formerly North American Royalties, Inc. Welfare Fund)
200 E. 8th St.
Chattanooga, TN 37402 (423) 265-3181
FAX: (423) 266-8459
Contact: Gordon L. Smith, III, Tr.

Established in 1966 in TN.
Donor(s): North American Royalties, Inc.
Financial data (yr. ended 12/31/01): Grants paid, $91,633; assets, $1,028,649 (M); gifts received, $500; expenditures, $101,030; qualifying distributions, $95,933.
Limitations: Giving limited to Chattanooga, TN.
Application information: Application forms are provided for scholarships. Scholarships are only for dependents of company employees. Application form not required.
Trustees: Larry Bowers, Lorie Mallchok, Frances Smith, Gordon L. Smith III, Chris Steger.
EIN: 626052490
Codes: CS, FD2, CD, GTI

50077
Del Greco Foundation, Inc.
c/o Albert Del Greco
8113 Poplar Wood Ln.
Nashville, TN 37221

Established in 1999 in TN.
Financial data (yr. ended 12/31/99): Grants paid, $91,000; assets, $11,188 (M); gifts received, $60,000; expenditures, $113,229; qualifying distributions, $91,000.
Limitations: Applications not accepted. Giving primarily in AL and UT.
Application information: Contributes only to pre-selected organizations.
Officer: Albert Del Greco, Mgr.
EIN: 364282670
Codes: FD2

50078
Martha Christine White Foundation, Inc.
P.O. Box 400
Winchester, TN 37398-0400
Contact: Martha P. Jordan, Secy.-Treas.

Established in 1996 in AL.
Financial data (yr. ended 12/31/01): Grants paid, $90,250; assets, $1,644,419 (M); expenditures, $114,525; qualifying distributions, $99,703.
Limitations: Giving primarily in AL.
Application information: Application form not required.
Officer and Directors:* Martha P. Jordan,* Secy.-Treas.; John E. Rochester, Rev. Carnes E. Summers.
EIN: 631106800
Codes: FD2

50079
The Samuel M. Fleming Foundation
1205 3rd Ave. N.
Nashville, TN 37208
Contact: Alden H. Smith, Jr., Secy.

Established in 1993 in TN.
Donor(s): Joanne Fleming Hayes.
Financial data (yr. ended 12/31/01): Grants paid, $90,000; assets, $2,382,955 (M); gifts received, $463,127; expenditures, $137,995; qualifying distributions, $103,345.
Limitations: Applications not accepted. Giving primarily in the Nashville, TN, area.
Application information: Contributes only to pre-selected organizations.
Officers: Samuel M. Fleming, Chair.; W. Lipscomb Davis, Jr., V.P.; Alden H. Smith, Jr., Secy.; Elizabeth B. Davie, Treas.
Trustees: Joanne Fleming Hayes, Samuel Fleming Wilt.
EIN: 582026295
Codes: FD2

50080
Robert Lee Weiss Foundation
c/o First Tennessee Bank, N.A., Trust Div.
800 S. Gay St.
Knoxville, TN 37995
Contact: Keith Keisling

Established in 1985 in TN.
Donor(s): Robert Lee Weiss, Jr.‡

Financial data (yr. ended 08/31/01): Grants paid, $88,500; assets, $2,585,319 (M); expenditures, $100,747; qualifying distributions, $92,649.
Limitations: Giving primarily in the eastern TN, area, with emphasis on Knoxville.
Application information: Application form required.
Officers: David Lantz, Mgr.; Robert McDonald, Mgr.; Rev. Thomas Russell Roddy, Mgr.
Trustee: First Tennessee Bank, N.A.
EIN: 621261218
Codes: FD2

50081
Murray C. & Jo P. Murphey Foundation, Inc.
c/o Murray C. Murphey
5100 Poplar Ave., Ste. 2216
Memphis, TN 38137

Established in 1992 in TN.
Donor(s): Murray C. Murphey.
Financial data (yr. ended 12/31/00): Grants paid, $88,000; assets, $107,834 (M); expenditures, $89,586; qualifying distributions, $89,586.
Limitations: Applications not accepted. Giving primarily in Memphis, TN.
Application information: Contributes only to pre-selected organizations.
Officers and Directors:* Murray C. Murphey,* Chair. and Pres.; Deborah K. White,* Secy.; Michael D. Murphey,* Treas.; Michael R. White.
EIN: 621497933
Codes: FD2

50082
House for Hope Foundation
1321 Murfreesboro Rd., No. 800
Nashville, TN 37217

Established in 2001.
Financial data (yr. ended 12/31/01): Grants paid, $87,550; assets, $22,912 (L); gifts received, $32,470; expenditures, $91,851; qualifying distributions, $87,550.
Limitations: Giving primarily in TN.
Officers: James Carbine, Pres.; Kim Dykes, V.P.; John Sheley, Secy.-Treas.
EIN: 621822790

50083
Civitan Child Welfare Auxiliary, Inc.
3712 Anderson Ave.
Chattanooga, TN 37412 (423) 886-2139
Application address: P.O. Box 339, Signal Mountain, TN 37377, tel.: (423) 886-2139;
E-mail: hheggie830327@comcast.net
Contact: Hunter D. Heggle, Chair.

Established in 1927.
Financial data (yr. ended 12/31/01): Grants paid, $87,357; assets, $1,384,584 (M); expenditures, $86,553; qualifying distributions, $78,770.
Limitations: Giving primarily in northern AL, northwest GA, and southeast TN.
Application information: Application form not required.
Officers: Hunter D. Heggle, Chair.; John F. Crisman, Secy.; Henry Crine, Treas.
Directors: Thilo H. Best, J. William Dietzen.
EIN: 626036153
Codes: FD2, GTI

50084
McKenzie Family Foundation
2 Union Sq.
1000 Tallan Bldg.
Chattanooga, TN 37402

Established in 1997 in TN.
Donor(s): Steve McKenzie, Brenda McKenzie.
Financial data (yr. ended 06/30/01): Grants paid, $87,230; assets, $17,214 (M); gifts received, $47,860; expenditures, $92,618; qualifying distributions, $87,230.
Limitations: Applications not accepted. Giving on a national basis.
Application information: Contributes only to pre-selected organizations.
Officers: Brenda McKenzie, Pres. and Treas.; Steve McKenzie, V.P. and Secy.
Director: John C. Stophel.
EIN: 621714714
Codes: FD2

50085
The Kathryn Carell Brown Foundation
c/o Equitable Trust Co.
800 Nashville City Ctr.
Nashville, TN 37211 (615) 780-9318
Contact: M. Kirk Scobey, Jr.

Established in 1997 in TN.
Donor(s): Kathryn Carell Brown.
Financial data (yr. ended 12/31/00): Grants paid, $86,666; assets, $1,241,523 (M); expenditures, $93,041; qualifying distributions, $85,843.
Limitations: Giving primarily in Nashville, TN.
Application information: Application form required.
Trustees: David H. Brown, Kathryn Carell Brown.
EIN: 626314878
Codes: FD2

50086
Horsehead Community Development Fund of Tennessee, Inc.
P.O. Box 626
Rockwood, TN 37854

Established in 1991 in TN.
Financial data (yr. ended 12/31/00): Grants paid, $86,300; assets, $126,248 (M); gifts received, $57,708; expenditures, $88,684; qualifying distributions, $86,300.
Limitations: Applications not accepted. Giving primarily in Roane County, TN.
Application information: Contributes only to pre-selected organizations.
Officers: James Henry, Chair.; Sherry Hoppe, Vice-Chair.; Edward B. Pemberton, Secy.; Douglas Wilson, Treas.
EIN: 621458185
Codes: FD2

50087
Wright Charitable Trust
c/o Carroll Bank & Trust
19510 W. Main St.
Huntingdon, TN 38344

Established in 1998.
Financial data (yr. ended 12/31/00): Grants paid, $86,020; assets, $2,551,677 (M); expenditures, $120,283; qualifying distributions, $85,646.
Limitations: Applications not accepted. Giving primarily in Huntington, TN.
Application information: Contributes only to pre-selected organizations.
Trustee: Carroll Bank and Trust.
EIN: 581947918
Codes: FD2

50088
The Joyce Foundation
c/o SunTrust Banks, Inc., Nashville, N.A., Trust Tax Dept.
P.O. Box 305110
Nashville, TN 37230-5110 (615) 748-5449
Contact: James Atwood

Established in 1985 in TN.
Donor(s): Kathryn Craig Henry.
Financial data (yr. ended 12/31/01): Grants paid, $86,000; assets, $16,774 (M); gifts received, $86,016; expenditures, $89,027; qualifying distributions, $86,929.
Limitations: Giving primarily in Nashville, TN.
Application information: Application form not required.
Trustee: SunTrust Banks, Inc.
EIN: 626177976
Codes: FD2

50089
J. Bransford Wallace Foundation
417 W. Tyne Blvd.
Nashville, TN 37205

Established in 1993 in TN.
Financial data (yr. ended 12/31/01): Grants paid, $85,800; assets, $396,370 (M); expenditures, $95,014; qualifying distributions, $87,232.
Limitations: Applications not accepted.
Application information: Contributes only to pre-selected organizations.
Trustee: J. Bransford Wallace.
EIN: 621551709
Codes: FD2

50090
The Warren S. Wurzburg, Sr. and Marjorie O. Wurzburg Foundation
c/o National Bank of Commerce, Trust Dept.
1 Commerce Sq.
Memphis, TN 38150-0001
Application address: 710 S. 4th St., Memphis, TN 38101-0710
Contact: Warren Wurzburg

Established in 1984 in TN.
Donor(s): Wurzburg, Inc., Steven M. Shapiro, Warren Wurzburg, Jr.
Financial data (yr. ended 12/31/00): Grants paid, $85,698; assets, $1,138,229 (M); gifts received, $25,750; expenditures, $98,398; qualifying distributions, $85,698.
Limitations: Giving limited to Memphis, TN.
Trustee: National Bank of Commerce.
EIN: 581544786
Codes: CS, FD2, CD

50091
The Edith Carell Johnson Foundation
4407 Iroquois
Nashville, TN 37205

Established in 1996 in TN.
Donor(s): Edith Carell Johnson.
Financial data (yr. ended 12/31/01): Grants paid, $85,500; assets, $1,154,507 (M); expenditures, $90,809; qualifying distributions, $86,477.
Limitations: Applications not accepted. Giving primarily in Nashville, TN.
Application information: Contributes only to pre-selected organizations.
Officer: Edith Carell Johnson, Chair.
Director: David B. Johnson.
EIN: 626314839
Codes: FD2

50092
The Powell Foundation
3622 Bristol Hwy.
Johnson City, TN 37601-1324
Contact: James J. Powell, Chair.

Established in 2000 in TN.
Donor(s): James J. Powell.
Financial data (yr. ended 12/31/01): Grants paid, $85,500; assets, $2,550,143 (M); expenditures, $115,950; qualifying distributions, $85,500.

50092—TENNESSEE

Officers and Directors:* James J. Powell, Chair. and Pres.; James J. Powell, Jr.,* V.P.; Gary F. Clayton, Secy.-Treas.; Jeffrey J. Powell, Michael W. Powell.
EIN: 621819796

50093
Brumit Family Charitable Foundation
112 S. Sycamore St.
Elizabethton, TN 37643-3328
Contact: Charles K. Brumit, Tr.

Established in 1999.
Donor(s): Charles K. Brumit.
Financial data (yr. ended 06/30/02): Grants paid, $83,125; assets, $885,803 (M); expenditures, $100,972; qualifying distributions, $83,125.
Trustees: Charles K. Brumit, John W. Brumit, Stephen W. Brumit.
EIN: 626363392

50094
Sophie Muller Trust
315 Deaderick St., 4th Fl.
Nashville, TN 37237-0401

Established in 1998 in TN.
Financial data (yr. ended 12/31/00): Grants paid, $83,101; assets, $1,400,017 (M); expenditures, $94,766; qualifying distributions, $83,874.
Limitations: Applications not accepted.
Application information: Contributes only to pre-selected organizations.
Trustee: AmSouth Bank.
EIN: 626149813
Codes: FD2

50095
Oliver & Evelyn Smith Foundation
7216 Wellington Dr., Ste. 1
Knoxville, TN 37919-5936 (423) 584-2000
Contact: Oliver A. Smith IV, V.P.

Established in 1987 in TN.
Financial data (yr. ended 03/31/02): Grants paid, $82,793; assets, $1,682,964 (M); expenditures, $134,333; qualifying distributions, $121,057.
Limitations: Giving primarily in Knoxville, TN.
Application information: Application form not required.
Officers: Richard D. Wynn, Pres.; Oliver A. Smith IV, V.P.; Carol Smith Tombras, Secy.; Diana Flaherty, Treas.
Director: Dooley Tombras.
EIN: 621310938
Codes: FD2

50096
Gail Latimer Foundation
1703 Stonewall Dr.
Union City, TN 38261-5919 (731) 885-1354

Established in 1998 in TN.
Donor(s): Gail M. Latimer.
Financial data (yr. ended 12/31/01): Grants paid, $81,529; assets, $51,084 (M); gifts received, $55,774; expenditures, $83,803; qualifying distributions, $81,084.
Limitations: Applications not accepted. Giving primarily in TN.
Application information: Contributes only to pre-selected organizations.
Officers and Directors:* Gail M. Latimer,* Pres.; William Bonn Latimer,* V.P.; John Warner,* Secy.
EIN: 621742273
Codes: FD2

50097
Doochin Family Charitable Trust
(Formerly Interstate Packaging Foundation Charitable Trust)
P.O. Box 789
White Bluff, TN 37187-0922 (615) 797-9000
Contact: Jerald Doochin, Tr.

Established in 1977.
Donor(s): Interstate Packaging Corp.
Financial data (yr. ended 04/30/01): Grants paid, $81,508; assets, $453,324 (M); expenditures, $83,782; qualifying distributions, $81,508.
Limitations: Giving primarily in TN.
Trustees: Jerald Doochin, Michael Doochin.
EIN: 621031459
Codes: CS, FD2, CD

50098
The Hohenberg Foundation, Inc.
159 E. Pkwy. N.
Memphis, TN 38104-3036 (901) 726-4413
Contact: Juliet H. Wischmeyer, Pres.

Established in 1976 in TN.
Financial data (yr. ended 10/31/01): Grants paid, $81,500; assets, $1,736,902 (M); expenditures, $103,915; qualifying distributions, $90,900.
Limitations: Applications not accepted. Giving primarily in Memphis, TN.
Officers and Directors:* Juliet H. Wischmeyer,* Pres.; Adam E. Hohenberg,* Secy.-Treas.; Laetitia H. Angliviel, Julien J. Hohenberg, Mary M.G. Hohenberg.
EIN: 620991218
Codes: FD2

50099
The Crittenden Foundation
J.C. Bradford & Co.
3100 West End Ave., Ste. 110
Nashville, TN 37203-5812
Contact: James C. Bradford, Jr.

Established in 1990 in TN.
Donor(s): Eleanor B. Currie.
Financial data (yr. ended 12/31/01): Grants paid, $81,000; assets, $1,625,177 (M); gifts received, $144,190; expenditures, $84,680; qualifying distributions, $82,261.
Limitations: Applications not accepted. Giving primarily in Nashville, TN.
Application information: Contributes only to pre-selected organizations.
Trust Committee: Eleanor B. Currie, Francis C. Currie, Francis C. Currie, Jr., James Bradford Currie.
EIN: 626234537
Codes: FD2

50100
James E. & Katharine B. Harwood Charitable Trust
6305 Humphreys Blvd., Ste. 207
Memphis, TN 38120-2378

Established in 1992 in TN.
Donor(s): James E. Harwood, Jr.
Financial data (yr. ended 12/31/00): Grants paid, $80,000; assets, $717,560 (M); expenditures, $84,760; qualifying distributions, $81,921.
Limitations: Applications not accepted. Giving primarily in TN.
Application information: Contributes only to pre-selected organizations.
Trustees: Katharine H. Gooch, James E. Harwood.
EIN: 582025944
Codes: FD2

50101
James H. Tharp Charitable Trust
c/o First Tennessee Bank, N.A., Trust Dept.
P.O. Box 84
Memphis, TN 38101-0084 (901) 681-2352
Contact: John Laughlin, Trust Off., First Tennessee Bank, N.A.

Established in 1972 in TN.
Financial data (yr. ended 11/30/01): Grants paid, $80,000; assets, $1,591,754 (M); expenditures, $93,237; qualifying distributions, $81,838.
Limitations: Giving primarily in Memphis, TN.
Application information: Application form not required.
Trustee: First Tennessee Bank, N.A.
EIN: 626105988
Codes: FD2

50102
Frizzell Foundation
1624 King College Rd.
Bristol, TN 37620

Established in 2001 in TN.
Financial data (yr. ended 12/31/01): Grants paid, $79,000; assets, $2,791 (M); gifts received, $82,500; expenditures, $79,725; qualifying distributions, $79,000.
Limitations: Applications not accepted.
Application information: Contributes only to pre-selected organizations.
Officers and Directors:* Ben M. Frizzell, Jr.,* Pres.; Patsy B. Frizzell,* V.P.
EIN: 621862490

50103
After God's Heart, Inc.
1801 Hickory Glen Rd.
Knoxville, TN 37932
Contact: Jan Kuban, Pres.

Established in 1999 in TN.
Donor(s): Daniel P. Kuban, Jan H. Kuban.
Financial data (yr. ended 12/31/01): Grants paid, $78,500; assets, $1,594,683 (M); gifts received, $21,068; expenditures, $102,728; qualifying distributions, $78,392.
Officers and Directors:* Jan H. Kuban,* Pres.; Daniel P. Kuban,* Secy.; Jeffrey R. Kuban, Kevin M. Kuban, Robert D. Kuban, Scott B. Kuban.
EIN: 621804034
Codes: FD2

50104
Bright-Martin Corporation
c/o Fletcher Bright Co.
537 Market St., Ste. 400
Chattanooga, TN 37402 (423) 755-8830
Contact: George T. Bright, Dir.

Established in 1997 in TN.
Financial data (yr. ended 12/31/00): Grants paid, $77,775; assets, $27,934 (M); gifts received, $38,945; expenditures, $80,596; qualifying distributions, $77,771.
Application information: Application form not required.
Directors: Anne Bright, George T. Bright, Clifford G. Martin, Garrison E. Martin, John G. Martin.
EIN: 621715632
Codes: FD2

50105
Daelansa Foundation
c/o Regions Bank
428 McCallie Ave.
Chattanooga, TN 37402

Established about 1983 in TN.

Financial data (yr. ended 12/31/01): Grants paid, $77,750; assets, $2,513,360 (M); expenditures, $138,563; qualifying distributions, $110,046.
Limitations: Applications not accepted. Giving primarily in FL and TN.
Application information: Contributes only to pre-selected organizations.
Officers and Trustees:* Anita J. Hamilton,* Co-Chair.; Sarah J. Shy,* Co-Chair.; Frank T. Hamilton,* Secy.; Carl J. Arnold, Mgr.; Regions Bank.
EIN: 581577718
Codes: FD2

50106
Adams Family Foundation II
801 Mooreland Ln.
Murfreesboro, TN 37128
Contact: W. Andrew Adams, Tr.

Established in 1993 in TN.
Donor(s): W. Andrew Adams.
Financial data (yr. ended 12/31/00): Grants paid, $75,690; assets, $1,524,895 (M); expenditures, $77,908; qualifying distributions, $75,828.
Limitations: Giving limited to the southeast, primarily in TN.
Trustees: Andrew Adams, Anthony A. Adams, Dorothy Adams, W. Andrew Adams, Andrea A. Brown.
EIN: 621515108
Codes: FD2

50107
The Hand Foundation, Inc.
c/o Oscar H. Brock
1426 Williams St., Ste. Q
Chattanooga, TN 37408 (423) 266-7028
E-mail: obrock@signalfinancial.com
Contact: Oscar H. Brock, Secy.-Treas.

Established around 1974.
Financial data (yr. ended 12/31/01): Grants paid, $75,354; assets, $1,273,475 (M); expenditures, $85,023; qualifying distributions, $83,801.
Limitations: Giving primarily in MD and TN.
Application information: Application form not required.
Officers and Directors:* Jean Geraghty,* Pres.; William E. Brock IV,* V.P.; Oscar H. Brock,* Secy.-Treas.; John Kruesi Brock, William E. Brock III, Laura Brock Doley, Robert S. Killebrew, Jr., John McDonald.
EIN: 237442979
Codes: FD2

50108
The Rich Foundation
95 White Bridge Rd., Ste. 404
Nashville, TN 37205

Established in 1996 in TN.
Financial data (yr. ended 06/30/02): Grants paid, $75,300; assets, $2,082,717 (M); gifts received, $300,000; expenditures, $78,640; qualifying distributions, $75,300.
Limitations: Applications not accepted. Giving primarily in TN.
Application information: Contributes only to pre-selected organizations.
Trustees: Patti R. Gordon, Amy Lucile Rich, David Tate Rich, John William Rich.
EIN: 621588498

50109
Patricia Werthan Uhlmann Foundation
800 Nashville City Center
Nashville, TN 37219-1743

Established in 1998 in TN.
Donor(s): Patricia W. Uhlmann.

Financial data (yr. ended 12/31/00): Grants paid, $75,000; assets, $652,931 (M); expenditures, $78,849; qualifying distributions, $78,249.
Limitations: Applications not accepted.
Application information: Contributes only to pre-selected organizations.
Officers: Patricia W. Uhlmann, Pres.; Heloise W. Kuhn, Secy.-Treas.
Director: John Uhlmann.
EIN: 621743716

50110
J. H. & Dorothy Shepherd Charitable Foundation
2000 1st Tennessee Bldg.
165 Madison Ave., Ste. 2000
Memphis, TN 38103 (901) 526-2000
Contact: Allan J. Wade, Tr.

Established in 1990 in TN.
Financial data (yr. ended 12/31/00): Grants paid, $73,500; assets, $2,066 (M); gifts received, $76,578; expenditures, $76,790; qualifying distributions, $76,790.
Limitations: Giving primarily in Memphis, TN.
Trustee: Allan J. Wade.
EIN: 626228490

50111
J. C. Garrett III Family Foundation
P.O. Box 488
Goodlettsville, TN 37072 (615) 859-5200
Contact: J.C. Garrett III, Tr.

Established in 1995 in TN.
Donor(s): J.C. Garrett III.
Financial data (yr. ended 12/31/01): Grants paid, $70,840; assets, $1,522,771 (M); expenditures, $83,131; qualifying distributions, $70,840.
Limitations: Giving primarily in TN.
Application information: Application form not required.
Trustees: J.C. Garrett III, John C. Garrett IV, Leslie Anne Garrett, Susan L. Garrett, Rachel Lenore Garrett McCloud.
EIN: 621577524

50112
Melrose Foundation, Inc.
P.O. Box 629
Knoxville, TN 37901-0629
Contact: Jackson G. Kramer, Dir.

Incorporated in 1945 in TN.
Financial data (yr. ended 12/31/01): Grants paid, $70,500; assets, $8,826,083 (M); expenditures, $245,128; qualifying distributions, $70,224.
Limitations: Giving primarily in Knoxville, TN.
Officers and Directors:* Edwin H. Rayson,* Pres.; Wayne R. Kramer, V.P. and Secy.-Treas.; Jackson G. Kramer, James G. Maloy, Cowan Rodgers III.
EIN: 626037984

50113
The Julia Carell Stadler Foundation
c/o Kirk Scobey
1109 Belle Meade Blvd.
Nashville, TN 37205

Established in 1997 in TN.
Donor(s): Julia Carell Stadler.
Financial data (yr. ended 12/31/00): Grants paid, $70,035; assets, $1,290,786 (M); expenditures, $63,105; qualifying distributions, $70,035.
Limitations: Applications not accepted. Giving primarily in Nashville, TN.
Application information: Contributes only to pre-selected organizations.
Officer: Julia Carell Stadler, Chair.
Board member: George B. Stadler.
EIN: 626314877

50114
Agape Foundation
725 Vail Ct.
Nashville, TN 37215

Established in 1995 in TN.
Donor(s): Helen King Cummings, Harvey R. Cummings.
Financial data (yr. ended 12/31/01): Grants paid, $70,000; assets, $1,813,141 (M); expenditures, $96,945; qualifying distributions, $70,000.
Limitations: Applications not accepted. Giving primarily in Nashville, TN.
Application information: Contributes only to pre-selected organizations.
Officers and Directors:* Helen King Cummings,* Pres.; Harvey R. Cummings,* Secy.-Treas.; Philip R. Patton.
EIN: 621586158

50115
The Morris Family Foundation
c/o John A. Morris
3401 West End Ave., Ste. 685
Nashville, TN 37203

Established in 1990 in TN.
Financial data (yr. ended 12/31/01): Grants paid, $70,000; assets, $1,324,469 (M); expenditures, $71,086; qualifying distributions, $70,000.
Limitations: Applications not accepted. Giving primarily in NY and TN.
Application information: Contributes only to pre-selected organizations.
Trustees: Alfred H. Morris, John A. Morris.
EIN: 581913577

50116
Mary Cortner Ragland Foundation
c/o SunTrust Banks, Inc.
P.O. Box 305110
Nashville, TN 37230-5110 (615) 748-5813
Contact: Kim Williams, Trust Off., SunTrust Banks, Inc.

Established in 1999 in TN.
Donor(s): Mary C. Ragland.‡
Financial data (yr. ended 06/30/01): Grants paid, $70,000; assets, $1,793,747 (M); gifts received, $451,579; expenditures, $84,345; qualifying distributions, $77,373.
Limitations: Giving primarily in Nashville, TN.
Trustee: SunTrust Banks, Inc.
EIN: 311684739

50117
Unaka Scholarship Foundation, Inc.
c/o Unaka Co., Inc.
P.O. Box 877
Greeneville, TN 37744-0877
Application address: 1500 Industrial Rd., Greeneville, TN 37745, tel.: (423) 639-1171
Contact: Dominick Jackson, Pres.

Financial data (yr. ended 06/30/01): Grants paid, $69,851; assets, $138,105 (M); expenditures, $69,898; qualifying distributions, $69,898.
Limitations: Giving primarily in SC and TN.
Application information: Application form required.
Officer: Mildred S. Buckles, Secy.
Directors: Larry Dunbar, Dominick Jackson.
EIN: 621530053
Codes: GTI

50118
The BBC Foundation
428 McCallie Ave.
Chattanooga, TN 37402

Financial data (yr. ended 12/31/01): Grants paid, $69,700; assets, $2,120,813 (M); expenditures, $81,599; qualifying distributions, $75,126.
Limitations: Applications not accepted. Giving primarily in Chattanooga, TN.
Application information: Contributes only to pre-selected organizations.
Officers and Trustees:* H. Clay Evans Johnson,* Chair.; Betsy J.F. Farmer,* Vice-Chair.; H. Clay Evans Johnson, Jr.,* Vice-Chair.; Barbara J. Prickett,* Vice-Chair.; Knox S. Farmer,* V.P.; Carl J. Arnold,* Secy.-Treas.
EIN: 581577719

50119
Mark Smith Charitable Foundation
2033 Richard Jones Rd.
Nashville, TN 37215

Established in 1999 in TN.
Financial data (yr. ended 03/31/01): Grants paid, $69,250; assets, $165,733 (M); expenditures, $73,227; qualifying distributions, $68,956.
Limitations: Applications not accepted. Giving primarily in TN.
Application information: Contributes only to pre-selected organizations.
Officers: Mark W. Smith, Pres.; Deborah D. Smith, Secy.
EIN: 621793172

50120
Hill Family Foundation
1755-D Lynnfield Rd., Ste. 142
Memphis, TN 38119 (901) 761-4664

Established in 2000 in TN.
Donor(s): Wilton D. Hill.
Financial data (yr. ended 12/31/01): Grants paid, $68,700; assets, $93,482 (M); expenditures, $68,764; qualifying distributions, $68,642.
Limitations: Giving primarily in Memphis, TN and surrounding areas of AR and MS.
Officers and Directors:* Wilton D. Hill,* Pres.; Andi F. Hill,* Secy.-Treas.; Kathryn L. Hill, S. Davidson Hill.
EIN: 621746910

50121
Mueller Brass Foundation
8285 Tournament Dr., Ste. 150
Memphis, TN 38125

Financial data (yr. ended 11/30/01): Grants paid, $67,307; assets, $118,153 (M); expenditures, $67,307; qualifying distributions, $67,216.
Limitations: Applications not accepted. Giving primarily in IL.
Application information: Contributes only to pre-selected organizations.
Directors: John Fonzo, Harvey Karp, Kent McKee, William O'Hagen, James H. Rourke.
EIN: 386055712

50122
John and Angela Shaheen Charitable Trust
200 N. Crest Rd.
Chattanooga, TN 37404

Established in 1999 in TN.
Donor(s): John A. Shaheen, Angela P. Shaheen.
Financial data (yr. ended 12/31/01): Grants paid, $66,438; assets, $125,554 (M); gifts received, $142,687; expenditures, $67,438; qualifying distributions, $66,438.

Trustees: Joe D. Goodson, Angela P. Shaheen, John A. Shaheen.
EIN: 626361671

50123
William A. Carson Foundation
c/o William A. Carson, II
130 N. Court Ave.
Memphis, TN 38112

Established in 1948 in IN.
Donor(s): William A. Carson.‡
Financial data (yr. ended 12/31/00): Grants paid, $65,500; assets, $484,963 (M); expenditures, $71,981; qualifying distributions, $65,500.
Limitations: Applications not accepted. Giving primarily in Evansville, IN.
Application information: Contributes only to pre-selected organizations.
Officers and Directors:* William A. Carson III,* Pres. and Treas.; Christopher S. Carson,* V.P.; Robert M. Becker,* Secy.
EIN: 356022740

50124
Frank and Virginia Rogers Foundation
(Formerly Speedwell Heritage Foundation)
P.O. Box 1646
Knoxville, TN 37901 (865) 523-8486
Contact: Virginia B. Rogers, Chair.

Established in 1973.
Financial data (yr. ended 12/31/01): Grants paid, $65,500; assets, $1,191,262 (M); expenditures, $76,709; qualifying distributions, $65,500.
Limitations: Giving primarily in Knoxville, TN.
Officers: Virginia B. Rogers, Chair.; Philip Scheurer, Pres.; Wayne Kramer, Secy.; William E. Pinkston, Treas.
Directors: Barbara Apking, Bobbye Dyslin, Benton E. Gates, Richard D. Rogers, Lindsay Young.
EIN: 237326907

50125
Reese Rule Charitable Foundation, Inc.
2033 Richard Jones Rd.
Nashville, TN 37215

Established in 1999 in TN.
Financial data (yr. ended 03/31/01): Grants paid, $63,794; assets, $169,684 (M); expenditures, $68,919; qualifying distributions, $63,794.
Limitations: Applications not accepted.
Application information: Contributes only to pre-selected organizations.
Officers: Reese L. Smith III, Pres.; Emily D. Smith, Secy.-Treas.
Trustees: Lyndsay Claire Smith, R. Lauren Smith.
EIN: 621793173

50126
The Lillian Foundation
c/o J.C. Bradford, Jr.
330 Commerce St.
Nashville, TN 37201

Established in 1990 in TN.
Donor(s): Eleanor Bradford Unitrust.
Financial data (yr. ended 12/31/01): Grants paid, $63,150; assets, $1,374,248 (M); gifts received, $144,190; expenditures, $64,073; qualifying distributions, $63,150.
Limitations: Applications not accepted.
Application information: Contributes only to pre-selected organizations.
Trust Committee Members: Bryan Robertson Bradford, James C. Bradford, Jr., James C. Bradford III, Lillian Robertson Bradford.
EIN: 626344538

50127
Card Foundation
P.O. Box 24
Hixson, TN 37343
Contact: Janice C. Henderson, Secy.-Treas.

Established in 1977 in TN.
Donor(s): J. Lewis Card, Sr., J. Lewis Card, Jr.
Financial data (yr. ended 11/30/99): Grants paid, $63,000; assets, $1,094,194 (M); expenditures, $73,334; qualifying distributions, $63,027.
Limitations: Giving primarily in Hamilton County and Chattanooga, TN.
Application information: Application form not required.
Officers: J. Lewis Card, Sr., Pres.; Rocelia O. Card, V.P.; Janice C. Henderson, Secy.-Treas.
EIN: 237326879

50128
The Chapman Foundation
c/o Steven Curtis Chapman
P.O. Box 120103
Nashville, TN 37212

Established in 1996 in TN.
Donor(s): Mary Beth Chapman, Steven Curtis Chapman.
Financial data (yr. ended 12/31/01): Grants paid, $62,850; assets, $66,479 (M); gifts received, $72,500; expenditures, $63,780; qualifying distributions, $63,773.
Limitations: Applications not accepted. Giving primarily in TN.
Application information: Contributes only to pre-selected organizations.
Officers and Committee Members:* Steven Curtis Chapman,* Chair.; Jeanie Kaserman,* Secy.-Treas.; Mary Beth Chapman.
EIN: 621631073

50129
The Vise Foundation
4337 Beekman Dr.
Nashville, TN 37215 (615) 665-0183
Contact: Harry Vise, Pres.

Established in 1986 in TN.
Donor(s): Harry Vise.
Financial data (yr. ended 12/31/01): Grants paid, $62,549; assets, $252,294 (M); expenditures, $65,295; qualifying distributions, $62,549.
Limitations: Giving primarily in Nashville, TN.
Officers and Directors:* Harry Vise,* Pres.; David Vise, Secy.-Treas.; Doris Vise.
EIN: 621301149

50130
The Sigel Family Charitable Trust
5691 Sycamore Grove Ln.
Memphis, TN 38119-2269
Contact: Andrew Sigel, Tr.

Established in 1986 in TN.
Donor(s): Andrew Sigel, Gary Sigel.
Financial data (yr. ended 12/31/01): Grants paid, $62,195; assets, $970,548 (M); expenditures, $64,068; qualifying distributions, $62,195.
Limitations: Giving primarily in New York, NY, and Memphis, TN.
Application information: Application form required.
Trustees: Andrew Sigel, Erika Sigel, Gary Sigel.
EIN: 581728810

50131
Wallace Foundation
P.O. Box 6004
Morristown, TN 37815-6004 (423) 586-5650
Contact: John D. Wallace, Pres.

Established in 1964.
Donor(s): John D. Wallace.
Financial data (yr. ended 06/30/02): Grants paid, $60,850; assets, $609,228 (M); gifts received, $124,411; expenditures, $64,650; qualifying distributions, $60,850.
Limitations: Giving primarily in TN.
Application information: Application form not required.
Officers: John D. Wallace, Pres.; Doyle M. Wallace, V.P.; Diane S. Gregs, Jr., Secy.; Cornelles Van Der Veloe, Treas.
EIN: 626048465

50132
Polly Boyd Scholarship Fund
702 Tallan Bldg.
2 Union Sq.
Chattanooga, TN 37402 (423) 756-0611
Contact: Joel W. Richardson, Jr., Tr.

Donor(s): R.J.R. Nabisco Foundation, John T. Lupton, Community Foundation of Greater Chattanooga, Inc., The Warren A. Stevens Trust.
Financial data (yr. ended 12/31/00): Grants paid, $58,500; assets, $637,557 (M); gifts received, $54,025; expenditures, $59,506; qualifying distributions, $58,771.
Limitations: Giving limited to TN.
Application information: Application form required.
Trustees: Llewellyn Boyd, Charles B. Chitty, Joel W. Richardson, Jr.
EIN: 626184352
Codes: GTI

50133
Precision Rubber Products Foundation, Inc.
104 Hartmann Dr.
Lebanon, TN 37087-8401

Donor(s): Precision Rubber Products.
Financial data (yr. ended 06/30/01): Grants paid, $57,750; assets, $1,255,809 (M); expenditures, $58,590; qualifying distributions, $58,590.
Limitations: Giving primarily in areas of company operations and affiliates.
Application information: Application form required for scholarships.
Officers and Board Members:* James Carroll,* Pres.; Lynn Winfree,* Secy.; Howard G. Gillette, Anita Huddleston, Jerry L. McFadden, Michael E. Midgett.
EIN: 310503347
Codes: CS, CD

50134
The Gertrude Jeckyl Charitable Foundation
(Formerly The Jeckyl Foundation)
c/o Sussman & Assocs.
1222 16th Ave. S., 3rd Fl.
Nashville, TN 37212

Established in 1992 in CA.
Donor(s): Bette Midler.
Financial data (yr. ended 07/31/01): Grants paid, $56,233; assets, $69,780 (M); gifts received, $118,000; expenditures, $56,413; qualifying distributions, $56,233.
Limitations: Applications not accepted.
Application information: Contributes only to pre-selected organizations.
Officers: Bette Midler, Pres.; Charles Sussman, Mgr.
EIN: 954385689

50135
Col. R. McDonald Gray Family Foundation, Inc.
8858 Cedar Springs Ln., Ste. 5000
Knoxville, TN 37923

Established in 1999 in TN.
Financial data (yr. ended 12/31/00): Grants paid, $55,762; assets, $650,764 (M); expenditures, $56,550; qualifying distributions, $55,318.
Limitations: Giving primarily in Knoxville, TN.
Officers: Dorothy Gray, Pres.; Don Gray, V.P.; Stan Sheldon, Secy.-Treas.
EIN: 621796048

50136
Higher Ground Foundation
c/o Titus International
1515 McBrien Rd.
Chattanooga, TN 37412-3103 (423) 867-7079
Contact: L.W. Nichols, Pres.

Established in 1986 in TN.
Donor(s): Jack H. Cornelius, Sue Cornelius.
Financial data (yr. ended 12/31/01): Grants paid, $55,700; assets, $13,378 (M); gifts received, $55,000; expenditures, $59,420; qualifying distributions, $56,625.
Limitations: Giving primarily in TN.
Application information: Application form not required.
Officers and Directors:* Sue Cornelius,* Chair.; L.W. Nichols,* Pres.; Marilyn F. Schneller,* Secy.; Lowell David Marcum,* Treas.
EIN: 581730029

50137
Gerald W. & Mary A. Phillips Family Charitable Foundation
505 Waxwood Dr.
Brentwood, TN 37027-5621

Established in 1998 in TN.
Donor(s): Gerald W. Phillips, Mary A. Phillips.
Financial data (yr. ended 12/31/01): Grants paid, $54,805; assets, $786,107 (M); expenditures, $61,513; qualifying distributions, $54,805.
Limitations: Applications not accepted. Giving primarily in TN.
Application information: Contributes only to pre-selected organizations.
Trustees: Gerald W. Phillips, Mary Ann Phillips.
EIN: 621744494

50138
Bradford Foundation
530 Belle Meade Blvd.
Nashville, TN 37205

Established in 1958 in TN.
Financial data (yr. ended 12/31/01): Grants paid, $54,750; assets, $1,748,354 (M); expenditures, $71,845; qualifying distributions, $54,860.
Limitations: Giving primarily in Nashville, TN.
Officers: James C. Bradford, Jr., Mgr.; Eleanor B. Currie, Mgr.
EIN: 626042470

50139
Ruth McBride Polk Trust
c/o SunTrust Banks, Inc.
P.O. Box 305110
Nashville, TN 37230-5110

Established in 1990 in TN.
Donor(s): Ruth McBride Polk.‡
Financial data (yr. ended 12/31/01): Grants paid, $54,328; assets, $1,347,151 (M); expenditures, $66,267; qualifying distributions, $56,213.
Limitations: Applications not accepted. Giving limited to TN.
Application information: Contributes only to pre-selected organizations.
Trustee: SunTrust Banks, Inc.
EIN: 626240011

50140
The L.A.M.P. Foundation
c/o Townes L. Osborn
409 Bearben Park Cir.
Knoxville, TN 37919-7448
Contact: Arthur W. Lavidge, Secy.-Treas.

Established in 1999 in TN.
Donor(s): Arthur W. Lavidge.
Financial data (yr. ended 12/31/01): Grants paid, $53,000; assets, $997,033 (M); expenditures, $54,830; qualifying distributions, $53,000.
Limitations: Giving primarily in Knoxville, TN.
Application information: Application form required.
Officers: Townes Lavidge Osborn, Pres.; R. Lyle Lavidge, V.P.; Arthur W. Lavidge, Secy.-Treas.
EIN: 621722567

50141
Henry Laird Smith Foundation
800 Nashville City Ctr.
Nashville, TN 37219-1743

Established in 1993 in TN.
Donor(s): Margaret Thompson Smith.
Financial data (yr. ended 12/31/01): Grants paid, $53,000; assets, $824,483 (M); expenditures, $61,947; qualifying distributions, $53,000.
Limitations: Applications not accepted. Giving primarily in Nashville, TN.
Application information: Contributes only to pre-selected organizations.
Trustees: Margaret T. Smith, Overton T. Smith, Equitable Trust Co.
EIN: 626271796

50142
The Gause Foundation
4363 W. Cherry Pl.
Memphis, TN 38117-3520

Established in 1995 in TN.
Donor(s): Dorothea O. Gause, Luther P. Gause.
Financial data (yr. ended 12/31/01): Grants paid, $52,855; assets, $1,006,670 (M); expenditures, $53,390; qualifying distributions, $52,855.
Limitations: Applications not accepted. Giving primarily in GA and TN.
Application information: Contributes only to pre-selected organizations.
Trustees: Sidney Gause Childress, Nan Gause Evans, Dorothea O. Gause, Luther P. Gause.
EIN: 626288610

50143
McGehee Family Foundation
700 Colonial Rd., Ste. 125
Memphis, TN 38117
Contact: James E. McGehee, III, Pres.

Established in 1999 in TN.
Donor(s): James E. McGehee, Jr.
Financial data (yr. ended 12/31/01): Grants paid, $52,350; assets, $888,825 (M); expenditures, $90,070; qualifying distributions, $52,350.
Limitations: Giving primarily in TN.
Officers: James E. McGehee III, Pres.; Andrew P. McGehee, V.P.; J. Clifton Paessler, Secy.; Stuart C. McGehee, Treas.
EIN: 621801291

50144
Pershing Yoakley & Associates Foundation
525 Portland St.
Knoxville, TN 37919

Donor(s): Edward V. Pershing.
Financial data (yr. ended 12/31/00): Grants paid, $51,656; assets, $6,803 (M); gifts received, $31,266; expenditures, $51,656; qualifying distributions, $51,656.
Limitations: Giving primarily in AL and TN.
Officers: D. Pace Porter, Pres.; Thomas M. Fisher, V.P.; Douglas A. Yoakley, Secy.
EIN: 621725360

50145
Maddox Family Foundation
c/o William S. Saville, AmSouth Bank
601 Market St., Trust Dept.
Chattanooga, TN 37402-4802
Contact: Helen G. Maddox, Grant Comm. Member

Established in 1997 in GA.
Donor(s): Helen G. Maddox, W. Henry Maddox III.
Financial data (yr. ended 12/31/01): Grants paid, $51,000; assets, $1,068,341 (M); expenditures, $65,500; qualifying distributions, $53,121.
Limitations: Giving primarily in GA.
Grant Committee: Nancy M. Lewallen, Carol G. Maddox, Helen G. Maddox, Helen M. Menefee.
Trustee: AmSouth Bank.
EIN: 586332618

50146
Ned R. McWherter Charitable Foundation, Inc.
P.O. Box 30
Dresden, TN 38225

Established in 1996 in TN.
Donor(s): Ned R. McWherter.
Financial data (yr. ended 12/31/00): Grants paid, $50,761; assets, $1,136,910 (M); expenditures, $72,047; qualifying distributions, $50,761.
Limitations: Applications not accepted. Giving primarily in MO and TN.
Application information: Contributes only to pre-selected organizations.
Officers: Ned R. McWherter, Pres.; Michael R. McWherter, V.P.; Madelyn B. Pritchett, Secy.
EIN: 621657841

50147
Victoria Owen Klein Foundation
P.O. Box 1728
Brentwood, TN 37024

Financial data (yr. ended 12/31/01): Grants paid, $50,000; assets, $696,873 (M); expenditures, $50,140; qualifying distributions, $50,000.
Limitations: Giving primarily in WA.
Trustees: Fred D. Bryan, Victoria Owen Klein.
EIN: 621839796

50148
The Margaret Ann and Walter Robinson Foundation
c/o The Equitable Trust Co.
511 Union St., Ste. 800
Nashville, TN 37219

Established in 1991 in TN.
Donor(s): Margaret Ann Craig Robinson.
Financial data (yr. ended 12/31/01): Grants paid, $50,000; assets, $1,058,326 (M); expenditures, $61,787; qualifying distributions, $50,000.
Limitations: Applications not accepted. Giving primarily in TN.
Application information: Contributes only to pre-selected organizations.

Trustees: Ann Robinson Kelly, Elizabeth Robinson Page, Emmie Robinson Rick, Margaret Ann Craig Robinson, Walter M. Robinson, Jr., Walter M. Robinson III.
EIN: 626249111

50149
Barbara Owen Smith Family Foundation
P.O. Box 1728
Brentwood, TN 37024-1728
Application address: 838 Brentview Dr., Nashville, TN 37220
Contact: Fred D. Bryan, Tr.

Financial data (yr. ended 12/31/01): Grants paid, $50,000; assets, $696,689 (M); expenditures, $50,180; qualifying distributions, $50,005.
Limitations: Giving primarily in TN.
Trustees: Fred D. Bryan, Barbara Owen Smith.
EIN: 621839695

50150
Cars for Kids Southern Style
245 Shanna Dr.
Selmer, TN 38375

Financial data (yr. ended 12/31/01): Grants paid, $48,450; assets, $33,403 (M); gifts received, $82,631; expenditures, $66,003; qualifying distributions, $48,450.
Limitations: Applications not accepted.
Application information: Contributes only to pre-selected organizations.
Officers: Larry Price, Pres.; Charles Coleman, V.P.; Theresa Robinson, Secy.
EIN: 621438499

50151
Roos Foundation
c/o Charles E. Roos
566 Mainstream Dr., Ste. 300
Nashville, TN 37228

Donor(s): Anne Roos, Charles Roos.
Financial data (yr. ended 12/31/01): Grants paid, $48,450; assets, $118,801 (M); expenditures, $49,136; qualifying distributions, $48,450.
Limitations: Applications not accepted. Giving primarily in Nashville, TN.
Application information: Contributes only to pre-selected organizations.
Officers: Charles Roos, Pres.; Anne Roos, V.P.
EIN: 621577658

50152
Lamberth Foundation of Mississippi, Inc.
100 James Blvd., No. F-5
Signal Mountain, TN 37377
Contact: Rev. Jamie Tynes

Donor(s): Mildred E. Lamberth.‡
Financial data (yr. ended 12/31/01): Grants paid, $48,000; assets, $478,581 (M); expenditures, $59,076; qualifying distributions, $51,805.
Limitations: Giving limited to the Heidelberg, MS, area.
Application information: Application form not required.
Officers: Carl J. Lambert, Pres.; Mark Rodgers, Secy.
Directors: Robert C. Hatcher, Richard P. Jahn, Jr.
EIN: 721359762

50153
The Bernard Lapides and Shirley W. Lapides Foundation
c/o National Bank of Commerce, Trust Div.
1 Commerce Sq.
Memphis, TN 38150
Additional address: c/o Bernard Lapides, 710 South St., Memphis, TN 38101-0710

Financial data (yr. ended 12/31/00): Grants paid, $47,600; assets, $1,819,726 (M); gifts received, $18,750; expenditures, $66,797; qualifying distributions, $47,600.
Limitations: Giving primarily in Memphis, TN.
Trustee: National Bank of Commerce.
EIN: 581556976

50154
Lindahl Foundation
c/o State Industries, Inc.
500 Bypass Rd.
Ashland City, TN 37015
Application address: c/o Scholarship Program Admins., Inc., 3314 West End Ave., Nashville, TN 37203-0916
Contact: Betty J. True, Secy.-Treas.

Established in 1990 in TN.
Donor(s): John R. Lindahl, Sr.
Financial data (yr. ended 07/31/00): Grants paid, $47,434; assets, $40,882 (M); gifts received, $7,015; expenditures, $54,449; qualifying distributions, $47,434.
Limitations: Giving limited to TN.
Application information: Application form required.
Officers: John R. Lindahl, Jr., Chair.; George L. Fehrmann, Vice-Chair.; Betty J. True, Secy.-Treas.
Trustees: Herbert W. Lindahl, R.D. Skelton, Larry T. Thrailkill.
EIN: 621420369
Codes: GTI

50155
The Volunteer Trust
c/o SunTrust Banks, Inc.
P.O. Box 305110
Nashville, TN 37230-5110
Additional address: 226 Capitol Blvd., Ste. 200, Nashville, TN 37219
Contact: Douglas Henry, Jr., Tr.

Established in 1986 in TN.
Donor(s): Kathryn Craig Henry.‡
Financial data (yr. ended 08/31/01): Grants paid, $47,000; assets, $28,380 (M); gifts received, $26,135; expenditures, $47,310; qualifying distributions, $47,148.
Limitations: Giving primarily in TN.
Trustee: Douglas Henry, Jr.
EIN: 626186274

50156
Paul Holbrook Trust
c/o SunTrust Banks, Inc.
P.O. Box 305110
Nashville, TN 37230-5110

Financial data (yr. ended 05/31/02): Grants paid, $46,520; assets, $1,102,328 (M); expenditures, $63,738; qualifying distributions, $46,520.
Limitations: Applications not accepted.
Application information: Contributes only to pre-selected organizations.
Trustee: SunTrust Banks, Inc.
EIN: 626187596

50157
The Sawyer Family Foundation, Inc.
343 Bunker Hill Rd.
Cookeville, TN 38501

Established in 1998 in GA.
Donor(s): Carl Sawyer, Marcia Sawyer.
Financial data (yr. ended 04/30/02): Grants paid, $46,452; assets, $639,493 (M); expenditures, $50,746; qualifying distributions, $46,452.
Limitations: Applications not accepted. Giving primarily in FL and GA.
Application information: Contributes only to pre-selected organizations.
Trustees: Carl B. Sawyer, Christy Renee Sawyer, Marcia K. Sawyer.
EIN: 582401467

50158
Hudson Foundation, Inc.
1615 Scholar Ave.
Chattanooga, TN 37406 (423) 624-2631
Contact: James C. Hudson, Jr., Pres.

Established in 1988 in TN.
Financial data (yr. ended 12/31/01): Grants paid, $46,100; assets, $125,593 (M); gifts received, $700; expenditures, $47,000; qualifying distributions, $46,100.
Limitations: Giving primarily in Chattanooga, TN.
Officers: James C. Hudson, Jr., Pres.; James C. Hudson III, V.P.; Steven T. Hudson, Secy.-Treas.
EIN: 621363739

50159
Dewey & Louise Martin Scholarship Fund
c/o AmSouth Bank
315 Deaderick St., 4th Fl.
Nashville, TN 37237-0401 (615) 736-6679
Contact: Renee Fredericksen

Established in 1998 in TN.
Financial data (yr. ended 12/31/01): Grants paid, $45,468; assets, $772,632 (M); expenditures, $53,054; qualifying distributions, $45,468.
Limitations: Giving primarily in Trousdale County, TN.
Application information: Application form available at Trousdale County High School, TN. Application form required.
Trustees: Tony Linville, Toby Woodmore, AmSouth Bank.
EIN: 621721707

50160
Arthur Hamilton Educational Trust Fund
c/o First Tennessee Bank, N.A.
P.O. Box 84
Memphis, TN 38101-0084

Financial data (yr. ended 12/31/01): Grants paid, $45,000; assets, $249,214 (M); expenditures, $48,417; qualifying distributions, $45,000.
Limitations: Giving limited to Dyer County, TN.
Trustee: First Tennessee Bank, N.A.
EIN: 626086530

50161
Reynolds Family Foundation
1105 Lynnwood Blvd.
Nashville, TN 37215

Established in 1999 in TN.
Donor(s): Lee Allen Reynolds.
Financial data (yr. ended 12/31/01): Grants paid, $45,000; assets, $965,543 (M); gifts received, $70,000; expenditures, $51,007; qualifying distributions, $45,000.
Limitations: Applications not accepted.
Application information: Contributes only to pre-selected organizations.

Officers: Lee Allen Reynolds, Pres.; Mary Elizabeth Reynolds, Secy.-Treas.
Director: David Allen Reynolds.
EIN: 621781092

50162
Tonya Memorial Foundation, Inc.
c/o SunTrust Banks, Inc.
736 Market St.
Chattanooga, TN 37402

Incorporated in 1949 in DE.
Donor(s): Burkett Miller.‡
Financial data (yr. ended 12/31/01): Grants paid, $44,653; assets, $4,263,807 (M); expenditures, $130,388; qualifying distributions, $107,984.
Limitations: Giving limited to the Chattanooga, TN, area.
Officers and Trustees:* H. James Hitching,* Chair.; Maurice H. Martin,* Pres.; Allen L. McCallie,* Secy.; H. Whitney Durand,* Treas.
EIN: 626042269

50163
The Hassell Charitable Foundation
P.O. Box 183
Clifton, TN 38425 (931) 676-3311
Additional tel.: (931) 676-3371
Contact: Autry Gobbell, Tr., or Martha Gobbell, Tr.

Established in 1982.
Financial data (yr. ended 12/31/00): Grants paid, $43,795; assets, $16,128,733 (M); expenditures, $273,622; qualifying distributions, $2,051,157; giving activities include $2,000,000 for programs.
Limitations: Giving limited to a 125-mile radius of Clifton, TN.
Application information: Application form required.
Trustees: Charles Cobb, Oliver Cobb, Autry Gobbell, Martha Gobbell, Stephen Gobbell.
EIN: 581485616
Codes: GTI

50164
Sreyas Foundation
4414 Tyne Blvd.
Nashville, TN 37215 (615) 292-7328
Contact: Lindy Sayers

Established in 1994 in TN.
Financial data (yr. ended 12/31/01): Grants paid, $43,755; assets, $374,993 (M); expenditures, $59,683; qualifying distributions, $43,755.
Limitations: Giving primarily in TN.
Trustees: Allen D. Lentz, J.H. Sayers, Jr., Lindy Sayers.
EIN: 626279182

50165
Phillips Family Foundation
c/o Judith P. Clevenger
406 Frazier Ave., Ste. D
Chattanooga, TN 37405 (423) 266-9777

Established in 2000 in TN.
Donor(s): John A. Phillips, Jr.
Financial data (yr. ended 01/31/02): Grants paid, $43,000; assets, $69,013 (M); gifts received, $50,582; expenditures, $43,157; qualifying distributions, $43,000.
Trustee: Judith P. Clevenger.
EIN: 621810351

50166
G. H. Weems Educational Fund
122 Debusk Ln.
Knoxville, TN 37922
Contact: William M. Slayden, Chair.

Established in 1939.

Financial data (yr. ended 12/31/00): Grants paid, $42,945; assets, $1,439,737 (M); expenditures, $64,136; qualifying distributions, $57,845; giving activities include $125 for loans to individuals.
Limitations: Giving primarily in Humphries, Dickson and Montgomery counties, TN.
Publications: Newsletter.
Application information: Application form required.
Officer and Trustees:* William M. Slayden II,* Chair.; Beth M. Slayden, Secy.; William M. Slayden III,* Exec. Dir.; Patricia S. Hollis, Verda McCurdy, Jamey McIntire, Lucile Monroe, John Lee Williams.
EIN: 626047271
Codes: GTI

50167
The Terry D. and Rosann B. Douglass Foundation
c/o Anne Sale
810 Innovation Dr.
Knoxville, TN 37932
Contact: Terry D. Douglass, Dir.

Established in 1994 in TN.
Financial data (yr. ended 12/31/01): Grants paid, $42,761; assets, $856,463 (M); gifts received, $244,050; expenditures, $43,799; qualifying distributions, $42,761.
Limitations: Giving primarily in Knoxville, TN.
Directors: Rosann B. Douglass, Terry D. Douglass.
EIN: 582068304

50168
Ahlstrom Foundation, Inc.
(Formerly Knowlton Brothers Foundation, Inc.)
Eastgate Town Ctr.
5600 Brainerd Rd., Ste. 100
Chattanooga, TN 37411

Financial data (yr. ended 03/31/01): Grants paid, $42,620; assets, $23,615 (M); expenditures, $42,699; qualifying distributions, $42,690.
Limitations: Giving limited to residents of TN.
Officers: Kari Kohonen, Pres. and Treas.; Dean Holbrook, Secy.
EIN: 156020264

50169
The Ashcraft Foundation, Inc.
6484 Robbins Ridge Ln.
Memphis, TN 38119

Financial data (yr. ended 12/31/99): Grants paid, $42,400; assets, $621,569 (L); expenditures, $47,433; qualifying distributions, $42,039.
Limitations: Applications not accepted. Giving primarily in TN.
Application information: Contributes only to pre-selected organizations.
Officers: Mary Lee McClain, Pres.; James G. Robbins, Secy.-Treas.
EIN: 626048445

50170
The Nancy and Victor S. Johnson, Jr. Foundation, Inc.
(Formerly Victor S. Johnson, Jr. Foundation, Inc.)
705 Murfreesboro Rd., Box 100255
Nashville, TN 37210-4521 (615) 748-3366
Application address: 703 Murfreesboro Rd., Nashville, TN 37210, tel.: (615) 748-3360
Contact: Lillian B. Jenkins, Secy.-Treas.

Donor(s): Victor S. Johnson, Jr., Nancy M. Johnson.
Financial data (yr. ended 12/31/01): Grants paid, $41,050; assets, $853,735 (M); expenditures, $45,572; qualifying distributions, $41,050.
Limitations: Giving primarily in Nashville, TN.

50170—TENNESSEE

Officers and Directors:* Victor S. Johnson, Jr.,* Pres.; Nancy M. Johnson,* V.P.; Lillian B. Jenkins,* Secy.-Treas.; Victor S. Johnson III.
EIN: 626073456

50171
Chattanooga Orthopedic Educational and Research Foundation
975 E. 3rd St., Box 260
Chattanooga, TN 37403 (423) 756-6623
Contact: Hugh P. Brown, M.D., Pres.

Donor(s): Hugh P. Brown, M.D., Channappa Chandra, M.D., Martin Redish, M.D., Robert Coddington, M.D., Paul M. Apyan, M.D., Marshall Jemison, M.D., John Nash, M.D.
Financial data (yr. ended 12/31/00): Grants paid, $40,781; assets, $102,140 (M); gifts received, $114,827; expenditures, $93,514; qualifying distributions, $84,113; giving activities include $43,366 for programs.
Limitations: Giving primarily in Chattanooga, TN.
Officers and Directors:* Hugh P. Brown, M.D.,* Pres.; Channappa Chandra, M.D.,* V.P.; William Aiken, Secy.; Paul Broadstone, M.D.,* Treas.; Robert Coddington, M.D., Martin H. Redish, M.D.
EIN: 237091528
Codes: GTI

50172
The Bonny Oaks Foundation
910 Brynwood Terr.
Chattanooga, TN 37415-3007 (423) 877-8201
Contact: Malcolm M. Adamson, Secy.-Treas.

Established in 1983.
Financial data (yr. ended 04/30/02): Grants paid, $40,684; assets, $859,237 (M); expenditures, $46,510; qualifying distributions, $40,684.
Limitations: Giving primarily in TN.
Publications: Financial statement.
Application information: Application form not required.
Officers and Directors:* David Nelson,* Pres.; Malcolm M. Adamson,* Secy.-Treas.; Roger Ingvalson, Morty Lloyd, Ray McLaurin, David Nelson, Stephen Pike, Mickey Robbins.
EIN: 621175793

50173
Carlos H. Cantu Family Foundation
2255 Johnson Rd.
Germantown, TN 38139
Contact: Carlos H. Cantu, Pres.

Established around 1994 in TN.
Donor(s): Carlos H. Cantu.
Financial data (yr. ended 12/31/01): Grants paid, $40,500; assets, $189,445 (M); gifts received, $51,831; expenditures, $41,577; qualifying distributions, $40,500.
Limitations: Giving primarily in Germantown and Memphis, TN, and TX.
Application information: Application form not required.
Officers and Directors:* Carlos H. Cantu, Pres.; Gloria L. Cantu, V.P.; Alberto T. Cantu,* Secy.; Carlos H. Cantu, Jr.,* Treas.; David S. Cantu, George A. Cantu, Lorenzo A. Cantu, Gloria A. Cantu Shrewsbury.
EIN: 621578086

50174
The Dodson Family Charitable Foundation, Inc.
115 E. Main St.
Gallatin, TN 37066-2801

Established in 2000 in TN.
Financial data (yr. ended 12/31/00): Grants paid, $40,000; assets, $780,768 (M); gifts received, $819,133; expenditures, $40,001; qualifying distributions, $39,984.
Limitations: Applications not accepted. Giving primarily in Gallatin, TN.
Application information: Contributes only to pre-selected organizations.
Officers and Directors:* William C. Hudgins,* Pres.; Wilda H. Dodson,* Secy.; Penn Ueoka Dodson, Susan Dodson Hiller.
EIN: 621808946

50175
Alice W. Jew Foundation
c/o Jack K. Byrd
111 Westwood Pl., Ste. 400
Brentwood, TN 37027

Established in 1995 in TN.
Donor(s): Alice W. Jew.‡
Financial data (yr. ended 04/30/02): Grants paid, $40,000; assets, $1,409,679 (M); expenditures, $187,975; qualifying distributions, $45,372.
Limitations: Applications not accepted. Giving primarily in TN.
Application information: Contributes only to pre-selected organizations.
Trustees: Jack K. Byrd, Roger Proctor, Leland Watts.
EIN: 621581405

50176
Stephen B. Smith Charitable Foundation, Inc.
2033 Richard Jones Rd.
Nashville, TN 37215

Established in 1999 in TN.
Donor(s): Marcella V. Smith.
Financial data (yr. ended 03/31/01): Grants paid, $40,000; assets, $200,244 (M); expenditures, $45,232; qualifying distributions, $40,000.
Limitations: Applications not accepted.
Application information: Contributes only to pre-selected organizations.
Officers: Stephen B. Smith, Pres.; Denise S. Smith, Secy.-Treas.
Trustee: John Stanford.
EIN: 621793679

50177
TCH Fort Foundation
c/o SunTrust Banks, Inc.
P.O. Box 305110
Nashville, TN 37230-5110 (615) 748-5813
Contact: Kim Williams

Established in 1999 in TN.
Financial data (yr. ended 09/30/01): Grants paid, $40,000; assets, $850,706 (M); expenditures, $60,292; qualifying distributions, $44,975.
Application information: Application form not required.
Trustee: SunTrust Banks, Inc.
EIN: 626356582

50178
The Schoenbaum Scholarship Foundation
(Formerly The Shoney's Foundation, Inc.)
c/o John Ploszkiewicz
1727 Elm Hill Pike
Nashville, TN 37210 (615) 231-2744

Established in 1992 in TN.
Financial data (yr. ended 06/30/01): Grants paid, $39,500; assets, $805,493 (M); expenditures, $56,693; qualifying distributions, $45,360.
Limitations: Giving limited to residents of TN.
Application information: Application form required.
Officers and Directors:* Betty J. Marshall,* Pres.; V. Michael Payne, V.P.; Wanda G. Parsons, Secy.; F.E. McDaniel, Treas.
EIN: 581992911
Codes: GTI

50179
M. & W. Waller Fund
c/o SunTrust Banks, Inc.
P.O. Box 305110
Nashville, TN 37230-5110 (615) 748-5813
Contact: Lee Ann Duvall

Financial data (yr. ended 12/31/01): Grants paid, $38,300; assets, $509,782 (M); expenditures, $44,529; qualifying distributions, $41,352.
Limitations: Giving primarily in TN.
Application information: Application form not required.
Trustee: SunTrust Banks, Inc.
EIN: 626049606

50180
Jesus Christ is Lord Ministries
P.O. Box 1266
Hendersonville, TN 37077-1266
(615) 824-2775
Contact: Donald R. Mercer, Tr.

Established in 1991 in TN.
Donor(s): Donald R. Mercer, Edith F. Mercer, Mercer Corp.
Financial data (yr. ended 07/31/01): Grants paid, $38,120; assets, $261,706 (M); gifts received, $52,003; expenditures, $91,913; qualifying distributions, $38,120.
Limitations: Giving primarily in FL, GA, and TN.
Trustees: Donald R. Mercer, Edith F. Mercer.
EIN: 621477389

50181
Garney B. Scott Jr. Family Foundation, Inc
c/o Garney B. Scott Jr.
1485 Scepter Ln.
Waverly, TN 37185

Established in 2000 in TN.
Donor(s): Garney B. Scott, Jr.
Financial data (yr. ended 12/31/01): Grants paid, $37,486; assets, $336,009 (M); expenditures, $38,646; qualifying distributions, $37,250.
Limitations: Applications not accepted. Giving primarily in TN.
Application information: Contributes only to pre-selected organizations.
Directors: Andrea C. Pennington, Carolyn M. Scott, Garney B. Scott, Jr.
EIN: 621841085

50182
The Viam Charitable and Educational Foundation, Inc.
142 Fairbanks Rd.
Oak Ridge, TN 37830-7078 (423) 482-2400
Contact: Huu D. Dinh, Dir.

Financial data (yr. ended 12/31/01): Grants paid, $37,390; assets, $132,939 (M); gifts received, $10,410; expenditures, $47,920; qualifying distributions, $37,390.
Application information: Application form required.
Directors: Huu D. Dinh, Nancy Pham-Dinh, Duykim Tran Nguyen.
EIN: 621603003

50183
The Watson Foundation, Inc.
c/o H.E. Mixon
4176 Lake Meadow Way
Louisville, TN 37777

Incorporated in 1956 in TN.

Donor(s): Fred H. Fain,‡ Henry N. Carmichael, Jr., F.W. Goddard,‡ Forrest I. Watson, John A. Ayres, Sr.,‡ Ira A. Watson, Eva M. Watson.
Financial data (yr. ended 12/31/01): Grants paid, $37,300; assets, $792,717 (M); gifts received, $2,000; expenditures, $39,153; qualifying distributions, $37,300.
Limitations: Applications not accepted. Giving primarily in KY and TN.
Application information: Contributes only to pre-selected organizations.
Officers and Directors:* Forrest I. Watson,* Chair.; Samuel A. Watson, Pres.; Jan Watson,* Secy.; Margery G. Watson.
EIN: 626045681

50184
Burton Family Foundation
610 Polo Run
Collierville, TN 38017
Contact: Dennis Burton, Pres.

Established in 1999 in TN.
Donor(s): Dennis Burton, Ellen Ann Burton.
Financial data (yr. ended 10/31/00): Grants paid, $37,000; assets, $6,527 (M); gifts received, $82,207; expenditures, $40,619; qualifying distributions, $37,000.
Officers and Directors:* Dennis Burton,* Pres. and Treas.; Ellen Ann Burton,* Secy.; Katina Gaines.
EIN: 364334244

50185
Dudley & Walter Morgan Foundation
210 Evelyn Ave.
Nashville, TN 37205-3308 (615) 383-8023
Contact: Dudley Morgan, Pres.

Established in 1994 in TN.
Donor(s): Dudley Morgan, Mrs. Dudley Morgan.
Financial data (yr. ended 11/30/01): Grants paid, $37,000; assets, $681,327 (M); gifts received, $300; expenditures, $46,671; qualifying distributions, $37,000.
Limitations: Giving primarily in Nashville, TN.
Application information: Application form not required.
Officers: Dudley Morgan, Pres.; William D. Morgan, Secy.
Trustee: Walter M. Morgan III.
EIN: 621585196

50186
Ira M. Gambill Medical Education Trust
c/o AmeriStar Investments & Trust
P.O. Box 1981
Kingsport, TN 37662
Contact: Randy Bell, V.P., AmeriStar Investments & Trust

Financial data (yr. ended 06/30/01): Grants paid, $36,500; assets, $693,216 (M); expenditures, $46,776; qualifying distributions, $41,455.
Limitations: Giving limited to Johnson County, TN.
Application information: Application form required.
Trustee: AmeriStar Investments & Trust.
EIN: 626186726
Codes: GTI

50187
Charlotte Fanning Foundation, Inc.
(Formerly Fanning Orphan School)
421 Cedarcliff Dr.
Antioch, TN 37013 (615) 361-1144
Contact: Norma Morefield

Financial data (yr. ended 05/31/02): Grants paid, $36,450; assets, $561,753 (M); gifts received, $300; expenditures, $45,634; qualifying distributions, $41,330.
Limitations: Giving primarily in Nashville, TN.
Officers: Philip C. Kelly, Pres.; Greg Hardeman, Secy.; Kathy Bell, Treas.
Trustees: Earl Dennis, Miles Ezell, Jr., Linda Hyne, Walt Leaver, Sr., Mary Jane Loden, Betty Mansfield, Lee Marsh, Jim B. McInteer, Winston Moore, Frank Outhier, Patricia Peek, David Sciortino.
EIN: 620541810
Codes: GTI

50188
McCoy Foundation Trust B
1277 E. Massey St.
Memphis, TN 38120-3233 (901) 681-2352
Contact: Norfleet R. Turner, Tr.

Financial data (yr. ended 12/31/01): Grants paid, $36,100; assets, $2,538,856 (M); expenditures, $36,625; qualifying distributions, $36,100.
Limitations: Giving primarily in Memphis, TN.
Trustees: Norfleet R. Turner.
EIN: 237099427

50189
Clark Foundation, Inc.
801 Broad St.
Chattanooga, TN 37402-2621 (423) 321-6310
Contact: George M. Clark, Jr., Pres.

Financial data (yr. ended 12/31/01): Grants paid, $35,805; assets, $787,739 (M); gifts received, $266; expenditures, $36,476; qualifying distributions, $35,455.
Limitations: Giving primarily in TN.
Application information: Application form not required.
Officers: George M. Clark, Jr., Pres. and Treas.; Carole M. Clark, V.P.; George M. Clark III, Secy.
EIN: 620695496

50190
E. Maurine Hawkins Memorial Scholarship Fund
c/o Trust Co. of Knoxville
P.O. Box 789
Knoxville, TN 37901-0789
Application address: c/o Tennessee High School, 1112 Edgemont Ave., Bristol, TN 37620, tel.: (423) 652-9317
Contact: Whitney Walling, Chair.

Financial data (yr. ended 12/31/01): Grants paid, $35,750; assets, $324,252 (M); expenditures, $38,967; qualifying distributions, $35,750.
Limitations: Giving limited to Bristol, TN.
Application information: Application form not required.
Officer and Trustees:* Whitney Walling,* Chair.; Tom Davenport, Nancy Dickerson, Jean Green, Nelson Pyle.
EIN: 621338535
Codes: GTI

50191
The Joseph and Lynn May Foundation
(Formerly The Dorothy and Dan May Foundation)
c/o Joseph L. May
424 Church St., Ste. 2000
Nashville, TN 37219

Established in 1991.
Financial data (yr. ended 12/31/00): Grants paid, $35,676; assets, $30,205 (M); gifts received, $40,973; expenditures, $36,837; qualifying distributions, $35,676.
Limitations: Applications not accepted. Giving limited to Nashville, TN.
Application information: Contributes only to pre-selected organizations.
Trustee: Joseph L. May.
EIN: 621434348

50192
Peggy and Lawrence West Foundation
204 Woodlake Dr.
Gallatin, TN 37066-4420

Established in 1999 in TN.
Donor(s): Lawrence West, Peggy West.
Financial data (yr. ended 07/31/01): Grants paid, $35,000; assets, $905,890 (M); gifts received, $203,910; expenditures, $47,096; qualifying distributions, $35,000.
Limitations: Giving primarily in TN.
Directors: Lawrence West, Peggy West.
EIN: 621748446

50193
Bass Charitable Trust
521 General Kershaw Dr.
Old Hickory, TN 37138

Established in 2000.
Financial data (yr. ended 12/31/00): Grants paid, $34,664; assets, $154 (M); gifts received, $33,225; expenditures, $34,713; qualifying distributions, $34,664.
Limitations: Applications not accepted. Giving primarily in TN.
Application information: Contributes only to pre-selected organizations.
Trustees: Bobby Bass, Sandra Bass.
EIN: 626366262

50194
Clyde W. Harrell Educational Fund
c/o AmSouth Bank
315 Deaderick St., 11th Fl.
Nashville, TN 37237-1101

Financial data (yr. ended 02/28/01): Grants paid, $34,000; assets, $427,250 (M); expenditures, $44,021; qualifying distributions, $34,765.
Limitations: Applications not accepted. Giving limited to residents of Hawkins County, TN.
Application information: Scholarship recipients are chosen by their high school principal with final approval by the AmSouth Bank Committee.
Trustee: AmSouth Bank.
EIN: 626085008
Codes: GTI

50195
The McReynolds Family Foundation
1133 N. Ocoee St.
Cleveland, TN 37311

Established in 1999 in TN.
Donor(s): William S. McReynolds, Anne B. McReynolds.
Financial data (yr. ended 12/31/01): Grants paid, $33,775; assets, $914,420 (M); gifts received, $269,556; expenditures, $35,186; qualifying distributions, $33,775.
Limitations: Applications not accepted.
Application information: Contributes only to pre-selected organizations.
Officers and Directors:* William S. McReynolds,* Pres. and Treas.; Anne B. McReynolds,* V.P.; Michael E. Callaway,* Secy.; Anne Reeves McReynolds, Kenneth McReynolds, William Jackson McReynolds II, George W. Thorogood, Jr., James O. Williams.
EIN: 621781438

50196
Capstone Foundation, Inc.
103 Powell Ct., Ste. 150
Brentwood, TN 37027

Established in 1998.
Financial data (yr. ended 12/31/00): Grants paid, $33,038; assets, $281 (L); gifts received, $19,500; expenditures, $34,654; qualifying distributions, $33,038.
Officer: Linda A. Pettit, Pres.
Director: Bettye W. Hawkins.
EIN: 621749796

50197
Robert and Evelyn Condra Foundation
(Formerly Robert M. Condra Foundation)
c/o Douglas J. Brown
211 Commerce St., Ste. 1000
Nashville, TN 37201
Application address: c/o Jim Sherrod, 1005 8th Ave. S., Nashville, TN 37203, tel.: (615) 254-5590

Financial data (yr. ended 12/31/01): Grants paid, $33,000; assets, $452,976 (M); expenditures, $42,078; qualifying distributions, $32,992.
Limitations: Giving primarily in SC and TN.
Application information: Application form not required.
Directors: Douglas J. Brown, Michael Clardy, Vera Johnson, Jim Sherrod.
EIN: 626025128

50198
The Patti R. Hart Family Foundation
(Formerly The Patti H. Kenney Family Foundation)
c/o H. Rodes Hart
612 10th Ave. N.
Nashville, TN 37203

Established in 1993 in TN.
Donor(s): H. Rodes Hart, Patti R. Hart.
Financial data (yr. ended 12/31/01): Grants paid, $33,000; assets, $8,225 (M); gifts received, $30,293; expenditures, $33,293; qualifying distributions, $33,000.
Limitations: Applications not accepted. Giving primarily in Nashville, TN.
Application information: Contributes only to pre-selected organizations.
Trustee: H. Rodes Hart.
EIN: 626262169

50199
The Roros Foundation
c/o Equitable Trust Company
511 Union St., Ste. 800
Nashville, TN 37219-1743

Established in 1997 in TN.
Donor(s): Kermit C. Stengel.
Financial data (yr. ended 12/31/01): Grants paid, $32,600; assets, $634,542 (M); gifts received, $82,000; expenditures, $36,317; qualifying distributions, $32,600.
Limitations: Applications not accepted.
Application information: Contributes only to pre-selected organizations.
Officers: Kermit C. Stengel, Jr., Pres.; Marc K. Stengel, V.P. and Secy.; Eric L. Stengel, V.P.
EIN: 621677764

50200
Holland Family Scholarship Foundation
(Formerly C.V. Holland, Maybelle Holland, & John Holland Scholarship Fund)
c/o AmSouth Bank
315 Deaderick St., 4th Fl.
Nashville, TN 37237-0401
Application address: 128 W. Lincoln St., Ste. B, Tullahoma, TN 37388
Contact: Doyle E. Richardson

Financial data (yr. ended 05/31/01): Grants paid, $32,500; assets, $562,127 (M); expenditures, $36,757; qualifying distributions, $32,393.
Limitations: Giving limited to residents of Tullahoma, TN.
Application information: Application form required.
Trustee: AmSouth Bank.
EIN: 626141452
Codes: GTI

50201
Julie & Marty Belz Charitable Foundation
5118 Park Ave., Ste. 249
Memphis, TN 38117

Established in 1999 in TN.
Donor(s): Martin S. Belz, Julianne P. Belz.
Financial data (yr. ended 12/31/01): Grants paid, $32,337; assets, $57,318 (M); expenditures, $32,357; qualifying distributions, $32,337.
Limitations: Applications not accepted. Giving primarily in Memphis, TN.
Application information: Contributes only to pre-selected organizations.
Officers: Martin S. Belz, Pres.; Julianne Belz, Secy.
EIN: 621713829

50202
Mattie Helen Elliott Scholarship Fund
900 S. Gay St., 3rd Fl.
Knoxville, TN 37902

Established in 1996.
Financial data (yr. ended 12/31/01): Grants paid, $32,168; assets, $798,633 (M); expenditures, $39,327; qualifying distributions, $32,168.
Limitations: Giving primarily in Somerset, KY.
Trustee: Marguerite Self.
EIN: 616222167

50203
The Clark Family Foundation
5050 Poplar Ave., Ste. 2200
Memphis, TN 38157-2202

Established in 1986 in TN.
Donor(s): William B. Clark.
Financial data (yr. ended 11/30/01): Grants paid, $32,100; assets, $6,745 (M); expenditures, $32,161; qualifying distributions, $32,100.
Limitations: Applications not accepted. Giving primarily in Memphis, TN.
Application information: Contributes only to pre-selected organizations.
Officers and Trustees:* William B. Clark, Jr.,* Pres.; Nicholas G. Clark,* Secy.-Treas.; George B. Clark, Diana Clark Gill.
EIN: 581698603

50204
The Jacquelyn D. Guthrie Foundation
511 Public Sq.
Springfield, TN 37172

Established in 1996 in TN.
Donor(s): Jacquelyn D. Guthrie.
Financial data (yr. ended 11/30/01): Grants paid, $31,750; assets, $839,888 (M); expenditures, $34,554; qualifying distributions, $31,750.
Limitations: Applications not accepted.
Application information: Contributes only to pre-selected organizations.
Trustee: Jacquelyn D. Guthrie.
EIN: 621669983

50205
Lucius E. Burch III Family Foundation
102 Woodmont Blvd., Ste. 320
Nashville, TN 37205-5251

Donor(s): Lucius E. Burch III.
Financial data (yr. ended 06/30/01): Grants paid, $31,100; assets, $420,261 (M); expenditures, $38,003; qualifying distributions, $31,100.
Limitations: Applications not accepted. Giving in the U.S., with an emphasis on TN.
Application information: Contributes only to pre-selected organizations.
Officers and Trustees:* Lucius E. Burch III,* Chair.; Anita V. Burch,* Secy.; Lucius E. Burch IV.
EIN: 621675760

50206
Flora Belle Moss & Bessie Abigail Moss Foundation
5100 Stage Rd., Ste. 4
Memphis, TN 38134-3199 (901) 377-0344
Contact: Carl R. Olsen, Tr.

Financial data (yr. ended 09/30/01): Grants paid, $30,500; assets, $529,101 (M); expenditures, $51,295; qualifying distributions, $30,500.
Limitations: Giving primarily in TN.
Grant Committee: Ronald K. Moore.
Trustee: Carl R. Olsen.
EIN: 626153838

50207
The Wolford Family Foundation
419 N. Market St., Ste. 210
Chattanooga, TN 37405

Established in 1995 in TN.
Donor(s): James L. Wolford.
Financial data (yr. ended 09/30/01): Grants paid, $30,500; assets, $84,822 (M); gifts received, $25,100; expenditures, $36,058; qualifying distributions, $30,500.
Limitations: Applications not accepted. Giving primarily in Chattanooga, TN.
Application information: Contributes only to pre-selected organizations.
Officers: Diane Wolford, Pres.; James L. Wolford, V.P. and Treas.; Richard W. Buhrman, Secy.
EIN: 621616951

50208
ACOM Tennessee-Japan Cultural Exchange Foundation
5105 S. National Dr.
Knoxville, TN 37914

Established in 1994 in TN.
Donor(s): Matsushita Electronic Components Corp. of America, Panasonic Industrial Co., Matsushita Electronic Components Co., Ltd.
Financial data (yr. ended 02/28/01): Grants paid, $30,124; assets, $345,113 (M); gifts received, $32,000; expenditures, $32,832; qualifying distributions, $30,754.
Limitations: Giving limited to residents of Knoxville, TN.
Application information: Unsolicited requests for funds not accepted.
Officers and Directors:* Hasutaka Kanamon, Co-Pres.; Naoki Kono,* Co-Pres.; Lawrence E. Levine, Secy.; Clark Brandon, Treas.; Terukazu Mori, Yvonne Scott, Toshihide Tominaga, Sam Venable.
EIN: 621558047

50209
The Mercy Foundation
3600 Franklin Rd.
Nashville, TN 37204

Established in 1998 in TN.
Donor(s): Scott L. Mercy.
Financial data (yr. ended 12/31/01): Grants paid, $29,500; assets, $1,756,100 (M); gifts received, $1,261,847; expenditures, $35,476; qualifying distributions, $29,500.
Limitations: Applications not accepted.
Application information: Contributes only to pre-selected organizations.
Trustees: Joy M. Mercy, Scott L. Mercy.
EIN: 626351496

50210
Jural Couey Carter Trust
c/o SunTrust Banks, Inc.
P.O. Box 305110
Nashville, TN 37230-5110

Financial data (yr. ended 10/31/01): Grants paid, $29,400; assets, $477,626 (M); expenditures, $35,659; qualifying distributions, $31,977.
Limitations: Applications not accepted.
Application information: Contributes only to pre-selected organizations.
Trustee: SunTrust Banks, Inc.
EIN: 581583888

50211
The Salmon Foundation
P.O. Box 240005
Memphis, TN 38124-0005

Donor(s): TVESCO, Inc.
Financial data (yr. ended 12/31/01): Grants paid, $29,275; assets, $604,591 (M); gifts received, $6,000; expenditures, $32,659; qualifying distributions, $29,275.
Limitations: Applications not accepted. Giving primarily in Memphis, TN.
Application information: Contributes only to pre-selected organizations.
Officers: John L. Salmon, Pres. and Secy.; Madeleine S. Hamm, Treas.
EIN: 621219453

50212
John M. and Arnold S. Jones Family Foundation
121 W. Summer St.
Greeneville, TN 37743
Application address: 100 Old Orchard Dr., Greeneville, TN 37743, tel.: (423) 638-4181
Contact: Gregg K. Jones, Secy.

Established in 2000.
Donor(s): John M. Jones, Arnold S. Jones.
Financial data (yr. ended 12/31/01): Grants paid, $29,250; assets, $544,849 (M); gifts received, $382,765; expenditures, $31,852; qualifying distributions, $29,250.
Officers: John M. Jones, Chair., Pres., and Mgr.; Gregg K. Jones, Secy.; John M. Jones IV, Treas.
Directors: Sarah J. Harbison, Alex S. Jones, Arnold S. Jones, Edith S. Jones.
EIN: 621839619

50213
Walters Foundation
P.O. Box 1238
Morristown, TN 37816-1238 (423) 586-4090
Contact: George H. Prater, Tr.

Financial data (yr. ended 12/31/01): Grants paid, $28,500; assets, $569,075 (M); gifts received, $2,400; expenditures, $29,700; qualifying distributions, $29,066.

Limitations: Applications not accepted. Giving primarily in Morristown, TN.
Application information: Contributes only to pre-selected organizations.
Trustees: Paul R. Capps, Dorothy P. Forry, George H. Prater, Sanford B. Prater, Tracy Prater, H. Scott Reams.
EIN: 626047267

50214
The Foundation for Cultural Enrichment
48 S. Jamestown Rd.
Cookeville, TN 38501-5435

Established in 1987 in TN.
Donor(s): James W. Barger.
Financial data (yr. ended 06/30/02): Grants paid, $28,427; assets, $245,906 (M); expenditures, $29,759; qualifying distributions, $28,427.
Limitations: Applications not accepted. Giving primarily in Fort Worth, TX.
Application information: Contributes only to pre-selected organizations.
Officers and Directors:* James W. Barger,* Pres.; David K. Morgan,* Treas.
EIN: 581778992

50215
Betsy Ross Foundation, Inc.
307 Jackson St.
Paris, TN 38242
Application address: P.O. Box 1262, Paris, TN 38242, tel.: (901) 642-6113
Contact: David B. Wilcox, Pres.

Established in 1993 in TN.
Donor(s): David B. Wilcox.
Financial data (yr. ended 11/30/01): Grants paid, $28,424; assets, $11,371 (M); gifts received, $38,500; expenditures, $29,427; qualifying distributions, $28,424.
Officers: David B. Wilcox, Pres.; John Fuqua, V.P.; J.R. Williams, Secy.
EIN: 621490795

50216
Lillian Rawles Educational Trust Fund
c/o First Citizens National Bank
P.O. Box 370
Dyersburg, TN 38025-0370 (901) 285-4410

Financial data (yr. ended 08/31/02): Grants paid, $28,391; assets, $459,824 (M); expenditures, $33,440; qualifying distributions, $28,391.
Limitations: Applications not accepted. Giving limited to TN.
Application information: Contributes only to pre-selected organizations.
Trustee: First Citizens National Bank.
EIN: 581468965

50217
Joseph K. Maloy & Marianne S. Maloy Foundation
c/o Kenneth H. Maloy
708 Thornwood Pl.
Kingsport, TN 37660-5037

Established in 1994 in TN.
Financial data (yr. ended 12/31/00): Grants paid, $28,234; assets, $539,325 (M); expenditures, $31,398; qualifying distributions, $28,234.
Limitations: Applications not accepted. Giving primarily in TN.
Application information: Contributes only to pre-selected organizations.
Officers: Kenneth Harrison Maloy, Pres.; Elizabeth Maloy Corrigan, V.P. and Secy.-Treas.; Susan Fosbury Maloy, V.P. and Secy.-Treas.
EIN: 621561982

50218
Woodbury Educational Foundation
P.O. Box 320
Woodbury, TN 37190-0323
Application address: 415 Lehman St., Woodbury, TN 37190, tel.: (615) 563-2431
Contact: Russell E. Myers, Secy.-Treas.

Established in 1986 in TN.
Financial data (yr. ended 05/31/01): Grants paid, $28,000; assets, $0 (M); expenditures, $31,066; qualifying distributions, $27,675.
Limitations: Giving limited to residents of Cannon County, TN.
Application information: Application form required.
Officers: Bobby D. Vance, Pres.; Richie Hunter, V.P.; Russell E. Myers, Secy.-Treas.
Directors: Carole Davenport, Joe Daniel Davenport, Janie King.
EIN: 620470043
Codes: GTI

50219
Hiram W. & Cecil J. Holtsford Scholarship Fund
P.O. Box 692
Lawrenceburg, TN 38464 (931) 762-6620
Contact: Charles Doerflinger, Tr.

Established in 1989 in TN.
Financial data (yr. ended 06/30/00): Grants paid, $27,892; assets, $594,157 (M); expenditures, $28,631; qualifying distributions, $28,290.
Limitations: Giving limited to Lawrence County, TN.
Application information: Application form required.
Trustees: Charles Doerflinger, Wayne Hairrell.
EIN: 626169638
Codes: GTI

50220
Speller Foundation
405 Oakleigh Hill
Nashville, TN 37215-5802 (615) 370-8165
Contact: Lawrence W. Speller, Tr.

Established in 1988 in TN.
Financial data (yr. ended 06/30/01): Grants paid, $27,798; assets, $226,966 (M); gifts received, $25,000; expenditures, $29,894; qualifying distributions, $27,708.
Limitations: Giving primarily in Nashville, TN.
Trustee: Lawrence W. Speller.
EIN: 621360614

50221
Martha W. Banker Charitable Trust
1033 Chancery Ln.
Nashville, TN 37215 (615) 665-1142
Contact: J. Barry Banker, Tr.

Established in 1995 in TN.
Financial data (yr. ended 12/31/00): Grants paid, $27,100; assets, $488,793 (M); gifts received, $2,000; expenditures, $32,261; qualifying distributions, $27,100.
Limitations: Giving primarily in TN.
Trustee: J. Barry Banker.
EIN: 626288471

50222
Sheffield Foundation
200 Sunnyside Dr.
Nashville, TN 37205

Established in 1994.
Donor(s): Frank B. Sheffield, Jr.
Financial data (yr. ended 06/30/01): Grants paid, $27,017; assets, $158,963 (M); expenditures, $28,330; qualifying distributions, $27,017.

50222—TENNESSEE

Limitations: Applications not accepted. Giving primarily in TN.
Application information: Contributes only to pre-selected organizations.
Officers and Trustees:* Carolyn P. Sheffield,* Pres. and Treas.; Frank B. Sheffield, Jr.,* Secy.; Deborah S. Bryan, Stephanie S. Sheffield.
EIN: 621586491

50223
Zoe Foundation
P.O. Box 159021
Nashville, TN 37215
Contact: S. Douglas Smith, Chair.

Established in 1994 in TN.
Financial data (yr. ended 12/31/00): Grants paid, $27,000; assets, $1,154,822 (M); expenditures, $40,600; qualifying distributions, $27,000.
Limitations: Giving primarily in TN.
Officer and Trustees:* S. Douglas Smith,* Chair.; Elizabeth S. Hill, Thomas J. Hill, Jr., Bryan Frazer Smith, C. David Smith, Carrie McDaniel Smith, Jeannie M. Smith, L. Caroline Smith, Nan F. Smith, Troy Jonathan Smith.
EIN: 626289289

50224
Matt H. Dobson Foundation
5340 N. Stanford Dr.
Nashville, TN 37215

Financial data (yr. ended 06/30/01): Grants paid, $26,330; assets, $767,890 (M); expenditures, $30,985; qualifying distributions, $26,845.
Limitations: Applications not accepted. Giving primarily in TN.
Application information: Contributes only to pre-selected organizations.
Officer: Matt H. Dobson IV, Mgr.
EIN: 626036159

50225
The Linda W. Dale Foundation
1414 Chickering Rd.
Nashville, TN 37215

Established in 1993 in TN.
Financial data (yr. ended 12/31/01): Grants paid, $26,304; assets, $111,296 (M); expenditures, $27,182; qualifying distributions, $26,304.
Limitations: Applications not accepted.
Application information: Contributes only to pre-selected organizations.
Trustees: Linda W. Dale, Robert V. Dale, Naomi Linda Dale Haddock, Lezley Dale Johnson.
EIN: 621528974

50226
Malco Charity Trust
P.O. Box 171809
Memphis, TN 38187-1809

Established in 1945 in TN.
Financial data (yr. ended 12/31/01): Grants paid, $26,100; assets, $2,535 (M); gifts received, $28,000; expenditures, $26,113; qualifying distributions, $26,113.
Limitations: Applications not accepted. Giving primarily in Memphis, TN.
Application information: Contributes only to pre-selected organizations.
Officer: Bill W. Blackburn, Cont.
Trustees: Herbert R. Levy, Richard L. Lightman.
EIN: 626065266

50227
The Partnership Foundation
250 E. Cherry Cir.
Memphis, TN 38117

Established in 1998 TN.

Donor(s): Diana C. Gill.
Financial data (yr. ended 12/31/01): Grants paid, $26,100; assets, $294,091 (M); gifts received, $25,000; expenditures, $26,344; qualifying distributions, $26,100.
Limitations: Applications not accepted.
Application information: Contributes only to pre-selected organizations.
Officers: John M. Gill, Pres.; Diana C. Gill, Secy.
Director: Karen D. Clark.
EIN: 621729566

50228
Bartlett-Patterson Corporation
c/o C. Ray Adams
119 S. Main St.
Greeneville, TN 37743

Established in 1998 in TN.
Donor(s): Patterson Bartlett.‡
Financial data (yr. ended 07/31/01): Grants paid, $26,013; assets, $1,929,563 (M); expenditures, $26,632; qualifying distributions, $26,013.
Officers: John Cartwright, Pres.; Gene Gaby, Secy.; C. Ray Adams, Treas.
EIN: 621706760

50229
Wilkins Charitable Trust
P.O. Box 280742
Memphis, TN 38168

Established in 1996 in TN.
Financial data (yr. ended 12/31/99): Grants paid, $25,789; assets, $250,426 (M); gifts received, $154,535; expenditures, $31,045; qualifying distributions, $25,789.
Limitations: Applications not accepted. Giving on a national basis, with emphasis on TN.
Application information: Contributes only to pre-selected organizations.
Trustees: Janalee Wilkins, Shawn Wilins.
EIN: 316542316

50230
Chai Foundation
812 Georgia Ave., Ste. 1000
Chattanooga, TN 37402

Donor(s): Morris Ellman, Mrs. Morris Ellman, Neil Ellman, Mrs. Neil Ellman.
Financial data (yr. ended 05/31/02): Grants paid, $25,500; assets, $541,221 (M); gifts received, $12,458; expenditures, $26,312; qualifying distributions, $25,500.
Limitations: Applications not accepted.
Application information: Contributes only to pre-selected organizations.
Officers and Trustees:* Neil Ellman,* Pres.; George Ellman,* V.P.; Mrs. Morris Ellman,* Secy.; Morris Ellman,* Treas.; Avi Ellman, Mrs. Harvis Skopp.
EIN: 626047060

50231
Winegardner Community Foundation, Inc.
8275 Tournament Dr., Ste. 144
Memphis, TN 38125
Contact: Roy E. Winegardner, Pres.

Established in 1990.
Donor(s): Roy E. Winegardner, John McDonnell, David Hirsch.
Financial data (yr. ended 08/31/01): Grants paid, $25,120; assets, $1,019,973 (M); expenditures, $46,855; qualifying distributions, $41,361.
Limitations: Giving primarily in Memphis, TN.
Application information: Application form required.

Officers and Directors:* Roy E. Winegardner,* Pres. and Treas.; William H.D. Fones, Jr.,* Secy.; Boyd L. Rhodes.
EIN: 581487801
Codes: GTI

50232
Yount Family Foundation
3901 West End Ave., Apt. 508
Nashville, TN 37205-1803

Established in 1990 in TN.
Donor(s): Thomas L. Yount.
Financial data (yr. ended 12/31/01): Grants paid, $25,060; assets, $151,029 (M); expenditures, $25,060; qualifying distributions, $25,060.
Limitations: Applications not accepted. Giving primarily in Nashville, TN.
Application information: Contributes only to pre-selected organizations.
Trustees: Nancy Hart Diehl Harvey, Robb S. Harvey, Margaret Yount Reis, Pamela Y. White, Jane W. Yount, Thomas L. Yount.
EIN: 626240044

50233
Lawrence Lewis Foundation
c/o National Bank of Commerce
1 Commerce Sq.
Memphis, TN 38150
Contact: Susan Drake

Donor(s): Joseph and Louise Lewis Trust.
Financial data (yr. ended 03/31/02): Grants paid, $25,016; assets, $1,080,853 (M); gifts received, $700,000; expenditures, $27,857; qualifying distributions, $25,016.
Limitations: Giving primarily in Memphis, TN.
Trustee: National Bank of Commerce.
EIN: 626269000

50234
The Laura Jo and Wayne Dugas Family Foundation
138 2nd Ave. N., Ste. 200
Nashville, TN 37201

Established in 1998 in TN.
Donor(s): Laura Jo Turner Dugas.
Financial data (yr. ended 12/31/01): Grants paid, $25,000; assets, $5,373,294 (M); gifts received, $1,839,577; expenditures, $27,006; qualifying distributions, $27,006.
Limitations: Applications not accepted. Giving primarily in FL.
Application information: Unsolicited requests for funds not accepted.
Trustees: Laura Jo Turner Dugas, Stephen H. Dugas, Wayne F. Dugas, Sr., Wayne F. Dugas, Jr., William S. Dugas.
EIN: 582426636

50235
The Vickers Foundation
640 Valley Forge Rd.
Cookeville, TN 38501

Established in 1998 in TN.
Donor(s): Larry E. Vickers.
Financial data (yr. ended 12/31/01): Grants paid, $25,000; assets, $521,273 (M); gifts received, $241,895; expenditures, $31,577; qualifying distributions, $25,000.
Limitations: Applications not accepted.
Application information: Contributes only to pre-selected organizations.
Trustee: Larry E. Vickers.
EIN: 621722201

50236
Foundation for Early Development
323 Lynnwood Blvd.
Nashville, TN 37205-2928

Established in 1987 in WA.
Donor(s): Michael Green.
Financial data (yr. ended 06/30/01): Grants paid, $24,674; assets, $95,990 (M); gifts received, $48; expenditures, $26,848; qualifying distributions, $24,674.
Limitations: Applications not accepted. Giving primarily in Nashville, TN and WA.
Application information: Contributes only to pre-selected organizations.
Officer: Michael Green, C.E.O.
EIN: 770166781

50237
Mimsye and Leon May Foundation
(Formerly Nashville Foundation)
230 Ensworth Ave.
Nashville, TN 37205-1922

Financial data (yr. ended 09/30/01): Grants paid, $24,100; assets, $447,004 (M); expenditures, $26,789; qualifying distributions, $24,100.
Limitations: Applications not accepted. Giving primarily in TN.
Officers: Leon May, Pres.; Jacob May, V.P.; Mimsye May, Secy.
EIN: 626037728

50238
Bruce & Susan Wohlfeld Family Foundation
507 Granny White Pike
Brentwood, TN 37027

Established in 1997.
Donor(s): Bruce Wohlfeld, Susan Wohlfeld.
Financial data (yr. ended 12/31/01): Grants paid, $24,076; assets, $500,318 (M); expenditures, $24,975; qualifying distributions, $24,076.
Limitations: Applications not accepted.
Application information: Contributes only to pre-selected organizations.
Officers and Directors:* Susan S. Wohlfeld,* Pres.; Anne L. Wohlfeld,* V.P.; Bryan J. Wohlfeld,* V.P.; Peter A. Silver,* Secy.; Bruce A. Wohlfeld,* Treas.; Steven L. Wohlfeld.
EIN: 411873763

50239
Katie Dean Foundation
c/o First Tennessee Bank, N.A., Trust Div.
800 S. Gay St.
Knoxville, TN 37995-1230 (865) 971-2165
Contact: K. Keisling, Trust Off., First Tennessee Bank, N.A., Trust Div.

Established in 1994 in TN.
Financial data (yr. ended 03/31/02): Grants paid, $24,065; assets, $650,410 (M); expenditures, $30,978; qualifying distributions, $24,065.
Limitations: Giving primarily in Knoxville, TN.
Trustee: First Tennessee Bank, N.A.
EIN: 626286984

50240
The John C. Fogerty Foundation
7009 Penbrook Dr.
Franklin, TN 37069-8408

Established in 1986 in CA.
Donor(s): John C. Fogerty.
Financial data (yr. ended 12/31/99): Grants paid, $24,000; assets, $725,012 (M); expenditures, $46,811; qualifying distributions, $24,000.
Limitations: Applications not accepted.
Application information: Contributes only to pre-selected organizations.

Officers: John C. Fogerty, Pres.; Robert G. Fogerty, Secy.-Treas.
EIN: 943031037

50241
Wills Memorial Foundation
c/o County Executive
1 N. Washington St.
Brownsville, TN 38012 (731) 772-1432

Financial data (yr. ended 06/30/01): Grants paid, $24,000; assets, $435,021 (M); expenditures, $27,332; qualifying distributions, $26,745.
Limitations: Giving limited to residents of Haywood County, TN.
Application information: Application form required.
Officer and Trustees:* John Sharpe,* Chair.; Dixon Hood, Pat Mann, Jr., Sandra Silverstein, Betty Smith, Christy Smith.
EIN: 620973997
Codes: GTI

50242
Myron Lewis Foundation
c/o National Bank of Commerce
1 Commerce Sq.
Memphis, TN 38150
Application address: c/o Susan Drake, National Bank of Commerce, Trust Division, 850 Ridgelake Rd., Ste. 101, Memphis, TN 38120, tel.: (910) 415-6403

Established in 1999 in TN.
Financial data (yr. ended 03/31/01): Grants paid, $23,826; assets, $1,083,840 (M); gifts received, $700,000; expenditures, $26,646; qualifying distributions, $23,826.
Trustee: National Bank of Commerce.
EIN: 621533710

50243
Pace Family Foundation
95 White Bridge Rd., Ste. 504
Nashville, TN 37205-1490 (615) 352-9600
Contact: Ronald D. Pace, Tr.

Donor(s): Derek M. Pace, Kevin D. Pace, Ronald D. Pace.
Financial data (yr. ended 09/30/01): Grants paid, $23,575; assets, $570,374 (M); gifts received, $284; expenditures, $25,811; qualifying distributions, $23,575.
Limitations: Giving primarily in Waverly, TN.
Trustees: Derek D. Pace, Kevin D. Pace, Ronald D. Pace.
EIN: 621665556

50244
Cathy L. Hodges Memorial Cancer Foundation
9724 Kingston Pike, Ste. 1000
Knoxville, TN 37922 (865) 690-5346
Contact: Bill A. Hodges, Pres.

Established in 1995 in TN.
Donor(s): Phillip Fulmer, Vicki Fulmer.
Financial data (yr. ended 06/30/01): Grants paid, $22,960; assets, $13,127 (M); gifts received, $28,498; expenditures, $23,409; qualifying distributions, $23,409.
Officers: Bill A. Hodges, Pres.; Dennis C. Overton, Secy. and Treas.
EIN: 621620282

50245
ARM Foundation
417 Davidson Rd.
Nashville, TN 37205-3134
Application address: Nashville City Ctr., Ste. 1500, 511 Union St., Nashville, TN 37219
Contact: Edwin Pyle

Established in 1990.
Financial data (yr. ended 10/31/01): Grants paid, $22,956; assets, $164,420 (M); expenditures, $26,193; qualifying distributions, $22,956.
Limitations: Giving limited to Nashville, TN.
Application information: Letter.
Directors: Adrianne Marianelli, Walter Marianelli.
EIN: 621443239

50246
Mervin Pregulman Foundation
1901 Riverfront Pkwy.
Chattanooga, TN 37408
Contact: Mervin Pregulman, Dir.

Established in 1998 in TN.
Donor(s): Mervin Pregulman.
Financial data (yr. ended 12/31/01): Grants paid, $22,675; assets, $282,540 (M); gifts received, $20,000; expenditures, $23,644; qualifying distributions, $22,675.
Directors: Betsy A. Pregulman, Helen S. Pregulman, John S. Pregulman, Mervin Pregulman, Mindy P. Pregulman, Robert J. Pregulman.
EIN: 626333937

50247
American Paper & Twine Company Charitable Trust
7400 Cockrill Bend Blvd.
Nashville, TN 37209 (615) 350-9000
Contact: Robert S. Doochin, Tr.

Donor(s): American Paper & Twine Co.
Financial data (yr. ended 12/31/01): Grants paid, $22,180; assets, $1,099 (M); gifts received, $22,000; expenditures, $22,271; qualifying distributions, $22,271.
Limitations: Giving primarily in Nashville, TN.
Trustees: Karen Doochin, Robert S. Doochin, William David Morris, Jason Ritchason.
EIN: 626046717
Codes: CS, CD

50248
Johnson Scholarship Foundation, Inc.
1002 Rolling Meadow Dr.
Mount Juliet, TN 37122 (615) 758-3617
Contact: Dan York, Treas.

Donor(s): Kerry Anderson, Neil Anderson, Roy Burch, Martha E. Butler.‡
Financial data (yr. ended 12/31/00): Grants paid, $21,804; assets, $226,423 (M); gifts received, $165; expenditures, $23,058; qualifying distributions, $23,058.
Limitations: Giving limited to Nashville, TN.
Officers: Roy Burch, Pres.; Paul Brown, V.P.; Paul Rodgers, Secy.; Dan York, Treas.
EIN: 626047142
Codes: GTI

50249
Maury County Historical Society
P.O. Box 147
Columbia, TN 38402-0147

Financial data (yr. ended 12/31/01): Grants paid, $21,000; assets, $744,456 (M); gifts received, $45; expenditures, $35,902; qualifying distributions, $21,000.
Limitations: Applications not accepted.

50249—TENNESSEE

Application information: Contributes only to pre-selected organizations.
Officers and Directors:* Alice Wright Algood,* Pres.; Robert Andrew Duncan,* V.P.; Irene Rawdon Dugger,* Recording Secy.; Mary Margaret Lovell,* Treas.; Jeanne Q. Cooper, Jennie Jo Hardison, Fred L. Hawkins, Jr., and 5 additional directors.
EIN: 237067714

50250
East Nashville Knights of Columbus Club, Inc.
c/o James L. Thiltgen
135 Ellington Pl.
Madison, TN 37115 (615) 860-3430

Financial data (yr. ended 06/30/01): Grants paid, $20,850; assets, $347,984 (M); expenditures, $21,216; qualifying distributions, $20,634.
Limitations: Giving limited to Madison and Nashville, TN.
Application information: Unsolicited requests for funds not accepted nor acknowledged.
Officers: Joseph H. Fricault, Pres.; Jack C. Webster, V.P.; James E. Tohill, Secy.; James L. Thiltgen, Treas.
Directors: Francis A. Bumpus, Stephen J. Pentecost, Clifford G. Reinert.
EIN: 621431787

50251
David G. Williamson, Jr. Foundation
401 W. Hillwood Dr.
Nashville, TN 37205-1340

Established in 1988 in TN.
Donor(s): Betty O. Williamson.
Financial data (yr. ended 12/31/01): Grants paid, $20,629; assets, $376,696 (M); expenditures, $21,783; qualifying distributions, $20,629.
Limitations: Applications not accepted. Giving on a national basis, with emphasis on the South.
Application information: Contributes only to pre-selected organizations.
Officers: Betty O. Williamson, Pres.; David G. Williamson III, Secy.
Directors: Mary Glynn Tucker, Beth Ann Williamson.
EIN: 621372451

50252
The Daniel Foundation
608 Vance Dr.
Bristol, TN 37620
Contact: James K. Daniel, Jr., Tr.

Established in 1999 in TN.
Donor(s): James K. Daniel.
Financial data (yr. ended 06/30/01): Grants paid, $20,391; assets, $293,291 (M); gifts received, $10,000; expenditures, $20,391; qualifying distributions, $20,334.
Trustees: James K. Daniel, James K. Daniel, Jr., Martha Daniel.
EIN: 621740358

50253
Covenant Foundation
P.O. Box 1822
Brentwood, TN 37024-1822

Established in 1999 in TN.
Donor(s): Donald G. Albright.
Financial data (yr. ended 12/31/01): Grants paid, $20,180; assets, $1,118 (M); gifts received, $21,192; expenditures, $21,452; qualifying distributions, $20,180.
Limitations: Giving primarily in TN.
Officers: Donald G. Albright, Pres.; Julie A. Albright, V.P. and Secy.-Treas.
Director: Donald M. Albright.

EIN: 621761994

50254
The Jarratt Foundation
314 Church St.
Nashville, TN 37201

Financial data (yr. ended 12/31/01): Grants paid, $20,100; assets, $297,885 (M); expenditures, $20,665; qualifying distributions, $20,100.
Officer and Directors:* Chris L. Jarratt, Pres.; Jeffrey A. Jarratt, James G. Lewis.
EIN: 621763218

50255
Haven Foundation, Inc.
P.O. Box 1044
Madison, TN 37116-1044

Donor(s): Thomas G. Scott, Mrs. Thomas G. Scott.
Financial data (yr. ended 12/31/01): Grants paid, $20,081; assets, $7,412 (M); gifts received, $29,590; expenditures, $30,636; qualifying distributions, $29,008.
Limitations: Giving on a national basis.
Trustees: Jack L. Hughes, Lou Hughes, Rebecca Scott, Thomas G. Scott.
EIN: 311501017

50256
Sam and DeLois Anderson Foundation
161 Cherokee St.
Kingsport, TN 37660-4307

Donor(s): Sam Anderson.
Financial data (yr. ended 03/31/01): Grants paid, $20,000; assets, $270,556 (M); gifts received, $20,000; expenditures, $21,573; qualifying distributions, $19,887.
Limitations: Applications not accepted. Giving primarily in NC.
Application information: Contributes only to pre-selected organizations.
Officers: Sam H. Anderson, Pres.; Jane A. Booher, V.P.; DeLois A. Dietrich, V.P.; DeLois H. Anderson, Secy.
EIN: 621744255

50257
Maude Parks Memorial Fund
1109 Graybar Ln.
Nashville, TN 37204
Contact: Norman Randolph Parks, Pres.

Financial data (yr. ended 12/31/01): Grants paid, $20,000; assets, $514,546 (M); expenditures, $25,653; qualifying distributions, $20,000.
Limitations: Giving on a national basis.
Application information: Application form not required.
Officers: Norman Randolph Parks, Pres.; Judith E. Parks, V.P.
EIN: 626042777

50258
The Lewis-Warburg Foundation
(Formerly The Riley-Ross Foundation)
401 Union St., 12th Fl.
Nashville, TN 37219

Established in 1998 in TN.
Donor(s): James G. Lewis.
Financial data (yr. ended 12/31/01): Grants paid, $19,800; assets, $534,877 (M); gifts received, $129,650; expenditures, $33,602; qualifying distributions, $19,721.
Officer: James G. Lewis, Pres.
Director: Linda Riley-Rountree.
EIN: 621721451

50259
The Ortale Family Foundation
104 Woodmont Blvd., Ste. 200
Nashville, TN 37205-2245

Established in 1996 in TN.
Donor(s): Buddy Ortale.
Financial data (yr. ended 11/30/01): Grants paid, $19,546; assets, $501,908 (M); expenditures, $20,261; qualifying distributions, $19,546.
Limitations: Applications not accepted.
Application information: Contributes only to pre-selected organizations.
Trustees: Buford H. Ortale, Cynthia C. Ortale.
EIN: 621664345

50260
Carrie Parks Wilson Trust
1109 Graybar Ln.
Nashville, TN 37204
Contact: Norman Randolph Parks, Pres.

Financial data (yr. ended 12/31/01): Grants paid, $19,400; assets, $737,585 (M); expenditures, $28,535; qualifying distributions, $19,400.
Limitations: Giving primarily in TN and TX.
Officers: Norman Randolph Parks, Pres.; Judith E. Parks, V.P. and Secy.
EIN: 596219246

50261
Frank J. B. and Emma S. Varallo Foundation
c/o Joseph Decosimo & Co.
Tallan Bldg., Ste. 1100
Chattanooga, TN 37402 (423) 756-7100

Established in 1989 in TN.
Donor(s): Frank J.B. Varallo, Emma S. Varallo.
Financial data (yr. ended 09/30/01): Grants paid, $19,333; assets, $252,045 (M); gifts received, $3,333; expenditures, $25,122; qualifying distributions, $19,333.
Limitations: Giving primarily in TN.
Trustees: Joseph F. Decosimo, Robert F. Decosimo, Joseph A. Schmissrauter, Jr., Emma S. Varallo, Frank J.B. Varallo.
EIN: 626225565

50262
MICO Foundation, Inc.
c/o Bank of America
633 Chestnut St.
Chattanooga, TN 37450
Contact: L. Putnam

Established in 1992 in TN.
Financial data (yr. ended 12/31/99): Grants paid, $19,291; assets, $387,896 (M); expenditures, $26,917; qualifying distributions, $19,291.
Application information: Application form not required.
Officer and Directors:* Margaret C. Oehmig,* Pres.; Marian O. Latimer, Randolph D. Oehmig, William C. Oehmig.
EIN: 621443316

50263
The O. G. Wollman, Dorothy Armstrong Wollman and Ella Armstrong Scholarship Fund
c/o AmSouth Bank
315 Deaderick St., 4th Fl.
Nashville, TN 37237-0401
Application address: c/o Rogers, Richardson, & Duncan, 128 W. Lincoln St., Ste. B, Tullahoma, TN 37388
Contact: Doyle E. Richardson, Comm. Member

Established in 1993 in TN.

Financial data (yr. ended 01/31/01): Grants paid, $19,200; assets, $394,701 (M); expenditures, $25,531; qualifying distributions, $19,791.
Limitations: Giving limited to residents of Tullahoma, TN.
Application information: Application form required.
Committee Members: Thomas P. Ballou, J.C. Eoff, Jr., Ann Hickerson Jennings, Doyle E. Richardson, Claude Snoddy.
Trustee: AmSouth Bank.
EIN: 626266551
Codes: GTI

50264
Love Gift Trust
c/o Frank J. Hall, Jr.
4646 Poplar Ave., Ste. 422
Memphis, TN 38117-4434

Established in 1990 in TN.
Financial data (yr. ended 12/31/00): Grants paid, $19,000; assets, $11,710 (M); expenditures, $19,150; qualifying distributions, $19,000.
Limitations: Applications not accepted. Giving primarily in TN.
Application information: Contributes only to pre-selected organizations.
Trustees: June H. Dixon, June Grace Hall, Susan H. Wilson.
EIN: 581888314

50265
Mike Curb Family Foundation
47 Music Sq. E.
Nashville, TN 37203

Established in 1998 in TN.
Donor(s): Mike Curb.
Financial data (yr. ended 07/31/01): Grants paid, $18,917; assets, $11,707,273 (M); gifts received, $6,500,020; expenditures, $105,871; qualifying distributions, $18,917.
Limitations: Applications not accepted. Giving primarily in Nashville, TN.
Application information: Contributes only to pre-selected organizations.
Officers and Directors:* Mike Curb,* Pres.; Tracy Moore,* Secy.; Linda Curb.
EIN: 954686920

50266
NGB Foundation
c/o E. Warner Bass
2700 1st American Ctr.
Nashville, TN 37238

Established in 1989 in TN.
Donor(s): Elizabeth R. Neff.‡
Financial data (yr. ended 12/31/01): Grants paid, $18,800; assets, $144,305 (M); expenditures, $21,013; qualifying distributions, $18,800.
Limitations: Applications not accepted. Giving primarily in NC and TN.
Application information: Contributes only to pre-selected organizations.
Trustees: E. Warner Bass, Margaret G. Bass, John T. Gregory IV.
EIN: 626223672

50267
F. P. Kendall Foundation
1 Union Sq., Ste. 700, Krystal Bldg.
Chattanooga, TN 37402-2515
Contact: Judy Kendall Hyde, Pres.

Financial data (yr. ended 12/31/01): Grants paid, $18,500; assets, $468,343 (M); expenditures, $21,787; qualifying distributions, $18,607.

Officers: F. Paul Kendall, Jr., Chair. and Treas.; Judy Kendall Hyde, Pres.; Peggy Kendall, V.P.; Ann Stephens, V.P.; Kay Kendall Butler, Secy.
EIN: 626041345

50268
Elizabeth Johnson McNutt Charitable Foundation
351 Grandview St.
Memphis, TN 38111
Contact: Charles McNutt, Tr.

Donor(s): Elizabeth McNutt.
Financial data (yr. ended 12/31/00): Grants paid, $18,292; assets, $286,015 (M); expenditures, $22,041; qualifying distributions, $18,292.
Trustees: Charles McNutt, Phoebe McNutt.
EIN: 626251086

50269
The Adams Family Foundation
c/o Alfred A. Adams
133 1/2 Public Sq.
Lebanon, TN 37087

Established in 1993.
Financial data (yr. ended 12/31/99): Grants paid, $17,875; assets, $256,597 (M); expenditures, $18,898; qualifying distributions, $17,875.
Limitations: Applications not accepted. Giving primarily in TN.
Application information: Contributes only to pre-selected organizations.
Trustees: Alfred A. Adams V, William Joseph Adams.
EIN: 626273372

50270
West Tennessee Young Farmers & Homemakers Leadership Development Corporation
c/o John Woolfolk
147 Bear Creek Pike
Columbia, TN 38401 (931) 388-7872

Financial data (yr. ended 12/31/01): Grants paid, $17,825; assets, $330,915 (M); expenditures, $19,376; qualifying distributions, $17,825.
Limitations: Giving primarily in TN.
Directors: Hugh Adams, Mike Brundige, Jim Byford, Charles Curtis, Linda Davis, Keith Fowler, Glynn Giffin, Jane May, Jim McKee, Steve Paschall, Tommy Patterson, Heather Winters.
EIN: 621542474

50271
Priscilla and Robert H. Siskin Charitable Trust
Republic Ctr.
633 Chestnut St., Ste. 1630
Chattanooga, TN 37450 (423) 267-4345

Established in 1998 in TN.
Donor(s): Robert H. Siskin, Priscilla Siskin.
Financial data (yr. ended 12/31/01): Grants paid, $17,724; assets, $315,685 (M); gifts received, $40; expenditures, $18,862; qualifying distributions, $17,724.
Trustee: Priscilla Siskin.
EIN: 626334609

50272
The Altenbern Foundation
1025 Chancery Ln. S.
Nashville, TN 37215-4523

Established in 1988 in TN.
Donor(s): Douglas C. Altenbern, Sr.
Financial data (yr. ended 12/31/00): Grants paid, $17,603; assets, $222,208 (M); expenditures, $23,523; qualifying distributions, $17,869.
Limitations: Applications not accepted. Giving primarily in TN.

Application information: Contributes only to pre-selected organizations.
Trustees: D. Phillips Altenbern, Douglas C. Altenbern, Sr., Douglas C. Altenbern, Jr., Werdna Lee Phillips Altenbern, Anne Altenbern Dobbs.
EIN: 581791916

50273
Will & Jane Harris Foundation
1411 Heritage Landing
Chattanooga, TN 37405

Donor(s): Jane A. Harris.
Financial data (yr. ended 11/30/01): Grants paid, $17,500; assets, $521,916 (M); expenditures, $20,194; qualifying distributions, $17,500.
Limitations: Applications not accepted. Giving primarily in Chattanooga, TN.
Application information: Contributes only to pre-selected organizations.
Officers and Trustees:* Jane A. Harris,* Chair.; G. Richard Hostetter,* Secy.; Carter J. Lynch,* Mgr.; Robert R. Evans, Raymond R. Murphy, Jr.
EIN: 581340046

50274
Urologic Cancer Foundation
828 N. Curtiswood Ln.
Nashville, TN 37204-4314

Established in 1988 in UT.
Donor(s): Jack D. Solomon.
Financial data (yr. ended 12/31/01): Grants paid, $17,500; assets, $273,249 (M); expenditures, $18,806; qualifying distributions, $17,500.
Limitations: Applications not accepted. Giving primarily in Nashville, TN.
Application information: Contributes only to pre-selected organizations.
Trustees: Richard H. Johnson II, Barbara B. Smith.
EIN: 742518380

50275
Sapphire Foundation
2524 Stones River Ct.
Nashville, TN 37214

Established in 1987 in TN.
Donor(s): Ruth Liddle.
Financial data (yr. ended 12/31/00): Grants paid, $17,000; assets, $394,988 (M); gifts received, $6,916; expenditures, $19,762; qualifying distributions, $17,000.
Limitations: Applications not accepted. Giving on a national basis.
Application information: Contributes only to pre-selected organizations.
Trustee: M.A. Henderson.
EIN: 621348330

50276
BGW Foundation
c/o Bobbie G. Winsett
107 Willow Crest St.
Goodlettsville, TN 37072-7040

Established in 2000 in TN.
Donor(s): Bobbie G. Winsett.
Financial data (yr. ended 12/31/01): Grants paid, $16,980; assets, $227,403 (M); expenditures, $17,650; qualifying distributions, $17,580.
Limitations: Applications not accepted. Giving primarily in Goodlettsville, TN.
Application information: Contributes only to pre-selected organizations.
Trustee: Bobbie G. Winsett.
EIN: 621824589

50277
The Toms Foundation
607 Market St., 9th Fl.
P.O. Box 2466
Knoxville, TN 37901-2466 (865) 544-3000
FAX: (865) 637-1709
Contact: Ronald L. Grimm, Chair.

Trust established in 1952 in TN.
Donor(s): W.P. Toms.‡
Financial data (yr. ended 06/30/99): Grants paid, $16,917; assets, $5,215,267 (M); expenditures, $287,566; qualifying distributions, $195,509; giving activities include $135,083 for programs.
Limitations: Giving primarily in eastern TN.
Publications: Annual report (including application guidelines).
Officers and Trustees:* Ronald L. Grimm,* Chair.; Dorothy B. Wilson,* Vice-Chair.; Thomas R. Ramsey III,* Secy.; Don McLean, Treas.; Janet Grimm, R. Brett Grimm, Mary Mayne Perry.
EIN: 626037668

50278
Elizabeth Chenoweth Foundation, Inc.
117 E. Washington St.
P.O. Box 1373
Paris, TN 38242-1373 (901) 642-1322
Contact: John Etheridge, Secy.-Treas.

Established around 1969.
Financial data (yr. ended 12/31/99): Grants paid, $16,800; assets, $288,028 (M); gifts received, $5,540; expenditures, $17,408; qualifying distributions, $16,669.
Limitations: Giving limited to Henry County, TN.
Application information: Application form required.
Officers and Directors:* Rick Kriesky,* Pres.; John Etheridge,* Secy.-Treas.; Thomas Beasley, Randy Stephens, Charles Wilson.
EIN: 237044756
Codes: GTI

50279
The Hunt Family Foundation of Nashville TN
716 Enquirer Ave.
Nashville, TN 37205

Established in 1997 in TN.
Donor(s): James V. Hunt.
Financial data (yr. ended 12/31/01): Grants paid, $16,700; assets, $172,889 (M); gifts received, $123,571; expenditures, $17,551; qualifying distributions, $16,700.
Limitations: Applications not accepted.
Application information: Contributes only to pre-selected organizations.
Officers: James V. Hunt, Sr., Pres.; Sally B. Hunt, V.P. and Secy.; James V. Hunt, Jr., Treas.
Trustees: Allan B. Hunt, Elizabeth S. Hunt.
EIN: 626317506

50280
Healing Stones Foundation
c/o George Bullard
P.O. Box 50276
Nashville, TN 37205-0276

Financial data (yr. ended 12/31/00): Grants paid, $16,468; assets, $1,335,957 (M); gifts received, $246,000; expenditures, $267,541; qualifying distributions, $197,191.
Limitations: Applications not accepted. Giving primarily in TN.
Application information: Contributes only to pre-selected organizations.
Officer: George Bullard, Pres.
EIN: 621633499

50281
Life Line International Charitable Trust
3500 Equestrian Way
Knoxville, TN 37921
Contact: Zane P. Vincent, Dir.

Established in 1999 in GA.
Donor(s): Life Line International Asset Management Co.
Financial data (yr. ended 12/31/01): Grants paid, $16,455; assets, $540,314 (M); gifts received, $111,898; expenditures, $37,673; qualifying distributions, $0.
Limitations: Giving primarily in GA.
Officer and Directors:* John E. Vincent,* Exec. Dir.; Zane P. Vincent.
EIN: 656249110
Codes: CS

50282
The Williams-King Foundation
(Formerly The Corrine W. Brothers Foundation)
800 Nashville City Ctr.
Nashville, TN 37219

Established in 1994 in TN.
Financial data (yr. ended 12/31/01): Grants paid, $16,350; assets, $241,121 (M); expenditures, $19,047; qualifying distributions, $16,350.
Limitations: Applications not accepted.
Application information: Contributes only to pre-selected organizations.
Trustees: Corinne K. Harrison, Clayton T. King, James R. King, Jr., Matthew A. King.
EIN: 621528972

50283
The Bristol Public Library Foundation
c/o Frank W. DeFriece, Jr.
113 Landmark Ln.
Bristol, TN 37620

Established in 1999 in TN.
Financial data (yr. ended 12/31/01): Grants paid, $16,051; assets, $508,504 (M); expenditures, $18,210; qualifying distributions, $16,051.
Limitations: Applications not accepted.
Application information: Contributes only to pre-selected organizations.
Trustees: William C. Burriss, Jr., Frank W. DeFriece, Jr., Roger L. Leonard.
EIN: 626360312

50284
The Donner Foundation
1005 Troy Ave.
Dyersburg, TN 38024-3242

Established in 1995 in TN.
Financial data (yr. ended 12/31/01): Grants paid, $16,000; assets, $416,109 (M); expenditures, $16,026; qualifying distributions, $16,000.
Limitations: Applications not accepted. Giving limited to Dyersburg, TN.
Application information: Contributes only to pre-selected organizations.
Officers and Trustees:* Richard W. Donner,* Admin.; Ralph G. Ross,* Mgr.; Mary E. Bloch, Suzanne Donner.
EIN: 621585887

50285
Ferrari Family Foundation
357 Riverside Dr., Ste. 140
Franklin, TN 37064

Established in 1997.
Donor(s): R. Keith Ferrari.
Financial data (yr. ended 12/31/01): Grants paid, $16,000; assets, $185,245 (M); expenditures, $14,505; qualifying distributions, $16,000.
Limitations: Applications not accepted. Giving primarily in AL and TN.
Application information: Contributes only to pre-selected organizations.
Officers: R. Keith Ferrari, Pres.; Kim Ferrari, Secy.
Director: L. Eugene Striegel.
EIN: 621689958

50286
The Howard and June F. Entman Charitable Trust
6037 Shady Grove Rd.
Memphis, TN 38120
Contact: Howard Entman, Tr.

Donor(s): Howard Entman, June F. Entman.
Financial data (yr. ended 12/31/01): Grants paid, $15,845; assets, $340,486 (M); expenditures, $16,209; qualifying distributions, $15,845.
Limitations: Giving primarily in Memphis, TN.
Trustees: Howard Entman, June F. Entman.
EIN: 581917668

50287
The Steward Foundation, Inc.
1242 Carl Seyfert Memorial Dr.
Brentwood, TN 37027-4108

Established in 1988 in NJ.
Donor(s): Andrew D. Lee, Diane L. Lee.
Financial data (yr. ended 12/31/01): Grants paid, $15,700; assets, $70,054 (M); expenditures, $16,654; qualifying distributions, $15,700.
Limitations: Applications not accepted. Giving primarily in NJ.
Application information: Contributes only to pre-selected organizations.
Officers and Directors:* Diane L. Lee,* Pres. and Secy.; Andrew D. Lee,* V.P. and Treas.; Richard T. Brown.
EIN: 222934500

50288
The Lackey Foundation, Inc.
230 3rd Ave. S.
Franklin, TN 37064

Established in 1999 in TN.
Donor(s): Douglas Lackey.
Financial data (yr. ended 12/31/01): Grants paid, $15,650; assets, $246,677 (M); expenditures, $16,363; qualifying distributions, $15,650.
Limitations: Applications not accepted.
Application information: Contributes only to pre-selected organizations.
Officers: Douglas Lackey, Pres. and Treas.; Sherron Lackey, V.P.; Scott Swedenburg, Secy.
EIN: 621790381

50289
Landmark Health Services, Inc.
424 Church St., 2800
Nashville, TN 37219-2386

Established in 1998 in TN.
Financial data (yr. ended 12/31/01): Grants paid, $15,400; assets, $502,491 (M); expenditures, $16,619; qualifying distributions, $15,400.
Director: J. Kelly Avery, M.D.
EIN: 621640122

50290
T. Franklin Cheek Jr. Scholarship Fund
227 Anthony St.
Ripley, TN 38063

Established in 2001 in TN.
Financial data (yr. ended 06/30/01): Grants paid, $15,000; assets, $811,405 (M); expenditures, $17,552; qualifying distributions, $15,000.
Application information: Application form required.

Board Members: Ronnie Tatum, Alan Wallace.
EIN: 621849625

50291
Reba McEntire Foundation
c/o Starstruck Entertainment, Inc.
40 Music Sq. W.
Nashville, TN 37203

Established in 1996 in TN.
Donor(s): Schools Now LLC, Reba McEntire, Meredith Corp.
Financial data (yr. ended 12/31/01): Grants paid, $15,000; assets, $2,991 (M); gifts received, $1,000; expenditures, $15,279; qualifying distributions, $15,000.
Limitations: Applications not accepted. Giving primarily in TN.
Application information: Contributes only to pre-selected organizations.
Trustees: Narvel Blackstock, Reba McEntire.
EIN: 621654248

50292
Roger B. & Evelyn W. Paddison Charitable Foundation
315 Dearderick St., 4th Fl.
Nashville, TN 37237-0401
Application address: c/o AmSouth Bank, P.O. Box 511, Knoxville, TN 37901

Established in 1996 in TN.
Donor(s): Evelyn Paddison Charitable Lead Trusts.
Financial data (yr. ended 12/31/01): Grants paid, $14,947; assets, $1,346,303 (M); gifts received, $240,000; expenditures, $22,915; qualifying distributions, $14,947.
Application information: Application form required.
Trustees: Mary Paddison James, AmSouth Bank.
EIN: 626310121

50293
The Bornblum Foundation
100 N. Main St., Ste. 3020
Memphis, TN 38103 (901) 525-5744
Contact: Alvin A. Gordon, Exec. Dir.

Established in 1991 in GA.
Donor(s): Bert Bornblum, David Bornblum.
Financial data (yr. ended 12/31/01): Grants paid, $14,820; assets, $3,153 (M); gifts received, $15,500; expenditures, $14,842; qualifying distributions, $14,820.
Limitations: Giving primarily in Memphis, TN.
Application information: Application form required.
Officer: Alvin A. Gordon, Exec. Dir.
Directors: Bert Bornblum, David Bornblum, Bruce L. Feldbaum.
EIN: 621448070

50294
Brayton Foundation
306 W. Court St.
Dyersburg, TN 38024-4645
Contact: Katherine Brayton, Tr.

Donor(s): L.O. Brayton & Co.
Financial data (yr. ended 12/31/01): Grants paid, $14,554; assets, $292,547 (M); expenditures, $17,736; qualifying distributions, $14,554.
Limitations: Giving primarily in TN.
Application information: Application form not required.
Trustees: John Brayton, Katherine Brayton, Joe Enoch, Hester Hill, Lucinda Jones, First Citizens National Bank.
EIN: 626090488

50295
The Joe and Velma DeWitt Foundation
1000 Tallan Bldg.
2 Union Sq.
Chattanooga, TN 37402-2500 (423) 756-3000
Contact: Glenn C. Stophel, Secy.-Treas.

Donor(s): Velma DeWitt Macguire.
Financial data (yr. ended 12/31/01): Grants paid, $14,500; assets, $168,083 (M); expenditures, $14,737; qualifying distributions, $14,500.
Limitations: Giving primarily in Chattanooga, TN.
Officers: Velma DeWitt Macguire, Pres.; Glenn C. Stophel, Secy.
Director: J.T. Wilson.
EIN: 584180022

50296
The Jarman Foundation
2100 Parkway Towers
Nashville, TN 37219

Established in 1937 in TN.
Donor(s): W. Maxey Jarman,‡ James Franklin Jarman.
Financial data (yr. ended 12/31/01): Grants paid, $14,100; assets, $217,409 (M); expenditures, $20,334; qualifying distributions, $14,100.
Limitations: Applications not accepted. Giving primarily in TN.
Application information: Contributes only to pre-selected organizations.
Trustee: Frank C. Ingraham.
EIN: 626039471

50297
Herbert and Mary Shainberg Foundation
(Formerly Herbert Shainberg Foundation)
c/o First Tennessee Bank, N.A.
P.O. Box 84
Memphis, TN 38101-0084

Donor(s): Mary Shainberg, Suzanne Shainberg, Terry Shainberg.
Financial data (yr. ended 01/31/02): Grants paid, $14,000; assets, $93,149 (M); expenditures, $16,913; qualifying distributions, $14,000.
Limitations: Giving primarily in Memphis, TN.
Trustee: First Tennessee Bank, N.A.
EIN: 626195785

50298
The Dixon Foundation
2401 Keith St., Ste. 101
Cleveland, TN 37311

Established in 2000 in TN.
Donor(s): H. Bernard Dixon.
Financial data (yr. ended 12/31/01): Grants paid, $13,621; assets, $1,686 (M); gifts received, $14,070; expenditures, $16,016; qualifying distributions, $13,621.
Limitations: Giving primarily in Cleveland, TN.
Officers: H. Bernard Dixon, Pres.; Starr S. Dixon, Treas.; Betty Benefield, Secy.
Directors: Valerie Dixon Babb, Candace Dixon Ramsey, Venessa Dixon Torrence.
EIN: 621821535

50299
Robert & Martha Fogelman Charitable Trust
6455 Poplar Ave.
Memphis, TN 38119

Established in 1981.
Donor(s): Robert F. Fogelman.
Financial data (yr. ended 11/30/01): Grants paid, $13,450; assets, $141,228 (M); gifts received, $10,560; expenditures, $19,359; qualifying distributions, $13,450.

Limitations: Applications not accepted. Giving primarily in Memphis, TN.
Application information: Contributes only to pre-selected organizations.
Officers and Trustees:* Catherine S. Fogelman,* Pres.; Martha H. Fogelman,* Secy.; Martha F. Fogelman, Robert F. Fogelman, Robert F. Fogelman II.
EIN: 586163005

50300
The Nicholson Foundation, Inc.
424 Church St., Ste. 1400
Nashville, TN 37219 (615) 726-3400
Contact: Alexander M. Nicholson, Jr., Pres.

Established in 1997 in TN.
Donor(s): Alexander M. Nicholson, Alexander M. Nicholson, Jr.
Financial data (yr. ended 12/31/01): Grants paid, $13,397; assets, $175,932 (M); expenditures, $15,498; qualifying distributions, $13,397.
Application information: Application form not required.
Officers: Alexander M. Nicholson, Chair.; Alexander M. Nicholson, Jr., Pres.; Laurie M. Nicholson, Secy.
EIN: 621685784

50301
Dolan Gardens Foundation
304 S. Palisades Dr.
Signal Mountain, TN 37377

Established in 1997 in TN.
Donor(s): Frances F. Jones.
Financial data (yr. ended 12/31/01): Grants paid, $13,000; assets, $312,895 (M); expenditures, $16,864; qualifying distributions, $13,000.
Limitations: Applications not accepted.
Application information: Contributes only to pre-selected organizations.
Officers: Frances F. Jones, Pres.; Leslie J. Dulin, Secy.; Thomas H. Jones, Jr., Treas.
EIN: 621686888

50302
Heritage Foundation, Inc.
914 N. Highland Ave.
Jackson, TN 38301-4431

Financial data (yr. ended 12/31/01): Grants paid, $12,868; assets, $272,710 (M); gifts received, $25,000; expenditures, $16,202; qualifying distributions, $12,868.
Limitations: Applications not accepted.
Application information: Contributes only to pre-selected organizations.
Officers: Thomas Jackson Weaver III, Pres.; Barbara McBride Weaver, V.P. and Secy.; Winston Truett, V.P. and Treas.; Frank McKinnie Weaver, V.P.; Marguerite McKinnie Weaver, V.P.
EIN: 581764982

50303
Hillwood Ministries, Inc.
1100 N.W. Rutland Rd.
Mount Juliet, TN 37122

Established in 1997 in TN.
Financial data (yr. ended 12/31/00): Grants paid, $12,814; assets, $62,443 (M); gifts received, $32,416; expenditures, $77,449; qualifying distributions, $12,814.
Officer: Robert Hill, Pres.
EIN: 621229011

50304
Walmac Foundation, Inc.
3617 Laurel Oak Ln.
Knoxville, TN 37931-1622 (865) 690-0737
Contact: Wallace A. Casnelli, Pres.

Donor(s): Wallace A. Casnelli.
Financial data (yr. ended 11/30/01): Grants paid, $12,693; assets, $174,616 (M); expenditures, $13,263; qualifying distributions, $12,693.
Limitations: Giving primarily in Knoxville, TN.
Officers: Wallace A. Casnelli, Pres.; Mary A. Casnelli, Secy.-Treas.
Directors: Charles S. White, Al Witt.
EIN: 621178718

50305
Huseby Family Foundation
301 Deerwood Ln.
Brentwood, TN 37027 (615) 661-8091
Contact: Robert Huseby, Pres.

Established in 1997 in TN.
Financial data (yr. ended 12/31/00): Grants paid, $12,436; assets, $300,217 (M); gifts received, $99,208; expenditures, $16,943; qualifying distributions, $12,436.
Officers: Robert Huseby, Pres.; Christina Huseby, Secy.
EIN: 621725069

50306
Josie M. Fitzhugh Trust f/b/o Josephine Circle
c/o Union Planters Bank, Trust Dept.
P.O. Box 387
Memphis, TN 38147 (901) 383-6200

Financial data (yr. ended 10/31/01): Grants paid, $12,400; assets, $223,428 (M); expenditures, $15,865; qualifying distributions, $13,959.
Limitations: Giving limited to Jackson, MS.
Trustee: Union Planters Bank.
EIN: 626035544
Codes: GTI

50307
Fresh Springs Foundation
1365 Cooks Valley Rd.
Kingsport, TN 37664

Established in 1996 in TN.
Donor(s): Jan McMurray, John McMurray.
Financial data (yr. ended 12/31/01): Grants paid, $12,344; assets, $30,883 (M); gifts received, $11,575; expenditures, $19,352; qualifying distributions, $15,236.
Limitations: Applications not accepted. Giving on a national and international basis.
Application information: Contributes only to pre-selected organizations.
Officers: Janice R. McMurray, Pres.; John M. McMurray, Secy.
Directors: Rev. Gale Hartley, Claude A. Marlowe, Jr., Ron Owens.
EIN: 621660294

50308
Mario C. & Grace Charles Education Foundation
c/o UBS Painewebber
310 W. End Ave., Ste. 150
Nashville, TN 37203

Established in 1999 in TN.
Financial data (yr. ended 10/31/01): Grants paid, $12,000; assets, $916,548 (M); expenditures, $44,918; qualifying distributions, $20,741.
Limitations: Applications not accepted.
Application information: Contributes only to pre-selected organizations.
Trustee: UBS Painewebber Trust Co.
EIN: 621762700

50309
Rosalie Conte Foundation
c/o AmSouth Bank
315 Deadbrick St., 11th Fl.
Nashville, TN 37237-1101
Application address: 1724 Chickering Rd., Nashville, TN 37215
Contact: Andrea Conte, Dir.

Established in 1989 in TN.
Donor(s): Andrea Conte.
Financial data (yr. ended 12/31/00): Grants paid, $12,000; assets, $348,207 (M); expenditures, $17,282; qualifying distributions, $12,132.
Limitations: Giving limited to residents of the Great Barrington, MA, area.
Application information: Application form required.
Directors: Andrea Conte, Carol Conte, Nicholas Conte, Sr., Nicholas Conte, Jr., Stephen Conte.
Trustee: AmSouth Bank.
EIN: 581849183
Codes: GTI

50310
Woosley Family Foundation Trust
c/o Harry Lee Woosley, III
4419 Warner Pl.
Nashville, TN 37205

Established in 1996 in TN.
Donor(s): Lula Woosley.
Financial data (yr. ended 12/31/01): Grants paid, $11,997; assets, $142,668 (M); expenditures, $12,445; qualifying distributions, $11,997.
Limitations: Applications not accepted.
Application information: Contributes only to pre-selected organizations.
Trustees: Harry Lee Woosley III, Jessica Delbridge Woosley.
EIN: 626311736

50311
The Christ Foundation
101 Abbeywood Dr.
Nashville, TN 37215-6145
Contact: John E. McDowell, Tr.

Established in 1993.
Donor(s): The Christ Foundation, John McDowell, Katherine McDowell.
Financial data (yr. ended 12/31/01): Grants paid, $11,918; assets, $117,633 (M); gifts received, $15,100; expenditures, $12,251; qualifying distributions, $11,918.
Limitations: Giving limited to TN.
Trustees: Joe L. Dick, Amanda McDowell, Curtis McDowell, John E. McDowell, Charles Webb.
EIN: 582071026

50312
Sandra Schatten Foundation
424 Church St., Ste. 1800
Nashville, TN 37219

Established in 2000 in TN.
Donor(s): Sandra Schatten.
Financial data (yr. ended 12/31/01): Grants paid, $11,750; assets, $194,850 (M); expenditures, $14,259; qualifying distributions, $11,750.
Limitations: Applications not accepted.
Application information: Contributes only to pre-selected organizations.
Trustees: Dwayne W. Barrett, Sandra Schatten.
EIN: 621814759

50313
Deaton Family Foundation
c/o Claude Terrell Deaton
25 Northumberland Dr.
Nashville, TN 37215

Established in 1993 in TN.
Donor(s): Claude T. Deaton III.
Financial data (yr. ended 12/31/01): Grants paid, $11,500; assets, $280,340 (M); gifts received, $5,000; expenditures, $12,442; qualifying distributions, $11,590.
Limitations: Applications not accepted. Giving primarily in Nashville, TN.
Application information: Contributes only to pre-selected organizations.
Officers: Claude T. Deaton III, Pres.; Gretchen Deaton, Secy.
Directors: Melissa D. Carrigan, Dana M. Deaton, Heather Deaton.
EIN: 621550299

50314
E. B. Coburn Scholarship Trust
c/o Brownsville Bank, Trust Dept.
P.O. Box 879
Brownsville, TN 38012-0879
Application address: c/o Gordon Perry, Haywood County High School, Brownsville, TN 38012

Established in 1989 in TN.
Financial data (yr. ended 12/31/00): Grants paid, $11,322; assets, $146,690 (L); expenditures, $12,662; qualifying distributions, $13,980.
Limitations: Giving limited to residents of Haywood County, TN.
Trustee: Brownsville Bank.
EIN: 626199961

50315
Caryn F. and Rudi E. Scheidt, Jr. Family Charitable Trust
6230 River Grove Cove
Memphis, TN 38120 (901) 680-9135
Contact: Rudi E. Scheidt, Jr., Tr.

Established in 1998 in TN.
Financial data (yr. ended 11/30/01): Grants paid, $11,300; assets, $143,564 (M); gifts received, $2,950; expenditures, $14,250; qualifying distributions, $11,300.
Limitations: Giving primarily in Memphis, TN.
Application information: Application form not required.
Trustees: Caryn F. Scheidt, Rudi E. Scheidt, Jr.
EIN: 626350877

50316
McKee Educational Foundation
214 Kennith Dr.
Nashville, TN 37207-3327 (615) 227-0309
Contact: C. William McKee, Tr.

Established in 1997 in TN.
Donor(s): James O. McKee.
Financial data (yr. ended 12/31/01): Grants paid, $11,000; assets, $150,027 (M); expenditures, $11,145; qualifying distributions, $11,000.
Application information: Application form required.
Trustees: Sharon Dezurick, C. William McKee, Michael C. McKee.
EIN: 911845996

50317
Joy Foundation
194 Spence Ln.
Nashville, TN 37210

Established in 2000 in TN.

Donor(s): Roy C. Flowers.
Financial data (yr. ended 06/30/02): Grants paid, $10,600; assets, $185,387 (M); gifts received, $72,924; expenditures, $11,160; qualifying distributions, $10,600.
Limitations: Applications not accepted.
Application information: Contributes only to pre-selected organizations.
Officers: Deborah Pittman, Pres.; Roy C. Flowers, Secy.-Treas.
EIN: 621827342

50318
Hattie G. Watkins Educational Fund
c/o Union Planters Bank, Trust Dept.
P.O. Box 387
Memphis, TN 38147 (901) 383-6200
Contact: Jason Eagle, Trust Off., Union Planters Bank

Financial data (yr. ended 10/31/01): Grants paid, $10,400; assets, $279,450 (M); expenditures, $16,259; qualifying distributions, $12,481.
Limitations: Giving primarily in TN.
Trustee: Union Planters Bank.
EIN: 626051024

50319
Held Foundation, Inc.
4108 Cherryton Dr.
Chattanooga, TN 37411-3712
Contact: George Held, Pres.

Established in 1992 in TN.
Donor(s): George Held, Peggy Held, Betty Held.
Financial data (yr. ended 12/31/00): Grants paid, $10,385; assets, $1 (M); expenditures, $11,284; qualifying distributions, $10,385.
Limitations: Giving primarily in Chattanooga, TN.
Application information: Application form not required.
Officers and Directors:* George Held,* Pres.; Mark Rogers, Secy.; Betty Held, Peggy Held.
EIN: 621487190

50320
Harkavy, Shainberg, Kosten & Pinstein Charitable Foundation
100 Peabody Pl., Ste. 1300
Memphis, TN 38103 (901) 761-1263
Contact: Michael D. Kaplan, Pres.

Donor(s): Allen C. Dunstan, Neil Harkavy, Ronald M. Harkavy, Michael D. Kaplan, Alan L. Kosten, Robert L. Pinstein, Raymond M. Shainberg.
Financial data (yr. ended 12/31/99): Grants paid, $10,069; assets, $347 (M); gifts received, $10,000; expenditures, $10,201; qualifying distributions, $10,069.
Officer and Directors:* Michael D. Kaplan,* Pres.; Ronald M. Harkavy, Raymond M. Shainberg.
EIN: 621610954

50321
ARCRUN, Inc.
P.O. Box 667
Dyersburg, TN 38024
Contact: Katherine Brayton, Tr.

Financial data (yr. ended 12/31/01): Grants paid, $10,035; assets, $103,115 (M); expenditures, $10,465; qualifying distributions, $10,035.
Limitations: Giving limited to residents of the AL and the Dyersburg, TN, area.
Application information: Forms supplied by ACRUN, Inc. Application form required.
Trustees: Elmer Bivens, Katherine Brayton, David Nunn.
EIN: 620988419

50322
Rainey Foundation
1021 N. Heritage Dr.
Maryville, TN 37803

Established in 1985 in TN.
Donor(s): John C. Rainey.
Financial data (yr. ended 07/31/01): Grants paid, $10,025; assets, $17,067 (M); expenditures, $10,621; qualifying distributions, $10,025.
Limitations: Applications not accepted. Giving limited to Maryville, TN.
Application information: Contributes only to pre-selected organizations.
Directors: Doris Rainey, John C. Rainey.
EIN: 621244141

50323
Mary E. Roark Scholarship Fund Trust
123 Public Sq.
Gallatin, TN 37066 (615) 452-5611
Contact: Nathan Harsh, Tr.

Financial data (yr. ended 12/31/01): Grants paid, $10,015; assets, $339,135 (M); expenditures, $11,427; qualifying distributions, $10,015.
Limitations: Giving limited to residents of TN.
Application information: Applications must include resume, grades, personal life history, and work background.
Trustee: Nathan Harsh.
EIN: 626289349
Codes: GTI

50324
Eleanor's Foundation, Inc.
4107 Franklin Rd.
Nashville, TN 37204

Established in 1997 in TN.
Donor(s): Suzanne M. Blackburn, Rick Blackburn.
Financial data (yr. ended 12/31/01): Grants paid, $10,000; assets, $12,300 (M); gifts received, $10,000; expenditures, $11,697; qualifying distributions, $10,000.
Limitations: Applications not accepted. Giving primarily in CA, MS and TN.
Application information: Contributes only to pre-selected organizations.
Officers: Suzanne M. Blackburn, Pres.; M.J. Herbison, Secy.
EIN: 621609534

50325
The C. Scott & Muriel S. Mayfield Family Foundation
220 Lynnwood Dr.
Athens, TN 37303-4141

Established in 1998.
Donor(s): Muriel S. Mayfield.
Financial data (yr. ended 12/31/01): Grants paid, $10,000; assets, $390,227 (M); gifts received, $100,000; expenditures, $13,322; qualifying distributions, $9,902.
Limitations: Applications not accepted. Giving primarily in TN.
Application information: Contributes only to pre-selected organizations.
Officers: Elaine M. Cathcart, Pres.; Muriel S. Mayfield, Secy.-Treas.
Directors: Clarice M. Baggett, C. Scott Mayfield, Jr.
EIN: 621740682

50326
The Mighty Oak Foundation, Inc.
4019 Breakwater Dr.
Hixson, TN 37343
Application address: 1 Park Pl., 6148 Lee Hwy. Ste. 103, Chahanuaga, TN, 37421, tel.: (423) 843-3891
Contact: Jeffery V. Curry, V.P.

Financial data (yr. ended 12/31/00): Grants paid, $10,000; assets, $4,000 (L); expenditures, $10,000; qualifying distributions, $0.
Limitations: Giving primarily in TN.
Officers: Jan Fulton, Pres.; Jeffery V. Curry, V.P.
EIN: 621723942

50327
Mildred T. Stahlman Education Foundation
c/o Vanderbilt University
A-0109 Medical Ctr. N.
Nashville, TN 37232

Established in 1988 in TN.
Donor(s): Mildred T. Stahlman, M.D.
Financial data (yr. ended 12/31/01): Grants paid, $10,000; assets, $23,814 (M); gifts received, $30,118; expenditures, $11,904; qualifying distributions, $9,945.
Limitations: Giving limited to residents of Humphreys County, TN.
Application information: Application form required.
Officers and Directors:* Mildred T. Stahlman, M.D.,* Pres.; Jeffrey T. Carr,* Secy.-Treas.; Robert Bell Cotton, M.D., James L. Long, Mary Angela Skelton, M.D.
EIN: 621379222
Codes: GTI

50328
Dudley Warren Family Foundation
3640 Knollwood Rd.
Nashville, TN 37215

Established in 1996 in TN.
Donor(s): Dudley W. Warner, Sara Warner.
Financial data (yr. ended 06/30/02): Grants paid, $10,000; assets, $512,574 (M); expenditures, $10,000; qualifying distributions, $10,000.
Limitations: Applications not accepted. Giving primarily in Nashville, TN.
Application information: Contributes only to pre-selected organizations.
Officers and Directors:* Dudley W. Warner,* Pres.; Beth G. Warner,* Secy.-Treas.; Sara Warner.
EIN: 621663740

50329
John W. Simpson, Jr. Foundation Fund
P.O. Box 869
Jasper, TN 37347

Financial data (yr. ended 01/01/01): Grants paid, $9,900; assets, $121,808 (M); expenditures, $1,388; qualifying distributions, $9,835.
Limitations: Giving limited to residents of Jasper, TN.
Application information: Application form required.
Officer: Edwin Z. Kelly, Jr., Treas.
Directors: Terry Gentle, Janie B. Lamb.
EIN: 626052488

50330
The Frank Z. Jemison, Jr. Foundation, Inc.
c/o 1 Union Pl.
35 Union Ave., Ste. 200
Memphis, TN 38103 (901) 544-1705
Contact: Frank Z. Jemison, Jr., Pres.

Established in 1984 in TN.

Donor(s): Frank Z. Jemison, Jr.
Financial data (yr. ended 07/31/01): Grants paid, $9,850; assets, $87,860 (M); expenditures, $10,450; qualifying distributions, $10,436.
Limitations: Giving primarily in Memphis, TN.
Officers and Directors:* Frank Z. Jemison, Jr.,* Pres.; Sandra L. Perkins,* Secy.; Michael Johnson, Treas.; S. Herbert Rhea, John W. Slater, Jr.
EIN: 581620146

50331
Sunlight Foundation
P.O. Box 150123
Nashville, TN 37215-0123

Established in 1999 in TN.
Donor(s): Deborah D. Sherman, Timothy J. Siktberg.
Financial data (yr. ended 12/31/01): Grants paid, $9,800; assets, $512,709 (M); gifts received, $260,568; expenditures, $11,685; qualifying distributions, $9,800.
Limitations: Applications not accepted.
Application information: Contributes only to pre-selected organizations.
Officers: Deborah D. Sherman, Pres.; Timothy J. Siktberg, Secy.
Director: Billie Don Sherman.
EIN: 621809916

50332
Perkins Charitable Trust
1011 W. Poplar, Ste. 3
Collierville, TN 38017

Established in 1996 in OH.
Donor(s): C.C. and C. Asset Managment Co.
Financial data (yr. ended 12/31/99): Grants paid, $9,385; assets, $263,362 (M); gifts received, $265,195; expenditures, $9,630; qualifying distributions, $9,385.
Limitations: Applications not accepted. Giving primarily in TN.
Application information: Contributes only to pre-selected organizations.
Trustees: Chad E. Perkins, Charles Perkins, Charles L. Perkins II.
EIN: 316541937

50333
Valerie Wright Memorial Foundation
1907 Light Tower Cir.
Hixson, TN 37343-3185

Established in 1985 in TN.
Donor(s): Louis S. Wright, Billie K. Wright.
Financial data (yr. ended 10/31/01): Grants paid, $9,000; assets, $89,933 (M); expenditures, $9,280; qualifying distributions, $9,000.
Limitations: Giving primarily in Chattanooga, TN.
Officers: Louis S. Wright, Pres. and Treas.; Andy Ashford, V.P.; Billie K. Wright, Secy.
Directors: Terry Atkin Cavett, Albert C. Kiser.
EIN: 621287485

50334
Janette Day Residuary Educational Trust
c/o Union Planters Bank, N.A.
P.O. Box 189
Jackson, TN 38302
Contact: Martha B. Peddy, Trust Off., Union Planters Bank, N.A.

Established in 1998 in TN.
Donor(s): Janette Day.‡
Financial data (yr. ended 10/31/01): Grants paid, $8,795; assets, $258,949 (M); expenditures, $13,255; qualifying distributions, $15,992.
Limitations: Giving limited to residents in Madison County, TN.
Trustee: Union Planters Bank.

EIN: 626356036

50335
Tennessee Foundation for Architecture
209 10th Ave. S., Ste. 506
Nashville, TN 37203
Application address: c/o Scholarship Comm., 530 Church St., Nashville, TN 37208

Established in 1985 in TN.
Financial data (yr. ended 12/31/01): Grants paid, $8,700; assets, $131,779 (M); gifts received, $750; expenditures, $12,462; qualifying distributions, $8,700.
Limitations: Giving limited to TN.
Officers and Directors:* Angie King,* Pres.; Eugene E. Burr, V.P.; Roy D. Shockley, Secy.; Sam E. DiCarlo, Treas.; Ken Brandenburg, Marleen K. Davis, D. Mark Freeman, David Hawkins, Kelly Headden, Gary B. Hilbert, David W. Leonard, Connie C. Wallace.
EIN: 581679107

50336
Ali Foundation, Inc.
c/o Subhi D. Ali
806 E. Main St.
Waverly, TN 37185-1814

Established in 1999.
Financial data (yr. ended 06/30/00): Grants paid, $8,640; assets, $4,218 (M); gifts received, $14,214; expenditures, $10,010; qualifying distributions, $10,010.
Officers: Subhi D. Ali, Pres.; Maysoon S. Ali, V.P. and Secy.; Yasmine S. Ali, Secy.-Treas.
EIN: 621784711

50337
Fred W. and Marion B. McPeake Family Foundation
612 16th St.
Knoxville, TN 37916

Established in 2000 in TN.
Financial data (yr. ended 06/30/01): Grants paid, $8,611; assets, $70 (M); gifts received, $9,461; expenditures, $9,350; qualifying distributions, $8,981.
Limitations: Applications not accepted. Giving primarily in Knoxville, TN.
Application information: Contributes only to pre-selected organizations.
Officers: Fred W. McPeake, Pres.; Marion B. McPeake, V.P.; Linda M. Shuler, V.P.; Linda Smith, Secy.
EIN: 621824739

50338
The Anne Bransford Wallace Foundation
c/o Deborah A. Kolarich, C.P.A.
3010 Poston Ave., Ste. 220
Nashville, TN 37203

Established in 1994 in TN.
Donor(s): Anne Bransford Wallace.
Financial data (yr. ended 12/31/00): Grants paid, $8,550; assets, $138,404 (M); expenditures, $9,257; qualifying distributions, $8,550.
Limitations: Applications not accepted.
Application information: Contributes only to pre-selected organizations.
Trustee: Anne Bransford Wallace.
EIN: 621551711

50339
The J. S. and J. R. King Foundation
4504 Hickory Hill Rd.
Kingsport, TN 37664

Established in 1997 in TN.
Donor(s): Jane S. King, John R. King.

Financial data (yr. ended 12/31/01): Grants paid, $8,200; assets, $363,426 (M); expenditures, $8,836; qualifying distributions, $8,200.
Limitations: Applications not accepted. Giving primarily in TN.
Application information: Contributes only to pre-selected organizations.
Officers and Directors:* John R. King, Pres., Treas. and Mgr.; Jane S. King,* Secy.; Jennifer K. Ferreira, John R. King III.
EIN: 621692084

50340
V. S. Johnson, Jr. Charitable Trust
703 Murfreesboro Rd.
Nashville, TN 37210

Financial data (yr. ended 12/31/00): Grants paid, $8,000; assets, $199,617 (M); expenditures, $8,310; qualifying distributions, $7,899.
Limitations: Applications not accepted. Giving primarily in the Northeast.
Application information: Contributes only to pre-selected organizations.
Trustee: Victor S. Johnson III.
EIN: 646171330

50341
The Calvert Family Foundation
110 Old Indian Hill Rd.
Greeneville, TN 37743

Financial data (yr. ended 12/31/01): Grants paid, $7,500; assets, $111,697 (M); expenditures, $9,831; qualifying distributions, $7,500.
Limitations: Applications not accepted. Giving primarily in Greeneville, TN.
Application information: Contributes only to pre-selected organizations.
Officers and Directors:* S.J. Clavert, Jr.,* Pres.; P.R. Calvert,* Secy.; Sam J. Calvert III, Melanie C. Coley.
EIN: 621659836

50342
Lambert & Mary Campbell Foundation
2809 12th Ave. S
Nashville, TN 37204
Application address: P.O. Box 40304, Nashville, TN 37204-0304, tel.: (615) 292-4739
Contact: Mark M. McInteer, Tr.

Financial data (yr. ended 12/31/01): Grants paid, $7,427; assets, $86,503 (M); expenditures, $7,566; qualifying distributions, $7,427.
Limitations: Giving primarily in TN.
Trustees: Billy L. Akin, Walter C. Leaver III, Jim Bill McInteer, Mark M. McInteer, Robert G. Neil.
EIN: 621180348

50343
Astre Foundation
(Formerly FDS Foundation)
P.O. Box 11325
Chattanooga, TN 37401
Contact: Franck C. Hughes, Tres.

Financial data (yr. ended 12/31/01): Grants paid, $7,400; assets, $104,621 (M); gifts received, $1,344; expenditures, $7,854; qualifying distributions, $7,329.
Limitations: Giving primarily in Chattanooga, TN.
Application information: Application form not required.
Officers: Mary L. Hughes, Chair.; David L. Hughes,* Pres.; Kathaleen Hughes,* Secy.; Frank C. Hughes, Treas.
Directors: Buckner L. Hughes, D'Arcy N. Hughes, Nat C. Hughes, Sam B. Hughes.
EIN: 621046446

TENNESSEE—50359

50344
Gherkin Foundation, Inc.
700 Krystal Bldg.
Chattanooga, TN 37402

Established in 1986 in TN.
Donor(s): Sharon Mills.
Financial data (yr. ended 12/31/01): Grants paid, $7,000; assets, $783,420 (M); expenditures, $9,288; qualifying distributions, $7,000.
Limitations: Giving primarily in the Chattanooga, TN, area.
Officers: Sharon Mills, Pres.; W.E. Landis, V.P. and Treas.; Shirley Miller, Secy.
EIN: 621289460
Codes: TN

50345
J. H. & Evelyn S. Hankins Foundation
1508 Washington Dr.
Lebanon, TN 37087

Financial data (yr. ended 12/31/01): Grants paid, $7,000; assets, $298,101 (M); expenditures, $7,682; qualifying distributions, $7,000.
Trustees: Brenda H. Callis, C. Edward Callis.
EIN: 621549282

50346
M. C. Hitchcock Foundation, Inc.
P.O. Box 400
Winchester, TN 37398-0400 (931) 962-1060
Contact: William Henry Agee, V.P.

Established in 1997.
Financial data (yr. ended 12/31/01): Grants paid, $7,000; assets, $127,169 (M); expenditures, $7,638; qualifying distributions, $488.
Officers: Mabel Claire Hitchcock, Pres.; William Henry Agee, V.P.; Jane M. Hitchcock, Secy.-Treas.
EIN: 631188980

50347
Jennie Harris Southall Memorial Trust
c/o First Farmers & Merchants Bank
P.O. Box 1148
Columbia, TN 38402-1148 (931) 388-3145

Established around 1961.
Financial data (yr. ended 12/31/01): Grants paid, $7,000; assets, $292,857 (M); expenditures, $8,750; qualifying distributions, $7,000.
Limitations: Giving primarily in Columbia, TN.
Trustee: First Farmers & Merchants Bank.
EIN: 237425275

50348
Ben-Glo Foundation, Inc.
1085 S. Bellevue Blvd.
Memphis, TN 38106-2344 (901) 774-2146
Contact: C.O. Daugherty, M.D., Pres.

Donor(s): C.O. Daugherty, M.D.
Financial data (yr. ended 12/31/99): Grants paid, $6,800; assets, $122,083 (M); gifts received, $152; expenditures, $6,800; qualifying distributions, $6,800.
Limitations: Giving primarily in MS and TN.
Officer: C.O. Daugherty, M.D., Pres.
EIN: 621086663

50349
Martha McCrory Foundation, Inc.
187 Mississippi Ave.
Sewanee, TN 37375 (931) 598-5881
Contact: Martha McCrory, Pres.

Established in 1999 in AL.
Donor(s): Martha McCrory.
Financial data (yr. ended 12/31/01): Grants paid, $6,750; assets, $240,090 (M); expenditures, $8,723; qualifying distributions, $6,750.

Officers: Martha McCrory, Pres.; Martha H. Didriksen, V.P.; Mary H. Hutmacher, V.P.; Priscilla C. Fort, Secy.-Treas.
EIN: 631229383

50350
James R. Meadows, Jr. Foundation
636 Grassmere Park Dr.
Nashville, TN 37211
Contact: James R. Meadows, Jr., Pres.

Financial data (yr. ended 12/31/00): Grants paid, $6,610; assets, $7,143 (M); expenditures, $7,122; qualifying distributions, $6,610.
Officers: James R. Meadows, Jr., Pres.; Patricia Williams, Secy.; Thomas Cole, Treas.
Trustee: Thomas Sherrard.
EIN: 621545923

50351
William N. Fry, Sr. Trust
c/o National Bank of Commerce
1 Commerce Sq.
Memphis, TN 38150

Financial data (yr. ended 10/31/00): Grants paid, $6,570; assets, $99,858 (M); expenditures, $8,016; qualifying distributions, $6,570.
Limitations: Applications not accepted. Giving limited to Memphis, TN.
Application information: Contributes only to pre-selected organizations.
Trustee: National Bank of Commerce.
EIN: 626042819

50352
Caritas Foundation
c/o Clay J. Jackson
P.O. Box 1869
Brentwood, TN 37027

Established in 1997 in TN.
Financial data (yr. ended 12/31/01): Grants paid, $6,550; assets, $150,478 (M); gifts received, $5,000; expenditures, $8,262; qualifying distributions, $6,550.
Limitations: Applications not accepted. Giving limited to Nashville, TN.
Application information: Contributes only to pre-selected organizations.
Trustee: Clay T. Jackson.
EIN: 621682892

50353
Barnabas Trust
3692 Summer Ave.
Memphis, TN 38122

Established in TN in 1997.
Donor(s): Lloyd G. Hansen.
Financial data (yr. ended 12/31/01): Grants paid, $6,500; assets, $261,588 (M); expenditures, $8,674; qualifying distributions, $6,500.
Limitations: Applications not accepted. Giving on a national and international basis.
Application information: Contributes only to pre-selected organizations.
Trustee: Lloyd G. Hansen.
EIN: 656228178

50354
Newell and Bettie Graham Foundation
728 E. Main St.
Union City, TN 38261

Established in 1999 in TN.
Donor(s): Newell Graham, Bettie Graham.
Financial data (yr. ended 12/31/01): Grants paid, $6,500; assets, $150,143 (M); expenditures, $6,604; qualifying distributions, $6,500.
Limitations: Applications not accepted.

Application information: Contributes only to pre-selected organizations.
Officers: R. Newell Graham, Pres.; Bettie Graham, Secy.
EIN: 621795977

50355
Ada Martin Scholarship Fund
c/o SunTrust Banks, Inc.
P.O. Box 305110
Nashville, TN 37230-5110
Contact: Scott Lindsey, Trust Off., SunTrust Banks, Inc.

Financial data (yr. ended 09/30/01): Grants paid, $6,176; assets, $205,946 (M); expenditures, $10,337; qualifying distributions, $8,101.
Limitations: Giving limited to residents of Hartsville County, TN.
Trustee: SunTrust Banks, Inc.
EIN: 626144039

50356
The Louise Bransford Frazer Foundation
420 Ellendale Dr.
Nashville, TN 37205 (615) 385-3727
Contact: Louise Bransford Frazer, Tr.

Established in 1994 in TN.
Donor(s): Louise Bransford Frazer.
Financial data (yr. ended 12/31/01): Grants paid, $6,100; assets, $80,281 (M); expenditures, $7,885; qualifying distributions, $6,049.
Trustees: Louise Bransford Frazer, Mellon Bank, N.A.
EIN: 626287926

50357
Aladdin Industries Employees Trust
703 Murfreesboro Rd.
Nashville, TN 37210-4521
Contact: L.B. Jenkins, Secy.

Donor(s): Aladdin Industries, Inc., Aladdin Industries, LLC.
Financial data (yr. ended 12/31/01): Grants paid, $6,000; assets, $144,605 (M); expenditures, $6,707; qualifying distributions, $6,000.
Limitations: Giving primarily in Nashville, TN.
Officer: L.B. Jenkins, Secy.
Trustees: V.S. Johnson III, F.R. Meyer.
EIN: 237107691
Codes: CS, CD

50358
The Harris Family Foundation
315 Deadrick St., 11th Fl.
Nashville, TN 37237-1101
Application Address: 6045 Sunrise Cir., Franklin TN, 37067
Contact: Frances T. Harris, Advisory Comm.

Established in 1999 in TN.
Donor(s): Frances Harris.
Financial data (yr. ended 12/31/01): Grants paid, $6,000; assets, $176,818 (M); expenditures, $7,478; qualifying distributions, $6,000.
Advisory Committee Members: Frances T. Harris, John T. Harris, T. Vance Little, Carole H. Sharp.
Trustee: AmSouth Bank.
EIN: 621792697

50359
King Foundation
1315 Belmeade Dr.
Kingsport, TN 37664

Donor(s): E. William King, John R. King, Margaret K. Norris.
Financial data (yr. ended 11/30/01): Grants paid, $6,000; assets, $99,815 (M); expenditures, $6,575; qualifying distributions, $6,000.

50359—TENNESSEE

Limitations: Applications not accepted. Giving primarily in TN.
Application information: Contributes only to pre-selected organizations.
Officers and Directors:* John R. King,* Pres.; E. William King,* V.P.; Margaret K. Norris,* Secy.
EIN: 626046495

50360
Nayla & George Nassar, Jr. Foundation
1700 1 Commerce Sq.
Memphis, TN 38103

Established in 1998 in TN.
Donor(s): George Nassar, Jr.
Financial data (yr. ended 12/31/01): Grants paid, $6,000; assets, $12,840 (M); expenditures, $6,304; qualifying distributions, $6,000.
Limitations: Applications not accepted.
Application information: Contributes only to pre-selected organizations.
Trustee: George Nassar, Jr.
EIN: 621764555

50361
The Sheperds Foundation
215 Derby Glen Ln.
Brentwood, TN 37027

Established in 2001.
Donor(s): C & M, LLC, Nacarato GMC Trucks, Inc.
Financial data (yr. ended 12/31/01): Grants paid, $6,000; assets, $144,534 (M); gifts received, $162,046; expenditures, $9,800; qualifying distributions, $130,503.
Limitations: Applications not accepted. Giving primarily in TN.
Application information: Contributes only to pre-selected organizations.
Officers: Michael J. Nacarato, Jr., Pres.; Teresa A. Nacarato, Secy.
Directors: Michael J. Nacarato, Sr., Michael J. Nacarato, III.
EIN: 621842982

50362
Anna Mary Bransford Lenderman Foundation
624 Enquirer Ave.
Nashville, TN 37205

Financial data (yr. ended 12/31/01): Grants paid, $5,950; assets, $92,227 (M); expenditures, $6,015; qualifying distributions, $5,950.
Limitations: Giving primarily in Nashville, TN.
Trustee: Anna M. Bransford Lenderman.
EIN: 626287930

50363
E. C. Baldonado Foundation
c/o Orlino Baldonado
10513 Hardin Valley Rd.
Knoxville, TN 37932-1502

Established in 1999 in TN.
Financial data (yr. ended 12/31/01): Grants paid, $5,850; assets, $1,538 (M); gifts received, $2,500; expenditures, $5,850; qualifying distributions, $5,850.
Directors: Estrella Baldonado, Orlino Baldonado.
EIN: 621768280

50364
The Academy Place Foundation
2302 Jefferson Ave.
Memphis, TN 38104

Established in 2000 in TN.
Donor(s): Robert Hunt, Eileen Hunt.
Financial data (yr. ended 12/31/01): Grants paid, $5,500; assets, $378,386 (M); gifts received, $269,863; expenditures, $7,814; qualifying distributions, $5,500.

Limitations: Applications not accepted.
Application information: Contributes only to pre-selected organizations.
Trustees: Eileen D. Hunt, Robert J. Hunt.
EIN: 626380345

50365
The Cyrus Feldman Memorial Trust
c/o Henry A. Feldman
173 California Ave.
Oak Ridge, TN 37830-4001

Established in 1990.
Financial data (yr. ended 11/30/01): Grants paid, $5,500; assets, $64,675 (M); gifts received, $50; expenditures, $5,608; qualifying distributions, $5,532.
Limitations: Applications not accepted. Giving limited to Oak Ridge, TN.
Application information: Contributes only to pre-selected organizations.
Trustees: Alice M. Feldman, Henry A. Feldman.
EIN: 043105618

50366
J. C. Freels Scholarship Awards Trust
c/o Union Planters Bank
P.O. Box 15993
Knoxville, TN 37901-5993

Financial data (yr. ended 12/31/01): Grants paid, $5,500; assets, $155,281 (M); expenditures, $8,015; qualifying distributions, $7,946.
Limitations: Giving limited to the Morristown, TN, area.
Application information: Unsolicited requests for funds not accepted.
Trustee: Union Planters Bank.
EIN: 626049363
Codes: GTI

50367
St. John's Orphanage
(also known as Knox Children's Foundation)
c/o First Tennessee Bank, N.A., Trust Div.
P.O. Box 1991
Knoxville, TN 37995-1230
Application address: 4110 Sutherland Ave., Knoxville, TN 37919, tel.: (865)584-1184
Contact: J. Finbarr Saunders, Jr., Secy.

Financial data (yr. ended 12/31/01): Grants paid, $5,500; assets, $931,054 (M); gifts received, $31,362; expenditures, $58,927; qualifying distributions, $5,500.
Limitations: Giving limited to Knox County, TN.
Application information: Application form required.
Officers: Fritz Schilling, Pres.; Robert Killefer, 1st V.P.; J. Finbarr Saunders, Jr., Secy.; Veda Bateman, Treas.; and 16 additional trustees.
Trustees: Peggy Addicks, First Tennessee Bank, N.A.
EIN: 626034309

50368
Thackston Family Foundation
c/o Edward Lee Thackston
2010 Priest Rd.
Nashville, TN 37215

Financial data (yr. ended 12/31/01): Grants paid, $5,300; assets, $180,272 (M); expenditures, $6,141; qualifying distributions, $6,141.
Directors: Gemma Kathleen Roberts, Edward Lee Thackston, Guy Carleton Thackston.
EIN: 621541568

50369
The Sherrill Foundation
713 Vail Ct.
Nashville, TN 37215-1849

Financial data (yr. ended 06/30/02): Grants paid, $5,200; assets, $24,573 (M); expenditures, $6,185; qualifying distributions, $5,096.
Limitations: Applications not accepted.
Application information: Contributes only to pre-selected organizations.
Officers: R. Parker Sherrill, Pres.; Robert Parker Sherrill, Jr., V.P.; Scott D. Sherrill, V.P.; Steve Renner, Secy.-Treas.
EIN: 621586458

50370
Cornerstone Foundation
c/o Tim A. Graham
1st Tennessee Plz., 800 S. Gay St., Ste. 1930
Knoxville, TN 37929
Application address: 7010 Oak Ridge Hwy., Knoxville, TN 37929, tel.: (865) 693-7000

Established in 1997 in TN.
Financial data (yr. ended 12/31/01): Grants paid, $5,185; assets, $3,197 (M); expenditures, $5,192; qualifying distributions, $5,185.
Trustee: Tim A. Graham.
EIN: 311497257

50371
Holland Family Foundation
2015 Clearfield Ln.
Chattanooga, TN 37405

Established in 1999 in TN.
Donor(s): Brice L. Holland, Lynn H. Holland.
Financial data (yr. ended 12/31/01): Grants paid, $5,000; assets, $137,022 (M); gifts received, $51,944; expenditures, $6,500; qualifying distributions, $5,000.
Limitations: Applications not accepted.
Application information: Contributes only to pre-selected organizations.
Officers: Brice H. Holland, Pres.; Lynn H. Holland, Secy.-Treas.
Directors: Bonnie H. Autry, Melody H. Barrow, Cheryl L. Lamb, Karla H. Ryan.
EIN: 621788704

50372
Lifewalk 2000
880 Madison Ave., Ste. 1001
Memphis, TN 38103

Established in 1998 in TN.
Financial data (yr. ended 12/31/00): Grants paid, $5,000; assets, $442 (M); gifts received, $9,847; expenditures, $9,739; qualifying distributions, $5,000.
Director: Preston D. Archer.
EIN: 621729383

50373
The James W. & Anne B. Reel Foundation
P.O. Box 3858
Johnson City, TN 37602-3858

Established in 1999 in TN.
Donor(s): James W. Reel.
Financial data (yr. ended 12/31/01): Grants paid, $5,000; assets, $97,891 (M); gifts received, $100,000; expenditures, $7,062; qualifying distributions, $5,000.
Limitations: Applications not accepted. Giving primarily in Greene County, TN.
Application information: Contributes only to pre-selected organizations.
Officers: James W. Reel, Pres.; Anne B. Reel, V.P.; Susanne C. Reel, Treas.

EIN: 621798716

50374
The Richardson Foundation
(Formerly T. C. H. Richardson Foundation)
c/o Equitable Trust Co.
800 Nashville City Ctr.
Nashville, TN 37219-1743

Established in 1983 in TN.
Donor(s): T.C.H. Jean Williams Trust.
Financial data (yr. ended 12/31/01): Grants paid, $5,000; assets, $530,620 (M); gifts received, $98,600; expenditures, $14,789; qualifying distributions, $5,000.
Limitations: Applications not accepted. Giving primarily in Nashville, TN.
Application information: Contributes only to pre-selected organizations.
Trustee: Equitable Trust Co.
Trust Committee Members: Jean Ellen R. Cheek, Gayle R. Eadie, Richard D. Holton, James S. Lattimore, Jr., Walter E. Richardson III.
EIN: 621179433

50375
Peary Wilemon National Cotton Ginners Scholarship Foundation, Inc.
1918 N. Pkwy.
Memphis, TN 38112
Application address: P.O. Box 820285, Memphis, TN 38182, tel.: (901) 274-9030
Contact: Bill M. Norman, Exec. V.P.

Established in 1995 in TN.
Financial data (yr. ended 02/28/01): Grants paid, $5,000; assets, $97,275 (M); expenditures, $5,124; qualifying distributions, $5,047.
Limitations: Giving primarily in MS and TX.
Application information: Application form required.
Officers: Bobby Greene, Chair.; Myrl Mitchell, Pres.; Bill M. Norman, Exec. V.P.; Richard Bransford, 1st V.P.; Michael Hooper, 2nd V.P.; Richard Holder, 3rd V.P.
Trustees: David Alderete, Jeff Ballentine, Bill Brooks, Sid Brough, John Edmonston, Carla Fuller, Kirk Gilkey, Lela Harvey, Randy Kennedy, Sam Leake, David Lingle, Larry McClendon, Murry McClintock, Mike McMinn, Van Murphy, George Perrow, Kirby Powell, Jimmy Roppolo, Bobby Todd, John Visic, Gene West, Robert Waters.
EIN: 621595279

50376
No Other Foundation
c/o John C. Stites, II
1080 S. Willow Ave.
Cookeville, TN 38501

Established in 1999 in TN.
Donor(s): American Buildings Co.
Financial data (yr. ended 03/31/02): Grants paid, $4,540; assets, $85,857 (M); expenditures, $6,303; qualifying distributions, $4,540.
Officers: John D. Stites II, Pres.; James R. Stites, V.P.; Rosemary Stites, Secy.
Trustees: Donnie Davidson, Sarah Davidson, Mary Stites.
EIN: 621790241
Codes: CS

50377
James C. Hailey Scholarship Trust Fund
132 Ware Dr.
McMinnville, TN 37110 (931) 668-5858
Contact: Pat Grissom-Young, Tr.

Financial data (yr. ended 12/31/01): Grants paid, $4,500; assets, $138,793 (M); expenditures, $5,196; qualifying distributions, $4,500.

Limitations: Giving limited to residents of Warren County, TN.
Application information: Application form required.
Trustees: John H. Biddle, Pat Grissom-Young, Jerry Hale, Ron Martin.
EIN: 621414161

50378
In His Name Foundation
1044 9th St.
Lawrenceburg, TN 38464

Established in 1998 in TN.
Financial data (yr. ended 12/31/99): Grants paid, $4,500; assets, $36,338 (M); gifts received, $20,000; expenditures, $4,500; qualifying distributions, $4,500.
Trustees: Kellie L. Dobias, Le'An R. Dobias, Matthew C. Dobias.
EIN: 621763817

50379
Tennessee Mortgage Bankers Association Education Trust Fund
P.O. Box 78612
Nashville, TN 37207-8612
Application address: 144 E-Market Pl. Blvd., Knoxville, TN 37922
Contact: Cathy Neubert, Pres.

Donor(s): Tennessee Mortgage Bankers Association.
Financial data (yr. ended 05/31/01): Grants paid, $4,500; assets, $99,888 (M); gifts received, $13,481; expenditures, $4,874; qualifying distributions, $4,500.
Limitations: Giving limited to residents of TN.
Application information: Application form required.
Officers: Cathy Neubert, Pres.; Jack M. Potts, Secy.; Steve Smith, Treas.
Directors: Samuel E. "Sam" Allen, James M. Beaty.
EIN: 621427379

50380
William M. Bell Foundation
8545 Cordes Cir.
Germantown, TN 38139 (901) 755-7174
Contact: Vallie Jo Witmer Bell, Mgr.

Financial data (yr. ended 06/30/02): Grants paid, $4,473; assets, $9,023 (M); expenditures, $5,232; qualifying distributions, $4,473.
Limitations: Giving limited to TN.
Officer: Vallie Jo Witmer Bell, Mgr.
EIN: 626046340

50381
Ella Rae Rupp Parks Memorial Fund
1109 Graybar Ln.
Nashville, TN 37204 (615) 297-9049
Contact: Norman Randolph Parks, Pres.

Established in 1996.
Donor(s): Norman L. Parks.
Financial data (yr. ended 12/31/01): Grants paid, $4,350; assets, $114,984 (M); expenditures, $6,222; qualifying distributions, $4,350.
Limitations: Giving primarily in TN and TX.
Application information: Application form not required.
Officers: Norman Randolph Parks, Pres.; Judith Elaine Parks, V.P.
EIN: 621638744

50382
Arthur Halle Memorial Foundation
2537 Germantown Rd. S.
Germantown, TN 38138

Financial data (yr. ended 12/31/01): Grants paid, $4,000; assets, $67,617 (M); expenditures, $5,942; qualifying distributions, $4,000.
Limitations: Applications not accepted. Giving primarily in Memphis, TN.
Application information: Contributes only to pre-selected organizations.
Officers and Trustees:* Jean H. Lewis,* Pres.; Margaret Halle, M.D.,* Secy.; A. Arthur Halle III, M.D.
EIN: 626045763

50383
Jasper Stark Trust Fund
108 Mulberry St.
Collierville, TN 38017
Application address: 305 Poplar View, Collierville, TN 38017, TL.: (901) 853-4781
Contact: Pam Wilson, Tr.

Financial data (yr. ended 12/31/01): Grants paid, $4,000; assets, $75,362 (M); expenditures, $4,654; qualifying distributions, $4,509.
Limitations: Giving limited to Collierville, TN.
Application information: Application form required.
Trustees: Robert Humphreys, Susan McCoy, Mike Neighbors, Tim Setherland, Pam Wilson.
EIN: 237378290
Codes: GTI

50384
The Kane Family Charitable Foundation
c/o SunTrust Banks, Inc.
P.O. Box 30511
Nashville, TN 37230-5110

Established in 1996 in TN.
Donor(s): Charles J. Kane, Rosemary Kane.
Financial data (yr. ended 12/31/01): Grants paid, $3,930; assets, $386,632 (M); expenditures, $4,834; qualifying distributions, $4,305.
Limitations: Applications not accepted.
Application information: Contributes only to pre-selected organizations.
Officers: Charles J. Kane, Pres.; Rosemary Kane, V.P.; Michael J. Kane, Secy.; Charles J. Kane, Jr., Treas.
EIN: 621657632

50385
The Shirley Foundation, Inc.
1716 Starmont Trail
Knoxville, TN 37909-1892

Established in 1987 in TN.
Donor(s): Paul K. Shirley, Nadine Shirley.
Financial data (yr. ended 06/30/02): Grants paid, $3,924; assets, $180,168 (M); gifts received, $20,001; expenditures, $4,113; qualifying distributions, $3,924.
Limitations: Applications not accepted.
Application information: Contributes only to pre-selected organizations.
Officers and Directors:* Paul K. Shirley,* Pres. and Treas.; Nadine L. Shirley,* V.P. and Secy.; Paula Melton, Sandra Seymour, William K. Shirley.
EIN: 581687407

50386
Cumberland Center for Justice and Peace, Inc.
P.O. Box 307
Sewanee, TN 37375 (931) 598-1486
Contact: Barbara Dykes, Treas.

Established in 1990 in TN.

Donor(s): Rev. John M. Gessell, Mary Jane Francis.
Financial data (yr. ended 12/31/01): Grants paid, $3,680; assets, $123,888 (M); gifts received, $6,394; expenditures, $13,569; qualifying distributions, $13,499.
Limitations: Giving primarily in TN.
Application information: Application form required.
Officers and Directors:* Phil Loney,* Chair.; Thomas Edward Camp,* Vice-Chair.; Julia Bordley,* Secy.; Barbara Dykes,* Treas.; Robin Hille, Exec. Dir.; A. Scott Bates, Ann M. Oliver, Dora Turner, and 11 additional directors.
EIN: 581871360

50387
Lilbourn Vurl Hammond Charitable Trust
5212 Riverbriar Rd.
Knoxville, TN 37919

Established in 1996.
Financial data (yr. ended 12/31/00): Grants paid, $3,532; assets, $184,655 (M); expenditures, $5,885; qualifying distributions, $3,532.
Limitations: Applications not accepted.
Application information: Contributes only to pre-selected organizations.
Trustees: Ann Hansen, The Trust Co.
EIN: 626304999

50388
Matthew H. Casey Memorial Scholarship Fund Trust
c/o Bobby G. Matthews
2815 Democrat Rd.
Memphis, TN 38118-1510 (901) 541-7373
Contact: Olen Lamar Spencer, Pres.

Established around 1979 in TN.
Financial data (yr. ended 12/31/99): Grants paid, $3,500; assets, $29,203 (M); expenditures, $3,783; qualifying distributions, $3,544.
Limitations: Giving limited to the Memphis, TN, area.
Application information: Application form required.
Officer and Trustees:* Olen Lamar Spencer,* Pres.; Curt Wagner.
EIN: 581354124

50389
Hart Charitable Trust
c/o John D. Houston
2 Union Sq., Tallan Bldg., Ste. 1205
Chattanooga, TN 37402
Application Address: 3003 Nurick Dr., Chattanooga, TN 37415
Contact: Carolyn R. Hart, Chair.

Donor(s): Carolyn R. Hart, Sibyl R. Robinson.
Financial data (yr. ended 06/30/01): Grants paid, $3,500; assets, $71,907 (M); gifts received, $10,061; expenditures, $4,167; qualifying distributions, $3,500.
Limitations: Giving primarily in Portland, OR, and Chattanooga, TN.
Officers: Carolyn R. Hart, Chair.; Geoff D. Hart, Vice-Chair.; Charles T. Hart, Secy.-Treas.
EIN: 626286248

50390
Mississippi State University Bass Memorial Loan Fund
c/o AmSouth Bank
315 Deaderick St., Ste. 0401
Nashville, TN 37237-0401
Application address: P.O. Box 23100, Jackson, MS 39225-3100, tel.: (601) 354-8116
Contact: Lorraine Bleakney, Trust Off., AmSouth Bank

Financial data (yr. ended 06/30/02): Grants paid, $3,396; assets, $89,125 (M); expenditures, $3,885; qualifying distributions, $3,396.
Limitations: Giving limited to Jackson, MS.
Trustee: AmSouth Bank.
EIN: 646020860

50391
DKS Foundation, Inc.
1101 Kermit Dr., Ste. 300
Nashville, TN 37217

Established in 1999 in TN.
Donor(s): David Shewmaker, Kelly Shewmaker.
Financial data (yr. ended 12/31/01): Grants paid, $3,370; assets, $66,772 (M); gifts received, $25; expenditures, $3,635; qualifying distributions, $3,370.
Trustees: David Shewmaker, Kelly Shewmaker.
EIN: 621803274

50392
Charles & Ann McCormick Charitable Trust
2041 Cages Bend Rd.
Gallatin, TN 37066

Established in 1996 in TN.
Donor(s): SRK Asset Managment Co.
Financial data (yr. ended 12/31/01): Grants paid, $3,110; assets, $503,341 (M); gifts received, $102,901; expenditures, $3,160; qualifying distributions, $3,110.
Limitations: Applications not accepted.
Application information: Contributes only to pre-selected organizations.
Trustees: Ann McCormick, Charles McCormick.
EIN: 316542328

50393
William C. Pallas, M.D. Foundation, Inc.
P.O. Box 1749
Chattanooga, TN 37401
Application address: 5251-C Hwy. 153, Ste. 158, Hixson, TN 37343-4910
Contact: William C. Pallas, M.D., Pres.

Financial data (yr. ended 11/30/01): Grants paid, $3,051; assets, $235,138 (M); expenditures, $4,206; qualifying distributions, $3,051.
Limitations: Giving primarily in Chattanooga, TN.
Application information: Application form not required.
Officers and Directors:* William C. Pallas, M.D.,* Pres. and Treas.; Katherine R. Pallas,* V.P. and Secy.; Christopher W. Pallas.
EIN: 620724674

50394
The Burkholder Family Foundation
4107 Legend Hall Dr.
Nashville, TN 37215-2420
Application address: 223 Madison St., Ste. 112, Madison, TN 37115

Established in 1991 in TN.
Donor(s): Linda M. Burkholder, H. Frank Burkholder, Jr.
Financial data (yr. ended 12/31/01): Grants paid, $3,022; assets, $57,470 (M); expenditures, $3,203; qualifying distributions, $3,022.
Limitations: Giving primarily in Nashville, TN.
Trustees: William H. Bradford, H. Frank Burkholder, Jr., Linda M. Burkholder.
EIN: 626249110

50395
Carthage Christian Church Scholarship Fund
812 E. Jefferson Ave.
Carthage, TN 37030
Contact: Kenneth Robinson, Chair.

Financial data (yr. ended 12/31/00): Grants paid, $3,000; assets, $112,054 (M); expenditures, $3,725; qualifying distributions, $3,000.
Limitations: Giving primarily in Smith County, TN.
Application information: Application form required.
Officer: Kenneth Robinson, Chair.
Trustees: Richard Brimm, Frances Robinson.
EIN: 621763601

50396
J. C. Eoff Scholarship Trust
c/o First National Bank of Tullahoma
P.O. Box 520
Tullahoma, TN 37388
Contact: Beth Welsh, Trust Off., First National Bank of Tullahoma

Established in 1995 in TN.
Financial data (yr. ended 12/31/01): Grants paid, $3,000; assets, $41,504 (M); gifts received, $6,141; expenditures, $3,590; qualifying distributions, $3,574.
Trustee: First National Bank.
EIN: 626289799

50397
J. W. Frierson Church of Christ Development Foundation
1310 Jefferson St.
Nashville, TN 37208-3041 (615) 329-9330
Contact: Milton A. Murray, Pres.

Financial data (yr. ended 12/31/01): Grants paid, $3,000; assets, $243,776 (M); expenditures, $118,715; qualifying distributions, $3,000.
Limitations: Giving primarily in Terrell, TX.
Officers: Milton A. Murray, Pres.; Alvin Adkinson, V.P.; Ernest Davis, Recording Secy.; D.E. Lanier, Financial Secy.
EIN: 620752890

50398
E. L. McConnell Foundation
c/o Mayfair United Methodist Church
1409 E. Center St.
Kingsport, TN 37664-2501

Established in 1997 in TN.
Donor(s): Holiday H. Smith.
Financial data (yr. ended 12/31/00): Grants paid, $3,000; assets, $108,735 (M); gifts received, $53,592; expenditures, $3,000; qualifying distributions, $3,000.
Limitations: Giving primarily in Kingsport, TN.
Application information: Applicants must be members of Mayfair United Methodist Church. Application form required.
Officers: Holiday H. Smith, Chair.; Johnsie W. Morgan, V.P. and Secy.; Steven R. Gossett, Treas.
EIN: 581708795

50399
James D. Shannon-Trinity Hospital Trust Fund
P.O. Box 489
Erin, TN 37061 (931) 289-4211
Contact: Jay Woodall, Tr.

Financial data (yr. ended 06/30/00): Grants paid, $3,000; assets, $84,112 (M); expenditures, $3,224; qualifying distributions, $3,000.

Limitations: Giving limited to the residents of Erin, TN, area.
Application information: Application form required.
Trustees: Gladys Anderson, Mark Beal, James Branson, Sam Clemmons, Jay Woodall.
EIN: 626170506

50400
TCH Henry Cannon Charitable Trust
c/o SunTrust Bank, Nashville, N.A.
P.O. Box 305110
Nashville, TN 37230-5110

Established in 1999 in TN.
Donor(s): Henry R. Cannon.
Financial data (yr. ended 10/31/01): Grants paid, $2,928; assets, $142,182 (M); gifts received, $59,901; expenditures, $5,706; qualifying distributions, $4,309.
Limitations: Applications not accepted.
Application information: Contributes only to pre-selected organizations.
Trustee: SunTrust Bank.
EIN: 311634955

50401
Brener-Barshay Foundation, Inc.
1061 Carter Dr.
Chattanooga, TN 37415-5601 (423) 875-8316
Contact: Max D. Brener, Pres.

Established in 1988 in TN.
Financial data (yr. ended 12/31/01): Grants paid, $2,871; assets, $51,799 (M); expenditures, $2,976; qualifying distributions, $2,871.
Limitations: Giving primarily in Chattanooga, TN.
Application information: Application form not required.
Officers and Directors:* Max D. Brener,* Pres.; Scott Brener,* V.P.; William Brener,* V.P.
EIN: 621350203

50402
Thomas R. Preston Charitable Purposes
c/o First Tennessee Bank, N.A.
701 Market St.
Chattanooga, TN 37402

Financial data (yr. ended 12/31/99): Grants paid, $2,836; assets, $62,266 (M); expenditures, $3,620; qualifying distributions, $2,836.
Limitations: Applications not accepted. Giving primarily in Chattanooga, TN.
Application information: Contributes only to pre-selected organizations.
Trustee: First Tennessee Bank, N.A.
EIN: 626034470

50403
Horatio B. and Willie J. Buntin Foundation
c/o Mary N. Wade
1645 Old Hillsboro Rd.
Franklin, TN 37069-4745

Established in 1989 in TN.
Donor(s): Willie J. Buntin.
Financial data (yr. ended 12/31/01): Grants paid, $2,700; assets, $1,826,843 (M); gifts received, $1,752,541; expenditures, $3,195; qualifying distributions, $3,195.
Limitations: Applications not accepted.
Application information: Contributes only to pre-selected organizations.
Officers: Mary N. Wade, Pres.; Lucille J. Nelson, Secy.
EIN: 626224481

50404
The Robert C. and Macon W. Hilton Foundation
1219 Chickering Rd.
Nashville, TN 37215-4519 (615) 292-6789
Contact: Robert C. Hilton, Pres.

Donor(s): Robert C. Hilton.
Financial data (yr. ended 06/30/01): Grants paid, $2,500; assets, $106,391 (M); gifts received, $1,400; expenditures, $2,620; qualifying distributions, $2,620.
Limitations: Giving primarily in Nashville, TN.
Officers and Trustees:* Robert C. Hilton,* Pres.; Macon W. Hilton,* Secy.-Treas.; Robert C. Hilton, Jr., Elizabeth H. Lasley.
EIN: 621306905

50405
Steve Nelson Ministries
1040 Brookside Dr.
Gallatin, TN 37066

Established in TN in 1997.
Financial data (yr. ended 12/31/01): Grants paid, $2,390; assets, $1 (M); expenditures, $2,543; qualifying distributions, $2,390.
Directors: Terry Edwards, Murry Keith, Rev. Steven S. Nelson.
EIN: 582059013

50406
John E. Mayfield Charitable Foundation
c/o John E. Mayfield
1280 Spring Valley Dr.
Pegram, TN 37143-5073

Established in 1996.
Donor(s): John E. Mayfield.
Financial data (yr. ended 12/31/01): Grants paid, $2,362; assets, $72,907 (M); gifts received, $49,221; expenditures, $2,362; qualifying distributions, $2,362.
Limitations: Giving primarily in Ashland City, TN.
Application information: Application form not required.
Trustee: John E. Mayfield.
EIN: 311473693

50407
Walter R. Courtenay Eagle Scout Trust Fund
5315 Meadowlake Rd.
Brentwood, TN 37027-5146

Established in 1990 in TN.
Donor(s): Raymond T. Throckmorton, Jr.
Financial data (yr. ended 12/31/00): Grants paid, $2,000; assets, $38,384 (M); expenditures, $2,528; qualifying distributions, $2,528.
Limitations: Giving limited to residents of TN.
Application information: Unsolicited requests for funds not accepted.
Trustee: Raymond T. Throckmorton, Jr.
EIN: 621465126

50408
Robert Stanley Foreign Language Scholarship Trust
c/o Cynthia S. Alkire
570 Vine St., Apt. 61
Chattanooga, TN 37403

Established in 1993.
Financial data (yr. ended 12/31/01): Grants paid, $2,000; assets, $22 (M); gifts received, $2,000; expenditures, $2,000; qualifying distributions, $2,002.
Limitations: Applications not accepted.
Trustee: Cynthia S. Alkire.
EIN: 550720883

50409
John M. and Ellen F. Webb Foundation, Inc.
88 Weblon Ln.
Sewanee, TN 37375

Established in 2000 in TN.
Donor(s): Ellen F. Webb.
Financial data (yr. ended 12/31/01): Grants paid, $2,000; assets, $79,234 (M); expenditures, $2,485; qualifying distributions, $1,995.
Limitations: Applications not accepted. Giving primarily in TN.
Application information: Contributes only to pre-selected organizations.
Officers: Ellen F. Webb, Pres.; Judith D. Webb, V.P.; Shipp H. Webb, Secy.
EIN: 621833869

50410
Roxbury Fund II
4400 Belmont Park Terr., No. 195
Nashville, TN 37215-3629 (615) 383-2784
Contact: Robert P. Sherman, Tr.

Financial data (yr. ended 12/31/01): Grants paid, $1,915; assets, $13,067 (M); expenditures, $2,340; qualifying distributions, $0.
Limitations: Giving primarily in Nashville, TN.
Application information: Application form not required.
Officer and Trustee:* Robert P. Sherman,* Mgr.
EIN: 581426699

50411
I.B. Tigrett Memorial Trust Fund
315 Deaderick St., 4th Fl.
Nashville, TN 37237-0401
Application address: c/o Jay Satterfield, AmSouth Bank, P.O. Box 309, Jackson, TN 38302

Financial data (yr. ended 12/31/01): Grants paid, $1,838; assets, $104,855 (M); expenditures, $5,998; qualifying distributions, $1,838.
Limitations: Giving limited to Madison County, TN.
Trustee: AmSouth Bank.
EIN: 626037886

50412
James B. & Grace Dean Havron Scholarship Trust
P.O. Box 757
Jasper, TN 37347-0757

Financial data (yr. ended 12/31/00): Grants paid, $1,800; assets, $38,674 (M); expenditures, $167; qualifying distributions, $1,800.
Limitations: Giving limited to TN.
Application information: Recipients are selected by the school faculty.
Officer and Trustees:* John W. Moore,* Mgr.; D. Havron, James B. Havron, Georgia Gore Taylor.
EIN: 581506089

50413
Joe F. Thomas Family Foundation
P.O. Box 41511
Memphis, TN 38174-1511

Donor(s): Kenneth D. Thomas.
Financial data (yr. ended 12/31/01): Grants paid, $1,700; assets, $0 (M); expenditures, $2,101; qualifying distributions, $1,690.
Limitations: Applications not accepted. Giving primarily in Memphis, TN.
Application information: Contributes only to pre-selected organizations.
Director: Edith B. Thomas.
EIN: 621135271

50414
Ruthe Edmondson Leyen Memorial Fund, Inc.
9735 Kingston Pike
Knoxville, TN 37922 (865) 691-2834
Contact: Thomas W. Harper, Secy.

Established in 2000 in TN.
Financial data (yr. ended 12/31/00): Grants paid, $1,575; assets, $17,323 (M); gifts received, $18,843; expenditures, $1,575; qualifying distributions, $1,575.
Officers: Sara E. Markey, Pres.; Thomas W. Harper, Secy.
Directors: Diana E. Covert, Daniel Edmondson, John Edmondson.
EIN: 311742587

50415
Red Kramer Workmens Circle Foundation, Inc.
c/o Joseph Jacobs
5384 Poplar Ave., Ste. 414
Memphis, TN 38119-3676 (901) 682-3775

Established in 1994 in TN.
Financial data (yr. ended 12/31/01): Grants paid, $1,530; assets, $129,218 (M); expenditures, $2,016; qualifying distributions, $1,530.
Limitations: Applications not accepted. Giving primarily in NY.
Application information: Contributes only to pre-selected organizations.
Officers and Director:* Ethel Kramer, Pres.; Ted M. Winestone, V.P. and Secy.; Joscelyn K. Winestone,* V.P.
EIN: 582046759

50416
Domini-Ashley Foundation
c/o Mark F. Ashley
1915 Hwy. 130 E.
Shelbyville, TN 37160-7244 (931) 684-4910

Established around 1986.
Financial data (yr. ended 09/30/99): Grants paid, $1,400; assets, $409,587 (M); gifts received, $1,223; expenditures, $14,904; qualifying distributions, $1,400.
Officers and Trustees:* Mark F. Ashley,* Pres.; Marty K. Ashley,* Secy.; Cynthia J. Ashley, John W. Ashley, Susan R. Ashley.
EIN: 237099401

50417
Watts Bar Teacher Training and Student Scholarship Mathematics and Science Trust Fund
c/o First National Bank & Trust Co.
P.O. Box 2000
Spring City, TN 37381

Financial data (yr. ended 12/31/01): Grants paid, $1,400; assets, $34,287 (M); expenditures, $1,545; qualifying distributions, $1,545.
Limitations: Giving limited to McMinn, Miegs, Rhea, Roane, counties, TN.
Officer and Directors:* Jack Cox,* Chair.; Carl DeBlonk, John Jewell, Jerry White.
EIN: 581626935

50418
TCH Walter Gasser Foundation
(Formerly Walter E. and Margaret Gasser Foundation)
c/o SunTrust Banks, Inc.
P.O. Box 305110
Nashville, TN 37230-5110

Financial data (yr. ended 01/31/02): Grants paid, $1,267; assets, $39,298 (M); expenditures, $2,890; qualifying distributions, $1,267.

Limitations: Applications not accepted. Giving limited to the Whites Creek, TN, area.
Application information: Unsolicited requests for funds not accepted.
Trustee: SunTrust Banks, Inc.
EIN: 581449298

50419
Cooper-Burchfield Foundation, Inc.
c/o Charles C. Burridge
3016 Hedrick St.
Nashville, TN 37203

Established in 1990 in TN; funded in fiscal 1992.
Donor(s): Margaret Cooper.
Financial data (yr. ended 06/30/01): Grants paid, $1,250; assets, $126,632 (M); expenditures, $2,522; qualifying distributions, $2,430.
Limitations: Giving primarily in Sevierville, TN.
Officers: Margaret Cooper, Pres.; Emily B. Kile, V.P.; Charles C. Burridge, Secy.-Treas.
EIN: 621465098

50420
The Smith Foundation Charitable Trust
1329 Candlewick Rd.
Knoxville, TN 37922
Contact: Marshall W. Smith, Tr.

Financial data (yr. ended 12/31/01): Grants paid, $1,135; assets, $17,821 (M); gifts received, $75; expenditures, $1,187; qualifying distributions, $1,135.
Limitations: Giving primarily in Knoxville, TN.
Trustees: Laura G. Smith, Marshall W. Smith.
EIN: 626295205

50421
Dorothy Dean Shelton Charitable Trust
P.O. Box 955
Soddy Daisy, TN 37384-0955

Established in 1998 in TN.
Donor(s): Dorothy Dean Shelton.
Financial data (yr. ended 12/31/01): Grants paid, $1,006; assets, $31,697 (M); expenditures, $1,177; qualifying distributions, $1,006.
Limitations: Applications not accepted.
Application information: Contributes only to pre-selected organizations.
Trustee: Dorothy Dean Shelton.
EIN: 626347942

50422
Octavus M. Eaves Foundation
217 Ridgefield Rd.
Memphis, TN 38111-6034

Established in 2000 in TN.
Donor(s): Octavus M. Eaves.‡
Financial data (yr. ended 12/31/00): Grants paid, $1,000; assets, $49,696 (M); gifts received, $60,000; expenditures, $2,294; qualifying distributions, $1,000.
Limitations: Giving primarily in NM.
Trustee: Linda E. Isbell.
EIN: 621822354

50423
Faith Foundation
6918 Shallowford Rd., Ste. 305
Chattanooga, TN 37421-1783 (423) 499-9863
Contact: Hugh F. Kendall, Pres.

Donor(s): Hugh F. Kendall, Kay M. Kendall.
Financial data (yr. ended 06/30/99): Grants paid, $1,000; assets, $6,094 (M); expenditures, $1,032; qualifying distributions, $1,000.
Limitations: Giving primarily in Signal Mountain, TN.
Application information: Application form not required.

Officers: Hugh F. Kendall, Pres.; Kay M. Kendall, Secy.
EIN: 621048738

50424
The James S. Frazer, III Foundation
420 Ellendale Dr.
Nashville, TN 37205 (615) 385-3727
Contact: James S. Frazer, III, Tr.

Established in 1994 in TN.
Donor(s): James S. Frazer III.
Financial data (yr. ended 12/31/01): Grants paid, $1,000; assets, $22,435 (M); expenditures, $1,998; qualifying distributions, $1,000.
Trustees: James S. Frazer III, Mellon Bank, N.A.
EIN: 626287925

50425
The C. A. Rawls Memorial Scholarship Foundation
39 S. Jackson St.
Brownsville, TN 38012 (901) 772-9283
Contact: Cynthia Bond, Chair.

Established in 1987 in TN.
Financial data (yr. ended 03/31/00): Grants paid, $1,000; assets, $6,194 (M); gifts received, $500; expenditures, $1,000; qualifying distributions, $1,000.
Limitations: Giving limited to Haywood County, TN.
Application information: Application form required.
Officer: Cynthia Bond, Chair.
Trustees: Maltimore Bond, Andrea Johnson, William Rawls.
EIN: 621311532

50426
W. H. Parks Scholarship Fund
First Citizens National Bank
1 Commerce Sq.
Dyersburg, TN 38025

Financial data (yr. ended 12/31/01): Grants paid, $800; assets, $15,101 (M); expenditures, $945; qualifying distributions, $800.
Limitations: Giving limited to the Dyersburg, TN, area.
Application information: Application form not required.
Trustee: First Citizens National Bank.
EIN: 626080592

50427
National Activity Education Organization
P.O. Box 5530
Sevierville, TN 37862 (865) 429-0717
Contact: Gail K. Buckner, Tr.

Established in 1986.
Financial data (yr. ended 06/30/00): Grants paid, $700; assets, $7,023 (M); gifts received, $1,000; expenditures, $6,774; qualifying distributions, $787.
Limitations: Giving primarily in Sevierville, TN.
Application information: Application form required.
Officers and Trustees:* Mary Anne Favale,* Pres.; Nancy Williams, Secy.; Kimberly Figueroa, Treas.; Pamela Bailey, Gail K. Buckner, Donna Calvo, Tonia Hooker.
EIN: 363319629

50428
The Bradshaw Family Foundation
P.O. Box 1166
Lebanon, TN 37088-1166

Donor(s): James C. Bradshaw.

Financial data (yr. ended 12/31/01): Grants paid, $650; assets, $360 (M); gifts received, $1,000; expenditures, $824; qualifying distributions, $650.
Limitations: Giving primarily in Lebanon, TN.
Officer and Trustees:* John Bradshaw,* Mgr.; James C. Bradshaw, Jr., Martha Ann Bradshaw.
EIN: 626270452

50429
J.M.M. Charitable Trust
253 Inez Dr.
Smyrna, TN 37167

Established in 1999.
Financial data (yr. ended 12/31/00): Grants paid, $640; assets, $28,572 (M); gifts received, $28,330; expenditures, $653; qualifying distributions, $640.
Limitations: Applications not accepted. Giving primarily in Nashville, TN.
Application information: Contributes only to pre-selected organizations.
Trustee: Jerry Matthews.
EIN: 626366272

50430
Tyrone Kuo Scholarship Award
c/o AmSouth Bank
315 Deaderick St., 11th Fl.
Nashville, TN 37237-1101

Financial data (yr. ended 09/30/01): Grants paid, $631; assets, $10,299 (M); expenditures, $651; qualifying distributions, $651.
Limitations: Giving limited to Kingsport, TN.
Application information: Unsolicited request for funds not accepted.
Trustees: Leland A. Davis, Chung-Ming Kuo, AmSouth Bank.
EIN: 626103277

50431
The Log College
P.O. Box 293081
Nashville, TN 37229-3081 (615) 833-7718
Contact: David Lutzweiler, Pres.

Financial data (yr. ended 12/31/01): Grants paid, $625; assets, $1,359 (M); gifts received, $2,000; expenditures, $2,215; qualifying distributions, $625.
Limitations: Giving on a national and international basis.
Officers: David Lutzweiler, Pres.; Lois V. Lutzweiler, Secy.-Treas.
EIN: 237017104

50432
Colonel Return Jonathan Meigs First Trust
c/o AmSouth Bank
315 Deaderick St., 4th Fl.
Nashville, TN 37237-0401

Financial data (yr. ended 12/31/01): Grants paid, $593; assets, $33,532 (M); expenditures, $1,915; qualifying distributions, $593.
Limitations: Applications not accepted. Giving limited to McMinn, Meigs and Rhea counties, TN.
Application information: Contributes only to pre-selected organizations.
Trustee: AmSouth Bank.
EIN: 626070182

50433
Cosby Charitable Trust
5719 Pinola Ave.
Bartlett, TN 38134

Established in 1998.
Financial data (yr. ended 12/31/00): Grants paid, $590; assets, $56,110 (M); gifts received, $67,686; expenditures, $1,642; qualifying distributions, $590.
Limitations: Applications not accepted.
Application information: Contributes only to pre-selected organizations.
Trustee: Ulysses Cosby.
EIN: 626343039

50434
M. J. Edwards Foundation
588 Vance Ave., Ste. 200
Memphis, TN 38126
Contact: Jesse H. Turner, Jr., Tr.

Established in 1999 in TN.
Donor(s): M.J. Edwards.
Financial data (yr. ended 02/28/02): Grants paid, $570; assets, $34,296 (M); gifts received, $15,000; expenditures, $575; qualifying distributions, $570.
Trustee: Jesse H. Turner, Jr.
EIN: 621808049

50435
Boote Family Foundation
131 Oakwood Dr.
Lewisburg, TN 37091

Donor(s): J. Owen Boote.
Financial data (yr. ended 12/31/99): Grants paid, $540; assets, $10,481 (M); gifts received, $508; expenditures, $692; qualifying distributions, $540.
Officer and Trustees:* J. Owen Boote, Jr.,* Chair.; Linda Boote Allen, Joseph Gerristen, Helen Boote Shivers.
EIN: 626229035

50436
Fred L. Cash Memorial Scholarship Fund
P.O. Box 591
Knoxville, TN 37901-0591
Application address: c/o Carol Scott, Guidance Counselor, West High School, 3326 Sutherland Ave., Knoxville, TN 37919

Financial data (yr. ended 12/31/00): Grants paid, $500; assets, $6,613 (M); expenditures, $500; qualifying distributions, $507.
Limitations: Giving limited to residents of Knoxville, TN.
Application information: Application form required.
Officers and Advisory Committee Members:* Charles A. Clark,* Chair.; Joseph J. Meyers,* Vice-Chair.; Donald A. Boatman,* Secy.; S.N Martin,* Treas.; Carol Scott, Donna Wright.
EIN: 621287479

50437
Bryan Gatlin Memorial Scholarship Trust
758 Memory Ln.
Collierville, TN 38017-1808
Application address: c/o Guidance Counselor, Collierville High School, 146 College St., Collierville, TN 38017, tel.: (901) 853-3310

Financial data (yr. ended 12/31/99): Grants paid, $500; assets, $11,561 (M); expenditures, $504; qualifying distributions, $500.
Limitations: Giving limited to Collierville, TN.
Trustees: Julie V. Gatlin, James A. Johnston, Kelly A. Johnston, Lois J. Johnston.
EIN: 621317419

50438
Elizabeth Stobaugh Pyle Foundation
2525 W. End Ave., Ste. 1500
Nashville, TN 37203-1423

Established in 1999 in TN.
Donor(s): Elizabeth Stobaugh Pyle.
Financial data (yr. ended 10/31/01): Grants paid, $500; assets, $30,103 (M); gifts received, $23,829; expenditures, $1,473; qualifying distributions, $1,303.
Limitations: Applications not accepted.
Application information: Contributes only to pre-selected organizations.
Officers and Directors:* Carolyn Pyle Crepps,* Pres.; Edwin S. Pyle,* Secy.; Duard F. Pyle, Jr., Jan Pyle Washington.
EIN: 621802664

50439
Carlotta Stewart Watson Scholarship Fund
3145 Hoskins Rd. EXT.
Memphis, TN 38111-2960 (901) 324-4984
Contact: Rutha D. Pegues

Financial data (yr. ended 06/30/01): Grants paid, $500; assets, $5,914 (M); expenditures, $500; qualifying distributions, $0.
Limitations: Giving limited to Shelby County, TN.
Application information: Application form required.
Trustees: George Clark, Rutha D. Pegues.
EIN: 237181567

50440
The Wildwood Foundation
c/o Sally Houston McDougall
406 W. Brookfield Dr.
Nashville, TN 37205-4408

Established in 1995 in TN.
Donor(s): Sally Houston McDougall.
Financial data (yr. ended 12/31/01): Grants paid, $450; assets, $12,281 (M); gifts received, $449; expenditures, $899; qualifying distributions, $450.
Limitations: Applications not accepted.
Application information: Contributes only to pre-selected organizations.
Trustee: Sally Houston McDougall.
EIN: 621585504

50441
Grace Unlimited Foundation
P.O. Box 247
Copperhill, TN 37317
Contact: Terry McDaniel, Exec. Dir.

Established in 2000.
Financial data (yr. ended 12/31/00): Grants paid, $350; assets, $215,468 (M); gifts received, $78,500; expenditures, $26,610; qualifying distributions, $350.
Limitations: Giving primarily in TN.
Officers: Nancy McDaniel, Exec. Dir.; Terry McDaniel, Exec. Dir.
EIN: 364388810

50442
The Charles F. Barker Foundation
4159 Forest Glen Dr.
Knoxville, TN 37919-5214

Established in 1986 in OH.
Donor(s): William Connell, Mrs. William Connell.
Financial data (yr. ended 12/31/99): Grants paid, $300; assets, $18,609 (M); gifts received, $1,044; expenditures, $300; qualifying distributions, $300.
Officers: William G. Connell, Pres.; Lynne Skiken, V.P.; Gail Gault Connell, Secy.-Treas.
EIN: 311195077

50443
Mooney Memorial Fund
c/o National Bank of Commerce, Trust Div.
1 Commerce Sq.
Memphis, TN 38103-1602
Contact: Behtany Goolsby, Trust Off., NBC

Financial data (yr. ended 12/31/00): Grants paid, $300; assets, $5,834 (M); expenditures, $429; qualifying distributions, $297.
Limitations: Giving primarily in the Memphis, TN, area.
Trustee: National Bank of Commerce.
EIN: 626033909

50444
Osteen Merit Foundation, Inc.
(also known as Merit Foundation, Inc.)
415 W. Poplar Ave.
Collierville, TN 38017-2533 (901) 853-2184
Contact: H. Thomas Brooks, Tr.

Financial data (yr. ended 06/30/01): Grants paid, $300; assets, $6,037 (M); expenditures, $323; qualifying distributions, $300.
Limitations: Giving limited to residents of Collierville, TN.
Application information: Application form required.
Trustees: H. Thomas Brooks, Catherine Hinton, Mike Teabbe.
EIN: 626041477

50445
Corinne T. Woolard Foundation
108 E. Brow Rd.
Lookout Mountain, TN 37350

Established in 1993 in TN.
Donor(s): Corinne T. Woolard.
Financial data (yr. ended 12/31/01): Grants paid, $260; assets, $5,101 (M); expenditures, $260; qualifying distributions, $260.
Limitations: Applications not accepted. Giving primarily in Lebanon, TN.
Application information: Contributes only to pre-selected organizations.
Trustees: Cheryl W. Stinnett, Donald S. Stinnett, Corinne T. Woolard.
EIN: 621524084

50446
If It's Meant to Be Foundation, Inc.
2409A Volunteer Pkwy.
Bristol, TN 37620-6802

Established in 2001 in TN.
Financial data (yr. ended 12/31/01): Grants paid, $257; assets, $865 (M); gifts received, $5,692; expenditures, $4,827; qualifying distributions, $4,827.
Directors: Mickey Baker, Ken Vance.
EIN: 621860208

50447
The Charles and Elaine Moore Family Foundation
5106 Pheasant Run Trail
Brentwood, TN 37027

Established in 1997.
Financial data (yr. ended 12/31/01): Grants paid, $244; assets, $3,330 (M); gifts received, $126; expenditures, $244; qualifying distributions, $244.
Officers: Charles Z. Moore, Chair.; Elaine P. Moore, Secy.
EIN: 626322129

50448
Philip D. Cooper Memorial Research Trust Fund, Inc.
711 Montclair Dr.
Johnson City, TN 37604

Financial data (yr. ended 12/31/01): Grants paid, $200; assets, $1,329 (M); gifts received, $600; expenditures, $1,802; qualifying distributions, $199.
Directors: Douglas R. Cooper, Victory L. Cooper, Whitney Anne Cooper.
EIN: 621785667

50449
Pentecostal International Missions for Christ
2180 N. Ocoee St.
Cleveland, TN 37311

Established in 1999.
Financial data (yr. ended 12/31/01): Grants paid, $200; assets, $512 (M); gifts received, $650; expenditures, $200; qualifying distributions, $200.
Officers: R. Jerome Shepherd, Pres.; Marcia Dunn Gilbert, Secy.
EIN: 581818881

50450
Ross Family Foundation
P.O. Box 669
Milan, TN 38358-0699

Established in 2000 in TN.
Donor(s): Tommy W. Ross, Thelma Ross.
Financial data (yr. ended 12/31/01): Grants paid, $200; assets, $13,227 (M); gifts received, $14,891; expenditures, $210; qualifying distributions, $200.
Limitations: Applications not accepted.
Application information: Contributes only to pre-selected organizations.
Trustees: Thelma T. Ross, Tommy W. Ross.
EIN: 626370390

50451
The Hendrix Educational Foundation
P.O. Box 547
Selmer, TN 38375-0547

Financial data (yr. ended 12/31/00): Grants paid, $150; assets, $15,867 (M); expenditures, $198; qualifying distributions, $150.
Limitations: Applications not accepted. Giving limited to residents of TN.
Application information: Unsolicited request for funds not accepted.
Officers and Directors:* Tom E. Hendrix,* Pres.; George L. Donaldson,* Secy.-Treas.; Bob J. Brooks.
EIN: 581371544

50452
William H. Frist Family Foundation
c/o Deborah Kolarich
3010 Poston Ave., Ste. 220
Nashville, TN 37203

Established in 1993 in TN.
Financial data (yr. ended 12/31/00): Grants paid, $100; assets, $2,054 (M); gifts received, $2; expenditures, $105; qualifying distributions, $100.
Limitations: Applications not accepted.
Application information: Contributes only to pre-selected organizations.
Trustees: Karyn M. Frist, William H. Frist.
EIN: 626271800

50453
The Brewer Charitable Foundation
414 Union St., Rm. 1600
P.O. Box 198062
Nashville, TN 37219

Donor(s): Leon P. Brewer.
Financial data (yr. ended 05/31/01): Grants paid, $30; assets, $55,429 (M); expenditures, $309; qualifying distributions, $309.
Limitations: Applications not accepted. Giving primarily in Collinwood, TN.
Application information: Contributes only to pre-selected organizations.
Officers and Directors:* Leon P. Brewer,* Pres.; Reva S. Brewer,* Secy.; Elizabeth B. McFall.
EIN: 621114343

50454
Allen Christian Foundation
754 Shady Grove Rd. S.
Memphis, TN 38120-3108

Established in 1986 in TN.
Donor(s): Donald C. Allen, Mary J. Allen.
Financial data (yr. ended 06/30/02): Grants paid, $0; assets, $735,263 (M); gifts received, $1,135; expenditures, $33,458; qualifying distributions, $33,458.
Limitations: Applications not accepted. Giving primarily in TN.
Application information: Contributes only to pre-selected organizations.
Officers: Donald C. Allen, Chair.; Dianne Guthrie, Pres.; Cynthia Castor, Secy.-Treas.
Trustees: Mary J. Allen, Emily Ashworth, Stephen Ashworth, Wade Messer, Tonya Palmer.
EIN: 621282992

50455
Association for the Care of Aging Population-The Care Foundation
(Formerly Association for the Care of Aging Population)
5901 Shelby Oaks Dr., Ste. 175
Memphis, TN 38134

Established in 1986.
Financial data (yr. ended 12/31/00): Grants paid, $0; assets, $2,327,168 (M); expenditures, $6,317; qualifying distributions, $0.
Limitations: Applications not accepted. Giving primarily in Memphis, TN.
Application information: Contributes only to pre-selected organizations.
Directors: Matthew T. Bond, George T. Johnson.
EIN: 621255712

50456
The Beasley Foundation
507 Martingale Ct.
Brentwood, TN 37027

Established in 1997 in TN.
Financial data (yr. ended 06/30/02): Grants paid, $0; assets, $588 (M); expenditures, $13; qualifying distributions, $0.
Limitations: Applications not accepted.
Application information: Contributes only to pre-selected organizations.
Trustees: Jeffrey P. Merkle, J. Allen Reynolds III.
EIN: 621623951

50457
Bellevue Volunteer Fire Department
136 Morton Mill Cir.
Nashville, TN 37221
Application address: 3314 W. End Ave., Ste. 102, Nashville, TN 37203

Financial data (yr. ended 12/31/01): Grants paid, $0; assets, $146,976 (M); expenditures, $6,380; qualifying distributions, $0.
Limitations: Giving primarily in Bellevue, TN.
Application information: Application form required.
Directors: Lou Farringer, Jim Melrose, Wayne Veach.
EIN: 621580555

50458
The John W. and Irene E. Bolam Charitable Trust
203 Proffitt Ridge Rd.
Mooresburg, TN 37811

Financial data (yr. ended 12/31/99): Grants paid, $0; assets, $4,116 (M); expenditures, $0; qualifying distributions, $0.
Officers: John W. Bolam, Pres.; Irene E. Bolam, V.P.
EIN: 621720497

50459
The Boult Family Foundation
c/o Reber M. Boult
424 Church St., 28th Fl.
Nashville, TN 37219

Established in 1999 in TN.
Financial data (yr. ended 12/31/99): Grants paid, $0; assets, $54,378 (M); gifts received, $54,358; expenditures, $0; qualifying distributions, $0.
Limitations: Applications not accepted.
Application information: Contributes only to pre-selected organizations.
Trustees: Reber F. Boult, Reber M. Boult, William Ralston Mason, Olivia Ann Boult Walling.
EIN: 626370501

50460
Bright Star International, Inc.
P.O. Box 120415
Nashville, TN 37212

Established in 2000.
Financial data (yr. ended 12/31/00): Grants paid, $0; assets, $337 (M); gifts received, $352; expenditures, $15; qualifying distributions, $0.
Officer and Directors:* Dawn Purtee,* Chair.; Barry Goldwater III, Steven Roads.
EIN: 731416872

50461
The Brock Family Foundation
P.O. Box 3625
Brentwood, TN 37024
Application address: 201 Seaboard Ln., Brentwood, TN 37064
Contact: Darlene Brock, Secy.-Treas.

Established in 1999 in TN.
Donor(s): Dan Brock, Darlene Brock.
Financial data (yr. ended 12/31/99): Grants paid, $0; assets, $227,228 (M); expenditures, $0; qualifying distributions, $0.
Officers: Dan Brock, Pres.; Darlene Brock, Secy.-Treas.
Directors: Clarence Brock, Greg Ham.
EIN: 621788820

50462
John M. Burnham & Margaret S. Burnham Charitable Foundation
1484 Burgess Falls Rd.
Cookeville, TN 38506-5627

Donor(s): John M. Burnham, Margaret S. Burnham.
Financial data (yr. ended 12/31/01): Grants paid, $0; assets, $4,266 (M); expenditures, $10; qualifying distributions, $0.
Limitations: Applications not accepted. Giving primarily in Cookeville, TN.
Application information: Contributes only to pre-selected organizations.
Trustees: John M. Burnham, Margaret S. Burnham.
EIN: 581752546

50463
J. W. Carell Family Foundation
4015 Travis Dr.
Nashville, TN 37211

Established in 2000.
Donor(s): James W. Carell.
Financial data (yr. ended 12/31/00): Grants paid, $0; assets, $456,001 (M); gifts received, $410,792; expenditures, $2,844; qualifying distributions, $0.
Trustees: Eileen Carell, James M. Carell, James W. Carell, Michael J. Carell, Richard P. Carell, Christine Ann Palmer.
EIN: 597168292

50464
Chattanooga Engineering Educational Fund, Inc.
P.O. Box 4031
Chattanooga, TN 37405

Established around 1979.
Financial data (yr. ended 12/31/99): Grants paid, $0; assets, $1,480 (M); gifts received, $1,480; expenditures, $0; qualifying distributions, $0.
Limitations: Giving primarily in Chattanooga, TN.
Officers: Greg Sedrick, Pres.; Ed Chapin, 1st V.P.; Lulu Copeland, 2nd V.P.; Phil Kazermersky, Secy.; Uwe Zitzow, Treas.
EIN: 581363310

50465
Ruth Q. Davis Foundation, Inc.
P.O. Box 400
Winchester, TN 37398-0400 (931) 962-1060
Contact: Henry Agee

Established in 1997.
Financial data (yr. ended 12/31/01): Grants paid, $0; assets, $4,347 (M); expenditures, $250; qualifying distributions, $0.
Officers: Ruth Q. Davis, Pres.; Sam Woody, V.P.; Norris F. Nay, Secy.-Treas.
EIN: 721367496

50466
J. C. Dellinger Memorial Foundation
125 Third Ave., N.
Franklin, TN 37064

Established in 1995 in TN.
Financial data (yr. ended 12/31/00): Grants paid, $0; assets, $283,386 (M); expenditures, $2,879; qualifying distributions, $0.
Limitations: Applications not accepted.
Application information: Contributes only to pre-selected organizations.
Trustees: Jolene C. Harms, Bell Hartley, John Hartley.
EIN: 311524723

50467
Arthur J. Dyer-Nashville Bridge Company Foundation, Inc.
315 Deaderick St., 4th Fl.
Nashville, TN 37237-0401

Financial data (yr. ended 12/31/01): Grants paid, $0; assets, $66,585 (M); expenditures, $1,354; qualifying distributions, $0.
Limitations: Applications not accepted.
Application information: Contributes only to pre-selected organizations.
Trustee: AmSouth Bank.
EIN: 510219417

50468
The Firm Foundation
104 John Arnold Ave.
Chattanooga, TN 37412

Established in 1995 in TN.
Donor(s): Dennis Bizzoco.
Financial data (yr. ended 12/31/01): Grants paid, $0; assets, $5,564 (M); gifts received, $6,210; expenditures, $6,261; qualifying distributions, $0.
Limitations: Applications not accepted.
Application information: Contributes only to pre-selected organizations.
Directors: Dennis Bizzoco, Leslie Bizzoco, Michael Jennings.
EIN: 621556289

50469
Garden Association, Inc.
55 1/2 1st. Ave. N.E.
Cleveland, TN 37364-0192

Established in 1998 in TN.
Donor(s): Harvey Templeton, Jr., Handly C. Templeton.
Financial data (yr. ended 12/31/01): Grants paid, $0; assets, $3,147,842 (M); expenditures, $43,491; qualifying distributions, $0.
Officer: Becky Templeton, Mgr.
EIN: 522153635

50470
Golightly Foundation, Inc.
1065 Morgan Keegan Twr.
50 N. Front St.
Memphis, TN 38103 (901) 577-1018
Contact: Ernest B. Williams III, Pres.

Established in 1955 in TN.
Financial data (yr. ended 12/31/01): Grants paid, $0; assets, $2,693,586 (M); expenditures, $2,938; qualifying distributions, $0.
Limitations: Giving primarily in AR and TN.
Application information: Application form not required.
Officer and Trustee:* Ernest B. Williams III,* Pres.
EIN: 626047757

50471
Violet Hampton Trust No. 2
c/o AmSouth Bank
315 Deaderick St., 4th Fl.
Nashville, TN 37237-0401
Contact: Joseph Chickey

Established in 2000 in TN.
Donor(s): Violet Hampton.‡
Financial data (yr. ended 12/31/01): Grants paid, $0; assets, $1,262,972 (M); expenditures, $13,334; qualifying distributions, $0.
Limitations: Giving limited to TN.
Application information: Application form required.
Trustee: AmSouth Bank.
EIN: 626373852

50472
Constance Harding Memorial Foundation
P.O. Box 261
Bristol, TN 37621-0261

Established in 2001 in AK.
Financial data (yr. ended 12/31/01): Grants paid, $0; assets, $8,904 (M); gifts received, $8,857; expenditures, $0; qualifying distributions, $0.
Limitations: Applications not accepted.
Application information: Contributes only to pre-selected organizations.
Officers: Norman Shelburne, Pres.; Joseph Jackson, Secy.; Elizabeth Barger, Treas.
EIN: 364453061

50473
The Kevin I. Hart Family Foundation
612 10th Ave. N.
Nashville, TN 37203

Established in 1993 in TN.
Financial data (yr. ended 12/31/00): Grants paid, $0; assets, $7,416 (M); gifts received, $128; expenditures, $128; qualifying distributions, $0.
Limitations: Applications not accepted.
Application information: Contributes only to pre-selected organizations.
Trustee: H. Rodes Hart.
EIN: 626262168

50474
Camilla & Zack Hubert Foundation, Inc.
2877 Curtis St.
Memphis, TN 38118-2636
Contact: Erika Sugarmon, Treas.

Financial data (yr. ended 12/31/01): Grants paid, $0; assets, $40,650 (M); gifts received, $87; expenditures, $275; qualifying distributions, $0.
Limitations: Giving primarily in GA.
Application information: Application form not required.
Officers and Trustees:* Edward Taylor III,* Pres.; Roslyn D. Blackeney, Secy.; Erika Sugarmon, Treas.; Benjamin Hubert.
EIN: 581311685

50475
Hypertension Institute Foundation
6375 Chickering Cir.
Nashville, TN 37215

Established in 1999 in TN.
Financial data (yr. ended 03/31/01): Grants paid, $0; assets, $77,909 (M); gifts received, $377,740; expenditures, $227,230; qualifying distributions, $0.
Directors: Jordan Asher, M.D., Laurie Hays, R.N., Mark C. Houston, M.D., Allen Naftilan, M.D., Linda Riley, R.N.
EIN: 621795666

50476
Life Care Foundation for Education Research
c/o John Wagner
P.O. Box 3480
Cleveland, TN 37320-3480 (423) 473-5858

Established in 1995.
Donor(s): Life Care Centers of America Inc., Forrest L. Preston.
Financial data (yr. ended 12/31/01): Grants paid, $0; assets, $2,538 (M); gifts received, $151; expenditures, $1,255; qualifying distributions, $0.
Limitations: Applications not accepted. Giving on a national basis.
Application information: Contributes only to pre-selected organizations.

Officers: Forrest L. Preston, Chair.; John Wagner, Pres.; John McMullan, Secy.; J. Michael Waddell, Treas.
Directors: Letitia Erdmann, Beecher Hunter, Susie Hutchings.
EIN: 621582584
Codes: CS, CD

50477
The Lifepoint Community Foundation
103 Powell Ct., Ste. 200
Brentwood, TN 37027

Established in 1999 in DE and TN.
Donor(s): LifePoint Hospitals, Inc.
Financial data (yr. ended 12/31/00): Grants paid, $0; assets, $2,232,500 (M); gifts received, $10,000; expenditures, $5,000; qualifying distributions, $0.
Limitations: Applications not accepted.
Application information: Contributes only to pre-selected organizations.
Officers and Directors:* James M. Fleetwood, Jr.,* Pres.; Neil D. Hemphill, V.P.; William F. Carpenter III,* Secy.; Kenneth C. Donahey, Treas.
EIN: 621794442

50478
The Ira A. Lipman Foundation
22 S. 2nd St.
Memphis, TN 38103-2695 (901) 522-6000
Contact: Ira A. Lipman, Tr.

Established in 1991 in TN.
Donor(s): Ira A. Lipman.
Financial data (yr. ended 11/30/01): Grants paid, $0; assets, $16,123 (M); expenditures, $0; qualifying distributions, $0.
Trustees: Gustave K. Lipman, Ira A. Lipman, Joshua S. Lipman, M. Benjamin Lipman.
EIN: 582026329

50479
The LJ Family Foundation
315 Deaderick St., 11th Fl.
Nashville, TN 37237-1101
Application address: 714 Cherokee Blvd., Knoxville, TN 37919
Contact: Wendell Jackson Long, Tr.

Established in 1999 in TN.
Donor(s): Wendell J. Long.
Financial data (yr. ended 06/30/01): Grants paid, $0; assets, $204,615 (M); gifts received, $100,000; expenditures, $1,773; qualifying distributions, $0.
Trustees: Frances Carlen Long, W. Jackson Long, Jr., Wendell Jackson Long, Loucinda Long-Inscoe.
EIN: 626352749

50480
The Master's Table, Inc.
620 Shelby St.
Bristol, TN 37620

Established in 2001 in TN.
Donor(s): Joseph A. Gregory.
Financial data (yr. ended 12/31/01): Grants paid, $0; assets, $12,640,000 (M); gifts received, $12,235,000; expenditures, $0; qualifying distributions, $0.
Limitations: Applications not accepted.
Application information: Contributes only to pre-selected organizations.
Officers: Joseph R. Gregory, Pres.; Lucinda J. Gregory, Secy.-Treas.
EIN: 621874715

50481
The W. W. Mebane Scholarships
c/o Carroll Bank & Trust
P.O. Box 889
Huntingdon, TN 38344

Established in 2001.
Financial data (yr. ended 12/31/01): Grants paid, $0; assets, $35,482 (M); gifts received, $2,285; expenditures, $227; qualifying distributions, $0.
Limitations: Applications not accepted.
Application information: Contributes only to pre-selected organizations.
Trustee: Carroll Bank & Trust.
EIN: 626381972

50482
Memphis and Shelby County Medical Foundation, Inc.
1067 Cresthaven Rd.
Memphis, TN 38119

Established in 1994 in TN.
Financial data (yr. ended 06/30/01): Grants paid, $0; assets, $483,390 (M); gifts received, $269,350; expenditures, $148,719; qualifying distributions, $148,719.
Limitations: Applications not accepted. Giving primarily in Memphis, TN.
Application information: Contribute only to pre-selected organizations.
Officers: Evelyn B. Ogle, M.D., Pres.; Rex A. Amonette, M.D., V.P.; Dennis A. Higdon, M.D., Secy.-Treas.
EIN: 626048069

50483
The Merwin Foundation, Inc.
c/o Fell Merwin
150 Hunters Ln.
Hendersonville, TN 37075

Established in 1999 in TN.
Donor(s): D. Fell Merwin, Lisa W. Merwin.
Financial data (yr. ended 12/31/00): Grants paid, $0; assets, $43,374 (M); gifts received, $18,613; expenditures, $250; qualifying distributions, $0.
Limitations: Applications not accepted.
Application information: Contributes only to pre-selected organizations.
Board Members: Otto Karl Jahrling, D. Fell Merwin, Lisa W. Merwin, Timothy L. Takas.
EIN: 621785447

50484
The Moore International Foundation
P.O. Box 141000
Nashville, TN 37214-1000

Financial data (yr. ended 12/31/01): Grants paid, $0; assets, $10,140 (M); expenditures, $0; qualifying distributions, $0.
Trustees: Peggy Jean Moore, Rachel M. Moore, Sam Moore, Samuel Joseph Moore.
EIN: 621586334

50485
The Mynatt Charitable Trust
3144 Heathstone Cove
Germantown, TN 38138

Established in 1997 in TN.
Donor(s): ARM Asset Mgmt. Co.
Financial data (yr. ended 12/31/99): Grants paid, $0; assets, $220,106 (L); expenditures, $0; qualifying distributions, $0.
Limitations: Applications not accepted. Giving primarily in Germantown, TN.
Application information: Contributes only to pre-selected organizations.
Trustees: Linda Mynatt, Robert Mynatt.

EIN: 316542310

50486
The E. C. & Lucile H. Nichols Charitable Trust
4420 Milesdale Ct.
Nashville, TN 37204-4127

Established in 1997.
Donor(s): Edward C. Nichols, Jr.
Financial data (yr. ended 12/31/01): Grants paid, $0; assets, $7 (M); expenditures, $0; qualifying distributions, $0.
Limitations: Giving primarily in TN.
Trustee: Edward C. Nichols, Jr.
EIN: 311520424

50487
The Pearl Foundation
1222 16th Ave. S., 3rd Fl.
Nashville, TN 37212
Contact: Janis Ian, Pres.

Established in 1999 in MI.
Financial data (yr. ended 12/31/01): Grants paid, $0; assets, $46,774 (M); gifts received, $23,500; expenditures, $29; qualifying distributions, $0.
Officer and Director: Janis Ian,* Pres. and Secy.-Treas.
EIN: 383477884

50488
PLC Educational Foundation, Inc.
P.O. Box 862
Kingston, TN 37763-0862

Established in 1987 in TN.
Donor(s): Professional Loss Control, Inc.
Financial data (yr. ended 04/30/01): Grants paid, $0; assets, $26,205 (M); gifts received, $49,800; expenditures, $26,484; qualifying distributions, $25,893; giving activities include $25,893 for programs.
Limitations: Applications not accepted. Giving primarily in MA.
Application information: Contributes only to pre-selected organizations.
Officers and Directors:* Kenneth W. Dungan,* Pres.; Opal B. Kristich,* Secy.; James B. Dewey, Philip Reichle.
EIN: 621272544
Codes: CS, CD

50489
Providence International, Inc.
(Formerly Addictions Ministries, Inc.)
c/o Wyatt, Tarrant & Combs
2525 West End Ave., Ste. 1500
Nashville, TN 37203

Established in 1999 in TN.
Donor(s): Julie Griggs, Glynn Griggs.
Financial data (yr. ended 12/31/00): Grants paid, $0; assets, $190,203 (M); gifts received, $1,606; expenditures, $3,312; qualifying distributions, $0.
Limitations: Applications not accepted.
Application information: Contributes only to pre-selected organizations.
Officers: Glynn Griggs, Pres.; Julie Griggs, Secy.-Treas.
EIN: 640734492

50490
Eleanor M. Robbins Foundation
6484 Robbins Ridge Ln.
Memphis, TN 38119

Established in 2000.
Donor(s): The Ashcroft Foundation, James G. Robbins.
Financial data (yr. ended 12/31/00): Grants paid, $0; assets, $451,092 (M); gifts received, $327,452; expenditures, $9,963; qualifying distributions, $0.
Limitations: Applications not accepted.
Application information: Contributes only to pre-selected organizations.
Officers: James G. Robbins, Pres.; Julia P. Robbins, V.P.; David P. Halle, Secy.-Treas.
EIN: 621826290

50491
Robinson Family Foundation, Inc.
4409 Chickering Ln.
Nashville, TN 37215-4914

Established in 2001 in TN.
Donor(s): Bailey Robinson III, Laura Robinson.
Financial data (yr. ended 12/31/01): Grants paid, $0; assets, $250,000 (M); gifts received, $250,000; expenditures, $0; qualifying distributions, $0.
Officers: Bailey P. Robinson III, Pres.; Laura Sue Robinson, Secy.
Directors: Eve Robinson Hanley, Glenn L. Hanley, James Thomas Harris, Tracey Robinson Harris, Bailey P. Robinson IV.
EIN: 621857048

50492
Miriam P. Schulman Foundation
111 Westwood Pl., Ste. 400
Brentwood, TN 37027

Established in 1999 in TN.
Financial data (yr. ended 11/30/01): Grants paid, $0; assets, $1,879 (M); expenditures, $504; qualifying distributions, $504.
Limitations: Applications not accepted.
Application information: Contributes only to pre-selected organizations.
Officers: James M. Schulman, Pres.; Robert E. Schulman, V.P.; James R. Mills, Secy.-Treas.
EIN: 621805165

50493
Shamblin Foundation
308 Seaboard Ln.
Franklin, TN 37067-8242
Contact: David Shamblin, Secy.

Established in 1997 in TN.
Donor(s): David G. Shamblin, Gwen H. Shamblin.
Financial data (yr. ended 12/31/01): Grants paid, $0; assets, $176,518 (M); expenditures, $694; qualifying distributions, $0.
Limitations: Giving primarily in Nashville, TN.
Officers: Gwen H. Shamblin, Pres.; David G. Shamblin, Secy.
EIN: 621692059

50494
Sharley Charitable Trust
5683 Ashley Sq. S.
Memphis, TN 38120

Established in 1996 in TN.
Donor(s): RNS Asset Management Co.
Financial data (yr. ended 12/31/99): Grants paid, $0; assets, $320,977 (L); expenditures, $0; qualifying distributions, $0.
Limitations: Applications not accepted.
Application information: Contributes only to pre-selected organizations.
Trustees: Nancy Sharley, Reginald Sharley.
EIN: 316542308

50495
Siegel Foundation
c/o SunTrust Banks, Inc.
P.O. Box 305110
Nashville, TN 37230-5110
Contact: Kim Williams

Established in 2000 in TN.
Financial data (yr. ended 12/31/00): Grants paid, $0; assets, $1,253,919 (M); gifts received, $1,177,399; expenditures, $5,021; qualifying distributions, $2,510.
Trustees: Charles Babb, Evelyn Hardison, Rollie Holden, Jr., Tom Newsom, John Rollyson, Kren Stoltz, Joe Swanson, Jr., Lara Womack, SunTrust Banks, Inc.
EIN: 311646336

50496
Chase Simpson Charitable Trust
4979 Ridge Park Dr.
Memphis, TN 38128

Established in 1997 in TN.
Financial data (yr. ended 12/31/99): Grants paid, $0; assets, $5,469 (L); expenditures, $0; qualifying distributions, $0.
Limitations: Applications not accepted. Giving primarily in TN.
Application information: Contributes only to pre-selected organizations.
Trustees: Elizabeth Simpson, Robert Simpson.
EIN: 626325239

50497
The Sparks Foundation
775 Ridge Lake Blvd.
Memphis, TN 38120 (901) 766-4600

Established in 2001 in TN.
Donor(s): Willard D. Sparks.
Financial data (yr. ended 12/31/01): Grants paid, $0; assets, $4,083,700 (M); gifts received, $4,087,095; expenditures, $0; qualifying distributions, $0.
Application information: Application form required.
Trustees: Robert D. Sparks, Willard R. Sparks.
EIN: 237029788

50498
Special Housing Services, Inc.
179 Belle Forest Cir.
Nashville, TN 37221

Financial data (yr. ended 06/30/02): Grants paid, $0; assets, $1,103,841 (M); gifts received, $28,384; expenditures, $86,841; qualifying distributions, $0.
Limitations: Applications not accepted. Giving primarily in Nashville, TN.
Application information: Contributes only to pre-selected organizations.
Officers: Don Bruno, Pres.; Cliff Reinert, V.P.; D. Kent Skinner, Treas.
EIN: 581524605

50499
J. Spencer Speed Scholarship Fund Foundation
1400 S. Germantown Rd.
Germantown, TN 38138-2205
(901) 759-3100
Contact: John M. Vines, Mgr.

Financial data (yr. ended 12/31/01): Grants paid, $0; assets, $92,699 (M); expenditures, $846; qualifying distributions, $0.
Officer: John M. Vines, Mgr.
Trustee: S. Terry Canale.
EIN: 626042839

50500
Larry & Donna Treadway Charitable Trust
1121 Bledsoe Dr.
Castalian Springs, TN 37031

Financial data (yr. ended 12/31/99): Grants paid, $0; assets, $26,723 (L); expenditures, $0; qualifying distributions, $0.
Limitations: Applications not accepted.
Application information: Contributes only to pre-selected organizations.
Trustees: Donna Treadway, Larry Treadway.
EIN: 626317360

50501
The David and Rebecca Winestone Memorial Foundation, Inc.
5515 Yates Cove
Memphis, TN 38120-2409
Application address: 5384 Poplar Ave., Ste. 414, Memphis, TN 38119-3676, tel.: (901) 682-3775; FAX: 682-3894
Contact: Shelby W. Baum, Secy.

Financial data (yr. ended 12/31/01): Grants paid, $0; assets, $64,423 (M); gifts received, $28,170; expenditures, $515; qualifying distributions, $0.
Application information: Application form required.
Officer: Shelby W. Baum, Secy.
Directors: Irving Friedman, Alvin A. Gordon, Marshall D. Gordon, Rebecca W. Hanover, David S. Winestone II, John S. Winestone, Joscelyn K. Winestone, Marie I. Winestone.
EIN: 626366746

50502
Wolftever Charitable Foundation
4900 Wilson Ave.
Signal Mountain, TN 37377
Application address: P.O. Box 2226, Umatilla, FL 32784
Contact: Paul John Kruesi, Jr., Tr.

Established in 2000 in TN.
Donor(s): Paul John Kruesi, Jr.
Financial data (yr. ended 09/30/01): Grants paid, $0; assets, $162,377 (M); expenditures, $0; qualifying distributions, $0.
Trustees: Marion Green Kruesi, Paul John Kruesi, Jr., Paul John Kruesi III, Starr K. Weekes.
EIN: 621834123

50503
Raymond Zimmerman Jewish Foundation
P.O. Box 150769
Nashville, TN 37215

Established in 1998 in TN.
Financial data (yr. ended 09/30/02): Grants paid, $0; assets, $2,503 (M); gifts received, $2,710; expenditures, $210; qualifying distributions, $0.
Limitations: Applications not accepted.
Application information: Contributes only to pre-selected organizations.
Trustee: Raymond Zimmerman.
EIN: 621620480

TEXAS

50504
Houston Endowment Inc.
600 Travis, Ste. 6400
Houston, TX 77002-3007 (713) 238-8100
FAX: (713) 238-8101; URL: http://www.houstonendowment.org
Contact: H. Joe Nelson III, Pres.

Incorporated in 1937 in TX.
Donor(s): Jesse H. Jones,‡ Mrs. Jesse H. Jones.‡
Financial data (yr. ended 12/31/01): Grants paid, $71,761,140; assets, $1,367,954,880 (M); expenditures, $80,648,379; qualifying distributions, $74,500,000.
Limitations: Giving primarily in Houston, TX; no grants outside the continental U.S.
Publications: Informational brochure (including application guidelines), annual report.
Application information: Grant payments of $20.7 million originally scheduled for 1999 were accelerated and paid in 1998. Application form not required.
Officers and Directors:* Milton Carroll,* Chair.; H. Joe Nelson III,* Pres.; Sheryl L. Johns, V.P., Treas., and C.F.O.; David L. Nelson, V.P., and Grant Dir.; D. Kent Anderson, Audrey Jones Beck, Jack S. Blanton, Harold Metts, Laurence E. Simmons, Melissa Jones Stevens, Rosie Zamora.
EIN: 746013920
Codes: FD, FM

50505
SBC Foundation
(Formerly Southwestern Bell Foundation)
130 E. Travis, Ste. 350
San Antonio, TX 78205 (210) 351-2218
Additional tel.: (800) 591-9663; FAX: (210) 351-2599; URL: http://www.sbc.com/corporate_citizenship/sbc_in_our_communities/sbc_foundation
Contact: Laura Sanford, Pres.

Established in 1984 in MO.
Donor(s): Southwestern Bell Corp., SBC Communications Inc.
Financial data (yr. ended 12/31/01): Grants paid, $69,111,239; assets, $536,184,004 (M); gifts received, $209,112,587; expenditures, $70,063,842; qualifying distributions, $69,111,239.
Limitations: Giving primarily in AR, CA, CT, IL, IN, KS, MI, MO, NV, OH, OK, TX, and WI.
Publications: Corporate giving report, application guidelines, informational brochure (including application guidelines).
Application information: Applications via the Internet are not accepted. Application form required.
Officers and Directors:* Bill Daley,* Chair.; Laura Sanford, Pres.; Hal Rainbolt, V.P. and Secy.; Mike Viola, V.P. and Treas.; Jim Ellis, Karen Jennings.
EIN: 431353948
Codes: CS, FD, CD, FM

50506
The Brown Foundation, Inc.
2217 Welch Ave.
Houston, TX 77019 (713) 523-6867
Application address: P.O. Box 130646, Houston, TX 77219-0646; FAX: (713) 523-2917; E-mail: bfi@brownfoundation.org; URL: http://www.brownfoundation.org
Contact: Nancy Pittman, Exec. Dir.

Incorporated in 1951 in TX.
Donor(s): Herman Brown,‡ Margarett Root Brown,‡ George R. Brown,‡ Alice Pratt Brown.‡
Financial data (yr. ended 06/30/01): Grants paid, $62,446,805; assets, $1,323,153,103 (M); expenditures, $67,448,193; qualifying distributions, $62,236,020.
Limitations: Giving primarily in TX, with emphasis on Houston.
Publications: Application guidelines, annual report (including application guidelines), informational brochure (including application guidelines).
Application information: Grant proposal guidelines are available upon request. Will consider one grant proposal per 12-month period from an organization. No grant funds pledged beyond the current year. Application form required.
Officers and Trustees:* M.S. Stude,* Chair.; Maconda Brown O'Connor,* Pres.; Isabel Brown Wilson,* 1st V.P.; Nancy Brown Negley,* V.P.; Louisa Stude Sarofim,* V.P.; John F. Fort III,* Secy.; Nancy Pittman, Exec. Dir.
EIN: 746036466
Codes: FD, FM

50507
Communities Foundation of Texas, Inc.
4605 Live Oak St.
Dallas, TX 75204 (214) 826-5231
FAX: (214) 823-7737; URL: http://www.cftexas.org
Contact: Jeverley R. Cook, Ph.D., V.P., Grants

Established in 1953 in TX; incorporated in 1960.
Financial data (yr. ended 06/30/01): Grants paid, $40,340,000; assets, $627,493,000 (M); gifts received, $14,690,000; expenditures, $50,337,000.
Limitations: Giving primarily in the Dallas, TX, area (for grants from unrestricted funds).
Publications: Program policy statement, application guidelines, financial statement, newsletter, annual report.
Application information: Proposals sent by FAX are not accepted. Application form not required.
Officers and Trustees:* Charles J. Wyly, Jr.,* Chair.; Milton P. Levy, Jr.,* Vice-Chair.; Edward M. Fjordbak,* Pres.; Jack Kinnebrew, C.O.O.; Jeverley R. Cook, Ph.D., V.P., Grants; Marcia Williams Godwin, V.P., Admin.; Cheryl Unis Mansour, V.P., Donor Rels.; J. Michael Redfearn, V.P., Finance; Thompson Sawyer, V.P., Investments; Philip O'Bryan Montgomery III,* Secy.; Linda Pitts Custard, Treas.; Ebby Halliday Acers, Tr. Emeritus; Ruth Sharp Altshuler, Chair. Emeritus; Daniel W. Cook III, Joseph M. Grant, Ph.D., Linda Brack McFarland, Lydia Haggar Novakov, Jere W. Thompson, Gifford Touchstone, Joel T. Williams III.
EIN: 750964565
Codes: CM, FD, FM

50508
ExxonMobil Foundation
(Formerly ExxonMobil Education Foundation)
5959 Las Colinas Blvd.
Irving, TX 75039-2298 (972) 444-1104
FAX: (972) 444-1405; URL: http://www.exxonmobil.com/contributions/index.html
Contact: Edward F. Ahnert, Pres.

Incorporated in 1955 in NJ as Esso Education Foundation; name changed to Exxon Education Foundation in 1972; current name adopted in 1999.
Donor(s): Exxon Corp., Exxon Mobil Corp., and affiliated companies.
Financial data (yr. ended 12/31/01): Grants paid, $39,667,911; assets, $70,171,738 (M); gifts received, $36,749,080; expenditures, $40,072,297; qualifying distributions, $40,057,297.
Publications: Annual report.
Application information: Applications are not encouraged. The foundation will accept 2-page letters of inquiry relating to project ideas that are consonant with the goals of its Mathematics Education or Elementary and Secondary School Improvement programs.
Officers and Trustees:* K.P. Cohen,* Chair.; Edward F. Ahnert, Pres.; A.E. Lawson, Exec. Dir.; C.T. Olson, V.P.; R.M. Cureton, Secy.; S.B.L. Penrose, Treas.; P.A. Hanson, Cont.; D.P. Bailey, D.L. Baird, Jr., F.W. Bass, J.C. Glaubig, A.M. Lopez, B.G. Macklin, R.V. Pisarczyk, F.A. Risch, F.B. Sprow, P.A. Wetz.
EIN: 136082357
Codes: CS, FD, CD, FM

50509
The Meadows Foundation, Inc.
Wilson Historic District
3003 Swiss Ave.
Dallas, TX 75204-6090 (214) 826-9431
Additional Tel.: (800) 826-9431; FAX: (214) 827-7042; E-mail: grants@mfi.org; URL: http://www.mfi.org
Contact: Bruce H. Esterline, V.P., Grants

Incorporated in 1948 in TX.
Donor(s): Algur Hurtle Meadows,‡ Virginia Meadows.‡
Financial data (yr. ended 12/31/01): Grants paid, $37,462,718; assets, $784,033,413 (M); expenditures, $46,577,035; qualifying distributions, $37,462,718; giving activities include $3,798,254 for program-related investments and $873,221 for programs.
Limitations: Giving limited to TX.
Publications: Annual report (including application guidelines), application guidelines.
Application information: An online grant application form is available on the foundation's Web site. Application form not required.
Officers and Directors:* Robert A. Meadows,* Chair.; Linda P. Evans,* C.E.O. and Pres.; Martha L. Benson, V.P., Treas. and C.F.O.; Michael E. Patrick, V.P. and C.I.O.; Bruce H. Esterline, V.P., Grants; Robert E. Weiss, V.P., Admin.; Emily J. Jones, Corp. Secy.; Evelyn Meadows Acton, Dir. Emeritus; John W. Broadfoot, J.W. Bullion, Dir. Emeritus; True Miller Campbell, Daniel H. Chapman, Judy B. Culbertson, John A. Hammack, Sally R. Lancaster, Dir. Emeritus; P. Mike McCullough, Curtis W. Meadows, Jr., Dir. Emeritus; Eric Richard Meadows, Mark A. Meadows, Michael L. Meadows, Sally C. Miller, Dir. Emeritus; William A. Nesbitt, G. Tomas Rhodus, Evy Kay Ritzen, Eloise Meadows Rouse, Dir. Emeritus; Dorothy C. Wilson, Dir. Emeritus; Stephen Wheeler Wilson.
EIN: 756015322

50509—TEXAS

Codes: FD, FM

50510
Sid W. Richardson Foundation
309 Main St.
Fort Worth, TX 76102 (817) 336-0494
URL: http://www.sidrichardson.org
Contact: Valleau Wilkie, Jr., Exec. Dir.

Established in 1947 in TX.
Donor(s): Sid W. Richardson,‡ and associated companies.
Financial data (yr. ended 12/31/01): Grants paid, $34,798,143; assets, $257,816,716 (M); gifts received, $257,817,000; expenditures, $37,691,314; qualifying distributions, $36,407,023; giving activities include $580,194 for programs.
Limitations: Giving limited to TX, with emphasis on Fort Worth for the arts and human services, and statewide for health and education.
Publications: Annual report (including application guidelines).
Application information: Application form required.
Officers and Directors:* Perry R. Bass,* Chair.; Edward P. Bass,* Pres.; Valleau Wilkie, Jr., Exec. V.P. and Exec. Dir.; Lee M. Bass,* V.P.; Nancy Lee Bass,* V.P.; Sid R. Bass,* V.P.; Jo Helen Rosacker, Secy.; M.E. Chappell,* Treas.
EIN: 756015828
Codes: FD, FM

50511
The Robert A. Welch Foundation
5555 San Felipe, Ste. 1900
Houston, TX 77056-2732 (713) 961-9884
FAX: (713) 961-5168; E-mail:
dittrich@welch1.org; URL: http://
www.welch1.org
Contact: Norbert Dittrich, Pres.

Established in 1954 in TX as a private foundation.
Donor(s): Robert A. Welch.‡
Financial data (yr. ended 08/31/01): Grants paid, $30,060,065; assets, $612,796,502 (M); expenditures, $34,503,021; qualifying distributions, $30,969,692; giving activities include $192,993 for programs.
Limitations: Giving limited to TX.
Publications: Annual report, application guidelines, newsletter.
Application information: To be eligible for consideration, an applicant must be a university, college or other educational institution within the state of TX. Application form required.
Officers and Directors:* Richard J.V. Johnson,* Chair. and C.E.O.; Charles W. Duncan, Jr.,* Vice-Chair.; Norbert Dittrich, Pres. and C.O.O.; J. Evans Attwell,* Secy.; Dennis Hendrix,* Treas.; Jack S. Josey, Chair. Emeritus.
EIN: 760343128
Codes: FD, FM, GTI

50512
Shell Oil Company Foundation
(Formerly Shell Companies Foundation, Inc.)
910 Louisiana, Ste. 4137
P.O. Box 2099
Houston, TX 77252 (713) 241-3616
FAX: (713) 241-3329; E-mail:
socfoundation@shellus.com; URL: http://
www.countonshell.com/community/
involvement/shell_foundation.html
Contact: B.L. McHam, V.P.

Incorporated in 1953 in NY.
Donor(s): Shell Oil Co., and other participating companies.
Financial data (yr. ended 12/31/01): Grants paid, $29,734,931; assets, $66,393,686 (M); expenditures, $34,697,557; qualifying distributions, $29,734,931.
Limitations: Giving primarily in areas of company operations in the U.S.
Publications: Corporate giving report (including application guidelines).
Application information: Scholarship programs administered through National Merit Scholarship Corp. Application form not required.
Officers and Directors:* R.J. Routs,* Pres.; B.L. McHam, V.P.; P.M. Loman, Secy.; G.R. Hullinger, Treas.; R.J. Decyk, P.M. Dreckman, J.R. Eagan, E.F. Gibson, M.F. Keeth, C.A. Lamboley, A.Y. Noojin, R.M. Restucci.
EIN: 136066583
Codes: CS, FD, CD, FM

50513
The Joe and Lois Perkins Foundation
2304 Midwestern Pkwy., Ste. 200
Wichita Falls, TX 76308 (940) 691-7770

Incorporated in 1941 in TX.
Donor(s): J.J. Perkins.‡
Financial data (yr. ended 12/31/00): Grants paid, $25,874,319; assets, $15,600 (M); expenditures, $26,087,087; qualifying distributions, $25,912,463.
Limitations: Applications not accepted. Giving primarily in TX.
Application information: Contributes only to pre-selected organizations.
Officers and Directors:* Joe N. Prothro,* Pres.; Elizabeth P. Prothro,* V.P.; Kathryn Prothro Yeager,* V.P.; K. Elizabeth Yeager,* Secy.; Mark H. Prothro,* Treas.; David H. Prothro.
EIN: 756012450
Codes: FD, FM

50514
Amon G. Carter Foundation
201 Main St., Ste. 1945
P.O. Box 1036
Fort Worth, TX 76102 (817) 332-2783
FAX: (817) 332-2787; E-mail:
jrobinson@agcf.org; URL: http://www.agcf.org
Contact: John H. Robinson, Exec. V.P., Grant Admin.

Incorporated in 1945 in TX.
Donor(s): Amon G. Carter,‡ N.B. Carter,‡ Star-Telegram Employees Fund, Carter Foundation Production Co.
Financial data (yr. ended 12/31/00): Grants paid, $17,167,151; assets, $335,901,614 (M); expenditures, $20,324,289; qualifying distributions, $17,346,759.
Limitations: Giving largely restricted to Fort Worth and Tarrant County, TX.
Publications: Program policy statement, application guidelines.
Application information: Grants outside local geographic area usually initiated by board. Application form not required.
Officers and Directors:* Ruth Carter Stevenson,* Pres.; W. Patrick Harris, Exec. V.P., Investments; John H. Robinson, Exec. V.P., Grant Admin.; Robert W. Brown, M.D.,* V.P.; Sheila B. Johnson,* Secy.; Mark L. Johnson,* Treas.; Kathy A. King, Cont.; Kate Johnson.
EIN: 756000331
Codes: FD, FM

50515
Albert & Bessie Mae Kronkosky Charitable Foundation
112 E. Pecan, Ste. 830
San Antonio, TX 78205 (210) 475-9000
Additional tel.: (888) 309-9001; FAX: (210) 354-2204; E-mail: kronfndn@kronkosky.org;
URL: http://www.kronkosky.org
Contact: Palmer Moe, Exec. Dir.

Established in 1991 in TX.
Donor(s): Albert Kronkosky,‡ Bessie Mae Kronkosky.
Financial data (yr. ended 12/31/01): Grants paid, $16,951,916; assets, $294,998,137 (M); expenditures, $20,001,442; qualifying distributions, $18,538,888.
Limitations: Giving limited to Bandera, Bexar, Comal, and Kendall counties, TX.
Publications: Application guidelines.
Application information: Application form required.
Trustee: Bank of America.
EIN: 746385152
Codes: FD, FM

50516
T. L. L. Temple Foundation
109 Temple Blvd., Ste. 300
Lufkin, TX 75901 (936) 639-5197
Contact: A. Wayne Corely, Exec. Dir.

Trust established in 1962 in TX.
Donor(s): Georgie T. Munz,‡ Katherine S. Temple.‡
Financial data (yr. ended 11/30/01): Grants paid, $15,014,915; assets, $319,332,383 (M); expenditures, $16,187,228; qualifying distributions, $14,695,225.
Limitations: Giving primarily in counties in TX constituting the East Texas Pine Timber Belt.
Publications: Application guidelines, program policy statement.
Application information: Application form required.
Officers and Trustees:* Arthur Temple III,* Chair.; Arthur Temple,* Chair. Emeritus; M.F. Zeagler, Cont.; A. Wayne Corley, Exec. Dir.; Ward R. Burke, Phillip M. Leach, H.J. Shands III, W. Temple Webber, Jr.
EIN: 756037406
Codes: FD, FM

50517
Covenant Foundation, Inc.
8122 Datapoint Dr., Ste. 1000
San Antonio, TX 78229
Contact: Franklin B. Stagg, Pres.

Established in 1991 in TX.
Donor(s): James R. Leininger, Cecelia A. Leininger.
Financial data (yr. ended 12/31/00): Grants paid, $14,341,693; assets, $54,854,362 (M); gifts received, $10,000; expenditures, $17,659,610; qualifying distributions, $14,260,550.
Limitations: Applications not accepted. Giving primarily in TX.
Application information: Contributes only to pre-selected organizations.
Officer and Directors:* Franklin B. Stagg,* Pres.; Thomas W. Lyles, Jr., Secy.; Charles A. Staffel,* Treas.; Brian Leininger, Cecelia A. Leininger, James R. Leininger, Tracy Leininger, Kelly Welch, Richard Welch, Robert Welch.
EIN: 742622129
Codes: FD, FM

50518
The Cullen Foundation
601 Jefferson, 40th Fl.
Houston, TX 77002 (713) 651-8837
E-mail: salexander@cullenfdn.org; URL: http://www.cullenfdn.org
Contact: Alan M. Stewart, Exec. Dir.

Trust established in 1947 in TX.
Donor(s): Hugh Roy Cullen,‡ Lillie Cullen.‡
Financial data (yr. ended 12/31/01): Grants paid, $14,001,667; assets, $240,000,000 (M); expenditures, $15,795,051; qualifying distributions, $14,144,150.
Limitations: Giving limited to TX, with emphasis on Houston.
Publications: Application guidelines.
Application information: Application form not required.
Officers and Directors:* Roy Henry Cullen,* Pres.; Isaac Arnold, Jr.,* V.P.; Wilhelmina E. Robertson,* Secy.; Alan M. Stewart, Exec. Dir. and Treas.; Bert L. Campbell, William H. Drushel, Jr.
EIN: 760647361
Codes: FD, FM

50519
The Burnett Foundation
(Formerly The Burnett-Tandy Foundation)
801 Cherry St., Box 16
Fort Worth, TX 76102-6881 (817) 877-3344
Contact: Thomas F. Beech, Exec. V.P.

Established in 1978 in TX.
Donor(s): Anne Burnett Tandy,‡ Ben Bird.
Financial data (yr. ended 12/31/01): Grants paid, $13,880,745; assets, $263,614,624 (M); expenditures, $14,582,162; qualifying distributions, $14,732,654; giving activities include $65,844 for programs.
Limitations: Giving primarily in the Fort Worth, TX, area.
Publications: Biennial report, program policy statement, application guidelines.
Application information: Application form required.
Officers and Trustees:* Anne W. Marion,* Pres.; Thomas F. Beech, Exec. V.P.; Edward R. Hudson, Jr.,* V.P. and Secy.-Treas.; Benjamin J. Fortson, Anne Windfohr Grimes, John L. Marion.
EIN: 751638517

50520
The Wortham Foundation
2727 Allen Pkwy., Ste. 1570
Houston, TX 77019 (713) 526-8849
FAX: (713) 526-7222; E-mail: bsnyder@wortham.org
Contact: Barbara J. Snyder, Grants Admin.

Trust established in 1958 in TX.
Donor(s): Gus S. Wortham,‡ Lyndall F. Wortham.‡
Financial data (yr. ended 09/30/01): Grants paid, $11,994,500; assets, $211,395,002 (M); expenditures, $13,764,529; qualifying distributions, $11,850,666.
Limitations: Giving limited to Houston and Harris County, TX.
Publications: Annual report, informational brochure (including application guidelines).
Application information: Please do not send bound copies of proposal. Application form required.
Officers and Trustees:* Fred C. Burns,* Chair.; Brady F. Carruth,* Pres.; R.W. Wortham III,* Secy.-Treas.; William V.H. Clarke, Cont.; James A. Elkins III, E.A. Stumpf III.
EIN: 741334356
Codes: FD, FM

50521
McCombs Foundation, Inc.
9000 Tesoro Dr., Ste. 122
San Antonio, TX 78217 (210) 821-6523
Contact: Gary V. Woods, Secy.-Treas.

Established in 1981 in TX.
Donor(s): Gary V. Woods, and members of the McCombs family, McCombs Family Charitable Lead Trust.
Financial data (yr. ended 12/31/00): Grants paid, $11,079,015; assets, $81,727,058 (M); gifts received, $23,577,996; expenditures, $13,117,865; qualifying distributions, $11,217,994.
Limitations: Giving primarily in TX.
Application information: Application form not required.
Officers: Billy J. McCombs, Pres.; Charline H. McCombs, V.P.; Gary V. Woods, Secy.-Treas.
EIN: 742204217

50522
The Dallas Foundation
900 Jackson St., Ste. 150
Dallas, TX 75202 (214) 741-9898
FAX: (214) 741-9848; E-mail: mjalonick@dallasfoundation.org; URL: http://www.dallasfoundation.org
Contact: Mary M. Jalonick, Exec. Dir.

Established in 1929 in TX.
Financial data (yr. ended 12/31/01): Grants paid, $11,040,866; assets, $91,938,196 (M); gifts received, $11,946,072; expenditures, $13,052,476.
Limitations: Giving limited to the City and County of Dallas, TX.
Publications: Annual report (including application guidelines), application guidelines, informational brochure, grants list, newsletter.
Application information: Application form not required.
Officer: Mary M. Jalonick, Exec. Dir.
Governors: J. McDonald Williams,* Chair.; Mary Evans Sias, Ph.D., Vice-Chair.; Deedie Potter Rose, Secy.; Dolores G. Barzune, Albert C. Black, Jr., John R. Castle, Walter J. Humann, Elizabeth A. Lang-Miers, John D. Solana, Ronald G. Steinhart.
Trustee Banks: Bank One, N.A., Bank of America, Compass Bank.
EIN: 752890371
Codes: CM, FD, FM

50523
USAA Foundation, a Charitable Trust
(Formerly USAA Foundation II, a Charitable Trust)
USAA Bldg.
9800 Fredericksburg Rd., D-3-E
San Antonio, TX 78288-3500 (210) 498-1225
Contact: Barbara B. Gentry, Trust Rep.

Established in 1994 in TX.
Donor(s): United Services Automobile Assn.
Financial data (yr. ended 06/30/01): Grants paid, $10,837,349; assets, $145,237,670 (M); expenditures, $11,264,192; qualifying distributions, $10,774,304.
Limitations: Applications not accepted. Giving primarily in AZ, CA, CO, Washington, DC, FL, TX, and VA.
Application information: Contributes only to pre-selected organizations.
Trust Representative: Barbara B. Gentry, Pres.
Trustee: USAA Federal Savings Bank.
EIN: 746423382
Codes: CS, FD, CD, FM

50524
The William Stamps Farish Fund
10000 Memorial Dr., Ste. 920
Houston, TX 77024
Contact: Martha F. Gerry, Pres.

Incorporated in 1951 in TX.
Donor(s): Libbie Rice Farish.‡
Financial data (yr. ended 06/30/01): Grants paid, $10,300,000; assets, $192,913,382 (M); expenditures, $10,715,677; qualifying distributions, $10,352,506.
Limitations: Giving primarily in Houston, TX.
Publications: Application guidelines.
Application information: Application form not required.
Officers and Trustees:* Martha Farish Gerry,* Pres.; Laura Farish Chadwick, V.P.; Caroline P. Rotan, Secy.; Terry W. Ward, Treas.; Cornelia G. Corbett.
EIN: 746043019
Codes: FD, FM

50525
Austin Community Foundation for the Capital Area, Inc.
(Formerly Austin Community Foundation)
P.O. Box 5159
Austin, TX 78763 (512) 472-4483
E-mail: info@austincommunityfoundation.org;
URL: http://www.austincommunityfoundation.org
Contact: Richard G. Slaughter, Exec. Dir.

Established in 1977 in TX.
Financial data (yr. ended 12/31/01): Grants paid, $10,271,612; assets, $53,788,077 (M); gifts received, $12,636,627; expenditures, $13,731,005.
Limitations: Giving limited to Travis County, TX, for discretionary grants.
Publications: Newsletter, program policy statement, application guidelines, annual report.
Application information: Grant guidelines publication describes sequenced application format to follow. Telephone for exact deadlines. Application form not required.
Officers and Board of Governors:* Dorothy J. Drummer,* Pres.; Richard G. Slaughter, Exec. Dir.; and 19 additional governors.
EIN: 741934031
Codes: CM, FD

50526
RGK Foundation
1301 W. 25th St., Ste. 300
Austin, TX 78705-4236 (512) 474-9298
FAX: (512) 474-7281; E-mail: jhampton@rgkfdn.org; URL: http://www.rgkfoundation.org
Contact: Jami Hampton, Grants Admin.

Incorporated in 1966 in TX.
Donor(s): George Kozmetsky, Ronya Kozmetsky.
Financial data (yr. ended 12/31/00): Grants paid, $10,140,537; assets, $108,483,771 (M); expenditures, $11,126,827; qualifying distributions, $1,038,888.
Publications: Informational brochure (including application guidelines).
Application information: Proposals for medical research must follow NIH guidelines. Application form required.
Officers and Trustees:* Gregory A. Kozmetsky,* Chair. and Pres.; Christina C. Collier, Exec. V.P.; Nadya Kozmetsky Scott,* V.P.; Cynthia H. Kozmetsky,* Secy.; Patricia A. Hayes, Charles Hurwitz, George Kozmetsky, Ronya Kozmetsky, Michael E. Patrick.
EIN: 746077587

50526—TEXAS

Codes: FD, FM

50527
Robert J. Kleberg, Jr. and Helen C. Kleberg Foundation
700 N. Saint Mary's St., Ste. 1200
San Antonio, TX 78205 (210) 271-3691
Contact: Robert L. Washington, Grants Coord.

Incorporated in 1950 in TX.
Donor(s): Helen C. Kleberg,‡ Robert J. Kleberg, Jr.‡
Financial data (yr. ended 12/31/00): Grants paid, $9,985,828; assets, $208,987,899 (M); expenditures, $11,389,214; qualifying distributions, $9,799,446.
Publications: Annual report, application guidelines.
Application information: Application form not required.
Officers and Directors:* Helen K. Groves,* Pres.; John D. Alexander, Jr.,* V.P. and Secy.; Emory A. Hamilton,* V.P. and Treas.; Helen C. Alexander,* V.P.; Caroline R. Alexander, John B. Carter, Jr., Henrietta A. George, Dorothy A. Matz, H. Virgil Sherrill.
EIN: 746044810
Codes: FD, FM

50528
John P. McGovern Foundation
2211 Norfolk St., Ste. 900
Houston, TX 77098-4044 (713) 661-4808
FAX: (713) 661-3031
Contact: John P. McGovern, M.D., Pres.

Established in 1961 in TX.
Donor(s): John P. McGovern, M.D.
Financial data (yr. ended 08/31/01): Grants paid, $9,451,286; assets, $197,269,019 (M); gifts received, $2,560,653; expenditures, $10,065,467; qualifying distributions, $9,727,071.
Limitations: Applications not accepted. Giving primarily in TX, with emphasis on Houston; giving also in the Southwest.
Application information: Contributes only to pre-selected organizations.
Officers and Directors: John P. McGovern, M.D.,* Pres.; Kathrine G. McGovern,* V.P. and Treas.; Gay Collette, Secy.; Orville L. Story.
EIN: 746053075
Codes: FD, FM

50529
Perry and Nancy Lee Bass Corporation
201 Main St., Ste. 2300
Fort Worth, TX 76102-3127

Established in 1989 in TX.
Donor(s): Perry R. Bass.
Financial data (yr. ended 06/30/01): Grants paid, $9,076,000; assets, $60,536,228 (M); gifts received, $1,300,000; expenditures, $10,127,560; qualifying distributions, $9,040,503.
Limitations: Applications not accepted. Giving primarily in Fort Worth, TX.
Application information: Contributes only to pre-selected organizations.
Officers and Directors:* Perry R. Bass,* Chair. and Pres.; Nancy Lee Bass,* Vice-Chair. and V.P.; W. Robert Cotham, V.P.; Gary W. Reese, V.P.; Valleau Wilkie, Jr., V.P.; Lee M. Bass,* Secy.-Treas.
EIN: 752308846
Codes: FD

50530
The Fondren Foundation
7 TCT 37
P.O. Box 2558
Houston, TX 77252-8037 (713) 216-4513
Contact: Martie Herrick

Trust established in 1948 in TX.
Donor(s): Mrs. W.W. Fondren, Sr.,‡ and others.
Financial data (yr. ended 10/31/01): Grants paid, $9,000,000; assets, $172,674,279 (M); expenditures, $10,889,248; qualifying distributions, $8,960,025.
Limitations: Giving primarily in TX, with emphasis on Houston.
Publications: Application guidelines.
Application information: Application form not required.
Officers and Trustees:* Leland T. Fondren, Chair.; Harper B. Trammell, Vice-Chair.; Catherine Underwood Murray, Secy.-Treas.; Doris Fondren Allday, R. Edwin Allday, Laura Fondren Trammell Baird, Ellanor Allday Beard, Celia Whitfield Crank, Bentley B. Fondren, Robert E. Fondren, Walter W. Fondren III, Walter W. Fondren IV, Marie Fondren Hall, Michael W. Springer, Carrie Trammell Sturges, Ann Gordon Trammell, David M. Underwood, David M. Underwood, Jr., Duncan K. Underwood, Lynda Knapp Underwood, Sue Trammell Whitfield, Susan T. Whitfield, W. Trammell Whitfield, William F. Whitfield, Sr., William F. Whitfield, Jr., Frances Fondren Wilson.
EIN: 746042565
Codes: FD, FM

50531
Albert and Margaret Alkek Foundation
1221 McKinney, Ste. 4525
Houston, TX 77010-2011 (713) 951-0019
FAX: (713) 951-0043
Contact: Sandra Bacak, Cont.

Established in 1996 in TX.
Donor(s): Albert B. Alkek,‡ Margaret M. Alkek.
Financial data (yr. ended 12/31/00): Grants paid, $8,935,625; assets, $211,208,729 (M); gifts received, $27,034; expenditures, $10,890,140; qualifying distributions, $8,959,558.
Limitations: Giving limited to TX.
Publications: Application guidelines.
Application information: Application form not required.
Officers and Directors:* Charles A. Williams,* Pres.; Scott B. Seaman,* Treas. and Exec. Dir.; Sandra Bacak, Cont.; Bobby R. Alford, Margaret M. Alkek, Daniel C. Arnold, Joe M. Bailey, Ralph D. Feigin, Dan B. Jones, John Moder, Margaret V. Williams, Randa D. Williams.
EIN: 760491186
Codes: FD, FM

50532
Clear Channel Communications Foundation
200 E. Basse Rd.
San Antonio, TX 78209

Established in 1999 in TX.
Donor(s): Clear Channel Communications, Inc.
Financial data (yr. ended 12/31/01): Grants paid, $8,669,669; assets, $10,190,774 (M); gifts received, $11,876,492; expenditures, $8,771,836; qualifying distributions, $8,771,836.
Limitations: Applications not accepted. Giving primarily in San Antonio, TX.
Application information: Contributes only to pre-selected organizations.
Officers and Directors:* L. Lowry Mays,* Pres.; Mark P. Mays,* V.P. and Secy.; Randall T. Mays,* V.P. and Treas.
EIN: 742908486
Codes: CS, FD, CD

50533
The Moody Foundation
2302 Post Office St., Ste. 704
Galveston, TX 77550 (409) 763-5333
FAX: (409) 763-5564; *URL:* http://www.moodyf.org
Contact: Peter M. Moore, Dir., Grants

Trust established in 1942 in TX.
Donor(s): William Lewis Moody, Jr.,‡ Libbie Shearn Moody.‡
Financial data (yr. ended 12/31/01): Grants paid, $8,277,161; assets, $926,916,215 (M); gifts received, $19,023,214; expenditures, $12,719,814; qualifying distributions, $10,666,090.
Limitations: Giving limited to TX.
Publications: Annual report, application guidelines.
Application information: Foundation will send application guidelines if project is of interest. For scholarship application form and submission deadlines contact Sandy Griffin. Application form not required.
Officers and Trustees:* Frances Moody Newman,* Chair.; Robert L. Moody,* Vice-Chair.; Ross Moody, Treas.; Harold C. MacDonald, Compt.; Frances Ann Moody, Exec. Dir.
EIN: 741403105
Codes: FD, FM, GTI

50534
San Antonio Area Foundation
110 Broadway, Ste. 230
San Antonio, TX 78205 (210) 225-2243
FAX: (210) 225-1980; *E-mail:* gift@saafdn.org;
URL: http://www.saafdn.org
Contact: Clarence R. "Reggie" Williams, C.E.O.

Established in 1964 in TX.
Financial data (yr. ended 12/31/01): Grants paid, $7,706,229; assets, $106,312,000 (M); gifts received, $13,846,803; expenditures, $1,778,887.
Limitations: Giving limited to Bexar County, TX, and surrounding counties, except when otherwise specified by donor.
Publications: Annual report, newsletter, application guidelines, financial statement, grants list, informational brochure.
Application information: Scholarship applications must be submitted to Bexar County Scholarship Clearinghouse, unless specifically designated by donor. Application form required.
Officers and Directors:* Clarence R. "Reggie" Williams, C.E.O. and Exec. Dir.; Marvin Forland, M.D.,* Pres.; Laura McNutt,* V.P.; Barbara Gentry,* Secy.; Raymond Carvajal,* Treas.; Janet Irwine, C.F.O.; John E. Banks, Jr., Michael D. Beldon, John Brazil, Ph.D., Rita Elizondo, Cathy Obriotti Green, Claudia Ladensohn, Joe Linson, Sherman P. Macdaniel, Lissa Martinez, Ommy Strauch, Pat L. Wilson, Mollie Zachry.
Trustee Banks: Broadway National Bank, JPMorgan Chase Bank, Bank of America, Merryl Lynch, Wells Fargo Bank, N.A., Frost National Bank, Bank One, N.A., UBS PaineWebber Inc.
EIN: 746065414
Codes: CM, FD, GTI

50535
The Cockrell Foundation
1600 Smith, Ste. 3900
Houston, TX 77002-7348 (713) 209-7500
Contact: M. Nancy Williams, Exec. V.P.

Trust established in 1957 in TX; incorporated in 1966.

Donor(s): Dula Cockrell,‡ Ernest Cockrell, Jr.,‡ Virginia H. Cockrell.‡
Financial data (yr. ended 12/31/01): Grants paid, $7,690,000; assets, $133,845,696 (M); expenditures, $8,588,690; qualifying distributions, $7,690,000.
Limitations: Giving primarily in Houston, TX.
Publications: Informational brochure (including application guidelines).
Application information: Application form not required.
Officers and Directors:* Ernest H. Cockrell,* Pres.; M. Nancy Williams, Exec. V.P.; Milton T. Graves,* V.P. and Assoc. Dir.; Douglas E. Bryant, Secy.-Treas.; David A. Cockrell, Advisory Dir.; Ernie D. Cockrell, Advisory Dir.; Janet S. Cockrell, Carol Cockrell Curran, Richard B. Curran, J. Webb Jennings III, Laura Jennings Turner.
EIN: 746076993
Codes: FD, FM

50536
Abell-Hanger Foundation
P.O. Box 430
Midland, TX 79702   (915) 684-6655
FAX: (915) 684-4474; E-mail:
AHF@abell-hanger.org; URL: http://www.abell-hanger.org
Contact: David L. Smith, Exec. Dir.

Incorporated in 1954 in TX.
Donor(s): George T. Abell,‡ Gladys H. Abell.‡
Financial data (yr. ended 06/30/02): Grants paid, $7,242,558; assets, $131,022,129 (M); expenditures, $8,314,580; qualifying distributions, $8,017,489.
Limitations: Giving limited to TX, with emphasis within the Permian Basin.
Publications: Annual report (including application guidelines).
Application information: Application form required.
Officers and Trustees:* Tevis Herd, Pres.; David L. Smith,* Exec. V.P.; Lester Van Pelt, Jr.,* V.P.; Herbert L. Cartwright III, Secy.-Treas.; Arlen L. Edgar, Jerome M. Fullinwider, Robert C. Leibrock, Clarence Scharbauer III, James I. Trott, Charles M. Younger, M.D.
EIN: 756020781
Codes: FD, FM

50537
The Gordon and Mary Cain Foundation
8 Greenway Plz., Ste. 702
Houston, TX 77046   (713) 960-9283
Contact: James D. Weaver, Pres.

Established in 1988 in TX.
Donor(s): Gordon A. Cain, Mary H. Cain.
Financial data (yr. ended 12/31/01): Grants paid, $7,165,668; assets, $133,275,328 (M); expenditures, $7,837,502; qualifying distributions, $7,221,991.
Limitations: Giving primarily in Houston, TX.
Publications: Application guidelines.
Application information: Application form not required.
Officers: Gordon A. Cain, Chair. and C.E.O.; James D. Weaver, Pres.; Mary H. Cain, V.P.; William A. McMinn, V.P.; Margaret W. Oehmig, V.P.; Sharyn A. Weaver, V.P.; William C. Oehmig, Secy.-Treas.
EIN: 760251558
Codes: FD, FM

50538
Dodge Jones Foundation
P.O. Box 176
Abilene, TX 79604   (915) 673-6429
Contact: Lawrence E. Gill, V.P., Grants Admin.

Incorporated in 1954 in TX.
Donor(s): Ruth Leggett Jones,‡ and others.
Financial data (yr. ended 12/31/00): Grants paid, $7,003,182; assets, $110,356,720 (M); expenditures, $8,314,855; qualifying distributions, $7,061,330.
Limitations: Giving primarily in Abilene, TX.
Application information: Application form not required.
Officers and Directors:* Julia Jones Matthews, Pres.; Joseph E. Canon,* Exec. V.P. and Exec. Dir.; Thomas R. Allen, V.P. and C.F.O.; Lawrence E. Gill, V.P., Grants Admin.; Linda Buckner, Secy.-Treas.; Joe B. Matthews, Kade L. Matthews.
EIN: 756006386
Codes: FD, FM

50539
Perot Foundation
12377 Merit Dr., Ste. 1700
Dallas, TX 75251   (972) 788-3000
Contact: Carolyn P. Rathjen, V.P.

Established in 1969 in TX.
Donor(s): H. Ross Perot.
Financial data (yr. ended 12/31/00): Grants paid, $6,886,195; assets, $39,443,352 (M); gifts received, $151,250; expenditures, $6,917,747; qualifying distributions, $6,872,244.
Limitations: Applications not accepted. Giving primarily in TX.
Application information: Contributes only to pre-selected organizations. Unsolicited requests for funds not considered. The scholarship program for children of graduates of the class of 1953 of the United States Naval Academy is no longer active.
Officers and Directors:* H. Ross Perot, Pres.; Carolyn P. Rathjen,* V.P.; Suzanne P. McGee, Nancy P. Mulford, H. Ross Perot, Jr., Katherine B. Perot, Margot B. Perot, John Thomas Walter, Jr.
EIN: 756093258
Codes: FD, FM

50540
Texas Instruments Foundation
7839 Churchill Way
Dallas, TX 75251   (972) 917-4505
Application address: P.O. Box 650311, M.S. 3906, Dallas, TX 75265; URL: http://www.ti.com/corp/docs/company/citizen/foundation/index.shtml
Contact: Ann Minnis, Grants Admin.

Trust established in 1951 in TX; incorporated in 1964.
Donor(s): Texas Instruments Inc., and wholly-owned subsidiaries.
Financial data (yr. ended 12/31/01): Grants paid, $6,799,585; assets, $23,764,464 (M); expenditures, $8,196,284; qualifying distributions, $6,886,599; giving activities include $93,983 for programs.
Limitations: Giving limited to plant site cities in TX: Attleboro, Austin, Dallas, Houston, Hunt Valley, Lubbock, Sherman, and Versailles.
Publications: Application guidelines.
Application information: Application for Founders' Prize by nomination only; application forms for Founders' Prize available from Liston M. Rice, Jr., Pres. Application form not required.
Officers and Directors:* Liston M. Rice, Jr.,* Pres.; Terri West,* V.P.; Cynthia Stewart, Secy.; William A. Aylesworth,* Treas.; Richard J. Agnich, Thomas Engibous, Steve Leven, Ann F. Minnis, James C. Mitchell, Phil Ritter, Bart Thomas.
EIN: 756038519
Codes: CS, FD, CD, FM

50541
Hillcrest Foundation
c/o Bank of America
P.O. Box 830241
Dallas, TX 75283-0241   (214) 209-1965
Contact: Daniel Kelly, V.P., Bank of America

Trust established in 1959 in TX.
Donor(s): Mrs. W.W. Caruth, Sr.‡
Financial data (yr. ended 05/31/01): Grants paid, $6,775,666; assets, $142,320,165 (M); expenditures, $7,626,246; qualifying distributions, $6,878,778.
Limitations: Giving limited to TX, with emphasis on Dallas County.
Publications: Application guidelines, informational brochure (including application guidelines).
Application information: Application form required.
Trustees: Harold Byrd, Jr., Bill W. Caruth III, Harry A. Shuford, Charles P. Storey, Bank of America.
EIN: 756007565
Codes: FD, FM

50542
Hoblitzelle Foundation
5956 Sherry Ln., Ste. 901
Dallas, TX 75225-6522   (214) 373-0462
URL: http://home.att.net/~hoblitzelle
Contact: Paul W. Harris, Exec. V.P.

Trust established in 1942 in TX; incorporated in 1953.
Donor(s): Karl St. John Hoblitzelle,‡ Esther T. Hoblitzelle.‡
Financial data (yr. ended 04/30/01): Grants paid, $6,694,347; assets, $131,795,263 (M); gifts received, $30,140; expenditures, $7,895,091; qualifying distributions, $7,200,396.
Limitations: Giving limited to TX, primarily Dallas.
Publications: Annual report (including application guidelines), program policy statement, newsletter.
Application information: Application form not required.
Officers and Directors:* Gerald W. Fronterhouse,* Chair.; George A. Shafer,* C.E.O. and Pres.; Paul W. Harris, Exec. V.P.; Donna C. Berry,* Secy.; Caren H. Prothro,* Treas.; Lillian M. Bradshaw, Dorothy R. Cullum, Linda P. Custard, Jerry Farrington, James W. Keay, William T. Solomon, Charles C. Sprague, M.D., Kern Wildenthal, M.D., Ph.D., J. McDonald Williams.
EIN: 756003984
Codes: FD, FM

50543
Reliant Resources Foundation
(Formerly Reliant Energy Foundation)
P.O. Box 4567
Houston, TX 77210   (713) 207-5155
Contact: Robert W. Gibbs, Jr., Pres.

Established in 1997 in TX.
Donor(s): Reliant Energy, Inc., Reliant Energy Ventures, Inc.
Financial data (yr. ended 12/31/00): Grants paid, $6,554,892; assets, $21,971,181 (M); gifts received, $363,736; expenditures, $6,611,458; qualifying distributions, $6,427,523.
Officers and Directors:* Don D. Jordan,* Co-Chair.; R.S. Steve Letbetter,* Co-Chair.; Robert W. Gibbs, Jr.,* Pres.; Hugh Rice Kelly, Secy.; Marc Killbride, Treas.; Lee W. Hogan, David M. McClanahan.

50543—TEXAS

EIN: 760537222
Codes: CS, FD, CD, FM

50544
Kimberly-Clark Foundation, Inc.
P.O. Box 619100
Dallas, TX 75261-9100 (972) 281-1200
Contact: Carolyn A. Mentesana, V.P.

Incorporated in 1952 in WI.
Donor(s): Kimberly-Clark Corp.
Financial data (yr. ended 12/31/00): Grants paid, $6,496,851; assets, $6,470,270 (M); gifts received, $10,335,947; expenditures, $6,650,393; qualifying distributions, $6,639,415.
Limitations: Giving primarily in communities where the company has operations; limited contributions to national organizations.
Publications: Annual report.
Application information: Request must be in writing, received by mail and addressed to the foundation's V.P. Application form required.
Officers and Directors:* Tina S. Barry, Pres.; Carolyn A. Mentesana, V.P.; Ron McCray, Secy.; W. Anthony Gamron,* Treas.; O. George Everbach, Wayne R. Sanders.
EIN: 396044304
Codes: CS, FD, CD, FM

50545
Greater Houston Community Foundation
4550 Post Oak Pl., Ste. 317
Houston, TX 77027-3106 (713) 960-1990
FAX: (713) 960-1994; E-mail:
lgardner@ghcf.org; URL: http://www.ghcf.org

Established in 1971 in TX.
Financial data (yr. ended 12/31/00): Grants paid, $6,471,926; assets, $52,262,075 (M); gifts received, $19,563,240; expenditures, $8,113,183.
Limitations: Giving limited to the Houston, TX, area.
Publications: Annual report, informational brochure (including application guidelines).
Officer: David M. Weekley, Chair.
EIN: 237160400
Codes: CM, FD

50546
Bass Foundation
309 Main St.
Fort Worth, TX 76102 (817) 336-0494
Contact: Valleau Wilkie, Jr., Exec. Dir.

Established in 1945 in TX.
Donor(s): Perry R. Bass, Lee M. Bass, Edward P. Bass, Sid Richardson Carbon and Gasoline Co., Perry R. Bass, Inc.
Financial data (yr. ended 12/31/01): Grants paid, $6,300,000; assets, $7,836,076 (M); expenditures, $6,397,373; qualifying distributions, $6,325,591.
Limitations: Applications not accepted. Giving primarily in Fort Worth, TX.
Application information: Contributes only to pre-selected organizations.
Officers and Directors:* Perry R. Bass,* Pres.; Edward P. Bass,* V.P.; Lee M. Bass,* V.P.; Nancy Lee Bass,* V.P.; Cynthia K. Alexander, Secy.-Treas.; Valleau Wilkie, Jr., Exec. Dir.
EIN: 756033983
Codes: FD, FM

50547
The Robert and Janice McNair Foundation
711 Louisiana St., 33rd Fl.
Houston, TX 77002-2734
Contact: Joanie Haley, Exec. Dir.

Established in 1988 in TX.
Donor(s): Robert McNair, Janice McNair.
Financial data (yr. ended 12/31/00): Grants paid, $6,083,945; assets, $12,955,967 (M); expenditures, $6,172,176; qualifying distributions, $6,140,412.
Limitations: Giving primarily in Houston, TX.
Publications: Informational brochure.
Officer: Joanie Haley, Exec. Dir.
Trustees: Janice McNair, Robert McNair.
EIN: 766050185
Codes: FD, FM

50548
M. D. Anderson Foundation
P.O. Box 2558
Houston, TX 77252-8037 (713) 216-4513
Contact: Charlene D. Slack, Secy.-Treas.

Trust established in 1936 in TX.
Donor(s): M.D. Anderson.‡
Financial data (yr. ended 12/31/00): Grants paid, $5,859,516; assets, $164,982,332 (M); expenditures, $6,429,450; qualifying distributions, $5,937,338.
Limitations: Giving limited to TX, primarily the Houston area.
Publications: Multi-year report, application guidelines.
Application information: Application form not required.
Officers: Gibson Gayle, Jr., Pres.; Uriel E. Dutton, V.P.; Charles W. Hall, V.P.; Jack Trotter, V.P.; Charlene D. Slack, Secy.-Treas.
EIN: 746035669
Codes: FD, FM

50549
Coastal Bend Community Foundation
The Six Hundred Bldg.
600 Leopard St., Ste. 1716
Corpus Christi, TX 78473 (361) 882-9745
FAX: (361) 882-2865; E-mail:
jmoloney@cbcfoundation.org; URL: http://www.cbcfoundation.org
Contact: Jim Moloney, Exec. Dir.

Established in 1980 in TX.
Financial data (yr. ended 12/31/01): Grants paid, $5,676,561; assets, $29,986,847 (L); gifts received, $3,938,178; expenditures, $6,508,709.
Limitations: Giving limited to Aransas, Bee, Jim Wells, Kleberg, Nueces, Refugio, and San Patricio counties, TX.
Publications: Grants list, informational brochure, application guidelines, annual report.
Application information: Cover form required. Application form required.
Officers and Directors:* T.D. Sells, Jr.,* Pres.; Ginger D. Fagen,* V.P.; Pat M. Eisenhauer,* V.P. Investments; Lou Adele May, Secy.-Treas.; Jim Moloney,* Exec. Dir.; Harry Lee Adams, Jr., Deb Bauer, Jeff Bell, Susie Bracht Black, Roberto Bosquez, M.D., Austin Brown, John Chapman, Lawrence Cornelius, Patricia Cypher, Joe DeLeon, Jr., Tom Dobson, Bill Finley, Jr., Lucien Flournoy, Joe Fulton, Paul R. Haas, Ed Harte, Mark H. Hulings, Dick Messbanger, Patty P. Mueller, Gorman Ritchie, Robert Rooke, Chela Storm, Norman P. Wilcox, Ivan Wilson, and 3 additional directors.
EIN: 742190039
Codes: CM, FD, GTI

50550
Rockwell Fund, Inc.
1330 Post Oak Blvd., Ste. 1825
Houston, TX 77056 (713) 629-9022
FAX: (713) 629-7702; E-mail:
mvogt@rockfund.org; URL: http://www.rockfund.org
Contact: Martha Vogt, Sr. Prog. Off.

Trust established in 1931; incorporated in 1949 in TX; merged with Rockwell Brothers Endowment, Inc. in 1981.
Donor(s): Members of the James M. Rockwell family.‡
Financial data (yr. ended 12/31/01): Grants paid, $5,655,860; assets, $115,411,552 (M); gifts received, $1,000; expenditures, $6,718,219; qualifying distributions, $6,139,861; giving activities include $100,000 for programs.
Limitations: Giving primarily in TX, with emphasis on Houston.
Publications: Annual report, application guidelines, grants list.
Application information: Applicants should not submit more than 1 proposal per year; Applications must include a 5-page written narrative, application form, and check list. Application form required.
Officers and Trustees:* R. Terry Bell,* Pres.; Mary Jo Loyd,* Secy.; Bennie Green,* Treas.; Helen N. Sterling, Tr. Emerita.
EIN: 746040258
Codes: FD, FM

50551
The George Foundation
PMB 310 Morton St., Ste. C
Richmond, TX 77469 (281) 342-6109
Additional address: 207 S. 3rd St., Richmond, TX 77469; URL: http://www.thegeorgefoundation.org
Contact: Dee Koch, Grants Off.

Trust established in 1945 in TX.
Donor(s): A.P. George,‡ Mamie E. George.‡
Financial data (yr. ended 12/31/00): Grants paid, $5,523,900; assets, $111,095,580 (M); expenditures, $9,233,059; qualifying distributions, $7,105,325; giving activities include $883,122 for programs.
Limitations: Giving primarily in Fort Bend County, TX.
Publications: Informational brochure.
Application information: The foundation acknowledges receipt of proposals within two weeks. During the review process, interviews and site visits are requested to better evaluate the proposal. The foundation will not consider a grant application from the same applicant, whether granted or denied, more frequently than once every twelve month period. Application form not required.
Officers and Trustees:* Lane Ward,* Chair.; Sandra G. Thompson, C.F.O.; Roland Adamson, Exec. Dir.; Charles H. Herder, William A. Little, Gene Reed, E.E. Reed, W. Lane Ward, Jr., Mike Wells.
EIN: 746043368
Codes: FD

50552
The Michael and Susan Dell Foundation
P.O. Box 163867
Austin, TX 78716-3867

Established in 1999 in TX.
Donor(s): Michael S. Dell.
Financial data (yr. ended 12/31/00): Grants paid, $5,475,861; assets, $224,270,856 (M);

expenditures, $10,339,538; qualifying distributions, $3,481,285.
Limitations: Applications not accepted. Giving primarily in Austin, TX.
Application information: Contributes only to pre-selected organizations.
Officers and Directors:* Michael S. Dell,* Pres.; Susan L. Dell,* 1st V.P.; Alexander Dell,* 2nd V.P.; Marc Lisker, Secy.; Tricia Dopieralski, Treas.
EIN: 364336415
Codes: FD

50553
El Paso Energy Foundation
(Formerly El Paso Natural Gas Foundation)
P.O. Box 2511
Houston, TX 77252-2511 (713) 420-2878
Application address: 1001 Louisiana, Houston, TX 77002
Contact: Karen King, Mgr.

Established in 1992 in TX.
Donor(s): El Paso Natural Gas Co.
Financial data (yr. ended 12/31/00): Grants paid, $5,427,182; assets, $11,957,306 (M); gifts received, $4,300,000; expenditures, $5,452,273; qualifying distributions, $5,426,185.
Limitations: Giving limited to AZ, NM, OK, TX, and UT.
Publications: Informational brochure (including application guidelines).
Application information: Application form required.
Officers and Directors:* William A. Wise,* Chair. and C.E.O.; Norma F. Dunn, Pres.; H. Brent Austin,* Exec. V.P. and C.F.O.; Britton White, Jr.,* Exec. V.P. and Genl. Counsel; Joel Richards III,* Exec. V.P.; C. Dana Rice, Sr. V.P. and Treas.; Jeffrey I. Beason, Sr. V.P. and Cont.; Basil R. Woller, Sr. V.P. and Gen. Aud.; Judy A. Vandgraff, Sr. V.P.; David L. Siddall, V.P., Corp. Secy. and Assoc. Genl. Counsel; Gregory W. Watkins, V.P.; Ralph Eads, John D. Hushon, Greg G. Jenkins, Robert G. Phillips, John W. Somerhalder II.
EIN: 742638185
Codes: CS, FD, CD, FM

50554
Community Foundation of North Texas
(Formerly The Community Foundation of Metropolitan Tarrant County)
Fort Worth Club Bldg.
306 W. 7th St., Ste. 306
Fort Worth, TX 76102 (817) 877-0702
FAX: (817) 877-1215; E-mail: hdowd@cfntx.org; URL: http://www.cfntx.org
Contact: Homer M. Dowd, Pres.

Established in 1981 in TX as a program of the United Way; status changed to independent community foundation in 1989.
Financial data (yr. ended 12/31/01): Grants paid, $5,343,311; assets, $97,033,486 (L); gifts received, $10,613,495; expenditures, $6,001,488.
Limitations: Giving primarily in northern TX.
Publications: Application guidelines, annual report, grants list, informational brochure.
Application information: Guidelines available on foundation Web site. Application form not required.
Officers and Directors:* Nicholas Martin, Jr.,* Chair.; Robert A. Ferguson,* Vice-Chair.; Homer M. Dowd,* Pres. and Exec. Dir.; Leslie Pope, V.P. Finance; Sally Werst McKeen,* Secy.; John Stevenson,* Treas.; L.D. Brightbill III, Benjamin Doskocil, Sr., Carol Dunaway, Crawford H. Edwards, Allen Hodges, Marty V. Leonard, Phillip W. McCrury, John Pergande, Edgar H. Schollmaier, E. Bruce Street, Martha S. Williams.
EIN: 752267767

Codes: CM, FD

50555
Hobby Family Foundation
2131 San Felipe
Houston, TX 77019-5620 (713) 521-1163
Contact: Jennifer Cole, Secy.

Established in 1995.
Donor(s): W.P. Hobby.
Financial data (yr. ended 12/31/00): Grants paid, $5,128,321; assets, $25,589,261 (M); expenditures, $5,256,918; qualifying distributions, $5,125,775.
Limitations: Giving primarily in TX.
Application information: Application form not required.
Officers and Trustees:* W.P. Hobby,* Pres.; Laura H. Beckworth,* V.P.; Diana P. Hobby,* V.P.; Paul W. Hobby, V.P.; Jennifer Cole, Secy.; Cathy Leeson, Treas.
EIN: 760489862
Codes: FD, FM

50556
The Eugene McDermott Foundation
3808 Euclid Ave.
Dallas, TX 75205 (214) 521-2924
Contact: Mrs. Mary McDermott Cook, Pres.

Incorporated in 1972 in TX; absorbed The McDermott Foundation in 1977.
Donor(s): Eugene McDermott,‡ Mrs. Eugene McDermott.
Financial data (yr. ended 08/31/01): Grants paid, $4,973,725; assets, $110,362,338 (M); expenditures, $5,164,191; qualifying distributions, $5,002,165.
Limitations: Giving primarily in Dallas, TX.
Application information: No printed material available. Application form not required.
Officers and Trustees:* Mary McDermott Cook,* Pres.; Charles E. Cullum,* V.P.; J.H. Cullum Clark, Mrs. Eugene McDermott, C.J. Thomsen.
Agent: Bank of America.
EIN: 237237919
Codes: FD, FM

50557
Vivian L. Smith Foundation
1900 W. Loop S., Ste. 1050
Houston, TX 77027-3207 (713) 986-8030
Contact: Amy Meckel

Established in 1981 in TX.
Donor(s): Vivian L. Smith.‡
Financial data (yr. ended 12/31/01): Grants paid, $4,795,000; assets, $74,974,878 (M); expenditures, $5,439,531; qualifying distributions, $4,813,874.
Publications: Application guidelines.
Application information: Application form not required.
Officers and Trustees:* Suzanne R. Benson,* Pres.; H. Devon Graham, Jr., V.P.; Janice R. Smith, Secy.-Treas.; H.L. Brown, Jr., Bobby Smith Cohn, Sandra Smith Dompier, Richard H. Skinner, Jack T. Trotter.
EIN: 760101380
Codes: FD, FM

50558
John S. Dunn Research Foundation
3355 W. Alabama, Ste. 720
Houston, TX 77098-1718 (713) 626-0368
Contact: Lloyd J. Gregory, Jr., M.D., Exec. V.P. and Medical Advisor

Established in 1985 in TX.
Donor(s): John S. Dunn, Sr.‡

Financial data (yr. ended 12/31/01): Grants paid, $4,718,346; assets, $97,868,336 (M); expenditures, $5,536,270; qualifying distributions, $4,988,191.
Limitations: Giving limited to TX.
Publications: Informational brochure (including application guidelines), application guidelines.
Application information: Application form not required.
Officers and Trustees:* John S. Dunn, Jr.,* Pres.; Lloyd J. Gregory, Jr., M.D.,* Exec. V.P. and Medical Advisor; C. Harold Wallace,* V.P. and Secy.; Milby Dow Dunn,* V.P. and Treas.; Dagmar Dunn Pickens Gipe,* V.P.; Charles W. Hall,* V.P.; J. Dickson Rogers,* V.P.
EIN: 741933660
Codes: FD, FM

50559
Swalm Foundation
11511 Katy Fwy., Ste. 430
Houston, TX 77079 (281) 497-5280
FAX: (281) 497-7340; URL: http://www.swalm.org
Contact: Mimi Minkoff, Secy., Admin. and Grant Mgr.

Established in 1980 in TX.
Donor(s): Beth C. Swalm, Dave C. Swalm, Texas Olefins Co.
Financial data (yr. ended 11/30/01): Grants paid, $4,710,947; assets, $79,695,598 (M); gifts received, $2,300,000; expenditures, $5,835,529; qualifying distributions, $5,185,884.
Limitations: Giving primarily in TX.
Publications: Application guidelines, financial statement, informational brochure (including application guidelines).
Application information: Application form required.
Officers and Directors:* Beth C. Swalm,* Chair.; Billy C. Ward,* C.E.O. and Pres.; Dave C. Swalm,* V.P.; Mimi Minkoff,* Secy., Admin. and Grant Mgr.; Mark C. Mendelovitz,* Treas.; Clark Swalm, Lisa Swalm, Valerie White.
EIN: 742073420
Codes: FD, FM

50560
The Effie and Wofford Cain Foundation
4131 Spicewood Springs Rd., Ste. A-1
Austin, TX 78759 (512) 346-7490
FAX: (512) 346-7491
Contact: Mrs. Lynn Fowler, Exec. Dir.

Incorporated in 1952 in TX.
Donor(s): Effie Marie Cain,‡ R. Wofford Cain.‡
Financial data (yr. ended 10/31/01): Grants paid, $4,468,033; assets, $95,664,554 (M); gifts received, $2,271,961; expenditures, $5,318,351; qualifying distributions, $4,865,251.
Limitations: Giving primarily in TX.
Publications: Application guidelines.
Application information: Organizations may re-apply for funding every other fiscal year. The foundation provides grants and contributions, on a highly selective basis, primarily to scientific/medical institutions and educational institutions. Substantially all of the grants and contributions are made to organizations with which the foundation has an existing historical relationship. Application form required.
Officers and Directors:* Franklin W. Denius,* Exec. V.P.; James B. Cain,* V.P.; John C. Cain,* V.P.; F. Wofford Denius,* V.P.; Charmaine D. McGill,* V.P.; Lynn Fowler, Secy.-Treas. and Exec. Dir.
EIN: 756030774
Codes: FD, FM

50561
Lee and Ramona Bass Foundation
309 Main St.
Fort Worth, TX 76102 (817) 336-0494
FAX: (817) 332-2176; E-mail:
cjohns@sidrichardson.org; URL: http://
www.sidrichardson.org/lrbf.htm
Contact: Valleau Wilkie, Jr., Exec. Dir.

Established in 1994 in TX.
Donor(s): Lee M. Bass.
Financial data (yr. ended 12/31/00): Grants paid, $4,316,500; assets, $42,148,101 (M); expenditures, $4,578,299; qualifying distributions, $4,334,262.
Limitations: Giving primarily in TX.
Publications: Annual report.
Application information: Application form not required.
Officers and Directors:* Lee M. Bass,* Pres. and Treas.; Ramona S. Bass,* V.P.; William P. Hallman, Jr.,* Secy.; Valleau Wilkie, Jr.,* Exec. Dir.
EIN: 752495163
Codes: FD, FM

50562
The Frank and Anyse Sue Mayborn Foundation
(Formerly Frank W. Mayborn Foundation)
10 S. 3rd St.
Temple, TX 76501-7619

Established in 1965 in TX.
Donor(s): Anyse Sue Mayborn.
Financial data (yr. ended 12/31/01): Grants paid, $4,300,778; assets, $13,947,785 (M); gifts received, $3,300,000; expenditures, $4,329,601; qualifying distributions, $4,291,393.
Limitations: Applications not accepted. Giving primarily in the central TX area.
Application information: Contributes only to pre-selected organizations.
Officers and Directors:* Anyse Sue Mayborn,* Pres. and Treas.; Jerry L. Arnold, Secy.; Jim D. Bowmer, Frank M. Burke, Jr.
EIN: 746067859
Codes: FD

50563
The CH Foundation
P.O. Box 94038
Lubbock, TX 79493-4038 (806) 792-0448
FAX: (806) 792-7824
Contact: Kay Sanford, Pres. and Grants Admin.

Established in 1976 in TX.
Donor(s): Christine DeVitt.‡
Financial data (yr. ended 12/31/01): Grants paid, $4,278,790; assets, $87,150,213 (M); expenditures, $5,674,932; qualifying distributions, $4,355,690.
Limitations: Giving primarily in Lubbock, TX and surrounding counties.
Publications: Grants list, application guidelines.
Application information: Application form not required.
Officers and Trustees:* Kay Sanford,* Pres. and Grants Admin.; Louise Willson Arnold,* V.P.; Don Graf,* Secy. and Exec. Dir.; Kevin McMahon,* Treas.; Nelda Thompson.
EIN: 751534816
Codes: FD, FM

50564
O'Donnell Foundation
100 Crescent Ct., Ste. 1660
Dallas, TX 75201-1884 (214) 871-5800
E-mail: info@odf.org; URL: http://www.odf.org
Contact: Carolyn R. Bacon, Exec. Dir.

Incorporated in 1957 in TX.
Donor(s): Peter O'Donnell, Jr., Edith Jones O'Donnell.
Financial data (yr. ended 11/30/01): Grants paid, $4,163,489; assets, $147,567,013 (M); gifts received, $650,000; expenditures, $5,568,685; qualifying distributions, $4,965,354.
Limitations: Giving primarily in TX.
Application information: Application form not required.
Officers and Directors:* Peter O'Donnell, Jr.,* Pres.; Rita C. Clements,* V.P.; Edith Jones O'Donnell,* Secy.-Treas.; Carolyn R. Bacon, Exec. Dir.; Duncan E. Boeckman, Philip O'B. Montgomery, Jr., M.D.
EIN: 756023326
Codes: FD, FM

50565
Leland Fikes Foundation, Inc.
3050 Lincoln Plz.
500 N. Akard St.
Dallas, TX 75201 (214) 754-0144
Contact: Nancy J. Solana, V.P., Research and Grant Admin.

Incorporated in 1952 in DE.
Donor(s): Leland Fikes,‡ Catherine W. Fikes.‡
Financial data (yr. ended 12/31/00): Grants paid, $4,085,900; assets, $75,784,531 (M); gifts received, $180,000; expenditures, $5,643,322; qualifying distributions, $4,336,801.
Limitations: Giving primarily in the Dallas, TX, area.
Publications: Application guidelines.
Application information: Submit proposal upon request. Application form not required.
Officers and Trustees:* Lee Fikes,* Pres. and Treas.; Nancy J. Solana, V.P., Research and Grant Admin. and Secy.; Amy L. Fikes,* V.P.; Brendan Fikes.
EIN: 756035984
Codes: FD, FM

50566
The Goldsbury Foundation
P.O. Box 460567
San Antonio, TX 78246-0567
Application address: 5121 Broadway, San Antonio, TX 78209, tel.: (210) 930-1251, ext. 12; E-mail: sfeldmann@goldsbury-foundation.org
Contact: Suzanne Mead Feldmann, Mgr.

Established in 1996 in TX.
Donor(s): Christopher Goldsbury, Jr.
Financial data (yr. ended 12/31/01): Grants paid, $4,060,257; assets, $10,699,427 (M); expenditures, $4,192,673; qualifying distributions, $4,173,588.
Limitations: Giving primarily in San Antonio, TX.
Application information: Application form not required.
Officers and Directors:* Christopher Goldsbury, Jr.,* Pres.; Rodney J. Sands,* V.P.; Richard A. Longoria Derby, Angela A. Goldsbury, John M. Lafferty, Ron Lichtenfeld, William Scanlon, Jr.
EIN: 742780083
Codes: FD

50567
Anne T. & Robert M. Bass Foundation
201 Main St., Ste. 2300
Fort Worth, TX 76102-3157 (817) 390-8400

Established in 1984 in TX.
Donor(s): Robert M. Bass.
Financial data (yr. ended 12/31/01): Grants paid, $3,954,270; assets, $18,489,539 (M); expenditures, $3,988,653; qualifying distributions, $3,949,227.
Limitations: Applications not accepted. Giving primarily in Fort Worth, TX.
Application information: Contributes only to pre-selected organizations.
Officers and Directors:* Anne T. Bass,* Pres.; Robert M. Bass,* V.P.; J. Taylor Crandall,* Secy.-Treas.
EIN: 752001892
Codes: FD

50568
Hamon Charitable Foundation
2626 Howell St., Ste. 905
Dallas, TX 75204

Established in 1998 in TX.
Donor(s): Nancy B. Hamon.
Financial data (yr. ended 12/31/01): Grants paid, $3,925,000; assets, $5,155,210 (M); expenditures, $4,314,791; qualifying distributions, $3,845,652.
Limitations: Applications not accepted. Giving primarily in TX.
Application information: Contributes only to pre-selected organizations.
Officers and Directors:* Nancy B. Hamon,* Pres.; Keith H. Perkins,* V.P. and Treas.; John L. Roach,* V.P.; Jennie M. Nash, Secy.
EIN: 752734057
Codes: FD

50569
Helen Jones Foundation, Inc.
P.O. Box 53665
Lubbock, TX 79453
Application address: 4603 92nd St., Lubbock, TX 79424, tel.: (806) 794-8078
Contact: Louise Arnold, Pres.

Established about 1984 in TX.
Donor(s): Helen DeVitt Jones.
Financial data (yr. ended 12/31/00): Grants paid, $3,891,500; assets, $95,815,138 (M); expenditures, $4,925,088; qualifying distributions, $1,908,423.
Limitations: Giving primarily in Lubbock, TX.
Application information: Application form not required.
Officers and Directors:* Louise Willson Arnold,* Pres.; James C. Arnold,* V.P.; Robert Neff Arnold,* Secy.; Randy L. Wright,* Treas.; Marianna Markham.
EIN: 751977748
Codes: FD

50570
Temple-Inland Foundation
303 S. Temple Dr.
P.O. Drawer 338
Diboll, TX 75941 (936) 829-1721
Contact: Evonne Nerren, Secy.-Treas.

Established in 1985 in TX.
Donor(s): Temple-Inland Inc.
Financial data (yr. ended 06/30/00): Grants paid, $3,808,323; assets, $78,747 (M); gifts received, $3,895,000; expenditures, $3,828,449; qualifying distributions, $3,828,449.
Limitations: Giving primarily in areas of company operations.
Officers and Directors:* Doyle R. Simmons,* Pres.; Roger B. Smart, V.P.; M. Richard Warner,* V.P.; Evonne Nerren, Secy.-Treas.; Kenneth R. Dubuque, Kenneth M. Jastrow II, Harold C. Maxwell, Jack C. Sweeny, Arthur Temple III.
EIN: 751977109
Codes: CS, FD, CD, FM, GTI

50571
The Abe and Annie Seibel Foundation
c/o Frost National Bank
P.O. Box 179
Galveston, TX 77553 (409) 763-1151
Contact: Janet L. Bertilino, Asst V.P. and Trust Off., Frost National Bank

Trust established in 1960 in TX.
Donor(s): Abe Seibel,‡ Annie Seibel.‡
Financial data (yr. ended 07/31/01): Grants paid, $3,597,017; assets, $37,426,142 (M); expenditures, $4,376,532; qualifying distributions, $4,019,460; giving activities include $3,597,017 for loans to individuals.
Limitations: Giving limited to graduates of TX high schools attending TX colleges and universities.
Publications: Application guidelines.
Application information: Application form required.
Directors: Phyllis Milstein, F.A. Odom.
Trustee: Frost National Bank.
EIN: 746035556
Codes: FD, GTI

50572
The L. J. Sevin Family Foundation
13455 Noel Rd., Ste. 1670
Dallas, TX 75240

Established in 2000 in NY.
Donor(s): L. J. Sevin.
Financial data (yr. ended 12/31/01): Grants paid, $3,575,000; assets, $405,849 (M); gifts received, $3,396,886; expenditures, $3,577,961; qualifying distributions, $3,574,504.
Limitations: Applications not accepted. Giving primarily in New Orleans, LA.
Application information: Contributes only to pre-selected organizations.
Trustees: Robert Paluck, Frederic A. Rubinstein, Jo D. Sevin, L. J. Sevin.
EIN: 137230889
Codes: FD

50573
Linda and Ken Lay Family
(Formerly Linda and Ken Lay Family Foundation)
2001 Kirby Dr., Ste. 1240
Houston, TX 77019
Contact: Holly Korman, Secy.

Established in 1994 in TX.
Financial data (yr. ended 12/31/00): Grants paid, $3,543,342; assets, $52,172,583 (M); gifts received, $14,542,683; expenditures, $3,853,374; qualifying distributions, $3,629,947.
Limitations: Applications not accepted. Giving primarily in TX.
Application information: Contributes only to pre-selected organizations; Unsolicited applications are not considered.
Officers and Directors:* Linda P. Lay,* Chair. and Pres.; Kenneth L. Lay,* V.P.; Holly Korman, Secy.; Robert R. Herrold, T. David Herrold, Mark K. Lay, Robyn Herrold-Lay Vermeil, Elizabeth A. Lay Vittor.
EIN: 760454168
Codes: FD

50574
The Cailloux Foundation
(also known as Floyd A. & Kathleen C. Cailloux Foundation)
P.O. Box 291276
Kerrville, TX 78029-1276 (830) 895-5222
FAX: (830) 895-5212; *E-mail:* info@cailouxfoundation.org; *URL:* http://www.cailouxfoundation.org
Contact: Barbara Gaither, Exec. Asst.

Established in 1994.
Donor(s): Floyd A. Cailloux,‡ Kathleen C. Cailloux.
Financial data (yr. ended 12/31/01): Grants paid, $3,409,259; assets, $65,487,971 (M); expenditures, $4,105,644; qualifying distributions, $3,605,540.
Limitations: Giving primarily in the TX Hill Country region.
Publications: Financial statement, program policy statement, application guidelines.
Application information: Application form required.
Officers and Directors:* F. O'Neil Griffin,* Chair.; W. Wayne Patterson,* Pres.; William R. Goertz,* V.P. and Secy.-Treas.; Jack Biegler.
EIN: 746422979
Codes: FD, FM

50575
The Priddy Foundation
807 8th St., Ste. 1010
Wichita Falls, TX 76301 (940) 723-8720
FAX: (940) 723-8656; *E-mail:* info@priddyfdn.org; *URL:* http://www.priddyfdn.org
Contact: Debbie C. White, Dir., Grants

Established in 1963 in TX.
Donor(s): Ashley H. Priddy,‡ Robert T. Priddy, Swannanoa H. Priddy,‡ Walter M. Priddy.‡
Financial data (yr. ended 12/31/01): Grants paid, $3,379,353; assets, $80,891,252 (M); gifts received, $1,603,482; expenditures, $4,068,168; qualifying distributions, $3,566,458.
Limitations: Giving primarily in an 120-mile radius of Wichita Falls, TX and within a 75-mile radius of Wichita Falls into OK.
Publications: Program policy statement, application guidelines, annual report (including application guidelines).
Application information: Application form required.
Officers and Trustees:* David Wolverton,* Pres.; Gale Richardson,* V.P.; Berneice Leath,* Secy.-Treas.; Debbie C. White, Dir., Grants; Rick Boone, Dick Bundy, Bill Daniel, Phyllis Hiraki, Martin Litteken, Nancy Marks, Jimmy Oakley, Betsy Priddy, Advisory Tr.; Randy Priddy, Advisory Tr.; Robert T. Priddy, Tr. Emeritus; Ruby Priddy, Advisory Tr.; Jesse Rogers, Ken Telg, Julia Whitmire, Beverly Williamson.
EIN: 756029882
Codes: FD

50576
The Ewing Halsell Foundation
711 Navarro St., Ste. 537
San Antonio, TX 78205 (210) 223-2640

Trust established in 1957 in TX.
Donor(s): Ewing Halsell,‡ Mrs. Ewing Halsell,‡ Grace F. Rider.‡
Financial data (yr. ended 06/30/00): Grants paid, $3,366,329; assets, $74,257,070 (M); expenditures, $4,303,386; qualifying distributions, $3,511,255.
Limitations: Giving limited to TX, with emphasis on southwestern TX, particularly San Antonio.
Publications: Biennial report (including application guidelines), program policy statement.
Application information: Application form not required.
Trustees: Gilbert M. Denman, Jr., Chair.; Edward H. Austin, Jr., Jean Deacy, Leroy G. Denman, Jr., Hugh A. Fitzsimmons, Jr.
EIN: 746063016
Codes: FD, FM

50577
Harold Simmons Foundation
3 Lincoln Ctr.
5430 LBJ Fwy., Ste. 1700
Dallas, TX 75240-2697 (972) 233-2134
Contact: Lisa Simmons Epstein, Pres.

Incorporated in 1988 in TX.
Donor(s): Contran Corp., NL Industries, Inc., and subsidiaries.
Financial data (yr. ended 12/31/99): Grants paid, $3,312,399; assets, $11,258,963 (M); gifts received, $2,800,000; expenditures, $3,337,220; qualifying distributions, $3,312,399.
Limitations: Giving limited to the Dallas and Fort Worth, TX, area.
Publications: Annual report, application guidelines.
Application information: Application form not required.
Officers and Directors:* Harold C. Simmons,* Chair.; Lisa Simmons Epstein,* Pres.; Steven L. Watson,* V.P. and Secy.; Eugene K. Anderson, Treas.; Keith A. Johnson, Cont.
EIN: 752222091
Codes: CS, FD, CD

50578
Bernard and Audre Rapoport Foundation
5400 Bosque Blvd., 245
Waco, TX 76710 (254) 741-0510
FAX: (254) 756-0510; *E-mail:* rapoport@texnet.net
Contact: Carole Jones, Fdn. Coord.

Established in 1988 in TX.
Donor(s): Audre Rapoport, Bernard Rapoport, Patricia Rapoport, Ronald B. Rapoport.
Financial data (yr. ended 12/31/00): Grants paid, $3,185,036; assets, $68,726,711 (M); expenditures, $3,971,274; qualifying distributions, $3,507,104.
Limitations: Giving on a national basis, with major emphasis on Waco, TX, including McKennan and surrounding counties; some support also in Israel.
Publications: Annual report, informational brochure (including application guidelines), newsletter, application guidelines.
Application information: Contact foundation for guidelines. Application form not required.
Officers and Trustees:* Bernard Rapoport,* Pres.; Audre Rapoport,* V.P.; Ronald B. Rapoport,* Secy.-Treas.; Maggie McCarthy, Exec. Dir.; James D. Chesney, Larry D. Jaynes, William A. Nesbitt, Kay Olson, Patricia W. Rapoport, Joel Schwartz.
EIN: 742479712
Codes: FD, FM

50579
The Cynthia & George Mitchell Foundation
10077 Grogan's Mill Rd., Ste. 475
The Woodlands, TX 77380
Application address: P.O. Box 5708, Austin, TX 78763-5708, tel.: (512) 474-8887
Contact: Meredith Mitchell Dreiss, Mgr.

Established in 1981.
Donor(s): Cynthia W. Mitchell, George P. Mitchell.

50579—TEXAS

Financial data (yr. ended 12/31/01): Grants paid, $3,162,500; assets, $13,358,010 (M); gifts received, $122,000; expenditures, $3,340,213; qualifying distributions, $3,340,213.
Limitations: Giving limited to TX.
Officers and Trustees:* George P. Mitchell,* Pres. and Treas.; Cynthia W. Mitchell,* V.P and Secy.; Meredith Mitchell Dreiss, Mgr.; Pamela K. Maguire, Mgr.; G. Scott Mitchell.
EIN: 742170127
Codes: FD

50580
The Hamill Foundation
1160 Dairy Ashford, Ste. 250
Houston, TX 77079 (281) 556-9581
FAX: (281) 556-0456; E-mail: cread@lconn.net
Contact: Charlie H. Read, Pres.

Established in 1969 in TX.
Donor(s): Marie G. Hamill,‡ Claud B. Hamill.‡
Financial data (yr. ended 12/31/01): Grants paid, $3,074,145; assets, $65,255,973 (M); expenditures, $4,463,365; qualifying distributions, $3,276,169.
Limitations: Applications not accepted. Giving primarily in Houston, TX.
Application information: Contributes only to pre-selected organizations.
Officers and Directors:* Charles D. McMurrey,* Chair.; Charlie H. Read,* C.E.O. and Pres.; Thomas H. Brown,* V.P., Secy., and Grants Dir.; Charles W. Snider,* V.P.; William T. Miller.
EIN: 237028238
Codes: FD

50581
Cooper Industries Foundation
600 Travis, Ste. 5800
Houston, TX 77002-1001 (713) 209-8607
Application address: P.O. Box 4446, Houston, TX 77210-4446, tel.: (713) 209-8800; FAX: (713) 209-8982; E-mail: info@cooperindustries.com; URL: http://www.cooperindustries.com/about/index.htm
Contact: Jennifer L. Evans, Secy. and Dir., Community Affairs

Incorporated in 1964; absorbed Crouse-Hinds Foundation in 1982; absorbed McGraw-Edison Foundation in 1985.
Donor(s): Cooper Industries, Inc., Gerda Kaudisch.‡
Financial data (yr. ended 12/31/01): Grants paid, $3,032,117; assets, $1,738,448 (M); expenditures, $3,044,765; qualifying distributions, $3,032,117.
Limitations: Giving in Houston, TX, and other communities of company operations in AL, AR, CA, CO, CT, FL, GA, IL, ME, MI, MO, MS, NC, NV, NY, OH, OR, PA, SC, TX, and WI.
Publications: Application guidelines, annual report.
Application information: Requests that are local in nature will be referred to the nearest local operation for recommendation. Application form not required.
Officers and Trustees:* H. John Riley, Jr.,* Chair.; Vicki B. Guennewig,* Pres.; Jennifer L. Evans, Secy. and Dir., Community Affairs; D. Bradley McWilliams,* Treas.; D.K. Schumacher.
EIN: 316060698
Codes: CS, FD, CD, FM

50582
The Clayton Fund, Inc.
c/o J.P. Morgan Private Bank
P.O. Box 2558
Houston, TX 77252-8037 (713) 216-4513
Contact: Charlene Slack

Trust established in 1952 in TX.
Donor(s): William L. Clayton,‡ Susan V. Clayton.‡
Financial data (yr. ended 12/31/00): Grants paid, $3,012,000; assets, $56,130,249 (M); expenditures, $3,527,117; qualifying distributions, $2,955,468.
Limitations: Giving primarily in TX.
Publications: Application guidelines.
Application information: Request application guidelines. Application form not required.
Officers and Trustees:* Burdine C. Johnson,* Pres.; William L. Garwood, Jr.,* V.P.; William C. Baker, J.P. Morgan Private Bank.
EIN: 760285764
Codes: FD

50583
Roy and Christine Sturgis Charitable and Educational Trust
c/o Bank of America
P.O. Box 830241
Dallas, TX 75283-0241 (214) 209-1965
Contact: Daniel J. Kelly, V.P., Bank of America

Established in 1981 in AR.
Donor(s): Christine Sturgis.‡
Financial data (yr. ended 09/30/00): Grants paid, $3,002,500; assets, $60,820,561 (M); expenditures, $3,656,005; qualifying distributions, $3,134,460.
Limitations: Giving primarily in AR and the Dallas, TX, area.
Publications: Application guidelines, program policy statement.
Application information: No personal interviews granted. Application form required.
Trustee Bank: Bank of America.
EIN: 756331832
Codes: FD, FM

50584
The Feldman Foundation
7800 Stemmons Fwy.
Dallas, TX 75247
Application address: P.O. Box 1046, Dallas, TX 75221
Contact: Robert L. Feldman, Tr.

Trust established in 1946 in TX.
Donor(s): Commercial Metals Co., and subsidiaries.
Financial data (yr. ended 12/31/01): Grants paid, $3,001,580; assets, $31,571,159 (M); gifts received, $1,054,137; expenditures, $3,507,461; qualifying distributions, $3,129,418.
Limitations: Giving primarily in NY and TX.
Application information: Application form not required.
Trustees: Daniel E. Feldman, Moses Feldman, Robert L. Feldman.
EIN: 756011578
Codes: CS, FD, CD, FM

50585
David Weekley Family Foundation
1111 N. Post Oak Rd.
Houston, TX 77055

Established in 1990.
Donor(s): David M. Weekley, Bonnie S. Weekley.
Financial data (yr. ended 12/31/99): Grants paid, $2,957,061; assets, $25,926,311 (M); gifts received, $8,947,519; expenditures, $2,997,004; qualifying distributions, $2,949,359.
Limitations: Applications not accepted. Giving primarily in Houston, TX.
Application information: Contributes only to pre-selected organizations.
Officers: David M. Weekley, Pres.; Weldon T. Weekley, Secy.; Bonnie S. Weekley, Treas.
EIN: 760324538
Codes: FD

50586
Sterling-Turner Foundation
(Formerly Turner Charitable Foundation)
815 Walker St., Ste. 1543
Houston, TX 77002-5724 (713) 237-1117
FAX: (713) 223-4638; E-mail: eyvonne@wt.net
Contact: Eyvonne Moser, Exec. Dir.

Incorporated in 1960 in TX.
Donor(s): Isla Carroll Turner,‡ P.E. Turner.‡
Financial data (yr. ended 12/31/00): Grants paid, $2,954,250; assets, $54,868,277 (M); expenditures, $3,298,845; qualifying distributions, $2,993,034.
Limitations: Giving limited to TX.
Publications: Application guidelines, annual report (including application guidelines).
Application information: Contact foundation for guidelines. Application form required.
Officers and Trustees:* T.R. Reckling III,* Pres.; Bert F. Winston, Jr.,* V.P.; Christiana R. McConn,* Secy.; Isla C. Reckling,* Treas.; Eyvonne Moser, Exec. Dir.; Thomas E. Berry, Blake W. Caldwell, Carroll R. Goodman, Chaille W. Hawkins, James S. Reckling, John B. Reckling, Stephen M. Reckling, T.R. "Cliffe" Reckling IV, Thomas K. Reckling, L. David Winston, Bert F. Winston III.
EIN: 741460482
Codes: FD

50587
Mamie McFaddin Ward Heritage Foundation
c/o Hibernia National Bank
P.O. Box 3928
Beaumont, TX 77704-3928
Contact: Jean Moncla, V.P. and Trust Off., Hibernia National Bank

Established in 1976 in TX.
Donor(s): Mamie McFaddin Ward.‡
Financial data (yr. ended 12/31/01): Grants paid, $2,924,790; assets, $33,188,671 (M); expenditures, $3,084,759; qualifying distributions, $2,910,932.
Limitations: Giving limited to Jefferson County, TX.
Publications: Application guidelines.
Application information: Application form required.
Trustees: Eugene H.B. McFaddin, James L.C. McFaddin, Jr., Ida M. Pyle, Rosine M. Wilson, Hibernia National Bank.
EIN: 746260525
Codes: FD

50588
El Paso Community Foundation
P.O. Box 272
El Paso, TX 79943-0272 (915) 533-4020
FAX: (915) 532-0716; E-mail: grants@epcf.org; URL: http://www.epcf.org
Contact: Janice W. Windle, Pres.

Incorporated in 1977 in TX.
Financial data (yr. ended 12/31/00): Grants paid, $2,828,028; assets, $99,399,763 (M); gifts received, $4,516,975; expenditures, $5,907,466.
Limitations: Giving limited to the El Paso, TX, area.
Publications: Annual report, application guidelines, newsletter, informational brochure.

Application information: Only 1 request per year per applicant will be considered by the board. Application form not required.
Officers and Directors:* Joe Alcantar, Jr.,* Chair.; Frances R. Axelson,* Vice-Chair.; Tommye Duncan,* Vice-Chair.; Janice W. Windle, Pres.; Virginia Kemendo, Exec. V.P.; Nestor Valencia, V.P., Plan.; Cathy Hill, V.P.; Carl E. Ryan, Secy.; Marylee Warwick,* Treas.; Margaret Varner Bloss, Yvonne Carrillo, Lillian Crouch, Mabel Fayant, Richard H. Feuille, Tom Hussmann, Jose Manuel Mascarenas, Don Melendez, Guillermo Ochoa, Rebeca Ramos, Mary Carmen Saucedo, Dorothy White.
EIN: 741839536
Codes: CM, FD

50589
Burlington Resources Foundation
(Formerly Burlington Resources/Meridian Oil Foundation)
5051 Westheimer St., Ste. 1400
Houston, TX 77050-2124 (713) 624-9366
Contact: Dee McBride, Admin.

Established in 1994.
Donor(s): Burlington Resources Inc.
Financial data (yr. ended 12/31/00): Grants paid, $2,804,803; assets, $10,905,678 (M); gifts received, $6,280,087; expenditures, $2,809,642; qualifying distributions, $2,804,803.
Limitations: Giving primarily in TX and elsewhere in the Southwest in areas of company locations.
Application information: Application form required.
Officers and Directors:* Bobby S. Shackouls,* Chair.; Gavin H. Smith,* Pres.; Steven J. Shapiro,* Sr. V.P. and C.F.O.; Joseph P. McCoy, Sr. V.P. and Cont.; L. David Hanower,* Sr. V.P.; Daniel D. Hawk, V.P. and Treas.; Frederick J. Plaeger II, Sr. V.P. and Genl. Counsel; Jeffery P. Monte, Corp. Secy.; Ernesto Gomez, Tax Off.
EIN: 760453686
Codes: CS, FD, CD

50590
Hatton W. Sumners Foundation for the Study and Teaching of Self Government, Inc.
(Formerly Hatton W. Sumners Foundation)
325 N. Saint Paul St., Ste. 3920
Dallas, TX 75201-3817 (214) 220-2128
Additional tel.: (214) 953-0737
Contact: Hugh C. Akin, Exec. Dir.

Trust established in 1949 in TX, became a Texas nonprofit corporation in 1998.
Financial data (yr. ended 12/31/00): Grants paid, $2,800,651; assets, $64,706,119 (M); gifts received, $11,050; expenditures, $3,762,323; qualifying distributions, $3,033,034.
Limitations: Giving primarily in TX and the southwestern states.
Publications: Application guidelines, informational brochure (including application guidelines).
Application information: Application form not required.
Officers and Trustees:* James Cleo Thompson, Jr.,* Chair.; Alfred Paul Murrah, Jr.,* Vice-Chair.; William C. Pannell,* Secy.; Thomas S. Walker,* Treas.; Hugh Clark Akin, Exec. Dir.; Gordon R. Carpenter, David Drumm, Pete Geren, David Long, Charles Moore.
EIN: 752734032
Codes: FD

50591
The Challenge Foundation
PMB 302
1900 Preston Road, No. 267
Plano, TX 75093 (972) 567-3573
FAX: (972) 867-3265; *E-mail:* information@challengefoundation.org; *URL:* http://www.challengefoundation.org
Contact: William M. Steinbrook, Jr., Exec. Dir.

Established in 1988 in GA.
Donor(s): John D. Bryan.
Financial data (yr. ended 12/31/00): Grants paid, $2,797,277; assets, $21,025,069 (M); gifts received, $4,317,225; expenditures, $3,197,451; qualifying distributions, $3,175,943.
Publications: Program policy statement, application guidelines.
Application information: Charter schools funded through Request For Proposal process. Application form required.
Officer: William Steinbrook, Jr., Exec. Dir.
Trustees: John D. Bryan, Martha Bryan.
EIN: 581817816
Codes: FD, FM

50592
M. G. and Lillie A. Johnson Foundation, Inc.
P.O. Box 2269
Victoria, TX 77902 (361) 575-7970
FAX: (361) 575-2264; *E-mail:* mgj@cox-internet.com
Contact: Robert Halepeska, Exec. V.P.

Incorporated in 1958 in TX.
Donor(s): M.G. Johnson,‡ Lillie A. Johnson.‡
Financial data (yr. ended 11/30/01): Grants paid, $2,781,905; assets, $51,612,794 (M); expenditures, $3,200,977; qualifying distributions, $2,788,137.
Limitations: Giving limited primarily to TX. Recent giving exclusively to the Texas Gulf Coast area, including Brazoria, Matagorda, Wharton, Colorado, Lavaca, Jackson, Calhoun, Victoria, DeWitt, Gonzales, Karnes, Bee, Goliad, Refugio, and Aransas counties.
Publications: Application guidelines.
Application information: Application form not required.
Officers and Trustees:* M.H. Brock,* Pres.; Robert Halepeska, Exec. V.P.; Lloyd Rust,* V.P.; Munson Smith,* Secy.; James Bouligny, Dick Koop, Jack R. Morrison, Terrell Mullins.
EIN: 746076961
Codes: FD

50593
Nelda C. and H. J. Lutcher Stark Foundation
P.O. Box 909
Orange, TX 77631-0909 (409) 883-3513
FAX: (409) 883-3530
Contact: Walter G. Riedel III, Chair.

Incorporated in 1961 in TX.
Donor(s): H.J. Lutcher Stark,‡ Nelda C. Stark.‡
Financial data (yr. ended 02/28/01): Grants paid, $2,669,101; assets, $180,492,769 (M); gifts received, $15,500,125; expenditures, $6,294,620; qualifying distributions, $5,575,624.
Limitations: Giving limited to southwestern LA, and TX.
Publications: Annual report, application guidelines.
Application information: Application form not required.
Officers and Trustees:* W.G. Riedel III,* Chair.; Eunice R. Benckenstein,* Vice-Chair.; Roy Wingate,* Secy.; Laurence R. David,* Treas.; R. Frederick Gregory, M.D., Clyde V. McKee, Jr., H.J. Lutcher Stark II.

EIN: 746047440
Codes: FD

50594
Lamar Bruni Vergara Trust
P.O. Box 734
Laredo, TX 78042-0734

Established in 1990 in TX.
Donor(s): Lamar Bruni Vergara.‡
Financial data (yr. ended 12/31/01): Grants paid, $2,664,206; assets, $57,442,992 (M); expenditures, $3,054,864; qualifying distributions, $2,664,206.
Limitations: Applications not accepted. Giving primarily in Laredo, TX.
Application information: Contributes only to pre-selected organizations.
Trustees: Solomon Casseb, Jr., J.C. Martin III.
EIN: 746374699
Codes: FD, FM

50595
Harry S. and Isabel C. Cameron Foundation
c/o Bank of America
P.O. Box 2518
Houston, TX 77252-2518
Contact: Diane Guiberteau

Established in 1966 in TX.
Donor(s): Isabel C. Cameron.‡
Financial data (yr. ended 06/30/01): Grants paid, $2,637,786; assets, $35,053,822 (M); expenditures, $2,968,246; qualifying distributions, $2,643,323.
Limitations: Giving primarily in TX, with emphasis on Houston.
Application information: Application form not required.
Directors: Priscilla Bormet, David W. Cameron, Sylvia J. Cameron, Estelle Cameron Maloney, Frances Cameron Miller.
Trustee: Bank of America.
EIN: 746073312
Codes: FD

50596
The Rogers Foundation
601 Chase Dr.
Tyler, TX 75701-9431 (903) 561-4041
Application address: P.O. Box 8799, Tyler, TX 75711
Contact: Robyn M. Rogers, Pres.

Established in 1986 in TX.
Donor(s): Robert M. Rogers.‡
Financial data (yr. ended 12/31/01): Grants paid, $2,569,167; assets, $43,693,587 (M); gifts received, $420,000; expenditures, $2,894,826; qualifying distributions, $2,546,989.
Limitations: Giving primarily in Tyler, TX.
Publications: Informational brochure (including application guidelines).
Application information: Application form required.
Officers and Directors:* Robyn M. Rogers,* Pres.; Sheryl Rogers Palmer,* V.P.; Paul W. Powell,* Treas.
EIN: 752143064
Codes: FD

50597
Perkins-Prothro Foundation
2304 Midwestern Pkwy., Ste. 200
Wichita Falls, TX 76308-2334 (940) 723-7163

Established in 1967.
Donor(s): Lois Perkins,‡ Charles N. Prothro, Elizabeth P. Prothro.
Financial data (yr. ended 12/31/00): Grants paid, $2,548,478; assets, $48,488,665 (M); gifts

50597—TEXAS

received, $9,386,884; expenditures, $2,789,727; qualifying distributions, $2,588,971.
Limitations: Applications not accepted. Giving limited to TX, with emphasis on Wichita Falls.
Application information: Contributes only to pre-selected organizations.
Officers and Trustees:* Joe N. Prothro,* Pres.; Elizabeth P. Prothro,* V.P.; Kathryn Prothro Yeager,* V.P.; K. Elizabeth Yeager,* Secy.; Mark H. Prothro,* Treas.; David H. Prothro.
EIN: 751247407
Codes: FD

50598
Dora Roberts Foundation
c/o Bank One, Texas, N.A.
P.O. Box 2050
Fort Worth, TX 76113 (817) 884-4442
Contact: Rick Piersall, V.P. and Trust Off., Bank One, Texas, N.A.

Trust established in 1948 in TX.
Donor(s): Dora Roberts.‡
Financial data (yr. ended 06/30/01): Grants paid, $2,522,454; assets, $40,798,084 (M); expenditures, $3,312,218; qualifying distributions, $2,831,791.
Limitations: Giving limited to TX, with emphasis on Big Spring.
Advisory Board: J.P. Taylor, Chair.; Lisa Canter, Roger Canter, Mrs. Horace Garrett, Bob Moore, Sue Garrett Partee, R.H. Weaver.
Trustee: Bank One, Texas, N.A.
EIN: 756013899
Codes: FD

50599
Albert & Ethel Herzstein Charitable Foundation
6131 Westview Dr.
Houston, TX 77055-5421 (713) 681-7868
E-mail: albertandethel@herzsteinfoundation.org;
URL: http://www.herzsteinfoundation.org
Contact: L. Michael Hajtman, Pres.

Established in 1965 in TX.
Donor(s): Albert H. Herzstein,‡ Ethel Avis Herzstein,‡ Sadie Herzstein Smith,‡ and members of the Herzstein family.
Financial data (yr. ended 12/31/00): Grants paid, $2,498,372; assets, $44,255,428 (M); gifts received, $2,286,131; expenditures, $2,982,658; qualifying distributions, $2,672,276.
Limitations: Giving primarily in TX.
Publications: Informational brochure (including application guidelines), application guidelines.
Application information: Application form not required.
Officer: L. Michael Hajtman, Pres.
Directors: Richard Loewenstern, George W. Strake, Jr., Nathan Topek, M.D.
EIN: 746070484
Codes: FD

50600
Helen Greathouse Charitable Trust
c/o Wells Fargo Bank Texas, N.A.
P.O. Box 1959
Midland, TX 79702

Established in 1997 in TX.
Financial data (yr. ended 12/31/01): Grants paid, $2,489,500; assets, $30,137,094 (M); expenditures, $3,004,311; qualifying distributions, $2,446,089.
Limitations: Giving primarily in TX.
Application information: Application form required.
Trustees: Joan Baskin, Joann Foster, Terry Maddox, John Younger, Wells Fargo Bank Texas, N.A.
EIN: 752691859

Codes: FD

50601
Strake Foundation
712 Main St., Ste. 3300
Houston, TX 77002-3210 (713) 216-2400
FAX: (713) 216-2401; *E-mail:* foundation@strake.org
Contact: George W. Strake, Jr., Pres.

Trust established in 1952 in TX; incorporated in 1983.
Donor(s): George W. Strake, Sr.,‡ Susan K. Strake,‡ George W. Strake, Jr., Susan S. Dilworth,‡ Georganna S. Parsley.
Financial data (yr. ended 12/31/01): Grants paid, $2,454,750; assets, $53,290,527 (M); expenditures, $2,797,748; qualifying distributions, $2,617,982.
Limitations: Giving primarily in TX, especially Houston; no grants outside the U.S.
Publications: Annual report (including application guidelines), application guidelines, informational brochure.
Application information: Application form required.
Officers and Directors:* George W. Strake, Jr.,* Pres. and Treas.; Paul L. Robison, Jr., Exec. Dir.
EIN: 760041524
Codes: FD, FM

50602
The M. S. Doss Foundation, Inc.
P.O. Box 1677
Seminole, TX 79360-1677 (915) 758-2770
Contact: Joe K. McGill, Pres.

Established in 1985 in TX.
Donor(s): M.S. Doss,‡ Meek Lane Doss,‡ Twin Mountain Supply, Inc.
Financial data (yr. ended 12/31/01): Grants paid, $2,388,044; assets, $53,439,176 (M); expenditures, $3,011,352; qualifying distributions, $2,522,902; giving activities include $73,918 for programs.
Limitations: Giving primarily in the eastern NM and western TX area; giving limited to Gaines County, TX, for scholarships.
Application information: Scholarship payments made directly to the college on behalf of named recipient. Application form required.
Officers and Trustees:* Joe K. McGill,* Chair. and Pres.; Richard Spraberry,* V.P.; Billie Thompson,* Secy.; Stuart Robertson,* Treas.; Julia Narvarte Romanow.
EIN: 751945227
Codes: FD

50603
Amarillo Area Foundation, Inc.
801 S. Fillmore, Ste. 700
Amarillo, TX 79101 (806) 376-4521
FAX: (806) 373-3656; *E-mail:* haf@aaf-hf.org;
URL: http://aaf-hf.org
Contact: Jim Allison, Pres. and Exec. Dir.

Established as a trust in 1957 in TX.
Financial data (yr. ended 12/31/00): Grants paid, $2,362,450; assets, $50,585,654 (M); gifts received, $4,225,128; expenditures, $3,225,319.
Limitations: Giving limited to the 26 northernmost counties of the TX Panhandle.
Publications: Annual report, application guidelines, newsletter.
Application information: Specific application format required. Application form required.
Officers and Directors:* Fay Moore,* Chair.; Bud Joyner,* 1st Vice-Chair.; Lilia Escajeda,* 2nd Vice-Chair.; Jim Allison, Pres. and Exec. Dir.; Julie Attebury,* Secy.; and 21 additional directors.

EIN: 750978220
Codes: CM, FD, FM, GTI

50604
The Looper Foundation
11757 Katy Freeway, Ste. 1400
Houston, TX 77079

Established in 1997 in TX.
Donor(s): Doris Looper, Terry Looper.
Financial data (yr. ended 06/30/01): Grants paid, $2,258,500; assets, $2,512,120 (M); gifts received, $806,121; expenditures, $2,282,083; qualifying distributions, $2,254,049.
Limitations: Applications not accepted. Giving primarily in Colorado Springs, CO.
Application information: Contributes only to pre-selected organizations.
Officers: Terry Looper, Pres. and Treas.; Doris Looper, V.P. and Secy.
EIN: 760330594
Codes: FD

50605
George and Mary Josephine Hamman Foundation
910 Travis St., Ste. 1990
Houston, TX 77002-5816 (713) 658-8345
URL: http://www.hammanfoundation.org
Contact: E. Alan Fritsche, Exec. Dir.

Incorporated in 1954 in TX.
Donor(s): Mary Josephine Hamman,‡ George Hamman.‡
Financial data (yr. ended 12/31/01): Grants paid, $2,241,500; assets, $56,654,713 (M); expenditures, $3,031,860; qualifying distributions, $2,427,647.
Limitations: Giving only in the state of TX for grants. Scholarships to high school seniors is limited to the immediate Houston area.
Publications: Application guidelines, financial statement.
Application information: Application form required.
Officers and Directors:* Henry R. Hamman,* Pres.; Anne H. Shepherd, Secy.; Charles D. Milby, Jr., Treas.; E. Alan Fritsche, Exec. Dir.; Mary M. Brown, Russell R. Hamman.
EIN: 746061447
Codes: FD, GTI

50606
John M. O'Quinn Foundation
(Formerly The O'Quinn Foundation)
3518 Travis, Ste. 200
Houston, TX 77002
Application address: 440 Louisiana, Houston,TX 77002, tel.: (713) 236-2659
Contact: John M. O'Quinn, Pres.

Established in 1986 in TX.
Donor(s): John M. O'Quinn.
Financial data (yr. ended 12/31/99): Grants paid, $2,230,158; assets, $51,549,713 (M); gifts received, $25,115,237; expenditures, $2,401,166; qualifying distributions, $2,281,143.
Limitations: Giving primarily in Houston, TX.
Application information: Application form not required.
Officers: John M. O'Quinn, Pres.; Robert A. Higley, Secy.-Treas.
Trustee: David Griffis.
EIN: 760206844
Codes: FD

50607
Harry S. Moss Heart Trust
c/o Bank of America
901 Main St., P.O. Box 830241
Dallas, TX 75283-0241   (214) 209-1965
Contact: Daniel J. Kelly, V.P., Bank of America

Trust established in 1973 in TX.
Donor(s): Harry S. Moss,‡ Florence M. Moss.‡
Financial data (yr. ended 09/30/00): Grants paid, $2,167,000; assets, $42,161,945 (M); expenditures, $2,434,097; qualifying distributions, $2,152,180.
Limitations: Giving limited to TX, with emphasis on Dallas County.
Publications: Application guidelines, program policy statement.
Application information: No new applications or grants through 2002; all funds are committed. Application form not required.
Trustee: Bank of America.
EIN: 756147501
Codes: FD

50608
Pauline Allen Gill Foundation
1901 N. Akard St.
Dallas, TX 75201   (214) 521-7243
Contact: Pauline G. Sullivan, Pres.

Established in 1975 in TX.
Donor(s): Pauline Allen Gill Sullivan.
Financial data (yr. ended 12/31/01): Grants paid, $2,116,145; assets, $31,721,111 (M); gifts received, $12,998; expenditures, $2,300,343; qualifying distributions, $2,114,100.
Limitations: Applications not accepted. Giving primarily in Dallas, TX.
Application information: Contributes only to pre-selected organizations.
Officers and Trustees:* Pauline Allen Gill Sullivan,* Pres. and Mgr.; B. Gill Clements,* V.P. and Treas.; Nancy Clements Seay,* V.P.; George E. Seay III, Secy.
EIN: 237431528
Codes: FD

50609
Community Foundation of Abilene
500 Chestnut, Ste. 1509
P.O. Box 1001
Abilene, TX 79604   (915) 676-3883
FAX: (915) 676-4206; *E-mail:* cfa@abilene.com; *URL:* http://www.abilene.com/communityfoundation
Contact: Nancy E. Jones, Pres.

Incorporated in 1985 in TX.
Financial data (yr. ended 06/30/00): Grants paid, $2,105,255; assets, $32,102,939 (M); expenditures, $2,613,008.
Limitations: Giving limited to the Abilene, TX, area.
Publications: Annual report, application guidelines, newsletter.
Application information: Call foundation for grant guidelines and deadline information. Application form not required.
Officers and Trustees:* Dave Copeland,* Chair.; Bob Surovik,* Vice-Chair.; Nancy E. Jones, Pres.; Bobbie Wolfe,* Treas.; Patti Holloway, Sam Reeves, and 10 additional trustees.
EIN: 752045832
Codes: CM, FD

50610
Hal & Charlie Peterson Foundation
515 Jefferson St.
P.O. Box 293870
Kerrville, TX 78029-3870   (830) 896-2262
FAX: (830) 896-2283; *E-mail:* hcpfdn@ktc.com
Contact: John Mosty, Secy.-Treas.

Established in 1944 in TX.
Donor(s): Hal Peterson,‡ Charlie Peterson.‡
Financial data (yr. ended 12/31/01): Grants paid, $2,083,782; assets, $52,714,417 (M); gifts received, $49,537; expenditures, $2,405,112; qualifying distributions, $2,218,232.
Limitations: Giving primarily in Kerr County, TX, and adjacent counties, and to state or national organizations with a local chapter in this area.
Publications: Informational brochure (including application guidelines), program policy statement, application guidelines.
Application information: Application form required.
Officers and Directors:* Scott Parker,* Pres.; W.H. Cowden, Jr.,* V.P.; John Mosty,* Secy.-Treas.; Charles H. Johnston, Nowlin McBryde, C.D. Peterson, James Stehling.
EIN: 741109626
Codes: FD, FM

50611
Caesar Kleberg Foundation for Wildlife Conservation
711 Navarro St., Ste. 535
San Antonio, TX 78205
FAX: (210) 223-3657
Contact: Leroy G. Denman, Jr., Tr.

Trust established about 1951 in TX.
Donor(s): Caesar Kleberg.‡
Financial data (yr. ended 12/31/00): Grants paid, $2,073,000; assets, $44,824,445 (M); gifts received, $2,500; expenditures, $2,705,421; qualifying distributions, $2,068,293.
Application information: Application form not required.
Trustees: Leroy G. Denman, Jr., Stephen J. Kleberg, Duane M. Leach.
EIN: 746038766
Codes: FD

50612
The Dell Foundation
Round Rock 1, Box 8045
1 Dell Way
Round Rock, TX 78682-9426
E-mail: the_dell_foundation@dell.com; *URL:* http://www.dell.com/dellfoundation
Contact: Michele Glaze

Established in 1995.
Donor(s): Dell Computer Corp.
Financial data (yr. ended 01/31/02): Grants paid, $2,059,760; assets, $11,565,003 (M); gifts received, $93,311; expenditures, $1,850,313; qualifying distributions, $2,059,760.
Limitations: Giving primarily in middle TN and central TX.
Publications: Application guidelines.
Application information: Only on-line applications accepted. Application form required.
Officers and Directors:* Thomas B. Green,* Chair.; Michele Moore,* Secy.; Kevin Nater, Treas.; Carl Everett, Alex Smith, Carl Stolle, Cathy Thompson, Brian Wood.
EIN: 742732496
Codes: CS, FD, CD

50613
T. J. Brown and C. A. Lupton Foundation, Inc.
Fort Worth Club Bldg.
306 W. 7th St., Ste. 309
Fort Worth, TX 76102

Incorporated in 1942 in TX.
Donor(s): T.J. Brown,‡ C.A. Lupton,‡ V.J. Earnhart, J.A. Gooch.
Financial data (yr. ended 12/31/00): Grants paid, $2,010,000; assets, $43,329,779 (M); expenditures, $2,341,877; qualifying distributions, $2,074,161.
Limitations: Applications not accepted. Giving primarily in Fort Worth, TX.
Application information: Contributes only to pre-selected organizations.
Officer and Directors:* Sam P. Woodson III,* Pres.; Tav Holmes Berry, Whitfield J. Collins, Charles Lupton Geren, Kit Tennison Moncrief, Lee Lupton Tennison, William E. Tucker.
EIN: 750992690
Codes: FD

50614
The J. S. Bridwell Foundation
807 8th St., Ste. 500
Wichita Falls, TX 76301-3365

Incorporated in 1949 in TX.
Donor(s): J.S. Bridwell,‡ Margaret B. Bowdle.
Financial data (yr. ended 12/31/01): Grants paid, $1,968,205; assets, $40,822,399 (M); expenditures, $2,151,183; qualifying distributions, $1,996,283.
Limitations: Applications not accepted. Giving primarily in Wichita Falls, TX.
Application information: Contributes only to pre-selected organizations.
Officers: Mac W. Cannedy, Jr., Pres.; Herbert B. Story, V.P.; Paul Schoppa, Jr., Secy.; Clifford G. Tinsley, Treas.
Directors: Ralph S. Bridwell, Terry M. Walker.
EIN: 756032988
Codes: FD

50615
Rose-Marie and Jack R. Anderson Foundation
c/o Neil R. Anderson
16475 Dallas Pkwy., Ste. 735
Addison, TX 75001-0682

Established in 1994 in TX.
Donor(s): Jack R. Anderson, Rose-Marie Anderson.
Financial data (yr. ended 12/31/00): Grants paid, $1,914,000; assets, $35,081,511 (M); expenditures, $1,999,342; qualifying distributions, $1,944,325.
Limitations: Applications not accepted. Giving on a national basis.
Application information: Contributes only to pre-selected organizations.
Officers and Directors:* Neil R. Anderson,* Pres. and Treas.; Rose-Marie Anderson,* Secy.; Jack R. Anderson, Gail Anderson Canizares, Barbara Anderson McDonald.
EIN: 752542403
Codes: FD

50616
Courtney S. Turner Charitable Trust
c/o Bank of America
P.O. Box 831041
Dallas, TX 75283-1041
Application address: c/o Bank of America, 1200 Main St., 14th Fl., Kansas City, MO, 64105, tel.: (816) 979-7481
Contact: David P. Ross, Sr. V.P., Bank of America

Established in 1986 in MO.
Donor(s): Courtney S. Turner.

Financial data (yr. ended 12/31/01): Grants paid, $1,912,907; assets, $34,149,209 (M); expenditures, $2,215,119; qualifying distributions, $2,039,982.
Limitations: Giving primarily in Atchison KS, and Kansas City, MO.
Application information: Application form not required.
Trustees: Daniel C. Weary, Bank of America.
EIN: 436316904
Codes: FD

50617
Carl B. and Florence E. King Foundation
5956 Sherry Ln., Ste. 620
Dallas, TX 75225
Contact: Carl Yeckel, Pres.

Incorporated in 1966 in TX.
Donor(s): Carl B. King,‡ Florence E. King,‡ Dorothy E. King.‡
Financial data (yr. ended 12/31/00): Grants paid, $1,907,429; assets, $49,127,096 (M); expenditures, $4,511,179; qualifying distributions, $3,168,741.
Limitations: Giving primarily in the Dallas, TX, area.
Publications: Program policy statement, application guidelines.
Application information: Application forms required for scholarships only and available from the Texas Interscholastic League and the Dallas YMCA. The foundation makes no direct scholarships or student loans to individuals.
Officers: Carl L. Yeckel, Pres.; Jack C. Phipps, V.P.; Thomas W. Vett, Secy.-Treas.
Directors: Arden R. Grover, William D. Jordan, Daniel P. Junkin.
EIN: 756052203
Codes: FD, GTI

50618
Elizabeth Huth Coates Charitable Foundation of 1992
c/o Broadway National Bank
P.O. Box 17001
San Antonio, TX 78217-0001
Contact: Nancy F. May, V.P. and Trust Off., Broadway National Bank

Established in 1993 in TX.
Donor(s): Elizabeth Huth Coates.‡
Financial data (yr. ended 12/31/01): Grants paid, $1,853,825; assets, $35,761,748 (M); expenditures, $1,960,684; qualifying distributions, $1,841,667.
Limitations: Giving primarily in San Antonio, TX.
Application information: Application form not required.
Trustee: Broadway National Bank.
EIN: 746399782
Codes: FD

50619
Reese Foundation
P.O. Box 1745
Austin, TX 78767-1745

Established in 1998 in TX.
Donor(s): Michael S. Reese, Pamela W. Reese.
Financial data (yr. ended 12/31/00): Grants paid, $1,833,333; assets, $3,034,056 (M); gifts received, $500,000; expenditures, $1,847,689; qualifying distributions, $1,833,333.
Limitations: Applications not accepted. Giving primarily in CA and TX.
Application information: Contributes only to pre-selected organizations.
Directors: Dawn Michelle Reese, Michael S. Reese, Pamela W. Reese.

EIN: 742883252
Codes: FD

50620
Morgan Charitable Foundation, Inc.
801 Laurel St.
Beaumont, TX 77701-2228 (409) 838-1000
Contact: Glen W. Morgan, Pres.

Established in 1998 in TX.
Donor(s): Glen W. Morgan.
Financial data (yr. ended 12/31/01): Grants paid, $1,825,500; assets, $442,779 (M); expenditures, $1,827,472; qualifying distributions, $1,825,202.
Limitations: Giving primarily in Beaumont, TX.
Application information: Application form not required.
Officer: Glen W. Morgan, Pres.
EIN: 760589391
Codes: FD

50621
The Summerlee Foundation
5956 Sherry Ln., Ste. 610
Dallas, TX 75225-8025 (214) 363-9000
FAX: (214) 363-1941; E-mail: info@summerlee.org; URL: http://www.summerlee.org
Contact: Melanie Lambert, V.P., for animal welfare, or John W. Crain, V.P., for Texas history

Established in 1988 in TX.
Donor(s): Annie Lee Roberts.‡
Financial data (yr. ended 06/30/01): Grants paid, $1,804,225; assets, $52,188,414 (M); expenditures, $3,072,176; qualifying distributions, $2,470,288.
Limitations: Giving primarily in TX.
Publications: Biennial report (including application guidelines), grants list, application guidelines.
Application information: Application form not required.
Officers and Directors:* Hon. David D. Jackson,* Pres.; Melanie Lambert,* V.P. and Treas.; John W. Crain,* V.P.; Lynne Starnes, Secy.; Ron Tyler.*
EIN: 752252355
Codes: FD

50622
George & Fay Young Foundation, Inc.
5520 LBJ Fwy., Ste. 540
Dallas, TX 75240 (972) 404-4001
FAX: (972) 385-8990
Contact: Carol Young Marvin, Pres.

Established in 1993 in TX as successor to George & Fay Young Charitable Foundation.
Donor(s): George Young,‡ Fay Cameron Young.‡
Financial data (yr. ended 11/30/01): Grants paid, $1,800,356; assets, $43,973,272 (M); gifts received, $3,807,018; expenditures, $2,291,495; qualifying distributions, $1,808,448.
Limitations: Giving primarily in Dallas and Fort Worth, TX.
Publications: Application guidelines.
Application information: Application form not required.
Officers and Directors:* Carol Young Marvin,* Pres.; Richard L. Ripley,* Secy.; John Franklin, John T. Green, L. Edward Marvin.
EIN: 752478225
Codes: FD

50623
Franklin Lindsay Student Aid Fund
c/o JPMorgan Chase Bank
P.O. Box 550
Austin, TX 78789-0001 (512) 479-2645
FAX: (512) 479-2656; E-mail: info@FranklinLindsay.org
Contact: JoAnn Parks, Admin. Off.

Trust established in 1957 in TX.
Donor(s): Franklin Lindsay.‡
Financial data (yr. ended 12/31/00): Grants paid, $1,784,677; assets, $18,056,645 (M); expenditures, $2,138,507; qualifying distributions, $2,086,186; giving activities include $1,784,677 for loans to individuals.
Limitations: Giving limited to loans for students at institutions of higher learning in TX.
Publications: Program policy statement, application guidelines, informational brochure.
Application information: Address completed application to appropriate loan committee member (depending on area of TX where student resides). Application form required.
Loan Committee: Charles Barnes, Alvin P. Bormann, Jr., M.H. Connelly, John D. Dollard, Jack W. Hall, William Hearn, Edgar Jablonowski, Fred Jones, James R. Kay, Michael Novak, Jan L. Patterson, Dorothy Ray, Alfred Rodriguez, Tookie Spoor, James W. Stegall, Mary Swanson.
Trustee: JPMorgan Chase Bank.
EIN: 746031753
Codes: FD, GTI

50624
The Burdine Johnson Foundation
P.O. Box 1230
Buda, TX 78610 (512) 312-1336
Contact: Robert C. Giberson, Tr.

Trust established in 1960 in TX.
Donor(s): Burdine C. Johnson, J.M. Johnson.
Financial data (yr. ended 12/31/00): Grants paid, $1,778,750; assets, $37,877,712 (M); expenditures, $1,880,873; qualifying distributions, $1,759,514.
Limitations: Giving primarily in TX.
Application information: Application form not required.
Trustees: Robert C. Giberson, William T. Johnson, Martha L. Mattox.
EIN: 746036669
Codes: FD

50625
The David Robinson Foundation
P.O. Box 780577
San Antonio, TX 78278 (210) 696-8061
FAX: (210) 696-7754

Established in 1992 in TX.
Donor(s): David Robinson, Valerie Robinson.
Financial data (yr. ended 08/31/00): Grants paid, $1,769,377; assets, $4,213,561 (M); gifts received, $133,212; expenditures, $1,795,121; qualifying distributions, $176,840.
Limitations: Giving primarily in San Antonio, TX.
Application information: Application form required.
Directors: David Robinson, Valerie R. Robinson.
EIN: 742644713
Codes: FD

50626
Halliburton Foundation, Inc.
2601 Beltline Rd.
Carrollton, TX 75006
Application address: 3600 Lincoln Plz., 500 N. Akard, Dallas, TX 75201
Contact: Celeste Colgan, V.P. and Secy.

Incorporated in 1965 in TX.
Donor(s): Halliburton Co., Brown & Root, Inc., and other subsidiaries.
Financial data (yr. ended 12/31/00): Grants paid, $1,746,644; assets, $15,679,123 (M); gifts received, $1,406,603; expenditures, $1,795,753; qualifying distributions, $1,776,688.
Limitations: Giving primarily in the Southwest, with emphasis on TX.
Application information: Application form not required.
Officers and Trustees:* David J. Lesar,* Pres.; Margaret E. Carriere,* V.P. and Secy.; Jerry H. Blurton, V.P. and Treas.; Susan S. Keith, Gary V. Morris.
EIN: 751212458
Codes: CS, FD, CD

50627
East Texas Communities Foundation, Inc.
(Formerly East Texas Area Foundation)
315 N. Broadway, Ste. 210
Tyler, TX 75702 (903) 533-0208
Application address: P.O. Box 1432, Tyler, TX 75710; FAX: (903) 533-0258; E-mail: etcf@tyler.net
Contact: Nancy Lamar, Pres. and Exec. Dir.

Established in 1989 in TX.
Financial data (yr. ended 12/31/99): Grants paid, $1,688,871; assets, $9,036,693 (M); gifts received, $6,172,696; expenditures, $1,857,145.
Limitations: Giving primarily in eastern TX.
Publications: Annual report, informational brochure, newsletter.
Application information: Application form not required.
Officers and Trustees:* Allen Burt,* Chair.; Nancy Lamar,* Pres.; Mike Allen, Secy.; Mel Lovelady,* Treas.; Elaine Biddle, Carl Bochow, Jeff Buford, Herb Buie, Linda Butter, Nelson Clyde IV, Bob Dobbs, Kevin Eltife, Dawn Franks, Bill Martin, Fred Nichols, John Payne, James Perkins, A.W. Riter, Jr., Sam Roosth, Sandy Shepard, Norman Shtofman, Fred Smith, Tom Smith.
EIN: 752309138
Codes: CM, FD

50628
The Waco Foundation
900 Austin Ave., Ste. 1000
Waco, TX 76701-1949 (254) 754-3404
FAX: (254) 753-2887; E-mail: info@wacofoundation.org or tomc@wacofoundation.org; URL: http://www.wacofoundation.org
Contact: Tom H. Collins, Jr., Exec. Dir.

Established in 1958 in TX.
Financial data (yr. ended 03/31/02): Grants paid, $1,667,440; assets, $40,248,102 (L); gifts received, $1,402,157; expenditures, $1,865,522.
Limitations: Giving limited to McLennan County, TX.
Publications: Annual report, grants list, informational brochure, program policy statement, application guidelines.
Application information: Application form required.
Officers and Directors:* Nelwyn Reagan,* Chair.; Hal Whitaker,* Vice-Chair.; Nancy Callan, Secy.; Tom H. Collins, Jr.,* Exec. Dir.; Rick Bostwick, Louis Englander, David Horner, Beth Mayfield, William R. Pakis, Art Pertile, Tom Salome.
EIN: 746054628
Codes: CM, FD

50629
Ernest L. Kurth, Jr. Charitable Foundation
P.O. Box 831041
Dallas, TX 75283
Application address: P.O. Box 1506, Lufkin, TX 75902-1506, tel.: (936) 632-6450
Contact: Wyatt Leinart, Tr.

Established in 1983.
Donor(s): Ernest L. Kurth.‡
Financial data (yr. ended 12/31/00): Grants paid, $1,657,322; assets, $26,503,761 (M); gifts received, $309,604; expenditures, $1,826,872; qualifying distributions, $1,644,603.
Limitations: Giving primarily in Angelina County, TX.
Application information: Application form required.
Directors: Mary Ann Adams, Lynn Fisher, James Gibbs, Trey Henderson, Henry Holubec, Sandra G. Kurth, Joe McElroy.
Trustees: Wyatt Leinart, Bank of America.
EIN: 751862248
Codes: FD

50630
Kelly Gene Cook, Sr. Charitable Foundation, Inc.
278 Waterford Way
Montgomery, TX 77356 (936) 449-6272
Application address: c/o Carolyn Bost, 1675 Lakeland Dr., Ste. 507, Jackson, MS 39216, tel.: (601) 981-1116; FAX: (936) 597-7783; Montgomery, TX FAX: (601) 981-1146; E-mail: Pegpool@aol.com, or kgccf@ayrix.net
Contact: Peggy Cook Pool, Pres.

Incorporated in 1986 in TX.
Donor(s): Kelly G. Cook,‡ Peggy Cook Pool.
Financial data (yr. ended 12/31/00): Grants paid, $1,631,003; assets, $35,975,941 (M); expenditures, $1,887,446; qualifying distributions, $1,714,816.
Limitations: Giving primarily in LA, MS, and TX.
Application information: Apply to the financial aid office at Millsaps College, the University of Mississippi, Mississippi State University, or the University of Southern Mississippi; the foundation makes final selection of recipients. Application form required.
Officers and Directors:* Peggy Cook Pool,* Pres.; Deborah Rochelle,* V.P.; JoAnn Mikell,* Secy.; Corbin Barnes,* Treas.; Robert Kneppler, Jr.
EIN: 760201807
Codes: FD, GTI

50631
Harris and Eliza Kempner Fund
2201 Market St., Ste. 601
Galveston, TX 77550-1529 (409) 762-1603
FAX: (409) 762-5435; E-mail: information@kempnerfund.org; URL: http://www.kempnerfund.org
Contact: Elaine R. Perachio, Exec. Dir.

Established in 1946 in TX.
Donor(s): Various interests and members of the Kempner family.
Financial data (yr. ended 12/31/01): Grants paid, $1,629,504; assets, $41,263,559 (M); gifts received, $6,128; expenditures, $1,903,883; qualifying distributions, $2,175,222; giving activities include $100,000 for program-related investments and $271,339 for loans to individuals.
Limitations: Giving primarily in Galveston County, TX.
Publications: Annual report (including application guidelines).
Application information: Computerized solicitations not considered. Student loans are restricted. Application form not required.
Officers and Trustees:* Robert L.K. Lynch,* Chair.; John Thornton Currie,* Vice-Chair.; Barbara Weston Sasser,* Secy.; Peter Kempner Thompson, M.D.,* Treas.; Elaine R. Perachio, Exec. Dir.; Hetta Towler Kempner, Isaac Herbert Kempner III, James Lee Kempner, Lyda Ann Quinn Thomas, Daniel Kempner Thorne.
EIN: 760680130
Codes: FD, GTI

50632
The Constantin Foundation
4809 Cole Ave., LB 127
Dallas, TX 75205-3578 (214) 522-9300
Contact: Betty S. Hillin, Exec. Dir.

Trust established in 1947 in TX.
Donor(s): E. Constantin, Jr.,‡ Mrs. E. Constantin, Jr.‡
Financial data (yr. ended 12/31/00): Grants paid, $1,617,300; assets, $43,358,309 (M); expenditures, $1,980,912; qualifying distributions, $1,658,923.
Limitations: Giving limited to Dallas County, TX.
Publications: Application guidelines.
Application information: Application form not required.
Officer: Betty S. Hillin, Exec. Dir.
Trustees: Henry C. Beck, Jr., Gene H. Bishop, Harvey Berryman Cash, Roy Gene Evans, Joseph Boyd Neuhoff, Joel T. Williams, Jr.
EIN: 756011289
Codes: FD

50633
The Ellwood Foundation
P.O. Box 550049
Houston, TX 77255 (713) 785-5507
Contact: H. Wayne Hightower, Tr.

Trust established in 1958 in TX.
Donor(s): D.C. Ellwood,‡ Irene L. Ellwood.‡
Financial data (yr. ended 09/30/01): Grants paid, $1,600,030; assets, $31,764,853 (M); expenditures, $1,824,890; qualifying distributions, $1,554,373.
Limitations: Giving primarily in the Houston, TX, area.
Application information: Application form not required.
Trustees: H. Wayne Hightower, H. Wayne Hightower, Jr., Raybourne Thompson, Jr.
EIN: 746039237
Codes: FD

50634
Margaret & James A. Elkins, Jr. Foundation
1166 First City Tower
1001 Fannin St.
Houston, TX 77002
Contact: Lauren Baird

Established in 1956 in TX.
Financial data (yr. ended 10/31/01): Grants paid, $1,598,500; assets, $27,981,226 (M); expenditures, $2,004,393; qualifying distributions, $1,598,500.
Limitations: Giving primarily in TX, with emphasis on the metropolitan Houston area.
Application information: Application form not required.
Trustees: J.A. Elkins, Jr., James A. Elkins III.
EIN: 746051746

50634—TEXAS

Codes: FD

50635
The Wolslager Foundation
P.O. Box 1191
San Angelo, TX 76902
FAX: (915) 486-9053
Contact: Shirley Rogers, Secy.-Treas.

Established in 1993.
Donor(s): J.W. Wolslager, Josephine S. Wolslager.‡
Financial data (yr. ended 12/31/01): Grants paid, $1,598,334; assets, $33,949,701 (M); gifts received, $153,213; expenditures, $1,879,609; qualifying distributions, $1,598,334.
Limitations: Giving limited to the Tucson and Huachaca areas, AZ, Las Cruces, NM, and San Angelo and El Paso, TX.
Application information: Application form not required.
Officers and Trustees:* J.W. Wolslager,* Pres.; Stephen J. Wolslager, V.P.; Shirley M. Rogers,* Secy.-Treas.; F.B. Murski, W. Truett Smith, J.W. Wolslager, Jr.
EIN: 752493763
Codes: FD

50636
Bell Trust
660 Preston Forest Ctr., Box 289
Dallas, TX 75230-2718 (972) 788-4151
Contact: Barry D. Packer, Exec. Tr.

Trust established in 1956 in TX.
Donor(s): R.S. Bell,‡ Katharine Bell.‡
Financial data (yr. ended 12/31/00): Grants paid, $1,584,969; assets, $24,729,600 (M); gifts received, $23,317; expenditures, $1,697,579; qualifying distributions, $1,616,435.
Application information: Application form not required.
Trustees: Barry D. Packer, Exec. Tr.; Betty Bell Muns, James N. Muns, John B. Muns, Barbara Bell Packer, C. Philip Slate, Harold Taylor.
EIN: 756020180
Codes: FD

50637
M. B. and Edna Zale Foundation
(Formerly The Zale Foundation)
3102 Maple Ave., Ste. 225
Dallas, TX 75201 (214) 855-0627
Contact: Leonard R. Krasnow, Pres.

Incorporated in 1951 in TX.
Donor(s): Members of the Zale family.
Financial data (yr. ended 12/31/01): Grants paid, $1,578,834; assets, $31,715,909 (M); gifts received, $328,107; expenditures, $2,388,133; qualifying distributions, $2,010,537.
Limitations: Giving primarily in FL, NY, and TX.
Publications: Annual report, program policy statement, application guidelines, informational brochure (including application guidelines).
Application information: Application form not required.
Officers and Trustees:* Donald Zale,* Chair.; Leonard R. Krasnow, Pres.; George Tobolowsky, Secy.-Treas.; Sheryl Falik, David Fields, Leo Fields, Dana Gerard, Janet Zale Giesse, Gloria Landsberg, Steven Landsberg, Margie Plough, Michael F. Romaine, Karen Seltzer, Julie Tobolowsky, Stanley Zale.
EIN: 756037429
Codes: FD

50638
Zimmer Family Foundation
5803 Glenmont
Houston, TX 77081 (713) 295-7200
Contact: David Edwab, Vice-Chair.

Established in 1992 in TX.
Donor(s): George Zimmer, Donna Zimmer, Robert E. Zimmer.
Financial data (yr. ended 12/31/99): Grants paid, $1,574,864; assets, $7,884,805 (M); expenditures, $1,598,275; qualifying distributions, $1,584,302.
Limitations: Giving primarily in CA and TX.
Officers: George Zimmer, Chair.; David Edwab, Vice-Chair.; Michael Conlon, Secy.; Gary Ckodre, Treas.
Trustees: Lynn Zimmer, Robert Zimmer.
EIN: 760370782
Codes: FD, GTI

50639
Caroline Wiess Law Foundation
2001 Kirby Dr., Ste. 713
Houston, TX 77019
Contact: Caroline W. Law, Pres.

Established in 1983 in TX.
Donor(s): Caroline Wiess Law.
Financial data (yr. ended 12/31/00): Grants paid, $1,559,927; assets, $27,662,924 (M); gifts received, $400,000; expenditures, $1,644,034; qualifying distributions, $1,555,554.
Limitations: Applications not accepted. Giving limited to Houston, TX.
Application information: Contributes only to pre-selected organizations.
Officers and Trustees:* Caroline W. Law,* Pres.; Jo Marsh,* V.P.; Peter C. Marzio,* V.P.; James A. Elkins III,* Secy.; Larry E. Wuebbels,* Treas.
EIN: 760077285
Codes: FD

50640
Dr. Bob and Jean Smith Foundation
(Formerly Bob Smith, M.D. Foundation)
3811 Turtle Creek Ctr.
No. 2150 LB 53
Dallas, TX 75219 (214) 521-3461
Contact: Sally Smith, Grant Coord. or Patty Smith, C.F.O.

Established in 1989 in TX.
Financial data (yr. ended 09/30/01): Grants paid, $1,553,664; assets, $27,136,316 (M); expenditures, $2,117,983; qualifying distributions, $1,620,975.
Limitations: Giving primarily in the Dallas, TX, area.
Publications: Application guidelines.
Application information: Application form not required.
Officers and Directors:* C.R. Smith, M.D.,* Chair. and C.E.O.; Jean K. Smith,* Vice-Chair.; Patty A. Smith,* Pres., Secy.-Treas. and C.F.O.; Marty S. Kelley, George A. Nicoud, Jr., Sally Smith, Scott R. Smith.
EIN: 510137245
Codes: FD

50641
The Robert R. and Kay M. Onstead Foundation
600 Travis, Ste. 6475
Houston, TX 77002-3007 (713) 227-5884
Contact: Robert R. Onstead, Pres.

Established in 1993 in TX.
Donor(s): Robert R. Onstead, Kay M. Onstead.
Financial data (yr. ended 12/31/01): Grants paid, $1,549,000; assets, $29,755,389 (M); gifts received, $747,883; expenditures, $1,728,926; qualifying distributions, $1,525,963.

Limitations: Giving primarily in TX.
Officers: Robert R. Onstead, Pres.; Kay M. Onstead, V.P.
Trustees: Ann Onstead Hill, R. Randall Onstead, Jr.
EIN: 760417998
Codes: FD

50642
Lowe Foundation
5151 San Felipe, Ste. 400
Houston, TX 77056-3607 (713) 622-5420
Contact: Barbara Hendry, Secy.

Established in 1988 in TX.
Donor(s): Erma Lowe,‡ Maralo, Inc., Mary Ralph Lowe.
Financial data (yr. ended 12/31/01): Grants paid, $1,531,118; assets, $29,658,304 (M); gifts received, $2,327,482; expenditures, $1,699,547; qualifying distributions, $1,526,283.
Limitations: Giving limited to TX.
Application information: Application form required.
Officers and Trustees:* Mary Ralph Lowe,* Pres.; Diana Strauss,* V.P.; Barbara Hendry, Secy.; Geoffrey Perrin, Treas.; Patricia Fleming, Melinda Perrin, Anita Stude, Clayton Yost.
EIN: 760262645
Codes: FD

50643
Providence Journal Charitable Foundation
400 S. Record St.
Dallas, TX 75202
Application address: 75 Fountain St., Providence, RI 02902
Contact: Board of Trustees

Trust established in 1956 in RI.
Donor(s): The Providence Journal Co.
Financial data (yr. ended 12/31/00): Grants paid, $1,515,567; assets, $17,296,020 (M); expenditures, $1,115,392; qualifying distributions, $1,502,135.
Limitations: Giving primarily in RI, with emphasis on Providence.
Trustees: Sandra J. Radcliffe, Henry D. Sharpe, Jr., Joel N. Stark, Howard G. Sutton, John W. Wall.
EIN: 056015372
Codes: CS, FD, CD

50644
The Nightingale Code Foundation
1001 McKinney, Ste. 1900
Houston, TX 77002 (713) 265-0270
Contact: Michael Zilkha

Established in 1998 in TX.
Donor(s): Michael Zilkha.
Financial data (yr. ended 12/31/00): Grants paid, $1,514,104; assets, $9,693,865 (M); expenditures, $1,574,322; qualifying distributions, $1,425,530.
Limitations: Applications not accepted. Giving primarily in New York, NY, and TX.
Officers: Michael Zilkha, Pres.; Joseph Romano, Secy.
Director: Cornelia O'Leary Zilkha.
EIN: 760574572
Codes: FD

50645
The Belo Foundation
(Formerly A. H. Belo Corporation Foundation)
400 S. Record St., Ste. 200
Dallas, TX 75202-4841 (214) 977-6661
Contact: Becky Odlozil, Exec. Dir.

Established in 1995 in TX as successor to The Dallas Morning News - WFAA Foundation.
Donor(s): A.H. Belo Corp., Belo Corp.

Financial data (yr. ended 12/31/00): Grants paid, $1,501,928; assets, $53,257,593 (M); expenditures, $2,212,610; qualifying distributions, $1,709,416.
Limitations: Giving primarily in areas of company operations, including Phoenix and Tucson, AZ, Riverside, CA, Louisville, KY, New Orleans, LA, Boise, ID, Charlotte, NC, Portland, OR, Providence, RI, Austin, Dallas-Fort Worth, Houston, and San Antonio, TX, the Hampton-Norfolk, VA, area, Spokane, and the Seattle-Tacoma area, WA.
Publications: Informational brochure, application guidelines.
Application information: Application form not required.
Officers and Trustees:* Burl Osborne,* Chair.; Judith Garret Segura,* Pres.; Becky Odlozil, Exec. Dir.; Robert W. Decherd, Ward L. Huey, Jr., James M. Moroney, Jr.
EIN: 752564365
Codes: CS, FD, CD

50646
Amon G. Carter Star-Telegram Employees Fund
P.O. Box 17480
Fort Worth, TX 76102 (817) 332-3535
Contact: Mrs. Nenetta Carter Tatum, Pres.

Established in 1945 in TX.
Donor(s): Fort Worth Star-Telegram, Amon G. Carter,‡ KXAS-TV, WBAP Radio.
Financial data (yr. ended 04/30/01): Grants paid, $1,491,669; assets, $31,392,491 (M); expenditures, $1,621,638; qualifying distributions, $1,561,934.
Limitations: Giving primarily in Tarrant County, TX.
Application information: Individual assistance available only to employees and children of employees of the Fort Worth Star-Telegram, KXAS-TV, and WBAP Radio. Application form not required.
Officers: Nenetta Carter Tatum, Pres.; Mark L. Johnson, V.P.; John H. Robinson, Secy.-Treas.
EIN: 756014850
Codes: CS, FD, CD, GTI

50647
Kinder Foundation, Inc.
(Formerly Richard D. Kinder Foundation, Inc.)
3355 Del Monte Dr.
Houston, TX 77019
Contact: Nancy G. Kinder, Pres.

Established in 1994 in TX.
Donor(s): Richard D. Kinder.
Financial data (yr. ended 12/31/01): Grants paid, $1,485,764; assets, $22,925,361 (M); expenditures, $1,559,205; qualifying distributions, $1,502,242.
Limitations: Applications not accepted. Giving primarily in Washington, DC, MO, NY and TX.
Application information: Contributes only to pre-selected organizations.
Officers: Richard D. Kinder, Chair.; Nancy G. Kinder, Pres.; Katherine Kinder Howes, V.P. and Secy.-Treas.
Director: Peggy B. Menchaca.
EIN: 760519073
Codes: FD

50648
Susan Vaughan Foundation, Inc.
(Formerly McAshan Foundation, Inc.)
c/o J. P. Morgan Private Bank
P.O. Box 2558
Houston, TX 77252-8037 (713) 216-4513
Contact: Charlene D. Slack; or Bill Askey, Trust Off., JP Morgan Private Bank

Trust established in 1952 in TX; reorganized in 1991 under current name.
Donor(s): Susan C. McAshan, Susan Vaughan Clayton Trust No. 1.
Financial data (yr. ended 12/31/99): Grants paid, $1,477,000; assets, $32,834,530 (M); expenditures, $1,740,874; qualifying distributions, $1,471,913.
Limitations: Giving limited to Houston and Austin, TX.
Publications: Application guidelines.
Application information: Application form not required.
Trustees: Susan C. Garwood, Duncan E. Osborne, Elizabeth B. Osborne.
EIN: 760285765
Codes: FD

50649
The Mattsson McHale Foundation
5301 Mary Anna Dr.
Austin, TX 78746 (512) 329-0410
Contact: Christine Mattsson, Dir.

Established in 1995 in TX.
Donor(s): John McHale.
Financial data (yr. ended 12/31/99): Grants paid, $1,469,250; assets, $24,709,841 (M); gifts received, $2,274; expenditures, $1,658,339; qualifying distributions, $1,469,250.
Limitations: Giving primarily in TX.
Application information: Application form not required.
Directors: Christine Mattsson, Sharon Mattsson, John McHale.
EIN: 752623152
Codes: FD

50650
Estill Foundation
4022 Lowman St.
Corpus Christi, TX 78411-3133
(361) 851-2813
Contact: Jeannette Holloway, Pres.

Established in 1976.
Donor(s): Gentry Estill,‡ Jeannette Holloway.
Financial data (yr. ended 09/30/00): Grants paid, $1,463,135; assets, $78,279 (M); gifts received, $1,555,548; expenditures, $1,491,480; qualifying distributions, $1,487,231.
Limitations: Giving primarily in TX.
Officers: Jeannette Holloway, Pres.; Alice K.E. Johnson, V.P.; Mary Maurer, Secy.-Treas.
EIN: 741892894
Codes: FD

50651
Ray C. Fish Foundation
2001 Kirby Dr., Ste. 1005
Houston, TX 77019 (713) 522-0741
Contact: Paula Hooton, Secy.

Incorporated in 1957 in TX.
Donor(s): Raymond Clinton Fish,‡ Mirtha G. Fish.‡
Financial data (yr. ended 06/30/01): Grants paid, $1,443,090; assets, $29,928,494 (M); gifts received, $91,737; expenditures, $2,075,230; qualifying distributions, $1,561,168.
Limitations: Giving primarily in TX, with emphasis on Houston.
Publications: Financial statement, informational brochure (including application guidelines), application guidelines.
Application information: Application form not required.
Officers and Trustees:* Barbara F. Daniel,* Pres.; Robert J. Cruikshank,* V.P.; James L. Daniel, Jr.,* V.P.; Paula Hooton,* Secy.; Christopher J. Daniel,* Treas.; Catherine Daniel.
EIN: 746043047
Codes: FD

50652
Marcus & Anne Rosenberg Foundation
12020 Excelsior Way
Dallas, TX 75230 (972) 934-1809
Contact: Marcus Rosenberg, Pres.

Established in 1986 in TX.
Donor(s): Anne Rosenberg, Marcus Rosenberg, Steve Rosenberg.
Financial data (yr. ended 12/31/01): Grants paid, $1,430,730; assets, $2,878,836 (M); expenditures, $1,491,797; qualifying distributions, $1,425,301.
Limitations: Giving primarily in New York, NY, and Dallas, TX.
Application information: Application form required.
Officers and Directors:* Marcus Rosenberg,* Pres.; Anne Rosenberg,* V.P.; Steven Rosenberg,* V.P.
EIN: 752141473
Codes: FD

50653
Hawn Foundation, Inc.
4809 Cole Ave., Ste 225
Dallas, TX 75205 (214) 219-4809
FAX: (214) 219-2809
Contact: Joe V. Hawn, Jr., Pres.

Incorporated in 1962 in TX.
Donor(s): Mildred Hawn,‡ W.R. Hawn,‡ Mary C. Hawn.‡
Financial data (yr. ended 08/31/01): Grants paid, $1,403,500; assets, $35,650,587 (M); gifts received, $4,021,320; expenditures, $1,646,287; qualifying distributions, $1,536,498.
Limitations: Giving primarily in TX, with emphasis on Dallas.
Application information: Application form not required.
Officers and Directors:* Joe V. Hawn, Jr.,* Pres.; Audrey N. Hawn, V.P.; John J. Patterson, Secy.; Edward A. Copley, William Russell Hawn, Jr., Grady Jordan, I.N. Taylor.
EIN: 756036761
Codes: FD

50654
The Hoglund Foundation
3729 Normandy
Dallas, TX 75205 (214) 526-6522
FAX: (214) 526-6465; E-mail: khc@hoglundfdtn.org; URL: http://www.hoglundfdtn.org
Contact: Mrs. Kelly H. Compton, Exec. Dir.

Established in 1989 in TX.
Donor(s): Forrest E. Hoglund.
Financial data (yr. ended 12/31/01): Grants paid, $1,392,562; assets, $44,898,978 (M); gifts received, $2,934,075; expenditures, $1,706,637; qualifying distributions, $1,500,467.
Limitations: Giving primarily in Dallas and Houston, TX.
Publications: Application guidelines.
Application information: Application form not required.

50654—TEXAS

Officers and Trustees:* Forrest E. Hoglund,* Chair.; Sally R. Hoglund,* V.P.; Kelly H. Compton,* Secy.-Treas. and Exec. Dir.; Shelly H. Dee, Kristy H. Robinson.
EIN: 752300978
Codes: FD

50655
Catto Charitable Foundation
110 E. Crockett St.
San Antonio, TX 78205-2612   (210) 222-2161
Contact: Jessica Hobby Catto, Pres.

Established in 1967.
Financial data (yr. ended 12/31/00): Grants paid, $1,361,500; assets, $29,841,208 (M); expenditures, $1,542,588; qualifying distributions, $1,574,298.
Officers and Directors:* Jessica Hobby Catto,* Pres.; Henry E. Catto, Jr.,* V.P.; Susan R. Farrimond, Secy.-Treas.
EIN: 742773632
Codes: FD, FM

50656
Huffington Foundation
700 Louisiana St., Ste. 2400
Houston, TX 77002
Application address: P.O. Box 4337, Houston, TX 77210-4337
Contact: Roy M. Huffington, Sr. Tr.

Established in 1987 in TX.
Donor(s): Terry L. Huffington, Michael Huffington, Roy M. Huffington.
Financial data (yr. ended 12/31/01): Grants paid, $1,349,000; assets, $24,438,615 (M); expenditures, $1,656,641; qualifying distributions, $1,344,226.
Limitations: Applications not accepted. Giving primarily in Houston, TX.
Application information: Contributes only to pre-selected organizations.
Trustees: Phyllis Gough Huffington, Roy M. Huffington, Terry L. Huffington.
EIN: 766040840
Codes: FD

50657
Baumberger Endowment
P.O. Box 6067
San Antonio, TX 78209-0067

Trust established in 1979 in TX.
Donor(s): Charles Baumberger, Jr.‡
Financial data (yr. ended 12/31/01): Grants paid, $1,336,813; assets, $27,357,784 (M); gifts received, $500; expenditures, $1,633,052; qualifying distributions, $1,495,067.
Limitations: Giving limited to residents of Bexar County, TX.
Publications: Program policy statement, application guidelines.
Application information: Contact high school counselor for guidelines; student must pick up application at high school counselor's office; no applications will be mailed. Application form required.
Officers: Jerome F. Weynand, Chair.; Ronald Schmidt, Vice-Chair.; Stanley H. Schmidt, Secy.; Cynthia A. Guyon, Exec. Dir.
Trustees: Frank W. Burk, Marilou M. Long.
EIN: 237225925
Codes: FD, GTI

50658
The Pauline Sterne Wolff Memorial Foundation
Texan Bldg.
333 W. Loop N., 4th Fl.
Houston, TX 77024
Application address: c/o JPMorgan Chase Bank, P.O. Box 2558, Houston, TX 77252, tel.: (713) 216-1451
Contact: Elizabeth Hickman

Incorporated in 1922 in TX.
Financial data (yr. ended 12/31/99): Grants paid, $1,331,500; assets, $29,740,592 (M); expenditures, $1,570,580; qualifying distributions, $1,323,431.
Limitations: Giving limited to TX, with emphasis on Harris County.
Officers: Henry J.N. Taub II, Pres.; Henry J.N. Taub, V.P. and Secy.-Treas.; Jenard M. Gross, V.P.; Regina J. Rogers, V.P.; Marc J. Shapiro, V.P.
EIN: 741110698
Codes: FD

50659
Edward & Helen Bartlett Foundation
(Formerly Edward E. Bartlett & Helen Turner Bartlett Foundation)
c/o Bank One Trust Co., N.A.
P.O. Box 2050
Fort Worth, TX 76113
Application address: c/o Bank One Trust Co., N.A., P.O. Box 1, Tulsa, OK 74193
Contact: Mike Bartel

Established in 1961 in OK.
Donor(s): Edward E. Bartlett.‡
Financial data (yr. ended 12/31/00): Grants paid, $1,321,283; assets, $32,893,016 (M); expenditures, $1,826,953; qualifying distributions, $1,365,370.
Limitations: Giving limited to OK.
Application information: Application form not required.
Trustees: H.O. Bartlett II, Harry Freeman, Bank One Trust Co., N.A.
EIN: 736092250
Codes: FD

50660
The Kincaid Foundation
125 E. John Carpenter Freeway, Ste. 190
Irving, TX 75062

Established in 1997 in TX.
Donor(s): Thomas R. Kincaid.
Financial data (yr. ended 12/31/01): Grants paid, $1,311,517; assets, $3,540,356 (M); expenditures, $1,399,295; qualifying distributions, $1,359,926.
Trustees: W. Richard Jones, Thomas R. Kincaid.
EIN: 752687930
Codes: FD

50661
Sarofim Foundation
2 Houston Ctr., Ste. 2907
Houston, TX 77010-1083   (713) 654-4484
Contact: Fayez Sarofim, Tr.

Established in 1968.
Donor(s): Fayez Sarofim, Louisa Stude Sarofim.
Financial data (yr. ended 06/30/01): Grants paid, $1,270,000; assets, $21,941,080 (M); gifts received, $250,000; expenditures, $1,281,351; qualifying distributions, $1,259,726.
Limitations: Giving primarily in NY and Houston, TX.
Application information: Application form not required.
Trustees: Christopher B. Sarofim, Fayez Sarofim, Raye G. White.
EIN: 237065248

Codes: FD

50662
AMR/American Airlines Foundation
P.O. Box 619616, M.D. 5656
Dallas, TX 75261-9616   (817) 967-3540
Application address for Miles for Kids in Need Program: c/o AMR Corp., Frequent Traveler Special Progs., P.O. Box 619616, M.D. 1396, Dallas, TX 75261-9616, tel.: (800) 882-8880; URL: http://www.amrcorp.com/corpinfo.htm
Contact: Timothy J. Doke, Secy.

Established in 1985 in TX.
Donor(s): AMR Corp., Flagship Charities, Chicago Charities.
Financial data (yr. ended 12/31/00): Grants paid, $1,265,434; assets, $1,843,169 (M); gifts received, $292,098; expenditures, $1,446,932; qualifying distributions, $1,445,446.
Limitations: Giving primarily in those communities where AMR operates a hub or has a major facility and/or employee base.
Publications: Application guidelines.
Application information: All requests for limited travel assistance through Miles for Kids in Need program must be referred through an approved nonprofit agency. Application form not required.
Officers and Directors:* Donald J. Carty,* Pres.; Thomas J. Kiernan,* V.P.; Timothy J. Doke,* Secy.; Gerald J. Aprey,* Treas.
EIN: 762086656
Codes: CS, FD, CD

50663
Kathleen Cailloux Family Foundation
c/o JPMorgan Chase Bank
P.O. Box 47531
San Antonio, TX 78265-7531   (210) 841-7011
Contact: John D. Rogers

Established in 1998 in TX.
Donor(s): Kathleen C. Cailloux.
Financial data (yr. ended 12/31/01): Grants paid, $1,250,000; assets, $19,527,865 (M); expenditures, $1,315,065; qualifying distributions, $1,244,547.
Limitations: Applications not accepted. Giving primarily in Galveston and Kerr counties, TX.
Application information: Unsolicited requests for funds not accepted.
Trustees: Robert S. Andresakis, Kenneth F. Cailloux, Sandy Cailloux, Blackie Heileman, Paula L. Heileman, JPMorgan Chase Bank.
EIN: 742857513
Codes: FD

50664
Louisa Stude Sarofim Foundation
1001 Fannin St., Ste. 4700
Houston, TX 77002

Established in 1991.
Financial data (yr. ended 12/31/01): Grants paid, $1,240,000; assets, $24,729,177 (M); expenditures, $1,364,352; qualifying distributions, $1,271,170.
Limitations: Applications not accepted. Giving primarily in TX.
Application information: Contributes only to pre-selected organizations.
Trustees: Mary L. Porter, Allison Sarofim, Christopher Sarofim, Louisa S. Sarofim.
EIN: 760347329
Codes: FD

50665
Oldham Little Church Foundation
5177 Richmond Ave., Ste. 1030
Houston, TX 77056-6701
Contact: Louis E. Finlay, Pres.

Trust established in 1949 in TX.
Donor(s): Morris Calvin Oldham.‡
Financial data (yr. ended 12/31/01): Grants paid, $1,237,800; assets, $24,810,272 (M); expenditures, $1,683,920; qualifying distributions, $1,471,343.
Limitations: Giving on a national basis.
Application information: Application form required.
Officers: Louis E. Finlay, Pres. and Treas.; David Chavanne, V.P.; Raymond E. Hankamer, V.P.; Carloss Morris, Jr., V.P.; James S. Riley, V.P.; Stewart Morris, Secy.
Trustees: Linda R. Dunham, Sadie Hodo.
EIN: 760465633
Codes: FD

50666
The Weiser Foundation
6601 Oak Hill Ct.
Fort Worth, TX 76132 (817) 390-8876
Application address: 2033 Windsor Pl., Fort Worth, TX, 76110
Contact: John M. Weiser, Pres.

Established in 1994 in TX.
Donor(s): John M. Weiser.
Financial data (yr. ended 12/31/99): Grants paid, $1,230,000; assets, $1,391,654 (M); gifts received, $440,000; expenditures, $1,232,184; qualifying distributions, $1,229,453.
Limitations: Giving primarily in TX.
Application information: Grants are made at the discretion of the Board of Directors.
Officers: John M. Weiser, Pres.; R. Douglas Wallace, V.P.; Terri L. Weiser, Secy.
EIN: 752561493
Codes: FD

50667
Tocker Foundation
3814 Medical Pkwy.
Austin, TX 78756-4002 (512) 452-1044
FAX: (512) 452-7690; E-mail: Grants@Tocker.org
Contact: Darryl Tocker, Exec. Dir.

Established in 1964 in TX.
Donor(s): Phillip Tocker,‡ Mrs. Phillip Tocker.‡
Financial data (yr. ended 11/30/99): Grants paid, $1,220,945; assets, $39,731,832 (M); gifts received, $1,000; expenditures, $1,565,318; qualifying distributions, $1,672,574.
Limitations: Giving primarily in TX.
Publications: Informational brochure (including application guidelines).
Application information: Application form required.
Officer: Darryl Tocker, Exec. Dir.
Directors: Mel Kunze, Barbara Tocker, Robert Tocker.
EIN: 756037871
Codes: FD

50668
Qurumbli Foundation
c/o William P. Hallman, Jr.
201 Main St., Ste. 3200
Fort Worth, TX 76102-3105

Established in 1991 in TX.
Donor(s): William P. Hallman, Jr.
Financial data (yr. ended 11/30/00): Grants paid, $1,218,246; assets, $710,140 (M); expenditures, $1,222,046; qualifying distributions, $1,217,836.
Limitations: Applications not accepted. Giving primarily in Fort Worth, TX.
Application information: Contributes only to pre-selected organizations.
Directors: Clive D. Bode, William P. Hallman, Jr., Mark L. Hart, Jr.
EIN: 752404804
Codes: FD

50669
Clara B. and W. Aubrey Smith Charitable Foundation
c/o Bank of America
P.O. Box 831041
Dallas, TX 75283-1041
Application address: c/o Bank of America, 330 W. Main St., Denison, TX 75020, tel.: (903) 465-2131
Contact: Linda Hunt

Established in 1985 in TX.
Donor(s): Clara Blackford Smith.‡
Financial data (yr. ended 06/30/01): Grants paid, $1,210,340; assets, $19,358,528 (M); expenditures, $1,390,069; qualifying distributions, $922,174.
Limitations: Giving primarily in Denison and Sherman,TX.
Application information: Application form required.
Directors: Ronnie Cole, Jerry Culpepper, Wayne E. Delaney, M.D., Jack Lilley.
Trustee: Bank of America.
EIN: 756314114
Codes: FD

50670
The Steve & Sarah Smith Family Foundation
P.O. Box 340667
Austin, TX 78734

Established in 2000 in TX.
Donor(s): Steve Smith.
Financial data (yr. ended 12/31/00): Grants paid, $1,200,000; assets, $18,127,229 (M); gifts received, $15,916,914; expenditures, $1,200,500; qualifying distributions, $1,200,000.
Limitations: Applications not accepted. Giving primarily in Austin and Fort Worth, TX.
Application information: Contributes only to pre-selected organizations.
Officers: Steve Smith, Pres.; Randall N. Williamson, V.P.; Lester J. Ducote, Secy.
Directors: Rachel H. Smith, Rayner H. Smith, Sarah R. Smith.
EIN: 742970009
Codes: FD

50671
Earl C. Sams Foundation, Inc.
101 N. Shoreline Dr., Ste. 602
Corpus Christi, TX 78401 (361) 888-6485
FAX: (361) 884-4241
Contact: Bruce S. Hawn, Pres.

Incorporated in 1946 in NY; reincorporated in 1988 in TX.
Donor(s): Earl C. Sams.‡
Financial data (yr. ended 12/31/01): Grants paid, $1,194,700; assets, $28,260,350 (M); expenditures, $1,663,500; qualifying distributions, $1,412,243.
Limitations: Giving primarily in southern TX.
Application information: Application form not required.
Officers and Directors:* Susan Hawn Yuras,* Chair. and V.P.; Bruce Sams Hawn,* C.E.O. and Pres.; Susan Ohnmacht, Secy.-Treas.; Nancy E. Hawn.
EIN: 741463151
Codes: FD

50672
The Zachry Foundation
P.O. Box 240130
San Antonio, TX 78224-0330
Application address: 310 S. Saint Mary's St., Ste. 2500, San Antonio, TX 78285, tel.: (210) 554-4663; FAX: (210) 554-4605
Contact: Pam O'Connor, Exec. Dir.

Incorporated in 1960 in TX.
Donor(s): H.B. Zachry Co.
Financial data (yr. ended 12/31/00): Grants paid, $1,191,500; assets, $10,494,340 (M); gifts received, $1,250,000; expenditures, $1,221,843; qualifying distributions, $1,187,775.
Limitations: Giving limited to TX; awards for the arts and humanities, health and social services, and K-12 education limited to San Antonio organizations.
Application information: Application form required.
Officers and Trustees:* J.P. Zachry,* Pres.; Murray L. Johnston, Jr.,* Secy.; Charles Ebrom,* Treas.; Pamela O'Connor, Exec. Dir.; H.B. Zachry, Jr., Mollie Steves Zachry.
EIN: 741485544
Codes: FD

50673
George W. Brackenridge Foundation
711 Navarro St., Ste. 535
San Antonio, TX 78205 (210) 224-1011
Contact: Gilbert M. Denman, Jr., Tr.

Trust established in 1920 in TX.
Donor(s): George W. Brackenridge.‡
Financial data (yr. ended 12/31/01): Grants paid, $1,184,882; assets, $27,603,708 (M); gifts received, $154; expenditures, $1,300,805; qualifying distributions, $1,210,048.
Limitations: Applications not accepted. Giving limited to TX.
Application information: All grants made on the foundation's own initiative.
Trustees: Gilbert M. Denman, Jr., Leroy G. Denman, Jr., John H. Moore.
EIN: 746034977
Codes: FD

50674
Lennox Foundation
P.O. Box 799900
Dallas, TX 75379-9900
Contact: David H. Anderson, Chair.

Incorporated in 1951 in IA.
Financial data (yr. ended 11/30/01): Grants paid, $1,178,450; assets, $20,757,512 (M); gifts received, $504,750; expenditures, $1,353,910; qualifying distributions, $1,178,450.
Limitations: Applications not accepted. Giving limited to areas of family involvement in CA, IA, ME, and TX.
Application information: Unsolicited requests for funds not accepted.
Officers and Trustees:* David H. Anderson,* Chair.; Robert W. Norris,* Vice-Chair.; Lynn B. Storey,* Secy.
EIN: 426053380
Codes: FD

50675
Alcon Foundation
6201 S. Freeway
Fort Worth, TX 76134
Contact: Mary K. Dulle, Co-Chair.

Established in 1962 in TX.
Donor(s): Alcon Laboratories, Inc.

50675—TEXAS

Financial data (yr. ended 12/31/01): Grants paid, $1,177,981; assets, $8,903 (M); gifts received, $1,184,750; expenditures, $1,177,520; qualifying distributions, $1,177,977.
Limitations: Giving on a national basis.
Application information: Application form not required.
Trustees: Mary K. Dulle, Co-Chair.; John A. Walters, Co-Chair.; C.A. Baker, J. Hiddemen, Fred Pettinato, Cary Rayment, T.R.G. Sear, Marvin Sulak.
EIN: 756034736
Codes: CS, FD, CD

50676
The Fasken Foundation
P.O. Box 162786
Austin, TX 78716-2786 (512) 708-1003
Contact: Andrew C. Elliott, Jr., Dir.

Incorporated in 1955 in TX.
Donor(s): Andrew A. Fasken,‡ Helen Fasken House,‡ Vickie Mallison,‡ Howard Marshall Johnson,‡ Ruth Shelton.‡
Financial data (yr. ended 12/31/00): Grants paid, $1,175,096; assets, $17,537,265 (M); expenditures, $1,944,217; qualifying distributions, $1,218,506.
Limitations: Giving limited to the Midland, TX, area.
Publications: Application guidelines.
Application information: Application form required.
Officers: Steven Fasken, Pres.; F. Andrew Fasken, V.P.
Trustees: Murray T. Fasken, William P. Franklin, Susan Fasken Hartin, Tevis Herd, B.L. Jones, Thomas E. Kelly, Gerald C. Nobles, Jr.
Director: Andrew C. Elliot, Jr.
EIN: 756023680
Codes: FD, GTI

50677
William A. and Elizabeth B. Moncrief Foundation
Moncrief Bldg.
950 Commerce St.
Fort Worth, TX 76102 (817) 336-7232
Contact: W.A. Moncrief, Jr., Pres.

Established in 1954.
Donor(s): W.A. Moncrief.‡
Financial data (yr. ended 09/30/01): Grants paid, $1,167,749; assets, $4,935,811 (M); expenditures, $1,216,131; qualifying distributions, $1,168,528.
Limitations: Giving primarily in TX.
Officers: W.A. Moncrief, Jr., Pres. and Mgr.; R.W. Moncrief, V.P.; C.B. Moncrief, Secy.-Treas.
EIN: 756036329
Codes: FD

50678
Navarro Community Foundation
P.O. Box 1035
Corsicana, TX 75151 (903) 874-4301
Contact: Bruce Robinson, Exec. Secy.-Treas.

Established in 1938 in TX.
Donor(s): Frank N. Drane.‡
Financial data (yr. ended 12/31/01): Grants paid, $1,156,704; assets, $18,224,859 (M); expenditures, $1,228,631; qualifying distributions, $1,149,041.
Limitations: Giving limited to Navarro County, TX.
Application information: Application form not required.
Officers: William Clarkson III, Chair.; C. David Campbell, M.D., 1st Vice-Chair.; O.L. Albritton, 2nd Vice-Chair.; Bruce Robinson, Exec. Secy.-Treas.

Trustees: C.L. Brown III, Lynn Cooper, Embry Ferguson, Gioia Keeney, Billie Love McFerran, Scott Middleton, Lynn Sanders, H.M. Settle III, M.D., John B. Stroud.
EIN: 750800663
Codes: FD

50679
The Stanford & Joan Alexander Foundation
1400 Post Oak Blvd., Ste. 900
Houston, TX 77056
Contact: Joan Alexander, Secy.

Established in 1986 in TX.
Donor(s): Stanford Alexander, Joan Alexander.
Financial data (yr. ended 12/31/01): Grants paid, $1,142,457; assets, $21,810,395 (M); gifts received, $1,424,375; expenditures, $1,159,610; qualifying distributions, $1,131,825.
Limitations: Applications not accepted. Giving primarily in Houston, TX.
Application information: Contributes only to pre-selected organizations.
Officers and Directors:* Stanford Alexander,* Pres. and Treas.; Joan Alexander,* V.P. and Secy.; Andrew M. Alexander, Melvin Dow.
EIN: 760204170
Codes: FD

50680
Ruth C. and Charles S. Sharp Foundation, Inc.
P.O. Box 1330
Lewisville, TX 75067

Incorporated in 1965 in TX.
Donor(s): Charles S. Sharp, Ruth Collins Sharp, Carr P. Collins Foundation.
Financial data (yr. ended 12/31/01): Grants paid, $1,136,765; assets, $20,990,870 (M); expenditures, $1,398,753; qualifying distributions, $1,202,369.
Limitations: Applications not accepted. Giving primarily in Dallas, TX.
Application information: Contributes only to pre-selected organizations.
Officers and Directors:* Ruth Sharp Altshuler,* Pres.; Sally S. Harris,* V.P.; Connie G. Romans, Treas.; Susan S. McAdam.
EIN: 756045366
Codes: FD

50681
Ralph L. Smith Foundation
c/o Bank of America, N.A.
P.O. Box 831041
Dallas, TX 75283-1041
Application address: c/o David P. Ross, Sr. V.P., Bank of America, 1200 Main St., Kansas City, MO 64105, tel.: (816) 979-7481

Trust established in 1952 in MO.
Donor(s): Harriet T. Smith,‡ Ralph L. Smith.‡
Financial data (yr. ended 12/31/01): Grants paid, $1,133,050; assets, $22,884,609 (M); expenditures, $1,297,812; qualifying distributions, $1,214,834.
Limitations: Giving primarily in the metropolitan Kansas City, MO, area.
Application information: Applications for grants will not be acknowledged.
Managers: Neil T. Dauthat, Harriet H. Dennison, E.M. Douthat III, Paul N. Douthat, Ralph L. Smith.
Trustee: Bank of America.
EIN: 446008508
Codes: FD

50682
The i2 Foundation, Inc.
11511 Luna Rd., Ste. 1400
Dallas, TX 75234 (469) 357-3117
FAX: (469) 357-7777; *E-mail:*
bindu_nambiar@i2.com; *URL:* http://www.i2foundation.org
Contact: Bindu Nambiar, Grants Coord.

Donor(s): i2 Technologies, Inc., John Hogge, Brian Kennedy, Lekha Singh, Hiten Varia.
Financial data (yr. ended 12/31/00): Grants paid, $1,125,912; assets, $15,281,137 (M); gifts received, $1,072,768; expenditures, $1,608,702; qualifying distributions, $1,573,639.
Limitations: Applications not accepted. Giving on a national and international basis.
Application information: Contributes only to pre-selected organizations.
Officers: Lekha Singh, Pres.; Robert Donohoo, Secy.; William Beecher, Treas.
Directors: Sarinder Chhabra, Melis Jones, Brian Kennedy, Dave Pace, Austin Thomas, Hiten Varia, Romesh Wadhwani.
EIN: 752764747
Codes: CS, FD, CD

50683
The Trull Foundation
404 4th St.
Palacios, TX 77465 (361) 972-5241
FAX: (361) 972-1109; *E-mail:*
info@trullfoundation.org; *URL:* http://www.trullfoundation.org
Contact: E. Gail Purvis, Exec. Dir.

Trust established in 1967 in TX.
Donor(s): R.B. Trull, Florence M. Trull,‡ Gladys T. Brooking, Jean T. Herlin, Laura Shiflett.
Financial data (yr. ended 12/31/00): Grants paid, $1,108,536; assets, $26,905,058 (M); expenditures, $1,407,150; qualifying distributions, $86,811.
Limitations: Giving primarily in southern TX, with emphasis on the Palacios, TX, area.
Publications: Biennial report (including application guidelines), application guidelines.
Application information: Proposals submitted by FAX not considered. Application form required.
Officers and Trustees:* Colleen Claybourn,* Chair.; Rose C. Lancaster,* Vice-Chair.; J. Fred Huitt,* Secy.-Treas.; E. Gail Purvis, Exec. Dir.; Cara P. Herlin, Jean T. Herlin, Sarah H. Olfers, R.B. Trull, R. Scott Trull.
EIN: 237423943
Codes: FD

50684
Neva and Wesley West Foundation
P.O. Box 7
Houston, TX 77001
Contact: Stuart W. Stedman, Tr.

Trust established in 1956 in TX.
Donor(s): Wesley West,‡ Mrs. Wesley West.
Financial data (yr. ended 12/31/00): Grants paid, $1,106,000; assets, $17,324,731 (M); expenditures, $1,419,005; qualifying distributions, $1,085,781.
Limitations: Applications not accepted. Giving primarily in TX.
Application information: Unsolicited requests for funds not accepted.
Trustees: Randolph L. Pullin, Betty Ann West Stedman, Stuart West Stedman.
EIN: 746039393
Codes: FD

50685
The Allbritton Foundation
5615 Kirby Dr., Ste. 310
Houston, TX 77005
Contact: Virginia L. White, Secy.-Treas.

Established in 1958 in TX.
Donor(s): Joe L. Allbritton.
Financial data (yr. ended 11/30/01): Grants paid, $1,080,988; assets, $8,804,131 (M); gifts received, $95,000; expenditures, $1,124,314; qualifying distributions, $1,102,042.
Limitations: Giving on a national basis.
Application information: Application form required.
Officers and Trustees:* Joe L. Allbritton,* Pres.; Barbara Allbritton,* V.P.; Robert L. Allbritton,* V.P.; Virginia L. White, Secy.-Treas.; Charles W. Hall, Lawrence I. Hebert.
EIN: 746051876
Codes: FD

50686
The Carolyn J. and Robert J. Allison, Jr. Family Foundation
17001 N. Chase Dr.
Houston, TX 77060

Established in 1997 in TX.
Donor(s): Carolyn J. Allison, Robert J. Allison.
Financial data (yr. ended 12/31/01): Grants paid, $1,064,888; assets, $692,140 (M); gifts received, $1,637,500; expenditures, $1,080,900; qualifying distributions, $1,052,069.
Limitations: Applications not accepted. Giving primarily in TX.
Application information: Contributes only to pre-selected organizations.
Officers: Robert J. Allison, Jr., Pres.; Jane S. Allison, Secy.; Carolyn J. Allison, Treas.
Directors: Ann A. Stanislaw, Amy A. Watkins.
EIN: 760539246
Codes: FD

50687
Bruce McMillan, Jr. Foundation, Inc.
P.O. Box 9
Overton, TX 75684 (903) 834-3148
Contact: Ralph Ward, Jr., Pres.

Trust established in 1951 in TX.
Donor(s): V. Bruce McMillan, M.D.,‡ Mary Moore McMillan.‡
Financial data (yr. ended 06/30/01): Grants paid, $1,050,191; assets, $20,306,968 (M); expenditures, $1,539,891; qualifying distributions, $1,076,528.
Limitations: Giving primarily in the Overton, TX, area.
Publications: Application guidelines.
Application information: Application form required.
Officers and Directors:* Drew R. Heard, Chair. and V.P.; John Rodgers Pope,* Vice-Chair. and V.P.; Ralph Ward, Jr., Pres. and Treas.; Pamela M. Merritt, Secy.; Judy Hale.
EIN: 750945924
Codes: FD, GTI

50688
Scurlock Foundation
700 Louisiana, Ste. 3920
Houston, TX 77002
Contact: Elizabeth B. Wareing, Pres.

Incorporated in 1954 in TX.
Donor(s): E.C. Scurlock,‡ Mrs. E.C. Scurlock, Scurlock Oil Co., D.E. Farnsworth,‡ J.S. Blanton, Mrs. J.S. Blanton, and other members of the Blanton family.
Financial data (yr. ended 12/31/00): Grants paid, $1,049,052; assets, $20,634,065 (M); gifts received, $6,327; expenditures, $1,179,347; qualifying distributions, $1,051,003.
Limitations: Giving primarily in TX, with emphasis on the Houston area.
Application information: Funds heavily committed. Application form not required.
Officers and Directors:* Elizabeth B. Wareing,* Pres.; Eddy S. Blanton,* V.P.; Jack S. Blanton, Jr.,* V.P.; Ken Fisher,* Secy.-Treas.; Jack S. Blanton, Sr.
EIN: 741488953
Codes: FD

50689
Scarborough-Linebery Foundation
(Formerly Tom & Evelyn Linebery Foundation)
4305 N. Garfield, No. 260
Midland, TX 79702 (915) 682-0357

Established in 1976 in TX.
Donor(s): Tom Linebery, Evelyn Linebery.
Financial data (yr. ended 06/30/01): Grants paid, $1,047,146; assets, $14,704,136 (M); expenditures, $1,188,059; qualifying distributions, $1,047,146.
Limitations: Giving primarily in NM.
Publications: Informational brochure (including application guidelines).
Officers and Directors:* C.C. Matthews,* Pres.; Bill Humphries,* V.P.; Doug Grimes,* Secy.-Treas.; Tom Linebery, Joe Max Walker.
EIN: 510187878
Codes: FD

50690
Permian Basin Area Foundation
550 W. Texas, Ste. 1260
P.O. Box 10424
Midland, TX 79702 (915) 682-4704
FAX: (915) 498-8999; *E-mail:* pbaf@mo.quik.com
Contact: John D. Swallow, C.E.O. and Pres.

Incorporated in 1989 in TX.
Financial data (yr. ended 12/31/01): Grants paid, $1,034,148; assets, $12,657,859 (M); gifts received, $2,500,000; expenditures, $835,035.
Limitations: Giving primarily in southeastern NM and the Permian Basin area of western TX.
Publications: Annual report, application guidelines, newsletter.
Application information: Application form required.
Officers and Governors:* K. Michael Conaway,* Chair.; Joan Baskin,* Vice-Chair.; John D. Swallow, C.E.O. and Pres.; Lorraine Perryman,* Secy.; A.J. Brune III,* Treas.; June Cowden, Robert H. Dawson, Tracy Elms, Grace King, LaDoyce Lambert, Tulsi Singh, M.D., Jimmy Stallings, Ray Stoker, Jr., Betsy Triplett-Hurt, Jack Wood.
EIN: 752295008
Codes: CM, FD

50691
D. D. Hachar Charitable Trust Fund
c/o Laredo National Bank
P.O. Box 59
Laredo, TX 78042-0059
FAX: (956) 724-8923

Established in 1980 in TX.
Donor(s): Lamar Bruni Vergara Trust.
Financial data (yr. ended 04/30/01): Grants paid, $1,033,133; assets, $18,780,762 (M); gifts received, $100,000; expenditures, $1,400,495; qualifying distributions, $1,153,211.
Limitations: Giving limited to Laredo and Webb County, TX, and surrounding areas.
Publications: Annual report, informational brochure, program policy statement, application guidelines.
Application information: Application form required for scholarships. Grants to organizations are limited. Application form required.
Advisor: Joaquin Gonzales Cigarroa, Jr., M.D.
Trustee: Laredo National Bank.
EIN: 742093680
Codes: FD, GTI

50692
Roy F. and Joann Cole Mitte Foundation
6500 River Pl. Blvd., Bldg. 1
Austin, TX 78730
Contact: Lisa Leach

Established in 1997 in TX.
Donor(s): Roy F. Mitte.
Financial data (yr. ended 12/31/00): Grants paid, $1,023,301; assets, $360,002,103 (M); gifts received, $18,903,732; expenditures, $2,225,880; qualifying distributions, $1,023,301.
Limitations: Applications not accepted. Giving primarily in San Marcos, TX.
Application information: Contributes only to pre-selected organizations.
Directors: John Barnett, Robert A. Bender, William Brown, Joseph Crowe, Lewis Gilcrease, David C. Hopkins, Joann Cole Mitte, M. Scott Mitte, Roy F. Mitte, Elizabeth Nash, Frank Parker, Eugene E. Payne, Scotter Read, Jerome Supple.
EIN: 742766058
Codes: FD

50693
The James M. Collins Foundation
8115 Preston Rd., Ste. 680
Dallas, TX 75225
Contact: Dorothy Collins, Pres.

Established in 1964 in TX.
Donor(s): James M. Collins.‡
Financial data (yr. ended 12/31/00): Grants paid, $1,012,003; assets, $26,084,172 (M); expenditures, $1,246,397; qualifying distributions, $1,081,664.
Limitations: Giving primarily in TX.
Officers: Dorothy Dann Collins Torbett, Pres.; Michael J. Collins, V.P.; Dorothy Collins Weaver, Secy.
EIN: 756040743
Codes: FD

50694
The Staubach Foundation
15601 Dallas Pkwy., Ste. 400
Addison, TX 75001 (972) 361-5011
Contact: Sharon Bell

Established in 1986 in TX.
Donor(s): Roger T. Staubach, Marsh & McLennan, Phillips Brokerage, Balloons Over Texas, Holloway-Staubach Co.
Financial data (yr. ended 05/31/01): Grants paid, $1,008,816; assets, $2,753,618 (M); gifts received, $24,421; expenditures, $1,088,110; qualifying distributions, $1,020,227.
Limitations: Giving primarily in Dallas, TX.
Officers and Trustees:* Roger T. Staubach,* Pres.; Marianne H. Staubach,* V.P.; James C. Leslie,* Secy.
EIN: 752123195
Codes: FD

50695
Nancy Ann Hunt and Ray L. Hunt Philanthropic Fund
(Formerly Nancy Ann Hunt and Ray L. Hunt Foundation)
1445 Ross at Field, Ste. 1700
Dallas, TX 75202-2785

Established in 1983 in TX.
Donor(s): Ray L. Hunt.
Financial data (yr. ended 12/31/99): Grants paid, $1,000,000; assets, $4,639,901 (M); expenditures, $1,011,867; qualifying distributions, $1,002,161.
Limitations: Applications not accepted. Giving primarily in Dallas, TX.
Application information: Contributes only to pre-selected organizations.
Officers and Directors:* Ray L. Hunt,* Pres. and Treas.; Richard A. Massman,* V.P. and Secy.; Nancy Ann Hunt,* V.P.
EIN: 751903084
Codes: FD

50696
The KLE Foundation
P.O. Box 163991
Austin, TX 78716-3991

Established in 1997 TX.
Donor(s): Lorraine Clasquin, Eric Harslem.
Financial data (yr. ended 12/31/01): Grants paid, $993,500; assets, $15,779,327 (M); expenditures, $1,079,562; qualifying distributions, $962,217.
Limitations: Applications not accepted.
Application information: Contributes only to pre-selected organizations.
Officers: Lorraine Clasquin, Pres.; Eric Harslem, V.P. and Secy.
Director: Kate Harslem.
EIN: 742860436
Codes: FD

50697
Unocal Foundation
14141 S.W. Freeway
Sugar Land, TX 77478
Application address: c/o Laurie Regelbrugge, Mgr., 1150 Connecticut Ave. N.W., Ste. 1025, Washington, DC 20036, tel.: (202) 367-2782
Contact: Gregory F. Huger, Pres.

Incorporated in 1962 in CA.
Donor(s): Unocal Corp.
Financial data (yr. ended 01/31/01): Grants paid, $961,615; assets, $2,143,443 (M); gifts received, $636,146; expenditures, $1,045,158; qualifying distributions, $961,521.
Limitations: Giving primarily in areas of parent company operations in CA, IL, and TX.
Publications: Annual report.
Application information: Application form required for employee-related scholarships.
Officers and Trustees:* George A. Walker,* Chair.; Gregory F. Huger, Pres.; Stephen L. Hayes, V.P.; Carl D. McAulay,* V.P.; Roberta E. Kass, Secy.; Darrell D. Chessum, Treas.; Joe D. Cecil, Andrew L. Fawthrop, Thomas E. Fisher, Brian W. G. Marcotte.
EIN: 956071812
Codes: CS, FD, CD, GTI

50698
Calvert K. Collins Family Foundation, Inc.
(Formerly Calvert K. Collins Foundation, Inc.)
1701 N. Hampton, Ste. A
DeSoto, TX 75115

Incorporated in 1962 in TX.
Donor(s): Carr P. Collins.
Financial data (yr. ended 12/31/99): Grants paid, $960,975; assets, $11,560,244 (M); expenditures, $1,207,890; qualifying distributions, $990,573.
Limitations: Applications not accepted. Giving primarily in Dallas, TX.
Application information: Contributes only to pre-selected organizations.
Officers and Directors:* Calvert K. Collins,* Pres.; Richard H. Collins,* V.P. and Treas.; Christy C. Moroch,* Secy.
EIN: 756011615
Codes: FD

50699
The Michael and Linda Mewhinney Foundation
4242 Cochran Chapel Rd.
Dallas, TX 75209

Established in 1999 in TX.
Donor(s): Michael Mewhinney, Linda Mewhinney.
Financial data (yr. ended 05/31/01): Grants paid, $957,522; assets, $1,825,226 (M); gifts received, $960,000; expenditures, $961,312; qualifying distributions, $957,522.
Limitations: Applications not accepted. Giving primarily in NY and TX.
Application information: Contributes only to pre-selected organizations.
Officers: Michael Mewhinney, Pres. and Treas.; Linda Mewhinney, Secy.
Director: James S. Mewhinney.
EIN: 752828954
Codes: FD

50700
Ruth & Ted Bauer Family Foundation
P.O. Box 1063
Houston, TX 77251 (713) 830-3400
Contact: Patricia N. Lewis, Exec. Dir.

Established in 1997 in TX.
Donor(s): Charles T. Bauer, Ruth J. Bauer.
Financial data (yr. ended 12/31/01): Grants paid, $946,800; assets, $16,807,689 (M); expenditures, $1,049,869; qualifying distributions, $997,750.
Application information: Application form not required.
Officers: Charles T. Bauer, Pres. and Treas.; Ruth J. Bauer, Exec. V.P. and Secy.; Charles Douglas Bauer, V.P.; Patricia N. Lewis, Exec. Dir.
EIN: 760537473
Codes: FD

50701
Chaney Family Foundation
2 S. Briar Hollow Ln., Unit 4
Houston, TX 77027
Contact: E. Thomas Chaney, Pres.

Established in 1994 in TX.
Donor(s): E. Thomas Chaney, Mrs. E. Thomas Chaney.
Financial data (yr. ended 09/30/01): Grants paid, $942,385; assets, $2,174,890 (M); expenditures, $971,696; qualifying distributions, $939,562.
Limitations: Applications not accepted. Giving primarily in TX.
Application information: Unsolicited requests for funds not accepted.
Officers and Directors:* E. Thomas Chaney,* Pres.; Carol Ann Chaney,* V.P.; Jeffrey C. Chaney, Julie E. Chaney.
EIN: 760451100
Codes: FD

50702
Semmes Foundation, Inc.
800 Navarro, Ste. 210
San Antonio, TX 78205 (210) 225-0887
FAX: (210) 226-9288; *URL:* http://www.semmesfoundation.org
Contact: Thomas R. Semmes, Pres.

Incorporated in 1952 in TX.
Donor(s): Douglas R. Semmes.‡
Financial data (yr. ended 12/31/01): Grants paid, $931,100; assets, $19,358,825 (M); gifts received, $45,738; expenditures, $1,078,850; qualifying distributions, $966,815.
Limitations: Giving primarily in the San Antonio, TX, area.
Application information: The overwhelming majority of grants are initiated by the directors of the foundation. Application form not required.
Officers and Directors:* Thomas R. Semmes,* Pres.; D.R. Semmes, Jr.,* V.P.; Carol Duffell, Secy.-Treas.; Lucian L. Morrison, Jr., Patricia Semmes.
EIN: 746062264
Codes: FD

50703
The Reaud Charitable Foundation, Inc.
801 Laurel St.
Beaumont, TX 77701 (409) 838-1000
Contact: Wayne A. Reaud

Established in 1989 in TX.
Donor(s): Wayne A. Reaud.
Financial data (yr. ended 12/31/01): Grants paid, $906,799; assets, $32,333,813 (M); gifts received, $5,000,000; expenditures, $1,081,129; qualifying distributions, $896,846.
Limitations: Giving primarily in Beaumont, TX.
Application information: Application form not required.
Officer: Jon A. Reaud, Exec. Dir.
EIN: 760291657
Codes: FD

50704
Myra Stafford Pryor Charitable Trust
c/o Frost National Bank
P.O. Box 2950
San Antonio, TX 78299 (210) 220-4011
Contact: William L. Clyborne, V.P.

Established in 1993.
Financial data (yr. ended 12/31/01): Grants paid, $903,451; assets, $23,888,062 (M); expenditures, $1,440,777; qualifying distributions, $903,451.
Limitations: Giving primarily in TX.
Application information: Application form not required.
Trustee: Frost National Bank.
EIN: 746417499
Codes: FD

50705
The Tobin Endowment
3316 Oakwell Ct.
San Antonio, TX 78218 (210) 224-1155
Contact: J. Bruce Bugg, Jr., Tr.

Established in 1999 in TX.
Financial data (yr. ended 12/31/00): Grants paid, $901,140; assets, $48,210,650 (M); gifts received, $13,438,143; expenditures, $1,326,464; qualifying distributions, $1,047,337.
Limitations: Giving primarily in NY and TX.
Trustees: J. Bruce Bugg, Jr., Leroy G. Denman, Jr.
EIN: 746478848
Codes: FD

50706
Scaler Foundation, Inc.
800 Gessner, Ste. 1260
Houston, TX 77024

Incorporated in 1954 in TX.
Donor(s): Eric Boissonnas.
Financial data (yr. ended 12/31/01): Grants paid, $890,221; assets, $26,714,780 (M); expenditures, $1,315,451; qualifying distributions, $890,221.
Limitations: Applications not accepted. Giving primarily in the U.S. and France.
Application information: Contributes only to pre-selected organizations.
Officers and Directors:* Eric Boissonnas,* Chair.; Nicolas N. Boissonnas,* Pres.; Jacques C. Boissonnas,* V.P.; Catherine B. Coste,* V.P.; Marvin A. Wurzer,* Secy.-Treas.; Sylvina Boissonnas, Glenn H. Johnson.
EIN: 746036684
Codes: FD

50707
Devary Durrill Foundation, Inc.
615 S. Upper Broadway
Corpus Christi, TX 78401
Contact: William R. Durrill, Pres.

Established in 1984 in TX.
Financial data (yr. ended 12/31/01): Grants paid, $887,653; assets, $9,657,448 (M); gifts received, $9,225; expenditures, $1,124,756; qualifying distributions, $915,155.
Limitations: Applications not accepted. Giving limited to Corpus Christi, TX.
Application information: Contributes only to pre-selected organizations.
Officers: William R. Durrill, Pres.; Shirley R. Durrill, Secy.-Treas.
Directors: Ginger Durrill, Melissa Durrill, Michele Durrill, William R. Durrill, Jr.
EIN: 742370613
Codes: FD

50708
The Charles W. Tate & Judy Spence Tate Charitable Foundation
3640 Del Monte
Houston, TX 77019
Additional address: c/o Carolyn Gruensfelder, 3858 Candlelite Ln., Fort Worth, TX 76109, tel: (817) 731-1496
Contact: Judy S. Tate, Tr.

Established in 1994.
Donor(s): Charles W. Tate.
Financial data (yr. ended 12/31/01): Grants paid, $887,000; assets, $6,205,316 (M); expenditures, $891,835; qualifying distributions, $887,000.
Limitations: Giving primarily in Houston, TX.
Application information: Application form not required.
Trustees: Charles W. Tate, Judy Spence Tate.
EIN: 137047916
Codes: FD

50709
The Patrick and Beatrice Haggerty Foundation
(Formerly Haggerty Foundation)
7028 Turtle Creek Blvd.
Dallas, TX 75205
Contact: Beatrice Haggerty, Pres.

Established in 1968 in TX.
Donor(s): Patrick E. Haggerty,‡ Beatrice M. Haggerty.
Financial data (yr. ended 12/31/01): Grants paid, $877,775; assets, $12,695,785 (M); expenditures, $1,001,255; qualifying distributions, $882,689.
Limitations: Giving primarily in Dallas County, TX.
Application information: Application form not required.
Officers: Beatrice M. Haggerty, Pres.; Patrick E. Haggerty, Jr., V.P.; Teresa Haggerty Parravano, Secy.; Michael G. Haggerty, Treas.
Trustees: Kathleen Haggerty, Sheila Haggerty Turner.
EIN: 752076387
Codes: FD

50710
Orange Memorial Hospital Corporation
P.O. Box 2954
Orange, TX 77631-2954
Application address: 1502 Stickland, Ste. 7, Orange, TX 77630, tel.: (409) 886-3848
Contact: Robert A. Walker, V.P.

Established around 1987.
Financial data (yr. ended 12/31/00): Grants paid, $873,244; assets, $7,292,584 (M); expenditures, $935,383; qualifying distributions, $873,244.
Limitations: Giving limited to Orange County, TX.
Application information: Application form required.
Officers and Directors:* Jim I. Graves,* Pres.; Robert A. Walker,* V.P.; Robert Cormier,* Secy.; Benjamin C. Thacker,* Treas.; Gerald Erhman, James Jones, Walter Ridel, Kenneth Roach, Jeannie Scalfano, Dan Syphrett.
EIN: 741303719
Codes: FD, GTI

50711
The Nancy C. & Jeffrey A. Marcus Foundation, Inc.
c/o Deborah Streufert
300 Crescent Ct., Ste. 600
Dallas, TX 75201
Contact: Heidi Bruster

Established in 1989 in TX.
Donor(s): Jeffrey A. Marcus, Nancy C. Marcus.
Financial data (yr. ended 12/31/01): Grants paid, $872,910; assets, $1,713,622 (M); gifts received, $75,000; expenditures, $876,175; qualifying distributions, $874,485.
Limitations: Applications not accepted. Giving primarily in Dallas, TX.
Application information: Contributes only to pre-selected organizations.
Directors: Cindy Mannes, Jeffrey A. Marcus, Nancy C. Marcus.
EIN: 752283302
Codes: FD

50712
The Morris Foundation
4545 Bellaire Dr. S., Ste. 3
Fort Worth, TX 76109

Established in 1986 in TX.
Donor(s): Jack B. Morris, Linda C. Morris.
Financial data (yr. ended 12/31/00): Grants paid, $861,495; assets, $17,916,785 (M); gifts received, $567,350; expenditures, $907,092; qualifying distributions, $844,328.
Limitations: Applications not accepted. Giving primarily in Fort Worth, TX.
Application information: Contributes only to pre-selected organizations.
Officer: Joseph A. Monteleone, Exec. Dir.
Trustees: Jack B. Morris, Linda C. Morris.
EIN: 752137184
Codes: FD

50713
Oliver Dewey Mayor Foundation
P.O. Box 1088
Sherman, TX 75091-1088 (903) 813-5105
E-mail: rpruitt@mail.bokf.com
Contact: Regina D. Pruitt, Asst. V.P.

Established in 1983 in TX.
Donor(s): Oliver Dewey Mayor.‡
Financial data (yr. ended 06/30/01): Grants paid, $854,380; assets, $18,793,637 (M); expenditures, $1,498,175; qualifying distributions, $891,668.
Limitations: Giving limited to Mayes County, OK and Grayson County, TX.
Publications: Application guidelines.
Application information: Application form required.
Board of Governors: Samuel W. Graber, Steve Jones, Dana Lamb, Tony J. Lyons, Darius Maggi.
EIN: 751864630
Codes: FD

50714
Paul J. Meyer Family Foundation
P.O. Box 7411
Waco, TX 76714-7411

Established in 1985 in TX.
Donor(s): Japale, Ltd., SMI International, Inc., Paul J. Meyer, Sr.
Financial data (yr. ended 12/31/99): Grants paid, $850,858; assets, $10,909,134 (M); gifts received, $1,986,093; expenditures, $1,584,369; qualifying distributions, $1,179,116.
Limitations: Giving primarily in Waco, TX.
Officers and Directors:* Paul J. Meyer, Sr.,* Pres.; Alice Jane Meyer,* V.P.; William A. Meyer,* V.P.; Joe E. Baxter,* Secy.-Treas.
EIN: 742357421
Codes: FD

50715
South Texas Charitable Foundation
P.O. Box 2549
Victoria, TX 77902-2549 (361) 573-4383
Contact: Rayford L. Keller, Secy.-Treas.

Established in 1981 in TX.
Donor(s): Maude O'Connor Williams.
Financial data (yr. ended 11/30/01): Grants paid, $850,000; assets, $14,953,435 (M); expenditures, $868,598; qualifying distributions, $841,900.
Limitations: Giving primarily in TX.
Application information: Application form not required.
Officers: Ann O.W. Harithas, Pres.; Michael S. Anderson, V.P.; Rayford L. Keller, Secy.-Treas.
EIN: 742148107
Codes: FD

50716
Vivian L. Smith Foundation for Neurological Research
(Formerly Vivian L. Smith Foundation for Restorative Neurology)
1900 W. Loop, S., Ste. 1050
Houston, TX 77027 (713) 622-8611
Contact: Betty Patrick

Established in 1981 in TX.
Donor(s): Vivian L. Smith.‡
Financial data (yr. ended 06/30/01): Grants paid, $841,151; assets, $13,239,695 (M); expenditures, $970,169; qualifying distributions, $855,415.
Application information: Application form not required.
Officers and Trustees:* R.A. Seale, Jr.,* Pres.; Suzanne R. Benson,* V.P. and Treas.; W.N. Finnegan III,* V.P.; Steven H. Gerdes,* Secy.; Delmer Q. Bowman, Sandra Smith Dompier, Dee S. Osborne, Virgil E. Vickery.

50716—TEXAS

EIN: 742139770
Codes: FD

50717
M. J. & Alice S. Neeley Foundation
306 W. 7th St., Ste. 616
Fort Worth, TX 76102-4906 (817) 336-3032
FAX: (817) 336-0535; E-mail:
neeleyfndn@aol.com
Contact: Columba S. Reid, Exec. Dir.

Established about 1983 in TX.
Donor(s): Alice S. Neeley,‡ M.J. Neeley.‡
Financial data (yr. ended 09/30/01): Grants paid, $840,500; assets, $1,435,779 (M); gifts received, $20,628; expenditures, $902,095; qualifying distributions, $886,777.
Limitations: Giving primarily in TX.
Application information: Application form not required.
Trustees: Kathleen Neeley, Marian N. Nettles, Columba S. Reid, Bank One, N.A.
EIN: 751911872
Codes: FD

50718
Martha, David & Bagby Lennox Foundation
228 6th St. S.E.
Paris, TX 75460
Application address: c/o Bracewell & Patterson, LP, 711 Louisiana St., Ste. 2900, Houston, TX 77002-2781
Contact: William P. Streng, Pres.

Established in 1985 in TX.
Donor(s): Martha Lennox,‡ David Lennox,‡ Bagby Lennox.‡
Financial data (yr. ended 12/31/01): Grants paid, $839,442; assets, $14,357,833 (M); expenditures, $1,236,424; qualifying distributions, $881,378.
Limitations: Giving limited to the northeast TX area.
Publications: Application guidelines.
Officers: William P. Streng, Pres.; Sam L. Hocker, V.P.
Director: Mary Clark.
EIN: 760157945
Codes: FD

50719
Meredith Foundation
P.O. Box 117
Mineola, TX 75773

Trust established in 1958 in TX.
Donor(s): Harry W. Meredith.‡
Financial data (yr. ended 12/31/00): Grants paid, $834,368; assets, $16,689,739 (M); expenditures, $949,469; qualifying distributions, $817,971.
Limitations: Applications not accepted. Giving limited to the Mineola, TX, area.
Publications: Program policy statement.
Application information: Contributes only to pre-selected organizations.
Officers: James Dear, Chair.; Coulter Templeton, Vice-Chair.; Ray Williams, Secy.-Treas.
Trustees: W.T. Harrison, J. Carl Norris.
EIN: 756024469
Codes: FD

50720
Jenesis Group
P.O. Box 637
Hurst, TX 76054 (817) 581-1999
FAX: (972) 999-4599; E-mail:
ktanner@jenesis.org; URL: http://www.jenesis.org
Contact: Julie Jensen, Tr.

Established in 1986 in TX.
Donor(s): R.J. Jensen.
Financial data (yr. ended 12/31/01): Grants paid, $832,693; assets, $12,794,221 (M); expenditures, $930,238; qualifying distributions, $926,467.
Limitations: Giving on a national basis.
Publications: Program policy statement, application guidelines.
Application information: Application form not required.
Trustees: Julie Jensen, and 6 additional trustees.
EIN: 756349718
Codes: FD

50721
The Thomas O. Hicks Family Foundation
200 Crescent Ct., Ste. 1600
Dallas, TX 75201

Established in 1994 in TX.
Donor(s): Thomas O. Hicks.
Financial data (yr. ended 11/30/01): Grants paid, $826,930; assets, $8,548,465 (M); gifts received, $690,980; expenditures, $838,394; qualifying distributions, $808,909.
Limitations: Applications not accepted. Giving primarily in Austin and Dallas, TX.
Application information: Contributes only to pre-selected organizations.
Officers: Thomas O. Hicks, Pres.; Cinda C. Hicks, V.P.
Director: Rebecca A. McConnell.
EIN: 752570214
Codes: FD

50722
The Tapeats Fund
P.O. Box 1063
Houston, TX 77251 (713) 830-3400
Contact: Patricia N. Lewis, Exec. Dir.

Established in 1993 in TX.
Donor(s): Robert H. Graham, Laurel A.W. Graham.
Financial data (yr. ended 12/31/01): Grants paid, $824,130; assets, $15,011,424 (M); expenditures, $1,053,283; qualifying distributions, $890,573.
Limitations: Giving primarily in TX, with emphasis on Houston.
Publications: Application guidelines.
Application information: Application form not required.
Officers: Robert H. Graham, Pres.; Laurel A.W. Graham, Exec. V.P.; David R. Graham, V.P.
Trustee: Whitney Laurel Graham.
EIN: 760412011
Codes: FD

50723
Gulf Coast Medical Foundation
P.O. Box 30
Wharton, TX 77488 (979) 532-0904
FAX: (979) 532-0904; E-mail:
mburnham@wcnet.net
Contact: Melissa M. Burnham, Exec. V.P.

Established in 1983 in TX; converted from Caney Valley Memorial Hospital and Gulf Coast Medical Center.
Financial data (yr. ended 12/31/00): Grants paid, $820,000; assets, $17,900,000 (M); expenditures, $1,200,000; qualifying distributions, $820,000.
Limitations: Giving primarily in Wharton, Matagorda, Jackson, Colorado, Fort Bend, and Brazoria counties, TX.
Application information: Application form required.
Officers and Trustees:* Guy F. Stonall III,* Pres.; Melissa M. Burnham, Exec. V.P.; Jack Moore,* V.P.; Max Rotholz, Secy.; Charles Davis, Treas.; R.B. Caraway, M.D., Bert Heubner, and 7 additional trustees.

EIN: 741285242
Codes: FD

50724
Harry W. Bass, Jr. Foundation
4809 Cole Ave., Ste. 250
Dallas, TX 75205 (214) 599-0300
FAX: (214) 599-0405; E-mail:
dcalhoun@airmail.net
Contact: F. David Calhoun, Dir., Grants

Established in 1983 in TX.
Donor(s): Harry W. Bass, Jr.‡
Financial data (yr. ended 12/31/01): Grants paid, $810,835; assets, $49,004,069 (M); expenditures, $10,664,057; qualifying distributions, $810,835.
Limitations: Giving primarily in the Dallas, and Fort Worth, TX, area.
Application information: Application form not required.
Officers and Trustees:* Doris L. Bass,* Pres.; F. David Calhoun,* V.P., Grants; Michael Calhoun,* V.P.; J. Michael Wylie.
EIN: 751876307
Codes: FD

50725
Miriam and Emmett McCoy Foundation
P.O. Box 1028
San Marcos, TX 78667-1028

Established in 1993 in TX.
Donor(s): Emmett F. McCoy, Miriam M. McCoy.
Financial data (yr. ended 12/31/01): Grants paid, $805,318; assets, $5,719,462 (M); gifts received, $300,000; expenditures, $822,421; qualifying distributions, $807,572.
Limitations: Applications not accepted. Giving primarily in TX.
Application information: Contributes only to pre-selected organizations.
Officers and Directors:* Emmett F. McCoy,* Pres.; Miriam M. McCoy,* V.P. and Treas.; Brenda M. Remme,* Secy.
EIN: 742686146
Codes: FD

50726
CFP Foundation
P.O. Box 1063
Houston, TX 77251 (713) 830-3400
Contact: Patricia N. Lewis, Exec. Dir.

Established in 1997 in TX.
Donor(s): Gary T. Crum, Sylvie P. Crum.
Financial data (yr. ended 12/31/01): Grants paid, $802,915; assets, $14,390,874 (M); gifts received, $11,483; expenditures, $932,668; qualifying distributions, $851,787.
Limitations: Applications not accepted. Giving primarily in TX.
Application information: Unsolicited requests for funds not accepted.
Officers: Gary T. Crum, Pres. and Treas.; Sylvie P. Crum, Exec. V.P.; Carol L. Drawe, V.P. and Secy.
EIN: 760537479
Codes: FD

50727
Norman H. Read 1985 Charitable Trust
c/o Amarillo National Bank
P.O. Box 1
Amarillo, TX 79105-0001 (806) 378-8341
Contact: David E. Byrd, Sr. V.P. & Trust Off., Amarillo National Bank

Established in 1994.
Financial data (yr. ended 06/30/01): Grants paid, $792,606; assets, $21,591,137 (M); expenditures, $1,407,876; qualifying distributions, $805,022.

Limitations: Applications not accepted. Giving primarily in Boston and Salem, MA.
Application information: Contributes only to pre-selected organizations.
Trustees: Nile L. Albright, M.D., Amarillo National Bank.
EIN: 752622754
Codes: FD

50728
Larry W. and Katherine S. Buck Foundation
820 Gessner Rd., Ste. 1355
Houston, TX 77024

Donor(s): Larry W. Buck.
Financial data (yr. ended 11/30/01): Grants paid, $788,210; assets, $499,369 (M); expenditures, $788,746; qualifying distributions, $783,017.
Limitations: Applications not accepted. Giving on a national basis, with emphasis on TX.
Application information: Contributes only to pre-selected organizations.
Trustees: Katherine S. Buck, Larry W. Buck.
EIN: 760168891
Codes: FD

50729
Tom C. White Foundation
900 Eighth St., Ste. 900
Wichita Falls, TX 76301 (940) 723-1660
Contact: David Harrell White, Tr.

Established in 1959 in TX.
Donor(s): Tommie O. White.‡
Financial data (yr. ended 12/31/01): Grants paid, $782,551; assets, $1,754,039 (M); expenditures, $788,856; qualifying distributions, $780,845.
Limitations: Giving limited to Wichita Falls, TX.
Application information: Application form not required.
Trustees: David Harrell White, David K. White, Gail M. White.
EIN: 756037052
Codes: FD

50730
Bob and Vivian Smith Foundation
1900 W. Loop S., Ste. 1050
Houston, TX 77027-3207 (713) 986-8030
Contact: Amy Meckel

Established about 1969.
Donor(s): R.E. Smith,‡ Vivian L. Smith.‡
Financial data (yr. ended 12/31/01): Grants paid, $781,539; assets, $11,600,985 (M); expenditures, $857,425; qualifying distributions, $784,005.
Limitations: Giving on a national basis.
Publications: Application guidelines.
Application information: Application form not required.
Officers and Trustees:* W.N. Finnegan III,* Pres.; Suzanne B. Benson, Secy.-Treas.; Bobby Smith Cohn, Sandra Smith Dompier.
EIN: 237029052
Codes: FD

50731
Cornerstone Christian Outreach, Inc.
1445 Ross at Field, Ste. 1700
Dallas, TX 75202-2785

Established in 1985 in TX.
Donor(s): June Hunt.
Financial data (yr. ended 12/31/99): Grants paid, $775,783; assets, $9,258,179 (M); gifts received, $59,322; expenditures, $996,500; qualifying distributions, $949,500.
Limitations: Applications not accepted.
Application information: Contributes only to pre-selected organizations.

Officers and Directors:* Ruth June Hunt,* Chair. and Pres.; Bradley S. Ray,* V.P.; Barbara Clark Cashion, Secy.-Treas.; William Randall Dodgen, Edward J. Drake, Sr., Joann Hummel, June Page.
EIN: 752045805
Codes: FD

50732
Lockheed Martin Missiles and Fire Control Employee Charity Fund
(Formerly Lockheed Martin Vought Systems Employee Charity Fund)
P.O. Box 650003, PT 42
Dallas, TX 75265-0003
Contact: Brent Berryman, Treas.

Established in 1994 in TX.
Donor(s): Lockheed Martin Corp.
Financial data (yr. ended 12/31/01): Grants paid, $773,210; assets, $275,889 (M); gifts received, $781,402; expenditures, $773,210; qualifying distributions, $773,210.
Limitations: Giving primarily in Dallas, Fort Worth, and Lufkin, TX, and Camden, AR.
Application information: Application form not required.
Officers: James F. Berry, Pres.; G.D. Troxel, Secy.; Brent Berryman, Treas.
Director: Tom Cunningham.
EIN: 752528901
Codes: CS, FD, CD

50733
Russell Hill Rogers Fund for the Arts
c/o Peggy Walker, Bank of America
P.O. Box 121
San Antonio, TX 78291
Application address: 4040 Broadway, Ste. 605, San Antonio, TX 78209, tel.: (210) 826-8781
Contact: Jean Rogers Winchell, Tr.

Established in 1986.
Financial data (yr. ended 12/31/00): Grants paid, $762,835; assets, $16,576,203 (M); expenditures, $936,438; qualifying distributions, $759,908.
Limitations: Giving limited to San Antonio, TX, metropolitan area.
Application information: Application form not required.
Trustees: Frank P. Christian, Barbara S. Condos, Robert Lende, Allan G. Paterson, Jr., Jean Rogers Winchell, Bank of America.
EIN: 742403914
Codes: FD

50734
J. Campbell Murrell Fund
8113 Hickory Creek Dr.
Austin, TX 78735
Contact: J. Campbell Murrell, Pres.

Established in 1997 in TX.
Donor(s): J. Campbell Murrell.
Financial data (yr. ended 12/31/01): Grants paid, $760,994; assets, $13,477,227 (M); expenditures, $774,721; qualifying distributions, $760,782.
Limitations: Applications not accepted. Giving primarily in Fort Worth, TX.
Application information: Contributes only to pre-selected organizations.
Officer: J. Campbell Murrell, Pres.
Directors: Guy Grace, Melinda Grace.
EIN: 752694405
Codes: FD

50735
Dorothy Richard Starling Foundation
P.O. Box 66709
Houston, TX 77266 (713) 739-7007
Application address: 2727 Allen Pkwy., Ste. 1700, Houston, TX 77019-2125
Contact: The Trustees

Foundation established in 1969 in TX.
Donor(s): Frank M. Starling.‡
Financial data (yr. ended 12/31/01): Grants paid, $760,000; assets, $31,575,560 (M); expenditures, $1,000,139; qualifying distributions, $796,250.
Application information: Program must relate to classical violin at highest levels. Application form not required.
Trustees: Dunham F. Jewett, Melinda M. Kacal, Alexander C. Speyer, Jr.
EIN: 746121656
Codes: FD

50736
The Webber Family Foundation
c/o JPMorgan Chase Bank
P.O. Box 550
Austin, TX 78789-0001 (512) 479-2678
E-mail: info@webberfoundation.org; URL: http://www.webberfoundation.org
Contact: Sonia Garza

Established in 1999 in TX.
Donor(s): Neil Webber, Noelie Alito.
Financial data (yr. ended 12/31/01): Grants paid, $758,297; assets, $5,840,310 (M); gifts received, $740,801; expenditures, $807,822; qualifying distributions, $774,774.
Limitations: Giving limited to Washington, DC, New Orleans, LA, and Austin, TX.
Officers: Neil Webber, Pres. and Treas.; Noelie Alito, V.P. and Secy.
Trustee: Eva Alito.
EIN: 742927126
Codes: FD

50737
Baker Hughes Foundation
3900 Essex Ln., Ste. 210
Houston, TX 77027-5133 (713) 439-8600
Contact: Isaac C. Kerridge, Exec. Dir.

Established in 1994 in TX.
Donor(s): Baker Hughes Inc.
Financial data (yr. ended 12/31/01): Grants paid, $754,082; assets, $128,766 (M); gifts received, $750,000; expenditures, $755,524; qualifying distributions, $755,411.
Limitations: Giving primarily in TX, with emphasis on Houston; limited giving nationally.
Officers and Trustees:* Michael E. Wiley,* Chair. and Pres.; G. Stephen Finley,* V.P. and Treas.; Alan R. Crain, Jr.,* V.P.; Greg Nakanishi,* V.P.; Sandra E. Alford, Secy.; Isaac C. Kerridge,* Exec. Dir.
EIN: 760441292
Codes: CS, FD, CD

50738
The Morning Star Family Foundation
5949 Sherry Ln., Ste. 1600
Dallas, TX 75225

Established in 1996 in TX.
Donor(s): John D. McStay, Mrs. John D. McStay, The Morning Star Family Limited Partnership.
Financial data (yr. ended 12/31/01): Grants paid, $753,583; assets, $10,511,300 (M); gifts received, $492,388; expenditures, $764,537; qualifying distributions, $759,311.
Limitations: Applications not accepted. Giving primarily in TX.
Application information: Contributes only to pre-selected organizations.

50738—TEXAS

Officers and Trustees:* Ellen McStay,* Pres.; John McStay,* Secy.; Dee Devlin, Eric Devlin, Judge McStay.
EIN: 752682211
Codes: FD

50739
The Kodosky Foundation
22 Cousteau Ln.
Austin, TX 78746
E-mail: kodoskyfoundation@austin.rr.com
Contact: Gail Kodosky, V.P. and Secy.

Established in 1996 in TX.
Donor(s): Gail T. Kodosky, Jeffrey L. Kodosky.
Financial data (yr. ended 12/31/01): Grants paid, $736,500; assets, $16,053,029 (M); expenditures, $753,114; qualifying distributions, $735,170.
Limitations: Applications not accepted. Giving primarily in TX.
Application information: Contributes only to pre-selected organizations.
Officers and Directors:* Jeffrey L. Kodosky,* Pres. and Treas.; Gail T. Kodosky,* V.P. and Secy.; Karen K. Tips, Laura L. Walterman.
EIN: 742802674
Codes: FD

50740
Shield-Ayres Foundation
115 E. Travis St., Ste. 1445
San Antonio, TX 78205-1693 (210) 224-8839
FAX: (210) 224-8987
Contact: Patricia Shield Ayres, Pres.

Established in 1977 in TX.
Donor(s): Fred W. Shield,‡ Robert M. Ayres, Jr., Patricia Shield Ayres.
Financial data (yr. ended 12/31/01): Grants paid, $728,100; assets, $14,266,142 (M); expenditures, $811,650; qualifying distributions, $718,298.
Limitations: Giving primarily in Austin and San Antonio, TX.
Publications: Annual report (including application guidelines).
Application information: Application form not required.
Officer and Trustees:* Patricia Shield Ayres,* Pres.; Margaret Bowers Ayres, Robert Atlee Ayres, Robert M. Ayres, Jr., Vera Ayres Bowen.
EIN: 741938157
Codes: FD

50741
John & Mildred Cauthorn Charitable Trust
P.O. Box 678
Sonora, TX 76950
Contact: Jessie Kerbow, Secy.

Established in 1985 in TX.
Donor(s): Mildred Cauthorn.‡
Financial data (yr. ended 12/31/01): Grants paid, $725,117; assets, $5,779,105 (M); expenditures, $1,141,817; qualifying distributions, $716,457.
Limitations: Giving limited to Sutton County, TX.
Application information: Application form not required.
Officer: Jessie Kerbow, Secy.
Trustees: Milton Cavaness, Michael V. Hale, Jo Ann Jones, Nelda Mayfield, Bob Teaff.
EIN: 751977779
Codes: FD

50742
Louetta M. Cowden Foundation
c/o Bank of America
P.O. Box 831041
Dallas, TX 75283-1041
Application address: c/o David P. Ross, Bank of America, 1200 Main St., 14th Fl., Kansas City, MO 64105, tel.: (816) 979-7481

Trust established in 1964 in MO.
Donor(s): Louetta M. Cowden.‡
Financial data (yr. ended 12/31/01): Grants paid, $717,200; assets, $14,829,191 (M); gifts received, $26,000; expenditures, $858,788; qualifying distributions, $751,503.
Limitations: Giving limited to MO, with an emphasis on the metropolitan Kansas City area.
Publications: Application guidelines.
Application information: Application form not required.
Trustees: Arthur Bowen, Bank of America.
EIN: 436052617
Codes: FD

50743
Dallas Seminary Foundation Vision Fund
3909 Swiss Ave.
Dallas, TX 75204-6411

Established in 1989 in TX.
Donor(s): David Cooke, Jeanette Cooke, Tom Miller, Gene Wooldridge, Don Johnson, Gwynn Johnson, Norm Miller, Robert Murchison.
Financial data (yr. ended 12/31/01): Grants paid, $715,171; assets, $1,836,746 (M); gifts received, $758,329; expenditures, $730,327; qualifying distributions, $715,171.
Limitations: Applications not accepted. Giving on a national basis, primarily in MI and TX.
Application information: Contributes only to pre-selected organizations.
Trustee: Dallas Seminary Foundation.
EIN: 752242740
Codes: FD

50744
The Curtis & Doris K. Hankamer Foundation
9039 Katy Freeway, Ste. 530
Houston, TX 77024-1623
Contact: Gregory A. Herbst

Established in 1981 in TX.
Donor(s): Doris K. Hankamer,‡ Earl Curtis Hankamer, Jr.‡
Financial data (yr. ended 12/31/99): Grants paid, $709,500; assets, $8,976,492 (M); expenditures, $891,921; qualifying distributions, $711,977.
Limitations: Applications not accepted. Giving primarily in Houston, TX.
Application information: Contributes only to pre-selected organizations.
Trustees: S. Terry Bracken, Earl C. Hankamer III, H. Scott Hunsaker.
EIN: 760022687
Codes: FD

50745
Rachel Lyman Charitable Trust
P.O. Box 831041
Dallas, TX 75283-1041

Established in 2000 in TX.
Donor(s): Rachel Lyman.‡
Financial data (yr. ended 07/31/01): Grants paid, $709,470; assets, $12,066,599 (M); gifts received, $12,689,497; expenditures, $757,488; qualifying distributions, $714,272.
Limitations: Applications not accepted. Giving on a national basis, with emphasis on TX, TN, AZ, and CA.
Application information: Contributes only to pre-selected organizations.
Trustee: Bank of America.
EIN: 527114493
Codes: FD

50746
Clements Foundation
1901 N. Akard St.
Dallas, TX 75201 (214) 720-0337
Contact: Shirley Warren

Established in 1968 in TX.
Financial data (yr. ended 12/31/01): Grants paid, $706,600; assets, $11,532,064 (M); expenditures, $781,830; qualifying distributions, $729,822.
Limitations: Giving primarily in the Dallas, TX, area.
Officers: William P. Clements, Jr., Pres.; B. Gill Clements, V.P.; Nancy Clements Seay, V.P.
EIN: 756065076
Codes: FD

50747
The M. R. & Evelyn Hudson Foundation
P.O. Box 2110
Keller, TX 76244
Contact: M.R. Hudson, Dir.

Established in 1992 in KS.
Donor(s): M.R. Hudson.
Financial data (yr. ended 11/30/01): Grants paid, $706,000; assets, $51,904,867 (M); gifts received, $56,378,379; expenditures, $2,016,887; qualifying distributions, $3,931,683.
Limitations: Applications not accepted. Giving primarily in KS, OK, and TX.
Application information: Contributes only to pre-selected organizations.
Directors: Evelyn Hudson, M.K. Hudson, M.R. Hudson.
EIN: 481107753
Codes: FD

50748
Amy Shelton McNutt Charitable Trust
153 Treeline Park, Ste. 300
San Antonio, TX 78209-1880
Contact: Carol Bruehler, Secy.

Established about 1983 in TX.
Donor(s): Amy Shelton McNutt.‡
Financial data (yr. ended 09/30/01): Grants paid, $703,069; assets, $14,075,957 (M); expenditures, $859,514; qualifying distributions, $777,243.
Limitations: Giving primarily in TX, with emphasis on San Antonio.
Application information: Application form not required.
Officer: Carol Bruehler, Secy.
Trustees: R.B. Cutlip, Jack Guenther, Courtney J. Walker.
EIN: 742298675
Codes: FD

50749
Shelton Family Foundation
P.O. Box 2791
Abilene, TX 79604-2791 (915) 676-7724
Contact: David L. Copeland, Pres.

Established in 1997 in TX.
Donor(s): Andrew B. Shelton.‡
Financial data (yr. ended 06/30/01): Grants paid, $702,120; assets, $91,702,819 (M); gifts received, $46,760,000; expenditures, $851,690; qualifying distributions, $804,561.
Limitations: Giving primarily in the west central TX area.
Application information: Application form required.

Officers and Directors:* David L. Copeland,* Pres. and Treas.; Larry D. Franklin,* V.P. and Secy.; Stanley P. Wilson,* V.P.; Andrew D. Durham, David R. Durham, Sindy S. Durham, Wendy H. Durham, Leonard R. Hoffman, Shay Shelton Hoffman, C. Christine Nicols, Ruby W. Shelton.
EIN: 752655885
Codes: FD

50750
AIM Foundation
11 Greenway Plz., Ste. 2600
Houston, TX 77046 (713) 830-3400
Contact: Patricia N. Lewis, Exec. Dir.

Established in 1997 in TX.
Donor(s): Robert H. Graham, AIM Management Group Inc.
Financial data (yr. ended 12/31/01): Grants paid, $696,312; assets, $10,830,283 (M); gifts received, $105,450; expenditures, $911,441; qualifying distributions, $899,963.
Limitations: Applications not accepted. Giving primarily in TX, with emphasis on Houston.
Application information: No new organizations accepted in 2003.
Officers: Charles T. Bauer, Pres.; Gary T. Crum, V.P.; Robert H. Graham, V.P.
Trustee: Judith C. Creel.
EIN: 760522586
Codes: CS, FD, CD

50751
The Partnership Foundation
c/o Jay Wagley
5944 Luther Ln., Ste. 700
Dallas, TX 75225

Established in 1999 in TX.
Financial data (yr. ended 12/31/01): Grants paid, $695,000; assets, $12,509,895 (M); expenditures, $753,598; qualifying distributions, $692,629.
Limitations: Applications not accepted.
Application information: Contributes only to pre-selected organizations.
Officers and Directors:* Anne Paxton Wagley,* Pres.; B. Allyn Copp,* V.P.; James F.P. Wagley,* V.P.; Mary Wagley Copp,* Secy.; Sue Wagley,* Treas.
EIN: 752796975
Codes: FD

50752
The Hicks Family Charitable Foundation
600 Congress Ave., Ste. 1400
Austin, TX 78701

Established in 1997 in TX.
Donor(s): R. Steven Hicks.
Financial data (yr. ended 04/30/01): Grants paid, $694,870; assets, $2,485,499 (M); gifts received, $250,000; expenditures, $709,203; qualifying distributions, $694,733.
Limitations: Applications not accepted. Giving primarily in TX.
Application information: Contributes only to pre-selected organizations.
Directors: Donna Stockton Hicks, R. Steven Hicks, Lew Little, Jr.
EIN: 742877054
Codes: FD

50753
The Powell Foundation
2121 San Felipe, Ste. 110
Houston, TX 77019-5600 (713) 523-7557
FAX: (713) 523-7553; E-mail: info@powellfoundation.org; URL: http://www.powellfoundation.org
Contact: Caroline J, Sabin, Exec. Dir.

Established in 1967 in TX.
Donor(s): Ben H. Powell, Jr.,‡ Kitty King Powell.
Financial data (yr. ended 12/31/01): Grants paid, $694,655; assets, $15,763,614 (M); expenditures, $891,765; qualifying distributions, $814,857.
Limitations: Giving primarily in Harris, Walker, and Travis counties, TX.
Publications: Informational brochure (including application guidelines).
Application information: Application guidelines available on website. Application form not required.
Officers and Trustees:* Nancy Powell Moore,* Pres., Treas. and Mgr.; Antonia Scott Day,* V.P. and Secy.; Ben H. Powell V,* V.P.; Marian Moore Casey, Molly N. Kidd, Katherine G. Osborne, Kitty King Powell.
EIN: 746104592
Codes: FD

50754
The Levine Family Foundation
2925 Briarpark Dr., Ste. 1160
Houston, TX 77042

Established in 1995 in TX.
Donor(s): Fred Levine, Robert G. Levine, Dana L. Levine, members of the Levine family.
Financial data (yr. ended 12/31/00): Grants paid, $694,387; assets, $810,709 (M); gifts received, $600,000; expenditures, $712,983; qualifying distributions, $687,506.
Limitations: Applications not accepted. Giving primarily in TX.
Application information: Contributes only to pre-selected organizations.
Officers: Robert G. Levine, Pres.; Dana L. Levine Guefen, V.P.; Julie G. Levine, Secy.
EIN: 760489145
Codes: FD

50755
The William A. and Madeline Welder Smith Foundation
P.O. Box 2558
Houston, TX 77252-8037

Established in 1992 in TX.
Donor(s): William A. Smith.‡
Financial data (yr. ended 06/30/01): Grants paid, $694,175; assets, $16,912,758 (M); gifts received, $17,000; expenditures, $917,657; qualifying distributions, $826,399.
Limitations: Applications not accepted. Giving primarily in TX, with emphasis on Houston.
Application information: Contributes only to pre-selected organizations.
Trustees: Joe E. Coleman, Ernestine Hooper, C.M. McGee, Joseph W. Royce, H. Michael Tyson, JPMorgan Chase Bank.
EIN: 766076267
Codes: FD

50756
The EDS Foundation
5400 Legacy Dr., H3-6F-47
Plano, TX 75024
URL: http://www.eds.com/foundation
Contact: Diane Spradin, Exec. Dir.

Established in 2000 in TX.
Donor(s): Electronic Data Systems Corp.

Financial data (yr. ended 12/31/01): Grants paid, $688,076; assets, $16,377,922 (M); expenditures, $763,152; qualifying distributions, $513,296.
Limitations: Giving on a worldwide basis.
Publications: Application guidelines, grants list, program policy statement.
Application information: Application form required.
Officers: Richard H. Brown, Pres.; Troy W. Todd, V.P.; Janice Jones, Secy.; Scott J. Krenz, Treas.; Diane Spradlin, Exec. Dir.
Directors: Albert J. Edmonds, Ray L. Hunt, Tom Mattia, Steve Smith, Myrna B. Vance.
EIN: 752859297
Codes: CS, FD, CD

50757
Daniel and Edith Ripley Foundation
c/o Mayor, Day, Caldwell, & Keeton
600 Travis St., Ste. 4200
Houston, TX 77002

Financial data (yr. ended 12/31/00): Grants paid, $683,407; assets, $24,222,604 (M); gifts received, $4,114,875; expenditures, $1,039,843; qualifying distributions, $6,495,933.
Limitations: Applications not accepted. Giving primarily in Houston, TX.
Application information: Contributes only to a pre-selected organization.
Officer: James Greenwood III, C.E.O.
EIN: 746049474
Codes: FD

50758
Roger L. and Laura D. Zeller Charitable Foundation
P.O. Box 13430
San Antonio, TX 78213 (210) 344-9211
Contact: Ronald J. Herrmann, Tr.

Established in 1991 in TX.
Donor(s): Laura D. Zeller,‡ Roger L. Zeller, Zeller Living Trust.
Financial data (yr. ended 12/31/01): Grants paid, $681,500; assets, $87,290 (M); gifts received, $300,000; expenditures, $682,605; qualifying distributions, $681,889.
Limitations: Giving limited to Bexar County, TX, with emphasis on San Antonio.
Application information: Application form required.
Trustees: David S. Herrmann, Karen H. Hermann, Ronald J. Herrmann.
EIN: 742610755
Codes: FD

50759
Young Family Charitable Foundation
15851 Dallas Pkwy., Ste. 925
Addison, TX 75001
Application address: 2121 San Jacinto St., Ste. 1150, Dallas, TX 75201-6771, tel.: (214)922-0238
Contact: M.J. Trusty, Regional Trust Mgr., Merrill Lynch Trust Co.

Established in 1997 in TX.
Donor(s): Charles Young, Diane Young.
Financial data (yr. ended 12/31/00): Grants paid, $667,200; assets, $1,596,344 (M); expenditures, $672,078; qualifying distributions, $668,621.
Limitations: Giving primarily in TX.
Advisory Committee: Charles Young, Diane Young.
Trustee: Merrill Lynch Trust Co.
EIN: 226705354
Codes: FD

50760
E. F. Von Seggern Charitable Foundation
P.O. Box 190851
Dallas, TX 75219-0851 (214) 559-3944
Contact: Dwight E. Saur, Jr., Dir.

Established in 1994 in TX.
Donor(s): E.F. Von Seggern.‡
Financial data (yr. ended 12/31/01): Grants paid, $660,000; assets, $10,397,153 (M); expenditures, $922,317; qualifying distributions, $756,898.
Limitations: Giving limited to Dallas, TX.
Trustee and Directors:* Dwight E. Saur, Jr.,* Tr.; John Fisher, M.D., James H.W. Jacks, Rogene Russell.
EIN: 752304039
Codes: FD

50761
Ultramar Diamond Shamrock Foundation
P.O. Box 696000
San Antonio, TX 78269-6000

Established in 1999 in TX.
Donor(s): Ultramar Diamond Shamrock Corp., Coca-Cola Southwest.
Financial data (yr. ended 12/31/00): Grants paid, $659,141; assets, $642,741 (M); gifts received, $1,374,380; expenditures, $666,342; qualifying distributions, $662,969.
Limitations: Applications not accepted. Giving primarily in OK and TX.
Application information: Contributes only to pre-selected organizations.
Officers: Jean Gaulin, Chair.; Tim Fretthold, Pres.; Tara Ford, V.P. and Secy.; Julie Klumpyan, V.P. and Treas.; Chris Havens, V.P.; Bill Klesse, V.P.
EIN: 742904514
Codes: CS, FD, CD

50762
The Clarence Westbury Foundation
(Formerly The Scaler Westbury Foundation)
2200 Post Oak Blvd., Ste. 707
Houston, TX 77056-4707

Established in 1999 in TX.
Financial data (yr. ended 12/31/00): Grants paid, $656,424; assets, $8,762,625 (M); expenditures, $831,429; qualifying distributions, $646,978.
Limitations: Applications not accepted. Giving on an international basis.
Application information: Contributes only to pre-selected organizations.
Officers and Directors:* Jacques C. Boissannos,* Pres.; Nicolas N. Boissannos,* V.P.; Catherine B. Coste,* V.P.; Marvin A. Wurzer, Secy.-Treas.
EIN: 760507294
Codes: FD

50763
The Muse Educational Foundation
200 Crescent Ct., Ste. 1600
Dallas, TX 75201 (214) 965-7911
Contact: John Muse and Mary Salazar

Established in 1999 in TX.
Donor(s): John R. Muse, Lyn R. Muse.
Financial data (yr. ended 12/31/00): Grants paid, $654,400; assets, $5,376,934 (M); expenditures, $657,320; qualifying distributions, $650,883.
Limitations: Giving primarily in TX.
Officers and Directors:* John R. Muse,* Pres. and Treas.; Lyn R. Muse, Exec. V.P.; Thomas O. Hicks, H. Rand Reynolds.
EIN: 752824936
Codes: FD

50764
Dave Coy Foundation
P.O. Box 121
San Antonio, TX 78291-0121 (210) 270-5371
Contact: Gregg E. Muenster, Sr. V.P., Bank of America

Established in 1992 in TX.
Financial data (yr. ended 07/31/01): Grants paid, $648,456; assets, $3,416,101 (M); expenditures, $703,656; qualifying distributions, $654,735.
Limitations: Giving primarily in Bexar County, TX.
Publications: Annual report.
Application information: Application form required.
Trustees: A.B. Crowther, Bank of America.
EIN: 746394909
Codes: FD

50765
Dian Graves Owen Foundation
400 N. Pine, Ste. 1000
Abilene, TX 79601

Established in 1996 in TX.
Donor(s): Dian Graves Owen.
Financial data (yr. ended 12/31/99): Grants paid, $644,824; assets, $15,266,451 (M); gifts received, $4,909,650; expenditures, $870,965; qualifying distributions, $651,644.
Limitations: Applications not accepted. Giving primarily in Abilene, TX.
Application information: Contributes only to pre-selected organizations.
Officers and Directors:* Dian Graves Owen,* Chair. and Treas.; Tucker S. Bridwell,* Pres.; Diane K. Nichols, Secy.; Deborah O. Carson.
EIN: 752682536
Codes: FD

50766
Watson W. Wise Foundation
(Formerly Watson W. Wise Foundation & Charitable Trust)
110 N. College, Ste. 1002
Tyler, TX 75702 (903) 531-9615

Established around 1967.
Donor(s): Watson W. Wise.‡
Financial data (yr. ended 12/31/00): Grants paid, $640,000; assets, $11,967,186 (M); expenditures, $755,495; qualifying distributions, $658,806.
Limitations: Giving primarily in TX, with emphasis on Tyler.
Application information: Application form not required.
Officers: Will A. Knight, Pres.; Calvin Clyde, Jr., V.P.
Trustees: Herman A. Engel, Emma F. Wise.
EIN: 756064539
Codes: FD

50767
The Matthew 6 Foundation
c/o William P. Glasgow
600 Congress Ave., Ste. 3000
Austin, TX 78701

Established in 1998.
Donor(s): William P. Glasgow.
Financial data (yr. ended 12/31/01): Grants paid, $630,000; assets, $479,567 (M); gifts received, $7,775; expenditures, $640,824; qualifying distributions, $632,048.
Limitations: Applications not accepted. Giving primarily in TX.
Application information: Contributes only to pre-selected organizations.
Officers: William P. Glasgow, Pres.; Kelly H. Glasgow, Secy.
Directors: Edwin Bauman, Chris Harkrider.
EIN: 742897518
Codes: FD

50768
The Joseph D. and Lillie H. Jamail Foundation
1200 Smith St., Ste. 1135
Houston, TX 77002 (713) 650-8544
Contact: Robert L. Jamail, Secy.-Treas.

Established in 1986 in TX.
Donor(s): Joseph D. Jamail, Lillie H. Jamail.
Financial data (yr. ended 12/31/01): Grants paid, $626,918; assets, $14,527,096 (M); expenditures, $670,165; qualifying distributions, $626,918.
Limitations: Giving limited to TX.
Application information: No videos accepted. Application form not required.
Officer and Trustees:* Robert L. Jamail,* Treas.; Joseph D. Jamail III, Lee H. Jamail, Randall Hage Jamail.
EIN: 760181247
Codes: FD

50769
The Pangburn Foundation
c/o Bank One, Texas, N.A.
P.O. Box 2050
Fort Worth, TX 76113 (817) 884-4151
Contact: Robert Lansford

Established in 1962 in TX.
Financial data (yr. ended 03/31/01): Grants paid, $626,500; assets, $8,343,602 (M); expenditures, $712,766; qualifying distributions, $636,919.
Limitations: Giving primarily in the Fort Worth, TX, area.
Trustee: Bank One Trust Co., N.A.
EIN: 756042630
Codes: FD

50770
The Lyons Foundation
1202A Dairy Ashford St.
Houston, TX 77079-3004 (281) 497-0332
Contact: R.A. Seale, Jr., Pres.

Established in 1961 in TX.
Donor(s): Richard T. Lyons,‡ Sammie Lyons,‡ Magalou W. Hestand Trust.
Financial data (yr. ended 12/31/01): Grants paid, $624,121; assets, $11,846,024 (M); expenditures, $712,438; qualifying distributions, $624,007.
Limitations: Giving primarily in Houston, TX.
Application information: Application form not required.
Officers: R.A. Seale, Jr., Pres.; Phil Peden, V.P.; James S. Prentice, Secy.-Treas.
EIN: 746038717
Codes: FD

50771
Robert E. and Evelyn McKee Foundation
P.O. Box 220599
5835 Cromo, Ste. 1
El Paso, TX 79913-2599 (915) 581-4025
FAX: (915) 833-3714; E-mail: mckee_foundation@msn.com; URL: http://www.mckeefoundation.org
Contact: Louis B. McKee, Pres.

Incorporated in 1952 in TX.
Donor(s): Robert E. McKee,‡ Evelyn McKee,‡ Robert E. McKee, Inc., The Zia Co.
Financial data (yr. ended 12/31/01): Grants paid, $618,312; assets, $7,520,629 (M); expenditures, $873,822; qualifying distributions, $700,878.
Limitations: Giving primarily in TX, with emphasis on El Paso.
Publications: Annual report (including application guidelines), program policy statement, application guidelines.

Application information: Application form not required.
Officers and Trustees:* Louis B. McKee,* Pres. and Treas.; Frances McKee Hays,* Sr. V.P.; Margaret McKee Lund,* Sr. V.P.; Helen Lund Yancey,* V.P. and Secy.; Charlotte McKee Cohen,* V.P.; Sharon Hays Herrera,* V.P.; David C. McKee,* V.P.; Nelson D. McKee, V.P.; Susan J. McKee, V.P.; Carolyn McKee Hughes, C. Steven McKee, James T. McKee, Philip Russell McKee, R. Brian McKee, H.A. Woods.
EIN: 746036675
Codes: FD

50772
Nancy and John Snyder Foundation
(Formerly Nancy and John Foundation)
201 Main St., Ste. 1450
Fort Worth, TX 76102-5356

Established in 1980.
Donor(s): John C. Snyder.
Financial data (yr. ended 11/30/01): Grants paid, $612,997; assets, $8,827,928 (M); expenditures, $701,152; qualifying distributions, $619,499.
Limitations: Applications not accepted. Giving primarily in Fort Worth, TX.
Application information: Contributes primarily to pre-selected organizations and individuals.
Officers and Directors:* John C. Snyder,* Pres.; Nancy T. Snyder,* V.P.; Rodney L. Waller,* Secy.-Treas.
EIN: 751737014
Codes: FD, GTI

50773
Lola Wright Foundation, Inc.
P.O. Box 1138
Georgetown, TX 78627-1138 (512) 869-2574
Austin tel.: (512) 255-5353
Contact: Patrick H. O'Donnell, Pres.

Incorporated in 1954 in TX.
Donor(s): Johnie E. Wright.‡
Financial data (yr. ended 12/31/01): Grants paid, $607,929; assets, $16,155,580 (M); expenditures, $844,309; qualifying distributions, $660,785.
Limitations: Giving limited to within a 50-mile radius of Austin, TX.
Publications: Annual report, application guidelines.
Application information: Application form not required.
Officers and Directors:* Patrick H. O'Donnell,* Pres.; Vivian E. Todd,* V.P.; Wilford Flowers,* Secy.-Treas.; Raffy Garza-Viscaino, Paul Hilgers, James Meyers, Carole Rylander.
EIN: 746054717
Codes: FD

50774
Buford Foundation
2501 Cedar Springs LB-5, Ste. 200
Dallas, TX 75201-1400

Established in 1998 in TX.
Donor(s): Linda C. Buford, Robert P. Buford.
Financial data (yr. ended 12/31/00): Grants paid, $607,200; assets, $3,742,587 (M); gifts received, $1,475,000; expenditures, $1,471,476; qualifying distributions, $1,319,036; giving activities include $638,531 for programs.
Limitations: Applications not accepted.
Application information: Contributes only to pre-selected organizations.
Officer: Robert P. Buford.
Directors: Linda C. Buford, John Castle, Thomas Luce III, J. Mcdonald Williams, Jack Willome.
EIN: 752791126
Codes: FD

50775
Mary Potishman Lard Trust
c/o Bank One, Texas, N.A.
600 Bailey Ave.
Fort Worth, TX 76107
Application address: 500 W. 7th St., Ste. 700, Fort Worth, TX 76102
Contact: Walker C. Friedman, Tr.

Trust established in 1968 in TX.
Donor(s): Mary P. Lard.‡
Financial data (yr. ended 12/31/01): Grants paid, $598,750; assets, $13,057,077 (M); expenditures, $738,173; qualifying distributions, $614,010.
Limitations: Giving primarily in TX, with emphasis on Fort Worth.
Trustees: Alan D. Friedman, Walker C. Friedman.
Agent: Bank One, Texas, N.A.
EIN: 756210697
Codes: FD

50776
Folsom Charitable Foundation, Inc.
16475 Dallas Pkwy., Ste. 800
Addison, TX 75001-6856

Established in 1984 in TX.
Donor(s): Margaret D. Folsom, Robert S. Folsom.
Financial data (yr. ended 12/31/01): Grants paid, $594,846; assets, $2,914,247 (M); expenditures, $609,597; qualifying distributions, $604,347.
Limitations: Applications not accepted. Giving primarily in TX.
Application information: Contributes only to pre-selected organizations.
Officers and Trustees:* Robert S. Folsom,* Pres.; Margaret D. Folsom,* V.P.; Haddon O. Winckler, Secy.-Treas.; Robert Stephen Folsom, Debra Folsom Jarma, Diane Folsom Miller.
EIN: 751862254
Codes: FD

50777
Mays Family Foundation
200 E. Basse Rd.
San Antonio, TX 78209

Established around 1994.
Donor(s): L. Lowry Mays, Mark Mays, Randall Mays.
Financial data (yr. ended 12/31/01): Grants paid, $588,954; assets, $38,372,004 (M); gifts received, $14,534,964; expenditures, $589,830; qualifying distributions, $589,830.
Limitations: Applications not accepted. Giving primarily in San Antonio, TX.
Application information: Contributes only to pre-selected organizations.
Officers and Directors:* Peggy P. Mays,* Pres.; Kathryn M. Johnson,* V.P.; L. Lowry Mays,* Treas.; Mark P. Mays, Randall T. Mays, Linda M. McCaul.
EIN: 742691624
Codes: FD

50778
Ed Haggar Family Foundation
16051 Addison Rd., Ste. 212
Addison, TX 75001
Application address: 6113 Lemmon Ave., Dallas, TX 75209, tel.: (214) 956-5245
Contact: E.R. Haggar, Dir.

Established in 1995 in TX.
Financial data (yr. ended 06/30/01): Grants paid, $587,864; assets, $8,496,695 (M); expenditures, $758,021; qualifying distributions, $586,473.
Limitations: Giving primarily in TX and, to a lesser extent, CA and CO.
Directors: E.R. Haggar, E.R. Haggar, Jr., James J. Haggar, John D. Haggar, Patricia A. Haggar, Mary A. Stedillie, Patricia J. Turner.

EIN: 752565413
Codes: FD

50779
Allen Lovelace Moore and Blanche Davis Moore Foundation
800 N. Shoreline Blvd.
S. Tower, Ste. 1702
Corpus Christi, TX 78401 (361) 885-0077
Contact: Paul C. Pearson III, Dir.

Established in 1993 in TX.
Donor(s): Blanche Davis Moore.‡
Financial data (yr. ended 03/31/01): Grants paid, $587,650; assets, $15,645,111 (M); gifts received, $375,000; expenditures, $905,677; qualifying distributions, $587,650.
Limitations: Giving primarily in the Corpus Christi, TX area.
Application information: Application form required.
Directors: Charles Harmon Davis, Rev. Joseph Homer Davis, Jr., Lorine Jones, Gary Leach, Paul C. Pearson III.
EIN: 742675281
Codes: FD

50780
Ralph H. & Ruth J. McCullough Foundation
1300 Post Oak Blvd., 20th Fl.
Houston, TX 77056-8000 (713) 986-7200
Contact: Joseph W. Royce, Secy.

Established in 1981 in TX.
Donor(s): Ralph H. McCullough,‡ Ruth J. McCullough.‡
Financial data (yr. ended 12/31/01): Grants paid, $586,000; assets, $14,219,961 (M); expenditures, $781,341; qualifying distributions, $717,521.
Limitations: Applications not accepted. Giving primarily in TX.
Application information: Contributes only to pre-selected organizations.
Officers and Trustees:* Joe E. Coleman,* Pres. and Treas.; James T. McCullough,* V.P.; Joseph W. Royce, Secy.; Jack H. Hooper, Dee S. Osborne, Anne M. Shallenberger, H. Michael Tyson.
EIN: 742177193
Codes: FD

50781
Theodore and Beulah Beasley Foundation, Inc.
3811 Turtle Creek Blvd., Ste. 940
Dallas, TX 75219-4490
Contact: Mary E. Beasley, Pres.

Incorporated in 1957 in TX.
Donor(s): Theodore P. Beasley.
Financial data (yr. ended 12/31/01): Grants paid, $585,325; assets, $13,694,186 (M); expenditures, $901,075; qualifying distributions, $663,068.
Limitations: Applications not accepted. Giving primarily in the Dallas, TX, area.
Application information: Contributes only to pre-selected organizations.
Officers: Mary E. Beasley, Pres.; Robert R. Beasley, V.P.; Vicki Vanderslice, V.P.; Linda Tinney, Secy.; Samuel Dashefsky, Treas. and Exec. Dir.
EIN: 756035806
Codes: FD

50782
The Simmons Foundation
109 N. Post Oak Ln., Ste. 220
Houston, TX 77024 (713) 268-8099
FAX: (713) 580-1850; *E-mail:* lmay@redstonecompanies.com
Contact: Linda K. May, Dir.

Established in 1993.
Donor(s): Gay A. Roane.

50782—TEXAS

Financial data (yr. ended 12/31/00): Grants paid, $585,250; assets, $12,255,859 (M); gifts received, $50,000; expenditures, $628,463; qualifying distributions, $568,345.
Limitations: Giving primarily in Harris County and Houston, TX.
Application information: Application form not required.
Officers and Directors:* David L. Solomon,* Pres.; David Shindeldecker,* V.P.; Linda May, Gay A. Roane.
EIN: 760398915
Codes: FD

50783
The Sidhu-Singh Family Foundation
2301 N. Greenville Ave., Ste. 150
Richardson, TX 75082

Established in 1999 in TX.
Donor(s): Sanjiv Sidhu, Lekha Singh.
Financial data (yr. ended 12/31/00): Grants paid, $584,540; assets, $2,764,505 (M); expenditures, $619,790; qualifying distributions, $567,064.
Limitations: Applications not accepted. Giving primarily in Dallas, TX.
Application information: Contributes only to pre-selected organizations.
Directors: Michael Held, Sanjiv Sidhu, Lekha Singh.
EIN: 752849866
Codes: FD

50784
The Ware Foundation
c/o Amarillo National Bank-Trust
P.O. Box 1
Amarillo, TX 79105-0001

Established in 1996 in TX.
Donor(s): B.T. Ware II, Richard C. Ware II, Mary S. Ware.
Financial data (yr. ended 12/31/00): Grants paid, $580,647; assets, $3,336,675 (M); gifts received, $678,992; expenditures, $631,235; qualifying distributions, $578,453.
Limitations: Applications not accepted. Giving primarily in TX.
Application information: Contributes only to pre-selected organizations.
Officer: B.T. Ware II, Pres.
Directors: Mary S. Ware, Richard C. Ware II, W.R. Ware.
EIN: 752662421
Codes: FD

50785
The Bryant & Nancy Hanley Foundation
5455 Northbrook
Dallas, TX 75220 (214) 665-1900
Contact: Bryant M. Hanley, Jr., Pres.

Established in 1996.
Donor(s): Bryant M. Hanley, Nancy Hanley.
Financial data (yr. ended 12/31/01): Grants paid, $578,393; assets, $4,107,012 (M); gifts received, $810,180; expenditures, $603,149; qualifying distributions, $568,406.
Limitations: Giving primarily in Dallas, TX.
Officers and Directors:* Bryant M. Hanley, Jr.,* Pres.; Nancy Hanley,* Secy.-Treas.; Barbara Hanley-Caldas, Sarah Hanley.
EIN: 752683075
Codes: FD

50786
University Park Civic Foundation, Inc.
3800 University Blvd.
Dallas, TX 75205

Financial data (yr. ended 12/31/00): Grants paid, $578,095; assets, $21,642 (M); gifts received, $50,765; expenditures, $578,095; qualifying distributions, $578,095.
Limitations: Applications not accepted.
Application information: Unsolicited requests for funds not accepted.
Officers: Harold Peek, Pres.; Olin B. Lane, Jr., V.P.; W. Richard Davis, Secy.-Treas.
EIN: 752215491
Codes: FD

50787
The Helm Foundation, Inc.
8 Greenway Plz., Rm. 718
Houston, TX 77046

Established in 1993 in TX.
Donor(s): Glora Bee Helm, Tair, Ltd.
Financial data (yr. ended 12/31/00): Grants paid, $577,234; assets, $8,623,752 (M); gifts received, $1,442,899; expenditures, $671,197; qualifying distributions, $577,561.
Limitations: Applications not accepted. Giving primarily in TX.
Application information: Contributes only to pre-selected organizations.
Officers and Directors:* Glora Bee Helm,* Chair.; Cyrus Vard Helm,* Pres.; Roger A. Anderson,* Exec. V.P.; David W. Welles,* Secy.
EIN: 760419884
Codes: FD

50788
The R. W. Fair Foundation
P.O. Box 689
Tyler, TX 75710 (903) 592-3811
Contact: Wilton H. Fair, Pres.

Trust established in 1936; incorporated in 1959 in TX.
Donor(s): R.W. Fair,‡ Mattie Allen Fair.‡
Financial data (yr. ended 12/31/00): Grants paid, $576,085; assets, $15,605,870 (M); expenditures, $1,159,019; qualifying distributions, $576,655.
Limitations: Giving primarily in the Southwest, with emphasis on TX.
Publications: Application guidelines.
Application information: Application form required.
Officers and Directors:* Wilton H. Fair,* Pres.; James W. Fair,* Sr. V.P.; Sam Bright,* V.P.; Wilma Stenhouse,* Secy.-Treas.; Herbert Buie, B.G. Hartley, Will A. Knight, B.B. Palmore.
EIN: 756015270
Codes: FD

50789
The Galtney Foundation
820 Gessner, Ste. 1000
Houston, TX 77024-4259
Contact: Joseph L. Moore, Dir.

Established in 1995 in TX.
Donor(s): William F. Galtney, Jr.
Financial data (yr. ended 12/31/99): Grants paid, $575,484; assets, $5,648 (M); gifts received, $12,500; expenditures, $577,253; qualifying distributions, $575,484.
Limitations: Giving primarily in TX.
Officers and Directors:* William F. Galtney, Jr.,* Pres.; Susanne W. Galtney,* Secy.-Treas.; Joseph L. Moore.
EIN: 760489358

50790
Marcia & Otto Koehler Foundation
c/o Bank of America
P.O. Box 121
San Antonio, TX 78291-0121 (210) 270-5371
Contact: Gregg Muenster, Sr. V.P., Bank of America

Established in 1980 in TX.
Donor(s): Marcia Koehler.‡
Financial data (yr. ended 07/31/01): Grants paid, $570,000; assets, $9,620,701 (M); expenditures, $727,704; qualifying distributions, $570,000.
Limitations: Giving limited to Bexar County, TX.
Publications: Annual report.
Application information: Application form required.
Trustee: Bank of America.
EIN: 742131195
Codes: FD

50791
Louis H. and Mary Patricia Stumberg Foundation
310 S. St. Mary's, Ste. 701
San Antonio, TX 78205 (210) 225-0243
FAX: (210) 225-2556
Contact: Louis H. Stumberg, Tr.

Established in 1989 in TX.
Donor(s): Louis H. Stumberg, Mary Pat Stumberg.
Financial data (yr. ended 12/31/01): Grants paid, $568,626; assets, $7,949,178 (M); gifts received, $30,000; expenditures, $615,006; qualifying distributions, $567,866.
Limitations: Giving primarily in San Antonio, TX.
Publications: Annual report.
Trustees: Diana M. Stumberg, Eric B. Stumberg, Louis H. Stumberg, Louis H. Stumberg, Jr., Mary Pat Stumberg.
EIN: 746367261
Codes: FD

50792
Minnie Stevens Piper Foundation
800 N.W. Loop 410, Ste. 200
San Antonio, TX 78216-5699 (210) 525-8494
FAX: (210) 341-6627; *E-mail:* mspf@mspf.org
Contact: Carlos Otero, Secy.

Incorporated in 1950 in TX.
Donor(s): Randall G. Piper,‡ Minnie Stevens Piper.‡
Financial data (yr. ended 12/31/01): Grants paid, $567,640; assets, $25,497,565 (M); gifts received, $343; expenditures, $1,737,134; qualifying distributions, $1,409,417; giving activities include $216,221 for loans to individuals and $301,280 for programs.
Limitations: Giving limited to TX; student loans limited to U.S. citizens residing in TX and attending TX educational institutions.
Publications: Occasional report, program policy statement.
Application information: Recipients of scholarship and professorship award programs must be nominated; nomination not necessary for student loans. Application form not required.
Officers and Directors:* John H. Wilson II,* Pres.; Michael J. Balint,* V.P.; Carlos Otero,* Secy. and Exec. Dir.; Martin R. Harris,* Treas.; Paul T. Curl, Lewis M. Fox, Kenneth Shumate, J. Burleson Smith.
EIN: 741292695
Codes: FD, GTI

50793
Riggs Benevolent Fund
P.O. Box 831041
Dallas, TX 75283-1041
Application address: c/o Bank of America, Private Client Group, P.O. Box 1681, Little Rock, AR 72203-1681, tel.: (501) 378-1626
Contact: Sandra K. Walker

Trust established in 1959 in AR.
Donor(s): members of the Riggs family, Robert G. Cress, Lamar W. Riggs Trust, J.A. Riggs Tractor Co., Inc.
Financial data (yr. ended 12/31/00): Grants paid, $561,300; assets, $6,705,944 (M); gifts received, $130,906; expenditures, $626,038; qualifying distributions, $559,601.
Limitations: Giving primarily in Little Rock, AR.
Application information: Unsolicited applications rarely produce a response.
Trustees: Robert G. Cress, John A. Riggs III, Bank of America.
EIN: 716050130
Codes: FD

50794
Howard Earl Rachofsky Foundation
8201 Preston Rd., Ste. 400
Dallas, TX 75225 (214) 890-8819
Contact: Dina H. Bardi, Secy.

Established in 1993 in TX.
Donor(s): Howard Earl Rachofsky.
Financial data (yr. ended 03/31/01): Grants paid, $559,503; assets, $267,416 (M); gifts received, $703,637; expenditures, $575,057; qualifying distributions, $570,566.
Limitations: Giving primarily in Dallas, TX.
Application information: Application form not required.
Officers: Howard Earl Rachofsky, Pres.; William C. Ward, V.P.; Dina H. Bardi, Secy.; Michael Massad, Treas.
EIN: 752481321
Codes: FD

50795
The Charitable Foundation of the Frost National Bank of San Antonio
c/o Frost National Bank
P.O. Box 2950
San Antonio, TX 78299
Application address: c/o Exec. Comm., Frost National Bank, 100 W. Houston St., San Antonio, TX 78205, tel.: (210) 220-4449
Contact: William Clyborne

Established around 1979.
Donor(s): The Frost National Bank.
Financial data (yr. ended 12/31/01): Grants paid, $559,418; assets, $738,571 (M); gifts received, $250,000; expenditures, $573,789; qualifying distributions, $559,129.
Limitations: Giving primarily in San Antonio, TX.
Trustee: Frost National Bank.
EIN: 742058155
Codes: CS, FD, CD

50796
Progress Foundation
P.O. Box 2950
San Antonio, TX 78299

Established in 1997 in TX.
Donor(s): Carlos Enrique Alvarez, Maria de Guadalupe Alvarez.
Financial data (yr. ended 09/30/01): Grants paid, $558,333; assets, $11,702,125 (M); expenditures, $722,841; qualifying distributions, $558,333.
Limitations: Applications not accepted. Giving in the U.S., primarily in Davidson, NC, and San Antonio, TX.
Application information: Contributes only to pre-selected organizations.
Trustee: Frost National Bank.
EIN: 746449471
Codes: FD

50797
Hope Pierce Tartt Scholarship Fund
P.O. Box 1964
Marshall, TX 75671
Contact: E.N. Smith, Jr., Chair.

Trust established in 1978 in TX.
Donor(s): Hope Pierce Tartt.‡
Financial data (yr. ended 05/31/01): Grants paid, $557,500; assets, $12,109,649 (M); expenditures, $658,279; qualifying distributions, $551,759.
Limitations: Giving primarily in Harrison, Panola, Marion, Rusk and Upshur counties, TX.
Publications: Program policy statement, application guidelines.
Application information: Students must contact financial aid offices of participating schools for application. Foundation does not select individuals for grants. Application form required.
Officers and Directors:* E.N. Smith, Jr.,* Chair.; Robert L. Duvall,* Secy.-Treas.; Howdy Dawson, Bushe Morgan.
EIN: 756263272
Codes: FD

50798
Ben E. Keith Foundation Trust
c/o Bank One, Texas, N.A.
600 Bailey Ave., TX1-3434
Fort Worth, TX 76107
Application address: P.O. Box 2050, Fort Worth, TX 76113, tel.: (817) 884-4151
Contact: Robert Lansford

Trust established in 1951 in TX.
Financial data (yr. ended 06/30/01): Grants paid, $556,800; assets, $16,123,119 (M); expenditures, $677,187; qualifying distributions, $563,158.
Limitations: Giving limited to TX.
Trustee: Bank One, Texas, N.A.
EIN: 756013955
Codes: FD

50799
The Marilyn Augur Family Foundation
(Formerly The Marilyn Augur Foundation)
3131 Turtle Creek Blvd., Ste. 1000
Dallas, TX 75219 (214) 522-5586
FAX: (214) 522-0245; *E-mail:* maf@waymark.net; *URL:* http://fdncenter.org/grantmaker/augur
Contact: Nancy Elizabeth Roberts, V.P.

Established in 1990 in TX; funded in 1991.
Donor(s): Marilyn Augur.
Financial data (yr. ended 12/31/00): Grants paid, $555,214; assets, $12,412,026 (M); expenditures, $844,352; qualifying distributions, $639,268.
Limitations: Giving primarily in Dallas, TX.
Application information: Application form required.
Officers and Trustees:* Marilyn Augur,* Pres.; Nancy Elizabeth Roberts, V.P.; Elizabeth T. Jones Turner,* V.P.; P. Mike McCullough,* Secy.; Margaret M. Augur Hancock,* Treas.
EIN: 752358239
Codes: FD

50800
The Neil and Elaine Griffin Foundation
301 Junction Hwy., Ste. 320
Kerrville, TX 78028
Application address: P.O. Box 1961, Kerrville, TX 78028, tel.: (830) 896-6667
Contact: Richard D. Griffin, Managing Tr.

Established in 1994 in TX.
Donor(s): F. O'Neil Griffin.
Financial data (yr. ended 09/30/01): Grants paid, $552,784; assets, $6,829,773 (M); gifts received, $600; expenditures, $634,221; qualifying distributions, $552,006.
Limitations: Giving limited to Kerrville, TX.
Application information: Scholarships are restricted to Kerr County High School graduates only. Application form required.
Directors: F. O'Neil Griffin, Richard D. Griffin.
EIN: 742729281
Codes: FD

50801
The Stanzel Family Foundation, Inc.
311 Baumgarten St.
Schulenburg, TX 78956 (979) 743-6559
Contact: Theodore E. Stanzel, Pres.

Established in 1989 in TX; funded in 1990.
Donor(s): Joseph Stanzel,‡ Victor Stanzel.‡
Financial data (yr. ended 07/31/01): Grants paid, $547,753; assets, $15,490,996 (M); gifts received, $777,563; expenditures, $794,543; qualifying distributions, $601,217.
Limitations: Giving limited to Schulenburg, Weimar, and La Grange, TX.
Application information: Application form required.
Officers: Theodore E. Stanzel, Pres.; Robert R. Stanzel, V.P.; Helen Niesner, Secy.; Ginger Bosl, Treas.
EIN: 742579827
Codes: FD, GTI

50802
Sunnyside Foundation, Inc.
8222 Douglas Ave., Ste. 501
Dallas, TX 75225-5936 (214) 692-5686
Contact: Joan McClendon, Exec. Dir.

Established in 1928 in TX.
Donor(s): I. Jalonick.‡
Financial data (yr. ended 12/31/99): Grants paid, $546,754; assets, $12,080,962 (M); gifts received, $426,661; expenditures, $698,860; qualifying distributions, $598,574.
Limitations: Giving limited to residents of TX.
Application information: Application form required.
Officers and Trustees:* Robert Forrest,* Pres.; Susan Hueffner,* V.P.; William R. Hays III, Treas.; Joan McClendon, Exec. Dir.; Linda Ozanne, Susan Williams.
EIN: 756037004
Codes: FD, GTI

50803
The Fleming Foundation
500 W. 7th St., Ste. 1007
Fort Worth, TX 76102-4732
Contact: G. Malcolm Louden, Asst. Secy.-Treas.

Incorporated in 1936 in TX.
Donor(s): William Fleming.‡
Financial data (yr. ended 12/31/01): Grants paid, $546,500; assets, $2,582,634 (M); expenditures, $603,764; qualifying distributions, $546,500.
Limitations: Giving primarily in TX, with emphasis on Fort Worth.
Application information: Application form not required.

50803—TEXAS

Officers: Mary D. Walsh, Pres.; F. Howard Walsh, Jr., Secy.-Treas.
Director: Gary Goble.
EIN: 756022736
Codes: FD

50804
International Medical Outreach, Inc.
902 Frostwood, No. 288
Houston, TX 77024
Contact: Todd Price, Pres.

Established in 1997 in TX.
Donor(s): Todd Price, Christian Alliance for Humanitarian Aid, Medical Bridges, Inc.
Financial data (yr. ended 12/31/00): Grants paid, $544,747; assets, $179,073 (M); gifts received, $430,620; expenditures, $635,232; qualifying distributions, $635,003.
Limitations: Giving on an international basis, with emphasis on the Ukraine.
Officers: Todd Price, Pres.; Susan Price, V.P.; Robert Liken, Secy.; Justin Osteen, Treas.
EIN: 760392915
Codes: FD

50805
B. B. Owen Trust
P.O. Box 830068
Richardson, TX 75083
Contact: Monty J. Jackson, Tr.

Trust established in 1974 in TX.
Donor(s): B.B. Owen.‡
Financial data (yr. ended 09/30/01): Grants paid, $537,440; assets, $13,878,336 (M); expenditures, $580,458; qualifying distributions, $637,220.
Limitations: Giving primarily in Dallas, TX.
Application information: Application form not required.
Trustees: Spencer Carver, Monty J. Jackson, Wendell W. Judd.
EIN: 751385809
Codes: FD

50806
Cyvia and Melvyn Wolff Foundation
P.O. Box 219169
Houston, TX 77218

Established in 1997 in TX.
Donor(s): Curtis Wolff, Cyvia G. Wolff, Melvyn L. Wolff.
Financial data (yr. ended 11/30/01): Grants paid, $537,400; assets, $1,155,272 (M); expenditures, $544,596; qualifying distributions, $535,832.
Limitations: Applications not accepted. Giving primarily in Houston, TX.
Application information: Contributes only to pre-selected organizations.
Officers: Melvyn L. Wolff, Pres. and Treas.; Cyvia G. Wolff, V.P. and Secy.
Trustee: Curtis Wolff.
EIN: 760556526
Codes: FD

50807
Marion Foundation
7751 San Felipe
Houston, TX 77063

Established in 2000 in TX.
Donor(s): Request Seismic Surveys, Ltd.
Financial data (yr. ended 12/31/00): Grants paid, $535,500; assets, $218,553 (M); gifts received, $668,200; expenditures, $535,520; qualifying distributions, $532,520.
Limitations: Applications not accepted. Giving primarily in Houston, TX and WY.
Application information: Contributes only to pre-selected organizations.

Officers and Directors:* Jesse R. Marion,* Pres.; Cathy A. Marion,* Secy.-Treas.; Mary A. Calannia.
EIN: 760635519
Codes: FD

50808
The Edward and Betty Marcus Foundation
8222 Douglas Ave., Ste. 680
Dallas, TX 75225 (214) 361-4681
FAX: (214) 941-3103; E-mail: bancroft@flash.net
Contact: M'Lou Bancroft, Exec. Dir.

Established about 1984 in TX.
Donor(s): Betty B. Marcus.‡
Financial data (yr. ended 12/31/99): Grants paid, $535,410; assets, $11,484,031 (M); expenditures, $697,350; qualifying distributions, $606,593.
Limitations: Giving limited to TX.
Publications: Biennial report, application guidelines.
Application information: Application form not required.
Officers and Trustees:* Melba Davis Whatley,* Chair.; Peter J. Blum,* Vice-Chair.; Carolyn Levy Clark,* Secy.-Treas.; Norine Haynes, Theodore S. Hochstim, Cary Shel Marcus, Richard C. Marcus.
EIN: 751989529
Codes: FD

50809
Joe and Louise Cook Foundation
505 Cherokee Dr.
Temple, TX 76504
Contact: Barbara Wendland, Pres.

Established in 1989 in TX.
Donor(s): Joe B. Cook,‡ Louise P. Cook.‡
Financial data (yr. ended 12/31/01): Grants paid, $535,041; assets, $9,165,573 (M); expenditures, $406,434; qualifying distributions, $536,520.
Limitations: Applications not accepted. Giving primarily in TX.
Application information: Contributes only to pre-selected organizations. Unsolicited applications not accepted.
Officers and Directors:* Barbara Wendland,* Pres.; C. Wendland,* V.P.; E. Wendland,* Treas.
EIN: 742541278
Codes: FD

50810
Meinig Family Foundation
3619 Nottingham St.
Houston, TX 77005
Contact: Kathy Geib, Tr.

Established in 1992 in OK.
Donor(s): Peter C. Meinig, Kathryn Geib.
Financial data (yr. ended 12/31/01): Grants paid, $534,914; assets, $9,504,789 (M); gifts received, $43,832; expenditures, $793,414; qualifying distributions, $532,394.
Limitations: Giving primarily in CO, NY, OK, and TX.
Publications: Application guidelines.
Application information: Currently only funding organizations with which board members have direct involvement. Application form not required.
Trustees: Kathryn Geib, Nancy E. Meinig, Peter C. Meinig, Anne Smalling, Sarah P. Snipes.
EIN: 731373991
Codes: FD

50811
The Charlotte and Donald Test Foundation
6123 Meadowcrest Dr.
Dallas, TX 75230
Application address: c/o John Wagner, 7502 Greenville Ave., Ste. 250, Dallas, TX 75231

Established in 1991 in TX.

Donor(s): Donald Test.
Financial data (yr. ended 12/31/01): Grants paid, $534,000; assets, $519,462 (M); expenditures, $536,761; qualifying distributions, $534,000.
Limitations: Giving on a national basis, primarily in Dallas, TX; giving also in Washington, DC, and TN.
Trustees: Charlotte C. Test, Donald Test.
EIN: 752407926
Codes: TN

50812
The Chilton Foundation Trust
c/o Bank of America
P.O. Box 830241
Dallas, TX 75283-0241 (214) 508-9446
Contact: Alice Rahlfs, V.P., Bank of America

Established in 1945 in TX.
Donor(s): Arthur L. Chilton,‡ Leonore Chilton.‡
Financial data (yr. ended 12/31/01): Grants paid, $530,139; assets, $11,378,260 (M); expenditures, $650,462; qualifying distributions, $542,677.
Limitations: Giving primarily in TX.
Application information: Application form not required.
Trustee: Bank of America.
EIN: 756006996
Codes: FD

50813
Christian Mission Concerns
P.O. Box 20815
Waco, TX 76702

Established in 1984 in TX.
Donor(s): Paul Piper, Sr., Paul Piper, Jr.
Financial data (yr. ended 12/31/01): Grants paid, $528,757; assets, $19,206,191 (M); gifts received, $4,773; expenditures, $858,077; qualifying distributions, $787,513; giving activities include $168,000 for loans.
Limitations: Applications not accepted. Giving primarily in Waco, TX.
Application information: Contributes only to pre-selected organizations.
Officers and Directors:* Kent Reynolds,* Pres.; Paul Piper, Jr.,* V.P.; H.H. Reynolds,* Secy.; J.D. Hudson,* Treas.
EIN: 742317938
Codes: FD

50814
The Waggoners Foundation
6605 Cypresswood Dr., Ste. 250
Spring, TX 77379

Established in 1993 in TX.
Donor(s): J. Virgil Waggoner, June Waggoner.
Financial data (yr. ended 12/31/01): Grants paid, $526,750; assets, $7,404,647 (M); expenditures, $691,630; qualifying distributions, $526,750.
Limitations: Applications not accepted. Giving primarily in Houston, TX.
Application information: Contributes only to pre-selected organizations.
Officers and Directors:* J. Virgil Waggoner,* Chair.; June Waggoner,* Vice-Chair.; J. Kevin Quisenberry, Exec. Admin.; Liz Quisenberry.
EIN: 760404981
Codes: FD

50815
Walsh Foundation
500 W. 7th St., Ste. 1007
Fort Worth, TX 76102 (817) 335-3741
Contact: G. Malcolm Louden, Secy.-Treas.

Established in 1956 in TX.
Donor(s): Mary D. Walsh, F. Howard Walsh, Sr.

Financial data (yr. ended 12/31/01): Grants paid, $523,990; assets, $4,888,548 (M); gifts received, $291,155; expenditures, $557,132; qualifying distributions, $520,114.
Limitations: Giving primarily in Fort Worth, TX.
Officers: F. Howard Walsh, Sr., Pres.; Mary D. Walsh, V.P.; G. Malcolm Louden, Secy.-Treas.
Director: F. Howard Walsh, Jr.
EIN: 756021726
Codes: FD

50816
The Friedkin Foundation
7701 Wilshire Pl. Dr.
Houston, TX 77040 (713) 744-3550
Contact: L. Michael Phelps, Asst. Secy.-Treas.

Established in 1990 in TX.
Donor(s): Thomas H. Friedkin.
Financial data (yr. ended 12/31/00): Grants paid, $519,000; assets, $208,456 (L); expenditures, $520,500; qualifying distributions, $519,000.
Limitations: Giving primarily in Houston, TX.
Officers and Directors:* Thomas H. Friedkin,* Pres.; Thomas Dan Friedkin,* Sr. V.P.; Frank X. Gruen,* Secy.-Treas.; Tomisu Friedkin Dawley, Susan J. Friedkin, Jerry H. Pyle.
EIN: 760324626
Codes: FD

50817
Mary Moody Northen Endowment
P.O. Box 1300
Galveston, TX 77553-1300 (409) 765-9770
Contact: Betty Massey, Exec. Dir.

Established in 1964.
Donor(s): Mary Moody Northen.‡
Financial data (yr. ended 12/31/00): Grants paid, $516,257; assets, $65,240,516 (M); expenditures, $2,883,419; qualifying distributions, $4,388,730; giving activities include $1,560,215 for programs.
Limitations: Giving limited to TX and VA.
Application information: Application form not required.
Officers and Directors:* Edward L. Protz,* Pres.; G. William Rider,* V.P. and Treas.; Robert L. Moody,* Secy.; Betty Jeanette Massey, Exec. Dir.
EIN: 751171741
Codes: FD

50818
Overlake Foundation, Inc.
P.O. Box 2549
Victoria, TX 77902-2548
Contact: Thomas Lane Keller, V.P. and Treas.

Incorporated in 1981 in TX.
Donor(s): Mary Alice Fitzpatrick.
Financial data (yr. ended 11/30/01): Grants paid, $514,981; assets, $7,793,452 (M); expenditures, $559,957; qualifying distributions, $514,140.
Limitations: Giving primarily in TX.
Application information: Application form not required.
Officers: Rayford Keller, Pres.; Donald J. Malouf, V.P. and Secy.; Thomas L. Keller, V.P. and Treas.
Directors: Michael Scott Anderson, Steven Craig Anderson.
EIN: 751793068
Codes: FD

50819
B.E.L.I.E.F. Foundation
(Formerly Janet Jarie Jensen Foundation)
6500 Beltline Rd., Ste. 170
Irving, TX 75063
Contact: Kim Tanner, Admin.

Established in 1997 in TX.
Donor(s): Janet Jarie Jensen.

Financial data (yr. ended 12/31/01): Grants paid, $514,842; assets, $2,411,918 (L); expenditures, $549,536; qualifying distributions, $346,543.
Limitations: Applications not accepted. Giving primarily in TX.
Application information: Contributes only to pre-selected organizations.
Trustee: Janet Jarie Jensen.
EIN: 752707934
Codes: FD

50820
The James R. Dougherty, Jr. Foundation
P.O. Box 640
Beeville, TX 78104-0640 (361) 358-3560
Contact: Daren R. Wilder, Asst. Secy.

Trust established in 1950 in TX.
Donor(s): James R. Dougherty,‡ Mrs. James R. Dougherty.‡
Financial data (yr. ended 11/30/01): Grants paid, $514,201; assets, $9,760,250 (M); gifts received, $2,080; expenditures, $608,778; qualifying distributions, $534,713.
Limitations: Giving primarily in TX.
Application information: Application form not required.
Officer and Trustees:* Mary Patricia Dougherty,* Secy.-Treas.; Rachel Carr, Kevin F. Dougherty, Erin Marcotte, Beatrice Rossi-Landi, Frances Carr Tapp, Ben F. Vaughan III, Genevieve Vaughan.
EIN: 746039858
Codes: FD

50821
Cora A. Hull Charitable Trust A
c/o Bank of America
P.O. Box 831041
Dallas, TX 75283-1041

Established in 1996 in MO.
Financial data (yr. ended 12/31/01): Grants paid, $511,312; assets, $4,079,417 (M); expenditures, $559,631; qualifying distributions, $517,514.
Limitations: Applications not accepted. Giving primarily in Kansas City, MO.
Application information: Contributes only to pre-selected organizations.
Trustee: Bank of America.
EIN: 431796792
Codes: FD

50822
David & Sharon Jamail Family Foundation
2303 River Hills Rd.
Austin, TX 78733

Established in 1997 in TX.
Financial data (yr. ended 12/31/00): Grants paid, $508,728; assets, $4,503,903 (M); expenditures, $639,230; qualifying distributions, $508,728.
Limitations: Applications not accepted. Giving primarily in Austin, TX.
Application information: Contributes only to pre-selected organizations.
Officers: David G. Jamail, Pres. and Treas.; Sharon Jamail, V.P. and Secy.
Trustee: Brian M. Wallace.
EIN: 742854045
Codes: FD

50823
The Ed and Evelyn Kruse Foundation
2512 Gun and Rod Rd.
Brenham, TX 77833

Established in 1997 in TX.
Donor(s): Edward F. Kruse, Evelyn D. Kruse.
Financial data (yr. ended 12/31/99): Grants paid, $508,260; assets, $548,293 (M); expenditures, $523,588; qualifying distributions, $507,939.

Limitations: Applications not accepted. Giving primarily in TX.
Application information: Contributes only to pre-selected organizations.
Officers and Directors:* Edward F. Kruse,* Pres.; Evelyn D. Kruse,* V.P.; Paul W. Kruse,* Secy.; William J. Rankin,* Treas.
EIN: 742833992
Codes: FD

50824
Westcott Foundation
100 Crescent Ct., Ste. 1620
Dallas, TX 75201-1884 (214) 777-5015
Contact: Jack T. Smith, Pres.

Established in 1989 in TX.
Donor(s): Carl Westcott, Jimmy Westcott.
Financial data (yr. ended 12/31/01): Grants paid, $507,659; assets, $5,555,723 (M); expenditures, $595,086; qualifying distributions, $542,006.
Limitations: Giving primarily in Dallas, TX.
Application information: Application form required.
Officers: Carl Westcott, Chair.; Jack T. Smith, Pres.; Jimmy Westcott, V.P.; Judy Ledoux, Secy.-Treas.
Directors: Diane Adler, Court Westcott.
EIN: 752304233
Codes: FD

50825
The Mankoff Family Foundation
(Formerly The Mankoff Charitable Foundation)
5950 Berkshire Ln., Ste. 550
Dallas, TX 75225
Contact: Joy S. Mankoff, Dir.

Established in 1997 in TX.
Donor(s): Joy S. Mankoff, Ronald M. Mankoff.
Financial data (yr. ended 12/31/00): Grants paid, $506,006; assets, $12,648,681 (M); gifts received, $60,000; expenditures, $690,715; qualifying distributions, $534,048.
Application information: Application form not required.
Directors: Douglas F. Mankoff, Jeffrey W. Mankoff, Joy S. Mankoff, Marcia Mankoff, Ronald M. Mankoff, Staci Mankoff.
EIN: 752739184
Codes: FD

50826
Janelle and Clifford Grum Foundation
P.O. Box 368
Diboll, TX 75941
Contact: Clifford J. Grum, Tr., or Dona Janelle Grum, Tr.

Established in 1993 in TX.
Donor(s): Clifford J. Grum, Dona Janelle Grum.
Financial data (yr. ended 06/30/01): Grants paid, $505,750; assets, $1,595,290 (M); gifts received, $555,437; expenditures, $514,146; qualifying distributions, $506,018.
Limitations: Giving primarily in eastern TX.
Trustees: Clifford J. Grum, Dona Janelle Grum.
EIN: 756454067
Codes: FD

50827
Plitt Southern Theatres, Inc. Employees Fund
c/o Joe S. Jackson
7502 Greenville Ave., Ste. 500
Dallas, TX 75231

Established in 1945 in TX.
Donor(s): Plitt Southern Theatres, Inc.
Financial data (yr. ended 12/31/00): Grants paid, $505,067; assets, $3,779,474 (M); expenditures, $563,473; qualifying distributions, $505,067.

Limitations: Applications not accepted. Giving primarily in TX.
Application information: Grants are awarded at the discretion of the trustees.
Officers and Trustees:* Joe S. Jackson,* Pres.; W.R. Curtis,* V.P. and Secy.; Roy H. Aaron, Raymond C. Fox, Henry G. Plitt.
EIN: 756037855
Codes: CS, FD, CD, GTI

50828
Schollmaier Foundation
3904 Arlan Ln.
Fort Worth, TX 76109-4705

Established in 1978.
Donor(s): Edgar H. Schollmaier, Rama L. Schollmaier.
Financial data (yr. ended 12/31/00): Grants paid, $502,875; assets, $9,497,222 (M); gifts received, $615,076; expenditures, $556,708; qualifying distributions, $495,620.
Limitations: Applications not accepted. Giving primarily in Fort Worth,TX.
Application information: Contributes only to pre-selected organizations.
Officers and Directors:* Rama L. Schollmaier, Pres. and Treas.; Edgar H. Schollmaier,* V.P.; Harry M. Brants,* Secy.
EIN: 751577328
Codes: FD

50829
Ed Rachal Foundation
500 N. Shoreline, Ste. 1002
Corpus Christi, TX 78471 (361) 881-9040
FAX: (361) 881-9885; E-mail: edrachal@edrachal.org; URL: http://www.edrachal.org
Contact: Paul D. Atheide, C.E.O.

Established in 1965 in TX.
Financial data (yr. ended 08/31/01): Grants paid, $501,633; assets, $41,022,239 (M); expenditures, $1,800,187; qualifying distributions, $772,745.
Limitations: Giving limited to TX.
Publications: Annual report, grants list.
Application information: Application form required.
Officers and Directors:* John D. White,* Chair.; Robert L. Walker,* Vice-Chair.; Paul D. Altheide,* C.E.O. and Secy.; Richard Schendel,* Treas.
EIN: 741116595
Codes: FD

50830
The Charles and Betty Urschel Foundation
153 Treeline Park, Ste. 300
San Antonio, TX 78209-1880

Established in 1960 in TX.
Donor(s): Elizabeth H. Urschel,‡ Jack Guenther, Valerie Urschel Guenther.
Financial data (yr. ended 07/31/01): Grants paid, $500,855; assets, $5,887,846 (M); expenditures, $519,584; qualifying distributions, $613,628; giving activities include $105,244 for programs.
Limitations: Applications not accepted. Giving primarily in the San Antonio, TX, area.
Application information: Contributes only to pre-selected organizations.
Officers: Valerie Urschel Guenther, Pres.; Jack Guenther, V.P. and Secy.-Treas.; Jack E. Guenther, Jr., V.P.; Abigail Kampmann, V.P.
EIN: 746053172
Codes: FD

50831
William M. Fuller Foundation
1010 W. Wall St.
Midland, TX 79701 (915) 683-5661

Financial data (yr. ended 12/31/01): Grants paid, $500,714; assets, $9,226,703 (M); expenditures, $652,888; qualifying distributions, $507,728.
Limitations: Applications not accepted. Giving primarily in Fort Worth and Midland, TX.
Application information: Contributes only to pre-selected organizations.
Officers: Marcia F. French, Pres. and Treas.; L.R. French, Jr., V.P.; William Fuller K. French, Secy.
Director: Dee J. Kelly.
EIN: 752335552
Codes: FD

50832
The Lillian H. and C. W. Duncan Foundation
c/o J.P. Morgan Private Bank
P.O. Box 2558-8037
Houston, TX 77252-8037 (713) 216-4513
E-mail: Charlene_Slack@chase.com; FAX: (713) 216-4599
Contact: Charlene Slack

Established in 1964 in TX.
Donor(s): C.W. Duncan.‡
Financial data (yr. ended 09/30/01): Grants paid, $500,600; assets, $7,041,776 (M); expenditures, $547,933; qualifying distributions, $518,333.
Limitations: Giving primarily in Houston, TX.
Publications: Application guidelines.
Application information: Application form not required.
Officers and Directors:* John H. Duncan,* Chair.; Charles W. Duncan, Jr.,* Pres.; Mary Anne Duncan Dingus,* V.P.; Robert J. "Pete" Faust,* Secy.-Treas.; Anne S. Duncan, Brenda Duncan, C.W. Duncan III, John H. Duncan, Jr., Jeaneane Duncan Marsh.
EIN: 746064215
Codes: FD

50833
Cary M. Maguire Foundation
1201 Elm St., Ste. 4000
Dallas, TX 75270

Established in 1975 in TX.
Donor(s): Cary M. Maguire.
Financial data (yr. ended 03/31/01): Grants paid, $500,056; assets, $1,655,125 (M); gifts received, $179,060; expenditures, $509,119; qualifying distributions, $502,639.
Limitations: Applications not accepted. Giving primarily in Washington, DC.
Application information: Contributes only to pre-selected organizations.
Officers and Directors:* Cary M. Maguire,* Pres.; Ann T. Maguire,* Secy.; Ann B. Maguire, J.R. Mobley.
EIN: 510169327
Codes: FD

50834
Jim M. Vaughn Foundation
(Formerly The Vaughn Foundation)
P.O. Box 550
Austin, TX 78789
Application address: 830 S. Beckham, Tyler, TX 75701, tel.: (903) 597-7652
Contact: Jim M. Vaughn, Dir.

Established in 1952 in TX.
Donor(s): Edgar H. Vaughn,‡ Lillie Mae Vaughn,‡ John Willie Bell Crut.
Financial data (yr. ended 12/31/01): Grants paid, $499,832; assets, $9,121,346 (M); gifts received, $31,456; expenditures, $580,958; qualifying distributions, $522,388.
Limitations: Giving primarily in Tyler, TX.
Application information: Application form not required.
Directors: James M. Vaughn, Jr., Jim M. Vaughn, JPMorgan Chase Bank.
EIN: 756008953
Codes: FD

50835
Todd Wagner Foundation
3008 Taylor St.
Dallas, TX 75226

Established in 2000 in TX.
Donor(s): Todd R. Wagner.
Financial data (yr. ended 12/31/00): Grants paid, $499,675; assets, $2,003,646 (M); gifts received, $2,666,757; expenditures, $677,186; qualifying distributions, $976,727; giving activities include $299,986 for loans.
Limitations: Giving primarily in CA, CO, and TX.
Officers and Directors:* Todd R. Wagner,* Pres.; Matthew J. Dolan, Secy.; Leslie W. Mcmahon,* Treas.; Marcia L. Wagner.
EIN: 912028112
Codes: FD

50836
The Ginger Murchison Foundation
c/o Bank of America
P.O. Box 831041
Dallas, TX 75283-1041

Established in 1993 in TX.
Donor(s): Virginia L. Murchison.
Financial data (yr. ended 12/31/01): Grants paid, $497,000; assets, $10,071,448 (M); expenditures, $532,580; qualifying distributions, $493,746.
Limitations: Applications not accepted. Giving primarily in TX.
Application information: Contributes only to pre-selected organizations.
Officers: Don Wills, Pres. and Treas.; James B. Cain, V.P. and Secy.
Agent: Bank of America.
EIN: 752482261
Codes: FD

50837
American Airlines Center Foundation, Inc.
Dallas Fort Worth Airport
P.O. Box 619616, MD 5575
Dallas, TX 75261-9616 (817) 963-8199
Contact: Timothy J. Doke

Established in 1999 in TX.
Donor(s): American Airlines, Inc., Dallas Basketball Ltd., Dallas Stars, LP.
Financial data (yr. ended 12/31/01): Grants paid, $493,246; assets, $563,443 (M); gifts received, $625,000; expenditures, $493,738; qualifying distributions, $493,121.
Limitations: Giving primarily in Dallas, TX.
Officers and Directors:* Donald J. Carty,* Pres.; James A. Beer,* V.P. and Treas.; Michael W. Gunn,* V.P.; Thomas O. Hicks,* V.P.
EIN: 752825468
Codes: CS, FD, CD

50838
G. A. C. Halff Foundation
745 E. Mulberry, Ste. 400
San Antonio, TX 78212
Contact: Thomas F. Bibb, V.P

Incorporated in 1951 in TX.
Donor(s): G.A.C. Halff.‡

Financial data (yr. ended 02/28/02): Grants paid, $490,000; assets, $7,773,369 (M); expenditures, $553,234; qualifying distributions, $488,718.
Limitations: Giving primarily in San Antonio, TX.
Publications: Application guidelines.
Application information: Application form not required.
Officers and Trustees:* Hugh Halff, Jr.,* Pres.; Thomas F. Bibb,* V.P. and Treas.; Catherine H. Edson,* Secy.; Roland R. Arnold, Thomas H. Edson, Marie M. Halff, Jerry O. Street, Stephanie H. Street.
EIN: 746042432
Codes: FD

50839
The Jerry & Kay Cox Foundation
6-C Lacewood
Houston, TX 77024-7412
Contact: Jerry S. Cox, Pres.

Established in 1996 in TX.
Donor(s): Jerry S. Cox.
Financial data (yr. ended 12/31/01): Grants paid, $486,667; assets, $6,315,569 (M); expenditures, $564,271; qualifying distributions, $484,709.
Limitations: Giving primarily in TX.
Application information: Application form not required.
Officers: Jerry S. Cox, Pres. and Treas.; Kay Cox, V.P. and Secy.
Directors: Courtney Ellen Cox, Joshua Paul Cox.
EIN: 760511052
Codes: FD

50840
The J. M. Haggar, Jr. Family Foundation
(Formerly The J. M. Haggar, Jr. Charitable Foundation)
16051 Addison Rd., Ste. 212
Addison, TX 75001
Application address: P.O. Box 8267, Dallas, TX 75205-8267
Contact: Ray Pyle

Established in 1997.
Donor(s): Joseph M. Haggar, Jr.
Financial data (yr. ended 06/30/01): Grants paid, $484,634; assets, $8,145,457 (M); expenditures, $540,230; qualifying distributions, $479,386.
Limitations: Giving primarily in TX.
Application information: Application form not required.
Directors: Marian H. Bryan, Isabell Haggar, J.M. Haggar, Jr., J.M. Hagger III, Lydia H. Novakov.
EIN: 752565414
Codes: FD

50841
Greathouse Foundation
P.O. Box 3739
Abilene, TX 79604 (915) 677-9121
Contact: Dewayne E. Chitwood, Exec. Dir.

Established in 1997 in TX.
Donor(s): Wes-Tex Drilling Co.
Financial data (yr. ended 12/31/01): Grants paid, $482,733; assets, $8,752,825 (M); expenditures, $523,465; qualifying distributions, $484,084.
Limitations: Giving primarily in Abilene, TX.
Application information: Application form not required.
Officers and Directors:* Marcella Greathouse, Pres.; Dewayne E. Chitwood,* V.P. and Exec. Dir.; Paul Cannon,* Secy.; Sharons Mcdonald,* Treas.
EIN: 752710208
Codes: FD

50842
The Salzman-Medica Foundation
8613 Mendocino Dr.
Austin, TX 78735-1420

Established in 1998 in TX.
Donor(s): John K. Medica, Megan S. Medica.
Financial data (yr. ended 12/31/00): Grants paid, $480,000; assets, $795,287 (M); gifts received, $1,201,702; expenditures, $480,259; qualifying distributions, $480,000.
Limitations: Applications not accepted. Giving on a national basis.
Application information: Contributes only to pre-selected organizations.
Directors: Angela Asbury, John K. Medica, Megan S. Medica.
EIN: 742881198
Codes: FD

50843
Serafy Foundation
205 W. Levee St.
Brownsville, TX 78520 (956) 564-5313
Contact: Nicholas T. Serafy, Tr.

Established in 1997 in TX.
Donor(s): Nicholas T. Serafy, Jean H. Serafy.
Financial data (yr. ended 11/30/00): Grants paid, $479,217; assets, $1,409,461 (M); gifts received, $262,210; expenditures, $493,453; qualifying distributions, $478,401.
Limitations: Giving primarily in Brownsville, TX.
Trustees: Jean H. Serafy, Nicholas T. Serafy, Nicholas T. Serafy, Jr.
EIN: 742861035
Codes: FD

50844
William S. & Lora Jean Kilroy Foundation
3700 Buffalo Speedway, Ste. 750
Houston, TX 77098 (713) 621-8221
Contact: Lora Jean Kilroy, Tr.

Established in 1985 in TX.
Donor(s): William S. Kilroy,‡ Lora Jean Kilroy.
Financial data (yr. ended 12/31/01): Grants paid, $478,192; assets, $10,499,132 (M); expenditures, $563,389; qualifying distributions, $491,875.
Limitations: Giving primarily in TX.
Application information: Donations made only to organizations known to trustees. Application form not required.
Trustee: Lora Jean Kilroy.
EIN: 760169904
Codes: FD

50845
Lubbock Area Foundation, Inc.
1655 Main, Ste. 209
Lubbock, TX 79401 (806) 762-8061
FAX: (806) 762-8551; E-mail: Kathy@lubbockareafoundation.org; URL: http://www.lubbockareafoundation.org
Contact: Kathleen Stocco, Exec. Dir.

Incorporated in 1980 in TX.
Financial data (yr. ended 12/31/01): Grants paid, $477,856; assets, $7,517,750 (M); gifts received, $832,188; expenditures, $728,840.
Limitations: Giving limited to Lubbock, TX, and the surrounding South Plains counties.
Publications: Newsletter, application guidelines, informational brochure, financial statement.
Application information: Application form not required.
Officers and Directors:* Steven Garrett, Pres.; Irasema Velasquez,* V.P.; Regina Johnston, Secy.-Treas.; Kathleen Stocco, Exec. Dir.; and 22 additional directors.
EIN: 751709180

Codes: CM, FD

50846
Rosemary Haggar Vaughan Family Foundation
10723 Preston Rd., No. 179
Dallas, TX 75230

Established in 1996.
Financial data (yr. ended 12/31/01): Grants paid, $477,750; assets, $8,925,595 (M); expenditures, $609,949; qualifying distributions, $524,248.
Limitations: Applications not accepted. Giving primarily in Dallas, TX.
Application information: Contributes only to pre-selected organizations.
Officers: Rosemary Vaughan, Pres.; Mary Lynn Vaughan, V.P.; Vicki Miller, Secy.-Treas.
EIN: 752577797
Codes: FD

50847
Katrine Menzing Deakins Charitable Trust
c/o Bank of America
P.O. Box 1317
Fort Worth, TX 76101-1317 (817) 390-6714
Contact: Eric Hyden, V.P., Bank of America

Established in 1987 in TX.
Financial data (yr. ended 03/31/02): Grants paid, $474,000; assets, $7,681,174 (M); expenditures, $534,402; qualifying distributions, $475,746.
Limitations: Giving limited to TX, with emphasis on Fort Worth.
Publications: Annual report (including application guidelines).
Trustee: Bank of America.
EIN: 756370503
Codes: FD

50848
Garvey Texas Foundation, Inc.
P.O. Box 9600
Fort Worth, TX 76147-2600
Contact: Shirley F. Garvey, Pres.

Incorporated in 1962 in TX.
Donor(s): James S. Garvey, Shirley F. Garvey, Garvey Foundation.
Financial data (yr. ended 12/31/01): Grants paid, $470,170; assets, $8,946,394 (M); expenditures, $523,483; qualifying distributions, $467,147.
Limitations: Giving primarily in CO, KS, NE, OK and TX.
Application information: Application form required.
Officers: Shirley F. Garvey, Pres.; James S. Garvey, V.P.; Richard F. Garvey, Secy.; Bedford L. Burgher, Treas.
EIN: 756031547
Codes: FD

50849
Alvin and Lucy Owsley Foundation
3000 1 Shell Plz.
910 Louisiana
Houston, TX 77002-4995 (713) 229-1272
Contact: Alvin Owsley, Jr., Tr.

Trust established in 1950 in TX.
Donor(s): Alvin M. Owsley,‡ Lucy B. Owsley.‡
Financial data (yr. ended 12/31/01): Grants paid, $465,655; assets, $7,894,548 (M); gifts received, $500; expenditures, $488,866; qualifying distributions, $459,722.
Limitations: Giving limited to TX.
Publications: Application guidelines.
Application information: Application form not required.
Trustees: Wendy Garrett, Alvin Owsley, Jr., David T. Owsley.
EIN: 756047221

Codes: FD

50850
Mays Foundation
914 S. Tyler St.
Amarillo, TX 79101
Contact: Troy M. Mays, Pres.

Established in 1965.
Donor(s): W.A. Mays and Agnes Mays Trust.
Financial data (yr. ended 07/31/01): Grants paid, $461,286; assets, $7,317,137 (M); gifts received, $3,844; expenditures, $679,807; qualifying distributions, $458,423.
Limitations: Giving primarily in TX.
Application information: Application form not required.
Officer and Trustees:* Troy M. Mays,* Pres.; Karra Mays Hill, Stacy Mays Sharp.
EIN: 751213346
Codes: FD

50851
McGovern Fund
(Formerly McGovern Fund for the Behavioral Sciences)
2211 Norfolk, Ste. 900
Houston, TX 77098-4044 (713) 661-4808
FAX: (713) 661-3031
Contact: John P. McGovern, M.D., Pres.

Established in 1979 in TX.
Donor(s): John P. McGovern Foundation.
Financial data (yr. ended 11/30/01): Grants paid, $461,200; assets, $745,832 (M); expenditures, $520,635; qualifying distributions, $510,590.
Limitations: Applications not accepted. Giving primarily in TX, with emphasis on Houston; giving also in the Southwest.
Application information: Contributes only to pre-selected organizations. Grants primarily initiated by the foundation.
Officers and Directors:* John P. McGovern, M.D.,* Chair. and Pres.; Kathrine G. McGovern,* V.P. and Treas.; Gay Collette,* Secy.; Orville L. Story.
EIN: 742086867
Codes: FD, FM

50852
Truman and Anita Arnold Foundation
2900 St. Michael Dr., 5th Fl.
Texarkana, TX 75503
Application address: P.O. Box 1481, Texarkana, TX 75504-1481
Contact: Truman Arnold and Anita Arnold, Trustees

Established in 1998 in TX.
Donor(s): Truman Arnold, Anita Arnold.
Financial data (yr. ended 12/31/00): Grants paid, $459,000; assets, $3,924,829 (M); gifts received, $434,695; expenditures, $504,715; qualifying distributions, $454,387.
Limitations: Giving primarily in Texarkana, TX.
Application information: Application form not required.
Trustees: Anita Arnold, Truman Arnold.
EIN: 710811364
Codes: FD

50853
Watson Family Foundation
10111 Richmond Ave., Ste. 225
Houston, TX 77042 (713) 690-4848
Contact: Charles L. Watson, Pres.

Established in 1994 in TX.
Donor(s): Charles L. Watson, Kim R. Watson.
Financial data (yr. ended 12/31/00): Grants paid, $458,469; assets, $9,608,727 (M); gifts received, $7,870,500; expenditures, $459,487; qualifying distributions, $458,403.
Limitations: Giving limited to Houston, TX.
Officers: Charles L. Watson, Pres.; Kim R. Watson, V.P. and Secy.-Treas.
Director: Billie M. Hogan.
EIN: 760420732
Codes: FD

50854
The Larry J. Martin Family Foundation
2100 W. Loop South, Ste. 1450
Houston, TX 77027

Established in 1998 in TX.
Donor(s): Larry J. Martin.
Financial data (yr. ended 12/31/00): Grants paid, $453,113; assets, $15,504 (M); gifts received, $415,890; expenditures, $455,094; qualifying distributions, $450,697.
Limitations: Applications not accepted.
Application information: Contributes only to pre-selected organizations.
Officers: Larry J. Martin, Pres.; Walter Montgomery Martin, V.P.; Monica Ann Martin McFarland, V.P.; Lana Nicole Martin Kimball, Secy.; Michael Sean Martin, Treas.
EIN: 760575272
Codes: FD

50855
Wilton & Effie Mae Hebert Foundation
P.O. Box 908
Port Neches, TX 77651 (409) 727-2345
Application address: 802 West Dr., Port Neches, TX 77651
Contact: Pauline Womack, Dir.

Established in 1992 in TX.
Donor(s): Wilton P. Hebert,‡ Effie Mae Hebert.‡
Financial data (yr. ended 12/31/01): Grants paid, $450,198; assets, $13,514,728 (M); expenditures, $667,937; qualifying distributions, $482,183.
Limitations: Giving primarily in TX.
Application information: Application form required.
Directors: Earl Black, James Black, Jimmy Foster, Joe Hebert, Ed Hughes, Joe Vernon, Pauline Womack.
EIN: 760065521
Codes: FD

50856
J. C. Penney Company Fund, Inc.
P.O. Box 10001
Dallas, TX 75301-8101 (972) 431-1349
E-mail: jsiegel@jcpenney.com; *URL:* http://www.jcpenneyinc.com/company/commrel/index.htm
Contact: Jeannette Siegel, V.P.

Established in 1984 in NY.
Donor(s): J.C. Penney Co., Inc., J.C. Penney Corp., Inc.
Financial data (yr. ended 03/31/01): Grants paid, $447,174; assets, $6,151,179 (M); expenditures, $449,179; qualifying distributions, $446,243.
Limitations: Giving on a national and local basis.
Publications: Financial statement.
Application information: Application guidelines available on website. Application form not required.
Officers and Directors:* G.L. Davis,* Chair.; R.M. Caldwell, Pres. and Exec. Dir.; J. Siegel, V.P.; Bob Hood, Secy.; W. Alcorn, Treas. and Cont.; and 5 additional directors.
EIN: 133274961
Codes: CS, FD, CD

50857
The Billie and Gillis Thomas Family Foundation
(Formerly The Thomas Foundation)
8333 Douglas Ave., Ste. 1414
Dallas, TX 75225-5821
Contact: Gillis Thomas, Pres.

Established in 1997 in TX.
Donor(s): H. Gillis Thomas, Billie D. Thomas.
Financial data (yr. ended 12/31/01): Grants paid, $445,000; assets, $2,108,802 (M); gifts received, $1,200,150; expenditures, $452,256; qualifying distributions, $445,144.
Limitations: Giving primarily in Dallas, TX.
Application information: Application form required.
Officers and Trustees:* H. Gillis Thomas,* Pres.; Billie D. Thomas,* V.P.; Robyn T. Conlon,* Secy.; Walter T. Shank, Treas.
EIN: 752721588
Codes: FD

50858
The Cimarron Foundation
c/o Chase Bank of TX
4401 N. Mesa St.
El Paso, TX 79902-1150 (915) 298-4221
Contact: Nina Holcomb

Established in 1987 in TX.
Donor(s): Woody L. Hunt.
Financial data (yr. ended 12/31/01): Grants paid, $443,747; assets, $3,951,265 (M); expenditures, $477,074; qualifying distributions, $449,333.
Limitations: Giving primarily in TX.
Officers and Trustees:* Woody L. Hunt,* Pres.; Gayle G. Hunt,* V.P.; Jack L. Hunt.
Manager: Chase Bank of Texas.
EIN: 742489868
Codes: FD

50859
The Duda Family Foundation
1 Galleria Twr.
13355 Noel Rd., LB3, Ste. 1315
Dallas, TX 75240-6603 (972) 934-2244
Contact: Steven F. Tabor

Established in 1997.
Donor(s): Fritz L. Duda, Mrs. Fritz L. Duda.
Financial data (yr. ended 12/31/01): Grants paid, $443,360; assets, $13,862,192 (M); expenditures, $515,852; qualifying distributions, $443,360.
Limitations: Giving on a national basis.
Trustees: Fritz L. Duda, Fritz L. Duda, Jr., James F. Duda, Mary L. Duda, Leigh A. Duda Scott, Lendy D. Duda Vail.
EIN: 436765664
Codes: FD

50860
Redman Foundation, Inc.
P.O. Box 861111
Plano, TX 75086-1111 (972) 633-1774
FAX: (972) 633-6422; *E-mail:* cdmartin@texoma.net
Contact: Carol Martin, Exec. Dir.

Established in 1951, reincorporated in 1995 in TX.
Financial data (yr. ended 12/31/01): Grants paid, $442,100; assets, $6,669,444 (M); expenditures, $479,129; qualifying distributions, $461,816.
Limitations: Giving primarily in Dallas and northern TX.
Application information: Application form not required.
Officers and Trustees:* William R. Wines,* Chair.; Carol Martin, Exec. Dir.; Kay Chafin, George Chapman, James Redman, Mrs. James Redman.
EIN: 752617664
Codes: FD

50861
The William and Marie Wise Family Foundation
c/o William A. Wise
1001 Louisiana, Ste. 30
Houston, TX 77002

Established in 1998 in TX.
Donor(s): William A. Wise.
Financial data (yr. ended 12/31/01): Grants paid, $441,554; assets, $2,216,805 (M); expenditures, $443,736; qualifying distributions, $440,902.
Limitations: Giving primarily in Boulder, CO, and Houston, TX.
Officers: Marie Figge Wise, Pres. and Treas.; William A. Wise, V.P. and Secy.
EIN: 311519664
Codes: FD

50862
McCrea Foundation
c/o Phoebe Muzzy
5005 Woodway, Ste. 210
Houston, TX 77056

Established in 1960 in VA.
Donor(s): Mary Corling McCrea.‡
Financial data (yr. ended 02/28/01): Grants paid, $440,490; assets, $7,429,915 (M); expenditures, $481,531; qualifying distributions, $446,921.
Limitations: Applications not accepted. Giving primarily in Portland, OR, Newport, RI, and Houston, TX.
Application information: Contributes only to pre-selected organizations.
Agent: Bank One, N.A.
EIN: 546052010
Codes: FD

50863
The Search Foundation
(Formerly The Sophia Foundation)
800 Gessner, Ste. 1260
Houston, TX 77024

Established in 1996 in TX.
Donor(s): Fondation Ventose.
Financial data (yr. ended 12/31/01): Grants paid, $439,948; assets, $7,502,853 (M); gifts received, $219,621; expenditures, $515,182; qualifying distributions, $439,948.
Limitations: Applications not accepted. Giving on a national and international basis.
Application information: Contributes only to pre-selected organizations.
Officers and Directors:* Roger Coste,* Chair.; Catherine B. Coste,* Pres.; Bertrand Coste,* V.P.; Stephane Coste,* V.P.; Marvin A. Wurzer, Secy.-Treas.
EIN: 760520202
Codes: FD

50864
Richmond Foundation
1009 Austin Hwy.
San Antonio, TX 78209-4729
Contact: Jack C. Richmond, Pres.

Established in 1998.
Donor(s): Jack C. Richmond, Mrs. Jack C. Richmond.
Financial data (yr. ended 12/31/00): Grants paid, $439,610; assets, $1,159,874 (M); gifts received, $954,938; expenditures, $440,615; qualifying distributions, $439,466.
Limitations: Giving primarily in San Antonio, TX.
Officers: Jack C. Richmond, Pres.; Laura G. Richmond, Secy.-Treas.
Directors: Clay P. Richmond, John M. Richmond, Steven J. Richmond.
EIN: 742895911
Codes: FD

50865
Flora Cameron Foundation
5701 Broadway, Ste. 106
San Antonio, TX 78209 (210) 824-8301
Contact: Flora C. Atherton, Pres.

Established in 1952 in TX.
Donor(s): Flora C. Atherton.
Financial data (yr. ended 08/31/01): Grants paid, $437,600; assets, $1,555,373 (M); expenditures, $453,350; qualifying distributions, $440,031.
Limitations: Giving primarily in TX.
Officers: Flora C. Atherton, Pres. and Treas.; John H. Crichton, V.P.; Gloria Labatt, Secy.
EIN: 746038681
Codes: FD

50866
The Vale-Asche Foundation
c/o Grant Comm.
2001 Kirby Dr., Ste. 1010
Houston, TX 77019-6081 (713) 520-7334

Incorporated in 1956 in DE.
Donor(s): Ruby Vale,‡ Fred B. Asche.‡
Financial data (yr. ended 11/30/01): Grants paid, $437,500; assets, $13,378,530 (M); expenditures, $478,144; qualifying distributions, $437,500.
Limitations: Giving primarily in Houston, TX.
Application information: Request reviewed mid-Aug. through Oct. Application form not required.
Officers: Mrs. Vale Asche Russell, Pres.; Asche Ackerman, 1st V.P.; Anna B. Leonard, 2nd V.P.; William E. Blummer, Secy.-Treas.
EIN: 516015320
Codes: FD

50867
College First Foundation
2121 Precinct Line Rd.
Hurst, TX 76054 (817) 656-3811
Application address: c/o Nancy Robinson, P.O. Box 2176, Hurst, TX 76054, tel.: (817) 428-4200
Contact: Nancy Robinson, Admin.

Established in 1996 in TX.
Donor(s): Ronald L. Jensen, Alliance for Affordable Healthcare Association, Inc.
Financial data (yr. ended 12/31/01): Grants paid, $437,000; assets, $316,058 (M); gifts received, $468,456; expenditures, $4,860,049; qualifying distributions, $485,562.
Limitations: Giving on a national basis.
Application information: Prospective recipients should submit a formal application to the scholarship program offered by the organization to which their parent is a member. Application form required.
Officers and Directors:* Jeff Jensen,* Pres.; Lou Anne Jensen,* V.P.; Alan D. Tracy,* Secy.-Treas.; Nancy Robinson, Admin.; Janet Jensen.
EIN: 752638941
Codes: FD, GTI

50868
Silverton Foundation, Inc.
701 Brazos St., Ste. 1400
Austin, TX 78701 (512) 485-1900

Established in 1999 in TX.
Donor(s): Silverton Partners, LP.
Financial data (yr. ended 01/31/01): Grants paid, $433,962; assets, $7,492,067 (M); gifts received, $10,158,030; expenditures, $562,151; qualifying distributions, $368,435.
Limitations: Giving in Australia and the U.S., with some emphasis on TX.
Officers: Pamela M. Ryan, Chair.; William P. Wood, Pres.; Andrew S. White, Secy.
EIN: 742936881
Codes: FD

50869
Cecilia Young Willard Helping Fund
c/o Broadway National Bank
P.O. Box 17001
San Antonio, TX 78217
Application address: P.O. Box 17001-Trust, San Antonio, TX 78217
Contact: Nancy F. May, C.T.F.A., V.P. and Trust Off., Broadway National Bank

Established in 1987 in TX.
Donor(s): Cecilia Young Willard Trust.
Financial data (yr. ended 05/31/01): Grants paid, $433,468; assets, $6,887,266 (M); expenditures, $473,594; qualifying distributions, $425,084.
Limitations: Giving primarily in MD, NC, and TX.
Application information: Funding limited primarily to those organizations that Dr. Willard contributed to during her lifetime. Grant requests are reviewed. Application form not required.
Trustee: Broadway National Bank.
EIN: 746350893
Codes: FD

50870
The O'Connor & Hewitt Foundation
(Formerly Dorothy O'Connor Foundation)
1 O'Connor Plz., Ste. 1100
Victoria, TX 77901-6549 (361) 578-6271
Contact: Robert J. Hewitt, Pres.

Established in 1989 in TX.
Donor(s): Dorothy Hanna O'Connor,‡ Dennis O'Connor,‡ Robert J. Hewitt.
Financial data (yr. ended 12/31/01): Grants paid, $433,100; assets, $13,238,498 (M); gifts received, $946,742; expenditures, $442,078; qualifying distributions, $433,100.
Limitations: Giving limited to the south TX area.
Officers: Robert J. Hewitt, Pres.; Robert J. Hewitt, Jr., V.P.; Robert L. Coffey, Secy.-Treas.
EIN: 742527227
Codes: FD

50871
The Beal Foundation
c/o Bank of America, Trust Dept.
P.O. Box 270
Midland, TX 79702-0270 (915) 685-2063
Additional address: c/o Spencer E. Beal, 104 S. Pecos, Midland, TX 79701, tel.: (915) 682-3753

Incorporated in 1962 in TX.
Donor(s): Carlton Beal, Keleen K. Beal, W.R. Davis.
Financial data (yr. ended 12/31/99): Grants paid, $431,000; assets, $6,198,001 (M); gifts received, $1,000,000; expenditures, $564,421; qualifying distributions, $431,000.
Limitations: Giving primarily in the Midland, TX, area.
Application information: 1st time applicants must complete longer application form. Application form required.
Officers: Carlton E. Beal, Jr., Chair.; Bill J. Hill, Secy.-Treas.
Trustees: Barry A. Beal, Keleen H. Beal, Kelly S. Beal, Spencer E. Beal, Larry Bell, Robert J. Cowen, Karlene Beal Garber, Steven C. Hofer, Ray Poage, Jane B. Ramsland.
EIN: 756034480
Codes: FD

50872
The Rosenthal Foundation
604 E. 4th St., Ste. 201
Fort Worth, TX 76102

Established in 1979.

Donor(s): E.M. Rosenthal.
Financial data (yr. ended 11/30/01): Grants paid, $429,956; assets, $3,015,055 (M); expenditures, $452,019; qualifying distributions, $431,544.
Limitations: Applications not accepted. Giving primarily in Fort Worth, TX.
Application information: Contributes only to pre-selected organizations.
Trustees: Marcia Cohen, E.M. Rosenthal, Rosalyn G. Rosenthal, William Rosenthal.
EIN: 751675127
Codes: FD

50873
Posey Family Foundation
15303 Dallas Pkwy., No. 800
Addison, TX 75001

Established in 1998 in TX.
Donor(s): Lee Posey, Sally Posey.
Financial data (yr. ended 03/31/01): Grants paid, $429,000; assets, $1,097,151 (M); expenditures, $436,838; qualifying distributions, $433,510.
Limitations: Applications not accepted. Giving on a national basis, with emphasis on TX.
Application information: Contributes only to pre-selected organizations.
Officers: Lee Posey, Pres.; Tim Smith, V.P.; Gina Betts, Secy.; Pattie Keath, Treas.
Directors: Jennifer L. Posey, Jill M. Posey, Sally Posey.
EIN: 752768325
Codes: FD

50874
The Brumley Foundation
P.O. Box 9294
Amarillo, TX 79105-9294 (806) 376-1555
FAX: (806) 376-1554
Contact: Marilyn Ault, Secy.-Treas.

Established in 1986 in TX.
Donor(s): Dixie Holland,‡ Frank J. Warren,‡ Vivian Warren.‡
Financial data (yr. ended 12/31/99): Grants paid, $427,673; assets, $14,401,073 (M); gifts received, $5,367,465; expenditures, $469,642; qualifying distributions, $427,673.
Limitations: Giving limited to the upper 26 counties of the Texas Panhandle, with preference to the population center (Amarillo) and Moore County.
Application information: Application form not required.
Officers and Directors:* Tom Clarence Warren,* Pres.; Stanley Harrison,* V.P.; Marilyn C. Ault,* Secy.-Treas.; Bruce Burnett, Ida Mae Gorseline, Dayle Tipton, Thomas Warren.
EIN: 752089705
Codes: FD

50875
The Humphreys Foundation
P.O. Box 550
Liberty, TX 77575-0550 (936) 336-3321
Contact: Doris Peters, Mgr.

Incorporated in 1957 in TX.
Donor(s): Geraldine Davis Humphreys.‡
Financial data (yr. ended 09/30/01): Grants paid, $425,500; assets, $8,090,135 (M); expenditures, $519,691; qualifying distributions, $437,497.
Limitations: Giving limited to TX.
Publications: Application guidelines.
Application information: Application form required.
Officers: Linda Bertman, Pres.; Claude C. Roberts, V.P. and Secy.; Louis Paine, V.P.
EIN: 746061381
Codes: FD

50876
Jack H. & William M. Light Charitable Trust
c/o Broadway National Bank
P.O. Box 17001
San Antonio, TX 78217
Contact: Nancy F. May, V.P. and Trust Off., Broadway National Bank

Established in 1998.
Donor(s): Jack H. Light,‡ William M. Light.‡
Financial data (yr. ended 12/31/01): Grants paid, $425,190; assets, $8,280,479 (M); gifts received, $39,963; expenditures, $468,715; qualifying distributions, $426,919.
Limitations: Giving primarily in Houston and San Antonio, TX.
Application information: Application form not required.
Trustee: Broadway National Bank.
EIN: 742874941
Codes: FD

50877
Crystelle Waggoner Charitable Trust
c/o Bank of America
P.O. Box 831041
Dallas, TX 75283-1041
Application address: P.O. Box 1317, Fort Worth, TX 76101
Contact: Darlene Mann, Sr. V.P., Bank of America

Established in 1982 in TX.
Donor(s): Crystelle Waggoner.‡
Financial data (yr. ended 06/30/01): Grants paid, $424,550; assets, $11,220,880 (M); expenditures, $647,169; qualifying distributions, $437,838.
Limitations: Giving limited to TX, especially Fort Worth and Decatur.
Publications: Annual report (including application guidelines).
Application information: Application form not required.
Trustee: Bank of America.
EIN: 751881219
Codes: FD

50878
Kolitz Family Foundation, Inc.
302 Red Cedar
San Antonio, TX 78230
Contact: Robert Kolitz, Pres.

Established in 2000 in TX.
Donor(s): Robert Kolitz, Sandora Kolitz.
Financial data (yr. ended 12/31/01): Grants paid, $420,000; assets, $611,703 (M); expenditures, $428,947; qualifying distributions, $420,000.
Officers: Robert Kolitz, Pres.; Sandora Kolitz, Secy.-Treas.
EIN: 650968813

50879
Vin & Caren Prothro Foundation
2304 Midwestern Pkwy., Ste. 200
Wichita Falls, TX 76308

Established in 2000 in TX.
Donor(s): Caren H. Prothro.
Financial data (yr. ended 12/31/01): Grants paid, $419,705; assets, $24,862,723 (M); gifts received, $17,500,000; expenditures, $468,019; qualifying distributions, $419,705.
Limitations: Applications not accepted.
Application information: Contributes only to pre-selected organizations.
Officers: Caren H. Prothro, Pres.; Vincent H. Prothro, V.P.; Nita C. Clark, Secy.; J. H. Cullum Clark, Treas.
EIN: 752911958

50880
Kalman & Ida Wolens Foundation
c/o Baker & McKenzie
2001 Ross Ave., Ste. 2300
Dallas, TX 75201
Contact: Cheryl Jerome Moore, Pres.

Established in 1972 in TX.
Donor(s): Louis Wolens.‡
Financial data (yr. ended 07/31/01): Grants paid, $416,880; assets, $5,256,267 (M); expenditures, $451,749; qualifying distributions, $418,914.
Limitations: Giving primarily in TX.
Application information: Application form not required.
Officers and Directors:* Dean Milkes,* Chair.; Cheryl Jerome Moore,* Pres.; Bette Miller,* V.P. and Treas.; Marjorie Milkes,* Secy.; Matt Dawson, Joe W. Milkes.
EIN: 237222516
Codes: FD

50881
John and Maurine Cox Foundation
c/o John Cox
P.O. Box 2217
Midland, TX 79702-2217

Established in 1994 in TX.
Donor(s): John L. Cox.
Financial data (yr. ended 12/31/01): Grants paid, $416,650; assets, $10,687,317 (M); gifts received, $1,000,000; expenditures, $419,650; qualifying distributions, $413,294.
Limitations: Applications not accepted. Giving limited to TX.
Application information: Contributes only to pre-selected organizations.
Trustees: John L. Cox, Kelly Cox, Maurine T. Cox.
EIN: 752536459
Codes: FD

50882
Visiting Nurse Association of Houston Foundation
2707 N. Loop W., Ste. 520
Houston, TX 77008

Established in 1996 in TX.
Donor(s): Vaughn, Nelson, Scarborough & McConnell, L.P.
Financial data (yr. ended 06/30/00): Grants paid, $414,134; assets, $9,735,754 (M); gifts received, $11,381; expenditures, $536,374; qualifying distributions, $448,271.
Limitations: Applications not accepted. Giving limited to Houston, TX.
Application information: Contributes only to pre-selected organizations.
Officers: Gloria Herman, Co-Pres.; Geri Wood, Ph.D., Co-Pres.; N. Joyce Punch, Secy.; Noel Graubart, Treas.
Directors: Mary Louise Chapman, James S. Diamonon, M.D., Jeannie Frazier, Sarah C. Helms, Shirley M. Gee Henry, R.N., Donald S. Huge, M.D., Shirley F. Hutchinson, R.N., Ph.D., David I. Lapin, Mary Linda Letbetter, Cheryl Levine, Ph.D., David Lummis, Marylou Robins, Ph.D., Elsa Tansey, Ph.D.
EIN: 760454511
Codes: FD

50883
Hahl Proctor Charitable Trust
c/o Bank of America
P.O. Box 270
Midland, TX 79702
Contact: Bill J. Hill, Account Mgr., Bank of America

Established in 1987 in TX.

Financial data (yr. ended 04/30/01): Grants paid, $414,000; assets, $8,332,064 (M); expenditures, $494,795; qualifying distributions, $420,921.
Limitations: Giving limited to Midland, TX.
Application information: Application form not required.
Trustee: Bank of America.
EIN: 756382699

50884
Dujay Charitable Foundation
c/o Hibernia National Bank
P.O. Box 3928
Beaumont, TX 77704
FAX: (409) 880-1437
Contact: Jean Moncla, V.P. and Trust Off., Hibernia National Bank

Established in 1994 in TX.
Donor(s): Eva Dujay.‡
Financial data (yr. ended 12/31/01): Grants paid, $412,019; assets, $6,116,031 (M); expenditures, $455,946; qualifying distributions, $409,058.
Limitations: Giving primarily in Jefferson County, TX.
Publications: Application guidelines.
Application information: Application form required.
Trustee: Hibernia National Bank.
EIN: 760416456
Codes: FD

50885
Fash Foundation
2504 Oakland Blvd.
Fort Worth, TX 76103-3235

Established in 1990 in TX.
Donor(s): Annie G. Fash,‡ Ralph E. Fash.
Financial data (yr. ended 12/31/01): Grants paid, $411,966; assets, $6,330,530 (M); expenditures, $420,787; qualifying distributions, $410,314.
Limitations: Applications not accepted. Giving primarily in Fort Worth, TX.
Application information: Contributes only to pre-selected organizations.
Officers: Ralph E. Fash, Pres.; Linda E. Bush, V.P.; Kirk Manning, Secy.; James L. Kaiser, Treas.
Director: Helen G. Kaiser.
EIN: 752327856
Codes: FD

50886
Hayes Family Charitable Foundation
9626 Melton Ln.
Frisco, TX 75034

Established in 1997 in TX.
Donor(s): William F. Hayes, Brenda W. Hayes.
Financial data (yr. ended 12/31/01): Grants paid, $411,000; assets, $1,015,376 (M); expenditures, $413,594; qualifying distributions, $410,918.
Limitations: Applications not accepted. Giving primarily in CO and TX.
Application information: Contributes only to pre-selected organizations.
Trustees: Brenda W. Hayes, William F. Hayes, Christie H. Sackett.
EIN: 752737791
Codes: FD

50887
Alice Kleberg Reynolds Meyer Foundation
c/o Frost National Bank
P.O. Box 2127
Austin, TX 78768 (512) 473-4803
E-mail: smcgillicuddy@frostbank.com
Contact: Sherry McGillicuddy, Exec. V.P.

Established in 1978 in TX.
Donor(s): Alice K. Meyer.‡

Financial data (yr. ended 12/31/01): Grants paid, $411,000; assets, $17,920,730 (M); expenditures, $461,935; qualifying distributions, $411,000.
Limitations: Giving limited to south central TX.
Publications: Grants list, application guidelines.
Application information: Application form not required.
Trustee: Frost National Bank.
EIN: 742847652
Codes: FD

50888
Will E. Coyote Foundation
301 Commerce St., Ste. 2975
Fort Worth, TX 76102

Established in 1998 in TX.
Donor(s): Geoffrey P. Raynor.
Financial data (yr. ended 12/31/01): Grants paid, $410,316; assets, $4,011,163 (M); gifts received, $4,409,000; expenditures, $420,403; qualifying distributions, $410,316.
Limitations: Applications not accepted.
Application information: Contributes only to pre-selected organizations.
Officers: Geoffrey P. Raynor, Pres.; Robert McCormick, V.P.; Kim Baldi, Secy.
EIN: 752765224

50889
Taub Foundation
Texan Bldg.
333 W. Loop N., 4th Fl.
Houston, TX 77024 (713) 688-2426

Incorporated in 1953 in TX.
Donor(s): Henry J.N. Taub, H. Ben Taub.
Financial data (yr. ended 06/30/01): Grants paid, $408,485; assets, $7,766,741 (M); expenditures, $427,405; qualifying distributions, $408,485.
Limitations: Applications not accepted. Giving primarily in TX.
Application information: Contributes only to pre-selected organizations.
Trustees: Gail Hendrix, H. Ben Taub, Henry J.N. Taub, Henry J.N. Taub II, Marcy E. Taub.
EIN: 746060216
Codes: FD

50890
The Decherd Foundation
400 S. Record St., 2nd Fl.
Dallas, TX 75202
Contact: Vickie S. King

Established in 1993 in TX.
Donor(s): Robert W. Decherd, Maureen H. Decherd.
Financial data (yr. ended 12/31/01): Grants paid, $406,500; assets, $6,026,274 (M); expenditures, $466,523; qualifying distributions, $396,489.
Limitations: Applications not accepted. Giving primarily in Dallas, TX.
Application information: Unsolicited requests for funds not accepted.
Officers: Robert W. Decherd, Chair.; Maureen H. Decherd, Pres.; William Bennett Cullum, Secy.-Treas.
EIN: 752507229
Codes: FD

50891
Bertha Foundation
P.O. Box 1110
Graham, TX 76450 (940) 549-1400
Contact: Alice Ann Street, Pres.

Established in 1967 in TX.
Donor(s): E. Bruce Street, M. Boyd Street.‡

Financial data (yr. ended 12/31/01): Grants paid, $402,406; assets, $9,864,824 (M); expenditures, $461,774; qualifying distributions, $409,544.
Limitations: Giving limited to Graham, TX.
Officers and Directors:* Alice Ann Street,* Pres.; J.R. Montgomery,* Secy.; Sandra Street Estess, E. Bruce Street, M.B. Street, Jr., Melissa Street York.
EIN: 756050023
Codes: FD

50892
The Frees Foundation
5373 W. Alabama, Ste. 404
Houston, TX 77056
FAX: (713) 623-6509; *E-mail:* freesfoundation@msn.com
Contact: Nancy Frees Fountain, Managing Dir.

Established in 1983 in TX.
Donor(s): C. Norman Frees, Shirley B. Frees.
Financial data (yr. ended 12/31/01): Grants paid, $402,044; assets, $10,318,048 (M); expenditures, $749,515; qualifying distributions, $601,577.
Limitations: Giving primarily in Houston, TX.
Publications: Annual report, grants list, application guidelines.
Application information: Application form required.
Officers and Directors:* Shirley B. Frees,* Pres.; Nancy Frees Fountain,* Secy. and Managing Dir.; Edmund M. Fountain, Jr.,* Treas.; Al Jensen.
EIN: 760053200
Codes: FD

50893
The Morris L. Lichtenstein, Jr. Foundation
210 S. Carancahua, Ste. 500
Corpus Christi, TX 78401
Application address: P.O. Box 2888, Corpus Christi, TX 78403, tel.: (512) 884-1961
Contact: Harry L. Marks, Tr.

Established in 1995 in TX.
Donor(s): Morris L. Lichtenstein, Jr.‡
Financial data (yr. ended 12/31/01): Grants paid, $401,350; assets, $8,166,266 (M); expenditures, $1,175,811; qualifying distributions, $441,090.
Limitations: Giving primarily in Corpus Christi, TX.
Trustees: Harry L. Marks, Marcia Marks, Charles W. Thomasson.
EIN: 742757309
Codes: FD

50894
The Ward Family Foundation
8201 Preston Rd., Ste. 400
Dallas, TX 75225-6201

Established in 1993 in TX.
Donor(s): William C. Ward, Cynthia R. Ward.
Financial data (yr. ended 12/31/01): Grants paid, $400,350; assets, $7,830,532 (M); expenditures, $404,464; qualifying distributions, $399,678.
Limitations: Applications not accepted. Giving primarily in TX.
Application information: Contributes only to pre-selected organizations.
Officers: William C. Ward, Pres.; Cynthia R. Ward, V.P. and Secy.; Katherine J. Ward, Treas.
EIN: 752514341
Codes: FD

50895
Jane and John Justin Foundation
P.O. Box 425
Fort Worth, TX 76101

Financial data (yr. ended 12/31/01): Grants paid, $400,000; assets, $8,720,377 (M); expenditures, $431,363; qualifying distributions, $400,000.
Limitations: Applications not accepted.

Application information: Contributes only to pre-selected organizations.
Officers: John S. Justin, Jr.,* Chair and Pres.; Jane C. Justin,* Vice-Chair and V.P.; J.T. Dickenson,* Secy.; Richard J. Savitz,* Treas.; Roy B. Topham, Exec. Dir.
Directors: Mary C. Justin, Dee J. Kelly.
EIN: 752442749

50896
Tennessee Titans Foundation
P.O. Box 844
Houston, TX 77001
Contact: K.S. Adams, Jr.

Established in 1999 in TN.
Donor(s): K.S. Adams, Jr., Mrs. K.S. Adams, Jr.
Financial data (yr. ended 12/31/01): Grants paid, $400,000; assets, $850,062 (M); gifts received, $199,610; expenditures, $457,119; qualifying distributions, $400,000.
Limitations: Giving limited to TN.
Application information: Application form not required.
Officers and Directors:* K.S. Adams, Jr.,* Pres.; John Adams Barrett,* V.P. and Treas.; Nancy N. Adams,* V.P.; Susan C. Lewis, Susan Adams Smith, Amy Adams Strunk.
EIN: 760611503
Codes: FD

50897
The Gil and Dody Weaver Foundation
1845 Woodall Rodgers Fwy., Ste. 1275
Dallas, TX 75201 (214) 999-9497
FAX: (214) 999-9496
Contact: William R. Weaver, M.D., Tr.

Established in 1980 in TX.
Donor(s): Galbraith McF. Weaver, Elizabeth Eudora Weaver.
Financial data (yr. ended 09/30/01): Grants paid, $396,100; assets, $16,088,019 (M); expenditures, $758,470; qualifying distributions, $408,174.
Limitations: Giving limited to LA, OK, and TX; emphasis on TX.
Publications: Application guidelines.
Application information: Application form not required.
Trustee: William R. Weaver, M.D.
EIN: 751729449
Codes: FD

50898
Bridgeway Charitable Foundation
5615 Kirby Dr., Ste. 518
Houston, TX 77005

Established in 2001 in TX.
Donor(s): Bridgeway Capital Mgmt.
Financial data (yr. ended 12/31/01): Grants paid, $395,047; assets, $281,607 (M); gifts received, $648,820; expenditures, $401,385; qualifying distributions, $394,802.
Limitations: Applications not accepted.
Application information: Contributes only to pre-selected organizations.
Officers and Directors:* John N.R. Montgomery,* Pres. and Treas.; Ann M. Montgomery,* V.P.; Joanna R. Schima,* Secy.
EIN: 760666069
Codes: FD

50899
William E. Scott Foundation
801 Cherry St., Ste. 2000
Fort Worth, TX 76102 (817) 336-2400
Contact: Robert W. Decker, Pres.

Incorporated in 1960 in TX.
Donor(s): William E. Scott.‡

Financial data (yr. ended 05/31/02): Grants paid, $394,751; assets, $17,053,058 (M); expenditures, $564,680; qualifying distributions, $417,417.
Limitations: Giving limited to LA, NM, OK, and TX, with emphasis on the Fort Worth-Tarrant County, TX, area.
Publications: Application guidelines.
Application information: Application form not required.
Officers and Directors:* Robert W. Decker,* Pres.; Raymond B. Kelly III,* V.P.
EIN: 756024661
Codes: FD

50900
The Kathryn O'Connor Foundation
1 O'Connor Plz., Ste. 1100
Victoria, TX 77901 (361) 578-6271
Contact: D.H. Braman, Jr., Pres.

Incorporated in 1951 in TX.
Donor(s): Kathryn S. O'Connor,‡ Tom O'Connor, Jr.,‡ Dennis O'Connor, Mary O'Connor Braman.‡
Financial data (yr. ended 12/31/00): Grants paid, $394,424; assets, $6,588,093 (M); gifts received, $16,429; expenditures, $422,612; qualifying distributions, $394,424.
Limitations: Giving limited to southern TX, with emphasis on Victoria and Refugio counties and surrounding area.
Publications: Annual report.
Application information: Application form not required.
Officers: D.H. Braman, Jr., Pres.; Venable B. Proctor, Secy.; Robert L. Coffey, Treas.
EIN: 746039415
Codes: FD

50901
C.I.O.S.
P.O. Box 20815
Waco, TX 76702-0815
Contact: Paul P. Piper, Jr., Tr.

Incorporated about 1952 in TN; corporation liquidated into a charitable trust in 1987.
Donor(s): Paul P. Piper, Sr., Mrs. Paul P. Piper, Paul P. Piper, Jr., Piper Industries, Inc.
Financial data (yr. ended 06/30/01): Grants paid, $389,345; assets, $123,854,226 (M); gifts received, $7,325; expenditures, $1,030,193; qualifying distributions, $8,884,934; giving activities include $8,516,628 for program-related investments.
Limitations: Applications not accepted. Giving on a national basis.
Application information: Contributes only to pre-selected organizations.
Trustees: Mary J. Piper, Paul P. Piper, Sr., Paul P. Piper, Jr., Pally Piper Richard.
EIN: 742472778
Codes: FD

50902
Meredith Private Foundation
70 Pascal Ln.
Austin, TX 78746

Established in 1998 in TX.
Donor(s): Lynn M. Meredith, Thomas J. Meredith.
Financial data (yr. ended 12/31/99): Grants paid, $386,650; assets, $14,056,048 (M); gifts received, $4,771,875; expenditures, $579,935; qualifying distributions, $386,650.
Limitations: Applications not accepted.
Application information: Contributes only to pre-selected organizations.
Directors: Kelley Guest, Kathryn Morgan Meredith, Lynn M. Meredith, Thomas J. Meredith.
EIN: 742882442

50903
The Prairie Foundation
303 W. Wall Ave., Ste. 1901
Midland, TX 79701-5116 (915) 683-1777
Contact: Benjamin L. Blake, Chair, Grants Comm.

Established in 1957 in TX.
Donor(s): David Fasken Special Trust, Barbara Fasken.
Financial data (yr. ended 12/31/01): Grants paid, $386,000; assets, $8,429,353 (M); expenditures, $420,617; qualifying distributions, $386,332.
Limitations: Giving primarily in the San Francisco Bay Area, CA and Midland and Odessa, TX.
Application information: Application form required.
Officers and Directors:* Robert T. Dickson,* Pres.; Norbert J. Dickman,* V.P.; Louis A. Bartha,* Secy.-Treas.; Benjamin L. Blake.
EIN: 756012458
Codes: FD

50904
Bryant Edwards Foundation, Inc.
807 8th St., 2nd Fl.
Wichita Falls, TX 76301-3381

Established in 1959.
Donor(s): Bryant Edwards.‡
Financial data (yr. ended 10/31/01): Grants paid, $385,000; assets, $8,199,284 (M); expenditures, $447,650; qualifying distributions, $393,328.
Limitations: Applications not accepted. Giving primarily in TX.
Application information: Contributes only to pre-selected organizations.
Officers and Directors:* Mac Cannedy, Jr.,* Pres.; Dennis D. Cannedy,* V.P.; Erwin Davenport,* Secy.; John W. Barfield,* Treas.
EIN: 756012973
Codes: FD

50905
The Rosewood Foundation
500 Crescent Ct., Ste. 300
Dallas, TX 75201

Established in 2000 in TX.
Donor(s): The Rosewood Corp.
Financial data (yr. ended 12/31/00): Grants paid, $383,903; assets, $21,686 (M); gifts received, $398,163; expenditures, $386,192; qualifying distributions, $382,086.
Limitations: Applications not accepted. Giving primarily in TX.
Application information: Contributes only to pre-selected organizations.
Officers and Trustees:* David K. Sands,* Pres.; Don W. Crisp,* V.P.; Patrick B. Sands,* Secy.; Laurie Sands Harrison,* Treas.; Schuyler B. Marshall IV, J.B. Sands, Stephen H. Sands.
EIN: 752827470
Codes: FD

50906
Bhupat and Jyott Mehta Family Foundation
738 Hwy. 6 S., Ste. 850
Houston, TX 77079-4033
Application address: c/o Janet Bertolino, U.S. National Bank, 2201 Market St., Galveston, TX 77553, tel.: (409) 770-7165

Established in 1996 in TX.
Donor(s): Rahul Mehta.
Financial data (yr. ended 09/30/01): Grants paid, $382,000; assets, $15,062,100 (M); gifts received, $280,784; expenditures, $442,239; qualifying distributions, $433,496; giving activities include $28,595 for loans to individuals.

Limitations: Giving primarily in Santa Clara, CA and Houston, TX.
Application information: Application form required.
Directors: Bhupat J. Mehta, Jainesh Mehta, Nisha B. Mehta, Rahul B. Mehta.
EIN: 760522455
Codes: FD

50907
J. W. Bagley Foundation
101 Firebird Cove
Lakeway, TX 78734

Established in 1994.
Financial data (yr. ended 12/31/01): Grants paid, $380,000; assets, $5,983,008 (M); gifts received, $66,559; expenditures, $430,075; qualifying distributions, $404,529.
Limitations: Applications not accepted. Giving primarily in MS.
Application information: Contributes only to pre-selected organizations.
Officers: Mark C. Bagley, Pres.; Sharon B. Wax, V.P.; Rocky Picasso, Secy.; Susan O. Huurman, Treas.
Trustees: James W. Bagley, Jean A. Bagley.
EIN: 742738464
Codes: FD

50908
J. A. and Isabel M. Elkins Foundation
1166 First City Tower
1001 Fannin St.
Houston, TX 77002
Contact: Lauren Baird

Trust established in 1956 in TX.
Financial data (yr. ended 08/31/01): Grants paid, $380,000; assets, $6,231,885 (M); expenditures, $380,975; qualifying distributions, $360,614.
Limitations: Giving primarily in TX, with emphasis on the metropolitan Houston area.
Application information: Application form not required.
Trustees: J.A. Elkins, Jr., J.A. Elkins III.
EIN: 746047894
Codes: FD

50909
V.H. McNutt Memorial Foundation
153 Treeline Park, Ste. 300
San Antonio, TX 78209-1880
Contact: Jack Guenther, Tr.

Trust established in 1960 in TX.
Donor(s): Amy McNutt.
Financial data (yr. ended 12/31/00): Grants paid, $379,200; assets, $9,494,964 (M); expenditures, $441,294; qualifying distributions, $406,011.
Limitations: Giving primarily in San Antonio, TX.
Trustees: Jack Guenther, Valerie Guenther.
EIN: 746035044
Codes: FD

50910
J. Edward & Helen M. C. Stern Foundation
c/o JPMorgan Chase Bank
P.O. Box 1290
Fort Worth, TX 76101-1290
Contact: Lynne Thomas

Established in 1992 in TX.
Donor(s): J. Edward Stern.‡
Financial data (yr. ended 12/31/00): Grants paid, $378,450; assets, $5,658,879 (M); expenditures, $433,390; qualifying distributions, $371,682.
Limitations: Giving primarily in TX.
Application information: Application packet mailed upon receipt of written request. Application form required.

Officer and Trustees:* Barbara Wheeler,* Chair.; Anthony Azar, Sharon Butterworth, Laurence Nickey, M.D., Carl Ryan.
EIN: 742652851
Codes: FD

50911
Mildred Dulaney Foundation
c/o Wells Fargo Bank Texas, N.A.
P.O. Box 2626
Waco, TX 76702-2626

Established in 1999 in TX.
Donor(s): Mildred Dulaney Living Trust.
Financial data (yr. ended 12/31/01): Grants paid, $375,945; assets, $3,185,569 (M); gifts received, $3,011,085; expenditures, $406,752; qualifying distributions, $372,179.
Limitations: Applications not accepted. Giving primarily in New York, NY, and TX.
Application information: Contributes only to pre-selected organizations.
Officers: Oliver McMahan, Chair.; Charles H. Dulaney, Vice-Chair.
Directors: Carl Avera, Sue Davis, Jeffrey P. Gholson, Lester Gibson, G. E. Middleton, John Miller, Frank Pete Rowe.
EIN: 760615843
Codes: FD

50912
Cora Foundation, Inc.
c/o J.P. Morgan Private Bank
P.O. Box 2558
Houston, TX 77252-2558 (713) 216-4513

Established in 1997 in TX.
Donor(s): Linda R. Ough, Steven T. Ough.
Financial data (yr. ended 12/31/01): Grants paid, $375,477; assets, $1,617,503 (M); expenditures, $404,681; qualifying distributions, $385,945.
Application information: Application form not required.
Officers: Steven T. Ough, Pres.; Linda R. Ough, Secy.-Treas.
Director: Bruce R. Ough.
EIN: 760528888
Codes: FD

50913
Otter Island Foundation
c/o Matthew R. Simmons
700 Louisiana, Ste. 5000
Houston, TX 77002

Established in 1993 in TX.
Donor(s): Matthew R. Simmons, Ellen Simmons.
Financial data (yr. ended 12/31/01): Grants paid, $374,627; assets, $4,388,646 (M); gifts received, $50,000; expenditures, $385,982; qualifying distributions, $371,514.
Limitations: Applications not accepted.
Application information: Contributes only to pre-selected organizations.
Officers and Director:* Matthew R. Simmons,* Pres.; Ellen C.L. Simmons, V.P. and Treas.; Shelly K. Daugherty, Secy.
EIN: 760421104
Codes: FD

50914
The Cecil and Ida Green Foundation
(Formerly The Green Foundation)
1700 Pacific Ave., Ste. 3300
Dallas, TX 75201-4693 (214) 969-1477
Contact: Rust E. Reid, V.P. and Secy.-Treas.

Established in 1958 in TX.
Donor(s): Cecil H. Green, Ida M. Green.‡
Financial data (yr. ended 12/31/01): Grants paid, $374,500; assets, $6,850,439 (M); gifts received, $75,000; expenditures, $408,969; qualifying distributions, $389,612.
Limitations: Giving primarily in the Dallas, TX, area; limited giving to specific institutions in Canada, England and Australia.
Application information: Application form not required.
Officers and Trustees:* Bryan Smith,* Pres.; Rust E. Reid,* V.P. and Secy.-Treas.; James E. Brooks, Philip O'B. Montgomery.
EIN: 752263168
Codes: FD

50915
CEMEX Foundation
(Formerly Southdown Foundation)
c/o Cemex, Inc., V.P., Human Resources
1200 Smith St., Ste. 2400
Houston, TX 77002-4486

Established in 1993.
Donor(s): Medusa Corp.
Financial data (yr. ended 12/31/00): Grants paid, $373,764; assets, $1,671,732 (M); expenditures, $395,259; qualifying distributions, $372,319.
Limitations: Giving primarily in areas of company operations in AL, CA, CO, FL, GA, IN, KY, MA, MI, MO, NJ, OH, PA, TN, TX, and VA.
Officers and Trustees:* Gilberto Perez,* Chair.; Clarence C. Comer, Pres.; Don E. Newquist, Secy.-Treas.; R. Frank Coddock, Jr., Stephen R. Miley, Andy Miller, David J. Repasz.
EIN: 346505254
Codes: CS, FD

50916
Community Foundation of the Texas Hill Country
(Formerly Kerrville Area Community Trust)
P.O. Box 291354
Kerrville, TX 78029-1354 (830) 896-8811
FAX: (830) 792-5956; *E-mail:* info@communityfoundation.net; *URL:* http://www.communityfoundation.net
Contact: Laura P. Lewis, Secy. and Exec. Dir.

Established in 1981 in TX.
Donor(s): Mary Bright,‡ Alma Dietert,‡ Ollie Mittack,‡ Joe Foy.
Financial data (yr. ended 12/31/01): Grants paid, $372,680; assets, $7,454,581 (L); gifts received, $3,271,704; expenditures, $534,077.
Limitations: Giving limited to the area generally known as the Texas Hill Country, including Center Point, Comfort, Fredericksburg, Hunt, Ingram, Kerrville and Medina.
Publications: Financial statement, grants list, informational brochure, newsletter, application guidelines, annual report.
Application information: Application form required.
Officers and Directors:* Kerwin Overby,* Pres.; Elizabeth Hughes,* V.P.; Laura P. Lewis,* Secy. and Exec. Dir.; Joan Dell Dolce,* Treas.; Charles Brownine, Sandy Calloux, Tim Crenwelge, Gary Crozier, Barbara F. Daniel, Stephen Fine, Bill Johnston, Sharon Joseph, A.C. Schwethelm.
EIN: 742225369
Codes: CM, FD

50917
RFS Foundation
c/o Wells Fargo, Trust Dept.
P.O. Drawer 913
Bryan, TX 77805-0913
Contact: Robert M. Schoolfield, Tr.

Established in 1977.
Donor(s): Ray E. Schoolfield,‡ Robert M. Schoolfield.

50917—TEXAS

Financial data (yr. ended 08/31/01): Grants paid, $372,076; assets, $98,942 (M); gifts received, $377,150; expenditures, $373,812; qualifying distributions, $369,311.
Limitations: Applications not accepted. Giving primarily in TX.
Application information: Contributes only to pre-selected organizations.
Trustees: Amy Schoolfield, Robert M. Schoolfield, Marcia Sue Schoolfield Spellman.
EIN: 741949935
Codes: FD

50918
Steven C. and Mary Sue Simon Family Foundation
4436 Potomac Ave.
Dallas, TX 75205

Established in 1996 in TX.
Donor(s): Mary Simon, Steven Simon, Ryan Simon.
Financial data (yr. ended 12/31/00): Grants paid, $372,000; assets, $5,250,612 (M); gifts received, $24,000; expenditures, $431,484; qualifying distributions, $400,253.
Limitations: Applications not accepted. Giving primarily in MN.
Application information: Contributes only to pre-selected organizations.
Officers: Mary Sue Simon, Pres.; Ryan Simon, Secy.; Steven C. Simon, Treas.
Directors: Hunter Simon, Stacey Soinski, Nicole Woods.
EIN: 412796392
Codes: FD

50919
The John D. Furst Foundation
200 Crescent Ct., Rm. 1600
Dallas, TX 75201

Established in 1997 in TX.
Donor(s): Jack D. Furst.
Financial data (yr. ended 12/31/00): Grants paid, $370,295; assets, $1,128,760 (M); gifts received, $1,471,000; expenditures, $370,295; qualifying distributions, $370,295.
Limitations: Applications not accepted. Giving primarily in TX.
Application information: Contributes only to pre-selected organizations.
Officers: John D. Furst, Chair.; Debra L. Furst, Pres. and Secy.-Treas.
Directors: John S. Furst, Robert S. Furst.
EIN: 752724923
Codes: FD

50920
Melbern G. and Susanne M. Glasscock Foundation
3203 Audley St.
Houston, TX 77098-1901
Application address: P.O. Box 22143, Houston, TX 77227, tel.: (713) 520-2903
Contact: Melbern G. Glasscock, Pres.

Established in 1992 in TX.
Donor(s): Melbern G. Glasscock, Susanne M. Glasscock.
Financial data (yr. ended 12/31/00): Grants paid, $370,000; assets, $15,302,120 (M); gifts received, $886,875; expenditures, $383,270; qualifying distributions, $354,066.
Limitations: Giving primarily in Houston, TX.
Application information: Application form not required.
Officers and Trustees:* Melbern G. Glasscock,* Pres. and Treas.; Susanne M. Glasscock,* V.P.; R.E. Bean, D.M. Glasscock, A.E. Wynn.

EIN: 760380195
Codes: FD

50921
Joan and Herb Kelleher Charitable Foundation
110 E. Crockett St.
San Antonio, TX 78205
FAX: (210) 223-3512; *E-mail:* jjrizzo@flash.net
Contact: Ruth K. Agather, Tr.

Established in 1997 in TX.
Donor(s): Herbert D. Kelleher, Joan N. Kelleher.
Financial data (yr. ended 12/31/01): Grants paid, $370,000; assets, $11,845,547 (M); gifts received, $4,296,600; expenditures, $571,484; qualifying distributions, $364,055.
Limitations: Giving limited to TX and WY.
Application information: Application form not required.
Trustees: Ruth K. Agather, David N. Kelleher, Herbert D. Kelleher, J. Michael Kelleher, Joan N. Kelleher, Julia K. Stacy.
EIN: 742833381
Codes: FD

50922
Wichita Falls Area Community Foundation
719 Scott Street, Ste. 414
Wichita Falls, TX 76301

Incorporated in TX in 2001.
Financial data (yr. ended 12/31/01): Grants paid, $365,240; assets, $3,782,611 (M); gifts received, $2,027,267; expenditures, $549,734.
Limitations: Giving primarily in KY, and Wichita Falls, TX.
Officers and Directors:* Gary H. Shores,* Chair.; Ray Clymer,* Vice-Chair.; H.E. Neale, C.E.O. and Pres.; Berneice Leath, Secy.-Treas.; D. Phil Bolin, T.M. Cornelius, John Hirschi, Pat Morgan, Robert T. Priddy, Joseph N. Sherrill, Jr., Kenneth Telg, David Wolverton, Kay Yeager.
EIN: 752817894
Codes: CM, FD

50923
Bill and Cecily Sun Foundation, Inc.
c/o Harper & Pearson Co., PC
1 Riverway W., Ste. 1000
Houston, TX 77056

Established in 2001 in TX.
Donor(s): Cecily R. Sun, William N. Sun.
Financial data (yr. ended 12/31/01): Grants paid, $364,196; assets, $1,413,073 (M); gifts received, $1,705,500; expenditures, $364,196; qualifying distributions, $364,196.
Limitations: Applications not accepted. Giving primarily in China; some giving in Houston, TX.
Application information: Contributes only to pre-selected organizations.
Officers: Cecily R. Sun, Pres.; William N. Sun, Secy.-Treas.
Director: Teresa L. Chou.
EIN: 760687982
Codes: FD

50924
The Schissler Foundation
(Formerly Schissler Charitable Foundation)
P.O. Box 11738
Spring, TX 77391-1738 (713) 626-3890
Contact: Richard P. Schissler, Pres.

Established in 1983.
Donor(s): Nancy R. Schissler, Richard P. Schissler.
Financial data (yr. ended 03/31/01): Grants paid, $364,000; assets, $409,563 (M); gifts received, $74,402; expenditures, $376,199; qualifying distributions, $366,829.
Limitations: Giving primarily in Houston, TX.

Application information: Application form not required.
Officers and Trustees:* Richard P. Schissler,* Pres.; Richard P. Schissler III, V.P.; Nancy Lynn Red, Secy.-Treas.; Laura Lee Jenkins, Nancy R. Schissler.
EIN: 760056884
Codes: FD

50925
Mechia Foundation
P.O. Box 1310
Beaumont, TX 77704-1310

Established in 1978.
Donor(s): Ben J. Rogers,‡ Julie Rogers,‡ Regina Rogers.
Financial data (yr. ended 12/31/01): Grants paid, $363,400; assets, $6,676,668 (M); gifts received, $150,628; expenditures, $387,855; qualifying distributions, $368,606.
Limitations: Applications not accepted. Giving primarily in Beaumont and Houston, TX.
Application information: Contributes only to pre-selected organizations.
Trustee: Regina Rogers.
EIN: 741948840
Codes: FD

50926
The Link Foundation
c/o H. David Hughes
111 Congress Ave., Ste. 1400
Austin, TX 78701
Contact: Joe W. Bratcher III, Pres.

Established in 1985 in TX.
Donor(s): Joe W. Bratcher III.
Financial data (yr. ended 12/31/01): Grants paid, $363,333; assets, $2,011,181 (M); gifts received, $102,737; expenditures, $376,941; qualifying distributions, $363,579.
Limitations: Giving on a national basis, with some emphasis on Austin, TX.
Officers: Joe W. Bratcher III, Pres. and Treas.; Brigid Anne Cockrum, V.P. and Secy.
Director: Elizbieta Szoka.
EIN: 742387802
Codes: FD

50927
Philip R. Jonsson Foundation
5781 Keller Springs Rd.
Dallas, TX 75248 (972) 380-6123
Application address: P.O. Box 795365,
Dallas, TX 75379-5365
Contact: Anne Marie Messier

Established in 1977 in TX.
Donor(s): Philip R. Jonsson.
Financial data (yr. ended 12/31/99): Grants paid, $362,619; assets, $8,426,900 (M); gifts received, $730,566; expenditures, $461,068; qualifying distributions, $362,619.
Limitations: Giving primarily in TX, with emphasis on Dallas.
Application information: Application form not required.
Officers: Kenneth B. Jonsson, Pres.; Eileen J. Lewis, 1st V.P.; Christina A. Jonsson, 2nd V.P.; Steven W. Jonsson, Secy.; Suzanne E. Jonsson, Treas.
EIN: 751552642
Codes: FD

50928
Meyer and Ida Gordon Foundation
1616 S. Voss Rd.
Houston, TX 77057

Incorporated in 1950 in TX.

Donor(s): Members of the Gordon family, Gordon's Jewelry Co.
Financial data (yr. ended 12/31/01): Grants paid, $362,500; assets, $7,135,186 (M); expenditures, $371,934; qualifying distributions, $362,500.
Limitations: Applications not accepted. Giving primarily in Houston, TX.
Application information: Contributes only to pre-selected organizations.
Officers: James C. Gordon, Pres.; Daniel P. Gordon, V.P.; Lowry W. Barfield, Secy.
EIN: 746046795
Codes: FD

50929
The West Endowment
P.O. Box 491
Houston, TX 77001
Contact: Coordinator of Grants

Established in 1995 in TX.
Financial data (yr. ended 12/31/99): Grants paid, $362,000; assets, $7,450,260 (M); expenditures, $393,789; qualifying distributions, $362,624.
Limitations: Giving primarily in TX, with emphasis on Harris County.
Officers and Directors:* W.R. Lloyd, Jr.,* Pres.; Robert H. Parsley,* V.P.; James A. Reichert,* V.P.; Margene West Lloyd,* Secy.; Barbara Keyes, Treas.
EIN: 760481204
Codes: FD

50930
Arline Guefen Foundation
49 Briar Hollow, No. 2201
Houston, TX 77027

Established in 1993 in TX.
Donor(s): Arline Guefen.
Financial data (yr. ended 06/30/01): Grants paid, $361,871; assets, $0 (M); expenditures, $363,884; qualifying distributions, $361,871.
Limitations: Applications not accepted. Giving limited to TX.
Application information: Contributes only to pre-selected organizations.
Trustee: Arline Guefen.
EIN: 760422707
Codes: FD

50931
Grogan Lord Foundation, Inc.
P.O. Box 649
Georgetown, TX 78627   (512) 930-4554
Contact: R. Griffin Lord

Established in 1992 in TX.
Donor(s): Sharon Lord Caskey, R. Griffin Lord, Grogan Lord, Ruth Joyce Hite.
Financial data (yr. ended 12/31/01): Grants paid, $360,000; assets, $4,590,374 (M); gifts received, $475,252; expenditures, $360,469; qualifying distributions, $357,368.
Limitations: Giving primarily in TX.
Application information: Application form required.
Officers: Grogan Lord, Pres.; Sharon Lord Caskey, V.P. and Secy.-Treas.
EIN: 742623948
Codes: FD

50932
The Denton A. Cooley Foundation
6624 Fannin, Ste. 2700
Houston, TX 77030   (713) 799-2700
Contact: K.M. Gerrie, Secy.

Incorporated in 1960 in TX.
Donor(s): Denton A. Cooley, M.D., Louise T. Cooley.
Financial data (yr. ended 11/30/01): Grants paid, $358,367; assets, $1,238,309 (M); gifts received, $270,000; expenditures, $367,367; qualifying distributions, $358,367.
Limitations: Giving primarily in the Houston, TX, area.
Application information: Application form not required.
Officers and Trustees:* Denton A. Cooley, M.D.,* Pres.; Louise T. Cooley,* V.P.; K.M. Gerrie,* Secy.; James Berardo,* Treas.
EIN: 746053213
Codes: FD

50933
Zephyr Foundation
4006 FM 1035
Wellington, TX 79095
FAX: (806) 447-5440; *E-mail:* vpwhite@count.net
Contact: Valerie White, Pres.

Established in 1996 in TX.
Donor(s): Dave Swalm, Beth Swalm.
Financial data (yr. ended 12/31/01): Grants paid, $356,800; assets, $7,379,505 (M); gifts received, $800,000; expenditures, $359,065; qualifying distributions, $356,800.
Limitations: Giving primarily in Collingsworth County, TX, and surrounding counties in the TX Panhandle.
Officers: Valerie White, Pres.; Pat White, V.P. and Secy.; Beth Swalm, V.P.
EIN: 752647195
Codes: FD

50934
Rosa May Griffin Foundation
P.O. Box 1790
Kilgore, TX 75663-1775
Contact: Dan Phillips, Secy.-Treas.

Incorporated in 1960 in TX.
Donor(s): Rosa May Griffin.‡
Financial data (yr. ended 12/31/01): Grants paid, $356,088; assets, $6,593,156 (M); expenditures, $426,505; qualifying distributions, $346,281.
Limitations: Giving limited to TX.
Publications: Program policy statement.
Application information: Application form not required.
Officers and Trustees:* Ebb Mobley, Pres.; Dan Phillips,* Secy.-Treas.; E.B. Mobley.
EIN: 756011866
Codes: FD

50935
Marlene Nathan Meyerson Family Foundation
2800 Post Oak Blvd., 61st Fl.
Houston, TX 77056-6102

Established in 1999 in TX.
Donor(s): Marlene N. Meyerson.
Financial data (yr. ended 12/31/01): Grants paid, $355,666; assets, $2,717,572 (M); gifts received, $607,650; expenditures, $371,298; qualifying distributions, $360,793.
Limitations: Applications not accepted. Giving primarily in Santa Fe, NM and TX.
Application information: Contributes only to pre-selected organizations.
Officers: Marlene Nathan Meyerson, Pres.; Marti Meyerson Hooper, V.P.; Marvin D. Nathan, V.P.
Directors: Brenda F. Brand, Elizabeth Glassman, Barry H. Margolis, Morton H. Meyerson.
EIN: 752797176
Codes: FD

50936
B. A. and Elinor Steinhagen Benevolent Trust
c/o Hibernia National Bank
P.O. Box 3928
Beaumont, TX 77704
FAX: (409) 880-1437
Contact: Jean Moncla, V.P. and Trust Off., Hibernia National Bank

Trust established in 1939 in TX.
Donor(s): B.A. Steinhagen,‡ Elinor Steinhagen.‡
Financial data (yr. ended 08/31/01): Grants paid, $354,184; assets, $6,685,697 (M); expenditures, $421,141; qualifying distributions, $354,184.
Limitations: Giving limited to Jefferson County, TX.
Publications: Application guidelines.
Application information: Application form required.
Trustee: Hibernia National Bank.
EIN: 746039544
Codes: FD

50937
Stemmons Foundation
P.O. Box 143127
Irving, TX 75014-3127   (972) 650-9162
Contact: Ann C. Carlisle, Secy.-Treas.

Established in 1963 in TX.
Financial data (yr. ended 12/31/01): Grants paid, $352,300; assets, $5,176,020 (M); expenditures, $370,559; qualifying distributions, $365,972.
Limitations: Giving primarily in Dallas, TX.
Publications: Application guidelines.
Application information: Application form not required.
Officers: Allison S. Simon, Pres.; Heinz K. Simon, V.P.; Jean H. Stemmons, V.P.; John M. Stemmons, Sr., V.P.; Ann C. Carlisle, Secy.-Treas. and Mgr.
EIN: 756039966
Codes: FD

50938
Paul Patton Charitable Trust
c/o Bank of America
P.O. Box 831041
Dallas, TX 75283-1041
Application address: c/o David P. Ross, Sr. V.P., Bank of America, N.A., 1200 Main St., 14th Fl., Kansas City, MO 64105; *Tel.:* (816) 979-7481

Established in 1989 in MO.
Financial data (yr. ended 12/31/01): Grants paid, $350,279; assets, $5,906,298 (M); expenditures, $441,585; qualifying distributions, $383,127.
Limitations: Giving primarily in the greater Kansas City, MO, area.
Trustees: William L. Evans, Jr., C. Ted McCarter, Bank of America.
EIN: 446009254
Codes: FD

50939
The Carmage & Martha Ann Walls Foundation
1050 Wilcrest Dr.
Houston, TX 77042

Financial data (yr. ended 06/30/01): Grants paid, $350,144; assets, $7,039,313 (M); expenditures, $434,806; qualifying distributions, $350,144.
Limitations: Applications not accepted. Giving primarily in AL, GA, and TX.
Application information: Contributes only to pre-selected organizations.
Officers and Trustees:* Lissa Walls Vahldiek,* Pres.; Byrd Cooper Walls,* V.P.; Martha Ann Walls,* V.P.; B. Leon Brown,* Secy.; Patricia Roberts, Secy.; John R. Allender,* Treas.
EIN: 760031815
Codes: FD

50940
Circle Bar Foundation
P.O. Box 791000
San Antonio, TX 78279-1000

Established in 1964 as John H. & Dela W. White Fund.
Donor(s): John H. White, Dela W. White.
Financial data (yr. ended 12/31/01): Grants paid, $350,000; assets, $6,756,823 (M); gifts received, $280,000; expenditures, $394,883; qualifying distributions, $335,581.
Limitations: Applications not accepted. Giving primarily in San Antonio, TX.
Application information: Contributes only to pre-selected organizations.
Officer: Dela W. White, Mgr.
Trustees: John H. White, Jr., Tuleta C. White.
EIN: 746063672
Codes: FD

50941
The Tom and Deborah Green Family Foundation
P.O. Box 5058
Austin, TX 78763-5058
FAX: (512) 474-7976; *E-mail:* amydavidson@austin.rr.com
Contact: Deborah Green

Established in 1999 in TX.
Donor(s): Thomas Green, Deborah Green.
Financial data (yr. ended 12/31/00): Grants paid, $349,258; assets, $915,078 (M); expenditures, $371,700; qualifying distributions, $339,382.
Limitations: Applications not accepted.
Application information: Contributes only to pre-selected organizations.
Officers: Thomas B. Green, Pres. and Treas.; Deborah B. Green, V.P. and Secy.
Director: Amy Laughlin.
EIN: 756563186
Codes: FD

50942
The W. K. Gordon, Jr. Foundation
201 Main St., Ste. 600
Fort Worth, TX 76102 (817) 339-1156
Contact: Bruce Petty, Secy.-Treas.

Established in 1997 in TX.
Donor(s): Anna Melissa Gordon.
Financial data (yr. ended 12/31/01): Grants paid, $349,000; assets, $5,314,992 (M); expenditures, $363,711; qualifying distributions, $354,740.
Limitations: Giving primarily in Albuquerque, NM, and Fort Worth, TX.
Application information: Application form not required.
Officers and Directors:* Anna Melissa Gordon,* Pres.; Marguerite Melissa Gordon,* V.P.; W.K. Gordon III,* V.P.; Bruce Petty,* Secy.-Treas.; Joel A. Gordon.
EIN: 752708533
Codes: FD

50943
Onward & Upward Initiative Charitable Trust
c/o James J. Jensen
2121 Precinct Line Rd.
Hurst, TX 76054
Application address: 850 Cannon Dr., Ste. 200, Hurst, TX 76054, tel.: (817) 428-4200
Contact: Kim Tanner, Admin.

Established in 1997 in TX.
Donor(s): James J. Jensen.
Financial data (yr. ended 12/31/01): Grants paid, $346,003; assets, $1,933,612 (M); expenditures, $626,624; qualifying distributions, $347,306.
Limitations: Giving on a national basis.
Trustee: James J. Jensen.

EIN: 752707910
Codes: FD

50944
CRC Foundation
7500 San Felipe, Ste. 860
Houston, TX 77063

Established in 1989 in TX.
Donor(s): Carrie P. Woliver, Ronald W. Woliver.
Financial data (yr. ended 12/31/99): Grants paid, $345,915; assets, $3,367,731 (M); expenditures, $367,375; qualifying distributions, $344,096.
Limitations: Applications not accepted. Giving limited to Houston, TX.
Application information: Contributes only to pre-selected organizations.
Trustees: Terry McDaniel, Carrie P. Woliver, Ronald W. Woliver.
EIN: 760285550
Codes: FD

50945
Lightner Sams Foundation, Inc.
5400 LBJ Freeway, Ste. 515
Dallas, TX 75240 (972) 458-8811
E-mail: foundation@lightnersams.org; *FAX:* (972) 458-8812
Contact: Larry Lightner, Pres.

Established in 1994 in TX.
Financial data (yr. ended 12/31/01): Grants paid, $345,330; assets, $11,445,854 (M); expenditures, $648,535; qualifying distributions, $345,330.
Limitations: Giving primarily in Dallas, TX.
Publications: Application guidelines.
Application information: Application form not required.
Officers and Trustees:* Larry F. Lightner,* Pres.; Sue B. Lightner,* V.P.; Earl Sams Lightner, Sr., Robin H. Lightner.
EIN: 752555622
Codes: FD

50946
The Aragona Family Foundation
(Formerly The Sandra and Joseph Aragona Family Foundation)
78 St. Stephens School Rd.
Austin, TX 78746 (512) 328-2178
Contact: Joseph C. Aragona, Pres.

Established in 1997 in TX.
Donor(s): Joseph C. Aragona, Sandra R. Aragona.
Financial data (yr. ended 12/31/01): Grants paid, $345,300; assets, $2,971,913 (M); gifts received, $897,058; expenditures, $391,531; qualifying distributions, $377,188.
Limitations: Giving primarily in Austin, TX.
Officers: Joseph C. Aragona, Pres.; Sandra R. Aragona, V.P.
Director: Jeffrey C. Garvey.
EIN: 742833147
Codes: FD

50947
Louis and Elizabeth Nave Flarsheim Charitable Foundation
c/o Bank of America
P.O. Box 831041
Dallas, TX 75283-1041
Application address: 1200 Main St., Kansas City, MO 64105, tel.: (816) 979-7481
Contact: David P. Ross, Sr. V.P., Bank of America

Established in 1980.
Donor(s): Louis Flarsheim, Elizabeth Flarsheim.
Financial data (yr. ended 11/30/01): Grants paid, $341,880; assets, $4,183,279 (M); expenditures, $391,306; qualifying distributions, $359,895.

Limitations: Giving primarily in the Kansas City, MO, area.
Application information: Application form not required.
Trustee: Bank of America.
EIN: 436223957
Codes: FD

50948
The Woodhill Foundation
11767 Katy Freeway, Ste. 375
Houston, TX 77079

Established in 2000 in TX.
Donor(s): James R. Woodhill, Louis R. Woodhill, Peter Schaeffer.
Financial data (yr. ended 12/31/00): Grants paid, $341,824; assets, $341,145 (M); gifts received, $185,497; expenditures, $531,827; qualifying distributions, $341,824.
Limitations: Applications not accepted. Giving primarily in CA and TX.
Officers and Directors:* James R. Woodhill,* Pres.; Louis R. Woodhill,* V.P.; Chirsty Albeck, Secy.-Treas.
EIN: 760644277
Codes: FD

50949
F. D. Orth Foundation
P.O. Drawer B
Falfurrias, TX 78355

Established in 2001 in TX.
Donor(s): Franklin D. Orth.
Financial data (yr. ended 12/31/01): Grants paid, $340,891; assets, $44,200 (M); gifts received, $388,367; expenditures, $350,628; qualifying distributions, $340,891.
Limitations: Giving primarily in TX.
Officers and Directors:* Franklin D. Orth,* Pres. and Treas.; Robert Scott,* V.P.; Debra A. Hutto,* Secy.
EIN: 742965759

50950
West Foundation
P.O. Box 1675
Wichita Falls, TX 76307-1675
Contact: Reece A. West, Pres.

Established in 1973 in TX.
Donor(s): Gordon T. West,‡ Ellen B. West,‡ Gordon T. West, Jr.
Financial data (yr. ended 09/30/01): Grants paid, $340,575; assets, $17,210,238 (M); expenditures, $447,659; qualifying distributions, $406,682.
Limitations: Applications not accepted. Giving limited to the Wichita Falls, TX, area.
Application information: Unsolicited requests for funds not accepted.
Officers and Trustees:* Reece A. West,* Pres.; Joseph N. Sherrill, Jr.,* V.P.; Gordon T. West, Jr.,* V.P.
EIN: 237332105
Codes: FD, GTI

50951
McNair Foundation
3340 Camp Bowie Blvd.
Fort Worth, TX 76107
Contact: D. Cal McNair, Pres.

Donor(s): D. Cal McNair.
Financial data (yr. ended 12/31/00): Grants paid, $340,275; assets, $767,388 (M); expenditures, $361,023; qualifying distributions, $336,212.
Limitations: Giving primarily in TX.
Application information: Application form not required.

Officers and Director:* D. Cal McNair, Pres.; Melissa J. McNair, V.P.; Darlene Kirkley,* Secy.
EIN: 752793683
Codes: FD

50952
Fleetwood Memorial Foundation, Inc.
501 S. Fielder Rd.
Arlington, TX 76013 (817) 261-2368
Contact: Tom Cravens, Chair.

Established in 1974.
Financial data (yr. ended 10/31/01): Grants paid, $339,000; assets, $4,789,554 (M); gifts received, $600; expenditures, $416,109; qualifying distributions, $364,417.
Limitations: Giving limited to TX.
Publications: Application guidelines, informational brochure.
Application information: Application form required.
Officers and Directors:* Tom Cravens,* Chair.; Nathan Robinett,* Vice-Chair.; William B. Jackson, Secy.-Treas.; W.W. Snider, Genl. Counsel; and 9 additional directors.
EIN: 510163324
Codes: FD, GTI

50953
Behmann Brothers Foundation
P.O. Box 271486
Corpus Christi, TX 78427-1486
(361) 265-0164
Contact: Charles L. Kosarek, Jr., Pres.

Established in 1979.
Donor(s): Arno W. Behmann,‡ Herman W. Behmann.‡
Financial data (yr. ended 06/30/01): Grants paid, $336,970; assets, $7,235,372 (M); expenditures, $391,372; qualifying distributions, $345,389.
Limitations: Giving primarily in southern TX.
Officers and Directors:* Charles L. Kosarek, Jr.,* Pres.; Frances R. Kosarek,* V.P.; Ross Mitchon,* Secy.; Willie J. Kosarek,* Treas.; T. Mark Anderson, John Lloyd Bluntzer, Karen K. Clark, Joshua Kosarek.
EIN: 742146739
Codes: FD

50954
MacDonald-Peterson Foundation
2929 Allen Pkwy., Ste. 2525
Houston, TX 77019-2153
Contact: Wm. Nathan Cabaniss, V.P. and Treas.

Established in 1995 in TX.
Financial data (yr. ended 12/31/01): Grants paid, $335,000; assets, $6,830,036 (M); expenditures, $401,061; qualifying distributions, $335,000.
Limitations: Giving primarily in TX.
Application information: Application form not required.
Officers: Philip M. Peterson, Pres.; Wm. Nathan Cabaniss, V.P. and Treas.; William T. Miller, Secy.
Directors: Diana MacDonald Moore, Erik G. Peterson.
EIN: 760430319
Codes: FD

50955
Nation Foundation (Corporation)
P.O. Box 180849
Dallas, TX 75218 (214) 388-5751
Contact: James Nation, Dir.

Established in 1999 in TX.
Donor(s): Oslin Nation, James Nation.
Financial data (yr. ended 01/31/01): Grants paid, $334,716; assets, $4,632,728 (M); gifts received, $220,091; expenditures, $334,799; qualifying distributions, $334,716.
Directors: Frieda Ashworth, James H. Nation, Oslin Nation.
EIN: 752791965
Codes: FD

50956
Palmer Foundation
2800 Post Oak Blvd.
Houston, TX 77056-6196
Application address: 5450 Transco Tower, Houston, TX 77056, tel.: (713) 960-7517
Contact: C. Robert Palmer, Pres.

Established in 1997 in TX.
Donor(s): C. Robert Palmer.
Financial data (yr. ended 12/31/01): Grants paid, $334,500; assets, $724,799 (M); gifts received, $300,000; expenditures, $337,142; qualifying distributions, $335,791.
Limitations: Giving primarily in TX.
Application information: Application form required.
Officers: C. Robert Palmer, Pres.; Rebecca T. Palmer, V.P.; Shelley P. Hayes, Secy.-Treas.
EIN: 760565827
Codes: FD

50957
Liatis Foundation
2707 Kipling
Houston, TX 77098 (713) 520-7600
FAX: (713) 520-7632
Contact: Steven Borick, Pres.

Established in 1993 in TX.
Donor(s): Juanita A. Borick.
Financial data (yr. ended 12/31/00): Grants paid, $333,958; assets, $8,407,604 (M); gifts received, $700,000; expenditures, $405,972; qualifying distributions, $321,296.
Limitations: Giving on a national basis.
Publications: Corporate giving report, application guidelines, financial statement.
Application information: Application form required.
Officers and Trustees:* Steven James Borick,* Pres.; Linda Susan Borick,* Secy.; Juanita A. Borick, Robert Allen Borick.
EIN: 760420275
Codes: FD

50958
Don A. Sanders Family Foundation
3100 Chase Twr.
Houston, TX 77002 (713) 250-4213
Contact: Don A. Sanders, Pres.

Established in 1997 in TX.
Donor(s): Don A. Sanders.
Financial data (yr. ended 12/31/01): Grants paid, $332,807; assets, $7,438 (M); expenditures, $339,008; qualifying distributions, $332,579.
Limitations: Applications not accepted. Giving primarily in Houston, TX.
Application information: Contributes only to pre-selected organizations.
Officers: Don A. Sanders, Pres.; Ben T. Morris, V.P.; Walter P. Zivley, Secy.; Jay F. Rea, Treas.
EIN: 760537031
Codes: FD

50959
Bob L. Herd Foundation
P.O. Box 9340
Tyler, TX 75711
Application address: 3901 Manhattan, Tyler, TX 75701, tel.: (903) 509-3456
Contact: Janice Thompson, Secy.-Treas.

Established in 1994 in TX.
Donor(s): Bob L. Herd.
Financial data (yr. ended 12/31/01): Grants paid, $332,000; assets, $6,680,023 (M); expenditures, $484,295; qualifying distributions, $386,092.
Limitations: Giving primarily in Tyler, TX.
Officers: Bob L. Herd, Pres.; Patsy L. Herd, V.P.; Janice Thompson, Secy.-Treas.
EIN: 752530305
Codes: FD

50960
Bergman-Davison-Webster Charitable Trust
2301 Israel Rd.
Livingston, TX 77351-2531 (936) 327-8642
Contact: Carolyn Davsion Nixon, Tr.

Established in 1996 in TX.
Financial data (yr. ended 06/30/01): Grants paid, $331,700; assets, $9,625,988 (M); expenditures, $427,841; qualifying distributions, $374,314.
Limitations: Giving limited to the cities of Corrigan and Livingston as well as Polk County, TX.
Application information: Application form not required.
Trustees: Donnis Bergman, Harry Bergman, James Bergman, Gene Bush, Carolyn Davison Nixon.
Director: Janet Bergman.
EIN: 760521612
Codes: FD

50961
G. R. White Trust
c/o Bank One, Texas, N.A.
600 Bailey Ave.
Fort Worth, TX 76107
Application address: c/o Bank One, Texas, N.A., P.O. Box 2050, Fort Worth, TX 76113, tel.: (817) 884-4165
Contact: Donald R. Smith

Established in 1965.
Donor(s): G.R. White.‡
Financial data (yr. ended 09/30/01): Grants paid, $331,534; assets, $7,025,838 (M); expenditures, $515,919; qualifying distributions, $333,804.
Limitations: Giving limited to TX.
Application information: Application form not required.
Trustee: Bank One, Texas, N.A.
EIN: 756094930
Codes: FD

50962
The Gorges Foundation
(Formerly Patty Gorges Foundation)
P.O. Box 3547
Harlingen, TX 78551-3547
Contact: Matt Gorges, Pres.

Established in 1993 in TX.
Donor(s): Matt F. Gorges, Patricia C. Gorges.
Financial data (yr. ended 12/31/00): Grants paid, $331,392; assets, $1,467,520 (M); expenditures, $336,963; qualifying distributions, $329,165.
Limitations: Giving primarily in Cameron County, TX.
Application information: Application form not required.
Officers and Trustees:* Matt F. Gorges,* Pres.; Patty Gorges,* Secy.-Treas.; Daniel Hightower.
EIN: 742690463

Codes: FD

50963
Joe Barnhart Foundation
1738 Sunset Blvd.
Houston, TX 77005-1714

Established in 1988 in TX.
Financial data (yr. ended 12/31/00): Grants paid, $330,342; assets, $24,717,702 (M); expenditures, $3,557,231; qualifying distributions, $3,228,169; giving activities include $2,802,358 for programs.
Limitations: Applications not accepted. Giving limited to Beeville, TX.
Application information: Contributes only to pre-selected organizations.
Trustees: Jack Bace, Walter S. Baker, Jr., Margaret Moser, Margaret Price, V. Richard Viebig, Jr.
EIN: 760261675
Codes: FD

50964
John S. and Dorothy Rule Ayres Fund
c/o Bank of America
P.O. Box 831041
Dallas, TX 75283-1041

Established in 1998 in MO.
Donor(s): John S. Ayres.‡
Financial data (yr. ended 12/31/01): Grants paid, $329,500; assets, $1,419,062 (M); expenditures, $419,445; qualifying distributions, $365,474.
Limitations: Applications not accepted. Giving primarily in Kansas City, MO.
Application information: Contributes only to pre-selected organizations.
Trustee: Bank of America.
EIN: 436808719
Codes: FD

50965
Carlson Family Foundation, Inc.
113 S. Gardenview St.
San Antonio, TX 78213
Contact: Thomas A. Norton, Treas.

Established in 2000 in NJ.
Financial data (yr. ended 12/31/00): Grants paid, $326,805; assets, $19,886,292 (M); expenditures, $476,313; qualifying distributions, $450,490.
Limitations: Applications not accepted. Giving on a national and international basis.
Application information: Unsolicited requests for funds not accepted.
Officers: John A. Norton, Pres.; Michael A. Norton, Secy.; Thomas A. Norton, Treas.
Directors: Elaine Boylen, John Lont, James M. Norton, Lenore C. Norton, Lenore "Trilby" Norton, Mary T. Norton, Paul S. Norton.
EIN: 311678303
Codes: FD

50966
The McLane Foundation
4001 Industrial Blvd.
Temple, TX 76504

Established in 2001 in TX.
Donor(s): Drayton McLane, Jr.
Financial data (yr. ended 12/31/01): Grants paid, $323,241; assets, $134,973 (M); gifts received, $460,000; expenditures, $325,027; qualifying distributions, $325,027.
Limitations: Applications not accepted. Giving limited to Cameron, TX.
Application information: Contributes only to pre-selected organizations.
Officers and Directors:* Drayton McLane, Jr.,* Pres.; G.W. Sanford, Jr.,* V.P.; Webster F. Stickney, Jr.,* Secy.-Treas.
EIN: 742990325

50967
King Ranch Family Trust
P.O. Drawer 911
Kingsville, TX 78363
Application address: P.O. Box 17777, San Antonio, TX 78217, tel.: (210) 822-2348; FAX: (512) 516-0616; E-mail: texpeg@aol.com
Contact: Richard M. Kleberg III

Trust established in 1946 in TX.
Donor(s): King Ranch Family.
Financial data (yr. ended 12/31/01): Grants paid, $322,094; assets, $6,601,664 (M); gifts received, $2,977; expenditures, $368,929; qualifying distributions, $329,875.
Limitations: Giving limited to TX, with emphasis on the Kingsville and Corpus Christi, area.
Publications: Annual report, application guidelines, financial statement, informational brochure (including application guidelines).
Application information: Application form not required.
Trustees: Leslie C. Clement, Richard M. Kleberg III.
EIN: 746044809
Codes: FD

50968
John and Florence Newman Foundation
112 E. Pecan, Ste. 2222
San Antonio, TX 78205 (210) 226-0371

Established in 1988 in TX.
Donor(s): Florence B. Newman.
Financial data (yr. ended 12/31/01): Grants paid, $321,550; assets, $13,264,125 (M); expenditures, $646,486; qualifying distributions, $351,321.
Limitations: Applications not accepted. Giving primarily in San Antonio, TX.
Application information: Contributes only to pre-selected organizations.
Directors: Ann J. Newman, John E. Newman, Jr., Thomas R. Semmes.
EIN: 742525348
Codes: FD

50969
David L. Tandy Foundation
P.O. Box 126377
Fort Worth, TX 76126
Application address: P.O. Box 101477, Fort Worth, TX 76185-1477
Contact: Erwin C. Whitney, Secy.

Established in 1968 in TX.
Financial data (yr. ended 05/31/01): Grants paid, $321,000; assets, $3,350,461 (M); expenditures, $332,355; qualifying distributions, $320,392.
Limitations: Giving primarily in TX, with emphasis on Fort Worth.
Officers and Directors:* Emmett E. Duemke,* Pres.; B.R. Roland,* V.P. and Treas.; A.R. Tandy, V.P.; Mrs. E.C. Whitney,* V.P.; P.N. Whitney, V.P.; T.L. Whitney,* V.P.; Erwin C. Whitney, Secy.
EIN: 756083140
Codes: FD

50970
The Walter M. Mischer & Mary A. Mischer Foundation
2727 N. Loop, W., Ste. 200
Houston, TX 77008 (713) 869-7800
Contact: Cherry York, Secy.-Treas.

Established in 1998 in TX.
Donor(s): Mary A. Mischer, Walter M. Mischer.
Financial data (yr. ended 12/31/99): Grants paid, $320,000; assets, $5,796,335 (M); expenditures, $398,836; qualifying distributions, $320,000.
Limitations: Giving primarily in Harris County, TX.
Application information: Application form required.
Officers: Walter M. Mischer, Pres.; John W. Storms, V.P.; Cherry York, Secy.-Treas.
EIN: 760574194

50971
Harry S. Moss Foundation
970 San Jacinto Twr.
2121 San Jacinto St.
Dallas, TX 75201 (214) 754-2984
Contact: Frank S. Ryburn, Pres.

Incorporated in 1952 in TX.
Donor(s): Harry S. Moss, Florence M. Moss, Moss Petroleum Co.
Financial data (yr. ended 11/30/01): Grants paid, $318,500; assets, $6,267,133 (M); expenditures, $367,413; qualifying distributions, $320,211.
Limitations: Giving primarily in the Dallas, TX, area.
Application information: Application form not required.
Officers: Frank S. Ryburn, Pres.; Mary Jane Ryburn, V.P. and Secy.-Treas.
EIN: 756036333
Codes: FD

50972
E. Paul and Helen Buck Waggoner Foundation, Inc.
P.O. Box 2130
Vernon, TX 76385
Contact: Gene W. Willingham, Secy.-Treas.

Incorporated in 1966 in TX.
Donor(s): E. Paul Waggoner,‡ Helen Buck Waggoner.‡
Financial data (yr. ended 04/30/01): Grants paid, $318,367; assets, $6,627,409 (M); expenditures, $331,388; qualifying distributions, $318,367.
Limitations: Applications not accepted. Giving primarily in TX.
Application information: Unsolicited requests for funds not accepted.
Officers: Electra Waggoner Biggs, Pres.; Helen Biggs Willingham, V.P.; Gene W. Willingham, Secy.-Treas.
EIN: 751243673
Codes: FD

50973
The Crain Foundation
P.O. Box 2146
Longview, TX 75606-2146 (903) 758-8276
Contact: Ann Lacy Crain, Pres.

Established in 1997 in TX.
Financial data (yr. ended 12/31/01): Grants paid, $317,760; assets, $4,675,597 (M); gifts received, $1,053,848; expenditures, $322,154; qualifying distributions, $317,760.
Officers and Directors:* Ann Lacy Crain,* Pres.; Rogers L. Crain,* V.P. and Secy.; B. Walter Crain III,* V.P. and Treas.; Ann Lacy Crain II,* V.P.; Neal Hawthorn, V.P.
EIN: 752698267
Codes: FD

50974
Summerfield G. Roberts Foundation
c/o Bank of America
P.O. Box 831041
Dallas, TX 75283-1041 (214) 363-9000
Contact: David Jackson, Tr.

Established in 1990 in TX.
Donor(s): Summerfield G. Roberts.‡
Financial data (yr. ended 03/31/01): Grants paid, $317,178; assets, $7,363,369 (M); expenditures, $407,547; qualifying distributions, $365,704.
Limitations: Giving limited to TX.

Publications: Application guidelines, financial statement.
Application information: Scholarship application forms provided by educational institutions must be completed by prospective award recipients. The foundation does not make the final selection of individuals receiving support.
Trustees: David Jackson, Bank of America.
EIN: 752341916
Codes: FD

50975
McIntosh Foundation
900 Rockmead, Ste. 132
Kingwood, TX 77339
Contact: David Russell, Dir.

Established in 1997 in TX.
Donor(s): Barbara J. McIntosh, Gerald M. McIntosh.
Financial data (yr. ended 08/31/01): Grants paid, $315,739; assets, $882,002 (M); expenditures, $447,650; qualifying distributions, $315,739.
Application information: Application form not required.
Directors: David Brass, Jan Hoff, Barbara J. McIntosh, Gerald M. McIntosh, David Russell, Tiffany Vasenius, Richard Ware.
EIN: 760553568
Codes: FD

50976
Gilliland Family Foundation
(Formerly Search Foundation)
550 S. Taylor, LB No. 249
Amarillo, TX 79101 (806) 374-8652
Contact: Sandra Gilliland, Pres.

Established in 1996 in TX.
Donor(s): Bill Gilliland, Sandra Gilliland.
Financial data (yr. ended 12/31/01): Grants paid, $314,569; assets, $5,797,566 (M); expenditures, $387,464; qualifying distributions, $334,475.
Limitations: Giving primarily in TX.
Application information: Application form required.
Officers: Sandra Gilliland, Pres. and Treas.; Robin Hall, V.P. and Secy.; Lori D'Atri, V.P.; Bill Gilliland, V.P.
EIN: 760181982
Codes: FD

50977
W. L. & Louise E. Seymour Foundation
201 E. Main St., 4th Fl.
El Paso, TX 79901 (915) 546-6515
Contact: Terry Crenshaw, Trust Off., JPMorgan Chase Bank

Established in 1983 in TX.
Donor(s): Louise E. Seymour.‡
Financial data (yr. ended 03/31/01): Grants paid, $313,907; assets, $5,360,344 (M); expenditures, $365,987; qualifying distributions, $326,865.
Limitations: Giving primarily in El Paso, TX.
Trustee: JPMorgan Chase Bank.
EIN: 746315820
Codes: FD

50978
The Marlene and J. O. Stewart, Jr. Foundation
c/o Ron F. Acton
7100 Westwind Dr., Ste. 210
El Paso, TX 79912
Contact: Ron Acton, Pres.

Established in 2000 in TX.
Donor(s): Marlene Stewart, James O. Stewart, Jr.
Financial data (yr. ended 12/31/01): Grants paid, $313,608; assets, $4,470,335 (M); expenditures, $545,109; qualifying distributions, $313,608.

Officers and Directors:* Ron F. Acton,* Pres.; Myron Brown,* V.P.; James O. Stewart, Jr.,* V.P.; James O. Stewart III,* V.P.; Marlene Stewart,* V.P.
EIN: 742958268

50979
W. P. & Bulah Luse Foundation
c/o Bank of America
P.O. Box 831041
Dallas, TX 75283-1041
Application address: c/o Bank of America, P.O. Box 830241, Dallas, TX 75283-0241, tel.: (214) 508-1989
Contact: Bill Arrington

Established in 1947 in TX.
Donor(s): Bulah Luse,‡ W.P. Luse.‡
Financial data (yr. ended 12/31/00): Grants paid, $313,500; assets, $8,851,348 (M); gifts received, $839; expenditures, $414,597; qualifying distributions, $317,841.
Limitations: Giving limited to TX.
Application information: Application form not required.
Trustees: James P. Bevans, Jack Burrell, George Wilken, Bank of America.
EIN: 756007639
Codes: FD

50980
Goodman-Abell Foundation
2550 N. Loop W., Ste. 750
Houston, TX 77056

Established in 1998 in TX.
Donor(s): G. Hughes Abell, Betsy G. Abell.
Financial data (yr. ended 02/28/01): Grants paid, $312,661; assets, $2,285,437 (M); gifts received, $616,802; expenditures, $373,108; qualifying distributions, $329,729.
Limitations: Applications not accepted. Giving primarily in TX.
Application information: Contributes only to pre-selected organizations.
Officers: Betsy G. Abell, Pres.; G. Hughes Abell, Secy.
Director: John B. Goodman.
EIN: 742869876
Codes: FD

50981
Nina Heard Astin Charitable Trust
c/o Wells Fargo Bank, N.A., Trust Dept.
P.O. Drawer 913
Bryan, TX 77805 (979) 776-5402
Scholarship application addresses: c/o Bryan High School Counselors, 3401 E. 29th St., Bryan, TX 77802, tel.: (979) 774-3273, or c/o A&M Consolidated High School, 701 W. Loop S., College Station, TX 77840, tel.: (979) 696-0544

Established around 1975.
Financial data (yr. ended 03/31/01): Grants paid, $312,000; assets, $7,051,244 (M); expenditures, $381,103; qualifying distributions, $313,444.
Limitations: Giving primarily in TX.
Application information: Application form required for scholarships.
Trustee: Wells Fargo Bank, N.A.
EIN: 741721901
Codes: FD, GTI

50982
Gaston Episcopal Hospital Foundation, Inc.
6331 Chesley
Dallas, TX 75214 (214) 820-3136
Contact: Charles Cooper, Secy.

Established in 1980 in TX.

Financial data (yr. ended 12/31/01): Grants paid, $310,063; assets, $5,919,876 (M); expenditures, $356,312; qualifying distributions, $354,579.
Limitations: Giving limited to TX.
Application information: Application form required.
Officers and Trustees:* Felix B. Goldman,* Pres.; W. Plack Carr, Jr.,* V.P.; Charles M. Cooper,* Secy.; Jon L. Mosle, Jr.,* Treas.; Neil D. Anderson, William David Barnett, M.D., Louis A. Beecherl, Jr., C. DeWitt Brown, Jr., Margaret Hunt Hill, Lawrence S. Pollock, Jr.
EIN: 751743288
Codes: FD

50983
Wal-Dot Foundation
7557 Rambler Rd., Ste. 1425
Dallas, TX 75231 (214) 891-5933
FAX: (214) 891-5979; E-mail: neuwalter@aol.com
Contact: Walter Neustadt, Jr., Pres.

Established in 1993 in OK.
Donor(s): Walter Neustadt, Jr., Dolores K. Neustadt.
Financial data (yr. ended 12/31/01): Grants paid, $309,630; assets, $5,975,602 (M); gifts received, $313,228; expenditures, $345,836; qualifying distributions, $320,254.
Limitations: Applications not accepted. Giving primarily in TX.
Application information: Contributes only to pre-selected organizations.
Officers and Directors:* Walter Neustadt, Jr.,* Pres.; Dolores K. Neustadt,* V.P.
EIN: 731414803
Codes: FD

50984
Dunagan Foundation, Inc.
P.O. Box 387
Monahans, TX 79756
FAX: (915) 943-2572; E-mail: dunagan@apex2000.net
Contact: Kathlyn C. Dunagan, Pres.

Established in 1976 in TX.
Donor(s): J. Conrad Dunagan,‡ Kathlyn C. Dunagan, John C. Dunagan.
Financial data (yr. ended 12/31/01): Grants paid, $309,425; assets, $4,315,659 (M); gifts received, $7,375; expenditures, $325,996; qualifying distributions, $307,161.
Limitations: Applications not accepted. Giving primarily in TX; limited support in CT, IL, and MO.
Application information: Contributes only to pre-selected organizations; unsolicited requests for funds not considered.
Officers and Board Members:* Kathlyn C. Dunagan,* Pres.; John C. Dunagan,* V.P.; Kathleen Dunagan,* Secy.; Richard J. Hoyer,* Treas.
EIN: 751561848
Codes: FD

50985
Jack & Judi Holmes Foundation
3257 Inwood Dr.
Houston, TX 77019-3227
Contact: John B. Holmes, Jr., Pres.

Established in 1999 in TX.
Donor(s): John B. Holmes, Jr., Judi McGee Holmes.
Financial data (yr. ended 12/31/00): Grants paid, $307,920; assets, $297,354 (M); gifts received, $300,000; expenditures, $310,172; qualifying distributions, $307,920.
Limitations: Giving on a national basis.

Officers and Directors:* John B. Holmes, Jr.,* Pres.; Judi McGee Holmes,* V.P.; John B. Holmes III, Ryland Holmes Sudduth.
EIN: 760559779
Codes: FD

50986
A. W. Riter, Jr. Family Foundation
c/o A.W. Riter, Jr.
110 N. College, Ste. 1406
Tyler, TX 75702-7244

Established in 1997 in TX.
Donor(s): A.W. Riter, Jr., Betty Jo B. Riter.
Financial data (yr. ended 12/31/01): Grants paid, $307,600; assets, $4,487,081 (M); expenditures, $328,890; qualifying distributions, $306,210.
Limitations: Applications not accepted. Giving primarily in Tyler, TX.
Application information: Contributes only to pre-selected organizations.
Officers: A.W. Riter, Jr., Pres.; A.W. Riter III, V.P.; Betty Jo B. Riter, V.P.; Melvin B. Lovelady, Secy.-Treas.
EIN: 752707712
Codes: FD

50987
B. M. Woltman Foundation
2525 N. Loop W., Ste. 102
Houston, TX 77008
Application address: c/o Lutheran Church, Missouri Synod, 7900 East Hwy. 290, Austin, TX 78724-2499
Contact: Rev. Kenneth Hennings, Exec. Dir

Trust established in 1948 in TX.
Donor(s): B.M. Woltman,‡ Woltman Furniture Co., and others.
Financial data (yr. ended 12/31/01): Grants paid, $307,000; assets, $5,915,815 (M); expenditures, $369,544; qualifying distributions, $313,076.
Limitations: Giving limited to TX.
Application information: Application forms provided for scholarships.
Officers and Trustees:* Mary McCanne Currin,* Pres.; Carloss Morris,* Secy.-Treas.; Rev. Donald G. Black, James E. Kellerman, Rev. James E. Linderman, R. Lynn Moers, Michael Richter, Ronald W. Rosenhagen.
EIN: 741402184
Codes: FD, GTI

50988
Navarro County Health Services Foundation
777 Main St.
Fort Worth, TX 76102
Additional application address: c/o Belvia Barham, Columbia Navarro Regional Hospital, West Hwy. 22, Corsicana, TX 75110, tel.: (903) 654-6810
Contact: JoAnn Means, Pres.

Financial data (yr. ended 12/31/00): Grants paid, $305,000; assets, $8,709,886 (M); expenditures, $355,433; qualifying distributions, $305,643.
Limitations: Giving to residents of Navarro County, TX, particularly in Corsicana.
Application information: Applications are accepted on a first come basis by Belvia Barham in the business office on Wednesdays from 1:00 PM to 4:00 PM. If you are unable to meet on Wed., an appointment will be necessary for an application to be taken. Application form required.
Officers: JoAnn H. Means, Pres.; David Campbell, V.P.; A.L. Atkiesson, Secy.
Trustees: Beth Bolen, James Chapman, Lynn Gill, Walker Lea, Bob Scott, Harrison Sloan.
EIN: 751767188
Codes: FD, GTI

50989
The Bob & Karen Wortham Charitable Foundation
801 Laurel
Beaumont, TX 77701 (409) 838-1000
Contact: Bob Wortham, Pres.

Established in 1999 in TX.
Donor(s): Bob Wortham.
Financial data (yr. ended 12/31/01): Grants paid, $304,650; assets, $453,324 (M); gifts received, $700,000; expenditures, $307,185; qualifying distributions, $307,089.
Limitations: Giving primarily in Beaumont, TX.
Application information: Application form not required.
Officer: Bob Wortham, Pres.
EIN: 760601063
Codes: FD

50990
Steve & Katherine Papermaster Family Foundation
701 Brazos, Ste. 500
Austin, TX 78701-3232

Financial data (yr. ended 12/31/99): Grants paid, $304,258; assets, $1,985,231 (M); gifts received, $370,305; expenditures, $388,768; qualifying distributions, $304,104.
Limitations: Applications not accepted.
Application information: Contributes only to pre-selected organizations.
Officers: Steven G. Papermaster, Pres.; Gail E. Papermaster, Secy.
Trustee: Katherine L. Papermaster.
EIN: 742832637
Codes: FD

50991
The Simpson Charitable Trust
c/o Phil Simpson
P.O. Box 100
Avinger, TX 75630-0100

Established in 2000 in TX.
Donor(s): Phil Simpson, Lorraine Hammerich Simpson.
Financial data (yr. ended 12/31/01): Grants paid, $303,923; assets, $4,699,714 (M); expenditures, $319,382; qualifying distributions, $301,624.
Limitations: Applications not accepted. Giving on a national basis.
Application information: Contributes only to pre-selected organizations.
Officers: Phil Simpson, Pres.; Lorraine Hammerich Simpson, V.P.; David Philip Simpson, Secy.; Patricia Taylor, Treas.
EIN: 756583001
Codes: FD

50992
The Raymond Dickson Foundation
P.O. Box 406
Hallettsville, TX 77964-0406 (361) 798-2531

Established in 1958 in TX.
Donor(s): Raymond Dickson,‡ Alton C. Allen.‡
Financial data (yr. ended 12/31/01): Grants paid, $302,718; assets, $6,864,189 (M); expenditures, $354,556; qualifying distributions, $302,718.
Limitations: Giving limited to TX.
Publications: Program policy statement, application guidelines.
Application information: Application form not required.
Officer and Trustees:* Wilbur Baber, Jr.,* Chair.; Curtis Gunn, Jr., Dunham F. Jewett, Lillian Moore Miller, Curtis T. Vaughan.
EIN: 746052983
Codes: FD

50993
The Eleanor and Frank Freed Foundation
700 Louisiana, Ste. 2550
Houston, TX 77002
Contact: Randall E. Evans, Secy.

Established in 1992 in TX.
Donor(s): Eleanor Freed Stern.‡
Financial data (yr. ended 09/30/01): Grants paid, $300,168; assets, $2,857,364 (M); gifts received, $193,000; expenditures, $345,251; qualifying distributions, $300,168.
Limitations: Applications not accepted. Giving primarily in Houston, TX.
Application information: Contributes only to pre-selected organizations. Unsolicited requests for funds not considered.
Officers: Randall E. Evans, Pres.; Gloria L. Herman, Secy.; Benjamin D. Rosenberg, Treas.
Trustees: William A. Camfield, Stephen M. Kaufman, Robert Loeb.
EIN: 760385085
Codes: FD

50994
Dr. Ralph and Marian Falk Foundation
(Formerly Dr. Ralph and Marian Falk Medical Research Foundation)
3007 Skyway Cir. N
Irving, TX 75038 (972) 659-9500

Established in 1974 in IL.
Donor(s): Marian C. Falk.
Financial data (yr. ended 12/31/01): Grants paid, $300,000; assets, $5,062,581 (M); expenditures, $339,258; qualifying distributions, $298,637.
Limitations: Giving primarily in the Dallas, TX, area.
Application information: Application form not required.
Officers and Directors:* Nicole F. Kohl,* Chair. and Treas.; Carol C. Fullinwider,* V.P.; Clayton Kohl,* V.P.; Atlee M. Kohl,* Secy.
EIN: 237380541
Codes: FD

50995
Killson Educational Foundation
c/o Bank of America
P.O. Box 831041
Dallas, TX 75283-1041
Application address: c/o Bank of America, P.O. Box 2518, Houston, TX 77252-2518, tel.: (713) 247-6773
Contact: Pam Bradley

Established in 1996 in TX.
Financial data (yr. ended 01/31/01): Grants paid, $300,000; assets, $3,823,701 (M); expenditures, $325,361; qualifying distributions, $304,566.
Limitations: Giving limited to TX.
Application information: Application form not required.
Trustee: Bank of America.
EIN: 752650791
Codes: FD

50996
Van De Walle Charitable Foundation
1100 Muirfield Vlg.
College Station, TX 77845-8938

Donor(s): Patricia Schoenemann.
Financial data (yr. ended 12/31/00): Grants paid, $300,000; assets, $1,970 (M); expenditures, $304,500; qualifying distributions, $300,000.
Limitations: Applications not accepted. Giving primarily in College Station, TX.
Application information: Contributes only to pre-selected organizations.

Trustees: Mark A. Schoenemann, Patricia V. Schoenemann, Elaine Thompson.
EIN: 742882560
Codes: FD

50997
Lizanell and Colbert Coldwell Foundation
c/o JPMorgan Chase Bank
P.O. Box 140
El Paso, TX 79980-0540 (915) 546-6515
Contact: Terry Crenshaw, V.P. and Trust Off., JPMorgan Chase Bank

Established in 1990 in TX.
Donor(s): Lizanell Coldwell.‡
Financial data (yr. ended 03/31/01): Grants paid, $299,700; assets, $5,203,682 (M); expenditures, $371,848; qualifying distributions, $313,447.
Limitations: Giving limited to TX, with emphasis on El Paso.
Trustees: William Collins, Laurence Nickey, M.D.
Administrator: JPMorgan Chase Bank.
EIN: 742576133
Codes: FD

50998
Robert D. & Catherine R. Alexander Foundation
4200 S. Hulen St., Ste. 617
Fort Worth, TX 76109-4913
Contact: R. Denny Alexander, Tr.

Established in 1962 in TX.
Donor(s): Catherine R. Alexander, R.D. Alexander Trust.
Financial data (yr. ended 12/31/01): Grants paid, $298,725; assets, $5,684,017 (M); expenditures, $376,416; qualifying distributions, $296,495.
Limitations: Giving primarily in Tarrant County, TX, with emphasis on Fort Worth.
Application information: Application form not required.
Trustees: Catherine R. Alexander, R. Denny Alexander.
EIN: 756012124
Codes: FD

50999
Ershel Franklin Charitable Trust
P.O. Box 790
Post, TX 79356 (806) 495-3579
Contact: Giles C. McCrary, Tr.

Established in 1985 in TX.
Financial data (yr. ended 12/31/01): Grants paid, $297,855; assets, $6,063,702 (M); expenditures, $307,455; qualifying distributions, $307,455.
Limitations: Applications not accepted. Giving primarily in TX.
Application information: Contributes only to pre-selected organizations.
Trustee: Giles C. McCrary.
EIN: 756305761
Codes: FD

51000
Hervey Foundation
P.O. Box 20000
El Paso, TX 79998
Application address: 1005 N. Mesa, El Paso, TX 79902, tel.: (915) 532-2621
Contact: Georgiana Garcia

Trust established in 1957 in TX.
Financial data (yr. ended 01/31/02): Grants paid, $296,950; assets, $5,414,259 (M); expenditures, $312,037; qualifying distributions, $293,834.
Limitations: Giving limited to El Paso, TX.
Publications: Annual report (including application guidelines).
Application information: Application form required.

Trustees: Hugh Frederick, Sherleen Lockhart Hervey, Eric D. Payne.
EIN: 746068068
Codes: FD

51001
The Gregory Fund
c/o Robert P. Gregory, Jr.
5777 Indian Cir.
Houston, TX 77057
Application address: c/o Banc One Corp, P.O. Box 2558, Houston, TX 77252-8037, tel.: (713) 216-4649
Contact: Judy Cook

Established in 1986 in TX.
Donor(s): Robert P. Gregory, Jr., Ann C. Gregory.
Financial data (yr. ended 12/31/01): Grants paid, $296,000; assets, $6,153,853 (M); expenditures, $302,728; qualifying distributions, $295,154.
Limitations: Giving primarily in TX.
Trustees: Ann C. Gregory, Robert P. Gregory, Jr.
EIN: 760170992
Codes: FD

51002
The Gale Foundation
2615 Calder St., Ste. 630
Beaumont, TX 77702

Donor(s): Edwin Gale.
Financial data (yr. ended 04/30/01): Grants paid, $292,730; assets, $7,613,184 (M); gifts received, $27,575; expenditures, $326,994; qualifying distributions, $321,567.
Limitations: Applications not accepted. Giving primarily in TX; some funding also in NY.
Application information: Contributes only to pre-selected organizations.
Trustee: Rebecca S. Gale.
EIN: 760009604
Codes: FD

51003
Albert L. Ueltschi Foundation
7701 Briarcrest Ct.
Irving, TX 75063

Established in 1997 in TX.
Donor(s): Albert L. Ueltschi.
Financial data (yr. ended 12/31/01): Grants paid, $292,000; assets, $7,572,165 (M); gifts received, $286,664; expenditures, $292,385; qualifying distributions, $291,927.
Limitations: Applications not accepted. Giving on a national basis.
Application information: Contributes only to pre-selected organizations.
Officer: Albert L. Ueltschi, Pres.
Directors: Nancy J. Gavin, Patricia L. Rickert, Anne Ueltschi, James T. Ueltschi.
EIN: 752709168
Codes: FD

51004
Sequor Foundation
c/o Burnside & Rishebarger, PLLC
8700 Tesoro Dr., Ste. 340
San Antonio, TX 78217
Application address: 211 W. Austin St., Marshall, TX 75670, tel.: (903) 938-8373
Contact: Richard M. Anderson

Established in 1998 in TX.
Financial data (yr. ended 06/30/01): Grants paid, $289,400; assets, $6,100,563 (M); expenditures, $409,321; qualifying distributions, $282,750.
Limitations: Giving primarily in CA and TX.
Officers: Joe Bradberry, Pres.; Arthur Milberger, V.P.; James Smith, Secy.-Treas.
EIN: 363783683

Codes: FD

51005
Ranger-Ryan Scholarship Foundation
10777 Westheimer Rd., Ste. 5N
Houston, TX 77042
Contact: Mary Ploog, Scholarship Mgmt. Svcs.

Established in 1990.
Donor(s): Ranger Insurance Co.
Financial data (yr. ended 12/31/00): Grants paid, $289,040; assets, $552,753 (M); gifts received, $4,852; expenditures, $272,092; qualifying distributions, $272,092.
Limitations: Giving limited to graduates of Ryan Middle School in Houston, TX.
Application information: Unsolicited requests for funds not accepted.
Officers: Philip J. Broughton, Pres.; Jerry B. Mackey, V.P.; Barbara P. Blasingame, Secy.; Michael P. Berry, Treas.
EIN: 760266492
Codes: CS, FD, CD, GTI

51006
Vanberg Family Foundation
PMB 255
6110 E. Mockingbird Ln.
Dallas, TX 75214
Contact: Anne M. Vanberg, Dir.

Established in 1990 in TX.
Donor(s): Harold E. Vanberg, Sr.,‡ Anne M. Vanberg.
Financial data (yr. ended 12/31/99): Grants paid, $287,691; assets, $4,920,608 (M); gifts received, $1,796,834; expenditures, $365,794; qualifying distributions, $277,957.
Limitations: Giving primarily in Dallas, TX.
Application information: Application form required.
Directors: Nancy Vanberg Brooks, Hawk Mesa Storm, Anne M. Vanberg.
EIN: 752342463
Codes: FD

51007
Bud Smith Foundation, Inc.
2200 Ross Ave., Ste. 3800
Dallas, TX 75201 (214) 999-1919
Contact: Henry J. Smith, Pres., or Jane M. Smith, V.P.

Established in 1997 in TX.
Donor(s): Henry J. Smith, Jane M. Smith.
Financial data (yr. ended 12/31/01): Grants paid, $286,216; assets, $53,259 (M); gifts received, $204,000; expenditures, $289,602; qualifying distributions, $286,215.
Limitations: Giving primarily in Amarillo and Dallas, TX.
Officers: Henry J. Smith, Pres.; Karen Smith Evans, V.P.; Lori Smith Love, V.P.; Jane M. Smith, V.P.; Robert C. Taylor, Secy.
EIN: 752681816
Codes: FD

51008
Dr. Leon Bromberg Charitable Trust Fund
2200 Market St., Ste. 710
Galveston, TX 77550-1532 (409) 762-5890
Contact: Charles G. Dibrell, Jr., Chair.

Established in 1985 in TX.
Donor(s): Leon Bromberg.‡
Financial data (yr. ended 04/30/01): Grants paid, $284,818; assets, $6,465,043 (M); expenditures, $428,609; qualifying distributions, $317,567.
Limitations: Giving in the U.S., with emphasis on Bryan, Galveston, Crockett and Houston, TX.

51008—TEXAS

Officers and Trustees:* Charles G. Dibrell, Jr.,* Chair.; Charles G. Dibrell III,* Secy.-Treas.
EIN: 760193007
Codes: FD

51009
Charles and Susan Gordon and Julia Gordon Gray Memorial Trust
c/o Frost National Bank
P.O. Box 2950
San Antonio, TX 78299-2950

Established in 1992 in TX.
Donor(s): Julia G. Gray.‡
Financial data (yr. ended 11/30/01): Grants paid, $283,342; assets, $4,891,044 (M); expenditures, $327,000; qualifying distributions, $280,586.
Limitations: Applications not accepted. Giving primarily in TX.
Application information: Contributes only to pre-selected organizations.
Trustee: Frost National Bank.
EIN: 746410729
Codes: FD

51010
W. B. Munson Foundation
c/o Bank One Trust Co., N.A.
8111 Preston Rd., Ste. 200
Dallas, TX 75225
Application address: c/o Bank One Trust Co., N.A., 200 N. Travis, Sherman, TX 75090, tel.: (903) 868-0701
Contact: Mary Anne Valentine

Trust established in 1943 in TX.
Financial data (yr. ended 12/31/00): Grants paid, $283,265; assets, $8,334,870 (M); expenditures, $352,272; qualifying distributions, $285,981.
Limitations: Giving limited to Grayson County, TX.
Application information: Applications not accepted for scholarships. Application form required.
Board of Governors: Margaret Bishop, Ben Munson IV, David M. Munson, Sr., David M. Munson, Jr., Peter K. Munson.
Trustee: Bank One Trust Co., N.A.
EIN: 756015068
Codes: FD

51011
Robert W. Knox, Sr. and Pearl Wallis Knox Charitable Foundation
c/o Bank of America
P.O. Box 831041, TX1-492-12-01
Dallas, TX 75283-1041
Application address: c/o Bank of America, P.O. Box 2518, Houston, TX 77252-2518
Contact: Bette Lehmberg, V.P., Bank of America

Established in 1964 in TX.
Donor(s): Robert W. Knox, Jr.‡
Financial data (yr. ended 08/31/01): Grants paid, $282,925; assets, $5,434,479 (M); expenditures, $331,353; qualifying distributions, $292,726.
Limitations: Giving primarily in Houston, TX.
Application information: Application form not required.
Trustee Bank: Bank of America.
EIN: 746064974
Codes: FD

51012
Inman Foundation
c/o Bobby R. Inman
3200 Riva Ridge Rd.
Austin, TX 78746

Established in 1997 in TX.
Donor(s): Bobby R. Inman.
Financial data (yr. ended 12/31/00): Grants paid, $282,524; assets, $3,539,666 (M); expenditures, $320,437; qualifying distributions, $282,524.
Limitations: Applications not accepted. Giving primarily in Austin, TX.
Application information: Contributes only to pre-selected organizations.
Officers: Bobby R. Inman, Pres. and Treas.; William C. Inman, V.P.; Nancy Inman, Secy.
EIN: 742833552
Codes: FD

51013
Bowers Foundation
P.O. Box 56048
Houston, TX 77256

Established in 1988 in TX.
Donor(s): Hugh R. Bowers, Ryn R. Bowers.
Financial data (yr. ended 12/31/01): Grants paid, $281,350; assets, $3,893,068 (M); expenditures, $283,773; qualifying distributions, $279,562.
Limitations: Applications not accepted. Giving primarily in TX.
Application information: Contributes only to pre-selected organizations.
Officers: Hugh R. Bowers, Pres.; Ryn R. Bowers, V.P.; C.M. Barth, Treas.
EIN: 760260739
Codes: FD

51014
Chinquapin Foundation
(Formerly MJR Fund)
4608 Meadowood Rd.
Dallas, TX 75220 (214) 350-7434
Contact: Margaret J. Rogers, Pres.

Donor(s): Margaret J. Rogers.
Financial data (yr. ended 12/31/01): Grants paid, $280,700; assets, $6,155,314 (M); gifts received, $6,018; expenditures, $342,403; qualifying distributions, $285,997.
Limitations: Giving primarily in CA.
Application information: Application form not required.
Officers: Margaret J. Rogers, Pres.; Laura Charlton Cole, V.P.; Emily Charlton Corrigan, Secy.; Erik Allen Charlton, Treas.
EIN: 752052571
Codes: FD

51015
The Charles and Betti Saunders Foundation
19 Willowron Dr.
Houston, TX 77024-7618 (713) 651-5374

Established in 1993 in TX.
Donor(s): Charles A. Saunders, Betti F. Saunders.
Financial data (yr. ended 06/30/01): Grants paid, $280,200; assets, $5,388,378 (M); expenditures, $286,497; qualifying distributions, $277,956.
Limitations: Giving primarily in TX.
Application information: Application form required.
Trustees: Cynthia S. Buggs, Shelly S. Eatherly, Melanie S. Mahoney, Betti F. Saunders, Charles A. Saunders, C. Stephen Saunders.
EIN: 760410069
Codes: FD

51016
The Carruth Foundation, Inc.
2727 Allen Pkwy., Ste. 1570
Houston, TX 77019-2125

Established in 1994 in TX.
Donor(s): Allen H. Carruth.
Financial data (yr. ended 01/31/01): Grants paid, $280,000; assets, $6,474,766 (M); gifts received, $390,922; expenditures, $280,644; qualifying distributions, $278,001.
Limitations: Applications not accepted. Giving primarily in Houston, TX.
Application information: Contributes only to pre-selected organizations.
Officers and Trustees:* Ethel G. Carruth,* Pres.; Brady F. Carruth,* Secy.; William V.H. Clarke, Treas.
EIN: 760439576
Codes: FD

51017
The Gorman Foundation
4040 Broadway, Ste. 615
San Antonio, TX 78209
Contact: Frances S. Coker, Secy.

Established in 1997.
Financial data (yr. ended 12/31/00): Grants paid, $279,434; assets, $4,790,388 (M); expenditures, $288,574; qualifying distributions, $281,561.
Limitations: Giving primarily in San Antonio, TX.
Officers: James W. Gorman, Jr., Pres.; Rowena C. Gorman, V.P.; Frances S. Coker, Secy.; David A. Gorman, Treas.
Director: Michael A. Schott.
EIN: 742822598
Codes: FD

51018
Ina Calkins Foundation
c/o Bank of America
P.O. Box 831041
Dallas, TX 75283-1041
Application address: P.O. Box 419119, Kansas City, MO 64141-6119, tel: 816-979-7481
Contact: David P. Ross, Sr. V.P.

Established in 2000 in MO.
Financial data (yr. ended 12/31/01): Grants paid, $278,221; assets, $6,321,085 (M); expenditures, $317,888; qualifying distributions, $280,098.
Limitations: Giving limited to organizations and residents of Kansas City, MO.
Trustee: Bank of America.
EIN: 526994869
Codes: FD

51019
The Waste Management Charitable Foundation, Inc.
(Formerly Wheelabrator Technologies Rust International Charitable Foundation, Inc.)
c/o Waste Management, Inc.
1001 Fannin St., Ste. 4000
Houston, TX 77002 (713) 512-6200
Contact: Marilyn Brown

Established in 1990 in TX.
Donor(s): Wheelabrator Technologies Inc.
Financial data (yr. ended 12/31/00): Grants paid, $278,150; assets, $9,306,679 (M); expenditures, $474,893; qualifying distributions, $399,234.
Limitations: Giving on a national basis, with some emphasis on TX.
Application information: Application form not required.
Officers: John M. Kehoe, Jr., Pres.; Richard S. Haak, Jr., Cont.
Director: Robert J. Gagalis.
EIN: 043073733
Codes: CS, FD, CD

51020
Leola W. and Charles H. Hugg Trust
c/o JPMorgan Chase Bank
P.O. Box 2558
Houston, TX 772527

Established in 1979.

Financial data (yr. ended 12/31/01): Grants paid, $277,825; assets, $4,950,854 (M); expenditures, $329,793; qualifying distributions, $291,910.
Limitations: Applications not accepted. Giving limited to Williamson County, TX.
Trustees: Richard Anderson, Sherri Babcock, JPMorgan Chase Bank.
EIN: 741907673
Codes: FD

51021
San Marcos Civic Foundation
P.O. Box 161687
Austin, TX 78716 (512) 328-6696
Contact: Susan Hinton, Tr.

Established in 1968 in TX.
Donor(s): H.Y. Price, Jr.,‡ Lois Pollard Price.‡
Financial data (yr. ended 12/31/01): Grants paid, $277,562; assets, $8,230,706 (M); expenditures, $568,628; qualifying distributions, $455,933.
Limitations: Giving primarily in Hays County, TX.
Publications: Newsletter, informational brochure.
Application information: Application form required.
Trustees: Mary Davis, Susan Hinton, Timothy M. Price.
EIN: 746109230
Codes: FD

51022
David & Gusta Rosenberg Family Foundation
7 Cheltenham Way
Dallas, TX 75230
Contact: David Rosenberg, Pres.

Established in 1986 in TX.
Donor(s): David Rosenberg, Gusta Rosenberg.
Financial data (yr. ended 12/31/01): Grants paid, $277,500; assets, $8,333,481 (M); expenditures, $278,364; qualifying distributions, $277,500.
Limitations: Giving primarily in Brooklyn, NY and Dallas, TX.
Application information: Application form required.
Officers and Directors:* David Rosenberg,* Pres.; Gusta Rosenberg,* V.P.; Ira W. Silverton,* V.P.
EIN: 752145757
Codes: FD

51023
Community Hospital Foundation, Inc.
13301 East Freeway, Ste. 307
Houston, TX 77015

Incorporated in 1986 in TX.
Financial data (yr. ended 05/31/01): Grants paid, $275,000; assets, $4,209,486 (M); expenditures, $318,577; qualifying distributions, $305,002.
Limitations: Applications not accepted. Giving primarily in TX.
Application information: Contributes only to pre-selected organizations.
Officers: Loren Rohr, Pres.; John Ward, V.P.; Edythe Tompson, Secy.; Patsy Simon, Treas.; Gerald Cobb, Fin. Off.
EIN: 741470290
Codes: FD

51024
James N. McCoy Foundation
5001 Ditto Ln.
Wichita Falls, TX 76302-3501

Established in 1995 in TX.
Donor(s): James N. McCoy.
Financial data (yr. ended 12/31/00): Grants paid, $274,030; assets, $6,790,351 (M); gifts received, $1,000,000; expenditures, $286,069; qualifying distributions, $267,535.

Limitations: Applications not accepted. Giving primarily in TX.
Application information: Contributes only to pre-selected organizations.
Officers and Trustees:* Carolyn Hays,* Pres.; Mark McCoy,* V.P.; R. Ken Hines,* Secy.-Treas.; Robert W. Goff, Jr.
EIN: 752587034
Codes: FD

51025
Helen Irwin Littauer Educational Trust
c/o Bank of America
P.O. Box 831041
Dallas, TX 75283-1041
Application address: P.O. Box 1317, Fort Worth, TX 76101, tel.: (817) 390-6921
Contact: Linda M. Metcalf, V.P., Bank of America

Established in 1969 in TX.
Financial data (yr. ended 04/30/01): Grants paid, $273,590; assets, $8,712,675 (M); expenditures, $355,599; qualifying distributions, $280,725.
Limitations: Giving primarily in TX.
Application information: Application form not required.
Trustee: Bank of America.
EIN: 237029857
Codes: FD

51026
Catalyst Foundation
1301 McKinney, Ste. 5100
Houston, TX 77010-3095
Contact: Charles H. Still, Secy.

Established in 1992.
Financial data (yr. ended 12/31/01): Grants paid, $271,156; assets, $5,733,644 (M); expenditures, $365,318; qualifying distributions, $307,198.
Limitations: Applications not accepted. Giving on a national basis.
Application information: Contributes only to pre-selected organizations.
Officers: Ken Suyama, Pres.; Yoshihiki Horio, V.P.; Charles H. Still, Secy.; Satoru Ohya, Treas.
EIN: 760383386
Codes: FD

51027
The Membery Foundation
607 Robin Dale Dr.
Austin, TX 78734

Established in 1988 in TX.
Donor(s): Willard M. Hanzlik, Cordelia H. Hanzlik.
Financial data (yr. ended 12/31/99): Grants paid, $268,630; assets, $655,549 (M); expenditures, $270,540; qualifying distributions, $266,648.
Limitations: Applications not accepted. Giving primarily in CA, ME, and MO.
Application information: Contributes only to pre-selected organizations.
Officers and Directors:* Willard M. Hanzlik,* Pres. and Treas.; Cordelia H. Hanzlik, V.P. and Secy.; Terri Lacy.
EIN: 760260974
Codes: FD

51028
Eula Mae and John Baugh Foundation
1390 Enclave Pkwy.
Houston, TX 77077

Established in 1995 in TX.
Donor(s): Eula Mae Baugh, John F. Baugh.
Financial data (yr. ended 12/31/01): Grants paid, $268,240; assets, $15,813,083 (M); expenditures, $313,720; qualifying distributions, $3,267,698; giving activities include $3,048,000 for loans.

Limitations: Applications not accepted. Giving primarily in TX.
Application information: Contributes only to pre-selected organizations.
Trustees: Eula Mae Baugh, John F. Baugh, E. James Lowrey, Jaqueline Morrison Moore, Barbara Baugh Morrison, Julia Morrison Ortiz.
EIN: 760457820
Codes: FD

51029
Rob and Bessie Welder Wildlife Foundation
P.O. Box 1400
Sinton, TX 78387-1400 (361) 364-2643
FAX: (361) 364-2650; *E-mail:* Welderwf@aol.com; *URL:* http://hometown.aol.com/welderwf/welderweb.html
Contact: Dr. D. Lynn Drawe, Dir.

Trust established in 1954 in TX.
Donor(s): R.H. Welder,‡ Mrs. R.H. Welder,‡ Edward H. & Winnie H. Smith Fellowship Trust Fund.
Financial data (yr. ended 12/31/01): Grants paid, $267,858; assets, $19,480,976 (M); gifts received, $30,108; expenditures, $1,426,196; qualifying distributions, $267,858.
Limitations: Giving primarily in the U.S.
Publications: Application guidelines, biennial report, informational brochure (including application guidelines).
Application information: Application guidelines available on website. Application form required.
Director: D. Lynn Drawe.
Trustees: H.C. Weil, John J. Welder V, Patrick H. Welder.
EIN: 741381321
Codes: FD, GTI

51030
The Kayser Foundation
600 Travis St., Ste. 3500
Houston, TX 77002-2910 (713) 226-1393
Contact: R. Bruce Laboon, Pres.

Incorporated in 1961 in TX.
Donor(s): Paul Kayser, Mrs. Paul Kayser.
Financial data (yr. ended 12/31/01): Grants paid, $267,189; assets, $4,886,127 (M); expenditures, $317,220; qualifying distributions, $283,100.
Limitations: Giving primarily in Houston, TX.
Officers: R. Bruce Laboon, Pres.; Jeff Love, V.P.; Kenneth Simon, Secy.-Treas.
EIN: 746050591
Codes: FD

51031
The Darla Moore Foundation
777 Main St., Ste. 2250
Fort Worth, TX 76102

Established in 1999 in TX.
Donor(s): Darla D. Moore.
Financial data (yr. ended 12/31/01): Grants paid, $264,500; assets, $589,067 (M); expenditures, $278,865; qualifying distributions, $266,144.
Limitations: Applications not accepted. Giving primarily in NY.
Application information: Contributes only to pre-selected organizations.
Officers: Darla Moore, Pres.; Melissa T. Parrish, Secy.-Treas.
EIN: 752825341
Codes: FD

51032
The Gill Foundation
1330 Post Oak Blvd., Ste. 1575
Houston, TX 77056

Established in 1997 in TX.

51032—TEXAS

Donor(s): Jack M. Gill, Linda C. Gill.
Financial data (yr. ended 11/30/01): Grants paid, $262,779; assets, $4,132,550 (M); expenditures, $393,222; qualifying distributions, $262,779.
Limitations: Applications not accepted. Giving primarily in CA and TX.
Application information: Contributes only to pre-selected organizations.
Officers: Jack M. Gill, Pres. and Treas.; Linda C. Gill, V.P. and Secy.
Directors: Jason A. Gill, Jefferson M. Gill, Tyler A. Gill, Jennifer L. Roberts.
EIN: 311506372
Codes: FD

51033
The Jesse H. & Susan R. Oppenheimer Foundation
711 Navarro, Ste. 620
San Antonio, TX 78205-1713

Established in 1964 in TX.
Donor(s): Jesse H. Oppenheimer, Susan R. Oppenheimer.
Financial data (yr. ended 12/31/01): Grants paid, $262,263; assets, $5,457,447 (M); gifts received, $13,857; expenditures, $305,268; qualifying distributions, $262,263.
Limitations: Applications not accepted. Giving limited to Bexar County, TX.
Application information: Contributes only to pre-selected organizations; all donations are trustee-generated. Unsolicited applications not considered.
Trustees: J. David Oppenheimer, Jesse H. Oppenheimer, Susan R. Oppenheimer.
EIN: 746032845
Codes: FD

51034
Paul and Mary Haas Foundation
P.O. Box 2928
Corpus Christi, TX 78403 (361) 887-6955
FAX: (361) 883-5992; *E-mail:* haasfdn@aol.com
Contact: Karen L. Wesson, Exec. Dir.

Trust established in 1954 in TX.
Donor(s): Paul R. Haas, Mary F. Haas.
Financial data (yr. ended 12/31/99): Grants paid, $262,230; assets, $3,351,499 (M); gifts received, $391,566; expenditures, $326,400; qualifying distributions, $279,407.
Limitations: Giving primarily in the Corpus Christi, TX, area.
Publications: Grants list, application guidelines, financial statement, informational brochure (including application guidelines).
Application information: Application form required.
Officers and Trustees:* Paul R. Haas,* Pres.; Rheta Haas Page,* Secy.; Mary F. Haas, Raymond P. Haas, Rene Haas.
EIN: 746031614
Codes: FD, GTI

51035
Ruth McLean Bowman Bowers Foundation
P.O. Box 12199
San Antonio, TX 78212-0199
Application address: 615 Belknap Pl., San Antonio, TX 78212, tel.: (210) 733-0911
Contact: Ruth McLean Bowers, Pres.

Established in 1956 in TX.
Donor(s): Ruth McLean Bowers.
Financial data (yr. ended 12/31/01): Grants paid, $262,000; assets, $5,664,116 (M); expenditures, $266,389; qualifying distributions, $262,000.
Limitations: Giving primarily in Washington, DC, NY, and TX.
Application information: Application form not required.
Officers and Trustees:* Ruth McLean Bowers,* Pres. and Treas.; William O. Bowers III,* V.P.; Marrs McLean Bowman,* Secy.; Beth Bowman Harper, Bonnie Bowman Korbell.
EIN: 746062585
Codes: FD

51036
Naomi and Martin Warren Family Foundation
c/o JPMorgan Chase Bank
P.O. Box 2558, 600 Travis St., 7th Fl.
Houston, TX 77252-2558 (713) 216-1451
Contact: Elizabeth C. Hickman

Established in 1998 in TX.
Donor(s): Geraldine Roper, Jim Roper, Andrew Spector, Helen Spector, Benjamin Warren, Joy Warren.
Financial data (yr. ended 12/31/00): Grants paid, $261,500; assets, $3,130,354 (M); expenditures, $296,350; qualifying distributions, $260,667.
Limitations: Giving primarily in NJ, New York, NY, and the greater Houston, TX, area.
Application information: Unsolicited requests for funds not accepted. Applications accepted by invitation only. Application form required.
Officers and Directors:* Naomi Warren,* Pres.; Geraldine Roper,* V.P.; Helen Spector,* V.P.; Benjamin Warren,* V.P.; Joy Warren,* V.P.
EIN: 760588400
Codes: FD

51037
Norbert H. Hardner Foundation
1706 W. 6th St.
Austin, TX 78703-4703

Established in 2000 in TX.
Donor(s): Norbert H. Hardner.‡
Financial data (yr. ended 12/31/01): Grants paid, $261,450; assets, $3,457,556 (M); gifts received, $515,000; expenditures, $389,877; qualifying distributions, $261,450.
Limitations: Applications not accepted. Giving primarily in PA.
Application information: Contributes only to pre-selected organizations.
Officers: Jared Hardner, Pres.; Sara Hardner Leon, V.P.; Rebecca Haverly, Secy.; Margaret Hardner, Treas.
EIN: 742952380
Codes: FD

51038
A Healing Touch Foundation
(Formerly Ruth M. Smith & Holly Smith Foundation)
c/o The Northern Trust Co.
2701 Kirby Dr.
Houston, TX 77098

Donor(s): Ruth McNair Smith.
Financial data (yr. ended 12/31/01): Grants paid, $260,900; assets, $2,835 (M); gifts received, $75,000; expenditures, $268,801; qualifying distributions, $261,581.
Limitations: Applications not accepted. Giving primarily in Houston, TX.
Application information: Contributes only to pre-selected organizations.
Trustees: Ruth McNair Smith, Northern Trust Bank of Texas.
EIN: 766080508
Codes: FD

51039
The Morton & Angela Topfer Family Foundation
c/o Charlene Heydinger
500 Plaza on the Lake
Austin, TX 78746

Established in 2000 in TX.
Donor(s): Angela Topfer, Morton Topfer.
Financial data (yr. ended 12/31/01): Grants paid, $259,486; assets, $62,502,132 (M); gifts received, $30,449,967; expenditures, $742,722; qualifying distributions, $381,451.
Trustees: Angela Topfer, Morton Topfer.
EIN: 742961304
Codes: FD

51040
The Roff Foundation
333 Clay St., Ste. 4300
Houston, TX 77002-4104 (713) 655-5312
Contact: J. Hugh Roff, Jr., Pres.

Established in 1995 in TX.
Donor(s): J. Hugh Roff, Jr., Ann Roff.
Financial data (yr. ended 12/31/01): Grants paid, $259,100; assets, $941,413 (M); expenditures, $276,671; qualifying distributions, $259,590.
Limitations: Giving limited to Houston, TX.
Officers: J. Hugh Roff, Jr., Pres.; Ann Roff, V.P.; Bessie Grahmann, Secy.-Treas.
Directors: Andrew W. Roff, Charles L. Roff, Elizabeth A. Roff, Jennifer L. Roff, John H. Roff III.
EIN: 760484703
Codes: FD

51041
Clifton C. and Henryetta C. Doak Charitable Trust
c/o Wells Fargo Bank Texas, N.A.
P.O. Drawer 913
Bryan, TX 77805 (979) 776-3267
Contact: Kenneth Loke, Trust Off., Wells Fargo Bank Texas, N.A.

Established in 1993 in TX.
Donor(s): Henryetta C. Doak.‡
Financial data (yr. ended 12/31/01): Grants paid, $258,800; assets, $4,055,197 (M); gifts received, $9,840; expenditures, $302,895; qualifying distributions, $249,817.
Limitations: Giving limited to the Brazos County, TX area.
Application information: Application form required.
Trustee: Wells Fargo Bank Texas, N.A.
EIN: 746402510
Codes: FD

51042
FSR Foundation
c/o Kanaly Trust Co.
4550 Post Oak Place Dr., Ste. 139
Houston, TX 77027

Established in 1989 in TX.
Donor(s): Fred S. Robertson III, Sara Kolin Robertson.
Financial data (yr. ended 12/31/01): Grants paid, $258,000; assets, $1,937,045 (M); expenditures, $285,863; qualifying distributions, $256,909.
Limitations: Giving primarily in TX.
Trustees: Fred S. Robertson III, Sara Kolin Robertson, Kanaly Trust Co.
EIN: 766053774
Codes: FD

51043
The Fruehauf Foundation
c/o Sentinel Trust
2001 Kirby Dr., Ste. 1210
Houston, TX 77019
Application address: c/o Dian Stallings, 100 Maple Park Blvd., Ste. 106, St. Clair Shores, MI 48081

Incorporated in 1968 in MI.
Donor(s): Barbara F. Bristol, Angela Fruehauf, Harvey C. Fruehauf, Jr., Susanne M. Fruehauf.
Financial data (yr. ended 12/31/01): Grants paid, $257,275; assets, $5,221,992 (M); expenditures, $295,796; qualifying distributions, $273,862.
Officers and Directors:* Harvey C. Fruehauf, Jr.,* Pres. and Treas.; Barbara F. Bristol,* V.P.; Frederick R. Keydel,* Secy.; Martha S. Fruehauf, Harvey B. Wallace II.
EIN: 237015744
Codes: FD

51044
Notsew Orm Sands Foundation
4212 San Felipe St., Ste. I
Houston, TX 77027-2902
Contact: Belinda Worley, Admin.

Established around 1995.
Financial data (yr. ended 12/31/99): Grants paid, $256,541; assets, $2,887,075 (M); expenditures, $291,383; qualifying distributions, $288,109.
Limitations: Applications not accepted.
Application information: Contributes only to pre-selected organizations.
Officers: Charles Burnett III, Pres. and Treas.; Miriam W. Burnett, V.P. and Secy.
EIN: 760455176
Codes: FD

51045
Martin Woodall Foundation, Inc.
4428 Park Ln.
Dallas, TX 75220

Established in 2000 in TX.
Donor(s): Martin Woodall.
Financial data (yr. ended 12/31/00): Grants paid, $255,500; assets, $954,816 (M); gifts received, $1,269,605; expenditures, $1,003,584; qualifying distributions, $265,247.
Limitations: Applications not accepted. Giving primarily in Dallas, TX.
Application information: Contributes only to pre-selected organizations.
Officers: Martin Woodall, Chair. and Secy.-Treas.; Chris A. Reasor, Pres. and Mgr.
Director: Russell Holloway.
EIN: 752857655
Codes: FD

51046
Guy I. Bromley Residuary Trust
c/o Bank of America
P.O. Box 831041
Dallas, TX 75283-1041
Application address: c/o David P. Ross, Bank of America, 1200 Main St., 14th Fl., Kansas City, MO 64141-7481, tel.: (816) 979-7481
Contact: David P. Ross, Sr. V.P., Bank of America

Established in 1964 in MO.
Donor(s): Guy I. Bromley.
Financial data (yr. ended 12/31/01): Grants paid, $254,747; assets, $6,984,073 (M); expenditures, $322,806; qualifying distributions, $268,866.
Limitations: Giving primarily in KS and MO.
Application information: Application form not required.
Trustee: Bank of America.
EIN: 436157236

Codes: FD

51047
Josephine Anderson Charitable Trust
c/o Amarillo National Bank
Plz. 1, P.O. Box 1
Amarillo, TX 79105 (806) 378-8342
Contact: James R. Garrison, V.P. and Trust Off.

Established in 1976.
Donor(s): Josephine Anderson.‡
Financial data (yr. ended 02/28/02): Grants paid, $254,500; assets, $7,517,131 (M); expenditures, $447,513; qualifying distributions, $280,918.
Limitations: Giving primarily in the TX Panhandle, with emphasis on Amarillo.
Officer and Trustees:* Imadell Carter,* Mgr.; Amarillo National Bank.
EIN: 751469596
Codes: FD

51048
Jordan Family Foundation
4301 Westside Dr., Ste. 100
Dallas, TX 75209-6546

Established in 1993.
Financial data (yr. ended 12/31/00): Grants paid, $253,700; assets, $877,757 (M); gifts received, $300,000; expenditures, $255,215; qualifying distributions, $254,596.
Limitations: Applications not accepted. Giving primarily in TX.
Application information: Contributes only to pre-selected organizations. Unsolicited requests for funds not accepted.
Officers and Trustees:* Edwin B. Jordan,* Pres.; Christopher G. Jordan,* V.P.; Edwin B. Jordan, Jr.,* V.P.; Louise C. Jordan,* V.P.; Anne Jordan Logan,* V.P.; Robert C. Sutton, C.F.O.
EIN: 752486085
Codes: FD

51049
Central Texas Foundation, Inc.
P.O. Box 1564
Brownwood, TX 76804 (915) 646-4443
Contact: Stuart S. Coleman, Pres.

Established in 1982 in TX.
Donor(s): James R. Beadel.‡
Financial data (yr. ended 12/31/01): Grants paid, $253,609; assets, $5,456,627 (M); expenditures, $276,433; qualifying distributions, $271,159.
Limitations: Giving limited to Brown County, TX, and immediate adjacent counties surrounding Brown County.
Publications: Application guidelines, financial statement.
Application information: Application form required.
Officers: Stuart Coleman, Pres.; Tom Munson, V.P.; Bob Beadel, Secy.-Treas.
Trustees: Don Jordan, Jr., Groner Pitts.
EIN: 751848800
Codes: FD

51050
Darrell and Susan Keith Foundation
c/o Darrell Keith
1705 W. 7th St.
Fort Worth, TX 76102

Established in 1998.
Donor(s): Darrell Keith, Susan Keith.
Financial data (yr. ended 12/31/00): Grants paid, $252,400; assets, $360,059 (M); expenditures, $256,392; qualifying distributions, $252,063.
Limitations: Applications not accepted. Giving primarily in TX.
Application information: Contributes only to pre-selected organizations.
Officers and Director:* Darrell Keith, Pres.; Susan Keith, V.P.; Courtney Keith,* Secy.
EIN: 752739505
Codes: FD

51051
I. D. & Marguerite Fairchild Foundation
P.O. Box 150143
Lufkin, TX 75915-0143 (936) 634-2771
Contact: C. James Haley, Jr., Pres.

Established in 1977 in TX.
Donor(s): Marguerite Fairchild.‡
Financial data (yr. ended 06/30/01): Grants paid, $252,000; assets, $4,198,343 (M); expenditures, $319,520; qualifying distributions, $277,520.
Limitations: Giving primarily in Angelina County, TX.
Application information: Application form not required.
Officers: C. James Haley, Jr., Pres.; Hilda Mitchell, V.P.; Mary Duncan, Secy.
EIN: 751572514
Codes: FD

51052
J. E. S. Edwards Foundation
4413 Cumberland Rd. N.
Fort Worth, TX 76116 (817) 737-6924
Contact: Jareen E. Schmidt, Pres.

Established in 1976 in TX.
Donor(s): Jareen E. Schmidt.
Financial data (yr. ended 07/31/01): Grants paid, $251,525; assets, $6,586,410 (M); expenditures, $298,548; qualifying distributions, $251,525.
Limitations: Giving primarily in Fort Worth, TX.
Application information: Grant requests outside of the Fort Worth, TX, area considered only if program is not available within Fort Worth. Application form not required.
Officers: Jareen E. Schmidt, Pres.; Stace Sewell, V.P.; Sheryl E. Bowen, Secy.-Treas.
EIN: 510173260
Codes: FD

51053
Lantana Education Charitable Foundation
c/o Richard C. Strauss
8401 N. Central Expwy., Ste. 350
Dallas, TX 75225 (214) 292-3410

Established in 2000 in TX.
Donor(s): Rayzor Ranch.
Financial data (yr. ended 12/31/01): Grants paid, $251,500; assets, $29,768 (M); gifts received, $281,731; expenditures, $253,413; qualifying distributions, $251,492.
Limitations: Giving primarily in TX.
Officers and Directors:* Richard C. Strauss,* Pres.; Mark R. Wagner,* V.P. and Secy.; John P. Wagner,* V.P.; Paul Farr,* Treas.
EIN: 752882214

51054
Formby Foundation
(Formerly The William and Katrine Formby Foundation)
3825 Lake Austin Blvd., No. 402
Austin, TX 78703

Established in 1992 in TX.
Donor(s): William Lee Formby, Katrine Sabine Formby.
Financial data (yr. ended 12/31/01): Grants paid, $251,100; assets, $415,142 (M); expenditures, $255,537; qualifying distributions, $251,910.
Limitations: Applications not accepted. Giving primarily in Austin, TX.

51054—TEXAS

Application information: Contributes only to pre-selected organizations.
Officers: William L. Formby, Pres. and V.P.; Katrine L. Formby, Secy.-Treas.
EIN: 742644571
Codes: FD

51055
The Miles Foundation, Inc.
1231 Greenway Dr., Ste. 1000
Irving, TX 75038-2595

Established in 1999 in TX.
Donor(s): Ellison Miles.
Financial data (yr. ended 12/31/00): Grants paid, $251,000; assets, $1,295,395 (M); gifts received, $1,500,000; expenditures, $251,870; qualifying distributions, $250,646.
Limitations: Applications not accepted.
Application information: Contributes only to pre-selected organizations.
Officers and Directors:* Ellison Miles, Chair.; Mike Russ,* Pres.; Jack Burdett,* V.P. and Treas.; Sherry Wilson,* Secy.; Oscar Cox, Richard Macomb.
EIN: 752739180
Codes: FD

51056
The Tapestry Foundation
1717 W. 6th St., Ste. 460
Austin, TX 78703-4778 (512) 314-0707
E-mail: mctmb@aol.com
Contact: Mary Carmel Borders, Pres.

Established in 1994 in MI.
Donor(s): Thomas P. Borders.
Financial data (yr. ended 12/31/01): Grants paid, $250,750; assets, $4,939,433 (M); expenditures, $301,845; qualifying distributions, $290,105.
Limitations: Applications not accepted. Giving primarily in the Louisville, KY, and Austin, TX, metropolitan areas; some giving also in MI, NH, and IN.
Application information: Contributes only to pre-selected organizations.
Officers: Mary Carmel Borders, Pres.; Joshua T. Borders, V.P.; Thomas P. Borders, Secy.-Treas.
Director: Samantha C. Borders.
EIN: 383196007
Codes: FD

51057
Texas Shiloh Foundation
18946 Redland Rd.
San Antonio, TX 78259

Established in 1998 in TX.
Donor(s): David Jones, Diana Jones.
Financial data (yr. ended 12/31/99): Grants paid, $250,032; assets, $402,456 (M); gifts received, $417,500; expenditures, $251,596; qualifying distributions, $250,032.
Limitations: Applications not accepted.
Application information: Contributes only to pre-selected organizations.
Officer and Director:* David Lynn Jones,* Pres. and Treas.
EIN: 742883718

51058
Carreker Family Foundation, Inc.
12201 Merit Dr.
Dallas, TX 75251-2258

Established in 2000 in TX.
Donor(s): John Denzil Carreker, Jr.
Financial data (yr. ended 12/31/01): Grants paid, $250,000; assets, $1,099,402 (M); expenditures, $280,058; qualifying distributions, $250,000.
Limitations: Applications not accepted.

Application information: Contributes only to pre-selected organizations.
Officers and Directors:* John Denzil Carreker, Jr.,* Pres.; Connie Brook Carreker,* Secy.-Treas.; Brenton Edward Carreker, Brook Lee Carreker, John D. Carreker, III.
EIN: 752910414

51059
Esping Family Foundation
2626 Cole Ave., Ste. 700
Dallas, TX 75204 (214) 849-9808
FAX: (214) 849-9823; *E-mail:* hesping@efoholdings.com
Contact: Heather Esping, Pres.

Established in 1997 in TX.
Donor(s): Perry E. Esping.‡
Financial data (yr. ended 12/31/01): Grants paid, $249,500; assets, $10,096,521 (M); expenditures, $363,657; qualifying distributions, $291,306.
Limitations: Giving primarily in TX.
Application information: Application form required.
Officers and Directors:* Heather H. Esping,* Pres. and Treas.; Jennifer A. Esping,* V.P. and Secy.; John E. Kirtland,* V.P. and Secy.; Darren Blanton, Kathryn R. Esping, William P. Esping.
EIN: 752702676
Codes: FD

51060
James L. & Kathryn Ketelsen Charitable Foundation
1100 Louisiana, Ste. 450
Houston, TX 77002-5222
Contact: James Ketelsen, Tr.

Established in 1998 in TX.
Donor(s): James L. Ketelsen.
Financial data (yr. ended 12/31/01): Grants paid, $249,323; assets, $820,827 (M); gifts received, $120,040; expenditures, $260,002; qualifying distributions, $250,955.
Limitations: Applications not accepted. Giving primarily in Houston, TX.
Application information: Unsolicited requests for funds not accepted.
Trustees: James L. Ketelsen, Kathryn Ketelsen.
EIN: 311601478
Codes: FD

51061
Educational Advancement Foundation
P.O. Box 1844
Austin, TX 78767-1844 (512) 469-3580
Application address: P.O. Box 924948, Houston, TX 77292-4948, tel.: (713) 621-1515
Contact: Earl C. Lairson, Tr.

Established in 1969 in TX.
Donor(s): Harry Lucas, Jr.
Financial data (yr. ended 12/31/01): Grants paid, $248,895; assets, $2,609,121 (M); gifts received, $810,576; expenditures, $782,191; qualifying distributions, $675,292.
Limitations: Giving primarily in TX.
Publications: Informational brochure, application guidelines.
Trustees: Hamilton Beazley, Earl C. Lairson, Alfred E. Leiser, M.D., Harry Lucas, Jr., James Moorhouse.
EIN: 237001761
Codes: FD

51062
Salute to Education, Inc.
c/o Ford Credit
P.O. Box 792230
San Antonio, TX 78279-2230
Application address: 110 Broadway, Ste. 220, San Antonio, TX 78205, tel.: (210) 225-3353

Donor(s): Richard S. Kane, Clarence Kahlig II, William P. Sims, Jr., Elizabeth Gillespie.
Financial data (yr. ended 12/31/00): Grants paid, $248,250; assets, $566,564 (M); gifts received, $412,400; expenditures, $285,824; qualifying distributions, $248,250.
Limitations: Giving primarily in TX.
Application information: Application form accompanied by faculty recommendation and copy of student's transcript. Application form required.
Officers: William P. Sims, Chair.; Clarence Kahlig II, Vice-Chair.; Steve Pollack, Treas.
Directors: Elizabeth Gillespie, Richard S. Kane, George Whitchurch.
EIN: 742661078
Codes: FD

51063
The Abe Zale Foundation
3102 Maple Ave., Ste. 225
Dallas, TX 75201 (214) 855-0628
Contact: Leonard R. Krasnow, Exec. Dir.

Established in 1995 in TX.
Financial data (yr. ended 12/31/01): Grants paid, $247,900; assets, $3,935,397 (M); expenditures, $578,546; qualifying distributions, $267,683.
Limitations: Applications not accepted. Giving primarily in TX.
Application information: Unsolicited requests for funds not accepted.
Officers: Donald Zale, Chair.; George Tobolowsky, Pres. and Treas.; Leonard R. Krasnow, Secy. and Exec. Dir.
EIN: 752580972
Codes: FD

51064
Angel Works Foundation, Inc.
14785 Preston Rd., Ste. 750
Dallas, TX 75254-6825

Established in 2000 in TX.
Donor(s): Nancy L. Albertini.
Financial data (yr. ended 12/31/01): Grants paid, $247,880; assets, $705 (M); gifts received, $254,135; expenditures, $253,925; qualifying distributions, $250,619.
Limitations: Applications not accepted. Giving primarily in Dallas, TX.
Application information: Contributes only to pre-selected organizations.
Officers and Directors:* Nancy L. Albertini,* Pres.; Steve J. Metzger,* V.P.; Michael D. Ginsberg,* Secy.-Treas.
EIN: 752865907
Codes: FD

51065
Early Foundation, Inc.
6319 Mimosa Ln.
Dallas, TX 75230
Contact: Jeannette B. Early, Pres.

Established in 1963 in TX.
Donor(s): Jeannette B. Early.
Financial data (yr. ended 05/31/01): Grants paid, $247,650; assets, $3,882,773 (M); expenditures, $286,168; qualifying distributions, $286,168.
Limitations: Giving primarily in Dallas, TX.
Application information: Application form required.

Officers: Jeannette B. Early, Pres.; Patti Rose Early Trippet, V.P. and Secy.-Treas.
Director: Edward A. Early.
EIN: 756011853
Codes: FD

51066
DeBusk Foundation
2089 N. Collins, Ste. 111
Richardson, TX 75080-2664 (972) 231-2313
FAX: (972) 231-5425; E-mail: mdebusk@swbell.com
Contact: Kari Washam, Secy.

Established in 1979.
Financial data (yr. ended 12/31/01): Grants paid, $247,269; assets, $5,127,264 (M); expenditures, $332,942; qualifying distributions, $246,570.
Limitations: Giving limited to TX.
Publications: Application guidelines.
Application information: Application form required.
Officers and Directors:* Patricia McNutt,* Pres.; Mike Tibbals,* V.P.; Kari Washam, Secy.; Keith Belcher,* Treas.; Diane Cooper, Manuel DeBusk, Sue Francis, Marty Webb.
EIN: 751671193
Codes: FD

51067
Spec's Charitable Foundation
(Formerly Carroll & Carolynn Jackson Charitable Foundation)
2410 Smith St.
Houston, TX 77006

Established in 1995 in TX.
Donor(s): Carolynn F. Jackson.
Financial data (yr. ended 12/31/00): Grants paid, $247,000; assets, $4,125,205 (M); expenditures, $436,341; qualifying distributions, $288,719; giving activities include $6,314 for programs.
Limitations: Applications not accepted. Giving primarily in TX.
Application information: Contributes only to pre-selected organizations.
Officers: Karen Lynn Rydman, Pres.; Robert J. Heisler, V.P.; John A. Rydman, V.P.; Lisa Rydman Elder, Secy.-Treas.
EIN: 760488033
Codes: FD

51068
MBC Foundation
9826 Marek Rd.
Houston, TX 77038 (713) 681-9213
Contact: Ralph S. Marek, Secy.

Established in 1968 in TX.
Donor(s): Members of the Marek family.
Financial data (yr. ended 12/31/99): Grants paid, $244,686; assets, $7,460,366 (M); gifts received, $2,210,986; expenditures, $3,269,574; qualifying distributions, $235,637.
Limitations: Applications not accepted. Giving primarily in Houston, TX.
Application information: Contributes only to pre-selected organizations.
Officers: John L. Marek, Pres.; William A. Marek, V.P. and Treas.; Ralph S. Marek, Secy.
Directors: Frances Marek, Martha Marek.
EIN: 746108373
Codes: FD2

51069
Jeffrey Keith Skilling Foundation
10 N. Briar Wood Ct.
Houston, TX 77019 (713) 853-6894
Contact: Jeffrey Keith Skilling, Tr.

Established in 1994 in TX.

Donor(s): Jeffrey Keith Skilling.
Financial data (yr. ended 12/31/00): Grants paid, $244,366; assets, $364,912 (M); expenditures, $251,829; qualifying distributions, $246,107.
Limitations: Giving primarily in Houston, TX.
Trustee: Jeffrey Keith Skilling.
EIN: 760560262
Codes: FD2

51070
Luttrell Trust
607 E. Abram St., Ste. 12B
Arlington, TX 76010

Established in 1959.
Donor(s): James Luttrell, George Ray Luttrell Trust, Will Ann Luttrell Trust.
Financial data (yr. ended 12/31/01): Grants paid, $244,125; assets, $5,994,438 (M); expenditures, $258,162; qualifying distributions, $245,719.
Limitations: Applications not accepted. Giving primarily in Dallas, Arlington, and Fort Worth, TX.
Application information: Contributes only to pre-selected organizations.
Trustee: James Luttrell.
EIN: 756036279
Codes: FD2

51071
Hackett Family Foundation
3372 Del Monte
Houston, TX 77019

Established in 1996 in TX.
Donor(s): James T. Hackett.
Financial data (yr. ended 12/31/00): Grants paid, $243,828; assets, $393,344 (M); gifts received, $114,216; expenditures, $251,126; qualifying distributions, $244,848.
Limitations: Applications not accepted. Giving on a national basis, with some emphasis on Houston, TX.
Application information: Contributes only to pre-selected organizations.
Officers and Directors:* James T. Hackett,* Pres.; Maureen O'Gara Hackett,* Secy.; Donald R. Sinclair.
EIN: 760522431
Codes: FD2

51072
Bessie I. Hofstetter Trust
P.O. Box 831041
Dallas, TX 75283-1041 (214) 508-2005
Contact: Bank of America, Trust Comm.

Trust established in 1934 in TX.
Donor(s): Bessie I. Hofstetter.
Financial data (yr. ended 06/30/01): Grants paid, $243,654; assets, $4,954,382 (M); expenditures, $281,949; qualifying distributions, $254,356.
Limitations: Giving primarily in Corsicana and Waxahachie, TX.
Trustee: Bank of America.
EIN: 756006485
Codes: FD2

51073
The PAL Foundation
103 Tomahawk Trail
San Antonio, TX 78232
Contact: Peter A. Leininger, Dir.

Established in 1993.
Financial data (yr. ended 12/31/01): Grants paid, $242,387; assets, $2,556,904 (M); expenditures, $257,203; qualifying distributions, $241,858.
Limitations: Applications not accepted. Giving primarily in TX.
Application information: Contributes only to pre-selected organizations.

Directors: Daniel E. Leininger, James R. Leininger, John H. Leininger, Peter A. Leininger.
EIN: 742692751
Codes: FD2

51074
Foundation for Southeast Texas, Inc.
700 North St.
Beaumont, TX 77701 (409) 833-5775
Application address: P.O. Box 3092, Beaumont, TX 77704; FAX: (409) 833-7885; E-mail: foundationset@IH2000.net
Contact: Carol Flahen, Exec. Dir.

Established in 1996 in TX.
Financial data (yr. ended 12/31/01): Grants paid, $242,383; assets, $5,577,650 (M); gifts received, $21,000; expenditures, $448,998.
Limitations: Giving limited to Hardin, Jefferson, and Orange counties, TX.
Publications: Annual report.
Application information: Application form required.
Officers: Dean Robinson, Pres.; Peg Towers, V.P.; Maurine Graj, Secy.; Shelton McClure, Treas.
Directors: Larry Beaulieu, Sandra Benski, Brown Claybar, David Cobble, Joe Domino, Jim Dunaway, and 18 additional diretors.
EIN: 760530567
Codes: CM, FD2

51075
Perrin Foundation
9338 Meadowbrook Dr.
Dallas, TX 75220

Established in 1993 in TX.
Donor(s): George M. Perrin.
Financial data (yr. ended 06/30/01): Grants paid, $241,238; assets, $2,457,457 (M); expenditures, $247,102; qualifying distributions, $244,694.
Limitations: Applications not accepted. Giving primarily in Dallas, TX.
Application information: Contributes only to pre-selected organizations.
Officers: George M. Perrin, Pres.; Dominique Perrin, V.P.
Trustee: Chuck Billings.
EIN: 752508292
Codes: FD2

51076
Michael and Rebecca Cemo Foundation
4015 Inverness Dr.
Houston, TX 77019

Established in 1997 in TX.
Donor(s): Michael J. Cemo, Rebecca A. Cemo.
Financial data (yr. ended 04/30/01): Grants paid, $240,735; assets, $9,498,305 (M); gifts received, $2,050,262; expenditures, $271,739; qualifying distributions, $244,526.
Limitations: Applications not accepted. Giving primarily in Houston, TX.
Application information: Contributes only to pre-selected organizations.
Officers and Directors:* Michael J. Cemo,* Pres. and Treas.; Rebecca A. Cemo,* V.P. and Secy.; Jason M. Cemo, Stephanie C. Cemo.
EIN: 760537009
Codes: FD2

51077
Hugh A. McAllister, Jr. Charitable Foundation
2500 City West Blvd., Ste. 1000
Houston, TX 77042

Established in 1997 in TX.
Donor(s): Hugh A. McAllister, Jr.

51077—TEXAS

Financial data (yr. ended 12/31/01): Grants paid, $240,500; assets, $5,029,206 (M); expenditures, $272,164; qualifying distributions, $237,610.
Limitations: Applications not accepted. Giving on a national basis, with emphasis on Washington, DC.
Application information: Contributes only to pre-selected organizations.
Officers: Hugh A. McAllister, Pres.; Angela McAllister, V.P. and Secy.; Dana Leigh McAllister, Treas.
EIN: 760556345
Codes: FD2

51078
Donald D. Hammill Foundation
8700 Shoal Creek Blvd.
Austin, TX 78757-6816   (512) 451-0784
E-mail: ddhfound@aol.com
Contact: Cindy Thigpen, Secy.-Treas.

Established in 1987 in TX.
Donor(s): Donald D. Hammill.
Financial data (yr. ended 12/31/01): Grants paid, $240,287; assets, $3,942,498 (M); expenditures, $310,774; qualifying distributions, $269,488.
Limitations: Giving primarily in the Austin and Travis County, TX, area; scholarships are given on a national basis.
Publications: Informational brochure.
Application information: Application guidelines available upon request. Application form required.
Officers: J. Lee Wiederholt, Pres.; Cindy Thigpen, Secy.-Treas.
Trustees: Donald D. Hammill, Stephen Larsen, Phyllis Newcomer, James Patton, Nils Pearson, Judith Voress.
EIN: 742499947
Codes: FD2, GTI

51079
The Florence Foundation
P.O. Box 830241
Dallas, TX 75283-0241   (214) 209-6486
Additional tel.: (214) 209-6414; FAX: (214) 209-1940
Contact: Gary Melle, Secy.

Established in 1956.
Donor(s): Fred F. Florence.‡
Financial data (yr. ended 11/30/01): Grants paid, $240,000; assets, $3,669,118 (M); expenditures, $272,507; qualifying distributions, $246,365.
Limitations: Giving primarily in Dallas, TX.
Publications: Application guidelines.
Application information: Application form required.
Officer and Members:* Cecile Florence Cook,* Chair.; David L. Florence, Helen Florence, Paul W. Harris, Sharon Florence McCandless, Gary E. Melle, Katherine Florence Parrish, Terry C. Pritchett, John T. Stuart, Denise G. Wickline.
Trustee: Bank of America.
EIN: 756008029
Codes: FD2

51080
Susman Family Foundation
1000 Louisiana St., Ste. 5100
Houston, TX 77002   (713) 653-7839

Established in 1998 in TX.
Donor(s): Stephen D. Susman.
Financial data (yr. ended 03/31/01): Grants paid, $238,921; assets, $3,836,282 (M); gifts received, $4,107,229; expenditures, $258,703; qualifying distributions, $239,838.
Limitations: Giving primarily in NY and TX.
Officers: Stephen D. Susman, Chair.; Ellen Susman, Pres. and Treas.; Brenda Tolar, Secy.

Directors: Stacy M. Kuhn, Harry P. Susman.
EIN: 760569093
Codes: FD2

51081
The Alkek and Williams Foundation
1221 McKinney, Ste. 4545
Houston, TX 77010-2011   (713) 658-8989
Contact: Charles A. Williams, Tr.

Established in 1996 in TX.
Donor(s): Margaret Alkek.
Financial data (yr. ended 12/31/99): Grants paid, $238,500; assets, $5,677,293 (M); gifts received, $1,189,219; expenditures, $263,870; qualifying distributions, $213,630.
Limitations: Giving primarily in TX.
Trustees: Margaret Alkek, Charles A. Williams, Margaret V. Williams, Randa D. Williams.
EIN: 766122587
Codes: FD2

51082
The ADR Foundation, Inc.
P.O. Box 118953
Carrollton, TX 75011-8953

Established in 1999 in TX.
Donor(s): Danny L. Dansby, Linda L. Dansby.
Financial data (yr. ended 12/31/01): Grants paid, $238,000; assets, $3,979,815 (M); expenditures, $248,597; qualifying distributions, $246,152.
Limitations: Applications not accepted. Giving primarily in TX.
Application information: Contributes only to pre-selected organizations.
Officers: Danny L. Dansby, Pres.; Linda L. Dansby, Secy.
Director: John Lawrence.
EIN: 752849058
Codes: FD2

51083
The Ralph and Genevieve B. Horween Foundation
Triad Bldg.
14887 Hwy. 105 W., Ste. 201
Montgomery, TX 77356

Established in 1993 in TX.
Financial data (yr. ended 12/31/01): Grants paid, $238,000; assets, $3,846,349 (M); expenditures, $242,484; qualifying distributions, $236,101.
Limitations: Applications not accepted. Giving primarily in TX and VA.
Application information: Contributes only to pre-selected organizations.
Officers: Frederick Stow, Pres.; Ralph Stow, V.P.; Stuart F. Chase, Secy.
EIN: 760401800
Codes: FD2

51084
The Schlegel Horizon Foundation
(Formerly Schlegal PeopleCare Heritage Horizon Foundation_)
4835 LBJ Fwy., Ste. 700
Dallas, TX 75244   (972) 404-0400
Contact: James R. Mitchell, Treas.

Established in 1994 in TX.
Donor(s): Myrna D. Schlegel, Robert J. Schlegel.
Financial data (yr. ended 09/30/01): Grants paid, $237,242; assets, $856,391 (M); gifts received, $10,000; expenditures, $243,309; qualifying distributions, $237,169.
Limitations: Giving primarily in TX.
Officers and Trustees:* Myrna D. Schlegel,* Pres.; James R. Mitchell,* V.P. and Treas.; Robert J. Schlegel,* Secy.; Robert K. Schlegel, Kimberly J. Schlegel.

EIN: 752567631
Codes: FD2

51085
The Paulos Foundation
6708 Ashbrook Dr.
Fort Worth, TX 76132

Established in 1990 in TX.
Donor(s): James J. Paulos.
Financial data (yr. ended 12/31/01): Grants paid, $236,525; assets, $5,348,497 (M); expenditures, $249,798; qualifying distributions, $232,586.
Limitations: Applications not accepted. Giving limited to Dallas, TX.
Application information: Contributes only to pre-selected organizations.
Officers: Flora P. Brewer, Chair. and Pres.; Angela D. Paulos, V.P. and Secy.
Directors: John J. Paulos, Sam G. Paulos.
EIN: 752353196
Codes: FD2

51086
Bosque Foundation
(Formerly Bosque Charitable Foundation)
5950 Cedar Springs Blvd., Ste. 210
Dallas, TX 75235-6803
Contact: Louis A. Beecherl, Jr., Tr.

Established in 1983 in TX.
Donor(s): Julia T. Beecherl, Louis A. Beecherl, Jr.
Financial data (yr. ended 12/31/01): Grants paid, $236,500; assets, $3,299,248 (M); expenditures, $239,488; qualifying distributions, $235,916.
Limitations: Giving primarily in TX.
Application information: Application form not required.
Trustees: John T. Beecherl, Julia T. Beecherl, Louis A. Beecherl, Jr., Louis A. Beecherl III, William C. Beecherl, Julianna Beecherl Davis, Mary Beecherl Dillard.
EIN: 756380232
Codes: FD2

51087
The Bill and Helen Crowder Foundation
P.O. Box 1421
La Porte, TX 77572
Contact: Helen S. Crowder, Pres.

Established in 1999 in TX.
Financial data (yr. ended 12/31/01): Grants paid, $236,000; assets, $4,440,615 (M); expenditures, $288,426; qualifying distributions, $284,788.
Limitations: Giving primarily in TX.
Officers: Helen S. Crowder, Pres.; James R. Keeney, Jr., Secy.
Directors: R.N. Domec, Marylyn Simms.
EIN: 760555573
Codes: FD2

51088
Woods Foundation
9000 Tesoro Dr., Ste. 122
San Antonio, TX 78217
Contact: Gary V. Woods, Pres.

Established in 2000 in TX.
Donor(s): Gary V. Woods.
Financial data (yr. ended 12/31/01): Grants paid, $235,100; assets, $384,273 (M); gifts received, $229,050; expenditures, $242,325; qualifying distributions, $235,100.
Officers: Gary V. Woods, Pres.; Glenda M. Woods, V.P.; Steven L. Cummings, Secy.
EIN: 742955600

51089
Nelson Puett Foundation
P.O. Box 9038
Austin, TX 78766 (512) 453-6611
Contact: Nelson Puett, Pres.

Established in 1955 in TX.
Donor(s): Nelson Puett, Nelson Puett Mortgage Co.
Financial data (yr. ended 02/28/01): Grants paid, $234,943; assets, $12,766,260 (M); gifts received, $938,125; expenditures, $275,096; qualifying distributions, $1,518,492; giving activities include $1,283,549 for loans.
Limitations: Giving primarily in TX.
Publications: Financial statement.
Application information: Information on scholarships available from individual high schools. Application form not required.
Officers: Nelson Puett, Pres.; Ruth B. Puett, V.P.; Janis Schultz, Secy.-Treas.
EIN: 746062365
Codes: FD2

51090
Worthing Scholarship Fund
c/o Bank of America
P.O. Box 831041
Dallas, TX 75283-1041
Scholarship application address: 119 East St., Houston, TX 77018-6545
Contact: Frank D. Wesley, Principal

Established in 1951 in TX.
Financial data (yr. ended 09/30/00): Grants paid, $234,750; assets, $5,903,194 (M); expenditures, $288,767; qualifying distributions, $267,498.
Limitations: Giving limited to Houston, TX.
Application information: Applications should include name, address, grades, family history and income.
Trustee: Bank of America.
EIN: 741160916
Codes: FD2

51091
GM Charitable Trust
1617 Galveston St.
Laredo, TX 78043
Contact: Guadalupe Martinez, Tr.

Established in 1996 in TX.
Donor(s): Guadalupe Martinez.
Financial data (yr. ended 12/31/01): Grants paid, $234,700; assets, $33,457 (M); gifts received, $20,000; expenditures, $234,939; qualifying distributions, $234,665.
Limitations: Giving primarily in TX.
Trustee: Guadalupe Martinez.
EIN: 526784976
Codes: FD2

51092
The Tolleson Family Foundation
5500 Preston Rd., Ste. 250
Dallas, TX 75205-1241

Established in 1994.
Financial data (yr. ended 12/31/01): Grants paid, $234,428; assets, $1,476,541 (M); expenditures, $241,213; qualifying distributions, $233,531.
Limitations: Applications not accepted. Giving primarily in TX.
Application information: Contributes only to pre-selected organizations.
Officers: Debra J. Tolleson, Pres.; John C. Tolleson, V.P.; Eric W. Bennett, Secy.-Treas.
EIN: 752567318
Codes: FD2

51093
George A. Robinson IV Foundation
5005 Riverway, Ste. 200
Houston, TX 77056
Contact: Robert S. Pulitzer, V.P.

Established in 1993.
Financial data (yr. ended 12/31/01): Grants paid, $234,000; assets, $4,102,022 (M); expenditures, $263,234; qualifying distributions, $228,892.
Limitations: Giving primarily in Houston, TX.
Application information: Application form not required.
Officers: George A. Robinson IV, Pres.; Robert S. Pulitzer, V.P. and Treas.; Henry J.N. Taub II, Secy.
EIN: 760399825
Codes: FD2

51094
The Greater El Paso Chamber of Commerce Foundation, Inc.
10 Civic Ctr. Plz.
El Paso, TX 79901 (915) 534-0500
Contact: Wes Jury, Pres.

Financial data (yr. ended 12/31/00): Grants paid, $232,805; assets, $7,679,746 (M); gifts received, $239,544; expenditures, $1,183,550; qualifying distributions, $465,611.
Limitations: Giving limited to the El Paso, TX, area.
Application information: Application form not required.
Officers and Directors:* Robert Brown, Co-Chair.; Al Martinez-Fonts,* Co-Chair.; Wes Jury, Pres.; Hugo Bustamante, Nathan Christian, Edward Egbert, M.D., Hugh Frederick, Dave Graham, Jim Haines, Don Henderson, Woody Hunt, Lisa Huzella, Jim Phillips, Gerald Rubin, Humberto Sambrano, J.O. Stewart.
EIN: 742236918
Codes: FD2

51095
The Gladys B. Foundation
2951 Marina Bay Dr., No. 130-338
League City, TX 77573

Established in 1992 in TX.
Donor(s): Warren Burnett, Kay Taylor Burnett.
Financial data (yr. ended 06/30/01): Grants paid, $232,500; assets, $809,045 (M); expenditures, $234,468; qualifying distributions, $231,907.
Limitations: Applications not accepted. Giving primarily in TX.
Application information: Contributes only to pre-selected organizations.
Officers: Warren Burnett, Pres.; Kay Taylor Burnett, Secy.
Director: Richard C. Abalos.
EIN: 760370448
Codes: FD2

51096
Ed Cox Foundation
2200 Ross Ave., Ste. 3200
Dallas, TX 75201

Established in 1985 in TX.
Donor(s): Elizabeth Cox,‡ Edwin L. Cox, Sr.
Financial data (yr. ended 12/31/01): Grants paid, $230,835; assets, $1,096,860 (M); expenditures, $259,667; qualifying distributions, $259,809.
Limitations: Applications not accepted. Giving primarily in Washington, DC and TX.
Application information: Contributes only to pre-selected organizations.
Officer and Trustees:* J. Oliver McGonigle,* Mgr.; Berry R. Cox, Edwin L. Cox, Sr., Edwin L. Cox, Jr., Chandler C. Mashek.
EIN: 752042913
Codes: FD2

51097
The Bosch Foundation
811 Dallas Ave.
Houston, TX 77002

Established in 1998 in TX.
Donor(s): Douglas Bosch.
Financial data (yr. ended 12/31/99): Grants paid, $230,758; assets, $185,392 (M); expenditures, $242,280; qualifying distributions, $230,758.
Officers and Directors:* Douglas B. Bosch,* Pres.; Kim Combs,* Secy.; John B. Barry.
EIN: 760590372

51098
The Holthouse Foundation for Kids
c/o Michael Holthouse
1800 West Loop S., Ste. 1875
Houston, TX 77027

Established in 2000 in TX.
Donor(s): Colleen Holthouse, Michael H. Holthouse.
Financial data (yr. ended 12/31/00): Grants paid, $230,500; assets, $12,859,164 (M); gifts received, $12,901,163; expenditures, $236,844; qualifying distributions, $228,698.
Limitations: Applications not accepted. Giving primarily in Houston, TX.
Application information: Contributes only to pre-selected organizations.
Officers: Michael H. Holthouse, Pres.; Richard H. Stein, Secy.-Treas.
Member: Colleen Holthouse.
EIN: 760620426
Codes: FD2

51099
The Bone Hill Foundation
4000 S. Medford Dr.
Lufkin, TX 75901

Established in 1991 in TX.
Financial data (yr. ended 12/31/01): Grants paid, $230,000; assets, $3,421,181 (M); expenditures, $289,268; qualifying distributions, $230,000.
Limitations: Applications not accepted. Giving limited to the Lufkin, TX, area.
Application information: Contributes only to pre-selected organizations.
Officers: Rick L. Campbell, Chair.; Frank E. Parker, Vice-Chair.; Ted A. Lankford, Treas.
Trustees: Dewey Howard, Gary D. Kronrad, Lisa McAdams, Bob Reeves.
EIN: 756279006
Codes: FD2

51100
Higgs Foundation
18303 Longmoor
Houston, TX 77084

Established in 1996 in TX.
Donor(s): William G. Higgs, Ann M. Higgs.
Financial data (yr. ended 11/30/01): Grants paid, $230,000; assets, $4,234,526 (M); gifts received, $3,102,454; expenditures, $255,476; qualifying distributions, $230,000.
Limitations: Applications not accepted.
Application information: Contributes only to pre-selected organizations.
Trustees: Ann M. Higgs, Gregory N. Higgs, William G. Higgs.
EIN: 760519824
Codes: FD2

51101
May H. Ilgenfritz Testamentary Trust
c/o Bank of America
P.O. Box 831041
Dallas, TX 75283-1041
Application address: c/o Virginia Swearingen, 717 W. 6th St., Sedalia, MO 65302

Trust established in 1941 in MO.
Financial data (yr. ended 12/31/01): Grants paid, $228,380; assets, $4,421,564 (M); expenditures, $295,722; qualifying distributions, $256,728.
Limitations: Giving limited to residents and organizations of Sedalia, MO.
Trustees: Virginia Swearingen, Bank of America.
EIN: 440663403
Codes: FD2, GTI

51102
The Robert and Shirley Phillips Family Foundation
P.O. Box 4503
Houston, TX 77210 (832) 676-5367
Contact: Robert G. Phillips, Pres.

Established in 1999 in TX.
Donor(s): Robert G. Phillips, Shirley J. Phillips.
Financial data (yr. ended 03/31/02): Grants paid, $226,905; assets, $840,707 (M); expenditures, $227,914; qualifying distributions, $227,079.
Limitations: Giving primarily in TX.
Officers and Directors:* Robert G. Phillips,* Pres. and Treas.; Shirley J. Phillips,* V.P. and Secy.; Brittany Phillips.
EIN: 760604378
Codes: FD2

51103
Herman & Patsy Smith Charitable Foundation
1903 Central Dr., Ste. 403
Bedford, TX 76021-5813 (817) 540-4942
Contact: Patsy Smith, Dir.

Established in 1996 in TX.
Donor(s): Patsy R. Smith.
Financial data (yr. ended 12/31/01): Grants paid, $226,800; assets, $3,792,398 (M); gifts received, $200,000; expenditures, $240,004; qualifying distributions, $222,619.
Limitations: Giving primarily in Washington, DC and TX.
Officers and Directors:* Patsy R. Smith,* Pres. and Treas.; Madelyn B. Ivey,* V.P. and Secy.; Betty Rush.
EIN: 752610418
Codes: FD2

51104
The Convergence Institute
1012 Weston Ln.
Austin, TX 78733

Established in 1998 in TX.
Donor(s): Mary K. Martin, Thomas B. Martin, Jr.
Financial data (yr. ended 12/31/99): Grants paid, $225,667; assets, $10,020,587 (M); expenditures, $300,120; qualifying distributions, $225,667.
Limitations: Applications not accepted. Giving primarily in TX.
Application information: Contributes only to pre-selected organizations.
Officers: Thomas B. Martin, Jr., Pres.; Mary K. Martin, Secy.
Trustees: Joseph Kivlin, Louise Kivlin, Helen Martin.
EIN: 742871700

51105
C. J. & Syble Fowlston Charitable Trust
P.O. Box 51259
Amarillo, TX 79124-1259 (806) 355-7640
Contact: Joyce Perkins, Tr.

Established in 1981.
Donor(s): Syble E. Fowlston,‡ C.J. Fowlston.‡
Financial data (yr. ended 12/31/00): Grants paid, $225,000; assets, $4,837,499 (M); expenditures, $365,028; qualifying distributions, $245,158.
Limitations: Giving limited to the 20 northernmost counties of the TX Panhandle.
Trustee: Joyce Perkins.
EIN: 756281596
Codes: FD2

51106
Tenneco Foundation
c/o Bank of America
P.O. Box 2518
Houston, TX 77252-2518
Contact: Pamela J. Bradley, V.P., Bank of America

Established in 1952.
Donor(s): Tenneco Inc., Tenneco Automotive Inc.
Financial data (yr. ended 12/31/00): Grants paid, $223,000; assets, $701,069 (M); expenditures, $250,891; qualifying distributions, $226,117.
Limitations: Giving primarily to residents of Houston, TX.
Application information: Unsolicited requests for funds not accepted or acknowledged.
Officers: Dana G. Mead, Chair. and C.E.O.; Belton K. Johnson, Chair.; M. Kathryn Eickhoff, Mgr.; Peter J. Flawn, Mgr.
EIN: 746037919
Codes: CS, FD2, CD, GTI

51107
Mary Kay Foundation
(Formerly Mary Kay Ash Charitable Foundation)
16251 Dallas Pkwy.
Dallas, TX 75248
Contact: Michael Lunceford, Tr.

Incorporated in 1969 in TX.
Donor(s): Mary Kay Ash.
Financial data (yr. ended 06/30/01): Grants paid, $222,625; assets, $3,184,750 (M); expenditures, $276,400; qualifying distributions, $222,625.
Limitations: Giving primarily in TX, with emphasis on Dallas.
Application information: Application form not required.
Trustees: Mary Kay Ash, Brad Glendening, Michael Lunceford.
EIN: 756081602
Codes: FD2

51108
Taylor S. Abernathy and Patti Harding Abernathy Charitable Trust
c/o Bank of America
P.O. Box 831041
Dallas, TX 75283-1041
Application address: P.O. Box 419119, Kansas City, MO 64141-6119, tel.: (816) 979-7481
Contact: David P. Ross, Sr. V.P., Bank of America

Established in 1988 in MO.
Financial data (yr. ended 12/31/01): Grants paid, $220,892; assets, $3,695,613 (M); expenditures, $267,126; qualifying distributions, $235,395.
Limitations: Giving primarily in the metropolitan Kansas City, MO, area.
Trustee: Bank of America.
EIN: 436343880
Codes: FD2

51109
Adler Foundation
910 Travis St., Ste. 1950
Houston, TX 77002-5809
E-mail: Louis@adlerventures.com
Contact: Louis K. Adler, Pres.

Established in 1982.
Financial data (yr. ended 06/30/01): Grants paid, $220,552; assets, $4,575,575 (M); expenditures, $225,105; qualifying distributions, $220,352.
Limitations: Applications not accepted. Giving primarily in Houston, TX.
Application information: Contributes only to pre-selected organizations.
Officers and Trustees:* Louis K. Adler,* Pres. and Treas.; Gail F. Adler,* V.P. and Secy.; Marc F. Adler, Robert M. Hopson.
EIN: 760001183
Codes: FD2

51110
The Tasajillo Charitable Trust
c/o O.S. Wyatt, Jr.
P.O. Box 56223
Houston, TX 77256

Established in 1997 in TX.
Financial data (yr. ended 12/31/01): Grants paid, $220,000; assets, $5,134,523 (M); expenditures, $230,461; qualifying distributions, $220,000.
Limitations: Applications not accepted. Giving primarily in TX.
Application information: Contributes only to pre-selected organizations.
Trustees: M. Truman Arnold, Bradford A. Wyatt, O.S. Wyatt, Jr.
EIN: 760537229
Codes: FD2

51111
The Truchard Foundation
3816 Hunterwood Pt.
Austin, TX 78746 (512) 327-8558

Established in 1997 in TX.
Donor(s): James J. Truchard, Lee I. Truchard.
Financial data (yr. ended 12/31/01): Grants paid, $220,000; assets, $4,351,268 (M); gifts received, $5,039; expenditures, $222,247; qualifying distributions, $219,685.
Limitations: Applications not accepted. Giving primarily in TX.
Application information: Contributes only to pre-selected organizations.
Officers and Directors:* James J. Truchard,* Pres.; Lee I. Truchard, V.P. and Treas.; Aimee C. Truchard, Anthony M. Truchard, John-Marcel E. Truchard, Michael James Truchard.
EIN: 742816894
Codes: FD2

51112
Still Water Foundation
3939 Bee Caves, Ste. C-100
Austin, TX 78746 (512) 328-1184
FAX: (512) 327-1940; *E-mail:* padminc@aol.com
Contact: Patti O'Meara, Managing Agent

Established in 1982 in NM.
Donor(s): Julia Matthews Wilkinson.
Financial data (yr. ended 12/31/01): Grants paid, $218,477; assets, $3,641,167 (M); expenditures, $310,313; qualifying distributions, $248,337.
Limitations: Applications not accepted. Giving primarily in TX.
Application information: The foundation has instituted a self-directed grantmaking policy, whereby only those organizations invited to submit proposals will be reviewed. Unsolicited requests for funds not accepted.

Directors: James Flieller, Duncan E. Osborne, Julia Matthews Wilkinson.
EIN: 850307646
Codes: FD2

51113
Harry and Anne Sager Foundation
c/o Kanaly Trust Co.
4550 Post Oak Pl. Dr., Ste. 139
Houston, TX 77027

Established in 1994 in TX.
Donor(s): Harry C. Sager, Anne Sager.
Financial data (yr. ended 09/30/01): Grants paid, $217,746; assets, $729,591 (M); expenditures, $218,900; qualifying distributions, $217,394.
Limitations: Giving primarily in TX and WY.
Directors: Andrew D. Kanaly, Anne Sager, Harry C. Sager, Elizabeth Sager Yates.
EIN: 760454743
Codes: FD2

51114
The LSG Charitable Foundation
c/o The Gottesman Co.
301 Congress Ave., No. 1390
Austin, TX 78701 (512) 320-5574

Established in 1998 in TX.
Donor(s): Sanford Lee Gottesman.
Financial data (yr. ended 12/31/01): Grants paid, $217,500; assets, $1,329,645 (M); gifts received, $220,000; expenditures, $219,003; qualifying distributions, $219,003.
Limitations: Applications not accepted. Giving primarily in Austin, TX.
Application information: Contributes only to pre-selected organizations.
Trustees: Lisa T. Gottesman, Sanford Lee Gottesman.
EIN: 742900154
Codes: FD2

51115
Rachael & Ben Vaughan Foundation
P.O. Box 2233
Austin, TX 78768-2233 (512) 477-4726
Application address: 515 Congress Ave., No. 2060, Austin TX, 78701; FAX: (512) 477-1437; E-mail: rbvf@swbell.net
Contact: William R. Ward, Jr.

Established in 1952 in TX.
Donor(s): Ben F. Vaughan, Jr.,‡ Rachael Vaughan.‡
Financial data (yr. ended 11/30/01): Grants paid, $216,650; assets, $4,834,548 (M); gifts received, $782,950; expenditures, $230,328; qualifying distributions, $222,430.
Limitations: Giving limited to southern and central TX.
Publications: Application guidelines, grants list.
Application information: Application form not required.
Officers and Trustees:* Ben F. Vaughan III,* Pres.; Ben F. Vaughan IV,* V.P.; Genevieve Vaughan,* V.P.; Daphne duPont Vaughan,* Secy.-Treas.
EIN: 746040479
Codes: FD2

51116
Sid Richardson Memorial Fund
309 Main St.
Fort Worth, TX 76102 (817) 336-0494
Contact: Jo Helen Rosacker, Admin.

Incorporated in 1965 in TX.
Donor(s): Sid W. Richardson.‡
Financial data (yr. ended 12/31/01): Grants paid, $216,550; assets, $5,845,138 (M); expenditures, $342,531; qualifying distributions, $297,572.
Limitations: Giving primarily in TX.

Publications: Newsletter.
Application information: Application form required.
Officers and Directors:* C.T. Floyd,* Pres.; Jo Helen Rosacker, Secy. and Admin.; Cynthia K. Alexander, Treas.; John Hogg, Robert E. Kolba.
EIN: 751220266
Codes: FD2, GTI

51117
The Anne Hendricks Bass Foundation
1801 Deepdale Dr.
Fort Worth, TX 76107-3517 (817) 735-1863
Contact: Anne H. Bass, Tr.

Established in 1997 in TX.
Donor(s): Anne H. Bass.
Financial data (yr. ended 12/31/01): Grants paid, $215,113; assets, $3,758,529 (M); expenditures, $216,743; qualifying distributions, $215,113.
Limitations: Giving primarily in NY.
Trustees: Anne H. Bass, Hyatt A. Bass, Samantha S. Bass.
EIN: 137117629
Codes: FD2

51118
Ann Berger Wolens Foundation
P.O. Box 2235
Corsicana, TX 75151-2235 (903) 874-2961
Contact: Dean Milkes, Tr.

Established in 1991.
Donor(s): Anne Berger Wolens.‡
Financial data (yr. ended 12/31/01): Grants paid, $212,945; assets, $3,789,239 (M); expenditures, $313,933; qualifying distributions, $212,945.
Limitations: Giving primarily in New York, NY, and TX.
Trustees: Matt Dawson, Dean Milkes.
EIN: 752328477

51119
Marti Foundation
1501-D N. Main St.
Cleburne, TX 76033-3869
Contact: Hoylene Harris, Mgr.

Established in 1988 in TX.
Donor(s): George W. Marti, Jo C. Marti.
Financial data (yr. ended 05/31/01): Grants paid, $212,565; assets, $583,348 (M); gifts received, $150,000; expenditures, $267,709; qualifying distributions, $217,974; giving activities include $5,000 for loans to individuals.
Limitations: Giving primarily in Johnson County, TX.
Application information: Application form required.
Officer: George W. Marti, Pres.
Director: Michelle Marti.
EIN: 752265837
Codes: FD2, GTI

51120
C. B. and Anita Branch Trust
103 Ranger Creek Rd.
Boerne, TX 78006

Established in 1995 in TX.
Donor(s): C.B. Branch,‡ Anita Branch.
Financial data (yr. ended 12/31/00): Grants paid, $212,500; assets, $5,819,707 (M); gifts received, $550,257; expenditures, $189,304; qualifying distributions, $217,372.
Limitations: Applications not accepted. Giving primarily in TX.
Application information: Contributes only to pre-selected organizations.
Trustees: Anita Branch, Kristi Branch, C. Stephen Fritsch.

EIN: 746431994
Codes: FD2

51121
Fain Foundation
807 8th St., Ste. 500
Wichita Falls, TX 76301-3381

Established in 1942 in TX.
Donor(s): Minnie Rhea Wood.
Financial data (yr. ended 12/31/01): Grants paid, $212,500; assets, $2,127,398 (M); expenditures, $218,105; qualifying distributions, $213,355.
Limitations: Applications not accepted. Giving primarily in Wichita Falls, TX.
Application information: Contributes only to pre-selected organizations.
Officers and Directors:* Minnie Rhea Wood,* Pres. and Treas.; Martha Fain,* V.P. and Secy.; Mac W. Cannedy, Jr., John M. Kelly, Ann K. Thompson.
EIN: 756016679
Codes: FD2

51122
Ken W. Davis Foundation
P.O. Box 3419
Fort Worth, TX 76113 (817) 332-4081
FAX: (817) 332-4095; E-mail: Tuck52@aol.com;
URL: http://fdncenter.org/grantmaker/davis
Contact: Alan Davis, V.P., Prog. Off.

Incorporated in 1954 in TX.
Donor(s): Members of the Ken W. Davis family.
Financial data (yr. ended 10/31/02): Grants paid, $212,000; assets, $4,598,296 (M); expenditures, $214,453; qualifying distributions, $212,000.
Limitations: Giving primarily in Fort Worth and Midland, TX.
Publications: Application guidelines, annual report.
Application information: National Network of Grantmakers Common Grant Application Form is accepted. Application form required.
Officers: Ken W. Davis, Jr., Pres.; John Taylor, V.P. and Secy.-Treas.; A.T. Davis, V.P., Prog. Off.; T.C. Davis, V.P.
Directors: Alana Marsh, Kay Davis Sellers.
EIN: 756012722
Codes: FD2

51123
Mosbacher Foundation, Inc.
c/o Mosbacher Properties
712 Main St., Ste. 2200
Houston, TX 77002-3290

Incorporated in 1948 in NY.
Donor(s): Emil Mosbacher, Gertrude Mosbacher, Emil Mosbacher, Jr.,‡ Barbara Mosbacher, Robert A. Mosbacher, Jr., A.W. Downing Mears, Jr., Diane Mosbacher, Kathryn Mosbacher, Lisa M. Mears, Robert A. Mosbacher.
Financial data (yr. ended 12/31/00): Grants paid, $211,629; assets, $1,361 (M); gifts received, $197,849; expenditures, $211,824; qualifying distributions, $211,824.
Limitations: Applications not accepted. Giving primarily in Houston, TX.
Application information: Contributes only to pre-selected organizations. Unsolicited requests for funds not considered.
Officers and Directors:* Robert A. Mosbacher, Jr.,* Pres. and Treas.; A.W. Downing Mears, Jr.,* V.P. and Secy.; W.R. Smith.
EIN: 136155392
Codes: FD2

51124
Sylvan T. Baer Foundation Trust
c/o Bank of America
P.O. Box 831041
Dallas, TX 75283-1041
Application address: c/o Fdn. of Jewish Federation of Greater Dallas, 7800 Northaven Rd., Ste. A, Dallas, TX 75230

Financial data (yr. ended 01/31/01): Grants paid, $210,592; assets, $4,419,225 (M); expenditures, $276,343; qualifying distributions, $213,897.
Limitations: Giving limited to Dallas, TX.
Application information: Applications handled through the Foundation of Jewish Federation of Greater Dallas.
Trustee: Bank of America.
EIN: 756044967
Codes: FD2

51125
Abe & Rae Weingarten Fund
700 Louisiana St., Ste. 3850
Houston, TX 77002
Contact: Stephen Lasher, Tr.

Established in 1964 in TX.
Financial data (yr. ended 06/30/01): Grants paid, $210,391; assets, $2,960,399 (M); expenditures, $216,368; qualifying distributions, $211,029.
Limitations: Applications not accepted. Giving primarily in Houston, TX.
Application information: Contributes only to pre-selected organizations.
Officer: Joan W. Schnitzer, Mgr.
Trustee: Stephen Lasher.
EIN: 746065115
Codes: FD2

51126
Pollock Foundation
2626 Howell St., Ste. 895
Dallas, TX 75204 (214) 871-7155
FAX: (214) 871-8158
Contact: Robert G. Pollock, Tr.

Established in 1955 in TX.
Donor(s): Lawrence S. Pollock, Sr.,‡ Lawrence S. Pollock, Jr.‡
Financial data (yr. ended 12/31/01): Grants paid, $207,997; assets, $15,655,750 (M); expenditures, $311,557; qualifying distributions, $210,247.
Limitations: Giving primarily in Dallas, TX.
Application information: Application form required.
Trustees: Lawrence S. Pollock III, Richard Pollock, Robert G. Pollock, Shirley Pollock.
EIN: 756011985
Codes: FD2

51127
The P Twenty-One Foundation
675 Bering Dr., Ste. 110
Houston, TX 77057 (713) 782-9897
Contact: Joseph W. Ryan, Pres.

Established in 2000 in TX.
Donor(s): Joseph W. Ryan, Yolanda V. Ryan.
Financial data (yr. ended 11/30/01): Grants paid, $207,000; assets, $4,251,263 (M); expenditures, $233,426; qualifying distributions, $217,704.
Limitations: Giving primarily in southern TX.
Officers and Directors:* Joseph W. Ryan,* Pres. and Treas.; Yolanda V. Ryan,* V.P. and Secy.; Minerva V. Campos.
EIN: 760628482
Codes: FD2

51128
Mary Smith Charitable Foundation
c/o Bank of America
P.O. Box 831041
Dallas, TX 75283-1041

Established in 1992 in TX.
Donor(s): Mary Ilo Smith.
Financial data (yr. ended 12/31/01): Grants paid, $206,050; assets, $3,157,036 (M); expenditures, $241,050; qualifying distributions, $210,747.
Limitations: Applications not accepted. Giving primarily in TX.
Application information: Contributes only to pre-selected organizations.
Trustee: Bank of America.
EIN: 742652604
Codes: FD2

51129
Friedel Family Foundation
5327 Valburn Cir.
Austin, TX 78731

Established in 1998 in AZ and TX.
Donor(s): Leonard L. Friedel, Phyllis J. Friedel.
Financial data (yr. ended 12/31/01): Grants paid, $205,485; assets, $3,220,548 (M); expenditures, $243,797; qualifying distributions, $206,973.
Limitations: Applications not accepted. Giving primarily in AZ and TX.
Application information: Contributes only to pre-selected organizations.
Directors: Leonard L. Friedel, Phyllis J. Friedel, Lynne F. Gellman, Randi F. Sherman.
EIN: 860938348
Codes: FD2

51130
Fay T. Barnes Scholarship Trust
c/o JPMorgan Chase Bank
P.O. Box 550
Austin, TX 78789-0001 (512) 479-2647
E-mail: sonia.Garza@chase.com
Contact: Sonia Garza, Trust Admin.

Established in 1982 in TX.
Financial data (yr. ended 12/31/01): Grants paid, $205,000; assets, $3,133,969 (M); expenditures, $245,666; qualifying distributions, $222,286.
Limitations: Giving limited to high school seniors in Williamson and Travis counties, TX.
Publications: Informational brochure (including application guidelines).
Application information: High school students in Williamson and Travis counties, TX, should contact high school counselors for application information. Application forms not available through Chase Bank of Texas, N.A. Application form required.
Trustee: JPMorgan Chase Bank.
EIN: 742256469
Codes: FD2, GTI

51131
The Edward & Brenda Martin Foundation
309 Harborside Cir.
Kemah, TX 77565

Donor(s): Edward E. Martin, Brenda A. Martin.
Financial data (yr. ended 12/31/00): Grants paid, $205,000; assets, $6,503 (M); expenditures, $205,121; qualifying distributions, $205,107.
Limitations: Applications not accepted.
Application information: Contributes only to pre-selected organizations.
Officers: Edward E. Martin, Jr., Pres.; Brenda A. Martin, Secy.; Andrew D. Kreston, Treas.
EIN: 760455300
Codes: FD2

51132
The Greentree Fund
5130 Green Tree
Houston, TX 77056

Established in 1968 in TX.
Donor(s): Nancy C. Allen.
Financial data (yr. ended 06/30/01): Grants paid, $204,772; assets, $4,880,310 (M); gifts received, $808,185; expenditures, $253,302; qualifying distributions, $206,415.
Limitations: Applications not accepted. Giving primarily in Houston, TX.
Application information: Contributes only to pre-selected organizations.
Trustees: Nancy C. Allen, Randolph F. Allen, Fayez Sarofim.
EIN: 237065240
Codes: FD2

51133
The Armand and Lynn Shapiro Family Foundation
c/o JPMorgan Chase Bank
P.O. Box 2558, Trust Dept.
Houston, TX 77252-2558

Established in 1998 in TX.
Donor(s): Armand S. Shapiro, Lynn P. Shapiro.
Financial data (yr. ended 12/31/01): Grants paid, $203,750; assets, $288,272 (M); gifts received, $105,364; expenditures, $205,811; qualifying distributions, $204,723.
Limitations: Applications not accepted. Giving primarily in TX.
Application information: Contributes only to pre-selected organizations.
Officers: Armand S. Shapiro, Pres.; Lynn P. Shapiro, V.P.
Director: Stefani Shapiro Golub.
EIN: 760563328
Codes: FD2

51134
William T. Vogt and Lorine E. Vogt Charitable Foundation
800 N. Shoreline Blvd., Ste. 2550 S.
Corpus Christi, TX 78401
Additional address: 558 W. Montgomery Ave., Havenford, PA 19041-1409, tel.: (610) 527-1650
Contact: Lorine E. Vogt, Tr.

Established in 1984 in PA.
Donor(s): Lorine E. Vogt, William T. Vogt.
Financial data (yr. ended 12/31/01): Grants paid, $203,750; assets, $2,671,264 (M); gifts received, $100,205; expenditures, $207,165; qualifying distributions, $203,250.
Limitations: Giving primarily in PA.
Publications: Financial statement.
Application information: Application form not required.
Trustees: Lorine E. Vogt, William T. Vogt.
EIN: 232339924
Codes: FD2

51135
Texas Home Health, Inc.
3120 Fannin St.
Beaumont, TX 77701-3902

Financial data (yr. ended 12/31/01): Grants paid, $203,000; assets, $9,255,328 (M); expenditures, $519,170; qualifying distributions, $203,000.
Limitations: Applications not accepted. Giving primarily in TX.
Application information: Contributes only to pre-selected organizations.
Officers: Charline Dauphin, Pres.; Stephen Abhsier, V.P. and Secy.; Robin Dauphin, Treas.
EIN: 237009052

Codes: FD2

51136
The Barnard Foundation
15 Greenway, Ste. 9D
Houston, TX 77046
Contact: Susan Young, V.P.

Established in 1997 in TX.
Donor(s): David P. Barnard.
Financial data (yr. ended 12/31/01): Grants paid, $202,548; assets, $1,214,291 (M); expenditures, $237,754; qualifying distributions, $212,860.
Limitations: Giving primarily in MI.
Officers: David P. Barnard, Pres.; David M. Barnard, V.P. and Treas.; Susan Young, V.P.; Patricia C. Barnard, Secy.
EIN: 760537476
Codes: FD2

51137
Tom C. & Mary B. Reitch Charitable Trust
c/o Bank of America
P.O. Box 831041
Dallas, TX 75283-1041
Application address: c/o Charitable Gift Planning, Texas Women's University, P.O. Box 425618, Denton, TX 76204-5618
Contact: Jane Erwin

Established in 2000 in TX.
Donor(s): Mary B. Reitch.‡
Financial data (yr. ended 12/31/01): Grants paid, $202,423; assets, $4,144,951 (M); expenditures, $247,255; qualifying distributions, $202,423.
Application information: Application form required.
Trustee: Bank of America.
EIN: 527033945

51138
The Douglass Foundation
330 Argyle Ave.
San Antonio, TX 78209 (210) 824-1149
Contact: Helen D. Douglass, V.P.

Established in 1984 in TX.
Donor(s): Donald J. Douglass.
Financial data (yr. ended 12/31/01): Grants paid, $202,100; assets, $3,669,552 (M); gifts received, $1,658; expenditures, $277,932; qualifying distributions, $213,006; giving activities include $336 for programs.
Limitations: Giving primarily in San Antonio, TX.
Application information: Application form not required.
Officers and Directors:* Donald J. Douglass,* Pres. and Treas.; Helen D. Douglass,* V.P.; Deborah K. Samuel, Secy.; Marylee D. Browning, Scott E. Douglass, Oran F. Logan, O.S. Simpson, Jr.
EIN: 742239830
Codes: FD2

51139
Slough Foundation Trust
P.O. Box 831041
Dallas, TX 75283-1041
Application address: P.O. Box 270, Midland, TX 79702, tel.: (915) 685-2073
Contact: John Peterson

Established in 1998 in TX.
Financial data (yr. ended 12/31/00): Grants paid, $201,367; assets, $4,388,725 (M); expenditures, $287,217; qualifying distributions, $208,267.
Limitations: Giving limited to residents of TX.
Application information: Application form required.
Trustee: Bank of America.
EIN: 911997459
Codes: FD2

51140
Sarah & Ernest Butler Family Fund
c/o Ernest C. Butler
7601 Rustling Rd.
Austin, TX 78731

Established in 1997.
Donor(s): Ernest C. Butler, Sarah Butler, Linda E. Butler, Robert E. Butler.
Financial data (yr. ended 12/31/01): Grants paid, $201,300; assets, $18,634,010 (M); gifts received, $15,509,748; expenditures, $202,451; qualifying distributions, $201,300.
Limitations: Giving primarily in Austin, TX.
Trustees: Ernest C. Butler, Linda Butler, Robert Butler, Sarah Butler.
EIN: 742852289
Codes: FD2

51141
Robert E. Hansen Family Foundation
c/o Baird, Kurtz, & Dobson
1360 Post Oak Blvd., Ste. 1900
Houston, TX 77056

Established in 1988 in TX.
Donor(s): Margaret W.H. Hansen.
Financial data (yr. ended 08/31/01): Grants paid, $201,203; assets, $3,370,788 (M); expenditures, $228,750; qualifying distributions, $199,929.
Limitations: Applications not accepted. Giving on a national basis.
Application information: Contributes only to pre-selected organizations.
Officers: Margaret W.H. Hansen, Pres. and Treas.; Alexander E. Hansen, V.P.; Laurie H. Saxton, Secy.-Treas.
EIN: 760259279
Codes: FD2

51142
HSD Charitable Trust
c/o Helen B. Davis
5500 Preston Rd., Ste. 320
Dallas, TX 75205

Established in 1992 in TX.
Donor(s): Wirt Davis II, Helen Buchanan Davis, Hannah Davis Cutshall.
Financial data (yr. ended 12/31/01): Grants paid, $201,000; assets, $3,452,720 (M); expenditures, $241,080; qualifying distributions, $201,000.
Limitations: Applications not accepted. Giving primarily in Dallas, TX.
Application information: Contributes only to pre-selected organizations.
Trustees: Hannah Davis Cutshall, Helen Buchanan Davis, Wirt Davis II.
EIN: 756433837
Codes: FD2

51143
Dalkowitz Charitable Trust
c/o Bank of America
P.O. Box 121
San Antonio, TX 78291-0121 (210) 270-5371
Contact: Gregg E. Muenster, Sr. V.P., Bank of America

Established in 1993 in TX.
Donor(s): Nathalie Dalkowitz.
Financial data (yr. ended 07/31/01): Grants paid, $200,700; assets, $2,533,421 (M); expenditures, $241,322; qualifying distributions, $205,522.
Limitations: Giving limited to Bexar County, TX.
Publications: Annual report.
Application information: Application form required.
Trustee: Bank of America.
EIN: 746410360
Codes: FD2

51144
Killam Family Foundation
P.O. Box 499
Laredo, TX 78042 (956) 724-7141
Contact: Radcliffe Killam, Tr.

Established in 1998 in TX.
Donor(s): Radcliffe Killam, Sue Killam, Michael Dileo, Tracy Dileo, David Killam.
Financial data (yr. ended 12/31/01): Grants paid, $200,675; assets, $589,155 (M); gifts received, $47,581; expenditures, $215,916; qualifying distributions, $200,675.
Limitations: Giving primarily in TX, with emphasis on Laredo.
Application information: Application form not required.
Trustees: Radcliffe Killam, Sue Killam.
EIN: 746473230
Codes: FD2

51145
Tom and Melba Harken Foundation, Inc.
8050 Eastex Fwy.
Beaumont, TX 77708 (409) 898-8906
Contact: Tom Harken, Pres.

Established in 1991 in TX.
Donor(s): Thomas L. Harken, Melba Harken.
Financial data (yr. ended 12/31/01): Grants paid, $200,525; assets, $177,925 (M); gifts received, $199,951; expenditures, $200,587; qualifying distributions, $200,525.
Limitations: Giving primarily in TX.
Application information: Application form not required.
Officers: Thomas L. Harken, Pres.; Melba Harken, V.P.; Thomas L. Harken, Jr., Secy.; Mark Hamilton Harken, Treas.
EIN: 760356036
Codes: FD2

51146
Hal & Diane Brierley Foundation
8401 N. Central Expwy., Ste. 1000, LB 37
Dallas, TX 75225 (214) 760-8700
Contact: Hal Brierley, Dir.

Established in 1999 in TX.
Donor(s): Hal Brierley, Diane M. Walden Brierley.
Financial data (yr. ended 12/31/00): Grants paid, $200,000; assets, $1,326,463 (M); expenditures, $207,198; qualifying distributions, $199,836.
Limitations: Giving primarily in Dallas, TX.
Application information: Application form required.
Directors: Diane M. Walden Brierley, Harold M. Brierley, Charles Cheatham.
EIN: 756563187
Codes: FD2

51147
Hassie Hunt Foundation, Inc.
1601 Elm St., Ste. 3400
Dallas, TX 75201-7254 (214) 922-1000
Contact: Margaret Hunt Hill, Secy.-Treas. or Danny R. Bowlin, V.P.

Established in 1975 in TX.
Donor(s): Hassie Hunt Trust.
Financial data (yr. ended 12/31/00): Grants paid, $200,000; assets, $1,929,641 (M); gifts received, $125,000; expenditures, $200,217; qualifying distributions, $198,472.
Limitations: Giving primarily in Dallas, TX.
Officers and Directors:* Lamar Hunt,* Pres.; Danny R. Bowlin,* V.P.; Margaret Hunt Hill,* Secy.-Treas.
EIN: 510229948
Codes: FD2

51148
The Jacob and Terese Hershey Foundation
2121 San Felipe, Ste. 124
Houston, TX 77019 (713) 529-7611
FAX: (713) 529-7613; E-mail: hbar@wt.net
Contact: Judith Boyce, Exec. Dir.

Established in 1961 in TX.
Donor(s): J.W. Hershey,‡ Terese T. Hershey, Gerald Smith,‡ Dell Butcher,‡ Peter S. Meyer.
Financial data (yr. ended 12/31/01): Grants paid, $198,400; assets, $2,830,427 (M); gifts received, $5,030; expenditures, $326,121; qualifying distributions, $248,197.
Limitations: Giving primarily in Houston, TX.
Publications: Application guidelines.
Application information: Application form not required.
Officers and Directors:* Terese T. Hershey,* Pres.; Ann Hamilton,* V.P.; Amie Rodnick,* Secy.; Peter S. Meyer,* Treas.; Judith Boyce, Exec. Dir.; Jeffrey Hershey, Olive S. Hershey, Arthur L. Storey, Jr.
EIN: 746039126
Codes: FD2

51149
Kathryn Murfee Endowment
2200 Post Oak Blvd., Ste. 320
Houston, TX 77056-4706 (713) 622-5855
Contact: June R. Nabb, Tr.

Established in 1981 in TX.
Financial data (yr. ended 08/30/01): Grants paid, $198,000; assets, $3,822,339 (M); expenditures, $399,591; qualifying distributions, $197,468.
Limitations: Giving limited to TX, with emphasis on Houston.
Application information: Application form required.
Trustees: Dan R. Japnet, June R. Nabb, James V. Walzel.
EIN: 760007237
Codes: FD2

51150
Ernest A. Mantzel Foundation
c/o Frost National Bank
P.O. Box 179
Galveston, TX 77553-0179
Appliction address: c/o Frost National Bank, P.O. Box 8210, Galveston, TX 77553, tel.: (409) 770-5665

Donor(s): Ernest A. Mantzel.‡
Financial data (yr. ended 12/31/01): Grants paid, $197,850; assets, $5,254,906 (M); gifts received, $12,064; expenditures, $253,579; qualifying distributions, $198,388; giving activities include $59,000 for loans to individuals.
Limitations: Giving limited to Galveston, TX.
Application information: Application form required.
Trustee: Frost National Bank.
Directors: Katherine Kankel, Harris L. Kempner, Jr., F.A. Odom.
EIN: 746155151
Codes: FD2

51151
The FHC Foundation
301 Commerce St., Ste. 1500
Fort Worth, TX 76102
Application address: 2512 Thomas Pl., Fort Worth, TX 76107

Established in 1996 in TN and TX.
Donor(s): Bobby F. Sammons, Lynda R. Sammons.
Financial data (yr. ended 12/31/01): Grants paid, $197,250; assets, $3,871,619 (M); expenditures, $203,816; qualifying distributions, $194,247.
Limitations: Giving primarily in UT.
Application information: Contact foundation for application guidelines.
Officers and Directors:* Bobby F. Sammons,* Pres. and Treas.; Lynda R. Sammons,* V.P. and Secy.; Elizabeth P. Sammons.
EIN: 621594775
Codes: FD2

51152
The Mary Cecile Chambers Scholarship Fund
(Formerly The Mary Cecile Chambers Charitable Trust)
c/o Moody National Bank
P.O. Box 1139
Galveston, TX 77553 (409) 765-5561
Contact: Larry Dundee, Sr. V.P. and Trust Off., Moody National Bank; Toby Sessions, V.P. and Trust Off.; or Renee Graham, Scholarship Coord.

Established in 1991 in TX as successor to Mary Cecile Chambers Scholarship Trust.
Donor(s): Mary Cecile Chambers Scholarship Trust.
Financial data (yr. ended 03/31/01): Grants paid, $197,000; assets, $5,453,311 (M); expenditures, $248,521; qualifying distributions, $229,347.
Limitations: Giving limited to TX residents.
Application information: 1st-year students are given priority over renewal grants. Application form required.
Trustee: Moody National Bank.
EIN: 766071425
Codes: FD2, GTI

51153
Brownsville Community Foundation, Inc.
275 Jose Marti Blvd., Ste. B
Brownsville, TX 78521

Established in 1997 in TX.
Financial data (yr. ended 12/31/00): Grants paid, $196,258; assets, $324,087 (L); gifts received, $589,747; expenditures, $424,828.
Limitations: Giving limited to Brownsville, TX.
Officers and Trustees:* Christine Burton, C.E.O; Mary Yturria, Pres.; Alice Wilson,* Secy.; Richard L. Burton,* Treas.; Antonio Garza, JPMorgan Chase Bank.
EIN: 742826613
Codes: CM

51154
Tassie & Constantine Nicandros Foundation
3040 Post Oak Blvd., Ste. 730
Houston, TX 77056

Established in 1996 in TX.
Financial data (yr. ended 12/31/00): Grants paid, $195,640; assets, $712,069 (M); expenditures, $206,260; qualifying distributions, $195,811.
Limitations: Applications not accepted. Giving primarily in Houston, TX.
Application information: Contributes only to pre-selected organizations.
Officer: Tassie Nicandros, Pres.
EIN: 760521683
Codes: FD2

51155
Allan C. King and Gloria G. King Foundation
800 Bering Dr., Ste. 305
Houston, TX 77057
Contact: Allan C. King, Pres.

Established in 1993.
Financial data (yr. ended 12/31/99): Grants paid, $195,555; assets, $2,415,214 (M); expenditures, $215,806; qualifying distributions, $195,915.
Limitations: Giving primarily in Houston, TX.
Application information: Application form not required.
Officers: Allan C. King, Pres.; Gloria G. King, V.P.
EIN: 760392430
Codes: FD2

51156
H. E. and Kate Dishman Charitable Foundation Trust
c/o Hibernia National Bank
P.O. Box 3928
Beaumont, TX 77704
FAX: (409) 880-1437
Contact: Jean Moncla, V.P. and Trust Off., Hibernia National Bank

Established in 1985 in TX.
Donor(s): H.E. Dishman,‡ Kate Dishman, The Dishman Foundation.
Financial data (yr. ended 12/31/01): Grants paid, $195,542; assets, $3,529,738 (M); expenditures, $235,209; qualifying distributions, $195,542.
Limitations: Giving primarily in Jefferson County, TX.
Publications: Application guidelines.
Application information: Application form required.
Trustee: Hibernia National Bank.
EIN: 766024806
Codes: FD2

51157
William & Sylvia Zale Foundation
c/o Joe Bock, CPA
P.O. Box 223566
Dallas, TX 75222-3566 (214) 987-4688

Established in 1951 in TX.
Donor(s): Eugene Zale, Sylvia Zale, Lew D. Zale.
Financial data (yr. ended 08/31/01): Grants paid, $195,250; assets, $3,642,212 (M); expenditures, $213,668; qualifying distributions, $211,866.
Limitations: Applications not accepted. Giving primarily in Dallas, TX.
Application information: Contributes only to pre-selected organizations.
Trustees: Eugene Zale, Lew D. Zale.
EIN: 756037591
Codes: FD2

51158
Lucy & Isadore B. Adelman Foundation
10440 N. Central Expwy., No. 1200
Dallas, TX 75231-2232
Contact: Murray P. Benenson

Established in 1981.
Donor(s): Lucy Adelman, Susan Adelman, Claudio Llanos.
Financial data (yr. ended 06/30/01): Grants paid, $194,960; assets, $1,927,498 (M); expenditures, $211,754; qualifying distributions, $194,960.
Limitations: Giving primarily in CA.
Officers: Susan Adelman, Pres. and Treas.; Shari Leinwand, V.P.; Claudio Llanos, Secy.
EIN: 751806018
Codes: FD2

51159
The Arch and Stella Rowan Foundation, Inc.
P.O. Box 8632
Fort Worth, TX 76124-0632 (817) 336-2679
FAX: (817) 336-2679
Contact: Alice B. Myatt, Secy.

Established in 1963 in TX.
Donor(s): Stella S. Rowan,‡ Arch H. Rowan.‡
Financial data (yr. ended 08/31/02): Grants paid, $194,930; assets, $3,237,225 (M); expenditures, $197,425; qualifying distributions, $194,930.
Limitations: Giving limited to TX.
Application information: Application form not required.

Officer: Alice B. Myatt, Secy.
EIN: 756030348
Codes: FD2

51160
Dee J. Kelly Foundation
201 Main St., Ste. 2500
Fort Worth, TX 76102 (817) 332-2500
Contact: Dee J. Kelly, Sr., Pres.

Established in 1990 in TX.
Donor(s): Dee J. Kelly, Sr.
Financial data (yr. ended 07/31/00): Grants paid, $193,500; assets, $451,231 (M); gifts received, $331,928; expenditures, $195,524; qualifying distributions, $193,428.
Limitations: Giving primarily in the Fort Worth, TX, area.
Officers: Dee J. Kelly, Sr., Pres.; Dee J. Kelly, Jr., V.P. and Secy.; Craig Kelly, V.P.
Director: Cynthia Barnes.
EIN: 752363975

51161
Simpson-Omohundro Foundation
(also known as Omohundro Educational Trust)
P.O. Box 2507
Beaumont, TX 77704

Established in 1988 in TX.
Donor(s): Helen Omohundro,‡ Ed Omohundro.‡
Financial data (yr. ended 12/31/01): Grants paid, $193,084; assets, $3,052,758 (M); expenditures, $233,801; qualifying distributions, $196,046.
Limitations: Applications not accepted. Giving limited to Flora, MS, and Beaumont, TX.
Application information: Contributes only to pre-selected organizations.
Trustees: Edward Connell, Paul Parker, Peter Boyd Wells III.
EIN: 760260102
Codes: FD2

51162
Henry & Tommy Lehmann Charitable Foundation
P.O. Box 223
Giddings, TX 78942 (979) 542-3636
Contact: Jake Jacobsen, Chair.

Established in 1997 in TX.
Financial data (yr. ended 09/30/01): Grants paid, $191,509; assets, $1,268,252 (M); expenditures, $196,076; qualifying distributions, $196,076.
Limitations: Giving limited to Lee County, TX.
Application information: Application form not required.
Officer: Jake Jacobsen, Chair.
Trustees: Elberta Emmons, Bob Tarrant, Douglas Thielemann, Rick Wahrmund.
EIN: 742805235
Codes: FD2

51163
The Quanex Foundation
c/o Quanex Corp.
1900 W. Loop S., Ste. 1500
Houston, TX 77027-3267

Incorporated in 1951 in IL.
Donor(s): Quanex Corp., LaSalle Steel Co.
Financial data (yr. ended 12/31/00): Grants paid, $191,509; assets, $6,903,170 (M); expenditures, $298,465; qualifying distributions, $191,509.
Limitations: Giving primarily in areas of company operations.
Application information: Application form not required.
Officers and Directors:* P.J. Giddens,* Pres.; T.M. Murphy, V.P.; V.E. Oechsle,* V.P.
EIN: 366065490

Codes: CS, FD2, CD

51164
Reuhl Family Foundation
5124 Tangle Ln.
Houston, TX 77056

Established in 1997 in TX.
Donor(s): Gerald G. Reuhl.
Financial data (yr. ended 12/31/01): Grants paid, $190,000; assets, $3,241,252 (M); expenditures, $223,588; qualifying distributions, $189,054.
Limitations: Applications not accepted. Giving primarily in TX.
Application information: Contributes only to pre-selected organizations.
Officers and Trustees:* Gerald G. Reuhl,* Pres. and Treas.; Ellen Ann Reuhl,* V.P. and Secy; Brooks McGee, Catherine Reuhl, Sarah Jane Reuhl.
EIN: 760559539
Codes: FD2

51165
The Damon Wells Foundation
2001 Kirby Dr., No. 806
Houston, TX 77019

Established in 1993 in TX.
Donor(s): Damon Wells, Jr.
Financial data (yr. ended 12/31/01): Grants paid, $189,400; assets, $3,682,923 (M); gifts received, $15,997; expenditures, $195,269; qualifying distributions, $189,990.
Limitations: Applications not accepted. Giving on a national basis.
Application information: Contributes only to pre-selected organizations.
Officers and Directors:* Damon Wells, Jr.,* Pres.; David M. Underwood,* V.P.; Anne M. Alexander,* Secy.; Carol Billups,* Treas.
EIN: 760419933
Codes: FD2

51166
The Robert & Jane Cizik Foundation
600 Travis St., Ste. 3628
Houston, TX 77002

Established in 1997 in TX.
Donor(s): Robert Cizik.
Financial data (yr. ended 12/31/01): Grants paid, $189,113; assets, $1,195,807 (M); expenditures, $216,259; qualifying distributions, $188,381.
Limitations: Applications not accepted. Giving primarily in Houston, TX.
Application information: Contributes only to pre-selected organizations.
Directors: Greg Cizik, Jane Morin Cizik, Paula J. Cizik, Peter Cizik, Robert Cizik, Robert M. Cizik, Myra Marsh.
EIN: 760528683
Codes: FD2

51167
Pardee Cancer Treatment Association of Greater Brazosport
490 This Way, Ste. 220
Lake Jackson, TX 77566-5142

Established in 1975.
Donor(s): Elsa Pardee Foundation.
Financial data (yr. ended 12/31/00): Grants paid, $187,990; assets, $240,392 (M); gifts received, $202,546; expenditures, $207,450; qualifying distributions, $207,370.
Limitations: Applications not accepted. Giving limited to residents of southern Brazoria County, TX.
Application information: Unsolicited requests for funds are not accepted; no telephone calls.

Officers and Directors:* Everett Stovall,* Chair.; Charles P. Quirk, Jr.,* Treas.; Bill Black, Joe R. Garrett, Michael Gemignani, Thomas Lunsford, Harold Nicoll.
EIN: 510169385
Codes: FD2, GTI

51168
The Dorset Foundation, Inc.
P.O. Box 1805
Sherman, TX 75091
Contact: Carolyn Fields, Pres.

Incorporated about 1957 in TX.
Donor(s): W.S. Dorset.‡
Financial data (yr. ended 12/31/00): Grants paid, $187,555; assets, $4,926,371 (M); expenditures, $206,631; qualifying distributions, $192,720.
Limitations: Giving primarily in Sherman, TX.
Officers: Carolyn Fields, Pres.; Bonner Sewell Ball, V.P.; Carolyn N. Sewell, Secy.
EIN: 756013384
Codes: FD2

51169
Shiloff Family Foundation
c/o Robert M. Shiloff
4171 N. Mesa St., Ste. B-100
El Paso, TX 79902

Established in 1994 in TX.
Financial data (yr. ended 12/31/01): Grants paid, $187,000; assets, $3,359,795 (M); expenditures, $218,851; qualifying distributions, $186,249.
Limitations: Applications not accepted. Giving primarily in the El Paso, TX area.
Application information: Contributes only to pre-selected organizations. Unsolicited requests for funds not accepted.
Officers and Directors:* Robert M. Shiloff,* Pres.; Robyn Shiloff Pragner, V.P.; Bryan Shiloff, V.P.; Stuart Shiloff, V.P.; Martin N. Colton, Secy.; Sara P. Shiloff.
EIN: 742691141
Codes: FD2

51170
ECG Foundation
c/o Bank of America, Trust Dept.
P.O. Box 908
Austin, TX 78781 (512) 397-2717
Contact: Amber Carden

Established in 1986 in TX.
Donor(s): Ellen Clayton Garwood.‡
Financial data (yr. ended 04/30/01): Grants paid, $185,742; assets, $3,557,200 (M); expenditures, $238,506; qualifying distributions, $194,818.
Limitations: Giving primarily in Austin, TX.
Application information: Funding limited to organizations which received grants in 1991. Application form required.
Officers: Howard Yancy, Pres.; William L. Garwood, Jr., V.P.; Mary Margaret Farabee, Secy.; Lew Little, Treas.
Trustee: Bank of America.
EIN: 742418070
Codes: FD2

51171
Robert Tucker Hayes Foundation, Inc.
(Formerly Earl Hayes Foundation, Inc.)
511 E. John Carpenter Fwy., Ste. 400
Irving, TX 75062 (972) 869-2860
Contact: Rick Blake, Pres.

Incorporated in 1949 in DE.
Donor(s): Frue Alline Hayes,‡ Robert T. Hayes.
Financial data (yr. ended 11/30/01): Grants paid, $185,700; assets, $0 (M); gifts received,

51171—TEXAS

$227,200; expenditures, $191,306; qualifying distributions, $191,026.
Limitations: Giving primarily in the Dallas, TX, area.
Application information: Application form not required.
Officers and Directors:* Rick Blake,* Pres.; Cynthia Blazejewski,* V.P.; Robert T. Hayes,* V.P.; Susie McQuade, Secy.; Douglas Dunlap,* Treas.
EIN: 756011537

51172
The South Coast Foundation
c/o JPMorgan Chase Bank
P.O. Box 550
Austin, TX 78789

Established in 1996.
Financial data (yr. ended 12/31/01): Grants paid, $185,700; assets, $1,766,570 (M); expenditures, $209,839; qualifying distributions, $187,907.
Limitations: Applications not accepted. Giving primarily in Austin, TX.
Application information: Contributes only to pre-selected organizations.
Officers: Walter A. Deroeck, Pres. and Treas.; Judith McAdams Deroeck, V.P. and Secy.
Directors: Kathryn Deroeck-Boykin, Melinda Deroeck, Walter B. Deroeck.
EIN: 742805139
Codes: FD2

51173
The Roach Foundation, Inc.
100 Throckmorton St., Ste. 480
Fort Worth, TX 76102

Established in 1999 in TX.
Donor(s): John V. Roach, Jean W. Roach.
Financial data (yr. ended 12/31/00): Grants paid, $184,798; assets, $3,388,238 (M); expenditures, $216,369; qualifying distributions, $170,475.
Limitations: Applications not accepted. Giving primarily in TX.
Application information: Contributes only to pre-selected organizations.
Officers: John V. Roach, Pres.; Jean W. Roach, V.P.; Amy Roach Callaway, Secy.; Lori Anne Roach, Treas.; Lou Ann Blaylock, Exec. Dir.
EIN: 752848244
Codes: FD2

51174
The Al Clark Family Foundation
c/o Nancy Palmieri
301 Commerce St., Ste. 1900
Fort Worth, TX 76102

Established in 1999 in TX.
Donor(s): Alvin W. Clark, Susan D. Clark.
Financial data (yr. ended 12/31/01): Grants paid, $184,400; assets, $395,278 (M); gifts received, $183,000; expenditures, $185,736; qualifying distributions, $184,317.
Limitations: Giving primarily in El Paso, TX.
Officers: Susan D. Clark, Pres.; Alvin W. Clark, V.P. and Secy.-Treas.; Delmar R. Clark, V.P.
EIN: 742920793
Codes: FD2

51175
Genevieve McDavitt Orsinger Foundation
24 Longsford
San Antonio, TX 78209   (210) 590-0535
Contact: Linda McDavitt, Exec. Dir.

Established in 1997 in TX.
Donor(s): Genevieve McDavitt.
Financial data (yr. ended 04/30/02): Grants paid, $183,766; assets, $4,524,255 (M); gifts received, $100,000; expenditures, $237,988; qualifying distributions, $194,868.
Limitations: Giving limited to Bexar County and central TX.
Publications: Informational brochure, application guidelines.
Application information: Application form required.
Directors: Linda McDavitt, Exec. Dir.; Howard Klein, Jr., Patricia Meyer, Genevieve McDavitt Orsinger.
EIN: 742832873
Codes: FD2

51176
The Gallagher Foundation
700 Louisiana St., 40th Fl.
Houston, TX 77002

Established in 2000 in TX.
Financial data (yr. ended 11/30/01): Grants paid, $183,575; assets, $2,907,907 (M); gifts received, $2,708,450; expenditures, $214,480; qualifying distributions, $183,575.
Officer and Directors:* Michael T. Gallagher,* Pres.; Paul Comstock, Joan D. Gallagher, Sean Gallagher, Pete Hidalgo, Shannon G. Smith, Byron Ubernosky.
EIN: 760662307

51177
Van Duyn Foundation
150 Gessner Rd., Unit 8D
Houston, TX 77024   (713) 228-1040
Contact: Theodore W. Van Duyn, Jr.

Established in 1997 in TX.
Financial data (yr. ended 12/31/01): Grants paid, $181,987; assets, $544,258 (M); expenditures, $182,784; qualifying distributions, $182,430.
Limitations: Giving primarily in NC.
Application information: Application form not required.
Trustees: Teresa Van Duyn, Theodore W. Van Duyn, Jr.
EIN: 766122231
Codes: FD2

51178
Millenium Opportunity Foundation
24420 Stuebner Airline Hwy.
Tomball, TX 77375-3120   (713) 355-6500
Contact: Robert Baldwin, Pres.

Established in 1999 in TX.
Donor(s): Robert Baldwin, Cathrine Baldwin.
Financial data (yr. ended 12/31/01): Grants paid, $181,647; assets, $1,322,648 (M); expenditures, $194,698; qualifying distributions, $181,110.
Limitations: Giving primarily in TX.
Officers and Trustees:* Robert H. Baldwin,* Pres.; Cathrine Baldwin,* Treas.; L. W. Scott.
EIN: 731567472
Codes: FD2

51179
The Stallings Foundation
3828 Beverly Dr.
Dallas, TX 75205

Established in 2000 in TX.
Donor(s): Robert Stallings, Mrs. Robert Stallings.
Financial data (yr. ended 12/31/01): Grants paid, $181,500; assets, $1,855,175 (M); gifts received, $50,000; expenditures, $239,917; qualifying distributions, $181,500.
Limitations: Applications not accepted.
Application information: Contributes only to pre-selected organizations.
Officers: Robert W. Stallings, Chair. and Pres.; Linda E. Stallings, V.P.; Keri Nutting, Secy.; Melissa Brutcher, Treas.
EIN: 752887491

51180
Alan and Ruby Riedel Foundation
803 Creekwood Way
Houston, TX 77024

Established in 1997 in TX.
Donor(s): Alan Riedel, Ruby Riedel.
Financial data (yr. ended 12/31/01): Grants paid, $181,211; assets, $286,603 (M); gifts received, $2,448; expenditures, $187,949; qualifying distributions, $181,211.
Limitations: Applications not accepted.
Application information: Contributes only to pre-selected organizations.
Officers: Alan Riedel, Pres. and Treas.; Ruby Riedel, V.P. and Secy.
Directors: Amy Riedel Bone, John Riedel, Ralph Riedel.
EIN: 311520973
Codes: TN

51181
Journey Charitable Foundation
9129 Briar Forest Dr.
Houston, TX 77024-7213

Established in 1998 in TX.
Donor(s): Francine M. Fleming.
Financial data (yr. ended 10/31/01): Grants paid, $180,400; assets, $3,151,644 (M); gifts received, $969,596; expenditures, $214,437; qualifying distributions, $183,405.
Limitations: Applications not accepted. Giving primarily in TX.
Application information: Contributes only to pre-selected organizations.
Trustees: Francine M. Fleming, Weldon Mikulik, Janice Oettmeier.
EIN: 760574341
Codes: FD2

51182
The Nathan J. Klein Fund
2211 Norfolk, Ste. 1050
Houston, TX 77098   (713) 533-4400
Contact: Edward J. Klein, Tr.

Established in 1953 in TX.
Donor(s): Nathan J. Klein, Almeda Harold Corp.
Financial data (yr. ended 12/31/01): Grants paid, $180,275; assets, $6,850,971 (M); expenditures, $278,675; qualifying distributions, $180,275.
Limitations: Giving primarily in Houston, TX.
Trustees: Edward J. Klein, Ernest Klein, Martha K. Lottman, Shirley K. Markey.
EIN: 746060543
Codes: FD2

51183
John & Mildred Holmes Family Foundation
c/o Legacy Trust Co.
P.O. Box 1471
Houston, TX 77251-1471   (713) 651-8800
Contact: Joe Untermeyer, Secy.-Treas.

Established in 1999 in TX.
Donor(s): Mildred McDannald Holmes.
Financial data (yr. ended 12/31/01): Grants paid, $180,000; assets, $3,506,883 (M); expenditures, $188,866; qualifying distributions, $179,191.
Limitations: Giving primarily in Austin, TX.
Application information: Application form required.
Officers: Mildred McDannald Holmes, Pres.; Lucy H. Johnson, V.P.; Joe Untermeyer, Secy.-Treas.

Directors: Betty Holmes, Mildred Marshall Holmes.
EIN: 311645204
Codes: FD2

51184
The Pemmy Smith Foundation
c/o Bank of America
P.O. Box 831041
Dallas, TX 75283-1041

Established in 1994 in TX.
Financial data (yr. ended 03/31/01): Grants paid, $180,000; assets, $3,141,659 (M); expenditures, $222,948; qualifying distributions, $189,438.
Limitations: Applications not accepted. Giving limited to the Galveston-Houston, TX, area.
Application information: Contributes only to pre-selected organizations.
Trustee: Bank of America.
EIN: 746096537
Codes: FD2

51185
The Community Foundation of Brazoria County, Texas
P.O. Box 2392
Angleton, TX 77516-2392 (979) 848-2628
FAX: (979) 848-0032; E-mail: cfbrzco@brazosport.edu; URL: http://www.cfbr.org
Contact: Vicki Kirby, Pres.

Established in 1994 in TX.
Financial data (yr. ended 06/30/01): Grants paid, $177,777; assets, $703,336 (L); gifts received, $255,329; expenditures, $220,728.
Limitations: Applications not accepted. Giving primarily in Brazoria County, TX.
Publications: Informational brochure, newsletter.
Application information: Unsolicited requests for funds not accepted.
Officers: Ron Jones, Chair.; Vicki Kirby, Pres. and Exec. Dir.; Jim Jarvie, V.P. Devel.; Juan Longoria, V.P. Finance; Suzanne Stofor, Secy.; Ken Smith, Treas.
EIN: 760427068
Codes: CM, FD2, GTI

51186
The de Compiegne-Wallace Foundation
P.O. Box 10808
Midland, TX 79702 (915) 682-5371
FAX: (915) 682-0512
Contact: Henri de Compiegne, Jr., Tr.

Established in 1994.
Financial data (yr. ended 12/31/01): Grants paid, $177,625; assets, $2,870,780 (M); expenditures, $182,109; qualifying distributions, $176,539.
Limitations: Applications not accepted. Giving primarily in NM and TX.
Application information: Contributes only to pre-selected organizations.
Trustees: Elise Wallace de Compiegne, Henri Joseph de Compiegne, Henri de Compiegne, Jr., Mary Wallace de Compiegne, Anne de Compiegne Lutz.
EIN: 752533153
Codes: FD2

51187
Tompkins Family Charitable Foundation, Inc.
711 Louisiana St., Ste. 2300
Houston, TX 77002
Contact: Jack I. Tompkins, Dir.

Established in 1997 in TX.
Donor(s): Jack I. Tompkins.
Financial data (yr. ended 12/31/01): Grants paid, $177,572; assets, $247,104 (M); gifts received, $150,000; expenditures, $178,547; qualifying distributions, $176,994.
Limitations: Giving primarily in TX.
Directors: Dorothy G. Tompkins, Jack I. Tompkins, Michael G. Tompkins.
EIN: 760522351
Codes: FD2

51188
The Christian Charitable Trust
P.O. Box 691328
Houston, TX 77269-1328

Established in 1992 in TX.
Donor(s): Richard L. Davis, Teresa Davis.
Financial data (yr. ended 12/31/99): Grants paid, $177,238; assets, $68,010 (M); expenditures, $184,264; qualifying distributions, $179,496.
Limitations: Applications not accepted. Giving in the U.S., with some emphasis on TX; giving also in Canada.
Application information: Contributes only to pre-selected organizations.
Officers: Janine Koch, Treas.; David T. White, Trust Admin.
Trustee: Richard L. Davis.
EIN: 760384972
Codes: FD2, GTI

51189
Gayle and Paul Stoffel Foundation
5949 Sherry Ln., Ste. 1465
Dallas, TX 75225

Established in 1997 in TX.
Donor(s): Paul Stoffel, Gayle Stoffel.
Financial data (yr. ended 12/31/00): Grants paid, $176,652; assets, $351,187 (M); gifts received, $2,582; expenditures, $178,376; qualifying distributions, $177,378.
Limitations: Applications not accepted. Giving primarily in Dallas, TX.
Application information: Contributes only to pre-selected organizations.
Officers: Paul Stoffel, Pres.; Gayle Stoffel, V.P.
EIN: 311542757
Codes: FD2

51190
The Glazer Foundation
14860 Landmark Blvd.
Dallas, TX 75240
Contact: Robert S. Glazer, Tr.

Established in 1958 in TX.
Donor(s): Robert S. Glazer.
Financial data (yr. ended 09/30/01): Grants paid, $176,600; assets, $2,314,059 (M); expenditures, $213,230; qualifying distributions, $176,118.
Limitations: Giving primarily in Dallas, TX.
Application information: Application form required.
Trustee: Robert S. Glazer.
EIN: 756012545
Codes: FD2

51191
Harris K. & Lois G. Oppenheimer Foundation
200 Patterson Ave., Apt. 612
San Antonio, TX 78209-6267
Contact: Lois G. Oppenheimer, Pres.

Established in 1984 in TX.
Financial data (yr. ended 06/30/01): Grants paid, $175,850; assets, $3,439,869 (M); expenditures, $199,775; qualifying distributions, $175,641.
Limitations: Applications not accepted. Giving primarily in San Antonio, TX.
Application information: Unsolicited requests for funds not accepted. Recipients are trustee generated.
Officers: Lois G. Oppenheimer, Pres.; Pauline O. Weisberg, V.P.; Claire O. O'Malley, Secy.-Treas.
EIN: 742347610
Codes: FD2

51192
The Graham and Carolyn Holloway Family Foundation
3405 Fox Meadows Dr.
Colleyville, TX 76034
E-mail: valerieh31@attbi.com
Contact: Valerie Holloway, V.P.

Established in 1994 in TX.
Donor(s): E. Graham Holloway, Carolyn G. Holloway.
Financial data (yr. ended 12/31/00): Grants paid, $175,000; assets, $4,229,095 (M); expenditures, $219,092; qualifying distributions, $175,000.
Limitations: Giving primarily in San Francisco, CA and TX.
Application information: Application form not required.
Officers: E. Graham Holloway, Chair. and Treas.; G. Scott Holloway, Pres.; Valerie L. Holloway, V.P.; Carolyn G. Holloway, Secy.
EIN: 752569765
Codes: FD2

51193
The Kimble Foundation
2201 Civic Cir., No. 713
Amarillo, TX 79109

Established in 1989 in TX.
Donor(s): V Heart Ranch, Inc.
Financial data (yr. ended 12/31/01): Grants paid, $175,000; assets, $3,345,478 (M); gifts received, $608,671; expenditures, $177,443; qualifying distributions, $147,134.
Limitations: Applications not accepted. Giving primarily in Amarillo, TX.
Application information: Contributes only to pre-selected organizations.
Officers: Lou N. Kimble, Pres.; John Satterstrom, V.P.; D.R. McGuire, Secy.-Treas.
Directors: O.M. Calhoun, L.G. McKinney.
EIN: 237041926

51194
John & Nevils Wilson Foundation
P.O. Drawer 97511
Wichita Falls, TX 76307-7511
FAX: (940) 322-8324
Contact: Joseph N. Sherrill, Jr., V.P.

Established in 1968 in TX.
Donor(s): J.H. Wilson.‡
Financial data (yr. ended 11/30/01): Grants paid, $174,886; assets, $3,638,812 (M); expenditures, $198,345; qualifying distributions, $176,291.
Limitations: Giving primarily in Wichita County, TX.
Application information: Telephone calls not accepted. Application form not required.
Officers and Trustees:* Evelyn Wilson Egan,* Pres.; Virginia Wilson Ewing,* V.P.; Joseph N. Sherrill, Jr.,* V.P.; Earle W. Crawford, David A. Kimbell.
EIN: 756080151
Codes: FD2

51195
Alma Morelock Charitable Trust
c/o Bank of America
P.O. Box 831041
Dallas, TX 75283-1041
Application address: 1200 Main St., 14th Fl., Kansas City, MO 64105, tel.: (816) 979-7481
Contact: David P. Ross, Sr. V.P., Bank of America

Established in 1987 in MO.
Financial data (yr. ended 12/31/01): Grants paid, $174,350; assets, $953,269 (M); expenditures, $198,385; qualifying distributions, $187,192.
Limitations: Giving limited to Kansas City, MO, and Emory, VA.
Trustee: Bank of America.
EIN: 446008586
Codes: FD2

51196
Jerry and Nanette Finger Foundation
520 Post Oak Blvd., Ste. 750
Houston, TX 77027

Established in 1986 in TX.
Donor(s): Jerry E. Finger, Nanette B. Finger, and other members of the Finger family.
Financial data (yr. ended 11/30/00): Grants paid, $174,345; assets, $1,337,096 (M); gifts received, $186,250; expenditures, $174,837; qualifying distributions, $174,837.
Limitations: Applications not accepted. Giving primarily in Aspen, CO, and Houston, TX.
Application information: Contributes only to pre-selected organizations.
Officers: Jerry E. Finger, Pres.; Nanette B. Finger, V.P.; Walter G. Finger, Secy.-Treas.; Jonathan S. Finger, Mgr.
EIN: 760209018
Codes: FD2

51197
The Campbell Foundation
P.O. Box 297
Abilene, TX 79604-0297
Contact: T.C. Campbell, Chair.

Established in 1978 in TX.
Donor(s): T.C. Campbell, Clara G. Campbell.
Financial data (yr. ended 12/31/01): Grants paid, $174,000; assets, $3,894,883 (M); gifts received, $120,000; expenditures, $179,000; qualifying distributions, $178,007.
Limitations: Giving primarily in the Abilene, TX, area.
Application information: Application form not required.
Officer and Trustees:* T.C. Campbell,* Chair. and Mgr.; Clara G. Campbell, Sarah Campbell, Howard Wilkins.
EIN: 756256881
Codes: FD2

51198
The Charles & Melissa Davis Charitable Foundation
4545 Post Oak Pl., Ste. 302
Houston, TX 77027-3105
Contact: Melissa Davis, Tr.

Established in 1997 in TX.
Donor(s): Charles N. Davis, Jr., Melissa M. Davis.
Financial data (yr. ended 12/31/01): Grants paid, $172,700; assets, $3,646,078 (M); expenditures, $177,649; qualifying distributions, $172,700.
Limitations: Giving primarily in Houston, TX.
Trustees: Charles N. Davis, Jr., Melissa M. Davis.
EIN: 760538400
Codes: FD2

51199
Fleming Endowment
1330 Post Oak Blvd., Ste. 3030
Houston, TX 77056-3019

Established in 1997.
Donor(s): George M. Fleming.
Financial data (yr. ended 10/31/00): Grants paid, $172,000; assets, $3,292,381 (M); expenditures, $204,093; qualifying distributions, $172,000.
Limitations: Applications not accepted. Giving primarily in TX.
Application information: Contributes only to pre-selected organizations.
Trustees: George M. Fleming, Scott Fleming.
EIN: 760555849

51200
South Plains Foundation, Inc.
511 Ave. K
Lubbock, TX 79408 (806) 792-9915
FAX: (806) 795-7671
Contact: Robert P. Anderson, Dir.

Established in 1989 in TX.
Financial data (yr. ended 06/30/01): Grants paid, $171,618; assets, $4,651,009 (M); expenditures, $249,365; qualifying distributions, $201,641.
Limitations: Giving limited to the Lubbock, TX, area.
Application information: Application form required.
Officers: William Miller, Pres.; Max L. Ince, V.P.; James Moore, Secy.-Treas.
Directors: Robert P. Anderson, William Armstrong, Sandy Ogletree.
EIN: 752294100
Codes: FD2

51201
Simon and Louise Henderson Foundation
P.O. Box 1365
Lufkin, TX 75902-1365 (936) 634-3448
Contact: Simon W. Henderson III, Pres.

Established in 1958 in TX.
Donor(s): Louise Henderson.‡
Financial data (yr. ended 12/31/01): Grants paid, $171,581; assets, $3,283,633 (M); expenditures, $198,107; qualifying distributions, $184,159.
Limitations: Giving primarily in eastern TX.
Application information: Application form not required.
Officers: Simon W. Henderson III, Pres.; Joie E. Henderson, V.P.; Joie Honea Henderson, Secy.-Treas.
Director: M.F. Zeagler.
EIN: 756022769
Codes: FD2

51202
Wolff-Toomim Foundation
109 N. Post Oak
Houston, TX 77024

Established in 1990 in TX.
Donor(s): David Toomim, Shirley Toomim.
Financial data (yr. ended 12/31/01): Grants paid, $170,542; assets, $38,477 (M); gifts received, $150,000; expenditures, $171,836; qualifying distributions, $170,496.
Limitations: Applications not accepted. Giving primarily in the Harris County, TX, area.
Application information: Contributes only to pre-selected organizations.
Trustees: David R. Toomim, Shirley W. Toomim, Cyvia Wolff, Melvyn L. Wolff.
EIN: 760324661
Codes: FD2

51203
Kane Charitable Foundation
9001 Leopard St.
Corpus Christi, TX 78409-2599
(361) 241-5000
Contact: Sam Kane, Tr.

Established in 1980 in TX.
Donor(s): Sam Kane Beef Processors, Inc.
Financial data (yr. ended 10/31/01): Grants paid, $170,060; assets, $196,718 (M); expenditures, $175,129; qualifying distributions, $170,960.
Limitations: Giving primarily in NY and TX.
Application information: Application form required.
Trustees: Aranka Kane, Bernard Kane, Esther Kane, Harold Kane, Jerry Kane, Sam Kane.
EIN: 742154323
Codes: FD2

51204
Bodhi Foundation
P.O. Box 4517
Austin, TX 78765-4517

Established in 1998 in TX.
Donor(s): David Lunsford.
Financial data (yr. ended 06/30/01): Grants paid, $170,053; assets, $874,560 (M); expenditures, $244,755; qualifying distributions, $164,737.
Limitations: Applications not accepted. Giving on a national basis.
Application information: Contributes only to pre-selected organizations.
Manager: David Lunsford.
Directors: Stephanie Lane, Peter Lunsford.
EIN: 742890569
Codes: FD2

51205
Crossroads Foundation
(Formerly Twin Pines Foundation)
116 Nottingham Dr.
Victoria, TX 77904-1710 (361) 573-9678
Contact: Noble M. Malik, Chair.

Established in 1995 in TX.
Financial data (yr. ended 12/31/01): Grants paid, $170,000; assets, $3,511,553 (M); expenditures, $176,371; qualifying distributions, $170,000.
Limitations: Giving primarily in Victoria County, TX, or adjacent counties.
Officers: Noble M. Malik, Chair.; D.F. Martinak, V.P.; John W. Harris, Secy.
Board Members: David Drost, Betty Hedgclough, Dan Hiller, Don Krueger, Joseph M. Long, M.D., Rev. Donald R. Ruppert.
EIN: 741382486
Codes: FD2

51206
The Sam and Sonia Wilson Family Foundation
5305 Western Hills Dr.
Austin, TX 78731

Established in 1995 in TX.
Donor(s): Sam Wilson, Sonia Wilson.
Financial data (yr. ended 11/30/01): Grants paid, $169,245; assets, $1,075,676 (M); expenditures, $171,560; qualifying distributions, $170,728.
Limitations: Applications not accepted. Giving primarily in Austin, TX.
Application information: Contributes only to pre-selected organizations.
Officers: Sam Wilson, Pres.; Sonia Wilson, V.P.
EIN: 742768520
Codes: FD2

51207
The Joan & Marvin Kaplan Foundation
(Formerly The Joan and Marvin Kaplan Family Charitable Foundation)
c/o Marvin Kaplan
339 Hunter's Trail
Houston, TX 77024

Established in 1986 in TX.
Donor(s): Marvin Kaplan, Joan Kaplan.
Financial data (yr. ended 12/31/01): Grants paid, $168,700; assets, $3,454,509 (M); gifts received, $309,144; expenditures, $195,189; qualifying distributions, $170,300.
Limitations: Applications not accepted. Giving primarily in Houston, TX.
Application information: Contributes only to pre-selected organizations.
Officers and Directors:* Marvin Kaplan,* Pres. and Treas.; Joan Kaplan,* V.P. and Secy.
EIN: 760205105
Codes: FD2

51208
Elizabeth L. and Russell F. Hallberg Foundation
(also known as E. L. & R. F. Hallberg Foundation)
c/o Bank One, Texas, N.A.
P.O. Box 2050
Fort Worth, TX 76113-2050
Additional address: 2705 S. Cooper St., Ste. 300, Arlington, TX 76015
Contact: Virginia Winkler, Tr.

Established in 1986 in TX.
Financial data (yr. ended 09/30/01): Grants paid, $168,125; assets, $4,183,871 (M); expenditures, $206,274; qualifying distributions, $176,028.
Limitations: Giving primarily in TX.
Trustees: Virginia Winkler, Bank One, Texas, N.A.
EIN: 756356892
Codes: FD2

51209
The Tim and Karen Hixon Foundation
315 E. Commerce St., Ste. 300
San Antonio, TX 78205
Contact: George C. Hixon, Pres.

Established in 1994 in TX.
Donor(s): Karen J. Hixon, George C. Hixon.
Financial data (yr. ended 12/31/01): Grants paid, $167,767; assets, $3,475,234 (M); expenditures, $194,769; qualifying distributions, $167,063.
Limitations: Applications not accepted. Giving primarily in TX.
Publications: Financial statement.
Application information: Contributes only to pre-selected organizations.
Officers and Directors:* George C. Hixon,* Pres.; Karen J. Hixon,* V.P.; Kimberly Owens, Secy.-Treas.; Bryan S. Hixon, George S. Hixon, Jack J. Spector.
EIN: 742730275
Codes: FD2

51210
Texas House Foundation
2208 W. 34th St.
Houston, TX 77018

Financial data (yr. ended 12/31/01): Grants paid, $167,500; assets, $3,399,680 (M); expenditures, $252,254; qualifying distributions, $167,500.
Limitations: Applications not accepted. Giving limited to TX.
Application information: Contributes only to pre-selected organizations.
Directors: Wyatt Heard, Joe Knauth, B.W. Payne, Chris Seager.
EIN: 760502916

51211
Sollie & Lilla McCreless Foundation for Christian Evangelism, Christian Missions, and Christian Education
745 E. Mulberry, Ste. 250
San Antonio, TX 78212 (210) 736-3199
Contact: Jimmie L. Joffe, Secy.

Established in 1958 in TX.
Donor(s): Sollie E. McCreless,‡ Lilla M. McCreless.‡
Financial data (yr. ended 12/31/01): Grants paid, $167,250; assets, $3,414,384 (M); expenditures, $204,866; qualifying distributions, $184,249.
Limitations: Giving on a national basis.
Publications: Program policy statement.
Application information: Application form not required.
Officers and Directors:* Frances Jean Sunderland,* Pres.; Robert B. Sunderland,* V.P.; Jimmie L. Joffe, Secy.; Elaine B. Hutzler, Treas.; Douglas E. Jividen, David W. Sunderland.
EIN: 741485541
Codes: FD2

51212
Clifton Foundation
215 Mary Ave., Ste. 306
Waco, TX 76701-2253 (254) 741-6400
Contact: James R. Clifton, Pres.

Established in 1997 in TX.
Donor(s): James R. Clifton, William L. Clifton, Jr., Mary Lacy Clifton Chase.
Financial data (yr. ended 12/31/99): Grants paid, $166,424; assets, $4,690,554 (M); expenditures, $166,538; qualifying distributions, $166,538.
Limitations: Applications not accepted. Giving primarily in Waco, TX.
Application information: Unsolicited requests for funds not accepted.
Officers and Directors:* James R. Clifton,* Pres.; William L. Clifton, Jr.,* V.P. and Treas.; Mary Lacy Clifton Chase.
EIN: 742832766
Codes: FD2

51213
William J. & Shirley G. Morgan Foundation
302 Lodge Hollow Ct.
Houston, TX 77024 (713) 789-8866
Contact: William J. Morgan, Mgr.

Established in 1979.
Donor(s): Shirley G. Morgan, William J. Morgan.
Financial data (yr. ended 11/30/01): Grants paid, $166,250; assets, $1,363,646 (M); gifts received, $4,498; expenditures, $174,548; qualifying distributions, $167,768.
Limitations: Giving primarily in TX.
Application information: Application form not required.
Officers: Shirley G. Morgan, Mgr.; William J. Morgan, Mgr.
EIN: 742076642
Codes: FD2

51214
The Crail Foundation
4511 Balcones Dr.
Austin, TX 78731

Established in 1996 in TX.
Donor(s): Kimberley B. Granger.
Financial data (yr. ended 12/31/01): Grants paid, $166,000; assets, $3,510,591 (M); expenditures, $207,312; qualifying distributions, $175,472.
Limitations: Applications not accepted. Giving limited to Austin, TX.
Application information: Contributes only to pre-selected organizations.

Officers and Directors:* Kimberley B. Granger,* Pres.; Peter J. Granger,* V.P. and Treas.; Duncan E. Osborne,* Secy.
EIN: 742797515
Codes: FD2

51215
Robert and Ruth Glaze Foundation
8111 Preston Rd., Ste. 707
Dallas, TX 75225-6315 (214) 750-4460
Contact: Robert E. Glaze, Pres.

Established in 1986 in TX.
Donor(s): Robert E. Glaze, Ruth T. Glaze.
Financial data (yr. ended 12/31/01): Grants paid, $165,210; assets, $3,548,707 (M); expenditures, $220,855; qualifying distributions, $195,828.
Limitations: Giving primarily in Dallas, TX.
Application information: Application form required.
Officers and Directors:* Robert E. Glaze,* Pres. and Treas.; Ruth T. Glaze,* V.P. and Secy.; Thomas R. Hurtekant.
EIN: 752102493
Codes: FD2

51216
The Keith and Mattie Stevenson Foundation
c/o Kanaly Trust Co.
4550 Post Oak Place Dr., Ste. 139
Houston, TX 77027
Contact: David Doll

Established in 1992 in TX.
Donor(s): Keith T. Stevenson, Mattie Stevenson.
Financial data (yr. ended 12/31/01): Grants paid, $165,000; assets, $2,871,083 (M); expenditures, $191,667; qualifying distributions, $164,191.
Limitations: Giving primarily in TX.
Application information: Application form not required.
Trustees: Keith T. Stevenson, Mattie Stevenson, Kanaly Trust Co.
EIN: 760366599
Codes: FD2

51217
K. H. Jordan Foundation
4242 Lomo Alto, No. N110
Dallas, TX 75219
Contact: Kathryn H. Jordan, Tr.

Established in 1999 in TX.
Donor(s): Kathryn H. Jordan.
Financial data (yr. ended 12/31/01): Grants paid, $164,500; assets, $7,111,440 (M); gifts received, $942,513; expenditures, $176,893; qualifying distributions, $131,876.
Limitations: Giving primarily in TX.
Trustee: Kathryn H. Jordan.
EIN: 752851443
Codes: FD2

51218
KPW Foundation
c/o Karyn Buchanan
600 Congress Ave., Ste. 200
Austin, TX 78701

Established in 1993 in TX.
Donor(s): Jerald Winetroub.
Financial data (yr. ended 11/30/01): Grants paid, $164,065; assets, $3,476,269 (M); expenditures, $218,051; qualifying distributions, $177,673.
Limitations: Applications not accepted. Giving primarily in Austin, TX.
Application information: Contributes only to pre-selected organizations.
Officers: Robert W. Hughes, Pres.; Kyle L. Hughes, 1st V.P.; Craig Hughes, 2nd V.P.; M. Gail Hughes, Secy.; Karyn Buchanan, Treas.

51218—TEXAS

EIN: 742707482
Codes: FD2

51219
Jack & Katherine Pearce Educational Foundation
c/o U.S. Bank
P.O. Box 8210
Galveston, TX 77553-8210 (409) 770-5665
Contact: Janet L. Bertolino, Trust Off., U.S. Bank

Established about 1950.
Financial data (yr. ended 12/31/01): Grants paid, $164,000; assets, $1,705,498 (M); expenditures, $194,686; qualifying distributions, $184,742; giving activities include $113,000 for loans to individuals.
Limitations: Giving limited to residents of Galveston, TX.
Publications: Informational brochure (including application guidelines).
Application information: Applications accepted Jan. 1 through Mar. 31 each year. Application form required.
Directors: Edward J. Patterson, Rev. Ronald Pogue, Albert Shannon.
Trustee: U.S. Bank.
EIN: 746035546
Codes: FD2, GTI

51220
The M. L. Shanor Foundation
P.O. Box 2370
Wichita Falls, TX 76307 (940) 761-2401
Contact: Frank W. Jarratt, Pres.

Established in 1963 in TX.
Donor(s): Harry Campsey, J.D. Huffaker, N.T.P. Co.
Financial data (yr. ended 12/31/01): Grants paid, $163,700; assets, $4,048,660 (M); gifts received, $52,110; expenditures, $241,174; qualifying distributions, $172,061.
Limitations: Giving primarily in TX, with emphasis on Cherokee, Wichita and Wilbarger counties.
Application information: Application form required for student loans.
Officers and Directors:* Frank W. Jarratt,* Pres.; Barbara Jarratt,* Secy.-Treas.; Alan J. Freeman, M.R. Klappenbach.
EIN: 756012834
Codes: FD2, GTI

51221
Franklin Family Foundation
P.O. Box 269
San Antonio, TX 78291

Established in 1999 in TX.
Donor(s): Larry D. Franklin, Charlotte A. Franklin.
Financial data (yr. ended 12/31/01): Grants paid, $163,366; assets, $610,764 (M); gifts received, $630,315; expenditures, $163,537; qualifying distributions, $163,366.
Limitations: Applications not accepted.
Application information: Contributes only to pre-selected organizations.
Officers and Directors:* Larry D. Franklin,* Pres. and Treas.; Charlotte A. Franklin,* V.P. and Secy.; Kristi Franklin Borchardt, Kelly Leigh Hardwick.
EIN: 742921587

51222
Marguerite Sours Foundation
P.O. Box 1419
Rockport, TX 78381-1419
Application address: 1021 N. Hwy. 35, Rockport, TX 78382
Contact: William G. Walston Sr., Pres.

Established around 1986.
Financial data (yr. ended 12/31/00): Grants paid, $162,220; assets, $3,430,269 (M); expenditures, $201,800; qualifying distributions, $172,200.
Limitations: Giving primarily in KS and TX.
Officers: William G. Walston, Sr., Pres.; Dale Stuckey, V.P.; Jackie Bauer, Secy.
EIN: 742425445
Codes: FD2

51223
The Pineywoods Foundation
P.O. Box 1647
Lufkin, TX 75902-1647 (936) 634-7444
Application address: 515 S. 1st St., Lufkin, TX 75901; FAX: (409) 634-7750
Contact: Bob Bowman, Secy.

Established in 1984 in TX.
Donor(s): The Southland Foundation.
Financial data (yr. ended 12/31/01): Grants paid, $162,113; assets, $2,923,838 (M); expenditures, $190,773; qualifying distributions, $174,859.
Limitations: Giving limited to Angelina, Cherokee, Houston, Jasper, Nacogdoches, Panola, Polk, Sabine, San Augustine, San Jacinto, Shelby, Trinity, and Tyler counties, TX.
Publications: Informational brochure, application guidelines.
Application information: Application form required.
Officers and Trustees:* John F. Anderson,* Chair.; Bob Bowman,* Secy.; George Henderson,* Treas.
EIN: 751922533
Codes: FD2

51224
The York Children's Foundation
8554 Katy Fwy., No. 208
Houston, TX 77024 (713) 984-5500
Contact: David F. Beck, Secy.-Treas.

Incorporated in 1991.
Donor(s): The York Group, Inc.
Financial data (yr. ended 12/31/99): Grants paid, $162,000; assets, $111,075 (M); gifts received, $213,600; expenditures, $164,395; qualifying distributions, $164,396.
Application information: Application can be obtained from a funeral director selling York's products. Application form required.
Officers and Trustees:* Gerald D. Runnels,* Pres.; David F. Beck,* Secy.-Treas.; Ed English, Jill Glasband, Paul Horvath, Bernard Mimms, Sr., Dennis Munderloth, George Paynil, Jim Peacock, Gerald Robbins, Lee Scott, Susan Tasca, Gary Trick.
EIN: 760353019
Codes: FD2

51225
Mike A. Myers Foundation
6310 Lemmon Ave., Ste. 200
Dallas, TX 75209

Established in 1982 in TX.
Donor(s): Mike A. Myers.
Financial data (yr. ended 12/31/00): Grants paid, $161,635; assets, $2,664,587 (M); gifts received, $441,213; expenditures, $204,239; qualifying distributions, $160,417.
Limitations: Giving primarily in Dallas, TX.
Application information: Application form not required.
Officers and Trustees:* Mike A. Myers,* Chair. and Pres.; Kathy Carver, Secy.; Joe Pipes, Treas.; Curtis W. Meadows, Jr., Alan D. Myers, Larry Temple, Carol M. Wilcox.
EIN: 751832130
Codes: FD2

51226
Horse Creek Trust
2001 Ross Ave., Ste. 2700 LB 155
Dallas, TX 75201
Contact: Allan G. Paterson

Established in 1986 in TX.
Donor(s): Esther Berry.
Financial data (yr. ended 03/31/01): Grants paid, $160,600; assets, $3,038,105 (M); expenditures, $193,346; qualifying distributions, $162,034.
Limitations: Applications not accepted. Giving primarily in San Antonio, TX.
Application information: Contributes only to pre-selected organizations.
Trustee: Allan G. Paterson.
EIN: 746340243
Codes: FD2

51227
Kleh Family Foundation
10811 Greenwillow, No. 25
Houston, TX 77035
Contact: William H. Kleh, Dir.

Established in 1997 in CO.
Donor(s): William H. Kleh, Patricia M. Kleh.
Financial data (yr. ended 12/31/01): Grants paid, $160,254; assets, $3,130,111 (M); gifts received, $300,000; expenditures, $200,347; qualifying distributions, $168,846.
Limitations: Giving on a national basis.
Officers: William H. Kleh, Chair. and Pres.; Patricia M. Kleh, V.P. and Secy.; Terri G. Rogers, V.P. and Treas.
Directors: Jack Kleh, Jeffrey Steele.
EIN: 911757481
Codes: FD2

51228
Oshman Foundation
P.O. Box 230234
Houston, TX 77223-8234

Established in 1958.
Donor(s): Oshman's Sporting Goods, Inc., Jeanette Oshman Efron.
Financial data (yr. ended 11/30/00): Grants paid, $158,847; assets, $5,816,923 (M); expenditures, $164,839; qualifying distributions, $159,797.
Limitations: Applications not accepted. Giving primarily in Houston, TX.
Application information: Contributes only to pre-selected organizations.
Officers: Jeanette Oshman, Pres.; Judy O. Margolis,* V.P.; Marilyn Oshman,* V.P.
Directors: Marvin Aronowitz, Alvin N. Lubetkin.
EIN: 746039864
Codes: CS, FD2, CD

51229
Sally & Bernard Fuchs Charitable Foundation
121 N. Post Oak Ln., Apt. 2206
Houston, TX 77024

Established in 1985 in TX.
Donor(s): Bernard Fuchs, Sally Fuchs.
Financial data (yr. ended 12/31/01): Grants paid, $158,812; assets, $105,883 (M); expenditures, $160,722; qualifying distributions, $159,732.
Limitations: Applications not accepted. Giving primarily in TX.
Application information: Contributes only to pre-selected organizations.
Officers: Bernard Fuchs, Pres. and Treas.; Roslyn Beth Fuchs Haikin, V.P. and Secy.
EIN: 760155368
Codes: FD2

51230
Feinberg Foundation, Inc.
4855 N. Mesa, Ste. 120
El Paso, TX 79912 (915) 541-7900
Contact: Stephen L. Feinberg, Pres.

Established in 1971.
Donor(s): Milton D. Feinberg, Stephen L. Feinberg, Sean Feinberg,‡ David C. Feinberg, William I. Feinberg.
Financial data (yr. ended 12/31/01): Grants paid, $158,637; assets, $2,528,956 (M); gifts received, $626,425; expenditures, $162,028; qualifying distributions, $162,028.
Limitations: Giving primarily in Santa Fe, NM and El Paso, TX.
Application information: Application form not required.
Officers: Stephen L. Feinberg, Pres.; Jack T. Chapman, V.P.; Andrew Feinberg, V.P.; Elisa Varela, Secy.-Treas.
EIN: 746039246
Codes: FD2

51231
The Luchsinger Family Foundation
3663 Inverness Dr.
Houston, TX 77019

Established in 1988 in TX.
Donor(s): Amelia D. Luchsinger, John W. Luchsinger.
Financial data (yr. ended 12/31/01): Grants paid, $157,750; assets, $1,807,636 (M); expenditures, $164,465; qualifying distributions, $157,562.
Limitations: Applications not accepted. Giving primarily in TX.
Application information: Contributes only to pre-selected organizations.
Officers and Trustees:* Amelia D. Luchsinger,* Pres.; Mary L. Castaneda,* V.P.; Patricia L. Ward,* V.P.; John W. Luchsinger,* Secy.-Treas.
EIN: 760254155
Codes: FD2

51232
First Command Educational Foundation
(Formerly USPA & IRA Educational Foundation)
P.O. Box 2387
Fort Worth, TX 76113-2387

Established in 1983 in TX.
Donor(s): Carroll H. Payne II, Freda J. Payne, Naomi Payne, Debra Payne, IRA, Inc.
Financial data (yr. ended 12/31/01): Grants paid, $157,466; assets, $75,428 (M); gifts received, $498,906; expenditures, $482,046; qualifying distributions, $428,168.
Application information: Applications are solicited by officers' wives clubs at local military installations. Application form required.
Officers and Directors:* Donaldson D. Frizzell,* Pres.; Philip G. Loignon, V.P.; Mira E. Murray, Secy.; Martin R. Durbin,* Treas.; Charles T. Bauer,* C.O.B.; M. Douglas Mays, Charles P. Nemfakos, Carroll H. Payne II, Charles H. Payne II.
EIN: 751973894
Codes: FD2, GTI

51233
Manning Foundation
c/o JPMorgan Chase Bank
P.O. Box 2558
Houston, TX 77252-8037 (713) 216-1451
FAX: (713) 216-2119; E-mail:
ElizabethHickman@chase.com
Contact: Elizabeth C. Hickman, V.P. and Trust Off.

Established in 1995 in TX.
Donor(s): William O. Manning.‡
Financial data (yr. ended 01/31/01): Grants paid, $157,140; assets, $3,375,256 (M); expenditures, $192,577; qualifying distributions, $166,135.
Limitations: Giving primarily in TX.
Publications: Application guidelines.
Application information: Application form not required.
Trustees: Nancy S. Robinson, Gerard H. Stafford, Jr., JPMorgan Chase Bank.
EIN: 766105634
Codes: FD2

51234
Hext Family Foundation, Inc.
5030 E. University Blvd., Ste. D102
Odessa, TX 79762 (915) 550-7527
Application address: P.O. Box 15038, Odessa TX, 79768; E-mail: mpalmer@airocom.net; URL: http://www.hextfoundation.com
Contact: Mark Palmer, V.P.

Established in 1998 in TX.
Donor(s): Bill Hext,‡ Jane Hext, Hext Management, LLC, Mark Palmer, Susan Palmer, Melinda Spencer, Tim Spencer.
Financial data (yr. ended 12/31/01): Grants paid, $155,499; assets, $4,338,801 (M); gifts received, $7,087; expenditures, $283,813; qualifying distributions, $253,961; giving activities include $14,645 for programs.
Limitations: Giving primarily in Permian Basin, TX.
Publications: Informational brochure (including application guidelines), program policy statement, grants list.
Application information: Application form required.
Officers: Jane Hext, Pres.; Mark Palmer, V.P., Treas. and Exec. Dir.; Melinda Spencer, V.P. and Secy.
Directors: Susan Palmer, Tim Spencer.
EIN: 752754667
Codes: FD2

51235
Sondra S. Terry Memorial Foundation
770 S. Post Oak Ln., Ste. 600
Houston, TX 77056

Established in 1999 in TX.
Donor(s): Deborah T. Kearns, Floyd M. Kearns.
Financial data (yr. ended 02/28/02): Grants paid, $155,000; assets, $286,076 (M); expenditures, $156,636; qualifying distributions, $155,000.
Limitations: Applications not accepted. Giving primarily in Houston, TX.
Application information: Contributes only to pre-selected organizations.
Officers and Directors:* Deborah T. Kearns,* Pres. and Treas.; Floyd M. Kearns,* V.P. and Secy.; Andrienne N. Kearns.
EIN: 311649999

51236
The Boone Foundation
4417 Lorraine Ave.
Dallas, TX 75205-3610

Established in 1994 in TX.
Donor(s): Cordelia F. Boone.
Financial data (yr. ended 12/31/01): Grants paid, $154,600; assets, $1,205,876 (M); gifts received, $500,000; expenditures, $159,554; qualifying distributions, $159,356.
Limitations: Applications not accepted.
Application information: Contributes only to pre-selected organizations.
Officers: Thomas K. Boone, Pres.; Cordelia F. Boone, V.P.
EIN: 752567121
Codes: FD2

51237
Coleman Foundation
615 Urban Loop
San Antonio, TX 78204

Established in 1991 in TX.
Donor(s): Bobby W. Coleman, Ann Coleman.
Financial data (yr. ended 12/31/01): Grants paid, $153,900; assets, $510,093 (M); gifts received, $159,000; expenditures, $165,507; qualifying distributions, $153,900.
Limitations: Applications not accepted. Giving limited to TX.
Application information: Contributes only to pre-selected organizations.
Officers: Bobby W. Coleman, Pres. and V.P.; Jack B. Phillips, Jr., Secy.-Treas.
EIN: 742610014
Codes: FD2

51238
The Gerd & Dorothy R. Miller Family Foundation
105 Riviera Dr.
San Antonio, TX 78213

Established in 1997 in TX.
Donor(s): Gerd Miller, Dorothy R. Miller.
Financial data (yr. ended 03/31/01): Grants paid, $153,586; assets, $212,782 (M); gifts received, $72,071; expenditures, $156,988; qualifying distributions, $153,006.
Limitations: Applications not accepted. Giving primarily in TX.
Application information: Contributes only to pre-selected organizations.
Directors: Dorothy R. Miller, Gerd Miller.
EIN: 742824377
Codes: FD2

51239
Trini and O. C. Mendenhall Foundation
8835 Stable Ln.
Houston, TX 77024

Established in 1998 in TX.
Financial data (yr. ended 12/31/00): Grants paid, $152,900; assets, $113,412 (M); gifts received, $100,000; expenditures, $157,632; qualifying distributions, $157,343.
Limitations: Applications not accepted. Giving primarily in TX.
Application information: Contributes only to pre-selected organizations.
Officers: Trinidad V. Mendenhall, Chair.; Oniel Mendenhall, Jr., Secy.
EIN: 760530965
Codes: FD2

51240
Belmont Foundation
545 E. John Carpenter Fwy., Ste. 1530
Irving, TX 75062-8110 (972) 831-1575

Established in 1993 in TX.
Donor(s): J. Ralph Ellis, Jr.
Financial data (yr. ended 12/31/01): Grants paid, $152,075; assets, $326,350 (M); gifts received, $155,057; expenditures, $153,720; qualifying distributions, $152,007.
Limitations: Applications not accepted. Giving limited to TX.
Application information: Contributes only to pre-selected organizations.
Trustee: J. Ralph Ellis.
EIN: 752503354
Codes: FD2

51241—TEXAS

51241
The William T. and Sally S. Slick Foundation
10603 S. Evers Park Dr.
Houston, TX 77024
Contact: William T. Slick, Jr., Pres.

Established in 1997 in TX.
Donor(s): Sally S. Slick, William T. Slick, Jr.
Financial data (yr. ended 12/31/01): Grants paid, $151,700; assets, $764,140 (M); gifts received, $20,935; expenditures, $159,856; qualifying distributions, $154,723.
Limitations: Applications not accepted. Giving primarily in Houston, TX.
Application information: Generally only contributes to pre-selected organizations.
Officers: William T. Slick, Jr., Chair.; Sally S. Slick, Secy.
Directors: Steven G. Slick, Susan S. Threatt.
EIN: 760538030
Codes: FD2

51242
The Roger and Rosemary Enrico Foundation
3831 Turtle Creek Blvd., No. 23B
Dallas, TX 75219

Established in 2000 in TX.
Donor(s): Roger A. Enrico.
Financial data (yr. ended 12/31/01): Grants paid, $151,500; assets, $3,041,924 (M); gifts received, $1,436,140; expenditures, $169,073; qualifying distributions, $140,235.
Limitations: Applications not accepted. Giving primarily in TX.
Application information: Contributes only to pre-selected organizations.
Officer: Terence C. Sullivan, Treas.
Directors: Aaron J. Enrico, Roger A. Enrico, Rosemary Enrico.
EIN: 752871636

51243
The Deason Foundation
2828 N. Haskell, 10th Fl.
Dallas, TX 75204

Established in 1997 in TX.
Donor(s): Darwin Deason.
Financial data (yr. ended 12/31/00): Grants paid, $151,369; assets, $3,955,340 (M); expenditures, $151,369; qualifying distributions, $151,193.
Limitations: Applications not accepted. Giving primarily in AR.
Application information: Contributes only to pre-selected organizations.
Officers: Darwin Deason, Pres. and Treas.; David W. Black, V.P. and Secy.; Douglas Deason, V.P.
EIN: 752715549
Codes: FD2

51244
GHS Foundation
2900 Weslayan, Ste. B
Houston, TX 77027
Contact: Nancy Cooke, V.P.

Established in 2000 in TX.
Donor(s): Gerald H. Smith, Fidelity Charitable Gift Trust.
Financial data (yr. ended 02/28/01): Grants paid, $151,000; assets, $4,316,157 (M); gifts received, $4,582,283; expenditures, $168,045; qualifying distributions, $151,000.
Limitations: Giving primarily in TX.
Application information: Application form not required.
Officers: Gerald H. Smith, Pres.; Nancy Hamlin Cooke, V.P. and Secy.-Treas.; Robert E. Hutson, V.P.
EIN: 760628970
Codes: FD2

51245
James Avery Charitable Foundation
P.O. Box 291367
Kerrville, TX 78029-1367

Established in 1992 in TX.
Donor(s): James Avery Craftsman, Inc.
Financial data (yr. ended 12/31/01): Grants paid, $150,000; assets, $1,592,619 (M); gifts received, $154,940; expenditures, $182,527; qualifying distributions, $178,368.
Limitations: Applications not accepted. Giving primarily in IL and TX.
Application information: Contributes only to pre-selected organizations.
Distribution Committee: Homer James Avery, Juana Estella Hollin-Avery.
Trustee: Christopher M. Avery.
EIN: 742627241
Codes: FD2

51246
Richard D. Bass Foundation
(Formerly The Bass Foundation)
4516 Wildwood Rd.
Dallas, TX 75209
FAX: (214) 351-6994
Contact: Barbara B. Moroney, Tr.

Established in 1945 in TX; in 1983, foundation split up into The Bass Foundation and Harry Bass Foundation.
Donor(s): Harry W. Bass, Sr.,‡ Mrs. Harry W. Bass, Sr.‡
Financial data (yr. ended 12/31/01): Grants paid, $150,000; assets, $2,792,908 (M); expenditures, $176,539; qualifying distributions, $149,261.
Limitations: Giving primarily in the metropolitan Dallas, TX, area, and the Salt Lake City, UT, area.
Application information: Application form not required.
Trustees: Alice W. Bass, Richard D. Bass, Barbara B. Moroney, Bonnie B. Smith.
EIN: 756013540
Codes: FD2

51247
The Butcher Fund
5623 Shady River
Houston, TX 77056 (713) 622-8987
Contact: Lorain S. Butcher, Pres.

Established in 1966.
Donor(s): E.D. Butcher.‡
Financial data (yr. ended 03/31/01): Grants paid, $150,000; assets, $2,821,765 (M); expenditures, $170,057; qualifying distributions, $156,950.
Limitations: Giving primarily in Houston, TX.
Application information: Application form not required.
Officers and Directors:* Lorain S. Butcher,* Pres. and Treas.; Allen D. Butcher,* V.P.; John E. Butcher,* V.P.; C. Boone Schwatzel,* Secy.; R. Ernest Butcher, Wanda M. Butcher, Anna Butcher Nemeti.
EIN: 746074669
Codes: FD2

51248
Martha Ann Cogdell Hospital Trust
c/o Bank One, Texas, N.A.
P.O. Box 2050
Fort Worth, TX 76113-2050 (817) 884-4151
Contact: Robert M. Lansford

Established in 1951.
Financial data (yr. ended 09/30/01): Grants paid, $150,000; assets, $2,485,192 (M); expenditures, $184,260; qualifying distributions, $157,369.
Limitations: Giving primarily in TX.
Trustee: Bank One, Texas, N.A.
EIN: 756013973
Codes: FD2

51249
Ben & Maytee Fisch Foundation
3715 Wynnwood Dr.
Tyler, TX 75701-9698
Contact: Maytee R. Fisch, Pres.

Established in 1997 in TX.
Donor(s): Ben Fisch, Maytee R. Fisch.
Financial data (yr. ended 05/31/01): Grants paid, $150,000; assets, $2,766,596 (M); expenditures, $162,407; qualifying distributions, $149,458.
Limitations: Giving primarily in TX.
Application information: Application form not required.
Officers and Directors:* Maytee R. Fisch,* Pres.; Ben Fisch,* V.P.; Martee F. Fuerst,* Secy.; Linda F. Fisch, Stephen E. Fisch, Jan F. Fuerst.
EIN: 752732192
Codes: FD2

51250
The Flohr Family Foundation
127 Grant Ave.
San Antonio, TX 78209
Contact: Bruce Flohr, Chair.

Established in 2000.
Donor(s): Bruce Flohr.
Financial data (yr. ended 02/28/02): Grants paid, $150,000; assets, $2,603,985 (M); expenditures, $193,554; qualifying distributions, $192,614.
Limitations: Giving primarily in TX.
Officers: Bruce Flohr, Chair.; Janet Flohr, Secy.
EIN: 742944303
Codes: FD2

51251
Harvey R. Houck, Jr. and Patricia W. Houck Foundation, Inc.
8811 Westheimer, Ste. 208
Houston, TX 77063

Established in 1994 in TX.
Donor(s): Harvey R. Houck, Jr., Patricia West Houck.
Financial data (yr. ended 12/31/01): Grants paid, $150,000; assets, $5,974,252 (M); expenditures, $152,128; qualifying distributions, $149,693.
Limitations: Applications not accepted. Giving limited to TX.
Application information: Contributes only to pre-selected organizations.
Officers and Directors:* Harvey R. Houck, Jr., Pres.; Patricia West-Houck,* V.P. and Secy.; Harriet Elizabeth Houck, V.P.; Liza Houck,* V.P.; Gordon B. Rose,* Treas.
EIN: 760435413
Codes: FD2

51252
MKB Foundation
P.O. Box 163064
Austin, TX 78716-3064

Established in 2001.
Donor(s): K & M Family Partners Ltd., Michael S. Bennett, Karen E. Bennett.
Financial data (yr. ended 12/31/01): Grants paid, $150,000; assets, $271,440 (M); gifts received, $23,325; expenditures, $150,074; qualifying distributions, $150,000.
Limitations: Applications not accepted.
Application information: Contributes only to pre-selected organizations.
Officers and Directors:* Michael S. Bennett,* Pres.; Karen E. Bennett,* Secy.-Treas.; Melissa A. Bennett.
EIN: 742979968

Codes: FD2

51253
The Spence Foundation
813 First Pl.
Tyler, TX 75702

Established in 1997 in TX.
Donor(s): Mary John Spence.
Financial data (yr. ended 10/31/01): Grants paid, $150,000; assets, $1,480,607 (M); gifts received, $220,200; expenditures, $152,454; qualifying distributions, $150,000.
Limitations: Applications not accepted. Giving primarily in Tyler, TX.
Application information: Contributes only to pre-selected organizations.
Officers: Mary John Spence, Pres.; Ralph Spence, Jr., V.P.; Judy Spence Tate, Secy.; Louise Spence Griffeth, Treas.
EIN: 752740118
Codes: FD2

51254
Patterson Foundation
c/o BancorpSouth, Trust Dept.
P.O. Box 5608
Texarkana, TX 75505-5608

Established in 1994 in TX.
Donor(s): Jessica B. Patterson.
Financial data (yr. ended 12/31/01): Grants paid, $149,849; assets, $1,807,324 (M); gifts received, $72,839; expenditures, $163,594; qualifying distributions, $148,176.
Limitations: Applications not accepted. Giving primarily in Texarkana, TX.
Application information: Contributes only to pre-selected organizations.
Officers: Jessica B. Patterson, Pres.; Nancy P. Troike, V.P.; Robert McDowell, Secy.-Treas.
EIN: 752561756
Codes: FD2

51255
Alice & David C. Bintliff Foundation
1001 Fannin, Ste. 722
Houston, TX 77002-6707

Established in 1959 in TX.
Donor(s): Alice J. Bintliff.
Financial data (yr. ended 12/31/01): Grants paid, $149,501; assets, $2,955,280 (M); expenditures, $166,501; qualifying distributions, $148,852.
Limitations: Applications not accepted. Giving primarily in Houston, TX.
Application information: Contributes only to pre-selected organizations.
Officers and Directors:* Raleigh W. Johnson, Jr.,* Chair.; Daniel C. Arnold,* Pres.; Beverly B. Arnold,* V.P.; Marjorie B. Johnson,* V.P.; Nancy L. Gafford, Secy.; Robert A. Weigle, Treas.
EIN: 746061437
Codes: FD2

51256
M. & A. McCullough Foundation
807 8th St., 2nd Fl.
Wichita Falls, TX 76301-3381

Established in 1955.
Donor(s): M.E. McCullough.
Financial data (yr. ended 12/31/01): Grants paid, $149,000; assets, $3,438,228 (M); expenditures, $157,315; qualifying distributions, $152,024.
Limitations: Applications not accepted. Giving primarily in Wichita Falls, TX.
Application information: Contributes only to pre-selected organizations.
Officers: Thomas E. McCullough, Pres. and Treas.; Linda McCullough Decker, V.P. and Secy.

EIN: 756021589
Codes: FD2

51257
Weatherspoon Charitable Foundation
3402 Hillview Dr.
Austin, TX 78703
Contact: Mary Bowden, Treas.

Established in 1988 in IA.
Donor(s): Margaret Weatherspoon.
Financial data (yr. ended 12/31/01): Grants paid, $149,000; assets, $2,767,505 (M); expenditures, $151,648; qualifying distributions, $149,332.
Application information: Unsolicited requests for funds not accepted. Application form not required.
Officers: Margaret Weatherspoon, Pres.; Jacqueline Reineke, V.P. and Secy.; Mary Bowden, Treas.
EIN: 421324028
Codes: FD2

51258
The Mark and Kathleen Watson Charitable Foundation
P.O. Box 6886
San Antonio, TX 78209-0886 (210) 824-4546
Contact: Mark E. Watson, Jr., Pres.

Established in 1997 in TX.
Donor(s): Mark Watson.
Financial data (yr. ended 09/30/01): Grants paid, $148,876; assets, $2,236,348 (M); gifts received, $1,000,000; expenditures, $163,013; qualifying distributions, $148,434.
Limitations: Giving primarily in San Antonio, TX.
Application information: Application form not required.
Officer: Mark E. Watson, Jr., Pres.
Trustee: F.B. Lyon III.
EIN: 742825092
Codes: FD2

51259
The Harold Farb Foundation
P.O. Box 27741
Houston, TX 77227-7741

Established in 1980.
Financial data (yr. ended 11/30/01): Grants paid, $148,080; assets, $917,891 (M); expenditures, $154,217; qualifying distributions, $148,009.
Limitations: Applications not accepted. Giving primarily in Houston, TX.
Application information: Contributes only to pre-selected organizations.
Trustee: Harold Farb.
EIN: 742150068
Codes: FD2

51260
Jay & Shirley Marks Foundation
10475 Southwest Fwy.
Houston, TX 77074-1101

Established in 1972.
Donor(s): Jay Marks, Shirley Marks.
Financial data (yr. ended 11/30/01): Grants paid, $147,552; assets, $81,414 (M); gifts received, $83,376; expenditures, $148,505; qualifying distributions, $146,801.
Limitations: Giving primarily in Houston, TX.
Application information: Application form not required.
Directors: Fran Lowe, Jay Marks, Lester Marks, Shirley Marks.
EIN: 237253928
Codes: FD2

51261
The Stuart Charitable Foundation
703 Kuhlman Rd.
Houston, TX 77024

Established in 1998 in TX.
Financial data (yr. ended 10/31/01): Grants paid, $147,550; assets, $2,260,120 (M); expenditures, $169,922; qualifying distributions, $147,051.
Limitations: Applications not accepted. Giving primarily in TX.
Application information: Contributes only to pre-selected organizations.
Officers and Directors:* Donald S. Jackson,* Pres.; Randolph Allen,* V.P.; Benton McGarrah,* V.P.; R. Kay Parker,* Secy.; Eugene Prior,* Treas.
EIN: 760554432
Codes: FD2

51262
The Shelton Foundation
P.O. Box 79092
Houston, TX 77024
Contact: John T. Shelton, Jr., Tr.

Established in 1989 in TX.
Donor(s): John Shelton.
Financial data (yr. ended 11/30/01): Grants paid, $147,360; assets, $753,647 (M); expenditures, $154,698; qualifying distributions, $153,776.
Limitations: Applications not accepted. Giving primarily in Baton Rouge, LA, and Houston, TX.
Officers and Trustees:* Rose Ann Shelton,* Pres.; Sharon Shelton,* V.P.; Shirley Merideth,* Secy.; John T. Shelton III,* Treas.; John T. Shelton, Jr.
EIN: 760294299
Codes: FD2

51263
The Virginia and L. E. Simmons Family Foundation
6600 JPMorgan Chase Tower
Houston, TX 77002-3007

Established in 1994 in TX.
Donor(s): L.E. Simmons, Virginia W. Simmons.
Financial data (yr. ended 12/31/01): Grants paid, $147,351; assets, $4,003,155 (M); expenditures, $150,027; qualifying distributions, $147,701.
Limitations: Applications not accepted. Giving primarily in TX.
Application information: Contributes only to pre-selected organizations.
Officers: L.E. Simmons, Pres.; Virginia W. Simmons, V.P.; Anthony F. Deluca, Secy.-Treas.
EIN: 760453177
Codes: FD2

51264
Mary A. Peterson Wyatt Charitable Trust
c/o Frost National Bank, Trust Dept.
P.O. Box 2950
San Antonio, TX 78299 (210) 220-4449
Contact: William Clyborne, Jr., V.P. and Trust Off., Frost National Bank

Established in 1999 in TX.
Financial data (yr. ended 12/31/01): Grants paid, $147,091; assets, $2,201,232 (M); expenditures, $174,944; qualifying distributions, $147,091.
Limitations: Giving primarily in TX.
Trustee: Frost National Bank.
EIN: 746474894

51265
The Robert & Mary Ann Cotham Foundation
201 Main St., Ste. 2300
Fort Worth, TX 76102

Established in 1995 in TX.
Donor(s): W. Robert Cotham, Mary Ann Cotham.

51265—TEXAS

Financial data (yr. ended 12/31/01): Grants paid, $147,062; assets, $356,389 (M); expenditures, $147,320; qualifying distributions, $147,062.
Limitations: Applications not accepted. Giving primarily in TX.
Application information: Contributes only to pre-selected organizations.
Officers and Directors:* W. Robert Cotham,* Pres.; Hugh T. Blevins, Jr.,* V.P.; Mary Ann Cotham,* Secy.-Treas.
EIN: 752572390
Codes: FD2

51266
The Mundy Family Foundation
11150 S. Wilcrest Dr., Ste. 300
Houston, TX 77099
Contact: Joe S. Mundy, Tr.

Established in 1996.
Donor(s): Joe S. Mundy, John T. Mundy.
Financial data (yr. ended 12/31/01): Grants paid, $147,000; assets, $0 (M); expenditures, $147,875; qualifying distributions, $147,000.
Limitations: Applications not accepted. Giving primarily in TX.
Application information: Unsolicited requests for funds not accepted.
Trustees: Frances S. Mundy, Joe S. Mundy, John T. Mundy, Marion E. Mundy, Sue E. Mundy.
EIN: 760520888
Codes: FD2

51267
Argyle Foundation
200 Concord Plz., Ste. 700
San Antonio, TX 78216-6941
Contact: Margo Marbut, Pres.

Established in 1997 in TX.
Donor(s): Bob Marbut, Margo Marbut.
Financial data (yr. ended 12/31/01): Grants paid, $146,900; assets, $1,664,726 (M); gifts received, $11,000; expenditures, $224,969; qualifying distributions, $176,445.
Limitations: Applications not accepted. Giving primarily in TX.
Application information: Unsolicited requests for funds not accepted.
Officers: Bob Marbut, Chair.; Margo Marbut, Pres.; Patricia Meyer, Secy.; Joann Bennett, Treas.
Director: Mike Marbut.
EIN: 742815647
Codes: FD2

51268
The Malachi Foundation
4665 Sweetwater Blvd., Ste. 105
Sugar Land, TX 77479
Contact: Brenda D. Taylor, Admin.

Established in 1994.
Donor(s): Gregory L. Feste, Dan Clearly, Chris Herndon, Curry Juneau, Michael Noonan, David Peterson, Clint Summers, Winston Dominique, Ron Goodler, John Havelka, Wayne Murray, Quailvalley Church, Malachi Financial Svcs.
Financial data (yr. ended 12/31/01): Grants paid, $146,740; assets, $314,202 (M); gifts received, $130,295; expenditures, $158,656; qualifying distributions, $158,490.
Limitations: Giving primarily in OK, TN, and TX.
Application information: Application form not required.
Officer and Trustee:* Gregory L. Feste,* Pres.
EIN: 760439471
Codes: FD2, GTI

51269
Abbott and Leslie Sprague Family Foundation
3451 Piping Rock Ln.
Houston, TX 77027-4112
Contact: J. Abbott Sprague, Pres.

Established in 1998 in TX.
Donor(s): J. Abbott Sprague, Leslie M. Sprague.
Financial data (yr. ended 06/30/01): Grants paid, $146,000; assets, $4,086,624 (M); expenditures, $150,917; qualifying distributions, $126,371.
Limitations: Giving primarily in Houston, TX.
Application information: Application form required.
Officers: J. Abbott Sprague, Pres. and Treas.; Leslie M. Sprague, V.P. and Secy.
Trustee: Seth Sprague.
EIN: 760569950
Codes: FD2

51270
The Susan and Jack Lapin Family Foundation
109 N. Post Oak Ln., Ste. 300
Houston, TX 77024

Established in 1997 in TX.
Financial data (yr. ended 11/30/01): Grants paid, $145,890; assets, $283,861 (M); expenditures, $149,924; qualifying distributions, $147,197.
Limitations: Applications not accepted. Giving primarily in TX.
Application information: Contributes only to pre-selected organizations.
Trustees: Jack Lapin, Susan K. Lapin.
EIN: 760527416
Codes: FD2

51271
Huthsteiner Fine Arts Trust
c/o JPMorgan Chase Bank
300 Crescent Ct., Ste. 400
Dallas, TX 75201 (877) 221-5363
Contact: Jeff Rea, V.P., JPMorgan Chase Bank

Established in 1980 in TX.
Donor(s): Robert and Pauline Huthsteiner Trust.
Financial data (yr. ended 07/31/02): Grants paid, $145,500; assets, $2,850,635 (M); expenditures, $172,433; qualifying distributions, $153,190.
Limitations: Giving primarily in El Paso, TX.
Application information: Application form not required.
Trustee: JPMorgan Chase Bank.
EIN: 746308412
Codes: FD2

51272
Taylor County Historical Foundation
400 Pine St., Ste. 1000
Abilene, TX 79601-5142

Established in 1999 in TX.
Financial data (yr. ended 12/31/01): Grants paid, $145,448; assets, $12,068 (M); gifts received, $156,960; expenditures, $146,343; qualifying distributions, $145,448.
Limitations: Applications not accepted.
Application information: Contributes only to pre-selected organizations.
Officers: Tucker S. Bridwell, Pres.; Dian G. Stai, V.P.; H.C. Zachary, Secy.; Joseph E. Canon, Treas.
EIN: 752802500

51273
The Sands Foundation
100 Crescent Ct., Ste. 1700
Dallas, TX 75201

Established in 1959 in TX.
Donor(s): Caroline Rose Hunt, Loyd B. Sands.‡
Financial data (yr. ended 12/31/00): Grants paid, $144,850; assets, $540,790 (M); expenditures, $79,776; qualifying distributions, $145,610.
Limitations: Applications not accepted. Giving primarily in Dallas, TX.
Application information: Contributes only to pre-selected organizations.
Officers: Caroline Rose Hunt, Pres.; Laurie Sands Harrison, V.P.; Stephen Hunt Sands, Secy.-Treas.
EIN: 756010788
Codes: FD2

51274
James M. Mansour Foundation
609 Castle Ridge Rd., Ste. 215
Austin, TX 78746 (512) 327-4454
Contact: James M. Mansour, Dir.

Established in 1998 in TX.
Donor(s): James M. Mansour.
Financial data (yr. ended 12/31/00): Grants paid, $144,609; assets, $1,117,903 (M); expenditures, $263,142; qualifying distributions, $143,549.
Limitations: Giving on a national basis.
Directors: Kevin D. Fowler, Rich W. Lusk, James M. Mansour, Randy L. McFadden, Kristi J. McIntyre, Paul Zito.
EIN: 311599571
Codes: FD2

51275
Gault-Hussey Charitable Trust
c/o Bank of America
P.O. Box 831041
Dallas, TX 75283-1041
Application address: P.O. Box 88, Topeka, KS 66601, tel.: (785) 295-9463
Contact: Rudy Wrenick, Jr., Sr. V.P., Bank of America

Established in 1980 in KS.
Financial data (yr. ended 11/30/01): Grants paid, $144,500; assets, $2,733,928 (M); expenditures, $169,717; qualifying distributions, $146,616.
Limitations: Giving primarily in northeast KS.
Application information: Application form not required.
Trustee: Bank of America.
EIN: 486237061
Codes: FD2

51276
The William H. and Lucille Williams Charitable Trust
c/o Bank of America
P.O. Box 831041
Dallas, TX 75283-1041

Established in 1994 in TX.
Donor(s): William H. Williams.‡
Financial data (yr. ended 12/31/01): Grants paid, $144,000; assets, $3,077,197 (M); expenditures, $194,312; qualifying distributions, $154,218.
Limitations: Applications not accepted. Giving limited to Houston, TX.
Application information: Contributes only to pre-selected organizations.
Trustee: Bank of America.
EIN: 766049170
Codes: FD2

51277
Brodsky Foundation
c/o Donald W. Brodsky
1100 Louisiana St., Ste. 1800
Houston, TX 77002

Established in 1966 in TX.
Donor(s): Alexander E. Brodsky, M.D.,‡ Ruth W. Brodsky.

Financial data (yr. ended 12/31/00): Grants paid, $142,855; assets, $3,140,407 (M); expenditures, $151,156; qualifying distributions, $141,661.
Limitations: Applications not accepted. Giving primarily in Houston, TX.
Application information: Contributes only to pre-selected organizations.
Officers: Ruth W. Brodsky, Pres.; Donald W. Brodsky, V.P. and Secy.-Treas.; James W. Brodsky, M.D., V.P.; Ellen Brodsky Gaber, V.P.
EIN: 746089484
Codes: FD2

51278
Andrew Delaney Foundation
2727 Allen Pkwy., Ste. 460
Houston, TX 77019
Contact: Andrew Delaney, Pres.

Established in 1988 in TX.
Donor(s): Andrew Delaney.
Financial data (yr. ended 12/31/01): Grants paid, $142,625; assets, $3,027,991 (M); gifts received, $2,308; expenditures, $173,157; qualifying distributions, $162,349.
Limitations: Applications not accepted. Giving primarily in TX.
Application information: Contributes only to pre-selected organizations.
Officers and Trustees:* Andrew Delaney,* Pres.; Janet L. Delaney,* V.P. and Secy.-Treas.; Pauline M. Delaney, James P. Lee, Antoinette R. Stapper.
EIN: 760265537
Codes: FD2

51279
A. J. and Jessie Duncan Foundation
c/o Harold Brown
201 Main St., Ste. 801
Fort Worth, TX 76102

Incorporated in 1955 in TX.
Donor(s): A.J. Duncan,‡ Jessie Duncan.‡
Financial data (yr. ended 02/28/01): Grants paid, $142,145; assets, $2,900,880 (M); expenditures, $176,730; qualifying distributions, $156,804.
Limitations: Giving primarily in TX.
Officers and Directors:* C. Harold Brown,* Pres.; Harold A. Brown,* V.P.; Christopher J. Pruitt,* Secy.-Treas.
EIN: 756018425
Codes: FD2

51280
Hill Country Community Foundation
P.O. Box 10
Burnet, TX 78611

Established in 1987 in TX.
Financial data (yr. ended 12/31/99): Grants paid, $142,059; assets, $1,396,882 (M); gifts received, $153,533; expenditures, $150,138.
Limitations: Giving limited to the Texas Hill Country area.
Officers: John Hoover, Pres.; Margaret Gross, Secy.; Cary Johnson, Treas.
EIN: 742452519
Codes: CM, FD2

51281
Potts and Sibley Foundation
P.O. Box 8907
Midland, TX 79708 (915) 686-8636
Contact: Robert W. Bechtel, Mgr.

Established in 1967 in TX.
Donor(s): Effie Potts Sibley Irrevocable Trust.
Financial data (yr. ended 07/31/01): Grants paid, $141,500; assets, $4,154,399 (M); expenditures, $302,339; qualifying distributions, $158,943.
Limitations: Giving primarily in TX.

Application information: Application form required.
Officer, Trustees and Directors:* Robert W. Bechtel,* Mgr. and Dir.; Allen G. McGuire, Dir.; Tom Scott, Dir.; D.J. Sibley, Jr., Dir.; Hiram Sibley, Dir.
EIN: 756081070
Codes: FD2

51282
Merrick Family Foundation
2716 Stanford Ave.
Dallas, TX 75225

Established in 1999 in TX.
Donor(s): Nicholas A. Merrick, Leslie T. Merrick.
Financial data (yr. ended 12/31/01): Grants paid, $141,210; assets, $280,444 (M); gifts received, $7,000; expenditures, $152,592; qualifying distributions, $142,865.
Limitations: Applications not accepted. Giving primarily in TX.
Application information: Contributes only to pre-selected organizations.
Officers: Nicholas A. Merrick, Pres.; Leslie T. Merrick, Secy.
Director: Judith L. Merrick.
EIN: 752851383
Codes: FD2

51283
M. K. Brown Foundation, Inc.
P.O. Box 581
Pampa, TX 79066-0662 (806) 669-6851
Contact: Bill W. Waters, Chair.

Established in 1960 in TX.
Donor(s): M.K. Brown.‡
Financial data (yr. ended 12/31/01): Grants paid, $140,560; assets, $3,481,896 (M); expenditures, $191,118; qualifying distributions, $148,192.
Limitations: Giving limited to the TX Panhandle area, with emphasis on Gray and Pampa County, TX.
Officers: Bill W. Waters, Chair.; William Jarrel Smith, Jr., Vice-Chair.; David E. Holt, Secy.
EIN: 756034058
Codes: FD2

51284
Navarro County Educational Foundation, Inc.
P.O. Box 3082
Corsicana, TX 75151
Application address: M.C. and Mattie Caston Scholarship Program, c/o Navarro College, 3200 W. 7th Ave., Corsicana, TX 75110

Established in 1988 in TX.
Financial data (yr. ended 12/31/01): Grants paid, $140,234; assets, $3,598,350 (M); expenditures, $165,874; qualifying distributions, $145,191.
Limitations: Giving limited to residents of Ellis, Freestone, Limestone, and Navarro counties, TX.
Application information: Submit a completed Navarro College application for admission, and a Caston Scholarship application. First priority will be given to Navarro County High School graduates. Application form required.
Officers: C. David Campbell, M.D., Pres.; Oliver Albritton, V.P.; Barbara Moe, Secy.-Treas.
Directors: Mickey Hillock, Larry Morrison, Tom White.
EIN: 752227788
Codes: FD2

51285
William E. and Natoma Pyle Harvey Charitable Trust
c/o Compass Bank
2001 Kirby, P.O. Box 4886
Houston, TX 77210-4886
Contact: Tom Collins

Established in 1990.
Financial data (yr. ended 12/31/01): Grants paid, $140,000; assets, $1,860,482 (M); expenditures, $170,615; qualifying distributions, $150,044.
Limitations: Giving primarily in Houston, TX.
Publications: Annual report.
Application information: Application form not required.
Trustee: Compass Bank.
EIN: 766060508
Codes: FD2

51286
Mike Hogg Fund
c/o JPMorgan Chase Bank
P.O. Box 2558
Houston, TX 77252-8037 (713) 216-4422
Application address: c/o JPMorgan Chase Bank, 600 Travis, Ste. 700, P.O. Box 2558, Houston, TX 77252-8037
Contact: Jana Reynolds

Established in 1959.
Financial data (yr. ended 12/31/01): Grants paid, $140,000; assets, $2,241,396 (M); expenditures, $164,803; qualifying distributions, $139,985.
Limitations: Applications not accepted. Giving primarily in Houston, TX.
Trustee: JPMorgan Chase Bank.
Advisors: John G. Batsakis, Gerald D. Dodd, Jr., John A. Murray.
EIN: 746033383
Codes: FD2

51287
The Sunshine Foundation
10000 N. Central Expwy., Ste. 1540
Dallas, TX 75231

Established in 1999 in TX.
Donor(s): Wayne G. Willems, Grace M. Willems.
Financial data (yr. ended 09/30/01): Grants paid, $140,000; assets, $2,040,630 (M); expenditures, $146,271; qualifying distributions, $140,070.
Limitations: Applications not accepted. Giving on a national basis.
Application information: Contributes only to pre-selected organizations.
Officers and Directors:* Wayne G. Willems,* Pres.; John R. Bauer,* Secy.; Grace M. Willems,* Treas.; David C. Willems, Jennifer L. Willems.
EIN: 752850271
Codes: FD2

51288
Gailo Trust
P.O. Box 2488
Bellaire, TX 77402-2488

Established in 1963 in TX.
Donor(s): Aaron J. Farfel.‡
Financial data (yr. ended 12/31/01): Grants paid, $139,750; assets, $2,320,020 (M); expenditures, $149,282; qualifying distributions, $142,699.
Limitations: Giving primarily in Houston, TX.
Trustee: Lois F. Stark.
EIN: 746054992
Codes: FD2

51289
The Barbara & Richard Raynor Medical Foundation
301 Commerce St., Ste. 2975
Fort Worth, TX 76102-4175

Established in 2000 in TX.
Financial data (yr. ended 12/31/01): Grants paid, $138,148; assets, $173,709 (M); expenditures, $138,534; qualifying distributions, $138,148.
Limitations: Applications not accepted.
Application information: Contributes only to pre-selected organizations.
Officers: Richard Raynor, Pres.; Dave Gillespie, Secy.; Geoffrey Raynor, Treas.
Directors: Kim Baldi, Barbara Raynor.
EIN: 752905762

51290
Brandenburg Life Foundation
4545 Biltmore Dr.
Frisco, TX 75034
E-mail: davidbra@sprynet.com
Contact: David Warren Brandenburg, Pres.

Established in 1996 in TX.
Donor(s): David Brandenburg, Inet, Inc., InterVoice, Inc.
Financial data (yr. ended 12/31/01): Grants paid, $138,075; assets, $3,148,332 (M); gifts received, $61,686; expenditures, $188,530; qualifying distributions, $183,746.
Limitations: Applications not accepted.
Application information: Contributes only to pre-selected organizations.
Officers and Directors:* David Warren Brandenburg,* Pres.; Diana Brandenburg,* V.P. and Secy.-Treas.; Geraldine Gurney.
EIN: 752651513
Codes: FD2

51291
The Krist Foundation
2525 Bay Area Blvd., Ste. 410
Houston, TX 77058 (281) 283-8500
Contact: Ronald D. Krist, Pres.

Established in 1998 in TX.
Donor(s): Ronald D. Krist.
Financial data (yr. ended 03/31/01): Grants paid, $138,075; assets, $780,281 (M); expenditures, $140,405; qualifying distributions, $137,670.
Limitations: Giving primarily in TX.
Officer and Directors:* Ronald D. Krist,* Pres.; Carole D. Krist, Karyn D. Krist, Kevin D. Krist, Scott C. Krist.
EIN: 311594569
Codes: FD2

51292
The Littlestar Foundation
c/o Deborah Jackson Littlestar
31721 Wild Oak Hill
Fair Oaks Ranch, TX 78015

Established in 1997 in CO.
Financial data (yr. ended 10/31/01): Grants paid, $137,895; assets, $2,114,076 (L); expenditures, $145,387; qualifying distributions, $137,257.
Limitations: Applications not accepted. Giving primarily in CO, IL and TX.
Application information: Contributes only to pre-selected organizations.
Officers: Deborah Jackson Littlestar, Pres. and Treas.; Mark Lynn Littlestar, V.P. and Secy.; Sharon K. Roshek, V.P.
EIN: 841441054
Codes: FD2

51293
Glenn & Dee Simmons Foundation, Inc.
5430 LBJ Fwy., Ste. 1700
Dallas, TX 75240-2697 (972) 450-4206
Contact: Sandra K. Myers, Secy.

Established in 1997 in TX.
Donor(s): Glenn R. Simmons.
Financial data (yr. ended 12/31/01): Grants paid, $137,400; assets, $151,747 (M); gifts received, $120,000; expenditures, $137,405; qualifying distributions, $137,363.
Limitations: Giving primarily in OK and TX.
Application information: Application form not required.
Officers: Glenn R. Simmons, Pres. and Treas.; Diane C. Simmons, V.P.; Sandra K. Myers, Secy.
EIN: 752738525

51294
Loring Cook Foundation
P.O. Box 1060
McAllen, TX 78505
Scholarship application address: c/o Counselor, McAllen Memorial High School, McAllen, TX 78501, tel.: (956) 686-5491

Incorporated in 1953 in TX.
Financial data (yr. ended 03/31/01): Grants paid, $137,236; assets, $4,002,895 (M); expenditures, $181,301; qualifying distributions, $138,444.
Limitations: Giving primarily in TX.
Application information: Application form required for scholarships.
Officers: Carolyn Cook Landrum, Chair.; Kathleen Cook Colins, Pres.; Samuel Dalton, V.P.; James W. Collins, Treas.
EIN: 746050063
Codes: FD2, GTI

51295
T. C. Lupton, Jr. Family Foundation
3811 Turtle Creek Blvd., LB 29
Dallas, TX 75219
Contact: Carol L. Huckin, Pres.

Established in 1994 in TX.
Donor(s): T.C. Lupton, Jr., Carolyn C. Lupton.
Financial data (yr. ended 06/30/01): Grants paid, $136,900; assets, $2,358,719 (M); gifts received, $100,000; expenditures, $159,959; qualifying distributions, $135,900.
Limitations: Applications not accepted. Giving primarily in Dallas, TX.
Application information: Contributes only to pre-selected organizations.
Officers: T.C. Lupton, Jr., Chair.; Carol L. Huckin, Pres.; Carolyn C. Lupton, Secy.
Directors: Laurie L. Liedtke, Tav C. Lupton III.
EIN: 752549244
Codes: FD2

51296
Denison Community Foundation
313 W. Woodard
Denison, TX 75020

Financial data (yr. ended 09/30/00): Grants paid, $136,875; assets, $151,172 (M); gifts received, $144,000; expenditures, $194,959.
Limitations: Giving limited to the Denison, TX area.
Officers: Carol Shaffer, Chair.; Anna McKinney, Pres. and Secy.; Kathy, Yates, Treas.
Board Members: Andrea Bratcher, Sherry Christie, Norman Gordon, Martha Landrum, Marsha Perkins, Donna Perry, Herman Ringler.
EIN: 752146358
Codes: CM, FD2

51297
Jere W. and Margaret D. Thompson Foundation
12225 Greenville Ave., Ste. 440
Dallas, TX 75243
Application address: 3838 Oak Lawn Ave., Ste. 1850, Dallas, TX 75219
Contact: Jere W. Thompson, Pres.

Established in 1997 in TX.
Donor(s): Jere W. Thompson, Margaret D. Thompson.
Financial data (yr. ended 12/31/00): Grants paid, $136,120; assets, $61,074 (M); gifts received, $65,213; expenditures, $139,120; qualifying distributions, $136,081.
Limitations: Giving primarily in TX.
Application information: Application form not required.
Officers: Jere W. Thompson, Pres.; Margaret D. Thompson, V.P.; Michael D. Thompson, Secy.; Dean A. Renkes, Treas.
EIN: 311527336
Codes: FD2

51298
Veritas Foundation, Inc.
602 W. 13th St.
Austin, TX 78701 (512) 472-1877
Contact: Diana Kay Crow, Pres.; or Deborah A. Grote, Secy.

Established in 1983 in TX.
Donor(s): Joe Crow.‡
Financial data (yr. ended 12/31/00): Grants paid, $136,079; assets, $2,537,779 (M); expenditures, $196,765; qualifying distributions, $171,299.
Limitations: Giving primarily in Austin, TX.
Application information: Application form not required.
Officers and Directors:* Diana Kay Crow,* Pres. and Exec. Dir.; J.A. Crow,* V.P.; Deborah A. Grote,* Secy.; Chris Crow,* Treas.
EIN: 742254024
Codes: FD2

51299
Foundation for the Advancement of Christianity
1213 Chatsworth Dr.
Colleyville, TX 76034-4272 (817) 498-8690
Contact: Burton H. Patterson, Tr.

Established in 1999 in TX.
Donor(s): Burton H. Patterson, Virginia L. Patterson.
Financial data (yr. ended 12/31/01): Grants paid, $135,720; assets, $2,363,289 (M); expenditures, $249,787; qualifying distributions, $135,720; giving activities include $30,000 for programs.
Limitations: Applications not accepted. Giving primarily in TX.
Application information: Unsolicited requests for funds not accepted.
Trustees: Burton H. Patterson, Frank W. Patterson, Virginia L. Patterson.
EIN: 742869512
Codes: FD2

51300
H. E. Stumberg, Sr. Orphans, Crippled Children & Handicapped Persons Trust
310 S. St. Mary's St., Ste. 701
San Antonio, TX 78205-3164
FAX: (210) 225-2556
Contact: Louis H. Stumberg, Tr.

Established in 1960 in TX.
Donor(s): Louis H. Stumberg, H. E. Stumberg.‡
Financial data (yr. ended 12/31/01): Grants paid, $135,600; assets, $2,440,502 (M); expenditures, $151,118; qualifying distributions, $144,493.
Limitations: Giving limited to Bexar County, TX.

Publications: Annual report.
Application information: Application form not required.
Trustees: Belle Stumberg Berg, Louis H. Stumberg, Jr., Louis H. Stumberg.
EIN: 746063272
Codes: FD2

51301
Fifth Avenue Foundation
801 Cherry St., Ste. 2100
Fort Worth, TX 76102 (817) 877-2814
FAX: (817) 877-2807
Contact: Whitfield J. Collins, Pres.

Established in 1979 in TX.
Donor(s): Pauline G. Evans.‡
Financial data (yr. ended 12/31/01): Grants paid, $135,500; assets, $1,294,060 (M); expenditures, $156,086; qualifying distributions, $140,465.
Limitations: Giving limited to local organizations in the Dallas-Fort Worth, TX, area and also to national organizations.
Application information: Application form not required.
Officers and Directors:* Whitfield J. Collins,* Pres.; Marie Harper,* V.P.
EIN: 751659424
Codes: FD2

51302
Essar Foundation
P.O. Box 1310
Beaumont, TX 77704-8311

Established in 1984 in TX.
Donor(s): S.J. Rogers.
Financial data (yr. ended 12/31/01): Grants paid, $135,460; assets, $716,396 (M); expenditures, $136,416; qualifying distributions, $134,922.
Limitations: Applications not accepted. Giving primarily in Beaumont, Hitchcock, and Houston, TX.
Application information: Contributes only to pre-selected organizations.
Trustees: Jordan Rogers, S.J. Rogers.
EIN: 760101655
Codes: FD2

51303
Reed Charitable Foundation
P.O. Box 2169
Frisco, TX 75034

Established in 1996 in TX.
Donor(s): Lyle D. Reed, Nellie Rosalie Reed.
Financial data (yr. ended 12/31/01): Grants paid, $135,000; assets, $2,639,476 (M); expenditures, $150,238; qualifying distributions, $135,000.
Limitations: Applications not accepted. Giving on a national basis.
Application information: Contributes only to pre-selected organizations.
Trustee: James W. Reed III.
Advisory Committee Members: Lyle D. Reed, Nellie Rosalie Reed.
EIN: 752663460
Codes: FD2

51304
Alpert Family Foundation
5301 Hollister, Ste. 300
Houston, TX 77040

Established in 1995 in TX.
Donor(s): Robert Alpert.
Financial data (yr. ended 11/30/00): Grants paid, $134,500; assets, $1,512,823 (M); expenditures, $150,469; qualifying distributions, $134,550.
Limitations: Applications not accepted. Giving primarily in TX.

Application information: Contributes only to pre-selected organizations.
Officers: Robert Alpert, Pres.; Hillary Harriman Alpert, V.P.; Linda Stanley, Secy.
EIN: 760421101
Codes: FD2

51305
Joe B. Foster Family Foundation
10000 Memorial Dr., Ste. 520
Houston, TX 77024
Contact: Joe B. Foster, Pres.

Established in 1998 in TX.
Donor(s): Joe B. Foster.
Financial data (yr. ended 04/30/01): Grants paid, $134,500; assets, $3,144,164 (M); expenditures, $155,067; qualifying distributions, $133,590.
Limitations: Applications not accepted. Giving primarily in Austin and Houston, TX.
Application information: Contributes only to pre-selected organizations.
Officer and Director:* Joe B. Foster,* Pres.
EIN: 760538109
Codes: FD2

51306
The Arch L. Ferguson Foundation
601 E. Abram St.
Arlington, TX 76010

Established in 1970.
Donor(s): Edwin V. Bonneau, Mrs. Edwin V. Bonneau, Snyder Church of Christ, Victoria Church of Christ.
Financial data (yr. ended 12/31/00): Grants paid, $134,372; assets, $6,512,729 (M); gifts received, $15,653; expenditures, $303,139; qualifying distributions, $261,212.
Limitations: Applications not accepted. Giving on a national and international basis.
Application information: Contributes only to pre-selected organizations and individuals.
Officers and Directors:* Wayne Hood,* Pres.; Gary Hood,* V.P. and Mgr.; Delos Johnson,* V.P.; Edwin V. Bonneau,* Secy.-Treas.; Quinton Gage, Scott Gage.
EIN: 237103241
Codes: FD2, GTI

51307
The Gray Foundation
P.O. Box 45
Houston, TX 77001

Established in approximately 1960 in TX.
Donor(s): Elaine H. Gray,‡ James A. Gray.‡
Financial data (yr. ended 08/31/01): Grants paid, $134,000; assets, $2,674,963 (M); expenditures, $146,362; qualifying distributions, $134,000.
Limitations: Applications not accepted. Giving primarily in LA and TX.
Application information: Contributes only to pre-selected organizations.
Officer: Emily Gray Elmore, Pres.
EIN: 746040504
Codes: FD2

51308
The Jackson Foundation
5005 Woodway, Ste. 200
Houston, TX 77056-1789 (713) 850-9033
Application address: P.O. Box 42808, Houston, TX 77242-2808; FAX: (713) 850-1527; E-mail: information@thejacksonfoundation.org; URL: http://www.thejacksonfoundation.org
Contact: Carol Deason, Secy.-Treas.

Established in 1998 in TX.

Financial data (yr. ended 09/30/01): Grants paid, $134,000; assets, $2,124,815 (M); expenditures, $206,663; qualifying distributions, $158,535.
Limitations: Giving primarily in TX.
Publications: Financial statement, grants list, application guidelines.
Application information: Application form required.
Officers and Directors:* Douglas Blake Jackson,* Pres.; Donald L. Blair,* V.P.; Paul Jornayvaz,* V.P.; Carol Deason,* Secy.-Treas.; Tom Martin.
EIN: 760554322
Codes: FD2

51309
The Boyd and Joan Kelley Charitable Foundation
516 Gazelle Trail
Harker Heights, TX 76548

Established in 1998.
Financial data (yr. ended 12/31/01): Grants paid, $133,532; assets, $2,809,587 (M); gifts received, $2,834,600; expenditures, $152,679; qualifying distributions, $133,532.
Limitations: Applications not accepted. Giving primarily in TX.
Application information: Contributes only to pre-selected organizations.
Officer and Trustee:* Oliver Kelly,* Mgr.
EIN: 742897733
Codes: FD2

51310
Ferguson Sports Foundation, Inc.
490 Park St.
Beaumont, TX 77704

Established in 1999 in TX.
Donor(s): Paul F. Ferguson, Jr.
Financial data (yr. ended 03/31/01): Grants paid, $132,869; assets, $96,798 (M); gifts received, $86,862; expenditures, $168,671; qualifying distributions, $161,671.
Limitations: Applications not accepted. Giving primarily in Beaumont, TX.
Application information: Contributes only to pre-selected organizations.
Officers: Paul F. Ferguson, Jr., Pres. and Secy.-Treas.; Kara L. Ferguson, V.P.
EIN: 760620856
Codes: FD2

51311
The Bonita and Jeff Garvey Family Foundation
701 Brazos St., Ste. 1400
Austin, TX 78701 (512) 485-1900
Contact: Jeff Garvey, Pres.

Established in 1999 in TX.
Donor(s): Jeff Garvey, Bonita Garvey.
Financial data (yr. ended 12/31/01): Grants paid, $132,279; assets, $826,851 (M); gifts received, $2,000; expenditures, $139,836; qualifying distributions, $132,024.
Limitations: Giving primarily in TX.
Officer: Jeff Garvey, Pres.
Directors: Joseph Aragona, Bonita Garvey.
EIN: 742933953
Codes: FD2

51312
Mariposa Foundation
221 W. 6th St., Ste. 1450
Austin, TX 78701-3403

Established in 1997 in TX.
Donor(s): Jack D. Howard, Jr.
Financial data (yr. ended 12/31/00): Grants paid, $132,183; assets, $147,129 (M); expenditures, $133,251; qualifying distributions, $132,183.

Limitations: Applications not accepted. Giving primarily in Austin, TX.
Application information: Contributes only to pre-selected organizations.
Officers: Jack D. Howard, Jr., Pres.; Julia Rankin Howard, V.P.
Director: Bradley Schlosser.
EIN: 742828019
Codes: FD2

51313
Julia and Albert Smith Foundation
c/o The Inwood Management LP
3100 Richmond Ave., Ste. 405
Houston, TX 77098 (713) 655-0383

Established in 1986 in TX.
Donor(s): Albert J. Smith III, Gwendolyn Smith, Albert J. Smith, Jr., Julia C. Smith.
Financial data (yr. ended 11/30/01): Grants paid, $132,000; assets, $3,002,807 (M); expenditures, $175,657; qualifying distributions, $136,922.
Limitations: Applications not accepted. Giving primarily in Houston, TX.
Application information: Contributes only to pre-selected organizations.
Officers and Directors:* Julia C. Smith, Pres.; Albert J. Smith, Jr., Secy.-Treas.; Julia Anne Stuckey,* Mgr.; Albert J. Smith III, William C. Smith.
EIN: 760207247
Codes: FD2

51314
Medallion Foundation, Inc.
24 Greenway Plz., Ste. 1509
Houston, TX 77046-2098

Established in 1984 in TX.
Donor(s): H.S. Finkelstein.
Financial data (yr. ended 09/30/01): Grants paid, $131,153; assets, $649,358 (M); expenditures, $392,284; qualifying distributions, $136,146.
Limitations: Applications not accepted. Giving on a national basis.
Application information: Contributes only to pre-selected organizations.
Officers and Directors:* Philip A. Donis,* Pres.; H.S. Finkelstein,* V.P. and Secy.-Treas.; Mark L. Entman,* V.P.; Robert J. Pilegee,* V.P.
EIN: 760141071
Codes: FD2

51315
LSF Foundation
3 Ourlane Pl.
Houston, TX 77024
Contact: Mark A. Frantz, Pres.

Established in 1996 in TX.
Donor(s): Lisa S. Frantz.
Financial data (yr. ended 06/30/01): Grants paid, $131,000; assets, $2,441,672 (M); gifts received, $6,000; expenditures, $141,384; qualifying distributions, $131,000.
Limitations: Giving primarily in TX, with emphasis on Houston.
Application information: Application form not required.
Officers: Mark A. Frantz, Pres.; Lisa S. Frantz, Secy.; Carol Cantrell, Treas.
EIN: 760506645
Codes: FD2

51316
Pat and Tom Frost Foundation
c/o Frost Financial Mgmt. Svcs.
P.O. Box 2950
San Antonio, TX 78299

Established in 1994 in TX.

Donor(s): Patricia H. Frost, Thomas C. Frost.
Financial data (yr. ended 12/31/01): Grants paid, $130,348; assets, $3,373,559 (M); gifts received, $30,470; expenditures, $153,926; qualifying distributions, $130,348.
Limitations: Applications not accepted. Giving primarily in San Antonio, TX.
Application information: Contributes only to pre-selected organizations.
Trustees: Patricia H. Frost, Thomas C. Frost.
EIN: 742699577
Codes: FD2

51317
L. A. Long Trust
c/o First National Bank
P.O. Box 540
Graham, TX 76450-0540
Application address: c/o School Board of Trustees, Graham Independent School District, Graham, TX 76450

Established in 1967 in TX.
Donor(s): L.A. Long.‡
Financial data (yr. ended 07/31/01): Grants paid, $130,343; assets, $601,995 (M); expenditures, $159,080; qualifying distributions, $145,119; giving activities include $130,343 for loans to individuals.
Limitations: Giving limited to residents of Young County, TX.
Trustee: First National Bank.
EIN: 750399970
Codes: GTI

51318
Davis Charitable Trust
c/o Northern Trust Bank of TX
600 Congress Ave., Ste. 1820
Austin, TX 78701

Established in 1997 in TX.
Donor(s): Ira Davis.‡
Financial data (yr. ended 12/31/00): Grants paid, $129,581; assets, $4,520,327 (M); gifts received, $2,564,908; expenditures, $167,491; qualifying distributions, $163,348.
Limitations: Applications not accepted. Giving primarily in Austin, TX.
Application information: Contributes only to pre-selected organizations.
Trustees: JPMorgan Chase Bank, Northern Trust Co. of Texas.
EIN: 746456780
Codes: FD2

51319
Marian Meaker Apteckar Foundation
c/o JPMorgan Chase Bank
P.O. Box 140
El Paso, TX 79980

Established in 1996 in TX.
Financial data (yr. ended 05/31/01): Grants paid, $129,446; assets, $2,336,513 (M); expenditures, $159,636; qualifying distributions, $146,048.
Limitations: Applications not accepted. Giving on a national basis with some emphasis on El Paso, TX.
Application information: Contributes only to pre-selected organizations.
Trustee: JPMorgan Chase Bank.
EIN: 742060589
Codes: FD2

51320
Michael L. Rosenberg Foundation
P.O. Box 794186
Dallas, TX 75379-4186

Established in 1997 in TX.

Donor(s): Sonia Rosenberg.
Financial data (yr. ended 12/31/99): Grants paid, $129,406; assets, $3,544,760 (M); gifts received, $550; expenditures, $156,868; qualifying distributions, $128,905.
Limitations: Applications not accepted. Giving primarily in TX.
Application information: Contributes only to pre-selected organizations.
Officers and Directors:* Michael L. Rosenberg,* Pres.; Lawrence Barzune, M.D.,* V.P.; Stanford M. Kaufman,* Secy.-Treas.
EIN: 752736174
Codes: FD2

51321
The Bob Gunn Foundation
P.O. Box 97508
Wichita Falls, TX 76308

Established in 2000 in TX.
Donor(s): Robert D. Gunn.
Financial data (yr. ended 12/31/00): Grants paid, $129,100; assets, $371,205 (M); gifts received, $500,000; expenditures, $129,100; qualifying distributions, $129,100.
Limitations: Applications not accepted. Giving primarily in Wichita Falls, TX.
Application information: Contributes only to pre-selected organizations.
Officer: Robert D. Gunn, Pres. and Secy.-Treas.
Directors: Vincent C. Gunn, William C. Gunn.
EIN: 752836910
Codes: FD2

51322
Forrest Foundation
P.O. Box 193, Rte. 2
Slaton, TX 79364
Contact: Lynn Forrest, Tr.

Established in 1953.
Financial data (yr. ended 06/30/01): Grants paid, $128,850; assets, $926,799 (M); expenditures, $157,102; qualifying distributions, $128,258.
Limitations: Giving primarily in TX.
Application information: Application form not required.
Trustees: Mary Jo English, Bernice Forrest, Lynn Forrest, Marianne F. Loveless, Jean McNeely.
EIN: 756021465
Codes: FD2

51323
Red River Valley Council for the Aid of Persons with Mental Problems, Inc.
Box 1015
Paris, TX 75461-1015 (903) 784-8035
Contact: Dub Bassett

Established in 1975 in TX.
Financial data (yr. ended 12/31/01): Grants paid, $128,772; assets, $3,039,062 (M); expenditures, $150,727; qualifying distributions, $132,482.
Limitations: Giving primarily in southeastern OK and northeastern TX.
Application information: Application form not required.
Officers and Members:* Bobby R. Walters,* Chair.; Joe Pogue, Vice-Chair.; L.W. Bassett, Jr.,* Treas.; and 11 additional board members.
EIN: 237455279
Codes: FD2

51324
Webber Foundation
2001 Kirby Dr., Ste. 1200
Houston, TX 77019 (713) 528-6875
Contact: W. Temple Webber, Jr., Pres.

Established in 1956.

Financial data (yr. ended 12/31/01): Grants paid, $128,700; assets, $711,806 (M); expenditures, $130,964; qualifying distributions, $128,550.
Limitations: Giving primarily in Houston, TX.
Application information: Application form not required.
Officers: W. Temple Webber, Jr., Pres.; Barbara C. Webber, V.P.; W. Temple Webber III, Secy.-Treas.
EIN: 756036145
Codes: FD2

51325
The Scott Petty Foundation
711 Navarro St., Ste. 235
San Antonio, TX 78205
Contact: Scott Petty, Jr., Dir.

Established in 1980 in TX.
Donor(s): Edwina H. Petty, O.S. Petty,‡ Scott Petty, Jr.
Financial data (yr. ended 11/30/01): Grants paid, $128,600; assets, $2,414,845 (M); expenditures, $170,775; qualifying distributions, $127,983.
Limitations: Applications not accepted. Giving primarily in San Antonio, TX.
Directors: Edwina H. Petty, Eleanor O. Petty, Scott Petty, Jr.
EIN: 742146978
Codes: FD2

51326
Ed and Gladys Hurley Trust Foundation
c/o Bank of America
P.O. Box 830241
Dallas, TX 75283-0241 (214) 209-6486
Contact: Gary E. Melle, Tr. Off., Bank of America

Established in 1957 in TX.
Donor(s): Ed E. Hurley.‡
Financial data (yr. ended 08/31/01): Grants paid, $128,500; assets, $2,868,651 (M); expenditures, $155,658; qualifying distributions, $134,012.
Limitations: Giving limited to TX.
Publications: Informational brochure (including application guidelines).
Application information: Loan applicants apply for funds through their respective schools. Application form required.
Trustee: Bank of America.
EIN: 756006961
Codes: FD2, GTI

51327
Kahng Foundation
c/o Choonja Kahng
9707 Crenata Cove
Austin, TX 78759-6267
Contact: Peter Kahng, Tr.

Established in 1998 in TX.
Donor(s): Choonja Kahng, Stephen Kahng.
Financial data (yr. ended 12/31/01): Grants paid, $128,350; assets, $1,314,319 (M); expenditures, $130,020; qualifying distributions, $128,350.
Limitations: Giving primarily in CA and MA.
Officer: Choonja Kahng, Pres.
Trustees: Peter Kahng, Stephen Kahng.
EIN: 742883492
Codes: FD2

51328
Edward G. and Kathryn E. Mader Foundation
c/o Bank of America
P.O. Box 831041
Dallas, TX 75283-1041
Application address: c/o Mader Foundation, P.O. Box 6645, Lee's Summit, MO 64064, URL: http://www.maderfoundation.org

Established in 2000 in MO.
Donor(s): Kathryn E. Mader, Kathryn E. Mader Trust.
Financial data (yr. ended 12/31/01): Grants paid, $128,010; assets, $2,559,653 (M); gifts received, $44,510; expenditures, $209,113; qualifying distributions, $13,159.
Limitations: Giving primarily in eastern Jackson County, MO.
Application information: Application form required.
Officers: Kathryn E. Mader, Chair. and Pres.; Janice Kay Mader, V.P.; John G. Mader, V.P.; Lisa Leeann Mader, V.P.; David A. Schaeffer, V.P.; Melissa D. Mader-Schaefer, Secy.; Michael J. Mader, Treas.
EIN: 431870924
Codes: FD2

51329
The Lester Foundation
5906 Green Tree Rd.
Houston, TX 77057-1416 (713) 782-7620
Contact: Earl L. Lester, Jr.

Established in 2000 in TX.
Donor(s): Earl L. Lester, Jr.
Financial data (yr. ended 12/31/01): Grants paid, $127,875; assets, $739,303 (M); gifts received, $513,286; expenditures, $141,255; qualifying distributions, $127,875.
Board Members: John I. Griffin, Linda L. Griffin, Earl L. Lester, Jr., Mary G. Lester.
EIN: 760640698

51330
Graham Benevolent Foundation
P.O. Box 1567
Graham, TX 76450

Established in 1928 in TX.
Donor(s): M.K. Graham.‡
Financial data (yr. ended 12/31/01): Grants paid, $127,700; assets, $2,451,005 (M); expenditures, $130,553; qualifying distributions, $130,553.
Limitations: Applications not accepted. Giving limited to Graham, TX.
Application information: Contributes only to pre-selected organizations.
Officers: N.D. Stovall, Jr., Pres.; E.S. Graham III, Secy.
EIN: 756022754
Codes: FD2

51331
Paul & Kathryn Redmon Family Foundation
6707 Barlett Rd.
Katy, TX 77493

Established in 1996 in TX.
Donor(s): Paul Redmon, Kathryn Redmon.
Financial data (yr. ended 11/30/01): Grants paid, $127,625; assets, $1,886,244 (M); gifts received, $1,765,975; expenditures, $150,392; qualifying distributions, $127,625.
Limitations: Applications not accepted. Giving primarily in Katy, TX.
Application information: Contributes only to pre-selected organizations.
Officer and Trustees:* Paul Redmon,* Mgr.; Kathryn Redmon.
EIN: 760515036
Codes: FD2

51332
Los Trigos Fund
c/o Gayle D. Fogelson
300 Crescent Ct., Ste. 920
Dallas, TX 75201-7851

Established in 1990 in TX.
Donor(s): Gayle D. Fogelson.
Financial data (yr. ended 12/31/00): Grants paid, $127,184; assets, $262,057 (M); expenditures, $144,414; qualifying distributions, $132,196.
Limitations: Applications not accepted. Giving on a national basis, primarily in NM and TX.
Application information: Contributes only to pre-selected organizations.
Officer and Trustee:* Gayle D. Fogelson,* Mgr.
EIN: 752339010
Codes: FD2

51333
Riepe Family Foundation
16025 Tahoe Ave.
Houston, TX 77040 (713) 466-9764
Contact: Randall S. Riepe, Pres.

Established in 1997 in TX.
Donor(s): Randall S. Riepe, Deanna L. Riepe.
Financial data (yr. ended 12/31/01): Grants paid, $127,000; assets, $1,049,439 (M); gifts received, $3,071; expenditures, $277,035; qualifying distributions, $127,000.
Officers: Randall S. Riepe, Pres. and Treas.; Deanna L. Riepe, V.P.; Christian S. Riefe, Secy.
EIN: 760538128

51334
The Poujol Foundation
8733 Daffodil
Houston, TX 77063 (713) 977-0610
Contact: Albert C. Poujol, Treas.

Financial data (yr. ended 06/30/01): Grants paid, $126,522; assets, $99,098 (M); gifts received, $100,500; expenditures, $126,556; qualifying distributions, $126,522.
Limitations: Giving primarily in TX.
Application information: For scholarships: two letters of recommendation from unrelated sources and estimate of the applicant's parents' income for the current and two preceding years.
Officers: Michael A. Poujol, Pres.; Melissa A. Poujol, V.P.; Angela G. Poujol, Secy.; Albert C. Poujol, Treas.
EIN: 311562146
Codes: FD2

51335
Diana and Richard C. Strauss Foundation
8401 N. Central Expwy., Ste. 350
Dallas, TX 75225 (214) 292-3400
Contact: Richard C. Strauss, Pres.

Established in 1997 in TX.
Donor(s): Richard C. Strauss, Diana Strauss, Jenifer Strauss, Staci Strauss, Tania Strauss.
Financial data (yr. ended 12/31/01): Grants paid, $126,500; assets, $162,301 (M); gifts received, $100,000; expenditures, $130,957; qualifying distributions, $127,125.
Limitations: Giving primarily in TX.
Application information: Application form required.
Officers and Directors:* Diana Strauss,* Chair. and Secy.; Richard C. Strauss,* Pres.; Jenifer Strauss,* V.P.; Staci Strauss,* V.P.; Tania Strauss,* V.P.; Ronald G. Steinhart.
EIN: 752734838
Codes: FD2

51336
The Eva and Marvin Womack Foundation
4305 Waterford Pl.
Austin, TX 78731

Established in 1997 in TX.
Donor(s): Eva Robuck Womack, R. Marvin Womack.
Financial data (yr. ended 12/31/01): Grants paid, $126,500; assets, $3,028,341 (M); gifts received,

51336—TEXAS

$438,460; expenditures, $128,636; qualifying distributions, $123,036.
Limitations: Applications not accepted. Giving on a national basis.
Application information: Contributes only to pre-selected organizations.
Officers and Directors:* R. Marvin Womack,* Pres.; Eva Robuck Womack,* Secy.; Deanna Lynn Womack, Michael Scott Womack.
EIN: 742831302
Codes: FD2

51337
The Kuli Family Foundation
c/o Alex S. Kuli
100 Congress Ave., Ste. 930
Austin, TX 78701

Established in 1997 in TX.
Donor(s): Alex S. Kuli, Gladys B. Kuli.
Financial data (yr. ended 12/31/01): Grants paid, $126,384; assets, $640,040 (M); expenditures, $131,862; qualifying distributions, $126,384.
Limitations: Applications not accepted. Giving on a national basis, with emphasis on ME and MN.
Application information: Contributes only to pre-selected organizations.
Officers: Alex S. Kuli, Pres.; Gladys B. Kuli, V.P.; Geoffery C. Kuli, Secy.
EIN: 742833211

51338
Eugene Straus Charitable Trust
c/o Bank of America
P.O. Box 830241
Dallas, TX 75283-1041 (214) 209-1965
Contact: Daniel J. Kelly, V.P., Bank of America

Trust established in 1975 in TX.
Donor(s): Eugene Straus.‡
Financial data (yr. ended 08/31/01): Grants paid, $126,000; assets, $2,114,299 (M); expenditures, $150,063; qualifying distributions, $128,074.
Limitations: Giving limited to Dallas County, TX.
Publications: Application guidelines.
Application information: Application form not required.
Trustee: Bank of America.
EIN: 756229249
Codes: FD2

51339
Charles Thomas & Mary Alice Pearson Educational Foundation
c/o Bank of America
P.O. Box 831041
Dallas, TX 75283-1041
Application address: c/o Jones & Jones, P.O. Box 1284, Fayetteville, AR 72702

Established around 1994 in AR.
Donor(s): Mary Alice Pearson, Mrs. Charles Turner.
Financial data (yr. ended 05/31/01): Grants paid, $125,500; assets, $1,554,127 (M); expenditures, $150,412; qualifying distributions, $128,266.
Limitations: Giving limited to Fayetteville, AR.
Trustee: Bank of America.
EIN: 710738555
Codes: FD2, GTI

51340
David D. & Nona S. Payne Foundation, Inc.
Hughes Bldg., Ste. 440-A
Pampa, TX 79065 (806) 665-9764
Application address: 2000 Charles St., Pampa, TX 79065, tel.: (806) 665-3488
Contact: Adelaide S. Colwell, Secy.

Established in 1980 in TX.
Donor(s): Nona S. Payne.‡

Financial data (yr. ended 06/30/02): Grants paid, $125,400; assets, $2,296,215 (M); expenditures, $144,840; qualifying distributions, $123,540.
Limitations: Giving primarily in the TX Panhandle area.
Publications: Financial statement, grants list.
Application information: Application form required.
Officers and Trustees:* Vanessa G. Buzzard,* Pres.; Rebecca L. Holmes,* V.P. and Treas.; Adelaide S. Colwell,* Secy.
EIN: 751736339
Codes: FD2

51341
Joseph Platt Turner, Jr. & Kathryn Moore Turner Foundation
3210 Slough Dr.
Temple, TX 76502-3980

Established in 1990 in TX.
Donor(s): Joseph Platt Turner, Jr., Kathryn Moore Turner.
Financial data (yr. ended 05/31/01): Grants paid, $125,000; assets, $934,319 (M); gifts received, $45,297; expenditures, $128,694; qualifying distributions, $124,768.
Limitations: Applications not accepted. Giving primarily in Mars Hill, TX.
Application information: Contributes only to pre-selected organizations.
Officers: J. Platt Turner, Pres.; Kathryn Moore Turner, V.P.; Mary K. Conner, Secy.; Martha T. Manley, Treas.
EIN: 742576598
Codes: FD2

51342
The John W. and Nellie Akin Foundation
(Formerly The Akin Foundation)
P.O. Box 3020
Lufkin, TX 75903-3020

Incorporated in 1948 in TX.
Donor(s): J.W. Akin.
Financial data (yr. ended 12/31/01): Grants paid, $124,700; assets, $0 (M); expenditures, $194,760; qualifying distributions, $124,700.
Limitations: Applications not accepted. Giving on a national basis, with some emphasis on TX.
Application information: Contributes only to pre-selected organizations.
Trustees: Harold Fite, Fred A. Hutson, Harold J. Pickup, Jr., James D. Yates.
EIN: 756036487
Codes: FD2

51343
Mercy International
304 Tower Dr.
San Antonio, TX 78232
Contact: John H. Leininger, Dir.

Established in 1992 in TX.
Donor(s): John H. Leininger, Diane J. Leininger.
Financial data (yr. ended 12/31/01): Grants paid, $124,197; assets, $2,273,586 (M); gifts received, $11,000; expenditures, $141,063; qualifying distributions, $124,197.
Limitations: Applications not accepted. Giving primarily in FL and TX.
Application information: Unsolicited requests for funds not accepted.
Directors: Diane J. Leininger, Jeffrey E. Leininger, John H. Leininger.
EIN: 742633786
Codes: FD2

51344
Wood Family Memorial Trust
P.O. Box 1338
Victoria, TX 77902 (361) 572-6539
Application address: 101 S. Main, Victoria, TX 77901
Contact: Richard T. "Terry" Cullen, Tr.

Established in 1981.
Financial data (yr. ended 11/30/01): Grants paid, $123,417; assets, $3,536,228 (M); expenditures, $160,720; qualifying distributions, $123,417.
Limitations: Giving primarily in Victoria, TX.
Application information: Application form required.
Trustees: Richard T. "Terry" Cullen, Elvin "Al" Koehn.
EIN: 746307476
Codes: FD2

51345
Gene Conley Foundation
c/o Wells Fargo Bank Texas, N.A.
P.O. Box 9129
Wichita Falls, TX 76308-9129 (940) 766-8310
Contact: Jerry Schnedorf, V.P., Well Fargo Bank Texas, N.A.

Established in 1989 in TX.
Financial data (yr. ended 12/31/01): Grants paid, $123,339; assets, $2,874,155 (M); expenditures, $141,107; qualifying distributions, $138,605.
Limitations: Giving primarily in northern TX.
Application information: Application form required.
Trustee: Wells Fargo Bank Texas, N.A.
Board Members: Mike Elvea, Sandy Goff, Barry Plaxco, Diane A. Prothro, David I. Ramsey, Joseph N. Sherrill, Jr., Stan S. West.
EIN: 752224430
Codes: FD2

51346
Hill Foundation
1601 Elm St., Ste. 5000
Dallas, TX 75201-7254
Contact: Lyda Hill, V.P.

Established in 1954.
Donor(s): Margaret Hunt Hill.
Financial data (yr. ended 02/28/01): Grants paid, $122,504; assets, $1,625,985 (M); expenditures, $123,962; qualifying distributions, $122,504.
Limitations: Applications not accepted. Giving primarily in Cold Springs, CO, and Dallas, TX.
Application information: Contributes only to pre-selected organizations.
Officers and Trustees:* Margaret Hunt Hill,* Chair. and Pres.; Lyda Hill, Vice-Chair. and V.P.; Alinda Wikert, Secy.-Treas.; Al G. Hill, Jr., M.E. Nugent.
EIN: 756010533
Codes: FD2

51347
The Carolyn and Mike Maples Foundation
2208 Windsor Rd.
Austin, TX 78703
Contact: Mike Maples, Tr.

Established in 2000 in TX.
Donor(s): Jane Carolyn Maples, Michael J. Maples.
Financial data (yr. ended 04/30/01): Grants paid, $122,435; assets, $1,301,972 (M); gifts received, $1,317,694; expenditures, $128,082; qualifying distributions, $122,435.
Limitations: Giving on a national basis, with some emphasis on TX.
Trustees: Jane Carolyn Maples, Michael J. Maples.
EIN: 916500136
Codes: FD2

51348
The New Covenant Foundation
1412 Main St., Ste. 905
Dallas, TX 75202

Established in 2000 in TX.
Donor(s): George E. Seay, Jr., George E. Seay III.
Financial data (yr. ended 12/31/01): Grants paid, $122,189; assets, $1,790,129 (M); gifts received, $10,000; expenditures, $136,620; qualifying distributions, $122,189.
Limitations: Applications not accepted. Giving primarily in TX.
Application information: Contributes only to pre-selected organizations.
Trustees: George E. Seay, Jr., George E. Seay III, Nancy C. Seay.
EIN: 752820210

51349
Esther McCulloch Dansby and Pauline McCulloch Grant Foundation, Inc.
P.O. Box 2643
Bryan, TX 77805-2643
Contact: Janie McDougal, Secy.

Established in 1988 in TX.
Donor(s): Esther McCulloch Dansby.‡
Financial data (yr. ended 12/31/01): Grants paid, $122,150; assets, $2,343,679 (M); expenditures, $137,467; qualifying distributions, $135,851.
Limitations: Giving primarily in TX.
Application information: Application form not required.
Officers: Pauline Grant Diebel, Pres.; Samuel N. Sharp, V.P.; Esther Jane Grant McDougal, Secy.-Treas.
Trustees: Phillip C. Diebel, Fain McDougal, Jr.
EIN: 742522314
Codes: FD2

51350
Louis and Allison Brandt Foundation
2001 Kirby Dr., Ste. 914
Houston, TX 77019

Established about 1983 in TX.
Donor(s): Louis K. Brandt, Allison Brandt.
Financial data (yr. ended 12/31/00): Grants paid, $122,000; assets, $2,020,110 (M); expenditures, $142,890; qualifying distributions, $123,229.
Limitations: Applications not accepted. Giving primarily in Harris County, TX.
Application information: Contributes only to pre-selected organizations.
Trustee: Louis K. Brandt.
EIN: 760069463

51351
Benjamin F. Johnston Foundation
P.O. Box 126377
Fort Worth, TX 76161-1337

Established in 1962 in DE and TX.
Financial data (yr. ended 02/28/01): Grants paid, $121,500; assets, $1,745,687 (M); expenditures, $125,240; qualifying distributions, $121,500.
Limitations: Applications not accepted. Giving primarily in Fort Worth, TX.
Application information: Contributes only to pre-selected organizations.
Officers: Sherwood Johnston, Pres.; Jesse Upchurch, V.P.; Wesley A. Roland, Secy.; Bill Roland, Treas.
EIN: 756024154
Codes: FD2

51352
Erving & Joyce Wolf Foundation
1001 Fannin St., Ste. 2000
Houston, TX 77002-6709

Donor(s): Erving Wolf, Joyce Wolf.
Financial data (yr. ended 02/28/01): Grants paid, $120,750; assets, $2,314,579 (M); expenditures, $137,025; qualifying distributions, $119,351.
Limitations: Applications not accepted. Giving primarily in NY and TX.
Application information: Contributes only to pre-selected organizations.
Officers and Directors:* Erving Wolf,* Pres.; Joyce Wolf,* V.P. and Secy.; M. Daniel Wolf,* Treas.; Diane R. Wolf, Mathew D. Wolf.
EIN: 237275662
Codes: FD2

51353
James D. and Kay Y. Moran Foundation
5500 Preston Rd., Ste. 390
Dallas, TX 75205   (214) 528-6483
Contact: Kay Moran McCord, Pres.

Established in 1989 in TX.
Donor(s): Geary Ellet, Kay Moran McCord.
Financial data (yr. ended 09/30/01): Grants paid, $120,500; assets, $1,974,570 (M); expenditures, $126,300; qualifying distributions, $124,667.
Limitations: Applications not accepted. Giving primarily in OK and TX.
Application information: Contributes only to pre-selected organizations.
Officers: Kay Moran McCord, C.E.O. and Pres.; Heather Moran, V.P.; Elberta Washburn, Secy.-Treas.
Director: E.W. Moran, Jr.
EIN: 752303252
Codes: FD2

51354
William and Salome Scanlan Foundation
112 E. Pecan St., 30th Fl.
San Antonio, TX 78205

Donor(s): John McAllen Scanlan.
Financial data (yr. ended 12/31/01): Grants paid, $120,166; assets, $901,391 (M); gifts received, $98,160; expenditures, $130,268; qualifying distributions, $122,902.
Limitations: Giving primarily in TX.
Trustee: John McAllen Scanlan.
EIN: 742697713
Codes: FD2

51355
Cal and Joyce Arnold Foundation Trust
3419 Westminster Ave.
Dallas, TX 75205

Established in 2001 in TX.
Donor(s): Cal Arnold, Joyce Arnold.
Financial data (yr. ended 12/31/01): Grants paid, $120,000; assets, $530,648 (M); gifts received, $691,406; expenditures, $128,208; qualifying distributions, $120,000.
Limitations: Applications not accepted. Giving primarily in Little Rock, AR.
Application information: Contributes only to pre-selected organizations.
Trustees: Calvin G. Arnold, Joyce Sue Arnold.
EIN: 626385273

51356
Victor & Peggy Creighton Charitable Trust
9311 San Pedro, Ste. 1200
San Antonio, TX 78216

Established in 2000.

Financial data (yr. ended 12/31/01): Grants paid, $120,000; assets, $2,601,256 (M); expenditures, $140,101; qualifying distributions, $120,000.
Limitations: Applications not accepted. Giving primarily in San Antonio, TX.
Application information: Contributes only to pre-selected organizations.
Trustee: Walter Mathis.
EIN: 746437206
Codes: FD2

51357
Karl Folkers Foundation for Biomedical and Clinical Research
816 Congress Ave., Ste. 1100
Austin, TX 78701-2443
Contact: Dick Curran, Exec. Dir.

Established in 1991.
Financial data (yr. ended 12/31/01): Grants paid, $120,000; assets, $2,285,555 (M); expenditures, $163,530; qualifying distributions, $120,000.
Limitations: Applications not accepted. Giving primarily in TX.
Application information: Contributes only to pre-selected organizations.
Officers: Richard Willis, V.P. and Secy.; Lee Baker, V.P. and Treas.; Dick Curran, Exec. Dir.
Directors: Alan Combs, Dir. of Pharmacology; William Shive, Dir. of Biochemistry; William Hilgers, Legal Counsel.
EIN: 742579336
Codes: FD2

51358
The Frill Foundation
4200 Chase Tower
600 Travis St.
Houston, TX 77002
Contact: William R. Lummis, Pres.

Established in 1997 in TX.
Donor(s): France B. Lummis, William R. Lummis.
Financial data (yr. ended 12/31/00): Grants paid, $120,000; assets, $2,767,066 (M); expenditures, $133,894; qualifying distributions, $126,947.
Limitations: Giving primarily in TX.
Officers: William R. Lummis, Pres. and Treas.; France B. Lummis, Sr. V.P. and Secy.; Frederick R. Lummis II, V.P.; Palmer Bradley Lummis, V.P.; Ransom C. Lummis, V.P.
EIN: 311505628
Codes: FD2

51359
The Rawley Foundation
c/o JPMorgan Chase Bank
P.O. Box 2558
Houston, TX 77252   (713) 216-4511
Additional address: c/o Stanley T. Rawley, 5400 Mesa Dr., Houston, TX 77028, tel.: (713) 635-4200

Established in 1997 in TX.
Financial data (yr. ended 12/31/01): Grants paid, $120,000; assets, $2,362,493 (M); gifts received, $172,544; expenditures, $138,309; qualifying distributions, $127,874.
Limitations: Giving primarily in Houston, TX.
Application information: Application form not required.
Trustees: Joyce S. Rawley, Stanley T. Rawley.
EIN: 766124547
Codes: FD2

51360
The Mazanec Foundation
302 Fall River Ct.
Houston, TX 77024

Established in 1996 in TX.

51360—TEXAS

Donor(s): George L. Mazanec, Elsa B. Mazanec.
Financial data (yr. ended 12/31/01): Grants paid, $119,320; assets, $344,201 (M); gifts received, $106,480; expenditures $122,477; qualifying distributions, $118,832.
Limitations: Applications not accepted. Giving primarily in Houston, TX.
Application information: Contributes only to pre-selected organizations.
Officers and Directors:* George L. Mazanec, Pres.; Elsa B. Mazanec, V.P. and Secy.; Robert Andrew Mazanec,* V.P.; John Charles Mazanec,* Treas.
EIN: 760521836
Codes: FD2

51361
Verne Cooper Foundation, Inc.
1400 W. Russell Ave.
Bonham, TX 75418 (903) 583-5574
Contact: Steve Mohundro, Secy.

Established in 1994 in TX.
Financial data (yr. ended 12/31/01): Grants paid, $119,193; assets, $2,274,621 (M); gifts received, $2,362; expenditures, $128,965; qualifying distributions, $123,938.
Limitations: Giving primarily in Fannin County, TX.
Application information: Application form required.
Officers and Trustees:* H.L. Milton,* Pres.; Mary Law, V.P.; Steve Mohundro,* Secy.; Hal Fowler, Hans Harjo, Bill Matthews.
EIN: 752547151
Codes: FD2, GTI

51362
Lillian Kaiser Lewis Foundation
c/o JPMorgan Chase Bank
P.O. Box 2558
Houston, TX 77252-8037 (713) 216-4513
Contact: Charlene D. Slack, Trust Off., JPMorgan Chase Bank

Established in 1966 in TX.
Donor(s): Lillian Kaiser Lewis.‡
Financial data (yr. ended 09/30/01): Grants paid, $119,000; assets, $2,082,625 (M); expenditures, $150,179; qualifying distributions, $127,000.
Limitations: Giving limited to the metropolitan Houston, TX, area.
Publications: Application guidelines.
Application information: Application form not required.
Trustees: G. Sidney Buchanan, Delores Wilkenfeld, JPMorgan Chase Bank.
EIN: 746076511
Codes: FD2

51363
Jack & Charlotte Owen Educational Scholarship Trust
c/o Hibernia National Bank
P.O. Box 451
Texarkana, TX 75504-0451

Established in 1991 in TX.
Financial data (yr. ended 12/31/01): Grants paid, $118,589; assets, $1,708,280 (M); expenditures, $137,766; qualifying distributions, $122,528.
Limitations: Giving limited to residents of Bowie County, TX.
Application information: Application form obtained through high school counselor. Application form required.
Trustee: Hibernia National Bank.
EIN: 756414441
Codes: FD2, GTI

51364
Angell Fund, Inc.
3130 S. Alameda St.
Corpus Christi, TX 78404-2506

Established in 1981.
Donor(s): James A. Ayers, M.D., Yvonne V. Ayers.
Financial data (yr. ended 12/31/01): Grants paid, $117,500; assets, $1,119,614 (M); gifts received, $98,538; expenditures, $118,387; qualifying distributions, $117,500.
Limitations: Applications not accepted. Giving primarily in Corpus Christi, TX.
Application information: Contributes only to pre-selected organizations.
Officers: James A. Ayers, M.D., Chair. and Pres.; Yvonne V. Ayers, V.P.
Trustee: Margaret Hoelscher.
EIN: 742160687

51365
The Oehmig Foundation
8 Greenway Plz., Ste. 702
Houston, TX 77046 (713) 877-8257
Contact: William C. Oehmig, C.E.O.

Established in 1988 in TX.
Donor(s): William C. Oehmig, Margaret W. Oehmig.
Financial data (yr. ended 12/31/01): Grants paid, $117,000; assets, $1,995,423 (M); expenditures, $141,379; qualifying distributions, $116,786.
Limitations: Giving primarily in TN and TX.
Officers: William C. Oehmig, C.E.O.; Margaret W. Oehmig, Pres.; Randolph D. Oehmig, Secy.-Treas.
EIN: 760260014
Codes: FD2

51366
Beryl Lowe Rice & John W. Rice Foundation
P.O. Box 539
Fowlerton, TX 78021 (830) 373-4489
Contact: Leighton Donnell, Dir.

Established in 2000 in TX.
Financial data (yr. ended 12/31/00): Grants paid, $115,903; assets, $522,138 (M); gifts received, $635,348; expenditures, $117,789; qualifying distributions, $117,715.
Limitations: Giving primarily in Alpine, TX.
Application information: Application form required.
Directors: Cydney C. Donnell, James L. Donnell, James L. Donnell, Jr., Leighton Donnell.
EIN: 742960699
Codes: FD2

51367
Shadywood Foundation
1001 Fannin St., Ste. 720
Houston, TX 77002-6707

Established in 1999 in TX.
Donor(s): Daniel C. Arnold, Beverly B. Arnold.
Financial data (yr. ended 12/31/01): Grants paid, $115,827; assets, $576,335 (M); expenditures, $129,546; qualifying distributions, $115,827.
Limitations: Applications not accepted. Giving primarily in TX.
Application information: Contributes only to pre-selected organizations.
Officers and Directors:* Daniel C. Arnold,* Chair.; Beverly B. Arnold,* Pres.; Steven D. Arnold,* V.P.; Alice A. Helms,* V.P.; Susan A. Marty, Robert A. Weigle.
EIN: 760592215
Codes: FD2

51368
Von Ehr Foundation
3510 Tree Trunk Trail
Richardson, TX 75082

Established in 1999 in TX.
Donor(s): James R. Von Ehr II.
Financial data (yr. ended 12/31/01): Grants paid, $115,500; assets, $2,681,626 (M); expenditures, $190,754; qualifying distributions, $114,587.
Limitations: Applications not accepted. Giving primarily in TX.
Application information: Contributes only to pre-selected organizations.
Officers and Directors:* James R. Von Her II,* Pres.; Gayla Von Ehr,* V.P. and Secy.-Treas.; James L. Halperin.
EIN: 752825954
Codes: FD2

51369
The Trammell Foundation
4265 San Felipe St., No. 603
Houston, TX 77027-3307 (713) 621-9325
Contact: Susan Trammell Whitfield, Vice-Chair.

Established in 1963 in TX.
Donor(s): W.B. Trammell, Ella F. Fondren 1982 Trust f/b/o Sue Trammell Whitfield.
Financial data (yr. ended 12/31/01): Grants paid, $115,000; assets, $2,263,635 (M); expenditures, $123,740; qualifying distributions, $115,199.
Limitations: Giving limited to Houston and the Harris County, TX, area.
Officers: Julia Delmey Trammel, Chair.; Laura Trammell Baird, Vice-Chair.; Celia Whitfield Crank, Secy.-Treas.
Board of Governors: Walter W. Fondren, Vanesa Garza, Carnie Trammell Sturges, Ann Gordon Trammell, Carolyn Green Trammell, Harper Bryan Trammell, Sue Trammell, Susan Trammell Whitfield, William F. Whitfield, Sr., William F. Whitfield, Jr.
EIN: 746057690
Codes: FD2

51370
Crump Family Foundation
P.O. Box 50820
Midland, TX 79710

Established in 1997 in TX.
Donor(s): E. Lea Crump, Melanie A. Crump.
Financial data (yr. ended 06/30/01): Grants paid, $114,500; assets, $255,357 (M); expenditures, $114,910; qualifying distributions, $114,500.
Limitations: Applications not accepted.
Application information: Contributes only to pre-selected organizations.
Officers: E. Lea Crump, Pres.; Melanie A. Crump, Secy.
EIN: 752737064

51371
Ralph A. Johnston Foundation, Inc.
P.O. Box 10
Burton, TX 77835-0010
Contact: Jerry J. Andrew, Pres.

Established in 1959 in TX; incorporated in 1963.
Donor(s): Ralph A. Johnston.‡
Financial data (yr. ended 05/31/02): Grants paid, $114,500; assets, $2,263,868 (M); expenditures, $121,969; qualifying distributions, $116,834.
Limitations: Giving primarily in the Houston, TX, area.
Application information: Funding very limited; few new grants awarded each year. Application form not required.
Officers and Directors:* Jerry J. Andrew,* Pres.; Lyle E. Carbaugh,* V.P. and Treas.; Cheryl Duff,*

Secy.; James J. Johnston, Jr., Jill Lewis, Dee S. Osborne, Gladys Watford.
EIN: 746051797
Codes: FD2

51372
The Dale and Deborah Ross Foundation
P.O. Box 17149
Sugar Land, TX 77496-7149 (281) 775-0100

Established in 1997 in TX.
Donor(s): Deborah H. Ross, R. Dale Ross.
Financial data (yr. ended 12/31/01): Grants paid, $114,443; assets, $638,648 (M); expenditures, $119,040; qualifying distributions, $114,443.
Limitations: Applications not accepted. Giving primarily in Houston, TX.
Application information: Contributes only to pre-selected organizations.
Officers: R. Dale Ross, Pres.; David J. Ross, V.P.; Michael A. Ross, V.P.; Deborah H. Ross, Secy.-Treas.
EIN: 760551779
Codes: FD2

51373
McKee Family Foundation, Inc.
4525 Beverly Dr.
Dallas, TX 75205

Established in 1997 in TX.
Donor(s): Cassandra M. McKee.
Financial data (yr. ended 12/31/99): Grants paid, $114,250; assets, $518,792 (M); expenditures, $115,835; qualifying distributions, $115,408.
Limitations: Applications not accepted. Giving primarily in Carrollton, TX.
Application information: Contributes only to pre-selected organizations.
Officers: Philip R. McKee, Pres.; Cassandra R. McKee, V.P.; Dennis Jameson, Secy.; Edward Easterling, Treas.
EIN: 752708394
Codes: FD2

51374
Dr. Ruskin C. & Karen Norman Family Foundation
7950 Floyd Curl Dr., Ste. 1001
San Antonio, TX 78229

Established in 1997 in TX.
Donor(s): Karen Norman, Ruskin C. Norman, M.D.
Financial data (yr. ended 06/30/01): Grants paid, $114,210; assets, $637,642 (M); expenditures, $115,558; qualifying distributions, $113,965.
Limitations: Applications not accepted. Giving primarily in TX.
Application information: Contributes only to pre-selected organizations.
Trustees: James C. Norman, Karen Norman, Ruskin C. Norman, M.D.
EIN: 742826677
Codes: FD2

51375
Fischer Foundation, Inc.
400 Main St., Ste. 905
Corpus Christi, TX 78401
Contact: Jeffrey S. Harris

Established in 1964 in TX.
Donor(s): Jerry E. Fischer.
Financial data (yr. ended 07/31/01): Grants paid, $113,850; assets, $57,323 (M); expenditures, $115,612; qualifying distributions, $113,850.
Limitations: Giving primarily in TX.
Officers: Jerry E. Fischer, Pres. and Treas.; Bill Fischer, V.P.; Mark Fischer, V.P.; Laura F. Smith, V.P.; Alice Ann Fischer, Secy.

Director: Betty F. Harris.
EIN: 746062598
Codes: FD2

51376
The John R. and Mary Margaret Clay Charitable Foundation
2617 Mockingbird Ct.
Fort Worth, TX 76109
Contact: John R. Clay, Pres.

Established in 1986 in TX.
Donor(s): John R. Clay.
Financial data (yr. ended 12/31/01): Grants paid, $112,793; assets, $1,905,586 (M); expenditures, $124,791; qualifying distributions, $116,273.
Limitations: Applications not accepted. Giving primarily in Fort Worth, TX.
Application information: Contributes only to pre-selected organizations. Funding limited to programs of personal interest to trustees.
Officers: John R. Clay, Pres.; Mary Margaret Clay, Secy.
EIN: 752055174
Codes: FD2

51377
Barney F. and Ellen L. Kogen Charitable Foundation
3131 Eastside, Ste. 120
Houston, TX 77098
Contact: W. Mark Moore, Pres.

Established in 1996 in TX.
Donor(s): Barney F. Kogen, Ellen L. Kogen.
Financial data (yr. ended 12/31/00): Grants paid, $112,399; assets, $116,319 (M); expenditures, $114,343; qualifying distributions, $112,399.
Limitations: Applications not accepted. Giving primarily in TX.
Application information: Contributes only to pre-selected organizations.
Officers: Barney F. Kogen, Chair.; W. Mark Moore, Pres.; Linda Gaines, V.P. and Secy.-Treas.
Director: Ellen L. Kogen.
EIN: 760495253
Codes: FD2

51378
Chrest Foundation, Inc.
6500 Beltline Rd., Ste. 170
Irving, TX 75063 (972) 999-4514
Contact: Lou Anne King Jensen

Established in 1999 in TX.
Donor(s): Jeffrey J. Jenses.
Financial data (yr. ended 12/31/01): Grants paid, $112,040; assets, $2,076,799 (M); gifts received, $31,063; expenditures, $160,036; qualifying distributions, $159,805.
Limitations: Giving primarily in Turkey.
Publications: Application guidelines, program policy statement.
Application information: Application form not required.
Officers and Directors:* Lou Anne King Jensen,* Pres.; Jeffrey J. Jensen,* V.P.; Cindy D. Pagel, Secy.; Gary L. Friedman,* Treas.
EIN: 752840026
Codes: FD2

51379
The George Grayson Foundation
800 E. Campbell Rd., Ste. 340
Richardson, TX 75081 (972) 424-9926

Established in 1990 in TX.
Donor(s): George D. Grayson.
Financial data (yr. ended 12/31/99): Grants paid, $111,762; assets, $431,569 (M); expenditures, $111,762; qualifying distributions, $107,325.

Limitations: Giving primarily in CA, TX, and VA.
Officers and Directors:* George D. Grayson,* Pres.; Kathy Bender Grayson,* V.P.; James E. Shepherd,* Secy.
EIN: 752375952
Codes: FD2

51380
Welborn-Payne Endowment Trust
c/o American State Bank
P.O. Box 1401
Lubbock, TX 79408-1401

Established in 1998 in TX.
Donor(s): Ernestine Payne-Welborn.
Financial data (yr. ended 12/31/01): Grants paid, $111,604; assets, $2,935,641 (M); gifts received, $116,333; expenditures, $304,789; qualifying distributions, $115,004.
Limitations: Applications not accepted. Giving primarily in Lubbock, TX.
Application information: Contributes only to pre-selected organizations.
Trustees: Ernestine Payne-Welborn, American State Bank.
EIN: 756435671
Codes: FD2

51381
The Fred & Louise Joachim Foundation
2308 W. 5th St.
Plainview, TX 79072 (806) 293-4287

Established in 1997.
Financial data (yr. ended 12/31/01): Grants paid, $111,000; assets, $2,529,055 (M); expenditures, $121,195; qualifying distributions, $111,000.
Limitations: Giving primarily in Plainview, TX.
Application information: Application form not required.
Trustees: Odis Sims, Don A. Williams.
EIN: 752695806
Codes: FD2

51382
David Rosenberg Children Foundation
6203 Turner Way
Dallas, TX 75230 (214) 696-2477
Contact: Oscar Rosenberg, Secy.-Treas.

Established in 1994.
Financial data (yr. ended 12/31/99): Grants paid, $111,000; assets, $781,171 (M); expenditures, $113,076; qualifying distributions, $109,929.
Limitations: Giving primarily in Dallas, TX.
Application information: Application form required.
Officers: Sheldon Rosenberg, Pres.; Bernard Rosenberg, V.P.; Oscar Rosenberg, Secy.-Treas.
EIN: 752518673
Codes: FD2

51383
Helen I. Little Education Trust
c/o Bank of America
P.O. Box 831041
Dallas, TX 75283-1041
Application address: c/o Christ Episcopal Church, 505 E. Commerce, Mexia, TX 76667, tel.: (254) 562-5918

Established in 1997 in TX.
Financial data (yr. ended 12/31/01): Grants paid, $110,845; assets, $1,553,348 (M); expenditures, $129,774; qualifying distributions, $109,321.
Limitations: Giving primarily in TX.
Trustee: Bank of America.
EIN: 756500051
Codes: FD2

51384
B. C. & Addie Brookshire Kleberg County Charitable Foundation
c/o Frost National Bank
P.O. Drawer 749
Corpus Christi, TX 78403 (361) 844-1055
Contact: Neal Powers

Established in 1958 in TX.
Financial data (yr. ended 06/30/01): Grants paid, $110,536; assets, $2,225,091 (M); expenditures, $124,149; qualifying distributions, $110,536.
Limitations: Giving limited to Kleberg County, TX.
Application information: Application form not required.
Trustee: Frost National Bank.
EIN: 746108397
Codes: FD2

51385
Trotter Education Foundation
109 N. Post Oak Ln., Ste.425
Houston, TX 77024 (713) 652-5750
Contact: J.T. Trotter, Pres.

Established in 1997 in TX.
Donor(s): J.T. Trotter, E.W. Kelly, Jr.
Financial data (yr. ended 11/30/01): Grants paid, $110,400; assets, $9,242 (M); gifts received, $75,997; expenditures, $110,631; qualifying distributions, $110,389.
Limitations: Applications not accepted. Giving primarily in Houston, TX.
Application information: Contributes only to pre-selected organizations.
Officers and Trustees:* J.T. Trotter,* Pres.; Richard E. Monroe, Jr.,* V.P. and Secy.-Treas.
EIN: 742209416
Codes: FD2

51386
Richard Spencer Lewis Memorial Foundation
c/o Jefferson State Bank
P.O. Box 5190
San Antonio, TX 78201-0190

Established in 1961 in TX.
Donor(s): A.J. Lewis,‡ Mrs. A.J. Lewis, and members and friends of the Lewis family.
Financial data (yr. ended 12/31/01): Grants paid, $110,000; assets, $2,180,489 (M); gifts received, $405; expenditures, $115,032; qualifying distributions, $109,354.
Limitations: Applications not accepted. Giving primarily in TX.
Application information: Contributes only to pre-selected organizations.
Officers and Trustees:* Linda Lewis McSween,* Pres.; A.J. Lewis, Jr.,* V.P. and Secy.-Treas.; Peggy Lewis, Paul E. McSween, Jr.
EIN: 746075376
Codes: FD2

51387
Ann Bradshaw Stokes Foundation
1436 W. Gray St., No. 543
Houston, TX 77019

Established in 1982 in TX.
Donor(s): Ann Bradshaw Stokes.‡
Financial data (yr. ended 12/31/01): Grants paid, $110,000; assets, $1,973,127 (M); expenditures, $121,497; qualifying distributions, $110,000.
Limitations: Applications not accepted. Giving limited to TX.
Application information: Individual recipients are chosen by beneficiary schools, not by the foundation itself.
Trustee: George Ann Stokes.
EIN: 751866981
Codes: FD2

51388
Jack and Annis Bowen Foundation
(Formerly The W. J. Bowen Foundation)
P.O. Box 1396-77251
2800 Post Oak Blvd., Level 4
Houston, TX 77056
Contact: W.J. Bowen, Pres.

Established in 1985 in TX.
Donor(s): W.J. Bowen, Annis H. Bowen.
Financial data (yr. ended 12/31/01): Grants paid, $109,950; assets, $1,692,556 (M); gifts received, $57,290; expenditures, $125,068; qualifying distributions, $116,862.
Limitations: Giving primarily in TX.
Application information: Application form not required.
Officers and Directors:* W.J. Bowen,* Pres. and Treas.; Annis H. Bowen,* V.P. and Secy.; Berry Dunbar Bowen, Barbara Bowen Cauble.
EIN: 760181972
Codes: FD2

51389
Dene Anton Foundation
(Formerly The Judge Roy and Dene Hofheinz Trust)
c/o Bank of America, Trust Dept.
P.O. Box 2518
Houston, TX 77252-2518 (713) 247-7435
Contact: Dene Hofheinz Anton, Tr.

Established in 1984 in TX.
Donor(s): Roy M. Hofheinz Charitable Foundation.
Financial data (yr. ended 09/30/99): Grants paid, $109,171; assets, $925,765 (M); expenditures, $125,912; qualifying distributions, $112,878.
Limitations: Giving primarily in CA.
Trustees: Dene Hofheinz Anton, Bank of America.
EIN: 760093912
Codes: FD2

51390
The Mag Foundation
P.O. Box 831041
Dallas, TX 75283-1041
Application address: P.O. Box 419119, Kansas City, MO 64141-6119
Contact: David P. Ross, Sr. V.P., Bank of America

Established in 1954 in MO.
Financial data (yr. ended 12/31/01): Grants paid, $109,000; assets, $2,241,382 (M); expenditures, $137,053; qualifying distributions, $115,494.
Limitations: Giving primarily in the metropolitan Kansas City, MO, area.
Application information: Application form not required.
Trustees: Myron Ellison, Geoffrey Oelsner, Jr., Helen Mag Wolcott, Bank of America.
EIN: 446012324
Codes: FD2

51391
James A. & Mayme H. Rowland Foundation
c/o Bank of America
P.O. Box 831041
Dallas, TX 75283-1041 (214) 559-6443
Contact: M.D. Hinyard, V.P., Bank of America

Established in 1956 in TX.
Financial data (yr. ended 12/31/01): Grants paid, $109,000; assets, $2,078,213 (M); expenditures, $129,758; qualifying distributions, $105,278.
Limitations: Giving primarily in Dallas, TX.
Application information: Application form not required.
Trustees: Susan Sowell Lyman, Mary Sowell Shelmire, Jason B. Sowell, Jr.
EIN: 756043988

Codes: FD2

51392
The Prentice Foundation
5100 San Felipe, Ste. 233E
Houston, TX 77056 (713) 850-0346
Contact: Cynthia R. Prentice, V.P.

Established in 1994 in TX.
Donor(s): F. David Prentice, Mrs. F. David Prentice.
Financial data (yr. ended 11/30/01): Grants paid, $108,891; assets, $1,472,268 (M); expenditures, $118,799; qualifying distributions, $108,891.
Limitations: Giving primarily in TX.
Officers: F. David Prentice, Pres. and Treas.; Cynthia R. Prentice, V.P. and Secy.
Director: Howard Shylman.
EIN: 760455526
Codes: FD2

51393
Saunders Foundation
7500 San Felipe St., Ste. 1070
Houston, TX 77024

Established in 1998 in TX.
Donor(s): Frederic M. Saunders, Mission-Heights Management Co., LTD.
Financial data (yr. ended 12/31/01): Grants paid, $108,550; assets, $566,400 (M); gifts received, $428,600; expenditures, $113,099; qualifying distributions, $110,022.
Limitations: Applications not accepted. Giving primarily in TX.
Application information: Contributes only to pre-selected organizations.
Directors: Meredith S. Mason, Fredric M. Saunders, Gayle D. Saunders, Stuart D. Saunders.
EIN: 760574880
Codes: FD2

51394
James Halperin Foundation
100 Highland Park Village, Ste. 200
Dallas, TX 75205

Established in 1989 in TX.
Donor(s): James L. Halperin.
Financial data (yr. ended 12/31/01): Grants paid, $108,450; assets, $2,036,239 (M); gifts received, $835; expenditures, $119,345; qualifying distributions, $108,450.
Limitations: Applications not accepted. Giving on a national basis.
Application information: Contributes only to pre-selected organizations.
Officers: James L. Halperin, Pres.; Abigail Halperin, V.P.; Majorie Halperin, Secy.
EIN: 752294319
Codes: FD2

51395
Curtis Martin Job Foundation
5500 Preston Rd., Ste. 250
Dallas, TX 75205
Contact: Curtis J. Martin, Jr., Pres.

Established in 1998 in TX.
Donor(s): Curtis James Martin, Jr.
Financial data (yr. ended 12/31/00): Grants paid, $108,060; assets, $938,904 (M); gifts received, $2,500; expenditures, $108,253; qualifying distributions, $108,060.
Limitations: Giving primarily in NY and PA.
Officers and Directors:* Curtis James Martin, Jr.,* Pres. and Treas.; Werner Scott,* V.P. and Secy.; Rochella C. Martin.
EIN: 752818747
Codes: FD2

51396
Fentress-Brown Foundation, Inc.
2121 S. Lamar Blvd., Ste. 202
Austin, TX 78704 (512) 442-1223
Contact: J. Tim Brown, Secy.-Treas.

Established in 1976.
Financial data (yr. ended 09/30/01): Grants paid, $108,000; assets, $1,768,096 (M); expenditures, $112,739; qualifying distributions, $107,104.
Limitations: Giving limited to Austin, Corsicana, and San Antonio, TX.
Officers and Trustees:* David Brown,* Chair.; Richard F. Brown,* Vice-Chair.; J. Tim Brown,* Secy.-Treas.
EIN: 510191739
Codes: FD2

51397
Clear Creek Education Foundation
15410 Poplar Springs Ln.
Houston, TX 77062 (281) 338-5823
Contact: Ava Lunsford, Liason

Established in 1997 in TX.
Donor(s): Houston Livestock Show and Rodeo, Longhorn Project Committee, The Boeing Co., Nova Chemicals U.S.A., Allied Signal.
Financial data (yr. ended 12/31/00): Grants paid, $107,841; assets, $171,833 (M); gifts received, $96,620; expenditures, $111,130; qualifying distributions, $108,800.
Limitations: Giving limited to Clear Creek, TX.
Publications: Occasional report.
Application information: Contributes only to Clear Creek Independent School District and projects benefiting Clear Creek Independent School District students. Application form required.
Directors: Hank Alston, Bill Bispeck, David Black, Jennifer Bowers, Jim Broughton, Jeffrey Carr, Rick Clapp, Lisa Clark, Ron Crowder, Melodye Davis, Hon. Louie Ditta, Roz Doyle, and 20 additional directors.
EIN: 760383447
Codes: FD2

51398
SK Foundation
2001 Kirby Dr., Ste. 901
Houston, TX 77019

Established in 1996 in TX.
Financial data (yr. ended 12/31/01): Grants paid, $107,575; assets, $1,568,687 (M); expenditures, $110,503; qualifying distributions, $107,575.
Limitations: Applications not accepted. Giving primarily in TX.
Application information: Contributes only to pre-selected organizations.
Officers: W.A. Stockard, Jr., Pres.; Sue Stockard Schaefer, V.P.; Jan Stockard Cato, Secy.-Treas.
EIN: 760500154

51399
Virginia & Robert Hobbs Charitable Trust
c/o JPMorgan Chase Bank
P.O. Box 1290
Fort Worth, TX 76101-1290
Contact: David S. Bucher

Established in 1998 in TX.
Financial data (yr. ended 06/30/01): Grants paid, $107,522; assets, $2,130,199 (M); expenditures, $119,755; qualifying distributions, $104,570.
Limitations: Giving primarily in Fort Worth, TX.
Trustee: JPMorgan Chase Bank.
EIN: 752773208
Codes: FD2

51400
William Wright Family Foundation
P.O. Box 1980
Vernon, TX 76385-1980

Established in 1998 in TX.
Donor(s): William E. Wright.
Financial data (yr. ended 12/31/01): Grants paid, $107,500; assets, $5,655,787 (M); gifts received, $4,313,708; expenditures, $110,596; qualifying distributions, $107,500.
Limitations: Applications not accepted. Giving primarily in Vernon, TX.
Application information: Contributes only to pre-selected organizations.
Officers and Directors:* William D. Wright,* Pres.; Betty J. Wright,* V.P.; William E. Wright,* Secy.-Treas.; Betty D. Bolton, James Bolton, Patricia L. Wright.
EIN: 752743584

51401
The Hook Family Foundation
2727 Allen Pkwy., Ste. 1601
Houston, TX 77019

Established in 1998 in TX.
Donor(s): Harold S. Hook.
Financial data (yr. ended 12/31/99): Grants paid, $107,375; assets, $2,002,160 (M); expenditures, $143,958; qualifying distributions, $110,114.
Limitations: Applications not accepted.
Application information: Contributes only to pre-selected organizations.
Officers: Harold S. Hook, Pres.; Joanne H. Hook, Secy.
EIN: 760574363
Codes: FD2

51402
Larry & Norma Price Family Charitable Foundation
824 E. Redd Rd., Ste. 1-A
El Paso, TX 79912

Established in 1998 in TX.
Donor(s): Larry R. Price, Norma Price.
Financial data (yr. ended 12/31/01): Grants paid, $107,021; assets, $17,729 (M); gifts received, $98,000; expenditures, $107,130; qualifying distributions, $107,011.
Limitations: Applications not accepted. Giving primarily in El Paso, TX.
Application information: Contributes only to pre-selected organizations.
Trustees: Larry R. Price, Norma Price.
EIN: 742819831
Codes: FD2

51403
The Pine Foundation
c/o H. David Hughes
111 Congress Ave., Ste. 1400
Austin, TX 78701 (512) 479-9730
Contact: Brigid Anne Cockrum, Pres.

Established in 1985 in TX.
Donor(s): Brigid Anne Cockrum.
Financial data (yr. ended 12/31/01): Grants paid, $107,000; assets, $1,550,045 (M); expenditures, $111,682; qualifying distributions, $108,885.
Limitations: Giving limited to the central TX area.
Application information: Application form not required.
Officers: Brigid Anne Cockrum, Pres.; James Bryant Cockrum, Secy.
Director: Wendy Albrecht.
EIN: 742387801
Codes: FD2

51404
Luke & Merle Soules Family Foundation
100 W. Houston St., No. 1500
San Antonio, TX 78205-1424

Established in 1999.
Donor(s): Luther H. Soules III.
Financial data (yr. ended 12/31/00): Grants paid, $107,000; assets, $1,908,264 (M); gifts received, $5,150; expenditures, $120,025; qualifying distributions, $106,435.
Limitations: Applications not accepted. Giving primarily in TX.
Application information: Contributes only to pre-selected organizations.
Directors: Terri Lynn Barnett, Andrea Marie Morrison, Joe Carlton Soules, Sr., Laura Nell Soules, Luther H. Soules III, Jimmy Blair Young, Jr.
EIN: 311675276
Codes: FD2

51405
Cielo Azul Foundation
3500 Ranch Rd., 620 N.
Austin, TX 78734

Established in 2000 in TX.
Donor(s): Betsy Blair, James Van Winkle.
Financial data (yr. ended 12/31/01): Grants paid, $106,982; assets, $2,699,224 (M); expenditures, $139,950; qualifying distributions, $111,953.
Limitations: Applications not accepted. Giving primarily in Austin, TX.
Application information: Contributes only to pre-selected organizations.
Officers and Directors:* Betsy Blair,* Pres.; James Van Winkle,* V.P. and Secy.-Treas.
EIN: 742982455
Codes: FD2

51406
George A. & Nancy P. Shutt Foundation
2 Turtle Creek Village
3838 Oak Lawn Ave., Ste. 707
Dallas, TX 75219-4508 (214) 521-0292
Contact: George A. Shutt, Pres.

Established in 1983 in TX.
Donor(s): George A. Shutt, Nancy P. Shutt.
Financial data (yr. ended 11/30/01): Grants paid, $106,637; assets, $2,579,174 (M); gifts received, $25,000; expenditures, $136,177; qualifying distributions, $112,762.
Limitations: Giving primarily in Dallas, TX.
Application information: Generally contributes to pre-selected organizations that meet IRS guidelines for non-profit organizations.
Officers: George A. Shutt, Pres.; Harriet Shutt Burrow, V.P.; Anne Shutt, V.P.
Director: Nancy P. Shutt.
EIN: 751856138
Codes: FD2

51407
Donald J. & Joan P. McNamara Foundation
c/o Donald J. McNamara
2200 Ross Ave., Ste. 4200W
Dallas, TX 75201

Established in 1997 in TX.
Donor(s): Donald J. McNamara.
Financial data (yr. ended 12/31/01): Grants paid, $106,452; assets, $190,822 (M); gifts received, $74,700; expenditures, $108,114; qualifying distributions, $106,039.
Limitations: Applications not accepted. Giving primarily in TX.
Application information: Contributes only to pre-selected organizations.

Officers and Trustees:* Donald J. McNamara,* Chair. and Pres.; Daniel A. Decker,* Secy.-Treas.; Joan P. McNamara.
EIN: 752696820
Codes: FD2

51408
Carl C. Anderson, Sr. and Marie Jo Anderson Charitable Foundation
c/o Bank of America
P.O. Box 831041
Dallas, TX 75283-1041
Application address: 1016 La Posada, Ste. 142, Austin, TX 78752, tel.: (512) 485-2285
Contact: Jennifer J. Bird, Tr.

Donor(s): Carl C. Anderson, Sr., Marie Jo Anderson.
Financial data (yr. ended 12/31/01): Grants paid, $106,000; assets, $18,511,126 (M); gifts received, $145,970; expenditures, $238,533; qualifying distributions, $106,000.
Limitations: Giving primarily in NM and TX.
Application information: Application form not required.
Trustees: Carl C. Anderson, Sr., Charles R. Batte III, Jennifer J. Bird, R. Russell Rager, Bank of America.
EIN: 746078530

51409
Carrie S. Orleans Trust
c/o Bank of America, N.A.
P.O. Box 831041
Dallas, TX 75283-1041 (214) 559-6470
Contact: Carrie Hilton

Financial data (yr. ended 06/30/01): Grants paid, $106,000; assets, $2,745,833 (M); expenditures, $132,066; qualifying distributions, $109,948.
Limitations: Giving limited to Dallas County, TX.
Trustee: Bank of America.
EIN: 756006730
Codes: FD2

51410
Sam Roosth Foundation
P.O. Box 2019
Tyler, TX 75710
Contact: Steven C. Roosth, V.P.

Established in 1953 in TX.
Donor(s): Members of the Roosth family.
Financial data (yr. ended 12/31/99): Grants paid, $106,000; assets, $1,753,927 (M); expenditures, $114,163; qualifying distributions, $106,367.
Limitations: Applications not accepted. Giving primarily in Tyler, TX.
Publications: Annual report.
Application information: Contributes only to pre-selected organizations.
Officers and Directors:* Wiley Roosth,* Pres.; Hyman Roosth, V.P.; Steven C. Roosth, V.P.; Sol Roosth,* Secy.-Treas.; Sam Roosth.
EIN: 756023828
Codes: FD2

51411
The D. Kent and Linda C. Anderson Foundation
12 E. Rivercrest
Houston, TX 77042 (713) 626-3431
Contact: D. Kent Anderson, Pres.

Established in 1997 in TX.
Donor(s): D. Kent Anderson.
Financial data (yr. ended 12/31/00): Grants paid, $105,350; assets, $558,399 (M); gifts received, $63,841; expenditures, $108,204; qualifying distributions, $104,913.
Limitations: Giving primarily in TX.
Officers and Directors:* D. Kent Anderson, Pres., V.P., and Treas.; Linda C. Anderson,* Secy.; Clarke Kent Anderson, Huntley C. Anderson, Whitney P. Anderson.
EIN: 760520696
Codes: FD2

51412
Harriet & Joe Foster Foundation
(Formerly Joe B. Foster Family Foundation)
325 Sugarberry Cir.
Houston, TX 77024
FAX: (713) 789-3061
Contact: Harriet R. Foster, Pres.

Established in 1995 in TX.
Financial data (yr. ended 12/31/01): Grants paid, $105,000; assets, $64,962 (M); gifts received, $106,169; expenditures, $106,345; qualifying distributions, $106,157.
Limitations: Applications not accepted. Giving primarily in the Houston, TX, area.
Application information: Contributes only to pre-selected organizations.
Officers: Harriet R. Foster, Pres. and Treas.; William Warren Foster, V.P.; D. Bryan Ruez, Secy.
Directors: Jennifer Kate Foster, Kenneth Knox Foster.
EIN: 760464978
Codes: FD2

51413
Salners Family Foundation
5644 Westheimer Rd., Ste. 505
Houston, TX 77056 (713) 263-7622
Contact: Shari Koziol

Established in 1997 in TX.
Donor(s): James L. Salners.
Financial data (yr. ended 12/31/00): Grants paid, $105,000; assets, $2,199,641 (M); expenditures, $139,750; qualifying distributions, $118,108.
Limitations: Giving primarily in Houston, TX.
Application information: Application form not required.
Officers and Directors:* James L. Salners,* Pres.; Sarah Johnson Salners,* Secy.; Lissa Dawn Wilson Debes,* Treas.
EIN: 760555234
Codes: FD2

51414
Stanford C. and Mary Clare Finney Foundation
8201 Preston Rd., Ste. 440
Dallas, TX 75225 (214) 890-8817
Contact: P.J. Vitruk

Established in 1999 in TX.
Donor(s): Stanford C. Finney, Jr., Mary Clare Finney.
Financial data (yr. ended 12/31/00): Grants paid, $104,775; assets, $926,970 (M); expenditures, $108,531; qualifying distributions, $104,829.
Limitations: Giving primarily in Dallas, TX.
Officers: Stanford C. Finney, Jr., C.E.O. and Pres.; Mary Clare Finney, Secy.
EIN: 752809984
Codes: FD2

51415
J. N. & Macie Edens Foundation
c/o Bank of America
P.O. Box 831041
Dallas, TX 75283-1041
Application address: c/o Bob Burris, 100 N. Main, Corsicana, TX 75110, tel.: (903) 654-3250

Established in 1991 in TX.
Donor(s): J.N. Edens, Jr. Trust.
Financial data (yr. ended 12/31/01): Grants paid, $104,674; assets, $2,035,216 (M); expenditures, $128,998; qualifying distributions, $106,501.
Limitations: Giving primarily in Corsicana, TX.
Application information: Application form not required.
Trustee: Bank of America.
EIN: 756413983
Codes: FD2

51416
J. B. & Margaret Blaugrund Foundation
4000 N. Stanton St.
El Paso, TX 79902

Established in 1958 in TX.
Donor(s): Joseph B. Blaugrund,‡ Margaret A. Blaugrund.‡
Financial data (yr. ended 07/31/01): Grants paid, $104,600; assets, $2,070,234 (M); expenditures, $109,497; qualifying distributions, $108,084.
Limitations: Applications not accepted. Giving primarily in, but not limited to TX, with emphasis on El Paso.
Application information: Contributes only to pre-selected organizations.
Officers: Yeta Ann Marks, Pres.; J. Alan Marks, Secy.-Treas.
EIN: 746040400
Codes: FD2

51417
Guadalupe Hills Foundation
P.O. Box 1076
Seguin, TX 78155

Established in 1996 in CA, DC, & TX.
Donor(s): First MAC Personal Trust.
Financial data (yr. ended 12/31/99): Grants paid, $103,970; assets, $841,983 (M); gifts received, $233,950; expenditures, $151,521; qualifying distributions, $103,970.
Limitations: Applications not accepted.
Application information: Contributes only to pre-selected organizations.
Managers: Charlotte Jaynes, Mikel Jaynes.
EIN: 522033975
Codes: FD2

51418
Hoeffner Foundation
P.O. Box 4726
Tyler, TX 75712-4726

Established in 1999 in TX.
Donor(s): Rex Hide, Inc.
Financial data (yr. ended 06/30/01): Grants paid, $103,900; assets, $1,599,645 (M); gifts received, $150,000; expenditures, $107,538; qualifying distributions, $103,163.
Limitations: Giving primarily in PA and TX.
Application information: Application form not required.
Officers: Sandra J. Hoeffner, Pres.; Noelle Hoeffner Barr, V.P.; Holly Jo Hoeffner Kaplan, V.P.; Heather Lynn Hoeffner, Secy.-Treas.
EIN: 752834784
Codes: FD2

51419
Lorraine and Alexander Dell Foundation
615 Shartle Cir.
Houston, TX 77024-5521

Established in 1998.
Financial data (yr. ended 11/30/01): Grants paid, $103,500; assets, $745,828 (M); expenditures, $104,766; qualifying distributions, $103,500.
Limitations: Applications not accepted.
Application information: Contributes only to pre-selected organizations.
Directors: Alexander Dell, Lorraine Dell.
EIN: 311581558
Codes: FD2

51420
Kenneth P. Gifford Foundation
c/o JPMorgan Chase Bank
P.O. Drawer 140
El Paso, TX 79980-0001
Contact: Terry Crenshaw

Established in 1977.
Financial data (yr. ended 09/30/99): Grants paid, $103,500; assets, $2,303,205 (M); expenditures, $132,168; qualifying distributions, $103,500.
Limitations: Giving primarily in El Paso County, TX.
Application information: Application form not required.
Trustee: JPMorgan Chase Bank.
EIN: 741977400
Codes: FD2

51421
Seegers Foundation
8222 Douglas Ave., Ste. 790
Dallas, TX 75225

Established in 1984 in TX.
Donor(s): Paul Ray Seegers, Phyllis Ann Seegers.
Financial data (yr. ended 12/31/01): Grants paid, $103,400; assets, $203,235 (M); gifts received, $137,350; expenditures, $104,275; qualifying distributions, $103,964.
Limitations: Giving primarily in Dallas, TX.
Officers: Phyllis Ann Seegers, Pres. and Treas.; Paul Ray Seegers, V.P.; Scott R. Seegars, V.P.; Santo Bisignano, Jr., Secy.
Trustee: David G. Glickman.
EIN: 752001868
Codes: FD2

51422
Schwartz Foundation
7598 N. Mesa St., Ste. 205
El Paso, TX 79912 (915) 845-4000
Contact: Scott M. Schwartz, Secy.

Established in 1999 in TX.
Donor(s): I.T. Schwartz, Susan Schwartz.
Financial data (yr. ended 12/31/01): Grants paid, $103,250; assets, $629,224 (M); expenditures, $103,961; qualifying distributions, $102,538.
Limitations: Giving primarily in El Paso, TX.
Officers: I.T. Schwartz, Pres.; Susan Schwartz, V.P.; Scott M. Schwartz, Secy.; Douglas A. Schwartz, Treas.
Director: Tania Schwartz.
EIN: 742900056
Codes: FD2

51423
The Sanders H. and Norma H. Campbell Charitable Foundation
6310 Lemon Ave., Ste. 275
Dallas, TX 75209

Established in 1998 in TX.
Financial data (yr. ended 12/31/00): Grants paid, $103,050; assets, $230,658 (M); gifts received, $177,184; expenditures, $103,050; qualifying distributions, $103,050.
Limitations: Applications not accepted.
Application information: Contributes only to pre-selected organizations.
Trustee: Norma H. Campbell.
EIN: 752769227
Codes: FD2

51424
Dougherty Foundation
P.O. Box 640
Beeville, TX 78104-0640 (361) 358-3560
Contact: Daren R. Wilder, Treas.

Established in 1940 in TX.
Donor(s): Genevieve T. Dougherty,‡ James R. Dougherty.‡
Financial data (yr. ended 07/31/01): Grants paid, $103,000; assets, $1,856,321 (M); expenditures, $106,816; qualifying distributions, $102,258.
Limitations: Giving primarily in southern TX.
Application information: 3-line executive summary should appear on first page of request. Application form not required.
Officer: Daren R. Wilder, Treas.
Trustees: Molly Dougherty, Frances Carr Tapp, Ben F. Vaughan III.
EIN: 746039859
Codes: FD2

51425
The Rodney H. and Judy E. Margolis Foundation
1400 Post Oak Blvd., Ste. 808
Houston, TX 77056-3009

Established in 1986 in TX.
Donor(s): Judy E. Margolis, Rodney H. Margolis.
Financial data (yr. ended 12/31/01): Grants paid, $103,000; assets, $658,680 (M); gifts received, $56,777; expenditures, $110,881; qualifying distributions, $103,848.
Limitations: Applications not accepted. Giving primarily in Houston, TX.
Application information: Contributes only to pre-selected organizations.
Officers: Rodney H. Margolis, Pres. and Treas.; Judy E. Margolis, V.P. and Secy.
EIN: 760208020
Codes: FD2

51426
Peach Mott Foundation, Inc.
P.O. Box 2549
Victoria, TX 77902-2549 (361) 573-4383
Contact: Thomas L. Keller, Secy.-Treas.

Established in 1994 in TX.
Donor(s): Michael Scott Anderson.
Financial data (yr. ended 11/30/01): Grants paid, $103,000; assets, $865,862 (M); gifts received, $113,850; expenditures, $103,239; qualifying distributions, $100,287.
Limitations: Giving primarily in TX.
Officers: Michael Scott Anderson, Pres.; Rayford L. Keller, V.P.; Thomas L. Keller, Secy.-Treas.
EIN: 742730037
Codes: FD2

51427
Hand in Hand Foundation
5150 Broadway, PMB 301
San Antonio, TX 78209-5710

Established in 1998 in TX.
Donor(s): Furr Investments, Ltd., Sunset Ridge Church, John Furr, Paula Furr.
Financial data (yr. ended 12/31/00): Grants paid, $102,408; assets, $390,249 (M); gifts received, $424,151; expenditures, $110,979; qualifying distributions, $102,408.
Limitations: Applications not accepted. Giving primarily in TX, Honduras, and Costa Rica.
Application information: Contributes only to pre-selected organizations.
Officers: John Furr, Pres. and Treas.; Dean Smith, V.P.; Paula Furr, Secy.
EIN: 742878386
Codes: CS, CD

51428
Southwest Medical Institute, Inc.
10300 N. Central Expwy., No. 230
Dallas, TX 75231

Donor(s): Kevin Gill, M.D.
Financial data (yr. ended 12/31/00): Grants paid, $102,310; assets, $0 (M); gifts received, $584,234; expenditures, $157,637; qualifying distributions, $102,310.
Limitations: Giving primarily in GA and TX.
Officers: Kevin Gill, M.D., Pres.; John F. Lown, V.P.
EIN: 752281441
Codes: FD2

51429
The Dennis and Jennie Hendrix Foundation
5400 Westheimer Ct.
Houston, TX 77056-5310

Established in 1994 in TX.
Donor(s): Dennis Hendrix, Jennie Hendrix.
Financial data (yr. ended 12/31/01): Grants paid, $101,860; assets, $1,177,143 (M); expenditures, $104,407; qualifying distributions, $101,574.
Limitations: Applications not accepted. Giving on a national basis.
Application information: Contributes only to pre-selected organizations.
Officers: Dennis R. Hendrix, Pres.; Jennie M. Hendrix, Secy.-Treas.
Directors: Natalie Hendrix Miller, Amy Hendrix Summers, Alisa Hendrix Sutor.
EIN: 760440413
Codes: FD2

51430
The Linda and Ronny Finger Foundation
c/o Legacy Trust Co.
P.O. Box 1471
Houston, TX 77251-1471

Established in 1999 in TX.
Donor(s): Linda K. Finger.
Financial data (yr. ended 06/30/01): Grants paid, $101,550; assets, $239,135 (M); gifts received, $387,885; expenditures, $106,359; qualifying distributions, $101,550.
Limitations: Applications not accepted. Giving primarily in Houston, TX.
Application information: Contributes only to pre-selected organizations.
Officer: Linda K. Finger, Pres.
Directors: Dee S. Osborne, J. Dickson Rogers.
EIN: 760610732
Codes: FD2

51431
The Works of Grace Foundation
3656 Maplewood Ave.
Dallas, TX 75205-2835

Established in 2000 in TX.
Donor(s): Theresa Castellano.
Financial data (yr. ended 12/31/01): Grants paid, $100,706; assets, $8,317,746 (M); expenditures, $117,507; qualifying distributions, $100,706.
Limitations: Applications not accepted.
Application information: Contributes only to pre-selected organizations.
Officers: Benjamin David Wood, Pres.; Theresa Castellano, V.P. and Treas.; Leslie Fundy, Secy.
EIN: 752906814

51432
Charles and Jennie Fermaturo Charitable Foundation
c/o Bank of America, N.A.
P.O. Box 831041
Dallas, TX 75283-1041
Application address: P.O. Box 419119, Kansas City, MO 64141-6119, tel.: (816) 979-7481
Contact: David P. Ross, Sr. V.P., Bank of America

Established in 1978 in MO.
Donor(s): Jennie Fermaturo Irrevocable Trust.
Financial data (yr. ended 12/31/01): Grants paid, $100,539; assets, $1,638,823 (M); expenditures, $130,546; qualifying distributions, $112,336.
Limitations: Giving primarily in the Kansas City, MO, area.
Application information: Application form not required.
Trustee: Bank of America.
EIN: 436213510
Codes: FD2

51433
The UTE Trail Ranch Foundation
(Formerly Covenant Trust)
1412 Main St., Ste. 905
Dallas, TX 75202

Established in 1982 in TX.
Donor(s): George E. Seay III, Nancy C. Seay, George E. Seay, Jr., Sarah S. Seay.
Financial data (yr. ended 12/31/01): Grants paid, $100,411; assets, $993,722 (M); gifts received, $22,234; expenditures, $121,759; qualifying distributions, $121,739.
Limitations: Applications not accepted. Giving primarily in TX.
Application information: Contributes only to pre-selected organizations. Unsolicited requests for funds not accepted.
Trustees: George E. Seay, Jr., George E. Seay III.
EIN: 237087227
Codes: FD2

51434
The Roy Gene and Pamela Evans Foundation
P.O. Box 601025
Dallas, TX 75360-1025

Established in 1989 in TX.
Donor(s): Roy Gene Evans, Pamela B. Evans.
Financial data (yr. ended 12/31/01): Grants paid, $100,204; assets, $2,020,372 (M); expenditures, $106,915; qualifying distributions, $100,204.
Limitations: Applications not accepted. Giving primarily in Dallas, TX.
Application information: Contributes only to pre-selected organizations.
Officers: Roy Gene Evans, Pres.; Pamela B. Evans, V.P. and Secy.
EIN: 752292043
Codes: FD2

51435
The Karakin Foundation
P.O. Box 2079
Abilene, TX 79604

Established in 1997 in TX.
Donor(s): Joseph B. Matthews, Julia Jones Matthews.
Financial data (yr. ended 12/31/01): Grants paid, $100,000; assets, $412,941 (M); expenditures, $107,699; qualifying distributions, $100,000.
Limitations: Applications not accepted.
Application information: Contributes only to pre-selected organizations.
Officers and Directors:* Joseph B. Matthews,* Pres.; Leroy Bolt,* V.P. and Treas.; David L. Buhrmann,* Secy.
EIN: 752692023

51436
The Leah Lee Adatto Kayem Foundation
10830 Old Katy Rd.
Houston, TX 77043

Established in 1998 in TX.
Donor(s): Leah Lee Adatto Kayem.
Financial data (yr. ended 04/30/01): Grants paid, $100,000; assets, $1,353,374 (M); expenditures, $103,363; qualifying distributions, $99,278.
Limitations: Applications not accepted. Giving primarily in Houston, TX.
Application information: Contributes only to pre-selected organizations.
Officers: Leah Lee Adatto Kayem, Pres.; Curtis R. Kayem, V.P.; Carol O'Kelly Kayem, Secy.-Treas.
EIN: 311601499
Codes: FD2

51437
Kuykendall Foundation
P.O. Box 6220
Lubbock, TX 79493-6220
Contact: John F. Schneider, Mgr.

Established in 1945.
Donor(s): George P. Kuykendall, Roger L. Kuykendall, Mary V. Kuykendall.
Financial data (yr. ended 12/31/01): Grants paid, $100,000; assets, $1,847,239 (M); expenditures, $107,261; qualifying distributions, $102,799.
Limitations: Giving primarily in Lubbock, TX.
Application information: Application form not required.
Officer and Trustees:* John F. Schneider,* Mgr.; Harry Mays, JoAnn Schneider, Karol K. Tarbox.
EIN: 756038612
Codes: FD2

51438
Marshal Verne Ross Foundation, Inc.
2200 Quail Hollow Dr.
Bryan, TX 77802-2919 (979) 776-1522
Contact: Mary Frances Ross, Pres.

Established in 1998 in TX.
Financial data (yr. ended 12/31/01): Grants paid, $100,000; assets, $1,583,166 (M); expenditures, $124,577; qualifying distributions, $99,413.
Limitations: Giving primarily in TX.
Officers: Mary Frances Ross, Pres.; Margaret Purvis, V.P.; Wendell Moore, Secy.-Treas.
Directors: Amanda Lee Ross, Marsha Frances Ross Shaer.
EIN: 742864663
Codes: FD2

51439
The Donald Monk Cancer Research Foundation
1120 Capital of Texas Hwy., S., Bldg 32
Austin, TX 78746

Established in 2001 in TX.
Financial data (yr. ended 12/31/01): Grants paid, $99,930; assets, $26,060 (M); gifts received, $187,340; expenditures, $161,280; qualifying distributions, $99,930.
Limitations: Applications not accepted. Giving primarily in CO.
Application information: Contributes only to pre-selected organizations.
Officers: Allison Minton, Pres.; Alan Andrews, Secy.
Directors: Nancy Cagle, Margaret Monk, Marilou Morrison, Thomas Slaga, Loretta Zapp.
EIN: 742996539

51440
David and Margaret Kilgore Foundation
3919 Southwestern Blvd.
Dallas, TX 75225-7034

Established in 1988 in TX.
Donor(s): David P. Kilgore, Margaret W. Kilgore.
Financial data (yr. ended 12/31/01): Grants paid, $99,910; assets, $732,003 (M); gifts received, $300,106; expenditures, $102,071; qualifying distributions, $99,974.
Limitations: Applications not accepted. Giving on a national basis.
Application information: Contributes only to pre-selected organizations.
Officers: David P. Kilgore, Chair.; Margaret W. Kilgore, Vice-Chair.
EIN: 752279050
Codes: FD2

51441
David B. Terk Foundation
12015 San Pedro Ave., Ste. 100
San Antonio, TX 78216 (210) 495-4545
FAX: (210) 494-7770

Established in 1992.
Financial data (yr. ended 12/31/99): Grants paid, $99,725; assets, $1,911,916 (M); gifts received, $37,935; expenditures, $108,768; qualifying distributions, $97,787.
Limitations: Applications not accepted. Giving primarily in TX.
Application information: Contributes only to pre-selected organizations.
Officers and Directors:* David B. Terk,* Pres.; Kristin R. Belt,* V.P.; Kimberly T. Murphy,* V.P.; Robert M. Shiloff,* Secy.-Treas.
EIN: 742640710
Codes: FD2

51442
The Dunham Charitable Foundation
c/o Woodway Financial Advisors
10000 Memorial Dr., Ste. 650
Houston, TX 77024

Established in 1997 in TX.
Donor(s): Archie Dunham, Linda Dunham.
Financial data (yr. ended 09/30/01): Grants paid, $99,500; assets, $783,264 (M); expenditures, $117,361; qualifying distributions, $101,378.
Limitations: Applications not accepted. Giving primarily in TX.
Application information: Contributes only to pre-selected organizations.
Officers and Directors:* Archie Dunham,* Pres.; Cary Dunham,* V.P.; Linda Dunham,* V.P.; Steve Dunham,* V.P.; Laura Shook,* V.P.
EIN: 760554767
Codes: FD2

51443
FINA Foundation
(Formerly American Petrofina Foundation)
P.O. Box 2159
Dallas, TX 75221-2159
Contact: J. Maria Martineau, Secy.

Incorporated in 1974 in TX.
Donor(s): FINA, Inc.
Financial data (yr. ended 12/31/01): Grants paid, $99,348; assets, $3,381,947 (M); expenditures, $101,201; qualifying distributions, $99,348.
Limitations: Giving primarily in TX, in areas where company employees reside.
Application information: Application form required for employee matching gifts. Grants are between $50 and $5,000; special restrictions applied to grants to higher education institutions.

Officers and Directors:* Ronald W. Haddock,* Pres.; Cullen M. Godfrey,* V.P.; Carla H. Meadows,* V.P.; J. Maria Martineau,* Secy.
EIN: 237391423
Codes: CS, FD2, CD

51444
Havens Foundation, Inc.
25132 Oakhurst, Ste. 210
Spring, TX 77386
Contact: Joe D. Havens, Pres.

Established in 1990 in TX.
Donor(s): Joe D. Havens, Margaret L. Havens.
Financial data (yr. ended 12/31/01): Grants paid, $99,100; assets, $1,747,494 (M); expenditures, $103,901; qualifying distributions, $103,901.
Limitations: Giving primarily in TX.
Application information: Application form required.
Officers and Directors:* Joe D. Havens,* Pres.; Kendra Wolf, Secy.-Treas.; Margaret L. Havens, Michael D. Havens, Nancy R. Hoff.
EIN: 760317434
Codes: FD2, GTI

51445
The Bettye & Murphy George Foundation
105 Loftin St.
Lufkin, TX 75904

Established in 1998 in TX.
Financial data (yr. ended 12/31/01): Grants paid, $99,000; assets, $1,405,423 (M); expenditures, $100,894; qualifying distributions, $99,491.
Limitations: Applications not accepted. Giving primarily in TX.
Application information: Contributes only to pre-selected organizations.
Officers: Randy George, Pres.; Trent Hicks, Secy.-Treas.
EIN: 752706694
Codes: FD2

51446
Rose Silverthorne Foundation
2940 N. O'Connor Rd., Ste. 125
Irving, TX 75062 (972) 252-4200
Contact: William B. Driscoll, Treas.

Established in 1994.
Donor(s): Mary R. Silverthorne.
Financial data (yr. ended 12/31/00): Grants paid, $98,841; assets, $2,748,612 (M); gifts received, $20,250; expenditures, $117,105; qualifying distributions, $11,272.
Limitations: Giving primarily to residents of TX.
Publications: Application guidelines.
Application information: Application form required.
Officers: Mary R. Silverthorne, Pres.; Bridget Russell, Secy.; William B. Driscoll, Treas.
EIN: 752669407
Codes: FD2

51447
The Riddle Foundation
6810 F.M. 1960 W., Ste. 200
Houston, TX 77069 (281) 444-9090
Contact: Don R. Riddle, Pres.

Established in 1994 in TX.
Donor(s): Don R. Riddle.
Financial data (yr. ended 12/31/99): Grants paid, $98,788; assets, $2,929,947 (M); gifts received, $500,000; expenditures, $100,899; qualifying distributions, $96,440.
Limitations: Giving primarily in Houston, TX.
Officers and Directors:* Don R. Riddle,* Pres.; Jenny L. Riddle,* V.P.; Stacy Riddle-Baumgartner,* Secy.; Todd Arlis Riddle,* Treas.
EIN: 760455477
Codes: FD2

51448
The Jamail Galveston Foundation
1200 Smith St., Ste. 1135
Houston, TX 77002
Contact: Robert L. Jamail

Established in 1992 in TX.
Donor(s): Joseph D. Jamail, Lillie H. Jamail.
Financial data (yr. ended 12/31/00): Grants paid, $98,500; assets, $3,559,070 (M); gifts received, $25,000; expenditures, $134,233; qualifying distributions, $96,480.
Limitations: Giving limited to the Galveston, TX area.
Application information: Videos not accepted. Application form not required.
Officers: Lillie H. Jamail, Pres. and Treas.; Donald P. Stevens, V.P.; John S. McEldowney, Secy.
EIN: 760370098

51449
The Malachi Fund
(Formerly The Elaine & Brad Bracewell Foundation)
2001 Kirby Dr.
Houston, TX 77019 (713) 529-1100
Contact: Brad Bracewell, Tr.

Established in 1998 in TX.
Donor(s): Brad Bracewell, Elaine Bracewell.
Financial data (yr. ended 12/31/00): Grants paid, $98,392; assets, $147,088 (M); expenditures, $106,252; qualifying distributions, $98,381.
Limitations: Giving primarily in Houston, TX.
Trustee: Brad Bracewell.
EIN: 311581961
Codes: FD2

51450
Joseph W. Gayden Memorial Foundation
1501 N. Banks
Pampa, TX 79065

Financial data (yr. ended 12/31/01): Grants paid, $98,338; assets, $1,526,825 (M); expenditures, $101,663; qualifying distributions, $99,088.
Limitations: Applications not accepted.
Application information: Contributes only to pre-selected organizations.
Officers: Henry Urbanczyk, Chair.; Robert L. Neslage, Vice-Chair.; Joe Martinez, Secy.-Treas.
Trustte: Bishop John Yanta.
EIN: 756155809
Codes: FD2

51451
The Boeckman Family Foundation
2911 Turtle Creek Blvd., Ste. 1240
Dallas, TX 75219-6256
Contact: Duncan E. Boeckman, V.P.

Established in 1998 in TX.
Donor(s): Elizabeth Mayer Boeckman, Duncan E. Boeckman.
Financial data (yr. ended 12/31/00): Grants paid, $98,170; assets, $5,184,020 (M); gifts received, $5,296,996; expenditures, $102,057; qualifying distributions, $102,027.
Limitations: Applications not accepted. Giving primarily in Santa Fe, NM and Dallas, TX.
Application information: Unsolicited requests for funds not accepted.
Officers and Trustees:* Elizabeth Mayer Boeckman,* Pres.; Duncan E. Boeckman,* V.P. and Secy.-Treas.; Kathryn Boeckman Howd.
EIN: 752766894
Codes: FD2

51452
A. S. Genecov Foundation
P.O. Box 132450
Tyler, TX 75713-2450
FAX: (903) 509-8866
Contact: Felicity Reedy

Established in 1955.
Donor(s): A.S. Genecov,‡ Hilda J. Genecov.‡
Financial data (yr. ended 12/31/01): Grants paid, $98,100; assets, $2,039,002 (M); expenditures, $98,139; qualifying distributions, $98,100.
Limitations: Applications not accepted. Giving limited to eastern TX.
Publications: Annual report.
Application information: Contributes only to pre-selected organizations.
Officers: Dennis D. Darryl, Mgr.; Terry Muntz Darryl, Mgr.; Maurine Genecov Muntz, Mgr.
EIN: 756023698
Codes: FD2

51453
Kline Family Foundation
5807 Deloache Ave.
Dallas, TX 75225

Established in 1997 in TX.
Donor(s): J. Peter Kline.
Financial data (yr. ended 12/31/01): Grants paid, $98,016; assets, $1,704,687 (M); expenditures, $106,825; qualifying distributions, $97,431.
Limitations: Applications not accepted. Giving primarily in TX, with emphasis on the Dallas-Fort Worth area.
Application information: Contributes only to pre-selected organizations.
Officer and Director:* J. Peter Kline,* Pres.
EIN: 752698214
Codes: FD2

51454
The Robert Schwan and Anne Kriescher Charitable Foundation
800 N. Shoreline Blvd., Ste. 900 N.
Corpus Christi, TX 78401-3709

Established in 1999 in TX.
Donor(s): Robert M. Tabone.
Financial data (yr. ended 12/31/00): Grants paid, $98,000; assets, $2,955,200 (M); gifts received, $70,000; expenditures, $217,466; qualifying distributions, $93,305.
Limitations: Applications not accepted. Giving primarily in TX.
Application information: Contributes only to pre-selected organizations.
Officers: Robert M. Tabone, Pres.; Helen M. Tabone, V.P.; Jean M. Tabone, Secy.; Michael J. Tabone, Treas.
Directors: Richard L. Leshin, Fr. Victor Scocco, Kathryn A. Tabone, Robert A. Tabone.
EIN: 742905939
Codes: FD2

51455
Kadane Foundation
P.O. Box 960
Wichita Falls, TX 76307-0960

Established in 1989 in TX.
Financial data (yr. ended 12/31/01): Grants paid, $97,375; assets, $1,168,156 (M); gifts received, $190,817; expenditures, $108,879; qualifying distributions, $108,879.
Limitations: Applications not accepted. Giving primarily in Wichita Falls, TX.
Application information: Contributes only to pre-selected organizations.
Officers: Billie Kirby, Pres.; Robert W. Goff, Jr., V.P.; Johanna Little, V.P.

51455—TEXAS

EIN: 752294608
Codes: FD2

51456
Castle Hills Schools Foundation, Inc.
4228 N. Central Expwy., Ste. 300
Dallas, TX 75206-6534

Donor(s): Castle Hills Development Corp., Weekley Homes, L.P., Wyndsor Custom Homes, Castle Hills Development Corp.
Financial data (yr. ended 12/31/00): Grants paid, $97,305; assets, $633,227 (M); gifts received, $354,370; expenditures, $97,438; qualifying distributions, $97,305.
Limitations: Applications not accepted. Giving primarily in TX.
Application information: Unsolicited requests for funds not accepted.
Officers: Christopher R. Bright, Pres. and Treas.; Clay V.N. Bright, V.P. and Secy.
Directors: Harvey R. Bright, Margaret Bright Vonder Hoya, Carol Bright Hunter.
EIN: 752732689
Codes: FD2

51457
The Sam D. Young Family Foundation
P.O. Box 2558
Houston, TX 77252-8037 (800) 367-6548
Contact: Sam D. Young, Jr., Pres.

Established in 1982 in TX.
Donor(s): Sam D. Young, Jr., Elizabeth Y. Taber.
Financial data (yr. ended 11/30/01): Grants paid, $97,260; assets, $616,641 (M); gifts received, $40,300; expenditures, $108,370; qualifying distributions, $98,217.
Limitations: Giving primarily in El Paso, TX.
Application information: Application form not required.
Officers: Sam D. Young, Jr., Pres.; Elizabeth Y. Taber, V.P.
EIN: 742272101
Codes: FD2

51458
Hazel Montgomery, M.D., Memorial Scholarship Trust
P.O. Box 8444
Tyler, TX 75711-8444
Application address: c/o Jack Crain, Superintendent, West Independent School District, 801 N. Reagan, West, TX 76691, tel.: (817) 826-3728

Established in 1997 in TX.
Donor(s): Hazel I. Montgomery.‡
Financial data (yr. ended 05/31/01): Grants paid, $96,538; assets, $1,486,618 (M); expenditures, $111,539; qualifying distributions, $96,538.
Trustee: Southside Bank.
EIN: 756498847
Codes: FD2

51459
Schulte Charitable Foundation
10943 N. Sam Houston Pkwy. W., Ste. 150
Houston, TX 77064

Established in 1994 in TX.
Donor(s): Johnie Schulte, Jr.
Financial data (yr. ended 12/31/00): Grants paid, $96,479; assets, $280,106 (M); gifts received, $8,500; expenditures, $100,909; qualifying distributions, $97,801.
Limitations: Applications not accepted. Giving primarily in TX.
Application information: Contributes only to pre-selected organizations.
Officers: Johnie Schulte, Jr., Pres.; Barbara Schulte, V.P. and Secy.-Treas.
EIN: 760455567
Codes: FD2

51460
The William and Phyllis Snyder Foundation
5 Carmarthen Ct.
Dallas, TX 75225

Established in 1999 in TX.
Donor(s): William B. Snyder, Phyllis G. Snyder.
Financial data (yr. ended 12/31/00): Grants paid, $96,444; assets, $170,492 (M); gifts received, $46; expenditures, $98,864; qualifying distributions, $96,444.
Limitations: Applications not accepted. Giving primarily in Iowa City, IA.
Application information: Contributes only to pre-selected organizations.
Officers: William B. Snyder, Pres. and Treas.; Phyllis G. Snyder, V.P. and Secy.
Director: Claudia K. Snyder.
EIN: 752847446
Codes: FD2

51461
James M. and Nancy J. Hoak Foundation
7037 Vassar Ave.
Dallas, TX 75205-1259

Established in 1990 in TX.
Donor(s): James M. Hoak, Nancy J. Hoak.
Financial data (yr. ended 11/30/01): Grants paid, $96,435; assets, $1,880,429 (M); expenditures, $125,625; qualifying distributions, $97,935.
Limitations: Applications not accepted. Giving primarily in Dallas, TX.
Application information: Contributes only to pre-selected organizations.
Officers: James M. Hoak, Pres. and Treas.; Nancy J. Hoak, V.P. and Secy.
EIN: 752357697
Codes: FD2

51462
The Harvey & Joyce Mitchell Family Foundation
5826 Farquhar
Dallas, TX 75209

Established in 1997 in TX.
Donor(s): Harvey R. Mitchell, Joyce Ann Mitchell.
Financial data (yr. ended 12/31/01): Grants paid, $96,430; assets, $249,351 (M); gifts received, $57,977; expenditures, $100,575; qualifying distributions, $98,640.
Limitations: Applications not accepted. Giving primarily in Dallas, TX.
Application information: Contributes only to pre-selected organizations.
Officers: Joyce Ann Mitchell, Pres.; Harvey R. Mitchell III, V.P.; Paul S. Mitchell, V.P.; Harvey R. Mitchell, Secy.-Treas.
EIN: 752681515
Codes: FD2

51463
GFT Associates
P.O. Box 5585
Austin, TX 78763

Established in 1991 in TX.
Donor(s): Balie J. Griffith, Beverly D. Griffith.
Financial data (yr. ended 12/31/01): Grants paid, $96,350; assets, $763,290 (M); gifts received, $120,000; expenditures, $98,009; qualifying distributions, $96,350.
Limitations: Applications not accepted. Giving primarily in Austin, TX.
Application information: Contributes only to pre-selected organizations.
Officers: Balie J. Griffith, Pres.; Stephen B. Griffith, V.P.; Beverly D. Griffith, Secy.
EIN: 742572771

51464
Don and Colletta McMillian Foundation
10497 Town & Country Way, Ste. 230
Houston, TX 77024-1118
Contact: Don F. McMillian, Chair.; or Colletta R. McMillian, Pres.

Established in 1991 in TX.
Donor(s): Don McMillian, Lolletta McMillian.
Financial data (yr. ended 11/30/01): Grants paid, $96,223; assets, $1,833,424 (M); gifts received, $169,111; expenditures, $111,602; qualifying distributions, $96,862.
Limitations: Giving primarily in Houston, TX.
Application information: Application form not required.
Officers and Trustees:* Don F. McMillian,* Chair.; Colletta R. McMillian,* Pres.; Don F. McMillian, Jr., Reid R. McMillian, Robert R. McMillian.
EIN: 760364247
Codes: FD2

51465
Art Happens
5501 Columbia Art Ctr.
Dallas, TX 75214

Established in 1998 in TX.
Donor(s): Kaleta Doolin.
Financial data (yr. ended 12/31/01): Grants paid, $96,150; assets, $1,402,063 (M); expenditures, $110,442; qualifying distributions, $96,150.
Limitations: Applications not accepted.
Application information: Contributes only to pre-selected organizations.
Officers: Kaleta Doolin, Pres.; Charles W. Doolin, V.P.; Earl L. Doolin, Secy.-Treas.
EIN: 752764775

51466
KWS Foundation
3756 Knollwood
Houston, TX 77019
Contact: Donald R. Sinclair, Pres.

Established in 1997 in TX.
Donor(s): Donald R. Sinclair.
Financial data (yr. ended 12/31/00): Grants paid, $96,000; assets, $623,594 (M); gifts received, $422; expenditures, $105,241; qualifying distributions, $94,830.
Limitations: Applications not accepted. Giving primarily in Houston, TX.
Application information: Contributes only to pre-selected organizations.
Officers: Donald R. Sinclair, Pres.; James T. Hackett, V.P.; Susan Lacy Sinclair, Secy.-Treas.
EIN: 760521970
Codes: FD2

51467
The Hevrdejs Foundation
8 Greenway Plz., Ste. 702
Houston, TX 77046 (713) 961-5110
Contact: Cathy Hevrdejs, Pres.

Established in 1988 in TX.
Donor(s): Frank J. Hevrdejs.
Financial data (yr. ended 12/31/00): Grants paid, $95,900; assets, $1,503,371 (M); expenditures, $124,944; qualifying distributions, $107,269.
Limitations: Giving primarily in TX.
Publications: Informational brochure (including application guidelines).
Application information: Application form not required.

Officers and Trustees:* Frank J. Hevrdejs,* Chair.; Catherine L. Hevrdejs,* Pres.; Phyllis C. Childress,* Secy.; Lynn T. Campbell, Ted Estess, David Fink.
EIN: 760267717
Codes: FD2

51468
The Goldfield Family Foundation
1850 Turbeville Rd.
Denton, TX 76210

Established in 2000 in TX.
Donor(s): Shirley M. Goldfield.
Financial data (yr. ended 12/31/00): Grants paid, $95,800; assets, $30,033 (M); gifts received, $135,188; expenditures, $100,024; qualifying distributions, $99,495.
Limitations: Applications not accepted. Giving primarily in New York, NY and Dallas, TX.
Application information: Contributes only to pre-selected organizations.
Officers: Shirley M. Goldfield, Pres.; Kirk Rimer, Secy.
EIN: 752823513
Codes: FD2

51469
Ennar Foundation
P.O. Box 1310
Beaumont, TX 77704-8311

Established in 1984 in TX.
Donor(s): N.J. Rogers.
Financial data (yr. ended 12/31/01): Grants paid, $95,755; assets, $188,839 (M); expenditures, $96,130; qualifying distributions, $95,628.
Limitations: Applications not accepted. Giving primarily in TX.
Application information: Contributes only to pre-selected organizations.
Trustee: N.J. Rogers.
EIN: 760101850
Codes: FD2

51470
Gilman and Gonzalez-Falla Theatre Foundation, Inc.
P.O. Box 18925
Corpus Christi, TX 78480 (361) 937-2520
Contact: Celso M. Gonzales, V.P.

Established in 1989 in TX.
Donor(s): Sondra and Charles Gilman, Jr. Foundation.
Financial data (yr. ended 12/31/01): Grants paid, $95,330; assets, $183,160 (M); gifts received, $295,408; expenditures, $301,515; qualifying distributions, $243,744.
Publications: Application guidelines.
Application information: Write for application. Application form required.
Officers: Sondra Gilman Gonzalez-Falla, Pres.; Celso M. Gonzalez, V.P.
EIN: 133463382
Codes: FD2, GTI

51471
The Toller Family Foundation
c/o Jo Ella Toller
22 Wincrest Falls Dr.
Cypress, TX 77429
E-mail: wtoller@msn.com

Established in 1997 in CT.
Donor(s): Jo Ella Toller, William R. Toller.
Financial data (yr. ended 12/31/01): Grants paid, $95,250; assets, $685,700 (M); expenditures, $103,323; qualifying distributions, $95,250.
Limitations: Applications not accepted. Giving primarily in AR, CT, OK, TX, and UT.

Application information: Contributes only to pre-selected organizations.
Officers: Jo Ella Toller, Pres.; Michelle D. Toller-Augustini, V.P. and Secy.; William R. Toller, Sr., V.P. and Treas.; Gregory A. Toller, V.P.; W. Robert Toller, Jr., V.P.
EIN: 061484189

51472
Harkins Foundation
P.O. Box 23075
Corpus Christi, TX 78403-3075
(361) 883-3022
Contact: Burt Harkins, Tr.

Established in 1969 in TX.
Financial data (yr. ended 10/31/00): Grants paid, $95,020; assets, $1,620,141 (M); expenditures, $100,310; qualifying distributions, $94,154.
Limitations: Giving primarily in TX.
Application information: Application form not required.
Trustees: Burt Harkins, Tim Harkins, Deirdre Richards, Mary Lee Sweeney.
EIN: 746124115
Codes: FD2

51473
The Victor J. Rogers Family Foundation
P.O. Box 1310
Beaumont, TX 77704-8311

Established in 1980 in TX.
Donor(s): Rogers Bros. Foundation, Inc., Victor J. Rogers.
Financial data (yr. ended 11/30/01): Grants paid, $94,881; assets, $487,926 (M); expenditures, $95,274; qualifying distributions, $94,669.
Limitations: Applications not accepted. Giving primarily in Beaumont, TX.
Application information: Contributes only to pre-selected organizations.
Officer: Fred L. Brown, Mgr.
Trustees: J.W. Rogers, Victor J. Rogers.
EIN: 742147665
Codes: FD2

51474
Morrison Trust
c/o Frost National Bank Trust Dept.
P.O. Box 2950
San Antonio, TX 78299-2950 (210) 220-4441
Contact: William L. Clyborne, Jr., V.P., Frost National Bank

Financial data (yr. ended 09/30/01): Grants paid, $94,782; assets, $3,488,456 (M); expenditures, $127,845; qualifying distributions, $111,602.
Limitations: Giving primarily in TX.
Trustee: Frost National Bank.
EIN: 746013340
Codes: FD2, GTI

51475
Holt Foundation
P.O. Box 207916
San Antonio, TX 78220-7916

Established in 1994 in TX.
Donor(s): Benjamin D. Holt, Jr., Holt Companies.
Financial data (yr. ended 11/30/01): Grants paid, $94,677; assets, $1,130,158 (M); gifts received, $41,279; expenditures, $95,375; qualifying distributions, $94,970.
Limitations: Applications not accepted. Giving primarily in San Antonio, TX.
Application information: Contributes only to pre-selected organizations.
Officers and Directors:* Peter M. Holt,* Pres.; Kenneth R. Kamp, V.P. and Secy.; David C.

Hennessee, Treas.; Anne Holt, Benjamin D. Holt, Jr., Benjamin D. Holt III.
EIN: 742728633
Codes: FD2

51476
C. N. and Maria Papadopoulos Charitable Foundation
3939 Hartsdale Dr.
Houston, TX 77063-6403
Contact: Helena P. Johnson

Established in 1999 in TX.
Donor(s): C.N. Papadopoulos.
Financial data (yr. ended 03/31/02): Grants paid, $94,640; assets, $1,886,220 (M); expenditures, $191,046; qualifying distributions, $94,640.
Limitations: Applications not accepted. Giving on a national basis, with emphasis on TX.
Application information: Contributes only to pre-selected organizations. Unsolicited requests for funds not accepted.
Officers and Directors:* C.N. Papadopoulos,* Pres. and Treas.; Maria Papadopoulos,* V.P.; Helena P. Johnson,* Secy.; Neofytos "Dean" Papadopoulos, William C. Papadopoulos, Christina P. Papandreau.
EIN: 760604133
Codes: FD2

51477
Unkefer Foundation
750 N. St. Paul St., 10th Fl.
Dallas, TX 75201

Established in 1999 in TX.
Donor(s): Ronald A. Unkefer, Terry L. Unkefer.
Financial data (yr. ended 12/31/01): Grants paid, $94,285; assets, $1,027,436 (M); expenditures, $99,210; qualifying distributions, $94,285.
Limitations: Applications not accepted.
Application information: Contributes only to pre-selected organizations.
Officers: Ronald A. Unkefer, Pres.; Terry L. Unkefer, Secy.
Director: Gary M. Lawrence.
EIN: 752794083
Codes: FD2

51478
Guinn Foundation, Inc.
1111 7th St.
Wichita Falls, TX 76301

Established in 1980 in TX.
Donor(s): Alfred B. Guinn, Patricia A. Guinn.
Financial data (yr. ended 12/31/01): Grants paid, $93,640; assets, $2,065,308 (M); gifts received, $68,940; expenditures, $95,618; qualifying distributions, $96,618.
Limitations: Applications not accepted. Giving primarily in TX.
Application information: Contributes only to pre-selected organizations.
Officers: Alfred B. Guinn, Pres. and Treas.; Patricia A. Guinn, V.P. and Secy.; Alfred Patrick Guinn, V.P.
EIN: 751735688
Codes: FD2

51479
Tellepsen Foundation
5425 Tupper Lake
Houston, TX 77056-1624

Financial data (yr. ended 12/31/01): Grants paid, $93,533; assets, $259,628 (M); gifts received, $50,000; expenditures, $94,206; qualifying distributions, $93,533.
Limitations: Applications not accepted. Giving primarily in Houston, TX.

Application information: Contributes only to pre-selected organizations.
Trustees: Karen Tellepsen Robinson, Howard T. Tellepsen, Jr., Tom Tellepsen II.
EIN: 741176983
Codes: FD2

51480
Cloyde & Ethel Lee Tracy Foundation
P.O. Box 1969
Victoria, TX 77902-1969
Contact: Munson Smith, Secy.

Established in 1984 in TX.
Donor(s): Ethel Lee Tracy.
Financial data (yr. ended 04/30/01): Grants paid, $93,500; assets, $1,635,254 (M); expenditures, $96,753; qualifying distributions, $93,500.
Limitations: Giving limited to Victoria, TX.
Officers: Melvin L. Roloff, Pres.; Munson Smith, Secy.; John McQuillen, Treas.
EIN: 742318575
Codes: FD2

51481
Confer-Creel Foundation
102 Cherrywood
Bellaire, TX 77401 (713) 664-2104
Contact: Rodney L. Creel

Established in 1997 in TX.
Donor(s): Judith C. Creel, Rodney L. Creel.
Financial data (yr. ended 04/30/01): Grants paid, $92,522; assets, $1,711,117 (M); expenditures, $102,904; qualifying distributions, $99,924.
Limitations: Giving on a national basis, with emphasis on LA and PA.
Application information: Application form required.
Officers: Jason Creel, Pres.; Judith C. Creel, Exec. V.P. and Secy.; Pamela B. Creel, V.P.; Rodney L. Creel, Treas.
EIN: 760536959
Codes: FD2

51482
The Liberty Street Foundation
8 Greenway Plz., Ste. 702
Houston, TX 77046

Established in 1988 in TX.
Donor(s): William R. Camp, Jr., Christy C. Camp.
Financial data (yr. ended 12/31/99): Grants paid, $92,500; assets, $840,411 (M); expenditures, $99,704; qualifying distributions, $92,500.
Limitations: Applications not accepted. Giving primarily in Nantucket, MA and Houston, TX.
Application information: Contributes only to pre-selected organizations.
Officers and Directors:* William R. Camp, Jr.,* Pres. and Treas.; Christy C. Camp,* V.P. and Secy.; Catherine C. Zammito.
EIN: 760257819
Codes: FD2

51483
Partridge Foundation
P.O. Drawer B
Kingsville, TX 78364
Contact: B. Waring Partridge, III, Pres.

Established in 1994 in TX.
Donor(s): B. Waring Partridge III.
Financial data (yr. ended 12/31/01): Grants paid, $92,500; assets, $1,611,630 (M); expenditures, $120,765; qualifying distributions, $92,500.
Limitations: Giving primarily in CT.
Application information: Request on organization letterhead.
Officers: B. Waring Partridge III, Pres. and Treas.; Julia A. Jitkoff, V.P. and Secy.

Director: Peter A. Noterman.
EIN: 742712637
Codes: FD2

51484
The Pieper Foundation
4265 San Felipe St., Ste. 1100
Houston, TX 77027-2912

Established in 1998 in TX.
Donor(s): W. Bernard Pieper, Mrs. W. Bernard Pieper.
Financial data (yr. ended 09/30/01): Grants paid, $92,350; assets, $1,280,051 (M); expenditures, $108,794; qualifying distributions, $91,755.
Limitations: Applications not accepted. Giving primarily in Houston, TX.
Application information: Contributes only to pre-selected organizations.
Trustees: Mary Lee Pieper Newman, Adele H. Pieper, Lynda Louise Pieper, W. Bernard Pieper.
EIN: 760552952
Codes: FD2

51485
The Lorenzo Family Foundation
333 Clay St., Ste. 4040
Houston, TX 77002

Established in 1997 in TX.
Donor(s): Francisco A. Lorenzo.
Financial data (yr. ended 12/31/00): Grants paid, $92,300; assets, $286,188 (M); gifts received, $60,000; expenditures, $96,990; qualifying distributions, $92,300.
Limitations: Applications not accepted. Giving primarily in MA and TX.
Application information: Contributes only to pre-selected organizations.
Directors: Francisco A. Lorenzo, Nicole P. Lorenzo, Sharon N. Lorenzo.
EIN: 760538228
Codes: FD2

51486
B. G. Byars Foundation
c/o Raymond W. Cozby, III
P.O. Box 2020
Tyler, TX 75710-2020 (903) 535-4200
E-mail: raymond.cozby@regions.com

Financial data (yr. ended 12/31/01): Grants paid, $92,250; assets, $133,887 (M); expenditures, $98,742; qualifying distributions, $92,250.
Limitations: Giving limited to residents of Smith County, TX.
Application information: Application form not required.
Trustees: Emily Elizabeth Byars Summers, Regions Bank.
EIN: 756011610
Codes: FD2

51487
Harvey & Mireille Katz Charitable Foundation
1250 W. Sam Houston Pkwy. S., Ste. 148
Houston, TX 77042

Established in 1997 in TX.
Financial data (yr. ended 12/31/01): Grants paid, $92,037; assets, $624,783 (M); expenditures, $97,470; qualifying distributions, $93,107.
Limitations: Applications not accepted.
Application information: Contributes only to pre-selected organizations.
Officers: Harvey Katz, Pres.; Audrey S. Wachsberg, V.P.; Mireille Katz, Secy.-Treas.
EIN: 760520066
Codes: FD2

51488
The Diana and Conrad Weil, Jr. Charitable Foundation
4600 Post Oak Pl., Ste. 152
Houston, TX 77027

Donor(s): Bertha Gordon Miller, Conrad S. Weil, Jr., Diana Miller Weil, I.L. and Bertha Gordon Miller Foundation, S. Conrad Weil.
Financial data (yr. ended 03/31/01): Grants paid, $91,995; assets, $442,951 (M); gifts received, $43,219; expenditures, $98,974; qualifying distributions, $93,090.
Limitations: Applications not accepted. Giving primarily in TX.
Application information: Contributes only to pre-selected organizations.
Officers: S. Conrad Weil, Jr., Pres. and Treas.; Diana Miller Weil, V.P. and Secy.
Trustee: Lauren Weil Friedman.
EIN: 760314718
Codes: FD2

51489
John and Linda Knox Family Foundation
10000 Memorial Dr., Ste. 330
Houston, TX 77024

Established in 1998 in TX.
Donor(s): John Knox, Linda S. Knox.
Financial data (yr. ended 12/31/01): Grants paid, $91,469; assets, $259,230 (M); expenditures, $95,412; qualifying distributions, $91,469.
Limitations: Applications not accepted.
Application information: Contributes only to pre-selected organizations.
Officers: John T. Knox, Jr., Pres.; Linda S. Knox, Secy.
Trustee: John T. Knox.
EIN: 760573833
Codes: FD2

51490
Sarah M. & Charles E. Seay Charitable Trust
300 Crescent Ct., Ste. 1370
Dallas, TX 75201-6923

Established in 1983 in TX.
Donor(s): Charles E. Seay, Sarah M. Seay.
Financial data (yr. ended 12/31/01): Grants paid, $91,293; assets, $4,945,652 (M); gifts received, $2,000,000; expenditures, $93,273; qualifying distributions, $91,293.
Limitations: Applications not accepted. Giving primarily in TX, with emphasis on Dallas.
Application information: Contributes only to pre-selected organizations. Unsolicited requests for funds not considered.
Trustees: Truman Kemper, Charles E. Seay, Charles E. Seay, Jr., Sarah M. Seay, Stephen M. Seay.
EIN: 751894505
Codes: FD2

51491
Sara & John Lindsey Foundation
3640 Willowick
Houston, TX 77019

Established in 1997 in TX.
Financial data (yr. ended 12/31/01): Grants paid, $91,258; assets, $1,014,166 (M); expenditures, $104,596; qualifying distributions, $91,258.
Officers: John H. Lindsey, Pres.; Sara H. Lindsey, V.P.
EIN: 760537238
Codes: FD2

51492
Heiligbrodt Family Foundation
11015 Landon Ln.
Houston, TX 77024

Donor(s): L. William Heiligbrodt, Corinne C. Heiligbrodt.
Financial data (yr. ended 12/31/00): Grants paid, $90,850; assets, $0 (M); gifts received, $88,325; expenditures, $91,491; qualifying distributions, $90,850.
Limitations: Giving primarily in TX.
Directors: George Champagne, Corinne C. Heiligbrodt, L. William Heiligbrodt.
EIN: 760372581
Codes: FD2

51493
Lydick Family Foundation
5161 San Felipe St., Ste. 320
P.O. Box 39
Houston, TX 77056 (713) 780-9203
Contact: J. Lee Lydick, Dir.

Established in 2000 in TX.
Donor(s): J. Lee Lydick.
Financial data (yr. ended 12/31/01): Grants paid, $90,834; assets, $1,744,271 (M); expenditures, $98,982; qualifying distributions, $90,834.
Directors: Anne Woodson Lydick, John Lee Lydick, John Lee Lydick, Jr., Robert Woodson Lydick.
EIN: 760662291

51494
Marjorie T. Walthall Perpetual Charitable Trust
112 W. Ridgewood Ct.
San Antonio, TX 78212-2342 (210) 822-5433
Contact: Paul T. Walthall, Tr.

Established in 1976 in TX.
Donor(s): Marjorie T. Walthall.
Financial data (yr. ended 12/31/00): Grants paid, $90,820; assets, $4,296,094 (M); expenditures, $137,393; qualifying distributions, $128,068.
Limitations: Giving primarily in San Antonio, TX.
Trustees: Marjorie Walthall Fry, Paul T. Walthall, Wilson J. Walthall III.
EIN: 510170313
Codes: FD2

51495
Franklin I. Brinegar Foundation
P.O. Box 600461
Dallas, TX 75360-0461
Application address: 3131 Maple Ave., Ste. 12B, Dallas, TX 75201, tel.: (214) 520-2559
Contact: Ralph F. Brinegar, Vice-Chair.

Established in 1960 in TX.
Donor(s): Franklin I. Brinegar.‡
Financial data (yr. ended 08/31/01): Grants paid, $90,534; assets, $1,528,619 (M); expenditures, $110,390; qualifying distributions, $90,048.
Limitations: Giving primarily in Dallas, TX.
Officers: Franklin I. Brinegar II, Chair.; Ralph F. Brinegar, Vice-Chair. and Treas.; Nan B. Matson, Secy.
Trustees: Mary M. Brinegar, Rosemary T. Brinegar, Carol B. Lowery.
EIN: 756023620
Codes: FD2

51496
Gabriel's Gifts Charitable Foundation
3333 Eastside St., Ste. 125G
Houston, TX 77098

Established in 2000.
Donor(s): Doreen James Wise.
Financial data (yr. ended 12/31/00): Grants paid, $90,250; assets, $160,695 (M); gifts received, $246,626; expenditures, $91,852; qualifying distributions, $91,852.
Limitations: Applications not accepted. Giving primarily in TX.
Application information: Contributes only to pre-selected organizations.
Officer: Doreen James Wise, Pres.
EIN: 760635336
Codes: FD2

51497
The Canseco Foundation
c/o Jorge Canseco
223 Inslee Ave.
San Antonio, TX 78209
Contact: Patricia C. Bruce, Pres.

Established in 1997 in TX.
Donor(s): Consuelo S. Canseco.‡
Financial data (yr. ended 12/31/01): Grants paid, $90,000; assets, $1,852,213 (M); expenditures, $94,353; qualifying distributions, $89,576.
Limitations: Giving primarily in Laredo and Webb County, TX.
Application information: Application form required.
Officers and Directors:* Patricia Canseco Bruce,* Pres.; Jorge E. Canseco,* Secy.-Treas.; Carlos M. Canseco, Francisco R. Canseco, Kim Canseco, Margarita Canseco Kantny, Cecilia Canseco Keck, Conti C. Meehan.
EIN: 742802328
Codes: FD2

51498
Opal G. Cox Charitable Trust
c/o Bank of America
P.O. Box 831041
Dallas, TX 75283-1041
Scholarship application addresses: c/o William J. Dube III, Office of Baylor Academic Scholarships and Financial Aid, Baylor Univ., Box 7028, Waco, TX 76798-7028, tel.: (254) 755-2611; or c/o David G. McQuitty, Dir. of Student Aid, Southwestern Baptist Theological Seminary, Box 22000, Fort Worth, TX 76122, tel.: (817) 923-1921

Established in 1982 in TX.
Donor(s): Opal G. Cox.‡
Financial data (yr. ended 08/31/01): Grants paid, $90,000; assets, $3,335,646 (M); expenditures, $140,501; qualifying distributions, $96,326.
Limitations: Giving primarily in TX.
Application information: Applications are available at financial aid office. Application form required.
Trustee: Bank of America.
EIN: 746307500
Codes: FD2, GTI

51499
Foundation for Kidney Transplantation
5 Lochtyne Cir.
Houston, TX 77024

Established in 1998 in TX.
Financial data (yr. ended 12/31/01): Grants paid, $90,000; assets, $2,550,517 (M); gifts received, $499,985; expenditures, $93,577; qualifying distributions, $90,000.
Limitations: Applications not accepted. Giving primarily in TX.
Application information: Contributes only to pre-selected organizations.
Officers: Helfried Liebling, Pres. and Treas.; Melissa Goldberg, V.P.; Brenda Goldberg, Secy.
EIN: 760551989
Codes: FD2

51500
Ollege and Minnie Morrison Foundation
c/o JPMorgan Chase Bank
P.O. Box 2558
Houston, TX 77252-8037 (713) 216-4513
Contact: Charlene D. Slack

Established in 1970.
Financial data (yr. ended 12/31/01): Grants paid, $90,000; assets, $1,811,573 (M); expenditures, $116,130; qualifying distributions, $91,158.
Limitations: Applications not accepted. Giving primarily in Livingston, TX.
Application information: Unsolicited requests for funds not considered.
Trustee: JPMorgan Chase Bank.
EIN: 237073336
Codes: FD2, GTI

51501
Parker Foundation
1020 N.E. Loop 410, Ste. 550
San Antonio, TX 78209

Incorporated in 1957 in TX.
Donor(s): Members of the Parker family, Joseph B. Parker, John M. Parker.
Financial data (yr. ended 03/31/01): Grants paid, $90,000; assets, $1,732,608 (M); expenditures, $103,528; qualifying distributions, $92,153.
Limitations: Applications not accepted. Giving primarily in the San Antonio, TX, area.
Application information: Contributes only to pre-selected organizations.
Officers and Directors:* Mary O. Parker,* Pres.; Camilla M. Parker, V.P.; Joseph B. Parker,* V.P.; John M. Parker,* Secy.-Treas.
EIN: 746040454
Codes: FD2

51502
The George G. & Alva Hudson Smith Foundation
P.O. Box 1245
Hillsboro, TX 76645-1245
Contact: Betty R. Dohoney, Pres.

Established in 1992 in TX.
Donor(s): Ruth S. Mooreman.‡
Financial data (yr. ended 06/30/01): Grants paid, $90,000; assets, $2,163,660 (M); expenditures, $116,818; qualifying distributions, $90,000.
Limitations: Giving limited to TX, with emphasis on the Hillsboro and Hill County areas.
Publications: Application guidelines.
Officers: Betty Ray Dohoney, Pres.; D'Ette Cowan, V.P.; Rev. Bob Moon, Secy.; Andrew L. Smith, Treas.
Director: John B. Tuggle.
EIN: 742653426
Codes: FD2

51503
Stillman-Lack Foundation
602 Wellesley Dr.
Houston, TX 77024-5507 (713) 479-1074
Contact: Jonathan Lack, Secy.-Treas.

Donor(s): Eli Stillman.‡
Financial data (yr. ended 07/31/01): Grants paid, $90,000; assets, $1,870,115 (M); gifts received, $1,585,623; expenditures, $177,134; qualifying distributions, $90,000.
Officer: Jonathan Lack, Secy.-Treas.
Trustees: Fredell Eichorn, Sharon Lack, Zella Silverman.
EIN: 746120167

51504
The Rosendo and Cheryl Parra Foundation
3725 Hunterwood Pt.
Austin, TX 78746-1305

Established in 1999 in TX.
Donor(s): Rosendo G. Parra, Cheryl L. Parra.
Financial data (yr. ended 12/31/01): Grants paid, $89,977; assets, $1,060,651 (M); expenditures, $95,360; qualifying distributions, $89,738.
Limitations: Applications not accepted. Giving on a national basis.
Application information: Contributes only to pre-selected organizations.
Directors: Michael Freiman, Cheryl L. Parra, Rosendo G. Parra.
EIN: 756563199
Codes: FD2

51505
RNC, Incorporated
13363 Southview Ln.
Dallas, TX 75240

Donor(s): Jeannie Pascale.
Financial data (yr. ended 12/31/00): Grants paid, $89,870; assets, $24,359 (M); gifts received, $85,000; expenditures, $91,371; qualifying distributions, $91,200.
Limitations: Applications not accepted. Giving on a national basis.
Application information: Contributes only to pre-selected organizations.
Officers: Robert N. Crawford, Pres. and Treas.; Cathy Middleton, V.P.; Jeannie Pascale, Secy.
EIN: 752539678
Codes: FD2

51506
The Legett Foundation
P.O. Box 1170
Clarendon, TX 79226-1170 (806) 874-5110
Contact: Kade L. Matthews, Pres.

Established in 1996 in TX.
Donor(s): Kade L. Matthews, Julia Jones Matthews.
Financial data (yr. ended 12/31/01): Grants paid, $89,706; assets, $1,231,670 (M); expenditures, $106,293; qualifying distributions, $89,706.
Limitations: Giving primarily in TX.
Officers: Kade L. Matthews, Pres.; John A. Matthews, Jr., V.P.; Joseph E. Cannon, Secy.-Treas.
EIN: 752696419

51507
Lulu Bryan Rambaud Charitable Trust
c/o Houston Trust Co.
1001 Fannin St., Ste. 1500
Houston, TX 77002-6707

Established in 1949 in TX.
Financial data (yr. ended 12/31/01): Grants paid, $89,600; assets, $1,519,721 (M); expenditures, $116,261; qualifying distributions, $98,525.
Limitations: Giving limited to Houston, TX.
Application information: Individuals are referred by Christ Church Cathedral, Houston, TX. Application form not required.
Trustees: James A. Elkins, Jr., Stuart A. Hellman, A.J. Hurt, Jr.
EIN: 746033114
Codes: FD2

51508
Stein Family Charitable Trust
c/o Bank of America
P.O. Box 831041
Dallas, TX 75283-1041
Application address: P.O. Box 1317, Fort Worth, TX 76101, tel.: (817) 390-6916
Contact: Joe B. Grissom, V.P., Bank of America

Established in 1983 in TX.
Donor(s): Harriet Stein,‡ Katie Stein,‡ Laura Stein,‡ and other members of the Stein family.
Financial data (yr. ended 02/28/01): Grants paid, $89,280; assets, $1,360,656 (M); expenditures, $98,258; qualifying distributions, $89,272.
Limitations: Giving primarily in the Dallas-Fort Worth, TX, area.
Publications: Annual report (including application guidelines).
Application information: Application form not required.
Trustee: Bank of America.
EIN: 756336289
Codes: FD2

51509
Galen T. Brown Foundation
c/o GCR Assocs.
13333 Westland E. Blvd., No. 203
Houston, TX 77041 (281) 890-2378
FAX: (713) 894-2566; *E-mail:* cmbregenze@bray.com
Contact: Craig C. Brown, Tr.

Established in 1988 in TX.
Donor(s): Galen T. Brown,‡ Robin G. Brown.
Financial data (yr. ended 12/31/00): Grants paid, $89,228; assets, $2,347,815 (M); gifts received, $1,650; expenditures, $149,272; qualifying distributions, $117,653.
Limitations: Giving primarily in Houston, TX and surrounding areas.
Application information: Application form not required.
Trustees: Craig C. Brown, Robin G. Brown.
EIN: 760254349
Codes: FD2

51510
The Jerry and Maury Rubenstein Foundation
2330 Holmes Rd.
Houston, TX 77051

Established in 2000 in TX.
Donor(s): Texas Pipe & Supply Co, Inc.
Financial data (yr. ended 05/31/02): Grants paid, $89,000; assets, $1,453,438 (M); gifts received, $690,628; expenditures, $90,097; qualifying distributions, $89,000.
Limitations: Applications not accepted. Giving primarily in Houston, TX.
Application information: Contributes only to pre-selected organizations.
Trustees: Jerry Rubenstein, Maury Rubenstein.
EIN: 316645608

51511
William and Evelyn Griffin Foundation
3207 Groveland
Houston, TX 77019 (713) 827-4870

Established in 1997 in TX.
Donor(s): Evelyn H. Griffin, William A. Griffin.
Financial data (yr. ended 12/31/01): Grants paid, $88,850; assets, $1,331,180 (M); expenditures, $95,720; qualifying distributions, $88,850.
Limitations: Applications not accepted. Giving primarily in GA; some giving also in CA and TX.
Application information: Contributes only to pre-selected organizations.
Officers and Directors:* Evelyn H. Griffin,* Pres.; G. Eyvonne Hairell, Secy.; William A. Griffin III.
EIN: 760538855

51512
The Ken and Teresa Rice Foundation
c/o Sentinel Trust Co.
2001 Kirby Dr., Ste. 1210
Houston, TX 77019-6018

Established in 2000 in TX.
Donor(s): Kenneth D. Rice, Teresa K. Rice.
Financial data (yr. ended 12/31/01): Grants paid, $88,196; assets, $1,784,511 (M); gifts received, $220,341; expenditures, $102,881; qualifying distributions, $88,196.
Limitations: Applications not accepted.
Application information: Contributes only to pre-selected organizations.
Officers and Directors:* Kenneth D. Rice,* Pres. and Treas.; Teresa K. Rice,* V.P. and Secy.; Susan Holmes-Burkart.
EIN: 760663652

51513
Bowden-Massey Foundation
P.O. Box 90436
San Antonio, TX 78209
E-mail: bowdenvm@aol.com
Contact: Charles L. Bowden, Pres.

Established in 1992 in TX.
Donor(s): Charles L. Bowden, Virginia M. Bowden.
Financial data (yr. ended 12/31/01): Grants paid, $87,750; assets, $800,000 (M); gifts received, $88,345; expenditures, $88,002; qualifying distributions, $88,000.
Limitations: Applications not accepted. Giving primarily in TX.
Publications: Annual report.
Application information: Unsolicited requests for funds not accepted.
Officers and Directors:* Charles L. Bowden,* Pres. and Treas.; Virginia M. Bowden,* V.P. and Secy.; Ellen M. Bowden, Sharon B. Davis.
EIN: 742637829
Codes: FD2

51514
The George and Anne Butler Foundation
12603 Pinerock Ln.
Houston, TX 77024
Contact: George V. Grainger, Pres.

Incorporated in 1956 in TX.
Donor(s): George A. Butler,‡ Anne G. Butler,‡ Houston Corp., McEvoy Co.
Financial data (yr. ended 12/31/00): Grants paid, $87,530; assets, $2,042,889 (M); expenditures, $149,345; qualifying distributions, $87,530.
Limitations: Applications not accepted. Giving primarily in Houston, TX.
Application information: Contributes only to pre-selected organizations.
Officers: George V. Grainger, Pres. and Treas.; Allen B. Grainger, Secy.
EIN: 746063429
Codes: FD2

51515
H. L. & Elizabeth M. Brown Foundation
P.O. Box 1030
Midland, TX 79702
Contact: H.L. Brown, Jr., Pres.

Established in 1981 in TX.
Donor(s): Elizabeth M. Brown Charitable Trust.
Financial data (yr. ended 12/31/01): Grants paid, $87,100; assets, $73,825 (M); gifts received,

$68,565; expenditures, $92,292; qualifying distributions, $90,495.
Limitations: Giving primarily in TX.
Application information: Application form required.
Officers: H.L. Brown, Jr., Pres.; Mary Jane B. Johndroe, V.P.; Annabelle E. Brown, Secy.
EIN: 751783643
Codes: FD2

51516
The Sanders Foundation
7777 Market Center Ave.
El Paso, TX 79912

Established in 1993.
Financial data (yr. ended 12/31/00): Grants paid, $87,000; assets, $1,747,324 (M); gifts received, $24,000; expenditures, $91,776; qualifying distributions, $87,000.
Limitations: Applications not accepted. Giving on a national basis.
Application information: Contributes only to pre-selected organizations.
Directors: Barry A. Kobren, Louann F. Sanders, William D. Sanders.
EIN: 742698726
Codes: FD2

51517
Ann B. Lancaster Memorial Foundation
305 Azalea Dr.
Grapevine, TX 76051

Established in 1985 in TX.
Donor(s): Baylor Medical Center.
Financial data (yr. ended 06/30/01): Grants paid, $86,775; assets, $2,042,720 (M); gifts received, $40,000; expenditures, $153,361; qualifying distributions, $90,228; giving activities include $3,285 for programs.
Limitations: Giving primarily in Grapevine, TX.
Officers: E.L. Lancaster, M.D., Pres.; Minnie Lee S. Lancaster, M.D., V.P. and Secy.
Directors: Charles L. Lancaster, Shirley Gage Moore, William Wilkerson.
EIN: 756061513
Codes: FD2

51518
The LBJ Nonprofit Corporation
114 W. 7th St., Ste. 300
Austin, TX 78701

Established in 1996 in TX.
Donor(s): The LBJ Family Foundation.
Financial data (yr. ended 12/31/99): Grants paid, $86,250; assets, $2,055,263 (M); expenditures, $107,249; qualifying distributions, $87,263.
Limitations: Applications not accepted. Giving primarily in TX.
Application information: Contributes only to pre-selected organizations.
Officers and Trustees:* Luci Baines Johnson,* Pres.; Nicole Marie Nugent Covert,* V.P.; Patrick Lyndon Nugent,* V.P.; Willyn Wahl, Secy.; Ian J. Turpin,* Treas.
EIN: 742715123
Codes: FD2

51519
Katz Foundation
P.O. Box 1438
Corpus Christi, TX 78403-1438
(361) 882-4371
Contact: Doris Katz, Tr.

Established in 1956 in TX.
Donor(s): Abe M. Katz,‡ Doris Katz.
Financial data (yr. ended 10/31/01): Grants paid, $86,033; assets, $1,388,479 (M); gifts received, $9,000; expenditures, $87,683; qualifying distributions, $85,322.
Limitations: Giving primarily in TX.
Application information: Application form not required.
Trustee: Doris Katz.
EIN: 746054042
Codes: FD2

51520
The Gonsoulin Charitable Trust
c/o Al A. Gonsoulin
10 Muirfield Way
Sugar Land, TX 77479-3966

Established in 1998 in TX.
Financial data (yr. ended 12/31/99): Grants paid, $85,950; assets, $7,958,308 (M); gifts received, $8,412,000; expenditures, $86,035; qualifying distributions, $8,837.
Limitations: Applications not accepted. Giving primarily in LA and TX.
Application information: Contributes only to pre-selected organizations.
Trustees: Al A. Gonsoulin, Gene J. Gonsoulin.
EIN: 766106726
Codes: FD2

51521
The Felvis Foundation
c/o David R. Graham
2413 Maconda Ln.
Houston, TX 77027

Established in 1997 in TX.
Donor(s): Robert H. Graham, Mrs. Robert H. Graham.
Financial data (yr. ended 12/31/01): Grants paid, $85,600; assets, $1,575,109 (M); expenditures, $103,556; qualifying distributions, $86,131.
Limitations: Applications not accepted. Giving primarily in TX.
Application information: Contributes only to pre-selected organizations.
Officers: David R. Graham, Pres.; Robert H. Graham, V.P.; Joanne C. Graham, Secy.-Treas.
EIN: 311519688
Codes: FD2

51522
Barber Foundation
133 Wall St.
Abilene, TX 79603
FAX: (915) 698-6860; *E-mail:* LHAMPTON@abilene.com
Contact: Harwell Barber, Mgr.

Established in 1966 in TX.
Donor(s): Harwell Barber, Rita Barber.‡
Financial data (yr. ended 12/31/01): Grants paid, $85,567; assets, $1,560,334 (M); gifts received, $91,707; expenditures, $91,707; qualifying distributions, $84,865.
Limitations: Giving primarily in Abilene, TX.
Application information: Application form not required.
Officer: Harwell Barber, Mgr.
Trustees: Carolyn Barber, Carolyn Barber Hampton.
EIN: 756067600
Codes: FD2

51523
Foresight Foundation
2404 Marlandwood Rd.
Temple, TX 76502
Application address: 3513 S.W. Dodgen Loop, Temple, TX 76502
Contact: Alan C. Jones, M.D., Pres.

Established in 1986 in TX.
Donor(s): Alan C. Jones, M.D., Lillian McKibbin.
Financial data (yr. ended 11/30/01): Grants paid, $85,500; assets, $968,994 (M); expenditures, $89,045; qualifying distributions, $84,972.
Limitations: Giving limited to central TX.
Publications: Informational brochure.
Application information: Application form not required.
Officer and Trustees:* Alan C. Jones, M.D.,* Pres. and Secy.; John M. Burrough, Charles Harrel, Steven C. Jones, Jennifer V. Schrup.
EIN: 742444567
Codes: FD2

51524
Katherine Butler Johnson Foundation
771 River Oaks Cir.
McKinney, TX 75069
Contact: Katherine Butler Johnson, Pres.

Established in 1997 in TX.
Donor(s): Claiborne H. Johnson, Jr.
Financial data (yr. ended 12/31/01): Grants paid, $85,500; assets, $652,171 (M); gifts received, $185,600; expenditures, $86,971; qualifying distributions, $85,500.
Limitations: Giving primarily in TX.
Officers and Directors:* Katherine Butler Johnson,* Pres. and Treas.; Elizabeth Johnson Keig,* Secy.; Claiborne H. Johnson III, Noran Johnson Reardon.
EIN: 742833152

51525
The MK2 Foundation
3389 Inwood Dr.
Houston, TX 77019
Contact: Max P. Watson, Jr., Dir.

Established in 1997.
Donor(s): Max P. Watson.
Financial data (yr. ended 12/31/01): Grants paid, $85,500; assets, $1,158,840 (M); gifts received, $22,000; expenditures, $85,500; qualifying distributions, $85,500.
Limitations: Giving primarily in Houston, TX.
Directors: Matthew C. Blackmon, Kay Greene Watson, Max P. Watson, Jr.
EIN: 760537908
Codes: FD2

51526
J. P. & Mary Jon Bryan Foundation
1221 Lamar, Ste. 1600
Houston, TX 77010
Contact: J.P. Bryan, Dir.

Established in 1993 in TX.
Donor(s): J.P. Bryan, M.J. Bryan.
Financial data (yr. ended 05/31/01): Grants paid, $85,396; assets, $1,661,144 (M); expenditures, $102,266; qualifying distributions, $88,656.
Limitations: Giving primarily in GA, NY and TX.
Application information: Application form required.
Directors: J.P. Bryan, John B. Bryan, M.J. Bryan.
EIN: 760406294
Codes: FD2

51527
The Warren Foundation, Inc.
6300 Ocean Dr.
Corpus Christi, TX 78412
Contact: Frank McMillan

Incorporated in 1955 in TX.
Donor(s): Guy I. Warren,‡ Mrs. Guy I. Warren.
Financial data (yr. ended 04/30/01): Grants paid, $85,205; assets, $2,086,419 (M); expenditures, $105,855; qualifying distributions, $95,016.

Limitations: Giving primarily in the Corpus Christi, TX, area.
Application information: Application form not required.
Officers: Richard Leshin, Pres.; Jefferson Bell, Jr., V.P.; Paula S. Waddle, Secy.; John Buckley, Treas.
Directors: Barbara Canales Black, Harvie Branscomb, Jr., John Chapman, Susan Dugan, Lucien Flouroy, Robert Furgason, Rosie Garza, Hon. Rene Haas, Fred Heldenfels IV, Harris A. Kaffie, Leon Loeb, Joseph P. Mueller, Alvaro J. Ramos, Guadalupe Rangel, Celika Storm.
EIN: 741262852
Codes: FD2

51528
The Harvest Foundation
P.O. Box 721402
Houston, TX 77272-1402

Established in 1991 in TX.
Donor(s): Daniel Waite, Sr., Mrs. Daniel Waite, Sr.
Financial data (yr. ended 09/30/01): Grants paid, $85,000; assets, $1,212,542 (M); expenditures, $207,738; qualifying distributions, $204,948.
Limitations: Applications not accepted. Giving primarily in TX.
Application information: Contributes only to pre-selected organizations. Funds fully committed; unsolicited requests for funds not considered.
Officers: Daniel Waite, Sr., Pres. and Treas.; Thomas E. Waite, V.P.; Susan W. Blanchfield, Secy.
EIN: 760352570
Codes: FD2

51529
Ralph B. Rogers Foundation
3601 Turtle Creek Blvd., Ste. 505
Dallas, TX 75219

Trust established in 1953 in TX.
Donor(s): Ralph B. Rogers.‡
Financial data (yr. ended 12/31/00): Grants paid, $85,000; assets, $940,941 (M); expenditures, $89,904; qualifying distributions, $85,000.
Limitations: Giving primarily in TX.
Application information: Application form not required.
Officers: Mary Neil Rogers, Pres.; Katherine Roberts, Secy.
Trustees: Frances Conroy, John B. Rogers, Richard G. Rogers, Robert D. Rogers, William E. Rogers.
EIN: 136153567
Codes: FD2

51530
The Beretta Foundation
123 Hubbard
San Antonio, TX 78209
FAX: (201) 805-8713; E-mail: jbt@txdirect.net

Established in 1968 in TX.
Donor(s): John King Beretta.‡
Financial data (yr. ended 06/30/01): Grants paid, $84,775; assets, $1,736,955 (M); expenditures, $255,356; qualifying distributions, $232,783.
Limitations: Giving limited to TX, with emphasis on San Antonio.
Publications: Program policy statement, application guidelines.
Application information: Application form not required.
Trustees: Jacqueline R. Beretta, Gilbert M. Denman.
EIN: 237014591
Codes: FD2

51531
Anne Duncan & C. W. Duncan, Jr. Foundation
600 Travis, Ste. 6100
Houston, TX 77002
Contact: Robert J. Faust, Secy.-Treas.

Established in 1964.
Financial data (yr. ended 09/30/01): Grants paid, $84,750; assets, $4,480,400 (M); expenditures, $85,241; qualifying distributions, $85,241.
Limitations: Giving primarily in TX and WY.
Application information: Application form not required.
Officers and Directors:* M.A. Dingus,* Chair.; C.W. Duncan, Jr.,* Pres.; A.S. Duncan,* V.P.; C.W. Duncan III,* V.P.; R.J. Faust,* Secy.-Treas.
EIN: 746064309
Codes: FD2

51532
Deangelis Family Foundation
701 Brazos St., Ste. 1400
Austin, TX 78701 (512) 485-1900
Contact: Ken and Jeri Deangelis

Established in 2000 in TX.
Donor(s): Ken Deangelis, Jeri Deangelis.
Financial data (yr. ended 12/31/01): Grants paid, $84,705; assets, $121,439 (M); expenditures, $93,755; qualifying distributions, $85,472.
Limitations: Giving primarily in Austin, TX.
Application information: Application form not required.
Officers: Jeri E. Deangelis, Pres. and Treas.; Kenneth P. Deangelis, V.P. and Secy.
Trustee: Jeffery C. Garvey.
EIN: 742955715
Codes: FD2

51533
The Suzy Mercado Scholarship Foundation
4400 Post Oak Pkwy., No. 1550
Houston, TX 77027
Application address: c/o Suzy Mercado, 2201 San Felipe, Houston, TX 77019

Established in 1997.
Donor(s): Thomas P. Tatham, Virginia S. Tatham.
Financial data (yr. ended 12/31/99): Grants paid, $84,594; assets, $1,638,531 (M); expenditures, $123,927; qualifying distributions, $84,594.
Limitations: Giving primarily in TX.
Officers: Thomas P. Tatham, Pres.; Virginia S. Tatham, V.P. and Secy.
EIN: 760543418
Codes: FD2

51534
The Zandan Foundation
(Formerly The 270 Foundation)
c/o Bank of America
P.O. Box 908
Austin, TX 78781 (512) 397-2257
Contact: Hutch Gregg

Established in 1997 in TX.
Donor(s): Nanci Fisher, Peter A. Zandan.
Financial data (yr. ended 12/31/01): Grants paid, $84,479; assets, $1,240,469 (M); expenditures, $101,393; qualifying distributions, $84,479.
Limitations: Giving primarily in Austin, TX.
Officers and Directors:* Peter A. Zandan,* Pres.; Nanci Lee Fisher,* Secy.; James A. Williams.
EIN: 742832788
Codes: FD2

51535
The Lomax Family Foundation
P.O. Box 542
Georgetown, TX 78627
E-mail: saint@alltel.net
Contact: Lee Lomax, Dir.

Established in 1998 in TX.
Donor(s): Arthur Lee Lomax, Connie Judith Lomax.
Financial data (yr. ended 12/31/00): Grants paid, $84,400; assets, $636,590 (M); gifts received, $235,969; expenditures, $92,685; qualifying distributions, $83,535.
Limitations: Applications not accepted. Giving primarily in NC and TX.
Application information: Contributes only to pre-selected organizations.
Directors: Arthur Lee Lomax, Connie Judith Lomax, Lawrence H. Nordinger III.
EIN: 742900491
Codes: FD2

51536
Joel & Cathy Richards Foundation
121 N. Post Oak Ln., Ste. 101
Houston, TX 77024

Established in 1997 in TX.
Donor(s): Cathy Richards, Joel Richards.
Financial data (yr. ended 12/31/01): Grants paid, $84,225; assets, $23,718 (M); gifts received, $98,210; expenditures, $90,574; qualifying distributions, $83,627.
Limitations: Applications not accepted. Giving primarily in TX.
Application information: Contributes only to pre-selected organizations.
Officers: Joel Richards III, Pres.; Emily Richards, V.P.; Catherine C. Richards, Secy.; Marni Richards, Treas.
Director: Matt Richards.
EIN: 760537444
Codes: FD2

51537
Wallace, Barbara & Kelly King Charitable Foundation
c/o Southwest Bank Trust
5950 Berkshire Ln., Ste. 405
Dallas, TX 75225-5846

Established in 1998 in TX.
Donor(s): Barbara King.
Financial data (yr. ended 12/31/01): Grants paid, $84,000; assets, $1,511,353 (M); expenditures, $147,872; qualifying distributions, $84,000.
Limitations: Applications not accepted. Giving limited to Dallas, TX.
Application information: Contributes only to pre-selected organizations.
Trustee: Southwest Bank Trust.
EIN: 752720794
Codes: FD2

51538
The Ryrie Foundation
3310 Fairmount St., Apt. 5D
Dallas, TX 75201-1232
Contact: Charles C. Ryrie, Tr.

Donor(s): Charles C. Ryrie.
Financial data (yr. ended 12/31/00): Grants paid, $84,000; assets, $2,067,038 (M); gifts received, $354,949; expenditures, $88,286; qualifying distributions, $84,000.
Limitations: Giving on a national basis.
Application information: Application form required.
Trustee: Charles C. Ryrie.
EIN: 752001540

Codes: FD2, GTI

51539
Billy & Dorothy Tucker Foundation
316 E. Lakewood St.
Nacogdoches, TX 75961

Established in 1996 in TX.
Donor(s): Dorothy E. Tucker.
Financial data (yr. ended 09/30/00): Grants paid, $84,000; assets, $1,501,133 (M); gifts received, $2,091; expenditures, $95,467; qualifying distributions, $84,374.
Limitations: Applications not accepted.
Application information: Contributes only to pre-selected organizations.
Officers: Dorothy E. Tucker, Pres.; Billy P. Tucker, V.P. and Secy.
Directors: Teddy Tucker Butts, Betsi Ann Tucker Chandler, William Cameron Tucker.
EIN: 752708928

51540
Garver Foundation
P.O. Box 541537
Houston, TX 77254-1537

Established in 1997 in TX.
Donor(s): C. Michael Garver.
Financial data (yr. ended 12/31/01): Grants paid, $83,950; assets, $1,728,776 (M); gifts received, $128,000; expenditures, $85,571; qualifying distributions, $83,914.
Limitations: Applications not accepted. Giving limited to Houston, TX.
Application information: Contributes only to pre-selected organizations.
Trustee: C. Michael Garver.
EIN: 760556696
Codes: FD2

51541
Worldwide Philanthropic Foundation
100 Brazos Point Dr.
Waco, TX 76705-5212 (254) 755-8833
Contact: Meredith Flynn, Pres.

Established in 1996.
Donor(s): Meredith Flynn, Timothy Flynn.
Financial data (yr. ended 12/31/99): Grants paid, $83,715; assets, $33,727 (M); gifts received, $75,420; expenditures, $103,263; qualifying distributions, $94,444.
Limitations: Giving on a national basis.
Application information: Application form not required.
Officers and Directors:* Meredith Flynn,* Pres.; Timothy Flynn,* V.P.; Rick Creel,* Secy.-Treas.; Jared Flynn, Shawnine Flynn.
EIN: 742774506
Codes: FD2

51542
Sharon Lee MacDonald Charitable Trust
c/o Compass Bank
P.O. Box 4886
Houston, TX 77210-4886

Established in 1974 in TX.
Financial data (yr. ended 12/31/01): Grants paid, $83,500; assets, $1,653,792 (M); expenditures, $125,672; qualifying distributions, $82,605.
Limitations: Applications not accepted. Giving primarily in CT, NY, and TX.
Application information: Contributes only to pre-selected organizations.
Trustee: Compass Bank.
EIN: 746203857
Codes: FD2

51543
The Prichard Family Foundation
P.O. Box 6396
Corpus Christi, TX 78466-6396

Established in 1998 in TX.
Donor(s): Lev and Ella Prichard Charitable Trust.
Financial data (yr. ended 06/30/01): Grants paid, $83,500; assets, $1,722,815 (M); gifts received, $892,521; expenditures, $101,307; qualifying distributions, $83,500.
Limitations: Applications not accepted. Giving primarily in TX.
Application information: Contributes only to pre-selected organizations.
Officers: Lev H. Prichard IV, Pres.; Paul Armes, V.P.; Margaret Elaine Prichard Fagan, Treas.
EIN: 742891651
Codes: FD2

51544
Anita A. Ray Foundation
c/o Bank of America
3301 Golden Rd.
Tyler, TX 75701

Established in 1997.
Financial data (yr. ended 09/30/01): Grants paid, $83,335; assets, $1,644,898 (M); expenditures, $91,131; qualifying distributions, $85,257.
Limitations: Applications not accepted. Giving primarily in Tyler, TX.
Application information: Contributes only to pre-selected organizations.
Officer: Anita A. Ray, Pres.
EIN: 752732082
Codes: FD2

51545
Louise L. Morrison Trust
c/o Frost National Bank, Trust Dept.
P.O. Box 2950
San Antonio, TX 78299-2950 (210) 220-4991
Contact: William T. Clyborne, Jr., V.P., Frost National Bank

Donor(s): Louise L. Morrison.‡
Financial data (yr. ended 09/30/01): Grants paid, $83,020; assets, $2,570,474 (M); expenditures, $106,079; qualifying distributions, $93,573.
Limitations: Giving limited to San Antonio, TX.
Trustee: Frost National Bank.
EIN: 741386236
Codes: FD2

51546
Mirza Trust of San Antonio
P.O. Box 22765
Houston, TX 77227-2765 (713) 524-4691

Donor(s): John M. Bennett Trust.
Financial data (yr. ended 12/31/01): Grants paid, $83,000; assets, $1,453,683 (M); gifts received, $21,382; expenditures, $104,393; qualifying distributions, $81,392.
Limitations: Giving limited to TX.
Application information: Application form not required.
Trustees: Shannon Bush, Bennett N. Easton, R.L. Easton, Natalie M. Ingram, Carolyn Jackson, John B. Lupe, Joella L. Mach, T.C. Musgrave III.
EIN: 746062411
Codes: FD2

51547
The Carol Winn and James Reed Dunaway Family Foundation, Inc.
1501 Merrimac Cir., Ste. 100
Fort Worth, TX 76107-6512

Established in 1999 in TX.

Donor(s): James R. Dunaway, Carol W. Dunaway.
Financial data (yr. ended 12/31/00): Grants paid, $82,955; assets, $1,462,127 (M); expenditures, $91,417; qualifying distributions, $82,955.
Limitations: Applications not accepted. Giving primarily in Fort Worth, TX.
Application information: Contributes only to pre-selected organizations.
Officers: Carol W. Dunaway, Co-Chair.; James R. Dunaway, Co-Chair.
Directors: Bryan Winn Dunaway, Christina Dunaway, Scott Michael Dunaway.
EIN: 752770176
Codes: FD2

51548
Minnie L. Maffett Scholarship Trust
c/o Bank of America
P.O. Box 831041
Dallas, TX 75283-1041
Scholarship application address: c/o Barbara Guandique, Office of Fin. Aid, Southern Methodist Univ., P.O. Box 750196, Dallas, TX 75275-0196, tel.: (214) 692-3417

Established in 1964 in TX.
Financial data (yr. ended 04/30/01): Grants paid, $82,933; assets, $1,329,049 (M); expenditures, $100,191; qualifying distributions, $87,122.
Limitations: Giving limited to residents of TX, with preference to Limestone County.
Application information: Applicant must supply an official transcript. Application form required.
Trustee: Bank of America.
EIN: 756037885
Codes: GTI

51549
Goodell Foundation
5927 Joyce Way
Dallas, TX 75225

Established in 1997 in TX.
Donor(s): Sol Goodell.
Financial data (yr. ended 12/31/01): Grants paid, $82,900; assets, $204,959 (M); expenditures, $84,214; qualifying distributions, $82,835.
Limitations: Applications not accepted. Giving primarily in Dallas, TX.
Application information: Contributes only to pre-selected organizations.
Officers and Directors:* Sol Goodell,* Pres.; Susan J. Goodell,* V.P.; P. Mike McCullough,* Secy.-Treas.
EIN: 752705912
Codes: FD2

51550
Hurwitz Family Foundation
5847 San Felipe, Ste. 2600
Houston, TX 77057

Established in 1992 in TX.
Donor(s): Charles Hurwitz, Barbara Hurwitz.
Financial data (yr. ended 12/31/01): Grants paid, $82,863; assets, $1,371,606 (M); gifts received, $85,000; expenditures, $82,890; qualifying distributions, $82,857.
Limitations: Applications not accepted. Giving primarily in New York, NY.
Application information: Contributes only to pre-selected organizations.
Officers: Charles Hurwitz, Pres.; Barbara Hurwitz, V.P.; Shawn M. Hurwitz, Secy.; David A. Hurwitz, Treas.
EIN: 760368521
Codes: FD2

51551
Ella M. Coile Foundation
c/o Bank of America, N.A.
P.O. Box 831041
Dallas, TX 75283-1041
Application address: c/o Bank of America, N.A., 1200 Main St., 14th Fl., Kansas City, MO 64105, tel.: (816) 979-7481
Contact: David P. Ross, Sr. V.P., Bank of America

Established in 1992 in MO.
Financial data (yr. ended 12/31/00): Grants paid, $82,500; assets, $7,306,489 (M); expenditures, $173,668; qualifying distributions, $656,572.
Limitations: Giving in KS and MO, with emphasis on the bi-state Kansas City area.
Trustees: Dorothy Cargyle, Julie Gatrost, Michael L. Gatrost.
EIN: 431595776
Codes: FD2

51552
Rowley Foundation
1601-121 N. Post Oak Ln., Ste. 2601
Houston, TX 77024-7141

Donor(s): Craig M. Rowley, Jean B. Rowley.
Financial data (yr. ended 12/31/01): Grants paid, $82,203; assets, $64,709 (M); gifts received, $68,415; expenditures, $86,364; qualifying distributions, $82,203.
Limitations: Applications not accepted. Giving primarily in Houston, TX.
Application information: Contributes only to pre-selected organizations.
Officers and Trustees:* Craig M. Rowley,* Pres.; Jean B. Rowley,* V.P. and Secy.-Treas.; Mary Frances Colt, John Steele Rowley, Michael Fitzgerald Rowley, Robert Mason Rowley.
EIN: 760015720

51553
L'Aiglon Foundation
P.O. Drawer B
Kingsville, TX 78364 (361) 595-0411
Contact: Julia A. Jitkoff, Dir.

Established in 1982 in TX.
Donor(s): Julia A. Jitkoff.
Financial data (yr. ended 09/30/01): Grants paid, $81,834; assets, $1,187,979 (M); expenditures, $93,768; qualifying distributions, $81,834.
Limitations: Giving on a national basis.
Directors: Linda M. Hahn, Julia A. Jitkoff, B. Waring Partridge III.
EIN: 742249409
Codes: FD2

51554
The Bookout Family Foundation
P. O. Box 61369
Houston, TX 77208
Contact: John F. Bookout, Jr., Pres.

Established in 1996 in TX.
Donor(s): John F. Bookout, Jr., Carolyn C. Bookout.
Financial data (yr. ended 12/31/01): Grants paid, $81,660; assets, $1,124,789 (M); gifts received, $243,550; expenditures, $85,065; qualifying distributions, $81,952.
Limitations: Applications not accepted. Giving primarily in TX.
Application information: Contributes only to pre-selected organizations.
Officers and Directors:* John F. Bookout, Jr.,* Pres.; John F. Bookout,* V.P.; Beverly Von Kurnatowski,* Secy.-Treas.; Carolyn C. Bookout, Adair Stevenson.
EIN: 760508684
Codes: FD2

51555
Clifford Foundation, Inc.
P.O. Box 1001
Corsicana, TX 75151
Contact: C.L. Brown III, Pres.

Established in 1993 in TX.
Donor(s): C.L. Brown III.
Financial data (yr. ended 06/30/01): Grants paid, $81,487; assets, $1,229,315 (M); gifts received, $159,632; expenditures, $83,041; qualifying distributions, $82,178.
Limitations: Giving limited to residents of Navarro County, TX.
Application information: Applicants must be current high school graduates from Navarro County, TX attending TX state supported schools only. Application form required.
Officers: C.L. Brown III, Pres.; John B. Stroud, V.P.; William S. Maupin, Secy.-Treas.
Scholarship Committee: Shari Carroll, Suzanne Laird, Claudia Lynn Murchison, Nellie Carr Thorogood.
EIN: 752506394
Codes: FD2, GTI

51556
M. C. Bowman Foundation
P.O. Box 831041
Dallas, TX 75283-1041

Established in 1994 in AR.
Financial data (yr. ended 12/31/01): Grants paid, $81,252; assets, $1,433,311 (M); expenditures, $99,450; qualifying distributions, $83,335.
Limitations: Applications not accepted. Giving limited to AR.
Application information: Contributes only to pre-selected organizations.
Trustee: Bank of America.
EIN: 582034959
Codes: FD2

51557
The Beck Foundation
15911 Booth Cir.
Leander, TX 78641-9679
Contact: Kenneth H. Beck, Pres.

Established in 1998 in TX.
Donor(s): Kenneth H. Beck, Joyce L. Beck.
Financial data (yr. ended 12/31/99): Grants paid, $81,164; assets, $145,248 (M); expenditures, $81,164; qualifying distributions, $81,164.
Limitations: Applications not accepted.
Application information: Contributes only to pre-selected organizations.
Officers and Directors:* Kenneth H. Beck,* Pres.; Joyce L. Beck,* V.P. and Secy.; Gwen E. Collman,* Treas.; Ross K. Beck.
EIN: 742900045
Codes: FD2

51558
Aron S. & Anaruth P. Gordon Foundation
2401 Fountain View Dr., Ste. 350
Houston, TX 77057

Established in 1968 in TX.
Donor(s): Aron S. Gordon, Anaruth P. Gordon.
Financial data (yr. ended 12/31/01): Grants paid, $81,100; assets, $1,766,637 (M); expenditures, $83,144; qualifying distributions, $78,955.
Limitations: Applications not accepted. Giving primarily in Houston, TX.
Application information: Contributes only to pre-selected organizations.
Trustees: Aron S. Gordon, Daniel P. Gordon.
EIN: 746109511
Codes: FD2

51559
Carl A. Davis & Lois E. Davis Religious & Charitable Trust
5177 Richmond Ave., Ste. 740
Houston, TX 77056

Established in 1990 in TX.
Donor(s): Carl A. Davis, Lois E. Davis.
Financial data (yr. ended 12/31/99): Grants paid, $81,000; assets, $1,461,512 (M); gifts received, $525,669; expenditures, $81,636; qualifying distributions, $80,475.
Limitations: Applications not accepted. Giving primarily in TX.
Application information: Contributes only to pre-selected organizations.
Trustee: Carl A. Davis.
EIN: 766066429
Codes: FD2

51560
The Westerman Foundation
15508 Wright Brothers Dr.
Addison, TX 75001

Established in 2000 in TX.
Donor(s): Laura J. Westerman.
Financial data (yr. ended 12/31/00): Grants paid, $81,000; assets, $189,863 (M); gifts received, $282,062; expenditures, $81,150; qualifying distributions, $81,000.
Limitations: Applications not accepted. Giving primarily in AL, Washington, DC, KS, LA, and TX.
Application information: Contributes only to pre-selected organizations.
Officers: Catherine Belden, Pres.; Lene Westerman Pecorari, V.P.; Laura J. Westerman, Secy.; Jon Silvertooth, Treas.
EIN: 752897679
Codes: FD2

51561
DLR Trust
5005 Riverway Dr., Ste. 350
Houston, TX 77056-2133

Donor(s): Adolph O. Susholtz, Bettiruth B. Susholtz.
Financial data (yr. ended 12/31/99): Grants paid, $80,809; assets, $2,108,623 (M); expenditures, $89,435; qualifying distributions, $80,809.
Limitations: Applications not accepted. Giving primarily in TX.
Application information: Contributes only to pre-selected organizations.
Trustees: Adolph O. Susholtz, Bettiruth B. Susholtz, Rodney D. Susholtz.
EIN: 746075064

51562
Ellen Knox Beck-MKB Foundation
(also known as MKB Foundation)
c/o Bank of America
P.O. Box 831041
Dallas, TX 75283-1041
Application address: P.O. Box 830259, Dallas, TX 75283-0259, tel.: (214) 508-6674
Contact: Susan Bullard

Established in 1975 in TX.
Financial data (yr. ended 05/31/01): Grants paid, $80,750; assets, $800,901 (M); expenditures, $88,810; qualifying distributions, $82,182.
Limitations: Giving limited to residents of Coleman County, TX.
Committee Members: Chris O. Knox, E. Beck Knox, Jack L. Knox.
Trustee: Bank of America.
EIN: 756233396
Codes: GTI

51563
Texas Bankers Foundation
203 W. 10th St.
Austin, TX 78701

Established in 1995 in TX.
Donor(s): Texas Bankers Association.
Financial data (yr. ended 05/31/00): Grants paid, $80,645; assets, $324,053 (M); gifts received, $1,356; expenditures, $98,402; qualifying distributions, $80,494.
Limitations: Giving primarily in areas of company operations in TX.
Officers: W. Philip Johnson, Chair.; Robert E. Harris, Secy.
Director: W.F. Smith, Jr.
EIN: 742602147

51564
James P. Grizzard Foundation
4747 Bellaire Blvd., Ste. 355
Bellaire, TX 77401

Established in 1976 in TX.
Donor(s): James P. Grizzard.
Financial data (yr. ended 12/31/99): Grants paid, $80,616; assets, $193,909 (M); expenditures, $98,690; qualifying distributions, $80,616.
Limitations: Applications not accepted. Giving primarily in Houston, TX.
Application information: Contributes only to pre-selected organizations.
Trustees: James M. Grizzard, Suzanne Grizzard Werner.
EIN: 741922094
Codes: FD2

51565
The Bergstrom Family Foundation
1715 Chesnut Grove Ln.
Kingwood, TX 77345
Contact: Stephen W. Bergstrom, Chair.

Established in 1997 in TX.
Donor(s): Stephen W. Bergstrom.
Financial data (yr. ended 12/31/99): Grants paid, $80,343; assets, $2,676,877 (M); expenditures, $86,415; qualifying distributions, $80,295.
Limitations: Applications not accepted. Giving primarily in TX.
Application information: Contributes only to pre-selected organizations.
Officers: Stephen W. Bergstrom, Chair. and Pres.; Debora Bergstrom, V.P. and Treas.; Wayne Bergstrom, Secy.
EIN: 760563582
Codes: FD2

51566
Abbas-E-Alamdar, Inc.
4295 San Felipe, Ste. 220
Houston, TX 77027

Established in 1998 in TX.
Donor(s): M.J. Ebrahim.
Financial data (yr. ended 12/31/99): Grants paid, $80,301; assets, $42,214 (L); gifts received, $70,270; expenditures, $80,566; qualifying distributions, $80,301.
Limitations: Applications not accepted. Giving primarily in Pakistan; some giving also for the benefit of the local area Islamic community.
Application information: Contributes only to pre-selected organizations.
Officers: Fayaz Merchant, Pres.; M.J. Ebrahim, Secy.; Naushad Kermali, Treas.
EIN: 760408377
Codes: FD2

51567
Morris Greenspun Foundation
3717 Maplewood Ave.
Dallas, TX 75205-2826 (214) 756-6189
Contact: Theodore S. Hochstim, Dir.

Established in 1964 in TX.
Financial data (yr. ended 12/31/01): Grants paid, $80,040; assets, $1,094,584 (M); expenditures, $95,606; qualifying distributions, $79,898.
Limitations: Giving primarily in Los Angeles, CA, New York, NY, and Dallas, TX.
Application information: Application form not required.
Directors: Iva G. Hochstim, Theodore S. Hochstim.
EIN: 756019227
Codes: FD2

51568
Ray & Nancy Bearden Family Foundation
16105 Chateau Ave.
Austin, TX 78734
Application address: c/o Donnelly & Desroches, 2500 Citywest Blvd., Ste. 1000, Houston, TX 77042, tel.: (713) 339-3960
Contact: Ray Bearden, Dir.

Established in 2000 in TX.
Donor(s): C. Ray Bearden, Nancy R. Bearden.
Financial data (yr. ended 12/31/01): Grants paid, $80,000; assets, $662,643 (M); gifts received, $4,830; expenditures, $90,537; qualifying distributions, $90,445.
Limitations: Giving primarily in TX.
Directors: C. Ray Bearden, Kerri A. Bearden, Matthew R. Bearden, Nancy R. Bearden, Brandon E. Pierce, Chad P. Pierce.
EIN: 742957665
Codes: FD2

51569
M. A. & Josephine R. Grisham Foundation
c/o Bank of Texas Trust Co.
2009 Independence Dr., Ste. 100
Sherman, TX 75090
Contact: Regina D. Pruitt

Established in 1965.
Financial data (yr. ended 07/31/01): Grants paid, $80,000; assets, $1,267,077 (M); expenditures, $90,195; qualifying distributions, $79,729.
Limitations: Giving primarily in CA, NY, and TX.
Application information: Unsolicited requests for funds not accepted. Application form not required.
Trustees: Mrs. Harwell Barber, Daniel Blinkoff, Susannah Blinkoff, Carol Hall Majzlin, Josephine Renzulli.
EIN: 756054079
Codes: FD2

51570
Rupe Foundation
3103 Carlisle St.
Dallas, TX 75204
Contact: Lee C. Ritchie, V.P.

Established in 1942 in TX.
Donor(s): Wabash Properties, Rupe Capital, Moore Investment Co.
Financial data (yr. ended 12/31/01): Grants paid, $80,000; assets, $2,280,881 (M); expenditures, $91,803; qualifying distributions, $80,987.
Limitations: Giving primarily in Dallas, TX.
Officers: Paula R. Dennard, Pres.; Lee C. Ritchie, V.P.; D. Gordon Rupe III, V.P.; Dennis L. Lutes, Secy.
EIN: 756022488
Codes: FD2

51571
Snell Charitable Foundation, Inc.
4008 Texas St.
Vernon, TX 76384

Established in 1997 in TX.
Financial data (yr. ended 12/31/00): Grants paid, $80,000; assets, $2,339,760 (M); expenditures, $97,325; qualifying distributions, $96,294.
Limitations: Applications not accepted. Giving primarily in TX.
Application information: Contributes only to pre-selected organizations.
Officers: Doris King Snell, Pres.; Sara Jane Wood, 1st V.P.; Robert D. Snell, 2nd V.P.; Ann S. Bumstead, Secy.
EIN: 752707017
Codes: FD2

51572
The Thirion Family Foundation
4308 Bennedict Ln.
Austin, TX 78746-1940

Established in 1997 in TX.
Donor(s): Walter T. Thirion.
Financial data (yr. ended 12/31/00): Grants paid, $79,976; assets, $171,211 (M); gifts received, $30,303; expenditures, $85,303; qualifying distributions, $83,485.
Limitations: Applications not accepted.
Application information: Contributes only to pre-selected organizations.
Officers and Directors:* Walter T. Thirion,* Pres. and Treas.; Lorraine Kay Thirion, V.P.-Secy.; Joel Rollins.
EIN: 742862429

51573
M. E. Singleton Scholarship Trust
P.O. Box 717
Waxahachie, TX 75168
Contact: George H. Singleton, Pres.

Donor(s): Jeannette S. Cloyd.
Financial data (yr. ended 07/31/01): Grants paid, $79,960; assets, $1,688,376 (M); expenditures, $87,315; qualifying distributions, $80,095.
Limitations: Giving primarily in TX.
Application information: Application form required.
Officers and Trustees:* George H. Singleton,* Pres.; Steven F. Chapman,* Secy.-Treas.; Albert Mims, David Montgomery, Terry Nichols, Mark Singleton, Mike Turner.
EIN: 756037399
Codes: FD2, GTI

51574
Texas Ministries, Inc.
29259 No Le Hace
Fair Oaks Ranch, TX 78015
Contact: Scott Felder, Dir.

Established in 1994.
Donor(s): Scott Felder.
Financial data (yr. ended 09/30/00): Grants paid, $79,800; assets, $59,859 (M); gifts received, $32,091; expenditures, $298,502; qualifying distributions, $79,765.
Limitations: Giving primarily in TX.
Application information: Application form not required.
Directors: Luis Bryce, Lori Felder, Scott Felder.
EIN: 742730310
Codes: FD2

51575—TEXAS

51575
The Foundation for All Creatures
c/o Robert L. Trimble
100 Crescent Ct., Ste. 250
Dallas, TX 75201 (214) 855-2960

Financial data (yr. ended 12/31/01): Grants paid, $79,700; assets, $390,320 (M); expenditures, $90,541; qualifying distributions, $79,700.
Directors: Janice E. Cibulka, Mary Mitchell Trimble, Robert L. Trimble.
EIN: 752793423

51576
Edward & Wilhelmina Ackerman Foundation
5956 Sherry Ln., Ste. 1600
Dallas, TX 75225

Established in 1996 in TX.
Donor(s): Edward M. Ackerman, Wilhelmina Ackerman.
Financial data (yr. ended 12/31/99): Grants paid, $79,540; assets, $1,899,231 (M); gifts received, $152,500; expenditures, $84,789; qualifying distributions, $78,453.
Limitations: Giving primarily in TX.
Directors: David B. Ackerman, Edward M. Ackerman, Wilhelmina Ackerman.
EIN: 752681488
Codes: FD2

51577
The Boshell Family Foundation
5220 Spring Valley Rd., Ste. 600
Dallas, TX 75240

Established in 1985.
Donor(s): Edward O. Boshell, Jr., Margie I. Boshell, Columbia General Corp.
Financial data (yr. ended 12/31/99): Grants paid, $79,250; assets, $1,005,336 (M); expenditures, $98,948; qualifying distributions, $78,734.
Limitations: Applications not accepted. Giving primarily in TX.
Application information: Contributes only to pre-selected organizations.
Officer and Trustees:* Edward O. Boshell, Jr.,* Mgr.; Alexander C. Boshell, Betsey B. Potter, Betsy Boshell Todd.
EIN: 756341019

51578
Amarillo Business Foundation
P.O. Box 389
Amarillo, TX 79105
Contact: Louise Ross, Dir.

Established in 1999 in TX.
Financial data (yr. ended 12/31/01): Grants paid, $79,167; assets, $3,453,010 (M); expenditures, $143,846; qualifying distributions, $79,167.
Limitations: Giving primarily in TX.
Officers: George Raffkind, Pres.; John F. Stradley, V.P.; Bill Ware, Secy.
Directors: Della Dunn, W. Wayne Hedrick, Ted Y. Lokey, John M. Pickett, Louise Ross, Ted F. Schuler, Jr., Edward R. Scott, Jr., Coyt Webb.
EIN: 752859752
Codes: FD2

51579
Heidemann-Wuest Foundation
26495 Natural Bridge Caverns Rd.
San Antonio, TX 78266-2671

Established in 1998 in TX.
Financial data (yr. ended 12/31/00): Grants paid, $79,117; assets, $1,174,883 (M); expenditures, $91,165; qualifying distributions, $82,095.
Limitations: Applications not accepted. Giving primarily in San Antonio, TX.
Application information: Contributes only to pre-selected organizations.
Trustees: Brad Wayne Wuest, Joye Wuest, Travis Reginald Wuest.
EIN: 742872706
Codes: FD2

51580
Lynne Murray, Sr. Educational Foundation
1400 Post Oak Blvd., Ste. 600
Houston, TX 77056 (713) 966-4444
Contact: Robert J. Piro, Tr.

Established in 1969 in TX.
Financial data (yr. ended 12/31/01): Grants paid, $79,100; assets, $1,793,378 (M); expenditures, $112,665; qualifying distributions, $79,100.
Limitations: Giving limited to the Houston, TX, area.
Trustee: Robert J. Piro.
EIN: 746137429
Codes: FD2

51581
Dr. Max & Dr. Susan Mitchell Foundation
2200 Smith-Barry, Ste. 150
Arlington, TX 76013

Established in 1998.
Financial data (yr. ended 06/30/01): Grants paid, $78,921; assets, $32,311 (M); gifts received, $80,000; expenditures, $78,921; qualifying distributions, $78,921.
Directors: Frederick P. Mesch, Allen B. Mitchell, Glen B. Mitchell, Jane M. Mitchell, Susan B. Mitchell.
EIN: 752814869
Codes: FD2

51582
Art and Eva Camunez Tucker Foundation
1414 N. Martin Luther King Blvd.
San Angelo, TX 76903
FAX: (915) 653-9643; *E-mail:* mikeskanic@aol.com
Contact: Eva Camunez Tucker, Pres.

Established in 1993 in TX.
Donor(s): Eva Camunez Tucker.
Financial data (yr. ended 12/31/01): Grants paid, $78,100; assets, $2,716,249 (M); expenditures, $80,442; qualifying distributions, $78,100.
Limitations: Applications not accepted. Giving primarily in TX.
Application information: Contributes only to pre-selected organizations.
Officers: Eva Camunez Tucker, Pres.; Terry Mikeska, V.P.
Trustees: Susan Campbell, J. Alvin Hay, Sr., Len Mertz, Charlie Powell.
EIN: 752490509
Codes: FD2

51583
Crosstone
7557 Rambler Rd., Ste. 1100
Dallas, TX 75231-2310

Donor(s): J.E. Headington, Catherine M. Headington.
Financial data (yr. ended 12/31/01): Grants paid, $78,069; assets, $70,297 (M); gifts received, $13,070; expenditures, $78,249; qualifying distributions, $78,219.
Limitations: Applications not accepted. Giving primarily in Neah Bay, WA.
Officers and Directors:* Catherine M. Headington,* Pres.; G.L. Headington, V.P.; T.C. Headington,* V.P.
EIN: 752541407

51584
Richard Warren Mithoff Family Charitable Foundation
3450 1 Allen Ctr.
Houston, TX 77002

Established in 1984.
Donor(s): Richard Warren Mithoff.
Financial data (yr. ended 12/31/99): Grants paid, $78,000; assets, $885,002 (M); gifts received, $349,375; expenditures, $78,244; qualifying distributions, $78,000.
Limitations: Applications not accepted. Giving primarily in Houston, TX.
Application information: Contributes only to pre-selected organizations.
Officers: Richard Warren Mithoff, Jr., Chair.; Virginia Mithoff, Secy.
Director: V. Richard Viebig, Jr.
EIN: 760094136
Codes: FD2

51585
Redwine Foundation
P.O. Box 391
San Angelo, TX 76902-0391

Established in 1992.
Donor(s): Bruce A. Redwine.
Financial data (yr. ended 06/30/01): Grants paid, $77,914; assets, $48,377 (M); gifts received, $50,807; expenditures, $85,305; qualifying distributions, $83,804.
Limitations: Giving primarily in TX.
Application information: Application form not required.
Trustees: Thomas E. Covington, Bruce A. Redwine, Michael D. Schall, Mary J. Warren, Robert R. Williams.
EIN: 752441030
Codes: FD2

51586
Irene Cafcalas Hofheinz Foundation
c/o Fred Hofheinz
6671 Southwest Fwy., Ste. 303
Houston, TX 77074-2284

Established about 1984 in TX.
Donor(s): Roy M. Hofheinz Charitable Foundation.
Financial data (yr. ended 12/31/01): Grants paid, $77,450; assets, $1,247,372 (M); expenditures, $101,171; qualifying distributions, $86,546.
Limitations: Applications not accepted. Giving primarily in Houston, TX.
Application information: Contributes only to pre-selected organizations.
Trustee: Fred Hofheinz.
EIN: 760083597
Codes: FD2

51587
Pat and Jane Bolin Family Foundation
2525 Kell Blvd., Ste. 510
Wichita Falls, TX 76308-1061
Application address: 8111 Preston Rd., Ste. 900, Dallas, TX 75225, tel.: (214) 369-1545
Contact: Pat S. Bolin, Pres.

Established in 1998.
Financial data (yr. ended 12/31/01): Grants paid, $77,250; assets, $850,632 (M); expenditures, $77,689; qualifying distributions, $76,340.
Limitations: Giving primarily in TX.
Application information: Application form not required.
Officers: Pat S. Bolin, Pres.; Jane R. Bolin, Secy.
EIN: 752769154
Codes: FD2

51588
Valero Scholarship Trust
c/o Valero Energy Corp. Employee Devel. Dept.
P.O. Box 500, Tax Dept.
San Antonio, TX 78292-0500
Application address: 1 Valero Pl., San Antonio, TX 78212-3186

Established in 1996 in TX.
Donor(s): Valero Energy Corp.
Financial data (yr. ended 12/31/00): Grants paid, $77,250; assets, $161,496 (M); gifts received, $72,700; expenditures, $83,931; qualifying distributions, $83,164.
Limitations: Giving primarily in areas of company operations.
Application information: Application form required.
Trustees: John D. Gibbons, Frost National Bank.
EIN: 746437579
Codes: CS, CD, GTI

51589
Morris & Ann Ashendorf Foundation, Inc.
8323 S.W. Freeway, Ste. 300
Houston, TX 77074-1688

Incorporated in 1985 in TX.
Donor(s): Kalman & Ida Wolens Foundation, Inc., H. Wesley Ashendorf.
Financial data (yr. ended 12/31/99): Grants paid, $77,115; assets, $1,515,345 (M); expenditures, $78,453; qualifying distributions, $77,115.
Limitations: Applications not accepted. Giving primarily in Houston, TX.
Application information: Contributes only to pre-selected organizations.
Officers: H. Wesley Ashendorf, Pres.; Carole S. Ashendorf, V.P.
EIN: 760121343
Codes: FD2

51590
Adolf & Kaethe Wechsler Memorial Foundation
c/o Bank of America, Trust Dept.
P.O. Box 831041
Dallas, TX 75283-1041 (214) 580-2411

Established in 1993 in TX.
Financial data (yr. ended 12/31/01): Grants paid, $77,000; assets, $1,243,620 (M); expenditures, $89,390; qualifying distributions, $82,799.
Limitations: Applications not accepted. Giving primarily in Galveston, TX.
Application information: Contributes only to pre-selected organizations.
Trustees: Barker Lain, Bank of America.
EIN: 760442309
Codes: FD2

51591
Jo Ann and Gary Petersen Charitable Fund
210 Hedwig Rd.
Houston, TX 77024

Established in 2000 in TX.
Donor(s): Jo Ann Petersen, Gary Petersen.
Financial data (yr. ended 12/31/01): Grants paid, $76,790; assets, $266,454 (M); expenditures, $80,544; qualifying distributions, $76,650.
Limitations: Applications not accepted. Giving primarily in TX.
Application information: Contributes only to pre-selected organizations.
Officers: Gary Petersen, Pres.; Jo Ann Petersen, Secy.-Treas.
Trustee: D. Martin Phillips.
EIN: 760664091
Codes: FD2

51592
Joanie and Ben Bentzin Family Foundation
8111 Two Coves Dr.
Austin, TX 78730-3122

Established in 1999 in TX.
Donor(s): Benson A.E. Bentzin, Joanie Schoener Bentzin.
Financial data (yr. ended 12/31/01): Grants paid, $76,639; assets, $1,149,050 (M); expenditures, $78,612; qualifying distributions, $76,935.
Limitations: Applications not accepted. Giving primarily in TX.
Application information: Contributes only to pre-selected organizations.
Officers and Directors:* Benson A.E. Bentzin,* Pres. and Treas.; Joanie Schoener Bentzin,* V.P. and Secy.
EIN: 742918462
Codes: FD2

51593
Dolly Vinsant Memorial Foundation
c/o McAllen National Bank
P.O. Box 5555
McAllen, TX 78502-5555
Application address: Route 6, Box 711, San Benito, TX 78586, tel.: (986) 399-2491
Contact: Richard H. Welch, Chair.

Established in 1997.
Financial data (yr. ended 09/30/01): Grants paid, $76,000; assets, $1,279,962 (M); expenditures, $91,844; qualifying distributions, $76,000.
Limitations: Giving primarily in TX.
Application information: Application form required.
Officers: Richard H. Welch, Chair.; Erwin W. Scott, Jr., Vice-Chair.; Irving R. Reiff, Secy.-Treas.
Directors: Mike Myers, Milton Phipps, Victor Trevino, Bob Turnburlinson, Charles Wilson.
EIN: 741143136
Codes: GTI

51594
Theodore P. Davis Charitable Trust
c/o JPMorgan Chase Bank
P.O. Box 550
Austin, TX 78789 (512) 479-2647
Contact: Sonia Garza, Trust Admin.

Established in 1987 in TX.
Financial data (yr. ended 12/31/01): Grants paid, $75,936; assets, $1,761,138 (M); expenditures, $107,536; qualifying distributions, $86,674.
Limitations: Giving limited to the metropolitan Austin, TX, area.
Application information: Application forms available Aug. 1 to Sept. 17. Application form required.
Trustees: Billy Ramsey, JPMorgan Chase Bank.
EIN: 746254895
Codes: FD2

51595
Harry R. Staley Charitable Trust A
c/o Bank of America
P.O. Box 831041
Dallas, TX 75283-1041

Established in 1995 in MO.
Financial data (yr. ended 12/31/01): Grants paid, $75,860; assets, $1,535,670 (M); expenditures, $108,908; qualifying distributions, $80,949.
Limitations: Applications not accepted. Giving primarily in LA, MN, MO, and NH.
Application information: Contributes only to pre-selected organizations.
Trustees: Nancy Laubach, Bank of America.
EIN: 436239849
Codes: FD2

51596
The Lende Foundation
701 N. St. Mary's St., Ste. 24
San Antonio, TX 78205

Established in 1978 in TX.
Donor(s): H.W. Lende, Jr., R.R. Lende, Elizabeth Lende.
Financial data (yr. ended 11/30/01): Grants paid, $75,843; assets, $1,766,667 (M); expenditures, $82,686; qualifying distributions, $80,651.
Limitations: Applications not accepted. Giving primarily in San Antonio, TX.
Application information: Contributes only to pre-selected organizations.
Officers: H.W. Lende, Jr., Pres. and Treas.; R.R. Lende, V.P.
EIN: 741985933
Codes: FD2

51597
The Andrew and Julie Alexander Foundation
2600 Citadel Plz. Dr., Ste. 300
Houston, TX 77008

Established in 1998 in TX.
Donor(s): Andrew Mark Alexander, Julie Alexander.
Financial data (yr. ended 12/31/01): Grants paid, $75,801; assets, $1,218,671 (M); expenditures, $79,118; qualifying distributions, $76,338.
Limitations: Applications not accepted. Giving primarily in TX.
Application information: Contributes only to pre-selected organizations.
Officers and Directors:* Andrew Mark Alexander,* Pres. and Treas.; Julie Alexander,* V.P. and Secy.; Martin Debrovner.
EIN: 760573347
Codes: FD2

51598
Sear Family Foundation
4301 County Rd. 707
Cleburne, TX 76031 (817) 790-5444
Contact: Timothy R.G. Sear, Pres.

Established in 1996 in TX.
Donor(s): Judith Sear, Timothy R.G. Sear.
Financial data (yr. ended 12/31/01): Grants paid, $75,676; assets, $525,592 (M); gifts received, $209,760; expenditures, $77,055; qualifying distributions, $75,676.
Limitations: Giving on a national basis.
Application information: Application form not required.
Officers and Directors:* Timothy R.G. Sear,* Pres.; Judith Sear,* Secy.-Treas.; Adam T.J. Sear, Charles D. Sear, Jason D. Sear, Katherine Sear.
EIN: 752673430
Codes: FD2

51599
The Andrews Foundation
2402 Westgate, Ste. 200
Houston, TX 77019 (713) 528-6571
Contact: Judith N. Andrews, V.P.

Established in 1998 in TX.
Donor(s): Judith N. Andrews, Richard J. Andrews, Rose Piller.
Financial data (yr. ended 04/30/01): Grants paid, $75,250; assets, $1,197,157 (M); gifts received, $1,630; expenditures, $96,301; qualifying distributions, $83,251.
Limitations: Giving primarily in TX.
Application information: Application form not required.
Officers and Directors:* Richard J. Andrews, Pres. and Treas.; Judith N. Andrews,* V.P. and Secy.; Rita N. Justice.

51599—TEXAS

EIN: 760537224
Codes: FD2

51600
Murrell Foundation
8350 N. Central Expy., Ste. G100
Dallas, TX 75206 (214) 363-3691
Contact: John R. Murrell, Pres.

Established in 1990 in TX.
Donor(s): John H. Murrell,‡ John R. Murrell, Mrs. John H. Murrell, Kelley A. Murrell.
Financial data (yr. ended 06/30/01): Grants paid, $75,173; assets, $242,351 (M); gifts received, $173,000; expenditures, $76,782; qualifying distributions, $75,162.
Limitations: Giving primarily in Dallas, TX.
Application information: Application form not required.
Officers and Directors:* John R. Murrell,* Pres.; J. Waddy Bullion,* V.P.; P. Mike McCullough,* V.P.; Charlene J. Murrell,* V.P.; Cathy Arrington, Secy.-Treas.; Curtis W. Meadows, Jr.
EIN: 752344755

51601
The Andrea Family Foundation
c/o Rudolph G. Andrea
5508 Linmore Ln.
Plano, TX 75093-7619

Established in 2000 in TX.
Donor(s): Rudolph G. Andrea, Christina M. Andrea.
Financial data (yr. ended 12/31/00): Grants paid, $75,000; assets, $1,191,221 (M); gifts received, $1,501,992; expenditures, $81,875; qualifying distributions, $75,000.
Application information: Application form required.
Officers and Directors:* Rudolph G. Andrea,* Pres. and Treas.; Christina M. Andrea,* V.P. and Secy.; William N. Gammill, Phillip Kushner.
EIN: 752861029

51602
J. Tom Eady Charitable Trust
c/o Corsicana National Bank & Trust
P.O. Box 624
Corsicana, TX 75151 (903) 654-4500
Contact: Gary Brown, Trust Off., Corsicana National Bank & Trust

Established in 2000 in TX.
Donor(s): John Thomas Eady.‡
Financial data (yr. ended 12/31/01): Grants paid, $75,000; assets, $10,061,668 (M); gifts received, $23,704; expenditures, $76,043; qualifying distributions, $75,000.
Trustee: Corsicana National Bank & Trust.
EIN: 756604134

51603
George and Patsy Eby Foundation
P.O. Box 91506
Austin, TX 78709
Contact: George A. Eby, Pres. or Patsy Ann Eby, V.P.

Established in 1998 in TX.
Donor(s): George Eby, Patsy Ann Eby.
Financial data (yr. ended 12/31/01): Grants paid, $75,000; assets, $1,377,605 (M); expenditures, $129,332; qualifying distributions, $74,203.
Limitations: Giving primarily in TX.
Application information: Application form required.
Officers and Directors:* George Andrew Eby III,* Pres.; Patsy Ann Eby,* V.P. and Treas.; Karen Lynn Eby,* Secy.; Colin Martin Eby.
EIN: 742860396

51604
Stinson Foundation
303 W. Wall St.
Midland, TX 79701
Application address: P.O. Box 270, Midland, TX 79702
Contact: Bill J. Hill, Pres.

Established in 1992.
Financial data (yr. ended 12/31/01): Grants paid, $75,000; assets, $1,191,739 (M); expenditures, $88,829; qualifying distributions, $76,100.
Limitations: Giving primarily in Permian Basin, TX.
Application information: Application form required.
Officers: Bill J. Hill, Pres.; John R. Peterson, V.P.; Jeff Morton, Secy.-Treas.
Trustee: Joe Julien.
EIN: 752391338

51605
Gold Foundation
8115 Preston Rd., Ste. 240
Dallas, TX 75225-6330

Established in 2000 in TX.
Donor(s): Alan Gold, Rita Sue Gold.
Financial data (yr. ended 12/31/01): Grants paid, $74,950; assets, $413,318 (M); gifts received, $122,790; expenditures, $77,641; qualifying distributions, $74,950.
Limitations: Giving primarily in TX.
Officer: Alan Gold, Pres.
Trustees: Mary Lee Broder, James J. Gold, Rita Sue Gold.
EIN: 752860360

51606
The Kimmelman Family Foundation
300 Crescent Ct., Ste. 400
Dallas, TX 75201

Established in 1997 in TX.
Donor(s): Enoch A. Kimmelman.
Financial data (yr. ended 12/31/01): Grants paid, $74,850; assets, $137,200 (M); gifts received, $100,000; expenditures, $77,084; qualifying distributions, $74,847.
Limitations: Applications not accepted. Giving primarily in El Paso, TX.
Application information: Contributes only to pre-selected organizations.
Trustee: JPMorgan Private Bank.
EIN: 742830623

51607
The Edward and Helen Oppenheimer Foundation
3435 Westheimer, Ste. 1506
Houston, TX 77027-5347

Established in 1993 in TX.
Donor(s): Edward Oppenheimer, Jr.
Financial data (yr. ended 12/31/01): Grants paid, $74,750; assets, $2,156,761 (M); gifts received, $225,679; expenditures, $102,466; qualifying distributions, $73,974.
Limitations: Applications not accepted. Giving limited to Houston, TX.
Application information: Contributes only to pre-selected organizations.
Officers and Trustees:* Edward Oppenheimer, Jr.,* Chair., Pres., and Treas.; Gloria L. Herman,* V.P.; Lee E. Herman,* Secy.; Carla A. Herman, Paul F. Herman.
EIN: 760403101

51608
Denman/Newman Foundation
c/o Linwood Newman
3443 Ella Lee Ln.
Houston, TX 77027-4101

Established in 1998 in TX.
Donor(s): Linwood D. Newman.
Financial data (yr. ended 12/31/00): Grants paid, $74,500; assets, $1,153,387 (M); expenditures, $75,765; qualifying distributions, $73,873.
Limitations: Applications not accepted. Giving primarily in TX.
Application information: Contributes only to pre-selected organizations.
Officer: Linwood D. Newman, Pres.
EIN: 311596627

51609
The Porter Foundation
2121 San Jacinto St., Ste. 2900
Dallas, TX 75201

Established in 1999 in TX.
Donor(s): David M. Porter.
Financial data (yr. ended 12/31/00): Grants paid, $74,500; assets, $27,402 (M); expenditures, $75,759; qualifying distributions, $74,469.
Limitations: Applications not accepted. Giving primarily in TX.
Application information: Contributes only to pre-selected organizations.
Officers: David M. Porter, Pres. and Treas.; Dana Deison Porter, V.P.; Nancy Porter Searway, Secy.
EIN: 752852344

51610
Crarey-Griest Charitable Trust
P. O. Box 831041
Dallas, TX 75283-1041

Established in 2001 in KS and MO.
Financial data (yr. ended 12/31/01): Grants paid, $74,343; assets, $1,187,813 (M); gifts received, $1,116,599; expenditures, $97,031; qualifying distributions, $76,299.
Limitations: Applications not accepted. Giving primarily in Topeka, KS.
Application information: Contributes only to pre-selected organizations.
Trustee: Bank of America.
EIN: 486290911

51611
J. A. Leppard Foundation Trust
2519 Waterford Dr.
San Antonio, TX 78217 (210) 824-2148
Contact: Harry James Fraser, Jr., Admin.

Established in 1980 in TX.
Donor(s): J.A. Leppard.‡
Financial data (yr. ended 12/31/01): Grants paid, $74,200; assets, $1,683,361 (M); expenditures, $93,728; qualifying distributions, $78,789.
Limitations: Giving primarily in TX.
Application information: Application form not required.
Officer and Trustees:* Harry James Fraser, Jr.,* Admin.; Whitney E. Booth, J.A. Leppard, Jr., George Poppas, Jr.
EIN: 742044159

51612
Mullen Foundation
P.O. Box 60
Alice, TX 78333-0060
Application address: 70 N. King St., Alice, TX 78332, tel.: (361) 664-5263
Contact: Robert R. Mullen III, Pres.

Established in 1950 in TX.

Donor(s): Robert R. Mullen III.
Financial data (yr. ended 12/31/01): Grants paid, $74,100; assets, $101,671 (M); expenditures, $74,128; qualifying distributions, $74,100.
Limitations: Giving primarily in TX.
Officers and Directors:* Robert R. Mullen III,* Pres.; Claudette Mullen,* V.P.; Maria Greenwell,* Secy.-Treas.; Ellen Crowley, R.Y. Wheeler.
EIN: 746046829

51613
Ben and Margaret Love Foundation
1800 Chase Tower
Houston, TX 77002 (713) 216-4010
Contact: Ben F. Love, Pres.

Established in 1986 in TX.
Donor(s): Ben F. Love, Margaret M. Love.
Financial data (yr. ended 12/31/00): Grants paid, $73,520; assets, $1,608,102 (M); expenditures, $79,716; qualifying distributions, $75,506.
Limitations: Giving primarily in Houston, TX.
Officers and Directors:* Ben F. Love,* Pres.; Margaret M. Love, V.P. and Secy.-Treas.; Jeff B. Love, Jan Love Simmons.
EIN: 760220082

51614
Del Barto-Tramonte Foundation, Inc.
2127 Broadway
P.O. Box 325
Galveston, TX 77553

Established in 1961.
Financial data (yr. ended 06/30/01): Grants paid, $73,500; assets, $1,861,026 (M); expenditures, $118,993; qualifying distributions, $89,734.
Limitations: Applications not accepted. Giving primarily in TX.
Application information: Contributes only to pre-selected organizations.
Officers: Sam G. Tramonte, Pres.; M.L. Cantrell, Secy.
EIN: 746050231

51615
Rushing Family Foundation
2737 82nd St.
Lubbock, TX 79423

Established in 2000 in TX.
Financial data (yr. ended 12/31/01): Grants paid, $73,425; assets, $1,531,356 (M); expenditures, $106,078; qualifying distributions, $73,425.
Limitations: Giving primarily in Lubbock, TX.
Officers: W.B. Rushing, Pres.; Don Rushing, V.P.; Ted Rushing, Secy.-Treas.
EIN: 752596401

51616
Felix L. and Jo Stehling Foundation
4040 Broadway, Ste. 420
San Antonio, TX 78209
Contact: James C. Worth, Pres.

Established in 1994 in TX.
Donor(s): Felix L. Stehling, Billie Jo Stehling.
Financial data (yr. ended 12/31/01): Grants paid, $73,100; assets, $562,528 (M); expenditures, $78,895; qualifying distributions, $71,970.
Limitations: Giving primarily in TX.
Officers: Felix L. Stehling, Chair.; James C. Worth, Pres. and Treas.; Lynn L. Moody, Secy.
Director: Billie Jo Stehling.
EIN: 742730197

51617
Anchorage Foundation of Texas
10 Waverly Ct.
Houston, TX 77005

Established in 1979.

Donor(s): Anne S. Bohnn.
Financial data (yr. ended 06/30/01): Grants paid, $72,940; assets, $3,405,205 (M); gifts received, $35,000; expenditures, $195,248; qualifying distributions, $190,345; giving activities include $81,909 for programs.
Limitations: Applications not accepted. Giving primarily in Houston, TX.
Application information: Contributes only to pre-selected organizations.
Officers: Anne S. Bohnn, Pres.; C. LeRoy Melcher, Secy.; Jody Blazek, Treas.
Directors: Marc Melcher, Pierre S. Melcher, P.M. Schlumberger.
EIN: 742071804

51618
Willingham Foundation
P.O. Box 831041
Dallas, TX 75283-1041
Application address: c/o E. Paul Bruechner, Bank of America, Trust Dept., 3301 Golden Rd., Tyler, TX 75701, tel.: (903) 510-5043

Established in 1961.
Financial data (yr. ended 12/31/00): Grants paid, $72,850; assets, $2,621,347 (M); gifts received, $264,702; expenditures, $99,185; qualifying distributions, $79,076.
Limitations: Giving limited to TX, with an emphasis on Smith County.
Officers: C. Harold Willingham, M.D., Pres.; Sara W. Bowyer, V.P.; Charles Lawrence Willingham, V.P.; John G. Payne, Secy.
Trustee: Bank of America.
EIN: 756035231

51619
Cleve H. Tandy Foundation
c/o D.C. Earley
4609 Pinehurst Dr. S.
Austin, TX 78747

Established in 1958.
Financial data (yr. ended 12/31/01): Grants paid, $72,700; assets, $1,461,232 (M); expenditures, $74,792; qualifying distributions, $72,064.
Limitations: Applications not accepted. Giving limited to TX.
Application information: Contributes only to pre-selected organizations.
Officers and Directors:* Douglas C. Earley,* Pres.; Judd M. Earley,* 1st V.P. and Treas.; Cleve M. Earley,* 2nd V.P. and Secy.; Annalyn Earley Bryant.
EIN: 746047828

51620
Kowitz Family Foundation
1901 N. Akard St.
Dallas, TX 75201-2305

Established in 1997 in TX.
Donor(s): Sarah Kowitz, David Kowitz.
Financial data (yr. ended 12/31/01): Grants paid, $72,400; assets, $740,589 (M); gifts received, $29,257; expenditures, $76,600; qualifying distributions, $72,400.
Limitations: Applications not accepted. Giving primarily in NY.
Application information: Unsolicited requests for funds not accepted.
Officers and Trustees:* David Kowitz,* Pres. and Treas.; Sarah Kowitz,* V.P. and Secy.; Julie Miller.
EIN: 752707561

51621
Timberlawn Psychiatric Research Foundation, Inc.
2750 Grove Hill Rd.
Dallas, TX 75227 (214) 388-0451
Contact: Ann Supina, Admin.

Reclassified as a private foundation in 2000.
Financial data (yr. ended 12/31/01): Grants paid, $72,004; assets, $4,142,628 (M); gifts received, $18,246; expenditures, $251,791; qualifying distributions, $159,725.
Limitations: Giving limited to the Dallas, TX, Metroplex area.
Offices: John T. Gossett, M.D., Chair.; Jerry M. Lewis, M.D., Chair.; Carlos W. Davis, Jr., Ph.D., Dir.; Ann Supina, Admin.
Trustees: Drew N. Bagot, Trammell Crow, Suzanne Settle Dees, Kenneth M. Dickson, and 11 additional trustees.
EIN: 751089368

51622
Marshall Formby Foundation
c/o Hale County State Bank, Trust Dept.
P.O. Box 970
Plainview, TX 79072
Contact: Garry A. Petras, Sr. V.P. and Trust Off., Hale County State Bank

Established in 1987 in TX.
Financial data (yr. ended 12/31/01): Grants paid, $72,000; assets, $1,126,233 (M); expenditures, $92,952; qualifying distributions, $72,000.
Limitations: Applications not accepted. Giving primarily in Plainview, TX.
Application information: Contributes only to pre-selected organizations.
Trustees: John Anderson, Tom Hamilton, Graddy Tunnell.
Agent: Hale County State Bank.
EIN: 752156614

51623
Tom and Pat Powers Foundation
18011 Hollywell Dr.
Houston, TX 77084
Contact: Thomas R. Powers, Pres.

Established in 1990 in TX.
Donor(s): Patsy G. Powers, Thomas R. Powers.
Financial data (yr. ended 05/31/01): Grants paid, $72,000; assets, $1,426,123 (M); expenditures, $76,060; qualifying distributions, $71,570.
Limitations: Applications not accepted. Giving primarily in Houston and Waco, TX.
Application information: Contributes only to pre-selected organizations.
Officers: Thomas R. Powers, Pres.; Matthew S. Powers, V.P.; Patsy G. Powers, Secy.
EIN: 760282108

51624
Sidwell Foundation
P.O. Box 9298
Amarillo, TX 79105-9298

Established in 1983 in TX.
Donor(s): Eugene C. Sidwell, Sarah Pauline Sidwell, Eugene R. Sidwell.
Financial data (yr. ended 06/30/01): Grants paid, $72,000; assets, $1,159,647 (M); gifts received, $16,314; expenditures, $83,206; qualifying distributions, $73,866.
Limitations: Applications not accepted. Giving primarily in TX; some funding nationally.
Application information: Contributes only to pre-selected organizations.
Trustees: Ann Sidwell Fatheree, Eugene R. Sidwell, Sarah Pauline Sidwell.
EIN: 751915561

51625
Warm Foundation
(Formerly Wayne M. Abramson Foundation)
1007 Balcones Dr.
Fredericksburg, TX 78624
Contact: Lori Abramson, Pres.

Established in 1980 in TX.
Donor(s): A.D. Abramson.‡
Financial data (yr. ended 12/31/01): Grants paid, $72,000; assets, $1,195,402 (M); gifts received, $7,199; expenditures $83,237; qualifying distributions, $72,820.
Limitations: Applications not accepted. Giving primarily in CA and WA.
Publications: Informational brochure.
Application information: Contributes only to pre-selected organizations.
Officers: Lori Abramson, Pres.; Kim Tieken, V.P.; Leslie Hontou, Secy.; Charlene McAllister Abramson, Treas.
EIN: 760064293

51626
Myer Family Charitable Foundation
3755 Capital of Texas Hwy. S.
Austin, TX 78704

Established in 1995.
Financial data (yr. ended 12/31/00): Grants paid, $71,950; assets, $1,375,911 (M); expenditures, $86,583; qualifying distributions, $73,897.
Limitations: Applications not accepted. Giving primarily in Austin, TX.
Application information: Contributes only to pre-selected organizations.
Officers: Robert L. Myer, Pres.; Carolyn K. Griffin, V.P. and Treas.; Sharon K. Myer, Secy.
EIN: 742765437

51627
The Tucker Foundation
P.O. Box 218
Katy, TX 77492-0218 (281) 391-2208
Contact: Dona Tucker Barker, Pres.

Established in 1987 in TX.
Donor(s): Dona Tucker Barker.
Financial data (yr. ended 05/31/01): Grants paid, $71,830; assets, $1,287,130 (M); expenditures, $105,643; qualifying distributions, $73,469.
Limitations: Giving primarily in CA and TX.
Officers: Dona Tucker Barker, Pres.; Gina Corsi, Secy.; Ida Banks, Treas.
EIN: 746053182

51628
Bess A. Wilkins Memorial Scholarship Fund
c/o Bank of America
P.O. Box 831041
Dallas, TX 75283
Contact: Barbara Davis, Tr. Off., Bank of America

Established in 1972 in AR.
Financial data (yr. ended 12/31/00): Grants paid, $71,793; assets, $1,318,546 (M); expenditures, $90,870; qualifying distributions, $71,793.
Limitations: Giving limited to Fordyce, AR.
Trustee: Bank of America.
EIN: 716084050

51629
Cadeaux, Inc.
1120 Empire Central Pl., Ste. 200
Dallas, TX 75247 (214) 688-0880
Contact: M.E. Moore, Jr., Pres.

Established in 1963.
Donor(s): Lillian G. Moore.
Financial data (yr. ended 09/30/99): Grants paid, $71,728; assets, $830,130 (M); expenditures, $74,486; qualifying distributions, $71,055.
Limitations: Giving primarily in Dallas, TX.
Officer: M.E. Moore, Jr., Pres. and V.P.
EIN: 756038070

51630
James C. & Elizabeth R. Conner Foundation
204 S. Wellington St.
Marshall, TX 75670-4056 (903) 938-0331
Contact: Robert L. Duvall, Chair.

Donor(s): Elizabeth Conner, James C. Conner.
Financial data (yr. ended 12/31/01): Grants paid, $71,659; assets, $3,935,027 (M); expenditures, $78,033; qualifying distributions, $73,359.
Limitations: Giving limited to U.S. citizens.
Application information: Application form required.
Officers: Robert L. Duvall, Chair.; Roger K. Jones, Vice-Chair.; R. Michael Hallum, Secy.
EIN: 752302882
Codes: GTI

51631
Flynn Family Foundation
200 Bluffcove
San Antonio, TX 78216

Established in 1994 in TX.
Donor(s): Patricia A. Flynn, Robert W. Flynn.
Financial data (yr. ended 12/31/01): Grants paid, $71,500; assets, $675,089 (M); expenditures, $72,870; qualifying distributions, $71,500.
Limitations: Applications not accepted. Giving on a national basis, with some emphasis on Washington, DC and TX.
Application information: Contributes only to pre-selected organizations.
Trustees: Patricia A. Flynn, Robert W. Flynn.
EIN: 746423178

51632
C. J. Wrightsman Educational Fund, Inc.
801 Cherry St., Ste. 2100
Fort Worth, TX 76102 (817) 332-9396
Contact: Whitfield J. Collins, Pres.

Established in 1965 in TX.
Donor(s): C.J. Wrightsman.‡
Financial data (yr. ended 07/31/01): Grants paid, $71,245; assets, $1,366,812 (M); expenditures, $90,283; qualifying distributions, $80,214.
Limitations: Giving limited to students attending TX institutions.
Application information: Applicants must be able to demonstrate financial need. Application form required.
Officers: Whitfield J. Collins, Pres.; Allan Howeth, V.P.; Harry E. Bartel, Secy.-Treas.
EIN: 756046853
Codes: GTI

51633
William J. & Genevieve H. Coonly Foundation
1280 Hawkins Blvd., Ste. 200
El Paso, TX 79925-4949
Application address: 717 Dover Ct., El Paso, TX 79932, tel.: (915) 584-4341
Contact: Genevieve H. Coonly, Dir.

Donor(s): William J. Coonly, Genevieve H. Coonly.
Financial data (yr. ended 11/30/00): Grants paid, $71,000; assets, $455,135 (M); expenditures, $72,250; qualifying distributions, $70,854.
Limitations: Giving primarily in El Paso, TX.
Directors: Genevieve H. Coonly, William J. Coonly.
EIN: 746063001

51634
Mildred & Lawrence Lieder Foundation
P.O. Box 267
Cypress, TX 77429 (281) 373-0855
Contact: Lawrence Anton Lieder, Tr.

Established in 1991 in TX.
Donor(s): Lawrence Anton Lieder, Mildred Hobbs Lieder.
Financial data (yr. ended 12/31/01): Grants paid, $71,000; assets, $799,634 (M); expenditures, $72,202; qualifying distributions, $71,814.
Limitations: Giving primarily in TX.
Trustees: Lawrence Allen Lieder, Lawrence Anton Lieder, Mildred Hobbs Lieder.
EIN: 760354931

51635
The Bobbie A. Atkinson Foundation
3424 Texas Blvd.
Texarkana, TX 75503-3248

Established in 1995 in TX.
Donor(s): Bobbie A. Atkinson.
Financial data (yr. ended 06/30/01): Grants paid, $70,811; assets, $1,573,560 (M); gifts received, $12,131; expenditures, $77,629; qualifying distributions, $73,962.
Limitations: Applications not accepted. Giving primarily in Texarkana, TX.
Application information: Contributes only to pre-selected organizations.
Officers: Robert McDowell, Pres.; Mark H. Lawley, V.P. and Secy.; Debbie Cox, V.P.; Kathy Powers, V.P.; Bobbie A. Atkinson, Treas.; Jauquita A. Hargus, Treas.
EIN: 752626803

51636
Merfish-Jacobson Foundation
P.O. Box 1937
Houston, TX 77251-1937
Contact: Rochelle M. Jacobson, Tr.

Established in 1988 in TX.
Donor(s): N. Merfish Plumbing Supply Co.
Financial data (yr. ended 12/31/01): Grants paid, $70,710; assets, $216,096 (M); gifts received, $60,652; expenditures, $71,634; qualifying distributions, $71,272.
Limitations: Giving primarily in Houston, TX.
Application information: Application form not required.
Trustees: Rochelle M. Jacobson, Abe Merfish, Gerald Merfish, Ida K. Merfish.
EIN: 760239810

51637
The Reed-George Foundation, Inc.
P.O. Drawer 310
Bastrop, TX 78602-0310 (512) 303-1649
Contact: Jill Green, Secy.-Treas.

Established in 1999 in TX.
Donor(s): Rita Reed George.
Financial data (yr. ended 12/31/01): Grants paid, $70,500; assets, $144,173 (M); expenditures, $70,500; qualifying distributions, $70,442.
Limitations: Giving primarily in TX.
Officers: Rita Reed George, Pres.; Jill Green, Secy.-Treas.
EIN: 752827105

51638
The Provincial Foundation
6346 Lupton Dr.
Dallas, TX 75225 (214) 369-0110
Contact: Joseph Mannes, Pres.

Established in 1958 in PA.

Financial data (yr. ended 01/31/01): Grants paid, $70,330; assets, $1,499,126 (M); expenditures, $84,077; qualifying distributions, $69,502.
Limitations: Giving primarily in NH, NY, PA and TX.
Publications: Annual report (including application guidelines).
Application information: Application form not required.
Officers: Joseph Mannes, Pres.; Andrew J. Mannes, V.P.; George L. Mannes, V.P.
EIN: 231422090

51639
The JBD Foundation
(Formerly The Jeaneane B. Duncan Foundation)
c/o JPMorgan Chase Bank
P.O. Box 2558
Houston, TX 77252-2558 (713) 216-1451
Contact: Sells Neuhaus, Secy.

Established in 1998 in TX.
Donor(s): Jeaneane B. Duncan.
Financial data (yr. ended 12/31/00): Grants paid, $70,250; assets, $2,048,306 (M); gifts received, $540,750; expenditures, $94,727; qualifying distributions, $70,250.
Limitations: Giving primarily in Houston, TX.
Officers: Jeaneane B. Duncan, Pres.; John H. Duncan, Jr., V.P.; Jeaneane Duncan Marsh, V.P.; Sells Neuhaus, Secy.
EIN: 760578785

51640
Chairman's Award Foundation
P.O. Box 4567
Houston, TX 77210
Contact: Preston Johnson

Donor(s): Reliant Energy Ventures, Inc.
Financial data (yr. ended 12/31/01): Grants paid, $70,200; assets, $974,338 (M); gifts received, $62,201; expenditures, $115,606; qualifying distributions, $70,200.
Limitations: Giving primarily in TX.
Application information: Unsolicited requests for funds not accepted.
Trustee: Preston Johnson.
EIN: 760321771
Codes: CS, GTI

51641
Gatewood-Hawkins Foundation
P.O. Box 608
Tyler, TX 75710

Established in 1999 in TX.
Donor(s): James F. Gatewood.
Financial data (yr. ended 12/31/01): Grants paid, $70,100; assets, $842,911 (M); gifts received, $10,599; expenditures, $70,250; qualifying distributions, $70,100.
Directors: James F. Gatewood, Virginia Hawkins Gatewood.
EIN: 752780310

51642
Marvin E. Finn Foundation, Inc.
Simley Bldg., 1515 N. Hwy. 281
P.O. Box 908
Marble Falls, TX 78654-0908 (830) 693-5736
Contact: Marvin E. Finn, Pres.

Established in 1983 in TX.
Donor(s): Marvin E. Finn.
Financial data (yr. ended 12/31/01): Grants paid, $70,000; assets, $1,275,089 (M); gifts received, $23,706; expenditures, $72,830; qualifying distributions, $70,000.
Limitations: Giving primarily in TX.

Application information: Application form required.
Officers and Directors:* Marvin E. Finn,* Pres.; Linda F. Finn,* Secy.; Gregory M. Finn, Wayne C. Thelen.
EIN: 742290608

51643
The Pacey Family Foundation
8410 Navidad Dr.
Austin, TX 78735

Established in 1998 in TX.
Donor(s): M. Susan Pacey, Russell H. Pacey.
Financial data (yr. ended 12/31/01): Grants paid, $70,000; assets, $1,501,393 (M); expenditures, $71,955; qualifying distributions, $70,000.
Limitations: Applications not accepted. Giving primarily in TX.
Application information: Contributes only to pre-selected organizations.
Officers: M. Susan Pacey, Pres.; Thomas D. Pacey, V.P.; Alicia J. Pacey, Secy.; Russell H. Pacey, Treas.
EIN: 742898359

51644
The T. J. and LaVerne Plunkett Foundation
P.O. Box 2573
Henderson, TX 75653-2573 (903) 657-6225
Contact: Bill Plunkett, Pres.

Established in 1996 in TX.
Donor(s): LaVerne Plunkett.‡
Financial data (yr. ended 12/31/01): Grants paid, $70,000; assets, $2,130,985 (M); gifts received, $803,809; expenditures, $78,804; qualifying distributions, $69,613.
Limitations: Giving primarily in TX.
Officers: William J. Plunkett, Pres.; Sue Ann Wooster, V.P.; Sarah L. Plunkett, Secy.; Tony Wooster, Treas.
EIN: 752651793

51645
The Norm & Carole Sonju Foundation
5402 Harbor Town
Dallas, TX 75287-7409

Established in 1995 in TX.
Donor(s): Norm Sonju, Carole Lynne Sonju.
Financial data (yr. ended 12/31/01): Grants paid, $70,000; assets, $1,009,597 (M); expenditures, $72,908; qualifying distributions, $69,707.
Limitations: Applications not accepted. Giving limited to Dallas, TX.
Application information: Contributes only to pre-selected organizations.
Officers and Directors:* Norm Sonju,* Pres.; Carole Lynne Sonju,* Secy.-Treas.; David Norman Sonju, Lynne Elisabeth Sonju, Scott Norman Sonju.
EIN: 752613104

51646
The Wiseda Foundation
P.O. Box 122269
Fort Worth, TX 76121-2269 (817) 737-2269
Contact: William S. Davis, Tr.

Established in 1976 in TX.
Donor(s): William S. Davis, Davoil, Inc.
Financial data (yr. ended 09/30/01): Grants paid, $70,000; assets, $882,701 (M); expenditures, $76,735; qualifying distributions, $69,645.
Limitations: Giving primarily in TX.
Application information: Application form not required.
Trustee: William S. Davis.
EIN: 751533548

51647
Tyler Foundation
2800 W. Mockingbird Ln.
Dallas, TX 75235 (214) 902-5000
E-mail: bmiller@tylertechnologies.com
Contact: Brian K. Miller, V.P. and Treas.

Established in 1971 in TX.
Donor(s): Tyler Corp., Tyler Technologies, Inc.
Financial data (yr. ended 12/31/01): Grants paid, $69,949; assets, $2,477,814 (M); expenditures, $104,296; qualifying distributions, $69,949.
Limitations: Giving primarily in Dallas, TX, or other locations where Tyler Technologies has facilities.
Application information: Application form not required.
Officers: John Yeaman, Jr., Chair. and Pres.; Brian K. Miller, V.P. and Treas.; Terri L. Alford, Secy.
EIN: 237140526
Codes: CS, CD

51648
Air Liquide America Foundation, Inc.
(Formerly Big Three Industries Foundation, Inc.)
c/o Tax Dept.
P.O. Box 460149, 21st Fl.
Houston, TX 77056-8149
Application address: c/o Citizens' Scholarship Foundation of America, P.O. Box 297, St. Peters, MN 56082

Established in 1993 in TX.
Donor(s): Air Liquide America Corp.
Financial data (yr. ended 12/31/01): Grants paid, $69,900; assets, $565 (M); gifts received, $76,580; expenditures, $76,836; qualifying distributions, $76,836.
Limitations: Applications not accepted. Giving on a national basis.
Application information: Unsolicited requests for funds not accepted.
Officers: Kenneth W. Miller, Pres.; John N. Baird, Secy.; Wayne F. Bowman, Treas.
Directors: Wanda Boldebuck, MaryJane Mudd, Gary Prezbindowski.
EIN: 760366343
Codes: CS, CD, GTI

51649
Children's Covenant Foundation, Inc.
c/o Charles A. Staffel
8122 Datapoint Dr., Ste. 900
San Antonio, TX 78229

Established in 1996 in TX.
Donor(s): James R. Leininger.
Financial data (yr. ended 12/31/01): Grants paid, $69,800; assets, $707,707 (M); expenditures, $80,086; qualifying distributions, $69,620.
Limitations: Applications not accepted. Giving primarily in Nashville, TN.
Application information: Contributes only to pre-selected organizations.
Officers and Directors:* Sam A. Brooks,* Pres.; Dan A. Brooks,* V.P.; Thomas W. Lyles, Secy.; Charles A. Staffel, Treas.; Cecelia A. Leininger, James R. Leininger.
EIN: 742604651

51650
Stuart-Griffin-Perlitz Foundation
(also known as Stuart-Griffin Foundation)
P.O. Box 293580
Kerrville, TX 78029 (830) 896-8964
Application address: P.O. Box 33580, Kerrville, TX 78029, tel.: (512) 896-8964
Contact: James R. Perlitz, Secy.-Treas.

Established in 1965.

Financial data (yr. ended 05/31/01): Grants paid, $69,750; assets, $1,424,706 (M); expenditures, $73,123; qualifying distributions, $68,725.
Limitations: Giving primarily in TX.
Officers: Lea Griffin Perlitz, Pres.; James R. Perlitz, Secy.-Treas.
EIN: 746066479

51651
IBC Foundation
1200 San Bernardo Ave.
Laredo, TX 78040

Established in 1999 in TX.
Financial data (yr. ended 12/31/01): Grants paid, $69,500; assets, $1,005,198 (M); gifts received, $306,000; expenditures, $71,606; qualifying distributions, $69,500.
Officers and Directors:* Dennis E. Nixon,* Pres.; Imelda Navarro, V.P. and Treas.; Luisa Benavides, Secy.; Richard Haynes, Antonio R. Sanchez, Jr.
EIN: 742902265

51652
Lula Hasam McAfee Foundation
c/o JPMorgan Chase Bank
201 E. Main, 4th Fl.
El Paso, TX 79901 (915) 546-6515
Contact: Terry Crenshaw

Established in 1974.
Financial data (yr. ended 07/31/01): Grants paid, $69,500; assets, $123,503 (M); expenditures, $90,866; qualifying distributions, $73,832.
Limitations: Giving limited to El Paso County, TX.
Trustee: JPMorgan Chase Bank.
EIN: 746109154

51653
Rena Fleming Foundation for Boys, Inc.
c/o Corsicana National Bank
P.O. Box 624
Corsicana, TX 75151
Contact: Gary D. Brown, Secy.-Treas.

Established in 1970 in TX.
Financial data (yr. ended 10/31/01): Grants paid, $69,350; assets, $1,898,344 (M); expenditures, $88,072; qualifying distributions, $79,637.
Limitations: Giving limited to Navarro County, TX.
Application information: Application form not required.
Officers: J.I. Walton, Pres.; Frank Murchison, V.P.; Gary D. Brown, Secy.-Treas.
Directors: C.L. Brown III, H.L. Hillock.
EIN: 751045968

51654
Armstrong Family Foundation
P.O. Box 6995
Lubbock, TX 79493-6995
Contact: William Armstrong, Pres.

Established in 1997 in TX.
Donor(s): William Armstrong.
Financial data (yr. ended 12/31/01): Grants paid, $69,274; assets, $515,861 (M); gifts received, $71,349; qualifying distributions, $69,274.
Limitations: Giving primarily in Lubbock,TX.
Officers: William Armstrong, Pres.; Mary Leigh Armstrong, V.P.; Robert William Armstrong, Secy.; Camilla Wideman, Treas.
EIN: 752707415

51655
M. C. Shook Trust
c/o San Angelo National Bank, Trust Dept.
P.O. Box 5291
San Angelo, TX 76902-5291 (915) 659-5998
Contact: David Byrd, Trust Off.

Established in 1955 in NY.
Donor(s): Melvin C. Shook.
Financial data (yr. ended 12/31/01): Grants paid, $69,115; assets, $1,313,864 (M); expenditures, $75,475; qualifying distributions, $69,115.
Limitations: Giving primarily in San Angelo, TX.
Application information: Application form not required.
Trustee: San Angelo National Bank.
EIN: 756022499

51656
The Rudman Foundation
1700 Pacific Ave., Ste. 4700
Dallas, TX 75201-4670
Contact: M.B. Rudman, Mgr.

Trust established in 1946 in TX.
Donor(s): I. Rudman,‡ Rose Rudman.
Financial data (yr. ended 12/31/01): Grants paid, $69,010; assets, $339,942 (M); expenditures, $77,989; qualifying distributions, $69,010.
Limitations: Giving primarily in TX.
Application information: Application form not required.
Officers and Trustees:* M.B. Rudman,* Mgr.; R.E. Sater,* Mgr.
EIN: 756020439

51657
L. D. Ormsby Charitable Foundation, Inc.
112 E. Pecan, Ste. 900
San Antonio, TX 78205 (210) 226-4157
Contact: C.B. Gregory, Jr., Exec. V.P.

Established in 1963 in TX.
Financial data (yr. ended 09/30/99): Grants paid, $69,000; assets, $2,091,653 (M); gifts received, $383; expenditures, $98,420; qualifying distributions, $67,509.
Limitations: Giving limited to San Antonio, TX.
Application information: Application form not required.
Officers and Board Members:* C.B. Gregory, Sr.,* Pres.; C.B. Gregory, Jr.,* Exec. V.P. and Secy.-Treas.; John W. Harris.
EIN: 741497772

51658
The Sholar Foundation
2808 Fairmount St., Ste. 250
Dallas, TX 75201 (214) 979-1100
Contact: Stephen S. Brookshire, Pres.

Established in 2000 in TX.
Donor(s): Gail S. Brookshire, Stephen S. Brookshire.
Financial data (yr. ended 12/31/01): Grants paid, $69,000; assets, $159,567 (M); gifts received, $95,000; expenditures, $70,395; qualifying distributions, $69,000.
Limitations: Giving primarily in Dallas, TX.
Application information: Application form not required.
Officers and Directors:* Stephen S. Brookshire,* Pres.; Gail S. Brookshire,* V.P. and Treas.; Jeffrey B. Brawner, Secy.
EIN: 752846540

51659
N. O. Simmons Foundation
167 E. Price Rd.
Brownsville, TX 78521

Established in 1997 in TX.
Financial data (yr. ended 12/31/01): Grants paid, $68,763; assets, $620,175 (M); expenditures, $69,445; qualifying distributions, $68,763.
Limitations: Applications not accepted.
Application information: Contributes only to pre-selected organizations.
Officers and Directors:* N.O. Simmons,* Pres.; Maria Lourdes Lara Simmons,* V.P.; Lourdes Simmons Kilgore,* Secy.-Treas.
EIN: 742807673

51660
The Peter and Anne Pratt Family Foundation
6255 Meadow Lake
Houston, TX 77057 (713) 626-0695
Contact: Scott Pratt, Secy.

Established in 1999.
Donor(s): Peter Pratt, Anne Pratt.
Financial data (yr. ended 08/31/01): Grants paid, $68,705; assets, $469,054 (M); gifts received, $237,006; expenditures, $103,122; qualifying distributions, $68,705.
Limitations: Giving primarily in Houston, TX.
Officers: Anne Pratt, Pres.; Scott Pratt, Secy.
Directors: James Bashaw, Kimberly Bashaw, Mason Bashaw, Catherine Pratt, Jospeh Pratt, Peter Pratt, Peter Pratt, Jr.
EIN: 760617763

51661
The Levant Foundation
600 Travis, Ste. 6800
Houston, TX 77002

Established in 1999 in TX.
Donor(s): Jamal Daniel.
Financial data (yr. ended 12/31/01): Grants paid, $68,647; assets, $2,342 (M); gifts received, $63,000; expenditures, $69,375; qualifying distributions, $68,647.
Limitations: Applications not accepted. Giving primarily in Lebanon, as well as in Houston, TX.
Application information: Contributes only to pre-selected organizations.
Officers and Directors:* Jamal Daniel,* Pres.; Dee S. Osborne,* Secy.; John Howland,* Treas.
EIN: 311637973

51662
Stephen Joel Weiss Charitable Foundation
150 W. Parker Rd., Ste. 305
Houston, TX 77076

Donor(s): Stephen Joel Weiss.
Financial data (yr. ended 12/31/01): Grants paid, $68,629; assets, $267,319 (M); gifts received, $82,500; expenditures, $84,272; qualifying distributions, $68,629.
Limitations: Applications not accepted. Giving primarily in Houston, TX.
Application information: Contributes only to pre-selected organizations.
Trustee: Stephen Joel Weiss.
EIN: 760538328

51663
The Nicole and Atlee Kohl Family Foundation
(Formerly The Atlee Kohl Family Foundation)
3007 Skyway Cir. N.
Irving, TX 75038-3524 (972) 659-9500
Contact: Bob Carter

Established in 1982.
Donor(s): Atlee Kohl, Nicole F. Kohl, Stewart Siebens.
Financial data (yr. ended 11/30/01): Grants paid, $68,325; assets, $1,487,044 (M); gifts received, $6,300; expenditures, $83,797; qualifying distributions, $70,998.
Limitations: Giving primarily in the Dallas, TX, area.
Application information: Application form not required.
Officers and Directors:* Atlee Kohl,* Pres.; Nicole F. Kohl,* V.P.; Carolyn Kohl, Clayton Kohl, Marian Kohl.

EIN: 363214720

51664
The Cipione Family Foundation, Inc.
411 Brazos St., No. 310
Austin, TX 78701

Established in 1999 in TX.
Donor(s): Claymon A. Cipione, Patricia A. Cipione, Cipione Charitable Lead Trust.
Financial data (yr. ended 12/31/01): Grants paid, $68,104; assets, $1,886,120 (M); gifts received, $107,397; expenditures, $119,802; qualifying distributions, $105,695.
Limitations: Applications not accepted. Giving primarily in Washington, DC and TX.
Application information: Contributes only to pre-selected organizations.
Officers: Claymon A. Cipione, Pres.; Patricia A. Cipione, V.P.; Lynette Cipione, Mgr.
EIN: 311663062

51665
Joe R. & Emilie F. Straus, Sr. Charitable Trust
P.O. Box 600
San Antonio, TX 78205
Contact: David J. Straus, Tr.

Established in 1978 in TX.
Donor(s): Joe R. Straus, Sr.,‡ David J. Straus, Joe R. Straus, Jr., Loci Straus.
Financial data (yr. ended 12/31/01): Grants paid, $68,103; assets, $1,084,400 (M); gifts received, $5,500; expenditures, $80,388; qualifying distributions, $67,636.
Limitations: Giving primarily in the San Antonio, TX, area.
Application information: Application form not required.
Trustees: David J. Straus, Joe R. Straus, Jr.
EIN: 741996914

51666
Edward H. Andrews Foundation
P.O. Box 130025
Houston, TX 77219-0025
Application address: c/o Terri Lacy, 600 Travis, Ste. 4200, Houston, TX 77002

Established in 1996 in TX.
Donor(s): Edward H. Andrews.
Financial data (yr. ended 07/31/02): Grants paid, $68,065; assets, $935,818 (M); expenditures, $74,097; qualifying distributions, $69,573.
Limitations: Giving on a national basis.
Application information: Application form required.
Officers: Edward H. Andrews, Pres.; Bruce McIntyre, V.P.
Director: Peter C. Maffitt.
EIN: 311514306

51667
The Planetary Trust
c/o Margaret J. Haley
7149 Hillgreen
Dallas, TX 75214-1933

Established in 1994 in TX.
Donor(s): John M. Haley, Margaret J. Haley.
Financial data (yr. ended 12/31/01): Grants paid, $67,820; assets, $494,243 (M); expenditures, $68,277; qualifying distributions, $67,820.
Limitations: Applications not accepted. Giving limited to TX.
Application information: Contributes only to pre-selected organizations.
Trustee: Margaret J. Haley.
EIN: 752567517

51668
Josephine Graf Foundation
4920 Briarwood Pl.
Dallas, TX 75209-2004
Contact: Joanne Stroud Bilby, Pres.

Donor(s): Joanne Stroud Bilby.
Financial data (yr. ended 11/30/99): Grants paid, $67,707; assets, $1,519,262 (M); expenditures, $68,280; qualifying distributions, $67,392.
Limitations: Applications not accepted. Giving on a national basis.
Application information: Contributes only to pre-selected organizations.
Officers and Directors:* Joanne Stroud Bilby,* Pres.; Joyce Mann,* V.P.; Ethan Stroud, Secy.-Treas.
EIN: 751187926

51669
The Anchorage Foundation, Inc.
P.O. Box 312109
New Braunfels, TX 78131-2109
(830) 629-8003
Contact: Pierre M. Schlumberger, Pres.

Financial data (yr. ended 12/31/01): Grants paid, $67,625; assets, $521,679 (M); expenditures, $75,032; qualifying distributions, $67,625.
Limitations: Giving primarily in TX.
Officers: Pierre M. Schlumberger, Pres.; Anne S. Bohnn, V.P. and Secy.-Treas.
Director: Jody Blazek.
EIN: 746036644

51670
Leon and Beatrice Obenhaus Grodhaus Foundation
420 Walnut St.
P.O. Box 867
Columbus, TX 78934
Contact: James H. Whitcomb, Secy.-Treas.

Established in 1984 in TX.
Financial data (yr. ended 12/31/01): Grants paid, $67,621; assets, $1,519,843 (M); expenditures, $74,793; qualifying distributions, $67,621.
Limitations: Giving limited to Weimar and Colorado counties, TX.
Application information: Application form not required.
Officer and Trustees:* James H. Whitcomb,* Secy.-Treas.; F.T. Barfield, Alfred Flournoy, Harvey Vornsand.
EIN: 746328959

51671
The Dean Foundation, Inc.
2626 Cole Ave., Ste. 400
Dallas, TX 75204-3073 (214) 665-9500
Contact: Jimmy Dean, Pres.

Established in 1995 in TX.
Donor(s): Jimmy Dean, Donna Dean.
Financial data (yr. ended 07/31/01): Grants paid, $67,618; assets, $2,011 (M); gifts received, $69,014; expenditures, $67,868; qualifying distributions, $67,618.
Limitations: Giving primarily in Richmond, VA.
Application information: Application form not required.
Officers: Jimmy Dean, Pres.; Donna Dean, Secy.-Treas.
Director: Stephen Conte.
EIN: 752637602

51672
Gayden Family Foundation
12222 Merit Dr., Ste. 1500
Dallas, TX 75251

Established in 1999 in TX.
Donor(s): William K. Gayden.
Financial data (yr. ended 12/31/01): Grants paid, $67,000; assets, $875,377 (M); gifts received, $397,890; expenditures, $68,540; qualifying distributions, $67,000.
Directors: Cynthia N. Gayden, William K. Gayden, Katherine G. Keenan, Elizabeth G. Williams.
EIN: 756563143

51673
The Payne-Madole Foundation
1201 Elm St., Ste. 5400
Dallas, TX 75270

Established in 1999 in TX.
Donor(s): Robert B. Payne, Virginia W. Payne.
Financial data (yr. ended 12/31/00): Grants paid, $67,000; assets, $451,773 (M); expenditures, $68,783; qualifying distributions, $66,346.
Limitations: Applications not accepted.
Application information: Contributes only to pre-selected organizations.
Trustees: Susan P. Madole, Marshall B. Payne, Robert B. Payne, Robert B. Payne, Jr., Virginia W. Payne.
EIN: 752854185

51674
The Robert L. and Barbara Zorich Family Foundation
307 Hickory Post Ln.
Houston, TX 77079

Established in 2000 in TX.
Donor(s): Barbara L. Zorich, Robert L. Zorich.
Financial data (yr. ended 12/31/01): Grants paid, $67,000; assets, $353,671 (M); expenditures, $72,839; qualifying distributions, $67,000.
Limitations: Applications not accepted.
Application information: Contributes only to pre-selected organizations.
Trustees: Barbara L. Zorich, Bret A. Zorich, Robert L. Zorich.
EIN: 760664404

51675
The Altman Family Foundation
6906 Norway Pl.
Dallas, TX 75230

Established in 1985 in TX.
Donor(s): Jack Altman, Ruth Altman.
Financial data (yr. ended 06/30/01): Grants paid, $66,818; assets, $838,113 (M); gifts received, $50,000; expenditures, $72,455; qualifying distributions, $66,818.
Limitations: Applications not accepted. Giving primarily in Dallas, TX.
Application information: Contributes only to pre-selected organizations.
Trustees: Jack Altman, Ruth Altman, Emanuel Rohan.
EIN: 752077004

51676
Mary B. & James K. Jennings Charitable Foundation
5830 Indian Trail
Houston, TX 77057

Established in 1997 in TX.
Donor(s): James K. Jennings, Jr., Mary B. Jennings.
Financial data (yr. ended 12/31/01): Grants paid, $66,775; assets, $560,648 (M); expenditures, $68,863; qualifying distributions, $67,356.
Limitations: Applications not accepted.
Application information: Contributes only to pre-selected organizations.

51676—TEXAS

Officers: James K. Jennings, Jr., Pres.; Elizabeth B. Jennings, V.P.; James K. Jennings III, V.P.; Mary B. Jennings, Secy.
EIN: 760534859

51677
The R. Vernon & Lynda Y. Peppard Foundation
(also known as The Peppard Foundation)
3131 McKinney Ave., LB 103
Dallas, TX 75204 (972) 985-0496

Established in 1987.
Donor(s): R. Vernon Peppard, Lynda Y. Peppard.
Financial data (yr. ended 12/31/01): Grants paid, $66,752; assets, $1,157,249 (M); expenditures, $67,139; qualifying distributions, $66,752.
Limitations: Applications not accepted. Giving primarily in AR and TX.
Application information: Contributes only to pre-selected organizations.
Trustees: Lynda Y. Peppard, R. Vernon Peppard.
EIN: 752154075

51678
F. V. Hall, Jr. & Marylou Hall Children's Crisis Foundation
c/o Bank of America
P.O. Box 831041
Dallas, TX 75283-1041
Application address: P.O. Box 60163, San Angelo, TX 76906-0163

Established in 1978 in TX.
Donor(s): F.V. Hall,‡ MaryLou Hall.‡
Financial data (yr. ended 04/30/01): Grants paid, $66,732; assets, $1,421,282 (M); expenditures, $74,296; qualifying distributions, $68,458.
Limitations: Giving limited to Tom Green County, TX.
Application information: Application form required.
Officers: Robert Grant, Mgr.; Susan Marshall, Mgr.; Craig Porter, Mgr.
Trustee: Bank of America.
EIN: 756260350
Codes: GTI

51679
The Gary and Lee Rosenthal Foundation
600 Travis St., Rm. 6110
Houston, TX 77002-3007

Established in 1994 in TX.
Donor(s): Gary L. Rosenthal, Lee H. Rosenthal.
Financial data (yr. ended 12/31/01): Grants paid, $66,666; assets, $802,922 (M); expenditures, $69,504; qualifying distributions, $66,666.
Limitations: Applications not accepted. Giving limited to Houston, TX.
Application information: Contributes only to pre-selected organizations.
Officers and Directors:* Gary L. Rosenthal,* Pres.; Lee H. Rosenthal,* V.P. and Secy.; Barry Margolis,* V.P. and Treas.
EIN: 760453685

51680
The Bertha Morere Trust
c/o Bank One Trust Co., N.A.
P.O. Box 2050
Fort Worth, TX 76113

Financial data (yr. ended 12/31/99): Grants paid, $66,585; assets, $826,376 (M); expenditures, $72,320; qualifying distributions, $66,173.
Limitations: Applications not accepted. Giving limited to New Orleans, LA, Boston, MA, St. Louis, MO, New York, NY, and Jeffersonville and Nashville, TN.
Application information: Contributes only to pre-selected organizations.

Trustee: Bank One, Louisiana, N.A.
EIN: 726056383

51681
Dan and Hermine Hemphill Charitable Foundation, Inc.
802 N. Washington
Odessa, TX 79761 (915) 332-0928
Contact: Hermine Hemphill, Pres.

Established in 1999 in TX.
Donor(s): Dan Hemphill, Hermine Hemphill.
Financial data (yr. ended 12/31/01): Grants paid, $66,457; assets, $1,679,337 (M); expenditures, $117,601; qualifying distributions, $66,457.
Application information: Application form required.
Officers and Directors:* Dan Hemphill,* Pres.; Uday Koya,* V.P.; Hermine Hemphill,* Secy.-Treas.
EIN: 752844681

51682
Katherine U. Sanders Foundation
c/o Ben T. Morris
600 Travis, 3100 Chase Tower
Houston, TX 77002

Established in 1998.
Financial data (yr. ended 12/31/01): Grants paid, $66,350; assets, $9,967 (M); gifts received, $4,027; expenditures, $70,559; qualifying distributions, $66,350.
Limitations: Applications not accepted. Giving primarily in Houston, TX.
Application information: Contributes only to pre-selected organizations.
Officers: Katherine U. Sanders, Pres.; Bert D. Sanders, V.P.; Walter P. Zivley, Secy.; Ben T. Morris, Treas.
EIN: 760563189

51683
El Paso County Salute to Education
4445 N. Mesa St., Ste. 121
El Paso, TX 79902-1107 (915) 532-1127
Application address: c/o Munoz Public Relations, 110 Broadway St., Ste. 220, San Antonio, TX 78205, tel.: (210) 225-3353

Established in 1998 in TX.
Donor(s): Ford Motor Credit Co., Ford Motor Co., Casa Ford, Inc., Shamaley Ford, Mesa Ford.
Financial data (yr. ended 12/31/00): Grants paid, $66,286; assets, $142,192 (M); gifts received, $114,070; expenditures, $66,477; qualifying distributions, $66,311.
Limitations: Giving limited to residents of El Paso and Hudspeth counties, TX.
Application information: Application form required.
Officers: Clay Lowenfield, Pres.; Jimmy Dick IV, V.P.; Paul Lee, Secy.; Gary Byrd, Treas.
Director: L.J. Shamaley.
EIN: 742871171
Codes: CS, CD

51684
Formosa Plastics Environmental Endowment Trust Fund
c/o First National Bank
P.O. Drawer 7
Port Lavaca, TX 77979-0007

Established around 1992.
Donor(s): Formosa Plastics Corp., Texas.
Financial data (yr. ended 12/31/01): Grants paid, $66,057; assets, $1,141,464 (M); expenditures, $74,997; qualifying distributions, $66,057.
Limitations: Giving limited to southern TX.
Application information: Application form required.

Trustees: W.H. Bauer, Jr., Jack Wu.
EIN: 746388418
Codes: CS, CD

51685
Symonds Foundation
P.O. Box 920919
Houston, TX 77292-0919

Established in 1955 in TX.
Financial data (yr. ended 10/31/01): Grants paid, $66,000; assets, $790,726 (M); expenditures, $73,402; qualifying distributions, $65,371.
Limitations: Applications not accepted. Giving on a national basis.
Application information: Contributes only to pre-selected organizations.
Trustees: Susan Symonds Bodin, J. Taft Symonds, Williston B. Symonds, Bank of America.
EIN: 746035953

51686
Tom C. & Mary B. Reitch Scholarship Trust
c/o Bank of America
P.O. Box 831041
Dallas, TX 75283-1041
Application address: c/o Mineola High School, 900 W. Patten St., Mineola, TX 75773, tel.: (903) 569-3000
Contact: Ms. Yvie Witt

Established in 2000 in TX.
Donor(s): Mary B. Reitch.‡
Financial data (yr. ended 12/31/01): Grants paid, $65,957; assets, $1,370,173 (M); expenditures, $87,046; qualifying distributions, $65,957.
Limitations: Giving primarily in Mineola, TX.
Application information: Application form required.
Trustee: Bank of America.
EIN: 527033946

51687
James S. Seneker Trust for Religious Education
c/o Bank of America
P.O. Box 831041
Dallas, TX 75283-1041
Seneker Scholarship Awards application address: c/o Financial Aid Off., Perkins School of Theology, Southern Methodist University, Dallas, TX 75275; The Schisler Graduate Awards application address: c/o Board of Higher Education and Ministry, The United Methodist Church, Office of Loans and Scholarships, P.O. Box 871, Nashville, TN 37202

Established in 1984 in TX.
Financial data (yr. ended 05/31/01): Grants paid, $65,936; assets, $2,298,308 (M); expenditures, $78,751; qualifying distributions, $68,298.
Limitations: Giving primarily in Dallas, TX.
Application information: Application form required.
Trustee: Bank of America.
EIN: 756318275

51688
Newman Foundation
700 El Paseo
Denton, TX 76205 (940) 566-0990
Contact: James K. Newman, Pres.

Established in 1996 in TX.
Donor(s): Gloria A. Newman, James K. Newman.
Financial data (yr. ended 12/31/01): Grants paid, $65,500; assets, $971,121 (M); expenditures, $68,088; qualifying distributions, $65,500.
Limitations: Applications not accepted. Giving primarily in TX, with emphasis on Denton.
Application information: Contributes only to pre-selected organizations.

Officers and Directors:* James K. Newman,* Pres. and Secy.-Treas.; Gloria A. Newman,* V.P.; Katherine E. Newman, Matthew L. Newman.
EIN: 752680607

51689
The Janszen Charitable Trust
P.O. Box 455
Hurst, TX 76053

Established in 1992.
Financial data (yr. ended 12/31/01): Grants paid, $65,150; assets, $236,810 (M); gifts received, $65,100; expenditures, $65,150; qualifying distributions, $65,150.
Limitations: Applications not accepted. Giving primarily in TX.
Application information: Contributes only to pre-selected organizations.
Trustee: James B. Morgan.
EIN: 756423830

51690
Stone Family Foundation
3001 Chatelaine Dr.
Austin, TX 78746

Donor(s): Paul D. Stone, Dianne M. Stone.
Financial data (yr. ended 12/31/01): Grants paid, $65,020; assets, $363,344 (M); gifts received, $430,270; expenditures, $65,056; qualifying distributions, $65,020.
Limitations: Applications not accepted. Giving limited to TX.
Application information: Contributes only to pre-selected organizations.
Officers and Directors:* Paul D. Stone,* Pres. and Treas.; Dianne M. Stone,* V.P. and Secy.; John L. Stone.
EIN: 742990932

51691
The Ninnie L. Baird Foundation
P.O. Box 9275
Fort Worth, TX 76147-2275
Contact: Byron R. Baird, Pres.

Established in 1998 in TX.
Donor(s): Byron R. Baird, C.B. Baird.
Financial data (yr. ended 12/31/01): Grants paid, $65,000; assets, $1,455,305 (M); gifts received, $100,000; expenditures, $75,155; qualifying distributions, $65,840.
Limitations: Giving primarily in TX.
Application information: Application form not required.
Officers: Byron R. Baird, Pres.; Debbie Baird, V.P.; P. Bradley Lummis, Secy.-Treas.
Directors: Harry Bruce Baird, John Engert, Stephanie R. Harvey, Janet B. Quisenberry, Greg B. Whitehead.
EIN: 752734849

51692
The Michael H. & Kathryn N. Jordan Family Foundation
c/o Kathryn J. Donaldsoney
3729 Stratford
Dallas, TX 75205
Contact: Michael H. Jordan, Pres.

Established in 1993 in TX.
Donor(s): Michael H. Jordan, Kathryn H. Jordan.
Financial data (yr. ended 12/31/01): Grants paid, $65,000; assets, $1,385,723 (M); gifts received, $99,632; expenditures, $139,782; qualifying distributions, $119,904.
Limitations: Giving on a national basis.
Application information: Application form not required.

Officers and Directors:* Michael H. Jordan,* Pres.; Kathryn H. Jordan,* V.P.; Stephen H. Jordan,* Secy.; Kathryn H. Donaldson,* Treas.
EIN: 752461017

51693
Kelley Family Foundation, Inc.
P.O. Box 51166
Amarillo, TX 79159-1166
Contact: Sharon K. Oeschger, Secy.

Established in 1991.
Financial data (yr. ended 12/31/01): Grants paid, $65,000; assets, $3,091,413 (M); expenditures, $100,488; qualifying distributions, $65,000.
Limitations: Applications not accepted. Giving primarily in Amarillo, TX.
Application information: Contributes only to pre-selected organizations. Unsolicited requests for funds not accepted.
Officers and Directors:* Hazel M. Kelley Wilson,* Chair.; Oliver Kendall Kelley,* Pres.; Sherry L. Kelley,* V.P.; Judy K. Morgan,* V.P.; Sharon K. Oeschger,* Secy.; George C. Sell,* Treas.; Jim Morgan, Lawrence A. Oeschger, Ross W. Wilson.
EIN: 752383584

51694
Miranda Leonard Foundation
500 Throckmorton, Ste. 1300
Fort Worth, TX 76102

Established in 1970.
Donor(s): Miranda Leonard.
Financial data (yr. ended 12/31/01): Grants paid, $65,000; assets, $1,249,541 (M); expenditures, $77,551; qualifying distributions, $65,000.
Limitations: Applications not accepted. Giving primarily in San Francisco, CA.
Application information: Contributes only to pre-selected organizations.
Officers and Trustees:* Jenkins Garrett,* Mgr.; Miranda Leonard,* Mgr.; Martha Leonard, G.W. Owens.
EIN: 237103778

51695
Sutton Family Foundation, Inc.
4311 Ravine Ridge Trail
Austin, TX 78746-1283

Established in 1998 in NJ and TX.
Donor(s): Mark Sutton, Dayna Sutton.
Financial data (yr. ended 07/31/01): Grants paid, $65,000; assets, $1,088,772 (M); gifts received, $163,620; expenditures, $65,065; qualifying distributions, $65,000.
Limitations: Applications not accepted.
Application information: Contributes only to pre-selected organizations.
Trustees: Kent Anderson, Dayna Sutton, Mark B. Sutton.
EIN: 742900064

51696
The Ross Foundation
P.O. Box 78
2121 Kirby Dr.
Houston, TX 77019
Contact: Ellen G. Ross, Dir.

Established in 1989 in TX.
Donor(s): David Ross III, Florence Shutts Ross.‡
Financial data (yr. ended 12/31/01): Grants paid, $64,570; assets, $957,881 (M); expenditures, $73,326; qualifying distributions, $64,870.
Limitations: Applications not accepted. Giving primarily in MA and TX.
Application information: Contributes only to pre-selected organizations.

Directors: David Ross III, David Ross IV, Ellen G. Ross.
EIN: 760286746

51697
The Abbott Foundation
9701 Eagle Rising Cove
Austin, TX 78730

Established in 1999 in TX.
Donor(s): Gary Abbott, Shawn Abbott.
Financial data (yr. ended 12/31/01): Grants paid, $64,500; assets, $999,090 (M); gifts received, $1,200; expenditures, $67,217; qualifying distributions, $64,500.
Limitations: Applications not accepted.
Application information: Contributes only to pre-selected organizations.
Officers: Gary Abbott, Pres.; Shawn Abbott, V.P.
EIN: 742940444

51698
The H. H. Weinert Foundation
P.O. Box 279
Austin, TX 78767-0279

Established in 1992 in TX.
Donor(s): Roland Blumberg, Jane Blumberg.
Financial data (yr. ended 12/31/01): Grants paid, $64,000; assets, $1,249,066 (M); expenditures, $81,006; qualifying distributions, $64,451.
Limitations: Applications not accepted. Giving primarily in TX.
Application information: Contributes only to pre-selected organizations.
Officers: Carla Blumberg, Pres. and Treas.; Donna Carter, V.P.; Molly Lamphear, Secy.
EIN: 742649437

51699
James A. Jackson Charitable Foundation
17827 Windflower Way, Apt. 101
Dallas, TX 75252

Established in 1994 in OH and TX.
Donor(s): James A. Jackson.
Financial data (yr. ended 12/31/99): Grants paid, $63,949; assets, $7,541 (M); gifts received, $286,767; expenditures, $279,256; qualifying distributions, $63,949.
Limitations: Applications not accepted.
Application information: Contributes only to pre-selected organizations.
Officers: James A. Jackson, Pres.; Calvin J. Lawshe, V.P.; Michael Scott Reeves, Secy.
EIN: 752552092

51700
Antonio Haghenbeck y de La Lama Foundation, Inc.
811 Caroline St.
Montgomery, TX 77356
Application address: 7130 Las Ventanas Dr., Austin, TX 78731, tel.: (512) 795-0450
Contact: Mary Jo Gutierrez, V.P.

Established in 1986 in TX.
Donor(s): Antonio Haghenbeck y de La Lama.‡
Financial data (yr. ended 11/30/01): Grants paid, $63,733; assets, $3,225,941 (M); expenditures, $868,301; qualifying distributions, $63,733.
Limitations: Giving primarily in Mexico.
Officers and Directors:* Carmela Rivero Jimenez,* Pres.; Mary Jo Gutierrez,* V.P. and Treas.; Cecilia Vega Leon.
EIN: 760227001

51701—TEXAS

51701
Wolff Family Charitable Foundation
20 Briar Hollow Ln.
Houston, TX 77027

Established in 1987 in TX.
Donor(s): David S. Wolff.
Financial data (yr. ended 12/31/00): Grants paid, $63,729; assets, $2,293,064 (M); expenditures, $85,311; qualifying distributions, $63,729.
Limitations: Applications not accepted. Giving on a national basis, with emphasis on TX.
Application information: Contributes only to pre-selected organizations.
Officers and Directors:* David S. Wolff,* Pres.; David L. Lane, V.P.; Elizabeth Toy Brodsky, Secy.; Mary C. Wolff.
EIN: 760236381

51702
Thompson Smith Foundation
6110 Covey Lane
Tyler, TX 75703

Established in 1992.
Donor(s): H. Thompson Smith.
Financial data (yr. ended 12/31/01): Grants paid, $63,615; assets, $1,142,095 (M); expenditures, $64,408; qualifying distributions, $63,615.
Limitations: Applications not accepted. Giving primarily in TX.
Application information: Contributes only to pre-selected organizations.
Officers: H. Thompson Smith, Pres.; Elizabeth Monroe Smith, V.P.; Paul Rogers Smith, V.P.; Anne Monroe Smith, Secy.-Treas.
EIN: 752441568

51703
The Alfred S. Gage Foundation
110 E. Crockett St.
San Antonio, TX 78205
E-mail: jjrizzo@flash.net
Contact: Roxana Catto Hayne, V.P.

Established in 1989 in TX.
Donor(s): Roxana Gage Catto.‡
Financial data (yr. ended 06/30/01): Grants paid, $63,400; assets, $2,729,347 (M); gifts received, $1,879,278; expenditures, $85,291; qualifying distributions, $65,791.
Limitations: Giving primarily in San Antonio, TX and the adjacent counties of Brewster and Presidio, TX.
Application information: Application form not required.
Officers and Directors:* Roxana Catto Hayne,* V.P. and Secy.; Joan Negley Kelleher,* V.P. and Treas.
EIN: 742553574

51704
Ken Marchant Foundation
2125 N. Josey Ln., Ste. 200
Carrollton, TX 75006
Contact: Ken E. Marchant, Dir.

Donor(s): Ken E. Marchant, Randall Marchant.
Financial data (yr. ended 06/30/01): Grants paid, $63,374; assets, $992,422 (M); gifts received, $15,000; expenditures, $67,915; qualifying distributions, $63,374.
Limitations: Giving primarily in OK and TX.
Directors: Donna M. Marchant, Ken E. Marchant.
EIN: 752001862

51705
I. A. Nehemiah Foundation
(Formerly Nehemiah Foundation)
c/o Bank of America
P.O. Box 831041
Dallas, TX 75283-1041
Application address: P.O. Box 26900, Albuquerque, NM 87125-6900, tel.: (505) 282-2546

Established in 1997 in NM.
Donor(s): V. June Broce.
Financial data (yr. ended 06/30/01): Grants paid, $63,000; assets, $1,365,735 (M); expenditures, $85,444; qualifying distributions, $64,294.
Limitations: Giving primarily in CA and Albuquerque, NM.
Officers: V. June Broce, Pres.; Jerry Hastey, Secy.; Betty Leonard, Treas.
EIN: 742833210

51706
Barrett Foundation
10611 Gawain Ln.
Houston, TX 77024-5513

Established in 1997 in TX.
Financial data (yr. ended 03/31/02): Grants paid, $62,939; assets, $371,253 (M); expenditures, $63,929; qualifying distributions, $62,939.
Officers: James N. Barrett, Pres. and Secy.; Eva Barrett, V.P.
Director: James N. Barrett III, Robert W. Barrett.
EIN: 760534826

51707
R. C. & Paris Blair Charitable Trust
518 Ave. H
Levelland, TX 79336

Established in 1986 in TX.
Financial data (yr. ended 12/31/01): Grants paid, $62,500; assets, $455,239 (M); expenditures, $74,520; qualifying distributions, $62,500.
Limitations: Applications not accepted. Giving limited to TX.
Application information: Contributes only to pre-selected organizations.
Trustee: Harold Phelan.
EIN: 752056392

51708
The Frank and Dorothy Bragg Charitable Trust
c/o Bank of America
P.O. Box 831041
Dallas, TX 75283-1041

Established in 1998 in TX.
Financial data (yr. ended 02/28/02): Grants paid, $62,375; assets, $1,377,645 (M); expenditures, $96,107; qualifying distributions, $62,375.
Limitations: Applications not accepted. Giving primarily in TX.
Application information: Contributes only to pre-selected organizations.
Trustee: Bank of America.
EIN: 756521856

51709
Clay and Louise Wood Charitable Foundation, Inc.
P.O. Box 711
Odessa, TX 79760

Established in 1999 in TX.
Donor(s): Clay Wood.
Financial data (yr. ended 06/30/01): Grants paid, $62,350; assets, $949,279 (M); expenditures, $96,570; qualifying distributions, $64,052.
Limitations: Applications not accepted. Giving primarily in Odessa, TX.

Application information: Contributes only to pre-selected organizations.
Officers: Clay Wood, Pres.; Donald E. Wood, V.P.; Jack Wood, V.P.; Louise Wood, V.P.; Gregory Wood, Secy.-Treas.
EIN: 752806006

51710
Red Oak Foundation
c/o Rebecca Brumley
3327 W. 7th St., Ste. C
Fort Worth, TX 76107-2714

Established in 1992.
Donor(s): I. Jon Brumley, Rebecca Brumley.
Financial data (yr. ended 12/31/01): Grants paid, $62,225; assets, $1,020,218 (M); gifts received, $180,000; expenditures, $125,858; qualifying distributions, $119,721.
Limitations: Applications not accepted. Giving primarily in TX.
Application information: Contributes only to pre-selected organizations.
Directors: Louis Baldwin, I. Jon Brumley, Rebecca Brumley.
EIN: 752382416

51711
Bratton Family Foundation
47 Valley Ridge Rd.
Fort Worth, TX 76107

Established in 1993 in TX.
Financial data (yr. ended 12/31/01): Grants paid, $62,090; assets, $286,519 (M); expenditures, $63,615; qualifying distributions, $62,090.
Limitations: Applications not accepted. Giving primarily in Fort Worth, TX.
Application information: Contributes only to pre-selected organizations.
Trustee: Douglas K. Bratton.
EIN: 752513615

51712
Blanche Mary Taxis Foundation
1800 Lincoln Plz.
Dallas, TX 75201-6616
Contact: Robert L. Dillard III, Secy.

Financial data (yr. ended 12/31/01): Grants paid, $62,000; assets, $895,228 (M); expenditures, $73,907; qualifying distributions, $62,000.
Limitations: Giving primarily in Dallas, TX.
Officers and Trustees:* Robert L. Dillard, Jr.,* Pres.; Lawrence W. Jackson,* V.P.; Robert L. Dillard III,* Secy.; H. Louis Nichols,* Treas.; Plez A. Transou, Hon. Dee Brown Walker.
EIN: 756012051

51713
Michael and Mary Kay Poulos Foundation
2121 Kirby Dr., Ste. 73
Houston, TX 77019

Established in 1994 in TX.
Donor(s): Michael J. Poulos, Mary Kay Poulos.
Financial data (yr. ended 12/31/01): Grants paid, $61,798; assets, $480,156 (M); gifts received, $166,600; expenditures, $75,164; qualifying distributions, $65,048.
Limitations: Applications not accepted. Giving limited to MA, NY, and TX.
Application information: Contributes only to pre-selected organizations.
Officers: Michael J. Poulos, Pres. and Treas.; Mary Kay Poulos, V.P. and Secy.
Director: Joseph S. Maniscalco.
EIN: 760455309

51714
Lillian Waltom Foundation
901 Oak St.
Jourdanton, TX 78026
Contact: W.F. Zuhlke, Jr., Tr.

Established in 1988 in TX.
Donor(s): Lillian Waltom.‡
Financial data (yr. ended 12/31/00): Grants paid, $61,795; assets, $1,270,723 (M); expenditures, $88,020; qualifying distributions, $62,312.
Limitations: Giving limited to residents of Atascosa County, TX.
Application information: Application form required.
Trustees: Leon Steinle, Houston Winters, Gerald Zuhlke, W.F. Zuhlke, Jr.
EIN: 742509618
Codes: GTI

51715
Ed and Mary Heath Foundation
P.O. Box 338
Tyler, TX 75710 (903) 597-7436
Contact: Charlotte Schaefers, Prog. Off.

Established in 1954 in TX.
Donor(s): J.E. Heath,‡ Mary M. Heath.‡
Financial data (yr. ended 12/31/01): Grants paid, $61,750; assets, $2,188,101 (M); expenditures, $243,620; qualifying distributions, $61,750.
Limitations: Giving limited to Smith County, TX.
Publications: Newsletter, occasional report.
Application information: Application form not required.
Officers and Directors:* W.R. Smith, Chair.; Gregg Bonham, Vice-Chair.; Jack Jackson,* Secy.-Treas.; Mike Massar, Charlotte Smith Shaefers, Margaret Smith, Charles White.
EIN: 756021506

51716
Hinnant Foundation, Inc.
c/o Berry A. Hinnant
4307 Emil Ave.
Amarillo, TX 79106-6028

Donor(s): Jerry H. Hinnant, Betty A. Hinnant.
Financial data (yr. ended 12/31/01): Grants paid, $61,671; assets, $34,907 (M); gifts received, $28,000; expenditures, $62,560; qualifying distributions, $61,671.
Limitations: Applications not accepted. Giving on an international basis.
Application information: Contributes only to pre-selected organizations.
Officers: Jerry H. Hinnant, Pres.; Cathy L. Smith, V.P.; Betty A. Hinnant, Secy.-Treas.
EIN: 751255069

51717
The McGee Foundation
1911 N. Lamar St., Ste. 300
Dallas, TX 75202
Contact: Brian Lee Modic, V.P.

Established in 1989 in TX.
Donor(s): Leonard K. McGee, Nancy C. McGee.
Financial data (yr. ended 12/31/01): Grants paid, $61,500; assets, $1,369,881 (M); expenditures, $61,554; qualifying distributions, $61,500.
Limitations: Applications not accepted. Giving primarily in Dallas, TX.
Application information: Contributes only to pre-selected organizations.
Officers and Directors:* Robert Lavie, Pres.; Brian L. Modic,* V.P. and Treas.; Patricia M. Laney, Secy.; David Andrew Jennings, Alexandra M. Lavie, Leonard K. McGee, Nancy C. McGee.
EIN: 752306054

51718
Levin Family Foundation
1301 Harbor View Dr.
Galveston, TX 77550

Established in 1997 in TX.
Donor(s): William C. Levin.
Financial data (yr. ended 06/30/02): Grants paid, $61,237; assets, $668,287 (M); expenditures, $85,228; qualifying distributions, $61,237.
Limitations: Applications not accepted. Giving limited to Galveston, TX.
Application information: Contributes only to pre-selected organizations.
Officers: William C. Levin, Pres.; Gerry Lee Hornstein, Secy.; Carol Lynn Cantin, Treas.
EIN: 760572174

51719
Rosemary & Tom Medders, Jr. Foundation
4245 Kemp. Blvd., Ste. 904
Wichita Falls, TX 76308-2830 (940) 692-6626
Contact: Rosemary M. Medders, Chair.

Established in 1975 in TX.
Donor(s): Rosemary M. Medders.
Financial data (yr. ended 06/30/01): Grants paid, $61,100; assets, $1,067,201 (M); expenditures, $77,303; qualifying distributions, $61,100.
Limitations: Giving primarily in TX.
Application information: Rarely considers unsolicited requests. Application form not required.
Officers and Trustees:* Rosemary M. Medders,* Chair.; Tom B. Medders III,* Vice-Chair.; Lewis Cadman, Secy.; Marilyn M. Winters.
EIN: 751491867

51720
Mildred Cabe Cook Foundation
3402 Texas Blvd.
Texarkana, TX 75503

Established in 1988 in TX.
Financial data (yr. ended 12/31/01): Grants paid, $61,000; assets, $1,303,502 (M); expenditures, $82,187; qualifying distributions, $61,000.
Limitations: Applications not accepted. Giving primarily in AR and TX.
Application information: Contributes only to pre-selected organizations.
Officers: Lucille T. Cook, Pres.; Anne C. Slicker, V.P.; Robert McDowell, Secy.-Treas.
EIN: 752252349

51721
The J. B. and Mary Lou Sandlin Family Foundation
5137 Davis Blvd.
North Richland Hills, TX 76180

Established in 2001 in TX.
Donor(s): Johnnie B. and Mary Lou Charitable Trust.
Financial data (yr. ended 12/31/01): Grants paid, $60,900; assets, $83,516 (M); gifts received, $123,986; expenditures, $63,756; qualifying distributions, $62,328.
Limitations: Applications not accepted.
Application information: Contributes only to pre-selected organizations.
Officer: Mary Lou Sandlin, Secy.-Treas.
Directors: J. Scott Sandlin, Michael A. Sandlin, Terry Lee Sandlin, Suzan M. Speight.
EIN: 752839017

51722
The Elbert W. Rogers Foundation
c/o Elizabeth Marr Lee
2020 Ross Ave.
Dallas, TX 75201

Established in 1998 in TX.
Financial data (yr. ended 12/31/01): Grants paid, $60,650; assets, $1,969,687 (M); expenditures, $109,146; qualifying distributions, $85,506; giving activities include $5,593 for programs.
Limitations: Applications not accepted. Giving primarily in Greenville, SC and TX.
Application information: Contributes only to pre-selected organizations.
Officers: Charles Marr, Chair.; Elizabeth Marr Lee, Pres.; Charles Lee, V.P.
EIN: 752774884

51723
Thomas Gilcrease Foundation
7314 Oak Manor Dr., No. 305
San Antonio, TX 78229-4530 (210) 375-7565
Contact: Barta Gilcrease Busby, Pres.

Incorporated in 1942 in OK.
Donor(s): Thomas Gilcrease.‡
Financial data (yr. ended 09/30/01): Grants paid, $60,500; assets, $1,356,723 (M); expenditures, $88,839; qualifying distributions, $60,500.
Limitations: Giving primarily in OK and TX.
Application information: Application form not required.
Officers: Barta Gilcrease Busby, Pres.; Peter D. Denney, V.P.; Eugene F. Gilcrease, V.P.; Jana Gilcrease, V.P.; Thomas G. Denney, Secy.-Treas.
EIN: 736009934

51724
Harry and Devera Lerman Educational Trust
c/o Cundiff, Rogers, Solt & Walker
6243 IH 10 W., Ste. 950
San Antonio, TX 78201-2022

Established in 1987 in TX.
Financial data (yr. ended 12/31/01): Grants paid, $60,417; assets, $978,524 (M); expenditures, $64,845; qualifying distributions, $60,417.
Limitations: Applications not accepted. Giving primarily in San Antonio, TX.
Application information: Contributes only to pre-selected organizations.
Trustees: Herman Cundiff, Cecil Schenker, Rabbi Samuel M. Stahl.
EIN: 746335132

51725
Kronick Charitable Trust
c/o Riverbend Properties G.P.
2501 Gravel Pl.
Fort Worth, TX 76118

Established in 1988.
Financial data (yr. ended 12/31/01): Grants paid, $60,395; assets, $2,504,959 (M); expenditures, $134,313; qualifying distributions, $60,395.
Limitations: Applications not accepted.
Application information: Contributes only to pre-selected organizations.
Trustee: Norman Kronick.
EIN: 990265277

51726
The Miller Foundation, Inc.
17341 Campbell Rd.
Dallas, TX 75252-5353

Established in 1994 in TX.
Donor(s): EnMark Gas Gathering, L.P.

Financial data (yr. ended 12/31/00): Grants paid, $60,350; assets, $372,399 (M); expenditures, $60,898; qualifying distributions, $60,350.
Limitations: Applications not accepted. Giving primarily in TX.
Application information: Contributes only to pre-selected organizations.
Officers: Rodney G. Miller, Pres.; Olivia A. Miller, Secy.
EIN: 752518345
Codes: CS, CD

51727
Sam and Marille Sparks East Town Osteopathic Foundation
8344 E. R.L. Thornton Fwy., Ste. 400
Dallas, TX 75228
Application address: 4224 Gus Thomason Rd., Dallas, TX 75150
Contact: Jim Yarbrough, Treas.

Established in 1988 in TX.
Financial data (yr. ended 12/31/01): Grants paid, $60,305; assets, $1,462,276 (M); expenditures, $81,906; qualifying distributions, $66,705.
Limitations: Giving primarily in Dallas, TX.
Officers: Richard Anderson, Chair.; Bill Stafford, Vice-Chair.; Dean Wierman, Secy.; Jim Yarbrough, Treas.
Directors: Frank Bradley, Jerry Diffee, Robert Sharp.
EIN: 752179453

51728
The Ann & Stephen Kaufman Family Foundation
c/o Stephen M. Kaufman
3 Riverway, Ste. 1350
Houston, TX 77056

Established in 1996 in TX.
Financial data (yr. ended 11/30/01): Grants paid, $60,250; assets, $865,623 (M); expenditures, $72,687; qualifying distributions, $60,250.
Limitations: Applications not accepted.
Application information: Contributes only to pre-selected organizations.
Trustees: Ann P. Kaufman, Stephen M. Kaufman.
EIN: 760524143

51729
Harry B. & Aileen B. Gordon Foundation
5847 San Felipe, Ste. 1675
Houston, TX 77057

Established in 1968 in TX.
Donor(s): Harry B. Gordon, Aileen B. Gordon.
Financial data (yr. ended 12/31/01): Grants paid, $60,055; assets, $1,567,491 (M); expenditures, $63,442; qualifying distributions, $60,380.
Limitations: Applications not accepted. Giving primarily in Houston, TX.
Application information: Contributes only to pre-selected organizations.
Trustees: Aileen B. Gordon, Harry B. Gordon.
EIN: 746109514

51730
The Richard J. and Victoria T. Agnich Foundation
19 Downs Lake Cir.
Dallas, TX 75230

Established in 1998 in TX.
Donor(s): Richard J. Agnich, Victoria T. Agnich, Robert Trescher, Mrs. Robert Trescher.
Financial data (yr. ended 05/31/01): Grants paid, $60,000; assets, $3,406,069 (M); gifts received, $1,535,392; expenditures, $116,640; qualifying distributions, $58,691.
Limitations: Applications not accepted. Giving primarily in Dallas, TX.
Application information: Contributes only to pre-selected organizations.
Trustees: Richard J. Agnich, Victoria T. Agnich.
EIN: 752817365

51731
Ruth R. Bettes Charitable Foundation
2600 Citadel Plz., Ste. 105
Houston, TX 77008-1041
Contact: John W. Wheat, Tr.

Established in 1986 in TX.
Donor(s): Ruth R. Bettes.‡
Financial data (yr. ended 12/31/00): Grants paid, $60,000; assets, $1,460,825 (M); expenditures, $108,290; qualifying distributions, $64,000.
Limitations: Applications not accepted. Giving primarily in TX.
Trustee: John W. Wheat.
EIN: 760159312

51732
Joseph and Bernice Margolin Foundation
2929 Post Oak, Ste. 509
Houston, TX 77056

Established in 1994 in TX.
Donor(s): Bernice Margolin.
Financial data (yr. ended 11/30/01): Grants paid, $60,000; assets, $879,812 (M); expenditures, $61,681; qualifying distributions, $61,681.
Limitations: Applications not accepted. Giving primarily in OR and TX.
Application information: Contributes only to pre-selected organizations.
Trustees: Allan Margolin, Bernice Margolin.
EIN: 760463240

51733
McDaniel Charitable Foundation
3235 Ave. L
Santa Fe, TX 77510-8568

Established in 1999 in TX.
Financial data (yr. ended 12/31/00): Grants paid, $60,000; assets, $11,511,878 (M); expenditures, $185,086; qualifying distributions, $60,000.
Limitations: Applications not accepted. Giving primarily in TX.
Application information: Contributes only to pre-selected organizations.
Officers: Mark A. Lyons, Pres.; Michelle Lyons-Spier, V.P.; Melissa Lyons-Gardner, Secy.
Directors: Stewart Campbell, William H. Frazier, Randall Harris, John W. Lyons, Jr.
EIN: 760538313

51734
The Torres Foundation
P.O. Box 461009
San Antonio, TX 78246-0267
Additional address: P.O. Box 171234, San Antonio, TX 78217
Contact: Joe H. Guerra, Treas.

Established in 1992 in KS.
Donor(s): Arturo Torres.
Financial data (yr. ended 08/31/01): Grants paid, $60,000; assets, $1,127 (M); gifts received, $282; expenditures, $65,205; qualifying distributions, $60,000.
Limitations: Applications not accepted.
Application information: Contributes only to pre-selected organizations.
Officers: Arturo Torres, Pres.; Maria Elena Flores-Cuellar, Secy.; Joe H. Guerra, Treas.
EIN: 742651074

51735
Patrick Wardlaw Family Foundation
4800 Lakewood Dr., Ste. 2A
Waco, TX 76710
Application address: P.O. Box 7792, Waco, TX 76714, tel.: (254) 741-1226
Contact: Patrick N. Wardlaw, Chair.

Established in 1999.
Donor(s): Patrick N. Wardlaw.
Financial data (yr. ended 06/30/01): Grants paid, $60,000; assets, $452,492 (M); gifts received, $269,392; expenditures, $61,981; qualifying distributions, $60,000.
Limitations: Giving primarily in AR and TX.
Officer: Patrick N. Wardlaw, Chair.
Directors: Rebecca Wardlaw Clark, Michael N. Wardlaw, Victoria Wardlaw.
EIN: 742938810

51736
The Fastow Family Foundation
333 Clay St., Ste. 1203
Houston, TX 77002

Established in 2000.
Donor(s): Andrew S. Fastow.
Financial data (yr. ended 12/31/01): Grants paid, $59,700; assets, $4,384,309 (M); expenditures, $174,345; qualifying distributions, $59,700.
Limitations: Applications not accepted. Giving primarily in Houston, TX.
Application information: Contributes only to pre-selected organizations.
Officer: Andrew S. Fastow, Pres. and Treas.
Trustees: Jana Kaplan, Lillianne P. Weingarten.
EIN: 760635090

51737
Glacier Christian Foundation, Inc.
P.O. Box 50065
Austin, TX 78763-0065

Established around 1989.
Donor(s): Jack D. Brown, M. Nell Brown.
Financial data (yr. ended 12/31/01): Grants paid, $59,685; assets, $483,576 (M); gifts received, $13,709; expenditures, $80,689; qualifying distributions, $59,407.
Limitations: Applications not accepted. Giving primarily in TX.
Application information: Contributes only to pre-selected organizations.
Officers: M. Nell Brown, Pres.; Jack D. Brown, V.P.
EIN: 742290095

51738
R. Leon Gibson and Mary F. Gibson Foundation
P.O. Box 1721
Kilgore, TX 75663   (903) 984-7987
Contact: Charles Watkins, Pres.

Established in 1990 in TX.
Donor(s): Mary F. Gibson.‡
Financial data (yr. ended 12/31/01): Grants paid, $59,500; assets, $1,180,393 (M); expenditures, $66,151; qualifying distributions, $59,500.
Limitations: Giving limited to TX.
Officers: Charles Watkins, Pres.; Harold G. Habenicht, Secy.-Treas.
Directors: Jeff Beck, Elizabeth Delashaw, Julie Hope, Robbie Hope.
EIN: 752340623

51739
The Currie Fund
520 Post Oak Blvd., Ste. 125
Houston, TX 77027   (713) 552-0033
Contact: Jack T. Currie, Pres.

Established in 1986.

Donor(s): Jack T. Currie.
Financial data (yr. ended 12/31/01): Grants paid, $59,394; assets, $1,074,116 (M); gifts received, $36,218; expenditures, $70,740; qualifying distributions, $59,394.
Limitations: Giving primarily in TX.
Officers and Trustees:* Jack T. Currie,* Pres.; Dorothy P. Currie,* Secy.; Harriss T. Currie, Laura T. Currie.
EIN: 760207466

51740
Paton Family Charitable Foundation
10 Intrepid Cir.
Rockwall, TX 75032-5750

Donor(s): Dariah L. Morgan, Bruce R. Paton, Pepsico, Inc.
Financial data (yr. ended 09/30/01): Grants paid, $59,301; assets, $8,491 (L); gifts received, $69,992; expenditures, $67,715; qualifying distributions, $59,301.
Limitations: Applications not accepted. Giving on a national basis, with emphasis on TX.
Application information: Contributes only to pre-selected organizations.
Officers: Bruce R. Paton, Pres.; Margaret R. Paton, V.P.; Bruce R. Paton, Jr., Secy.; Jennifer Paton Stacey, Treas.
Directors: Dariah L. Morgan, Zachary B. Stacey.
EIN: 752735104

51741
The Barrow Family Foundation
5847 San Felipe, Ste. 3830
Houston, TX 77057

Established in 1986 in TX.
Donor(s): Janice H. Barrow, Thomas D. Barrow.
Financial data (yr. ended 12/31/01): Grants paid, $59,300; assets, $1,225,146 (M); expenditures, $72,380; qualifying distributions, $59,300.
Limitations: Applications not accepted. Giving on a national basis.
Application information: Contributes only to pre-selected organizations.
Officers and Trustees:* Thomas D. Barrow,* Pres.; Janice H. Barrow,* Secy.; Elizabeth B. Brueggeman,* Treas.; Kenneth T. Barrow, Theodore H. Barrow, Barbara Barrow McCelvey.
EIN: 760205381

51742
Martin W. & Bettie J. Halsell Foundation
4341 Potomac Ave.
Dallas, TX 75205-2628
Contact: Harriet Halsell, Tr.

Established in 1987 in TX.
Donor(s): Harriet Halsell.
Financial data (yr. ended 12/31/01): Grants paid, $59,000; assets, $979,891 (M); gifts received, $5; expenditures, $61,313; qualifying distributions, $58,723.
Limitations: Giving primarily in TX.
Trustees: Samuel W. Graber, Harriet Halsell, Lamar C. Jackson.
EIN: 756363533

51743
Garland D. Rhoads Foundation
c/o Bank of America
100 N. Main
Corsicana, TX 75110 (903) 654-3252

Financial data (yr. ended 03/31/02): Grants paid, $58,966; assets, $556,538 (M); expenditures, $69,714; qualifying distributions, $58,966.
Limitations: Giving primarily in Corsicana, TX.
Application information: Application form not required.

Trustee: Bank of America.
EIN: 756047011

51744
Margaret T. Morris Foundation
c/o Bank of America
P.O. Box 831041
Dallas, TX 75283-1041

Established in 1991 in TX.
Donor(s): Margaret T. Morris.‡
Financial data (yr. ended 12/31/00): Grants paid, $58,950; assets, $65,762 (M); expenditures, $62,816; qualifying distributions, $60,589.
Limitations: Giving limited to residents of Houston, TX.
Application information: Application form required.
Selection Committee: Beverly Clark, Sylvia Cornell, Marilyn Finer-Collins, Janice Foster.
Trustee: Bank of America.
EIN: 766072038
Codes: GTI

51745
Masters Family Foundation
433 E. Las Colinas Blvd., Ste. 1290
Irving, TX 75039
Contact: Micky Jo Masters, Chair.

Established in 1990 in TX.
Donor(s): James L. Masters.
Financial data (yr. ended 12/31/99): Grants paid, $58,933; assets, $185,711 (M); expenditures, $58,933; qualifying distributions, $58,787.
Limitations: Giving limited to residents of Hopkins County, TX.
Officers: Micky Jo Masters, Chair.; James L. Masters III, Pres.
Director: Chad Young.
EIN: 752323131

51746
Rhema Foundation
117 Lilac Ln.
San Antonio, TX 78209-5256

Established in 1984 in TX.
Donor(s): John W. Hunter.
Financial data (yr. ended 11/30/01): Grants paid, $58,900; assets, $1,866,357 (M); expenditures, $107,296; qualifying distributions, $58,900.
Limitations: Applications not accepted. Giving primarily in San Antonio, TX.
Application information: Contributes only to pre-selected organizations.
Officers and Directors:* John W. Hunter,* Pres.; Paula P. Hunter,* Secy.; Courtney Ashley Hunter Wooten.
EIN: 742368887

51747
The Jerold B. Katz Foundation
10101 Harwin, Ste. 100
Houston, TX 77036 (713) 779-2003
Contact: Evan H. Katz, C.E.O.

Established in 1980 in TX.
Donor(s): Jerold B. Katz.
Financial data (yr. ended 11/30/00): Grants paid, $58,875; assets, $1,488,833 (M); gifts received, $7,770; expenditures, $66,437; qualifying distributions, $60,265.
Limitations: Giving primarily in TX.
Application information: The foundation has discontinued awarding scholarships to the general public. Application form not required.
Officers and Trustees:* Evan H. Katz,* C.E.O. and Pres.; Robert M. Gross,* Sr. V.P. and Secy.-Treas.; Lissy B. Katz, Exec. V.P. and C.O.O.; Martin M. Katz.

EIN: 742164970

51748
Pharaoh C. Thompson Foundation
902 Neuhaus Tower
200 S. 10th St.
McAllen, TX 78501-4857

Established in 1953.
Donor(s): Charles E. Thompson,‡ Charles E. Thompson, Jr.
Financial data (yr. ended 12/31/01): Grants paid, $58,864; assets, $1,280,554 (M); expenditures, $61,286; qualifying distributions, $58,864.
Limitations: Applications not accepted. Giving primarily in TX.
Application information: Contributes only to pre-selected organizations.
Officer: Charles E. Thompson, Jr., Mgr.
EIN: 746062450

51749
Maida Davis Turtle Charitable Trust
c/o Frost National Bank, Trust Dept.
P.O. Box 2950
San Antonio, TX 78299-2950 (210) 220-4620
Contact: Courtney Newton, Trust Off., Frost National Bank

Established in 1978 in TX.
Financial data (yr. ended 07/31/02): Grants paid, $58,763; assets, $1,078,703 (M); expenditures, $73,587; qualifying distributions, $58,763.
Limitations: Giving primarily in San Antonio, TX.
Trustee: Frost National Bank.
EIN: 746275950

51750
Newcastle Scholarship Trust
c/o First National Bank, Trust Dept.
P.O. Box 540
Graham, TX 76450
Contact: Ted Boedecker, Sr. V.P. and Trust Off., First National Bank

Established in 1989 in TX.
Donor(s): Clarence B. Daniels.‡
Financial data (yr. ended 06/30/01): Grants paid, $58,752; assets, $328,016 (M); expenditures, $62,663; qualifying distributions, $60,450.
Limitations: Giving limited to residents of Young County, TX.
Application information: Application form not required.
Trustee: First National Bank.
EIN: 752299986
Codes: GTI

51751
Chaney Foundation
1800 W. Loop S., Ste. 700
Houston, TX 77027-3261
FAX: (713) 499-1218
Contact: Leslie Daneford

Established in 1993 in TX.
Donor(s): Diane R. Chaney, John D. Chaney.
Financial data (yr. ended 12/31/01): Grants paid, $58,000; assets, $684,271 (M); expenditures, $63,059; qualifying distributions, $58,000.
Limitations: Applications not accepted. Giving primarily in Houston, TX.
Application information: Contributes only to pre-selected organizations.
Officers and Trustees:* John D. Chaney,* Pres., V.P. and Treas.; Diane R. Chaney,* Secy.; Ruth C. Burke.
EIN: 760399351

51752
Richard Stodder Charitable Foundation
c/o Bank of America
700 Louisiana St., Ste. 2550
Houston, TX 77002

Established in 1986 in TX.
Donor(s): Richard H. Stodder.‡
Financial data (yr. ended 06/30/02): Grants paid, $58,000; assets, $1,210,270 (M); gifts received, $32,200; expenditures, $64,219; qualifying distributions, $58,000.
Limitations: Applications not accepted. Giving primarily in Houston, TX.
Application information: Contributes only to pre-selected organizations.
Officers: Randall E. Evans, Chair.; Susanne W. Evans, V.P.; Elaine Jameson, Treas.
EIN: 760129714

51753
The Gurvetch Foundation
c/o Bank of America, N.A.
P.O. Box 831041
Dallas, TX 75283-1041
Application address: P.O. Box 832408, Dallas, TX 75283-1041, tel.: (214) 209-1905
Contact: Cindy Miller, Trust Off., Bank of America

Financial data (yr. ended 12/31/01): Grants paid, $57,840; assets, $1,090,303 (M); expenditures, $72,577; qualifying distributions, $57,840.
Limitations: Giving primarily in Dallas, TX.
Trustees: Neil J. O'Brien, Bank of America.
EIN: 237034054

51754
H. E. and Ruby Pelz Trust 2
(Formerly Ruby Pelz Foundation)
P.O. Box 1496
Marshall, TX 75671-1496
Application address: P.O. Box 1386, Marshall, TX 75671, tel.: (903) 938-6611
Contact: William A. Abney, Tr.

Established in 1991 in TX.
Financial data (yr. ended 05/31/02): Grants paid, $57,790; assets, $1,033,750 (M); expenditures, $65,352; qualifying distributions, $57,790.
Limitations: Giving primarily in Marshall, TX.
Officer: Cary M. Abney, Secy.
Trustees: Ruben K. Abney, William A. Abney, Martha Key.
EIN: 746392477

51755
Baker Family Foundation
2245 Christopher Ln.
Burleson, TX 76028

Established in 1997 in TX.
Financial data (yr. ended 12/31/01): Grants paid, $57,750; assets, $1,546,727 (M); expenditures, $59,595; qualifying distributions, $57,750.
Limitations: Applications not accepted. Giving primarily in TX.
Application information: Contributes only to pre-selected organizations.
Officers and Directors:* Charles A. Baker,* Pres. and Treas.; Josephine K. Baker,* Secy.; A. Xavier Baker,* Mgr.
EIN: 752705831

51756
Parker Trust
c/o Bank of America
P.O. Box 831041
Dallas, TX 75283
Contact: Pat Meziere, Trust Off., Bank of America

Financial data (yr. ended 12/31/01): Grants paid, $57,646; assets, $1,005,199 (M); expenditures, $69,530; qualifying distributions, $57,646.
Limitations: Giving limited to Kay County, OK.
Trustee: Bank of America.
EIN: 736262880

51757
Gates of Chai
201 Main St., Ste. 1100
Fort Worth, TX 76102

Established in 1984.
Donor(s): Marcia P. Kurtz.
Financial data (yr. ended 09/30/01): Grants paid, $57,500; assets, $1,000,120 (M); expenditures, $73,406; qualifying distributions, $64,429.
Limitations: Applications not accepted. Giving primarily in TX.
Application information: Contributes only to pre-selected organizations.
Officers and Directors:* Marcia P. Kurtz,* Pres.; Richard Spellman,* V.P.; Marvin E. Blum,* Secy.-Treas.
EIN: 752002419

51758
Hollomon-Price Foundation
3860 W. Northwest Hwy., Ste. 111
Dallas, TX 75220

Established in 1999 in TX.
Donor(s): Wayne Hollomon Price.
Financial data (yr. ended 09/30/01): Grants paid, $57,400; assets, $936,087 (M); gifts received, $299,666; expenditures, $67,885; qualifying distributions, $67,886.
Limitations: Applications not accepted. Giving primarily in TX.
Application information: Contributes only to pre-selected organizations.
Officer: John Bellett, Pres.
Directors: Eugene Bailey, John R. Bauer, Nancy Bellett, Michael Jon Deppe, Samantha Echols Hollomon, Thaddeus Van Alen Hollomon, Van Alen Hollomon, Michael David Price, Wayne Hollomon Price.
EIN: 752850527

51759
The E. P. Woodruff Charitable Trust
309 N. Fisk Ave.
Brownwood, TX 76801 (915) 646-2821
Contact: Darrell E. Haynes, Tr.

Established in 1998 in TX.
Donor(s): Darrell E. Haynes.
Financial data (yr. ended 12/31/01): Grants paid, $57,250; assets, $1,343,977 (M); gifts received, $250; expenditures, $74,121; qualifying distributions, $57,250.
Limitations: Giving limited to TX.
Officer: Judy Snow, Secy.
Trustees: Darrell E. Haynes, Priscilla Monson, W. Gene Porter, William G. Shaw, Rowland Winn.
EIN: 756545874

51760
Daisy Foundation
1 Winners Cir.
Houston, TX 77024
Contact: Joel V. Staff, Chair.

Established in 1998 in TX.
Donor(s): Joel V. Staff, Mary Martha Staff.
Financial data (yr. ended 12/31/01): Grants paid, $57,000; assets, $425,784 (M); gifts received, $32,472; expenditures, $65,559; qualifying distributions, $57,000.
Limitations: Giving primarily in CA and TX.
Officers: Joel V. Staff, Chair.; Mary Martha Staff, Pres.; Jennifer Staff Johnson, Secy.; Julia Staff Barrett, Treas.
EIN: 760568991

51761
Denman Foundation
139 Hickory Dr.
Houston, TX 77024

Established in 1997 in TX.
Donor(s): Ernestine N. Palmer, Ronald O. Palmer.
Financial data (yr. ended 12/31/01): Grants paid, $57,000; assets, $1,333,812 (M); expenditures, $59,137; qualifying distributions, $57,000.
Limitations: Applications not accepted. Giving primarily in TX.
Application information: Contributes only to pre-selected organizations.
Directors: Douglas E. Clark, Ernestine N. Palmer, Ronald O. Palmer.
EIN: 311573295

51762
Douglas W. Sankey Foundation, Inc.
4808 Post Oak Timber Dr.
Houston, TX 77056

Established in 1998 in TX.
Donor(s): Margaret R. Sankey.
Financial data (yr. ended 03/31/02): Grants paid, $57,000; assets, $1,299,096 (M); expenditures, $58,555; qualifying distributions, $57,000.
Limitations: Applications not accepted. Giving primarily in TX.
Application information: Contributes only to pre-selected organizations.
Officers and Directors:* Margaret R. Sankey,* Pres.; Kimberly S. Young,* Secy.
EIN: 760572067

51763
Farris Foundation
P.O. Box 61407
Houston, TX 77208-1407
Contact: George R. Farris, Dir.

Established in 1986 in TX.
Donor(s): George R. Farris.
Financial data (yr. ended 12/31/01): Grants paid, $56,500; assets, $147,385 (M); expenditures, $59,302; qualifying distributions, $56,500.
Limitations: Giving limited to Houston, TX.
Directors: George R. Farris, Madelyn Doherty Farris, Thomas K. Farris.
EIN: 760201222

51764
The McMullen Foundation
(Formerly Roswald & Jo Ann McMullen Foundation)
7 S. Lakemist Harbour Pl.
The Woodlands, TX 77381

Donor(s): Roswald K. McMullen, Jo Ann McMullen.
Financial data (yr. ended 06/30/01): Grants paid, $56,500; assets, $242 (M); gifts received, $12,500; expenditures, $57,705; qualifying distributions, $56,500.
Limitations: Applications not accepted. Giving primarily in TX.
Application information: Contributes only to pre-selected organizations.

Officers and Trustees:* Roswald K. McMullen,* Pres. and Treas.; Nanette Joiner,* V.P. and Secy.; William H. Caudill.
EIN: 760046259

51765
Tom and Carolyn Hamilton Family Foundation
c/o Woodway Financial Advisors
10000 Memorial Dr., Ste. 650
Houston, TX 77024

Established in 1998 in TX.
Financial data (yr. ended 05/31/02): Grants paid, $56,250; assets, $965,655 (M); expenditures, $65,506; qualifying distributions, $56,250.
Limitations: Applications not accepted.
Application information: Contributes only to pre-selected organizations.
Officers: Carolyn E. Hamilton, Pres.; Thomas M. Hamilton, V.P. and Secy.-Treas.
Directors: Brett A. Hamilton, Janet J. Hamilton, Scott T. Hamilton.
EIN: 760573521

51766
Josephine & J. A. Wheeler Memorial Foundation
c/o Security Bank
P.O. Box Drawer AA
Ralls, TX 79357
Contact: Gene McLaughlin, Tr.

Established in 1992.
Financial data (yr. ended 12/31/00): Grants paid, $56,185; assets, $1,047,413 (M); expenditures, $83,439; qualifying distributions, $56,185.
Limitations: Giving primarily in TX.
Application information: Application form not required.
Trustees: Gene McLaughlin, Walker Watkins.
EIN: 752485347

51767
The King's Ministry, Inc.
5051 Westheimer, Ste. 725
Houston, TX 77056

Established in 1996 in TX.
Donor(s): Alfred F. DeBellas, Alfred F. DeBellas, Jr., Mrs. Alfred F. DeBellas, Jr.
Financial data (yr. ended 12/31/99): Grants paid, $56,141; assets, $8,486 (M); gifts received, $80,630; expenditures, $134,992; qualifying distributions, $133,124; giving activities include $19,369 for programs.
Limitations: Applications not accepted. Giving primarily in CA and FL.
Application information: Contributes only to pre-selected organizations.
Officer: Denise DeBellas, Pres.
Directors: Alfred F. DeBellas, Jr., Marty Sammona, Monroe Thompson.
EIN: 760513654

51768
The Boyd Morse Foundation
c/o Margolis, Phipps & Wright
1400 Post Oak Blvd., Ste. 900
Houston, TX 77056-3009

Established in 1999 in TX.
Donor(s): Laura Boyd, Brinkley Morse.
Financial data (yr. ended 12/31/01): Grants paid, $56,000; assets, $1,298,857 (M); expenditures, $59,465; qualifying distributions, $56,000.
Limitations: Applications not accepted.
Application information: Contributes only to pre-selected organizations.
Officers and Directors:* Laura Boyd,* Pres.; Lucille Boyd,* V.P. and Treas.; Brinkley Morse,* Secy.
EIN: 760605572

51769
W. J. & Lela Budwine Foundation, Inc.
3502 Edgewood Dr.
Amarillo, TX 79109-4036

Established in 1997 in TX.
Donor(s): Lela Budwine, W.J. Budwine.
Financial data (yr. ended 06/30/01): Grants paid, $56,000; assets, $1,358,684 (M); gifts received, $31,346; expenditures, $60,390; qualifying distributions, $56,626.
Limitations: Applications not accepted. Giving primarily in TX.
Application information: Contributes only to pre-selected organizations.
Officers: W.J. Budwine, Pres.; Wayne Budwine, V.P.; Milton Wing, Secy.-Treas.
EIN: 760520860

51770
The Robert L. and Jean Clarke Family Foundation
711 Louisiana St., Ste. 2900
Houston, TX 77002
Contact: Robert L. Clarke, Dir.

Established in 1996 in TX.
Donor(s): Robert L. Clarke, Jean T. Clarke.
Financial data (yr. ended 12/31/01): Grants paid, $56,000; assets, $1,044,062 (M); expenditures, $58,400; qualifying distributions, $55,048.
Limitations: Giving primarily in NM and TX.
Application information: Application form not required.
Directors: Jean T. Clarke, Robert L. Clarke, R. Logan Clarke, Jr.
EIN: 760522676

51771
Warren Skaaren Charitable Trust
c/o W. Amon Burton, Jr.
1306 Guadalupe St.
Austin, TX 78701

Donor(s): Warren Skaaren.‡
Financial data (yr. ended 12/31/01): Grants paid, $56,000; assets, $1,008,332 (M); gifts received, $18,688; expenditures, $84,236; qualifying distributions, $56,000.
Limitations: Applications not accepted. Giving primarily in Austin, TX.
Application information: Contributes only to pre-selected organizations.
Trustee: W. Amon Burton, Jr.
EIN: 742619296

51772
Hubert E. Clift Foundation
2710 W. Alabama
Houston, TX 77098 (713) 973-1918
Application address: 1462 Campbell Rd., Ste. 100, Houston, TX 77055
Contact: T.E. Kennerly, Secy.-Treas.

Established in 1965 in TX.
Donor(s): Jeannette E. Clift George.
Financial data (yr. ended 12/31/01): Grants paid, $55,800; assets, $651,511 (M); expenditures, $66,792; qualifying distributions, $55,800.
Limitations: Giving primarily in Houston, TX.
Application information: Application form not required.
Officers and Trustees:* Jeannette E. Clift George,* Pres.; T.E. Kennerly,* Secy.-Treas.; Robert W. Goodman, Jr., James Scofield.
EIN: 746072539

51773
From the Father with Love
c/o Kim L. De Los Santos
8122 Datapoint Dr., Ste. 900
San Antonio, TX 78229

Established in 1982 in TX.
Donor(s): Thomas W. Lyles, Jr., Lisa A. Lyles.
Financial data (yr. ended 11/30/01): Grants paid, $55,707; assets, $458,315 (M); gifts received, $100,000; expenditures, $66,081; qualifying distributions, $55,707.
Limitations: Applications not accepted. Giving primarily in TX.
Application information: Contributes only to pre-selected organizations.
Directors: Kim L. De Los Santos, Lisa A. Lyles, Thomas W. Lyles, Jr.
EIN: 742862627

51774
Edgar A. & Ruth E. Robinson Family Foundation
2001 Ross Ave., Ste. 2700
Dallas, TX 75201

Established in 1997 in TX.
Donor(s): Edgar A. Robinson, Ruth E. Robinson.
Financial data (yr. ended 12/31/01): Grants paid, $55,600; assets, $2,133,415 (M); gifts received, $1,074,330; expenditures, $68,635; qualifying distributions, $55,600.
Limitations: Applications not accepted.
Application information: Unsolicited requests for funds not accepted.
Officer and Directors:* Edgar A. Robinson,* Pres.; Jeffrey M. Robinson, Laurie K. Robinson, Ruth E. Robinson.
EIN: 752703246

51775
William O. & Louise H. Mullins Foundation Trust
c/o Amarillo National Bank, Trust Dept.
P.O. Box 1
Amarillo, TX 79105-0001

Established in 1987 in TX.
Financial data (yr. ended 12/31/01): Grants paid, $55,575; assets, $1,165,154 (M); expenditures, $73,874; qualifying distributions, $55,575.
Limitations: Giving primarily in Amarillo, TX.
Application information: Contributes only to pre-selected organizations. Scholarship recipients are chosen by the college.
Trustee: Amarillo National Bank.
EIN: 756353107

51776
Joe Lewis & Vivian Lewis Scholarship
P.O. Box 1028
Marshall, TX 75671-1028

Financial data (yr. ended 12/31/01): Grants paid, $55,345; assets, $1,184,749 (M); expenditures, $81,037; qualifying distributions, $54,804.
Limitations: Applications not accepted. Giving primarily in Marshall and Hawkins, TX.
Application information: Contributes only to pre-selected organizations.
Trustees: Jean Birmingham, Sebetha Jenkins, Ora Asa Johnson, Jr., Hibernia National Bank.
EIN: 752796384

51777
Rotto Family Foundation
16 Autumn Crescent Dr.
The Woodlands, TX 77381-5157
(281) 364-8396
Contact: Barbara L. Rotto, Secy.

Established in 1999 in TX.

Donor(s): Richard L. Rotto, Barbara L. Rotto.
Financial data (yr. ended 12/31/01): Grants paid, $55,300; assets, $532,273 (M); expenditures, $56,951; qualifying distributions, $55,300.
Limitations: Giving primarily in the Southwest, with emphasis on NM.
Officers and Directors:* Richard L. Rotto,* Pres.; Barbara L. Rotto,* Secy.; L. Michele Rotto Bulla, Donal P. Rotto, Richard K. Rotto, Sue L. Rotto.
EIN: 760596600

51778
Crawford and Hattie Jackson Foundation
c/o Briggs & Veselka Co.
6565 W. Loop S., Ste. 800
Bellaire, TX 77401

Established in 1997 in TX.
Financial data (yr. ended 12/31/00): Grants paid, $55,250; assets, $1,408,097 (M); expenditures, $72,004; qualifying distributions, $55,250.
Limitations: Applications not accepted. Giving primarily in TX.
Application information: Contributes only to pre-selected organizations.
Officers: Hattie Jackson, Pres.; J. Steven Awalt, V.P.; Rooney C. Koenig, V.P.; Brenda McGraw, Secy.
EIN: 760526233

51779
Wilma Donohue Moleen Foundation
c/o JPMorgan Chase Bank
P.O. Box 140
El Paso, TX 79980
Application address: c/o Terry Crenshaw, 201 E. Main Dr., El Paso, TX 79901, tel.: (915) 546-6515

Established in 1993 in TX.
Financial data (yr. ended 05/31/02): Grants paid, $55,150; assets, $1,098,961 (M); gifts received, $14,000; expenditures, $86,306; qualifying distributions, $55,150.
Limitations: Giving limited to southwest TX and southern NM.
Trustee: JPMorgan Chase Bank.
EIN: 746409404

51780
The Sutherlin-Martin Foundation
3616 Maplewood Ave.
Dallas, TX 75205

Established in 2000 in TX.
Donor(s): Todd Martin, Martha Martin.
Financial data (yr. ended 12/31/01): Grants paid, $55,140; assets, $102,051 (M); gifts received, $100,191; expenditures, $55,640; qualifying distributions, $55,140.
Directors: Martha Martin, Todd Martin, Eric Sutherlin, Vilda Sutherlin.
EIN: 752898909

51781
The Jack S. and Donna P. Josey Foundation
(Formerly The Josey Foundation)
2001 Kirby Dr., Ste. 1002
Houston, TX 77019

Established in 1983.
Donor(s): Jack S. Josey.
Financial data (yr. ended 12/31/00): Grants paid, $55,055; assets, $690,618 (M); expenditures, $93,277; qualifying distributions, $55,055.
Limitations: Applications not accepted. Giving primarily in Houston, TX.
Application information: Contributes only to pre-selected organizations.
Trustees: Donna P. Josey, Jack S. Josey, Joseph Oscar Neuhoff, III.
EIN: 760057364

51782
Formosa Plastics Religious Trust
c/o First National Bank
P.O. Drawer 7
Port Lavaca, TX 77979-0007
Contact: William H. Bauer, Jr., Tr.

Established in 1995 in TX.
Donor(s): Formosa Plastics Corp., Texas.
Financial data (yr. ended 12/31/01): Grants paid, $55,005; assets, $1,134,333 (M); expenditures, $61,463; qualifying distributions, $55,005.
Limitations: Giving limited to Calhoun, Jackson, and Victoria counties, TX.
Trustees: William H. Bauer, Jr., Jack Wu.
EIN: 746432974
Codes: CS, CD

51783
Maxine Curtis Foundation
P.O. Box 780242
San Antonio, TX 78278-0242
Contact: D.R. Freiling, Treas.

Established in 1995 in TX.
Financial data (yr. ended 09/30/01): Grants paid, $55,000; assets, $1,682,348 (M); gifts received, $41,333; expenditures, $63,763; qualifying distributions, $55,000.
Officers: Scott Mullen, Pres.; Frank Dansby, V.P.; William Klutz, V.P.; Donald Willis, V.P.; D.R. Freiling, Treas.
EIN: 742760667

51784
Pipe Line Contractors Association Scholarship Foundation
1700 Pacific Ave., Ste. 4100
Dallas, TX 75201-4675
Application address: c/o Scholarship Management Svcs., 1505 Riverview Rd., P.O. Box 297, St. Peter, MN 56082, tel.: (507) 931-1682

Donor(s): Henkels & McCoy, Inc., Otis Eastern Service, Inc., Sheehan Pipe Line Construction Co., Ozzie's Pipeline Padder, Inc., Mustang Tractor & Equipment Co., Welded Construction Co., Associated Pipe Line Contractors, Inc., H.C. Price Co., Key Enterprises, Inc., Pipeline Inspection Co., Ltd.
Financial data (yr. ended 12/31/01): Grants paid, $55,000; assets, $466,375 (M); gifts received, $17,300; expenditures, $70,019; qualifying distributions, $59,688.
Limitations: Giving primarily in areas of company operations.
Application information: Application form required.
Officers and Scholarship Committee Members:* H. Charles Price,* Chair.; J. Patrick Tielborg, Secy.; Bob Johnston,* Dir.; Paul Somerville,* Dir.; Paul Evans, Doug Fabick.
EIN: 752744096

51785
Uplands Foundations
6310 Belmont St.
Houston, TX 77005-3402

Established in 2000 in TX.
Donor(s): Gay M. Rogers.
Financial data (yr. ended 12/31/01): Grants paid, $55,000; assets, $841,864 (M); expenditures, $56,831; qualifying distributions, $55,000.
Limitations: Applications not accepted.
Application information: Contributes only to pre-selected organizations.
Trustee: Gay M. Rogers.
EIN: 760662839

51786
C. L. Rowan Charitable & Educational Fund, Inc.
1204 B W. 7th St.
Fort Worth, TX 76102   (817) 332-5000
Contact: Brent R. Hyder, Pres.

Established in 1954 in TX.
Donor(s): Merle M. Rowan.
Financial data (yr. ended 10/31/00): Grants paid, $54,888; assets, $1,376,448 (M); expenditures, $61,920; qualifying distributions, $61,920.
Limitations: Giving primarily in the Dallas-Fort Worth, TX, area.
Officers and Directors:* Brent R. Hyder,* Pres.; Whitney H. More,* Secy.; Martha R. Hyder,* Treas.; Kelly R. Greenwell, Heward Hultgren.
EIN: 756009661
Codes: GTI

51787
The Rita Crocker Clements Foundation
6930 Turtle Creek Blvd.
Dallas, TX 75205   (214) 739-8514
Contact: Rita Crocker Clements, Tr.

Established in 1995 in TX.
Donor(s): Rita Crocker Clements.
Financial data (yr. ended 12/31/01): Grants paid, $54,772; assets, $246,275 (M); expenditures, $56,631; qualifying distributions, $54,772.
Limitations: Giving limited to Dallas, TX.
Trustees: Rita Crocker Clements, Barbara Bass Moroney, Bonnie Bass Smith.
EIN: 752553491

51788
True Firm Foundation
4040 Broadway, Ste. 420
San Antonio, TX 78209
Contact: James C. Worth, Pres.

Established in 1998 in TX.
Donor(s): James C. Worth, Jane S. Worth.
Financial data (yr. ended 12/31/01): Grants paid, $54,750; assets, $51,395 (M); gifts received, $82,000; expenditures, $54,837; qualifying distributions, $54,750.
Officers: James C. Worth, Pres.; Jane S. Worth, V.P. and Secy.
Directors: Timothy A. Watt, Brian D. Worth.
EIN: 742900409

51789
Barnabas Foundation
4236 Beverly Dr.
Dallas, TX 75205-3021

Established in 1998 in TX.
Donor(s): Dale P. Jones, Anita C. Jones.
Financial data (yr. ended 12/31/01): Grants paid, $54,645; assets, $615,021 (M); gifts received, $10,000; expenditures, $65,145; qualifying distributions, $54,645.
Limitations: Applications not accepted.
Application information: Contributes only to pre-selected organizations.
Officers and Directors:* Dale P. Jones,* Pres.; Lee Anna Jones Lackey,* V.P.; Leisa Raye Jones Winters,* V.P.; Anita C. Jones,* Secy.; Brandon Lackey, Jimmy Winters.
EIN: 752708264

51790
Bill & Hazel Cordell Foundation
P.O. Box 1793
Quitman, TX 75783   (903) 763-1226
Contact: Jesse A. Cordell, Tr.

Donor(s): Jesse A. Cordell.

Financial data (yr. ended 11/30/01): Grants paid, $54,556; assets, $396,014 (M); expenditures, $58,530; qualifying distributions, $56,448.
Limitations: Giving primarily in TX.
Trustee: Jesse A. Cordell.
EIN: 760330598
Codes: GTI

51791
Cornerstone Foundation
1424 Belaire Dr.
Roanoke, TX 76262-8951

Established in 2000 in TX.
Donor(s): Ronald N. Lewandowski, Dianne G. Lewandowski.
Financial data (yr. ended 12/31/01): Grants paid, $54,500; assets, $4,002 (M); gifts received, $46,000; expenditures, $54,560; qualifying distributions, $54,500.
Limitations: Giving primarily in TX.
Trustees: Dianne G. Lewandowski, Ronald N. Lewandowski.
EIN: 752909300

51792
Irving & Jeanne Lang Mathews Trust
200 Patterson, Ste. 908
San Antonio, TX 78209-6269

Established in 1997 in TX.
Donor(s): Jeanne Lang Mathews.
Financial data (yr. ended 06/30/01): Grants paid, $54,333; assets, $212,157 (M); gifts received, $27,166; expenditures, $54,333; qualifying distributions, $53,623.
Limitations: Applications not accepted. Giving primarily in NY and TX.
Application information: Contributes only to pre-selected organizations.
Officers: Jeanne Lang Mathews, Pres.; Neil Boldrick, Jr., V.P.; Sylvan Stephen Lang, Secy.-Treas.
EIN: 742815404

51793
Roane M. Lacy Family Foundation
8001 Fish Pond Rd.
Waco, TX 76710-1087 (254) 776-8733
Contact: Roane M. Lacy, Jr., Tr.

Established in 1994.
Donor(s): Roane M. Lacy, Jr.
Financial data (yr. ended 12/31/01): Grants paid, $54,167; assets, $514,863 (M); gifts received, $26,000; expenditures, $54,287; qualifying distributions, $54,167.
Application information: Application form not required.
Trustees: Ann M. Lacy, Benjamin C. Lacy, Roane M. Lacy, Jr.
EIN: 742729741

51794
Floyd R. Carlson Charitable Trust
c/o JPMorgan Chase Bank
P.O. Box 550
Austin, TX 78789

Established in 1988 in TX.
Donor(s): Floyd R. Carlson.‡
Financial data (yr. ended 12/31/01): Grants paid, $54,141; assets, $918,923 (M); expenditures, $70,659; qualifying distributions, $54,141.
Limitations: Giving limited to TX.
Trustees: Lester "Doak" Fling, Robert Griffith, Tommy Nelson, JPMorgan Chase Bank.
EIN: 746355588

51795
Penrose Foundation
c/o J. Thomas Schieffer
777 Main St., Ste. 3250
Fort Worth, TX 76102 (817) 332-1328
Contact: Sharon Schieffer Mayes, Dir.

Established in 1993 in TX.
Donor(s): Patricia P. Schieffer, J. Thomas Schieffer.
Financial data (yr. ended 12/31/00): Grants paid, $54,050; assets, $1,269,828 (M); gifts received, $24,149; expenditures, $73,620; qualifying distributions, $58,603.
Limitations: Giving primarily in Fort Worth, TX.
Application information: Scholarship applicants must include transcripts, test scores, letters of recommendation, an essay and parents' tax returns.
Officers and Directors:* Patricia P. Schieffer,* Pres.; J. Thomas Schieffer,* V.P.; Carmen Rios,* Secy.; Sharon Schieffer Mayes.
EIN: 752456902
Codes: GTI

51796
The Dan Kirkland Wells Foundation
P.O. Box 39
Rogers, TX 76569

Donor(s): Stephen A. Wells.
Financial data (yr. ended 11/30/01): Grants paid, $54,045; assets, $1,161,657 (M); expenditures, $55,169; qualifying distributions, $54,045.
Limitations: Applications not accepted. Giving limited to TX.
Application information: Contributes only to pre-selected organizations.
Officers: James K. Wells, Chair.; Stephen A. Wells, Pres.; Judy K. Wells, Secy.-Treas.
EIN: 751822990

51797
The Bible Tract & Missionary Society
4506 Crescent Lakes Cir.
Sugar Land, TX 77479
Contact: R.L. Nohr, Pres.

Established in 1942 in TX.
Financial data (yr. ended 12/31/99): Grants paid, $54,010; assets, $1,055,898 (M); expenditures, $60,965; qualifying distributions, $54,010; giving activities include $189,500 for loans to individuals.
Limitations: Applications not accepted. Giving primarily in TX.
Application information: Unsolicited requests for funds not considered.
Officers: R.L. Nohr, Pres.; J.B. Clooney, 1st V.P.; J.F. Faulkner, 2nd V.P.; Ron Brown, Secy.-Treas.
Trustees: A. Griffin, Glen Lemon, Mike Levy, John Preston.
EIN: 746043926

51798
Hygeia Foundation
720 S. F St.
Harlingen, TX 78550 (956) 423-2050
Contact: H. Lee Richards, Tr.

Established in 1953 in TX.
Donor(s): Hygeia Dairy Co.
Financial data (yr. ended 03/31/01): Grants paid, $54,000; assets, $638,232 (M); expenditures, $60,005; qualifying distributions, $54,000.
Limitations: Giving primarily in southern TX.
Application information: Application form not required.
Trustees: James D. Purl, Jr., H. Lee Richards, Merry K. Richards.
EIN: 746047054
Codes: CS, CD

51799
Minnie Patton Scholarship Foundation Trust
c/o Bank of America
P.O. Box 831041
Dallas, TX 75283-0241 (214) 209-1905
Application address: c/o Cindy Williams, P.O. Box 832408, Dallas, TX 75283-2408, tel.: (214) 209-1905

Established in 1983 in TX.
Donor(s): Minnie K. Patton.‡
Financial data (yr. ended 01/31/02): Grants paid, $54,000; assets, $982,835 (M); expenditures, $99,006; qualifying distributions, $60,121.
Limitations: Giving limited to Dallas County, TX.
Publications: Program policy statement.
Application information: Application form required.
Trustee: Bank of America.
EIN: 756318876
Codes: GTI

51800
Henderson-Wessendorff Foundation
P.O. Box 669
Richmond, TX 77469
Contact: Loise H. Wessendorff, Pres.

Established in 1956 in TX.
Donor(s): Loise J. Henderson.‡
Financial data (yr. ended 12/31/01): Grants paid, $53,965; assets, $9,207,339 (M); expenditures, $354,456; qualifying distributions, $345,629.
Limitations: Giving primarily in TX.
Officers: Loise H. Wessendorff, Pres. and Treas.; Joe C. Wessendorff, V.P. and Secy.; James A. Elkins, Jr., V.P.; Joe Darst Robinson, V.P.
Trustee: Jack Moore.
EIN: 746047149

51801
Robert S. & Joyce Pate Capper Charitable Foundation
48 Valley Ridge Rd.
Fort Worth, TX 76107-3109
Contact: Robert S. Capper, Tr.

Established in 1997 in TX.
Donor(s): Joyce Pate Capper, Robert S. Capper.
Financial data (yr. ended 12/31/01): Grants paid, $53,755; assets, $596,221 (M); gifts received, $61,168; expenditures, $56,301; qualifying distributions, $53,574.
Trustees: Joyce Pate Capper, Robert S. Capper.
EIN: 752692199

51802
Walter Benona Sharp Memorial Foundation
c/o Bank of America
P.O. Box 831041
Dallas, TX 75283-1041

Established in 1953 in TX.
Donor(s): Sharp Family Trust, Honey Sharp Lippmann.
Financial data (yr. ended 12/31/01): Grants paid, $53,750; assets, $56,626 (M); gifts received, $75,000; expenditures, $58,704; qualifying distributions, $53,750.
Limitations: Giving primarily in Houston, TX.
Trustees: Honey S. Lippman, Dudley C. Sharp, Jr., Julia S. Vergara, Bank of America.
EIN: 746033150

51803
The Burrow Foundation, Inc.
2020 Stonewalk Dr.
Houston, TX 77056-4220

Established in 1986 in TX.
Donor(s): Harold Burrow, Vassa Burrow.

51803—TEXAS

Financial data (yr. ended 11/30/01): Grants paid, $53,645; assets, $333,355 (M); expenditures, $54,174; qualifying distributions, $54,033.
Limitations: Applications not accepted. Giving primarily in Houston, TX.
Application information: Contributes only to pre-selected organizations.
Officers: Vassa Burrow, Pres.; Kathy Burrow Vermillion, V.P.; Harold Burrow, Jr., Treas.
Trustees: Harry W. Burrow, Larry W. Burrow.
EIN: 760206830

51804
Formosa Plastics Corporation, Texas-Calhoun High School Scholarship Foundation, Inc.
c/o Calhoun County School District, Superintendent
525 N. Commerce St.
Port Lavaca, TX 77979-3034 (361) 552-9728

Established in 1992 in TX.
Donor(s): Formosa Plastics Corp., Texas.
Financial data (yr. ended 12/31/01): Grants paid, $53,617; assets, $1,062,680 (M); gifts received, $8,957; expenditures, $54,857; qualifying distributions, $54,239.
Limitations: Giving limited to residents of Calhoun County, TX.
Application information: Application form required.
Officers: Richard Bothe, Pres.; Randy Smith, V.P.; Edward W. Wilson, Secy.-Treas.
Directors: Jesse Briseno, Leta Callaway, Rene Flores, Pat Herren, Larry Korenek, Mike McGuire, Larry Nichols, Edward Presley, Brenda Wilson.
EIN: 742634043
Codes: CS, CD, GTI

51805
Rochelle and Max Levit Family Foundation
P.O. Box 14200
Houston, TX 77221-4200

Established in 1998 in TX.
Donor(s): Max S. Levit.
Financial data (yr. ended 12/31/01): Grants paid, $53,577; assets, $982,479 (M); expenditures, $55,669; qualifying distributions, $53,577.
Limitations: Applications not accepted.
Application information: Contributes only to pre-selected organizations.
Officers: Max S. Levit, Pres.; Rochelle Levit, Secy.
EIN: 760574404

51806
The Lundeen Foundation, Inc.
8501 Navidad Dr.
Austin, TX 78735-1456
FAX: (512) 306-0528
Contact: Allan J. Lundeen, Pres. and Barbara S. Lundeen, Secy.

Established in 1988 in TX.
Donor(s): Allan J. Lundeen, Barbara S. Lundeen.
Financial data (yr. ended 12/31/01): Grants paid, $53,460; assets, $424,768 (M); gifts received, $1,448; expenditures, $59,550; qualifying distributions, $53,460.
Limitations: Giving primarily in TX.
Application information: Unsolicited requests for funds not accepted.
Officers and Directors:* Allan J. Lundeen,* Pres. and Treas.; Barbara S. Lundeen,* Secy.; David Lundeen, William Lundeen.
EIN: 760265276

51807
The Pamela H. and Joseph M. Dealey, Jr. Foundation
4332 Fairfax Ave.
Highland Park, TX 75205-3027
(972) 574-8080
Contact: Joseph M. Dealey, Jr., Pres.

Established in 1998 in TX.
Financial data (yr. ended 12/31/00): Grants paid, $53,350; assets, $203,212 (M); expenditures, $57,660; qualifying distributions, $54,519.
Limitations: Giving primarily in Dallas, TX.
Officers: Joseph M. Dealey, Jr., Pres.; Pamela H. Dealey, Secy.
Trustee: Stuart M. Bumpas.
EIN: 752751716

51808
Vandal and Winifred Mercer Texas A & M Educational Foundation
c/o U.S. Bank
P.O. Box 8210
Galveston, TX 77553 (409) 770-5665
Contact: Janet Bertolino, Asst. V.P., U.S. Bank

Established in 1995.
Financial data (yr. ended 12/31/00): Grants paid, $53,250; assets, $1,241,747 (M); expenditures, $71,142; qualifying distributions, $64,990; giving activities include $53,250 for loans to individuals.
Limitations: Giving limited to TX residents, with preference given to residents of Galveston County.
Application information: Application form required.
Trustee: U.S. Bank.
EIN: 760472391

51809
Fentress Foundation
P.O. Box 8359
Waco, TX 76714-8359
Contact: Sara Humphreys Warren, Secy.-Treas.

Established in 1959 in TX.
Financial data (yr. ended 08/31/01): Grants paid, $53,200; assets, $1,140,263 (M); gifts received, $42,804; expenditures, $76,232; qualifying distributions, $53,200.
Limitations: Applications not accepted. Giving limited to the Waco, TX area.
Application information: Contributes only to pre-selected organizations.
Officers and Trustees:* Clara Lacy Fentress,* Pres.; Sara Humphreys Warren,* Secy.-Treas.
EIN: 746048267

51810
Dr. George H. Kilpatrick Memorial Trust
c/o JPMorgan Chase Bank
P.O. Box 47531
San Antonio, TX 78265-7531 (210) 841-7042
Contact: Al Leach

Financial data (yr. ended 12/31/01): Grants paid, $53,199; assets, $1,082,020 (M); expenditures, $69,192; qualifying distributions, $53,199.
Application information: Application form not required.
Trustee: JPMorgan Chase Bank.
EIN: 746032524

51811
The Lee & Carolyn Goodman Foundation
1701 River Run Rd., Ste. 203
Fort Worth, TX 76107

Established in 1986.
Financial data (yr. ended 12/31/01): Grants paid, $53,195; assets, $2,102 (M); gifts received, $48,800; expenditures, $54,159; qualifying distributions, $53,195.
Limitations: Applications not accepted. Giving limited to TX.
Application information: Contributes only to pre-selected organizations.
Trustee: Lee Goodman, Jr.
EIN: 752078655

51812
Carol J. and R. Denny Alexander Foundation
4200 S. Hulen St., Ste. 617
Fort Worth, TX 76109-4911
Contact: R. Denny Alexander, Tr.

Established in 1998.
Donor(s): Carol J. Alexander, R. Denny Alexander.
Financial data (yr. ended 12/31/01): Grants paid, $53,130; assets, $809,077 (M); expenditures, $58,392; qualifying distributions, $52,941.
Limitations: Giving primarily in Fort Worth, TX.
Application information: Application form required.
Trustees: Carol J. Alexander, R. Denny Alexander.
EIN: 752769254

51813
Music Foundation of San Antonio, Inc.
11918 Vance Jackson Rd.
San Antonio, TX 78230-1444 (210) 696-1973
Contact: Robin Abraham, Pres.

Established in 1997 in TX.
Financial data (yr. ended 12/31/00): Grants paid, $53,034; assets, $1,050,471 (M); gifts received, $5,881; expenditures, $73,700; qualifying distributions, $70,319.
Limitations: Giving limited to San Antonio, TX.
Application information: Application form required.
Officers: Robin Abraham, Pres.; Peggy Abraham, V.P.; Phyllis Abbas, Secy.-Treas.
EIN: 742828454
Codes: GTI

51814
The Jeff D. Sandefer Foundation
515 Congress Ave., Ste. 1875
Austin, TX 78701

Established in 1997 in TX.
Donor(s): Jeff D. Sandefer.
Financial data (yr. ended 12/31/00): Grants paid, $53,000; assets, $989,220 (M); expenditures, $56,950; qualifying distributions, $53,000.
Limitations: Applications not accepted. Giving primarily in Austin, TX.
Application information: Contributes only to pre-selected organizations.
Officers: Jeff D. Sandefer, Pres.; John Owens, Secy.
Directors: John B. Lawson, Michael L. Riordan, John R. Rutherford.
EIN: 742804730

51815
The RR Family Foundation
2001 Kirby Dr., Ste. 610
Houston, TX 77019

Established in 1998 in TX.
Donor(s): Risher Randall, Fairfax Randall.
Financial data (yr. ended 12/31/01): Grants paid, $52,814; assets, $1,777,743 (M); expenditures, $54,681; qualifying distributions, $52,814.
Limitations: Applications not accepted. Giving primarily in TX.
Application information: Contributes only to pre-selected organizations.
Officers: Risher Randall, Pres.; Fairfax Crow Randall, V.P. and Secy.; Risher Randall, Jr., V.P. and Treas.

EIN: 760574955

51816
Joe K. Jones Family Foundation, Inc.
c/o David M. Spector
604 N. Bell Ave.
Denton, TX 76201

Established in 1995 in TX.
Donor(s): Joe K. Jones, Joyce A. Jones.
Financial data (yr. ended 10/31/01): Grants paid, $52,504; assets, $17,470 (M); gifts received, $50,000; expenditures, $55,333; qualifying distributions, $52,504.
Limitations: Applications not accepted. Giving primarily in AR, FL, and TX.
Application information: Contributes only to pre-selected organizations.
Officers and Directors:* Joyce A. Jones,* Pres.; Pam Jones,* V.P.; Will Jones,* V.P.; Robert J. Widmer, Jr.,* Secy.; David M. Spector,* Treas.; Roy P. Anderson, Joe K. Jones.
EIN: 752622578

51817
The Living Barnabas Foundation
8401 N. Central Expwy., Ste. 340
Dallas, TX 75225

Established in 1997 in TX.
Donor(s): D. Gorman, L. Gorman.
Financial data (yr. ended 12/31/01): Grants paid, $52,500; assets, $2,426,645 (M); expenditures, $56,747; qualifying distributions, $52,500.
Limitations: Applications not accepted. Giving primarily in Orlando, FL, and Dallas and Plano, TX.
Application information: Contributes only to pre-selected organizations.
Officers: D. Gorman, Pres.; L. Gorman, V.P.
EIN: 752720037

51818
Helping Hands Foundation
P.O. Box 897
Point Blank, TX 77364

Established in 1999.
Donor(s): John Stefan.
Financial data (yr. ended 12/31/00): Grants paid, $52,425; assets, $21,290 (M); gifts received, $53,288; expenditures, $54,599; qualifying distributions, $2,174.
Limitations: Applications not accepted. Giving on an international basis.
Application information: Contributes only to pre-selected organizations.
Officers: John Stefan, Mgr.; Lois Stefan, Mgr.
EIN: 760613044

51819
Vick Charitable Foundation
6417 Pemberton Dr.
Dallas, TX 75230

Established in 1997 in TX.
Donor(s): Mike Vick, Gretchen Vick.
Financial data (yr. ended 12/31/01): Grants paid, $52,100; assets, $197,356 (M); expenditures, $53,715; qualifying distributions, $53,644.
Limitations: Applications not accepted. Giving primarily in Dallas, TX.
Application information: Contributes only to pre-selected organizations.
Officers and Directors:* Michael Vick,* Pres.; Gretchen P. Vick,* V.P. and Secy.; Alice N. Vick.
EIN: 732729784

51820
Stephen Warren Miles and Marilyn Ross Miles Foundation
(Formerly Regency Foundation)
2550 N. Loop W., Ste. 400
Houston, TX 77092

Established in 1980.
Donor(s): Stephen Warren Miles, Marilyn Ross Miles.
Financial data (yr. ended 11/30/01): Grants paid, $52,044; assets, $1,013,239 (M); expenditures, $57,973; qualifying distributions, $52,044.
Limitations: Giving primarily in TX.
Application information: Write for application form. Application form required.
Officers and Directors:* Stephen Warren Miles,* Pres. and Treas.; Marilyn Ross Miles,* V.P. and Secy.; Edward Ross Miles, Stephen Warren Miles, Jr.
EIN: 742187638

51821
The Bradbury Dyer Foundation
500 Crescent Ct., Ste. 260
Dallas, TX 75201 (214) 871-3773
Contact: Bradbury Dyer III, Pres.

Established in 1995.
Donor(s): Bradbury Dyer III.
Financial data (yr. ended 12/31/01): Grants paid, $52,000; assets, $1,175,097 (M); gifts received, $19,000; expenditures, $56,855; qualifying distributions, $53,531.
Limitations: Giving on a national basis.
Officers and Trustees:* Bradbury Dyer III,* Pres.; Nancy Anne Dyer,* Secy.
EIN: 752629363

51822
The Polemanakos Foundation
c/o JPMorgan Chase Bank
P.O. Box 2558
Houston, TX 77252 (713) 216-4865

Established in 1964 in TX.
Financial data (yr. ended 12/31/01): Grants paid, $52,000; assets, $1,163,829 (M); expenditures, $74,910; qualifying distributions, $52,000.
Limitations: Giving primarily in TX.
Officer: Tom Lykos, Mgr.
Trustee: JPMorgan Chase Bank.
EIN: 746064811

51823
Rollins M. & Amalie L. Koppel Foundation
P.O. Box 2878
Harlingen, TX 78551 (956) 425-2000
Contact: Terry Wadkins, Secy.-Treas.

Financial data (yr. ended 12/31/01): Grants paid, $51,955; assets, $417,240 (M); expenditures, $57,400; qualifying distributions, $51,955.
Limitations: Giving primarily in TX.
Officers: Rollins M. Koppel, Pres.; Amalie L. Koppel, V.P.; Terry Wadkins, Secy.- Treas.
EIN: 742863028

51824
The Reilly Family Foundation
c/o The Ballpark
1000 Ballpark Way, Ste. 304
Arlington, TX 76011 (817) 265-2364
FAX: (817) 265-0537

Established in 1996 in TX.
Donor(s): John C. Franklin, Stars for Children.
Financial data (yr. ended 12/31/01): Grants paid, $51,885; assets, $575,190 (M); gifts received, $105,769; expenditures, $87,247; qualifying distributions, $77,814.
Limitations: Giving primarily in Fort Worth, TX.
Application information: Application form required.
Officers and Trustees:* Michael A. Reilly,* Chair.; T.W. Reilly III,* Pres.; Diana Allison, Cynthia Anderson, Robert Barnes, John C. Franklin, R.J. Grogan, Jr., Verna L. Riddles, Richard D. Trubitt.
EIN: 752366809

51825
Daniel B. Deupree Foundation
P.O. Box 345
Bonham, TX 75418
Application address: Rte. 3 Box 259B, Bonham, TX 75418, tel.: (903) 961-3001
Contact: Lisa Hicks

Established in 1981 in TX.
Financial data (yr. ended 12/31/01): Grants paid, $51,834; assets, $1,576,326 (M); expenditures, $62,168; qualifying distributions, $53,513.
Limitations: Giving primarily to residents of Fannin County, TX.
Application information: Application form required.
Trustees: Bryon Caylor, Joe Deupree, Janie Eller, James R. Hicks, Mary Law.
EIN: 759033769
Codes: GTI

51826
The Steve Elkington Foundation, Inc.
13131 Champions Dr., Ste. 206
Houston, TX 77069 (281) 880-6400
Contact: Dana J. Carter, V.P.

Established in 2000 in TX.
Donor(s): Ebco Land Development, LTD.
Financial data (yr. ended 12/31/01): Grants paid, $51,500; assets, $68,885 (M); gifts received, $67,265; expenditures, $73,482; qualifying distributions, $51,500.
Application information: Application form not required.
Officers: Steve J. Elkington, Chair. and Pres.; Lisa D. Elkington, V.P. and Secy.; Dana J. Carter, V.P. and Treas.
EIN: 760660008

51827
Minchen-Beville Foundation
c/o JPMorgan Chase Bank
P.O. Box 2558
Houston, TX 77252-8037 (713) 216-1457

Established in 1992 in TX.
Donor(s): Ruth Minchen.‡
Financial data (yr. ended 12/31/01): Grants paid, $51,498; assets, $1,425,703 (M); expenditures, $79,323; qualifying distributions, $51,498.
Limitations: Giving limited to Georgetown, TX.
Trustees: Richard L. Anderson, Robert K. Fowler, Jr., Gwen S. Morrison, JPMorgan Chase Bank.
EIN: 766063590

51828
Biba and Jon Parker Foundation
530 Woodbend Ln.
Houston, TX 77079-6851

Established in 1993 in TX.
Donor(s): Jonathan E. Parker, Vivian C. Parker.
Financial data (yr. ended 12/31/01): Grants paid, $51,414; assets, $750,064 (M); gifts received, $10,000; expenditures, $53,691; qualifying distributions, $51,414.
Limitations: Applications not accepted. Giving on a national basis.
Application information: Contributes only to pre-selected organizations.

51828—TEXAS

Trustees: Elois Parker Meachum, Jonathan E. Parker, Jonathan Edward Parker, Jr., Marian Louise Parker, Vivian C. Parker.
EIN: 760431146

51829
James R. Crane Foundation
15350 Vickery Dr.
Houston, TX 77032

Established in 1999 in TX.
Donor(s): James R. Crane.
Financial data (yr. ended 12/31/00): Grants paid, $51,405; assets, $968,115 (M); expenditures, $51,405; qualifying distributions, $51,405.
Limitations: Applications not accepted. Giving primarily in Houston, TX.
Application information: Contributes only to pre-selected organizations.
Directors: James R. Crane, Ronald Franklin, Douglas Seckel.
EIN: 760626224

51830
Lewis H. Pool Foundation
P.O. Box 1316
Carthage, TX 75633-7316 (903) 694-2878
Contact: Inez P. Pool, Tr.

Established in 1988 in TX.
Donor(s): Inez P. Pool, Philip R. Pool.
Financial data (yr. ended 09/30/01): Grants paid, $51,220; assets, $1,058,850 (M); expenditures, $52,679; qualifying distributions, $51,220.
Limitations: Giving primarily in the Panola County, TX, area.
Trustees: Carolyn Pool, Inez P. Pool, Matthew C. Pool, Molly K. Pool, Philip R. Pool.
EIN: 752254591

51831
The Trier Family Foundation
8826 Stable Crest Blvd.
Houston, TX 77024

Established in 1999 in TX.
Donor(s): Clayton Trier, Virginia Trier.
Financial data (yr. ended 12/31/00): Grants paid, $51,050; assets, $289,004 (M); expenditures, $60,053; qualifying distributions, $50,983.
Limitations: Applications not accepted. Giving primarily in TX.
Application information: Contributes only to pre-selected organizations.
Officers and Directors:* Virginia Trier,* Pres.; Evelyn Trier,* V.P.; Clayton Trier,* Secy.-Treas.
EIN: 760555166

51832
Robert & Janis Birchall Foundation
3456 Ocean Dr.
Corpus Christi, TX 78411 (361) 853-6330
Contact: Janis L. Birchall, M.D., Pres.

Established in 1997 in TX.
Donor(s): Janis L. Birchall, M.D.
Financial data (yr. ended 12/31/01): Grants paid, $51,000; assets, $741,723 (M); expenditures, $68,775; qualifying distributions, $51,000.
Limitations: Giving primarily in TX.
Officers and Directors:* Janis L. Birchall, M.D.,* Pres.; Rita A. Mueller,* V.P.; Luann Suckley,* Secy.; Peter B. Suckley,* Treas.
EIN: 742853757

51833
Nancy and Paul Flum Foundation
4302 Noble Oak Trail
Houston, TX 77059

Established in 1993.

Financial data (yr. ended 12/31/01): Grants paid, $51,000; assets, $1,030,258 (M); expenditures, $53,602; qualifying distributions, $51,142.
Limitations: Applications not accepted. Giving limited to MO, primarily in St. Louis.
Application information: Contributes only to pre-selected organizations.
Officer and Trustees:* Leslie Flum Uljee,* Exec. Dir.; Paul L. Flum.
EIN: 436474901

51834
The B. Holman Foundation
8311 San Benito Way
Dallas, TX 75218-4312

Established in 2001 in TX.
Donor(s): Beulah A. Holman.
Financial data (yr. ended 12/31/01): Grants paid, $51,000; assets, $804,718 (M); gifts received, $1,018,017; expenditures, $630,245; qualifying distributions, $51,000.
Limitations: Applications not accepted.
Application information: Contributes only to pre-selected organizations.
Directors: Mary M. Brinegar, Beulah A. Holman, Barbara T. Renfro.
EIN: 752910322

51835
Jacque Vaughn Charitable Trust
(Formerly Jacque Vaughn Wilson Charitable Trust)
P.O. Box 97511
Wichita Falls, TX 76307

Established in 1988 in TX.
Donor(s): Wilson Drilling Corp., Jacque Vaughn Wilson.‡
Financial data (yr. ended 06/30/02): Grants paid, $51,000; assets, $3,183,255 (M); expenditures, $84,354; qualifying distributions, $51,000.
Limitations: Applications not accepted. Giving limited to Wichita Falls, TX.
Application information: Contributes only to pre-selected organizations.
Trustee: Joseph N. Sherrill, Jr.
EIN: 756379527
Codes: CS, CD

51836
Vasco McCoy, Jr. Foundation
3424 Texas Blvd.
Texarkana, TX 75503

Donor(s): Vasco McCoy, Jr.
Financial data (yr. ended 12/31/01): Grants paid, $50,980; assets, $494,243 (M); gifts received, $46,000; expenditures, $52,545; qualifying distributions, $50,980.
Limitations: Applications not accepted. Giving primarily in Texarkana, TX.
Application information: Contributes only to pre-selected organizations.
Trustees: Alice Anderson, Betty Anderson Haisten, Pamela McCoy, Vasco McCoy, Jr.
EIN: 237325476

51837
The Vaughan Foundation
P.O. Box 17258
San Antonio, TX 78217 (210) 352-1300
Contact: Curtis T. Vaughan, Jr., Pres.

Established in 1947 in TX.
Donor(s): Curtis T. Vaughan, Jr., Vaughan & Sons, Inc.
Financial data (yr. ended 12/31/01): Grants paid, $50,937; assets, $194,631 (M); gifts received, $5,852; expenditures, $51,029; qualifying distributions, $50,869.

Limitations: Applications not accepted. Giving primarily in San Antonio, TX.
Application information: Contributes only to pre-selected organizations. Unsolicited requests for funds not considered.
Officers and Directors:* Curtis T. Vaughan, Jr.,* Pres.; Vaughan B. Meyer,* V.P.; Curtis T. Vaughan III, Secy.-Treas.; Elizabeth Bishop, Ben Foster, Jr., Norman Harwell, Nell Herff, George C. Vaughan, Richard S. Vaughan, Robert L. Vaughan.
EIN: 746040833

51838
Fred and Ann Margolin Foundation
10515 Lennox Ln.
Dallas, TX 75229-5415
Contact: Ann Margolin, Pres.

Established in 1995 in TX.
Donor(s): Ann Margolin, Fred Margolin.
Financial data (yr. ended 12/31/00): Grants paid, $50,833; assets, $456,430 (M); gifts received, $182,909; expenditures, $54,168; qualifying distributions, $50,833.
Limitations: Giving limited to Dallas, TX.
Officer: Ann E. Margolin, Pres.
Trustees: James Epstein, Fred Margolin.
EIN: 752568875

51839
Greene Family Foundation
(Formerly Aubrey M. Costa Foundation)
4635 Park Ln.
Dallas, TX 75220-2524

Established in 1968 in TX.
Donor(s): Aubrey M. Costa.‡
Financial data (yr. ended 12/31/01): Grants paid, $50,650; assets, $592,530 (M); expenditures, $56,881; qualifying distributions, $50,650.
Limitations: Applications not accepted. Giving primarily in TX.
Application information: Contributes only to pre-selected organizations.
Trustees: Edward C. Greene, Milton J. Greene.
EIN: 756085394

51840
Dooley Family Foundation
2575 Ashley St.
Beaumont, TX 77702 (409) 842-1381
Contact: Arthur Rhew Dooley, Jr.

Established in 1997 in TX.
Financial data (yr. ended 03/31/02): Grants paid, $50,626; assets, $314,628 (M); gifts received, $18,061; expenditures, $54,906; qualifying distributions, $50,626.
Officers and Trustee:* Arthur Rhew Dooley, Jr.,* Pres.; Sally Conway Dooley, Secy.-Treas.
EIN: 760536719

51841
The Larry and Pat McNeil Foundation
P.O. Box 779
Corpus Christi, TX 78403-0779
(361) 882-2001
Contact: L.A. McNeil, Tr.

Established in 1979 in TX.
Donor(s): Laurence A. McNeil, Kathryn B. McNeil.
Financial data (yr. ended 11/30/01): Grants paid, $50,600; assets, $677,735 (M); gifts received, $100,000; expenditures, $59,497; qualifying distributions, $50,600.
Limitations: Giving primarily in Corpus Christi, TX.
Trustees: Kathryn B. McNeil, L.A. McNeil.
EIN: 742083817

51842
The Eurice M. Bass Foundation
428 E. Preston Glen
Gunter, TX 75058-9511

Established in 1998 in TX.
Donor(s): Eurice M. Bass.
Financial data (yr. ended 12/31/00): Grants paid, $50,500; assets, $2,482,890 (M); expenditures, $109,064; qualifying distributions, $97,538.
Limitations: Applications not accepted.
Application information: Contributes only to pre-selected organizations.
Officers: Eurice M. Bass, Pres.; Claude Miller, V.P.; Linda M. Simms, Secy.
EIN: 752739565

51843
Pauline and Austin Neuhoff Charitable Trust
4005 Glenwick Ln.
Dallas, TX 75205

Financial data (yr. ended 12/31/01): Grants paid, $50,496; assets, $106,596 (M); gifts received, $26,491; expenditures, $51,800; qualifying distributions, $50,496.
Limitations: Applications not accepted. Giving primarily in TX.
Application information: Contributes only to pre-selected organizations.
Trustees: Austin P. Neuhoff, Pauline S. Neuhoff.
EIN: 756511775

51844
Eos Foundation Trust
(Formerly Gwendolyn Weiner Charitable Foundation)
P.O. Box 121938
Fort Worth, TX 76121

Established in 1990 in TX.
Donor(s): Lucile Weiner, Gwendolyn Weiner.
Financial data (yr. ended 09/30/01): Grants paid, $50,310; assets, $1,033,706 (M); gifts received, $235,060; expenditures, $51,639; qualifying distributions, $50,310.
Limitations: Applications not accepted.
Application information: Contributes only to pre-selected organizations.
Trustees: Susan Boyle, Nina Pruitt, Gwendolyn Weiner.
EIN: 756417110

51845
Shirley and David Toomim Foundation
109 N. Post Oak Ln., Ste. 300
Houston, TX 77024
Application address: 5315 Pine St., Bellaire, TX 77401, tel.: (713) 662-7784
Contact: Bruce M. Levy, Tr.

Established in 1999 in TX.
Financial data (yr. ended 12/31/01): Grants paid, $50,300; assets, $894,274 (M); expenditures, $58,965; qualifying distributions, $50,300.
Limitations: Giving primarily in Houston, TX.
Trustees: Bruce M. Levy, Ellen F. Robinson, Roddy Toomim.
EIN: 760585077

51846
Bertha Z. Ellis Trust
c/o Bank of America
P.O. Box 831041
Dallas, TX 75283-1041
Application address: c/o Bob Burris, 100 N. Main St., Corsicana, TX 75110, tel.: (903) 654-3254

Financial data (yr. ended 03/31/02): Grants paid, $50,206; assets, $487,004 (M); expenditures, $58,988; qualifying distributions, $50,206.
Limitations: Giving primarily in TX.
Trustee: Bank of America.
EIN: 756296558

51847
Louis and Miriam Rosenbaum Foundation
315 E. Rim Rd.
El Paso, TX 79902

Established in 1994 in TX.
Donor(s): Louis Rosenbaum, Miriam Rosenbaum.
Financial data (yr. ended 12/31/01): Grants paid, $50,161; assets, $436,460 (M); gifts received, $52,500; expenditures, $71,357; qualifying distributions, $50,161.
Limitations: Applications not accepted. Giving primarily in El Paso, TX.
Application information: Contributes only to pre-selected organizations.
Officer: Louis Rosenbaum, Mgr.
EIN: 742664769

51848
Solomon D. & Victoria David Foundation
P.O. Box 310005
New Braunfels, TX 78131-0005

Financial data (yr. ended 09/30/01): Grants paid, $50,150; assets, $930,429 (M); expenditures, $61,048; qualifying distributions, $61,048.
Limitations: Applications not accepted. Giving primarily in TX.
Application information: Contributes only to pre-selected organizations.
Officers: S.D. David, Jr.,* Pres.; Horace B. Hill,* Treas.
EIN: 741608274

51849
Black Family Foundation
P.O. Box 7907
Horseshoe Bay, TX 78657

Established in 1998 in CT.
Donor(s): C. Robert Black.
Financial data (yr. ended 12/31/01): Grants paid, $50,000; assets, $1,028,684 (M); gifts received, $489,405; expenditures, $57,322; qualifying distributions, $50,000.
Limitations: Applications not accepted. Giving primarily in TX.
Application information: Contributes only to pre-selected organizations.
Officers: C. Robert Black, Pres.; Kevin Robert Black, V.P.; Susan Black Handley, V.P.; Billie Black, Secy.
EIN: 066463395

51850
Jarlath O. & Evelyn H. Edwards Foundation
9137 Briar Forest Dr.
Houston, TX 77024-7222

Established in 1997.
Donor(s): Evelyn H. Edwards.
Financial data (yr. ended 04/30/02): Grants paid, $50,000; assets, $476,245 (M); expenditures, $51,339; qualifying distributions, $50,000.
Limitations: Applications not accepted.
Officers: Evelyn H. Edwards, Pres.; Christine A. Edwards, V.P. and Treas.; Jeanne M. Edwards, Secy.
EIN: 760537323

51851
The Seawell Elam Foundation
P.O. Box 5335
Austin, TX 78763 (512) 476-0715
Contact: Robert Elam Roth, Dir.

Established in 1992 in TX.
Donor(s): Belle P. Elam.
Financial data (yr. ended 12/31/01): Grants paid, $50,000; assets, $3,382,747 (M); expenditures, $83,944; qualifying distributions, $50,000.
Limitations: Giving primarily in TX.
Application information: Application form required.
Directors: Durell M. Roth, Elizabeth Elam Roth, Robert Elam Roth.
EIN: 742637039

51852
The Gerald J. Ford Foundation, Inc.
200 Crescent Ct., Ste. 1350
Dallas, TX 75201

Established in 1997 in TX.
Financial data (yr. ended 12/31/01): Grants paid, $50,000; assets, $728,451 (M); expenditures, $53,000; qualifying distributions, $51,035.
Limitations: Applications not accepted. Giving primarily in TX.
Application information: Contributes only to pre-selected organizations.
Officers and Directors:* Gerald J. Ford,* Pres.; Nancy J. Foederer, Secy.; Christie S. Flanagan, Carl B. Webb.
EIN: 752729818

51853
Frankel Family Foundation, Inc.
(Formerly The Leonard R. Frankel Family Foundation)
2 Houston Ctr., Ste. 3020
Houston, TX 77010

Established in 1991 in TX.
Financial data (yr. ended 12/31/01): Grants paid, $50,000; assets, $933,046 (M); expenditures, $53,771; qualifying distributions, $51,889.
Limitations: Applications not accepted. Giving primarily in Houston, TX.
Application information: Contributes only to pre-selected organizations.
Officers: Russell M. Frankel, Chair.; Sherry G. Frankel, V.P.; Marvin D. Nathan, Secy.
Trustee: Barry H. Margolis.
EIN: 760354825

51854
Highlands Foundation
P.O. Box 820606
Dallas, TX 75382

Established in 2000 in TX.
Donor(s): John Albers.
Financial data (yr. ended 12/31/01): Grants paid, $50,000; assets, $395,999 (M); expenditures, $70,091; qualifying distributions, $50,000.
Limitations: Giving primarily in Edina, MN.
Officers: John Albers, Pres. and Treas.; Janet Albers, V.P. and Secy.
EIN: 752781492

51855
Knapp Foundation
118 E. Tyler Ave.
Harlingen, TX 78550
Application address: P.O. Box 69, Harlingen, TX 78552, tel.: (956) 423-1370
Contact: Chris Cooley

Established in 1952.
Donor(s): F.E. Knapp, J.A. Knapp.
Financial data (yr. ended 12/31/01): Grants paid, $50,000; assets, $984,499 (M); expenditures, $53,229; qualifying distributions, $50,000.
Limitations: Giving primarily in TX.
Application information: Application form not required.
Directors: F.E. Knapp, Jr., J.A. Knapp, Jr.
EIN: 746060544

51856
The Maby/King Foundation
147 Hickory Ridge Dr.
Houston, TX 77024

Established in 1997 in TX.
Financial data (yr. ended 12/31/01): Grants paid, $50,000; assets, $916,761 (M); gifts received, $74,000; expenditures, $52,725; qualifying distributions, $51,611.
Limitations: Applications not accepted.
Application information: Contributes only to pre-selected organizations.
Officers: Kevin C. King, Pres.; Monica Maby King, V.P. and Secy.
Director: H. Bradley Whatley.
EIN: 311577190

51857
The Mariposa Charitable Foundation
4004 Sycamore Ln.
Allen, TX 75002

Established in 2001 in TX.
Donor(s): Cathy E. Colburn, Roger J. Colburn.
Financial data (yr. ended 12/31/01): Grants paid, $50,000; assets, $158,009 (M); gifts received, $207,730; expenditures, $51,602; qualifying distributions, $49,981.
Limitations: Applications not accepted. Giving primarily in Dallas, TX.
Application information: Contributes only to pre-selected organizations.
Officers: Roger J. Colburn, Pres. and Treas.; Cathy E. Colburn, V.P. and Secy.
Trustee: Rose Mary Spooner.
EIN: 752910504

51858
McBee Family Foundation
705 San Antonio St.
Austin, TX 78701 (512) 476-2386
Contact: Sue Brandt McBee, Pres.

Established in 2000 in TX.
Donor(s): Sue Brandt McBee.
Financial data (yr. ended 12/31/01): Grants paid, $50,000; assets, $588,457 (M); gifts received, $5,745; expenditures, $51,945; qualifying distributions, $50,000.
Application information: Application form not required.
Officers: Sue Brandt McBee, Pres.; Robert McBee, Secy.-Treas.
Trustee: Marilyn Moore.
EIN: 742981871

51859
Florence and William K. McGee, Jr. Family Foundation
5957 Crab Orchard
Houston, TX 77057-1421 (713) 780-7886

Financial data (yr. ended 12/31/01): Grants paid, $50,000; assets, $909,303 (M); expenditures, $53,253; qualifying distributions, $50,000.
Officers and Directors:* William K. McGee,* Pres. and Treas.; Florence H. McGee,* V.P. and Secy.; Thomas Wells McGee, William Wells McGee.
EIN: 760585804

51860
James and Sally Nation Foundation
P.O. Box 180849
Dallas, TX 75218 (214) 388-5751

Established in 2001 in TX.
Donor(s): James Nation, Sally Nation.
Financial data (yr. ended 12/31/01): Grants paid, $50,000; assets, $418,708 (M); gifts received, $465,000; expenditures, $50,000; qualifying distributions, $50,000.
Directors: Frieda Ashworth, James Nation, Sally Nation.
EIN: 752942544

51861
Jack & Nannerl H. Ryan Foundation
c/o Ann E. O'Neal
2004 Wing Point
Plano, TX 75093

Established in 1983.
Donor(s): Ann E. O'Neal.
Financial data (yr. ended 09/30/01): Grants paid, $50,000; assets, $908,644 (M); expenditures, $52,219; qualifying distributions, $50,000.
Limitations: Applications not accepted. Giving primarily in TX.
Officer and Directors:* Ann E. O'Neal,* Exec. Dir.; Gayle Allison, D. Michael O'Neal.
EIN: 751944774

51862
The Skiles Foundation
6039 Glendora Ave.
Dallas, TX 75230

Established in 1999 in TX.
Donor(s): Elwin L. Skiles, Jr.
Financial data (yr. ended 12/31/01): Grants paid, $50,000; assets, $869,626 (M); expenditures, $83,974; qualifying distributions, $50,000.
Limitations: Applications not accepted.
Application information: Contributes only to pre-selected organizations.
Officers and Trustees:* Elwin L. Skiles, Jr.,* Pres. and Treas.; Ann Skiles McGinty,* V.P. and Secy.; Sarah Skiles Zachry,* V.P.
EIN: 752845190

51863
Vinson & Elkins L.L.P. Scholarship Foundation
2300 First City Twr.
1001 Fannin St., Ste. 2300
Houston, TX 77002-6710
Contact: Stacy Sims

Established in 1994 in TX.
Donor(s): Vinson & Elkins L.L.P.
Financial data (yr. ended 12/31/01): Grants paid, $50,000; assets, $0 (M); gifts received, $47,500; expenditures, $50,000; qualifying distributions, $50,000.
Limitations: Giving limited to residents of Houston, TX.
Application information: Application form required.
Officers and Directors:* David T. Hedges, Jr.,* Pres.; Yolanda C. Knull,* V.P.; John W. Spire, Treas.; W.H. Drushel.
EIN: 760428361
Codes: CS, CD, GTI

51864
W. T. Yett Charitable Foundation
c/o Frost National Bank, Trust Dept.
P.O. Box 2950
San Antonio, TX 78299-2950

Established in 1991 in TX.
Financial data (yr. ended 12/31/00): Grants paid, $50,000; assets, $918,060 (M); expenditures, $68,396; qualifying distributions, $50,762.
Limitations: Giving limited to residents of Blanco County, TX.
Application information: Application form not required.
Trustee: Frost National Bank.
EIN: 742640368
Codes: GTI

51865
Ralph Buchanan Albaugh Trust
c/o Bank of America
P.O. Box 831041
Dallas, TX 75283-1041
Application address: c/o Lindy Dehn, Methodist Home, Waco, TX 76702, tel.: (254) 753-0181

Financial data (yr. ended 12/31/01): Grants paid, $49,878; assets, $1,474,151 (M); expenditures, $63,593; qualifying distributions, $55,494.
Limitations: Giving primarily in Waco, TX.
Application information: Application form required.
Trustees: Jack Kyle Daniels, Jerry Major, Scott Wallace, Bank of America.
EIN: 746041694
Codes: GTI

51866
Ralph Wilson Plastics Employees Scholarship Fund
600 General Bruce Dr.
Temple, TX 76501-5199
Application address: c/o Selection Comm., P.O. Box 625, Temple, TX 76503-0625, tel.: (254) 207-6360
Contact: Dan Case, Tr.

Established in 1966 in TX.
Donor(s): Ralph Wilson Plastics Co.
Financial data (yr. ended 06/30/01): Grants paid, $49,875; assets, $1,173,928 (M); gifts received, $23,215; expenditures, $61,388; qualifying distributions, $51,314.
Limitations: Giving limited to residents of Temple, TX.
Application information: Scholarships are awarded for 1 year only and may be renewed. Application form required.
Officers: Cynthia Sharp, Pres.; Brenda White, V.P.; Charlene Harvey, Secy.; Jake Herndon, Treas.
Trustee: Dan Case.
EIN: 746245026
Codes: CS, CD, GTI

51867
The Everhart Foundation
11910 Greenville Ave., Ste. 400
Dallas, TX 75243

Established in 1991 in TX.
Donor(s): John P. Everhart.
Financial data (yr. ended 12/31/01): Grants paid, $49,622; assets, $49,437 (M); gifts received,

$64,873; expenditures, $50,674; qualifying distributions, $49,622.
Limitations: Applications not accepted. Giving limited to TX.
Application information: Contributes only to pre-selected organizations.
Trustees: R. Allen Dodgen, Anita C. Everhart, John P. Everhart.
EIN: 752362397

51868
Earl and Ann Morris Family Foundation
7600 W. Tidwell, Ste. 110
Houston, TX 77040

Donor(s): Earl E. Morris.
Financial data (yr. ended 11/30/01): Grants paid, $49,589; assets, $158,066 (M); gifts received, $25,000; expenditures, $50,481; qualifying distributions, $49,589.
Limitations: Applications not accepted.
Application information: Contributes only to pre-selected organizations.
Officers and Directors:* Earl Morris,* Pres.; Janie Herring, Secy.; Allen McGee, Treas.; Donald G. Ezzell, Stephanie G. Ezzell, Elizabeth A. Martens, Steven R. Martens, Ann Morris.
EIN: 760556003

51869
Four Cedars Foundation, Inc.
c/o Frost National Bank
P.O. Box 2950
San Antonio, TX 78299

Established in 1998 in WI.
Donor(s): William P. Rogers.
Financial data (yr. ended 05/31/01): Grants paid, $49,500; assets, $1,683,333 (M); expenditures, $64,901; qualifying distributions, $49,500.
Limitations: Applications not accepted. Giving primarily in Duluth, MN.
Application information: Contributes only to pre-selected organizations.
Trustees: James L. Banks, Robert D. Banks, Jr., Joel S. Cooper, Mark D. Johnson, William P. Rogers.
Agent: Frost National Bank.
EIN: 391945362

51870
Roy Scholarship Fund
c/o JPMorgan Chase Bank
P.O. Box 47531
San Antonio, TX 78265-7531
Application addresses: c/o Senior Counselor, Westlake High School, 4100 Westbank Dr., Austin, TX 78746, tel.: (512) 328-4100; c/o Senior Counselor, Stephen F. Austin High School, 1715 W. 1st St., Austin, TX 78703, tel.: (512) 474-5977
Contact: Sonia Garza

Financial data (yr. ended 03/31/02): Grants paid, $49,500; assets, $895,742 (M); expenditures, $69,779; qualifying distributions, $55,010.
Limitations: Giving limited to Austin, TX.
Application information: Recipients are chosen by selection committee. Application form not required.
Trustee: JPMorgan Chase Bank.
EIN: 746086969
Codes: GTI

51871
Mr. and Mrs. James A. Stroud Foundation
14160 Dallas Pkwy., Ste. 300
Dallas, TX 75240 (972) 770-5600
Contact: James A. Stroud, C.E.O. and Secy.

Established in 1998 in TX.
Donor(s): Lynn M. Stroud.
Financial data (yr. ended 12/31/01): Grants paid, $49,295; assets, $499,091 (M); expenditures, $58,383; qualifying distributions, $49,295.
Limitations: Giving primarily in Dallas, TX.
Officers: James A. Stroud, C.E.O. and Secy.; Lynn M. Stroud, Pres. and Treas.
EIN: 752763113

51872
The Greg and Mari Marchbanks Family Foundation
600 Congress Ave., Ste. 200
Austin, TX 78701

Established in 1998 in TX.
Donor(s): Gregory S. Marchbanks, Mari S. Marchbanks.
Financial data (yr. ended 12/31/01): Grants paid, $49,233; assets, $1,433,003 (M); expenditures, $62,220; qualifying distributions, $51,242.
Limitations: Applications not accepted. Giving primarily in Austin, TX.
Application information: Contributes only to pre-selected organizations.
Officers: Gregory S. Marchbanks, Pres.; Mari S. Marchbanks, V.P.; Tyson S. Feaster, Secy.
EIN: 742862373

51873
R. & T. Robertson Foundation
600 Leopard St., Ste. 1800
Corpus Christi, TX 78473-0038
Contact: Amy Robertson Ehrman, Pres.

Financial data (yr. ended 11/30/01): Grants paid, $49,000; assets, $340,266 (M); expenditures, $49,566; qualifying distributions, $49,000.
Limitations: Giving primarily in Corpus Christi, TX.
Officers: Amy Robertson Ehrman, Pres.; Marie A. Robertson, V.P.
Director: Roland C. Robertson.
EIN: 742224591

51874
Louis & Millie Kocurek Charitable Foundation
c/o Bank of America
P.O. Box 831041
Dallas, TX 75283-1041

Financial data (yr. ended 11/30/01): Grants paid, $48,512; assets, $1,028,544 (M); expenditures, $62,280; qualifying distributions, $48,512.
Limitations: Applications not accepted. Giving primarily in AK, NY, TX and WI.
Application information: Contributes only to pre-selected organizations.
Trustee: Bank of America.
EIN: 746306747

51875
Robert J. Potter Foundation
1901 N. Akard St.
Dallas, TX 75201

Established in 1996 in TX.
Donor(s): Robert J. Potter.
Financial data (yr. ended 12/31/01): Grants paid, $48,288; assets, $98,259 (M); gifts received, $700; expenditures, $48,981; qualifying distributions, $48,288.
Limitations: Applications not accepted.
Application information: Contributes only to pre-selected organizations.
Officers and Trustees:* Robert J. Potter,* Pres. and Treas.; Mary E. Edmiston,* Secy.; Peter P. Smith.
EIN: 752680882

51876
Tom C. Barnsley Foundation
c/o Bank of America
P.O. Box 931041
Dallas, TX 75283-1041

Established in 1977.
Financial data (yr. ended 12/31/01): Grants paid, $48,000; assets, $646,613 (M); expenditures, $63,019; qualifying distributions, $47,495.
Limitations: Giving limited to the Crane County, TX, area.
Advisors: Debbie Cowden, Vonna Johnson, Bill Teague.
Trustees: V.H. VanHorn, Bank of America.
EIN: 756248739
Codes: GTI

51877
First Fruits, Inc.
P.O. Box 53068
Lubbock, TX 79453 (806) 863-2231
Contact: William S. Stewart, Pres.

Donor(s): William S. Stewart.
Financial data (yr. ended 12/31/99): Grants paid, $47,814; assets, $6,912 (M); gifts received, $51,678; expenditures, $49,479; qualifying distributions, $47,814.
Limitations: Giving on a national basis, with some emphasis on TX.
Officers: William S. Stewart, Pres.; Samuel C. Stewart, V.P.; Sarah Stewart, Secy.-Treas.
EIN: 751819290

51878
The Riklin Charitable Trust
1100 N.E. Loop 410, Ste. 730
San Antonio, TX 78209

Established in 2000 in TX.
Financial data (yr. ended 12/31/01): Grants paid, $47,769; assets, $2,849,870 (M); gifts received, $455,613; expenditures, $80,008; qualifying distributions, $79,867.
Limitations: Applications not accepted. Giving primarily in San Antonio, TX.
Application information: Contributes only to pre-selected organizations.
Trustee: Arthur L. Riklin.
EIN: 746493929

51879
The Charles E. Jacobs Foundation
P.O. Box 1178
Albany, TX 76430

Established in 2000 in TX.
Financial data (yr. ended 12/31/01): Grants paid, $47,617; assets, $655,482 (M); expenditures, $63,865; qualifying distributions, $47,617.
Limitations: Applications not accepted. Giving primarily in Albany, TX.
Application information: Contributes only to pre-selected organizations.
Officers: Glenn A. Picquet, Pres.; Dan Neff, V.P. and Treas.; Marcia Carol Brewer Jacobs, Secy.
EIN: 752859040

51880
Howard Family Foundation
7230 Acacia Dr.
Leander, TX 78641

Established in 2000 in TX.
Donor(s): Mark Eugene Howard II, Irma Funderburk Howard, Joel Eugene Howard.
Financial data (yr. ended 12/31/01): Grants paid, $47,500; assets, $97,603 (M); gifts received, $82,482; expenditures, $50,896; qualifying distributions, $47,500.

51880—TEXAS

Limitations: Applications not accepted.
Application information: Contributes only to pre-selected organizations.
Officers: Mark Eugene Howard II, Pres.; Irma Funderburk Howard, V.P.; Joel Eugene Howard, Secy.-Treas.
EIN: 742976962

51881
Lents Foundation
600 Travis St., Ste. 6110
Houston, TX 77002-3007

Donor(s): Mary Frances Hunsicker Lents, Max R. Lents.
Financial data (yr. ended 12/31/01): Grants paid, $47,350; assets, $1,048,376 (M); gifts received, $255,503; expenditures, $54,118; qualifying distributions, $47,973.
Limitations: Applications not accepted. Giving primarily in Houston, TX.
Application information: Contributes only to pre-selected organizations.
Trustees: Ann Lents, John Lents, Murphy K. Lents.
EIN: 746083129

51882
Ralph & Pat Morgan Foundation
3507 Glenwood Ave.
Wichita Falls, TX 76308

Established in 1999 in TX.
Donor(s): Ralph W. Morgan, Patricia M. Morgan.
Financial data (yr. ended 12/31/01): Grants paid, $47,300; assets, $193,498 (M); expenditures, $51,429; qualifying distributions, $47,300.
Limitations: Applications not accepted. Giving primarily in TX.
Application information: Contributes only to pre-selected organizations.
Trustees: Robert W. Goff, Jr., Patricia M. Morgan, Ralph W. Morgan.
EIN: 752853874

51883
F. A. & Blanche Wood Heitmann Foundation
c/o JPMorgan Chase Bank
P.O. Box 2558
Houston, TX 77252-2558

Established in 1954.
Financial data (yr. ended 06/30/01): Grants paid, $47,105; assets, $653,710 (M); expenditures, $53,564; qualifying distributions, $49,150.
Limitations: Applications not accepted. Giving primarily in Houston, TX.
Application information: Contributes only to pre-selected organizations.
Trustees: Marian S. Cheatham, Robert F. Strange, Robert F. Strange, Jr., JPMorgan Chase Bank.
EIN: 746037341

51884
Margaret C. B. & S. Spencer N. Brown Foundation, Inc.
P.O. Box 7832
Waco, TX 76714-7832

Established in 1983.
Donor(s): Margaret Boyce Brown, S. Spencer Brown, Sr., National Diversified.
Financial data (yr. ended 12/31/01): Grants paid, $47,020; assets, $2,106,357 (M); gifts received, $57,500; expenditures, $60,127; qualifying distributions, $58,240.
Limitations: Applications not accepted. Giving primarily in TX.
Application information: Contributes only to pre-selected organizations.
Officers: S. Spencer Brown, Sr., Pres.; S. Spencer Brown, Jr., V.P.; Margaret Boyce Brown, Secy.

Trustees: Maria Stanton Brown, Stanton Boyce Brown, Margaret Brown Lewis, ExTraCo Banks.
EIN: 746046197

51885
Christopher Brownlee Memorial Trust
2211 Blackberry Dr.
Richardson, TX 75082 (972) 699-3540
Contact: Kathy Brownlee, Tr.

Established in 1996.
Financial data (yr. ended 12/31/00): Grants paid, $47,000; assets, $67,770 (M); gifts received, $79,783; expenditures, $65,669; qualifying distributions, $47,000.
Application information: Application form not required.
Trustees: Kathy Brownlee, Mark Brownlee.
EIN: 752201339

51886
Justin Paul Foundation, Inc.
6700 The Outer Ave.
Leander, TX 78641-9384 (512) 259-8738
Additional tel.: (512) 346-7490; FAX: (512) 260-8173
Contact: Harvey L. Walker, Pres.

Established in 1981 in TX.
Donor(s): Harvey L. Walker, Martha J. Walker, Ovada M. Pounders.
Financial data (yr. ended 12/31/01): Grants paid, $47,000; assets, $977,277 (M); expenditures, $48,735; qualifying distributions, $47,000.
Limitations: Giving primarily in OK and TX.
Application information: Donors initiate about 50 percent of contacts. Application form required.
Officers and Directors:* Harvey L. Walker,* Pres. and Treas.; Martha J. Walker,* V.P. and Secy.; Kenneth P. Pounders,* V.P.; Marty Barbieri, Betty Flores, Claudell Thomas, Terry W. Walker.
EIN: 751801580

51887
The Moor Foundation
c/o JPMorgan Chase Bank
201 E. Main Dr., 4th Fl.
El Paso, TX 79901
Contact: Terry Crenshaw, Trust Off., JPMorgan Chase Bank

Financial data (yr. ended 06/30/01): Grants paid, $47,000; assets, $768,956 (M); expenditures, $50,706; qualifying distributions, $50,373.
Limitations: Giving limited to El Paso, TX.
Trustee: JPMorgan Chase Bank.
EIN: 746033984

51888
The Leiser Family Foundation, Inc.
2200 Ross Ave., Ste. 3700
Dallas, TX 75201-2770

Established in 1997 in TX.
Donor(s): Thomas A. Leiser.
Financial data (yr. ended 12/31/00): Grants paid, $46,875; assets, $176,320 (M); gifts received, $2,571; expenditures, $47,547; qualifying distributions, $46,875.
Limitations: Applications not accepted.
Application information: Contributes only to pre-selected organizations.
Officer and Directors:* Thomas A. Leiser,* Pres.; Roger Fuller, Phyllis F. Leiser.
EIN: 752737278

51889
Emma F. Jacobs Foundation
301 Glenwood Dr.
Houston, TX 77007

Established in 2000 in TX.

Donor(s): Emma F. Jacobs.
Financial data (yr. ended 12/31/01): Grants paid, $46,853; assets, $293,921 (M); expenditures, $51,543; qualifying distributions, $46,853.
Limitations: Giving primarily in Houston, TX.
Officers: Emma F. Jacobs, Pres.; Bobby Lowe, V.P.; Kelle Dement, Secy.-Treas.
EIN: 760629500

51890
The Harding Foundation
Harding Fdn. Bldg.
P.O. Box 130, 5th and Hidalgo
Raymondville, TX 78580 (956) 689-2706
FAX: (956) 698-5740
Contact: Mrs. Glenn W. Harding, Corresponding Secy.

Incorporated in 1947 in TX.
Donor(s): W.A. Harding,‡ Laura V. Harding.‡
Financial data (yr. ended 12/31/00): Grants paid, $46,750; assets, $1,214,307 (M); expenditures, $206,543; qualifying distributions, $92,123.
Application information: Application form required.
Officers and Directors:* Glenn W. Harding,* Pres.; Martin Dale Harding,* V.P.; Dorothy Harding Parr,* Secy.; Mrs. Glenn W. Harding, Corresponding Secy.
EIN: 746025883
Codes: GTI

51891
Edith & Gaston Hallam Foundation No. 2
1805 Record Crossing
Dallas, TX 75235

Donor(s): Edith Hallam, Gaston Hallam.
Financial data (yr. ended 11/30/01): Grants paid, $46,700; assets, $997,904 (M); expenditures, $47,904; qualifying distributions, $46,700.
Limitations: Applications not accepted. Giving primarily in Dallas, TX.
Application information: Contributes only to pre-selected organizations.
Officer: Robert G. Hallam, Chair.
Trustee: Howard P. Hallam.
EIN: 237048873

51892
Mary Dinn Reynolds Methodist Foundation
P.O. Box 210
Alice, TX 78333

Financial data (yr. ended 12/31/01): Grants paid, $46,500; assets, $973,187 (M); expenditures, $51,156; qualifying distributions, $46,500.
Limitations: Applications not accepted. Giving primarily in Alice, TX.
Application information: Contributes only to pre-selected organizations.
Officers and Trustees:* W.J. Tiller,* Chair.; Carolyn Merritt, Secy.; John Burris, Treas.; Bill Acker, Rev. Peter Aguilar, Kirk Baxter, L.C. Johnston, Clyde Wright.
EIN: 746085324

51893
Joe Ward & Jean Hanson Educational Trust
P.O. Box 2050
Fort Worth, TX 76113

Financial data (yr. ended 03/31/00): Grants paid, $46,400; assets, $908,191 (M); expenditures, $53,379; qualifying distributions, $46,400.
Trustee: Bank One, Oklahoma, N.A.
EIN: 736301424

51894
Ming K. Jeang Foundation
3911 Roaring Rapids
Houston, TX 77059 (281) 286-0803
Contact: Ming K. Jeang, M.D., Pres.

Established in 1994 in TX.
Donor(s): Ming K. Jeang, M.D.
Financial data (yr. ended 11/30/01): Grants paid, $46,283; assets, $1 (M); expenditures, $47,857; qualifying distributions, $46,283.
Officers: Ming K. Jeang, M.D., Pres.; Kuan-Teh Jeang, Ph.D., V.P.; Shao-Shang Hwang Jeang, Secy.
EIN: 760454594

51895
Earl Snelling Public Property Beautification Trust
P.O. Box 789
Lufkin, TX 75902-0789 (936) 633-2197
Contact: Danny Roper, Tr.

Financial data (yr. ended 12/31/01): Grants paid, $46,231; assets, $598,303 (M); expenditures, $54,393; qualifying distributions, $46,231.
Limitations: Giving limited to Angelina County, TX.
Directors: Anna B. Connell, Howard Daniel, Mary L. Duran.
Trustee: Danny Roper.
EIN: 752674946

51896
Martha Sue Byrd Foundation
c/o John Wommack
8214 Westchester Dr., Ste. 500
Dallas, TX 75225-6111

Established in 2000 in TX.
Donor(s): Martha Sue Byrd.
Financial data (yr. ended 12/31/01): Grants paid, $46,198; assets, $143,600 (M); expenditures, $47,764; qualifying distributions, $46,198.
Limitations: Applications not accepted.
Application information: Contributes only to pre-selected organizations.
Trustees: Martha Sue Byrd, John R. Wommack.
EIN: 752894658

51897
Louise B. Belsterling Foundation of the Dallas Garden Club, Inc.
P.O. Box 802601
Dallas, TX 75380
Application address: c/o Mrs. David M. Munson, 7000 Park Ln., Dallas, TX 75225

Financial data (yr. ended 05/31/02): Grants paid, $46,014; assets, $658,689 (M); gifts received, $32,850; expenditures, $55,535; qualifying distributions, $46,014.
Limitations: Giving limited to College Station, Lubbock, and Richardson, TX.
Application information: Application form required.
Officers: Mrs. James H. Shelton, Pres.; Mrs. Louise Dunklin, V.P.; Mrs. Tie Davis, Secy.; Mrs. Robert H. Bliss, Treas.
EIN: 751375644

51898
Tilman & Paige Fertitta Family Foundation
1510 W. Loop S., 8th Fl.
Houston, TX 77027

Established in 2000 in TX.
Donor(s): Landry's Seafood Restaurants, Inc., Landry's Restaurants, Inc.
Financial data (yr. ended 12/31/01): Grants paid, $46,000; assets, $420,888 (M); gifts received, $172,500; expenditures, $50,905; qualifying distributions, $45,999.
Limitations: Applications not accepted. Giving primarily in Houston, TX.
Application information: Contributes only to pre-selected organizations.
Officers: Tilman J. Fertitta, Pres.; Paige Fertitta, V.P.; Steve Scheinthal, Secy.
EIN: 760626357
Codes: CS, CD

51899
Margaret Mosher Phillips Foundation
7506 Currin Dr.
Dallas, TX 75230-3630 (214) 368-3796
Contact: Margaret Louise Rosenlund, Tr.

Financial data (yr. ended 12/31/01): Grants paid, $46,000; assets, $857,632 (M); expenditures, $52,750; qualifying distributions, $46,000.
Limitations: Giving primarily in Dallas, TX.
Trustees: Janice K. Dauterman, Jack E. Rosenlund, Margaret Louise Rosenlund.
EIN: 751709181

51900
Thelma Emil and Edmund Fahrenkamp Memorial Trust
c/o Bank One, Texas, N.A.
P.O. Box 2050
Fort Worth, TX 76113-2050 (817) 884-4248
Contact: Jay Bartley, Trust Off., Bank One, Texas, N.A.

Established in 1994 in TX.
Financial data (yr. ended 05/31/01): Grants paid, $45,500; assets, $778,810 (M); expenditures, $55,615; qualifying distributions, $48,096.
Limitations: Giving primarily in Fort Worth, TX.
Trustee: Bank One Texas, N.A.
EIN: 756466013

51901
The Wise Family Foundation
213 Mesa Dr.
Gatesville, TX 76528

Donor(s): Charles D. Wise, Mary A. Wise, Thelma Smith.‡
Financial data (yr. ended 12/31/01): Grants paid, $45,493; assets, $616,722 (M); expenditures, $48,282; qualifying distributions, $45,493.
Limitations: Applications not accepted.
Application information: Contributes only to pre-selected organizations.
Trustees: Charles D. Wise, Charles R. Wise, Mary A. Wise, Mary K. Wise.
EIN: 766084279

51902
Betty Stieren Kelso Foundation
640 Ivy Ln.
San Antonio, TX 78209-2827
Contact: Betty Kelso, Pres.

Established in 1986 in TX.
Donor(s): Betty Kelso.
Financial data (yr. ended 12/31/01): Grants paid, $45,478; assets, $950,614 (M); expenditures, $53,930; qualifying distributions, $45,478.
Limitations: Giving limited to San Antonio, TX.
Application information: Application form required.
Officers: Betty Kelso, Pres.; Robert Kelso, V.P.; Barry Roberts, Secy.-Treas.
EIN: 742442790

51903
Pease Family Charitable Trust
4717 Fletcher Ave.
Fort Worth, TX 76107

Established in 1994.
Donor(s): Herbert L. Pease, Sr.
Financial data (yr. ended 12/31/01): Grants paid, $45,300; assets, $77,209 (M); gifts received, $100,000; expenditures, $46,275; qualifying distributions, $45,300.
Limitations: Applications not accepted. Giving primarily in TX.
Application information: Contributes only to pre-selected organizations.
Trustees: Herbert L. Pease, Sr., Herbert L. Pease, Jr., Mary V. Pease.
EIN: 756466399

51904
Paul F. and Virginia J. Engler Foundation
P.O. Box 3050
Amarillo, TX 79116-3050

Established in 1990 in TX.
Donor(s): Members of the Engler family.
Financial data (yr. ended 12/31/01): Grants paid, $45,182; assets, $1,057,720 (M); expenditures, $45,864; qualifying distributions, $45,182.
Limitations: Applications not accepted. Giving on a national basis.
Application information: Contributes only to pre-selected organizations.
Officers: Paul F. Engler, Chair.; Roxann Schwertner, Secy.; Mike Engler, Treas.
EIN: 752356449

51905
Grits Foundation
5005 Woodway Dr., Ste. 200
Houston, TX 77056-1789 (713) 850-7702
Contact: George A. Peterkin, Jr., Pres.

Established in 1997 in TX.
Financial data (yr. ended 12/31/01): Grants paid, $45,000; assets, $1,019,424 (M); gifts received, $373,813; expenditures, $48,898; qualifying distributions, $45,000.
Limitations: Giving primarily in Houston, TX.
Application information: Application form not required.
Officers and Directors:* George A. Peterkin, Jr.,* Pres.; Nancy G. Peterkin,* V.P. and Secy.; John T. Peterkin,* Treas.; Susan Peterkin Hey, Lynn Peterkin.
EIN: 311505617

51906
The Niland Foundation
(Formerly The ZBH Foundation)
c/o Nona F. Niland, M.D.
324 Eanes School Rd.
Austin, TX 78746

Established in 1998 in TX.
Donor(s): Nona F. Niland.
Financial data (yr. ended 05/31/00): Grants paid, $45,000; assets, $1,289,408 (M); gifts received, $3,421; expenditures, $84,040; qualifying distributions, $47,232.
Limitations: Applications not accepted. Giving primarily in Austin, TX.
Application information: Contributes only to pre-selected organizations.
Directors: Mary Elizabeth Niland, Nona F. Niland, P. Barry Niland.
EIN: 742881646

51907
Shelby Tengg Foundation for Heart and Cancer Research
c/o Bank of America
P.O. Box 831041
Dallas, TX 75283-1041

Established in 1998 in TX.
Donor(s): Shelby Rae Tengg.
Financial data (yr. ended 12/31/01): Grants paid, $45,000; assets, $828,826 (M); expenditures, $54,883; qualifying distributions, $45,000.
Limitations: Applications not accepted.
Application information: Contributes only to pre-selected organizations.
Trustee: Bank of America.
EIN: 311603107

51908
The Winston Family Foundation
7627 River Point Dr.
Houston, TX 77063

Established in 1997 in TX.
Donor(s): Barbara W. Winston, Blake W. Winston, Phillip W. Winston.
Financial data (yr. ended 12/31/00): Grants paid, $45,000; assets, $878,808 (M); expenditures, $56,151; qualifying distributions, $45,000.
Limitations: Applications not accepted.
Application information: Contributes only to pre-selected organizations.
Officers and Directors:* Barbara W. Winston,* Pres. and Treas.; Blake W. Winston,* V.P. and Secy.; Camille Hawkins, Rosalind W. Newton, Bert F. Winston III, David Winston, Phillip W. Winston.
EIN: 760555351

51909
Farison Fund for Engineering Education Trust
P.O. Box 831041
Dallas, TX 75283-1041

Established in 1999 in AR.
Financial data (yr. ended 04/30/02): Grants paid, $44,931; assets, $936,552 (M); expenditures, $57,057; qualifying distributions, $44,931.
Limitations: Applications not accepted. Giving primarily in Fayetteville, AR.
Application information: Contributes only to pre-selected organizations.
Trustee: Bank of America.
EIN: 527038659

51910
Cox & Smith Foundation
c/o Cox & Smith Incorporated, Exec. Dir.
112 E. Pecan St., Ste. 1800
San Antonio, TX 78205 (210) 554-5500

Established in 1989 in TX.
Donor(s): Cox & Smith Inc.
Financial data (yr. ended 12/31/01): Grants paid, $44,885; assets, $63,267 (M); gifts received, $52,000; expenditures, $44,885; qualifying distributions, $44,885.
Limitations: Giving primarily in San Antonio, TX.
Application information: Application form not required.
Officers: Dan G. Webster III, Pres.; Paul H. Smith, Secy.
EIN: 742524104
Codes: CS, CD

51911
Last Resort, Inc.
P.O. Box 142432
Austin, TX 78714-2432 (512) 386-5000
Contact: William B. Crouch, Jr., Pres.

Donor(s): William B. Crouch, Jr., Raymond Z. Tyx, Joe Zern.
Financial data (yr. ended 09/30/01): Grants paid, $44,844; assets, $68,598 (M); gifts received, $45,885; expenditures, $60,982; qualifying distributions, $60,966; giving activities include $15,502 for programs.
Limitations: Giving primarily in Austin, TX.
Officers and Directors:* William B. Crouch, Jr.,* Pres.; Dan Snyder,* V.P.; Michael Petty, Secy.; Joseph Zern,* Treas.; Alton Carter, Rick Hull, Gary Nauert, Al Simmons, Ray Tyx.
EIN: 742714534

51912
Antonio Gonzalez Sr. Charitable Trust Fund
4220 San Bernardo Ave.
Laredo, TX 78040

Established in 1999 in TX.
Donor(s): Aurora Gonzalez.‡
Financial data (yr. ended 12/31/01): Grants paid, $44,822; assets, $527,004 (M); gifts received, $2,338; expenditures, $51,302; qualifying distributions, $45,293.
Limitations: Applications not accepted.
Application information: Contributes only to pre-selected organizations.
Trustee: Roberto Gonzalez.
EIN: 912144204

51913
Ron and Ella Lee Lassiter Foundation
11115 Wickwood
Houston, TX 77024 (713) 827-3813
Contact: Ronald C. Lassiter, Chair.

Established in 1997 in TX.
Donor(s): Ronald C. Lassiter, Ella Lee Lassiter.
Financial data (yr. ended 12/31/01): Grants paid, $44,805; assets, $556,029 (M); expenditures, $60,905; qualifying distributions, $44,805.
Application information: Application form not required.
Officers and Directors:* Ronald C. Lassiter,* Chair. and Pres.; Ella Lee Lassiter,* Secy.; J. Philip Friesen, James M. Lassiter.
EIN: 760556328

51914
J. Frank Dobie Library Trust
JPMorgan Chase Bank
P.O. Box 550
Austin, TX 78789-0001
Application address: 302 N. Main, Victoria, TX 77901
Contact: James B. Stewart, Chair., Awards Comm.

Established in 1975 in TX.
Donor(s): Willie Belle Coker, J. Frank Dobie.
Financial data (yr. ended 11/30/01): Grants paid, $44,800; assets, $871,057 (M); expenditures, $60,886; qualifying distributions, $43,936.
Limitations: Giving limited to TX.
Application information: Only public libraries in Texas serving a population of 15,000 or less are eligible to apply.
Officer and Awards Committee Members:* James B. Stewart,* Chair.; Marty Taylor, Sarah Widener.
Trustee: JPMorgan Chase Bank.
EIN: 746245335

51915
Collins-Binkley Foundation, Inc.
3304 Tanglewood Trail
Fort Worth, TX 76109-2633

Established in 1980.
Donor(s): William W. Collins, Jr., Margaret B. Collins.
Financial data (yr. ended 12/31/01): Grants paid, $44,750; assets, $1,547,865 (M); gifts received, $350,537; expenditures, $47,496; qualifying distributions, $44,750.
Limitations: Applications not accepted. Giving limited to TX.
Application information: Contributes only to pre-selected organizations.
Officers and Trustees:* William W. Collins, Jr.,* Pres. and Treas.; Margaret B. Collins,* V.P. and Secy.; William W. Collins III, Ann Collins Florsheim.
EIN: 751740333

51916
SDMS Educational Foundation
c/o Donald F. Haydon
12770 Coit Rd., Ste. 708
Dallas, TX 75251 (972) 239-7367
URL: http://www.sdms.org/foundation/gems.asp

Established in 1989. Classified as a company-sponsored operating foundation.
Donor(s): Diasonics, Inc., Advanced Technology Labs, American Institute of Ultra Sound, Phillips Ultra Sound, Inc., Radiation Measurement, Inc., Society of Diagnostic Medical Sonographers, Acuson, Eastman Kodak Co., Siemens Corp., Sony Corp. of America, Toshiba Medical Systems, Bracco Diagnostics, Inc., DuPont Pharm. Medical Imaging.
Financial data (yr. ended 12/31/00): Grants paid, $44,700; assets, $551,707 (M); gifts received, $70,722; expenditures, $135,464; qualifying distributions, $101,666.
Application information: Applicant must include two letters of recommendation and essay on goals. Application form required.
Officers: Jean Lea Spitz, Pres.; Robert G. Magner, Jr., V.P.; Pamela Foy, Treas.; Dawn Sanchez, Exec. Dir.
Directors: Joan Baker, Philip Bendick, Carolyn Coffin.
EIN: 752262610
Codes: GTI

51917
McFadin Foundation
c/o Lee "Nick" McFadin, Jr.
1250 N.E. Loop 410, Ste. 400
San Antonio, TX 78209

Established in 1997 in TX.
Donor(s): Lee N. "Nick" McFadin, Jr.
Financial data (yr. ended 12/31/01): Grants paid, $44,650; assets, $1,136,607 (M); expenditures, $45,845; qualifying distributions, $44,650.
Officers: Lee N. "Nick" McFadin, Jr., Pres.; Terry McFadin, V.P.; Lee N. "Nick" McFadin III, Secy.-Treas.
EIN: 742834099

51918
The Earthman Foundation
2240 Chilton Rd.
Houston, TX 77019

Established in 1998 in TX.
Donor(s): Michael R. Earthman, Betsy W. Earthman.
Financial data (yr. ended 12/31/00): Grants paid, $44,600; assets, $840,065 (M); expenditures, $49,153; qualifying distributions, $44,600.

Limitations: Applications not accepted.
Application information: Contributes only to pre-selected organizations.
Officers and Directors:* Michael R. Earthman,* Pres. and Treas.; Betsy W. Earthman,* V.P. and Secy.; Emily W. Earthman, Micheal G. Earthman, Richard W. Earthman.
EIN: 311614070

51919
Merrymac-McKinley Foundation, Inc.
2311 Cedar Springs, Ste. 405
Dallas, TX 75201   (214) 922-9033
Contact: Mark C. McKinley, Dir.

Donor(s): John K. McKinley.
Financial data (yr. ended 12/31/01): Grants paid, $44,569; assets, $1,002,493 (M); expenditures, $49,375; qualifying distributions, $46,616.
Limitations: Giving on a national basis, with emphasis on AL.
Directors: Helen H. McKinley, John K. McKinley, Mark C. McKinley.
EIN: 742457886

51920
Lynn and Joel Brochstein Foundation, Inc.
(Formerly Brochstein Foundation)
11530 Main St.
Houston, TX 77025

Established in 1975 in TX.
Donor(s): Brochsteins, Inc., Architectural Woodwork Corp., Joel Brochstein, Lynn Brochstein.
Financial data (yr. ended 10/31/01): Grants paid, $44,532; assets, $912,276 (M); expenditures, $47,720; qualifying distributions, $44,532.
Limitations: Applications not accepted. Giving primarily in TX.
Application information: Contributes only to pre-selected organizations.
Trustees: Joel Brochstein, Lynn Brochstein.
EIN: 746039346
Codes: CS, CD

51921
The Judith and Henry Sauer Charitable Foundation
Henry A. Sauer, Jr.
503 Westminster
Houston, TX 77024   (713) 467-1237
Contact: Judy Sauer, Pres.

Established in 1994 in TX.
Donor(s): Judy Sauer.
Financial data (yr. ended 12/31/01): Grants paid, $44,500; assets, $641,505 (M); expenditures, $48,851; qualifying distributions, $44,500.
Limitations: Giving limited to Houston, TX.
Officers and Directors:* Judy Sauer,* Pres.; Henry Sauer,* Secy.-Treas.; Elizabeth C. Sauer, Ellen Sauer, Henry Sauer III.
EIN: 760425579

51922
Stan & Suzanne St. Pierre Foundation
11 Treasure Cove
The Woodlands, TX 77381

Established in 1998 in TX.
Financial data (yr. ended 12/31/01): Grants paid, $44,236; assets, $873,146 (M); expenditures, $47,965; qualifying distributions, $44,236.
Officers: Stan St. Pierre, Pres. and Treas.; Suzanne St. Pierre, V.P. and Secy.
Director: Julie St. Pierre.
EIN: 760575422

51923
James & Dorothy Doss Foundation, Inc.
P.O. Box 388
Weatherford, TX 76086-0388

Established in 1972 in TX.
Donor(s): James Doss.
Financial data (yr. ended 12/31/01): Grants paid, $44,203; assets, $1,535,446 (M); gifts received, $229,905; expenditures, $58,219; qualifying distributions, $44,203.
Limitations: Applications not accepted. Giving primarily in TX.
Application information: Contributes only to pre-selected organizations.
Officers: Dorothy Doss, Pres.; Nancy Knight, Secy.-Treas.
EIN: 756170120

51924
Pierce Runnells Foundation
3900 Essex, Ste. 1100
Houston, TX 77027   (713) 627-2390
Contact: Pierce Runnells, Pres.

Established in 1996 in TX.
Donor(s): Pierce Runnells.
Financial data (yr. ended 12/31/01): Grants paid, $44,000; assets, $1,110,167 (M); gifts received, $40,050; expenditures, $59,005; qualifying distributions, $44,000.
Limitations: Giving primarily in TX.
Officers and Directors:* Pierce Runnells,* Pres. and Treas.; Colin Phillips,* V.P.; Kate Thompson,* Secy.; Clive Runnells, Nancy M. Runnells.
EIN: 760512606

51925
David and Betty Sacks Foundation Trust
c/o Bank of America
P.O. Box 831041
Dallas, TX 75283-1041
Application address: P.O. Box 121, San Antonio, TX 78291-0121, tel.: (210) 270-5371
Contact: Gregg Muenster, Trust Off., Bank of America

Established in 1999 in TX.
Donor(s): David R. Sacks.‡
Financial data (yr. ended 12/31/01): Grants paid, $44,000; assets, $814,231 (M); expenditures, $54,965; qualifying distributions, $44,000.
Limitations: Giving primarily in TX.
Application information: Application form required.
Trustee: Bank of America.
EIN: 746417564

51926
Nina Astin Winkler Charitable Trust
c/o Wells Fargo Bank, N.A.
P.O. Drawer 913
Bryan, TX 77805   (979) 776-5402

Established in 1992.
Financial data (yr. ended 03/31/00): Grants paid, $44,000; assets, $1,498,670 (M); expenditures, $64,512; qualifying distributions, $50,307.
Limitations: Giving primarily in Bryan, TX.
Application information: Application form not required.
Trustee: Wells Fargo Bank, N.A.
EIN: 746265322

51927
The WWJD Foundation
12770 Merit Dr., Ste. 400
Dallas, TX 75251

Established in 1997 in TX.
Donor(s): R. Thomas Miller.

Financial data (yr. ended 12/31/01): Grants paid, $44,000; assets, $1,017,198 (M); gifts received, $25,000; expenditures, $46,628; qualifying distributions, $44,000.
Limitations: Applications not accepted.
Application information: Contributes only to pre-selected organizations.
Trustees: J.D. Jones II, Melissa Miller Jones, Mable S. Miller, Monika Elaine Miller, R. Thomas Miller.
EIN: 752739093

51928
Yowell Family Foundation
P.O. Box 2330
Harker Heights, TX 76548

Established in 1998 in TX.
Donor(s): Sheryl L. Anderson, Mike Helm, Deborah Yowell Farley, William H. Yowell, Johnnie L. Yowell.
Financial data (yr. ended 12/31/00): Grants paid, $43,950; assets, $165,586 (M); gifts received, $21,000; expenditures, $44,733; qualifying distributions, $43,950.
Limitations: Applications not accepted. Giving primarily in TX.
Application information: Contributes only to pre-selected organizations.
Directors: Sheryl L. Anderson, Deborah Yowell Farley, Johnnie L. Yowell, William H. Yowell.
EIN: 742877232

51929
Formosa Plastics Memorial Medical Center Trust
c/o First National Bank
P.O. Drawer 7
Port Lavaca, TX 77979
URL: http://www.fpcusa.com

Established in 1995 in TX.
Donor(s): Formosa Plastics Corp., Texas.
Financial data (yr. ended 12/31/01): Grants paid, $43,721; assets, $545,943 (M); expenditures, $46,814; qualifying distributions, $43,721.
Limitations: Applications not accepted. Giving limited to Fort Lavaca, TX.
Application information: Contributes only to pre-selected organizations.
Trustees: William H. Bauer, Jr., Jack Wu, First National Bank.
EIN: 746432975
Codes: CS, CD

51930
The Swaim-Gause-Rucker Foundation
(Formerly Swaim-Gause-Rucker Foundation of Mart, Texas)
c/o Wells Fargo Bank Texas, N.A.
P.O. Box 2626
Waco, TX 76702-2626   (254) 714-6160
Application address: c/o First Baptist Church, Mart, TX 76664
Contact: Rev. Tim Watson, Tr.

Established around 1979.
Financial data (yr. ended 12/31/00): Grants paid, $43,601; assets, $1,302,210 (M); gifts received, $800; expenditures, $59,614; qualifying distributions, $51,092; giving activities include $51,092 for programs.
Limitations: Giving limited to Mart, TX.
Trustees: Herman Duhr, Jr., Clyde Martin, Tommy Sanders, Paul Thronburg, Rev. Tim Watson, Wells Fargo Bank Texas, N.A.
EIN: 742054306

51931
The Kevin and Lesley Lilly Foundation
3424 Robinhood
Houston, TX 77005-2228
Application address: 600 Travis, Ste. 3700,
Houston, TX 77002
Contact: Kevin J. Lilly, Pres.

Established in 1996 in TX.
Donor(s): Kevin J. Lilly.
Financial data (yr. ended 07/31/01): Grants paid, $43,579; assets, $380,003 (M); gifts received, $96,075; expenditures, $54,111; qualifying distributions, $43,579.
Limitations: Giving primarily in TX.
Officers and Directors:* Kevin J. Lilly,* Pres. and Treas.; Lesley K. Lilly,* V.P. and Secy.; Joseph W. Thomson.
EIN: 311518662

51932
N. D. & Mary Redmon Foundation, Inc.
P.O. Box 88
Tulia, TX 79088-0088 (806) 995-3528
Contact: George J. Jennings, Jr., Dir.

Financial data (yr. ended 12/31/01): Grants paid, $43,500; assets, $931,699 (M); expenditures, $55,447; qualifying distributions, $43,500.
Limitations: Giving primarily in the Swisher County, TX, area.
Application information: Application form required.
Directors: Kenneth B. Godwin, George J. Jennings, Jr.
EIN: 751333002

51933
Dallas Cotton Exchange Trust
c/o JPMorgan Chase Bank
P.O. Box 660197
Dallas, TX 75266-0197

Financial data (yr. ended 12/31/00): Grants paid, $43,350; assets, $162,029 (M); expenditures, $51,756; qualifying distributions, $44,880.
Limitations: Applications not accepted. Giving primarily in TX.
Trustees: Eduardo Esteve, Joe Ferguson, Heinz Mollsen, JPMorgan Chase Bank.
EIN: 756009995

51934
Alford H. Hermann Family Foundation, Inc.
267 Alamo Country Club
318 Diana Dr.
Alamo, TX 78516

Donor(s): Nancy S. Hermann.
Financial data (yr. ended 12/31/01): Grants paid, $43,250; assets, $1,085,481 (M); expenditures, $52,137; qualifying distributions, $42,489.
Limitations: Applications not accepted. Giving primarily in TX and WI.
Application information: Contributes only to pre-selected organizations.
Officers: Nancy S. Hermann, Pres.; Kurt C. Hermann, V.P.; Rosemarie Davis, Secy.; Roger A. Hermann, Treas.
Director: John R. Poirier.
EIN: 391950647

51935
Harl & Evelyn Mansur Foundation
P.O. Box 8106
Wichita Falls, TX 76307-8106 (940) 767-2778
Contact: Harl D. Mansur Jr., Treas.

Donor(s): Evelyn L. Mansur, Harl D. Mansur, Jr.
Financial data (yr. ended 12/31/01): Grants paid, $43,130; assets, $562,930 (M); expenditures, $49,493; qualifying distributions, $43,130.
Limitations: Giving primarily in TX.
Officers: Evelyn L. Mansur, Pres.; Cline L. Mansur, V.P.; Harl D. Mansur, Jr., Treas.
EIN: 756085383

51936
A. I. and Manet Schepps Foundation, Inc.
(Formerly Schepps Charitable Foundation, Inc.)
4608 Valerie St.
Bellaire, TX 77401 (713) 667-6649
Contact: A.I. Schepps, Pres.

Established in 1962 in TX.
Donor(s): A.I. Schepps.
Financial data (yr. ended 12/31/01): Grants paid, $43,114; assets, $2,843,615 (M); gifts received, $1,179; expenditures, $58,321; qualifying distributions, $50,718.
Limitations: Applications not accepted. Giving primarily in Houston, TX.
Application information: Contributes only to pre-selected organizations.
Officers: A.I. Schepps, Pres.; Nancy Brand, Secy.; Manet Schepps, Treas.
Director: Gilda Sprung.
EIN: 746050262

51937
The Henley Foundation
49 Briar Hollow, No. 1902
Houston, TX 77027 (713) 743-4326
Contact: Ernest J. Henley, Pres.

Established in 1998.
Donor(s): Ernest J. Henley.
Financial data (yr. ended 12/31/00): Grants paid, $43,029; assets, $191,265 (M); expenditures, $47,978; qualifying distributions, $42,915.
Officers: Ernest J. Henley, Pres.; Barbara M. Henley, V.P.
Trustees: Allan M. Henley, Davis C. Henley.
EIN: 760587893

51938
Peggy and Bill Shiffick Charitable Foundation
3614 Montrose Blvd., Ste. 505
Houston, TX 77006 (713) 688-1635
Contact: William Shiffick, Tr.

Established in 1996 in TX.
Donor(s): Margaret Shiffick, William Shiffick.
Financial data (yr. ended 12/31/01): Grants paid, $43,000; assets, $126,389 (M); gifts received, $50,000; expenditures, $44,660; qualifying distributions, $43,000.
Limitations: Giving limited to TX.
Application information: Application form not required.
Trustees: Christine Herrforth Groccia, Margaret Herrforth Shiffick, William Shiffick.
EIN: 766112561

51939
Hazel & Henry S. Grace Foundation
3705 Maplewood Ave.
Wichita Falls, TX 76308-2129
Contact: Kenneth C. Armstrong, Secy.-Treas.

Donor(s): Hazel H. Grace.
Financial data (yr. ended 09/30/01): Grants paid, $42,850; assets, $779,550 (M); expenditures, $57,756; qualifying distributions, $42,850.
Limitations: Giving limited to Wichita Falls, TX.
Officers: Carla Edwards, Pres.; Kenneth C. Armstrong, Secy.-Treas.
EIN: 751762642

51940
Raymond & Susan Brochstein Foundation
11530 Main St.
Houston, TX 77025

Donor(s): Raymond Brochstein, Susan Brochstein.
Financial data (yr. ended 11/30/01): Grants paid, $42,760; assets, $3,120,256 (M); expenditures, $47,804; qualifying distributions, $43,055.
Limitations: Applications not accepted. Giving limited to Houston, TX.
Application information: Contributes only to pre-selected organizations.
Trustees: Raymond Brochstein, Susan Brochstein.
EIN: 760039176

51941
His Right Hand Foundation
301 Commerce St., Ste. 1600
Fort Worth, TX 76102 (817) 332-1600
Contact: Beth Brewer

Established in 1997 in TX.
Donor(s): Scott M. Kleberg.
Financial data (yr. ended 12/31/00): Grants paid, $42,711; assets, $336,286 (M); gifts received, $4,000; expenditures, $42,868; qualifying distributions, $42,724.
Officers and Trustee:* Scott M. Kleberg, Pres.; Julie M. Kleberg, V.P.; Edward E. Hartline,* Secy.
EIN: 760542713

51942
Henry & Elizabeth Donaghey Foundation
c/o Bank of Texas Trust Co.
P.O. Box 1088
Sherman, TX 75091-1088

Established in 1984 in TX.
Donor(s): Elizabeth Donaghey.‡
Financial data (yr. ended 12/31/01): Grants paid, $42,603; assets, $560,061 (M); expenditures, $49,709; qualifying distributions, $43,563.
Limitations: Giving limited to TX.
Application information: Application form required.
Trustee: Bank of Texas Trust Co.
EIN: 751937116
Codes: GTI

51943
Arnold Foundation
c/o Jim Arnold, Jr.
406 Sterzing St.
Austin, TX 78704

Donor(s): Jim Arnold, Jr., Patrice J. Arnold, Jessamine J. Arnold.
Financial data (yr. ended 12/31/99): Grants paid, $42,575; assets, $1,365,971 (M); gifts received, $800,000; expenditures, $43,165; qualifying distributions, $42,043.
Limitations: Applications not accepted. Giving limited to Austin, TX.
Application information: Contributes only to pre-selected organizations.
Officers and Directors:* Jim Arnold, Jr.,* Pres.; Patrice J. Arnold,* V.P. and Secy.-Treas.
EIN: 742295878

51944
David B. Hendricks II Foundation
31626 Huffsmith-Dobbin Rd.
Magnolia, TX 77354

Established in 1999.
Financial data (yr. ended 12/31/01): Grants paid, $42,500; assets, $778,922 (M); expenditures, $45,410; qualifying distributions, $42,500.
Officer: David B. Hendricks, Pres.
EIN: 760619640

51945
The Wayne Family Foundation
2801 Turtle Creek Blvd., No. 5E
Dallas, TX 75219 (214) 520-7709
Contact: Sue Wayne, Pres.

Established in 1999 in TX.
Financial data (yr. ended 12/31/01): Grants paid, $42,500; assets, $1,206,389 (M); expenditures, $63,224; qualifying distributions, $42,500.
Limitations: Giving primarily in Dallas, TX.
Publications: Grants list, newsletter.
Officers: Susan Wayne, Pres.; Marcy Grace Rippel, V.P.; Jonathan Wayne, V.P.; Ernestine Wayne, Treas.
EIN: 752792518

51946
Sue and Chuck Farmer Foundation
14 Serena
San Antonio, TX 78248-2440

Established in 1993 in TX.
Financial data (yr. ended 12/31/01): Grants paid, $42,450; assets, $41,671 (M); expenditures, $72,832; qualifying distributions, $56,367.
Limitations: Applications not accepted. Giving primarily in TX.
Officers: Earle Munns, Pres.; David Plemons, Secy.-Treas.
EIN: 752500937
Codes: GTI

51947
Helen Freeborn Kerr Charitable Foundation
c/o Bank of America, Trust Div.
P.O. Box 831041
San Antonio, TX 78283-1041
Application address: P.O. Box 121, San Antonio, TX 78291, tel.: (210) 270-5378
Contact: Gregg Muenster, Trust Off., Bank of America

Established in 1992 in TX.
Donor(s): Helen Freeborn Kerr.‡
Financial data (yr. ended 12/31/01): Grants paid, $42,441; assets, $1,389,380 (M); expenditures, $58,002; qualifying distributions, $45,250.
Limitations: Giving primarily in TX.
Application information: Application form required.
Trustee: Bank of America.
EIN: 742670337

51948
William Jesse Godwin Foundation
P.O. Box 739
Whitesboro, TX 76273
Contact: Gene Bryan, Pres.

Established in 1963.
Donor(s): Godwin Foundation Trusts.
Financial data (yr. ended 12/31/01): Grants paid, $42,439; assets, $0 (M); gifts received, $59,179; expenditures, $52,090; qualifying distributions, $42,439.
Limitations: Giving limited to Grayson County, TX.
Application information: For scholarship assistance, send a letter including tuition cost, room and board fees, major field of study, and student's future plans. Application form required.
Officers and Trustees:* Gene Bryan, Pres.; Cary Bryan,* V.P.; Bonnie Patterson, Secy.; Ricky Patterson, Ralph A. Porter, Ronald Raney.
EIN: 756036128
Codes: GTI

51949
S. T. & Margaret D. Harris Foundation
3428 St. Johns Dr.
Dallas, TX 75205-2906

Established in 1961 in TX.
Donor(s): S.T. Harris, Margaret D. Harris.
Financial data (yr. ended 10/31/01): Grants paid, $42,375; assets, $864,525 (M); expenditures, $45,011; qualifying distributions, $42,375.
Limitations: Applications not accepted. Giving primarily in Dallas, TX.
Application information: Contributes only to pre-selected organizations.
Officers and Directors:* S.T. Harris,* Pres.; Hallie Harris,* Secy.; Richard E. Harns, Pamela Harris McCoy.
EIN: 237118609

51950
Gray-Pampa Foundation, Inc.
412 Combs-Worley Bldg.
Pampa, TX 79065
Application address: 401 Combs-Worley Bldg., Pampa, TX 79065, tel.: (806) 669-3191
Contact: Wesley Green, Chair.

Established in 1954.
Financial data (yr. ended 12/31/01): Grants paid, $42,150; assets, $1,750,459 (M); gifts received, $2,049; expenditures, $45,929; qualifying distributions, $42,150.
Limitations: Giving limited to the Panhandle of TX, with emphasis on Gray and Pampa counties.
Officer and Trustees:* Wesley Green,* Chair.; Kenneth W. Fields, Bill W. Waters, Floyd Watson.
EIN: 756021715

51951
The Beall Foundation
5300 Miramar Ln.
Colleyville, TX 76034

Established in 2000 in TX.
Financial data (yr. ended 12/31/01): Grants paid, $42,063; assets, $439,130 (M); gifts received, $4,320; expenditures, $43,056; qualifying distributions, $42,063.
Limitations: Giving primarily in OK.
Directors: Fallis A. Beall, Robert S. Beall, Shelley A. Beall.
EIN: 752850868

51952
Florence S. Ducey Charitable Trust
c/o JPMorgan Chase Bank
P.O. Box 2558
Houston, TX 77252-2558

Established in 1965.
Financial data (yr. ended 09/30/01): Grants paid, $42,000; assets, $699,061 (M); expenditures, $54,863; qualifying distributions, $41,932.
Limitations: Applications not accepted. Giving primarily in Houston, TX.
Application information: Contributes only to pre-selected organizations.
Trustee: JPMorgan Chase Bank.
EIN: 746071454

51953
The Howard Hallam Family Foundation
1805 Record Crossing
Dallas, TX 75235-6200 (214) 634-1500
Contact: Howard Hallam, Pres.

Established in 1993 in TX.
Donor(s): Howard Hallam.
Financial data (yr. ended 12/31/01): Grants paid, $41,800; assets, $517,407 (M); expenditures, $45,751; qualifying distributions, $41,800.
Limitations: Giving primarily in Dallas, TX.
Officers: Howard Hallam, Pres.; Fanchon Hallam, V.P.; Rhonda Harden, Secy.-Treas.
EIN: 752448134

51954
Tecumseh Foundation
(Formerly William Watt Matthews Foundation)
2701 Scenic Dr.
Austin, TX 78703-1038 (512) 474-9974
Contact: Terry Matthews, Pres.

Established in 1997 in TX.
Donor(s): Julia Jones Matthews, James A. Matthews, John J. Matthews.
Financial data (yr. ended 12/31/01): Grants paid, $41,800; assets, $794,388 (M); gifts received, $16,061; expenditures, $47,162; qualifying distributions, $41,800.
Limitations: Giving primarily in TX, with emphasis on Austin.
Officers and Directors:* Terry Matthews,* Pres.; John J. Matthews,* V.P.; James A. Matthews, Jr.,* Secy.; John A. Matthews, Jr.,* Treas.; Kade L. Matthews.
EIN: 742807652

51955
Foundation of First Fruits
c/o Stephen J. Vancura
3302 Walnut Cir.
Harker Heights, TX 76548

Established in 1997 in TX.
Donor(s): Lydia A. Vancura, Stephen J. Vancura.
Financial data (yr. ended 12/31/01): Grants paid, $41,715; assets, $7,687 (M); gifts received, $48,500; expenditures, $43,015; qualifying distributions, $41,715.
Limitations: Applications not accepted. Giving primarily in TX.
Application information: Contributes only to pre-selected organizations.
Officers and Directors:* Stephen J. Vancura,* Pres.; Lydia A. Vancura,* Secy.; Carolyn Rhew.
EIN: 742797454

51956
Robert Allen Mann Foundation
P.O. Box 8436
Waco, TX 76714-8436 (254) 757-2424
Contact: Robert A. Mann, Chair.

Established in 1976.
Donor(s): Robert A. Mann.
Financial data (yr. ended 12/31/01): Grants paid, $41,666; assets, $61,400 (M); gifts received, $16,000; expenditures, $42,281; qualifying distributions, $41,572.
Limitations: Applications not accepted. Giving primarily in Waco, TX.
Application information: Contributes only to pre-selected organizations.
Officers: Robert A. Mann, Chair. and Pres.; David W. Mann, V.P.; Annie Laurie Miller, Secy.-Treas.
EIN: 741885309

51957
Herbert Blair Irrevocable Trust
P.O. Box 831041
Dallas, TX 75283-1041

Established in 1999 in AR.
Financial data (yr. ended 12/31/01): Grants paid, $41,570; assets, $1,195,573 (M); expenditures, $56,791; qualifying distributions, $41,570.
Limitations: Applications not accepted. Giving primarily in AR.
Application information: Contributes only to pre-selected organizations.
Trustee: Bank of America.

EIN: 716174983

51958
M. E. Hart Foundation
P.O. Box 50076
Austin, TX 78763-0076

Established in 1989 in TX.
Financial data (yr. ended 12/31/00): Grants paid, $41,500; assets, $2,370,074 (M); gifts received, $176,272; expenditures, $65,839; qualifying distributions, $60,617.
Limitations: Applications not accepted. Giving primarily in CT, NY, and TX; some giving also in Canada.
Application information: Contributes only to pre-selected organizations.
Officers: Sally H. Sheehy, Pres.; Mark B. Schreiber, Secy.; Ronald G. Mueller, Treas.
EIN: 742509577

51959
Reflections Foundation
6109 FM 390 N.
Brenham, TX 77833

Donor(s): Felix Covington, Joyce Covington.
Financial data (yr. ended 11/30/01): Grants paid, $41,496; assets, $3,214,525 (M); gifts received, $2,464,190; expenditures, $51,009; qualifying distributions, $41,496.
Limitations: Applications not accepted. Giving primarily in TX and VA.
Application information: Contributes only to pre-selected organizations.
Manager: Felix W. Covington.
EIN: 742859519

51960
Vetter Foundation
5333 Walnut Hill Ln.
Dallas, TX 75229-6620 (214) 368-5680
Contact: Edward O. Vetter, Tr.

Donor(s): Edward O. Vetter.
Financial data (yr. ended 12/31/01): Grants paid, $41,467; assets, $1,041,202 (M); gifts received, $76,125; expenditures, $48,818; qualifying distributions, $41,940.
Limitations: Giving primarily in the Dallas, TX, area.
Trustees: Edward O. Vetter, Sally Vetter.
EIN: 756038164

51961
Bill & Katie Weaver Charitable Trust
1845 Woodall Rogers Fwy., Ste. 1275
Dallas, TX 75201
Contact: William R. Weaver, M.D., Tr.

Donor(s): William R. Weaver.
Financial data (yr. ended 11/30/01): Grants paid, $41,443; assets, $1,049,799 (M); expenditures, $60,784; qualifying distributions, $41,443.
Limitations: Giving primarily in Dallas, TX.
Publications: Application guidelines.
Application information: Application form not required.
Trustees: Katie M. Weaver, William R. Weaver, M.D.
EIN: 752001841

51962
Kinzie Scholarship Foundation
P.O. Box 37
Lindale, TX 75771-0037

Donor(s): Earl C. Kinzie.
Financial data (yr. ended 12/31/01): Grants paid, $41,367; assets, $911,080 (M); gifts received, $3,711; expenditures, $42,756; qualifying distributions, $41,367.
Limitations: Applications not accepted. Giving limited to McPherson, KS, and TX.
Application information: Contributes only to pre-selected organizations.
Trustee: Earl C. Kinzie.
EIN: 237058959

51963
The Gayle H. & Peter Bickers Foundation
3814 Doris Dr.
Amarillo, TX 79109

Established in 1998.
Donor(s): Peter Bickers, Gayle Bickers.
Financial data (yr. ended 12/31/01): Grants paid, $41,305; assets, $208,182 (M); gifts received, $129,391; expenditures, $46,891; qualifying distributions, $41,305.
Officers and Directors:* Gayle Bickers,* Pres.; Peter Bickers,* V.P. and Secy.-Treas.; Margaret A. Bickers.
EIN: 752788931

51964
The Thomas C. & Carolyn W. Walker Family Foundation
3510 Turtle Creek Blvd., Ste. 10-A
Dallas, TX 75219 (214) 953-7552
Contact: Thomas C. Walker, Chair.; or Carolyn W. Walker, Dir.

Donor(s): Carolyn W. Walker, Thomas C. Walker.
Financial data (yr. ended 12/31/01): Grants paid, $41,000; assets, $377,399 (M); gifts received, $205,100; expenditures, $57,678; qualifying distributions, $41,000.
Limitations: Giving on a national basis, with emphasis on Dallas, TX.
Officer: Thomas C. Walker, Chair.
Directors: James B. Harrell, Carolyn W. Walker.
EIN: 311501965

51965
Clampitt Foundation
c/o Foundation Mgr.
9207 Ambassador Row
Dallas, TX 75247-4695 (214) 638-3300

Established in 1964.
Donor(s): Maxwell A. Clampitt.
Financial data (yr. ended 12/31/01): Grants paid, $40,925; assets, $1,234,416 (M); expenditures, $41,735; qualifying distributions, $40,925.
Limitations: Giving primarily in Dallas, TX.
Officers and Director:* Maxwell A. Clampitt,* Pres.; Richard Clampitt, V.P.; Don Gay, Secy.; Don Clampitt, Treas.
EIN: 756034280

51966
Coker Foundation
1701 Hermann Dr., Unit 504
Houston, TX 77004-7346
Contact: Newton J. Coker, Tr.

Established in 1998 in TX.
Financial data (yr. ended 06/30/02): Grants paid, $40,920; assets, $1,078,373 (M); expenditures, $55,621; qualifying distributions, $40,920.
Limitations: Giving primarily in GA, with emphasis on Canton and Houston, TX.
Trustees: Esther G. Coker, Josephine R. Coker, Melba G. Coker, Newton J. Coker, Reagan R. Coker, Walter G. Coker.
EIN: 311621660

51967
Earnest & Beth Gammage Charitable Foundation
5555 Del Monte, Ste. 705
Houston, TX 77056-4117

Donor(s): T. Earnest Gammage, T. Earnest Gammage, Jr.
Financial data (yr. ended 03/31/01): Grants paid, $40,914; assets, $1 (M); expenditures, $40,914; qualifying distributions, $40,914.
Limitations: Applications not accepted. Giving primarily in KY and TX.
Application information: Contributes only to pre-selected organizations.
Trustees: Beth M. Gammage, T. Earnest Gammage, Jr.
EIN: 237000769

51968
The Stanton Foundation
10000 Memorial, Ste. 310
Houston, TX 77024-3420

Established in 1986 in TX.
Financial data (yr. ended 12/31/01): Grants paid, $40,850; assets, $360,435 (M); gifts received, $50,000; expenditures, $49,961; qualifying distributions, $40,850.
Limitations: Applications not accepted. Giving primarily in Houston, TX.
Application information: Contributes only to pre-selected organizations.
Officers: R. John Stanton, Jr., Pres.; Katherine W. Stanton, V.P.; S. Stuart Hellman, Secy.-Treas.
EIN: 760208595

51969
Fired Up Foundation
3555 Ranch Rd.
Austin, TX 78734

Established in 1999.
Financial data (yr. ended 12/31/01): Grants paid, $40,759; assets, $12,345 (M); gifts received, $82,550; expenditures, $70,488; qualifying distributions, $40,759.
Officer: Sheri Strehle, V.P.
EIN: 742933083

51970
Pyle Memorial Trust
c/o First State Bank of Gainesville
P.O. Box 10
Gainesville, TX 76241

Established in 1994.
Financial data (yr. ended 12/31/99): Grants paid, $40,757; assets, $791,383 (M); expenditures, $49,643; qualifying distributions, $40,757.
Limitations: Applications not accepted. Giving primarily in TX.
Application information: Contributes only to pre-selected organizations.
Trustee: First State Bank of Gainesville.
EIN: 756463015

51971
Inez B. & H. E. McCarley Foundation Trust
Plz. 1, Box 1
Amarillo, TX 79105 (806) 378-8333
Contact: Jacque Branch, Trust Officer, Amarillo National Bank

Established in 1983 in TX.
Financial data (yr. ended 01/31/02): Grants paid, $40,725; assets, $743,287 (M); expenditures, $49,137; qualifying distributions, $42,658.
Limitations: Giving limited to Pampa, TX.
Advisory Council: Cliff Bickerstaff, Jacque Branch, Charles White, Randy White.

Trustee: Amarillo National Bank.
EIN: 756308044

51972
Don L. Holden Foundation, Inc.
1094 Southwoods Dr.
Fredericksburg, TX 78624 (830) 997-4489
Contact: Don L. Holden, Pres.

Donor(s): Don L. Holden.
Financial data (yr. ended 11/30/01): Grants paid, $40,682; assets, $821,881 (M); gifts received, $9,615; expenditures, $43,740; qualifying distributions, $40,682.
Limitations: Giving primarily in TX.
Officer: Don L. Holden, Pres.
Trustees: J.D. Davis, Jewell Holden.
EIN: 746048619

51973
A. Earl & Frances E. Ziegler Foundation
c/o A. Earl Ziegler
P.O. Box 25402
Dallas, TX 75225

Established in 1990 in TX.
Donor(s): A. Earl Ziegler, Frances E. Ziegler.
Financial data (yr. ended 12/31/01): Grants paid, $40,600; assets, $411,466 (M); expenditures, $41,553; qualifying distributions, $40,600.
Limitations: Applications not accepted. Giving primarily in Norman, OK.
Application information: Contributes only to pre-selected organizations.
Officers and Trustees:* A. Earl Ziegler,* Pres.; Frances E. Ziegler,* Secy.-Treas.; Margaret Gay Downing.
EIN: 752334594

51974
LDB Foundation
8122 Datapoint Dr., Ste. 900
San Antonio, TX 78229

Established in 1997 in TX.
Donor(s): Sam A. Brooks.
Financial data (yr. ended 12/31/01): Grants paid, $40,575; assets, $1,676,867 (M); gifts received, $1,160,263; expenditures, $66,898; qualifying distributions, $40,575.
Limitations: Applications not accepted.
Application information: Contributes only to pre-selected organizations.
Officers and Directors:* Linda D. Brooks,* Pres.; Sam A. Brooks,* V.P.; Thomas V. Lyles, Secy.; Charles A. Staffel, Treas.; Daniel A. Brooks, E. Ashley Brooks.
EIN: 742829433

51975
Coastal Bend Foundation, Inc.
140 W. Cleveland Blvd.
Aransas Pass, TX 78336-2766 (361) 758-7568
Contact: Tom Andrews, Exec. Dir.

Established in 1988 in TX.
Financial data (yr. ended 12/31/01): Grants paid, $40,500; assets, $2,188,974 (M); gifts received, $1,030; expenditures, $78,166; qualifying distributions, $56,980.
Limitations: Giving limited to within 15 miles of Aransas Pass, TX.
Application information: Application form required.
Officer: Tom Andrews, Exec. Dir.
Directors: Charles Benbow, Frank Hametner, Jan Pate, Wendell Roberts, Craig Smith.
EIN: 742129257

51976
The Nancy and Clive Runnells Foundation
3900 Essex Ln., Ste. 1100
Houston, TX 77027 (713) 627-2390
Contact: Clive Runnells, Pres.

Established in 2000 in TX.
Donor(s): Clive Runnells, Nancy Runnells.
Financial data (yr. ended 12/31/01): Grants paid, $40,310; assets, $202,987 (M); gifts received, $51,950; expenditures, $55,684; qualifying distributions, $40,310.
Officers and Directors:* Clive Runnells,* Pres.; Patty Young, Secy.; Nancy Runnells, Pierce Runnells.
EIN: 760608321

51977
Wacker Foundation
10848 Strait Ln.
Dallas, TX 75229 (214) 373-3308
Contact: John A. Wacker, Pres.

Established in 1975 in TX.
Donor(s): John A. Wacker, Lee Ida Wacker.
Financial data (yr. ended 06/30/00): Grants paid, $40,259; assets, $901,453 (M); gifts received, $53,676; expenditures, $60,375; qualifying distributions, $45,131.
Application information: Application form not required.
Officers and Directors:* John A. Wacker,* Pres.; Bernard Rimland, Ph.D.,* V.P.; Lee Ida Wacker,* Secy.-Treas.; Donald R. Davis, Ph.D., Robert Noble, M.D., Hugh D. Riordan, M.D.
EIN: 237412635
Codes: GTI

51978
Donnell Foundation
P.O. Box 5003
Wichita Falls, TX 76307-5003
Contact: Barry B. Donnell, Tr.

Donor(s): Sam Donnell, Barry B. Donnell.
Financial data (yr. ended 12/31/01): Grants paid, $40,252; assets, $1,064,833 (M); expenditures, $46,521; qualifying distributions, $40,252.
Limitations: Giving primarily in Wichita Falls, TX.
Trustees: Barry B. Donnell, Sam Donnell.
EIN: 756064428

51979
Friedman Family Foundation
14999 Preston Rd., No. D212-PMB314
Dallas, TX 75240

Established in 2000 in TX.
Donor(s): Lawrence J. Friedman, Janelle R. Friedman.
Financial data (yr. ended 12/31/01): Grants paid, $40,150; assets, $151,544 (M); expenditures, $40,150; qualifying distributions, $40,150.
Limitations: Applications not accepted.
Application information: Contributes only to pre-selected organizations.
Officer: Janelle R. Friedman, Pres. and Secy.-Treas.
Director: Lawrence J. Friedman.
EIN: 752910316

51980
Berry R. Cox Family Foundation
2200 Ross Ave., Ste. 3200
Dallas, TX 75201-2741

Established in 2000 in TX.
Donor(s): Berry R. Cox.
Financial data (yr. ended 12/31/01): Grants paid, $40,104; assets, $3,158,934 (M); gifts received, $1,004,000; expenditures, $127,657; qualifying distributions, $40,104.
Limitations: Applications not accepted.
Application information: Contributes only to pre-selected organizations.
Officers and Trustees:* Richard J. Gass,* Pres.; Todd Kesterton, Secy.-Treas.; Berry R. Cox, Jeanne T. Cox.
EIN: 752864400

51981
J. Y. Sanders Foundation
c/o Bank One, Louisiana
P.O. Box 2050
Fort Worth, TX 76113
Additional address: c/o Bank One, Louisiana, N.A., P.O. Box 91210, Baton Rouge, LA 70821

Established in 1983.
Financial data (yr. ended 12/31/99): Grants paid, $40,060; assets, $1,414,816 (M); expenditures, $48,332; qualifying distributions, $40,396.
Limitations: Giving primarily in LA.
Trustee: Bank One, Louisiana, N.A.
EIN: 726106652

51982
Andrews Family Foundation
1 Sugar Creek Center Blvd., Ste. 970
Sugar Land, TX 77478

Established in 2000 in TX.
Donor(s): A. Glynn Andrews, Laurie Andrews.
Financial data (yr. ended 12/31/01): Grants paid, $40,000; assets, $516,655 (M); expenditures, $56,826; qualifying distributions, $40,000.
Limitations: Applications not accepted.
Application information: Contributes only to pre-selected organizations.
Officers: A. Glynn Andrews, Pres.; Laurie Andrews, V.P.; Shawn Forshage, V.P.; Ginger Hanna, V.P.; Jay F. Rea, Treas.
EIN: 760664008

51983
Celia Berwin Memorial Foundation
6035 Forest Shadow
San Antonio, TX 78240-3355
Application address: HRC Box 10, Big Foot, TX 78005
Contact: Victor J. Sobrino, V.P.

Financial data (yr. ended 12/31/01): Grants paid, $40,000; assets, $759,439 (M); expenditures, $48,997; qualifying distributions, $41,952.
Limitations: Giving primarily in San Antonio, TX.
Officers and Trustees:* John Harris,* Pres.; Victor J. Sobrino,* V.P.; Susan Peters,* Secy.; Janie Mann,* Treas.; Dottie Sobrino.
EIN: 746074127

51984
The Mr. & Mrs. Joe W. Bratcher, Jr. Foundation
c/o H. David Hughes
1400 Franklin Plz., 111 Congress Ave.
Austin, TX 78701
Contact: Joe W. Bratcher, Jr., Pres.

Established in 1985 in TX.
Donor(s): Joe W. Bratcher, Jr., Mrs. Joe W. Bratcher, Jr.
Financial data (yr. ended 12/31/01): Grants paid, $40,000; assets, $222,514 (M); expenditures, $41,486; qualifying distributions, $41,118.
Limitations: Giving primarily in Austin, TX.
Officers: Joe W. Bratcher, Jr., Pres.; Rhobie K. Bratcher, Secy.
Director: Joe W. Bratcher III.
EIN: 742387803

51985
Bybee Foundation
c/o Robert W. Bybee
5550 Harvest Hill Rd., No. 269
Dallas, TX 75230

Established in 1989 in TX.
Financial data (yr. ended 12/31/01): Grants paid, $40,000; assets, $628,378 (M); expenditures, $43,459; qualifying distributions, $7,459.
Limitations: Applications not accepted. Giving primarily in TX.
Application information: Contributes only to pre-selected organizations.
Officer and Director:* Robert W. Bybee,* Pres. and Exec. Dir.
EIN: 760292426

51986
The John W. and Alida M. Considine Foundation
5100 San Felipe, Ste. 222E
Houston, TX 77056-3611

Established in 1994 in TX.
Donor(s): James F. Considine.
Financial data (yr. ended 12/31/01): Grants paid, $40,000; assets, $1,360,716 (M); expenditures, $75,943; qualifying distributions, $40,000.
Limitations: Applications not accepted. Giving primarily in TX.
Application information: Contributes only to pre-selected organizations.
Officers: James F. Considine, Pres. and Treas.; W. Clarke Gomley, V.P. and Secy.
Director: Lawrence A. Rubenstein.
EIN: 760453135

51987
Dehan Family Foundation
c/o Steve Dehan
3700 Winding Creek Dr.
Austin, TX 78735

Established in 1997 in TX.
Donor(s): Steve Dehan, Alison Dehan.
Financial data (yr. ended 12/31/00): Grants paid, $40,000; assets, $1,206,935 (M); gifts received, $402,162; expenditures, $42,854; qualifying distributions, $39,811.
Limitations: Applications not accepted. Giving primarily in TX.
Application information: Contributes only to pre-selected organizations.
Officers and Directors:* Stephen E. Dehan,* Pres. and Treas.; Alison Dehan,* V.P. and Secy.; Susan Dehan.
EIN: 742807323

51988
Kids, Inc. Foundation
c/o Amarillo National Bank
2201 S.E. 27th Ave.
Amarillo, TX 79103

Established in 1994 in TX.
Donor(s): Ronald A. Ingram.‡
Financial data (yr. ended 12/31/01): Grants paid, $40,000; assets, $501,568 (M); expenditures, $43,308; qualifying distributions, $40,000.
Limitations: Applications not accepted.
Application information: Contributes only to pre-selected organizations.
Officer: Bill Countiss, Pres.
Directors: Vanessa Buzzard, Michael David, Dave Taylor, Lewis N. Thomas.
EIN: 756252673

51989
Kohn-Hutter Trust Estate
c/o JPMorgan Chase Bank
P.O. Box 550, 700 Lavaca
Austin, TX 78789 (512) 472-5461
Application address: c/o Sonia Garza, Lutheran Campus Ministry University Center, 2100 San Antonio, Austin, TX 78705

Established in 1995 in TX.
Financial data (yr. ended 09/30/01): Grants paid, $40,000; assets, $827,077 (M); expenditures, $62,435; qualifying distributions, $49,519.
Limitations: Giving limited to Austin, TX.
Application information: Application form required.
Trustee: JPMorgan Chase Bank.
EIN: 746312816

51990
The Mills Dennis Family Foundation
P.O. Box 27967
Austin, TX 78755-7967

Donor(s): Bonnie K. Mills.
Financial data (yr. ended 12/31/01): Grants paid, $40,000; assets, $625,035 (M); gifts received, $26,202; expenditures, $57,554; qualifying distributions, $40,000.
Limitations: Applications not accepted.
Application information: Contributes only to pre-selected organizations.
Officers: Bonnie K. Mills, Pres. and Treas.; Spencer P. Dennis, V.P. and Secy.
EIN: 742877137

51991
NASA College Scholarship Fund, Inc.
NASA Johnson Space Ctr.
2101 NASA Rd. 1
Houston, TX 77058
Contact: Thomas Sullivan, Ph.D.

Established in 1982.
Donor(s): Kennedy Space Center Alumia League.
Financial data (yr. ended 12/31/00): Grants paid, $40,000; assets, $597,875 (M); gifts received, $21,906; expenditures, $43,072; qualifying distributions, $42,357.
Limitations: Giving on a national basis.
Officers: Teresa R. Sullivan, Pres. and Treas.; Scott Wood, V.P.; Candace Hunt, Secy.; Gail Hammond, Treas.
Directors: Nancy A. Abell, Edward A. Frankle, Gregory W. Hayes, Joseph S. Heyman, James R. Jaax, James M. Kennedy, Steven R. Nagel, Michael L. Richardson, Nancy G. Robertson.
EIN: 760039071
Codes: GTI

51992
The O'Dell Foundation
2345 Bering Dr., Ste. 412
Houston, TX 77057

Established in 1998 in TX.
Donor(s): John O'Dell, Holly O'Dell.
Financial data (yr. ended 11/30/00): Grants paid, $40,000; assets, $2,508 (M); gifts received, $201,532; expenditures, $42,849; qualifying distributions, $42,849.
Limitations: Applications not accepted. Giving primarily in Houston, TX.
Application information: Contributes only to pre-selected organizations.
Officers: John O'Dell, Pres.; Holly O'Dell, V.P. and Secy.
Directors: Catherine O'Dell, Monica O'Dell.
EIN: 760600930

51993
Turvey Family Foundation
371 Tynebridge Ln.
Houston, TX 77024-7427

Established in 1997 in TX.
Donor(s): Marie W. Turvey.
Financial data (yr. ended 12/31/00): Grants paid, $40,000; assets, $742,664 (M); expenditures, $51,443; qualifying distributions, $40,000.
Limitations: Applications not accepted.
Application information: Contributes only to pre-selected organizations.
Directors: Teresa E. Turvey Blesie, Anne M. Turvey, Christine E. Turvey, David E. Turvey, Harry D. Turvey, Marie W. Turvey, Sarah C. Turvey, Thomas P. Turvey.
EIN: 760536783

51994
The James A. "Bill" & L. Doris Williams Scholarship Foundation
c/o Bank of Houston
P.O. Box 8306
Houston, TX 77288-8306 (713) 529-4881
Contact: William P. Traylor, Tr.

Established in 1989 in TX.
Donor(s): L. Doris Williams.‡
Financial data (yr. ended 12/31/01): Grants paid, $40,000; assets, $1,043,386 (M); expenditures, $63,829; qualifying distributions, $40,000.
Limitations: Giving limited to TX.
Application information: Application form required.
Trustees: John G. Heard, William P. Traylor.
EIN: 760249241

51995
J.F. Charitable Endowment, Inc.
c/o Bank One, Texas, N.A.
3211 38th St.
Lubbock, TX 79413
Contact: Donna Griffis, Dir.

Established in 1988.
Financial data (yr. ended 09/30/01): Grants paid, $39,885; assets, $141,822 (M); expenditures, $42,775; qualifying distributions, $39,885.
Limitations: Giving limited to TX.
Directors: Dan Griffis, Donna Griffis, Michael Weiss.
Trustee: Bank One, Texas, N.A.
EIN: 752213977

51996
John L. Whitmire Foundation
10101 S.W. Freeway, Ste. 380
Houston, TX 77074

Established in 1999 in TX.
Donor(s): The Whitmire Foundation.
Financial data (yr. ended 12/31/01): Grants paid, $39,841; assets, $131,082 (M); expenditures, $43,289; qualifying distributions, $39,841.
Officers: John L. Whitmire, Pres.; Judy Morgan, V.P.; Marcella Jo Francis, Secy.-Treas.
Directors: Richard L. Whitmire, Ronald P. Whitmire.
EIN: 760595569

51997
The O'Neill Foundation
c/o Sean P. O'Neill
5114 Holly Terrace Dr.
Houston, TX 77056

Established in 1997 in TX.
Donor(s): Brian O'Neill, Kathryn O'Neill.
Financial data (yr. ended 12/31/01): Grants paid, $39,750; assets, $792,951 (M); gifts received,

$502,920; expenditures, $47,635; qualifying distributions, $39,750.
Limitations: Applications not accepted.
Application information: Contributes only to pre-selected organizations.
Officers: Brian E. O'Neill, Pres. and Treas.; Kathryn T. O'Neill, V.P. and Secy.; Sean Paul O'Neill, V.P.
EIN: 760517919

51998
Edward C. Raymund Charitable Foundation
1136 N. Cottonwood Dr.
Richardson, TX 75080-3762 (972) 644-3634
Contact: Patricia A. Raymund

Established in 1998 in TX.
Donor(s): Edward C. Raymund.
Financial data (yr. ended 12/31/01): Grants paid, $39,724; assets, $785,056 (M); expenditures, $45,017; qualifying distributions, $39,724.
Limitations: Giving primarily in CA.
Officer and Directors:* Patricia A. Raymund,* Pres.; Ruth Hemming, Robert Lund, Edward C. Raymund.
EIN: 752765658

51999
The Larry and Annette Sondock Foundation
5027 Heatherglen Dr.
Houston, TX 77096-4215

Established in 1985 in TX.
Donor(s): Annette Sondock, Larry Sondock.
Financial data (yr. ended 11/30/01): Grants paid, $39,505; assets, $265,548 (M); gifts received, $20,450; expenditures, $40,537; qualifying distributions, $39,505.
Limitations: Applications not accepted. Giving on a national basis.
Application information: Contributes only to pre-selected organizations.
Trustees: Annette Sondock, Larry Sondock.
EIN: 760170655

52000
Visible Changes Educational Foundation
1303 Campbell Rd.
Houston, TX 77055

Established in 1990.
Financial data (yr. ended 12/31/01): Grants paid, $39,477; assets, $485,523 (M); expenditures, $40,863; qualifying distributions, $39,477.
Limitations: Applications not accepted. Giving limited to residents of TX.
Application information: Unsolicited requests for funds not accepted.
Officer: John McCormack, Mgr.
EIN: 760303682
Codes: GTI

52001
Ella B. Thompson Trust
c/o Bank of America
P.O. Box 831041
Dallas, TX 75283-1041

Financial data (yr. ended 12/31/00): Grants paid, $39,200; assets, $776,097 (M); expenditures, $48,162; qualifying distributions, $42,041.
Limitations: Applications not accepted. Giving limited to residents of Galveston County, TX.
Trustee: Bank of America.
EIN: 746082981
Codes: GTI

52002
Barbara Bass Moroney Foundation, Inc.
4516 Wildwood
Dallas, TX 75209

Established in 1992 in OK.
Donor(s): Barbara Bass Moroney.
Financial data (yr. ended 12/31/01): Grants paid, $39,000; assets, $389,251 (M); gifts received, $25,000; expenditures, $39,826; qualifying distributions, $39,000.
Limitations: Applications not accepted.
Application information: Contributes only to pre-selected organizations.
Directors: Andrew S. Hartman, Barbara Bass Moroney, James M. Moroney III, Bonnie Bass Smith.
EIN: 731416208

52003
The Nowiczewski Foundation
22 Royal Dalton Cir.
Conroe, TX 77304

Established in 1998.
Donor(s): Joe Nowiczewski.
Financial data (yr. ended 03/31/02): Grants paid, $39,000; assets, $462,281 (M); gifts received, $52,530; expenditures, $41,005; qualifying distributions, $39,000.
Officers and Directors:* Joseph Nowiczewski,* Pres. and Treas.; Paula Nowiczewski,* Secy.; Joseph Paul Nowiczewski.
EIN: 760569596

52004
The Masel S. Quinn Foundation
c/o David H. Crockett
13802 Shavano Pt.
San Antonio, TX 78230-5832

Established in 2000 in TX.
Donor(s): Masel S. Quinn.
Financial data (yr. ended 12/31/01): Grants paid, $39,000; assets, $1,093,352 (M); gifts received, $745,000; expenditures, $83,957; qualifying distributions, $39,000.
Limitations: Applications not accepted. Giving primarily in TX.
Application information: Contributes only to pre-selected organizations.
Officers: David H. Crockett, Pres.; Thomas H. Crockett, V.P.; Robert T. Crockett, Secy.-Treas.
EIN: 742982707

52005
Carole and Gene Chambers Foundation
110 E. Sherwood Dr.
Alvin, TX 77511

Established in 1988 in TX.
Donor(s): Carole Barrett Chambers, Eugene Carroll Chambers.
Financial data (yr. ended 09/30/01): Grants paid, $38,925; assets, $864,093 (M); gifts received, $1,290; expenditures, $41,015; qualifying distributions, $38,925.
Limitations: Applications not accepted. Giving primarily in TX.
Application information: Contributes only to pre-selected organizations.
Officers: Carole Barrett Chambers, Pres. and Treas.; Eugene Carroll Chambers, V.P. and Secy.
EIN: 760262887

52006
The Grant Family Fund
1025 Bamar Ln.
Galveston, TX 77554-7166

Established in 1991 in TX.
Donor(s): J. Andrew Grant, Eleanor C. Grant.
Financial data (yr. ended 11/30/01): Grants paid, $38,827; assets, $923,618 (M); expenditures, $39,955; qualifying distributions, $38,830.
Limitations: Applications not accepted. Giving primarily in TX.
Application information: Contributes only to pre-selected organizations.
Officers: J. Andrew Grant, Pres.; Julian A. Grant, V.P.; Eleanor C. Grant, Secy.-Treas.
Directors: Brian A. Grant, Dean E. Grant.
EIN: 760355665

52007
Hixon Family Foundation
114 Rio Bravo
San Antonio, TX 78232

Established in 1998 in TX.
Financial data (yr. ended 12/31/00): Grants paid, $38,700; assets, $303,900 (M); gifts received, $155,000; expenditures, $40,230; qualifying distributions, $38,700.
Limitations: Applications not accepted.
Application information: Contributes only to pre-selected organizations.
Officers: Steve Hixon, Pres. and Treas.; Martha Hixon, V.P. and Secy.
Director: Jolene Bryant Davis.
EIN: 742882611

52008
Friedman-Grossman Family Foundation
2002 Sunset Blvd.
Houston, TX 77005-1651
Contact: Ellin Friedman Grossman, Pres.

Established in 1995 in TX.
Donor(s): Bassami R. Friedman.‡
Financial data (yr. ended 12/31/01): Grants paid, $38,666; assets, $376,275 (M); expenditures, $44,885; qualifying distributions, $38,666.
Officers and Trustees:* Ellin Friedman Grossman,* Pres. and Treas.; Robert G. Grossman,* V.P. and Secy.; Jennifer Grossman Albert.
EIN: 760518834

52009
James T. and Claudette M. Rodgers Foundation
c/o James T. Rodgers, III
11902 Knobcrest Dr.
Houston, TX 77070-2410

Established in 1990 in TX.
Donor(s): Claudette M. Rodgers, James T. Rodgers.
Financial data (yr. ended 12/31/01): Grants paid, $38,620; assets, $619,224 (M); expenditures, $39,481; qualifying distributions, $38,620.
Limitations: Applications not accepted. Giving primarily in Houston, TX.
Application information: Contributes only to pre-selected organizations.
Officer and Directors:* James T. Rodgers III,* Pres.; Claudette M. Rodgers, James T. Rodgers IV.
EIN: 760331607

52010
Craig and Kathryn Hall Foundation
(Formerly Hall Foundation for Individual Opportunity)
6801 Gaylord Pkwy., Ste. 100
Frisco, TX 75034

Established in 1979 in MI and TX.
Donor(s): Craig Hall.
Financial data (yr. ended 08/31/01): Grants paid, $38,538; assets, $198,714 (M); gifts received, $91,563; expenditures, $38,639; qualifying distributions, $38,639.
Limitations: Giving primarily in Dallas, TX.

52010—TEXAS

Directors: Donald L. Braun, Craig Hall.
EIN: 382275211

52011
The Langford Family Foundation
2716 Barton Creek Blvd., No. 1923
Austin, TX 78735

Established around 1995.
Donor(s): John J. Langford, Judith A. Langford.
Financial data (yr. ended 12/31/01): Grants paid, $38,500; assets, $0 (M); gifts received, $791; expenditures, $39,181; qualifying distributions, $38,500.
Limitations: Applications not accepted. Giving primarily in Pittsburg, KS, and Austin, TX.
Application information: Contributes only to pre-selected organizations.
Officer and Directors:* John J. Langford,* Pres. and Treas.; Brad Langford, Lisa A. Pepin.
EIN: 742729726

52012
The Meyer Foundation, Inc.
10915 Walwick
Houston, TX 77024-7627
Application address: 5402 Chevy Chase, Houston, TX 77024, tel.: (713) 668-2369
Contact: Joseph F. Meyer, IV, Secy.

Established in 1999 in TX.
Donor(s): Joseph F. Meyer III, Rosemary Meyer.
Financial data (yr. ended 12/31/01): Grants paid, $38,500; assets, $1,298,064 (M); gifts received, $146,611; expenditures, $64,596; qualifying distributions, $38,500.
Officers: Rosemary Meyer, Pres.; Lucy Mitchell, V.P.; Joseph F. Meyer IV, Secy.; Joseph F. Meyer III, Treas.
Trustees: C. Fred Meyer, Ken B. Meyer.
EIN: 760613316

52013
J. F. Seinsheimer, Jr. Charitable Foundation
2115 Winnie St.
Galveston, TX 77550

Established in 1998 in TX.
Donor(s): J.F. Seinsheimer III.
Financial data (yr. ended 06/30/02): Grants paid, $38,500; assets, $617,657 (M); expenditures, $49,685; qualifying distributions, $38,500.
Limitations: Applications not accepted.
Application information: Contributes only to pre-selected organizations.
Officer and Directors:* J.F. Seinsheimer III,* Chair. and Pres.; Virginia Seisheimer Grief, Secy.; Robert L. Seinsheimer, Treas.; J.F. Seinsheimer, Jr., J.F. Seinsheimer VI.
EIN: 760609508

52014
R. H. & Esther F. Goodrich Foundation
P.O. Box 1148
Houston, TX 77251-1148 (713) 659-3680
Contact: Hugh R. Goodrich, Pres.

Donor(s): Hugh R. Goodrich.
Financial data (yr. ended 12/31/01): Grants paid, $38,300; assets, $862,380 (M); expenditures, $40,001; qualifying distributions, $38,300.
Limitations: Giving on a national basis.
Officers: Hugh R. Goodrich, Pres.; Thomas E. Berry, V.P. and Secy.; Priscilla G. Timpson, 1st V.P.; Thomas W. McBath, Secy.-Treas.
EIN: 746068252

52015
Heart of Texas Community Foundation
c/o Wells Fargo Bank Texas, N.A.
P.O. Box 291308, MAC T 5630-011
Kerrville, TX 78029-1308 (830) 792-1703
FAX: (830) 792-6960; *E-mail:* wesley.d.dorman@norwest.com
Contact: Wes Dorman, Trust Mgr., Wells Fargo Bank Texas, N.A.

Established in 1994 in TX.
Financial data (yr. ended 12/31/00): Grants paid, $38,203; assets, $1,513,161 (M); gifts received, $37,412; expenditures, $77,713.
Limitations: Applications not accepted. Giving limited to TX.
Application information: Contributes only to pre-selected organizations.
Trustee: Wells Fargo Bank Texas, N.A.
Distribution Committee: Virgil Justice, Tom Terrell, Kit Werlein.
EIN: 746414639
Codes: CM

52016
Live Oak Foundation
P.O. Box 1202
George West, TX 78022 (512) 449-2508
Contact: Alfred West Ward, Pres.

Established in 1980 in TX.
Donor(s): Alfred West Ward.
Financial data (yr. ended 12/31/01): Grants paid, $38,193; assets, $676,371 (M); expenditures, $46,933; qualifying distributions, $40,363.
Limitations: Giving primarily in southern TX.
Application information: Applicants should submit a brief resume of academic qualifications.
Officers: Alfred West Ward, Pres.; Rose Thomas, Secy.-Treas.
EIN: 742119731
Codes: GTI

52017
Hollyfield Foundation
P.O. Box 66722
Houston, TX 77266 (713) 523-6900

Established in 1994 in TX.
Financial data (yr. ended 12/31/00): Grants paid, $38,075; assets, $2,431,131 (M); expenditures, $241,222; qualifying distributions, $62,258; giving activities include $24,182 for programs.
Limitations: Applications not accepted. Giving primarily in Houston, TX.
Application information: Contributes only to pre-selected organizations.
Officers: K. Wayne Bockman, Chair.; Janice M. Brunjes, 1st Vice-Chair.; Clair Koepsel, 2nd Vice-Chair.; Donald Shipwith, Secy.; D. Gregory Barbutti, Treas.
Directors: Terrance Baggott, Paul Carter, Kerri J. Dorman, Gordon R. Goss, Larry Lingle, Terri L. Richardson, Floyd W. Robinson, David West, Mark Wood.
EIN: 760404874

52018
Anne and Don Fizer Foundation
1360 Post Oak Blvd., Ste., 1600
Houston, TX 77056

Established in 1999 in TX.
Donor(s): Don E. Fizer.
Financial data (yr. ended 12/31/01): Grants paid, $38,000; assets, $17,579 (M); gifts received, $3,195; expenditures, $40,124; qualifying distributions, $38,890.
Officer: Don E. Fizer, Pres.
Director: D. Dudley Oldham.
EIN: 760599693

52019
The Frank and Brenda Gallagher Family Foundation
1517 Nantucket Dr.
Houston, TX 77057

Established in 1999 in TX.
Financial data (yr. ended 12/31/01): Grants paid, $38,000; assets, $750,339 (M); gifts received, $1,000; expenditures, $45,012; qualifying distributions, $38,000.
Limitations: Applications not accepted.
Application information: Contributes only to pre-selected organizations.
Officers: Frank P. Gallagher, Chair. and Secy.; Brenda J. Gallagher, Pres. and Treas.
Directors: Kathryn E. Gallagher, Lisa Gallagher Williamson.
EIN: 760611575

52020
The John T. Shea Charitable Foundation
c/o JPMorgan Chase Bank
P.O. Box 2558
Houston, TX 77252-8037 (713) 216-3444
Contact: Rebecca Bushkuhl, Trust Off., JPMorgan Chase Bank

Donor(s): John T. Shea.
Financial data (yr. ended 06/30/01): Grants paid, $38,000; assets, $848,237 (M); expenditures, $53,137; qualifying distributions, $44,641.
Limitations: Giving primarily in Houston, TX.
Trustee: JPMorgan Chase Bank.
EIN: 746038652

52021
Edith & Herbert Stehberg Charitable Trust
8204 Elmbrook, Ste. 190
Dallas, TX 75247-4013

Financial data (yr. ended 08/31/01): Grants paid, $38,000; assets, $664,796 (M); expenditures, $48,038; qualifying distributions, $44,288.
Limitations: Applications not accepted. Giving primarily in TX.
Application information: Contributes only to pre-selected organizations.
Trustee: Joe Ratner, C.P.A.
EIN: 751780936

52022
Sweet Mercies Foundation
c/o Joe & Judy Aufman
3726 Inwood Dr.
Houston, TX 77019

Established in 1997 in TX.
Donor(s): Judy Aufman, Jody Hawk.
Financial data (yr. ended 12/31/01): Grants paid, $37,911; assets, $641,703 (M); gifts received, $4,024; expenditures, $57,686; qualifying distributions, $37,911.
Limitations: Applications not accepted. Giving primarily in TX.
Application information: Contributes only to pre-selected organizations.
Officers: Joe Aufman, Pres.; Judy Aufman, V.P.; Jody Hawk, Secy.-Treas.
EIN: 760522437

52023
Tess White Foundation, Inc.
9614 Hillview Dr.
Dallas, TX 75231-1527 (214) 348-7505
Contact: Richard Delong, V.P.

Established in 1999.
Donor(s): Tess White.

Financial data (yr. ended 04/30/02): Grants paid, $37,900; assets, $799,930 (M); expenditures, $43,275; qualifying distributions, $37,900.
Limitations: Giving limited to Dallas, TX.
Officers: Tess White, Pres.; Richard Delong, V.P.; Frank E. McLain, V.P.; William Pierce, V.P.
EIN: 752816516

52024
Hegi Family Foundation
3318 Hanover St.
Dallas, TX 75225

Established in 1987 in TX.
Donor(s): Frederick B. Hegi, Jr.
Financial data (yr. ended 12/31/01): Grants paid, $37,825; assets, $1,375,634 (M); gifts received, $202,186; expenditures, $42,064; qualifying distributions, $37,825.
Limitations: Applications not accepted. Giving primarily in Dallas, TX.
Application information: Contributes only to pre-selected organizations.
Officers: Frederick B. Hegi, Jr., Pres.; Margie Ann Hegi, V.P.; Louise Backa, Secy.-Treas.
EIN: 752217565

52025
FLM Foundation
348 E. San Antonio St.
New Braunfels, TX 78130

Established in 1990 in TX.
Financial data (yr. ended 12/31/01): Grants paid, $37,500; assets, $737,799 (M); expenditures, $47,210; qualifying distributions, $36,458.
Limitations: Applications not accepted. Giving primarily in New Braunfels, TX.
Application information: Contributes only to pre-selected organizations.
Officer: Bob R. Kiesling, Pres.
EIN: 742585077

52026
The Henry B. Tippie Foundation
c/o Henry B. Tippie
P.O. Box 26557
Austin, TX 78755-0557

Established in 1998 in TX.
Donor(s): Henry B. Tipple.
Financial data (yr. ended 12/31/01): Grants paid, $37,500; assets, $664,771 (M); expenditures, $39,032; qualifying distributions, $37,500.
Limitations: Applications not accepted.
Application information: Contributes only to pre-selected organizations.
Officers: Henry B. Tippie, Chair., C.E.O., and Pres.; Patricia B. Tippie, Sr. Vice-Chair., V.P., and Secy.; Henry B. Tippie III, Vice-Chair.; L. Joseph Panico III, Treas.
Trustees: Linda T. Forrest, Helen T. Smith.
EIN: 742880664

52027
Upchurch Foundation
500 Main St., Ste. 600
Fort Worth, TX 76102

Established in 1993.
Donor(s): Jesse L. Upchurch.
Financial data (yr. ended 12/31/01): Grants paid, $37,500; assets, $431,291 (M); expenditures, $40,783; qualifying distributions, $37,500.
Limitations: Applications not accepted.
Application information: Contributes only to pre-selected organizations.
Officers and Directors:* Jesse L. Upchurch,* Pres.; Jesse L. Upchurch, Jr.,* V.P. and Secy.; Kenneth J. Upchurch,* V.P.
EIN: 752514029

52028
Commonwealth Foundation
P.O. Box 2102
El Paso, TX 79951-2102

Financial data (yr. ended 06/30/02): Grants paid, $37,450; assets, $431,309 (M); expenditures, $45,274; qualifying distributions, $37,450.
Limitations: Applications not accepted. Giving primarily in El Paso, TX.
Application information: Contributes only to pre-selected organizations.
Officers: Frances H. Weaver, Pres. and Treas.; Sharon A. Fashing, V.P.; Diania Minica, Secy.
EIN: 746047137

52029
John B. & Ethel Templeton Fund
c/o Bank of America
P.O. Box 831041
Dallas, TX 75283-1041

Donor(s): John B. Templeton, Ethel Templeton.
Financial data (yr. ended 12/31/01): Grants paid, $37,300; assets, $728,455 (M); expenditures, $43,990; qualifying distributions, $37,300.
Limitations: Applications not accepted. Giving limited to Austin, TX.
Officers: John B. Templeton IV,* Chair.; Robert Todd Templeton, Secy.
Directors: Debra Templeton, Laura Templeton.
EIN: 756024268

52030
Michael B. Morrow Foundation
8615 Stable Crest Blvd.
Houston, TX 77024
Contact: Connie Morrow, Dir.

Established in 1994 in TX.
Donor(s): John W. Morrow, Jr., Mrs. John W. Morrow, Jr.
Financial data (yr. ended 06/30/01): Grants paid, $37,290; assets, $596,272 (M); expenditures, $50,467; qualifying distributions, $37,290.
Directors: Connie Morrow, John W. Morrow, Jr., John W. Morrow III, Scott Morrow, Kellye Prostko, Marlene Stirl.
EIN: 760454125

52031
Raymond & Mary G. Rogstad Foundation
c/o Wells Fargo Bank Texas, N.A.
P.O. Box 2626
Waco, TX 76702-2626

Established in 1996 in TX.
Donor(s): Mary G. Rogstad.‡
Financial data (yr. ended 12/31/01): Grants paid, $37,179; assets, $747,375 (M); expenditures, $45,905; qualifying distributions, $37,179.
Limitations: Applications not accepted.
Application information: Contributes only to pre-selected organizations.
Trustee: Wells Fargo Bank Texas, N.A.
EIN: 746433550

52032
James & Margaret Earthman Foundation, Inc.
P.O. Box 8181
Galveston, TX 77553

Established in 1995 in TX.
Donor(s): James B. Earthman III, Margaret G. Earthman.
Financial data (yr. ended 12/31/01): Grants paid, $37,169; assets, $483,813 (M); gifts received, $90,000; expenditures, $38,697; qualifying distributions, $37,169.
Officers: James B. Earthman III, Pres.; Margaret G. Earthman, Secy.

Director: Addie M. Earthman.
EIN: 760487098

52033
The Lallinger Family Charitable Foundation
2121 Kirby Dr., Ste. 52
Houston, TX 77019-6065 (713) 961-2637

Financial data (yr. ended 12/31/99): Grants paid, $37,160; assets, $2,538,412 (M); gifts received, $210,000; expenditures, $43,280; qualifying distributions, $35,299.
Application information: Application form not required.
Officer: Michael Lallinger, Chair. and Pres.
EIN: 760574234

52034
Sunbelt Foundation
P.O. Box 791967
San Antonio, TX 78279-1967 (210) 349-3835
Contact: Christine M. Kotzur, Treas.

Established in 1993 in TX.
Financial data (yr. ended 12/31/01): Grants paid, $37,099; assets, $775,687 (M); expenditures, $51,399; qualifying distributions, $37,099.
Limitations: Giving primarily in San Antonio, TX.
Officers: Daniel A. Bennett, Pres. and Secy.; Barbara Peters, V.P.; Edgar M. Duncan, Secy.; Christine M. Kotzur, Treas.
EIN: 742686448

52035
Robert and Cecilia Hawk Citizenship Foundation
c/o PMB
519 Interstate 30, Ste. 704
Rockwall, TX 75087-5408 (972) 722-9218
Contact: Robert Hawk, Pres.

Established in 1995 in TX.
Donor(s): Robert Hawk.
Financial data (yr. ended 12/31/01): Grants paid, $36,972; assets, $772,220 (M); gifts received, $103,000; expenditures, $41,820; qualifying distributions, $36,753.
Limitations: Giving limited to residents of Rockwall, TX.
Application information: Application form required.
Officers: Robert Hawk, Pres.; Cecilia Hawk, Secy.-Treas.
Directors: Harold Evanson, Ken Jones, James Randolph, Cindy Tayhem, Jerry Vincent.
EIN: 752617169
Codes: GTI

52036
Neal C. and Cheryl L. Small Family Foundation
4031 W. Plano Pkwy., Ste. 100-D
Plano, TX 75093

Donor(s): Neal C. Small, Cheryl L. Small.
Financial data (yr. ended 06/30/01): Grants paid, $36,885; assets, $142,689 (M); gifts received, $7,227; expenditures, $90,175; qualifying distributions, $36,885.
Limitations: Applications not accepted. Giving primarily in Dallas, TX.
Officers: Neal C. Small, Pres.; Cheryl L. Small, Secy.
EIN: 752147156

52037
Lipnick Foundation
1717 St. James Pl., Ste. 245
Houston, TX 77056-3405

Donor(s): Elton S. Lipnick.

Financial data (yr. ended 11/30/01): Grants paid, $36,856; assets, $157,939 (M); expenditures, $37,028; qualifying distributions, $36,856.
Limitations: Applications not accepted. Giving primarily in Houston, TX.
Application information: Contributes only to pre-selected organizations.
Trustee: Elton S. Lipnick.
EIN: 746088087

52038
The Mitchell L. and Miriam Lewis Barnett Charitable Trust
300 N. Coit Rd., Ste. 1005
Richardson, TX 75080
Contact: Mitchell Barnett, Tr. or Miriam Lewis Barnett, Tr.

Donor(s): Mitchell L. Barnett, Miriam Lewis Barnett.
Financial data (yr. ended 07/31/01): Grants paid, $36,820; assets, $222,711 (M); gifts received, $115,000; expenditures, $39,567; qualifying distributions, $39,448.
Limitations: Giving primarily in Dallas, TX.
Application information: Application form not required.
Trustees: Darren L. Barnett, Miriam Lewis Barnett, Mitchell L. Barnett.
EIN: 756292944

52039
David E. Bloxom, Sr. Foundation
3954 Angus Dr.
Fort Worth, TX 76116

Established in 1999 in TX.
Donor(s): David E. Bloxom.
Financial data (yr. ended 12/31/00): Grants paid, $36,650; assets, $152,942 (M); gifts received, $180; expenditures, $93,645; qualifying distributions, $36,650.
Limitations: Applications not accepted.
Application information: Contributes only to pre-selected organizations.
Officer and Directors:* Roger B. Letz,* Pres.; David E. Bloxom, Bonnie D. Dowdy.
EIN: 752793902

52040
The Steves Foundation
(Formerly Marshall T. Steves Foundation)
P.O. Drawer S
San Antonio, TX 78211

Donor(s): Marshall T. Steves.
Financial data (yr. ended 02/28/02): Grants paid, $36,650; assets, $28,953 (M); gifts received, $60,000; expenditures, $36,823; qualifying distributions, $36,650.
Limitations: Applications not accepted. Giving primarily in San Antonio, TX.
Application information: Contributes only to pre-selected organizations.
Trustees: Edward Steves, Marshall T. Steves.
EIN: 746063267

52041
Joanne Stroud Bilby Foundation
4920 Briarwood Pl.
Dallas, TX 75209-2004 (214) 357-3939
Contact: Joanne Stroud Bilby, Pres.

Established in 1986 in TX.
Donor(s): Joanne Stroud Bilby.
Financial data (yr. ended 12/31/01): Grants paid, $36,606; assets, $360,173 (M); gifts received, $1,205; expenditures, $38,552; qualifying distributions, $35,790.
Limitations: Giving on a national basis.

Application information: Application form not required.
Officers: Joanne Stroud Bilby, Pres.; Natasha Stroud, V.P.; Eric M. Stroud, Secy.-Treas.
EIN: 752153006

52042
Nesbitt Memorial Trust
P.O. Box 297
Columbus, TX 78934-0297
Application address: 4004 Windsor Ave., Dallas, TX 75205-1747, tel.: (979) 732-5719
Contact: John H. Massey, Tr.

Established in 1987 in TX.
Financial data (yr. ended 12/31/01): Grants paid, $36,606; assets, $505,475 (M); expenditures, $37,244; qualifying distributions, $36,606.
Limitations: Giving limited to Columbus, TX.
Trustee: John H. Massey.
EIN: 742452261

52043
Mustang Foundation
P.O. Box 78
Cleburne, TX 76033 (817) 556-3255
Contact: Lowell Smith, Jr., Pres.

Established in 1999 in TX.
Financial data (yr. ended 12/31/01): Grants paid, $36,550; assets, $917,756 (M); gifts received, $35,000; expenditures, $43,164; qualifying distributions, $36,550.
Limitations: Giving primarily in TX.
Application information: Application form required.
Officers and Trustees:* Lowell Smith, Jr.,* Pres.; Pam Watson, Secy.-Treas.; Randy Denton, Sue Denton, Dolores M. Hullum, Marilyn S. King, Mike Lehrmann, Sue Ann Smith, Wade Wallace.
EIN: 752815383

52044
The Ann & Stephen Kaufman Foundation
c/o Stephen M. Kaufman
3 Riverway, Ste. 1350
Houston, TX 77056

Established in 1997 in TX.
Financial data (yr. ended 11/30/01): Grants paid, $36,440; assets, $668,408 (M); expenditures, $45,083; qualifying distributions, $36,440.
Limitations: Applications not accepted. Giving primarily in TX.
Application information: Contributes only to pre-selected organizations.
Trustees: Ann P. Kaufman, Stephen M. Kaufman.
EIN: 760526003

52045
The Trice Foundation
7750 N. MacArthur Blvd., Ste. 120
Irving, TX 75063
Application address: 3030 LBJ Freeway, Ste.150, Dallas, TX 75234
Contact: Susan Elizabeth Trice, Pres.

Established in 1996 in TX.
Financial data (yr. ended 12/31/00): Grants paid, $36,425; assets, $558,991 (M); expenditures, $46,426; qualifying distributions, $41,425.
Limitations: Giving primarily in TX.
Officers: Susan Elizabeth Trice, Pres.; Mary Beth Trice, V.P.; Betsy Ann Trice, Secy.-Treas.
EIN: 752681839

52046
W. C. Fuller Educational Trust
c/o Bank of America
P.O. Box 831041
Dallas, TX 75283-1041
Application addresses: c/o Southern Methodist University, Office of Financial Aid, P.O. Box 196, SMU, Dallas, TX 75275, tel.: (214) 692-3417; c/o Paul Quinn College, Dir., Financial Aid or Chair. of Admissions and Financial Aid Comm., Dallas, TX 75241

Financial data (yr. ended 10/31/01): Grants paid, $36,408; assets, $708,149 (M); expenditures, $44,195; qualifying distributions, $37,941.
Limitations: Giving limited to Dallas, TX.
Application information: Application form required.
Trustee: Bank of America, N.A.
EIN: 756234718
Codes: GTI

52047
Good News Foundation
8355 Evangeline Ln.
Beaumont, TX 77706 (409) 866-3672
Application address: Rt 1, Box 812, Newton, TX 75966, tel.: (409) 565-4802
Contact: Daniel S. Ayres, V.P.

Established in 1999 in TX.
Financial data (yr. ended 09/30/01): Grants paid, $36,385; assets, $17,930 (M); expenditures, $38,039; qualifying distributions, $37,192.
Limitations: Giving primarily in Colorado Springs, CO and TX.
Officers and Directors:* David H. Ayers,* Pres.; Daniel S. Ayres,* V.P; Carol D. Ayres,* Secy.; Angeline A. Ayers,* Treas.; William D. Maxey, Leon R. Pettis.
EIN: 760621984

52048
Fernandes Family Foundation
3535 Gillespie Ave., Ste. 6D
Dallas, TX 75219

Established in 1990 in TX.
Donor(s): Gary J. Fernandes.
Financial data (yr. ended 12/31/01): Grants paid, $36,245; assets, $1,885 (M); gifts received, $26,400; expenditures, $38,245; qualifying distributions, $36,245.
Limitations: Applications not accepted. Giving on a national basis, with emphasis on TX.
Application information: Contributes only to pre-selected organizations.
Officers: Gary J. Fernandes, Pres.; Sandra F. Fernandes, V.P.; Jennifer Fernandes McGill, Secy.-Treas.
EIN: 752335691

52049
George F. & Mary L. Leone Foundation
4100 Hildring Dr. E.
Fort Worth, TX 76109 (817) 926-0558
Contact: George F. Leone, Tr.

Donor(s): George F. Leone, Mary L. Leone.
Financial data (yr. ended 12/31/01): Grants paid, $36,200; assets, $932,230 (M); expenditures, $39,959; qualifying distributions, $36,200.
Limitations: Giving primarily in the Dallas-Fort Worth, TX, area.
Trustee: George F. Leone.
EIN: 751574708

52050
Kelly Family Foundation
(Formerly Stephen P. and Sandra Lu Kelly Foundation)
9 Stonebrook Ct.
Brownwood, TX 76801-6036 (915) 643-3561
Contact: Sandra Kelly, Pres.

Established in 1989 in TX.
Donor(s): Stephen P. Kelly, M.D., Sandra Kelly.
Financial data (yr. ended 08/31/01): Grants paid, $36,130; assets, $303,363 (M); expenditures, $36,742; qualifying distributions, $36,472.
Limitations: Giving primarily in Brown County, TX.
Application information: Applicant must include account of academic qualifications.
Officers: Sandra Kelly, Pres.; Stephen P. Kelly, M.D., V.P.
EIN: 752298202
Codes: GTI

52051
The Brighter Sky Foundation
222 Primrose Pl.
San Antonio, TX 78209

Established in 1998 in TX.
Donor(s): Camilla Ritchey.
Financial data (yr. ended 04/30/02): Grants paid, $36,018; assets, $868,958 (M); expenditures, $37,276; qualifying distributions, $36,018.
Limitations: Applications not accepted.
Application information: Contributes only to pre-selected organizations.
Officers and Directors:* Camilla Ritchey,* Pres.; Alexander Adell,* V.P.; Roy Adell,* Secy.
EIN: 742831546

52052
William N. & Lenore K. Burke Family Foundation
39 Mott Ln.
Houston, TX 77024

Established in 1997 in TX.
Donor(s): William N. Burke, Lenore K. Burke.
Financial data (yr. ended 12/31/01): Grants paid, $36,000; assets, $231,018 (M); expenditures, $36,605; qualifying distributions, $36,000.
Limitations: Applications not accepted. Giving primarily in Houston, TX.
Application information: Contributes only to pre-selected organizations.
Officers: William N. Burke, Chair. and Pres.; Lenore K. Burke, Secy.-Treas.
EIN: 760536565

52053
John W. & M. Irene Loots Charitable Foundation
c/o J. Victor Samuels
3555 Timmons Ln., Ste. 1440
Houston, TX 77027

Established in 1997 in TX.
Donor(s): Margaret Irene Loots Trust.
Financial data (yr. ended 12/31/00): Grants paid, $36,000; assets, $684,381 (M); expenditures, $49,381; qualifying distributions, $34,195.
Limitations: Applications not accepted. Giving primarily in Houston, TX.
Application information: Contributes only to pre-selected organizations.
Trustee: J. Victor Samuels.
EIN: 731503997

52054
O'Brien Foundation
P.O. Box 1052
Refugio, TX 78377-1052
Contact: John Morgan O'Brien, Pres.

Financial data (yr. ended 12/31/01): Grants paid, $36,000; assets, $725,421 (M); expenditures, $37,062; qualifying distributions, $36,000.
Limitations: Giving primarily in TX.
Officer: John Morgan O'Brien, Pres.
EIN: 746062067

52055
Charles B. and Jean G. Smith Family Foundation, Inc.
1348 Creekford Dr.
Sugar Land, TX 77478-3965

Established in 1994 in TX.
Financial data (yr. ended 12/31/01): Grants paid, $36,000; assets, $1,499,454 (M); gifts received, $67,345; expenditures, $36,000; qualifying distributions, $36,000.
Limitations: Applications not accepted. Giving primarily in TN and TX.
Application information: Contributes only to pre-selected organizations.
Officers and Directors:* Charles B. Smith, Jr.,* Pres.; Jean G. Smith,* V.P. and Secy.; Gina Lynne Faughtenbery, Karen L. Miller, Stephen E. Schuster.
EIN: 760456680

52056
Carleton Speed Family Foundation
P.O. Box 22383
Houston, TX 77227
Application address: 6565 W. Loop S., Ste. 800, Bellaire, TX 77401
Contact: Howard Startzman, Tr.

Established in 1995 in TX.
Financial data (yr. ended 12/31/01): Grants paid, $36,000; assets, $925,967 (M); expenditures, $54,986; qualifying distributions, $36,000.
Limitations: Giving primarily in Brookshire, TX.
Application information: Application form required.
Trustees: R.J. Eccles, Howard Startzman, David R. Streit.
EIN: 760485459

52057
Texas Knights Templar Educational Foundation
(Formerly Templar Educational Foundation)
507 S. Harwood St.
Dallas, TX 75201
Contact: Eldon Brooks

Established in 1993.
Financial data (yr. ended 12/31/01): Grants paid, $36,000; assets, $983,979 (M); gifts received, $20,000; expenditures, $58,108; qualifying distributions, $34,735.
Limitations: Giving primarily in TX.
Application information: Application form required.
Officer: Leonard O. Pierce, Chair.
Directors: Jerry N. Kirby, Roland J. Maddox, R. Furman Vinson, B.J. Young.
EIN: 752234779
Codes: GTI

52058
Midgley Foundation
c/o George Midgley
1209 Springwood Ct.
Euless, TX 76040-5959

Donor(s): Marion Midgley.
Financial data (yr. ended 12/31/01): Grants paid, $35,900; assets, $36,083 (M); expenditures, $38,538; qualifying distributions, $35,900.
Limitations: Applications not accepted.
Application information: Contributes only to pre-selected organizations.
Officers: George Midgley, Pres.; Marion Midgley, V.P.
EIN: 752547717

52059
Dossett Fund
P.O. Box 1339
Waco, TX 76703
Contact: Walter B. Dossett, Jr., Pres.

Donor(s): Walter B. Dossett, Jr., Reeder Dossett.
Financial data (yr. ended 04/30/02): Grants paid, $35,800; assets, $106,784 (M); gifts received, $11,000; expenditures, $37,433; qualifying distributions, $35,308.
Limitations: Giving primarily in Waco, TX.
Officers: Walter B. Dossett, Jr., Pres.; Reeder Dossett, V.P.; Mrs. Walter B. Dossett, Jr., Secy.-Treas.
EIN: 746056370

52060
A. M. Pate, Jr. Charitable Trust
c/o Bank of America
P.O. Box 831041
Dallas, TX 75283-1041
Application address: P.O. Box 1317, Fort Worth, TX 76101
Contact: Tom Ross

Financial data (yr. ended 06/30/02): Grants paid, $35,800; assets, $733,051 (M); expenditures, $43,818; qualifying distributions, $35,800.
Limitations: Giving primarily in Fort Worth, TX.
Trustee: Bank of America.
EIN: 752510793

52061
Annie M. & Clarke A. Polk Foundation
Drawer 399
Chappell Hill, TX 77426 (979) 836-3499

Donor(s): Annie M. Polk, Clarke A. Polk.
Financial data (yr. ended 06/30/99): Grants paid, $35,750; assets, $706,942 (M); gifts received, $90,207; expenditures, $37,682; qualifying distributions, $35,750.
Limitations: Giving primarily in Harris and Washington counties, TX.
Application information: Personal interview. Application form required.
Trustees: Evelyn Boatwright, John Boatwright, Ann Polk Hinton, Mary T. Middlebrooks, Tom Middlebrooks, Annie M. Polk, Clarke A. Polk.
EIN: 742293811
Codes: GTI

52062
Earl H. Burrough Scholarship Trust
c/o Bank of America
P.O. Box 831041
Dallas, TX 75283-1041

Established in 1996 in TX.
Financial data (yr. ended 12/31/01): Grants paid, $35,670; assets, $642,976 (M); expenditures, $42,177; qualifying distributions, $36,682.
Limitations: Applications not accepted. Giving primarily in TX.
Application information: Contributes only to pre-selected organizations.
Trustee: Bank of America.
EIN: 746345413

52063
Charles Jago Elder Foundation
P.O. Box 52430
Houston, TX 77052-2430
Contact: John W. Elder, Pres.

Established in 1986 in TX.
Donor(s): John W. Elder, Virginia J. Elder.
Financial data (yr. ended 09/30/01): Grants paid, $35,650; assets, $750,354 (M); gifts received, $61,775; expenditures, $40,504; qualifying distributions, $35,650.
Limitations: Giving primarily in Houston, TX.
Officers: John W. Elder, Pres.; Virginia J. Elder, V.P.
Trustee: Averill H. Mortimer.
EIN: 760234657

52064
KSM Mission Foundation, Inc.
4515 Cornell St.
Amarillo, TX 79109
Application address: 3919 Gatewood, Amarillo, TX 79109
Contact: Phil Sweeney, Pres.

Established in 1987 in TX.
Financial data (yr. ended 09/30/01): Grants paid, $35,600; assets, $1,241,755 (M); gifts received, $105,000; expenditures, $36,878; qualifying distributions, $35,600.
Limitations: Giving limited to Amarillo, TX.
Application information: Application form not required.
Officers: Phil Sweeney, Pres.; Billy Burr, V.P.; Don Abston, Secy.-Treas.
EIN: 752075030

52065
Elva J. Johnston Foundation
770 S. Post Oak Ln., Ste. 600
Houston, TX 77056

Financial data (yr. ended 11/30/01): Grants paid, $35,500; assets, $863,004 (M); expenditures, $43,328; qualifying distributions, $40,445.
Limitations: Applications not accepted. Giving limited to TX.
Application information: Contributes only to pre-selected organizations.
Trustees: Elva J. Johnston, Carolyn Josey Young, John H. Young.
EIN: 760057287

52066
Robert H. & Anita Q. Lawe Foundation
3701 Kirby Dr., Ste. 1112
Houston, TX 77098-3925 (713) 528-7480
Contact: Robert H. Lawe, Pres.

Donor(s): Robert H. Lawe.
Financial data (yr. ended 12/31/99): Grants paid, $35,450; assets, $490,968 (M); expenditures, $38,008; qualifying distributions, $35,050.
Limitations: Giving on a national basis, with emphasis on Houston, TX.
Application information: Application form not required.
Officers: Robert H. Lawe, Pres.; Anita Q. Lawe, Secy.
EIN: 760312167

52067
Breunig Family Foundation
8144 Walnut Hill, Ste. 987
Dallas, TX 75231

Established in 1998 in TX.
Donor(s): Mary M. Breunig, Robert P. Breunig.
Financial data (yr. ended 12/31/01): Grants paid, $35,300; assets, $701,402 (M); expenditures, $42,235; qualifying distributions, $35,300.
Limitations: Applications not accepted. Giving primarily in TX.
Application information: Contributes only to pre-selected organizations.
Director: Mary M. Breunig.
EIN: 752793180

52068
Sondra Nelson Pace Foundation
2011 N. Collins, Ste. 607
Richardson, TX 75080 (972) 671-3388
Contact: Ray H. Pace, Chair.

Donor(s): Ray H. Pace.
Financial data (yr. ended 12/31/01): Grants paid, $35,211; assets, $910,573 (M); gifts received, $134,431; expenditures, $49,196; qualifying distributions, $35,211.
Limitations: Giving primarily in TX.
Application information: Application form not required.
Officers: Ray H. Pace, Co-Chair.; Sondra Nelson Pace, Co-Chair.; Keli Cullen, Vice-Chair.; Keren Fetner, Vice-Chair.
EIN: 752789090

52069
E. A. & Kaye Durham Foundation
P.O. Box 1339
Corpus Christi, TX 78403

Established in 1996.
Donor(s): Kaye Durham Holt.
Financial data (yr. ended 12/31/00): Grants paid, $35,201; assets, $1,306,631 (M); expenditures, $60,295; qualifying distributions, $35,201.
Officers: Kaye Durham Holt, Pres.; Mary Durham Clark, V.P.; Edith Durham Sapp, V.P.; Ella C. Baker, Secy.; Eleanor Dunnam, Treas.
EIN: 742785892

52070
Krips Family Foundation
8 Patrick Ct.
Houston, TX 77024 (713) 968-2746
Contact: William M. Krips, Pres.

Established in 1997 in TX.
Donor(s): Judy H. Krips, William M. Krips.
Financial data (yr. ended 12/31/01): Grants paid, $35,060; assets, $704,586 (M); expenditures, $35,579; qualifying distributions, $35,060.
Officers: William M. Krips, Pres. and Treas.; Judy H. Krips, V.P.; Kathryn E. Krips, Secy.
EIN: 760555636

52071
Bernard S. and Ellen C. Appel Charitable Foundation
4917 Ranch View Rd.
Fort Worth, TX 76109-3117

Established in 1996.
Donor(s): Bernard S. Appel, Ellen C. Appel.
Financial data (yr. ended 12/31/01): Grants paid, $35,056; assets, $10,252 (M); gifts received, $31,900; expenditures, $35,734; qualifying distributions, $35,056.
Limitations: Applications not accepted. Giving primarily in Fort Worth, TX.
Application information: Contributes only to pre-selected organizations.
Directors: Bernard S. Appel, Ellen C. Appel, Steven E. Katten.
EIN: 752678012

52072
Holt Atherton Education Foundation
300 Convert St., Ste. 2500
San Antonio, TX 78205-3714 (210) 227-7591
Addictional application addresses: c/o Stevenson Atherton, 1250 N.E. Loop 410, San Antonio, TX 78209, tel.: (210) 826-4222, or c/o Geary Atherton, 355 Arcadia Pl., San Antonio, TX 78209, tel.: (210) 826-6283
Contact: James N. Martin, Tr.

Financial data (yr. ended 06/30/01): Grants paid, $35,000; assets, $640,264 (M); expenditures, $43,485; qualifying distributions, $33,978.
Limitations: Giving primarily in TX.
Trustees: Geary Atherton, Stevenson Atherton, James N. Martin.
EIN: 742087236

52073
The Dimmitt Foundation
301 Commerce St., Ste. 1500
Fort Worth, TX 76102-4115 (817) 877-1088
Contact: Katie D. Garrison, V.P.

Established in 1995 in TX.
Donor(s): Kate M. Dimmitt Charitable Remainder Unitrust No. 2, Kate M. Dimmitt.
Financial data (yr. ended 12/31/01): Grants paid, $35,000; assets, $643,777 (M); gifts received, $10,000; expenditures, $61,870; qualifying distributions, $35,000.
Limitations: Giving primarily in San Antonio, TX.
Officers: Kate M. Dimmitt, Pres.; Katie D. Garrison, V.P.
Director: Robert S. McClaren.
EIN: 742739657

52074
The Gardner Foundation
110 Parkwood Ct.
Austin, TX 78746-5486

Established in 1999 in TX.
Donor(s): Richard J. Gardner, Colleen E. Gardner.
Financial data (yr. ended 12/31/00): Grants paid, $35,000; assets, $926,296 (M); expenditures, $45,553; qualifying distributions, $35,000.
Limitations: Applications not accepted.
Application information: Contributes only to pre-selected organizations.
Officers and Directors:* Richard J. Gardner,* Chair. and Pres.; Colleen E. Gardner,* Secy.; Mark E. Thannisch,* Treas.
EIN: 742939678

52075
Jacquelyn E. Niehuss Foundation
c/o Bank of America
P.O. Box 831041
Dallas, TX 75283-1041
Application address: P.O. Box 1317, Fort Worth, TX 76101
Contact: Joe Grissom, V.P.and Trust Off., Bank of America

Financial data (yr. ended 06/30/02): Grants paid, $35,000; assets, $528,565 (M); expenditures, $38,942; qualifying distributions, $35,000.
Limitations: Giving primarily in Denton, TX.
Trustee: Bank of America.
EIN: 751607759

52076
The Thurman Family Foundation
c/o Gerald A. Thurman
14034 Cameron Rd.
Manor, TX 78653

Established in 1997 in TX.

Financial data (yr. ended 12/31/01): Grants paid, $35,000; assets, $21,723 (M); gifts received, $16,863; expenditures, $35,605; qualifying distributions, $35,000.
Limitations: Applications not accepted.
Application information: Contributes only to pre-selected organizations.
Officers and Directors:* Gerald A. Thurman,* Pres.; Carolyn A. Thurman,* Secy.; Kyle Glenn Thurman, Shawn Kevin Thurman.
EIN: 742793231

52077
Andrew F. & Barbara Veres Charitable Trust
2715 Quenby St.
West University Place, TX 77005

Established in 2000 in TX.
Donor(s): Andrew F. Veres, Barbara Veres.
Financial data (yr. ended 12/31/01): Grants paid, $34,975; assets, $317,224 (M); gifts received, $100,000; expenditures, $36,836; qualifying distributions, $34,975.
Limitations: Applications not accepted. Giving primarily in Dayton, OH.
Application information: Contributes only to pre-selected organizations.
Trustee: Andrew F. Veres.
EIN: 766166971

52078
Stanley and Linda Marcus Foundation
(Formerly Nonesuch Foundation)
300 Crescent Ct., Ste. 875
Dallas, TX 75201
Contact: Stanley Marcus, Pres.

Donor(s): Stanley Marcus.
Financial data (yr. ended 01/31/02): Grants paid, $34,825; assets, $151,460 (M); expenditures, $37,122; qualifying distributions, $34,825.
Limitations: Giving primarily in Dallas, TX.
Officers and Trustees:* Stanley Marcus,* Pres.; Richard Marcus,* V.P.; Linda Marcus,* Secy.-Treas.
EIN: 756037706

52079
Ann Lents and J. David Heaney Foundation
600 Travis, Ste. 6110
Houston, TX 77002

Established in 1994 in TX.
Donor(s): Ann Lents, J. David Heaney II.
Financial data (yr. ended 12/31/01): Grants paid, $34,763; assets, $576,585 (M); expenditures, $35,916; qualifying distributions, $34,763.
Limitations: Applications not accepted. Giving primarily in Houston, TX.
Application information: Contributes only to pre-selected organizations.
Officers: J. David Heaney II, Pres.; Murphy K. Lents, V.P. and Secy.; Ann Lents, V.P. and Treas.
EIN: 760453371

52080
B.K.S. Family Charitable Foundation, Inc.
(Formerly Shirley Family Foundation)
4731 Wildwood Rd.
Dallas, TX 75209 (214) 522-0149
Contact: Bernedene Kay Brunnier, Pres.

Established in 1989 in TX.
Donor(s): William A. Shirley, Jr.
Financial data (yr. ended 12/31/01): Grants paid, $34,700; assets, $639,556 (M); expenditures, $41,759; qualifying distributions, $34,700.
Limitations: Giving on a national basis.

Application information: Application form required.
Officer and Directors:* Bernedene Kay Brunnier,* Pres.; Bernedene Sara Shirley, Marjorie Sterling Shirley, William Peyton Shirley.
EIN: 752304410

52081
Bour Memorial Scholarship Fund
c/o Bank of America
P.O. Box 831041
Dallas, TX 75283-1041
Application address: P.O. Box 419119, Kansas City, MO 64141-6119, tel.: (816) 979-7481
Contact: David P. Ross, Sr. V.P., Bank of America

Financial data (yr. ended 12/31/01): Grants paid, $34,700; assets, $663,149 (M); expenditures, $39,718; qualifying distributions, $36,721.
Limitations: Giving limited to Lafayette County, MO.
Application information: Application available at Lafayette County schools. Application form required.
Distribution Committee: Joe Aull, Robert Florence, Sonny Oetting, Edie Rector.
Trustee: Bank of America.
EIN: 436225461
Codes: GTI

52082
Alwine Classen Memorial Scholarship Fund
c/o Frost National Bank
P.O. Box 2950
San Antonio, TX 78299
Contact: Susan T. Palmer, V.P., Frost National Bank

Financial data (yr. ended 06/30/02): Grants paid, $34,630; assets, $546,074 (M); expenditures, $42,046; qualifying distributions, $34,630.
Limitations: Giving primarily in TX.
Trustee: Frost National Bank.
EIN: 742267729

52083
Marguerite R. Edwards Scholarship Trust
c/o Union Planters Bank
P.O. Box 232
Alvin, TX 77512-0232
Application address: c/o Principal, Alvin High School, 802 S. Johnson, Alvin, TX 77511, tel.: (281) 585-6224

Financial data (yr. ended 07/31/01): Grants paid, $34,100; assets, $649,096 (M); expenditures, $45,396; qualifying distributions, $35,468.
Limitations: Giving limited to Alvin, TX.
Application information: Application form required.
Trustee: Union Planters Bank.
EIN: 746216234
Codes: GTI

52084
Wallace Shields Immediate Charitable Trust
c/o Bank of America
P.O. Box 831041
Dallas, TX 75283-1041

Established in 1995 in KS.
Financial data (yr. ended 12/31/01): Grants paid, $34,017; assets, $550,760 (M); expenditures, $40,443; qualifying distributions, $35,676.
Limitations: Applications not accepted. Giving primarily in KS and MO.
Application information: Contributes only to pre-selected organizations.

Trustees: Una Johann, Jon Root, Bank of America.
EIN: 486338331

52085
Aaron Forman Trust
c/o Frost National Bank
P.O. Box 179
Galveston, TX 77553

Financial data (yr. ended 10/31/01): Grants paid, $34,000; assets, $776,201 (M); expenditures, $43,955; qualifying distributions, $33,479.
Limitations: Applications not accepted. Giving limited to Galveston, TX.
Application information: Contributes only to pre-selected organizations.
Trustees: Doris Wechter Pryzant, Frost National Bank.
EIN: 746284810

52086
The Alex and Sally Halff Family Foundation
206 Sir Arthur Ct.
San Antonio, TX 78213

Established in 1998 in TX.
Donor(s): Alex Halff, Sally Halff.
Financial data (yr. ended 12/31/01): Grants paid, $34,000; assets, $843,099 (M); gifts received, $1,943; expenditures, $48,103; qualifying distributions, $32,749.
Limitations: Applications not accepted. Giving primarily in San Antonio, TX.
Application information: Contributes only to pre-selected organizations.
Directors: Mindi H. Alterman, Alex Halff, Elizabeth R. Halff, Glenn A. Halff, Harry A. Halff, James A. Halff, Sally Halff.
EIN: 742900229

52087
The Jarmon Foundation
c/o Judy Jarmon
5344 Blake Dr.
Plano, TX 75093

Established in 1993.
Financial data (yr. ended 12/31/01): Grants paid, $34,000; assets, $4,543 (M); gifts received, $25,000; expenditures, $34,002; qualifying distributions, $34,000.
Limitations: Applications not accepted. Giving primarily in TX.
Application information: Contributes only to pre-selected organizations.
Officers: Evelyn Ponder, Secy.; Cyndy Hudgins, Treas.
Directors: Jo Jarmon, Judy Jarmon.
EIN: 752466916

52088
The Eugene & Felice Malloy Foundation
2101 Polk
Houston, TX 77003-4319

Established in 1995 in TX.
Donor(s): Dennis M. Malloy, Felice L. Malloy.
Financial data (yr. ended 12/31/00): Grants paid, $34,000; assets, $1,161,223 (M); expenditures, $38,438; qualifying distributions, $34,000.
Limitations: Applications not accepted. Giving limited to TX.
Application information: Contributes only to pre-selected organizations.
Officers and Directors:* Dennis M. Malloy,* Pres.; Michele A. Malloy,* Secy.; Felice L. Malloy,* Treas.
EIN: 760480582

52089
M. D. Matthews Foundation
c/o Margolis, Phipps & Wright, PC
1400 Post Oak Blvd., No. 900
Houston, TX 77056-3009

Established in 1986 in TX.
Donor(s): M.D. Matthews.
Financial data (yr. ended 12/31/01): Grants paid, $34,000; assets, $609,358 (M); gifts received, $100,130; expenditures, $38,920; qualifying distributions, $34,000.
Limitations: Applications not accepted. Giving primarily in TX.
Application information: Contributes only to pre-selected organizations.
Trustee: M.D. Matthews.
EIN: 760206458

52090
Spears Charitable Trust
2710 Ave. Q
Lubbock, TX 79405-1446
Contact: Harrell Spears, Tr.

Donor(s): Harrell Spears.
Financial data (yr. ended 12/31/01): Grants paid, $34,000; assets, $574,569 (M); gifts received, $47,600; expenditures, $34,606; qualifying distributions, $16,756.
Limitations: Giving primarily in GA and TX.
Trustee: Harrell Spears.
EIN: 752445912

52091
Shelton Family Foundation
P.O. Box 291107
Kerrville, TX 78029-1107 (830) 896-8280
Contact: Fronie K. Shelton, Pres.

Donor(s): Robert R. Shelton.‡
Financial data (yr. ended 09/30/01): Grants paid, $33,898; assets, $154,698 (M); gifts received, $51,017; expenditures, $36,226; qualifying distributions, $33,898.
Limitations: Giving primarily in TX.
Officers and Directors:* Fronie K. Shelton,* Pres.; Edward E. Hartline,* Secy.
EIN: 742225673

52092
V. M. Ehlers Foundation
(Formerly V. M. Ehlers Memorial Fund, Inc.)
6813 Comanche Trail
Austin, TX 78732 (512) 266-2573
URL: http://www.twua.org/vmehlers.htm
Contact: Sam L. Warrington, Tr.

Established in 1959 in TX.
Donor(s): Texas Water Utilities Association, Texas Public Works Association, Water Environment Association of Texas.
Financial data (yr. ended 06/30/01): Grants paid, $33,885; assets, $397,914 (M); gifts received, $73,978; expenditures, $34,655; qualifying distributions, $34,271.
Limitations: Giving limited to residents of TX.
Application information: Application form required.
Officer and Trustees:* Robert A. McMillon,* Chair.; Daniel C. Allen, Ronald H. Bearden, David M. Cochran, Gordon Koblitz, William T. Manning, Debbie McReynolds.
EIN: 746062790
Codes: GTI

52093
Salome Foundation
100 Elm St.
Waco, TX 76703 (254) 756-6661
Contact: Tommy G. Salome, Mgr.

Established in 1995.
Donor(s): Tommy G. Salome.
Financial data (yr. ended 12/31/01): Grants paid, $33,841; assets, $604,103 (M); expenditures, $39,685; qualifying distributions, $33,673.
Limitations: Giving primarily in Waco, TX.
Officer: Tommy G. Salome, Mgr.
EIN: 742767798

52094
Tim & Suzanne Word Foundation
P.O. Box 310330
New Braunfels, TX 78131

Established in 1997 in TX.
Donor(s): Suzanne Zachry Word, Timothy Dean Word.
Financial data (yr. ended 12/31/01): Grants paid, $33,812; assets, $628,426 (M); gifts received, $47,032; expenditures, $34,510; qualifying distributions, $33,812.
Limitations: Applications not accepted.
Application information: Contributes only to pre-selected organizations.
Directors: Bryan Carl Word, Forrest Roark Word, Mary Amber Word, Patrick Zachry Word, Suzanne Zachry Word, Timothy Dean Word, Timothy Dean Word III.
EIN: 742831668

52095
JEM Foundation
700 Louisiana St., Ste. 3920
Houston, TX 77002-2731

Established in 1997 in TX.
Donor(s): Jack S. Blanton, Jr.
Financial data (yr. ended 12/31/01): Grants paid, $33,793; assets, $529,734 (M); expenditures, $45,141; qualifying distributions, $33,793.
Limitations: Applications not accepted. Giving primarily in Houston, TX.
Application information: Contributes only to pre-selected organizations.
Officers and Directors:* Jack S. Blanton, Jr.,* Chair., Pres. and Treas.; Leslie D. Blanton,* V.P. and Secy.; Elizabeth B. Wareing.
EIN: 760534530

52096
Mark Deering Foundation
c/o John F. Sheehy, Jr.
510 N. Valley Hills Dr., Ste. 500
Waco, TX 76710-6077
Application address: 4700 Westchester Dr., Waco, TX 76710, tel.: (254) 772-5263
Contact: Msgr. Mark Deering, Dir.

Established in 1995.
Donor(s): Mark Deering.
Financial data (yr. ended 12/31/01): Grants paid, $33,750; assets, $268,757 (M); gifts received, $10,330; expenditures, $35,478; qualifying distributions, $33,417.
Limitations: Giving limited to residents of Waco, TX.
Directors: Virginia G. Cawthron, Msgr. Mark Deering, John F. Sheehy, Jr., Gary B. Young, Kenneth J. Young.
EIN: 742726640
Codes: GTI

52097
Curtis Foundation, Inc.
P.O. Box 4299
Longview, TX 75606-4299 (903) 235-4786
Contact: James R. Curtis, Jr., Pres.

Donor(s): James R. Curtis, Sr.
Financial data (yr. ended 12/31/01): Grants paid, $33,719; assets, $502,699 (M); expenditures, $37,010; qualifying distributions, $33,719.
Limitations: Giving primarily in Longview, TX.
Application information: Application form not required.
Officers: James R. Curtis, Jr., Pres.; Sue Curtis, V.P.
EIN: 756011622

52098
John R. & Susan Landon Alford Foundation
P.O. Box 67
Henderson, TX 75652

Financial data (yr. ended 06/30/01): Grants paid, $33,600; assets, $792,424 (M); expenditures, $41,180; qualifying distributions, $33,600.
Limitations: Giving primarily in Rusk County, TX.
Officers: Landon Alford, Pres.; David Alford, V.P.; Julianna Brightwell, Secy.-Treas.
Directors: Mary Frances Alford, Phyllis Alford, John R. Alford, Jr., Milton McGee, Bess Rayford.
EIN: 756025997

52099
The DGBB Foundation
1341 W. Mockingbird, No. 700 W
Dallas, TX 75247-6905
Contact: David G. Rogers, Tr.

Established in 1997 in TX.
Donor(s): Ralph Rogers.
Financial data (yr. ended 12/31/01): Grants paid, $33,500; assets, $811,536 (M); expenditures, $35,313; qualifying distributions, $33,500.
Limitations: Applications not accepted. Giving primarily in NY, TX, and the New England area.
Application information: Contributes only to pre-selected organizations.
Trustees: Mary B. Rhoades, David G. Rogers, James B. Rogers, Robert D. Rogers.
EIN: 752707012

52100
The M. B. Esstman Family Charitable Foundation
225 Steeplechase Dr.
Irving, TX 75062-3847 (972) 718-4155

Established in 1997 in TX.
Financial data (yr. ended 12/31/01): Grants paid, $33,466; assets, $328,115 (M); expenditures, $42,968; qualifying distributions, $33,466.
Directors: Bryan R. Esstman, Julie M Esstman, Michael B. Esstman.
EIN: 752734172

52101
McPherson Family Foundation
221 W. Olmos Dr.
San Antonio, TX 78212
Contact: Jean L. McPherson, Pres.

Established in 1997 in TX.
Donor(s): Jean L. McPherson.
Financial data (yr. ended 12/31/01): Grants paid, $33,350; assets, $76,345 (M); expenditures, $36,449; qualifying distributions, $33,350.
Officer: Jean L. McPherson, Pres.
Director: Douglas A. McPherson.
EIN: 742832964

52102
Sherrill Family Foundation, Inc.
200 S. 10th St.
McAllen, TX 78501

Established in 1992 in TX.
Financial data (yr. ended 12/31/01): Grants paid, $33,330; assets, $723,985 (M); expenditures, $37,207; qualifying distributions, $33,330.
Limitations: Applications not accepted. Giving primarily in TX.
Application information: Contributes only to pre-selected organizations.
Officers: Deborah McDaniel, Pres.; Betty Ann Killingsworth, V.P.
EIN: 742638559

52103
The Jeff and Karen DeHaan Charitable Trust
3602 Wyatt Ln.
Texarkana, TX 75503

Established in 1991 in TX.
Donor(s): Jeff DeHaan, Karen DeHaan.
Financial data (yr. ended 12/31/01): Grants paid, $33,100; assets, $47,799 (M); gifts received, $50,000; expenditures, $33,180; qualifying distributions, $33,100.
Limitations: Applications not accepted. Giving on a national basis.
Application information: Contributes only to pre-selected organizations.
Trustees: Jeff DeHaan, Karen DeHaan.
EIN: 752369660

52104
The Richard D. Shiney Charitable Trust
c/o Bank Of America
P.O. Box 831041
Dallas, TX 75283-1041
Application address: c/o Ruby Wrenick, P.O. Box 88, Topeka, KS 66601, tel.: (785) 295-3463

Established in 2000 in KS.
Donor(s): Richard D. Shiney Trust.
Financial data (yr. ended 01/31/02): Grants paid, $33,021; assets, $889,974 (M); expenditures, $46,206; qualifying distributions, $33,021.
Limitations: Giving primarily in KS.
Trustee: Bank Of America.
EIN: 527059226

52105
The Bunny Love Foundation
c/o Anne Davidson
9930 Strait Ln.
Dallas, TX 75220-2045

Donor(s): Anne Davidson.
Financial data (yr. ended 12/31/01): Grants paid, $33,000; assets, $515,904 (M); gifts received, $4,935; expenditures, $39,250; qualifying distributions, $33,000.
Limitations: Applications not accepted. Giving primarily in Dallas, TX.
Application information: Contributes only to pre-selected organizations.
Officers and Directors:* Anne L. Davidson,* Pres. and Treas.; Rita Davidson,* V.P.; Beth Mates,* Secy.
EIN: 752705851

52106
David and Eula Wintermann Foundation
P.O. Box 337
Eagle Lake, TX 77434-0337 (979) 234-5551
Additional telephone number: (713) 228-7273
Contact: Jack Johnson, Pres.

Donor(s): Wintermann Marital Trust.
Financial data (yr. ended 09/30/01): Grants paid, $33,000; assets, $285,407 (M); gifts received, $170,219; expenditures, $31,504; qualifying distributions, $16,000.
Limitations: Giving limited to residents of TX.
Officers: Jack Johnson, Pres.; Donald N. Bendy, V.P.; Steve K. Balas, Secy.
EIN: 760082100
Codes: GTI

52107
Frank A. & Gladys F. Chamberlin Scholarship Fund
c/o Bank of America
P.O. Box 831041
Dallas, TX 75283-1041
Application address: c/o Office of Financial Aid, Tarleton State Univ., Stephenville, TX 76401

Financial data (yr. ended 07/31/01): Grants paid, $32,900; assets, $921,599 (M); expenditures, $40,510; qualifying distributions, $35,003.
Limitations: Giving limited to residents of Earth County, TX.
Application information: Application form required.
Trustee: Bank of America.
EIN: 756234715

52108
The Central Texas Foundation for the Support of Montessori Education
2211 Sunny Slope Dr.
Austin, TX 78703

Donor(s): Suzanne Carper.
Financial data (yr. ended 12/31/99): Grants paid, $32,876; assets, $2,157 (M); gifts received, $35,000; expenditures, $33,199; qualifying distributions, $32,876.
Limitations: Applications not accepted.
Application information: Contributes only to pre-selected organizations.
Officer and Directors:* Suzanne Carper,* Secy.-Treas.; Fleur A. Christensen, Diana Duane, Tina Juarez, Marvin Kelly, Ian Ratiu, Carlos Valdez.
EIN: 742863065

52109
T. Ragan Ryan Foundation, Inc.
3 Knipp Rd.
Houston, TX 77024 (713) 782-2229
Contact: Thoms C. Ryan, Secy.-Treas.

Established in 1994.
Donor(s): Emily D. Ryan, Thoms C. Ryan.
Financial data (yr. ended 12/31/00): Grants paid, $32,685; assets, $273,206 (M); expenditures, $32,808; qualifying distributions, $32,685.
Application information: Application form not required.
Officers: Kemper D. Ryan, Pres.; Emily D. Ryan, V.P.; Thoms C. Ryan, Secy.-Treas.
Directors: Jan B. Dryselius, Mary D. Dryselius.
EIN: 760421278

52110
Richard E. Gnade Charitable Trust
c/o Frost National Bank
P.O. Box 2950
San Antonio, TX 78299-2950
Contact: Susan T. Palmer, V.P., and Trust Off., Frost National Bank

Established in 1984 in TX.
Financial data (yr. ended 10/31/01): Grants paid, $32,682; assets, $632,376 (M); expenditures, $45,825; qualifying distributions, $37,104.
Limitations: Giving limited to residents of Bandera County, TX.
Trustee: Frost National Bank.
EIN: 746032311
Codes: GTI

52111
The Meek Foundation
205 N. Main St.
Winnsboro, TX 75494
Application address: P.O. Box 86, Fredericksburg, TX 78624
Contact: Paul D. Meek, Pres.

Established in 1986 in TX.
Donor(s): Betty R. Meek, Paul D. Meek.
Financial data (yr. ended 06/30/02): Grants paid, $32,603; assets, $398,696 (M); expenditures, $46,790; qualifying distributions, $32,603.
Limitations: Giving primarily in TX.
Application information: Application form not required.
Officers and Directors:* Paul D. Meek,* Pres.; Leon Oliver,* V.P.
EIN: 752148014

52112
Susan Long Skilling Foundation
5333 Doliver Dr.
Houston, TX 77056-2315 (713) 355-5454
Contact: Susan Lowe, Pres.

Established in 1998 in TX.
Donor(s): Susan Lowe.
Financial data (yr. ended 12/31/00): Grants paid, $32,525; assets, $491,392 (M); expenditures, $40,887; qualifying distributions, $32,525.
Officer: Susan Lowe, Pres. and Secy.-Treas.
EIN: 760560164

52113
The Hartnett Foundation
4504 Winewood Ct.
Colleyville, TX 76034

Established in 1997.
Donor(s): Stephen P. Hartnett.
Financial data (yr. ended 05/31/02): Grants paid, $32,523; assets, $587,308 (M); expenditures, $32,599; qualifying distributions, $32,523.
Officers: Hollis M. Greenlaw, Pres.; Julie Stephenson, Secy.-Treas.
Directors: Richard P. Hartnett, Sandra Hartnett, Stephen P. Hartnett.
EIN: 752708291

52114
The W. R. Burgess Foundation
c/o Clyde A. Pine, Jr.
100 N. Stanton St., Ste. 1700
El Paso, TX 79901-1448

Established in 1986 in TX.
Donor(s): W.R. Burgess.
Financial data (yr. ended 06/30/02): Grants paid, $32,500; assets, $778,571 (M); expenditures, $35,590; qualifying distributions, $32,500.
Limitations: Applications not accepted. Giving on a national basis.
Application information: Contributes only to pre-selected organizations.
Officers: W.R. Burgess, Pres. and Secy.; Clyde A. Pine, Jr., V.P. and Treas.
EIN: 742443002

52115
Jarl P. & Naydene K. Johnson Charitable Foundation
5626 Netherland Ct.
Dallas, TX 75229-5567
Application address: c/o Theodore Lustig, 13601 Preston Rd., Ste. 800E, Dallas, TX 75240, tel.: (800) 878-7822
Contact: Jarl Johnson, Dir.

Established in 1999 in TX.
Donor(s): Jarl P. Johnson, Naydene K. Johnson.

Financial data (yr. ended 12/31/01): Grants paid, $32,500; assets, $3,082 (M); gifts received, $25,000; expenditures, $32,500; qualifying distributions, $32,500.
Limitations: Giving primarily in OK and TX.
Directors: Karen L. Castle, Gary A. Johnson, Jarl P. Johnson, Naydene K. Johnson, Kelley L. Vogt, Marilyn Johnson Wark.
EIN: 752833932

52116
Dennis R. Meals Charitable Foundation
3221 Collingsworth, Ste. 200
Fort Worth, TX 76107-6582

Established in 1985 in TX.
Donor(s): Dennis R. Meals.
Financial data (yr. ended 12/31/01): Grants paid, $32,500; assets, $701,895 (M); expenditures, $37,665; qualifying distributions, $32,500.
Limitations: Applications not accepted. Giving primarily in TX.
Application information: Contributes only to pre-selected organizations.
Officers: Dennis R. Meals, Pres.; Jamelia L. Meals, Secy.
Directors: Elizabeth Anne Meals, Jennifer Denise Meals.
EIN: 752075800

52117
The Dan and Martha Lou Beaird Foundation
c/o Dan L. Beaird
5121 McKinney Ave.
Dallas, TX 75205

Established in 2001 in TX.
Donor(s): Dan Beaird, Martha Lou Beaird.
Financial data (yr. ended 12/31/01): Grants paid, $32,375; assets, $10,174 (M); gifts received, $42,641; expenditures, $32,467; qualifying distributions, $32,375.
Limitations: Applications not accepted.
Application information: Contributes only to pre-selected organizations.
Officers and Directors:* Dan L. Beaird,* Pres.; Martha Lou Beaird,* Secy.; Benjamin H. Beaird, Gayden B. Breckwoldt, John R. Hudson.
EIN: 752943958

52118
Pellets Foundation, Inc.
1101 Capital TX Hwy. S Bldg. K
Austin, TX 78746

Established in 1999 in TX.
Financial data (yr. ended 12/31/01): Grants paid, $32,340; assets, $361,556 (M); gifts received, $2,000; expenditures, $32,427; qualifying distributions, $32,340.
Limitations: Applications not accepted.
Application information: Contributes only to pre-selected organizations.
Officers: Carmen Creixell, V.P.; Mike Wylie, Secy.; Lourdes Kaufmann, Treas.
EIN: 742930551

52119
Eugene & Johnnye Mae Stevens Trust
c/o Bank of America, N.A.
P.O. Box 831041
Dallas, TX 75283-1041

Established in 1996 in TX.
Financial data (yr. ended 12/31/01): Grants paid, $32,302; assets, $522,729 (M); expenditures, $39,967; qualifying distributions, $32,302.
Limitations: Applications not accepted. Giving primarily in San Antonio, TX.
Application information: Contributes only to pre-selected organizations.

Trustee: Bank of America.
EIN: 746367999

52120
Tony and Lillian Dona Foundation
3600 Hanover St.
Dallas, TX 75225-7210

Established in 1998.
Donor(s): Anthony Wayne Dona, Lillian Yee Dona.
Financial data (yr. ended 12/31/01): Grants paid, $32,260; assets, $214,054 (M); gifts received, $14,825; expenditures, $34,635; qualifying distributions, $32,260.
Application information: Application form not required.
Officers: Anthony Wayne Dona, Pres. and Treas.; Lillian Yee Dona, V.P. and Secy.
Director: Bernadette D. Ashcraft.
EIN: 752770051

52121
Ray McCauley Charitable Trust
1009 Lakeshore Dr.
Mesquite, TX 75149

Financial data (yr. ended 12/31/01): Grants paid, $32,200; assets, $648,991 (M); expenditures, $44,841; qualifying distributions, $32,200.
Limitations: Applications not accepted. Giving primarily in Minneapolis, MN and Dallas, TX.
Application information: Contributes only to pre-selected organizations.
Trustee: Robert L. Hanby.
EIN: 756210299

52122
William Z. Hayes Foundation
c/o Bank of America
P.O. Box 831041
Dallas, TX 75283-1041

Financial data (yr. ended 01/31/02): Grants paid, $32,053; assets, $657,504 (M); expenditures, $39,243; qualifying distributions, $32,053.
Limitations: Giving primarily in TX.
Application information: Application form required.
Trustee: Bank of America.
EIN: 756245477

52123
Norman and Nancy Brinker Charitable Foundation
16 Robledo Dr.
Dallas, TX 75230

Established in 1997 in TX.
Donor(s): Norman E. Brinker.
Financial data (yr. ended 12/31/01): Grants paid, $32,025; assets, $566,837 (M); expenditures, $38,140; qualifying distributions, $33,562.
Limitations: Applications not accepted.
Application information: Contributes only to pre-selected organizations.
Officer and Director:* Nancy Brinker,* Pres.
EIN: 752668952

52124
Baron & Darlene Cass Family Foundation
5005 LBJ Fwy., Lockbox 119
Dallas, TX 75244

Established in 1993 in TX.
Donor(s): A. Baron Cass III.
Financial data (yr. ended 12/31/00): Grants paid, $31,990; assets, $371,945 (M); expenditures, $32,026; qualifying distributions, $31,990.
Limitations: Applications not accepted. Giving primarily in Dallas, TX.

Application information: Contributes only to pre-selected organizations.
Trustee: A. Baron Cass III.
EIN: 756453922

52125
The Elliot H. Matthews Foundation, Inc.
1415 Louisiana, Ste. 2220
Houston, TX 77002
Contact: Terrance P. Baggott, Chair.

Established in 1995 in TX.
Donor(s): Elliott H. Matthew.
Financial data (yr. ended 12/31/00): Grants paid, $31,925; assets, $345,592 (M); expenditures, $37,028; qualifying distributions, $31,925.
Limitations: Applications not accepted. Giving limited to Austin, TX.
Application information: Contributes only to pre-selected organizations.
Officers: Terrance P. Baggott, Chair.; K. Wayne Bockman, Vice-Chair.; Floyd W. Robinson, Jr., Secy.
EIN: 760364900

52126
Belin Foundation
2438 Windmill Dr.
Richmond, TX 77469-1256

Established in 1985 in TX.
Donor(s): J.B. Land Co., Inc., James Bruce Belin, Jr., Mary Ann Belin.
Financial data (yr. ended 10/31/01): Grants paid, $31,900; assets, $4,133,722 (M); expenditures, $58,972; qualifying distributions, $31,900.
Limitations: Applications not accepted. Giving primarily in Houston, TX.
Application information: Contributes only to pre-selected organizations.
Officers: James Bruce Belin, Jr., Pres.; Mary Ann Belin, V.P. and Secy.; Gregory Bruce Belin, V.P. and Treas.
EIN: 760163560

52127
William L. Mosher Foundation
11452 Strait Ln.
Dallas, TX 75229-2955
Contact: Emily E. Mosher, Tr.

Established in 1991 in TX.
Financial data (yr. ended 12/31/00): Grants paid, $31,850; assets, $657,207 (M); expenditures, $32,609; qualifying distributions, $31,850.
Limitations: Giving primarily in Dallas, TX.
Application information: Application form not required.
Trustees: Emily E. Mosher, William L. Mosher, Jr.
EIN: 751709187

52128
H. J. Diffenbaugh Trust for University of Illinois
c/o Bank of America
P.O. Box 831041
Dallas, TX 75283-1041
Application address: c/o David P. Ross, Sr. V.P., Bank of America, P.O. Box 419119, 14 W. 10th St., Kansas City, MO 64141-6119, tel.: (816) 979-7481

Financial data (yr. ended 12/31/01): Grants paid, $31,820; assets, $548,215 (M); expenditures, $36,408; qualifying distributions, $33,147.
Limitations: Giving limited to residents of MO.
Trustee: Bank of America.
EIN: 446008350
Codes: GTI

52129
The T. F. & J. Y. Shao Foundation
5868 Bridle Bend Ct.
Plano, TX 75093

Established in 2000 in TX.
Donor(s): Tzu Fann Shao.
Financial data (yr. ended 12/31/01): Grants paid, $31,700; assets, $462,702 (M); gifts received, $63,100; expenditures, $39,632; qualifying distributions, $32,039.
Limitations: Applications not accepted. Giving primarily in western China.
Application information: Contributes only to pre-selected organizations.
Officers: Tzu Fann Shao, Pres. and Treas.; Jeannie J.Y. Shao, V.P. and Secy.
Trustees: Wei Ann Bay, Wei Li Shao, Wei Ming Shao.
EIN: 752897359

52130
Madelyne M. and Edward D. McCarty Foundation, Inc.
4255 Westway Pl.
Dallas, TX 75205

Established in 1996 in TX.
Donor(s): Madelyne M. McCarty.
Financial data (yr. ended 12/31/01): Grants paid, $31,500; assets, $337,254 (M); expenditures, $34,841; qualifying distributions, $31,500.
Limitations: Applications not accepted.
Application information: Contributes only to pre-selected organizations.
Officers: Martha M. Kimmerling, Pres. and Tres.; James Warren Murphy, V.P. and Secy.
Director: Madelyne M. McCarty.
EIN: 752670222

52131
Plantowsky Family Foundation
4922 Holly
Bellaire, TX 77401

Established in 1999 in TX.
Donor(s): Scott R. Plantowsky, Joy K. Plantowsky.
Financial data (yr. ended 12/31/01): Grants paid, $31,450; assets, $572,464 (M); expenditures, $35,576; qualifying distributions, $33,510.
Limitations: Applications not accepted. Giving limited to Houston, TX.
Application information: Contributes only to pre-selected organizations.
Officers: Scott R. Plantowsky, Pres.; Joy K. Plantowsky, Secy.-Treas.
Director: Sam L. Susser.
EIN: 760625289

52132
W. W. Lynch Foundation
1845 Woodall Rodgers Fwy., Ste. 1600, LB-16
Dallas, TX 75201
Contact: William W. Lynch, Jr., Tr.

Established in 1957 in TX.
Donor(s): Martha H. Lynch.
Financial data (yr. ended 12/31/01): Grants paid, $31,400; assets, $675,700 (M); expenditures, $32,815; qualifying distributions, $31,400.
Limitations: Giving primarily in the Dallas-Fort Worth, TX, area.
Application information: Application form not required.
Trustees: Harry H. Lynch, Martha H. Lynch, William W. Lynch, Jr.
EIN: 756037212

52133
J. Paul Craig Foundation
c/o Amarillo National Bank, Trust Dept.
P.O. Box 1
Amarillo, TX 79105-0001 (806) 378-8334

Established in 1976.
Donor(s): Gertrude Craig,‡ J. Paul Craig,‡ Norah Craig.‡
Financial data (yr. ended 09/30/01): Grants paid, $31,327; assets, $617,718 (M); expenditures, $37,566; qualifying distributions, $31,327.
Limitations: Applications not accepted. Giving limited to the Panhandle area of TX, with emphasis on Amarillo.
Distribution Committee Members: Cliff Bickerstaff, J. Walter Browers, L.R. Hamner, Jr., William K. Irwin, Warren Jordan.
Trustee: Amarillo National Bank.
EIN: 756196164

52134
Carson Foundation
1032 Townplace St.
Houston, TX 77057-1942
Application address: Frank Abraham, c/o Student Aid Foundation Enterprises, 800 Commerce St., Houston, TX 77002

Established in 1997.
Financial data (yr. ended 12/31/01): Grants paid, $31,275; assets, $651,873 (M); gifts received, $120,000; expenditures, $45,310; qualifying distributions, $45,310.
Limitations: Giving primarily in TX.
Officers and Directors:* C. Neal Carson,* Pres.; William R. Zweifel,* Secy.; Lynn P. Chavarria,* Treas.
EIN: 760535539

52135
Bill & Jan Foundation
4245 Kemp Blvd., Ste. 408
Wichita Falls, TX 76308
Contact: W.M. Thacker, Jr., Pres.

Donor(s): W.M. Thacker, Jr., Jane A. Thacker.
Financial data (yr. ended 11/30/01): Grants paid, $31,230; assets, $600,242 (M); gifts received, $140,000; expenditures, $31,978; qualifying distributions, $63,362.
Limitations: Giving primarily in Wichita Falls, TX.
Officers and Directors:* W.M. Thacker, Jr.,* Pres.; John W. Kable,* V.P.; Jane A. Thacker,* Secy.-Treas.; Jeffrey W. Thacker, Thomas T. Thacker, William R. Thacker.
EIN: 751800162

52136
The White Odenthal Foundation
c/o Sherry G. Odenthal
35 W. Terrace Dr.
Houston, TX 77007

Established in 1997 in TX.
Donor(s): Britton White, Sherry Odenthal.
Financial data (yr. ended 12/31/01): Grants paid, $31,210; assets, $271,985 (M); gifts received, $90,100; expenditures, $31,460; qualifying distributions, $31,210.
Limitations: Applications not accepted.
Application information: Contributes only to pre-selected organizations.
Officers: Sherry G. Odenthal, Pres.; Britton White, V.P.; Jennifer R. White, V.P.; Britton White, Jr., Secy.-Treas.
EIN: 760537777

52137
The Carl and Phyllis Detering Foundation
3028 Washington Ave.
Houston, TX 77007-6029

Established in 1989 in TX.
Donor(s): Carl A. Detering, Sr.
Financial data (yr. ended 12/31/00): Grants paid, $31,150; assets, $432 (M); gifts received, $30,500; expenditures, $32,338; qualifying distributions, $31,150.
Limitations: Applications not accepted. Giving primarily in Houston, TX.
Application information: Contributes only to pre-selected organizations.
Officers: Carl A. Detering, Sr., Pres.; William C. Detering, V.P. and Secy.; Carl A. Detering, Jr., V.P. and Treas.
EIN: 760284834

52138
Frances Hollis Palmros Trust
c/o Bank One, Texas, N.A.
P.O. Box 2050
Fort Worth, TX 76113-2050 (817) 884-4151
Contact: Bob Lansford

Established in 1990 in TX.
Financial data (yr. ended 06/30/00): Grants paid, $31,102; assets, $602,673 (M); expenditures, $40,027; qualifying distributions, $31,102.
Limitations: Giving primarily in Fort Worth, TX.
Trustee: Bank One, Texas, N.A.
EIN: 756398182

52139
Lykes-Knapp Family Fund
(Formerly J. M. Lykes Family Foundation)
910 Travis St., Ste. 2200
Houston, TX 77002

Established in 1997 in TX.
Donor(s): Breck L. Knapp, Christopher L. Knapp, James M. L. Grace, R. Randall Grace, Jr., Genevieve K. O'Sullivan, A. John Knapp, Jr.
Financial data (yr. ended 12/31/00): Grants paid, $31,065; assets, $460,157 (M); gifts received, $3,493; expenditures, $38,027; qualifying distributions, $30,173.
Limitations: Applications not accepted. Giving on a national basis, with emphasis on TX.
Application information: Contributes only to pre-selected organizations.
Officer: Christopher L. Knapp, Pres.
Directors: Breckenridge L. Knapp, Genevieve K. O'Sullivan.
EIN: 760411686

52140
Robert K. and Marie B. Hutchings Foundation
817 Kuhlman Rd.
Houston, TX 77024

Financial data (yr. ended 12/31/01): Grants paid, $31,000; assets, $882,093 (M); gifts received, $100; expenditures, $37,774; qualifying distributions, $31,000.
Limitations: Applications not accepted. Giving limited to Galveston, TX.
Application information: Contributes only to pre-selected organizations.
Officers: Robert K. Hutchings, Pres.; John H. Hutchings, V.P.; William S. Moss, Jr., Secy.-Treas.
EIN: 760454957

52141
Michael and Diane Rosenberg Family Foundation
c/o Darrell Cain
5580 Peterson Ln., Ste. 250
Dallas, TX 75240

Established in 1996 in FL and TX.
Donor(s): Barbara Diane Rosenberg, Michael N. Rosenberg.
Financial data (yr. ended 11/30/01): Grants paid, $31,000; assets, $584,719 (M); gifts received, $26,097; expenditures, $38,794; qualifying distributions, $31,000.
Limitations: Applications not accepted.
Application information: Contributes only to pre-selected organizations.
Officers: Michael N. Rosenberg, Pres.; Barbara Diane Rosenberg, Secy.-Treas.
Trustees: Allison D. Rosenberg, Glen I. Rosenberg.
EIN: 752696894

52142
Helen Gertrude Sparks Charitable Trust
(also known as Sparks Charitable Trust)
c/o Bank of America
P.O. Box 831041
Dallas, TX 75283-1041
Application address: P.O. Box 1317, Fort Worth, TX 76101, tel.: (817) 390-6918
Contact: Melissa M. Kirtley, Trust Off.

Financial data (yr. ended 05/31/01): Grants paid, $31,000; assets, $749,363 (M); expenditures, $39,217; qualifying distributions, $31,000.
Limitations: Giving limited to the Fort Worth, TX, area.
Trustee: Bank of America.
EIN: 756167997

52143
The Whitley Charitable Foundation
301 Brazos St.
Austin, TX 78701
Contact: Ronald Jones, Pres.

Established in 1990 in TX.
Donor(s): Ronald Jones.
Financial data (yr. ended 12/31/01): Grants paid, $30,936; assets, $722,389 (M); gifts received, $6,150; expenditures, $32,281; qualifying distributions, $30,936.
Limitations: Applications not accepted. Giving primarily in Austin, TX.
Application information: Contributes only to pre-selected organizations.
Officers: Ronald Jones, Pres.; Johnny G. Jones, V.P.; Wilma Jones, Secy.-Treas.
EIN: 742588216

52144
Fairfield Foundation
4008 Shannon Ln.
Dallas, TX 75205-1737 (214) 528-5943
Contact: Anne Giles Kimbrough, Pres.

Established in 1980 in TX.
Donor(s): Arch P. Kimbrough,‡ William A. Sholten III.
Financial data (yr. ended 12/31/01): Grants paid, $30,800; assets, $511,987 (M); gifts received, $7,000; expenditures, $33,057; qualifying distributions, $30,800.
Limitations: Giving primarily in IL.
Officers and Trustees:* Anne Giles Kimbrough,* Pres.; Elizabeth L. Kimbrough,* V.P.; Lucy G. Kimbrough,* V.P.; Leslie K. Sholten,* V.P.; William A. Sholten III,* Secy.-Treas.
EIN: 751746196

52145
The Leon & Sandra Weiner Foundation, Inc.
121 N. Post Oak Blvd., No. 2301
Houston, TX 77024

Financial data (yr. ended 08/31/01): Grants paid, $30,775; assets, $785,485 (M); gifts received, $6,618; expenditures, $36,600; qualifying distributions, $30,775.
Limitations: Applications not accepted. Giving primarily in Houston, TX.
Application information: Contributes only to pre-selected organizations.
Officers: Sandra Weiner, Pres.; Leon Weiner, Secy.
EIN: 746049467

52146
Gaither Foundation
No. 2 Kitty Hawk W. St.
Richmond, TX 77469-9710

Established in 1995 in TX.
Financial data (yr. ended 12/31/01): Grants paid, $30,700; assets, $480,792 (M); expenditures, $31,650; qualifying distributions, $30,700.
Limitations: Applications not accepted. Giving primarily in Houston, TX.
Application information: Contributes only to pre-selected organizations.
Officers: Orville D. Gaither, Pres.; Mary M. Gaither, V.P.; Donna G. Guerrero, Secy.-Treas.
EIN: 760457657

52147
The Buzbee Foundation
c/o James Buzbee
503 N.W. 7th Ave.
Mineral Wells, TX 76067

Established in 1999 in TX.
Donor(s): James M. Buzbee, Erna Mae Buzbee.
Financial data (yr. ended 12/31/01): Grants paid, $30,500; assets, $785,748 (M); gifts received, $614,284; expenditures, $32,478; qualifying distributions, $30,500.
Limitations: Applications not accepted.
Application information: Contributes only to pre-selected organizations.
Trustees: Erna Mae Buzbee, James Bradford Buzbee, James Meredith Buzbee, Carla Suzanne Buzbee Osborn, Lelynn Kay Buzbee Wilson.
EIN: 752819095

52148
The J. Paul Grayson Foundation
1701 N. Greenville Ave., Ste. 702
Richardson, TX 75081

Established in 1990 in TX.
Donor(s): J. Paul Grayson.
Financial data (yr. ended 12/31/01): Grants paid, $30,500; assets, $1,629,120 (M); expenditures, $54,126; qualifying distributions, $32,900.
Limitations: Applications not accepted. Giving primarily in TX.
Application information: Contributes only to pre-selected organizations.
Officers and Directors:* J. Paul Grayson,* Pres.; Marleen Grayson Aaron,* V.P.; James E. Shepherd,* Secy.
EIN: 752379425

52149
Tom E. Turner Family Foundation
P.O. Box 171720
San Antonio, TX 78217
Application address: 1777 N.E. Loop 410, San Antonio, TX 78217, tel.: (210) 821-5900
Contact: Fred Turner, Dir.

Established in 2000 in TX.
Donor(s): Tom E. Turner, Brenda Turner.
Financial data (yr. ended 12/31/00): Grants paid, $30,475; assets, $1,913,811 (M); gifts received, $1,936,400; expenditures, $30,517; qualifying distributions, $30,475.
Limitations: Giving primarily in San Antonio, TX.
Application information: Application form not required.
Directors: Monroe Spears, Brenda Turner, Fred Turner, Tom E. Turner.
EIN: 742936734

52150
The Sedmak-Wooten Family Foundation
5 Cousteau Ln.
Austin, TX 78746

Established in 1999 in TX.
Donor(s): Jon S. Sedmak, Jr., Noralee Wooten Sedmak.
Financial data (yr. ended 12/31/00): Grants paid, $30,444; assets, $1,652,125 (M); gifts received, $37,000; expenditures, $67,950; qualifying distributions, $12,800.
Limitations: Applications not accepted. Giving primarily in Washington, DC and Austin, TX.
Application information: Contributes only to pre-selected organizations.
Officers and Directors:* Noralee Wooten Sedmak,* Pres. and Treas.; Jon S. Sedmak, Jr.,* V.P. and Secy.; Alyssa Caryn Sedmak, Jonathan Matthew Sedmak, Nicole Christine Sedmak.
EIN: 742919300

52151
The K. & L. Trimmer Foundation
6628 Castle Pines Dr.
Plano, TX 75093

Established in 1999 in TX.
Donor(s): Ken Trimmer, Linda Trimmer.
Financial data (yr. ended 12/31/01): Grants paid, $30,409; assets, $516,515 (M); expenditures, $34,509; qualifying distributions, $30,409.
Limitations: Applications not accepted. Giving primarily in Dallas, TX.
Application information: Contributes only to pre-selected organizations.
Directors: Sharon Rhine, Ken Trimmer, Linda Trimmer.
EIN: 752835373

52152
Louis & Madlyn Barnett Living Charitable Foundation
P.O. Box 11739
Fort Worth, TX 76110-0739
Contact: Laurie Werner, Tr.

Established in 1966.
Financial data (yr. ended 12/31/01): Grants paid, $30,384; assets, $1,184,819 (M); expenditures, $54,536; qualifying distributions, $30,384.
Limitations: Giving primarily in New York, NY and Fort Worth, TX.
Application information: Application form not required.
Trustees: Louis H. Barnett, Madlyn B. Barnett, R. Bernstein, Laurie B. Werner.
EIN: 751855078

52153
J. L. and Marion Jackson Foundation
6404 Williams Pkwy.
Dallas, TX 75205

Established in 1986 in TX.
Donor(s): J.L. Jackson, Mrs. J.L. Jackson.
Financial data (yr. ended 10/31/01): Grants paid, $30,315; assets, $333,128 (M); gifts received,

$25,000; expenditures, $39,371; qualifying distributions, $30,315.
Limitations: Applications not accepted. Giving primarily in Dallas, TX.
Application information: Contributes only to pre-selected organizations.
Officers: J.L. Jackson, Pres.; Marion V. Jackson, V.P.
Director: J. Leslie Jackson III.
EIN: 752147155

52154
The Bayou Charitable Trust
c/o JPMorgan Chase Bank
P.O. Box 2558
Houston, TX 77252-8037 (713) 216-4649
Contact: Judy Cook, Trust Off., JPMorgan Chase Bank

Established in 1992 in TX.
Donor(s): Charles H. Gregory, Jane H. Gregory.
Financial data (yr. ended 12/31/01): Grants paid, $30,300; assets, $623,370 (M); expenditures, $39,616; qualifying distributions, $30,300.
Limitations: Giving limited to TX.
Trustees: Charles H. Gregory, Jane H. Gregory, JPMorgan Chase Bank.
EIN: 766079369

52155
Bill Pace Cogdell Charitable Trust
2005 W. Missouri
Midland, TX 79701

Financial data (yr. ended 12/31/00): Grants paid, $30,288; assets, $1,296,578 (M); gifts received, $1,444; expenditures, $89,388; qualifying distributions, $30,288.
Limitations: Applications not accepted.
Application information: Contributes only to pre-selected organizations.
Trustees: John E. Gunter, Carol C. Subia.
EIN: 752737902

52156
Lubbock Chamber of Commerce Foundation
1301 Broadway St., Ste. 101
Lubbock, TX 79401
Contact: Eddie McBride

Financial data (yr. ended 09/30/00): Grants paid, $30,288; assets, $9,536 (M); expenditures, $30,479; qualifying distributions, $30,288; giving activities include $109 for programs.
Limitations: Giving primarily in Lubbock, TX.
Officer: Steve Massengale, Pres.
EIN: 752081274

52157
The Andress Foundation
P.O. Box 5198
Abilene, TX 79608-5198 (915) 698-5560
Application address: P.O. Box 6735, Abilene, TX 79608
Contact: Tony D. Andress, Jr., Pres.

Established in 1977 in TX.
Donor(s): Tony D. Andress, Sr.
Financial data (yr. ended 11/30/01): Grants paid, $30,200; assets, $1,316,825 (M); gifts received, $4,800; expenditures, $105,224; qualifying distributions, $103,258.
Limitations: Giving primarily in western TX, with emphasis on Abilene.
Officers and Directors:* Tony D. Andress, Jr.,* Pres.; Tony D. Andress, Sr.,* V.P. and Secy.; Kellie Andress Alegre, Ashley D. Andress.
EIN: 751577382

52158
George F. and Ann Harris Bellows Foundation
c/o Maddox, Maddox, Thomson, & Assocs.
5851 San Felipe, Ste. 700
Houston, TX 77057
Contact: Lawrence E. Maddox

Established in 1998 in TX.
Donor(s): George F. Bellows.
Financial data (yr. ended 12/31/01): Grants paid, $30,000; assets, $246,816 (M); gifts received, $4,725; expenditures, $36,355; qualifying distributions, $30,000.
Limitations: Giving primarily in Houston, TX.
Directors: George F. Bellows, Marilyn L. Bellows, Wayne H. Bellows, Karey Dubiel Dye, Lawrence J. Fossi.
EIN: 760588143

52159
Mr. & Mrs. James R. Blake Foundation
500 W. 7th St., Ste. 1213
Fort Worth, TX 76102

Donor(s): Loraine B. Cummins, James R. Blake, Mrs. James R. Blake.
Financial data (yr. ended 12/31/01): Grants paid, $30,000; assets, $629,520 (M); expenditures, $36,414; qualifying distributions, $30,000.
Limitations: Applications not accepted. Giving primarily in AZ and TX.
Application information: Contributes only to pre-selected organizations.
Officers: James R. Blake, Pres.; Dianna Way, Exec. Secy.; Cornelia C. Blake, Secy.-Treas.
EIN: 752139051

52160
McGinnis & Bettie Clark Foundation
6231 Queenswood
Houston, TX 77008

Established in 1998 in TX.
Donor(s): Bettie Clark, McGinnis Clark.
Financial data (yr. ended 12/31/01): Grants paid, $30,000; assets, $298,128 (M); gifts received, $116,464; expenditures, $35,567; qualifying distributions, $30,000.
Limitations: Applications not accepted. Giving primarily in Houston, TX.
Application information: Contributes only to pre-selected organizations.
Officers: McGinnis Clark, Pres.; Bettie Clark, V.P.; Paul W. Clark, Secy.-Treas.
Director: Carl W. Clark.
EIN: 760581346

52161
Ellis Family Foundation
3828 W. Davis St., Ste. 308/N355
Conroe, TX 77304 (936) 582-6556
Contact: Floyd E. Ellis, Pres.

Established in 1997 in TX.
Donor(s): Floyd E. Ellis.
Financial data (yr. ended 12/31/01): Grants paid, $30,000; assets, $625,346 (M); expenditures, $42,073; qualifying distributions, $30,000.
Limitations: Giving primarily in TX and WY.
Officer: Floyd E. Ellis, Pres.; David Kipp Ellis, V.P.; Valerie A. Jochen, V.P.; Marley J. Richards, V.P.; V. Diane Ellis, Secy.-Treas.
EIN: 311556165

52162
The Carolyn Grant Fay Fund
c/o Carolyn Grant Fay
P.O. Box 66309
Houston, TX 77266-6309

Established in 1993 in TX.
Donor(s): Carolyn Grant Fay.
Financial data (yr. ended 06/30/01): Grants paid, $30,000; assets, $322,141 (M); expenditures, $30,543; qualifying distributions, $30,000.
Limitations: Applications not accepted.
Application information: Contributes only to pre-selected organizations.
Directors: Marie Bel Fay Evnochides, Carolyn Grant Fay, John Spencer Fay, Carolyn Randall Fay Yocum.
EIN: 760388662

52163
The Glanville Family Foundation
c/o Glanville Family Interests
8 Greenway Plz., Ste. 702
Houston, TX 77046
Contact: Nancy H. Glanville, Pres.

Established in 1985 in NY.
Donor(s): James W. Glanville,‡ Nancy H. Glanville.
Financial data (yr. ended 06/30/02): Grants paid, $30,000; assets, $665,182 (M); expenditures, $32,927; qualifying distributions, $30,000.
Limitations: Giving on a national basis, with some emphasis on CA and TX.
Application information: Application form not required.
Officers and Directors:* Nancy H. Glanville,* Pres.; John H. Glanville,* V.P.; Thomas S. Glanville,* V.P.; Michael Powers, Secy.-Treas.; Charles D. Glanville, Robert E. Glanville.
EIN: 133284981

52164
The Thelma B. Goans Endowment, Inc.
1574 Common Dr.
El Paso, TX 79936 (915) 595-2600
Contact: Anthony Burdett, C.P.A.

Established in 1994 in TX.
Donor(s): Jacqueline Hudson Pippen.‡
Financial data (yr. ended 09/30/01): Grants paid, $30,000; assets, $162,829 (M); expenditures, $31,902; qualifying distributions, $30,000.
Limitations: Giving primarily in El Paso, TX.
Officers: Diane McGee, Pres.; Barbara Crews, V.P.; Gayle Millard, V.P.; Rachel Klein, Secy.; Chris Hopp, Treas.
Trustee: El Paso Veterinary Medical Assn.
EIN: 742729597

52165
Virginia Heacock Charitable Foundation
2500 City W. Blvd., No. 125
Houston, TX 77027-9006

Established in 1995 in TX.
Donor(s): Virginia Fern Heacock.
Financial data (yr. ended 12/31/01): Grants paid, $30,000; assets, $549,799 (M); gifts received, $50,556; expenditures, $31,699; qualifying distributions, $30,000.
Limitations: Applications not accepted.
Application information: Contributes only to pre-selected organizations.
Trustee: Virginia Fern Heacock.
EIN: 760487824

52166
Hensel Family Foundation
P.O. Box 3008
Humble, TX 77347-3008

Established in 1999 in TX.
Donor(s): Scott C. Hensel, Constance V. Hensel, Scott C. Hensel II, Alba M. Jessop.
Financial data (yr. ended 12/31/01): Grants paid, $30,000; assets, $620,357 (M); gifts received,

$652,409; expenditures, $30,809; qualifying distributions, $30,000.
Limitations: Applications not accepted.
Application information: Contributes only to pre-selected organizations.
Trustees: Constance V. Hensel, Scott C. Hensel, Scott C. Hensel II, Alba M. Jessop.
EIN: 760564239

52167
C. H. & K. B. Johnson Foundation
771 River Oaks Cir.
McKinney, TX 75069
Contact: Claiborne H. Johnson, Jr., Pres.

Established in 1992 in TX.
Donor(s): Claiborne H. Johnson, Jr., Katherine B. Johnson.
Financial data (yr. ended 12/31/01): Grants paid, $30,000; assets, $139,970 (M); expenditures, $31,110; qualifying distributions, $30,000.
Limitations: Applications not accepted. Giving primarily in Charleston, SC.
Application information: Unsolicited requests for funds not accepted. Contributes only to pre-selected organizations.
Officers and Directors:* Claiborne H. Johnson, Jr.,* Pres.; Katherine B. Johnson,* V.P.; Elizabeth J. Keig,* Secy.
EIN: 752424255

52168
The Carolyn S. and Tommie E. Lohman Foundation
10000 Memorial Dr., Ste. 520
Houston, TX 77024

Established in 1994 in TX.
Financial data (yr. ended 12/31/01): Grants paid, $30,000; assets, $362,296 (M); expenditures, $32,775; qualifying distributions, $30,000.
Limitations: Applications not accepted. Giving primarily in TX.
Application information: Contributes only to pre-selected organizations.
Officers: Carolyn S. Lohman, Pres.; Tommie E. Lohman, V.P and Secy.-Treas.
Directors: Caroline Lohman Agrella, Amber Lohman Gray.
EIN: 752571005

52169
Ruth Jones MacDonald Charitable Trust
770 S. Post Oak Ln., Ste. 630
Houston, TX 77056-1965

Established in 1998 in TX.
Financial data (yr. ended 06/30/01): Grants paid, $30,000; assets, $564,110 (M); expenditures, $40,724; qualifying distributions, $29,915.
Limitations: Applications not accepted. Giving primarily in Brookshire, TX.
Application information: Contributes only to pre-selected organizations.
Trustee: Bruce C. Arendale.
EIN: 766143209

52170
The J. B. and Hazel McAdams Foundation
4245 N. Central Expwy.
Dallas, TX 75205-4252
Contact: Polly Lou Moore, Pres.

Established in 1980 in TX.
Financial data (yr. ended 11/30/01): Grants paid, $30,000; assets, $100,359 (M); expenditures, $30,280; qualifying distributions, $30,000.
Limitations: Giving primarily in Dallas, TX.
Application information: Application form not required.

Officers: Polly Lou Moore, Pres.; Jack W. Hawkins, V.P.; Denise Turner, Secy.-Treas.
Directors: Dorman Shockley, Shirley Shockley.
EIN: 751736359

52171
The Hakeem Olajuwon Foundation
6420 Hillcroft St., Ste. 218
Houston, TX 77081-3103

Established in 1999.
Donor(s): Hakeem Olajuwon.
Financial data (yr. ended 12/31/00): Grants paid, $30,000; assets, $7,677,118 (M); gifts received, $5,800,000; expenditures, $34,065; qualifying distributions, $30,000.
Limitations: Applications not accepted.
Application information: Contributes only to pre-selected organizations.
Officer: Hakeem Olajuwon, Pres.
Directors: Jamal Asafi, Tajudeen Olajuwon.
EIN: 760626200

52172
Roy & Ellen Quillin Foundation Trust
c/o Frost National Bank
P.O. Box 2950
San Antonio, TX 78299 (210) 220-5955
Contact: William Clyborne, V.P., Frost National Bank

Financial data (yr. ended 07/31/01): Grants paid, $30,000; assets, $728,089 (M); expenditures, $39,388; qualifying distributions, $33,645.
Limitations: Giving primarily in San Antonio, TX.
Trustee: Frost National Bank.
EIN: 746228489

52173
River Creek Foundation
19C Smiser Smith Rd.
Boerne, TX 78006

Established in 1994 in TX.
Donor(s): Pyramid Manufacturing, Gary L. Jennings, Patsy R. Jennings.
Financial data (yr. ended 12/31/01): Grants paid, $30,000; assets, $136,062 (M); expenditures, $30,000; qualifying distributions, $30,000.
Limitations: Applications not accepted.
Application information: Contributes only to pre-selected organizations.
Officers: Gary L. Jennings, Pres.; Patsy R. Jennings, V.P.
EIN: 760455378

52174
The W. Morgan & Lou Claire Rose Trust
c/o J. Powell
391 Landa St.
New Braunfels, TX 78130

Financial data (yr. ended 12/31/01): Grants paid, $30,000; assets, $803,902 (M); expenditures, $31,097; qualifying distributions, $30,000.
Trustees: John Powell, Mary Powell.
EIN: 746471295

52175
George & Magnolia Willis Sealy Foundation
c/o Bank of America
P.O. Box 1500
Galveston, TX 77553

Financial data (yr. ended 12/31/01): Grants paid, $30,000; assets, $392,838 (M); expenditures, $38,821; qualifying distributions, $30,000.
Limitations: Giving primarily in TX.
Trustee: Bank of America.
EIN: 760157356

52176
Texas Newspaper Foundation
718 W. 5th St.
Austin, TX 78701

Established in 1991 in TX.
Donor(s): Roy J. Eaton.
Financial data (yr. ended 05/31/02): Grants paid, $30,000; assets, $215,580 (M); gifts received, $26,008; expenditures, $35,278; qualifying distributions, $30,000.
Limitations: Applications not accepted.
Application information: Contributes only to pre-selected organizations.
Officers and Trustees:* Roy J. Eaton,* Pres.; Fred V. Barbee, Jr.,* Treas.; Larry Crabtree, Sarah Greene, Larry Jackson, Phil Major, Roy McQueen, Sally Richards, Jerry Tidwell.
EIN: 237399356

52177
Warthog Charitable Foundation
7902 Woodridge
San Antonio, TX 78209

Donor(s): Charles W. Robinson, Jr.
Financial data (yr. ended 12/31/01): Grants paid, $30,000; assets, $879,751 (M); gifts received, $18,180; expenditures, $38,396; qualifying distributions, $30,000.
Limitations: Applications not accepted.
Application information: Contributes only to pre-selected organizations.
Trustees: Charles W. Robinson, Sr., Charles W. Robinson, Jr., Cynthia Robinson.
EIN: 742821059

52178
Texas Alpha Endowment Fund, Inc.
P.O. Box 27233
Austin, TX 78755-2233

Financial data (yr. ended 06/30/01): Grants paid, $29,950; assets, $37,689 (M); gifts received, $57,225; expenditures, $39,948; qualifying distributions, $29,950.
Limitations: Giving primarily in TX.
Officers: Chase McCurry, Pres.; Arthur Ranch, V.P.; Keys Curry, Secy.-Treas.
EIN: 742560499

52179
Maureen Connolly Brinker Tennis Foundation, Inc.
(Formerly Maureen Connolly Brinker Girls' Tennis Foundation, Inc.)
5419 Wateka Dr.
Dallas, TX 75209 (214) 357-1604
Contact: Mrs. Frank Jeffett, Pres.

Established in 1969.
Donor(s): Phillip Morris.
Financial data (yr. ended 04/30/01): Grants paid, $29,878; assets, $3,181,680 (M); gifts received, $34,032; expenditures, $372,098; qualifying distributions, $198,936; giving activities include $364,582 for programs.
Limitations: Giving primarily in Dallas, TX.
Officer: Mrs. Frank A. Jeffett, Pres.
Trustees: Norman Brinker, Robert C. Taylor.
EIN: 237040481

52180
Gus & Ethel Wolters Foundation Trust
c/o Frost National Bank
P.O. Box 2950
San Antonio, TX 78299 (210) 220-4457
Contact: Steve W. Barker, V.P., Frost National Bank

Financial data (yr. ended 08/31/01): Grants paid, $29,700; assets, $717,783 (M); expenditures, $40,668; qualifying distributions, $33,880.
Limitations: Giving limited to TX.
Application information: Contact Shriner High School or St. Pauls High School for application information. Application form required.
Trustee: Frost National Bank.
EIN: 742335544
Codes: GTI

52181
Longaker Foundation
12 Cypress Ridge Ln.
Sugar Land, TX 77479

Established in 2000 in TX.
Donor(s): Bruce Longaker.
Financial data (yr. ended 12/31/01): Grants paid, $29,640; assets, $390,222 (M); expenditures, $33,473; qualifying distributions, $29,438.
Limitations: Applications not accepted. Giving primarily in TX.
Application information: Contributes only to pre-selected organizations.
Officers and Directors:* Bruce Longaker,* Pres.; Sherri Loeffelholz,* Secy.; Jennifer Maxheimer.
EIN: 760664608

52182
The Tuschman Foundation
(Formerly The Julia Love Tuschman Foundation)
7670 Woodway, Ste. 120
Houston, TX 77063-1501 (713) 706-4000
FAX: (713) 706-4002; E-mail:
j.tusch@worldnet.att.net
Contact: John S. Tuschman, Tr.

Established in 1983 as The Fund for Matching Endowments; name changed in 1989 to The Julia Love Tuschman Foundation. In 1995, the foundation name was changed to The Tuschman Foundation.
Donor(s): Julia Love Tuschman.‡
Financial data (yr. ended 12/31/01): Grants paid, $29,533; assets, $546,821 (M); gifts received, $130,723; expenditures, $31,472; qualifying distributions, $29,533.
Limitations: Giving primarily in CO.
Trustees: Margaret Love DeVinney, John S. Tuschman.
EIN: 760082433

52183
The Kensan Trust
101 Westcott St., No. 501
Houston, TX 77007-7030

Established in 1994 in TX.
Donor(s): Cia Kensan Devan.
Financial data (yr. ended 12/31/00): Grants paid, $29,500; assets, $704,733 (M); expenditures, $31,045; qualifying distributions, $29,500.
Limitations: Applications not accepted.
Application information: Contributes only to pre-selected organizations.
Trustee: Cia Kensan Devan.
EIN: 766099805

52184
Brentham Foundation
510 N. Loop 121
Belton, TX 76513

Established in 1993 in TX.
Donor(s): Jerry D. Brentham.
Financial data (yr. ended 12/31/01): Grants paid, $29,480; assets, $475,217 (M); expenditures, $42,850; qualifying distributions, $29,480.
Limitations: Applications not accepted. Giving limited to TX.
Application information: Contributes only to pre-selected organizations.
Officers: Jerry D. Brentham, Pres.; Donnie L. Brentham, Secy.-Treas.
Trustees: Jerry Bawcom, Andy Davis, Kenneth W. Johnson, Ralph Masters, Larry Thompson.
EIN: 741946795

52185
Louise Briley Leake Charitable Trust
P.O. Box 2050
Fort Worth, TX 76113

Established in 1996 in ID.
Donor(s): Louise Briley Leake.‡
Financial data (yr. ended 12/31/99): Grants paid, $29,225; assets, $1,342,383 (M); expenditures, $46,261; qualifying distributions, $29,225.
Limitations: Applications not accepted. Giving limited to LA.
Application information: Contributes only to pre-selected organizations.
Trustee: Bank One Trust Co., N.A.
EIN: 726166273

52186
Help Our Students Succeed Foundation
3131 N. Hwy. 161
Irving, TX 75062 (972) 257-1244

Donor(s): Hoss Equipment Co.
Financial data (yr. ended 12/31/01): Grants paid, $29,049; assets, $24 (M); gifts received, $29,988; expenditures, $29,979; qualifying distributions, $29,049.
Application information: Application form required.
Officers and Directors:* Gregg M. Hoss,* Pres.; Andrew J. Speer III,* Secy.
EIN: 752622539
Codes: GTI

52187
The Olmsted-Taylor Foundation, Inc.
P.O. Box 1049
Dallas, TX 75221-1049 (972) 239-4699

Established in 1995 in TX.
Donor(s): Olmsted-Kirk Paper Co.
Financial data (yr. ended 12/31/01): Grants paid, $29,000; assets, $735,881 (M); gifts received, $610,610; expenditures, $29,131; qualifying distributions, $29,000.
Limitations: Applications not accepted. Giving primarily in Dallas, TX.
Trustees: Betty Moss Olmsted, Gail Bonneau Olmsted, Robert M. Olmsted, Jr., Betty Olmsted Taylor, John Taylor.
EIN: 752575065

52188
Roberta K. Randall Charitable Foundation
c/o Roberta K. Avery
P.O. Box 16936
Sugar Land, TX 77496-6936

Donor(s): Roberta K. Randall.
Financial data (yr. ended 12/31/01): Grants paid, $29,000; assets, $493,837 (M); gifts received, $1,120; expenditures, $33,180; qualifying distributions, $29,000.
Limitations: Applications not accepted. Giving primarily in TX.
Application information: Contributes only to pre-selected organizations.
Officers and Trustees:* Robert K. Avery,* Pres.; Lester T. Lothman,* V.P.; Elsie Maris,* Secy.-Treas.; John R. Craig IV, Courtney Maris.
EIN: 760555899

52189
The Minnie Quickenstedt Underwood Foundation
c/o Bank of America
P.O. Box 831041
Dallas, TX 75283-1041
Application address: c/o Trinity University, Scholarship Board, 715 Stadium Dr., San Antonio, TX 78284

Financial data (yr. ended 08/31/00): Grants paid, $29,000; assets, $283,024 (M); expenditures, $31,770; qualifying distributions, $29,320.
Limitations: Giving limited to San Antonio, TX.
Application information: Application form required.
Trustees: Mrs. Arch S. Underwood, Fred Q. Underwood, Harris F. Underwood, Bank of America.
EIN: 756049861

52190
The Lee and Edith Kidd Family Foundation
P.O. Box 1359
Denver City, TX 79323

Established in 2000 in TX.
Donor(s): Lee M. Kidd, Edith M. Kidd.
Financial data (yr. ended 12/31/01): Grants paid, $28,873; assets, $1,115,702 (M); expenditures, $29,317; qualifying distributions, $28,873.
Limitations: Applications not accepted. Giving primarily in TX.
Application information: Contributes only to pre-selected organizations.
Officers: Lee M. Kidd, Pres. and Treas.; Edith M. Kidd, V.P. and Secy.
Directors: Marilyn Kae Kidd, Marla Gene Kidd, Suzi Parker, Margaret Robertson.
EIN: 752877959

52191
Maynard Foundation
P.O. Box 9062
Amarillo, TX 79105-9062 (806) 374-3063
Contact: John C. Maynard, Pres.

Financial data (yr. ended 11/30/01): Grants paid, $28,750; assets, $648,485 (M); expenditures, $30,492; qualifying distributions, $28,750.
Limitations: Giving primarily in the southwestern U.S.
Officers: John C. Maynard, Pres.; Virginia I. Maynard, Secy.-Treas.
EIN: 756056417

52192
Neustadt Charitable Foundation
111 N. Wynden Estate Ct.
Houston, TX 77056 (713) 940-2804
Contact: Jean Neustadt, Jr., Pres.

Established in 1965 in OK.
Donor(s): Allan Neustadt, Doris W. Neustadt,‡ Jean Neustadt,‡ Joan Neustadt Weil, Walter Neustadt, Jr.
Financial data (yr. ended 12/31/01): Grants paid, $28,570; assets, $536,939 (M); expenditures, $31,946; qualifying distributions, $28,570.
Limitations: Giving primarily in OK and TX.

Application information: Application form not required.
Officers and Directors:* Jean Neustadt, Jr., Chair.; Bruce Neustadt,* Pres.; Marc Neustadt,* Secy.; Joseph Neustadt, Treas.
EIN: 736100346

52193
Haggerty Family Foundation
c/o Michael Haggerty
1102 W. 6th St.
Austin, TX 78703

Established in 1997 in TX.
Financial data (yr. ended 02/28/02): Grants paid, $28,500; assets, $370,026 (M); expenditures, $33,976; qualifying distributions, $28,500.
Limitations: Applications not accepted.
Application information: Contributes only to pre-selected organizations.
Officers and Directors:* Michael Haggerty,* Pres.; Jean Haggerty,* Secy.; Beatrice Haggerty.
EIN: 742834429

52194
The Horlock Foundation
1200 Post Oak Blvd., Ste. 430
Houston, TX 77056-3104 (713) 621-1981
Contact: Roy M. Horlock, Pres.

Established in 1980.
Donor(s): Roy M. Horlock.
Financial data (yr. ended 11/30/01): Grants paid, $28,500; assets, $489,284 (M); gifts received, $100,000; expenditures, $31,085; qualifying distributions, $28,500.
Limitations: Giving primarily in Houston and Fort Worth, TX.
Application information: Application form required.
Officer and Directors:* Roy M. Horlock,* Pres., V.P., and Secy.-Treas.; Peggy Horlock Dickerson, Bradley C. Hunter Horlock, Roy M. Horlock, Jr., Brenda E. Horlock Jewett, Nancy Horlock Lisenby, Kathy Horlock Morgan.
EIN: 742155927

52195
Stribling Funding Corporation
(Formerly Charitable Funding Corporation)
40 W. Twohig Ave., Ste. 412
San Angelo, TX 76903-6406 (915) 655-0133
Contact: Ben Stribling, Dir.

Established in 1988.
Financial data (yr. ended 09/30/01): Grants paid, $28,367; assets, $956,128 (M); expenditures, $35,763; qualifying distributions, $28,367.
Limitations: Giving limited to TX.
Directors: Ben Stribling, Beverly Stribling, Robert Stribling.
EIN: 742488373

52196
Maria Boswell Flake Home for Old Women
1001 Fannin St., Ste. 700
Houston, TX 77002-6777
Application address: 225 Houston Club Bldg., 811 Rusk St., Houston, TX 77002-2811, tel.: (713) 223-8061
Contact: Mrs. R. Dean Graves, Pres.

Established in 1910 in TX.
Financial data (yr. ended 12/31/01): Grants paid, $28,063; assets, $879,383 (M); expenditures, $56,024; qualifying distributions, $36,084.
Limitations: Giving limited to TX.
Officer and Trustees:* Mrs. R. Dean Graves,* Pres.; Mrs. Robert A. Bell, Thomas E. Berry, Mrs. W. Jeffrey Paine.
EIN: 741395692

52197
J. M. Wood Foundation
c/o Harelik & Fields, LLP
P.O. Box 8135
Waco, TX 76714-8135
Application address: P.O. Box 8434, Waco, TX, 76714-8434
Contact: Doris W. Wood, Pres.

Incorporated in 1957 in TX.
Donor(s): J. Carroll Wood, Doris W. Wood.
Financial data (yr. ended 01/31/01): Grants paid, $28,002; assets, $583,695 (M); expenditures, $33,069; qualifying distributions, $28,002.
Limitations: Giving on a national basis.
Officers: Doris W. Wood, Pres.; Joe C. Wood, Jr., V.P. and Secy.-Treas.
EIN: 746041784

52198
The Gilmore Foundation
1231 Lumpkin Rd.
Houston, TX 77043 (713) 468-8778
Contact: Susan G. Johnson, Tr.

Established in 1990 in TX.
Donor(s): Virginia Gilmore.
Financial data (yr. ended 09/30/01): Grants paid, $28,000; assets, $133,888 (M); expenditures, $30,289; qualifying distributions, $28,000.
Limitations: Giving primarily in Houston, TX.
Application information: Application form not required.
Trustee: Susan G. Johnson.
EIN: 760004867

52199
The Frances Gunn Family Foundation
811 6th St.
Wichita Falls, TX 76301

Established in 2000 in TX.
Donor(s): Frances E. Gunn.
Financial data (yr. ended 12/31/01): Grants paid, $28,000; assets, $492,784 (M); expenditures, $28,081; qualifying distributions, $28,000.
Limitations: Applications not accepted.
Application information: Contributes only to pre-selected organizations.
Directors: Frances E. Gunn, William C. Gunn.
EIN: 752912868

52200
The JHB Family Foundation
1901 N. Akard St.
Dallas, TX 75201

Established in 1991 in CA.
Donor(s): James E. Bass, Hong Z. Bass.
Financial data (yr. ended 12/31/01): Grants paid, $28,000; assets, $407,283 (M); expenditures, $31,300; qualifying distributions, $28,000.
Limitations: Applications not accepted.
Application information: Contributes only to pre-selected organizations.
Officers: James E. Bass, Pres.; Carolyn Dee Forman, V.P.; Bonnie Bass Smith, V.P.; Hong Z. Bass, Secy.
EIN: 954351345

52201
The Range Family Foundation
15 E. Greenway Plz., Ste. 18F
Houston, TX 77046-1501 (713) 355-8189
Contact: Walter K. Range, Jr., Pres.

Established in 2000 in TX.
Donor(s): Walter K. Range, Jr.
Financial data (yr. ended 12/31/01): Grants paid, $28,000; assets, $468 (M); expenditures, $28,245; qualifying distributions, $28,000.

Limitations: Giving primarily in New Orleans, LA, and Houston, TX.
Officers and Directors:* Walter K. Range, Jr.,* Pres. and Treas.; Leigh M. Williamson,* V.P.; Katharine F. Jewell,* Secy.
EIN: 311688436

52202
The Rundell Foundation
2200 Ross Ave., Ste. 4660W
Dallas, TX 75201-2765

Established in 1998 in TX.
Donor(s): Sylvia Rundell.
Financial data (yr. ended 12/31/01): Grants paid, $28,000; assets, $612,462 (M); expenditures, $44,089; qualifying distributions, $28,000.
Limitations: Applications not accepted.
Application information: Contributes only to pre-selected organizations.
Trustees: C.A. Rundell, Matthew H. Rundell, Pamela Rundell, Stephen A. Rundell, Sylvia Rundell.
EIN: 752768626

52203
R. F. and Jessie Shaw Foundation, Inc.
P.O. Box 1375
Henderson, TX 75653-1375

Established in 1985 in TX.
Donor(s): Marilyn Bonner Lane, Charles H. Richardson, Gene Shaw Richardson.
Financial data (yr. ended 09/30/01): Grants paid, $28,000; assets, $572,289 (M); expenditures, $35,922; qualifying distributions, $28,000.
Limitations: Applications not accepted. Giving limited to Henderson and Wichita Falls, TX.
Application information: Contributes only to pre-selected organizations.
Officers: Charles H. Richardson, Pres.; Marilyn Shaw Lane, V.P.; Gene Shaw Richardson, Secy.-Treas.; Stayton M. Bonner, Jr., Mgr.
EIN: 752070377

52204
Stewart Scholarship Foundation
c/o Debbie Wilson
1980 Post Oak Blvd., Ste. 910
Houston, TX 77056

Financial data (yr. ended 12/31/01): Grants paid, $28,000; assets, $4,631 (M); gifts received, $24,000; expenditures, $28,025; qualifying distributions, $28,000.
Officers: Nita Nanks, Pres.; Max Crisp, V.P. and Treas.
EIN: 760462905

52205
Blanche G. Terry Educational Trust
Citizens National Bank
400 W. Collin St.
Corsicana, TX 75110-5124 (903) 874-1700
Contact: Larry Turner

Financial data (yr. ended 05/31/02): Grants paid, $27,950; assets, $625,501 (M); expenditures, $35,067; qualifying distributions, $28,875.
Limitations: Giving limited to Navarro County, TX.
Application information: Application form required.
Trustee: Citizens National Bank.
EIN: 756173637
Codes: GTI

52206
The Donsky Foundation
5223 Braesheather Dr.
Houston, TX 77096-4107

Established in 1968 in TX.

Donor(s): Abe H. Donsky.
Financial data (yr. ended 12/31/01): Grants paid, $27,760; assets, $547,924 (M); gifts received, $23,679; expenditures, $28,458; qualifying distributions, $28,194.
Limitations: Applications not accepted. Giving primarily in Houston, TX.
Application information: Contributes only to pre-selected organizations.
Officers: Dana Solomon, Pres. and Treas.; Andrew Solomon, V.P. and Secy.
Director: Rex Solomon.
EIN: 746104789

52207
Peter P. and Bonnie B. Smith Foundation
1901 N. Akard St.
Dallas, TX 75201

Established in 1991 in TX.
Donor(s): Bonnie B. Smith, Peter P. Smith.
Financial data (yr. ended 12/31/01): Grants paid, $27,750; assets, $747,285 (M); expenditures, $33,467; qualifying distributions, $27,750.
Limitations: Applications not accepted. Giving primarily in Dallas, TX.
Application information: Contributes only to pre-selected organizations.
Officers: Bonnie B. Smith, Pres. and Treas.; Peter P. Smith, V.P. and Secy.
Trustee: Barbara Bass Maroney.
EIN: 752401292

52208
Pansy Yturria Kimbro Foundation
122 Chester St., No. 1
San Antonio, TX 78209

Established in 1998 in TX.
Financial data (yr. ended 08/31/01): Grants paid, $27,744; assets, $87,506 (M); gifts received, $30,000; expenditures, $29,332; qualifying distributions, $27,675.
Limitations: Applications not accepted. Giving primarily in San Antonio, TX.
Application information: Contributes only to pre-selected organizations.
Officers: Marion Y. Kimbro, Pres. and Treas.; Ray Smith, Jr., V.P. and Secy.; Marion Leonor Smith Zacarias, V.P.
EIN: 742872961

52209
The Metcalf Foundation
5212 Briar Tree
Dallas, TX 75248

Established in 1997 in TX.
Donor(s): Creative Information Systems, LLC, Norma Jean Metcalf, Richard I. Metcalf.
Financial data (yr. ended 12/31/01): Grants paid, $27,737; assets, $453,285 (M); expenditures, $29,329; qualifying distributions, $27,737.
Limitations: Applications not accepted.
Application information: Contributes only to pre-selected organizations.
Officer and Trustees:* Richard I. Metcalf,* V.P.; Guy H. Kerr, Norma Jean Metcalf.
EIN: 752727773

52210
The Straddlefork Foundation
600 Congress Ave., Ste. 1820
Austin, TX 78701-3626 (512) 479-2623
Contact: Richard D. Miller, Secy.-Treas.

Established in 1994 in TX.
Donor(s): Leila C. Wynn.
Financial data (yr. ended 12/31/01): Grants paid, $27,700; assets, $353,453 (M); expenditures, $34,320; qualifying distributions, $27,700.

Officers and Directors:* Leila C. Wynn,* Pres.; Richard D. Miller, Secy.-Treas.; Margaret Wynn Fortier, John Kesner, Anne Wynn Weissinger, Martha Wynn Weissinger, William Thomas Wynn II.
EIN: 742726777

52211
Trube Foundation
P.O. Box 629
Galveston, TX 77553
Application address: 802 Rosenberg, Galveston, TX 77550, tel.: (409) 763-2481
Contact: Michael B. Hughes, Tr.

Established in 1988 in TX.
Financial data (yr. ended 12/31/00): Grants paid, $27,700; assets, $715,383 (M); expenditures, $36,281; qualifying distributions, $27,700.
Limitations: Giving primarily in Galveston, TX.
Application information: Application form required.
Trustee: Michael B. Hughes.
EIN: 760231582

52212
Beth Rowell Mead Educational Trust
c/o Tyler Bank & Trust, N.A.
P.O. Box 2020
Tyler, TX 75710-2020
Application address: P.O. Box 486, Jefferson, TX 75657, tel.: (903) 665-7700
Contact: Suzanne Benefield, Tr.

Financial data (yr. ended 09/30/01): Grants paid, $27,550; assets, $670,259 (M); expenditures, $40,781; qualifying distributions, $36,258.
Limitations: Giving limited to residents of Cass, Gregg, Harrison, Marion, Morris, and Upshure counties, TX.
Application information: Application form required.
Trustees: Suzanne Benefield, Jesse M. DeWare IV, Regions Bank.
EIN: 756310255
Codes: GTI

52213
Ishvarphemi Foundation
P.O. Box 2009
Lubbock, TX 79408
Contact: M.I. Patel, Secy.

Established in 1999 in TX.
Donor(s): M.I. Patel, I.C. Patel.
Financial data (yr. ended 12/31/01): Grants paid, $27,486; assets, $106,426 (M); gifts received, $53,354; expenditures, $27,958; qualifying distributions, $27,486.
Limitations: Giving primarily in TX.
Officers: I.C. Patel, Pres.; M.I. Patel, Secy.
EIN: 752828460

52214
Samuel Bass Foundation, Inc.
8720 Canyon Dr.
Dallas, TX 75209

Established in 1999 in TX.
Donor(s): Kyle J. Bass.
Financial data (yr. ended 12/31/01): Grants paid, $27,375; assets, $102,876 (M); gifts received, $44,743; expenditures, $27,554; qualifying distributions, $27,375.
Limitations: Applications not accepted.
Application information: Contributes only to pre-selected organizations.
Officer: Kyle J. Bass, Mgr.
EIN: 752851419

52215
Crooker Charitable Foundation, Inc.
c/o John H. Crooker
1301 McKinney, Ste. 5100
Houston, TX 77010

In 1991 the foundation changed from a trust to a corporation.
Donor(s): John H. Crooker, Jr.
Financial data (yr. ended 03/31/02): Grants paid, $27,370; assets, $432,721 (M); gifts received, $18,000; expenditures, $29,251; qualifying distributions, $27,370.
Limitations: Applications not accepted. Giving primarily in Houston, TX.
Application information: Contributes only to pre-selected organizations.
Officers and Directors:* Robert W. Crooker,* Pres.; Kay B. Crooker,* V.P.; Barry S. Hunsaker, Jr.,* Secy.; J. Alec Mize,* Treas.; John H. Crooker, Jr.
EIN: 760331968

52216
The Brookview Foundation
4842 Brookview Dr.
Dallas, TX 75220

Established in 1962 in TX.
Donor(s): Henri L. Bromberg, Jr.,‡ Janice M. Bromberg.
Financial data (yr. ended 12/31/00): Grants paid, $27,290; assets, $1 (M); gifts received, $7; expenditures, $35,980; qualifying distributions, $27,290.
Limitations: Applications not accepted. Giving primarily in Dallas, TX.
Publications: Annual report.
Application information: Contributes only to pre-selected organizations.
Officers and Directors:* Janice M. Bromberg,* V.P.; Ruth Coker Green,* Secy.
EIN: 756013541

52217
The Joan and Howard Katz Family Foundation
210 W. 6th St., Ste. 1300
Fort Worth, TX 76102

Established in 1999 in TX.
Financial data (yr. ended 12/31/01): Grants paid, $27,250; assets, $209,404 (M); expenditures, $30,308; qualifying distributions, $27,250.
Limitations: Applications not accepted.
Application information: Contributes only to pre-selected organizations.
Officers: Howard Katz, Pres.; Joan Katz, V.P.; Carolyn Bernell, Secy.-Treas.
EIN: 752851845

52218
Abe and Irene Levine Trust
c/o Citizens State Bank
P.O. Box 600
Sealy, TX 77474-9990 (979) 885-3571
Contact: Leroy Zapalac, Tr.

Established in 1994 in TX.
Donor(s): Irene Levine.‡
Financial data (yr. ended 07/31/01): Grants paid, $27,200; assets, $1,940,439 (M); gifts received, $773,707; expenditures, $55,093; qualifying distributions, $27,200.
Limitations: Giving limited to residents of Sealy, TX.
Application information: Application form required.
Trustees: Hubert Odom, Leroy Zapalac.
EIN: 766100223

52219
Howard J. & Dorothy Adleta Foundation
c/o JPMorgan Chase Bank
300 Crescent Ct., Ste. 400
Dallas, TX 75201

Financial data (yr. ended 09/30/01): Grants paid, $27,166; assets, $363,287 (M); expenditures, $33,452; qualifying distributions, $28,002.
Limitations: Giving primarily in NY and TN.
Trustee: JPMorgan Chase Bank.
EIN: 756010244

52220
Robert L. and Sara Lou Cargill Charitable Trust
4701 Alta Mesa Blvd.
Fort Worth, TX 76133-6112

Established in 1987 in TX.
Donor(s): Robert L. Cargill, Sara Lou Cargill.
Financial data (yr. ended 12/31/01): Grants paid, $27,150; assets, $438,441 (M); gifts received, $1,076; expenditures, $31,060; qualifying distributions, $27,150.
Limitations: Applications not accepted. Giving primarily in OK and TX.
Application information: Contributes only to pre-selected organizations.
Trustees: Robert L. Cargill, Sara Lou Cargill.
EIN: 756365424

52221
Rotheudt/Dizinger Foundation
c/o H.W. Rotheudt and P. Dizinger
3701 Montrose Blvd.
Houston, TX 77006-4623

Established in 1990 in TX.
Donor(s): Vee Pak, Inc.
Financial data (yr. ended 06/30/01): Grants paid, $27,136; assets, $823,567 (M); expenditures, $36,670; qualifying distributions, $32,009.
Limitations: Applications not accepted. Giving primarily in Houston, TX.
Application information: Contributes only to pre-selected organizations.
Officers: Hans Willi Rotheudt, Pres.; Ditas Saints, Secy.-Treas.
EIN: 760324026

52222
Rildia Bee O'Bryan Cliburn Foundation
23 Westover Rd.
Fort Worth, TX 76107-3104

Donor(s): Van Cliburn, Spencer Hays.
Financial data (yr. ended 12/31/01): Grants paid, $27,100; assets, $2,167 (M); gifts received, $27,900; expenditures, $27,140; qualifying distributions, $27,100.
Limitations: Applications not accepted. Giving primarily in Fort Worth, TX.
Application information: Contributes only to pre-selected organizations.
Trustees: Nancy Lee Bass, Perry R. Bass, Raymond Boswell, Van Cliburn, Marcia Fuller French.
EIN: 133123730

52223
W. H. & Mary Ellen Cobb Charitable Trust
c/o Bank of America
P.O. Box 831041
Dallas, TX 75283-1041

Established in 1996 in TX.
Donor(s): W.H. and Mary Ellen Cobb Trust.
Financial data (yr. ended 12/31/01): Grants paid, $27,051; assets, $2,696,907 (M); gifts received, $1,805,954; expenditures, $61,198; qualifying distributions, $27,051.
Limitations: Applications not accepted.
Application information: Contributes only to pre-selected organizations.
Trustee: Bank of America.
EIN: 756488084

52224
The Freckles Foundation
c/o Anne H. Bushman
1202A Dairy Ashford
Houston, TX 77079-3004

Established in 1995 in TX.
Donor(s): Anne H. Bushman.
Financial data (yr. ended 12/31/01): Grants paid, $27,000; assets, $300,070 (M); gifts received, $10,000; expenditures, $31,539; qualifying distributions, $27,000.
Limitations: Applications not accepted. Giving primarily in Poughkeepsie, NY.
Application information: Contributes only to pre-selected organizations.
Officers: Anne H. Bushman, Pres.; Robert P. Bushman III, V.P.; R.A. Seale, Jr., Secy.-Treas.
EIN: 760486385

52225
The Wooldridge Foundation
7808 Glenshannon Ct.
Dallas, TX 75225

Established in 1999 in TX.
Donor(s): Raymond E. Woolridge.
Financial data (yr. ended 12/31/01): Grants paid, $27,000; assets, $457,345 (M); expenditures, $30,598; qualifying distributions, $27,000.
Limitations: Applications not accepted.
Application information: Contributes only to pre-selected organizations.
Officer and Directors:* Raymond E. Woolridge,* Chair.; Adrienne Leigh Woolridge, Ann Woolridge, Bradley E. Woolridge, P. Zachary Woolridge, Patricia Anne Woolridge, Peter Lasch Woolridge, Rebecca Ann Woolridge.
EIN: 311671698

52226
Hertzel and Suzy Finesilver Charitable Trust
c/o Lynn F. Crystal
P.O. Box 1658
San Antonio, TX 78296

Donor(s): Mrs. H. Finesilver.
Financial data (yr. ended 12/31/01): Grants paid, $26,800; assets, $202,415 (M); expenditures, $28,761; qualifying distributions, $26,800.
Limitations: Applications not accepted. Giving primarily in San Antonio, TX.
Application information: Contributes only to pre-selected organizations.
Trustee: Lynn F. Crystal.
EIN: 746409630

52227
The Hewitt Foundation, Inc.
8 Greeway Plz., Ste. 718
Houston, TX 77046

Established in 1998 in TX.
Donor(s): Jeffrey J. Hewitt, Naomi Hewitt.
Financial data (yr. ended 12/31/01): Grants paid, $26,760; assets, $90,165 (M); expenditures, $27,112; qualifying distributions, $26,760.
Limitations: Applications not accepted. Giving primarily in Houston, TX.
Application information: Contributes only to pre-selected organizations.
Officers and Directors:* Jeffrey J. Hewitt,* Pres.; Naomi Hewitt,* V.P.
EIN: 760550921

52228
The Donachie Foundation
730 1 Energy Sq.
Dallas, TX 75206
Contact: Judith A. Watson, Secy.-Treas.

Established in 1995 in TX.
Donor(s): Robert J. Donachie, Sr.
Financial data (yr. ended 12/31/01): Grants paid, $26,755; assets, $558,660 (M); gifts received, $50,000; expenditures, $52,402; qualifying distributions, $26,755.
Officers: Robert J. Donachie, Sr., Pres.; Ann Donachie, V.P.; Mark R. Donachie, V.P.; Robert J. Donachie, Jr., V.P.; Judith A. Watson, Secy.-Treas.
EIN: 752622987

52229
Hardin Foundation for Wichita County
P.O. Drawer 97511
Wichita Falls, TX 76307-7511
Application address: Kathy Pennartz, Financial Aid Office, c/o Midwestern State Univ., 3400 Taft Blvd., Wichita Falls, TX 76308
Contact: Joseph N. Sherrill, Jr., Chair.

Established in 1934 in TX.
Financial data (yr. ended 12/31/01): Grants paid, $26,716; assets, $609,270 (M); expenditures, $35,691; qualifying distributions, $26,716.
Limitations: Giving primarily in Wichita County, TX.
Application information: Application form for scholarship required.
Officer Trustees:* Joseph N. Sherrill, Jr.,* Chair.; R. Caven Crosnoe.
EIN: 751106480

52230
Nella Foundation, Inc.
651 Bering Dr., Ste. 1103
Houston, TX 77057-2135
Contact: Sheila K. Gilmore, Secy.-Treas.

Established in 1961.
Financial data (yr. ended 10/31/01): Grants paid, $26,693; assets, $293,855 (M); expenditures, $28,274; qualifying distributions, $27,258.
Limitations: Giving primarily in TX.
Officers: Stuart E. Fischbach, Pres.; Michael D. Gilmore, V.P.; Sheila K. Gilmore, Secy.-Treas.
EIN: 136117728

52231
Robert & Joanne Williams Foundation, Inc.
14611 Westway Ln.
Houston, TX 77077

Established in 1998 in TX.
Donor(s): Robert Williams, Joanne Williams.
Financial data (yr. ended 12/31/01): Grants paid, $26,610; assets, $632,591 (M); expenditures, $68,613; qualifying distributions, $26,610.
Limitations: Applications not accepted.
Application information: Contributes only to pre-selected organizations.
Trustees: Joanne M. Williams, Lara J. Williams, Robert H. Williams.
EIN: 760590354

52232
The Tomblin Family Foundation
210 Barton Springs Rd., Ste. 550
Austin, TX 78704

Established in 2000.
Donor(s): Anthony Tomblin.
Financial data (yr. ended 12/31/01): Grants paid, $26,600; assets, $647,362 (M); expenditures, $34,379; qualifying distributions, $26,600.
Limitations: Applications not accepted.

Application information: Contributes only to pre-selected organizations.
Officers: Anthony W. Tomblin, Pres.; Rebecca Tomblin, Secy.
EIN: 742983762

52233
Fort Worth Police Officers' Award Foundation
P.O. Box 17659
Fort Worth, TX 76102

Established in 1987 in TX.
Donor(s): Burlington Northern Railroad.
Financial data (yr. ended 12/31/01): Grants paid, $26,542; assets, $918,898 (M); gifts received, $20,170; expenditures, $67,017; qualifying distributions, $26,542.
Limitations: Giving primarily in TX.
Application information: Unsolicited requests for funds not considered or acknowledged.
Officers: Lynn Fuller, Chair.; Joyce Pate Capper, Vice-Chair.; Jim Lattimore, Treas.
Trustees: Larry Anpin, Bill Burton, Marvin Champlin, Ray Gilley, James Green, John Joyce, Tom Law, Jr., John McMillan, Gregory Miller, Bill Schmidt, Rommi Terrill.
EIN: 751744211
Codes: GTI

52234
Boswell Family Foundation
263 S. Bay Dr.
Bullard, TX 75757-8948
Contact: Jean S. Boswell, Pres.

Established in 1997 in TX.
Donor(s): Jean S. Boswell.
Financial data (yr. ended 12/31/00): Grants paid, $26,500; assets, $277,531 (M); expenditures, $31,494; qualifying distributions, $26,500.
Limitations: Giving primarily in San Antonio, TX.
Application information: Application form not required.
Officers: Jean S. Boswell, Pres.; Henry O. Boswell, V.P.; David J. Smith, Secy.-Treas.
Directors: Henry O. Boswell III, Diane E. McGowen, Laura J. Schultze, Mary G. Smith.
EIN: 752705283

52235
The Evans Foundation
6780 Abrams Rd., No. 207
Dallas, TX 75231-7172 (214) 343-4477
Contact: Herbert Craig Evans, Secy.-Treas.

Established in 1989 in TX.
Donor(s): Jack W. Evans, Sr., Imogene Evans.
Financial data (yr. ended 12/31/01): Grants paid, $26,500; assets, $523,624 (M); expenditures, $27,760; qualifying distributions, $26,500.
Limitations: Giving primarily in Dallas, TX.
Application information: Application form required.
Officers and Directors:* Roy Gene Evans,* Pres.; Jack W. Evans, Jr.,* V.P.; Herbert Craig Evans,* Secy.-Treas.; Imogene Evans.
EIN: 752304232

52236
Jackson Family Foundation
3623 Norfolk Rd.
Fort Worth, TX 76109-3513

Donor(s): J.I. Jackson.
Financial data (yr. ended 11/30/01): Grants paid, $26,500; assets, $501,869 (M); expenditures, $28,610; qualifying distributions, $27,050.
Limitations: Applications not accepted. Giving primarily in Fort Worth, TX.
Application information: Contributes only to pre-selected organizations.

Trustees: Susan Jackson Davis, Mary Jackson Stone.
EIN: 751675348

52237
Family Values, Inc.
1980 Post Oak Blvd., Ste. 2300
Houston, TX 77056

Established in 1998 in TX.
Donor(s): Murray W. Burns, L. Jeanne Burns.
Financial data (yr. ended 12/31/00): Grants paid, $26,485; assets, $485,105 (M); expenditures, $32,848; qualifying distributions, $26,485.
Limitations: Applications not accepted.
Application information: Contributes only to pre-selected organizations.
Officers: Murray W. Burns, Pres.; L. Jeanne Burns, Secy.-Treas.
EIN: 760557944

52238
Rogers Brothers Foundation, Inc.
595 Orleans St.
P.O. Box 1310
Beaumont, TX 77704

Incorporated in 1961 in TX.
Donor(s): Members of the Rogers family.
Financial data (yr. ended 11/30/01): Grants paid, $26,455; assets, $59,346 (M); expenditures, $26,486; qualifying distributions, $26,455.
Limitations: Applications not accepted. Giving primarily in TX.
Application information: Contributes only to pre-selected organizations.
Officers: Victor J. Rogers, Pres.; Sol J. Rogers, V.P.; Nate J. Rogers, Secy.-Treas.
EIN: 746063588

52239
Anne F. Lyster Charitable Foundation
c/o JPMorgan Chase Bank
500 E. Border St.
Arlington, TX 76010

Established in 1997 in TX.
Donor(s): Anne F. Lyster.‡
Financial data (yr. ended 12/31/01): Grants paid, $26,396; assets, $467,389 (M); expenditures, $35,882; qualifying distributions, $26,396.
Limitations: Applications not accepted. Giving primarily in TX.
Application information: Contributes only to pre-selected organizations.
Trustees: Dan Klein, JPMorgan Chase Bank.
EIN: 752683562

52240
John W. and Ann K. Johnson Foundation
3355 W. Alabama, Ste. 400
Houston, TX 77098

Established in 1997 in TX.
Donor(s): John W. Johnson.
Financial data (yr. ended 12/31/01): Grants paid, $26,300; assets, $516,074 (M); gifts received, $21,000; expenditures, $28,542; qualifying distributions, $26,300.
Officers and Trustee:* Ann K. Johnson,* Pres.; Christopher B. Johnson, V.P.; Kimball Johnson, V.P.; Ruth M. Johnson, V.P.; John W. Johnson, Secy.-Treas.
EIN: 760535844

52241
Lynwood Foundation
7171 Harwin, Ste. 210
Houston, TX 77036

Donor(s): Fong Chun Huang.

Financial data (yr. ended 12/31/01): Grants paid, $26,200; assets, $959,788 (M); gifts received, $25,000; expenditures, $26,212; qualifying distributions, $26,212.
Limitations: Applications not accepted. Giving primarily in Houston, Tx.
Application information: Contributes only to pre-selected organizations.
Officers: Fong Chun Huang, Pres.; John Lin, Secy.; Juei Huei Lai, Treas.
EIN: 760665538

52242
Joan and Keys Curry Foundation
29 Farnham Pk.
Houston, TX 77024

Established in 1989 in TX.
Donor(s): Keys Curry, Joan Curry.
Financial data (yr. ended 12/31/01): Grants paid, $26,084; assets, $641,363 (M); gifts received, $25,000; expenditures, $31,448; qualifying distributions, $26,084.
Limitations: Applications not accepted. Giving primarily in TX.
Application information: Contributes only to pre-selected organizations.
Trustees: Joan F. Curry, Keys A. Curry, Jr., Keys A. Curry III.
EIN: 766058156

52243
Inasmuch Trust
4029 Hearthstone Dr.
Mesquite, TX 75150-4583

Established in 1993 in TX.
Donor(s): C.R. Golsworthy.
Financial data (yr. ended 12/31/01): Grants paid, $26,067; assets, $448,131 (M); gifts received, $54,990; expenditures, $48,036; qualifying distributions, $27,622.
Limitations: Applications not accepted.
Application information: Contributes only to pre-selected organizations.
Trustees: D.S. Christopher, Ruth Christopher.
EIN: 766091242

52244
Charles Meyer Trust
c/o U.S. National Bank
P.O. Box 179
Galveston, TX 77553
Application address: c/o Rabbi, Temple B'nai Israel, 3008 Ave. O, Galveston, TX 77550

Financial data (yr. ended 05/31/00): Grants paid, $26,062; assets, $513,510 (M); expenditures, $33,011; qualifying distributions, $26,101.
Limitations: Giving limited to Galveston, TX.
Directors: Janet Bertilino, F.A. Odom, Rabbi, Temple B'nai Israel.
Trustee: Frost National Bank.
EIN: 746035534
Codes: GTI

52245
Chris and Kim Thomas Foundation
P.O. Box 810258
Dallas, TX 75381-0258

Established in 2000 in TX.
Donor(s): Christopher J. Thomas, Kim M. Thomas.
Financial data (yr. ended 12/31/00): Grants paid, $26,044; assets, $739,716 (M); gifts received, $887,344; expenditures, $26,228; qualifying distributions, $26,044.
Limitations: Applications not accepted. Giving primarily in TX.
Application information: Contributes only to pre-selected organizations.

52245—TEXAS

Directors: Richard C. Kang, Christopher J. Thomas, Kim M. Thomas.
EIN: 752886982

52246
Mary Hobbs Griffith Foundation
c/o Wells Fargo Bank Texas, N.A.
1 O'Connor Plz.
Victoria, TX 77902-6502

Financial data (yr. ended 10/31/01): Grants paid, $26,000; assets, $832,464 (M); expenditures, $65,655; qualifying distributions, $26,000.
Limitations: Applications not accepted. Giving primarily in San Antonio, Skidmore, and Sinton, TX.
Application information: Contributes only to pre-selected organizations.
Trustee: Wells Fargo Bank Texas, N.A.
EIN: 237000801

52247
Scott Murray Foundation, Inc.
3900 Barnett St.
Fort Worth, TX 76103-1400
Contact: Scott Murray, Tr.

Established in 1995.
Donor(s): Scott Murray.
Financial data (yr. ended 12/31/01): Grants paid, $25,990; assets, $10,498 (M); gifts received, $26,587; expenditures, $26,521; qualifying distributions, $25,990.
Trustees: Carole Murray, Scott Murray.
EIN: 752553020

52248
The Emmett G. Donegan Foundation
c/o Emmett G. Donegan
P.O. Box 429
Seguin, TX 78155

Established in 1987 in TX.
Donor(s): Emmett G. Donegan.
Financial data (yr. ended 12/31/01): Grants paid, $25,894; assets, $445,398 (M); gifts received, $25,000; expenditures, $27,253; qualifying distributions, $25,894.
Limitations: Applications not accepted. Giving primarily in Seguin, TX.
Application information: Contributes only to pre-selected organizations.
Trustees: Lester L. Brawner, Craig Donegan, Emmett G. Donegan, Nelson Donegan, Scott Donegan.
EIN: 746357764

52249
Johnson Family Foundation
HC 15, Box 427
Junction, TX 76849-9500 (915) 446-2150
Contact: Dennis Heap, Pres.

Established in 1994 in TX.
Financial data (yr. ended 12/31/01): Grants paid, $25,750; assets, $255,752 (M); gifts received, $48,690; expenditures, $43,659; qualifying distributions, $43,513.
Limitations: Giving limited to residents of Kimble County, TX.
Application information: Application form required.
Officers and Directors:* Jayne Johnson,* Pres.; Larry Crenwelge,* V.P.; Geraldine Durbon,* Secy.; John Rhodes.
EIN: 752568312

52250
The Douglas Charitable Foundation
c/o Donald D. Patteson, Jr.
1212 Potomac Dr.
Houston, TX 77057-1920

Established in 1994 in TX.
Donor(s): Donald D. Patteson, Jr.
Financial data (yr. ended 12/31/00): Grants paid, $25,649; assets, $77,333 (M); gifts received, $21,420; expenditures, $26,945; qualifying distributions, $25,845.
Limitations: Applications not accepted. Giving primarily in Houston, TX.
Application information: Unsolicited requests for funds not accepted.
Officers: Donald D. Patteson, Jr., Pres. and Treas.; L. Paige Mays, V.P.; Donald D. Patteson III, V.P.; Lindsay Michele Patteson, V.P.; Paula M. Patteson, V.P.
Directors: Buddy F. Mays, Susan H. Patteson.
EIN: 760450668

52251
Camp Normal Benevolent Foundation, Inc.
P.O. Box 3412
Longview, TX 75606

Financial data (yr. ended 12/31/00): Grants paid, $25,625; assets, $436,273 (M); expenditures, $42,634; qualifying distributions, $25,424.
Limitations: Applications not accepted. Giving primarily in TX.
Application information: Contributes only to pre-selected organizations.
Directors: Bobby Anderson, Medro Barnes, George Brittain, E. Grace Derrick, Alford Jones, Varee Jones McDaniel.
EIN: 751554759

52252
Joan N. Weil Charitable Trust
11930 Tavel Cir.
Dallas, TX 75230 (972) 239-6832
Contact: Joan N. Weil, Tr.

Established in 1997 in TX.
Donor(s): Neustadt Charitable Foundation.
Financial data (yr. ended 12/31/01): Grants paid, $25,580; assets, $523,600 (M); expenditures, $31,407; qualifying distributions, $25,580.
Trustees: Andrea Aranson, Jan Leeds, Taylor Mitchell, Joan N. Weil.
EIN: 311537937

52253
Lucy Dupree Hayes Trust
c/o Bank of America
P.O. Box 831041
Dallas, TX 75283-1041

Donor(s): Lucy Dupree Hayes.‡
Financial data (yr. ended 01/31/02): Grants paid, $25,556; assets, $528,598 (M); expenditures, $32,327; qualifying distributions, $25,556.
Limitations: Giving primarily in TX.
Application information: Application form required.
Trustees: John Scovell, W. Dean Willis, Bank of America.
EIN: 756259210

52254
Sanchez Family Foundation
(Formerly Antonio R. Sanchez, Jr. & Maria J. Sanchez Foundation)
1920 Sandman St.
Laredo, TX 78041

Donor(s): Antonio R. Sanchez, Jr.

Financial data (yr. ended 12/31/01): Grants paid, $25,539; assets, $178,027 (M); gifts received, $29,480; expenditures, $33,755; qualifying distributions, $25,539.
Limitations: Applications not accepted.
Application information: Contributes only to pre-selected organizations.
Officers: Antonio R. Sanchez, Pres.; Maria J. Sanchez, 1st V.P.; Frank Guerra, V.P. and Secy.-Treas.
EIN: 742835977

52255
The Tom and Sylvia Boyer Foundation
P.O. Box 3011
Amarillo, TX 79116-3011

Established in 1999.
Donor(s): Tom Boyer, Sylvia Boyer.
Financial data (yr. ended 12/31/00): Grants paid, $25,523; assets, $492,988 (M); gifts received, $381,684; expenditures, $30,229; qualifying distributions, $24,924.
Limitations: Applications not accepted.
Application information: Contributes only to pre-selected organizations.
Officers and Directors:* Tom Boyer,* Pres. and Treas.; Sylvia Boyer,* Secy.; Melissa Boyer.
EIN: 752849331

52256
Burns Family Foundation
10 Stillforest St.
Houston, TX 77024-7518
Contact: John Burns, Tr.

Established in 1994 in TX.
Financial data (yr. ended 12/31/01): Grants paid, $25,500; assets, $83,258 (M); expenditures, $26,583; qualifying distributions, $25,500.
Limitations: Giving primarily in TX.
Trustee: John Burns.
EIN: 760454689

52257
Jack and Carolyn Little Family Foundation
5847 San Felipe, Ste., 3920
Houston, TX 77057

Established in 1999 in TX.
Donor(s): Jack E. Little, Carolyn H. Little.
Financial data (yr. ended 12/31/01): Grants paid, $25,500; assets, $412,674 (M); expenditures, $42,012; qualifying distributions, $25,500.
Limitations: Applications not accepted.
Application information: Contributes only to pre-selected organizations.
Officers: Jack E. Little, Chair.; Carolyn H. Little, Pres.; Jack E. Little, Jr., Secy.; Allison L. English, Treas.
EIN: 760624255

52258
Dorsey McCrory Trust for Gonzales County, TX
P.O. Box 826
Gonzales, TX 78629
Application address: c/o Waelder ISD Counselor, 105 Ave. C, Waelder, TX 78959, tel.: (830) 788-7151

Established in 1994 in TX.
Donor(s): Dorsey McCrory.‡
Financial data (yr. ended 10/31/00): Grants paid, $25,500; assets, $542,356 (M); expenditures, $29,722; qualifying distributions, $29,440.
Limitations: Giving limited to residents of Waelder, TX.
Application information: Application form required.
Trustees: Hon. David Bird, J.D. Gray, Jr., Pastor Joe F. Howard, James Kelso, Pat McCrory.

EIN: 746414650
Codes: GTI

52259
Lena & Harry Turner Foundation
c/o Bank of America
P.O. Box 831041
Dallas, TX 75283-1041
Application address: 110 S.W. 2nd St., Grand Prairie, TX 75050-5603
Contact: Marshall Sutton, Tr., or Lee D. Herring, Tr.

Established in 1952 in TX.
Financial data (yr. ended 12/31/00): Grants paid, $25,484; assets, $593,719 (M); expenditures, $54,341; qualifying distributions, $27,983.
Limitations: Giving primarily in TX.
Application information: Application form not required.
Trustees: Lee D. Herring, Marshall Sutton, Bank of America.
EIN: 237416737
Codes: GTI

52260
Hibbs Family Foundation
c/o Billy J. Braly, C.P.A.
P.O. Box 6687
Tyler, TX 75711-6687

Established in 1999 in TX.
Donor(s): Billy E. Hibbs, Sr., Billy E. Hibbs, Jr., Claims Administrative Services, Hibbs-Hallmark & Company.
Financial data (yr. ended 12/31/01): Grants paid, $25,435; assets, $560,040 (M); gifts received, $198,650; expenditures, $29,400; qualifying distributions, $25,435.
Limitations: Applications not accepted. Giving primarily in Tyler, TX.
Application information: Contributes only to pre-selected organizations.
Officers and Directors:* Eugenia A. Hibbs,* Pres.; Billy E. Hibbs, Jr.,* V.P. and Secy.; Billy E. Hibbs, Sr.,* V.P.; Teresa W. Hibbs.
EIN: 752851757

52261
David & Catherine Mincberg Charitable Foundation
9660 Hillcroft, Ste. 433
Houston, TX 77096

Established in 1986 in TX.
Donor(s): David M. Mincberg.
Financial data (yr. ended 12/31/00): Grants paid, $25,354; assets, $542,806 (M); expenditures, $26,740; qualifying distributions, $25,354.
Limitations: Applications not accepted. Giving primarily in Houston, TX.
Application information: Contributes only to pre-selected organizations.
Trustees: Catherine A. Mincberg, David M. Mincberg.
EIN: 760224179

52262
The Edith and Robert Zinn Foundation
3400 Bissonnet, Ste. 250
Houston, TX 77005 (713) 838-2900
Contact: Robert Zinn, Tr.

Established in 1997 in TX.
Donor(s): Edith Zinn, Robert Zinn.
Financial data (yr. ended 12/31/00): Grants paid, $25,350; assets, $770,615 (M); expenditures, $28,470; qualifying distributions, $24,778.
Application information: Application form not required.
Trustees: Edith Zinn, Robert Zinn.

EIN: 760524140

52263
The Emilie & Phil Schepps Foundation
10221 Hollow Way
Dallas, TX 75229-6636 (214) 265-7691
Contact: Phillip J. Schepps, Dir.

Established in 1997 in TX.
Donor(s): Emilie K. Schepps, Phillip J. Schepps.
Financial data (yr. ended 12/31/01): Grants paid, $25,300; assets, $432,520 (M); gifts received, $41,997; expenditures, $40,330; qualifying distributions, $25,300.
Application information: Application form required.
Directors: Emilie K. Schepps, Joseph W. Schepps, Phillip J. Schepps.
EIN: 752737172

52264
Anne Lamkin Kinder Foundation, Inc.
2121 Kirby Dr., Ste. 123
Houston, TX 77019-6068 (713) 523-7994
Contact: Anne Lamkin Kinder, Pres.

Established in 1994 in TX.
Donor(s): Anne Lamkin Kinder.
Financial data (yr. ended 12/31/01): Grants paid, $25,274; assets, $752,359 (M); expenditures, $25,970; qualifying distributions, $25,274.
Limitations: Giving primarily in Houston, TX.
Officers: Anne Lamkin Kinder, Pres.; Robert E.L. Lamkin III, V.P.; Katherine Anne Kinder, Secy.
EIN: 760519074

52265
Bruce and Pamela Earthman Foundation
c/o Bruce Earthman
P.O. Box 130469
Houston, TX 77219-0469

Financial data (yr. ended 11/30/01): Grants paid, $25,250; assets, $345,726 (M); gifts received, $24,972; expenditures, $30,814; qualifying distributions, $25,250.
Trustees: Bruce Earthman, Pamela Earthman.
EIN: 766112239

52266
The H. H. McJunkin, Jr. Foundation
111 W. Spring Valley Rd.
Richardson, TX 75083-0160
Contact: Herbert H. McJunkin, Jr., Pres.

Established in 1998 in TX.
Financial data (yr. ended 12/31/01): Grants paid, $25,200; assets, $304,339 (M); expenditures, $26,205; qualifying distributions, $25,200.
Officers: Herbert H. McJunkin, Jr., Pres.; Bradford D. McJunkin, V.P. and Secy.; Kirk E. McJunkin, V.P. and Treas.
EIN: 752795350

52267
The Arnold and Suzanne Miller Foundation
5701 Woodway, Ste. 324
Houston, TX 77057

Donor(s): Bertha Gordon Miller, I.L. and Bertha Gordon Miller Foundation.
Financial data (yr. ended 03/31/02): Grants paid, $25,163; assets, $1,161,040 (M); expenditures, $27,421; qualifying distributions, $25,163.
Limitations: Applications not accepted. Giving primarily in Houston, TX.
Application information: Contributes only to pre-selected organizations.
Officers and Trustees:* Arnold M. Miller,* Pres.; Arnold M. Miller, Jr.,* V.P. and Secy.; Suzanne S. Miller,* Treas.
EIN: 760314951

52268
Claire V. Smith Charitable Foundation
c/o San Angelo National Bank, Trust Dept.
P.O. Box 2558
Houston, TX 77252-2558

Financial data (yr. ended 12/31/01): Grants paid, $25,124; assets, $416,180 (M); expenditures, $33,294; qualifying distributions, $25,124.
Limitations: Applications not accepted. Giving limited to TX.
Application information: Contributes only to pre-selected organizations.
Trustee: San Angelo National Bank.
EIN: 746078188

52269
David & Leslie Lawson Family Foundation
5928 Bent Creek Trail
Dallas, TX 75252

Established in 1998.
Financial data (yr. ended 12/31/01): Grants paid, $25,100; assets, $577,746 (M); gifts received, $75,052; expenditures, $25,156; qualifying distributions, $25,100.
Officers and Directors:* David R. Lawson,* Pres.; David C. Lawson,* V.P.; Leslie L. Lawson, Secy.-Treas.; Natalie Dooley, Matthew Lawson.
EIN: 752794838

52270
Hattie Zurfluh Scholarship Fund
c/o Wells Fargo Bank Texas, N.A.
P.O. Box 2626
Waco, TX 76702 (254) 714-6160

Established in 1989 in TX.
Donor(s): Hattie Zurfluk.‡
Financial data (yr. ended 12/31/00): Grants paid, $25,100; assets, $538,633 (M); expenditures, $29,874; qualifying distributions, $26,687.
Limitations: Giving limited to residents of Waco, TX.
Application information: Application form required.
Trustee: Wells Fargo Bank Texas, N.A.
EIN: 746370513
Codes: GTI

52271
Angels Among Us Foundation
P.O. Box 591508
Houston, TX 77259

Established in 1999 in TX.
Donor(s): Brenda G. Chapman.
Financial data (yr. ended 12/31/01): Grants paid, $25,000; assets, $459,300 (M); expenditures, $31,495; qualifying distributions, $25,000.
Limitations: Applications not accepted. Giving primarily in Houston, TX.
Application information: Contributes only to pre-selected organizations.
Officers and Directors:* Brenda G. Chapman,* Chair.; Lisa L. Ennis,* Secy.; Catherine L. Berry.
EIN: 760584410

52272
Vaughn T. Baird Foundation
c/o Vaughn T. Baird
401 N. 3rd St.
Temple, TX 76501

Established in 1994 in TX.
Donor(s): Vaughn T. Baird.
Financial data (yr. ended 12/31/01): Grants paid, $25,000; assets, $770,885 (M); expenditures, $37,344; qualifying distributions, $25,000.
Limitations: Applications not accepted. Giving primarily in TX.

52272—TEXAS

Application information: Contributes only to pre-selected organizations.
Officers: Vaughn T. Baird, Pres.; Joyce Baird, V.P.; Curtis D. Logan, V.P.; Thomas Baird, Secy.-Treas.
EIN: 742729905

52273
The Roger & Cynthia Borgelt Family Foundation
614 S. Capital of Texas Hwy.
Austin, TX 78746-5204

Established in 1997.
Financial data (yr. ended 12/31/01): Grants paid, $25,000; assets, $469,685 (M); gifts received, $76; expenditures, $27,476; qualifying distributions, $25,000.
Trustees: Cynthia A. Borgelt, Roger W. Borgelt.
EIN: 742833214

52274
S. S. Chern Foundation for Mathematical Research
8010 Harbor Pt.
Houston, TX 77071

Donor(s): May Chu.
Financial data (yr. ended 12/31/01): Grants paid, $25,000; assets, $704,377 (M); gifts received, $70,000; expenditures, $25,503; qualifying distributions, $25,000.
Limitations: Applications not accepted.
Application information: Contributes only to pre-selected organizations.
Officers and Trustees:* May Chu,* Pres. and Treas.; Susan Butler, Secy.; T.T. Chao, C.W. Chu, Phillip Griffiths, Isador M. Singer, Fred Tuthill, Zhong-xian Zhao.
EIN: 760531135

52275
Corgan Family Foundation
8619 Breakers Pt.
Dallas, TX 75243

Established in 2000 in TX.
Donor(s): C. Jack Corgan, Carol Corgan.
Financial data (yr. ended 12/31/00): Grants paid, $25,000; assets, $46,093 (M); gifts received, $75,000; expenditures, $29,047; qualifying distributions, $25,000.
Limitations: Applications not accepted. Giving primarily in Dallas, TX.
Application information: Contributes only to pre-selected organizations.
Officers: C. Jack Corgan, Pres.; Carol Corgan, V.P. and Treas.; Colin Corgan, Secy.
EIN: 752894393

52276
Edwards Charitable Foundation
7 Winners Cir.
Houston, TX 77024-3417 (713) 293-3434

Established in 1996 in TX.
Donor(s): Gary Edwards, Margaret Edwards.
Financial data (yr. ended 12/31/01): Grants paid, $25,000; assets, $460,849 (M); gifts received, $91,910; expenditures, $29,877; qualifying distributions, $25,000.
Limitations: Applications not accepted.
Application information: Contributes only to pre-selected organizations.
Officers: Gary W. Edwards, Pres. and Treas.; Margaret L. Edwards, V.P.-Secy.; Christy L. Hall, V.P.; Debbie L. Hance, V.P.
EIN: 760502902

52277
Hazel Bennett Falconer Goddard Foundation
c/o Jean K. Polchinski
5471 Darnell St.
Houston, TX 77096-1245 (713) 664-9872

Donor(s): Hazel B. Falconer Goddard.
Financial data (yr. ended 12/31/01): Grants paid, $25,000; assets, $46,933 (M); expenditures, $26,650; qualifying distributions, $25,000.
Limitations: Giving limited to Falls County, TX.
Application information: Application form required.
Officers: Richard H. Bennett, Pres. and Treas.; Ben T. Bennett, V.P. and Secy.
Director: Jean K. Polchinski.
EIN: 742240606

52278
The Dixie S. Jones Foundation
c/o Willetta Stellmacher
6243 La Vista Dr.
Dallas, TX 75214-4346 (214) 821-2920

Established in 1995 in TX.
Donor(s): Dixie S. Jones.‡
Financial data (yr. ended 12/31/01): Grants paid, $25,000; assets, $467,719 (M); expenditures, $26,453; qualifying distributions, $24,733.
Limitations: Giving primarily in Dallas, TX.
Trustee: Willetta Stellmacher.
EIN: 752602369

52279
The Lehmkuhl Foundation
2029 Diamond Springs Dr.
Houston, TX 77077-1934

Established in 1995 in TX.
Donor(s): Robert E. Lehmkuhl, Mary Ann Lehmkuhl.
Financial data (yr. ended 12/31/01): Grants paid, $25,000; assets, $341,679 (M); gifts received, $40; expenditures, $27,486; qualifying distributions, $27,486.
Limitations: Applications not accepted. Giving primarily in East St. Louis, IL.
Application information: Contributes only to pre-selected organizations.
Officers: Robert E. Lehmkuhl, Pres.; Mary Ann Lehmkuhl, V.P.; Mary Carol Lehmkuhl, Secy.-Treas.
EIN: 760484794

52280
The Lauro Lopez Family Foundation
10300 Heritage, Ste. 211
San Antonio, TX 78216

Established in 2000 in TX.
Donor(s): Lauro Lopez, Jr.
Financial data (yr. ended 12/31/01): Grants paid, $25,000; assets, $104,951 (M); gifts received, $122,852; expenditures, $28,585; qualifying distributions, $25,000.
Limitations: Applications not accepted. Giving primarily in Laredo, TX.
Application information: Contributes only to pre-selected organizations.
Officers: Lauro Lopez, Jr., Chair. and Pres.; Claudia A. Guerra, V.P. and Treas.; Chris L. Guerra, Secy.
EIN: 742982191

52281
The Matthews Family Foundation
745 E. Mulberry Ave., Ste. 700
San Antonio, TX 78212-3166

Established in 2000 in TX and IL.
Donor(s): Lawrence R. Matthews.‡

Financial data (yr. ended 12/31/01): Grants paid, $25,000; assets, $1,806,183 (M); expenditures, $54,399; qualifying distributions, $25,000.
Limitations: Applications not accepted.
Application information: Contributes only to pre-selected organizations.
Trustees: Alan R. Matthews, David C. Matthews, Graham W. Matthews, Warren L. Matthews, Wilson H. Matthews.
EIN: 364327734

52282
The Ogg Family Foundation
18723 Campbell Rd.
Dallas, TX 75252

Established in 1999 in TX.
Donor(s): Carol Ogg, Charles K. Ogg.
Financial data (yr. ended 12/31/00): Grants paid, $25,000; assets, $80,196 (M); expenditures, $32,599; qualifying distributions, $25,000.
Limitations: Applications not accepted.
Application information: Contributes only to pre-selected organizations.
Officers: Carol Ogg, Pres.; Charles K. Ogg, V.P. and Secy.-Treas.
EIN: 752850147

52283
The PSH Foundation
2777 Allen Parkway
Houston, TX 77019

Established in 2001 in TX.
Donor(s): Patti S. Harrison.
Financial data (yr. ended 05/31/02): Grants paid, $25,000; assets, $8,164,218 (M); gifts received, $8,014,603; expenditures, $156,236; qualifying distributions, $25,000.
Limitations: Applications not accepted.
Application information: Contributes only to pre-selected organizations.
Officers: Patti S. Harrison, Pres.; Mary J. Hamilton, V.P.
Trustees: Barbara Willard, Dale A. Dossey.
EIN: 760683559

52284
J. L. Williams Foundation, Inc.
P.O. Box 797464
Dallas, TX 75379 (972) 624-1414
Contact: Julia Underwood, Treas.

Established in 2000.
Donor(s): J.L. Williams.
Financial data (yr. ended 12/31/01): Grants paid, $25,000; assets, $981,237 (M); expenditures, $32,574; qualifying distributions, $25,000.
Limitations: Giving primarily in Dallas, TX.
Officers and Trustees:* J.L. Williams,* Chair. and Pres.; Joe Pipes,* Secy.; Julia Underwood, Treas.; Frederic Wagner, Jonell H. Williams.
EIN: 752671320

52285
Bob & Anna Wright Family Foundation
P.O. Box 1980
Vernon, TX 76385-1980

Established in 1998 in TX.
Donor(s): Wright Family Foundation, Robert L. Wright.
Financial data (yr. ended 12/31/01): Grants paid, $25,000; assets, $526,355 (M); expenditures, $27,597; qualifying distributions, $25,000.
Limitations: Applications not accepted. Giving primarily in Vernon, TX.
Application information: Contributes only to pre-selected organizations.

Directors: Cheryl Anne Henry, Anna L. Wright, Janet Gail Wright, Robert Kelly Wright, Robert L. Wright.
EIN: 752743582

52286
Chaparral Foundation
P.O. Box 130
Midland, TX 79702 (915) 684-5591

Established in 1997 in TX.
Financial data (yr. ended 12/31/01): Grants paid, $24,950; assets, $1,438,932 (M); expenditures, $24,950; qualifying distributions, $24,950.
Limitations: Giving primarily in TX.
Officer: J.H. Herd, Pres.
EIN: 752707574

52287
Movelda E. Rhine Scholarship Trust
1200 W. University Dr., Ste. 150
Denton, TX 76201
Contact: Judd B. Holt, Tr.

Established in 1998 in TX.
Financial data (yr. ended 12/31/00): Grants paid, $24,950; assets, $302,027 (M); expenditures, $33,789; qualifying distributions, $24,724.
Limitations: Giving primarily in TX.
Application information: Application form required.
Trustee: Judd B. Holt.
EIN: 756519984

52288
J. M. Parker Foundation
2 Village Dr., Ste. 408
Abilene, TX 79606 (915) 698-7366
Contact: James M. Parker, Pres.

Established in 1998 in TX.
Donor(s): James M. Parker, Cynthia Parker.
Financial data (yr. ended 12/31/00): Grants paid, $24,900; assets, $675,119 (M); gifts received, $159,016; expenditures, $25,741; qualifying distributions, $24,900.
Limitations: Giving primarily in TX.
Officers: James M. Parker, Pres.; Kelly Kinard, V.P. and Secy.; Jimmy M. Parker, V.P.; Cynthia A. Parker, Treas.
EIN: 752736419

52289
B.J.C. Charitable Foundation
11455 Fallbrook Dr., Ste. 202
Houston, TX 77065

Established in 1999 in TX.
Financial data (yr. ended 12/31/01): Grants paid, $24,855; assets, $105,890 (M); gifts received, $20,000; expenditures, $26,334; qualifying distributions, $24,855.
Trustees: Joseph Chen, Margaret Lewis, Regina L. Lewis.
EIN: 760626173

52290
Epstein Family Foundation, Inc.
5430 LBJ Fwy.
Dallas, TX 75240-2697 (972) 450-4232
Contact: Lisa Simmons Epstein, Pres.

Established in 1999 in TX.
Donor(s): Lisa Simmons Epstein.
Financial data (yr. ended 12/31/01): Grants paid, $24,750; assets, $103,180 (M); gifts received, $25,000; expenditures, $24,866; qualifying distributions, $24,750.
Limitations: Giving primarily in Dallas, TX.
Application information: Application form not required.

Officers and Directors:* Lisa Simmons Epstein,* Pres. and Treas.; A. Andrew R. Louis,* Secy.; Serena S. Connelly.
EIN: 752851439

52291
Frances & Josephine Holley Educational Trust
c/o Bank of America
P.O. Box 831041
Dallas, TX 75283-1041

Established in 1966 in TX.
Donor(s): Josephine Holley.‡
Financial data (yr. ended 08/31/01): Grants paid, $24,700; assets, $504,534 (M); expenditures, $29,180; qualifying distributions, $25,773.
Limitations: Giving primarily to residents of Dallas County, AL, and Dallas County, TX.
Trustee: Bank of America.
EIN: 756048241

52292
Thomas J. Gordon Foundation
P.O. Box 572055
Houston, TX 77257-2055

Donor(s): Thomas J. Gordon.
Financial data (yr. ended 12/31/01): Grants paid, $24,678; assets, $1,000 (M); gifts received, $25,000; expenditures, $24,800; qualifying distributions, $24,678.
Limitations: Applications not accepted. Giving primarily in Houston, TX.
Application information: Contributes only to pre-selected organizations.
Trustees: Daniel P. Gordon, James C. Gordon, Thomas J. Gordon.
EIN: 237040493

52293
Margaret Chesley Memorial Fund
P.O. Box 1000
Bellville, TX 77418-1000 (979) 865-9151
Contact: Elroy E. Kiecke, Tr.

Established in 1954.
Donor(s): Josephine C. Zeiske.‡
Financial data (yr. ended 12/31/01): Grants paid, $24,573; assets, $1 (M); gifts received, $36,749; expenditures, $25,165; qualifying distributions, $24,573.
Limitations: Giving limited to TX.
Trustee: Elroy E. Kiecke.
EIN: 746044407

52294
James & Eva Mayer Foundation
P.O. Box 328
Plainview, TX 79073-0328 (806) 296-6304
Additional tel.: (806) 291-8100
Contact: Gene V. Owen, Chair.

Established in 1987 in TX.
Donor(s): Eva H. Mayer.‡
Financial data (yr. ended 12/31/01): Grants paid, $24,500; assets, $5,135,429 (L); expenditures, $107,478; qualifying distributions, $24,500.
Limitations: Giving primarily in TX.
Publications: Application guidelines.
Officer and Trustees:* Gene V. Owen,* Chair.; Paul Lyle, David Wilder.
EIN: 756360908

52295
Linn Foundation
121 N. Post Oak Ln., Ste. 1101
Houston, TX 77024

Established in 2000 in TX.
Donor(s): Roger Linn, Lois Linn.
Financial data (yr. ended 12/31/01): Grants paid, $24,325; assets, $417,807 (M); gifts received, $29,365; expenditures, $26,513; qualifying distributions, $24,325.
Limitations: Applications not accepted.
Application information: Contributes only to pre-selected organizations.
Directors: Lois Linn, Roger Linn.
EIN: 311728452

52296
George Ball Charity Association
c/o Bank of America
P.O. Box 831041
Dallas, TX 75283-1041

Financial data (yr. ended 12/31/01): Grants paid, $24,250; assets, $496,754 (M); expenditures, $30,692; qualifying distributions, $24,250.
Limitations: Applications not accepted. Giving primarily in Galveston, TX.
Application information: Contributes only to pre-selected organizations.
Officers: John H. Hutchings, Pres.; John W. Kelso, V.P.; Brenda L. Hutchings, Secy.-Treas.
Trustees: Jeremy S. Davis, Michael Doherty, Susan Eckle, C.D. Gauss.
EIN: 746035096

52297
Berean Foundation
P.O. Box 15248
Amarillo, TX 79105

Donor(s): E. Jay O'Keefe.
Financial data (yr. ended 12/31/01): Grants paid, $24,236; assets, $114,801 (M); gifts received, $1,200; expenditures, $24,538; qualifying distributions, $24,236.
Limitations: Applications not accepted. Giving on a national basis.
Application information: Contributes only to pre-selected organizations.
Officers: E. Jay O'Keefe, Pres.; Nanne O. Jones, V.P.; Mary Ann O'Keefe, Secy.
EIN: 751820163

52298
Clara Lou Vena Siros Foundation
c/o Laredo National Bank
P.O. Box 59
Laredo, TX 78042-0059 (956) 723-1151

Financial data (yr. ended 12/31/01): Grants paid, $24,200; assets, $720,061 (M); expenditures, $39,499; qualifying distributions, $31,809.
Limitations: Giving limited to Laredo and Webb counties, TX.
Application information: Scholarships awarded only to those whose annual family income does not exceed $65,000. Application form required.
Trustees: Charles B. Dickinson, Laredo National Bank.
EIN: 742574458
Codes: GTI

52299
G. Bedell Moore Memorial Fund
P.O. Box 831130
Richardson, TX 75083-1130 (972) 231-6771
Contact: Gregory B. Moore, III, Tr.

Financial data (yr. ended 12/31/01): Grants paid, $24,185; assets, $565,206 (M); expenditures, $39,676; qualifying distributions, $24,185.
Limitations: Giving primarily in TX.
Trustees: W. Lewis Hart, C. Douglas Moore, Gregory B. Moore III, Gregory B. Moore IV, J. Burleson Smith.
EIN: 746043420

52300
John & Mary O'Brien Foundation for Academic Excellence
P.O. Box 9598
Amarillo, TX 79105
Application address: 800 Monroe, Amarillo, TX 79105, tel.: (806) 372-3877
Contact: Fay Moore, Treas.

Established in 1986 in TX.
Donor(s): Fay Moore, Blake O'Brien, Bob G. Moore, W.H. "Bill" O'Brien, Jay O'Brien, Lucy O'Brien, Alice O'Brien, John G. O'Brien.
Financial data (yr. ended 12/31/01): Grants paid, $24,088; assets, $343,644 (M); gifts received, $15,000; expenditures, $25,616; qualifying distributions, $23,825.
Limitations: Giving limited to the Amarillo, TX, area.
Application information: Interview required. Application form not required.
Officers and Directors:* Blake O'Brien,* Pres.; Alice O'Brien,* V.P.; Bob G. Moore,* Secy.; Fay Moore,* Treas.; Jane O'Brien, Jay O'Brien, John G. O'Brien, Shannon O'Brien, Susie O'Brien, W.H. "Bill" O'Brien.
EIN: 752156810
Codes: GTI

52301
Mary Pearl Bolton Trust
c/o Bank of America
P.O. Box 831041
Dallas, TX 75283-1041

Established in 2001.
Donor(s): Mary Pearl Bolton.
Financial data (yr. ended 12/31/01): Grants paid, $24,069; assets, $908,919 (M); gifts received, $773,517; expenditures, $26,240; qualifying distributions, $16,240.
Limitations: Applications not accepted. Giving primarily in Topeka, KS.
Trustee: Bank of America.
EIN: 527136611

52302
The Calhoun Foundation
251 S. Seguin Ave.
New Braunfels, TX 78130

Established in 1997 in TX.
Donor(s): Evelyn C. Calhoun.
Financial data (yr. ended 12/31/01): Grants paid, $24,000; assets, $996,492 (M); gifts received, $10,796; expenditures, $34,442; qualifying distributions, $24,000.
Limitations: Applications not accepted. Giving primarily in TX.
Application information: Contributes only to pre-selected organizations.
Officers: Gary D. Mathis, Pres.; James R. Rector, V.P.; James R. Boldt, Secy.-Treas.
EIN: 742804468

52303
Alfred A. & Tia Juana Drummond Foundation
c/o Bank One Trust Co., N.A.
P.O. Box 2050
Fort Worth, TX 76113

Financial data (yr. ended 10/31/01): Grants paid, $24,000; assets, $458,376 (M); expenditures, $32,002; qualifying distributions, $25,161.
Limitations: Giving limited to Marshall County, OK.
Application information: Selection is made by a Scholarship Committee at each participating public high school. Application form not required.
Trustee: Bank One Trust Co., N.A.
EIN: 731157648

Codes: GTI

52304
Kirk Edwards Foundation
2264 Hollyhill Dr.
Denton, TX 76205

Established in 1966 in TX.
Donor(s): A.B. Kirk Edwards.‡
Financial data (yr. ended 10/31/01): Grants paid, $24,000; assets, $3,291,846 (M); expenditures, $66,793; qualifying distributions, $28,543.
Limitations: Applications not accepted. Giving primarily in Henrietta, TX.
Application information: Contributes only to pre-selected organizations.
Officers and Trustees:* Carolyn Sullivan,* Pres.; Herbert B. Story,* V.P.; Elizabeth Young,* Secy.; David J. Welch,* Treas.; Frank Gibson, George Slagle.
EIN: 756054922

52305
The Adams Foundation
2525 Stemmons Fwy.
Dallas, TX 75207-2401

Established in 1997 in TX.
Donor(s): John L. Adams, Suzanne L. Adams.
Financial data (yr. ended 12/31/01): Grants paid, $23,950; assets, $433,831 (M); gifts received, $15,000; expenditures, $25,541; qualifying distributions, $23,950.
Limitations: Applications not accepted. Giving primarily in TX.
Application information: Contributes only to pre-selected organizations.
Officers: John L. Adams, Pres. and Treas.; Suzanne L. Adams, V.P. and Secy.
Directors: Elise L. Adams, John R. Adams.
EIN: 752738717

52306
Wayne H. Garrison Charitable Trust
c/o BancorpSouth, Trust Dept.
P.O. Box 5608
Texarkana, TX 75505

Established in 1994 in TX.
Donor(s): Wayne H. Garrison.‡
Financial data (yr. ended 12/31/01): Grants paid, $23,750; assets, $394,168 (M); expenditures, $28,469; qualifying distributions, $24,271.
Limitations: Applications not accepted. Giving primarily in Texarkana AR, and Texarkana, TX.
Application information: Contributes only to pre-selected organizations.
Trustee: BankcorpSouth.
EIN: 756462811

52307
Ruthy and Steven Rosenberg Charitable Foundation
12124 Madeleine Cir.
Dallas, TX 75230
Contact: Steven P. Rosenberg, Pres.

Established in 1991 in TX.
Donor(s): Steven P. Rosenberg, Ruthy F. Rosenberg.
Financial data (yr. ended 12/31/01): Grants paid, $23,619; assets, $185,553 (M); expenditures, $26,652; qualifying distributions, $23,619.
Limitations: Giving primarily in NY and TX.
Application information: Application form required.
Officers and Directors:* Steven P. Rosenberg,* Pres.; Marcus Rosenberg,* V.P.; Ruthy F. Rosenberg,* Secy.-Treas.
EIN: 752376470

52308
The Norris Foundation
1001 Eagles Landing Blvd.
Oak Point, TX 75068

Established in 2000 in TX.
Donor(s): Jill E. Norris, Warren Lee Norris.
Financial data (yr. ended 12/31/01): Grants paid, $23,500; assets, $330,160 (M); gifts received, $26,000; expenditures, $26,957; qualifying distributions, $26,093.
Limitations: Applications not accepted. Giving primarily in TX.
Application information: Contributes only to pre-selected organizations.
Officers: Jill E. Norris, Mgr.; Warren Lee Norris, Mgr.
Trustee: Pat C. Beaird.
EIN: 742465853

52309
Faith Charities, Inc.
449 Louisiana Pkwy.
Corpus Christi, TX 78404-1707

Established in 1996.
Donor(s): Laudadio Polymers, Inc.
Financial data (yr. ended 12/31/01): Grants paid, $23,400; assets, $2,256 (M); gifts received, $19,317; expenditures, $23,500; qualifying distributions, $23,400.
Limitations: Applications not accepted.
Application information: Contributes only to pre-selected organizations.
Officers: Paul D. Laudadio, Pres. and Treas.; Daphne J. Laudadio, V.P.; Tracey Valez, Secy.
Directors: Cornelius M. Hayes III, Fay Laudadio, Paul H. Laudadio.
EIN: 742797643

52310
Bolton Foundation
P.O. Box 2448
Waco, TX 76703-2448 (254) 772-1173
Contact: Catherine Bolton Brown, Pres.

Financial data (yr. ended 06/30/01): Grants paid, $23,350; assets, $425,032 (M); expenditures, $23,475; qualifying distributions, $23,350.
Limitations: Giving primarily in TX.
Officers: Catherine Bolton Brown, Pres.; Barbara Blake, V.P.; Willard E. Brown III, Secy.-Treas.
EIN: 746043299

52311
The Thomas and Sandra Hunt Foundation
6830 Hunt Ln.
Brookshire, TX 77423-9270

Established in 2000 in TX.
Donor(s): Thomas N. Hunt, Sandra J. Hunt.
Financial data (yr. ended 12/31/01): Grants paid, $23,250; assets, $336,013 (M); expenditures, $31,483; qualifying distributions, $23,250.
Limitations: Applications not accepted.
Application information: Contributes only to pre-selected organizations.
Trustees: Sandra J. Hunt, Thomas N. Hunt.
EIN: 760656591

52312
Albert L. McKay Charitable Trust for Underprivileged Children
2522 Calder Ave.
Beaumont, TX 77702-1930

Established in 1988 in TX.
Financial data (yr. ended 12/31/00): Grants paid, $23,200; assets, $680,808 (M); expenditures, $83,273; qualifying distributions, $59,463; giving activities include $60,073 for programs.

Limitations: Applications not accepted.
Application information: Contributes only to pre-selected organizations.
Trustees: R.J. Demahy, Marshall Cooper, Carlton Wood.
EIN: 766047458

52313
Wukasch Foundation
3960 Del Monte Dr.
Houston, TX 77019   (713) 788-5454
Contact: Don C. Wukasch, Pres.

Financial data (yr. ended 12/31/01): Grants paid, $23,189; assets, $750,005 (M); expenditures, $56,519; qualifying distributions, $23,189.
Application information: Application form not required.
Officers: Don C. Wukasch, Pres.; Ann Elizabeth Wukasch, V.P.; Barry C. Wukasch, V.P.; Walter Charles Wukasch, V.P.; Linda T. Wukasch, Secy.-Treas.; Pamela C. Speir, Exec. Dir.
EIN: 760501629

52314
The Denker Foundation
c/o Peter J. Denker & Charron R. Denker
2001 Ross Ave., Ste. 2700
Dallas, TX 75201-2936

Established in 1995 in TX.
Donor(s): Charron R. Denker, Peter J. Denker.
Financial data (yr. ended 12/31/01): Grants paid, $23,150; assets, $460,462 (M); gifts received, $6,500; expenditures, $25,537; qualifying distributions, $23,150.
Limitations: Applications not accepted. Giving primarily in TX.
Application information: Contributes only to pre-selected organizations.
Trustees: Charron R. Denker, Peter J. Denker.
EIN: 752623836

52315
Camp Trust
P.O. Box 1139
Cameron, TX 76520-1139
Application address: 803 E. 7th St., Cameron, TX 76520, tel.: (254) 697-6622
Contact: James D. Camp, Dir.

Established in 1992 in TX.
Donor(s): James D. Camp, Patricia A. Camp.
Financial data (yr. ended 12/31/01): Grants paid, $23,120; assets, $146,278 (M); expenditures, $23,675; qualifying distributions, $23,120.
Limitations: Giving limited to TX.
Application information: Application form not required.
Directors: David P. Camp, James D. Camp, James M. Camp, Patricia A. Camp, Carolyn Camp Hux.
EIN: 746399790

52316
The Linbeck Foundation
3810 W. Alabama St.
Houston, TX 77027-5294
Application address: P.O. Box 22500, Houston, TX 77227-2500, tel.: (713) 621-2350
Contact: Carolyn Noack, Secy.

Financial data (yr. ended 12/31/01): Grants paid, $23,100; assets, $303,138 (M); expenditures, $29,066; qualifying distributions, $23,100.
Limitations: Giving primarily in Houston, TX.
Application information: Application form not required.
Officers: Patti Ruth Linbeck, Pres.; Carolyn Noack, Secy.
Trustees: Patricia Linbeck Doyle, Dewayne E. Hahn, Constance Baird Linbeck, Suzanne Linbeck Reynolds.
EIN: 742198931

52317
The Mr. and Mrs. Robert J. Stetson Foundation
12240 Inwood Rd., Ste. 200
Dallas, TX 75244

Financial data (yr. ended 12/31/01): Grants paid, $23,100; assets, $355,832 (M); expenditures, $33,857; qualifying distributions, $23,100.
Officers: Robert J. Stetson, Pres.; Cindy Forester, V.P. and Secy.; Robert Chess Abernathy Stetson, Treas.
EIN: 752709237

52318
Robert Houston & Hollyanne Frances Farris Foundation
P.O. Box 1870
Harlingen, TX 78551-1870

Established in 1997 in TX.
Donor(s): Robert R. Farris, Robin Farris.
Financial data (yr. ended 12/31/01): Grants paid, $23,099; assets, $737,133 (M); gifts received, $99,000; expenditures, $24,850; qualifying distributions, $23,099.
Limitations: Applications not accepted.
Application information: Contributes only to pre-selected organizations.
Officer and Director:* Robert R. Farris,* Pres.; Robin Farris, Secy.-Treas.; Jonathan Brad Farris.
EIN: 742855935

52319
Charles & Katherine Moore Foundation
6840 Mossvine Cir.
Dallas, TX 75240

Financial data (yr. ended 12/31/01): Grants paid, $23,071; assets, $108,121 (M); expenditures, $23,911; qualifying distributions, $23,071.
Limitations: Applications not accepted. Giving primarily in Dallas, TX.
Application information: Contributes only to pre-selected organizations.
Trustees: Charles M. Moore III, Marvin F. Moore.
EIN: 756036330

52320
Eunice Corinne Mikeska Trust
c/o Commercial National Bank, Trust Dept.
P.O. Box 400
Beeville, TX 78104-0400

Financial data (yr. ended 12/31/01): Grants paid, $23,068; assets, $618,511 (M); expenditures, $29,450; qualifying distributions, $23,068.
Limitations: Applications not accepted. Giving limited to Beeville, TX.
Trustee: Commercial National Bank.
EIN: 742189947

52321
Harriett M. Cunningham Charitable Fund
1000 Goodhue Bldg.
Beaumont, TX 77701   (409) 832-7080
Contact: Donald L. Boudreaux, Secy.

Established in 1989.
Financial data (yr. ended 12/31/01): Grants paid, $23,000; assets, $700,944 (M); expenditures, $60,306; qualifying distributions, $23,000.
Limitations: Giving primarily in TX.
Officer and Directors:* Donald L. Boudreaux,* Secy. and Mgr.; Joe N. Jersild.
EIN: 760273663

52322
William Gano Houstoun Foundation
P.O. Box 27112
Austin, TX 78755-2112
Contact: James W. Houstoun, Dir.

Established in 1988 in TX.
Donor(s): James W. Houstoun.
Financial data (yr. ended 11/30/01): Grants paid, $23,000; assets, $353,960 (M); gifts received, $30,828; expenditures, $26,534; qualifying distributions, $22,610.
Limitations: Giving primarily in Austin, TX.
Directors: James W. Houstoun, Jeri K. Houstoun, Terry McDaniel.
EIN: 742522686

52323
Jackson-Haack Family Foundation
221 Magnolia Dr.
Coppell, TX 75019-3283

Established in 1995 in CA and TX.
Donor(s): Charles L. Jackson, Clara H. Jackson.
Financial data (yr. ended 11/30/01): Grants paid, $22,947; assets, $567,097 (M); expenditures, $40,741; qualifying distributions, $22,947.
Limitations: Applications not accepted. Giving primarily in CA, OR, and TX.
Application information: Contributes only to pre-selected organizations.
Officers and Directors:* Clara H. Jackson,* Pres.; Michelle Miller,* V.P.; Charles L. Jackson,* Secy.-Treas.
EIN: 752559696

52324
Renee Malca Cadour Corn Charitable Foundation
10017 Regal Park Ln., Ste. 105
Dallas, TX 75230   (214) 369-1802
Contact: Ida J. Corn, Tr.

Established in 1998 in TX.
Financial data (yr. ended 12/31/01): Grants paid, $22,750; assets, $674,042 (M); expenditures, $31,125; qualifying distributions, $22,750.
Trustees: Ida J. Corn, Marilyn Corn, Rise Corn.
EIN: 731543969

52325
John H. and Marjorie N. Glasgow Foundation
3650 Piping Rock Ln.
Houston, TX 77027-4117

Established in 1999 in TX.
Donor(s): Marjorie N. Glasgow, John H. Glasgow.
Financial data (yr. ended 12/31/00): Grants paid, $22,650; assets, $397,227 (M); expenditures, $25,900; qualifying distributions, $22,650.
Officers: Marjorie N. Glasgow, Pres.; John H. Glasgow, V.P.
Director: Lori N. Leeder.
EIN: 760609709

52326
Gatewood Family Foundation
16211 Park 10th Pl.
Houston, TX 77084
Contact: E. Michael Gatewood, Pres.

Established in 1999 in TX.
Donor(s): E. Michael Gatewood.
Financial data (yr. ended 12/31/01): Grants paid, $22,500; assets, $584,770 (M); gifts received, $455,000; expenditures, $26,761; qualifying distributions, $22,500.
Limitations: Giving limited to the Houston, TX area.
Officer: E. Michael Gatewood, Pres.

52326—TEXAS

Directors: Cindy L. Gatewood, Kristen J. Gatewood.
EIN: 760595111

52327
Marshall Foundation
c/o Jon Marshall
777 N. Eldridge
Houston, TX 77079

Established in 1997.
Donor(s): Jon Marshall, Gene V. Marshall.
Financial data (yr. ended 12/31/01): Grants paid, $22,500; assets, $350,439 (M); expenditures, $23,445; qualifying distributions, $22,500.
Limitations: Giving primarily in OK.
Officer: Jon Marshall, Pres.
EIN: 760537578

52328
Sursum Corda Foundation
c/o Joseph W. Bitter
446 County Rd. 115
Edna, TX 77957-4650
Contact: Joseph W. Bitter, Tr.

Donor(s): Joseph W. Bitter, Mary Ann Bitter.
Financial data (yr. ended 12/31/01): Grants paid, $22,500; assets, $327,663 (M); gifts received, $5,875; expenditures, $23,309; qualifying distributions, $22,500.
Trustees: Joseph W. Bitter, Mary Ann Bitter, Patrick Bitter.
EIN: 742833600

52329
Livermore Religious Trust
c/o Wells Fargo Bank Texas, N.A.
P.O. Box 10517
Lubbock, TX 79408-0517
Application address: c/o Don Schroeder, Trust Off., Wells Fargo Bank Texas, N.A., 1500 Broadway, Lubbock, TX 79401, tel.: (806) 767-7308

Financial data (yr. ended 12/31/01): Grants paid, $22,471; assets, $286,642 (M); expenditures, $27,560; qualifying distributions, $24,141.
Limitations: Giving limited to Lubbock, TX.
Trustees: John Crews, Wells Fargo Bank Texas, N.A.
EIN: 756017528

52330
The Sol B. & Annette Weiner Foundation, Inc.
434 Hunterwood Dr.
Houston, TX 77024-6936

Financial data (yr. ended 06/30/01): Grants paid, $22,185; assets, $675,100 (M); gifts received, $472,940; expenditures, $23,427; qualifying distributions, $22,185.
Limitations: Applications not accepted.
Application information: Contributes only to pre-selected organizations.
Officers: Sol B. Weiner, Pres.; Annette Weiner, Secy.
EIN: 237004544

52331
Paula Martin Jones Charities, Inc.
P.O. Box 191
Kilgore, TX 75663

Donor(s): Ruben S. Martin III.
Financial data (yr. ended 12/31/99): Grants paid, $22,172; assets, $327,269 (M); gifts received, $91,690; expenditures, $145,341; qualifying distributions, $88,883; giving activities include $114,623 for programs.
Limitations: Applications not accepted.

Application information: Contributes only to pre-selected organizations.
Officers and Directors:* Ruben S. Martin III,* Pres.; R.S. Martin, Jr.,* V.P.; Margaret G. Martin,* Secy.; Bill Bankston, W.D. O'Neal.
EIN: 752326989

52332
Charles Downey Charitable Trust
P.O. Box 831041
Dallas, TX 75283-1041

Established in 1998 in TX.
Financial data (yr. ended 12/31/01): Grants paid, $22,156; assets, $570,132 (M); expenditures, $27,149; qualifying distributions, $23,280.
Limitations: Applications not accepted.
Application information: Contributes only to pre-selected organizations.
Trustee: Bank of America.
EIN: 746432041

52333
Guess Foundation
800 Navarro St.
San Antonio, TX 78205-1723
Contact: Milton Guess, Pres.

Established in 1999 in TX.
Financial data (yr. ended 12/31/01): Grants paid, $22,000; assets, $30,371 (M); expenditures, $22,121; qualifying distributions, $22,080.
Officer: Milton Guess, Pres.
Directors: Sally Guess, Shanna Lindner.
EIN: 742898878

52334
The Craven Family Foundation
c/o PADM, Inc.
3939 Bee Cave Rd., Ste. C-1
Austin, TX 78746

Established in 1998 in TX.
Financial data (yr. ended 12/31/01): Grants paid, $22,000; assets, $745,660 (M); expenditures, $30,116; qualifying distributions, $22,000.
Limitations: Applications not accepted.
Application information: Contributes only to pre-selected organizations.
Officers: Donald Allen Craven, Jr., Pres. and Treas.; Donald Allen Craven, Sr., V.P.; Tiffany Aldrich Craven, Secy.
EIN: 742903652

52335
The Joe M. & Doris R. Dealey Family Foundation
8333 Douglas Ave., Ste. 1575
Dallas, TX 75225
Contact: Russell E. Dealey, Pres.

Established in 1995 in TX.
Donor(s): Doris Dealey.
Financial data (yr. ended 12/31/00): Grants paid, $22,000; assets, $564,492 (M); expenditures, $35,129; qualifying distributions, $22,000.
Officers: Russell E. Dealey, Pres. and Treas.; Pamela Dealey Campbell, V.P. and Secy.
Trustees: Stuart M. Bumpas, Branson K. Bywaters, Joseph M. Dealey, Jr., W.C. Smellage.
EIN: 752611909

52336
T. F. and C. M. Hastings Foundation, Inc.
14254 Misty Meadows Ln.
Houston, TX 77079-3183 (281) 497-3255
Contact: Thomas F. Hastings, Sr., Pres.

Established in 1998 in TX.
Donor(s): Thomas F. Hastings, Sr., Catherine Mary Hasings.

Financial data (yr. ended 03/31/01): Grants paid, $22,000; assets, $469,844 (M); expenditures, $26,797; qualifying distributions, $22,000.
Officers and Directors:* Thomas F. Hastings, Sr.,* Pres.; C.M. Hastings,* Secy.
EIN: 760571073

52337
The James Foundation Charitable Trust
c/o First National Bank of Abilene, Trust Dept.
P.O. Box 701
Abilene, TX 79604

Financial data (yr. ended 12/31/01): Grants paid, $22,000; assets, $332,113 (M); gifts received, $390; expenditures, $25,964; qualifying distributions, $22,000.
Limitations: Giving primarily in TX.
Application information: Application form not required.
Trustee: First National Bank of Abilene.
EIN: 756306453

52338
Rosenquist Family Foundation
9700 McIntyre Cir.
Austin, TX 78734

Established in 1999 in TX.
Donor(s): Lance A. Rosenquist.
Financial data (yr. ended 12/31/01): Grants paid, $22,000; assets, $328,201 (M); expenditures, $22,989; qualifying distributions, $22,000.
Limitations: Applications not accepted. Giving primarily in TX.
Application information: Contributes only to pre-selected organizations.
Trustees: Deborah J. Rosenquist, Lance A. Rosenquist.
EIN: 742902139

52339
Wakefield Foundation
100 E. 29th St., 3131B
Bryan, TX 77802-3907 (979) 589-3774
Contact: T. Parten Wakefield, Jr., Pres.

Established in 1993 in TX.
Donor(s): T. Parten Wakefield, Jr.
Financial data (yr. ended 12/31/00): Grants paid, $22,000; assets, $362,180 (M); expenditures, $23,431; qualifying distributions, $23,432.
Limitations: Giving primarily in TX.
Officers: T. Parten Wakefield, Jr., Pres. and V.P.; Linda Taylor, Secy.-Treas.
Director: Frank G. Anderson III.
EIN: 742659382

52340
Marguerite R. Edwards Civic Improvement & Activity Trust
c/o Union Planters Bank
P.O. Box 232
Alvin, TX 77512-0232
Application address: c/o Mayor of Alvin City, 216 Sealy St., Alvin, TX 77511, tel.: (281) 388-4200

Financial data (yr. ended 07/31/01): Grants paid, $21,834; assets, $389,108 (M); expenditures, $29,909; qualifying distributions, $22,893.
Limitations: Giving limited to the Alvin, TX, area.
Application information: Application form required.
Trustee: Union Planters Bank.
EIN: 746216233

52341
Pullen Family Foundation
5436 North Crest
Fort Worth, TX 76107 (817) 732-4170
Contact: Weston C. Pullen, III, Tr.

Established in 1994 in CT.
Donor(s): Weston C. Pullen III.
Financial data (yr. ended 12/31/00): Grants paid, $21,812; assets, $69,573 (M); expenditures, $21,812; qualifying distributions, $21,812.
Trustee: Weston C. Pullen III.
EIN: 061417246

52342
McGlothlin Foundation
c/o Patsy Moran
P.O. Box 89
Abilene, TX 79604-3579

Donor(s): Ray McGlothlin, Jr.
Financial data (yr. ended 12/31/01): Grants paid, $21,800; assets, $780,422 (M); expenditures, $25,173; qualifying distributions, $21,800.
Limitations: Applications not accepted. Giving primarily in TX.
Application information: Contributes only to pre-selected organizations.
Officers and Directors:* Ray McGlothlin, Jr.,* Pres.; Eric L. Oliver, V.P. and Secy.; Wilson C. Orr,* Treas.; Hal McGlothlin, Jack V. McGlothlin.
EIN: 756061282

52343
R. B. Price Family Foundation
201 E. Main St., Ste. 1521
El Paso, TX 79901-1334

Financial data (yr. ended 12/31/01): Grants paid, $21,736; assets, $416,099 (M); expenditures, $22,105; qualifying distributions, $21,736.
Limitations: Applications not accepted. Giving primarily in Albuquerque, NM, and El Paso, TX.
Officers: Barbara Price Curlin, Pres. and Mgr.; Dudley Price, V.P.; Jack V. Curlin, Secy.-Treas. and Mgr.
EIN: 746067200

52344
Robert Ashley and Margaret Looney McAllen Charitable Foundation
1800 E. Hwy. 83
Weslaco, TX 78596-8356 (956) 968-9288
Contact: Robert A. McAllen, Pres.

Established in 1992 in TX.
Donor(s): Robert A. McAllen, Margaret L. McAllen.
Financial data (yr. ended 12/31/01): Grants paid, $21,728; assets, $175,368 (M); gifts received, $7,500; expenditures, $22,513; qualifying distributions, $21,979.
Limitations: Giving primarily in TX.
Officers: Robert A. McAllen, Pres.; Margaret L. McAllen, V.P. and Secy.
Director: Forrest L. Jones.
EIN: 742663275

52345
Coulter and Lily Rush Hoppess Foundation, Inc.
1301 McKinney St., Ste. 3550
Houston, TX 77010-3053

Established in 2000 in TX.
Donor(s): Lily Rush Hoppess.
Financial data (yr. ended 12/31/01): Grants paid, $21,705; assets, $468,761 (M); expenditures, $25,018; qualifying distributions, $21,705.
Limitations: Applications not accepted.
Application information: Contributes only to pre-selected organizations.
Officers: Karl C. Hoppess, Pres.; Nancy Rush Forrester, Secy.
Directors: Judith Walker Hood, Martha Helen Hoppess.
EIN: 760614246

52346
Corpus Christi Exploration Company Foundation
P.O. Box 779
Corpus Christi, TX 78403-0779
(361) 882-2001
Contact: Leslie W. Dunn, Secy.-Treas.

Established in 1981 in TX.
Donor(s): Corpus Christi Exploration Co.
Financial data (yr. ended 11/30/01): Grants paid, $21,700; assets, $332,909 (M); expenditures, $22,939; qualifying distributions, $22,135.
Limitations: Giving primarily in Corpus Christi and Houston, TX.
Application information: Application form not required.
Officers: Paul R. Haas, Pres.; Laurence A. McNeil, V.P.; Leslie W. Dunn, Secy.-Treas.
EIN: 742161696
Codes: CS, CD

52347
The Giardini Foundation
6103 Valley Forge, Unit C
Houston, TX 77057
Contact: Mary Ann Giardini, Secy.-Treas.

Established in 1993 in TX.
Donor(s): Carl P. Giardini, Mary Ann Giardini.
Financial data (yr. ended 12/31/01): Grants paid, $21,700; assets, $324,742 (M); gifts received, $153,478; expenditures, $24,292; qualifying distributions, $21,700.
Limitations: Giving primarily in Bradford, PA.
Officers: Carl P. Giardini, Pres.; Mary Ann Giardini, Secy.-Treas.
EIN: 760410855

52348
R. Q. & L. A. Seely Charitable Trust
(Formerly Roger Q. & Lovye A. Seely Trust)
c/o Bank of America
P.O. Box 831041
Dallas, TX 75283-1041
Application address: c/o C.T. Griffin, Superintendent, Wortham Independent School District, P.O. Box 247, Wortham, TX 76695, tel.: (817) 765-3678

Financial data (yr. ended 02/28/02): Grants paid, $21,700; assets, $457,156 (M); expenditures, $27,307; qualifying distributions, $22,662.
Limitations: Giving limited to the Wortham, TX, area.
Application information: Application form required.
Trustee: Bank of America.
EIN: 756069098
Codes: GTI

52349
Lena Snell Helm Charitable Trust
c/o Bank of America
P.O. Box 831041
Dallas, TX 75283-1041

Established in 1995 in TX.
Donor(s): Lena Helm Charitable Trust.
Financial data (yr. ended 12/31/01): Grants paid, $21,660; assets, $383,651 (M); expenditures, $25,388; qualifying distributions, $21,660.
Limitations: Applications not accepted. Giving primarily in Clifton, TX.
Application information: Contributes only to pre-selected organizations.
Trustee: Bank of America.
EIN: 756465300

52350
Allen & Janice Lackey Foundation
1623 Scenic Shore Dr.
Kingwood, TX 77345-1903 (281) 360-3033
Contact: S. Allen Lackey, Tr.

Established in 1997.
Donor(s): S. Allen Lackey, Janice S. Lackey.
Financial data (yr. ended 12/31/01): Grants paid, $21,625; assets, $57,717 (M); expenditures, $22,860; qualifying distributions, $21,614.
Limitations: Giving primarily in Houston, TX.
Application information: Application form not required.
Trustees: Janice S. Lackey, S. Allen Lackey.
EIN: 766121154

52351
McEwen-Deck Foundation, Inc.
130 Hogan Dr.
Lake Kiowa, TX 76240-9557 (940) 665-4221
Contact: Lucy B. Deck, Pres.

Financial data (yr. ended 02/28/02): Grants paid, $21,541; assets, $441,803 (M); expenditures, $23,397; qualifying distributions, $21,541.
Limitations: Giving primarily in Wichita, KS.
Officers: Lucy B. Deck, Pres.; James C. Belknap, V.P.; Steve Deck, Treas.; Clark Nelson, Secy.
EIN: 486105172

52352
Esphahanian Foundation
10811 Hunters Forest
Houston, TX 77024-5417
Contact: Ramona K. Esphahanian, Dir.

Established in 1998 in TX.
Donor(s): Esphahanian Family Partnership, Ltd.
Financial data (yr. ended 12/31/00): Grants paid, $21,500; assets, $112,401 (M); expenditures, $24,075; qualifying distributions, $21,500.
Directors: Cyrus Esphahanian, Ramona K. Esphahanian, Vanita Esphahanian.
EIN: 760606798

52353
Tucker Foundation
P.O. Box 600667
Dallas, TX 75360-0667 (214) 526-7268
Contact: Pebble Fry

Financial data (yr. ended 12/31/01): Grants paid, $21,500; assets, $444,818 (M); expenditures, $31,025; qualifying distributions, $21,500.
Limitations: Giving limited to the Dallas, TX, area.
Application information: Application form not required.
Trustees: M. Robert Blakeney, Betty B. Tucker, Rosalie Tucker.
EIN: 756014646

52354
Carol Tyrrell Kyle Foundation
P.O. Box 15068
San Antonio, TX 78212-5068

Established in 1989 in TX.
Financial data (yr. ended 06/30/01): Grants paid, $21,435; assets, $431,138 (M); expenditures, $23,908; qualifying distributions, $21,435.
Limitations: Applications not accepted. Giving primarily in TX.
Application information: Contributes only to pre-selected organizations.
Trustee: Emilie Kyle Chenault.
EIN: 746372892

52355
The Estevez Christian Foundation
6402 Palacio Dr.
Amarillo, TX 79109-5115

Established in 1989 in TX.
Donor(s): Roberto Estevez, M.D.
Financial data (yr. ended 12/31/01): Grants paid, $21,314; assets, $365,605 (M); expenditures, $23,013; qualifying distributions, $21,189.
Limitations: Applications not accepted. Giving in the U.S., primarily in TX.
Application information: Contributes only to pre-selected organizations.
Directors: Daniel Dominguez, Anahid Estevez, Elizabeth Estevez, Laura Estevez, Leonardo Estevez, Roberto Estevez, M.D.
EIN: 752302835

52356
Conn Appliances Charitable Foundation, Inc.
3295 College St.
Beaumont, TX 77701
Additional address: P.O. Box 2358, Beaumont, TX 77704, tel.: (409) 835-3496

Established in 1976 in TX.
Donor(s): Conn Appliance, Inc.
Financial data (yr. ended 11/30/01): Grants paid, $21,280; assets, $969 (M); gifts received, $20,000; expenditures, $21,880; qualifying distributions, $21,880.
Limitations: Giving primarily in TX.
Application information: Application form required.
Officers: Thomas J. Frank, Pres.; C.W. Frank, Secy.-Treas.
EIN: 741884559
Codes: CS, CD, GTI

52357
Terrell Foundation
c/o Stephenville Bank and Trust Co.
P.O. Box 998
Stephenville, TX 76401

Financial data (yr. ended 12/31/01): Grants paid, $21,252; assets, $418,536 (M); expenditures, $24,972; qualifying distributions, $21,252.
Limitations: Giving limited to Stephenville, TX.
Application information: Application form not required.
Officer and Trustees:* C.H. McGuire,* Chair.; Penny Elliott, Barbara Nix, J.C. Terrell.
EIN: 756036585

52358
Annu Foundation
7 Lakewood Ct.
Lufkin, TX 75901-7319

Donor(s): J.S. Chandra.
Financial data (yr. ended 12/31/01): Grants paid, $21,250; assets, $386,716 (M); gifts received, $2,006; expenditures, $27,058; qualifying distributions, $21,250.
Directors: J. Steven Awalt, J.S. Chandra, Rodney C. Koenig, Kent H. McMahan, E. John R. Samuel.
EIN: 752768009

52359
The South Odessa Community Foundation
c/o American State Bank
P.O. Box 4797
Odessa, TX 79760

Established in 1998 in TX.
Donor(s): Ameripol Synpol Corp.
Financial data (yr. ended 12/31/01): Grants paid, $21,210; assets, $397,712 (M); expenditures, $24,127; qualifying distributions, $21,083.

Limitations: Giving primarily in Ector County, TX.
Application information: Application form required.
Trustees: Gene Collins, Frank Drace, American State Bank.
EIN: 752739500
Codes: CS, CD

52360
Volney E. Dibrell Charitable Trust
c/o Frost National Bank
P.O. Box 2950
San Antonio, TX 78299
Contact: William Clyborne, V.P., Frost National Bank

Established in 1992 in TX.
Financial data (yr. ended 03/31/01): Grants paid, $21,205; assets, $968,027 (M); expenditures, $37,714; qualifying distributions, $26,580.
Limitations: Giving limited to TX.
Trustee: Frost National Bank.
EIN: 746396825

52361
The Durham Foundation
c/o Patricia Durham
5419 Garden Village Dr.
Kingwood, TX 77339-1262

Financial data (yr. ended 12/31/01): Grants paid, $21,165; assets, $210,969 (M); expenditures, $24,110; qualifying distributions, $21,165.
Limitations: Applications not accepted. Giving limited to Houston, TX.
Application information: Contributes only to pre-selected organizations.
Trustees: Mary R. Amburn, Patricia Durham, Betty Pritchett.
EIN: 237185881

52362
The Jensen Family Foundation
4006 Beltline Rd., Ste. 250
Addison, TX 75001-4371

Established in 1999 in TX.
Donor(s): Robert L. Jensen.
Financial data (yr. ended 12/31/01): Grants paid, $21,100; assets, $273,067 (M); gifts received, $9,640; expenditures, $22,593; qualifying distributions, $21,100.
Limitations: Applications not accepted. Giving primarily in Iowa City, IA, and Dallas, TX.
Application information: Contributes only to pre-selected organizations.
Trustee: Robert L. Jensen.
EIN: 752837226

52363
Bedford W. Sipes Memorial Student Loan Fund
c/o Wells Fargo Bank Texas, N.A.
P.O. Box 900
Corpus Christi, TX 78403
Contact: Deborah A. Tamez, V.P. and Trust Off., Wells Fargo Bank, N.A.

Established in 1984 in TX.
Financial data (yr. ended 02/28/02): Grants paid, $21,100; assets, $263,362 (M); expenditures, $25,507; qualifying distributions, $22,123; giving activities include $21,100 for loans to individuals.
Limitations: Giving limited to Sinton, TX.
Application information: Application form required.
Trustee: Wells Fargo Bank Texas, N.A.
EIN: 746321954
Codes: GTI

52364
The Michael Baker Family Foundation
3322 Albans Rd.
Houston, TX 77005-2104

Established in 1999 in TX.
Financial data (yr. ended 12/31/01): Grants paid, $21,000; assets, $407,996 (M); expenditures, $23,672; qualifying distributions, $22,040.
Limitations: Applications not accepted.
Application information: Contributes only to pre-selected organizations.
Officers: Michael A. Baker, Chair.; Randall E. Evans, Pres.; Dwight A. Baker, V.P.; Emily J. Baker, Secy.; Cullen R. Evans, Treas.
EIN: 760608473

52365
T. B. Butler Foundation
P.O. Box 55
Tyler, TX 75710-0055   (903) 596-6336
Contact: Carole Wilson, Pres.

Established in 1997 in TX.
Financial data (yr. ended 12/31/01): Grants paid, $21,000; assets, $637,761 (M); gifts received, $117,660; expenditures, $26,526; qualifying distributions, $21,000.
Limitations: Giving primarily in Tyler, TX.
Officers: Carole Wilson, Pres.; Nelson Clyde III, V.P.; Lloyd Wilson, Secy.
Directors: Eloise Clyde Chandler, Carrie Clark, Thomas Clyde.
EIN: 752737670

52366
Beverly & Leonard Martin Foundation
338 Fawnlake
Houston, TX 77079-7348

Established in 1996 in TX.
Donor(s): Leonard Martin.
Financial data (yr. ended 12/31/01): Grants paid, $21,000; assets, $327,462 (M); expenditures, $21,281; qualifying distributions, $21,000.
Limitations: Applications not accepted.
Application information: Contributes only to pre-selected organizations.
Officer: Leonard Martin, Pres.
EIN: 311497868

52367
Mackenzie Foundation
c/o Floyd Mackenzie
P.O. Box 333
San Marcos, TX 78667-0333

Financial data (yr. ended 12/31/01): Grants paid, $20,910; assets, $194,726 (M); gifts received, $16,330; expenditures, $20,910; qualifying distributions, $20,910.
Officer: Floyd Mackenzie, Pres.
Directors: Diana Mackenzie, Donna Nelson, Rosemarie Sregner.
EIN: 742897307

52368
Joe E. Davis Foundation
3457 Curry Ln.
Abilene, TX 79606-2229   (915) 692-8200
Contact: Joe E. Davis, Dir.

Established in 1993 in TX.
Donor(s): Skinny's, Inc.
Financial data (yr. ended 12/31/01): Grants paid, $20,860; assets, $1,010,312 (M); gifts received, $20,000; expenditures, $36,127; qualifying distributions, $20,860.
Limitations: Giving primarily in Abilene, TX.
Directors: Billie J. Davis, Bo S. Davis, David C. Davis, Joe Bob Davis, Joe E. Davis.

EIN: 752497580

52369
The Norris Foundation
P.O. Box 121888
Arlington, TX 76006-7888
Contact: Robert W. Norris, Tr.

Established in 1998.
Financial data (yr. ended 12/31/99): Grants paid, $20,739; assets, $100 (M); gifts received, $21,000; expenditures, $20,785; qualifying distributions, $20,038.
Trustees: Robert W. Norris, Robin K. Norris.
EIN: 752756673

52370
Majorie Markham Page McAnespy Charitable Foundation, Inc.
P.O. Box 101026
Fort Worth, TX 76185 (817) 870-1057

Established in 1993.
Donor(s): Marjorie McAnespy.
Financial data (yr. ended 12/31/01): Grants paid, $20,600; assets, $336,439 (M); expenditures, $21,320; qualifying distributions, $20,600.
Limitations: Applications not accepted. Giving limited to TX.
Application information: Contributes only to pre-selected organizations.
Directors: Donald R. Barg, Marjorie McAnespy, Louis Page, Markham L. Page, Sandra Page, Frank Tupper Smith, Jr.
EIN: 752492225

52371
Coin B. Frederick & Erin Frederick Powers Trust
P.O. Box 29004
Kerrville, TX 78028-9004
Application address: c/o Security State Bank & Trust Co., 607 N. Main, Boerne, TX 78006

Established in 1995 in TX.
Donor(s): Erin F. Powers.‡
Financial data (yr. ended 11/30/01): Grants paid, $20,520; assets, $443,971 (M); expenditures, $26,555; qualifying distributions, $20,520.
Limitations: Giving primarily in Bourne, TX.
Application information: Application form required.
Trustees: Frank Y. Hill, Jr., Security State Bank & Trust Co.
EIN: 746435766

52372
Harry W. Hamilton Foundation
P.O. Box 1099
Sinton, TX 78387-1099
Application address: 1014 Santa Fe, Corpus Christi, TX 78404
Contact: Diana W. Hamilton, Pres.

Donor(s): Diana W. Hamilton.
Financial data (yr. ended 09/30/01): Grants paid, $20,500; assets, $515,085 (M); expenditures, $21,184; qualifying distributions, $20,500.
Limitations: Giving limited to residents of San Patricio County, TX.
Application information: Application form not required.
Officers: Diana W. Hamilton,* Pres.; Diana T. Morrison, V.P.; Hughes Thomas, Secy.; Jane H. McKee, Treas.
Trustees: Jeanne T. Talley, Richard P. Thomas.
EIN: 742338471

52373
The Helen Hodges Educational Charitable Foundation
c/o American State Bank, Trust Dept.
P.O. Box 1401
Lubbock, TX 79408 (806) 767-7000
Contact: Marion Bryant, Trust Off., American State Bank

Financial data (yr. ended 12/31/01): Grants paid, $20,500; assets, $408,944 (M); expenditures, $25,252; qualifying distributions, $20,851.
Limitations: Giving limited to Lubbock, TX.
Trustees: Robert Baker, Kay Fletcher, Betsy Jones, Connie Nicholson.
EIN: 510183778
Codes: GTI

52374
Kickapoo Springs Foundation
2030 Loop 306
San Angelo, TX 76904 (915) 949-2877
Contact: John A. Matthews, Jr., Pres.

Established in 1997 in TX.
Donor(s): John A. Matthews, Jr.
Financial data (yr. ended 12/31/01): Grants paid, $20,400; assets, $533,682 (M); expenditures, $20,462; qualifying distributions, $20,400.
Officers: John A. Matthews, Jr., Pres.; Kade L. Matthews, V.P.; Joseph B. Matthews, Secy.-Treas.
EIN: 752684716

52375
Lockett Foundation
P.O. Box 1331
Vernon, TX 76385-1331

Donor(s): Aubrey L. Lockett.
Financial data (yr. ended 12/31/01): Grants paid, $20,330; assets, $420,909 (M); expenditures, $24,687; qualifying distributions, $20,330.
Limitations: Applications not accepted. Giving primarily in TX.
Application information: Contributes only to pre-selected organizations.
Officers: Linda Lockett Cheslak, Pres.; Michael N. Underwood, V.P. and Secy.-Treas.
Trustees: Mae Belle Belew, Robert Lightfoot, Dan R. Nowlin.
EIN: 751534079

52376
Roman & Sonia Lubetzky Foundation
13275 Hunters Lark
San Antonio, TX 78230-2017 (210) 344-8229

Established in 1999.
Donor(s): Roman Lubetzky, Sonia Americus Lubetzky.
Financial data (yr. ended 12/31/00): Grants paid, $20,245; assets, $33,864 (M); expenditures, $22,056; qualifying distributions, $20,233.
Limitations: Giving on a national basis, with some emphasis in Washington, DC, New York, NY, and San Antonio, TX.
Officers: Roman Lubetzky, Pres.; Sioma Lubetzky, V.P. and Treas.; Illeana Katzenelson, V.P.; Daniel Lubetzky, V.P.; Tamara Stavinsky, V.P.; Sonia Americus Lubetzky, Secy.
EIN: 742885220

52377
Davidson Foundation
P.O. Box 1315
Marshall, TX 75671-1315
Contact: Robert L. Duvall, Secy.-Treas.

Established in 1956 in TX.
Donor(s): Hon. T. Whitfield Davidson.‡

Financial data (yr. ended 12/31/01): Grants paid, $20,200; assets, $1,016,359 (M); expenditures, $131,149; qualifying distributions, $20,700.
Limitations: Giving primarily in Diana and Marshall, TX.
Publications: Annual report, informational brochure.
Application information: Application form not required.
Officers: Hon. William J. Cornelius, Chair.; Robert L. Duvall, Secy.-Treas.
Trustees: Billy J. Davidson, Hon. J. Rodney Gilstrap, Ben C. Newman, William M. Runnels.
EIN: 756038584

52378
The Rider Family Fund
2 Dansby Dr.
Galveston, TX 77551

Established in 1991 in TX.
Donor(s): Gail Rider, G. William Rider.
Financial data (yr. ended 12/31/01): Grants paid, $20,150; assets, $444,171 (M); gifts received, $26,840; expenditures, $21,245; qualifying distributions, $20,150.
Limitations: Applications not accepted. Giving limited to Galveston, TX.
Application information: Contributes only to pre-selected organizations.
Officers: G. William Rider, Pres.; Tiffany Rider Parmenter, V.P.; Knox Rider, V.P.; Gail Rider, Secy.-Treas.
EIN: 760349036

52379
The Gregory-Johnstone Charitable Trust
c/o JPMorgan Chase Bank
P.O. Box 2558
Houston, TX 77252-8037 (713) 216-4966
Contact: Karen Burton, Trust Off., JPMorgan Chase Bank

Established in 1992 in TX.
Donor(s): Lillian G. Johnstone.
Financial data (yr. ended 12/31/01): Grants paid, $20,115; assets, $361,644 (M); expenditures, $28,958; qualifying distributions, $20,115.
Limitations: Giving on a national basis.
Trustees: Alan D. Johnstone, Lillian G. Johnstone, JPMorgan Chase Bank.
EIN: 766080218

52380
The Lanward Foundation
747 Coeur D'Alene Cir.
El Paso, TX 79922-2132
Contact: Cheryl A. McCown, Pres.

Financial data (yr. ended 12/31/01): Grants paid, $20,100; assets, $568,079 (M); expenditures, $34,034; qualifying distributions, $20,100.
Limitations: Giving primarily in El Paso, TX.
Officer: Cheryl A. McCown, Pres.
Trustees: Aneica Azar, Charles M. McCown.
EIN: 746080683

52381
Marcus Foundation
616 FM 1960 W., Ste. 210
Houston, TX 77090

Established in 1997 in TX.
Donor(s): Marvin Steve Bordelon.
Financial data (yr. ended 06/30/01): Grants paid, $20,100; assets, $81,604 (M); gifts received, $12,000; expenditures, $20,595; qualifying distributions, $20,087.
Limitations: Applications not accepted. Giving primarily in TX.

52381—TEXAS

Application information: Contributes only to pre-selected organizations.
Officers: Marvin Steve Bordelon, Pres.; Carolyn G. Bordelon, V.P. and Secy.; Seth M. Bordelon, Treas.
EIN: 760548299

52382
The Monroe Foundation, Inc.
P.O. Box 1425
Midland, TX 79702 (915) 683-6296

Established in 1991 in TX.
Donor(s): E.R. Monroe, H. Kathleen Monroe.
Financial data (yr. ended 12/31/01): Grants paid, $20,050; assets, $17,218 (M); expenditures, $20,070; qualifying distributions, $20,050.
Limitations: Applications not accepted. Giving primarily in Midland, TX.
Application information: Contributes only to pre-selected organizations.
Officers: E.R. Monroe, Pres.; H. Kathleen Monroe, V.P.; Bob W. Dutton, Secy.-Treas.
EIN: 752365852

52383
William and Ella Owens Medical Research Foundation
8452 Fredericksburg Rd., PMB 197
San Antonio, TX 78229-3317

Established in 1998 in TX.
Donor(s): William C. Owens, Sr.
Financial data (yr. ended 12/31/01): Grants paid, $20,050; assets, $1,241,183 (M); gifts received, $18; expenditures, $27,588; qualifying distributions, $20,050.
Limitations: Applications not accepted.
Application information: Contributes only to pre-selected organizations.
Trustees: William C. Ownes, Sr., William C. Owens, Jr.
EIN: 742884415

52384
Zachary Bell Foundation
6030 Woodland Dr.
Dallas, TX 75225

Established in 1999.
Financial data (yr. ended 12/31/01): Grants paid, $20,000; assets, $1 (M); gifts received, $25,000; expenditures, $20,000; qualifying distributions, $20,000.
Officers: Betty Jo Bell, Pres.; David Bell, Treas.
Director: Mary Meadow.
EIN: 752828264

52385
Davis Family Foundation
c/o John R. Davis
6703 Flanary Ln.
Dallas, TX 75252

Established in 1990 in TX.
Donor(s): John R. Davis, Sherri N. Davis.
Financial data (yr. ended 12/31/01): Grants paid, $20,000; assets, $160,874 (M); expenditures, $20,207; qualifying distributions, $20,000.
Limitations: Applications not accepted. Giving primarily in TX.
Application information: Contributes only to pre-selected organizations.
Officers and Directors:* John R. Davis,* Chair. and Pres.; John J. Kickham,* V.P.; Sherri N. Davis,* Secy.; Jack O. Norman.
EIN: 752371645

52386
The James Lee and Annanette Harper Family Foundation
120 Sunrise Cir.
Wimberley, TX 78676 (512) 847-8653

Financial data (yr. ended 12/31/01): Grants paid, $20,000; assets, $480,336 (M); gifts received, $20,000; expenditures, $32,324; qualifying distributions, $31,564.
Officers: James L. Harper, Pres. and Treas.; Annanette Harper, V.P. and Secy.
Trustees: Carol Harper, Heather L. Harper, James L. Harper, Jr., Paul D. Harper, Sandy Harper, Jill J. McMillan, Toney D. McMillan.
EIN: 742861135

52387
Mrs. G. R. Hawes Foundation, Inc.
6565 W. Loop S., Ste. 800
Bellaire, TX 77401-3505

Established in 1980.
Financial data (yr. ended 11/30/01): Grants paid, $20,000; assets, $471,809 (M); expenditures, $25,991; qualifying distributions, $20,000.
Limitations: Applications not accepted. Giving primarily in Wharton County, TX.
Application information: Contributes only to pre-selected organizations.
Officers and Directors:* Johnny J. Veselka,* Pres.; William A. Cline, V.P.; Rev. Joseph A. Koebel,* V.P.; John L. Roades, Secy.-Treas.
EIN: 742139756

52388
The Kosberg Foundation Charitable Trust
3040 Post Oak Blvd., Ste. 700
Houston, TX 77056

Donor(s): J. Livingston Kosberg, Saranne R. Kosberg.
Financial data (yr. ended 12/31/01): Grants paid, $20,000; assets, $1,765,955 (M); gifts received, $16,000; expenditures, $24,710; qualifying distributions, $20,000.
Limitations: Applications not accepted. Giving primarily in GA, NY and TX.
Application information: Contributes only to pre-selected organizations.
Directors: Lori K. Blumenthal, Robin Kosberg Elkin, J. Livingston Kosberg, Saranne R. Kosberg, Wendy Kosberg Starr.
EIN: 766023602

52389
The Frann Gordon Lichtenstein Foundation
1B West Oak Dr. N.
Houston, TX 77056-2119

Established in 1994 in TX.
Donor(s): Frann G. Lichtenstein.
Financial data (yr. ended 12/31/01): Grants paid, $20,000; assets, $386,238 (M); expenditures, $24,108; qualifying distributions, $20,000.
Limitations: Applications not accepted.
Application information: Contributes only to pre-selected organizations.
Officer: Frann Gordon Lichtenstein, Pres. and Treas.
Directors: Gregg G. Lichtenstein, Jill Lichtenstein Deutser.
EIN: 760283490

52390
Joe T. and Billie Carole McMillan Charitable Foundation
10810 Pine Bayou
Houston, TX 77024
Contact: Joe T. McMillan, Pres.

Established in 1998 in TX.
Donor(s): Joe T. McMillan, Billie Carole McMillan.
Financial data (yr. ended 12/31/01): Grants paid, $20,000; assets, $34,455 (M); expenditures, $21,841; qualifying distributions, $20,000.
Officers: Joe T. McMillan, Pres.; Billie Carole McMillan, V.P.; Linda McMillan Smith, Secy.; Daniel T. McMillan, Treas.
EIN: 760591353

52391
The Charles Oglesby and Donna Atchison Oglesby Charitable Trust
5404 Huckleberry Ln.
Houston, TX 77056-2715

Established in 2000 in TX.
Donor(s): Charles Oglesby, Donna Oglesby.
Financial data (yr. ended 12/31/00): Grants paid, $20,000; assets, $5,714 (M); gifts received, $26,663; expenditures, $20,805; qualifying distributions, $20,000.
Limitations: Applications not accepted. Giving primarily in Houston, TX.
Application information: Contributes only to pre-selected organizations.
Trustees: Charles Oglesby, Donna Oglesby.
EIN: 760643789

52392
The Pryor Foundation, Inc.
8515 Greenville Ave., Ste. N-108
Dallas, TX 75243-7011
Application address: 14 Hodgehaven Cir., Bloomington, IL 61704
Contact: Roger Pryor, Grant Coord.

Established in 1990 in TX.
Donor(s): Katherine Pryor, James T. Pryor, Ruth C. Pryor.
Financial data (yr. ended 01/31/02): Grants paid, $20,000; assets, $187,187 (M); expenditures, $24,254; qualifying distributions, $20,000.
Limitations: Giving primarily in TX.
Publications: Informational brochure (including application guidelines).
Application information: Application form required.
Officers and Directors:* Ruth C. Pryor,* Pres.; Cay Bolin,* V.P.; G. Ward Beaudry,* Treas.; Mike Fisher, Robert Livesay, Eldon Steele.
EIN: 752317653

52393
Shell Education Foundation
1 Shell Plz., P.O. Box 4749
Houston, TX 77210
Application address: P.O. Box 2099, Houston, TX, tel.: (713) 241-1595
Contact: Betty Lynn McHam, Pres.

Established in 1999 in TX.
Donor(s): Shell Oil Company Foundation.
Financial data (yr. ended 12/31/00): Grants paid, $20,000; assets, $0 (M); expenditures, $20,000; qualifying distributions, $20,000.
Limitations: Giving primarily in TX.
Officers and Directors:* Betty Lynn McHam,* Pres.; Frances Rabbe, Secy.; Scott Philbrook, Treas.; D. Young.
EIN: 760616117
Codes: CS

52394
Alex and Kim Smith Family Foundation, Inc.
248 Addie Roy Rd., Ste. C203
Austin, TX 78746

Established in 2001 in TX.
Donor(s): Alex C. Smith, Kim E. Smith.
Financial data (yr. ended 12/31/01): Grants paid, $20,000; assets, $1,689,402 (M); gifts received, $1,747,250; expenditures, $22,168; qualifying distributions, $20,000.
Limitations: Applications not accepted. Giving primarily in Austin, TX.
Application information: Contributes only to pre-selected organizations.
Officers: Alex C. Smith, Pres.; Kim E. Smith, V.P.; Melissa Anderson, Secy.-Treas.
EIN: 743000930

52395
John G. Thomas Family Foundation
1851 Hwy. 180 E.
Breckenridge, TX 76424

Established in 2000 in TX.
Donor(s): John G. Thomas.
Financial data (yr. ended 12/31/01): Grants paid, $20,000; assets, $382,796 (M); expenditures, $20,085; qualifying distributions, $20,000.
Limitations: Applications not accepted.
Application information: Contributes only to pre-selected organizations.
Officers: John G. Thomas, Pres. and Treas.; Brian C. Thomas, V.P.; Gregory Thomas, Secy.
EIN: 752878872

52396
The Tims Foundation
428 Timber Bay Ct.
Azle, TX 76020-0000 (817) 238-0706
Contact: Jerry L. Tims, Tr.

Established in 1985 in TX.
Donor(s): Jerry L. Tims.
Financial data (yr. ended 09/30/01): Grants paid, $20,000; assets, $701,786 (M); gifts received, $63,733; expenditures, $22,963; qualifying distributions, $20,000.
Limitations: Giving primarily in TX.
Trustee: Jerry L. Tims.
EIN: 756333692

52397
The Wildlife Heritage Foundation of Texas
6231 Treaschwig Rd.
Spring, TX 77373 (281) 209-1048
Contact: William O. Carter, Pres.

Established in 2000 in TX.
Financial data (yr. ended 12/31/01): Grants paid, $20,000; assets, $722,961 (M); gifts received, $400,000; expenditures, $20,304; qualifying distributions, $20,000.
Application information: Application form not required.
Officers: William O. Carter, Pres.; Ellen E. Carter, V.P. and Secy.
EIN: 760655673

52398
The Worthington Foundation
24 Eaton Sq.
Houston, TX 77027 (713) 572-0745

Established in 1999 in TX.
Donor(s): David W. Worthington.
Financial data (yr. ended 12/31/01): Grants paid, $20,000; assets, $591,785 (M); expenditures, $25,051; qualifying distributions, $20,000.
Limitations: Applications not accepted.

Application information: Contributes only to pre-selected organizations.
Officers and Directors:* David W. Worthington,* Pres. and Treas.; Barry W. Eastland,* V.P.; Jennifer W. Edwards,* V.P.; Page W. Arlt,* Secy.
EIN: 760626345

52399
Mason Brown Family Foundation, Inc.
5900 Willow Ln.
Dallas, TX 75230

Established in 2000 in TX.
Donor(s): Barbara L. Brown, Mason C. Brown.
Financial data (yr. ended 12/31/01): Grants paid, $19,930; assets, $569,128 (M); gifts received, $300,000; expenditures, $20,023; qualifying distributions, $19,930.
Limitations: Applications not accepted. Giving primarily in TX.
Application information: Contributes only to pre-selected organizations.
Officer: Mason C. Brown, Jr., Pres.
Directors: Barbara L. Brown, Mason C. Brown III, Miriam C. Brown, Michael A. Richard.
EIN: 752905171

52400
Archer Community Foundation
P.O. Box 877
Archer City, TX 76351 (940) 574-2489
E-mail: info@archercity.org

Established in 1997 in TX.
Financial data (yr. ended 09/30/00): Grants paid, $19,902; assets, $428,082 (M); gifts received, $406,112; expenditures, $138,931; giving activities include $115,988 for programs.
Limitations: Giving primarily in TX.
Officers: Ward Campbell, Pres.; Gary Bessinger, Vice-Pres.; Jerry Phillips, Secy.-Treas.
Directors: Abby Abernathy, Mike Castles, Deanna Cowan, Robert Kitchell.
EIN: 752604400
Codes: CM

52401
The M. L. Mayfield and Jessie Star Mayfield Foundation
4119 Tasslewood Ln.
Houston, TX 77014-1820
Contact: Charles F. Presley

Financial data (yr. ended 12/31/01): Grants paid, $19,900; assets, $517,287 (M); expenditures, $25,690; qualifying distributions, $24,218.
Limitations: Giving primarily in TX.
Trustees: Manning B. Mayfield, Pamalette S. Mayfield.
EIN: 760133546
Codes: GTI

52402
San Antonio A & M Club Foundation
6205 West Ave.
San Antonio, TX 78213-2315
Contact: Jim Whiteaker, Scholarship Admin.

Financial data (yr. ended 12/31/01): Grants paid, $19,800; assets, $574,925 (M); gifts received, $61,091; expenditures, $164,160; qualifying distributions, $54,818.
Limitations: Giving limited to individuals of Bexar County, TX.
Application information: Application form required.
Officers: Jeffrey T. Richter, Pres.; Fred L. May, 1st V.P.; John Neely, 2nd V.P.; Bob Sims, Secy.-Treas.
Directors: Tony L. Kaman, John R. Lane, Terrell Miller, John A. Stasney, Dean Williams, and 4 additional directors.

EIN: 742247729
Codes: GTI

52403
Tom & Lilian Grinnan Wilkinson Trust
309 N. Fisk Ave.
Brownwood, TX 76801-2971
Application address: P.O. Box 1147, Brownwood, TX 76804, tel.: (915) 646-6581
Contact: John A. Thomason, Tr.

Established in 1988 in TX.
Financial data (yr. ended 12/31/00): Grants paid, $19,750; assets, $324,630 (M); expenditures, $24,304; qualifying distributions, $19,750.
Limitations: Giving limited to TX, with preference to Brown County.
Application information: Application form required.
Trustees: John Lee Blagg, Darrell F. Haynes, John A. Thomason.
EIN: 756373248

52404
Lawler Foundation
c/o Carol M. Lawler
P.O. Box 2558
Humble, TX 77347

Donor(s): Carol M. Lawler, William L. Lawler.
Financial data (yr. ended 11/30/00): Grants paid, $19,657; assets, $114,263 (M); expenditures, $26,169; qualifying distributions, $19,482.
Limitations: Applications not accepted. Giving limited to residents of Houston, TX area.
Application information: Scholarship applicants selected by high school counselors.
Officer: Carol M. Lawler, Pres. and Mgr.
EIN: 760386450
Codes: GTI

52405
The Edward and Carol Esstman Foundation
1400 DAnbury Dr.
Mansfield, TX 76063-3845

Established in 2001 in TX.
Donor(s): Edward H. Esstman, Carol J. Esstman.
Financial data (yr. ended 12/31/01): Grants paid, $19,570; assets, $297,321 (M); gifts received, $409,100; expenditures, $24,034; qualifying distributions, $19,570.
Limitations: Applications not accepted.
Application information: Contributes only to pre-selected organizations.
Officers and Directors:* Edward H. Esstman,* Pres.; Carol J. Esstman,* Secy.-Treas.; Anglea E. Esstman.
EIN: 912111408

52406
The Bruckner Family Foundation, Inc.
2412 Teckla Blvd.
Amarillo, TX 79106

Donor(s): B.M. Bruckner, Sr.
Financial data (yr. ended 12/31/01): Grants paid, $19,560; assets, $313,036 (M); gifts received, $17,000; expenditures, $22,905; qualifying distributions, $20,405.
Limitations: Applications not accepted. Giving primarily in TX.
Application information: Contributes only to pre-selected organizations.
Officers: B.M. Bruckner, Jr., Pres.; Willie Mae Bruckner, Secy.-Treas.
EIN: 751686688

52407
Baxter-Whalen Family Foundation
17 Ellicott Way
Sugar Land, TX 77479

Established in 2000.
Donor(s): Enron Corp., John Clifford Baxter,‡ Carol Baxter.
Financial data (yr. ended 12/31/01): Grants paid, $19,500; assets, $496,986 (M); gifts received, $300,000; expenditures, $26,054; qualifying distributions, $19,500.
Limitations: Giving primarily in GA, NY, TX, and VA.
Application information: Unsolicited request for funds not accepted.
Officers: John Clifford Baxter, C.E.O. and Pres.; Carol L. Whalen, Secy.
Director: Margo Baxter.
EIN: 760648553
Codes: CS, CD

52408
The Kanaly Foundation
c/o Kanaly Trust Co. Inc.
4550 Post Oak Place Dr., Ste. 139
Houston, TX 77027
Contact: Jeffrey C. Kanaly, Tr.

Established in 1992 in TX.
Donor(s): Kanaly Trust Co. Inc., E. Deane Kanaly, Virginia L. Kanaly.
Financial data (yr. ended 12/31/01): Grants paid, $19,500; assets, $856,267 (M); gifts received, $237,301; expenditures, $23,094; qualifying distributions, $19,500.
Limitations: Giving limited to Norman, OK.
Application information: Application form not required.
Trustees: Andrew D. Kanaly, E. Deane Kanaly, Jeffrey C. Kanaly, Steven P. Kanaly, Virginia L. Kanaly.
EIN: 760381632
Codes: CS, CD

52409
Swan C. Norby Scholarship Fund
c/o Bank of America
P.O. Box 831041
Dallas, TX 75283-1041
Application address: c/o Grandview Lions Club-College Scholarship, Grandview, MO 64030

Established in 1996 in MO.
Donor(s): Dorothy B. Norby.‡
Financial data (yr. ended 12/31/01): Grants paid, $19,500; assets, $389,257 (M); expenditures, $24,748; qualifying distributions, $21,040.
Limitations: Giving primarily in Grandview, MO.
Application information: Application form required.
Trustee: Bank of America.
EIN: 431763633
Codes: GTI

52410
Sure Foundation, Inc.
P.O. Box 910
Pasadena, TX 77501-0910 (713) 943-7777
Contact: John H. Moon, Sr., Tr.

Established in 1987 in TX.
Donor(s): John H. Moon, Sr.
Financial data (yr. ended 12/31/01): Grants paid, $19,500; assets, $534,401 (M); expenditures, $19,877; qualifying distributions, $19,500.
Limitations: Giving primarily in Pasadena, TX.
Trustees: Jean Fogg, A. Rose Moon, John H. Moon, Sr., John H. Moon, Jr.
EIN: 760219600

52411
Jack Wesley McCain Trust
P.O. Box 660
Sweetwater, TX 79556

Financial data (yr. ended 12/31/00): Grants paid, $19,498; assets, $527,013 (M); expenditures, $26,151; qualifying distributions, $19,498.
Limitations: Applications not accepted. Giving primarily in Abilene, TX.
Application information: Contributes only to pre-selected organizations.
Trustee: First National Bank.
EIN: 756528801

52412
E. O. Elam Scholarship Trust Fund
c/o Hail & Co., PC
P.O. Box 111
Hamilton, TX 76531
Application address: P.O. Box 311, Hamilton, TX 76531, tel.: (254) 386-8937
Contact: Robert W. Witzsche, Tr.

Financial data (yr. ended 12/31/01): Grants paid, $19,408; assets, $315,012 (M); expenditures, $19,643; qualifying distributions, $197,210.
Limitations: Giving limited to residents of Hamilton County, TX.
Trustees: Jack Davidson, Pam Eilers, Ramon L. Haile, David Lengefeld, Robert W. Witzsche.
EIN: 746306225
Codes: GTI

52413
The Byron and Rosemary Clayton Foundation
639 Oakbend Dr.
Coppell, TX 75019-2478

Established in 1996 in TX.
Donor(s): Byron W. Clayton, Rosemary Clayton.
Financial data (yr. ended 12/31/01): Grants paid, $19,400; assets, $281,455 (M); expenditures, $23,480; qualifying distributions, $19,400.
Limitations: Applications not accepted.
Application information: Contributes only to pre-selected organizations.
Officers and Directors:* Byron W. Clayton,* Pres.; Rosemary Clayton,* Secy.-Treas.; Bernice Nichols.
EIN: 752680636

52414
Mountain Top International
1109 Ave. G.
Rosenberg, TX 77471

Established in 1998.
Donor(s): Gerald Pate, Bob Morris.
Financial data (yr. ended 12/31/01): Grants paid, $19,400; assets, $694 (M); gifts received, $10,078; expenditures, $19,407; qualifying distributions, $19,400.
Limitations: Applications not accepted. Giving primarily in OK and TX.
Application information: Unsolicited requests for funds not accepted.
Directors: Bobby E. Morris, Ramona Morris, Victor Tibbets.
EIN: 760569471

52415
The Barakat Foundation
c/o Haynes and Boone, LLP
901 Main St., Ste. 3100
Dallas, TX 75202-3789 (214) 651-5000

Established in 1987 in TX.
Donor(s): Hamida Alireza, Haji Abdullah Alireza, Gilbert Carr.

Financial data (yr. ended 12/31/00): Grants paid, $19,337; assets, $164,383 (M); gifts received, $63,500; expenditures, $32,036; qualifying distributions, $31,980.
Application information: Application form required.
Officers and Directors:* Hamida Alireza,* Pres. and V.P.; Tarik A. Alireza,* Secy.-Treas.; Bryanne Alireza, Ghassan Alireza, Marianne Alireza, Betty Lussier.
EIN: 752249402
Codes: GTI

52416
Blake W. Brockermeyer Charitable Foundation
P.O. Box 4160
Fort Worth, TX 76164-0160

Established in 1999 in TX.
Donor(s): Blake W. Brockermeyer.
Financial data (yr. ended 12/31/01): Grants paid, $19,300; assets, $6,910 (M); expenditures, $22,728; qualifying distributions, $19,300.
Limitations: Applications not accepted.
Application information: Contributes only to pre-selected organizations.
Officers: Blake W. Brockermeyer, Pres.; Kristy C. Brockermeyer, V.P.; Kae B. Brockermeyer, Secy.-Treas.
EIN: 752817578

52417
Henry Foundation, Inc.
12720 Hillcrest Rd., Ste. 419
Dallas, TX 75230 (972) 458-0826
Contact: Brenda J. Sluyter, Pres.

Donor(s): Margaret E. Sluyter.
Financial data (yr. ended 12/31/01): Grants paid, $19,200; assets, $382,599 (M); expenditures, $22,241; qualifying distributions, $19,200.
Limitations: Giving primarily in Dallas, TX.
Application information: Application form not required.
Officers and Directors:* Brenda J. Sluyter,* Pres.; Thomas H. Cantrill,* V.P. and Treas.; Robert J. Philippon,* V.P.; Erma K. Davies,* Secy.
EIN: 756017790

52418
Bernard and Shirley Weingarten Charitable Trust
P.O. Box 56244
Houston, TX 77256

Established in 1992 in TX.
Donor(s): Bernard Weingarten.
Financial data (yr. ended 12/31/01): Grants paid, $19,200; assets, $315,928 (M); expenditures, $20,748; qualifying distributions, $19,200.
Limitations: Applications not accepted. Giving primarily in Houston, TX.
Application information: Contributes only to pre-selected organizations.
Officers: Bernard Weingarten, Pres.; Janet Weingarten Battista, Secy.; Linda Weingarten Kates, Treas.
EIN: 760385651

52419
The Hersh Foundation
125 E. John Carpenter Fwy., Ste. 600
Irving, TX 75062

Established in 1997 in TX.
Donor(s): Julie K. Hersch, Kenneth A. Hersch.
Financial data (yr. ended 12/31/01): Grants paid, $19,020; assets, $28,296 (M); gifts received, $8,728; expenditures, $20,370; qualifying distributions, $19,020.
Limitations: Applications not accepted.

Application information: Contributes only to pre-selected organizations.
Officers: Kenneth A. Hersh, Pres. and Treas.; Julie K. Hersh, V.P. and Secy.
Trustee: Richard L. Covington.
EIN: 752720646

52420
Laurance H. Armour, Jr. & Margot Boyd Armour Family Foundation
c/o L.H. Armour, Jr.
3555 Timmons Ln., Ste. 730
Houston, TX 77027

Financial data (yr. ended 11/30/01): Grants paid, $19,000; assets, $531,906 (M); expenditures, $23,415; qualifying distributions, $23,415.
Limitations: Applications not accepted. Giving primarily in TX.
Application information: Contributes only to pre-selected organizations.
Trustee: Laurance H. Armour, Margot B. Armour.
EIN: 366218249

52421
Mattie-Jennie Fund Trust
c/o Frost National Bank, Trust Dept.
P.O. Box 2950
San Antonio, TX 78299 (210) 220-4449
Contact: William C. Clyborne, V.P., Frost National Bank

Financial data (yr. ended 04/30/02): Grants paid, $19,000; assets, $433,539 (M); expenditures, $25,476; qualifying distributions, $19,000.
Limitations: Giving limited to TX.
Trustee: Frost National Bank.
EIN: 746318942

52422
Frederic J. and Dorothea Oppenheimer Foundation
5170 Broadway, Ste. 25
San Antonio, TX 78209-5730
Contact: Frederic J. Oppenheimer, Pres.

Established in 1984 in TX.
Donor(s): Frederic J. Oppenheimer, Dorothea C. Oppenheimer.
Financial data (yr. ended 12/31/01): Grants paid, $19,000; assets, $569,621 (M); expenditures, $26,561; qualifying distributions, $19,000.
Limitations: Giving primarily in San Antonio, TX.
Officers: Frederic J. Oppenheimer, Pres.; Lucille O. Travis, V.P.; Dorothea C. Oppenheimer, Secy.-Treas.
EIN: 742336644

52423
Lura Sira Sanders Trust
(Formerly AGT Trust)
7001 Preston Rd., Ste. 410
Dallas, TX 75205 (214) 522-8004
Contact: M. Robert Blakeney, Tr.

Financial data (yr. ended 05/31/01): Grants paid, $19,000; assets, $352,713 (M); expenditures, $25,252; qualifying distributions, $19,000.
Limitations: Giving limited to Dallas, TX.
Trustees: M. Robert Blakeney, Marietta Johnson.
EIN: 756045901

52424
The Teal Foundation
2700 Post Oak Blvd., Ste. 1440
Houston, TX 77056

Established in 1986 in TX.
Donor(s): Ruby R. Graham, Sarah F. Jackson.
Financial data (yr. ended 12/31/01): Grants paid, $19,000; assets, $410,735 (M); gifts received, $25,000; expenditures, $19,149; qualifying distributions, $19,000.
Limitations: Applications not accepted. Giving limited to TX.
Application information: Contributes only to pre-selected organizations.
Trustees: Ruby R. Graham, Sarah F. Jackson, Alfred J. Thorpe.
EIN: 766033961

52425
George Trimble Special Need Trust
c/o Bank of America
P.O. Box 831041
Dallas, TX 75283-1041
Application address: P.O. Drawer 814, El Dorado, KS 67042, tel.: (316) 321-4444
Contact: Rod Ziegler, Trust Off., Bank of America

Established in 1993 in KS.
Financial data (yr. ended 12/31/01): Grants paid, $19,000; assets, $379,971 (M); expenditures, $23,999; qualifying distributions, $20,236.
Limitations: Giving limited to the Butler County, KS.
Application information: Special need applicants may choose to send a letter rather than an application. Application form required.
Trustees: Bank of America.
EIN: 486319821
Codes: GTI

52426
The Clee and Olivia Elliott Children's Foundation
13355 Noel Rd., Ste. 250
Dallas, TX 75240

Financial data (yr. ended 12/31/00): Grants paid, $18,959; assets, $381,238 (M); gifts received, $16,955; expenditures, $21,744; qualifying distributions, $18,959.
Directors: Clayton C. Elliott, Anne Lewis, David Wells.
EIN: 752719413

52427
Harold D. & Betty Jo Owen Foundation
6248 Camp Bowie Blvd.
Fort Worth, TX 76116-5525

Financial data (yr. ended 12/31/01): Grants paid, $18,850; assets, $395,589 (M); expenditures, $50,974; qualifying distributions, $18,850.
Trustee: H. Dean Owen, Jr.
EIN: 751633142

52428
The Jon T. and Sheridan M. Hansen Charitable Foundation
1029 Los Jardines Cir.
El Paso, TX 79912

Established in 1999 in TX.
Financial data (yr. ended 12/31/01): Grants paid, $18,800; assets, $137,196 (M); expenditures, $23,175; qualifying distributions, $18,800.
Limitations: Applications not accepted.
Application information: Contributes only to pre-selected organizations.
Officers and Directors:* Jon T. Hansen,* Pres.; Derek E. Hansen,* V.P.; Helen C. Hansen,* V.P.; Sheridan M. Hansen,* Secy.; Thomas W. Hansen,* Treas.
EIN: 742941648

52429
The Jones Family Charitable Trust
c/o Albert Jones
P.O. Box 892
Hewitt, TX 76643-0892

Established in 1994 in TX.
Donor(s): Hazel M. Jones.
Financial data (yr. ended 12/31/01): Grants paid, $18,700; assets, $1 (M); gifts received, $10,000; expenditures, $19,963; qualifying distributions, $18,700.
Limitations: Applications not accepted. Giving primarily in TX.
Application information: Contributes only to pre-selected organizations.
Trustee: Hazel M. Jones, Steve Jones.
EIN: 746416395

52430
The Amini Foundation
8000 IH-10 W., Ste. 820
San Antonio, TX 78230 (210) 349-1600
Contact: Margaret Amini, Pres.

Established in 1987 in TX.
Donor(s): K.K. Amini, Margaret Amini, Rex Amini, Sue Amini-Minor.
Financial data (yr. ended 12/31/01): Grants paid, $18,650; assets, $398,712 (M); expenditures, $19,022; qualifying distributions, $19,022.
Limitations: Giving primarily in San Antonio, TX.
Officers and Trustees:* Margaret Amini,* Pres.; Sue Amini-Minor,* V.P. and Secy.-Treas.; Michael Amini.
EIN: 742482592

52431
The J. L. Hodges Family Foundation
11771 Quail Creek Dr.
Houston, TX 77070
Contact: James L. Hodges, Treas.

Established in 1988 in TX.
Donor(s): James L. Hodges, Craig Hodges.
Financial data (yr. ended 12/31/00): Grants paid, $18,600; assets, $114,814 (M); gifts received, $4,250; expenditures, $19,049; qualifying distributions, $18,576.
Limitations: Giving on an international basis.
Application information: Application form not required.
Officers: Deolva B. Hodges, Pres.; S. Craig Hodges, 1st V.P.; Richard L. Hodges, 2nd V.P.; Jill H. Parsons, Secy.; James L. Hodges, Treas.
EIN: 760265720

52432
David B. Lack Family Foundation, Inc.
P.O. Box 2088
Victoria, TX 77902
Contact: David B. Lack, Pres.

Donor(s): Melvin Lack, David B. Lack.
Financial data (yr. ended 12/31/01): Grants paid, $18,550; assets, $118,715 (M); expenditures, $19,229; qualifying distributions, $18,550.
Limitations: Giving limited to TX.
Officers: David B. Lack, Pres.; Jay Lack, V.P.; Jane S. Lack, Secy.; Melvin Lack, Treas.
EIN: 742000289

52433
The Collier Foundation
P.O. Box 1401
Lubbock, TX 79408 (806) 763-7061
Contact: W.R. Collier, Tr.

Donor(s): W.R. Collier, Robert F. Collier.
Financial data (yr. ended 12/31/01): Grants paid, $18,525; assets, $249,706 (M); gifts received,

$27,150; expenditures, $23,896; qualifying distributions, $18,525.
Limitations: Giving limited to TX.
Application information: Application form required.
Trustees: Robert F. Collier, W.R. Collier.
EIN: 752005401

52434
Max and Madaline Broude Charitable Foundation
309 W. 7th St., Ste. 1100
Fort Worth, TX 76102

Established in 1990.
Donor(s): John S. Broude, Judy Rosenblum.
Financial data (yr. ended 12/31/01): Grants paid, $18,500; assets, $174,774 (M); gifts received, $5,417; expenditures, $19,882; qualifying distributions, $18,500.
Limitations: Applications not accepted. Giving primarily in TX.
Application information: Contributes only to pre-selected organizations.
Officer and Directors:* John S. Broude,* Pres.; Max R. Broude, Sylvia Broude, Judy Rosenblum.
EIN: 752355178

52435
Leo & Inez Dunkin McDonald Charitable Trust
c/o Bank of America
P.O. Box 831041
Dallas, TX 75283-1041
Application address: c/o Bank of America, 100 N. Main St., Corsicana, TX 75110, tel.: (903) 654-3251

Financial data (yr. ended 12/31/01): Grants paid, $18,500; assets, $496,045 (M); expenditures, $22,328; qualifying distributions, $18,500.
Limitations: Giving primarily in Mexia, TX.
Application information: Application form not required.
Trustee: Bank of America.
EIN: 756361602

52436
White Memorial Trust
c/o JPMorgan Chase Bank
P.O. Box 660197
Dallas, TX 75266-0197 (214) 965-4446

Financial data (yr. ended 12/31/00): Grants paid, $18,461; assets, $293,612 (M); expenditures, $24,030; qualifying distributions, $19,802.
Limitations: Giving limited to TX.
Trustees: John W. Digings, William J. Donald, Ron Windham, JPMorgan Chase Bank.
EIN: 756010010

52437
Ho-Chou Family Foundation
3601 34th St.
Lubbock, TX 79410

Established in 1999 in TX.
Financial data (yr. ended 12/31/00): Grants paid, $18,444; assets, $279,905 (M); gifts received, $145,403; expenditures, $32,224; qualifying distributions, $0.
Limitations: Giving primarily in Lubbock, TX.
Trustees: Jui Lien Ho, Ming Tao Ho, Jui Jung Kuo.
EIN: 752820267

52438
Donald E. Blackketter Educational & Charitable Foundation
115 E. 3rd St.
Shamrock, TX 79079-2337

Established in 1956 in TX.
Donor(s): Donald E. Blackketter.
Financial data (yr. ended 12/31/01): Grants paid, $18,400; assets, $338,729 (M); expenditures, $18,613; qualifying distributions, $18,400.
Limitations: Applications not accepted. Giving primarily in TX.
Application information: Contributes only to pre-selected organizations.
Trustee: Donald E. Blackketter.
EIN: 756020153

52439
The Crump Foundation
8710 Ashridge Pk.
Spring, TX 77379 (281) 376-8544
Contact: Marjorie A. Crump, Pres.

Established in 1994 in TX.
Donor(s): Richard K. Crump.
Financial data (yr. ended 07/31/01): Grants paid, $18,400; assets, $436,980 (M); gifts received, $13,240; expenditures, $21,458; qualifying distributions, $18,400.
Limitations: Giving primarily in Houston, TX.
Officers: Marjorie A. Crump, Pres. and Treas.; Richard K. Crump, V.P. and Secy.
EIN: 760453687

52440
Bess L. Rayford Foundation
P.O. Box 1009
Henderson, TX 75653-1009

Donor(s): Bess L. Rayford.
Financial data (yr. ended 09/30/01): Grants paid, $18,400; assets, $437,185 (M); gifts received, $300; expenditures, $21,837; qualifying distributions, $18,400.
Officer: Bess L. Rayford, Pres. and Treas.
EIN: 311583091

52441
The Kahn Education Foundation
5950 Berkshire Ln., Ste. 1050
Dallas, TX 75225 (214) 369-6209
Contact: Sherian Minczewski

Established in 1996 in TX.
Donor(s): Stephen S. Kahn.
Financial data (yr. ended 12/31/01): Grants paid, $18,350; assets, $2,162,702 (M); expenditures, $43,846; qualifying distributions, $18,350.
Limitations: Giving primarily in TX.
Trustees: Stephen S. Kahn, Sherian L. Minczewski, Sallie A. Scanlan.
EIN: 752667164

52442
Tex-Trude Charities, Inc.
Tex-Trude, Inc.
2001 Sheldon Rd.
Channelview, TX 77530-2685 (281) 452-5961
Contact: Don L. Lueken, Tr.

Established in 1988 in TX.
Donor(s): Tex-Trude, Inc.
Financial data (yr. ended 12/31/01): Grants paid, $18,250; assets, $167,472 (M); gifts received, $40,000; expenditures, $18,250; qualifying distributions, $18,250.
Limitations: Giving primarily in Houston, TX.
Trustees: Don L. Lueken, C.M. Nettles, Charles M. Nettles.
EIN: 760250950
Codes: CS, CD

52443
John and Pamela Beckert Family Foundation
10000 N. Central Expwy., Ste. 1400
Dallas, TX 75231

Established in 1998 in TX.
Donor(s): John A. Beckert, Pamela Beckert.
Financial data (yr. ended 12/31/01): Grants paid, $18,215; assets, $289,957 (M); expenditures, $19,566; qualifying distributions, $18,215.
Limitations: Applications not accepted. Giving primarily in Dallas, TX.
Application information: Contributes only to pre-selected organizations.
Directors: John A. Beckert, Pamela Beckert, Richard N. Beckert.
EIN: 752769489

52444
First Federal Community Foundation
630 Clarksville St.
Paris, TX 75460
Contact: Richard M. Amis, Tr.

Established in 1997 in TX.
Financial data (yr. ended 12/31/01): Grants paid, $18,200; assets, $553,589 (M); gifts received, $95,000; expenditures, $19,310; qualifying distributions, $18,200.
Limitations: Giving primarily in TX.
Trustees: Richard M. Amis, E. Sims Norment, Tim Taylor.
EIN: 752716310

52445
Lorin Boswell Foundation
c/o Lorin Boswell, Jr.
6706 Camp Bowie Blvd.
Fort Worth, TX 76116 (817) 377-4218

Financial data (yr. ended 11/30/01): Grants paid, $18,094; assets, $190,589 (M); expenditures, $19,234; qualifying distributions, $18,094.
Limitations: Applications not accepted. Giving primarily in Tarrant County, TX.
Application information: Contributes only to pre-selected organizations.
Officers: Gayle B. Gordon, Pres.; T. Patrick Gordon, Jr., V.P.; Lorin Boswell, Jr., Secy.
EIN: 237418086

52446
Quiet Foundation
12221 Merit Dr., Ste. 1500
Dallas, TX 75251

Financial data (yr. ended 12/31/01): Grants paid, $18,063; assets, $3,765 (M); gifts received, $8,199; expenditures, $27,615; qualifying distributions, $18,063.
Limitations: Applications not accepted.
Application information: Contributes only to pre-selected organizations.
Officers: R. Allen Angel, Pres. and Treas.; Jeff D. Reeter, V.P. and Secy.
EIN: 752568792

52447
Dr. Richard C. and Esther Bellamy Educational Trust
c/o First Liberty National Bank
P.O. Box 10109
Liberty, TX 77575-7609
Application address: 1900 Sam Houston, Liberty, TX 77575, tel.: (936) 336-6471
Contact: Charles W. Fisher, Jr., Trust Off., First Liberty National Bank

Established in 1981.
Financial data (yr. ended 12/31/00): Grants paid, $18,000; assets, $974,571 (M); expenditures, $62,841; qualifying distributions, $51,756.
Limitations: Giving limited to Liberty County, TX.
Application information: Application form required.
Trustee: First Liberty National Bank.
EIN: 766002566
Codes: GTI

52448
Howell Foundation
3711 San Felipe Rd.
Houston, TX 77027

Established in 1975 in TX.
Donor(s): Evelyn E. Howell, Paul N. Howell.
Financial data (yr. ended 12/31/01): Grants paid, $18,000; assets, $522,134 (M); expenditures, $18,802; qualifying distributions, $18,000.
Limitations: Applications not accepted. Giving primarily in TX.
Application information: Contributes only to pre-selected organizations.
Trustees: Charles W. Hall, Bradley N. Howell, David L. Howell, Douglas W. Howell, Evelyn E. Howell, Steven K. Howell, Thomas M. Wright.
EIN: 237421916

52449
L. L. & Eva M. Lentz Charitable Trust
c/o Frost National Bank
P.O. Box 2950
San Antonio, TX 78299-2950
Application address: 100 W. Houston, San Antonio, TX 78205, tel.: (210) 220-4449
Contact: William L. Clyborne, V.P., Frost National Bank

Financial data (yr. ended 12/31/01): Grants paid, $18,000; assets, $386,837 (M); expenditures, $23,268; qualifying distributions, $18,000.
Limitations: Giving primarily in TX.
Trustee: Frost National Bank.
EIN: 746174799

52450
The Porchey Family Foundation
7 Stillforest
Houston, TX 77024-7518

Established in 1988 in TX.
Donor(s): Barbara P. Porchey, David V. Porchey.
Financial data (yr. ended 12/31/01): Grants paid, $18,000; assets, $148,015 (M); gifts received, $1,117; expenditures, $20,467; qualifying distributions, $18,000.
Limitations: Applications not accepted. Giving primarily in Houston, TX.
Application information: Contributes only to pre-selected organizations.
Officers and Trustees:* Barbara P. Porchey,* Pres.; David V. Porchey,* Secy.-Treas.; Elizabeth Fay Porchey, Robert Virgil Porchey, Susan Louise Porchey, Kimberly Porchey Richter.
EIN: 760257820

52451
Alphonse Siros Charitable Trust
P.O. Box 818
Laredo, TX 78042-0818

Financial data (yr. ended 12/31/00): Grants paid, $18,000; assets, $802,560 (M); expenditures, $29,609; qualifying distributions, $19,225.
Limitations: Applications not accepted. Giving primarily in Laredo, TX.
Application information: Contributes only to pre-selected organizations.
Trustee: Charles B. Dickinson, C.P.A.
EIN: 746357816

52452
The Duddlesten Foundation
12 E. Greenway Plz., Ste. 701
Houston, TX 77046-1203 (713) 268-7532
FAX: (713) 532-7169
Contact: Wayne B. Duddlesten, Dir.

Donor(s): Wayne B. Duddlesten.
Financial data (yr. ended 12/31/01): Grants paid, $17,900; assets, $97,140 (M); expenditures, $19,434; qualifying distributions, $17,900.
Limitations: Giving primarily in TX.
Directors: Elizabeth S. Duddlesten, Wayne B. Duddlesten.
EIN: 760003093

52453
Nancy & Paul Pressler Foundation
5118 Holly Terr.
Houston, TX 77056

Donor(s): Nancy Pressler, Paul Pressler.
Financial data (yr. ended 12/31/01): Grants paid, $17,875; assets, $6,213 (M); gifts received, $23,000; expenditures, $18,850; qualifying distributions, $17,875.
Limitations: Applications not accepted.
Application information: Contributes only to pre-selected organizations.
Officers and Trustees:* Paul Pressler,* Chair.; Nancy Pressler,* Vice-Chair.; Anne P. Csorba, Jean P. Visy.
EIN: 237002002

52454
The Bechtel Fund
610 E. Holland Ave.
Alpine, TX 79830 (915) 837-5861
Contact: J. Shaw Skinner, Treas.

Financial data (yr. ended 07/31/01): Grants paid, $17,825; assets, $303,267 (M); expenditures, $19,138; qualifying distributions, $17,825.
Limitations: Giving limited to Brewster, Presidio and Jeff Davis County, TX.
Application information: Application form required.
Officers: Fannie Weston, Pres.; Wayne Sheehan, V.P.; Robert Halpern, Secy.; J. Shaw Skinner, Treas.
Director: Kimball Miller.
EIN: 742683303

52455
Coast Foundation, Inc.
P.O. Drawer A
Dickinson, TX 77539-2001

Donor(s): W.G. Hall.
Financial data (yr. ended 09/30/01): Grants paid, $17,815; assets, $102,785 (M); gifts received, $2,600; expenditures, $19,086; qualifying distributions, $19,043.
Limitations: Applications not accepted. Giving primarily in TX.
Application information: Contributes only to pre-selected organizations.
Officers: C.F. Hall, Pres.; S.L. Hall, V.P. and Secy.
Director: S.L. Hall.
EIN: 746087573

52456
The Dugan Foundation
1415 Louisiana St., Ste. 3100
Houston, TX 77002-7353

Established in 2000.
Donor(s): Nortex Corp.
Financial data (yr. ended 12/31/01): Grants paid, $17,800; assets, $281,263 (M); gifts received, $150,000; expenditures, $18,993; qualifying distributions, $18,393.
Limitations: Applications not accepted.
Application information: Contributes only to pre-selected organizations.
Directors: A.W. Dugan, Lydia P. Dugan.
EIN: 760649328
Codes: CS, CD

52457
Aaron Rashti Family Foundation, Inc.
P.O. Box 101296
Fort Worth, TX 76185 (817) 732-3120
Contact: Aaron Rashti, Pres.

Established in 1993 in TX.
Donor(s): Aaron Rashti.
Financial data (yr. ended 12/31/01): Grants paid, $17,760; assets, $479,787 (M); gifts received, $25,030; expenditures, $18,932; qualifying distributions, $17,760.
Limitations: Giving primarily in TX.
Officer: Aaron Rashti, Pres.
EIN: 752437335

52458
Hall Brothers Trust - Ed G. Hall Estate
P.O. Box 68
Brownwood, TX 76801
Application address: 205 North Ctr., Brownwood, TX 76801, tel.: (915) 646-2621
Contact: Rex Bessent, Tr.

Financial data (yr. ended 12/31/00): Grants paid, $17,750; assets, $438,183 (M); expenditures, $27,308; qualifying distributions, $17,750.
Limitations: Giving limited to Brown County, TX.
Trustees: Rex Bessent, L.M. Burney, Sr., W. Gene Porter.
EIN: 756020040

52459
The Pettinger Foundation, Inc.
305 S. Jupiter, Ste. 100
Allen, TX 75002

Established in 1998 in TX.
Donor(s): Hedwig Pettinger, Wesley Pettinger.
Financial data (yr. ended 08/31/00): Grants paid, $17,740; assets, $74,904 (M); gifts received, $50,000; expenditures, $22,563; qualifying distributions, $21,476.
Officers: Wesley Pettinger, Pres.; Hedwig Pettinger, V.P.; Brandon Pitts, Treas.
EIN: 752768241

52460
Lloyd Bolding Family Foundation
1121 N. Longview
Kilgore, TX 75662 (903) 983-2086
Contact: Lloyd Bolding, Pres.

Financial data (yr. ended 12/31/01): Grants paid, $17,550; assets, $296,137 (M); expenditures, $20,177; qualifying distributions, $17,550.
Limitations: Giving primarily in Kilgore and Longview, TX.
Officers: Lloyd Bolding, Pres.; Evelyn Bolding, V.P. and Secy.
Directors: Beth Bolding, Bo Bolding, Jeff Bolding, Tami Bolding.
EIN: 752792859

52461
Kenneth and Cherrie Garrett Foundation
6100 Southwest Blvd., Ste. 250
Fort Worth, TX 76109-3930

Established in 2000 in TX.
Donor(s): Cherrie Garrett, Kenneth Garrett.
Financial data (yr. ended 12/31/01): Grants paid, $17,550; assets, $1,281,907 (M); gifts received, $631,215; expenditures, $28,142; qualifying distributions, $17,550.
Limitations: Applications not accepted.
Application information: Contributes only to pre-selected organizations.
Officers: Cherrie Garrett, Pres.; Chris Athon, V.P.; Diane Hawkins, V.P.; Kenneth Garrett, Secy.-Treas.
EIN: 752900252

52462
Norman & Maureen Norwood Foundation
13401 S.W. Fwy., Ste. 201
Sugar Land, TX 77478

Donor(s): Norman Norwood.
Financial data (yr. ended 12/31/01): Grants paid, $17,550; assets, $190,753 (M); expenditures, $18,721; qualifying distributions, $17,550.
Limitations: Applications not accepted. Giving on a national basis, with emphasis on TX.
Application information: Contributes only to pre-selected organizations.
Trustees: Maureen Norwood, Norman Norwood.
EIN: 741916262

52463
Walzel-Frick Foundation, Inc.
5212 Briar Dr. E.
Houston, TX 77056-1102

Established in 1999 in TX.
Donor(s): F. Alan Frick.
Financial data (yr. ended 12/31/00): Grants paid, $17,530; assets, $32,836 (M); expenditures, $22,556; qualifying distributions, $17,530.
Limitations: Applications not accepted. Giving primarily in MI and TX.
Application information: Contributes only to pre-selected organizations.
Officers: F. Alan Frick, Pres.; Cheryl Walzel, Secy.-Treas.
Director: Max Hendrick.
EIN: 760616075

52464
The Bock Foundation
44 Pascal Ln.
Austin, TX 78746

Established in 1999 in TX.
Donor(s): William G. Bock, Cynthia L. Bock.
Financial data (yr. ended 12/31/01): Grants paid, $17,500; assets, $289,419 (M); gifts received, $1,135; expenditures, $30,586; qualifying distributions, $17,500.
Limitations: Applications not accepted.
Application information: Contributes only to pre-selected organizations.
Officers: Cynthia L. Bock, Pres. and Treas.; William G. Bock, V.P. and Secy.
EIN: 742939296

52465
Texas Industries Foundation
c/o Texas Industries Scholarship Coord.
1341 W. Mockingbird Ln., Ste. 700
Dallas, TX 75247-6913

Incorporated in 1965 in TX.
Donor(s): Texas Industries, Inc.
Financial data (yr. ended 12/31/01): Grants paid, $17,500; assets, $1,970 (M); gifts received, $17,500; expenditures, $17,500; qualifying distributions, $17,500.
Limitations: Applications not accepted. Giving primarily in LA and TX.
Officers and Directors:* R.D. Rogers,* Pres.; R.M. Fowler,* V.P. and Treas.; James R. McCraw, V.P.; Robert C. Moore,* Secy.; R. Alpert.
EIN: 756043179
Codes: CS, CD, GTI

52466
Windham Foundation
c/o Vacek, Lange & Westerfield, PC
11 Greenway Plz., Ste. 1524
Houston, TX 77046

Donor(s): Lynn Burke Windham, Jr.
Financial data (yr. ended 12/31/01): Grants paid, $17,500; assets, $771,313 (M); expenditures, $21,244; qualifying distributions, $17,500.
Limitations: Giving primarily in TX.
Application information: Application form not required.
Officers: Lynn Burke Windham III, Pres.; Mary Amanda Wigginton, V.P.; Ellen Windham, V.P.; Betty Gladys Windham, Secy.
EIN: 742073691

52467
George F. Sunkel Foundation
P.O. Box 1001
Clarksville, TX 75426-1001 (903) 427-3163
Contact: M.K. Russell, Jr., Secy.

Financial data (yr. ended 07/31/02): Grants paid, $17,450; assets, $294,606 (M); expenditures, $22,472; qualifying distributions, $17,450.
Limitations: Giving primarily in Clarksville, TX.
Officers: Joseph L. Frank, Jr., Pres.; M.K. Russell, Jr., Secy. and Mgr.
EIN: 756082991

52468
Frank H. and June Smith Dotterweich Memorial Trust
P.O. Box 1414
Kingsville, TX 78364-1414

Established in 1992 in TX.
Financial data (yr. ended 12/31/01): Grants paid, $17,400; assets, $606,102 (M); expenditures, $29,126; qualifying distributions, $17,400.
Limitations: Applications not accepted. Giving primarily in TX.
Trustees: Ben A. Glusing, Richard A. Neville, Douglas E. Vannoy, Morgan Dean Witter Trust Co.
EIN: 746385370

52469
Joseph and Martye Rubin Foundation
(Formerly Joseph Rubin Foundation)
2 Elm Ct.
San Antonio, TX 78209 (210) 375-2021
Contact: Joseph Paul Rubin, Tr.

Financial data (yr. ended 08/31/01): Grants paid, $17,400; assets, $336,758 (M); expenditures, $18,639; qualifying distributions, $17,400.
Limitations: Giving primarily in San Antonio, TX.
Trustees: James A. Rubin, Joseph Paul Rubin.
EIN: 746041430

52470
The Green Foundation, Inc.
918 Southwind
Port Arthur, TX 77640

Established in 1988 in TX.
Donor(s): Andrew Green, Joyce M. Green.
Financial data (yr. ended 09/30/01): Grants paid, $17,343; assets, $1,004,516 (M); gifts received, $203,417; expenditures, $23,674; qualifying distributions, $18,233.
Limitations: Applications not accepted. Giving primarily in TX.
Application information: Contributes only to pre-selected organizations.
Officers: Andrew Green, Pres.; Joyce M. Green, Secy.-Treas.
Directors: John B. McClane, Glen Whitley.
EIN: 752256928

52471
John P. Hayes Charitable Trust
3510 Turtle Creek Blvd., Apt. 11E
Dallas, TX 75219-5544

Established in 1986 in TX.
Donor(s): John P. Hayes, Margaret B. Hayes.
Financial data (yr. ended 12/31/99): Grants paid, $17,205; assets, $50,851 (M); gifts received, $9,775; expenditures, $18,509; qualifying distributions, $17,205.
Limitations: Applications not accepted. Giving primarily in Dallas, TX.
Application information: Contributes only to pre-selected organizations.
Trustees: John P. Hayes, Margaret B. Hayes, Timothy M. Hayes.
EIN: 752143642

52472
The James W. Aston Foundation
(Formerly The Aston Foundation)
c/o Bank of America
P.O. Box 831041
Dallas, TX 75283-1041
Application address: c/o C.W. Beard, 5500 Preston Rd., Ste. B, Dallas, TX 75205

Established in 1961.
Donor(s): James W. Aston.‡
Financial data (yr. ended 09/30/01): Grants paid, $17,200; assets, $261,911 (M); expenditures, $21,242; qualifying distributions, $18,264.
Limitations: Giving primarily in TN and TX.
Trustee: Bank of America.
EIN: 756008534

52473
Abe & Peggy J. Levy Foundation
2525 S. Shore Blvd., Ste. 410
League City, TX 77573

Financial data (yr. ended 12/31/00): Grants paid, $17,055; assets, $1,412,488 (M); expenditures, $24,213; qualifying distributions, $17,055.
Limitations: Giving primarily in Galveston, TX.
Trustees: William C. Ansell, James Kessler, Darryl Levy, Stanley A. Levy, Keith W. McFatridge, Jr., Marilyn McFatridge.
EIN: 766083712

52474
Lloyd M. Bentsen Foundation
P.O. Box 593
Mission, TX 78573-0593 (956) 686-7426
Contact: Betty Bentsen Winn, V.P.

Financial data (yr. ended 11/30/01): Grants paid, $17,000; assets, $307,524 (M); expenditures, $19,028; qualifying distributions, $17,000.
Limitations: Giving primarily in TX.
Application information: Application form not required.
Officers: Donald L. Bentsen, Pres.; Betty Bentsen Winn, V.P.
EIN: 742244153

52475
Dunlap Foundation
2514 Westgate
Houston, TX 77019

Established in 1998 in TX.
Financial data (yr. ended 12/31/01): Grants paid, $17,000; assets, $240,690 (M); expenditures, $19,500; qualifying distributions, $17,000.
Trustees: James L. Dunlap, James R. Dunlap.
EIN: 911976048

52476
J. C. Ferguson Foundation, Inc.
4526 E. University, Bldg. 2, Ste. D
Odessa, TX 79762
Application address: 3800 E. 42nd St., Ste. 405, Odessa, TX 79726, tel.: (915) 362-4341
Contact: Fayette F. Griffin, Dir.

Financial data (yr. ended 06/30/02): Grants paid, $17,000; assets, $653,958 (M); gifts received,

$510,000; expenditures, $17,289; qualifying distributions, $17,000.
Limitations: Giving primarily in TX.
Directors: Fayette F. Griffin, Frank Morris, Jimmie Todd.
EIN: 752539175

52477
Dr. Howard M. Siegler Foundation, Inc.
2201 W. Holcombe, Ste. 245
Houston, TX 77030

Established in 1997 in TX.
Donor(s): Toinette Siegler.
Financial data (yr. ended 12/31/99): Grants paid, $17,000; assets, $691,265 (M); expenditures, $17,569; qualifying distributions, $11,933.
Limitations: Applications not accepted.
Application information: Contributes only to pre-selected organizations.
Directors: Don Schlossberg, Howard Shulman, Toinette A. Siegler.
EIN: 760537979

52478
Spinal Conquest Foundation
P.O. Box 743
Dalhart, TX 79022

Established in 1999 in TX.
Financial data (yr. ended 12/31/01): Grants paid, $16,813; assets, $1 (M); expenditures, $17,469; qualifying distributions, $16,813.
Limitations: Applications not accepted.
Application information: Contributes only to pre-selected organizations.
Directors: Justin Koehler, Kelcey Koehler, Kortney Koehler, Mike Koehler, Sharon Koehler.
EIN: 752820139

52479
Lloyd-Bland Foundation
14319 Hughes Ln.
Dallas, TX 75254-8501

Established in 2001 in TX.
Donor(s): Marcea Bland Lloyd, Edwin O. Lloyd.
Financial data (yr. ended 12/31/01): Grants paid, $16,650; assets, $35,266 (M); gifts received, $67,630; expenditures, $16,873; qualifying distributions, $16,650.
Limitations: Applications not accepted. Giving primarily in Dallas, TX.
Application information: Contributes only to pre-selected organizations.
Officers: Marcea Bland Lloyd, Pres. and Treas.; Edwin O. Lloyd, V.P. and Secy.
Trustee: Beatriz Bland.
EIN: 752912179

52480
KFFH, Inc.
2445 North Blvd.
Houston, TX 77098

Established in 2000 in TX.
Donor(s): Frost Family.
Financial data (yr. ended 03/31/01): Grants paid, $16,600; assets, $1,556,023 (M); gifts received, $1,560,000; expenditures, $17,022; qualifying distributions, $16,600.
Limitations: Applications not accepted. Giving primarily in Orlando, FL.
Application information: Contributes only to pre-selected organizations.
Officers: Mark Klein, Pres.; Timothy Klein, V.P.; Kathryn Klein, Secy.
EIN: 760657129

52481
Roland & Jane Blumberg Foundation
200 N. River St., Ste. 100
Seguin, TX 78155
Contact: Hilmar D. Blumberg, Pres. or Joe H. Bruns, Secy.-Treas.

Financial data (yr. ended 09/30/01): Grants paid, $16,500; assets, $321,325 (M); expenditures, $21,877; qualifying distributions, $16,500.
Limitations: Giving primarily in Seguin, TX.
Application information: Application form not required.
Officers and Directors:* Hilmar D. Blumberg,* Pres.; Edward A. Blumberg,* V.P.; Joe H. Bruns,* Secy.-Treas.
EIN: 741983329

52482
Marie Roper Foundation
2016 Bentwater Dr.
Montgomery, TX 77356

Established in 1997 in TX.
Donor(s): A. Hardy Roper.
Financial data (yr. ended 04/30/02): Grants paid, $16,500; assets, $280,252 (M); gifts received, $8,500; expenditures, $19,085; qualifying distributions, $16,500.
Trustees: A. Hardy Roper, Andrew H. Roper, Martin E. Roper.
EIN: 760537055

52483
The George H. & Mary Morgan Sullivan Charitable Foundation
2211 Colonial Pkwy.
Fort Worth, TX 76109

Established in 1996 in TX.
Donor(s): George H. Sullivan, Mary Morgan Sullivan.
Financial data (yr. ended 12/31/01): Grants paid, $16,400; assets, $400,131 (M); gifts received, $30,000; expenditures, $17,782; qualifying distributions, $16,400.
Limitations: Applications not accepted. Giving primarily in TX.
Application information: Contributes only to pre-selected organizations.
Officer and Trustees:* George H. Sullivan,* Pres.; Mary Morgan Sullivan.
EIN: 752682021

52484
Collins/Fisher Foundation
2200 Ross Ave., Ste. 4600W
Dallas, TX 75201
Application address: 1501 K St. N.W., Ste. 100, Washington, DC 20005

Established in 2001 in TX.
Donor(s): James M. Collins Foundation.
Financial data (yr. ended 12/31/01): Grants paid, $16,350; assets, $5,865,806 (M); expenditures, $65,136; qualifying distributions, $65,136.
Limitations: Giving on a national basis, with some emphasis on Washington, DC.
Officers: Nancy Collins Fisher, Chair. and Pres.; Richard W. Fisher, Vice-Chair. and Treas.; Jan McMinn, Secy.
EIN: 311736933

52485
H. J. Diffenbaugh Trust for Kansas University
c/o Bank of America
P.O. Box 831041
Dallas, TX 75283-1041
Application address: c/o David P. Ross, Sr. V.P., Bank of America, P.O. Box 419119, Kansas City, MO 64141-6119, tel.: (816) 979-6119

Financial data (yr. ended 12/31/01): Grants paid, $16,350; assets, $273,919 (M); expenditures, $21,860; qualifying distributions, $17,942.
Limitations: Giving limited to residents of MO.
Application information: Applicants must be enrolled at Kansas University.
Trustee: Bank of America.
EIN: 446008349
Codes: GTI

52486
Mike & Jean Phillips Charitable Foundation
3200 Southwest Fwy., Ste. 3400
Houston, TX 77027-7528

Established in 1996 in TX.
Donor(s): Jean Phillips, Michael Phillips.
Financial data (yr. ended 12/31/01): Grants paid, $16,333; assets, $87,484 (M); gifts received, $9,357; expenditures, $17,227; qualifying distributions, $16,333.
Limitations: Applications not accepted.
Application information: Contributes only to pre-selected organizations.
Officer and Directors:* Michael Phillips,* Pres.; Jean Phillips.
EIN: 760511489

52487
Warner Foundation
2106 Golden Pond Dr.
Kingwood, TX 77345 (281) 360-8286
Contact: Darrell G. Warner, Pres.

Established in 1996 in TX.
Donor(s): Darrell G. Warner, Hilda R. Warner.
Financial data (yr. ended 12/31/01): Grants paid, $16,300; assets, $94,203 (M); gifts received, $20,061; expenditures, $19,082; qualifying distributions, $16,300.
Application information: Application form not required.
Officers and Directors:* Darrell G. Warner,* Pres.; Hilda R. Warner,* Secy.-Treas.; Ann W. Henrichsen, William D. Warner.
EIN: 760509976

52488
Southeast Texas A & M Foundation
c/o Leonard Forey
P.O. Box 12161
Beaumont, TX 77726-2161

Financial data (yr. ended 12/31/00): Grants paid, $16,165; assets, $42,608 (M); gifts received, $28,820; expenditures, $28,041; qualifying distributions, $16,165.
Limitations: Giving limited to residents of Chambers, Jefferson, and Hardin counties, TX.
Application information: Application form required.
Officers: Ed Collins, Pres.; Peggy Parigi, Secy.; Sam C. Parigi, Jr., Treas.
Directors: Gordon Birdwell, F.O. "Gator" Dollinger, Burton French, Lewis Hiltpold, Tom Natho, Harvey Randolph, Charlie Schultz, David Spacek, Malcolm Williams, Michael Wolf.
EIN: 760300907

52489
The M. C. Batey Trust
P.O. Box 831041
Dallas, TX 75283-1041
Application address: c/o Office of Development and College Relations, Tyler Junior College, P.O. Box 9020, Tyler, TX 75711, tel.: (903) 510-2200

Established in 1992 in TX.
Financial data (yr. ended 08/31/01): Grants paid, $16,155; assets, $299,164 (M); expenditures, $21,438; qualifying distributions, $16,155.
Limitations: Giving limited to residents of Smith County, TX.
Application information: Application form required.
Committee Members: Bill Crowe, Whit Riter, James C. Wynne.
Trustee: Bank of America.
EIN: 756435461

52490
The Jeffrey A. Carter Foundation
13531 Hughes Pl.
Dallas, TX 75240-5334

Established in 1994.
Donor(s): Jeffrey A. Carter.
Financial data (yr. ended 12/31/00): Grants paid, $16,000; assets, $371,010 (M); gifts received, $4,744; expenditures, $17,398; qualifying distributions, $16,000.
Limitations: Applications not accepted. Giving primarily in Dallas, TX.
Application information: Contributes only to pre-selected organizations.
Directors: Susan Fodor Bishop, Jeffrey A. Carter, Randy J. Carter.
EIN: 752571811

52491
The Rosalie and Bettie Cartwright Foundation
2911 Ferndale Pl.
Houston, TX 77098-1117
Contact: Bettie Cartwright, Pres.

Established in 1994 in TX.
Financial data (yr. ended 12/31/00): Grants paid, $16,000; assets, $274,105 (M); gifts received, $10,000; expenditures, $19,518; qualifying distributions, $17,381.
Limitations: Giving primarily in TX.
Officers: Bettie Cartwright, Pres. and Treas.; Joiner Cartwright, Jr., V.P.; Colin E. Kennedy, Secy.
EIN: 760460233

52492
Florence Oeding Estate Trust
506 Simpson St.
P.O. Box 324
Schulenburg, TX 78956-0324 (979) 743-3750
Contact: Paul Huser, Tr.

Established in 1975 in TX.
Financial data (yr. ended 12/31/01): Grants paid, $16,000; assets, $228,501 (M); expenditures, $17,519; qualifying distributions, $16,594.
Limitations: Giving primarily in TX.
Trustee: Paul Huser.
EIN: 746247707

52493
Rubenfeld Family Foundation
3122 Robinhood
Houston, TX 77005

Established in 1993 in TX.
Donor(s): Sheldon Rubenfeld, M.D., Linda S. Rubenfeld.
Financial data (yr. ended 09/30/01): Grants paid, $16,000; assets, $242,709 (M); gifts received, $50,000; expenditures, $19,197; qualifying distributions, $16,000.
Limitations: Applications not accepted. Giving primarily in Houston, TX.
Application information: Contributes only to pre-selected organizations.
Officers: Sheldon Rubenfeld, M.D., Pres. and Treas.; Linda S. Rubenfeld, V.P. and Secy.
Trustee: Allen Applebaum.
EIN: 760421521

52494
S.D. Scholarship Fund
(Formerly Champion International Corporation)
c/o Donohue Industries Inc.
P.O. Box 1149, Hwy. 103 E.
Lufkin, TX 75902-0149

Donor(s): Champion International Corp., Donohue Industries Inc., Abitibi Consolidated.
Financial data (yr. ended 08/31/01): Grants paid, $16,000; assets, $120,518 (M); gifts received, $4,000; expenditures, $16,500; qualifying distributions, $16,000.
Limitations: Giving primarily in TX.
Application information: Application form required.
Officers and Directors:* Paula Parish, Secy.; W.C. Durham,* Treas.; C.M. Wright, Mgr.; J.M. Comer, Glenn Wallace.
Scholarship Selection Committee Members: Langston Kerr, Frank Leathers.
EIN: 742077273
Codes: CS, CD, GTI

52495
The Scott R. Wheaton Foundation
P.O. Box 2050
Fort Worth, TX 76113 (817) 884-4448

Financial data (yr. ended 12/31/99): Grants paid, $16,000; assets, $361,207 (M); expenditures, $19,517; qualifying distributions, $16,000.
Officers: Mary Jane Wheaton Morse, Pres.; Steven F. Wheaton, V.P.; Scott R. Wheaton, Jr., Secy.-Treas.
Directors: Clayton Morse, Gretchen Wheaton.
Trustee: Bank One Trust Co., N.A.
EIN: 721405288

52496
The Jim L. Peterson Foundation
P.O. Box 1338
Goliad, TX 77963-1338

Established in 1986.
Donor(s): Jim L. Peterson.
Financial data (yr. ended 12/31/01): Grants paid, $15,986; assets, $150,065 (M); gifts received, $6,500; expenditures, $37,893; qualifying distributions, $15,986.
Limitations: Applications not accepted. Giving primarily in TX.
Application information: Contributes only to pre-selected organizations.
Trustee: Jim L. Peterson.
EIN: 742467974

52497
Irby N. & Marion H. Taylor Foundation
7105 Fern Meadow Cir.
Dallas, TX 75248-5603
Application address: 1620 Villanova, Richardson, TX 75081
Contact: Thomas H. Taylor, Tr.

Donor(s): Irby N. Taylor, Marion H. Taylor.
Financial data (yr. ended 11/30/01): Grants paid, $15,850; assets, $269,760 (M); gifts received, $521; expenditures, $16,427; qualifying distributions, $15,850.
Limitations: Giving primarily in Dallas, TX.
Trustees: Patricia T. Canavan, Marion H. Taylor, Thomas H. Taylor.
EIN: 756053890

52498
Kevin and Kyle Witt Memorial
c/o Russell A. Witt
P.O. Box 866932
Plano, TX 75086-6932

Established in 1997.
Donor(s): Russell Witt, Alexandra Witt.
Financial data (yr. ended 11/30/01): Grants paid, $15,850; assets, $512,548 (M); gifts received, $108,653; expenditures, $24,488; qualifying distributions, $15,850.
Limitations: Applications not accepted.
Application information: Contributes only to pre-selected organizations.
Officers and Directors:* Russell Witt, Jr.,* Pres.; Cheryl Witt,* V.P.; Alexandra Witt,* Secy.; Richard Witt, Treas.
EIN: 752738631

52499
Bud & Norma Johnson Family Foundation, Inc.
3371 Forest Glen Dr.
Denton, TX 76205
Contact: Norma Johnson, Pres.

Established in 1999 in TX.
Donor(s): Arthur "Bud" Johnson, Norma Johnson.
Financial data (yr. ended 12/31/01): Grants paid, $15,800; assets, $468,510 (M); gifts received, $74,790; expenditures, $19,423; qualifying distributions, $15,800.
Limitations: Giving primarily in TX.
Officers and Directors:* Norma Johnson,* Pres.; Arthur "Bud" Johnson,* Secy.-Treas.; Cynthia Lynn Johnson, Jeffrey J. Johnson.
EIN: 752852191

52500
The Prentiss Foundation
3890 W. Northwest Hwy., Ste. 400
Dallas, TX 75220

Established in 1988 in TX.
Donor(s): Michael V. Prentiss, Patricia Prentiss.
Financial data (yr. ended 12/31/01): Grants paid, $15,750; assets, $973,131 (M); expenditures, $15,788; qualifying distributions, $15,750.
Limitations: Applications not accepted. Giving primarily in Dallas, TX.
Application information: Contributes only to pre-selected organizations.
Officers and Director:* Michael V. Prentiss,* Pres.; Dennis J. DuBois, V.P.; Robin Grout, Treas.
EIN: 752255757

52501
The Uhr Family Foundation
(Formerly The Jonathan W. Uhr Family Foundation)
2626 Cole Ave., Ste. 400
Dallas, TX 75204
Application address: 12311 Shiremont, Dallas, TX 75230
Contact: Jonathan W. Uhr, Pres.

Established in 1987 in TX.
Donor(s): Jonathan W. Uhr.
Financial data (yr. ended 12/31/00): Grants paid, $15,729; assets, $402,326 (M); expenditures, $17,923; qualifying distributions, $15,729.
Limitations: Giving on a national basis.
Application information: Application form not required.
Officers: Jonathan W. Uhr, Pres.; Jacqueline Louise Guise, V.P.; Sarita Uhr, Secy.-Treas.
EIN: 752158090

52502
Richard and Barbara S. Nelson Foundation
13614 Havershire Ln.
Houston, TX 77079-3406

Established in 1997 in TX.
Donor(s): Barbara S. Nelson.
Financial data (yr. ended 12/31/00): Grants paid, $15,610; assets, $1 (M); gifts received, $721; expenditures, $16,521; qualifying distributions, $15,610.
Limitations: Applications not accepted.
Application information: Contributes only to pre-selected organizations.
Officer: Barbara S. Nelson, Pres.
EIN: 760549839

52503
Norman H. Helms, Jr. Charitable Foundation
2801 Windsor Ln.
Port Neches, TX 77651

Established in 2000 in TX.
Donor(s): Norman H. Helms, Jr.
Financial data (yr. ended 12/31/01): Grants paid, $15,600; assets, $1,575 (M); gifts received, $5,239; expenditures, $16,736; qualifying distributions, $15,600.
Limitations: Applications not accepted. Giving primarily in TX.
Application information: Contributes only to pre-selected organizations.
Trustees: Betty Helms, Norman H. Helms, Jr.
EIN: 760646532

52504
The National We Care Foundation
4101 International Pkwy.
Carrollton, TX 75007

Financial data (yr. ended 12/31/01): Grants paid, $15,600; assets, $45,191 (M); expenditures, $25,664; qualifying distributions, $19,807.
Limitations: Applications not accepted.
Application information: Contributes only to pre-selected organizations.
Officers: Peter Gudmundsson, Pres.; Shawn Whalen Shinn, V.P.; Brad Heles, Secy.-Treas.; Robert Johnston, Genl. Counsel.
Board Member: Dave Smith.
EIN: 752402958

52505
Bradford-Nye Trust
P.O. Box 359
Tyler, TX 75710-0359 (903) 597-8311
Application address: c/o First Baptist Church, 300 W. Ferguson St., P.O. Box 277, Tyler, TX 75710, tel.: (903) 597-4436
Contact: Dorothy Land, Scholarship Comm.

Financial data (yr. ended 12/31/01): Grants paid, $15,500; assets, $166,356 (M); expenditures, $16,230; qualifying distributions, $15,380.
Limitations: Giving limited to Smith County, TX.
Application information: Application form required.
Trustees: Tracey Crawford, John H. Minton, Wendell Pool.
EIN: 756329248
Codes: GTI

52506
Ken and Martha Bruner Foundation
P.O. Box 820331
Fort Worth, TX 76182-0331
Application address: 529 Circle View Dr. N., Hurst, TX 76054, tel.: (817) 282-1716
Contact: Kenneth L. Bruner, Pres.

Established in 1990 in TX.
Donor(s): Kenneth L. Bruner, Martha M. Bruner.
Financial data (yr. ended 12/31/01): Grants paid, $15,500; assets, $384,072 (M); gifts received, $15,000; expenditures, $16,404; qualifying distributions, $15,500.
Limitations: Giving primarily in Fort Worth, TX.
Officers and Directors:* Kenneth L. Bruner,* Pres.; Martha M. Bruner,* V.P. and Secy.-Treas.
EIN: 752356469

52507
Spencer Charitable Foundation
600 Leopard St., Ste. 2000
Corpus Christi, TX 78473

Established in 1998 in TX.
Donor(s): Jack W. Spencer, Deanna June Spencer.
Financial data (yr. ended 09/30/01): Grants paid, $15,500; assets, $398,070 (M); gifts received, $3,530; expenditures, $19,894; qualifying distributions, $15,500.
Limitations: Applications not accepted.
Application information: Contributes only to pre-selected organizations.
Officers and Directors:* Jack W. Spencer,* Pres.; Deanna June Spencer,* V.P.; Charlotte Spencer Stacy,* Secy.; Andre M. Spencer,* Treas.
EIN: 742900267

52508
The Molbeck Family Foundation
3424 Ella Lee
Houston, TX 77027

Established in 1998 in TX.
Donor(s): John Molbeck, Teresa Molbeck.
Financial data (yr. ended 11/30/01): Grants paid, $15,388; assets, $18,246 (M); expenditures, $15,388; qualifying distributions, $15,388.
Limitations: Applications not accepted.
Application information: Contributes only to pre-selected organizations.
Directors: Ashlie M. Molbeck, John N. Molbeck, Sr., John N. Molbeck, Jr., Kristin L. Molbeck, Teresa A. Molbeck.
EIN: 760584993

52509
Giles Family Foundation
P.O. Box 230253
Houston, TX 77223

Established in 1990 in TX.
Donor(s): Joanne R. Giles.
Financial data (yr. ended 05/31/02): Grants paid, $15,305; assets, $276,445 (M); expenditures, $20,357; qualifying distributions, $15,305.
Limitations: Applications not accepted. Giving on a national basis, with emphasis on TX.
Application information: Contributes only to pre-selected organizations.
Officers: Robert N. Giles, Pres.; David L. Giles, V.P.; Douglas L. Giles, Secy.; Joanne R. Giles, Treas.
Trustee: David L. Giles.
EIN: 760312730

52510
Texas School of Business Educational Foundation
6363 Richmond
Houston, TX 77057

Established in 1991 in TX.
Donor(s): Joseph A. Aufman, Judith A. Aufman.
Financial data (yr. ended 12/31/00): Grants paid, $15,300; assets, $156,688 (M); expenditures, $17,035; qualifying distributions, $15,221.
Limitations: Giving limited to residents of TX.
Application information: Application form required.
Officer: W. Kevin Keller, Pres.
Trustee: James E. Tucker, Jr.
EIN: 760354909

52511
Tina E. Bangs Foundation
727 Bunker Hill, No. 10
Houston, TX 77024
Contact: Molly E. Shanks, Pres.

Established in 1994 in TX.
Donor(s): Tina E. Bangs.
Financial data (yr. ended 07/31/01): Grants paid, $15,250; assets, $229,560 (M); expenditures, $15,565; qualifying distributions, $15,250.
Officers: Molly E. Shanks, Pres.; Don E. Fizer, V.P.; Barbara Stanley, Secy.-Treas.
EIN: 760445886

52512
The Texas Area Fund Foundation, Inc.
c/o East Texas National Bank, Trust Dept.
P.O. Box 770
Palestine, TX 75802

Established in 1999 in TX.
Financial data (yr. ended 12/31/00): Grants paid, $15,250; assets, $350,163 (M); gifts received, $39,934; expenditures, $358,289.
Limitations: Giving limited to Palestine, TX.
Officers: Jackson Hanks, Pres.; Larry Womack, V.P.; Bob McKelvey, Secy.; Phil Jenkins, Treas.
Trustees: Kathy Rainbolt, Tucker Royall, Fernando Varela.
EIN: 752834546
Codes: CM

52513
The Cleaves and Mae Rhea Foundation
6100 Western Pl., Ste. 910
Fort Worth, TX 76107

Established in 1997 in TX.
Donor(s): C. Rhea Thompson, J. Andy Thompson.
Financial data (yr. ended 12/31/01): Grants paid, $15,248; assets, $1,224,214 (M); expenditures, $23,994; qualifying distributions, $15,248.
Limitations: Applications not accepted. Giving primarily in Chesterfield and St. Louis, MO, and CA.
Application information: Contributes only to pre-selected organizations.
Officers: J. Andy Thompson, Pres.; Nancy S. Thompson, Secy.-Treas.
Directors: Christopher S. Thompson, C. Rhea Thompson, Heather Thompson, John A. Thompson, Jr., Wendy Thompson.
EIN: 752709116

52514
Kathryn Coye Leach Trust
c/o Bank One Trust Co., N.A.
P.O. Box 2050
Fort Worth, TX 76113-2050 (817) 884-4181
Contact: Lee Price

Established in 1998.
Financial data (yr. ended 08/31/01): Grants paid, $15,241; assets, $296,968 (M); expenditures, $17,349; qualifying distributions, $15,241.
Trustee: Bank One Trust Co., N.A.
EIN: 756496933

52515
The Turney Foundation
P.O. Box 1496
Marshall, TX 75671-1496 (903) 938-9255
Contact: Cary M. Abney, Mgr.

Financial data (yr. ended 12/31/01): Grants paid, $15,215; assets, $371,932 (M); expenditures, $23,331; qualifying distributions, $15,215.

52515—TEXAS

Limitations: Giving limited to Harrison County, TX.
Officers: Louis W. Kariel, Jr., Pres.; Cary M. Abney, Mgr.
EIN: 751043523

52516
Bruce B. Dice Foundation
c/o Bruce B. Dice
14405 Walters Rd., Ste. 400
Houston, TX 77014

Donor(s): Bruce B. Dice.
Financial data (yr. ended 05/31/02): Grants paid, $15,203; assets, $65,307 (M); expenditures, $16,139; qualifying distributions, $15,203.
Limitations: Applications not accepted.
Application information: Contributes only to pre-selected organizations.
Officers: Bruce B. Dice, Chair.; Kevin B. Dice, Pres.; Kirk Brian Dice, Secy.-Treas.
Director: Karen Dice Clemens.
EIN: 760538023

52517
The Herrmann Family Charitable Foundation
P.O. Box 13430
San Antonio, TX 78213
Contact: Ronald J. Herrmann, Tr.

Established in 1994 in TX.
Donor(s): Ronald J. Herrmann, Karen H. Herrmann.
Financial data (yr. ended 12/31/01): Grants paid, $15,172; assets, $1,358,832 (M); gifts received, $110,000; expenditures, $16,187; qualifying distributions, $113,627; giving activities include $508 for programs.
Limitations: Giving primarily in TX.
Application information: Application form not required.
Trustees: David S. Herrmann, Karen H. Herrmann, Ronald J. Herrmann.
EIN: 742715033

52518
The Miller Assistance Fund
c/o Hibernia National Bank
P.O. Box 3928
Beaumont, TX 77704-3928
Application address: c/o The Rabbi of Temple Emanuel, P.O. Box 423, Beaumont, TX 77704-0423

Donor(s): Rudolph C. Miller.‡
Financial data (yr. ended 06/30/00): Grants paid, $15,050; assets, $108,119 (M); expenditures, $16,687; qualifying distributions, $16,616.
Limitations: Giving limited to the Beaumont, TX, area.
Application information: Application form not required.
Committee Members: Paul Kessler, Leonard M. Mothner.
Trustee: Hibernia National Bank.
EIN: 746255231
Codes: GTI

52519
The Mayde Waddell Butler Foundation
P.O. Box 1127
Rosenberg, TX 77471

Donor(s): Mayde W. Butler.
Financial data (yr. ended 11/30/01): Grants paid, $15,000; assets, $190,201 (M); expenditures, $16,572; qualifying distributions, $15,000.
Limitations: Applications not accepted. Giving primarily in TX.
Application information: Contributes only to pre-selected organizations.
Officer: William C. Butler, Pres.

Trustees: Robert Frank, Douglas A. Heath, Lester T. Lothman.
EIN: 766058535

52520
Raymond J. Dusek Foundation
4218 Crescent Dr.
Granbury, TX 76049-5386

Financial data (yr. ended 12/31/01): Grants paid, $15,000; assets, $1,318 (M); expenditures, $15,383; qualifying distributions, $15,000.
Limitations: Giving primarily in Wichita Falls, TX.
Application information: Application form not required.
Officers: Raymond J. Dusek, Jr., Pres.; David D. Dusek, V.P.; Karen K. Dusek, Secy.-Treas.
EIN: 736112407

52521
El Paso County Medical Society Foundation
1301 Montana Ave.
El Paso, TX 79902-5530 (915) 533-0940
Contact: Patricia Slaughter, Exec. Dir.

Financial data (yr. ended 12/31/01): Grants paid, $15,000; assets, $25,610 (M); expenditures, $15,000; qualifying distributions, $0.
Limitations: Giving limited to El Paso County, TX.
Officers: Branch Criage, M.D., Pres.; Rajendra Marwah, M.D., V.P.; Luis Acosta, M.D., Secy.; Eric Sides, M.D., Treas.
EIN: 237004287

52522
Grizzle Family Foundation
2316 Steel St.
Houston, TX 77098-5610 (713) 324-2966
Contact: J. David Grizzle, Pres.

Established in 1998 in TX.
Donor(s): Anne F. Grizzle, J. David Grizzle.
Financial data (yr. ended 12/31/01): Grants paid, $15,000; assets, $463,526 (M); gifts received, $5,000; expenditures, $15,616; qualifying distributions, $15,000.
Limitations: Giving primarily in NY and TX.
Officers: J. David Grizzle, Pres.; Anne F. Grizzle, V.P.
EIN: 760556358

52523
The Hurd Foundation
1200 Golden Key, Ste. 340
El Paso, TX 79925
Application address: 752 De Leon, El Paso, TX 79912, tel.: (915) 581-9003
Contact: Lacy Justice, Tr.

Established in 1993 in TX.
Donor(s): Stephen C. Hurd.
Financial data (yr. ended 12/31/01): Grants paid, $15,000; assets, $372,980 (M); expenditures, $20,833; qualifying distributions, $15,000.
Limitations: Giving limited to Austin, TX.
Application information: Application form required.
Officers: Stephen C. Hurd, Pres.; Susan O. Hurd, Secy.-Treas.
Trustee: Lacy Justice.
EIN: 742690698

52524
The John Paul Marcum Foundation
1800 Norwood, Ste. 104
Hurst, TX 76054 (817) 268-1156
Contact: Jerry B. Jackson, Tr.

Established in 1997 in TX.
Donor(s): John Paul Marcum.‡

Financial data (yr. ended 12/31/01): Grants paid, $15,000; assets, $67,051 (M); expenditures, $15,120; qualifying distributions, $15,000.
Trustee: Jerry B. Jackson.
EIN: 752700548

52525
The Mitchell Foundation
3900 Dallas Pkwy., Ste. 500
Plano, TX 75093

Established in 1998 in TX.
Financial data (yr. ended 12/31/00): Grants paid, $15,000; assets, $291,255 (M); expenditures, $7,982; qualifying distributions, $15,000.
Officers: Lee Roy Mitchell, Pres.; Robert Copple, V.P.; Tandy Mitchell, Secy.
EIN: 752769798

52526
Robert L. Moody Foundation
2302 Postoffice St., Ste. 702
Galveston, TX 77550-1981 (409) 763-6461
Contact: Robert L. Moody, Dir.

Donor(s): Robert L. Moody.
Financial data (yr. ended 08/31/02): Grants paid, $15,000; assets, $218,338 (M); expenditures, $15,853; qualifying distributions, $15,000.
Limitations: Giving primarily in Galveston, TX.
Directors: Ann McLeod Moody, Robert L. Moody, Frances Moody Newman.
EIN: 746054531

52527
Onstead Foundation
600 Travis, Ste. 6475
Houston, TX 77002 (713) 227-5884
Contact: Robert R. Onstead, V.P.

Donor(s): Robert R. Onstead, Charles M. Onstead.
Financial data (yr. ended 12/31/01): Grants paid, $15,000; assets, $195,515 (M); gifts received, $40,267; expenditures, $15,267; qualifying distributions, $15,000.
Limitations: Giving limted to Ellis County, TX.
Officers: Charles Onstead, Pres.; Robert R. Onstead, V.P.; Dixie Murff, Secy.-Treas.
EIN: 752760633

52528
The Squibb Family Foundation
2 Cransbrook Ct.
Dallas, TX 75225-2466

Established in 1997 in TX.
Donor(s): Charles E. Squibb.
Financial data (yr. ended 12/31/01): Grants paid, $15,000; assets, $312,370 (M); expenditures, $16,353; qualifying distributions, $15,000.
Limitations: Applications not accepted. Giving primarily in Dallas, TX.
Application information: Contributes only to pre-selected organizations.
Officers: Charles E. Squibb, Pres.; Carl Randall Squibb, V.P.; Mary Margaret Utsman, V.P.; Martha Dale Squibb, Secy.
EIN: 752690855

52529
Waycaster Foundation
6235 Woods Bridge Way
Houston, TX 77007-7042

Established in 1993 in TX.
Donor(s): Billy W. Waycaster, Patricia M. Waycaster.
Financial data (yr. ended 12/31/01): Grants paid, $15,000; assets, $190,763 (M); expenditures, $15,513; qualifying distributions, $15,000.
Limitations: Applications not accepted. Giving limited to Houston, TX.

Application information: Contributes only to pre-selected organizations.
Trustees: Billy W. Waycaster, Kimberly Waycaster, Patricia M. Waycaster.
EIN: 766093624

52530
Western European Architecture Foundation
306 W. Sunset, Ste. 550
San Antonio, TX 78209
Contact: P.J. Fleming, Pres.

Established in 1989 in TX.
Donor(s): George Parker, Jr., Parker Foundation.
Financial data (yr. ended 12/31/01): Grants paid, $15,000; assets, $3,350 (M); expenditures, $208,960; qualifying distributions, $177,243.
Limitations: Giving on a national basis.
Officer and Directors:* P.J. Fleming,* Pres.; Carol Fleming, Richard Halter.
EIN: 742553016
Codes: GTI

52531
Whitener Family Foundation
c/o C. Cleve Whitener
901 S. 1st St.
Abilene, TX 79602-1502 (915) 670-9660

Established in 1996 in TX.
Donor(s): C. Cleve Whitener, Lauren Engineers & Constructors, Inc., Mary R. Whitener.
Financial data (yr. ended 12/31/01): Grants paid, $15,000; assets, $285,886 (M); gifts received, $50,000; expenditures, $15,185; qualifying distributions, $15,111.
Limitations: Applications not accepted. Giving primarily in GA.
Application information: Contributes only to pre-selected organizations.
Directors: Alan K. Davis, C. Cleve Whitener, Mary Rebecca Whitener.
EIN: 752681790

52532
Ellen Hamilton Wilkerson Educational Trust
c/o F.C. Witherspoon
3701 Kirby, Ste. 716
Houston, TX 77098-3921
Application address: 5667 Lynbrook Dr., Houston, TX 77056
Contact: John H. Wilkerson, Tr.

Established in 1994 in TX.
Donor(s): Ellen H. Wilkerson.
Financial data (yr. ended 12/31/01): Grants paid, $15,000; assets, $353,212 (M); expenditures, $16,982; qualifying distributions, $15,000.
Limitations: Giving primarily in TX.
Trustees: Jack Daniel, Mary Kempner Daniel, Page Kempner Lummis, Richard Lummis, Seth A. McMeans, Edward Morris Wilkerson, Ellen H. Wilkerson, John Hamilton Wilkerson, Sr.
EIN: 760452803

52533
Melba C. Wynne Foundation
c/o Bank of America
P.O. Box 831041
Dallas, TX 75283-1041
Application address: c/o Bank of America, P.O. Box 830259, Dallas, TX 75283-0259, tel.: (214) 508-6759
Contact: Nancy Knapp, Trust Off., Bank of America

Financial data (yr. ended 02/28/01): Grants paid, $15,000; assets, $532,982 (M); expenditures, $37,033; qualifying distributions, $19,553.
Limitations: Giving primarily in Houston, TX.
Trustee: Bank of America.

EIN: 760281311

52534
The Claude & Mae Moss Charities, Inc.
534 Pine St., Ste. 102
Abilene, TX 79601-5130
Application address: 1850 Elmwood Dr., Abilene, TX 79605
Contact: Richard L. Spalding, Sr., Pres.

Financial data (yr. ended 12/31/01): Grants paid, $14,932; assets, $441,846 (M); expenditures, $22,708; qualifying distributions, $14,932.
Limitations: Giving limited to Abilene, TX.
Officers: Richard L. Spalding, Sr., Pres.; Gordon Asbury, Jr., V.P. and Secy.-Treas.
Director: Richard L. Spalding, Jr.
EIN: 752008057

52535
Vietnam Forum Foundation
2318 Steel St.
Houston, TX 77098

Established in 1998 in TX.
Financial data (yr. ended 12/31/01): Grants paid, $14,800; assets, $44,839 (M); gifts received, $32,300; expenditures, $15,133; qualifying distributions, $14,800.
Limitations: Applications not accepted.
Application information: Contributes only to pre-selected organizations.
Officers: Kien Pham, Chair.; Vy Ton, Vice-Chair.; Tri Pham, Pres.; To-Ann Pham, Treas.
EIN: 760398917

52536
Mary L. & William J. Osher Foundation
12015 Surrey Ln.
Houston, TX 77024-5011

Established in 1993 in TX.
Donor(s): William J. Osher.
Financial data (yr. ended 12/31/01): Grants paid, $14,750; assets, $261,271 (M); gifts received, $56,920; expenditures, $15,750; qualifying distributions, $14,750.
Limitations: Applications not accepted. Giving primarily in New York, NY and Houston, TX.
Application information: Contributes only to pre-selected organizations.
Director: William J. Osher.
EIN: 766085721

52537
Vance D. & Mary Lee Raimond Foundation
P.O. Box 1870
Harlingen, TX 78551-1870

Established in 1997 in TX.
Donor(s): Vance D. Raimond.
Financial data (yr. ended 12/31/01): Grants paid, $14,720; assets, $4,202,950 (M); gifts received, $3,762,048; expenditures, $24,362; qualifying distributions, $14,720.
Limitations: Applications not accepted. Giving primarily in Harlingen, TX.
Application information: Contributes only to pre-selected organizations.
Officers and Directors:* Robert R. Farkis,* Pres.; Betty R. Farkis,* Secy.-Treas.
EIN: 742859693

52538
Blankinship 1991 Foundation, Inc.
c/o Herbert H. Blankinship
P.O. Box 51270
Midland, TX 79710-1270

Established in 1991 in TX.
Donor(s): Herbert H. Blankinship, V. Elizabeth Blankinship.

Financial data (yr. ended 12/31/01): Grants paid, $14,710; assets, $385,367 (M); gifts received, $90,458; expenditures, $28,160; qualifying distributions, $14,710.
Limitations: Applications not accepted. Giving primarily in Midland, TX.
Application information: Contributes only to pre-selected organizations.
Officers: Herbert H. Blankinship, Pres.; V. Elizabeth Blankinship, V.P.; Barbra J. Grafa, Secy.; Bob W. Dutton, Treas.
EIN: 752395220

52539
Harry Arnote Charitable Foundation
c/o Bank of America
P.O. Box 831041
Dallas, TX 75283-1041
Application address: 2 S. Main St., Liberty, MO 64068
Contact: John M. Crossett

Financial data (yr. ended 06/30/02): Grants paid, $14,700; assets, $429,606 (M); expenditures, $23,057; qualifying distributions, $14,700.
Limitations: Giving limited to Clay County, MO.
Trustees: Jon M. Krebs, Richard Logerwell, Dennis Nicely.
EIN: 446012919

52540
Bulah Peery Memorial Scholarship Fund
Box 515
Booker, TX 79005-0515 (806) 658-4551
Contact: Daryl Pitts, Dir.

Financial data (yr. ended 07/31/01): Grants paid, $14,700; assets, $344,550 (M); gifts received, $4,789; expenditures, $16,084; qualifying distributions, $14,700.
Limitations: Giving limited to the Booker, TX, area.
Application information: Applicant must present proof of enrollment in a college in the U.S.
Directors: Kenda Burdick, Darrie Francis, Diana Hoover, John Kaufman, Mike Lee, Kayla Parvin, Daryl Pitts, Kent Sims.
EIN: 756038523
Codes: GTI

52541
Everson Family Foundation
P.O. Box 17149
Sugar Land, TX 77496-7149 (281) 775-0102

Established in 1997 in TX.
Donor(s): Jacquelyn R. Everson, Lloyd K. Everson.
Financial data (yr. ended 12/31/01): Grants paid, $14,650; assets, $166,757 (M); expenditures, $14,862; qualifying distributions, $14,650.
Officers and Directors:* Lloyd K. Everson,* Pres.; Brent A. Everson,* V.P.; Jennifer A. Everson,* V.P.; Kara E. Everson,* V.P.; Jacquelyn R. Everson,* Secy.-Treas.
EIN: 760554082

52542
Cathy Block Scholarship Fund
4413 Willow Way
Fort Worth, TX 76133

Established in 1993.
Financial data (yr. ended 12/31/01): Grants paid, $14,601; assets, $86,356 (M); gifts received, $33,732; expenditures, $27,923; qualifying distributions, $14,601.
Limitations: Applications not accepted.
Application information: Contributes only to pre-selected organizations.
Trustees: Cathy Block, Stanley Block, John N. Mangieri.
EIN: 756452194

52543
ABBA Foundation
P.O. Box 11044
Midland, TX 79702-8044

Established in 1997.
Donor(s): Alan E. Byars, Barbara M. Byars.
Financial data (yr. ended 12/31/01): Grants paid, $14,595; assets, $356,912 (M); expenditures, $22,277; qualifying distributions, $14,595.
Limitations: Applications not accepted.
Application information: Contributes only to pre-selected organizations.
Officers: Alan E. Byars, Pres.; Alan E. Byars, Jr., V.P.; Elizabeth Anne Byars, V.P.; Barbara M. Byars, Secy.-Treas.
EIN: 752723256

52544
The Jennings Foundation Trust
P.O. Box 55901
Houston, TX 77255-5901

Established in 1986 in TX.
Donor(s): Edwin J. Jennings, Colleen A. Jennings.
Financial data (yr. ended 12/31/00): Grants paid, $14,523; assets, $5,639 (M); expenditures, $14,707; qualifying distributions, $14,523.
Limitations: Applications not accepted. Giving primarily in Houston, TX.
Application information: Contributes only to pre-selected organizations.
Trustees: Colleen A. Jennings, Edwin J. Jennings.
EIN: 766034715

52545
Raymond E. Buck Foundation, Inc.
622 Roaring Springs Dr.
Fort Worth, TX 76114

Financial data (yr. ended 12/31/01): Grants paid, $14,500; assets, $250,097 (M); expenditures, $17,335; qualifying distributions, $14,500.
Limitations: Giving primarily in Fort Worth, TX.
Officer and Directors:* Katherine Buck McDermott,* Chair. and Pres.; Roy E. McDermott, J. Howard Shelton, Grover Swift, W.R. Watt, Jr.
EIN: 756029883

52546
KLN Foundation
819 Independence Pkwy.
Southlake, TX 76092

Established in 1997 in TX.
Donor(s): Donald H. Neustadt, Karen L. Neustadt.
Financial data (yr. ended 12/31/01): Grants paid, $14,500; assets, $515,630 (M); expenditures, $15,392; qualifying distributions, $14,500.
Limitations: Applications not accepted. Giving primarily in Arlington, TX.
Application information: Contributes only to pre-selected organizations.
Officers: Karen L. Neustadt, Pres.; Kristin Fay Ingalis, Secy.; Donald H. Neustadt, Treas.
EIN: 752710712

52547
The Massey Family Charitable Trust
650 Colonial Dr.
Abilene, TX 79603

Established in 1989 in TX.
Donor(s): Cleber J. Massey, Patricia A. Massey.
Financial data (yr. ended 12/31/01): Grants paid, $14,500; assets, $370,431 (M); gifts received, $70,000; expenditures, $15,702; qualifying distributions, $14,500.
Limitations: Applications not accepted. Giving primarily in Abilene, TX.
Application information: Contributes only to pre-selected organizations.
Trustees: Cleber J. Massey, Patricia A. Massey.
EIN: 756394613

52548
Glazer Family Fund
P.O. Box 809013
Dallas, TX 75380-9013

Financial data (yr. ended 10/31/01): Grants paid, $14,475; assets, $258,818 (M); expenditures, $14,649; qualifying distributions, $14,475.
Limitations: Applications not accepted. Giving primarily in the Dallas, TX, area.
Application information: Contributes only to pre-selected organizations.
Trustees: Bennett Glazer, Frances Glazer.
EIN: 756016938

52549
James M. Voss Charitable Trust
5412 FM 535
Cedar Creek, TX 78612-3417
Contact: Mary J. Voss, Tr.

Established in 1993 in TX.
Financial data (yr. ended 12/31/01): Grants paid, $14,450; assets, $285,831 (M); expenditures, $17,216; qualifying distributions, $14,450.
Trustee: Mary J. Voss.
EIN: 746409415

52550
Foulkrod Foundation
2423 Pebble Beach Dr.
League City, TX 77573-6418

Financial data (yr. ended 12/31/01): Grants paid, $14,400; assets, $682,441 (M); expenditures, $16,125; qualifying distributions, $14,400.
Application information: Application form not required.
Trustees: Chris Foulkrod, Dan Foulkrod, Jay Foulkrod, Kay Foulkrod.
EIN: 386078317

52551
The Wallace L. & Sidney H. Hall Foundation
5956 Sherry Ln., Ste. 1810
Dallas, TX 75225

Established in 1997 in TX.
Donor(s): Sydney H. Hall, Wallace L. Hall.
Financial data (yr. ended 12/31/00): Grants paid, $14,354; assets, $33,137 (M); gifts received, $5,470; expenditures, $17,337; qualifying distributions, $14,354.
Limitations: Applications not accepted.
Application information: Contributes only to pre-selected organizations.
Officers and Directors:* Wallace L. Hall,* Pres. and Treas.; Sydney H. Hall,* V.P. and Secy.; George H. Hall, Wallace L. Hall, Jr., Sydney A. Jordaan.
EIN: 752688301

52552
Woolworth Scholarship Fund
P.O. Box 729
San Angelo, TX 76902-0729
Application addresses: c/o Counselor's Office, San Angelo Central High School, 100 Cottonwood St., San Angelo, TX 76901, tel.: (915) 658-3511; or c/o Lakeview High School, 900 E. 43 St., San Angelo, Texas 76903, tel.: (915) 659-3500

Financial data (yr. ended 12/31/99): Grants paid, $14,250; assets, $337,409 (M); expenditures, $18,659; qualifying distributions, $14,582.
Limitations: Giving limited to San Angelo, TX.
Application information: Application form required.
Trustees: Joe Gonzales, Lamar Kopecky, Joe Munoz, Ralph Wilson.
EIN: 756185995

52553
Carleen & Alde Fridge Foundation
c/o JPMorgan Chase Bank
P.O. Box 2558
Houston, TX 77252-8037
Application address: c/o David M. Wax, Exec. Dir., Houston Symphony Orchestra, 615 Louisiana St., Houston, TX 77002, tel.: (713) 224-4240

Financial data (yr. ended 12/31/01): Grants paid, $14,242; assets, $365,046 (M); expenditures, $23,068; qualifying distributions, $14,242.
Limitations: Giving limited to Houston, TX.
Trustee: JPMorgan Chase Bank.
EIN: 746179001

52554
Martin H. and Helen M. Wikierak Charitable Trust
c/o Wells Fargo Bank Texas, N.A.
P.O. Box 2138
Fort Worth, TX 76113-2138

Established in 1995 in TX.
Financial data (yr. ended 12/31/01): Grants paid, $14,225; assets, $264,488 (M); expenditures, $18,177; qualifying distributions, $14,225.
Limitations: Applications not accepted. Giving primarily in Tarrant County, TX.
Application information: Contributes only to pre-selected organizations.
Trustee: Wells Fargo Bank Texas, N.A.
EIN: 756488132

52555
James H. Davis Foundation, Inc.
805 Tree Haven Ct.
Highland Village, TX 75077-6495

Established in 1995 in TX.
Financial data (yr. ended 12/31/01): Grants paid, $14,200; assets, $163,548 (M); expenditures, $14,497; qualifying distributions, $14,200.
Limitations: Applications not accepted. Giving primarily in TX.
Application information: Contributes only to pre-selected organizations.
Officers: M. Winston Rhea, Pres.; Charlotte D. Rhea, V.P.; Deborah J. Rhea, Secy.; James W. Rhea, Treas.
EIN: 752579777

52556
Riggs Family Foundation
c/o Leonard M. Riggs, Jr.
1717 Main St., Ste. 5200
Dallas, TX 75201-7365

Established in 1998 in TX.
Financial data (yr. ended 12/31/01): Grants paid, $14,150; assets, $464,923 (M); expenditures, $17,953; qualifying distributions, $14,150.
Limitations: Applications not accepted.
Application information: Contributes only to pre-selected organizations.
Directors: Leonard M. Riggs, Jr., Peggy A. Riggs, Chuck Robison.
EIN: 752765743

52557
Arthur F. Lind Scholarship Fund
P.O. Box 215
Ganado, TX 77962-0215
Application address: c/o Ganado Independent School District, Ganado, TX 77962, tel.: (512) 771-3482

Financial data (yr. ended 03/31/01): Grants paid, $14,115; assets, $107,558 (M); expenditures, $18,807; qualifying distributions, $15,040.
Limitations: Giving limited to residents of Ganado, TX.
Application information: Application form required.
Scholarship Committee: L.L. Duckett, A.J. Scott.
EIN: 742618872
Codes: GTI

52558
Ike & Fannie Sablosky Foundation
c/o Bank of America
P.O. Box 831041
Dallas, TX 75283-1041

Established in 1956 in TX.
Financial data (yr. ended 04/30/01): Grants paid, $14,100; assets, $889,790 (M); expenditures, $18,682; qualifying distributions, $14,100.
Limitations: Applications not accepted. Giving primarily in Dallas, TX.
Application information: Contributes only to pre-selected organizations.
Trustee: Bank of America.
EIN: 756007998

52559
Nagel Foundation
5225 Katy Freeway, Ste. 600
Houston, TX 77007

Established in 1997 in TX.
Donor(s): Alfred F. Nagel.
Financial data (yr. ended 12/31/01): Grants paid, $14,050; assets, $98,247 (M); expenditures, $15,300; qualifying distributions, $14,050.
Limitations: Applications not accepted. Giving primarily in Memphis, TN.
Application information: Contributes only to pre-selected organizations.
Officers: Alfred F. Nagel, Pres.; Audrey D. Cecko, Secy.; Kim Pandak, Treas.
EIN: 311513006

52560
Montgomery County Community Foundation
c/o Bert Lynch
P.O. Box 2548
Conroe, TX 77305

Donor(s): Eric J. Bauer, Mrs. Eric J. Bauer.
Financial data (yr. ended 12/31/00): Grants paid, $14,044; assets, $456,504 (M); gifts received, $394,071; expenditures, $28,447; qualifying distributions, $14,044.
Limitations: Applications not accepted. Giving primarily in Montgomery County, TX.
Application information: Contributes only to pre-selected organizations.
Officers and Directors:* Lloyd Carll,* Pres.; Nancy Dossey,* Secy.; Jill Vaughn,* Treas.; Jerry Creighton, Don Gebert, Jan Hofer-Rowe, David Lusk, Bert Lynch, Foster Madeley, Julie Martineau, George Sowers, John Wiesner.
EIN: 760082098
Codes: TN

52561
The Devnick Foundation
c/o Allyson J. Allen
3631 Turkey Creek Dr.
Austin, TX 78730-3709

Established in 1998 in TX.
Donor(s): William M. Allen, Allyson J. Allen.
Financial data (yr. ended 12/31/01): Grants paid, $14,000; assets, $279,978 (M); expenditures, $13,357; qualifying distributions, $14,000.
Limitations: Giving primarily in Austin, TX.
Directors: Allyson Jayne Allen, William Mark Allen, Teresa J. Hamm.
EIN: 742900450

52562
Verna Lilly Dodd Scholarship Trust
c/o Bank One, Louisiana, N.A.
P.O. Box 2050
Fort Worth, TX 76113
Application address: c/o W.T. Blackwell, Mer Rouge Methodist Church, P.O. Box 400, Mer Rouge, LA 71261

Established in 1986 in LA.
Financial data (yr. ended 05/31/00): Grants paid, $14,000; assets, $281,573 (M); expenditures, $17,820; qualifying distributions, $13,928.
Limitations: Giving primarily to residents of Morehouse Parish, LA.
Application information: Application form required.
Trustee: Bank One Louisiana, N.A.
EIN: 726118421
Codes: GTI

52563
Hand Foundation
8500 Cypresswood Dr., Ste. 201
Spring, TX 77379

Established in 1984 in TX.
Donor(s): Donald E. Hand, Mandolin Investments, Inc.
Financial data (yr. ended 12/31/01): Grants paid, $14,000; assets, $554,468 (M); gifts received, $32,000; expenditures, $16,177; qualifying distributions, $14,000.
Limitations: Applications not accepted. Giving primarily in Houston, TX.
Application information: Contributes only to pre-selected organizations.
Trustees: Donald E. Hand, Donald E. Hand, Jr.
EIN: 760114173

52564
Frank & Marilyn Richardson Family Foundation
2001 Kirby, Ste. 504
Houston, TX 77019

Established in 1998 in TX.
Donor(s): Frank H. Richardson.
Financial data (yr. ended 04/30/01): Grants paid, $14,000; assets, $659,832 (M); gifts received, $100,000; expenditures, $28,711; qualifying distributions, $14,000.
Limitations: Applications not accepted. Giving primarily in Houston, TX.
Application information: Contributes only to pre-selected organizations.
Officer and Directors:* Frank H. Richardson,* Pres.; Marilyn D. Richardson, Scott H. Richardson, Stacey Richardson.
EIN: 760538271

52565
Schopfer Charitable Trust
P.O. Box 154358
Waco, TX 76715 (254) 829-0064

Established in 1997 in TX.
Financial data (yr. ended 12/31/01): Grants paid, $14,000; assets, $245,400 (M); expenditures, $19,230; qualifying distributions, $14,000.
Limitations: Applications not accepted.
Application information: Contributes only to pre-selected organizations.
Trustee: Curtis L. Brown.
EIN: 746443812

52566
Wicker-Weir Foundation
P.O. Box 64980-850
Dallas, TX 75206-0980 (214) 528-0321
Contact: Jay A. Comstock, Mgr.

Established in 1990 in TX.
Donor(s): Dan R. Weir, Martha J. Weir.
Financial data (yr. ended 12/31/00): Grants paid, $14,000; assets, $303,852 (M); expenditures, $15,332; qualifying distributions, $14,000.
Limitations: Giving primarily in Dallas, TX.
Application information: The foundation generally selects recipients from approximately 30 pre-selected organizations.
Officers and Directors:* Dan R. Weir,* Pres.; J. Blake Weir,* V.P.; J. Brad Weir,* V.P.; J. Brooks Weir,* V.P.; Martha J. Weir,* Secy.; Jay A. Comstock, Mgr.
EIN: 752293062

52567
Sheppard Community Foundation of Navarro County, Texas
(Formerly E. M. Sheppard Foundation)
c/o Joe B. Brooks
Rte. 1, Box 289
Frost, TX 76641-9759

Established in 1996 in TX.
Donor(s): E.M. Sheppard.‡
Financial data (yr. ended 12/31/01): Grants paid, $13,800; assets, $397,524 (M); gifts received, $45,043; expenditures, $15,723; qualifying distributions, $13,800.
Limitations: Applications not accepted. Giving primarily in Frost, TX.
Application information: Contributes only to pre-selected organizations.
Officers: Joe B. Brooks, Pres. and Treas.; Myra Lee McCain, Secy.
Directors: Jimmie L. Alexander, Ronald D. Brown, Sandra R. Dowd, Clifford E. Williams.
EIN: 742782886

52568
Paul and Carol Horvitz Foundation
150 Sugarberry Cir.
Houston, TX 77024 (713) 784-5086
Contact: Paul Horvitz, Pres.

Established in 1999 in TX.
Donor(s): Paul Horvitz, Carol Horvitz.
Financial data (yr. ended 05/31/02): Grants paid, $13,760; assets, $214,626 (M); gifts received, $202,250; expenditures, $19,175; qualifying distributions, $13,760.
Limitations: Giving primarily in TX.
Officers: Paul Horvitz, Pres.; Steven Horvitz, V.P.; Carol Horvitz, Secy.; Marica Cohen, Treas.
EIN: 311660848

52569
Smith Family Foundation
c/o Sidney R. Smith
207 S. Washington
Livingston, TX 77351-3442

Established in 1993 in TX.
Donor(s): Edythe A. Smith, Sidney R. Smith.
Financial data (yr. ended 12/31/01): Grants paid, $13,750; assets, $763,447 (M); expenditures, $16,259; qualifying distributions, $13,750.
Limitations: Applications not accepted. Giving primarily in Livingston, TX.
Application information: Contributes only to pre-selected organizations.
Trustees: Edythe A. Smith, Fred M. Smith, Robert M. Smith, Sidney R. Smith.
EIN: 766084284

52570
Wakefield Family Foundation
6151 Los Felinos Cir.
El Paso, TX 79912
Application address: 2829 Montana Ave., Ste. 201, El Paso, TX 79903, tel.: (915) 566-9305
Contact: Betty Ruth Wakefield, Tr.

Established in 1984 in TX.
Donor(s): Betty Ruth Wakefield.
Financial data (yr. ended 06/30/02): Grants paid, $13,700; assets, $250,688 (M); expenditures, $14,948; qualifying distributions, $13,700.
Limitations: Giving primarily in the El Paso, TX, area.
Trustees: Sallie Baggett, Adair Margo, Betty Ruth Wakefield, Cornelius William Wakefield.
EIN: 742386522

52571
Abagail Robertson Trust
c/o Bank of America
P.O. Box 831041
Dallas, TX 75283-1041
Application address: c/o Gene Jennings, P.O. Box 1681, Little Rock, AR 72203

Financial data (yr. ended 12/31/01): Grants paid, $13,550; assets, $362,820 (M); expenditures, $19,930; qualifying distributions, $13,550.
Limitations: Giving limited to AR.
Trustees: Mary L. Ratcliffe, Bank of America.
EIN: 716049864

52572
Karl A. Nielson and Karen J. Nielson Scholarship Fund
c/o First State Bank
P.O. Box 247
Spearman, TX 79081
Application addresses: c/o Glenda Guthrie, Counselor, Spearman High School, 403 E. 11th St., Spearman, TX 79081, tel.: (806) 659-2584; c/o Kathy Potts, Principal, Gruver High School, P.O. Box 747, Gruver, TX 79040, tel.: (806) 733-2477; c/o Bill Anderson, Principal, Tekamah-Herman Community Schools, 112 N. 13th, Tekamah, NE 68601

Financial data (yr. ended 12/31/01): Grants paid, $13,535; assets, $220,616 (M); expenditures, $16,055; qualifying distributions, $15,677.
Limitations: Giving limited to Tekamah, NE, and Gruver and Spearman, TX.
Application information: Application form required.
Trustee: First State Bank.
EIN: 752065409
Codes: GTI

52573
Acid Maltase Deficiency Association, Inc.
P.O. Box 700248
San Antonio, TX 78270-0248

Established in 1995 in TX.
Donor(s): Marylyn M. House, Randall H. House.
Financial data (yr. ended 09/30/01): Grants paid, $13,500; assets, $135,083 (M); gifts received, $38,985; expenditures, $15,415; qualifying distributions, $15,415; giving activities include $660 for programs.
Limitations: Applications not accepted. Giving on a national basis.
Application information: Contributes only to pre-selected organizations.
Officers and Directors:* Randall H. House,* Pres.; Mark H. Miller,* V.P.; Marylyn M. House,* Secy.-Treas.
EIN: 742760695

52574
Mildred L. Ayres Trust
c/o Bank of America
P.O. Box 831041
Dallas, TX 75283-1041
Application address: 1200 Main St., 14th Fl., Kansas City, MO 64105, tel.: (816) 979-7481
Contact: David P. Ross, Sr. V.P., Bank of America

Financial data (yr. ended 12/31/01): Grants paid, $13,500; assets, $324,867 (M); expenditures, $17,650; qualifying distributions, $16,078.
Limitations: Giving limited to residents of MO.
Application information: Application form required.
Trustee: Bank of America.
EIN: 446008191
Codes: GTI

52575
Arthur M. Miller Fund
c/o Bank of America
P.O. Box 831041
Dallas, TX 75283-1041 (214) 209-3364

Established in 1990 in KS.
Financial data (yr. ended 12/31/01): Grants paid, $13,500; assets, $437,863 (M); expenditures, $18,167; qualifying distributions, $14,962.
Limitations: Giving primarily in Wichita, KS.
Application information: Application form not required.
Trustee: Bank of America.
EIN: 481077714
Codes: GTI

52576
Gardner W. Heidrick, Jr. and Joan G. Heidrick Foundation
10430 Memorial Dr.
Houston, TX 77024
Contact: Garnder W. Heidrick, Jr., Pres.

Established in 1998.
Donor(s): Gardner W. Heidrick, Jr.
Financial data (yr. ended 04/30/02): Grants paid, $13,445; assets, $166,839 (M); expenditures, $15,181; qualifying distributions, $13,445.
Limitations: Giving primarily in IL and TX.
Officer: Gardner W. Heidrick, Jr., Pres.
Director: Joan Heidrick.
EIN: 760538057

52577
Edwin M. Jones Foundation, Inc.
Milam Bldg.
115 E. Travis St., Ste. 404
San Antonio, TX 78205-1604

Financial data (yr. ended 12/31/01): Grants paid, $13,445; assets, $258,735 (M); gifts received, $500; expenditures, $13,560; qualifying distributions, $13,445.
Limitations: Applications not accepted. Giving limited to San Antonio, TX.
Application information: Contributes only to pre-selected organizations.
Officers: Van Lewis, Pres.; E.O. Sarratt III, V.P. and Treas.; B.F. Youngblood III, Secy.
EIN: 746036562

52578
Carl B. Rechner Foundation
c/o Bank of America
P.O. Box 831041
Dallas, TX 75283-1041
Application address: 1200 Main St., 14th Fl., Kansas City, MO 64105, tel.: (816) 979-7481
Contact: David P. Ross, Sr. V.P., Bank of America

Financial data (yr. ended 12/31/01): Grants paid, $13,400; assets, $238,184 (M); expenditures, $18,972; qualifying distributions, $15,347.
Limitations: Giving primarily in Boston, MA.
Trustee: Bank of America.
EIN: 446012403

52579
J. W. Vandeveer Foundation, Inc.
1825 W. Mockingbird Ln.
Dallas, TX 75235

Donor(s): J.W. Vandeveer.
Financial data (yr. ended 12/31/01): Grants paid, $13,350; assets, $453 (M); gifts received, $13,000; expenditures, $13,486; qualifying distributions, $13,350.
Limitations: Applications not accepted. Giving primarily in TX.
Application information: Contributes only to pre-selected organizations.
Officer and Directors:* J.W. Vandeveer,* Pres.; E.J. Chupik, Steve Jackson.
EIN: 751710672

52580
Wolens Federation
513 E. 7th Ave.
P.O. Box 2235
Corsicana, TX 75151-2235 (903) 874-2961
Contact: Dean Milkes, Pres.

Financial data (yr. ended 08/31/99): Grants paid, $13,325; assets, $460,250 (M); gifts received, $2,400; expenditures, $20,459; qualifying distributions, $13,325.
Limitations: Giving primarily in TX.
Officers: Dean Milkes, Pres.; Ethan Milkes, V.P. and Treas.; Marjorie Milkes, Secy.
EIN: 756036674

52581
Paul & Alta Cates Religious Foundation Trust
c/o Plains National Bank
P.O. Box 271
Lubbock, TX 79408-1469

Donor(s): Alta Bowers Cates, Paul Cates Trust.
Financial data (yr. ended 12/31/01): Grants paid, $13,310; assets, $90,575 (M); gifts received, $6,000; expenditures, $14,694; qualifying distributions, $13,964.
Limitations: Giving primarily in TX.

Application information: Application form not required.
Trustees: Alta Bowers Cates, Alta Ada Cates Williams, Plains National Bank.
EIN: 756017531

52582
The Dixie and Cedric Wenger 1994 Foundation
8610 N. New Braunfels Ave., Ste. 101
San Antonio, TX 78217 (210) 829-1300
Contact: Robert A. Martin, Tr.

Established in 1994 in TX.
Donor(s): Olga Starnes Kuhn Wenger.
Financial data (yr. ended 12/31/01): Grants paid, $13,300; assets, $218,188 (M); expenditures, $16,361; qualifying distributions, $13,300.
Limitations: Giving primarily in TX.
Application information: Application form not required.
Trustees: David J. Doherty, Gloria Lamascus, Robert A. Martin, Sue C. Ortman, Olga Starnes Kuhn Wenger.
EIN: 742719361

52583
Elfarouq Foundation
2800 Post Oak Blvd.
5310 Transco Tower
Houston, TX 77056
Application address: c/o Admin. Office, 1207 Conrad Sauer, Houston, TX 77043, tel.: (713) 465-2020

Established in 1997 in TX.
Donor(s): Omar Megerisi, Tristar Holdings, Inc.
Financial data (yr. ended 12/31/00): Grants paid, $13,267; assets, $4,741,975 (M); gifts received, $968,604; expenditures, $458,658; qualifying distributions, $458,658.
Application information: Application form required.
Officers and Directors:* Omar Megerisi,* Pres.; Masaud Baaba,* V.P.; Edward Hartline,* Secy.-Treas.; Hakeem Olajuwon.
EIN: 760527335

52584
Helen R. Kahn Endowment Trust
c/o Bank of America
P.O. Box 831041
Dallas, TX 75283-1041
Application address: c/o Sandra K. Walker, Tr. Off., Bank of America, P.O. Box 1681, Little Rock, AR 72203

Financial data (yr. ended 12/31/00): Grants paid, $13,266; assets, $1 (M); expenditures, $14,850; qualifying distributions, $13,266.
Limitations: Giving limited to AR.
Trustee: Bank of America.
EIN: 716082075

52585
Jacquite L. Patterson Memorial Scholarship Trust Fund
1507 Alta Mira Dr.
Killeen, TX 76541-8247
Application address: c/o Scholarship Comm., Killeen High School, Killeen, TX 76541

Established in 1989 in TX.
Donor(s): Jacquite L. Patterson.‡
Financial data (yr. ended 06/30/00): Grants paid, $13,169; assets, $13,325 (M); expenditures, $13,325; qualifying distributions, $13,325.
Limitations: Giving limited to residents of Killeen, TX.
Application information: Application form not required.
Trustee: Willa Jean Budden.

EIN: 746370889

52586
Dougherty Carr Foundation
P.O. Box 60010
Corpus Christi, TX 78466-0010
(361) 852-6472
Contact: May D. King, Tr.

Established in 1991 in TX as successor to Dougherty-Carr Arts Foundation.
Donor(s): May D. King.
Financial data (yr. ended 12/31/01): Grants paid, $13,154; assets, $345,431 (M); gifts received, $104,272; expenditures, $19,538; qualifying distributions, $13,154.
Limitations: Giving in the U.S., primarily in Corpus Christi, TX.
Trustee: May D. King.
EIN: 742607564

52587
David C. DeMartini Foundation
11714 Spriggs Way
Houston, TX 77024

Established in 1999 in TX.
Donor(s): David C. DeMartini.
Financial data (yr. ended 12/31/01): Grants paid, $13,000; assets, $51,927 (M); expenditures, $13,776; qualifying distributions, $13,000.
Limitations: Applications not accepted.
Application information: Contributes only to pre-selected organizations.
Officers and Directors:* David C. DeMartini,* Pres. and Treas.; Carol D. Moss,* Secy.; Joan Bisagno.
EIN: 760610810

52588
Marvy Finger Family Foundation
99 Detering St., Ste. 200
Houston, TX 77007

Established in 1999 in TX.
Donor(s): Marvy A. Finger.
Financial data (yr. ended 12/31/00): Grants paid, $13,000; assets, $1,016,155 (M); gifts received, $750,453; expenditures, $25,000; qualifying distributions, $13,000.
Limitations: Applications not accepted.
Application information: Contributes only to pre-selected organizations.
Officers: Marvy A. Finger, Pres. and Treas.; Jill F. Jewett, V.P.; Gordon Pilmer, Secy.
EIN: 760625865

52589
Garitty Charity Association
c/o Citizens National Bank
400 W. Collin St.
Corsicana, TX 75110 (903) 874-1700

Financial data (yr. ended 03/31/02): Grants paid, $13,000; assets, $567,152 (M); expenditures, $16,351; qualifying distributions, $13,000.
Limitations: Giving primarily in Corsicana, TX.
Officers: William Clarkson, Chair.; Embry Ferguson, Vice-Chair.; Lynn Sanders, Secy.
Trustees: John Smith, John B. Stroud.
EIN: 237161021

52590
Gratitude Foundation
(Formerly The Fisher Peeples Foundation)
P.O. Box 1669
Austin, TX 78767-1669

Financial data (yr. ended 12/31/01): Grants paid, $13,000; assets, $285,670 (M); expenditures, $17,170; qualifying distributions, $13,000.
Officer: Sharon G. Jones.

EIN: 742834026

52591
Green Umbrella Corporation
416 Main St.
Kerrville, TX 78028 (830) 896-5688
Contact: Lorrie Ferris, Dir.

Established in 2000 in TX.
Donor(s): Lorrie Ferris.
Financial data (yr. ended 12/31/01): Grants paid, $13,000; assets, $214,549 (M); expenditures, $20,735; qualifying distributions, $17,759.
Limitations: Giving primarily in TX.
Directors: Helen Eisaman, Lorrie Ferris, Bertha Templeton.
EIN: 237385847

52592
Vivian Holmes Charitable Trust
c/o Frost National Bank, Trust Dept.
P.O. Box 2950
San Antonio, TX 78299-2950
Contact: Linda Namestnik, Trust Off., Frost National Bank

Donor(s): Vivian Holmes.‡
Financial data (yr. ended 11/30/01): Grants paid, $13,000; assets, $917,254 (M); expenditures, $22,680; qualifying distributions, $13,000.
Limitations: Giving limited to TX.
Trustee: Frost National Bank.
EIN: 746267294

52593
Wallie Lock Charitable Foundation
1901 Dawn Dr.
Georgetown, TX 78628-3303 (512) 477-9535
Contact: James A. Porfirio, Tr.

Established in 1991 in TX.
Financial data (yr. ended 12/31/01): Grants paid, $13,000; assets, $471,174 (M); expenditures, $21,132; qualifying distributions, $13,000.
Limitations: Giving primarily in TX.
Trustees: Kenneth A. Jones, James A. Porfirio, J.D. Thomas.
EIN: 742591783

52594
Daniel Jackson Mckenzie Scholarship Foundation
1445 Ross Ave., LB 224
Dallas, TX 75202-2812

Established in 1998 in TX.
Financial data (yr. ended 12/31/01): Grants paid, $13,000; assets, $303,243 (M); expenditures, $16,814; qualifying distributions, $13,000.
Limitations: Applications not accepted.
Application information: Contributes only to pre-selected organizations.
Trustee: Wells Fargo Bank, N.A.
EIN: 756063653

52595
The Dick and Judy Perkins Charitable Foundation
10855 Beinhorn Rd.
Houston, TX 77024-3000 (713) 783-7880
Contact: Richard Douglas Perkins, Pres.

Established in 1996 in TX.
Donor(s): Judith W. Perkins, Richard Douglas Perkins.
Financial data (yr. ended 12/31/01): Grants paid, $13,000; assets, $160,383 (M); gifts received, $15,800; expenditures, $17,080; qualifying distributions, $13,000.
Limitations: Giving primarily in Houston, TX.
Application information: Application form required.

52595—TEXAS

Officers and Directors:* Richard Douglas Perkins,* Pres. and Treas.; Judith Ann Watson Perkins,* V.P. and Secy.; Keith Douglas Perkins, Stephanie Celeste Perkins.
EIN: 760514006

52596
Henry C. Schulte and Virginia M. Schulte Foundation
34179 FM 1577
San Benito, TX 78586

Established in 1998 in TX.
Donor(s): Henry C. Schulte, Virginia M. Schulte.
Financial data (yr. ended 12/31/01): Grants paid, $13,000; assets, $295,572 (M); expenditures, $14,054; qualifying distributions, $13,000.
Limitations: Applications not accepted.
Application information: Contributes only to pre-selected organizations.
Officers: Henry C. Schulte, Chair.; John Stephen Randall, Jr., Pres.; Virginia M. Schulte, Secy.-Treas.
EIN: 742882225

52597
Sheppard Foundation
c/o Darrell W. Cain
5580 Peterson Ln., Ste. 250
Dallas, TX 75240

Established in 1996 in TX and FL.
Donor(s): Daisy G. Sheppard, Stanley A. Sheppard, Marcia Sheppard.
Financial data (yr. ended 11/30/01): Grants paid, $13,000; assets, $213,246 (M); expenditures, $15,795; qualifying distributions, $13,000.
Limitations: Applications not accepted. Giving primarily in AL and FL.
Application information: Contributes only to pre-selected organizations.
Officers and Directors:* Stanley A. Sheppard,* Pres.; Marcia Sheppard,* Secy.-Treas.; Lee L. Sheppard, Stanley A. Sheppard, Jr.
EIN: 752679645

52598
D., G., R. & R. Taylor Family Foundation, Inc.
1418 Country Club Rd.
Arlington, TX 76013

Established in 1999 in TX.
Donor(s): G. Dale Taylor.
Financial data (yr. ended 12/31/01): Grants paid, $13,000; assets, $29,073 (M); expenditures, $13,598; qualifying distributions, $13,000.
Limitations: Applications not accepted.
Application information: Contributes only to pre-selected organizations.
Director: G. Dale Taylor.
EIN: 752851894

52599
El Sacrificio
P.O. Box 441
Pearsall, TX 78061

Financial data (yr. ended 12/31/01): Grants paid, $12,827; assets, $257,025 (M); expenditures, $90,829; qualifying distributions, $12,827.
Officers: Modesta A. Salazar, Pres.; Juan Davila, V.P.; Anita Garza, Secy.; Simon Salazar, Treas.
EIN: 741926791
Codes: TN

52600
Keith M. Orme Charitable Foundation, Inc.
c/o Keith M. Orme
112 Geneseo Rd.
San Antonio, TX 78209-5912

Established in 1996 in TX.
Donor(s): Annette W. Orme.

Financial data (yr. ended 12/31/01): Grants paid, $12,805; assets, $203,893 (M); expenditures, $17,088; qualifying distributions, $12,805.
Limitations: Applications not accepted. Giving primarily in San Antonio, TX.
Application information: Contributes only to pre-selected organizations.
Officers: Keith M. Orme, Pres.; Pat V. Orme, V.P.
Director: R. Marlene Merritt.
EIN: 742772038

52601
John Herman Hasenbeck Charitable Trust
500 Elizabeth Rd.
San Antonio, TX 78209   (210) 225-5964
Contact: George A. Olson, Tr.

Financial data (yr. ended 12/31/01): Grants paid, $12,750; assets, $880,369 (M); expenditures, $55,525; qualifying distributions, $55,525.
Limitations: Giving primarily in Bexar County, TX.
Trustee: George A. Olson.
EIN: 746327096

52602
Kercheville Foundation
P.O. Box 696010
San Antonio, TX 78269-6010

Donor(s): Joe B. Kercheville, Ann E. Kercheville.
Financial data (yr. ended 12/31/01): Grants paid, $12,735; assets, $318,825 (M); gifts received, $70,111; expenditures, $17,896; qualifying distributions, $12,735.
Limitations: Applications not accepted.
Application information: Contributes only to pre-selected organizations.
Director: Ann E. Kercheville.
EIN: 742863080

52603
Martha Jane & James Edward Anthony Foundation, Inc.
7900 Monticello Dr.
Granbury, TX 76049

Donor(s): James E. Anthony.
Financial data (yr. ended 12/31/00): Grants paid, $12,712; assets, $449,629 (M); gifts received, $31,195; expenditures, $18,867; qualifying distributions, $12,357.
Limitations: Applications not accepted. Giving primarily in TX.
Application information: Contributes only to pre-selected organizations.
Officers: Martha Jane Anthony, Pres.; James E. Anthony, V.P.
EIN: 237025284

52604
The TCB Charitable Trust
19307 Puget Ln.
Spring, TX 77388

Established in 1997 in TX.
Financial data (yr. ended 12/31/99): Grants paid, $12,682; assets, $203,150 (M); gifts received, $28,310; expenditures, $13,275; qualifying distributions, $17,774.
Limitations: Applications not accepted.
Application information: Contributes only to pre-selected organizations.
Trustee: Troy C. Bonin.
EIN: 766119755

52605
Theodore H. & Annette G. Strauss Foundation
c/o Theodore H. Strauss
5914 Desco Dr.
Dallas, TX 75225-1603

Established in 1997 in TX.

Donor(s): Theodore H. Strauss, Annette G. Strauss.
Financial data (yr. ended 06/30/01): Grants paid, $12,600; assets, $561,735 (M); gifts received, $10,239; expenditures, $15,925; qualifying distributions, $12,600.
Limitations: Applications not accepted. Giving primarily in Dallas, TX.
Application information: Contributes only to pre-selected organizations.
Officer: Theodore H. Strauss, Pres.
EIN: 752738391

52606
Westheimer Foundation, Inc.
4700 Kirby Dr.
Houston, TX 77098-5004

Financial data (yr. ended 12/31/01): Grants paid, $12,580; assets, $12,618 (M); expenditures, $12,682; qualifying distributions, $12,580.
Limitations: Applications not accepted.
Application information: Contributes only to pre-selected organizations.
Officers: Ben Hurwitz, Pres.; Barry Weinberger, V.P. and Secy.
EIN: 746083139

52607
Ace World Foundation
10200 Jacksboro Hwy.
Fort Worth, TX 76135

Established in 2000 in TX.
Financial data (yr. ended 12/31/01): Grants paid, $12,500; assets, $14,517 (M); gifts received, $20,971; expenditures, $12,500; qualifying distributions, $12,500.
Limitations: Applications not accepted.
Application information: Contributes only to pre-selected organizations.
Officers: Linda S. Ghanemi, Pres.; Melissa Kroll, Secy.
Directors: Linda Cornwell, Nancy Romo, Robert D. Vought.
EIN: 752853030

52608
The Gladys D. Bevil Charitable Trust
1150 N. 11th St.
Beaumont, TX 77702-1207   (409) 838-3755
Contact: Larry L. Mills, Tr.

Established in 1998 in TX.
Donor(s): Gladys D. Bevil.
Financial data (yr. ended 06/30/01): Grants paid, $12,500; assets, $578,984 (M); gifts received, $50,000; expenditures, $26,115; qualifying distributions, $12,500.
Trustees: Bettye Cook, Claude J. Herpin, Larry L. Mills.
EIN: 766138930

52609
Moshana Foundation
P.O. Box 9788
Austin, TX 78766-9788

Donor(s): Milton T. Smith, Helen G. Smith.
Financial data (yr. ended 06/30/01): Grants paid, $12,500; assets, $464,534 (M); gifts received, $35,050; expenditures, $17,286; qualifying distributions, $12,500.
Limitations: Applications not accepted. Giving primarily in Austin, TX.
Application information: Contributes only to pre-selected organizations.
Officers and Directors:* Milton T. Smith,* Chair. and Pres.; Helen G. Smith,* Secy.-Treas.; Paul F. Gardner, Tina S. Gardner, Todd Gardner, Brian Karotkin, Leslie Karotkin, Lonnie S. Karotkin, Michael Karotkin.

EIN: 237022232

52610
The Joseph Bailey Obering Foundation
8117 Preston Rd., Ste. 520
Dallas, TX 75225 (214) 378-6642

Established in 1991 in TX.
Donor(s): Joseph B. Obering.
Financial data (yr. ended 12/31/01): Grants paid, $12,500; assets, $406,700 (M); gifts received, $266,502; expenditures, $15,091; qualifying distributions, $12,500.
Limitations: Applications not accepted.
Application information: Contributes only to pre-selected organizations.
Officers and Directors:* Joseph B. Obering,* Pres.; Guy Dietrich,* Secy.; Earl Fain III,* Treas.
EIN: 752369400

52611
Power Service Products Foundation
c/o Eddie M. Kramer
513 Peaster Hwy.
Weatherford, TX 76086 (817) 599-9486

Established in 1997 in TX. Classified as a private operating foundation in 1998.
Donor(s): Power Service Products, Inc.
Financial data (yr. ended 12/31/01): Grants paid, $12,500; assets, $151 (M); gifts received, $12,730; expenditures, $12,727; qualifying distributions, $12,525.
Limitations: Applications not accepted.
Application information: Contributes only to pre-selected organizations.
Officers: Eddie M. Kramer, Pres. and Treas.; Patricia A. Kramer, V.P.
Directors: Amanda C. Kramer, Jeffrey J. Kramer, Ruth B. Swain.
EIN: 752693125
Codes: CS

52612
The Julie & John Thornton Family Foundation
701 Brazos St., Ste. 1400
Austin, TX 78701 (512) 485-1900
Contact: John Thornton, Pres., and Julie Thornton, V.P.

Established in 2000 in TX.
Donor(s): Julie Thornton, John Thornton.
Financial data (yr. ended 12/31/01): Grants paid, $12,500; assets, $274,909 (M); gifts received, $3,600; expenditures, $14,760; qualifying distributions, $12,500.
Application information: Application form not required.
Officers: John Thornton, Pres. and Treas.; Julie Thornton, V.P. and Secy.
Trustee: Blaine Wesner.
EIN: 742945416

52613
The Joe & Mary Upshaw Family Foundation
651 E. Highland St.
Southlake, TX 76092-8681

Established in 1996.
Donor(s): Mary Upshaw.
Financial data (yr. ended 12/31/00): Grants paid, $12,500; assets, $213,123 (M); expenditures, $16,022; qualifying distributions, $12,500.
Limitations: Applications not accepted. Giving on a national basis.
Application information: Contributes only to pre-selected organizations.
Trustees: Mary Jo Milner, Hugh Gene Upshaw, Mary Upshaw, Richard Evermond Upshaw.
EIN: 752685047

52614
Charles Warnken, Sr. Memorial College Scholarship Fund
P.O. Drawer B
Pleasanton, TX 78064
Application address: P.O. Box 276, Poth, TX 78147
Contact: Catherine W. Bertrand, Mgr.

Financial data (yr. ended 06/30/01): Grants paid, $12,500; assets, $177,020 (M); expenditures, $16,466; qualifying distributions, $12,500.
Limitations: Giving limited to Poth, TX.
Officers: Catherine W. Bertrand, Mgr.; Carol W. Jung, Mgr.; Charles H. Warnken, Jr., Mgr.; James V. Warnken, Mgr.
EIN: 742213880

52615
John 3:16 Frontier Mission
P.O. Box 1397
Mission, TX 78573 (956) 585-1292
Contact: Ken Esau, Pres.

Donor(s): Ken Esau.
Financial data (yr. ended 12/31/01): Grants paid, $12,490; assets, $82,441 (M); gifts received, $13,361; expenditures, $12,542; qualifying distributions, $12,459.
Limitations: Giving primarily in TX.
Officers and Trustees:* Ken Esau,* Pres.; Paul Wohlgemuth, V.P.; George Carpenter,* Secy.; Duane Gibson,* Treas.; Ron Petsch.
EIN: 742399991

52616
Max and Dorothy F. Baggerly Charitable Trust
50 St. Andrews Dr.
Amarillo, TX 79124

Established in 1997.
Donor(s): Dorothy F. Baggerly, Max W. Baggerly.
Financial data (yr. ended 12/31/01): Grants paid, $12,475; assets, $1,483 (M); expenditures, $12,475; qualifying distributions, $12,295.
Limitations: Applications not accepted. Giving primarily in TX.
Application information: Contributes only to pre-selected organizations.
Trustees: Dorothy F. Baggerly, Max W. Baggerly.
EIN: 752682175

52617
The Blackwell Foundation
5606 Cavanaugh St.
Houston, TX 77021-3802 (713) 643-6577
Contact: L.D. Blackwell, Mgr.

Established in 1999 in TX.
Donor(s): L.D. Blackwell.
Financial data (yr. ended 05/31/01): Grants paid, $12,470; assets, $333,260 (M); expenditures, $23,404; qualifying distributions, $12,470.
Application information: Application form required.
Officer and Trustees:* L.D. Blackwell,* Mgr.; Karen Blackwell.
EIN: 760610529

52618
The Bozeman Foundation
6161 Savoy Dr., Ste. 222
Houston, TX 77036-3326

Donor(s): Quest Petrochemical Co.
Financial data (yr. ended 05/31/02): Grants paid, $12,435; assets, $142,021 (M); expenditures, $14,459; qualifying distributions, $12,435.
Limitations: Applications not accepted. Giving primarily in Washington, DC, and TX.
Application information: Contributes only to pre-selected organizations.
Officers: Beth Bozeman, Pres.; Brett Bozeman, V.P.; Bryan Bozeman, Secy.-Treas.
EIN: 760312732

52619
Richard & Sandy Beckert Foundation
14901 Quorum Dr., Ste. 850
Dallas, TX 75240

Financial data (yr. ended 12/31/00): Grants paid, $12,400; assets, $163,432 (M); expenditures, $12,550; qualifying distributions, $12,400.
Officers: Richard Beckert, Pres.; Sandra Beckert, Secy.
EIN: 752769082

52620
Faulkner Family Foundation
700 Crystal Mountain Dr.
Austin, TX 78733-6117

Established in 1998 in TX.
Donor(s): Von D. Faulkner, Dorsi F. Faulkner.
Financial data (yr. ended 12/31/01): Grants paid, $12,400; assets, $39,510 (M); expenditures, $12,891; qualifying distributions, $12,400.
Limitations: Applications not accepted.
Application information: Contributes only to pre-selected organizations.
Trustees: Dorsi F. Faulkner, Von D. Faulkner.
EIN: 742871792

52621
Logos Foundation
P.O. Box 2281
Wimberley, TX 78676

Financial data (yr. ended 12/31/00): Grants paid, $12,338; assets, $330,956 (M); expenditures, $14,886; qualifying distributions, $12,338.
Limitations: Applications not accepted.
Application information: Contributes only to pre-selected organizations.
Officers and Directors:* James E. Chisholm,* Pres.; Joan F. Chisholm,* Secy.-Treas.
EIN: 742883369

52622
The Jorge and Guadalupe Rodriguez Family Foundation
1949 W. Paisano
El Paso, TX 79922

Established in 1995 in TX.
Donor(s): Guadalupe Rodriguez, Jorge Rodriguez.
Financial data (yr. ended 12/31/00): Grants paid, $12,300; assets, $136,781 (M); expenditures, $22,388; qualifying distributions, $12,300.
Limitations: Applications not accepted. Giving primarily in El Paso, TX.
Application information: Contributes only to pre-selected organizations.
Officers: Guadalupe Rodriguez, Pres.; Jorge Rodriguez, V.P.; Blake Barrow, Secy.-Treas.
EIN: 742761446

52623
Carroll and John B. Goodman Foundation
2550 North Loop W., Ste. 750
Houston, TX 77092

Established in 1992 in TX.
Donor(s): John B. Goodman, Carroll R. Goodman.
Financial data (yr. ended 06/30/01): Grants paid, $12,250; assets, $5,903 (M); expenditures, $17,370; qualifying distributions, $12,114.
Limitations: Applications not accepted. Giving primarily in Houston, TX.
Application information: Contributes only to pre-selected organizations.

52623—TEXAS

Officers: John B. Goodman, Pres.; Carroll R. Goodman, Secy.
EIN: 760411893

52624
Braverman Family Charitable Foundation
1100 N. Main St.
San Antonio, TX 78212

Established in 1999 in TX.
Donor(s): Sheldon P. Braverman, Phyllis Braverman.
Financial data (yr. ended 12/31/00): Grants paid, $12,244; assets, $926,846 (M); gifts received, $2,750; expenditures, $20,166; qualifying distributions, $12,244.
Limitations: Applications not accepted. Giving primarily in NJ, NY, and TX.
Application information: Contributes only to pre-selected organizations.
Officers and Directors:* Sheldon P. Braverman,* Pres. and Treas.; Phyllis Braverman,* Secy.; Susan Gail B. Blumenthal, Richard M. Braverman, Stuart E. Braverman.
EIN: 742940220

52625
Beulah Thornton Leith Charitable Trust
c/o Bank of America
P.O. Box 831041
Dallas, TX 75283-1041

Established in 1995 in TX.
Financial data (yr. ended 06/30/01): Grants paid, $12,192; assets, $417,361 (M); expenditures, $18,455; qualifying distributions, $12,192.
Limitations: Applications not accepted.
Application information: Contributes only to pre-selected organizations.
Trustee: Bank of America.
EIN: 766051842

52626
James & Lillian Lockerd Foundation
c/o Citizens National Bank
400 W. Collins St.
Corsicana, TX 75110 (903) 872-1700
Contact: Lynn Sanders, Trust Off., Citizens National Bank

Financial data (yr. ended 12/31/01): Grants paid, $12,069; assets, $322,123 (M); expenditures, $15,490; qualifying distributions, $13,450.
Limitations: Applications not accepted.
Application information: Contributes only to pre-selected organizations.
Trustee: Citizens National Bank.
EIN: 756476031

52627
Delfina & Josefina Alexander Family Foundation
1620 Corpus Christi St.
Laredo, TX 78043

Established in 1998 in TX.
Donor(s): Delfina E. Alexander, Josefina A. Gonzalez.
Financial data (yr. ended 12/31/00): Grants paid, $12,000; assets, $258,169 (M); expenditures, $12,459; qualifying distributions, $12,000.
Limitations: Applications not accepted. Giving primarily in Laredo, TX.
Application information: Contributes only to pre-selected organizations.
Directors: Delfina E. Alexander, Josefina A. Gonzalez.
EIN: 742876837

52628
Apache Foundation
c/o Goerge J. Morgenthaler
2000 Post Oak Blvd., Ste. 100
Houston, TX 77056-4400

Established in 1960 in MN.
Donor(s): Apache Corporation, and subsidiaries.
Financial data (yr. ended 12/31/00): Grants paid, $12,000; assets, $285,342 (M); gifts received, $295,961; expenditures, $54,235; qualifying distributions, $79,679.
Limitations: Applications not accepted. Giving primarily in MN.
Application information: Contributes only to pre-selected organizations.
Officers and Directors:* Raymond Plank,* Chair.; G. Steven Farris,* Pres.; George J. Morgenthaler,* V.P. and Secy.; Roger B. Plank, V.P. and C.F.O.; Thomas L. Mitchell, V.P. and Cont.; Matthew W. Dundrea, V.P. and Treas.; Michael S. Bahorich, V.P.; Robert J. Dye, V.P.; Lisa A. Floyd, V.P.; Anthony R. Lentini, Jr., V.P.; Floyd R. Price, V.P.; Jon W. Sauer, V.P.; Daniel L. Schaeffer, V.P.; Cheri L. Peper, Secy.
EIN: 416031039
Codes: CS, CD

52629
Banks Charitable Trust
14827 Preston Rd., Ste. 605
Dallas, TX 75240

Financial data (yr. ended 12/31/00): Grants paid, $12,000; assets, $582,956 (M); gifts received, $190,784; expenditures, $46,784; qualifying distributions, $12,000.
Limitations: Applications not accepted. Giving primarily in TX.
Application information: Contributes only to pre-selected organizations.
Trustees: Joe Feagin, Sharon Feagin.
EIN: 756483645

52630
Rosalie & Joiner Cartwright, Jr. Foundation
306 Blalock Rd.
Houston, TX 77024-6515
Contact: Joiner Cartwright, Jr., Dir.

Established in 1994 in TX.
Financial data (yr. ended 12/31/01): Grants paid, $12,000; assets, $1,298,919 (M); gifts received, $13,403; expenditures, $20,884; qualifying distributions, $12,000.
Limitations: Giving on a national basis.
Directors: Bettie Cartwright, Joiner Cartwright, Jr., Gloria Hui.
EIN: 760460235

52631
Davis Family Foundation
5430 Ursula Ln.
Dallas, TX 75229

Established in 1998 in TX.
Donor(s): Howard Davis.
Financial data (yr. ended 12/31/01): Grants paid, $12,000; assets, $77,982 (M); gifts received, $7,500; expenditures, $12,373; qualifying distributions, $12,000.
Limitations: Giving primarily in MT.
Trustees: Howard Davis, Laurel Davis, Sharon Davis.
EIN: 311589361

52632
Robert K. Franklin, Jr. Foundation
c/o Olivia Dee Franklin
3831 Turtle Creek Blvd., Ste. 5A
Dallas, TX 75219-4411

Financial data (yr. ended 12/31/01): Grants paid, $12,000; assets, $235,178 (M); expenditures, $13,303; qualifying distributions, $12,000.
Limitations: Applications not accepted. Giving primarily in Houston, TX.
Application information: Contributes only to pre-selected organizations.
Officers: Olivia Dee Franklin, Pres. and Treas.; Irene Franklin White, V.P. and Secy.; Robert K. Franklin III, V.P.
EIN: 741480046

52633
Sol & Fannie Halff Memorial Fund
c/o Frost National Bank
P.O. Box 2950
San Antonio, TX 78299-2950
Contact: William Clyborne, V.P. and Trust Off., Frost National Bank

Financial data (yr. ended 12/31/01): Grants paid, $12,000; assets, $201,643 (M); expenditures, $15,269; qualifying distributions, $12,000.
Limitations: Giving primarily in San Antonio, TX.
Trustee: Frost National Bank.
EIN: 746032172

52634
Lewelling Family Foundation, Inc.
P.O. Box 253
Argyle, TX 76226-5310

Established in 1999.
Donor(s): Charles Lowelling, Eileen Lowelling.
Financial data (yr. ended 04/30/02): Grants paid, $12,000; assets, $194,660 (M); expenditures, $12,500; qualifying distributions, $12,000.
Limitations: Giving primarily in Dallas, TX.
Officers: Eileen Lewelling, Pres.; John Charles Lewelling, V.P.; James Hunter Lewelling, Secy.-Treas.
EIN: 752809951

52635
Thomas G. & Nancy J. Macrini Foundation
8607 Stable Crest Blvd.
Houston, TX 77024

Established in 2000 in TX.
Donor(s): Nancy J. Macrini, Thomas G. Macrini.
Financial data (yr. ended 12/31/01): Grants paid, $12,000; assets, $735,138 (M); gifts received, $721,073; expenditures, $14,816; qualifying distributions, $12,000.
Limitations: Applications not accepted. Giving primarily in Houston, TX.
Application information: Contributes only to pre-selected organizations.
Officers: Thomas G. Macrini, Pres.; Nancy J. Macrini, V.P. and Secy.
Director: John A. Macrini.
EIN: 760641778

52636
Mutual Benefit Foundation
P.O. Box 1089
Navasota, TX 77868-1089 (936) 894-2435
Contact: Willa Layne Lowe, Pres.

Financial data (yr. ended 12/31/00): Grants paid, $12,000; assets, $342,342 (M); expenditures, $19,354; qualifying distributions, $12,000.
Limitations: Giving primarily in TX.
Application information: Application form required.

IN THIS SECTION, WITHIN EACH STATE, FOUNDATIONS ARE LISTED IN DESCENDING ORDER BY TOTAL GRANTS PAID

Officers and Directors:* Willa Layne Lowe,* Pres.; Majorie Trimm,* Secy.-Treas.; Joe A. Airola, Mary Lou Epps, Clinton F. Morse.
EIN: 746001303

52637
Southeast Fort Worth Juvenile Enhancement Foundation
P.O. Box 15420
Fort Worth, TX 76119

Established in 2000 in TX.
Donor(s): Bruce Conti, Lee Ann Conti.
Financial data (yr. ended 12/31/01): Grants paid, $12,000; assets, $12,978 (M); expenditures, $14,750; qualifying distributions, $12,000.
Limitations: Giving primarily in Fort Worth, TX.
Officers and Directors:* Bruce Conti,* Pres.; Lee Ann Conti,* Secy.; Bob Conti.
EIN: 752889054

52638
The Jarrell and Shirley Rubinett Family Foundation
3004 Belmont Cir.
Austin, TX 78703

Established in 1995 in TX.
Donor(s): Jarrell D. Rubinett, Shirley A. Rubinett.
Financial data (yr. ended 11/30/01): Grants paid, $11,995; assets, $259,845 (M); expenditures, $13,851; qualifying distributions, $11,995.
Trustees: Benita G. Rubinett, Gordon M. Rubinett, Jarrell D. Rubinett, Lynn E. Rubinett, Shirley A. Rubinett.
EIN: 742767179

52639
Leila E. Webb Trust
P.O. Box 2857
Abilene, TX 79604

Financial data (yr. ended 12/31/00): Grants paid, $11,970; assets, $384,912 (M); expenditures, $17,130; qualifying distributions, $11,970.
Limitations: Applications not accepted. Giving primarily in TX.
Application information: Contributes only to pre-selected organizations.
Trustee: State National Bank.
EIN: 756534931

52640
The Mission Religious Charitable Trust
521 Delia Dr.
Longview, TX 75601

Donor(s): Keith Parker.
Financial data (yr. ended 12/31/00): Grants paid, $11,948; assets, $8,753 (M); expenditures, $12,068; qualifying distributions, $11,948.
Limitations: Giving primarily in Longview, TX.
Officer: Keith Parker, Mgr.
EIN: 752795919

52641
Worrall Foundation
6342 La Vista Dr.
Dallas, TX 75214

Established in 2000 in TX.
Donor(s): Jessie Elizabeth Mills.
Financial data (yr. ended 12/31/01): Grants paid, $11,905; assets, $223,596 (M); expenditures, $23,687; qualifying distributions, $11,905.
Limitations: Applications not accepted.
Application information: Contributes only to pre-selected organizations.
Officers and Directors:* Gerald Worrall III,* Pres.; Norma J. Worrall,* Secy.; Jan M. Worrall,* Treas.; Gerald Worrall II.
EIN: 752886782

52642
W. R. Hammond Foundation
c/o Wells Fargo Bank Texas, N.A.
P.O. Box 9129
Wichita Falls, TX 76308

Established in 1998 in TX.
Donor(s): W.R. Hammond Trust.
Financial data (yr. ended 12/31/00): Grants paid, $11,838; assets, $238,304 (M); expenditures, $12,840; qualifying distributions, $11,713.
Limitations: Giving primarily in TX and UT.
Application information: Unsolicited request for fund not accepted.
Trustee: Wells Fargo Bank Texas, N.A.
EIN: 756524028

52643
The Cherry Family Foundation
2326 River Rack Trail
Kingwood, TX 77345

Established in 2001 in DE.
Donor(s): Rhenn Cherry, Teresa Cherry.
Financial data (yr. ended 12/31/01): Grants paid, $11,750; assets, $2,940 (M); gifts received, $15,000; expenditures, $12,189; qualifying distributions, $11,750.
Limitations: Applications not accepted.
Application information: Contributes only to pre-selected organizations.
Directors: Rhenn Cherry, Teresa Cherry.
EIN: 760685876

52644
The Lyda Hill Foundation
1601 Elm St., Ste. 3400
Dallas, TX 75201-7254 (214) 922-1000
Contact: Michael E. Nugent, Secy.

Established in 1997 in TX.
Donor(s): Lyda Hill.
Financial data (yr. ended 11/30/01): Grants paid, $11,750; assets, $133,017 (M); gifts received, $20,000; expenditures, $23,792; qualifying distributions, $11,750.
Officers: Lyda Hill, Pres.; Graham McFarlane, V.P.; Michael E. Nugent, Secy.; Mike Cockrell, Treas.
EIN: 752708838

52645
Eric Harborne Foundation
P.O. Box 40647
Fort Worth, TX 76140-0647 (817) 790-3868
Contact: Brooks Bradley, C.E.O.

Established in 1999 in TX.
Donor(s): Eric G. Harborne.
Financial data (yr. ended 12/31/01): Grants paid, $11,749; assets, $174,084 (M); gifts received, $5,979; expenditures, $24,469; qualifying distributions, $11,749.
Officer: Brooks Bradley, C.E.O.
Directors: Mark Bradley, Eric G. Harborne.
EIN: 752814926

52646
The Bortunco Foundation
P.O. Box 14214
Houston, TX 77221-4214 (713) 799-1200
Contact: Gilbert M. Turner, Chair.

Financial data (yr. ended 07/31/01): Grants paid, $11,720; assets, $99,968 (M); gifts received, $500; expenditures, $12,000; qualifying distributions, $11,720.
Limitations: Giving primarily in Houston, TX.
Trustees: Gilbert M. Turner, Chair.; Dale Kornegay, Claydene K. Turner.
EIN: 746105634

52647
San Angelo National Community Foundation
(Formerly San Angelo Community Foundation)
301 W. Beauregard Ave.
San Angelo, TX 76903 (915) 659-5900
Contact: Mike Boyd, Secy.-Treas.

Established in 1996 in TX.
Donor(s): Texas Commerce Bank-San Angelo, N.A.
Financial data (yr. ended 12/31/01): Grants paid, $11,702; assets, $17,407 (M); expenditures, $13,803; qualifying distributions, $11,702.
Limitations: Giving limited to TX.
Officers: Dal DeWess, Chair.; Robert Pate, V.P.; Mike Boyd, Secy.-Treas.
EIN: 762608076

52648
Marjorie E. Evans Foundation
8787 Tallyho Rd.
Houston, TX 77061-3420

Established in 1996 in TX.
Donor(s): Marjorie E. Evans.
Financial data (yr. ended 09/30/01): Grants paid, $11,633; assets, $9,019 (M); gifts received, $6,800; expenditures, $18,708; qualifying distributions, $11,633.
Limitations: Applications not accepted. Giving primarily in Houston, TX.
Application information: Contributes only to pre-selected organizations.
Officers: Marjorie E. Evans, Pres. and Treas.; Donald W. Taft, V.P.; Jacquelyn C. Clark, Secy.
EIN: 760515460

52649
James Burns Ewart Memorial Trust
c/o Bank of America
P.O. Box 831041
Dallas, TX 75283-1941

Financial data (yr. ended 12/31/01): Grants paid, $11,570; assets, $249,855 (M); expenditures, $14,012; qualifying distributions, $11,570.
Limitations: Applications not accepted. Giving limited to AR.
Application information: Contributes only to pre-selected organizations.
Trustee: Bank of America.
EIN: 716049951

52650
M. B. Ahmed Family Foundation
10 Homeplace Ct.
Arlington, TX 76016
Contact: M.B. Ahmed, Pres.

Established in 2000.
Donor(s): M.B. Ahmed.
Financial data (yr. ended 12/31/01): Grants paid, $11,521; assets, $445,344 (M); gifts received, $63,350; expenditures, $15,966; qualifying distributions, $11,521.
Limitations: Giving on a national and international basis.
Officer: M.B. Ahmed, Pres.
EIN: 752840134

52651
Clift Brannon Evangelistic Association
P.O. Box 1441
Longview, TX 75606

Financial data (yr. ended 12/31/99): Grants paid, $11,500; assets, $56,882 (M); gifts received, $44,613; expenditures, $44,704; qualifying distributions, $0.
Limitations: Applications not accepted.

Application information: Contributes only to pre-selected organizations.
Officers: Clifton Brannon, Pres.; Ola Ruth Brannon, Secy.-Treas.
Directors: Beverly Brown, Madeline Jones.
EIN: 751449916

52652
The Foster Foundation
540 Camino Real
El Paso, TX 79922

Financial data (yr. ended 05/31/02): Grants paid, $11,500; assets, $270,630 (M); expenditures, $11,693; qualifying distributions, $11,500.
Limitations: Applications not accepted. Giving limited to El Paso, TX.
Application information: Contributes only to pre-selected organizations.
Trustees: Charles H. Foster, Mary R. Foster, Rita O. Foster.
EIN: 746063790

52653
The Gilmer Foundation, Inc.
420 Sweeten St.
Rocksprings, TX 78880

Established in 1993.
Donor(s): Claud Gilmer, Gary C. Gilmer.
Financial data (yr. ended 12/31/99): Grants paid, $11,500; assets, $470,405 (M); gifts received, $305,025; expenditures, $12,719; qualifying distributions, $11,397.
Limitations: Applications not accepted. Giving primarily in TX.
Directors: Carson C. Gilmer, Claud Gilmer, Gary C. Gilmer.
EIN: 742661419

52654
The McLean Foundation
c/o Woodway Financial Advisors
10000 Memorial Dr., Ste. 650
Houston, TX 77024
Contact: Katherine S. McLean, Pres.

Established in 1995 in TX.
Donor(s): Katherine S. McLean.
Financial data (yr. ended 11/30/01): Grants paid, $11,500; assets, $261,374 (M); expenditures, $16,421; qualifying distributions, $11,500.
Limitations: Giving primarily in Houston, TX.
Application information: Application form not required.
Officers: Katherine S. McLean, Pres.; Kelley M. Bennett, V.P. and Secy.; John M. McLean, V.P. and Treas.
EIN: 760499308

52655
The Pedernales Electric Cooperative Scholarship Fund
201 S. Ave. F
Johnson City, TX 78636

Established in 1998.
Donor(s): Pedernales Electric Cooperative.
Financial data (yr. ended 12/31/01): Grants paid, $11,500; assets, $12,724 (M); gifts received, $8,421; expenditures, $11,914; qualifying distributions, $11,496.
Limitations: Applications not accepted.
Officers: Toni Reyes, Pres.; John Houser, V.P.; Melinda Armbuster, Secy.
EIN: 742897600

52656
Morris & Birdie Rauch Foundation
4211 Southwest Freeway, Ste. 200
Houston, TX 77027-7229
Application address: P.O. Box 270415, Houston, TX 77277-0415
Contact: Gerald Rauch, Tr.

Donor(s): Veda Mae Glesby, Gerald Rauch, Leonard Rauch.
Financial data (yr. ended 02/28/02): Grants paid, $11,500; assets, $127,451 (M); expenditures, $11,832; qualifying distributions, $11,500.
Limitations: Giving primarily in Houston, TX.
Application information: Application form required.
Trustees: Veda Mae Glesby, Gerald Rauch, Leonard Rauch.
EIN: 746045123

52657
Select Educational Trust
(Formerly Select Minority Trust)
P.O. Box 278
Sulphur Springs, TX 75483
Contact: Larry F. Bridges III, Tr.

Financial data (yr. ended 12/31/01): Grants paid, $11,500; assets, $374,012 (M); expenditures, $11,750; qualifying distributions, $11,540.
Limitations: Giving primarily in Sulphur Springs, TX.
Application information: Application form not required.
Trustees: Larry F. Bridges III, James S. Johnson, Carolyn Keys Stuart.
EIN: 756058883
Codes: GTI

52658
Spertus Family Foundation
5300 Bee Caves Rd., Bldg. 1, Ste. 220
Austin, TX 78746-5232

Financial data (yr. ended 12/31/01): Grants paid, $11,500; assets, $260,952 (M); expenditures, $14,994; qualifying distributions, $11,500.
Limitations: Applications not accepted. Giving primarily in Chicago, IL.
Application information: Contributes only to pre-selected organizations.
Officers: Herman Spertus, Pres.; William Gross, V.P.; Philip Spertus, V.P.; R. Jeanne Steig, V.P.
EIN: 363139665

52659
Indira and Om Singla Family Foundation
529 Oak Crest Dr.
Coppell, TX 75019-4082

Established in 2000 in TX.
Donor(s): Indira Singla, Om Singla.
Financial data (yr. ended 12/31/01): Grants paid, $11,446; assets, $1 (M); expenditures, $14,530; qualifying distributions, $11,446.
Limitations: Giving primarily in Dallas, TX.
Trustees: Indira Singla, Om Singla.
EIN: 752855375

52660
Reecie and Opal Jones Trust Foundation
1170 W. Frey St.
Stephenville, TX 76401-2922

Established in 1986 in TX.
Donor(s): Reecie R. Jones, Opal Jones.
Financial data (yr. ended 12/31/01): Grants paid, $11,440; assets, $346,749 (M); gifts received, $40,000; expenditures, $12,293; qualifying distributions, $11,440.

Limitations: Applications not accepted. Giving primarily in Stephenville, TX.
Application information: Contributes only to pre-selected organizations.
Officer and Trustees:* Reecie R. Jones,* Chair.; Larry Chew, Linda Chew, Opal Jones.
EIN: 756361079

52661
George and Claudette Hatfield Foundation, Inc.
206 S. Town E. Blvd.
Mesquite, TX 75149-2010
Application address: 1 Shadydale Ln., Rockwall, TX, 75087, tel.: (972) 268-7625, Ext. 127
Contact: George R. Hatfield, Pres.

Established in 1997 in TX.
Donor(s): Claudette Hatfield, George R. Hatfield.
Financial data (yr. ended 12/31/99): Grants paid, $11,326; assets, $189,827 (M); gifts received, $29,031; expenditures, $27,772; qualifying distributions, $27,596.
Limitations: Giving primarily in TX.
Application information: Application form required.
Officers and Directors:* George R. Hatfield,* Pres.; John G. Hatfield,* V.P.; Susan Wheelis,* V.P.; Claudette Hatfield,* Secy.-Treas.
EIN: 752706578

52662
Lewis and Joan Lowenstein Foundation
(Formerly Lewis Lowenstein Foundation)
14 Greenway Plz., Ste. 17R
Houston, TX 77046

Donor(s): Lewis A. Lowenstein.
Financial data (yr. ended 11/30/01): Grants paid, $11,175; assets, $341,794 (M); expenditures, $14,157; qualifying distributions, $13,477.
Limitations: Applications not accepted. Giving primarily in Houston, TX.
Application information: Contributes only to pre-selected organizations.
Trustee: Lewis A. Lowenstein.
EIN: 237002857

52663
The D. Lynd and Terri K. McGowan Foundation
c/o Sheila D. McCarn
11 Mott Ln.
Houston, TX 77024-7315   (713) 974-3592
Contact: Nora M. McGowan, Pres.

Established in 1991 in TX.
Donor(s): Nora M. McGowan.
Financial data (yr. ended 06/30/02): Grants paid, $11,132; assets, $198,234 (M); gifts received, $15,322; expenditures, $11,600; qualifying distributions, $11,132.
Limitations: Giving primarily in Houston, TX.
Officers: Nora M. McGowan, Pres.; John E. McGowan, V.P.; Marvin E. Conrad, Secy.; Sheila D. McCarn, Treas.
EIN: 760308875

52664
Jacqmin Foundation
642 Koui Ct.
Bastrop, TX 78602

Established in 1997 in TX.
Donor(s): Alice Jacqmin, Harris Jacqmin.
Financial data (yr. ended 12/31/01): Grants paid, $11,100; assets, $74,150 (M); gifts received, $1,000; expenditures, $11,470; qualifying distributions, $11,100.
Limitations: Applications not accepted.
Application information: Contributes only to pre-selected organizations.
Officer: Alice Jacqmin, Pres.

Directors: David Jacqmin, Harris Jacqmin, Debra Kramer.
EIN: 742840925

52665
Aged & Indigent Old Folks of El Paso County Foundation
c/o JPMorgan Chase Bank
201 E. Main Dr., 4th Fl.
El Paso, TX 79901 (915) 546-6515
Contact: Terry Crenshaw

Financial data (yr. ended 06/30/02): Grants paid, $11,000; assets, $943,217 (M); expenditures, $25,978; qualifying distributions, $11,000.
Limitations: Giving limited to El Paso County, TX.
Trustee: JPMorgan Chase Bank.
EIN: 746033945

52666
The Benton Family Foundation
8615 Pasture View Ln.
Houston, TX 77024

Established in 1998 in TX.
Donor(s): F. Fox Benton, Jr., Lizinka Benton.
Financial data (yr. ended 12/31/00): Grants paid, $11,000; assets, $224,096 (M); expenditures, $17,763; qualifying distributions, $11,146.
Limitations: Applications not accepted.
Application information: Contributes only to pre-selected organizations.
Officers: F. Fox Benton, Jr., Pres. and Treas.; Lizinka Benton, V.P. and Secy.
EIN: 760537349

52667
Carrie Morton Brown Foundation
c/o JPMorgan Chase Bank
201 E. Main Dr., 4th Fl.
El Paso, TX 79901 (915) 546-6515

Financial data (yr. ended 06/30/02): Grants paid, $11,000; assets, $658,180 (M); expenditures, $21,053; qualifying distributions, $11,000.
Limitations: Giving limited to El Paso County, TX.
Trustee: JPMorgan Chase Bank.
EIN: 742111392

52668
H. J. Diffenbaugh Trust for Baker University
c/o Bank of America
P.O. Box 831041
Dallas, TX 75283-1041
Application address: Bank of America, P.O. Box 419119, Kansas City, MO 64141-6119, tel.: (816) 979-7481
Contact: David P. Ross, Sr. V.P., Bank of America

Financial data (yr. ended 12/31/01): Grants paid, $11,000; assets, $254,418 (M); expenditures, $16,628; qualifying distributions, $12,619.
Limitations: Giving limited to residents of MO.
Trustee: Bank of America.
EIN: 446008351
Codes: GTI

52669
The Grace W. Dobson Family Foundation
4600 Parkdale Dr.
Corpus Christi, TX 78411
Contact: Thomas E. Dobson, Tr.

Established in 1999 in TX.
Donor(s): Grace W. Dobson, members of the Dobson family, Whataburger, Inc.
Financial data (yr. ended 09/30/01): Grants paid, $11,000; assets, $532,978 (M); gifts received, $271,097; expenditures, $16,071; qualifying distributions, $11,000.
Limitations: Giving primarily in AZ, FL, and TX.
Application information: Application form required.
Trustees: Hugh Carlton Dobson, Mary Lynne Dobson, Thomas E. Dobson.
EIN: 742935744

52670
The Foundation for Dreamers
11218 N. Lamar
Austin, TX 78753
Application address: 825 County Rd. 48, Gatesville, TX 76528, tel.: (254) 248-1841
Contact: Mary Traverse, Secy.-Treas.

Established in 1995 in TX.
Donor(s): Douglas S. Richards, Jr.
Financial data (yr. ended 12/31/00): Grants paid, $11,000; assets, $116,562 (M); gifts received, $95,635; expenditures, $18,897; qualifying distributions, $14,586.
Limitations: Giving primarily in AZ, CA and TX.
Application information: Application form required.
Officers: Douglas S. Richards, Jr., Pres.; Mary Traverse, Secy.-Treas.
Director: Curtis Cripe.
EIN: 742736860

52671
The Hamilton Charitable & Educational Foundation, Inc.
c/o Roger D. Aksamit
1130 Banks St.
Houston, TX 77006-6134

Established in 2000 in TX.
Donor(s): Roger D. Aksamit, Barbara Aksamit.
Financial data (yr. ended 12/31/01): Grants paid, $11,000; assets, $10,050 (M); gifts received, $3,500; expenditures, $11,204; qualifying distributions, $11,000.
Limitations: Applications not accepted.
Application information: Contributes only to pre-selected organizations.
Officers and Directors:* Roger D. Aksamit,* Pres.; Barbara Aksamit,* Secy.; Frank R. Aksamit.
EIN: 760644162

52672
Kochi Foundation
4372 Faculty Ln.
Houston, TX 77004

Established in 2000 in TX.
Donor(s): Jay Kochi, Mrs. Jay Kochi.
Financial data (yr. ended 12/31/01): Grants paid, $11,000; assets, $110,047 (M); gifts received, $70,000; expenditures, $11,776; qualifying distributions, $11,000.
Limitations: Applications not accepted.
Application information: Contributes only to pre-selected organizations.
Directors: Jay Kochi, Mrs. Jay Kochi.
EIN: 760663329

52673
The Martin Family Foundation
c/o Harelik & Fields
P.O. Box 8135
Waco, TX 76714-8135

Established in 1991 in TX.
Financial data (yr. ended 06/30/02): Grants paid, $11,000; assets, $144,446 (M); expenditures, $14,384; qualifying distributions, $11,000.
Limitations: Applications not accepted.
Application information: Contributes only to pre-selected organizations.
Officers: James Forrest Martin, Pres.; James Wesley Martin, Secy.-Treas.
EIN: 742615882

52674
The W. T. & Louise J. Moran Foundation
2727 Allen Pkwy., Ste. 1650
Houston, TX 77019-2125
Contact: R. Robert Mullins, Tr.

Established in 1997 in TX.
Donor(s): Mrs. W.T. Moran.
Financial data (yr. ended 12/31/00): Grants paid, $11,000; assets, $3,818,622 (M); gifts received, $2,000,000; expenditures, $33,350; qualifying distributions, $11,000.
Limitations: Giving primarily in Houston, TX.
Application information: Application form not required.
Officers and Trustees:* Louise J. Moran,* Pres.; Allen L. Jogerst,* V.P.; C.W. Sunday,* V.P.; Randall E. Evans,* Secy.; R. Robert Mullins,* Treas.
EIN: 760513027

52675
Robert and Willora Oglesby Foundation, Inc.
1409 N. Waterview
Richardson, TX 75080-3970 (972) 238-4722
Contact: Robert K. Oglesby, Dir.

Donor(s): Barbara Jackson, Gerry Smith, Angela Smith, Michael Seay, Jan Seay.
Financial data (yr. ended 12/31/01): Grants paid, $11,000; assets, $228,984 (M); gifts received, $32,970; expenditures, $12,474; qualifying distributions, $10,925.
Directors: Danny Hawk, Robert K. Oglesby, Robert K. Oglesby, Jr., Willora Oglesby.
EIN: 752468388

52676
The Romsdahl Foundation
4530 Verone St.
Bellaire, TX 77401-5514

Established in 1997 in TX.
Financial data (yr. ended 11/30/01): Grants paid, $11,000; assets, $223,317 (M); expenditures, $12,823; qualifying distributions, $11,000.
Limitations: Applications not accepted.
Application information: Contributes only to pre-selected organizations.
Officers: Marvin M. Romsdahl, Pres.; Christine A. Romsdahl, Secy.; Virginia M. Romsdahl, Treas.
EIN: 760554765

52677
Weir Foundation
P.O. Box 720158
Dallas, TX 75372-0158
Contact: Michael L. Clubb, Secy.

Financial data (yr. ended 02/28/01): Grants paid, $11,000; assets, $408,374 (M); gifts received, $132,751; expenditures, $11,980; qualifying distributions, $11,000.
Limitations: Giving primarily in TX.
Officers: J. Ray Weir, C.E.O. and Pres.; Patsy Moore, C.O.O. and V.P.; Michael L. Clubb, Secy.
Director: Jack Brady.
EIN: 751943678

52678
Woods Family Charitable Foundation
4719 E. Twin Lakes Dr.
Tyler, TX 75704-5415
Contact: Edward G. Woods, Pres.

Established in 1998 in TX.
Financial data (yr. ended 12/31/01): Grants paid, $11,000; assets, $192,065 (M); expenditures, $13,485; qualifying distributions, $11,000.
Limitations: Giving primarily in IA and MO.

Officers: Edward G. Woods, Pres.; Susan Gail Sutton, V.P.; Linda Louise Rose, Secy.; Norma L. Woods, Treas.
Director: Laura Lynn Sanders.
EIN: 760575266

52679
Patricia Clare McGuire Foundation
3435 Westheimer Rd., Ste. 1604
Houston, TX 77027-5355

Established in 1983 in TX.
Financial data (yr. ended 12/31/01): Grants paid, $10,925; assets, $223,214 (M); expenditures, $10,925; qualifying distributions, $10,925.
Limitations: Applications not accepted. Giving primarily in Houston, TX.
Application information: Contributes only to pre-selected organizations.
Trustee: Bernard Z. Lee.
EIN: 760057006

52680
Morning Star Foundation
c/o Sallie Tucker Anderson
P.O. Box 129
Calvert, TX 77837-0306

Established in 1985 in TX.
Donor(s): Sallie Tucker Anderson, Wesley E. Anderson.
Financial data (yr. ended 12/31/01): Grants paid, $10,880; assets, $301,258 (M); expenditures, $12,966; qualifying distributions, $10,880.
Limitations: Applications not accepted. Giving limited to TX.
Application information: Contributes only to pre-selected organizations.
Officers and Trustees:* Sallie Tucker Anderson,* Pres. and Treas.; Wesley E. Anderson,* V.P. and Secy.; William Townsend Anderson, Catherine Jane Anderson Manterola.
EIN: 742373236

52681
Alfredo Cisneros Del Moral Foundation, Inc.
735 E. Guenther St.
San Antonio, TX 78210-1235

Established in 1999 in TX.
Financial data (yr. ended 12/31/01): Grants paid, $10,868; assets, $263,744 (M); gifts received, $3,100; expenditures, $12,980; qualifying distributions, $10,868.
Limitations: Giving primarily in San Francisco, CA.
Officers: Sandra Cisneros, Pres.; Susan Bergholz, V.P.; Eve Porter, Secy.
EIN: 742866648

52682
The JB Foundation, Inc.
4415 Lago Vienta
Austin, TX 78734

Established in 2000 in IN.
Financial data (yr. ended 12/31/01): Grants paid, $10,850; assets, $6,895 (M); gifts received, $87,961; expenditures, $101,454; qualifying distributions, $10,850.
Limitations: Applications not accepted. Giving primarily in Indianapolis, IN.
Application information: Contributes only to pre-selected organizations.
Officers and Directors:* Jason Belser,* Pres.; Sarita Belser,* Secy.; Evelyn Belser,* Treas.
EIN: 352107049

52683
Ellen B. DeMar Trust
c/o Bank of America
P.O. Box 831041
Dallas, TX 75283-1041

Financial data (yr. ended 06/30/01): Grants paid, $10,800; assets, $157,935 (M); expenditures, $19,569; qualifying distributions, $11,780.
Limitations: Giving limited to Dallas County, TX.
Application information: Application form required.
Trustee: Bank of America.
EIN: 756007283

52684
The Whitehurst Foundation
400 N. Tower Dr.
San Antonio, TX 78232

Established in 1997 in TX.
Donor(s): John Whitehurst.
Financial data (yr. ended 12/31/01): Grants paid, $10,800; assets, $209,667 (M); expenditures, $11,885; qualifying distributions, $10,800.
Limitations: Applications not accepted. Giving primarily in San Antonio, TX.
Application information: Contributes only to pre-selected organizations.
Director: John Whitehurst.
EIN: 742833742

52685
The Midyett Family Foundation
2211 Sutton Pl.
Richardson, TX 75080
Contact: Robert Midyett, Jr., Tr.

Established in 1994 in TX.
Donor(s): Robert B. Midyett, Jr., Vicki A. Midyett.
Financial data (yr. ended 11/30/01): Grants paid, $10,764; assets, $249,748 (M); expenditures, $12,386; qualifying distributions, $10,764.
Limitations: Giving primarily in TX.
Application information: Application form not required.
Officers and Trustees:* Robert B. Midyett, Jr.,* Pres.; Vicki A. Midyett,* Secy.-Treas.; Michelle L. Midyett, Cathey Midyett Wiederecht.
EIN: 752570373

52686
Dewane Family Charitable Foundation
c/o Patrick E. Dewane
308 Sawgrass Cir.
Lufkin, TX 75901-7503

Established in 1997.
Donor(s): Patrick E. Dewane, Jane E. Dewane.
Financial data (yr. ended 12/31/01): Grants paid, $10,723; assets, $165,264 (M); expenditures, $11,703; qualifying distributions, $10,723.
Limitations: Applications not accepted.
Application information: Contributes only to pre-selected organizations.
Officers: Patrick E. Dewane, Pres.; Jane E. Dewane, V.P. and Secy.
Director: Christopher P. Dewane.
EIN: 752707960

52687
Hudgins Fund
1014 S. Travis St.
Amarillo, TX 79101-3026
Contact: Jack S. Hudgins, Pres.

Established in 1999 in TX.
Donor(s): Jack S. Hudgins, Marlene Hoge Hudgins, Jack S. Hudgins, Jr.
Financial data (yr. ended 12/31/01): Grants paid, $10,625; assets, $331,922 (M); gifts received, $21,800; expenditures, $11,218; qualifying distributions, $10,314.
Officers: Jack S. Hudgins, Pres.; Jack S. Hudgins, Jr., V.P.; Marlene Hoge Hudgins, V.P.; Julie Hudgins Morris, V.P.
EIN: 752853493

52688
William C. and Antoinette M. Childs Foundation
1351 Lower Turtle Creek Rd.
Kerrville, TX 78028
Contact: William C. Childs, Pres.

Established in 1997 in TX.
Donor(s): Antoinette Childs, William C. Childs.
Financial data (yr. ended 12/31/01): Grants paid, $10,600; assets, $97,404 (M); expenditures, $10,609; qualifying distributions, $10,600.
Officers: William C. Childs, Pres. and Treas.; Antoinette Childs, V.P. and Secy.
EIN: 760358285

52689
Christian-American Citizens, Inc.
(Formerly Sutton Fund)
12146 Midlake Dr.
Dallas, TX 75218-1354

Donor(s): Robert C. Sutton.
Financial data (yr. ended 03/31/02): Grants paid, $10,600; assets, $7,441 (M); expenditures, $10,970; qualifying distributions, $10,600.
Limitations: Applications not accepted. Giving primarily in TX.
Application information: Contributes only to pre-selected organizations.
Trustees: Rhey Standlee, Nancy Sutton, Robert C. Sutton.
EIN: 751242083

52690
Buehring Family Foundation
P.O. Box 8546
Greenville, TX 75404

Established in 1999 in TX.
Donor(s): E. Fred Buehring.‡
Financial data (yr. ended 12/31/01): Grants paid, $10,550; assets, $433,727 (M); gifts received, $365,643; expenditures, $14,693; qualifying distributions, $10,550.
Limitations: Applications not accepted. Giving primarily in TX.
Application information: Contributes only to pre-selected organizations.
Officers: Cary F. Buehring, V.P.; Kelley D. Fincher, Secy.
EIN: 752836286

52691
Jennifer Lynn Stroud Foundation
14160 Dallas Pkwy., Ste. 300
Dallas, TX 75240 (972) 770-5600
Contact: James A. Stroud, Chair.

Established in 1996 in TX.
Donor(s): James A. Stroud, Lynn M. Stroud.
Financial data (yr. ended 12/31/01): Grants paid, $10,533; assets, $55,174 (M); gifts received, $6,010; expenditures, $13,655; qualifying distributions, $10,533.
Limitations: Giving primarily in TX.
Officers: James A. Stroud, Chair.; Lynn M. Stroud, C.E.O.
EIN: 752635767

52692
Crawford Missionary Foundation
3809 N. Main St.
Victoria, TX 77901-2611

Donor(s): Kenneth V. Crawford, Audrey M. Crawford.
Financial data (yr. ended 12/31/01): Grants paid, $10,475; assets, $2,672 (M); gifts received, $10,000; expenditures, $10,475; qualifying distributions, $10,475.
Limitations: Applications not accepted. Giving primarily in TX.
Director: Audrey M. Crawford.
EIN: 742881315

52693
The Cy and Dee Dee Richards Foundation
c/o Knopp & Hardcastle, PC
615 N. Upper Broadway, Ste. 770
Corpus Christi, TX 78477-0088
(361) 883-8999
Contact: Kacy Richards, Secy.-Treas.

Established in 1991 in TX.
Donor(s): Deirdre Harkins Richards, Cyrus F. Richards III.
Financial data (yr. ended 12/31/00): Grants paid, $10,405; assets, $281,347 (M); expenditures, $16,128; qualifying distributions, $10,405.
Limitations: Giving primarily in TX.
Officers: Deirdre Harkins Richards, Pres.; Cyrus F. Richards III, V.P.; Kacy Richards, Secy.-Treas.
EIN: 742643099

52694
Coale Foundation
408 Seawind
Austin, TX 78734-4444

Donor(s): George B. Coale, Mary R. Coale.
Financial data (yr. ended 12/31/01): Grants paid, $10,350; assets, $93,802 (M); expenditures, $10,702; qualifying distributions, $10,350.
Limitations: Applications not accepted. Giving primarily in Austin, TX.
Application information: Contributes only to pre-selected organizations.
Officers: George B. Coale III, M.D., Pres.; Robert D. Coale, V.P.; Mary R. Coale, Secy.-Treas.
EIN: 741607413

52695
Anvil Foundation
1341 Oak Harbor Blvd.
Azle, TX 76020-4917

Financial data (yr. ended 12/31/01): Grants paid, $10,340; assets, $16 (M); gifts received, $10,000; expenditures, $10,340; qualifying distributions, $10,340.
Limitations: Applications not accepted. Giving primarily in Fort Worth, TX.
Officer and Directors:* Patricia Craus,* Pres.; Jeanette C. Baker.
EIN: 237213444

52696
C. J. White Foundation
5005 Woodway Dr., Ste. 220
Houston, TX 77056-1711

Financial data (yr. ended 09/30/01): Grants paid, $10,320; assets, $112,086 (M); expenditures, $11,261; qualifying distributions, $10,320.
Limitations: Giving primarily in Houston, TX.
Officers: C.J. White III, Pres. and Treas.; R.J. Wax, V.P.; Barbara N. White, V.P.
EIN: 742147537

52697
The Harvie & Mary Jo Branscomb Fund
(Formerly Corpus Christi Community Fund)
3817 S. Alameda St., Ste. B
Corpus Christi, TX 78411

Financial data (yr. ended 10/31/01): Grants paid, $10,300; assets, $107 (M); expenditures, $10,735; qualifying distributions, $10,300.
Limitations: Applications not accepted. Giving primarily in Corpus Christi, TX.
Application information: Contributes only to pre-selected organizations.
Trustee: Harvie Branscomb, Jr.
EIN: 746412259

52698
Carl E. Kessler Family Foundation
P.O. Box C
Mineral Wells, TX 76068

Established in 1994 in TX.
Donor(s): Carl E. Kessler.
Financial data (yr. ended 12/31/01): Grants paid, $10,300; assets, $360,881 (M); gifts received, $95,000; expenditures, $12,914; qualifying distributions, $10,300.
Officer: Carl E. Kessler, Pres.
EIN: 752567397

52699
Lartigue Family Foundation
227 Dawns Edge Dr.
Montgomery, TX 77356-5945

Established in 2000 in TX.
Donor(s): Henry J. Lartigue, Kaye F. Lartigue.
Financial data (yr. ended 12/31/01): Grants paid, $10,250; assets, $120,340 (M); expenditures, $14,410; qualifying distributions, $10,250.
Limitations: Applications not accepted.
Application information: Contributes only to pre-selected organizations.
Officers and Trustees:* Henry J. Lartigue, Jr.,* Chair. and Pres.; Kaye F. Lartigue,* Secy.; Henry Lartigue III.
EIN: 760647096

52700
Houston Osteopathic Foundation
1603 N. Main St.
Pearland, TX 77581-5117 (281) 464-6291
Application address: c/o Grant Comm., 9225 Katy Fwy., Ste. 201, Houston, TX 77021, tel.: (713) 464-6291
Contact: Robert L. Murphy, Pres.

Incorporated in 1975 in TX.
Financial data (yr. ended 12/31/01): Grants paid, $10,200; assets, $1,143,638 (M); expenditures, $52,531; qualifying distributions, $40,214.
Limitations: Giving limited to TX.
Officers: Robert L. Murphy, Pres.; Lanny Vlasek, Secy.; Marguerite J. Badger, Treas.
Directors: David Armbruster, Dewey Campbell, Bill Coltharp, E.P. Gemmer, Jr., Hunter Harang, J. Dean Knox, Joe Martin, Carl V. Mitten, Robert Prangle, David Suffian.
EIN: 742426837
Codes: GTI

52701
Thornton Foundation
2700 W. Pafford St.
Fort Worth, TX 76110-5893 (817) 926-3327
Contact: Lloyd Thornton, Pres.

Donor(s): Lloyd Thornton.
Financial data (yr. ended 12/31/00): Grants paid, $10,150; assets, $40,491 (M); expenditures, $10,250; qualifying distributions, $10,197.

Limitations: Giving primarily in Fort Worth, TX.
Application information: Application form not required.
Officer: Lloyd Thornton, Pres.
EIN: 756022530

52702
The Von Rosenberg Foundation
8502 Dashwood Dr.
Houston, TX 77036-4716

Established in 1996 in TX.
Donor(s): Edgar L. Von Rosenberg.
Financial data (yr. ended 10/31/01): Grants paid, $10,100; assets, $53,448 (M); gifts received, $40,000; expenditures, $11,196; qualifying distributions, $10,100.
Director: Edgar L. Von Rosenberg, Jean L. Von Rosenberg, Michael K. Von Rosenberg.
EIN: 760520143

52703
DeWetter Family Charitable Foundation
833 Cherry Hill Ln.
El Paso, TX 79912-3324 (915) 584-8700

Established in 1986 in CA.
Donor(s): Peter DeWetter, Margaret B. DeWetter.
Financial data (yr. ended 12/31/01): Grants paid, $10,050; assets, $350,564 (M); expenditures, $17,694; qualifying distributions, $13,539.
Limitations: Applications not accepted. Giving primarily in El Paso, TX.
Application information: Contributes only to pre-selected organizations.
Officer: Margaret B. DeWetter, Pres. and Secy.
Directors: Charles Safford DeWetter, David Brooks DeWetter, Robert Emerson DeWetter.
EIN: 954078374

52704
The Hyde Foundation
6300 Ridglea Pl., Ste. 1018
Fort Worth, TX 76116-5778
Contact: Patricia Hyde, Pres.

Financial data (yr. ended 12/31/01): Grants paid, $10,040; assets, $224,545 (M); gifts received, $10,000; expenditures, $10,681; qualifying distributions, $10,040.
Limitations: Giving limited to the Dallas-Fort Worth, TX, area.
Officers and Trustees:* Patricia Hyde,* Pres.; C. Brodie Hyde II,* V.P. and Treas.; C. Brodie Hyde III,* Secy.; Sylvia F. Hyde.
EIN: 751812716

52705
The Almond Foundation
305 W. Academy St.
Del Rio, TX 78840-5906

Established in 2001 in TX.
Donor(s): Carolyn Kay Almond.
Financial data (yr. ended 12/31/01): Grants paid, $10,000; assets, $100,700 (M); gifts received, $110,000; expenditures, $10,000; qualifying distributions, $10,000.
Limitations: Applications not accepted. Giving primarily in CA.
Application information: Contributes only to pre-selected organizations.
Officers: Judith Skutch Whitson, V. P.; Gloria Wapnick, Secy.; Beverly Mcneff, Treas.; Carolyn Kay Almond, Mgr.
EIN: 743008087

52706
Jon C. Beal, Jr. Memorial Trust
1611 Country Rd. 2
Lubbock, TX 79423-0103
Contact: Arlen W. Hastings, Tr.

Donor(s): Jon Beal.
Financial data (yr. ended 12/31/01): Grants paid, $10,000; assets, $118,024 (M); gifts received, $10,177; expenditures, $10,081; qualifying distributions, $9,940.
Limitations: Giving limited to Fredonia, KS.
Trustee: Arlen W. Hastings.
EIN: 480959834
Codes: GTI

52707
The Gretchen S. Bryan Charitable Foundation
4265 San Felipe, Ste. 1413
Houston, TX 77027

Established in 1994 in TX.
Donor(s): J. Shelby Bryan.
Financial data (yr. ended 12/31/01): Grants paid, $10,000; assets, $257,388 (M); expenditures, $10,690; qualifying distributions, $10,000.
Limitations: Applications not accepted. Giving primarily in New York, NY.
Application information: Contributes only to pre-selected organizations.
Trustees: J. Shelby Bryan, Anthony T. Constantino, Jack DiMartino.
EIN: 760474090

52708
Cordua Family Foundation
1800 Post Oak Blvd., Ste. 200
Houston, TX 77056

Established in 1998 in TX.
Donor(s): Michael Cordua, Lucia Cordua.
Financial data (yr. ended 12/31/00): Grants paid, $10,000; assets, $3,527 (M); gifts received, $10,000; expenditures, $10,151; qualifying distributions, $10,000.
Limitations: Applications not accepted. Giving primarily in Houston, TX.
Application information: Contributes only to pre-selected organizations.
Officers and Directors:* Michael Cordua,* Pres.; Lucia Cordua, V.P.; Edward Hartline, Secy.-Treas.
EIN: 760557172

52709
Eleanor Crook Foundation
227 N. Mitchell St.
San Marcos, TX 78666

Financial data (yr. ended 11/30/01): Grants paid, $10,000; assets, $74,479 (M); gifts received, $17,200; expenditures, $10,676; qualifying distributions, $10,000.
Officers: Eleanor Crook, Pres. and Treas.; William H. Crook, Jr, V.P. and Secy.; Mary Elizabeth Crook, V.P.; Noel C. Moored, V.P.
EIN: 742857866

52710
Dortch Foundation
6335 W. Northwest Hwy., No. 1916
Dallas, TX 75225 (214) 696-3301
Contact: H. Wayne Dortch, Pres.

Established in 1997 in TX.
Donor(s): H. Wayne Dortch, Alice M. Dortch.
Financial data (yr. ended 12/31/01): Grants paid, $10,000; assets, $218,608 (M); gifts received, $18,131; expenditures, $11,216; qualifying distributions, $10,000.
Limitations: Giving primarily in TX.

Officers and Directors:* H. Wayne Dortch,* Pres.; Alice M. Dortch,* V.P.; Marlene D. Thomson,* V.P.
EIN: 752737449

52711
Foundation of Joseph
601 N.W. Loop 410, Ste. 104
San Antonio, TX 78216-5595
Contact: Peter M. Wolverton, Tr.

Donor(s): Betty Wolverton, Peter M. Wolverton.
Financial data (yr. ended 12/31/01): Grants paid, $10,000; assets, $188,628 (M); gifts received, $10,167; expenditures, $11,075; qualifying distributions, $10,000.
Trustees: Gene Allen, John R. Hannah, Monica Hayes, Betty Wolverton, Peter M. Wolverton.
EIN: 742767267

52712
The Glass-Belmont Foundation
4431 Lymbar Dr.
Houston, TX 77096
Contact: Nancy L. Glass, Secy.-Treas.

Established in 1999 in TX.
Donor(s): John W. Belmont, Nancy L. Glass.
Financial data (yr. ended 11/30/01): Grants paid, $10,000; assets, $66,677 (M); gifts received, $42,213; expenditures, $18,278; qualifying distributions, $10,000.
Officers: John W. Belmont, Pres.; J. Arnold Glass, V.P.; Nancy L. Glass, Secy.-Treas.
EIN: 311699626

52713
Mike and Dian Hutchison Family Foundation
101 Cantor Gait
San Antonio, TX 78231

Established in 2000 in TX.
Donor(s): Hutchison Supply Company, William M. Hutchison.
Financial data (yr. ended 12/31/01): Grants paid, $10,000; assets, $188,606 (M); gifts received, $100,000; expenditures, $10,593; qualifying distributions, $9,981.
Limitations: Applications not accepted.
Application information: Contributes only to pre-selected organizations.
Officers and Directors:* William M. Hutchison,* Pres.; Dian D. Hutchison,* V.P.; Lisa M. Youngblood, Secy.; Mike Wylie, Treas.; Curtis R. Hutchison.
EIN: 742982407
Codes: CS

52714
The Loucks Family Foundation
26001 Masters Pkwy.
Spicewood, TX 78669-3038 (830) 798-2995

Established in 2001 in TX.
Donor(s): Larry K. Loucks, Patricia M. Loucks.
Financial data (yr. ended 12/31/01): Grants paid, $10,000; assets, $124,734 (M); gifts received, $117,290; expenditures, $12,294; qualifying distributions, $11,600.
Officers: Larry K. Loucks, Pres. and Treas.; Patricia M. Loucks, V.P. and Secy.
Trustees: Clay A. Loucks, Travis P. Loucks.
EIN: 742971030

52715
The Susie Swindle McDonough Foundation
4420 Lorraine Ave.
Dallas, TX 75205-3611

Established in 2000 in TX.
Donor(s): Susie Swindle McDonough.

Financial data (yr. ended 12/31/01): Grants paid, $10,000; assets, $204,099 (M); expenditures, $12,459; qualifying distributions, $10,000.
Limitations: Giving primarily in Dallas, TX.
Officers: Susie Swindle McDonough, Pres.; Samuel Frierson McDonough, Jr., Secy.
EIN: 756579990

52716
The Rose Foundation
(also known as The Political Science Fund)
5808 Annapolis St.
Houston, TX 77005-2412
Contact: Kent L. Tedin, Pres.

Financial data (yr. ended 03/31/02): Grants paid, $10,000; assets, $65,929 (M); expenditures, $10,828; qualifying distributions, $10,000.
Limitations: Giving primarily in Houston, TX.
Officers: Kent L. Tedin, Pres.; Donald S. Lute, Secy.; Richard Murray, Treas.
EIN: 760228422

52717
Victoria Livestock Show Foundation, Inc.
209 Dundee St.
Victoria, TX 77904

Established in 1994 in TX.
Financial data (yr. ended 04/30/01): Grants paid, $10,000; assets, $41,597 (M); gifts received, $12,929; expenditures, $11,221; qualifying distributions, $10,000.
Application information: Application form required.
Officer and Director:* Leesa Brown,* Pres.
EIN: 742712669

52718
The Steele-Trigger Foundation for Humanitarian Causes
3106 Lookout Ln.
Austin, TX 78746

Donor(s): Katherine M. Steele, Jeffrey M. Trigger.
Financial data (yr. ended 12/31/99): Grants paid, $10,000; assets, $9,090 (M); gifts received, $7,000; expenditures, $10,137; qualifying distributions, $10,000.
Limitations: Applications not accepted. Giving primarily in Dallas, TX.
Application information: Contributes only to pre-selected organizations.
Trustees: Katherine M. Steele, Jeffrey M. Trigger.
EIN: 752160463

52719
C. S. Watson Scholarship Foundation
(also known as Clara Stewart Watson Foundation)
P.O. Box 831041
Dallas, TX 75283-1041

Financial data (yr. ended 08/31/01): Grants paid, $10,000; assets, $795,333 (M); expenditures, $15,893; qualifying distributions, $12,306.
Limitations: Giving limited to Dallas and Tarrant counties, TX.
Trustee: Bank of America.
EIN: 756064730
Codes: GTI

52720
The Wolf Benevolent Trust
c/o Secured Trust Bank
1909 S. Bway., Ste. 100
Tyler, TX 75701 (903) 597-4611
Contact: Kathy Gerash

Established in 1986 in TX.
Donor(s): Dorothy M. Wolf.

Financial data (yr. ended 04/30/00): Grants paid, $9,882; assets, $122,266 (M); gifts received, $4,000; expenditures, $11,927; qualifying distributions, $10,556.
Limitations: Giving primarily in TX.
Officer: Dorothy M. Wolf, Mgr.
Trustee: Secured Trust Bank.
EIN: 752089226

52721
Leola M. Osborn Trust
c/o Bank of America
P.O. Box 831041
Dallas, TX 75283
Application address: c/o Bank of America, Trust Dept., 3rd and Grand, Ponca City, OK 74601, tel.: (580) 767-8243

Financial data (yr. ended 12/31/01): Grants paid, $9,844; assets, $115,586 (M); expenditures, $15,341; qualifying distributions, $9,844.
Limitations: Giving limited to residents of the Tonkawa, OK, area.
Trustee: Bank of America.
EIN: 736169571

52722
The Beasley Foundation
4717 Harley Ave.
Fort Worth, TX 76107-3713
Contact: Clifton H. Beasley, Jr., Tr.

Donor(s): Harold Beasley.
Financial data (yr. ended 12/31/01): Grants paid, $9,770; assets, $207,524 (M); expenditures, $10,827; qualifying distributions, $9,770.
Limitations: Giving primarily in Little Rock, AR, and the Dallas/Fort Worth, TX, area.
Trustee: Clifton H. Beasley, Jr.
EIN: 751575719

52723
Courson Family Endowment Fund
P.O. Box 809
Perryton, TX 79070 (806) 435-3122
Contact: Joyce G. Courson, Pres.

Financial data (yr. ended 12/31/01): Grants paid, $9,712; assets, $217,898 (M); expenditures, $9,943; qualifying distributions, $9,712.
Limitations: Giving limited to TX.
Officer: Joyce G. Courson, Pres.
EIN: 752276117

52724
B & B Foundation
8101 Boat Club Rd., No. 330
Fort Worth, TX 76179

Financial data (yr. ended 09/30/01): Grants paid, $9,700; assets, $94,000 (M); gifts received, $94,000; expenditures, $17,941; qualifying distributions, $9,700.
Limitations: Applications not accepted. Giving primarily in TX.
Application information: Contributes only to pre-selected organizations.
Officers: Gary J. Baker, Pres.; Deborra L. Baker, Secy. - Treas.
Director: Michael W. Kemp.
EIN: 752813025

52725
The Vaughan B. Meyer Foundation
P.O. Box 6985
San Antonio, TX 78209 (210) 824-0136
Contact: Vaughan B. Meyer, Pres.

Established in 1996 in TX.
Donor(s): Vaughan B. Meyer.
Financial data (yr. ended 06/30/01): Grants paid, $9,700; assets, $56,907 (M); expenditures, $10,870; qualifying distributions, $9,683.
Limitations: Giving primarily in San Antonio, TX.
Officers: Vaughan B. Meyer, Pres.; Beverly V. Meyer, V.P.; Catherine M. Lange, Secy.-Treas.
EIN: 742789402

52726
Semmler Fund, Inc.
803 Link Dr., No. 11A
Duncanville, TX 75116

Established in 1994 in TX.
Donor(s): Russell C. Semmler, Brigitte Semmler.
Financial data (yr. ended 12/31/01): Grants paid, $9,700; assets, $175,168 (M); expenditures, $12,267; qualifying distributions, $9,700.
Limitations: Applications not accepted. Giving on a national basis.
Application information: Contributes only to pre-selected organizations.
Directors: Brigitte Semmler, Russell C. Semmler, Jay K. Stevenson.
EIN: 752570120

52727
Urban Vision Foundation, Inc.
1500 Citywest Blvd., Ste. 450
Houston, TX 77042
Contact: John T. Jones, Pres.

Donor(s): John T. Jones, Al Hassler.
Financial data (yr. ended 12/31/01): Grants paid, $9,689; assets, $44,140 (M); gifts received, $20,854; expenditures, $14,708; qualifying distributions, $9,689.
Limitations: Giving primarily in Houston, TX.
Officers: John T. Jones, Pres.; Lisa Jones, Secy.
Director: Al Hassler.
EIN: 760554508

52728
Cecil D. Parker Family Foundation
3705 Maplewood Ave.
Wichita Falls, TX 76308
Contact: Kenneth C. Armstrong, Pres.

Established in 2000.
Donor(s): Cecil D. Parker.‡
Financial data (yr. ended 06/20/01): Grants paid, $9,589; assets, $1,176,747 (M); gifts received, $1,313,882; expenditures, $25,675; qualifying distributions, $11,882.
Officers: Kenneth C. Armstrong, Pres.; Robert W. Goff, Jr., V.P.; Douglas C. Armstrong, Secy.
EIN: 752804289

52729
Jack Zubowski Foundation
3196 Produce Row
Houston, TX 77023 (713) 921-4161
Contact: Paul Zubowski, Treas.

Established in 1994.
Donor(s): Gale Zubowski.
Financial data (yr. ended 12/31/00): Grants paid, $9,529; assets, $226,450 (M); expenditures, $11,124; qualifying distributions, $9,529.
Limitations: Giving primarily in TX.
Officers: Gale Zubowski, Pres.; Helene Kuperman, Secy.; Paul Zubowski, Treas.
EIN: 742690863

52730
H. W. Perkins Foundation
1324 Lyndhurst Cir.
Bryan, TX 77802-1157
Application address: 12830 Hillcrest Rd., Ste. 111, Dallas, TX 75230
Contact: Harrie P.W. Perkins, Dir.

Financial data (yr. ended 10/31/01): Grants paid, $9,525; assets, $218,781 (M); expenditures, $14,903; qualifying distributions, $9,525.
Limitations: Giving primarily in TX.
Application information: Application form not required.
Director: Harrie P.W. Perkins.
EIN: 746312717

52731
Cotter Family Foundation
5627 Morningside Ave.
Dallas, TX 75206

Established in 1999.
Donor(s): Brandon Cotter, Amy Cotter.
Financial data (yr. ended 10/31/01): Grants paid, $9,521; assets, $301,358 (M); expenditures, $83,515; qualifying distributions, $9,521.
Limitations: Giving primarily in TX.
Officers: Amy Lane Cotter, Pres.; R. Brandon Cotter, Secy.
EIN: 752845680

52732
Wiley & Lauretta Baker Family Foundation
c/o Wiley Baker
1407 9th St.
Shallowater, TX 79363

Established in 1998 in MT.
Financial data (yr. ended 12/31/01): Grants paid, $9,500; assets, $384,767 (M); expenditures, $10,185; qualifying distributions, $443.
Limitations: Applications not accepted.
Application information: Contributes only to pre-selected organizations.
Directors: Lauretta Baker, Wiley Baker.
EIN: 810508870

52733
The Ewing Family Foundation
2712 Fenwick Ln.
Plano, TX 75093-3436 (972) 867-7944
Contact: John W. Ewing, Dir.

Established in 1999 in TX.
Donor(s): John W. Ewing.
Financial data (yr. ended 12/31/01): Grants paid, $9,500; assets, $546,295 (M); gifts received, $4,559; expenditures, $20,024; qualifying distributions, $9,500.
Limitations: Giving primarily in Dallas, TX.
Application information: Application form not required.
Directors: Carlos Ewing Elliot, Elizabeth Ewing, John W. Ewing, Mark W. Ewing.
EIN: 752845908

52734
Jackson County Foundation
1601 Rio Grande, Ste. 450
Austin, TX 78701-1149 (512) 474-2120
Contact: William N. Patman, Tr. or Carrin M. Patman, Tr.

Financial data (yr. ended 12/31/01): Grants paid, $9,500; assets, $98,648 (M); expenditures, $9,585; qualifying distributions, $9,500.
Limitations: Giving primarily in Jackson and Travis counties, TX.
Trustees: Carrin M. Patman, William N. Patman.
EIN: 746049009

52735
The Willard and Ruth Johnson Charitable Foundation
c/o Willard M. Johnson
P.O. Box 27727
Houston, TX 77227

Established in 1992 in TX.
Financial data (yr. ended 12/31/01): Grants paid, $9,500; assets, $161,250 (M); gifts received, $10,000; expenditures, $9,725; qualifying distributions, $9,500.
Limitations: Applications not accepted. Giving primarily in Houston, TX.
Application information: Contributes only to pre-selected organizations.
Trustees: David M. Johnson, John W. Johnson, Ruth Mayer Johnson, Willard M. Johnson, Mary Anne Johnson Lindley.
EIN: 760386599

52736
John and Ilene Kennedy Foundation
1401 Slaydon St.
Henderson, TX 75654-4270 (903) 657-3121
Contact: Ilene D. Kennedy, Pres.

Established in 1996 in TX.
Donor(s): Ilene D. Kennedy.
Financial data (yr. ended 12/31/01): Grants paid, $9,500; assets, $219,469 (M); expenditures, $11,464; qualifying distributions, $9,500.
Limitations: Giving primarily in AL and TX.
Officers: Ilene D. Kennedy, Pres.; John I. Kennedy, Jr., V.P.
Director: Linda L. Kennedy.
EIN: 752642065

52737
Wu Shu-Lien King Charitable Foundation
5125 Runnin River Dr.
Plano, TX 75093

Established in 1998 in CA.
Donor(s): Wu Shu-Lien King.
Financial data (yr. ended 12/31/01): Grants paid, $9,500; assets, $298,862 (M); expenditures, $34,188; qualifying distributions, $9,500.
Limitations: Applications not accepted. Giving primarily in TX.
Application information: Contributes only to pre-selected organizations.
Officer and Director:* Wu Shu-Lien King,* Pres. and Secy.-Treas.
EIN: 770492184

52738
The Gilbert and Thyra Plass Arts Foundation, Inc.
914 Park Ln.
Bryan, TX 77802-4357 (979) 846-3976
Contact: Gilbert N. Plass, Tr.; or Thyra N. Plass, Tr.

Established in 1990 in TX.
Donor(s): Gilbert N. Plass, Thyra N. Plass.
Financial data (yr. ended 12/31/01): Grants paid, $9,500; assets, $395,231 (M); gifts received, $12,000; expenditures, $15,448; qualifying distributions, $9,500.
Limitations: Giving limited to TX.
Application information: Application form not required.
Trustees: Paul Parrish, Gilbert N. Plass, Thyra N. Plass, William Rogers, Mary Evelyn Tielking.
EIN: 742570709

52739
J. Harry Tappan and Winnie Converse Tappan Charitable Trust
Bank of America Plz.
300 Convent St., 25th Fl.
San Antonio, TX 78205-3716 (210) 225-5964
Contact: George A. Olson, Trust Off., Bank of America

Established in 1988 in TX.
Financial data (yr. ended 12/31/01): Grants paid, $9,500; assets, $463,156 (M); expenditures, $47,930; qualifying distributions, $9,500.
Limitations: Giving limited to TX, with emphasis on the San Antonio area.
Trustee: George A. Olson.
EIN: 746360833

52740
Bhandara Foundation
6060 Richmond Ave., Ste. 380
Houston, TX 77057

Established in 1996 in TX.
Donor(s): Feroze Bhandara, Shernaz Bhandara.
Financial data (yr. ended 11/30/01): Grants paid, $9,450; assets, $75,560 (M); expenditures, $10,016; qualifying distributions, $9,450.
Limitations: Giving primarily in TX.
Trustees: Feroze Bhandara, Shernaz Bhandara.
EIN: 760522768

52741
W. H. Francis Foundation
P.O. Box 7500-401
Dallas, TX 75209-0500

Established in 1956 in TX.
Financial data (yr. ended 09/30/01): Grants paid, $9,445; assets, $442,898 (M); expenditures, $32,719; qualifying distributions, $31,179.
Limitations: Applications not accepted. Giving primarily in Dallas, TX.
Application information: Contributes only to pre-selected organizations.
Trustee: James B. Francis.
EIN: 756015940

52742
The Siemer Foundation
63 Downs Lake Cir.
Dallas, TX 75230-1900
Application address: 2200 Ross Ave., Ste. 1600, Dallas, TX 75201-6778, tel.: (214) 840-7000
Contact: Clemens H. Siemer, Pres.

Established in 1997 in TX.
Donor(s): Clemens H. Siemer.
Financial data (yr. ended 12/31/01): Grants paid, $9,350; assets, $187,656 (M); expenditures, $10,205; qualifying distributions, $9,350.
Officers: Clemens H. Siemer, Pres.; Mary Rita Siemer, V.P. and Secy.
EIN: 752739020

52743
K Clinic Foundation
421 E. Airport Fwy.
Irving, TX 75062

Financial data (yr. ended 12/31/01): Grants paid, $9,335; assets, $8,932 (L); gifts received, $18,485; expenditures, $9,803; qualifying distributions, $9,335.
Officers: Sarkis J. Kechejian, Pres.; Nishan J. Kechejian, Secy.
Director: Gregory Kechejian.
EIN: 752795776

52744
Mae V. Alright Charitable Trust
c/o Wells Fargo Bank Texas, N.A.
40 N.E. Loop 410, Ste. 20
San Antonio, TX 78216

Financial data (yr. ended 12/31/01): Grants paid, $9,279; assets, $166,740 (M); expenditures, $13,064; qualifying distributions, $10,626.
Limitations: Applications not accepted.
Application information: Contributes only to pre-selected organizations.
Trustee: Wells Fargo Bank Texas, N.A.
EIN: 746351908

52745
George B. and Irene Lindler Foundation
7811 Oak Vista Ln.
Houston, TX 77087-5443 (713) 644-4203
Contact: Joyce Lindler, Pres.

Established in 1980 in TX.
Donor(s): Irene B. Lindler.‡
Financial data (yr. ended 12/31/00): Grants paid, $9,250; assets, $1,718,476 (M); expenditures, $49,918; qualifying distributions, $32,762.
Limitations: Giving primarily in Houston, TX.
Officers: Joyce Lindler, Pres.; William S. Broughton, V.P. and Secy.
Board Members: Helen Beyer, Bobbie Henderson, John Veseika.
EIN: 742121178

52746
The Gerrie Foundation
3910 Rockledge Dr.
Austin, TX 78731 (512) 345-1485
Contact: Robert E. Gerrie, Pres.

Established in 2000 in TX.
Donor(s): Robert E. Gerrie, Margaret M. Gerrie.
Financial data (yr. ended 08/31/01): Grants paid, $9,200; assets, $9,671 (M); gifts received, $24,169; expenditures, $12,085; qualifying distributions, $9,200.
Officers: Robert E. Gerrie, Pres.; Jay Gerrie, Secy.; Margaret M. Gerrie, Treas. and Exec. Dir.
Directors: Susan M. Davis, Linda L. Stafford.
EIN: 742974287

52747
Bill & Norma Jaquess Charitable Foundation
300 MacArthur Ct.
Irving, TX 75061

Established in 2000 in TX.
Donor(s): Billy R. Jaquess, Norma L. Jaquess.
Financial data (yr. ended 12/31/01): Grants paid, $9,200; assets, $1 (M); gifts received, $50,000; expenditures, $13,867; qualifying distributions, $9,200.
Officers: Billy R. Jaquess, Pres. and Treas.; Norma L. Jaquess, V.P. and Secy.
EIN: 752905419

52748
The Columbus Community Hospital Foundation, Inc.
P.O. Box 297
Columbus, TX 78934-0297

Financial data (yr. ended 04/30/02): Grants paid, $9,153; assets, $212,505 (M); gifts received, $3,115; expenditures, $9,310; qualifying distributions, $9,153.
Limitations: Applications not accepted. Giving limited to Columbus, TX.
Application information: Contributes only to a pre-selected organization.
Officers: Patti Hill, Pres.; Pierce Arthur, Treas.
Director: Robin Garcia.

EIN: 742464333

52749
Furr Foundation, Inc.
c/o Henry B. Furr
1273 Canterbury Dr.
Abilene, TX 79602 (915) 676-8189
Contact: Oneta R. Furr, Secy.

Established in 1995.
Donor(s): H. Bedford Furr, Oneta R. Furr.
Financial data (yr. ended 12/31/01): Grants paid, $9,087; assets, $200,003 (M); gifts received, $50,029; expenditures, $59,456; qualifying distributions, $9,087.
Application information: Application form required.
Officers: H. Bedford Furr, Pres.; Oneta R. Furr, Secy.
Directors: William L. Cook, Jr., Myrn Horn Hall.
EIN: 752605002

52750
James K. B. & Audrey Calais Nelson Foundation
1990 Post Oak Blvd., Ste. 2410
Houston, TX 77056
Contact: James K.B. Nelson, Pres.

Established in 1998 in TX.
Donor(s): J.K.B. Nelson, Audrey C. Nelson.
Financial data (yr. ended 12/31/01): Grants paid, $9,075; assets, $832 (M); gifts received, $5,000; expenditures, $9,811; qualifying distributions, $9,075.
Limitations: Giving primarily in Houston, TX.
Officers and Directors:* James K.B. Nelson,* Pres. and Treas.; Audrey C. Nelson,* V.P. and Secy.; Felicia C. Nelson.
EIN: 760553531

52751
The M. W. and Fair Miller Foundation, Inc.
200 W. 5th St.
Bonham, TX 75418-4303 (903) 583-5574
Contact: Walter L. Sisk, Jr., Tr.

Financial data (yr. ended 12/31/99): Grants paid, $9,036; assets, $245,290 (M); expenditures, $10,044; qualifying distributions, $9,305.
Limitations: Giving limited to Fannin County, TX.
Trustees: Jerry Hopson, Walter L. Sisk, Jr., Tyler Todd.
EIN: 752260316

52752
Bradshaw Foundation
1616 Voss, Ste. 650
Houston, TX 77057-2625 (713) 783-2291
Contact: Samuel K. Bradshaw, Pres.

Established in 1990 in TX.
Donor(s): Samuel K. Bradshaw, Linda M. Bradshaw.
Financial data (yr. ended 12/31/01): Grants paid, $9,000; assets, $178,080 (M); gifts received, $108; expenditures, $9,083; qualifying distributions, $9,000.
Limitations: Giving primarily in MO.
Officers and Trustees:* Samuel K. Bradshaw,* Pres.; Linda M. Bradshaw,* V.P.; Kent S. Bradshaw,* Secy.-Treas.; Carol K. Castleman.
EIN: 760306413

52753
May Chu Enterprises Charity
6527 Parkriver Crossing
Sugar Land, TX 77479-5922

Established in 2000 in TX.
Donor(s): May Chu.‡

Financial data (yr. ended 06/30/02): Grants paid, $9,000; assets, $139,919 (M); expenditures, $10,234; qualifying distributions, $9,000.
Limitations: Applications not accepted. Giving primarily in Houston, TX.
Application information: Contributes only to pre-selected organizations.
Trustees: Christian Sue Chuang, Mun-Shan Lee, Li-Ling Lin, Mei Winden, Jein-Fong Yu.
EIN: 760649458

52754
Dorflinger Foundation
c/o Glen V. Dorflinger
8800 Woodway Dr., Apt. 6
Houston, TX 77063-2300

Established in 1998 in TX.
Financial data (yr. ended 12/31/01): Grants paid, $9,000; assets, $195,373 (M); gifts received, $46,510; expenditures, $9,355; qualifying distributions, $9,355.
Limitations: Applications not accepted. Giving primarily in Houston, TX.
Application information: Contributes only to pre-selected organizations.
Trustees: Glen V. Dorflinger, Peter G. Dorflinger, Phyllis F. Dorflinger.
EIN: 760562740

52755
GO Foundation
P.O. Box 65045
Lubbock, TX 79464-5045 (806) 784-0117

Donor(s): George Q. Offutt, Linda N. Offutt.
Financial data (yr. ended 12/31/01): Grants paid, $9,000; assets, $31,024 (M); gifts received, $6,110; expenditures, $9,345; qualifying distributions, $9,000.
Limitations: Applications not accepted. Giving primarily in TX.
Application information: Contributes only to pre-selected organizations.
Officers: George Q. Offutt, Pres.; Linda N. Offutt, V.P. and Secy.; Bradley Q. Offutt, V.P.; Brian K. Offutt, V.P.
EIN: 752768304

52756
God's Share Foundation, Inc.
P. O. Box 681001
Houston, TX 77268-1001

Established in 1997 in TX.
Donor(s): Dudley Warner, Sharlet Warner.
Financial data (yr. ended 12/31/01): Grants paid, $9,000; assets, $105,207 (M); gifts received, $5,000; expenditures, $11,495; qualifying distributions, $9,000.
Limitations: Applications not accepted.
Application information: Contributes only to pre-selected organizations.
Officers: Dudley Warner, Pres.; Sharlet Warner, V.P.; Misty Lark Warner, Secy.-Treas.
EIN: 760538014

52757
The Father Bernard C. Goertz Scholarship Trust Fund
585 Shiloh Rd.
Bastrop, TX 78602-3769
Contact: Fr. Bernard Goertz

Established in 1998.
Donor(s): Fr. Bernard Goertz.
Financial data (yr. ended 12/31/99): Grants paid, $9,000; assets, $199,474 (M); expenditures, $9,643; qualifying distributions, $14,067; giving activities include $4,610 for loans to individuals.

Application information: Application form required.
Officer: Minnie Bartsch, Chair.
EIN: 760577575

52758
Harry A. & Cleo S. Kollmyer Foundation
(Formerly Harry A. & Cleo S. Kollmyer Memorial Foundation)
22 E. Ave. B
San Angelo, TX 76903

Established in 1993 in TX.
Donor(s): Steve Kollmyer, Joe Kollmyer.
Financial data (yr. ended 12/31/01): Grants paid, $9,000; assets, $165,456 (M); expenditures, $9,921; qualifying distributions, $9,000.
Limitations: Applications not accepted. Giving limited to San Angelo, TX.
Application information: Contributes only to pre-selected organizations.
Trustees: Joe Kollmyer, Steve Kollmyer.
EIN: 756435038

52759
Jan & J. Venn Leeds Foundation
10807 Atwell Dr.
Houston, TX 77096-4939

Established in 1997 in TX.
Donor(s): Jan Audrey Norvell Leeds, J. Venn Leeds, Jr.
Financial data (yr. ended 04/30/02): Grants paid, $9,000; assets, $268,639 (M); expenditures, $11,033; qualifying distributions, $9,000.
Limitations: Applications not accepted. Giving primarily in TX.
Application information: Contributes only to pre-selected organizations.
Officers: Jan Audrey Norvell Leeds, Pres.; J. Venn Leeds, V.P. and Secy.; David Venn Leeds, Treas.
EIN: 760537395

52760
The Tom and Frances Slone Charitable Foundation
4705 Shadycreek Ln.
Colleyville, TX 76034-4735

Established in 2000 in TX.
Donor(s): Tom Slone, Frances Slone.
Financial data (yr. ended 12/31/01): Grants paid, $9,000; assets, $205,702 (M); gifts received, $57,735; expenditures, $12,128; qualifying distributions, $9,000.
Limitations: Applications not accepted.
Application information: Contributes only to pre-selected organizations.
Officers: Tom Slone, Pres.; Frances Slone, V.P.
EIN: 752906950

52761
Robert B. Taylor Educational Trust
P.O. Box 28629
San Antonio, TX 78228-0629
Application address: c/o Financial Aid Off., St. Phillip's College, San Antonio, TX 78228, tel.: (210) 531-3272

Established around 1992.
Financial data (yr. ended 12/31/99): Grants paid, $9,000; assets, $677,833 (M); expenditures, $10,515; qualifying distributions, $10,349.
Limitations: Giving limited to residents of San Antonio, TX.
Application information: Application form required.
Trustees: Juan Armendariz, Ford Nielsen.
EIN: 746364769
Codes: GTI

52762
The Open Hand Fund, Inc.
1901 N.W. Military, Ste. 100
San Antonio, TX 78213

Financial data (yr. ended 11/30/01): Grants paid, $8,982; assets, $42,616 (M); expenditures, $9,593; qualifying distributions, $8,982.
Limitations: Applications not accepted. Giving primarily in San Antonio, TX.
Application information: Contributes only to pre-selected organizations.
Officers and Trustees:* Eleanor Siegal,* Pres.; Erna A. Epstein,* V.P.; Pablo Siegal,* Secy.-Treas.
EIN: 746062570

52763
The Max and Isabell Herzstein Foundation
5100 San Felipe St., No. 241 E
Houston, TX 77056-3619

Established in 1986 in TX.
Financial data (yr. ended 09/30/01): Grants paid, $8,950; assets, $290,462 (M); expenditures, $10,500; qualifying distributions, $8,950.
Limitations: Applications not accepted. Giving limited to Houston, TX.
Application information: Contributes only to pre-selected organizations.
Trustees: Isabell Herzstein, Max H. Herzstein.
EIN: 760201215

52764
The Naasson K. & Florrie S. Dupre Permanent Educational Scholarship Fund Trust
c/o American State Bank
P.O. Box 1401
Lubbock, TX 79408-1401 (806) 767-7000
Application address: c/o Dean of Agriculture, Texas Tech University, Lubbock, TX 79409, tel.: (806) 742-2808

Financial data (yr. ended 12/31/00): Grants paid, $8,900; assets, $185,507 (M); expenditures, $11,553; qualifying distributions, $10,055.
Limitations: Giving limited to residents of Lubbock, TX.
Application information: Application form required.
Officer: Bryan Limmer, Mgr.
Trustee: American State Bank.
EIN: 756103694
Codes: GTI

52765
Jeff Austin Trust
P.O. Box 951
Jacksonville, TX 75766-0951 (903) 586-1526
Contact: Ronny E. Lee, Tr.

Donor(s): Jeff Austin, Sr.
Financial data (yr. ended 12/31/00): Grants paid, $8,875; assets, $91,835 (M); gifts received, $3,375; expenditures, $9,125; qualifying distributions, $8,875.
Limitations: Giving primarily in TX.
Officers: Jeff Austin, Jr., Chair.; Joe Terrell, Vice-Chair.; Ronny E. Lee, Secy.-Treas.
Trustees: Jane Chapman, Herbert Riley.
EIN: 756033802

52766
Leasure Foundation
185 IH-45 N.
Huntsville, TX 77320-3548

Established in 1998.
Financial data (yr. ended 12/31/00): Grants paid, $8,865; assets, $179,900 (M); gifts received, $17,040; expenditures, $17,040; qualifying distributions, $8,865.

Limitations: Applications not accepted.
Application information: Contributes only to pre-selected organizations.
Director: F. Daniel Leasure.
EIN: 760590972

52767
Winkelmann Charitable Foundation
c/o Samuel A. Winkelmann, Jr.
830 S. Mason Rd., Ste. A-7
Katy, TX 77450-3885

Donor(s): Samuel A. Winkelmann, Jr.
Financial data (yr. ended 04/30/01): Grants paid, $8,850; assets, $276,003 (M); gifts received, $50,000; expenditures, $11,588; qualifying distributions, $8,850.
Limitations: Applications not accepted. Giving limited to TX.
Application information: Contributes only to pre-selected organizations.
Officers: Samuel A. Winkelmann, Jr., Pres.; Terry L. Diggers, V.P.; Donald Bogy, Secy.-Treas.
EIN: 760450020

52768
Ruth Snyder Trust
c/o Wells Fargo Bank Texas, N.A., Trust Dept.
P.O. Box 10517
Lubbock, TX 79408-3517 (806) 293-1311

Donor(s): M.R. Snyder,‡ Ruth Snyder.‡
Financial data (yr. ended 12/31/00): Grants paid, $8,750; assets, $240,850 (M); expenditures, $12,043; qualifying distributions, $10,003.
Limitations: Giving limited to Plainview, TX.
Application information: Application form required.
Trustee: Wells Fargo Bank Texas, N.A.
EIN: 756324447

52769
Corner Light Foundation, Inc.
5119 Haydenbend Cir.
Grapevine, TX 76051

Established in 1998.
Donor(s): Gwynn McGregor, Alan McGregor.
Financial data (yr. ended 12/31/01): Grants paid, $8,650; assets, $121,426 (M); expenditures, $12,214; qualifying distributions, $8,650.
Limitations: Applications not accepted.
Application information: Contributes only to pre-selected organizations.
Officer: Gwynn McGregor, Pres.
Directors: Clint Fraser, Alan McGregor.
EIN: 752738527

52770
Mary Luccock Livermore Foundation
4920 S. Loop 289, Ste. 107
Lubbock, TX 79414
Application address: 1713 31st St., Lubbock, TX 79411, tel.: (806) 744-8166
Contact: Jane Livermore, Pres.

Donor(s): Mary L. Livermore.‡
Financial data (yr. ended 11/30/01): Grants paid, $8,592; assets, $592,407 (M); expenditures, $99,747; qualifying distributions, $30,166.
Limitations: Giving primarily in Lubbock, TX.
Officers and Trustees:* Jane Livermore,* Mgr.; Nan K. Woolam,* Secy.; Jana Sanders.
EIN: 751623098

52771
Norman J. and Evelyn S. Luke Foundation
13727 Tosca Ln.
Houston, TX 77079-7019

Established in 1987 in TX.
Donor(s): Norman J. Luke, Evelyn S. Luke.

Financial data (yr. ended 11/30/01): Grants paid, $8,585; assets, $454,103 (M); expenditures, $14,723; qualifying distributions, $8,585.
Limitations: Applications not accepted. Giving primarily in TX.
Application information: Contributes only to pre-selected organizations.
Trustees: Evelyn S. Luke, Norman J. Luke.
EIN: 760250936

52772
Eula Carter & Graham Smith Memorial Scholarship Fund
201 N. Kaufman St.
P.O. Box 985
Mount Vernon, TX 75457

Established in 1988 in TX.
Financial data (yr. ended 12/31/01): Grants paid, $8,569; assets, $449,524 (M); gifts received, $1,000; expenditures, $28,076; qualifying distributions, $15,096.
Limitations: Giving primarily in Mount Vernon, TX.
Trustees: J.H. Connally, B.F. Hicks, Virginia O'Donnell.
EIN: 756364952
Codes: GTI

52773
Longview Foundation, Inc.
P.O. Box 626
Longview, TX 75606-0626

Financial data (yr. ended 12/31/00): Grants paid, $8,569; assets, $416,105 (M); expenditures, $10,494; qualifying distributions, $8,569.
Limitations: Giving limited to the Longview, TX, area.
Application information: Application form required.
Officers: Blackshear Jameson, Pres.; Mrs. Blackshear Jameson, V.P.
Trustees: Jacqueline Simpson, Mrs. Dozier Skipper.
EIN: 756037353

52774
Goedecke Foundation
904 Glendale St.
Hallettsville, TX 77964

Financial data (yr. ended 12/31/01): Grants paid, $8,550; assets, $97,924 (M); expenditures, $12,698; qualifying distributions, $8,550.
Limitations: Applications not accepted. Giving limited to TX.
Application information: Contributes only to pre-selected organizations.
Officers and Directors:* Otto E. Goedecke,* Pres.; Margret Goedecke,* Secy.; Waltraut G. Duckworth.
EIN: 746047283

52775
The Thompson Foundation
3838 Oak Lawn Ave., No. 1850
Dallas, TX 75219
Contact: John P. Thompson, Tr.

Financial data (yr. ended 12/31/00): Grants paid, $8,550; assets, $4,011 (M); expenditures, $8,728; qualifying distributions, $8,550.
Limitations: Giving primarily in Dallas, TX.
Application information: Application form not required.
Trustees: Jere W. Thompson, Joe C. Thompson, Jr., John P. Thompson.
EIN: 756021210

52776
Khushalani Foundation
8126 Rebawood Dr.
Humble, TX 77346-1751

Established in 1992 in TX.
Donor(s): Ashok I. Khushalani, Susan J. Khushalani.
Financial data (yr. ended 12/31/01): Grants paid, $8,546; assets, $59,279 (M); gifts received, $39,461; expenditures, $22,208; qualifying distributions, $8,546.
Limitations: Applications not accepted. Giving primarily in TX.
Application information: Contributes only to pre-selected organizations.
Officers and Directors:* Ashok I. Khushalani,* Pres. and Treas.; Susan J. Khushalani,* Secy.; Mohan I. Khushalani.
EIN: 760345480

52777
Dr. & Mrs. Paul Pierce Memorial Foundation
c/o Bank of America, Trust Dept.
P.O. Box 831041
Dallas, TX 75283-1041
Application address: P.O. Box 830241, Dallas, TX 75283-0241

Established in 1963.
Financial data (yr. ended 04/30/01): Grants paid, $8,521; assets, $594,218 (M); expenditures, $17,399; qualifying distributions, $8,521.
Limitations: Giving limited to TX.
Application information: Application form not required.
Trustee: Bank of America.
EIN: 756029209

52778
The Grogan Family Foundation, Inc.
12 Fossil Rd.
Weatherford, TX 76087-8626 (817) 594-4245
Contact: Roy J. Grogan, Pres.

Donor(s): Roy J. Grogan.
Financial data (yr. ended 12/31/01): Grants paid, $8,520; assets, $116,043 (M); gifts received, $4,000; expenditures, $9,013; qualifying distributions, $8,520.
Limitations: Giving primarily in TX.
Application information: Application form not required.
Officers: Roy J. Grogan, Pres.; Roy J. Grogan, Jr., V.P.; Jeanne Grogan, Secy.-Treas.
Trustee: Georganne G. Catalani, Jeanne Grogan Milton.
EIN: 751840845

52779
Robert L. & Mary Frances Cattoi Family Foundation
7350 Palado Dr.
Dallas, TX 75240

Established in 2000 in TX.
Donor(s): Robert L. Cattoi.
Financial data (yr. ended 12/31/01): Grants paid, $8,500; assets, $3,069 (M); expenditures, $19,477; qualifying distributions, $8,500.
Limitations: Applications not accepted.
Application information: Contributes only to pre-selected organizations.
Officers: Robert L. Cattoi, Pres.; Robert J. Cattoi, V.P. and Secy.-Treas.; David C. Cattoi, V.P.; Carol Cattoi Lanning, V.P.
EIN: 752889024

52780
Douglas R. DeCluitt Foundation
3135 Franklin Ave.
Waco, TX 76710-7317
Contact: Douglas R. DeCluitt, Pres.

Donor(s): Douglas R. DeCluitt.
Financial data (yr. ended 12/31/01): Grants paid, $8,500; assets, $151,374 (M); gifts received, $1,000; expenditures, $8,851; qualifying distributions, $8,500.
Limitations: Giving primarily in NH and TX.
Officers: Douglas R. DeCluitt, Pres. and Treas.; Christopher D. DeCluitt, Secy.
Director: Sherri L. Nunley.
EIN: 742402303

52781
Michael Hoctor Foundation, Inc.
3 Courtlandt Pl.
Houston, TX 77006 (713) 526-7447
Contact: Michael Hoctor, Dir.

Established in 1997.
Donor(s): Michael Hoctor.
Financial data (yr. ended 12/31/01): Grants paid, $8,500; assets, $33,340 (M); expenditures, $8,500; qualifying distributions, $8,500.
Limitations: Giving primarily in Houston, TX.
Application information: Application form required.
Director: Michael Hoctor.
EIN: 760556797

52782
Irani Family Foundation
5035 W. Bellfort
Houston, TX 77035

Established in 1997 in TX.
Donor(s): Dinshaw Irani, Katie D. Irani.
Financial data (yr. ended 03/31/00): Grants paid, $8,500; assets, $202,144 (M); expenditures, $9,010; qualifying distributions, $8,500.
Limitations: Applications not accepted.
Application information: Contributes only to pre-selected organizations.
Director: Katie D. Irani.
EIN: 760542834

52783
Hazel Vaughn Leigh Trust
c/o Frost National Bank
P.O. Box 16509
Fort Worth, TX 76162-0509

Financial data (yr. ended 12/31/99): Grants paid, $8,500; assets, $706,599 (M); expenditures, $21,722; qualifying distributions, $10,872.
Limitations: Applications not accepted. Giving primarily in Fort Worth, TX.
Trustee: Frost National Bank.
EIN: 756476114

52784
Overbid Property Trust
110 N. Lamont St.
Aransas Pass, TX 78336
Application address: 307 S. Lamont, Aransas Pass, TX 78336
Contact: Richard D. Hatch, Tr.

Established in 1931.
Financial data (yr. ended 12/31/01): Grants paid, $8,500; assets, $195,423 (M); expenditures, $9,751; qualifying distributions, $8,500.
Limitations: Giving limited to Aransas Pass, TX.
Trustees: Frank Hametner, Richard D. Hatch, Charles Marshall, Meredith Moore.
EIN: 237222332

52785
The James R. and Lela M. Porter Foundation
58 Red Sable Dr.
The Woodlands, TX 77380

Established in 1998 in TX.
Donor(s): James R. Porter, Lela A. Porter.
Financial data (yr. ended 12/31/01): Grants paid, $8,500; assets, $220,619 (M); expenditures, $14,898; qualifying distributions, $8,500.
Limitations: Applications not accepted.
Application information: Contributes only to pre-selected organizations.
Officers: James R. Porter, Pres.; Lela M. Porter, Secy.-Treas.
EIN: 760589798

52786
The Swabado Family Foundation
2402 Twin Grove
Kingwood, TX 77339-2531 (281) 354-2155
Contact: William R. Swabado, Tr.

Established in 1994 in TX.
Donor(s): William R. Swabado.
Financial data (yr. ended 12/31/01): Grants paid, $8,450; assets, $42 (M); gifts received, $8,965; expenditures, $9,556; qualifying distributions, $8,450.
Trustees: Betty L. Swabado, Tanya L. Swabado, William R. Swabado.
EIN: 760434068

52787
The Father Joe Znotas Memorial Scholarship Fund
3010 Lyons Rd.
Austin, TX 78702-3639
Contact: Rev. Msgr. Lonnie Reyes, Pres.

Financial data (yr. ended 12/31/99): Grants paid, $8,450; assets, $9,256 (M); gifts received, $6,260; expenditures, $104,496; qualifying distributions, $8,450.
Limitations: Giving limited to residents of Austin, TX.
Application information: Application form required.
Officer and Trustee:* Rev. Msgr. Lonnie Reyes,* Pres.
EIN: 742157960

52788
Klinck Foundation, Inc.
P.O. Box 700
McAllen, TX 78505 (956) 631-3333
Contact: Jan M. Klinck, Dir.

Established in 1986 in TX.
Donor(s): Jan M. Klinck, Gary K. Klinck.
Financial data (yr. ended 12/31/01): Grants paid, $8,390; assets, $166,318 (M); expenditures, $8,497; qualifying distributions, $8,390.
Limitations: Giving primarily in TX.
Directors: Gary K. Klinck, Jan M. Klinck, Hollis Rankin III.
EIN: 742445901

52789
Kathleen Jones Alexander Foundation
505 S. Main St., Ste. 105
San Antonio, TX 78204-1207

Donor(s): W. McIlwaine Thompson, Jr.
Financial data (yr. ended 12/31/00): Grants paid, $8,350; assets, $231,995 (M); gifts received, $10,000; expenditures, $9,040; qualifying distributions, $8,350.
Limitations: Applications not accepted. Giving primarily in VA.

IN THIS SECTION, WITHIN EACH STATE, FOUNDATIONS ARE LISTED IN DESCENDING ORDER BY TOTAL GRANTS PAID

Application information: Contributes only to pre-selected organizations.
Directors: Elsie Thompson, W. McIlwaine Thompson, Jr.
EIN: 746039211

52790
The "Green Bar Bill" Hillcourt Trust
1001 Fannin, Ste. 3700
Houston, TX 77002-6797 (713) 754-6205
Contact: Nelson R. Block, Tr.

Established in 1996 in TX.
Financial data (yr. ended 12/31/00): Grants paid, $8,344; assets, $193,574 (M); expenditures, $10,182; qualifying distributions, $8,344.
Application information: Application form not required.
Officer and Trustees:* Joe Quick,* Treas.; Nelson R. Block, Scott B. Clabaugh, Joe Davis, Paul Y. Dunn.
EIN: 166415434

52791
Paul & Barbara Black Foundation
500 N. Water St., No. 1000 S.
Corpus Christi, TX 78471 (361) 882-3153
Contact: Paul P. Black

Established in 1997 in TX.
Donor(s): Paul Black, Barbara Black.
Financial data (yr. ended 12/31/00): Grants paid, $8,324; assets, $200,000 (M); gifts received, $5,500; expenditures, $8,673; qualifying distributions, $8,324.
Limitations: Giving primarily in Corpus Christi, TX.
Officer and Directors:* Paul P. Black,* Mgr.; Barbara C. Black.
EIN: 742877634

52792
Lumry Family Foundation
9900 N. Central Expwy., Ste. 525
Dallas, TX 75231

Established in 1999 in TX.
Donor(s): Immunology Research Institute, Schering-Plough Corp., Health Education Alliance, Pfizer Inc.
Financial data (yr. ended 12/31/01): Grants paid, $8,280; assets, $289,171 (M); gifts received, $130,395; expenditures, $20,841; qualifying distributions, $8,280.
Limitations: Applications not accepted. Giving primarily in TX.
Application information: Contributes only to pre-selected organizations.
Officers: William R. Lumry, Pres.; Rozalia N. Lumry, V.P.; Raymond H. Lumry, Secy.
EIN: 752802707

52793
Files Foundation
P.O. Box 429
Anahuac, TX 77514-0429 (409) 267-3171
Contact: Douglas M. Cameron, Pres.

Donor(s): Douglas M. Cameron.
Financial data (yr. ended 12/31/00): Grants paid, $8,259; assets, $118,239 (M); gifts received, $38,365; expenditures, $8,460; qualifying distributions, $8,259.
Limitations: Giving primarily in Anhuac, TX.
Publications: Application guidelines, financial statement, program policy statement.
Application information: Application form required.
Officers: Douglas M. Cameron, Pres.; Edward B. Stephenson, V.P.; James Earl Weaver, Secy.-Treas.
Trustees: Lance Wade Cameron, Warren G. Clark, Jr.
EIN: 741921896

52794
John Steven Kellett Foundation
P.O. Box 66574
Houston, TX 77266-6574

Established in 1992 in TX.
Donor(s): John Steven Kellett.
Financial data (yr. ended 03/31/01): Grants paid, $8,250; assets, $27,273 (M); gifts received, $10,268; expenditures, $9,097; qualifying distributions, $8,250.
Limitations: Applications not accepted. Giving primarily in TX.
Application information: Contributes only to pre-selected organizations.
Officers: John Steven Kellett, Pres. and Exec. Dir.; E. Donald Gordon, 1st V.P.; Denise O'Doherty, 2nd V.P.; Donald Skipwith, Secy.; Kathy Hubbard, Treas.
EIN: 760387959

52795
Louis M. Alpern & Laura K. Alpern Foundation
2201 N. Stauton St.
El Paso, TX 79902

Established around 1995.
Donor(s): Louis M. Alpern, Laura K. Alpern.
Financial data (yr. ended 12/31/00): Grants paid, $8,200; assets, $119,569 (M); expenditures, $10,085; qualifying distributions, $8,200.
Limitations: Applications not accepted. Giving primarily in CA, MA, and TX.
Trustees: Laura K. Alpern, Louis M. Alpern.
EIN: 746422347

52796
Taylor Family Foundation
4149 Ranier Ct.
Fort Worth, TX 76109-5026

Established in 1979 in TX.
Donor(s): Bob Benjamin Taylor, Linda R. Taylor, Solomon Taylor, Thomas M. Taylor.
Financial data (yr. ended 12/31/01): Grants paid, $8,200; assets, $793,049 (M); expenditures, $11,185; qualifying distributions, $8,200.
Limitations: Applications not accepted. Giving primarily in Fort Worth, TX.
Application information: Contributes only to pre-selected organizations.
Trustees: Annette B. Taylor, Bob Benjamin Taylor, Linda R. Taylor, Solomon Taylor, Thomas M. Taylor.
EIN: 751665622

52797
Alice Wasserman Library Trust
c/o First National Bank
P.O. Drawer 7
Port Lavaca, TX 77979-0007

Established in 1996 in TX.
Donor(s): Alice Wasserman.
Financial data (yr. ended 12/31/01): Grants paid, $8,200; assets, $163,831 (M); expenditures, $9,132; qualifying distributions, $8,200.
Trustee: First National Bank.
EIN: 746433411

52798
Carol H. & Richard F. Harris Foundation
7 Lorrie Lake Ln.
Houston, TX 77024

Established in 1999 in TX.
Donor(s): Richard F. Harris.
Financial data (yr. ended 12/31/99): Grants paid, $8,100; assets, $97,353 (M); gifts received, $94,688; expenditures, $13,234; qualifying distributions, $8,100.
Limitations: Applications not accepted.
Application information: Contributes only to pre-selected organizations.
Officers and Directors:* Richard F. Harris,* Pres. and Treas.; Carol H. Harris,* V.P.; Rachel F. Harris.
EIN: 760600320

52799
The Marks Charitable Foundation
952 Echo Ln., Ste. 300
Houston, TX 77024
Contact: J. Stephen Marks, III, Tr.

Established in 1994 in TX.
Donor(s): J. Stephen Marks III.
Financial data (yr. ended 12/31/01): Grants paid, $8,008; assets, $766,077 (M); gifts received, $491,637; expenditures, $12,903; qualifying distributions, $8,008.
Trustees: J. Stephen Marks III, Mary Lynn Marks, Leonard B. Rosenberg.
EIN: 760293820

52800
Alpha Epsilon Boule Education Foundation
c/o H. Ron White
1999 Bryan St., Ste. 2300
Dallas, TX 75201
Application address: c/o H.B. Bell, 6626 Harvest Glen, Dallas, TX 75248, tel.: (972) 233-7102

Established in 1994 in TX.
Financial data (yr. ended 12/31/01): Grants paid, $8,000; assets, $28,849 (M); gifts received, $38,116; expenditures, $9,974; qualifying distributions, $9,974.
Limitations: Giving limited to residents of TX.
Application information: Application form required.
Officers: H.B. Bell, Chair.; Charles Mitchell, Vice-Chair.; Wright Lassiter, Secy.; Robert L. Price, Treas.
EIN: 752541844

52801
Ballew Foundation
17624 Woods Edge
Dallas, TX 75287

Established in 1998.
Donor(s): Joe Ballew.
Financial data (yr. ended 12/31/00): Grants paid, $8,000; assets, $202,861 (M); gifts received, $91,743; expenditures, $11,906; qualifying distributions, $8,000.
Limitations: Applications not accepted.
Application information: Contributes only to pre-selected organizations.
Officer: Joe Ballew, Chair.
EIN: 752806799

52802
Curing the Old Age Disease Society
811 Dallas St., Ste. 1015
Houston, TX 77002-5912 (713) 654-0194
Contact: Miller W. Quarles, Pres.

Established in 1990.
Donor(s): Miller W. Quarles.
Financial data (yr. ended 11/30/00): Grants paid, $8,000; assets, $107 (M); gifts received, $13,103; expenditures, $14,843; qualifying distributions, $6,843.
Limitations: Giving primarily in Worcester, MA.
Officer and Directors:* Miller W. Quarles,* Pres.; Penny Q. Beauchamp, James A. Harrison, Mary Lynn Hunt, Brenda Linn, and 10 additional directors.
EIN: 760362624

52803
Maud and Jack Eddy Foundation Trust
P.O. Box 998
Lampasas, TX 76550-0998 (512) 556-3601
Contact: Geron B. Crumley, Tr. or Melba Shimko, Tr.

Established in 1995 in TX.
Donor(s): Maud Eddy.‡
Financial data (yr. ended 12/31/00): Grants paid, $8,000; assets, $213,014 (M); expenditures, $8,672; qualifying distributions, $22,535.
Limitations: Giving limited to residents of Lampasas, TX.
Application information: Application form required.
Trustees: Geron B. Crumley, Melba Shimko.
EIN: 746422083

52804
The Dewuse Guyton Foundation
31 Lana Ln.
Houston, TX 77027

Established in 1987 in TX.
Donor(s): Dewuse Guyton, Jr., Martha K. Guyton.
Financial data (yr. ended 12/31/01): Grants paid, $8,000; assets, $54,980 (M); expenditures, $8,000; qualifying distributions, $8,000.
Limitations: Applications not accepted. Giving primarily in Houston, TX.
Application information: Contributes only to pre-selected organizations.
Trustees: Dewuse Guyton, Jr., Martha K. Guyton.
EIN: 760242303

52805
Eric G. Hirsch Memorial Trust
5297 Sycamore Valley Ln.
Navasota, TX 77868-6019
Application address: c/o Joyce Finch, Klein Forest High School, 11400 Misty Valley, Houston, TX 77066

Donor(s): Marjorie S. Hirsch.
Financial data (yr. ended 12/31/01): Grants paid, $8,000; assets, $102,590 (M); gifts received, $260; expenditures, $8,259; qualifying distributions, $8,105.
Limitations: Giving limited to Houston, TX.
Application information: Application form required.
Trustees: Wayne F. Collins, Harold E. Colvard, Marjorie S. Hirsch.
EIN: 760148604
Codes: GTI

52806
The Hornish Family Foundation
c/o Harry Kester Hornish, Jr.
7333 Westover
Waco, TX 76710
Contact: Harry K. Hornish, Jr., Dir.

Established in 2000 in TX.
Donor(s): Harry Kester Hornish, Jr.
Financial data (yr. ended 12/31/01): Grants paid, $8,000; assets, $54,332 (M); gifts received, $62,000; expenditures, $8,986; qualifying distributions, $8,000.
Limitations: Giving primarily in TX.
Directors: Harry Kester Hornish, Jr., Janet Carver Hornish, Jennifer Dawn Hornish, Ryam Palmer Hornish.
EIN: 742982809

52807
James K. Laroe, Jr. Memorial Foundation
1901 N. Akard St.
Dallas, TX 75201-2305
Application address: P.O. Box 69, Terrell, TX 75160
Contact: Betty C. Laroe, Pres.

Established in 2000 in TX.
Donor(s): Betty C. Laroe.
Financial data (yr. ended 12/31/01): Grants paid, $8,000; assets, $136,133 (M); expenditures, $8,010; qualifying distributions, $8,000.
Application information: Application form not required.
Officers and Trustees:* Betty C. Laroe,* Pres.; James K. Laroe,* V.P. and Secy.; Daniel J. Laroe,* Treas.
EIN: 752909582

52808
Emma Matula Estate
c/o Paul Huser
P.O. Box 324, 506 Simpson St.
Schulenberg, TX 78956-0324
Application address: c/o Schulenberg Independent School District, 517 North St., Schulenberg, TX 78956, tel.: (979) 743-3448
Contact: Mike Bonner, Super.

Donor(s): Emma Matula.‡
Financial data (yr. ended 12/31/00): Grants paid, $8,000; assets, $182,050 (M); expenditures, $8,808; qualifying distributions, $8,308.
Limitations: Giving limited to Schulenburg, TX.
Application information: Application form not required.
Trustee: Paul Huser.
EIN: 746233606

52809
Cecile Moeschle Scholarship Trust
c/o Regions Bank
P.O. Box 2392
Longview, TX 75606-2392

Established in 1986 in TX.
Financial data (yr. ended 12/31/99): Grants paid, $8,000; assets, $239,779 (M); expenditures, $10,983; qualifying distributions, $0.
Limitations: Giving primarily to residents of Longview, TX.
Application information: Application form required.
Trustee: Regions Bank.
EIN: 756349280

52810
Normandy Foundation
P.O. Box 118227
Carrollton, TX 75011-8227

Established in 1998 in TX.
Donor(s): Donna C. Rohling, Edward J. Rohling.
Financial data (yr. ended 12/31/01): Grants paid, $8,000; assets, $53,437 (M); expenditures, $9,165; qualifying distributions, $8,000.
Limitations: Applications not accepted.
Application information: Contributes only to pre-selected organizations.
Officers and Trustees:* Donna C. Rohling,* Pres.; Edward J. Rohling,* V.P. and Treas.
EIN: 752769151

52811
Ted Pian Family Memorial Fund
c/o Marilyn Pian Schnitzer
6947 Desco Dr.
Dallas, TX 75225-1718

Financial data (yr. ended 09/30/01): Grants paid, $8,000; assets, $88,554 (M); expenditures, $8,581; qualifying distributions, $8,000.
Limitations: Applications not accepted. Giving limited to Dallas, TX.
Application information: Contributes only to pre-selected organizations.
Trustee: Marilyn Pian Schnitzer.
EIN: 756012454

52812
Sisters Four Charity, Inc.
c/o Alan Davis
2449 Innisbrook Dr.
Abilene, TX 79606

Donor(s): Peter Norton.
Financial data (yr. ended 12/31/01): Grants paid, $8,000; assets, $12,738 (M); gifts received, $5,300; expenditures, $8,544; qualifying distributions, $8,000.
Limitations: Applications not accepted. Giving primarily in TX.
Application information: Contributes only to pre-selected organizations.
Directors: Jean Norton, Kathryn Norton, Peter Norton.
EIN: 752512654

52813
Luda Belle Walker Foundation
803 Jefferson Ave.
Lufkin, TX 75904-3725 (936) 634-2771
Contact: C. James Haley, Jr., Tr.

Donor(s): Lida Belle Walker.
Financial data (yr. ended 12/31/01): Grants paid, $8,000; assets, $211,584 (M); gifts received, $59,560; expenditures, $8,500; qualifying distributions, $8,000.
Limitations: Giving primarily in the Angelina County, TX area.
Trustees: Virginia R. Allen, Anna Beth Connell, C. James Haley, Jr.
EIN: 752745568

52814
The Robert and Kelmor Wallace Charitable Foundation
P.O. Box 691267
San Antonio, TX 78269-1267
Contact: Robert G. Wallace, Tr.

Established in 1999 in TX and OK.
Donor(s): Robert G. Wallace, Kelmore Wallace.
Financial data (yr. ended 12/31/01): Grants paid, $8,000; assets, $168,335 (M); gifts received, $14,186; expenditures, $12,157; qualifying distributions, $8,000.
Trustees: Kelmore Wallace, Robert G. Wallace.
EIN: 311663883

52815
M. S. Wright, Sr. Charitable Foundation
P.O. Box 9
Nacogdoches, TX 75963-0009

Donor(s): Thomas W. Wright, Joe A. Wright.
Financial data (yr. ended 12/31/01): Grants paid, $7,947; assets, $13,945 (M); expenditures, $8,676; qualifying distributions, $7,947.
Limitations: Applications not accepted. Giving primarily in Nacogdoches, TX.
Application information: Contributes only to pre-selected organizations.

52815—TEXAS

Trustees: Joe A. Wright, Thomas W. Wright.
EIN: 756038167

52816
Elmer McKenney Scholarship Trust
P.O. Box 831041
Dallas, TX 75283-1041
Application addresses: c/o Marilyn Cluck, Sr. Counselor, Abilene High School, 842 N. 6th, Abilene, TX 79603, tel.: (915) 677-1444; c/o Isabel Anderson, 3639 Sayles Blvd., Abilene, TX 79602, tel.: (915) 691-1000; or c/o Billie McKeever, 600 North Ave. E., Haskell, TX 79521, tel.: (940) 864-2848

Established in 1987 in TX.
Financial data (yr. ended 07/31/01): Grants paid, $7,930; assets, $171,659 (M); expenditures, $12,907; qualifying distributions, $11,442.
Limitations: Giving limited to residents of Abilene, TX.
Application information: Application form required.
Trustee: Bank of America.
EIN: 756319992
Codes: GTI

52817
Michael Alan Wolf Fund
3710 Rawlins, Ste. 970
Dallas, TX 75219 (214) 823-9941
Contact: Howard B. Wolf, Tr.

Financial data (yr. ended 04/30/99): Grants paid, $7,897; assets, $1,286 (M); expenditures, $7,897; qualifying distributions, $7,826.
Limitations: Giving primarily in Dallas, TX.
Trustee: Howard B. Wolf.
EIN: 756028678

52818
The Betty & Sheldon Greenberg Charitable Foundation
6640 Eastex Fwy., Ste. 111
Beaumont, TX 77708-4319 (409) 898-1580
Contact: Sheldon Greenberg, Tr.

Financial data (yr. ended 12/31/00): Grants paid, $7,875; assets, $97,907 (M); expenditures, $8,553; qualifying distributions, $7,875.
Limitations: Giving primarily in Beaumont, TX.
Trustee: Sheldon Greenberg.
EIN: 742164634

52819
BEK International, Inc.
1209 Wedgewood Dr.
El Paso, TX 79925-7628

Established in 1999 in TX.
Donor(s): BEK Medical & Specialty Shop.
Financial data (yr. ended 08/31/01): Grants paid, $7,852; assets, $43,301 (M); gifts received, $19,384; expenditures, $10,313; qualifying distributions, $9,155.
Limitations: Giving primarily in TX.
Application information: Unsolicited requests for funds not accepted.
Directors: Joel Silva, Dora Williams, Larry Williams.
Trustee: Joel Silva.
EIN: 742940556
Codes: CS

52820
J. H. DeVault Foundation
2929 Post Oak Blvd., Ste. 1606
Houston, TX 77056

Donor(s): J.H. DeVault, Juanita DeVault, David DeVault, Jerry DeVault.
Financial data (yr. ended 11/30/01): Grants paid, $7,820; assets, $71,563 (M); gifts received, $45,000; expenditures, $8,660; qualifying distributions, $7,820.
Limitations: Applications not accepted. Giving primarily in Houston, TX.
Application information: Contributes only to pre-selected organizations.
Officers: J.H. DeVault, Pres.; David DeVault, V.P.; Jerry DeVault, V.P.; Juanita DeVault, V.P.
EIN: 237332789

52821
James and Lynn Erickson Family Foundation
6713 Lake Shore Rd.
Garland, TX 75044

Established in 1999.
Financial data (yr. ended 12/31/01): Grants paid, $7,819; assets, $5,757 (M); gifts received, $11,000; expenditures, $9,574; qualifying distributions, $7,819.
Limitations: Applications not accepted.
Application information: Contributes only to pre-selected organizations.
Director: James Erickson.
EIN: 311669291

52822
Grafa Family Foundation, Inc.
P.O. Box 51270
Midland, TX 79710

Established in 1991 in TX.
Donor(s): Carroll B. Grafa III, Barbra J. Grafa.
Financial data (yr. ended 12/31/01): Grants paid, $7,780; assets, $1,641 (M); gifts received, $7,500; expenditures, $57; qualifying distributions, $7,780.
Limitations: Giving primarily in TX.
Officers: Carroll B. Grafa III, Pres.; Bob W. Dutton, V.P.; Barbra J. Grafa, Secy.-Treas.
EIN: 752395218

52823
The Earlane & Sam Croom Foundation
1421 Winrock Blvd.
Houston, TX 77057-1729 (713) 467-1606
Contact: Earlane B. Croom, Tr.

Established in 2000 in TX.
Donor(s): Earlane B. Croom.
Financial data (yr. ended 12/31/01): Grants paid, $7,750; assets, $41,597 (M); expenditures, $9,257; qualifying distributions, $7,750.
Limitations: Giving primarily in Houston, TX.
Trustees: Thomas E. Berry, Earlane B. Croom, Sam G. Croom, Jr.
EIN: 760645570

52824
Ed Stedman Foundation
2965 IH 10 E., Ste. 201
Beaumont, TX 77704-2111 (409) 924-0328
Contact: Ed Stedman, Jr., Tr.

Donor(s): Ed Stedman, Jr.
Financial data (yr. ended 03/31/02): Grants paid, $7,653; assets, $122,968 (M); expenditures, $10,772; qualifying distributions, $7,653.
Limitations: Giving limited to Beaumont, TX.
Trustees: Tony L. Chauveaux, Ed Stedman, Jr., Ed Stedman III.
EIN: 746199874

52825
Charles & Lois Marie Bright Foundation
420 North St.
Nacogdoches, TX 75961
Application address: 920 University Dr., Nacogdoches, TX 75961
Contact: Billy J. Earley

Established in 1997 in TX.
Donor(s): Charles R. Bright.
Financial data (yr. ended 09/30/01): Grants paid, $7,632; assets, $212,962 (M); gifts received, $100,000; expenditures, $7,650; qualifying distributions, $7,627.
Officers: Billy J. Earley, Pres.; Gayla Mize, V.P.; C. Byron Smith, Secy.-Treas.
EIN: 752717755

52826
The FitzGerald Foundation
P.O. Box 5046
Abilene, TX 79608-5046
Application address: 1141 Butternut St., Abilene, TX 79602, tel.: (915) 677-7346
Contact: Norman D. FitzGerald, Dir.

Donor(s): Norman D. FitzGerald.
Financial data (yr. ended 11/30/01): Grants paid, $7,575; assets, $22,974 (M); expenditures, $8,507; qualifying distributions, $7,575.
Directors: Gerald Texas FitzGerald, Norman D. FitzGerald, Norman Scott FitzGerald, Leland G. Kelley.
EIN: 756036748

52827
Mary Helen Campbell Foundation
2201 County Rd., Ste. 164
Lueders, TX 79533-2219

Established in 1999 in TX.
Donor(s): Mary Helen Campbell.
Financial data (yr. ended 12/31/01): Grants paid, $7,528; assets, $221,019 (M); gifts received, $100,372; expenditures, $7,722; qualifying distributions, $7,528.
Limitations: Applications not accepted.
Application information: Contributes only to pre-selected organizations.
Officers and Directors:* Mary Helen Campbell,* Pres. and Secy.-Treas.; Bailey F. Campbell,* V.P.; Jay L. Arnold, Steve Nance, Bob Peddy.
EIN: 752849273

52828
R. M. Kleberg Research Foundation
P.O. Box 911
Kingsville, TX 78363
Application address: P.O. Box 17777, San Antonio, TX 78217, tel.: (210) 822-2348
Contact: Richard M. Kleberg III, Secy.-Treas.

Financial data (yr. ended 12/31/01): Grants paid, $7,507; assets, $169,542 (M); expenditures, $9,155; qualifying distributions, $7,507.
Limitations: Giving primarily in College Station, TX.
Officers: R.G. Sugden, V.P.; Richard M. Kleberg III, Secy.-Treas.
Directors: Stephen J. Kleberg, Alice Meyer, Katherine B. Reynolds, James L. Yarborough.
EIN: 746061385

52829
CLC Foundation
2901 First City Tower
Houston, TX 77002
Application address: c/o Citizens Bank, Clovis, NM 88101, tel.: (505) 769-1911
Contact: Lucille N. Laughlin, Pres.

Established in 1994 in TX.
Donor(s): John L. Carter.
Financial data (yr. ended 12/31/00): Grants paid, $7,500; assets, $147,587 (M); gifts received, $14,674; expenditures, $7,922; qualifying distributions, $7,312.
Limitations: Giving primarily in NM and TX.
Officers: Lucile N. Laughlin, Pres.; John L. Carter, V.P. and Secy.-Treas.
EIN: 761032112

52830
The Hatchett Foundation
6510 Abrams Rd., No. 215
Dallas, TX 75231

Established in 1998 in TX.
Donor(s): Hatchett Capital Group, Inc., R.J. Hatchett III.
Financial data (yr. ended 12/31/00): Grants paid, $7,500; assets, $252,359 (M); gifts received, $60,000; expenditures, $10,027; qualifying distributions, $7,500.
Limitations: Applications not accepted. Giving primarily in AL.
Application information: Contributes only to pre-selected organizations.
Officers: Richard J. Hatchett III,* Pres.; Richard J. Hatchett IV, V.P.; Colleen C. Hatchett, Secy.
Trustees: Catherine C. Hatchett, E. Larkin Hatchett.
EIN: 752803709

52831
The Blake T. Liedtke Family Foundation
700 Milam, 13th Fl., N. Tower
Houston, TX 77002

Established in 1997 in TX.
Donor(s): Blake T. Liedtke.
Financial data (yr. ended 12/31/01): Grants paid, $7,500; assets, $56,969 (M); expenditures, $7,586; qualifying distributions, $7,500.
Limitations: Applications not accepted.
Application information: Contributes only to pre-selected organizations.
Officers and Directors:* Blake T. Liedtke,* Pres. and Treas.; Laurie L. Liedtke,* V.P. and Secy.; Terri Lacy,* V.P.
EIN: 760549845

52832
The Lon & Susan Smith Family Foundation
143 Park Hill Dr.
San Antonio, TX 78212

Established in 1997 in TX.
Donor(s): Lon S. Smith, M.D., Susan Smith.
Financial data (yr. ended 12/31/01): Grants paid, $7,500; assets, $49,868 (M); expenditures, $8,788; qualifying distributions, $7,500.
Limitations: Applications not accepted.
Application information: Contributes only to pre-selected organizations.
Officers and Directors:* Lon S. Smith, M.D.,* Pres.; Susan Smith,* Secy.; R.C. Norman.
EIN: 742820956

52833
Texas Neurosciences Foundation
4410 Medical Dr., Ste. 600
San Antonio, TX 78229

Established in 1996 in TX.

Financial data (yr. ended 12/31/01): Grants paid, $7,500; assets, $119,657 (M); expenditures, $8,065; qualifying distributions, $7,500.
Limitations: Applications not accepted. Giving primarily in San Antonio, TX.
Application information: Contributes only to pre-selected organizations.
Officers: Thomas Kingman, M.D., Pres.; Wesley W. O. Krueger, M.D., Secy.; Warren Neely, M.D., Treas.
EIN: 742539380

52834
Wendland Trust
P.O. Box 40
Temple, TX 76503-0040
Contact: Erroll Wendland, Tr.

Financial data (yr. ended 12/31/01): Grants paid, $7,500; assets, $139,266 (M); expenditures, $7,708; qualifying distributions, $7,500.
Limitations: Giving primarily in TX.
Trustees: Bobbye Lee Godbey, Erroll Wendland.
EIN: 746048638

52835
The Paul & Shelia Schlosberg Family Foundation
6254 Preston Creek Dr.
Dallas, TX 75240-3518

Established in 2000 in TX.
Financial data (yr. ended 12/31/01): Grants paid, $7,475; assets, $637 (M); expenditures, $8,795; qualifying distributions, $7,475.
Directors: Sandra Chapman, Paul E. Schlosberg, Shelia Schlosberg.
EIN: 752892724

52836
J. W. and Eula Carter Scholarship Fund in Memory of Newt Bryson
P.O. Box 787
Mount Vernon, TX 75457-0787

Established in 1988 in TX.
Financial data (yr. ended 12/31/99): Grants paid, $7,450; assets, $111,414 (M); expenditures, $8,460; qualifying distributions, $7,376.
Limitations: Applications not accepted. Giving limited to Mount Vernon, TX.
Application information: Unsolicited requests for funds not accepted.
Trustees: J.H. Connally, B.F. Hicks, Virginia O'Donnell.
EIN: 756364951

52837
Judge Thornton Foundation
P.O. Box 192
Trinity, TX 75862-0192 (936) 594-2185
Contact: Jimmie Thornton, Pres.

Established in 1997 in TX.
Donor(s): Jimmie Thornton.
Financial data (yr. ended 12/31/01): Grants paid, $7,400; assets, $50,754 (M); gifts received, $7,000; expenditures, $7,654; qualifying distributions, $7,400.
Limitations: Giving primarily in Trinity County, TX.
Application information: Application form required.
Officers and Directors:* Jimmie Thornton,* Pres.; Cinda Norsworthy,* Secy.; Betty Wright.
EIN: 752704872

52838
Albert & Lena Hirschfeld Charitable Trust B
c/o Bank of America
P.O. Box 831041
Dallas, TX 75283-1041
Application address: P.O. Box 121, San Antonio, TX 78291-0121, tel.: (210) 270-5378

Financial data (yr. ended 12/31/01): Grants paid, $7,376; assets, $131,048 (M); expenditures, $10,105; qualifying distributions, $7,376.
Limitations: Giving primarily in San Antonio, TX.
Directors: Genl. A.B. Crowther, Lufkin Gilliland, Morris Spector, M.D.
Trustee: Bank of America.
EIN: 746264720

52839
The George & Elizabeth Haikin Foundation
8616 Lafonte St.
Houston, TX 77024

Financial data (yr. ended 12/31/01): Grants paid, $7,367; assets, $136,485 (M); expenditures, $8,278; qualifying distributions, $7,367.
Limitations: Applications not accepted. Giving primarily in Houston, TX.
Application information: Contributes only to pre-selected organizations.
Officer: Mike Haikin, Pres.
EIN: 746047174

52840
Williams Foundation
c/o Holly L. Spellman
5210 Dana Leigh Dr.
Houston, TX 77066-1732

Financial data (yr. ended 07/31/01): Grants paid, $7,315; assets, $253,549 (M); expenditures, $12,561; qualifying distributions, $7,315.
Limitations: Applications not accepted. Giving primarily in IN.
Application information: Contributes only to pre-selected organizations.
Trustees: Joyce Holtkamp, Nita McNealy, Max Niemeyer, Tom Niemeyer, Warren Patitz, Holly Spellman.
EIN: 356088864

52841
M. Scott Kraemer & Joyce Whiting Kraemer Family Foundation
7703 Valley View Ln.
Houston, TX 77074-5326

Established in 1993 in TX.
Donor(s): M. Scott Kraemer.
Financial data (yr. ended 12/31/01): Grants paid, $7,210; assets, $9,911 (M); gifts received, $9,000; expenditures, $7,575; qualifying distributions, $7,210.
Limitations: Giving primarily in TX.
Application information: Application form not required.
Officers: M. Scott Kraemer, Pres. and Treas.; Joyce Whiting Kraemer, V.P. and Secy.; Sandra McCauley, V.P.
EIN: 760393442

52842
The Martin Foundation
P.O. Box 8836
Horseshoe Bay, TX 78657-8836

Established in 1994 in TX.
Financial data (yr. ended 06/30/01): Grants paid, $7,200; assets, $1,636 (M); gifts received, $9,385; expenditures, $7,796; qualifying distributions, $7,200.
Limitations: Applications not accepted.

52842—TEXAS

Application information: Contributes only to pre-selected organizations.
Officer: Samuel A. Martin, Pres.
EIN: 760354906

52843
Appoline & Simeon Patout Foundation
217 E. Washington Ave.
Navasota, TX 77868
Application address: c/o Directors, 3512 J. Patout Burns Rd., Jeanerette, LA 70544, tel.: (337) 276-4592

Established in 1990 in LA.
Financial data (yr. ended 07/31/01): Grants paid, $7,200; assets, $111,292 (M); gifts received, $16,473; expenditures, $7,323; qualifying distributions, $7,200.
Limitations: Giving limited to residents of LA.
Application information: Application form required.
Directors: Anne Wall Bowman, Mary Burns, Patout Burns, Louise Dunn, Edwin S. Patout, Feather Rivers Patout, Jared Patout, Susan Crawford Patout.
EIN: 581888278

52844
Greer Garson Endowment Fund
c/o Bank of America
P.O. Box 831041
Dallas, TX 75283-1041
Application address: c/o Dean, Meadows School of the Arts, S.M.U., Dallas, TX 75205, tel.: (214) 692-2600

Donor(s): Greer Garson Fogelson.
Financial data (yr. ended 05/31/02): Grants paid, $7,053; assets, $201,926 (M); expenditures, $10,693; qualifying distributions, $8,263.
Limitations: Giving limited to Dallas, TX.
Trustee: Bank of America.
EIN: 756270099

52845
The Charlotte and Jamil Azzam Foundation
c/o Kanaly Trust Co.
4550 Post Oak Pl. Dr., Ste. 139
Houston, TX 77027-3163

Established in 1992 in TX.
Donor(s): Charlotte Azzam, Jamil Azzam.
Financial data (yr. ended 12/31/01): Grants paid, $7,000; assets, $1,860,140 (M); expenditures, $30,287; qualifying distributions, $8,161.
Limitations: Applications not accepted. Giving primarily in Houston, TX.
Application information: Contributes only to pre-selected organizations.
Officers: Charlotte Azzam, Mgr.; Jamil Azzam, Mgr.
Trustee: Kanaly Trust Co.
EIN: 760364245

52846
Bruce Family Foundation
1082 Los Jardines Cir.
El Paso, TX 79912-1941
Contact: Harry L. Bruce, Pres.

Established in 2000 in TX.
Donor(s): Harry Bruce, Patricia Bruce.
Financial data (yr. ended 12/31/01): Grants paid, $7,000; assets, $133,995 (M); expenditures, $10,670; qualifying distributions, $7,000.
Officers: Harry L. Bruce, Pres.; Marcia Bruce, V.P. and Secy.; Patricia Bruce, V.P. and Secy.; Steve Bruce, V.P. and Treas.
EIN: 742963528

52847
CLC Foundation
2901 First City Twr.
Houston, TX 77002-6760
Application address: c/o Citizens Bank, Clovis, NM 88101, tel.: (505) 769-1911
Contact: Lucile N. Laughlin, Pres.

Established in 1984 in TX.
Donor(s): John L. Carter.
Financial data (yr. ended 12/31/01): Grants paid, $7,000; assets, $162,381 (M); gifts received, $6,819; expenditures, $7,287; qualifying distributions, $7,000.
Limitations: Giving limited to residents of Clovis, NM.
Officers: Lucile N. Laughlin, Pres.; John L. Carter, V.P. and Secy.-Treas.
EIN: 760132112

52848
The Estes Foundation
c/o Carl Estes, II
5010 Longmont Dr.
Houston, TX 77056-2416

Established in 1995 in TX.
Donor(s): Mrs. Joe E. Estes.
Financial data (yr. ended 12/31/99): Grants paid, $7,000; assets, $176,252 (M); expenditures, $7,133; qualifying distributions, $7,050.
Limitations: Applications not accepted. Giving primarily in Houston, TX.
Application information: Contributes only to pre-selected organizations.
Officers: Carroll Estes, Pres.; Duskie Estes, V.P.; Gay G. Estes, Secy.; Carl Estes II, Treas.
EIN: 760474136

52849
Gil Memorial Scholarships, Inc.
2109 Plantation Ln.
Plano, TX 75093
Contact: Linda Nelson, Dir.

Established in 1991 in TX.
Donor(s): Linda Nelson, Robert Nelson.
Financial data (yr. ended 12/31/01): Grants paid, $7,000; assets, $137,196 (M); gifts received, $25,000; expenditures, $7,032; qualifying distributions, $6,979.
Limitations: Giving primarily to residents of Plano, TX.
Application information: Applicants must have 12 hours in credits at an accredited university and a 2.7 GPA. Application form required.
Directors: Frances Lease, Linda Nelson, Robert Nelson.
EIN: 752389081

52850
Ida Morris Charitable Trust
217 Village Cir.
Waco, TX 76710
Contact: Helen Clark, Tr.

Financial data (yr. ended 01/31/02): Grants paid, $7,000; assets, $21,563 (M); expenditures, $11,174; qualifying distributions, $7,000.
Limitations: Giving limited to Waco, TX.
Trustee: Helen Clark.
EIN: 741959187

52851
Joseph & Clifford Nelson Murphy Charitable Foundation, Inc.
P.O. Box 940
Marshall, TX 75671 (903) 935-9331

Established in 1992 in TX.
Donor(s): Mrs. Clifford Nelson Murphy.
Financial data (yr. ended 12/31/01): Grants paid, $7,000; assets, $173,823 (M); gifts received, $25,898; expenditures, $8,048; qualifying distributions, $7,000.
Limitations: Applications not accepted. Giving primarily in TX.
Application information: Contributes only to pre-selected organizations.
Officers: Mary M. Daughety, Pres.; J. Rick McMinn, V.P.; Charles Nelson, Secy.
EIN: 752359694

52852
The Stai Family Foundation
c/o Harlan C. Stai
11 Hudson Cir.
Houston, TX 77024-7254

Established in 1997 in TX.
Donor(s): Harlan C. Stai.
Financial data (yr. ended 12/31/00): Grants paid, $7,000; assets, $95,913 (M); expenditures, $10,395; qualifying distributions, $7,000.
Limitations: Applications not accepted. Giving primarily in Houston, TX.
Application information: Contributes only to pre-selected organizations.
Officers: Harlan C. Stai, Pres.; Aaron Stai, V.P.; Dian G. Owen, Secy.
EIN: 760537918

52853
Waco Citizens Foundation
P.O. Box 1277
Waco, TX 76703-1277

Donor(s): Harriette L. Lacy.
Financial data (yr. ended 12/31/00): Grants paid, $7,000; assets, $117,297 (M); expenditures, $7,496; qualifying distributions, $7,000.
Limitations: Applications not accepted. Giving primarily in Waco, TX.
Application information: Contributes only to pre-selected organizations.
Officer: Harriette L. Lacy, Pres.
Directors: Donald R. Howe, Sr., Thomas L. Lacy, Sr., Walter G. Lacy, William D. Lacy.
EIN: 746044021

52854
Gray & Patricia Wakefield Charitable Foundation
614 Hunters Grove Ln.
Houston, TX 77024 (713) 224-9661
Contact: Gray C. Wakefield, Tr.

Financial data (yr. ended 06/30/01): Grants paid, $7,000; assets, $174,844 (M); expenditures, $7,050; qualifying distributions, $7,000.
Limitations: Giving primarily in Houston, TX.
Application information: Application form not required.
Trustees: Gray C. Wakefield, Patricia R. Wakefield.
EIN: 746104638

52855
Everett E. and Orabeth K. Woods Foundation
P.O. Box 5749
Abilene, TX 79605
Contact: Benjamin K. Woods, V.P.

Established in 1992 in TX.
Donor(s): Woods Clinical Management.
Financial data (yr. ended 09/30/01): Grants paid, $7,000; assets, $109,743 (M); gifts received, $5,899; expenditures, $10,002; qualifying distributions, $7,000.
Officers: Everett E. Woods, Pres.; Benjamin K. Woods, V.P.; Donald E. Woods, V.P.; Orabeth K. Woods, V.P.
EIN: 752212157

52856
The Young Family Foundation
115 W. Putnam
Ganado, TX 77962
Application addresses: c/o Ganado High School, 510 W. Devers, Ganado, TX 77962; c/o Louise High School, 408 2nd St., Louise, TX 77455; c/o Tidehaven High School, P.O. Box 159, El Maton, TX 77440

Established in 2000 in TX.
Financial data (yr. ended 09/30/01): Grants paid, $7,000; assets, $947,211 (M); gifts received, $1,100,000; expenditures, $18,774; qualifying distributions, $18,774.
Limitations: Giving limited to residents of TX.
Application information: Applications available at each high school counselor's office. Application form required.
Officers: Raymond Young, Pres.; Royce Young, V.P.; Paula Young Kacer, Secy.-Treas.
Directors: Barbara Larson, Carleen Olson, Bill Silliman, John Stockton.
EIN: 742979295

52857
Bamberger Ranch Conservancy
2341 Blue Ridge Dr.
Johnson City, TX 78636-9707 (830) 868-7303
Contact: J. David Bamberger, Pres.

Established in 1994 in TX.
Donor(s): J. David Bamberger.
Financial data (yr. ended 11/30/01): Grants paid, $6,990; assets, $207,484 (M); gifts received, $13,675; expenditures, $19,152; qualifying distributions, $6,990.
Limitations: Giving primarily in San Antonio and Austin, TX.
Officers and Directors:* J. David Bamberger,* Pres.; David K. Bamberger,* V.P.; Margaret Campbell, James Rhoades, and 3 additional directors.
EIN: 742729929

52858
Debra Marie Lugar Memorial Foundation
18954 FM 2252
Garden Ridge, TX 78266-2703
(210) 651-6783
Contact: Garry M. Lugar, Dir.

Established in 2000 in TX.
Donor(s): Garrich Industries, Inc.
Financial data (yr. ended 12/31/00): Grants paid, $6,937; assets, $55,165 (M); gifts received, $25,000; expenditures, $6,937; qualifying distributions, $6,937.
Limitations: Giving primarily in San Antonio, TX.
Application information: Application form not required.
Directors: Susan Braden, Garry M. Lugar, Karen S. Lugar.
EIN: 742906811
Codes: CS

52859
The Costello Foundation
717 James Dr.
Richardson, TX 75080

Donor(s): John Patrick Costello, Sr.
Financial data (yr. ended 12/31/01): Grants paid, $6,900; assets, $148,610 (M); expenditures, $7,923; qualifying distributions, $6,900.
Limitations: Applications not accepted. Giving primarily in Dallas, TX.
Application information: Contributes only to pre-selected organizations.
Trustees: Collen Armstrong, John Patrick Costello, Jr.

EIN: 756021713

52860
Lewis Foundation
39 Elkins Lake
Huntsville, TX 77340

Financial data (yr. ended 12/31/00): Grants paid, $6,900; assets, $223,619 (M); gifts received, $132,861; expenditures, $10,491; qualifying distributions, $6,833.
Limitations: Applications not accepted.
Application information: Contributes only to pre-selected organizations.
Officer: Roy Lewis, Mgr.
EIN: 912135736

52861
The Jerry and Becky Lindauer Family Foundation
600 Congress Ave., Ste. 200
Austin, TX 78701

Established in 1999 in TX.
Donor(s): Jerry Lindauer, Becky Lindauer.
Financial data (yr. ended 12/31/01): Grants paid, $6,850; assets, $3,511 (M); gifts received, $8,085; expenditures, $8,667; qualifying distributions, $6,850.
Limitations: Applications not accepted.
Application information: Contributes only to pre-selected organizations.
Officers: Jerry Lindauer, Pres.; Becky Lindauer, V.P.
EIN: 742938546

52862
Stephens Foundation
400 Oak St.
P.O. Box 9129
Graham, TX 76450-2522 (940) 549-0050
Contact: Ronald Stephens, V.P.

Donor(s): Ronald Stephens, Bruce Stephens.
Financial data (yr. ended 09/30/01): Grants paid, $6,850; assets, $139,820 (M); expenditures, $6,976; qualifying distributions, $6,850.
Limitations: Giving primarily in Graham, TX.
Officers: Barbara Stephens, Pres.; Bruce Stephens, V.P.; Ronald Stephens, V.P.; B.L. Williams, Secy.-Treas.
EIN: 510169342

52863
Dean Allen Willis Foundation
c/o Suzanne Willis
P.O. Box 1046
Perryton, TX 79070

Established in 1996 in TX.
Donor(s): Barry Willis.
Financial data (yr. ended 12/31/01): Grants paid, $6,842; assets, $137,862 (M); gifts received, $2,561; expenditures, $7,360; qualifying distributions, $6,842.
Limitations: Applications not accepted. Giving primarily in Perryton, TX.
Application information: Contributes only to pre-selected organizations.
Officers and Directors:* Suzanne Willis,* Pres.; Barry Willis,* V.P.; Brent Allen,* Secy.-Treas.; Manon E. Childers, M.D., Lawrence Ellzey.
EIN: 752680569

52864
Betts Foundation
c/o Byrleen K. Terry
730 Fonville Dr.
Marlin, TX 76661-2826
Application address: 615 Perry St., Marlin, TX 76661, tel.: (254) 883-2616
Contact: Louise Dugat, Pres.

Financial data (yr. ended 12/31/00): Grants paid, $6,750; assets, $170,685 (M); expenditures, $8,418; qualifying distributions, $6,750.
Limitations: Giving limited to Falls County, TX.
Application information: Application form not required.
Officers: Louise Dugat, Pres.; Jackie Wasserman, V.P.; Virginia Torbett, Secy.; Byrleen Terry, Admin.
EIN: 751014070

52865
Anthony Family Foundation
12770 Coit Rd., Ste. 1170
Dallas, TX 75251

Established in 1996 in TX.
Donor(s): Cynthia S. Anthony, R. Jay Anthony.
Financial data (yr. ended 12/31/01): Grants paid, $6,700; assets, $2,080 (M); expenditures, $7,224; qualifying distributions, $6,700.
Limitations: Applications not accepted.
Application information: Contributes only to pre-selected organizations.
Officers and Directors:* R. Jay Anthony,* Pres.; Cynthia S. Anthony,* V.P. and Secy.-Treas.; James Kevin Flynn.
EIN: 752681504

52866
Lipsitz Foundation
(Formerly Melvin A. Lipsitz Family Foundation)
c/o Melvin A. Lipsitz
P.O. Box 1175
Waco, TX 76703-1175

Established in 1990 in TX.
Donor(s): Melvin Lipsitz, Jr.
Financial data (yr. ended 12/31/01): Grants paid, $6,675; assets, $48,468 (M); gifts received, $4,000; expenditures, $7,600; qualifying distributions, $6,658.
Limitations: Applications not accepted. Giving primarily in Waco, TX.
Officers: Melvin A. Lipsitz, Pres.; Lynne Lipsitz, V.P.; Lee Gundlach, Secy.-Treas.
EIN: 742587599

52867
The Balcony Foundation, Inc.
4935 Cape Coral Dr.
Dallas, TX 75287
Contact: Ronald Simmons, Pres.

Established in 1999 in TX.
Donor(s): Ronald Simmons.
Financial data (yr. ended 12/31/00): Grants paid, $6,661; assets, $39,707 (M); expenditures, $6,661; qualifying distributions, $6,661.
Officers: Ronald Simmons, Pres.; Justin Simmons, V.P.; Lisa Simmons, Secy.-Treas.
EIN: 752852957

52868
Kuglen Foundation
c/o Craig C. Kuglen
1310 Rockcliff Rd.
Austin, TX 78746-1205

Established in 1998 in TX.
Donor(s): Craig C. Kuglen.

52868—TEXAS

Financial data (yr. ended 04/30/02): Grants paid, $6,550; assets, $26,818 (M); expenditures, $6,863; qualifying distributions, $6,550.
Limitations: Applications not accepted. Giving primarily in TX.
Application information: Contributes only to pre-selected organizations.
Officer: Craig C. Kuglen, Pres. and Mgr.
EIN: 742832878

52869
The Jessie A. Leak Private Foundation
2304 Avalon Pl.
Houston, TX 77019

Established in 1997 in TX.
Financial data (yr. ended 12/31/01): Grants paid, $6,525; assets, $720 (M); gifts received, $6,240; expenditures, $7,955; qualifying distributions, $6,525.
Limitations: Applications not accepted.
Application information: Contributes only to pre-selected organizations.
Trustee: Jessie A. Leak.
EIN: 562059774

52870
The Foundation for Church Growth
2710 Farmers Branch Ln.
Farmers Branch, TX 75234 (972) 247-0219
Contact: Edwin V. Bonneau, Pres.

Established in 1993 in TX.
Donor(s): Edwin V. Bonneau.
Financial data (yr. ended 12/31/01): Grants paid, $6,500; assets, $800,180 (M); expenditures, $11,543; qualifying distributions, $6,500.
Limitations: Giving primarily in TX.
Officers and Directors:* Edwin V. Bonneau,* Pres.; Todd O. Bonneau,* V.P.; Barbara J. Bonneau,* Secy.-Treas.; Julie L. Bonneau, Rene Watten, Steven P. Watten.
EIN: 752181549

52871
Walter J. & Ada B. Kreager Memorial Scholarship Fund
c/o Hibernia National Bank
P.O. Box 3928
Beaumont, TX 77704
Application address: c/o Lana Walsh, Port Neches High School, 1401 Merriman St., Port Neches, TX 77651

Established in 1996 in TX.
Donor(s): Ada Belle Kreager.‡
Financial data (yr. ended 05/31/01): Grants paid, $6,500; assets, $249,415 (M); expenditures, $10,037; qualifying distributions, $9,955.
Limitations: Giving limited to the Groves and Port Neches, TX, area.
Application information: Application form required.
Trustee: Hibernia National Bank.
EIN: 760504933

52872
The Nancy Ruth Fund
3713 Wood Rail Dr.
Plano, TX 75074

Established in 2000 in TX.
Donor(s): Lorraine K. Darley, Henry M. Darley.
Financial data (yr. ended 10/31/01): Grants paid, $6,500; assets, $101,212 (M); gifts received, $131,676; expenditures, $11,579; qualifying distributions, $8,538.
Limitations: Applications not accepted.
Application information: Contributes only to pre-selected organizations.

Officers: Lorraine K. Darley, C.E.O.; Laura B. Darley, V.P.; Andrew D. Hansen, Secy.; Henry M. Darley, C.F.O.
EIN: 752907236

52873
The Parten Foundation
808 Travis St., Ste. 1453
Houston, TX 77002

Incorporated in 1962 in TX.
Donor(s): John R. Parten, Grace P. Thomas,‡ Jubal R. Parten.‡
Financial data (yr. ended 03/31/01): Grants paid, $6,500; assets, $873,609 (M); expenditures, $18,942; qualifying distributions, $6,500.
Limitations: Applications not accepted. Giving primarily in TX.
Application information: Contributes only to pre-selected organizations.
Officers and Directors:* John R. Parten,* Pres.; Robert F. Pratka,* V.P. and Treas.; Valerie Coulter, Secy.
EIN: 746043490

52874
Reitmeier Charitable Foundation
16022 Gore Grass Ct.
Spring, TX 77379-2931

Donor(s): Georgan W. Reitmeier, R. Thomas Reitmeier.
Financial data (yr. ended 12/31/01): Grants paid, $6,500; assets, $104,983 (M); expenditures, $6,500; qualifying distributions, $6,500.
Limitations: Applications not accepted. Giving on a national basis.
Application information: Contributes only to pre-selected organizations.
Trustees: Georgan W. Reitmeier, R. Thomas Reitmeier.
EIN: 741902119

52875
Rooke Foundation, Inc.
P.O. Box 610
Woodsboro, TX 78393-0610
Contact: Robert E. Rooke, Jr., V.P.

Financial data (yr. ended 12/31/01): Grants paid, $6,500; assets, $196,094 (M); expenditures, $6,695; qualifying distributions, $6,695.
Limitations: Giving limited to Refugio County, TX.
Application information: Applications available at Refugio County high schools, TX. Application form required.
Officers and Directors:* Frank J. Scanio, Jr.,* Pres.; Norma R. Canfield,* V.P.; Robert E. Rooke, Jr.,* V.P.
EIN: 746003460
Codes: GTI

52876
IHS Foundation
30435 Hwy, 281 N.
Bulverde, TX 78163

Financial data (yr. ended 12/31/01): Grants paid, $6,480; assets, $971 (M); gifts received, $7,240; expenditures, $6,500; qualifying distributions, $6,480.
Trustees: Barbara Barnett, Thomas Jones, William M. Parham.
EIN: 742804021

52877
Brooks Family Charitable Trust
2901 Morton St.
Fort Worth, TX 76107-2925

Established in 1986 in TX.
Donor(s): Bill R. Brooks.

Financial data (yr. ended 12/31/01): Grants paid, $6,450; assets, $231,698 (M); expenditures, $6,769; qualifying distributions, $6,450.
Limitations: Applications not accepted. Giving limited to Fort Worth, TX.
Application information: Contributes only to pre-selected organizations.
Trustees: Betty J. Brooks, Bill R. Brooks, Kelly Brooks Keller.
EIN: 756333715

52878
Mike and Myrtle Michael Charitable Trust
c/o Wells Fargo Bank Texas, N.A.
P.O. Drawer 913
Bryan, TX 77805-0913 (979) 776-3267

Established in 1998 in TX.
Donor(s): M. Michael.‡
Financial data (yr. ended 05/31/02): Grants paid, $6,416; assets, $120,508 (M); expenditures, $9,352; qualifying distributions, $6,416.
Limitations: Giving primarily in TX.
Trustee: Wells Fargo Bank Texas, N.A.
EIN: 742915277

52879
The Campana Foundation, Inc.
Rte. 1, Box 269M
George West, TX 78022 (361) 566-2244
Contact: Jean Martin, Pres.

Donor(s): T.J. Martin, Jr., Angela Martin, Jeff Martin.
Financial data (yr. ended 12/31/01): Grants paid, $6,414; assets, $5,106 (M); gifts received, $3,895; expenditures, $7,107; qualifying distributions, $6,414.
Application information: Application form not required.
Officers: Jean Martin, Pres.; T.J. Martin, Jr., Secy.-Treas.
Director: M.M. Martin.
EIN: 742385761

52880
Woodell Foundation, Inc.
10951 Beinhorn Rd.
Houston, TX 77024-4517

Financial data (yr. ended 04/30/01): Grants paid, $6,410; assets, $50,242 (M); expenditures, $7,946; qualifying distributions, $6,410.
Officers: Leewood Woodell, Pres.; Thomas Woodell, Secy.-Treas.
EIN: 760538344

52881
Redstone Summit Foundation
P.O. Box 631327
Houston, TX 77263-1327
Contact: K.T. Synder, II, Pres.

Established in 1997 in TX.
Donor(s): K.T. Snyder II, Karen G. Snyder.
Financial data (yr. ended 12/31/01): Grants paid, $6,400; assets, $73,437 (M); expenditures, $7,609; qualifying distributions, $6,400.
Officers and Directors:* K.T. Snyder II,* Pres.; Karen G. Synder,* Secy.; John R. Boyer, Jr.
EIN: 760533496

52882
Richard and Kathy Burrow Vermillion Foundation, Inc.
2001 Kirby Dr., Ste. 715
Houston, TX 77019-6033

Established in 2000.
Donor(s): The Burrow Foundation, Inc.
Financial data (yr. ended 11/30/01): Grants paid, $6,400; assets, $9,800 (M); gifts received,

$10,000; expenditures, $6,570; qualifying distributions, $6,570.
Limitations: Applications not accepted.
Application information: Contributes only to pre-selected organizations.
Trustees: Benjamin Robert Vermillion, C. Richard Vermillion, Jr., C. Richard Vermillion III, Kathy Burrow Vermillion.
EIN: 760631338

52883
Lynn & Armin Cantini Friendship Trust
4724 Sherman Blvd.
Galveston, TX 77551

Established in 1997 in TX.
Donor(s): Lynn L. Cantini, Armin Cantini.
Financial data (yr. ended 06/30/02): Grants paid, $6,394; assets, $124,573 (M); expenditures, $8,188; qualifying distributions, $6,394.
Limitations: Applications not accepted.
Application information: Contributes only to pre-selected organizations.
Trustees: Armin Cantini, Lynn L. Cantini.
EIN: 760575325

52884
Howard Trout Foundation
12335 Kingsride Ln., No. 147
Houston, TX 77024-4116 (713) 973-1364
Contact: Howard James Trout, Dir.

Financial data (yr. ended 12/31/01): Grants paid, $6,375; assets, $69,689 (M); expenditures, $6,375; qualifying distributions, $6,375.
Limitations: Giving primarily in Lufkin and Houston, TX.
Directors: Douglas E. Clark, Howard James Trout.
EIN: 742191428

52885
Beard Fund
510 W. Davis St.
Dallas, TX 75208
Contact: Frances Jeanette Beard, Tr.

Donor(s): Frances Jeanette Beard.
Financial data (yr. ended 08/31/00): Grants paid, $6,361; assets, $133,062 (M); expenditures, $8,979; qualifying distributions, $6,361.
Limitations: Giving limited to TX.
Trustees: David Glenn Beard, Frances Jeanette Beard.
EIN: 756029095

52886
The Franklin P. and Mildred A. Azpell Foundation
3200 Riverfront Dr., Ste. 100
Fort Worth, TX 76107
Contact: Roger M. Norman, Tr.

Established in 2001 in TX.
Donor(s): Mildred A. Azpell.‡
Financial data (yr. ended 12/31/01): Grants paid, $6,345; assets, $286,274 (M); gifts received, $280,000; expenditures, $12,205; qualifying distributions, $6,345.
Trustee: Roger M. Norman.
EIN: 756593173

52887
P & R Foundation
c/o Philip K. Dady
109 Royal View Rd.
Salado, TX 76571-5468

Financial data (yr. ended 12/31/01): Grants paid, $6,345; assets, $14,179 (M); gifts received, $20,000; expenditures, $6,368; qualifying distributions, $6,368.
Limitations: Giving primarily in TX.

Trustee: Philip K. Dady.
EIN: 746496946

52888
Harold B. & Eleanor M. Cameron Foundation, Inc.
2818 Pounds Ave.
Tyler, TX 75701

Established in 1997 in TX.
Financial data (yr. ended 06/30/02): Grants paid, $6,300; assets, $92,492 (M); gifts received, $9,703; expenditures, $6,650; qualifying distributions, $6,300.
Limitations: Applications not accepted. Giving primarily in Troup, TX.
Application information: Contributes only to pre-selected organizations.
Officers: Harold B. Cameron, Pres.; Eleanor M. Cameron, V.P.; Howard B. Cameron, Jr., Secy.-Treas.
EIN: 752699508

52889
T. B. Maston Foundation
(Formerly T. B. Maston Scholarship Foundation)
333 N. Washington Ave.
Dallas, TX 75246-1798 (214) 828-5190

Donor(s): Wayne Barnes.
Financial data (yr. ended 12/31/01): Grants paid, $6,300; assets, $340,344 (M); gifts received, $15,450; expenditures, $36,009; qualifying distributions, $6,300.
Limitations: Giving primarily in Fort Worth, TX.
Officers: Jimmy Allen, Chair.; David Morgan, Vice-Chair.; Leta Tillman, Secy.; Joe Haag, Treas.
EIN: 752117002

52890
The Mercedes M. Murphy Foundation
6550 Fannin St., Ste. 2323
Houston, TX 77030-2717 (713) 795-4300
Contact: Edward C. Murphy, M.D., Pres.

Donor(s): Edward C. Murphy, M.D.
Financial data (yr. ended 12/31/01): Grants paid, $6,300; assets, $2,161 (M); gifts received, $8,345; expenditures, $6,919; qualifying distributions, $6,919.
Limitations: Giving primarily in TX and VA.
Officers: Edward C. Murphy, M.D., Pres.; Irene A. Sachs, Secy.
EIN: 760150340
Codes: TN

52891
Edwards Foundation
5114 McKinney Ave., Ste. 309
Dallas, TX 75205-2902

Donor(s): J. Brian Edwards.‡
Financial data (yr. ended 12/31/99): Grants paid, $6,277; assets, $172,555 (M); expenditures, $7,323; qualifying distributions, $7,072.
Limitations: Applications not accepted. Giving primarily in TX.
Application information: Contributes only to pre-selected organizations.
Trustees: D. Van Edwards, Frances J. Smith.
EIN: 726012729

52892
Freedom Foundation
14275 Midway Rd., Ste. 220-27
Addison, TX 75001

Established in 1998 in TX.
Donor(s): Robert W. Canterbury, Hollis B. Canterbury.

Financial data (yr. ended 12/31/01): Grants paid, $6,259; assets, $7,524 (M); expenditures, $53,854; qualifying distributions, $6,259.
Limitations: Applications not accepted. Giving primarily in Dallas, TX.
Application information: Contributes only to pre-selected organizations.
Officers: Michael D. Canterbury, Pres.; Anneliese Adams Canterbury, Secy.
Directors: Hollis B. Canterbury, Robert W. Canterbury, Dennis W. Lewis.
EIN: 752790350

52893
The Richard and Angela Armitage Family Foundation
5 Pascal Ln.
Austin, TX 78746 (512) 329-9051

Established in 2001 in TX.
Donor(s): Angela V. Armitage, Richard J. Armitage.
Financial data (yr. ended 12/31/01): Grants paid, $6,250; assets, $105,067 (M); gifts received, $116,098; expenditures, $12,678; qualifying distributions, $11,928.
Limitations: Giving on a national basis, with emphasis on TX.
Officers: Richard J. Armitage, Pres. and Treas.; Angela V. Armitage, V.P. and Secy.
Trustee: David J. Armitage.
EIN: 743000470

52894
First Christian Church of Throckmorton Receivership
(Formerly First Chirstian Church of Throckmorton Trust)
P.O. Box 540
Graham, TX 76450-0540 (940) 549-2040
Contact: Ted Boedeker, Sr. V.P. & Trust Off., First National Bank

Established in 1997 in TX.
Financial data (yr. ended 12/31/01): Grants paid, $6,152; assets, $233,805 (M); gifts received, $780; expenditures, $8,737; qualifying distributions, $6,152.
Limitations: Giving limited to TX.
Application information: Application form required.
Trustee: First National Bank.
EIN: 756451027

52895
Laura & Bob Higley Foundation
6339 Belmont St.
Houston, TX 77005

Established in 1996 in TX.
Donor(s): Laura C. Higley, Robert A. Higley.
Financial data (yr. ended 12/31/01): Grants paid, $6,100; assets, $18,535 (M); gifts received, $400; expenditures, $6,400; qualifying distributions, $6,100.
Trustees: Laura C. Higley, Laura Lee Higley, Robert A. Higley.
EIN: 760522712

52896
Terri Volter Memorial Foundation
18814 Racquet Ridge Rd.
Humble, TX 77346-8212
Contact: Terrell V. Volter, Pres.

Established in 1999 in TX.
Donor(s): Terrell V. Volter, Eva M. Volter.
Financial data (yr. ended 12/31/01): Grants paid, $6,100; assets, $1,591 (M); gifts received, $6,500; expenditures, $9,405; qualifying distributions, $6,100.

52896—TEXAS

Application information: Application form required.
Officer and Directors:* Terrell V. Volter,* Pres.; Eva M. Volter, Keema L. Volter.
EIN: 760606290

52897
Dr. Edith F. Bondi Foundation
3350 McCue, Ste. 903
Houston, TX 77056-7109
Contact: Edith F. Bondi, Pres.

Donor(s): Edith F. Bondi.
Financial data (yr. ended 12/31/00): Grants paid, $6,000; assets, $154,614 (M); expenditures, $6,004; qualifying distributions, $6,000.
Limitations: Giving primarily in NY and TX.
Officers: Edith F. Bondi, Pres.; Michael S. Parmet, V.P.
EIN: 760285812

52898
Maureen Connolly Brinker Cancer Fund, Inc.
2911 Turtle Creek Blvd., No. 1010
Dallas, TX 75219 (214) 528-1590
Contact: Robert C. Taylor, Tr.

Financial data (yr. ended 04/30/02): Grants paid, $6,000; assets, $144,644 (M); expenditures, $6,929; qualifying distributions, $6,000.
Limitations: Giving primarily in Dallas, TX.
Trustees: Norman Brinker, Robert C. Taylor.
EIN: 751328729

52899
The John Aure Buesseler and Cathryn Anne Hansen Buesseler Foundation
3305 59th St.
Lubbock, TX 79413-5517

Established in 2000 in TX.
Donor(s): John Aure Buesseler, Cathryn Anne Hansen Buesseler.
Financial data (yr. ended 12/31/01): Grants paid, $6,000; assets, $23,814 (M); gifts received, $16,200; expenditures, $16,200; qualifying distributions, $6,000.
Limitations: Applications not accepted.
Application information: Contributes only to pre-selected organizations.
Officers: John Aure Buesseler, Pres.; Frank R. Buesseler, V.P.; Cathryn Anne Hansen Buesseler, Secy.-Treas.
EIN: 752816028

52900
Cargill Foundation
P.O. Box 992
Longview, TX 75606-0992
Contact: Robert L. Cargill, Jr., Dir.

Financial data (yr. ended 11/30/01): Grants paid, $6,000; assets, $101,218 (M); expenditures, $6,316; qualifying distributions, $5,966.
Limitations: Giving primarily in Longview, TX.
Directors: Pauline W. Cargill, Robert L. Cargill, Jr.
EIN: 752085807

52901
Collin County Adult Literacy Council
P.O. Box 490
Allen, TX 75013

Financial data (yr. ended 06/30/99): Grants paid, $6,000; assets, $1,247 (M); gifts received, $4,200; expenditures, $6,367; qualifying distributions, $6,000.
Limitations: Giving primarily in TX.
Application information: Application form not required.
Officers: Pat Guess, Pres.; Sue Compton, V.P.; Barbara Pettis, Secy.; Barbara Ridley, Treas.

EIN: 752008683

52902
Ida Fay Cowden Foundation
P.O. Box 482
Midland, TX 79702-0482 (915) 684-6311
Contact: Wright E. Cowden, Jr., Pres.

Financial data (yr. ended 05/31/00): Grants paid, $6,000; assets, $248,413 (M); expenditures, $10,796; qualifying distributions, $10,796; giving activities include $4,796 for programs.
Limitations: Giving primarily in Midland, TX.
Application information: Application form not required.
Officers and Directors:* Wright E. Cowden, Jr.,* Pres.; Carolyn G. Cowden,* V.P.; Loyd Whitley,* V.P.
EIN: 756035889

52903
Daugherty Fund
7027 Fisher Rd.
Dallas, TX 75214-1914 (214) 823-4433
Contact: Paul E. Daugherty, Jr., Pres.

Financial data (yr. ended 12/31/01): Grants paid, $6,000; assets, $123,723 (M); expenditures, $6,634; qualifying distributions, $6,000.
Limitations: Giving primarily in MA and TX.
Officers and Directors:* Paul E. Daugherty, Jr.,* Pres.; Mary Scott Daugherty,* V.P.; Linda M. Daugherty,* Secy.-Treas.
EIN: 760007726

52904
C. O. Fenner Charitable Foundation
c/o Garland R. Sandhop
608 N. Wells St.
Edna, TX 77957-2719
Application address: c/o Cathy Marek, Tr., 119 Newport Dr., Victoria, TX 77904

Established in 1994.
Financial data (yr. ended 06/30/01): Grants paid, $6,000; assets, $110,786 (M); expenditures, $6,045; qualifying distributions, $5,943.
Limitations: Giving primarily in Jackson County, TX.
Trustees: Charlie Fenner, Paul Holm, Janet Miller, Garland R. Sandhop.
EIN: 746422483

52905
Lynn B. and Dorothy Griffith Charitable Foundation
P.O. Box 976
Waxahachie, TX 75168-0976 (972) 937-0502
Contact: Lynn G. Winborne, Dir.

Established in 1985 in TX.
Financial data (yr. ended 06/30/00): Grants paid, $6,000; assets, $116,317 (M); expenditures, $6,135; qualifying distributions, $6,135.
Limitations: Giving limited to the Waxahachie, TX, area.
Application information: Application form required.
Directors: Dan E. Morton, Parker, Lynn G. Winborne, M.G. Winborne.
EIN: 756336325

52906
Helmle-Shaw Foundation
9411 Cadman Ct.
Houston, TX 77096-4206 (713) 782-7730
Contact: Judith Helmle Shaw, Secy.

Established in 1994 in TX.
Financial data (yr. ended 12/31/00): Grants paid, $6,000; assets, $242,275 (M); gifts received, $98,074; expenditures, $7,247; qualifying distributions, $6,000.
Officers: Roy C. Shaw, Jr., Pres.; Judith Helmle Shaw, Secy.
EIN: 760420414

52907
Judy's Foundation
828 W. 6th St.
Austin, TX 78703

Established in 2000 in TX.
Donor(s): Judith L. Trabulsi.
Financial data (yr. ended 10/31/01): Grants paid, $6,000; assets, $177,009 (M); gifts received, $232,554; expenditures, $7,167; qualifying distributions, $6,000.
Limitations: Applications not accepted.
Application information: Contributes only to pre-selected organizations.
Officer and Trustees:* Judith L. Trabulsi,* Dir.; Kimberly Lynn Strama Cohen, Julie Ann O'Neill, Kevin Richard O'Neill, Richard Keith Strama, Thomas Mark Strama, Blake Evans Trabulsi, Genevieve Paige Trabulsi.
EIN: 746498006

52908
The Jake and Nina Kamin Foundation
1 Sugar Creek Ctr. Blvd., Ste. 890
Sugar Land, TX 77478
Contact: Jake Kamin, Pres.

Established in 1986 in TX.
Donor(s): Jake Kamin.
Financial data (yr. ended 12/31/01): Grants paid, $6,000; assets, $102,635 (M); expenditures, $8,941; qualifying distributions, $6,000.
Limitations: Giving primarily in Houston, TX.
Officers: Jake Kamin, Pres.; Sanford A. Weiner, V.P.; Dulane Bourdeau, Secy.; Frank Mandola, Treas.
EIN: 760206841

52909
Louise Knight Scholarship Trust
P.O. Box 925
Madisonville, TX 77864-0924
Contact: Roger Knight, Jr., Tr.

Established in 1990 in TX.
Donor(s): Roger Knight, Jr.
Financial data (yr. ended 12/31/00): Grants paid, $6,000; assets, $37,348 (M); gifts received, $6,000; expenditures, $6,000; qualifying distributions, $6,000.
Limitations: Giving limited to Madisonville, TX.
Application information: Application form required.
Trustee: Roger Knight, Jr.
EIN: 746387730

52910
M. B. Krupp Foundation
4500 Hastings Dr.
El Paso, TX 79903-1914

Financial data (yr. ended 12/31/01): Grants paid, $6,000; assets, $370,501 (M); gifts received, $230,000; expenditures, $7,305; qualifying distributions, $6,000.
Limitations: Applications not accepted. Giving primarily in El Paso, TX.
Application information: Contributes only to pre-selected organizations.
Officer: Maxine M. Krupp, Pres. and Treas.
EIN: 741562995

52911
Lee Family Charitable Trust
P.O. Box 545
Bandera, TX 78003
Contact: Donald D. Lee, Tr. or Roberta K. Lee, Tr.

Donor(s): Donald D. Lee, Karen Lee, Roberta K. Lee.
Financial data (yr. ended 08/31/01): Grants paid, $6,000; assets, $176,134 (M); expenditures, $6,568; qualifying distributions, $6,000.
Limitations: Giving primarily in TX.
Trustees: Donald D. Lee, Roberta K. Lee.
EIN: 742077025

52912
Brady and Pauline Lowe Charitable Trust
2313 Broadway
Lubbock, TX 79401

Established in 2000 in TX.
Donor(s): Brady Lowe, Pauline Lowe.
Financial data (yr. ended 12/31/01): Grants paid, $6,000; assets, $119,836 (M); gifts received, $84,167; expenditures, $6,000; qualifying distributions, $6,000.
Limitations: Applications not accepted. Giving primarily in TX.
Application information: Contributes only to pre-selected organizations.
Trustees: Larry K. Lowe, Loretta D. Lowe.
EIN: 742959690

52913
Henry George Mackintosh Foundation
2129 Wroxton Rd.
Houston, TX 77005

Established in 1994 in TX.
Donor(s): Peter D. Mackintosh, Evangeline Mackintosh.
Financial data (yr. ended 12/31/01): Grants paid, $6,000; assets, $140,985 (M); expenditures, $8,668; qualifying distributions, $6,000.
Limitations: Applications not accepted. Giving primarily in AR and TX.
Application information: Contributes only to pre-selected organizations.
Directors: Alex Cantu, Evangeline Mackintosh, Peter D. Mackintosh, Rob Roy Mackintosh.
EIN: 760445888

52914
Meat Cutters Educational Trust
UFCW Region 5
1701 W. Northwest Hwy., Ste. 200
Grapevine, TX 76051
Application address: c/o UFCW Scholarship Prog., Office of Education, 1775 K St., N.W., Washington, DC 20006

Established in 1984 in TX.
Financial data (yr. ended 12/31/01): Grants paid, $6,000; assets, $204,541 (M); expenditures, $10,034; qualifying distributions, $8,399.
Limitations: Giving limited to AR, KS, LA, MO, OK, and TX.
Publications: Informational brochure (including application guidelines).
Application information: SAT or ACT scores required. Application form not required.
Trustees: Joseph P. Chicoine, Paulia Weaver, Bank One, Texas, N.A.
EIN: 752035368
Codes: GTI

52915
The W. L. and Barbara Nix Charitable Foundation
c/o W.L. Nix
P.O. Box 1316
Stephenville, TX 76401-1316

Established in 1993 in TX.
Donor(s): W.L. Nix, Barbara Nix.
Financial data (yr. ended 12/31/01): Grants paid, $6,000; assets, $121,491 (M); expenditures, $7,052; qualifying distributions, $6,000.
Limitations: Applications not accepted. Giving limited to TX.
Application information: Contributes only to pre-selected organizations.
Trustees: Barbara Nix, Beverlee Nix, W.L. Nix, William K. Nix.
EIN: 752507408

52916
Oshman's Sports Partnership Foundation
2302 Maxwell Ln.
Houston, TX 77023

Established in 1996 in TX.
Donor(s): Carol Mann, Glimcher Properties Limited Partnership, Robust International, Inc., Sporting Goods Manufacturers Association.
Financial data (yr. ended 03/31/01): Grants paid, $6,000; assets, $409 (M); gifts received, $5,000; expenditures, $6,000; qualifying distributions, $6,000.
Limitations: Giving primarily in TX.
Directors: Carolyn S. Agriesti, Susan Blackwood, Carol Mann, Marilyn Oshman.
EIN: 760506862

52917
Charles Y. C. Pak Foundation
7107 Churchill Way
Dallas, TX 75230-1906

Established in 1988 in TX.
Donor(s): Charles Y.C. Pak, Vitel, Inc.
Financial data (yr. ended 12/31/01): Grants paid, $6,000; assets, $971,903 (M); gifts received, $16,000; expenditures, $8,998; qualifying distributions, $6,000.
Limitations: Applications not accepted. Giving primarily in IL and Dallas, TX.
Application information: Contributes only to pre-selected organizations.
Officers and Trustees:* Charles Y.C. Pak,* Pres.; Jane Pak, Secy.; James T. Bland, Neill Walsdorf.
EIN: 752267679

52918
Carlos G. Parker Foundation
1015 Cecelia St.
Taylor, TX 76574 (512) 352-2314
Contact: Thomas G. Parker, Tr.

Financial data (yr. ended 12/31/00): Grants paid, $6,000; assets, $67,702 (M); gifts received, $500; expenditures, $6,528; qualifying distributions, $6,000.
Limitations: Giving primarily in TX.
Trustees: Ray Condra, C. Dale Parker, Steve Parker, Thomas G. Parker.
EIN: 741916263

52919
Peterson Foundation
P.O. Box 140165
Dallas, TX 75214-0165

Financial data (yr. ended 04/30/00): Grants paid, $6,000; assets, $9,618 (M); gifts received, $13,582; expenditures, $6,711; qualifying distributions, $6,000; giving activities include $6,000 for loans.
Limitations: Applications not accepted.
Application information: Contribute only to pre-selected organizations.
Directors: K. Peterson, L. Peterson, O. Peterson, V. Sonne-Peterson.
EIN: 541828936

52920
Pioneer Natural Resources Scholarship Foundation
(Formerly Parker & Parsley Scholarship Foundation)
5205 N. O'Connor Blvd., Ste. 1400
Irving, TX 75039 (972) 444-9001
Contact: Larry N. Paulsen, V.P.

Established in 1992 in TX.
Donor(s): Parker & Parsley Petroleum Co., Norris Sucker Rods.
Financial data (yr. ended 12/31/01): Grants paid, $6,000; assets, $34,518 (M); expenditures, $6,000; qualifying distributions, $6,000.
Limitations: Giving primarily to residents of TX.
Application information: Application form required.
Officers and Directors:* Scott D. Sheffield,* Pres.; Larry N. Paulsen, V.P.; Mark L. Withrow,* Secy.
EIN: 752443728
Codes: CS, GTI

52921
The Read & Pate Foundation, Inc.
2911 Turtle Creek Blvd., No. 1010
Dallas, TX 75219

Financial data (yr. ended 12/31/01): Grants paid, $6,000; assets, $232,243 (M); expenditures, $21,334; qualifying distributions, $6,000.
Limitations: Giving limited to TX.
Application information: Students are nominated by eligible schools.
Trustees: Robert Hogue, Russell M. Stanley, James Pat Wood.
EIN: 237352744

52922
Timmerman Foundation, Inc.
P.O. Box 789
Pflugerville, TX 78691
Contact: Theodore R. Timmerman, Pres.

Established in 1986 in TX.
Financial data (yr. ended 12/31/01): Grants paid, $6,000; assets, $68,265 (M); gifts received, $6,500; expenditures, $12,612; qualifying distributions, $6,000.
Limitations: Giving primarily in TX.
Officers: Theodore R. Timmerman, Pres.; Marlene Timmerman, V.P.; Timothy Timmerman, Secy.-Treas.
EIN: 742459364

52923
Edward P. & Raye G. White Charitable Trust
2 Houston Ctr., Ste. 2907
Houston, TX 77010-1083 (713) 654-4484
Contact: Raye G. White, Tr.

Donor(s): Edward P. White, Raye G. White.
Financial data (yr. ended 12/31/01): Grants paid, $6,000; assets, $125,336 (M); gifts received, $3,500; expenditures, $6,386; qualifying distributions, $6,000.
Limitations: Giving primarily in Houston, TX.
Trustees: Fayez Sarofim, Edward P. White, Raye G. White.
EIN: 760205506

52924
Rotary International-John Burns Memorial Foundation
(Formerly Uvalde Rotary Club-John Burns Memorial)
605 E. Main St.
Uvalde, TX 78801-5716
Application address: 221 W. Mesquite St., Uvalde, TX 78801, tel.: (830) 278-2475
Contact: John Harrell, Pres.

Financial data (yr. ended 06/30/02): Grants paid, $5,950; assets, $92,075 (M); expenditures, $6,280; qualifying distributions, $5,950.
Limitations: Giving limited to Uvalde, TX.
Officers: John Harrell, Pres.; Leslie Laffere, V.P.; Henry Casel, Secy.; W.A. Kessler, Jr., Treas.
EIN: 746046125

52925
B. C. & Gladys L. Drinkard Foundation, Inc.
P.O. Box 1564
Brownwood, TX 76804-1564 (915) 646-4443
Contact: Mary E. Beniteau Bell

Established in 1985 in TX.
Financial data (yr. ended 12/31/01): Grants paid, $5,940; assets, $126,844 (M); expenditures, $7,210; qualifying distributions, $7,131.
Limitations: Giving limited to Brown County, TX.
Officers: Robert Porter, Chair.; Tom Munson, Vice-Chair.; Greg Doods, Secy.; Priscilla Monson, Treas.
EIN: 752054014

52926
Arlene & Jerome Leibs Fund
11607 St. Michaels Dr.
Dallas, TX 75230

Donor(s): Arlene Leibs, Jerome S. Leibs.
Financial data (yr. ended 10/31/01): Grants paid, $5,935; assets, $58,756 (M); gifts received, $15,000; expenditures, $5,978; qualifying distributions, $5,935.
Limitations: Applications not accepted. Giving primarily in Dallas, TX.
Application information: Contributes only to pre-selected organizations.
Trustee: Arlene Leibs.
EIN: 756027789

52927
Third Order Missionaries of Charity Universal Fraternity of the Word
5985 Meadow Way
Beaumont, TX 77707-1833

Donor(s): Fr. Angelo Scolozzi.
Financial data (yr. ended 12/31/00): Grants paid, $5,901; assets, $182,914 (M); gifts received, $71,427; expenditures, $33,841; qualifying distributions, $123,900.
Limitations: Applications not accepted.
Application information: Contributes only to pre-selected organizations.
Officers: Fr. Angelo Scolozzi, Pres.; Rhea A. Hudson, V.P.; Nancy Svestka, Secy.-Treas.
EIN: 760526538

52928
The Robertson-Finley Foundation
P.O. Box 967
Houston, TX 77001

Established in 1999 in TX.
Donor(s): Daniel R. Finley.
Financial data (yr. ended 12/31/01): Grants paid, $5,876; assets, $2,245 (M); gifts received, $6,500; expenditures, $7,631; qualifying distributions, $5,876.

Limitations: Applications not accepted.
Application information: Contributes only to pre-selected organizations.
Trustee: Daniel R. Finley.
EIN: 760598999

52929
The Shuttee Foundation
(Formerly David A. & Karen M. Shuttee Foundation)
6815 Hunters Glen
Dallas, TX 75205 (214) 855-8825
Application address: 300 Crescent Ct., Ste. 100, Dallas, TX 75201
Contact: David A. Shuttee, Pres.

Donor(s): David A. Shuttee.
Financial data (yr. ended 12/31/01): Grants paid, $5,845; assets, $3,294 (M); gifts received, $5,500; expenditures, $6,259; qualifying distributions, $5,845.
Limitations: Giving primarily in TX.
Application information: Application form required.
Officers and Directors:* David A. Shuttee,* Pres.; Karen M. Shuttee, V.P. and Secy.-Treas.; Steven K. Meyer.
EIN: 752433971

52930
The Hodges Foundation
P.O. Box 2995
Abilene, TX 79604 (915) 677-1374

Donor(s): Eddie V. Hodges.
Financial data (yr. ended 12/31/01): Grants paid, $5,807; assets, $384,821 (M); expenditures, $28,988; qualifying distributions, $5,807.
Limitations: Applications not accepted. Giving primarily in Abilene, TX.
Application information: Contributes only to pre-selected organizations.
Trustees: Eddie V. Hodges, Nelda R. Hodges.
EIN: 756329970

52931
Peter Andrew Sunseri Scholarship Fund
c/o Frost National Bank
P.O. Box 179
Galveston, TX 77553-0179 (409) 770-7165
Contact: Janet Bertolino, Trust Off., Frost National Bank

Donor(s): Andrea Sunseri, Carroll Sunseri.
Financial data (yr. ended 12/31/01): Grants paid, $5,800; assets, $152,056 (M); gifts received, $1,000; expenditures, $7,868; qualifying distributions, $7,811.
Limitations: Giving limited to residents of Galveston, TX.
Application information: Application form required.
Directors: Stephanie Doyle, Peter Moore, Stephen Stubbs, Andrea Sunseri, Carolyn Sunseri.
Trustee: Frost National Bank.
EIN: 766029110

52932
The O.H.B. Foundation
1800 St. James Pl., Ste. 200
Houston, TX 77056

Donor(s): Alfred W. Lasher, Jr.
Financial data (yr. ended 12/31/01): Grants paid, $5,793; assets, $5,411 (M); expenditures, $5,909; qualifying distributions, $5,793.
Limitations: Applications not accepted. Giving primarily in FL, NY, and TX.
Application information: Contributes only to pre-selected organizations.

Trustees: Christy E. Jones, Alfred W. Lasher, Jr., Jeanne See Lasher.
EIN: 226019837

52933
Catherine N. and Robert P. Teten Charitable Trust
100 Congress Ave., Ste. 700
Austin, TX 78701-2752
Contact: William T. Teten, Tr.

Financial data (yr. ended 12/31/00): Grants paid, $5,775; assets, $114,495 (M); expenditures, $6,362; qualifying distributions, $5,715.
Limitations: Giving limited to the Southwest, with emphasis on TX.
Trustees: Robert Paul Teten, Jr., William T. Teten.
EIN: 746383898

52934
George Rounds Trust
c/o Ethel B. Pierce
617 Marshall
West Columbia, TX 77486-4047
(979) 345-2591
Contact: Royce Arnold, Tr.

Financial data (yr. ended 12/31/99): Grants paid, $5,752; assets, $122,655 (M); expenditures, $10,884; qualifying distributions, $5,132.
Limitations: Giving limited to residents of the West Columbia, TX, area.
Application information: Application form required.
Trustee: Royce Arnold.
EIN: 746062601

52935
Margaret & Trammell Crow Educational Foundation
c/o ACU Station
P.O. Box 29120
Abilene, TX 79699-9120
Application address: c/o Gene Linder, P.O. Box 3812, Abilene, TX 79604

Donor(s): Trammell Crow Co., Tramell Crow Residential Companies.
Financial data (yr. ended 05/31/01): Grants paid, $5,750; assets, $119,994 (M); expenditures, $7,315; qualifying distributions, $5,660.
Limitations: Giving limited to residents of Abilene, TX.
Application information: Application form required.
Trustee: Abilene Christian University.
EIN: 756308221

52936
The Lynch Foundation
333 Morningside Dr.
San Antonio, TX 78209

Established in 1958.
Financial data (yr. ended 11/30/01): Grants paid, $5,750; assets, $225,805 (M); expenditures, $6,098; qualifying distributions, $5,750.
Limitations: Applications not accepted. Giving primarily in TX.
Application information: Contributes only to pre-selected organizations.
Trustee: Alice A. Lynch.
EIN: 746031487

52937
Dexion Foundation, Inc.
P.O. Box 20099
Houston, TX 77225-0099 (713) 664-5664
Contact: K.D. Charalampous, M.D., Dir.

Donor(s): K.D. Charalampous, M.D.

Financial data (yr. ended 12/31/01): Grants paid, $5,735; assets, $104,875 (M); expenditures, $6,315; qualifying distributions, $5,735.
Limitations: Giving primarily in Houston,TX.
Director: K.D. Charalampous, M.D.
EIN: 741534420

52938
Mike Harvey Foundation
P.O. Box 446
Tyler, TX 75710-1147

Financial data (yr. ended 12/31/01): Grants paid, $5,701; assets, $52,864 (M); expenditures, $6,584; qualifying distributions, $5,701.
Limitations: Applications not accepted. Giving primarily in Tyler, TX.
Application information: Contributes only to pre-selected organizations.
Officers: Mike J. Harvey, Jr., Pres.; Richard Harvey, V.P.
EIN: 756080973

52939
John H. Lee Foundation
4200 Chase Twr.
Houston, TX 77002
Contact: John A. Lee, Tr.

Established in 1995 in TX.
Donor(s): John H. Lee.
Financial data (yr. ended 12/31/01): Grants paid, $5,700; assets, $121,337 (M); gifts received, $30,000; expenditures, $12,645; qualifying distributions, $5,700.
Limitations: Giving limited to Houston, TX.
Trustees: James H. Lee, John A. Lee, John H. Lee, Margaret K. Lee, Suzanne C. Lee.
EIN: 760476999

52940
McEvoy Foundation
P.O. Box 810219
Dallas, TX 75381-0219

Financial data (yr. ended 06/30/01): Grants paid, $5,700; assets, $139,904 (M); expenditures, $5,700; qualifying distributions, $5,700.
Limitations: Applications not accepted. Giving primarily in Houston, TX.
Application information: Contributes only to pre-selected organizations.
Trustees: Susan McEvoy Maner, A. Patrick McEvoy, Sr., Joan S. McEvoy.
EIN: 751692847

52941
The Peter G. & Marjorie A. Behr Private Charitable Foundation
c/o Kanaly Trust Co.
4550 Post Oak Pl. Dr., Ste. 139
Houston, TX 77027-3106 (713) 626-9483

Donor(s): Peter G. Behr, Marjorie A. Behr.
Financial data (yr. ended 12/31/01): Grants paid, $5,675; assets, $101,745 (M); expenditures, $7,981; qualifying distributions, $6,304.
Limitations: Giving primarily in VT.
Application information: Application form not required.
Trustees: Christopher E. Behr, Marjorie A. Behr, Peter G. Behr, Kanaly Trust Co.
EIN: 760209482

52942
The Levit-Setzer Family Foundation
P.O. Box 14200
Houston, TX 77221-4200

Established in 1998 in TX.
Donor(s): Leah S. Levit.
Financial data (yr. ended 12/31/01): Grants paid, $5,651; assets, $516,302 (M); expenditures, $7,714; qualifying distributions, $5,651.
Limitations: Applications not accepted. Giving primarily in Houston, TX.
Application information: Contributes only to pre-selected organizations.
Officers: Milton H. Levit, Chair.; Leah S. Levit, Pres.; Jill L. Talisman, V.P. and Secy.; Gerald A. Levit, V.P. and Treas.
EIN: 760569827

52943
Sophie & William Steinkamp Education Trust
c/o Bank of America
P.O. Box 831041
Dallas, TX 75283-1041
Application address: c/o Trust Admin., Bank of America, P.O. Box 1681 (W-6), Little Rock, AR 72203

Financial data (yr. ended 03/31/00): Grants paid, $5,625; assets, $169,289 (M); expenditures, $9,319; qualifying distributions, $5,625.
Limitations: Giving limited to residents of Pulaski County, AR.
Trustee: Bank of America.
EIN: 716123582
Codes: GTI

52944
The Thomas W. Garner Foundation
1111 N. Loop W., Ste. 1100
Houston, TX 77008

Donor(s): Thomas W. Garner.
Financial data (yr. ended 12/31/01): Grants paid, $5,600; assets, $24,004 (M); expenditures, $5,725; qualifying distributions, $5,600.
Limitations: Applications not accepted. Giving primarily in TX.
Application information: Contributes only to pre-selected organizations.
Officers and Trustees:* Thomas W. Garner,* Pres.; J. Ron Young,* V.P. and Secy.; Judith Arndt Garner.
EIN: 760208031

52945
Christian Commerce Corporation
P.O. Box 924264
Houston, TX 77292-4264
Contact: Ralph DeVore, Dir.

Financial data (yr. ended 12/31/00): Grants paid, $5,596; assets, $30,467 (M); gifts received, $42,937; expenditures, $46,265; qualifying distributions, $5,596.
Directors: Floyd V. Bryan, Brenda DeVore, Ralph DeVore, Kimberly Yorloff.
EIN: 751952244

52946
George Snively Research Foundation
P.O. Box 2203
Odessa, TX 79760

Financial data (yr. ended 09/30/99): Grants paid, $5,560; assets, $0 (M); expenditures, $5,560; qualifying distributions, $5,560.
Officers and Directors:* Richard G. Snyder, Ph.D., Pres.; Paul Appel, Secy.; Channing L. Ewing, M.D.,* Treas.; Harold A. Fenner, Jr.,* Mgr.; William C. Chilcot, Ph.D.
Board Member: Daniel J. Thomas, M.D.
EIN: 113118238

52947
Agape Foundation
P.O. Box 1226
Donna, TX 78537-1226
Contact: James E. Fitzgerald, Pres.

Donor(s): Jack Archer.
Financial data (yr. ended 09/30/01): Grants paid, $5,533; assets, $1,117 (M); gifts received, $5,225; expenditures, $5,968; qualifying distributions, $5,968.
Limitations: Giving primarily in Mexico.
Officers: James E. Fitzgerald, Pres.; Glen Johnson, V.P.; Deborah Fitzgerald, Mgr.
EIN: 237431519
Codes: GTI

52948
The Wece B. and Martha A. Johnson Foundation
c/o Martha A. Johnson
1402 Mary Lee Ln.
Longview, TX 75601
Application address: c/o Longview Bank & Trust, P.O. Box 3188, Longview, TX 75606, tel.: (903) 237-5578
Contact: Bob Dyer, V.P.

Established in 1997 in TX.
Donor(s): Martha A. Johnson.
Financial data (yr. ended 12/31/01): Grants paid, $5,530; assets, $45,605 (M); gifts received, $40,000; expenditures, $5,538; qualifying distributions, $5,530.
Officers: Martha A. Johnson, Pres.; Bob Dyer, V.P.; Denise Harper, Secy.; Sally Brown, Treas.
Directors: Mark Abernathy, Howard P. Coghlan, David Crowson, and 2 additional directors.
EIN: 752659420

52949
Jesse T. & Jodie E. King Foundation
c/o John T. King
13418 Kingsride Ln.
Houston, TX 77079-3431

Established in 1995 in TX.
Donor(s): John T. King.
Financial data (yr. ended 12/31/01): Grants paid, $5,502; assets, $18,854 (M); gifts received, $6,650; expenditures, $5,568; qualifying distributions, $5,502.
Limitations: Applications not accepted. Giving primarily in TX.
Application information: Contributes only to pre-selected organizations.
Officers: John T. King, Pres.; Kathryn King Coleman, V.P.; Carolyn King Waller, V.P.
EIN: 760474227

52950
The Attwell Foundation
1001 Fannin St., Ste. 3415
Houston, TX 77002

Established in 2000 in TX.
Donor(s): J. Evans Attwell.
Financial data (yr. ended 12/31/01): Grants paid, $5,500; assets, $596,890 (M); gifts received, $159,820; expenditures, $5,500; qualifying distributions, $5,500.
Limitations: Applications not accepted.
Application information: Contributes only to pre-selected organizations.
Officer: J. Evans Attwell, Chair.
Directors: Emily St. Clare Attwell, Evans Scott Attwell, John Thomason Attwell, Mary Petersen Attwell, Mary Virginia Attwell, Carol Peterson Attwell Rowntree.
EIN: 760658600

52951
Craig C. Brown Foundation
13333 Westland E. Blvd., Ste. 203
Houston, TX 77041
Contact: Craig C. Brown, Dir.

Donor(s): Craig C. Brown, Marline C. Brown.
Financial data (yr. ended 12/31/00): Grants paid, $5,500; assets, $240,564 (M); expenditures, $7,334; qualifying distributions, $5,500.
Limitations: Giving limited to TX.
Directors: Craig C. Brown, Marline C. Brown, Robin G. Brown.
EIN: 760453555

52952
Jerry & Lucille Donnelly Scholarship Trust
c/o Bank of America
P.O. Box 831041
Dallas, TX 75283-1041
Application address: Kay Tennant, c/o Bank of America, P.O. Box 830259, Dallas, TX 75283-0259, tel.: (800) 257-0332

Financial data (yr. ended 12/31/01): Grants paid, $5,500; assets, $138,894 (M); expenditures, $9,322; qualifying distributions, $7,604.
Limitations: Giving primarily to residents of Blackwell, OK.
Trustee: Bank of America.
EIN: 731119304

52953
Bob & Angelina Dorsey Foundation
1101-02 Uptown Park Blvd.
Houston, TX 77056 (713) 621-4241
Contact: Bob R. Dorsey, Pres.

Donor(s): Bob R. Dorsey, Angelina Dorsey.
Financial data (yr. ended 12/31/00): Grants paid, $5,500; assets, $60,490 (M); expenditures, $5,500; qualifying distributions, $5,500.
Limitations: Giving primarily in Austin, TX.
Officers: Bob R. Dorsey, Pres.; Ellen Dorsey, Secy.
EIN: 741886825

52954
Jennifer Hicks Memorial Fund
700 Louisiana St., Ste. 1700
Houston, TX 77002-2722
Application address: 11551 Raintree Cir., Houston, TX 77024
Contact: Taylor M. Hicks, Jr., Dir.

Established in 1999 in TX.
Donor(s): Taylor M. Hicks, Jr., Mrs. Taylor M. Hicks, Jr.
Financial data (yr. ended 12/31/01): Grants paid, $5,500; assets, $1,175 (M); expenditures, $6,000; qualifying distributions, $6,000.
Application information: Application form not required.
Directors: Pam Hicks, Taylor M. Hicks, Jr., Teri Lacy.
EIN: 760598735

52955
Stephen and Debra Hix Family Foundation
5580 Peterson Ln., Ste. 250
Dallas, TX 75240

Established in 2001 in TX and NC.
Donor(s): Debra Hix, Stephen G. Hix.
Financial data (yr. ended 12/31/01): Grants paid, $5,500; assets, $161,162 (M); gifts received, $153,560; expenditures, $12,479; qualifying distributions, $5,500.
Limitations: Applications not accepted. Giving primarily in KY.
Application information: Contributes only to pre-selected organizations.

Officers: Stephen G. Hix, Pres.; Debra Hix, Secy.
Director: Mark T. Hix.
EIN: 621846054

52956
St. Clair Family Foundation, Inc.
c/o Darrell W. Cain
5580 Peterson Ln., Ste. 250
Dallas, TX 75240

Established in 2000 in TX.
Donor(s): John St. Clair, Janette St. Clair.
Financial data (yr. ended 12/31/01): Grants paid, $5,500; assets, $94,674 (M); gifts received, $5,200; expenditures, $7,050; qualifying distributions, $5,500.
Limitations: Applications not accepted.
Application information: Contributes only to pre-selected organizations.
Officers: John St. Clair, Pres.; Janette St. Clair, Secy.
EIN: 752894978

52957
SRW Foundation, Inc.
2008 Homedale Dr.
Austin, TX 78704

Donor(s): Sarah Weddington.
Financial data (yr. ended 12/31/01): Grants paid, $5,491; assets, $44,093 (M); expenditures, $5,677; qualifying distributions, $5,491.
Limitations: Applications not accepted. Giving primarily in Austin, TX.
Application information: Contributes only to pre-selected organizations.
Trustees: Doyle Ragle, Sarah Weddington.
EIN: 742594853

52958
Robert Craige Means Foundation
P.O. Box 207
Valentine, TX 79854

Financial data (yr. ended 12/31/99): Grants paid, $5,453; assets, $163,784 (M); expenditures, $7,271; qualifying distributions, $7,271.
Limitations: Applications not accepted. Giving on a national basis.
Application information: Contributes only to pre-selected organizations.
Officer: Alfred Means, Pres.
EIN: 746066214

52959
Florence, Inc.
5555 Del Monte Dr., Ste. 604
Houston, TX 77056

Financial data (yr. ended 08/31/01): Grants paid, $5,440; assets, $90,121 (M); expenditures, $6,065; qualifying distributions, $5,962.
Limitations: Applications not accepted. Giving primarily in TX.
Application information: Contributes only to pre-selected organizations.
Officers: Florence Diamond, Pres. and Mgr.; Stuart Diamond, V.P.; Neal Diamond, Secy.
EIN: 237379575

52960
Steele Charitable Foundation
1710 Mykawa Rd.
Pearland, TX 77581 (281) 485-8339
Contact: Erin M. Steele, Secy.

Financial data (yr. ended 12/31/01): Grants paid, $5,426; assets, $86,434 (M); gifts received, $25,000; expenditures, $6,024; qualifying distributions, $5,426.
Limitations: Giving primarily in the Pearland and south TX area.

Officers: Robert S. Steele, Pres.; Erin M. Steele, Secy.; John Deterling, Treas.
EIN: 760556143

52961
The Keith & Carol Brown Family Foundation
c/o Keith L. Brown
11 Auburn Pl.
San Antonio, TX 78209

Established in 2000 in TX.
Donor(s): Keith L. Brown.
Financial data (yr. ended 12/31/01): Grants paid, $5,400; assets, $20,023 (M); expenditures, $5,781; qualifying distributions, $5,400.
Limitations: Applications not accepted. Giving primarily in Denver, CO and San Antonio, TX.
Application information: Contributes only to pre-selected organizations.
Officer: Keith L. Brown, Pres.
EIN: 742959911

52962
E & M Foundation, Inc.
P.O. Box 77215
Houston, TX 77215

Established in 1998.
Donor(s): Chen Wang.
Financial data (yr. ended 12/31/99): Grants paid, $5,400; assets, $74,411 (M); gifts received, $7,000; expenditures, $5,400; qualifying distributions, $5,400.
Limitations: Applications not accepted.
Application information: Contributes only to pre-selected organizations.
Directors: Grace Shieh, Emily Wang, Ming Y. Wang.
EIN: 760509216

52963
Ferron Family Foundation
400 N. Sam Houston Pkwy., Ste. 400
Houston, TX 77060
Contact: Martin R. Ferron, Dir.

Established in 1999 in TX.
Donor(s): Martin R. Ferron.
Financial data (yr. ended 12/31/00): Grants paid, $5,400; assets, $24,970 (M); expenditures, $7,498; qualifying distributions, $5,545.
Director: Martin R. Ferron.
EIN: 760432191

52964
Regina Gross Fund
6901 Helsem Way
Dallas, TX 75230-1920

Financial data (yr. ended 12/31/01): Grants paid, $5,397; assets, $116,087 (M); expenditures, $6,162; qualifying distributions, $5,397.
Limitations: Applications not accepted. Giving primarily in TX.
Application information: Contributes only to pre-selected organizations.
Trustees: Florence G. Ziegler, Regina G. Ziegler, Rosilene G. Ziegier, Ruthann G. Ziegler.
EIN: 756027498

52965
Jack and Diane Eckels Charity Fund
45 Briar Hollow Ln., Ste. 10
Houston, TX 77027-9311

Donor(s): Jack P. Eckels, Diane D. Eckels.
Financial data (yr. ended 11/30/01): Grants paid, $5,215; assets, $50,990 (M); expenditures, $5,289; qualifying distributions, $5,215.
Limitations: Applications not accepted. Giving primarily in Houston, TX.

Application information: Contributes only to pre-selected organizations.
Trustees: Diane D. Eckels, Jack P. Eckels.
EIN: 760591466

52966
Gilpatrick Scholarship Trust
P.O. Box 247
Spearman, TX 79081
Application addresses: c/o Glenda Guthrie, Spearman High School, 403 E. 11th St., Spearman, TX 79081, tel.: (806) 659-2584; c/o Kathy Potts, Gruver High School, P.O. Box 747, Gruver, TX 79040, tel.: (806) 733-2477

Established in 2000.
Donor(s): Evelyn Mae Gilpatrick.‡
Financial data (yr. ended 12/31/00): Grants paid, $5,215; assets, $780,488 (M); gifts received, $776,766; expenditures, $8,252; qualifying distributions, $8,100.
Limitations: Giving limited to residents of Hansford County, TX.
Application information: Application form required.
Trustee: First State Bank.
EIN: 311687792

52967
Amical Foundation
5080 Spectrum Dr., Ste. 805 W.
Addison, TX 75001

Donor(s): Donald J. Phillips.
Financial data (yr. ended 12/31/01): Grants paid, $5,200; assets, $146,886 (M); expenditures, $8,933; qualifying distributions, $5,200.
Limitations: Applications not accepted.
Application information: Contributes only to pre-selected organizations.
Directors: David Denison, Donald J. Phillips, Judith Lynn Sullivan.
EIN: 752736902

52968
Mary Lola Bradstreet Brewer Community Foundation
505 W. 5th St.
Clifton, TX 76634

Financial data (yr. ended 12/31/01): Grants paid, $5,200; assets, $127,824 (M); expenditures, $5,230; qualifying distributions, $5,200.
Limitations: Applications not accepted. Giving primarily in TX.
Application information: Contributes only to pre-selected organizations.
Officers and Directors:* Jim B. Smith,* Chair.; Dee Anna Nichols,* Secy.; Janice E. Belvin,* Treas.; Jerry Smith.
EIN: 742323922

52969
Philip & Barbara Hankins Charitable Trust
1801 Lavaca, No. 14J
Austin, TX 78701 (512) 476-7944
Contact: Barbara S. Hankins, Tr.

Donor(s): Philip C. Hankins.
Financial data (yr. ended 12/31/01): Grants paid, $5,130; assets, $80,243 (M); expenditures, $5,646; qualifying distributions, $5,130.
Limitations: Giving primarily in Austin, TX.
Trustees: John E. Beard, Barbara S. Hankins, Philip C. Hankins.
EIN: 237050263

52970
Cassorla Charitable Trust
7201 Winecup Hollow
Austin, TX 78750

Established in 1993 in SC.
Financial data (yr. ended 12/31/00): Grants paid, $5,124; assets, $10,584 (M); expenditures, $5,139; qualifying distributions, $5,124.
Limitations: Applications not accepted. Giving on a national basis.
Application information: Contributes only to pre-selected organizations.
Trustees: Elie Cassorla, Judith Cassorla.
EIN: 576155125

52971
Farris Family Foundation
c/o E2 Communications, Inc.
6404 International Pkwy., Ste. 1200
Plano, TX 75093
Application address: 8333 Douglas Ave., Ste. 550, Dallas, TX 75225; Tel: (214) 368-7470
Contact: Jeffrey L. Farris, Dir.

Established in 1997 in TX.
Donor(s): Jeffrey L. Farris, Beverly H. Farris.
Financial data (yr. ended 12/31/00): Grants paid, $5,100; assets, $224,295 (M); expenditures, $7,148; qualifying distributions, $5,100.
Limitations: Giving primarily in Dallas, TX.
Directors: Beverly H. Farris, Jeffrey L. Farris, Nathaniel Herron.
EIN: 752708088

52972
Nierling Family Scholarship Jamestown College Trust
200 Crescent Ct., Ste. 900
Dallas, TX 75201-7837

Established in 1999 in ND.
Donor(s): Richard B. Nierling.
Financial data (yr. ended 12/31/00): Grants paid, $5,029; assets, $318,441 (M); gifts received, $104,803; expenditures, $5,029; qualifying distributions, $4,155.
Limitations: Applications not accepted. Giving primarily in Jamestown, ND.
Application information: Contributes only to pre-selected organizations.
Trustee: Richard B. Nierling.
EIN: 912004883

52973
The Louise Barekman Memorial Foundation
c/o Bank of America
P.O. Box 831041
Dallas, TX 75283-1041
Application address: c/o C. Lincoln Williston, Exec. Dir., Texas Medical Assn., 1801 N. Lamar Blvd., Austin, TX 78701

Financial data (yr. ended 08/31/01): Grants paid, $5,000; assets, $88,738 (M); expenditures, $7,484; qualifying distributions, $5,968.
Limitations: Giving limited to Austin, Dallas, and Fort Worth, TX.
Application information: Application form required.
Trustee: Bank of America.
EIN: 756030210

52974
Nancy and Roman Boruta Family Foundation
14 Windermere Ln.
Houston, TX 77063

Established in 1999 in TX.
Donor(s): Nancy Boruta, Roman Boruta.

Financial data (yr. ended 12/31/01): Grants paid, $5,000; assets, $57,873 (M); expenditures, $10,272; qualifying distributions, $7,230.
Limitations: Applications not accepted. Giving primarily in Houston, TX.
Application information: Contributes only to pre-selected organizations.
Officers: Nancy Boruta, Pres.; Roman Boruta, V.P.
Director: Judy Bozeman.
EIN: 760616296

52975
Adriance Finch Foundation
411 Shadywood Rd.
Houston, TX 77057

Established in 1999 in TX.
Financial data (yr. ended 12/31/01): Grants paid, $5,000; assets, $17,318 (M); gifts received, $4,500; expenditures, $5,835; qualifying distributions, $5,000.
Trustee: Hubert B. Finch.
EIN: 760611550

52976
For Love of the Arts Foundation, Inc.
1956 Shepherd Ranch Rd.
Fredericksburg, TX 78624

Established in 2000 in TX.
Financial data (yr. ended 12/31/01): Grants paid, $5,000; assets, $105,443 (M); expenditures, $6,065; qualifying distributions, $5,000.
Limitations: Applications not accepted. Giving primarily in Fredericksburg, TX.
Application information: Contributes only to pre-selected organizations.
Officers: Steve Shepherd, Pres.; Rene Brooks Cameron, Secy.
EIN: 742948245

52977
Stevie Glazer Nurses Fund
14860 Landmark Blvd.
Dallas, TX 75240

Financial data (yr. ended 05/31/01): Grants paid, $5,000; assets, $42,284 (M); expenditures, $5,023; qualifying distributions, $4,964.
Limitations: Applications not accepted. Giving limited to TX.
Application information: Contributes only to pre-selected organizations.
Officer: Frances Glazer, Mgr.
EIN: 756023508

52978
Rosalie and Billy Goldberg Foundation
6100 Corporate Dr., Ste. 500
Houston, TX 77036-3483

Financial data (yr. ended 12/31/01): Grants paid, $5,000; assets, $1 (M); gifts received, $5,000; expenditures, $5,925; qualifying distributions, $5,000.
Limitations: Giving primarily in LA and TX.
Officers and Trustees:* Billy B. Goldberg,* Pres. and Treas.; Diane Goldberg Levy,* V.P.; Frank S. Goldberg,* V.P.; Mark Goldberg,* V.P.; Richard E. Goldberg,* V.P.; Rosalie A. Goldberg,* Secy.
EIN: 760089083

52979
Good Earth Foundation
(Formerly S.E. Foundation)
c/o Lawrence E. Maddox
5851 San Felipe, No. 700
Houston, TX 77057
Contact: Sonja H. Earthman, Pres.

Established in 1994.
Donor(s): Sonja H. Earthman.

52979—TEXAS

Financial data (yr. ended 04/30/02): Grants paid, $5,000; assets, $392,808 (M); expenditures, $14,605; qualifying distributions, $5,000.
Limitations: Giving primarily in Houston, TX.
Officers: Sonja H. Earthman, Pres. and Treas.; Lawrence E. Maddox, Secy.
Directors: Amy Elaine Earthman Cardwell, Lannie Gayle Earthman, Mary Louise Earthman, Robert Lawrence Earthman, Jr.
EIN: 760447921

52980
Hildenbrand Foundation
P.O. Box 61229
Houston, TX 77208

Established in 2001 in TX.
Donor(s): Jeffrey Hildenbrand, Melinda Hildenbrand.
Financial data (yr. ended 12/31/01): Grants paid, $5,000; assets, $1,495,000 (M); gifts received, $1,500,000; expenditures, $5,000; qualifying distributions, $5,000.
Limitations: Applications not accepted.
Application information: Contributes only to pre-selected organizations.
Officers: Jeffrey D. Hildenbrand, Pres. and Treas.; Melinda B. Hildenbrand, V.P. and Secy.
Director: Jean-Paul Budinger.
EIN: 760699250

52981
H. H. and Edna Houseman Charitable Trust
c/o Hibernia National Bank - Beaumont
P.O. Box 3928
Beaumont, TX 77704-3928

Established in 1999 in TX.
Donor(s): Edna Houseman.
Financial data (yr. ended 12/31/01): Grants paid, $5,000; assets, $93,582 (M); expenditures, $7,562; qualifying distributions, $4,969.
Limitations: Applications not accepted. Giving primarily in TX.
Application information: Contributes only to pre-selected organizations.
Trustees: Edna Houseman, Robert Houseman, Hibernia National Bank.
EIN: 760636804

52982
Lacerte Charitable Foundation
(Formerly Joyce & Lawrence Lacerte Charitable Foundation)
5950 Sherry Ln., Ste. 900
Dallas, TX 75225 (214) 346-7000
Contact: Lawrence Lacerte, Pres.

Established in 1997 in TX.
Donor(s): Joyce Lacerte, Lawrence Lacerte.
Financial data (yr. ended 12/31/01): Grants paid, $5,000; assets, $73,670 (M); expenditures, $6,843; qualifying distributions, $5,000.
Limitations: Giving primarily in Dallas, TX.
Application information: Application form not required.
Officers and Directors:* Lawrence Lacerte,* Pres. and Treas.; Joyce Lacerte,* V.P. and Secy.; Lena Baca.
EIN: 752681517

52983
Lupuloff-Barth Foundation
P.O. Box 56048
Houston, TX 77256-6048

Established in 1989 in TX.
Donor(s): Carin Marcy Barth, Todd F. Barth.
Financial data (yr. ended 12/31/01): Grants paid, $5,000; assets, $116,769 (M); gifts received, $2,500; expenditures, $5,011; qualifying distributions, $5,000.
Limitations: Applications not accepted. Giving primarily in TX.
Application information: Contributes only to pre-selected organizations.
Officers: Carin Marcy Barth, Pres.; Todd F. Barth, V.P. and Secy.-Treas.
EIN: 760288218

52984
The Catherine Terrell McCartney Foundation
c/o James W. McCartney
3201 1st City Tower
Houston, TX 77002

Established in 1997 in TX.
Donor(s): James W. McCartney.
Financial data (yr. ended 12/31/01): Grants paid, $5,000; assets, $177,134 (M); expenditures, $6,236; qualifying distributions, $5,000.
Limitations: Applications not accepted. Giving primarily in TX.
Application information: Contributes only to pre-selected organizations.
Officers and Directors:* James W. McCartney,* Pres.; Margaret Jane Moore, Secy.; Susan McCartney Finnegan, Catherine McCartney Miller, James W. McCartney V.
EIN: 760536585

52985
W. H. Miekow Educational Trust
322 Preston St.
Columbus, TX 78934-1942

Financial data (yr. ended 12/31/01): Grants paid, $5,000; assets, $106,709 (M); expenditures, $5,240; qualifying distributions, $5,000.
Limitations: Applications not accepted. Giving primarily in TX.
Application information: Contributes only to pre-selected organizations.
Trustee: William N. Miekow.
EIN: 746297462

52986
J. A. R. Moseley Foundation, Inc.
P.O. Box 429
Jefferson, TX 75657-0429
Contact: Col. King Sain, Pres.

Financial data (yr. ended 12/31/01): Grants paid, $5,000; assets, $82,156 (M); expenditures, $5,297; qualifying distributions, $5,000.
Limitations: Giving limited to Marion County, TX.
Application information: Application form not required.
Officers: Col. King Sain, Pres.; Imogene Bass, Secy.-Treas.
EIN: 237104689

52987
National Society for Parent-Child Development
1111 Herman Dr., No. 29E
Houston, TX 77004

Established in 1989 in TX.
Donor(s): Robert Katz, Walter Katz.
Financial data (yr. ended 04/30/02): Grants paid, $5,000; assets, $24,440 (M); gifts received, $21,226; expenditures, $5,000; qualifying distributions, $5,000.
Limitations: Applications not accepted. Giving limited to Houston, TX.
Application information: Contributes only to pre-selected organizations.
Directors: Milton Boniuk, E.J. Farge, Tom Moore.
EIN: 760252078

52988
Nichols Scholarship Foundation, Inc.
9700 Richmond Ave., Ste. 255
Houston, TX 77042 (281) 492-7477
Contact: Rebecca U. Nichols, Pres.

Established in 1999 in TX.
Donor(s): W.S. Nichols III, William A. Paulea.
Financial data (yr. ended 12/31/00): Grants paid, $5,000; assets, $29,336 (M); gifts received, $2,500; expenditures, $5,734; qualifying distributions, $4,965.
Limitations: Giving to residents of Tyler County, TX.
Officers: Rebecca U. Nichols, Pres.; W.S. Nichols III, V.P.; Michael W. Nichols, Secy.-Treas.
EIN: 760603435

52989
Nipul Foundation
2213 Whitney Ln.
McKinney, TX 75070

Established in 2000 in TX.
Donor(s): Pulin R. Patel, Shriti P. Patel.
Financial data (yr. ended 12/31/01): Grants paid, $5,000; assets, $368,845 (M); gifts received, $290,250; expenditures, $5,074; qualifying distributions, $5,000.
Directors: Kanan Patel, Pulin R. Patel, Shriti P. Patel.
EIN: 752913028
Codes: TN

52990
The O'Hare Family Private Foundation
2905 Popano Cove
Austin, TX 78746-1974

Established in 1999 in TX.
Donor(s): W. Scott O'Hare.
Financial data (yr. ended 12/31/01): Grants paid, $5,000; assets, $373,158 (M); expenditures, $7,288; qualifying distributions, $5,768.
Limitations: Applications not accepted.
Application information: Contributes only to pre-selected organizations.
Officers: W. Scott O'Hare, Pres.; Kathryn Angell Sackett O'Hare, V.P. and Secy.
Director: Jody Cole.
EIN: 752802946

52991
Clive and Kathryn Runnells Foundation
c/o Jonathan E. Kemmerer
600 W. 8th St., Ste. 800
Austin, TX 78701

Established in 1994 in TX.
Donor(s): Clive Runnells, Kathryn Long Runnells.
Financial data (yr. ended 12/31/00): Grants paid, $5,000; assets, $260,989 (M); expenditures, $5,645; qualifying distributions, $5,000.
Limitations: Applications not accepted. Giving primarily in Austin, TX.
Application information: Contributes only to pre-selected organizations.
Directors: Jonathan E. Kemmerer, Clive Runnells III, Kathryn Long Runnells.
EIN: 742721433

52992
Crutcher and Vickie Scott Foundation
c/o ACU Sta.
P.O. Box 8244
Abilene, TX 79699
Contact: Gaston Welborn

Established in 1990 in TX.

Financial data (yr. ended 05/31/01): Grants paid, $5,000; assets, $105,789 (M); expenditures, $5,720; qualifying distributions, $5,000.
Limitations: Giving limited to male residents of Abilene, TX.
Application information: Application form required.
Trustee: Abilene Christian University.
EIN: 752294967

52993
Sink Foundation, Inc.
2425 WLS, Ste. 200
Houston, TX 77027 (713) 661-2320
Contact: James M. Sink, Pres.

Established in 1998 in TX.
Donor(s): James M. Sink, Susan W. Sink.
Financial data (yr. ended 03/31/01): Grants paid, $5,000; assets, $90,114 (M); expenditures, $6,076; qualifying distributions, $5,000.
Officers and Directors:* James M. Sink,* Pres.; Susan W. Sink,* Secy.
EIN: 760575208

52994
Strickland Foundation Trust
3 Stones Spring Cir.
The Woodlands, TX 77381

Established in 2000.
Financial data (yr. ended 12/31/00): Grants paid, $5,000; assets, $232,367 (M); gifts received, $280,663; expenditures, $5,000; qualifying distributions, $5,000.
Limitations: Applications not accepted. Giving primarily in The Woodlands, TX.
Application information: Contributes only to pre-selected organizations.
Officers: Donald R. Strickland, Mgr.; Reba G. Strickland, Mgr.
EIN: 766155554

52995
Lindsey and May Tape Foundation
2116 Thompson Hwy., Ste. F1
Richmond, TX 77469

Financial data (yr. ended 11/30/01): Grants paid, $5,000; assets, $23,518 (M); gifts received, $10,000; expenditures, $5,000; qualifying distributions, $5,000.
Limitations: Applications not accepted.
Application information: Contributes only to pre-selected organizations.
Officers: May W. Tape, Pres.; Joe L. Tape, V.P. and Treas.
EIN: 760588528

52996
Texas Prairieland Foundation
P.O. Box 1135
Albany, TX 76430

Established in 1998 in TX.
Donor(s): Lynne J. Woodward, Lynne J. Teinert.
Financial data (yr. ended 12/31/01): Grants paid, $5,000; assets, $511,040 (M); gifts received, $199,974; expenditures, $11,752; qualifying distributions, $5,000.
Limitations: Applications not accepted. Giving primarily in TX.
Application information: Contributes only to pre-selected organizations.
Officer and Director:* Lynne J. Teinert,* Pres.
EIN: 752797205

52997
The Triquetra Foundation
10 Inwood Oaks Dr.
Houston, TX 77024

Established in 1999 in TX.
Donor(s): Scott D. Josey, Holly H. Josey.
Financial data (yr. ended 08/31/00): Grants paid, $5,000; assets, $18,050 (M); gifts received, $23,050; expenditures, $5,000; qualifying distributions, $0.
Limitations: Applications not accepted.
Officers: Scott D. Josey, Pres.; Keith D. Josey, V.P.; Holly H. Josey, Secy.-Treas.
EIN: 742933775

52998
Verfred Foundation
c/o Vernon R. Brockett
8206 Whippoorwill Dr.
Waco, TX 76712
Application address: 2700 Cresthill Cir., Waco, TX 76710-1016

Financial data (yr. ended 12/31/01): Grants paid, $5,000; assets, $123,091 (M); expenditures, $5,821; qualifying distributions, $5,000.
Limitations: Giving primarily in TX.
Officers: George E. Brockett, Pres.; Charles R. Brockett, Secy.
EIN: 221714111

52999
Warren Foundation
17314 State Hwy. 249, Ste. 200
Houston, TX 77064-1140
Contact: J.N. Warren, Mgr.

Donor(s): J.N. Warren.
Financial data (yr. ended 12/31/01): Grants paid, $5,000; assets, $149,096 (M); expenditures, $5,758; qualifying distributions, $5,000.
Limitations: Giving primarily in TX.
Officer: J.N. Warren, Mgr.
Trustees: Edwin K. Hunter, John P. Melko.
EIN: 726197916

53000
The Jeff and Bonnie Whitman Foundation
12308 Shiremont Dr.
Dallas, TX 75230-2240

Established in 1998 in TX.
Donor(s): Jeffrey Whitman, Bonnie Whitman.
Financial data (yr. ended 12/31/00): Grants paid, $5,000; assets, $202,166 (M); gifts received, $2,200; expenditures, $18,670; qualifying distributions, $5,000.
Directors: Augusta Whitman, Bonnie Whitman.
EIN: 752823240

53001
Barbara and Grant Woodard Foundation
3115 W. Loop S., Ste. 39
Houston, TX 77027
Contact: Grant C. Woodard, Pres.

Established in 1998 in TX.
Donor(s): Grant Woodard.
Financial data (yr. ended 12/31/01): Grants paid, $5,000; assets, $114,517 (M); gifts received, $45,000; expenditures, $5,805; qualifying distributions, $5,000.
Officers: Grant C. Woodard, Pres.; Laura Woodard Devinney, V.P. and Treas.; Douglas Woodard, V.P.; G. Martin Woodard, V.P.; Robin Woodard Weening, Secy.
EIN: 760576106

53002
The Mary Bonham Educational Trust
P.O. Box 1007
Sulphur Springs, TX 75483-1007
Application address: 315 Jefferson, Sulphur Springs, TX 75482
Contact: Carl D. Bryan, Tr.

Established in 1994.
Financial data (yr. ended 12/31/99): Grants paid, $4,982; assets, $101,757 (M); expenditures, $5,080; qualifying distributions, $5,018.
Limitations: Giving primarily to residents in Sulphur Springs, TX.
Trustees: Mary Bonham, Carl D. Bryan, Paul Glover, Rhonda Shing, Judy Tipping.
EIN: 756454600

53003
San Angelo Surgery Residents' Trust
102 N. Magdalen
San Angelo, TX 76903

Financial data (yr. ended 12/31/01): Grants paid, $4,950; assets, $1 (M); gifts received, $23,000; expenditures, $23,076; qualifying distributions, $4,950.
Director: John S. Cargile.
EIN: 756429939

53004
Flournoy Davis Manzo Child Development Foundation
4107 Ruskin St.
Houston, TX 77005

Established in 1992 in TX.
Financial data (yr. ended 12/31/01): Grants paid, $4,920; assets, $100,397 (M); expenditures, $6,851; qualifying distributions, $4,920.
Limitations: Applications not accepted. Giving primarily in Houston, TX.
Application information: Contributes only to pre-selected organizations.
Trustees: Craig Joyce, Molly A. Joyce, Evelyn W. Wooten.
EIN: 760390166

53005
The T. D. & Joy Howell Foundation
P.O. Box 1228
Marshall, TX 75671-1228
Contact: T.D. Howell, Pres.

Established in 1997 in TX.
Donor(s): T.D. Howell, Inc.
Financial data (yr. ended 12/31/00): Grants paid, $4,905; assets, $1,368 (M); gifts received, $6,000; expenditures, $4,905; qualifying distributions, $4,905.
Limitations: Giving limited to residents of Harrison County, TX.
Officers: T.D. Howell, Pres.; Steve Howell, Secy.
Directors: Joy Howell, Leslie Howell.
EIN: 752704078

53006
Carol K. Engler Foundation
2 Gunn Ct.
Amarillo, TX 79106-4158 (806) 467-1048

Established in 1992 in TX.
Financial data (yr. ended 12/31/01): Grants paid, $4,904; assets, $1,159 (M); gifts received, $5,000; expenditures, $5,054; qualifying distributions, $4,904.
Limitations: Applications not accepted. Giving primarily in Amarillo, TX.
Application information: Contributes only to pre-selected organizations.

Officers and Directors:* Carol K. Engler, Pres.; Matthew P. Engler,* Secy.-Treas.; Sara S. Cady, Jennifer L. Engler, Mark A. Engler, Michael J. Engler, Teresa E. Raizen.
EIN: 752403435

53007
Jack and Nancy Munson Foundation
8217 Forest Ridge Dr.
Waco, TX 76712-2405 (254) 772-5453
Contact: Jack G. Munson, Pres.

Established in 2000 in TX.
Donor(s): Jack G. Munson, Nancy J. Munson.
Financial data (yr. ended 12/31/01): Grants paid, $4,900; assets, $33,373 (M); gifts received, $25,170; expenditures, $6,821; qualifying distributions, $4,900.
Limitations: Giving primarily in Waco, TX.
Officers and Directors:* Jack G. Munson,* Pres. and Treas.; Nancy J. Munson,* V.P. and Secy.; James R. Munson.
EIN: 742978284

53008
Mildred & Dave Moore Educational Trust
P.O. Box 546
Linden, TX 75563-0546

Financial data (yr. ended 12/31/01): Grants paid, $4,855; assets, $107,334 (M); expenditures, $5,110; qualifying distributions, $5,110.
Limitations: Applications not accepted. Giving limited to TX.
Application information: Contributes only to pre-selected organizations.
Trustee: John R. Rountree.
EIN: 756395334

53009
The Cornerstone Foundation
356 Couch Rd.
Lorena, TX 76655-3115 (254) 857-3218
Contact: Gregory A. Vaughn, Tr.

Donor(s): Gregory A. Vaughn, Mary Ann Vaughn.
Financial data (yr. ended 12/31/01): Grants paid, $4,825; assets, $9,889 (M); expenditures, $4,901; qualifying distributions, $4,825.
Trustees: Gregory A. Vaughn, Mary Ann Vaughn.
EIN: 746346832

53010
Dawson O. and Allison B. George Foundation
1360 Post Oak Blvd., Ste. 1440
Houston, TX 77056

Donor(s): Allison B. George, Dawson O. George III.
Financial data (yr. ended 12/31/01): Grants paid, $4,752; assets, $108,356 (M); gifts received, $1,500; expenditures, $6,459; qualifying distributions, $4,752.
Limitations: Applications not accepted. Giving primarily in TX.
Application information: Contributes only to pre-selected organizations.
Officers: Dawson O. George III, Pres.; Allison B. George, Secy.
Trustees: Douglas Barrett Orme George, Emily Allison George, Kathryn G. Murray.
EIN: 760508308

53011
The Cottrell Foundation, Inc.
5930 E. Royal Ln., Ste. 266
Dallas, TX 75230 (214) 631-4247
Contact: Isabell Cottrell, Pres.

Established around 1988.
Donor(s): Pro-Line Corp.
Financial data (yr. ended 12/31/00): Grants paid, $4,633; assets, $986 (M); gifts received, $6,000; expenditures, $6,099; qualifying distributions, $5,749.
Limitations: Giving primarily in TX.
Application information: Application form not required.
Officer: Isabell Cottrell, Pres.
EIN: 752222138

53012
Raymon Lee Thomas Trust
HCR 2, Box 136
Kress, TX 79052 (806) 864-3564
Contact: Clifton Thomas, Tr.

Financial data (yr. ended 11/30/99): Grants paid, $4,605; assets, $65,928 (M); expenditures, $4,843; qualifying distributions, $4,605.
Limitations: Giving primarily in NM and TX.
Trustees: Hazel Nelson, Clifton Thomas, Warren Thomas.
EIN: 757154731

53013
Terese Lynn Atkins Foundation
P.O. Box 1566
Denton, TX 76202-1566
Application address: c/o Michael J. Whitten, 218 N. Elm St., Denton, TX 76201, tel.: (940) 383-1618
Contact: Shirley C. Ottman, Dir.

Established in 1988 in TX.
Donor(s): Mark Howard Atkins, Mark H. Atkins.
Financial data (yr. ended 12/31/01): Grants paid, $4,600; assets, $100,480 (M); expenditures, $5,163; qualifying distributions, $4,600.
Limitations: Giving primarily in Denton, TX.
Directors: Mark Howard Atkins, Steven L. Lee, Joseph H. Marino, Shirley C. Ottman.
EIN: 752262144

53014
Kickham Foundation
16051 Addison Rd., Ste. 212
Addison, TX 75001-5369
Contact: R. Kevin Chisholm

Established in 1989 in TX.
Donor(s): Members of the Kickham family.
Financial data (yr. ended 12/31/00): Grants paid, $4,575; assets, $61,432 (M); gifts received, $5,275; expenditures, $4,625; qualifying distributions, $4,575.
Limitations: Giving primarily in Westbury, NY.
Officers: Agnes D. Kickham, Pres.; John J. Kickham, V.P.
EIN: 752287558

53015
Julie Ann Jones Memorial Theological Scholarship Trust
P.O. Box 382
Brenham, TX 77834-0382 (979) 836-4679
Contact: James R. Jones, Tr. or Sally M. Jones, Tr.

Financial data (yr. ended 12/31/01): Grants paid, $4,550; assets, $245,514 (M); gifts received, $3,765; expenditures, $5,016; qualifying distributions, $4,550.
Limitations: Giving limited to the Washington County, TX, area.
Application information: Application form not required.
Trustees: James R. Jones, Sally M. Jones, Pastor, First United Methodist Church.
EIN: 742219724

53016
Emmett and Geri Donegan Foundation
P.O. Box 429
Seguin, TX 78156-0429

Established in 1999 in TX.
Donor(s): Emmett G. Donegan, Geraldine Donegan.
Financial data (yr. ended 12/31/01): Grants paid, $4,505; assets, $2,349 (M); expenditures, $4,867; qualifying distributions, $4,505.
Limitations: Applications not accepted.
Application information: Contributes only to pre-selected organizations.
Trustees: Craig Donegan, Emmett G. Donegan, Geraldine Donegan, Brian Thomas.
EIN: 742916886

53017
Bannerman Foundation
2903 Tarry Trail
Austin, TX 78703

Established in 2000 in TX.
Donor(s): Dealey Decherd Herndon.
Financial data (yr. ended 12/31/01): Grants paid, $4,500; assets, $2,183,158 (M); gifts received, $264,375; expenditures, $8,654; qualifying distributions, $4,500.
Officers: David Herndon, Pres.; Benjamin David Herndon, V.P.; Bryan Derek Herndon, Secy.; Dealey Decherd Herndon, Treas.
EIN: 742982730

53018
R. E. L. Howard Trust
2601 Bellefontaine, Ste. C108
Houston, TX 77025

Financial data (yr. ended 07/31/01): Grants paid, $4,500; assets, $105,800 (M); expenditures, $7,121; qualifying distributions, $4,500.
Limitations: Applications not accepted. Giving primarily in Houston, TX.
Application information: Contributes only to pre-selected organizations.
Trustees: Betty Reinhardt, Michael Reinhardt.
EIN: 746241552

53019
A. B. Kempel Memorial Fund
c/o Regions Bank, Trust Dept.
P.O. Box 2020
Tyler, TX 75710
Application addresses: c/o Judy Poe, Grafton High School, Riverside Dr., Grafton, WV 26354; c/o Nathan Hollis, John Tyler High School; 1120 N. N.W. Loop 323, Tyler, TX 75702

Financial data (yr. ended 11/30/00): Grants paid, $4,500; assets, $125,461 (M); expenditures, $6,434; qualifying distributions, $4,934.
Limitations: Giving limited to Tyler, TX, and Grafton, WV.
Application information: Application form not required.
Trustee: Regions Bank.
EIN: 256081029

53020
The Laurel Foundation
4803 Crestway Dr.
Austin, TX 78731-4714

Financial data (yr. ended 12/31/01): Grants paid, $4,500; assets, $92,595 (M); expenditures, $6,440; qualifying distributions, $4,500.
Limitations: Applications not accepted. Giving primarily in Austin, TX.
Application information: Contributes only to pre-selected organizations.

Directors: Helen Skaaren, Liz Viola, Tom Viola.
EIN: 742448353

53021
Looney-Montgomery Foundation
(Formerly Montgomery Foundation)
P.O. Box 118
Edinburg, TX 78540-0118

Donor(s): Cullen R. Looney.
Financial data (yr. ended 12/31/01): Grants paid, $4,500; assets, $255,881 (M); gifts received, $100,000; expenditures, $5,270; qualifying distributions, $4,500.
Limitations: Giving limited to the lower Rio Grande Valley area in TX.
Officer: Cullen R. Looney, Pres.; Carol L. Looney, Secy.
EIN: 746050563

53022
Mallard-Turner Memorial Scholarship Trust
c/o First State Bank of Uvalde
P.O. Box 1908
Uvalde, TX 78802-1908 (830) 278-6231
Contact: Robert K. Baen, Sr.V.P., First State Bank of Uvalde

Established in 1990 in TX.
Donor(s): Estelle Turner Mallard.
Financial data (yr. ended 12/31/99): Grants paid, $4,500; assets, $148,632 (M); expenditures, $5,986; qualifying distributions, $5,345.
Limitations: Giving limited to Uvalde County, TX.
Application information: Applications can be obtained at Southwest Texas Junior College, Uvalde, TX 78801. Application form required.
Trustee: First State Bank of Uvalde.
EIN: 746384709

53023
Velma & Gatewood Newberry Foundation
3508 Windsor Rd.
Austin, TX 78703 (512) 472-1417
Contact: Camille M. Shannon, Tr.

Financial data (yr. ended 10/31/01): Grants paid, $4,500; assets, $100,586 (M); expenditures, $6,326; qualifying distributions, $4,500.
Limitations: Giving primarily in TX.
Trustees: Carole N. Roberson, Camille M. Shannon.
EIN: 746057050

53024
Ward County Council for Handicapped Children, Inc.
819 S. Allen St.
P.O. Box 238
Monahans, TX 79756-0238 (915) 943-4004
Contact: Bob Mobley, Compt.

Financial data (yr. ended 12/31/99): Grants paid, $4,500; assets, $172,250 (M); gifts received, $5,000; expenditures, $10,739; qualifying distributions, $8,954.
Limitations: Giving limited to Ward County, TX.
Application information: Application form required.
Officers: Don Huey, Pres.; Mary Adair, Secy.; Beverly Huey, Treas.
EIN: 751100663

53025
John C. & Nan K. Willett Foundation
6102 Olive Grove Ct.
Kingwood, TX 77345
Contact: John C. Willett, Pres.

Established in 1999 in TX.
Donor(s): John C. Willett.
Financial data (yr. ended 12/31/01): Grants paid, $4,500; assets, $97,873 (M); gifts received, $4,500; expenditures, $9,361; qualifying distributions, $4,500.
Officers: John C. Willett, Pres.; Nan K. Willett, V.P. and Secy.
Director: Amy Nan Willett Thelander.
EIN: 760626310

53026
David & Jeannette Lipson Trust
c/o U.S. National Bank
P.O. Box 179
Galveston, TX 77550
Application address: c/o U.S. National Bank, 2201 Market St., Galveston, TX 77550, tel.: (409) 763-1151
Contact: Janet Bertilino

Established in 1989 in TX.
Donor(s): David Lipson, Jeanette Lipson.
Financial data (yr. ended 12/31/01): Grants paid, $4,496; assets, $158,423 (M); expenditures, $10,194; qualifying distributions, $4,496.
Limitations: Giving primarily to female residents of Galveston, TX.
Application information: Application form required.
Directors: Mary Frances Heins, Rabbi James L. Kessler, Richard Toledo.
EIN: 746125212

53027
Willie Motis C.B.M., U.S.N. Foundation
226 W. Oak
West, TX 76691-1443 (254) 826-5303
Contact: Jake T. Tucker, Tr.

Financial data (yr. ended 12/31/01): Grants paid, $4,480; assets, $163,228 (M); expenditures, $11,399; qualifying distributions, $4,480.
Limitations: Giving limited to West, TX.
Trustee: Jake T. Tucker.
EIN: 742315684

53028
Hollifield Family Foundation
3527 Sleepy Hollow
Amarillo, TX 79121

Established in 2001 in TX.
Donor(s): James Hollifield.
Financial data (yr. ended 12/31/01): Grants paid, $4,448; assets, $96,097 (M); gifts received, $10,000; expenditures, $6,559; qualifying distributions, $4,448.
Limitations: Applications not accepted.
Application information: Contributes only to pre-selected organizations.
Trustee: James Hollifield.
Directors: Julie Hollifield, Thomas Hollifield, Timothy Hollifield.
EIN: 656358251

53029
Estrella Charitable Trust
929 E. Contour Dr.
San Antonio, TX 78212

Established in 1998 in TX.
Financial data (yr. ended 06/30/02): Grants paid, $4,431; assets, $6,499 (M); gifts received, $2,800; expenditures, $4,451; qualifying distributions, $4,431.
Limitations: Applications not accepted.
Application information: Contributes only to pre-selected organizations.
Trustees: Leonard Cockerill, Margaret Netemeyer.
EIN: 742858545

53030
Folkerson Foundation
c/o Wallace Vernon
P.O. Box 935
Killeen, TX 76540
Application address: 600 Indian Trail, Ste. 101, Harker Heights, TX 76548, tel.: (254) 690-7300
Contact: Cecile L. Folkerson, V.P.

Financial data (yr. ended 10/31/01): Grants paid, $4,387; assets, $282,761 (M); expenditures, $4,387; qualifying distributions, $4,387.
Limitations: Giving primarily in TX.
Officers: Douglas Folkerson, Pres.; Cecile Folkerson, V.P.; Don Folkerson, 2nd V.P.; Jan Folkerson, 2nd V.P.; Gene Silverblatt, Secy.; Wallace Vernon, Treas.
EIN: 742688916

53031
Michael P. and Eunice M. Massad Foundation, Inc.
5429 LBJ Fwy., Ste. 550
Dallas, TX 75240

Established in 1992 in TX.
Financial data (yr. ended 12/31/00): Grants paid, $4,370; assets, $92,438 (M); gifts received, $9,188; expenditures, $4,370; qualifying distributions, $4,370.
Limitations: Applications not accepted.
Application information: Contributes only to pre-selected organizations.
Officers: Michael P. Massad, Pres. and Treas.; Eunice M. Massad, V.P.; Michael P. Massad, Jr., Secy.
EIN: 752410924

53032
Staggs Family Foundation
9502 Chapel Down
Austin, TX 78729

Established in 1999 in TX.
Donor(s): David M. Staggs, Barbara Staggs.
Financial data (yr. ended 12/31/01): Grants paid, $4,360; assets, $224,460 (M); expenditures, $5,991; qualifying distributions, $4,360.
Officers: David M. Staggs, Pres.; Barbara Staggs, V.P.
EIN: 742938938

53033
Henderson County Medical Society Education Fund, Inc.
P.O. Box 1398
Athens, TX 75751 (903) 675-6671
Contact: Sherry Marshall

Established in 1996 in TX.
Financial data (yr. ended 12/31/00): Grants paid, $4,350; assets, $51,727 (M); expenditures, $4,617; qualifying distributions, $4,326.
Application information: Application form required.
Officers: Douglas Curran, M.D., Pres.; Ted Mettetal, M.D., V.P.; Harold Smitson, M.D., Secy.; Diane David, Treas.
Director: Donna Pugh.
EIN: 752590065

53034
Bible Based Ministries
P.O. Box 8911
Fort Worth, TX 76124-0911

Financial data (yr. ended 12/31/01): Grants paid, $4,325; assets, $7,499 (M); gifts received, $21,928; expenditures, $22,936; qualifying distributions, $4,325.

53034—TEXAS

Limitations: Applications not accepted. Giving primarily in TX.
Application information: Contributes only to pre-selected organizations.
Directors: Harold Davis, William L. Latham, Don Leaman, Richard Martin, Don Miller, Mary Purcell.
EIN: 751169800

53035
Guadalupe Rodriguez Charitable Foundation
615 E. Schuster Ave., Ste. 1
El Paso, TX 79902-4360

Established in 1999 in TX.
Donor(s): Guadalupe Rodriguez.
Financial data (yr. ended 12/31/01): Grants paid, $4,300; assets, $171,911 (M); expenditures, $14,626; qualifying distributions, $4,300.
Limitations: Applications not accepted. Giving primarily in El Paso, TX.
Application information: Contributes only to pre-selected organizations.
Officers and Directors:* Guadalupe Rodriguez,* Pres.; Hector M. Zavaleta,* V.P.; George W. Butterworth,* Secy.-Treas.
EIN: 912071839

53036
The Wilton Foundation
P.O. Box 790
Lamesa, TX 79331
Application address: 611 N. 2nd St., Lamesa, TX 79331-5415, tel.: (806) 872-5426
Contact: Scott Leonard, Tr.

Established in 1999 in TX.
Donor(s): Robert S. Wilton.
Financial data (yr. ended 06/30/01): Grants paid, $4,300; assets, $36,815 (M); gifts received, $37,837; expenditures, $4,310; qualifying distributions, $4,298.
Limitations: Giving primarily in TX.
Trustees: Scott L. Leonard, R. Dale Newberry, Carter T. Schildknecht.
EIN: 752856276

53037
The Perkins Foundation
1312 Brook Hollow Way
Bryan, TX 77802-1125 (979) 779-0375
Contact: Beth Price, Tr.

Financial data (yr. ended 11/30/01): Grants paid, $4,294; assets, $288,338 (M); expenditures, $4,924; qualifying distributions, $4,294.
Limitations: Giving primarily in Bryan, TX.
Trustees: Judith Perkins McMurtry, Harrie Perkins, Mrs. M.G. Perkins, Beth Price.
EIN: 746106375

53038
Earl W. and Hazel C. Pierson Foundation
1245 Country Rd. 400
Dime Box, TX 77853
Contact: Jerry M. Armstrong, V.P.

Established in 1993 in TX.
Donor(s): Hazel C. Pierson.‡
Financial data (yr. ended 12/31/01): Grants paid, $4,250; assets, $7,872 (M); expenditures, $4,368; qualifying distributions, $4,250.
Limitations: Giving primarily in Houston, TX.
Application information: Application form not required.
Officers: Marion B. Armstrong, Pres.; Jerry M. Armstrong, V.P. and Treas.; Jack Manning, Secy.
Directors: Terri Armstrong, Frank A. Borreca, Gloria Borreca, Phyllis Sorsby.
EIN: 760394931

53039
Robert A. Josey Foundation
711 William St., Ste. 402
Houston, TX 77002-1176

Donor(s): Robert A. Josey II.
Financial data (yr. ended 12/31/01): Grants paid, $4,200; assets, $58,759 (M); expenditures, $4,618; qualifying distributions, $4,200.
Limitations: Applications not accepted. Giving primarily in Houston, TX.
Application information: Contributes only to pre-selected organizations.
Trustees: Jack S. Josey, Lenoir M. Josey II, Robert A. Josey II.
EIN: 741942017

53040
Bernard E. and Marjorie J. Crocker Foundation
2606 Country Sq.
San Antonio, TX 78209 (210) 824-7835
Contact: Marjorie J. Crocker, Pres.

Established in 2000 in TX.
Donor(s): Marjorie J. Crocker.
Financial data (yr. ended 12/31/01): Grants paid, $4,122; assets, $40,291 (M); expenditures, $4,315; qualifying distributions, $4,122.
Limitations: Giving on a national basis, with emphasis on TX.
Application information: Application form not required.
Officers: Marjorie J. Crocker, Pres.; David E. Crocker, V.P.; Nancy R. Yale, Secy.-Treas.
EIN: 742945919

53041
Coventry Foundation
710 Waugh Dr., Ste. 200
Houston, TX 77019-2006

Established in 1999 in TX.
Donor(s): Chris Minnick, Penny Minnick.
Financial data (yr. ended 02/28/01): Grants paid, $4,107; assets, $192,248 (M); gifts received, $175,326; expenditures, $7,264; qualifying distributions, $7,248.
Limitations: Applications not accepted. Giving primarily in Houston, TX.
Directors: Stephen L. Brochstein, R.L. "Pat" Denison, Chris Minnick, Penny Minnick.
EIN: 760593057

53042
Dallas Bankers Wives Charitable Trust
c/o Bank of America
P.O. Box 831041
Dallas, TX 75283-1041
Application address: c/o Dean's Office, Texas Women's University, 304 Administration Dr., Denton, TX 76201

Financial data (yr. ended 04/30/00): Grants paid, $4,100; assets, $104,465 (M); gifts received, $595; expenditures, $4,157; qualifying distributions, $4,638.
Limitations: Giving limited to Denton, TX.
Application information: Application form required.
Trustee: Bank of America.
EIN: 756064548

53043
Judd & Cynthia Oualline Foundation
217 Mayerling
Houston, TX 77024-6423 (713) 781-1224
Contact: Cynthia S. Oualline, Pres.

Donor(s): Cynthia Oualline.

Financial data (yr. ended 12/31/99): Grants paid, $4,100; assets, $188,691 (M); expenditures, $7,624; qualifying distributions, $4,100.
Limitations: Giving primarily in Houston, TX.
Officers: Cynthia S. Oualline, Pres. and Treas.; Judd Oualline, Jr., V.P. and Secy.
EIN: 760523986

53044
The Harris Franklin Pearson Private Foundation Trust
P.O. Box 470068
Fort Worth, TX 76147

Donor(s): Harris Franklin Pearson.
Financial data (yr. ended 12/31/01): Grants paid, $4,100; assets, $181,599 (M); gifts received, $5,000; expenditures, $5,121; qualifying distributions, $4,100.
Limitations: Giving primarily in Fort Worth, TX.
Officer and Trustee:* Harris Franklin Pearson,* Pres.
EIN: 752639980

53045
Thomas W. Hughen School Trust
c/o Wells Fargo Bank Texas, N.A.
40 N.E. Loop 410, Ste. 20
San Antonio, TX 78216

Financial data (yr. ended 12/31/00): Grants paid, $4,065; assets, $156,112 (M); expenditures, $10,101; qualifying distributions, $4,885.
Limitations: Applications not accepted.
Application information: Contributes only to pre-selected organizations.
Trustee: Wells Fargo Bank Texas, N.A.
EIN: 746041629

53046
Katten Family Charitable Foundation
3706 Windmill Hill
Waco, TX 76710

Donor(s): Edwin M. Kattan.
Financial data (yr. ended 12/31/01): Grants paid, $4,025; assets, $48,852 (M); expenditures, $4,025; qualifying distributions, $4,025.
Directors: Doris Q. Kattan, Edwin M. Kattan, Steven E. Kattan.
EIN: 742832881

53047
Midwestern State University Holland-King Foundation
P.O. Box 9129
Wichita Falls, TX 76308
Application address: c/o Midwestern State University, School Relations Office, 3410 Taft, Wichita Falls, TX 76308; Tel.: (940) 397-4651
Contact: Anne Opperman

Financial data (yr. ended 12/31/99): Grants paid, $4,003; assets, $158,515 (M); expenditures, $5,955; qualifying distributions, $4,190.
Trustee: Kristin Morris.
EIN: 756452384

53048
William H. Bowen Educational Charitable Foundation
5646 Milton St., Ste. 900
Dallas, TX 75206-3995
Contact: Patrick M. Sullivan, Pres.

Established in 1989 in TX.
Donor(s): William H. Bowen.‡
Financial data (yr. ended 11/30/01): Grants paid, $4,000; assets, $152,847 (M); expenditures, $7,631; qualifying distributions, $4,000.

Officers and Directors:* Patrick M. Sullivan,* Pres.; Guy U. Griffeth,* V.P.; Janis Huddelston,* Secy.; Marlene Z. Franklin,* Treas.
EIN: 752303984

53049
DJDM Foundation
6006 Sjolander Rd.
Baytown, TX 77521

Established in 1998 in TX.
Donor(s): Joe L. Moore, Debra P. Moore.
Financial data (yr. ended 12/31/01): Grants paid, $4,000; assets, $54,148 (M); gifts received, $41,714; expenditures, $4,014; qualifying distributions, $4,000.
Officers: David L. Moore, Pres.; Debra P. Moore, Secy.; Joe L. Moore, Treas.
EIN: 760590748

53050
Hope Foundation
P.O. Box 801901
Dallas, TX 75380-1901

Donor(s): Calvin D. Stoltzfus, Beverly A. Stoltzfus.
Financial data (yr. ended 12/31/00): Grants paid, $4,000; assets, $70,719 (M); gifts received, $70,000; expenditures, $4,628; qualifying distributions, $619.
Limitations: Applications not accepted.
Application information: Contributes only to pre-selected organizations.
Trustees: Beverly A. Stoltzfus, Calvin D. Stoltzfus.
EIN: 756526146

53051
Houston Geological Society Foundation
7457 Harwin, Ste. 301
Houston, TX 77036-2190 (713) 524-7040

Established in 1984 in TX.
Financial data (yr. ended 06/30/00): Grants paid, $4,000; assets, $132,646 (M); gifts received, $2,980; expenditures, $4,234; qualifying distributions, $4,000.
Limitations: Giving primarily in TX.
Application information: Application form required.
Officers: Hugh Hardy, Chair.; John A. Adamick, Secy.; David Fontaine, Treas.
EIN: 760138744

53052
M. C. Jackson, Sr. Family Foundation
c/o P.J. Fleming, C.P.A.
306 W. Sunset Rd., No. 119
San Antonio, TX 78209
Contact: Holly Jackson, Pres.

Established in 1998 in TX.
Donor(s): Jackson Family Charitable Tr.
Financial data (yr. ended 12/31/01): Grants paid, $4,000; assets, $710,010 (M); gifts received, $263,721; expenditures, $53,439; qualifying distributions, $4,000.
Limitations: Giving primarily in Fayetteville, GA, and Fredericksburg, TX.
Officer and Directors:* Holly Jackson,* Pres.; P.J. Fleming, Mell C. Jackson, Jr.
EIN: 742878478

53053
The Dorothy and Jim Kronzer Foundation
3000 Weslayan, Ste. 375
Houston, TX 77027-5753
Application address: 723 Patterson St., Austin, TX 78703
Contact: Kimberlee Kronzer O'Brien, Pres.

Established in 2000 in TX.
Donor(s): Dorothy B. Kronzer.
Financial data (yr. ended 12/31/01): Grants paid, $4,000; assets, $466,067 (M); expenditures, $4,000; qualifying distributions, $4,000.
Application information: Application form not required.
Officers and Directors:* Dorothy B. Kronzer, Chair.; Kimberlee Kronzer O'Brien,* Pres.; Walter James Kronzer III,* V.P. and Secy.; Kathryn Elaine Steele Kronzer, John Stafford O'Brien.
EIN: 311703357

53054
Ethel Brown Nicholson Fund
c/o Woodway Financial Advisors
10000 Memorial Dr.
Houston, TX 77024

Established in 1995 in TX.
Donor(s): Ethel Brown Nicholson.
Financial data (yr. ended 12/31/01): Grants paid, $4,000; assets, $62,771 (M); expenditures, $4,525; qualifying distributions, $4,000.
Limitations: Applications not accepted.
Application information: Contributes only to pre-selected organizations.
Trustee: Ethel Brown Nicholson.
EIN: 760389803

53055
Robert B. Park Estate Trust
c/o Roy W. Twombly
22 N. Charleston Ct.
Sugar Land, TX 77478-3655

Financial data (yr. ended 12/31/01): Grants paid, $4,000; assets, $221,553 (M); expenditures, $9,443; qualifying distributions, $4,000.
Limitations: Applications not accepted. Giving primarily in Cleveland, OH, and Houston, TX.
Application information: Contributes only to pre-selected organizations.
Trustee: Roy W. Twombly.
EIN: 746049276

53056
Renwick Family Foundation
9521 Windy Hall Rd.
Dallas, TX 75238
Application address: c/o Northern Trust, 5540 Preston Rd., Dallas, TX 75205-2637

Established in 2000 in TX.
Donor(s): Mary P. Renwick, William K. Renwick.
Financial data (yr. ended 12/31/01): Grants paid, $4,000; assets, $192,529 (M); gifts received, $725; expenditures, $8,301; qualifying distributions, $4,000.
Limitations: Giving limited to LA.
Application information: Application form required.
Officers: Mary P. Renwick, Co-Chair.; William K. Renwick, Co-Chair.; W. Kenneth Renwick, Jr., Secy.; Steven P. Renwick, Treas.
EIN: 756589482

53057
The Ithaka Foundation
c/o James V. Baird
600 Travis St., Ste. 4200
Houston, TX 77002
Application address: 24020 Old Hundred Rd., Dickerson, MD 20842-9665, tel.: (703) 575-3142
Contact: David Langstaff, Pres.

Established in 1997 in TX.
Donor(s): David Langstaff.
Financial data (yr. ended 12/31/01): Grants paid, $3,965; assets, $75,855 (M); expenditures, $11,731; qualifying distributions, $3,965.
Officers: David H. Langstaff, Pres. and Treas.; Cynthia Shauer Langstaff, V.P. and Secy.
Director: Lee M. Langstaff.
EIN: 760555608

53058
Bennett & Marion Glazer Foundation, Inc.
c/o Bennett Glazer
14860 Landmark Blvd.
Dallas, TX 75254

Established in 2001 in TX.
Donor(s): Bennett Glazer.
Financial data (yr. ended 12/31/01): Grants paid, $3,950; assets, $240,760 (M); expenditures, $3,953; qualifying distributions, $3,950.
Trustees: Bennett Glazer, Marion Glazer.
EIN: 752916887

53059
Callejo-Botello Foundation Charitable Trust
4314 N. Central Expwy.
Dallas, TX 75206-6536 (214) 741-6710
Contact: William F. Callejo, Tr.

Donor(s): Adelfa B. Callejo, William F. Callejo.
Financial data (yr. ended 12/31/01): Grants paid, $3,925; assets, $195,733 (M); expenditures, $4,145; qualifying distributions, $3,925.
Limitations: Giving primarily in TX.
Application information: Application form required.
Trustees: Adelfa B. Callejo, William F. Callejo, P.C. Lam.
EIN: 751678195
Codes: GTI

53060
Barkett Family Foundation, Inc.
5580 Peterson Ln., Ste. 250
Dallas, TX 75240

Established in 1997 in FL and TX.
Donor(s): George A. Barkett, Sue T. Barkett.
Financial data (yr. ended 11/30/01): Grants paid, $3,900; assets, $65,638 (M); gifts received, $20,000; expenditures, $5,235; qualifying distributions, $3,900.
Limitations: Applications not accepted.
Application information: Contributes only to pre-selected organizations.
Officers: George A. Barkett, Pres.; Sue T. Barkett, Secy.-Treas.
Directors: Andrea T. Barkett, G. Doughlas Barkett.
EIN: 582372150

53061
The Adam and Rebecca Beshara Foundation, Inc.
300 Crescent Ct., Ste. 800
Dallas, TX 75201

Established in 2000 in TX.
Donor(s): Jeffrey A. Marcus, Mrs. Jeffrey A. Marcus.
Financial data (yr. ended 12/31/01): Grants paid, $3,879; assets, $202,619 (M); gifts received, $25,000; expenditures, $6,684; qualifying distributions, $3,879.
Limitations: Applications not accepted. Giving primarily in Dallas, TX.
Application information: Contributes only to pre-selected organizations.
Officers: Rebecca Marcus Beshara, Pres.; Adam Beshara, V.P.; Nancy C. Marcus, Secy.; Jeffrey A. Marcus, Treas.
EIN: 752895615

53062
Foundation for Positive Growth, Inc.
2050 N. Stemmons Fwy., Ste. 174-F
Dallas, TX 75342

Established in 1995 in TX.
Financial data (yr. ended 12/31/01): Grants paid, $3,846; assets, $1 (M); gifts received, $3,500; expenditures, $4,315; qualifying distributions, $3,846.
Limitations: Giving primarily in TX.
Officer: Alvin Roy Granoff, Pres.
EIN: 752322523

53063
Hudiburg Foundation, Inc.
7769 Grapevine Hwy.
Fort Worth, TX 76180   (817) 498-2400
Contact: John R. Payne, Pres.

Established in 1972 in TX.
Donor(s): Lorene A. Hudiburg.
Financial data (yr. ended 12/31/01): Grants paid, $3,800; assets, $251,830 (M); expenditures, $6,570; qualifying distributions, $3,800.
Limitations: Giving limited to Fort Worth, TX.
Officers: John R. Payne, Pres.; Lorene A. Hudiburg, V.P.; W.E. Voss, Treas.
EIN: 237394498

53064
The Inge Foundation
207 S. Brazos St.
Granbury, TX 76048

Established in 2000 in TX.
Donor(s): Charles Inge, Dominique Inge.
Financial data (yr. ended 12/31/01): Grants paid, $3,750; assets, $1,489,432 (M); gifts received, $1,447,493; expenditures, $10,169; qualifying distributions, $3,750.
Trustees: Charles Inge, Dominique Inge, Rust E. Reid.
EIN: 752913283

53065
The Colburn-Pledge Music Scholarship Foundation
101 Cardinal Ave.
San Antonio, TX 78209   (210) 824-8785
Contact: Joycelyn H. Rudeloff, Secy.

Financial data (yr. ended 06/30/00): Grants paid, $3,700; assets, $35,003 (M); expenditures, $3,836; qualifying distributions, $3,836.
Limitations: Giving limited to TX.
Application information: Application form required.
Officers: Shirley Frederic, Pres.; Mary Ruth Leonard, V.P.; Joycelyn H. Rudeloff, Secy.; Eric Brahinsky, Treas.
Directors: Donna Kole, Richard Kole.
EIN: 742346339

53066
Debs and Vernelle Gamblin Foundation
P.O. Box 8685
Horseshoe Bay, TX 78657-8685

Established in 1997 in TX.
Donor(s): Debs Gamblin.
Financial data (yr. ended 12/31/01): Grants paid, $3,700; assets, $30,125 (M); gifts received, $200; expenditures, $3,856; qualifying distributions, $3,700.
Limitations: Applications not accepted.
Application information: Contributes only to pre-selected organizations.
Officers and Directors:* Debs Gamblin,* Pres.; Vernelle Gamblin,* Secy.-Treas.
EIN: 742829931

53067
Sam and Margaret Lee Foundation
P.O. Box 1550
Roanoke, TX 76262-1550

Established in 1992 in TX.
Financial data (yr. ended 12/31/01): Grants paid, $3,657; assets, $4,715 (M); gifts received, $3,000; expenditures, $4,032; qualifying distributions, $3,657.
Officers: Sam W. Lee, Chair. and Treas.; Margaret B. Lee, Vice-Chair.; Billy G. Ragsdale, Secy.
EIN: 752444739

53068
Frances Patterson Trust
c/o Bank of America
P.O. Box 831041
Dallas, TX 75283-1041
Application address: c/o Bank of America, P.O. Box 830259, Dallas, TX 75283-0259, tel.: (800) 257-0332

Financial data (yr. ended 12/31/01): Grants paid, $3,646; assets, $136,247 (M); expenditures, $5,905; qualifying distributions, $4,754.
Limitations: Giving limited to residents of Fredonia, KS.
Trustee: Bank of America.
EIN: 446008159
Codes: GTI

53069
Morris & Ann Kagan Foundation
8801 Knight Rd.
Houston, TX 77054   (713) 748-2000
Contact: Lawrence Kagan, Pres.

Donor(s): Morris Kagan, Lawrence Kagan.
Financial data (yr. ended 12/31/01): Grants paid, $3,600; assets, $70,292 (M); expenditures, $4,348; qualifying distributions, $3,600.
Officer and Director:* Lawrence Kagan,* Pres.
EIN: 746068035

53070
C. H. & Elaine Warnken, Jr. Charitable Trust
P.O. Drawer B
Pleasanton, TX 78064

Established in 1989 in TX.
Donor(s): Charles H. Warnken, Jr., Elaine Warnken.
Financial data (yr. ended 11/30/01): Grants paid, $3,600; assets, $138,046 (M); expenditures, $6,328; qualifying distributions, $3,600.
Limitations: Applications not accepted. Giving primarily in TX.
Application information: Contributes only to pre-selected organizations.
Trustees: Byron Warnken, Charles H. Warnken, Jr., Elaine Warnken, James Warnken, Kurt Warnken.
EIN: 742554309

53071
William B. Ward Midwestern University Scholarship Fund Trust
c/o Wells Fargo Bank Texas, N.A.
P.O. Box 9129
Wichita Falls, TX 76308
Application address: c/o Midwestern State University, 3440 Taft Blvd., Wichita Falls, TX 76308-2095

Financial data (yr. ended 09/30/01): Grants paid, $3,526; assets, $116,079 (M); expenditures, $6,112; qualifying distributions, $3,526.
Limitations: Giving limited to Wichita Falls, TX.
Application information: Application form required.
Trustee: Wells Fargo Bank Texas, N.A.
EIN: 756155842

53072
Jim Black Memorial Scholarship Trust
c/o Regions Bank
P.O. Box 2020
Tyler, TX 75710
Application address: c/o Robert E. Lee High School, 411 E. Southeast Loop 323, Tyler, TX 75701, tel.: (903) 561-3911

Financial data (yr. ended 12/31/01): Grants paid, $3,500; assets, $71,893 (M); expenditures, $5,217; qualifying distributions, $3,500.
Limitations: Giving limited to Tyler, TX.
Application information: Application form required.
Trustee: Regions Bank.
EIN: 756265235
Codes: GTI

53073
Joe H. & Mary Lee Bryant Foundation
c/o American State Bank
P.O. Box 1401
Lubbock, TX 79408-1401   (806) 767-7000
Contact: Bryan Limmer, V.P.

Donor(s): Mary Lee Bryant.
Financial data (yr. ended 12/31/01): Grants paid, $3,500; assets, $76,148 (M); expenditures, $5,262; qualifying distributions, $3,500.
Limitations: Giving primarily in Lubbock, TX.
Officer and Trustees:* Bryan Limmer,* V.P.; Joe Sam Bryant, American State Bank.
EIN: 756054494

53074
Rusty & Susan Burnett Foundation
202 Vanderpool, Ste. 34
Houston, TX 77024

Established in 1997 in TX.
Donor(s): Rusty Burnett, Susan Burnett.
Financial data (yr. ended 12/31/01): Grants paid, $3,500; assets, $42,416 (M); expenditures, $3,540; qualifying distributions, $3,500.
Officers: Rusty Burnett, Pres.; Susan Burnett, V.P.; Joe Walk, V.P.
EIN: 760556476

53075
William and Louise Doering Charitable Foundation
5 Parliment Pl.
Dallas, TX 75225

Established in 1986 in TX.
Donor(s): William L. Crofford, Jr., Elizabeth L. Crofford.
Financial data (yr. ended 12/31/01): Grants paid, $3,500; assets, $57,983 (M); expenditures, $3,541; qualifying distributions, $3,500.
Limitations: Applications not accepted. Giving primarily in Ponca City, OK, and Dallas, Galveston and Houston, TX.
Application information: Contributes only to pre-selected organizations.
Officers and Directors:* William L. Crofford, Jr.,* Pres.; Elizabeth Louise Crofford,* V.P.; Jonathan M. Crofford, V.P.; Theodore W. Crofford, V.P.; Jennifer Crofford Freeman,* Secy.
EIN: 752147143

53076
Yrma Cleveland Jones Trust
2016 Coggin Ave.
Brownwood, TX 76801
Contact: John A. Thomason, Tr.

Financial data (yr. ended 12/31/00): Grants paid, $3,500; assets, $84,489 (M); expenditures, $4,990; qualifying distributions, $3,500.
Limitations: Giving limited to Brown County, TX.
Trustees: Patti Jordan, John A. Thomason, Helen Wesson.
EIN: 237162526

53077
K & E Fund, Inc.
2200 Post Oak Blvd., Ste. 707
Houston, TX 77056-4707

Donor(s): Katherine R. Johnson.
Financial data (yr. ended 12/31/01): Grants paid, $3,500; assets, $2,771 (M); gifts received, $5,000; expenditures, $4,432; qualifying distributions, $3,500.
Limitations: Applications not accepted. Giving primarily in Houston, TX.
Application information: Contributes only to pre-selected organizations.
Officers and Directors:* Glenn H. Johnson,* Pres. and Treas.; Diana E. Johnson,* V.P. and Secy.; Jessica Len Miller.
EIN: 746040532

53078
Dennis O'Connor III Foundation
106 W. Juan Linn
Victoria, TX 77901 (361) 572-9638
Contact: Louise O'Connor, Pres.

Established in 1997 in TX.
Donor(s): Jim Johnstone, Junie Johnstone.
Financial data (yr. ended 12/31/01): Grants paid, $3,500; assets, $67,064 (M); expenditures, $4,845; qualifying distributions, $3,500.
Officers and Directors:* Louise S. O'Connor,* Pres.; Virginia Drake Liebermann,* V.P.; Clay S. O'Connor,* Secy.; Thomas Donald O'Connor,* Treas.; Laurie House O'Connor.
EIN: 742804523

53079
Spradlin Foundation, Inc.
500 S. Rusk St.
Kilgore, TX 75662 (903) 984-3629
Contact: Ronald E. Spradlin, III, Pres.

Established in 2000 in TX.
Donor(s): Ronald E. Spradlin.
Financial data (yr. ended 12/31/01): Grants paid, $3,500; assets, $89,484 (M); expenditures, $6,655; qualifying distributions, $3,430.
Limitations: Giving primarily in Kilgore, TX.
Application information: Application form not required.
Officers: Ronald E. Spradlin III, Pres.; Eric Brian Marcott, V.P.; Nan Shertzer White, Secy.-Treas.
EIN: 752910442

53080
Oshman Family Foundation
4350 Ocean Dr., Ste. 505
Corpus Christi, TX 78412
Contact: Joseph Oshman, Pres.

Established in 2000 in TX.
Donor(s): Joseph Oshman, Dorothy Oshman.
Financial data (yr. ended 12/31/01): Grants paid, $3,480; assets, $224,963 (M); gifts received, $1,250; expenditures, $5,399; qualifying distributions, $3,480.
Officers: Joseph Oshman, Pres.; Dorothy Oshman, 1st V.P.; Robert D. Oshman, 2nd V.P.; Steven Oshman, 3rd V.P.; Sandra Lee Oshman, Secy.; Scot H. Oshman, Treas.
EIN: 742979529

53081
David Noel Pritsker Foundation, Inc.
3820 Park Pl.
Addison, TX 75001
Contact: Hildegarde M. Pritsker, Tr.

Financial data (yr. ended 01/31/02): Grants paid, $3,476; assets, $40,088 (M); expenditures, $3,983; qualifying distributions, $3,476.
Limitations: Giving primarily in Dallas, TX.
Trustee: Hildegarde M. Pritsker.
EIN: 751748587

53082
AFTL Ambassadors for the Lord Ministries
1505 Churchill Way
Rowlett, TX 75088-6036

Established in 1991.
Financial data (yr. ended 12/31/01): Grants paid, $3,470; assets, $222 (M); gifts received, $5,294; expenditures, $5,642; qualifying distributions, $3,470; giving activities include $2,008 for programs.
Officer: K.I. Thomas, Pres.
Directors: Diana Ellis, Johnson Abraham Roulett.
EIN: 752374437

53083
Vincent C. and Ann K. Gunn Foundation
P.O. Box GOCO
Wichita Falls, TX 76307 (940) 723-5585

Established in 1990 in TX.
Donor(s): Vincent C. Gunn.
Financial data (yr. ended 12/31/01): Grants paid, $3,464; assets, $210,365 (M); expenditures, $7,097; qualifying distributions, $3,464.
Limitations: Applications not accepted. Giving primarily in Wichita Falls, TX.
Application information: Contributes only to pre-selected organizations.
Officers: Vincent C. Gunn, Pres. and Treas.; Ann K. Gunn, V.P. and Secy.
Director: Donald J. Hupp.
EIN: 752361496

53084
Ruth & Roy Schapira Family Fund
1600 Westway Blvd.
McAllen, TX 78501-4254 (956) 686-3248

Donor(s): Roy Schapira, Ruth Schapira.
Financial data (yr. ended 09/30/01): Grants paid, $3,461; assets, $39,919 (M); expenditures, $4,206; qualifying distributions, $3,461.
Limitations: Applications not accepted. Giving primarily in TX.
Application information: Contributes only to pre-selected organizations.
Trustees: Roy Schapira, Ruth Schapira.
EIN: 746088062

53085
The Hyatt Anne Bass Foundation
201 Main St., Ste. 2300
Fort Worth, TX 76102-3105 (817) 390-8400

Established in 1994 in TX.
Donor(s): Perry R. Bass.
Financial data (yr. ended 12/31/01): Grants paid, $3,400; assets, $48,653 (M); expenditures, $4,157; qualifying distributions, $3,400.
Limitations: Applications not accepted. Giving limited to Fort Worth, TX.
Application information: Contributes only to pre-selected organizations.
Officers and Directors:* Sid R. Bass,* Pres.; Perry R. Bass,* V.P.; W. Robert Cotham, 2nd V.P.; Nancy Lee Bass,* Secy.-Treas.
EIN: 752554448

53086
The Samantha Sims Bass Foundation
c/o W. Robert Cotham
201 Main St., Ste. 2300
Fort Worth, TX 76102-3105 (817) 390-8400

Established in 1994 in TX.
Donor(s): Perry R. Bass.
Financial data (yr. ended 12/31/01): Grants paid, $3,400; assets, $48,625 (M); expenditures, $4,157; qualifying distributions, $3,400.
Limitations: Applications not accepted. Giving limited to Fort Worth, TX.
Application information: Contributes only to pre-selected organizations.
Officers and Directors:* Sid R. Bass,* Pres.; Perry R. Bass,* V.P.; W. Robert Cotham, 2nd V.P.; Nancy Lee Bass,* Secy.-Treas.
EIN: 752554447

53087
The Sid Richardson Bass H Foundation
c/o W. Robert Cotham
201 Main St., Ste. 2300
Fort Worth, TX 76102-3105 (817) 390-8400

Established in 1994 in TX.
Donor(s): Perry R. Bass.
Financial data (yr. ended 12/31/01): Grants paid, $3,400; assets, $48,624 (M); expenditures, $4,157; qualifying distributions, $3,395.
Limitations: Applications not accepted. Giving limited to Fort Worth, TX.
Application information: Contributes only to pre-selected organizations.
Officers and Directors:* Sid R. Bass,* Pres.; Perry R. Bass,* V.P.; W. Robert Cotham, 2nd V.P.; Nancy Lee Bass,* Secy.-Treas.
EIN: 752554449

53088
The Sid Richardson Bass S Foundation
c/o W. Robert Cotham
201 Main St., Ste. 2300
Fort Worth, TX 76102-3105

Established in 1994 in TX.
Donor(s): Perry R. Bass.
Financial data (yr. ended 12/31/01): Grants paid, $3,400; assets, $48,654 (M); expenditures, $4,157; qualifying distributions, $3,395.
Limitations: Applications not accepted. Giving limited to Fort Worth, TX.
Application information: Contributes only to pre-selected organizations.
Officers and Directors:* Sid R. Bass,* Pres.; Perry R. Bass,* V.P.; W. Robert Cotham, 2nd V.P.; Nancy Lee Bass,* Secy.-Treas.
EIN: 752554450

53089
Sherer Family Foundation
5580 Peterson Ln., Ste. 250
Dallas, TX 75240

Established in 1999 in TX and AL.
Donor(s): Jerald M. Sherer, Billie C. Sherer.
Financial data (yr. ended 12/31/01): Grants paid, $3,400; assets, $76,876 (M); gifts received, $26,522; expenditures, $5,009; qualifying distributions, $3,400.
Limitations: Applications not accepted. Giving primarily in Austin, TX.

Application information: Contributes only to pre-selected organizations.
Officers and Directors:* Jerald M. Sherer,* Pres.; Billie C. Sherer,* Secy.-Treas.; Susan S. Henley, Lisa S. Reed.
EIN: 311645491

53090
The Edward Perry Bass Foundation
201 Main St., Ste. 2300
Fort Worth, TX 76102-3105

Established in 1994 in TX.
Donor(s): Perry R. Bass.
Financial data (yr. ended 12/31/01): Grants paid, $3,300; assets, $48,729 (M); expenditures, $4,057; qualifying distributions, $3,300.
Limitations: Applications not accepted. Giving limited to Fort Worth, TX.
Application information: Contributes only to pre-selected organizations.
Officers and Directors:* Edward P. Bass,* Pres.; Perry R. Bass,* V.P.; W. Robert Cotham, 2nd V.P.; Nancy Lee Bass,* Secy.-Treas.
EIN: 752554451

53091
The Ramona Frates Bass Foundation
c/o W. Robert Cotham
201 Main St., Ste. 2300
Fort Worth, TX 76102 (817) 390-8400

Established in 1994 in TX.
Donor(s): Perry R. Bass.
Financial data (yr. ended 12/31/01): Grants paid, $3,300; assets, $48,716 (M); expenditures, $4,057; qualifying distributions, $3,300.
Limitations: Applications not accepted. Giving limited to Fort Worth, TX.
Application information: Contributes only to pre-selected organizations.
Officers and Directors:* Lee M. Bass,* Pres.; Perry R. Bass,* V.P.; W. Robert Cotham,* 2nd V.P.; Nancy Lee Bass,* Secy.-Treas.
EIN: 752554445

53092
The Sophie Seeligson Bass Foundation
c/o W. Robert Cotham
201 Main St., Ste. 2300
Fort Worth, TX 76102 (817) 390-8400

Established in 1994 in TX.
Financial data (yr. ended 12/31/01): Grants paid, $3,300; assets, $48,710 (M); expenditures, $4,057; qualifying distributions, $3,300.
Limitations: Applications not accepted. Giving limited to Fort Worth, TX.
Application information: Contributes only to pre-selected organizations.
Officers and Directors:* Lee M. Bass,* Pres.; Perry R. Bass,* V.P.; W. Robert Cotham,* 2nd V.P.; Nancy Lee Bass,* Secy.-Treas.
EIN: 752554446

53093
The Perry Richardson Bass II Foundation
c/o W. Robert Cotham
201 Main St., Ste. 2300
Fort Worth, TX 76102

Established in 1994 in TX.
Donor(s): Perry R. Bass.
Financial data (yr. ended 12/31/01): Grants paid, $3,300; assets, $48,715 (M); expenditures, $4,057; qualifying distributions, $3,295.
Limitations: Applications not accepted. Giving limited to TX.
Application information: Contributes only to pre-selected organizations.

Officers and Directors:* Lee M. Bass,* Pres.; Perry R. Bass,* V.P.; W. Robert Cotham, 2nd V.P.; Nancy Lee Bass,* Secy.-Treas.
EIN: 752554452

53094
Hubbard Family Foundation, Inc.
6221 Colleyville Blvd., Ste. 150
Colleyville, TX 76034

Established in 2000 in TX.
Donor(s): Vance M. Hubbard.
Financial data (yr. ended 12/31/01): Grants paid, $3,300; assets, $637,658 (M); expenditures, $3,440; qualifying distributions, $3,300.
Limitations: Applications not accepted.
Application information: Contributes only to pre-selected organizations.
Officers: Vance M. Hubbard, Pres.; Albert M. Suarez, V.P.
Director: Valerie Hubbard.
EIN: 752764879

53095
The Wells Texas Foundation, Inc.
13635 Perthshire Rd.
Houston, TX 77079-5938

Financial data (yr. ended 12/31/01): Grants paid, $3,300; assets, $102,978 (M); gifts received, $5,200; expenditures, $5,164; qualifying distributions, $3,300.
Limitations: Applications not accepted.
Application information: Contributes only to pre-selected organizations.
Officers and Directors:* Kenneth F. Wells,* Pres. and Treas.; Sibyl R. Wells,* V.P. and Secy.; Sharon Wells Rosenfeld, David K. Wells.
EIN: 760574582

53096
The Sinclair Foundation
5749 Swiss Ave.
Dallas, TX 75214-4638 (214) 969-8595
Contact: Judson Mark Sinclair, Tr.

Established in 1986 in TX.
Donor(s): Judson Mark Sinclair.
Financial data (yr. ended 12/31/01): Grants paid, $3,265; assets, $5,123 (M); gifts received, $4,000; expenditures, $3,276; qualifying distributions, $3,276.
Limitations: Giving primarily in Dallas, TX.
Trustee: Judson Mark Sinclair.
EIN: 756350967

53097
Friedman Foundation
800 Bering Dr., Ste. 210
Houston, TX 77057

Established in 1998 in TX.
Donor(s): Esther Blonstein.
Financial data (yr. ended 12/31/99): Grants paid, $3,250; assets, $1,330,191 (M); gifts received, $188,847; expenditures, $14,976; qualifying distributions, $2,875.
Limitations: Applications not accepted. Giving primarily in Houston, TX.
Application information: Contributes only to pre-selected organizations.
Officers: Esther Friedman Blonstein, Pres.; Morton Cohn, V.P.; J. Kent Friedman, Secy.-Treas.
EIN: 311629811

53098
A. D. Myers Memorial Fund
P.O. Box 55
Olney, TX 76374 (940) 564-5616
Contact: David Ickert, Tr.

Financial data (yr. ended 12/31/00): Grants paid, $3,250; assets, $2,018 (M); expenditures, $3,282; qualifying distributions, $3,282.
Limitations: Giving primarily in TX.
Trustee: David A. Ickert.
EIN: 751588787

53099
Thomas Memorial Trust
c/o Bank of America
P.O. Box 831041
Dallas, TX 75283-1041

Established in 1997 in AR.
Financial data (yr. ended 12/31/99): Grants paid, $3,250; assets, $119,047 (M); gifts received, $2,648; expenditures, $6,093; qualifying distributions, $3,429.
Trustee: Bank of America.
EIN: 626329992

53100
Luckens/McAdams Foundation
4609 Edgemont Dr.
Austin, TX 78731-5225
Contact: Diana Claire McAdams, Dir.

Established in 1997 in TX.
Donor(s): Diana Claire McAdams, Bennet J. Luckens.
Financial data (yr. ended 11/30/01): Grants paid, $3,247; assets, $93,216 (M); expenditures, $3,729; qualifying distributions, $3,247.
Limitations: Giving primarily in Austin, TX.
Directors: Bennet J. Luckens, Diana Claire McAdams, Nancy Reeves McAdams.
EIN: 742828028

53101
The Richardson Foundation
1901 N. Akard St.
Dallas, TX 75201
Application address: P.O. Box 1619, Lindale TX 75771
Contact: Gene A. Richardson, Sr., Pres.

Established in 1997 in TX.
Donor(s): Gene A. Richardson, Sr., Mary C. Richardson.
Financial data (yr. ended 12/31/01): Grants paid, $3,232; assets, $54,700 (M); expenditures, $3,844; qualifying distributions, $3,232.
Application information: Application form not required.
Officers and Trustees:* Gene A. Richardson, Sr.,* Pres. and Treas.; Gene A. Richardson, Jr.,* V.P. and Secy.; Mary C. Richardson.
EIN: 752707547

53102
Junick Foundation
5622 Bayou Glen Rd.
Houston, TX 77056

Donor(s): June C. Anderson.
Financial data (yr. ended 11/30/01): Grants paid, $3,200; assets, $62,882 (M); expenditures, $3,755; qualifying distributions, $3,200.
Limitations: Applications not accepted. Giving limited to Houston, TX.
Application information: Contributes only to pre-selected organizations.
Officers: June C. Anderson, Pres.; Christine C. Moseley, V.P.
EIN: 760135407

53103
Walker Foundation
6315 Park Ln.
Dallas, TX 75225

Donor(s): John M. Walker, Sr.‡
Financial data (yr. ended 12/31/00): Grants paid, $3,200; assets, $20,452 (M); gifts received, $20,000; expenditures, $3,200; qualifying distributions, $3,200.
Limitations: Applications not accepted. Giving primarily in Dallas, TX.
Application information: Contributes only to pre-selected organizations.
Officers: John M. Walker, Jr., Pres.; Carol V. Walker, V.P.; Allen Walker, Secy.-Treas.
EIN: 756066143

53104
Jack G. Davis Memorial Foundation
P.O. Box 277
Mart, TX 76664-0277 (254) 876-2686
Contact: Sue C. Davis, Pres.

Established in 1987 in TX.
Financial data (yr. ended 12/31/99): Grants paid, $3,150; assets, $7,684 (M); gifts received, $5,650; expenditures, $3,158; qualifying distributions, $3,156.
Limitations: Giving limited to Mart, TX.
Officers: Sue C. Davis, Pres.; Clayton A. Davis, V.P.; Erin B. Davis, V.P.; Mary Frances Davis, Secy.; Philip C. Davis, Treas.
EIN: 760252079

53105
The Landreth Foundation
306 W. 7th St., Ste. 504
Fort Worth, TX 76102

Donor(s): Mary Adele Smith Trust.
Financial data (yr. ended 12/31/01): Grants paid, $3,130; assets, $85,662 (M); expenditures, $4,391; qualifying distributions, $3,130.
Limitations: Applications not accepted.
Application information: Contributes only to pre-selected organizations.
Officers: Edward L. Smith, Pres. and Treas.; William A. Landreth, Jr., V.P. and Secy.
EIN: 752567937

53106
Robert & Ruby Priddy Charitable Trust
807 8th St., Ste. 600
Wichita Falls, TX 76301

Established in 2000 in TX.
Donor(s): Robert T. Priddy.
Financial data (yr. ended 12/31/01): Grants paid, $3,100; assets, $49,077 (M); gifts received, $200,026; expenditures, $155,673; qualifying distributions, $153,362.
Limitations: Applications not accepted. Giving primarily in PA and TX.
Application information: Contributes only to pre-selected organizations.
Officer: Robert T. Priddy, Chair.
Directors: Richard H. Bundy, Berneice R. Leath, Joseph N. Sherrill, Jr., David Wolverton.
EIN: 752924748

53107
Yager Foundation, Inc.
P.O. Box 419
Caldwell, TX 77836-0419 (979) 567-3212
Contact: Henrietta W. Yager, Pres.

Established in 1968 in TX.
Donor(s): B.T. Yager, Jr., Henrietta W. Yager.
Financial data (yr. ended 10/31/01): Grants paid, $3,100; assets, $1,004,958 (M); expenditures, $9,121; qualifying distributions, $4,100.
Limitations: Giving primarily in TX.
Application information: Application form not required.
Officer and Directors:* Henrietta W. Yager,* Pres.; Ann Yager Chapman,* V.P.; Katherine Yager Rogers,* V.P.; Craig Blum,* Secy.-Treas.; B.T. Yager.
EIN: 237055782

53108
The Diagnostic Clinic of Houston Medical Foundation
(Formerly Frederick R. Lummis Medical Foundation)
6448 Fannin St.
Houston, TX 77030 (713) 797-9191
Contact: W.T. Arnold, M.D., Pres.

Financial data (yr. ended 08/31/01): Grants paid, $3,061; assets, $212,326 (M); gifts received, $10,370; expenditures, $13,876; qualifying distributions, $3,061.
Limitations: Giving limited to TX.
Application information: Application form not required.
Officers: W.T. Arnold, M.D., Pres.; E. Infante, M.D., V.P.; L.L. Travis, M.D., Secy.; D.C. Solcher, M.D., Treas.
EIN: 746061783

53109
K. S. Adams, Jr. Foundation
P.O. Box 844
Houston, TX 77001 (713) 881-3442
Contact: W.R. Scofiled

Donor(s): The Houston Oilers, Inc., K.S. Adams, Jr.
Financial data (yr. ended 06/30/01): Grants paid, $3,000; assets, $1,543 (M); gifts received, $117,200; expenditures, $118,959; qualifying distributions, $3,000.
Limitations: Giving primarily in Houston, TX.
Application information: Application form not required.
Trustees: K.S. Adams, Jr., Nancy N. Adams, John Barrett, Steve Underwood.
EIN: 746070101

53110
The Brinkley Foundation
6525 Woodcreek Ln.
North Richland Hills, TX 76180
(817) 281-2067
Contact: Charles C. Brinkley, Tr.

Donor(s): Charles C. Brinkley.
Financial data (yr. ended 09/30/01): Grants paid, $3,000; assets, $72,252 (M); expenditures, $4,166; qualifying distributions, $3,382.
Limitations: Giving primarily in TX.
Application information: Application form not required.
Trustees: C. Michael Brinkley, Charles C. Brinkley, Mary P. Brinkley.
EIN: 752080794

53111
Caprock Foundation, Inc.
3411 Knoxville Ave.
Lubbock, TX 79413

Established in 1997 in TX.
Donor(s): Marciano Morales.
Financial data (yr. ended 12/31/01): Grants paid, $3,000; assets, $3,700 (M); gifts received, $7,000; expenditures, $3,570; qualifying distributions, $3,000.
Limitations: Applications not accepted.
Application information: Contributes only to pre-selected organizations.
Officers: Marciano Morales, Pres.; Martha Morales, Secy.
EIN: 752697916

53112
Cedars Foundation
10301 County Rd., Ste. 1016
Burleson, TX 76028

Established in 1996 in TX.
Donor(s): Nabil Aboukhair.
Financial data (yr. ended 12/31/01): Grants paid, $3,000; assets, $316 (M); gifts received, $2,800; expenditures, $3,040; qualifying distributions, $3,000.
Limitations: Applications not accepted.
Application information: Contributes only to pre-selected organizations.
Officers and Directors:* Nabil Aboukhair,* Pres.; Ragida Aboukhair,* Secy.-Treas.; Joseph Ashkar.
EIN: 752653638

53113
Jack and Phyllis Curtis Foundation
P.O. Box 1901
Pampa, TX 79066-1901

Established in 2000 in TX.
Donor(s): Phyllis R. Curtis.
Financial data (yr. ended 12/31/01): Grants paid, $3,000; assets, $91,444 (M); gifts received, $75,000; expenditures, $3,500; qualifying distributions, $3,000.
Limitations: Applications not accepted.
Application information: Contributes only to pre-selected organizations.
Officers: Joe E. Curtis, Pres.; Jack T. Curtis, Jr., V.P.; Ellen Brister, Secy.; Terry Wilemon, Treas.
EIN: 752897872

53114
Davidson Perpetual Charitable Trust
1280 Hawkins Blvd., Ste. 200
El Paso, TX 79925-4988 (915) 593-1280

Financial data (yr. ended 12/31/01): Grants paid, $3,000; assets, $112,687 (M); expenditures, $3,656; qualifying distributions, $3,000.
Limitations: Applications not accepted. Giving primarily in TX.
Application information: Contributes only to pre-selected organizations.
Directors: Bruce G. Bixler, Burton H. Patterson, Frances M. Davidson Strickland.
EIN: 742771403

53115
Emmiedoc Foundation, Inc.
3636 Amherst Ave.
Dallas, TX 75225-7421

Established in 1999 in TX.
Financial data (yr. ended 12/31/01): Grants paid, $3,000; assets, $109,536 (M); gifts received, $2,000; expenditures, $3,150; qualifying distributions, $3,000.
Officers and Directors:* Lea Fassler,* Pres. and Treas.; Thomas McConnell,* V.P. and Secy.; Scott Fassler, Anne Koch, John B. Koch, Allen McConnell, Dierdre McConnell, Marianne McConnell.
EIN: 752854599

53116
Hertha Issleib Foundation
335 E. Ramsey
San Antonio, TX 78216 (210) 342-1142
Contact: Lutz Issleib, Pres.

Financial data (yr. ended 12/31/00): Grants paid, $3,000; assets, $368,355 (M); expenditures, $3,328; qualifying distributions, $3,000.
Limitations: Giving primarily in TX.
Officers: Lutz Issleib, Pres. and Secy.; Helen Wade Buescher, V.P. and Treas.
Directors: Rosemarie Bittner, Mrs. Gene Issleib.
EIN: 746041167

53117
Laura B. Jackson Charitable Trust
c/o Leah K. Darby
P.O. Box 351
Longview, TX 75606-0351 (903) 663-6363
Contact: John N. Darby, Tr.

Established in 1992.
Donor(s): John N. Darby, Leah K. Darby.
Financial data (yr. ended 12/31/00): Grants paid, $3,000; assets, $59,038 (M); gifts received, $1,785; expenditures, $3,469; qualifying distributions, $2,906.
Limitations: Giving limited to resident in TX.
Application information: Application form required.
Trustees: Anne Elizabeth Darby, J. Miles Darby, John N. Darby, Leah K. Darby.
EIN: 756437403

53118
Arnold J. and Irene B. Kocurek Family Foundation, 1986
P.O. Box 1600
San Antonio, TX 78296
Contact: Arnold J. Kocurek, Mgr.

Established in 1986 in TX.
Donor(s): Arnold J. Kocurek, Irene B. Kocurek.
Financial data (yr. ended 02/28/01): Grants paid, $3,000; assets, $41,531 (M); expenditures, $4,985; qualifying distributions, $3,000.
Limitations: Giving limited to TX, with emphasis on San Antonio.
Application information: Application form not required.
Officers: Arnold J. Kocurek, Mgr.; Irene B. Kocurek, Mgr.
Trustee: Frost National Bank.
EIN: 746345100

53119
Kwan Charitable Foundation
5 Crosslands Rd.
Fort Worth, TX 76132-1005 (817) 737-5427
Contact: William L.G. Kwan, Pres.

Donor(s): William L.G. Kwan, Juliet Kwan.
Financial data (yr. ended 12/31/01): Grants paid, $3,000; assets, $46,464 (M); expenditures, $3,612; qualifying distributions, $3,000.
Application information: Application form not required.
Officers: William L.G. Kwan, Pres.; Juliet Kwan, Secy.-Treas.
Directors: Jason William Kwan, William James Kwan.
EIN: 752703398

53120
Nona S. Payne Charitable Trust
2000 Charles
Pampa, TX 79065
Application address: c/o Dir., Pampa High School Choir or Band, Pampa High School, 111 E. Harvester St., Pampa, TX 79065, tel.: (806) 669-2681

Donor(s): Nona S. Payne.‡
Financial data (yr. ended 09/30/00): Grants paid, $3,000; assets, $70,664 (M); gifts received, $39,990; expenditures, $3,330; qualifying distributions, $3,000.
Limitations: Giving limited to Pampa, TX.
Trustees: Adelaide S. Colwell, Phil B. Gentry, Randy F. Watson.
EIN: 751688261

53121
Frances Ramsey Scholarship Memorial Fund
14911 Dancers Image
San Antonio, TX 78248
Contact: Ann Adams, Tr.

Financial data (yr. ended 07/31/99): Grants paid, $3,000; assets, $53,395 (M); gifts received, $305; expenditures, $3,426; qualifying distributions, $3,426.
Limitations: Giving primarily in LA, OK, and TX.
Application information: Application form required.
Trustees: Ann Adams, Patty Cast, Beverly Seal.
EIN: 731136414

53122
The Sheedy Foundation
6003 Pine Forest Rd.
Houston, TX 77057-1431 (713) 654-4484

Established in 1997 in TX.
Donor(s): Charles E. Sheedy, Ellen G. Sheedy.
Financial data (yr. ended 12/31/01): Grants paid, $3,000; assets, $64,371 (M); gifts received, $1,532; expenditures, $3,757; qualifying distributions, $3,000.
Officers and Directors:* Charles E. Sheedy,* Pres.; Ellen G. Sheedy,* V.P. and Secy.-Treas.; Elizabeth A. Sheedy, V.P.
EIN: 760537763

53123
Tommy B. and Lucille Jackson Slaughter Foundation
c/o Tommy B. Slaughter
806 E. Bowie St.
Marshall, TX 75670-4208

Established in 1995 in TX.
Donor(s): Tommy B. Slaughter.
Financial data (yr. ended 12/31/99): Grants paid, $3,000; assets, $171,708 (M); gifts received, $107,100; expenditures, $3,235; qualifying distributions, $3,068.
Limitations: Applications not accepted. Giving primarily in Nacogdoches, TX.
Application information: Contributes only to pre-selected organizations.
Officers: Tommy B. Slaughter, Chair.; Robert L. Duvall, Secy.
Director: James Kroll.
EIN: 752588004

53124
Southwest Meat Foundation, Inc.
(Formerly Southwest Meat Packers Foundation, Inc.)
4103 S. Texas Ave., No. 101
Bryan, TX 77802

Financial data (yr. ended 06/30/01): Grants paid, $3,000; assets, $50,671 (M); gifts received, $5,962; expenditures, $11,306; qualifying distributions, $3,000.
Limitations: Applications not accepted. Giving primarily in TX.
Application information: Contributes only to pre-selected organizations.
Officers: Bob Ondrusek, Pres.; Vinson Kirchner, V.P.; Joe Harris, Ph.D., Secy.; Bob Ondersek, Treas.
Trustee: Jason Beyer, Charlie Booth.
EIN: 752010092

53125
Valley Diagnostic Medical Foundation
2200 Haine Dr.
Harlingen, TX 78550
Application address: P.O. Box 2187, Harlingen, TX 78551, tel.: (956) 421-7200
Contact: Joseph D. Dougherty, M.D., Pres.

Established in 1983 in TX.
Financial data (yr. ended 06/30/01): Grants paid, $3,000; assets, $91,081 (M); gifts received, $200; expenditures, $3,450; qualifying distributions, $3,000.
Limitations: Giving limited to the Rio Grande Valley, TX, area.
Officer and Trustees:* Joseph D. Dougherty, M.D.,* Pres.; Garner Klein, M.D., Catherine Owens.
EIN: 742291844

53126
Kathy J. Welch and John T. Unger Foundation
816 Kipling St.
Houston, TX 77006-4313 (713) 524-8725

Donor(s): Kathy J. Welch, John T. Unger.
Financial data (yr. ended 12/31/00): Grants paid, $3,000; assets, $45,627 (M); gifts received, $3,009; expenditures, $3,106; qualifying distributions, $3,000.
Officers: Kathy J. Welch, Pres.; John T. Unger, V.P.
Director: Richard S. Snell.
EIN: 760573337

53127
Westchester Foundation
306 W. Sunset Rd., Ste. 119
San Antonio, TX 78209
Contact: Daniel R. Fleming, Mgr.

Established in 1999 in TX.
Donor(s): Laura B. Revitz.
Financial data (yr. ended 12/31/00): Grants paid, $3,000; assets, $57,111 (M); expenditures, $3,000; qualifying distributions, $2,991.
Officer: Daniel R. Fleming, Mgr.
Directors: James K. Crowley, Laura C. Kiser, Laura B. Revitz.
EIN: 742947871

53128
Bruce & Gladys Wright Charitable Trust
P.O. Box 596
Edna, TX 77957
Application address: c/o Peggy Burnside, Edna High School Counselor, 1307 W. Gayle St., Edna, TX 77957, tel.: (361) 782-5255

Established in 1999 in TX.
Financial data (yr. ended 09/30/01): Grants paid, $3,000; assets, $154,726 (M); gifts received,

$100,000; expenditures, $3,083; qualifying distributions, $3,083.
Limitations: Giving limited to TX.
Application information: Application form required.
Officers: Joe Ryan, Pres.; Dennis Ray, V.P.; John Shutt, Secy.-Treas.
Trustees: Gary Covin, Carol McDonald.
EIN: 316647955

53129
Chantal Foundation
P.O. Box 5369
Galveston, TX 77554-0369

Established in 1999 in TX.
Donor(s): Heida Thurlow.
Financial data (yr. ended 11/13/00): Grants paid, $2,944; assets, $213,533 (M); gifts received, $400,000; expenditures, $4,821; qualifying distributions, $2,944.
Limitations: Applications not accepted. Giving primarily in Houston, TX.
Application information: Contributes only to pre-selected organizations.
Officers: Heida Thurlow, Chair.; Golda Jacobs, Secy.; Michael McNeely, Treas.
EIN: 760625499

53130
Don Dickerman Ministries, Inc.
333 Patricia Ln.
Bedford, TX 76022-7312

Donor(s): Arnold Pair.
Financial data (yr. ended 12/31/01): Grants paid, $2,900; assets, $32,693 (M); gifts received, $85,531; expenditures, $55,863; qualifying distributions, $52,084; giving activities include $52,084 for programs.
Officers and Directors:* Joe Tanner,* Pres.; Bobby Adkins,* V.P.; Amy Normand,* Secy.; Richard Schneck,* Treas.; Ty Alford, Rev. Don Dickerman.
EIN: 752120183

53131
Harry & Becky Gibson Family Foundation
4418 Denmere Ct.
Humble, TX 77345

Established in 1998 in TX.
Donor(s): Harry T. Gibson.
Financial data (yr. ended 12/31/00): Grants paid, $2,900; assets, $57,011 (M); expenditures, $3,127; qualifying distributions, $2,900.
Trustees: Becky Gibson, Harry T. Gibson.
EIN: 760565577

53132
Ruth K. Shartle & Sara Lee Taylor Latin American Educational Aid Foundation
8923 Briar Forest Dr.
Houston, TX 77024
Contact: Marcia Taylor

Financial data (yr. ended 01/31/99): Grants paid, $2,891; assets, $14,723 (M); expenditures, $3,621; qualifying distributions, $2,884.
Limitations: Giving primarily in Houston, TX.
Trustees: Gretchen Shartle Sabin, Martin J. Taylor III.
EIN: 746081284

53133
The Boyd Foundation Charitable Trust
2700 Post Oak Blvd., Ste. 1400
Houston, TX 77056-5705 (713) 877-8400
Contact: J. Michael Boyd, Tr.

Established in 1995 in LA.
Donor(s): J. Michael Boyd.

Financial data (yr. ended 12/31/01): Grants paid, $2,850; assets, $112,440 (M); gifts received, $47,000; expenditures, $2,918; qualifying distributions, $2,845.
Limitations: Applications not accepted. Giving limited to residents of LA.
Application information: Unsolicited requests for funds not accepted.
Trustee: J. Michael Boyd.
EIN: 760204169

53134
The Virginia and Lester Clark Foundation
(Formerly The Lester Clark Foundation)
P.O. Box 752
Breckenridge, TX 76424 (254) 559-2246
Contact: David Clark, Pres.

Financial data (yr. ended 03/31/02): Grants paid, $2,820; assets, $61,490 (M); expenditures, $3,098; qualifying distributions, $2,920.
Limitations: Giving primarily in TX.
Officers: David Clark, Pres.; Barrett Clark, V.P.; Virginia Clark, V.P.; Rena Goldsmith, Secy.-Treas.
EIN: 756049011

53135
Sam and Cathy Manning Foundation
c/o Sam B. Manning
5323 Livingstone Ave.
Dallas, TX 75209

Donor(s): Cathy L. Manning, Sam B. Manning.
Financial data (yr. ended 12/31/01): Grants paid, $2,800; assets, $69,020 (M); gifts received, $4,086; expenditures, $3,675; qualifying distributions, $2,800.
Limitations: Applications not accepted.
Application information: Contributes only to pre-selected organizations.
Directors: Cathy L. Manning, Sam B. Manning, Wesley B. Manning.
EIN: 752702997

53136
J. K. Olsen Foundation, Inc.
1437 Pecan Hill Dr.
Stephenville, TX 76401

Established in 1999 in TX.
Donor(s): Kenneth C. Olsen, Judy E. Olsen.
Financial data (yr. ended 12/31/01): Grants paid, $2,800; assets, $105,771 (M); gifts received, $2,800; expenditures, $3,696; qualifying distributions, $2,800.
Limitations: Applications not accepted.
Application information: Contributes only to pre-selected organizations.
Officers: Kenneth C. Olsen, Pres.; Judy E. Olsen, Secy.-Treas.
Director: Ronnie C. McClure, Ph.D.
EIN: 760626853

53137
Simecheck Family Foundation
741 W. Creekside Dr.
Houston, TX 77024

Established in 1999 in TX.
Donor(s): Don M. Simecheck.
Financial data (yr. ended 12/31/01): Grants paid, $2,794; assets, $29,971 (M); gifts received, $1,294; expenditures, $4,395; qualifying distributions, $2,794.
Limitations: Applications not accepted.
Application information: Contributes only to pre-selected organizations.
Officers and Directors:* Don M. Simecheck,* Pres. and Treas.; Marjorie M. Simecheck,* V.P. and Secy.; Craig M. Simecheck.
EIN: 760610345

53138
Clara Lagow Scholarship Fund
2319 Warner Rd.
Fort Worth, TX 76110-1755
Contact: La Nelle Douglass, Tr.

Donor(s): Legal Secretaries Association.
Financial data (yr. ended 04/30/01): Grants paid, $2,771; assets, $30,795 (M); gifts received, $385; expenditures, $3,268; qualifying distributions, $3,268.
Limitations: Giving primarily in TX.
Application information: Applicant must include transcript and two letters of recommendation.
Trustees: La Nelle Douglass, La Voice Meier, Amelda Perritt.
EIN: 752358026

53139
Ruth A. Cantrall Trust
c/o Bank of America
P.O. Box 831041
Dallas, TX 75283-1041
Application address: P.O. Box 419119, Kansas City, MO 64141, tel.: (816) 979-7481
Contact: David P. Ross, Sr. V.P. and Trust Off., Bank of America

Financial data (yr. ended 12/31/01): Grants paid, $2,708; assets, $117,854 (M); expenditures, $4,025; qualifying distributions, $3,371.
Limitations: Giving limited to KS.
Trustee: Bank of America.
EIN: 486208276
Codes: GTI

53140
Maria Esther Salinas Foundation
5177 Richmona Ave., Ste. 265
Houston, TX 77056-6703
Application address: 5611 Oak Trail, Houston, TX 77091, tel.: (713) 682-6373
Contact: Esther Salinas Kana, Chair.

Financial data (yr. ended 12/31/99): Grants paid, $2,665; assets, $10,698 (M); gifts received, $8,065; expenditures, $3,190; qualifying distributions, $3,190.
Limitations: Giving limited to TX.
Application information: Application form required.
Officers: Esther Salinas Kana, Chair.; Edward E. Salinas, Pres.; Robert J. Salinas, V.P.; Patricia Salinas Wiles, Secy.; Luis L. Salinas, Treas.
EIN: 760345099

53141
Barney M. and Hester Kent Scholarship Fund and Trust, Inc.
321 N. 15th St.
Corsicana, TX 75110
Contact: Gary Brown, Trust Off., Corsicana National Bank

Established in 1999 in TX.
Financial data (yr. ended 12/31/01): Grants paid, $2,600; assets, $55,539 (M); expenditures, $3,493; qualifying distributions, $2,600.
Trustee: Corsicana National Bank.
EIN: 752736858

53142
Rotary Club of Lubbock Foundation
c/o Marjan Wilkins
1603 W. Loop 289
Lubbock, TX 79416 (806) 785-3030

Established in 1998.
Donor(s): Rotary Club of Lubbock.
Financial data (yr. ended 06/30/02): Grants paid, $2,600; assets, $44,549 (M); gifts received, $300;

expenditures, $3,147; qualifying distributions, $2,600.
Limitations: Giving primarily in Lubbock, TX.
Officers and Directors:* Morris Wilkes,* Pres.; Gene Tate,* 1st V.P.; Scott Fanning,* 2nd V.P.; Donna Eagan,* Secy.; Randy Wright, Treas.; Gary Bell, Jim Carpenter, Chester Golightly, Gerald O. Griffin, David Hester, Regina Johnston, Charles Joplin, Dick Moser, Tom Nichols, Fran Scott.
EIN: 752765212

53143
Chambers-Schoellkopt-Trim Scholarship Foundation
c/o Boys & Girls Club of Greater Dallas, Inc.
4816 Worth St.
Dallas, TX 75246
Contact: Craig Price

Established in 1990 in TX.
Donor(s): Boys and Girls Clubs of Greater Dallas, Inc.
Financial data (yr. ended 12/31/00): Grants paid, $2,588; assets, $64,321 (M); gifts received, $600; expenditures, $3,060; qualifying distributions, $2,552.
Limitations: Giving limited to residents of the greater Dallas, TX, area.
Application information: Application form required.
Officers: Jim Chambers, Pres.; John L. Schoellkopf, V.P.; Lloyd Harris, Secy.-Treas.
EIN: 752213989

53144
Lucille Hanus Gondran Foundation, Inc.
2102 Mechanic, Ste. 300
Galveston, TX 77550

Financial data (yr. ended 12/31/01): Grants paid, $2,553; assets, $193,733 (M); expenditures, $2,753; qualifying distributions, $2,553.
Limitations: Applications not accepted. Giving primarily in Galveston, TX.
Application information: Contributes only to pre-selected organizations.
Officer: James B. Earthman, Pres.
EIN: 760343370

53145
The Waggoner-Welch Charitable Foundation
130 Painted Bunting Ln.
Georgetown, TX 78628-4401 (512) 864-3951
Contact: James L. Bolton, Tr.

Established in 1995 in TX.
Donor(s): Louise Waggoner.
Financial data (yr. ended 12/31/01): Grants paid, $2,550; assets, $51,297 (M); expenditures, $3,651; qualifying distributions, $2,550.
Limitations: Giving primarily in Waco, TX.
Trustees: Betty Duane Bolton, James L. Bolton.
EIN: 756486538

53146
K. R. and Laura Miller Foundation
(Formerly K. R. Miller Foundation)
2202 E. Airline, Ste. A
Victoria, TX 77901

Established in 2000 in TX.
Donor(s): K.R. Miller.
Financial data (yr. ended 12/31/01): Grants paid, $2,538; assets, $50,025 (M); expenditures, $2,549; qualifying distributions, $2,538.
Directors: Dennis Heller, Michael Maraggia, Darrell Sklar.
EIN: 742941588

53147
John F. Austin Scholarship Fund
P.O. Box 1246
Dickinson, TX 77539-1246
Application address: c/o Dickinson High School, Dickinson, TX 77539, tel.: (281) 584-6800

Donor(s): Mitchell M. Dale.
Financial data (yr. ended 12/31/00): Grants paid, $2,500; assets, $42,891 (M); expenditures, $2,706; qualifying distributions, $2,631.
Limitations: Giving limited to Dickinson, TX.
Application information: Application form required.
Officer and Trustees:* Jasper J. Liggio,* Chair.; Mitchell M. Dale, Robert B. Holly.
EIN: 742179881

53148
Dennis Barger Foundation
P.O. Box 239
Dallas, TX 75221-0239
Contact: Jess T. Hay, Tr.

Financial data (yr. ended 04/30/01): Grants paid, $2,500; assets, $31,687 (M); gifts received, $165; expenditures, $3,575; qualifying distributions, $3,575.
Limitations: Giving primarily in Highland Village, TX.
Trustees: Robert T. Enloe III, Ned Harris, Jess T. Hay.
EIN: 751302078

53149
Bestway Rentals Edwin Anderson Scholarship Foundation, Inc.
7800 Stemmons Fwy.
Dallas, TX 75247

Established in 2001 in TX.
Donor(s): Bestway, Inc.
Financial data (yr. ended 12/31/01): Grants paid, $2,500; assets, $10,613 (M); gifts received, $13,250; expenditures, $2,640; qualifying distributions, $2,570.
Limitations: Applications not accepted. Giving primarily in AL.
Application information: Unsolicited requests for funds not accepted.
Officers and Directors:* Teresa A. Sheffield,* Pres.; Beth A. Durrett,* Secy.; Vincent Jarbo.
EIN: 752901174
Codes: CS

53150
The Bob and Cathleen Davis Foundation
11503 Wendover Ln.
Houston, TX 77024-5222

Established in 2000 in TX.
Financial data (yr. ended 12/31/01): Grants paid, $2,500; assets, $859,234 (M); gifts received, $435,510; expenditures, $2,500; qualifying distributions, $2,500.
Officers and Directors:* Robert C. Davis,* Pres.; Cathleen Gilley Davis,* Secy.; Jeffrey Lee Sarff,* Treas.; Brian Ted Davis, Victoria Gilley Davis.
EIN: 760664836

53151
Foundation for Research on Bi-Polar Psychology, Inc.
125 Running Water
Georgetown, TX 78628
Contact: J.W. Thomas, Chair.

Financial data (yr. ended 12/31/01): Grants paid, $2,500; assets, $27,212 (M); expenditures, $4,048; qualifying distributions, $2,500.

Limitations: Giving primarily in Houston, TX.
Application information: Application form required.
Officers: J.W. Thomas, Chair.; Thomas J. Thomas, Vice-Chair.; Martha J. Thomas, Secy.
EIN: 752001741

53152
Homann and Homann Charitable Trust
P.O. Box 65
Junction, TX 76849-0065
Contact: Bryan C. Booth, Tr.

Established in 1995 in TX.
Donor(s): James C. Cherry.
Financial data (yr. ended 12/31/99): Grants paid, $2,500; assets, $501 (M); gifts received, $2,115; expenditures, $2,536; qualifying distributions, $2,536.
Limitations: Giving primarily in TX.
Application information: Application form not required.
Trustee: Bryan C. Booth.
EIN: 752570086

53153
Howard H. Klein Foundation
10515 Rodgers Rd.
Houston, TX 77070-1626
Contact: Lori Klein Quinn, Secy.-Treas.

Established in 1987 in TX.
Donor(s): Roxanne Shaw.
Financial data (yr. ended 12/31/00): Grants paid, $2,500; assets, $40,950 (M); expenditures, $2,611; qualifying distributions, $2,500.
Limitations: Giving primarily in Austin, TX.
Application information: Application form required.
Officers and Trustees:* Jed Shaw,* Pres.; Roxanne Shaw,* V.P.; Lori Klein Quinn,* Secy.-Treas.
EIN: 760236778

53154
Jules Lauve, Jr. Catholic School Scholarship Trust
P.O. Box 16986
Galveston, TX 77552-6986

Established in 1999 in TX.
Financial data (yr. ended 12/31/01): Grants paid, $2,500; assets, $42,628 (M); expenditures, $2,585; qualifying distributions, $2,500.
Limitations: Applications not accepted. Giving primarily in TX.
Application information: Contributes only to pre-selected organizations.
Officers: Juliet Staudt, Pres.; Darcy Overton, Secy.-Treas.
EIN: 766135908

53155
James E. & Elizabeth D. Lewis Foundation
3632 McFarlin Blvd.
Dallas, TX 75205

Established in 1997.
Donor(s): Elizabeth D. Lewis, James E. Lewis.
Financial data (yr. ended 12/31/01): Grants paid, $2,500; assets, $46,054 (M); expenditures, $2,584; qualifying distributions, $2,500.
Limitations: Applications not accepted.
Application information: Contributes only to pre-selected organizations.
Officers and Directors:* James E. Lewis,* Pres.; Elizabeth D. Lewis,* Secy.-Treas.; David G. Little.
EIN: 752671047

53156
John & Ruth Michener Foundation
301 Commerce St., Ste. 3500
Fort Worth, TX 76102 (817) 878-0505
Contact: John W. Michener, Jr., Tr.

Donor(s): John W. Michener, Jr.
Financial data (yr. ended 12/31/00): Grants paid, $2,500; assets, $109,441 (M); expenditures, $2,993; qualifying distributions, $2,500.
Limitations: Giving primarily in Fort Worth, TX.
Trustee: John W. Michener, Jr.
EIN: 752001859

53157
The Kathrine M. and James H. Milam Family Charities, Inc.
c/o Mary H. Whiteside
3626 Armstrong Pkwy.
Dallas, TX 75205

Established in 1998 in TX.
Donor(s): Jane Henry.
Financial data (yr. ended 12/31/01): Grants paid, $2,500; assets, $52,064 (M); gifts received, $50,081; expenditures, $2,500; qualifying distributions, $2,500.
Officers: Mary M. Whiteside, Pres. and Treas.; James Henry Whiteside, V.P.; Mary Jane Witeside, Secy.
EIN: 752738414

53158
The Owen Foundation
P.O. Box 270473
Houston, TX 77277-0473

Established in 2000 in TX.
Donor(s): Vivien Owen.
Financial data (yr. ended 12/31/01): Grants paid, $2,500; assets, $241 (M); gifts received, $5,084; expenditures, $4,700; qualifying distributions, $4,700.
Limitations: Applications not accepted.
Application information: Contributes only to pre-selected organizations.
Director: Vivien Owen.
EIN: 316649359

53159
Chandubhai Patel Foundation
2302 Sherbrooke Ln.
McKinney, TX 75070

Established in 2001 in TX.
Donor(s): Achal R. Patel, Nisha A. Patel.
Financial data (yr. ended 12/31/01): Grants paid, $2,500; assets, $71,265 (M); gifts received, $75,300; expenditures, $4,805; qualifying distributions, $2,500.
Limitations: Applications not accepted. Giving primarily in London, England.
Application information: Contributes only to pre-selected organizations.
Directors: Achal R. Patel, Nisha A. Patel, Ravindrabhai C. Patel.
EIN: 752913029

53160
The Peninsula Foundation
5555 Morningside Dr., Ste. 209-C
Houston, TX 77005 (713) 528-0366
Application address: c/o Guidance Dept., Menominee High School, 2101 8th St., Menominee, MI 49858, tel.: (906) 863-7814

Donor(s): Ame Vennema,‡ Catherine S. Vennema.
Financial data (yr. ended 12/31/00): Grants paid, $2,500; assets, $23,059 (M); expenditures, $2,738; qualifying distributions, $2,500.
Limitations: Giving limited to Menominee, MI.

Application information: Application form required.
Trustees: Margaret K. Lemen, John Vennema, Peter A. Vennema, Linda V. White.
EIN: 742028228

53161
Kathleen L. Rand Scholarship Trust
c/o Bank of America
P.O. Box 831041
Dallas, TX 75283-1041
Application address: c/o Bank of America, 303 Roma St. N.W., 7th Fl., Albuquerque, NM 87103
Contact: Betsy Garber

Financial data (yr. ended 12/31/01): Grants paid, $2,500; assets, $34,547 (M); expenditures, $3,890; qualifying distributions, $3,171.
Limitations: Giving limited to Raton, NM.
Application information: Recipients are selected by a committee of the Raton Public School System.
Trustee: Bank of America.
EIN: 850312986

53162
Reed Engineering Group Employees Scholarship
2424 Stutz Dr., Ste. 400
Dallas, TX 75235-6500
Application address: c/o Meredith & Assoc., 2621 W. Airport Fwy., Ste. 101, Irving, TX 75062-6096

Established in 1997 in TX.
Donor(s): Reed Engineering Group, Inc.
Financial data (yr. ended 09/30/01): Grants paid, $2,500; assets, $57,423 (M); gifts received, $15,577; expenditures, $6,077; qualifying distributions, $5,750.
Application information: Application form required.
Officers: Ron Reed, Pres.; Sarah Reed, V.P.; Whitney Smith, Secy.-Treas.
EIN: 752728400
Codes: CS, CD

53163
The Springmeyer Foundation
6404 Sewanee
Houston, TX 77005

Established in 2000 in TX.
Donor(s): Jeff N. Springmeyer, Amie J. Springmeyer.
Financial data (yr. ended 12/31/01): Grants paid, $2,500; assets, $1,362,582 (M); gifts received, $1,019,590; expenditures, $8,149; qualifying distributions, $2,500.
Limitations: Applications not accepted.
Application information: Contributes only to pre-selected organizations.
Officers and Directors:* Jeff N. Springmeyer,* Pres. and Treas.; Amie J. Springmeyer,* V.P. and Secy.; Craig R. Springmeyer.
EIN: 760664848

53164
Jay Vanderpool Scholarship Fund
c/o U.S. National Bank
P.O. Box 179
Galveston, TX 77553-0179

Established in 1987 in TX.
Donor(s): Harold Y. Vanderpool, Natalie A. Vanderpool, Harold J. Vanderpool.
Financial data (yr. ended 12/31/01): Grants paid, $2,500; assets, $58,893 (M); expenditures, $2,500; qualifying distributions, $2,500.
Limitations: Applications not accepted. Giving limited to Galveston County, TX.

Application information: Contributes only to pre-selected organizations.
Advisory Committee: Nathalie A. Vanderpool Bartle, Katherine Provost, Harold Y. Vanderpool, Jon Y. Vanderpool.
EIN: 766038758

53165
The Ed and Catherine Max Foundation
c/o Phillip Ryan
4118 Shore Front Dr.
Fort Worth, TX 76135-9486 (817) 237-4306
Contact: Catherine Max

Financial data (yr. ended 12/31/00): Grants paid, $2,496; assets, $1 (M); expenditures, $2,521; qualifying distributions, $2,496.
Limitations: Giving primarily in TX.
Trustee: Phillip Ryan.
EIN: 752263203

53166
Helen Patterson Scholarship Trust
c/o Charles L. Hagwood, Jr.
P.O. Box 105
Junction, TX 76849-0105 (915) 446-3391
Contact: Jon T. Murr, Tr.

Financial data (yr. ended 12/31/01): Grants paid, $2,451; assets, $19,317 (M); expenditures, $2,601; qualifying distributions, $2,491.
Limitations: Giving limited to residents of Junction, TX.
Application information: Application form required.
Trustees: Jim Barker, Jon T. Murr, Rob Roy Spiller.
EIN: 746063656

53167
Barton B. Wallace, Jr. Fund
4328 Windsor Pkwy.
Dallas, TX 75205

Financial data (yr. ended 08/31/01): Grants paid, $2,450; assets, $5,330 (M); gifts received, $4,000; expenditures, $2,731; qualifying distributions, $2,450.
Limitations: Applications not accepted.
Application information: Contributes only to pre-selected organizations.
Trustee: Barton B. Wallace, Jr.
EIN: 756053850

53168
Reno O. Schumann Educational Trust
c/o First Protestant Church
172 W. Coll St.
New Braunfels, TX 78130-5108
(830) 609-7729

Financial data (yr. ended 12/31/99): Grants paid, $2,425; assets, $212,001 (M); gifts received, $175,000; expenditures, $3,209; qualifying distributions, $2,404.
Limitations: Giving limited to New Braunfels, TX.
Trustees: Craig Harris, Daryl Higgins, Tom Purdum.
EIN: 746248871

53169
Bess A. Bates Trust
c/o Wells Fargo Bank Texas, N.A.
P.O. Box 2088
San Angelo, TX 76902-2088

Established in 1994 in TX.
Financial data (yr. ended 12/31/00): Grants paid, $2,406; assets, $34,420 (M); expenditures, $4,553; qualifying distributions, $2,372.
Limitations: Applications not accepted.
Application information: Contributes only to pre-selected organizations.

Trustee: Wells Fargo Bank Texas, N.A.
EIN: 756392485

53170
Vikram J. Bajaj Memorial Trust
2704 Glassboro Cir.
Arlington, TX 76015-1438

Donor(s): Bhushan D. Bajaj, Sudesh A. Bajaj.
Financial data (yr. ended 01/31/02): Grants paid, $2,400; assets, $52,553 (M); expenditures, $3,084; qualifying distributions, $2,400.
Limitations: Applications not accepted. Giving primarily in Arlington, TX.
Application information: Contributes only to pre-selected organizations.
Trustees: Bhushan D. Bajaj, Sudesh A. Bajaj.
EIN: 751980895

53171
The Vicky and Tim Harkins Foundation
5934 S. Staples, Ste. 214
Corpus Christi, TX 78413
Contact: Vicky S. Harkins, Secy.-Treas.

Established in 1991 in TX.
Donor(s): H. Timothy Harkins, Vicky S. Harkins.
Financial data (yr. ended 12/31/00): Grants paid, $2,400; assets, $450,052 (M); expenditures, $6,029; qualifying distributions, $2,400.
Limitations: Giving primarily in TX.
Application information: Application form not required.
Officers: H. Timothy Harkins, Pres.; Vicky S. Harkins, Secy.-Treas.
EIN: 752411242

53172
Rudolph C. & Byrdie Miller Scholarship Fund
c/o Hibernia National Bank
P.O. Box 3928
Beaumont, TX 77704 (409) 880-1432
Contact: Josie Gonzales, Trust Off., Hibernia National Bank

Financial data (yr. ended 06/30/01): Grants paid, $2,400; assets, $47,859 (M); expenditures, $3,743; qualifying distributions, $3,726.
Limitations: Giving limited to residents of Beaumont, TX, area.
Application information: Applicants are recommended by Beaumont Rotary Club, Beaumont Lions Club, Kiwanis Club, and the Boy Scouts.
Trustee: Hibernia National Bank.
EIN: 746255229

53173
The Collins Family Foundation
3135 Renker Dr.
San Antonio, TX 78217 (210) 653-0900
Contact: Jay C. Collins, Pres.

Established in 1986 in TX.
Donor(s): Jay C. Collins, Margaret L. Collins.
Financial data (yr. ended 12/31/01): Grants paid, $2,381; assets, $41,425 (M); gifts received, $2,955; expenditures, $2,457; qualifying distributions, $2,381.
Limitations: Giving primarily in TX.
Officers: Jay C. Collins, Pres.; Margaret L. Collins, V.P. and Secy.; James M. Collins, Sr., Treas.
EIN: 742442493

53174
Elmer and Myrtle Oliver Family Charitable Foundation
110 Shoreacras
La Porte, TX 77571 (281) 471-4090
Contact: Marianne Oliver Williams, Tr.

Established in 1994 in TX.
Donor(s): Marianne Oliver Williams.
Financial data (yr. ended 12/31/01): Grants paid, $2,350; assets, $149,217 (M); expenditures, $2,696; qualifying distributions, $2,350.
Limitations: Giving primarily in TX.
Trustee: Marianne Oliver Williams.
EIN: 760455335

53175
Monahans American Legion Post 473 Scholarship Trust
P.O. Box 410
Monahans, TX 79756 (915) 943-7561

Financial data (yr. ended 12/31/01): Grants paid, $2,307; assets, $64,743 (M); expenditures, $4,020; qualifying distributions, $2,307.
Limitations: Applications not accepted.
Application information: Contributes only to pre-selected organizations.
Officer: Jack Forga, C.F.O.
EIN: 756505724

53176
E. D. Farmer Relief Fund
c/o County Judge's Office
1 Courthouse Sq.
Weatherford, TX 76086
Contact: Don Duffield, Tr.

Financial data (yr. ended 12/31/01): Grants paid, $2,306; assets, $137,532 (M); expenditures, $2,887; qualifying distributions, $2,306.
Limitations: Giving primarily in Weatherford, TX.
Application information: Recipients generally referred by local police.
Trustees: Don Duffield, L. Owen Henderson, Mark Riley.
EIN: 756027759

53177
George W. Dickinson & Edythe W. Dickinson Trust Fund
c/o Wells Fargo Bank
40 N.E. Loop 410, Ste. 20
San Antonio, TX 78216

Financial data (yr. ended 12/31/01): Grants paid, $2,264; assets, $70,950 (M); expenditures, $5,800; qualifying distributions, $4,286.
Limitations: Applications not accepted.
Application information: Contributes only to pre-selected organizations.
Trustee: Wells Fargo Bank, N.A.
EIN: 746348758

53178
Allison Educational Trust
P.O. Box 798
Sonora, TX 76950-0798
Contact: Jo Ann Jones

Financial data (yr. ended 12/31/99): Grants paid, $2,251; assets, $102,844 (M); expenditures, $3,213; qualifying distributions, $2,351.
Limitations: Giving limited to the residents of Sonora, TX.
Application information: Application form required.
Trustees: John Childers, Armer Earwood, Carla Garner.
EIN: 237124306

53179
The Ackels Foundation
2777 Stemmons Fwy.
Dallas, TX 75207

Established in 1994 in TX.
Donor(s): Lawrence E. Ackels.
Financial data (yr. ended 12/31/01): Grants paid, $2,250; assets, $37,347 (M); gifts received, $600; expenditures, $2,250; qualifying distributions, $2,250.
Limitations: Giving primarily in Dallas, TX.
Officers: Lawrence E. Ackels, Pres.; Larry Ackels, Jr., V.P.; Henry Ackels, Secy.-Treas.
EIN: 752487277

53180
Foundation for a Compassionate Society Donation Fund
P.O. Box 3138
Austin, TX 78764-3138
Contact: Genevieve Vaughan, Pres.

Established in 1992 in TX.
Donor(s): Genevieve Vaughan.
Financial data (yr. ended 12/31/00): Grants paid, $2,250; assets, $4,049 (M); gifts received, $3,600; expenditures, $2,637; qualifying distributions, $2,250.
Officer: Genevieve Vaughan, Pres.
Directors: Frieda Werden, Marjorie West First.
EIN: 760363037

53181
McRae-Fleming, Inc.
10333 Richmond Ave., Ste. 860
Houston, TX 77042

Donor(s): Elsie V. McRae.
Financial data (yr. ended 12/31/01): Grants paid, $2,250; assets, $15,645 (M); expenditures, $2,813; qualifying distributions, $2,250.
Limitations: Giving primarily in Houston, TX.
Officers and Trustees:* Elsie V. McRae,* Pres.; Cody McRae,* V.P.; Blanche Parks,* Secy.; Misty McRae,* Treas.
EIN: 760131051

53182
New Braunfels Rotary Club Scholarship Fund
P.O. Box 310587
New Braunfels, TX 78131-0587
Application address: c/o David Lamon, P.O. Box 311160, New Braunfels, TX 78131-1160

Financial data (yr. ended 06/30/01): Grants paid, $2,250; assets, $82,646 (M); gifts received, $2,550; expenditures, $2,290; qualifying distributions, $2,250.
Limitations: Giving limited to residents of TX.
Application information: Application form required.
Officers and Directors:* Lee Edwards,* Pres.; Jill Curtis,* Secy.; Lena Daugherty, Treas.; Freddie Cervera, Ivonne Day, Robbie Hinson, Kent Hofstadt.
EIN: 742438204

53183
Becher Family Foundation
3 Aberdeen Crossing
The Woodlands, TX 77381-5174

Established in 1999 in TX.
Donor(s): Andrew Becher.
Financial data (yr. ended 12/31/00): Grants paid, $2,200; assets, $43,618 (M); expenditures, $6,516; qualifying distributions, $6,516.
Officer: Andrew Becher, Pres.
EIN: 760625933

53184
Till Charitable Trust
1111 Festival Dr.
Houston, TX 77062

Established in 1997 in TX.
Financial data (yr. ended 12/31/99): Grants paid, $2,150; assets, $43,684 (M); expenditures, $4,352; qualifying distributions, $4,352.
Officer: Thomas A. Till, Exec. Dir.

EIN: 760521317

53185
Myrtle A. Gunter Memorial Trust
c/o Wells Fargo Texas, N.A.
P.O. Box 2088
San Angelo, TX 76902-2088

Financial data (yr. ended 09/30/01): Grants paid, $2,139; assets, $64,976 (M); expenditures, $3,570; qualifying distributions, $2,139.
Limitations: Applications not accepted. Giving limited to San Angelo, TX.
Application information: Contributes only to pre-selected organizations.
Trustee: Wells Fargo Bank Texas, N.A.
EIN: 756291262

53186
Evans Swann Memorial Community Trust
c/o Bank of America
P.O. Box 831041
Dallas, TX 75283-1041
Application addresses: c/o Travis County Medical Society, P.O. Box 4679, Austin, TX 78765; c/o F.M. Pearce, 601 Medical Pk. Twr., Austin, TX 78705; c/o Rotary Club of Austin, Rotary Scholarship, 111 E. 1st St., Austin, TX 78701

Financial data (yr. ended 12/31/00): Grants paid, $2,100; assets, $180,921 (M); expenditures, $6,082; qualifying distributions, $3,308.
Limitations: Giving limited to Travis County, TX.
Application information: Application form required.
Trustee: Bank of America.
EIN: 746103394

53187
Far West Foundation, Inc.
5102 29th Dr., Ste. A
Lubbock, TX 79407

Financial data (yr. ended 09/30/01): Grants paid, $2,100; assets, $42,767 (M); expenditures, $2,246; qualifying distributions, $2,195.
Limitations: Applications not accepted. Giving limited to Lubbock, TX.
Application information: Contributes only to pre-selected organizations.
Officers and Trustee:* David L. Teague,* Pres.; Betty Teague, Secy.-Treas.
EIN: 756022308

53188
Ichthus Foundation
403 Lazy Bluff
San Antonio, TX 78216 (210) 735-1516
Contact: J. Michael Wilkes, Pres.

Established in 1993 in TX.
Financial data (yr. ended 12/31/01): Grants paid, $2,100; assets, $96,910 (M); gifts received, $30,000; expenditures, $2,579; qualifying distributions, $2,100.
Limitations: Giving on a national basis.
Application information: Application form not required.
Officers: J. Michael Wilkes, Pres. and Treas.; John L. Wilkes, V.P.; Ruth N. Wilkes, Secy.
EIN: 742684295

53189
Sam Rayburn Foundation
P.O. Box 309
Bonham, TX 75418-0309 (903) 583-2444
Application address: 800 W. Sam Rayburn Dr., Bonham, TX 75418
Contact: H.G. Dulaney, Tr.

Established around 1972 in TX.

Financial data (yr. ended 12/31/00): Grants paid, $2,100; assets, $25,625 (M); gifts received, $194; expenditures, $2,100; qualifying distributions, $0.
Limitations: Giving limited to Bonham, TX.
Officers and Trustees:* Dee J. Kelly,* Chair.; Edward H. Phillips,* Secy.-Treas.; Don E. Carleton, David Cole, H.G. Dulaney, Martha R. Dye, Ralph Hall.
EIN: 750984560

53190
Ruth Anderson Kimbell Foundation
P.O. Box 94903
Wichita Falls, TX 76308-0903

Established in 1992 in TX.
Donor(s): Ruth Anderson Kimbell Charitable Trust.
Financial data (yr. ended 12/31/01): Grants paid, $2,082; assets, $663,715 (M); gifts received, $80,000; expenditures, $3,555; qualifying distributions, $2,082.
Limitations: Applications not accepted. Giving primarily in Wichita Falls, TX.
Application information: Contributes only to pre-selected organizations.
Officers: David A. Kimbell, Pres.; Mike Elyea, V.P. and Treas.; Pat Hensley, Secy.
EIN: 752371260

53191
J. Newton Rayzor Foundation
1204 W. University Dr., Ste. 400
Denton, TX 76201-1771 (940) 387-8711
FAX: (940) 566-1591
Contact: Philip A. Baker, V.P.

Donor(s): Rayzor Investments, Ltd.
Financial data (yr. ended 09/30/00): Grants paid, $2,050; assets, $435,298 (M); gifts received, $300,000; expenditures, $3,061; qualifying distributions, $2,529.
Limitations: Giving primarily in TX.
Officer and Trustees:* Phillip A. Baker,* V.P. and Treas.; June Rayzor Elliott, John H. Fant, Evelyn Rayzor Nienhuis.
EIN: 237327814

53192
Constance E. McCaughan Charitable Trust
600 Leopard St., Ste. 2000
Corpus Christi, TX 78473

Established in 1992 in TX.
Donor(s): Constance E. McCaughan.‡
Financial data (yr. ended 02/28/01): Grants paid, $2,003; assets, $651,177 (M); expenditures, $5,256; qualifying distributions, $2,003.
Limitations: Applications not accepted. Giving primarily in Corpus Christi, TX.
Application information: Contributes only to pre-selected organizations.
Trustee: Robert C. Fancher.
EIN: 746400039

53193
Shaheen Abdullah Charitable Trust Fund
P.O. Box 347
Dalhart, TX 79022-0347

Established in 1996 in TX.
Donor(s): A.S. Abdullah.
Financial data (yr. ended 12/31/01): Grants paid, $2,000; assets, $54,186 (M); gifts received, $75; expenditures, $2,002; qualifying distributions, $2,000.
Trustee: A.S. Abdullah.
EIN: 752677509

53194
Trent Boydstun Scholarship Fund
1406 Clubview Ct.
Arlington, TX 76013-1004 (817) 461-8560
Contact: Helen Boydstun, Secy.

Financial data (yr. ended 12/31/99): Grants paid, $2,000; assets, $9,237 (M); gifts received, $300; expenditures, $2,025; qualifying distributions, $2,018.
Limitations: Giving primarily in Arlington, TX.
Application information: Application form required.
Officers and Directors:* Dwayne Boydstun,* Pres.; Margaret A. Gibbs,* V.P.; Helen Boydstun,* Secy.
EIN: 752082521

53195
R. S. Bradshaw, Jr. Scholarship Trust
c/o Texas Foundries, Inc.
P.O. Box 831041
Dallas, TX 75283-1041
Application address: c/o Personnel Mgr., Texas Foundries, Inc., Box 3718, Lufkin, TX 75903

Established in 1989 in TX.
Donor(s): Texas Foundries, Inc.
Financial data (yr. ended 06/30/01): Grants paid, $2,000; assets, $48,930 (M); expenditures, $3,070; qualifying distributions, $2,523.
Limitations: Giving limited to residents of TX.
Application information: Application form required.
Officer: Phillip DeWitt, Pres.
Trustee: Bank of America.
EIN: 756390739
Codes: CS, CD

53196
Harry & Rose Caplovitz Medical Award Fund
860 Country Ln.
Houston, TX 77024-3106

Financial data (yr. ended 12/31/99): Grants paid, $2,000; assets, $29,289 (M); expenditures, $2,183; qualifying distributions, $2,183.
Limitations: Applications not accepted. Giving primarily in New Orleans, LA, and Houston, TX.
Application information: Recipients are selected by faculty committee.
Trustees: Coleman D. Caplovitz, M.D., Kenneth Kates.
EIN: 760029286

53197
Diekemper Family Foundation, Inc.
P.O. Box 2453
Lubbock, TX 79408 (806) 762-4186
Contact: Lou Dunn Diekemper, Pres.

Established in 2000 in TX.
Donor(s): Lou Dunn Diekemper.
Financial data (yr. ended 12/31/01): Grants paid, $2,000; assets, $930,929 (M); gifts received, $90,000; expenditures, $18,166; qualifying distributions, $2,000.
Limitations: Giving primarily in Lubbock, TX.
Officers: Lou Dunn Diekemper, Pres.; Kara Mia Diekemper, V.P.; Diane Burchard, Secy.; Lou Ann Bergstein, Treas.
EIN: 752883998

53198
Emma Loyd Eaton Charitable Trust
2301 Cedar Springs, Ste. 150
Dallas, TX 75201

Established in 1999 in TX.
Donor(s): Emma Loyd Eaton.‡

53198—TEXAS

Financial data (yr. ended 12/31/01): Grants paid, $2,000; assets, $40,514 (M); expenditures, $2,833; qualifying distributions, $1,988.
Limitations: Applications not accepted.
Application information: Contributes only to pre-selected organizations.
Trustee: Gordon Peterson.
EIN: 752822069

53199
Alice Taylor Gray Foundation
P.O. Box 179
Galveston, TX 77553

Established in 1998 in TX.
Financial data (yr. ended 12/31/01): Grants paid, $2,000; assets, $32,157 (M); gifts received, $2,000; expenditures, $2,633; qualifying distributions, $2,000.
Trustee: Frost National Bank.
EIN: 766137958

53200
The Hoffinger-Lowe Foundation
2639 Sutton Ct.
Houston, TX 77027 (713) 621-2778
Contact: Ellen Hoffinger-Lowe, Pres.

Established in 1993 in TX.
Donor(s): Richard Lowe, Ellen Lowe.
Financial data (yr. ended 12/31/00): Grants paid, $2,000; assets, $35,554 (M); expenditures, $3,409; qualifying distributions, $1,986.
Limitations: Giving limited to TX.
Officers: Ellen Hoffinger-Lowe, Pres.; Richard Lowe, V.P.
Trustee: Gary Lowe.
EIN: 760313825

53201
Fred W. Linton Educational Scholarship Fund, Inc.
P.O. Box 2009
Texas City, TX 77592-2009

Financial data (yr. ended 06/30/99): Grants paid, $2,000; assets, $10,788 (M); expenditures, $2,099; qualifying distributions, $2,099.
Limitations: Giving primarily in Texas City, TX.
Application information: Application form required.
Officer: Emkin Linton, Pres.
EIN: 237174516

53202
McGaha Foundation
4245 Kemp Blvd., Ste. 408
Wichita Falls, TX 76308

Donor(s): Ruth McGaha.
Financial data (yr. ended 12/31/01): Grants paid, $2,000; assets, $207,518 (M); gifts received, $99,773; expenditures, $2,534; qualifying distributions, $2,000.
Limitations: Applications not accepted. Giving primarily in TX.
Application information: Contributes only to pre-selected organizations.
Officers: Ruth McGaha, Pres.; Herbert E. Smith, Jr., V.P.; W.M. Thacker, Jr., Secy.; Gary Shores, Treas.
Director: Herbert B. Story.
EIN: 756017848

53203
The Dale McLain Family Scholarship Fund
c/o FirstBank Southwest
P.O. Box 929
Perryton, TX 79070-0929 (806) 435-3676

Financial data (yr. ended 12/31/01): Grants paid, $2,000; assets, $22,886 (M); expenditures, $2,735; qualifying distributions, $1,992.
Limitations: Giving limited to residents of Perryton, TX.
Application information: Application form not required.
Trustee: FirstBank Southwest.
Advisory Board: Doug Burke, Joe Gibson, Bruce Julian, Scott McGarraugh, Dale McLain.
EIN: 756312159

53204
Stanley H. Peavy Benevolent Foundation
c/o Stanley H. Peavy, Jr.
423 4th St.
Graham, TX 76450

Donor(s): Stanley H. Peavy, Jr., Sandra Peavy.
Financial data (yr. ended 12/31/01): Grants paid, $2,000; assets, $29,704 (M); expenditures, $2,328; qualifying distributions, $2,108.
Limitations: Applications not accepted. Giving primarily in TX.
Officers: Sandra Peavy, Pres.; Stanley H. Peavy III, V.P.; Stanley H. Peavy, Jr., Secy.-Treas.
EIN: 756013150

53205
Edwin & Lee Peterson Fund
c/o Bank of America
P.O. Box 831041
Dallas, TX 75283-1041

Financial data (yr. ended 12/31/01): Grants paid, $2,000; assets, $1 (M); expenditures, $3,135; qualifying distributions, $2,000.
Limitations: Applications not accepted. Giving primarily in Denison, TX.
Application information: Contributes only to pre-selected organizations.
Trustee: Bank of America.
EIN: 736018291

53206
Mark Thomas Price, II Memorial Music Fund
2506 Bandelier Dr.
Houston, TX 77080-3811 (713) 462-0090
Contact: Claire B. Tapscott, Secy.-Treas.

Established in 1989 in TX.
Financial data (yr. ended 12/31/01): Grants paid, $2,000; assets, $33,050 (M); gifts received, $250; expenditures, $2,166; qualifying distributions, $1,984.
Limitations: Giving limited to residents of Harris County, TX.
Officers: Mark T. Price, Pres.; Claire B. Tapscott, Secy.-Treas.
EIN: 760286838

53207
Lillian Thorp Shelhorn Foundation
5036 Radbrook Pl.
Dallas, TX 75220

Established in 1997 in TX.
Donor(s): James J. O'Neill, Elizabeth J. O'Neill.
Financial data (yr. ended 12/31/01): Grants paid, $2,000; assets, $36,038 (M); gifts received, $272; expenditures, $2,747; qualifying distributions, $1,989.
Limitations: Applications not accepted. Giving limited to Dallas, TX.
Application information: Contributes only to pre-selected organization.
Officers: James J. O'Neill, Pres.; Elizabeth J. O'Neill, V.P. and Treas.; Frank Thorp, V.P.; John Thorp, V.P.
EIN: 311523295
Codes: TN

53208
Smart-Wallace Educational Trust
415 N.E. 4th Ave.
Mineral Wells, TX 76067
Contact: Carla Hay, Tr.

Financial data (yr. ended 12/31/00): Grants paid, $2,000; assets, $17,410 (M); gifts received, $199; expenditures, $2,245; qualifying distributions, $2,000.
Limitations: Giving limited to residents of Mineral Wells, TX.
Application information: Application form required.
Trustees: Kathy Boswell, Margaret Colton, Herman Fitts, Carla Hay.
EIN: 756085142

53209
The Snappy Foundation
412 Lovett Blvd.
Houston, TX 77006-4019

Established in 1999 in TX.
Donor(s): J. Christopher Holland, Cathleen W. Holland.
Financial data (yr. ended 12/31/01): Grants paid, $2,000; assets, $39,573 (M); expenditures, $2,424; qualifying distributions, $2,000.
Limitations: Applications not accepted.
Application information: Contributes only to pre-selected organizations.
Officers and Directors:* J. Christopher Holland,* Pres. and Treas.; Cathleen W. Holland,* V.P. and Secy.; Gerry D. Wolfe.
EIN: 760624798

53210
The Steelhammer Family Foundation
2100 W. Loop S., Ste. 1400
Houston, TX 77027

Established in 1999 in TX.
Donor(s): Robert H. Steelhammer.
Financial data (yr. ended 06/30/01): Grants paid, $2,000; assets, $8,209 (M); gifts received, $3,500; expenditures, $2,500; qualifying distributions, $2,000.
Limitations: Applications not accepted.
Application information: Contributes only to pre-selected organizations.
Officers: Robert H. Steelhammer, Pres.; Judith Steelhammer, Secy.
EIN: 760624687

53211
Wolf-Casper Fund
3710 Rawlins, Ste. 970
Dallas, TX 75219 (214) 823-9941
Contact: Howard B. Wolf, Tr.

Donor(s): Howard B. Wolf, Lois Wolf.
Financial data (yr. ended 07/31/99): Grants paid, $1,985; assets, $66,843 (M); expenditures, $2,321; qualifying distributions, $1,985.
Limitations: Giving primarily in Dallas, TX.
Trustees: Howard B. Wolf, Lois Wolf.
EIN: 756051924

53212
Shelter the Children
6607 Shelton Home Ct.
Arlington, TX 76017-0733

Established in 1999 in TX.
Financial data (yr. ended 12/31/01): Grants paid, $1,980; assets, $16,642 (M); gifts received, $141,000; expenditures, $1,980; qualifying distributions, $1,980.
Limitations: Applications not accepted.
Application information: Contributes only to pre-selected organizations.
Officers and Directers:* Glen D. Harrison,* Pres.; Teddilynn Wilson, Secy.-Treas.
Director: Stephen D. Harrison.
EIN: 752520689

53213
The Williams Foundation
923 N.W. Loop 281
Longview, TX 75604-2918

Financial data (yr. ended 10/31/01): Grants paid, $1,975; assets, $8,207 (M); expenditures, $2,013; qualifying distributions, $1,975.
Limitations: Applications not accepted. Giving primarily in CA and TX.
Application information: Contributes only to pre-selected organizations.
Trustees: James A. Kirkland, T. John Ward, Paul E. Williams.
EIN: 751800737

53214
Val Verde Friends of the Arts
P.O. Box 411456
Del Rio, TX 78841-1456
Application address: 525 S. Main St., Ste. 505, Del Rio, TX 78840-581, tel.: (830) 775-0561
Contact: Ernest L. Worley, Jr., Treas.

Established in 1998 in TX.
Financial data (yr. ended 09/30/02): Grants paid, $1,942; assets, $2,108 (M); gifts received, $1,600; expenditures, $2,518; qualifying distributions, $1,942.
Limitations: Giving primarily in Val Verde County, TX.
Officers: Helen Dengler, Chair.; Dwight Brown, Vice Chair.; Annelies Castro-Rios, Secy.; Ernest L. Worley, Jr., Treas.
Directors: Humberto Aguirre, Judy Burks, Wilburine Campbell, Roberto Fernandez, Gene Frank, Didi Kolkebeck, and 13 other directors.
EIN: 742328818

53215
Roy & Ila Meinecke Charitable Foundation
P.O. Box 154
Bellville, TX 77418-0154

Established in 2000 in TX.
Financial data (yr. ended 12/31/00): Grants paid, $1,904; assets, $113,326 (M); gifts received, $55,000; expenditures, $1,904; qualifying distributions, $1,904.
Limitations: Applications not accepted. Giving primarily in Bellville, TX.
Application information: Contributes only to pre-selected organizations.
Trustees: Perry L. Marek, Fritz Nelius, Bruce Ueckert, James H. Wyatt.
EIN: 742160129

53216
Tom Moore Community Music Foundation
1007 W. Cottage
Houston, TX 77009

Financial data (yr. ended 12/31/00): Grants paid, $1,850; assets, $46,092 (M); expenditures, $2,184; qualifying distributions, $1,850.
Limitations: Applications not accepted. Giving primarily in Houston, TX.
Application information: Contributes only to pre-selected organizations.
Officers: Peter H. Squire, Pres.; David Elliot, V.P.; Robbie MacIver, Secy.; Stan Brewer, Treas.
EIN: 760348160

53217
Leonard S. Roth Foundation
2215 Avalon Pl.
Houston, TX 77019

Established in 1988 in TX.
Donor(s): Leonard S. Roth.
Financial data (yr. ended 11/30/01): Grants paid, $1,850; assets, $39,174 (M); gifts received, $15,236; expenditures, $2,396; qualifying distributions, $1,850.
Limitations: Applications not accepted.
Application information: Contributes only to pre-selected organizations.
Trustee: Leonard S. Roth.
EIN: 760265462

53218
The E. Earle & Lottie Marie MacDonald Scholarship Fund
P.O. Box 1259
Mission, TX 78572-1259
Application address: P.O. Box 1257, Mission, TX 78572, tel.: (956) 585-4835
Contact: James M. Blankenbaker, Tr.

Financial data (yr. ended 05/31/99): Grants paid, $1,800; assets, $34,062 (M); expenditures, $3,020; qualifying distributions, $3,020.
Limitations: Giving limited to Mission, TX.
Trustee: James M. Blankenbaker.
EIN: 741957489

53219
Nelson Family Foundation
c/o Anna K. Nelson
5 E. Wedgemere Cir.
The Woodlands, TX 77381-4190

Established in 1997 in TX.
Donor(s): Anna K. Nelson, Eric B. Nelson.
Financial data (yr. ended 12/31/01): Grants paid, $1,800; assets, $37,909 (M); gifts received, $1,230; expenditures, $2,118; qualifying distributions, $1,800.
Limitations: Applications not accepted. Giving primarily in Washington, DC and Tampa, FL.
Application information: Contributes only to pre-selected organizations.
Trustees: Anna K. Nelson, Eric B. Nelson.
EIN: 766127484

53220
George B. Kirkpatrick Charitable Trust
c/o Wells Fargo Bank Texas, N.A.
40 N.E. Loop 410, Ste. 201
San Antonio, TX 78216

Financial data (yr. ended 12/31/01): Grants paid, $1,756; assets, $87,012 (M); expenditures, $5,282; qualifying distributions, $2,175.
Limitations: Applications not accepted.
Application information: Contributes only to pre-selected organizations.
Trustee: Wells Fargo Bank Texas, N.A.
EIN: 746442622

53221
Chapel Lamb
1707 Todd Trail
College Station, TX 77845

Established in 2000 in TX.
Financial data (yr. ended 12/31/00): Grants paid, $1,750; assets, $4,499 (M); gifts received, $7,589; expenditures, $3,127; qualifying distributions, $0.
Limitations: Giving on a national basis; some giving to Japan.
Officers: Ryoichi Wada, Chair.; Chiaki Wada, Vice-Chair.
EIN: 742950596

53222
R. L. & Phyllis Glazer Foundation, Inc.
14860 Landmark Blvd.
Dallas, TX 75254

Established in 2001 in TX.
Donor(s): R.L. Glazer.
Financial data (yr. ended 12/31/01): Grants paid, $1,734; assets, $230,629 (M); expenditures, $3,080; qualifying distributions, $1,734.
Trustees: Phyllis Glazer, R.L. Glazer.
EIN: 752916889

53223
Kristy M. Landers Memorial Scholarship
803 W. 7th St.
Muleshoe, TX 79347

Financial data (yr. ended 12/31/01): Grants paid, $1,700; assets, $22,653 (M); gifts received, $675; expenditures, $1,750; qualifying distributions, $1,700.
Limitations: Giving limited to residents of Muleshoe, TX.
Officers: Max Crittendon, Chair.; Mike Holt, Vice-Chair.; Nina Landers, Secy.-Treas.
EIN: 752267762

53224
The Ed & Josie Toogood Foundation
c/o William E. Toogood
10264 Timber Trail Dr.
Dallas, TX 75229-6063

Established in 1997 in TX.
Financial data (yr. ended 12/31/01): Grants paid, $1,674; assets, $32,824 (M); expenditures, $1,778; qualifying distributions, $1,674.
Limitations: Applications not accepted.
Application information: Contributes only to pre-selected organizations.
Officers: W.E. Toogood, Pres.; Mary Josephine Toogood, V.P.
Directors: Anne Marie Bristol-White, John Stanley.
EIN: 752738976

53225
Youth Board of Port Arthur
c/o Wells Fargo Bank, N.A.
P.O. Box 4441
Houston, TX 77210-4441
Application address: c/o Port Arthur Independent School District, 735 5th St., Port Arthur, TX 77640, tel.: (409) 985-9383

Financial data (yr. ended 12/31/00): Grants paid, $1,645; assets, $39,147 (M); expenditures, $2,798; qualifying distributions, $1,645.
Limitations: Giving limited to Port Arthur, TX.
Application information: Application form required.
Trustee: Wells Fargo Bank, N.A.
EIN: 740641617

53226
Adair-Turnbull Memorial Trust Fund
813 8th St., Ste. 550
Wichita Falls, TX 76301-3318 (940) 322-9900

Financial data (yr. ended 10/31/01): Grants paid, $1,600; assets, $25,569 (M); gifts received, $55; expenditures, $1,680; qualifying distributions, $1,642.
Limitations: Giving primarily in Wichita Falls, TX.
Application information: Application form required.
Trustee: Ewell Cason.
EIN: 751783623

53227
James and Susan Martin Charitable Trust
c/o Martin, Drought & Torres, Inc.
300 Convent, Ste. 2500
San Antonio, TX 78205
Contact: James N. Martin, Tr.

Established in 1997 in TX.
Donor(s): James N. Martin, Susan H. Martin.
Financial data (yr. ended 12/31/01): Grants paid, $1,600; assets, $42,148 (M); expenditures, $2,140; qualifying distributions, $1,600.
Limitations: Giving primarily in TX.
Trustees: Alyson N. Martin, Andrea V. Martin, James N. Martin, Susan H. Martin.
EIN: 742821490

53228
The Phillips Foundation, Inc.
P.O. Box 3489
Corpus Christi, TX 78463-3489

Established in 1997 in TX.
Donor(s): C.W. Phillips.
Financial data (yr. ended 11/30/00): Grants paid, $1,600; assets, $2,878 (M); expenditures, $1,689; qualifying distributions, $1,600.
Limitations: Giving on an international basis; primarily South Africa.
Officers and Directors:* C.W. Phillips,* Pres. and Treas.; Peggy J. Phillips,* 1st V.P.; Pamela Sue Landers,* 2nd V.P.; Deborah D. Keeble, Daniel T. Richter, Thomas M. Schroeder, William T. Simmons.
EIN: 742862037

53229
The Jim and Lynn Moroney Family Foundation
c/o James M. Moroney, Jr.
P.O. Box 655237
Dallas, TX 75265-5237

Established in 1996 in TX.
Donor(s): James M. Moroney, Jr., Lynn Moroney.
Financial data (yr. ended 12/31/01): Grants paid, $1,550; assets, $31,545 (M); gifts received, $6,072; expenditures, $2,786; qualifying distributions, $1,550.
Limitations: Applications not accepted. Giving primarily in Dallas, TX.
Application information: Contributes only to pre-selected organizations.
Officers: James M. Moroney, Jr., Pres.; Lynn Moroney, V.P.; James M. Moroney III, Secy.-Treas.
EIN: 752608813

53230
Donald R. Watkins Memorial Foundation, Inc.
1200 Binz St., Ste. 130
Houston, TX 77004-6925

Established in 1998 in TX.
Financial data (yr. ended 12/31/99): Grants paid, $1,525; assets, $322,705 (M); gifts received, $1,225,668; expenditures, $1,044,632; qualifying distributions, $1,061,901; giving activities include $1,043,107 for programs.
Officers: Zinetta A. Burney, Pres.; Gregory W. Elzie, V.P.; Mary Brown-Redmond, Secy.; Sharyon Gathe, Treas.
Directors: Steven L. Applewhite, Dorothy Bartley, James K. Ellis, Martha Kelly, Roland R. Rousseve, Eric W. Staggers, Victor Villareal, Barbara Wright-Boyle.
EIN: 760519450

53231
Dianne & Duffey Albright Foundation
P.O. Box 589
Port Aransas, TX 78373

Established in 2000.
Donor(s): Duffey Albright, Dianne Albright.
Financial data (yr. ended 12/31/01): Grants paid, $1,500; assets, $21,848 (M); expenditures, $2,885; qualifying distributions, $1,500.
Officers: Dianne Albright, Pres.; Duffey Albright, V.P.; Elyse Albright, Secy.; Dawn Albright, Treas.
Directors: Eve Albright, Amy Navarro.
EIN: 742946900

53232
David Bowen Memorial Scholarship, Inc.
Rte. 4, Box 34
Yoakum, TX 77995

Financial data (yr. ended 12/31/99): Grants paid, $1,500; assets, $41,597 (M); expenditures, $1,586; qualifying distributions, $0.
Application information: Application form not required.
Officer: Catherine M. Thigpen, Treas.
EIN: 760341733

53233
The Brockman Foundation
(Formerly The Robert T. Brockman Charitable Foundation)
6700 Hollister
Houston, TX 77040-5345

Established in 1987 in TX.
Donor(s): Universal Computer Systems, Inc., Universal Computer Consulting, Inc., Universal Computer Network, Inc.
Financial data (yr. ended 12/31/00): Grants paid, $1,500; assets, $961,974 (M); expenditures, $3,072; qualifying distributions, $1,500.
Limitations: Applications not accepted. Giving primarily in TX.
Application information: Contributes only to pre-selected organizations.
Officers and Directors:* Robert T. Brockman,* Pres.; Dorothy K. Brockman,* V.P.; Robert Burnett, Secy.-Treas.; Alfred J. Thorpe.
EIN: 760239422

53234
Hakka Cultural Education Foundation of Houston, Inc.
9100 Park W. Dr.
Houston, TX 77063-4104

Established in 1995 in TX.
Financial data (yr. ended 12/31/99): Grants paid, $1,500; assets, $55,519 (M); gifts received, $10,280; expenditures, $10,410; qualifying distributions, $10,410.
Limitations: Giving primarily in Houston, TX.
Application information: Application form required.
Officer: David C. Lai, Chair.; Henry W. Yang, Vice Chair.
Director: Philip Chung, David Lai.
EIN: 760471541

53235
KPMG Peat Marwick Foundation Southwest/Dallas
200 Crescent Ct., Ste. 300
Dallas, TX 75201-1885

Established in 1995 in TX.
Donor(s): C.H. Moore, William G. Cummins, Thomas A. Reedy, Richard J. Sabolik, Christine T. St. Claire, Gregory B. Tomlinson, Mark A. Springer, Larry Lott.
Financial data (yr. ended 12/31/01): Grants paid, $1,500; assets, $6,477 (M); expenditures, $1,759; qualifying distributions, $1,500.
Limitations: Applications not accepted. Giving primarily in TX.
Application information: Contributes only to pre-selected organizations.
Officers: C.H. Moore, Pres.; Gary M. Choate, V.P.; Charles F. Thomas, Secy.-Treas.
EIN: 752621023

53236
The Lack Foundation
470 Mariners Dr.
Kemah, TX 77565-2261

Established in 1944 in TX.
Donor(s): Fredell Eichhorn, Sanford Lack, Zella Silverman.
Financial data (yr. ended 12/31/00): Grants paid, $1,500; assets, $74,683 (M); expenditures, $1,591; qualifying distributions, $1,500.
Limitations: Giving primarily in TX.
Application information: Application form not required.
Officers: Stephen Lack, Pres.; Fredell Eichhorn, V.P.; Heather Jack, Secy.-Treas.
EIN: 746047167

53237
Pauline Smith Marshall Memorial Scholarship Fund, Inc.
Rte. 1, Box 267A
Buna, TX 77612 (409) 994-3395
Application address: c/o Buna Consolidated Independent School District, Buna, TX 77612, tel.: (409) 994-5101
Contact: Jasper C. Smith, Jr., Chair.

Financial data (yr. ended 11/30/01): Grants paid, $1,500; assets, $25,066 (M); expenditures, $1,965; qualifying distributions, $1,965.
Limitations: Giving limited to residents of Buna, TX.
Application information: Application form required.
Officer and Trustees:* Jasper C. Smith, Jr.,* Chair.; Dorothy Smith, Jerry E. Smith, Joan Smith, Larkin A. Smith.
EIN: 760251589

53238
Morillon Family Foundation
c/o William L. Morillon, III
24822 Lakebriar Dr.
Katy, TX 77494-1809

Financial data (yr. ended 12/31/01): Grants paid, $1,500; assets, $2,741 (M); gifts received, $2,000; expenditures, $1,702; qualifying distributions, $1,500.
Trustees: Marie A. Morillon, WIlliam L. Morillon III.
EIN: 760589224

53239
Olivares Foundation
1601 N. Travis
Sherman, TX 75090

Established in 1997 in TX.
Financial data (yr. ended 12/31/01): Grants paid, $1,500; assets, $23,932 (M); expenditures, $1,760; qualifying distributions, $1,500.
Trustees: Gayle P. Olivares, Rebecca Louise Olivares, Michael E. Snyder, C.P.A.
EIN: 752724223

53240
Herman Pieper Charitable Trust
P.O. Box 311059
New Braunfels, TX 78131-1059
Application address: 457 Landa, Ste. H, New Braunfels, TX 78130
Contact: Jayne E. Jochec, Tr.

Established in 1990 in TX.
Financial data (yr. ended 12/31/99): Grants paid, $1,500; assets, $139,185 (M); gifts received, $8,861; expenditures, $6,887; qualifying distributions, $6,887.
Limitations: Giving limited to New Braunfels, TX.
Trustees: Jayne E. Jochec, Helen M. Villarreal.
EIN: 746375682

53241
The Nelta Buie Ray and Donald Lee Ray Foundation
P.O. Box 32
Diana, TX 75640

Established in 1999 in TX.
Donor(s): Donald Lee Ray, Nelta Buie Ray.
Financial data (yr. ended 12/31/01): Grants paid, $1,500; assets, $11,004 (M); gifts received, $1,500; expenditures, $4,305; qualifying distributions, $1,500.
Limitations: Applications not accepted.
Application information: Contributes only to pre-selected organizations.
Officers and Directors:* Donald Lee Ray,* Mgr.; Nelta Buie Ray,* Mgr.; Rebecca Ray Buckner, Russell Lane Ray, Laura Ray Sorrell.
EIN: 752860566

53242
Dorothy Sinz/Muckleroy Charitable Foundation
8925 Memorial Dr.
Houston, TX 77024

Established in 1997 in TX.
Donor(s): Dorothy Sinz.
Financial data (yr. ended 12/31/00): Grants paid, $1,500; assets, $134,747 (M); expenditures, $1,500; qualifying distributions, $1,328.
Limitations: Applications not accepted. Giving primarily in TX.
Application information: Contributes only to pre-selected organizations.
Officers: Dorothy Sinz, Pres. and Secy.; Michael Muckleroy, V.P.
EIN: 760538011

53243
White Mountain Institute
(Formerly Ambulatory Anesthesia Research Foundation)
2704 Welborn St., Apt. F
Dallas, TX 75219

Established around 1987.
Financial data (yr. ended 09/30/01): Grants paid, $1,500; assets, $1,964,403 (M); gifts received, $455,324; expenditures, $22,342; qualifying distributions, $1,500.
Limitations: Applications not accepted. Giving on a national basis.
Application information: Contributes only to pre-selected organizations.
Officers: Paul E. White, M.D., Pres.; Linda D. White, Secy. and C.F.O.
EIN: 770094396

53244
Albert E. & Myrtle Gunn York Trust
c/o Wells Fargo Bank Texas, N.A.
P.O. Box 511
Victoria, TX 77902-0511

Financial data (yr. ended 12/31/01): Grants paid, $1,500; assets, $672,612 (M); expenditures, $10,717; qualifying distributions, $1,500.
Limitations: Giving primarily in Victoria, TX.
Trustee: Wells Fargo Bank Texas, N.A.
EIN: 746446490

53245
ACE Foundation - Trinity Lyceum
(Formerly The Arlington Cultural and Education Foundation and Trinity Lyceum)
305 S. West St.
Arlington, TX 76010

Donor(s): Carlton Reid, Bernice Reid.
Financial data (yr. ended 12/31/01): Grants paid, $1,449; assets, $486,375 (M); gifts received, $46,094; expenditures, $102,800; qualifying distributions, $0.
Limitations: Applications not accepted. Giving primarily in TX.
Application information: Contributes only to pre-selected organizations.
Officers: Dawna Alsobrook, Pres.; Gena Turner, Secy.; Down Carter, Treas.; Carlton Reld, Bernice Reld.
EIN: 752147456

53246
Colonel Ruth Broe Scholarship Fund
c/o Marine Military Academy
320 Iwo Jima Blvd.
Harlingen, TX 78550-3627 (956) 423-6006

Financial data (yr. ended 12/31/01): Grants paid, $1,445; assets, $28,472 (M); expenditures, $1,461; qualifying distributions, $1,447.
Limitations: Giving limited to Harlingen, TX.
Application information: Application form required.
Trustee: Dan Lanoue.
EIN: 336002174

53247
American College of Hyperbaric Medicine
P.O. Box 25914-130
Houston, TX 77265

Established in 1996 in TX.
Financial data (yr. ended 04/30/00): Grants paid, $1,410; assets, $17,125 (M); expenditures, $18,913; qualifying distributions, $1,410.
Limitations: Applications not accepted.
Application information: Contributes only to pre-selected organizations.
Officers: Tom Bozzuto, Pres.; David Youngblood, V.P.; Donn Bowers, Secy. Treas.
EIN: 752166886

53248
Fiona Rose Murphy Foundation
2520 Cedar Elm
Plano, TX 75075

Established in 2001 in TX.
Financial data (yr. ended 12/31/01): Grants paid, $1,404; assets, $7,655 (M); gifts received, $9,156; expenditures, $1,501; qualifying distributions, $1,501.
Officers and Directors:* Lois M. Murphy,* Pres.; Michael Martin Murphy,* V.P.; Pink L. Murphy,* Secy.-Treas.
EIN: 752920385

53249
Carol And Jack McGuire Foundation
747 Grandview Pl.
San Antonio, TX 78209 (210) 821-6755
Contact: Carol & John T. McGuire

Established in 2000 in TX.
Donor(s): Carol McGuire, John T. McGuire.
Financial data (yr. ended 12/31/01): Grants paid, $1,304; assets, $639,895 (M); gifts received, $350,000; expenditures, $11,318; qualifying distributions, $1,304.
Limitations: Applications not accepted.
Application information: Contributes only to pre-selected organizations.
Directors: Carol McGuire, John T. McGuire.
EIN: 742979027

53250
William E. Armentrout Foundation
c/o William E. Armentrout
3805 Gillon Ave.
Dallas, TX 75205-3114

Established in 1998 in TX.
Donor(s): William E. Armentrout.
Financial data (yr. ended 12/31/01): Grants paid, $1,300; assets, $25,731 (M); expenditures, $1,314; qualifying distributions, $1,300.
Limitations: Applications not accepted. Giving primarily in Dallas, TX.
Application information: Contributes only to pre-selected organizations.
Officers and Directors:* William E. Armentrout, Chair. and Pres.; Charles D. Armentrout,* V.P. and Treas.; Dennis L. Lutes,* Secy.; Elizabeth R. Kaye, Lee C. Ritchie.
EIN: 752750535

53251
Musselman Family Charitable Foundation
P.O. Box 10609
Midland, TX 79702

Established in 1996 in TX.
Donor(s): Henry G. Musselman.
Financial data (yr. ended 07/31/01): Grants paid, $1,300; assets, $71 (M); expenditures, $1,551; qualifying distributions, $1,300.
Limitations: Applications not accepted.
Application information: Contributes only to pre-selected organizations.
Officer: Henry G. Musselman, Pres.
EIN: 752708768

53252
The Dale and Barbara Reed Charitable Foundation
1115 Yorkshire Dr.
Carrollton, TX 75007

Established in 2000 in TX.
Financial data (yr. ended 12/31/01): Grants paid, $1,284; assets, $27,409 (M); gifts received, $21,096; expenditures, $1,349; qualifying distributions, $1,284.
Officers: Dale R. Reed, Pres. and Treas.; Barbara L. Reed, V.P. and Secy.
EIN: 752903857

53253
Madge B. & Felix H. Watson Foundation
c/o Wells Fargo Bank Texas, N.A.
P.O. Box 9129
Wichita Falls, TX 76308-9129

Established in 1999 in TX.
Financial data (yr. ended 12/31/01): Grants paid, $1,276; assets, $953,515 (M); gifts received, $883,728; expenditures, $9,472; qualifying distributions, $1,276.
Limitations: Applications not accepted.
Application information: Contributes only to pre-selected organizations.
Trustee: Wells Fargo Bank Texas, N.A.
EIN: 752852810

53254
The ACR Foundation
43 N. Lakemist Harbour Pl.
Spring, TX 77381-3344

Established in 2000 in TX.
Donor(s): Al Reese, Jr., Caryl R. Reese.
Financial data (yr. ended 12/31/01): Grants paid, $1,250; assets, $1 (M); gifts received, $2,500; expenditures, $1,755; qualifying distributions, $1,250.
Limitations: Applications not accepted. Giving primarily in TX.
Application information: Contributes only to pre-selected organizations.
Officers and Directors:* Al Reese, Jr.,* Pres.; Caryl R. Reese,* Secy.-Treas.; David G. Dunlap.
EIN: 760648796

53255
Anderson Family Foundation
1401 Avenue Q
Lubbock, TX 79401-3819
Application address: c/o American State Bank, P.O. Box 1401, Lubbock, TX 79408, tel.: (806) 767-7000
Contact: Steve Exter, Tr.

Established in 2000 in TX.
Financial data (yr. ended 12/31/01): Grants paid, $1,250; assets, $46,981 (M); expenditures, $2,055; qualifying distributions, $1,250.
Trustee: Steve Exter.
EIN: 752840787

53256
Mohr Foundation, Inc.
(Formerly E. B. Mohr Foundation, Inc.)
4700 Kelsey Rd.
Dallas, TX 75229-6506

Financial data (yr. ended 12/31/01): Grants paid, $1,250; assets, $1 (M); expenditures, $4,800; qualifying distributions, $1,250.
Limitations: Applications not accepted. Giving primarily in TX.
Application information: Contributes only to pre-selected organizations.
Officers and Directors:* Lady George Mohr,* Pres. and Secy.; Robert E. Mohr,* V.P. and Treas.; Preston D. Morton.
EIN: 756022705

53257
Arthur K. and June D. Smith Foundation
1505 S. Blvd.
Houston, TX 77006-6335

Established in 1998 in TX.
Donor(s): Arthur K. Smith, June D. Smith.
Financial data (yr. ended 12/31/99): Grants paid, $1,250; assets, $30,644 (M); gifts received, $12,016; expenditures, $1,819; qualifying distributions, $1,443.

Limitations: Applications not accepted.
Application information: Contributes only to pre-selected organizations.
Trustees: Arthur K. Smith, June D. Smith.
EIN: 760573022

53258
Army Lodge-Thagard Foundation, Inc.
P.O. Box 8084
San Antonio, TX 78208   (210) 226-7962
Contact: Jose N. Guerra, Sr., Pres.

Financial data (yr. ended 05/31/99): Grants paid, $1,225; assets, $25,543 (M); expenditures, $1,266; qualifying distributions, $1,225.
Limitations: Giving primarily in TX.
Officers: Jose N. Guerra, Sr., Pres.; Mario G. Vargas, V.P.; Eldie E. Ebner, Secy.; Ronald C. Gehring, Treas.
Board Members: Richard F. Adaszczyk, William B. Sessums.
EIN: 746105633

53259
Cecile Curlin Autrey Ham Bluebonnet Memorial and Scholarship Corporation
P.O. Box 163690
Austin, TX 78716-3690
Application address: P.O. Box 896, Austin, TX 78767, tel.: (512) 474-4200
Contact: Jeff W. Autrey, Dir.

Established in 1991 in TX.
Donor(s): Bill Ham.
Financial data (yr. ended 07/31/01): Grants paid, $1,225; assets, $33,465 (M); gifts received, $814; expenditures, $2,039; qualifying distributions, $1,225.
Limitations: Giving primarily in TX.
Directors: Jeff W. Autrey, Bill Ham.
EIN: 742610431

53260
Lifshutz Fund, Inc.
215 W. Travis St.
San Antonio, TX 78205   (210) 226-6221
Contact: Lawrence Torres, Treas.

Financial data (yr. ended 04/30/02): Grants paid, $1,210; assets, $9,952 (M); expenditures, $1,510; qualifying distributions, $1,210.
Limitations: Giving primarily in San Antonio, TX.
Officers: Bernard Lifshutz, Pres.; Lawrence Torres, Treas.
EIN: 746063335

53261
Carter Fund, Inc.
6395 Hilldale Ct.
Fort Worth, TX 76116   (817) 732-0136
Contact: Gerald C. Meehan, Pres.

Donor(s): Gerald C. Meehan.
Financial data (yr. ended 09/30/01): Grants paid, $1,200; assets, $85,614 (M); expenditures, $17,669; qualifying distributions, $1,200.
Limitations: Giving primarily in Chippewa Falls, WI.
Application information: Application form not required.
Officers and Director:* Gerald C. Meehan,* Pres.; Bill Lee, V.P.
EIN: 756015634

53262
Frost Foundation
1415 Louisiana St., Ste. 2220
Houston, TX 77002
Application address: c/o Southampton Medical Group, 4110 Greenbriar St., Ste. 200, Houston, TX 77098
Contact: Shannon Schroder, Dir.

Established in 1999 in TX.
Financial data (yr. ended 12/31/00): Grants paid, $1,200; assets, $44,427 (M); gifts received, $1,500; expenditures, $1,294; qualifying distributions, $1,247.
Directors: Terrance Baggott, Bruce G. Garrison, Scott Holman, Bill Lee, Shannon Schroder.
EIN: 760587800

53263
Houston Hispanic Chamber of Commerce Educational Foundation
2900 Woodridge, Ste. 312
Houston, TX 77087

Established in 1999 in TX.
Financial data (yr. ended 12/31/00): Grants paid, $1,200; assets, $17,567 (M); expenditures, $7,433; qualifying distributions, $1,200.
Limitations: Applications not accepted. Giving primarily in Houston, TX.
Application information: Contributes only to pre-selected organizations.
Directors: Lupe Fraga, Yolanda Londono, Jose Adan Trevino.
EIN: 760405427

53264
David S. McLure Scholarship Fund
1200 Smith, Ste. 1400
Houston, TX 77002
Application address: c/o Senior Counselor, Bellaire High School, Bellaire, TX 77401, tel.: (713) 667-2064

Financial data (yr. ended 05/31/00): Grants paid, $1,200; assets, $20,470 (M); gifts received, $1,100; expenditures, $1,265; qualifying distributions, $1,265.
Limitations: Giving limited to the Bellaire, TX, area.
Application information: Application form required.
Officers: Barry W. Adkins, Pres.; Jean Price, Secy.
Trustees: Joel P. Kay, Charles Wells.
EIN: 760132791

53265
The Cutlass Foundation
P.O. Box 48427
Watauga, TX 76148-0427
Contact: Johnie E. Paslay, Tr.

Donor(s): Paslay Trust.
Financial data (yr. ended 12/31/00): Grants paid, $1,189; assets, $211 (M); gifts received, $1,300; expenditures, $1,208; qualifying distributions, $0.
Limitations: Giving primarily in Fort Worth, TX.
Trustee: Johnie E. Paslay.
EIN: 752791918

53266
Billie Grace Foundation, Inc.
7880 San Felipe St., Ste. 111
Houston, TX 77063-1683   (713) 952-7111
Contact: Charles K. Stephenson, Dir.

Established in 1986 in TX.
Donor(s): Charles K. Stephenson.
Financial data (yr. ended 04/30/02): Grants paid, $1,183; assets, $6,710 (M); gifts received, $100;

expenditures, $1,483; qualifying distributions, $1,183.
Limitations: Giving primarily in Houston, TX.
Application information: Application form not required.
Director: Charles K. Stephenson.
EIN: 742444753

53267
04Arts Foundation
410 E. Arsenal
San Antonio, TX 78204 (210) 226-1101
Contact: Penelope Speier, Pres.

Established in 1995 in TX.
Donor(s): Penelope Gallagher, William Gallagher.
Financial data (yr. ended 12/31/01): Grants paid, $1,172; assets, $16,793 (M); gifts received, $151,396; expenditures, $186,915; qualifying distributions, $1,172.
Limitations: Giving primarily in TX.
Application information: Application form not required.
Officers: Penelope Speier, Pres.
Directors: Wendy W. Atwell, Jon Cochran, Peter Holt, Linda Pace, Alexandra Ruth Weil.
EIN: 742730665

53268
Rejuvenation Outreach Ministries
P.O. Box 60124
Fort Worth, TX 76115

Financial data (yr. ended 11/03/01): Grants paid, $1,153; assets, $0 (M); gifts received, $9,223; expenditures, $1,910; qualifying distributions, $1,153.
Officers: Alice V. Miller, Pres.; Priscilla Jackson, V.P.; Sergio Jackson, Secy.-Treas.
EIN: 752847802

53269
Munoz Christian Foundation, Inc.
P.O. Box 128
Sullivan City, TX 78595-0128
Contact: Frank Munoz, Mgr.

Donor(s): Frank Munoz, Jon Munoz.
Financial data (yr. ended 12/31/01): Grants paid, $1,150; assets, $1 (M); gifts received, $7,267; expenditures, $7,494; qualifying distributions, $1,150.
Limitations: Giving primarily in TX.
Officers: David Munoz, Mgr.; Frank Munoz, Mgr.; Mary Munoz, Mgr.
EIN: 237374255

53270
Champaben Himatlal Sangani Charitable Foundation
2224 Highpoint Dr.
Carrollton, TX 75007

Established in 1999 in TX.
Donor(s): Bharat H. Sangani, Smita Sangani.
Financial data (yr. ended 11/30/01): Grants paid, $1,150; assets, $92,124 (M); gifts received, $1,000; expenditures, $1,458; qualifying distributions, $1,150.
Limitations: Applications not accepted.
Application information: Contributes only to pre-selected organizations.
Officers and Directors:* Bharat H. Sangani,* Pres.; Suresh Sangani,* V.P.; Smita Sangani,* Secy.; Himathal Sangani,* Treas.; Kiran Sangani.
EIN: 752792697

53271
Adams Vision Foundation
1124 Holly Dr.
Carrollton, TX 75010 (972) 394-6859
FAX: (972)394-6859; E-mail: fmsigrp@onlinetodat.com
Contact: G. Edward Adams, Exec. Tr.

Established in 1997 in TX.
Donor(s): Brenda J. Adams, G. Edward Adams, Wendy J. Adams.
Financial data (yr. ended 12/31/00): Grants paid, $1,111; assets, $8,689 (M); gifts received, $3,900; expenditures, $3,226; qualifying distributions, $1,111; giving activities include $25 for programs.
Limitations: Giving primarily in TX.
Publications: Annual report.
Application information: Application form required.
Trustees: Brenda J. Adams, G. Edward Adams, Wendy J. Adams.
EIN: 752687417

53272
Josephine & Forrest Hood Scholarship Fund
2000 N. Conway
Mission, TX 78572-0873
Contact: Charles G. Zey, Tr.

Financial data (yr. ended 12/31/01): Grants paid, $1,100; assets, $47,440 (M); expenditures, $1,479; qualifying distributions, $1,100.
Limitations: Giving limited to residents of Mission, TX.
Application information: Recipients are selected by teachers committee at Mission High School.
Trustees: Medardo De Leon, Charles G. Zey.
EIN: 237087680

53273
Port Arthur Respiratory Disease Trust
(Formerly Port Arthur Unit Texas Tuberculosis Association)
P.O. Box 2307
Port Arthur, TX 77643-2307 (409) 983-4533
Contact: Banker Phares, Tr.

Financial data (yr. ended 06/30/02): Grants paid, $1,093; assets, $20,876 (M); expenditures, $2,408; qualifying distributions, $1,468.
Limitations: Giving limited to Port Arthur, TX.
Application information: Application form required.
Trustee: Banker Phares.
EIN: 746090724

53274
Ward Fund
(Formerly Joe L. Ward Company, Ltd. Charitable Trust)
P.O. Box 7551
Waco, TX 76714-7551

Financial data (yr. ended 12/31/01): Grants paid, $1,050; assets, $21,901 (M); expenditures, $1,076; qualifying distributions, $1,050.
Limitations: Applications not accepted. Giving primarily in Waco, TX.
Application information: Contributes only to pre-selected organizations.
Trustee: Joe L. Ward, Jr.
EIN: 746047138
Codes: TN

53275
One Hundred Club of El Paso
c/o Larry Stockton
2829 Montana Ave., Ste. 201
El Paso, TX 79903-2496 (915) 566-9305
Contact: Larry Stockton

Financial data (yr. ended 03/31/02): Grants paid, $1,020; assets, $67,530 (M); expenditures, $2,310; qualifying distributions, $1,020.
Limitations: Giving limited to El Paso, TX.
Officers: Betty C. Farah, Pres.; George Janzen, V.P.; William Mounce, V.P.
EIN: 237361555

53276
American State Bank Endowed Scholarship Fund for Nursing (LCU and St. Mary's)
c/o American State Bank
1401 Ave. Q
Lubbock, TX 79408-1401
Application address: c/o Lubbock Christian Univ., Div. of Nursing, 5601 W. 19th St., Lubbock, TX 79407

Established in 1993 in TX.
Donor(s): American State Bank.
Financial data (yr. ended 12/31/01): Grants paid, $1,000; assets, $22,039 (M); expenditures, $1,360; qualifying distributions, $1,245.
Limitations: Giving limited to Lubbock, TX.
Application information: Application form required.
Trustee: American State Bank.
EIN: 752474107
Codes: CS, CD

53277
The Blessing Fund Foundation
605 Oak Ln.
Liberty Hill, TX 78642 (512) 515-6044
Contact: Jeanne P. Lindquist, Tr.

Established in 2000 in TX.
Donor(s): Douglas L. Lindquist.
Financial data (yr. ended 12/31/00): Grants paid, $1,000; assets, $3,084 (M); gifts received, $4,000; expenditures, $1,029; qualifying distributions, $1,029.
Limitations: Giving primarily in TX.
Application information: Application form required.
Trustees: Douglas L. Lindquist, Jeanne P. Lindquist.
EIN: 746488591

53278
Buster Brown Memorial Scholarship Fund
2112 W. Front St.
Tyler, TX 75702
Contact: Alice Emmons, Secy.

Financial data (yr. ended 12/31/01): Grants paid, $1,000; assets, $51,688 (M); expenditures, $1,280; qualifying distributions, $1,280.
Limitations: Giving primarily to students residing in TX.
Officers: Gehrie Aten, Co-Chair.; Robert Aten, Co-Chair.; Alice Emmons, Secy.
EIN: 752402922

53279
Virginia Bryan Trust for Aid to the Blind
P.O. Box 162562
Austin, TX 78716-2562 (512) 263-4323

Established in 1994 in LA.
Financial data (yr. ended 04/30/02): Grants paid, $1,000; assets, $142,101 (M); expenditures, $38,866; qualifying distributions, $1,000.
Limitations: Applications not accepted.

53279—TEXAS

Application information: Contributes only to pre-selected organizations.
Trustees: John N. Bryan, Sandra Bryan.
EIN: 582084465

53280
Chris Byrd Memorial Music Scholarship Charitable Trust
25587 Magnolia Rd.
Hockley, TX 77447

Established in 1999 in TX.
Financial data (yr. ended 05/31/01): Grants paid, $1,000; assets, $16,769 (L); gifts received, $6,025; expenditures, $1,759; qualifying distributions, $1,000.
Limitations: Giving primarily in TX.
Trustees: Michael L. Byrd, Peggy Ann Byrd, Phillip T. Raddin.
EIN: 760607832

53281
Raul S. Cantu Family Foundation
c/o Raul S. Cantu
343 W. Houston St., Ste. 912
San Antonio, TX 78205-2109

Established in 1997 in TX.
Donor(s): Raul S. Cantu.
Financial data (yr. ended 12/31/99): Grants paid, $1,000; assets, $2,774 (M); expenditures, $1,923; qualifying distributions, $1,923.
Limitations: Applications not accepted. Giving primarily in San Antonio, TX.
Application information: Contributes only to pre-selected organizations.
Officers: Raul S. Cantu, Pres.; Maria E. Cantu, V.P.; Raul S. Cantu, Sr., V.P.; Richard Cantu, V.P.
EIN: 742849213

53282
Crowder Family Foundation
9806 Inwood Rd.
Dallas, TX 75220

Established in 2000 in TX.
Donor(s): Kevin Crowder, Karen Crowder.
Financial data (yr. ended 12/31/00): Grants paid, $1,000; assets, $5,054 (M); gifts received, $6,500; expenditures, $1,447; qualifying distributions, $1,000.
Limitations: Applications not accepted. Giving primarily in Dallas, TX.
Application information: Contributes only to pre-selected organizations.
Officers: Kevin Crowder, Pres. and Treas.; Karen Crowder, V.P. and Secy.
EIN: 311704739
Codes: TN

53283
Rex Cumming Foundation, Inc.
5375 Waneta Dr.
Dallas, TX 75209

Established in 2000 in TX.
Donor(s): Rex Barron Cumming.
Financial data (yr. ended 06/30/02): Grants paid, $1,000; assets, $11,423 (M); gifts received, $10,000; expenditures, $5,814; qualifying distributions, $1,000.
Officers: Rex Barron Cumming, Pres.; Jacqueline Cumming McKay, Secy.; Linda J. Harrison, Treas.
EIN: 752894512

53284
C. E. Doolin Foundation
c/o Earl L. Doolin
6411 Northaven Rd.
Dallas, TX 75230-3015

Financial data (yr. ended 12/31/01): Grants paid, $1,000; assets, $6,103 (M); gifts received, $1,000; expenditures, $1,005; qualifying distributions, $1,000.
Officers: Earl L. Doolin, Pres.; Kaleta Doolin, V.P.; Charles W. Doolin, Secy.
EIN: 752775603

53285
Doulos Foundation
P.O. Box 1600
San Antonio, TX 78296

Donor(s): D.R. Freiling.
Financial data (yr. ended 12/31/00): Grants paid, $1,000; assets, $640,122 (M); gifts received, $5,390; expenditures, $2,542; qualifying distributions, $1,000.
Limitations: Applications not accepted. Giving primarily in San Antonio, TX.
Application information: Contributes only to pre-selected organizations.
Trustee: D.R. Freiling.
EIN: 742232566

53286
Gary W. Evans Scholarship Trust
8352 County Rd. 410
Navasota, TX 77868-9609

Financial data (yr. ended 03/31/00): Grants paid, $1,000; assets, $9,204 (M); gifts received, $26; expenditures, $1,026; qualifying distributions, $1,000.
Limitations: Applications not accepted. Giving limited to Navasota, TX.
Trustees: James M. Evans, James R. Evans, Ruby D. Evans.
EIN: 742224238

53287
Maurice W. Fox Memorial Scholarship Trust
2412 County Rd. 334
Burnet, TX 78611-4970
Application address: 629 Wyassup Rd., North Stonineton, CT 06359
Contact: Nelda S. Fox Nardone, Tr.

Financial data (yr. ended 12/31/00): Grants paid, $1,000; assets, $4,209 (M); gifts received, $1,000; qualifying distributions, $1,000.
Limitations: Giving limited to residents of North Stonington, CT.
Application information: Application form not required.
Trustees: Sam R. Elam, Nelda S. Fox Nardone.
EIN: 066241133

53288
Golden Rule Foundation
P.O. Box 250
Premont, TX 78375-0250

Established in 1997 in TX.
Donor(s): BC Restaurants, Inc., Bowen Enterprises, Inc.
Financial data (yr. ended 12/31/01): Grants paid, $1,000; assets, $89,268 (M); gifts received, $50,000; expenditures, $1,300; qualifying distributions, $1,000.
Officer: Jennifer J. Bowen, Pres.
EIN: 742701169

53289
Mike Howard Memorial Scholarship Trust
3101 Garland
Decatur, TX 76234
Application address: c/o Principal, Paradise High School, Paradise, TX 76073

Financial data (yr. ended 05/31/01): Grants paid, $1,000; assets, $20,834 (M); gifts received, $270; expenditures, $1,183; qualifying distributions, $1,183.
Limitations: Giving limited to residents of Paradise, TX.
Application information: Application form required.
Trustee: Joyce Ennis.
EIN: 756375964

53290
Jericho Road Ministries
118 W. Cheryl St.
Longview, TX 75604

Donor(s): Charles Bachtell, Dorothy Bachtell.
Financial data (yr. ended 12/31/01): Grants paid, $1,000; assets, $115 (M); gifts received, $1,400; expenditures, $2,690; qualifying distributions, $1,000.
Limitations: Giving primarily in TX.
Officers: Eddie Napps, Pres.; Mary W. Napps, Secy.
Director: Larry Rehnquist.
EIN: 752609555
Codes: TN

53291
Ed B. Johnson, Jr. Scholarship Trust Fund
P.O. Box 540
Graham, TX 76450-0540
Application address: c/o Exec. Dir., Texas A&M Univ. Development Fund, College Station, TX 77841

Financial data (yr. ended 12/31/99): Grants paid, $1,000; assets, $26,641 (M); expenditures, $1,777; qualifying distributions, $1,400.
Limitations: Giving limited to TX.
Application information: Application form required.
Trustee: First National Bank.
EIN: 756272205

53292
Kaamna Foundation
c/o Bhagwan I. Bhatia
6614 Muirfield Cir.
Plano, TX 75093

Financial data (yr. ended 12/31/01): Grants paid, $1,000; assets, $1 (M); gifts received, $1,000; expenditures, $1,000; qualifying distributions, $1,000.
Limitations: Applications not accepted. Giving primarily in India.
Directors: Bhagwan I. Bhatia, Shashi B. Bhatia, Ramesh Singh.
EIN: 752370281

53293
The L & M Charitable Foundation, Inc.
550 W. Texas Ave., Ste. 945
Midland, TX 79701

Established in 2000 in TX.
Financial data (yr. ended 12/31/01): Grants paid, $1,000; assets, $2,107,166 (M); gifts received, $2,200,000; expenditures, $4,792; qualifying distributions, $1,000.
Limitations: Applications not accepted.
Application information: Contributes only to pre-selected organizations.

Officer and Directors:* Richard T. McMillan,* Pres.; Jan Late McMillan, Kirstin Elizabeth McMillan.
EIN: 752874187

53294
Dennis W. McCarthy Foundation
7670 Woodway Dr., Ste. 220
Houston, TX 77063

Established in 1991 in TX.
Financial data (yr. ended 12/31/01): Grants paid, $1,000; assets, $1 (M); expenditures, $1,050; qualifying distributions, $1,000.
Limitations: Applications not accepted. Giving primarily in TX.
Officers: Dennis W. McCarthy, Pres.; Karen Carney, V.P.; Del McCarthy, V.P.; Connie Sigel, V.P.
EIN: 760340904

53295
McDavid Foundation, Inc.
4616 Tryon Rd.
Longview, TX 75605
Application address: 3129 Sleepy Hollow Rd., Falls Church, VA 22042
Contact: Jane C. Harvey, Pres.

Financial data (yr. ended 06/30/01): Grants paid, $1,000; assets, $23,473 (M); expenditures, $1,175; qualifying distributions, $1,000.
Limitations: Giving limited to residents of TX.
Application information: Application form required.
Officer: Jane C. Harvey, Pres.
Directors: Ross McDavid, Robert G. Rogers.
EIN: 752517945

53296
June A. and Peter G. McGuire Family Foundation
5910 N. Central Expwy., Ste. 1355
Dallas, TX 75206

Donor(s): Peter G. McGuire, June A. McGuire.
Financial data (yr. ended 12/31/00): Grants paid, $1,000; assets, $61,508 (M); expenditures, $1,015; qualifying distributions, $1,000.
Limitations: Applications not accepted. Giving primarily in Dallas, TX.
Application information: Contributes only to pre-selected organizations.
Officers and Directors:* Peter G. McGuire,* Pres. and Treas.; June A. McGuire,* V.P. and Secy.; Timothy P. Tehan.
EIN: 752754570

53297
Lavoy and Anne Moore Charitable Foundation
P.O. Box 448
Conroe, TX 77305-0448

Financial data (yr. ended 12/31/01): Grants paid, $1,000; assets, $174,896 (M); gifts received, $4,000; expenditures, $2,844; qualifying distributions, $1,000.
Officers and Trustees:* Arrol Lavoy Moore,* Pres.; Ann G. Moore,* V.P.; Susan Moore Pokorski,* Secy.; Bonnie Moore Hanley,* Treas.; Nancy Moore McLemore.
EIN: 760562352

53298
The Munn Educational Charitable Trust
P.O. Box 65
Junction, TX 76849-0065 (915) 446-2531
Contact: Rob Roy Spiller, Tr.

Financial data (yr. ended 12/31/99): Grants paid, $1,000; assets, $9,302 (M); expenditures, $1,061; qualifying distributions, $1,055.
Limitations: Giving limited to Junction, TX.
Application information: Application form required.
Trustees: Bryan Booth, L.R. Hawkins, Rob Roy Spiller.
EIN: 742330487

53299
Gogineni Sri Ranganayakamma Charitable Foundation
c/o L. Prasad M. Vemulapalli
1026 River Glen W.
San Antonio, TX 78216

Established in 1995 in TX.
Donor(s): L. Prasad M. Vemulapalli, Sudha Vemulapalli.
Financial data (yr. ended 12/31/01): Grants paid, $1,000; assets, $22,809 (M); expenditures, $1,080; qualifying distributions, $1,000.
Limitations: Applications not accepted.
Application information: Contributes only to pre-selected organizations.
Officers and Directors:* L. Prasad M. Vemulapalli,* Pres.; Sudha Vemulapalli,* Secy.; Ravi Prasad Vemulapalli.
EIN: 742769389

53300
Olga Schawe Trust
c/o Wells Fargo Bank Texas, N.A.
40 N.E. Loop 410, Ste. 20
San Antonio, TX 78216

Financial data (yr. ended 12/31/01): Grants paid, $1,000; assets, $36,384 (M); expenditures, $1,914; qualifying distributions, $1,318.
Limitations: Applications not accepted. Giving primarily in TX.
Application information: Unsolicited requests for funds not accepted.
Trustees: Wells Fargo Bank Texas, N.A.
EIN: 756187611

53301
Schoenvogel Family Foundation, Inc.
23 Forest Dr.
College Station, TX 77840-2312

Established in 1998 in TX.
Financial data (yr. ended 12/31/01): Grants paid, $1,000; assets, $16,026 (M); expenditures, $1,153; qualifying distributions, $1,000.
Limitations: Applications not accepted.
Application information: Contributes only to pre-selected organizations.
Officer: Clarence W. Schoenvogel, Pres.
EIN: 742885548

53302
Stephenson-Perona Athletic Scholarship
706 Kelly St.
Fairfield, TX 75840-0238
Application address: c/o Don Posey, Principal, Fairfield High School, Fairfield, TX 75840, tel.: (903) 389-4177

Financial data (yr. ended 06/30/99): Grants paid, $1,000; assets, $53,033 (M); gifts received, $2,451; expenditures, $2,283; qualifying distributions, $2,283.
Limitations: Giving limited to Fairfield, TX.
Application information: Application form required.
Officers: Christina Perona, Secy.; Richard White, Treas.; John R. Perona, Admin.
EIN: 742177081

53303
Evin Thayer Scholarship Fund
2643 Colquitt St.
Houston, TX 77098
Contact: Evin Thayer, Pres.

Financial data (yr. ended 08/31/00): Grants paid, $1,000; assets, $2,552 (M); gifts received, $44,855; expenditures, $43,870; qualifying distributions, $43,870; giving activities include $42,870 for programs.
Limitations: Giving limited to the greater Houston, TX, area.
Officers: Evin Thayer, Pres.; Todd J. Ramos, Secy.
EIN: 760591037

53304
The Cathy and Dwight Thompson Foundation
1230 Yaupon Valley Rd.
Austin, TX 78746

Established in 1999 in TX.
Donor(s): Catherine P. Thompson.
Financial data (yr. ended 12/31/00): Grants paid, $1,000; assets, $1,377,029 (M); gifts received, $708,983; expenditures, $1,000; qualifying distributions, $1,000.
Limitations: Applications not accepted.
Application information: Contributes only to pre-selected organizations.
Officers: Dwight D. Thompson, Pres.; Debra Paxton, V.P.; Catherine P. Thompson, Secy.-Treas.
EIN: 756563188

53305
Vietnam Veterans of Southeast Texas
5115 Dawn Dr.
Beaumont, TX 77706-6807

Established in 1992 in TX.
Financial data (yr. ended 12/31/01): Grants paid, $1,000; assets, $5,003 (M); gifts received, $6,157; expenditures, $1,350; qualifying distributions, $1,000.
Limitations: Giving primarily to residents of Beaumont, TX.
Application information: No grants paid in 1998. Application form required.
Officers: Robert Matherne, Pres.; Chester Lafley, V.P.; Mary Ann Burbidge, Secy.; Thomas C. Gibson, Treas.
EIN: 760363885

53306
Waco Founder Lions Foundation
1716 N. 42nd St.
Waco, TX 76710 (254) 776-5341

Established in 1989.
Financial data (yr. ended 06/30/01): Grants paid, $1,000; assets, $33,433 (M); gifts received, $130; expenditures, $1,184; qualifying distributions, $1,000.
Limitations: Giving primarily in TX.
Officers: Tim Nemec, Pres.; Bob Kinney, 1st V.P.; Curtis Holland, 2nd V.P.; C.C. Sirkel, Jr., 3rd V.P.; John Householder, Secy.; Sam Griffin, Treas.
EIN: 742567483

53307
The Weber Family Foundation
c/o Timothy M. & Donna H. Weber
2901 Stanford Ave.
Dallas, TX 75225

Established in 1999 in TX.
Donor(s): Timothy M. Weber, Donna H. Weber.
Financial data (yr. ended 12/31/01): Grants paid, $1,000; assets, $157,229 (M); gifts received, $44,720; expenditures, $5,358; qualifying distributions, $1,000.

Limitations: Giving primarily in Dallas, TX.
Directors: Anthony R. Weber, Donna H. Weber, Timothy M. Weber.
EIN: 752853347

53308
David Alan Wetsel Medical Assistance Fund for Persons with AIDS
4202 Tomberra Way
Dallas, TX 75220-5051
Contact: Carole Wetsel, Pres.

Established in 1994 in TX.
Financial data (yr. ended 11/30/00): Grants paid, $1,000; assets, $0 (M); expenditures, $2,327; qualifying distributions, $1,000; giving activities include $1,000 for programs.
Application information: Application form required.
Officers and Directors:* Carole Wetsel,* Pres.; Lisa W. Otero,* V.P. and Treas.; David P. Parry,* Secy.
EIN: 752569015

53309
Imogene Woolverton Educational Trust
c/o Peggy Haldeman
7216 FM 1266
Mabank, TX 75147

Established in 2000.
Financial data (yr. ended 12/31/01): Grants paid, $1,000; assets, $26,631 (M); expenditures, $1,000; qualifying distributions, $982.
Trustees: Max Callahan, Sandra Dunlap, Peggy Haldeman, Billy Montgomery, Maxie Turner.
EIN: 752877768

53310
Ruben Foundation
1818 Old Oak Dr.
Arlington, TX 76012

Donor(s): B. Hochstein, R. Hochstein.
Financial data (yr. ended 11/30/01): Grants paid, $978; assets, $30,893 (M); gifts received, $4,300; expenditures, $2,957; qualifying distributions, $978.
Limitations: Applications not accepted. Giving primarily in TX.
Application information: Contributes only to pre-selected organizations.
Trustees: B. Hochstein, R. Hochstein.
EIN: 751575295

53311
Austin Alpha Foundation
2111 Chicon St.
Austin, TX 78722-2430
Contact: Samuel E. Robertson, Chair.

Established around 1984.
Financial data (yr. ended 12/31/01): Grants paid, $960; assets, $146,860 (M); gifts received, $9,015; expenditures, $20,770; qualifying distributions, $960.
Limitations: Giving primarily in TX.
Officers and Directors:* Samuel E. Robertson,* Chair.; Kenneth Evans, Treas.; Allen M. Johnson, Secy.; Charles Atkins.
EIN: 742220579

53312
Edgar and Linda Perry Foundation
9390 Research Blvd., Ste. 1-410
Austin, TX 78759

Donor(s): Edgar Perry, Linda Perry.
Financial data (yr. ended 05/31/00): Grants paid, $925; assets, $427,011 (M); gifts received, $142,000; expenditures, $36,760; qualifying distributions, $13,108; giving activities include $11,942 for programs.
Limitations: Applications not accepted. Giving primarily in TX.
Application information: Contributes only to pre-selected organizations.
Officer: Edgar Perry, Pres. and Treas.
Directors: Chris Perry, Linda Perry, Ryan Perry.
EIN: 742335903

53313
Eternal Church of Christ, Inc.
5120 Urban Crest Rd.
Dallas, TX 75227-1552

Financial data (yr. ended 12/31/01): Grants paid, $909; assets, $15 (M); gifts received, $965; expenditures, $964; qualifying distributions, $909.
Limitations: Giving primarily in TX.
Trustee: Jack Barnes.
EIN: 751575940

53314
Citation Foundation
5070 S. Collins, Ste. 207
Arlington, TX 76018 (817) 992-9122
Contact: Larry D. Singley, Tr.

Established in 2000.
Financial data (yr. ended 12/31/00): Grants paid, $905; assets, $20,195 (M); gifts received, $22,600; expenditures, $905; qualifying distributions, $905.
Limitations: Giving primarily in Arlington, TX.
Trustees: Larry D. Singley, Shelia G. Singley.
EIN: 912172428

53315
Lenora L. Allen - Marie Herring Memorial Trust
(also known as Allen-Herring Memorial Trust)
c/o Bank One Trust Co., N.A.
P.O. Box 2050
Fort Worth, TX 76113
Application address: P.O. Box 21116, Shreveport, LA 71154-0001
Contact: Stephen Vickers, Trust Off., Bank One, Trust Co., N.A.

Financial data (yr. ended 12/31/99): Grants paid, $900; assets, $92,828 (M); expenditures, $5,426; qualifying distributions, $1,111.
Limitations: Giving limited to Caddo and De Soto parishes, LA.
Trustee: Bank One Trust Co., N.A.
EIN: 726028842

53316
Dr. Garcia's Share
P.O. Box 821388-314
Dallas, TX 75382-1388

Established in 1990.
Donor(s): Catalina E. Garcia.
Financial data (yr. ended 09/30/01): Grants paid, $900; assets, $1,501 (M); gifts received, $2,325; expenditures, $2,338; qualifying distributions, $900.
Limitations: Giving primarily in TX.
Application information: Application form not required.
Officer and Directors:* Catalina E. Garcia,* Exec. Dir.; Rollin Gary.
EIN: 752283332

53317
Southwest Digestive Diseases Foundation
5242 Park Ln.
Dallas, TX 75220
Contact: Clara L. Campbell, Pres.

Established in 1970 in TX.
Donor(s): Claire P. Campbell, Clara L. Campbell, Hugh P. Campbell, Sr.‡
Financial data (yr. ended 12/31/01): Grants paid, $900; assets, $643,709 (M); expenditures, $2,587; qualifying distributions, $900.
Limitations: Giving primarily in Dallas, TX.
Officers: Clara L. Campbell, Pres.; Claire P. Campbell, V.P.; Hugh P. Campbell, Jr., Secy.
Director: Carol Ann Campbell Conway.
EIN: 237086925

53318
The W. I. & Inez Davis Foundation
107 John C. Rogers Dr.
Center, TX 75935

Established in 1994 in TX.
Financial data (yr. ended 12/31/01): Grants paid, $875; assets, $9,443 (M); expenditures, $940; qualifying distributions, $875.
Limitations: Applications not accepted.
Application information: Contributes only to pre-selected organizations.
Trustees: Neilson Davis, Cynthia D. Griffin, Guy W. Griffin.
EIN: 752574976

53319
Dlabal Foundation
P.O. Box 163237
Austin, TX 78730 (512) 346-2050
Contact: Paul W. Dlabal, M.D., Tr.

Established in 1996 in TX.
Donor(s): Paul Dlabal, M.D.
Financial data (yr. ended 12/31/99): Grants paid, $875; assets, $74,254 (M); gifts received, $19,217; expenditures, $3,979; qualifying distributions, $875.
Application information: Application form not required.
Trustee: Paul W. Dlabal, M.D.
EIN: 742766923

53320
Simon Kratzenstein Fund
155 Kush Ln.
Corpus Christi, TX 78404-1611

Donor(s): Madelyn Posner Loeb.
Financial data (yr. ended 08/31/01): Grants paid, $865; assets, $15,784 (M); expenditures, $1,047; qualifying distributions, $865.
Limitations: Applications not accepted. Giving primarily in Corpus Christi, TX.
Application information: Contributes only to pre-selected organizations.
Trustee: Madelyn Posner Loeb.
EIN: 746052493

53321
Chinese Benevolent Society of El Paso
P.O. Box 971866
El Paso, TX 79997-1866

Established in 1985 in TX.
Financial data (yr. ended 12/31/01): Grants paid, $850; assets, $37,866 (M); expenditures, $6,983; qualifying distributions, $832.
Limitations: Giving limited to El Paso, TX.
Officers and Directors:* M.T. Lam,* Chair.; Maureen Lam,* Pres. and V.P.; Martha Yee,* Secy.; Gene Wong,* Treas.; Shinping Chiji, Ben K. Chow, Seam Chow, H.S. Oey, Paul Quon, Carmen Sang.
EIN: 237064037

53322
S. J. Cook Foundation Charitable Trust
214 S. Rike St.
Farmersville, TX 75442

Donor(s): Wilma Howell.

Financial data (yr. ended 12/31/99): Grants paid, $825; assets, $21,882 (M); gifts received, $6,860; expenditures, $1,118; qualifying distributions, $1,100.
Limitations: Giving primarily in Farmersville, TX.
Trustees: Edwin O. Cartwright, Wilma C. Howell.
EIN: 752708604

53323
National Center for Dispute Settlement
2777 Stemmons Fwy., Ste. 1452
Dallas, TX 75207-2235

Established in 1996 in MI.
Financial data (yr. ended 12/31/01): Grants paid, $800; assets, $2,991,056 (M); expenditures, $4,764,341; qualifying distributions, $204,085.
Limitations: Applications not accepted.
Application information: Contributes only to pre-selected organizations.
Officer: Edward Hartfield, Exec. Dir.
EIN: 521540079

53324
Elburt Fund
c/o Burton Gilliland
P.O. Box 600106
Dallas, TX 75360-0106

Donor(s): Burton Gilliland, Eloise Gilliland.
Financial data (yr. ended 08/31/01): Grants paid, $750; assets, $28,032 (M); expenditures, $1,383; qualifying distributions, $750.
Limitations: Applications not accepted. Giving primarily in the Dallas and Fort Worth, TX, areas.
Application information: Contributes only to pre-selected organizations.
Trustees: Jean Gilliland Elliott, Burton Gilliland, Eloise Gilliland, Ann B. Gilliland Roberts.
EIN: 756015670

53325
Fugit Gospel Foundation, Inc.
412 N. Texas Ave.
Odessa, TX 79761-5198

Donor(s): Gerald K. Fugit.
Financial data (yr. ended 09/30/01): Grants paid, $750; assets, $58,618 (M); gifts received, $1,430; expenditures, $1,911; qualifying distributions, $1,911.
Limitations: Giving primarily in TX.
Officers and Directors:* Gerald K. Fugit,* Pres.; Deborah Fugit,* V.P.; Bette Fugit,* Secy.
EIN: 751327349

53326
Lang Charities, Inc.
332 W. Sunset Rd., Ste. 10
San Antonio, TX 78209

Financial data (yr. ended 12/31/01): Grants paid, $750; assets, $14,273 (M); expenditures, $2,012; qualifying distributions, $750.
Limitations: Applications not accepted. Giving limited to San Antonio, TX.
Application information: Contributes only to pre-selected organizations.
Trustees: Neil Boldrick, Jr., Stephen Lang, Jeanne Mathews.
EIN: 746047889

53327
Luminaria Charitable Foundation
5207 Shady River Dr.
Houston, TX 77056

Established in 1999 in TX.
Donor(s): John S. Parsley.
Financial data (yr. ended 12/31/00): Grants paid, $750; assets, $11,009 (M); expenditures, $1,313; qualifying distributions, $750.

Limitations: Applications not accepted. Giving primarily in Houston, TX.
Application information: Contributes only to pre-selected organizations.
Officers: John S. Parsley, Pres. and Treas.; Nancy Nolan Parsley, V.P.; Deborah A. Peacock, Secy.
EIN: 760608192

53328
Marrs McLean Scholarship Trust
P.O. Box 65
Junction, TX 76849-0065 (915) 446-2531
Contact: L.R. Hawkins, Tr.

Donor(s): Fred L. Dill, Sr.
Financial data (yr. ended 12/31/01): Grants paid, $750; assets, $22,742 (M); expenditures, $827; qualifying distributions, $790.
Limitations: Giving limited to Junction, TX.
Application information: Application form required.
Trustees: K. Cowsert, L.R. Hawkins, John R. Loeffler.
EIN: 746062589

53329
L. R. Sharp, Jr. Foundation
7236 Alexander Dr.
Dallas, TX 75214 (214) 821-9237

Financial data (yr. ended 12/31/01): Grants paid, $750; assets, $30,441 (M); expenditures, $840; qualifying distributions, $746.
Limitations: Giving limited to residents of Panola County, TX.
Officer: Thomas H. Sharp, Mgr.
EIN: 752197579

53330
Trotter Foundation
1215 Rock Springs Rd.
Duncanville, TX 75137-2839

Financial data (yr. ended 12/31/01): Grants paid, $735; assets, $14,314 (M); expenditures, $743; qualifying distributions, $735.
Limitations: Applications not accepted. Giving primarily in TX.
Application information: Contributes only to pre-selected organizations.
Officers: Ide P. Trotter, Pres. and Treas.; Ruth T. Penick, V.P.; Luella H. Trotter, Secy.
EIN: 752201352

53331
The Oneal Foundation
4245 Kemp, Ste. 920
Wichita Falls, TX 76308

Donor(s): Cora Maud Oneal.
Financial data (yr. ended 07/31/99): Grants paid, $722; assets, $19,079 (M); expenditures, $1,513; qualifying distributions, $722.
Limitations: Applications not accepted. Giving primarily in TX.
Application information: Contributes only to pre-selected organizations.
Trustee: James H. Hard, Jr.
EIN: 756059633

53332
Ophthalmic Research Foundation
11025 Granbury Cove
Temple, TX 76502
Contact: Henry Hacker, Tr.

Financial data (yr. ended 12/31/01): Grants paid, $700; assets, $1,524 (M); expenditures, $715; qualifying distributions, $700.
Trustees: Henry Hacker, Hope Schuyler Hacker.
EIN: 223693261

53333
Mary Ida Carpenter School Fund
2700 W. 15th St.
Plano, TX 75075-7524
Contact: John Muns, Pres.

Donor(s): Mr. Carpenter.‡
Financial data (yr. ended 10/31/01): Grants paid, $650; assets, $10,367 (M); expenditures, $737; qualifying distributions, $650.
Limitations: Giving limited to resident of Plano, TX.
Officers and Directors:* John Muns,* Pres.; Mary Beth King,* V.P.; Duncan Webb,* Secy.; Gary Base, Allan Bird, Scott Carpenter, Ralph Snow, Melody Timinsky, and 4 additional directors.
EIN: 756253207

53334
The Cody Ryan Hutson Foundation
P.O. Box 2149
Longview, TX 75606

Established in 1989 in TX.
Financial data (yr. ended 06/30/00): Grants paid, $645; assets, $26,557 (M); gifts received, $1,385; expenditures, $645; qualifying distributions, $645.
Limitations: Giving limited to TX.
Application information: Application form required.
Officer: Sally Bodenheim Maledon, Pres.
Director: James I. Calk.
EIN: 752304040

53335
The Kings Foundation
P.O. Box 27333
Austin, TX 78755-2333

Donor(s): William Daniel Burleson, David L. Ferguson, Danaye Properties.
Financial data (yr. ended 12/31/99): Grants paid, $615; assets, $11,826 (M); gifts received, $2,662; expenditures, $914; qualifying distributions, $914.
Limitations: Applications not accepted. Giving primarily in TX.
Application information: Contributes only to pre-selected organizations.
Officers and Directors:* William Daniel Burleson,* Pres. and Treas.; David L. Ferguson,* V.P.; Faye B. Horton,* V.P.
EIN: 742412375

53336
M. S. Wells Paducah Scholarship Fund
c/o Fort Worth National Bank
P.O. Box 310
Paducah, TX 79248-0310

Financial data (yr. ended 12/31/99): Grants paid, $613; assets, $10,343 (M); expenditures, $692; qualifying distributions, $613.
Limitations: Giving limited to Paducah, TX.
Application information: Application form not required.
Trustees: John Ferguson, Lindy Jordan, Randall Ryan.
EIN: 756057014

53337
Alpha Xi Delta Foundation of Texas, Inc.
13630 Littlecrest Ln.
Dallas, TX 75234
Application address: 1230 Eagle Rock Cove, Austin, TX 75750
Contact: Maridy Dandeneau

Financial data (yr. ended 12/31/99): Grants paid, $600; assets, $17,735 (M); gifts received, $100; expenditures, $619; qualifying distributions, $613.
Limitations: Giving limited to residents of TX.

53337—TEXAS

Officers: Mrs. Ronnie Erwin, Pres.; Mrs. Jeffrey Caffee, V.P.; Michele Johnson, Secy.; Mrs. Ronald Doerler, Treas.
EIN: 746053460

53338
Buddy Johnson Memorial Scholarship
8308 Tecumseh Dr.
Austin, TX 78753-5745 (512) 339-9000
Contact: Chloe R. Johnson, Chair.

Established in 1991 in TX.
Financial data (yr. ended 12/31/01): Grants paid, $600; assets, $2,549 (M); expenditures, $605; qualifying distributions, $600.
Limitations: Giving limited to residents of TX.
Application information: Application form required.
Officers: Chloe R. Johnson, Chair.; Julia Moake, Vice-Chair.; Kaye Wilson, Secy.-Treas.
EIN: 742638186

53339
Lomond Foundation
3122 San Sebastian Dr.
Carrollton, TX 75006 (972) 436-4595
Contact: Michael C. Donohoe, Tr.

Established in 1999 in TX.
Financial data (yr. ended 12/31/01): Grants paid, $600; assets, $12,504 (M); gifts received, $12,000; expenditures, $605; qualifying distributions, $600.
Application information: Application form required.
Trustee: Michael C. Donohoe.
EIN: 752849478

53340
Henry L. and Josephine Smith Scholarship Foundation, Inc.
207 N.E. 7th Ave.
Mineral Wells, TX 76067 (940) 325-6858
Contact: Rev. Henry L. Smith, Sr., Pres.

Established in 1988 in TX.
Financial data (yr. ended 12/31/01): Grants paid, $600; assets, $4,521 (M); gifts received, $845; expenditures, $609; qualifying distributions, $600.
Limitations: Giving limited to TX.
Officers: Rev. Henry L. Smith, Sr., Pres.; Henry L. Smith, Jr., V.P.; Lilian Small, Secy.; Harry Small, Treas.
EIN: 752220834

53341
Elma Dill Russell Spencer Foundation
c/o Jefferson State Bank
P.O Box 5190
San Antonio, TX 78201

Financial data (yr. ended 12/31/01): Grants paid, $575; assets, $12,029 (M); expenditures, $2,039; qualifying distributions, $575.
Limitations: Applications not accepted. Giving limited to San Antonio, TX.
Application information: Contributes only to pre-selected organizations.
Officers and Trustees:* Steve C. Lewis,* Pres. and Treas.; Ralph Langley,* V.P.; Marion Schroeder, Secy.; Emerson Banack.
EIN: 746060515

53342
Stevens Family Charitable Foundation
204 Walter St.
Yoakum, TX 77995-1720

Established in 1993 in TX.
Donor(s): Effie Stevens.

Financial data (yr. ended 12/31/99): Grants paid, $575; assets, $24,237 (M); expenditures, $1,100; qualifying distributions, $575.
Limitations: Applications not accepted. Giving primarily in southern TX.
Application information: Contributes only to pre-selected organizations.
Officers: Effie Stevens, Pres.; Ardie Ray Stevens, V.P. and Treas.; Zenith Stevens, Secy.
EIN: 742676026

53343
Crosby Foundation
c/o Gary C. Smith, C.P.A.
5935 Old Bullard Rd., Ste. 204
Tyler, TX 75703

Financial data (yr. ended 11/30/01): Grants paid, $560; assets, $10,393 (M); gifts received, $18; expenditures, $569; qualifying distributions, $560.
Limitations: Applications not accepted.
Application information: Contributes only to pre-selected organizations.
Trustee: Dexter Crosby.
EIN: 237164679

53344
The Maxine Henley Scholarship Fund
P.O. Drawer 836
George West, TX 78022
Application address: c/o Selection Comm., P.O. Drawer L., George West, TX 78022

Financial data (yr. ended 12/31/01): Grants paid, $550; assets, $15,698 (M); gifts received, $50; expenditures, $550; qualifying distributions, $550.
Limitations: Giving limited to George West, TX.
Application information: Application form required.
Trustees: Travis L. Martin, David Nicholson, J.R. Schneider.
EIN: 742311275

53345
Parker Family Foundation
P.O. Box MWH
Wichita Falls, TX 76307-7509
Application address: P.O. Box 285, Byers, TX 76357
Contact: Joe J. Parker, Jr., V.P.

Financial data (yr. ended 06/30/02): Grants paid, $550; assets, $22,200 (M); expenditures, $961; qualifying distributions, $550.
Limitations: Giving primarily in TX.
Application information: Application form not required.
Officers: Joe J. Parker, Sr., Pres. and Treas.; Joseph N. Sherrill, Jr., V.P. and Secy.; Joe J. Parker, Jr., V.P.
EIN: 751554760

53346
Clark Cancer Foundation
4024 Virginia Pine Dr.
Carrollton, TX 75010 (972) 459-5909
Contact: Theresia D. Clark, Tr.

Established in 2000 in TX.
Donor(s): Theresia D. Clark.
Financial data (yr. ended 12/31/00): Grants paid, $520; assets, $4,608 (M); gifts received, $10,000; expenditures, $871; qualifying distributions, $871.
Limitations: Giving primarily in Dallas, TX.
Application information: Application form required.
Trustees: Leonard A. Clark, Theresia D. Clark.
EIN: 752849603

53347
American Society for Hispanic Art Historical Studies
(also known as ASHAHS)
c/o Southern Methodist University
Division of Art History, Owen 1630
Dallas, TX 75275-0356
Contact: Pamela A. Patton, Secy.

Established in 1974.
Financial data (yr. ended 12/31/01): Grants paid, $500; assets, $1,457 (M); expenditures, $1,388; qualifying distributions, $0.
Limitations: Giving on a national basis.
Officer and Executive Committee Members:*
Pamela A. Patton,* Secy.; Karen R. Mathews, Susan V. Webster.
EIN: 510163990

53348
Bedrock Foundation
c/o James C. Smith
8235 Douglas Ave., Ste. 420
Dallas, TX 75225

Established in 2000 in TX.
Donor(s): James C. Smith, Cynthia F. Smith.
Financial data (yr. ended 12/31/01): Grants paid, $500; assets, $1,557,076 (M); gifts received, $900,000; expenditures, $505; qualifying distributions, $500.
Limitations: Applications not accepted.
Application information: Contributes only to pre-selected organizations.
Officers and Trustees:* James C. Smith,* Pres.; Cynthia F. Smith,* V.P.; James F. Gallivan,* Secy.-Treas.
EIN: 752903853

53349
Kenneth C. English Family Foundation
6 Glenmeadow Ct.
Dallas, TX 75225

Established in 2001 in TX.
Donor(s): Kenneth C. English.
Financial data (yr. ended 12/31/01): Grants paid, $500; assets, $1,000,125 (M); gifts received, $1,000,000; expenditures, $774; qualifying distributions, $500.
Limitations: Applications not accepted. Giving primarily in TX.
Application information: Contributes only to pre-selected organizations.
Officers: Kenneth C. English, Pres. and Treas.; Mamie English, V.P.; Wanda K. Gass, Secy.
EIN: 752967910

53350
A. B. Gilbert Foundation
89606 Interstate Hwy. 20
Santo, TX 76472-3815
Application address: P.O. Box 127, Santo, TX 76472-0127
Contact: A.B. Gilbert, Dir.

Established in 1998 in TX.
Donor(s): A.B. Gilbert.
Financial data (yr. ended 12/31/01): Grants paid, $500; assets, $207,329 (M); expenditures, $2,155; qualifying distributions, $500.
Application information: Application form required.
Director: A.B. Gilbert.
EIN: 752825884

53351
Crystal Gomes Sunshine Foundation for Academic Excellence
P.O. Box 15650
Amarillo, TX 79105
Application address: 21573 E. Illinois, Rt. 116, Farmington, IL 61531, tel.: (309) 245-2559
Contact: Crystal A. Gomes, Tr.

Established in 2000 in IL and TX.
Financial data (yr. ended 12/31/01): Grants paid, $500; assets, $51,845 (M); gifts received, $1,000; expenditures, $787; qualifying distributions, $500.
Limitations: Giving limited to Fulton, Knox, Peoria, and Tazewell counties, IL, and the top 26 counties of the TX panhandle region.
Application information: Application form required.
Trustees: J. Michael Connor, Crystal A. Gomes.
EIN: 752863570

53352
Angela Marie Hussenoeder Memorial
2220 Westcreek Ln., Ste. 91E
Houston, TX 77027

Established in 2000 in TX.
Financial data (yr. ended 12/31/00): Grants paid, $500; assets, $4,537 (M); gifts received, $5,802; expenditures, $875; qualifying distributions, $3,778.
Limitations: Applications not accepted. Giving primarily in NE.
Officer: Stefan A. Hussenoeder, Mgr.
Directors: Guenter Hussenoeder, Sabrina King.
EIN: 760623323

53353
The Insurance Alliance Foundation
(Formerly Houstoun, Woodard, Gentle, Tomforde & Anderson, Inc.)
1776 Yorktown St., Ste. 200
Houston, TX 77056

Established in 2000 in TX.
Donor(s): The Insurance Alliance.
Financial data (yr. ended 06/30/01): Grants paid, $500; assets, $120,466 (M); gifts received, $125,000; expenditures, $1,782; qualifying distributions, $500.
Limitations: Applications not accepted. Giving primarily in Washington, DC.
Application information: Contributes only to pre-selected organizations.
Officers: James W. Tomforde, Pres.; Rock N. Houstoun, V.P.; E. Bryan Gentle, Secy.-Treas.
EIN: 760655083
Codes: CS, TN

53354
John and Elizabeth Kassab Foundation
c/o Bruce Kassab
P.O. Box 852268
Mesquite, TX 75185-2268

Established in 1999.
Donor(s): John Kassab.
Financial data (yr. ended 12/31/01): Grants paid, $500; assets, $6,789 (M); expenditures, $2,952; qualifying distributions, $500.
Limitations: Applications not accepted.
Application information: Contributes only to pre-selected organizations.
Trustee: Bruce Kassab.
EIN: 752827077

53355
Nasjiwan Kooner Foundation
5516 Lindsey Dr.
Plano, TX 75093

Established in 2001 in TX.
Donor(s): Karanjit S. Kooner.
Financial data (yr. ended 12/31/01): Grants paid, $500; assets, $11,466 (M); gifts received, $26,015; expenditures, $12,436; qualifying distributions, $12,436.
Limitations: Applications not accepted.
Application information: Contributes only to pre-selected organizations.
Director: Karanjit S. Kooner.
EIN: 752886612

53356
The Lord's Fund
c/o Jenkens & Gilchrist
1800 Frost Bank Twr.
San Antonio, TX 78205 (210) 246-5648
FAX: (210) 246-5999
Contact: Larry Berkman, Secy.-Treas.

Established in 1997 in TX.
Donor(s): William Lance Berkman.
Financial data (yr. ended 12/31/00): Grants paid, $500; assets, $101,393 (M); gifts received, $80; expenditures, $1,461; qualifying distributions, $500.
Limitations: Giving primarily in TX.
Officer: Larry Berkman, Secy.-Treas.
Trustees: Cynthia Ann Berkman, William Lance Berkman, George Cozart.
EIN: 742879125

53357
Troy Post Foundation
10455 N. Central Expwy., Ste. 109-212
Dallas, TX 75231 (972) 661-9003
Contact: Troy V. Post, Chair.

Donor(s): Troy Post.
Financial data (yr. ended 12/31/01): Grants paid, $500; assets, $7,236 (M); expenditures, $956; qualifying distributions, $500.
Limitations: Giving primarily in Dallas, TX.
Officers and Directors:* Troy V. Post,* Chair.; E. Lou Post,* Pres.; John A. Post,* Secy.; Richard P. Catalano,* Treas.
EIN: 756041926

53358
The Presbyterian Church Local Fund
(also known as Pierce and Marguerite Hoggett Scholarship Fund)
P.O. Box 82
Junction, TX 76849-0082
Application address: 105 Valley View, Junction, TX 76849, tel.: (915) 446-3554
Contact: Charles L. Hagood, Jr., Tr.

Financial data (yr. ended 12/31/01): Grants paid, $500; assets, $9,246 (M); expenditures, $548; qualifying distributions, $536.
Limitations: Giving limited to Junction, TX.
Application information: Application form required.
Trustees: Charles L. Hagood, Jr., Jack C. Hoggett, Jack C. Hoggett, Jr.
EIN: 742232542

53359
The Benjamin V. Salazar Memorial Fund
6317 Ridgewood Dr.
Amarillo, TX 79109-6542

Financial data (yr. ended 12/31/00): Grants paid, $500; assets, $108 (M); gifts received, $600; expenditures, $801; qualifying distributions, $500.

Limitations: Applications not accepted. Giving limited to Amarillo, TX.
Application information: Unsolicited requests for funds not accepted.
Officers and Directors:* Joyce Chuachingco, M.D.,* Pres.; Judi Synek,* Secy.; Helen Botsonis, Arturo Carrillo, M.D., Janice Cross, Ibis Galatas Gutierrez, M.D., Ramon Lopez, M.D., Dean Maglinte, M.D.
EIN: 752468846

53360
Beulah Voigt Memorial Scholarship
6958 Walling Ln.
Dallas, TX 75231-7308 (214) 343-1898
Contact: Kimberly Brannon, Pres.

Established in 1998 in TX.
Donor(s): Kimberly Brannon, Joe Brannon.
Financial data (yr. ended 12/31/00): Grants paid, $500; assets, $3,547 (M); expenditures, $764; qualifying distributions, $764.
Limitations: Giving primarily in Peotone, IL.
Application information: Application form required.
Officers and Directors:* Kimberly Brannon,* Pres.; Joe Brannon, Secy.; Doug Bohnsack, Kathy Bohnsack, Janet Robbins, Mary Robbins, Tim Robbins, Kris Roberson.
EIN: 752833425

53361
James Sterling Schalk Memorial Trust
P.O. Box 1680
Wichita Falls, TX 76307

Financial data (yr. ended 09/30/01): Grants paid, $488; assets, $11,475 (M); expenditures, $488; qualifying distributions, $488.
Limitations: Applications not accepted.
Application information: Contributes only to pre-selected organizations.
Trustees: John T. Schalk, Susan Schalk.
EIN: 752018511

53362
The John & Stephen Appleton Foundation, Inc.
6801 Snider Plz., Ste. 220
Dallas, TX 75205

Established in 1986 in TX.
Donor(s): John S. Appleton, Stephen Appleton.
Financial data (yr. ended 12/31/01): Grants paid, $487; assets, $19,412 (M); expenditures, $1,480; qualifying distributions, $487.
Limitations: Giving primarily in the greater metropolitan Dallas, TX, area.
Application information: No phone solicitations; applicants must be affiliated or administered by the Presbyterian Church. Application form required.
Directors: Deborah S. Appleton, John S. Appleton, Gina D. Gibbs.
EIN: 752172075

53363
The Robert A. & Marianne S. Gwinn Family Foundation
3321 Beverly Dr.
Dallas, TX 75205 (214) 698-4100
Contact: Robert A. Gwin, Pres.

Established in 1998 in TX.
Financial data (yr. ended 12/31/00): Grants paid, $400; assets, $400,525 (M); gifts received, $27,525; expenditures, $5,983; qualifying distributions, $5,681.
Officers: Robert A. Gwin, Pres.; Marianne S. Gwinn, V.P.; Stephen W. Gwinn, Secy.-Treas.
EIN: 752769152

53364
Virginia Gallogly Levine Trust
c/o John R. Gallogly
51 S. Piney Plains Cir.
The Woodlands, TX 77382-1134

Financial data (yr. ended 12/31/01): Grants paid, $400; assets, $12,218 (M); expenditures, $409; qualifying distributions, $409.
Limitations: Applications not accepted. Giving limited to MS.
Application information: Unsolicited requests for funds not accepted.
Trustees: John R. Gallogly, Sr. M. Poulinus Oakes, Sr. Elise Todd.
EIN: 646173980

53365
Catherine C. Wahrmund Foundation
297 Airport Ridge
Kerrville, TX 78028-1750
Contact: Catherine C. Wahrmund, Pres.

Financial data (yr. ended 12/31/00): Grants paid, $400; assets, $4,415 (M); expenditures, $425; qualifying distributions, $425.
Limitations: Giving primarily in Yelm, WA.
Officers: Catherine C. Wahrmund, Pres.; Robert Wahrmund, Treas.
Trustees: Jane Diaz de Leon, Anne Wahrmund, Jeff Wahrmund.
EIN: 742860558

53366
The Arthur R. and Joanne W. Stark Foundation
HC 16 Box 103
Medina, TX 78055

Established in 1999 in TX.
Donor(s): Arthur R. Stark, Joanne W. Stark.
Financial data (yr. ended 12/31/01): Grants paid, $362; assets, $6,323 (M); expenditures, $676; qualifying distributions, $362.
Limitations: Applications not accepted.
Application information: Contributes only to pre-selected organizations.
Trustees: Cheryl W. Hogan, Jan S. McLaughlin, Arthur R. Stark III.
EIN: 742938322

53367
Beauchamp Foundation
2333 Bellefontaine Blvd.
Houston, TX 77030

Established in 2000 in TX.
Donor(s): Gary V. Beauchamp, Marian Wilfert Beauchamp.
Financial data (yr. ended 12/31/01): Grants paid, $350; assets, $302,603 (M); gifts received, $5,000; expenditures, $4,500; qualifying distributions, $350.
Limitations: Applications not accepted.
Application information: Contributes only to pre-selected organizations.
Officers: Gary V. Beauchamp, Pres. and Treas.; Marian Wilfert Beauchamp, V.P. and Secy.
Director: Cheryl Colletta Fasullo.
EIN: 760663469

53368
Cytopathnet
3118 Glenmere Ct.
Carrollton, TX 75007 (800) 421-5991
Contact: Jana C. Sullinger, M.D., Dir.

Established in 1998.
Donor(s): Jana C. Sullinger, M.D.
Financial data (yr. ended 12/31/99): Grants paid, $350; assets, $20,992 (M); gifts received, $1,282; expenditures, $7,309; qualifying distributions, $350.
Director: Jana C. Sullinger, M.D.
EIN: 752758673

53369
Sinclair Foundation
532 Sandbend Dr.
Kerrville, TX 78028
Application address: 534 Sandbend Dr., Kerrville, TX 78028, tel.: (800) 442-8659
Contact: T.A. Sinclair, M.D., Pres.

Donor(s): T.A. Sinclair, M.D.
Financial data (yr. ended 12/31/01): Grants paid, $350; assets, $1,796 (M); gifts received, $7,500; expenditures, $102,351; qualifying distributions, $350.
Limitations: Giving primarily in Houston, TX.
Officers and Trustees:* T.A. Sinclair, M.D.,* Pres.; Elizabeth Flowers,* Secy.; Marjorie Woods,* Treas.; Ann Cox, Fagan A. Cox, Lucille Sinclair, T.A. Sinclair III, Lynn Zarr.
EIN: 741553549

53370
Jesus Is Lord Ministries
P.O. Box 210805
Dallas, TX 75211

Financial data (yr. ended 12/31/01): Grants paid, $349; assets, $768 (M); gifts received, $599; expenditures, $564; qualifying distributions, $564; giving activities include $215 for programs.
Officer: Emmanuel Adelowo, Secy.
EIN: 752870283

53371
Michael and Patricia Daves Foundation
5200 Keller Springs Rd., Ste. 231
Dallas, TX 75248

Established in 2000 in TX.
Financial data (yr. ended 12/31/01): Grants paid, $300; assets, $4,317 (M); gifts received, $3,000; expenditures, $406; qualifying distributions, $300.
Limitations: Giving primarily in TX.
Directors: Don Michael Daves, Patricia Nell Daves, Paul Lee Daves, Donna Michelle Lima.
EIN: 752872124

53372
Anne E. Dugger Scholarship Fund
c/o Frost National Bank
P.O. Box 2950
San Antonio, TX 78299-2950
Application address: c/o Anne Mahon, Counselor, New Braunfels High School, New Braunfels, TX 78130

Financial data (yr. ended 12/31/99): Grants paid, $300; assets, $11,171 (M); expenditures, $682; qualifying distributions, $496.
Limitations: Giving limited to New Braunfels, TX.
Application information: Application form required.
Trustee: Frost National Bank.
EIN: 746120178

53373
Forus Foundation
706 Birch Brook
Leander, TX 78641 (512) 260-6696
Contact: Kandace K. Lindquist, Tr.

Established in 2000 in TX.
Financial data (yr. ended 12/31/00): Grants paid, $300; assets, $464 (M); gifts received, $900; expenditures, $456; qualifying distributions, $456.
Application information: Application form required.
Trustees: Kandace K. Lindquist, Marc D. Lindquist.

EIN: 742974703

53374
Charles R. and Martha B. Hall Family Foundation
5580 Peterson Ln., Ste. 250
Dallas, TX 75240

Established in 2001 in TX and AL.
Donor(s): Charles R. Hall, Martha B. Hall.
Financial data (yr. ended 12/31/01): Grants paid, $300; assets, $13,675 (M); gifts received, $20,000; expenditures, $6,325; qualifying distributions, $300.
Limitations: Applications not accepted.
Application information: Contributes only to pre-selected organizations.
Officers: Charles R. Hall, Pres.; Martha B. Hall, Secy.
Directors: Charles Kevin Hall, Jennifer L. Jacks, Karen E. Mcintyre.
EIN: 621856628

53375
The J. C. and Sue Lee Foundation
6000 Augusta Cir.
College Station, TX 77845

Established in 1996 in TX.
Financial data (yr. ended 12/31/01): Grants paid, $300; assets, $139,299 (M); expenditures, $600; qualifying distributions, $300.
Director: Alfred Ian Lee.
EIN: 742804948

53376
The Russell Scott Redwine Memorial Scholarship Fund
HCR 1, Box 77
Friona, TX 79035
Contact: Harrol Redwine, Chair.

Established in 1988 in TX.
Financial data (yr. ended 04/30/00): Grants paid, $300; assets, $9,232 (M); gifts received, $45; expenditures, $300; qualifying distributions, $300.
Limitations: Giving limited to the Lazbuddie, TX, area.
Application information: Contact Lazbuddie Independent School District for application form.
Officers and Trustees:* Harrol Redwine,* Chair.; Susan Cage,* Secy.-Treas.; Hardy Carlyle Lazbuddie, Melvin Morris, Vickie Morris-Lazbuddie.
EIN: 752239378

53377
Dr. Patel Family Charitable Trust
P.O. Box 2231
Vernon, TX 76385-2231 (940) 552-9901
Contact: James E. Smith, Chair.

Donor(s): Babu M. Patel.
Financial data (yr. ended 12/31/01): Grants paid, $262; assets, $17,718 (M); gifts received, $1,250; expenditures, $526; qualifying distributions, $383.
Limitations: Giving limited to Vernon, TX.
Application information: Application form required.
Officer and Trustees:* James E. Smith,* Chair.; Douglas C. Jeffrey III, Kenny Railsback.
EIN: 752743357

53378
Charitable Assistance Life Foundation
P.O. Box 7813
Dallas, TX 75209-7813

Established around 1970.
Financial data (yr. ended 12/31/00): Grants paid, $250; assets, $852,913 (M); gifts received,

$5,000; expenditures, $957,850; qualifying distributions, $432,522.
Limitations: Applications not accepted.
Application information: Contributes only to pre-selected organizations.
Officers: V.E. Tipton, Chair.; Gary L. Tipton, Pres.; Adrienne Dukes, V.P.
EIN: 751325579

53379
JSCS Ford Foundation
1210 Krist Dr.
Houston, TX 77055-7524

Financial data (yr. ended 12/31/01): Grants paid, $250; assets, $229,895 (M); gifts received, $33,500; expenditures, $21,365; qualifying distributions, $250.
Officers and Directors:* J. Steve Ford,* Pres.; Cynthia S. Ford,* Secy.; John S. Ford, Jr.
EIN: 760556101

53380
Fred & Mable R. Parks Foundation
811 Rusk, Ste. 1750
Houston, TX 77002-2814 (713) 222-6251
Contact: Debra Marfin, Tr.

Donor(s): Fred Parks.‡
Financial data (yr. ended 12/31/01): Grants paid, $250; assets, $7,914 (M); expenditures, $1,000; qualifying distributions, $250.
Limitations: Giving primarily in Houston, TX.
Application information: Application form required.
Officers and Trustees:* Sloan B. Blair,* V.P.; Ann Stallings,* V.P.; Debra Marfin, Virginia McClintock.
EIN: 760122692

53381
Eddie and Daisy Richardson Foundation, Inc.
c/o James R. McMinn
P.O. Box 940
Marshall, TX 75671-0940 (903) 935-9331

Established in 1994.
Financial data (yr. ended 12/31/01): Grants paid, $250; assets, $9,821 (M); gifts received, $220; expenditures, $469; qualifying distributions, $250.
Limitations: Applications not accepted. Giving primarily in TX.
Application information: Contributes only to pre-selected organizations.
Officers: Daisy D. Richardson, Pres.; J. Rodney Gilstrap, V.P.; J. Rick McMinn, Secy.
EIN: 752553871

53382
Harlan and Amy Korenvaes Family Foundation
4271 Bordeaux Ave.
Dallas, TX 75205

Established in 2000.
Donor(s): Harlan B. Korenvaes, Amy B. Korenvaes.
Financial data (yr. ended 12/31/01): Grants paid, $246; assets, $4,741 (M); expenditures, $246; qualifying distributions, $246.
Limitations: Applications not accepted.
Application information: Contributes only to pre-selected organizations.
Officers and Directors:* Harlan B. Korenvaes,* Pres.; Amy B. Korenvaes,* Secy.; Harold Ames.
EIN: 752902691

53383
Charles C. Matthews Foundation
c/o Charles C. Matthews
P.O. Box 427
Carthage, TX 75633-0427

Financial data (yr. ended 12/31/01): Grants paid, $206; assets, $5,768 (M); gifts received, $2,000; expenditures, $356; qualifying distributions, $206.
Limitations: Giving primarily in the Carthage, TX, area.
Trustees: John W. Conway, Jimmy D. Payne, Raymond C. Schieffer, Robert M. Underwood.
EIN: 752741045

53384
The Ellen Fabiano Educational Foundation
c/o Michael H. Pellegrino
5524 Cold Spring Dr.
Arlington, TX 76017

Established in 2000 in TX.
Financial data (yr. ended 12/31/01): Grants paid, $200; assets, $1,039 (M); expenditures, $200; qualifying distributions, $200.
Directors: Joseph A. Pellegrino, Michael H. Pellegrino, Theresa J. Pellegrino.
EIN: 752836383

53385
William S. Kilroy Lung Foundation
1221 McKinney St., Ste. 2850
Houston, TX 77010-2008 (713) 651-0101
Contact: Lora Jean Kilroy, Chair.

Established in 1999 in TX.
Donor(s): Lora Jean Kilroy.
Financial data (yr. ended 12/31/01): Grants paid, $200; assets, $121,905 (M); gifts received, $200; expenditures, $2,578; qualifying distributions, $200.
Officers and Directors:* Lora Jean Kilroy, Chair. and Pres.; Steven D. Brown, M.D.,* Secy.; W.S. Kilroy, Jr.,* Treas.
EIN: 311674337

53386
Vicknair Family Foundation
c/o Tommy Jude Vicknair
1618 Lake Wilderness Ln.
Kingwood, TX 77345-1879
Application address: 86 N. Bethany Bend Cir., The Woodlands, TX 77382, tel.: (281) 297-1100
Contact: Mitchell W. Vicknair, Dir.

Established in 1999.
Financial data (yr. ended 12/31/01): Grants paid, $200; assets, $2,283 (M); gifts received, $1,180; expenditures, $880; qualifying distributions, $200.
Directors: Carol F. Vicknair, Mitchell W. Vicknair, Steven S. Vicknair, Tommy J. Vicknair.
EIN: 760619171

53387
Schwartz Charitable Foundation
P.O. Box 701039
Houston, TX 77270-1039 (713) 868-2828
Contact: Jean Schwartz Ladin, Mgr.

Financial data (yr. ended 12/31/01): Grants paid, $160; assets, $3,057 (M); expenditures, $649; qualifying distributions, $160.
Limitations: Giving limited to Houston, TX.
Application information: Application form not required.
Officer and Trustees:* Jean Schwartz Ladin,* Mgr.; Ida Schwartz, David Weintraub.
EIN: 746095660

53388
Howard Carlyle Memorial Scholarship Fund
P.O. Box 122
Lazbuddie, TX 79053

Established in 1989.
Financial data (yr. ended 04/30/01): Grants paid, $150; assets, $4,247 (M); gifts received, $50; expenditures, $150; qualifying distributions, $150.
Limitations: Giving primarily in Lazbuddie, TX.
Application information: Unsolicited requests for funds not accepted.
Officer and Trustees:* Hardy Carlyle,* Chair.; Carl Bodiford, Thelma Coffee, Gwen Warren.
EIN: 752298279

53389
The Marshall P. and Maryelaine Cline Charitable Foundation
5419 Bent Tree Dr.
Dallas, TX 75248 (972) 931-0856
Contact: Marshall P. Cline, Tr.

Established in 1995 in NY.
Donor(s): Marshall P. Cline.
Financial data (yr. ended 12/31/99): Grants paid, $105; assets, $0 (L); expenditures, $1,902; qualifying distributions, $200.
Application information: Application form not required.
Trustees: Marshall P. Cline, Maryelaine Cline, David Pearce.
EIN: 161494667

53390
Arthur and Philamena Baird Family Foundation
19 Exbury Way
Houston, TX 77056

Established in 2000 in TX.
Donor(s): Arthur L. Baird, Philamena Baird.
Financial data (yr. ended 12/31/01): Grants paid, $100; assets, $64,863 (M); gifts received, $26,552; expenditures, $879; qualifying distributions, $100.
Officers: Philamena Baird, Pres.; Arthur L. Baird, V.P. and Treas.; Krista Mathis, Secy.
EIN: 760652465

53391
The Baylor Family Foundation
6629 Golf Dr.
Dallas, TX 75205

Financial data (yr. ended 12/31/01): Grants paid, $100; assets, $100 (M); gifts received, $100; expenditures, $100; qualifying distributions, $100.
Trustee: Jim Harrell.
EIN: 752853599

53392
Helen Garmany Foundation
1756 Oakland Blvd.
Fort Worth, TX 76103

Established in 2000 in TX.
Donor(s): Helen Garmany.
Financial data (yr. ended 04/30/02): Grants paid, $100; assets, $626,321 (M); expenditures, $38,497; qualifying distributions, $38,497.
Limitations: Applications not accepted.
Application information: Contributes only to pre-selected organizations.
Directors: Anthony D. Barrick, E.E. Barrick, Helen Garmany.
EIN: 752880507

53393
The Phil and Linda Hardberger Foundation
319 W. Hollywood Ave.
San Antonio, TX 78212

Established in 2000 in TX.
Donor(s): Phillip D. Hardberger, Linda M. Hardberger.
Financial data (yr. ended 12/31/01): Grants paid, $100; assets, $681,091 (M); expenditures, $11,710; qualifying distributions, $100.
Limitations: Applications not accepted.
Application information: Contributes only to pre-selected organizations.
Officers: Phillip D. Hardberger, Pres.; Linda M. Hardberger, V.P. and Secy.-Treas.
Director: Amy Hardberger.
EIN: 742980009

53394
Bill and Mary Hughes Family Foundation
12518 Winding Brook Ln.
Houston, TX 77024-4927

Established in 2000 in TX.
Donor(s): William J. Hughes, Mary Alice Knight Hughes.
Financial data (yr. ended 12/31/01): Grants paid, $100; assets, $17,240 (M); gifts received, $10,000; expenditures, $140; qualifying distributions, $100.
Limitations: Applications not accepted.
Application information: Contributes only to pre-selected organizations.
Directors: John M. Hughes, Mary Alice Knight Hughes, William J. Hughes.
EIN: 760657484

53395
Patrick W. Price Foundation
306B N. Edward Gary
San Marcos, TX 78666-5708

Established in 1997 in TX.
Financial data (yr. ended 12/31/01): Grants paid, $100; assets, $17 (M); gifts received, $100; expenditures, $100; qualifying distributions, $100.
Trustees: Kimberly C. Ford, Patrick Webb Price.
EIN: 742824719

53396
Truett and Rita Smith Foundation
c/o Kanaly Trust Co.
4550 Post Oak Place Dr., Ste. 139
Houston, TX 77027

Established in 1999 in TX.
Donor(s): Truett Smith, Rita Smith.
Financial data (yr. ended 12/31/01): Grants paid, $100; assets, $137 (M); gifts received, $400; expenditures, $830; qualifying distributions, $100.
Trustees: C. Truett Smith, Rita Emily Anne Smith, Kanaly Trust Co.
EIN: 766032912

53397
The Turley Family Foundation
5105 Lakehill Court
Dallas, TX 75220-2161

Established in 2000 in TX.
Financial data (yr. ended 12/31/01): Grants paid, $100; assets, $913 (M); expenditures, $100; qualifying distributions, $100.
Officers and Trustees:* Windle Turley,* Pres. and Treas.; Shirley Turley,* V.P. and Secy.; M. Linda Turley, Ronald W. Turley.
EIN: 752887784

53398
E. C. Westervelt Trust
P.O. Box 9317
Corpus Christi, TX 78469 (361) 884-4949
Contact: Grace Knox Flato, Tr.

Financial data (yr. ended 12/31/00): Grants paid, $100; assets, $18,116 (M); expenditures, $100; qualifying distributions, $100.
Limitations: Giving primarily in TX.
Trustees: Edwin F. Flato III, Grace Knox Flato.
EIN: 746047805

53399
The Swiren Pollans Charitable Foundation
860 Hwy. 96 S.
Silsbee, TX 77656

Financial data (yr. ended 12/31/01): Grants paid, $75; assets, $12,446 (M); expenditures, $426; qualifying distributions, $75.
Limitations: Applications not accepted. Giving on a national basis.
Application information: Contributes only to pre-selected organizations.
Officers and Directors:* Paula Pollans,* Pres.; John Steve Eppes,* V.P. and Secy.-Treas.
EIN: 363045425

53400
Budek Family Foundation, Inc.
5580 Peterson Ln., Ste. 250
Dallas, TX 75240

Established in 2000 in TX and FL.
Donor(s): Gary Budek, Paula Budek.
Financial data (yr. ended 12/31/01): Grants paid, $70; assets, $421 (M); gifts received, $640; expenditures, $1,109; qualifying distributions, $70.
Limitations: Applications not accepted.
Application information: Contributes only to pre-selected organizations.
Officers: Gary M. Budek, Pres.; Paula J. Budek, Secy.
Director: Julie M. Budek.
EIN: 752864970

53401
Geneva Rogers Foundation, Inc.
P.O. Box 1052
Perryton, TX 79070-1052

Established in 1992.
Donor(s): O.C. Rogers.
Financial data (yr. ended 12/31/00): Grants paid, $61; assets, $24,427 (M); expenditures, $1,691; qualifying distributions, $61.
Limitations: Applications not accepted.
Application information: Contributes only to pre-selected organizations.
Officers: O.C. Rogers, Pres.; Glenna M. Rogers, V.P.; Suzanne Pointer, Secy.-Treas.
EIN: 752428139

53402
The Thompson Charitable Foundation
P.O. Box 111
Hamilton, TX 76531-0111

Established in 1999 in TX.
Financial data (yr. ended 12/31/01): Grants paid, $52; assets, $1,071 (M); gifts received, $75; expenditures, $78; qualifying distributions, $52.
Trustee: Joe Thompson.
EIN: 742908267

53403
Golden Rule Foundation
1660 S. Stemmons Fwy., Ste. 290
Lewisville, TX 75067
Contact: Lea Ann Leslie, Tr.

Established in 1998 in TX.
Financial data (yr. ended 12/31/00): Grants paid, $50; assets, $780 (M); gifts received, $900; expenditures, $356; qualifying distributions, $356.
Application information: Application form required.
Trustees: Gary K. Leslie, Lea Ann Leslie.
EIN: 752790882

53404
The Hunsucker Family Foundation
150 Gessener, Ste. 12E
Houston, TX 77024

Established in 1996 in TX.
Donor(s): Robert D. Hunsucker.
Financial data (yr. ended 11/30/01): Grants paid, $50; assets, $339 (M); expenditures, $194; qualifying distributions, $194.
Limitations: Applications not accepted.
Application information: Contributes only to pre-selected organizations.
Trustees: Marjorie E. Hunsucker, Tara Gayle Hunsucker.
EIN: 766123063

53405
Thomas Michael Parker Foundation
3303 24th St.
Lubbock, TX 79410-2130

Established in 2000 in DE.
Financial data (yr. ended 10/31/01): Grants paid, $50; assets, $1,000 (M); gifts received, $1,733; expenditures, $733; qualifying distributions, $683.
Limitations: Applications not accepted. Giving primarily in Lubbock, TX.
Application information: Contributes only to pre-selected organizations.
Director: Thomas Michael Parker.
EIN: 311753058

53406
Calvert Foundation
5402 Westerham St.
Fulshear, TX 77441

Established in 1998 in TX.
Financial data (yr. ended 12/31/01): Grants paid, $42; assets, $623 (M); expenditures, $212; qualifying distributions, $42.
Directors: Joyce Davis, Lou Davis, Kent Kilbourne, Lila Kilbourne.
EIN: 760585491

53407
DSH Foundation
(also known as Dorothy S. Hines Foundation)
2800 Post Oak Blvd., Ste. 5000
Houston, TX 77056-6190

Financial data (yr. ended 09/30/01): Grants paid, $42; assets, $614 (M); expenditures, $155; qualifying distributions, $42.
Limitations: Applications not accepted.
Trustees: Dorothy S. Hines, Jeffrey C. Hines.
EIN: 766014187

53408
Streng Charitable Foundation, Inc.
c/o William P. Streng
1903 Dunstan Rd.
Houston, TX 77005-1619

Donor(s): Louisa E. Streng, William P. Streng.

Financial data (yr. ended 12/31/00): Grants paid, $15; assets, $55,298 (M); gifts received, $100; expenditures, $15,000; qualifying distributions, $15.
Officers and Directors:* William P. Streng,* Pres. and Treas.; John E. Streng,* V.P.; Sarah B. Streng,* V.P.; Louisa E. Streng,* Secy.
EIN: 761515234

53409
Abutrab Foundation
701 Legacy Dr., Apt. 2224
Plano, TX 75023-2240

Established in 2000 in TX.
Donor(s): Mohammad Rashad Ali.
Financial data (yr. ended 12/31/01): Grants paid, $0; assets, $103,270 (M); gifts received, $1,750; expenditures, $175; qualifying distributions, $0.
Directors: Mohammad Abid Ali, Mohammad Rashad Ali, Mohammad Sajid Ali.
EIN: 752913031
Codes: TN

53410
The David Lawrence Albert Foundation
P.O. Box 790490
San Antonio, TX 78279-6841

Established in 2000 in TX.
Donor(s): Carl A. Albert.
Financial data (yr. ended 12/31/01): Grants paid, $0; assets, $2,521 (M); expenditures, $2,028; qualifying distributions, $0.
Limitations: Applications not accepted.
Application information: Contributes only to pre-selected organizations.
Officers and Directors:* Carl A. Albert,* Pres.; Matthew Albert,* Secy.; Elisa Albert.
EIN: 742910369

53411
Jose Antonio Alvarez Alonso Scholarship Fund
c/o Al Horan, Caltex Petroleum Corp.
P.O. Box 619500
Dallas, TX 75261-9500
Application address: Juan Antonio Ortega, c/o Repsol Petroleo, S.A., Paseo de la Castellana, Ste., 278/280, Madrid, Spain 28046

Donor(s): Respol Petroleo, S.A.
Financial data (yr. ended 12/31/01): Grants paid, $0; assets, $162,352 (M); expenditures, $2,621; qualifying distributions, $1,000.
Limitations: Giving on a national and international basis.
Trustees: A.W. Horan, Juan Antonio Ortega.
EIN: 510190586

53412
Amarandon Charitable Foundation, Inc.
1821 Yuam St.
Houston, TX 77004

Established in 2000 in TX.
Donor(s): Ronald A. Meadows.‡
Financial data (yr. ended 12/31/01): Grants paid, $0; assets, $287,552 (M); expenditures, $0; qualifying distributions, $0.
Limitations: Applications not accepted.
Application information: Contributes only to pre-selected organizations.
Directors: Margie L. Beecher, Jayne M. Frederick, Randle H. Meadows.
EIN: 742959087

53413
Ambassadors of God Foundation
1800 Norwood, Ste. 104
Hurst, TX 76054-3000
Contact: Jerry B. Jackson, Tr.

Established in 1999 in TX.
Financial data (yr. ended 12/31/00): Grants paid, $0; assets, $13,270 (M); gifts received, $10,000; expenditures, $2,000; qualifying distributions, $0.
Trustee: Jerry B. Jackson.
EIN: 752836220

53414
The Ansary Foundation
c/o Hon. Hushang Ansary
1000 Louisiana, Ste. 5900
Houston, TX 77002
Contact: Kenneth G. Hochman

Established in 1998.
Donor(s): Hushang Ansary.
Financial data (yr. ended 12/31/01): Grants paid, $0; assets, $1,116,238 (M); expenditures, $0; qualifying distributions, $0.
Application information: Application form not required.
Trustee: Hushang Ansary.
EIN: 760548330

53415
The Neal A. Askew Family Foundation
P.O. Box 1988
Wimberley, TX 78676

Established in 1999 in TX.
Financial data (yr. ended 12/31/00): Grants paid, $0; assets, $3,060 (M); gifts received, $3,060; expenditures, $0; qualifying distributions, $0.
Officer: Neal A. Askew, Pres.
EIN: 586399200

53416
Associated Plumb-Heat-Cool Contractors Of Tx Charitable and Education
505 E. Huntland Dr., Ste. 170
Austin, TX 78752
Contact: Nancy Jones

Established in 2001 in TX.
Donor(s): Plumbing Education Council of Texas, Inc.
Financial data (yr. ended 12/31/01): Grants paid, $0; assets, $130,498 (M); gifts received, $129,000; expenditures, $0; qualifying distributions, $0.
Application information: Application form required.
Trustees: Robert Bentivegna, Steve Burch, Albert Hollub.
EIN: 742942085

53417
Aubrey Library Foundation
c/o Jayne Clark
P.O. Box 613
Aubrey, TX 76227

Financial data (yr. ended 11/30/99): Grants paid, $0; assets, $94,464 (M); expenditures, $3,689; qualifying distributions, $0.
Officers and Directors:* Jayne Clark,* Pres.; Hal Rachal, Jr., V.P. and Secy.-Treas.; Margaret Teves.
EIN: 752682346

53418
Austin Fairchild Art Foundation
101 W. 6th St., Ste. 803
Austin, TX 78701

Established in 2001.
Donor(s): Dennis R. Mcdaniel.

Financial data (yr. ended 12/31/01): Grants paid, $0; assets, $28,674 (M); gifts received, $34,114; expenditures, $5,449; qualifying distributions, $0.
Trustee: Dennis R. McDaniel.
EIN: 751983753

53419
The AV Foundation
701 Brazos St., Ste. 1400
Austin, TX 78701 (512) 485-1900
Contact: Joseph C. Aragona, V.P.

Established in 2000 in TX.
Donor(s): AV Partners VI, LP, AVP Management Svcs., Inc.
Financial data (yr. ended 12/31/01): Grants paid, $0; assets, $97,250 (M); expenditures, $2,550; qualifying distributions, $0.
Application information: Application form not required.
Officers: John D. Thornton, Pres.; Joseph C. Aragona, V.P.; Blaine F. Wesner, Secy.-Treas.
Trustees: Kenneth P. Deanagelis, Edward E. Olkkola.
EIN: 742969590

53420
Jalane Baker Foundation
P.O. Box 515432
Dallas, TX 75251

Established in 1999 in TX.
Donor(s): Jalane Baker.
Financial data (yr. ended 08/31/01): Grants paid, $0; assets, $99,272 (M); gifts received, $50,000; expenditures, $0; qualifying distributions, $0.
Limitations: Applications not accepted.
Application information: Contributes only to pre-selected organizations.
Directors: Jalane Baker, James M. Baker, Patsy L. Baker, Jamie Sirman.
EIN: 752827817

53421
Baker Foundation of Burleson, Inc.
117 E. Ellison
Burleson, TX 76028
Application address: P.O. Box 309, Burleson, TX 76097-0309, tel.: (817) 295-2202
Contact: Howard Walton Baker, Pres.

Established in 1998 in TX.
Donor(s): Howard Walton Baker.
Financial data (yr. ended 12/31/01): Grants paid, $0; assets, $220,817 (M); gifts received, $192; expenditures, $1,577; qualifying distributions, $0.
Limitations: Giving primarily in Burleson, TX.
Officers: Howard Walton Baker, Pres.; Harold Ray Booth, V.P. and Secy.; Jeffrey Scott Rasco, Treas.
EIN: 752739558

53422
The Barker Foundation
105 W. 8th St.
Austin, TX 78701

Established in 2001 in TX.
Donor(s): The Barker Family Charitable Trust.
Financial data (yr. ended 12/31/01): Grants paid, $0; assets, $59,945 (M); gifts received, $70,445; expenditures, $2,450; qualifying distributions, $1,470.
Limitations: Applications not accepted.
Application information: Contributes only to pre-selected organizations.
Officers: Kirby G. Barker III, Pres.; Kyle E. Barker, Secy.-Treas.
Director: Joel Perison.
EIN: 742957926

53423
Barnes Charitable Foundation, Inc.
P.O. Box 12768
Odessa, TX 79768

Established in 1996 in TX.
Financial data (yr. ended 12/31/01): Grants paid, $0; assets, $9,311 (M); gifts received, $3,000; expenditures, $458; qualifying distributions, $0.
Limitations: Applications not accepted. Giving primarily in TX.
Application information: Contributes only to pre-selected organizations.
Officers: Bob C. Barnes, Pres.; Earlene Barnes, V.P.; Dorothy Mitchell, Secy.
EIN: 752625727

53424
Sam R. and Malcolm Monroe Barnes Foundation
P.O. Box 1851
Trinity, TX 75862-1851

Established in 1994 in TX.
Donor(s): Daniel T. Barnes.
Financial data (yr. ended 12/31/01): Grants paid, $0; assets, $1 (M); gifts received, $444,450; expenditures, $664; qualifying distributions, $0.
Officers: Dan T. Barnes, Pres.; Sally B. Edmonds, Secy.; Elizabeth A. Barnes, Treas.
EIN: 752570146

53425
Louise S. and W. H. Bauer Charitable Endowment Trust
c/o First National Bank
P.O. Drawer 7
Port Lavaca, TX 77979
Application address: 1101 Hwy. 35 S., Port Lavaca, TX 77979-5198

Established in 2001.
Financial data (yr. ended 12/31/01): Grants paid, $0; assets, $489,125 (M); expenditures, $209; qualifying distributions, $0.
Limitations: Giving limited to Calhoun County, TX.
Trustee: W. H. Bauer, Jr.
EIN: 316666379

53426
The Baxter Trust
c/o Frost National Bank
P.O. Box 1315
Houston, TX 77251-1315

Donor(s): Murphy H. Baxter.
Financial data (yr. ended 12/31/01): Grants paid, $0; assets, $4,518,894 (M); gifts received, $300,000; expenditures, $61,364; qualifying distributions, $0.
Limitations: Applications not accepted. Giving primarily in MD and Houston, TX.
Application information: Contributes only to pre-selected organizations.
Trustee: Kelly Baxter, Guilford Jones, Jack Martin, M.D., Lucian L. Morrison, Ray G. Petty.
EIN: 760174893

53427
Bayless Foundation
106 W. Houston St.
Cleveland, TX 77327

Established in 2000.
Financial data (yr. ended 12/31/00): Grants paid, $0; assets, $1 (M); expenditures, $0; qualifying distributions, $0.
Officer: D. Bayless, Mgr.
EIN: 766166075

53428
Beaird Family Foundation
18039 Windtop Ln.
Dallas, TX 75287

Established in 2000 in TX.
Donor(s): Pat C. Beaird, Colleen C. Beaird.
Financial data (yr. ended 12/31/00): Grants paid, $0; assets, $20,000 (M); gifts received, $20,000; expenditures, $0; qualifying distributions, $0.
Limitations: Applications not accepted.
Application information: Contributes only to pre-selected organizations.
Officers: Colleen C. Beaird, Mgr.; Pat C. Beaird, Mgr.
Trustee: Steven M. Lugar.
EIN: 752912647

53429
The Richard J. and Pamela Behrens Foundation
4450 Sigma Rd., Ste. 130
Dallas, TX 75244-4529

Established in 2001 in TX.
Donor(s): Pamela Behrens.
Financial data (yr. ended 12/31/01): Grants paid, $0; assets, $35,002 (M); gifts received, $35,000; expenditures, $0; qualifying distributions, $0.
Limitations: Applications not accepted.
Application information: Contributes only to pre-selected organizations.
Officers: Pamela Behrens, Pres.; Patricia T. Dryden, V.P.; Patricia Sari-Spear, Secy.-Treas.
EIN: 752955065

53430
Mary and Jeff Bell Foundation
710 Buffalo St., Ste. 100
Corpus Christi, TX 78401
Contact: Jeff Bell, Tr.

Established in 1997 in TX.
Donor(s): Jeff Bell.
Financial data (yr. ended 11/30/01): Grants paid, $0; assets, $1,453 (M); expenditures, $314; qualifying distributions, $0.
Trustee: Jeff Bell.
EIN: 742855870

53431
The Berman Family Foundation
1471 Red Hawk Rd.
Wimberley, TX 78676

Established in 2001 in TX.
Donor(s): David Berman, Ellen Berman.
Financial data (yr. ended 12/31/01): Grants paid, $0; assets, $71,042 (M); gifts received, $68,136; expenditures, $66; qualifying distributions, $0.
Limitations: Applications not accepted.
Application information: Contributes only to pre-selected organizations.
Officers: David S. Berman, Pres.; Ellen T. Berman, V.P.; James B. Gregory, Secy.-Treas.
EIN: 743023778

53432
Biehl Foundation
5200 Hollister
Houston, TX 77040-6298
Contact: Vernon Bain, Tr.

Financial data (yr. ended 12/31/01): Grants paid, $0; assets, $129,335 (M); expenditures, $48; qualifying distributions, $0.
Limitations: Giving primarily in TX.
Application information: Application form not required.
Trustees: Vernon Bain, Lindy Ellason.
EIN: 746063301

53433
R. D. Bierne Trust Fund
c/o Bank of America
P.O. Box 831041
Dallas, TX 75283-1041

Financial data (yr. ended 12/31/01): Grants paid, $0; assets, $88,947 (M); expenditures, $3,314; qualifying distributions, $1,349.
Limitations: Applications not accepted. Giving limited to TX.
Application information: Contributes only to pre-selected organizations.
Trustee: Bank of America.
EIN: 756017999

53434
Blossom Foundation
c/o Col. Paul Applin
2406 Pemberton Pkwy.
Austin, TX 78703

Established in 2000.
Donor(s): Genevieve Vaughn.
Financial data (yr. ended 12/31/01): Grants paid, $0; assets, $694,589 (M); gifts received, $12,100; expenditures, $25,867; qualifying distributions, $0.
Limitations: Applications not accepted.
Application information: Contributes only to pre-selected organizations.
Officer and Trustees:* Col. Paul Applin,* C.F.O.; Wynette Barton, Jan Carlson, Jennifer Knauth, Cynthia Tincher.
EIN: 742915725

53435
Bonner-Price Student Loan Fund Trust
c/o Wells Fargo Bank Texas, N.A., Trust Dept.
P.O. Box 10517
Lubbock, TX 79408-3517

Financial data (yr. ended 12/31/00): Grants paid, $0; assets, $894,046 (M); expenditures, $51,592; qualifying distributions, $76,553; giving activities include $67,000 for loans to individuals.
Limitations: Giving primarily in TX.
Application information: Applicant must be enrolled at McMurry College, TX. Application form required.
Trustee: Wells Fargo Bank Texas, N.A.
EIN: 726084752
Codes: GTI

53436
Charles T. & Katie B. Brackins Scholarship Foundation
(Formerly Brackins Scholarship Foundation)
c/o Bank of America
P.O. Box 831041
Dallas, TX 75283-1041

Financial data (yr. ended 06/30/01): Grants paid, $0; assets, $22,302 (M); expenditures, $996; qualifying distributions, $842.
Limitations: Giving limited to Dallas, TX.
Application information: Application form required.
Trustee: Bank of America.
EIN: 756010057

53437
Brittingham Conservation Foundation
12377 Merit Dr., Ste. 220
Dallas, TX 75251

Established in 2000 in TX.
Donor(s): John G. Brittingham.
Financial data (yr. ended 12/31/00): Grants paid, $0; assets, $904 (M); gifts received, $5,000; expenditures, $4,111; qualifying distributions, $0.

Officers: John G. Brittingham, Pres.; Pat C. Beaird, Secy.
Trustee: Christine M. Brittingham.
EIN: 752888360

53438
The George K. and Eleanor Jane Broady Family Opportunity Foundation
1301 Waters Ridge Dr.
Lewisville, TX 75057
Contact: George K. Broady, Dir.

Established in 1997 in TX.
Donor(s): George K. Broady.
Financial data (yr. ended 12/31/01): Grants paid, $0; assets, $274,214 (M); expenditures, $0; qualifying distributions, $0.
Limitations: Giving primarily in Conway, AR and Dallas, TX.
Director: George K. Broady.
EIN: 752739287

53439
The Brodsky Charitable Foundation Trust
5223 Royal Ln.
Dallas, TX 75229

Established in 2000.
Financial data (yr. ended 12/31/00): Grants paid, $0; assets, $225,432 (M); expenditures, $0; qualifying distributions, $0.
Officer: Frederick Brodsky, Pres.
EIN: 752849127

53440
William A. Brookshire Foundation
7825 Park Place Blvd.
Houston, TX 77087
Contact: Bob McKinley

Established in 1998 in TX.
Donor(s): William A. Brookshire.
Financial data (yr. ended 06/30/01): Grants paid, $0; assets, $1,665,706 (M); gifts received, $400,005; expenditures, $11,315; qualifying distributions, $44,500.
Application information: Application form not required.
Officers and Directors:* William A. Brookshire,* Pres.; Lori Brookshire-Garrison,* V.P.; Pamela McKinley,* Secy.-Treas.
EIN: 760594307

53441
The Brownstone Institute
P.O. Box 185373
Fort Worth, TX 76181-0373
Contact: Philip S. Rushing, Tr.

Established in 1998.
Financial data (yr. ended 12/31/99): Grants paid, $0; assets, $497 (M); gifts received, $1,100; expenditures, $0; qualifying distributions, $0.
Trustee: Philip S. Rushing.
EIN: 756527292

53442
Burch-Setton Student Loan Fund
c/o Wells Fargo Bank Texas, N.A.
P.O. Box 10517
Lubbock, TX 79408-3517 (806) 293-1311
Application address: c/o Board of Stewards, First United Methodist Church, 1001 W. 7th St., Plainview, TX 79072, tel.: (806) 293-3658
Contact: Sherrie Gibson

Established in 1968 in TX.
Financial data (yr. ended 12/31/00): Grants paid, $0; assets, $1,237,233 (M); expenditures, $75,548; qualifying distributions, $175,065; giving activities include $171,000 for loans to individuals.

Limitations: Giving limited to residents of Briscoe, Castro, Floyd, Hale, Lamb and Swisher counties, TX.
Application information: Application form required.
Trustee: Wells Fargo Bank Texas, N.A.
EIN: 756056226
Codes: GTI

53443
Edward G. Bustin Charitable Trust
c/o JPMorgan Chase Bank
P.O. Box 660197
Dallas, TX 75266-0197

Established in 1994 in TX.
Financial data (yr. ended 12/31/01): Grants paid, $0; assets, $806,808 (M); expenditures, $10,047; qualifying distributions, $7,534.
Trustee: JPMorgan Chase Bank.
EIN: 756528726

53444
Charles C. Butt Foundation
P.O. Box 839999
San Antonio, TX 78283-3999

Established in 1997 in TX.
Donor(s): Charles C. Butt.
Financial data (yr. ended 12/31/00): Grants paid, $0; assets, $47,145 (M); expenditures, $0; qualifying distributions, $0.
Limitations: Applications not accepted.
Application information: Contributes only to pre-selected organizations.
Officers: Charles C. Butt, Pres.; Debra Salge, Secy.
EIN: 311537197

53445
Faith P. & Charles L. Bybee Foundation - A Trust
P.O. Box 82
Round Top, TX 78954-0082

Established in 1970 in TX.
Donor(s): Faith P. Bybee,‡ Charles L. Bybee.‡
Financial data (yr. ended 12/31/99): Grants paid, $0; assets, $1,806,547 (M); gifts received, $70,254; expenditures, $164,528; qualifying distributions, $33,599; giving activities include $148,196 for programs.
Limitations: Giving primarily in TX.
Officers and Trustees:* Barry Moore,* Pres.; Barbara Vilutis,* Secy.-Treas.; Percival Beacroft, Ernesto Caldeira, Joe N. Westerlage, Jr.
EIN: 741917686

53446
Wilson K. & Roslyn R. Cadman Charitable Trust
c/o Bank of America
P.O. Box 831041
Dallas, TX 75283-1041
Application address: c/o Pamela J. Beim, Bank of America, P.O. Box 1122, Wichita, KS 76201-1122, tel.: (316) 261-2111

Established in 2000 in KS.
Donor(s): Wilson K. Cadman, Rosalyn R. Cadman.
Financial data (yr. ended 11/30/01): Grants paid, $0; assets, $244,097 (M); gifts received, $250,000; expenditures, $1,861; qualifying distributions, $863.
Limitations: Giving primarily in the Wichita, KS, area.
Trustees: Wilson K. Cadman, Bank of America.
EIN: 527136577

53447
Ralph G. Campbell and Jeroleen Johnson Campbell Foundation, Inc.
2525 Ridgmar Blvd., No. 200A
Fort Worth, TX 76116-4582

Established in 1993 in TX.
Donor(s): Ralph G. Campbell, Jeroleen J. Campbell.
Financial data (yr. ended 12/31/01): Grants paid, $0; assets, $21 (M); expenditures, $633; qualifying distributions, $0.
Limitations: Applications not accepted.
Application information: Contributes only to pre-selected organizations.
Officers: Jeroleen J. Campbell, V.P.; Coleman D. Nichols, Secy.-Treas.
Director: Charles A. Garrett.
EIN: 752501287

53448
Jesse W. Cannon Scholarship Foundation
c/o Bank of America
P.O. Box 831041
Dallas, TX 75283-1041
Application address: P.O. Box 1284, Fayetteville, AR 72702-1284, tel.: (501) 443-4313
Contact: Lewis D. Jones, Dir.

Financial data (yr. ended 04/30/01): Grants paid, $0; assets, $2,261,581 (M); expenditures, $28,798; qualifying distributions, $126,167; giving activities include $123,026 for loans to individuals.
Limitations: Giving limited to AR.
Application information: Application form required for student loans.
Directors: Lewis D. Jones, Curtis Shipley.
Trustee: Bank of America.
EIN: 716099820
Codes: GTI

53449
Caring About the Children
326 Sterling Browning Rd.
San Antonio, TX 78232-1220

Established in 2000.
Financial data (yr. ended 12/31/00): Grants paid, $0; assets, $1,470 (M); gifts received, $2,977; expenditures, $1,507; qualifying distributions, $0.
Officers: Bob Rogers, Pres.; Bruce Swearingen, V.P.; Thomas W. Lyles, Jr., Secy.; Mark Gremmer, Treas.
EIN: 742930976

53450
The C. L. Carlile Foundation
P.O. Box 1287
Big Spring, TX 79721-1287

Established in 2001 in TX.
Financial data (yr. ended 12/31/01): Grants paid, $0; assets, $2,002 (M); gifts received, $2,000; expenditures, $0; qualifying distributions, $0.
Officers: Cleo L. Carlile, Pres.; Thelma L. Carlile, Secy.-Treas.
Director: Deanna Gross.
EIN: 752961579

53451
Carpe Vita Foundation
8828 N. Stemmons Fwy., No. 106
Dallas, TX 75247

Established in 1999.
Donor(s): Marcos Rodriguez.
Financial data (yr. ended 12/31/99): Grants paid, $0; assets, $5,000,000 (M); gifts received,

53451—TEXAS

$5,000,000; expenditures, $0; qualifying distributions, $0.
Officer: James Anderson, V.P.
Directors: Charles Hart, Laurie J. Martin, Robert C. Moore, Eugene Pleasant, Marcos A. Rodriguez, Sonya Nance Rodriguez.
EIN: 311629840

53452
J. Celli Charitable Trust Fund
P.O. Box 831041
Dallas, TX 75283-1041

Established in 1997 in TX.
Financial data (yr. ended 03/31/02): Grants paid, $0; assets, $714,739 (M); expenditures, $11,608; qualifying distributions, $0.
Limitations: Applications not accepted. Giving primarily in TX and VA.
Application information: Contributes only to pre-selected organizations.
Trustee: Bank of America.
EIN: 311521680

53453
Chatham Hill Foundation
P.O. Box 542647
Dallas, TX 75354   (214) 351-2121

Established in 1994 in TX.
Donor(s): The Florida Co., Joe C. Thompson, Jr.
Financial data (yr. ended 12/31/01): Grants paid, $0; assets, $2,144,364 (M); gifts received, $1,002,000; expenditures, $72,419; qualifying distributions, $0.
Limitations: Giving primarily in TX.
Officers: Joe C. Thompson, Jr., Pres.; Joe C. Thompson III, V.P.; Dorothy K. Thompson, Treas.
EIN: 752532557

53454
Circum-Pacific Council for Energy and Mineral Resources, Inc.
5100 Westheimer, Ste. 500
Houston, TX 77056-5591

Financial data (yr. ended 12/31/99): Grants paid, $0; assets, $63,868 (M); gifts received, $15,000; expenditures, $12,234; qualifying distributions, $12,234; giving activities include $12,234 for programs.
Trustee: John A.T. Reinemund.
EIN: 953173820

53455
Concordia Foundation
12 Boulevard Green
Bellaire, TX 77401

Established in 1997 in TX.
Donor(s): James Haskins, Nancy Haskins.
Financial data (yr. ended 11/30/01): Grants paid, $0; assets, $27,347 (M); gifts received, $10,000; expenditures, $481; qualifying distributions, $0.
Limitations: Applications not accepted.
Application information: Contributes only to pre-selected organizations.
Trustees: James Haskins, Nancy Haskins.
EIN: 760554979

53456
Cornudas Mountain Foundation
1016 E. Rio Grande Ave.
El Paso, TX 79902-4617

Financial data (yr. ended 12/31/01): Grants paid, $0; assets, $204,105 (M); gifts received, $10,964; expenditures, $2,755; qualifying distributions, $0.
Limitations: Applications not accepted.
Application information: Contributes only to pre-selected organizations.

Officers and Trustees:* James R. Magee,* Pres.; James McCall,* V.P.; Susan Wente,* Secy.-Treas.; Barbara Kemble.
EIN: 742571541

53457
Corpus Christi Roxie Armytage Cancer Fund Trust
c/o Nueces County Medical Society
1000 Morgan Ave.
Corpus Christi, TX 78404
Contact: Nina Sisley, Pres.

Financial data (yr. ended 03/31/02): Grants paid, $0; assets, $29,275 (M); expenditures, $778; qualifying distributions, $0.
Limitations: Giving limited to southern TX.
Officer: Nina Sisley, Pres.
Trustee: Nueces County Medical Society.
EIN: 746039014

53458
James and Molly Crownover Family Foundation
c/o James W. Crownover
909 Fannin St., 2 houston Ctr., Ste. 3675
Houston, TX 77010

Established in 2001 in TX.
Donor(s): James Crownover, Molly Crownover.
Financial data (yr. ended 12/31/01): Grants paid, $0; assets, $454,984 (M); gifts received, $462,344; expenditures, $0; qualifying distributions, $0.
Officer: James W. Crownover.
EIN: 760700578

53459
Cunningham Fund
P.O. Box 701178
Dallas, TX 75370

Donor(s): Gloria M. Cunningham.
Financial data (yr. ended 09/30/01): Grants paid, $0; assets, $538 (M); expenditures, $150; qualifying distributions, $0.
Limitations: Applications not accepted. Giving primarily in TX.
Application information: Contributes only to pre-selected organizations.
Trustees: Gloria M. Cunningham, Hugh M. Cunningham, Jr.
EIN: 756015628

53460
The Covar & Eugene Dabezies Family Foundation, Inc.
4306 89th St.
Lubbock, TX 79423-2904

Established in 2000 in TX.
Financial data (yr. ended 12/31/01): Grants paid, $0; assets, $1,028 (M); gifts received, $250; expenditures, $250; qualifying distributions, $0.
Officers: Eugene J. Dabezies, Pres.; Eugene J. Dabezies, Jr., V.P.; Alice Jeppe Dabezies Madsen, V.P.; Joyce Covar Dabezies White, V.P.; Covar J. Dabezies, Secy.-Treas.
EIN: 752904171

53461
The Dalkys Foundation
1 Smithdale Ct.
Houston, TX 77024

Established in 2001 in TX.
Donor(s): David R. Miller, Lisa E. Miller.
Financial data (yr. ended 12/31/01): Grants paid, $0; assets, $992,239 (M); gifts received, $1,002,591; expenditures, $0; qualifying distributions, $0.
Limitations: Applications not accepted.

Application information: Contributes only to pre-selected organizations.
Officers and Directors:* David R. Miller, Pres.; George E. Jochetz III,* V.P.; Lisa E. Miller,* V.P.
EIN: 030373301

53462
Deacon & Brothers Foundation
4343 Carter Creek Pkwy., Ste. 102
Bryan, TX 77802
Contact: Ernest V. Bruchez, Pres.

Established in 2000 in TX.
Financial data (yr. ended 12/31/01): Grants paid, $0; assets, $45,742 (M); expenditures, $2,006; qualifying distributions, $0.
Limitations: Giving limited to the Bryan and College Station, TX, area.
Officers: Ernest V. Bruchez, Pres.; Jay Goss, V.P.; William S. Thornton, Jr., Secy.
EIN: 742774003

53463
Defenbaugh Family Foundation
6 Twilight Glen Ct.
The Woodlands, TX 77381

Established in 1999 in TX.
Donor(s): Mary B. Defenbaugh.
Financial data (yr. ended 12/31/01): Grants paid, $0; assets, $364,909 (M); expenditures, $291; qualifying distributions, $0.
Limitations: Applications not accepted.
Application information: Contributes only to pre-selected organizations.
Officers: Brad G. Defenbaugh, Pres.; Deborah A. Defenbaugh, V.P.; Mary B. Defenbaugh, Secy.-Treas.
EIN: 760624951

53464
Richard and Marion Dewey Family Foundation
c/o Richard B. Dewey
702 Bryson Way
Southlake, TX 76092

Established in 2000 in TX.
Donor(s): Richard B. Dewey.
Financial data (yr. ended 12/31/01): Grants paid, $0; assets, $229,569 (M); gifts received, $7,853; expenditures, $7,474; qualifying distributions, $0.
Limitations: Applications not accepted.
Application information: Contributes only to pre-selected organizations.
Officer: Richard B. Dewey, Pres.
EIN: 752879287

53465
David H. Dewhurst Foundation
109 N. Post Oak Ln., Ste. 540
Houston, TX 77024

Established in 1993.
Financial data (yr. ended 12/31/01): Grants paid, $0; assets, $100,275 (M); expenditures, $2,829; qualifying distributions, $0.
Limitations: Applications not accepted. Giving limited to TX.
Application information: Contributes only to pre-selected organizations.
Officers: David H. Dewhurst, Pres.; John E. Lyle, V.P.; Eugene H. Dewhurst, Secy.-Treas.
EIN: 760420739

53466
Enrico & Sandra di Portanova Charitable Foundation
P.O. Box 27285
Houston, TX 77227-7285

Established in 1993 in TX.

Financial data (yr. ended 03/31/01): Grants paid, $0; assets, $214,748 (M); gifts received, $200,559; expenditures, $2,028; qualifying distributions, $0.
Limitations: Applications not accepted. Giving primarily in NY and TX.
Application information: Contributes only to pre-selected organizations.
Officers and Directors:* Gregory R. Hovas,* Pres.; Lewis M. Linn,* V.P.; Carla S. Hovas,* Secy.-Treas.
EIN: 760408460

53467
Albert & Mary Dick Charitable Trust
c/o Wells Fargo Bank Texas, N.A.
P.O. Box 511
Victoria, TX 77902
Contact: Betty Zoe, Trust Off., Wells Fargo Bank Texas, N.A.

Established in 1991 in TX.
Donor(s): Albert Dick.
Financial data (yr. ended 12/31/01): Grants paid, $0; assets, $11,420 (M); expenditures, $464; qualifying distributions, $0.
Limitations: Giving primarily in the Gulf Coast area of TX.
Trustees: Betty Zoe, Wells Fargo Bank Texas, N.A.
EIN: 746388649

53468
Mary Louise Dobson Foundation
c/o Dwight D. King
2120 Newton St.
Wharton, TX 77488 (979) 282-7000
Contact: Dwight D. King, Dir.

Established in 2001 in TX.
Donor(s): Mary Louise Dobson.
Financial data (yr. ended 12/31/01): Grants paid, $0; assets, $1,184,784 (M); expenditures, $792; qualifying distributions, $0.
Directors: Mary Louise Dobson, Dwight D. King, Jane Dobson Rice.
EIN: 760690889

53469
Douglas Foundation
3024 N. Sylvania Ave.
Fort Worth, TX 76111-3012 (817) 838-6371
Contact: John A. Burgoyne, Tr.

Established in 1999.
Financial data (yr. ended 12/31/99): Grants paid, $0; assets, $100 (M); gifts received, $100; expenditures, $0; qualifying distributions, $0.
Trustee: John A. Burgoyne.
EIN: 912051860

53470
The Duncan Foundation
c/o A. Baker Duncan
311 3rd St.
San Antonio, TX 78205-1900

Donor(s): A. Baker Duncan.
Financial data (yr. ended 02/28/02): Grants paid, $0; assets, $1,089 (M); gifts received, $400; expenditures, $336; qualifying distributions, $0.
Limitations: Applications not accepted. Giving on a national basis.
Application information: Contributes only to pre-selected organizations.
Officers: A. Baker Duncan, Pres.; A. Baker Duncan III, V.P.; Richard W. Duncan, Secy.
EIN: 746060667

53471
John and Mary Eads Foundation
952 Echo Ln., No. 920
Houston, TX 77024

Established in 2001 in TX.
Donor(s): John Eads, Mary Lane Lawson Eads.
Financial data (yr. ended 12/31/01): Grants paid, $0; assets, $499,049 (M); gifts received, $495,507; expenditures, $58; qualifying distributions, $0.
Limitations: Applications not accepted.
Application information: Contributes only to pre-selected organizations.
Officers: John Eads, Pres. and Treas.; Mary Lane Lawson Eads, V.P. and Secy.
Director: Ralph Eads III.
EIN: 760698202

53472
East Texas Rails to Trails, Inc.
401 E. Front St., No. 230
Tyler, TX 75702

Established in 1996 in TX.
Financial data (yr. ended 12/31/00): Grants paid, $0; assets, $92,182 (M); expenditures, $0; qualifying distributions, $0.
Limitations: Applications not accepted.
Application information: Contributes only to pre-selected organizations.
Officers: Delia Meese, Pres.; Jarvie Stroupe, V.P.; George Anthony, Secy.-Treas.
EIN: 752365302

53473
Travis H. and Gladys Edwards Foundation
c/o Lewis Farmer
P.O. Box 716
Olney, TX 76374-0716

Established in 2001 in TX.
Donor(s): Travis H. Edwards.‡
Financial data (yr. ended 12/31/01): Grants paid, $0; assets, $651,155 (M); gifts received, $665,159; expenditures, $0; qualifying distributions, $0.
Trustees: Lewis Farmer, Luke Lunn, Robert McQuerry.
EIN: 752934621

53474
M. C. Edwards Trust
c/o JPMorgan Chase Bank
201 E. Main Dr., 4th Fl.
El Paso, TX 79901-1340 (915) 546-6515
Contact: Terry Crenshaw, Trust Off., JPMorgan Chase Bank

Financial data (yr. ended 06/30/02): Grants paid, $0; assets, $167,837 (M); expenditures, $5,461; qualifying distributions, $0.
Limitations: Giving limited to El Paso County, TX.
Trustee: JPMorgan Chase Bank.
EIN: 746033979

53475
The Craig Eiland Against the Odds Charitable Trust Foundation, Inc.
6 Tradewinds Dr.
Galveston, TX 77554 (409) 744-7756
Contact: David Herrin, Tr.

Established in 1994 in TX.
Financial data (yr. ended 12/31/01): Grants paid, $0; assets, $978 (M); expenditures, $120; qualifying distributions, $0.
Application information: Application form required.
Trustee: David M. Herrin.
EIN: 760421791

53476
W. N. and Jane Enger Foundation, Inc.
10672 County Rd. 3909
Athens, TX 75751-3863

Established in 2000 in TX.
Donor(s): William R. Enger.
Financial data (yr. ended 12/31/00): Grants paid, $0; assets, $20,395 (M); gifts received, $20,000; expenditures, $0; qualifying distributions, $22,098.
Officers: William R. Enger, Pres.; Dennis Nolley, Secy.
Director: Bruce Odom.
EIN: 752895683

53477
Enterprise TFL Foundation
c/o Texas Bank
2525 Ridgmar Blvd., Ste. 100
Fort Worth, TX 76116 (817) 735-0948
Contact: Edward T. Fritz, Secy.-Treas.

Established in 1997 in IL.
Financial data (yr. ended 12/31/01): Grants paid, $0; assets, $117,679 (M); expenditures, $3,369; qualifying distributions, $0.
Limitations: Giving primarily in IL and TX.
Officers: Susan M. Mullins, Pres.; Margret A. Frank, V.P.; Edward T. Fritz, Secy.-Treas.
EIN: 364128410

53478
Face Foundation
6655 Travis St., Ste. 900
Houston, TX 77030-1332

Established in 1995 in TX.
Donor(s): Todd Smith, Demeirio Boulafendis, Margaret Uthman.
Financial data (yr. ended 07/31/00): Grants paid, $0; assets, $306 (M); gifts received, $500; expenditures, $1,409; qualifying distributions, $659; giving activities include $659 for programs.
Limitations: Applications not accepted. Giving primarily in Atlanta, GA.
Application information: Contributes only to pre-selected organizations.
Officers: Russell W.H. Kridel, Pres.; James Kridel, Jr., V.P.; Steven C. Kaufer, Secy.
EIN: 760477832

53479
Fannin Charitable Foundation, Inc.
901 Waterfall Way, Ste. 205
Richardson, TX 75080

Established in 2000 in TX.
Financial data (yr. ended 12/31/01): Grants paid, $0; assets, $5,204 (M); expenditures, $0; qualifying distributions, $0.
Officers: Brent Fannin, Pres. and Treas.; Cindy Fannin, V.P.; Michael Fannin, Secy.
EIN: 752906147

53480
The Thomas Kinder and Martha W. Farris Charitable Foundation, Inc.
800 W. Kentucky
Floydada, TX 79235

Established in 1999 in TX.
Financial data (yr. ended 12/31/01): Grants paid, $0; assets, $4,357 (M); expenditures, $407; qualifying distributions, $0.
Officers: Martha W. Farris, Pres.; George R. Farris, V.P.; John C. Farris, V.P.; Elizabeth Farris Figari, V.P.; T.K. Farris, Jr., Secy.-Treas.
EIN: 752832647

53481
Homoiselle & Albert Fay Foundation
515 Houston Ave.
Houston, TX 77007-7793 (713) 227-5251
Contact: Albert B. Fay, Jr., Tr.

Established in 1961 in TX.
Donor(s): Albert B. Fay, Jr.,‡ Homoiselle H. Fay.‡
Financial data (yr. ended 11/30/01): Grants paid, $0; assets, $871 (M); expenditures, $80; qualifying distributions, $0.
Limitations: Giving primarily in TX.
Trustees: Albert B. Fay, Jr., Marion Fay Monsen.
EIN: 746056613

53482
Felter Foundation, Inc.
4704-A E. Cesar Chavez
Austin, TX 78702

Established in 1999 in TX.
Financial data (yr. ended 12/31/01): Grants paid, $0; assets, $3,389 (M); gifts received, $300; expenditures, $5; qualifying distributions, $0.
Officers: Patricia E. Felter, Pres.; Brenda Horton, Secy.-Treas.
Directors: Patrick O'Keefe, Richard Shanks.
EIN: 742862478

53483
Kittie Nelson Ferguson Foundation
c/o Frost National Bank
P.O. Box 1600
San Antonio, TX 78296

Established in 2001 in TX.
Donor(s): Kittie & Rugeley Ferguson Family Foundation.
Financial data (yr. ended 11/30/01): Grants paid, $0; assets, $3,525,013 (M); gifts received, $2,847,500; expenditures, $0; qualifying distributions, $0.
Limitations: Applications not accepted.
Application information: Contributes only to pre-selected organizations.
Trustees: Kittie Nelson Ferguson, Frost National Bank.
EIN: 743018259

53484
Rugeley Ferguson Foundation
c/o Frost Bank
P.O. Box 1600
San Antonio, TX 78296

Established in 2000 in TX.
Financial data (yr. ended 11/30/01): Grants paid, $0; assets, $1,510,720 (M); expenditures, $0; qualifying distributions, $0.
Limitations: Applications not accepted.
Application information: Contributes only to pre-selected organizations.
Trustees: H. Rugeley Ferguson, Frost National Bank.
EIN: 743018256

53485
Flowserve Foundation
(Formerly Duriron Foundation)
c/o Flowserve Corp.
222 W. Las Colinas Blvd., Ste. 1500
Irving, TX 75039-5421 (972) 443-6500
Contact: Kathleen McVey, Treas.

Established in 1983 in OH. Merger of BW/IP, Inc. and Durco International Inc. in 1997.
Donor(s): The Duriron Co., Inc., Durco International Inc., Flowserve Corp., BW/IP, Inc.
Financial data (yr. ended 12/31/99): Grants paid, $0; assets, $753 (M); expenditures, $1,130; qualifying distributions, $0.

Limitations: Giving primarily in areas of company operations, with emphasis on Dayton, OH, and Cookeville, TN.
Publications: Application guidelines.
Application information: Application form not required.
Officers and Trustees:* C. Scott Greer,* Pres.; Ronald F. Shuff,* V.P. and Secy.; Renee Hornbaker, V.P.; Kathleen McVey,* Treas.
EIN: 311080064
Codes: CS, CD

53486
The Food Foundation
1925 Cedar Springs Rd., Ste. 101
Dallas, TX 75201

Established in 2000 in TX.
Financial data (yr. ended 12/31/00): Grants paid, $0; assets, $8,165 (M); gifts received, $340; expenditures, $4,348; qualifying distributions, $12,513; giving activities include $2,523 for programs.
Limitations: Applications not accepted.
Application information: Contributes only to pre-selected organizations.
Officers: Philip J. Romano, Chair., C.E.O., and Pres.; Philip M. Parsons, Secy.-Treas.
EIN: 752911547

53487
For the Love of Animals Foundation, Inc.
311 Morris Tivydale Rd.
Fredericksburg, TX 78624

Established in 2000 in TX.
Financial data (yr. ended 12/31/01): Grants paid, $0; assets, $94,027 (M); gifts received, $1,300; expenditures, $35,055; qualifying distributions, $0.
Limitations: Applications not accepted. Giving primarily in Fredericksburg, TX.
Application information: Contributes only to pre-selected organizations.
Officers: Deborah Smithdeal, C.E.O.; Charles Smithdeal, Pres.; Jonathan Godfrey, Treas.
EIN: 742948246

53488
Foundation for International Understanding, Health and Education, Inc.
2626 Foliage Green Dr.
Kingwood, TX 77339-1007

Established in 2001 in TX.
Financial data (yr. ended 12/31/01): Grants paid, $0; assets, $1,500 (M); gifts received, $1,500; expenditures, $1,500; qualifying distributions, $1,500.
Officers and Directors:* C. Justina Chen,* Pres. and Treas.; Victor Chen,* V.P.; Niangue Joseph.
EIN: 043650493

53489
4L Foundation
7601 Newhall Ln.
Austin, TX 78746

Established in 1999 in TX.
Donor(s): David K. Lockett, Marsha M. Lockett.
Financial data (yr. ended 12/31/00): Grants paid, $0; assets, $244,149 (M); gifts received, $250,000; expenditures, $0; qualifying distributions, $0.
Limitations: Applications not accepted.
Application information: Contributes only to pre-selected organizations.
Officers and Directors:* David K. Lockett,* Pres. and Treas.; Marsha M. Lockett,* Secy.; Jay D. Lockett.
EIN: 742973277

53490
Leonard and Teresa Friedman Foundation
1 Greenway Plaza, Ste. 850
Houston, TX 77046-0196

Established in 2000 in TX.
Donor(s): Leonard Edward Friedman, Teresa H. Friedman.
Financial data (yr. ended 12/31/00): Grants paid, $0; assets, $46,031 (M); gifts received, $46,469; expenditures, $0; qualifying distributions, $0.
Limitations: Applications not accepted.
Application information: Contributes only to pre-selected organizations.
Officers and Directors:* Teresa H. Friedman,* Pres.; Leonard Edward Friedman,* V.P.; Michael Lawrence Friedman,* Secy.-Treas.; David Alan Friedman, Kenneth Scott Friedman, Laurie Bain Friedman, Melissa Schindell Friedman.
EIN: 760598286

53491
The Bayard and Cornelia Friedman Fund
1305 Shady Oaks Ln.
Fort Worth, TX 76107

Established in 2001 in TX.
Donor(s): Cornelia C. Friedman.
Financial data (yr. ended 12/31/01): Grants paid, $0; assets, $101,385 (M); gifts received, $101,249; expenditures, $0; qualifying distributions, $0.
Limitations: Applications not accepted.
Application information: Contributes only to pre-selected organizations.
Officers: Cornelia Cheney Friedman, Pres.; Alan D. Friedman, V.P.; Cornelia "Nita" Friedman, V.P.; Walker C. Friedman, Secy.; Harry B. Friedman II, Treas.
EIN: 752886727

53492
Friends of the Adolphus Sterne Home, Inc.
211 Lanana St.
Nacogdoches, TX 75961
Contact: Robert P. Blount, Pres.

Established in 2001 in TX.
Financial data (yr. ended 12/31/01): Grants paid, $0; assets, $29,585 (M); gifts received, $29,034; expenditures, $11; qualifying distributions, $0.
Limitations: Giving primarily in Nacagooches, TX.
Officers: Robert P. Blount, Pres.; John C. Hill, V.P.; Sarah Alice Millard, Secy.; Raymond E. Gilmore, Treas.
EIN: 751807003

53493
G. Architecture Foundation
1250 N.E. Loop 410, Ste. 335
San Antonio, TX 78209

Established in 1999 in TX.
Donor(s): William J. Gallagher.
Financial data (yr. ended 12/31/00): Grants paid, $0; assets, $2,400 (M); expenditures, $0; qualifying distributions, $0.
Limitations: Applications not accepted.
Application information: Contributes only to pre-selected organizations.
Officer and Directors:* William J. Gallagher,* Pres.; William H.B. Gallagher, Augusta B. Rosser.
EIN: 742918095

53494
Andree & Jean Gaulin Foundation
9901 IH-10 W., Ste. 250
San Antonio, TX 78230

Established in 2001 in TX.

Financial data (yr. ended 11/30/01): Grants paid, $0; assets, $5 (M); gifts received, $5; expenditures, $0; qualifying distributions, $0.
Trustees: Jean Gaulin, Andree Leboeuf.
EIN: 066519973

53495
The Genesis Foundation
1700 Columbine Ln.
Leander, TX 78641 (512) 259-9630
Contact: Scott Lindquist, Tr.

Established in 2000 in TX.
Financial data (yr. ended 12/31/00): Grants paid, $0; assets, $116 (M); expenditures, $9; qualifying distributions, $0.
Application information: Application form required.
Trustees: Laura Lindquist, Scott Lindquist.
EIN: 742960429

53496
Christine Gibson Scholarship Fund
215 State Hwy., 75 South
Fairfield, TX 75840

Established in 2000 in TX.
Donor(s): Roger Gibson.
Financial data (yr. ended 12/31/01): Grants paid, $0; assets, $7,636 (M); gifts received, $7,211; expenditures, $0; qualifying distributions, $0.
Trustees: Alwyn Gibson, Danny Gibson, Gregory Gibson, Roger Gibson.
EIN: 752849840

53497
Jules D. Gosseaux Foundation, Inc.
c/o Jules D. Gosseaux
2321 W. Expressway 83
McAllen, TX 78503

Established in 2001 in TX.
Donor(s): Jules D. Gosseaux.
Financial data (yr. ended 12/31/01): Grants paid, $0; assets, $20,002 (M); gifts received, $20,000; expenditures, $0; qualifying distributions, $0.
Officers: Jules D. Gosseaux, Pres.; Tony L. Talbott, Secy.; C. Wesley Kittleman, Treas.
EIN: 742992668

53498
Charles & Phyllis Gottlieb Memorial
c/o Phyllis Gottlieb
2805 W. 4th St.
Cameron, TX 76520-3050

Established in 2001.
Financial data (yr. ended 12/31/01): Grants paid, $0; assets, $125 (M); gifts received, $125; expenditures, $0; qualifying distributions, $0.
Trustee: Phyllis Gottlieb.
EIN: 756591323

53499
GRB Foundation
(Formerly Buford Foundation)
6125 Paluxy Dr., Bldg. 13
Tyler, TX 75703

Financial data (yr. ended 12/31/01): Grants paid, $0; assets, $200,882 (M); expenditures, $91; qualifying distributions, $0.
Limitations: Applications not accepted. Giving limited to Tyler, TX.
Application information: Contributes only to pre-selected organizations.
Officers: Robert Buford, Pres.; Beryl Berry, Secy.-Treas.
Trustee: Geoffrey Buford.
EIN: 751938482

53500
Greensheet Educational Foundation, Inc.
2601 Main St.
Houston, TX 77002-9201

Established in 1997.
Donor(s): Helen Gordon.
Financial data (yr. ended 03/31/02): Grants paid, $0; assets, $450 (M); gifts received, $17,598; expenditures, $278,233; qualifying distributions, $0; giving activities include $278,233 for programs.
Officers: Kathleen Douglass, Chair.; Bill Chaney, Secy.
Directors: Rebecca Blakeley, Helen Gordon.
EIN: 760536008

53501
The Gregory Foundation
13535 Grandmaster Piece Ln.
Houston, TX 77041-5535

Established in 1993 in TX.
Donor(s): Louis Gregory, Linda Lorelle Gregory.
Financial data (yr. ended 12/31/00): Grants paid, $0; assets, $990 (M); expenditures, $459; qualifying distributions, $0.
Limitations: Applications not accepted. Giving primarily in Houston, TX.
Application information: Contributes only to pre-selected organizations.
Trustees: Linda Lorelle Gregory, Louis Gregory.
EIN: 760418673

53502
Grevish Fund
c/o Cecil L. Smith
P.O. box 25169
Dallas, TX 75225

Established in 2001 in TX.
Financial data (yr. ended 12/31/01): Grants paid, $0; assets, $100 (M); gifts received, $1,500; expenditures, $0; qualifying distributions, $0.
Officers: Gregory A. Smith, Pres.; Cecil L. Smith, Vicki S. Farrow, Sherry S. Welton.
EIN: 752940201

53503
Kittie Nash Groce Trust
301 Dance Dr.
West Columbia, TX 77486

Established in 1996.
Financial data (yr. ended 12/31/00): Grants paid, $0; assets, $961,960 (M); expenditures, $38,355; qualifying distributions, $0.
Limitations: Applications not accepted. Giving primarily in West Columbia, TX.
Application information: Contributes only to pre-selected organization.
Trustees: John Damon, Roy Ledbetter, John Phillips.
EIN: 746226677

53504
Virginia & Christian Groneman Charitable Trust
P.O. Drawer 913
Bryan, TX 77805

Established in 2001 in TX.
Donor(s): Virginia Groneman.‡
Financial data (yr. ended 12/31/01): Grants paid, $0; assets, $539,001 (M); gifts received, $570,540; expenditures, $2,487; qualifying distributions, $0.
Limitations: Applications not accepted.
Application information: Contributes only to pre-selected organizations.
Trustee: Wells Fargo Bank.
EIN: 316652642

53505
John E. Guida Foundation
P.O. Box 24503
Houston, TX 77229

Established in 2000 in TX.
Donor(s): John E. Guida.
Financial data (yr. ended 11/30/01): Grants paid, $0; assets, $192,872 (M); gifts received, $248,107; expenditures, $10,107; qualifying distributions, $0.
Limitations: Applications not accepted.
Application information: Contributes only to pre-selected organizations.
Officers: John E. Guida, Pres. and Treas.; John S. Guida, V.P.; Laraine Guida McIntyre, Secy.
EIN: 760664874

53506
Ha'le Animal Rehabilitation of Texas
(Formerly United States Special Services)
2502 Canterbury Dr.
Carrollton, TX 75006-1607

Donor(s): Madolyn Congdon.
Financial data (yr. ended 12/31/01): Grants paid, $0; assets, $128,635 (M); expenditures, $9,420; qualifying distributions, $9,272.
Limitations: Applications not accepted. Giving primarily in TX.
Application information: Contributes only to pre-selected organizations.
Officers: Ryan Stewart, Pres.; Sharon Stewart, V.P.; Kathy Norton, Secy.
EIN: 751596640

53507
Haby Charitable Trust
P.O. Box 5247
San Angelo, TX 76902-5247
Contact: Homer H. Haby, Tr.

Donor(s): Homer H. Haby.
Financial data (yr. ended 12/31/01): Grants paid, $0; assets, $6,538 (M); expenditures, $14; qualifying distributions, $0.
Limitations: Giving primarily in San Angelo, TX.
Application information: Application form not required.
Trustees: H. Howard Haby, Homer H. Haby.
EIN: 746046851

53508
The Houston and Michelle Hall Foundation
5956 Sherry Ln., Ste. 1810
Dallas, TX 75225-8029

Established in 2000 in TX.
Donor(s): G. Houston Hall, Michelle D. Hall.
Financial data (yr. ended 12/31/00): Grants paid, $0; assets, $1,000,000 (M); gifts received, $1,000,000; expenditures, $0; qualifying distributions, $0.
Limitations: Applications not accepted.
Application information: Contributes only to pre-selected organizations.
Officers: G. Houston Hall, Pres. and Treas.; Michelle D. Hall, V.P. and Secy.
EIN: 755915750

53509
Sue Smith Harrison Family Foundation
5848 Diamond Point Cir.
El Paso, TX 79912

Established in 1999 in OK and TX.
Donor(s): Sue Smith Harrison.
Financial data (yr. ended 05/31/01): Grants paid, $0; assets, $74,382 (M); expenditures, $0; qualifying distributions, $0.
Limitations: Applications not accepted.

53509—TEXAS

Application information: Contributes only to pre-selected organizations.
Trustees: Gail K. Guerra, Michael E. Guerra, Stephanie L. Guerra, Susan H. Guerra, Steven T. Harrison.
EIN: 731569188

53510
Hauferma Foundation
5300 Town & Country Blvd., Ste. 300
Frisco, TX 75034-6898

Established in 2000 in TX.
Donor(s): TIV Operations Group, Inc., David Wayne Larsen, Victoria Coates Larsen.
Financial data (yr. ended 12/31/00): Grants paid, $0; assets, $535,850 (M); gifts received, $551,000; expenditures, $15,543; qualifying distributions, $15,543.
Limitations: Applications not accepted.
Application information: Contributes only to pre-selected organizations.
Officers: Michael Andrew Ladwig, Pres. and Treas.; David Wayne Larsen, Exec. V.P.; Victoria Coates Larsen, V.P.; Andrew J. Bensko, Secy.
EIN: 752854354
Codes: CS, CD

53511
Harry A. Haverlah Foundation
c/o East Texas National Bank
P.O. Box 770
Palestine, TX 75802

Established in 1967 in TX.
Donor(s): Harry A. Haverlah.‡
Financial data (yr. ended 12/31/01): Grants paid, $0; assets, $205,687 (M); gifts received, $1,660; expenditures, $41,822; qualifying distributions, $24,719; giving activities include $10,999 for loans to individuals.
Limitations: Giving limited to Anderson County, TX.
Application information: Application form required.
Officers and Directors:* Harry L. Brown,* Pres.; Jessie Kraus,* Secy.; Joe C. Crutcher, L.L. Davis, Stewart Kenderdine.
EIN: 751242215
Codes: GTI

53512
Heller Family Foundation
4501 Henning Dr.
Austin, TX 78738-1626 (512) 263-1666
Contact: Andrew R. Heller, Dir.

Established in 2000 in TX.
Donor(s): Andrew R. Heller, Mary Ann Heller.
Financial data (yr. ended 10/31/01): Grants paid, $0; assets, $460,496 (M); gifts received, $469,066; expenditures, $0; qualifying distributions, $0.
Application information: Application form not required.
Directors: Andrew R. Heller, Mary Ann Heller, Lawrence R. Paton.
EIN: 742983472

53513
The Henriksen Foundation
8831 Stable Ln.
Houston, TX 77024
Contact: Ronald W. Henriksen, Dir.

Established in 1998 in TX.
Donor(s): Ronald W. Henriksen.
Financial data (yr. ended 06/30/01): Grants paid, $0; assets, $1,105,051 (M); expenditures, $3,743; qualifying distributions, $0.
Limitations: Giving primarily in TX.

Directors: Ronald W. Henriksen, Russell C. Henriksen, Sheri C. Henriksen.
EIN: 760588346

53514
George Hervey Foundation
6261 Camino Allegre
El Paso, TX 79912

Financial data (yr. ended 12/31/00): Grants paid, $0; assets, $802 (L); expenditures, $17; qualifying distributions, $0.
Limitations: Giving primarily in El Paso, TX.
Trustee: Bette Hervey Becker.
EIN: 746046839

53515
Hill Country Student Help
P.O. Box 1092
Fredericksburg, TX 78624 (830) 997-9865
Contact: Helen V. Birck, Secy.-Treas.

Financial data (yr. ended 12/31/00): Grants paid, $0; assets, $714,863 (M); expenditures, $7,666; qualifying distributions, $29,627; giving activities include $19,938 for loans to individuals.
Limitations: Giving limited to residents of Gillespie County, TX.
Application information: Application form required.
Officers and Directors:* Edward F. Stein, Jr.,* Pres.; Curtis Cameron,* V.P.; Helen V. Birck,* Secy.-Treas.; John Benson, Mark Bierschwale, John R. Metzger, J. Hardin Perry.
EIN: 741473060
Codes: GTI

53516
Hoap Foundation (USA)
c/o Shair Baz Hakemy
1120 Harbor Haven
Southlake, TX 76092

Established in 2000 in TX.
Donor(s): Shair Baz Hakemy.
Financial data (yr. ended 12/31/00): Grants paid, $0; assets, $5,000 (M); gifts received, $5,000; expenditures, $0; qualifying distributions, $0.
Limitations: Applications not accepted.
Application information: Contributes only to pre-selected organizations.
Directors: Kamal Daya, Shair Baz Hakemy, Mohammad Y. Hakemy.
EIN: 752838314

53517
Patsy B. Hollandsworth Family Foundation
P.O. Box 1632
Longview, TX 75606-1632
Contact: Harriet W. Courington, Pres.

Established in 1996.
Donor(s): Patsy B. Hollandworth.
Financial data (yr. ended 12/31/01): Grants paid, $0; assets, $5,992,506 (M); expenditures, $1,091; qualifying distributions, $0.
Officers and Directors:* Harriet W. Courington,* Pres. and Treas.; William H. Wilson,* V.P.; Alyce Kay Garrett,* Secy.
EIN: 752655126

53518
James T. & Jan L. Hoover Family Foundation
8015 Shoal Creek Blvd., Ste. 100
Austin, TX 78757

Established in 2000 in TX.
Donor(s): James T. Hoover, Jan L. Hoover.
Financial data (yr. ended 12/31/00): Grants paid, $0; assets, $85,125 (M); gifts received, $86,625; expenditures, $0; qualifying distributions, $0.
Limitations: Applications not accepted.

Application information: Contributes only to pre-selected organizations.
Officers: James T. Hoover, Pres. and Treas.; Jan L. Hoover, V.P. and Secy.
Director: Anne L. Hess.
EIN: 742929251

53519
Frank W. and Gladys G. Hornbrook Scholarship Fund
c/o Broadway National Bank, Trust Dept.
P.O. Box 17001
San Antonio, TX 78217
Application address: c/o Guidance Counselor, Alamo Heights High School, 6900 Broadway, San Antonio, TX 78209, tel.: (210) 820-8875

Donor(s): Gladys B. Hornbrook.‡
Financial data (yr. ended 12/31/99): Grants paid, $0; assets, $309,611 (M); gifts received, $250,000; expenditures, $2,855; qualifying distributions, $0.
Limitations: Giving limited to residents of San Antonio, TX.
Trustee: Broadway National Bank.
EIN: 742881302

53520
The Carolyn Hortenstine Foundation
329 Shasta Dr.
Houston, TX 77024
Contact: Carolyn B. Hortenstine, Pres.

Established in 1992 in TX.
Donor(s): Bardsdale Hortenstine, Carolyn B. Hortenstine.
Financial data (yr. ended 04/30/01): Grants paid, $0; assets, $18,892 (M); expenditures, $1,847; qualifying distributions, $0.
Limitations: Giving limited to Houston, TX.
Officers: Carolyn B. Hortenstine, Pres.; Bardsdale Hortenstine, V.P. and Treas.; Terri Lacy, Secy.
EIN: 760420961

53521
Huddleston Foundation
1 Houston Ctr., 1221 McKinney, Ste. 3700
Houston, TX 77010

Established in 2001 in TX.
Donor(s): B.P. Huddleston, Flora M. Huddleston.
Financial data (yr. ended 12/31/01): Grants paid, $0; assets, $98,333 (M); gifts received, $100,000; expenditures, $16; qualifying distributions, $0.
Limitations: Applications not accepted.
Application information: Contributes only to pre-selected organizations.
Officers and Directors:* B.P. Huddleston,* Pres.; Peter D. Huddleston,* V.P.; Lisa H. Currie,* Secy.; Flora M. Huddleston,* Treas.; W. Paul Huddleston.
EIN: 760589041

53522
G. C. Hudson Youth Foundation
(Formerly Jake Hudson Youth Foundation)
c/o Bank of America
P.O. Box 831041
Dallas, TX 75283-1041
Application address: Trust Committee, c/o Bank of America, 100 N. Main St., Trust Dept., Corsicana, TX, 75110, tel.: (903) 654-3254

Financial data (yr. ended 07/31/01): Grants paid, $0; assets, $87,820 (M); expenditures, $2,147; qualifying distributions, $0.
Limitations: Giving primarily in Corsicana and Navarro County, TX.
Trustee: Bank of America.
EIN: 756082593

53523
Arthur C. Hughes Foundation Trust
c/o Bank of America
P.O. Box 831041
Dallas, TX 75283-1041 (214) 508-1978

Financial data (yr. ended 09/30/01): Grants paid, $0; assets, $107,220 (M); expenditures, $3,645; qualifying distributions, $0.
Limitations: Applications not accepted. Giving primarily in Dallas, TX.
Application information: Contributes only to pre-selected organizations.
Trustee: Bank of America.
EIN: 756007061

53524
The Ruth Ray Hunt Foundation
1445 Ross at Field, Ste. 1700
Dallas, TX 75202-2785

Established in 1981 in TX.
Financial data (yr. ended 06/30/01): Grants paid, $0; assets, $13,486 (M); expenditures, $421; qualifying distributions, $327.
Limitations: Applications not accepted. Giving primarily in TX.
Application information: Contributes only to pre-selected organizations.
Officers and Directors:* Ray L. Hunt,* Pres.; Richard A. Massman,* V.P. and Secy.; Barbara Clark Cashion, Treas.; Walter J. Humann.
EIN: 751726227

53525
Elton M. Hyder, Jr. Charitable Fund, Inc.
(Formerly Elton M. Hyder, Jr. Charitable & Educational Fund, Inc.)
1204-B West 7th St.
Fort Worth, TX 76102
Contact: Brent Hyder, Pres.

Established in 1959 in TX.
Donor(s): Elton M. Hyder, Jr.,‡ Merle M. Rowan.
Financial data (yr. ended 10/31/01): Grants paid, $0; assets, $3,581,250 (M); expenditures, $28,919; qualifying distributions, $0.
Officers and Director:* Brent Hyder,* Pres.; Whitney Hyder More, V.P.; Martha R. Hyder, Treas.
EIN: 756005547

53526
The Isaac I Foundation
1 Birchmont Ln.
Dallas, TX 75230
Application address: c/o Ron E. Rinard, 2701 Hibernia St., Dallas, TX 75204, tel.: (214) 979-0553

Established in 2001 in TX.
Donor(s): Ron E. Rinard.
Financial data (yr. ended 12/31/01): Grants paid, $0; assets, $1,000,935 (M); gifts received, $1,000,000; expenditures, $8,433; qualifying distributions, $0.
Application information: Application form not required.
Directors: Cecilia M. Rinard, Ronald E. Rinard, John R. Stoika.
EIN: 752965575

53527
The Jam Foundation
P.O. Box 130906
The Woodlands, TX 77393-0906

Established in 2000.
Financial data (yr. ended 12/31/00): Grants paid, $0; assets, $210,000 (M); gifts received, $210,000; expenditures, $0; qualifying distributions, $0.
Limitations: Applications not accepted.
Application information: Contributes only to pre-selected organizations.
Trustees: Jeffery Geuther, Marjorie Geuther.
EIN: 760669987

53528
Jenkins Charitable Trust
15623 Forest Run Dr.
Cypress, TX 77429

Established in 1998.
Financial data (yr. ended 12/31/99): Grants paid, $0; assets, $340 (L); gifts received, $340; expenditures, $0; qualifying distributions, $0.
Limitations: Applications not accepted.
Application information: Contributes only to pre-selected organizations.
Trustees: Kerney John Jenkins, Leah M. Jenkins.
EIN: 766142465

53529
JLH Foundation
1035 Diary Ashford, Ste. 115
Houston, TX 77079

Established in 2001 in TX.
Donor(s): Donna L. Sheppard-Hern, Trigeant, Ltd.
Financial data (yr. ended 12/31/01): Grants paid, $0; assets, $60,399 (M); gifts received, $23,904; expenditures, $4,292; qualifying distributions, $0.
Officers and Directors:* Paula A. Hern,* Chair.; Ellis Tudzin,* Secy.-Treas.; Tom Barbour.
EIN: 760666945

53530
John & Nedra Johnson Charitable Foundation
c/o G.L. Geary
9330 LBJ Fwy.
Dallas, TX 75243

Established in 2001 in TX.
Financial data (yr. ended 12/31/01): Grants paid, $0; assets, $675,664 (M); expenditures, $0; qualifying distributions, $0.
Trustees: A. Shawn Johnson, Holly Johnson West.
EIN: 752905570

53531
Louise G. and Jack P. Jones Foundation
5028 Bellaire Dr. S.
Fort Worth, TX 76109

Established in 2001.
Financial data (yr. ended 12/31/01): Grants paid, $0; assets, $9,547 (M); gifts received, $9,500; expenditures, $240; qualifying distributions, $0.
Limitations: Applications not accepted.
Application information: Contributes only to pre-selected organizations.
Officers: Jack P. Jones, Pres.; Louise G. Jones, Secy.-Treas.
Directors: Steven A. Jones, David A. Jones.
EIN: 752919362

53532
Dee and Florence Jones Scholarship Fund
102 Hobbs St.
San Angelo, TX 76903-7906 (915) 653-3701
Contact: Kenneth Thomas, Tr.

Financial data (yr. ended 12/31/01): Grants paid, $0; assets, $6,597 (M); expenditures, $112; qualifying distributions, $0.
Limitations: Giving primarily in San Angelo, TX.
Application information: Application form required.
Trustees: Constance Thomas, Kenneth Thomas.
EIN: 752026855

53533
Edith Irby Jones, M.D. Foundation
c/o Joseph Mason
2601 Prospect St.
Houston, TX 77004-7737

Established in 1999 in TX.
Financial data (yr. ended 12/31/99): Grants paid, $0; assets, $1,000 (M); gifts received, $1,000; expenditures, $0; qualifying distributions, $0.
Directors: Edith I. Jones, Joseph Mason.
EIN: 760601145

53534
Lenoir M. Josey Foundation
4202 Yoakum Blvd.
Houston, TX 77006-5418

Donor(s): Lenoir M. Josey II.
Financial data (yr. ended 12/31/01): Grants paid, $0; assets, $3,140 (M); expenditures, $2; qualifying distributions, $0.
Limitations: Applications not accepted. Giving primarily in Austin, TX.
Application information: Contributes only to pre-selected organizations.
Trustees: Jack S. Josey, Lenoir M. Josey II, Robert A. Josey II.
EIN: 237435545

53535
Joshua Foundation
10203 Birchridge Dr., Ste. 400
Humble, TX 77338

Established in 1996 in TX.
Donor(s): Henry O. Harper, Jr.
Financial data (yr. ended 12/31/00): Grants paid, $0; assets, $207,035 (M); gifts received, $525,291; expenditures, $120; qualifying distributions, $0.
Limitations: Applications not accepted. Giving primarily in TX.
Application information: Contributes only to pre-selected organizations.
Directors: Carolyn F. Harper, Christi M. Harper, Henry O. Harper, Jr.
EIN: 760483771

53536
Journey Foundation
4909 Orchard Dr.
Sachse, TX 75048

Established in 1999 in TX.
Financial data (yr. ended 12/31/99): Grants paid, $0; assets, $100 (M); expenditures, $0; qualifying distributions, $0.
Limitations: Applications not accepted.
Application information: Contributes only to pre-selected organizations.
Trustees: Rebecca A. Jernigan, Thomas K. Jernigan, Sr.
EIN: 752796143

53537
W. D. Kelley Foundation
(Formerly W. D. Kelley Charitable Trust)
c/o Grants Committee
707 Rock St.
Georgetown, TX 78626 (512) 863-2575
FAX: (512) 863-2576
Contact: Dale Illig, Exec. Dir.

Established in 1996 in TX.
Financial data (yr. ended 12/31/01): Grants paid, $0; assets, $1,000 (M); expenditures, $0; qualifying distributions, $0.
Limitations: Giving primarily within 50 miles of Georgetown, TX.

Application information: Application form not required.
Officer: Dale Illig, Exec. Dir.
EIN: 743007226

53538
Dr. and Mrs. Hugh A. Kennedy Foundation
802 N. Carancahua St., Ste. 1270
Corpus Christi, TX 78470-0184
Contact: Martin C. Davis, Pres.

Established in 2001 in TX.
Donor(s): Hugh A. Kennedy,‡ Margaret T. Kennedy.‡
Financial data (yr. ended 12/31/01): Grants paid, $0; assets, $13,097,751 (M); gifts received, $8,827,405; expenditures, $43,970; qualifying distributions, $0.
Officers and Directors:* Martin C. Davis,* Pres.; Avalee Byrd,* V.P.; James Roach,* Secy.; Jake Henry,* Treas.
EIN: 742983794

53539
The Klein Foundation
500 W. Texas, Ste. 1230
Midland, TX 79701
Application address: c/o MJ Summer Camp, 4550 Post Oak Pl., Ste. 150, Houston, TX 77027-3106, tel.: (713) 877-8104

Established in 1995 in TX.
Donor(s): Michael L. Klein.
Financial data (yr. ended 12/31/99): Grants paid, $0; assets, $13,165 (M); expenditures, $1,493; qualifying distributions, $0.
Limitations: Giving primarily to residents of Houston and Midland, TX.
Application information: Application form required.
Officers and Trustees:* Michael L. Klein,* Pres.; Jeanne Lee Klein,* V.P. and Secy.-Treas.; Jacquelyn Klein Brown, Eric Klein, Quincy James Lee, Zachry Steven Lee.
EIN: 752555667

53540
Theodore A. Kowitz Memorial Foundation
c/o Mary E. Edmiston
1901 N. Akard St.
Dallas, TX 75201-2305

Donor(s): David Kowitz.
Financial data (yr. ended 12/31/01): Grants paid, $0; assets, $10,767 (M); gifts received, $1; expenditures, $124; qualifying distributions, $0.
Limitations: Applications not accepted. Giving primarily in Middletown, NY.
Officers: David Kowitz, Pres. and Treas.; Eric Millep, Secy.
Trustees: Julie Kowitz, Ellen Miller.
EIN: 752619264

53541
The Heather Lang Foundation
HC 70, Box 148
Lohn, TX 76852-9714

Established in 2000.
Financial data (yr. ended 12/31/01): Grants paid, $0; assets, $0 (M); expenditures, $413; qualifying distributions, $0.
Officers and Directors:* Elmer N. Lang,* Pres.; Linda Lang,* Secy.-Treas.; Elmer N. Lang, Jr., Jeremy D. Lang.
EIN: 311694530

53542
Julian G. Lange Family Foundation I
7 Elmcourt St.
San Antonio, TX 78209-2811
Contact: Richard A. Lange, Tr.

Established in 1999 in TX.
Donor(s): Julian G. Lange.‡
Financial data (yr. ended 12/31/01): Grants paid, $0; assets, $1,436,461 (M); gifts received, $94,018; expenditures, $1,849; qualifying distributions, $0.
Limitations: Giving limited to OH.
Application information: Applications not accepted until 2005.
Trustee: Richard A. Lange.
EIN: 311663386

53543
The Susan and Jack Lapin Foundation
c/o Jack Lapin
109 N. Post Oak Ln., Ste. 300
Houston, TX 77024

Established in 1996 in TX.
Donor(s): Jean Kaufman.‡
Financial data (yr. ended 11/30/01): Grants paid, $0; assets, $252,200 (M); expenditures, $3,382; qualifying distributions, $0.
Limitations: Applications not accepted.
Application information: Contributes only to pre-selected organizations.
Trustees: Jack Lapin, Susan K. Lapin.
EIN: 760527414

53544
The Lattimore Foundation
1700 Redbud Blvd., Ste. 400
McKinney, TX 75069

Established in 1999 in TX.
Financial data (yr. ended 12/31/99): Grants paid, $0; assets, $402,421 (M); expenditures, $0; qualifying distributions, $0.
Limitations: Applications not accepted.
Application information: Contributes only to pre-selected organizations.
Directors: John Victor Lattimore, Jr., Oscar Paige, Bishop James Stanton.
EIN: 752850578

53545
James Allbritain Lawson Charitable Trust
P.O. Box 831041
Dallas, TX 75283-1041

Established in 2001 in MO.
Donor(s): James Lawson Unitrust.
Financial data (yr. ended 12/31/01): Grants paid, $0; assets, $2,055,751 (M); gifts received, $2,236,714; expenditures, $18,517; qualifying distributions, $3,656.
Limitations: Giving limited to Livingston County, MO.
Trustee: Bank of America.
EIN: 436225310

53546
The LeTourneau Foundation
4300 S. Business 281
Edinburg, TX 78539-9699
Contact: Roy S. LeTourneau, Pres.

Incorporated in 1935 in CA.
Donor(s): Robert G. LeTourneau,‡ Mrs. Robert G. LeTourneau.
Financial data (yr. ended 12/31/01): Grants paid, $0; assets, $197,214 (M); expenditures, $72,962; qualifying distributions, $0.
Limitations: Giving on a national basis.

Officers and Directors:* Roy S. LeTourneau,* Pres.; Randy LeTourneau,* Secy.-Treas.
EIN: 756001947

53547
Lewis Foundation
P.O. Box 9910
College Station, TX 77842

Established in 1999 in TX.
Financial data (yr. ended 12/31/99): Grants paid, $0; assets, $101,249 (M); gifts received, $101,249; expenditures, $0; qualifying distributions, $0.
Limitations: Applications not accepted.
Application information: Contributes only to pre-selected organizations.
Officer: Roy Lewis, Mgr.
EIN: 742936403

53548
Marion and Cadell S. Liedtke Family Charitable Foundation
P.O. Box 1389
Midland, TX 79702

Established in 1996 in TX.
Donor(s): Cadell S. Liedtke.
Financial data (yr. ended 07/31/01): Grants paid, $0; assets, $1,355 (M); expenditures, $323; qualifying distributions, $0.
Limitations: Applications not accepted. Giving primarily in TX.
Application information: Contributes only to pre-selected organizations.
Officers and Directors:* Cadell S. Liedtke,* Pres.; Marion Liedtke,* Secy.; Leslie J. Liedtke.
EIN: 752708769

53549
Lugar Family Foundation
12377 Merit Dr., Ste. 220
Dallas, TX 75251

Established in 2000 in TX.
Donor(s): Steven M. Lugar, Gari B. Lugar.
Financial data (yr. ended 12/31/00): Grants paid, $0; assets, $329,624 (M); gifts received, $327,284; expenditures, $0; qualifying distributions, $0.
Limitations: Applications not accepted.
Application information: Contributes only to pre-selected organizations.
Officers: Gari B. Lugar, Mgr.; Steven M. Lugar, Mgr.
Trustee: Pat C. Beaird.
EIN: 752912021

53550
The MacGregor Foundation
8306 Bell Mountain Dr.
Austin, TX 78730-2826

Established in 2000 in TX.
Financial data (yr. ended 12/31/01): Grants paid, $0; assets, $800,618 (M); gifts received, $804,684; expenditures, $4,184; qualifying distributions, $0.
Limitations: Applications not accepted.
Application information: Contributes only to pre-selected organizations.
Officers: Douglas B. MacGregor, Pres. and Treas.; Michael Y. MacGregor, Secy.
Directors: Elizabeth L. Looney, Katharine J. Loughlin.
EIN: 742983728

53551
Make an Impact Charitable Foundation
4320 N. Beltline Rd.
Irving, TX 75038

Established in 2001 in TX.
Donor(s): CCISTECH Inc., Dana Ballinger, Jim Mills, Dickson Perry.
Financial data (yr. ended 12/31/01): Grants paid, $0; assets, $40,424 (M); gifts received, $40,424; expenditures, $0; qualifying distributions, $0.
Limitations: Applications not accepted.
Application information: Contributes only to pre-selected organizations.
Trustees: Dana Ballinger, Dickson Perry, Raul Toledo.
EIN: 010557469
Codes: CS

53552
Marett-Tillman Charitable Trust
P.O. Box 780841
San Antonio, TX 78278-0841

Established in 1987 in TX.
Donor(s): V. Stanley Marett, Susan E. Marett.
Financial data (yr. ended 12/31/01): Grants paid, $0; assets, $40,057 (M); expenditures, $153; qualifying distributions, $0.
Limitations: Applications not accepted. Giving on a national basis.
Application information: Contributes only to pre-selected organizations.
Trustees: Susan E. Marett, V. Stanley Marett.
EIN: 756353039

53553
Mayfield Foundation, Inc.
P.O. Box 570365
Houston, TX 77257-0365

Established in 1996 in TX.
Donor(s): Jack H. Mayfield, Jr.
Financial data (yr. ended 12/31/01): Grants paid, $0; assets, $5 (M); expenditures, $257; qualifying distributions, $0.
Limitations: Applications not accepted. Giving primarily in TX.
Application information: Contributes only to pre-selected organizations.
Officers: Jack H. Mayfield, Jr., Pres.; Don W. Pisklak, Treas.
EIN: 760495695

53554
The McHenry Tichenor Foundation
724 N. Sam Houston Blvd.
San Benito, TX 78586-5265

Established in 2001 in AZ.
Donor(s): Jean Tichenor.
Financial data (yr. ended 12/31/01): Grants paid, $0; assets, $252,460 (M); gifts received, $166,975; expenditures, $13,119; qualifying distributions, $0.
Limitations: Applications not accepted.
Application information: Contributes only to pre-selected organizations.
Officers: Susan Ander, Pres. and Treas.; Jean Tichenor, V.P.; Elizabeth S. Waynick, Secy.
EIN: 861033389

53555
Shirley & William S. McIntyre Foundation
12222 Merit Dr., Ste. 1660
Dallas, TX 75251

Established in 2000 in TX.
Donor(s): Shirley C. McIntyre, William S. McIntyre, International Risk Management.

Financial data (yr. ended 06/30/01): Grants paid, $0; assets, $144,917 (M); gifts received, $267,919; expenditures, $0; qualifying distributions, $0.
Limitations: Applications not accepted.
Application information: Contributes only to pre-selected organizations.
Officers: Shirley C. McIntyre, Pres.; William S. McIntyre, V.P.
EIN: 752910339

53556
McKinster Charitable Foundation
40 Crown Pl.
Richardson, TX 75080-1603

Established in 1998 in TX.
Financial data (yr. ended 12/31/01): Grants paid, $0; assets, $191,260 (M); expenditures, $2,429; qualifying distributions, $0.
Limitations: Applications not accepted.
Application information: Contributes only to pre-selected organizations.
Trustee: Frank J. Whitworth.
EIN: 752729296

53557
Medical Arts Foundation, Inc.
P.O. Box 841
Corsicana, TX 75151-0841

Financial data (yr. ended 12/31/01): Grants paid, $0; assets, $83,987 (M); gifts received, $70; expenditures, $3,591; qualifying distributions, $0.
Limitations: Applications not accepted.
Application information: Contributes only to pre-selected organizations.
Officer and Trustees:* Kent Rodgers, M.D.,* Chair.; Joseph M. Glicksman, M.D., Neal Green, M.D., Scott Middleton, M.D., John Nelson, M.D.
EIN: 751581285

53558
Nettie Millhollon Educational Trust Estate
P.O. Box 643
Stanton, TX 79782 (915) 756-2261
Contact: Debbie Thompson, Office Mgr.

Trust established in 1963 in TX.
Donor(s): Nettie Millhollon.‡
Financial data (yr. ended 06/30/00): Grants paid, $0; assets, $3,281,960 (M); expenditures, $145,605; qualifying distributions, $278,754; giving activities include $280,149 for loans to individuals.
Limitations: Giving limited to residents of TX.
Application information: Applicants must be TX residents pursuing a BA degree. Interview required; only makes student loans. Application form required.
Officers and Trustees:* Claude Ray Glaspie,* Chair.; Mary Belle Keaton,* Vice-Chair.; Beverley North,* Secy.-Treas.; Charles Blocker, Rodger Burch, Kyle Kendall, W.E. Morrow, Eddie Odom.
EIN: 756024639
Codes: GTI

53559
Mission Ministries, Inc.
2818 Simondale Dr.
Fort Worth, TX 76109

Established in 1995 in TX.
Donor(s): John M. Holland.
Financial data (yr. ended 12/31/00): Grants paid, $0; assets, $0 (M); expenditures, $1,706; qualifying distributions, $1,706.
Limitations: Applications not accepted.
Application information: Contributes only to pre-selected organizations.

Trustees: Leslie D. Fry, Corrie J. Holland, James R. Holland, John M. Holland, Gaylord Sturgess.
EIN: 752623029

53560
The Ronald E. Moore Foundation
(Formerly Ronald E. & Alexandra Moore Foundatioon)
2711 Park Hill Dr.
Fort Worth, TX 76109-1424

Donor(s): Ronald E. Moore, Alexandra Moore.
Financial data (yr. ended 12/31/01): Grants paid, $0; assets, $474,344 (M); gifts received, $17,934; expenditures, $8; qualifying distributions, $0.
Limitations: Applications not accepted. Giving in the U.S., primarily in TX, NY, CA, and Washington, DC; some giving also in South America.
Application information: Contributes only to pre-selected organizations.
Officer: Ronald E. Moore, Pres.
EIN: 752392367

53561
Felix and Angela Morales Memorial Foundation
2901 Canal St.
Houston, TX 77003

Established in 1994 in TX.
Donor(s): Angela Morales.
Financial data (yr. ended 12/31/00): Grants paid, $0; assets, $75,730 (M); gifts received, $94,830; expenditures, $16,199; qualifying distributions, $15,212.
Limitations: Applications not accepted. Giving primarily in TX.
Application information: Unsolicited requests for funds not accepted.
Officers and Directors:* Richard C. Vara,* Pres.; Christina Morales Krasnick,* Secy.-Treas.; Felix Fraga, Herlinda Garcia, Adrian Nieto, Minerva Perez, Lolene Smith.
EIN: 760428633

53562
Morse Family Foundation, Inc.
c/o JPMorgan Chase Bank
P.O. Box 550
Austin, TX 78789-0001 (512) 479-2627
E-mail: scott.deneen@jpmorgan.com; cecilia.rohloff@jpmorgan.com
Contact: Scott Deneen, V.P., JPMorgan Chase Bank

Established in 1997 in TX.
Donor(s): Estelle Morse.
Financial data (yr. ended 12/31/00): Grants paid, $0; assets, $977,890 (M); expenditures, $14,774; qualifying distributions, $0.
Limitations: Applications not accepted. Giving primarily in Austin, TX.
Publications: Financial statement.
Application information: Contributes only to pre-selected organizations.
Officers: Scott N. Morse, Pres.; Frederic C. Morse III, V.P.; Mary Morse, Secy.-Treas.
EIN: 742637207

53563
Mildred S. & Edward J. Mosher Foundation
P.O. Box 22383
Houston, TX 77227-2383 (713) 626-7830
Contact: Jean Mosher Kendall, Secy.-Treas.

Donor(s): Edward J. Mosher.
Financial data (yr. ended 09/30/01): Grants paid, $0; assets, $624,388 (M); expenditures, $9,370; qualifying distributions, $0.
Application information: Application form required.

53563—TEXAS

Officers: E. Blake Mosher, Pres.; Susan Rowan, V.P.; Jean Mosher Kendall, Secy.-Treas.
EIN: 237435543

53564
Clifton F. Mountain Foundation
2028 Albans Rd.
Houston, TX 77005

Established in 1997 in TX.
Donor(s): Bristol, Myer, Squibb.
Financial data (yr. ended 12/31/99): Grants paid, $0; assets, $155,632 (M); gifts received, $150,000; expenditures, $64,359; qualifying distributions, $64,359; giving activities include $54,111 for programs.
Officers: Clifton F. Mountain, Pres.; Kay E. Hermes, Secy.-Treas.
Director: Lawrence M. Hermes.
EIN: 760491659

53565
The Mouton Foundation
102 Kirkwood Ct.
Sugar Land, TX 77478
Contact: John O. Mouton, Tr.

Established in 1990 in TX.
Donor(s): John O. Mouton, Carole J. Mouton.
Financial data (yr. ended 12/31/01): Grants paid, $0; assets, $2,506 (M); expenditures, $600; qualifying distributions, $0.
Trustees: Carole J. Mouton, Ian A. Mouton, Jeremy A. Mouton, John O. Mouton.
EIN: 760324344

53566
The National Tax Research Committee
(Formerly Betty & Jack Trotter Foundation)
109 N. Post Oak Ln., Ste. 425
Houston, TX 77024

Financial data (yr. ended 12/31/01): Grants paid, $0; assets, $146,940 (M); expenditures, $2,568; qualifying distributions, $0.
Limitations: Applications not accepted. Giving on a national basis.
Application information: Contributes only to pre-selected organizations.
Officers: James A. Reichert, Pres.; Richard W. Fairchild, Jr., V.P. and Secy.-Treas.
EIN: 760052457

53567
New Braunfels Community Chorale
410 Saddle Tree Dr.
New Braunfels, TX 78130

Financial data (yr. ended 12/31/01): Grants paid, $0; assets, $7,719 (M); gifts received, $660; expenditures, $9,980; qualifying distributions, $0.
Limitations: Applications not accepted. Giving primarily in New Braunfels, TX.
Officers: Ann Young, Pres.; Maxine Perry, V.P.; Ken Devillier, Treas.
EIN: 742398955

53568
The New Mavericks Foundation
2909 Taylor St.
Dallas, TX 75226-1909
Contact: Allegra East, Exec. Dir.

Established in 2000 in TX.
Donor(s): Dallas Basketball Limited, Dallas Mavericks Foundation.
Financial data (yr. ended 06/30/01): Grants paid, $0; assets, $494,817 (M); gifts received, $494,817; expenditures, $0; qualifying distributions, $0.
Application information: Application form required.

Officers: Terdema L. Ussery, Pres.; Floyd Jahner, V.P. and Treas.; Cheryl Karalla, Secy.; Allegra East, Exec. Dir.
Directors: Brian Cuban, Jeff Cuban, Mark Cuban, Lois Evans, Joy Nelson, Tiffany Stewart, Gretchen Minyard Williams, Martin Woodall.
EIN: 311767408
Codes: CS

53569
Newport-Van Everdingen Foundation
5000 Montrose Blvd., Ste. 20
Houston, TX 77006

Established in 2000 in TX.
Financial data (yr. ended 12/31/00): Grants paid, $0; assets, $5,000 (M); gifts received, $5,000; expenditures, $0; qualifying distributions, $0.
Officer: Patrick Newport, Pres.
EIN: 752913007

53570
Bryan Nichols Scholarship Trust
c/o Citizens National Bank of Milam County
118 S. Houston
Cameron, TX 76520

Established in 2001 in TX.
Donor(s): R. Bryan Nichols.
Financial data (yr. ended 12/31/01): Grants paid, $0; assets, $123,425 (M); gifts received, $119,693; expenditures, $1,881; qualifying distributions, $1,264.
Limitations: Applications not accepted.
Application information: Contributes only to pre-selected organizations.
Trustee: Citizens National Bank of Milam County.
EIN: 746438292

53571
Nierling United Presbyterian Church Trust
200 Crescent Ct., Ste. 1200
Dallas, TX 75201-7837

Established in 1999 in ND.
Donor(s): Richard D. Nierling.‡
Financial data (yr. ended 12/31/99): Grants paid, $0; assets, $58,528 (M); gifts received, $60,000; expenditures, $0; qualifying distributions, $0.
Limitations: Applications not accepted.
Application information: Contributes only to pre-selected organizations.
Trustee: Richard B. Nierling.
EIN: 912004884

53572
Nierling-Jamestown Hospital Trust
200 Crescent Ct., Ste. 1200
Dallas, TX 75201-7837

Established in 1999 in ND.
Financial data (yr. ended 12/31/00): Grants paid, $0; assets, $58,699 (M); gifts received, $60,000; expenditures, $0; qualifying distributions, $0.
Limitations: Applications not accepted.
Application information: Contributes only to pre-selected organizations.
Trustee: Richard B. Nierling.
EIN: 912004888

53573
Nine Eleven Foundation
5050 Woodway Dr., Apt. 8P
Houston, TX 77056 (713) 621-3899
Contact: Hilda Askanase, Tr.

Donor(s): Hilda Askanase.
Financial data (yr. ended 12/31/01): Grants paid, $0; assets, $50,221 (M); expenditures, $750; qualifying distributions, $0.
Limitations: Giving primarily in Houston, TX.
Trustee: Hilda Askanase.

EIN: 746104597

53574
Northside Music School, Inc.
11918 Vance Jackson Rd.
San Antonio, TX 78230

Established in 2000 in TX.
Donor(s): Robin Abraham, Peggy Abraham.
Financial data (yr. ended 12/31/00): Grants paid, $0; assets, $31,518 (M); gifts received, $50,651; expenditures, $19,427; qualifying distributions, $31,224.
Limitations: Applications not accepted.
Application information: Contributes only to pre-selected organizations.
Officers: Robin Abraham, Pres.; Peggy Abraham, V.P.; Phyllis Abbas, Secy.-Treas.
EIN: 742930001

53575
NRKC Drug Dog Fund, Inc.
P.O. Box 466
Cleburne, TX 76033

Established in 2000.
Financial data (yr. ended 12/31/01): Grants paid, $0; assets, $1 (M); gifts received, $615; expenditures, $2,030; qualifying distributions, $0.
Officers: Mary Hogan, Pres.; George Willis, V.P.; Betty J. Epperson, Secy.; Ginger Pugh, Treas.
Directors: Bruce Barnes, Roland G. Bartlett, Willis Pipes, Betty Stiles, Laurie Telfair.
EIN: 752895800

53576
The O'Brien and Sager Charitable Trust
c/o Kanaly Trust Co.
4550 Post Oak Place Dr., Ste. 139
Houston, TX 77027-3163

Established in 1999 in TX.
Donor(s): Brian E. O'Brien, Sandra L. O'Brien, Harry C. Sager, Anne H. Sager.
Financial data (yr. ended 12/31/01): Grants paid, $0; assets, $295,316 (M); gifts received, $162,388; expenditures, $6,798; qualifying distributions, $0.
Limitations: Applications not accepted.
Application information: Contributes only to pre-selected organizations.
Trustees: Brian E. O'Brien, Sandra L. O'Brien, Anne H. Sager, Harry C. Sager, Kanaly Trust Co.
EIN: 760603800

53577
Michael O'Connor and Karen L. O'Connor Foundation
c/o Phillip Plant
800 N. Shoreline Blvd., Ste. 2200S
Corpus Christi, TX 78401

Established in 2001 in TX.
Financial data (yr. ended 12/31/01): Grants paid, $0; assets, $1,018 (M); gifts received, $1,000; expenditures, $0; qualifying distributions, $0.
Limitations: Applications not accepted.
Application information: Contributes only to pre-selected organizations.
Officers: Michael A. O'Connor, Pres.; Phillip M. Plant, V.P.; Karen L. O'Connor, Secy.; Alfred B. Jones, Jr., Treas.
EIN: 742969840

53578
Ott Charitable Foundation
3689 Inwood Dr.
Houston, TX 77019-3023

Established in 2000 in TX.
Donor(s): David A. Ott, Pamela F. Ott.

Financial data (yr. ended 12/31/00): Grants paid, $0; assets, $9,856 (M); gifts received, $9,856; expenditures, $0; qualifying distributions, $0.
Limitations: Applications not accepted.
Application information: Contributes only to pre-selected organizations.
Officers: David A. Ott, Pres.; Pamela F. Ott, Secy.-Treas.
EIN: 760664063

53579
The Paisano Foundation
2020 Mercantile Tower, MT239
Corpus Christi, TX 78477

Donor(s): Edwin Singer, Patsy Dunn Singer.
Financial data (yr. ended 12/31/01): Grants paid, $0; assets, $316 (M); expenditures, $0; qualifying distributions, $0.
Limitations: Applications not accepted. Giving primarily in Corpus Christi, TX.
Application information: Contributes only to pre-selected organizations.
Trustee: Edwin Singer.
EIN: 237393207

53580
Palacios Community Foundation
P.O. Box 880
Palacios, TX 77465

Established in 2000 in TX.
Donor(s): Palacios Campsite Assoc.
Financial data (yr. ended 12/31/01): Grants paid, $0; assets, $712,354 (M); expenditures, $15,162; qualifying distributions, $0.
Limitations: Applications not accepted.
Application information: Contributes only to pre-selected organizations.
Officers: Marvin L. Curtis, Pres.; Leonard Lamar, V.P. and Treas.; Thomas Holsworth, Secy.
EIN: 760590386

53581
Y. H. Pao Foundation
330 N. Sam Houston Pkwy., E., Ste. 190
Houston, TX 77060 (281) 591-8881
Contact: Yih-Ho "Michael" Pao, Pres.

Established in 1989.
Donor(s): Yih-Ho "Michael" Pao.
Financial data (yr. ended 03/31/99): Grants paid, $0; assets, $48,863 (M); expenditures, $838; qualifying distributions, $0.
Officers and Directors:* Yih-Ho "Michael" Pao,* Pres.; Russell T. Smith, V.P.; Joanne Pao,* Secy.-Treas.
EIN: 943113172

53582
The Parker Charitable Foundation
1 Plaza Sq.
Port Arthur, TX 77642

Established in 2001 in TX.
Donor(s): Carl Parker.
Financial data (yr. ended 12/31/01): Grants paid, $0; assets, $10,142 (M); gifts received, $10,000; expenditures, $0; qualifying distributions, $0.
Trustee: Carl Parker.
EIN: 311681983

53583
Roy & M. Permenter Charitable Trust
P.O. Box 3928
Beaumont, TX 77704

Established in 2001 in TX.
Financial data (yr. ended 12/31/01): Grants paid, $0; assets, $509,996 (M); gifts received, $513,165; expenditures, $4,783; qualifying distributions, $0.

Trustee: Hibernia National Bank.
EIN: 760694948

53584
Christina Petrash Trust
703 Lyons Ave.
P.O. Box 118
Schulenburg, TX 78956-0118

Financial data (yr. ended 12/31/01): Grants paid, $0; assets, $135,954 (M); expenditures, $6,295; qualifying distributions, $0.
Limitations: Applications not accepted. Giving limited to Schulenburg, TX.
Application information: Contributes only to pre-selected organizations.
Trustees: Elmer Kobza, Gerald Kobza.
EIN: 746245233

53585
Philadelphia Foundation
4141 Mendenhall Dr.
Dallas, TX 75244
Contact: Susan Yelderman, Secy.

Established in 1985 in CA.
Donor(s): Mark Yelderman, Susan Yelderman.
Financial data (yr. ended 11/30/99): Grants paid, $0; assets, $67,380 (M); expenditures, $178; qualifying distributions, $178.
Limitations: Giving primarily in TX.
Application information: Applicant must include transcript and statement of financial need.
Officers: Mark Yelderman, Pres.; Susan Yelderman, Secy.
Director: David Roper.
EIN: 942995658

53586
Phillips Family Foundation
130 Plantation Rd.
Houston, TX 77024

Established in 2001 in TX.
Donor(s): D. Martin Phillips, Liane M. Phillips.
Financial data (yr. ended 12/31/01): Grants paid, $0; assets, $304,961 (M); gifts received, $305,000; expenditures, $187; qualifying distributions, $0.
Limitations: Applications not accepted.
Application information: Contributes only to pre-selected organizations.
Trustees: Gary R. Petersen, D. Martin Phillips, Liane M. Phillips.
EIN: 750590214

53587
Pine Family Foundation
c/o Ray Pine
401 W. 37th St.
Austin, TX 78705
Application address: 1000 Jo Jo Rd., Pensacola, FL 32514
Contact: Sharron P. Catledge, Secy.

Established in 1994 in TX.
Donor(s): Ray Pine.
Financial data (yr. ended 12/31/99): Grants paid, $0; assets, $978,361 (M); expenditures, $53,745; qualifying distributions, $53,558.
Limitations: Giving on a national basis, with emphasis on AL and NY.
Application information: Application form required.
Officers: Gwendolyn Pine, Chair. and Treas.; Ray Pine, Pres.; Kay Sousares, V.P.; Sharron Catledge, Secy.
EIN: 742697612

53588
The Pogue Family Foundation
P.O. Box 1920
Dallas, TX 75221

Established in 2000 in TX.
Donor(s): Jeffrey Blake Pogue, David Brent Pogue, Blair Matthew Pogue, A. Mack Pogue.
Financial data (yr. ended 12/31/00): Grants paid, $0; assets, $4,010,934 (M); gifts received, $4,036,500; expenditures, $25,618; qualifying distributions, $0.
Limitations: Applications not accepted.
Application information: Contributes only to pre-selected organizations.
Officer: Nancy Davis, Secy.
Directors: William C. Cooper, B. Jack Pogue, Blair Matthew Pogue, David Brent Pogue, Jean Pogue, Jeffrey Blake Pogue, Mack Pogue, Robert C. Taylor.
EIN: 752894071

53589
Poindexter Foundation
1100 Louisiana St., Ste. 5400
Houston, TX 77002

Established in 1993 in TX.
Donor(s): John B. Poindexter.
Financial data (yr. ended 12/31/01): Grants paid, $0; assets, $55,138 (M); gifts received, $1,541; expenditures, $3,220; qualifying distributions, $0.
Limitations: Applications not accepted. Giving limited to TX.
Application information: Contributes only to pre-selected organizations.
Officers and Trustees:* John B. Poindexter,* Pres.; Paul B. Clemenceau,* V.P. and Secy.; Stephen Magee, V.P. and Treas.; E. Philip Cannon.
EIN: 760388498

53590
Potterhouse Foundation
5001 S. Hulen, Ste. 106
Fort Worth, TX 76132 (817) 346-4416
Contact: A.E. Dumois, Dir.

Donor(s): A.E. Dumois.
Financial data (yr. ended 05/31/02): Grants paid, $0; assets, $222,291 (M); gifts received, $20,000; expenditures, $696; qualifying distributions, $0.
Limitations: Giving primarily in Fort Worth, TX.
Application information: Application form required.
Directors: A.E. Dumois, Sherry Lynn Dumois.
EIN: 751824677

53591
John C. & Leona Numsen Price Scholarship Trust
c/o Compass Bank
5840 W. Northeast Hwy.
Dallas, TX 75225
Contact: Thelma Williams, Trust Off., Compass Bank

Financial data (yr. ended 05/31/01): Grants paid, $0; assets, $85,492 (M); expenditures, $1,002; qualifying distributions, $0.
Limitations: Giving limited to Palestine, TX.
Application information: Application form required.
Trustee: Compass Bank.
EIN: 746311868

53592
Les and Mary Puckett Children's Foundation
c/o J. Lester Puckett
5201 Evergreen St.
Bellaire, TX 77401-4921

Established in 1999 in TX.

53592—TEXAS

Donor(s): J. Lester Puckett, Mary B. Puckett.
Financial data (yr. ended 12/31/01): Grants paid, $0; assets, $4,717 (M); gifts received, $1,392; expenditures, $1,522; qualifying distributions, $0.
Limitations: Applications not accepted.
Application information: Contributes only to pre-selected organizations.
Officers: J. Lester Puckett, Pres. and Treas.; Mary B. Puckett, V.P. and Secy.
EIN: 760626026

53593
Ragsdale Foundation
575 Comal Ave.
New Braunfels, TX 78130 (830) 625-9362

Established in 1998 in TX.
Donor(s): Gary D. Mathis.
Financial data (yr. ended 12/31/01): Grants paid, $0; assets, $164,344 (M); gifts received, $100,000; expenditures, $1,707; qualifying distributions, $0.
Limitations: Applications not accepted.
Application information: Contributes only to pre-selected organizations.
Officer and Director:* Paul C. Ragsdale,* Pres., V.P., and Secy.-Treas.
EIN: 742862267

53594
The Ronald Rapoport Foundation
c/o Bernard Rapoport
5400 Bosque, Ste. 245
Waco, TX 76710 (254) 741-0510

Established in 2001 in TX.
Donor(s): Bernard Rapoport.
Financial data (yr. ended 12/31/01): Grants paid, $0; assets, $50,001 (M); gifts received, $50,000; expenditures, $0; qualifying distributions, $0.
Officers and Trustees:* Ronald Rapoport,* Chair.; Patricia Rapoport,* Pres.; Bernard Rapoport,* V.P.; Larry D. Jaynes,* Secy.; Audre Rapoport,* Treas.; and 5 additional trustees.
EIN: 742872414

53595
Sylvia Ratner Foundation
1 Amber Glen
San Antonio, TX 78257-1251

Established in 2000 in TX.
Donor(s): Paul Ratner, M.D.
Financial data (yr. ended 11/30/01): Grants paid, $0; assets, $119,396 (M); gifts received, $150,044; expenditures, $104; qualifying distributions, $0.
Limitations: Applications not accepted.
Application information: Contributes only to pre-selected organizations.
Officers: Paul Ratner, M.D., Pres. and Secy.; Marc Ratner, V.P.; Sybil Ratner, V.P.
EIN: 742983190

53596
The RDN and PRN Foundation
(Formerly Nasher Foundation)
P.O. Box 829007
Dallas, TX 75382-9007
Contact: Raymond D. Nasher, Pres.

Established in 1965 in TX.
Donor(s): Raymond D. Nasher.
Financial data (yr. ended 12/31/01): Grants paid, $0; assets, $4,770,387 (M); expenditures, $1,272; qualifying distributions, $194.
Limitations: Applications not accepted. Giving primarily in Dallas, TX.
Application information: Contributes only to pre-selected organizations.
Officers: Raymond D. Nasher, Pres.; Byron A. Parker, Treas.

EIN: 751183763

53597
Dora Bastiani Redmon Memorial Research Foundation
5223 Contour Pl.
Houston, TX 77096

Established in 1997 in TX.
Financial data (yr. ended 12/31/00): Grants paid, $0; assets, $129,604 (M); gifts received, $9,517; expenditures, $89,582; qualifying distributions, $0.
Officers and Directors:* Agile H. Redmon, Jr., M.D.,* Pres.; Laura L. Sommerville, M.D.,* V.P.; E. William Langley,* Secy.-Treas.; Gailen D. Marshall, M.D., Marshall E. McCabe, M.D., James J. Redmon, John G. Redmon.
EIN: 760537347

53598
The Richey Family Charitable Foundation
3700 S. Stonebridge
McKinney, TX 75070

Established in 1994 in AL.
Financial data (yr. ended 12/31/01): Grants paid, $0; assets, $50 (M); expenditures, $0; qualifying distributions, $0.
Limitations: Applications not accepted.
Application information: Contributes only to pre-selected organizations.
Officers: Linda Richey Graves, Pres.; Robert Earl Richey, V.P.; Christopher Keith Richey, Secy.-Treas.
EIN: 631133330

53599
L. E. Richey Foundation, Inc.
3003 S. Loop W., Ste. 510
Houston, TX 77054

Established in 1997 in TX.
Donor(s): L.E. Richey.
Financial data (yr. ended 12/31/01): Grants paid, $0; assets, $2,159,738 (M); gifts received, $40,000; expenditures, $70,103; qualifying distributions, $0.
Limitations: Applications not accepted. Giving primarily in TX.
Application information: Contributes only to pre-selected organizations.
Officers: L.E. Richey, Pres.; Todd R. Richey, V.P.; Lisa K. Brockett, Secy.-Treas.
EIN: 760555299

53600
Adan A. Rios Foundation
4007 Shallow Pond Ct.
Sugar Land, TX 77479-2427
Contact: Adan A. Rios, M.D., Pres.

Established in 1998 in TX.
Financial data (yr. ended 12/31/01): Grants paid, $0; assets, $2,274 (M); gifts received, $32,189; expenditures, $36,089; qualifying distributions, $0.
Limitations: Giving primarily in Houston, TX.
Officers: Adan A. Rios, M.D., Pres. and Treas.; Jorge R. Quesada, M.D., V.P. and Secy.
Director: Patricia Salvato, M.D.
EIN: 760587814

53601
The Robbins Foundation
P.O. Box 22086
Houston, TX 77227-2086

Established in 2000 in TX.
Financial data (yr. ended 12/31/00): Grants paid, $0; assets, $249,945 (M); expenditures, $0; qualifying distributions, $0.

Trustees: Gregory A. Herbst, William K. Robbins, Jr.
EIN: 311535162

53602
Elizabeth Dennis Rockwell Foundation
3617 Yoakum Blvd., Apt. 4
Houston, TX 77006-4248

Established in 1994 in TX.
Donor(s): Elizabeth D. Rockwell.
Financial data (yr. ended 12/31/01): Grants paid, $0; assets, $29,354 (M); expenditures, $50; qualifying distributions, $50.
Limitations: Applications not accepted.
Application information: Contributes only to pre-selected organizations.
Trustee: Elizabeth D. Rockwell.
EIN: 760439414

53603
The Rodriguez Foundation
8828 N. Stemmons Freeway, Ste. 106
Dallas, TX 75247

Established in 1999 in TX.
Financial data (yr. ended 12/31/00): Grants paid, $0; assets, $931,067 (M); expenditures, $9,052; qualifying distributions, $0.
Officer: James Anderson, V.P.
Directors: Marcos A. Rodriguez, Sonya Nance Rodriguez.
EIN: 752737734

53604
Sacre Family Foundation, Inc.
c/o Ronald A. Britton
3100 North A, The Rohill Bldg. No. 200
Midland, TX 79705-5305 (915) 686-0022

Established in 1994 in TX.
Financial data (yr. ended 12/31/01): Grants paid, $0; assets, $38,708 (M); gifts received, $10,000; expenditures, $21; qualifying distributions, $0.
Limitations: Applications not accepted. Giving primarily in Midland, TX.
Application information: Contributes only to pre-selected organizations.
Officers: Susan A. Britton, Pres.; Bob W. Dutton, V.P.; Ronald A. Britton, Secy.-Treas.
EIN: 752543743

53605
San Antonio Foundation for Excellence
141 Lavaca St.
San Antonio, TX 78210-1039

Established in 1998 in TX.
Donor(s): H.E. Butt Grocery Co.
Financial data (yr. ended 12/31/00): Grants paid, $0; assets, $0 (M); expenditures, $1,622; qualifying distributions, $1,622.
Limitations: Applications not accepted. Giving primarily in San Antonio, TX.
Officers: Diana Lam, Pres.; Margaret Mireles, V.P.; Julian H. Trevino, Secy.-Treas.
EIN: 742861587
Codes: GTI

53606
The Omar Abu Sarris Memorial Trust
P.O. Box 157
Sherman, TX 75091-0157

Established around 1994.
Donor(s): Ibrahim Abu Sarris, High Enterprises, Inc.
Financial data (yr. ended 12/31/01): Grants paid, $0; assets, $914 (M); expenditures, $0; qualifying distributions, $0.
Limitations: Giving limited to Sherman, TX.
Trustee: Ibrahim Abu Sarris.

EIN: 756453919

53607
The Evalee C. Schwarz Charitable Trust for Education
c/o JPMorgan Chase Bank
P.O. Box 2558
Houston, TX 77252-2558
Contact: Patricia Kasprzak, V.P. and Trust Off., JPMorgan Chase Bank

Established in 1997 in TX.
Donor(s): Evalee C. Schwarz.‡
Financial data (yr. ended 08/31/01): Grants paid, $0; assets, $4,047,292 (M); gifts received, $261,500; expenditures, $209,474; qualifying distributions, $271,350; giving activities include $271,350 for loans to individuals.
Limitations: Giving on a national basis.
Application information: Application form required.
Loan Committee Members: Ross Hardy, Donald Joiner, David Keilson.
Trustee: JPMorgan Chase Bank.
EIN: 766129622

53608
The Sharma Foundation
2301 N. Greenville Ave., Ste. 150
Richardson, TX 75082

Established in 2000 in TX.
Donor(s): Bianca Sharma.
Financial data (yr. ended 12/31/00): Grants paid, $0; assets, $5,046,343 (M); gifts received, $5,130,000; expenditures, $102,582; qualifying distributions, $0.
Limitations: Applications not accepted.
Application information: Contributes only to pre-selected organizations.
Officer: Bianca Sharma, Pres.
Director: Michael R. Held.
EIN: 752857275

53609
The Sherman Foundation
11767 Katy Freeway, Ste. 230
Houston, TX 77079

Established in 2000.
Financial data (yr. ended 12/31/00): Grants paid, $0; assets, $100 (M); expenditures, $0; qualifying distributions, $0.
Officer: Jim Sherman, Mgr.
EIN: 912136222

53610
Shield Foundation
367 Park Ridge
Boerne, TX 78006

Established in 2000 in TX.
Donor(s): Harold J. Lees.
Financial data (yr. ended 12/31/00): Grants paid, $0; assets, $300,858 (M); gifts received, $300,000; expenditures, $0; qualifying distributions, $0.
Limitations: Applications not accepted.
Application information: Contributes only to pre-selected organizations.
Directors: Ken Burton, Jr., Harold J. Lees, Robin B. Lees.
EIN: 742975776

53611
Andrea Rudd Skibell Family Foundation
6210 Raintree Ct.
Dallas, TX 75240

Established in 1995.

Financial data (yr. ended 12/31/00): Grants paid, $0; assets, $949 (M); expenditures, $30; qualifying distributions, $0.
Officers: Andrea Rudd Skibell, Pres.; Leslie Rudd, V.P. and Treas.; Richard Skibell, Secy.
EIN: 752623022

53612
Slavik Charitable Foundation
209 N. Allen St.
Edna, TX 77957 (361) 782-3246
Contact: Charles M. Slavik, Sr., Tr., or Emma Slavik, Tr.

Established in 1993.
Donor(s): Charles M. Slavik, Sr., Emma Slavik.
Financial data (yr. ended 06/30/01): Grants paid, $0; assets, $65,525 (M); expenditures, $5,083; qualifying distributions, $0.
Limitations: Giving primarily in Jackson County, TX.
Trustees: Garland R. Sandhop, Charles M. Slavik, Sr., Charles M. Slavik, Jr., Emma Slavik, Thomas Slavik.
EIN: 742682888

53613
Louise Bowers Slentz Foundation, Inc.
P.O. Box 662
Pampa, TX 79066-0662

Donor(s): Louise P. Slentz.
Financial data (yr. ended 12/31/01): Grants paid, $0; assets, $1,757 (M); expenditures, $69; qualifying distributions, $0.
Limitations: Applications not accepted.
Application information: Contributes only to pre-selected organizations.
Officer: Louise P. Slentz, Pres.
EIN: 752666611

53614
The Martha Small Foundation
2727 Allen Pkwy., Ste. 1300
Houston, TX 77019

Established in 1992.
Donor(s): James R. Moriarty.
Financial data (yr. ended 12/31/01): Grants paid, $0; assets, $49 (M); expenditures, $0; qualifying distributions, $0.
Limitations: Applications not accepted.
Application information: Contributes only to pre-selected organizations.
Officers: James R. Moriarty, Pres. and Treas.; Cynthia R. Moriarty, V.P. and Secy.
Director: Stephen M. Hackerman.
EIN: 760380576

53615
Barbara B. & William T. Smith Charitable Trust
c/o Kanaly Trust Co.
4550 Post Oak Place Dr., Ste. 139
Houston, TX 77027 (800) 882-8723

Financial data (yr. ended 11/30/01): Grants paid, $0; assets, $80,075 (M); expenditures, $3,774; qualifying distributions, $0.
Limitations: Giving primarily in TX.
Trustee: Kanaly Trust Co.
EIN: 766084385

53616
Smith Trust
3214 39th St.
Lubbock, TX 79413 (806) 799-5600
Contact: L. Edwin Smith, Tr.

Donor(s): L. Edwin Smith.
Financial data (yr. ended 12/31/01): Grants paid, $0; assets, $34,805 (M); expenditures, $321; qualifying distributions, $0.

Limitations: Giving limited to Lubbock, TX.
Trustees: L. Edwin Smith, Ruth H. Smith.
EIN: 756082816

53617
Jack and Doris Smothers and Mary Ann Bruni Memorial Foundation
P.O. Box 17001
San Antonio, TX 78217

Established in 2000 in TX.
Financial data (yr. ended 09/30/01): Grants paid, $0; assets, $1,063,981 (M); gifts received, $1,063,981; expenditures, $0; qualifying distributions, $0.
Limitations: Applications not accepted.
Application information: Contributes only to pre-selected organizations.
Officers: Mary Ann Bruni, Pres.; Frances T. Farenthold, Secy.
Director: Philip Knox Key.
EIN: 742950058

53618
Sonship Ministries, Inc.
2610 S. Harrison St.
Amarillo, TX 79109-2536

Financial data (yr. ended 12/31/00): Grants paid, $0; assets, $3,120 (M); gifts received, $40; expenditures, $761; qualifying distributions, $761; giving activities include $560 for programs.
Limitations: Applications not accepted.
Application information: Contributes only to pre-selected organizations.
Officers: Robert W. Bauman, Jr., Pres. and Treas.; Vana Eller, V.P.; Larry Latham, V.P.; Michelle Bauman, Secy.
EIN: 942708064

53619
James E. Sowell Foundation
3131 McKinney, Ste. 200
Dallas, TX 75204-2482 (214) 871-3320
Contact: Keith Martin, Secy.-Treas.

Established in 1997 in TX.
Donor(s): James E. Sowell.
Financial data (yr. ended 12/31/01): Grants paid, $0; assets, $752,801 (M); expenditures, $2,422; qualifying distributions, $0.
Officers: James E. Sowell, Pres.; Elizabeth Sowell, V.P.; Keith Martin, Secy.-Treas.
Director: Larry James.
EIN: 752641436

53620
Spirit Line Foundation
c/o Barton W. Dailey
1747 Citadel Plz., Ste. 206
San Antonio, TX 78209-1017

Financial data (yr. ended 12/31/99): Grants paid, $0; assets, $262 (M); gifts received, $911; expenditures, $1,039; qualifying distributions, $1,039; giving activities include $769 for programs.
Officers: Barton W. Dailey, Pres.; Nancy Dailey, V.P. and Secy.
EIN: 742747784

53621
Spokes for Folks
4037 Druid Ln.
Dallas, TX 75205 (214) 890-8960
E-mail: schwartzcj@aol.com; URL: http://www.spokesforfolks.org
Contact: Cindy Schwartz, Secy.-Treas.

Established in 2000 in TX.
Donor(s): Mrs. Carl H. Westcott, Nabisco, Inc.

53621—TEXAS

Financial data (yr. ended 05/31/01): Grants paid, $0; assets, $10,759 (M); gifts received, $13,128; expenditures, $2,372; qualifying distributions, $909.
Limitations: Giving primarily in TX.
Officers and Directors:* Armond Schwartz III,* Pres.; Cindy Schwartz,* Secy.-Treas.; Pam Jackson, Jeanie Laube, Jeffrey Marcus, Sally Rosenberg.
EIN: 311726515

53622
Paul R. Stalnaker, M.D. Trust
P.O. Box 8306
Houston, TX 77288-8306
Application address: c/o D.C. Allensworth, M.D., Zeta Phi Chi Benefit Assn., Univ. of Texas Medical Branch, Galveston, TX 77550
Contact: William P. Traylor, Tr.

Financial data (yr. ended 12/31/00): Grants paid, $0; assets, $1,729,872 (M); expenditures, $53,851; qualifying distributions, $0.
Limitations: Giving limited to Galveston, TX.
Application information: Unsolicited requests for funds not considered or acknowledged. Application form required.
Trustees: Stephen R. Lewis, M.D., William P. Traylor, Edward L. Wall, M.D.
EIN: 746238103
Codes: GTI

53623
C. R. Stem Foundation
2264 Valley Mill
Carrollton, TX 75006-1936 (972) 418-8930
Contact: Randall E. Stem

Established in 2000 in TX.
Donor(s): Randall E. Stem.
Financial data (yr. ended 12/31/00): Grants paid, $0; assets, $100 (M); gifts received, $100; expenditures, $0; qualifying distributions, $0.
Application information: Application form required.
Trustee: Randall E. Stem.
EIN: 752871440

53624
Madlin Stevenson Foundation
2513 S. Gessner, Ste. 334
Houston, TX 77063

Established in 2001 in TX.
Donor(s): Madlin Stevenson.‡
Financial data (yr. ended 12/31/01): Grants paid, $0; assets, $476,625 (M); gifts received, $559,500; expenditures, $0; qualifying distributions, $0.
Limitations: Applications not accepted.
Application information: Contributes only to pre-selected organizations.
Trustees: Kathleen Cynthia Pickett-Stevenson, Donald E. Stevenson, Keith T. Stevenson, Mattie Stevenson.
EIN: 760664265

53625
Freddie Lewis Stoepler Trust
P.O. Box 915
Eden, TX 76837
Application address: c/o High School counselor, Eden High School, Eden, TX 76837

Donor(s): Freddie Lewis Stoepher.‡
Financial data (yr. ended 12/31/01): Grants paid, $0; assets, $295,159 (M); expenditures, $2,890; qualifying distributions, $6,000; giving activities include $6,000 for loans to individuals.
Limitations: Giving primarily in TX.
Application information: Unsolicited requests for funds not considered or acknowledged.

Trustee: Tommy Kelso.
EIN: 752387244
Codes: GTI

53626
E. & B. Sullivan Foundation
1258 Renoir Dr.
Dallas, TX 75230

Donor(s): John M. Draughon.
Financial data (yr. ended 12/31/01): Grants paid, $0; assets, $317,205 (M); expenditures, $434; qualifying distributions, $0.
Limitations: Giving primarily in TX.
Officers and Trustees:* John M. Draughon,* Pres.; Patricia D. Akin,* V.P.; Cathy Ann Draughon,* V.P.; Beverly A. Draughon,* Secy.; JoAnn D. Draughon,* Treas.
EIN: 760208033

53627
Robert J. and Elizabeth A. Symon Family Foundation
4314 Bretton Bay Ln.
Dallas, TX 75287

Established in 1998 in TX.
Donor(s): Robert J. Symon, Elizabeth A. Symon.
Financial data (yr. ended 12/31/01): Grants paid, $0; assets, $580,586 (M); expenditures, $33,812; qualifying distributions, $0.
Limitations: Applications not accepted. Giving primarily in TX; some giving also in NY, NJ, and VA.
Application information: Contributes only to pre-selected organizations.
Trustees: Elizabeth A. Symon, Robert J. Symon.
EIN: 752793751

53628
The Tatham Foundation
4400 Post Oak Pkwy., No. 1600
Houston, TX 77027

Established in 1998 in TX.
Donor(s): Thomas P. Tatham.
Financial data (yr. ended 12/31/00): Grants paid, $0; assets, $0 (M); gifts received, $100; expenditures, $400; qualifying distributions, $0.
Limitations: Applications not accepted. Giving primarily in Houston, TX.
Application information: Contributes only to pre-selected organizations.
Officers: Thomas P. Tatham, Pres.; Virginia S. Tatham, V.P. and Secy.
EIN: 760543419

53629
Tau Trustees Educational Foundation, Inc.
6122 Riverview Way
Houston, TX 77057

Donor(s): R.C. Connor, M.G. Sweeney.
Financial data (yr. ended 12/31/00): Grants paid, $0; assets, $14,024 (M); expenditures, $759; qualifying distributions, $759.
Limitations: Giving limited to Austin, TX.
Application information: Application form required.
Officers: Robert T. Sabom, Pres.; Timothy J. Herman, V.P.
EIN: 751886641

53630
Tears Foundation
5326 Spanish Oak Dr.
Houston, TX 77066-2821

Established in 1999 in TX.
Donor(s): Linda Pugh.

Financial data (yr. ended 08/31/00): Grants paid, $0; assets, $5,513 (M); gifts received, $5,975; expenditures, $196; qualifying distributions, $0.
Limitations: Applications not accepted.
Application information: Contributes only to pre-selected organizations.
Officer and Directors:* Linda Pugh,* Pres.; Rita Ruckert, Annette Smith.
EIN: 760624950

53631
The Telos Foundation
P.O. Box 294045
Kerrville, TX 78029-4045

Established in 1987 in TX.
Financial data (yr. ended 12/31/01): Grants paid, $0; assets, $14,709 (M); gifts received, $45,039; expenditures, $37,863; qualifying distributions, $0.
Limitations: Applications not accepted. Giving primarily in Tarpon Springs, FL.
Application information: Contributes only to pre-selected organizations.
Trustees: Daniel L. Schoen, Doris L. Schoen, Ivan L. Schoen.
EIN: 760228672

53632
Texas Cardiac Arrhythmia Research Foundation
3705 Medical Pkwy., Ste. 550
Austin, TX 78705

Established in 1998 in TX.
Financial data (yr. ended 12/31/99): Grants paid, $0; assets, $118,527 (M); gifts received, $284,174; expenditures, $295,020; qualifying distributions, $0; giving activities include $293,030 for programs.
Limitations: Applications not accepted.
Application information: Contributes only to pre-selected organizations.
Officers: Robert C. Canby, M.D., Pres.; Rodney P. Horton, M.D., V.P.; Debbie Cardinal, Secy.
Director: Fr. Fred Bomar.
EIN: 742890365

53633
Texas Consortium for Physical Therapy Clinical Education, Inc.
c/o UTMB/SAHS, Dept. of Phys. Therapy
301 University Blvd.
Galveston, TX 77555-1028

Financial data (yr. ended 08/31/01): Grants paid, $0; assets, $30,843 (L); expenditures, $20,390; qualifying distributions, $1,404; giving activities include $14,472 for programs.
Limitations: Applications not accepted. Giving limited to TX.
Application information: Contributes only to pre-selected organizations.
Officers: Tom Turturro, Chair.; Carolyn Utsey, Treas.
Trustee: Robert C. Hall.
EIN: 752150192

53634
Allie L. Thomas Memorial, Inc.
c/o J.B. Hall
214 W. 9th St.
San Angelo, TX 76903-5328

Established in 2000 in TX.
Financial data (yr. ended 07/31/01): Grants paid, $0; assets, $2,800 (M); expenditures, $0; qualifying distributions, $0.
Trustee: J.B. Hall.
EIN: 752609472

53635
Robert J. Thorne Charitable and Educational Trust
1472 N. Hampton Rd.
DeSoto, TX 75115

Donor(s): R.J. Thorne.‡
Financial data (yr. ended 12/31/01): Grants paid, $0; assets, $124,973 (M); expenditures, $6,134; qualifying distributions, $3,067.
Limitations: Applications not accepted. Giving limited to Dallas, TX.
Application information: Contributes only to pre-selected organizations.
Trustee: Roy L. Thorne.
EIN: 237143153

53636
Thorne-Sigmund Fund
1472 N. Hampton Rd., Ste. 108
DeSoto, TX 75115-3001 (972) 224-7221

Financial data (yr. ended 12/31/01): Grants paid, $0; assets, $42,267 (M); expenditures, $4,000; qualifying distributions, $0.
Limitations: Giving primarily in Dallas, TX.
Trustee: Roy L. Thorne.
EIN: 237047332

53637
Richard D. & Emily G. Tinsley Foundation
2935 Ferndale St.
Houston, TX 77098-1117

Established in 1998.
Financial data (yr. ended 12/31/01): Grants paid, $0; assets, $8,383 (M); expenditures, $1,296; qualifying distributions, $0.
Limitations: Applications not accepted.
Application information: Contributes only to pre-selected organizations.
Officers and Directors:* Richard D. Tinsley,* Pres.; Emily G. Tinsley,* Secy.-Treas.; Robyn Lynn Tinsley.
EIN: 760598843

53638
Solomon & Rebecca Topletz Scholarship
7509 Inwood Rd., No. 301
Dallas, TX 75209-4098
Contact: H.M. Topletz, Tr.

Financial data (yr. ended 12/31/01): Grants paid, $0; assets, $44,260 (M); expenditures, $2,600; qualifying distributions, $135.
Limitations: Giving limited to Dallas, TX.
Application information: Application form required.
Trustees: L.T. Edwards, H.M. Topletz, J.M. Topletz.
EIN: 751866087

53639
Jim & Eva Marie Tranum Family Foundation
2707 Creekside Dr.
Temple, TX 76502-3144

Established in 2000 in TX.
Donor(s): Jim Tranum, Eva Marie Tranum.
Financial data (yr. ended 12/31/01): Grants paid, $0; assets, $23,586 (M); expenditures, $96; qualifying distributions, $0.
Limitations: Applications not accepted.
Application information: Contributes only to pre-selected organizations.
Officers: Jim Tranum, Pres.; Eva Marie Tranum, Secy.-Treas.
EIN: 742947363

53640
Trebing Memorial Scholarship Fund
c/o Bank of America
P.O. Box 831041
Dallas, TX 75283-1041 (800) 357-7094
Contact: Mark Whitson, Trust Off., Bank of America

Financial data (yr. ended 12/31/00): Grants paid, $0; assets, $24,579 (M); gifts received, $24,579; expenditures, $2,422; qualifying distributions, $192.
Limitations: Giving limited to Little Rock, AR.
Trustee: Bank of America.
EIN: 710552818

53641
The Trisla Foundation
800 Bering Dr., Ste. 270
Houston, TX 77057-2130 (713) 784-1105

Financial data (yr. ended 12/31/01): Grants paid, $0; assets, $308 (M); expenditures, $0; qualifying distributions, $0.
Officers: T.R. Reckling III, Chair.; Isla Carroll Reckling, Vice-Chair.; Thomas Kelly Reckling, Secy.; Randa Reckling Roach, Treas.
EIN: 760563568

53642
Tillman Trotter Foundation
109 North Post Oak Ln.
Houston, TX 77024-7749

Established in 1959 in TX.
Financial data (yr. ended 03/31/02): Grants paid, $0; assets, $246 (M); expenditures, $162; qualifying distributions, $0.
Limitations: Applications not accepted. Giving primarily in Houston, TX.
Application information: Contributes only to pre-selected organizations.
Officer: J.T. Trotter, Mgr.
EIN: 746042221

53643
The Underwood Foundation
909 Fannin, No. 850
Houston, TX 77010-1005

Established in 1997 in TX.
Donor(s): David Underwood, Lynda Underwood.
Financial data (yr. ended 12/31/00): Grants paid, $0; assets, $10,091,485 (M); expenditures, $36,329; qualifying distributions, $0.
Limitations: Applications not accepted.
Application information: Contributes only to pre-selected organizations.
Officers and Directors:* David K. Underwood,* Pres. and Treas.; Lynda Underwood,* V.P. and Secy.; Catherine Underwood Murray, David K. Underwood, Jr., Duncan R. Underwood.
EIN: 760528032

53644
James M. Vaughn, Jr. Foundation Fund
c/o JPMorgan Chase Bank
700 Lavaca St.
Austin, TX 78701-3109
Application address: 2235 Brentwood Dr., Houston, TX 77019
Contact: James M. Vaughn, Jr., Pres.

Established about 1971 in TX.
Financial data (yr. ended 12/31/00): Grants paid, $0; assets, $1,477,076 (M); expenditures, $20,719; qualifying distributions, $0.
Limitations: Giving primarily in TX.
Officers: James M. Vaughn, Jr., Pres.; Sally Vaughn, V.P.; Jan Werner, Secy.-Treas.
EIN: 237166546

Codes: GTI

53645
Joy & Anne Wagner Foundation
620 S. Taylor St.
Amarillo, TX 79101-2436

Donor(s): T.J. Wagner III.
Financial data (yr. ended 05/31/02): Grants paid, $0; assets, $56,505 (M); expenditures, $802; qualifying distributions, $0.
Limitations: Applications not accepted. Giving primarily in TX.
Application information: Contributes only to pre-selected organizations.
Trustees: Glen Brosier, J. Scott Brosier, T.J. Wagner III.
EIN: 756080148

53646
William Blair and Glen E. Waltrip Family Foundation
1929 Allen Pkwy., 12th Fl.
Houston, TX 77019 (713) 525-9130
FAX: (713) 525-5555
Contact: William Blair Waltrip, Pres.

Established in 1998.
Donor(s): William Blair, Glen E. Waltrip, Robert L. Waltrip.
Financial data (yr. ended 05/31/02): Grants paid, $0; assets, $402,808 (M); gifts received, $3,325; expenditures, $2,519; qualifying distributions, $0.
Limitations: Giving primarily in Galveston and Houston, TX.
Application information: Application form not required.
Officers: William Blair Waltrip, Pres.; Glen E. Waltrip, V.P.; Catherine L. Waltrip, Secy.; Elizabeth B. Waltrip, Treas.
Director: Robert L. Waltrip.
EIN: 311614316

53647
The Waltrip-McGee Foundation
1929 Allen Pkwy., 12th Fl.
Houston, TX 77019 (713) 525-6264
FAX: (713) 525-5555
Contact: Robert L. Waltrip, Pres.

Established in 1998.
Donor(s): Robert L. Waltrip.
Financial data (yr. ended 04/30/02): Grants paid, $0; assets, $819,522 (M); gifts received, $10,625; expenditures, $2,473; qualifying distributions, $0.
Limitations: Giving primarily in Galveston and Houston, TX.
Application information: Application form not required.
Officers: Robert L. Waltrip, Pres.; Wanda A. McGee, V.P.; W. Blair Waltrip, V.P.; Robert L. Waltrip, Jr., Secy.-Treas.
Directors: Holly Waltrip Benson, Claire H. Waltrip, Glen E. Waltrip.
EIN: 311608714

53648
Darren and Sara Ward Family Foundation
119 Fleetwood Cove
Coppell, TX 75019

Established in 2000 in TX.
Donor(s): Jerry D. Ward.
Financial data (yr. ended 12/31/00): Grants paid, $0; assets, $133,510 (M); gifts received, $133,651; expenditures, $151; qualifying distributions, $0.
Limitations: Applications not accepted.
Application information: Contributes only to pre-selected organizations.

53648—TEXAS

Officers and Directors:* Jerry D. Ward,* Pres.; Sara I. Ward,* Secy.-Treas.
EIN: 752912259

53649
James D. and Nelda M. Whatley Foundation
P.O. Box 6266
Corpus Christi, TX 78466-6266
Contact: James D. Whatley, Pres.

Established in 1986 in TX.
Donor(s): James D. Whatley.
Financial data (yr. ended 11/30/99): Grants paid, $0; assets, $1,692 (M); gifts received, $617; expenditures, $617; qualifying distributions, $617.
Limitations: Giving primarily in Corpus Christi, TX.
Officer and Trustees:* James D. Whatley,* Pres.; Esmerella Cantu, Dana Stump.
EIN: 742440851

53650
Whetstone Mountain Foundation
2602 Kings Forest Dr.
Kingwood, TX 77339

Established in 2001 in TX.
Donor(s): John J. Johnson.
Financial data (yr. ended 12/31/01): Grants paid, $0; assets, $100,000 (M); gifts received, $100,500; expenditures, $500; qualifying distributions, $0.
Officers: Nancy T. Johnson, Pres.; John J. Johnson, V.P.; Sara C. Johnson, Secy.-Treas.
EIN: 760691948

53651
Wynn Douglas White Foundation
130 Houston Ave.
Weatherford, TX 76086

Established in 2000.
Donor(s): Robert D. White, Carolynn S. White.
Financial data (yr. ended 12/31/01): Grants paid, $0; assets, $13,883 (M); gifts received, $15,000; expenditures, $1,180; qualifying distributions, $0.
Officers: Carolynn S. White, Pres. and Treas.; Robert D. White, V.P. and Secy.
Directors: Jeffrey S. McCarty, Irma A. Moore, Anita White.
EIN: 752865426

53652
Virginia K. Whitmire Foundation
c/o Terri Lacy
600 Travis St., Ste. 4200
Houston, TX 77002

Established in 1999 in TX.
Donor(s): The Whitmire Foundation.
Financial data (yr. ended 12/31/01): Grants paid, $0; assets, $265,406 (M); gifts received, $1,604; expenditures, $4,545; qualifying distributions, $0.
Officers: Virginia K. Whitmire, Pres.; Richard L. Whitmire, V.P.; Ronald P. Whitmire, V.P.; Marcella J. Francis, Secy.-Treas.
EIN: 760595568

53653
Wichita Falls University Kiwanis Foundation, Inc.
P.O. Box 2421
Wichita Falls, TX 76307

Financial data (yr. ended 09/30/01): Grants paid, $0; assets, $20,135 (M); gifts received, $2,500; expenditures, $0; qualifying distributions, $0.
Limitations: Applications not accepted. Giving primarily in Indianapolis, IN.
Application information: Contributes only to pre-selected organizations.

Officers: John Rhoads, Pres.; Elmer Emory, Pres.-Elect; Dennis Probst, V.P.; Loyd Huckaby, Secy.; Doug Cox, Treas.
Directors: Bob Aldrich, Bryan Alexander, Judy Darnell, Bob Gragg, Paul Irwin, Doug James.
EIN: 751398039

53654
Wiggins Foundation
3838 Oak Lawn Ave., Ste. 700
Dallas, TX 75219

Financial data (yr. ended 03/31/02): Grants paid, $0; assets, $52,394 (M); gifts received, $22,024; expenditures, $1,005; qualifying distributions, $0.
Limitations: Applications not accepted. Giving primarily in Dallas, TX.
Application information: Contributes only to pre-selected organizations.
Trustees: Peter N. Wiggins III, William R. Wiggins.
EIN: 756026405

53655
The Williams Foundation
P.O. Box 522
Grapevine, TX 76051
Application address: 106 Stoney Ridge Rd., Azle, TX 76020-1000, tel.: (817) 448-9144
Contact: James Elmo Lutz, Tr.

Financial data (yr. ended 12/31/99): Grants paid, $0; assets, $31,780 (M); gifts received, $18,025; expenditures, $0; qualifying distributions, $1,496.
Trustee: James Elmo Lutz.
EIN: 752784320

53656
Paul J. Williams Foundation
c/o Joyce K. Fields
3300 N. A, Ste. 8-125
Midland, TX 79705

Established in 1997 in TX.
Donor(s): Paul J. Williams.
Financial data (yr. ended 12/31/00): Grants paid, $0; assets, $1,037,999 (M); gifts received, $3,000; expenditures, $38,147; qualifying distributions, $3,151.
Limitations: Applications not accepted. Giving primarily in TX.
Application information: Contributes only to pre-selected organizations.
Officers: Joyce K. Fields, Pres. and Treas.; Royce D. Fields, V.P.; Jim Ed Miller, Secy.
EIN: 752610617

53657
Williams-Chadwick Fund
111 Brittany Dr.
San Antonio, TX 78212

Established in 1993 in TX.
Financial data (yr. ended 12/31/01): Grants paid, $0; assets, $1 (M); gifts received, $1,000; expenditures, $1,025; qualifying distributions, $0.
Officers and Directors:* Donald F. Williams,* Pres.; Barbara N. Williams,* V.P.; Mary Burke Williams,* Secy.; George M. Williams, Jr.,* Treas.
EIN: 742691912

53658
The Winspear Foundation
4815 Brookview Dr.
Dallas, TX 75220

Established in 2001 in TX.
Donor(s): William W. Winspear.
Financial data (yr. ended 12/31/01): Grants paid, $0; assets, $10,000 (M); gifts received, $10,500; expenditures, $500; qualifying distributions, $500.
Limitations: Applications not accepted.

Application information: Contributes only to pre-selected organizations.
Trustees: Donald W. Winspear, Malcolm G. Winspear, William W. Winspear.
EIN: 306001989

53659
The Winston Charitable Foundation
P.O. Box 248
Hunt, TX 78024-0248
Contact: Bert F. Winston, Jr., Pres.

Established in 1998 in TX.
Donor(s): Bert F. Winstion, Jr.
Financial data (yr. ended 12/31/01): Grants paid, $0; assets, $108,464 (M); expenditures, $2,822; qualifying distributions, $0.
Officers and Directors:* Bert F. Winston, Jr.,* Pres.; Lynn David Winston,* V.P.; Chaille Winston Hawkins,* Secy.
EIN: 742877210

53660
Lita Witt Music Foundation, Inc.
2426 W. 10th
Dallas, TX 75211
Contact: Russel J. Carver, Pres.

Donor(s): Lita Witt.
Financial data (yr. ended 12/31/01): Grants paid, $0; assets, $70,113 (M); gifts received, $468; qualifying distributions, $0.
Limitations: Giving primarily in TX.
Officers: Russel J. Carver, Pres.; Lynell Peek, V.P.; George Cooper, Secy.-Treas.
EIN: 752092675

53661
WNPC Foundation
200 E. Basse Rd.
San Antonio, TX 78209

Established in 2001 in TX.
Donor(s): James Wilmott, Robert Schiller, Robert S. Pitts, Jr., J. Dale Harvey II, Paul R. Davis, Christopher J. Brahm, Randall T. Mays.
Financial data (yr. ended 12/31/01): Grants paid, $0; assets, $68,581 (M); gifts received, $70,000; expenditures, $1,517; qualifying distributions, $0.
Limitations: Applications not accepted.
Application information: Contributes only to pre-selected organizations.
Officers and Directors:* Randall T. Mays,* Pres.; J. Dale Harvey III,* Secy.; Robert S. Pitts, Jr.,* Treas.; and 6 additional directors.
EIN: 743015796

53662
Clarence & Lynn Wolfe Foundation
1501 N. Bank
Pampa, TX 79065

Established in 2001 in TX.
Financial data (yr. ended 12/31/01): Grants paid, $0; assets, $4,989 (M); gifts received, $5,000; expenditures, $391; qualifying distributions, $0.
Officers: Clarence Wolfe, Pres.; Lynn Wolfe, Secy.
Director: Phil Vanderpool.
EIN: 752961803

53663
The Woodward Family Foundation
5390E Royal Ln., MB No. 173
Dallas, TX 75229-6631

Established in 2000 in TX.
Donor(s): Stanley M. Woodward.
Financial data (yr. ended 12/31/00): Grants paid, $0; assets, $1,563,172 (M); gifts received, $1,491,461; expenditures, $0; qualifying distributions, $0.
Limitations: Applications not accepted.

Application information: Contributes only to pre-selected organizations.
Directors: Robert G. Kipp, Judy A. Woodward, Stanley M. Woodward.
EIN: 752912129

53664
Workplace Toxics Foundation
825 Montrose Dr.
Port Neches, TX 77651-2228

Financial data (yr. ended 12/31/01): Grants paid, $0; assets, $43,844 (M); gifts received, $43,844; expenditures, $3,961; qualifying distributions, $0.

Limitations: Giving primarily in TX.
Officers: Eugene Rasheta, Pres.; E.W. Dickey, V.P.; Kathy Gray, Secy.-Treas.
EIN: 760316150

53665
Wrage Foundation
c/o Jack Ohlrich
P.O. Box 310242
New Braunfels, TX 78131

Financial data (yr. ended 03/31/02): Grants paid, $0; assets, $26,130 (M); expenditures, $592; qualifying distributions, $0.

Limitations: Applications not accepted. Giving primarily in TX.
Application information: Contributes only to pre-selected organizations.
Trustees: John B. Gunn, Jr., Kay Wrage Gunn, Jack Ohlrich.
EIN: 741157469

UTAH

53666
The George S. and Dolores Dore Eccles Foundation
Deseret Bldg.
79 S. Main St., 12th Fl.
Salt Lake City, UT 84111 (801) 246-5331
Contact: Lisa Eccles, Exec. Dir.

Incorporated in 1958 in UT; absorbed Lillian Ethel Dufton Charitable Trust in 1981.
Donor(s): George S. Eccles.‡
Financial data (yr. ended 12/31/01): Grants paid, $35,968,790; assets, $586,134,060 (M); gifts received, $1,156; expenditures, $38,610,093; qualifying distributions, $36,392,802.
Limitations: Giving primarily in the intermountain area, particularly UT.
Application information: Application form required.
Officers and Directors:* Spencer F. Eccles,* Pres.; Alonzo W. Watson, Jr.,* V.P., Secy. and Gen. Counsel; Robert M. Graham, Treas.; Lisa Eccles, Exec. Dir.
EIN: 876118245
Codes: FD, FM

53667
The Jon and Karen Huntsman Foundation
c/o Huntsman, Inc.
500 Huntsman Way
Salt Lake City, UT 84108-1235

Established in 1988 in UT.
Donor(s): Jon M. Huntsman.
Financial data (yr. ended 12/31/00): Grants paid, $10,591,500; assets, $63,116,348 (M); gifts received, $900,000; expenditures, $11,004,164; qualifying distributions, $11,569,081; giving activities include $980,159 for program-related investments.
Limitations: Applications not accepted. Giving on a national basis.
Application information: Contributes only to pre-selected organizations.
Officers and Trustees:* Jon M. Huntsman,* Pres.; Christena Durham,* V.P.; David H. Huntsman,* V.P.; James H. Hunstman,* V.P.; Jon M. Huntsman, Jr.,* V.P.; Karen H. Huntsman,* V.P.; Paul C. Huntsman,* V.P.; Jennifer H. Parkin,* V.P.; Robert B. Lence,* Secy.; Richard P. Durham, David Gardner, Jim Huffman, Kathleen H. Huffman, Brynn B. Huntsman, Cheryl Ann W. Huntsman, Marianne M. Huntsman, Mary K. Huntsman, Michelle R. Huntsman, Peter R. Huntsman, David Parkin.
EIN: 742521914
Codes: FD, FM

53668
Emma Eccles Jones Foundation
c/o Wells Fargo Bank Northwest, N.A.
P.O. Box 628
Salt Lake City, UT 84110-0628
(801) 246-5363
Application address: c/o Clark P. Giles, P.O. Box 45385, Salt Lake City, UT 84145-0385, tel.: (801) 532-1500; FAX: (801) 532-7543
Contact: Clark P. Giles

Established in 1972 in UT.
Donor(s): Emma Eccles Jones.‡
Financial data (yr. ended 08/31/01): Grants paid, $7,394,500; assets, $122,729,446 (M); expenditures, $7,873,318; qualifying distributions, $7,504,060.
Limitations: Applications not accepted. Giving primarily in UT.
Application information: No grants anticipated being made incident to unsolicited requests until 2007.
Committee Members: Clark P. Giles, Chair.; Horace T. Clemm, Vice-Chair.; Robert A. Hatch, Secy.; Spencer F. Eccles, Frederick Q. Lawson.
Trustee Bank: Wells Fargo Bank Northwest, N.A.
EIN: 876155073
Codes: FD, FM

53669
S. J. & Jessie E. Quinney Foundation
P.O. Box 45385
Salt Lake City, UT 84145-0385
Contact: Herbert C. Livsey, Dir.

Established about 1982 in UT.
Donor(s): S.J. Quinney.‡
Financial data (yr. ended 12/31/00): Grants paid, $7,045,634; assets, $106,227,150 (M); expenditures, $7,477,423; qualifying distributions, $7,065,287.
Limitations: Applications not accepted. Giving limited to UT.
Application information: Contributes only to pre-selected organizations. The foundation solicits funding requests. Unsolicited requests for funding not considered.
Directors: James W. Freed, Clark P. Giles, Frederick Q. Lawson, Janet Q. Lawson, Peter Q. Lawson, Herbert C. Livsey, Stephen B. Nebeker, David E. Quinney, Jr., JoAnne L. Shrontz, Alonzo W. Watson, Jr.
EIN: 870389312
Codes: FD, FM

53670
Stewart Education Foundation
(Formerly Donnell B. and Elizabeth Dee Shaw Stewart Educational Foundation)
c/o First Security Bank of Utah, N.A.
P.O. Box 9936
Ogden, UT 84409 (801) 626-9531
Additional address: 802 Whispering Oaks Rd., Ogden, UT 84403
Contact: J.D. Lampros, Chair.; Mary Barker, Secy. for applications

Established in 1977 in UT.
Donor(s): Elizabeth D.S. Stewart.‡
Financial data (yr. ended 12/31/01): Grants paid, $5,615,610; assets, $102,589,129 (M); expenditures, $5,948,974; qualifying distributions, $5,799,260.
Limitations: Giving primarily in Ogden, UT.
Application information: Application form required.
Officers: Jack D. Lampros, Chair.; Dean W. Hurst, Co-Vice-Chair.; C.W. Stromberg, Co-Vice-Chair.
Members: Mary Barker, Rex Child, Kristen Hurst-Hyde, Jamie Shenefelt, Richard Stromberg.
Trustee: First Security Bank of Utah, N.A.
EIN: 876179880
Codes: FD, FM

53671
Dr. W. C. Swanson Family Foundation, Inc.
2955 Harrison Blvd., Ste. 201
Ogden, UT 84403 (801) 392-0360
Additional tel.: (801) 530-0360; FAX: (801) 392-0429; E-mail: SFF@swanfound.org; Lynda@swanfound.org
Contact: Lynda Murphy, Grants Admin.

Established in 1977; incorporated in 1999.
Donor(s): W.C. Swanson.‡

Financial data (yr. ended 12/31/00): Grants paid, $4,161,406; assets, $53,759,376 (M); gifts received, $1,083,652; expenditures, $7,244,387; qualifying distributions, $6,328,848; giving activities include $649,266 for programs.
Limitations: Giving primarily in UT, with emphasis on Weber County and Ogden City.
Publications: Newsletter, application guidelines, informational brochure.
Application information: Must complete application and provide all requested information. Application form required.
Advisory Board and Directors:* W. Charles Swanson,* Chair. and C.E.O.; Cindy Purcell, Pres.; Annabel Hofer,* Exec. V.P.; Lew Costley,* Secy.; Michael Fosmark, Robert Marguardt.
EIN: 870578540
Codes: FD, FM

53672
The Worth of a Soul Foundation
P.O. Box 434
Orem, UT 84058-0434

Established in 2000 in UT.
Donor(s): Dialogic Systems Corp.
Financial data (yr. ended 12/31/01): Grants paid, $3,528,978; assets, $103,426,743 (M); expenditures, $5,154,837; qualifying distributions, $3,236,504.
Limitations: Applications not accepted. Giving primarily in Provo, UT.
Application information: Contributes only to pre-selected organizations.
Trustees: Val Kreidel, Lewena Noorda, Raymond J. Noorda.
EIN: 870649164
Codes: CS, FD

53673
The Ashton Family Foundation
251 River Park Dr., Ste. 350
Provo, UT 84604
Application address: c/o Ralph Rasmussen, P.O. Box 432, Provo, UT 84603
Contact: Alan C. Ashton, Tr.

Established in 1993 in UT.
Donor(s): Alan C. Ashton.
Financial data (yr. ended 12/31/00): Grants paid, $3,346,142; assets, $33,946,521 (M); gifts received, $7,000; expenditures, $3,644,852; qualifying distributions, $3,346,142.
Limitations: Giving primarily in UT.
Trustees: Alan C. Ashton, Brigham Ashton, Eliza Ashton, Elizabeth Ashton, Karen Ashton, Morgan Ashton, Samuel Ashton, Spencer Ashton, Stephanie Ashton, Traci Ashton, Emily Ann Eddington, Paul Eddington, Allison Norton, Toby Norton, Amy Jo Young, Chad Young.
EIN: 870480108
Codes: FD

53674
Blake M. and Nancy L. Roney Foundation
75 W. Center St.
Provo, UT 84601-4432

Established in 1996 in UT.
Donor(s): Blake M. Roney, Nancy L. Roney.
Financial data (yr. ended 12/31/99): Grants paid, $3,002,400; assets, $970,934 (M); gifts received, $75,969; expenditures, $3,002,680; qualifying distributions, $3,002,400.
Limitations: Applications not accepted. Giving limited to UT.
Application information: Contributes only to pre-selected organizations.
Trustees: Blake M. Roney, Nancy L. Roney.
EIN: 870565402

Codes: FD

53675
Willard L. Eccles Charitable Foundation
P.O. Box 58198
Salt Lake City, UT 84158-0198
(801) 463-9580
FAX: (801) 463-9748; E-mail: wleccles@evoskis.com; URL: http://www.wleccles.org
Contact: Stephen E. Denkers, Secy.

Established in 1981 in UT.
Financial data (yr. ended 03/31/01): Grants paid, $2,598,807; assets, $47,525,918 (M); expenditures, $2,847,054; qualifying distributions, $2,736,462.
Limitations: Giving primarily in UT, with emphasis in the Ogden area.
Application information: Application form required.
Officer and Committee Members:* Stephen E. Denkers,* Secy.; Susan Coit, William E. Coit, M.D., Barbara E. Coit-Yeager, Julie E. Denkers, Stephen G. Denkers, Susan E. Denkers, Ann Goss.
Trustees: David Buckmen, First Security Bank of Utah, N.A.
EIN: 942759395
Codes: FD

53676
R. Harold Burton Foundation
(Formerly R. Harold Burton Private Foundation)
P.O. Box 58477
Salt Lake City, UT 84158 (801) 715-7141
FAX: (801) 364-6783; URL: http://www.rharoldburtonfoundation.org
Contact: Richard G. Horne, Exec. Dir.

Established in 1987 in UT.
Donor(s): Robert Harold Burton.‡
Financial data (yr. ended 12/31/01): Grants paid, $2,317,882; assets, $40,951,984 (M); expenditures, $2,733,725; qualifying distributions, $2,378,127.
Limitations: Giving primarily in Salt Lake County, UT.
Publications: Application guidelines.
Application information: Applications must be in by deadline. Application form required.
Members: Judith Burton Moyle, Chair.; Frederick A. Moreton, Jr., Vice-Chair.; Richard Robert Burton, Mike Moreton, Rebecca Moyle, Wood Moyle.
Trustee: First Security Bank of Utah, N.A.
EIN: 742425567
Codes: FD

53677
Marriner S. Eccles Foundation
701 Deseret Bldg.
79 S. Main St.
Salt Lake City, UT 84111
E-mail: mseccles@xmission.com
Contact: Shannon K. Toronto

Established in 1973 in Utah.
Donor(s): Marriner S. Eccles.‡
Financial data (yr. ended 03/31/02): Grants paid, $2,172,334; assets, $36,488,522 (M); expenditures, $2,357,749; qualifying distributions, $2,253,003.
Limitations: Giving limited to UT.
Application information: Guidelines revised annually, E-mail for revised guidelines in Nov. Application form required.
Officers and Committee Members:* Spencer F. Eccles, Chair.; Alonzo W. Watson, Jr.,* Secy.; C. Hope Eccles, James M. Steele, Elmer D. Tucker.
Trustee: Wells Fargo Bank, N.A.

EIN: 237185855
Codes: FD

53678
Tanner Charitable Trust
1930 S. State St.
Salt Lake City, UT 84115 (801) 486-2430

Incorporated in 1965 in UT.
Donor(s): Obert C. Tanner.
Financial data (yr. ended 12/31/01): Grants paid, $2,014,600; assets, $6,274,914 (M); expenditures, $2,042,453; qualifying distributions, $2,021,762.
Limitations: Applications not accepted. Giving primarily in Salt Lake City, UT.
Application information: Contributes only to pre-selected organizations.
Officer and Trustees:* Carolyn T. Irish,* Chair.; Kent H. Murdock, Grace A. Tanner.
EIN: 876125059
Codes: FD

53679
W. Jeffrey & Molly T. Knowles Family Foundation
4394 N. Stafford Ct.
Provo, UT 84604

Established in 1999 in UT.
Donor(s): W. Jeffrey Knowles, Molly T. Knowles.
Financial data (yr. ended 12/31/00): Grants paid, $1,864,886; assets, $0 (M); gifts received, $9,725; expenditures, $1,894,611; qualifying distributions, $1,848,056.
Limitations: Applications not accepted. Giving primarily in UT.
Application information: Contributes only to pre-selected organizations.
Trustees: Molly T. Knowles, W. Jeffrey Knowles.
EIN: 870643950
Codes: FD

53680
Marie Eccles Caine Charitable Foundation
P.O. Box 628
Salt Lake City, UT 84110
Application address: 324 N. 500 E., Brigham City, UT 84302
Contact: Manon C. Russell, Comm. Member, or Dan C. Russell, Comm. Member

Established in 1981 in UT.
Donor(s): Marie Eccles Caine.‡
Financial data (yr. ended 05/31/01): Grants paid, $1,794,912; assets, $32,948,732 (M); gifts received, $13,392; expenditures, $1,900,499; qualifying distributions, $1,821,524.
Limitations: Giving primarily in Logan and Cache County, UT.
Application information: Application form not required.
Committee Members: Dan C. Russell, Manon C. Russell, George R. Wanlass, Kathryn C. Wanlass.
Trustee: Wells Fargo Bank, N.A.
EIN: 942764258
Codes: FD

53681
The Katherine W. Dumke and Ezekiel R. Dumke, Jr. Foundation
P.O. Box 776
Kaysville, UT 84037 (801) 544-4626
E-mail: kwd@fndtn.org
Contact: Denise R. Johnsen, Off. Mgr.

Established in 1988 in UT.
Donor(s): Ezekiel R. Dumke, Jr.
Financial data (yr. ended 12/31/01): Grants paid, $1,789,539; assets, $27,571,563 (M); expenditures, $1,858,289; qualifying distributions, $1,778,077.

Limitations: Giving limited to the intermountain area, with emphasis on UT.
Publications: Application guidelines.
Application information: Application form required.
Officers and Trustees:* Katherine W. Dumke,* Pres.; Katherine E. Thornton,* V.P.; Ezekiel R. Dumke, Jr.,* Secy.-Treas.
Grants Committee Member: Andrea S. Dumke.
EIN: 870461899
Codes: FD

53682
Val A. Browning Charitable Foundation
c/o First Security Bank of Utah, N.A.
P.O. Box 628
Salt Lake City, UT 84110-0628
Application address: P.O. Box 9930, Ogden, UT 84409, tel.: (801) 626-9533
Contact: Mary Barker

Established in 1975 in UT.
Donor(s): Val A. Browning.
Financial data (yr. ended 12/31/01): Grants paid, $1,651,039; assets, $31,815,006 (M); expenditures, $1,794,977; qualifying distributions, $1,692,895.
Limitations: Giving primarily in UT.
Application information: Application form not required.
Officers: John Val Browning, Chair.; Orville Rex Child, Secy.
Directors: Bruce W. Browning, Carol B. Dumke, Judith B. Jones.
Trustee: First Security Bank of Utah, N.A.
EIN: 876167851
Codes: FD

53683
The ALS Foundation
584 S. State St.
Orem, UT 84058

Established in 1994 in UT.
Financial data (yr. ended 06/30/01): Grants paid, $1,228,000; assets, $25,161,283 (M); gifts received, $10,000; expenditures, $1,470,926; qualifying distributions, $1,228,000.
Limitations: Applications not accepted. Giving primarily in UT, especially Provo and Salt Lake City.
Application information: Contributes only to pre-selected organizations.
Trustees: Gaylord K. Swim, Katherine M. Swim, Roger C. Swim.
EIN: 870514581
Codes: FD

53684
Janet Q. Lawson Foundation
P.O. Box 45385
Salt Lake City, UT 84145-0385

Established around 1991 in UT.
Donor(s): Emma Eccles Jones,‡ Janet Q. Lawson.
Financial data (yr. ended 12/31/00): Grants paid, $1,175,000; assets, $21,908,761 (M); expenditures, $1,291,366; qualifying distributions, $1,188,673.
Limitations: Applications not accepted. Giving limited to UT, with emphasis on Salt Lake City.
Application information: Contributes only to pre-selected organizations.
Advisory Committee and Trustees:* Frederick Q. Lawson,* Advisor; Janet Q. Lawson,* Advisor; Peter Q. Lawson, Advisor; Herbert C. Livsey,* Advisor; JoAnne L. Shrontz, Advisor.
EIN: 870481508
Codes: FD

53685
Thrasher Research Fund
15 E. South Temple St., 3rd Fl.
Salt Lake City, UT 84150 (801) 240-4753
FAX: (801) 240-1625; E-mail: bussej@thrasherresearch.org; URL: http://www.thrasherresearch.org
Contact: Julia L. Busse

Established in 1977 in UT.
Donor(s): E.W. "Al" Thrasher.
Financial data (yr. ended 12/31/99): Grants paid, $1,163,008; assets, $48,904,522 (M); expenditures, $1,422,594; qualifying distributions, $1,615,472.
Limitations: Giving on a national and international basis.
Publications: Biennial report (including application guidelines), informational brochure (including application guidelines).
Application information: Guidelines are available on website, and should be viewed before submitting any applications. Application form required.
Officers and Executive Committee:* Keith B. McMullin,* Chair.; Harold Brown,* Vice-Chair.; E.W. "Al" Thrasher,* Vice-Chair.; A. Dean Byrd, Pres.; Katherine Boswell, Aileen H. Clyde, Isaac C. Ferguson, Clayton S. Huber, John M. Matsen, Sandra Rogers, Mary Anne Q. Wood.
EIN: 876179851
Codes: FD

53686
Edwin & Leah Battson Foundation
c/o Deseret Trust Co.
P.O. Box 11558
Salt Lake City, UT 84147-1558

Financial data (yr. ended 12/31/01): Grants paid, $1,076,800; assets, $509,106 (M); gifts received, $1,048,600; expenditures, $1,083,719; qualifying distributions, $1,078,315.
Limitations: Applications not accepted. Giving primarily in UT.
Application information: Contributes only to pre-selected organizations.
Trustee: Clinton E. Patterson.
EIN: 237073414
Codes: TN

53687
Dr. Ezekiel R. and Edna Wattis Dumke Foundation
P.O. Box 776
Kaysville, UT 84037 (801) 497-9474
E-mail: erd@fndtn.org
Contact: Denise R. Johnsen, Office Mgr.

Incorporated in 1959 in UT.
Financial data (yr. ended 12/31/01): Grants paid, $1,053,040; assets, $19,684,018 (M); expenditures, $1,186,093; qualifying distributions, $1,060,887.
Limitations: Giving limited to the western region of the U.S., with emphasis on ID, MT, NM, UT, and WY.
Publications: Application guidelines.
Application information: Application form required.
Officers and Directors:* Edmund E. Dumke,* Pres.; Claire Dumke Ryberg,* V.P.; Nancy Healy Schwanfelder,* Secy.; E. Michelle Praggastic, Treas.; Ezekiel R. Dumke, Jr., Andrea Dumke Manship, Betsy Thornton.
EIN: 876119783
Codes: FD

53688
Frederick Q. Lawson Foundation
P.O. Box 45385
Salt Lake City, UT 84145-0385
(801) 532-1500

Established around 1991.
Donor(s): Emma Eccles Jones,‡ Frederick Q. Lawson.
Financial data (yr. ended 12/31/99): Grants paid, $1,005,000; assets, $19,297,374 (M); expenditures, $1,100,209; qualifying distributions, $1,011,902.
Limitations: Applications not accepted. Giving primarily in Salt Lake City, UT.
Application information: Contributes only to pre-selected organizations.
Advisory Committee and Trustees:* Frederick Q. Lawson,* Advisor; Herbert C. Livsey,* Advisor.
EIN: 870481510
Codes: FD

53689
Ruth Eleanor Bamberger and John Ernest Bamberger Memorial Foundation
136 S. Main, Ste. 418
Salt Lake City, UT 84101 (801) 364-2045
Contact: Eleanor Roser, Member

Incorporated in 1947 in UT.
Donor(s): Ernest Bamberger,‡ Eleanor F. Bamberger.‡
Financial data (yr. ended 12/31/01): Grants paid, $995,857; assets, $25,892,584 (M); expenditures, $1,226,632; qualifying distributions, $1,060,114.
Limitations: Giving primarily in UT.
Application information: Interview required for scholarship applicants. Application form not required.
Members: Clarence Bamberger, Jr., Julie Barrett, Carol Olwell, Eleanor Roser, Roy W. Simmons.
EIN: 876116540
Codes: FD, GTI

53690
The One Foundation
75 W. Center St.
Provo, UT 84601-4432

Established in 1998 in UT.
Donor(s): Blake M. Roney, Nancy L. Roney.
Financial data (yr. ended 12/31/01): Grants paid, $953,180; assets, $1,677,147 (M); gifts received, $23,861; expenditures, $955,473; qualifying distributions, $951,605.
Limitations: Applications not accepted. Giving primarily in Palo Alto, CA.
Trustees: Keith R. Halls, Blake M. Roney, Nancy L. Roney.
EIN: 870576575
Codes: FD

53691
The GFC Foundation
584 S. State St.
Orem, UT 84058

Established in 1994 in UT.
Donor(s): Katherine Swim.
Financial data (yr. ended 06/30/01): Grants paid, $952,066; assets, $22,176,487 (M); expenditures, $1,230,441; qualifying distributions, $952,066.
Limitations: Applications not accepted. Giving primarily in, but not limited to, UT, especially Provo and Salt Lake City.
Application information: Contributes only to pre-selected organizations.
Trustees: Gaylord K. Swim, Lauralyn B. Swim.
EIN: 870529248
Codes: FD

53692
The B. W. Bastian Foundation
51 West Ctr., Ste. 755
Orem, UT 84057

Established in 1997 in UT.
Financial data (yr. ended 12/31/99): Grants paid, $910,850; assets, $17,517,270 (M); gifts received, $3,485,699; expenditures, $1,105,945; qualifying distributions, $941,630.
Limitations: Applications not accepted. Giving primarily in UT.
Application information: Contributes only to pre-selected organizations.
Trustee: Bruce W. Bastian, Brent Erklens, Rich Ith, Michael S. Marriott.
EIN: 841378232
Codes: FD

53693
Lawrence T. and Janet T. Dee Foundation
P.O. Box 58767
Salt Lake City, UT 84158 (801) 246-5363
Application address: c/o David L. Buchman, V.P., and Relationship Mgr., Wells Fargo Bank Northwest, N.A., P.O. Box 25491, Salt Lake City, UT 84125
Contact: Thomas D. Dee III, Vice-Chair.

Established in 1971 in UT.
Donor(s): L.T. Dee,‡ Janet T. Dee.‡
Financial data (yr. ended 12/31/01): Grants paid, $806,300; assets, $13,698,205 (M); expenditures, $874,901; qualifying distributions, $815,754.
Limitations: Giving primarily in Salt Lake City and Ogden, UT.
Publications: Application guidelines.
Application information: Application form not required.
Officers and Directors:* Thomas D. Dee II,* Chair.; David L. Dee,* Vice-Chair.; Thomas D. Dee III,* Vice-Chair.
Trustee: Wells Fargo Bank Northwest, N.A.
EIN: 876150803
Codes: FD

53694
The Salt Lake Foundation
9 Exchange Pl., Ste. 959
Salt Lake City, UT 84111 (801) 533-0820
Contact: F. Wayne Elggren, Treas.

Financial data (yr. ended 06/30/00): Grants paid, $804,493; assets, $3,573,773 (M); gifts received, $1,040,766; expenditures, $953,829.
Limitations: Giving primarily in UT, with emphasis on Salt Lake City.
Officers: Clark P. Giles, Exec. Chair.; Thomas Christensen, Jr., Chair.; F. Wayne Elggren, Treas.; Scott W. Lee, Counsel.
Board Members: Franklin K. Brough, Ph.D., Deanna T. Clark, Nancy N. Mathews, Stewart Ogden.
EIN: 742526626
Codes: CM, FD

53695
Eccles Family Foundation
(Formerly Spencer F. & Cleone P. Eccles Family Foundation)
c/o David L. Buchman, Wells Fargo Bank Northwest, N.A.
P.O. Box 628
Salt Lake City, UT 84125

Established in 1993 in UT.
Donor(s): Spencer F. Eccles, Hope Eccles Behlf.‡
Financial data (yr. ended 06/30/01): Grants paid, $772,932; assets, $17,282,279 (M); gifts received, $1,400,017; expenditures, $807,309; qualifying distributions, $777,002.

Limitations: Applications not accepted. Giving primarily in Ogden and Salt Lake City, UT.
Application information: Contributes only to pre-selected organizations.
Trustee: Wells Fargo Bank Northwest, N.A.
EIN: 876227329
Codes: FD

53696
The James R. Greenbaum, Jr. Family Foundation
432 E. Oak Forest Rd.
Salt Lake City, UT 84103

Established in 1991 in UT.
Donor(s): James R. Greenbaum, Jr.
Financial data (yr. ended 12/31/00): Grants paid, $740,746; assets, $1,826,870 (M); expenditures, $764,061; qualifying distributions, $739,370.
Limitations: Applications not accepted. Giving primarily in Salt Lake City, UT.
Application information: Contributes only to pre-selected organizations.
Trustee: James R. Greenbaum, Jr.
EIN: 876217358
Codes: FD

53697
Dialysis Research Foundation
5575 S. 500 E.
Ogden, UT 84405

Established in 1984.
Financial data (yr. ended 12/31/01): Grants paid, $670,345; assets, $2,992,366 (M); expenditures, $864,717; qualifying distributions, $671,853.
Limitations: Giving primarily in UT.
Application information: The foundation no longer awards grants to individual patients.
Officers and Board Members: Dave Trimble,* Chair.; H.J. Orme,* Vice-Chair.; Mark Lindsay,* Secy.-Treas.; Ruth Brockman, Fred Galvez, Mardee Hagen, Leo N. Harris, Kelvin Jackson, Mary Jo Jones, Phil K. Robinson, Schelly Schenk, Harry Senekjian, M.D.
EIN: 942819009
Codes: FD, GTI

53698
The Juniata Foundation, Inc.
c/o Pitchfork Mgmt., Inc.
P.O. Box 157
Midvale, UT 84047

Established in 1997 in WY and UT.
Donor(s): Robert E. Cook.
Financial data (yr. ended 12/31/01): Grants paid, $662,195; assets, $72,032 (M); expenditures, $984,623; qualifying distributions, $885,268.
Limitations: Applications not accepted. Giving on a national basis.
Application information: Contributes only to pre-selected organizations.
Directors: Paula J. Brooks, Camberly G. Cook, Chadwick W. Cook, Robert E. Cook.
EIN: 522018882
Codes: FD

53699
The Louis Scowcroft Peery Charitable Foundation
P.O. Box 1207
Bountiful, UT 84011-1207

Established in 1990 in UT.
Donor(s): Louis S. Peery, Janet P. Peery.
Financial data (yr. ended 12/31/00): Grants paid, $640,000; assets, $39,144,956 (M); gifts received, $41,016,975; expenditures, $1,035,737; qualifying distributions, $749,638.
Limitations: Applications not accepted. Giving primarily in Ogden, UT.
Application information: Contributes only to pre-selected organizations.
Officers: Leslie Ann Peery Howa, Mgr.; Paul T. Kunz, Mgr.; Jeffrey S. Peery, Mgr.
EIN: 870483734
Codes: FD

53700
M. Bastian Family Foundation
51 W. Center St., Ste. 305
Orem, UT 84057 (801) 225-2455
Contact: McKay S. Matthews

Established in 1993 in UT.
Donor(s): Melanie L. Bastian.
Financial data (yr. ended 12/31/99): Grants paid, $627,000; assets, $6,290,088 (M); expenditures, $639,622; qualifying distributions, $635,716.
Limitations: Giving primarily in UT, with emphasis on Provo, and VA, with emphasis on Alexandria.
Application information: Application form required.
Trustee: Melanie L. Bastian, McKay S. Matthews.
EIN: 876225255
Codes: FD

53701
The Mary Elizabeth Dee Shaw Charitable Trust
c/o Wells Fargo Bank Northwest, N.A.
P.O. Box 628
Salt Lake City, UT 84110
Application address: P.O. Box 9936, Ogden, UT 84409, tel.: (801) 626-9533
Contact: Jack D. Lampros, Chair., or Mary L. Barker, Secy.

Trust established in 1959 in UT.
Donor(s): Mary Elizabeth Dee Shaw.‡
Financial data (yr. ended 12/31/99): Grants paid, $620,000; assets, $15,007,783 (M); expenditures, $739,414; qualifying distributions, $675,279.
Limitations: Applications not accepted. Giving limited to UT.
Application information: Funds largely committed for the next 10 years.
Officers and Directors:* Jack D. Lampros,* Chair.; Dean W. Herst,* Vice-Chair.; C.W. Stromberg,* Vice-Chair.; Mary L. Barker,* Secy.; O. Rex Child,* Treas.
Trustees: Thomas D. Dee II, Joseph F. Hansen, Wells Fargo Bank Northewest, N.A.
EIN: 876116370

53702
Henry W. & Leslie M. Eskuche Charitable Foundation
c/o U.S. Bank
15 W. South Temple, Ste. 200
Salt Lake City, UT 84101 (801) 534-6268
FAX: (801) 534-6208
Contact: Russell J. Johnson, V.P. and Mng. Dir., U.S. Bank

Established in 1978.
Donor(s): Leslie M. Eskuche.‡
Financial data (yr. ended 02/28/01): Grants paid, $583,046; assets, $8,058,206 (M); expenditures, $665,124; qualifying distributions, $591,362.
Limitations: Giving primarily in UT.
Advisory Committee: Paula Julander, Tracy D. Smith, Peggy Stock.
Trustee: U.S. Bank.
EIN: 876179296
Codes: FD

53703
Hayward Family Foundation
(Formerly Nancy Eccles & Homer M. Hayward Foundation)
c/o Wells Fargo Bank Northwest, N.A.
P.O. Box 25491
Salt Lake City, UT 84125
Contact: David L. Buchman

Established in 1993 in UT.
Donor(s): Nancy Eccles Hayward.
Financial data (yr. ended 06/30/01): Grants paid, $574,000; assets, $12,053,905 (M); gifts received, $250,086; expenditures, $597,333; qualifying distributions, $577,037.
Limitations: Applications not accepted. Giving on a national basis.
Application information: Contributes only to pre-selected organizations. Unsolicited requests for funds not accepted.
Trustee: Wells Fargo Bank Northwest, N.A.
EIN: 876227330
Codes: FD

53704
The Bourne-Spafford Foundation
10584 S. 700 E. No. 244
Sandy, UT 84070-0943 (801) 277-5111
Contact: David R. Spafford, Tr.

Established in 1994 in UT.
Donor(s): David R. Spafford, Susan B. Spafford.
Financial data (yr. ended 12/31/01): Grants paid, $500,000; assets, $4,783,561 (M); gifts received, $327,220; expenditures, $557,459; qualifying distributions, $500,000.
Limitations: Giving primarily in Salt Lake City, UT.
Trustees: David R. Spafford, Susan B. Spafford.
EIN: 870533046
Codes: FD

53705
Herbert I. and Elsa B. Michael Foundation
c/o U.S. Bank
15 W. South Temple, Ste. 200
Salt Lake City, UT 84101 (801) 534-6085
FAX: (801) 534-6208
Contact: Russell Johnson, V.P.

Established in 1950 in UT.
Donor(s): Elsa B. Michael.‡
Financial data (yr. ended 09/30/01): Grants paid, $487,677; assets, $7,028,683 (M); expenditures, $569,158; qualifying distributions, $498,693.
Limitations: Giving primarily in UT.
Application information: Application form required.
Trustees: Peter Billings, Jr., Hal N. Swenson, U.S. Bank.
Advisory Committee: Richard Howe, Bernard Machen, Tracy D. Smith.
EIN: 876122556
Codes: FD

53706
Robert I. Wishnick Foundation
(Formerly The Witco Foundation)
P.O. Box 681869
Park City, UT 84068
Contact: William Wishnick, Pres.

Incorporated in 1951 in IL.
Donor(s): William Wishnick.
Financial data (yr. ended 12/31/01): Grants paid, $456,020; assets, $7,716,934 (M); expenditures, $490,547; qualifying distributions, $462,314.
Limitations: Applications not accepted. Giving on a national basis.
Application information: Contributes only to pre-selected organizations.

53706—UTAH

Officers and Directors:* William Wishnick,* Pres.; Lisa Wishnick,* V.P.; Robert L. Bachner,* Secy.; Simeon Brinberg, Ami Jo Gibson, Gina Grossman.
EIN: 136068668
Codes: FD

53707
Steven J. and Kalleen Lund Foundation
75 W. Center St.
Provo, UT 84601-4432

Established in 1996 in UT.
Donor(s): Kalleen Lund, Steven J. Lund.
Financial data (yr. ended 12/31/01): Grants paid, $436,199; assets, $476,450 (M); expenditures, $436,589; qualifying distributions, $436,199.
Limitations: Applications not accepted. Giving primarily in UT.
Application information: Contributes only to pre-selected organizations.
Trustees: Kalleen Lund, Steven J. Lund.
EIN: 870565417

53708
Ben B. and Iris M. Margolis Foundation
(Formerly Ben B. and Iris M. Margolis Foundation for Medical Research)
c/o Wells Fargo Bank Northwest, N.A.
P.O. Box 25491
Salt Lake City, UT 84125 (801) 350-5583
Contact: Julie Webster

Established in 1979 in UT.
Donor(s): Iris M. Margolis,‡ Ben B. Margolis.‡
Financial data (yr. ended 03/31/01): Grants paid, $412,273; assets, $8,314,868 (M); expenditures, $461,960; qualifying distributions, $427,337.
Limitations: Giving primarily in Salt Lake City, UT.
Application information: Application form not required.
Trustee: First Security Bank of Utah, N.A.
EIN: 876180864
Codes: FD

53709
The SPAN Foundation
559 West 500 South
Bountiful, UT 84010
Contact: Lynn G. Robbins, Tr.

Established in 1992 in UT.
Donor(s): Lynn G. Robbins.
Financial data (yr. ended 12/31/01): Grants paid, $385,595; assets, $6,062,330 (M); gifts received, $1,063,959; expenditures, $470,575; qualifying distributions, $385,468.
Limitations: Giving primarily in UT.
Publications: Financial statement.
Application information: Application form not required.
Trustee: Lynn G. Robbins.
Director: Jan E. Robbins.
EIN: 876220698
Codes: FD

53710
Raymond Family Foundation
c/o Wells Fargo Bank Northwest, N.A.
P.O. Box 25491
Salt Lake City, UT 84125 (801) 246-1436
Contact: David L. Buchman

Established in 1996 in UT.
Donor(s): Mary R. Redmond, Mary R. Raymond Charitable Lead Trust, Robert Raymond Foundation, Inc.
Financial data (yr. ended 12/31/01): Grants paid, $342,420; assets, $12,826,618 (M); gifts received, $250,000; expenditures, $422,358; qualifying distributions, $380,315.

Limitations: Giving on a national basis, with emphasis on CA, ME, NY, PA, and UT.
Application information: Application form not required.
Trustee: Wells Fargo Bank Northwest, N.A.
EIN: 566502391
Codes: FD

53711
The Skolnick Foundation
1553 Connecticut Dr.
Salt Lake City, UT 84103
Contact: Angela A. Skolnick, Tr.

Established in 1996 in UT.
Donor(s): Angela A. Skolnick, Mark H. Skolnick.
Financial data (yr. ended 12/31/01): Grants paid, $335,618; assets, $4,571,403 (M); gifts received, $3; expenditures, $339,826; qualifying distributions, $326,670.
Limitations: Giving primarily in Salt Lake City, UT.
Application information: Application form not required.
Trustees: Angela A. Skolnick, Giancarlo Skolnick, Joshua Skolnick, Mark H. Skolnick.
EIN: 870567067
Codes: FD

53712
Junior E. & Blanche B. Rich Foundation
c/o Wells Fargo Bank Northwest, N.A.
P.O. Box 628
Salt Lake City, UT 84110-0628
Application address: 2826 Pierce Ave., Ogden, UT 84409

Established in 1975 in UT.
Financial data (yr. ended 12/31/01): Grants paid, $312,457; assets, $4,734,306 (M); expenditures, $343,099; qualifying distributions, $328,392.
Limitations: Giving primarily in Weber County, UT.
Application information: Application form not required.
Officer: Sharon Rich Lewis, Chair.
Directors: Lynne Rich Lichfield, Carolyn Rich Nebeker, Edward B. Rich.
Trustee: Wells Fargo Bank Northwest, N.A.
EIN: 876173654
Codes: FD

53713
The Will Ascend Foundation
1331 N. Hidden Quail Cove
Farmington, UT 84025

Established in 1999 in UT.
Donor(s): Gary Williams, Deborah Williams.
Financial data (yr. ended 12/31/01): Grants paid, $310,020; assets, $435,712 (M); gifts received, $401; expenditures, $310,973; qualifying distributions, $309,810.
Limitations: Applications not accepted. Giving primarily in UT.
Application information: Contributes only to pre-selected organizations.
Trustees: Deborah Williams, Gary Williams.
EIN: 870644841
Codes: FD

53714
National Council on Employment Policy
2130 Ridgewood Way
Bountiful, UT 84010 (801) 296-9380
Contact: Garth L. Mangum, Secy.-Treas.

Established around 1967.
Financial data (yr. ended 06/30/01): Grants paid, $294,700; assets, $238,744 (M); gifts received, $324,966; expenditures, $586,631; qualifying distributions, $586,478.

Limitations: Applications not accepted. Giving primarily in OH and UT.
Application information: Contributes only to pre-selected organizations.
Officers: Marion Pines, Chair.; Garth L. Mangum, Secy.-Treas.
EIN: 520845420
Codes: FD

53715
Steiner Foundation, Inc.
505 E. South Temple St.
Salt Lake City, UT 84102-1061
(801) 328-8831
Contact: Kevin K. Steiner, Pres.

Established in 1959 in UT.
Donor(s): Steiner Corp.
Financial data (yr. ended 06/30/00): Grants paid, $280,897; assets, $4,048,410 (M); expenditures, $297,602; qualifying distributions, $285,096.
Limitations: Giving primarily in UT.
Application information: Application form not required.
Officers: Kevin K. Steiner, Pres.; Timothy L. Weiler, Secy.
EIN: 876119190
Codes: CS, FD, CD

53716
C. Scott and Dorothy E. Watkins Charitable Foundation
1935 E. Vine St., Ste. 260
Salt Lake City, UT 84121

Established in 1992.
Financial data (yr. ended 12/31/01): Grants paid, $275,000; assets, $5,079,799 (M); expenditures, $283,737; qualifying distributions, $275,000.
Limitations: Applications not accepted. Giving primarily in UT.
Application information: Contributes only to pre-selected organizations.
Trustees: Alonzo A. Hinckley, Jay Rasmussen, Gary Watkins.
EIN: 876218993
Codes: FD

53717
The Lighthouse Foundation
c/o Call Hartle & Co.
350 S. 400 E., Ste. 201
Salt Lake City, UT 84111 (801) 596-9999
Contact: Dennis R. Webb, Tr.

Established in 1992 in UT.
Donor(s): Dennis R. Webb.
Financial data (yr. ended 12/31/00): Grants paid, $274,511; assets, $611,316 (M); gifts received, $10,000; expenditures, $281,034; qualifying distributions, $273,058.
Limitations: Giving primarily in Salt Lake City, UT.
Application information: Application form not required.
Trustee: Dennis R. Webb.
EIN: 876220829
Codes: FD

53718
The Eric T. and Elizabeth C. Jacobsen Foundation
4764 Sagebrush Rd.
Park City, UT 84098

Established in 2000 in UT.
Donor(s): Eric T. Jacobsen, Elizabeth C. Jacobsen.
Financial data (yr. ended 12/31/01): Grants paid, $265,000; assets, $3,714,997 (M); gifts received, $2,110; expenditures, $323,678; qualifying distributions, $278,531.

Limitations: Applications not accepted. Giving primarily in St. Louis, MO and Helena, MT.
Application information: Contributes only to pre-selected organizations.
Trustees: Elizabeth C. Jacobsen, Eric T. Jacobsen.
EIN: 870661833
Codes: FD

53719
Simmons Family Foundation
c/o Elizabeth Watkins, Exec. Dir.
10 E. South Temple, Ste. 1000
Salt Lake City, UT 84133
E-mail: ewatkins@simmonsmedia.com

Established in 1986 in UT.
Donor(s): Roy W. Simmons.
Financial data (yr. ended 11/30/01): Grants paid, $258,625; assets, $6,585,590 (M); gifts received, $1,089,200; expenditures, $291,858; qualifying distributions, $285,679.
Limitations: Giving primarily in UT.
Publications: Application guidelines.
Application information: Application form required.
Trustees: Elizabeth S. Hoke, David E. Simmons, Harris Simmons, L.E. Simmons, Matthew R. Simmons, Julia S. Watkins.
EIN: 133420599
Codes: FD

53720
Semnani Foundation
60 E. South Temple, Ste. 2200
Salt Lake City, UT 84111 (801) 321-7725
Contact: Koshrow B. Semnani, Tr.

Established in 1991 in UT.
Donor(s): Khosrow B. Semnani.
Financial data (yr. ended 12/31/00): Grants paid, $245,215; assets, $19,414,980 (M); gifts received, $2,293,390; expenditures, $353,395; qualifying distributions, $245,215.
Limitations: Giving primarily in UT.
Trustees: Nolan Karras, Shirin Kia, Ghazelah Semnani, Khosrow B. Semnani.
EIN: 742639794
Codes: FD2

53721
Samuel C. & Myra G. Powell Foundation
c/o First Security Bank of Utah, N.A.
P.O. Box 628
Salt Lake City, UT 84110-0628
Application address: c/o Mary Barker, First Security Bank, P.O. Box 9936, Ogden, UT 84409, tel.: (801) 626-9531
Contact: Samuel Barker, Chair.

Established in 1974 in UT.
Financial data (yr. ended 12/31/00): Grants paid, $245,174; assets, $5,585,775 (M); expenditures, $320,866; qualifying distributions, $296,047.
Limitations: Giving primarily in Ogden and Salt Lake City, UT.
Application information: Application form not required.
Officers: Samuel Barker, Chair.; Charles H. Barker, Vice-Chair.
Directors: Mary L. Barker, Orville Rex Child, Jack D. Lampros.
Trustee: First Security Bank of Utah, N.A.
EIN: 876163275
Codes: FD2

53722
Annie Taylor Dee Foundation
P.O. Box 58767
Salt Lake City, UT 84158 (801) 246-5363
Application address: c/o David L. Buchman, V.P. and Relationship Mgr., Wells Fargo Bank Northwest, N.A., Institutional Trust, P.O. Box 25491, Salt Lake City, UT 84125
Contact: Thomas D. Dee III, Vice-Chair.

Trust established in 1961 in UT.
Donor(s): Maude Dee Porter,‡ Annie T. Dee.‡
Financial data (yr. ended 12/31/01): Grants paid, $222,500; assets, $3,533,821 (M); expenditures, $242,460; qualifying distributions, $226,645.
Limitations: Giving limited to UT, with emphasis on Ogden.
Application information: Application form required.
Officers and Directors:* Thomas D. Dee II,* Chair.; David L. Dee,* Vice-Chair.; Thomas D. Dee III,* Vice-Chair.
Trustee: Wells Fargo Bank Northwest, N.A.
EIN: 876116380
Codes: FD2

53723
Castle Foundation
c/o U.S. Bank Trust Co.
15 W. South Temple, Ste 200
Salt Lake City, UT 84101 (801) 534-6085
FAX: (801) 534-6208
Contact: F. Lynn Baldwin, V.P., U.S. Bank Trust Co.

Established in 1953 in UT.
Financial data (yr. ended 06/30/01): Grants paid, $214,900; assets, $3,997,828 (M); expenditures, $253,015; qualifying distributions, $218,995.
Limitations: Giving limited to UT, with emphasis on Salt Lake City.
Application information: Application form required.
Trustee: U.S. Bank, N.A.
EIN: 876117177
Codes: FD2

53724
Esther Foundation, Inc.
1716 N. Meadowlark Rd.
Orem, UT 84057
Contact: L. Graig Taylor, Pres.

Established in 1994 in UT.
Financial data (yr. ended 06/30/01): Grants paid, $208,543; assets, $3,444,436 (M); gifts received, $9,254; expenditures, $296,536; qualifying distributions, $157,620.
Limitations: Applications not accepted.
Application information: Unsolicited requests for funds not accepted.
Officers: L. Graig Taylor, Pres.; Kevin L. Simister, V.P.; John L. Valentine, Secy.
EIN: 870532890
Codes: FD2

53725
Odyssey Foundation
P.O. Box 712320
Salt Lake City, UT 84171-2320
Application address: 2437 Faretto Ln., Reno, NV 89511
Contact: Eric Roberts, Pres.

Established in 1999 in NV.
Donor(s): Frank Roberts, Jean Roberts.
Financial data (yr. ended 12/31/01): Grants paid, $196,000; assets, $3,625,625 (M); expenditures, $214,824; qualifying distributions, $195,273.
Limitations: Giving primarily in CA, CO, NV, and WA.
Publications: Newsletter.
Application information: Application form required.
Officers and Trustees:* Frank Roberts,* C.E.O.; Eric Roberts,* Pres.; Don Roberts,* V.P.; Jeff Peck,* Secy.-Treas.; Katherine Farrell, Doug Roberts, Jean Roberts.
EIN: 880436019
Codes: FD2

53726
Spencer F. & Cleone P. Eccles Foundation
c/o Wells Fargo Bank Northwest, N.A.
P.O. Box 25491
Salt Lake City, UT 84125
Contact: David L. Buchman

Established in 1993 in UT.
Donor(s): Hope Eccles Behlf,‡ Spencer F. Eccles.
Financial data (yr. ended 06/30/99): Grants paid, $192,916; assets, $15,367,077 (M); expenditures, $216,241; qualifying distributions, $452,107.
Limitations: Applications not accepted. Giving limited to Salt Lake City, UT.
Application information: Contributes only to pre-selected organizations.
Trustee: Wells Fargo Bank Northwest, N.A.
EIN: 876226329
Codes: FD2

53727
The Force for Good Foundation
75 W. Center St.
Provo, UT 84601-4432

Established in 1998 in UT.
Donor(s): Diamond Technology Partners, Inc., Newspaper Association of America, Noriaki Okamoto.
Financial data (yr. ended 12/31/99): Grants paid, $192,696; assets, $331,313 (M); gifts received, $523,882; expenditures, $219,220; qualifying distributions, $192,629.
Limitations: Applications not accepted.
Application information: Contributes only to pre-selected organizations.
Officer: Blake M. Romey, Chair. and Pres.
EIN: 870577244
Codes: FD2

53728
Paul Q. Callister Foundation, Inc.
(Formerly Louise E. Callister Foundation)
2005 S. 300 W.
Salt Lake City, UT 84115

Incorporated in 1958 in UT.
Donor(s): Paul Q. Callister, Mary B. Callister.
Financial data (yr. ended 06/30/01): Grants paid, $181,500; assets, $3,818,110 (M); expenditures, $232,397; qualifying distributions, $186,750.
Limitations: Giving primarily in Salt Lake City, UT.
Directors: Andrew Callister, Jan Callister, Paul Q. Callister, Sara McConkie, Jeanne C. Thorne.
EIN: 876118299
Codes: FD2

53729
Carlyle and Delta Harmon Scholarship Foundation
(Formerly Harmon Women's Scholarship Fund)
2481 W. 1425 S.
Syracuse, UT 84075
Contact: Richard McDermott

Established in 1997 in UT.
Donor(s): Carlyle Harmon Irrevocable Trust.
Financial data (yr. ended 12/31/99): Grants paid, $176,135; assets, $1,237,173 (M); expenditures, $200,188; qualifying distributions, $175,953.
Limitations: Giving primarily in UT.

53729—UTAH

Application information: Request application form from fund. Application form required.
Board Members: K. Coles, G. Cornia, I. Ferguson, R. Hansen, A. Harris, L. Lund, R. McDermott, K. Stocks, C. Thompson.
EIN: 870508363
Codes: FD2

53730
William E. Slaughter, Jr. Foundation, Inc.
59 S. Main St., PMB 144
Moab, UT 84532

Incorporated in 1959 in MI.
Donor(s): William E. Slaughter, Jr.‡
Financial data (yr. ended 12/31/01): Grants paid, $171,000; assets, $0 (M); expenditures, $189,970; qualifying distributions, $169,667.
Limitations: Applications not accepted. Giving primarily in AZ, HI, and UT.
Application information: Contributes only to pre-selected organizations.
Officers and Directors:* Kent C. Slaughter,* Pres. and Secy.; Gloria Slaughter,* V.P.; William E. Stillwater,* V.P.; William A. Corbett, C.F.O.
EIN: 386065616
Codes: FD2

53731
The Steve Young Family Foundation
559 W. 500 S. St.
Bountiful, UT 84010

Established in 1993 in UT.
Donor(s): J. Steven Young.
Financial data (yr. ended 12/31/00): Grants paid, $170,800; assets, $969,653 (M); expenditures, $177,602; qualifying distributions, $170,422.
Limitations: Giving on a national basis.
Trustee: J. Steven Young.
EIN: 870517242
Codes: FD2

53732
The Zions Bancorporation Foundation
1 S. Main St., Ste. 1380
Salt Lake City, UT 84111-1909

Established in 1997 in UT.
Donor(s): Zions Bancorporation.
Financial data (yr. ended 12/31/00): Grants paid, $167,867; assets, $4,076,687 (M); expenditures, $167,867; qualifying distributions, $166,731.
Limitations: Applications not accepted. Giving primarily in Salt Lake City, UT.
Application information: Contributes only to pre-selected organizations.
Officer and Trustee:* Harris Simmons,* Pres.
EIN: 841411938
Codes: CS, FD2, CD

53733
Questar Corporation Arts Foundation
180 E. 1st South St.
P.O. Box 45433
Salt Lake City, UT 84145-0433
(801) 324-5435
FAX: (801) 324-5483; *E-mail:* janb@questar.com
Contact: Jan Bates, Dir., Community Affairs

Established in 1991 in UT.
Donor(s): Questar Corp.
Financial data (yr. ended 12/31/01): Grants paid, $157,776; assets, $3,060,797 (M); gifts received, $162,000; expenditures, $163,543; qualifying distributions, $156,840.
Limitations: Applications not accepted. Giving limited to UT.
Application information: Contributes only to pre-selected organizations.

Officer and Trustees:* R.D. Cash,* Chair.; Connie C. Holbrook, Stephen E. Parks.
EIN: 870489086
Codes: CS, FD2, CD

53734
Questar Corporation Educational Foundation
180 E. 1st South St.
P.O. Box 45433
Salt Lake City, UT 84145-0433
(801) 324-5435
FAX: (801) 324-5483; *E-mail:* janb@questar.com
Contact: Janice Bates, Dir., Community Affairs

Established in 1988 in UT.
Donor(s): Questar Corp.
Financial data (yr. ended 12/31/01): Grants paid, $157,776; assets, $3,060,797 (M); gifts received, $162,000; expenditures, $163,543; qualifying distributions, $156,840.
Limitations: Applications not accepted. Giving limited to areas of company service in AZ, CO, OK, TX, UT, and WY.
Application information: Contributes only to pre-selected organizations.
Officer and Trustees:* R.D. Cash,* Chair.; Connie C. Holbrook, Stephen E. Parks.
EIN: 870461487
Codes: CS, FD2, CD

53735
First Security Foundation
P.O. Box 628
Salt Lake City, UT 84110-0628

Established in 1952 in UT.
Donor(s): First Security Corporation.
Financial data (yr. ended 12/31/01): Grants paid, $157,600; assets, $3,579,619 (M); expenditures, $170,187; qualifying distributions, $157,724.
Limitations: Applications not accepted. Giving limited to ID, NM, NV, OR, UT, and WY.
Application information: Contributes only to pre-selected organizations.
Officers and Trustees:* Spencer F. Eccles,* Pres.; Eileen C. Hansen, Secy.; Verna Lee Johnston, Treas.; First Security Bank, N.A.
EIN: 876118149
Codes: CS, TN

53736
Brent and Bonnie Jean Beesley Foundation
95 E. Tabernacle St., Ste. 200
St. George, UT 84770 (435) 628-0433
Contact: Brent Beesley, Tr.

Established in 1996 in UT.
Donor(s): Bonnie Jean Beesley, Brent Beesley, Heritage Holding Company.
Financial data (yr. ended 12/31/01): Grants paid, $152,350; assets, $3,017,547 (M); gifts received, $391,020; expenditures, $158,212; qualifying distributions, $155,281.
Limitations: Giving primarily in UT.
Trustees: Bonnie Jean Beesley, Brent Beesley, Laura Jean Beesley, Brian D. Chadaz, Brad L. Hales.
EIN: 870568595
Codes: FD2

53737
Child Family Foundation
2301 S. 300 W.
Salt Lake City, UT 84115

Established in 1997 in VT.
Donor(s): William H. Child.
Financial data (yr. ended 12/31/01): Grants paid, $150,000; assets, $3,607,062 (M); expenditures, $150,091; qualifying distributions, $150,000.

Limitations: Applications not accepted. Giving primarily in UT.
Application information: Contributes only to pre-selected organizations.
Officers: William H. Child, Pres.; William Steven Child, V.P.; Susan Kathleen Markham, Secy.; Patricia Ann Child, Treas.
EIN: 841407793
Codes: FD2

53738
Plateau Native American Foundation
P.O. Box 628
Salt Lake City, UT 84110-0628

Established in 1998 in ID.
Donor(s): Michael Adams.
Financial data (yr. ended 12/31/01): Grants paid, $143,000; assets, $2,423,281 (M); gifts received, $50; expenditures, $169,143; qualifying distributions, $154,201.
Limitations: Applications not accepted.
Application information: Contributes only to pre-selected organizations.
Trustee: Wells Fargo Bank Northwest, N.A.
EIN: 876240442
Codes: FD2

53739
Meldrum Foundation
1808 Mohawk Way
Salt Lake City, UT 84108

Established in 2000 in UT.
Donor(s): Peter D. Meldrum.
Financial data (yr. ended 12/31/01): Grants paid, $142,250; assets, $2,659,026 (M); gifts received, $17; expenditures, $199,512; qualifying distributions, $134,667.
Limitations: Applications not accepted. Giving primarily in Salt Lake City, UT.
Application information: Contributes only to pre-selected organizations.
Officers and Trustees:* Catherine R. Meldrum,* Secy.-Treas.; Peter D. Meldrum,* Exec. Dir.; Annette Meldrum, Christopher S. Meldrum.
EIN: 870657244
Codes: FD2

53740
Dinesh and Kalpana Patel Foundation
P.O. Box 58887
Salt Lake City, UT 84158-0887

Established in 1994 in UT.
Donor(s): Dinesh C. Patel.
Financial data (yr. ended 12/31/01): Grants paid, $138,237; assets, $937,869 (M); gifts received, $3,200; expenditures, $163,271; qualifying distributions, $137,700.
Limitations: Applications not accepted. Giving primarily in UT.
Application information: Contributes only to pre-selected organizations.
Trustees: Dinesh C. Patel, Kalpana D. Patel, Kiran C. Patel.
EIN: 870532423
Codes: FD2

53741
Ralph Nye Charitable Foundation
1646 29th St.
Ogden, UT 84403 (801) 621-3508
Contact: Alan Nye, Tr.

Established in 1981 in UT.
Donor(s): Ralph Nye.‡
Financial data (yr. ended 12/31/01): Grants paid, $137,000; assets, $2,665,544 (M); expenditures, $235,536; qualifying distributions, $137,000.

Limitations: Giving primarily in Weber County, UT.
Application information: Application form not required.
Trustees: Holly N. Bauman, Margaret M. Black, Alan Nye, Bret Nye, Fred M. Nye, Gregory B. Nye, Jay C. Nye, Robert R. Nye, Rodger A. Nye, Denice N. Rouady.
EIN: 942765986
Codes: FD2

53742
Harris H. and Amanda P. Simmons Foundation
1038 N.E. Capitol Blvd.
Salt Lake City, UT 84103

Established in 1997 in UT.
Donor(s): Harris H. Simmons.
Financial data (yr. ended 12/31/00): Grants paid, $135,016; assets, $2,747,931 (M); expenditures, $135,664; qualifying distributions, $135,190.
Limitations: Applications not accepted. Giving primarily in UT.
Application information: Contributes only to pre-selected organizations.
Trustee: Harris H. Simmons.
EIN: 841411937
Codes: FD2

53743
John and Marcia Price Family Foundation
35 Century Pkwy.
Salt Lake City, UT 84115 (801) 486-3911
Contact: Martin G. Peterson, Exec. Dir.

Established in 1997 in UT.
Financial data (yr. ended 12/31/01): Grants paid, $132,200; assets, $2,456,136 (M); gifts received, $800; expenditures, $144,593; qualifying distributions, $130,190.
Limitations: Giving primarily in UT.
Application information: Application form not required.
Officer and Directors:* Martin G. Peterson,* Exec. Dir.; Deirdra Price, John Steven Price, Marcia Price, Jennifer Price Wallin.
Trustee: John Price.
EIN: 841402027
Codes: FD2

53744
The Bryson Foundation
3800 Sherwood Dr.
Provo, UT 84604

Established in 1996 in UT.
Donor(s): R. Craig Bryson, Kathleen D. Bryson.
Financial data (yr. ended 12/31/01): Grants paid, $131,250; assets, $593,776 (M); expenditures, $135,339; qualifying distributions, $131,250.
Limitations: Applications not accepted. Giving limited to UT.
Application information: Contributes only to pre-selected organizations.
Trustees: Kathleen D. Bryson, R. Craig Bryson.
EIN: 871367935
Codes: FD2

53745
Edith Dee Green Foundation
c/o First Security Bank of Utah, N.A.
P.O. Box 30007
Salt Lake City, UT 84130
Mailing address: 1521 E. Wasatch Dr., Ogden, UT 84403
Contact: Mrs. Harold J. Mack, Mgr.

Established in 1969.
Financial data (yr. ended 12/31/01): Grants paid, $129,400; assets, $2,656,588 (M); expenditures, $145,536; qualifying distributions, $135,111.

Limitations: Applications not accepted. Giving limited to Ogden, UT.
Application information: Unsolicited requests for funds not accepted, funds currently committed.
Officers and Trustees:* Harold J. Mack,* Mgr.; Melva B. Mack,* Mgr.; First Security Bank of Utah, N.A.
EIN: 876149837
Codes: FD2

53746
Mitchell and June Morris Foundation
5200 Highland Dr., No. 202
Salt Lake City, UT 84117

Established in 1994 in UT.
Donor(s): G. Mitchell Morris, June Morris.
Financial data (yr. ended 12/31/01): Grants paid, $126,168; assets, $1,893,088 (M); expenditures, $127,784; qualifying distributions, $126,168.
Limitations: Applications not accepted. Giving primarily in Salt Lake City, UT.
Application information: Contributes only to pre-selected organizations.
Trustees: G. Mitchell Morris, June Morris.
EIN: 870529714

53747
Joseph and Evelyn Rosenblatt Charitable Fund
(Formerly Joseph and Evelyn Rosenblatt Charitable Trust, Inc.)
Eagle Gate Tower
60 E. South Temple, Ste. 620
Salt Lake City, UT 84111

Established in 1959.
Donor(s): Joseph Rosenblatt,‡ Evelyn Rosenblatt, Toby Rosenblatt.
Financial data (yr. ended 12/31/01): Grants paid, $125,424; assets, $3,432,490 (M); gifts received, $29,456; expenditures, $139,164; qualifying distributions, $125,424.
Limitations: Applications not accepted. Giving primarily in Salt Lake City, UT.
Application information: Contributes only to pre-selected organizations.
Officers and Directors:* Toby Rosenblatt,* Pres. and Secy.; Evelyn Rosenblatt,* V.P.; Norman Rosenblatt, V.P.
EIN: 876122725
Codes: FD2

53748
The Alan and Jeanne Hall Foundation
4155 Harrison Blvd., Ste. 300
Ogden, UT 84403

Established in 1999 in UT.
Donor(s): Alan E. Hall, Jeannie Hall.
Financial data (yr. ended 12/31/01): Grants paid, $121,767; assets, $2,643,285 (M); gifts received, $242,000; expenditures, $128,206; qualifying distributions, $123,585.
Limitations: Applications not accepted.
Application information: Contributes only to pre-selected organizations.
Officer: Alan E. Hall, Pres.
Trustees: Aaron Hall, Adam Hall, Eric Hall, Jeannie Hall, Laura West.
EIN: 870644251
Codes: FD2

53749
McGillis Charitable Foundation
3068 S. 1030 W.
Salt Lake City, UT 84119-3343

Established in 1986 in UT.
Donor(s): Richard L. McGillis, Joanne S. McGillis.

Financial data (yr. ended 12/31/01): Grants paid, $119,445; assets, $907,858 (M); expenditures, $120,560; qualifying distributions, $238,890.
Limitations: Applications not accepted. Giving primarily in Salt Lake City, UT.
Application information: Contributes only to pre-selected organizations.
Trustees: Roger McGillis, Mary Ann O'Connell, Evan R. Terry.
EIN: 870437797
Codes: FD2

53750
The Zaphiropoulos Foundation
c/o Renn Zaphiropoulos
P.O. Box 1022
Cedar City, UT 84721

Established in 1994 in UT.
Donor(s): Renn Zaphiropoulos, Marie Zaphiropoulos.
Financial data (yr. ended 12/31/01): Grants paid, $118,165; assets, $79,882 (M); expenditures, $119,728; qualifying distributions, $118,165.
Limitations: Applications not accepted. Giving primarily in UT.
Application information: Contributes only to pre-selected organizations.
Officers: Renn Zaphiropoulos, Pres.; Marie Zaphiropoulos, Secy.-Treas.
EIN: 870525302

53751
The Marion D. and Maxine C. Hanks Foundation, Inc.
Judge Bldg.
8 E. Broadway, Ste. 520
Salt Lake City, UT 84111 (801) 364-7705
Contact: Phyllis Warnick, Secy.

Established in 1993 in UT.
Donor(s): Hyrum Smith, Dick Winwood, Robert Bennett.
Financial data (yr. ended 12/31/01): Grants paid, $116,934; assets, $1,875,811 (M); gifts received, $5,600; expenditures, $167,034; qualifying distributions, $116,934.
Limitations: Giving primarily in Salt Lake City, UT.
Officer: Phyllis Warnick, Secy.
EIN: 870503758
Codes: FD2, GTI

53752
Judelson Family Foundation
P.O. Box 887
Park City, UT 84060

Established in 1996 in IL.
Donor(s): Joan Judelson, Robert Judelson.
Financial data (yr. ended 12/31/01): Grants paid, $116,350; assets, $651,455 (M); expenditures, $125,243; qualifying distributions, $119,302.
Limitations: Giving primarily in Park City and Salt Lake City, UT.
Officers: Robert Judelson, Pres.; Joan Judelson, Treas.
EIN: 364116388
Codes: FD2

53753
Delonne Anderson Family Foundation
559 W. 500th St. S.
Bountiful, UT 84010
Application address: c/o Margaret F. Anderson, P.O. Box 284, Etna, WY 83127

Established in 1997 in UT.
Donor(s): Margaret F. Anderson.
Financial data (yr. ended 12/31/01): Grants paid, $115,960; assets, $782,941 (M); expenditures, $125,742; qualifying distributions, $116,521.

53753—UTAH

Limitations: Giving primarily in UT.
Application information: Application form not required.
Trustees: Gary C. Anderson, Margaret F. Anderson, Steven C. Anderson, Margaret K. Steed.
EIN: 841407748
Codes: FD2

53754
The Cherokee & Walker Foundation
1245 E. Brickyard Rd., Ste.350
Salt Lake City, UT 84106 (801) 463-6161
Contact: Shane Peery, Tr.

Established in 1999 in UT.
Financial data (yr. ended 12/31/00): Grants paid, $113,667; assets, $147,309 (M); gifts received, $254,850; expenditures, $118,341; qualifying distributions, $113,667.
Trustees: Gregg T. Christensen, Connie Jenkins, James W. Jenkins, Shane R. Peery.
EIN: 870635720
Codes: FD2

53755
The Howard Foundation
3288 N. Brookside Dr.
Provo, UT 84604

Established in 1997 in UT.
Financial data (yr. ended 12/31/01): Grants paid, $111,850; assets, $1,416,892 (M); gifts received, $197,656; expenditures, $113,982; qualifying distributions, $111,420.
Limitations: Applications not accepted. Giving primarily in UT.
Application information: Contributes only to pre-selected organizations.
Trustees: Andrew L. Howard, Fred D. Howard, Jackson B. Howard, Holly Strachan.
EIN: 742712082
Codes: FD2

53756
The SFK Family Foundation
10584 S. 700 E., No. 222
Sandy, UT 84070 (801) 550-6610
Contact: Spencer F. Kirk, Tr.

Established in 1996 in UT.
Donor(s): Spencer F. Kirk.
Financial data (yr. ended 12/31/01): Grants paid, $111,475; assets, $9,542 (M); expenditures, $114,936; qualifying distributions, $111,475.
Limitations: Giving primarily in UT.
Application information: Application form not required.
Trustees: Kristen C. Kirk, Spencer F. Kirk.
EIN: 870564748

53757
Flamm Family Foundation
P.O. 712258
Salt Lake City, UT 84119-2258
(801) 453-1700
Contact: Robert Hunter

Established in 1997 in UT.
Donor(s): Jeffrey Flamm, Nancy Flamm.
Financial data (yr. ended 12/31/01): Grants paid, $110,211; assets, $2,002,380 (M); expenditures, $131,023; qualifying distributions, $119,503.
Limitations: Giving primarily in UT.
Trustees: Jeffrey Flamm, Nancy Flamm.
EIN: 846312928
Codes: FD2

53758
Wheeler Foundation
(Formerly Wheeler Machinery Foundation)
4899 W. 2100 S.
West Valley City, UT 84120 (801) 974-0388
Contact: Don M. Wheeler, Tr.

Established in 1992 in UT.
Donor(s): Don M. Wheeler.
Financial data (yr. ended 11/30/01): Grants paid, $110,150; assets, $2,378,575 (M); expenditures, $112,320; qualifying distributions, $111,320.
Limitations: Giving primarily in Salt Lake City, UT.
Trustees: Thomas Clark, Susan Holt, Alison Jensen, Don M. Wheeler, Katherine Younker.
EIN: 870503163
Codes: FD2

53759
MSL Family Foundation, Ltd.
2826 Pierce Ave.
Ogden, UT 84403 (801) 394-2407
Contact: Sharon R. Lewis, Dir.

Established in 1997 in IL.
Donor(s): O. Marvin Lewis, Sharon R. Lewis.
Financial data (yr. ended 12/31/00): Grants paid, $109,615; assets, $492 (M); gifts received, $109,815; expenditures, $111,868; qualifying distributions, $109,615.
Limitations: Applications not accepted.
Application information: Contributes only to pre-selected organizations.
Directors: O. Marvin Lewis, Sharon R. Lewis.
EIN: 841407828
Codes: FD2

53760
South Eden Foundation
7814 S. Pheasant Wood Dr.
Sandy, UT 84093-6291 (801) 532-1500
Contact: Jane A. Kennedy, Pres.

Established in 1998 in UT.
Donor(s): Jane A. Kennedy.
Financial data (yr. ended 12/31/00): Grants paid, $107,470; assets, $115,608 (M); gifts received, $171,179; expenditures, $108,409; qualifying distributions, $107,411.
Officers and Trustees:* Jane A. Kennedy,* Pres.; Anne H. Kennedy,* Secy.-Treas.; Roxane F. Anderson.
EIN: 870579749
Codes: FD2

53761
Douglas & Shelley Felt Family Foundation
2835 Pierce Ave.
Ogden, UT 84403

Established in 1999 in IL.
Donor(s): Douglas P. Felt, Shelley L. Felt.
Financial data (yr. ended 12/31/01): Grants paid, $107,300; assets, $912,575 (M); gifts received, $1,061,290; expenditures, $124,498; qualifying distributions, $107,264.
Limitations: Applications not accepted.
Application information: Contributes only to pre-selected organizations.
Officers: Douglas P. Felt, Pres.; Shelley L. Felt, Secy.
EIN: 364291148
Codes: FD2

53762
Donnell B. and Elizabeth Dee Shaw Stewart Foundation
c/o First Security Bank, N.A.
P.O. Box 628
Salt Lake City, UT 84110-0628
Application address: c/o First Security Bank of Utah, N.A., P.O. Box 9936, Ogden, UT 84409, tel.: (801) 626-9531
Contact: Mary Barker, Secy.

Financial data (yr. ended 12/31/01): Grants paid, $107,237; assets, $1,931,302 (M); expenditures, $128,706; qualifying distributions, $116,317.
Limitations: Giving limited to Ogden, UT.
Officers: Jack D. Lampros, Chair.; Dean W. Hurst, Co-Vice-Chair.; C. William Stromberg, Co-Vice-Chair.; Mary Barker, Secy.; O. Rex Child, Treas.
Trustee: First Security Bank Of Utah, N.A.
EIN: 876160658
Codes: FD2

53763
Art Works for Kids
6182 Field Rose Dr.
Salt Lake City, UT 84121-1568

Established in 1995 in UT.
Donor(s): Gary Crocker, Tim Fenton, Ralph Johnson, James Lee Sorenson, Joseph Sorenson, Brent & BonnieJean Beesley Foundation.
Financial data (yr. ended 07/31/01): Grants paid, $105,000; assets, $235,056 (M); gifts received, $282,621; expenditures, $262,510; qualifying distributions, $262,329.
Limitations: Applications not accepted.
Application information: Contributes only to pre-selected organizations.
Directors: Lisa Cluff, Shauna Johnson, Beverley Sorenson, James Lee Sorenson.
EIN: 870553478
Codes: FD2

53764
The Bennett W. Anderson Family Foundation
1023 E. 760 S.
Orem, UT 84097

Established in 1999 in UT.
Donor(s): Bennett W. Anderson.
Financial data (yr. ended 12/31/00): Grants paid, $104,471; assets, $131,875 (M); gifts received, $104,471; expenditures, $104,471; qualifying distributions, $104,471.
Limitations: Applications not accepted. Giving primarily in UT.
Application information: Contributes only to pre-selected organizations.
Officers: Bennett W. Anderson, Pres.; Rochelle T. Anderson, Secy.
EIN: 870643710
Codes: FD2

53765
Robert F. Orr Charitable Foundation
2871 Sunny Slopes Dr.
Park City, UT 84060

Established in 2001 in UT.
Donor(s): Robert F. Orr.
Financial data (yr. ended 12/31/01): Grants paid, $100,642; assets, $509,597 (M); gifts received, $610,000; expenditures, $100,709; qualifying distributions, $100,642.
Limitations: Applications not accepted. Giving primarily in Rupert, ID.
Application information: Contributes only to pre-selected organizations.

Officers and Directors:* Robert F. Orr,* Pres.; Kelli Lundgren,* Secy.-Treas.; Gregory R. Orr, Troy J. Orr.
EIN: 870680982
Codes: FD2

53766
Matthew B. Ellis Foundation
P.O. Box 526185
Salt Lake City, UT 84152

Established in 1997 in UT.
Financial data (yr. ended 12/31/01): Grants paid, $100,001; assets, $1,818,565 (M); expenditures, $103,624; qualifying distributions, $103,329.
Limitations: Applications not accepted. Giving limited to Ogden, UT.
Application information: Contributes only to pre-selected organizations.
Trustees: Daniel H. Ellis, Elaine Ellis, W. Hague Ellis.
EIN: 841395103
Codes: FD2

53767
Kennecott Utah Copper Visitors Center Charitable Foundation
P.O. Box 6001
Magna, UT 84044-6001
E-mail: cononell@kennecott.com
Contact: Louie Cononelos, Pres.

Established in 1994 in UT.
Donor(s): Kennecott Utah Copper Corp., Mrs. Herb Babcock.
Financial data (yr. ended 12/31/00): Grants paid, $100,000; assets, $238,334 (M); gifts received, $112,045; expenditures, $102,627; qualifying distributions, $99,024.
Limitations: Giving primarily in Salt Lake and Tooele counties, UT.
Publications: Informational brochure (including application guidelines), grants list.
Application information: Application form not required.
Officers and Trustees:* Louis J. Cononelos,* Pres.; Julie A. Cummings,* Secy.-Treas.; Norm Fitzgerald, Rev. Stan Herba, Max Hogan, Ruben Mesa, Connie Mockizuki, Chris Robison, Scott Whipple.
EIN: 870560044
Codes: CS, FD2, CD

53768
Preston G. Hughes Foundation, Inc.
912 N. Main St.
Spanish Fork, UT 84660-1714
Contact: Preston G. Hughes, C.E.O.

Established in 1963 in UT.
Financial data (yr. ended 12/31/01): Grants paid, $96,059; assets, $2,887,946 (M); expenditures, $111,526; qualifying distributions, $100,952.
Limitations: Applications not accepted. Giving primarily in UT.
Application information: Unsolicited requests for funds not accepted.
Officers: Preston G. Hughes, C.E.O.; J. Preston Hughes, Pres.; Maurice M. Hughes, V.P.; Barbara E. Bowen, Secy.
EIN: 876122482
Codes: FD2

53769
C. Comstock Clayton Foundation
c/o Wells Fargo Bank Northwest, N.A.
P.O. Box 25491
Salt Lake City, UT 84125
Application address: 3468 Santa Rosa Dr., Salt Lake City, UT 84109
Contact: Mary Lynne Hansen, Vice-Chair.

Established in 1968.
Financial data (yr. ended 12/31/01): Grants paid, $96,000; assets, $1,744,026 (M); expenditures, $109,420; qualifying distributions, $101,659.
Limitations: Giving primarily in Salt Lake City, UT.
Application information: Application form required.
Officers: Hope Eccles, Chair.; Mary Lynne Hansen, Vice-Chair.
Board Member: Marcia Daneman.
EIN: 237007241
Codes: FD2

53770
The Jones Family Charitable Foundation
344 W. Pleasant View Dr.
Ogden, UT 84414-2118

Established in 1993 in UT.
Donor(s): Leon L. Jones, Judith B. Jones.
Financial data (yr. ended 12/31/01): Grants paid, $95,000; assets, $1,488,237 (M); gifts received, $198,960; expenditures, $96,365; qualifying distributions, $94,295.
Limitations: Applications not accepted. Giving primarily in UT.
Application information: Contributes only to pre-selected organizations.
Officers and Trustee:* Amelia C. Jones, Mgr.; Ezra Thomas Jones,* Mgr.; Judith B. Jones, Mgr.; L.C. Allen Jones, Mgr.; Leon L. Jones,* Mgr.
EIN: 876223972
Codes: FD2

53771
Charles Redd Foundation
P.O. Box 247
La Sal, UT 84530
Application address: c/o Beverly Woods, 1425 N. 1200 W., Mapleton, UT 84664
Contact: Robert Byron Redd, Tr.

Established in 1971 in UT.
Financial data (yr. ended 12/31/01): Grants paid, $94,250; assets, $2,969,675 (M); expenditures, $123,228; qualifying distributions, $94,250.
Limitations: Giving primarily in southwestern CO and southeastern UT.
Application information: Application form not required.
Trustees: Robert Clegg, Rebecca Lambert, Regina Mitchell, Katheryn Mullins, Maraley Rasmussen, Regina Rasmussen, Annaley Redd, Charles Hardy Redd, Paul Redd, Robert Byron Redd, Debbie Stevens, Beverly Woods.
EIN: 876148176

53772
Robert W. Keener and Barbara J. Keener Foundation
P.O. Box 9360
Salt Lake City, UT 84109

Established in 1995 in UT.
Donor(s): Robert W. Keener, Barbara J. Keener.
Financial data (yr. ended 05/31/01): Grants paid, $93,865; assets, $1,162,009 (M); expenditures, $106,137; qualifying distributions, $97,642.
Limitations: Applications not accepted. Giving on a national basis.
Application information: Contributes only to pre-selected organizations.

Trustees: Daniel D. Garner IV, Robert W. Keener.
EIN: 876232895
Codes: FD2, GTI

53773
John A. & Telitha E. Lindquist Foundation
3408 Washington Blvd.
Ogden, UT 84401-4108
Contact: Robert E. Lindquist, Dir.

Established in 1994 in UT.
Donor(s): John A. Lindquist, Telitha E. Lindquist.
Financial data (yr. ended 12/31/01): Grants paid, $92,400; assets, $2,251,239 (M); expenditures, $97,681; qualifying distributions, $97,681.
Limitations: Giving limited to northern UT.
Officers: Kathryn Lindquist, Pres.; Peter N. Lindquist, Secy.; Steven E. Lindquist, C.F.O.
Directors: Laurie L. Babilis, Telitha L. Greiner, John E. Lindquist, Robert E. Lindquist.
EIN: 870530598
Codes: FD2

53774
Alvin Christenson Family Organization
P.O. Box 11085
Salt Lake City, UT 84111

Established in 1979 in UT.
Donor(s): Richard A. Christenson.
Financial data (yr. ended 12/31/01): Grants paid, $91,194; assets, $917,599 (M); expenditures, $98,266; qualifying distributions, $91,184.
Limitations: Applications not accepted. Giving limited to Salt Lake City, UT.
Application information: Contributes only to pre-selected organizations.
Officer: Richard A. Christenson, Pres.
EIN: 870328114
Codes: FD2, GTI

53775
Bamberger-Allen Health and Educational Foundation
163 S. Main St.
Salt Lake City, UT 84111

Established in 1969 in UT.
Financial data (yr. ended 12/31/00): Grants paid, $90,623; assets, $1,697,522 (M); expenditures, $91,099; qualifying distributions, $90,240.
Limitations: Applications not accepted. Giving limited to Salt Lake City, UT.
Application information: Contributes only to pre-selected organizations.
Officer: David W. Bernolfo, Pres.
Directors: Clarence Bamberger, Jr., Stephen C. Bamberger, Marie D. Bernolfo.
EIN: 237035442
Codes: FD2

53776
Eldred Sunset Manor Foundation, Inc.
P.O. Box 1387
Provo, UT 84603
Application address: 190 W. 800 N., Ste. 100, Provo, UT 84601
Contact: Sidney S. Gilbert, Pres.

Established in 1965.
Financial data (yr. ended 12/31/01): Grants paid, $86,202; assets, $1,622,453 (M); expenditures, $89,921; qualifying distributions, $85,684.
Limitations: Giving primarily in UT.
Application information: Application form required.
Officer: Sidney S. Gilbert, Pres.
EIN: 870232411
Codes: FD2

53777
Val A. Green and Edith D. Green Foundation
4615 W. 200 South
West Point, UT 84015

Established in 1997 in UT.
Donor(s): Edith D. Green, Val A. Green.
Financial data (yr. ended 03/31/02): Grants paid, $83,000; assets, $1,428,802 (M); expenditures, $119,412; qualifying distributions, $83,000.
Limitations: Applications not accepted. Giving primarily in UT.
Application information: Contributes only to pre-selected organizations.
Trustees: Edith D. Green, Val A. Green, Johnny E. Willis.
EIN: 841407030
Codes: FD2

53778
JEPS Foundation
PMB 133
2274 S. 1300 E., No. G-15
Salt Lake City, UT 84106-2814
Contact: Randolph C. Speers, Tr.

Established in 1994 in UT.
Financial data (yr. ended 12/31/01): Grants paid, $82,900; assets, $1,059,742 (M); gifts received, $60,000; expenditures, $87,427; qualifying distributions, $82,900.
Limitations: Giving limited to UT.
Application information: Application form not required.
Trustees: Catherine Aloia, Margaret Aloia, Jennifer P. Speers, Randolph C. Speers.
EIN: 870536246
Codes: FD2

53779
Donald D. & Elaine F. Davis Trust
966 Wintook Dr.
Ivins, UT 84738-6438

Established in 1986 in VA.
Donor(s): Donald D. Davis, Elaine F. Davis.
Financial data (yr. ended 12/31/01): Grants paid, $82,174; assets, $110,174 (M); gifts received, $156,760; expenditures, $83,747; qualifying distributions, $82,174.
Limitations: Applications not accepted. Giving primarily in MD, VA, and VT.
Application information: Contributes only to pre-selected organizations.
Trustees: Donald D. Davis, Elaine F. Davis.
EIN: 541398502
Codes: FD2

53780
Staheli Foundation
2726 E. Wasatch Dr., Ste. 22
Salt Lake City, UT 84108
Contact: Donald L. Staheli, Pres.

Established in 1997 in DE.
Donor(s): Donald L. Staheli.
Financial data (yr. ended 09/30/01): Grants paid, $78,100; assets, $2,059,364 (M); expenditures, $84,692; qualifying distributions, $80,259.
Limitations: Giving primarily in UT.
Application information: Application form required.
Officers: Donald L. Staheli, Pres.; Afton Staheli, Secy.
EIN: 311551307
Codes: FD2

53781
Medforte Research Foundation
803 N. 300 W.
Salt Lake City, UT 84103

Established in 1993 in UT.
Financial data (yr. ended 12/31/00): Grants paid, $75,308; assets, $1,903,606 (M); expenditures, $590,411; qualifying distributions, $77,264.
Limitations: Applications not accepted. Giving primarily in UT and VA.
Application information: Contributes only to pre-selected organizations.
Officers: Stewart Grow, Pres.; Darrell Deem, V.P. and Treas.; Dee Olsen, Secy.
Director: Ross Kelly Thueson.
EIN: 742519343
Codes: FD2

53782
Pope Foundation
693 Hobblecreek Rd.
Springville, UT 84663
Contact: Louis M. Pope

Established in 1997 in UT.
Donor(s): Louis M. Pope.
Financial data (yr. ended 12/31/99): Grants paid, $74,275; assets, $575,277 (M); gifts received, $16,000; expenditures, $78,756; qualifying distributions, $74,725.
Limitations: Giving primarily in NY and UT.
Board Members: Lisa Holmberg, Troy Holmberg, Christine C. Pope, Eric Pope, Jeff Pope, Krista Pope, Louis M. Pope, Louis M. Pope II, Natalie Pope.
EIN: 841372268

53783
Edward L. Burton Foundation
P.O. Box 9313
Salt Lake City, UT 84109

Established in 1955.
Financial data (yr. ended 12/31/00): Grants paid, $74,000; assets, $1,449,860 (M); expenditures, $75,549; qualifying distributions, $73,530.
Limitations: Applications not accepted. Giving limited to Salt Lake City, UT.
Application information: Contributes only to pre-selected organizations.
Trustees: Richard R. Burton, Fred A. Moreton, Jr.
EIN: 876117938

53784
John & Dora Lang Charitable Foundation
c/o U.S. Bank
15 W. South Temple, Ste. 200
Salt Lake City, UT 84101 (801) 534-6205
Contact: Russell Johnson, V.P., U.S. Bank

Established in 1960 in UT.
Financial data (yr. ended 09/30/01): Grants paid, $74,000; assets, $1,107,960 (M); expenditures, $88,345; qualifying distributions, $76,059.
Limitations: Giving primarily in Salt Lake City, UT.
Trustee: U.S. Bank, N.A.
EIN: 876115493

53785
The Achelis Foundation
P.O. Box 71342
Salt Lake City, UT 84171
Contact: Steve Achelis, Tr.

Established in 1990 in UT.
Donor(s): Steven B. Achelis, Denise J. Achelis.
Financial data (yr. ended 06/30/01): Grants paid, $73,108; assets, $1,491,517 (M); gifts received, $30,000; expenditures, $84,368; qualifying distributions, $83,429.
Limitations: Giving primarily in Salt Lake City, UT.
Application information: Application form not required.
Trustee: Steven B. Achelis.
EIN: 870481479

53786
The Rodney H. and Carolyn Brady Foundation
c/o Wells Fargo Bank Northwest, N.A.
P.O. Box 25491
Salt Lake City, UT 84125
Contact: David L. Buchman

Established in 1989 in UT.
Financial data (yr. ended 12/31/01): Grants paid, $72,500; assets, $1,138,454 (M); expenditures, $83,767; qualifying distributions, $78,683.
Limitations: Giving primarily in UT.
Application information: Application form not required.
Trustee: First Security Bank of Utah, N.A.
EIN: 742571965

53787
Arthur J. & Mable Poulton Kirk/Lavern Kirk & Joseph W. Stam Foundation
c/o Zions First National Bank
P.O. Box 30880
Salt Lake City, UT 84130-0880

Established in 1999 in UT.
Financial data (yr. ended 12/31/00): Grants paid, $72,203; assets, $1,983,046 (M); gifts received, $1,785,834; expenditures, $83,812; qualifying distributions, $75,016.
Limitations: Applications not accepted. Giving primarily in Salt Lake City, UT.
Application information: Contributes only to pre-selected organizations.
Trustee: Zions First National Bank.
EIN: 870639861

53788
Clark Family Foundation
1400 S. Foothill Dr., Ste. 110
Salt Lake City, UT 84106

Established in 1997 in UT.
Financial data (yr. ended 12/31/01): Grants paid, $70,381; assets, $1,790,466 (M); expenditures, $208,906; qualifying distributions, $70,381.
Limitations: Applications not accepted. Giving primarily in UT.
Application information: Contributes only to pre-selected organizations.
Officers: Mike Clark, Chair.; Seth Jarvis, Vice-Chair.; Mary Beth Clark, Secy.
EIN: 870562732

53789
The Don-Kay-Clay Cash Foundation
377 E. Canyon Oak Way
Salt Lake City, UT 84103

Established in 1997 in UT.
Donor(s): Roy Don Cash, Sondra Kay Cash.
Financial data (yr. ended 12/31/01): Grants paid, $67,255; assets, $2,037,006 (M); gifts received, $259,798; expenditures, $69,816; qualifying distributions, $67,255.
Limitations: Applications not accepted. Giving primarily in TX and UT.
Application information: Contributes only to pre-selected organizations.
Officers: Roy Don Cash, Pres.; Clay Collin Cash, V.P.; Sondra Kay Cash, Secy.-Treas.
EIN: 841381970

53790
Harold & Ruth Dance Charitable Foundation
1044 N. 1600 E.
Logan, UT 84321

Donor(s): Harold W. Dance, Ruth B. Dance.
Financial data (yr. ended 12/31/01): Grants paid, $66,000; assets, $610,320 (M); gifts received, $68,100; expenditures, $68,291; qualifying distributions, $66,000.
Limitations: Applications not accepted. Giving limited to Logan, UT.
Application information: Contributes only to pre-selected organizations.
Trustees: Harold W. Dance, Ruth B. Dance.
EIN: 870440689

53791
Harry S. Sloane Foundation
50 W. 300 S., Ste. 150
Salt Lake City, UT 84101-2006

Established in 1993 in UT.
Donor(s): Harry S. Sloane.
Financial data (yr. ended 02/28/02): Grants paid, $62,500; assets, $1,257,804 (M); gifts received, $9,639; expenditures, $96,484; qualifying distributions, $62,500.
Limitations: Applications not accepted. Giving primarily in UT.
Application information: Contributes only to pre-selected organizations.
Directors: Brent R. Armstrong, Lynn M. Carlson, Harry S. Sloane.
EIN: 870505864

53792
Beaver Creek Foundation
1292 E. 5375 S.
Ogden, UT 84403

Established in 1999 in UT.
Donor(s): O. Kelly Wheat, Barbara M. Wheat.
Financial data (yr. ended 09/30/01): Grants paid, $60,760; assets, $1,080,584 (M); expenditures, $74,503; qualifying distributions, $60,760.
Limitations: Applications not accepted. Giving primarily in UT.
Application information: Contributes only to pre-selected organizations.
Trustees: Barbara M. Wheat, O. Kelly Wheat.
EIN: 876246187

53793
Reese C. Anderson Charitable Trust
c/o Wells Fargo Bank Northwest, N.A.
P.O. Box 25491
Salt Lake City, UT 84125
Contact: David L. Buchman

Established in 1988 in UT.
Financial data (yr. ended 06/30/02): Grants paid, $60,000; assets, $989,493 (M); expenditures, $70,495; qualifying distributions, $60,000.
Limitations: Giving primarily in Salt Lake City, UT.
Application information: Application form not required.
Trustee: Wells Fargo Bank Northwest, N.A.
EIN: 742528227

53794
The Reinhold Foundation
P.O. Box 600
Layton, UT 84041

Established in 1997 in UT.
Financial data (yr. ended 12/31/00): Grants paid, $60,000; assets, $2,455,734 (M); expenditures, $124,625; qualifying distributions, $60,000.
Trustees: Rena R. Qualls, Rand F. Reinhold, Reed F. Reinhold, Robb F. Reinhold.

EIN: 870565581

53795
The W. Hague & Sue J. Ellis Foundation
P.O. Box 526185
Salt Lake City, UT 84152-6185

Established in 1997.
Donor(s): W. Hague Ellis.
Financial data (yr. ended 12/31/00): Grants paid, $59,602; assets, $1,077,249 (M); expenditures, $60,212; qualifying distributions, $59,345.
Limitations: Applications not accepted. Giving primarily in UT.
Application information: Contributes only to pre-selected organizations.
Trustees: Sue Ellis, W. Hague Ellis.
EIN: 871393756

53796
The Mark Family Foundation
P.O. Box 11564
Salt Lake City, UT 84147-0564
(801) 578-9103
Contact: Jack A. Mark, Dir.

Established in 1995 in UT.
Donor(s): Anne E. Mark.
Financial data (yr. ended 08/31/01): Grants paid, $59,000; assets, $0 (M); expenditures, $60,057; qualifying distributions, $58,934.
Limitations: Giving primarily in Salt Lake City, UT.
Application information: Application form not required.
Directors: Anne E. Mark, Jack A. Mark, Craig T. Vincent.
EIN: 870545204

53797
Argyle Family Foundation
1172 S. 1180 E.
Spanish Fork, UT 84660-5911

Financial data (yr. ended 12/31/01): Grants paid, $57,898; assets, $481,927 (M); expenditures, $61,617; qualifying distributions, $57,898.
Limitations: Applications not accepted. Giving primarily in UT.
Application information: Contributes only to pre-selected organizations.
Trustees: Clint B. Argyle, Sherry Argyle.
EIN: 870628938

53798
The Helaman Foundation
11 Quietwood Ln.
Sandy, UT 84092-4845
Contact: David J. Lyon, Tr.

Donor(s): Edward D. Smith.
Financial data (yr. ended 12/31/99): Grants paid, $56,900; assets, $9,507 (M); gifts received, $63,000; expenditures, $56,900; qualifying distributions, $56,900.
Limitations: Giving primarily in the western U.S., particularly to residents of AZ, CO, ID, and UT.
Application information: Application form not required.
Trustees: David J. Lyon, Edward D. Smith.
EIN: 311234291

53799
King Family Foundation
3863 E. Brockbank Dr.
Salt Lake City, UT 84124-3956

Established in 1997.
Donor(s): Warren P. King, Florence K. King.
Financial data (yr. ended 12/31/01): Grants paid, $56,140; assets, $898,425 (M); expenditures, $62,260; qualifying distributions, $56,140.

Limitations: Applications not accepted. Giving primarily in Salt Lake City, UT.
Application information: Contributes only to pre-selected organizations.
Trustee: Warren P. King.
EIN: 841390525

53800
Thomas A. & Lucille B. Horne Foundation
(Formerly Horne Foundation)
P.O. Box 955
Centerville, UT 84014
Contact: Lance K. Tempest

Donor(s): Susan S. Horne, Thomas B. Horne.
Financial data (yr. ended 12/31/01): Grants paid, $55,000; assets, $1,253,325 (M); gifts received, $50,000; expenditures, $65,069; qualifying distributions, $55,000.
Limitations: Applications not accepted. Giving limited to Salt Lake City, UT.
Application information: Contributes only to pre-selected organizations.
Trustees: Briony Horne, Susan S. Horne, Thomas P. Horne.
EIN: 942594430

53801
The Errol P. Eernisse Family Foundation
c/o Wells Fargo Bank Northwest, N.A.
P.O. Box 628
Salt Lake City, UT 84110-0628
Application address: c/o Wells Fargo Bank Northwest, N.A., 299 S. Main St., 8th Fl., Salt Lake City, UT 84111, tel.: (801) 246-1327
Contact: Fred Walton

Established in 1997 in UT.
Donor(s): Errol P. Eernisse.
Financial data (yr. ended 09/30/01): Grants paid, $50,000; assets, $848,000 (M); expenditures, $57,229; qualifying distributions, $53,191.
Limitations: Giving primarily in SD and UT.
Trustee: Wells Fargo Bank Northwest, N.A.
EIN: 876239794

53802
The Kenneth & Joanne Mayne Foundation
4683 Sagebrush Rd.
Park City, UT 84098 (435) 645-3990
Contact: Kenneth R. Mayne

Established in 1999 in UT.
Donor(s): Kenneth R. Mayne, Joanne Mayne.
Financial data (yr. ended 12/31/00): Grants paid, $50,000; assets, $1,005,392 (M); expenditures, $50,000; qualifying distributions, $50,000.
Trustees: Lynn M. Bushman, Joanne B. Mayne, Kenneth R. Mayne.
EIN: 870644461

53803
Trish's Foundation
c/o Wells Fargo Bank Northwest, N.A.
P.O. Box 628
Salt Lake City, UT 84110-0628
Application address: c/o Wells Fargo Northwest Bank, N.A., 79 S. Main, 3rd Fl., Salt Lake City, UT 84111
Contact: Patricia F. Hawley, Chair.

Established in 2000 in WY.
Donor(s): Patricia F. Hawley.
Financial data (yr. ended 12/31/01): Grants paid, $50,000; assets, $280,830 (M); gifts received, $90,000; expenditures, $53,367; qualifying distributions, $50,000.
Officer: Patricia F. Hawley, Chair.
EIN: 870667145

53804
The Deyhle Foundation
2293 Walker Ln.
Salt Lake City, UT 84117

Established in 1997 in UT.
Donor(s): Kenneth C. Deyhle.
Financial data (yr. ended 12/31/00): Grants paid, $46,437; assets, $860,699 (M); gifts received, $22,996; expenditures, $57,132; qualifying distributions, $46,437.
Limitations: Applications not accepted.
Application information: Contributes only to pre-selected organizations.
Officers: Kenneth C. Deyhle, Pres.; Gloria Deyhle, V.P.; Stuart Fredman, Secy.; Judith Martin, Treas.
Directors: Scott Deyhle, Stevenson G. Smith.
EIN: 870576102

53805
The Keystone Foundation
7069 S. Highland Dr., Ste. 100
Salt Lake City, UT 84121 (801) 942-2625
Contact: Richard G. Winwood, Dir.

Established in 1994 in UT.
Donor(s): Richard I. Winwood.
Financial data (yr. ended 12/31/01): Grants paid, $45,225; assets, $94,565 (M); expenditures, $46,872; qualifying distributions, $45,225.
Limitations: Giving primarily in UT.
Application information: Application form required.
Trustee: Richard I. Winwood.
Director: Richard G. Winwood.
Administration Committee: George R. Badger, Julie R. Badger, Judith A. Winwood, Valerie J. Winwood.
EIN: 876228583

53806
Aquarius Plateau Foundation
c/o Richard T. Beard
10 E. South Temple, Ste. 900
Salt Lake City, UT 84133

Established in 1994 in UT.
Donor(s): David Mock.
Financial data (yr. ended 12/31/00): Grants paid, $45,000; assets, $170,308 (M); expenditures, $47,772; qualifying distributions, $45,000.
Limitations: Applications not accepted. Giving primarily in MT and UT.
Application information: Contributes only to pre-selected organizations.
Officers: David Mock, Pres.; Martin Mock, V.P.
Trustee: Richard T. Beard.
EIN: 870532648

53807
Stephen G. and Susan E. Denkers Family Foundation
2792 Foothill Dr.
Ogden, UT 84403

Established in 2000 in UT.
Donor(s): Stephen G. Denkers, Susan E. Denkers.
Financial data (yr. ended 09/30/01): Grants paid, $45,000; assets, $14,927,396 (M); gifts received, $19,195,105; expenditures, $62,205; qualifying distributions, $54,070.
Limitations: Applications not accepted.
Application information: Contributes only to pre-selected organizations.
Trustees: Julie Denkers-Bishop, Stephen E. Denkers, Stephen G. Denkers, Susan E. Denkers.
EIN: 870659552

53808
The Kolob Foundation
c/o Randy Jay Green
423 Wakara Way, Ste. 212
Salt Lake City, UT 84108 (801) 583-8811

Established in 1995 in UT.
Donor(s): Randy J. Green, Pat Hemingway.
Financial data (yr. ended 12/31/00): Grants paid, $44,603; assets, $180,448 (M); gifts received, $70,922; expenditures, $48,264; qualifying distributions, $44,603.
Limitations: Giving primarily in Salt Lake City, UT.
Application information: Application form required.
Trustees: Ron Anderson, Penelope Umber Green, Randy J. Green, Pat Hemingway, Garth Mangum, Scott Rasmussen.
Director: Don Ulmer.
EIN: 876231892

53809
Help Every Living Person
6000 S. Fashion Blvd., No. 200
Salt Lake City, UT 84107 (801) 269-9988
Contact: Alma Hansen, Tr.

Established in 1986.
Donor(s): Rob Haertel, Alma Hansen.
Financial data (yr. ended 12/31/01): Grants paid, $43,883; assets, $1,805,777 (M); expenditures, $110,910; qualifying distributions, $43,883.
Limitations: Giving primarily in UT.
Application information: Application form required.
Trustees: Rob Haertel, Alma Hansen, Karen Hansen.
EIN: 870442225

53810
Aaron A. Hofmann Foundation, Inc.
455 S. 300 E., Ste. 300
Salt Lake City, UT 84111

Established in 1995 in UT.
Donor(s): Aaron A. Hofmann.
Financial data (yr. ended 12/30/01): Grants paid, $43,500; assets, $773,176 (M); gifts received, $316,823; expenditures, $49,123; qualifying distributions, $43,500.
Limitations: Applications not accepted. Giving primarily in Dallas, TX and Salt Lake City, UT.
Application information: Contributes only to pre-selected organizations.
Trustees: Aaron A. Hofmann, Corinne Hofmann, Suzanne Johanson.
EIN: 870552765

53811
Arlen B. Crouch Family Foundation
2566 Barcelona Dr.
Sandy, UT 84093
Contact: Arlen B. Crouch, Dir.

Established in 1993 in UT.
Donor(s): Arlen B. Crouch.
Financial data (yr. ended 12/31/01): Grants paid, $42,290; assets, $796,461 (M); expenditures, $52,262; qualifying distributions, $42,290.
Limitations: Giving primarily in ID and UT.
Directors: Audra Crouch Clegg, Alan Blair Crouch, Arlen B. Crouch, Arlen Ben Crouch II, Derrel R. Crouch, Robin C. Putnam.
EIN: 876225332

53812
Bowers Foundation
c/o Wells Fargo Bank Northwest, N.A.
P.O. Box 628
Salt Lake City, UT 84110-0628
Application address: c/o Wells Fargo Bank Northwest, N.A., P.O. Box 7, Twin Falls, ID 83303, tel.: (208) 736-1207
Contact: Mike Hagl, Trust Off., Wells Fargo Bank Northwest, N.A.

Established in 1991 in ID.
Financial data (yr. ended 03/31/02): Grants paid, $42,000; assets, $516,444 (M); expenditures, $50,984; qualifying distributions, $42,000.
Limitations: Giving limited to Twin Falls, ID.
Directors: Gary L. Garnand, Janet Key, Robert Seibel.
Trustee: Wells Fargo Bank Northwest, N.A.
EIN: 826071839

53813
Youth Tennis Foundation of Utah
P.O. Box 2009
Salt Lake City, UT 84110

Established in 1999 in UT.
Donor(s): All About Coins, Eccles Foundation.
Financial data (yr. ended 12/31/00): Grants paid, $41,686; assets, $600,430 (M); gifts received, $32,465; expenditures, $42,411; qualifying distributions, $41,686.
Limitations: Applications not accepted.
Application information: Contributes only to pre-selected organizations.
Officer: David L. Freed, Secy.-Treas.
Trustees: John Freed, Jane Hinckley, Jasmine Rich, Josephine Rose.
EIN: 876121880

53814
The Hellenic Foundation
P.O. Box 112223
Salt Lake City, UT 84147-2223
Contact: John F. Grove, Jr., Tr.

Donor(s): York Graphic Services, Inc., John F. Grove, Jr.
Financial data (yr. ended 06/30/01): Grants paid, $41,489; assets, $647,742 (M); expenditures, $51,788; qualifying distributions, $41,272.
Limitations: Giving primarily to residents of PA and UT.
Trustees: John F. Grove, Jr., Teresa I. Grove.
EIN: 222536161
Codes: CS, CD, GTI

53815
Iron Mountain Foundation
510 Payday Dr.
Park City, UT 84060-6700 (435) 649-7393
Contact: Franklin D. Richards, Jr., Chair.

Established in 1987 in UT.
Donor(s): Franklin D. Richards, Jr.
Financial data (yr. ended 12/31/01): Grants paid, $41,275; assets, $494,456 (M); expenditures, $50,196; qualifying distributions, $41,275.
Limitations: Giving primarily in UT.
Officers and Trustees:* Franklin D. Richards, Jr.,* Chair.; Kathryn L. Richards,* Secy.; Lance S. Richards,* Treas.; Peter Baron, Rinda R. Baron, James Hawkins, Lisa Hawkins, Franklin D. Richards III, Heidi Richards, Lisa B. Richards, Shawn C. Richards, Tracy Richards, Charles L. Sharp, Rachael Sharp, Andrea Thompson, Jeff Van Minde, Mary Van Minde.
EIN: 840440750

53816
Edward Low Memorial Trust
c/o Wells Fargo Bank Northwest, N.A.
P.O. Box 628
Salt Lake City, UT 84110-0628
Application address: Linda Lane c/o Wells Fargo Bank Northwest, N.A., P.O. Box 2618, Boise, ID 88701

Established in 1985 in ID.
Financial data (yr. ended 12/31/01): Grants paid, $41,000; assets, $749,909 (M); expenditures, $46,918; qualifying distributions, $43,577.
Limitations: Giving primarily in ID.
Trustee: Wells Fargo Bank Northwest, N.A.
EIN: 826062075

53817
The Bowers Foundation
P.O. Box 628
Salt Lake City, UT 84110-0628
Application address: c/o First Security Bank of Idaho, P.O. Box 7 Twin Falls, Idaho 83303, tel.: (208) 736-1207
Contact: Mike Hagl

Established in 1994 in ID.
Financial data (yr. ended 03/31/00): Grants paid, $40,000; assets, $693,798 (M); expenditures, $50,147; qualifying distributions, $45,552.
Directors: Curtis H. Eaton, Gary L. Garnand, Janet Key, Robert Seibel.
Trustee: First Security Bank, N.A.
EIN: 826075694

53818
The Scott W. & Betsy D. Thornton Family Foundation
P.O. Box 776
Kaysville, UT 84037

Established in 1997 in UT.
Donor(s): Betsy D. Thornton, Scott W. Thornton.
Financial data (yr. ended 12/31/01): Grants paid, $39,600; assets, $654,647 (M); gifts received, $5; expenditures, $41,863; qualifying distributions, $39,600.
Limitations: Applications not accepted. Giving primarily in Salt Lake City, UT.
Application information: Contributes only to pre-selected organizations.
Officer and Trustees:* Scott W. Thornton,* Pres.; April Thornton, Betsy D. Thornton.
EIN: 841409425

53819
The Headlee Family Foundation
4222 W. Old Orchard Rd.
Cedar Hills, UT 84062
Contact: Richard Headlee, Pres.

Established in 1995 in UT.
Donor(s): Richard H. Headlee.
Financial data (yr. ended 12/31/01): Grants paid, $39,339; assets, $296,017 (M); expenditures, $41,016; qualifying distributions, $39,339.
Limitations: Applications not accepted. Giving on a national basis.
Application information: Unsolicited requests for funds not accepted.
Officers and Trustees:* Richard Headlee, Pres. and Treas.; Mary Headlee,* V.P.; Kathy Barnard, Secy.; Howard Headlee,* Treas.
EIN: 870532544

53820
The Saul Breton Foundation
50 Shadow Ridge
P.O. Box 680366
Park City, UT 84068-0366 (435) 645-8645
Contact: Neil Breton, Pres.

Established in 1982 in CA.
Donor(s): Style Up of California, Inc., Kayo of California, Inc., Gary Rochelle.
Financial data (yr. ended 03/31/01): Grants paid, $39,050; assets, $349,260 (M); gifts received, $840; expenditures, $40,645; qualifying distributions, $38,574.
Limitations: Giving primarily in CA and Park City, UT.
Officers: Neil Breton, Pres.; Gail Breton, Secy.; Jana Hadany, Treas.
EIN: 953778252

53821
The Eaton Foundation
P.O. Box 980428
Park City, UT 84098-0428

Financial data (yr. ended 12/31/00): Grants paid, $38,490; assets, $257,238 (M); gifts received, $2,450; expenditures, $38,864; qualifying distributions, $38,490.
Limitations: Applications not accepted. Giving limited to UT.
Application information: Contributes only to pre-selected organizations.
Officers and Trustees:* Mark E. Eaton,* Pres.; Mary T. Eaton,* V.P.; Robin M. Szubielski,* Secy.-Treas.
EIN: 870517223

53822
George Q. Morris Foundation
c/o D. Mills
333 E. 400 S., Ste. 102
Salt Lake City, UT 84111-2988

Financial data (yr. ended 10/31/01): Grants paid, $38,450; assets, $2,168,264 (M); expenditures, $58,513; qualifying distributions, $38,450.
Limitations: Giving primarily in UT.
Trustees: Linda Kidd, Gabrielle Wood, Robin Wood.
EIN: 876119401

53823
The Bloomberg Foundation
P.O. Box 1915
Park City, UT 84060

Established in 1997 in NY & UT.
Donor(s): The Bloomberg Foundation.
Financial data (yr. ended 12/31/99): Grants paid, $37,785; assets, $577,643 (M); gifts received, $700; expenditures, $41,417; qualifying distributions, $34,097.
Limitations: Applications not accepted. Giving primarily in UT.
Application information: Contributes only to pre-selected organizations.
Officer: John I. Bloomberg, Pres.
EIN: 841421924

53824
The Paradox of Egoistic Hedonism Foundation
1223 W. Chavez Dr.
South Jordan, UT 84095

Established in 1997 in UT.
Donor(s): Sara Lichfield.
Financial data (yr. ended 12/31/01): Grants paid, $37,245; assets, $306,090 (M); gifts received, $20,080; expenditures, $55,945; qualifying distributions, $37,245.
Limitations: Applications not accepted.
Application information: Contributes only to pre-selected organizations.
Trustees: Aaron Rich Lichfield, Lynne Rich Lichfield, Sara Lichfield.
EIN: 841409402

53825
M. S. George and J. R. Foster Foundation
c/o Wells Fargo Bank Northwest, N.A.
P.O. Box 628
Salt Lake City, UT 84110-0628
Application address: c/o Wells Fargo Bank Northwest, N.A., P.O. Box 874, Lewiston, ID, 83501, tel.: (209) 799-6223

Established in 1996 in ID.
Financial data (yr. ended 12/31/01): Grants paid, $36,901; assets, $518,204 (M); expenditures, $48,036; qualifying distributions, $44,087.
Limitations: Giving limited to ID.
Trustees: Jack R. Foster, Mae J. Foster, Wells Fargo Bank Northwest, N.A.
EIN: 826081015

53826
The Belliston Family Foundation
2714 N. 880 E.
Provo, UT 84604-4077

Established in 1999 in UT.
Financial data (yr. ended 12/31/01): Grants paid, $36,700; assets, $128 (M); gifts received, $42,185; expenditures, $42,303; qualifying distributions, $36,700.
Trustees: Angus N. Belliston, Carl Belliston, James Belliston, Nathan Belliston, Ruth E. Belliston, Kathryn Bened, Anne Curtis, Camille Dowler, Janine Ruff.
EIN: 870641274

53827
Samuel A. & Richard D. Movitz Foundation
2343 Cottonwood Ln.
Salt Lake City, UT 84117

Donor(s): Richard D. Movitz.
Financial data (yr. ended 12/31/00): Grants paid, $36,500; assets, $1,898 (M); gifts received, $38,400; expenditures, $36,783; qualifying distributions, $36,500.
Limitations: Applications not accepted. Giving limited to UT.
Application information: Contributes only to pre-selected organizations.
Officers: Richard D. Movitz, Pres.; Eileen R. Movitz, Secy.
EIN: 876123492

53828
James R. and Barbara S. Clark Foundation
5860 S. Holladay Blvd.
Salt Lake City, UT 84121

Established in 1999 in UT.
Donor(s): James R. Clark.
Financial data (yr. ended 12/31/01): Grants paid, $36,475; assets, $1,021 (M); gifts received, $20,000; expenditures, $36,498; qualifying distributions, $36,470.
Limitations: Applications not accepted. Giving primarily in UT.
Application information: Contributes only to pre-selected organizations.
Officers: James R. Clark, Chair., Pres. and Treas.; Barbara S. Clark, V.P. and Secy.; Christopher J. Clark, V.P.; Elizabeth P. Clark, V.P.
EIN: 870638090

53829
Richards Memorial Medical Foundation
2020 E. 3300 S., No. 26
Salt Lake City, UT 84109

Financial data (yr. ended 10/31/01): Grants paid, $35,889; assets, $740,890 (M); expenditures, $37,241; qualifying distributions, $35,889.
Limitations: Giving primarily in UT.
Officers: Clark G. Richards, Pres.; Sidney J. Mulcock, Secy.
EIN: 876118168

53830
The Archer Family Charitable Corporation
P.O. Box 58031
Salt Lake City, UT 84158-0031
Contact: John D. Archer, Tr.

Established in 1991 in UT.
Donor(s): John D. Archer.
Financial data (yr. ended 12/31/01): Grants paid, $35,759; assets, $582,273 (M); expenditures, $38,804; qualifying distributions, $35,759.
Limitations: Giving primarily in Salt Lake City, UT.
Trustees: John D. Archer, Elizabeth Archer Williams.
EIN: 870491844

53831
Robert S. Carter Foundation, Inc.
6000 Oakhill Dr.
Salt Lake City, UT 84121 (801) 278-2074
Contact: Robert S. Carter, Pres.

Donor(s): Robert S. Carter.
Financial data (yr. ended 06/30/02): Grants paid, $35,500; assets, $508,883 (M); expenditures, $37,507; qualifying distributions, $35,500.
Limitations: Giving primarily in Salt Lake City, UT.
Application information: Application form not required.
Officers: Robert S. Carter, Pres.; Thomas A. Carter, V.P.; Roberta Carter, Secy.
Trustee: Edward G. Richards.
EIN: 870289003

53832
Colemere Foundation, Inc.
(Formerly M. & J. Colemere Foundation, Inc.)
632 E. 230 N.
American Fork, UT 84003
Application address: 120 E. 300 N., Provo, UT 84603
Contact: John L. Valentine, Secy.

Established in 2000.
Donor(s): Michael G. Colemere.
Financial data (yr. ended 12/31/01): Grants paid, $35,000; assets, $1,857,963 (M); gifts received, $66,365; expenditures, $35,000; qualifying distributions, $35,000.
Limitations: Applications not accepted. Giving primarily in UT.
Application information: Contributes only to pre-selected organizations.
Officers: Von Landon, Pres.; Bryan Tod, V.P.; John L. Valentine, Secy.
EIN: 870666264

53833
The Keoh Family Foundation
4201 Mt. Olympus Way
Salt Lake City, UT 84124

Established in 1997 in UT.
Financial data (yr. ended 12/31/01): Grants paid, $34,825; assets, $861,169 (M); expenditures, $44,012; qualifying distributions, $34,825.
Limitations: Applications not accepted.

Application information: Contributes only to pre-selected organizations.
Trustees: Joann O. Keller, Richard H. Keller.
EIN: 841399116

53834
The Stan and Sandy Checketts Foundation
350 W. 2500 N.
Logan, UT 84341
Contact: Stan Checketts, Pres.

Established in 1998 in UT.
Donor(s): Stan Checketts, Sandy Checketts.
Financial data (yr. ended 12/31/99): Grants paid, $34,712; assets, $1,207,808 (M); gifts received, $8,736; expenditures, $44,106; qualifying distributions, $38,890.
Limitations: Giving primarily in UT.
Officers: Stan Checketts, Pres.; Chris Checketts, V.P.; Sandy Checketts, Secy.
EIN: 870622407

53835
My Brother's Keeper Foundation
9090 S. Sandy Pkwy.
Sandy, UT 84070
Application address: 9090 Despain Way, Sandy, UT 84093
Contact: Leslie P. Layton, Tr.

Established in 1998 in UT.
Donor(s): Alan S. Layton, Leslie P. Layton.
Financial data (yr. ended 12/31/01): Grants paid, $34,648; assets, $17,178 (M); gifts received, $21,808; expenditures, $36,456; qualifying distributions, $34,645.
Application information: Application form required.
Trustees: Alan S. Layton, Leslie P. Layton.
EIN: 870579029

53836
Brigham Young University Common Fund Private Foundation
P.O. Box 11558
Salt Lake City, UT 84147-0558

Established in 1995.
Financial data (yr. ended 12/31/01): Grants paid, $33,925; assets, $660,681 (M); expenditures, $39,155; qualifying distributions, $33,925.
Limitations: Applications not accepted. Giving limited to UT.
Application information: Contributes only to pre-selected organizations.
Trustee: Deseret Trust Co., N.A.
EIN: 870533795

53837
Wadman Foundation
397 W. 4125 N.
Pleasant View, UT 84414-1154

Established in 1998 in UT.
Donor(s): V. Jay Wadman.
Financial data (yr. ended 12/31/01): Grants paid, $33,239; assets, $184,529 (M); gifts received, $80,000; expenditures, $33,591; qualifying distributions, $33,239.
Limitations: Applications not accepted. Giving primarily in UT.
Application information: Contributes only to pre-selected organizations.
Officer: V. Jay Wadman, Pres.
EIN: 841392243

53838
Intermountain Electrical Association Education Fund Scholarship Program
(also known as IEA Educational Scholarship Program)
2125 W. 2300 S.
West Valley City, UT 84119-2017
Contact: Klaas DeBoer

Established in 1988 in UT.
Donor(s): Intermountain Electrical Association.
Financial data (yr. ended 12/31/01): Grants paid, $33,000; assets, $589,044 (M); gifts received, $12,748; expenditures, $35,632; qualifying distributions, $35,632.
Limitations: Applications not accepted. Giving primarily in the Salt Lake City, UT, area.
Application information: Unsolicited requests for funds not considered or acknowledged.
Selection Committee: Reed Gardner, Victoria Gilbert, Tim Homer, Weslee Klein, Rick Stock, Leesa Winger.
EIN: 742520009
Codes: GTI

53839
The Stephen M. & Claire D. Ryberg Family Foundation
2159 S. 700 E., Ste. 200
Salt Lake City, UT 84106

Established in 1997 in UT.
Financial data (yr. ended 12/31/01): Grants paid, $32,933; assets, $492,429 (M); expenditures, $34,669; qualifying distributions, $32,933.
Limitations: Applications not accepted.
Application information: Contributes only to pre-selected organizations.
Officer and Trustees:* Stephen M. Ryberg,* Pres.; Claire D. Ryberg, Emily Ryberg.
EIN: 841409429

53840
Kenneth P. & Sally Rich Burbidge Foundation
4391 S. Parkview Dr.
Salt Lake City, UT 84124-3435
(801) 277-9416
Contact: Sally Rich Burbidge, Chair.

Established in 1998.
Donor(s): Sally Rich Burbidge.
Financial data (yr. ended 12/31/01): Grants paid, $32,644; assets, $528,596 (M); expenditures, $37,178; qualifying distributions, $32,644.
Officers: Sally Rich Burbidge, Chair.; Clark R. Burbidge, Treas.; Karin B. Cook, Co-Secy.; Jill B. Wiscomb, Co-Secy.
EIN: 870622260

53841
Gunnell Family Foundation
c/o Robert Hunter
P.O. Box 712258
Salt Lake City, UT 84171-2258

Financial data (yr. ended 12/31/01): Grants paid, $31,500; assets, $413,488 (M); expenditures, $41,268; qualifying distributions, $31,500.
Limitations: Giving primarily in UT.
Application information: Application form required.
Trustees: Kaye Gunnell, Ronald Gunnell.
EIN: 846312818

53842
EBJ & MSJ Foundation
c/o Ran D. Jones
4837 W. 4000 S.
Hooper, UT 84315-9633

Established in 1994 in MI.

Financial data (yr. ended 12/31/01): Grants paid, $30,654; assets, $307,505 (M); expenditures, $35,156; qualifying distributions, $30,654.
Limitations: Applications not accepted. Giving primarily in UT.
Application information: Contributes only to pre-selected organizations.
Officers: Edwin B. Jones, Pres. and Treas.; Mildred S. Jones, V.P. and Secy.
EIN: 383210186

53843
Help Other People Everywhere
6000 S. Fashion Blvd., Ste. 200
Murray, UT 84107
Contact: Rob Haertel, Tr.

Established in 1997 in UT.
Donor(s): Rob Haertel.
Financial data (yr. ended 06/30/02): Grants paid, $30,347; assets, $2,011,748 (M); expenditures, $73,540; qualifying distributions, $30,347.
Limitations: Applications not accepted. Giving primarily in UT.
Application information: Contributes only to pre-selected organizations.
Trustees: Ann Haertel, Rob Haertel, Ron Haertel, Sherrie Haertel, Mark Richards.
EIN: 841423527

53844
David Farmer Family Foundation
10454 Edinburgh Dr.
Highland, UT 84003

Established in 1995 in UT.
Donor(s): Dave Farmer.
Financial data (yr. ended 12/31/01): Grants paid, $30,205; assets, $18,475 (M); gifts received, $4,000; expenditures, $31,496; qualifying distributions, $30,205.
Limitations: Applications not accepted.
Application information: Contributes only to pre-selected organizations.
Trustees: Dave Farmer, Pam Farmer.
EIN: 870549324

53845
Goodwill Family Foundation
9500 S. 500 W., No. 208
Sandy, UT 84070

Donor(s): Goodwill Family.
Financial data (yr. ended 12/31/01): Grants paid, $29,131; assets, $5,638 (M); gifts received, $33,000; expenditures, $29,153; qualifying distributions, $29,131.
Limitations: Giving primarily in UT.
Trustees: Janet Engar, Dorothy P. Goodwill, Wilford W. Goodwill.
EIN: 870561863

53846
The Tom and Mary Norris Foundation
P.O. Box 45000
Salt Lake City, UT 84145 (801) 756-5955
Contact: A. Dennis Norton

Established in 1997 in UT.
Donor(s): Mary E. Norris.
Financial data (yr. ended 05/31/02): Grants paid, $28,442; assets, $1,173,298 (M); gifts received, $11,220; expenditures, $40,312; qualifying distributions, $28,442.
Limitations: Giving primarily in UT.
Trustees: Dennis A. Hullinger, Mary E. Norris, Joan H. Norton.
EIN: 841395794

53847
John B. Goddard Family Foundation
1788 Whispering Oaks Dr.
Ogden, UT 84403

Established in 1997 in UT.
Donor(s): John B. Goddard.
Financial data (yr. ended 12/31/01): Grants paid, $27,437; assets, $704,299 (M); expenditures, $36,569; qualifying distributions, $28,633.
Limitations: Applications not accepted. Giving primarily in UT.
Application information: Contributes only to pre-selected organizations.
Officer: John B. Goddard, Pres.
EIN: 841406997

53848
Michael P. Dixon Charitable Foundation
c/o Lynn Dixon
311 S. State St., Ste. 460
Salt Lake City, UT 84111 (801) 364-9262
Contact: Melissa Epperson, Secy.-Treas.

Established in 2000 in UT.
Donor(s): P. Lynn Dixon, Michael Dixon.‡
Financial data (yr. ended 12/31/01): Grants paid, $27,370; assets, $150,772 (M); gifts received, $5,605; expenditures, $37,675; qualifying distributions, $34,791.
Limitations: Giving primarily in Salt Lake City, UT.
Officers: P. Lynn Dixon, Pres.; Melissa Epperson, Secy.-Treas.
Trustees: Jennifer Dixon, Rona E. Dixon.
EIN: 870661243

53849
The Neal & Sherrie Savage Family Foundation
5250 S. 300 W., Ste. 200
Salt Lake City, UT 84106

Established in 2000 in UT.
Donor(s): Savage Industries, Inc.
Financial data (yr. ended 12/31/01): Grants paid, $27,070; assets, $2,264 (M); expenditures, $27,136; qualifying distributions, $27,064.
Limitations: Applications not accepted. Giving primarily in New York, NY and Salt Lake City, UT.
Application information: Contributes only to pre-selected organizations.
Officers and Trustees:* Gregory James Savage,* Pres.; Nathan Neal Savage,* Secy.-Treas.; Anna Savage Benedict, Melissa Ann Clayton, Malinda Savage Melville, Emilee Jayne Savage.
EIN: 870651828
Codes: CS

53850
The Gibbons Foundation
(Formerly Garco Foundation)
P.O. Box 526299
Salt Lake City, UT 84125-6299

Financial data (yr. ended 12/31/01): Grants paid, $26,000; assets, $540,072 (M); expenditures, $28,068; qualifying distributions, $26,000.
Limitations: Applications not accepted. Giving primarily in Salt Lake City, UT.
Application information: Contributes only to pre-selected organizations.
Officers: P.M. Gibbons, Pres.; William A. Gibbons, Secy.
Directors: Valli Durham, Victoria Hoagland.
EIN: 876127255

53851
The Jones Family Scholarship Foundation, Inc.
1694 E. Whispering Oaks Dr.
Ogden, UT 84403

Established in 1998 in FL.

Donor(s): Clifford L. Jones.
Financial data (yr. ended 12/31/99): Grants paid, $25,824; assets, $17,677 (M); gifts received, $20,000; expenditures, $26,204; qualifying distributions, $25,824.
Limitations: Applications not accepted.
Application information: Contributes only to pre-selected organizations.
Officers: Clifford L. Jones, Pres.; Linda L. Jones, Secy.; Jeffrey E. Jones, Treas.
EIN: 593543623

53852
Richard and Leola Hagman Foundation
P.O. Box 540561
North Salt Lake, UT 84054-0561

Established in 1997.
Donor(s): Richard P. Hagman.
Financial data (yr. ended 12/31/01): Grants paid, $25,000; assets, $46,078 (M); gifts received, $18,800; expenditures, $25,091; qualifying distributions, $25,000.
Limitations: Applications not accepted. Giving primarily in Salt Lake City, UT.
Application information: Contributes only to pre-selected organizations.
Officer and Trustees:* Leola M. Hagman,* Pres.; Judy Graham, Karroll Ann McIntyre.
EIN: 870510176

53853
The Dee Livingood Foundation
4774 S. 1300 W.
Riverdale, UT 84405

Donor(s): Lorraine H. Livingood.
Financial data (yr. ended 12/31/01): Grants paid, $25,000; assets, $198,946 (M); expenditures, $26,693; qualifying distributions, $25,000.
Limitations: Applications not accepted. Giving primarily in Ogden, UT.
Application information: Contributes only to pre-selected organizations.
Trustees: James W. Brown, Jack D. Livingood, Lorraine H. Livingood, William L. Smith, Stephen C. Spurlock.
EIN: 841371248

53854
Nebeker Family Foundation
1750 Kershaw St.
Ogden, UT 84403-0532

Established in 1999.
Financial data (yr. ended 12/31/01): Grants paid, $24,994; assets, $70 (M); gifts received, $25,116; expenditures, $24,994; qualifying distributions, $24,994.
Limitations: Applications not accepted. Giving primarily in NE.
Application information: Contributes only to pre-selected organizations.
Trustees: Adam R. Nebeker, Carolyn R. Nebeker, Conrad H. Nebeker, Jason R. Nebeker, Jonathan R. Nebeker, Michael R. Nebeker.
EIN: 870609294

53855
George T. Hansen Foundation
P.O. Box 17714
Salt Lake City, UT 84117
Contact: Mark B. Hansen, Secy.-Treas.

Financial data (yr. ended 03/31/01): Grants paid, $24,725; assets, $305,873 (M); expenditures, $25,963; qualifying distributions, $24,725.
Limitations: Giving primarily in Salt Lake City, UT.
Application information: Application form not required.

53855—UTAH

Officers: George T. Hansen, Jr., Pres.; George T. Hansen III, V.P.; Mark B. Hansen, Secy.-Treas.
EIN: 876123187

53856
B & L Foundation
2281 N. 1430 E.
Provo, UT 84604-2169
Contact: Mark M. Lewis, Pres.

Established in 1985 in UT.
Donor(s): Mark M. Lewis.
Financial data (yr. ended 09/30/00): Grants paid, $23,897; assets, $1,160,904 (M); gifts received, $9,008; expenditures, $88,853; qualifying distributions, $87,583; giving activities include $53,061 for programs.
Limitations: Giving primarily in Salt Lake City, UT.
Officers: Mark M. Lewis, Pres.; Fae B. Lewis, Secy.
Trustee: Wynn B. Bartholomew.
EIN: 742425299

53857
Dr. John C. & Bliss L. Hubbard Foundation
c/o Wells Fargo Bank Northwest, N.A.
299 S. Main St., 8th Fl.
Salt Lake City, UT 84101
Application address: c/o Financial Aid Office, College of Medicine, University of Utah, University & 200 S., Salt Lake City, UT 84132, tel.: (801) 581-2121

Financial data (yr. ended 12/31/01): Grants paid, $23,358; assets, $614,155 (M); expenditures, $30,889; qualifying distributions, $25,908.
Limitations: Giving limited to Salt Lake City, UT.
Scholarship Committee: J. Leon Sorenson, Walter Stevens, Ph.D., Harold Weight.
Trustee: Wells Fargo Bank Northwest, N.A.
EIN: 876120904

53858
Robert A. Patterson and Barbara M. Patterson Family Memorial Foundation
c/o Wells Fargo Bank Northwest, N.A.
P.O. Box 628
Salt Lake City, UT 84110
Application address: c/o Mary L. Barker, Trust Off., Wells Fargo Bank Northwest, N.A., P.O. Box 9936, Ogden, UT 84409, tel.: (801) 626-9533

Established in 1986 in UT.
Financial data (yr. ended 12/31/01): Grants paid, $23,246; assets, $433,447 (M); gifts received, $14,598; expenditures, $27,928; qualifying distributions, $23,246.
Limitations: Giving primarily in Salt Lake City, UT.
Officer and Directors:* Barbara H. Patterson,* Chair.; Elizabeth Patterson, Robert M. Patterson, James A. Rich, Joanne P. Rich, Margaret P. Sargent, William Sargent, Brent C. Sonnenberg.
Trustee: Wells Fargo Bank Northwest, N.A.
EIN: 876199706

53859
Diwal Foundation
2556 Sherwood Dr.
Salt Lake City, UT 84108
Contact: Waldo C. Perkins, Tr.

Established in 1997 in UT.
Donor(s): Waldo C. Perkins.
Financial data (yr. ended 12/31/01): Grants paid, $22,744; assets, $139,459 (M); expenditures, $23,918; qualifying distributions, $22,744.
Limitations: Giving primarily in AZ and UT.
Trustees: Fred Healey, Stephanie P. Lake, Melanie P. Meinzer, Bret D. Perkins, Daniel H. Perkins, Diane D. Perkins, Matthew B. Perkins, Suzette Perkins, Waldo C. Perkins.

EIN: 841404394

53860
Roger Leland Goudie Foundation
P.O. Box 628
Salt Lake City, UT 84110-0628
Application address: 61 S. Main, 4th Fl., Salt Lake City, UT 84111, tel.: (801) 246-5363
Contact: David Buchman

Established in 1999 in UT.
Donor(s): Roger Leland Goudie Trust.
Financial data (yr. ended 12/31/01): Grants paid, $22,450; assets, $537,185 (M); expenditures, $28,361; qualifying distributions, $22,450.
Limitations: Giving primarily in Salt Lake City, UT.
Trustee: First Security Bank, N.A.
EIN: 876245528

53861
The Thomas H. and Carolyn L. Fey Family Foundation
P.O. Box 684020
Park City, UT 84060-4020
Contact: Thomas H. Fey, V.P.

Established in 1994 in UT.
Donor(s): Carolyn L. Fey, Thomas H. Fey, Caroline H. Fey, Josephine H. Fey, Thomas H. Fey, Jr.
Financial data (yr. ended 12/31/01): Grants paid, $21,606; assets, $356,246 (M); expenditures, $25,781; qualifying distributions, $21,606.
Officers and Trustees:* Josephine B. Fey,* Pres.; Caroline H. Fey, V.P. and Secy.; Thomas H. Fey, V.P. and Treas.; Carolyn L. Fey,* V.P.; Thomas H. Fey, Jr., V.P.
EIN: 870532783

53862
Sunrise Foundation of America
8472 S. Taos Dr.
Sandy, UT 84093

Established in 1999 in UT.
Donor(s): Sharyn Johnson.
Financial data (yr. ended 09/30/01): Grants paid, $21,280; assets, $428,380 (M); expenditures, $31,335; qualifying distributions, $21,280.
Limitations: Applications not accepted.
Application information: Contributes only to pre-selected organizations.
Trustee: Sharyn Johnson.
EIN: 870638727

53863
The Ammon Foundation
91 West 4750 North
Provo, UT 84604

Established in 1999 in UT.
Donor(s): RMA, Inc.
Financial data (yr. ended 12/31/01): Grants paid, $21,198; assets, $705 (M); gifts received, $15,210; expenditures, $21,198; qualifying distributions, $21,198.
Limitations: Applications not accepted. Giving primarily in Salt Lake City, UT.
Application information: Contributes only to pre-selected organizations.
Trustees: Robert H. Anderson, Robert Michael Anderson.
EIN: 870622411

53864
Arthur J. and Lavern Kirk Stam Memorial Trust
c/o Zions First National Bank
P.O. Box 30880
Salt Lake City, UT 84130-0880

Established in 1999 in UT.
Donor(s): Lavern Kirk Stam.‡

Financial data (yr. ended 12/31/01): Grants paid, $20,727; assets, $390,834 (M); expenditures, $30,371; qualifying distributions, $20,727.
Limitations: Applications not accepted. Giving primarily in Salt Lake City, UT.
Application information: Contributes only to pre-selected organizations.
Trustee: Zions First National Bank.
EIN: 870639862

53865
The Philip G. McCarthey Family Foundation
327 S. Denver St.
Salt Lake City, UT 84111-3002

Financial data (yr. ended 12/31/00): Grants paid, $19,000; assets, $179,110 (M); expenditures, $19,188; qualifying distributions, $19,000.
Trustees: Philip G. McCarthey, Sandra W. McCarthey, Thomas K. McCarthey, Jr.
EIN: 870624010

53866
Sandra N. Tillotson Foundation
75 W. Center St.
Provo, UT 84601-4432

Established in 1996 in UT.
Donor(s): Sandra N. Tillotson.
Financial data (yr. ended 12/31/01): Grants paid, $19,000; assets, $387,243 (M); gifts received, $12,400; expenditures, $19,400; qualifying distributions, $19,000.
Limitations: Applications not accepted. Giving primarily in UT.
Application information: Contributes only to pre-selected organizations.
Trustee: Sandra N. Tillotson.
EIN: 870565395

53867
James LeVoy Sorenson Foundation
2511 S.W. Temple St.
Salt Lake City, UT 84115
Contact: Gloria Smith

Established in 1986 in UT.
Donor(s): James LeVoy Sorenson.
Financial data (yr. ended 12/31/01): Grants paid, $18,935; assets, $3,358,285 (M); expenditures, $18,935; qualifying distributions, $18,935.
Limitations: Giving primarily in Salt Lake City, UT.
Application information: Applications submitted early in the year have a better chance of funding. Application form not required.
Trustees: James Lee Sorenson, James LeVoy Sorenson.
EIN: 870440827

53868
Donald E. Crabtree Charitable Trust Fund
c/o Wells Fargo Bank Northwest, N.A.
P.O. Box 628
Salt Lake City, UT 84110-0628
Application address: c/o Wells Fargo Bank Northwest, N.A., P.O. Box 7, Twin Falls, ID 83303
Contact: Mike Hagl, Trust Off., Wells Fargo Bank Northwest, N.A.

Financial data (yr. ended 12/31/01): Grants paid, $18,694; assets, $361,343 (M); expenditures, $24,168; qualifying distributions, $21,413.
Limitations: Giving primarily in Moscow, ID.
Application information: Application form not required.
Trustee: Wells Fargo Bank Northwest, N.A.
EIN: 826056615

53869
Craig S. Tillotson Foundation
75 W. Center St.
Provo, UT 84601-4432

Established in 1997 UT.
Donor(s): Craig S. Tillotson.
Financial data (yr. ended 12/31/01): Grants paid, $18,428; assets, $555,262 (M); gifts received, $25,428; expenditures, $18,648; qualifying distributions, $18,428.
Limitations: Applications not accepted. Giving primarily in Salt Lake City, UT.
Application information: Contributes only to pre-selected organizations.
Trustees: Lee M. Brower, Craig S. Tillotson.
EIN: 870567144

53870
Charles Maxfield Parrish and Gloria F. Parrish Foundation
1030 Military Dr.
Salt Lake City, UT 84105-1714
Contact: Charles Maxfield Parrish, Chair.; or Gloria F. Parrish, Tr.

Established in 1992 in UT.
Donor(s): Charles Maxfield Parrish, Gloria F. Parrish.
Financial data (yr. ended 12/31/01): Grants paid, $18,000; assets, $851,649 (M); gifts received, $30,000; expenditures, $46,786; qualifying distributions, $18,000.
Limitations: Giving primarily in UT and WY.
Application information: Application form not required.
Officer and Trustees:* Charles Maxfield Parrish,* Chair.; Charles Bryan Parrish, Gloria F. Parrish.
EIN: 870490763

53871
Gary E. Stevenson Foundation
370 Abbey Ln.
Providence, UT 84332
Application Address: 387 W. Center, Orem, UT 84057, tel.: (801) 222-9700
Contact: Steven R. Skabelund, Tr.

Established in 1996 in UT.
Financial data (yr. ended 12/31/00): Grants paid, $18,000; assets, $552,137 (M); expenditures, $23,120; qualifying distributions, $18,000.
Trustee: Steven R. Skabelund.
EIN: 870533500

53872
The Lift Foundation
673 Ridgewood Cir.
Farmington, UT 84025

Established in 1999 in UT.
Donor(s): G. Andrew Barfuss.
Financial data (yr. ended 12/31/01): Grants paid, $17,400; assets, $257,691 (M); expenditures, $24,219; qualifying distributions, $17,400.
Limitations: Applications not accepted.
Application information: Contributes only to pre-selected organizations.
Officer: G. Andrew Barfuss, Pres.
Trustees: Joseph A. Barfuss, Julie Barfuss.
EIN: 870648103

53873
The Utah Motorsports Foundation
764 W. South Temple
Salt Lake City, UT 84104

Established in 1999 in UT.
Financial data (yr. ended 12/31/99): Grants paid, $17,261; assets, $20,865 (M); gifts received, $41,957; expenditures, $21,092; qualifying distributions, $21,092.
Limitations: Applications not accepted.
Application information: Unsolicited requests for funds not accepted.
Trustees: Mike Chapman, Kent Knowley, Terry Nish, Pat Sullivan.
EIN: 870628481

53874
Laurena B. and John H. Marshall Foundation
c/o Wells Fargo Bank Northwest, N.A.
P.O. Box 628
Salt Lake City, UT 84110-0628
Application address: c/o Wells Fargo Bank Northwest, N.A., P.O. Box 7, Twin Falls, ID 83303

Established in 1995 in ID.
Financial data (yr. ended 12/31/01): Grants paid, $16,403; assets, $369,644 (M); expenditures, $22,956; qualifying distributions, $19,692.
Limitations: Giving limited to Twin Falls, ID.
Trustee: Wells Fargo Bank Northwest, N.A.
EIN: 826080736

53875
West High Alumni Association
241 N. 300 W.
Salt Lake City, UT 84103
Application address: 3345 Bountiful Blvd., UT 84010-4465
Contact: Virginia Horton, Secy.-Treas.

Established in 1997 in UT.
Financial data (yr. ended 06/30/02): Grants paid, $16,300; assets, $58,233 (M); gifts received, $23,546; expenditures, $26,705; qualifying distributions, $16,300.
Officers: G. Ray Hale, Pres.; Dennis Vancampen, V.P.; Virginia Horton, Secy.-Treas.
EIN: 870456938

53876
Kenneth O. Melby Family Foundation
4725 S. Holladay Blvd., Ste. 210
Salt Lake City, UT 84117

Established in 1993 in UT.
Donor(s): Kenneth O. Melby.
Financial data (yr. ended 12/31/01): Grants paid, $15,900; assets, $340,014 (M); gifts received, $36,792; expenditures, $16,863; qualifying distributions, $15,900.
Limitations: Applications not accepted. Giving primarily in UT.
Application information: Contributes only to pre-selected organizations.
Officers: Kenneth O. Melby, Pres.; Cheryl Melby, V.P.; Karen Teerlink, Secy.; Alan Melby, Treas.
EIN: 870517013

53877
Blaine N. & Barbara W. Harmon Charitable Foundation
1436 Devonshire Dr.
Salt Lake City, UT 84108

Established in 1997 in UT.
Financial data (yr. ended 12/31/01): Grants paid, $15,500; assets, $134,593 (M); gifts received, $30,000; expenditures, $15,578; qualifying distributions, $15,500.
Limitations: Applications not accepted.
Application information: Contributes only to pre-selected organizations.
Officers: Blaine N. Harmon, Pres.; Barbara W. Harmon, Secy.-Treas.
Trustee: Teresa Wariner.
Directors: Nancy Harmon, Deborah Katter, Stacy Ogden.
EIN: 870621509

53878
Clarence and Ruth Birrer Foundation
c/o First Security Bank
P.O. Box 628
Salt Lake City, UT 84110-0628

Established in 1995 in ID.
Financial data (yr. ended 12/31/01): Grants paid, $15,471; assets, $334,043 (M); expenditures, $20,756; qualifying distributions, $15,471.
Limitations: Giving limited to Minidoka County, ID.
Trustee: First Security Bank, N.A.
EIN: 826081013

53879
The Reza Ali Khazeni Memorial Foundation
P.O. Box 11705
Salt Lake City, UT 84147-0705

Donor(s): Reza Ali Khazeni, Shireen Khazeni.
Financial data (yr. ended 12/31/01): Grants paid, $15,250; assets, $271,354 (M); gifts received, $8,825; expenditures, $15,405; qualifying distributions, $15,250.
Limitations: Applications not accepted. Giving primarily in Salt Lake City, UT.
Officers: Reza H. Khazeni, Pres.; Javed T. Khazeni, V.P.; Shireen Khazeni, V.P.; Ray Kingston, V.P.
EIN: 870503877

53880
Escalante Natural History Association
c/o Robin Venuti
170 N. Center St.
Escalante, UT 84726

Established in 1996 in NV and UT.
Financial data (yr. ended 12/31/99): Grants paid, $15,128; assets, $138,697 (M); gifts received, $37,733; expenditures, $23,928; qualifying distributions, $21,285.
Limitations: Giving limited to Escalante, UT.
Trustees: Michael Ingram, Dal R. Liston, Robin F. Venuti.
EIN: 880331379

53881
Diana S. Ellis Foundation
2632 Foothill Dr.
Ogden, UT 84403-0528

Donor(s): Diana S. Ellis.
Financial data (yr. ended 12/31/01): Grants paid, $15,000; assets, $300,241 (M); expenditures, $25,793; qualifying distributions, $15,000.
Limitations: Applications not accepted.
Application information: Contributes only to pre-selected organizations.
Trustee: Diana S. Ellis.
EIN: 870609445

53882
The Jinda/Lon Foundation
P.O. Box 981330
Park City, UT 84098
Contact: Robert F. Marasco, Mgr.

Established in 2000.
Donor(s): Robert F. Marasco.
Financial data (yr. ended 12/31/01): Grants paid, $15,000; assets, $3,171 (M); gifts received, $10,000; expenditures, $15,132; qualifying distributions, $15,000.
Limitations: Giving primarily in Omaha, NE and UT.
Officer: Robert F. Marasco, Mgr.
EIN: 870656724

53883
Claire E. Lindholm & George Lindholm Fund
c/o Zions First National Bank
P.O. Box 30880
Salt Lake City, UT 84130

Financial data (yr. ended 08/31/02): Grants paid, $14,433; assets, $365,311 (M); expenditures, $20,011; qualifying distributions, $14,433.
Limitations: Applications not accepted. Giving limited to Salt Lake City, UT.
Application information: Contributes only to pre-selected organizations.
Trustee: Zions First National Bank.
EIN: 876126939

53884
Bertin Family Foundation
1879 Ridgehollow Dr.
Bountiful, UT 84010-1016

Established in 1999 in UT.
Donor(s): Kim C. Bertin.
Financial data (yr. ended 12/31/01): Grants paid, $14,250; assets, $1,293,921 (M); gifts received, $503,838; expenditures, $17,400; qualifying distributions, $14,250.
Limitations: Applications not accepted. Giving primarily in UT.
Application information: Contributes only to pre-selected organizations.
Directors: Alex M. Bertin, Elizabeth Bertin, James A. Bertin, Jennifer Bertin, Kim C. Bertin, Michelle Bertin, Stephanie Bertin.
EIN: 870638640

53885
Dadiva Foundation
2159 S. 700 E., Ste. 200
Salt Lake City, UT 84106

Established in 1997 in UT.
Financial data (yr. ended 12/31/99): Grants paid, $13,730; assets, $646,688 (M); gifts received, $1,300; expenditures, $16,005; qualifying distributions, $13,597.
Limitations: Applications not accepted.
Application information: Contributes only to pre-selected organizations.
Trustees: Angela S. Dumke, Ezekiel R. Dumke III, Katherine W. Dumke.
EIN: 871407002

53886
The Robert E. Schocker Charitable Foundation
1798 S.W. Temple St., Ste. 200
Salt Lake City, UT 84115-1869

Established in 2000 in UT.
Donor(s): Robert E. Schocker.
Financial data (yr. ended 12/31/01): Grants paid, $13,700; assets, $727 (M); gifts received, $9,000; expenditures, $13,700; qualifying distributions, $13,700.
Limitations: Applications not accepted.
Application information: Contributes only to pre-selected organizations.
Trustees: Pattie Schocker, Robert E. Schocker, Robert Schocker, Jr.
EIN: 870644723

53887
M. Lynn Bennion Foundation, Inc.
c/o Wells Fargo Bank Iowa, N.A.
P.O. Box 628
Salt Lake City, UT 84110-0628
Application address: c/o John W. Bennion, 908 E. South Temple, Salt Lake City, UT 84102

Established in 1996 in UT.
Financial data (yr. ended 06/30/02): Grants paid, $13,000; assets, $199,637 (M); expenditures, $16,669; qualifying distributions, $13,000.
Limitations: Giving primarily in Salt Lake City, UT.
Trustees: John W. Bennion, Katherine Annette B. Clark, Rebecca Lindsay B. Glade, Carolyn B. Heaton, Wells Fargo Bank Iowa, N.A.
EIN: 870562664

53888
Anderson Family Foundation
c/o John R. Anderson
1939 S. 300 W., Ste. 200
Salt Lake City, UT 84115-7200

Donor(s): G.W. Anderson, Ida Lee Anderson.
Financial data (yr. ended 12/31/01): Grants paid, $12,982; assets, $277,701 (M); expenditures, $14,068; qualifying distributions, $12,982.
Limitations: Applications not accepted. Giving primarily in Denver, CO and Salt Lake City, UT.
Application information: Contributes only to pre-selected organizations.
Officers and Trustees:* John R. Anderson,* Pres.; Ida Lee Anderson,* V.P.; Keith R. Anderson, Secy.; J. Floyd Hatch,* Treas.
EIN: 870384626

53889
Scott R. Watterson Foundation
560 S. 1000 East
Logan, UT 84321
Application address: 1149 West Center St., Orem, UT 84057
Contact: Steven R. Skabelund

Established in 1994 in UT.
Financial data (yr. ended 12/31/00): Grants paid, $12,500; assets, $587,134 (M); expenditures, $17,961; qualifying distributions, $0.
Trustee: Scott R. Watterson.
EIN: 870533499

53890
The Robert W. Hemelgarn Memorial Foundation
c/o Ronald R. Hemelgarn
4725 S. Holladay Blvd., Ste. 210
Salt Lake City, UT 84117-5400

Established in 1998 in UT.
Donor(s): Ronald R. Hemelgarn.
Financial data (yr. ended 12/31/01): Grants paid, $12,433; assets, $23,134 (M); gifts received, $2,715; expenditures, $13,105; qualifying distributions, $12,433.
Limitations: Applications not accepted.
Application information: Contributes only to pre-selected organizations.
Officers: Ronald R. Hemelgarn, Pres.; Helen F. Hemelgarn, V.P.; Rhonda Hemelgarn, Secy.; Amy Hemelgarn, Treas.
EIN: 931216871

53891
Edith Dee Green Charitable Trust A
c/o First Security Bank of Utah, N.A.
P.O. Box 628
Salt Lake City, UT 84110-0628
Application address: c/o Dee Ann Nye, Chair., 1270 E. 34th St, Ogden, UT 84401

Financial data (yr. ended 12/31/01): Grants paid, $12,366; assets, $115,269 (M); expenditures, $14,603; qualifying distributions, $12,366.
Limitations: Giving limited to Ogden, UT.
Officer: Dee Ann Nye, Chair.
Trustee: First Security Bank of Utah, N.A.
EIN: 876121930

53892
Harold W. Ritchey Family Foundation
c/o Wells Fargo Bank Northwest, N.A.
P.O. Box 628
Salt Lake City, UT 84130
Application address: Harold W. Ritchey, 1756 Doxey, Ogden, UT 84403

Established in 1989 in UT.
Financial data (yr. ended 06/30/01): Grants paid, $12,300; assets, $262,141 (M); expenditures, $15,824; qualifying distributions, $12,300.
Limitations: Giving primarily in Ogden, UT.
Trustee: Wells Fargo Bank Northwest, N.A.
EIN: 742552549

53893
Brooke Brennan and Denice Renee Roney Foundation
75 W. Center St.
Provo, UT 84601-4432

Established in 1996 in UT.
Donor(s): Brooke B. Roney, Denice R. Roney.
Financial data (yr. ended 12/31/01): Grants paid, $12,293; assets, $478,834 (M); expenditures, $12,293; qualifying distributions, $12,293.
Limitations: Applications not accepted. Giving limited to UT.
Application information: Contributes only to pre-selected organizations.
Trustee: Denice Renee Roney.
EIN: 870565401

53894
Evergreen Foundation
3325 N. University Ave., No. 100
Provo, UT 84604

Established in 1996 in UT.
Donor(s): J. David Tanner.
Financial data (yr. ended 12/31/01): Grants paid, $12,179; assets, $2,754 (M); gifts received, $4,232; expenditures, $12,564; qualifying distributions, $12,179.
Limitations: Applications not accepted.
Application information: Contributes only to pre-selected organizations.
Trustees: J. David Tanner, Natalie R. Tanner.
EIN: 870552245

53895
Murray Rotary Club Foundation
c/o Karren, Hendrix & Assocs. C.P.A.
111 E. Broadway, Ste. 360
Salt Lake City, UT 84111
Application address: c/o W. Henry Pond, 6355 Westridge, Murray, UT 84107

Established in 1997 in UT.
Financial data (yr. ended 12/31/00): Grants paid, $12,000; assets, $19,105 (M); gifts received, $14,983; expenditures, $12,015; qualifying distributions, $11,997.
Limitations: Giving primarily in Sonora, Mexico.
Officers: W. Henry Pond, Pres.; Joyce Anderson, V.P.
Directors: Brent Barnum, R. Gayle Holman, Guy Jardine.
EIN: 870493080

53896
Moreton Family Foundation
c/o Edward B. Moreton
P.O. Box 58139
Salt Lake City, UT 84158-0139
Application address: P.O. Box 8139, Salt Lake City, UT 84108, tel.: (801) 531-1234

Financial data (yr. ended 12/31/01): Grants paid, $11,300; assets, $207,087 (M); expenditures, $12,855; qualifying distributions, $12,458.
Limitations: Giving limited to UT.
Trustees: Edward B. Moreton, Wells Fargo Bank Northwest, N.A.
EIN: 876133476

53897
Edna Childs Charitable Trust
c/o First Security Bank of Utah, N.A.
P.O. Box 628
Salt Lake City, UT 84110-0628
Application address: c/o Mike Hagl, First Security Bank, P.O. Box 7, Twin Falls, ID 83303-0007

Established in 1993.
Financial data (yr. ended 12/31/01): Grants paid, $11,225; assets, $258,917 (M); expenditures, $15,684; qualifying distributions, $11,225.
Limitations: Giving primarily in Twin Falls, ID.
Application information: Application form not required.
Trustee: First Security Bank, N.A.
EIN: 826052159

53898
The Elation Foundation
(Formerly The Epiphany Foundation)
1223 W. Chavez Dr.
South Jordan, UT 84095

Financial data (yr. ended 12/31/01): Grants paid, $11,151; assets, $136,825 (M); gifts received, $10,090; expenditures, $17,238; qualifying distributions, $11,151.
Limitations: Applications not accepted.
Application information: Contributes only to pre-selected organizations.
Trustees: Emily Lichfield Cannon, Scott C. Cannon, Kathryn Lichfield.
EIN: 870571966

53899
Crosland Family Foundation, Inc.
1497 Beverly Dr.
Ogden, UT 84403-0414
Contact: Jack W. Crosland III, Pres.

Established in 1998 in UT.
Donor(s): Lois B. Crosland.
Financial data (yr. ended 12/31/01): Grants paid, $11,050; assets, $199,632 (M); expenditures, $11,050; qualifying distributions, $11,050.
Officers: Jack W. Crosland III, Pres.; Sandra L. Crosland, V.P.; Ashley C. Nilsen, Secy.; C. W. Crosland, Treas.
EIN: 870622259

53900
Ng Foundation, Inc.
6053 S. 2300 E.
Salt Lake City, UT 84121

Donor(s): Nathaniel Goodman.
Financial data (yr. ended 12/31/01): Grants paid, $11,000; assets, $186,561 (M); gifts received, $25,212; expenditures, $11,306; qualifying distributions, $11,000.
Limitations: Applications not accepted.
Application information: Contributes only to pre-selected organizations.
Officers: Nathaniel Goodman, Pres.; Howard S. Landa, Secy.
Trustees: Jean Bailard, Jack Goodman, Kathryn Reynolds.
EIN: 870640709

53901
Quass Family Foundation
c/o Dallan W. Quass
63 W. Oakridge Dr.
Elk Ridge, UT 84651-4504

Established in 1999 in UT.
Donor(s): Dallan W. Quass, Solveig C. Quass.
Financial data (yr. ended 12/31/01): Grants paid, $10,750; assets, $6,308 (M); gifts received, $12,000; expenditures, $10,750; qualifying distributions, $10,750.
Trustees: Dallan W. Quass, Solveig C. Quass, Ronald G. Worsham.
EIN: 311655535

53902
C. Walker and Bonnie Cross Foundation
(Formerly Elias G. Cross, Sr. and Florence Hoxer Cross Foundation)
c/o First Security Bank of Utah, N.A.
P.O. Box 628
Salt Lake City, UT 84110-0628
Application address: c/o Mary L. Barker, Trust Off., First Security Bank of Utah, P.O. Box 9936, Ogden, UT 84409, tel.: (801) 626-9531

Established in 1985 in UT.
Donor(s): Florence H. Cross.
Financial data (yr. ended 12/31/01): Grants paid, $10,500; assets, $249,819 (M); expenditures, $14,908; qualifying distributions, $10,500.
Limitations: Giving primarily in Ogden, UT.
Officer and Trustees:* C. Walker Cross,* Chair.; Mary L. Barker, Samuel H. Barker, Orville Rex Child, Jack D. Lampros, First Security Bank of Utah, N.A.
EIN: 742352585

53903
Edward Lincoln and Bessie Boyce Gillmor Foundation
1235 E. 200 S., Ste. 503
Salt Lake City, UT 84102

Established in 1997 in UT.
Donor(s): Florence J. Gillmor.
Financial data (yr. ended 12/31/01): Grants paid, $10,240; assets, $379,542 (M); gifts received, $101,380; expenditures, $10,240; qualifying distributions, $10,240.
Limitations: Applications not accepted.
Application information: Contributes only to pre-selected organizations.
Officers: Florence J. Gillmor, Pres.; Robert M. Graham, Secy.-Treas.
Trustee: Helen C. Olbin.
EIN: 870483666

53904
Rouch Foundation
(Formerly A. P. and Louise Rouch Boys Foundation)
c/o Wells Fargo Bank Northwest, N.A.
P.O. Box 628
Salt Lake City, UT 84110-0628
Application address: c/o Wells Fargo Bank Northwest, N.A., P.O. Box 7, Twin Falls, ID 83303, tel.: (208) 736-1207

Established around 1979.
Financial data (yr. ended 12/31/01): Grants paid, $10,142; assets, $256,636 (M); expenditures, $14,822; qualifying distributions, $12,811.
Limitations: Giving primarily to residents of the Twin Falls, ID, area.
Application information: Application form not required.
Trustee: Wells Fargo Bank Northwest, N.A.
EIN: 826005152
Codes: GTI

53905
Melling Family Charitable Foundation
3081 E. Whitewater Dr.
Salt Lake City, UT 84121-1562

Established in 2000.
Donor(s): George D. Melling.
Financial data (yr. ended 12/31/01): Grants paid, $10,000; assets, $218,817 (M); expenditures, $12,846; qualifying distributions, $10,000.
Trustees: Amy Melling Avendano, George D. Melling, Nancy H. Melling, Thomas G. Melling.
EIN: 870663843

53906
Moore Family Foundation
5252 N. Edgewood Dr., Ste. 350
Provo, UT 84604

Established in 1999 in UT.
Donor(s): Margaret E. Moore.
Financial data (yr. ended 12/31/00): Grants paid, $10,000; assets, $99,892 (M); gifts received, $598; expenditures, $12,503; qualifying distributions, $10,000.
Limitations: Applications not accepted.
Application information: Contributes only to pre-selected organizations.
Trustees: Barbara J. Moore Collen, Jacqueline V. Moore, Margaret E. Moore, P. Richard Moore.
EIN: 870642459

53907
Bert L. Neal & Lulu M. Neal Foundation
P.O. Box 628
Salt Lake City, UT 84110-0628
Application address: c/o Mary Barker, Tr., P.O. Box 9936, Ogden, UT 84409, tel.: (801) 626-9531

Established in 1986 in UT.
Financial data (yr. ended 12/31/01): Grants paid, $9,900; assets, $256,036 (M); expenditures, $14,087; qualifying distributions, $9,900.
Limitations: Giving primarily in Ogden, UT.
Officer: Ralph W. Mitchell, Chair.
Trustees: Mary L. Barker, Samuel H. Barker, Orville Rex Child, Jack D. Lampros, Wells Fargo Bank Northwest, N.A.
EIN: 876161267

53908
John A. and Bonita G. Hopkin Family Society
c/o John Hopkin
480 E. 90 N.
Orem, UT 84097-5610

Established in 1991.
Donor(s): John A. Hopkin.
Financial data (yr. ended 12/31/01): Grants paid, $9,838; assets, $120,507 (M); gifts received, $11,700; expenditures, $16,960; qualifying distributions, $9,838.
Limitations: Applications not accepted.
Application information: Contributes only to pre-selected organizations.
Officers: John A. Hopkin, Chair. and Pres.; J. Arden Hopkin, V.P.; Bonita G. Hopkin, Secy.-Treas.
EIN: 742490613

53909
The Ninigret Foundation, Inc.
1700 S. 4650 W.
Salt Lake City, UT 84104-5310

Established in 1997 in UT.
Donor(s): Marion M. Abood.
Financial data (yr. ended 03/31/02): Grants paid, $9,760; assets, $33,807 (M); gifts received, $9,528; expenditures, $9,879; qualifying distributions, $9,760.
Limitations: Applications not accepted.
Application information: Contributes only to pre-selected organizations.
Directors: Marion M. Abood, Randolph G. Abood, Alan S. Fitter.
EIN: 841383523

53910
Snow, Christensen & Martineau Foundation
c/o Snow, Christensen & Martineau
P.O. Box 45000
Salt Lake City, UT 84145

Established in 1988 in UT.
Donor(s): Snow, Christensen & Martineau.
Financial data (yr. ended 12/31/01): Grants paid, $9,600; assets, $360,110 (M); expenditures, $14,361; qualifying distributions, $9,600.
Limitations: Applications not accepted. Giving limited to Salt Lake City, UT.
Application information: Contributes only to pre-selected organizations.
Officers and Trustees:* Ryan E. Tibbitts,* Pres.; John E. Gates,* Secy.-Treas.; R. Brent Stephens.
EIN: 870450634
Codes: CS, CD

53911
Ray, Quinney & Nebeker Foundation
P.O. Box 45385
Salt Lake City, UT 84145-0385

Donor(s): Ray, Quinney & Nebeker Law Firm, P.C.
Financial data (yr. ended 12/31/00): Grants paid, $9,500; assets, $395,929 (M); gifts received, $1,600; expenditures, $9,808; qualifying distributions, $9,558.
Limitations: Applications not accepted. Giving limited to UT, with emphasis on Provo and Salt Lake City.
Application information: Contributes only to pre-selected organizations.
Trustees: Clark P. Giles, Herbert C. Livsey, Stephen B. Nebeker, Alonzo W. Watson, Jr.
EIN: 870389313
Codes: CS, CD

53912
The Harold E. and Joyce A. Tornquist Charitable Foundation, Inc.
c/o Cheryl Craig
15 W. Sq. Temple, No. 200
Salt Lake City, UT 84101

Established in 1992 in UT.
Donor(s): Joyce A. Tornquist.
Financial data (yr. ended 12/31/01): Grants paid, $9,150; assets, $88,294 (M); gifts received, $258; expenditures, $12,518; qualifying distributions, $9,150.
Limitations: Applications not accepted. Giving primarily in Salt Lake City, UT.
Application information: Contributes only to pre-selected organizations.
Officer: Joyce A. Tornquist, Pres.
Directors: Robert R. Crawford, Eleanore Jorgensen.
EIN: 870504339

53913
James Family Foundation
462 N., 800 W.
Lindon, UT 84042-1219

Established in 1999 in UT.
Donor(s): Michael James, Juli James.
Financial data (yr. ended 12/31/01): Grants paid, $9,020; assets, $113,318 (M); gifts received, $4,655; expenditures, $9,650; qualifying distributions, $9,020.
Limitations: Applications not accepted.
Application information: Contributes only to pre-selected organizations.
Trustees: Joseph James, Juli James, Michael James.
EIN: 870637968

53914
Leah B. and H. Whitney Felt Foundation
c/o Leah B. Felt
3955 Parkview Dr.
Salt Lake City, UT 84124-2323

Established in 1998 in UT.
Financial data (yr. ended 12/31/01): Grants paid, $9,000; assets, $106,489 (M); expenditures, $9,066; qualifying distributions, $9,000.
Limitations: Applications not accepted.
Application information: Contributes only to pre-selected organizations.
Officers: Leah B. Felt, Pres.; George B. Felt, Secy.-Treas.
Trustees: Louise F. Christensen, Edward B. Felt, James W. Felt, Marion F. Watson.
EIN: 870617488

53915
F. F. and C. C. Sawyer Foundation
(Formerly Sawyer Private Foundation)
P.O. Box 628
Salt Lake City, UT 84110-0628
Application address: P.O. Box 9936, Ogden, UT 84401
Contact: Mary L. Barker, Tr., Wells Fargo Bank Northwest, N.A.

Established in 1988 in UT.
Donor(s): Clair Cleo Sawyer.
Financial data (yr. ended 12/31/01): Grants paid, $9,000; assets, $236,378 (M); expenditures, $12,913; qualifying distributions, $11,332.
Limitations: Giving primarily in Logan, UT.
Officer and Trustees:* Samuel H. Barker,* Chair.; Mary L. Barker, Orville Rex Child, J.E. Ted Johnston, Jack D. Lampros, Wells Fargo Bank Northwest, N.A.
EIN: 742495766

53916
The Children's Health Foundation
333 Main St.
P.O. Box 5000
Park City, UT 84060 (435) 649-2221

Established in 1986 in UT.
Donor(s): Randall K. Fields, Debra J. Fields, Mrs. Fields' Original Cookies, Inc., Vallarta Cuatro Ltd.
Financial data (yr. ended 12/31/01): Grants paid, $8,836; assets, $64,765 (M); gifts received, $8,686; expenditures, $10,996; qualifying distributions, $8,836.
Limitations: Applications not accepted. Giving on a national basis.
Application information: Contributes only to pre-selected organizations.
Officers: Debra J. Fields, Chair.; Randall K. Fields, Pres.; Edward L. Clissold, Secy.
EIN: 742450465
Codes: CS

53917
Livelihood Assistance Foundation
(Formerly The Gus and Lulie Family Foundation)
1632 South 200 E.
Orem, UT 84058

Established in 2000 in UT.
Donor(s): Angus Blackham, Lula Belle Blackham, M. Scott Blackham.
Financial data (yr. ended 12/31/01): Grants paid, $8,545; assets, $75,396 (M); gifts received, $14,318; expenditures, $9,460; qualifying distributions, $8,545.
Limitations: Applications not accepted. Giving in UT, and the Phillipines.
Application information: Contributes only to pre-selected organizations.
Officers: Angus Blackham, Pres.; M. Scott Blackham, Secy.; Lula Belle Blackham, Treas.
EIN: 870657386

53918
Heaps Family Foundation
243 W. 1925 N.
Orem, UT 84057

Established in 1999 in UT.
Donor(s): David O. Heaps, Marianne F. Heaps.
Financial data (yr. ended 12/31/00): Grants paid, $8,500; assets, $796,495 (M); gifts received, $9,657; expenditures, $23,249; qualifying distributions, $1,008.
Limitations: Applications not accepted.
Application information: Contributes only to pre-selected organizations.
Trustees: David O. Heaps, Marianne F. Heaps.
EIN: 870643525

53919
Haynes Foundation
c/o Eugene H. Butler
2919 Indian Hills Dr.
Provo, UT 84604-4332

Established in 1998.
Donor(s): Eugene H. Butler.
Financial data (yr. ended 12/31/01): Grants paid, $7,944; assets, $3,000 (M); gifts received, $8,175; expenditures, $8,049; qualifying distributions, $8,049.
EIN: 870573142

53920
Beta Gamma of Alpha Delta Pi Foundation
c/o Wells Fargo Bank Northwest, N.A.
P.O. Box 628
Salt Lake City, UT 84110
Application address: c/o University of Utah, Beta Gamma Scholarship Fund, P.O. Box 30007, Salt Lake City, UT 84130

Financial data (yr. ended 06/30/02): Grants paid, $7,500; assets, $121,639 (M); expenditures, $9,410; qualifying distributions, $7,500.
Limitations: Giving primarily in UT.
Application information: Application forms available at University of Utah. Application form required.
Officers and Directors:* Mary Graham,* Pres.; Emma Lou Moray,* V.P.; Claudette K. Dill,* Secy.; Elaine S. Anderson, Fay S. Ellison, Carolyn Felix, Jackie Norton.
Trustee: Wells Fargo Bank Northwest, N.A.
EIN: 742499740

53921
The Foundation for Indian Development
P.O. Box 1395
Provo, UT 84603
Contact: Marcia Johns

Established in 1999 in UT.
Donor(s): Cordell M. Andersen.
Financial data (yr. ended 12/31/99): Grants paid, $7,306; assets, $20,331 (M); gifts received, $24,883; expenditures, $15,513; qualifying distributions, $15,513.
Officer: Reid B. Johns, Exec. Dir.
EIN: 237072445

53922
James Moyle Genealogical & Historical Association
1958 Browning Ave.
Salt Lake City, UT 84108
Contact: Alice C. Marsh, Secy.-Treas.

Financial data (yr. ended 12/31/01): Grants paid, $7,150; assets, $24,727 (M); gifts received, $9,219; expenditures, $8,253; qualifying distributions, $7,150.
Limitations: Giving primarily in Salt Lake City, UT.
Officer and Directors:* Alice C. Marsh,* Secy.-Treas.; Helen Clair Jones, H.D. Moyle.
EIN: 876118795

53923
Jerald E. Mason and Miriam Peterson Mason Foundation
c/o Wiggins & Co.
3434 Washington Blvd., Ste. 303
Ogden, UT 84401-4100 (801) 627-2710
Contact: John E. Mason, Tr.

Established in 1993 in UT.
Financial data (yr. ended 09/30/01): Grants paid, $7,000; assets, $175,491 (M); expenditures, $8,217; qualifying distributions, $7,000.
Limitations: Giving primarily in UT.
Trustees: Elizabeth M. Bergquist, Cynthia M. Galecki, John E. Mason, Catherine M. Sims.
EIN: 876224895

53924
Melba McKenzie Charitable Trust
P.O. Box 30880
Salt Lake City, UT 84130-0880

Financial data (yr. ended 12/31/01): Grants paid, $7,000; assets, $178,057 (M); expenditures, $11,711; qualifying distributions, $7,000.
Limitations: Applications not accepted. Giving primarily in GA.
Application information: Contributes only to pre-selected organizations.
Trustee: Zions First National Bank.
EIN: 876236955

53925
The Reagan Foundation
1775 N. Warm Springs Rd.
Salt Lake City, UT 84116
Contact: William K. Reagan, Tr.

Established in 1998 in UT.
Donor(s): William K. Reagan.
Financial data (yr. ended 12/31/01): Grants paid, $7,000; assets, $358,535 (M); gifts received, $101,411; expenditures, $7,127; qualifying distributions, $7,000.
Trustees: Daniel A. Reagan, Julia Louise Oslowitz Reagan, William K. Reagan.
EIN: 870607740

53926
The Argyle Foundation
5369 Legacy Hill Dr.
West Jordan, UT 84084 (801) 975-9411
Contact: Shane V. Argyle, Pres.

Financial data (yr. ended 12/31/01): Grants paid, $6,828; assets, $386,715 (M); gifts received, $246,000; expenditures, $7,828; qualifying distributions, $6,828.
Limitations: Giving primarily in Salt Lake City, UT.
Officers: Shane V. Argyle, Pres.; Heidi B. Argyle, V.P.; Clint B. Argyle, Off.
EIN: 870618694

53927
Fabian and Clendenin Charitable Foundation
P.O. Box 510210
Salt Lake City, UT 84151
Application address: c/o Jay B. Bell, 215 S. State St., Ste. 1200, Salt Lake City, UT 84111, tel.: (801) 531-8900

Established in 1993.
Financial data (yr. ended 09/30/01): Grants paid, $6,708; assets, $8,744 (M); expenditures, $6,788; qualifying distributions, $6,708.
Limitations: Giving primarily in Salt Lake City, UT.
Trustee: P.C. Fabian.
EIN: 870510416

53928
The Heather and Don Stone Charitable Foundation
6649 S. Verano Cir.
West Jordan, UT 84084-6642

Established in 1986 in UT.
Financial data (yr. ended 12/31/99): Grants paid, $6,315; assets, $1,833 (M); gifts received, $6,025; expenditures, $6,489; qualifying distributions, $6,488; giving activities include $6,090 for programs.
Limitations: Applications not accepted. Giving primarily in UT.
Application information: Contributes only to pre-selected organizations.
Trustees: Donald F. Stone, Heather M. Stone.
EIN: 870442164

53929
WTF Foundation
1034 N. Chartwell Ct.
Salt Lake City, UT 84103

Established in 2000 in UT.
Financial data (yr. ended 12/31/01): Grants paid, $6,218; assets, $6,059 (M); gifts received, $12,000; expenditures, $6,300; qualifying distributions, $6,218.
Officers: Sen-Wan Fang, Pres.; Theresa S. Fang, V.P.
EIN: 870643999

53930
American Dream Foundation
1180 28th St.
Ogden, UT 84403

Established in 1999 in UT.
Donor(s): Karl Malone Foundation for Kids.
Financial data (yr. ended 12/31/99): Grants paid, $6,000; assets, $17,104 (M); gifts received, $23,520; expenditures, $6,466; qualifying distributions, $6,000.
Limitations: Applications not accepted.
Application information: Contributes only to pre-selected organizations.
Officers: John A. Gullo, Pres.; Karen Gullo, Secy.
Trustee: Harlan P. Schmitt.
EIN: 311642351

53931
Quintus C. Babcock Memorial Fund
5620 Highland Dr.
Salt Lake City, UT 84121-1303
Application address: c/o Dir. of Student Fin. Planning, Upper Iowa Univ., Fayette, IA 52142, tel.: (319) 425-5200

Financial data (yr. ended 12/31/01): Grants paid, $6,000; assets, $98,087 (M); expenditures, $6,686; qualifying distributions, $0.
Limitations: Giving limited to residents of the Fayette, IA, area.
Application information: Applicant must be enrolled at Upper Iowa University. Application form required.
Trustees: Alice T. Koempel, Donald R. Wilson.
EIN: 426075871
Codes: GTI

53932
Tobias - a Private Foundation
57 W. 200 S., Ste. 300
Salt Lake City, UT 84101-1633

Donor(s): Don S. Domgaard.
Financial data (yr. ended 12/31/01): Grants paid, $5,979; assets, $120,337 (M); gifts received, $6,000; expenditures, $5,980; qualifying distributions, $5,979.
Limitations: Applications not accepted.
Application information: Contributes only to pre-selected organizations.
Directors: Don S. Domgaard, Dorothy R. Domgaard.
EIN: 870568963

53933
The Slaymaker Family Foundation
6777 Vista Grande Dr.
Salt Lake City, UT 84121

Donor(s): Scott R. Slaymaker, Barbara Slaymaker.
Financial data (yr. ended 12/31/01): Grants paid, $5,900; assets, $131,172 (M); gifts received, $40,800; expenditures, $47,929; qualifying distributions, $5,900.
Limitations: Applications not accepted. Giving primarily in Salt Lake City, UT.
Application information: Contributes only to pre-selected organizations.
Trustees: Suzanne Bronzati, Barbara Slaymaker, Eric E. Slaymaker, Scott R. Slaymaker.
EIN: 841403563

53934
Utah Vision Foundation, Inc.
2319 S. Highland Dr.
Salt Lake City, UT 84106-2810

Established in 1997 in UT.
Donor(s): Colorado Vision Services, Inc.
Financial data (yr. ended 12/31/00): Grants paid, $5,792; assets, $129,193 (M); expenditures, $6,817; qualifying distributions, $5,792.
Limitations: Applications not accepted.
Application information: Contributes only to pre-selected organizations.
Officers: William Bogus, Pres.; Bill Codner, Secy.-Treas.
Directors: Ken Hooton, David Maihda, James Sargent.
EIN: 841381472

53935
Victoria Foundation
861 N. 1100 E.
Orem, UT 84097

Established in 1999 in UT.

53935—UTAH

Financial data (yr. ended 12/31/01): Grants paid, $5,700; assets, $236 (M); gifts received, $1,502; expenditures, $5,716; qualifying distributions, $5,716.
Officers and Trustees:* Kif Augustine Adams,* Pres.; Stirling Adams,* V.P. and Secy.-Treas.; Kent Wilson Adams, Matthew Adams.
EIN: 870626096

53936
Cora T. Hayward Educational Fund
c/o Zions First National Bank
1 Main St.
Salt Lake City, UT 84111-1909

Financial data (yr. ended 12/31/01): Grants paid, $5,400; assets, $117,055 (M); expenditures, $8,657; qualifying distributions, $5,400.
Limitations: Applications not accepted. Giving limited to UT.
Application information: Unsolicited requests for funds not accepted.
Trustee: Zions First National Bank.
EIN: 876137122

53937
Good Knightzz Foundation
3269 Danish Springs Cove
Sandy, UT 84093

Established in 2001 in UT.
Donor(s): Matthew Koch, Ann Koch.
Financial data (yr. ended 12/31/01): Grants paid, $5,382; assets, $6,987 (M); gifts received, $15,560; expenditures, $8,573; qualifying distributions, $5,828.
Trustees: Ann Koch, Matthew Koch.
EIN: 870681962

53938
The CJM Johnson-Muir Family Foundation
65 Lone Peak Dr.
Alpine, UT 84004

Established in 1994.
Donor(s): The Alpine Foundation.
Financial data (yr. ended 12/31/01): Grants paid, $5,317; assets, $94,472 (M); expenditures, $5,717; qualifying distributions, $5,317.
Limitations: Applications not accepted.
Application information: Contributes only to pre-selected organizations.
Trustees: H. Kent Johnson, Vicki J. Muir.
EIN: 870534291

53939
Edith Dee Green Charitable Trust C
c/o Wells Fargo Bank Northwest, N.A.
P.O. Box 628
Salt Lake City, UT 84110-0628
Application Address: c/o Mary Barker, Trust Off., Wells Fargo Bank Northwest, N.A., P.O. Box 9936, Ogden, UT 84409, tel.: (801) 626-9531

Financial data (yr. ended 12/31/01): Grants paid, $5,200; assets, $125,284 (M); expenditures, $74,587; qualifying distributions, $6,238.
Limitations: Giving limited to Ogden, UT.
Trustee: Wells Fargo Bank Northwest, N.A.
EIN: 876121932

53940
Tim Hixson Memorial Scholarship Trust
c/o Wells Fargo Bank Northwest, N.A.
299 S. Main St.
Salt Lake City, UT 84111
Application address: c/o Utah High School Hockey Assoc., P.O. Box 1213, Bountiful, UT 84011

Established in 1996 in UT.
Financial data (yr. ended 12/31/01): Grants paid, $5,110; assets, $71,947 (M); expenditures, $7,458; qualifying distributions, $6,319.
Limitations: Giving primarily in Centerville, UT.
Application information: Application form required.
Trustee: Wells Fargo Bank Northwest, N.A.
EIN: 876226810

53941
The Garff & Kim Cannon Foundation
235 S. 200 E.
Farmington, UT 84025

Established in 1994 in UT.
Donor(s): Garff G. Cannon, Kim H. Cannon.
Financial data (yr. ended 12/31/00): Grants paid, $5,099; assets, $14,741 (M); gifts received, $2,000; expenditures, $6,747; qualifying distributions, $5,099.
Limitations: Applications not accepted. Giving limited to Salt Lake City, UT.
Application information: Contributes only to pre-selected organizations.
Trustees: Garff G. Cannon, Kim H. Cannon.
EIN: 876225354

53942
Questar Corporation Native American Scholarship Foundation
180 E. 1st St. S.
P.O. Box 45433
Salt Lake City, UT 84145-0433

Established in 1998 in UT.
Financial data (yr. ended 12/31/01): Grants paid, $5,000; assets, $64,277 (M); expenditures, $5,095; qualifying distributions, $5,000.
Limitations: Applications not accepted. Giving primarily in Tempe, AZ.
Application information: Contributes only to pre-selected organizations.
Officer and Trustees:* R.D. Cash,* Chair.; Connie C. Holbrook, D.N. Rose.
EIN: 870623588

53943
The T. Luke Savage Family Foundation
5250 S. 300 W., Ste. 200
Salt Lake City, UT 84106

Established in 2000 in UT.
Donor(s): Savage Industries, Inc.
Financial data (yr. ended 12/31/01): Grants paid, $5,000; assets, $46,626 (M); expenditures, $5,008; qualifying distributions, $4,988.
Limitations: Applications not accepted.
Application information: Contributes only to pre-selected organizations.
Officers and Trustees:* T. Luke Savage,* Pres.; Todd Savage,* V.P.; Susan Savage,* Secy.-Treas.; Lorrie Savage Gilbert, Lisa Savage, Matthew Trent Savage, Terrence Savage, Troy Savage, Ty Savage.
EIN: 870651831
Codes: CS

53944
Edith Dee Green Charitable Trust B
c/o First Security Bank of Utah, N.A.
P.O. Box 628
Salt Lake City, UT 84110-0628
Application address: c/o Mary Barker, P.O. Box 9936, Ogden, UT 84409, tel.:(801) 626-9531

Financial data (yr. ended 12/31/01): Grants paid, $4,800; assets, $120,590 (M); expenditures, $7,017; qualifying distributions, $4,800.
Limitations: Giving primarily in UT.
Trustee: First Security Bank of Utah, N.A.
EIN: 876121931

53945
Gaddis U.S.R.F. Foundation
675 E. 2100 S., Ste. 150
Salt Lake City, UT 84106

Established in 1994 in UT.
Donor(s): James Gaddis, Barbara Gaddis.
Financial data (yr. ended 12/31/01): Grants paid, $4,775; assets, $61,929 (M); gifts received, $5,000; expenditures, $4,840; qualifying distributions, $4,775.
Limitations: Applications not accepted.
Application information: Contributes only to pre-selected organizations.
Officers: James Gaddis, Pres.; Barbara Gaddis, V.P.
EIN: 870284063

53946
J. M. & R. J. Horrigan Foundation
(also known as John M. Horrigan and Rosalind J. Horrigan Charitable Foundation)
c/o First Security Bank of Utah, N.A.
P.O. Box 628
Salt Lake City, UT 84110
Application address: 15 S. Main, Logan, UT 84321
Contact: Stan Norton, Dir.

Established in 1987 in UT.
Donor(s): Rosalind J. Horrigan.
Financial data (yr. ended 06/30/01): Grants paid, $4,600; assets, $96,415 (M); expenditures, $6,451; qualifying distributions, $4,600.
Limitations: Giving primarily in UT.
Application information: Application form not required.
Officer and Directors:* Bonnie Lee Horrigan-Slade,* Chair.; Cathleen M. Harper, Charles Metten, Patricia Horrigan Metten, Lisa S. Miller, Stan Norton.
Trustee: First Security Bank of Utah, N.A.
EIN: 742493471

53947
The Alvin E. Malstrom Foundation
9325 S. 700 E.
Sandy, UT 84070-6202

Established in 1997 in UT.
Financial data (yr. ended 12/31/01): Grants paid, $4,500; assets, $7,218 (M); gifts received, $9,000; expenditures, $4,500; qualifying distributions, $4,500.
Limitations: Applications not accepted.
Application information: Contributes only to pre-selected organizations.
Officers: Alvin E. Malstrom, Pres.; James B. Zupan, V.P.; Martin J. Pezely, Secy.; Mike Steele, Treas.
EIN: 870471168

53948
Etta Smout McDonald Charitable Trust
c/o Wells Fargo Bank Northwest, N.A.
P.O. Box 628
Salt Lake City, UT 84110
Application address: P.O. Box 9936, Ogden, UT 84409, tel.: (801) 626-9531
Contact: Mary Barker, Trust Off., Wells Fargo Bank Northwest, N.A.

Financial data (yr. ended 12/31/01): Grants paid, $4,236; assets, $104,302 (M); expenditures, $6,235; qualifying distributions, $4,236.
Limitations: Giving primarily in Ogden, UT.
Trustee: Wells Fargo Bank Northwest, N.A.
EIN: 876154687

53949
Leland B. & Dora T. Flint Foundation
c/o Victor K. Cummings
10 Rollingwood Ln.
Sandy, UT 84092

Financial data (yr. ended 12/31/01): Grants paid, $4,150; assets, $74,079 (M); expenditures, $4,966; qualifying distributions, $4,150.
Limitations: Applications not accepted. Giving primarily in UT.
Application information: Contributes only to pre-selected organizations.
Officers: Bonnie Talbot, Pres.; Patricia F. Knapp, V.P.; Susan F. Beaudoin, Secy.; James R. Beaudoin, Treas.
Director: Beverly F. Holman.
EIN: 876125176

53950
Howard & Betty Clark Foundation
3013 Sherwood Dr.
Salt Lake City, UT 84108

Established in 1997 in UT.
Donor(s): Betty B. Clark, Howard S. Clark.
Financial data (yr. ended 12/31/01): Grants paid, $4,130; assets, $207,474 (M); gifts received, $4,644; expenditures, $4,543; qualifying distributions, $4,130.
Limitations: Applications not accepted.
Application information: Contributes only to pre-selected organizations.
Trustees: Betty B. Clark, Howard S. Clark.
EIN: 841410684

53951
Dreamweaver Foundation
1816 Prospector Ave., Ste. 202
Park City, UT 84060 (435) 658-1188
Contact: John B. Benear, II, Tr.

Established in 2000 in UT.
Donor(s): John B. Benear.
Financial data (yr. ended 12/31/00): Grants paid, $4,000; assets, $5,729,954 (M); gifts received, $24,285,013; expenditures, $104,576; qualifying distributions, $90,922.
Trustee: John B. Benear II.
Administration Committee: Bradford Bond, Katy Lillquist.
EIN: 870648469

53952
Wells-Spencer Foundation
170 N. Center St.
Escalante, UT 84726
Application address: P.O. Box 520, Escalante, UT 84726
Contact: Frank P. Venuti, Tr.

Financial data (yr. ended 12/31/99): Grants paid, $4,000; assets, $17,512 (M); expenditures, $4,000; qualifying distributions, $4,000.
Limitations: Giving limited to Escalante, UT.
Trustees: Annalee Robinson Knudsen, Camille Snakegear, V.R. Spencer, F.P. Venuti.
EIN: 880327720

53953
Twelve Lawrence Trust
c/o James A. Fielding
1452 E. Sherman Ave.
Salt Lake City, UT 84105

Financial data (yr. ended 01/31/02): Grants paid, $3,950; assets, $61,871 (M); expenditures, $6,847; qualifying distributions, $3,950.
Limitations: Applications not accepted. Giving primarily in the Northeast.
Application information: Contributes only to pre-selected organizations.
Officer and Trustee:* Amy J. Fielding,* Mgr.
EIN: 046086444

53954
The Beth L. "Daryl" Davis Charitable Foundation
c/o Beth L. Davis
1029 E. 600 S.
Salt Lake City, UT 84102-3828
(801) 534-1496

Established in 1992 in UT.
Donor(s): Beth L. Davis.
Financial data (yr. ended 12/31/01): Grants paid, $3,850; assets, $81,203 (M); expenditures, $4,404; qualifying distributions, $3,850.
Limitations: Giving on a national basis.
Trustees: Beth L. Davis, Judy DeWaal, Donna A. King.
EIN: 870503468

53955
The Preparedness Foundation
190 E. Main St.
Midway, UT 84049

Established in 1999 in UT.
Donor(s): Harry R. Weyandt, Vickie L. Weyandt.
Financial data (yr. ended 12/31/00): Grants paid, $3,825; assets, $147,319 (M); expenditures, $10,529; qualifying distributions, $3,825.
Limitations: Applications not accepted.
Application information: Contributes only to pre-selected organizations.
Trustees: Harry R. Weyandt, Vickie L. Weyandt.
EIN: 870653938

53956
Kenneth C. Savage Family Foundation
c/o Savage Industries, Inc.
5250 S. 300 W., Ste. 200
Salt Lake City, UT 84107

Established in 2000 in UT.
Donor(s): Savage Industries, Inc.
Financial data (yr. ended 12/31/01): Grants paid, $3,600; assets, $47,996 (M); expenditures, $3,637; qualifying distributions, $3,588.
Limitations: Applications not accepted.
Application information: Contributes only to pre-selected organizations.
Officers and Trustees:* John K. Savage,* Pres.; Shannon Savage Magleby,* V.P.; Colleen Savage Smith,* V.P.; Carolyn Savage Wright,* V.P.; LaRae T. Savage,* Secy.-Treas.; Kenneth C. Savage.
EIN: 870651832
Codes: CS

53957
PRD Private Foundation
2914 Skyridge Cir.
Salt Lake City, UT 84109

Established in 1986 in UT.
Donor(s): Philip R. Dykstra, Martha H. Dykstra.
Financial data (yr. ended 12/31/01): Grants paid, $3,450; assets, $53,521 (M); expenditures, $3,634; qualifying distributions, $3,450.
Limitations: Applications not accepted. Giving primarily in UT.
Application information: Contributes only to pre-selected organizations.
Trustees: Martha H. Dykstra, Philip R. Dykstra.
EIN: 870440810

53958
Sjinc Foundation
c/o Luke H. Ong, PC
P.O. Box 1207
Bountiful, UT 84011-1207

Established in 2001 in UT.
Donor(s): Phillip M. Adams.
Financial data (yr. ended 12/31/01): Grants paid, $3,000; assets, $523,571 (M); gifts received, $526,000; expenditures, $3,000; qualifying distributions, $3,000.
Limitations: Applications not accepted.
Application information: Contributes only to pre-selected organizations.
Directors: Analecia Adams, Jacob R. Adams, Jason P. Adams, Jeremy T. Adams.
Trustees: Phillip M. Adams, Suann P. Adams.
EIN: 870686375

53959
Ogden Masonic Relief Board
P.O. Box 141
Ogden, UT 84402-0141

Financial data (yr. ended 12/31/01): Grants paid, $2,620; assets, $54,940 (M); expenditures, $3,178; qualifying distributions, $2,620.
Limitations: Applications not accepted. Giving primarily in UT.
Application information: Contributes only to pre-selected organizations.
Officers: Raymond F. White, Chair.; William F. Wade, Vice-Chair.; Maurice Nelson, Secy.-Treas.
EIN: 876120020

53960
Dale and Alice Ballard Charitable Foundation
(Formerly Ballard Charitable Foundation)
P.O. Box 628
Salt Lake City, UT 84110-0628

Established in 1997 in UT.
Financial data (yr. ended 10/31/01): Grants paid, $2,300; assets, $47,947 (M); expenditures, $3,587; qualifying distributions, $2,300.
Limitations: Applications not accepted.
Application information: Contributes only to pre-selected organizations.
Trustee: First Security Bank, N.A.
EIN: 876237645

53961
Keith A. Pedersen Family Organization
1915 W. 9640 S.
South Jordan, UT 84095

Donor(s): Keith A. Pederson.
Financial data (yr. ended 12/31/01): Grants paid, $2,300; assets, $43 (M); gifts received, $5,758; expenditures, $5,778; qualifying distributions, $2,300.
Limitations: Applications not accepted. Giving limited to UT.
Application information: Contributes only to pre-selected organizations.
Officers: Keith A. Pedersen, Pres.; Michael K. Pederson, V.P.; Cindy Aston, Secy.
EIN: 742378373

53962
Dohas Foundation
321 N. Mall Dr., Ste. I-201
St. George, UT 84790
Application address: 1134 E. 900 S., No. 15, St. George, UT 84790
Contact: Wilda A. Steed, Dir.

Established in 1999.
Financial data (yr. ended 12/31/01): Grants paid, $2,250; assets, $180,567 (M); gifts received,

$23,094; expenditures, $25,905; qualifying distributions, $3,980.
Director: Wilda A. Steed.
EIN: 841389408

53963
Irvin L. Warnock Scholarship
c/o W. Paul Warnock
6333 S. Seville Rd.
Salt Lake City, UT 84121-2115
Application address: P.O. Box 570021, Sigurd, UT 84657
Contact: Robert E. Warnock, Pres.

Established in 1994 in UT.
Donor(s): Arda Jean Christensen.
Financial data (yr. ended 12/31/00): Grants paid, $2,250; assets, $25,786 (M); gifts received, $2,505; expenditures, $2,452; qualifying distributions, $2,141.
Limitations: Giving limited to Richfield, UT.
Application information: Application form required.
Officers: Robert E. Warnock, Pres.; Arda Jean Christensen, V.P.; W. Paul Warnock, Treas.
EIN: 870515592

53964
Memory Grove Foundation, Inc.
c/o John Jansen
248 Canyon Rd.
Salt Lake City, UT 84103

Established in 1996 in UT.
Financial data (yr. ended 12/31/01): Grants paid, $2,222; assets, $139,245 (M); gifts received, $25,460; expenditures, $4,864; qualifying distributions, $2,222.
Limitations: Applications not accepted.
Application information: Contributes only to pre-selected organizations.
Officers: Bart Davis, Pres.; Bettie Bogart, Secy.; John Jansen, Treas.
EIN: 742448336

53965
Lawyers Endowment for Accident Prevention
6925 Union Park Ctr., Ste. 210
Midvale, UT 84047-4137

Financial data (yr. ended 12/31/01): Grants paid, $2,012; assets, $7,537 (M); gifts received, $8,110; expenditures, $2,101; qualifying distributions, $2,012.
Limitations: Applications not accepted. Giving primarily in UT.
Application information: Contributes only to pre-selected organizations.
Officer: Scott D. Brown, Pres.
EIN: 742561476

53966
Eleanor F. Bamberger Charitable Trust
136 S. Main St., Ste. 418
Salt Lake City, UT 84101-1601
Contact: William H. Olwell, Mgr.

Donor(s): Ernest Bamberger.‡
Financial data (yr. ended 12/31/99): Grants paid, $2,000; assets, $14,278 (M); expenditures, $2,623; qualifying distributions, $2,000.
Limitations: Giving limited to Salt Lake City, UT.
Officers: William H. Olwell, Mgr.; Eleanor Roser, Mgr.
EIN: 876119070

53967
Bank One, Utah Scholarship Trust
(Formerly William E. Myrick Scholarship Trust)
c/o Bank One, Utah, N.A.
80 W. Broadway, Ste. 202
Salt Lake City, UT 84101
Application address: c/o University of Utah, College of Business, 1202 Park Bldg., Salt Lake City, UT 844112

Established in 1974 in UT.
Donor(s): William E. Myrick.‡
Financial data (yr. ended 11/30/99): Grants paid, $2,000; assets, $16,894 (M); gifts received, $60; expenditures, $3,140; qualifying distributions, $2,000.
Limitations: Giving limited to Salt Lake City, UT.
Application information: Application form required.
Trustee: Bank One, Utah, N.A.
EIN: 876164360

53968
Catalyst Foundation
215 S. State St., Ste. 1170
Salt Lake City, UT 84111 (801) 532-7900
Contact: J. Lynn Dougan, Tr.

Established in 2000 in UT.
Donor(s): J. Lynn Dougan.
Financial data (yr. ended 12/31/01): Grants paid, $2,000; assets, $450,990 (M); expenditures, $2,494; qualifying distributions, $2,000.
Application information: Application form not required.
Officers and Trustees:* Diana Lady Dougan,* Chair. and Pres.; Gavin M. Dougan,* Secy.; Elena Lady Minton,* Treas.; J. Lynn Dougan.
EIN: 870666762

53969
Glen Nilson Family Foundation
P.O. Box 712
American Fork, UT 84003

Established in 1995 in UT.
Donor(s): Dave Farmer.
Financial data (yr. ended 12/31/01): Grants paid, $1,900; assets, $26,100 (M); expenditures, $1,900; qualifying distributions, $1,900.
Limitations: Applications not accepted.
Application information: Contributes only to pre-selected organizations.
Trustees: Glen Nilson, Raeanne Nilson.
EIN: 870549323

53970
J. Ralph MacFarlane Foundation
c/o Wells Fargo Bank Northwest, N.A.
P.O. Box 628
Salt Lake City, UT 84110-0628
Application address: P.O. Box 9936, Ogden, UT 84409, tel.: (801) 626-9531
Contact: Mary Barker, Trust Off., Wells Fargo Bank Northwest, N.A.

Donor(s): J. Ralph MacFarlane, M.D.
Financial data (yr. ended 12/31/01): Grants paid, $1,861; assets, $48,971 (M); expenditures, $3,131; qualifying distributions, $1,861.
Limitations: Giving limited to NY.
Trustees: Brook M. Karrington, J. Garrett McFarlane, J. Ralph MacFarlane, M.D., Roger T. MacFarlane, Sharon F. MacFarlane, Wells Fargo Bank Northwest, N.A.
EIN: 742353461

53971
O Du Schone Foundation
4552 Zarahemla Dr.
Salt Lake City, UT 84124-4000

Established in 1999 in UT.
Financial data (yr. ended 12/31/01): Grants paid, $1,780; assets, $71 (M); gifts received, $1,700; expenditures, $1,930; qualifying distributions, $1,780.
Limitations: Giving on a national basis, with emphasis on UT.
Trustee: Norbert F. Neumann.
EIN: 870626230

53972
The Haslem Family Foundation
1160 N. 800 W.
Orem, UT 84057

Established in 2001 in UT.
Donor(s): Keith Haslem.
Financial data (yr. ended 12/31/01): Grants paid, $1,600; assets, $1,550 (M); gifts received, $6,700; expenditures, $5,150; qualifying distributions, $5,150.
Limitations: Applications not accepted.
Application information: Contributes only to pre-selected organizations.
Officer: Keith Haslem, Pres.
EIN: 870668291

53973
Hallstrom Foundation, Inc.
c/o Andrew Nelson
P.O. Box 9662
Salt Lake City, UT 84109

Financial data (yr. ended 08/31/01): Grants paid, $1,500; assets, $224,641 (M); expenditures, $3,499; qualifying distributions, $1,500.
Limitations: Applications not accepted. Giving primarily in Charlottesville, VA.
Application information: Contributes only to pre-selected organizations.
Officers: Andres R. Nelson, Pres.; Ron Reeves, V.P.; Andrew R. Nelson, Secy.; Stephenson Jackson, Treas.
EIN: 396078202

53974
Wilfred C. Johnson Scholarship Trust f/b/o Lewis & Clark State College
c/o Wells Fargo Bank Northwest, N.A.
P.O. Box 628
Salt Lake City, UT 84110-0628
Application address: c/o Scholarship Coord., Lewis & Clark State College, Lewiston, ID 83501

Established in 1989 in ID.
Financial data (yr. ended 12/31/01): Grants paid, $1,500; assets, $71,495 (M); expenditures, $4,355; qualifying distributions, $3,154.
Limitations: Giving limited to residents of ID.
Application information: Application form required.
Trustee: Wells Fargo Bank Northwest, N.A.
EIN: 820373595

53975
Julie & Tane Williams Family Foundation
141 2nd Ave., Ste. 904
Salt Lake City, UT 84103-2305

Established in 1999 in IL.
Financial data (yr. ended 12/31/00): Grants paid, $1,460; assets, $836 (M); gifts received, $1,460; expenditures, $1,460; qualifying distributions, $1,460.
Limitations: Applications not accepted.

Application information: Contributes only to pre-selected organizations.
Officer: Julie L. Williams, Pres.
EIN: 870622970

53976
S. Rex and Joan T. Lewis Foundation
4382 Vintage Dr.
Provo, UT 84604-5678

Established in 1996 in UT.
Donor(s): Joan T. Lewis, S. Rex Lewis.
Financial data (yr. ended 12/31/01): Grants paid, $1,450; assets, $667,858 (M); gifts received, $87,778; expenditures, $2,273; qualifying distributions, $1,450.
Limitations: Applications not accepted. Giving primarily in UT.
Application information: Contributes only to pre-selected organizations.
Officer and Trustee: S. Rex Lewis,* Pres.
EIN: 841368580

53977
Vernon M. & Maree C. Buehler Charitable Foundation
c/o Vernon M. Buehler
1790 Country Club Dr.
Logan, UT 84321-4304

Established in 1991.
Donor(s): Vernon M. Buehler.
Financial data (yr. ended 12/31/01): Grants paid, $1,120; assets, $574,776 (M); gifts received, $127,223; expenditures, $2,506; qualifying distributions, $1,120.
Limitations: Giving primarily in Rexburg, ID, and UT.
Trustees: Vernon M. Buehler, Harold W. Dance.
EIN: 876216355

53978
W. David & Gay Etta Hemingway Foundation
84 Ricks Creek Way
Centerville, UT 84014

Established in 1996 in UT.
Donor(s): W. David Hemingway.
Financial data (yr. ended 12/31/99): Grants paid, $1,100; assets, $14,328 (M); gifts received, $41,600; expenditures, $31,889; qualifying distributions, $31,839.
Application information: Application form not required.
Trustees: Gay Etta Hemingway, Ryan Hemingway, W. David Hemingway.
EIN: 841369593

53979
Garth B. Last Charitable Foundation
216 W. St. George Blvd., Ste. C
St. George, UT 84770-3350
Contact: Dell V. McDonald, Pres.

Financial data (yr. ended 12/31/01): Grants paid, $1,100; assets, $53,760 (M); gifts received, $18,006; expenditures, $5,486; qualifying distributions, $1,100.
Application information: Application form required.
Officer and Trustees:* Dell V. McDonald,* Pres.; Bradley G. Last, Shirlee K. Last, Mary E. McDonald.
EIN: 870526622

53980
Clinical Research Associates Foundation
3707 N. Canyon Rd., Ste. 6
Provo, UT 84604-4590 (801) 226-2121
Contact: Rella P. Christensen, Tr.

Financial data (yr. ended 12/31/01): Grants paid, $1,000; assets, $25,186 (M); expenditures, $1,000; qualifying distributions, $1,000.
Limitations: Giving limited to Salt Lake City, UT.
Trustees: Gordon J. Christensen, Rella P. Christensen.
EIN: 942785527

53981
Glasmann Dudley Foundation
P.O. Box 40
Oakley, UT 84055

Established in 2000 in UT.
Donor(s): Susan Glasmann.
Financial data (yr. ended 12/31/01): Grants paid, $1,000; assets, $90,953 (M); gifts received, $9,741; expenditures, $4,785; qualifying distributions, $1,000.
Officer: Susan Glasmann, Pres.
Directors: Arielle Dudley, Richard W. Dudley, Daniel John Glasmann, Staci Glasmann.
EIN: 870666255

53982
Raines Foundation
8847 S. Sunridge Dr.
Sandy, UT 84093

Established in 2001 in UT.
Donor(s): Christine A. Raines.
Financial data (yr. ended 12/31/01): Grants paid, $1,000; assets, $92,107 (M); gifts received, $96,000; expenditures, $4,057; qualifying distributions, $4,057.
Limitations: Applications not accepted.
Application information: Contributes only to pre-selected organizations.
Officers and Trustees:* Christine A. Raines,* Chair., Pres., and Secy.-Treas.; William M. Raines IV,* V.P.
EIN: 870685648

53983
Harold W. and Artie Jepson Reeve Foundation
85 E. 300 S., No. 91-4
Hurricane, UT 84737
Application address: c/o Rob Golding, Principal, Hurricane High School, Hurricane, UT 84737

Established in 1987 in UT.
Financial data (yr. ended 12/31/99): Grants paid, $1,000; assets, $20,503 (M); gifts received, $1,000; expenditures, $1,000; qualifying distributions, $994.
Limitations: Giving limited to residents of Hurricane, UT.
Application information: Application form not required.
Trustees: Eldrow Reeve, Gilbert Reeve, Leo Reeve.
EIN: 742494813

53984
David Randolph and Elva Singleton Seely Scholarship Foundation
3145 S. 9100 West
Cedar City, UT 84720-6701
Application address: c/o Brent Arnold, Principal, Emery County High School, Castle Dale, UT 84513, tel.: (801) 381-2689

Established in 1989 in UT.
Financial data (yr. ended 12/31/01): Grants paid, $1,000; assets, $24,234 (M); expenditures, $1,118; qualifying distributions, $986.
Limitations: Giving limited to residents of Emery County, UT.
Application information: Applicants must be enrolled at Emery County High School, UT.
Officer and Trustees:* Jean Reeve,* Pres.; Eldon Reeve, Harold Randolph Reeve, Marjorie S. Reeve.
EIN: 742508732

53985
The Suitter Axland Foundation
(Formerly The Suitter Axland Armstrong & Hanson Foundation)
175 S.W. Temple St., Ste. 700
Salt Lake City, UT 84101-1480
(801) 532-7300
Contact: Frances H. Suitter, Tr.

Donor(s): Suitter Axland & Hanson, P.C.
Financial data (yr. ended 03/31/02): Grants paid, $930; assets, $76,563 (M); expenditures, $983; qualifying distributions, $930.
Limitations: Giving primarily in Salt Lake City, UT.
Trustees: Michael W. Homer, Carl F. Huefner, Frances H. Suitter.
EIN: 870484418
Codes: CS, CD

53986
The Arvin and Kathryn Grant Family Foundation
615 E. 3460 N.
Provo, UT 84604-4624

Established in 1999 in UT.
Donor(s): Marilyn J. Grant.
Financial data (yr. ended 12/31/00): Grants paid, $900; assets, $13,709 (M); gifts received, $14,400; expenditures, $900; qualifying distributions, $900.
Limitations: Giving primarily in UT.
Trustee: Marilyn J. Grant.
EIN: 870678460

53987
The Sherman and Judith Butters Foundation
2652 Bridgeport Ave.
Salt Lake City, UT 84121-5603

Established in 1988 in UT.
Donor(s): Sherman L. Butters.
Financial data (yr. ended 12/31/01): Grants paid, $875; assets, $105,259 (M); expenditures, $1,358; qualifying distributions, $875.
Limitations: Applications not accepted. Giving primarily in Salt Lake City, UT.
Application information: Contributes only to pre-selected organizations.
Trustees: Judith Butters, Sherman L. Butters.
EIN: 870460785

53988
Coombs Charitable Foundation
124 S. 600 E., Ste. 100
Salt Lake City, UT 84102

Established in 1986 in UT.
Donor(s): Jack R. Coombs, Margaret V. Coombs.
Financial data (yr. ended 11/30/01): Grants paid, $825; assets, $20,809 (M); gifts received, $8,000; expenditures, $5,568; qualifying distributions, $825.
Limitations: Applications not accepted. Giving primarily in UT.
Application information: Contributes only to pre-selected organizations.
Trustees: Jack R. Coombs, John Michael Coombs, Margaret V. Coombs.
EIN: 870441871

53989
C. Dean & Dottie M. Packer Charitable Foundation
3630 N. Little Rock Dr.
Provo, UT 84604-5261

Donor(s): C. Dean Packer, Dottie M. Packer.
Financial data (yr. ended 11/30/01): Grants paid, $750; assets, $44,484 (M); expenditures, $949; qualifying distributions, $750.
Limitations: Applications not accepted. Giving limited to UT.
Application information: Contributes only to pre-selected organizations.
Trustees: C. Dean Packer, Dottie M. Packer.
EIN: 942807858

53990
Edward H. Southwick, Jr. Foundation
(Formerly Happiness Foundation)
1675 N. 200 W., No. 9B
Provo, UT 84604 (801) 377-2177
Contact: Ronald W. Vigoren, Tr.

Established in 1988 in UT.
Donor(s): Edward H. Southwick, Jr.
Financial data (yr. ended 03/31/02): Grants paid, $750; assets, $14,957 (M); expenditures, $1,050; qualifying distributions, $750.
Limitations: Giving on a national basis.
Application information: Application form not required.
Directors: Althea S. Southwick, Edward H. Southwick, Sr., Edward H. Southwick, Jr.
Trustee: Ronald W. Vigoren.
EIN: 742504743

53991
The Craig Mortensen Family Foundation
1339 E. Bryan Ave.
Salt Lake City, UT 84105 (801) 975-9411
Contact: Craig Mortensen, Pres.

Established in 2000 in UT.
Donor(s): Craig Mortensen, Deanna Mortensen.
Financial data (yr. ended 12/31/00): Grants paid, $639; assets, $99,361 (M); gifts received, $100,000; expenditures, $639; qualifying distributions, $639.
Limitations: Giving primarily in Salt Lake City, UT.
Officers: Craig Mortensen, Pres.; Deanna Mortensen, V.P.
Director: Randy Sellers.
EIN: 870645857

53992
Lupine Foundation, Inc.
921 E. La Casa Dr.
Sandy, UT 84094

Established in 2001 in UT.
Donor(s): J. Bradley Simons, Shawn Simons.
Financial data (yr. ended 12/31/01): Grants paid, $556; assets, $26,818 (M); gifts received, $30,000; expenditures, $3,219; qualifying distributions, $556.
Officers: Shawn Simons, Pres.; Angelene T. Simons, V.P.; Joan Simons, Secy.
Directors: J. Bradley Simons, Jerry Simons, Kyle D. Simons.
EIN: 870679493

53993
The Dennis L. Crockett Family Foundation
c/o Reed L. Benson
2862 E. 9800 S.
Sandy, UT 84092

Donor(s): Dennis L. Crockett.
Financial data (yr. ended 12/31/01): Grants paid, $500; assets, $1,482,885 (M); gifts received, $3,000; expenditures, $58,601; qualifying distributions, $500.
Limitations: Applications not accepted. Giving primarily in Salt Lake City, UT.
Application information: Contributes only to pre-selected organizations.
Directors: Dennis L. Crockett, Teri L. Crockett, Dwight Egan, Kay Godfrey, John Hewlett.
EIN: 870517270

53994
Ernest J. & Norma Miller Foundation
P.O. Box 305
Hyrum, UT 84319

Established in 1997 in UT.
Donor(s): Ernest J. Miller.
Financial data (yr. ended 12/31/01): Grants paid, $418; assets, $9,707 (M); expenditures, $433; qualifying distributions, $418.
Limitations: Applications not accepted.
Application information: Contributes only to pre-selected organizations.
Officers and Trustees:* Ernest J. Miller,* Pres.; Norma Miller,* V.P.; John E. Clay,* Secy.-Treas.; Bruce L. Gittins.
EIN: 870524866

53995
Osborne & Janice Call Foundation
1108 E. 3250 N.
Ogden, UT 84414-1842
Contact: Lance M. Call, Mgr.

Financial data (yr. ended 12/31/00): Grants paid, $400; assets, $38,594 (M); expenditures, $1,285; qualifying distributions, $400.
Limitations: Giving limited to Pocatello, ID, and Salt Lake City, UT.
Officers and Trustees:* Janice M. Taylor,* Pres.; Lance M. Call,* Mgr.; Sharon Anderson, Jay Call, Candace Young.
EIN: 510206046

53996
Utah Junior Tennis Foundation, Inc.
5280 S. Commerce Dr., Ste. E-100
Salt Lake City, UT 84107

Financial data (yr. ended 12/31/00): Grants paid, $350; assets, $48,445 (M); gifts received, $33,058; expenditures, $39,214; qualifying distributions, $350.
Limitations: Applications not accepted. Giving primarily in UT.
Application information: Unsolicited requests for funds not accepted.
Officers: Steve Hard, Pres.; Larry Erickson, V.P.; Bill Jensen, Secy.; Brent Gray, Treas.; Linda Vincent, Mgr.
EIN: 870457864

53997
Earl M. and Corinne N. Wunderli Family Foundation
8010 Hunters Meadow Cir.
Sandy, UT 84093-6289
Contact: Earl M. Wunderli, Tr.

Established in 1999.
Donor(s): Earl M. Wunderli, Corinne N. Wunderli.
Financial data (yr. ended 12/31/01): Grants paid, $300; assets, $24,286 (M); gifts received, $10,313; expenditures, $316; qualifying distributions, $300.
Trustees: Suzanne Larsen, Corinne N. Wunderli, Earl M. Wunderli.
EIN: 870633866

53998
George Lamont Richards Foundation
2315 E. 1300 S.
Salt Lake City, UT 84108-1940

Donor(s): George Lamont Richards.
Financial data (yr. ended 12/31/00): Grants paid, $275; assets, $2,436 (M); expenditures, $496; qualifying distributions, $275.
Limitations: Applications not accepted. Giving primarily in UT.
Application information: Contributes only to pre-selected organizations.
Officer: George Lamont Richards, Pres.
EIN: 876166330

53999
The Morgan Groesbeck Foundation
175 S. Main St., Ste. 900
Salt Lake City, UT 84111 (801) 363-6176

Established in 1998 in UT.
Donor(s): Morgan Limited Partnership.
Financial data (yr. ended 12/31/99): Grants paid, $92; assets, $6,439 (M); expenditures, $1,373; qualifying distributions, $107; giving activities include $92 for programs.
Application information: Application form required.
Trustees: Karen Matthews, Daisy Morgan, John Morgan, Jr.
EIN: 870577202

54000
James G. Morrison Foundation
c/o Wells Fargo Bank Northwest, N.A.
P.O. Box 628
Salt Lake City, UT 84111
Contact: W. John Lamborn, Trust Off., Wells Fargo Bank Northwest, N.A.

Financial data (yr. ended 08/31/01): Grants paid, $3; assets, $33 (M); expenditures, $3; qualifying distributions, $3.
Limitations: Giving limited to Salt Lake City, UT.
Application information: Application form not required.
Trustee: Wells Fargo Bank Northwest, N.A.
EIN: 942775551

54001
Judy K. Allen Family Foundation
57 W. 200 South, Ste. 300
Salt Lake City, UT 84101-1633

Established in 2001 in UT.
Financial data (yr. ended 12/31/01): Grants paid, $0; assets, $75,000 (M); gifts received, $75,000; expenditures, $1; qualifying distributions, $0.
Limitations: Applications not accepted. Giving primarily in UT.
Application information: Contributes only to pre-selected organizations.
Officer: Judy K. Allen, Mgr.
Trustee: L. Diane Dixon.
EIN: 800027793

54002
David H. Anderson Foundation, Inc.
333 W. 2230, N., Ste. 333
Provo, UT 84604

Established in 2001.
Donor(s): Bill Anderson.
Financial data (yr. ended 12/31/01): Grants paid, $0; assets, $38,945 (M); gifts received, $40,771; expenditures, $1,826; qualifying distributions, $40,179; giving activities include $40,179 for programs.
Limitations: Applications not accepted.

Application information: Contributes only to pre-selected organizations.
Officer: Bill Anderson, Mgr.
EIN: 870640951

54003
Jean & Jack Andreasen Animal Home
2395 S. 150 E.
Bountiful, UT 84010-5670 (801) 942-6027
Contact: John R. Andreasen, Tr.

Donor(s): John R. Andreasen, Jean Andreasen.
Financial data (yr. ended 12/31/01): Grants paid, $0; assets, $16,212 (M); expenditures, $566; qualifying distributions, $0.
Limitations: Giving primarily in Salt Lake City, UT.
Trustee: John R. Andreasen.
EIN: 942786986

54004
The Baker Family Ancestral Trust
1262 N. 475 E.
Orem, UT 84097

Established in 2000 in UT.
Donor(s): Reeves Wilmer Baker, Sharey Ann Baker.
Financial data (yr. ended 12/31/01): Grants paid, $0; assets, $4,546 (M); expenditures, $2,800; qualifying distributions, $0.
Limitations: Applications not accepted.
Application information: Contributes only to pre-selected organizations.
Trustees: Reeves Wilmer Baker, Sharey Ann Baker.
EIN: 876247745

54005
Hyrum S. Bouck and Cora Staker Bouck Family Organization
6112 Shirl St.
Salt Lake City, UT 84123-5379

Established in 1998 in UT.
Financial data (yr. ended 12/31/00): Grants paid, $0; assets, $1,455 (M); gifts received, $1,387; expenditures, $1,865; qualifying distributions, $1,865.
Officer: Dina A. Tuttle, Pres.
Directors: Bill J. Bouck, Brian L. Bouck, Denza Iverson, Jana Remy, Nedva Stephensen.
EIN: 870575068

54006
The Michael and Judi Bourne Foundation
2285 E. Walker Ln.
Salt Lake City, UT 84117 (801) 550-6610
Contact: Pam Jenkins

Established in 1998 in UT.
Donor(s): David R. Spafford.
Financial data (yr. ended 12/31/01): Grants paid, $0; assets, $396 (M); expenditures, $1; qualifying distributions, $0.
Trustees: Judi Bourne, Michael Bourne.
EIN: 870569583

54007
The Bourne-Waldo Foundation
2285 E. Walker Ln.
Salt Lake City, UT 84117 (801) 550-6610
Application address: 10854 S. 700 E., Ste. 222, Sandy, UT 84070
Contact: Pam Jenkins

Established in 1998 in UT.
Donor(s): David R. Spafford.
Financial data (yr. ended 12/31/01): Grants paid, $0; assets, $396 (M); expenditures, $1; qualifying distributions, $0.
Trustees: Peter Waldo, Stephanie Waldo.
EIN: 870569461

54008
Boys and Girls Club of S.L. Youth Developmental Foundation
675 E. 2100 S., No. 270
Salt Lake City, UT 84106

Established in 2001.
Financial data (yr. ended 12/31/01): Grants paid, $0; assets, $388,516 (M); expenditures, $0; qualifying distributions, $0.
Limitations: Applications not accepted.
Application information: Contributes only to pre-selected organizations.
Directors: David Nelson, Jim Jensen, Sam Williams.
EIN: 870677008

54009
The Bringing Hope Foundation
(Formerly Greenbacks Bringing Hope Foundation)
P.O. Box 27157
Salt Lake City, UT 84127 (801) 977-7777
FAX: (801) 977-7799; E-mail: info@bringinghope.net; URL: http://www.bringinghope.net

Established in 1998.
Donor(s): Greenbacks, Inc., Nine West Shoes.
Financial data (yr. ended 06/30/01): Grants paid, $0; assets, $160,421 (M); gifts received, $355,004; expenditures, $228,261; qualifying distributions, $228,233; giving activities include $228,200 for programs.
Limitations: Applications not accepted. Giving primarily in UT.
Application information: Contributes only to pre-selected organizations.
Officers and Directors:* Brent L. Bishop,* Pres.; Karen Mecham,* Secy. and Exec. Dir.; Richard Wolfley,* Treas.; David J. Asay, Joe Franceschi, Mark K. Holland, JoAnn B. Seghini, Jane Shock, Olene S. Walker.
EIN: 870609687
Codes: CS, CD

54010
Dick Burton Foundation
5955 Fardown Ct.
Holladay, UT 84121-1417

Established in 2000.
Donor(s): Richard R. Burton.
Financial data (yr. ended 06/30/01): Grants paid, $0; assets, $295,315 (M); gifts received, $62,450; expenditures, $100; qualifying distributions, $0.
Limitations: Applications not accepted.
Application information: Contributes only to pre-selected organizations.
Officers: Richard R. Burton, Chair.; Herald O. Johnson, Exec. Dir.
Directors: Harold Cannon, Teresa Jordon, Michael Riordan, Mike Stewart.
EIN: 870659848

54011
Collester Foundation
783 El Dorado Ct.
Leeds, UT 84746

Donor(s): Johanna P. Collester.
Financial data (yr. ended 12/31/01): Grants paid, $0; assets, $193,726 (M); expenditures, $1,070; qualifying distributions, $0.
Limitations: Applications not accepted.
Application information: Contributes only to pre-selected organizations.
Officer and Trustees:* Johanna P. Collester,* Pres.; Kurt A. Johnson, Roger P. McDivitt.
EIN: 870562480

54012
Albert J. Colton Foundation
77 W. 200 South, Ste. 400
Salt Lake City, UT 84101

Established in 1991 in UT.
Donor(s): Elizabeth W. Colton, Fabian S. Clendenin, Uarda S. Wright.
Financial data (yr. ended 11/30/01): Grants paid, $0; assets, $105,701 (M); gifts received, $47,679; expenditures, $2,118; qualifying distributions, $0.
Limitations: Applications not accepted. Giving primarily in Salt Lake City, UT.
Application information: Contributes only to pre-selected organizations.
Trustee: Thomas Christensen, Jr.
Administrative Committee: William H. Adams, Elizabeth W. Colton.
EIN: 870492249

54013
Stephen G. Covey Family Association, Inc.
1400 E. Parkview Dr.
Provo, UT 84604
Application address: 3355 N. University Ave., Ste. 200, Provo, UT 84604, tel.: (801) 377-9515
Contact: Stephen R. Covey, Tr.

Financial data (yr. ended 12/31/01): Grants paid, $0; assets, $47,744 (M); gifts received, $800; expenditures, $1,561; qualifying distributions, $0.
Limitations: Giving primarily in UT.
Trustees: John M.R. Covey, Stephen M.R. Covey, Stephen R. Covey, Cynthia Haller.
EIN: 870321445

54014
The John D. Eccles & Vera E. Eccles Family Foundation
1509 E. 4700 S.
Ogden, UT 84403

Established in 1990 in UT.
Donor(s): John D. Eccles, Vera E. Eccles.
Financial data (yr. ended 12/31/01): Grants paid, $0; assets, $1,270,177 (M); gifts received, $50,010; expenditures, $179,760; qualifying distributions, $0.
Limitations: Giving primarily in UT.
Officers: David Eccles, Mgr.; Vera E. Eccles, Mgr.; Sarah E. Taylor, Mgr.
EIN: 870478574

54015
Buddy and Dorothy C. Elliott Foundation
5010 S. 2125 W.
Roy, UT 84067-2511

Established in 1999 in UT.
Financial data (yr. ended 12/31/01): Grants paid, $0; assets, $1,131 (M); expenditures, $0; qualifying distributions, $0.
Limitations: Applications not accepted. Giving primarily in Salt Lake City, UT.
Application information: Contributes only to pre-selected organizations.
Officers: Buddy Elliott, Pres.; Michael Jon Elliot, V.P.; Barbara Ann Elliott Hinds, V.P.
EIN: 841367864

54016
Esse Quam Videri Foundation
1223 W. Chavez Dr.
South Jordan, UT 84095

Established in 1997 in UT.
Donor(s): Lynne Rich Lichfield, Diana Lichfield.
Financial data (yr. ended 12/31/01): Grants paid, $0; assets, $436,872 (M); gifts received, $8,082; expenditures, $23,559; qualifying distributions, $0.

54016—UTAH

Limitations: Applications not accepted. Giving primarily in UT.
Application information: Contributes only to pre-selected organizations.
Trustees: Diana Lichfield, Lynne Rich.
EIN: 870570969

54017
The Fagergren Family Foundation
388 E. Thousand Oaks Cir.
Salt Lake City, UT 84124

Established in 1996 in UT.
Financial data (yr. ended 12/31/00): Grants paid, $0; assets, $94,027 (M); expenditures, $143; qualifying distributions, $0.
Trustees: Shirley G. Fagergren, William C. Fagergren.
EIN: 870540728

54018
Festival City Foundation
P.O. Box 1103
Cedar City, UT 84721

Established in 1999 in UT.
Financial data (yr. ended 12/31/00): Grants paid, $0; assets, $816 (M); gifts received, $520,000; expenditures, $1,609,439; qualifying distributions, $0.
Officers: Fred C. Adams, Co-Pres.; Joe Melling, Co-Pres.
Trustee: Jyl Shuler.
EIN: 870621269

54019
Foundation for Change
1790 N. State St.
Orem, UT 84057

Established in 1999 in UT.
Financial data (yr. ended 12/31/00): Grants paid, $0; assets, $586 (M); gifts received, $100,351; expenditures, $112,196; qualifying distributions, $0.
Limitations: Applications not accepted.
Application information: Contributes only to pre-selected organizations.
Officers: T.O. Paul Harper, Pres.; Randy K. Hardman, V.P.; P. Scott Richards, Secy.
EIN: 870578534

54020
Simon Soul Sun Goe Foundation
98 N. Main St.
Brigham City, UT 84302 (435) 723-3404
Contact: Simon Soul Sun Goe, Pres.

Established in 1996 in UT.
Financial data (yr. ended 12/31/01): Grants paid, $0; assets, $1 (M); expenditures, $114; qualifying distributions, $0.
Officers and Trustee:* Simon Soul Sun Goe,* Pres.; Fred R. Burr, Secy.-Treas.
EIN: 870568432

54021
The D. Forrest Greene & Gerda M. Greene Foundation
1456 Penrose Dr.
Salt Lake City, UT 84103

Established in 2000 in UT.
Donor(s): Gloria Pitt, David H. Greene, Susan Parkinson, Randi Greene, Enid Greene.
Financial data (yr. ended 12/31/00): Grants paid, $0; assets, $122,411 (M); gifts received, $111,638; expenditures, $0; qualifying distributions, $0.
Trustees: Enid Greene, Mark S. Hawks, Susan Parkinson.
EIN: 943382293

54022
Keith Ray and Anna Lisa Massaro Halls Foundation
75 W. Center St.
Provo, UT 84601-4432

Established in 1996.
Donor(s): Anna Lisa Massaro Halls, Keith Ray Halls.
Financial data (yr. ended 12/31/01): Grants paid, $0; assets, $105,004 (M); expenditures, $200; qualifying distributions, $0.
Limitations: Applications not accepted. Giving primarily in UT.
Application information: Contributes only to pre-selected organizations.
Trustees: Anna Lisa Massaro Halls, Keith Ray Halls.
EIN: 870565430

54023
W. P. Harlin Foundation
10259 S. Grayboulder Ct.
Sandy, UT 84092

Established in 2001 in UT.
Donor(s): Catherine L. Harlin.
Financial data (yr. ended 12/31/01): Grants paid, $0; assets, $30,000 (M); gifts received, $30,000; expenditures, $0; qualifying distributions, $0.
Limitations: Applications not accepted.
Application information: Contributes only to pre-selected organizations.
Trustee: Catherine Harlin.
EIN: 870686972

54024
The Harris Family Foundation
6075 Spring Canyon Rd.
Ogden, UT 84403

Established in 1997 in UT.
Donor(s): R. Robert Harris.
Financial data (yr. ended 12/31/01): Grants paid, $0; assets, $190,676 (M); expenditures, $2,853; qualifying distributions, $0.
Limitations: Applications not accepted.
Application information: Contributes only to pre-selected organizations.
Trustees: Marcia P. Harris, R. Robert Harris, Carl Wolfram.
EIN: 841426110

54025
Hetzel Hoellein Family Foundation
1475 33rd St.
Ogden, UT 84403-1301

Established in 2001 in UT.
Donor(s): James Hoellein, Joanne Hoellein.
Financial data (yr. ended 12/31/01): Grants paid, $0; assets, $3,080,640 (M); gifts received, $2,994,412; expenditures, $500; qualifying distributions, $0.
Limitations: Applications not accepted.
Application information: Contributes only to pre-selected organizations.
Officers: James Hoellein, Pres.; Joanne Hoellein, V.P.
EIN: 870678568

54026
Blaine T. & Barbara H. Hudson Private Foundation
1241 N. Fort Canyon Rd.
Alpine, UT 84004 (801) 756-1596
Contact: Blaine T. Hudson, Pres.

Established in 2000 in UT.

Financial data (yr. ended 12/31/00): Grants paid, $0; assets, $5,030 (M); gifts received, $5,000; expenditures, $0; qualifying distributions, $0.
Officers: Blaine T. Hudson, Pres.; Barbara H. Hudson, V.P.
Director: Mark B. Hudson.
EIN: 870660697

54027
Joseph Educational Foundation
3521 N. University Ave., No. 200
Provo, UT 84604-5149

Established in 1989.
Financial data (yr. ended 12/31/01): Grants paid, $0; assets, $9,190 (M); gifts received, $6,024; expenditures, $2,276; qualifying distributions, $0.
Trustees: Reid E. Bankhead, Douglas W. Morrison, Susan B. Morrison.
EIN: 870469833

54028
Frederick R. Lawson Foundation
P.O. Box 45385
Salt Lake City, UT 84145-0385

Established in 2000 in UT.
Donor(s): Frederick R. Lawson.
Financial data (yr. ended 12/31/00): Grants paid, $0; assets, $56,424 (M); gifts received, $53,063; expenditures, $0; qualifying distributions, $0.
Limitations: Applications not accepted.
Application information: Contributes only to pre-selected organizations.
Trustees: Clark P. Giles, Frederick R. Lawson, Frederick Q. Lawson, Peter Q. Lawson, Herbert C. Livsey, JoAnne L. Shrontz.
EIN: 870663253

54029
MesoAmerican Research Foundation
350 S. 400 E., Ste. 201
Salt Lake City, UT 84111-2934

Donor(s): The Lighthouse Foundation, SPAN.
Financial data (yr. ended 12/31/01): Grants paid, $0; assets, $37,984 (M); gifts received, $141,936; expenditures, $140,511; qualifying distributions, $0.
Officers: Tim M. Tucker, Pres.; Dennis R. Webb, V.P.; Lynn G. Robbins, Secy.-Treas.
EIN: 860731046

54030
Mishler Family Research, Inc.
556 N. 500 E.
Orem, UT 84097

Established in 2000 in UT.
Financial data (yr. ended 12/31/01): Grants paid, $0; assets, $4,805 (M); gifts received, $4,750; expenditures, $1,883; qualifying distributions, $0.
Director: Hal Mishler.
EIN: 870626064

54031
Charles & Gail Muskavitch Foundation
P.O. Box 628
Salt Lake City, UT 84110
Application address: c/o Lynn James, P.O. Box 20160, Long Beach, CA 90801-3160

Established in 2001 in CA.
Donor(s): Charles Muskavitch, Gail Muskavitch.
Financial data (yr. ended 12/31/01): Grants paid, $0; assets, $296,744 (M); gifts received, $284,283; expenditures, $1,397; qualifying distributions, $0.
Officers: Gail Muskavitch, Pres.; Timothy Woodall, Secy.-Treas.
Director: Charles Muskavitch.
EIN: 680466474

54032
The Pacile Family Foundation
8826 Hidden Oak Dr.
Salt Lake City, UT 84121

Established in 2000 in UT.
Donor(s): Pacile Investments, LLC.
Financial data (yr. ended 12/31/01): Grants paid, $0; assets, $2,426 (M); expenditures, $862; qualifying distributions, $212.
Limitations: Applications not accepted. Giving primarily in CA.
Application information: Contributes only to pre-selected organizations.
Officers: Raymond R. Pacile, Pres.; Theresa M. Pacile, V.P.; L. Allyson Ralphs, Secy.-Treas.
EIN: 870655206
Codes: CS

54033
Plum Tree Foundation
c/o Walter J. Plumb, III
809 E. Edgehill Rd.
Salt Lake City, UT 84103

Established in 1999.
Donor(s): Walter J. Plumb III.
Financial data (yr. ended 12/31/99): Grants paid, $0; assets, $188,000 (M); gifts received, $188,000; expenditures, $0; qualifying distributions, $0.
Trustee: Walter J. Plumb III.
EIN: 870624604

54034
Providence Foundation
2498 Walker Ln.
Salt Lake City, UT 84117

Established in 2000 in UT.
Donor(s): Patricia H. Falk.
Financial data (yr. ended 12/31/00): Grants paid, $0; assets, $21,152 (M); gifts received, $20,264; expenditures, $0; qualifying distributions, $0.
Limitations: Applications not accepted.
Application information: Contributes only to pre-selected organizations.
Officer: Patricia H. Falk, Chair.
Director: Jayne B. Clifford.
Trustees: Gregory N. Barrick, M. Ray Walker.
EIN: 870666125

54035
Redhill Foundation
c/o Stephen R. Covey
3355 N. University Ave., Ste. 200
Provo, UT 84604-6604 (801) 377-9215

Established in 1998 in UT.
Donor(s): Stephen R. Covey, Sandra M. Covey.
Financial data (yr. ended 12/31/01): Grants paid, $0; assets, $49,590 (M); expenditures, $551; qualifying distributions, $0.
Application information: Application form not required.
Trustees: Colleen Covey Brown, Maria Covey Cole, David M.R. Covey, Sandra M. Covey, Sean M. Covey, Stephen M.R. Covey, Stephen R. Covey, Cynthia Covey Haller, Catherine Covey Sagers.
EIN: 870572202

54036
James W. and Carolyn O. Ritchie Foundation
P.O. Box 127
Heber City, UT 84032
Contact: James W. Ritchie, Pres.

Established in 1995 in UT.
Donor(s): James W. Ritchie.
Financial data (yr. ended 12/31/01): Grants paid, $0; assets, $437,741 (M); expenditures, $903; qualifying distributions, $0.
Officer: James W. Ritchie, Pres.
EIN: 870541154

54037
The Roderick Earl Ross Memorial Foundation
P.O. Box 2460
Salt Lake City, UT 84110-2460
(801) 579-3400
Contact: R. Earl Ross, Secy.

Established around 1971.
Financial data (yr. ended 09/30/01): Grants paid, $0; assets, $138,587 (M); expenditures, $647; qualifying distributions, $0.
Limitations: Giving primarily in UT.
Officers and Trustees:* E. Rod Ross,* Pres.; Diane Gandre,* V.P.; Raymond Earl Ross,* Secy.
EIN: 237083407

54038
Silver Foundation
P.O. Box 628
Salt Lake City, UT 84110-0628

Incorporated in 1959 in CO.
Donor(s): Bernard Silver, Harold F. Silver, Ruth S. Silver, Silver Corp.
Financial data (yr. ended 12/31/01): Grants paid, $0; assets, $58,135 (M); expenditures, $3,911; qualifying distributions, $0.
Limitations: Applications not accepted. Giving limited to Denver, CO.
Application information: Contributes only to pre-selected organizations.
Officers: Cherry B. Silver, Pres.; Cannon F. Silver, V.P.; Bernard Silver, Secy.-Treas.
EIN: 846036560

54039
Hugh C. Smith Foundation
c/o Gilbert & Stewart
190 W. 800 N., No. 100
Provo, UT 84601

Donor(s): Hugh C. Smith.
Financial data (yr. ended 12/31/01): Grants paid, $0; assets, $4,355 (M); expenditures, $0; qualifying distributions, $0.
Limitations: Applications not accepted. Giving primarily in Orem, UT.
Application information: Contributes only to pre-selected organizations.
Officer: Paul C. Smith, Secy.
EIN: 237071347

54040
Chester A. Stewart Charitable Trust
c/o Wells Fargo Bank Northwest, N.A.
180 S. Main St.
Salt Lake City, UT 84101

Established in 2001 in UT.
Donor(s): Chester A. Stewart.‡
Financial data (yr. ended 05/31/01): Grants paid, $0; assets, $224,019 (M); gifts received, $213,542; expenditures, $875; qualifying distributions, $219.
Limitations: Applications not accepted.
Application information: Contributes only to pre-selected organizations.
Trustee: Wells Fargo Bank Northwest, N.A.
EIN: 870670154

54041
Van Cott, Bagley, Cornwall & McCarthy Foundation
50 S. Main St., Ste. 1600
Salt Lake City, UT 84144

Established in 1988 in UT.
Financial data (yr. ended 12/31/01): Grants paid, $0; assets, $17 (M); expenditures, $0; qualifying distributions, $0.
Officers: Stephen D. Swindle, Pres.; Brent J. Giaugue, V.P.; J. Keith Adams, Secy.-Treas.
Trustee: David E. Salisbury.
EIN: 870455136

54042
Wheelwright Family Charitable Foundation
1550 E. Weber Canyon Rd., Box 21
Oakley, UT 84055

Established in 2001 in UT.
Donor(s): The Steven C. Wheelwright Trust, The Margaret S. Wheelwright Trust.
Financial data (yr. ended 12/31/01): Grants paid, $0; assets, $4,681 (M); gifts received, $20,000; expenditures, $15,387; qualifying distributions, $0.
Trustees: Melinda W. Brown, S. Douglas Brown, Marianne W. Lewis, Mick Lewis, Kristen W. Taylor, Robert M. Taylor, Margaret S. Wheelwright, Nancy H. Wheelwright, Spencer D. Wheelwright, Steven C. Wheelwright.
EIN: 870672839

54043
George B. and Oma E. Wilcox and Gibbs M. and Catherine W. Smith Charitable Foundation
123 N. Flint St.
Kaysville, UT 84037

Established in 2000 in UT.
Donor(s): George W. Wilcox Marital Trust, Oma E. Wilcox.
Financial data (yr. ended 12/31/00): Grants paid, $0; assets, $1,717,476 (M); gifts received, $1,619,501; expenditures, $434; qualifying distributions, $0.
Limitations: Applications not accepted.
Application information: Contributes only to pre-selected organizations.
Trustees: E. Lynn Hansen, Catherine W. Smith, Gibbs M. Smith.
EIN: 870665162

54044
The Roger R. Williams Foundation for Family Prevention of Heart Disease
1339 W. Palmer Park Ln.
South Jordan, UT 84095

Established in 1998 in UT.
Financial data (yr. ended 12/31/00): Grants paid, $0; assets, $45,158 (M); expenditures, $3,335; qualifying distributions, $3,336.
Limitations: Applications not accepted.
Application information: Contributes only to pre-selected organizations.
Trustees: Paul Hopkins, Jean Marc Lalonel, Susan Stephenson, Thomas Williams.
EIN: 870622406

VERMONT

54045
Vermont Community Foundation
3 Court St.
P.O. Box 30
Middlebury, VT 05753 (802) 388-3355
FAX: (802) 388-3398; E-mail: vcf@vermontcf.org; URL: http://www.vermontcf.org
Contact: Faith I. Brown

Established in 1986 in VT.
Financial data (yr. ended 12/31/01): Grants paid, $8,147,265; assets, $62,817,882 (L); gifts received, $9,636,391; expenditures, $8,147,265.
Limitations: Giving limited to VT.
Publications: Annual report, multi-year report, application guidelines, financial statement, grants list, informational brochure (including application guidelines), program policy statement, occasional report.
Application information: Proposal summary form required. Application form not required.
Officers and Directors:* John H. Marshall,* Chair.; Richard C. White,* Vice-Chair.; Charles R. Cummings,* Secy.; Alec Webb,* Treas.; Lawrence H. Bruce, Jr., John T. Ewing, Deborah W. Granquist, Cornelius D. Hogan, Ellen Kahler, George E. Little, Jr., Lisa Lorimer, Carolyn C. Roberts, John F. Taylor, Vicky Young.
EIN: 222712160
Codes: CM, FD

54046
Ben Cohen Charitable Trust
c/o GHP Advisors, PC
P.O. Box 5550
Burlington, VT 05402-5550
Application address: 38 Wildwood Dr., Essex Junction, VT 05452
Contact: Duane Peterson, Mgr.

Established in 2000 in VT.
Donor(s): Bennet R. Cohen.
Financial data (yr. ended 10/31/01): Grants paid, $4,500,000; assets, $3,089,041 (M); gifts received, $7,500,000; expenditures, $4,510,522; qualifying distributions, $4,500,000.
Limitations: Giving on a national basis.
Application information: Application form not required.
Trustee: Bennet R. Cohen.
Officer: Duane Peterson, Mgr.
EIN: 030368595
Codes: FD

54047
Ben & Jerry's Foundation, Inc.
30 Community Dr.
South Burlington, VT 05403 (802) 846-1500
URL: http://www.benjerry.com/foundation/index.html
Contact: Debby Kessler, Admin. Asst.

Established in 1985 in NY.
Donor(s): Ben & Jerry's Homemade Inc.
Financial data (yr. ended 12/31/01): Grants paid, $1,824,994; assets, $5,864,790 (M); gifts received, $1,429,857; expenditures, $1,897,574; qualifying distributions, $1,824,994.
Limitations: Giving limited to the U.S. and its territories.
Publications: Annual report, application guidelines, grants list.
Application information: Preliminary application must be submitted 8 weeks prior to any deadline to be considered for that deadline. Full proposals accepted following foundation invitation only. Accepts NNG Common Grant Application; however, applicant must contact foundation before submitting. Do not submit proposals via FedEx or express mail. Application form required.
Officers and Trustees:* Jerry Greenfield,* Pres.; Elizabeth Bankowski,* Secy.; Jeffrey Furman,* Treas.; Rebecca Golden, Fdn. Dir.
EIN: 030300865
Codes: CS, FD, CD

54048
General Educational Fund, Inc.
c/o Merchants Trust Co.
P.O. Box 8490
Burlington, VT 05402
Contact: Linda Fischer Livingstone, Trust Admin.

Incorporated in 1918 in VT.
Donor(s): Emma Eliza Curtis,‡ Lorenzo E. Woodhouse.‡
Financial data (yr. ended 07/31/01): Grants paid, $861,569; assets, $25,307,262 (M); gifts received, $2,622; expenditures, $946,188; qualifying distributions, $851,569.
Limitations: Giving limited to VT residents.
Application information: Applicants must apply through Vermont Student Assistance Corp. Application form required.
Officer: Geoffrey Hesslink, Pres.
Trustees: Joseph Boutin, Michael Tuttle.
EIN: 036009912
Codes: FD, GTI

54049
Lintilhac Foundation
886 North Gate Rd.
Shelburne, VT 05482 (802) 985-4106
FAX: (802) 985-3725
Contact: Crea S. Lintilhac, Pres.

Established in 1975.
Donor(s): Claire Malcolm Lintilhac.‡
Financial data (yr. ended 12/31/00): Grants paid, $770,969; assets, $18,876,756 (M); gifts received, $702,733; expenditures, $977,444; qualifying distributions, $832,417.
Limitations: Giving primarily in north central VT, including Chittenden, Lamoille, and Washington counties.
Publications: Biennial report.
Application information: Application form not required.
Officers and Directors:* Crea S. Lintilhac,* Pres.; Philip M. Lintilhac,* V.P. and Secy.; Raeman P. Sopher,* Treas.
EIN: 510176851
Codes: FD

54050
Frank M. & Olive E. Gilman Foundation
c/o Frank Gilman, Gilman Office Ctr.
220 Holiday Dr., No. 27
White River Junction, VT 05001
(802) 295-3358

Established in 1991 in VT; funded in 1992.
Donor(s): Frank Gilman, Olive Gilman.
Financial data (yr. ended 12/31/01): Grants paid, $576,900; assets, $11,206,253 (M); expenditures, $588,783; qualifying distributions, $583,965.
Limitations: Giving limited to Grafton County, NH, and Orange and Windsor counties, VT.
Officers: Frank Gilman, Pres.; Brenda Jones, V.P.; Reginald Jones, V.P.; Elizabeth Jones, Secy.-Treas.
EIN: 030330527
Codes: FD

54051
Vermont Foundation for Children & Families
208 Flynn Ave.
Burlington, VT 05401

Established in 1998 in VT.
Financial data (yr. ended 12/31/01): Grants paid, $483,640; assets, $5,168,667 (M); expenditures, $526,522; qualifying distributions, $483,758.
Limitations: Applications not accepted. Giving primarily in Burlington, VT.
Application information: Contributes only to pre-selected organizations.
Officers: David Austin, Chair.; Charles H. Stringer, Pres.; Kathleen A. Coates, Secy.-Treas.
Directors: Mark Baglini, Gerri Bloomberg, Dorothea Hanna, Myron Sopher.
EIN: 223030227
Codes: FD

54052
Terry F. Allen Family Charitable Trust
256 Fuller Mountain Rd.
Ferrisburg, VT 05456

Established in 1997.
Donor(s): Terry F. Allen.
Financial data (yr. ended 12/31/00): Grants paid, $453,263; assets, $759,136 (M); expenditures, $514,395; qualifying distributions, $448,472.
Limitations: Applications not accepted. Giving primarily in VT.
Application information: Contributes only to pre-selected organizations.
Director: Terry F. Allen.
EIN: 046837908
Codes: FD

54053
William T. & Marie J. Henderson Foundation, Inc.
P.O. Box 600
Stowe, VT 05672
Contact: William T. Henderson, Pres.

Established in 1968 in NJ.
Financial data (yr. ended 11/30/01): Grants paid, $408,300; assets, $2,545,691 (M); expenditures, $448,032; qualifying distributions, $410,601.
Limitations: Applications not accepted. Giving primarily in NJ.
Application information: Contributes only to pre-selected organizations.
Officer and Trustees:* William T. Henderson,* Pres.; John T. Magnier, Marie J. Magnier, Regina Mathews.
EIN: 226033693
Codes: FD

54054
Charles P. Ferro Foundation
25 Bayview St.
Burlington, VT 05401 (802) 660-2765
E-mail: bonnie.ferro@verizon.net
Contact: Bonnie Ferro, Co-Exec. Dir.

Established in 1993.
Financial data (yr. ended 12/31/01): Grants paid, $316,250; assets, $8,447,462 (M); expenditures, $387,991; qualifying distributions, $316,250.
Limitations: Giving on a national basis.
Directors: Bonnie Ferro, Co-Exec. Dir.; Marianne Ferro, Co-Exec. Dir.
Trustees: Anthony V. Curto, Vera Dosky, Patrick Ferro, Shirley Ferro, Edward Friedhoff.
EIN: 223253710
Codes: FD

54055
Tarrant Family Foundation
c/o Fairholt
570 S. Prospect St.
Burlington, VT 05401 (802) 860-6188
Contact: Ronald L. Roberts

Established in 1996.
Donor(s): Richard Tarrant.
Financial data (yr. ended 12/31/99): Grants paid, $250,000; assets, $4,685,045 (M); expenditures, $257,829; qualifying distributions, $249,890.
Limitations: Giving primarily in VT, with emphasis in Chittenden County.
Officers: Amy E. Tarrant, Pres.; Jeremiah Tarrant, V.P. and Treas.; Richard E. Tarrant, Secy.
EIN: 061468923
Codes: TN

54056
Mortimer R. Proctor Trust
c/o Chittenden Trust Co.
P.O. Box 729
Rutland, VT 05702-0729
Contact: Jeanne Gilbert

Established around 1978.
Financial data (yr. ended 12/31/01): Grants paid, $224,232; assets, $3,998,119 (M); expenditures, $287,677; qualifying distributions, $222,682.
Limitations: Giving limited to Proctor, VT.
Application information: Application form required.
Trustee: Chittenden Trust Co.
EIN: 036020099
Codes: FD2

54057
Carris Corporate Foundation, Inc.
(Formerly The Carris Reels Fund)
P.O. Box 696
Rutland, VT 05702-0696

Established in 1990.
Donor(s): Carris Reels, Inc., Bridge Manufacturing, Inc., Vermont Tubbs, Inc.
Financial data (yr. ended 12/31/01): Grants paid, $216,952; assets, $149,814 (M); gifts received, $130,034; expenditures, $220,533; qualifying distributions, $216,853.
Limitations: Applications not accepted. Giving primarily in VT.
Application information: Contributes only to pre-selected organizations.
Officers: William Carris, Pres.; Barbara Carris, V.P.; Thomas Dowling, Secy.; David Fitz-Gerald, Treas.
EIN: 030326934
Codes: CS, FD2, CD

54058
Alcyon Foundation
c/o Frederick H. West
P.O. Box 1015, Prospect St.
Manchester, VT 05254

Established in 1994 in DE.
Donor(s): Lucile E. Dupont Flint, Frederick H. West, Mrs. Frederick H. West.
Financial data (yr. ended 12/31/01): Grants paid, $208,550; assets, $4,056,682 (M); gifts received, $74,955; expenditures, $225,403; qualifying distributions, $219,403.
Limitations: Applications not accepted. Giving primarily in VT.
Application information: Contributes only to pre-selected organizations.
Officers: Frederick H. West, Pres. and Treas.; Constance F. West, V.P. and Secy.
EIN: 510355030
Codes: FD2

54059
The Kelsey Trust
c/o Vermont Community Foundation
P.O. Box 30
Middlebury, VT 05753 (802) 388-3355
Contact: Judy Dunning, Grants Mgr.

Established in 1988 in MA.
Donor(s): Sally P. Johnson.
Financial data (yr. ended 06/30/01): Grants paid, $205,815; assets, $4,220,534 (M); gifts received, $107,000; expenditures, $228,446; qualifying distributions, $209,979.
Limitations: Giving limited to the Lake Champlain Valley Drainage Basin region: the eastern Adirondacks in NY, and western VT, north of Rutland.
Publications: Program policy statement, application guidelines, occasional report.
Application information: Application form required.
Trustees: Paula D. Johnson, Sally P. Johnson, Stephen P. Johnson.
EIN: 046609917
Codes: FD2

54060
G.D.S. Legacy Foundation, Inc.
80 Ordway Shore Rd.
Shelburne, VT 05482 (802) 985-2998
Contact: Peter D. Swift, Tr.

Established in 2000 in VT.
Donor(s): Peter D. Swift.
Financial data (yr. ended 12/31/01): Grants paid, $200,000; assets, $4,384,172 (M); gifts received, $550,500; expenditures, $259,930; qualifying distributions, $211,930.
Limitations: Giving primarily in Washington, DC, NY, and VT.
Trustees: Ted Cronin, William G. Post, Jr., Peter D. Swift.
EIN: 030368174
Codes: FD2

54061
Maya Educational Foundation
P.O. Box 38, Rte. 106
South Woodstock, VT 05071 (802) 457-1199
E-mail: mayaedfund@aol.com
Contact: Christopher Lutz, Tr.

Established in 1993 in VT.
Donor(s): Christopher Lutz.
Financial data (yr. ended 12/31/01): Grants paid, $178,605; assets, $400,266 (M); gifts received, $285,587; expenditures, $201,673; qualifying distributions, $178,605.
Limitations: Applications not accepted. Giving primarily in Guatemala.
Officers and Trustees:* Victor Montejo,* Pres.; Brenda Rosenbaum,* V.P.; Armando Alfonzo, Christopher Lutz, Ian Lutz, Sarah Lutz, Marilyn M. Moors, Kay Warren.
EIN: 030335159
Codes: FD2, GTI

54062
Copley Fund
22 Portland St.
Morrisville, VT 05661 (802) 888-2000
Application address: P.O. Box 696, Morrisville, VT 05661
Contact: Richard C. Sargent, Tr.

Established in 1969 in VT.
Financial data (yr. ended 12/31/01): Grants paid, $168,432; assets, $3,681,471 (M); expenditures, $207,057; qualifying distributions, $168,432.
Limitations: Giving limited to Lamoille County, VT.
Trustees: Robert Parker, Richard C. Sargent.
EIN: 036006013
Codes: FD2, GTI

54063
Oakland Foundation, Inc.
P.O. Box 491
Stowe, VT 05672-0491 (802) 253-5115
Application address: P.O. Box 3680, Parkersburg, WV 26103; FAX: (802) 253-6877; E-mail: oakland@oak.org
Contact: Katherine Lutz Coppock, Pres.

Established in 1996 in VT and WV.
Donor(s): Veronica Sammel Lutz.‡
Financial data (yr. ended 12/31/01): Grants paid, $151,517; assets, $3,729,603 (M); expenditures, $189,177; qualifying distributions, $151,517.
Limitations: Giving primarily in VT and WV.
Publications: Annual report, application guidelines.
Application information: Application form required.
Officers and Directors:* Katherine Lutz Coppock,* Pres. and Treas.; John S. Lutz,* V.P.; Elizabeth S. Lutz,* Secy.
EIN: 550754353
Codes: FD2

54064
NSB Foundation, Inc.
c/o Northfield Savings Bank
33 S. Main St.
Northfield, VT 05663 (802) 485-5291
URL: http://www.enorthfield.com
Contact: Carol Holt, Secy.

Established in 2000 in VT.
Donor(s): Northfield Savings Bank.
Financial data (yr. ended 12/31/01): Grants paid, $140,700; assets, $968,773 (M); gifts received, $170,300; expenditures, $170,006; qualifying distributions, $146,813.
Limitations: Giving limited to central VT.
Application information: Application form required.
Officers: Leo C. Laferriere, Pres.; Carol Holt, Secy.; Wayne Kowalski, Treas.
Directors: G. William Ellis, Anne L. Gould, Charles E. Haynes, Charles E. Mason.
EIN: 311713065
Codes: CS, FD2, CD

54065
Frank and Brinna Sands Foundation
c/o Conrad Reining
319 Caldwell Rd.
East Thetford, VT 05043

Established in 1996 in VT.
Donor(s): Brinna B. Sands, Frank E. Sands II.
Financial data (yr. ended 11/30/01): Grants paid, $135,250; assets, $2,080,500 (M); gifts received, $91,422; expenditures, $148,117; qualifying distributions, $142,001.
Limitations: Applications not accepted. Giving primarily in CT and VT.
Application information: Contributes only to pre-selected organizations.
Officers and Directors:* Brinna B. Sands,* Pres.; Frank E. Sands II,* V.P. and Secy.; Jennifer B. Kitchel, Conrad Reining.
EIN: 043342111
Codes: FD2

54066
Merchants Bank Foundation, Inc.
c/o Merchants Bank
275 Kennedy Dr.
South Burlington, VT 05403-6785
(802) 658-3400
Contact: Jennifer Varin, Treas.

Established in 1967 in VT.
Donor(s): Merchants Bancshares, Inc., Merchants Bank.
Financial data (yr. ended 08/31/01): Grants paid, $129,084; assets, $1,150,331 (M); gifts received, $125,000; expenditures, $143,416; qualifying distributions, $129,084.
Limitations: Giving primarily in VT.
Publications: Application guidelines.
Application information: Contact closest neighboring branch of Merchants Bank for application. Application form required.
Officers and Trustees:* Thomas S. Leavitt,* Chair.; Joseph L. Boutin,* Pres.; Jennifer L. Varin,* Treas.; Pamela P. Steece, Susan B. Thibeault, Kim G. Wood.
EIN: 036016628
Codes: CS, FD2, CD

54067
Warner Home for Little Wanderers
4 Forest Hill Dr.
St. Albans, VT 05478
Contact: Donna Roby, Treas.

Financial data (yr. ended 04/30/01): Grants paid, $127,255; assets, $1,658,942 (M); gifts received, $77,914; expenditures, $139,260; qualifying distributions, $127,998.
Limitations: Giving limited to Franklin County, VT.
Application information: Applicants must be a resident of Franklin County, VT, under the age of 21.
Officers: Julia Cahill, Pres.; Kay Ready, V.P.; Verna Kelley, Secy.; Donna Roby, Treas.
EIN: 030179439
Codes: FD2, GTI

54068
Pecor Family Foundation
King St. Dock
Burlington, VT 05401-5258 (802) 864-9804
Contact: Henry T. Sorrell, Treas.

Established in 1983 in VT.
Donor(s): Lake Champlain Cable T.V., Richmond Cable T.V.
Financial data (yr. ended 06/30/01): Grants paid, $126,967; assets, $577,064 (M); gifts received, $125,000; expenditures, $132,103; qualifying distributions, $132,103.
Limitations: Applications not accepted. Giving limited to VT.
Application information: Contributes only to pre-selected organizations.
Officers and Directors:* Ray C. Pecor,* Pres.; Jean G. Pecor,* V.P.; Henry T. Sorrell,* Treas.; Raymond C. Pecor III, Alan Sylvester.
EIN: 030287699
Codes: FD2

54069
The Redducs Chartered Foundation Corp.
c/o Fred Tiballi & Assoc., PC
120 Pine St.
Burlington, VT 05401
Contact: Frederick P. Tiballi, Exec. Dir.

Established in 1998 in FL and VT.
Donor(s): Mary Gale Scudder, Edward Scudder, Jr., Edward Scudder III, Katherine Scudder Tiballi.
Financial data (yr. ended 12/31/01): Grants paid, $126,000; assets, $4,366,299 (M); expenditures, $202,000; qualifying distributions, $171,456.
Limitations: Giving primarily in CA and VT.
Application information: Application form not required.
Officers and Directors:* Edward Scudder, Jr.,* Chair.; Katherine Scudder Tiballi,* Vice-Chair.; Edward Scudder III,* Pres.; Mary Gale Scudder,* V.P.; Robert F. Scudder,* V.P.; Fred Tiballi, Exec. Dir.
EIN: 650840245
Codes: FD2

54070
Green Mountain Coffee Roasters Foundation
33 Coffee Ln.
Waterbury, VT 05676
Contact: John Winter, Admin.

Established in 2000 in VT.
Donor(s): Robert Stiller.
Financial data (yr. ended 09/30/01): Grants paid, $124,361; assets, $14,281 (M); gifts received, $143,486; expenditures, $130,147; qualifying distributions, $128,187.
Officers: Robert Stiller, Pres.; Robert Britt, V.P. and Secy.; Paul Comey, V.P.; John Winter, Admin.
EIN: 030341004
Codes: FD2

54071
A. H. Rubenfeld Fund, Inc.
P.O. Box 8
Shelburne, VT 05482
Contact: John A. Kern, Mgr.

Established in 1951.
Donor(s): Mrs. Aaron H. Rubenfeld.‡
Financial data (yr. ended 12/31/01): Grants paid, $123,900; assets, $2,704,244 (M); expenditures, $169,723; qualifying distributions, $134,714.
Limitations: Applications not accepted. Giving primarily in San Francisco and San Diego, CA.
Application information: Contributes only to pre-selected organizations.
Officers and Directors:* Irving J. Kern,* Pres.; John A. Kern,* Treas. and Mgr.
EIN: 136161136
Codes: FD2

54072
The Geist Foundation
842 Dorset West Rd.
Dorset, VT 05251
Contact: Madeline R. Bloom, Tr.

Incorporated about 1959 in NJ.
Donor(s): Irving Geist.‡
Financial data (yr. ended 09/30/01): Grants paid, $104,430; assets, $602,943 (M); expenditures, $119,360; qualifying distributions, $111,214.
Limitations: Giving primarily in NJ and NY.
Application information: Application form not required.
Trustees: Alan K. Bloom, Jeffrey Bloom, Madeline R. Bloom.
EIN: 226059859
Codes: FD2

54073
The Lynchpin Foundation, Inc.
c/o Stewart E. Read
P.O. Box 7
Peru, VT 05152

Established n 1999 in VT.
Donor(s): Signa L. Mills.
Financial data (yr. ended 08/31/01): Grants paid, $100,700; assets, $43,378 (M); expenditures, $109,646; qualifying distributions, $100,689.
Limitations: Applications not accepted.
Application information: Contributes only to pre-selected organizations.
Officers: Signa L. Read, Pres.; Susan R. Cronin, V.P.; Sandra L. Read, V.P.; John H. Williams II, Secy.; Stewart W. Read, Treas.
EIN: 030358659
Codes: FD2

54074
The Arthur H. Scott Memorial Trust
c/o Chittenden Bank, Trust Dept.
2 Burlington Sq., P.O. Box 820
Burlington, VT 05402

Established in 1990 in VT.
Financial data (yr. ended 12/31/01): Grants paid, $97,976; assets, $1,512,590 (M); expenditures, $101,335; qualifying distributions, $87,502.
Limitations: Applications not accepted. Giving limited to residents of Chelsea, Hinesburg, and Northfield, VT.
Application information: Contributes only to pre-selected organizations.
Trustee: Chittenden Bank.
EIN: 036047004
Codes: FD2, GTI

54075
The Morris and Bessie Altman Foundation
P.O. Box 458
Shelburne, VT 05482 (802) 985-9943
Contact: Peter Stern, Dir.

Established in 1989 in VT.
Donor(s): P. Stern Charitable Remainder Trust, Peter Stern.
Financial data (yr. ended 06/30/01): Grants paid, $93,100; assets, $1,212,999 (M); expenditures, $116,547; qualifying distributions, $93,100.
Limitations: Giving primarily in VT.
Directors: Abbi Stern, Marjorie Stern, Peter Stern, Robert Stern, Sarena Stern.
EIN: 030323120
Codes: FD2

54076
George A. Dascomb Charitable Trust
P.O. Box 22
Bellows Falls, VT 05101-0022
Application address: 5 Hyde St., Bellows Falls, VT 05101
Contact: Paul Brandon, Tr.

Established in 1931 in VT.
Financial data (yr. ended 12/31/01): Grants paid, $92,102; assets, $3,031,351 (M); expenditures, $112,572; qualifying distributions, $92,102.
Limitations: Giving limited to Westminster, VT.
Application information: Application form not required.
Trustees: Paul Brandon, George Dascomb III, Daniel Higgins.
EIN: 036005799
Codes: FD2

54077
McKenzie Family Charitable Trust
c/o J. Michael McKenzie
P.O. Box 285
Putney, VT 05346

Established in 1993 in VT.
Donor(s): J. Michael McKenzie.
Financial data (yr. ended 12/31/01): Grants paid, $90,711; assets, $1,809,618 (M); expenditures, $96,755; qualifying distributions, $91,763.
Limitations: Applications not accepted. Giving primarily in NJ and VT.
Application information: Contributes only to pre-selected organizations.
Trustee: J. Michael McKenzie.

EIN: 226596096
Codes: FD2

54078
John L. Norris, Jr. & Barbara Norris Allen Charitable Foundation
P.O. Box 145
Lyndonville, VT 05851

Established in 1995 in VT.
Donor(s): John L. Norris, Jr.
Financial data (yr. ended 12/31/01): Grants paid, $89,000; assets, $1,591,095 (M); gifts received, $234,800; expenditures, $99,872; qualifying distributions, $88,798.
Limitations: Applications not accepted.
Application information: Contributes only to pre-selected organizations.
Officers: John L. Norris, Jr., Pres. and Treas.; Barbara Norris Allen, V.P.; Charles C. Allen III, Secy.
EIN: 030346151
Codes: FD2

54079
Lamson-Howell Foundation, Inc.
2968 Fish Hill Rd.
Randolph, VT 05060
Contact: Hannah Jeffery, Pres.

Established about 1972.
Donor(s): Samuel L. Howell.‡
Financial data (yr. ended 09/30/01): Grants paid, $88,980; assets, $20,104 (M); gifts received, $110,209; expenditures, $91,060; qualifying distributions, $88,304.
Limitations: Giving limited to Randolph, VT, and contiguous towns.
Application information: Application form not required.
Officers and Trustees:* Hannah Jeffery,* Pres.; Robert J. Lamson,* Secy.; Karl Miller,* Treas.; Steven Dimick.
EIN: 036010574
Codes: FD2

54080
Meadowhill Fund, Inc.
c/o John Rosenthal
210 Holmes Rd.
Charlotte, VT 05445

Donor(s): Morton Rosenthal.
Financial data (yr. ended 12/31/01): Grants paid, $88,315; assets, $1,333,714 (M); gifts received, $500,000; expenditures, $90,227; qualifying distributions, $87,465.
Limitations: Applications not accepted. Giving primarily in NY.
Application information: Contributes only to pre-selected organizations.
Officers: John Rosenthal, Pres.; Jane Goldman, V.P.; Sarah Hart, Treas.; Judy Rosenthal, Treas.
EIN: 136140942
Codes: FD2

54081
The Robert Fleming & Jane Howe Patrick Foundation, Inc.
P.O. Box 234
Charlotte, VT 05445 (802) 865-8322
E-mail: adantzscher@cs.com
Contact: Adam B. Dantzscher, Exec. Dir.

Established in 1988 in VT.
Donor(s): Harriet S. Patrick.
Financial data (yr. ended 06/30/01): Grants paid, $87,830; assets, $1,976,128 (M); expenditures, $129,569; qualifying distributions, $87,830.
Limitations: Giving limited to VT.
Application information: Application form not required.
Officers and Directors:* Harriet S. Patrick,* Pres.; Richard Cunningham,* V.P.; Adam B. Dantzscher,* Secy.-Treas. and Exec. Dir.; C. Dennis Hill, Glen A. Wright.
EIN: 030317962
Codes: FD2

54082
The WELD Foundation
c/o J. David Shenk
P.O. Box 1092
Manchester, VT 05254

Established in 1992.
Donor(s): Willis W. Shenk, Elsie S. Shenk.
Financial data (yr. ended 12/31/00): Grants paid, $86,750; assets, $2,335,544 (M); gifts received, $16,286; expenditures, $104,094; qualifying distributions, $86,750.
Limitations: Applications not accepted. Giving primarily in Lancaster County, PA.
Application information: Contributes only to pre-selected organizations.
Officers: Willis W. Shenk, Chair.; J. David Shenk, Pres.; Elsie S. Shenk, V.P. and Secy.; Mary Louise Shenk, Treas.
EIN: 232680871
Codes: FD2

54083
Courtney Buffum Family Foundation
40 George St.
P.O. Box 638
Burlington, VT 05402 (802) 863-3494
FAX: (802) 865-9747
Contact: John P. Cain

Established in 1997 in DE and VT.
Donor(s): Victoria U. Buffum.
Financial data (yr. ended 12/31/01): Grants paid, $82,500; assets, $1,342,148 (M); expenditures, $105,965; qualifying distributions, $82,500.
Limitations: Giving primarily in VT.
Publications: Application guidelines.
Application information: Application form not required.
Officers: Courtney Buffum, Pres.; Victoria U. Buffum, Treas.
EIN: 043359381
Codes: FD2

54084
The Hughes Family Foundation, Inc.
P.O. Box 246
Norwich, VT 05055-0246
Application address: 102 Maple Hill Rd., Norwich, VT 05055-0246, tel.: (802) 295-4286
Contact: James Hughes, Dir.

Established in 1998 in VT.
Donor(s): James Hughes, Elizabeth Hughes.
Financial data (yr. ended 12/31/01): Grants paid, $74,700; assets, $410,269 (M); gifts received, $82,326; expenditures, $75,699; qualifying distributions, $74,700.
Limitations: Giving primarily in NH and OH.
Directors: Harriette Hughes Griffin, Elizabeth S. Hughes, James A. Hughes, James S. Hughes, Timothy Hughes, M.D., Sharon Hughes Young.
EIN: 030356395

54085
Sinex Education Foundation, Inc.
c/o Donald F. Sinex
R.R. 1, Box 4388
Rutland, VT 05701-9233

Established in 1998 in VT.
Donor(s): Donald F. Sinex.
Financial data (yr. ended 12/31/01): Grants paid, $68,780; assets, $1,130,021 (M); expenditures, $68,780; qualifying distributions, $68,780.
Limitations: Applications not accepted. Giving primarily in Rutland, VT.
Application information: Contributes only to pre-selected organizations.
Trustees: Donald F. Sinex, Karen Wurster, Thomas P. Zarrilli.
EIN: 030356063

54086
The Jerry Greenfield & Elizabeth Skarie Foundation
2779 South St.
Williston, VT 05495

Established in 2000 in VT.
Donor(s): Jerry Greenfield, Elizabeth Skarie.
Financial data (yr. ended 12/31/01): Grants paid, $68,550; assets, $551,944 (M); gifts received, $100,350; expenditures, $68,900; qualifying distributions, $68,550.
Limitations: Applications not accepted.
Application information: Contributes only to pre-selected organizations.
Directors: Jerry Greenfield, Elizabeth Skarie, Frederick K. Thaler.
EIN: 311738299

54087
Marvin L. and Norma J. Hathaway Foundation, Inc.
204 Perry Lea Rd.
Waterbury, VT 05676

Donor(s): Marvin Hathaway, Norma Hathaway.
Financial data (yr. ended 12/31/01): Grants paid, $67,395; assets, $1,073,744 (M); expenditures, $80,458; qualifying distributions, $67,162.
Limitations: Applications not accepted. Giving primarily in VT.
Application information: Contributes only to pre-selected organizations.
Trustees: Lynn H. Bortree, Marvin Hathaway, Norma Hathaway, Robert Sloan.
EIN: 526908571

54088
Maverick Lloyd Foundation
(Formerly Maverick Foundation)
c/o Arthur Berndt
P.O. Box 99
Sharon, VT 05065

Established in 1995 in IL.
Donor(s): Georgia Lloyd.‡
Financial data (yr. ended 12/31/00): Grants paid, $64,000; assets, $1,279,424 (M); gifts received, $856,840; expenditures, $85,777; qualifying distributions, $64,000.
Limitations: Applications not accepted. Giving on a national basis.
Application information: Contributes only to pre-selected organizations.
Trustee: Arthur Berndt.
EIN: 367093389

54089
William and Gayle Chorske Family Foundation
198 Garvin Hill Rd.
Woodstock, VT 05091 (802) 457-3932
Contact: William W. Chorske, Pres.

Established in 1997 in VT.
Donor(s): William W. Chorske.
Financial data (yr. ended 12/31/01): Grants paid, $57,701; assets, $1,327,998 (M); gifts received, $1,573; expenditures, $69,011; quaifying distributions, $59,649.

54089—VERMONT

Limitations: Giving primarily in Woodstock, VT; giving also in Boston, MA, and Minneapolis, MN.
Officers: William W. Chorske, Pres.; Gayle O. Chorske, Secy.-Treas.
Directors: Matthew J. Chorske, Michael W. Chorske, Anne Marie Stuzin.
EIN: 043382941

54090
Everett H. Wyman Trust B Memorial Fund
c/o Chittenden Bank
P.O. Box 820
Burlington, VT 05402

Established in 1992 in VT.
Financial data (yr. ended 12/31/01): Grants paid, $55,903; assets, $1,442,289 (M); expenditures, $69,173; qualifying distributions, $55,903.
Limitations: Applications not accepted. Giving primarily in VT.
Application information: Contributes only to pre-selected organizations.
Trustee: Vermont National Bank.
EIN: 030337672

54091
The Panjandrum Foundation
c/o C&S Wholesale
Old Ferry Rd.
Brattleboro, VT 05302
Application address: P.O. Box 821, Brattleboro, VT 05302
Contact: William Hamlin, Treas.

Established in 1999.
Donor(s): Richard Cohen, Janet Cohen.
Financial data (yr. ended 12/31/01): Grants paid, $55,000; assets, $1,332,540 (M); expenditures, $74,989; qualifying distributions, $55,000.
Officer: William Hamlin, Treas.
Trustees: Janet L. Cohen, Richard B. Cohen.
EIN: 036069606

54092
Green Mountain Fund, Inc.
10 Machia Hill Rd.
Westford, VT 05494-9603 (802) 879-0288
E-mail: gmfps@together.net; *URL:* http://homepages.together.net/~gmfps
Contact: Will Miller, Secy.-Treas.

Established in 1988 in VT.
Donor(s): Charles MacMartin.
Financial data (yr. ended 12/31/01): Grants paid, $53,650; assets, $49,266 (M); expenditures, $55,163; qualifying distributions, $34,442.
Limitations: Giving limited to the Champlain Valley Watershed, NY and VT.
Publications: Informational brochure (including application guidelines).
Application information: Does not contribute to organizations with budgets over $100,000. Application form required.
Officers and Directors:* Ann Lipsitt,* Pres.; Beth Mintz, V.P.; Will Miller,* Secy.
EIN: 030316083
Codes: TN

54093
Wolf Kahn & Emily Mason Foundation, Inc.
P.O. Box 2314
Brattleboro, VT 05303-2314

Established in 1998 in NY.
Donor(s): Wolf Kahn, Emily Mason.
Financial data (yr. ended 08/31/01): Grants paid, $50,475; assets, $487,690 (M); gifts received, $204,438; expenditures, $52,982; qualifying distributions, $50,475.
Limitations: Applications not accepted. Giving primarily in NY.

Application information: Contributes only to pre-selected organizations.
Trustees: Wolf Kahn, Emily Mason.
EIN: 134036532

54094
Mount Laurel Foundation, Inc.
(Formerly Mount Laurel School, Inc.)
c/o Factory Point National Bank of Manchester
Main St.
Manchester Center, VT 05255
Contact: G. Frederick Zeller, Jr., Pres.

Financial data (yr. ended 06/30/01): Grants paid, $49,350; assets, $1,015,032 (M); gifts received, $65,960; expenditures, $59,320; qualifying distributions, $48,740.
Limitations: Giving limited to the Manchester, VT, area.
Officers: David Lewis, Pres.; David Pardo, V.P.; Karin Hegedus, Secy.; Marcia Fagan, Treas.
EIN: 036004154

54095
George W. Mergens Foundation
P.O. Box 633
Milton, VT 05468 (802) 862-6770
Application address: P.O. Box 718, Milton, VT 05468, tel.: (802) 893-4854
Contact: Paul Mergens, Pres.

Established in 1994 in VT.
Donor(s): Paul Mergens, Mary Mergens-Loughran.
Financial data (yr. ended 08/31/01): Grants paid, $48,500; assets, $1,060,857 (M); expenditures, $51,630; qualifying distributions, $47,918.
Limitations: Giving primarily in VT.
Application information: Application form not required.
Officers: Paul Mergens, Pres.; Lenora Mergens, V.P.; Mary Mergens-Loughran, Secy.
EIN: 030345055

54096
Hildegard Durfee Scholarship Fund
c/o Charles R. Cummings
P.O. Box 677
Brattleboro, VT 05302-0677

Established in 1991 in VT.
Donor(s): Hildegard Durfee.
Financial data (yr. ended 12/31/01): Grants paid, $42,750; assets, $693,177 (M); gifts received, $807; expenditures, $50,417; qualifying distributions, $44,894.
Limitations: Giving limited to residents of Windham County, VT.
Application information: Application form required.
Trustees: Richard Carroll, Charles R. Cummings, Sandra Pearson.
EIN: 226546128
Codes: GTI

54097
Wegner Family Foundation
c/o Arthur & Patricia Wegner
223 Orchard Shore
Colchester, VT 05446-1877

Established in 1992 in CT.
Financial data (yr. ended 12/31/01): Grants paid, $42,500; assets, $162,771 (M); expenditures, $42,523; qualifying distributions, $42,362.
Limitations: Applications not accepted. Giving primarily in CT, KS, and VT.
Application information: Contributes only to pre-selected organizations.
Trustees: Arthur Wegner, Elisabeth Wegner, Meleda Wegner, Patricia Wegner.
EIN: 226579803

54098
Fletcher Farm Foundation, Inc.
P.O. Box 4
Ludlow, VT 05149-0020

Established in 1941.
Financial data (yr. ended 08/31/01): Grants paid, $39,996; assets, $0 (L); expenditures, $133,063; qualifying distributions, $160,687.
Limitations: Applications not accepted.
Application information: Contributes only to pre-selected organizations.
Officers and Trustees:* John J. Collins, Jr.,* Pres.; Barbara LeMire,* V.P.; Martin Nitka,* Treas.; Douglas LeMire, Exec. Dir.; Mary Barton, Steve Birge, Sharon E.P. Bixley, R. Alden Blodgett, Jonathan Bouton, Thornton Burnet, Jr., Kevin M. Davis, Robert Evans, Robert Fletcher, David Harlow, Jerome Mayer, Jean Morrill, Don Pratt, David Stearns, Charlotte Summer.
EIN: 036007183

54099
Trustees of Chester Academy
c/o Banknorth Investment Management Group, N.A.
P.O. Box 595
Williston, VT 05495-0595

Financial data (yr. ended 03/31/00): Grants paid, $37,400; assets, $771,841 (M); expenditures, $44,789; qualifying distributions, $37,805.
Limitations: Giving limited to residents of Chester, VT.
Application information: Scholarship recipients are selected by the Board of Trustees. Application form not required.
Trustee: Banknorth Investment Management Group, N.A.
EIN: 036007034
Codes: GTI

54100
Lawrence H. Bernstein Foundation
20 Rose Hill Rd.
Woodstock, VT 05091

Financial data (yr. ended 12/31/01): Grants paid, $36,281; assets, $149,648 (M); expenditures, $36,702; qualifying distributions, $36,238.
Limitations: Applications not accepted. Giving primarily in VT.
Application information: Contributes only to pre-selected organizations.
Trustee: Lawrence H. Bernstein.
EIN: 046773334

54101
Eleanor White Trust
c/o Banknorth Investment Management Group, N.A.
P.O. Box 595
Williston, VT 05495-0595
Contact: Richard S. Smith, Tr.

Financial data (yr. ended 12/31/01): Grants paid, $36,000; assets, $567,430 (M); gifts received, $28,487; expenditures, $45,636; qualifying distributions, $42,711.
Limitations: Giving limited to residents of Fair Haven, VT.
Application information: Letter. Application form required.
Trustees: Keyser, Crowley, Carrol, George, Meub, Banknorth Investment Management Group, N.A.
EIN: 036004915
Codes: GTI

54102
Crosby Foundation, Inc.
153 Main St.
P.O. Box 517
Brattleboro, VT 05302 (802) 254-4588
Contact: Robert T. Gannett, Treas.

Financial data (yr. ended 05/31/01): Grants paid, $35,552; assets, $683,649 (M); expenditures, $46,015; qualifying distributions, $38,336.
Limitations: Giving limited to Windham County, VT.
Officers and Trustees:* Crosby B. Perry,* Pres.; Robert T. Gannett,* Treas.; John H. Carnahan, Betsy H. Neumeister.
EIN: 036005648

54103
Westford Forestry Foundation, Ltd.
c/o Herrick, Ltd.
72 Main St.
Burlington, VT 05401-8419
Application address: P.O. Box 2727, Underhill, VT 05489-0272, tel.: (802) 899-2957
Contact: Marthe J. Kruse, V.P.

Financial data (yr. ended 12/31/01): Grants paid, $34,754; assets, $607,153 (M); expenditures, $40,833; qualifying distributions, $34,754.
Limitations: Giving primarily in VT.
Officers: Christian A. Kruse, Pres.; Marthe J. Kruse, V.P.; Lori J. Ruple, Secy.
Directors: Louis Beaulieu, Bendeicte Dodge, Michael Snyder.
EIN: 030357996

54104
South Lake Champlain Trust, Inc.
c/o Chittenden Bank
P.O. Box 820
Burlington, VT 05402
Application address: 3 Gorham Ln., Middlebury, VT 05753, tel.: (802) 388-7609
Contact: Robert E. Collins, Advisory Comm. Member

Established in 1993 in VT.
Financial data (yr. ended 12/31/01): Grants paid, $34,642; assets, $928,355 (M); expenditures, $51,419; qualifying distributions, $34,642.
Limitations: Giving limited to VT.
Application information: Application form required.
Advisory Committee Members: Robert E. Collins, Wilson MacIntire, Calvin Staudt, Jr.
EIN: 223090826

54105
John R. & Grace D. Hogle Wildlife Sanctuary Trust
c/o Banknorth Investment Management Group, N.A.
P.O. Box 595
Williston, VT 05495

Established in 1998 in VT.
Financial data (yr. ended 12/31/99): Grants paid, $30,213; assets, $798,191 (M); expenditures, $44,629; qualifying distributions, $30,336.
Limitations: Applications not accepted.
Application information: Contributes only to pre-selected organizations.
Trustees: Charles R. Cummings, Banknorth Investment Management Group, N.A.
EIN: 036064921

54106
Salina Lewis Aylor Scholarship Fund
c/o Banknorth Investment Management Group, N.A.
P.O. Box 595
Williston, VT 05495

Financial data (yr. ended 12/31/01): Grants paid, $29,611; assets, $382,522 (M); expenditures, $32,262; qualifying distributions, $29,611.
Limitations: Applications not accepted.
Application information: Contributes only to pre-selected organizations.
Trustee: Banknorth Investment Management Group, N.A.
EIN: 036067065

54107
Sid & Cecelia Lance Family Foundation
P.O. Box 305
Northfield, VT 05663 (802) 485-3888

Donor(s): Cecelia Lance.
Financial data (yr. ended 12/31/00): Grants paid, $29,517; assets, $959,177 (M); gifts received, $70,000; expenditures, $49,154; qualifying distributions, $29,517.
Limitations: Giving primarily in VT.
Officers: Debra Miller, Mgr.; Randy Miller, Mgr.
Trustee: Cecelia Lance.
EIN: 953738539

54108
The Foundation for Pediatrics and Pediatric Hematology and Oncology, Inc.
1370 Spear St.
Charlotte, VT 05445

Established in 1998 in VT.
Financial data (yr. ended 12/31/01): Grants paid, $29,000; assets, $197,207 (M); gifts received, $24,000; expenditures, $29,105; qualifying distributions, $29,000.
Officers: Joseph Dickerman, Pres.; Jennifer Dickerman, Secy,.
Directors: James Dickerman, Laura Dickerman.
EIN: 030358619

54109
Schultz-Blackwell Trust
3779 Center Rd.
East Montpelier, VT 05651-4103

Established in 1994 in VT.
Donor(s): Marilyn S. Blackwell, Edward S. Blackwell III.
Financial data (yr. ended 12/31/01): Grants paid, $28,500; assets, $598,718 (M); expenditures, $29,351; qualifying distributions, $28,500.
Limitations: Applications not accepted. Giving primarily in VT.
Application information: Contributes only to pre-selected organizations.
Trustees: Edward S. Blackwell III, Marilyn S. Blackwell.
EIN: 036059731

54110
E. Dante Bogni Trust
c/o Banknorth Investment Management Group, N.A.
P.O. Box 595
Williston, VT 05495

Financial data (yr. ended 12/31/00): Grants paid, $28,099; assets, $1,218,387 (M); expenditures, $37,766; qualifying distributions, $28,399.
Limitations: Giving limited to residents of Barre and Montpelier, VT.
Application information: Applicants must be students of Spaulding High School or Montpelier High School, VT. Include list of accomplishments in the areas of mathematics, science, and community involvement with application and return to guidance office.
Trustee: Banknorth Investment Management Group, N.A.
EIN: 036044565

54111
Nordic Educational Trust
P.O. Box 895
Shelburne, VT 05482-0895
Contact: Ross R. Anderson, Pres.

Established in 1988 in VT.
Donor(s): Ross R. Anderson, The Nordic Group, Inc.
Financial data (yr. ended 12/31/00): Grants paid, $27,750; assets, $374,937 (M); gifts received, $1,000; expenditures, $40,964; qualifying distributions, $27,750.
Limitations: Giving limited to Chittenden and Grand Isle counties, VT.
Application information: Application form required.
Officers and Trustees: Ross R. Anderson, Pres.; Gail E. Anderson, Secy.; Ian Anderson, Deirdre Anderson.
Directors: Gerard A. Asselin, Tim Jermon, David Machavern, Tim Taft, Nancy Zahniser.
EIN: 222975012
Codes: GTI

54112
Frank F. England Scholarship Fund
c/o Community National Bank
289 N. Main St.
Barre, VT 05641
Application addresses: c/o Guidance Off., Northfield High School, Northfield, VT 05663, tel.: (802) 485-8644; or c/o Lucinda Buck Conti, 5 Burnside Ave., Barre, VT 05641

Financial data (yr. ended 12/31/00): Grants paid, $27,270; assets, $115,055 (M); gifts received, $401; expenditures, $29,326; qualifying distributions, $27,270.
Limitations: Giving limited to residents of Northfield, VT.
Application information: Application form required.
Scholarship Committee Members: Angela McLean, Lucinda Buck Conti.
Trustees: Katherine E. Buck, Northfield Savings Bank, Community National Bank.
EIN: 036054992

54113
John R. Wilson Scholarship Trust
c/o Banknorth Investment Management Group, N.A.
P.O. Box 595
Williston, VT 05495-0595
Application address: c/o D. Rodman Thomas, Trust Off., 500 Main St., Bennington, VT 05201

Donor(s): Mrs. Wilson.
Financial data (yr. ended 12/31/01): Grants paid, $26,600; assets, $473,727 (M); expenditures, $29,754; qualifying distributions, $27,496.
Limitations: Giving limited to Bennington County, VT.
Application information: Application form required.
Trustee: Banknorth Investment Management Group, N.A.
EIN: 036016072
Codes: GTI

54114
Anne Slade Frey Charitable Trust
P.O. Box 1310
Montpelier, VT 05601 (802) 223-1000
Contact: Bernard Lambek, Tr.

Established in 1992 in VT.
Donor(s): Anne Slade Frey.‡
Financial data (yr. ended 12/31/01): Grants paid, $26,000; assets, $350,742 (M); gifts received, $990; expenditures, $29,566; qualifying distributions, $26,000.
Limitations: Giving primarily in NH and VT.
Application information: Application form required.
Trustees: Nancy Cressman, Sara Goodman, Bernard Lambek, Valerie Mullen, Grace Paley, Briane Pinkson, Jim Schley, Nina Swaim.
EIN: 026090073

54115
Ethel Peabody Trust f/b/o Various Charities
c/o Banknorth Investment Management Group, N.A.
P.O. Box 595, Banknorth Group
Williston, VT 05495-0595

Established in 1989 in VT.
Donor(s): Ethel M. Peabody Trust.
Financial data (yr. ended 12/31/01): Grants paid, $25,093; assets, $675,238 (M); expenditures, $29,518; qualifying distributions, $25,093.
Limitations: Applications not accepted. Giving limited to Franklin County, VT.
Application information: Contributes only to pre-selected organizations.
Trustee: Banknorth Investment Management Group, N.A.
EIN: 036050543

54116
Olin Scott Fund, Inc.
407 Main St.
P.O. Box 1208
Bennington, VT 05201 (802) 447-1096
FAX: (802) 447-8560
Contact: Melvin A. Dyson, Dir.; or Melinda L. Dickie, Exec. Dir.

Incorporated in 1920 in VT.
Donor(s): Olin Scott.‡
Financial data (yr. ended 06/30/00): Grants paid, $25,000; assets, $3,541,363 (M); expenditures, $140,711; qualifying distributions, $207,027; giving activities include $114,500 for loans to individuals.
Limitations: Giving limited to residents of Bennington County, VT.
Application information: Application form required.
Officers and Trustees:* Kelton B. Miller,* Pres. and Treas.; Robert E. Cummings, Jr.,* V.P. and Secy.; Melinda L. Dickie,* Exec. Dir.; Melvin A. Dyson.
EIN: 036005697
Codes: GTI

54117
Bryant Chucking Grinder Company Charitable Foundation
53 Cutler Dr.
Springfield, VT 05156 (802) 885-5812
Contact: Richard H. Dexter, II, Treas.

Established around 1954.
Donor(s): Alan E. Stubbs.
Financial data (yr. ended 12/31/01): Grants paid, $24,850; assets, $970,149 (M); expenditures, $28,206; qualifying distributions, $24,850.
Limitations: Giving primarily in New England.
Officers and Trustees:* James V. Halvorsen,* Pres.; John Stahura, V.P.; David Shuffleberg, Secy.; Richard H. Dexter II,* Treas.; Victor Dzewaltowski, Claire Hatch, Robert Mitchell.
EIN: 036009332

54118
Adamant Community Cultural Foundation, Inc.
1241 Haggett Rd.
Adamant, VT 05640-0026
Contact: Frank A. Suchomel, Jr., Pres.

Donor(s): Frank A. Suchomel, Jr., Michael John Suchomel, James P. McLaughlin,‡ Ivy T. Keele.‡
Financial data (yr. ended 03/31/02): Grants paid, $24,200; assets, $199,620 (M); gifts received, $181,700; expenditures, $172,525; qualifying distributions, $145,268; giving activities include $121,066 for programs.
Limitations: Giving limited to the Adamant, VT, area.
Application information: Application form not required.
Officers: Frank A. Suchomel, Jr., Pres.; Michael John Suchomel, V.P., and Secy.-Treas.
EIN: 030286063

54119
Margaret E. C. Vuilemenot Revocable Trust
c/o Banknorth Investment Management Group, N.A.
P.O. Box 595
Williston, VT 05495-0595

Financial data (yr. ended 12/31/01): Grants paid, $22,752; assets, $1,025,976 (M); expenditures, $34,765; qualifying distributions, $22,752.
Limitations: Applications not accepted. Giving primarily in Washington, DC.
Application information: Contributes only to pre-selected organizations.
Trustee: Banknorth Investment Management Group, N.A.
EIN: 046602854

54120
The Keelan Family Foundation
3302 Vermont Rte. 7A
Arlington, VT 05250-8875
Application address: 549 Rte. 313 W., Arlington, VT 05250, tel.: (802) 375-2721
Contact: Verrall Keelan, Chair.

Established in 1988 in VT.
Financial data (yr. ended 12/31/00): Grants paid, $21,176; assets, $338,997 (M); expenditures, $22,425; qualifying distributions, $21,176.
Limitations: Giving primarily in NY and VT.
Officer: Verrall Keelan, Chair.
Trustees: Dennis Filippi, Kelly Filippi, Donald Keelan, Peter Keelan.
EIN: 141691901

54121
Ellen M. Willard Trust
c/o Robert T. Gannet
P.O. Box 517, 153 Main ST.
Brattleboro, VT 05302-0517
Contact: Robert T. Gannett, Tr.

Financial data (yr. ended 12/31/01): Grants paid, $21,000; assets, $520,741 (M); expenditures, $24,051; qualifying distributions, $23,186.
Limitations: Giving primarily in the southeastern Windham County, VT, area.
Application information: Application form not required.
Trustees: Robert T. Gannett, John A. Wallace, Jeanette White.
EIN: 036005923

54122
Erral A. Vaile & Evelyn L. Cleaveland Scholarship Fund
P.O. Box 820
Burlington, VT 05402
Application address: c/o Bertie Sprague, Principal, Brattleboro Union District No. 6 High School, Fairground Rd., Brattleboro, VT 05301

Established in 1994 in VT.
Donor(s): Erral Vaile.‡
Financial data (yr. ended 12/31/01): Grants paid, $20,815; assets, $416,613 (M); expenditures, $26,127; qualifying distributions, $20,815.
Limitations: Giving limited to residents of Brattleboro, VT.
Application information: Family financial statements, student's high school transcript, and two letters of recommendation required.
Trustee: Vermont National Bank.
EIN: 030343444
Codes: GTI

54123
William A. Morse Fund
c/o Banknorth Investment Management Group, N.A.
P.O. Box 595
Williston, VT 05495-0595
Application address: c/o Dora Powers, R.R. 2, Box 239-D, West Brattleboro, VT 05301

Financial data (yr. ended 12/31/01): Grants paid, $20,360; assets, $344,739 (M); expenditures, $23,521; qualifying distributions, $20,696.
Limitations: Giving limited to Brattleboro, South Newfane, and Williamsville, VT.
Application information: Application form required.
Trustee: Banknorth Investment Management Group, N.A.
EIN: 036004778
Codes: GTI

54124
Edwald Fund Trust
c/o Chettenden Trust Co.
P.O. Box 820
Burlington, VT 05402-0820

Established in 1993 in VT.
Financial data (yr. ended 12/31/01): Grants paid, $19,057; assets, $361,456 (M); expenditures, $23,384; qualifying distributions, $19,057.
Limitations: Applications not accepted. Giving limited to Putney, VT.
Application information: Contributes only to pre-selected organizations.
Trustee: Chittenden Trust Co.
EIN: 036057087

54125
William & Glenna James Scholarship Fund
c/o Banknorth Investment Management Group, N.A.
P.O. Box 595, Banknorth Group
Williston, VT 05495-0595
Application address: c/o Banknorth Investment Mgmt. Group, N.A., 89 Merchants Row, Rutland, VT 05701

Established in 1998 in VT.
Financial data (yr. ended 12/31/01): Grants paid, $19,040; assets, $471,700 (M); expenditures, $22,282; qualifying distributions, $20,032.
Limitations: Giving limited to residents of Proctor, VT.
Application information: Application form not required.
Trustee: Banknorth Investment Management Group, N.A.

EIN: 036064491
Codes: GTI

54126
The Byrne Fund for Wildwood, Inc.
c/o Robert E. Snyder
331 Olcott Dr., L3
White River Junction, VT 05001
Contact: Pam Byrne Gentek

Donor(s): John J. Byrne.
Financial data (yr. ended 12/31/00): Grants paid, $18,500; assets, $1,932,984 (M); gifts received, $1,003,221; expenditures, $21,931; qualifying distributions, $21,931.
Limitations: Giving primarily in Wildwood, NJ.
Application information: Application form required.
Officers and Directors:* James A. Byrne,* Pres.; Stephen S. Rubins,* V.P. and Secy.; Robert E. Snyder, Treas.
EIN: 061563592

54127
Dorothy S. Hastings Student Aid Fund
(also known as Hastings Student Aid Fund)
c/o Banknorth Investment Management Group, N.A.
P.O. Box 595
Williston, VT 05495-0595
Application address: 89 Merchants Row, Rutland, VT 05701

Established in 1989 in VT.
Donor(s): Dorothy Hastings.‡
Financial data (yr. ended 03/31/02): Grants paid, $17,500; assets, $587,108 (M); gifts received, $4,200; expenditures, $20,755; qualifying distributions, $18,417.
Limitations: Giving limited to residents of the Barton, VT, area, including Orleans County.
Publications: Program policy statement, application guidelines, informational brochure, financial statement, grants list.
Application information: Application form required.
Trustee: Banknorth Investment Management Group, N.A.
EIN: 036048694
Codes: GTI

54128
Five Twenty-Five Foundation, Inc.
c/o P. William Polk, Jr.
P.O. Box 65
Londonderry, VT 05148

Financial data (yr. ended 12/31/01): Grants paid, $17,050; assets, $191,825 (M); expenditures, $22,343; qualifying distributions, $19,001.
Limitations: Applications not accepted. Giving primarily in VT.
Application information: Contributes only to pre-selected organizations.
Officers: P. William Polk, Jr., Pres.; Nancy C. Polk, V.P.
EIN: 036016000

54129
The Tillie & William Blumstein Family Foundation, Inc.
(Formerly William Blumstein Family Foundation)
P.O. Box 1000
Killington, VT 05751
Contact: Timmie Rome, Dir.

Financial data (yr. ended 12/31/01): Grants paid, $16,465; assets, $315,047 (M); expenditures, $20,278; qualifying distributions, $18,269.
Limitations: Giving primarily in NY.
Directors: Kyver Blumstein, Timmie Rome.

EIN: 132608346

54130
VARA Educational Foundation, Inc.
619 Varney Hill Rd.
Starksboro, VT 05487 (802) 453-2755
Contact: Steve Kelly, Treas.

Financial data (yr. ended 07/31/00): Grants paid, $16,157; assets, $192,872 (M); gifts received, $13,920; expenditures, $18,750; qualifying distributions, $16,079.
Limitations: Giving limited to residents of VT.
Officers and Directors:* Lenny Britton,* Pres.; Wendy Neal,* V.P.; Duncan Brettell,* Secy.; Steve Kelly,* Treas.
EIN: 237336991

54131
Periwinkle Foundation, Inc.
481 Cemetery Hill Rd.
Guilford, VT 05301

Established in 1999 in VT.
Donor(s): Ray C. Walker, Jeanne Cowan Walker.
Financial data (yr. ended 12/31/01): Grants paid, $16,090; assets, $45,251 (M); gifts received, $33,015; expenditures, $17,117; qualifying distributions, $16,090.
Limitations: Applications not accepted. Giving primarily in VT.
Application information: Contributes only to pre-selected organizations.
Officers and Director:* Krista Whetstone, Pres.; Ray C. Walker,* Secy.; Jeanne Cowan Walker, Treas.
EIN: 030362094

54132
Walter Hayes, Sr., Beulah Buffum Hayes & Walter H. Hayes, Jr. Foundation
(also known as The Hayes Foundation)
P.O. Box 129
Wallingford, VT 05773 (802) 446-2877

Donor(s): Walter H. Hayes, Jr.‡
Financial data (yr. ended 12/31/00): Grants paid, $15,020; assets, $617,562 (M); gifts received, $37,010; expenditures, $78,117; qualifying distributions, $62,097; giving activities include $10,900 for programs.
Limitations: Giving limited to Rutland County, VT.
Application information: Application form required.
Officers: Carl L. Buffum, Jr., Chair.; Joan Aleshire, V.P.; Julia Chamberlain, Secy.; Richard J. Dundas, Treas.
EIN: 030284264
Codes: GTI

54133
Douglas C. Howe & Frank E. Shivers Revocable Trust
c/o Samara Foundation of VT, Inc.
P.O. Box 1263
Burlington, VT 05402-1263
Contact: Bill Lippert, Exec. Dir.

Established in 1999 in VT.
Donor(s): Douglas C. Howe.
Financial data (yr. ended 12/31/01): Grants paid, $14,286; assets, $241,892 (M); expenditures, $20,198; qualifying distributions, $14,286.
Limitations: Giving primarily in VT.
Application information: Application form required.
Officer: Bill Lippert, Exec. Dir.
Trustee: Samara Foundation of VT, Inc.
EIN: 226713515

54134
The Krzyzowa/Kreisau Foundation, Inc.
c/o H. Von Moltke
249 Hopson Rd.
Norwich, VT 05055

Donor(s): Lenore Von Huelsen Ponto.
Financial data (yr. ended 12/31/01): Grants paid, $14,032; assets, $4,210 (M); gifts received, $8,325; expenditures, $24,980; qualifying distributions, $14,032.
Limitations: Applications not accepted.
Application information: Contributes only to pre-selected organizations.
Officers: Helmuth C. Von Moltke, Pres.; Mark Huessy, Secy.; Lenore Von Huelsen Ponto, Treas.
Director: Arnold Steinhardt.
EIN: 030335376

54135
Micah Fund, Inc.
c/o Paul L. Kendall
487 Kendall Rd.
Braintree, VT 05060

Donor(s): Paul L. Kendall, Sharon K. Rives.
Financial data (yr. ended 12/31/01): Grants paid, $11,400; assets, $243,567 (M); expenditures, $13,348; qualifying distributions, $11,400.
Limitations: Applications not accepted. Giving primarily in New York, NY.
Application information: Contributes only to pre-selected organizations.
Officers: Paul L. Kendall, Pres. and Treas.; Sharon K. Rives, V.P. and Secy.
Trustee: Vivian Longo.
EIN: 133152979

54136
Ivan W. and Bernice K. Burnham Educational Foundation
c/o Banknorth Investment Management Group, N.A.
P.O. Box 595, Tax Dept.
Williston, VT 05495-0595 (802) 879-2285
Application address: c/o Cathy Doty, The Stratevest Group, N.A., 89 Merchants Row, Rutland, VT 05701

Financial data (yr. ended 12/31/01): Grants paid, $11,354; assets, $364,096 (M); expenditures, $13,876; qualifying distributions, $11,354.
Limitations: Giving limited to the Waterbury, VT, area.
Trustee: Banknorth Investment Management Group, N.A.
EIN: 036016085

54137
Bergeron Family Foundation
P.O. Box 4397
Burlington, VT 05406
Application address: 38 Elm St., Wellesley, MA 02481
Contact: Paul Bergeron, Tr.

Established in 2001 in VT.
Donor(s): Urban Bergeron, Pauline Bergeron.
Financial data (yr. ended 12/31/01): Grants paid, $11,000; assets, $1,060,212 (M); gifts received, $1,020,043; expenditures, $23,463; qualifying distributions, $11,000.
Limitations: Giving primarily in Burlington, VT.
Trustees: Jay Bergeron, John J. Bergeron, Paul U. Bergeron, Urban L. Bergeron, Jane B. Guyette.
EIN: 030370623

54138
Charles & Olivina Perron Memorial Trust
(also known as Charles A. Perron Memorial Trust f/b/o Graduates of High School Serving the City of North Adams)
c/o Banknorth Investment Management Group, N.A.
P.O. Box 595
Williston, VT 05495
Application address: c/o Banknorth Investment Management Group, N.A., 99 West St., Pittsfield, MA 01201
Contact: Paula Hilchey

Established in 1985 in MA.
Financial data (yr. ended 12/31/01): Grants paid, $10,400; assets, $172,857 (M); expenditures, $13,561; qualifying distributions, $11,372.
Limitations: Giving limited to North Adams, MA.
Trustee: Banknorth Investment Management Group, N.A.
EIN: 222672860
Codes: GTI

54139
Atrium Society
P.O. Box 816
Middlebury, VT 05753 (800) 848-6021
Contact: Jean Webster-Doyle, Pres.

Established in 1984 in CA.
Donor(s): Jean Webster-Doyle, Albert Gordon, Laurance S. Rockefeller, Terrence Webster-Doyle.
Financial data (yr. ended 12/31/00): Grants paid, $10,215; assets, $148,499 (M); gifts received, $149,000; expenditures, $102,244; qualifying distributions, $104,671; giving activities include $76,109 for programs.
Limitations: Giving primarily in CT and FL.
Application information: Application form not required.
Officers: Jean Webster-Doyle, Pres.; Terrence Webster-Doyle, V.P. and Secy.; Felicity Doyle, Treas.
EIN: 770015182

54140
Clayton Brown Scholarship Fund
c/o Chittenden Bank
P.O. Box 820, 2 Burlington Sq.
Burlington, VT 05402

Financial data (yr. ended 12/31/01): Grants paid, $9,682; assets, $201,188 (M); expenditures, $14,677; qualifying distributions, $9,602.
Limitations: Applications not accepted. Giving limited to residents of VT.
Application information: Unsolicited requests for funds not accepted.
Trustee: Chittenden Bank.
EIN: 036020016

54141
Howfirma Foundation
P.O. Box 417
Woodstock, VT 05091-0417
Contact: Gary R. Brown, Tr.

Established about 1983 in VT.
Donor(s): Frank H. Teagle, Jr.‡
Financial data (yr. ended 12/31/01): Grants paid, $9,400; assets, $564,099 (M); expenditures, $58,936; qualifying distributions, $9,336.
Limitations: Giving limited to the Woodstock, VT, area.
Application information: Application form required.
Trustee: Gary R. Brown.
EIN: 222495072

54142
Arthur G. Eastman Memorial Scholarship Fund
c/o Chittenden Bank
P.O. Box 820
Burlington, VT 05402
Application address: c/o Katherine James, Guidance Dir., Whitingham High School, Jacksonville, VT 05342, tel.: (802) 368-2929

Financial data (yr. ended 12/31/01): Grants paid, $8,940; assets, $157,649 (M); expenditures, $11,880; qualifying distributions, $8,836.
Limitations: Giving limited to residents of Jacksonville, VT.
Application information: Application form required.
Trustee: Chittenden Bank.
EIN: 030279845
Codes: GTI

54143
Jared Tamler Memorial Fund
c/o Julie Tamler Schottland
P.O. Box 8345
Brattleboro, VT 05304

Established in 1995 in VT.
Donor(s): Jonathan Tamler Schottland, Julie Tamler Schottland, Nettie Tamler.
Financial data (yr. ended 03/31/02): Grants paid, $8,900; assets, $132,271 (M); expenditures, $9,688; qualifying distributions, $9,230.
Limitations: Giving primarily in VT.
Officer: Julie Tamler Schottland, Pres.
Directors: Jonathan Tamler Schottland, Nettie Tamler.
EIN: 030346657

54144
Dunham-Mason Foundation, Inc.
P.O. Box 517
Brattleboro, VT 05301-0517 (802) 245-4588
Contact: Robert T. Gannett, Treas.

Financial data (yr. ended 12/31/01): Grants paid, $8,450; assets, $200,102 (M); expenditures, $12,173; qualifying distributions, $10,029.
Limitations: Giving primarily in Windham County, VT.
Application information: Application form required.
Officers and Trustees:* John M. Dunham,* Pres.; Whitney Mason Germon,* V.P.; Robert T. Gannett,* Treas.
EIN: 036004687

54145
Martin & Emma Butters Memorial Scholarship Fund
P.O. Box 303
Barton, VT 05822 (802) 525-3766
Contact: William Boyd Davies, Tr.

Financial data (yr. ended 12/31/00): Grants paid, $7,600; assets, $99,702 (M); expenditures, $8,621; qualifying distributions, $8,621.
Limitations: Giving limited to residents of Orleans County, VT.
Application information: Application form required.
Trustee: William Boyd Davies.
EIN: 036044769

54146
Margaret McNeil Charity Trust
c/o Banknorth Investment Management Group, N.A.
P.O. Box 595, Tax Dept.
Williston, VT 05495

Established in 1990 in MA.
Financial data (yr. ended 12/31/01): Grants paid, $7,315; assets, $282,948 (M); expenditures, $11,500; qualifying distributions, $8,629.
Limitations: Applications not accepted. Giving primarily in MA.
Application information: Unsolicited requests for funds not accepted.
Trustee: Banknorth Investment Management Group, N.A.
EIN: 046662754

54147
Abraham Noveck Scholarship Trust
c/o Banknorth Investment Management Group, N.A.
P.O. Box 594, Banknorth, Tax Dept.
Williston, VT 05495-0595
Application address: Sharry Rutken, Trust Off., Banknorth Investment Management Group, N.A., 500 Main St., Bennington, VT 05201

Established in 1992 in VT.
Financial data (yr. ended 03/31/99): Grants paid, $7,263; assets, $129,437 (M); expenditures, $9,530; qualifying distributions, $7,824.
Limitations: Giving limited to residents of Bennington, VT.
Trustee: Banknorth Investment Management Group, N.A.
EIN: 036049622

54148
Natural Areas Fund, Ltd.
c/o Paul L. Kendall
487 Kendall Rd.
Braintree, VT 05060

Donor(s): Paul L. Kendall, Sharon K. Rives.
Financial data (yr. ended 12/31/01): Grants paid, $7,000; assets, $295,407 (M); expenditures, $9,934; qualifying distributions, $7,101.
Limitations: Applications not accepted. Giving primarily in VT.
Application information: Contributes only to pre-selected organizations.
Officers: Paul L. Kendall, Pres. and Treas.; Sharon K. Rives, V.P. and Secy.
Trustee: M. Dickey Drysdale.
EIN: 133124697

54149
The Louise Breason May Foundation, Inc.
c/o Edgar May
Muckross Rd.
Springfield, VT 05156

Financial data (yr. ended 12/31/01): Grants paid, $6,750; assets, $204,796 (M); gifts received, $10,890; expenditures, $6,750; qualifying distributions, $6,750.
Limitations: Giving primarily in VT.
Officer and Director:* Edgar May,* Pres.
EIN: 030221568

54150
The Moser Foundation
433 Sperry Rd.
Cornwall, VT 05753

Established in 1987 in MD.
Donor(s): Thomas A. Moser, Virginia H. Moser.
Financial data (yr. ended 12/31/01): Grants paid, $6,485; assets, $95,843 (M); expenditures, $7,369; qualifying distributions, $6,485.
Limitations: Applications not accepted. Giving primarily in Middlebury, VT.
Application information: Contributes only to pre-selected organizations.
Directors: Thomas A. Moser, Virginia H. Moser.
EIN: 521557339

54151
Mary G. Voght Trust
(Formerly Voght Scholarship Fund)
c/o Banknorth Investment Management Group, N.A.
P.O. Box 595
Williston, VT 05495

Established in 1987 in MA.
Financial data (yr. ended 12/31/01): Grants paid, $6,150; assets, $209,355 (M); expenditures, $10,076; qualifying distributions, $7,056.
Limitations: Applications not accepted. Giving limited to Lee, MA.
Trustee: Banknorth Investment Management Group, N.A.
EIN: 046555019
Codes: GTI

54152
V. Faith Edmunds Scholarship Trust
c/o Banknorth Investment Management Group, N.A.
P.O. Box 595
Williston, VT 05495-0595
Application address: Principal of People's Academy, Rd. No. 3, Box 40, Morrisville, VT 05661

Established in 1992 in VT.
Financial data (yr. ended 12/31/01): Grants paid, $6,000; assets, $117,847 (M); expenditures, $7,114; qualifying distributions, $6,329.
Limitations: Giving limited to residents of Morristown, VT.
Trustee: Banknorth Investment Management Group, N.A.
EIN: 946443878
Codes: GTI

54153
Essex Classical Institute
62 Learned Dr.
Westford, VT 05494

Financial data (yr. ended 12/31/01): Grants paid, $6,000; assets, $164,004 (L); expenditures, $6,809; qualifying distributions, $6,809.
Limitations: Applications not accepted. Giving limited to residents of Essex, VT.
Application information: Applicants chosen and submitted by Essex High School.
Officers: Grant Corsom, Pres.; Barbara Chapin, 1st V.P.; Gilbert Myers, 2nd V.P.; George Clapp, Secy.; John Duby, Treas.
EIN: 036006448
Codes: GTI

54154
Dolphine LaFleur Scholarship Fund
(Formerly Dolphine LaFleur Scholarship Fund f/b/o Middlebury Union High School District No. 3)
c/o Chittenden Bank, Trust Dept.
P.O. Box 820
Burlington, VT 05402

Financial data (yr. ended 12/31/00): Grants paid, $5,225; assets, $107,005 (M); expenditures, $7,317; qualifying distributions, $5,146.
Limitations: Applications not accepted. Giving limited to residents of Burlington, VT.
Trustee: Chittenden Bank.
EIN: 036045279

54155
Dr. R. Winthrop Davison Scholarship Trust
c/o Banknorth Investment Management Group, N.A.
P.O. Box 595
Williston, VT 05495-0595

Financial data (yr. ended 04/30/00): Grants paid, $5,100; assets, $133,894 (M); expenditures, $7,212; qualifying distributions, $5,208.
Limitations: Applications not accepted. Giving limited to residents of the Hinsdale, VT, area.
Application information: Recipient selected by Hinsdale High School Comm.
Trustee: Banknorth Investment Management Group, N.A.
EIN: 036004738

54156
Harris & Frances Block Foundation, Inc.
c/o Betsy Chodorkoff
491 Ennis Hill Rd.
Marshfield, VT 05658

Established in 2001 in VT.
Donor(s): Carol Maurer.
Financial data (yr. ended 12/31/01): Grants paid, $5,000; assets, $160,235 (M); gifts received, $143,906; expenditures, $7,701; qualifying distributions, $5,000.
Officers: Carol Maurer, Pres.; Nancy M. Sluys, V.P.; Diane Maurer Schatz, Secy.; Betsy M. Chodorkoff, Treas. and Exec. Dir.
EIN: 311784246

54157
Sylvia M. Hayes Trust
c/o Community National Bank
289 N. Main St
Barre, VT 05641 (802) 485-8644
Application address: c/o Northfield High School, Northfield, VT 05663, tel.: (802) 485-8644
Contact: Reed Korrow, Scholarship Comm. Member

Financial data (yr. ended 12/31/00): Grants paid, $5,000; assets, $109,862 (M); gifts received, $90; expenditures, $6,672; qualifying distributions, $5,000.
Limitations: Giving limited to residents of Northfield, VT.
Application information: Application form required.
Trustee: Northfield Savings Bank.
Scholarship Committee: Jack Cashman, Reed Korrow, Deborah J. Partlow.
EIN: 036055393

54158
Robert P., Marguerite W. and Jerold King Memorial Scholarship
c/o Chittenden Bank
P.O. Box 820
Burlington, VT 05402
Application address: c/o Bertie Sprague, Principal, Brattleboro Union District No. 6 High School, Fairground Rd., Brattleboro, VT 05301

Established in 1989 in VT.
Financial data (yr. ended 12/31/01): Grants paid, $4,127; assets, $102,129 (M); expenditures, $6,440; qualifying distributions, $4,127.
Limitations: Giving limited to the Brattleboro, VT, area.
Application information: Application form required.
Trustee: Chittenden Bank.
EIN: 030318248

54159
Blind Artisans of Vermont, Inc.
110 Chestnut St.
Brattleboro, VT 05301-6579
Contact: Joann H. Nichols, Treas.

Financial data (yr. ended 06/30/01): Grants paid, $4,105; assets, $92,531 (M); expenditures, $5,689; qualifying distributions, $4,285; giving activities include $4,005 for programs.
Limitations: Giving limited to residents of VT.
Officers: Harriet Hall, Pres.; Michael Richman, V.P.; Heidi Pfau, Secy.; Joann H. Nichols, Treas.
Trustees: Tom Frank, Robert A. Green, John Hall.
EIN: 030181806

54160
Edward A. Lyon Trust
c/o Banknorth Investment Management Group, N.A.
P.O. Box 595, Banknorth Group, Tax Dept.
Williston, VT 05495-0595
Application address: c/o Rev. Peter Hanson, Trinity Lutheran Church, 43 Western Ave., Brattleboro, VT, 05301

Financial data (yr. ended 06/30/01): Grants paid, $4,000; assets, $150,349 (M); expenditures, $5,044; qualifying distributions, $4,151.
Limitations: Giving limited to the Windham County, VT, area.
Application information: Application form required.
Trustee: Banknorth Investment Management Group, N.A.
EIN: 036006845

54161
Alice E. Morton Memorial Scholarship Fund
c/o Banknorth Investment Management Group, N.A.
P.O. Box 595
Williston, VT 05495-0595 (802) 879-2285
Application address: c/o Bellows Free Academy, Main St., St. Albans, VT 05478, tel.: (802) 527-7576

Financial data (yr. ended 12/31/01): Grants paid, $4,000; assets, $129,555 (M); expenditures, $5,515; qualifying distributions, $4,477.
Limitations: Giving primarily in St. Albans, VT.
Application information: Application form required.
Trustee: Banknorth Investment Management Group, N.A.
EIN: 036005300
Codes: GTI

54162
The Mann Family Foundation
P.O. Box 28
Vernon, VT 05354

Established in 1998.
Financial data (yr. ended 12/31/01): Grants paid, $3,800; assets, $66,589 (M); expenditures, $7,946; qualifying distributions, $3,800.
Officers and Directors:* John R. Mann, Jr.,* Pres.; J. Christopher Mann,* V.P.; M. Beatrice Mann,* Secy.-Treas.
EIN: 030357311

54163
Harry E. Clark Scholarship Trust
c/o Banknorth Investment Management Group, N.A.
P.O. Box 595
Williston, VT 05495-0595

Financial data (yr. ended 04/30/00): Grants paid, $3,500; assets, $66,000 (M); expenditures, $4,107; qualifying distributions, $3,539.
Limitations: Applications not accepted. Giving limited to residents of Brattleboro, VT.
Trustee: Banknorth Investment Management Group, N.A.
EIN: 036007371

54164
Betty and Raymond Howard Scholarship Memorial Fund
25 Kingman St.
P.O. Box 320
St. Albans, VT 05478

Financial data (yr. ended 12/31/00): Grants paid, $3,437; assets, $125,283 (M); expenditures, $5,332; qualifying distributions, $3,437.
Limitations: Applications not accepted. Giving limited to residents of St. Albans, VT.
Application information: Recipient chosen by school faculty.
Trustee: Peoples Trust Co.
EIN: 036047459

54165
Public Domain Foundation
P.O. Box 430
Wilder, VT 05088
FAX: (802) 295-6250; E-mail: lizs@pdfoundation.org; URL: http://www.pdfoundation.org
Contact: Elizabeth Sunde, Exec. Dir.

Established in 1971 in NY.
Financial data (yr. ended 12/31/00): Grants paid, $3,100; assets, $108,376 (M); gifts received, $6,195; expenditures, $12,275; qualifying distributions, $3,100.
Limitations: Giving on a national basis.
Application information: Giving primarily to pre-selected organizations. Applicants may send letter via website.
Officers and Directors:* Noel Paul Stookey,* Pres.; Elizabeth Sunde,* Exec. Dir.
EIN: 237125049

54166
The Family Foundation Works
c/o Good Works Farm
P.O. Box 207
Townshend, VT 05353

Established in 1997 in CT.
Donor(s): Robert F. Works, John A. Works.
Financial data (yr. ended 12/31/01): Grants paid, $3,000; assets, $52,725 (M); expenditures, $3,212; qualifying distributions, $3,000.
Limitations: Applications not accepted.
Application information: Contributes only to pre-selected organizations.
Officers and Trustees:* John A. Works,* Secy.; Robert F. Works,* Treas.
EIN: 061485215

54167
Keal Foundation
c/o Jacobs, Morrisette, Marchand & Assoc.
P.O. Box 385
Burlington, VT 05402
Application address: P.O. Box 647, Orange, VA 22960, tel.: (540) 672-9023

Donor(s): Caryll M. Pott.
Financial data (yr. ended 12/31/99): Grants paid, $3,000; assets, $241,467 (M); gifts received, $425; expenditures, $3,425; qualifying distributions, $3,000.
Limitations: Giving limited to Essex, VT.
Application information: Application form required.
Trustees: Andrew W. Pott, Caryll M. Pott, Earll M. Pott, Leslie F. Pott, Kim S. Ward.
EIN: 030280402

54168
Stranahan Memorial Fund
c/o Peoples Trust Co.
P.O. Box 320
St. Albans, VT 05478 (802) 524-2196

Financial data (yr. ended 12/31/00): Grants paid, $3,000; assets, $68,534 (M); gifts received, $200; expenditures, $4,118; qualifying distributions, $3,000.
Limitations: Giving limited to St. Albans, VT.
Trustee: Peoples Trust Co.
EIN: 036009634

54169
Munsell Family Foundation
872 Grassy Brook Rd.
Brookline, VT 05345 (802) 254-3990
Contact: Mark L. Munsell, Tr.

Established in 2000 in VT.
Donor(s): Mark L. Munsell, Georgia M. Munsell.
Financial data (yr. ended 12/31/01): Grants paid, $2,950; assets, $72,727 (M); gifts received, $41,040; expenditures, $3,365; qualifying distributions, $2,950.
Limitations: Giving primarily in VT.
Application information: Application form not required.
Trustees: Georgia M. Munsell, Mark L. Munsell.
EIN: 030368072

54170
Annie T. Smith Mercy Fund
R.F.D. No. 1
Randolph, VT 05060-9801 (802) 234-9135
Contact: Barbara Pinello, Tr.

Financial data (yr. ended 12/31/99): Grants paid, $2,948; assets, $204,682 (M); expenditures, $3,146; qualifying distributions, $3,201.
Limitations: Giving limited to the Randolph, VT, area.
Trustee: Barbara Pinello.
EIN: 036005853

54171
Jean & Ruth Aseltine Fund
c/o Peoples Trust Co.
P.O. Box 320
St. Albans, VT 05478
Application address: c/o Reginald Godin, Bellows Free Academy of St. Albans, S. Main St., St. Albans, VT 05478, tel.: (802) 527-6402

Financial data (yr. ended 12/31/00): Grants paid, $2,826; assets, $95,284 (M); expenditures, $4,497; qualifying distributions, $2,804.
Limitations: Giving limited to residents of St. Albans, VT.
Trustee: Peoples Trust Co.

EIN: 036037928

54172
Robert T. Arnold Scholarship Trust Fund
c/o Banknorth Investment Management Group, N.A.
P.O. Box 595
Williston, VT 05495
Application address: c/o Superintendent, Adams Schools, 125 Savory Rd., Adams, MA 01220

Financial data (yr. ended 12/31/01): Grants paid, $2,800; assets, $43,485 (M); expenditures, $4,674; qualifying distributions, $3,394.
Limitations: Giving primarily in the Pittsfield, MA, area.
Trustee: Banknorth Investment Management Group, N.A.
EIN: 046141729
Codes: GTI

54173
Mildred M. Keefe Trust
c/o Chittenden Bank
P.O. Box 399
Bellows Falls, VT 05101

Financial data (yr. ended 12/31/01): Grants paid, $2,454; assets, $58,917 (M); expenditures, $4,270; qualifying distributions, $2,454.
Limitations: Applications not accepted. Giving primarily in Bellows Falls, VT.
Application information: Contributes only to a pre-selected organization.
Trustee: Chittenden Bank.
EIN: 036040490

54174
Buzz McDermott Scholarship Fund, Inc.
c/o Mary Ann McDermott Reynolds
336 Vermont, Rte. 105
Sheldon, VT 05483-9642
Application address: c/o Sally Bashaw, EFHS, Enosburg Falls, VT 05450, tel.: (802) 933-7777

Established in 1995 in VT.
Financial data (yr. ended 05/31/00): Grants paid, $2,100; assets, $32,841 (M); expenditures, $5,521; qualifying distributions, $2,100.
Application information: Application form required.
Officers: Madeline J. McDermott, Pres.; Peter J. McDermott, V.P.; Mary Ann McDermott Reynolds, Secy.-Treas.
EIN: 030349977

54175
Arlington Community Public Health Nursing Service, Inc.
c/o Lynn Williams
P.O. Box 62
Arlington, VT 05250-0062

Financial data (yr. ended 12/31/00): Grants paid, $2,075; assets, $376,331 (M); gifts received, $7,220; expenditures, $22,904; qualifying distributions, $18,594; giving activities include $15,085 for programs.
Limitations: Applications not accepted. Giving limited to Arlington, Sandgate, and Sunderland, VT.
Officers and Trustees:* Marge Hanson,* Pres.; Kathleen Morse,* V.P.; Rebecca Parks,* Corr. Secy.; Bobby O'Dea,* Secy.; Pat Carpenter, Martha Culler, and 24 additional trustees.
EIN: 030186323

54176
Reginald L. Blair Memorial Fund
c/o Douglas Moore
P.O. Box 201
Sharon, VT 05065
Application address: c/o Howe Hill, Sharon, VT 05065, tel.: (802) 763-7081
Contact: Vivian Moore, Pres.

Established in 1996 in VT.
Donor(s): Reginald L. Blair.
Financial data (yr. ended 12/31/00): Grants paid, $2,000; assets, $65,769 (M); expenditures, $2,252; qualifying distributions, $2,000.
Limitations: Giving primarily in Sharon, VT.
Application information: Application form required.
Officers: Vivian Moore, Pres.; Douglas Moore, V.P. and Secy.; Pamela Brackett, Treas.
Director: Philip Pomerville.
EIN: 030349878

54177
Per Kristiansen Memorial Scholarship Fund
20 S. Crest Dr.
Burlington, VT 05401 (802) 951-9325
Contact: Eileen G.C. Kristiansen, Treas.

Financial data (yr. ended 12/31/01): Grants paid, $2,000; assets, $15,813 (M); expenditures, $2,000; qualifying distributions, $2,000.
Limitations: Giving limited to residents of Milton, VT.
Application information: Application form required.
Officers: Gertrude Kristiansen, Pres.; Paul Kristiansen, V.P.; Linda Kristiansen, Secy.; Eileen G.C. Kristiansen, Treas.
EIN: 582423121

54178
Shefali Batra Foundation
c/o Narain D. Batra
Dickinson Dr.
Northfield Falls, VT 05664

Donor(s): Narain D. Batra.
Financial data (yr. ended 12/31/01): Grants paid, $1,830; assets, $7,274 (M); gifts received, $2,125; expenditures, $1,839; qualifying distributions, $1,830.
Limitations: Applications not accepted. Giving primarily in VT.
Application information: Contributes only to pre-selected organizations.
Trustees: Narain D. Batra, Nikhil N. Batra, Thakar Devi Batra, Varsha M. Batra.
EIN: 030333950

54179
The Educational Design Foundation
P.O. Box 25, 66 Old Coach Rd.
Norwich, VT 05055

Incorporated in 1991 in VT.
Donor(s): Elizabeth B. Carlson.
Financial data (yr. ended 12/31/01): Grants paid, $1,498; assets, $44,181 (M); expenditures, $2,318; qualifying distributions, $2,318; giving activities include $820 for programs.
Limitations: Applications not accepted. Giving primarily in VT.
Application information: Contributes only to pre-selected organizations.
Officers and Directors:* Elizabeth B. Carlson,* Pres.; Robert F. Carlson,* Secy.; Christopher C. Badger.
EIN: 030331005

54180
John T. Theodore Scholarship Fund
c/o Banknorth Investment Management Group, N.A.
P.O. Box 595, Banknorth Group
Williston, VT 05495-0595
Application address: c/o Bellows Free Academy, Main St., St. Albans, VT 05478

Financial data (yr. ended 10/31/01): Grants paid, $1,398; assets, $51,284 (M); expenditures, $1,726; qualifying distributions, $1,398.
Limitations: Giving limited to St. Albans, VT.
Trustee: Banknorth Investment Management Group, N.A.
EIN: 036010212

54181
The Richard A. Morton Foundation
c/o Richard A. Morton
P.O. Box 800, Vermont National Bank
Brattleboro, VT 05302-0800

Financial data (yr. ended 03/31/01): Grants paid, $1,376; assets, $1 (M); expenditures, $1,654; qualifying distributions, $1,376.
Limitations: Applications not accepted. Giving primarily in Orchard Park, NY.
Application information: Contributes only to pre-selected organizations.
Trustee: Richard A. Morton.
EIN: 166723787

54182
The Michael and Zarifa Ziter Memorial Trust
c/o Banknorth Investment Management Group, N.A.
P.O. Box 595, Banknorth Group
Williston, VT 05495-0595
Application address: c/o Society of St. Edmund, 270 Winooski Park, Colchester, VT 05439

Financial data (yr. ended 01/31/02): Grants paid, $1,329; assets, $74,107 (M); expenditures, $2,681; qualifying distributions, $1,329.
Limitations: Giving limited to Colchester, VT.
Trustee: Banknorth Investment Management Group, N.A.
EIN: 036043815

54183
The Helene Spoehr and Edgar E. Clarke Foundation, Inc.
237 Thaddeus Stevens Rd.
Peacham, VT 05862 (802) 592-3130
URL: http://www.scfdn.org
Contact: Grace DiNapoli

Established in 1999 in VT.
Donor(s): Helene D. Spoehr, Edgar E. Clarke.
Financial data (yr. ended 12/31/01): Grants paid, $1,310; assets, $238,116 (M); gifts received, $250; expenditures, $53,378; qualifying distributions, $24,812.
Limitations: Giving primarily in NH and VT.
Officers: Helene D. Spoehr, Pres.; Edgar E. Clarke, Secy.-Treas.
Director: Samantha Green.
EIN: 030361051

54184
McIndoe Falls Academy
P.O. Box 24
Barnet, VT 05821
Contact: Karolyn Farman, Chair.

Financial data (yr. ended 12/31/00): Grants paid, $800; assets, $229,527 (M); gifts received, $40; expenditures, $38,402; qualifying distributions, $9,157; giving activities include $26,145 for programs.
Limitations: Giving limited to residents in Barnet, VT.
Officers: Karolyn Farman, Chair.; Larry Thomas, Pres.
EIN: 030185087

54185
Mr. & Mrs. Gordon C. Trudeau Scholarship Fund
c/o Banknorth Investment Management Group, N.A.
P.O. Box 595, Banknorth, Tax Dept.
Williston, VT 05495-0595
Application address: c/o Bellows Free Academy, Main St., St. Albans, VT 05478, tel.: (802) 527-7576

Financial data (yr. ended 12/31/99): Grants paid, $720; assets, $13,681 (M); expenditures, $1,206; qualifying distributions, $1,049.
Limitations: Giving limited to residents of Winooski, VT.
Trustee: Banknorth Investment Management Group, N.A.
EIN: 237425793

54186
Eloise L. Myers Trust
(Formerly Steadman-Myers Memorial Fund)
c/o Banknorth Investment Management Group, N.A.
P.O. Box 595, Banknorth Group
Williston, VT 05495

Established in 1994 in MA.
Financial data (yr. ended 12/31/99): Grants paid, $700; assets, $13,393 (M); expenditures, $3,138; qualifying distributions, $1,668.
Limitations: Applications not accepted.
Trustee: Banknorth Investment Management Group, N.A.
EIN: 046309089

54187
Marion L. Hagar Memorial Scholarship Fund
P.O. Box 303
Barton, VT 05822-0303 (802) 525-3766
Contact: William Boyd Davies, Tr.

Established in 1987 in VT.
Financial data (yr. ended 12/31/01): Grants paid, $500; assets, $20,255 (M); expenditures, $1,101; qualifying distributions, $1,101.
Limitations: Giving limited to residents of VT.
Application information: Application form required.
Trustee: William Boyd Davies.
EIN: 222816135

54188
Dr. Claude A. Loftis Memorial Scholarship Fund
c/o Banknorth Investment Management Group, N.A.
P.O. Box 595
Williston, VT 05495-0595
Application address: c/o Bellows Free Academy, S. Main St., St. Albans, VT 05478

Financial data (yr. ended 05/31/02): Grants paid, $350; assets, $12,472 (M); expenditures, $573; qualifying distributions, $423.
Limitations: Giving limited to residents of St. Albans, VT.
Application information: Admission application from student's intended school and financial statement.
Trustee: Banknorth Investment Management Group, N.A.
EIN: 036023478

54189
Tricia E. Pettis Memorial Scholarship Fund
c/o Sheila B. Pettis
R.R. Box 3915, Pettis Rd.
Fair Haven, VT 05743

Established in 1996 in VT.
Financial data (yr. ended 06/30/00): Grants paid, $200; assets, $4,801 (L); gifts received, $250; expenditures, $219; qualifying distributions, $300.
Limitations: Giving to residents of Fair Haven, VT.
Trustees: Sheila B. Pettis, Stacy L. Pettis, Stephanie A. Pettis.
EIN: 030353594

54190
Sunset Ridge Charitable Trust
R.R. 2, Box 99
Bethel, VT 05032

Established in 2001 in VT.
Financial data (yr. ended 12/31/01): Grants paid, $131; assets, $2,256 (M); gifts received, $996; expenditures, $173; qualifying distributions, $0.
Limitations: Giving primarily in Bethel, VT.
Trustees: John Kreider, Vickie Kreider.
EIN: 036069386

54191
Alice Baber Art Fund, Inc.
P.O. Box 185
Jamaica, VT 05343

Established in 1989 in NY.
Donor(s): Alice Baber.‡
Financial data (yr. ended 12/31/01): Grants paid, $0; assets, $440,877 (M); gifts received, $6,337; expenditures, $122,369; qualifying distributions, $93,324.
Limitations: Giving primarily in CT, NY and VT.
Officer and Directors:* Beth A. Meachem,* Exec. Dir.; Elaine Beckwith, Laura Berry, Virginia T. Nelson.
EIN: 133511667

54192
Alger D. Beal Foundation
c/o Chittenden Bank
P.O. Box 820, 2 Burlington Sq.
Burlington, VT 05402

Established in 1989 in VT.
Donor(s): Alger D. Beal.‡
Financial data (yr. ended 12/31/00): Grants paid, $0; assets, $2,530 (M); expenditures, $1,603; qualifying distributions, $0.
Limitations: Applications not accepted. Giving limited to VT.
Application information: Contributes only to pre-selected organizations.
Trustees: Jacobs, McLintock & Scanlon, Chittenden Bank.
EIN: 223020006

54193
Charlie Burchard Memorial Trust
40 George St.
P.O. Box 638
Burlington, VT 05402-0638
Contact: Daniel L. Burchard, Tr.

Financial data (yr. ended 12/31/00): Grants paid, $0; assets, $50,177 (M); gifts received, $1,640; expenditures, $240; qualifying distributions, $240.
Limitations: Giving primarily in VT.
Trustees: Lisa Boudah, Steve Boudah, Daniel L. Burchard, Jane Burchard, John Burchard, John B. Burchard, Sara B. Burchard, Vicki Burchard.
EIN: 036048114

54194
The Jack and Dorothy Byrne Foundation, Inc.
c/o Robert E. Snyder
331 Olcott Dr., Ste. L3
White River Junction, VT 05001-9263
Contact: Dorothy M. Byrne, Pres.

Established in 1999 in DE.
Financial data (yr. ended 12/31/00): Grants paid, $0; assets, $205,409 (M); gifts received, $111,221; expenditures, $7,896; qualifying distributions, $7,896.
Officers and Directors:* Dorothy M. Byrne,* Pres.; John J. Byrne,* V.P.; Robert E. Snyder,* Secy.-Treas.; Christina M. Baltz.
EIN: 030363118

54195
The Canaan Foundation for Christian Education
c/o Richard Broggi
P.O. Box 366
Bridgewater Corners, VT 05035

Established in 1990 in VT.
Donor(s): Valley Bible Church.
Financial data (yr. ended 12/31/99): Grants paid, $0; assets, $482,262 (M); gifts received, $500; expenditures, $4,271; qualifying distributions, $4,271.
Limitations: Applications not accepted. Giving primarily in NH and VT.
Application information: Contributes only to pre-selected organizations.
Officers: Richard Broggi, Chair.; Charles Marrin, Secy.; Robert Oberkotter, Treas.
Trustees: Richard Heim, Bill Shaw, Betsy Warren, Don Wemple.
EIN: 222996387

54196
Charles Cooper Industrial School
c/o Laraine B. Smith, Chittenden Trust Co.
87 West St.
Rutland, VT 05701
Application address: c/o Dorothy Smith, 255 Union St., Bennington, VT 05201

Established in 1913 in VT.
Financial data (yr. ended 12/31/01): Grants paid, $0; assets, $1,243,528 (M); expenditures, $22,998; qualifying distributions, $85,440; giving activities include $74,800 for loans to individuals.
Limitations: Giving primarily to residents of Bennington County, VT.
Application information: Application form required.
Officers: Norma McShane, Pres.; Elizabeth Winter, V.P.; Susan Sage Wiskoski, Secy.; Laraine B. Smith, Treas.
EIN: 036010636
Codes: GTI

54197
The James L. FitzGerald Charitable Foundation, Inc.
3302 Vermont Rt. 7A
Arlington, VT 05250-8875

Established in 2000 in VT.
Donor(s): James L. FitzGerald.
Financial data (yr. ended 12/31/01): Grants paid, $0; assets, $100,000 (M); gifts received, $100,000; expenditures, $0; qualifying distributions, $0.
Officers: James L. FitzGerald, Pres.; Catharine B. Fairbanks, V.P.; Dennis A. Filippi, Secy.-Treas.
EIN: 030371569

54198
International Network of Resource Information Centers
P.O. Box 572
Windsor, VT 05089-0572

Established in 1985 in NH.
Donor(s): Donella H. Meadows, System Consulting, Inc., John A. Harris IV, Summit Foundation, Kathy Beys, Joan Davis, Rocky Mountain Institute, Sustainability Institute.
Financial data (yr. ended 12/31/01): Grants paid, $0; assets, $60,734 (M); gifts received, $77,472; expenditures, $48,356; qualifying distributions, $39,995; giving activities include $41,221 for programs.
Limitations: Applications not accepted. Giving on an international basis.
Application information: Contributes only to pre-selected organizations.
Officers and Directors:* Dennis L. Meadows, Pres. and Exec. Secy.; Gillian Martin Mehers,* Secy.; Wim Hafkamp,* Treas.; Zoltan Lontay, Aromar Revi, Jelel Ezzine, Nanda Gilden.
EIN: 222599815

54199
Bernice Jenkins Foundation, Inc.
c/o Amy J. Leavitt
4304 High Pastures Rd.
Woodstock, VT 05091-8116

Established in 2001 in VT.
Donor(s): Amy J. Leavitt.
Financial data (yr. ended 12/31/01): Grants paid, $0; assets, $100,000 (M); gifts received, $100,000; expenditures, $0; qualifying distributions, $0.
Limitations: Applications not accepted.
Application information: Contributes only to pre-selected organizations.
Trustee: Amy J. Leavitt.
EIN: 043612409

54200
Anthony C. Marro Memorial Trust
c/o Vermont National Bank
P.O. Box 800
Brattleboro, VT 05302

Established in 1993 in VT.
Donor(s): Anthony C. Marro.‡
Financial data (yr. ended 12/31/01): Grants paid, $0; assets, $451,439 (M); expenditures, $23,775; qualifying distributions, $0.
Limitations: Applications not accepted. Giving primarily in Ludlow, VT.
Application information: Contributes only to pre-selected organizations.
Trustees: Donald Laundry, Vermont National Bank.
EIN: 036056812

54201
C. Y. Oatway Foundation, Inc.
P.O. Box 62
South Pomfret, VT 05067-0062

Established in 1984 in CT.
Donor(s): Francis C. Oatway.
Financial data (yr. ended 11/30/01): Grants paid, $0; assets, $47,892 (M); expenditures, $0; qualifying distributions, $0.
Limitations: Giving on an international basis.
Officers: Ann T. Oatway, Pres.; Francis C. Oatway, Secy.-Treas.
Directors: Karen O. Crowley, Andrew C. Oatway, Christopher M. Oatway, Stephen F. Oatway.
EIN: 222581227

54202
Lord Rudolph Spanier Foundation, Inc.
P.O. Box 237
Cambridge, VT 05444-0237

Established in 2001 in VT.
Financial data (yr. ended 12/31/01): Grants paid, $0; assets, $6,864,000 (M); gifts received, $7,006,000; expenditures, $0; qualifying distributions, $0.
Officer: Ricard F. Spanier, Pres.

EIN: 223809595

54203
Vermont Dental Foundation
100 Dorset St., Ste. 18
South Burlington, VT 05403 (802) 864-0115
Contact: Peter Taylor, Exec. Dir.

Financial data (yr. ended 12/31/01): Grants paid, $0; assets, $5,883 (M); expenditures, $88; qualifying distributions, $0.

Officer: Peter Taylor, Exec. Dir.
Directors: Paul Averill, Phil Ehert, Judith Fisch, Karen Parolin, Brian Riggie, John Sinclair.
EIN: 030303902

VIRGIN ISLANDS

54204
The Beck Family Foundation, Inc.
4127 La Grande Princess, Ste. 304 A
Christainsted St. Croix, VI 00820

Established in 1999 in IL.
Donor(s): Robert N. Beck, Georgena M. Beck.
Financial data (yr. ended 12/31/01): Grants paid, $100,500; assets, $1,154,521 (M); gifts received, $72,200; expenditures, $100,650; qualifying distributions, $100,494.
Limitations: Applications not accepted. Giving primarily in IL.
Application information: Contributes only to pre-selected organizations.
Directors: Georgena M. Beck, Robert N. Beck, Guy R. Youman.
EIN: 364322305
Codes: FD2

54205
Peter Gruber Foundation
6000 Estate Charlotte Amalie, Ste. 4
St. Thomas, VI 00802   (340) 775-8035
Additional address: P.O. Box 503210, St. Thomas, VI 00805; FAX: (340) 775-8040; E-mail: pat@petergruberfoundation.org; URL: http://www.petergruberfoundation.org
Contact: Patricia Murphy, Pres.

Established in 1993 in CA.
Donor(s): Aberdeen, L.P., Peter J. Gruber.
Financial data (yr. ended 12/31/00): Grants paid, $43,875; assets, $10,536,677 (M); gifts received, $3,914,576; expenditures, $550,470; qualifying distributions, $220,645.
Limitations: Giving primarily in VI.
Application information: Application form not required.
Officers and Directors:* Peter J. Gruber, Pres.; Patricia Ann Murphy, V.P. and Secy.; Juanita Young,* Exec. Dir.; Luiz Fraga, Roberto Gasparini, Howard Hertz, Gary P. Kaplan, Hurdle H. Lea III.
EIN: 943185248

54206
Sidney Lee Dream Foundation
P.O. Box 130
Christiansted, VI 00821-0130
Contact: Sidney Lee, Dir.

Established in 1994.
Donor(s): Sidney Lee.
Financial data (yr. ended 12/31/99): Grants paid, $41,444; assets, $0 (L); expenditures, $41,444; qualifying distributions, $41,337.
Limitations: Giving on a national basis.
Directors: Phillip Lee, Sidney Lee, Candy Ward.
EIN: 660480642

54207
St. Croix Benjamin Foundation Scholarship Program, Inc.
4007 Estate Diamond Ruby
St. Croix, VI 00823

Established in 1998 in St. Croix.
Donor(s): Claude A. "Bennie" Benjamin.‡
Financial data (yr. ended 12/31/99): Grants paid, $36,000; assets, $1,388 (M); expenditures, $36,140; qualifying distributions, $36,140.
Limitations: Giving primarily in VI.
Officers: Walter J. M. Pedersen, Jr., Chair.; Magda B. Finch, V.P.; Emily Harris, Secy.
Director: James S. Glenn.
EIN: 660485162

54208
Humphrey Foundation
9003 Gentle Winds
Christiansted, VI 00820

Established in 1999 in VI.
Financial data (yr. ended 12/31/01): Grants paid, $9,200; assets, $89,179 (M); gifts received, $5,000; expenditures, $9,900; qualifying distributions, $9,200.
Limitations: Applications not accepted. Giving primarily in RI and the Virgin Islands.
Application information: Contributes only to pre-selected organizations.
Trustees: Marilyn Humphrey, William Humphrey.
EIN: 311624936

VIRGINIA

54209
The Whitaker Foundation
1700 N. Moore St., Ste. 2200
Rosslyn, VA 22209 (703) 528-2430
E-mail: info@whitaker.org; URL: http://www.whitaker.org
Contact: Peter G. Katona, Sc.D., C.E.O. and Pres.

Trust established in 1975 in NY.
Donor(s): U.A. Whitaker,‡ Helen F. Whitaker.‡
Financial data (yr. ended 12/31/01): Grants paid, $66,489,481; assets, $303,436,655 (M); expenditures, $71,353,595; qualifying distributions, $70,205,914.
Limitations: Giving limited to the U.S. and Canada for Biomedical Engineering Research and Special Opportunity Awards Programs; Regional Program limited to Collier County, FL; other programs are limited to the U.S.
Publications: Annual report (including application guidelines), program policy statement, informational brochure (including application guidelines), application guidelines.
Application information: The foundation has begun phasing out its grant programs to coincide with its planned closing in 2006. Application form not required.
Officers: Peter G. Katona, C.E.O. and Pres.; James A. Frost, V.P., Finance; John H. Linehan, Ph.D., V.P.; Wolf W. von Maltzahn, Ph.D., V.P., Biomedical Engineering.
Committee Members: G. Burtt Holmes, O.D., Chair.; William R. Brody, M.D., Ph.D., Ruth Whitaker Holmes, Ph.D., Thomas A. Holmes, James E. Kielley, Harold A. McInnes, Portia Whitaker Shumaker.
Trustee: The Chase Manhattan Bank, N.A.
EIN: 222096948
Codes: FD, FM

54210
Freddie Mac Foundation
M.S. A-40
8250 Jones Branch Dr.
McLean, VA 22102 (703) 918-8888
FAX: (703) 918-8895; E-mail: freddiemac__foundation@freddiemac.com; URL: http://www.freddiemacfoundation.org
Contact: Cheryl Clark, Dir., Foundation Giving

Established in 1990 in VA.
Donor(s): Federal Home Loan Mortgage Corp.
Financial data (yr. ended 12/31/01): Grants paid, $16,971,756; assets, $29,525,420 (M); gifts received, $20,855,320; expenditures, $21,335,092; qualifying distributions, $21,157,245.
Limitations: Giving primarily in Washington, DC; VA, in the counties of Arlington, Fairfax, Loudoun and Prince William and the cities of Alexandria, Falls Church, Manassas Park, and Leesburg; and MD, in the counties of Charles, Frederick, Howard, Montgomery, and Prince George's. Funding is also available for statewide initiatives in MD and VA and programs that are national in scope. Funding in Atlanta, GA, Chicago, IL, Dallas, TX, Los Angeles, CA, and New York, NY, is by invitation only.
Publications: Annual report, application guidelines, newsletter, grants list, informational brochure.
Application information: Requests for grants greater than $50,000 are by invitation only. Application form required.

Officers and Directors:* Leland C. Brendsel,* Chair.; Maxine B. Baker,* Pres. and C.E.O.; Catherine E. Dee, C.F.O.; Dionisia Bejarano Coffman, Tracy Hagen Mooney, Gregory J. Parseghian, Ronald Poe, Donald J. Schuenke, Clarice Dibble Walker.
EIN: 541573760
Codes: CS, FD, CD, FM

54211
The Case Foundation
(Formerly The Stephen Case Foundation)
P.O. Box 10700
McLean, VA 22102
Contact: Pamela McGraw, Sr. V.P., Strategic Planning and Outreach

Established in 1997 in VA.
Donor(s): Stephen M. Case.
Financial data (yr. ended 12/31/00): Grants paid, $13,890,628; assets, $88,956,725 (M); gifts received, $11,346,875; expenditures, $14,777,765; qualifying distributions, $14,554,938.
Limitations: Applications not accepted.
Application information: Contributes only to pre-selected organizations.
Officers and Directors:* Stephen M. Case,* Chair.; Jean Case,* Pres.; John Agee, Exec. V.P.; Jerry Dovalis, Sr. V.P., Strategic Rels.; Pam McGraw, Sr. V.P., Strategic Planning and Outreach; Shannon Rosser, Secy.-Treas.
EIN: 541848791
Codes: FD, FM

54212
Aimee and Frank Batten, Jr. Foundation
150 W. Brambleton Ave.
Norfolk, VA 23510

Established in 1998 in VA.
Donor(s): Frank Batten, Jr.
Financial data (yr. ended 12/31/00): Grants paid, $13,225,685; assets, $60,703,578 (M); gifts received, $51,751; expenditures, $13,908,038; qualifying distributions, $12,709,513.
Limitations: Applications not accepted.
Application information: Contributes only to pre-selected organizations.
Officer and Director:* Frank Batten, Jr.,* Pres. and Secy.-Treas.
EIN: 541879266
Codes: FD, FM

54213
The Community Foundation Serving Richmond & Central Virginia
(Formerly Greater Richmond Community Foundation)
7325 Beaufant Springs Dr., Ste. 210
Richmond, VA 23225 (804) 330-7400
FAX: (804) 330-5992; URL: http://www.tcfrichmond.org
Contact: Darcy S. Oman, Pres.

Established in 1968 in VA.
Financial data (yr. ended 12/31/01): Grants paid, $9,511,100; assets, $138,979,384 (M); gifts received, $30,517,764; expenditures, $10,640,791.
Limitations: Giving limited to residents of metropolitan Richmond, the tri-cities area, including Hopewell, Colonial Heights, and Petersburg, and Chesterfield, Hanover, and Henrico counties, VA.
Publications: Annual report, application guidelines, biennial report.
Application information: R.E.B. Awards for Teaching Excellence forms available in Jan. from participating schools. Application form required.

Officers and Directors:* E. Armistead Talman, M.D., Chair.; Robert F. Norfleet, Jr.,* Vice-Chair.; Darcy S. Oman,* Pres.; Waller Horsley, Secy.; Thomas S. Word, Jr.,* Secy.; Joseph L. Antrim III, Treas.; Jeannie P. Baliles, Austin Brockenbrough III, Denise P. Dickerson, William M. Gottwald, M.D., John L. McElroy, Jr., Michele A.W. McKinnon, Delores Z. Pretlow, Walter S. Robertson III, Gilbert M. Rosenthal, Fred T. Tattersall, Barbara B. Ukrop, Erwin H. Will, Jr., J. James Zocco, M.D.
EIN: 237009135
Codes: CM, FD, GTI

54214
Doudera Family Foundation
2940 N. Lynnhaven Rd., Ste. 200
Virginia Beach, VA 23452

Established in 1996.
Donor(s): Ralph J. Doudera.
Financial data (yr. ended 12/31/00): Grants paid, $7,573,444; assets, $9,484,901 (M); gifts received, $2,144,468; expenditures, $8,382,605; qualifying distributions, $7,543,555.
Limitations: Applications not accepted.
Application information: Contributes only to pre-selected organizations.
Officers and Director:* Ralph J. Doudera,* Pres. and Secy-Treas.; Richard C. Mapp III, V.P.
EIN: 541817654
Codes: FD

54215
Mustard Seed Foundation, Inc.
3330 N. Washington Blvd., Ste. 100
Arlington, VA 22201 (703) 524-5620
FAX: (703) 524-5643; URL: http://www.msfdn.org
Contact: Craig E. Nauta, Exec. V.P.

Established in 1983 in SC.
Donor(s): Eileen H. Bakke, Dennis W. Bakke, and members of the Bakke and Harvey families.
Financial data (yr. ended 12/31/00): Grants paid, $7,307,985; assets, $6,500,000 (M); gifts received, $3,135,217; expenditures, $7,861,085; qualifying distributions, $7,307,985.
Limitations: Giving on a national and international basis.
Publications: Annual report, application guidelines.
Application information: Application must be recommended by a board member before being considered. Application form required.
Officers and Directors:* Eileen H. Bakke,* Chair.; Dennis W. Bakke,* Pres.; Craig E. Nauta, Exec. V.P. and Secy.; Craig Nauta, Exec. V.P.; Paul O. Pearson,* Treas.; Brandon Bakke, Diana Bakke, K. Brian Bakke, Raymond J. Bakke, Helen C. Harvey, William B. Harvey, W. Brantley Harvey, Margaret Laffitte, Tuck Laffitte, Dan Thompson.
Junior Board: Margaret Bakke, Chair.; Dennis Bakke, Jr., Peter Bakke, Rachel Bakke, Jordan Carrier, W. Brantley Harvey IV, Helen Laffitte, M. Tucker Laffitte IV, Tylor Nauta, Carolyn Thompson, Daniel Thompson.
EIN: 570748914
Codes: FD, FM

54216
The Norfolk Foundation
1 Commercial Pl., Ste 1410
Norfolk, VA 23510-2113 (757) 622-7951
FAX: (757) 622-1751; E-mail:
info@norfolkfoundation.org; URL: http://
www.norfolkfoundation.org
Contact: Angelica D. Light, Pres.

Established in 1950 in VA by resolution and declaration of trust.
Financial data (yr. ended 12/31/01): Grants paid, $5,986,311; assets, $137,398,667 (M); gifts received, $5,079,964; expenditures, $6,736,700.
Limitations: Giving limited to Norfolk, VA, and a 50-mile area from its boundaries.
Publications: Annual report (including application guidelines), application guidelines, informational brochure, newsletter, financial statement, grants list.
Application information: Application form required for scholarships only; applications available Dec. 1.
Board Members: Joshua P. Darden, Jr., Chair.; Toy D. Savage, Jr., Vice-Chair.; Angelica D. Light, Pres.; John O. Wynne, Treas.; Jean C. Bruce, H.P. McNeal, Kurt M. Rosenbach, Martha M. Williams.
EIN: 540722169
Codes: CM, FD, FM, GTI

54217
Robins Foundation
1021 E. Cary St., 8th Fl.
Richmond, VA 23219 (804) 697-6917
Application address: P.O. Box 1124, Richmond, VA 23218; URL: http://
www.robins-foundation.org
Contact: William L. Roberts, Jr., Exec. Dir.

Established in 1957 in VA.
Donor(s): E. Claiborne Robins.‡
Financial data (yr. ended 12/31/01): Grants paid, $5,354,844; assets, $105,793,893 (M); expenditures, $6,286,038; qualifying distributions, $5,551,172.
Limitations: Giving primarily in Richmond, VA.
Publications: Application guidelines, annual report.
Application information: Application form required.
Officers and Directors:* Betty Robins Porter,* Pres.; E. Claiborne Robins, Jr., V.P.; E. Bruce Heilman,* Secy.; Reginald N. Jones,* Treas.; William L. Roberts, Jr., Exec. Dir.; Lewis T. Booker, Ann Carol Marchant, Lora M. Robins.
EIN: 540784484
Codes: FD, FM

54218
The Mary Morton Parsons Foundation
P.O. Box 85678
Richmond, VA 23285-5678
Contact: Mr. Hugh K. Leary, Exec. Dir.

Established in 1988 in VA.
Donor(s): Mary Morton Parsons.‡
Financial data (yr. ended 12/31/01): Grants paid, $5,035,000; assets, $88,571,808 (M); expenditures, $5,433,650; qualifying distributions, $5,014,579.
Limitations: Giving primarily in Richmond, VA.
Publications: Application guidelines.
Application information: Application form not required.
Officers and Directors:* Joseph L. Antrim III,* Pres. and Treas.; Charles F. Witthoefft,* V.P. and Secy.; Hugh K. Leary, Exec. Dir.; William C. Day, Mrs. Palmer P. Garson, E. Atwill Gilman, Thurston R. Moore.
EIN: 541530891

Codes: FD, FM

54219
The Robert G. Cabell III and Maude Morgan Cabell Foundation
P.O. Box 85678
Richmond, VA 23285-5678 (804) 780-2050
Contact: John B. Werner, Exec. Dir.

Incorporated in 1957 in VA.
Donor(s): Robert G. Cabell III,‡ Maude Morgan Cabell.‡
Financial data (yr. ended 12/31/01): Grants paid, $4,656,000; assets, $90,158,385 (M); expenditures, $4,693,978; qualifying distributions, $4,616,594.
Limitations: Giving limited to VA.
Publications: Application guidelines, informational brochure (including application guidelines).
Application information: Application form not required.
Officers and Directors:* J. Read Branch,* Pres. and Treas.; Edmund A. Rennolds, Jr.,* V.P.; Charles Cabell,* Secy.; John B. Werner, Exec. Dir.; Joseph L. Antrim III, J. Read Branch, Jr., Patteson Branch, Jr., John B. Cabell, Elizabeth Cabell Jennings, Mary Z. Zeugner.
EIN: 546039157
Codes: FD, FM

54220
The Batten Foundation
150 W. Brambleton Ave.
Norfolk, VA 23510-2018

Established in 1988 in VA.
Donor(s): Frank Batten.
Financial data (yr. ended 06/30/01): Grants paid, $4,314,034; assets, $25,956,732 (M); gifts received, $3,854,034; expenditures, $4,424,040; qualifying distributions, $4,289,040.
Limitations: Applications not accepted. Giving primarily in VA.
Application information: Contributes only to pre-selected organizations.
Officer: Frank Batten, Pres. and Treas.
EIN: 541451569
Codes: FD, FM

54221
SunTrust Foundation MidAtlantic
(Formerly Crestar Foundation)
c/o SunTrust Banks, Inc.
919 E. Main St.
Richmond, VA 23219 (804) 782-7907
Contact: Brenda L. Skidmore, Pres.

Established in 1973 in VA.
Donor(s): Crestar Bank, and other affiliates of Crestar Financial Corp., SunTrust Bank.
Financial data (yr. ended 12/31/01): Grants paid, $3,901,502; assets, $6,561,137 (M); gifts received, $4,000,000; expenditures, $3,903,807; qualifying distributions, $3,901,502.
Limitations: Giving limited to VA and communities served by bank affiliates.
Publications: Informational brochure.
Application information: Application form not required.
Officers: Brenda L. Skidmore, Pres.; Shirley Swartwout, Secy.-Treas.
EIN: 237336418
Codes: CS, FD, CD, FM

54222
WorldCom Foundation
(Formerly MCI WorldCom Foundation)
22001 Loudoun County Pkwy., Bldg. G1-3
Ashburn, VA 20147
FAX: (703) 886-0094
Contact: Caleb M. Schutz, Dir.

Established in 1986 in DC.
Donor(s): MCI Communications Corp., MCI WORLDCOM, Inc., WorldCom, Inc.
Financial data (yr. ended 12/31/00): Grants paid, $3,898,880; assets, $2,177,047 (M); gifts received, $2,734,216; expenditures, $7,615,953; qualifying distributions, $7,610,698.
Limitations: Applications not accepted.
Publications: Occasional report.
Application information: The foundation gives cash grants and limited in-kind products and services to premiere nonprofit organizations for innovative programs that align with its mission. Funds are disbursed through a request for proposal process offered to selected nonprofit organizations. Due to this proactive strategy the foundation does not review proposals at this time.
Directors: Vinton G. Cerf, Robert B. Hartnett, Bert C. Robert, Jr., Michael H. Salsbury, Caleb M. Schutz.
EIN: 510294683
Codes: CS, FD, CD, FM

54223
Massey Foundation
4 N. 4th St., Ste. 100
Richmond, VA 23219 (804) 643-3506
Contact: William E. Massey, Jr., Pres.

Established in 1958 in VA.
Donor(s): A.T. Massey Coal Co., Inc.
Financial data (yr. ended 11/30/01): Grants paid, $3,240,000; assets, $58,256,100 (M); expenditures, $3,605,708; qualifying distributions, $3,237,125.
Limitations: Giving primarily in VA, particularly Richmond.
Officers and Directors:* William E. Massey, Jr.,* Pres.; William Blair Massey,* V.P. and Secy.; E. Morgan Massey,* Treas.; Craig L. Massey, William Blair Massey, Jr.
EIN: 546049049
Codes: FD, FM

54224
Beazley Foundation, Inc.
3720 Brighton St.
Portsmouth, VA 23707-1788 (757) 393-1605
FAX: (757) 393-4708; E-mail:
beazley@norfolk.infi.net
Contact: Richard S. Bray, Pres.

Incorporated in 1948 in VA.
Donor(s): Fred W. Beazley,‡ Marie C. Beazley,‡ Fred W. Beazley, Jr.‡
Financial data (yr. ended 12/31/01): Grants paid, $2,947,056; assets, $65,909,671 (M); expenditures, $4,160,987; qualifying distributions, $3,529,346; giving activities include $336,783 for programs.
Limitations: Giving primarily in the South Hampton Roads area, VA.
Publications: Annual report, application guidelines, program policy statement.
Application information: Application form not required.
Officers and Trustees:* Richard S. Bray,* Pres.; P. Ward Robinett, Jr.,* Secy.; Leroy T. Canoles, Jr., Diane Pomeroy Griffin, William H. Hodges, Lawrence W. I'Anson, Jr.,* W. Ashton Lewis, Whitney G. Saunders.
EIN: 540550100

Codes: FD, FM

54225
The Horace G. Fralin Charitable Trust
P.O. Box 20069
Roanoke, VA 24018 (540) 774-4415
Contact: W. Heywood Fralin, Tr.

Established in 1989 in VA.
Financial data (yr. ended 12/31/00): Grants paid, $2,929,363; assets, $42,885,881 (M); gifts received, $9,951,671; expenditures, $3,545,526; qualifying distributions, $2,929,363.
Limitations: Giving primarily in Roanoke, VA.
Application information: Application form not required.
Manager and Trustee: W. Heywood Fralin.
EIN: 541509505
Codes: FD

54226
Landmark Communications Foundation
(Formerly Landmark Charitable Foundation)
150 W. Brambleton Ave.
Norfolk, VA 23510 (757) 446-2011
FAX: (757) 446-2489; E-mail: lhyatt@lcimedia.com
Contact: Linda S. Hyatt, V.P.

Incorporated in 1953 in VA.
Donor(s): Landmark Communications, Inc., The Virginian-Pilot, Greensboro News Co., Times-World Corp., KLAS-TV, WTVF-News Channel 5 Network, Capital Gazette.
Financial data (yr. ended 12/31/00): Grants paid, $2,739,555; assets, $55,227,887 (M); gifts received, $1,032,345; expenditures, $3,150,167; qualifying distributions, $2,897,086.
Limitations: Giving primarily in communities served by a Landmark company in Greensboro, NC, Las Vegas, NV, Nashville, TN, and the Hampton Roads and Roanoke, VA, areas.
Publications: Informational brochure (including application guidelines), application guidelines.
Application information: Application form not required.
Officers and Directors:* Frank Batten,* Chair.; Decker Anstrom,* Pres.; Linda S. Hyatt,* V.P. and Exec. Dir.; Richard F. Barry III,* V.P. and Treas.; Guy Friddell,* Secy.; D.R. Carpenter III, Frank Batten, Jr., R. Bruce Bradley, Richard A. Fraim, L. Govan King, Donald H. Patterson, Jr., Deborah Turner, Wendy Zomparelli.
EIN: 546038902
Codes: CS, FD, CD

54227
Charles E. Smith Family Foundation
2345 Crystal Dr.
Arlington, VA 22202

Established in 1963 in VA.
Donor(s): Charles E. Smith,‡ Robert H. Smith, Robert P. Kogod.
Financial data (yr. ended 02/28/01): Grants paid, $2,735,375; assets, $52,644,296 (M); gifts received, $13,186,239; expenditures, $2,765,455; qualifying distributions, $2,736,443.
Limitations: Applications not accepted. Giving primarily in the greater Washington, DC, area, MD, VA, NJ, and NY.
Application information: Contributes only to pre-selected organizations.
Officers and Directors:* Robert P. Kogod,* V.P.; Robert H. Smith, Secy.-Treas.; Arlene R. Kogod, Clarice R. Smith.
EIN: 311570183
Codes: FD

54228
The Alleghany Foundation
450 W. Main St.
P.O. Box 1176
Covington, VA 24426 (540) 962-0970
FAX: (540) 962-1170; E-mail: Allegfnd@aol.com
Contact: Lewis M. Nelson, Jr., Exec. Dir.

Established in 1995 in VA; converted from the sale of Alleghany Regional Hospital Corporation to Columbia/HCA Healthcare Corp.
Financial data (yr. ended 05/31/02): Grants paid, $2,557,310; assets, $47,190,047 (M); expenditures, $3,073,303; qualifying distributions, $2,726,459.
Limitations: Giving primarily in Alleghany County, Covington, and Clifton Forge, VA.
Publications: Annual report, informational brochure (including application guidelines).
Application information: Application form not required.
Officers and Directors:* James D. Snyder,* Pres.; James I. Dill,* V.P.; Patrick H. Winston, Jr.,* Secy.; Lewis M. Nelson, Jr.,* Treas. and Exec. Dir.; William J. Ellis, Harrison L. Fridley, Jr., Jack A. Hammond, Charles Kahle, George J. Kostel, Wallace C. Nunley, John G. Sanders, Ward W. Stevens III, Anne L. Wright.
EIN: 541027400
Codes: FD

54229
Catherine Filene Shouse Foundation
(Formerly The CFS Foundation)
127 S. Fairfax St., No. 400
Alexandria, VA 22314 (703) 549-1055
Contact: Camille D. Warren, Secy.

Established in 1989 in VA.
Donor(s): Catherine F. Shouse.‡
Financial data (yr. ended 12/31/00): Grants paid, $2,552,000; assets, $10,449,566 (M); gifts received, $8,600; expenditures, $2,682,067; qualifying distributions, $2,571,124.
Limitations: Applications not accepted. Giving primarily in the eastern U.S.
Application information: Applications are by invitation only.
Directors: Alice F. Emerson, G. William Miller, Camille D. Warren.
EIN: 541497757
Codes: FD

54230
Gannett Foundation, Inc.
(Formerly Gannett Communities Fund/Gannett Co., Inc.)
7950 Jones Branch Dr.
McLean, VA 22107 (703) 854-6069
FAX: (703) 854-2002; E-mail: isimpson@gcil.gannett.com; URL: http://www.gannettfoundation.org
Contact: Irma Simpson, Mgr.

Established in 1991 in VA.
Donor(s): Gannett Co., Inc.
Financial data (yr. ended 12/27/00): Grants paid, $2,526,364; assets, $47,480,286 (M); gifts received, $17,671,405; expenditures, $2,679,557; qualifying distributions, $2,447,812.
Limitations: Giving limited to organizations in Gannett-served communities, including the U.S., Canada, and the U.S. territory of Guam.
Publications: Annual report, corporate report, informational brochure (including application guidelines).
Application information: Application form required.
Officers and Directors:* John J. Curley,* Chair.; Douglas H. McCorkindale,* Pres.; Millicent A. Feller, V.P.; Larry F. Miller, V.P.; Thomas L. Chapple, Secy.; Gracia C. Martore, Treas.
EIN: 541568843
Codes: CS, FD, CD, FM

54231
Norfolk Southern Foundation
P.O. Box 3040
Norfolk, VA 23514-3040 (757) 629-2881
E-mail: dhwyld@nscorp.com; URL: http://www.nscorp.com/nscorp/html/foundation.html
Contact: Deborah H. Wyld, Exec. Dir.

Established in 1983 in VA.
Donor(s): Norfolk Southern Corp.
Financial data (yr. ended 12/31/01): Grants paid, $2,439,976; assets, $5,589,961 (M); gifts received, $3,738,178; expenditures, $2,545,559; qualifying distributions, $2,446,664.
Limitations: Giving restricted to 22-state operating territory of Norfolk Southern Corp.
Publications: Application guidelines, annual report, program policy statement.
Application information: Application form not required.
Officers: David R. Goode, Chair., C.E.O. and Pres.; Kathryn B. McQuade, V.P.; L.I. Prillaman, Jr., V.P.; Stephen C. Tobias, V.P.; Henry C. Wolf, V.P.; Reginald J. Chaney, Secy.; Marta Stewart, Treas.; Deborah H. Wyld, Exec. Dir.
EIN: 521328375
Codes: CS, FD, CD

54232
The Klaassen Family Private Foundation
(Formerly The Klaassen Family Foundation)
9050 Falls Run Rd.
McLean, VA 22102-1005

Established in 1997 in MD.
Donor(s): Paul J. Klaassen, Teresa J. Klaassen.
Financial data (yr. ended 12/31/00): Grants paid, $2,330,950; assets, $3,947,026 (M); gifts received, $185,000; expenditures, $2,348,122; qualifying distributions, $2,324,623.
Limitations: Applications not accepted. Giving primarily in VA.
Application information: Contributes only to pre-selected organizations.
Trustees: Diane Doumas, Paul J. Klaassen, Teresa M. Klaassen.
EIN: 526860099
Codes: FD

54233
The Pittman Family Foundation
249 Springvale Rd.
Great Falls, VA 22066

Established in 1997.
Donor(s): Robert W. Pittman.
Financial data (yr. ended 04/30/00): Grants paid, $2,317,910; assets, $4,609,566 (M); gifts received, $3,492,375; expenditures, $2,347,755; qualifying distributions, $2,297,450.
Limitations: Applications not accepted. Giving on a national basis, with emphasis on New York, NY.
Application information: Contributes only to pre-selected organizations.
Trustee: Robert W. Pittman.
EIN: 541876548
Codes: FD

54234
Parker Foundation
500 Forest Ave.
Richmond, VA 23229 (804) 285-5416
FAX: (804) 285-5450; E-mail: mmyers@chesapke.com; URL: http://www.parkerfoundation.org
Contact: Malcolm J. Myers, Dir.

Established in 1995 in VA.
Financial data (yr. ended 06/30/00): Grants paid, $2,204,162; assets, $110,497 (M); gifts received, $120,596; expenditures, $2,258,107; qualifying distributions, $2,254,120.
Limitations: Giving on a national basis.
Application information: Application form required.
Officers and Directors:* R. Jerry Parker, Jr.,* Pres.; Deana A. Parker,* Secy.-Treas.; Fritz Kling, Exec. Dir.; David Dwight, Malcolm J. Myers, Robert S. Parker, Jr.
EIN: 541770265
Codes: FD

54235
The Riverside Foundation Charitable Trust
305 Harrison St., S.E., 3rd Fl.
Leesburg, VA 20175
Application address: c/o The Riverside Foundation, P.O. Box 20266, Washington, DC 20041, tel.: (703) 448-0100
Contact: Grace McCrane, Admin. Asst.

Established in 1998.
Donor(s): The Trimble Revocable Living Trust.
Financial data (yr. ended 12/31/00): Grants paid, $2,164,813; assets, $16,529,022 (M); gifts received, $2,408; expenditures, $2,280,706; qualifying distributions, $2,184,004.
Limitations: Giving on a national basis.
Application information: Applicants should submit statement describing how organization has participated in religious ministry to the handicapped.
Officers and Directors:* Daniel D. Smith,* Pres.; Sharon R. Berry,* V.P.; Charles W. Colson,* Treas.; F. Carroll Brown, Carl F.H. Henry, Joni Erickson Tada, Ralph Veerman.
EIN: 546417931
Codes: FD

54236
Theresa A. Thomas Memorial Foundation
NationsBank Ctr.
1111 E. Main St., 21st Fl.
Richmond, VA 23219
Application address: P.O. Box 1122, Richmond, VA 23218, tel.: (804) 697-1200
Contact: Charles L. Reed, Pres.

Established in 1975.
Donor(s): George D. Thomas.‡
Financial data (yr. ended 08/31/00): Grants paid, $2,150,525; assets, $11,455,623 (M); expenditures, $2,224,928; qualifying distributions, $2,166,299.
Limitations: Giving primarily in VA.
Officers and Directors:* Charles L. Reed,* Pres. and Treas.; James C. Roberts,* V.P.; Richard L. Grier, Secy.
EIN: 510146629
Codes: FD

54237
The United Company Charitable Foundation
(Formerly United Coal Company Charitable Foundation)
P.O. Box 1280
Bristol, VA 24203-1280

Established in 1986 in VA.
Donor(s): United Coal Co., Inc., Burton Fletcher.
Financial data (yr. ended 12/31/01): Grants paid, $2,012,132; assets, $3,417,585 (M); gifts received, $1,602,400; expenditures, $2,031,072; qualifying distributions, $2,012,132.
Limitations: Applications not accepted. Giving primarily in TN and VA.
Application information: Contributes only to pre-selected organizations.
Officers: James W. McGlothlin, Pres.; Wayne L. Bell, Secy.; Lois A. Clarke, Treas.
EIN: 541390453
Codes: CS, FD, CD

54238
The Bryant Foundation
P.O. Box 1239
Stephens City, VA 22655 (540) 868-2183
Contact: Arthur H. Bryant II, Pres.

Established about 1949.
Donor(s): J.C. Herbert Bryant.‡
Financial data (yr. ended 12/31/00): Grants paid, $1,903,680; assets, $15,391,043 (M); expenditures, $1,999,900; qualifying distributions, $1,903,680.
Limitations: Giving primarily in VA.
Application information: Application form not required.
Officers: Arthur H. Bryant II, Pres. and Treas.; Arthur H. Bryant, Jr., Secy.
Trustee: Alexander W. Neal, Jr.
EIN: 546032840
Codes: FD

54239
Patricia and Douglas Perry Foundation
P.O. Box 869
Virginia Beach, VA 23451-2521

Established in 1993 in VA.
Donor(s): J. Douglas Perry, Patricia W. Perry.
Financial data (yr. ended 12/31/00): Grants paid, $1,902,812; assets, $4,791,099 (M); expenditures, $1,911,619; qualifying distributions, $1,902,812.
Limitations: Giving limited to residents of Virginia Beach and Norfolk, VA.
Application information: Application form required.
Officers: Patricia W. Perry, Pres.; Brandon D. Perry, V.P.; J. Douglas Perry, Treas.
Director: J. Christopher Perry.
EIN: 541691140
Codes: FD

54240
Thomas F. and Kate Miller Jeffress Memorial Trust
c/o Bank of America, Private Client Group
P.O. Box 26688
Richmond, VA 23261-6688 (804) 788-3698
FAX: (804) 788-2700
Contact: Dr. Richard B. Brandt, Advisor

Established in 1981 in VA.
Donor(s): Robert M. Jeffress.‡
Financial data (yr. ended 06/30/01): Grants paid, $1,870,764; assets, $32,408,864 (M); gifts received, $42,603; expenditures, $2,102,216; qualifying distributions, $1,888,254.
Limitations: Giving limited to VA.
Publications: Informational brochure (including application guidelines).
Application information: Application form not required.
Trustee: Bank of America.
Advisor: Richard B. Brandt, Ph.D.
Allocations Committee: Lawrence Blanchard, M.D., Cary Gresham, Thomas Haas, Ph.D., W. David Haress, Austin L. Roberts.
EIN: 546094925
Codes: FD

54241
Circuit City Foundation
9950 Mayland Dr.
Richmond, VA 23233-1464 (804) 527-4000
Contact: Jane Gurganus

Established in 1962 in VA.
Donor(s): Circuit City Stores, Inc., Wards Co., Inc.
Financial data (yr. ended 02/28/01): Grants paid, $1,700,986; assets, $2,048,005 (M); gifts received, $3,000,000; expenditures, $1,853,686; qualifying distributions, $1,852,541.
Limitations: Applications not accepted. Giving limited to areas of company operations.
Application information: Does not encourage unsolicited requests.
Trustees: Robert L. Burrus, Jr., Frances A. Lewis, Hyman Meyers, Frances H. Rosi, Richard L. Sharp, Edward Villanueva, Alan L. Wurtzel.
Scholarship Committee: Adrienne Bank, Grace Harris.
EIN: 546048660
Codes: CS, FD, CD, GTI

54242
Virginia Environmental Endowment
3 James Ctr.
1051 E. Cary St., Ste. 1400
Richmond, VA 23219 (804) 644-5000
Mailing address: P.O. Box 790, Richmond, VA 23218-0790; E-mail: info@vee.org; URL: http://www.vee.org
Contact: Gerald P. McCarthy, Exec. Dir.

Incorporated in 1977 in VA.
Donor(s): Allied Chemical Corp., Bethlehem Steel Corp., FMC Corp., Wheeling-Pittsburgh Steel Corp., Hauni Richmond, Inc., IR International, Inc.
Financial data (yr. ended 03/31/01): Grants paid, $1,689,318; assets, $17,372,200 (M); expenditures, $1,883,857; qualifying distributions, $1,689,318.
Limitations: Giving limited to KY and WV for the Ohio and Kanawha River Valleys Program and VA for the Virginia Program and Mini-Grant Program.
Publications: Annual report (including application guidelines), informational brochure (including application guidelines).
Application information: Application procedures and proposal requirements listed on website and in annual report. Application form not required.
Officers and Directors:* Dixon M. Butler,* Pres.; Alson H. Smith, Jr.,* Sr. V.P.; Gerald P. McCarthy, Secy. and Exec. Dir.; Paul U. Elbling,* Treas.; Robert M. Freeman, Linwood Holton, Nina Randolph, Robert B. Smith, Jr.
EIN: 541041973
Codes: FD

54243
Marietta McNeill Morgan & Samuel Tate Morgan, Jr. Foundation
c/o Bank of America
P.O. Box 26688
Richmond, VA 23261 (804) 788-2963
Contact: Elizabeth D. Seaman, Advisor

Trust established in 1967 in VA.
Donor(s): Marietta McNeill Morgan,‡ Samuel T. Morgan, Jr.‡
Financial data (yr. ended 06/30/01): Grants paid, $1,639,200; assets, $21,709,740 (M); expenditures, $1,828,703; qualifying distributions, $1,656,270.
Limitations: Giving limited to VA.
Publications: Informational brochure (including application guidelines).

Application information: Application form not required.
Trustee: Bank of America.
EIN: 546069447
Codes: FD

54244
The Beirne Carter Foundation
1802 Bayberry Ct., Ste. 301
Richmond, VA 23226-3773   (804) 521-0272
FAX: (804) 521-0274; E-mail:
bcarterfn@aol.com; URL: http://
www.bcarterfdn.org

Established in 1986 in VA.
Donor(s): Beirne B. Carter.‡
Financial data (yr. ended 12/31/00): Grants paid, $1,638,135; assets, $35,345,841 (M); expenditures, $1,940,357; qualifying distributions, $1,725,593.
Limitations: Giving primarily in VA.
Publications: Informational brochure (including application guidelines).
Application information: See Web site for list of items needed in proposal.
Officers: Mary Ross Carter Hutcheson, Pres.; Kenneth Laughon, V.P.; Talfourd H. Kemper, Secy.-Treas.
EIN: 541397827
Codes: FD

54245
William Petrach Charitable Trust
c/o Kay Mclaughlin
1750 Tysons Blvd., Ste. 1800
McLean, VA 22102

Established in 1999 in VA.
Financial data (yr. ended 12/31/99): Grants paid, $1,595,585; assets, $358,638 (M); gifts received, $1,932,904; expenditures, $1,600,519; qualifying distributions, $1,595,585.
Limitations: Applications not accepted. Giving on a national basis.
Application information: Contributes only to pre-selected organizations.
Trustee: Kay McLaughlin.
EIN: 912047013
Codes: FD

54246
The Pauley Family Foundation
c/o S.F. Pauley
314 Saint David's Ln.
Richmond, VA 23221

Established in 1993 in VA.
Donor(s): Stanley F. Pauley, Dorothy A. Pauley.
Financial data (yr. ended 12/31/00): Grants paid, $1,577,500; assets, $15,680,391 (M); expenditures, $1,694,664; qualifying distributions, $1,572,521.
Limitations: Applications not accepted. Giving primarily in Richmond, VA.
Application information: Contributes only to pre-selected organizations.
Officers: Stanley F. Pauley, Chair.; Dorothy A. Pauley, Pres. and Treas.; Katharine Pauley Hickok, V.P.; Lorna Pauley Jordan, V.P.; W. Birch Douglass III, Secy.
EIN: 541685158
Codes: FD

54247
The Flagler Foundation
(Formerly The Clisby Charitable Trust)
P.O. Box 8690
Richmond, VA 23226-0690
FAX: (804) 285-6560
Contact: Louise L. Foster, Pres.

Incorporated in 1963 in VA.
Donor(s): Jessie Kenan Wise.‡
Financial data (yr. ended 12/31/00): Grants paid, $1,494,947; assets, $26,906,400 (M); expenditures, $1,547,119; qualifying distributions, $1,500,567.
Limitations: Giving primarily in FL, with emphasis on St. Augustine, and in VA, with emphasis on Richmond.
Publications: Informational brochure (including application guidelines).
Application information: Receipt of proposals acknowledged. Application form not required.
Officers and Directors:* Louise L. Foster,* Pres.; Bradford B. Sauer,* V.P. and Treas.; Janet P. Lewis,* V.P.; Lewis B. Pollard, V.P.; Pam J. Royer, Secy.; Janet Lewis Sauer, B. Briscoe White III, Kenan Lewis White.
EIN: 546051282
Codes: FD

54248
Richard S. Reynolds Foundation
1403 Pemberton Rd., Ste. 102
Richmond, VA 23233   (804) 740-7350
FAX: (804) 740-7807; E-mail:
VPRSRFDN@aol.com
Contact: Victoria Pitrelli, Exec. Dir.

Incorporated in 1955 in VA.
Donor(s): David P. Reynolds, Julia L. Reynolds.‡
Financial data (yr. ended 06/30/01): Grants paid, $1,456,780; assets, $39,562,412 (M); gifts received, $38,526; expenditures, $1,729,962; qualifying distributions, $1,483,979.
Limitations: Giving primarily in VA.
Application information: Application form not required.
Officers and Directors:* David P. Reynolds,* Pres.; Mrs. Glenn R. Martin,* V.P.; Richard S. Reynolds III,* Secy.; William G. Reynolds, Jr.,* Treas.; Victoria Pitrelli, Exec. Dir.
EIN: 546037003
Codes: FD

54249
The Ukrop Foundation
600 Southlake Blvd.
Richmond, VA 23236-3922   (804) 327-7521
Contact: Gail Long

Established in 1983 in VA.
Donor(s): Ukrop's Super Markets, Inc.
Financial data (yr. ended 06/30/01): Grants paid, $1,453,617; assets, $12,300,969 (M); gifts received, $460,257; expenditures, $1,601,459; qualifying distributions, $1,444,244.
Limitations: Giving primarily in the greater Richmond, VA, area.
Application information: Application form not required.
Officers and Directors:* James E. Ukrop,* Pres.; Robert S. Ukrop,* V.P.; David J. Naquin,* Secy.-Treas.
EIN: 541206389
Codes: CS, FD, CD

54250
The Jackson Foundation
104 Shockoe Slip, Ste. 2B
Richmond, VA 23219-4125   (804) 644-5735
FAX: (804) 644-5736; E-mail:
linda@jacksonf.org or pat@jacksonf.org; URL:
http://www.jacksonf.org
Contact: Linda Buchanan, Admin., or Patricia M. Asch, Exec. Dir.

Established in 1981 in VA.
Donor(s): Andrew J. Asch, Jr.‡
Financial data (yr. ended 11/30/01): Grants paid, $1,427,601; assets, $17,083,801 (M); expenditures, $1,589,282; qualifying distributions, $1,417,149.
Limitations: Giving primarily in the metropolitan Richmond, VA, area.
Publications: Informational brochure (including application guidelines).
Application information: Application form required.
Officers and Directors:* Anthony James Asch,* Pres. and Treas.; Thomas A. Asch,* Secy.; Patricia M. Asch, Exec. Dir.; Linda Buchanan, W. Birch Douglass III.
EIN: 541186114
Codes: FD

54251
Perry Foundation, Inc.
P.O. Box 558
Charlottesville, VA 22902   (804) 977-5679
Contact: Francis H. Fife, Pres., or Stephanie Seech

Incorporated in 1946 in VA.
Donor(s): Hunter Perry,‡ Lillian Perry Edwards.‡
Financial data (yr. ended 12/31/00): Grants paid, $1,400,315; assets, $28,002,300 (M); expenditures, $1,520,626; qualifying distributions, $1,398,678.
Limitations: Giving primarily in VA, with emphasis on Albemarle County and Charlottesville.
Application information: Application form not required.
Officers and Trustees:* Francis H. Fife,* Pres.; Gary C. Mcgee,* V.P.; Susan M. Cabell,* Secy.; Edward D. Tayloe II,* Treas.; Roberta F. Brownfield, Suzanne Staton.
EIN: 546036446
Codes: FD

54252
Freiheit Foundation
1660 International Dr., Ste. 470
McLean, VA 22102
Contact: Peter Nguyen

Established in 1989 in MI.
Donor(s): Erik D. Prince, Joan Prince, Edgar D. Prince, Elsa D. Prince, Prince Holding Corp.
Financial data (yr. ended 06/30/01): Grants paid, $1,297,450; assets, $2,896,743 (M); gifts received, $2,500,000; expenditures, $1,305,215; qualifying distributions, $1,297,412.
Limitations: Applications not accepted. Giving primarily in Washington, DC, MI, and VA.
Application information: Contributes only to pre-selected organizations.
Officers: Erik D. Prince, Pres.; George Mokhiber, Secy.; Joan Prince, Treas.
EIN: 382902413
Codes: FD

54253—VIRGINIA

54253
Elis Olsson Memorial Foundation
c/o Dennis I. Belcher
P.O. Box 397
Richmond, VA 23218-0397 (804) 843-3300
Application address: P.O. Box 311, West Point, VA 23181

Established in 1966 in VA.
Donor(s): Inga Olsson Nylander,‡ Signe Maria Olsson.‡
Financial data (yr. ended 12/31/00): Grants paid, $1,291,623; assets, $26,651,154 (M); gifts received, $28,885; expenditures, $1,475,410; qualifying distributions, $1,347,037.
Limitations: Giving primarily in VA.
Officers and Directors:* Sture G. Olsson,* Pres.; Shirley C. Olsson,* V.P.; Dennis I. Belcher, Secy.-Treas.; Lisa Olsson Armstrong, Anne Olsson Loebs, Inga Olsson Rogers, Charles Elis Olsson.
EIN: 546062436
Codes: FD

54254
The Edward W. and Betty Knight Scripps Foundation
1360 Eagle Hill Farm
Charlottesville, VA 22901 (804) 973-3345
Contact: Gregory A. Robbins, V.P., Fin.

Established in 1987 in VA.
Donor(s): Betty Knight Scripps Harvey, Scripps League Newspapers, Inc.
Financial data (yr. ended 04/30/00): Grants paid, $1,290,000; assets, $6,724,230 (M); gifts received, $2,050,000; expenditures, $1,348,645; qualifying distributions, $1,331,822.
Limitations: Giving on a national basis.
Application information: Application form required.
Officers and Directors:* Betty Scripps Harvey,* Pres. and Treas.; Gregory A. Robbins,* V.P., Fin. and Secy.; Frederick W. Ahalt.
EIN: 541426826
Codes: FD

54255
Herndon Foundation
P.O. Box 995
Goochland, VA 23063

Established in 1965 in VA.
Donor(s): Floyd D. Gottwald, Jr.
Financial data (yr. ended 12/31/00): Grants paid, $1,286,789; assets, $18,364,362 (M); gifts received, $26,619; expenditures, $1,390,220; qualifying distributions, $1,272,221.
Limitations: Applications not accepted. Giving primarily in the Richmond, VA, area.
Application information: Contributes only to pre-selected organizations.
Officer: James T. Gottwald, Jr., Mgr.
Trustees: Elisabeth S. Gottwald, Floyd D. Gottwald, Jr.
EIN: 546060809
Codes: FD

54256
The Joco Foundation
1833 Joco Ln.
Moneta, VA 24121
Contact: Dianne E.H. Wilcox, Pres.

Established in 1990 in VA.
Donor(s): Reid Jones, Jr.‡
Financial data (yr. ended 12/31/99): Grants paid, $1,225,045; assets, $5,925,373 (M); expenditures, $1,556,919; qualifying distributions, $1,216,012.
Limitations: Giving primarily in VA.
Officer and Directors:* Diane E.H. Wilcox,* Pres. and Secy.-Treas.; Judy Jarrells, William J. Killinger.
EIN: 541552388
Codes: FD

54257
Alexander Berkeley Carrington, Jr. and Ruth S. Carrington Charitable Trust
c/o American National Bank and Trust Co.
P.O. Box 191
Danville, VA 24541
Contact: E. Budge Kent, Jr.

Established in 1985 in VA.
Donor(s): Alexander Berkeley Carrington,‡ Ruth Simpson Carrington.‡
Financial data (yr. ended 02/28/02): Grants paid, $1,130,392; assets, $21,502,321 (M); expenditures, $1,381,538; qualifying distributions, $1,135,629.
Limitations: Applications not accepted. Giving primarily in Danville, VA.
Application information: Contributes only to pre-selected organizations.
Trustees: B. Carrington Bidgood, James W. Perkinson, R. Lee Yancey, American National Bank and Trust Co. of Danville.
EIN: 546223108
Codes: FD

54258
The Kellar Family Foundation
P.O. Box 1178
Alexandria, VA 22313-1178

Established in 1997 in VA.
Donor(s): Arthur Kellar.
Financial data (yr. ended 02/28/02): Grants paid, $1,103,600; assets, $14,490,893 (M); expenditures, $1,280,003; qualifying distributions, $1,120,134.
Limitations: Applications not accepted. Giving primarily in VA.
Application information: Contributes only to pre-selected organizations.
Officers: Arthur Kellar, Pres. and Treas.; Elizabeth Kellar, Secy.
Directors: Judith C. Kellar Box, Nathan Box, Mary K. Kellar.
EIN: 522026425
Codes: FD

54259
W. C. English Foundation
c/o English Construction Co.
P.O. Box P7000
Lynchburg, VA 24505
Contact: Mrs. L.T. English, Tr.

Trust established in 1954 in VA.
Donor(s): Members of the English family.
Financial data (yr. ended 05/31/01): Grants paid, $1,088,666; assets, $28,520,935 (M); expenditures, $1,234,346; qualifying distributions, $1,061,136; giving activities include $67,211 for loans.
Limitations: Giving primarily in VA.
Trustees: Joan E. Allen, Beverly E. Dalton, Louise T. English, Margaret E. Lester, Suzanne E. Morse.
EIN: 546061817
Codes: FD

54260
The Titmus Foundation, Inc.
P.O. Box 10
Sutherland, VA 23885-0010 (804) 265-5834
Contact: Edward B. Titmus, Pres.

Incorporated in 1945 in VA.
Donor(s): Edward Hutson Titmus, Sr.‡
Financial data (yr. ended 01/31/01): Grants paid, $1,085,399; assets, $24,410,900 (M); expenditures, $1,226,734; qualifying distributions, $1,133,302.
Limitations: Giving primarily in VA.
Application information: No applications should be submitted in Jan. and Feb. Application form not required.
Officers: Edward B. Titmus, Pres.; Edward H. Titmus III, Exec. V.P.; William D. Allen II, V.P.; George B. Willis, V.P.; Kimberly T. Przybyl, Secy.; John J. Muldowney, Treas.
EIN: 546051332
Codes: FD

54261
The Mars Foundation
6885 Elm St.
McLean, VA 22101-3810 (703) 821-4900
FAX: (703) 448-9678
Contact: Sue Martin, Asst. Secy.

Incorporated in 1956 in IL.
Donor(s): Mars, Inc.
Financial data (yr. ended 12/31/01): Grants paid, $1,080,000; assets, $8,608,113 (M); gifts received, $600,000; expenditures, $975,701; qualifying distributions, $1,095,037.
Application information: Application form required.
Officers: Jacqueline B. Mars, Pres.; Forrest E. Mars, Jr., V.P.; John F. Mars, V.P.; Otis O. Otih, Secy.-Treas.
EIN: 546037592
Codes: CS, FD, CD

54262
William A. Hazel Family Foundation
c/o William A. Hazel
P.O. Box 600, 4305 Hazel Park Ct.
Chantilly, VA 20151-0600

Established in 2000 in VA.
Donor(s): William A. Hazel.
Financial data (yr. ended 12/31/01): Grants paid, $1,044,000; assets, $90,047 (M); gifts received, $10,044,544; expenditures, $1,056,544; qualifying distributions, $1,047,291.
Limitations: Applications not accepted. Giving primarily in VA.
Application information: Contributes only to pre-selected organizations.
Officers and Directors: William A. Hazel,* Pres.; Jay B. Keyser,* Secy.-Treas.; B. Daniel Hazel, David L. Hazel, Eleanor C. Hazel, William A. Hazel, Jr., Ruth Hazel, Jeannie H. Soltesz.
EIN: 541977626
Codes: FD

54263
Portsmouth General Hospital Foundation
360 Crawford St.
Portsmouth, VA 23704 (757) 391-0000
E-mail: pghfdn@pilot.infi.net; *URL:* http://www.pghfoundation.org
Contact: Alan E. Gollihue, C.E.O. and Pres.

Established in 1987 in VA as the Seller's Trust; converted through the sale of Portsmouth General Hospital, Inc. to Tidewater Health Care, Inc.; fully funded in 1988.
Financial data (yr. ended 06/30/02): Grants paid, $937,226; assets, $14,031,130 (M); expenditures, $1,261,985; qualifying distributions, $1,174,137.
Limitations: Giving limited to healthcare programs in Portsmouth, VA.
Publications: Application guidelines.
Application information: Application form not required.
Directors: Phyllis F. Bricker, Susan Taylor Hansen, William L. Harding, R. Scott Morgan, Karl S. Morristte, Brennan J. O'Connor, Horace S. Savage,

Jr., Harry L. Short, Burle U. Stromberg, Kevin D. Wilson, M.D., Nancy G. Wren.
EIN: 541463392
Codes: FD

54264
Foundation for Roanoke Valley, Inc.
310 1st St., Ste. 1150
P.O. Box 1159
Roanoke, VA 24006 (540) 985-0204
FAX: (540) 982-8175; *E-mail:* FRV@rev.net
Contact: Alan E. Ronk, Secy. and Exec. Dir.

Established in 1988 in VA; funded in 1990.
Financial data (yr. ended 06/30/01): Grants paid, $925,638; assets, $15,887,381 (M); gifts received, $1,095,536; expenditures, $1,337,804.
Limitations: Giving primarily in the greater Roanoke Valley, VA, area, with emphasis on Roanoke, Botetourt, Craig, Franklin and Rockbridge counties, VA.
Publications: Informational brochure, annual report, newsletter.
Application information: Application form required.
Officers and Governors:* Michael E. Warner,* Chair.; William A. Nash,* Vice-Chair.; Alan E. Ronk, Secy. and Exec. Dir.; James B. Lee,* Treas.; Carolyn C. Alley, Mary K. Bickford, Nan L. Coleman, Walter M. Dixon, Jr., Joy D. Frantz, Mason Haynesworth, James N. Hinson, Talfourd H. Kemper, Barbara B. Lemon, J. Lee E. Osborne, Peter A. Ostaseski, Douglas E. Pierce, M.D., Harry S. Rhodes, Garnett E. Smith, John B. Williamson III.
EIN: 541959458
Codes: CM, FD

54265
The Memorial Foundation for Children
P.O. Box 8450
Richmond, VA 23226
Contact: Elizabeth D. Seaman, Grants Coord.

Established about 1934 in VA.
Donor(s): Alexander S. George,‡ Elizabeth Strother Scott.‡
Financial data (yr. ended 12/31/01): Grants paid, $892,950; assets, $17,356,515 (M); expenditures, $910,343; qualifying distributions, $902,972.
Limitations: Giving limited to the Richmond, VA, area.
Publications: Informational brochure (including application guidelines).
Application information: Application form required.
Officers: Mrs. Richard A. Minardi, Jr., Pres.; Mrs. Paul B. Cosentino, V.P.; Mrs. J. Garrett Horsley, Corr. Secy.; Mrs. E. Armistead Talman, Treas.
EIN: 540536103
Codes: FD

54266
The Anne Lee Ueltschi Foundation
c/o The Private Consulting Group
1400 N. 14th St.
Arlington, VA 22209

Established in 1998 in DE.
Financial data (yr. ended 12/31/01): Grants paid, $892,916; assets, $513,047 (M); gifts received, $40,500; expenditures, $893,245; qualifying distributions, $893,001.
Limitations: Applications not accepted. Giving primarily in VA.
Application information: Contributes only to pre-selected organizations.
Officer: Anne Lee Ueltschi, Pres.
EIN: 061519387
Codes: FD

54267
Richard and Caroline T. Gwathmey Memorial Trust
c/o Bank of America
P.O. Box 26688
Richmond, VA 23261 (804) 788-3698
FAX: (804) 788-2700
Contact: Dr. Richard B. Brandt, Trust Advisor

Established in 1981 in VA.
Donor(s): Elizabeth G. Jeffress.‡
Financial data (yr. ended 06/30/01): Grants paid, $887,800; assets, $15,623,271 (M); expenditures, $1,006,852; qualifying distributions, $897,440.
Limitations: Giving limited to VA.
Publications: Informational brochure (including application guidelines), application guidelines.
Application information: Application form not required.
Trustee: Bank of America.
Advisor: Richard B. Brandt.
Allocations Committee: Lawrence E. Blanchard, Cary Gresham, Thomas Haas, David Harless, Austin L. Roberts.
EIN: 546191586
Codes: FD

54268
Geoffrey Gund Foundation
c/o Nancy Thibideaux
8484 Westpark Dr.
McLean, VA 22102
Application address: 40 E. 94th St., Apt. 28-E, New York, NY 10128
Contact: Geoffrey Gund, Tr.

Established in 1987 in DC.
Donor(s): Geoffrey Gund.
Financial data (yr. ended 06/30/01): Grants paid, $880,949; assets, $31,680,504 (M); gifts received, $3,000,000; expenditures, $1,267,217; qualifying distributions, $886,249.
Limitations: Giving primarily in NY, and Groton, MA.
Application information: Application form not required.
Trustees: Geoffrey Gund, Donald Kozusko, James O'Hara, KeyBank, N.A.
EIN: 521509128
Codes: FD

54269
Northern Virginia Community Foundation
8283 Greensboro Dr.
McLean, VA 22102 (703) 917-2600
FAX: (703) 902-3564; *E-mail:* jmkreutter@erols.com
Contact: Janet Miller Kreutter, Pres.

Incorporated in 1978 in VA.
Financial data (yr. ended 06/30/02): Grants paid, $880,114; assets, $12,604,300 (M); gifts received, $5,901,954; expenditures, $1,706,245.
Limitations: Giving limited to northern VA.
Publications: Annual report, financial statement, informational brochure, occasional report, newsletter, grants list, informational brochure (including application guidelines).
Application information: Application form required.
Officers and Directors:* Lavern J. Chatman,* Chair.; Janet Miller Kreutter,* Pres.; F. Weller Meyer,* Secy.; Robert Y. Hottle, Treas.; Robert Hickey,* Gen. Counsel; George Albright, C.G. Appelby, Leigh-Alexandra Basha, Lynn Alexis Lee Corey, John J. Dillon, Richard Duvall, James B. Graham, David Johnson, Dan Krevere, A. Paul Lanzillotta, Rodney W. Mateer, James E. Thomas III, Anthony R. Tringale, Dean Unemoto, Paul G. Veith, James M. Wordsworth.

EIN: 510232459
Codes: CM, FD, GTI

54270
The Glenstone Foundation
8404 Parham Ct.
McLean, VA 22102

Established in 1995 in VA.
Donor(s): Mitchell P. Rales.
Financial data (yr. ended 12/31/00): Grants paid, $876,920; assets, $34,521,605 (M); gifts received, $17,154,844; expenditures, $1,393,829; qualifying distributions, $879,211.
Limitations: Applications not accepted.
Application information: Contributes only to pre-selected organizations.
Officers and Director:* Mitchell P. Rales,* Chair.; Michael G. Ryan, Pres.; Joseph O. Bunting III, V.P.; Teresa L.C. Baldwin, Secy.-Treas.
EIN: 541739159
Codes: FD

54271
Universal Leaf Foundation
Hamilton and Broad Sts.
P.O. Box 25099
Richmond, VA 23260 (804) 359-9311
Contact: Nancy G. Powell, Mgr., Corp. Rels.

Established in 1975 in VA.
Donor(s): Universal Leaf Tobacco Co., Inc.
Financial data (yr. ended 06/30/01): Grants paid, $874,135; assets, $17,135,734 (M); expenditures, $962,443; qualifying distributions, $853,231.
Limitations: Giving primarily in VA.
Publications: Financial statement.
Application information: Application form not required.
Officers and Directors:* H.H. Harrell,* Pres.; Nancy G. Powell, V.P.; Catherine H. Claiborne, Secy.; Karen M.L. Whelan, Treas.; George C. Freeman, Genl. Counsel; A.B. King, C.A. Lelong, J.H. Starkey III, W.L. Taylor.
EIN: 510162337
Codes: CS, FD, CD

54272
The McGlothlin Foundation
P.O. Box 669
Bristol, VA 24203-0669 (276) 645-5370
Contact: Thomas D. McGlothlin, Pres.

Established in 1998 in VA.
Donor(s): Woodrow W. McGlothlin.
Financial data (yr. ended 12/31/01): Grants paid, $851,667; assets, $24,505,787 (M); expenditures, $1,131,679; qualifying distributions, $923,360.
Limitations: Giving in the southeastern U.S., with special emphasis to eastern KY, southwest VA, and northeast TN.
Publications: Informational brochure.
Officers: Woodrow W. McGlothlin, Chair. and C.E.O.; Thomas D. McGlothlin, Pres.; Michael D. McGlothlin, Secy.; James W. McGlothlin, Treas.
EIN: 541907305
Codes: FD

54273
The Genan Foundation
P.O. Box 5386
Charlottesville, VA 22905

Established in 1986 in VA.
Donor(s): Anne R. Worrell, T. Eugene Worrell.
Financial data (yr. ended 12/31/01): Grants paid, $849,000; assets, $2,466,167 (M); gifts received, $1,488,924; expenditures, $855,886; qualifying distributions, $849,454.
Limitations: Applications not accepted. Giving primarily in VA.

54273—VIRGINIA

Application information: Contributes only to pre-selected organizations.
Officers and Directors:* T. Eugene Worrell,* Chair.; Anne R. Worrell,* Pres.; Judith S. Coleman, Secy.; Andrew J. Dralopoli, Treas.
EIN: 541393561
Codes: FD

54274
Camp Foundation
P.O. Box 813
Franklin, VA 23851 (757) 562-3439
Contact: Bobby B. Worrell, Exec. Dir.

Incorporated in 1942 in VA.
Donor(s): James L. Camp,‡ P.D. Camp,‡ and their families.
Financial data (yr. ended 12/31/01): Grants paid, $816,917; assets, $19,241,001 (M); expenditures, $846,119; qualifying distributions, $826,746.
Limitations: Giving primarily in the city of Franklin, and Southampton and Isle of Wight counties, VA.
Publications: Application guidelines.
Application information: 4-year scholarships awarded to graduating high school seniors who are residents of the City of Franklin or the counties of Southampton and Isle of Wight. Application form not required.
Officers and Directors:* Robert C. Ray,* Chair.; Sol W. Rawls, Jr.,* Pres.; Westbrook Parker,* V.P.; John M. Camp, Jr.,* Treas.; Bobby B. Worrell,* Exec. Dir.; John M. Camp III, W.M. Camp, Jr., Clifford A. Cutchins III, William W. Cutchins, Randy B. Drake, John R. Marks, Paul Camp Marks, J. Edward Moyler, Jr., John D. Munford, S. Waite Rawls, Jr., J.E. Ray III, Richard E. Ray, Toy D. Savage, Jr.
EIN: 546052488
Codes: FD, GTI

54275
The Taubman Foundation
(Formerly Arthur & Grace W. Taubman Foundation, Inc.)
2965 Colonnade Dr., Ste. 300
Roanoke, VA 24018

Established around 1958.
Donor(s): Advance Stores Co., Inc., Nicholas F. Taubman.
Financial data (yr. ended 12/31/01): Grants paid, $816,500; assets, $109,970 (M); gifts received, $354,306; expenditures, $816,512; qualifying distributions, $816,512.
Limitations: Applications not accepted. Giving on a national basis, with emphasis on VA, primmarily in Roanoke, and Philadelphia, PA.
Application information: Unsolicited requests for funds not accepted.
Officers: Nicholas F. Taubman, Pres. and Secy.-Treas.; Eugenia L. Taubman, V.P.; Grace W. Taubman, V.P.
EIN: 546052861
Codes: FD, GTI

54276
Minnie & Bernard Lane Foundation
c/o Mrs. Bernard Lane
414 Washington St.
Altavista, VA 24517
Mailing address: P.O. Box 359, Altavista, VA 24517; Tel./FAX: (804) 369-6663
Contact: Cindy Jester, Admin. Asst.

Established in 1957 in VA.
Donor(s): Bernard B. Lane,‡ Minnie B. Lane.
Financial data (yr. ended 03/31/01): Grants paid, $815,590; assets, $8,719,109 (M); gifts received, $270,880; expenditures, $941,643; qualifying distributions, $813,941.
Limitations: Applications not accepted. Giving primarily in Campbell County, VA, for new projects.
Application information: Unsolicited requests for funds not accepted; funds fully committed.
Trustees: Minnie B. Lane, R.L. Short.
EIN: 546052404
Codes: FD

54277
The George and Carol Olmsted Foundation
103 W. Broad St., Ste. 330
Falls Church, VA 22046-4237
FAX: (703) 536-5020;
E-mail:scholars@olmstedfoundation.org; URL: http://www.olmstedfoundation.org
Contact: RADM Larry R. Marsh, Exec. V.P.

Incorporated in 1960 in VA.
Donor(s): George Olmsted.‡
Financial data (yr. ended 12/31/01): Grants paid, $792,952; assets, $32,302,317 (M); gifts received, $14,832,730; expenditures, $1,304,497; qualifying distributions, $1,195,026.
Limitations: Applications not accepted. Giving on a national basis.
Publications: Annual report, informational brochure.
Application information: Qualified military officers apply through their respective Military Service; funds largely committed.
Officers and Directors:* Amb. David S. Smith,* Chair.; Howard Hussing,* C.E.O. and Pres.; RADM Larry R. Marsh, Exec. V.P.; Joseph McManus, Secy.-Treas.; Maj. Genl. Bruce K. Scott, ADM. Carlisle A.H. Trost.
EIN: 546049005
Codes: FD, GTI

54278
WestWind Foundation
(Formerly The Caribbean-American Children's Foundation)
241 Rosemont Farm Way
Charlottesville, VA 22903-7200

Established in 1987 in DC.
Donor(s): Edward M. Miller.
Financial data (yr. ended 12/31/00): Grants paid, $733,475; assets, $10,023,666 (M); gifts received, $3,956,600; expenditures, $753,654; qualifying distributions, $725,147.
Limitations: Applications not accepted. Giving on a national basis, with emphasis on VA, ME, MA, and NY.
Application information: Contributes only to pre-selected organizations.
Trustees: Edward M. Miller, Janet H. Miller.
EIN: 526358830
Codes: FD

54279
Wrinkle in Time Foundation, Inc.
P.O. Box 306
The Plains, VA 20198-0306

Established in 1980 in NY.
Donor(s): A.B. Currier.
Financial data (yr. ended 12/31/01): Grants paid, $729,000; assets, $8,714,652 (M); expenditures, $796,787; qualifying distributions, $934,920.
Limitations: Giving primarily in VA.
Application information: Application form not required.
Officer and Board Member:* Andrea B. Currier,* Chair. and Pres.
EIN: 222351518
Codes: FD

54280
Carson Lee Fifer Foundation, Inc.
3601 Tupelo Pl.
Alexandria, VA 22304 (703) 712-5343
Contact: Carson Lee Fifer, Jr., Pres.

Financial data (yr. ended 12/31/00): Grants paid, $717,694; assets, $2,000 (M); expenditures, $728,945; qualifying distributions, $717,395.
Limitations: Giving primarily in Alexandria, VA.
Officers: Carson Lee Fifer, Jr., Pres.; Margaret Fifer Davenport, V.P.; Marilie F. Dewey, Secy.-Treas.
EIN: 540830140
Codes: FD

54281
Roy R. Charles Charitable Trust Two
c/o Davenport & Co.
P.O. Box 85678
Richmond, VA 23285-5678
Contact: Thomas N.P. Johnson, III, Tr.

Established in 1999 in VA.
Donor(s): Roy R. Charles Trust.
Financial data (yr. ended 12/31/01): Grants paid, $714,453; assets, $14,072,809 (M); gifts received, $280,603; expenditures, $854,756; qualifying distributions, $711,598.
Limitations: Giving primarily in VA.
Trustees and Distribution Committee:* Lawrence M. Cox, Angie Newman Johnson, Margaret Johnson, Thomas N.P. Johnson, Jr., Thomas N.P. Johnson III.
EIN: 546445977
Codes: FD

54282
W. Miller Richardson Trust
c/o Street, Street, Street, Scott of Bowman
P.O. Box 2100
Grundy, VA 24614 (276) 935-2128
Contact: S. T. Mullins, Tr.

Established in 1997 in VA.
Financial data (yr. ended 12/31/99): Grants paid, $707,113; assets, $1,795,139 (M); gifts received, $747,422; expenditures, $727,262; qualifying distributions, $706,779.
Limitations: Giving limited to the town of Grundy and Buchanan county, VA.
Trustee: S.T. Mullins.
EIN: 546436722
Codes: FD

54283
The Guilford Foundation
P.O. Box 13439
Richmond, VA 23225-8439

Established in 1987 in VA.
Donor(s): Ann K. Kirby,‡ Roger H.W. Kirby, Annette S. Kirby, Wade H.O. Kirby, James W. Kirby, Jr.
Financial data (yr. ended 12/31/01): Grants paid, $693,767; assets, $13,784,740 (M); gifts received, $36,094; expenditures, $785,237; qualifying distributions, $694,292.
Limitations: Applications not accepted. Giving in the U.S., with emphasis on VA; some giving also in England.
Application information: Contributes only to pre-selected organizations.
Officers and Directors:* Roger H.W. Kirby,* Pres.; William W. Harsh,* V.P.; Annette S. Kirby,* Secy.; Thomas M. Crowder,* Treas.; Frank C. Page,* Exec. Dir.; Wade H.O. Kirby.
EIN: 541423873
Codes: FD

54284
Bama Works Foundation
c/o PFM
310 Old Ivy Way, No. 301
Charlottesville, VA 22903

Established in 1998 in VI.
Financial data (yr. ended 12/31/01): Grants paid, $684,000; assets, $3,492 (M); gifts received, $310; expenditures, $684,406; qualifying distributions, $684,000.
Limitations: Applications not accepted. Giving primarily in Charlottesville, VA.
Application information: Contributes only to pre-selected organizations.
Directors: Carter A. Beauford, R. Coran Capshaw, John Hofnsby, David J. Matthews, Leroi H. Moore, Stefan Lessard, Boyd C. Tinsley.
EIN: 541893960
Codes: FD

54285
Stern Family Fund
(Formerly Philip M. Stern Family Fund)
P.O. Box 1590
Arlington, VA 22210-0890 (703) 527-6692
FAX: (703) 527-5775; E-mail: sternfund@starpower.net; URL: http://www.sternfund.org
Contact: Elizabeth Collaton, Exec. Dir.

Established in 1959 in DC; reorganized in 1994.
Donor(s): Philip M. Stern.‡
Financial data (yr. ended 06/30/01): Grants paid, $664,750; assets, $2,883,751 (M); expenditures, $764,309; qualifying distributions, $698,231.
Limitations: Giving limited to the U.S.
Publications: Application guidelines, grants list, informational brochure (including application guidelines).
Application information: Telephone inquiries and FAX submissions are discouraged, cover page format provided by NNG Common Grant Application section I cover page; see website for copy. Application form required.
Officers and Directors:* David M. Stern,* Pres.; Tracey Hughes,* V.P. and Secy.; Elizabeth Collaton, Exec. Dir.; Michael Caudell-Feagan, Alan Morrison, Sidney Wolfe.
EIN: 526037658
Codes: FD

54286
Trost Family Foundation, Inc.
11 River Rd.
Richmond, VA 23226-3310
Contact: Peter A. Trost III, Dir.

Established in 1997 in VA.
Donor(s): Peter A. Trost III.
Financial data (yr. ended 12/31/00): Grants paid, $642,533; assets, $1,131,654 (M); gifts received, $12,529; expenditures, $671,922; qualifying distributions, $642,533.
Application information: Application form not required.
Directors: Linda K. Trost, Peter A. Trost III, Byron E. Vaught, Dana T. Vaught.
EIN: 541850548
Codes: FD

54287
Estes Foundation
P.O. Box C
Chester, VA 23831-0318
Contact: Controller

Established in 1969 in VA.
Donor(s): C.E. Estes.
Financial data (yr. ended 12/31/01): Grants paid, $632,572; assets, $13,700,520 (M); expenditures, $699,279; qualifying distributions, $626,673.
Limitations: Applications not accepted. Giving primarily in VA.
Application information: Contributes only to pre-selected organizations.
Officers: C.E. Estes, Pres. and Treas.; Barbara Dodson, Secy.
Director: Martha E. Grover.
EIN: 237045252
Codes: FD

54288
Fredericksburg Savings Charitable Foundation
P.O. Box 748
400 George St.
Fredericksburg, VA 22404
Contact: Peggy J. Newman, Dir.

Established in 1998 in DE and VA.
Donor(s): Virginia Capital Bancshares, Inc.
Financial data (yr. ended 12/31/01): Grants paid, $610,838; assets, $14,819,379 (M); expenditures, $640,971; qualifying distributions, $618,253.
Limitations: Giving primarily in VA.
Application information: Application form required.
Directors: William M. Anderson, Jr., Lawrence A. Davies, Samuel C. Harding, Jr., Duval Q. Hicks, Jr., Peggy J. Newman.
EIN: 541913172
Codes: CS, FD, CD

54289
The Cecil and Irene Hylton Foundation, Inc.
5593 Mapledale Plz.
Dale City, VA 22193-4527
Contact: Malcolm W. Cook, Treas.

Established in 1989 in VA.
Donor(s): Cecil D. Hylton,‡ The First Grandchildren's Charitable Trust, The Second Grandchildren's Charitable Trust, Irene V. Hylton Charitable Lead Trust, The Second Childrens Charitable Trust.
Financial data (yr. ended 12/31/00): Grants paid, $610,700; assets, $45,270,964 (M); gifts received, $9,724,406; expenditures, $919,531; qualifying distributions, $643,155.
Limitations: Giving primarily in Prince William County, VA; funding also in northern VA, and metropolitan Washington County; giving on a national basis for land conservation and ecology.
Officers and Directors:* Conrad C. Hylton,* Pres.; George A. Halfpap,* Secy.; Malcolm W. Cook,* Treas.; Cecil D. Hylton, Jr., Cecilia M. Hylton.
EIN: 521633658
Codes: FD

54290
The Bansal Foundation
1861 International Dr.
McLean, VA 22102
Contact: Sanjeev K. Bansal, Tr.

Established in 1998 in MA and VA.
Donor(s): Sanjeev K. Bansal.
Financial data (yr. ended 12/31/01): Grants paid, $601,740; assets, $10,632,755 (M); expenditures, $606,610; qualifying distributions, $601,740.
Limitations: Giving on a national basis.
Application information: Application form required.
Trustee: Sanjeev K. Bansal.
EIN: 541933631
Codes: FD

54291
Mitsubishi Electric America Foundation
1560 Wilson Blvd., Ste. 1150
Arlington, VA 22209 (703) 276-8240
FAX: (703) 276-8260; E-mail: colleen.maher@meus.mea.com; URL: http://www.meaf.org
Contact: Colleen Maher, Prog. Off.

Established in 1991 in DC.
Donor(s): Mitsubishi Electric Corp., and its U.S. subsidiaries.
Financial data (yr. ended 12/31/00): Grants paid, $591,310; assets, $20,047,449 (M); expenditures, $1,080,636; qualifying distributions, $865,015.
Limitations: Giving on a national basis, with emphasis on areas of company operations.
Publications: Biennial report (including application guidelines), informational brochure (including application guidelines), grants list.
Application information: Telephone calls during the application process are discouraged. Application form not required.
Officers and Directors:* Kiyoshi Kawakami,* Pres.; Alan P. Olschwang, Secy.; Hiroki Yoshimatsu, Treas.; Rayna Aylward,* Exec. Dir.; Roger Barna, Cayce Blanchard, Bruce Brenizer, Christal Henderson, Melissa Ordaz, Perry Pappous, David Rebmann, Dick Schulenberg, Ichiro Taniguchi.
EIN: 521700855
Codes: CS, FD, CD

54292
The Collis/Warner Foundation, Inc.
c/o Nicholas D. Perrins
201 N. Union St., Ste. 360
Alexandria, VA 22314-2642

Established in 1997 in VA.
Donor(s): Lisa D. Collis, Mark R. Warner.
Financial data (yr. ended 12/31/00): Grants paid, $589,000; assets, $7,051,692 (M); gifts received, $2,000; expenditures, $623,219; qualifying distributions, $601,068; giving activities include $11,549 for programs.
Limitations: Applications not accepted. Giving primarily in Alexandria and Arlington, VA.
Application information: Contributes only to pre-selected organizations.
Officers and Directors:* Mark R. Warner,* Pres. and Treas.; Lisa D. Collis,* V.P. and Secy.
EIN: 541854416
Codes: FD

54293
The Charles Delmar Foundation
2 Skyline Pl., Ste. 1304
5203 Leesburg Pike
Falls Church, VA 22041
Contact: Mareen D. Hughes, Pres.

Established in 1957 in DC.
Donor(s): Charles Delmar,‡ Roland H. Delmar,‡ Elizabeth A. Delmar,‡ Mareen D. Hughes.
Financial data (yr. ended 12/31/01): Grants paid, $583,250; assets, $9,333,917 (M); expenditures, $618,808; qualifying distributions, $589,848.
Limitations: Giving primarily in Washington, DC; giving also in Latin America.
Application information: Application form not required.
Officers and Trustees:* Mareen D. Hughes,* Pres.; R. Bruce Hughes,* Secy.-Treas.
EIN: 526035345
Codes: FD

54294
The Rice Family Foundation
4378 Montreux Rd.
Warrenton, VA 20187

Established in 2001 in VA.
Donor(s): Paul Rice, Gina Rice.
Financial data (yr. ended 12/31/01): Grants paid, $562,456; assets, $5,646,212 (M); gifts received, $4,267,000; expenditures, $562,456; qualifying distributions, $562,456.
Limitations: Applications not accepted. Giving limited to VA.
Application information: Contributes only to pre-selected organizations.
Officers: Gina Rice, Pres. and Treas.; Paul Rice, V.P. and Secy.
EIN: 542055867

54295
The Palmer Foundation
4781 Williamsburg Blvd.
Arlington, VA 22207
E-mail:
patricia.sullivan@thepalmerfoundation.org;
URL: http://www.thepalmerfoundation.org
Contact: Patricia Sullivan, V.P.

Established in 1990 in IL.
Donor(s): Rogers Palmer,‡ Mary Palmer.‡
Financial data (yr. ended 12/31/01): Grants paid, $556,250; assets, $13,979,716 (M); gifts received, $233,481; expenditures, $663,718; qualifying distributions, $610,540.
Limitations: Applications not accepted.
Application information: Unsolicited requests for funds not accepted.
Officers and Directors:* Mary P. Enroth,* Pres.; Leonard G. Enroth,* V.P.; Susan Enroth,* V.P.; Karen E. Lischick,* V.P.; Patricia Sullivan,* V.P.; Jay L. Owen,* Secy.-Treas.
EIN: 363700897
Codes: FD

54296
Mark and Catherine Winkler Foundation
4900 Seminary Rd., Ste. 900
Alexandria, VA 22311 (703) 998-0400
Contact: Lynne S. Ball, Asst. Treas.

Established about 1964 in VA.
Donor(s): Catherine Winkler, Mark Winkler,‡ Catherine W. Herman.
Financial data (yr. ended 01/31/01): Grants paid, $547,440; assets, $1,593,984 (M); gifts received, $525,000; expenditures, $559,564; qualifying distributions, $554,806.
Limitations: Giving primarily in northern VA.
Publications: Application guidelines.
Application information: Accepts WG Common Grant Application Format. Application form required.
Officers: Catherine W. Herman, Chair.; Kathleen W. Wennesland, Pres.; Margaret Hecht, V.P.; Corolyn W. Thomas, Secy.
Director: Kim S. Wennesland.
EIN: 546054383
Codes: FD

54297
Three Swallows Foundation
12608 Wycklow Dr.
Clifton, VA 20124

Established in 1981 in VA.
Financial data (yr. ended 10/31/01): Grants paid, $545,545; assets, $3,323,721 (M); expenditures, $1,827,116; qualifying distributions, $615,930.
Limitations: Applications not accepted. Giving on a national basis, with some emphasis on CO.

Application information: Contributes only to pre-selected organizations.
Officers and Directors:* Paul N. Temple, Pres.; D. Barry Abell,* Treas.; Marc Abell, Pamela T. Abell, Rebecca Abell, James Brown, Monique Brown, Thomas Brown, Lise Temple Greenberg, Steven Greenberg, G. Michael Moore, Diane E. Temple, Nancy L. Temple, Robin R. Temple, Thomas D. Temple.
EIN: 521234546
Codes: FD

54298
LandAmerica Foundation
(Formerly Lawyers Title Foundation)
c/o Lawyers Title Insurance Corp.
P.O. Box 27567
Richmond, VA 23261 (804) 267-8330
Contact: W. Riker Purcell, Secy.

Established in 1952 as Richmond Corporation Foundation.
Donor(s): Lawyers Title Insurance Corp.
Financial data (yr. ended 12/31/00): Grants paid, $544,337; assets, $49,583 (M); gifts received, $550,000; expenditures, $544,337; qualifying distributions, $544,298.
Limitations: Giving primarily in areas of company operations.
Application information: Application form required.
Officer and Trustees:* W. Riker Purcell,* Secy.; Janet A. Alpert, H. Randolph Former, Charles H. Foster, Jr., Julie McClellan.
EIN: 546031167
Codes: CS, FD, CD

54299
CAP Charitable Foundation USA
1160 Pepsi Pl., No. 306-B
Charlottesville, VA 22901-0807
(804) 964-1588
URL: http://www.ronbrown.org
Contact: Michael Mallory, Pres.

Established in 1986 in DE.
Financial data (yr. ended 12/31/01): Grants paid, $537,414; assets, $96,541 (M); gifts received, $1,194,610; expenditures, $1,376,332; qualifying distributions, $964,461.
Limitations: Giving on a national basis.
Publications: Newsletter, informational brochure.
Application information: Application form required.
Officer: Michael Mallory, Pres.
EIN: 541832314
Codes: FD

54300
Gottwald Foundation
P.O. Box 955
Goochland, VA 23063

Established in 1957.
Donor(s): Floyd D. Gottwald, Sr.,‡ Floyd D. Gottwald, Jr.
Financial data (yr. ended 12/31/01): Grants paid, $528,649; assets, $11,036,215 (M); expenditures, $592,708; qualifying distributions, $516,396.
Limitations: Applications not accepted. Giving primarily in VA.
Application information: Contributes only to pre-selected organizations.
Officers: F.D. Gottwald, Jr., Pres.; James T. Gottwald,* V.P.; Bruce C. Gottwald, Secy.-Treas.
EIN: 546040560
Codes: FD

54301
Bedford Falls Foundation
6501 Menlo Rd.
McLean, VA 22101-3012

Established in 1997 in VA.
Donor(s): William Conway.
Financial data (yr. ended 12/31/01): Grants paid, $513,824; assets, $479,992 (M); expenditures, $513,832; qualifying distributions, $513,555.
Limitations: Applications not accepted.
Application information: Contributes only to pre-selected organizations.
Trustees: Joanne Conway, William E. Conway.
EIN: 526834462
Codes: FD

54302
Washington Forrest Foundation
2300 9th St. S., Ste. GR-1
Arlington, VA 22204 (703) 920-3688
FAX: (703) 920-0130; *E-mail:* washforr@aol.com
Contact: Deborah G. Lucckese, Exec. Dir.

Incorporated in 1968 in VA.
Donor(s): Benjamin M. Smith,‡ Charlotte Smith Gravett,‡ Virginia N. Smith.‡
Financial data (yr. ended 06/30/01): Grants paid, $510,115; assets, $12,954,863 (M); expenditures, $928,164; qualifying distributions, $528,647.
Limitations: Giving primarily in northern VA, with emphasis on south Arlington.
Publications: Program policy statement, grants list.
Application information: The foundation uses the WRAG Common Grant Application (modified for small proposals). Application form required.
Officers and Directors:* Margaret S. Peete,* Pres.; Deborah Lucckese,* V.P.; Leslie Ariail,* Secy.; Benjamin M. Smith, Jr.,* Treas.; Allison Erdle, Benjamin C. Gravett, David D. Peete, Jr.
EIN: 237002944
Codes: FD

54303
Andrew H. & Anne O. Easley Trust
(also known as The Easley Foundation)
c/o Wachovia Bank, N.A. Charitable Funds Dept.
P.O. Box 27602
Richmond, VA 23261 (804) 697-6901
Contact: Secy., The Easley Foundation

Established in 1968 in VA.
Donor(s): Andrew H. Easley.‡
Financial data (yr. ended 06/30/01): Grants paid, $508,498; assets, $407,887,389 (M); expenditures, $569,284; qualifying distributions, $508,031.
Limitations: Giving limited to the central VA, area, within a 30-mile radius of Lynchburg.
Publications: Application guidelines.
Application information: Application form not required.
Trustee: Wachovia Bank, N.A.
EIN: 546074720
Codes: FD

54304
The Lucy Pannill Sale Foundation
231 E. Church St., 5th Fl.
Martinsville, VA 24112
Contact: Dirs.

Established in 1994 in VA.
Donor(s): Lucy Pannill Sale.
Financial data (yr. ended 05/31/02): Grants paid, $507,997; assets, $2,798,778 (M); expenditures, $581,702; qualifying distributions, $527,002.
Limitations: Giving primarily in Martinsville, VA.
Officer and Directors:* Joseph R. Cobbe,* Pres.; John B. LaFaye, Lucy P. Sale.
EIN: 541726783

Codes: FD

54305
The George W. Logan Charitable Foundation
P.O. Box 1190
Salem, VA 24153-1190

Donor(s): George W. Logan.
Financial data (yr. ended 12/31/01): Grants paid, $499,850; assets, $545,156 (M); gifts received, $5,000; expenditures, $501,325; qualifying distributions, $496,455.
Limitations: Applications not accepted. Giving primarily in Roanoke, VA.
Application information: Contributes only to pre-selected organizations.
Officers and Director:* George W. Logan,* Pres.; Patra F. Bedwell, Secy.
EIN: 541902872
Codes: FD

54306
Ludington, Inc.
P.O. Box 12641
Roanoke, VA 24027

Established in 1984.
Financial data (yr. ended 12/31/01): Grants paid, $478,472; assets, $8,954,424 (M); expenditures, $502,845; qualifying distributions, $494,057.
Limitations: Applications not accepted. Giving primarily in Washington, DC, and New York, NY.
Application information: Contributes only to pre-selected organizations.
Directors: Philip Abbey, Emily Parrino, Greta Tisdale.
EIN: 311128833
Codes: FD

54307
The Batten-Rolph Foundation
Rte. 22, Box 226
Keswick, VA 22947

Established in 1997 in VA.
Donor(s): Dorothy B. Rolph.
Financial data (yr. ended 12/31/01): Grants paid, $477,298; assets, $5,368,629 (M); expenditures, $491,854; qualifying distributions, $475,488.
Limitations: Applications not accepted. Giving primarily in VA.
Application information: Contributes only to pre-selected organizations.
Officers: Dorothy B. Rolph, Pres.; Colin M. Rolph, V.P.; Susan R. Colpitts, Secy.
EIN: 541864288
Codes: FD

54308
The Funger Foundation, Inc.
1650 Tysons Blvd., No. 620
McLean, VA 22102

Established in 1998 in MD.
Donor(s): Morton Funger, Norma Lee Funger, Yetta K. Cohen.‡
Financial data (yr. ended 12/31/01): Grants paid, $473,765; assets, $6,642,161 (M); gifts received, $167,928; expenditures, $492,372; qualifying distributions, $473,765.
Limitations: Applications not accepted. Giving primarily in the eastern U.S., with emphasis on Washington, DC and MD.
Application information: Contributes only to pre-selected organizations.
Officers: Morton Funger, Pres.; Norma Lee Funger, Secy.-Treas.
Directors: C. Richard Beyda, Keith Parker Funger, William Scott Funger, Lydia Joy McClain, Melanie Fail Nichols.
EIN: 541893307

Codes: FD

54309
Charlottesville-Albemarle Foundation
114 4th St., S.E.
P.O. Box 1767
Charlottesville, VA 22902 (804) 296-1024
FAX: (804) 296-2503
Contact: John R. Redick, Exec. Dir.

Established in 1967 in VA; first grants distribution in 1972.
Financial data (yr. ended 12/31/00): Grants paid, $459,892; assets, $4,261,039 (M); gifts received, $31,634; expenditures, $681,189.
Limitations: Giving limited to the Charlottesville and Albemarle, VA, areas, within a fifty-mile radius.
Publications: Annual report, application guidelines, informational brochure (including application guidelines), newsletter.
Application information: Application form required.
Officers and Directors:* Lucius H. Bracey, Jr.,* Chair.; Shelah Scott,* Vice-Chair.; John R. Redick, Exec. Dir.; and 20 additional directors.
EIN: 546068643
Codes: CM, FD

54310
The William H., John G., and Emma Scott Foundation
c/o Davenport & Co.
P.O. Box 85678
Richmond, VA 23285-5678
Contact: Hugh K. Leary, Exec. Dir.

Incorporated in 1956 in VA.
Donor(s): John G. Scott,‡ Emma Scott Taylor.‡
Financial data (yr. ended 09/30/01): Grants paid, $435,000; assets, $10,544,105 (M); expenditures, $515,864; qualifying distributions, $435,000.
Limitations: Giving limited to VA, with strong emphasis on Richmond.
Publications: Application guidelines.
Application information: Scholarship program has been discontinued. Application form not required.
Officers and Trustees:* Robert F. Norfleet, Jr.,* Pres.; C. Cotesworth Pinckney,* V.P.; Edwin P. Munson,* Secy.; Hugh K. Leary, Treas. and Exec. Dir.; W. Hill Brown III, Susanne B. Crump, Charles M. Guthridge, E. Bryson Powell.
EIN: 540648772
Codes: FD

54311
Chase Foundation of Virginia
c/o Derwood S. Chase, Jr.
300 Preston Ave., Ste. 403
Charlottesville, VA 22902-5091

Established in 1995 in VA.
Donor(s): Derwood S. Chase, Jr.
Financial data (yr. ended 12/31/01): Grants paid, $425,000; assets, $9,977,386 (M); gifts received, $1,570,799; expenditures, $479,070; qualifying distributions, $432,470.
Limitations: Applications not accepted. Giving on a national basis.
Application information: Contributes only to pre-selected organizations.
Trustees: Alehandro A. Chafuen, Cheryl O. Chase, Derwood S. Chase, Jr., Gabriela C. Chase, Johanna B. Chase, Stuart F. Chase, John C. Goodman, Walter E. Williams.
EIN: 541770697
Codes: FD

54312
The Dalis Foundation
c/o Goodman & Co.
1 Commercial Pl., Ste. 800
Norfolk, VA 23510

Established in 1956.
Donor(s): M. Dan Dalis.‡
Financial data (yr. ended 05/31/01): Grants paid, $422,600; assets, $9,041,962 (M); expenditures, $504,960; qualifying distributions, $436,039.
Limitations: Applications not accepted. Giving primarily in Norfolk, VA.
Application information: Contributes only to pre-selected organizations.
Officers: Joan D. Martone, Pres. and Treas.; Sandra W. Norment, V.P.
EIN: 546046229
Codes: FD

54313
Greater Lynchburg Community Trust
c/o Central Fidelity National Bank Bldg., 19th Fl.
P.O. Box 714
Lynchburg, VA 24505 (434) 845-6500
FAX: (434) 845-6530; E-mail: glct@inmind.com;
URL: http://www.lynchburgtrust.org
Contact: Kenneth S. White, Pres.

Established as a community trust in 1972 in VA.
Financial data (yr. ended 09/30/01): Grants paid, $420,345; assets, $14,532,394 (M); gifts received, $1,613,215; expenditures, $696,865.
Limitations: Giving limited to Lynchburg and Bedford City, and Amherst, Bedford, and Campbell counties, VA.
Publications: Application guidelines, program policy statement, annual report, informational brochure, newsletter.
Application information: Application form not required.
Officers and Directors:* Samuel P. Cardwell,* Chair.; John P. Eckert,* Chair., Distribs. Comm.; Yuille Holt III,* Chair., Investment Comm.; Terry Hall Jamerson,* Vice-Chair.; Kenneth S. White, Pres.; Shanda K. Rowe, Secy.; William F. Quillian, Jr., Advisor; Elliot S. Schewel, Advisor; Stuart J. Turille, Advisor; W. Starke Camden, Robert H. Gillian, Joyce Houck, Joseph C. Knakal, Jr., Amy Ray, Irma Seiferth, Benny R. Shrader, James W. Sublett, Jr., Daniel B. Sweeney, John A. Watts, Jr., T. Ashby Watts III.
Trustee Banks: B.B. & T., SunTrust Banks, Inc., Wachovia Bank, N.A., Bank of America.
EIN: 546112680
Codes: CM, FD

54314
The Overton and Katherine Dennis Fund
c/o SunTrust Banks, Inc.
P.O. Box 85159
Richmond, VA 23285-5159 (804) 782-5230
Contact: Mgr.

Established in 1987 in VA as successor trust to Dennis Fund.
Financial data (yr. ended 05/31/01): Grants paid, $414,100; assets, $7,974,830 (M); expenditures, $459,418; qualifying distributions, $411,626.
Limitations: Giving primarily in VA, with emphasis on Richmond.
Officers and Directors:* Overton D. Dennis, Jr.,* Pres.; Philip H. Webb,* Treas.; Janet D. Branch, Elizabeth O. Dennis, Janet Jackson Dennis.
EIN: 541418161
Codes: FD

54315—VIRGINIA

54315
The Gladys and Franklin Clark Foundation
c/o Gilbert A. Bartlett, Pres.
P.O. Box 47
Williamsburg, VA 23187

Established in 1992 in VA.
Donor(s): Gladys & Franklin Clark Revocable Trust.
Financial data (yr. ended 12/31/01): Grants paid, $412,400; assets, $7,628,121 (M); expenditures, $570,688; qualifying distributions, $437,324.
Limitations: Applications not accepted. Giving primarily in Williamsburg, VA.
Application information: Contributes only to pre-selected organizations.
Officers and Directors:* Gilbert A. Bartlett,* Pres.; L. Alvin Garrison, Jr.,* Secy.; Joseph W. Montgomery,* Treas.
EIN: 541640751
Codes: FD

54316
North Shore Foundation
NationsBank Ctr., Rm. 1420
Norfolk, VA 23510
Contact: Joshua P. Darden, Jr., Pres.

Established in 1982 in VA.
Donor(s): Constance S. duPont Darden.
Financial data (yr. ended 04/30/01): Grants paid, $408,500; assets, $830 (M); gifts received, $173,561; expenditures, $410,394; qualifying distributions, $410,374.
Limitations: Giving primarily in VA.
Application information: Application form not required.
Officers and Directors:* Joshua P. Darden, Jr.,* Pres. and Treas.; Irene D. Field,* Secy.; Constance S. duPont Darden.
EIN: 521296293
Codes: FD

54317
The Lincoln-Lane Foundation
207 Granby St., Ste. 302
Norfolk, VA 23510 (757) 622-2557
FAX: (757) 623-2698
Contact: Margaret B. Belvin, Admin. Asst.

Incorporated in 1928 in VA.
Donor(s): John H. Rogers.‡
Financial data (yr. ended 07/31/01): Grants paid, $408,200; assets, $9,496,158 (M); gifts received, $5,500; expenditures, $630,233; qualifying distributions, $516,306.
Limitations: Giving limited to permanent residents of the Tidewater, VA, area.
Publications: Application guidelines, program policy statement.
Application information: New applications available starting Sept. 1. Application form required.
Officers and Directors:* Charles E. Jenkins II,* Pres.; Edith G. Grandy,* V.P., Secy.-Treas., and Exec. Dir.; Ruth P. Acra, John M. Ankerson, Patricia P. Cavender, Walter M. Moore IV.
EIN: 540601700
Codes: FD, GTI

54318
The Alison J. & Ella W. Parsons Foundation
999 Waterside Dr., Ste. 1700
Norfolk, VA 23510 (757) 622-3366
Application address: P.O. Box 3460, Norfolk, VA 23514, additional tel.: (757) 629-0666
Contact: Marie Achtemeier Finch, Admin.

Established in 1984 in VA.
Donor(s): Alison J. Parsons,‡ Ella W. Parsons.‡
Financial data (yr. ended 04/30/02): Grants paid, $407,500; assets, $7,576,881 (M); expenditures, $472,293; qualifying distributions, $421,709.
Limitations: Giving limited to the South Hampton Roads area (Portsmouth, Chesapeake, Virginia Beach, Suffolk and Norfolk,) VA.
Publications: Application guidelines.
Application information: 3-year hiatus between funded grant and new application. Application form not required.
Officers and Directors:* William K. Butler II,* Pres.; Howard L. Brantly,* V.P.; Robert C. Nusbaum,* Secy.-Treas.; Jane P. Batten, Constance C. Laws.
EIN: 541253938
Codes: FD

54319
The Wellspring Foundation
(Formerly The Stone Foundation)
c/o Investors Records Corp.
614 E. High St.
Charlottesville, VA 22902
Mailing address: Canal St. Sta., P.O. Box 276, New York, NY 10012, tel./FAX: (212) 226-1992; E-mail: wllsprg@aol.com
Contact: Kelly Seshimo, Secy.

Established in 1985 in NY.
Donor(s): Diana B. Clark, James Clark.‡
Financial data (yr. ended 12/31/99): Grants paid, $400,500; assets, $3,374,593 (M); gifts received, $171,511; expenditures, $410,295; qualifying distributions, $400,500.
Limitations: Giving primarily in New York, NY.
Application information: Application form not required.
Officers: Kelly Seshimo, Secy.; Benjamin Brewster, Treas.
Trustees: Ashley S. Pettus, Brewster W. Pettus, Elise S. Pettus.
EIN: 133457878
Codes: FD

54320
DPC Community Foundation
(Formerly Danville Community Foundation)
530 Main St., Ste. 302
P.O. Box 1039
Danville, VA 24543 (434) 793-0884
FAX: (434) 793-6489; E-mail: dpccf@gamewood.net; URL: http://www.dpccf.org
Contact: Debra L. Dodson, Exec. Dir.

Established in 1996 in VA.
Financial data (yr. ended 06/30/01): Grants paid, $400,202; assets, $10,933,915 (M); gifts received, $1,743,191; expenditures, $586,124.
Limitations: Giving primarily in Caswell County, NC, and Danville and Pittsylvania County, VA.
Publications: Annual report, grants list, newsletter, informational brochure, application guidelines.
Application information: Application form required.
Officers and Directors:* Dugan W. Maddux,* Pres.; P. Niles Daly, Secy.; L. Samuel Saunders, Treas.; Debra L. Dodson, Exec. Dir.
EIN: 541823141
Codes: CM, FD

54321
The Roller-Bottimore Foundation
c/o Bank of America
P.O. Box 26688
Richmond, VA 23261-6688 (804) 788-2963
Contact: Elizabeth D. Seaman, Advisor, Bank of America

Established in 1981.
Donor(s): Elizabeth R. Bottimore.‡
Financial data (yr. ended 12/31/01): Grants paid, $397,000; assets, $8,688,947 (M); expenditures, $474,918; qualifying distributions, $411,676.
Limitations: Giving primarily in central VA.
Publications: Informational brochure (including application guidelines).
Application information: Application form not required.
Officers and Directors:* Henry Spalding, Jr.,* Pres.; Lucy P. Summerell,* V.P.; John Thomas King,* Treas.
EIN: 541201084
Codes: FD

54322
Holt Family Foundation, Inc.
9107 Carterham Rd.
Richmond, VA 23229

Established in 1997 in VA.
Donor(s): B. Stuart Holt III.
Financial data (yr. ended 12/31/01): Grants paid, $396,492; assets, $272,484 (M); expenditures, $400,439; qualifying distributions, $397,325.
Limitations: Applications not accepted. Giving primarily in VA.
Application information: Contributes only to pre-selected organizations.
Officers and Directors:* Stephanie Holt,* V.P.; B. Stuart Holt III, Mgr.; Gary Withoefft.
EIN: 541850514
Codes: FD

54323
Thomas L. Leivesley, Jr. Foundation
c/o Robert L. Bradshaw, Jr.
204 S. Jefferson St., No. 200
Roanoke, VA 24011

Established in 2001 in VA.
Donor(s): Thomas L. Leivesley.‡
Financial data (yr. ended 12/31/01): Grants paid, $390,856; assets, $416,201 (M); gifts received, $783,824; expenditures, $393,713; qualifying distributions, $390,856.
Limitations: Applications not accepted. Giving primarily in Blacksburg and Roanoke, VA.
Application information: Contributes only to pre-selected organizations.
Trustees: Linda K. Howard, Robert I. Howard, Jr., The Trust Company of Virginia.
EIN: 546471433
Codes: FD

54324
The Bob Wiser Charitable Foundation Trust
9685-D Main St.
Fairfax, VA 22031-3745

Established in 1994 in VA.
Donor(s): Bob Wiser.
Financial data (yr. ended 06/30/01): Grants paid, $388,465; assets, $864,279 (M); gifts received, $1,100,000; expenditures, $388,807; qualifying distributions, $388,672.
Limitations: Applications not accepted. Giving primarily in VA.
Application information: Contributes only to pre-selected organizations.
Trustees: Irving L. Greenspon, Rhonda J. MacDonald, Nancy B. Padgett.
EIN: 546372531
Codes: FD

54325
The Truland Foundation
3330 Washington Blvd.
Arlington, VA 22201 (703) 516-2600
E-mail: rtruland@truland.com
Contact: Robert W. Truland, Tr.

Trust established in 1954 in VA.
Donor(s): Truland Systems Corp., and members of the Truland family.
Financial data (yr. ended 03/31/01): Grants paid, $388,282; assets, $2,697,908 (M); gifts received, $500,000; expenditures, $403,449; qualifying distributions, $397,402.
Limitations: Giving primarily in VA.
Application information: Application form not required.
Trustees: Alice O. Truland, Robert W. Truland.
EIN: 546037172
Codes: CS, FD, CD

54326
John J. McDonald, Jr. & Marian J. McDonnell Charitable Foundation
8401 Brookewood Ct.
McLean, VA 22102

Established in 1996 in VA.
Donor(s): John J. McDonnell, Jr., Marian J. McDonnell.
Financial data (yr. ended 11/30/01): Grants paid, $386,578; assets, $2,109,258 (M); gifts received, $364,000; expenditures, $431,744; qualifying distributions, $386,578.
Limitations: Applications not accepted.
Application information: Contributes only to pre-selected organizations.
Officers and Directors:* John J. McDonnell, Jr.,* Pres.; Marian J. McDonnell,* V.P. and Secy.
EIN: 541828698

54327
George and Effie Seay Memorial Trust
c/o Bank of America
P.O. Box 26688
Richmond, VA 23261-6688 (804) 788-2963
Contact: Elizabeth D. Seaman, Advisor

Trust established in 1957 in VA.
Donor(s): George J. Seay,‡ Effie L. Seay.‡
Financial data (yr. ended 06/30/01): Grants paid, $386,505; assets, $3,516,512 (M); expenditures, $440,059; qualifying distributions, $393,561.
Limitations: Giving limited to VA.
Publications: Informational brochure (including application guidelines).
Application information: Application form not required.
Trustee: Bank of America.
EIN: 546030604
Codes: FD

54328
Emily S. and Coleman A. Hunter Trust
c/o SunTrust Banks, Inc.
P.O. Box 27385
Richmond, VA 23261-7385

Established in 1985 in VA.
Donor(s): Coleman A. Hunter,‡ Emily S. Hunter.‡
Financial data (yr. ended 02/28/02): Grants paid, $385,935; assets, $6,696,699 (M); expenditures, $425,911; qualifying distributions, $385,935.
Limitations: Applications not accepted. Giving limited to VA, with emphasis on Richmond.
Application information: Contributes only to pre-selected organizations.
Trustee: SunTrust Banks, Inc.
EIN: 546219496

54329
Datatel Scholars Foundation
4375 Fair Lakes Ct.
Fairfax, VA 22033 (703) 968-9000
Additional tel.: (800) 486-4332; FAX: (703) 968-4573; E-mail: scholars@datatel.com; URL: http://www.datatel.com/scholars.htm

Established in 1991 in VA.
Donor(s): Datatel, Inc.
Financial data (yr. ended 12/31/01): Grants paid, $383,721; assets, $243,290 (M); gifts received, $339,051; expenditures, $383,901; qualifying distributions, $383,642.
Limitations: Giving on a national and international basis.
Publications: Application guidelines.
Application information: Students requesting applications from the foundation must indicate the name of the college or university to determine eligibility. Applications mailed directly to the foundation not considered; each institution forwards up to 2 applications to the foundation for consideration. Application form required.
Officers and Directors:* E.G. Kendrick, Jr.,* Chair.; H. Russell Griffith,* Pres.; Jane H. Roth, Secy. and Exec. Dir.; Vernon H. Hollidge,* Treas.; Thomas R. Davidson.
EIN: 541604129
Codes: CS, FD, CD, GTI

54330
Weissberg Foundation
c/o Marvin Weissberg
1901 N. Moore St., Ste. 803
Arlington, VA 22209 (703) 276-7500
FAX: (703) 276-1770; E-mail: ideboissiere@weissbergcorp.com
Contact: Ilene DeBoissiere, Exec. Dir.

Established in 1988 in VA.
Donor(s): Marvin F. Weissberg.
Financial data (yr. ended 12/31/01): Grants paid, $379,735; assets, $5,000,000 (M); gifts received, $306,000; expenditures, $457,921; qualifying distributions, $414,122.
Limitations: Giving primarily in the metropolitan Washington, DC, area.
Publications: Grants list, application guidelines.
Application information: Application form not required.
Officers and Directors:* Marvin F. Weissberg,* Pres.; Nina V. Weissberg,* V.P.; Barbara T. Napolitano,* Secy.; Martin Heyert,* Treas.; Ilene C. DeBoissiere,* Exec. Dir.; Wallace K. Babington, Weslie M. Weissberg.
EIN: 541475954
Codes: FD

54331
The J. Edwin Treakle Foundation, Inc.
P.O. Box 1157
Gloucester, VA 23061 (804) 693-0881
Contact: John Warren Cooke, Pres. and Genl. Mgr.

Incorporated in 1963 in VA.
Donor(s): J. Edwin Treakle.‡
Financial data (yr. ended 04/30/02): Grants paid, $365,000; assets, $7,273,959 (M); expenditures, $1,249,304; qualifying distributions, $413,435.
Limitations: Giving primarily in VA.
Application information: Application form required.
Officers and Directors:* John W. Cooke,* Pres. and General Mgr.; Harry E. Dunn,* V.P. and Treas.; Cynthia B. Horsley,* Secy.; Nancy Powell.
EIN: 546051620
Codes: FD

54332
The Edgar A. Thurman Charitable Foundation for Children
c/o SunTrust Banks, Inc.
P.O. Box 27385
Richmond, VA 23261-7385
Application address: c/o SunTrust Banks, Inc., P.O. Box 13888, Roanoke, VA 24038, tel.: (540) 982-3076
Contact: Carolyn McCoy

Trust established in 1952 in VA.
Donor(s): Edgar A. Thurman.‡
Financial data (yr. ended 06/30/01): Grants paid, $362,750; assets, $7,485,385 (M); expenditures, $402,363; qualifying distributions, $357,086.
Limitations: Giving limited to VA, with emphasis on the Roanoke area.
Publications: Program policy statement, application guidelines.
Application information: Application form required.
Trustee: SunTrust Banks, Inc.
EIN: 546113281
Codes: FD

54333
Rangeley Educational Fund
c/o SunTrust Banks, Inc., Tax Svcs.
P.O. Box 27385
Richmond, VA 23261-7385 (703) 666-8243
Contact: Gladys Setliff

Established about 1968 in VA.
Donor(s): William H. Rangeley.‡
Financial data (yr. ended 10/31/01): Grants paid, $362,300; assets, $3,379,011 (M); expenditures, $393,230; qualifying distributions, $381,226; giving activities include $362,300 for loans to individuals.
Limitations: Giving primarily in the city of Martinsville, and Henry and Franklin counties, VA.
Publications: Application guidelines.
Application information: Interviews usually required. Application form required.
Trustee: SunTrust Banks, Inc.
EIN: 546077906
Codes: FD, GTI

54334
Tara Foundation, Inc.
P.O. Box 1850
Middleburg, VA 20118 (540) 687-8884
Contact: Mary Painter

Donor(s): Magalen O. Bryant.
Financial data (yr. ended 12/31/01): Grants paid, $343,156; assets, $4,787,635 (M); gifts received, $600; expenditures, $357,160; qualifying distributions, $342,398.
Limitations: Giving on a national basis.
Officers and Directors:* Magalen C. Webert,* Pres.; John C.O. Bryant,* V.P.; John Gordon,* Secy.-Treas.; Magalen O. Bryant, Michael R. Crane, W. Carey Crane III, Kristiane W. Graham.
EIN: 541596203
Codes: FD

54335
Elizabeth Ireland Graves Charitable Trust
Rt. 1, Box 116
Bremo Bluff, VA 23022

Established in 1998 in VA.
Financial data (yr. ended 12/31/01): Grants paid, $343,016; assets, $11,489,224 (M); expenditures, $359,859; qualifying distributions, $343,016.
Trustee: Sayre O. Graves.
EIN: 546421160

54336
The Marion & Robert Rosenthal Family Foundation
c/o Donald Bavely
1100 S. Glebe Rd.
Arlington, VA 22204 (703) 553-4300
Contact: Robert M. Rosenthal, Pres.

Established in 1995 in VA.
Donor(s): Marion Rosenthal, Robert M. Rosenthal.
Financial data (yr. ended 12/31/00): Grants paid, $342,700; assets, $7,062,119 (M); expenditures, $364,903; qualifying distributions, $330,996.
Limitations: Applications not accepted. Giving primarily in Washington, DC and VA.
Application information: Contributes only to pre-selected organizations.
Officers and Directors:* Robert M. Rosenthal,* Pres.; Jane R. Cafritz,* V.P.; Marion Rosenthal,* V.P.; Nancy Rosenthal,* Secy.; Brooke R. Peterson,* Treas.
EIN: 541740285
Codes: FD

54337
Gang Family Foundation
11006 Sweet Meadow Dr.
Oakton, VA 22124

Established in 1998 in VA.
Donor(s): David Gang.
Financial data (yr. ended 12/31/00): Grants paid, $337,870; assets, $2,448,701 (M); expenditures, $363,142; qualifying distributions, $334,065.
Limitations: Applications not accepted. Giving on a national basis, with emphasis on CT and Washington, DC.
Application information: Contributes only to pre-selected organizations.
Officer: David Gang, Mgr.
EIN: 541922206
Codes: FD

54338
Frances Chapin Foundation
5416 Flintlock Ln., S.W.
Roanoke, VA 24014

Incorporated in 1966 in NJ.
Donor(s): Frances C. Crook.‡
Financial data (yr. ended 03/31/01): Grants paid, $332,500; assets, $6,267,868 (M); expenditures, $363,575; qualifying distributions, $300,343.
Limitations: Applications not accepted. Giving primarily in AZ, FL, and VA.
Application information: Contributes only to pre-selected organizations.
Officer and Director:* Thomas O. Maxfield III,* Pres.
EIN: 226087456
Codes: FD

54339
Portsmouth Community Foundation
P.O. Box 1394
Portsmouth, VA 23705 (757) 397-5424
FAX: (757) 397-7948; *E-mail:* portscomfound@picusnet.org; *URL:* http://www.thepcf.org
Contact: Judith E. Luffman, Exec. Dir.

Established in 1965 in VA.
Financial data (yr. ended 12/31/01): Grants paid, $330,190; assets, $3,871,415 (M); gifts received, $885,037; expenditures, $437,385.
Limitations: Giving limited to within a 50 mile radius of Portsmouth, VA.
Publications: Annual report (including application guidelines), application guidelines, financial statement, grants list, informational brochure, newsletter.
Application information: Application form required.
Officers: Albert J. Taylor, Chair.; Palmer Rutherford, Jr., Vice-Chair.; Philip M. Rudisill, Treas.; Judith E. Luffman, Exec. Dir.
EIN: 546062589
Codes: CM, FD

54340
AMDG Charitable Foundation
746 Walker Rd., Ste. 10-110
Great Falls, VA 22066
Contact: Mark Ryland, Pres.

Established in 1999 in DE.
Donor(s): Mark Ryland.
Financial data (yr. ended 12/31/01): Grants paid, $329,770; assets, $301,571 (M); gifts received, $636,232; expenditures, $339,582; qualifying distributions, $339,582.
Limitations: Giving on a national and international basis.
Officer: Mark Ryland, Pres.
EIN: 912016505
Codes: FD

54341
Smyth Foundation
P.O. Box 714
Nellysford, VA 22958-0476
FAX: (804) 361-1773
Contact: H. Gordon Smyth, Tr.

Established in 1990 in DE.
Donor(s): H. Gordon Smyth.
Financial data (yr. ended 12/31/01): Grants paid, $328,757; assets, $3,751,682 (M); gifts received, $28,000; expenditures, $358,196; qualifying distributions, $334,228.
Limitations: Applications not accepted. Giving primarily in central VA.
Application information: Contributes only to pre-selected organizations.
Trustees: H. Gordon Smyth, Mary R. Smyth.
EIN: 516178707
Codes: FD

54342
Bill Usery Labor Management Relations Foundation
2231 Crystal Dr.
Arlington, VA 22202
Contact: W.J. Usery, Jr., Chair.

Established in 1985 in DC.
Donor(s): W.J. Usery, Jr.
Financial data (yr. ended 01/31/01): Grants paid, $326,500; assets, $3,815,853 (M); gifts received, $300,000; expenditures, $412,742; qualifying distributions, $389,533.
Limitations: Giving primarily in GA.
Officers: W.J. Usery, Chair.; Melvin Usery, Vice-Chair.
Trustee: Doug Henne.
EIN: 521390822
Codes: FD

54343
National Association of Chain Drug Stores Education Foundation, Inc.
413 N. Lee St.
Alexandria, VA 22314 (703) 549-3001
Additional address: P.O. Box 1417-D49, Alexandria, VA 22313; *URL:* http://www.nacds.org
Contact: Ronald L. Ziegler, Pres.

Established in 1974 in VA.
Donor(s): Rorer Pharmaceutical Corp., PCS, Inc., Burroughs Wellcome Co., National Assn. of Chain Drug Stores.
Financial data (yr. ended 06/30/01): Grants paid, $324,764; assets, $1,919,860 (M); gifts received, $1,236,140; expenditures, $506,451; qualifying distributions, $406,451.
Limitations: Giving on a national basis.
Publications: Occasional report.
Application information: Application form required.
Officers: Ronald L. Ziegler, Pres.; Donald L. Mahor, V.P.; Sandra Kay Jung, Secy.; R. James Huber, Treas.
Directors: Donald D. Beeler, Leonard A. Genovese, Gerald Heller, Alan B. Levin, Frank A. Newman, Stephen D. Roath, Thomas Ryan.
EIN: 510144922
Codes: FD

54344
W. Russell and Norma Ramsey Foundation, Inc.
1001 19th St. N., 18th Fl.
Arlington, VA 22209-1710

Established in 1993 in VA.
Donor(s): W. Russell Ramsey, Norma Ramsey.
Financial data (yr. ended 06/30/01): Grants paid, $323,362; assets, $347,544 (M); expenditures, $329,562; qualifying distributions, $323,006.
Limitations: Applications not accepted. Giving primarily in the Washington, DC, area, including MD and VA.
Application information: Contributes only to pre-selected organizations.
Directors: Norma Ramsey, W. Russell Ramsey, Ned S. Scherer.
EIN: 521853713
Codes: FD

54345
The Ratner Family Foundation
2815 Hartland Rd.
Falls Church, VA 22043

Established in 1990 in VA.
Donor(s): Creative Hairdressers, Inc., and its subsidiaries.
Financial data (yr. ended 12/31/01): Grants paid, $321,493; assets, $132,495 (M); gifts received, $350,000; expenditures, $321,622; qualifying distributions, $321,493.
Limitations: Applications not accepted. Giving primarily in the metropolitan Washington, DC, area, and MD.
Application information: Contributes only to pre-selected organizations.
Officers: Dennis F. Ratner, Pres.; Warren A. Ratner, Secy.
EIN: 541527670
Codes: FD

54346
Lind Lawrence Foundation
c/o L.P. Martin and Co.
4132 Innslake Dr.
Glen Allen, VA 23060-3307
Contact: Lee P. Martin, Jr., Tr.

Established in 1973 in VA.
Donor(s): Lind Lawrence.‡
Financial data (yr. ended 09/30/01): Grants paid, $316,233; assets, $7,316,662 (M); expenditures, $384,315; qualifying distributions, $319,302.
Limitations: Giving primarily in Los Angeles, CA and Richmond, VA.
Trustees: Fred J. Bernhardt, Jr., Lee P. Martin, Jr.
EIN: 237310359
Codes: FD

54347
E. Carlton Wilton Foundation
c/o E. Carlton Wilton
10625 Patterson Ave.
Richmond, VA 23233-4748

Established in 1997 in VA.
Donor(s): E. Carlton Wilton.
Financial data (yr. ended 12/31/01): Grants paid, $308,400; assets, $1,445,889 (M); expenditures, $312,697; qualifying distributions, $308,400.
Limitations: Applications not accepted. Giving primarily in VA.
Application information: Contributes only to pre-selected organizations.
Officers: E. Carlton Wilton, Chair.; E. Carlton Wilton, Jr., Pres.; Peggy W. Laramore, Secy.-Treas.
Director: Betty L. Wilton.
EIN: 546050387
Codes: FD

54348
The Connors Foundation, Inc.
P.O. Box 7317
Alexandria, VA 22307-0317 (703) 683-4367
E-mail: JConnors@aol.com
Contact: Julia B. Connors, V.P.

Established in 1999.
Donor(s): Michael M. Connors, Julia B. Connors.
Financial data (yr. ended 12/31/01): Grants paid, $305,818; assets, $16,233,073 (M); gifts received, $5,574,683; expenditures, $313,405; qualifying distributions, $306,585.
Application information: Accepts Common Grant Application Form of the National Network of Grantmakers.
Officers: Michael M. Connors, Pres.; Julia B. Connors, V.P.
Directors: Patrick E. Connors, Kathleen C. Mueller.
EIN: 522204597
Codes: FD

54349
Daughters of Union Veterans of the Civil War, 1861-1865, D.C. Department
5129 Smith Midland Ln.
Midland, VA 22728 (540) 439-2779
Contact: Elizabeth Williams, Treas.

Financial data (yr. ended 12/31/00): Grants paid, $304,865; assets, $348,474 (M); gifts received, $103; expenditures, $329,610; qualifying distributions, $303,937.
Limitations: Giving primarily in the metropolitan Washington, DC, area, including VA and MD, and in Springfield, IL.
Application information: Application forms required for educational awards.
Officers: Pat Kotteman, Pres.; Grace Clifford, Sr. V.P.; Muriel Scott, Jr. V.P.; Dorothy Cloud, Secy.; Elizabeth Williams, Treas.
EIN: 530227401
Codes: FD

54350
The Jesse & Rose Loeb Foundation, Inc.
c/o B.B. & T.
P.O. Box 93
Warrenton, VA 20186 (540) 349-3474
Contact: Thomas H. Kirk, Pres.

Established in 1991 in VA.
Donor(s): Rose Loeb.
Financial data (yr. ended 09/30/02): Grants paid, $302,100; assets, $8,683,525 (M); gifts received, $206,372; expenditures, $357,641; qualifying distributions, $310,598.
Limitations: Giving primarily in Warrenton, VA.
Application information: Application form not required.
Officer and Directors:* Thomas H. Kirk,* Pres.; Frank E. Continetti, G. Wayne Eastham, Sue Ann Meek, Fred G. Wayland, Jr.
EIN: 541604839
Codes: FD

54351
The Ochsman Foundation, Inc.
1650 Tysons Blvd., Ste. 620
McLean, VA 22102

Established in 1998 in MD.
Donor(s): Ralph Ochsman, Meurice C. Ochsman, Yetta K. Cohen.‡
Financial data (yr. ended 12/31/01): Grants paid, $298,460; assets, $7,573,494 (M); gifts received, $50,000; expenditures, $308,896; qualifying distributions, $298,460.
Limitations: Applications not accepted. Giving primarily in the eastern U.S., with emphasis on Washington, DC, MD, and New York, NY.
Application information: Contributes only to pre-selected organizations.
Officers: Ralph Ochsman, Pres.; Meurice C. Ochsman, Secy.-Treas.
Directors: C. Richard Beyda, Bruce David Ochsman, Jeffrey Wayne Ochsman, Michael Paul Ochsman.
EIN: 541893317
Codes: FD

54352
The Kington Foundation, Inc.
201 N. Union St., Ste. 300
Alexandria, VA 22314-2642 (703) 519-3036
Contact: Allison Cryor, Pres.

Established in 1997 in VA.
Donor(s): Ann A. Kington, Mark J. Kington.
Financial data (yr. ended 11/30/01): Grants paid, $298,000; assets, $1,885,247 (M); expenditures, $427,072; qualifying distributions, $300,163.
Limitations: Giving primarily in Washington, DC and VA.
Application information: Application form required.
Officer: Allison W. Cryor, Pres.
Directors: Ann A. Kington, Mark J. Kington.
EIN: 541831668
Codes: FD

54353
Eugene Holt Foundation
P.O. Box 1120
Richmond, VA 23218-1120 (804) 783-1010
Contact: Ivor Massey, Jr., Pres.

Established in 1966.
Financial data (yr. ended 08/31/01): Grants paid, $292,750; assets, $1,726,195 (M); expenditures, $307,269; qualifying distributions, $292,511.
Limitations: Giving primarily in Richmond, VA.
Application information: Application form not required.
Officers: Ivor Massey, Jr., Pres.; Alina Massey, V.P.; Ivor Nickolas Massey, V.P.; Annegrett Massey, Treas.
EIN: 540802044
Codes: FD

54354
Edward P. Evans Foundation
P.O. Box 46, Rte. 602
Casanova, VA 20139
Contact: Edward P. Evans, Tr.

Established in 1983 in VA.
Donor(s): Edward P. Evans.
Financial data (yr. ended 11/30/01): Grants paid, $287,514; assets, $40,426,953 (M); expenditures, $325,669; qualifying distributions, $293,888.
Limitations: Giving primarily in MA and VA.
Application information: Application form not required.
Trustees: Edward P. Evans, Robert S. Evans, Dorsey R. Gardner, Charles J. Queenan, Jr.
EIN: 256232129
Codes: FD

54355
James A. Meador Trust
305 Blvd.
Salem, VA 24153

Established in 1995.
Donor(s): James A. Meador.‡
Financial data (yr. ended 07/31/01): Grants paid, $287,500; assets, $5,255,904 (M); expenditures, $344,461; qualifying distributions, $287,500.
Limitations: Giving primarily in VA.
Application information: Application form not required.
Trustee: Smyth M. Meador.
EIN: 546279092
Codes: FD

54356
Noland Memorial Foundation
P.O. Box 971
Newport News, VA 23607

Established in 1955.
Donor(s): Members of the Noland family.
Financial data (yr. ended 12/31/01): Grants paid, $284,350; assets, $6,793,248 (M); gifts received, $112,456; expenditures, $384,860; qualifying distributions, $284,350.
Limitations: Giving primarily in VA.
Application information: Application form not required.
Officers and Trustees:* Lloyd U. Noland, Jr.,* Pres.; J. David Grose, Secy.-Treas.; Anne Noland Edwards, Jane K. Noland, Lloyd U. Noland III, Susan C. Noland.
EIN: 546048597
Codes: FD

54357
KFL Foundation
c/o K. Logue
512 Arnon Lake Dr.
Great Falls, VA 22066

Established in 1999 in VA.
Donor(s): Kenneth F. Logue.
Financial data (yr. ended 12/31/01): Grants paid, $280,056; assets, $87,781 (M); gifts received, $216,000; expenditures, $282,232; qualifying distributions, $281,784.
Limitations: Applications not accepted. Giving primarily in Washington, DC and NJ.
Application information: Contributes only to pre-selected organizations.
Officer and Director:* Kenneth F. Logue,* Pres.
EIN: 541950966
Codes: FD

54358
HRH Charitable Foundation
4951 Lake Brook Dr., Ste. 500
Glen Allen, VA 23060

Established in 1995 in VA.
Donor(s): Hilb, Rogal and Hamilton Co.
Financial data (yr. ended 12/31/01): Grants paid, $279,190; assets, $8,841 (M); gifts received, $492,979; expenditures, $279,735; qualifying distributions, $0.
Limitations: Giving primarily in VA.
Officers and Directors:* Andrew L. Rogal, Pres.; Timothy J. Korman,* V.P.; Walter L. Smith,* Secy.; Carolyn Jones, Treas.

54358—VIRGINIA

EIN: 541757380
Codes: CS, FD, CD

54359
Cartledge Charitable Foundation, Inc.
4235 Electric Rd., S.W., Ste. 100
Roanoke, VA 24014-4145 (540) 776-7000
Contact: George B. Cartledge, Jr., Pres.

Established in 1960 in VA.
Donor(s): Olive M. Cartledge.
Financial data (yr. ended 08/31/01): Grants paid, $277,415; assets, $84,149 (M); gifts received, $161,449; expenditures, $277,527; qualifying distributions, $277,401.
Limitations: Giving primarily in VA.
Officers: George B. Cartledge, Jr., Pres.; Robert H. Bennett, Secy.
EIN: 546044831
Codes: FD

54360
The Virginia Beach Foundation
P.O. Box 4629
Virginia Beach, VA 23454 (757) 422-5249
Application address: 1604 W. Hilltop Exec. Ctr., Ste. 308, Virginia Beach, VA 23451; FAX: (757) 422-1849; E-mail: mainoffice@vabeachfoundation.org; URL: http://www.vabeachfoundation.org
Contact: Ted Clarkson, Exec. Dir.

Incorporated in 1987 in VA.
Financial data (yr. ended 09/30/01): Grants paid, $271,365; assets, $8,688,188 (M); gifts received, $3,425,414; expenditures, $848,437.
Limitations: Giving primarily within a 60-mile radius of Virginia Beach, VA.
Publications: Annual report, newsletter, application guidelines, financial statement, informational brochure, grants list.
Application information: Project report and site visit for evaluation required. Application form required.
Officers and Directors:* Robert C. Goodman, Jr.,* Chair.; Macon F. Brock,* 1st Vice-Chair.; Mrs. Robin D. Ray,* 2nd Vice-Chair.; Margaret G. Campbell,* Secy.; Dennis R. Deans,* Treas.; and 12 additional directors.
EIN: 541553631
Codes: CM, FD

54361
James A. Meador Foundation
305 Blvd.
Salem, VA 24153
Application addresses: c/o Guidance Office, Staunton River High School, Rte. 4, Box 732, Moneta, VA 24121, tel.: (540) 947-2867; c/o Salem High School, 400 Spartan Dr., Salem, VA 24153, tel.: (540) 387-2437; c/o Glenvar High School, 4549 Malus Dr., Salem, VA 24153, tel.: (540) 387-6536

Financial data (yr. ended 12/31/01): Grants paid, $270,200; assets, $4,270,477 (M); expenditures, $313,658; qualifying distributions, $268,942.
Limitations: Giving primarily in VA, with emphasis on Moneta and Roanoke.
Application information: Application form required.
Officers: S.M. Meador, Pres.; Susan Tinsley, V.P.; J.H. Meador, Secy.-Treas.
EIN: 540795438
Codes: FD

54362
The Retired Officers Association Scholarship Fund
201 N. Washington St.
Alexandria, VA 22314-2539 (703) 838-8163
Additional tel.: (800) 245-8762, ext. 169; URL: http://www.troa.org
Contact: Laurie Wavering, Admin.

Established in 1993 in VA.
Donor(s): Alf A. Jorgenson, Edna Richman, Evelyn C. Fickessen, Warren H. Metzner, John T. Barham, Fride Shoemaker, Gladys Larson, Mary W. Beresford, Herman R. Muns, Mrs. Herman R. Muns, Larry Smith, Dan Crozier,‡ Ethel Kastantt.
Financial data (yr. ended 12/31/01): Grants paid, $258,500; assets, $23,648,560 (M); gifts received, $2,065,647; expenditures, $337,804; qualifying distributions, $4,073,696; giving activities include $3,862,072 for loans to individuals.
Publications: Application guidelines, financial statement.
Application information: Online application available on website. Application form required.
Officers and Directors:* Joseph Hoar,* Chair.; Michael A. Nelson,* Pres.; Peter C. Wylie,* Secy.; Richard P. Cuevoni,* Chair., Scholarship Fund; Glenn R. Zauber,* Comp.; John F. Dunn, John L. Finan, Karen S. Rankin, Paul P. Sova.
EIN: 541659039
Codes: FD, GTI

54363
The Yorkshire Foundation
4 Tennis Rd.
Charlottesville, VA 22901 (804) 293-8516
Contact: Sarah Dandridge, Secy.

Established in 1998 in VA.
Financial data (yr. ended 12/31/00): Grants paid, $255,400; assets, $899,216 (M); expenditures, $259,875; qualifying distributions, $253,246.
Limitations: Giving primarily in Charlottesville, VA.
Officers and Directors:* Victor M. Dandridge, Jr.,* Pres. and Treas.; Sarah A. Dandridge,* Secy.
EIN: 541886874
Codes: FD

54364
Danville Lions Foundation, Inc.
c/o John B. Hall, Jr.
121 Wilton Ave.
Danville, VA 24541

Established in 1993 in VA.
Donor(s): Grant Charitable Trust.
Financial data (yr. ended 06/30/99): Grants paid, $253,319; assets, $1,094,611 (M); expenditures, $253,379; qualifying distributions, $253,125.
Limitations: Giving primarily in VA.
Officers: David Clark, Pres.; Wayne A. Smith, Secy.; Jerry R. Buckner, Treas.
Directors: John B. Hall, Jr., Frank King, Jack Soyars, David Torbert.
EIN: 541722900
Codes: FD

54365
Susan Bailey & Sidney Buford Scott Endowment Trust
P.O. Box 1575
Richmond, VA 23218-1575

Established in 1958.
Donor(s): Sidney Buford Scott.
Financial data (yr. ended 12/31/00): Grants paid, $252,259; assets, $27,152 (M); gifts received, $1,774; expenditures, $253,345; qualifying distributions, $250,677.
Limitations: Applications not accepted. Giving primarily in Richmond, VA.
Application information: Contributes only to pre-selected organizations.
Trustees: Sidney Buford Scott, Susan Buford Scott.
EIN: 546048451
Codes: FD

54366
Art and Annie Sandler Foundation, Inc.
448 Viking Dr., Ste. 220
Virginia Beach, VA 23452

Established in 1996 in VA.
Donor(s): Arthur B. Sandler.
Financial data (yr. ended 06/30/01): Grants paid, $251,819; assets, $1,208,993 (M); expenditures, $260,127; qualifying distributions, $239,185.
Limitations: Giving primarily in MA and VA.
Officers: Arthur B. Sandler, Pres.; Steven B. Sandler, V.P.; Annie L. Sandler, Secy.
EIN: 541850741
Codes: FD

54367
Ivakota Association, Inc.
c/o CMC, Inc.
901 N. Pitt St.
Alexandria, VA 22314 (703) 836-3344
Contact: Louis B. Rodenberg, Jr., Secy.-Treas.

Established in 1919 in VA.
Donor(s): Kate Waller Barrett.‡
Financial data (yr. ended 12/31/99): Grants paid, $251,500; assets, $5,370,715 (M); expenditures, $311,794; qualifying distributions, $257,047.
Limitations: Giving primarily in Alexandria, VA.
Publications: Grants list, program policy statement, application guidelines.
Application information: Application form not required.
Officers and Directors:* David M. Burke,* Pres.; Douglas G. Lindsay, V.P.; Louis B. Rodenberg, Jr.,* Secy.-Treas.; George Caldwell, Viola G. Pope, Stephen Rideout, Martha Saylor.
EIN: 540505919
Codes: FD

54368
Catherine J. McGinnis Family Foundation
c/o Daniel L. McGinnis
P.O. Box 1290
Leesburg, VA 20177-1290

Established in 1997 in VA.
Donor(s): Daniel L. McGinnis, Arlene M. McGinnis.
Financial data (yr. ended 12/31/00): Grants paid, $250,000; assets, $3,603,582 (M); gifts received, $5,549; expenditures, $260,738; qualifying distributions, $221,097.
Limitations: Applications not accepted. Giving primarily in VA; funding also in New York, NY.
Application information: Contributes only to pre-selected organizations.
Trustees: Arlene M. McGinnis, Daniel L. McGinnis, Erin M. Meitzler, Kelly A. Royston, Colleen M. Sniegocki.
EIN: 541850520
Codes: FD

54369
Harrison Family Foundation, Inc.
1000 Flowerdew Hundred Rd.
Hopewell, VA 23860

Established in 1993 in VA.
Donor(s): David A. Harrison III.
Financial data (yr. ended 09/30/01): Grants paid, $247,500; assets, $4,017,704 (M); expenditures, $254,608; qualifying distributions, $245,137.

Limitations: Applications not accepted. Giving primarily in Greenwich, CT, and Richmond, VA.
Application information: Contributes only to pre-selected organizations.
Officers and Directors:* David A. Harrison III,* Chair.; David A. Harrison IV, Pres.; Marjorie H. Webb,* Treas.; Ann L.H. Armstrong, George A. Harrison, Mary T.H. Keevil.
EIN: 541692935
Codes: FD

54370
Chesapeake Corporation Foundation
1021 E. Cary St.
P.O. Box 2350
Richmond, VA 23218-2350 (804) 697-1000
Contact: J.P. Causey, Jr.

Established in 1955 in VA.
Donor(s): Chesapeake Corp.
Financial data (yr. ended 12/31/01): Grants paid, $235,171; assets, $1,617,138 (M); expenditures, $244,750; qualifying distributions, $239,170.
Limitations: Giving primarily in areas of company operations.
Publications: Application guidelines.
Application information: Employee-related scholarships are administered by the Educational Testing Service; call or write for application and guidelines. Application form not required.
Trustees: Frances W. Boroughs, J.P. Causey, Jr., J. Carter Fox, Louis K. Matherne, Bruce M. Pinover, Brenda L. Skidmore, E.M. Valentine.
EIN: 540605823
Codes: CS, FD2, CD

54371
The Hastings Trust
5629 George Washington Hwy., Ste. C
Yorktown, VA 23692 (757) 722-2801
Contact: Robert C. Hastings, Tr.

Established in 1964 in VA.
Donor(s): Charles E. Hastings,‡ Mary C. Hastings.‡
Financial data (yr. ended 12/31/01): Grants paid, $233,005; assets, $2,288,848 (M); expenditures, $246,633; qualifying distributions, $234,999.
Limitations: Applications not accepted. Giving primarily in VA.
Application information: Contributes only to pre-selected organizations.
Trustees: John A. Hastings, Robert C. Hastings, Carol Sanders.
EIN: 546040247
Codes: FD2

54372
The Columbus Phipps Foundation
P.O. Box 26606
Richmond, VA 23261-6606
Application address: P.O. Box 113, Clintwood, VA 24228, tel.: (540) 926-8152
Contact: Paul D. Buchanan, Tr.

Established in 1993 in VA.
Donor(s): Beulah G. Phipps.
Financial data (yr. ended 03/31/01): Grants paid, $232,225; assets, $3,986,878 (M); gifts received, $6,875; expenditures, $293,831; qualifying distributions, $249,744.
Limitations: Giving limited to Dickenson County, VA.
Application information: Application form required.
Trustees: Carol P. Buchanan, Paul D. Buchanan, William R. McFall.
Advisory Committee: Phyllis Davidson, Betty Jo Dodson, Rita F. Justice.
Director: Kenneth M. Smith.
EIN: 546338751

Codes: FD2, GTI

54373
Elbert H., Evelyn J. and Karen H. Waldron Charitable Foundation, Inc.
P.O. Box 20069
Roanoke, VA 24018-0503
Contact: Karen H. Waldron, Pres.

Established in 1982 in VA.
Donor(s): Elbert H. Waldron,‡ Evelyn J. Waldron.
Financial data (yr. ended 12/31/01): Grants paid, $228,083; assets, $1,137,929 (M); gifts received, $233,653; expenditures, $232,795; qualifying distributions, $228,574.
Limitations: Applications not accepted. Giving limited to VA.
Application information: Contributes only to pre-selected organizations.
Officers and Director:* Karen H. Waldron,* Pres.; Shawn A. Ricci, V.P.; Rebecca F. Rosenberg, Secy.-Treas.
EIN: 521289232
Codes: FD2

54374
The Lipman Foundation
(Formerly The Eric and Jeanette Lipman Foundation)
5310 Riverside Dr.
Richmond, VA 23225

Established in 1985 in VA.
Donor(s): Eric M. Lipman,‡ Jeanette S. Lipman.
Financial data (yr. ended 12/31/01): Grants paid, $226,666; assets, $8,738,238 (M); gifts received, $331,784; expenditures, $325,713; qualifying distributions, $241,511.
Limitations: Applications not accepted. Giving primarily in Richmond, VA.
Application information: Contributes only to pre-selected organizations.
Officers: Jeanette S. Lipman, Pres.; W. Birch Douglass III, V.P.
EIN: 541360375
Codes: FD2

54375
The Wolf Foundation
c/o Rockhill Farm
Rte. 702 at 709
The Plains, VA 20198

Established in 1998 in VA.
Donor(s): Stephen M. Wolf.
Financial data (yr. ended 12/31/01): Grants paid, $225,650; assets, $422,934 (M); expenditures, $230,838; qualifying distributions, $225,650.
Limitations: Applications not accepted. Giving primarily in VA.
Application information: Contributes only to pre-selected organizations.
Trustees: Delores E. Wolf, Stephen M. Wolf.
EIN: 367236923
Codes: FD2

54376
Do'Ikyte Foundation
21570 Schoolhouse Ct.
Ashburn, VA 20148-5018
Application address: 575 Station Rd., Amherst, MA 01002-3418, tel.: (413) 256-4255
Contact: Thomas R. Asher, Secy.

Established in 1993 in DC.
Donor(s): Daniel Solomon, Lillian Cohen Solomon Trust.
Financial data (yr. ended 12/31/00): Grants paid, $225,000; assets, $12,715,244 (M); gifts received, $11,111,000; expenditures, $239,829; qualifying distributions, $234,456.

Limitations: Giving primarily in CA and NY.
Application information: Application form not required.
Officers and Directors:* Daniel Solomon,* Pres.; Jane Solomon,* V.P.; Thomas R. Asher,* Secy.; Liza Albright, Treas.
EIN: 043198227
Codes: FD2

54377
Beverly W. & Hampton O. Powell Charitable Foundation
P.O. Box 60
Altavista, VA 24517
Contact: John E. Lane, III, Pres.

Established in 1996 in VA.
Donor(s): B.W. & H.O. Powell Char. Lead Annuity Trust.
Financial data (yr. ended 12/31/01): Grants paid, $222,500; assets, $32,533 (M); gifts received, $225,000; expenditures, $225,942; qualifying distributions, $220,251.
Limitations: Giving primarily in VA, with emphasis on Altavista.
Officers: John E. Lane III, Pres.; T.J. Wilkinson, Jr., V.P.; Robert H. Gilliam, Jr., Secy.-Treas.
EIN: 541776363
Codes: FD2

54378
The Donald and Nancy L. Delaski Foundation
605 Deerfield Pond Ct.
Great Falls, VA 22066

Established in 1998 in VA.
Donor(s): Donald Delaski, Nancy L. Delaski.
Financial data (yr. ended 12/31/01): Grants paid, $215,241; assets, $2,906,031 (M); expenditures, $222,891; qualifying distributions, $214,730.
Limitations: Applications not accepted. Giving on a national basis.
Application information: Contributes only to pre-selected organizations.
Officers and Directors:* Donald Delaski,* Pres.; Nancy L. Delaski,* Secy.-Treas.
EIN: 541902570
Codes: FD2

54379
Janet Stone Jones Foundation
c/o Investors' Records Corp.
614 E. High St.
Charlottesville, VA 22902
Contact: Russell J. Bell, Secy.

Established in 1978 in NY.
Donor(s): Janet Stone Jones Charitable Lead Trust.
Financial data (yr. ended 12/31/00): Grants paid, $214,325; assets, $27,315 (M); gifts received, $103,910; expenditures, $217,325; qualifying distributions, $213,559.
Limitations: Giving primarily in the northeastern U.S.
Officer: Russell J. Bell, Secy.
Directors: Whitney Brewster Armstrong, Benjamin Brewster, Janet Brewster York.
EIN: 132988287
Codes: FD2

54380
The Taylor Foundation
6969 Tidewater Dr.
Norfolk, VA 23509 (757) 857-6081
Application address: P.O. Box 2556, Norfolk, VA 23501
Contact: Robert T. Taylor, V.P.

Trust established in 1951 in VA.
Donor(s): Members of the Taylor family.

54380—VIRGINIA

Financial data (yr. ended 12/31/01): Grants paid, $213,250; assets, $2,502,553 (M); expenditures, $253,081; qualifying distributions, $233,294.
Limitations: Giving primarily in the Southeast, with emphasis on NC and VA.
Application information: Application form not required.
Officers and Trustees:* Leslie M. Taylor,* Pres.; Robert T. Taylor,* V.P.; Tom Bennett, Cliff Cutchins, Susan T. Kirkpatrick.
EIN: 540555235
Codes: FD2

54381
Ukrop's Educational Foundation
c/o Select. Comm.
600 Southlake Blvd.
Richmond, VA 23236   (804) 379-7373

Established in 1996 in VA.
Financial data (yr. ended 03/31/02): Grants paid, $212,000; assets, $3,779,460 (M); expenditures, $242,436; qualifying distributions, $219,623.
Limitations: Giving primarily in VA.
Application information: High school seniors and college students must provide an official school transcript, SAT scores, and a letter of recommendation.
Officers: Robert S. Kelley, Pres.; Brian K. Jackson, Secy.; David J. Naquin, Treas.
Directors: Joseph Edward Ukrop, Nancy Jo Ukrop, Robert S. Ukrop.
EIN: 541777866
Codes: FD2, GTI

54382
Mitford Children's Foundation
P.O. Box 127
Esmont, VA 22937

Established in 1997 in NC.
Donor(s): Jan Karon.
Financial data (yr. ended 12/31/01): Grants paid, $211,954; assets, $312,257 (M); gifts received, $182,706; expenditures, $217,120; qualifying distributions, $211,954.
Limitations: Applications not accepted.
Application information: Contributes only to pre-selected organizations.
Officers: Jan Karon, Pres.; Barry D. Setzer, Secy.-Treas.
EIN: 911876317
Codes: FD2

54383
Tad Beck Fund
P.O. Box 1566
Lexington, VA 24450
FAX: (540) 258-1227; E-mail: tebjr@att.net
Contact: T.E. Beck, Jr., Pres.; Ann M. Beck, V.P.; or Avent C. Beck, Secy.

Incorporated in 1968 in DE.
Donor(s): T.E. Beck, Jr., Ann M. Beck, Avent C. Beck, T.E. Beck III,‡ Beck Foundation.
Financial data (yr. ended 12/31/01): Grants paid, $210,500; assets, $2,672,719 (M); gifts received, $205,000; expenditures, $220,608; qualifying distributions, $220,608.
Limitations: Applications not accepted. Giving primarily in Washington, DC, NE, SD, and VA.
Application information: Contributes only to pre-selected organizations.
Officers and Directors:* T.E. Beck, Jr.,* Pres.; Ann M. Beck,* V.P.; Avent C. Beck,* Secy.; John C. Beck,* Treas.
EIN: 476057394
Codes: FD2

54384
Kanter Family Foundation
8000 Towers Crescent Dr., Ste. 1070
Vienna, VA 22182-2700   (703) 448-7688
Contact: Joel S. Kanter, Pres.

Established in 1989 in IL.
Donor(s): Burton W. Kanter,‡ Joshua S. Kanter, Joel S. Kanter.
Financial data (yr. ended 10/31/01): Grants paid, $205,346; assets, $5,896,281 (M); gifts received, $7,977; expenditures, $264,250; qualifying distributions, $232,516.
Limitations: Giving primarily in Washington, DC, Chicago, IL, and VA.
Application information: Application form not required.
Officers: Joel S. Kanter, Pres.; Naomi Kanter, V.P.; Joshua S. Kanter, Treas.
EIN: 363682199
Codes: FD2

54385
The John D. Evans Foundation
Waterford Farm
P.O. Box 1082
Middleburg, VA 20118-1082   (540) 687-6099
Contact: John D. Evans

Established in 1993.
Donor(s): John D. Evans, Falcon Communications, Inc.
Financial data (yr. ended 09/30/01): Grants paid, $203,435; assets, $9,780,792 (M); expenditures, $330,526; qualifying distributions, $269,915.
Limitations: Giving primarily in VA.
Officers and Directors:* John D. Evans,* Pres.; Edward J. Beckwith,* Secy.; Jack Porter,* Treas.
EIN: 541685616
Codes: FD2

54386
Pincus Paul Charitable Trust
7 Downtown Plz. Shopping Ctr.
Norfolk, VA 23510-2828   (757) 627-4286
Contact: B. Leonard Laibstain, Tr.

Established in 1991 in VA.
Donor(s): Pincus Paul.‡
Financial data (yr. ended 12/31/01): Grants paid, $203,275; assets, $2,946,559 (M); expenditures, $223,968; qualifying distributions, $215,028.
Limitations: Giving primarily in VA.
Trustees: Rosalind L. Gamsey, B. Leonard Laibstain, Harry Laibstain.
EIN: 546313478
Codes: FD2

54387
Steve and Toni Sandler Foundation, Inc.
448 Viking Dr., Ste. 220
Virginia Beach, VA 23452

Established in 1996 in VA.
Donor(s): Steven B. Sandler.
Financial data (yr. ended 06/30/01): Grants paid, $203,095; assets, $1,751,758 (M); expenditures, $207,581; qualifying distributions, $202,136.
Limitations: Giving primarily in VA.
Officers: Steven B. Sandler, Pres.; Arthur B. Sandler, V.P.; Toni Sandler, Secy.
EIN: 541850740
Codes: FD2

54388
Central Newspapers Foundation
c/o Gannett Co., Inc.
1100 Wilson Blvd., Ste. 2100
Arlington, VA 22234-2299

Incorporated in 1935 in IN.
Donor(s): Central Newspapers, Inc., Eugene S. Pulliam, Indianapolis Newspapers, Inc., Phoenix Newspapers, Inc.
Financial data (yr. ended 04/30/01): Grants paid, $202,500; assets, $32,000 (M); gifts received, $100,000; expenditures, $207,797; qualifying distributions, $207,797.
Limitations: Applications not accepted. Giving primarily in AZ and IN.
Publications: Informational brochure.
Application information: Contributes only to pre-selected organizations.
Officers and Directors:* Susan Clark Johnson,* Pres.; Evan Ray,* V.P.; Gracia C. Matore, Treas.
EIN: 356013720
Codes: CS, FD2, CD, GTI

54389
The Des Plaines Publishing Charitable Trust
P.O. Box 1045
Fairfax, VA 22030-1045
FAX: (703) 352-7653
Contact: H. Robert Rhoden, Tr.

Established in 1985 in VA.
Donor(s): James A. Linen IV.‡
Financial data (yr. ended 09/30/01): Grants paid, $202,161; assets, $2,705,374 (M); expenditures, $248,467; qualifying distributions, $202,161.
Limitations: Applications not accepted. Giving on a national basis.
Application information: Contributes only to pre-selected organizations.
Trustees: Mark Batterson, Rev. Judson E. Childress, Jr., Rev. William N. Ilnisky, Pastor H. Robert Rhoden.
EIN: 546231578
Codes: FD2

54390
Carrington Family Foundation
P.O. Box 10549
Lynchburg, VA 24506-0549   (434) 582-5640
E-mail: lisa.taylor@consolidatedshoe.com
Contact: Richard A. Carrington III, Pres.

Established in 2000 in VA.
Financial data (yr. ended 12/31/01): Grants paid, $200,000; assets, $1,517,173 (M); gifts received, $200,000; expenditures, $202,352; qualifying distributions, $1,999,998.
Limitations: Giving primarily in Lynchburg and surrounding areas of VA.
Application information: Application form required.
Officers: Richard A. Carrington III, Pres.; Sandra S. Carrington, Secy.-Treas.
Directors: Bruce J. Carrington, Charles L. Carrington, John H. Carrington, William A. Carrington.
EIN: 541989401
Codes: FD2

54391
Charlotte's Web
c/o Ann L. & Matthew T. Weir
1100 Crest Ln.
McLean, VA 22101

Established in 1997 in MD.
Donor(s): Ann Weir.
Financial data (yr. ended 06/30/01): Grants paid, $200,000; assets, $4,221,931 (M); expenditures, $206,970; qualifying distributions, $188,652.
Limitations: Applications not accepted. Giving primarily in Andover, NH.
Application information: Contributes only to pre-selected organizations.
Trustees: Ann Weir, Matthew Weir.
EIN: 522007855

Codes: FD2

54392
C. E. Richardson Benevolent Foundation
202 N. Washington Ave.
P.O. Box 1120
Pulaski, VA 24301-1120 (540) 980-6628
Additional tel.: (540) 980-1704
Contact: Betty S. King, Secy.

Established in 1979.
Financial data (yr. ended 05/31/01): Grants paid, $200,000; assets, $4,634,867 (M); expenditures, $232,407; qualifying distributions, $219,361.
Limitations: Giving limited to VA.
Publications: Program policy statement, application guidelines.
Application information: Application form required.
Officer: Betty S. King, Secy.
Trustees: James D. Miller, Annie S. Muire, James C. Turk.
EIN: 510227549
Codes: FD2

54393
Arlington Community Foundation
2525 Wilson Blvd.
Arlington, VA 22201 (703) 243-4785
FAX: (703) 243-4796; *URL:* http://www.arlcf.org

Established in 1991 in VA.
Financial data (yr. ended 12/31/01): Grants paid, $195,918; assets, $4,874,393 (M); gifts received, $523,872; expenditures, $4,724,387.
Limitations: Giving limited to the Arlington, VA, area.
Publications: Annual report, program policy statement, financial statement, informational brochure, application guidelines, multi-year report, newsletter.
Application information: Application form, information and deadlines available on Web site. Application form required.
Officers and Trustees:* Donald O. Manning,* Pres.; Sidney G. Simmonds,* V.P.; Anne D. Stewart,* Secy.; Thomas P. Jennings,* Treas.; Vicki Kirkbride, Exec. Dir.; Leslie Ariail, Ellen M. Bozman, Stephen Caruthers, William D. Dolan III, Todd Endo, Robert H. Hawthorne, Hon. Claude M. Hilton, Jonathan C. Kinney, John G. Milliken, Hon. William T. Newman, Jr., Charles McDonnell Radigan, Lola C. Reinsch, Pamela Galloway Tabb, Raul Torres, and 7 additional trustees.
EIN: 541602838
Codes: CM, FD2

54394
J. L. Camp Foundation, Inc.
203 Southampton Rd.
Franklin, VA 23851 (757) 562-4272
Contact: James L. Camp IV, Pres.

Incorporated in 1946 in VA.
Donor(s): J.L. Camp, Jr.,‡ Mrs. J.L. Camp, Jr.,‡ James L. Camp III.‡
Financial data (yr. ended 12/31/01): Grants paid, $195,627; assets, $3,692,959 (M); expenditures, $218,828; qualifying distributions, $199,633.
Limitations: Giving primarily in VA.
Application information: Application form not required.
Officers and Directors:* James L. Camp IV,* Pres.; Toy D. Savage, Jr.,* V.P.; Douglas B. Ellis,* Secy.-Treas.
EIN: 540742940
Codes: FD2

54395
The Sergei Federov Foundation
1751 Pinnacle Dr., Ste. 1500
McLean, VA 22102

Financial data (yr. ended 12/31/00): Grants paid, $195,083; assets, $1,859,365 (M); gifts received, $1,000; expenditures, $240,384; qualifying distributions, $195,083.
Limitations: Giving primarily in MI.
Officers: Sergei Fedorov, Pres.; Victor Fedorov, V.P.; Sergei Kournikov, V.P.; Frank Zecca, Treas.
Directors: Philip De Picciotto, Michael D. Luit.
EIN: 383437116
Codes: FD2

54396
George, Clarence & Dorothy Shaffer Charitable Foundation
8621 Clydesdale Rd.
Springfield, VA 22151-1428
Alternative address: c/o James S. Regan, 1866 Neumann Way, Crofton, MD 21114-2113
Contact: Vera Schleeter, Pres.

Established in 1998 in VA.
Donor(s): Dorothy S. Shaffer.‡
Financial data (yr. ended 08/31/01): Grants paid, $195,000; assets, $3,317,622 (M); expenditures, $244,785; qualifying distributions, $193,838.
Limitations: Giving primarily in Washington, DC, and MD.
Officers and Directors:* Vera Schleeter,* Pres. and Treas.; James S. Regan,* V.P and Secy.
EIN: 541856732
Codes: FD2

54397
Living Stones Foundation
(Formerly William & Elizabeth Powell Family Foundation)
10050 White Shop Rd.
Culpeper, VA 22701 (540) 547-4532

Donor(s): William B. Powell, Elizabeth S. Powell.
Financial data (yr. ended 12/31/01): Grants paid, $193,910; assets, $554,732 (M); gifts received, $160,000; expenditures, $202,828; qualifying distributions, $193,910.
Limitations: Applications not accepted. Giving on a national basis.
Application information: Contributes only to pre-selected organizations.
Officers: William B. Powell, Pres.; Elizabeth S. Powell, Secy.; William C. Powell, Treas.
EIN: 521270668

54398
William B. Thalhimer, Jr. and Family Foundation
1513 Hearthglow Ln.
Richmond, VA 23233 (804) 330-7400
Contact: Robert L. Thalhimer, V.P.

Incorporated in 1953 in VA.
Donor(s): William B. Thalhimer, Jr., Barbara J. Thalhimer.
Financial data (yr. ended 10/31/01): Grants paid, $190,000; assets, $3,994,793 (M); gifts received, $495,000; expenditures, $222,841; qualifying distributions, $199,642.
Limitations: Applications not accepted. Giving primarily in VA.
Application information: Unsolicited requests for funds not accepted.
Officers and Directors:* William B. Thalhimer III,* Chair.; William B. Thalhimer, Jr.,* Chair. Emeritus; Barbara Thalhimer,* Pres.; Robert L. Thalhimer,* V.P.; Barbara J. Thalhimer,* Secy.-Treas.; Adam R. Thalhimer, S. Elizabeth Thalhimer, Staton L. Thalhimer.
EIN: 546047110

Codes: FD2

54399
Christian Heritage Foundation
(Formerly Christian Heritage Foundation of Virginia, Inc.)
P.O. Box 138
Forest, VA 24551
Application address: P.O. Box 228, Forest, VA 24551
Contact: Jimmy N. Thomas, Sr., Pres.

Established around 1986 in VA.
Donor(s): Glen Thomas, Jimmy N. Thomas, Jr., Jimmy N. Thomas, Sr., Daniel A. Reber.
Financial data (yr. ended 12/31/00): Grants paid, $188,926; assets, $4,232,394 (M); expenditures, $717,853; qualifying distributions, $188,926.
Limitations: Giving primarily in Lynchburg, VA.
Officers and Directors:* Jimmy N. Thomas, Sr.,* Pres.; Mary T. Thomas,* Pres.; Daniel A. Reber,* Treas.; Janis O. Reber,* Treas.
EIN: 541362173
Codes: FD2

54400
Rouse-Bottom Foundation
115 Harbor Dr.
Hampton, VA 23661-3301
Contact: Viola K. Wood, Admin. Asst.

Established in 1989 in VA.
Donor(s): Dorothy Bottom.‡
Financial data (yr. ended 12/31/01): Grants paid, $186,000; assets, $3,348,588 (M); expenditures, $214,007; qualifying distributions, $189,464.
Limitations: Giving primarily in VA, with emphasis on the Lower Peninsula and Tidewater areas.
Application information: Giving strictly limited to the foundation's fields of interest; funds are committed mainly to a core group of grantees. Application form not required.
Officers and Directors:* Raymond B. Bottom, Jr.,* Pres.; Dorothy Rouse-Bottom,* Secy.-Treas.; Lewis T. Booker, Jesse R. Forst, M. Whitney Gilkey, Lester Migdal.
EIN: 541521527
Codes: FD2

54401
Adele M. Thomas Charitable Foundation, Inc.
304 Buxton Rd.
Falls Church, VA 22046 (703) 533-9566
Contact: John V. Thomas, Pres.

Established in 2000 in VA.
Donor(s): Adele M. Thomas Trust.
Financial data (yr. ended 12/31/01): Grants paid, $184,055; assets, $4,959,051 (M); gifts received, $607,434; expenditures, $194,919; qualifying distributions, $192,905.
Limitations: Giving primarily in CA and VA.
Application information: Application form not required.
Officers and Directors:* John V. Thomas,* Pres.; Euncie W. Thomas,* V.P.
EIN: 311704650
Codes: FD2

54402
The Robert and Mary Haft Foundation, Inc.
2924 Telestar Ct.
Falls Church, VA 22042 (703) 645-8800
Contact: Robert M. Haft, Pres.

Established in 1997 in MD.
Donor(s): Mary Z. Haft, Robert M. Haft.
Financial data (yr. ended 12/31/00): Grants paid, $183,675; assets, $688,074 (M); expenditures, $199,250; qualifying distributions, $190,462.

54402—VIRGINIA

Officers: Robert M. Haft, Pres.; Mary Z. Haft, V.P.
EIN: 522034198
Codes: FD2

54403
The William M. Backer Foundation, Inc.
7181 Smitten Farm Ln.
The Plains, VA 20198
Contact: William M. Backer, Pres.

Established in 1990 in DE.
Donor(s): William M. Backer.
Financial data (yr. ended 07/31/01): Grants paid, $183,400; assets, $4,115,891 (M); gifts received, $19,365; expenditures, $238,429; qualifying distributions, $183,400.
Limitations: Applications not accepted. Giving in the U.S., with emphasis on VA.
Application information: Contributes only to pre-selected organizations.
Officers: William M. Backer, Pres. and Treas.; Philip S. Reiss, Secy.
EIN: 133579157
Codes: FD2

54404
The Adele A. and Harold J. Westbrook Foundation, Inc.
3512 Robious Forest Way
Midlothian, VA 23113
Application address: P.O. Box 664, Midlothian, VA 23113, tel.: (804) 594-0187
Contact: Joan Clarke, Secy.

Established in 1999 in SC and VA.
Donor(s): Edward J. Westbrook.
Financial data (yr. ended 12/31/01): Grants paid, $183,000; assets, $1,594,469 (M); gifts received, $61,262; expenditures, $233,809; qualifying distributions, $222,970.
Limitations: Giving on a national basis, with emphasis on the South.
Application information: Application form required.
Officers and Directors:* Edward J. Westbrook,* Pres. and Treas.; Charles J. Westbrook,* V.P.; Harold J. Westbrook,* V.P.; Richard Westbrook,* V.P.; Joan W. Clarke,* Secy. and Exec. Dir.
EIN: 571075664
Codes: FD2

54405
Luck Stone Foundation, Inc.
P.O. Box 29682
Richmond, VA 23229   (804) 784-3335
Contact: C.S. Luck III, Pres.

Established in 1966 in VA.
Donor(s): Luck Stone Corp.
Financial data (yr. ended 10/31/00): Grants paid, $182,150; assets, $5,319,954 (M); expenditures, $226,689; qualifying distributions, $182,150.
Limitations: Giving primarily in VA.
Application information: Application form not required.
Officers: C.S. Luck III, Pres.; Joseph Andrews, Jr., Secy.; J.H. Parker III, Treas.
EIN: 546064982
Codes: CS, FD2, CD

54406
The Whitney and Anne M. Stone Foundation
c/o Investors' Records Corp.
614 E. High St.
Charlottesville, VA 22902
Contact: David J. Wood, Jr., Tr.; or Joseph M. Wood II, Tr.

Established in 1986 in VA.
Donor(s): Anne M. Stone.‡

Financial data (yr. ended 12/31/00): Grants paid, $182,000; assets, $4,193,110 (M); expenditures, $216,419; qualifying distributions, $182,000.
Limitations: Giving primarily in VA.
Officer: Russell J. Bell, Secy.
Trustees: David J. Wood, Jr., Joseph M. Wood II.
EIN: 133394681
Codes: FD2

54407
Silver Foundation
1201 Central Park Blvd.
Fredericksburg, VA 22401

Established in 1990 in VA.
Donor(s): Carl D. Silver, Larry D. Silver.
Financial data (yr. ended 04/30/01): Grants paid, $181,147; assets, $3,346 (M); gifts received, $183,873; expenditures, $182,207; qualifying distributions, $182,207.
Limitations: Applications not accepted.
Directors: Paul S. Elkin, Carl D. Silver, Larry D. Silver.
EIN: 541556341
Codes: FD2

54408
De Beaumont Foundation, Inc.
c/o James B. Sprague, M.D.
1515 Chain Bridge Rd., Ste. G-20
McLean, VA 22101-4421

Established in 1999 in MA.
Donor(s): Pierre De Beaumont.
Financial data (yr. ended 10/31/01): Grants paid, $180,000; assets, $55,467 (M); gifts received, $53,329; expenditures, $184,004; qualifying distributions, $179,980.
Limitations: Applications not accepted. Giving primarily in NY.
Application information: Contributes only to pre-selected organizations.
Officers: James Sprague, Pres.; Murray Brennan, V.P.; Leroy Parker, Secy.-Treas.
Director: Pierre De Beaumont.
EIN: 043467074
Codes: FD2

54409
Paul H. Pusey Foundation
1806 Chantilly St.
Richmond, VA 23230
Application address: P.O. Box 8446, Richmond, VA 23226, tel.: (804) 353-7821
Contact: Paul H. Pusey, Jr., Pres.

Established in 1969.
Donor(s): Paul H. Pusey, Jr., Vernelle B. Pusey.
Financial data (yr. ended 12/31/01): Grants paid, $179,605; assets, $4,047,343 (M); gifts received, $162,531; expenditures, $224,471; qualifying distributions, $199,462.
Limitations: Giving primarily in Richmond, VA.
Officers: Paul H. Pusey, Jr., Pres. and Treas.; Patricia P. Pusey, V.P.; Vernelle B. Pusey, Secy.
EIN: 237043682
Codes: FD2

54410
William Whidbee Sale and Virginia B. Sale Foundation
P.O. Box 1308
Bassett, VA 24055

Established in 1984 in VA.
Donor(s): Virginia B. Sale.
Financial data (yr. ended 12/31/00): Grants paid, $179,500; assets, $3,376,284 (M); gifts received, $54,691; expenditures, $212,715; qualifying distributions, $178,933.

Limitations: Applications not accepted. Giving limited to VA.
Application information: Contributes only to pre-selected organizations.
Officers: Virginia B. Sale, Pres.; Jane B. Spilman, V.P.; H.B. Meador, Jr., Secy.-Treas.
Directors: Lucy B. Andrews, John D. Bassett III, Minnie Lane, Robert H. Spilman.
EIN: 541273433
Codes: FD2

54411
R. W. & F. S. Cabaniss Foundation
1911 W. Main St.
Richmond, VA 23220
Contact: R.W. Cabaniss, Jr., V.P. and Secy.

Established in 1983.
Donor(s): Florence S. Cabaniss Charitable Lead Trust.
Financial data (yr. ended 12/31/00): Grants paid, $178,500; assets, $2,149,279 (M); gifts received, $269,833; expenditures, $190,915; qualifying distributions, $177,370.
Limitations: Giving primarily in GA and VA.
Officers: Richard J. Cabaniss, Pres. and Treas.; R.W. Cabaniss, Jr., V.P. and Secy.
Director: William V. Cabaniss.
EIN: 541250647
Codes: FD2

54412
The Patricia L. Rickert Foundation
c/o The Private Consulting Group
1400 N. 14th St.
Arlington, VA 22209

Established in 1998 in DE.
Donor(s): Albert L. Veltschi, Patricia Rickert.
Financial data (yr. ended 12/31/00): Grants paid, $177,856; assets, $2,034,869 (M); gifts received, $193,008; expenditures, $177,856; qualifying distributions, $177,693.
Limitations: Applications not accepted.
Application information: Contributes only to pre-selected organizations.
Officer: Patricia L. Rickert, Pres.
EIN: 061519383
Codes: FD2

54413
David Strouse Blount Educational Foundation
c/o SunTrust Banks, Inc.
P.O. Box 27385
Richmond, VA 23261-7385
Application address: 510 S. Jefferson St., Roanoke, VA, tel.: (540) 982-3076
Contact: Caroline McCoy

Established in 1973 in VA.
Financial data (yr. ended 03/31/01): Grants paid, $177,000; assets, $2,814,338 (L); expenditures, $197,739; qualifying distributions, $175,348.
Limitations: Giving limited to residents of VA.
Application information: Application form required.
Trustee: SunTrust Banks, Inc.
EIN: 546111717
Codes: FD2, GTI

54414
Macananny Foundation
7113 Hillwood Ct.
Spotsylvania, VA 22553

Established around 1994 in VA.
Donor(s): Raymond E. Macananny.
Financial data (yr. ended 06/30/01): Grants paid, $176,000; assets, $1,076,591 (M); gifts received, $351,217; expenditures, $232,524; qualifying distributions, $194,263.

IN THIS SECTION, WITHIN EACH STATE, FOUNDATIONS ARE LISTED IN DESCENDING ORDER BY TOTAL GRANTS PAID

Limitations: Applications not accepted. Giving primarily in VA.
Application information: Contributes only to pre-selected organizations.
Officers: Raymond E. Macananny, Sr., Pres.; Wendy R. Richters, Secy.-Treas.
EIN: 541741042
Codes: FD2

54415
The Joffe Family Foundation, Inc.
110 Catoctin Cir. S.E.
P.O. Box 1294
Leesburg, VA 20177
Contact: Pete Melchione

Established in 1986 in MD.
Donor(s): David Joffe.
Financial data (yr. ended 11/30/01): Grants paid, $175,800; assets, $22,481 (M); gifts received, $185,000; expenditures, $176,800; qualifying distributions, $175,768.
Limitations: Applications not accepted. Giving primarily in FL.
Application information: Contributes only to pre-selected organizations.
Officers: David Joffe, Pres. and Treas.; Scott Joffe, V.P. and Secy.
EIN: 521489595
Codes: FD2

54416
W.W. Whitlock Foundation
P.O. Box 130
Mineral, VA 23117 (540) 864-5451
Contact: W.W. Whitlock, Pres.

Established around 1980.
Donor(s): John D. Whitlock, Jane W. Sisk.
Financial data (yr. ended 12/31/00): Grants paid, $174,931; assets, $3,219,814 (M); expenditures, $212,101; qualifying distributions, $175,447.
Limitations: Giving primarily in VA.
Officers: W.W. Whitlock, Pres.; John D. Whitlock, V.P.; Eula D. Whitlock, Secy.; Jane W. Sisk, Treas.
EIN: 521532383
Codes: FD2

54417
ShenTel Foundation
c/o Shenandoah Telecommunications Co.
P.O. Box 459
Edinburg, VA 22824
Contact: Christopher E. French, Pres.

Established in 1990 in VA.
Donor(s): Shenandoah Telecommunications Co.
Financial data (yr. ended 12/31/00): Grants paid, $174,820; assets, $2,849,556 (M); expenditures, $229,937; qualifying distributions, $173,738.
Limitations: Giving primarily in the service area of Shenandoah Telecommunications Co. and its affiliates.
Application information: Application form required.
Officers: Christopher E. French, Pres.; Laurence F. Paxton, V.P., Finance; Noel M. Borden, Secy.; Dick D. Bowman, Treas.
Directors: Ken L. Burch, Grover M. Holler, Jr., Harold Morrison, Jr., Zane Neff, James E. Zerkel.
EIN: 541549765
Codes: CS, FD2, CD

54418
Rives C. Minor & Asalie M. Preston Educational Fund, Inc.
P.O. Box 274
Charlottesville, VA 22902-0274
Contact: Brian P. Menard, Exec. Dir.

Established in 1982 in VA.
Donor(s): Bernice M. Hargis,‡ Asalie M. Preston,‡ Glenna C. Minor.‡
Financial data (yr. ended 02/28/01): Grants paid, $174,488; assets, $2,399,031 (M); gifts received, $1,200; expenditures, $235,897; qualifying distributions, $207,360.
Limitations: Giving limited to high school students of Albemarle County, and Charlottesville, VA.
Application information: Applications available through guidance counselors at participating public high schools in Albemarle County, and Charlottesville, VA. Unsolicited applications not considered. Application form required.
Officers and Directors:* Garrett M. Smith,* Pres.; Mary Carter,* Secy.-Treas.; Brian P. Menard, Exec. Dir.; Mary Ann Elwood, Rev. Raymond A. Hailes, Grace Tinsley.
EIN: 521279007
Codes: FD2, GTI

54419
The Praxis Foundation
(Formerly The James B. and Bruce R. Murray, Jr. Foundation)
0 Court Sq.
Charlottesville, VA 22902-5144
(434) 971-8080
Contact: James B. Murray, Jr., Pres.

Established in 1996 in VA.
Donor(s): James B. Murray, Jr.
Financial data (yr. ended 12/31/01): Grants paid, $172,700; assets, $4,319,228 (M); expenditures, $177,200; qualifying distributions, $170,754.
Limitations: Giving primarily in VA.
Officers and Directors:* James B. Murray, Jr.,* Pres.; Bruce R. Murray,* Secy.
EIN: 541830546
Codes: FD2

54420
The Hanlon Foundation
746 Walker Rd., PMB 10-186
Great Falls, VA 22066

Established in 1999 in VA.
Donor(s): Richard E. Hanlon, Pamela Y. Hanlon.
Financial data (yr. ended 12/31/01): Grants paid, $170,729; assets, $2,220,508 (M); expenditures, $204,507; qualifying distributions, $202,035.
Limitations: Applications not accepted. Giving on a national basis, with emphasis on the greater metropolitan Washington, DC, area, including MD and VA.
Application information: Contributes only to pre-selected organizations.
Directors: Joanna Brooke Hurley, Exec. Dir.; Alexander B. Hanlon, Pamela Y. Hanlon, Patrick R. Hanlon, Richard E. Hanlon, Sarah L. Hanlon, Benjamin R. Hurley.
EIN: 541974562
Codes: FD2

54421
Metropolitan Health Foundation, Inc.
700 W. Grace St.
Richmond, VA 23220 (804) 775-4100
Contact: Charles P. Winkler, M.D., Pres.

Established in 1984 in VA.
Financial data (yr. ended 12/31/01): Grants paid, $165,040; assets, $2,906,891 (M); expenditures, $204,692; qualifying distributions, $169,268.
Limitations: Giving primarily in the Richmond, VA, area.
Officers: Charles P. Winkler, M.D., Pres.; Charles P. Cardwell III, M.D., V.P.; Malcolm E. Ritsch, Jr., Secy.-Treas.
Director: Edmond A. Hooker, Jr., M.D.
EIN: 510186144
Codes: FD2

54422
Duvahl Ridgway Hull and Andrew W. Hull Charitable Foundation
c/o McGuire, Woods, LLP
P.O. Box 397
Richmond, VA 23218

Established in 1991 in VA.
Donor(s): Duvahl Ridgway Hull.
Financial data (yr. ended 06/30/01): Grants paid, $164,428; assets, $3,667,015 (M); gifts received, $782,991; expenditures, $186,151; qualifying distributions, $164,428.
Limitations: Applications not accepted. Giving limited to VA.
Application information: Contributes only to pre-selected organizations.
Officers and Directors:* Mary Hull Swiers,* Pres.; Patricia P. Cormier,* V.P.; Karen W. Chichster,* Secy.; S. Cabell Dudley, Jr.,* Treas.; T.L. Plunkett, Jr.
EIN: 541567947
Codes: TN

54423
Theodore H. & Nancy Price Foundation, Inc.
c/o Theodore W. Price
901 E. Bryd St., W. Twr., 6th Fl.
Richmond, VA 23219

Established around 1980.
Donor(s): Theodore W. Price.
Financial data (yr. ended 03/31/01): Grants paid, $164,050; assets, $1,103,805 (M); gifts received, $214,276; expenditures, $173,743; qualifying distributions, $162,365.
Limitations: Applications not accepted. Giving primarily in Richmond, VA.
Application information: Contributes only to pre-selected organizations.
Officers: Theodore W. Price, Pres.; G.P. Messiqua, V.P.; C.B. Price, Secy.
EIN: 136199406
Codes: FD2

54424
The English Foundation
(Formerly The English Foundation-Trust)
1522 Main St.
Altavista, VA 24517
Contact: E.R. English, Jr., Tr.

Established in 1956 in VA.
Donor(s): E.R. English, Sr.‡
Financial data (yr. ended 12/31/01): Grants paid, $163,700; assets, $3,014,527 (M); expenditures, $206,475; qualifying distributions, $163,015.
Limitations: Giving limited to the Campbell County, VA, area.
Publications: Annual report.
Application information: Application form required for scholarships. Only Altavista High School students are eligible. Application form required.
Trustees: E.R. English, Jr., Rita T. English, Sarah F. Simpson.
EIN: 546036409
Codes: FD2, GTI

54425
Gauri Ambegaonkar Foundation
1591 Spring Gate Dr., Unit 3116
McLean, VA 22102-3449
Application address: 11250 N. Port Washington Rd., Mequon, WI 53092, tel.: (414) 243-4141
Contact: Prakash Ambegaonkar, Tr.

Established in 1987 in WI.

54425—VIRGINIA

Donor(s): Prakash Ambegaonkar, Sunandini Ambegaonkar.
Financial data (yr. ended 12/31/00): Grants paid, $162,310; assets, $3,162,560 (M); expenditures, $182,923; qualifying distributions, $165,865.
Trustees: Prakash Ambegaonkar, Sunandini Ambegaonkar.
EIN: 391602182
Codes: FD2

54426
Harry Bramhall Gilbert Charitable Trust
700 Oriole Dr., Rm. 213
Virginia Beach, VA 23451
URL: http://fdncenter.org/grantmaker/gilbert
Contact: Stuart D. Glasser, Tr.

Established in 1993 in VA.
Donor(s): Leonore K. Gilbert.‡
Financial data (yr. ended 12/31/01): Grants paid, $161,000; assets, $3,645,369 (M); expenditures, $195,518; qualifying distributions, $178,084.
Limitations: Giving primarily in Chesapeake, Norfolk, and Virginia Beach, VA.
Application information: Application form not required.
Trustees: Stuart D. Glasser, Robert E. Larson.
EIN: 541674360
Codes: FD2

54427
The Mann T. Lowry Foundation
406 W. Franklin St.
Richmond, VA 23220 (804) 643-3512
Contact: George R. Hinnant, Pres.

Established in 1996 in VA.
Donor(s): Sara Lowry.‡
Financial data (yr. ended 12/31/00): Grants paid, $161,000; assets, $3,057,392 (M); gifts received, $64,927; expenditures, $305,235; qualifying distributions, $160,237.
Limitations: Giving limited to VA.
Application information: Application form not required.
Officer and Director:* George R. Hinnant,* Pres.
EIN: 546402823
Codes: FD2

54428
Caruthers Foundation, Inc.
4600 N. Fairfax Dr., Ste. 1000
Arlington, VA 22203 (703) 524-8811
Contact: Dana J. Snyder, Tr.

Established in 1979.
Donor(s): Preston C. Caruthers, Jeanne B. Caruthers.
Financial data (yr. ended 04/30/01): Grants paid, $158,850; assets, $267,206 (M); gifts received, $90,000; expenditures, $159,764; qualifying distributions, $158,769.
Limitations: Giving primarily in VA.
Trustees: Jeanne B. Caruthers, Lynn E. Caruthers, Preston C. Caruthers, Stephen P. Caruthers, Donald J. Creasy, Dana J. Snyder.
EIN: 510248560
Codes: FD2

54429
HJH Foundation
P.O. Box 228
Forest, VA 24551
Application address: 1055 Fallen Oaks Ln., Lynchburg, VA 24503, tel.: (434) 525-1028
Contact: Jimmy N. Thomas, Jr., Pres.

Established in 2000 in VA.
Donor(s): Jimmy N. Thomas, Jr.
Financial data (yr. ended 12/31/01): Grants paid, $158,130; assets, $377,803 (M); gifts received, $64,500; expenditures, $160,717; qualifying distributions, $159,893.
Limitations: Giving primarily in VA.
Officers and Directors:* Jimmy N. Thomas, Jr.,* Pres.; Rhonda P. Thomas,* Secy.-Treas.; Jimmy N. Thomas.
EIN: 542009003
Codes: FD2

54430
Staunton Augusta Waynesboro Community Foundation
(also known as SAW Community Foundation)
1100 W. Broad St.
Waynesboro, VA 22980 (540) 932-7878
FAX: (540) 932-7539; *E-mail:* sawfdtn@cfw.com;
URL: http://www.cfw.com/~sawfdtn
Contact: Joi E. Brown, Exec. Dir.

Established in 1992.
Donor(s): H.D. "Buz" Dawbarn.‡
Financial data (yr. ended 12/31/01): Grants paid, $156,795; assets, $3,710,059 (M); gifts received, $1,653,644; expenditures, $254,725.
Limitations: Giving limited to Augusta County, Nelson County, Staunton, and Waynesboro, VA.
Publications: Informational brochure, annual report (including application guidelines), financial statement, grants list, newsletter.
Application information: Application form required.
Officers and Directors:* Ben Melnyczuk,* Pres.; Beverly S. "Cheri" Moran,* V.P.; David Deering,* Secy.-Treas.; Joi E. Brown,* Exec. Dir.; C. Phillip Barger, Benham Black, Harold Cook, Lynn Diveley, Thomas Gorsuch, Pamela T. Huggins, Martin Lightsey, William McIntyre, P. William Moore, Jr., Donald A. Mostrorocco, Jr., Richard Schilling, Edward Stemmler, Robert A. Sullivan, Jennifer Vela, Wesley Wampler.
EIN: 541647385
Codes: CM, FD2

54431
Campbell Hoffman Foundation
9893 Georgetown Pike, PMB 805
Great Falls, VA 22066 (703) 757-7772
E-mail: jknox@campbellhoffman.org; *URL:* http://www.campbellhoffman.org
Contact: JoAnn Pearson Knox, Exec. Dir.

Established in 1995 in VA.
Donor(s): Jane Campbell.‡
Financial data (yr. ended 12/31/00): Grants paid, $156,230; assets, $2,371,847 (M); gifts received, $65,450; expenditures, $223,304; qualifying distributions, $157,858.
Limitations: Applications not accepted. Giving primarily in the greater Washington, DC, area.
Application information: Contributes only to pre-selected organizations.
Officers: John Williams, Pres.; JoAnn P. Knox, Exec. Dir.
Trustees: Brian Davis, David Gagen, Elizabeth Henderson, Carol Jameson, Lynda Joseph, Steve Kariya.
EIN: 541724558
Codes: FD2

54432
The Reinhart Foundation
8900 Brennan Rd.
Richmond, VA 23229

Established in 2000 in VA.
Donor(s): Myron Reinhart.
Financial data (yr. ended 12/31/01): Grants paid, $155,197; assets, $9,077,791 (M); gifts received, $55,588; expenditures, $314,751; qualifying distributions, $155,197.
Officer: Myron H. Reinhart, Chair. and Pres.
Directors: William L. Reinhart, Cynthia R. Richards.
EIN: 542001451
Codes: FD2

54433
Graphic Arts Education and Research Foundation
1899 Preston White Dr.
Reston, VA 20191 (703) 264-7200
E-mail: gaerf@npes.org; *URL:* http://www.npes.org/gaerf/home.html
Contact: Regis J. Delmontagne, Pres.

Established in 1984 in VA.
Donor(s): Graphic Arts Show Co., Inc.
Financial data (yr. ended 12/31/00): Grants paid, $155,171; assets, $1,733,248 (M); gifts received, $394,548; expenditures, $491,489; qualifying distributions, $155,171.
Limitations: Giving on a national basis.
Publications: Annual report, informational brochure, application guidelines.
Application information: Application form required.
Officers: Raymond W. Lawton, Chair.; Gerald Nathe, Vice-Chair.; Regis J. Delmontagne, Pres.; Ray W. Roper, Secy.; I. Greg Van Wert, Treas.
Directors: Donald Duncanson, Robert E. Murphy, James R. Schultz.
EIN: 521321169
Codes: FD2

54434
The Marie A. Dornhecker Revocable Trust
308 Cedar Lakes Dr., 2nd Fl.
Chesapeake, VA 23322-8343

Financial data (yr. ended 12/31/01): Grants paid, $155,000; assets, $751,544 (M); expenditures, $167,803; qualifying distributions, $157,015; giving activities include $2,015 for programs.
Limitations: Applications not accepted.
Application information: Contributes only to pre-selected organizations.
Trustee: Basnight Kinser.
EIN: 546440456
Codes: FD2

54435
The J. Henry Kegley Foundation
P.O. Box 1689
Bristol, VA 24203-1689

Established in 2000 in VA.
Financial data (yr. ended 12/31/00): Grants paid, $152,309; assets, $2,449,879 (M); gifts received, $2,678,935; expenditures, $161,758; qualifying distributions, $161,758.
Limitations: Giving primarily in VA.
Trustees: Homer A. Jones, Jr., George M. Warren, Jr.
EIN: 546445584
Codes: FD2

54436
The Malek Family Charitable Trust
1259 Crest Ln.
McLean, VA 22101

Established in 1995 in VA.
Donor(s): Frederic V. Malek.
Financial data (yr. ended 12/31/99): Grants paid, $151,039; assets, $1,903,323 (M); gifts received, $143,058; expenditures, $157,945; qualifying distributions, $150,836.
Limitations: Applications not accepted. Giving on a national basis.
Application information: Contributes only to pre-selected organizations.

Trustees: Frederic V. Malek, Frederic W. Malek, Marlene Malek, Michelle Malek.
EIN: 546373070
Codes: FD2

54437
The Brock Foundation
c/o Macon Brock, Jr.
1506 Duke of Windsor Rd.
Virginia Beach, VA 23454-2504

Established in 1998 in VA.
Donor(s): Macon F. Brock, Jr.
Financial data (yr. ended 12/31/00): Grants paid, $150,125; assets, $2,692,772 (M); gifts received, $1,456,472; expenditures, $151,364; qualifying distributions, $149,955.
Limitations: Applications not accepted.
Application information: Contributes only to pre-selected organizations.
Officers and Directors:* Macon F. Brock, Jr.,* Pres.; Joan P. Brock,* Secy.-Treas.; Macon F. Brock III, Kathryn Brock Everett, Christine Brock McCammon.
EIN: 541902235
Codes: FD2

54438
Hazel T. and George G. Carman Trust
c/o Bank of America, N.A.
P.O. Box 26606
Richmond, VA 23261-6606 (804) 788-3698
Application address: c/o Bank of America, N.A., P.O. Box 26903, Richmond, VA 23261, tel.: (804) 788-2964
Contact: Richard B. Brandt, Dir.

Established in 1988 in VA.
Financial data (yr. ended 08/31/01): Grants paid, $150,000; assets, $2,581,821 (M); expenditures, $178,751; qualifying distributions, $157,227.
Limitations: Applications not accepted. Giving primarily in Charlottesville, VA.
Application information: Grants are 10 years in duration. No new proposals will be accepted.
Director: Richard B. Brandt.
Trustee: Bank of America.
EIN: 546264240
Codes: FD2

54439
Fatherree Foundation
206 Gun Club Rd.
Richmond, VA 23221 (804) 359-5863
Contact: Anne W. Kenny, Pres.

Established around 1969 in VA.
Financial data (yr. ended 12/31/01): Grants paid, $150,000; assets, $2,637,828 (M); expenditures, $173,181; qualifying distributions, $151,656.
Limitations: Giving primarily in Richmond, VA.
Officers and Directors:* Anne W. Kenny,* Pres.; John C. Kenny,* Secy.; Kathryn B. Kenny Codd, Anne B. Kenny.
EIN: 546087147
Codes: FD2

54440
Charles G. Thalhimer and Family Foundation
600 E. Main St.
Richmond, VA 23219-2441 (804) 648-0103
Contact: Charles G. Thalhimer, Pres.

Established in 1976 in VA.
Donor(s): Members of the Thalhimer family.
Financial data (yr. ended 10/31/01): Grants paid, $149,230; assets, $2,754,110 (M); expenditures, $181,827; qualifying distributions, $151,274.
Limitations: Giving primarily in VA.
Application information: Application form not required.

Officers and Directors:* Charles G. Thalhimer,* Pres.; Rhoda R. Thalhimer,* Exec. V.P.; Charles G. Thalhimer, Jr.,* V.P. and Secy.; Harry R. Thalhimer,* V.P. and Treas.
EIN: 546047108
Codes: FD2

54441
The Sharp Foundation
P.O. Box 42333
Richmond, VA 23242-2333

Established in 1989 in VA.
Donor(s): Richard L. Sharp.
Financial data (yr. ended 12/31/00): Grants paid, $147,600; assets, $13,225,977 (M); gifts received, $8,826,250; expenditures, $181,398; qualifying distributions, $147,847.
Limitations: Applications not accepted. Giving primarily in Richmond, VA.
Application information: Contributes only to pre-selected organizations.
Officer: Richard L. Sharp, Pres. and Treas.
EIN: 541526891
Codes: FD2

54442
Hunt Family Fund
5841 Whitehall Rd.
Zanoni, VA 23191

Established in 1998.
Donor(s): William O. & Jeannette P. Hunt Foundation.
Financial data (yr. ended 12/31/00): Grants paid, $145,200; assets, $2,637,867 (M); gifts received, $103,110; expenditures, $160,494; qualifying distributions, $144,443.
Limitations: Applications not accepted. Giving primarily in VA.
Application information: Contributes only to pre-selected organizations.
Officers: Robert P. Hunt, Pres. and Treas.; Barbara B. Hunt, Secy.
EIN: 311604788
Codes: FD2

54443
C. W. Gooch, Jr. Charitable Trust
c/o SunTrust Banks, Inc.
P.O. Box 27385
Richmond, VA 23261-7385
Application address: Advisory Comm., c/o SunTrust Banks, Inc., P.O. Box 678, Lynchburg, VA 24505

Established in 1968 in VA.
Financial data (yr. ended 04/30/01): Grants paid, $144,600; assets, $2,803,829 (M); expenditures, $167,071; qualifying distributions, $143,009.
Limitations: Giving primarily in MD and VA.
Trustee: SunTrust Banks, Inc.
EIN: 546074371
Codes: FD2

54444
Houff Foundation
P.O. Box 220
Weyers Cave, VA 24486 (540) 234-9233
Contact: Dwight E. Houff, Secy.

Established in 1979.
Donor(s): Cletus E. Houff, Houff Transfer, Inc., Charlotte R. Houff.‡
Financial data (yr. ended 12/31/01): Grants paid, $142,460; assets, $4,630,674 (M); expenditures, $160,818; qualifying distributions, $142,460.
Limitations: Giving primarily in the Shenandoah Valley, VA, area.
Application information: Application form not required.

Officers: Roxie White, Pres.; Douglas Houff, V.P.; Dwight E. Houff, Secy.
EIN: 540236893
Codes: FD2

54445
The John B., Anna Augusta C. and George H. Hinton Memorial Fund
c/o Wachovia Bank, N.A. Charitable Funds Group 41046
P.O. Box 27602
Richmond, VA 23261 (804) 697-6901
Contact: Mary Jo Tull, V.P., Wachovia Bank, N.A.

Established in 1984 in VA.
Financial data (yr. ended 08/31/01): Grants paid, $141,900; assets, $2,950,736 (M); expenditures, $161,336; qualifying distributions, $151,761.
Limitations: Giving limited to King George, Lancaster, Northumberland, Richmond, and Westmoreland counties, VA.
Application information: Application form not required.
Directors: Ammon G. Dunton, Sr., W. Emory Lewis, Jr.
Trustee: Wachovia Bank, N.A.
EIN: 546033088
Codes: FD2

54446
The Robert P. and Arlene R. Kogod Family Foundation
2345 Crystal Dr., 10th Fl.
Arlington, VA 22202

Established in 1998 in VA.
Donor(s): Arlene R. Kogod, Robert P. Kogod, Charles E. Smith Mgmt., Inc.
Financial data (yr. ended 12/31/00): Grants paid, $141,807; assets, $209,674 (M); gifts received, $100,000; expenditures, $153,341; qualifying distributions, $141,807; giving activities include $130,245 for programs.
Limitations: Applications not accepted.
Application information: Contributes only to a pre-selected organizations.
Officers and Directors:* Robert P. Kogod,* Pres.; E. Matthew Hause, V.P. and Treas.; Arlene R. Kogod,* Secy.
EIN: 541813660
Codes: FD2

54447
The Melton Arts Foundation
2086 Hunters Crest Way
Vienna, VA 22181
Contact: William N. Melton, Pres.

Established in 1992 in VA.
Donor(s): William N. Melton.
Financial data (yr. ended 11/30/01): Grants paid, $141,500; assets, $75,409 (M); gifts received, $140,000; expenditures, $142,912; qualifying distributions, $141,500.
Limitations: Giving primarily in Washington, DC.
Application information: Independent screening board reviews all applications.
Officers and Directors:* William N. Melton,* Pres. and Treas.; Patricia S. Smith,* V.P. and Secy.
EIN: 541648543
Codes: FD2

54448
The Catesby Foundation
P.O. Box 500
The Plains, VA 20198-0500 (540) 253-5358
Contact: Casey Linehan

Established in 1971 in VA.
Donor(s): Richard R. Ohrstrom.‡

54448—VIRGINIA

Financial data (yr. ended 12/31/01): Grants paid, $140,000; assets, $2,714,148 (M); gifts received, $20,189; expenditures, $155,927; qualifying distributions, $145,646.
Limitations: Applications not accepted. Giving on a national basis.
Application information: Contributes only to pre-selected organizations.
Officers: George L. Ohrstrom II, Pres.; Mark J. Ohrstrom, V.P.; Kenneth M. Ohrstrom, Secy.; Barnaby A. Ohrstrom, Treas.
EIN: 237149750
Codes: FD2

54449
Page Family Foundation
6715 Arlington Blvd.
Falls Church, VA 22042
FL tel.: (561) 347-1252
Contact: William H. Page, Pres.

Established in 1992 in DC.
Donor(s): William H. Page.
Financial data (yr. ended 12/31/00): Grants paid, $140,000; assets, $3,466,553 (M); expenditures, $178,583; qualifying distributions, $136,265.
Limitations: Giving primarily in Washington, DC.
Officers: William H. Page, Pres.; William J. Page, Secy.-Treas.
Director: W. Raymond Page.
EIN: 541595128
Codes: FD2

54450
Helen G. Gifford Foundation
(Formerly The Lee A. & Helen G. Gifford Foundation)
2568 Ocean Shore Ave.
Virginia Beach, VA 23451
E-mail: bhearst@aol.com
Contact: William A. Hearst, Pres.

Established in 1997 in VA.
Donor(s): Helen G. Gifford.‡
Financial data (yr. ended 02/28/02): Grants paid, $138,981; assets, $2,083,424 (M); expenditures, $176,800; qualifying distributions, $138,534.
Limitations: Applications not accepted. Giving primarily in Norfolk, VA.
Application information: Contributes only to pre-selected organizations.
Officers and Directors:* William A. Hearst,* Pres.; Zelma G. Rivint,* Exec. V.P.; Patricia Rowland,* 1st V.P.; Jennifer Mizroch,* 2nd V.P.; Michael E. Barney,* Secy.; Joseph B. Hearst,* Treas.
EIN: 541850266
Codes: FD2

54451
First Hospital Corp. Private Foundation
240 Corporate Blvd., Ste. 400
Norfolk, VA 23502 (757) 459-5100
Contact: Ronald I. Dozoretz, Pres.

Established in 1992 in VA.
Donor(s): First Hospital Corp.
Financial data (yr. ended 06/30/01): Grants paid, $137,850; assets, $754,864 (M); gifts received, $396,189; expenditures, $165,714; qualifying distributions, $137,850.
Limitations: Giving primarily in Washington, DC and VA.
Officers and Directors:* Ronald I. Dozoretz, M.D.,* Pres. and Mgr.; Beth Dozoretz,* V.P.; Shari D. Friedman,* V.P.; Renee D. Strelitz,* V.P.; Michael Smith,* Secy.
EIN: 541674740
Codes: CS, FD2, CD

54452
Eugene Holt Massey Charitable Trust
P.O. Box 1120
Richmond, VA 23218 (804) 783-1010
Contact: Eugene Holt Massey, Tr.

Established in 1996 in VA.
Donor(s): Anne Holt Massey, Eugene Holt Massey.
Financial data (yr. ended 01/31/01): Grants paid, $135,000; assets, $1,573,396 (M); expenditures, $142,642; qualifying distributions, $133,920.
Limitations: Giving primarily in PA.
Trustee: Eugene Holt Massey.
EIN: 311558397
Codes: FD2

54453
New Society Fund
P.O. Box 17367
Arlington, VA 22216
Contact: G. Cameron Duncan, Jr., Pres.

Established in 1998 in VA.
Financial data (yr. ended 12/31/01): Grants paid, $134,500; assets, $1,796,839 (M); expenditures, $154,617; qualifying distributions, $135,235.
Limitations: Applications not accepted. Giving on a national basis.
Application information: Contributes only to pre-selected organizations.
Officers and Directors:* G. Cameron Duncan, Jr.,* Pres. and Treas.; Susan Mithan Duncan,* Secy.; Lucia Bowie Duncan.
EIN: 541847581

54454
Dan River Foundation
P.O. Box 261
Danville, VA 24543-0261 (804) 799-4912

Incorporated in 1957 in VA.
Donor(s): Dan River Inc.
Financial data (yr. ended 12/31/00): Grants paid, $133,770; assets, $2,196,987 (M); expenditures, $159,062; qualifying distributions, $159,062.
Limitations: Giving on a national basis, with emphasis on New York, NY, and Danville, VA.
Application information: Application form not required.
Officers and Directors:* Joseph L. Lanier, Jr.,* Pres.; Richard L. Williams,* V.P.; Harry L. Goodrich, Secy.; Barry F. Shea,* Treas.; Joseph C. Bouknight, E. Linwood Wright.
EIN: 546036112
Codes: CS, FD2, CD

54455
Bushkin Family Foundation
1650 Tysons Blvd., Ste. 200
McLean, VA 22102
Contact: Arthur A. Bushkin, Chair.; and Kathryn K. Bushkin, Pres.

Established in 1999 in VA.
Donor(s): Arthur Bushkin, Kathryn Bushkin.
Financial data (yr. ended 12/31/01): Grants paid, $132,000; assets, $1,845,668 (M); expenditures, $139,158; qualifying distributions, $131,833.
Limitations: Giving primarily in Washington, DC.
Officers: Arthur A. Bushkin, Chair. and C.E.O.; Kathryn K. Bushkin, Pres.
EIN: 541962183
Codes: FD2

54456
Homer & Mabel Derrick Foundation
P.O. Box 1111
Lexington, VA 24450-1111
Contact: H.E. Derrick, Jr., Tr.

Established in 1995 in VA.

Financial data (yr. ended 12/31/01): Grants paid, $131,478; assets, $2,796,940 (M); expenditures, $164,447; qualifying distributions, $146,929.
Limitations: Giving primarily in Lexington, VA.
Trustees: Betsy C. Anderson, H.E. Derrick, Jr., H.D. Morris, Mary D. Wofford.
EIN: 541587458
Codes: FD2

54457
Seagears Family Foundation
9909 Evenstar Ln.
Fairfax Station, VA 22039
Contact: Marilyn Neff Seagears, Pres.

Established in 1998 in VA.
Financial data (yr. ended 12/31/01): Grants paid, $131,300; assets, $1,965,104 (M); expenditures, $147,519; qualifying distributions, $133,959.
Limitations: Applications not accepted. Giving on a national basis, with emphasis on NY and the greater metropolitan Washington, DC, area, including MD and VA.
Application information: Contributes only to pre-selected organizations.
Officers and Directors:* Marilyn Neff Seagears,* Pres.; Murray W. Seagears,* Secy.-Treas.; Joanne N. Arbaugh.
EIN: 541899835
Codes: FD2

54458
American Woodmark Foundation, Inc.
3102 Shawnee Dr.
Winchester, VA 22601 (540) 665-9129
Contact: Brenda K. Dupont, Secy.-Treas.

Established in 1995 in VA.
Donor(s): American Woodmark Corp.
Financial data (yr. ended 04/30/01): Grants paid, $130,625; assets, $316,404 (M); gifts received, $144,670; expenditures, $131,657; qualifying distributions, $130,920.
Limitations: Giving limited to GA, VA, and WV, in areas of company operations.
Application information: Application form required.
Officers and Directors:* David Blount,* Chair.; Brenda K. Dupont,* Secy.-Treas.; D. Robert Taylor.
EIN: 541759773
Codes: CS, FD2, CD

54459
Armond & Rose Caplan Foundation
500 E. Main St., Ste. 1424
Norfolk, VA 23510 (757) 623-1062
Contact: Armond R. Caplan, Pres.; or Rose Caplan, V.P.

Established in 1977 in VA.
Donor(s): Armond R. Caplan, Rose J. Caplan.
Financial data (yr. ended 09/30/01): Grants paid, $130,597; assets, $2,523,377 (M); gifts received, $92,000; expenditures, $132,154; qualifying distributions, $129,330.
Limitations: Giving primarily in Norfolk, VA.
Officers and Directors:* Armond R. Caplan,* Pres.; Rose J. Caplan,* V.P.; James M. Caplan, Secy.; Stephen R. Caplan, Treas.
EIN: 510217380
Codes: FD2

54460
The Franklin Federal Foundation
4501 Cox Rd.
Glen Allen, VA 23060

Established in 2000 in VA.
Financial data (yr. ended 09/30/01): Grants paid, $130,000; assets, $1,051,508 (M); gifts received,

$475,000; expenditures, $134,531; qualifying distributions, $130,000.
Limitations: Applications not accepted. Giving primarily in VA.
Application information: Contributes only to pre-selected organizations.
Officers and Directors:* Richard T. Wheeler, Jr.,* Pres.; William E.W. Frayser, Jr., V.P.; Donald F. Marker, Secy.-Treas.; James B. Boume, Jr., Delmar L. Brown, William E.W. Frayser, Sr., Elizabeth W. Robertson, Percy Wootton.
EIN: 541996321
Codes: FD2

54461
Wise Foundation
P.O. Box 557
Marshall, VA 20116-0557
Contact: Lewis B. Pollard, Pres.

Established in 1999 in VA.
Donor(s): Mary L.F. Wiley.
Financial data (yr. ended 12/31/01): Grants paid, $129,500; assets, $5,062,514 (M); expenditures, $274,007; qualifying distributions, $129,500.
Limitations: Giving limited to VA.
Officers and Directors:* Lewis B. Pollard,* Pres. and Secy.-Treas.; Lewis S. Wiley,* V.P.
EIN: 541942771
Codes: FD2

54462
The Ron and Maryjane Dolan Charitable Trust
11801 Norwood Rd.
Wingina, VA 24599-3047

Established in 1999 in VA.
Donor(s): Ronald V. Dolan, Maryjane Tousignant-Dolan.
Financial data (yr. ended 12/31/00): Grants paid, $128,626; assets, $362,620 (M); expenditures, $132,016; qualifying distributions, $128,479.
Limitations: Applications not accepted. Giving primarily in VA.
Application information: Contributes only to pre-selected organizations.
Trustees: Ronald V. Dolan, Maryjane Tousignant-Dolan.
EIN: 546462216
Codes: FD2

54463
Lacy Foundation
P.O. Box 3084
Martinsville, VA 24115-3084

Established in 1980 in VA.
Financial data (yr. ended 08/31/01): Grants paid, $126,000; assets, $2,224,577 (M); expenditures, $150,717; qualifying distributions, $130,125.
Limitations: Applications not accepted. Giving limited to NC and VA.
Application information: Contributes only to pre-selected organizations.
Officers and Directors:* Frank M. Lacy, Jr.,* Pres.; Margaret A. James,* V.P.; Mary L. Cobbe,* Secy.
EIN: 521205924
Codes: FD2

54464
The William D. Euille Foundation, Inc.
P.O. Box 1911
Alexandria, VA 22313-1911
Application address: 3040 Colvin St., Alexandria, VA 22314, tel.: (703) 751-7970
Contact: William D. Euille, Pres.

Established in 1998 in VA.
Donor(s): William D. Euille.
Financial data (yr. ended 12/31/00): Grants paid, $125,400; assets, $214,061 (M); gifts received, $77,665; expenditures, $130,221; qualifying distributions, $125,184.
Limitations: Giving primarily in Alexandria, VA.
Officers: William D. Euille, Pres.; Charles S. Major III, Secy.; Jamie A. Brusick, Treas.
EIN: 541876127
Codes: FD2

54465
Thomas Jeffress Memorial, Inc.
c/o Bank of America
P.O. Box 26606
Richmond, VA 23261-6606 (804) 788-2058
Application address: P.O. Box 26903, Richmond, VA 23261, tel.: (804) 788-2852
Contact: Thomas C. Gresham, Secy.-Treas.

Established in 1947.
Financial data (yr. ended 12/31/00): Grants paid, $125,000; assets, $1,902,434 (M); expenditures, $148,497; qualifying distributions, $125,215.
Limitations: Giving limited to Richmond, VA.
Officers: J. Stewart Bryan III, Pres.; Henry C. Spalding, Jr., V.P.; Thomas C. Gresham, Secy.-Treas.
EIN: 540742494
Codes: FD2

54466
L. Dudley Walker Foundation
c/o SunTrust Banks, Inc.
P.O. Box 27385, HDQ 5905
Richmond, VA 23261-7385
Application address: c/o SunTrust Banks, Inc., 510 S. Jefferson St., Roanoke, VA 24112-4417, tel.: (540) 982-3002

Established in 1985 in VA.
Donor(s): L. Dudley Walker.
Financial data (yr. ended 03/31/01): Grants paid, $125,000; assets, $1,626,827 (M); expenditures, $134,316; qualifying distributions, $124,103.
Limitations: Giving primarily in VA.
Officer: L. Dudley Walker, Pres.
EIN: 521422410
Codes: FD2

54467
St. Roberto Bellarmin Foundation
258 E. High St.
Charlottesville, VA 22902-5178

Established in 1987.
Donor(s): Niklas Schrenck von Notzing.
Financial data (yr. ended 12/31/01): Grants paid, $124,753; assets, $148,781 (M); gifts received, $23,841; expenditures, $128,324; qualifying distributions, $126,066.
Limitations: Applications not accepted. Giving primarily in the U.S. and Europe.
Application information: Contributes only to pre-selected organizations.
Officer: Niklas Schrenck, Pres.
EIN: 541407053
Codes: FD2

54468
WMCD Charitable Foundation
c/o Craig L. Rascoe
P.O. Box 1320
Richmond, VA 23218-1320

Established in 1994 in VA.
Donor(s): Julious P. Smith, Jr.
Financial data (yr. ended 12/31/01): Grants paid, $123,308; assets, $80,842 (M); gifts received, $154,000; expenditures, $123,508; qualifying distributions, $123,508.
Limitations: Applications not accepted. Giving primarily in Richmond, VA.
Application information: Contributes only to pre-selected organizations.
Officers and Directors:* Calvin Fowler,* Pres.; Julious P. Smith, Jr., V.P.; Craig L. Rascoe,* Secy.-Treas.; Randolph Lickey.
EIN: 541700227
Codes: FD2

54469
Robert H. Smith Family Foundation
2345 Crystal Dr.
Arlington, VA 22202

Established in 1987 in VA.
Donor(s): Robert H. Smith, Clarice R. Smith.
Financial data (yr. ended 11/30/01): Grants paid, $123,225; assets, $16,752 (M); gifts received, $127,060; expenditures, $125,604; qualifying distributions, $124,267.
Limitations: Applications not accepted. Giving primarily in Washington, DC.
Application information: Contributes only to pre-selected organizations.
Officers: Robert H. Smith, Pres. and Treas.; Clarice R. Smith, V.P. and Secy.
Directors: David B. Smith, Michelle Smith, Steven C. Smith.
EIN: 521502273
Codes: FD2

54470
Marc E. Leland Foundation
1001 19th St. N., Ste. 1700
Arlington, VA 22209 (703) 351-9000
Contact: Marc E. Leland, C.E.O.

Established in 1986 in CA.
Donor(s): Marc E. Leland.
Financial data (yr. ended 12/31/01): Grants paid, $122,515; assets, $246,179 (M); gifts received, $23,577; expenditures, $125,182; qualifying distributions, $122,430.
Limitations: Giving primarily in Washington, DC, and Baltimore, MD.
Application information: Application form not required.
Officers and Directors:* Marc E. Leland,* C.E.O.; Olivia Leland,* Secy.; Natasha Leland,* C.F.O.
EIN: 954078342
Codes: FD2

54471
The George & Grace Dragas Foundation
4538 Bonney Rd.
Virginia Beach, VA 23462-3818
(757) 490-0161
Contact: Helen E. Dragas, Dir.

Established in 1990 in VA.
Donor(s): George Dragas, Jr.
Financial data (yr. ended 12/31/01): Grants paid, $122,425; assets, $2,454,551 (M); gifts received, $150,000; expenditures, $139,206; qualifying distributions, $135,574.
Limitations: Applications not accepted. Giving primarily in Norfolk, VA.
Application information: Contributes only to pre-selected organizations.
Directors: Grace V. Dragas, Helen E. Dragas, Mary D. Shearin, Jennifer D. Stedfast, Anita D. Weaver.
EIN: 541569136
Codes: FD2

54472
Bassett Furniture Industries Foundation
P.O. Box 626
Bassett, VA 24055

Established in 1992 in VA.
Donor(s): Bassett Furniture Industries, Inc.

54472—VIRGINIA

Financial data (yr. ended 11/30/01): Grants paid, $121,500; assets, $1,943,252 (M); expenditures, $121,976; qualifying distributions, $121,976.
Limitations: Applications not accepted. Giving primarily in NC and VA.
Application information: Contributes only to pre-selected organizations.
Officers and Directors:* Robert H. Spilman,* Pres.; Jay R. Hervey, Secy.; Grover S. Elliot,* Treas.
EIN: 541652381
Codes: CS, FD2, CD

54473
The Robey W. Estes Family Foundation
c/o Robey W. Estes, Jr.
P.O. Box 25612
Richmond, VA 23260 (804) 353-1900

Established in 1996 in VA.
Donor(s): Robey W. Estes, Sr.
Financial data (yr. ended 12/31/01): Grants paid, $120,505; assets, $1,814,220 (M); gifts received, $150,000; expenditures, $147,308; qualifying distributions, $123,135.
Limitations: Applications not accepted. Giving primarily in Richmond, VA.
Application information: Contributes only to pre-selected organizations.
Officers and Directors:* Robey W. Estes, Sr.,* Pres.; Robey W. Estes, Jr.,* V.P. and Secy.-Treas.; Mary Sue Estes Donahue,* V.P.; Carolyn C. Estes,* V.P.
EIN: 541821053
Codes: FD2

54474
The James and Kerri Scott Foundation
(Formerly The James F. Scott Foundation)
P.O. Box 8048
Charlottesville, VA 22906-8048

Established in 1997 in VA.
Donor(s): James F. Scott.
Financial data (yr. ended 12/31/00): Grants paid, $120,306; assets, $1,924,718 (M); expenditures, $139,070; qualifying distributions, $125,717.
Limitations: Applications not accepted. Giving primarily in Washington, DC, and VA.
Application information: Contributes only to pre-selected organizations.
Officer: James F. Scott, Pres. and Secy.
EIN: 541843312
Codes: FD2

54475
The Elmwood Fund
P.O. Box 85678
Richmond, VA 23285-5678
Contact: E.A. Rennolds, Jr., Pres.

Established in 1970 in VA.
Financial data (yr. ended 12/31/01): Grants paid, $119,000; assets, $2,290,184 (M); expenditures, $142,551; qualifying distributions, $119,000.
Limitations: Giving primarily in NY, TN and Richmond, VA.
Officers: E.A. Rennolds, Jr., Pres.; Mary Z. Rennolds, V.P.
Directors: Walter Dotts, Zayde R. Dotts.
EIN: 237075321
Codes: FD2

54476
Jack Kent Cooke Foundation
44115 Woodridge Pkwy., Ste. 200
Lansdowne, VA 20176
E-mail: jck@jackkentcookefoundation.org; *URL:* http://www.jackkentcookefoundation.org
Contact: Matthew J. Quinn, Exec. Dir.

Established in 1997 in VA. The foundation became active in 2000.
Donor(s): Jack Kent Cooke.
Financial data (yr. ended 05/31/02): Grants paid, $116,976; assets, $210,044,850 (M); gifts received, $124,850,000; expenditures, $2,604,872; qualifying distributions, $2,630,054.
Limitations: Giving on a national basis to applicants for high school and college scholarships; graduate scholarships awarded to students from or attending college in Washington, DC, MD, and VA.
Publications: Application guidelines, informational brochure (including application guidelines).
Application information: Application guidelines available on foundation Web site. Application form required.
Officers and Directors:* Mark Pollak, Pres.; Wanda G. Wiser,* Secy.; Mark Birmingham, Treas. and C.F.O.; Matthew Quinn, Exec. Dir.; John Kent Cooke, Sr., Gregory R. Dillon, Stuart A. Haney, Linda King, Howard B. Soloway.
EIN: 541896244
Codes: FD2

54477
Friedman, Billings & Ramsey Charitable Foundation, Inc.
1001 19th St. N., 18th Fl.
Arlington, VA 22209

Established in 1992 in DE and DC.
Donor(s): Friedman, Billings, Ramsey & Co., Inc., Emanuel Friedman, Kindy French, Eric Billings, Marianne Billings, Eric Generous.
Financial data (yr. ended 09/30/01): Grants paid, $116,880; assets, $5,580 (M); gifts received, $122,750; expenditures, $121,392; qualifying distributions, $116,880.
Limitations: Applications not accepted. Giving primarily in the Washington, DC, area, including MD and VA.
Application information: Contributes only to pre-selected organizations.
Directors: Eric J. Billings, Emanuel Friedman, W. Russell Ramsey.
EIN: 521802675
Codes: CS, FD2, CD

54478
B. Wilson Porterfield Foundation
30 W. Franklin Rd., Ste. 504
Roanoke, VA 24011
Contact: Bittle W. Porterfield III, Pres.

Established in 1990 in VA.
Financial data (yr. ended 12/31/01): Grants paid, $114,817; assets, $701,698 (M); expenditures, $118,921; qualifying distributions, $114,667.
Limitations: Giving primarily in Roanoke, VA.
Officers: Bittle W. Porterfield III, Pres. and Treas.; Charlotte K. Porterfield, V.P. and Secy.
EIN: 541549784
Codes: FD2

54479
NTELOS Foundation
(Formerly CFW Communications Foundation)
P.O. Box 1990
Waynesboro, VA 22980 (540) 946-3511
Contact: Carl A. Rosberg, Pres.

Established in 1990 in VA.
Donor(s): CFW Communications Co., Clifton Forge-Waynesboro Telephone Co., NTELOS Inc.
Financial data (yr. ended 12/31/01): Grants paid, $114,114; assets, $2,924,466 (M); expenditures, $135,248; qualifying distributions, $114,969.
Limitations: Giving primarily in VA.
Officers and Directors:* J.S. Quarforth,* Chair. and C.E.O.; Carl A. Rosberg,* Pres.; M.B. Moneymaker, V.P. and Secy.-Treas.; D.R. Maccarelli, V.P.; P.H. Arnold, W. Wayt Gibbs V, John B. Mitchell, J.N. Neff.
EIN: 541552737
Codes: CS, FD2, CD

54480
Duncan McRae Cocke Charitable Trust
P.O. Box 379
Williamsburg, VA 23187
Contact: Vernon M. Geddy, III, Tr.

Established in 1995 in VA.
Donor(s): Duncan McCrae Cocke.‡
Financial data (yr. ended 12/31/00): Grants paid, $112,100; assets, $59,826 (M); expenditures, $115,376; qualifying distributions, $112,005.
Limitations: Giving limited to VA.
Application information: Application form required.
Trustee: Vernon M. Geddy III.
EIN: 546374600
Codes: FD2

54481
The BRI Foundation, Inc.
c/o MJW
6402 Arlington Blvd., Ste. 1130
Falls Church, VA 22042-2300

Established in 1997 in VA.
Donor(s): Catherine C. Dorrier, Frank L. Hurley.
Financial data (yr. ended 04/30/01): Grants paid, $112,000; assets, $1,716,773 (M); expenditures, $129,185; qualifying distributions, $109,212.
Limitations: Applications not accepted. Giving primarily in Washington, DC, Boston, MA, and Baltimore, MD.
Application information: Contributes only to pre-selected organizations.
Officers: Frank L. Hurley, Chair.; Catharine C. Dorrier, Pres.; John Hurley, Secy.-Treas.
Director: Clara Hurley.
EIN: 541848984
Codes: FD2

54482
Retail Merchants Foundation
2412 Langhorne Rd.
Lynchburg, VA 24501

Established in 1997 in VA.
Financial data (yr. ended 12/31/01): Grants paid, $111,634; assets, $1,205,329 (M); gifts received, $274,206; expenditures, $138,598; qualifying distributions, $132,253.
Limitations: Giving primarily in VA.
Officers: David M. Somers, Chair; Jerry W. Morcom, Vice-Chair.; Roland K. Peters, Secy.-Treas.
Directors: Gene D. Gallagher, Charles Hammer.
EIN: 541824054
Codes: FD2

54483
The Robert B. Livy Charitable Trust
c/o Bank of America
P.O. Box 26606
Richmond, VA 23261-6606 (804) 788-3023
Contact: Chris Thomas, Trust Off., Bank of America

Established in 1991 in VA.
Financial data (yr. ended 07/31/01): Grants paid, $110,500; assets, $236,667 (M); gifts received, $90,000; expenditures, $118,936; qualifying distributions, $111,200.
Limitations: Applications not accepted. Giving primarily in VA.
Application information: Unsolicited requests for funds are not accepted.
Trustee: Bank of America.
EIN: 546319223
Codes: FD2

54484
The AWA Family Foundation
c/o Arthur Arundel
13873 Park Center Rd., Ste. 301
Herndon, VA 20171

Established in 1991 in VA.
Donor(s): Arthur W. Arundel.
Financial data (yr. ended 06/30/01): Grants paid, $110,360; assets, $1,399,281 (M); expenditures, $142,453; qualifying distributions, $120,233.
Limitations: Applications not accepted. Giving primarily in VA.
Application information: Contributes only to pre-selected organizations.
Officers: Arthur W. Arundel, Pres.; Leigh Schilling, Secy.
EIN: 541607743
Codes: FD2

54485
J. V. Schiro-Zavela Foundation
1223 Earnestine St.
McLean, VA 22101

Established in 1993 in MD.
Donor(s): Schiro Fund, Inc.
Financial data (yr. ended 12/31/01): Grants paid, $109,300; assets, $2,354,462 (M); expenditures, $116,248; qualifying distributions, $108,911.
Application information: Application form not required.
Trustees: Jean L. Schiro-Zavela, Vance S. Zavela.
EIN: 521802117
Codes: FD2

54486
Julian G. Lange Family Foundation II
P.O. Box 5
White Stone, VA 22578
Application address: 856 Barcarmil Way, Naples, FL 34110
Contact: Julie L. Peyton, Tr.

Established in 1999.
Financial data (yr. ended 06/30/01): Grants paid, $108,200; assets, $1,907,390 (M); expenditures, $131,763; qualifying distributions, $128,929.
Limitations: Giving primarily in the southwest OH area, with emphasis on Dayton and Oxford.
Trustee: Julie L. Peyton.
EIN: 311663389
Codes: FD2

54487
Alan & Esther Fleder Foundation
500 E. Main St., Ste. 1424
Norfolk, VA 23510 (757) 623-1062
Contact: Alan Fleder, Pres.

Established in 1977 in VA.
Donor(s): Alan Fleder, Esther Fleder.
Financial data (yr. ended 09/30/01): Grants paid, $105,800; assets, $2,300,655 (M); gifts received, $100,000; expenditures, $108,849; qualifying distributions, $104,554.
Limitations: Giving primarily in Norfolk, VA.
Application information: Application form not required.
Officers and Directors:* Alan Fleder,* Pres.; Marie Gordon, Secy.; Lawrence Fleder,* Treas.
EIN: 510217379
Codes: FD2

54488
The Herget Family Charitable Foundation
6216 Berkeley Rd.
Alexandria, VA 22307

Established in 1999 in VA.
Donor(s): R. Philip Herget III.
Financial data (yr. ended 12/31/01): Grants paid, $104,917; assets, $1,629,477 (M); expenditures, $117,242; qualifying distributions, $104,376.
Limitations: Applications not accepted. Giving primarily in Alexandria, VA.
Application information: Contributes only to pre-selected organizations.
Officers and Directors:* Anne S. Herget,* Pres.; R. Philip Herget III,* Secy.
EIN: 541968720
Codes: FD2

54489
Petersburg Methodist Home for Girls
P.O. Box 1688
Petersburg, VA 23805-0688
Contact: Barbara Moore, Secy.-Treas.

Established in 1976 in VA.
Financial data (yr. ended 12/31/01): Grants paid, $104,400; assets, $3,687,053 (M); expenditures, $145,849; qualifying distributions, $144,104.
Limitations: Giving limited to residents of Southside, VA.
Application information: Application form required.
Officers: Howard D. Brown, Pres.; Barbara W. Moore, Secy.-Treas.
Directors: Henry Brigstock, Frances Phillips, David H. Reames, Jr., Mark H. Stevens, Emily Walker, Erick F. Yarchin, Jr.
EIN: 540542500
Codes: FD2, GTI

54490
Sunningdale Charitable Trust
c/o Roland H. Parker
5 Rock Pointe Ln., Ste. 150
Warrenton, VA 20186

Financial data (yr. ended 12/31/00): Grants paid, $104,250; assets, $150,635 (M); gifts received, $119,921; expenditures, $104,964; qualifying distributions, $104,250.
Limitations: Applications not accepted. Giving primarily in FL.
Application information: Contributes only to pre-selected organizations.
Trustee: Roland H. Parker.
EIN: 521219238
Codes: FD2

54491
Beckett Charitable Foundation
437 N. Lee St.
Alexandria, VA 22313 (703) 836-7400
Contact: Randolph H. Watts, Tr.

Established in 1982 in VA.
Financial data (yr. ended 12/31/01): Grants paid, $104,000; assets, $1,922,907 (M); expenditures, $152,534; qualifying distributions, $103,276.
Limitations: Giving primarily in VA.
Trustee: Randolph H. Watts.
EIN: 541188521
Codes: FD2

54492
The Burford Leimenstoll Foundation, Inc.
2956 Hathaway Rd., Apt. 712
Richmond, VA 23225-1734

Established in 1991 in VA.
Donor(s): Betty Sams Christian.
Financial data (yr. ended 12/31/01): Grants paid, $103,920; assets, $1,406,607 (M); gifts received, $12,855; expenditures, $116,775; qualifying distributions, $103,920.
Limitations: Applications not accepted. Giving on a national basis.
Application information: Contributes only to pre-selected organizations.
Officers and Director:* Betty Sams Christian,* Pres.; Ben R. Lacy IV, Secy.
EIN: 541608741

54493
Emma May Ridgeway Charitable Trust
c/o Farmers & Merchants Trust Co.
P.O. Box 2800
Winchester, VA 22604

Established in 1983 in VA.
Financial data (yr. ended 07/31/01): Grants paid, $102,609; assets, $1,652,897 (M); expenditures, $119,528; qualifying distributions, $104,722.
Limitations: Giving primarily in the Winchester, VA, area.
Application information: Application form not required.
Trustee: Farmers & Merchants Trust Co.
EIN: 546202908
Codes: FD2

54494
The Jane and Robert Salzer Foundation
1349 MacBeth St.
McLean, VA 22102-2768
Contact: Thomas B. Salzer, Treas.

Established in 1987 in VA.
Donor(s): Lawrence Greenwald.‡
Financial data (yr. ended 12/31/01): Grants paid, $102,435; assets, $1,296,779 (M); expenditures, $108,295; qualifying distributions, $102,435.
Limitations: Giving on a national basis.
Officers: Jane Salzer, Pres.; Thomas Salzer, Treas.
EIN: 236856148
Codes: FD2

54495
Gordon R. Larson Foundation
c/o G. Larson & Old Dominion Trust Co.
100 E. Main St., Ste. 200
Norfolk, VA 23510

Established in 1998 in VA.
Donor(s): Gordon R. Larson, Old Dominion Trust Co.
Financial data (yr. ended 12/31/01): Grants paid, $101,585; assets, $1,717,766 (M); expenditures, $125,534; qualifying distributions, $100,919.

54495—VIRGINIA

Limitations: Applications not accepted. Giving primarily in VA.
Application information: Contributes only to pre-selected organizations.
Trustees: Gordon R. Larson, Old Dominion Trust Co.
EIN: 541895344
Codes: FD2

54496
Martha & William Adams Scholarship Trust
c/o SunTrust Banks, Inc., Tax Svcs. HDQ 5905
P.O. Box 27385
Richmond, VA 23261-7385
Additional address: 10 S. Jefferson St., Ste. 1400, Roanoke, VA 24038-4125
Contact: Talfourd H. Kemper, Tr.

Incorporated in 1985 in VA.
Donor(s): William B. Adams.‡
Financial data (yr. ended 11/30/01): Grants paid, $100,000; assets, $1,963,698 (M); expenditures, $117,425; qualifying distributions, $107,098.
Limitations: Giving primarily in VA.
Trustees: Talfourd H. Kemper, SunTrust Banks, Inc.
EIN: 521329899
Codes: FD2

54497
Best Products Foundation
c/o McGuire, Woods, Battle & Boothe, LLP
P.O. Box 397
Richmond, VA 23218

Established in 1967 in VA.
Donor(s): Best Products Co., Inc.
Financial data (yr. ended 01/31/02): Grants paid, $100,000; assets, $88,940 (M); expenditures, $106,416; qualifying distributions, $100,000.
Limitations: Applications not accepted. Giving primarily in areas of company operations.
Application information: Contributes only to pre-selected organizations. New proposals are not currently accepted.
Officers and Directors:* Frances A. Lewis,* Pres.; Robert L. Burrus, Jr.,* Secy.-Treas.; W. Edward Clingman, Jr.
EIN: 237139981
Codes: CS, CD

54498
Joshua P. and Elizabeth D. Darden Foundation
1420 NationsBank Ctr.
1 Commercial Pl.
Norfolk, VA 23510
Contact: Holley Darden, Secy.

Established in 1993 in VA.
Donor(s): Joshua P. Darden.
Financial data (yr. ended 12/31/01): Grants paid, $100,000; assets, $1,612,181 (M); expenditures, $121,620; qualifying distributions, $100,000.
Limitations: Giving primarily in Southampton Roads, VA.
Publications: Application guidelines.
Application information: Application form required.
Officers and Directors:* Joshua P. Darden,* Pres.; Holley Darden,* Secy.; Audrey Darden, Elizabeth D. Darden.
EIN: 541661365
Codes: FD2

54499
Ingersoll Family Foundation
713 Potomac Knolls Dr.
McLean, VA 22102

Established in 2000 in VA.
Financial data (yr. ended 06/30/02): Grants paid, $100,000; assets, $50,131 (M); gifts received, $150,000; expenditures, $100,350; qualifying distributions, $100,000.
Limitations: Applications not accepted.
Application information: Contributes only to pre-selected organizations.
Trustee: William Boley Ingersoll.
EIN: 541994813

54500
Lucille and Bruce Lambert Charitable Foundation, Inc.
c/o J. T. Butler
2100 Powhatan St.
Falls Church, VA 22043-1940

Established in 1999.
Financial data (yr. ended 12/31/00): Grants paid, $100,000; assets, $6,293,204 (M); gifts received, $505,738; expenditures, $268,905; qualifying distributions, $100,000.
Limitations: Applications not accepted. Giving on a national basis, with some emphasis on VA.
Application information: Contributes only to pre-selected organizations.
Officers and Directors:* J.T. Butler,* Pres.; George P. Levendis,* Secy.; Jay C. Brockman, Cyndi Butler, Harold M. Lambert.
EIN: 541898273
Codes: FD2

54501
Virginia Beach Rescue Squad Foundation, Inc.
P.O. Box 1234
Virginia Beach, VA 23451-0234

Financial data (yr. ended 12/31/00): Grants paid, $100,000; assets, $1,688,842 (M); gifts received, $48,420; expenditures, $141,873; qualifying distributions, $100,000.
Limitations: Applications not accepted. Giving limited to Virginia Beach, VA.
Application information: Contributes only to a pre-selected organization.
Officers: Littleton C. Hudgins, Chair.; Peter A. Agelasto III, Pres.; W. Shepherd Drewry, V.P.; Diane Stanton Monroe, Secy.; F.W. Twyman III, Treas.
EIN: 510242962
Codes: TN

54502
Ralph Stowers Scholarship
c/o Bank of Tazewell County Trust
P.O. Box 687
Tazewell, VA 24651-0687

Established in 1997.
Financial data (yr. ended 12/31/01): Grants paid, $99,778; assets, $2,036,920 (M); expenditures, $113,652; qualifying distributions, $98,747.
Limitations: Applications not accepted. Giving primarily in Tazewell County, VA.
Application information: Unsolicited requests for funds not accepted.
Trustee: Bank of Tazewell County Trust.
EIN: 546309437
Codes: FD2

54503
Scripture Truth Foundation
P.O. Box 339
Fincastle, VA 24090-0339

Established in 1980 in VA.
Donor(s): Morris V. Brodsky, Dorothy Brodsky, Scripture Truth Book Co.
Financial data (yr. ended 12/31/01): Grants paid, $99,750; assets, $68,611 (M); gifts received, $150,400; expenditures, $100,446; qualifying distributions, $99,750.
Limitations: Applications not accepted. Giving on a national basis.
Officers and Directors:* Philip G. Brodsky,* Pres.; Judith O. Brodsky,* Secy.-Treas.; and 8 additional directors.
EIN: 541117672
Codes: FD2

54504
Arenstein Foundation
c/o Keiter, Stehens
P.O. Box 32066
Richmond, VA 23294-2066

Established in 1979 in VA.
Donor(s): David Arenstein.
Financial data (yr. ended 01/31/02): Grants paid, $99,315; assets, $1,471,306 (M); expenditures, $137,984; qualifying distributions, $99,315.
Limitations: Applications not accepted. Giving primarily in Richmond, VA.
Application information: Contributes only to pre-selected organizations.
Officers and Directors:* Marjorie W. Arenstein,* Chair.; Richard Arenstein,* Pres.; Joan Arenstein,* V.P.; Judith Arenstein,* Secy.-Treas.
EIN: 541128232
Codes: FD2

54505
Fun Foundation
263 McLaws Cir., Ste. 104
Williamsburg, VA 23188

Established in 1978.
Donor(s): John C. Jamison.
Financial data (yr. ended 02/28/01): Grants paid, $98,200; assets, $649,548 (M); gifts received, $68,587; expenditures, $99,720; qualifying distributions, $97,632.
Limitations: Applications not accepted. Giving primarily in VA.
Application information: Contributes only to pre-selected organizations.
Trustees: Carol S. Jamison, John C. Jamison, Kelly Jamison Supplee.
EIN: 132961419
Codes: FD2

54506
TTL Foundation
1167 Presidential Cir.
Forest, VA 24551
Contact: Glen N. Thomas, Pres.

Established in 2000 in VA.
Donor(s): Glen N. Thomas, Teresa H. Thomas.
Financial data (yr. ended 12/31/01): Grants paid, $97,800; assets, $361,539 (M); expenditures, $101,574; qualifying distributions, $98,896.
Limitations: Giving primarily in VA.
Officer: Glen N. Thomas, Pres.
Directors: Jimmy N. Thomas, Teresa H. Thomas.
EIN: 542008793
Codes: FD2

54507
Koenig Private Foundation, Inc.
c/o Reed, Smith, et al.
3110 Fairview Park Dr., Ste. 1400
Falls Church, VA 22042

Established in 2000 in VA.
Donor(s): Ann M. Koenig Charitable Trust.
Financial data (yr. ended 12/31/01): Grants paid, $97,191; assets, $2,994,900 (M); gifts received, $55,843; expenditures, $206,658; qualifying distributions, $97,191.
Limitations: Applications not accepted.
Application information: Contributes only to pre-selected organizations.

Officers and Directors:* Duane W. Beckhorn,* Pres.; Patrick M. Buehler,* V.P., C.O.O., and Secy.; Kenneth H. Reese,* Treas.
EIN: 542010650

54508
John Stewart Bryan Memorial Foundation
1802 Bayberry Ct., Ste. 301
Richmond, VA 23226 (804) 285-7700
Contact: J. Stewart Bryan III, Pres.

Established in 1946 in VA.
Financial data (yr. ended 12/31/01): Grants paid, $97,000; assets, $718,892 (M); expenditures, $106,139; qualifying distributions, $96,972.
Limitations: Giving primarily in VA.
Application information: Application form not required.
Officers and Directors:* J. Stewart Bryan III,* Pres.; Florence Bryan Fowlkes,* Secy.; Mary T.B. Perkins,* Treas.
EIN: 237425357
Codes: FD2

54509
The Levmar Foundation, Inc.
P.O. Box 938
Herndon, VA 20172
Contact: Margarita Volftsun, Pres.

Established in 1998 in VA.
Donor(s): Lev Volftsun, Margarita Volftsun.
Financial data (yr. ended 12/31/01): Grants paid, $96,200; assets, $3,137,232 (M); expenditures, $136,212; qualifying distributions, $92,932.
Limitations: Applications not accepted. Giving primarily in NY and VA.
Application information: Contributes only to pre-selected organizations.
Officer: Margarita Volftsun, Pres.
Directors: Amy Rosenblatt Lui, Lev Volftsun.
EIN: 510387146
Codes: FD2

54510
Tuberculosis Foundation of Virginia, Inc.
3803 Sunbreeze Cir., Ste. 202
Roanoke, VA 24018 (540) 985-8108
Application address: P.O. Box 13727, Roanoke, VA 24036, tel.: (540) 224-5065
Contact: Robert Manetta, Secy.

Established in 1920 in VA.
Financial data (yr. ended 03/31/02): Grants paid, $96,000; assets, $2,013,884 (M); expenditures, $117,759; qualifying distributions, $97,478.
Limitations: Giving limited to VA.
Application information: Application form not required.
Officers: Robert L.A. Keeley, M.D., Pres.; Robert B. Manetta, Secy.
Trustees: Scott Arnold, M.D., Graham H. Bourhill, M.D., James A. Ford, Robert C. Keeley, M.D.
EIN: 540799918
Codes: FD2

54511
The Nettie L. Wiley and Charles L. Wiley Foundation
P.O. Box 126
Irvington, VA 22480-0126
Application address: P.O. Box 320, Irvington, VA 22480-0420
Contact: Thomas A. Gosse, Treas.

Established in 1981 in VA.
Donor(s): Nettie L. Lokey Wiley.
Financial data (yr. ended 12/31/01): Grants paid, $96,000; assets, $1,863,450 (M); gifts received, $100,000; expenditures, $102,603; qualifying distributions, $97,923.

Limitations: Giving primarily in VA.
Application information: Application form not required.
Officers: Nettie L. Wiley, Pres.; Gloria C. Conley, V.P.; B.H.B. Hubbard III, Secy.; Thomas A. Gosse, Treas.
EIN: 521231771
Codes: FD2

54512
T. David Fitz-Gibbon Charitable Trust
P.O. Box 85678
Richmond, VA 23285
Contact: Thomas N.P. Johnson III, Pres.

Established in 1983 in VA.
Donor(s): T. David Fitz-Gibbon.‡
Financial data (yr. ended 06/30/01): Grants paid, $94,431; assets, $1,676,262 (M); expenditures, $132,348; qualifying distributions, $94,219.
Limitations: Giving primarily in VA.
Application information: Limited amount of funds available due to long-term commitments. Application form not required.
Officers and Trustees:* Thomas Nelson Page Johnson, Jr.,* Chair.; Thomas Nelson Page Johnson III,* Pres.; William M. Walsh, Jr.
EIN: 521272224
Codes: FD2

54513
Fund for Innovation and Public Service
c/o William Drayton
1200 N. Nash St.
Arlington, VA 22209-3616

Financial data (yr. ended 12/31/01): Grants paid, $94,345; assets, $1,755,333 (M); gifts received, $5,933; expenditures, $101,069; qualifying distributions, $94,345.
Limitations: Applications not accepted.
Publications: Occasional report.
Application information: Contributes only to pre-selected organizations.
Officer: William Drayton, Pres. and Treas.
Directors: Ann Simon Hadley, Steven Hadley, David C. Oxman.
EIN: 133384072
Codes: FD2

54514
The Horton Foundation
P.O. Box 587
Charlottesville, VA 22902

Established in 1999 in VA.
Financial data (yr. ended 12/31/00): Grants paid, $94,000; assets, $104,999 (M); gifts received, $17,487; expenditures, $95,537; qualifying distributions, $95,481.
Limitations: Applications not accepted. Giving on a national basis, with emphasis on VA.
Application information: Contributes only to pre-selected organizations.
Officers and Directors:* David J. Matthews,* Pres.; Francis Jane Matthews,* Treas.; April R. Fletcher, Mgr.; R. Coran Capshaw, Beth Neville Evans, Pamela S. Horowitz.
EIN: 541890166
Codes: FD2

54515
The Gradison Foundation
1031 Savile Ln.
McLean, VA 22101
Contact: Willis D. Gradison, Jr., Pres.

Established in 1959.
Donor(s): Willis D. Gradison, Jr.

Financial data (yr. ended 12/31/01): Grants paid, $93,695; assets, $1,879,515 (M); expenditures, $112,556; qualifying distributions, $93,975.
Limitations: Giving primarily in Washington, DC, Cincinnati, OH, and VA.
Application information: Application form not required.
Officers and Trustees:* Willis D. Gradison, Jr.,* Pres. and Treas.; Margaret Gradison,* V.P. and Secy.; Joan Coe,* V.P.; Robin Gradison,* V.P.; Wendy Gradison,* V.P.; Beth Lyon,* V.P.
EIN: 316032172
Codes: FD2

54516
Betty J. Burrows and David H. Burrows Charitable Trust
P.O. Box 18124
Roanoke, VA 24014
Application address: 2307 Stanley Ave., Roanoke, VA 24014, tel.: (540) 345-9346
Contact: W.J. Burrows, Tr.

Established in 1987 in VA.
Donor(s): Betty J. Burrows, David H. Burrows.
Financial data (yr. ended 12/31/01): Grants paid, $93,500; assets, $821,628 (M); expenditures, $97,423; qualifying distributions, $95,255.
Limitations: Giving primarily in Roanoke, VA.
Trustees: Beverly B. Burleson, Wiley Jackson Burrows.
EIN: 546242930
Codes: FD2

54517
The W. M. Jordan Company Charitable Foundation
11010 Jefferson Ave.
Newport News, VA 23601-0337
(757) 596-6341

Established in 1996 in VI.
Donor(s): W.M. Jordan Company, Inc.
Financial data (yr. ended 12/31/01): Grants paid, $93,050; assets, $131,044 (M); gifts received, $120,000; expenditures, $93,076; qualifying distributions, $93,042.
Limitations: Giving primarily in VA.
Trustees: John R. Lawson, Thomas M. Shelton.
EIN: 546407107
Codes: CS, FD2

54518
The Richfood Foundation
8258 Richfood Rd.
Mechanicsville, VA 23116 (804) 746-6000
Contact: Fdn. Mgr.

Established in 1995 in VA.
Financial data (yr. ended 04/30/01): Grants paid, $92,334; assets, $149,444 (M); gifts received, $143,815; expenditures, $122,293; qualifying distributions, $120,750.
Limitations: Giving primarily in Richmond, VA.
Application information: Application form not required.
Officers: Gary Zimmerman, Pres.; Sharon Hooper, Secy.
EIN: 541813921
Codes: FD2

54519
John G. & Jean R. Gosnell Foundation, Inc.
(Formerly John G Gosnell Foundation, Inc.)
8130 Boone Blvd.
Vienna, VA 22182-2640

Established in 1996.
Donor(s): John G. Gosnell.
Financial data (yr. ended 10/31/01): Grants paid, $92,000; assets, $1,227,534 (M); gifts received,

54519—VIRGINIA

$400,663; expenditures, $107,431; qualifying distributions, $91,140.
Limitations: Applications not accepted. Giving primarily in Bethesda, MD.
Application information: Contributes only to pre-selected organizations.
Officers: John G. Gosnell, Pres. and Treas.; Susan G. Brown, V.P. and Secy.; Teresa G. Doggett, V.P.
EIN: 541829618
Codes: FD2

54520
Haymarket Lodge Charitable Foundation, Inc.
P.O. Box 313
Haymarket, VA 20168-0313

Established in 1993 in VA.
Financial data (yr. ended 12/31/00): Grants paid, $91,876; assets, $274,283 (M); expenditures, $163,939; qualifying distributions, $91,876.
Limitations: Applications not accepted. Giving primarily in VA.
Application information: Contributes only to pre-selected organizations.
Officers: Charles B. Darley, Pres.; Edward E. Groff, Secy.; Wayne W. Grindle, Treas.
Directors: Michael D. Kerns, Donald J. Kerr.
EIN: 541679008
Codes: FD2

54521
Windhorse Foundation
(Formerly The Salem Family Foundation)
590 Peter Jefferson Pkwy., Ste. 250
Charlottesville, VA 22911-4628
(804) 817-8204
Contact: David A. Salem, Tr.

Established in 1992 in MA.
Donor(s): David A. Salem, Richard M. Salem.
Financial data (yr. ended 12/31/01): Grants paid, $91,870; assets, $4,879,311 (M); gifts received, $1,000; expenditures, $208,885; qualifying distributions, $99,044.
Limitations: Applications not accepted. Giving primarily in CO.
Application information: Contributes only to pre-selected organizations.
Trustees: David A. Salem, Richard M. Salem.
EIN: 046707664
Codes: FD2

54522
The Better Living Foundation
P.O. Box 7627
Charlottesville, VA 22906-7627
(804) 973-4333
Contact: Richard L. Nunley, Pres.

Established in 1985 in VA.
Donor(s): Richard L. Nunley, Julia G. Nunley.
Financial data (yr. ended 12/31/00): Grants paid, $91,850; assets, $1,295,580 (M); gifts received, $130,025; expenditures, $105,923; qualifying distributions, $92,781.
Limitations: Giving primarily in Charlottesville, VA.
Officers and Directors:* Richard L. Nunley,* Pres.; Julia G. Nunley,* Secy.-Treas.; Caroline B. Nunley, John Nunley.
EIN: 541324304
Codes: FD2

54523
The Rau Foundation, Inc.
1250 Washington St., Ste. 817
Alexandria, VA 22314 (703) 838-2848
Contact: J. Alton Boyer, Secy.

Established in 1960 in DC.

Financial data (yr. ended 12/31/01): Grants paid, $91,025; assets, $1,835,922 (M); expenditures, $94,799; qualifying distributions, $181,224.
Limitations: Giving primarily in Washington, DC, and NY.
Application information: Application form not required.
Officers and Trustees:* Cynthia R. Boyer, Chair. and Treas.; Robin R. Henry,* Pres.; J. Alton Boyer,* Secy.
EIN: 546037137
Codes: FD2

54524
Hebrew Fund for the Aged of Richmond, Virginia
1111 E. Main St.
Richmond, VA 23219
Contact: David E. Constine, III, Pres.

Financial data (yr. ended 12/31/00): Grants paid, $90,567; assets, $1,399,236 (M); gifts received, $9,567; expenditures, $100,368; qualifying distributions, $99,121.
Limitations: Giving limited to Richmond, VA.
Application information: Application form not required.
Officers: David E. Constine III, Pres.; Harold P. Straus, V.P.; James Yoffy, Secy.; Neil Kessler, Treas.
Board Members: Louis O. Bowman, Jr., Mark Eisenmann, Jr., Steven Markel, Howard F. Marks, Sydney Meyers, Gilbert Rosenthal, William H. Schwarzschild III, Marshall Wishnack.
EIN: 510237242
Codes: FD2

54525
The Watkins Family Charitable Foundation
9211 Forest Hill Ave., Ste. 105
Richmond, VA 23235-6874 (804) 272-2202

Established in 1997 in VA.
Donor(s): Hays T. Watkins, H. Thomas Watkins III.
Financial data (yr. ended 12/31/00): Grants paid, $90,450; assets, $1,207,481 (M); gifts received, $196,124; expenditures, $95,127; qualifying distributions, $90,450.
Limitations: Applications not accepted. Giving primarily in VA.
Application information: Contributes only to pre-selected organizations.
Trustees: Philip A. Huss, Betty J. Watkins, H. Thomas Watkins III, Hays T. Watkins.
EIN: 541873256
Codes: FD2

54526
Carrie S. Camp Foundation, Inc.
P.O. Box 557
Franklin, VA 23851-0057
Contact: L. Clay Camp, Jr., Secy.

Incorporated about 1949 in VA.
Donor(s): Edith Clay Camp.
Financial data (yr. ended 12/31/00): Grants paid, $90,000; assets, $1,349,937 (M); expenditures, $95,671; qualifying distributions, $88,134.
Limitations: Giving primarily in VA.
Application information: Application form not required.
Officers: L. Clay Camp, Sr., Pres.; Barbara P. Camp, V.P.; L. Clay Camp, Jr., Secy.; Mildred M. Branche, Treas.
Director: Carrie Camp Gibbons.
EIN: 546052446
Codes: FD2

54527
The Edward H. & Virginia K. Gunst Foundation
P.O. Box 26606
Richmond, VA 23261-6606
Application address: c/o Bank of America, N.A., P.O. Box 26688, Richmond, VA 23261-6688, tel.: (804) 788-2674

Established in 2000 in VA.
Donor(s): Edward H. Gunst, Virginia K. Gunst, Edward Ross Moyer, Catherine M. Williams.
Financial data (yr. ended 12/31/01): Grants paid, $90,000; assets, $1,784,726 (M); expenditures, $154,397; qualifying distributions, $90,000.
Limitations: Giving primarily in Richmond, VA.
Trustees: Edward Ross Moyer, Catherine M. Williams.
EIN: 546476990

54528
The Edward H. Lane Foundation
c/o SunTrust Banks, Inc., Tax Svcs.
P.O. Box 27385
Richmond, VA 23261-7385
Application address: P.O. Box 209, Altavista, VA 24517, tel.: (804) 369-5641
Contact: John Edward Lane III, Tr.

Established in 1956 in VA.
Donor(s): Lane Co.
Financial data (yr. ended 11/30/01): Grants paid, $90,000; assets, $1,475,535 (M); expenditures, $100,042; qualifying distributions, $89,899.
Limitations: Giving primarily in VA.
Officer: David Jones, V.P. and Mgr.
Trustees: B.B. Lane, E.H. Lane, John Edward Lane III.
EIN: 546040095
Codes: FD2

54529
C. Kenneth Wright Foundation
(Formerly Wright Foundation)
P.O. Box 4433
Glen Allen, VA 23058-4433
Application address: P.O. Box 604, Richmond, VA 23218
Contact: C.K. Wright, Pres.

Donor(s): C.K. Wright, Basic Rent A Car Co.
Financial data (yr. ended 02/28/01): Grants paid, $89,900; assets, $1,500,818 (M); gifts received, $158,341; expenditures, $213,013; qualifying distributions, $89,855.
Limitations: Giving primarily in Richmond, VA.
Officers: C.K. Wright, Pres.; Richard L. Grier, Secy.; F. Elmore Butler, Treas.
EIN: 541064037
Codes: FD2

54530
Margaret Walker Purinton Foundation
c/o Gary L. Vickers
P.O. Box 1408
Charlottesville, VA 22902-1408

Established in 1997 in VA.
Donor(s): Margaret Purinton.
Financial data (yr. ended 12/31/00): Grants paid, $89,000; assets, $1,783,639 (M); gifts received, $468,896; expenditures, $93,010; qualifying distributions, $89,000.
Limitations: Applications not accepted. Giving primarily in MA and VA.
Application information: Contributes only to pre-selected organizations.
Officers: Margaret Walker Purinton, Pres.; Anne Davis Purinton, V.P.; Betsey Alden Purinton, V.P.
EIN: 541841603
Codes: FD2

54531
The Bondi Foundation
c/o Rich Walsh
1660 International Dr., Ste. 2133
McLean, VA 22102

Established in 1998 in DE.
Donor(s): Geoffrey C. Bible.
Financial data (yr. ended 12/31/00): Grants paid, $88,500; assets, $5,178,136 (M); gifts received, $1,114,075; expenditures, $100,513; qualifying distributions, $86,757.
Limitations: Giving primarily in NY.
Officers: Kim Margaret Bible, Pres.; Sara Curtis McDonald Bible, V.P.; Geoffrey Cyril Maitland Bible, Secy.; Thomas William Bible, Treas.
EIN: 134015931

54532
Kathryn & W. Harry Schwarzschild Fund
P.O. Box 27602
Richmond, VA 23261 (804) 697-6905
Application address: P.O. Box 1320, Richmond, VA 23210, tel.: (804) 783-6489
Contact: W. Harry Schwarzschild III, Pres.

Established in 1957.
Donor(s): W. Harry Schwarzschild, Jr.
Financial data (yr. ended 12/31/01): Grants paid, $88,300; assets, $1,801,557 (M); expenditures, $125,227; qualifying distributions, $88,300.
Limitations: Giving primarily in Richmond, VA.
Application information: Application form not required.
Officers: W. Harry Schwarzschild III, Pres. and Treas.; Kathryn E. Schwarzschild, V.P. and Secy.; Kathryn S. Brown, V.P.
EIN: 546035733
Codes: FD2

54533
H. C. Hofheimer II Family Foundation
828 Gravdon Ave.
Norfolk, VA 23507-1502
Contact: Henry Clay Hofheimer II, Pres.

Established in 1958.
Donor(s): H.C. Hofheimer II, Wesley Wright, Jr.
Financial data (yr. ended 03/31/02): Grants paid, $88,250; assets, $1,568,324 (M); expenditures, $89,810; qualifying distributions, $88,157.
Limitations: Applications not accepted. Giving primarily in VA.
Application information: Contributes only to pre-selected organizations.
Officers and Directors:* H. Clay Hofheimer II,* Pres.; Linda H. Kaufman,* V.P.; Wesley Wright, Jr.,* Secy.-Treas.; Clay H. Barr, Elise H. Wright.
EIN: 546036164
Codes: FD2

54534
The Clovelly Foundation
337 Clovelly Rd.
Richmond, VA 23221

Established in 1998 in VA.
Donor(s): Thomas N. Allen, Rebecca L. Allen.
Financial data (yr. ended 12/31/01): Grants paid, $88,000; assets, $1,591,963 (M); expenditures, $106,104; qualifying distributions, $89,198.
Limitations: Applications not accepted. Giving primarily in VA.
Application information: Contributes only to pre-selected organizations.
Officers and Directors:* Thomas N. Allen,* Pres.; Rebecca L. Allen,* Secy.-Treas.
EIN: 541900970
Codes: FD2

54535
The Stephen G. and Thelma S. Yeonas Foundation
6867 Elm St., Ste. 210
McLean, VA 22101-3623
Application address: 7450 Old Maple Sq., McLean, VA 22102, tel.: (703) 883-0202
Contact: Stephen G. Yeonas, Pres.

Donor(s): Stephen G. Yeonas, Thelma S. Yeonas.
Financial data (yr. ended 03/31/02): Grants paid, $87,709; assets, $494,921 (M); gifts received, $126,494; expenditures, $88,952; qualifying distributions, $87,709.
Limitations: Giving on a national basis.
Application information: Application form not required.
Officers: Stephen G. Yeonas, Pres.; Thelma S. Yeonas, V.P.; Stephanie Y. Ellis, Secy.; Stephen G. Yeonas, Jr., Treas.
EIN: 541399466
Codes: FD2

54536
W.E.D. Educational Fund
c/o Martin Mooradian
5532 G. Hempstead Way
Springfield, VA 22151
Application addresses: c/o George M. Dunyan, 3807 Charles Stewart Dr., Fairfax, VA 22033, or c/o St. Mary Armenian Apostolic Church, P.O. Box 39224, Washington, DC 20016; URL: http://members.aol.com/wedfund/index.html

Established in 1998.
Donor(s): William E. Docter,‡ Yervant Hekimian.‡
Financial data (yr. ended 12/31/00): Grants paid, $87,500; assets, $1,367,031 (M); expenditures, $111,610; qualifying distributions, $98,405.
Limitations: Giving limited to residents of Washington, DC.
Application information: Application form required.
Trustee: Ara Avedisian.
EIN: 526904529
Codes: FD2

54537
Robert G. Atkins Educational Trust
c/o B.B. & T., Trust Tax Dept.
P.O. Box 5228
Martinsville, VA 24115 (276) 666-3130
Additional tel.: (276) 666-3290; E-mail: lteegen@bbandt.com
Contact: Lorrie Teegen, V.P., B.B. & T.

Established in 1998 in VA.
Financial data (yr. ended 12/31/01): Grants paid, $87,000; assets, $1,472,557 (M); gifts received, $56; expenditures, $104,872; qualifying distributions, $86,687.
Application information: Application form required.
Trustee: B.B. & T.
EIN: 546426032
Codes: FD2

54538
J. R. Lester Educational Fund
c/o SunTrust Banks, Inc.
P.O. Box 27385
Richmond, VA 23261-7385
Application address: P.O. Box 491, Martinsville, VA 24115, tel.: (540) 666-8316
Contact: Frances Blankenship, Asst. V.P. and Trust Off., SunTrust Banks, Inc.

Established in 1958 in VA.
Donor(s): J.R. Lester.‡
Financial data (yr. ended 12/31/01): Grants paid, $86,075; assets, $613,844 (M); expenditures, $95,823; qualifying distributions, $86,075; giving activities include $86,075 for loans to individuals.
Limitations: Giving limited to Henry and Franklin counties, and Martinsville, VA.
Application information: Interview is required. Application form required.
Trustee: SunTrust Banks, Inc.
EIN: 546031460
Codes: FD2, GTI

54539
EastWest Foundation
(Formerly The Fenchuk Foundation)
14700 Village Square Pl.
Midlothian, VA 23113

Established in 1986 in VA.
Donor(s): Gary W. Fenchuk.
Financial data (yr. ended 09/30/01): Grants paid, $85,612; assets, $3,465 (M); gifts received, $80,160; expenditures, $85,744; qualifying distributions, $85,743.
Limitations: Applications not accepted. Giving primarily in VA.
Application information: Contributes only to pre-selected organizations.
Officer and Director:* Gary W. Fenchuk,* Pres.
EIN: 541391171
Codes: FD2

54540
Mitchell Foundation
c/o Norris E. Mitchell
P.O. Box 311
McLean, VA 22101-0311

Donor(s): Norris E. Mitchell.
Financial data (yr. ended 12/31/01): Grants paid, $85,000; assets, $114 (M); gifts received, $85,000; expenditures, $85,000; qualifying distributions, $85,000.
Limitations: Applications not accepted. Giving primarily in Oakton, VA.
Application information: Contributes only to pre-selected organizations.
Trustee: Norris E. Mitchell.
EIN: 541852192

54541
Barry S. and Evelyn M. Strauch Foundation, Inc.
1113 Langley Ln.
McLean, VA 22101-2230
FAX: (703) 356-2613
Contact: Evelyn M. Strauch, Pres.

Established in 1986 in VA.
Donor(s): Barry S. Strauch, M.D., Evelyn Strauch.
Financial data (yr. ended 09/30/01): Grants paid, $84,925; assets, $1,591,450 (M); gifts received, $50,389; expenditures, $106,272; qualifying distributions, $90,714.
Limitations: Applications not accepted. Giving primarily in Washington, DC, FL, and VA.
Application information: Contributes only to pre-selected organizations. Unsolicited requests for funds not considered.
Officers and Directors:* Evelyn Strauch,* Pres. and Treas.; Barry S. Strauch, M.D.,* Secy.
EIN: 541407386
Codes: FD2

54542
Dreaming Hand Foundation
8 Dogwood Ln.
Charlottesville, VA 22901

Established in 2000 in VA.
Donor(s): Kay F. Bechtel, Stefan D. Bechtel.
Financial data (yr. ended 12/31/01): Grants paid, $84,100; assets, $47,892 (M); gifts received,

54542—VIRGINIA

$1,703; expenditures, $94,395; qualifying distributions, $84,100.
Limitations: Applications not accepted. Giving primarily in Charlottesville, VA.
Application information: Contributes only to pre-selected organizations.
Officers: Stefan D. Bechtel, Pres.; Kay F. Bechtel, Secy.-Treas.
EIN: 542014866
Codes: FD2

54543
Tidewater Builders Association Scholarship Foundation, Inc.
2117 Smith Ave.
Chesapeake, VA 23320 (757) 420-2434
E-mail: tbamail@infi.net; URL: http://www.tbaonline.org/scholarships.html
Contact: Susan Hytry

Established in 1965 in VA.
Financial data (yr. ended 12/31/01): Grants paid, $84,000; assets, $1,007,584 (M); gifts received, $111,054; expenditures, $156,008; qualifying distributions, $132,807; giving activities include $132,957 for programs.
Limitations: Giving limited to the South Hampton Roads, VA, area and the eastern shore of VA only.
Application information: Application form required.
Officers: Jeffrey W. Ainslie, Chair.; Robert A. Widener, Pres.; Joseph C. Robinson, 1st V.P.; John C. Napolitano, 2nd V.P.; A. Ward Wiley, Assoc. V.P.; Robert W. Tyler, Secy.; John W. Iuliano III, Treas.
EIN: 546057730
Codes: FD2, GTI

54544
The Williams Family Foundation
2849 Meadowview Rd.
Falls Church, VA 22042-1310

Established in 1997 in VA.
Donor(s): F. Everett Williams, Mary Agnes Williams.
Financial data (yr. ended 12/31/00): Grants paid, $83,750; assets, $1,505,358 (M); gifts received, $549,549; expenditures, $101,039; qualifying distributions, $83,750.
Limitations: Applications not accepted. Giving primarily in GA.
Application information: Contributes only to pre-selected organizations.
Officers: Frank E. Williams, Jr., Pres.; Harold A. Williams, V.P.; Frank E. Williams III, Secy.-Treas.
EIN: 541861951
Codes: FD2

54545
The Town Foundation
P.O. Box 62503
Virginia Beach, VA 23466

Established in 1988 in VA.
Financial data (yr. ended 12/31/99): Grants paid, $81,803; assets, $1,813,882 (M); expenditures, $92,659; qualifying distributions, $91,363.
Limitations: Applications not accepted. Giving primarily in VA.
Application information: Contributes only to pre-selected organizations.
Officers: Alan S. Mirman, Pres.; Kay Egan, V.P.; Roberta Baker, Secy.; Bruce Longman, Treas.
EIN: 541442707
Codes: FD2

54546
The Ronald I. Dozoretz Foundation
c/o Linda A. Brown
240 Corporate Blvd., Ste. 400
Norfolk, VA 23502-4948

Established in 1998.
Donor(s): Ronald I. Dozoretz, M.D.
Financial data (yr. ended 12/31/01): Grants paid, $81,800; assets, $1,156,394 (M); expenditures, $100,211; qualifying distributions, $100,211.
Limitations: Applications not accepted. Giving primarily in Washington, DC, MD, and VA.
Application information: Contributes only to pre-selected organizations.
Officer and Director:* Ronald I. Dozoretz, M.D.,* Pres. and Secy.
EIN: 541922422
Codes: FD2

54547
Morton G. & Nancy P. Thalhimer Foundation, Inc.
(Formerly Morton G. & Ruth W. Thalhimer Foundation)
P.O. Box 523
Richmond, VA 23218-0523
Application address: 801 E. Main St., Ross Bldg., Ste. 1114, Richmond, VA 23219, tel.: (804) 225-0027
Contact: Morton G. Thalhimer, Jr., Pres.

Established in 1959 in VA.
Donor(s): Morton G. Thalhimer, Jr.
Financial data (yr. ended 12/31/01): Grants paid, $81,389; assets, $970,376 (M); expenditures, $84,013; qualifying distributions, $82,898.
Limitations: Giving primarily in VA.
Application information: Application form not required.
Officer and Directors:* Morton G. Thalhimer, Jr.,* Pres.; Waller H. Horsley, Nancy P. Thalhimer.
EIN: 546042097
Codes: FD2

54548
The Cochran Family Foundation
P.O. Drawer 1268
Staunton, VA 24402-1268

Established in 1997 in VA.
Donor(s): George M. Cochran, Lee S. Cochran.
Financial data (yr. ended 04/30/00): Grants paid, $80,800; assets, $834,607 (M); expenditures, $91,338; qualifying distributions, $80,305.
Limitations: Applications not accepted.
Application information: Contributes only to pre-selected organizations.
Directors: G. Moffett Cochran, George M. Cochran, H.C. Stuart Cochran, Lee S. Cochran.
Trustee: Planters Bank & Trust Co. of VA.
EIN: 546414870

54549
Muse Family Foundation
c/o John Rocovich
P.O. Box 13606
Roanoke, VA 24035 (540) 774-8800

Established in 1998 in VA.
Donor(s): Leonard Muse, Elizabeth Muse.
Financial data (yr. ended 12/31/00): Grants paid, $80,500; assets, $604,359 (M); gifts received, $136; expenditures, $89,020; qualifying distributions, $80,143.
Limitations: Applications not accepted. Giving primarily in VA.
Application information: Contributes only to pre-selected organizations.
Officer: Elizabeth H. Muse, Pres. and Secy.-Treas.
EIN: 541898099

Codes: FD2

54550
The Foster Family Foundation
11351 Random Hills Rd.
Fairfax, VA 22030-6081
Application address: 1001 Crest Ln., McLean, VA 22101
Contact: Betty Flanders Foster, Pres.

Established in 1998 in VA.
Donor(s): Betty Flanders Foster, Wesley Foster, Jr.
Financial data (yr. ended 12/31/01): Grants paid, $80,000; assets, $1,690,453 (M); expenditures, $108,523; qualifying distributions, $80,000.
Limitations: Applications not accepted. Giving on a national and international basis.
Application information: Contributes only to pre-selected organizations.
Officers and Directors:* Betty Flanders Foster,* Pres. and Secy.-Treas.; Heather Hanks,* V.P. and Secy.; Philip Rodney Lawrence, Jr.,* V.P. and Treas.; P. Wesley Foster, Jr.,* V.P.; P. Wesley Foster III,* V.P.; Amanda Foster Spahr,* V.P.; George W. Spahr,* V.P.
EIN: 541902260
Codes: FD2

54551
Safety Systems Foundation
2841 Woodlawn Ave.
Falls Church, VA 22042

Established in 1966 in NY.
Donor(s): William J. Murray, Claire Nader.
Financial data (yr. ended 12/31/00): Grants paid, $79,500; assets, $1,430,195 (M); expenditures, $83,404; qualifying distributions, $78,513.
Limitations: Applications not accepted. Giving on a national basis.
Application information: Contributes only to pre-selected organizations.
Trustees: Laura Milleron, Claire Nader.
EIN: 136220387
Codes: FD2

54552
The Carolyn and John Snow Foundation
122 Tempsford Ln.
Richmond, VA 23226

Established in 1997.
Donor(s): Carolyn Snow, John Snow.
Financial data (yr. ended 12/31/00): Grants paid, $78,750; assets, $295,483 (M); gifts received, $104,352; expenditures, $78,941; qualifying distributions, $78,622.
Officers: John W. Snow, Pres.; Carolyn K. Snow, Secy.
Director: Christopher H. Snow.
EIN: 541852262
Codes: FD2

54553
Troan Foundation, Inc.
c/o Erik Troan
620 Preston Pl.
Charlottesville, VA 22903

Established in 2000 in NC.
Donor(s): Erik W. Troan.
Financial data (yr. ended 12/31/01): Grants paid, $78,600; assets, $2,169,281 (M); gifts received, $144,720; expenditures, $127,657; qualifying distributions, $78,253.
Limitations: Applications not accepted. Giving primarily in NC.
Application information: Contributes only to pre-selected organizations.
Officers: Erik W. Troan, Chair. and Pres.; Brigid V. Troan, Secy.-Treas.

Director: Lawrence Edward Troan.
EIN: 562203535
Codes: FD2

54554
The Jane and Arthur Flippo Foundation
P.O. Box 38
Doswell, VA 23047

Established in 1988 in VA.
Donor(s): Arthur P. Flippo.
Financial data (yr. ended 12/31/00): Grants paid, $76,964; assets, $600,564 (M); expenditures, $80,996; qualifying distributions, $79,422.
Limitations: Applications not accepted. Giving primarily in VA.
Application information: Contributes only to pre-selected organizations.
Officers and Directors:* Arthur P. Flippo,* Pres.; Jane M. Flippo,* Secy.-Treas.
EIN: 541479553
Codes: FD2

54555
B.F. Foundation
P.O. Box 1179
Grundy, VA 24614 (276) 935-2994
Contact: Mrs. Gaynell S. Fowler, Pres.

Established in 1986 in VA.
Donor(s): F.B. Fowler, Gaynell Fowler.
Financial data (yr. ended 12/31/01): Grants paid, $76,500; assets, $1,295,742 (M); expenditures, $83,282; qualifying distributions, $76,500.
Limitations: Giving primarily in VA; some giving in KY and TN.
Officer and Directors:* Mrs. Gaynell Fowler,* Pres.; S.T. Mullins, H.A. Street, Dawneda F. Williams.
EIN: 541388355
Codes: FD2

54556
Fary Memorial Scholarship Fund
P.O. Box 485
Tappahannock, VA 22560 (804) 443-3368
FAX: (804) 443-9303
Contact: William L. Lewis, Admin.

Established in 1998.
Financial data (yr. ended 12/31/00): Grants paid, $76,358; assets, $0 (M); expenditures, $191,817; qualifying distributions, $128,705.
Limitations: Giving limited to the residents of VA.
Application information: Application form available from guidance counselor or the Scholarship Fund. Application form required.
Officer: William L. Lewis, Admin.
EIN: 541827276
Codes: FD2

54557
Hanno Family Foundation, Inc.
8180 Greensboro Dr., Ste. 450
McLean, VA 22102 (703) 748-2610
Contact: James J. Bruyette

Established in 1998 in VA.
Donor(s): Marshall W. Hanno.
Financial data (yr. ended 12/31/01): Grants paid, $75,950; assets, $314,559 (M); expenditures, $82,808; qualifying distributions, $75,950.
Limitations: Giving primarily in FL.
Officers: Marshall W. Hanno, Pres.; Lori L. Hanno, V.P.
Director: Kenneth W. Brown.
EIN: 541921087
Codes: FD2

54558
The Media General Foundation
333 E. Grace St.
P.O. Box 85333
Richmond, VA 23293-0001

Established in 1979 in VA.
Donor(s): Media General, Inc.
Financial data (yr. ended 12/31/00): Grants paid, $75,300; assets, $1,388,840 (M); expenditures, $75,300; qualifying distributions, $75,300; giving activities include $1,359,681 for programs.
Limitations: Applications not accepted. Giving primarily in VA.
Application information: Contributes only to pre-selected organizations.
Officers and Director:* J. Stewart Bryan III,* Pres.; G.L. Mahoney, Secy.; Marshall N. Morton, Treas.
EIN: 510235902
Codes: CS, FD2, CD

54559
The John Jay Hopkins Foundation
c/o McGuire, Woods, Battle & Boothe, LLP
1750 Tyson Blvd., Ste. 1800
McLean, VA 22102
Contact: Lianne H. Conger, Pres., or Philip Tierney, Secy.

Established in 1954 in DC.
Donor(s): John J. Hopkins.‡
Financial data (yr. ended 12/31/00): Grants paid, $75,250; assets, $1,763,179 (M); expenditures, $92,935; qualifying distributions, $82,750.
Limitations: Applications not accepted. Giving primarily in the metropolitan Washington, DC, area and VA.
Publications: Annual report.
Application information: Contributes only to pre-selected organizations. Unsolicited requests for funds not considered.
Officers and Trustees:* Lianne H. Conger,* Pres.; Philip Tierney,* Secy.; Clement E. Conger,* Treas.; Jay A. Conger, Shelly L. Conger, Harry Teeter.
EIN: 526036649
Codes: FD2

54560
Hooker Educational Foundation
c/o B.B. & T.
P.O. Box 5228
Martinsville, VA 24115
Application address: c/o Dir., Personnel, Hooker Furniture Corp., P.O. Box 4708, Martinsville, VA 24115
Contact: Thomas S. Word, Jr., Asst. Secy.

Established in 1991 in VA.
Donor(s): Hooker Furniture Corp., Mabel B. Hooker, J. Clyde Hooker, A. Frank Hooker, Jr.
Financial data (yr. ended 12/31/01): Grants paid, $75,000; assets, $1,178,779 (M); gifts received, $46,178; expenditures, $86,365; qualifying distributions, $76,799.
Limitations: Giving primarily in FL, NC, TN, and VA.
Application information: Applicant must include transcripts, college board scores and letters of recommendation. Application form required.
Officers and Directors:* E. Larry Ryder,* Pres.; Paul B. Toms, Jr.,* Secy.; Jack R. Palmer,* Treas.; Deborah T. Lawless.
EIN: 541583948
Codes: CS, CD, GTI

54561
Delman Mortenson Charitable Foundation
2001 Marthas Rd.
Alexandria, VA 22307

Established in 1994 in VA.

Donor(s): Edward Delman, Edith Delman.
Financial data (yr. ended 11/30/01): Grants paid, $75,000; assets, $1,457,610 (M); gifts received, $86,050; expenditures, $76,658; qualifying distributions, $74,592.
Limitations: Applications not accepted. Giving on a national basis.
Application information: Contributes only to pre-selected organizations.
Trustee: Edward Delman.
EIN: 541739798

54562
Ralph & Leo Rosenthal Foundation
12 Dillton Dr.
Richmond, VA 23233
Application address: c/o Waller R. Staples, 909 E. Main St., Richmond, VA 23219

Established in 1957.
Financial data (yr. ended 12/31/01): Grants paid, $75,000; assets, $1,484,991 (M); expenditures, $77,310; qualifying distributions, $75,000.
Limitations: Giving primarily in Richmond, VA.
Officers: Barbara R. Peskin, Pres. and Mgr.; Jeffrey L. Peskin, Mgr.
EIN: 546036891

54563
The Manuel H. & Mary Johnson Foundation
(Formerly Manuel H. Johnson Foundation)
7521 Old Dominion Dr.
McLean, VA 22102-2500
Contact: Manuel Johnson, Pres.

Established in 1994 in VA.
Donor(s): Manuel Johnson.
Financial data (yr. ended 12/31/00): Grants paid, $74,600; assets, $1,203,890 (M); gifts received, $50,000; expenditures, $74,790; qualifying distributions, $74,200.
Officer: Manuel Johnson, Pres.
EIN: 541737123

54564
The Seilheimer Foundation
P.O. Box 511
Orange, VA 22960-0301
Contact: Charles H. Seilheimer, Jr., Pres.

Established in 1998 in VA.
Donor(s): Mary Louise Seilheimer.
Financial data (yr. ended 12/31/00): Grants paid, $72,975; assets, $525,096 (M); expenditures, $74,708; qualifying distributions, $72,754.
Limitations: Giving primarily in VA.
Application information: Application form not required.
Officers: Charles H. Seilheimer, Jr., Pres.; Mary Louise Seilheimer, V.P.
EIN: 541921692

54565
William M. Camp Foundation
P.O. Box 557
Franklin, VA 23851-0557 (757) 562-7424
Contact: William M. Camp, Jr., Pres.

Established in 1999 in VA.
Financial data (yr. ended 12/31/01): Grants paid, $72,650; assets, $1,267,869 (M); expenditures, $76,174; qualifying distributions, $72,650.
Limitations: Giving primarily in VA.
Officers: William M. Camp, Jr., Pres.; Carrie Luanne Camp, Secy.; Mildred M. Branche, Treas.
EIN: 541821978

54566
Herbert E. & Marion K. Bragg Foundation
c/o SunTrust Banks, Inc.
P.O. Box 27385
Richmond, VA 23261-7385
Scholarship application address: c/o Carolyn McCoy, 510 S. Jefferson St., Roanoke, VA 24011

Established around 1991 in VA.
Financial data (yr. ended 10/31/01): Grants paid, $72,000; assets, $1,565,755 (M); expenditures, $94,628; qualifying distributions, $85,187.
Limitations: Giving limited to ME and VA.
Application information: Application form required.
Trustees: Robert A. Garland, SunTrust Banks, Inc.
EIN: 546313244
Codes: GTI

54567
Meyers-Krumbein Foundation, Inc.
5208 W. Shore Rd.
Midlothian, VA 23112
Application address: 211 South Wilton Rd., Richmond, VA 23226
Contact: Hyman Meyers, Pres.

Established in 1957.
Financial data (yr. ended 12/31/01): Grants paid, $72,000; assets, $34,918 (M); gifts received, $96,000; expenditures, $72,201; qualifying distributions, $72,000.
Limitations: Giving limited to Richmond, VA.
Officers: Hyman Meyers, Pres.; S. Sidney Meyers, V.P. and Secy.; Nathaniel Krumbein, V.P. and Treas.
EIN: 540799473

54568
Virginia Sargeant Reynolds Foundation
c/o J.S. Reynolds, Jr.
7 Oak Ln.
Richmond, VA 23226
Application address: 5621 Cary Street Rd., Richmond, VA 23226
Contact: Virginia Sargeant Reynolds, Chair.

Established in 1991 in VA.
Donor(s): Virginia Sargeant Reynolds.
Financial data (yr. ended 12/31/01): Grants paid, $72,000; assets, $1,815,198 (M); gifts received, $50,000; expenditures, $83,803; qualifying distributions, $73,777.
Limitations: Giving primarily in Richmond, VA.
Officers: Virginia Sargeant Reynolds, Chair.; J.S. Reynolds, Jr., Pres.; Waller H. Horsely, Secy.-Treas.
Directors: Austin Brockengrough III, Richard Roland Reynolds.
EIN: 541595360

54569
Weaver-Fagan Memorial Fund
NationsBank Bldg.
1 W. Queensway, Ste. 200
Hampton, VA 23669
Contact: Patrick B. McDermott, Tr.

Established in 1990 in VA.
Financial data (yr. ended 12/31/00): Grants paid, $72,000; assets, $1,700,431 (M); expenditures, $84,414; qualifying distributions, $79,202.
Limitations: Giving limited to residents of Hampton, VA.
Application information: Application form required.
Trustee: Patrick B. McDermott.
EIN: 541560569
Codes: GTI

54570
The Semper Charitable Foundation, Inc.
627 Innsbruck
Great Falls, VA 22066

Donor(s): William J. Agee, Mary Cunningham Agee.
Financial data (yr. ended 08/31/01): Grants paid, $71,950; assets, $1,140,746 (M); expenditures, $92,469; qualifying distributions, $71,950.
Limitations: Applications not accepted.
Application information: Contributes only to pre-selected organizations.
Officers and Directors:* Mary Cunningham Agee,* Pres.; William J. Agee,* V.P.
EIN: 133190113

54571
Catherine Moore Abbitt Foundation
901 Riverside Dr.
Newport News, VA 23606

Established in 1999 in VA.
Donor(s): Catherine M. Abbitt.
Financial data (yr. ended 05/31/01): Grants paid, $71,767; assets, $76,116 (M); expenditures, $72,539; qualifying distributions, $71,767.
Limitations: Applications not accepted.
Application information: Contributes only to pre-selected organizations.
Officer: Joan D. Aaron, Secy.
Trustees: Catherine M. Abbitt, Richard F. Abbitt, Emily A. Woodrum.
EIN: 546434848

54572
Farmers National Bancorp Private Foundation
8400 Arlington Blvd. Plz. 1
Falls Church, VA 22042-2399
Application address: c/o Board of Directors, 5 Church Cir., Annapolis, MD 21401

Established in 1984 in MD.
Donor(s): Farmers National Bank of Maryland.
Financial data (yr. ended 12/31/99): Grants paid, $71,500; assets, $543,951 (M); expenditures, $72,366; qualifying distributions, $71,158.
Limitations: Giving primarily in central and southern Anne Arundel County, and the eastern shore of MD.
Application information: Application form not required.
Committee Members: Louis Hyatt, M. Virginia Meredith, Charles L. Schelberg, William W. Simmons, John M. Suit II.
Trustee: Farmers Bank of Maryland.
EIN: 521342346
Codes: CS, CD

54573
The Greenstone Foundation
c/o Gerald W. Vesper
6712 Blantyre Rd.
Warrenton, VA 20186

Established in 1989 in VA.
Donor(s): Jocelyn Arundel Sladen.
Financial data (yr. ended 12/31/01): Grants paid, $71,500; assets, $31,376 (M); gifts received, $12,000; expenditures, $72,603; qualifying distributions, $71,767.
Limitations: Applications not accepted. Giving on a national basis.
Application information: Contributes only to pre-selected organizations.
Officers: Jocelyn Arundel Sladen,* Pres. and Treas.; Anne Alexander Rowley, V.P.; Jocelyn Alexander Kirk, Secy.
Director: Marjorie S. Arundel.
EIN: 541531482

54574
Ella O. Latham Trust
P.O. Box 27385
Richmond, VA 23261-7385
Application address: c/o SunTrust Banks, Inc., 15th and New York Ave., N.W., Washington, DC 20005
Contact: Susan C. Ruppert, Trust Off., SunTrust Banks, Inc.

Established in 1986 in DC.
Financial data (yr. ended 12/31/00): Grants paid, $71,200; assets, $2,186,488 (M); expenditures, $89,346; qualifying distributions, $71,896.
Limitations: Giving limited to Washington, DC.
Trustee: SunTrust Banks, Inc.
EIN: 526045742

54575
Thistle Foundation
500 E. Main St., Ste. 1510
Norfolk, VA 23510 (757) 624-2600
Contact: James L. Miller, Tr.

Established in 1986 in VA.
Donor(s): James H. Parker,‡ Ellen D. Parker.
Financial data (yr. ended 12/31/00): Grants paid, $70,500; assets, $859,280 (M); gifts received, $84,408; expenditures, $75,591; qualifying distributions, $70,500.
Limitations: Applications not accepted. Giving primarily in Norfolk, VA.
Application information: Contributes only to pre-selected organizations.
Trustees: James L. Miller, Ellen D. Parker, Grace F. Tazwell.
EIN: 541396531

54576
The Batavia Foundation
925 Towlston Rd.
McLean, VA 22102
Application address: c/o Arun K. Batavia, Pres, P.O. Box 10863, McLean, VA 22102, tel.: (703) 914-4300

Established in 1998 in VA.
Donor(s): Arun K. Batavia.
Financial data (yr. ended 12/31/01): Grants paid, $69,815; assets, $53,245 (M); expenditures, $68,815; qualifying distributions, $69,758.
Limitations: Giving primarily in VA.
Officers and Directors:* Arun K. Batavia,* Pres. and Treas.; Cathie F. Batavia,* V.P. and Secy.
EIN: 541906213

54577
Diken Foundation
1 James Ctr.
901 E. Cary St.
Richmond, VA 23219

Established in 1986 in VA.
Donor(s): Kenneth H. Trout.
Financial data (yr. ended 12/31/01): Grants paid, $69,150; assets, $155,907 (M); expenditures, $70,521; qualifying distributions, $69,150.
Limitations: Applications not accepted. Giving primarily in Baltimore, MD.
Application information: Contributes only to pre-selected organizations.
Directors: Diana M. Trout, Kenneth H. Trout.
EIN: 541394376

54578
The Patricia M. Kluge Foundation
3414 Ellerslie Dr.
Charlottesville, VA 22902-7734 (804) 961-9009
Contact: Patricia M. Kluge, Pres.

Established in 1995 in VA.
Donor(s): Patricia M. Kluge.
Financial data (yr. ended 12/31/01): Grants paid, $69,149; assets, $1,556,564 (M); gifts received, $10,045; expenditures, $114,462; qualifying distributions, $45,206.
Limitations: Giving primarily in Charlottesville, VA.
Application information: Application form not required.
Officer and Directors:* Patricia M. Kluge,* Pres.; Robert M. Huff, Mara S. Sierocinski.
EIN: 541803094

54579
The Violet H. Greco Foundation, Inc.
P.O. Box 1428
Suffolk, VA 23439

Established in 1997 in VA.
Financial data (yr. ended 06/30/00): Grants paid, $68,500; assets, $4,945,644 (M); gifts received, $4,536,264; expenditures, $86,021; qualifying distributions, $67,132.
Limitations: Applications not accepted. Giving primarily in Portsmouth, VA.
Application information: Contributes only to pre-selected organizations.
Officers: Richard R. Harris, Pres.; Frances Sledge, Secy.
Directors: Charlotte R. Jones, Chris Jones, Clarence L. Ringler.
Advisor: Robert Thorndike, Financial Advisor.
EIN: 541859728

54580
Ray Rowe 1988 Trust for Animals
41 E. Bellafonte Ave.
Alexandria, VA 22301-1442 (703) 836-7036
Contact: Duncan Forbes, Tr.

Established in 1988 in CA.
Donor(s): Raymond S. Rowe.‡
Financial data (yr. ended 12/31/99): Grants paid, $68,250; assets, $1,132,445 (M); expenditures, $80,403; qualifying distributions, $68,250.
Publications: Occasional report.
Application information: Application form not required.
Trustee: Duncan F. Forbes.
EIN: 956885584

54581
Island Sunrise Foundation, Inc.
c/o Lochnau, Inc.
P.O. Box 1850
Middleburg, VA 20118 (540) 687-8884
Contact: Mary Painter

Established in 1997 in MI.
Donor(s): James W. Webert, Magalen W. Webert.
Financial data (yr. ended 12/31/99): Grants paid, $68,000; assets, $505,386 (M); gifts received, $160,643; expenditures, $75,388; qualifying distributions, $67,931.
Officers: Magalen W. Webert, Pres.; James W. Webert, V.P.; Philip S. Lawrence.
EIN: 383351882

54582
Biomedical Research Foundation
2830 Shore Dr.
Virginia Beach, VA 23451

Financial data (yr. ended 06/30/01): Grants paid, $67,800; assets, $18,231 (M); expenditures, $74,839; qualifying distributions, $65,299.
Limitations: Applications not accepted. Giving primarily in AZ and TX.
Application information: Contributes only to pre-selected organizations.
Officers: Jordan U. Gutterman, Pres.; Julian H. Gutterman, Secy.-Treas.
EIN: 541429678
Codes: GTI

54583
Lawrence J. Goldrich Foundation
6477 College Park Sq., Ste. 306
Virginia Beach, VA 23464-3685
FAX: (757) 424-1435
Contact: Lawrence J. Goldrich, Pres.

Established in 1954 in NY.
Donor(s): Leslie Berger,‡ Lawrence J. Goldrich, Executive Park Co.
Financial data (yr. ended 12/31/01): Grants paid, $67,727; assets, $1,632,944 (M); expenditures, $69,874; qualifying distributions, $67,727.
Limitations: Giving primarily in NC, NY, and VA.
Application information: Application form not required.
Officer: Lawrence J. Goldrich, Pres.
Directors: I. William Berger, Andrew J. Goldrich, Janice Goldrich, Vicki Goldrich.
EIN: 116038035

54584
Emerson G. & Dolores G. Reinsch Foundation
2040 Columbia Pike
Arlington, VA 22204 (703) 920-3600
Contact: Lola C. Reinsch, Tr.

Established in 1964 in VA.
Financial data (yr. ended 12/31/01): Grants paid, $67,519; assets, $1,969,407 (M); expenditures, $71,635; qualifying distributions, $67,519.
Limitations: Giving primarily in northern VA.
Application information: Recipients of continuing grants need not resubmit an application. Application form not required.
Trustees: Paul F. Neff, Lola C. Reinsch.
EIN: 546055396

54585
Eric and Marianne Billings Foundation, Inc.
1001 19th St., 18th Fl.
Arlington, VA 22209

Established in 1993 in VA.
Donor(s): Eric Billings, Marianne Billings.
Financial data (yr. ended 06/30/01): Grants paid, $66,085; assets, $3,538 (M); gifts received, $59,700; expenditures, $69,105; qualifying distributions, $66,085.
Limitations: Applications not accepted. Giving primarily in Washington, DC.
Application information: Contributes only to pre-selected organizations.
Directors: Eric Billings, Marianne Billings, Ned S. Scherer.
EIN: 521853715

54586
John and Mary Camp Foundation
217 Meadow Lane
Franklin, VA 23851

Established in 1999 in VA.

Financial data (yr. ended 12/31/00): Grants paid, $66,000; assets, $1,146,689 (M); expenditures, $68,631; qualifying distributions, $66,000.
Limitations: Applications not accepted. Giving primarily in Raleigh, NC.
Application information: Contributes only to pre-selected organizations.
Officer: John M. Camp, Jr., Pres. and Secy.-Treas.
Directors: Olive C. Johnson, Virginia C. Smith.
EIN: 541920701

54587
LTG Foundation, Inc.
140 Park St., Ste. 101
Vienna, VA 22180 (703) 830-3373
Contact: Christopher Bayer, Exec. Dir.

Established in 1999 in VA.
Donor(s): James P. Massa, Susan E.F. Massa.
Financial data (yr. ended 09/30/01): Grants paid, $66,000; assets, $173,234 (M); gifts received, $76,000; expenditures, $138,529; qualifying distributions, $134,687.
Limitations: Giving primarily in NC.
Application information: Unsolicited requests for funds not accepted.
Officers: James P. Massa, Pres.; Susan E.F. Massa, V.P.; Thomas H. Campbell, Secy.; Christopher Bayer, Exec. Dir.
Directors: Russell Harris, Robert G. Topping.
EIN: 541965158

54588
Noland Company Foundation
2700 Warwick Blvd.
Newport News, VA 23607 (757) 928-9000

Established in 1962 in VA.
Donor(s): Noland Co.
Financial data (yr. ended 12/31/01): Grants paid, $65,948; assets, $875,173 (M); gifts received, $102,500; expenditures, $72,330; qualifying distributions, $65,948.
Limitations: Applications not accepted. Giving primarily in VA.
Application information: Contributes only to pre-selected organizations.
Officers: Lloyd U. Noland III, Pres.; Arthur P. Henderson, Jr., V.P.; John E. Gullett, Secy.
EIN: 540754191
Codes: CS, CD

54589
The Rice Foundation, Inc.
30 W. Franklin Rd., Ste. 504
Roanoke, VA 24011
Contact: Bittle W. Porterfield, III, Pres.

Established in 1984 in VA.
Donor(s): Bittle W. Porterfield III.
Financial data (yr. ended 12/31/01): Grants paid, $65,842; assets, $72,692 (M); gifts received, $73,866; expenditures, $67,042; qualifying distributions, $65,840.
Limitations: Giving primarily in Roanoke, VA.
Officers: Bittle W. Porterfield III, Pres. and Treas.; Charlotte K. Porterfield, V.P. and Secy.
EIN: 541249423

54590
Tigris Rivanna Foundation
c/o Thomas H. Jones
400 Balbion Dr.
Earlysville, VA 22936

Established in 1999 in VA.
Donor(s): Thomas H. Jones.
Financial data (yr. ended 01/31/02): Grants paid, $65,450; assets, $32,585 (M); gifts received, $77,187; expenditures, $66,174; qualifying distributions, $65,450.

54590—VIRGINIA

Limitations: Applications not accepted.
Application information: Contributes only to pre-selected organizations.
Officers and Directors:* Thomas H. Jones,* Pres.; Stephanie Hanna Jones,* V.P.; Diana Foster-Jones,* Secy.-Treas.; Christopher Foster Jones.
EIN: 541944505

54591
Virginia Concrete Foundation, Inc.
P.O. Box 666
Springfield, VA 22150-0666 (703) 354-7100
Contact: C.J. Shepherdson, Pres.

Established in 1962 in VA.
Donor(s): Concrete Concrete Co., Virginia Concrete Co.
Financial data (yr. ended 12/31/01): Grants paid, $65,400; assets, $1,347,295 (M); gifts received, $120,000; expenditures, $73,358; qualifying distributions, $65,400.
Limitations: Giving limited to northern VA, with emphasis on Alexandria, Arlington, and Fairfax counties.
Application information: Scholarship applicants must reside in northern VA for at least 4 years immediately preceding their nomination by the faculty of their high school. Application form required.
Officers: C.J. Shepherdson, Pres.; C.J. Shepherdson, Jr., Secy.; J.R. Johnson, Treas.
EIN: 546052942
Codes: GTI

54592
The Pruden Foundation
P.O. Box 3312
Suffolk, VA 23439-3312 (757) 539-6261
Contact: Peter D. Pruden, III, Dir.

Established in 1972 in VA.
Donor(s): Peter D. Pruden, Jr., Peter D. Pruden, Sr.‡
Financial data (yr. ended 02/28/02): Grants paid, $65,260; assets, $1,541,887 (M); expenditures, $65,627; qualifying distributions, $65,260.
Limitations: Giving primarily in Suffolk, VA.
Application information: Application form not required.
Directors: Thomas F. Buz Hofler, Brook Pruden, Peter D. Pruden, Jr., Peter D. Pruden III, Bobby Ralph, Whitney Saunders, Frank E. Sheffer.
EIN: 540923448

54593
Mabel Burroughs Tyler Foundation
999 Waterside Dr., Ste. 1925
Norfolk, VA 23510-3307 (757) 623-2491
Contact: Frederick V. Martin, Treas.

Established in 1994 in VA.
Financial data (yr. ended 01/31/02): Grants paid, $65,000; assets, $1,163,088 (M); expenditures, $75,955; qualifying distributions, $65,000.
Limitations: Giving primarily in Norfolk, VA.
Application information: Unsolicited requests for funds not accepted.
Officer and Directors:* Frederick V. Martin,* Treas.; Calvert Tyler Lester, Eleanor Tyler Stanton.
EIN: 541707734

54594
James L. and Mary Jane Bowman Charitable Trust
P.O. Box 480
Stephens City, VA 22655
Contact: James L. Bowman, Tr.

Established in 1997 in VA.
Donor(s): James L. Bowman.
Financial data (yr. ended 12/31/01): Grants paid, $64,131; assets, $2,705,076 (M); expenditures, $66,096; qualifying distributions, $64,131.
Limitations: Giving primarily in VA.
Application information: Application form not required.
Trustees: James L. Bowman, Beverley B. Shoemaker.
EIN: 546412915

54595
Ewing Family Foundation
c/o Charles B. Ewing, Jr.
1322 Merchant Ln.
McLean, VA 22101 (703) 356-3521

Established in 1997 in VA.
Donor(s): Betty G. Ewing, Charles B. Ewing, Jr.
Financial data (yr. ended 12/31/00): Grants paid, $64,000; assets, $1,284,750 (M); expenditures, $76,522; qualifying distributions, $62,233.
Limitations: Applications not accepted. Giving primarily in Washington, DC, Philadelphia, PA, and Falls Church, VA.
Application information: Contributes only to pre-selected organizations.
Officers and Directors:* Charles B. Ewing, Jr.,* Pres.; John C. Ewing,* Secy.-Treas.; Betty G. Ewing, Cynthia L. Ewing, Sarah E. Sagarese.
EIN: 541845641

54596
E. R. Warner McCabe Testamentary Trust - Virginia
(Formerly Society of Cincinnati - Virginia Trust)
c/o SunTrust Banks, Inc.
P.O. Box 27385
Richmond, VA 23261-7385
Application address: c/o Andrew H. Christian, Chair., McCabe Schol. Comm., P.O. Box 1357, Richmond, VA 23211

Established in 1974 in VA.
Financial data (yr. ended 07/31/01): Grants paid, $64,000; assets, $1,290,190 (L); expenditures, $77,134; qualifying distributions, $63,372.
Limitations: Giving primarily in the South.
Trustee: SunTrust Banks, Inc.
Scholarship Committee: Andrew H. Christian, Chair.
EIN: 546131246
Codes: GTI

54597
Dreyfus Foundation
106B 83rd St.
Virginia Beach, VA 23451

Established in 1997 in VA.
Donor(s): Mark Dreyfus.
Financial data (yr. ended 12/31/01): Grants paid, $63,500; assets, $703,530 (M); gifts received, $365,347; expenditures, $65,509; qualifying distributions, $63,500.
Limitations: Applications not accepted.
Application information: Contributes only to pre-selected organizations.
Officers and Directors:* Alfred Dreyfus,* Pres.; Mildred Dreyfus,* Secy.; Mark Dreyfus,* Treas.; Claudia Dreyfus Levi.
EIN: 541851411

54598
Abraham S. Ende Research Foundation
121 S. Market St.
Petersburg, VA 23803 (804) 733-8771

Established in 1965 in VA.
Donor(s): Milton Ende, Norman Ende.
Financial data (yr. ended 08/31/01): Grants paid, $63,000; assets, $256 (M); gifts received, $63,025; expenditures, $63,000; qualifying distributions, $63,000.
Limitations: Applications not accepted.
Application information: Contributes only to pre-selected organizations.
Officer: Milton Ende, Pres.
Trustees: Frederick I. Ende, M.D., Leigh Ende, M.D., Norman Ende, M.D.
EIN: 540762350

54599
The David and Janet Brashear Foundation
4350 N. Fairfax Dr., Ste., 820
Arlington, VA 22203
Contact: David M. Brashear, Chair.; or Janet M. Brashear, Pres.

Established in 1999.
Donor(s): David M. Brashear, Janet M. Brashear.
Financial data (yr. ended 12/31/01): Grants paid, $62,970; assets, $194,334 (M); expenditures, $65,213; qualifying distributions, $62,970.
Limitations: Giving primarily in Washington, DC, PA, and VA.
Officers and Trustees:* David M. Brashear,* Chair.; Janet M. Brashear,* Pres.
EIN: 541951078

54600
The Drescher Foundation
1000 Wilson Blvd., Ste. 700
Arlington, VA 22209 (703) 525-1101
Contact: Jared Drescher, Dir.

Established in 1983 DC and VA.
Donor(s): Jared Drescher.
Financial data (yr. ended 12/31/01): Grants paid, $62,822; assets, $541,720 (M); expenditures, $64,870; qualifying distributions, $63,643.
Limitations: Giving primarily in CO, the Washington, DC, area, including MD, and NY.
Directors: Irene Drescher, Jared Drescher, Dana Harrison.
EIN: 541257908

54601
Patricia E. Bassett & John D. Bassett III Foundation
P.O. Box 110
Galax, VA 24333

Donor(s): John D. Bassett III.
Financial data (yr. ended 08/31/01): Grants paid, $62,451; assets, $855,861 (M); gifts received, $25,000; expenditures, $70,214; qualifying distributions, $63,602.
Limitations: Applications not accepted. Giving on a national basis.
Application information: Contributes only to pre-selected organizations.
Officers: John D. Bassett III, Pres.; Ellen Bassett, V.P.; John D. Bassett IV, V.P.; Wyatt P. Bassett, V.P.; E. Ashton Poole, V.P.; Frances B. Poole, V.P.; Patricia E. Bassett, Secy.
EIN: 237066445

54602
A. D. & A. L. Morgan Memorial Scholarship Fund
c/o PaineWebber, Inc.
1 Columbus Ctr.
Virginia Beach, VA 23462
Application address: c/o Old Dominion Univ., Financial Aid Office, 121 Old Administration Bldg., Norfolk, VA 23529-0052

Financial data (yr. ended 12/31/99): Grants paid, $62,200; assets, $1,097,627 (M); expenditures, $74,839; qualifying distributions, $63,508.
Limitations: Giving limited to Tidewater, VA.

Application information: Application form required.
Trustees: Steve Fitzgerald, Trina H. Marson, George Webb, Douglas B. Williams.
EIN: 540309320
Codes: GTI

54603
Robert M. Darby Foundation, Inc.
(Formerly Patricia & Robert M. Darby Foundation)
c/o Guidance Off.
4733 Sperryville Pike
Woodville, VA 22749 (540) 987-8373
Contact: Robert M. Darby, Pres.

Established in 1990 in VA.
Donor(s): Robert M. Darby, Patricia Darby.
Financial data (yr. ended 12/31/01): Grants paid, $60,516; assets, $401,026 (M); expenditures, $61,923; qualifying distributions, $60,516.
Limitations: Giving limited to Rappahannock County, VA.
Application information: Application form required.
Officer: Robert M. Darby, Pres.
EIN: 541548288

54604
The Augusta Foundation
P.O. Box 324
Staunton, VA 24402-0324

Established in 1992 in VA.
Donor(s): John A. Zinn, Jr., Mary M. Gibbs.
Financial data (yr. ended 12/31/01): Grants paid, $60,288; assets, $50,229 (M); expenditures, $60,922; qualifying distributions, $60,288.
Limitations: Applications not accepted. Giving primarily in Staunton, VA.
Application information: Contributes only to pre-selected organizations.
Officers: John A. Zinn, Jr., Pres. and Treas.; Mary M. Gibbs, V.P. and Secy.
EIN: 541646582

54605
The Monford D. and Lucy L. Custer Foundation
407 S. Washington St.
Winchester, VA 22601
Contact: Linda C. Russell, Pres.

Established in 1997 in VA.
Financial data (yr. ended 12/31/01): Grants paid, $60,000; assets, $1,183,007 (M); expenditures, $69,920; qualifying distributions, $60,000.
Application information: Application form not required.
Officers and Directors:* Linda C. Russell,* Pres. and Secy.; Monford D. Custer III,* V.P. and Treas.; Ellen C. Morgan,* V.P.; Susan C. Sanders,* V.P.
EIN: 541839172

54606
Clifford D. and Virginia S. Grim Educational Fund
(Formerly Clifford D. Grim and Virginia S. Grim Educational Fund)
c/o First Union National Bank, VA
P.O. Box 14061
Roanoke, VA 24038-4061

Established around 1965.
Financial data (yr. ended 07/31/01): Grants paid, $60,000; assets, $1,360,994 (M); gifts received, $60,640; expenditures, $71,404; qualifying distributions, $60,000.
Limitations: Giving limited to the Winchester, VA, area.
Application information: Application form required.

Trustee: First Union National Bank of Virginia.
EIN: 546046865
Codes: GTI

54607
E. R. Warner McCabe Testamentary Trust - Georgia
(Formerly Society of Cincinnati, Georgia Trust)
c/o SunTrust Banks, Inc.
P.O. Box 27385
Richmond, VA 23261-7385
Application address: c/o Col. Ford P. Fuller, Jr., Chair., McCabe Schol. Comm., Society of Cincinnati State of Georgia, Savannah, GA 31406

Established in 1976.
Financial data (yr. ended 07/31/01): Grants paid, $60,000; assets, $1,308,387 (M); expenditures, $72,541; qualifying distributions, $59,295.
Limitations: Giving primarily to residents in the South.
Trustee: SunTrust Banks, Inc.
EIN: 546131247
Codes: GTI

54608
L. J. Sanford Trust f/b/o Church of St. Matthew and St. Timothy
c/o William F. Sanford, Jr.
2030 Wingfield Rd.
Charlottesville, VA 22901

Established in 1994 in VA.
Financial data (yr. ended 12/31/01): Grants paid, $60,000; assets, $1,350,754 (M); expenditures, $72,885; qualifying distributions, $60,000.
Limitations: Applications not accepted. Giving limited to New York, NY.
Application information: Contributes only to pre-selected organizations specified in the governing instrument.
Trustee: William F. Sanford, Jr.
EIN: 656142833
Codes: TN

54609
Virginia Commonwealth University Charitable Trust
8730 Higginbotham Pl.
Richmond, VA 23229

Donor(s): Inez A. Caudill.
Financial data (yr. ended 12/31/01): Grants paid, $60,000; assets, $813,008 (M); expenditures, $77,486; qualifying distributions, $60,000.
Limitations: Applications not accepted.
Application information: Contributes only to pre-selected organizations.
Trustees: L. Michael Gracik, Jr., Anthony E. Smith.
EIN: 546453690

54610
The Rugaber Family Fund
c/o Walter F. Rugaber
P.O. Box 938
Meadows of Dan, VA 24120-0938

Established in 1995.
Donor(s): Walter F. Rugaber.
Financial data (yr. ended 12/31/01): Grants paid, $59,800; assets, $1,080,839 (M); gifts received, $3,363; expenditures, $64,699; qualifying distributions, $59,800.
Limitations: Applications not accepted. Giving primarily in VA.
Application information: Contributes only to pre-selected organizations.
Directors: Sally S. Rugaber, Walter F. Rugaber.
EIN: 541771747

54611
The Varney Foundation
7849 Montvale Way
McLean, VA 22102

Established in 1994 in VA.
Donor(s): Robert C. Varney, Sandra D. Varney.
Financial data (yr. ended 12/31/01): Grants paid, $59,376; assets, $129,955 (M); gifts received, $10,000; expenditures, $60,319; qualifying distributions, $60,069.
Limitations: Applications not accepted. Giving on a national basis.
Application information: Contributes only to pre-selected organizations.
Officers and Directors:* Robert C. Varney,* Pres.; Sandra D. Varney,* Secy.
EIN: 541741120

54612
Clarke Hook Foundation
14506-E Lee Rd.
Chantilly, VA 20151-1635

Established in 1997 in VA.
Donor(s): F. David Clarke, Helen H. Clarke.
Financial data (yr. ended 12/31/01): Grants paid, $59,000; assets, $1,323,455 (M); gifts received, $200,000; expenditures, $66,571; qualifying distributions, $59,000.
Officers: Carol S. Whalen, Pres.; Helen C. Helton, V.P.; Thomas J. O'Hara, Jr., Secy.-Treas.
Directors: F. David Clarke, Helen H. Clarke.
EIN: 541868557

54613
Henry J. Fox Fund
c/o Reitberger, Pollekoff & Kozak, PC
8133 Leesburg Pike No. 550
Vienna, VA 22182
Application address: 4831 Park Ave., Bethesda, MD 20816, tel.: (301) 229-8576
Contact: Leslie Kefauver, Tr.

Donor(s): Charlotte Fox.
Financial data (yr. ended 12/31/01): Grants paid, $58,216; assets, $1,393,763 (M); expenditures, $70,278; qualifying distributions, $58,216.
Limitations: Giving primarily in Washington, DC, and FL.
Trustees: Charlotte Fox, Leslie Kefauver.
EIN: 526036472

54614
The Spahr Foundation
8500 Idylwood Valley Pl.
Vienna, VA 22182 (703) 289-9577
Contact: Thomas P. Spahr, Pres.

Established in 1999 in VA.
Donor(s): Thomas P. Spahr.
Financial data (yr. ended 12/31/01): Grants paid, $58,000; assets, $178,806 (M); expenditures, $61,789; qualifying distributions, $58,000.
Officers: Thomas P. Spahr, Pres.; Catherine M. Spahr, V.P.
EIN: 541968286

54615
The Mitchell Petersen Family Foundation
1775 Jamieson Ave., Ste. 210
Alexandria, VA 22314

Established in 1998.
Donor(s): Nancy Mitchell Petersen.
Financial data (yr. ended 09/30/01): Grants paid, $57,997; assets, $1,804,352 (M); expenditures, $175,053; qualifying distributions, $57,997.
Limitations: Giving primarily in Alexandria, VA.
Trustee: Nancy Mitchell Petersen.
EIN: 526942243

54616
The Harry D. Forsyth Foundation
c/o William P. Harris
P.O. Box 1276
Lynchburg, VA 24505

Established in 1992 in VA.
Donor(s): William P. Harris, Elizabeth F. Harris.
Financial data (yr. ended 12/31/01): Grants paid, $57,850; assets, $224,768 (M); gifts received, $57,030; expenditures, $58,686; qualifying distributions, $57,799.
Limitations: Applications not accepted. Giving primarily in Lynchburg, VA.
Application information: Contributes only to pre-selected organizations.
Trustees: William R. Chambers, Jr., Elizabeth Forsyth Harris, Lyall F. Harris, William P. Harris, Elizabeth Logan Harris-Cruz, Paul E. Sackett, Jr., Anne Frank Harris Slaughter.
EIN: 541635001

54617
Barnabas Ministries Foundation
1125 West Ave.
Richmond, VA 23220
Application address: 400 W. Franklin St., Richmond, VA 23220
Contact: Lucy B. Marsden, Dir.

Established in 2000.
Donor(s): Warren P. Hottle.
Financial data (yr. ended 12/31/00): Grants paid, $57,577; assets, $35,345 (M); gifts received, $72,977; expenditures, $63,900; qualifying distributions, $63,900.
Limitations: Giving primarily in VA.
Officers: Franklin Gillis, Pres.; Jeffrey S. Cribbs, Jr., Secy.; Warren P. Hottle, Treas.
Director: Lucy Marsden Hottle, William Huddleston.
EIN: 541972267

54618
W. E. McGuire Charitable Foundation, Inc.
c/o William M. Waldrop, M.D.
1112 Westover Ave.
Norfolk, VA 23507

Established in 1964.
Donor(s): Margaret Cutshall.‡
Financial data (yr. ended 10/31/01): Grants paid, $57,500; assets, $1,216,892 (M); expenditures, $66,758; qualifying distributions, $57,500.
Limitations: Applications not accepted. Giving primarily in the Minneapolis and St. Paul, MN, area, NC, and VA.
Application information: Contributes only to pre-selected organizations.
Officers and Directors:* Shirley M. Rhees,* Pres.; William McGuire Waldrop, M.D.,* V.P. and Treas.; David Jerome Rhees,* Secy.; Susan Waldrop Donckers, Jean M. Waldrop.
EIN: 540761802

54619
Warden Family Foundation
4332 Alfriends Trail
Virginia Beach, VA 23455 (757) 499-4020
Application address: P.O. Box 13109, Norfolk, VA 23506
Contact: Cyrus Dolph, IV

Established in 1998 in VA.
Donor(s): Doratha Warden.
Financial data (yr. ended 12/31/01): Grants paid, $57,375; assets, $1,845,193 (M); expenditures, $85,768; qualifying distributions, $57,375.
Limitations: Giving primarily in VA.
Officers: William B. Warden, Pres.; Sandra S. Warden, Secy.-Treas.
Directors: Jeffrey B. Warden, Mark R. Warden, Susan C. Warden, William S. Warden.
EIN: 541901227

54620
J. M. and E. H. Laprade Educational Trust
c/o SunTrust Banks, Inc.
P.O. Box 27385
Richmond, VA 23261-7385

Financial data (yr. ended 12/31/00): Grants paid, $57,000; assets, $803,734 (M); expenditures, $62,030; qualifying distributions, $57,978; giving activities include $57,000 for loans to individuals.
Limitations: Giving primarily in Martinsville, VA and surrounding counties.
Application information: Application form required.
Trustee: SunTrust Banks, Inc.
EIN: 546396348

54621
The Brandt Foundation
201 Fox Meadow Ln.
Winchester, VA 22602-2339 (540) 665-9100
Contact: William F. Brandt, Jr., Pres.

Donor(s): William F. Brandt, Jr.
Financial data (yr. ended 12/31/01): Grants paid, $56,900; assets, $1,450,749 (M); gifts received, $107,071; expenditures, $57,676; qualifying distributions, $56,900.
Limitations: Giving primarily in Winchester, VA.
Officers and Directors:* William F. Brandt, Jr.,* Pres. and Treas.; Elaine K. Brandt,* Secy.
EIN: 541392294

54622
McWick Technology Foundation, Inc.
3200 Glenwood Pl.
Falls Church, VA 22041
Contact: Kathleen McBride, Tr.

Established in 1996.
Donor(s): Kathleen McBride, Larry Rudwick.
Financial data (yr. ended 09/30/01): Grants paid, $56,833; assets, $497,651 (M); expenditures, $60,099; qualifying distributions, $56,833.
Trustees: Kathleen McBride, Michael Rhoades, Larry Rudwick.
EIN: 311483977

54623
George & Frances Armour Foundation, Inc.
c/o Stephen Wainger
1205 Cedar Point Dr.
Virginia Beach, VA 23451

Incorporated in 1957 in NY.
Donor(s): George L. Armour, Frances Armour.‡
Financial data (yr. ended 03/31/02): Grants paid, $56,000; assets, $1,210,162 (M); expenditures, $79,616; qualifying distributions, $56,000.
Limitations: Applications not accepted. Giving primarily in NY and VA.
Application information: Contributes only to pre-selected organizations.
Officers: Elizabeth Wainger, Pres.; Stephen Wainger, V.P. and Secy.-Treas.; Georgia Wainger, V.P.
EIN: 136155619

54624
The Harry F. Flippo and Margaret M. Flippo Foundation
57 S. Main St.
NationsBank Bldg., Ste. 401
Harrisonburg, VA 22801-3730
(540) 433-0932
Contact: Betty S. Leach, Dir.

Established in 1996 in VA.
Donor(s): Margaret Flippo.
Financial data (yr. ended 12/31/01): Grants paid, $56,000; assets, $1,632,905 (M); gifts received, $433,243; expenditures, $76,243; qualifying distributions, $55,706.
Limitations: Giving limited to VA.
Directors: Mensel Dean, Kevin Derr, Margaret Flippo, Betty S. Leach.
EIN: 541804597

54625
The Unalane Foundation
c/o Italo H. Ablondi
209 Prince St.
Alexandria, VA 22314-3313

Established in 1990 in VA.
Donor(s): Italo H. Ablondi.
Financial data (yr. ended 12/31/01): Grants paid, $55,620; assets, $726,830 (M); expenditures, $55,869; qualifying distributions, $55,620.
Limitations: Applications not accepted. Giving primarily in NY and VA.
Application information: Contributes only to pre-selected organizations.
Officers and Directors:* Italo H. Ablondi,* Pres. and Treas.; Unalane C. Ablondi,* V.P. and Secy.; Bruno Cappellini, Albert Giambelli, Leigh Helvie, J. Frank Osha.
EIN: 541522859

54626
Appreciation of Earth and Animal Foundation, Inc.
20292 Foggy Bottom Rd.
Bluemont, VA 20135-2130
Contact: Nancy L. Cooper, Pres.

Established in 1993 in GA.
Donor(s): Nancy L. Cooper.
Financial data (yr. ended 06/30/01): Grants paid, $55,600; assets, $1,174,435 (M); expenditures, $59,520; qualifying distributions, $58,334.
Limitations: Giving primarily in Washington, DC, FL, MD, and VA.
Officers and Directors:* Nancy L. Cooper,* Pres.; Nell C. Stager,* V.P.; Robert B. Dale III,* Secy.-Treas.; Nettie L. Cooper.
EIN: 541687076

54627
Louis P. & Lela Busch Foundation
101 Brookstone Ct.
Yorktown, VA 23693

Established in 1997 in VA.
Financial data (yr. ended 04/30/01): Grants paid, $55,000; assets, $1,229,508 (M); expenditures, $79,211; qualifying distributions, $55,000.
Limitations: Applications not accepted. Giving primarily in VA and the Pacific Northwest.
Application information: Contributes only to pre-selected organizations.
Directors: Lela E. Busch, Peter R. Eshleman, Scott A. Eshleman, Mary Ann Navarre, B. Marilyn Walter.
EIN: 541837593

54628
Homer A. and Ida S. Jones Trust
P.O. Box 1689
Bristol, VA 24203-1689

Established in 1983 in TN.
Donor(s): Homer A. Jones, Jr.
Financial data (yr. ended 11/30/01): Grants paid, $54,950; assets, $1,105,787 (M); gifts received, $38,215; expenditures, $56,885; qualifying distributions, $54,950.
Limitations: Applications not accepted.

Application information: Contributes only to pre-selected organizations.
Trustees: Homer A. Jones, Jr., Ida S. Jones.
EIN: 581535978

54629
The Cosgive Foundation
1360 Beverly Rd., Ste. 205
McLean, VA 22101 (703) 734-8555

Established in 1988 in VA.
Financial data (yr. ended 12/31/01): Grants paid, $54,775; assets, $336,710 (M); expenditures, $55,789; qualifying distributions, $54,775.
Limitations: Giving primarily in VA.
Trustees: Jacquelyn W. Coston, Otis D. Coston.
EIN: 541448945

54630
The Nettleton Foundation
P.O. Box 13606
Roanoke, VA 24035-3606

Established in 1984 in VA.
Financial data (yr. ended 12/31/01): Grants paid, $54,700; assets, $1,667,124 (M); expenditures, $66,603; qualifying distributions, $65,974.
Limitations: Applications not accepted. Giving limited to Staunton, VA.
Application information: Contributes only to pre-selected organizations.
Director: John G. Rocovich, Jr.
EIN: 521303298

54631
William M. Cage Library Trust
321 William St.
Fredericksburg, VA 22401
Contact: John C. Cowan, Tr.

Established in 1993.
Donor(s): William M. Cage.‡
Financial data (yr. ended 12/31/01): Grants paid, $54,582; assets, $1,283,196 (M); expenditures, $64,824; qualifying distributions, $54,582.
Limitations: Giving limited to VA.
Trustee: John C. Cowan.
EIN: 546350104

54632
The Hirschler Foundation
P.O. Box 8616
Richmond, VA 23226

Donor(s): Edward S. Hirschler, Elizabeth W. Hirschler.
Financial data (yr. ended 05/31/02): Grants paid, $54,490; assets, $1,024,930 (M); expenditures, $60,336; qualifying distributions, $54,490.
Limitations: Giving primarily in Richmond, VA.
Officer: Anne H. Long, Pres.
EIN: 546036828

54633
The Sugarman Family Foundation
2200 Wilson Blvd., 102-337
Arlington, VA 22201-3324

Established in 1995 in VA.
Donor(s): Joan G. Sugarman.
Financial data (yr. ended 12/31/01): Grants paid, $54,400; assets, $376,845 (M); expenditures, $66,706; qualifying distributions, $54,400.
Limitations: Applications not accepted. Giving on a national basis.
Application information: Contributes only to pre-selected organizations.
Officers and Directors:* Joan G. Sugarman,* Pres. and Treas.; Janet Sugarman Isaacs,* V.P. and Secy.; Edward J. Beckwith, Paul H. Feinberg, Joel Sugarman, Laurence Sugarman, Nancy Sugarman.
EIN: 541776858

54634
Dennis David Syposs Charitable Trust
P.O. Box 150126
Alexandria, VA 22315

Established in 1994 in DC.
Financial data (yr. ended 12/31/01): Grants paid, $54,320; assets, $483,138 (M); expenditures, $81,922; qualifying distributions, $54,320.
Limitations: Applications not accepted. Giving primarily in Sylmar, CA; some giving also in Washington, DC, and VA.
Application information: Contributes only to pre-selected organizations.
Trustee: Sandra J. Mullikin.
EIN: 526731597

54635
Watson-Galbraith Charitable Foundation
2362 Glen Echo Farm
Charlottesville, VA 22911 (804) 978-1415
Application address: 1900 Arlington Blvd., Ste. B, Charlottesville, VA 22903
Contact: Arthur A. Watson, Jr.

Established in 1996 in IL.
Donor(s): Arthur A. Watson, Jr.
Financial data (yr. ended 12/31/01): Grants paid, $54,000; assets, $107,219 (M); expenditures, $57,330; qualifying distributions, $55,504.
Limitations: Giving primarily in VA.
Officers and Directors:* Rachel L. Galbraith,* Pres.; Arthur A. Watson,* V.P.; Rebecca Galbraith.
EIN: 541835654

54636
Carneal-Drew Foundation
c/o Meade A. Spotts, V.P.
6061 River Rd.
Richmond, VA 23226
Contact: A.C. Spotts III, Pres.

Established in 1963.
Financial data (yr. ended 09/30/01): Grants paid, $53,940; assets, $1,044,764 (M); expenditures, $86,883; qualifying distributions, $53,940.
Limitations: Giving limited to VA.
Application information: Scholarship applicants must submit a resume of academic qualifications. Application form not required.
Officers: A.C. Spotts III, Pres. and Mgr.; Meade A. Spotts, V.P.; Courtland Spotts, Treas.
EIN: 546051095

54637
The Community Foundation of the New River Valley
P.O. Box 6009
Christiansburg, VA 24068
Contact: Andrew Morikawa, Exec. Dir.

Established in 1995 in VA.
Financial data (yr. ended 12/31/00): Grants paid, $53,564; assets, $793,708 (M); gifts received, $508,666; expenditures, $182,106.
Limitations: Giving primarily in VA.
Officers: Donald L. Michelson, Pres.; Stephen E. Wagner, V.P.; R.B. Crawford, Secy.; Marilyn Buhyhoff, Treas.; Andrew Morikawa, Exec. Dir.
EIN: 541740455
Codes: CM

54638
Peace, Love & Joy, Inc.
c/o Arman Simone
8511 Rogues Rd.
Warrenton, VA 20187-8347

Established in 1984 in CT.
Donor(s): Arman R. Simone.
Financial data (yr. ended 12/31/01): Grants paid, $53,314; assets, $214,455 (M); gifts received, $65,000; expenditures, $55,236; qualifying distributions, $53,314.
Limitations: Applications not accepted.
Application information: Contributes only to pre-selected organizations.
Officers: Arman R. Simone, Pres.; Louis G. Strasser, Treas.
EIN: 222559525

54639
The James W. Perkins Memorial Trust
c/o Payne, Gates, Farthing and Rodd, PC
999 Waterside Dr., Ste. 1515
Norfolk, VA 23510-3309 (757) 640-1500
Contact: C. Arthur Robinson II, Tr.

Established in 1990 in VA.
Donor(s): Mildred Perkins.‡
Financial data (yr. ended 12/31/00): Grants paid, $53,000; assets, $590,412 (M); expenditures, $75,296; qualifying distributions, $52,238.
Limitations: Giving primarily in VA.
Publications: Annual report.
Application information: Application form required.
Trustee: C. Arthur Robinson II.
EIN: 546271058
Codes: GTI

54640
Mary & Perry Thompson Educational Trust
c/o First Virginia Bank
P.O. Box 638
Fredericksburg, VA 22404
Application address: 1001 Princess Anne St., Fredericksburg, VA 22401
Contact: Michael J. Gannon, Trust Off., First Virginia Bank

Established in 1993.
Financial data (yr. ended 10/31/99): Grants paid, $53,000; assets, $1,135,440 (M); expenditures, $63,391; qualifying distributions, $52,652.
Limitations: Giving limited to residents of Fredericksburg, Spotsylvania and Stafford, VA.
Directors: Bruce D. Adkins, Nick Cadwallender, Sam C. Harding, Jr.
EIN: 546330780
Codes: GTI

54641
The Charles M. Caravati Foundation
931 Broad St. Rd.
Manakin Sabot, VA 23103
Contact: Charles Caravati, Jr., Tr.

Established in 1992 in VA.
Donor(s): Charles M. Caravati, Sr.,‡ Charles M. Caravati, Jr.
Financial data (yr. ended 03/31/02): Grants paid, $52,500; assets, $858,932 (M); gifts received, $54,551; expenditures, $54,798; qualifying distributions, $52,500.
Limitations: Giving primarily in VA.
Officer: Betty N. Caravati, Secy.-Treas.
Trustees: Charles Caravati, Jr., Charles M. Caravati III.
EIN: 546312421

54642
The Hausfeld Family Charitable Foundation
c/o Michael Hausfeld
9207 Coronado Terr.
Fairfax, VA 22031

Established in 2001 in VA.
Donor(s): Michael D. Hausfeld, Marilyn Hausfeld.
Financial data (yr. ended 12/31/01): Grants paid, $52,500; assets, $547,660 (M); gifts received,

54642—VIRGINIA

$600,000; expenditures, $52,500; qualifying distributions, $52,500.
Limitations: Applications not accepted. Giving primarily in Washington, DC.
Application information: Contributes only to pre-selected organizations.
Directors: Marilyn Hausfeld, Michael D. Hausfeld.
EIN: 311677290

54643
Evelyn E. & Richard J. Gunst Foundation
c/o Jerry Jenkins
5000 Monument Ave.
Richmond, VA 23230-0883

Established in 2000 in VA.
Donor(s): Richard J. Gunst.
Financial data (yr. ended 12/31/01): Grants paid, $52,200; assets, $968,560 (M); expenditures, $83,061; qualifying distributions, $52,200.
Limitations: Applications not accepted. Giving primarily in Richmond, VA.
Application information: Contributes only to pre-selected organizations.
Officers and Directors:* Richard J. Gunst,* Pres.; Janet D. Sheridan,* V.P.; Jerry W. Jenkins,* Secy.-Treas.
EIN: 541988873

54644
The Givens Foundation
1720 S. Military Hwy.
Chesapeake, VA 23320-2612
Contact: Edward J. Reed, Pres.

Established in 2000 in VA.
Donor(s): Edward J. Reed.
Financial data (yr. ended 12/31/01): Grants paid, $51,790; assets, $11,270 (M); expenditures, $51,815; qualifying distributions, $51,790.
Application information: Application form required.
Officers and Directors:* Edward J. Reed,* Pres.; Jeri G. Long,* V.P.; Janice G. Reed,* Secy.-Treas.
EIN: 542016468

54645
The Krumbein Foundation
c/o Ronald J. Norris, PC
4104 E. Parham Rd.
Richmond, VA 23228 (804) 672-8500

Established in 1981.
Donor(s): Charles Krumbein, Bruce Slater, Joyce Slater, Lee B. Krumbein, Michael M. Krumbein, Nathaniel Krumbein, Amy M. Krumbein, Susan Kornstein, Jane Keiser, Cynthia Krumbein.
Financial data (yr. ended 04/30/00): Grants paid, $51,300; assets, $438,032 (M); gifts received, $126,675; expenditures, $55,225; qualifying distributions, $51,300.
Limitations: Giving primarily in MA, NY, and VA.
Officers and Directors:* Amy M. Krumbein,* Pres.; Lee B. Krumbein,* V.P.; Michael M. Krumbein,* V.P.; Nathaniel Krumbein,* Secy.-Treas.; Jack Paul Fine, Malcolm Kalman, Jules Minter.
EIN: 541173621

54646
Hamilton Family Foundation Charitable Trust
5516 Falmouth St., Ste. 302
Richmond, VA 23230 (804) 285-7700
Contact: Helen H. Hamilton, Tr., or James C. Hamilton, Tr.

Established in 1996 in VA.
Financial data (yr. ended 12/31/01): Grants paid, $51,158; assets, $888,940 (M); gifts received, $343; expenditures, $53,338; qualifying distributions, $51,158.

Application information: Application form not required.
Trustees: Helen H. Hamilton, James C. Hamilton.
EIN: 546402636

54647
Mary Ratrie Wick Family Foundation
300 Virginia Ave.
Richmond, VA 23226 (804) 358-7452
Contact: Mary Ratrie Wick, Pres.

Established in 1997 in VA.
Donor(s): Mary Ratrie Wick.
Financial data (yr. ended 12/31/01): Grants paid, $51,026; assets, $775,288 (M); expenditures, $51,165; qualifying distributions, $51,026.
Limitations: Giving primarily in the Richmond, VA area.
Officers: Mary Ratrie Wick, Pres.; John H. Wick III, Secy.
EIN: 541850378

54648
The Dorothy-Ann Foundation
516 S. Henry St.
Williamsburg, VA 23185

Established in 1999 in VA.
Donor(s): Darwin O'Ryan Curtis, Darwin O'Ryan Curtis Charitable Lead Annunity Trust.
Financial data (yr. ended 12/31/01): Grants paid, $50,900; assets, $2,123,963 (M); gifts received, $179,789; expenditures, $112,041; qualifying distributions, $50,900.
Limitations: Applications not accepted. Giving primarily in Atlanta, GA.
Application information: Contributes only to pre-selected organizations.
Officers: Darwin O'Ryan Curtis, Pres.; Vernon M. Geddy, Jr., V.P.; Vernon M. Geddy III, Secy.-Treas.
EIN: 541965966

54649
Trub Family Foundation
c/o Aaron D. Trub
115 71st St.
Virginia Beach, VA 23451-2006

Established in 1998 in VA.
Donor(s): Sara Trub.
Financial data (yr. ended 12/31/01): Grants paid, $50,817; assets, $463,867 (M); expenditures, $57,178; qualifying distributions, $50,817.
Officers: Aaron D. Trub, Pres.; Sara R. Trub, Secy.-Treas.
EIN: 541922665

54650
The Irwin P. Edlavitch Foundation, Inc.
185 Chain Bridge Rd.
McLean, VA 22101

Established in 1998 in VA.
Financial data (yr. ended 12/31/01): Grants paid, $50,500; assets, $608,958 (M); expenditures, $56,452; qualifying distributions, $50,489.
Limitations: Applications not accepted. Giving primarily in Washington, DC, MD, and New York, NY.
Application information: Contributes only to pre-selected organizations.
Officers and Directors:* Irwin P. Edlavitch,* Pres.; Stefan F. Tucker,* Secy.; Stanley P. Snyder,* Treas.
EIN: 541907348

54651
Frederic Scott Bocock & Roberta Bryan Bocock Trust
P.O. Box 1575
Richmond, VA 23218 (804) 780-3273
Contact: Frederic S. Bocock, Tr.

Donor(s): Frederic S. Bocock, Roberta B. Bocock.
Financial data (yr. ended 12/31/01): Grants paid, $50,379; assets, $313,513 (M); gifts received, $20,000; expenditures, $55,606; qualifying distributions, $51,594.
Limitations: Giving primarily in VA.
Trustees: Frederic S. Bocock, Roberta B. Bocock.
EIN: 546051067

54652
The Claude Moore Charitable Foundation
P.O. Box 208
Oakton, VA 22124
Contact: Jesse B. Wilson III, Tr.

Established in 1987.
Donor(s): Claude Moore.‡
Financial data (yr. ended 12/31/99): Grants paid, $50,370; assets, $95,426,589 (M); expenditures, $536,850; qualifying distributions, $353,959; giving activities include $66,713 for program-related investments.
Limitations: Giving primarily in VA.
Application information: Application form not required.
Officer: J. Hamilton Lambert, Exec. Dir.
Trustees: Peter A. Arnston, Leigh B. Middleditch, Jr., Verlin W. Smith, Jesse B. Wilson III.
EIN: 521558571

54653
The Florence and Hyman Meyers Family Foundation
c/o Stanley H. Meyers
1606 Stoneycreek Dr.
Richmond, VA 23233

Established in 1995 in VA.
Donor(s): Hyman Meyers 1995 Charitable Lead Unitrust.
Financial data (yr. ended 12/31/00): Grants paid, $50,030; assets, $569,585 (M); gifts received, $229,946; expenditures, $50,995; qualifying distributions, $50,030.
Limitations: Applications not accepted. Giving on a national basis, with emphasis on the East Coast.
Application information: Contributes only to pre-selected organizations.
Officers and Directors:* Stanley H. Meyers,* Pres.; Janet S. Meyers,* Secy.; Donald C. Meyers, Janet M. Meyers, Prema M. Meyers, Mark A. Pollak.
EIN: 541738015

54654
Berni Family Charitable Foundation
7808 Preakness Ln.
Fairfax Station, VA 22039

Financial data (yr. ended 06/30/02): Grants paid, $50,000; assets, $272,762 (M); expenditures, $51,852; qualifying distributions, $50,000.
Limitations: Applications not accepted.
Application information: Contributes only to pre-selected organizations.
Trustees: John V. Adams, Mary B. Adams.
EIN: 541843093

54655
The Hitt Foundation, Inc.
2704 Dorr Ave.
Fairfax, VA 22031-4901

Established in 1999 in VA.

Donor(s): Myrtle Lee Hitt.
Financial data (yr. ended 12/31/01): Grants paid, $50,000; assets, $944,240 (M); expenditures, $69,437; qualifying distributions, $50,000.
Limitations: Applications not accepted.
Application information: Contributes only to pre-selected organizations.
Officers: Russell A. Hitt, Pres.; Brett R. Hitt, V.P.; James Millar, Secy.-Treas.
EIN: 541963708

54656
Marion Park Lewis Foundation for the Arts
P.O. Box 3300
Winchester, VA 22604-3300

Established in 1992 in VA.
Donor(s): Marion P. Lewis.
Financial data (yr. ended 12/31/01): Grants paid, $50,000; assets, $2,551,349 (M); gifts received, $2,596,631; expenditures, $54,448; qualifying distributions, $50,000.
Limitations: Applications not accepted. Giving limited to Winchester, VA.
Officers: Marion P. Lewis, Pres.; John P. Lewis, V.P.; David P. Lewis, Secy.; Howard P. Lewis, Treas.
EIN: 541620612

54657
Susan Lynde Phipps Foundation, Inc.
6045 Wilson Blvd
Arlington, VA 22205

Established in 2001.
Donor(s): Susan Lynde Duval Phipps.
Financial data (yr. ended 12/31/01): Grants paid, $50,000; assets, $907,341 (M); gifts received, $988,974; expenditures, $52,772; qualifying distributions, $50,000.
Limitations: Applications not accepted. Giving primarily in NY.
Application information: Contributes only to pre-selected organizations.
Officers: Susan Lynde Duval Phipps, Pres.; Claire Graham, V.P.; Daniel H. Duval, Secy.; Karen K. Duval, Treas.
EIN: 542015339

54658
The Evans-Gilruth Foundation
(also known as The Lew Evans Foundation)
7076 Glanamman Way
Warrenton, VA 20187-4171 (540) 341-4730
Contact: L.J. Evans, Jr., Dir.

Financial data (yr. ended 09/30/01): Grants paid, $49,983; assets, $78,076 (M); gifts received, $41,650; expenditures, $59,018; qualifying distributions, $55,482; giving activities include $5,499 for programs.
Limitations: Giving on a national basis.
Directors: John Carr, Philip Culbertson, L.J. Evans, Jr., Georgene Gilruth.
EIN: 521349405

54659
Richard & Shelley Birnbaum Family Foundation
10480 Cherokee Rd.
Richmond, VA 23235-1007

Established in 2000 in VA.
Donor(s): Richard S. Birnbaum, Shelley G. Birnbaum.
Financial data (yr. ended 12/31/01): Grants paid, $49,679; assets, $234,835 (M); gifts received, $170,678; expenditures, $51,029; qualifying distributions, $49,679.
Trustees: Richard S. Birnbaum, Shelley G. Birnbaum.
EIN: 546480217

54660
Charles B. Richardson Family Foundation
162 Old Forest Cir.
Winchester, VA 22602-6626
Contact: Charles B. Richardson, Pres. and Treas.

Established in 1999 in VA.
Donor(s): Elizabeth B. Richardson,‡ Charles B. Richardson.
Financial data (yr. ended 12/31/01): Grants paid, $49,427; assets, $914,823 (M); expenditures, $69,442; qualifying distributions, $49,427.
Limitations: Giving primarily in Urbana, VA.
Application information: Application form not required.
Officers: Charles B. Richardson, Pres. and Treas.; Margaret N. Richardson, Secy.
Directors: Anne K. Richardson, Thomas P. Richardson.
EIN: 541931421

54661
Alice D. & Frank J. Ix, Jr. Charitable Trust
1021 E. Cary St.
Richmond, VA 23219
Contact: Benjamin S. Bates Jr.

Financial data (yr. ended 12/31/01): Grants paid, $49,100; assets, $334,527 (M); expenditures, $54,150; qualifying distributions, $50,588.
Limitations: Giving primarily in NC, NJ, and VA.
Trustees: Frank J. Ix III, Jerome Ix, Wachovia Bank, N.A.
EIN: 546037882

54662
Inez Duff Bishop Charitable Trust
c/o Wachovia Bank, N.A.
1021 E. Cary St., 4th Fl.
Richmond, VA 23219
E-mail: karen.buchanan@wachovia.com
Contact: Karen N. Buchanan, V.P., Wachovia Bank, N.A.

Established in 1976.
Donor(s): Inez Duff Bishop.‡
Financial data (yr. ended 12/31/99): Grants paid, $48,700; assets, $2,033,245 (M); expenditures, $50,448; qualifying distributions, $50,448.
Limitations: Giving primarily in Charlottesville, VA.
Trustee: Wachovia Bank, N.A.
EIN: 546163110

54663
Herbert & Annie Carlton Foundation
7416 Forest Hill Ave.
Richmond, VA 23235-1528 (804) 272-3556
Contact: Z. Greene Hollowell, Jr., Treas.

Donor(s): Z. Greene Hollowell, Jr.
Financial data (yr. ended 08/31/01): Grants paid, $48,600; assets, $113,592 (M); gifts received, $9,684; expenditures, $51,772; qualifying distributions, $50,503.
Limitations: Giving primarily in the Richmond, VA, area.
Officers: Carolyn C. Hollowell, Pres.; Phillip C. Hollowell, V.P.; Martha A. Hollowell, Secy.; Z. Greene Hollowell, Jr., Treas. and Mgr.
EIN: 237092739

54664
All Saints' Scholarship Fund
999 Waterside Dr., Ste. 2200
Norfolk, VA 23510

Financial data (yr. ended 03/31/99): Grants paid, $48,550; assets, $1,395,533 (M); gifts received, $20,000; expenditures, $56,024; qualifying distributions, $48,550.

Limitations: Giving limited to Virginia Beach, VA.
Application information: Application form required.
Officer: Kim Short, Pres.
Director: Eric C. Hodeen.
EIN: 541643750

54665
Louis M. & Sally B. Kaplan Foundation
c/o Louis M. Kaplan
P.O. Box 3587
Alexandria, VA 22302-0587

Financial data (yr. ended 12/31/01): Grants paid, $48,416; assets, $426,394 (M); expenditures, $52,917; qualifying distributions, $48,416.
Limitations: Applications not accepted. Giving primarily in CO, Washington, DC, MD, and VA.
Application information: Contributes only to pre-selected organizations.
Trustees: Louis M. Kaplan, Sally B. Kaplan, Arthur Mason.
EIN: 521279681

54666
The Dr. Robert R. Bowen Foundation
P.O. Box 3011, Rivermont Sta.
Lynchburg, VA 24503-0011
Contact: C. Burton Gerhardt, Tr.

Established in 1994 in VA.
Donor(s): Robert Bowen.
Financial data (yr. ended 12/31/01): Grants paid, $48,400; assets, $969,556 (M); gifts received, $28,000; expenditures, $49,894; qualifying distributions, $48,400.
Limitations: Giving primarily in Lynchburg, VA.
Trustees: David L. Bowen, Rebecca P. Bowen, Robert R. Bowen, William P. Bowen, C. Burton Gerhardt.
EIN: 541738251

54667
Andrea Doudera Foundation
378 Claymont Dr.
Earlysville, VA 22936

Established in 2000 in VA.
Donor(s): Andrea D. Doudera.
Financial data (yr. ended 12/31/01): Grants paid, $48,400; assets, $50,095 (M); gifts received, $50,550; expenditures, $49,455; qualifying distributions, $48,400.
Limitations: Applications not accepted.
Application information: Contributes only to pre-selected organizations.
Officer and Director:* Andrea D. Doudera,* Pres.and Secy.
EIN: 541993169

54668
Neal J. Patten Foundation
12350 Jefferson Ave., Ste. 300
Newport News, VA 23602

Donor(s): Donald N. Patten.
Financial data (yr. ended 12/31/01): Grants paid, $47,950; assets, $955,895 (M); gifts received, $2,000; expenditures, $54,674; qualifying distributions, $47,950.
Limitations: Applications not accepted. Giving primarily in Newport News, VA.
Application information: Contributes only to pre-selected organizations.
Officers and Directors:* Donald J. Patten,* Pres.; Neal J. Patten,* V.P.; Martha H. Patten,* Secy.; Brooks Patten McElwain, Bradford N. Patten.
EIN: 546053958

IN THIS SECTION, WITHIN EACH STATE, FOUNDATIONS ARE LISTED IN DESCENDING ORDER BY TOTAL GRANTS PAID

54669
F. W. Johnston Foundation
c/o SunTrust Banks, Inc., Trust Tax Svcs.
P.O. Box 27385
Richmond, VA 23261-6665

Established in 1999 in VA.
Financial data (yr. ended 12/31/01): Grants paid, $47,828; assets, $1,773,294 (M); gifts received, $204; expenditures, $66,200; qualifying distributions, $48,611.
Limitations: Giving primarily in the Giles County and the Roanoke Valley areas of VA.
Application information: Application form not required.
Trustee: SunTrust Banks, Inc.
EIN: 546456401

54670
Harris Foundation
c/o H. Hiter Harris, III
6315 3 Chopt Rd.
Richmond, VA 23226

Established in 1997 in VA.
Donor(s): Elizabeth Harris, H. Hiter Harris, Jr., H. Hiter Harris III, Jil W. Harris.
Financial data (yr. ended 12/31/01): Grants paid, $47,500; assets, $358,489 (M); gifts received, $21,454; expenditures, $49,895; qualifying distributions, $47,500.
Limitations: Applications not accepted. Giving primarily in Richmond, VA.
Application information: Contributes only to pre-selected organizations.
Officers: H. Hiter Harris III, Pres.; Jil W. Harris, Secy.-Treas.
Director: Elizabeth T. Harris.
EIN: 541844579

54671
Berglund Foundation
1824 Williamson Rd., N.W.
Roanoke, VA 24012-5298 (540) 344-1461
Contact: R. Gene McGuire

Established in 1988 in VA.
Donor(s): Berglund Chevrolet, Inc.
Financial data (yr. ended 04/30/00): Grants paid, $47,428; assets, $556,661 (M); gifts received, $350,000; expenditures, $48,272; qualifying distributions, $47,428.
Limitations: Giving primarily in VA.
Officers: Bruce Farrell, Pres.; Anne Feazelle, Secy.
Director: Robert Harper.
EIN: 541475736

54672
The Kline Foundation
1028 Park Ave.
P.O. Box 1266
Norton, VA 24273-1014

Established in 1952.
Financial data (yr. ended 04/30/00): Grants paid, $46,500; assets, $975,031 (M); expenditures, $59,769; qualifying distributions, $46,500.
Limitations: Applications not accepted. Giving primarily in southwestern VA.
Application information: Contributes only to pre-selected organizations.
Officers: Harold E. Armsey, Pres.; John W. Litton, V.P.; M. Bardin Thrower, Jr., Secy.-Treas.
Trustees: George E. Culbertson, Glenn E. Teasley.
EIN: 546035703

54673
Logan III Charitable Fund
c/o McGuire, Woods, Battle & Bootlie, LLP
P.O. Box 397
Richmond, VA 23218-0397

Established in 1992 in VA.
Donor(s): Joseph D. Logan III, Laura B. Logan.
Financial data (yr. ended 12/31/01): Grants paid, $46,068; assets, $791,229 (M); expenditures, $48,079; qualifying distributions, $46,068.
Limitations: Applications not accepted. Giving primarily in VA.
Application information: Contributes only to pre-selected organizations.
Officers and Directors:* Joseph D. Logan III,* Pres.; Anna Clayton Logan,* V.P.; Laura B. Logan,* Secy.
EIN: 541646850

54674
The Barr Foundation
142 W. Olney Rd.
Norfolk, VA 23510
Contact: Clay H. Barr, Pres.

Established in 1996 in VA.
Donor(s): Clay H. Barr.
Financial data (yr. ended 06/30/02): Grants paid, $46,000; assets, $639,041 (M); gifts received, $50,120; expenditures, $59,521; qualifying distributions, $46,000.
Officer and Directors:* Clay H. Barr,* Pres.; Phillipa E. Barr, Elena B. Baum.
EIN: 311518708

54675
Public Safety Research Institute
2841 Woodlawn Ave.
Falls Church, VA 22042

Donor(s): Ralph Nader.
Financial data (yr. ended 12/31/99): Grants paid, $46,000; assets, $1,696,458 (M); gifts received, $46,221; expenditures, $48,063; qualifying distributions, $46,000.
Limitations: Applications not accepted. Giving on a national basis.
Application information: Contributes only to pre-selected organizations.
Directors: Ralph Nader, Diana Shaker, Edmund Shaker.
EIN: 520888196

54676
Vaughan Foundation
P.O. Box 1489
Galax, VA 24333
Application address: c/o Vaughan Furniture Co., Inc., 1 Railroad Ave., Galax, VA 24333, tel.: (703) 236-6111
Contact: John B. Vaughan, Pres.

Donor(s): Vaughan Furniture Co., Inc.
Financial data (yr. ended 09/30/01): Grants paid, $45,590; assets, $411,968 (M); gifts received, $50,000; expenditures, $46,816; qualifying distributions, $45,590.
Limitations: Giving primarily in VA.
Officers and Directors:* John B. Vaughan,* Pres.; T. George Vaughan,* Exec. V.P.; William B. Vaughan,* V.P.; Raymond L. Hall, Jr.,* Secy.
EIN: 541295313
Codes: CS, CD

54677
W. Howard & Lena E. Meador Charitable Trust
(Formerly Meador Charitable Trust)
305 Boulevard
Salem, VA 24153

Donor(s): James A. Meador.
Financial data (yr. ended 05/31/02): Grants paid, $45,500; assets, $768,982 (M); expenditures, $54,074; qualifying distributions, $45,500.
Limitations: Applications not accepted. Giving primarily in Moneta and Roanoke, VA.
Application information: Contributes only to pre-selected organizations.
Trustee: Smyth M. Meador.
EIN: 546132963

54678
Napolitano Family Foundation, Inc.
4425 Corporation Ln., Ste. 400
Virginia Beach, VA 23462-2903
(757) 490-3141
Contact: Frederick J. Napolitano, Mgr.

Donor(s): Frederick J. Napolitano.
Financial data (yr. ended 12/31/01): Grants paid, $45,345; assets, $459,177 (M); gifts received, $32,583; expenditures, $45,999; qualifying distributions, $45,345.
Limitations: Giving primarily in VA.
Officer and Trustee:* Frederick J. Napolitano,* Mgr.
EIN: 541310946

54679
Mabel H. Flory Charitable Trust
c/o First Virginia Bank
6400 Arlington Blvd., Plz. 1
Falls Church, VA 22042-2399 (703) 241-4843
Contact: Charles J. Conner, Jr.

Established in 1979 in VA.
Financial data (yr. ended 06/30/00): Grants paid, $45,267; assets, $869,413 (M); expenditures, $55,325; qualifying distributions, $44,472.
Limitations: Giving primarily in Washington, DC, and VA.
Trustee: First Virginia Bank.
EIN: 546207168

54680
The Randolph and Susan Reynolds Foundation
8605 River Rd.
Richmond, VA 23229-8301

Established in 2000 in VA.
Donor(s): Randolph N. Reynolds.
Financial data (yr. ended 12/31/01): Grants paid, $45,000; assets, $965,810 (M); expenditures, $70,437; qualifying distributions, $45,000.
Limitations: Applications not accepted.
Application information: Contributes only to pre-selected organizations.
Officers and Directors:* Randolph N. Reynolds,* Pres.; Susan Van Reypen Reynolds,* Secy.; Robert Gray Reynolds,* Treas.; Randolph N. Reynolds, Jr., William G. Reynolds, Jr.
EIN: 542015791

54681
The Neel Foundation
1157 Chain Bridge Rd.
McLean, VA 22101-2215 (703) 356-3866
Contact: Samuel E. Neel, Pres.

Donor(s): Samuel E. Neel, Mary W. Neel.
Financial data (yr. ended 12/31/01): Grants paid, $44,700; assets, $1,036,782 (M); gifts received, $99,400; expenditures, $48,256; qualifying distributions, $44,700.
Limitations: Giving on a national basis.

Officers and Directors:* Samuel E. Neel,* Pres.; Mary Neel West,* V.P.; James A. Neel,* Secy.; Mary W. Neel,* Treas.
EIN: 540761588

54682
Clark Scholarship Trust
(also known as Grace W. Clark, Thomas R. & Elsie T. Clark Scholarship Trust)
c/o Bank of America
P.O. Box 600
Lynchburg, VA 24505 (804) 528-2483
Contact: Bruce Love, V.P, Bank of America

Established in 1984 in VA.
Financial data (yr. ended 12/31/99): Grants paid, $44,500; assets, $2,038,327 (M); gifts received, $1,461; expenditures, $76,369; qualifying distributions, $46,604.
Limitations: Giving primarily to residents of Halifax County, VA.
Application information: Application form required.
Committee Members: Elodia Brade, Michaeleen Palmore.
Trustee: Bank of America.
EIN: 540907369
Codes: GTI

54683
KVA Foundation
1202 Pebbleton Ln.
Lynchburg, VA 24503
Contact: Kent Van Allen, Jr., Tr.

Established in 1997 in VA.
Donor(s): Kent Van Allen, Jr.
Financial data (yr. ended 01/31/02): Grants paid, $44,474; assets, $805,552 (M); expenditures, $46,925; qualifying distributions, $44,474.
Trustees: Katherine F. Van Allen, Kent Van Allen, Jr.
EIN: 541838819

54684
E. Polk Kellam Foundation, Inc.
P.O. Box 246
Belle Haven, VA 23306-0246
Contact: E. Polk Kellam, Jr., Treas.

Established in 1991 in VA.
Donor(s): Amine Cosby Kellam.
Financial data (yr. ended 06/30/01): Grants paid, $44,368; assets, $889,245 (M); expenditures, $45,366; qualifying distributions, $43,572.
Limitations: Giving limited to the Eastern Shore area of VA.
Officers: Amine C. Kellam, Pres.; Caramine K. Holcomb, Secy.; E. Polk Kellam, Jr., Treas.
EIN: 541605207

54685
Lolly Cohen Foundation, Inc.
P.O. Box 779
Virginia Beach, VA 23451
Contact: Myron J. Cohen, Pres.

Established in 1996 in VA.
Donor(s): Myron J. Cohen.
Financial data (yr. ended 06/30/01): Grants paid, $44,350; assets, $660,056 (M); gifts received, $47,796; expenditures, $49,874; qualifying distributions, $44,350.
Limitations: Giving primarily in VA.
Officers and Directors:* Myron J. Cohen,* Pres.; Betsy H. Cohen,* V.P.; James H. Cohen,* V.P.; Andrew Cohen,* Secy.
EIN: 311534603

54686
The Linhart Foundation
12050 W. Broad St.
Richmond, VA 23233
Contact: J. Theodore Linhart, Pres.

Donor(s): T. Lindemann.‡
Financial data (yr. ended 12/31/99): Grants paid, $44,067; assets, $1,272,050 (M); gifts received, $497,686; expenditures, $51,137; qualifying distributions, $44,067.
Limitations: Giving limited to Richmond, VA.
Officers: J. Theodore Linhart, Pres. and Secy.; Marilyn Moses, Treas.
Directors: C.F. Johnson, E.K. Johnson.
EIN: 540846082
Codes: GTI

54687
D. Baker Ames Charitable Foundation
c/o SunTrust Banks, Inc.
P.O. Box 27385
Richmond, VA 23261-7385
Application address: c/o Nancy Shumadine, Trust Off., SunTrust Banks, Inc., P.O. Box 2642, Norfolk, VA 23501, tel.: (757) 624-5524

Established in 1986 in VA.
Financial data (yr. ended 05/31/01): Grants paid, $43,800; assets, $769,379 (M); expenditures, $51,832; qualifying distributions, $43,800.
Limitations: Giving primarily in VA.
Trustees: Arthur D. Liles, Burke W. Margulies, SunTrust Banks, Inc.
EIN: 546034951
Codes: GTI

54688
L. & M. Meador Scholarship Trust
c/o Bank of America
P.O. Box 26606
Richmond, VA 23261-6606
Application address: c/o George Taylor, Bank of America, P.O. Box 14111, Roanoke, VA 24038, tel.: (540) 265-3174

Established in 1995.
Financial data (yr. ended 05/31/00): Grants paid, $43,462; assets, $1,448,973 (M); gifts received, $220; expenditures, $61,138; qualifying distributions, $47,160.
Limitations: Giving limited to residents of Norton, and Wise County, VA.
Application information: Application form required.
Trustee: Bank of America.
EIN: 546385104

54689
Jay and Maria Rappaport Foundation
12016 Sugarland Valley Dr.
Herndon, VA 20170 (703) 265-1989

Established in 1998 in CA.
Donor(s): Jay Rappaport, Maria Rappaport.
Financial data (yr. ended 12/31/01): Grants paid, $43,225; assets, $72,305 (M); expenditures, $43,265; qualifying distributions, $43,225.
Officer: Jay Rappaport, Pres.
EIN: 541924136

54690
Clarence L. Robey 1958 Trust
(Formerly Clarence L. Robey Foundation)
c/o First Virginia Bank, Trust Dept.
P.O. Box 27736
Richmond, VA 23261-7736
Application address: c/o Board of Directors, P.O. Box 181, Purcellville, VA 22132
Contact: A.M. Mike Peery, Vice-Chair.

Established in 1958 in VA.
Donor(s): Clarence L. Robey.‡
Financial data (yr. ended 12/31/99): Grants paid, $42,250; assets, $1,078,221 (M); expenditures, $51,325; qualifying distributions, $42,250.
Limitations: Giving primarily in Purcellville and Loudon County, VA.
Application information: Application form not required.
Officers and Directors:* Edward E. Nichols, Jr.,* Chair.; A.M. Mike Peery, Vice.-Chair.; Nancy Marsh, Margaret Vaughn, Arthur A. Welch, Doris L. Whitman.
EIN: 136047411

54691
The O'Keeffe Foundation
P.O. Box 675
Tazewell, VA 24651 (540) 988-6700

Established in 1997 in VA.
Donor(s): Virginia B. Gillespie.
Financial data (yr. ended 11/30/01): Grants paid, $42,000; assets, $846,527 (M); gifts received, $9,000; expenditures, $43,999; qualifying distributions, $42,000.
Trustees: George W. Williams, Kate G. Williams.
EIN: 541821108

54692
The Racoosin Family Foundation
c/o Mitchell Racoosin
6819 Elm St.
McLean, VA 22102

Established in 2000 in VA.
Donor(s): Harlene Racoosin, Marshall W. Racoosin Trust.
Financial data (yr. ended 12/31/01): Grants paid, $42,000; assets, $508,287 (M); gifts received, $60,953; expenditures, $45,572; qualifying distributions, $41,831.
Trustees: Kathy Racoosin, Mitchell Racoosin.
EIN: 527055720

54693
The Shepherd Foundation
739 Thimble Shoals Blvd., Ste. 704
Newport News, VA 23606

Established in 2000 in VA.
Financial data (yr. ended 12/31/00): Grants paid, $42,000; assets, $1,694,407 (M); gifts received, $625,690; expenditures, $91,095; qualifying distributions, $75,947.
Limitations: Applications not accepted. Giving primarily in VA.
Application information: Contributes only to pre-selected organizations.
Trustee: Stephen J. Matteucci.
EIN: 546455383

54694
The Rosenthal Foundation
(Formerly Samuel & Gilbert Rosenthal Foundation)
P.O. Box 6813
Richmond, VA 23230 (804) 359-3995
Contact: Gilbert M. Rosenthal, Pres.

Established in 1957 in VA.

54694—VIRGINIA

Donor(s): Standard Drug Co., Fanny S. Rosenthal.
Financial data (yr. ended 12/31/01): Grants paid, $41,500; assets, $704,928 (M); expenditures, $43,132; qualifying distributions, $41,500.
Limitations: Giving primarily in Richmond, VA.
Officers: Gilbert M. Rosenthal, Pres.; Jerry S. Rosenthal, V.P.; Thomas G. Rosenthal, V.P.; Fanny S. Rosenthal, Secy.-Treas.
EIN: 546037143

54695
J. Harvie Wilkinson, Jr. Charitable Foundation Trust
c/o SunTrust Banks, Inc.
P.O. Box 27385
Richmond, VA 23261-7385
Application address: 78 Westham Green, 300 Ridge Rd., Richmond, VA 23229
Contact: Letitia N. Wilkinson, Tr.

Financial data (yr. ended 12/31/01): Grants paid, $41,500; assets, $712,332 (M); expenditures, $49,608; qualifying distributions, $41,500.
Limitations: Giving primarily in Richmond, VA.
Trustees: Letitia N. Wilkinson, SunTrust Banks, Inc.
EIN: 546041350

54696
The Bob and Barbara Williams Foundation
2551 River Rd. W.
Maidens, VA 23102-2605 (804) 775-1809

Established in 1996 in VA.
Donor(s): Barbara Jane Drexel Williams, Robert C. Williams.
Financial data (yr. ended 12/31/01): Grants paid, $41,324; assets, $275,791 (M); expenditures, $43,419; qualifying distributions, $41,324.
Limitations: Giving primarily in Oxford, OH and VA.
Officers: Robert C. Williams, Pres. and Treas.; Elizabeth Slone Schneider, V.P.; Barbara Jane Drexel Williams, V.P.
EIN: 541826822

54697
The Rashkind Family Foundation
4529 E. Honey Grove Rd., Ste. 307
Virginia Beach, VA 23455-6087

Established in 1987 in VA.
Donor(s): Alan B. Rashkind, Michael P. Rashkind, Lisbeth R. Hartzell, Julian Rashkind, Eleanor B. Rashkind.
Financial data (yr. ended 12/31/01): Grants paid, $41,300; assets, $805,405 (M); gifts received, $50,000; expenditures, $45,473; qualifying distributions, $41,300.
Limitations: Applications not accepted. Giving primarily in MA and VA.
Application information: Contributes only to pre-selected organizations.
Officers: Eleanor B. Rashkind,* Pres.; Alan B. Rashkind,* V.P.; Michael P. Rashkind,* V.P.; Julian Rashkind,* Secy.
EIN: 541449316

54698
The Richard J. Dwyer, Jr. & Mary B. Dwyer Charitable Foundation Trust
c/o Richard J. Dwyer, Jr.
1615 N. Frost St.
Alexandria, VA 22304

Established in 1996 in VA.
Donor(s): Mary B. Dwyer, Richard J. Dwyer, Jr.
Financial data (yr. ended 06/30/02): Grants paid, $41,000; assets, $116,607 (M); gifts received, $60,000; expenditures, $41,921; qualifying distributions, $41,000.

Limitations: Applications not accepted. Giving primarily in VA.
Application information: Contributes only to pre-selected organizations.
Trustees: Mary B. Dwyer, Paul B. Dwyer, Richard J. Dwyer, Jr., Thomas A. Dwyer, Nancy D. McKenzie.
EIN: 541815672

54699
The George and Judith Handjinicolaou Foundation
1598 Maddux Ln.
McLean, VA 22101

Donor(s): George Handjinicolaou, Judith Handjinicolaou.
Financial data (yr. ended 09/30/01): Grants paid, $41,000; assets, $171,364 (M); gifts received, $65,000; expenditures, $43,447; qualifying distributions, $41,000.
Limitations: Applications not accepted.
Application information: Contributes only to pre-selected organizations.
Trustees: George Handjinicolaou, Judith Handjinicolaou.
EIN: 541965291

54700
St. Paul's Church Home
c/o St. Paul's Episcopal Church
815 E. Grace St.
Richmond, VA 23219

Established in 1861 in VA.
Financial data (yr. ended 12/31/01): Grants paid, $40,944; assets, $1,200,191 (M); expenditures, $44,029; qualifying distributions, $43,069.
Limitations: Giving limited to the metropolitan Richmond, VA, area.
Publications: Application guidelines.
Application information: Application form required.
Officers and Directors:* Mary Ann Ready,* Pres.; Stephen C. Micas,* Secy.; Carol McCoy,* Treas.
EIN: 546048630
Codes: GTI

54701
Jane & Gunby Treakle Charitable & Educational Foundation, Inc.
P.O. Box 420
Irvington, VA 22480-0420
Application address: c/o Director, P.O. Box 1419, Kilmarnock, VA 22482

Established in 1978 in VA.
Donor(s): H. Jane Treakle.‡
Financial data (yr. ended 11/30/01): Grants paid, $40,750; assets, $1,006,450 (M); expenditures, $66,828; qualifying distributions, $60,099.
Limitations: Giving primarily in VA.
Application information: Application form required.
Officer: R. Frederick Baensch, Pres.
Director: John A. Christopher.
EIN: 510215563
Codes: GTI

54702
Watterson Foundation
c/o John S. Watterson, III
1326 Pendleton Ct.
Charlottesville, VA 22901

Financial data (yr. ended 12/31/01): Grants paid, $40,700; assets, $850,344 (M); expenditures, $44,709; qualifying distributions, $40,700.
Limitations: Applications not accepted. Giving primarily in OH and VA.

Application information: Contributes only to pre-selected organizations.
Officers and Directors:* Wayt T. Watterson,* Pres.; John S. Watterson III,* V.P.; Stuart G. Watterson,* Secy.-Treas.
EIN: 346520026

54703
The Luminescence Foundation, Inc.
c/o Samuel B. Gunter
5 N. Hamilton St.
Middleburg, VA 20117

Established in 2000 in DE.
Donor(s): Zohar Ben-Dov.
Financial data (yr. ended 12/31/01): Grants paid, $40,500; assets, $774,446 (M); gifts received, $238,500; expenditures, $66,382; qualifying distributions, $40,500.
Limitations: Applications not accepted. Giving on an international basis, primarily in Kenya; giving also in NY and VA.
Application information: Contributes only to pre-selected organizations.
Officers and Directors:* Zohar Ben-Dov,* Pres.; Lisa Ben-Dov,* V.P.; Samuel B. Gunter, Secy.-Treas.; Ariella Ben-Dov, Tamar Ben-Dov Brufsky.
EIN: 541989253

54704
Community Foundation of the Rappahannock River Region, Inc.
P.O. Box 208
Fredericksburg, VA 22404

Financial data (yr. ended 06/30/00): Grants paid, $40,415; assets, $1,260,355 (M); gifts received, $1,129,563; expenditures, $131,082.
Officers: Homer Hite, Pres.; Keith L. Wampler, Pres.-Elect.; Beverly G. King, Secy.; William J. Kinnamon, Treas.
Directors: G. William Beale, Gerald A. Bellotti, Ronald W. Branscome, and 17 additional directors.
EIN: 541843987
Codes: CM

54705
The Layman Family Foundation
(Formerly Roanoke & Botetourt Telephone Foundation)
1000 Roanoke Rd.
P.O. Box 174
Daleville, VA 24083 (540) 992-2211
Contact: J. Allen Layman, Secy.-Treas.

Established in 1990 in VA; founded as Roanoke & Botetourt Telephone Foundation.
Donor(s): Roanoke & Botetourt Telephone Co., R&B Communications Foundation, Inc., The Layman Family Foundation.
Financial data (yr. ended 12/31/01): Grants paid, $40,196; assets, $686,271 (M); expenditures, $43,360; qualifying distributions, $40,045.
Limitations: Giving limited to Botetourt County, VA.
Application information: Application form not required.
Officers: Ira D. Layman, Pres.; J. Allen Layman, Secy.-Treas.
EIN: 541556638
Codes: CS, CD

54706
Scott & Stringfellow Educational Foundation
P.O. Box 1575
Richmond, VA 23218-1575
Contact: Bradley H. Gunter, Secy.

Established in 1993 in VA.

Donor(s): Scott & Stringfellow, Inc., Peter R. Kellogg.
Financial data (yr. ended 12/31/00): Grants paid, $40,050; assets, $1,320,131 (M); gifts received, $60,000; expenditures, $42,450; qualifying distributions, $40,050.
Limitations: Giving primarily in areas of company operations.
Publications: Informational brochure.
Application information: Application form required.
Officers and Directors:* Frederic S. Bocock,* Pres.; Robert F. Allen,* V.P.; Franklin B. Heiner,* V.P.; Bradley H. Gunter,* Secy.; Mike D. Johnston,* Treas.; Steven C. Delaney, Charles E. Mintz.
EIN: 541669283
Codes: CS, CD, GTI

54707
Educational and Benevolent Foundation of Peoples Mutual
c/o The Virginia Baptist Fdn.
P.O. Box 17035
Richmond, VA 23226

Established in 1995 in VA.
Donor(s): Peoples Mutual Telephone Co.
Financial data (yr. ended 12/31/01): Grants paid, $40,000; assets, $685,595 (M); gifts received, $173; expenditures, $46,220; qualifying distributions, $39,791.
Limitations: Giving limited to Danville and Richmond, VA.
Trustee: Virginia Baptist Foundation.
EIN: 541779633
Codes: CS, CD

54708
The Penrod Foundation
2809 S. Lynnhaven Rd., Ste. 350
Virginia Beach, VA 23452

Established in 1999 in VA.
Financial data (yr. ended 12/31/01): Grants paid, $40,000; assets, $22,572 (M); expenditures, $40,078; qualifying distributions, $40,000.
Limitations: Applications not accepted.
Application information: Contributes only to pre-selected organizations.
Trustees: E.A. Heidt, Sr., E.A. Heidt, Jr., Carl Gade, Louis LaGasse.
EIN: 541969024

54709
James P. & Frankie C. Carpenter Foundation
c/o Hantzmon, Wiebel & Co.
P.O. Box 1408
Charlottesville, VA 22902-1408

Established in 1997 in VA.
Donor(s): Frankie C. Carpenter.‡
Financial data (yr. ended 12/31/01): Grants paid, $39,500; assets, $861,194 (M); expenditures, $47,700; qualifying distributions, $39,500.
Limitations: Applications not accepted.
Application information: Contributes only to pre-selected organizations.
Directors and Trustees: Henry D. Aylor, J. Howard Carpenter, Edward L. Dean, Jeffrey C. Early, Michael D. Hale.
EIN: 541613842

54710
The Frederick and Elizabeth Singer Foundation
674 Ad Hoc Rd.
Great Falls, VA 22066

Donor(s): Frederick G.I. Singer, Elizabeth A. Singer.
Financial data (yr. ended 06/30/02): Grants paid, $39,193; assets, $939 (M); expenditures, $40,338; qualifying distributions, $39,193.
Limitations: Applications not accepted.
Application information: Contributes only to pre-selected organizations.
Trustee: Elizabeth A. Singer.
EIN: 541935247

54711
Mary Louise Old Andrews Trust
c/o Bank of America
P.O. Box 26606
Richmond, VA 23261-6606

Established in 1989 in VA by court order.
Donor(s): Mary Louise Old Andrews.
Financial data (yr. ended 01/31/01): Grants paid, $38,868; assets, $1,493,219 (M); expenditures, $50,889; qualifying distributions, $42,950.
Limitations: Applications not accepted. Giving limited to VA.
Application information: Contributes only to pre-selected organizations.
Trustee: Bank of America.
EIN: 546276317

54712
The Wilkerson Family Charitable Trust
c/o Virginia Baptist Foundation
P.O. Box 17035
Richmond, VA 23226

Established in 1998 in VA.
Financial data (yr. ended 12/31/01): Grants paid, $38,771; assets, $918,143 (M); gifts received, $163; expenditures, $46,844; qualifying distributions, $38,771.
Trustee: Virginia Baptist Foundation.
EIN: 541900342

54713
Tidewater Research Foundation, Inc.
c/o Edward M. Holland
P.O. Box 985
Arlington, VA 22216-0985

Donor(s): Edwin T. Holland, Edward M. Holland.
Financial data (yr. ended 06/30/02): Grants paid, $38,506; assets, $162,738 (M); expenditures, $53,829; qualifying distributions, $38,506.
Limitations: Applications not accepted. Giving primarily in VA.
Application information: Contributes only to pre-selected organizations.
Officers: Virginia M. Beeton, V.P.; Edward M. Holland, Secy. and Mgr.
EIN: 237038968

54714
Virgil L. Frantz Charitable Trust
P.O. Box 18174
Roanoke, VA 24014-0812

Established in 1979 in VA.
Donor(s): Virgil L. Frantz.‡
Financial data (yr. ended 12/31/01): Grants paid, $38,400; assets, $91,442 (M); expenditures, $41,450; qualifying distributions, $41,060.
Limitations: Applications not accepted. Giving primarily in VA.
Application information: Contributes only to pre-selected organizations.
Trustees: Wanda Frantz Elliott, J. Bouldin Frantz, Alexander I. Saunders.
EIN: 510233131

54715
Notes Family Foundation, Inc.
c/o Joel Notes
77 Eagle Point Rd.
Lancaster, VA 22503-2451

Established in 1999 in VA.
Donor(s): Joel Notes, Wanda Notes.
Financial data (yr. ended 12/31/01): Grants paid, $38,008; assets, $91,212 (M); expenditures, $40,730; qualifying distributions, $38,008.
Limitations: Applications not accepted. Giving primarily in VA.
Application information: Contributes only to pre-selected organizations.
Officers: Joel Notes, Pres.; Wanda Notes, Secy.
EIN: 541967341

54716
Sanjiv and Cindy T. Kaul Foundation
2020 Wingfield Rd.
Charlottesville, VA 22901

Established in 1998 in VA.
Financial data (yr. ended 12/31/01): Grants paid, $38,000; assets, $538,479 (M); gifts received, $90,500; expenditures, $43,960; qualifying distributions, $38,000.
Limitations: Applications not accepted.
Application information: Contributes only to pre-selected organizations.
Directors: Cindy T. Kaul, Sanjiv Kaul.
EIN: 541908216

54717
Neal and Jane Freeman Foundation, Inc.
P.O. Box 2169
Vienna, VA 22183-2169

Established in 1990 in DE and NY.
Donor(s): Neal B. Freeman, Jane Freeman.
Financial data (yr. ended 11/30/01): Grants paid, $37,500; assets, $663,957 (M); gifts received, $100,000; expenditures, $38,048; qualifying distributions, $37,071.
Limitations: Applications not accepted. Giving on a national basis, with emphasis on Washington, DC, and VA.
Application information: Contributes only to pre-selected organizations.
Officers: Neal B. Freeman, Pres.; Jane Freeman, Secy.-Treas.
Director: James B. Freeman.
EIN: 133603615

54718
Spartan Foundation
P.O. Box 14125
Roanoke, VA 24038-4125

Established in 1999 in VA.
Donor(s): J. McBroom.
Financial data (yr. ended 12/31/01): Grants paid, $37,374; assets, $84,002 (M); expenditures, $40,336; qualifying distributions, $37,374.
Officers: William A. Nash, Pres.; Lucille M. Saunders, Secy.; Alexander I. Saunders, Treas.
Director: Ronald Deneweth.
EIN: 541947173

54719
AMB Foundation
P.O. Box 710695
Herndon, VA 20170-0695
E-mail: ambfoundation@aol.com
Contact: Anne J. Wells, Pres.

Established in 1998 in IL.
Donor(s): Anne J. Wells.

54719—VIRGINIA

Financial data (yr. ended 12/31/99): Grants paid, $37,200; assets, $1,077,782 (M); expenditures, $39,592; qualifying distributions, $39,140.
Limitations: Giving on a national basis.
Officers and Directors:* Anne J. Wells,* Pres.; Theodore E. Wells,* V.P.; Marie W. Sloane,* Secy.-Treas.; Finbarr C. Sloane.
EIN: 364188235

54720
The J. & E. Berkley Foundation
P.O. Box 425
Ivy, VA 22945

Established in 2000 in VA.
Donor(s): Jean B. Baum.
Financial data (yr. ended 09/30/01): Grants paid, $37,200; assets, $893,761 (M); expenditures, $60,611; qualifying distributions, $37,200.
Limitations: Giving primarily in VA.
Officers: Jean B. Baum, Pres.; Lawrence J. Martin, Secy.-Treas.
EIN: 541978980

54721
Boyd Foundation
P.O. Box 64458
Virginia Beach, VA 23464

Financial data (yr. ended 12/31/01): Grants paid, $37,100; assets, $715,751 (M); gifts received, $2,293; expenditures, $45,744; qualifying distributions, $37,100.
Limitations: Applications not accepted. Giving primarily in Virginia Beach, VA.
Application information: Contributes only to pre-selected organizations.
Officers and Directors:* Joseph W. Boyd,* Pres.; Joseph W. Boyd, Jr.,* V.P.
EIN: 521344225

54722
Augusta Schultz Grubbs Charitable Trust
P.O. Drawer 635
Clifton Forge, VA 24422-0635
Application address: c/o Scholarship Comm., Alleghany High School, 1 Mountaineer Dr., Covington, VA 24426

Established in 1999 in VA.
Financial data (yr. ended 05/31/00): Grants paid, $37,000; assets, $1,472,387 (M); expenditures, $68,614; qualifying distributions, $147,270.
Limitations: Giving limited to residents of Alleghany, VA.
Trustee: James D. Snyder.
EIN: 541902317

54723
Standish Family Foundation
P.O. Box 1408
Charlottesville, VA 22902-1408
(804) 296-2156
Contact: L. Peyton Humphrey, Dir.

Established in 1997 in VA.
Donor(s): Joan M. Standish, Robert N. Standish.
Financial data (yr. ended 12/31/01): Grants paid, $37,000; assets, $666,992 (M); expenditures, $41,615; qualifying distributions, $37,000.
Officers and Directors:* Joan M. Standish,* Pres.; Robert N. Standish,* V.P.; Elizabeth S. Sackson, Secy.-Treas.; L.P. Humphrey.
EIN: 541877545

54724
The Cors Foundation
8300 Arlington Blvd., Ste. G-2
Fairfax, VA 22031
Application address: 7413 Georgetown Ct., McLean, VA 22102, tel.: (703) 827-0735

Donor(s): Allan D. Cors, Darleen Cors.
Financial data (yr. ended 12/31/01): Grants paid, $36,675; assets, $1,146,671 (M); expenditures, $53,609; qualifying distributions, $36,593.
Limitations: Giving primarily in Washington, DC and VA.
Officers and Directors:* Allan D. Cors,* Pres. and Treas.; Darleen Cors,* V.P. and Secy.; Brian G. Cors, Darcy S. Cors, Amy E. Flinn.
EIN: 541965260

54725
The George R. & Evelyn W. Brothers Trust
c/o Bank of America
P.O. Box 26606
Richmond, VA 23261-6903
Application address: c/o Bank of America, P.O. Box 26903, Richmond, VA 23261, tel.: (804) 788-2883
Contact: Charles C. Conway, Trust Off., Bank of America

Financial data (yr. ended 12/31/99): Grants paid, $36,665; assets, $461,536 (M); gifts received, $206; expenditures, $37,436; qualifying distributions, $36,665.
Limitations: Giving on a national basis, with emphasis on the East Coast.
Trustee: Bank of America.
EIN: 546031003

54726
Trolinger Trust
c/o SunTrust Banks, Inc.
P.O. Box 27385
Richmond, VA 23261
Application address: P.O. Box 3064, 1st St. Stn., Radford, VA 24141
Contact: John I. Barton, Chair.

Established in 1971.
Financial data (yr. ended 06/30/00): Grants paid, $36,616; assets, $2,179,390 (M); expenditures, $63,859; qualifying distributions, $39,828.
Limitations: Giving limited to Montgomery County, Radford, and other southwestern VA counties and cities.
Officer and Advisory Board Members:* John I. Barton,* Chair. and Secy.; Kermit L. Grim, H.M. Harvey, H.H. Shelburne, David A. Young.
Trustee: SunTrust Banks, Inc.
EIN: 546110451
Codes: GTI

54727
Cyrus Katzen Foundation, Inc.
P.O. Box 1040
Baileys Crossroads, VA 22041-0040
Contact: Cyrus Katzen, Tr.

Established in 1991 in MD.
Donor(s): Cyrus Katzen.
Financial data (yr. ended 11/30/01): Grants paid, $36,500; assets, $2,891,214 (M); gifts received, $560,000; expenditures, $39,352; qualifying distributions, $36,500.
Limitations: Giving primarily in Washington, DC.
Trustee: Cyrus Katzen.
EIN: 521756979

54728
The Marshall Miller Foundation
No. 6 Windsor Cir. Dr.
Bluefield, VA 24605-9685 (540) 322-4485
Contact: Marshall S. Miller, Tr.

Established in 1996 in VA.
Donor(s): Marshall S. Miller.
Financial data (yr. ended 06/30/02): Grants paid, $36,200; assets, $546,772 (M); expenditures, $41,648; qualifying distributions, $36,200.
Limitations: Giving primarily in WV.
Application information: Application form not required.
Trustees: Marshall S. Miller, Sharon H. Miller, Tracy M. Paine.
EIN: 541829427

54729
The William & Catherine Owens Foundation, Inc.
c/o Dexter Rumsey
P.O. Box 720
Irvington, VA 22480-0720

Donor(s): William F. Owens.
Financial data (yr. ended 06/30/02): Grants paid, $36,000; assets, $743,360 (M); expenditures, $46,676; qualifying distributions, $36,000.
Limitations: Applications not accepted. Giving primarily in VA.
Application information: Contributes only to pre-selected organizations.
Officers and Directors:* Dexter Rumsey,* Pres.; Sturie Sigfred,* V.P.; Ralph Weil,* Secy.-Treas.
EIN: 526036018

54730
Richard T. Liebhaber and Kirsten E. Liebhaber Family Foundation, Inc.
P.O. Box 8210
McLean, VA 22106-8210

Established in 1997 VA.
Financial data (yr. ended 12/31/01): Grants paid, $35,640; assets, $111,240 (M); expenditures, $40,165; qualifying distributions, $35,640.
Directors: Kirsten E. Liebhaber, Richard L. Liebhaber, Richard T. Liebhaber.
EIN: 541825174

54731
The Brown Foundation
2620 E. Gretna Rd.
Gretna, VA 24557 (804) 656-2528
Contact: Richard K. Brown, Tr.

Established in 2000 in VA.
Donor(s): Richard K. Brown, Ann F. Brown.
Financial data (yr. ended 12/31/01): Grants paid, $35,250; assets, $992,596 (M); gifts received, $150,000; expenditures, $39,790; qualifying distributions, $35,250.
Application information: Application form not required.
Trustees: Ann F. Brown, Richard K. Brown.
EIN: 316653585

54732
Nachman-Marks Foundation
9130 W. Broad St.
P.O. Box 5264
Richmond, VA 23294-5264 (804) 527-1515
Contact: Lawrence L. Nachman, Pres.

Established in 1989 in VA.
Donor(s): Rosalie Nachman.
Financial data (yr. ended 09/30/01): Grants paid, $35,101; assets, $287,218 (M); expenditures, $37,751; qualifying distributions, $35,101.
Limitations: Giving primarily in Richmond, VA.

Application information: Application form not required.
Officers: Lawrence L. Nachman, Pres.; Rosalie Nachman, V.P.
EIN: 541515951

54733
Rona M. & Erwin B. Drucker Charitable Trust, Inc.
301 Hiden Blvd.
Newport News, VA 23606

Established in 2000 in VA.
Donor(s): Erwin A. Drucker.
Financial data (yr. ended 12/31/01): Grants paid, $35,095; assets, $191,140 (M); gifts received, $82,000; expenditures, $36,870; qualifying distributions, $35,095.
Limitations: Applications not accepted. Giving primarily in VA.
Application information: Contributes only to pre-selected organizations.
Officers and Directors:* Erwin B. Drucker,* Pres.; David E.M. Drucker,* V.P.; Wendy C. Drucker,* V.P.
EIN: 541977954

54734
Florence S. Patton Foundation
P.O. Box 35792
Richmond, VA 23235-0792

Financial data (yr. ended 12/31/01): Grants paid, $35,030; assets, $736,304 (M); expenditures, $37,666; qualifying distributions, $35,030.
Limitations: Applications not accepted. Giving primarily in Erie, PA, and Richmond, VA.
Application information: Contributes only to pre-selected organizations.
Trustees: Franklin S. Patton, John S. Patton.
EIN: 256063741

54735
Charles C. Skinner & Ruth H. Skinner Memorial Trust
125 St. Paul's Blvd., Ste. 600
Norfolk, VA 23510 (757) 640-7535
Contact: James B. Covington, Tr.

Established in 1985 in VA.
Donor(s): Charles C. Skinner.‡
Financial data (yr. ended 08/31/01): Grants paid, $35,021; assets, $950,330 (M); expenditures, $51,991; qualifying distributions, $41,296.
Limitations: Giving limited to VA.
Trustees: James B. Covington, Melvin R. Green, Paul B. Watlington.
EIN: 546228993

54736
B.D.H. Foundation
c/o Robert L. Hintz
10002 Walsham Ct.
Richmond, VA 23233

Established in 1986 in VA.
Donor(s): Robert L. Hintz.
Financial data (yr. ended 12/31/00): Grants paid, $35,000; assets, $765,576 (M); gifts received, $15,000; expenditures, $42,401; qualifying distributions, $35,048.
Limitations: Applications not accepted. Giving limited to Richmond, VA.
Application information: Contributes only to pre-selected organizations.
Trustees: P. Michael Giftos, Gloria M. Hintz, Robert L. Hintz.
EIN: 546244738

54737
Margaret Spilman Bowden Foundation
c/o South Pickett Farm
P.O. Box 166
Warrenton, VA 20188 (540) 347-1376
Contact: Maximilian A. Tufts, Jr., V.P.

Established in 1993 in VA.
Donor(s): Margaret S. Bowden.
Financial data (yr. ended 12/31/00): Grants paid, $35,000; assets, $659,923 (M); expenditures, $43,979; qualifying distributions, $34,613.
Limitations: Giving primarily in Warrenton, VA.
Officers: Sally S. Tufts, Pres.; Maximilian A. Tufts, Jr., V.P.; Elizabeth W. Gookin, Secy.
EIN: 541685754

54738
Charles Fund, Inc.
c/o Bank of America
P.O. Box 26606
Richmond, VA 23261-6606
Application address: c/o Mr. Richmond, Jr., Richmond and Fishburne, P.O. Box 559, Charlottesville, VA 22902, tel.: (804) 977-8590

Donor(s): Edward C. Eisenhart.
Financial data (yr. ended 12/31/99): Grants paid, $35,000; assets, $1,045,863 (M); expenditures, $56,756; qualifying distributions, $35,000.
Limitations: Giving primarily in Charlottesville, VA, and Rochester, NY.
Application information: Application form not required.
Officers and Directors:* Edward C. Eisenhart,* Pres. and Treas.; Richard H. Eisenhart,* V.P. and Secy.; Sarah A. Eisenhart,* V.P.; Mrs. William H. Morris.
EIN: 168064401

54739
The W. C. English Scholarship Foundation
P.O. Box P7000
Lynchburg, VA 24505-7000

Established in 1993 in VA.
Financial data (yr. ended 12/31/01): Grants paid, $35,000; assets, $411,057 (M); expenditures, $26,658; qualifying distributions, $35,104.
Limitations: Giving limited to residents of VA.
Application information: Application form required.
Officers and Directors:* A. Douglas Dalton, Jr.,* Pres.; Beverly E. Dalton,* Secy.-Treas.
EIN: 541658362
Codes: GTI

54740
The Felucca Fund
(Formerly The Elizabeth Ballantine and Paul Leavitt Foundation)
1113 Basil Rd.
McLean, VA 22101-1803

Established in 1999 in DE.
Financial data (yr. ended 12/31/01): Grants paid, $35,000; assets, $274,457 (M); gifts received, $111,882; expenditures, $36,402; qualifying distributions, $35,000.
Officers: Elizabeth Ballantine, Pres.; Paul Leavitt, Secy.-Treas.
EIN: 541903806

54741
Romans Twelve
3614 Oval Dr.
Alexandria, VA 22305-1148

Donor(s): C. Eugene Steuerle, Norma L. Steuerle.
Financial data (yr. ended 11/30/01): Grants paid, $35,000; assets, $766,515 (M); gifts received, $75,000; expenditures, $38,473; qualifying distributions, $35,000.
Limitations: Applications not accepted. Giving primarily in Alexandria, VA.
Application information: Contributes only to pre-selected organizations.
Officers: Norma L. Steuerle, Pres.; Frederick T. Pusarelli, V.P.; C. Eugene Steuerle, Secy.-Treas.
EIN: 541215697

54742
The Frazier Foundation
10702 Perrin Cir.
Spotsylvania, VA 22553

Established in 2000.
Donor(s): Gary W. Frazier.
Financial data (yr. ended 06/30/01): Grants paid, $34,750; assets, $1,229,503 (M); gifts received, $125,072; expenditures, $37,986; qualifying distributions, $34,750.
Limitations: Applications not accepted.
Application information: Contributes only to pre-selected organizations.
Officer: Gary W. Frazier, Pres.
EIN: 541993898

54743
Lonza L. Rush Testamentary Trust
(Formerly R. Roy Rush Trust)
c/o SunTrust Banks, Inc.
P.O. Box 27385
Richmond, VA 23261
Application address: c/o Carolyn McCoy, SunTrust Banks, Inc., P.O. Box 13888, Roanoke, VA 24018, tel.: (540) 982-3014

Established in 1987 in VA.
Donor(s): R. Roy Rush.‡
Financial data (yr. ended 02/28/02): Grants paid, $34,500; assets, $1,073,177 (M); expenditures, $43,901; qualifying distributions, $34,543.
Limitations: Giving limited to residents of VA.
Trustee: SunTrust Banks, Inc.
EIN: 546138578

54744
The Carol M. and Charles G. Thalhimer, Jr. Foundation
23 Ampthill Rd.
Richmond, VA 23226-2232

Established in 1999 in VA.
Donor(s): Charles G. Thalhimer, Jr.
Financial data (yr. ended 12/31/01): Grants paid, $34,500; assets, $733,652 (M); gifts received, $629,305; expenditures, $35,798; qualifying distributions, $34,500.
Limitations: Giving primarily in Richmond, VA.
Officers: Charles G. Thalhimer, Jr., Pres.; Carol M. Thalhimer, Secy.
EIN: 546460302

54745
The Robert and Bessie Carter Foundation
830 E. Main St., Ste. 1700
Richmond, VA 23219-2725

Donor(s): Robert Carter,‡ Bessie B. Carter.
Financial data (yr. ended 06/30/01): Grants paid, $34,394; assets, $383,950 (M); gifts received, $24,750; expenditures, $40,466; qualifying distributions, $39,233.
Limitations: Applications not accepted. Giving primarily in VA.
Application information: Contributes only to pre-selected organizations.
Trustees: Andrew B. Carter, Bessie B. Carter, John B. Carter, Robert H. Carter II.
EIN: 541254224

54746
Michael & Eleanor Pinkert Family Foundation
705 Potomac Knolls Dr.
McLean, VA 22102-1421

Established in 1990 in VA.
Donor(s): Michael S. Pinkert, Eleanor A. Pinkert.
Financial data (yr. ended 12/31/01): Grants paid, $34,110; assets, $759,259 (M); expenditures, $40,350; qualifying distributions, $34,110.
Limitations: Applications not accepted. Giving primarily on the East Coast, with some emphasis on the greater metropolitan Washington, DC, area, including MD and VA.
Application information: Contributes only to pre-selected organizations.
Officers: Michael S. Pinkert, Pres.; Eleanor A. Pinkert, V.P. and Secy.
EIN: 541579981

54747
Amory S. Carhart Memorial Fund Trust
c/o Warrenton Hunt
P.O. Box 972
Warrenton, VA 20188
Contact: Mrs. F.B. Higginson, Tr.

Financial data (yr. ended 12/31/00): Grants paid, $33,863; assets, $594,610 (M); gifts received, $15,726; expenditures, $36,371; qualifying distributions, $33,267.
Limitations: Giving primarily in Warrenton, VA.
Trustees: Alfred C. Griffin, Feroline B. Higginson, Laura Van Roijen, Sally S. Tufts.
EIN: 237418084
Codes: GTI

54748
The Woodward Foundation, Inc.
c/o Carol D. Woodward
3600 W. Broad St.
Richmond, VA 23230-4915

Established in 1980.
Financial data (yr. ended 12/31/01): Grants paid, $33,500; assets, $818,944 (M); expenditures, $35,466; qualifying distributions, $33,500.
Limitations: Applications not accepted. Giving primarily in Sarasota, FL and Richmond, VA.
Application information: Contributes only to pre-selected organizations.
Officers and Directors:* John E. Woodward, Jr.,* Pres.; Carol D. Woodward,* V.P. and Secy.-Treas.
EIN: 541154689

54749
The Evelyn F. James Foundation
c/o G.S. Shackelford
P.O. Box 2768
Roanoke, VA 24001-2768

Established in 1993 in VA.
Donor(s): Evelyn F. James.
Financial data (yr. ended 12/31/01): Grants paid, $33,334; assets, $470,795 (M); expenditures, $38,174; qualifying distributions, $32,761.
Limitations: Applications not accepted. Giving primarily in Roanoke, VA.
Application information: Contributes only to pre-selected organizations.
Officers and Directors:* G. Scott Shackelford,* Pres.; Parker S. Crosland,* Secy.-Treas.; Walter M. Dixon, Jr.
EIN: 541662984

54750
Charles & Doris Koons Foundation
(Formerly C. V. & D. C. Koons Foundation)
c/o Wachovia Bank, N.A.
1751 Pinnacle Dr., N. Twr., 3rd Fl., VA 1895
McLean, VA 22102

Established in 1997 in DC.
Financial data (yr. ended 03/31/02): Grants paid, $33,257; assets, $1,363,449 (M); expenditures, $47,664; qualifying distributions, $34,007.
Limitations: Applications not accepted. Giving primarily in Washington, DC.
Application information: Contributes only to pre-selected organizations.
Trustee: First Union National Bank.
EIN: 566497724

54751
The Jacquemin Family Foundation, Inc.
8614 Westwood Ctr. Dr., Ste. 650
Vienna, VA 22182 (703) 917-0707
Contact: John M. Jacquemin, Pres.

Established in 1997 in VA.
Donor(s): John M. Jacquemin.
Financial data (yr. ended 12/31/01): Grants paid, $33,060; assets, $1,188,356 (M); expenditures, $47,029; qualifying distributions, $33,060.
Limitations: Giving primarily in Washington, DC, ME, and VA.
Officers and Directors:* John M. Jacquemin,* Pres.; Tracie Jensen Jacquemin, Secy.; Claude Jacquemin.
EIN: 541887187

54752
The Bullard Family Foundation
P.O. Box 26606
Richmond, VA 23261-6606
Application address: c/o Sarah Kay, 1111 E. Main St., 12th Fl., Richmond, VA 23219

Established in 1997 in VA.
Donor(s): Carolyn N. Bullard, John B. Bullard III.
Financial data (yr. ended 12/31/01): Grants paid, $33,000; assets, $668,301 (M); gifts received, $159,460; expenditures, $37,807; qualifying distributions, $33,000.
Limitations: Giving primarily in Richmond, VA.
Application information: Application form not required.
Officer and Director:* Carolyn N. Bullard,* Pres.
EIN: 541850814

54753
The Martin and Jody Grass Charitable Foundation
5000 Ocean Front Ave.
Virginia Beach, VA 23451

Donor(s): The Grass Family Foundation.
Financial data (yr. ended 12/31/01): Grants paid, $33,000; assets, $1,360,559 (M); expenditures, $47,062; qualifying distributions, $33,000.
Limitations: Applications not accepted.
Application information: Contributes only to pre-selected organizations.
Officers: Martin L. Grass, Pres. and Treas.; Jody H. Gras, V.P. and Secy.
EIN: 542000520

54754
Earle J. Schlarb Scholarship Trust
c/o Jeffrey G. Lenhart
P.O. Box 1287
Harrisonburg, VA 22801

Established in 1997 in VA.
Donor(s): Earle J. Schlarb.‡
Financial data (yr. ended 12/31/01): Grants paid, $32,992; assets, $808,866 (M); expenditures, $43,309; qualifying distributions, $34,578.
Limitations: Applications not accepted. Giving limited to residents of VA.
Trustee: Jeffrey G. Lenhart.
EIN: 546405104

54755
Fred C. Ridgeway Charitable Trust
c/o F & M Bank, Trust Dept.
P.O. Box 2800
Winchester, VA 22604 (540) 665-4200

Financial data (yr. ended 12/31/01): Grants paid, $32,753; assets, $566,942 (M); expenditures, $39,770; qualifying distributions, $32,753.
Limitations: Giving primarily in Frederick County, VA, and Berkley County, WV.
Application information: Application form not required.
Trustee: F & M Trust Co.
EIN: 546118268

54756
The R & P Charitable Trust
214 Berkshire Rd.
Richmond, VA 23221-3239

Established in 1986 in VA.
Donor(s): A. Paul Funkhouser.
Financial data (yr. ended 12/31/00): Grants paid, $32,751; assets, $2,059 (M); gifts received, $34,533; expenditures, $32,890; qualifying distributions, $32,751.
Limitations: Applications not accepted. Giving limited to VA.
Application information: Contributes only to pre-selected organizations.
Trustees: A. Paul Funkhouser, Eleanor R. Funkhouser.
EIN: 541395216

54757
Gordon C. Willis Charitable Trust
4754 Old Rocky Mount Rd.
Roanoke, VA 24014
Application address: P.O. Box 8425, Roanoke, VA 24014, tel.: (540) 774-1696
Contact: Martin Willis, Tr.; or Gordon Willis, Jr., Tr.

Established in 1995 in VA.
Donor(s): Gordon C. Willis.
Financial data (yr. ended 12/31/01): Grants paid, $32,550; assets, $0 (L); expenditures, $38,804; qualifying distributions, $33,025.
Trustees: Gordon C. Willis, Gordon C. Willis, Jr., Martin R. Willis.
EIN: 546391031

54758
Margaret Grattan Weaver Foundation
c/o Donald E. Showalter
P.O. Box 20028
Harrisonburg, VA 22801

Established in 1997 in VA.
Financial data (yr. ended 12/31/99): Grants paid, $32,117; assets, $1,046,160 (M); expenditures, $51,920; qualifying distributions, $32,022.
Limitations: Applications not accepted. Giving primarily in VA.
Application information: Contributes only to pre-selected organizations.
Directors: Martha B. Caldwell, George G. Grattan IV, Donald E. Showalter, Robert H. Strickler.
EIN: 541848339

54759
Paul W. Cronin Charitable Trust
c/o Rees. Broome & Diaz, PC
8133 Leesburg Pike, Ste. 900
Vienna, VA 22182-2702
Application address: P.O. Box 5162, Andover, MA 01810-0821
Contact: John P. Cronin, Tr.

Established in 1997 in VA.
Donor(s): Paul W. Cronin.‡
Financial data (yr. ended 12/31/01): Grants paid, $32,103; assets, $482,976 (M); expenditures, $70,469; qualifying distributions, $32,103.
Limitations: Giving primarily to residents of Andover, Lawrence, Methuer, and North Andover, MA.
Trustee: John P. Cronin.
Directors: Frank J. Dyer, Stephen P. Stapinsky.
EIN: 043402953

54760
The Charles Rowe Family Foundation
P.O. Box 754
Fredericksburg, VA 22404

Established in 1997.
Donor(s): Charles S. Rowe, Sr.
Financial data (yr. ended 12/31/01): Grants paid, $32,000; assets, $420,010 (M); gifts received, $170,638; expenditures, $34,330; qualifying distributions, $32,000.
Limitations: Applications not accepted.
Application information: Contributes only to pre-selected organizations.
Officer and Directors:* Charles S. Rowe, Sr.,* Pres. and Secy.; Ashley R. Gould, Charles S. Rowe, Jr., Timothy D. Rowe.
EIN: 541878918

54761
Camp Kiwanis Foundation, Inc.
2934 W. Main St.
Waynesboro, VA 22980-9556
Application address: 141 Huntington Pl., Waynesboro, VA 22980, tel.: (540) 943-1728
Contact: Bill Pfost, Chair.

Established in 1990 in VA.
Financial data (yr. ended 09/30/01): Grants paid, $31,867; assets, $229,046 (M); expenditures, $35,134; qualifying distributions, $31,867.
Limitations: Giving limited to Augusta and Waynesboro counties, VA.
Officers and Directors:* Bill Pfost,* Chair.; John Kiger, Secy.; Tom Wagner, Treas.; Gerald A. Jeutter, Ellis Kimbrough, John Leeth, Steven Scoggin.
EIN: 541490890

54762
The Next Generation Foundation
8321 Old Courthouse Rd., Ste. 300
Vienna, VA 22182-3817

Established in 2000 in ME.
Donor(s): Evelyn S. Offutt.
Financial data (yr. ended 12/31/01): Grants paid, $31,800; assets, $1,188,149 (M); gifts received, $1,000,000; expenditures, $32,755; qualifying distributions, $31,800.
Limitations: Applications not accepted.
Application information: Contributes only to pre-selected organizations.
Officer: Evelyn S. Offutt, Pres. and Secy.-Treas.
Directors: Anthony J. Offutt, Mary Offutt.
EIN: 010539770

54763
McGregor Links Foundation
3520 Duff Dr.
Falls Church, VA 22041

Established in 1997 in VA.
Donor(s): Madelyn P. Jennings.
Financial data (yr. ended 12/31/01): Grants paid, $31,500; assets, $1,322,487 (M); gifts received, $497; expenditures, $35,115; qualifying distributions, $31,500.
Limitations: Applications not accepted. Giving primarily in Washington, DC, NY, and VA.
Application information: Contributes only to pre-selected organizations.
Officers and Directors:* Madelyn P. Jennings,* Pres. and Treas.; Karen Hague Regan,* V.P.; Richard L. Clapp,* Secy.
EIN: 522069762

54764
The Parseghian Family Foundation
c/o Gregory J. Parseghian
8403 Brookewood Ct.
McLean, VA 22102

Established around 1994.
Financial data (yr. ended 12/31/01): Grants paid, $31,500; assets, $84,721 (M); expenditures, $34,500; qualifying distributions, $31,500.
Limitations: Applications not accepted.
Application information: Contributes only to pre-selected organizations.
Trustees: Christine Parseghian, Gregory J. Parseghian.
EIN: 137054876

54765
The Beath Foundation
c/o American Express, Tax & Bu. Svcs. Inc.,
3957 Westerre Pkwy., Ste. 160
Richmond, VA 23233

Financial data (yr. ended 12/31/01): Grants paid, $31,441; assets, $1,023,602 (M); expenditures, $38,858; qualifying distributions, $31,441.
Limitations: Applications not accepted.
Application information: Contributes only to pre-selected organizations.
Officers and Directors:* Jessica Beath,* Chair.; L.T. Christian,* Pres.; George M. Peters,* V.P. and Treas.; George Allen III, Eleanor Cox.
EIN: 541726845

54766
The Sacks/Louie Family Charitable Foundation
c/o Jonathan Sacks and Evelyn Louie
397 Patowhack Ct.
Great Falls, VA 22066-3031

Established in 1999 in VA.
Donor(s): Jonathan E. Sacks, Evelyn Louie.
Financial data (yr. ended 12/31/00): Grants paid, $31,315; assets, $711,845 (M); gifts received, $224,588; expenditures, $33,485; qualifying distributions, $31,049.
Limitations: Applications not accepted.
Application information: Contributes only to pre-selected organizations.
Trustees: Evelyn Louie, Jonathan E. Sacks.
EIN: 541938520

54767
Huff, Poole & Mahoney Foundation, Inc.
c/o Kevin Rack
4705 Columbus St., Ste. 100
Virginia Beach, VA 23462-6749

Established in 1998 in VA.
Financial data (yr. ended 12/31/01): Grants paid, $31,247; assets, $60 (M); gifts received, $31,247; expenditures, $31,247; qualifying distributions, $31,247.
Officers: Albert H. Poole, Pres.; Glen A. Huff, V.P.; Kevin B. Rack, Secy.-Treas.
Directors: Jeffrey F. Brooke, Reeves W. Mahoney, Robert F. McDonnell, John D. Radd, Tim M. Richardson, Stephen R. Romine, David N. Ventker, Stephen Wainger, David M. Zobel.
EIN: 541882539

54768
Marasco Newton Whittaker Foundation
2801 Clarendon Blvd., Ste. 100
Arlington, VA 22201 (703) 516-9100
URL: http://www.marasconewton.com/community_involvement/m_n_w_foundation
Contact: Jim Whittaker, Pres.

Established in 2000 in VA.
Donor(s): The Marasco Newton Group, Ltd.
Financial data (yr. ended 12/31/02): Grants paid, $31,239; assets, $14,236 (M); gifts received, $48,366; expenditures, $42,918; qualifying distributions, $32,052.
Limitations: Giving primarily in Arlington, VA.
Officers: James R. Whittaker, Pres.; Amy L. Marasco, V.P.; David A. Newton, Treas.
EIN: 311680869
Codes: CS

54769
J. Kenneth Timmons Irrevocable Trust
3260 Greywalls Ct.
Powhatan, VA 23139
Application address: c/o Greyfield Farm, Midlothian, VA 23113, tel.: (804) 794-6905
Contact: Marion F. Timmons, Tr.

Donor(s): J.Kenneth Timmons, Marion F. Timmons.
Financial data (yr. ended 11/30/00): Grants paid, $31,200; assets, $608,989 (M); gifts received, $196,257; expenditures, $32,126; qualifying distributions, $31,200.
Limitations: Giving primarily in Richmond, VA.
Trustees: J.K. Timmons, Marion F. Timmons.
EIN: 546193875

54770
Cedars Foundation, Inc.
40123 Bond St., Box 55
Waterford, VA 20197

Established in 1999 in DE and VA.
Donor(s): W. Bowman Cutter.
Financial data (yr. ended 12/31/99): Grants paid, $31,000; assets, $303,129 (M); gifts received, $334,772; expenditures, $31,182; qualifying distributions, $31,000.
Limitations: Applications not accepted.
Application information: Contributes only to pre-selected organizations.
Director: W. Bowman Cutter III.
EIN: 223651734

54771
Miriam P. Truesdell Trust
c/o Bank of America
P.O. Box 26606
Richmond, VA 23261-6606

Financial data (yr. ended 06/30/99): Grants paid, $30,901; assets, $969,937 (M); expenditures, $50,057; qualifying distributions, $31,671.
Limitations: Applications not accepted. Giving primarily in Waynesboro, VA.
Application information: Contributes only to pre-selected organizations.
Trustee: Bank of America.
EIN: 546158239

54772
Alexandria Rotary Foundation
P.O. Box 20271-1271
Alexandria, VA 22320-1271
Contact: John C. McCune, Jr., Treas.

Established in 1989 in VA.
Donor(s): The Rotary Club of Alexandria, VA.
Financial data (yr. ended 06/30/01): Grants paid, $30,750; assets, $187,882 (M); gifts received, $56,120; expenditures, $37,870; qualifying distributions, $30,750.
Limitations: Giving primarily in Alexandria, VA.
Officers: Katherine L. Morrison, Pres.; Paul Vander Myde, 1st V.P.; Stephen W. Gesham, 2nd V.P.; Leon A. Duncan, Secy.; John C. McCune, Jr., Treas.
Directors: John R. Allen, Thomas S. Field, Jr., Jesse J. Hernandez, Loretta S. Sebastian.
EIN: 541545015

54773
The George M. Neall II and Clara B. Neall Charitable Foundation Trust
c/o Rhonda J. MacDonald
7730 Arlen St.
Annandale, VA 22003
Application address: c/o First Virginia Bank, 6400 Arlington Blvd., Falls Church, VA 22042

Established in 1993 in VA.
Donor(s): George M. Neal II.
Financial data (yr. ended 06/30/02): Grants paid, $30,600; assets, $546,934 (M); expenditures, $34,358; qualifying distributions, $30,600.
Limitations: Giving primarily in Cambridge, MD, and Springfield, VA.
Trustees: George M. Neall II, First Virginia Bank.
EIN: 541621683

54774
Baer Foundation, Inc.
7084 Piedmont Dr.
Rapidan, VA 22733
Contact: Karla B. Baer, Secy.-Treas.

Donor(s): Albert M. Baer.‡
Financial data (yr. ended 12/31/01): Grants paid, $30,550; assets, $546,888 (M); expenditures, $33,797; qualifying distributions, $30,550.
Limitations: Giving primarily in VA.
Officer: Karla B. Baer, Pres.
EIN: 136082026

54775
Julian H. & Ruth D. Dymacek Foundation
914 Rolling Path Rd.
Louisa, VA 23093-2516 (540) 894-0993
Contact: Kenneth M. Lancaster, V.P.

Established in 1989 in VA.
Donor(s): Ruth D. Dymacek.
Financial data (yr. ended 11/30/00): Grants paid, $30,500; assets, $527,189 (M); expenditures, $41,460; qualifying distributions, $30,285.
Limitations: Giving primarily in Bumpass, VA.
Officers: Joseph M. Dymacek, Pres.; Kenneth M. Lancaster, V.P.; John D. Whitlock, Secy.-Treas.
EIN: 541511138

54776
Edward R. Kengla Foundation, Inc.
c/o Alexandria American Legion Post 24
P.O. Box 402
Alexandria, VA 22313

Established in 1991 in VA.
Financial data (yr. ended 12/31/00): Grants paid, $30,500; assets, $628,315 (M); expenditures, $31,253; qualifying distributions, $30,115.

Limitations: Giving limited to the Alexandria, VA, area.
Application information: Application form required for scholarship.
Directors: Daniel J. Burke, H. Warden Foley, Calvin Reid.
EIN: 541826229

54777
Tillin Foundation
1705 Chesterford Way
McLean, VA 22101

Established in 2000 in VA.
Donor(s): Hansford T. Johnson, Linda A. Johnson.
Financial data (yr. ended 12/31/01): Grants paid, $30,325; assets, $73,206 (M); gifts received, $53,819; expenditures, $32,924; qualifying distributions, $30,325.
Limitations: Applications not accepted.
Application information: Contributes only to pre-selected organizations.
Officers: Hansford T. Johnson, Pres.; Linda A. Johnson, Secy.-Treas.
EIN: 541981797

54778
Robert Blair Foundation
6177 St. Andrews Ln.
Richmond, VA 23226

Established in 1997 in VA.
Donor(s): Margaret M. Farinholt.
Financial data (yr. ended 12/31/01): Grants paid, $30,200; assets, $190,341 (M); gifts received, $49,830; expenditures, $38,186; qualifying distributions, $30,200.
Limitations: Applications not accepted.
Application information: Contributes only to pre-selected organizations.
Officers and Directors:* Margaret M. Farinholt,* Pres.; M.B. Farinholt, Secy.; Robert M. Farinholt, Treas.
EIN: 541879517

54779
Cornwell-Bireley Family Charitable Trust
c/o Gary Cornwell
314 Brierwood Dr.
Bluefield, VA 24605

Established in 1990 in VA.
Donor(s): Gary Cornwell, Laura Cornwell.
Financial data (yr. ended 06/30/01): Grants paid, $30,180; assets, $360,127 (M); gifts received, $50,000; expenditures, $30,520; qualifying distributions, $29,924.
Limitations: Applications not accepted. Giving primarily in Bluefield, VA.
Application information: Contributes only to pre-selected organizations.
Trustees: Charles Bireley, Gary Cornwell, Laura Cornwell, Katherine Plouff.
EIN: 546305643

54780
Blue Dot Foundation
8404 Parham Ct.
McLean, VA 22102

Established in 1997 in VA.
Donor(s): Steven W. Rales.
Financial data (yr. ended 12/31/99): Grants paid, $30,000; assets, $267,479 (M); gifts received, $212,000; expenditures, $335,990; qualifying distributions, $334,165; giving activities include $330,165 for programs.
Limitations: Applications not accepted. Giving primarily in MA.
Application information: Contributes only to pre-selected organizations.

Officers: Steven M. Rales, Chair.; Edward B. Tasch, C.E.O. and Pres.; Michael G. Ryan, V.P. and Secy.; Teresa L.C. Baldwin, V.P. and Treas.
Directors: Thomas F. Kennelly, Christine P. Rales, Gregory J. Whitehead.
EIN: 541842403

54781
Boris Margolin Foundation, Inc.
505 Birkdale Ct.
Yorktown, VA 23693 (757) 873-0376
Contact: Samuel Margolin, Pres.

Financial data (yr. ended 11/30/01): Grants paid, $30,000; assets, $613,248 (M); expenditures, $39,606; qualifying distributions, $30,000.
Limitations: Giving primarily in NJ, NY, and VA.
Officers: Samuel Margolin, Pres.; Ira Margolin, V.P.; Miriam Jaffe, Secy.-Treas.
EIN: 136133173

54782
The James F. Mitchell-Paul C. Kiernan Foundation for Medical Education and Research
(Formerly The James F. Mitchell Foundation for Medical Education and Research)
c/o Raymond Hunt
2205 Lofty Heights Pl.
Reston, VA 20191-1716
Contact: Paul D. Kiernan, Pres.

Financial data (yr. ended 12/31/01): Grants paid, $30,000; assets, $961,200 (M); expenditures, $71,140; qualifying distributions, $30,000.
Limitations: Giving primarily in Washington, DC, and Rochester, MN.
Application information: Application form not required.
Officers: Paul D. Kiernan, Pres.; Eugene M. Thore, V.P.
EIN: 530228399

54783
The Nancy Anne Charitable Foundation
9960 Lake Occoquan Dr.
Manassas, VA 20111

Established in 2000 in VA.
Donor(s): Nancy Anthony.
Financial data (yr. ended 06/30/02): Grants paid, $30,000; assets, $202,203 (M); expenditures, $35,094; qualifying distributions, $30,000.
Limitations: Applications not accepted.
Application information: Contributes only to pre-selected organizations.
Trustee: Nancy Anthony.
EIN: 546481608

54784
The Sam and Reba Sandler Family Foundation
c/o Nathan Benson
P.O. Box 8790
Virginia Beach, VA 23450-8790

Established in 1989 in VA.
Donor(s): Samuel Sandler.
Financial data (yr. ended 06/30/01): Grants paid, $30,000; assets, $99,042 (M); expenditures, $64,283; qualifying distributions, $30,000.
Limitations: Applications not accepted. Giving limited to VA.
Application information: Contributes only to pre-selected organizations.
Officers: Steven Sandler, Pres.; Arthur B. Sandler, V.P.; Sheri C. Sandler, Secy.
EIN: 541552922

54785
The Thomas Hospice
P.O. Box 2510
Midlothian, VA 23112-8510 (804) 897-3656
Contact: Barbara D. Hughes, Pres.

Established in 1996 in VA.
Donor(s): Eureka J. Traylor.‡
Financial data (yr. ended 03/31/02): Grants paid, $29,960; assets, $542,197 (M); gifts received, $25,861; expenditures, $67,129; qualifying distributions, $29,960.
Limitations: Giving limited to the metropolitan Richmond, VA, area.
Officers and Directors:* Barbara D. Hughes,* Pres.; Betty W. Stinson,* V.P.; Dorothy C. Cronk, Secy.; Louise D. Hartz,* Treas.; Betty P. Puritt.
EIN: 541798090

54786
Clarence L. Robey Charitable Trust
(Formerly Clarence L. Robey Testamentary Charitable Trust)
c/o First Virginia Bank
6400 Arlington Blvd. Plz. 1, Ste. 840
Falls Church, VA 22042
Application address: c/o Board of Directors, P.O. Box 181, Purcellville, VA 22132

Financial data (yr. ended 12/31/99): Grants paid, $29,700; assets, $790,849 (M); expenditures, $36,349; qualifying distributions, $29,376.
Limitations: Giving primarily in VA.
Application information: Application form not required.
Officers: Edward E. Nicholls, Jr., Chair.; A.M. Mike Perry, Vice-Chair.
Directors: Nancy Marsh, Margaret Vaughn, Arthur A. Welch, Doris L. Whitman.
EIN: 546138649

54787
Andrew and Martha Sanford Scholarship Foundation
P.O. Box 1958
Kilmarnock, VA 22482-1958
Application address: P.O. Box 26311, Richmond, VA 23260-6311

Established in 1990 in VA.
Donor(s): A.J. Sanford.‡
Financial data (yr. ended 12/31/00): Grants paid, $29,625; assets, $526,638 (M); expenditures, $35,313; qualifying distributions, $29,508.
Limitations: Giving limited to residents of Lancaster, Northumberland, Richmond, and Westmoreland counties, VA.
Application information: Application form required.
Committee Members: Frank E. English, Jr., Pamela J. Fawyer, Barbara K. McNeal, M. Duncan Minton, Jr.
EIN: 546295578
Codes: GTI

54788
Old Dominion Box Company Foundation, Inc.
P.O. Box 680
Lynchburg, VA 24505-0680 (434) 929-6701
Contact: Wayne Lankford

Established in 1951.
Donor(s): Old Dominion Box Co., Dillard Investment Corp., Little Rock Packaging Co., Inc., Hall Town Paperboard Co., Palmetto Box Co.
Financial data (yr. ended 11/30/01): Grants paid, $29,300; assets, $565,798 (M); expenditures, $131,416; qualifying distributions, $29,300.
Limitations: Giving primarily in Lynchburg, VA.
Application information: Application form not required.

Officers: Frank H. Buhler, Pres.; Michael O. Buhler, V.P.; Amy Buhler, Secy.-Treas.
EIN: 546036792
Codes: CS, CD

54789
Frederick P. & Mary Buford Hitz Trust, Inc.
208 S. Saint Asaph St.
Alexandria, VA 22314-3744

Established in 1968.
Donor(s): Frederick P. Hitz, Mary Buford Hitz.
Financial data (yr. ended 12/31/01): Grants paid, $29,291; assets, $14,643 (M); gifts received, $40,010; expenditures, $30,216; qualifying distributions, $29,291.
Limitations: Applications not accepted. Giving primarily in the Washington, DC, area, including VA.
Application information: Contributes only to pre-selected organizations.
Trustees: Frederic S. Bocock, Frederick P. Hitz, Mary Buford Hitz.
EIN: 546076815

54790
The Micawber Foundation, Inc.
13530 Stonegate Rd.
Midlothian, VA 23113

Donor(s): Needham B. Whitfield.
Financial data (yr. ended 12/31/01): Grants paid, $29,050; assets, $488,724 (M); expenditures, $31,031; qualifying distributions, $29,050.
Limitations: Applications not accepted. Giving primarily in VA.
Application information: Contributes only to pre-selected organizations.
Officers: Needham B. Whitfield, Pres.; Maha S. Whitfield, Secy.
Director: Julia W. Auerbach.
EIN: 061004777

54791
Nepeni Foundation
c/o SunTrust Banks, Inc.
P.O. Box 27385
Richmond, VA 23261-7385

Donor(s): Neil H. McElroy.‡
Financial data (yr. ended 12/31/01): Grants paid, $29,000; assets, $402,289 (M); expenditures, $30,804; qualifying distributions, $29,000.
Limitations: Applications not accepted. Giving primarily in Washington, DC.
Application information: Contributes only to pre-selected organizations.
Trustee: SunTrust Banks, Inc.
EIN: 316065583

54792
The Pittston Foundation
c/o The Pittston Co.
P.O. Box 18100
Richmond, VA 23226-8100

Established in 1997 in VA.
Donor(s): The Pittston Co.
Financial data (yr. ended 12/31/01): Grants paid, $29,000; assets, $595,884 (M); expenditures, $29,000; qualifying distributions, $28,928.
Limitations: Applications not accepted. Giving limited to Glen Allen, VA.
Application information: Contributes only to pre-selected organizations.
Officers and Directors:* Michael T. Dan,* Pres.; Frank T. Lennon,* V.P.; Austin F. Reed,* Secy.; James B. Hartough,* Treas.
EIN: 541815655
Codes: CS, CD

54793
Ray Rowe Trust for Animals No. 2
41 E. Bellefonte Ave.
Alexandria, VA 22301-1442 (703) 836-7036
Contact: Duncan F. Forbes, Tr.

Established in 1986 in CA.
Financial data (yr. ended 12/31/99): Grants paid, $29,000; assets, $391,672 (M); expenditures, $33,549; qualifying distributions, $28,961.
Limitations: Giving on a national basis.
Application information: Application form required.
Trustee: Duncan F. Forbes.
EIN: 956858457

54794
Argyll Foundation
P.O. Box 1408
Charlottesville, VA 22902-1408
Application address: P.O. Box 756, Culpepper, VA 22701-0756, tel.: (540) 825-0681
Contact: Louisa Ann Campbell, Pres.

Financial data (yr. ended 12/31/01): Grants paid, $28,803; assets, $463,941 (M); gifts received, $30,129; expenditures, $30,295; qualifying distributions, $28,803.
Limitations: Giving primarily in VA.
Officer and Director:* Louisa Ann Campbell,* Pres. and Secy.-Treas.
EIN: 541847081

54795
The Mary W. Bowers Charitable Trust
c/o Bank of America
P.O. Box 26606
Richmond, VA 23261-6903 (804) 788-2963

Financial data (yr. ended 12/31/99): Grants paid, $28,500; assets, $750,065 (M); expenditures, $35,268; qualifying distributions, $28,500.
Limitations: Giving primarily in Richmond, VA.
Trustee: Bank of America.
EIN: 546095877

54796
The O'Shaughnessy-Hurst Memorial Foundation, Inc.
87 Lee Hwy.
Warrenton, VA 20186

Donor(s): Mary Hurst O'Shaughnessy.
Financial data (yr. ended 12/31/01): Grants paid, $28,400; assets, $667,033 (M); gifts received, $35,000; expenditures, $51,202; qualifying distributions, $30,425.
Limitations: Applications not accepted. Giving primarily in Vienna, VA.
Application information: Contributes only to pre-selected organizations.
Officers and Directors:* Robert W. Dech,* Mgr.; Kathy Poorbaugh,* Treas.; William Soza.
EIN: 541394736

54797
The Peebles Family Foundation
P.O. Box 368
Ordinary, VA 23131-0368

Established around 1995.
Donor(s): David L. Peebles.
Financial data (yr. ended 12/31/01): Grants paid, $28,400; assets, $208,737 (M); gifts received, $128; expenditures, $30,771; qualifying distributions, $28,400.
Limitations: Applications not accepted.
Application information: Contributes only to pre-selected organizations.
Trustees: David L. Peebles, Mary A. Peebles.
EIN: 546372252

54798
The Bionetics Corporation Charitable Trust
11833 Canon Blvd., Ste. 100
Newport News, VA 23606

Established in 1987 in VA.
Donor(s): Bionetics Corp.
Financial data (yr. ended 12/31/01): Grants paid, $28,220; assets, $27,996 (M); gifts received, $20,167; expenditures, $28,283; qualifying distributions, $28,220.
Limitations: Applications not accepted. Giving primarily in VA.
Application information: Contributes only to pre-selected organizations.
Officers: Charles J. Stern, Pres.; Janice M. Kennard, V.P.
EIN: 596263704
Codes: CS, CD, GTI

54799
The Douglas Y. Hicks Charitable Foundation
c/o Bank of America
P.O. Box 26606
Richmond, VA 23261-6606

Established in 1998 in VA.
Financial data (yr. ended 08/31/00): Grants paid, $28,000; assets, $324,602 (M); expenditures, $35,626; qualifying distributions, $30,197.
Limitations: Applications not accepted. Giving primarily in Newport News, VA.
Application information: Contributes only to pre-selected organizations.
Trustee: Bank of America.
EIN: 546446266

54800
Vitreus Foundation
c/o Thomas C. Mac Avoy
494 Ednam Cir.
Charlottesville, VA 22903

Established in 1997 in VA.
Donor(s): Thomas C. Macavoy.
Financial data (yr. ended 12/31/01): Grants paid, $28,000; assets, $777,819 (M); gifts received, $54,411; expenditures, $31,272; qualifying distributions, $28,000.
Limitations: Applications not accepted. Giving primarily in CA and GA.
Application information: Contributes only to pre-selected organizations.
Officers: Thomas C. Macavoy, Pres.; Margaret Macavoy, Secy.-Treas.
EIN: 541829869

54801
Blechman-David Foundation, Inc.
301 Hiden Blvd., Ste. 200
Newport News, VA 23606 (757) 595-4500
Contact: E.D. David, Chair.

Established in 1997.
Donor(s): E.D. David, E.B. David.
Financial data (yr. ended 12/31/01): Grants paid, $27,865; assets, $1,125,637 (M); gifts received, $354,940; expenditures, $31,119; qualifying distributions, $27,865.
Limitations: Giving primarily in VA.
Officer: E.D. David, Chair.
Directors: E.B. David, J.W. David.
EIN: 541839135

54802
El Sawy Family Foundation
9408 Fairpine Ln.
Great Falls, VA 22066-2109

Established in 1994 in VA.
Donor(s): Abdel Hamid A. El Sawy, Soraya O. El Sawy.
Financial data (yr. ended 12/31/01): Grants paid, $27,843; assets, $514,419 (M); gifts received, $17,500; expenditures, $40,173; qualifying distributions, $27,843.
Limitations: Applications not accepted. Giving on an international basis, with emphasis on Cairo, Egypt.
Application information: Contributes only to pre-selected organizations.
Trustees: Abdel Hamid A. El Sawy, Soraya O. El Sawy.
EIN: 541740687

54803
Josephine Kugel Foundation, Inc.
6016 Claiborne Dr.
McLean, VA 22101

Donor(s): Robert B. Kugel, Dorothy B. Kugel.
Financial data (yr. ended 12/31/01): Grants paid, $27,825; assets, $454,414 (M); gifts received, $10,320; expenditures, $29,942; qualifying distributions, $27,825.
Limitations: Applications not accepted. Giving on a national basis, with emphasis on the East.
Application information: Contributes only to pre-selected organizations.
Officers and Directors:* Robert B. Kugel,* Pres.; Gretchen Kugel,* V.P.; Dorothy B. Kugel,* Secy.-Treas.; Jennie L. Kugel, Rebecca A. Kugel.
EIN: 476046285

54804
Gilbert Heritage Foundation
734 S. 21st St.
Arlington, VA 22202

Established in 1986 in VA.
Donor(s): Daniel D. Gilbert.
Financial data (yr. ended 12/31/01): Grants paid, $27,550; assets, $538,556 (M); expenditures, $28,605; qualifying distributions, $27,550.
Limitations: Applications not accepted. Giving on a national basis.
Application information: Contributes only to pre-selected organizations.
Trustees: Daniel D. Gilbert, Alice Petree.
EIN: 541394375

54805
Reed and Jeanne Larson Foundation
105 Robert Cole Ct.
Williamsburg, VA 23185-3385

Established in 1987 in VA.
Donor(s): Reed Larson.
Financial data (yr. ended 06/30/01): Grants paid, $27,500; assets, $554,889 (M); gifts received, $7,000; expenditures, $28,625; qualifying distributions, $27,500.
Limitations: Applications not accepted. Giving on a national basis.
Application information: Contributes only to pre-selected organizations.
Officers and Trustees:* Reed Larson,* Chair.; M. Jeanne Larson,* Secy.
EIN: 541443620

54806
Gerald F. Smith Scholarship Foundation
P.O. Box 3588
Winchester, VA 22604-2586

Established in 1995 in VA.
Financial data (yr. ended 12/31/00): Grants paid, $27,500; assets, $2,373 (M); gifts received, $10,000; expenditures, $27,822; qualifying distributions, $322.
Limitations: Giving primarily in PA, VA, and VT.
Application information: Unsolicited requests for funds not accepted.
Officers and Directors:* Gerald F. Smith,* Pres.; Michael A. Smith,* V.P.; Gerald F. Smith, Jr., Secy.-Treas.
EIN: 541725608

54807
Isabel Duncan Hatchett Foundation
125 Parkway Dr.
Newport News, VA 23606

Financial data (yr. ended 12/31/01): Grants paid, $27,365; assets, $56,235 (M); expenditures, $28,786; qualifying distributions, $27,365.
Limitations: Applications not accepted. Giving primarily in Newport News, VA.
Application information: Contributes only to pre-selected organizations.
Directors: Ann Duncan, Isabel Duncan Hatchett, Philip L. Hatchett.
EIN: 541526651

54808
Hampton Foundation
P.O. Box 397
Richmond, VA 23218
Application address: P.O. Box 298, Sperryville, VA 22740, tel.: (540) 987-8511
Contact: James W. Fletcher, III, Pres.

Financial data (yr. ended 12/31/01): Grants paid, $27,342; assets, $621,632 (M); expenditures, $32,914; qualifying distributions, $28,811.
Limitations: Giving primarily in VA.
Officers and Directors:* James W. Fletcher III,* Pres.; James P. Jamison,* V.P.; Frances A. Foster,* Secy.-Treas.
EIN: 546054035

54809
The Blocker Foundation
P.O. Box 14219
Norfolk, VA 23518-0219 (757) 583-4040
Contact: S. Frank Blocker, Pres.

Established in 1982.
Financial data (yr. ended 07/31/01): Grants paid, $26,993; assets, $3,218,833 (M); expenditures, $28,573; qualifying distributions, $26,998.
Limitations: Giving primarily in Norfolk, VA.
Officers and Directors:* S. Frank Blocker, Jr.,* Pres.; Mariam B. Lawler,* Secy.; M. Ward Cole, Frederick V. Martin.
EIN: 541217447

54810
Elisabeth Reed Carter Trust
1806 Park Ave.
Richmond, VA 23220-2821

Donor(s): Elisabeth Reed Carter.
Financial data (yr. ended 12/31/01): Grants paid, $26,525; assets, $558,644 (M); expenditures, $27,960; qualifying distributions, $27,286.
Limitations: Applications not accepted. Giving primarily in Richmond, VA.
Application information: Contributes only to pre-selected organizations.
Trustee: Elisabeth Reed Carter.
EIN: 546052216

54811
Parker Carson Foundation
c/o The Trust Co. of VA
9030 Stony Point Pkwy., Ste. 300
Richmond, VA 23235-1936

Established in 1997 in VA.
Donor(s): Lucile Swift Miller.

Financial data (yr. ended 12/31/01): Grants paid, $26,350; assets, $861,817 (M); expenditures, $37,023; qualifying distributions, $26,790.
Limitations: Applications not accepted. Giving primarily in VA.
Application information: Contributes only to pre-selected organizations.
Officer and Director:* Lucile Swift Miller,* Pres. and Secy.
EIN: 541875279

54812
J. Preston Levis Charitable Foundation
P.O. Box 1256
Middleburg, VA 20118-1256
Contact: John P. Levis, Jr., Pres.

Established in 2000 in VA.
Donor(s): John P. Levis, Jr.
Financial data (yr. ended 12/31/01): Grants paid, $26,200; assets, $682,099 (M); gifts received, $25,059; expenditures, $43,631; qualifying distributions, $26,200.
Limitations: Giving primarily in VA.
Officers and Directors:* John P. Levis, Jr., Pres.; John P. Levis III, V.P.; Margot L. Thompson,* Secy.-Treas.; C. Langhorne Washburn, Helen C. Wiley.
EIN: 541991015

54813
Miller Foundation, Inc.
(Formerly Saunders-Miller Foundation, Inc.)
P.O. Box 11674
Richmond, VA 23230-0074

Financial data (yr. ended 12/31/01): Grants paid, $25,650; assets, $424,687 (M); expenditures, $30,436; qualifying distributions, $25,650.
Limitations: Giving primarily in VA.
Officers and Directors:* Scott S. Miller,* Pres. and Treas.; J. Clifford Miller III,* Secy.-Treas.; Collins Denny III, Clifford Miller Yonce.
EIN: 540761553

54814
Lucy E. Meiller Educational Trust
c/o SunTrust Banks, Inc.
P.O. Box 27385
Richmond, VA 23261-7385
Application address: P.O. Box 13888, Roanoke, VA 24038
Contact: Carolyn McCoy, Trust Off., SunTrust Banks, Inc.

Established in 1986 in VA.
Financial data (yr. ended 08/31/01): Grants paid, $25,500; assets, $522,568 (M); expenditures, $30,858; qualifying distributions, $26,050.
Limitations: Giving limited to residents of VA.
Trustee: SunTrust Banks, Inc.
EIN: 546238746
Codes: GTI

54815
The Rosenblatt Foundation
6106 Greenlawn Ct.
Springfield, VA 22152

Established in 2000 in VA.
Donor(s): Melvin Rosenblatt.
Financial data (yr. ended 12/31/01): Grants paid, $25,347; assets, $56,620 (M); gifts received, $67,300; expenditures, $26,097; qualifying distributions, $25,347.
Limitations: Applications not accepted.
Application information: Contributes only to pre-selected organizations.
Director: Melvin Rosenblatt.
EIN: 541987576

54816
The Grace Curtis & Priscilla O'Hara Foundation, Inc.
3923 Old Lee Hwy., 62B
Fairfax, VA 22030

Established in 2000 in VA.
Donor(s): William O. Snead III.
Financial data (yr. ended 12/31/01): Grants paid, $25,300; assets, $711,629 (M); gifts received, $212,689; expenditures, $28,353; qualifying distributions, $25,300.
Limitations: Applications not accepted.
Application information: Contributes only to pre-selected organizations.
Directors: Erin O'Hara Snead, Patrick Gallagher Snead, Priscilla O'Hara Snead, william O. Snead III.
EIN: 542014975

54817
The Culbertson Foundation
420 Ivy Farm Dr.
Charlottesville, VA 22901

Established in 1998 in VA.
Donor(s): Alan N. Culbertson.
Financial data (yr. ended 12/31/99): Grants paid, $25,078; assets, $14,040 (M); gifts received, $28,170; expenditures, $25,665; qualifying distributions, $25,074.
Limitations: Applications not accepted.
Application information: Contributes only to pre-selected organizations.
Trustees: Alan N. Culbertson, Sharon P. Culbertson.
EIN: 550723776

54818
The Chad Campana Memorial Foundation
10300 Attems Way
Glen Allen, VA 23060

Established in 1997 in VA.
Financial data (yr. ended 12/31/01): Grants paid, $25,000; assets, $1,544,580 (M); gifts received, $1,775; expenditures, $118,322; qualifying distributions, $25,000.
Limitations: Applications not accepted.
Application information: Contributes only to pre-selected organizations.
Officer: James E. Campana, Secy.-Treas.; Sherry L. Campana, Exec. Dir.
Directors: Craig P. Campana, Tracie C. Meadows.
EIN: 550755313

54819
The David and Sylvia Krug Memorial Foundation
(Formerly Krug Memorial Foundation)
130 Business Park Dr.
Virginia Beach, VA 23462

Established in 1980 in VA.
Financial data (yr. ended 03/31/02): Grants paid, $25,000; assets, $800,168 (M); expenditures, $39,626; qualifying distributions, $25,000.
Limitations: Applications not accepted. Giving limited to VA.
Application information: Contributes only to pre-selected organizations.
Trustees: Herbert M. Pearlman, Miriam Weisberg, Samuel I. White.
EIN: 541049343

54820
Androus Foundation, Inc.
P.O. Box 7494
Alexandria, VA 22307

Donor(s): Arthur T. Androus.

Financial data (yr. ended 12/31/01): Grants paid, $24,750; assets, $515,747 (M); expenditures, $37,740; qualifying distributions, $24,750.
Limitations: Applications not accepted. Giving primarily in VA; some giving also in Athens, Greece.
Application information: Contributes only to pre-selected organizations.
Officer and Directors:* Deborah Androus,* Pres.; Catherine Androus, Theodore S. Androus, Sotiris Koukis, Lynne A. Smith, Jean Androus Woodman.
EIN: 526054135

54821
The Christian Mission Foundation
c/o A. G. Edwards & Sons
P.O. Box 13788
Roanoke, VA 24037

Established in 1993 in VA.
Financial data (yr. ended 12/31/01): Grants paid, $24,500; assets, $447,209 (M); gifts received, $4,725; expenditures, $25,433; qualifying distributions, $24,500.
Limitations: Applications not accepted. Giving primarily in VA.
Application information: Contributes only to pre-selected organizations.
Officers: Beverly T. Fitzpatrick, Jr., Pres.; William S. Moses, V.P.; Broaddus C. Fitzpatrick, Secy.; Robert H. Kulp, Treas.
Directors: Sara S. Airheart, Barbara B. Lemon, Dixie Morris.
EIN: 546044761

54822
Anna C. & R. J. Green Scholarship Fund
c/o Bank of America
P.O. Box 26606
Richmond, VA 23261
Application addresses: c/o Superintendent of Schools, Greenville, VA 24440, or c/o Principal, Greenville City School, Emporia, VA 23847

Financial data (yr. ended 12/31/99): Grants paid, $24,200; assets, $177,396 (M); expenditures, $26,308; qualifying distributions, $24,200.
Limitations: Giving limited to the Emporia and Greenville, VA, areas.
Trustee: Bank of America.
EIN: 546053477

54823
Charles L. Perkins, Sr. Charitable Trust, Inc.
8430-H Lee Hwy.
Fairfax, VA 22031

Established in 1989 in VA.
Donor(s): Charles L. Perkins, Sr.
Financial data (yr. ended 12/31/01): Grants paid, $24,075; assets, $180,634 (M); gifts received, $25,500; expenditures, $24,890; qualifying distributions, $24,075.
Limitations: Applications not accepted. Giving primarily in VA.
Application information: Contributes only to pre-selected organizations.
Trustees: Marian Cook, John P. Cummins III, Charles L. Perkins.
EIN: 540674478

54824
George Andreas Foundation, Inc.
c/o George C. Andreas
187 Chain Bridge Rd.
McLean, VA 22102

Established in 1993 in VA.
Donor(s): George C. Andreas, Ursula Andreas.
Financial data (yr. ended 12/31/00): Grants paid, $24,000; assets, $718,888 (L); gifts received,

$620,000; expenditures, $27,501; qualifying distributions, $23,964.
Limitations: Applications not accepted. Giving primarily in Washington, DC, and New York, NY.
Application information: Contributes only to pre-selected organizations.
Officers: George C. Andreas, Pres. and Treas.; Christopher Andreas, V.P.; Ursula Andreas, V.P.
EIN: 541691040

54825
The Cornelius J. Coakley Family Foundation, Inc.
(Formerly The John Kevin Coakley Foundation, Inc.)
7732 Lee Hwy.
Falls Church, VA 22042 (703) 573-0540
Application address: 4960 Old Dominion Dr., Arlington, VA 22207
Contact: Ellen P. Coakley, Pres.

Established in 1997 in VA.
Financial data (yr. ended 12/31/01): Grants paid, $23,930; assets, $560,099 (M); expenditures, $26,014; qualifying distributions, $23,930.
Limitations: Giving primarily in VA.
Officers and Directors:* Ellen P. Coakley,* Pres. and Secy.; Maria Coakley David,* Treas.; Cornelius J. Coakley, Liam F. Coakley, Michael D. Coakley.
EIN: 541851618

54826
The Taylor Foundation
P.O. Box 366
Reedville, VA 22539
Contact: George A. Taylor, Dir.

Established in 2000 in VA.
Donor(s): George A. Taylor, Cynthia C. Taylor.
Financial data (yr. ended 12/31/00): Grants paid, $23,800; assets, $10,563 (M); gifts received, $35,000; expenditures, $24,617; qualifying distributions, $23,800.
Limitations: Giving limited to VA.
Application information: Application form not required.
Officer: Cynthia C. Taylor, Pres.
Directors: Valarie J. Molin, Phyllis L. Neal, Julia P. Pritchard, H. Joseph Shepherd, George A. Taylor.
EIN: 541989593

54827
C. Neil and Carolyn S. Norgren Foundation
(Formerly Norsut Foundation)
3319 Marsden Point
Keswick, VA 22947-9133
Contact: Carolyn S. Norgren, Pres. and Treas.

Established in 1989 in CO.
Donor(s): Carl A. Norgren Foundation.
Financial data (yr. ended 12/31/01): Grants paid, $23,600; assets, $240,737 (M); expenditures, $26,531; qualifying distributions, $23,981.
Limitations: Applications not accepted. Giving primarily in CO.
Application information: Contributes only to pre-selected organizations.
Officer: Carolyn S. Norgren, Pres. and Treas.
EIN: 841120788

54828
Klingstein Foundation
c/o Fred Koontz
P.O. Box 1124
Harrisonburg, VA 22801-1124

Financial data (yr. ended 12/31/01): Grants paid, $23,500; assets, $482,389 (M); expenditures, $48,561; qualifying distributions, $23,500.

Limitations: Applications not accepted. Giving primarily in VA.
Application information: Contributes only to pre-selected organizations.
Officers: Donald H. Koontz, Pres.; Robert E. Gillette, V.P.; Fred Koontz, Secy.-Treas.
EIN: 546052224

54829
Plymale Foundation
c/o Wachovia Bank, N.A.
P.O. Box 27602
Richmond, VA 23261
Application address: c/o Mary Jo Tull, Trust Off., Wachovia Bank, N.A., 1021 E. Cary St., Richmond, VA 23219, tel.: (804) 697-6901

Established in 1963 in VA.
Donor(s): R.E. Plymate.‡
Financial data (yr. ended 12/31/99): Grants paid, $23,500; assets, $1,276,503 (M); expenditures, $25,451; qualifying distributions, $25,451.
Limitations: Giving limited to the Lynchburg, VA, area.
Application information: Application form not required.
Trustee: Wachovia Bank, N.A.
EIN: 546047324

54830
Adelman Family Foundation
7230 Forest Hill Ave.
Richmond, VA 23225-1524

Established in 1995 in VA.
Financial data (yr. ended 12/31/01): Grants paid, $23,000; assets, $544,049 (M); expenditures, $25,115; qualifying distributions, $23,000.
Limitations: Applications not accepted. Giving primarily in Charlottesville, VA.
Application information: Contributes only to pre-selected organizations.
Directors: Graham Adelman, Hilda Adelman, Louis Adelman.
EIN: 541746176

54831
The Boxwood Foundation
William B. Grover, III
9171 Hunt Club Ln.
Mechanicsville, VA 23111

Established in 1985 in VA.
Donor(s): Spotswood W. Box.
Financial data (yr. ended 03/31/02): Grants paid, $23,000; assets, $385,507 (M); expenditures, $27,171; qualifying distributions, $23,000.
Limitations: Applications not accepted. Giving primarily in SC.
Application information: Contributes only to pre-selected organizations.
Trustee: Spotswood W. Box.
EIN: 541377539

54832
The Waltie Fund
1771 Shallowell Rd.
Manakin Sabot, VA 23103-2334

Established in 1991 in VA.
Donor(s): W.N. Street, Jr., J. Randall Street, Mrs. J. Randall Street.
Financial data (yr. ended 12/31/01): Grants paid, $23,000; assets, $452,588 (M); gifts received, $8,000; expenditures, $23,322; qualifying distributions, $23,000.
Limitations: Applications not accepted. Giving primarily in VA, with emphasis on Richmond; some giving also in MD.
Application information: Contributes only to pre-selected organizations.

Officer: J. Randall Street, Pres. and Treas.
Directors: Charles Dixon Kendrick, Marjorie James Street Mitchell, William Henry Street, Jr.
EIN: 541582312

54833
Bernard J. & Charlotte E. Blommer Foundation
2440 Simmons Gap Rd.
Free Union, VA 22940-9802
Contact: Elizabeth Blommer, Tr. or Marguerite J. Saule, Tr.

Financial data (yr. ended 12/31/00): Grants paid, $22,950; assets, $432,766 (M); expenditures, $23,966; qualifying distributions, $23,964.
Limitations: Giving on a national basis.
Application information: Application form not required.
Trustees: Elizabeth Blommer, Marguerite J. Saule.
EIN: 366064571

54834
Teresa and Kathleen Strickland Memorial Fund, Inc.
3035 Holmes Run Rd.
Falls Church, VA 22042-4305

Established in 1997 in VA.
Donor(s): Henry E. Strickland, Muriel B. Strickland.
Financial data (yr. ended 12/31/01): Grants paid, $22,660; assets, $115,631 (M); expenditures, $23,029; qualifying distributions, $23,029.
Limitations: Applications not accepted.
Application information: Contributes only to pre-selected organizations.
Officers: Henry E. Strickland, Pres.; Muriel B. Strickland, Secy.
Director: Elizabeth S. Larson.
EIN: 541833949

54835
The Elm Foundation, Inc.
c/o Earl L. Mielke, Jr.
10127 Hillington Ct.
Vienna, VA 22182

Established in 1999 in VA.
Donor(s): Earl L. Mielke, Jr., Mildred K. Mielke.
Financial data (yr. ended 09/30/01): Grants paid, $22,405; assets, $250,865 (M); gifts received, $175,813; expenditures, $25,967; qualifying distributions, $22,405.
Limitations: Applications not accepted.
Application information: Contributes only to pre-selected organizations.
Officers: Earl L. Mielke, Jr., Pres. and Treas.; Mildred K. Mielke, Secy.
EIN: 541967463

54836
Donald P. King Foundation
218 Gun Club Rd.
Richmond, VA 23221-3335 (804) 353-6009
Contact: Donald P. King, Pres.

Donor(s): Donald P. King.
Financial data (yr. ended 11/30/01): Grants paid, $22,341; assets, $415,797 (M); expenditures, $32,146; qualifying distributions, $22,341.
Limitations: Giving primarily in VA.
Application information: Application form not required.
Officer: Donald P. King, Pres.
EIN: 546040036

VIRGINIA—54848

54837
Wards Corner Lions Club Charity Foundation, Inc.
P.O. Box 1037
Norfolk, VA 23501-1037
Contact: Charles T. Saunders, Secy.-Treas.

Financial data (yr. ended 06/30/02): Grants paid, $22,285; assets, $447,828 (M); gifts received, $3,440; expenditures, $22,657; qualifying distributions, $22,285.
Limitations: Giving limited to southern VA.
Officers and Trustees:* Bill Davis,* Pres.; Edward Kosjer,* V.P.; Charles T. Saunders, Secy.-Treas.
Directors: Richard Arnold, Berry Jacobs, Kerke Johnson, Chip Rogers, Orville Sarratt, Earl Spencer, Richard Stephens, Brodie Williams.
EIN: 541141818

54838
Robert Todd Carter Foundation
640 Dove Cir.
Bluefield, VA 24605   (276) 322-4451
Contact: Estelle Carter Johnson, Pres.

Established in 2000 in VA.
Donor(s): Juanita F. Carter.‡
Financial data (yr. ended 08/31/01): Grants paid, $22,000; assets, $386,006 (M); gifts received, $386,020; expenditures, $22,014; qualifying distributions, $22,000.
Limitations: Giving primarily in VA.
Application information: Application form not required.
Officers: Estelle Carter Johnson, Pres.; Sara Carter Odum, Secy.
Trustees: Robert Estil Carter, Betty Sue Schaughency, Mary Lou Smith.
EIN: 542012658

54839
Irving May & Edith H. May Foundation
5516 Falmouth St., Ste. 302
Richmond, VA 23230
Application address: 305 N.W. 22nd St., Delray Beach, FL 33444
Contact: Edith May Lebet, Pres.

Financial data (yr. ended 11/30/01): Grants paid, $21,800; assets, $360,392 (M); expenditures, $24,429; qualifying distributions, $21,800.
Limitations: Giving primarily in Philadelphia, PA.
Officers: Edith May Lebet, Pres.; Ralph A. May, Secy.; Bernard J. Herbst, Treas.
Directors: Frank E. Hahn, Jr., Margaret B. Hahn.
EIN: 546045912

54840
The Ridgeview-Seder Foundation
4114 N. Ridgeview Rd.
Arlington, VA 22207

Established in 1999 in VA.
Donor(s): Herman J. Obermayer, Betty Nan L. Obermayer.
Financial data (yr. ended 12/31/99): Grants paid, $21,746; assets, $24,362 (M); gifts received, $55,296; expenditures, $30,934; qualifying distributions, $26,741; giving activities include $4,995 for programs.
Limitations: Applications not accepted.
Application information: Contributes only to pre-selected organizations.
Officers: Herman J. Obermayer, Pres. and Treas.; Betty Nan L. Obermayer, Secy.
EIN: 912089594

54841
The Quin Family Foundation
1901 N. Fort Myer Dr., Ste. 1100
Arlington, VA 22209-1688

Established in 1998 in DE.
Donor(s): Whayne S. Quin.
Financial data (yr. ended 12/31/01): Grants paid, $21,725; assets, $5,363 (M); gifts received, $27,929; expenditures, $25,136; qualifying distributions, $21,725.
Limitations: Applications not accepted.
Application information: Contributes only to pre-selected organizations.
Officers: Whayne S. Quin, Pres.; Ursula K. Quin, Exec. V.P. and Secy.-Treas.; David W. Quin, V.P.; Margaret W. Quin, V.P.
EIN: 510385868

54842
Klaus Foundation
3607 Mayland Ct.
Richmond, VA 23233-1409   (804) 270-7401
Contact: Philip W. Klaus, Sr., Pres.

Donor(s): Philip W. Klaus, Jr.
Financial data (yr. ended 10/31/01): Grants paid, $21,646; assets, $365,329 (M); expenditures, $22,551; qualifying distributions, $21,646.
Limitations: Giving primarily in Richmond, VA.
Officers and Directors:* Philip W. Klaus, Sr.,* Pres. and Treas.; Nathalie Klaus,* V.P.; Susan L. Klaus,* V.P.; Edward S. Hirschler, Jr.,* Secy.; Philip W. Klaus, Jr.,* Secy.
EIN: 546036181

54843
Calvert & Sally Simmons Foundation
111 Oronoco St.
Alexandria, VA 22314

Established in 1990 in VA.
Donor(s): Calvert W. Simmons, Sally Dyson Simmons.
Financial data (yr. ended 09/30/01): Grants paid, $21,587; assets, $43,698 (M); gifts received, $35,852; expenditures, $24,736; qualifying distributions, $21,587.
Limitations: Applications not accepted. Giving primarily in the metropolitan Washington, DC, area, including MD and VA.
Application information: Contributes only to pre-selected organizations.
Officers: Calvert W. Simmons, Pres. and Treas.; Sally Dyson Simmons, Secy.
Director: Roger Machanic.
EIN: 541567705

54844
MAIHS Foundation
1209 Riverside Dr.
Newport News, VA 23606

Donor(s): Richard F. Abbitt, Carolyn S. Abbitt.
Financial data (yr. ended 07/31/01): Grants paid, $21,350; assets, $407,208 (M); gifts received, $33,320; expenditures, $22,480; qualifying distributions, $21,350.
Limitations: Applications not accepted. Giving primarily in Newport News, VA.
Application information: Contributes only to pre-selected organizations.
Officers and Directors:* Carolyn S. Abbitt,* Pres.; Richard F. Abbitt,* Pres.
EIN: 521441636

54845
The Tintagel Charitable Foundation
666 Tintagel Ln.
McLean, VA 22101-1835
E-mail: joans@msn.com

Established in 1998 in VA.
Donor(s): Joan H. Smith, T. Eugene Smith.
Financial data (yr. ended 12/31/01): Grants paid, $21,350; assets, $21,362 (M); expenditures, $22,122; qualifying distributions, $21,350.
Limitations: Applications not accepted. Giving primarily in Washington, DC and northern VA.
Application information: Contributes only to pre-selected organizations.
Trustees: Joan H. Smith, T. Eugene Smith.
EIN: 541897430

54846
The Sam and Marion Golden Helping Hand Foundation, Inc.
(Formerly Virginia Scrap Iron & Metal Co. Charitable Foundation, Inc.)
c/o Industrial & Mill Suppliers, Inc.
P.O. Box 8278
Roanoke, VA 24014-0278   (540) 343-3667
Contact: Sam Golden, Pres.

Donor(s): Virginia Scrap Iron & Metal Co., Inc., Industrial & Mill Suppliers, Inc.
Financial data (yr. ended 12/31/01): Grants paid, $21,325; assets, $378,159 (M); gifts received, $16,000; expenditures, $21,802; qualifying distributions, $21,474.
Limitations: Giving primarily in VA.
Officers and Directors:* Sam Golden,* Pres.; Marion Golden,* V.P.; Mary Ann Ward,* Secy-Treas.
EIN: 546050920
Codes: CS, CD

54847
District Lodge No. 3, Sons of Norway Foundation
(Formerly District Lodge No. 3, Sons of Norway Charitable Trust)
c/o Robert E. Norton
922 Dellwood Dr.
Vienna, VA 22180-6121

Financial data (yr. ended 12/31/99): Grants paid, $21,250; assets, $343,482 (M); gifts received, $17,060; expenditures, $23,255; qualifying distributions, $22,270.
Limitations: Applications not accepted. Giving primarily in FL and NY.
Trustees: Alan Arneson, David Dunlop, Ardis R. Gythfeldt, Auden Gythfeldt.
EIN: 237150690
Codes: GTI

54848
Hummel Schimmer Memorial Foundation
12148 Falls Way
Clifton, VA 20124
Contact: William E. Hummel, Chair.

Established in 1989 in VA.
Donor(s): William E. Hummel.
Financial data (yr. ended 11/30/01): Grants paid, $20,825; assets, $996 (M); gifts received, $10,000; expenditures, $20,930; qualifying distributions, $20,825.
Limitations: Giving primarily in VA.
Officer: William E. Hummel, Chair.
EIN: 541549783

54849
B. M. Stanton Foundation
c/o SunTrust Banks, Inc.
P.O. Box 27385
Richmond, VA 23261-7385
Application address: c/o Diane S. Monroe, 1317 Kingfisher Ct., Virginia Beach, VA 23451

Financial data (yr. ended 12/31/01): Grants paid, $20,700; assets, $557,132 (M); expenditures, $22,343; qualifying distributions, $20,700.
Limitations: Giving primarily in Virginia Beach, VA.
Officer and Directors:* Diane S. Monroe,* Chair.; Dorothy Mannix, Robert Stanton.
Trustee: SunTrust Banks, Inc.
EIN: 546191995

54850
A. A. Beiro Family Foundation
c/o Alexander A. Beiro
P.O. Box 1912
Alexandria, VA 22313-1912

Donor(s): Alexander A. Beiro.
Financial data (yr. ended 12/31/01): Grants paid, $20,500; assets, $264,124 (M); gifts received, $5,396; expenditures, $21,652; qualifying distributions, $20,500.
Limitations: Applications not accepted.
Application information: Contributes only to pre-selected organizations.
Directors: Alexander A. Beiro, Christopher J. Beiro, Ruth B. Dale, Jenni B. Reveille.
EIN: 541828045

54851
Greer Foundation, Inc.
50 Floyd Ave.
Rocky Mount, VA 24151

Donor(s): T. Keister Greer.
Financial data (yr. ended 12/31/99): Grants paid, $20,400; assets, $300,000 (M); gifts received, $20,400; expenditures, $20,400; qualifying distributions, $20,400.
Officers and Directors:* T. Keister Greer,* Pres.; Alexander I. Saunders,* V.P. and Secy.; Elizabeth T. Greer,* V.P.; Wendy S. Funderburk,* Treas.
EIN: 541936154

54852
Richard E. Olivieri Family Foundation, Inc.
4425 Corporation Ln., Ste. 400
Virginia Beach, VA 23462-2903

Donor(s): Richard E. Olivieri.
Financial data (yr. ended 12/31/01): Grants paid, $20,233; assets, $137,580 (M); gifts received, $17,583; expenditures, $20,929; qualifying distributions, $20,233.
Limitations: Applications not accepted. Giving limited to VA.
Application information: Contributes only to pre-selected organizations.
Officers and Director:* Richard E. Olivieri,* Pres. and Treas.; Maureen Olivieri, V.P. and Secy.
EIN: 541308959

54853
The RECO Foundation
710 Hospital St.
P.O. Box 25189
Richmond, VA 23260-5189 (804) 644-2800
Contact: Robert C. Courain, Pres.

Donor(s): RECO Constructors, Inc.
Financial data (yr. ended 09/30/01): Grants paid, $20,100; assets, $619,621 (M); gifts received, $20,000; expenditures, $26,409; qualifying distributions, $25,228.

Limitations: Giving primarily in areas of company operations.
Application information: Application form required.
Officers and Directors:* Robert C. Courain, Jr.,* Pres. and Treas.; Ruth C. Courain,* Secy.; Allen C. Goolsby III, Frank G. Louthan, Jr.
EIN: 546039609
Codes: CS, CD

54854
Davis Library, Inc.
c/o B.B. & T.
P.O. Box 5228
Martinsville, VA 24115
Application address: 912 Uniontown Rd., Westminster, MD 21157
Contact: Loring B. Yingling, Treas.

Financial data (yr. ended 12/31/01): Grants paid, $20,000; assets, $346,910 (M); expenditures, $24,774; qualifying distributions, $20,000.
Limitations: Giving limited to Carroll County, MD.
Officers: S. Ray Hollinger, Pres.; R. Neal Hoffman, V.P.; Edwin Shauck, Secy.; Loring B. Yingling, Treas.
Directors: John Moores, Priscilla C. Teeter, Lloyd B. Thomas, Carroll Yingling.
EIN: 520573216

54855
John C. Echols Memorial Fund
c/o Bank of America
P.O. Box 26606
Richmond, VA 23261-6903 (804) 528-2489
Contact: Pamela Mitchell, Trust Off., Bank of America

Financial data (yr. ended 12/31/99): Grants paid, $20,000; assets, $381,073 (M); gifts received, $1,999; expenditures, $24,157; qualifying distributions, $20,000.
Limitations: Giving primarily in VA.
Trustee: Bank of America.
EIN: 546063415

54856
Galliford-Mulard Foundation
2325 Shore Sands Ct.
Virginia Beach, VA 23451

Established in 1997 in VA; funded in 1998.
Donor(s): Genieve Galliford.
Financial data (yr. ended 06/30/02): Grants paid, $20,000; assets, $303,637 (M); expenditures, $34,110; qualifying distributions, $20,000.
Officer: Genieve Galliford, Pres.
EIN: 541874552

54857
The Geary-O'Hara Trust
1412 N. Meade St.
Arlington, VA 22209

Established in 1999 in VA.
Financial data (yr. ended 06/30/01): Grants paid, $20,000; assets, $338,097 (M); gifts received, $350,000; expenditures, $22,242; qualifying distributions, $20,000.
Limitations: Applications not accepted.
Application information: Contributes only to pre-selected organizations.
Trustee: John O'Hara.
EIN: 546461550

54858
Holcomb Family Foundation
P.O. Box 206
Cross Junction, VA 22625

Established in 1986 in VA.
Financial data (yr. ended 12/31/99): Grants paid, $20,000; assets, $192,192 (M); gifts received, $44; expenditures, $20,931; qualifying distributions, $20,000.
Limitations: Applications not accepted. Giving primarily in Winchester, VA.
Application information: Contributes only to pre-selected organizations.
Officer: Mary Jo Stout, Pres. and Secy.-Treas.
Directors: Keith A. Holcomb, Steven J. Holcomb.
EIN: 541386760

54859
Hampton Roads Health Coalition, Inc.
(Formerly Tidewater Health Coalition, Inc.)
287 Independence BLVD.
Virginia Beach, VA 23462

Financial data (yr. ended 09/30/01): Grants paid, $19,800; assets, $137,585 (M); gifts received, $453,876; expenditures, $472,092; qualifying distributions, $238,468.
Limitations: Applications not accepted.
Application information: Contributes only to pre-selected organizations.
Officers: Lindsay Rettie, Pres.; Dennis Turner, V.P.; D. Kaltenmark, Secy.-Treas.; B. Wallace, Exec. Dir.
Directors: Walter Grubbs, Nancy Hicks, Nancy Kennedy, Debbie Kerzel, Matt Manock, H. McHorney, Jr., Leslie Messick.
EIN: 541271014

54860
The Roffman Foundation
P.O. Box 17723
Richmond, VA 23226
Contact: Lawrence E. Roffman, Pres.

Donor(s): Lawrence E. Roffman.
Financial data (yr. ended 06/30/02): Grants paid, $19,704; assets, $151,856 (M); gifts received, $5,000; expenditures, $21,079; qualifying distributions, $19,704.
Limitations: Giving primarily in Richmond, VA.
Officer: Lawrence E. Roffman, Pres.
EIN: 526063707

54861
The Ben D. Conley Charitable & Educational Foundation
c/o Chesapeake Bank, Trust Dept.
P.O. Box 1419
Kilmarnock, VA 22482-1419
Contact: Ben D. Conley, Pres.

Donor(s): Ben D. Conley.
Financial data (yr. ended 11/30/01): Grants paid, $19,600; assets, $715 (M); gifts received, $19,231; expenditures, $20,861; qualifying distributions, $19,600.
Limitations: Giving limited to Lancaster and Northumberland counties, VA.
Officers: Ben D. Conley, Pres.; James Conley, V.P.; Jean H. Light, Secy.; Thomas A. Gosse, Treas.
Director: B.H.B. Hubbard.
EIN: 541398809

54862
The Jennifer Foundation
407 Virginia Ave.
Alexandria, VA 22302

Established in 1997 in IL.
Donor(s): David Phillips, Sr.
Financial data (yr. ended 12/31/01): Grants paid, $19,500; assets, $363,547 (M); expenditures, $22,834; qualifying distributions, $19,500.
Limitations: Applications not accepted. Giving on a national basis, with emphasis on MA and NC.
Application information: Contributes only to pre-selected organizations.

Officers: David Phillips, Jr., Pres.; Nancy Phillips, V.P.; Ruth Ann Phillips, Secy.; David Phillips, Sr., Treas.
EIN: 364159009

54863
The B. Scott & Brenda D. White Foundation
Rt. 2 Box 181 A
Castlewood, VA 24224-9780   (540) 738-8234
Contact: B. Scott White, Tr.

Established in 1997 in VA.
Donor(s): B. Scott White, Brenda D. White.
Financial data (yr. ended 11/30/00): Grants paid, $19,500; assets, $543,255 (M); expenditures, $25,551; qualifying distributions, $24,594; giving activities include $6,051 for programs.
Trustees: B. Scott White, Brenda D. White.
EIN: 546409173

54864
The EMBA Foundation, Inc.
5 Woodduck Rd.
Lexington, VA 24450-2232   (540) 463-3702
Contact: Gloria Smitka, V.P.

Established in 1988 in VA.
Donor(s): Milton Amayun, Raija Amayun, Gloria Smitka, Michael Smitka, Grace Keller, Clarence Amayun.
Financial data (yr. ended 12/31/01): Grants paid, $19,486; assets, $68,486 (M); gifts received, $17,284; expenditures, $20,420; qualifying distributions, $19,486.
Limitations: Giving limited to the northern Philippines.
Application information: Application form required.
Officers: Grace Keller, Pres.; Gloria Smitka, V.P.; Michael Smitka, Secy.-Treas.
Directors: Clarence Amayon, Milton Amayun, Olin Amayun.
EIN: 541458064

54865
Aztec Foundation
P.O. Box 16126
Alexandria, VA 22302

Established in 1988 in VA.
Donor(s): Joseph V. Braddock.
Financial data (yr. ended 12/31/01): Grants paid, $19,453; assets, $757,353 (M); expenditures, $52,668; qualifying distributions, $19,453.
Limitations: Giving primarily in Washington, DC and VA.
Application information: Application form not required.
Trustees: Bertha S. Braddock, Joseph Anthony Braddock, Joseph V. Braddock, Robert Braddock.
EIN: 541490266

54866
The Willard A. Van Engel Fellowship, Inc.
c/o VIMS, Dir.
P.O. Box 1346
Gloucester Point, VA 23062

Established in 1987 in VA.
Donor(s): Willard A. Van Engel.
Financial data (yr. ended 06/30/00): Grants paid, $19,246; assets, $237,935 (M); gifts received, $1,780; expenditures, $29,256; qualifying distributions, $19,246.
Limitations: Giving limited to Gloucester Point, VA.
Application information: Application form required.
Officers: Eugene Burreson, Pres.; Robert J. Burne, V.P.; Richard M. Foard, Secy.; Robert E. Harris, Jr., Treas.

EIN: 541401233
Codes: GTI

54867
The Kentland Foundation, Inc.
c/o Kentland Farms
P.O. Box 879
Berryville, VA 22611   (540) 955-1268

Incorporated about 1966 in MD.
Donor(s): Otis Beall Kent.‡
Financial data (yr. ended 12/31/01): Grants paid, $18,750; assets, $18,692,988 (M); expenditures, $2,529,865; qualifying distributions, $226,714.
Limitations: Applications not accepted. Giving primarily in Washington, DC, MD, and VA.
Application information: Contributes only to pre-selected organizations.
Officers: Helene Walker, Pres.; Sheila Stedman, Exec. V.P.; William Loren, V.P.; Jack Walker, Secy.-Treas.
EIN: 526070323

54868
Edward D. Barlow Foundation
845 Castile Pl.
Richmond, VA 23233

Established in 2000 in VA.
Donor(s): Edward D. Barlow.
Financial data (yr. ended 12/31/01): Grants paid, $18,688; assets, $2,652 (M); gifts received, $10,000; expenditures, $18,819; qualifying distributions, $18,688.
Limitations: Applications not accepted.
Application information: Contributes only to pre-selected organizations.
Directors: Edward D. Barlow, Edward Barlow II, Richard L. Grier.
EIN: 541988746

54869
The Lenasa Foundation, Inc.
c/o J. Asa Whitt
P.O. Box 32112
Richmond, VA 23294

Established in 1958 in VA.
Donor(s): J. Asa Whitt, Lena M. Whitt.
Financial data (yr. ended 07/31/01): Grants paid, $18,622; assets, $104,720 (M); expenditures, $19,265; qualifying distributions, $18,622.
Limitations: Applications not accepted. Giving primarily in VA.
Application information: Contributes only to pre-selected organizations.
Officers: Lena M. Whitt, Pres.; J. Asa Whitt, Treas.
Director: Joseph A. Whitt, Jr.
EIN: 541648229

54870
Rae Foundation
813 Colony Bluff Pl.
Richmond, VA 23233-5561

Established in 1998 in MI.
Donor(s): Brad A. Evans.
Financial data (yr. ended 12/31/01): Grants paid, $18,500; assets, $43,213 (M); gifts received, $50,000; expenditures, $19,985; qualifying distributions, $18,500.
Limitations: Applications not accepted. Giving on a national basis.
Application information: Contributes only to pre-selected organizations.
Directors: Brad A. Evans, Susan L. Evans.
EIN: 383436217

54871
Rogers Foundation, Inc.
9229 Arlington Blvd., Ste. 258
Fairfax, VA 22031

Donor(s): William F. Rogers.
Financial data (yr. ended 09/30/01): Grants paid, $18,500; assets, $494,108 (M); gifts received, $4,500; expenditures, $23,100; qualifying distributions, $18,500.
Limitations: Applications not accepted. Giving primarily in AR and VA.
Application information: Contributes only to pre-selected organizations.
Officers: William F. Rogers, Pres.; Rev. Carl L. Nissen, Secy.; Allen Hildreth, Treas.
EIN: 541248101

54872
Windcrest Foundation, Inc.
2082 Bowmans Mill Rd.
Middletown, VA 22645
Contact: Susanne H. Blount, Pres.

Established in 1997 in VA.
Donor(s): David L. Blount.
Financial data (yr. ended 12/31/01): Grants paid, $18,500; assets, $579,668 (M); expenditures, $21,039; qualifying distributions, $18,500.
Officers: Susanne H. Blount, Pres.; David L. Blount, V.P. and Secy.-Treas.
EIN: 541847897

54873
Emma E. Bogart Trust Fund
c/o Bank of America
P.O. Box 26606
Richmond, VA 23261

Financial data (yr. ended 06/30/00): Grants paid, $18,449; assets, $380,198 (M); expenditures, $21,397; qualifying distributions, $18,777.
Limitations: Applications not accepted. Giving limited to Petersburg, VA.
Application information: Contributes only to pre-selected organizations.
Trustee: Bank of America.
EIN: 546194559

54874
Wilbur H. Palmer Trust
c/o Bank of America
P.O. Box 26606
Richmond, VA 23261

Financial data (yr. ended 12/31/99): Grants paid, $18,296; assets, $406,522 (M); expenditures, $22,684; qualifying distributions, $18,296.
Limitations: Applications not accepted. Giving primarily in VA.
Application information: Contributes only to pre-selected organizations.
Trustee: Bank of America.
EIN: 546159009

54875
The Robert M. and Joyce A. Johnson Foundation
1611 Aerie Ln.
McLean, VA 22101-4662

Established in 1998 in VA.
Donor(s): Robert M. Johnson, Joyce A. Johnson.
Financial data (yr. ended 06/30/02): Grants paid, $18,220; assets, $246,354 (M); expenditures, $20,575; qualifying distributions, $18,220.
Limitations: Applications not accepted. Giving primarily in Washington, DC.
Application information: Contributes only to pre-selected organizations.
Officer: Robert M. Johnson, Pres.
Directors: Stanley L. Berlinsky, Joyce A. Johnson.

54875—VIRGINIA

EIN: 742887331

54876
Portsmouth Children's Home, Inc.
P.O. Box 399
Portsmouth, VA 23705
Application address: 3441 Bridge Rd., Suffolk, VA 23435
Contact: Thomas Moore, Pres.

Established in 1989 in VA.
Financial data (yr. ended 12/31/01): Grants paid, $18,190; assets, $727,429 (M); expenditures, $32,098; qualifying distributions, $18,190.
Limitations: Giving primarily in Portsmouth, VA.
Officers and Directors:* Thomas Moore,* Pres.; William H. Oast III,* V.P.; J.H. Hardin,* Secy.; David Todd,* Treas.; Ted Masters, Don Williams.
EIN: 541449277

54877
R. and M. Fink Family Trust
15365 Worth Ct.
Centreville, VA 20120

Established in 1999 in VA.
Donor(s): Mary Fink, Richard H. Fink.
Financial data (yr. ended 12/31/01): Grants paid, $18,100; assets, $148,492 (M); gifts received, $50,000; expenditures, $21,112; qualifying distributions, $18,100.
Limitations: Applications not accepted.
Application information: Contributes only to pre-selected organizations.
Directors: Mary Fink, Richard H. Fink.
EIN: 546466359

54878
Pendleton Construction Corporation Foundation
c/o Pendleton Construction Corp.
P.O. Box 549
Wytheville, VA 24382 (276) 228-8601
Contact: William N. Pendleton, Dir.

Donor(s): Pendleton Construction Corp.
Financial data (yr. ended 12/31/01): Grants paid, $18,100; assets, $89,185 (M); expenditures, $19,033; qualifying distributions, $18,022.
Limitations: Giving primarily in Wythe County, VA.
Application information: Application form not required.
Directors: Edmund Pendleton, Jr., William N. Pendleton.
EIN: 540846282
Codes: CS, CD

54879
Celia Kleinfeld Krichman Charitable Trust
c/o Edward S. Stein
P.O. Box 3789
Norfolk, VA 23514

Established in 1995.
Financial data (yr. ended 12/31/99): Grants paid, $18,080; assets, $317,329 (M); expenditures, $23,429; qualifying distributions, $17,984.
Limitations: Applications not accepted. Giving primarily in VA.
Application information: Contributes only to pre-selected organizations.
Trustee: Edward S. Stein.
EIN: 546388303

54880
Randolph W. Church, Jr. Charitable Trust
5114 Forsgate Pl.
Fairfax, VA 22030-4507

Established in 1998.
Donor(s): Randolph W. Church.
Financial data (yr. ended 12/31/01): Grants paid, $18,000; assets, $1 (M); expenditures, $18,200; qualifying distributions, $18,000.
Trustee: Randolph W. Church.
EIN: 546431526

54881
The Commerce Bank Foundation
c/o B.B. & T.
P.O. Box 5228
Martinsville, VA 24115

Established in 1992 in VA.
Donor(s): Commerce Bank of Virginia Beach.
Financial data (yr. ended 12/31/01): Grants paid, $18,000; assets, $377,747 (M); expenditures, $23,410; qualifying distributions, $17,941.
Limitations: Applications not accepted. Giving limited to the Virginia Beach, VA, area.
Application information: Contributes only to pre-selected organizations.
Directors: G. Robert Aston, McLenore Birdsong, Jr., Thomas C. Broyles, Arthur L. Cherry, J.W. Whiting Chisman, Jr., Dorothy M. Doumar, Andrew S. Fine, W. Ashton Lewis.
Trustee: B.B. & T.
EIN: 541647252
Codes: CS, CD

54882
SMACNA College of Fellows Foundation
P.O. Box 221230
Chantilly, VA 20151-1230 (703) 803-2980
Contact: Ronald D. Lewis

Donor(s): Sheet Metal and Air Conditioning National Association (SMACNA).
Financial data (yr. ended 12/31/01): Grants paid, $18,000; assets, $194,724 (M); gifts received, $58,258; expenditures, $18,060; qualifying distributions, $18,060.
Limitations: Giving primarily in areas of company operations.
Application information: Application form required.
Officers and Governors: Bruce J. Stockwell, Chair.; Clinton A. Gowan, Vice-Chair.; Robert J. Fenlon, F.W. Know, David M. McKenney, Donald G. Romano, Robert A. Zill, Sr.
EIN: 521538775
Codes: GTI

54883
Eugene Walters Family Foundation
161 Business Park Dr.
Virginia Beach, VA 23462-1129

Established in 1986 in VA.
Donor(s): Eugene Walters.
Financial data (yr. ended 11/30/01): Grants paid, $18,000; assets, $290,685 (M); expenditures, $19,505; qualifying distributions, $18,000.
Limitations: Applications not accepted. Giving primarily in VA.
Application information: Contributes only to pre-selected organizations.
Officers and Directors:* Eugene Walters,* Pres.; Barbara W. Doherman,* V.P.; Linda Croker, Treas.
EIN: 541402087

54884
Monacan Foundation
33 Runswick Dr.
Richmond, VA 23233

Established in 1996 in VA.
Donor(s): Collins Denny III, Rebecca M. Denny.
Financial data (yr. ended 12/31/01): Grants paid, $17,976; assets, $12,697 (M); gifts received, $20,791; expenditures, $18,244; qualifying distributions, $18,219.
Officers: Collins Denny III, Pres.; Anne C. Denny, Treas.
Director: Rebecca M. Denny.
EIN: 311478155

54885
W. B. Shafer, Jr. Memorial Trust
403 Boush St., Ste. 300
Norfolk, VA 23510

Established in 1992 in VA.
Donor(s): W. B. Sharer.
Financial data (yr. ended 08/31/01): Grants paid, $17,617; assets, $332,680 (M); expenditures, $26,034; qualifying distributions, $17,617.
Limitations: Applications not accepted. Giving primarily in Norfolk, VA.
Application information: Contributes only to pre-selected organizations.
Committee Members: Lawrence Goldrich, Chair.; Mary Bulman, James Roy Smith.
Trustee: Gordon B. Tayloe, Jr.
EIN: 546330779

54886
Walter C. & Ella Rawls Educational Trust
c/o SunTrust Banks, Inc.
P.O. Box 27385
Richmond, VA 23261-7385

Financial data (yr. ended 06/30/00): Grants paid, $17,500; assets, $437,032 (M); expenditures, $22,549; qualifying distributions, $19,837.
Limitations: Giving limited to residents of Gates, NC and Forest Glen, Kennedy, Suffolk and Sussex, VA.
Application information: Contact local high schools in Suffolk, Forest Glen, Kennedy, and Suffolk, VA, and Gates, NC, for application information. Application form required.
Advisory Committee: Cleveland M. Hawkins, John Hicks, Elwood Lewis, M.D., Joyce Trump, Charles Turner, Jane York.
Trustee: SunTrust Banks, Inc.
EIN: 546053305
Codes: GTI

54887
Irene & Tucker Grigg Foundation
c/o S. Tucker Grigg, Jr.
119 Shockoe Slip
Richmond, VA 23219-4121

Established in 1993 in VA.
Donor(s): S. Tucker Grigg, Jr., Irene S. Grigg.
Financial data (yr. ended 12/31/01): Grants paid, $17,128; assets, $463,591 (M); expenditures, $17,368; qualifying distributions, $17,128.
Limitations: Applications not accepted. Giving primarily in GA and VA.
Application information: Contributes only to pre-selected organizations.
Officer: S. Tucker Grigg, Jr., Pres.
Directors: Eleanor A. Grigg, S. Tucker Grigg III.
EIN: 541694119

54888
CHI Eagle Foundation
P.O. Box 13109
Norfolk, VA 23506-3109 (757) 466-0464
Contact: Cyrus A. Dolph, IV, Secy.

Established in 1987 in VA.
Financial data (yr. ended 12/31/01): Grants paid, $17,125; assets, $100,395 (M); gifts received, $19,746; expenditures, $20,554; qualifying distributions, $17,990.
Limitations: Giving primarily in VA.
Officers and Directors:* James R. Chisman,* Pres. and Treas.; Anne A. Chisman,* V.P. and Secy.; Cyrus A. Dolph IV,* Secy.

EIN: 541438465

54889
The William G. Reynolds, Jr. Charitable Foundation
8401 Patterson Ave., Ste. 105
Richmond, VA 23229 (804) 281-4660

Established in 1998 in VA.
Financial data (yr. ended 12/31/01): Grants paid, $17,110; assets, $330,857 (M); expenditures, $21,800; qualifying distributions, $17,110.
Limitations: Applications not accepted. Giving primarily in VA.
Application information: Contributes only to pre-selected organizations.
Trustees: Susan C. Armstrong, Mary L. Mason, William G. Reynolds, Jr.
EIN: 541900372

54890
James Randolph & Estelle Joyce Charitable Trust
P.O. Box 4311
Martinsville, VA 24115-4311

Financial data (yr. ended 12/31/00): Grants paid, $16,750; assets, $25,943 (M); expenditures, $17,035; qualifying distributions, $0.
Trustee: James Randolph.
EIN: 546439824

54891
The Van Brimer Family Foundation
c/o Eggleston Smith
460 McLaws Cir., Ste. 120
Williamsburg, VA 23185

Established in 1997 in VA.
Financial data (yr. ended 04/30/02): Grants paid, $16,700; assets, $305,661 (M); expenditures, $21,354; qualifying distributions, $16,700.
Limitations: Applications not accepted. Giving primarily in VA.
Application information: Contributes only to pre-selected organizations.
Directors: Erica Van Brimer Goldfarb, H. Winn Van Brimer, Jane W. Van Brimer, R. Hugh Van Brimer.
EIN: 541850906

54892
The Bane Foundation
c/o Eugene M. Bane, Jr.
P.O. Box 1538
Salem, VA 24153

Established in 1994 in VA.
Financial data (yr. ended 12/31/01): Grants paid, $16,500; assets, $489,604 (M); gifts received, $1,500; expenditures, $17,309; qualifying distributions, $16,500.
Limitations: Applications not accepted. Giving primarily in VA.
Application information: Contributes only to pre-selected organizations.
Officers and Directors:* Eugene M. Bane, Jr.,* Pres.; Elizabeth S. Stanley,* Secy.-Treas.
EIN: 541716303

54893
Sue W. Massie Trust
c/o Bank of America, N.A.
P.O. Box 26606
Richmond, VA 23261-6606
Application address: c/o William Massie Smith, Jr., 418 E. Water St., Charlottesville, VA 22902, tel.: (703) 296-2161

Financial data (yr. ended 06/30/99): Grants paid, $16,500; assets, $285,942 (M); expenditures, $19,556; qualifying distributions, $17,203.
Limitations: Giving primarily in Richmond, VA.

Trustee: Bank of America.
EIN: 546030503

54894
The Norton Charitable Foundation
3066 Gatehouse Plz.
Falls Church, VA 22042
Contact: Howard R. Norton III, Tr.

Financial data (yr. ended 09/30/01): Grants paid, $16,285; assets, $47 (M); gifts received, $5,000; expenditures, $16,285; qualifying distributions, $16,285.
Limitations: Giving primarily in Washington, DC and VA.
Trustees: Howard R. Norton III, Gerald H. Sherman.
EIN: 231626996

54895
Vision Charitable Trust
356 Copperfield Ln.
Herndon, VA 20170-5310

Established in 2000.
Financial data (yr. ended 12/31/00): Grants paid, $16,005; assets, $8,328 (M); gifts received, $23,601; expenditures, $16,090; qualifying distributions, $16,005.
Limitations: Applications not accepted. Giving primarily in Herndon, VA.
Application information: Contributes only to pre-selected organizations.
Trustees: Hany Salah, Mona Salah.
EIN: 546465120

54896
Bridgers/Short Foundation
c/o Richard T. Short
P.O. Box 933
Virginia Beach, VA 23451

Established in 1997 in VA.
Donor(s): Beverly B. Short, Richard T. Short.
Financial data (yr. ended 12/31/01): Grants paid, $16,000; assets, $640,426 (M); expenditures, $24,865; qualifying distributions, $16,000.
Limitations: Applications not accepted.
Application information: Contributes only to pre-selected organizations.
Officers and Directors:* Beverly B. Short,* Pres.; Richard T. Short,* V.P.; Marc T. Short,* Secy.-Treas.; Katherine L.S. Franta, James F. Short.
EIN: 541871352

54897
Das Charitable Foundation
6717 Holford Ln.
Springfield, VA 22152

Established in 1999 in DE.
Donor(s): B.R. Das, Saroj Das.
Financial data (yr. ended 06/30/01): Grants paid, $16,000; assets, $175,143 (M); gifts received, $50,000; expenditures, $16,210; qualifying distributions, $16,000.
Limitations: Applications not accepted.
Application information: Contributes only to pre-selected organizations.
Officers and Directors:* B.R. Das,* Pres.; Saroj R. Das,* Secy.-Treas.; Sandeep Das.
EIN: 510395118

54898
The O. B. Falls and Elizabeth L. Falls Foundation
600 E. Main St., Ste. 2400
Richmond, VA 23219
Contact: Donald L. Falls, Secy.

Established in 1999 in VA.
Financial data (yr. ended 12/31/01): Grants paid, $16,000; assets, $835,001 (M); gifts received,

$6,400; expenditures, $35,264; qualifying distributions, $16,000.
Officers and Directors:* Elizabeth L. Falls,* Pres.; Donald L. Falls, Secy.; Harriet F. Burnett, Marti DiBianco, Susan Fegley.
EIN: 541949243

54899
Emma Scott Taylor Education Trust
6620 W. Broad St., Ste. 300
Richmond, VA 23230
Contact: Austin Brockenbrough III, Tr., or Robert F. Norfleet, Tr.

Financial data (yr. ended 01/31/00): Grants paid, $16,000; assets, $300,052 (M); expenditures, $16,279; qualifying distributions, $15,884.
Limitations: Giving primarily in VA.
Trustees: Austin Brockenbrough III, Robert F. Norfleet.
EIN: 546072251

54900
The INRA Foundation
2300 Cedarfield Pkwy., Ste. 363
Richmond, VA 23223

Established in 1990 in VA.
Donor(s): Inez G. Roop, Ralph G. Roop.
Financial data (yr. ended 12/31/01): Grants paid, $15,973; assets, $220,514 (M); expenditures, $16,989; qualifying distributions, $15,973.
Limitations: Applications not accepted. Giving primarily in VA.
Application information: Contributes only to pre-selected organizations.
Officers: Ralph G. Roop, Pres.; Inez G. Roop, Secy.
EIN: 541531156

54901
Chinese Society for Women's Studies, Inc.
2907 Strathaven Pl.
Vienna, VA 22181-5915
Contact: Wu Xu

Established in 1997 in NY.
Donor(s): The Ford Foundation.
Financial data (yr. ended 06/30/02): Grants paid, $15,805; assets, $32,936 (M); gifts received, $30,150; expenditures, $39,911; qualifying distributions, $15,805.
Officers: Ping-Chun Husing, Co-Chair.; Yanmei Wei, Co-Chair.; Zongmin Li, Treas.
EIN: 113169060

54902
Naccash Foundation, Inc.
8501 Lewinsville Rd.
McLean, VA 22102-2210 (703) 734-9198
Contact: Rt. Rev. Joseph F. Francavilla, Pres.

Established in 1995.
Financial data (yr. ended 12/31/01): Grants paid, $15,640; assets, $694,074 (M); gifts received, $7,820; expenditures, $52,422; qualifying distributions, $15,640.
Limitations: Giving primarily in CA; some giving also in Washington, DC, MD, and VA.
Application information: Application form required.
Officers: Rt. Rev. Joseph F. Francavilla, Pres.; Rt. Rev. Charles Aboody, Secy.
EIN: 541560773

54903
J. P. Yancey Foundation
P.O. Box 1487
Newport News, VA 23601-0487
(757) 595-3306
Contact: Robert E. Yancey, Pres.

Financial data (yr. ended 05/31/02): Grants paid, $15,575; assets, $309,714 (M); expenditures, $16,499; qualifying distributions, $15,575.
Limitations: Giving primarily in VA.
Application information: Awards usually less than $1,000.
Officers and Directors:* Robert E. Yancey,* Pres.; Eloise A. Yancey,* Treas.
EIN: 546041815

54904
Allstadt Hardin Foundation
11570 Greenwich Point Rd.
Reston, VA 20194

Established in 2000 in VA.
Donor(s): Louis W. Allstadt.
Financial data (yr. ended 12/31/01): Grants paid, $15,500; assets, $522,465 (M); gifts received, $2,730; expenditures, $29,585; qualifying distributions, $15,500.
Limitations: Applications not accepted.
Application information: Contributes only to pre-selected organizations.
Officers: Louis W. Allstadt, Pres. and Treas.; Melinda G. Hardin, V.P. and Secy.
Directors: John A. Allstadt, Max H. Allstadt.
EIN: 542014941

54905
Lawson-Fierbaugh Foundation
(Formerly The Lawson-Fierbaugh Foundation)
P.O. Box 8400
Bristol, VA 24203

Established in 1987 in VA.
Donor(s): Joseph W. Lawson, Sr.
Financial data (yr. ended 11/30/01): Grants paid, $15,350; assets, $405,313 (M); expenditures, $17,079; qualifying distributions, $15,350.
Limitations: Applications not accepted. Giving primarily in VA.
Application information: Contributes only to pre-selected organizations.
Trustees: Joseph W. Lawson, Sr., Marguerite F. Lawson.
EIN: 626207011

54906
Smith Evans Foundation, Inc.
3027 John Marshall Dr.
Arlington, VA 22207-1339

Established in 1996 in VA.
Donor(s): Ernest P. Evans.
Financial data (yr. ended 12/31/01): Grants paid, $15,300; assets, $832,115 (M); expenditures, $62,246; qualifying distributions, $15,300.
Limitations: Applications not accepted.
Application information: Contributes only to pre-selected organizations.
Officers and Trustees:* Geoffrey O. Lindstrom,* Pres.; Donald L. Green,* V.P. and Secy.; Robert A. Foster,* Treas.
EIN: 541779569

54907
The Scherer Foundation
c/o J. Hamilton Scherer, Jr.
309 Oak Ln.
Richmond, VA 23226

Established in 1998 in VA.
Donor(s): J. Hamilton Scherer, Jr., Dorn Ellison Scherer.
Financial data (yr. ended 12/31/01): Grants paid, $15,272; assets, $72,434 (M); expenditures, $16,282; qualifying distributions, $15,114.
Limitations: Applications not accepted. Giving primarily in VA.
Application information: Contributes only to pre-selected organizations.
Officers and Directors:* Dorn Ellison Scherer,* Pres.; J. Hamilton Scherer, Jr.,* Secy.-Treas.
EIN: 541922686

54908
The Fitzgerald Foundation, Inc.
14367 Round Lick Ln.
Centreville, VA 20120
Contact: Susan Fitzgerald, Pres.

Established in 1996 in VA.
Donor(s): Michael Fitzgerald, Susan Fitzgerald.
Financial data (yr. ended 06/30/01): Grants paid, $15,127; assets, $210,592 (M); gifts received, $132,382; expenditures, $19,825; qualifying distributions, $15,127.
Limitations: Giving primarily in VA.
Officers: Susan Fitzgerald, Pres. and Secy.-Treas.; Michael Fitzgerald, V.P.
EIN: 541829850

54909
Birdsong Trust Fund
c/o W.R. Savage III
P.O. Box 1876
Suffolk, VA 23439-1876 (757) 539-3474
Application address: c/o Suffolk Iron Works, Suffolk, VA 23434, tel.: (757) 539-2353
Contact: John C. Harrell, Pres.

Donor(s): Birdsong Corp.
Financial data (yr. ended 12/31/01): Grants paid, $15,125; assets, $905,696 (M); gifts received, $10,000; expenditures, $24,432; qualifying distributions, $15,125.
Limitations: Giving limited to the Suffolk, VA, area.
Officers and Trustees:* John C. Harrell,* Pres.; W.R. Savage III,* Secy.; Jack W. Nurney,* Treas.
EIN: 546039845
Codes: CS, CD

54910
The Walter Franklin and Dorothy G. Covington Foundation
1036 Queenstown Rd.
Lancaster, VA 22503

Established in 2000 in VA.
Financial data (yr. ended 12/31/01): Grants paid, $15,000; assets, $632,639 (M); expenditures, $20,433; qualifying distributions, $15,000.
Limitations: Applications not accepted.
Application information: Contributes only to pre-selected organizations.
Committee Members: Margie Gano, Sally Shackleford, Reginald V. Shaw.
Director: A. Wayne Saunders.
EIN: 541986978

54911
Floyd W. Harris Foundation for Personal Evangelism, Inc.
6817 Alpine Dr.
Annandale, VA 22003

Established in 1986 in VA.
Donor(s): Floyd W. Harris.
Financial data (yr. ended 12/31/00): Grants paid, $15,000; assets, $1,379,256 (M); gifts received, $1,300,096; expenditures, $32,653; qualifying distributions, $15,000.
Limitations: Applications not accepted. Giving primarily in Richmond, VA.
Application information: Contributes only to pre-selected organizations.
Officers and Directors:* Floyd W. Harris,* Pres.; Charles H. Burton,* Secy.; Richard F. Harris, Nimrod McNair.
EIN: 541384875

54912
The Abe & Kathyrn Selsky Foundation, Inc.
c/o RPK
8133 Leesburg Pike, Ste. 550
Vienna, VA 22182 (703) 506-9700
Contact: Gary M. Abramson, Pres.

Established in 1996 in MD.
Donor(s): Abe Selsky.
Financial data (yr. ended 12/31/00): Grants paid, $15,000; assets, $344,797 (M); gifts received, $6,750; expenditures, $19,507; qualifying distributions, $15,000.
Officers: Gary M. Anderson, Pres. and Treas.; Lisa Reich Dillion, V.P.; Beth Rubinstein, V.P.; Ronald D. Abramson, Secy.
EIN: 522006783

54913
The David A. Trevillian Charitable Trust
c/o William J. Irvin
600 E. Main St., 20th Fl.
Richmond, VA 23219

Established in 1994 in VA.
Financial data (yr. ended 12/31/01): Grants paid, $15,000; assets, $108,690 (M); expenditures, $88,358; qualifying distributions, $15,000.
Limitations: Applications not accepted. Giving limited to Richmond, VA.
Application information: Contributes only to pre-selected organizations.
Trustee: William J. Irvin.
EIN: 546381596

54914
Winston O. Weaver Family Foundation, Inc.
P.O. Box 808
Harrisonburg, VA 22803

Established in 1985 in VA.
Donor(s): Winston O. Weaver, Sr.,‡ Rockingham Construction Co.
Financial data (yr. ended 12/31/01): Grants paid, $14,950; assets, $194,256 (M); gifts received, $18,305; expenditures, $21,854; qualifying distributions, $14,950.
Limitations: Applications not accepted. Giving primarily in Harrisonburg, VA.
Application information: Contributes only to pre-selected organizations.
Officers and Directors:* Phyllis L. Weaver,* Pres.; Winston O. Weaver, Jr.,* V.P.; M. Steven Weaver,* Secy.; M. Gregory Weaver,* Treas.
EIN: 541342706

54915
The Danwell Foundation
775 Allen Rd.
Earlysville, VA 22936-1868

Established in 1997 in VA.
Donor(s): Harry A. Wellons, Jr., Florence Lee Wellons.
Financial data (yr. ended 12/31/01): Grants paid, $14,917; assets, $280,211 (M); gifts received, $14,928; expenditures, $16,097; qualifying distributions, $14,917.
Limitations: Applications not accepted. Giving primarily in VA.
Application information: Contributes only to pre-selected organizations.

VIRGINIA—54927

Officer: Harry A. Wellons, Jr., Pres.
Director: Florence Lee Wellons.
EIN: 541850966

54916
Brent Family Foundation
909 E. Main St., Ste. 1200
Richmond, VA 23219-3095

Established in 1997 in VA.
Donor(s): Virginia M. Brent.
Financial data (yr. ended 12/31/01): Grants paid, $14,750; assets, $368,314 (M); expenditures, $16,312; qualifying distributions, $14,750.
Limitations: Applications not accepted.
Application information: Contributes only to pre-selected organizations.
Officers and Directors:* Virginia M. Brent,* Pres.; A. Mason Brent,* Secy.; Virginia Brent Hailes, Maria Brent Jones, Robert Brent Peek, Elizabeth Marshall Brent Waterman.
EIN: 541846029

54917
Loupassi Foundation
2601 Park Ave.
Richmond, VA 23220-2645

Established in 1999 in VA.
Donor(s): Manuel G. Loupassi.
Financial data (yr. ended 12/31/01): Grants paid, $14,705; assets, $267,584 (M); gifts received, $100,000; expenditures, $14,835; qualifying distributions, $14,705.
Limitations: Applications not accepted.
Application information: Contributes only to pre-selected organizations.
Officer: Manuel G. Loupassi, Mgr.
EIN: 541947904

54918
Nathan's Gift Foundation
4455 Royal Oak Dr., S.W.
Roanoke, VA 24018 (540) 989-1021
Contact: Bayard Harris, Pres.

Financial data (yr. ended 12/31/01): Grants paid, $14,683; assets, $29,460 (M); gifts received, $10,793; expenditures, $14,785; qualifying distributions, $14,683.
Limitations: Giving primarily in VA.
Application information: Application form not required.
Officers: Bayard Harris, Pres. and Treas.; Rebecca Harris, Secy.
EIN: 541696419

54919
The Amy Elizabeth Lauth Foundation
c/o Robert M. McNichols
3333 Peters Creek Rd.
Roanoke, VA 24019 (540) 366-0622

Established in 1997 in VA.
Donor(s): Mary Elyn McNichols, Robert McNichols.
Financial data (yr. ended 12/31/01): Grants paid, $14,637; assets, $180,897 (M); gifts received, $67,136; expenditures, $16,928; qualifying distributions, $14,637.
Officer: Robert M. McNichols, Pres. and Secy.-Treas.
EIN: 541849835

54920
John T. & Mary O'Brien Gibson Foundation
c/o Becker Tax Svcs.
3318 Dauphine Dr.
Falls Church, VA 22042-3725
Application address: 4830 Glenbrook Rd. N.W., Washington, DC 20016, tel.: (202) 362-3412
Contact: Mary O'Brien Gibson, Dir.

Donor(s): John T. Gibson, Mary O'Brien Gibson.
Financial data (yr. ended 12/31/01): Grants paid, $14,500; assets, $201,496 (M); gifts received, $50,000; expenditures, $14,586; qualifying distributions, $14,500.
Limitations: Giving primarily in the Washington, DC, area.
Director: Mary O'Brien Gibson.
EIN: 237004394

54921
Mecklenburg Scholarship Association, Inc.
504 E. 2nd St.
Chase City, VA 23924-1716 (434) 372-5353
Contact: A. Duke Reid, Secuy.-Treas.

Donor(s): Mary Roberts Pritchet Trust Fund, A.E. Wills Memorial Trust.
Financial data (yr. ended 05/31/01): Grants paid, $14,500; assets, $30,797 (M); gifts received, $15,819; expenditures, $16,727; qualifying distributions, $16,727.
Limitations: Giving limited to Chase City, VA; loans limited to Mecklenburg County, VA.
Application information: Application form required.
Officers and Directors:* W.S. Hundley, Jr.,* Pres.; Clarence O. Johnson,* V.P.; A. Duke Reid, Secy.-Treas.; Mrs. W.J. Cary, Thomas C. Emory, Ed Hall, Mrs. W.G. Moody, Mrs. Randall Suslick, Mrs. Dan M. Tucker.
EIN: 546040510
Codes: GTI

54922
Youth Opportunities Unlimited
600 Southlake Blvd.
Richmond, VA 23236
Application address: c/o Gail Long, Dir., Community Devel., 930 Stony Point Pkwy., Ste. 350, Richmond, VA 23235, tel.: (804) 379-7350

Established in 1992 in VA.
Donor(s): Ukrop's Super Markets, Inc., Richfood, Inc.
Financial data (yr. ended 12/31/01): Grants paid, $14,500; assets, $368,516 (M); expenditures, $10,683; qualifying distributions, $15,425.
Limitations: Giving primarily in VA.
Officers and Directors:* James E. Ukrop,* Pres. and Secy.; David J. Naquin,* V.P.; Robert S. Ukrop.
EIN: 541615588
Codes: CS, CD

54923
The Joan H. Moore Charitable Trust
P.O. Box 17035
Richmond, VA 23226

Established in 1998 in VA.
Financial data (yr. ended 12/31/01): Grants paid, $14,340; assets, $66,739 (M); expenditures, $14,921; qualifying distributions, $14,340.
Limitations: Applications not accepted. Giving primarily in Richmond, VA.
Application information: Contributes only to pre-selected organizations.
Trustee: Virginia Baptist Foundation.
EIN: 546443407

54924
The Robert and Luise Patterson Family Foundation
700 Tiber Ln.
Richmond, VA 23226

Established in 1997 in VA.
Donor(s): Robert H. Patterson, Jr.
Financial data (yr. ended 12/31/01): Grants paid, $14,300; assets, $27,302 (M); gifts received, $30,052; expenditures, $15,612; qualifying distributions, $14,300.
Limitations: Applications not accepted.
Application information: Contributes only to pre-selected organizations.
Officers and Directors:* Robert H. Patterson, Jr.,* Pres. and Treas.; Luise W. Patterson,* V.P. and Secy.; India Patterson Gregory, Margaret Patterson Mansfield, Robert H. Patterson III.
EIN: 541867031

54925
The Herndon Fortnightly Club
c/o Margaret Cyrus
P.O. Box 55
Herndon, VA 20172

Established around 1995.
Financial data (yr. ended 02/28/02): Grants paid, $14,203; assets, $276,284 (M); gifts received, $346; expenditures, $18,264; qualifying distributions, $14,203.
Limitations: Applications not accepted.
Application information: Contributes only to pre-selected organizations.
Officers: Nancy Jordon, Pres.; Thelma Hubert, V.P.; Nancy Jordon, Recording Secy.; Martha Rogers, Corr. Secy.; Margaret Cyrus, Treas.; Josephine E. Burns, Caroline Myres.
Director: Virginia Clarity.
EIN: 546052342

54926
LF & C Foundation
c/o Randolph F. Totten
P.O. Box 1535
Richmond, VA 23218-1535 (804) 788-8281

Established in 1997 in VA.
Financial data (yr. ended 12/31/01): Grants paid, $14,200; assets, $290,240 (M); expenditures, $16,635; qualifying distributions, $14,200.
Limitations: Giving primarily in Richmond, VA.
Application information: Application form not required.
Officers and Directors:* Virginia H. Totten,* Pres.; Randolph F. Totten, V.P. and Secy.; Caroline M. Totten, Fitz R. Totten, Louise G. Totten.
EIN: 541810269

54927
Mildred Alderson Trust
P.O. Box 17035
Richmond, VA 23226

Established in 1997 in VA.
Donor(s): Mildred Alderson.‡
Financial data (yr. ended 12/31/01): Grants paid, $14,000; assets, $275,475 (M); expenditures, $16,556; qualifying distributions, $14,000.
Limitations: Applications not accepted. Giving primarily in Annandale, VA.
Application information: Contributes only to pre-selected organizations.
Trustee: Virginia Baptist Foundation.
EIN: 546426438

54928—VIRGINIA

54928
Fannie & Milton Friedman Family Foundation
850 Jamestown Crescent
Norfolk, VA 23508 (757) 489-8381
Contact: Fannie G. Friedman, Pres.

Established in 1994.
Donor(s): Fannie G. Friedman.
Financial data (yr. ended 12/31/01): Grants paid, $14,000; assets, $748,606 (M); expenditures, $14,725; qualifying distributions, $14,000.
Limitations: Giving limited to VA.
Officers: Fannie G. Friedman, Pres.; Leslie H. Friedman, Secy.-Treas.
EIN: 541741509

54929
Agnes C. Robinson Trust
c/o SunTrust Banks, Inc.
P.O. Box 27385
Richmond, VA 23261-7385
Application address: 15th & New York Ave., N.W., Washington, DC 20005
Contact: Lori Anne Caumeil, Trust Off., SunTrust Banks, Inc.

Donor(s): Agnes C. Robinson.‡
Financial data (yr. ended 12/31/01): Grants paid, $14,000; assets, $281,753 (M); expenditures, $16,970; qualifying distributions, $14,000.
Limitations: Giving limited to the metropolitan Washington, DC, area.
Trustee: SunTrust Banks, Inc.
EIN: 526027469

54930
Sisters Foundation
435 Big Sky Trail
Blacksburg, VA 24060-8809

Financial data (yr. ended 12/31/01): Grants paid, $13,996; assets, $1 (M); gifts received, $15,670; expenditures, $14,470; qualifying distributions, $13,996.
Officers: Mary Jo Putney, Pres.; John Rekus, V.P.; Estill Putney, Secy.-Treas.
EIN: 541799752

54931
Binswanger Glass Foundation
7700 Hill Dr.
Richmond, VA 23225-1929
Contact: Millard I. Binswanger, Jr., Pres.

Donor(s): Binswanger Glass Co.
Financial data (yr. ended 12/31/01): Grants paid, $13,900; assets, $408,625 (M); expenditures, $14,868; qualifying distributions, $14,384.
Limitations: Giving primarily in Kansas City, MO, and Richmond, VA.
Officers and Directors:* Millard I. Binswanger, Jr.,* Pres. and Mgr.; Ellen B. Nolan, V.P.; Betsy W. Binswanger,* Secy.-Treas.; Katherine Grubb.
EIN: 546036349
Codes: CS, CD

54932
Phyllis P. Hayman Foundation, Inc.
6424 Woodville Dr.
Falls Church, VA 22044

Established in 1996.
Financial data (yr. ended 12/31/01): Grants paid, $13,628; assets, $166,189 (M); expenditures, $14,006; qualifying distributions, $13,628.
Limitations: Applications not accepted.
Application information: Contributes only to pre-selected organizations.
Officers and Directors:* Phyllis Hayman,* Pres. and Treas.; Robert Hayman,* V.P.; Sandye Hayman Needle,* Secy.

EIN: 541783703

54933
The Berger Foundation
1760 Reston Pkwy., Ste. 503
Reston, VA 20190-3303

Donor(s): Irving D. Berger.
Financial data (yr. ended 12/31/01): Grants paid, $13,400; assets, $58,053 (M); gifts received, $15,000; expenditures, $15,532; qualifying distributions, $13,400.
Limitations: Applications not accepted. Giving primarily in the Washington, DC, area, including MD and VA.
Application information: Contributes only to pre-selected organizations.
Trustee: Lyn K. Berger.
EIN: 526070520

54934
Nicholas A. Somma Scholarship Fund
9023 Forest Hill Ave.
Richmond, VA 23235-3054
Application address: c/o Chair., Scholarship Comm., Highland Springs High School, 15 S. Oak Ave., Highland Springs, VA 23075, tel.: (804) 737-6681

Established in 1987 in VA.
Financial data (yr. ended 06/30/01): Grants paid, $13,369; assets, $500,352 (M); expenditures, $23,538; qualifying distributions, $12,808.
Limitations: Giving limited to the Highland Springs, VA, area.
Application information: Application form required.
Director: Charles A. Somma, Jr.
EIN: 541393792
Codes: GTI

54935
The Legum-Bangel Foundation, Inc.
101 Mill Rd., Ste. B
Yorktown, VA 23693

Established in 1996 in VA.
Donor(s): Edith Nachman Legum.
Financial data (yr. ended 12/31/01): Grants paid, $13,303; assets, $261,639 (M); expenditures, $14,490; qualifying distributions, $13,303.
Limitations: Applications not accepted.
Application information: Contributes only to pre-selected organizations.
Officer: Sue Anne K. Bangel, Pres.
Trustees: William M. Bangel, Billie Bangel Eisner, Marc R. Eisner, James C. Smith, Jr., Eve Bangel Ware, Michael B. Ware.
EIN: 541792544

54936
C. Arthur Ware Testamentary Charitable Trust
1161 Arthur Ware Trail
South Boston, VA 24592-6928 (804) 572-2411
Contact: Charles A. Ware, Jr., Tr.

Established in 1995 in VA.
Financial data (yr. ended 12/31/01): Grants paid, $13,265; assets, $260,600 (M); expenditures, $17,694; qualifying distributions, $13,265.
Limitations: Giving primarily in VA.
Trustee: Charles A. Ware, Jr.
EIN: 546377165

54937
Snead Foundation
P.O. Box 9
Washington, VA 22747
Contact: Rayner V. Snead, Tr.

Establish in 1997 in VA.
Donor(s): Rayner V. Snead, Lois D. Snead.

Financial data (yr. ended 12/31/01): Grants paid, $13,237; assets, $277,411 (M); gifts received, $20,000; expenditures, $14,234; qualifying distributions, $13,237.
Limitations: Giving primarily in Washington, VA.
Trustees: Dana S. Adamson, Elizabeth S. Hewitt, Lois D. Snead, Rayner V. Snead, Rayner V. Snead, Jr., Samuel D. Snead, William T. Snead.
EIN: 541846301

54938
The Clyde W. and Mary O. Henley Trust
4025 Indian Trail
Suffolk, VA 23434-7338
Application adrress: 434 W. Washington St., Suffolk, VA 23434-5360, tel.: (757) 925-3763
Contact: Christopher B. Robinson, Tr.

Established in 1999 in VA.
Financial data (yr. ended 12/31/99): Grants paid, $13,234; assets, $461,828 (M); gifts received, $463,698; expenditures, $23,397; qualifying distributions, $13,234.
Trustee: Christopher B. Robinson.
EIN: 311651681

54939
The Grace Trust
219 Parsons Point Ln.
Edinburg, VA 22824-3124
Contact: Rev. James D. Bailey, Tr.

Financial data (yr. ended 07/31/01): Grants paid, $13,100; assets, $306,970 (M); expenditures, $15,158; qualifying distributions, $15,158.
Limitations: Giving primarily in VA.
Trustees: Rev. James D. Bailey, Judith C. Bailey.
EIN: 546299823

54940
Rixey Street Foundation, Inc.
3869 N. Rixey St.
Arlington, VA 22207

Donor(s): Thomas P. Jennings.
Financial data (yr. ended 12/31/01): Grants paid, $13,080; assets, $289,178 (M); gifts received, $3,800; expenditures, $13,815; qualifying distributions, $13,080.
Limitations: Applications not accepted.
Application information: Contributes only to pre-selected organizations.
Officer: Shelley C. Jennings, Pres.
EIN: 541842020

54941
The Junot Foundation
c/o Mark J. Ohrstrom
P.O. Box 500
The Plains, VA 20198-0500

Established in 1997 in DE and VA.
Donor(s): Mark J. Ohrstrom.
Financial data (yr. ended 12/31/01): Grants paid, $13,000; assets, $247,313 (M); expenditures, $14,904; qualifying distributions, $13,000.
Limitations: Applications not accepted.
Application information: Contributes only to pre-selected organizations.
Officer: Mark J. Ohrstrom, Pres.
EIN: 133930921

54942
Wolf Run Foundation, Inc.
301 Hiden Blvd.
Newport News, VA 23606
Application address: 7900 Wolf Run Hills Rd., Fairfax Station, VA 22039, tel.: (703) 239-2616
Contact: Franklin O. Blechman, Jr., Co-Pres.

Donor(s): Franklin O. Blechman, Jr., Jane Blechman.

Financial data (yr. ended 12/31/00): Grants paid, $12,941; assets, $472,327 (M); gifts received, $394,628; expenditures, $16,128; qualifying distributions, $12,941.
Limitations: Giving on a national basis, with some emphasis on the East Coast.
Officers: Franklin O. Blechman, Jr., Co-Pres.; Jane Blechman, Co-Pres.; J.W. David, Secy.
EIN: 541839134

54943
Fenton Foundation
2819 N. Parham Rd., Ste. 110
Richmond, VA 23294 (804) 747-4547
Contact: Eppa Hunton, Pres.

Financial data (yr. ended 12/31/01): Grants paid, $12,800; assets, $256,304 (M); expenditures, $21,445; qualifying distributions, $13,000.
Limitations: Giving primarily in NC and VA.
Application information: Application form not required.
Officers and Trustee:* Eppa Hunton,* Pres. and Treas.; Mary P. Hunton, Secy.
EIN: 546032866

54944
Schilthuis Family Foundation
2704 Old Point Dr.
Richmond, VA 23233-2160

Donor(s): Jan J. Schilthuis, Martha F. Schilthuis.
Financial data (yr. ended 12/31/01): Grants paid, $12,550; assets, $122,296 (M); expenditures, $13,252; qualifying distributions, $12,550.
Limitations: Applications not accepted. Giving on a national basis, with emphasis on WA.
Application information: Contributes only to pre-selected organizations.
Officers: Jan J. Schilthuis, Pres.; Martha F. Schilthuis, Treas.
EIN: 841099922

54945
Rufus Harrell Scholarship Trust
101 43rd St.
Virginia Beach, VA 23451-2501

Established in 1996 in VA.
Financial data (yr. ended 12/31/01): Grants paid, $12,545; assets, $162,014 (M); expenditures, $12,645; qualifying distributions, $12,545.
Trustee: James P. Harrell.
EIN: 541789047

54946
The Dobranski Foundation, Inc.
P.O. Box 26066
Alexandria, VA 22313

Established in 1999.
Donor(s): Anthony Dobranski.
Financial data (yr. ended 12/31/01): Grants paid, $12,500; assets, $349,323 (M); gifts received, $132,000; expenditures, $13,530; qualifying distributions, $12,500.
Limitations: Applications not accepted.
Application information: Contributes only to pre-selected organizations.
Officer: Anthony Dobranski, Pres.
EIN: 541964689

54947
The Newbern Foundation
2343 Highland Farm Rd.
Roanoke, VA 24019

Established in 2000 in VA.
Donor(s): Jess Newbern III.
Financial data (yr. ended 12/31/01): Grants paid, $12,500; assets, $369,684 (M); gifts received, $125,003; expenditures, $23,463; qualifying distributions, $12,500.
Officers: Jess Newbern III, Pres. and Treas.; J. Cason Newbern, V.P. and Secy.; Brook Newbern Roncinske, V.P.; Kelly Newbern Van Aken, V.P.
EIN: 542016695

54948
The Starke Foundation
9800 Mayland Dr.
Richmond, VA 23233 (804) 673-3810
Contact: Russell F. Starke, II, Pres.

Financial data (yr. ended 12/31/01): Grants paid, $12,500; assets, $363,768 (M); expenditures, $14,189; qualifying distributions, $12,500.
Limitations: Giving primarily in VA.
Officers: Russell F. Starke II, Pres.; Thomas J. Starke IV, V.P.; Terry S. Tosh, Treas.
EIN: 546038056

54949
Blechman-Morenoff Foundation, Inc.
301 Hiden Blvd., Ste. 200
Newport News, VA 23606-2939
(757) 595-4500
Contact: Judith B. Morenoff, Pres.

Established in 2000 in VA.
Financial data (yr. ended 12/31/01): Grants paid, $12,484; assets, $231,350 (M); expenditures, $12,821; qualifying distributions, $12,484.
Limitations: Giving primarily in Washington, DC, MD, and VA.
Officers and Directors: Judith B. Morenoff, Pres. and Chair.; Edward Morenoff,* Secy.-Treas.; Daniel T. Morenoff, David L. Morenoff, Lisa B. Morenoff, Richard A. Morenoff.
EIN: 541839136

54950
Falls Run Family Foundation
1200 N. Nash St., No. 1126
Arlington, VA 22209

Donor(s): Emanuel Rouvelas, Marilyn Rouvelas.
Financial data (yr. ended 12/31/01): Grants paid, $12,315; assets, $122,422 (M); gifts received, $15,917; expenditures, $16,764; qualifying distributions, $12,315.
Limitations: Giving primarily in the greater Washington, DC, area, including parts of MD and VA.
Officers: Marilyn Rouvelas, Pres.; Mary Rouvelas, Secy.; Larry Rouvelas, Treas.
Director: Emanuel Rouvelas.
EIN: 521491159

54951
The Fisher Foundation
1921 McVitty Rd.
Salem, VA 24153-7405

Established in 1989 in VA.
Donor(s): Richard H. Fisher.
Financial data (yr. ended 12/31/01): Grants paid, $12,267; assets, $434,474 (M); expenditures, $14,450; qualifying distributions, $12,267.
Limitations: Applications not accepted. Giving primarily in Roanoke Valley, VA.
Application information: Contributes only to pre-selected organizations.
Officers: Richard H. Fisher, Pres.; Anne Andrews, Secy.-Treas.
Board Member: Gwynn Franklin.
EIN: 541537005

54952
Irene Leache Memorial Trust
7336 Shirland Ave.
Norfolk, VA 23505
Application address: 1421 W. Princess Anne Rd., Norfolk, VA 23507
Contact: Carter Grandy Scott, Pres.

Donor(s): Mrs. Louis I. Jaffe.
Financial data (yr. ended 04/30/02): Grants paid, $12,250; assets, $584,085 (M); gifts received, $225; expenditures, $16,553; qualifying distributions, $12,250.
Limitations: Giving limited to the Tidewater, VA, area.
Officers: Carter Grandy Scott, Pres.; Kate Prinkley, V.P.; Clara Wolcott, Treas.
EIN: 546042364

54953
Central Soup Society of Philadelphia
c/o H. Coyne
1007 Turkey Run Rd.
McLean, VA 22101

Financial data (yr. ended 12/31/01): Grants paid, $12,000; assets, $255,594 (M); expenditures, $14,741; qualifying distributions, $12,000.
Limitations: Applications not accepted. Giving primarily in Philadelphia, PA; some giving also in Washington, DC.
Application information: Contributes only to pre-selected organizations.
Officers: Michael G. Mercer, Pres.; Robert M. Howard, Secy.; Helen M. McLean, Treas.
Directors: Elizabeth Cooper Cocharan, Susan McInnes Howard, Richard Paullin.
EIN: 236238324

54954
William T. Oxenham Foundation
11300 Midlothian Tpke.
Richmond, VA 23235
Contact: William Wheeler, Pres.

Established in 1998 in VA.
Financial data (yr. ended 12/31/01): Grants paid, $12,000; assets, $275,955 (M); expenditures, $13,787; qualifying distributions, $12,000.
Officers: William E. Wheeler, Pres. and Treas.; Nancy O. Wheeler, V.P.; John O. Wheeler, Secy.
EIN: 541880739

54955
The Ruby Rowe Thomas Scholarship Trust
P.O. Box 388
Gloucester Point, VA 23062-0388
(804) 642-6111
Contact: Jeffery W. Shaw, Tr.

Established in 1999 in VA.
Donor(s): Blanche R. Trombley.
Financial data (yr. ended 12/31/01): Grants paid, $12,000; assets, $150,060 (M); expenditures, $14,061; qualifying distributions, $12,000.
Limitations: Giving to graduating seniors of Gloucester High School, VA.
Application information: Applicants should submit Free Application for Federal Student Aid (FAFSA), transcript, and letters of recommendation.
Trustees: Jeffrey W. Shaw, Michael T. Soberick.
EIN: 546460652

54956 — VIRGINIA

54956
Strasburg Community Scholarship Trust Fund, Inc.
c/o First Bank
112 W. King St.
Strasburg, VA 22657
Contact: Directors

Financial data (yr. ended 12/31/01): Grants paid, $11,952; assets, $250,891 (M); expenditures, $13,940; qualifying distributions, $11,952.
Limitations: Giving limited to residents of Strasburg, VA.
Application information: Application form required.
Officers: John D. Hodson, Chair.; Dennis A. Dysart, Secy.-Treas.
Directors: Cheryl E. Bradford, Eddie Campbell, Jr., Leota Eastep, Pieter Greeff, Richard Kleese, Peggy Simon.
EIN: 541727339
Codes: GTI

54957
The H & H Foundation
210 E. Main St.
Richmond, VA 23219-2474 (804) 769-2629
Contact: Hilton W. Goodwyn, Jr., Treas.

Financial data (yr. ended 10/31/01): Grants paid, $11,810; assets, $275,811 (M); expenditures, $12,262; qualifying distributions, $11,810.
Limitations: Giving primarily in VA.
Application information: Application form not required.
Officers and Trustees:* Robert A. Goodwyn, Sr.,* Pres.; Veronica S. Bond,* Secy.; Hilton W. Goodwyn, Jr.,* Treas. and Mgr.
EIN: 546062840

54958
The Brooke Byers Charitable Trust
1213 Merchant Ln.
McLean, VA 22101

Established in 1999 in NY and VA.
Donor(s): Dorothy H. Hirshon,‡ Brooke Byers.
Financial data (yr. ended 12/31/01): Grants paid, $11,767; assets, $77,217 (M); gifts received, $750; expenditures, $12,517; qualifying distributions, $11,767.
Limitations: Applications not accepted.
Application information: Contributes only to pre-selected organizations.
Trustee: Brooke Byers.
EIN: 223686296

54959
The Susan S. and James B. Neligan Charitable Trust
985 Barracks Farm Rd.
Charlottesville, VA 22901

Established in 1988 in VA.
Donor(s): James B. Neligan, Susan S. Neligan.
Financial data (yr. ended 12/31/00): Grants paid, $11,600; assets, $19,074 (M); expenditures, $12,314; qualifying distributions, $11,600.
Limitations: Applications not accepted. Giving primarily in Charlottesville and Roanoke, VA.
Application information: Contributes only to pre-selected organizations.
Trustees: James B. Neligan, Susan S. Neligan.
EIN: 546248655

54960
The Robert and Dorothy Doumar Foundation
P.O. Box 1873
Norfolk, VA 23501-1873

Established in 2000 in VA.
Donor(s): Robert G. Doumar, Dorothy M. Doumar.
Financial data (yr. ended 12/31/01): Grants paid, $11,545; assets, $32,144 (M); gifts received, $1,924; expenditures, $13,969; qualifying distributions, $11,545.
Limitations: Applications not accepted.
Application information: Contributes only to pre-selected organizations.
Officers: Robert G. Doumar, Pres.; Dorothy M. Doumar, Secy.-Treas.
EIN: 542017412

54961
Louis Snyder Foundation
P.O. Box 2688
Virginia Beach, VA 23450-2688

Financial data (yr. ended 06/30/02): Grants paid, $11,450; assets, $131,005 (M); gifts received, $850; expenditures, $11,546; qualifying distributions, $11,450.
Limitations: Applications not accepted. Giving primarily in Norfolk and Virginia Beach, VA.
Application information: Contributes only to pre-selected organizations.
Officers: Robin Brickell, Pres.; Tammy Murphy, V.P.; Louis D. Snyder, Secy.-Treas.
EIN: 546039790

54962
Hollymar Foundation, Inc.
201A Royal St. S.E.
Leesburg, VA 20175

Established in 2000 in VA.
Donor(s): Randall S. Coppersmith.
Financial data (yr. ended 12/31/01): Grants paid, $11,365; assets, $78,907 (M); expenditures, $12,333; qualifying distributions, $11,365.
Limitations: Applications not accepted.
Application information: Contributes only to pre-selected organizations.
Officer and Directors:* Elizabeth M. Coppersmith,* Exec. Dir.; Randall S. Coppersmith.
EIN: 541980386

54963
The Dymer Foundation
c/o W. Bates Chappell
267 Dymer Beach Dr.
White Stone, VA 22578

Established in 1999 in VA.
Donor(s): W. Bates Chappell.
Financial data (yr. ended 03/31/02): Grants paid, $11,250; assets, $19,839 (M); gifts received, $684; expenditures, $12,010; qualifying distributions, $11,250.
Limitations: Applications not accepted. Giving on a national basis, with some emphasis on VA.
Application information: Contributes only to pre-selected organizations.
Trustees: Margaret C. Chappell, W. Bates Chappell, William B. Chappell, Jr.
EIN: 546457604

54964
Trinity Forum Foundation
7902 Westpark Dr., Ste. A
McLean, VA 22102-4202

Established in 1999 in VA.
Donor(s): Alonzo MacDonald.
Financial data (yr. ended 12/31/00): Grants paid, $11,122; assets, $543,853 (M); gifts received, $202,546; expenditures, $23,724; qualifying distributions, $11,122.
Limitations: Applications not accepted. Giving primarily in McLean, VA.
Application information: Contributes only to pre-selected organizations.
Officer: Alonzo MacDonald, Chair.
Directors: Mark Berner, Robert Gorham, Henry Smith, Rolf Towe.
EIN: 541612640

54965
Bob Fleigh Foundation, Inc.
1748 Founder's Hill S.
Williamsburg, VA 23185-7616
Application address: 1321 Oak Hill Ave., Hagerstown, MD 21742
Contact: Margery E. Fleigh, V.P.

Financial data (yr. ended 12/31/01): Grants paid, $11,115; assets, $271,897 (M); expenditures, $13,806; qualifying distributions, $11,115.
Limitations: Giving primarily in MD.
Officers: Nancy F. Daugherty, Pres.; Margery E. Fleigh, V.P.; Sandra Tillou, Secy.
EIN: 596143048

54966
Carlyle C. Goodson Foundation
404 Industry Dr.
Hampton, VA 23661-1382 (757) 826-9325
Contact: Carlyle C. Goodson, Tr.

Financial data (yr. ended 11/30/01): Grants paid, $11,100; assets, $77,424 (M); gifts received, $10,000; expenditures, $12,000; qualifying distributions, $11,100.
Limitations: Giving primarily in VA.
Trustee: Carlyle C. Goodson.
EIN: 541279905

54967
The Phibbs Family Charitable Trust
P.O. Box 155
Dayton, VA 22821-0155 (540) 879-9806
Contact: Carle S. Phibbs, Tr.

Established in 1998 in VA.
Donor(s): Carle S. Phibbs.
Financial data (yr. ended 12/31/01): Grants paid, $11,100; assets, $90,338 (M); expenditures, $11,260; qualifying distributions, $11,100.
Limitations: Giving primarily in VA.
Trustees: Elizabeth Phibbs Gentry, Allen M. Phibbs, Carle S. Phibbs, Jill Phibbs Wright.
EIN: 546421676

54968
Credit Marketing & Management Association Foundation
(Formerly CMMA Foundation)
P.O. Box 680
Vinton, VA 24179-0680
Contact: Ronald W. Ernest, Pres.

Established in 1996 in VA.
Donor(s): Credit Marketing & Management Assn.
Financial data (yr. ended 12/31/01): Grants paid, $11,000; assets, $202,509 (M); expenditures, $17,605; qualifying distributions, $13,349.
Limitations: Giving primarily in VA.
Officer: Ronald W. Ernest, Pres.
Directors: Garland Kidd, Larry Poteat, William H. Tuttle II, Wylie E. Walton.
EIN: 541779684
Codes: CS, CD

54969
Hooker Foundation
c/o American National Bank & Trust Co.
P.O. Box 191
Danville, VA 24543

Financial data (yr. ended 12/31/01): Grants paid, $11,000; assets, $205,148 (M); gifts received,

$1,000; expenditures, $13,473; qualifying distributions, $11,000.
Limitations: Applications not accepted. Giving primarily in Martinsville, VA.
Application information: Contributes only to pre-selected organizations.
Officers: J. Clyde Hooker, Jr., Pres.; Sandra Prillaman, Secy.
Directors: I.M. Groves, Jr., Frank Hooker, Jr., Paul B. Toms, Jr.
EIN: 237046126

54970
Satori Foundation
(Formerly The Rock Creek Foundation)
8404 Parham Ct.
McLean, VA 22102

Established in 1994 in VA.
Donor(s): Steven M. Rales.
Financial data (yr. ended 12/31/00): Grants paid, $11,000; assets, $22,715,396 (M); expenditures, $362,158; qualifying distributions, $11,000.
Limitations: Applications not accepted. Giving primarily in Washington, DC.
Application information: Contributes only to pre-selected organizations.
Officers and Directors:* Steven M. Rales,* Chair.; Michael G. Ryan, Pres.; Joseph O. Bunting III, V.P.; Teresa L.C. Baldwin, Secy.-Treas.; Christine P. Rales.
EIN: 541739160

54971
Specialized Carriers & Rigging Foundation
2750 Prosperity Ave., Ste. 620
Fairfax, VA 22031-4312 (703) 698-0291
Contact: N. Eugene Brymer, Exec. V.P.

Established in 1995.
Financial data (yr. ended 12/31/00): Grants paid, $11,000; assets, $475,551 (M); gifts received, $128,267; expenditures, $33,229; qualifying distributions, $17,758.
Limitations: Giving on a national basis.
Application information: Application form required.
Officers: N. Eugene Brymer, Exec. V.P.; Maryellen Lorenz, Treas.
Directors: Harold Anderson, Marilyn Bragg, John Claftin, Terry Emmert, Anne Koenig, and 30 additional directors.
EIN: 521272278

54972
Charles Robertson Foundation
4200 Oxford Cir. E.
Richmond, VA 23221
Contact: Charles H. Robertson, Jr., Pres.

Established in 1987 in VA.
Donor(s): Charles Robertson.
Financial data (yr. ended 08/31/99): Grants paid, $10,950; assets, $259,028 (M); expenditures, $12,881; qualifying distributions, $11,604.
Limitations: Giving primarily in Richmond, VA.
Officers: Charles H. Robertson, Jr., Pres.; Michael Robertson, Secy.
EIN: 541445906

54973
Henry F. Stern, Jr. Foundation
7301 Forest Ave., Ste. 105
Richmond, VA 23226

Established in 1989 in VA.
Donor(s): Henry F. Stern, Jr.
Financial data (yr. ended 12/31/01): Grants paid, $10,930; assets, $1,352 (M); gifts received, $12,183; expenditures, $11,795; qualifying distributions, $10,930.

Limitations: Applications not accepted. Giving primarily in VA.
Application information: Contributes only to pre-selected organizations.
Officers and Director:* Henry F. Stern, Jr.,* Pres.; William W. Flowers, Secy.-Treas.
EIN: 621417227

54974
5P Foundation
8713 Butterfield Ave.
Richmond, VA 23229

Established in 1999 in VA.
Donor(s): Subhash Pahuja.
Financial data (yr. ended 12/31/00): Grants paid, $10,900; assets, $252,698 (M); gifts received, $81,283; expenditures, $11,668; qualifying distributions, $10,900.
Limitations: Applications not accepted.
Application information: Contributes only to pre-selected organizations.
Officers: Kamini Pahuja, Pres.; Subhash Pahuja, Secy.-Treas.
Director: Gargi Pahuja.
EIN: 541967934

54975
Ira Byram Foundation, Inc.
2319 S. Queen St.
Arlington, VA 22202 (703) 920-8610
Contact: Bernice M. Byram, Pres.

Financial data (yr. ended 11/30/01): Grants paid, $10,895; assets, $34,657 (M); expenditures, $34,240; qualifying distributions, $10,895.
Limitations: Giving primarily in the metropolitan Washington, DC, area.
Officers: Bernice M. Byram, Pres.; Kathy McNamara, V.P.; Susan B. Stephens, Treas.
EIN: 526055753

54976
Lacopo Family Foundation
1216A Ingleside Ave.
McLean, VA 22101-2815

Established in 2000 in VA.
Donor(s): John D. Lacopo.
Financial data (yr. ended 12/31/01): Grants paid, $10,750; assets, $39,029 (M); gifts received, $533; expenditures, $13,740; qualifying distributions, $10,750.
Limitations: Applications not accepted.
Application information: Contributes only to pre-selected organizations.
Officers and Directors:* John D. Lacopo,* Co-Pres.; Sylvia G. Lacopo,* Co-Pres.; Caren D. Eaton,* Secy.; Evan A. Lacopo,* Treas.
EIN: 542008860

54977
The Ramon W. Breeden, Jr. Foundation
560 Lynnhaven Pkwy.
Virginia Beach, VA 23452 (757) 486-1000
Contact: Ramon W. Breeden, Jr., Pres.

Financial data (yr. ended 12/31/01): Grants paid, $10,700; assets, $63,995 (M); expenditures, $11,588; qualifying distributions, $10,700.
Limitations: Giving primarily in Virginia Beach, VA.
Officer: Ramon W. Breeden, Jr., Pres. and Treas.
EIN: 541167246

54978
Gilgit Charitable Trust
c/o Jack Spain, Jr.
P.O. Box 1535
Richmond, VA 23218-1535

Established in 1988 in VA.

Donor(s): Mary R. Spain.
Financial data (yr. ended 12/31/99): Grants paid, $10,500; assets, $259,275 (M); expenditures, $10,948; qualifying distributions, $10,948.
Limitations: Applications not accepted. Giving primarily in Richmond, VA.
Application information: Contributes only to pre-selected organizations.
Trustees: Jack Spain, Jr., John H. Spain, Mary R. Spain, Sidney H. Spain.
EIN: 521601996

54979
Eppa Hunton, Jr. Trust
c/o Bank of America
P.O. Box 26606
Richmond, VA 23261-6606 (804) 788-2963
Contact: Elizabeth D. Seaman, Trust Off., Bank of America

Donor(s): Eppa Hunton, Jr.‡
Financial data (yr. ended 06/30/00): Grants paid, $10,500; assets, $282,501 (M); expenditures, $15,819; qualifying distributions, $12,190.
Limitations: Giving limited to Richmond, VA.
Trustee: Bank of America.
EIN: 546030457

54980
Arthur E. & Clara M. Morrissette Foundation, Inc.
4503 Carlby Ln.
Alexandria, VA 22309
Application address: P.O. Box 15625, Alexandria, VA 22309

Established in 1997 in VA.
Donor(s): Clara M. Morrissette.
Financial data (yr. ended 12/31/01): Grants paid, $10,500; assets, $1,226,528 (M); expenditures, $11,567; qualifying distributions, $10,775.
Limitations: Giving limited to Washington, DC, MD and VA.
Officers and Directors:* Clara M. Morrissette,* Pres.; Kenneth Morrissette,* Secy.-Treas.; Arthur E. Morrissette.
EIN: 541851621

54981
Earl D. Leader Charitable Foundation, Inc.
5 Shapiro Ct.
Newport News, VA 23606-4400

Established in 1997 in VA.
Donor(s): Robert J. Frank.
Financial data (yr. ended 12/31/01): Grants paid, $10,280; assets, $129,779 (M); expenditures, $11,467; qualifying distributions, $10,280.
Limitations: Applications not accepted.
Application information: Contributes only to pre-selected organizations.
Officers: Robert J. Frank, Pres.; Romayne L. Frank, Secy.
EIN: 541870916

54982
Cole-Birches Foundation
5786 Valley View Dr.
Alexandria, VA 22310
Contact: Barry Cole, Pres.

Established in 1999 in MI.
Financial data (yr. ended 12/31/01): Grants paid, $10,000; assets, $266,965 (M); expenditures, $18,061; qualifying distributions, $10,000.
Officer: Barry Cole, Pres.
EIN: 383420905

54983
The Samuel & Robert Decker Foundation
1313 Dolley Madison Blvd., No. 204
McLean, VA 22101

Established in 1987.
Donor(s): David G. Decker, John G. Decker, Elaine Decker-Rosensweig.
Financial data (yr. ended 12/31/01): Grants paid, $10,000; assets, $674,416 (M); expenditures, $12,864; qualifying distributions, $10,000.
Limitations: Applications not accepted. Giving primarily in Washington, DC.
Application information: Contributes only to pre-selected organizations.
Trustees: David G. Decker, John G. Decker, Elaine Decker-Rosensweig.
EIN: 521532867

54984
Garden Writers Foundation, Inc.
10210 Leatherleaf Ct.
Manassas, VA 20111-4245
Application address: 264 Sherburne Cove, Cordova, TN 38018
Contact: Jim Browne, Dir.

Established in 1989 in AK.
Financial data (yr. ended 12/31/01): Grants paid, $10,000; assets, $175,324 (M); gifts received, $21,514; expenditures, $12,089; qualifying distributions, $10,000.
Limitations: Giving on a national basis.
Officers and Directors:* Alecia Troy,* Chair.; Bill Novak, Secy.; Robert Lagasse, Treas.; Jim Browne, Mary Callister Buley, Ruina Judd, Judy Lowe, Jeff Lowenfels, Paul Peterson.
EIN: 592933359

54985
The Sarah Elizabeth Howard Foundation
2109 Wakefield Ct.
Alexandria, VA 22307

Established in 1999 in VA.
Donor(s): William B. Howard, Julia M. Howard.
Financial data (yr. ended 12/31/01): Grants paid, $10,000; assets, $218,693 (M); gifts received, $2,320; expenditures, $10,125; qualifying distributions, $10,000.
Limitations: Applications not accepted.
Application information: Contributes only to pre-selected organizations.
Officers: William B. Howard, Pres.; Julia M. Howard, Secy.-Treas.
EIN: 541966936

54986
May Foundation
1229 Perry William Dr.
McLean, VA 22101

Donor(s): Gene H. May.
Financial data (yr. ended 06/30/02): Grants paid, $10,000; assets, $15,866 (M); gifts received, $25,000; expenditures, $10,000; qualifying distributions, $10,000.
Limitations: Applications not accepted. Giving primarily in VA.
Application information: Contributes only to pre-selected organizations.
Trustees: Barbara A. May, Gene H. May.
EIN: 546063721

54987
Cleo Lawson Mitchell Scholarship
P.O. Box 687
Tazewell, VA 24651
Application address: c/o Graham High School, Bluefield, VA 24605, tel.: (540) 326-1235
Contact: Bill Kinser, Chair., or Charlotte Viers, Treas.

Financial data (yr. ended 06/30/01): Grants paid, $10,000; assets, $245,355 (M); expenditures, $11,896; qualifying distributions, $10,000.
Limitations: Giving limited to Tazewell County, VA.
Officers and Trustees:* Bill Kinser,* Chair.; Charlotte Viers,* Treas.; Carol Hart.
EIN: 237179494

54988
T. Wayne Mostiler Foundation
1309 Windsor Point Rd.
Norfolk, VA 23509-1311

Financial data (yr. ended 04/30/02): Grants paid, $10,000; assets, $28,292 (M); expenditures, $10,694; qualifying distributions, $10,000.
Limitations: Applications not accepted. Giving primarily in the Norfolk, VA, area.
Application information: Contributes only to pre-selected organizations.
Trustees: Barbara C. Mostiler, T. Wayne Mostiler.
EIN: 521336919

54989
N. B. Shingleton Scholarship Fund
P.O. Box 551
Winchester, VA 22604-0551
Contact: Glenn R. Burdick, Admin.

Financial data (yr. ended 12/31/01): Grants paid, $10,000; assets, $100,169 (M); expenditures, $10,537; qualifying distributions, $10,464.
Limitations: Giving limited to residents of VA.
Officer: Glenn R. Burdick, Admin.
EIN: 237039441

54990
The John D. Tickle Foundation
c/o John D. Tickle
P.O. Box 1689
Bristol, VA 24203-1689

Established in 1989 in TN.
Donor(s): John D. Tickle.
Financial data (yr. ended 11/30/01): Grants paid, $10,000; assets, $508,648 (M); expenditures, $16,810; qualifying distributions, $10,000.
Limitations: Applications not accepted.
Application information: Contributes only to pre-selected organizations.
Trustee: John D. Tickle.
EIN: 541507449

54991
Lagos Family Foundation
11401 Ivy Home Pl.
Richmond, VA 23233

Established in 2000 in VA.
Donor(s): William J. Lagos, Ann D. Lagos.
Financial data (yr. ended 12/31/01): Grants paid, $9,950; assets, $101,977 (M); gifts received, $5,000; expenditures, $15,559; qualifying distributions, $9,950.
Limitations: Applications not accepted.
Application information: Contributes only to pre-selected organizations.
Officers: William J. Lagos, Pres.; Christopher J. Lagos, V.P.; William J. Lagos, Jr., V.P.; Ann D. Lagos, Secy.; Kathryn M. Lagos, Treas.
EIN: 542015119

54992
Ed & Lillian Hillger Charitable Trust
c/o Virginia Baptist Foundation
P.O. Box 17035
Richmond, VA 23226

Established in 1996 in VA.
Financial data (yr. ended 12/31/01): Grants paid, $9,684; assets, $217,746 (M); expenditures, $12,265; qualifying distributions, $9,684.
Trustee: Virginia Baptist Foundation.
EIN: 911812670

54993
Nansemond Charitable Foundation, Inc.
453 W. Washington St.
Suffolk, VA 23434 (757) 539-3421
Contact: Jack W. Webb, Jr., V.P.

Donor(s): Nansemond Insurance Svcs., Nansemond Insurance Agency.
Financial data (yr. ended 08/31/01): Grants paid, $9,600; assets, $183,816 (M); gifts received, $5,500; expenditures, $10,622; qualifying distributions, $9,600.
Limitations: Giving primarily in Suffolk, VA.
Application information: Application form required.
Officers and Directors:* Jack W. Webb, Sr.,* Pres.; Jack W. Webb, Jr.,* V.P.; Faye N. Webb,* Secy.; Jay A. Dorschel,* Treas.; Stephen L. Huber, Joseph N. Webb.
EIN: 541291449
Codes: CS, CD, GTI

54994
Hope for Children
1501 Brookmeade Pl.
Vienna, VA 22182
Contact: David W. Faeder, Dir.

Established in 1997 in VA.
Donor(s): David W. Faeder.
Financial data (yr. ended 12/31/00): Grants paid, $9,450; assets, $147,132 (M); expenditures, $10,183; qualifying distributions, $9,450.
Limitations: Giving primarily in Vienna, VA.
Directors: David W. Faeder, Gus Faeder, Margie Faeder.
EIN: 541876485

54995
Marks Foundation, Inc.
9023 Wood Sorrel Dr.
Richmond, VA 23229 (804) 282-0161
Contact: Howard F. Marks, Pres.

Financial data (yr. ended 12/31/01): Grants paid, $9,398; assets, $169,534 (M); expenditures, $10,254; qualifying distributions, $9,398.
Limitations: Giving primarily in Richmond, VA.
Officers: Howard F. Marks, Pres.; Patricia R. Marks, V.P.
EIN: 546053504

54996
Rama Devi and Beharilal Digambar Jain Foundation
c/o Pushpa Rani Jain
606 Fairway Dr.
Bluefield, VA 24605

Established in 1994 in VA.
Donor(s): Pushpa Rani Jain.
Financial data (yr. ended 12/31/01): Grants paid, $9,351; assets, $186,863 (M); gifts received, $2,853; expenditures, $9,935; qualifying distributions, $9,351.
Limitations: Giving on a national basis.
Application information: Application form required.

Officers: Rama Devi Jain, Pres.; Pushpa Rani Jain, Secy.-Treas.
EIN: 541726264

54997
Blackburn Foundation, Inc.
201 N. Union St., Ste. 340
Alexandria, VA 22314-2642 (703) 519-3703
Contact: James W. Blackburn, Jr., Pres.

Financial data (yr. ended 10/31/01): Grants paid, $9,350; assets, $311,861 (M); expenditures, $13,549; qualifying distributions, $9,350.
Limitations: Giving on a national basis, with emphasis on VA.
Officers and Trustees:* James W. Blackburn, Jr.,* Pres. and Secy.-Treas.; Richard F. Blackburn,* V.P.
EIN: 526036199

54998
Alton Carlton & Martha C. Elder Charitable Trust
c/o Bank of America
P.O. Box 26606
Richmond, VA 23261-6606

Established in 1994 in VA.
Donor(s): Alton Carlton Elder.‡
Financial data (yr. ended 11/30/00): Grants paid, $9,241; assets, $389,907 (M); gifts received, $188; expenditures, $12,404; qualifying distributions, $10,220.
Limitations: Applications not accepted. Giving limited to VA.
Application information: Contributes only to pre-selected organizations.
Trustee: Bank of America.
EIN: 546371097

54999
Edith L. Mudd Charitable Trust
c/o B.B. & T., Trust Dept.
P.O. Box 5228
Martinsville, VA 24115

Established in 1994 in VA.
Donor(s): Edith L. Mudd.‡
Financial data (yr. ended 02/28/02): Grants paid, $9,228; assets, $455,250 (M); expenditures, $13,208; qualifying distributions, $9,228.
Limitations: Applications not accepted. Giving primarily in VA.
Application information: Contributes only to pre-selected organizations.
Trustee: B.B. & T.
EIN: 546354120

55000
Martin Family Charitable Trust
c/o Martin R. William
2725 River Rd.
Virginia Beach, VA 23454-1210

Donor(s): William R. Martin.
Financial data (yr. ended 12/31/01): Grants paid, $9,115; assets, $14,463 (M); expenditures, $9,153; qualifying distributions, $9,115.
Limitations: Applications not accepted. Giving primarily in VA.
Application information: Contributes only to pre-selected organizations.
Trustee: William R. Martin.
EIN: 546434875

55001
Herbert Fried Foundation
c/o Herbert Fried, Jr.
P.O. Box 70307
Richmond, VA 23255-0307

Financial data (yr. ended 12/31/01): Grants paid, $9,050; assets, $235,262 (M); expenditures, $12,653; qualifying distributions, $9,050.
Limitations: Applications not accepted. Giving primarily in Richmond, VA.
Application information: Contributes only to pre-selected organizations.
Officers and Directors:* Jane C. Fried,* Pres. and Treas.; Herbert Fried, Jr.,* V.P. and Secy.; Robert C. Wendt.
EIN: 546038211

55002
The Ennio and Rosa Corte Foundation, Inc.
P.O. Box 445
Bluefield, VA 24605 (540) 326-3938
Contact: Rosa Corte, Pres.

Established in 1999 in VA.
Donor(s): Rosa Corte.
Financial data (yr. ended 12/31/01): Grants paid, $9,000; assets, $304,314 (M); gifts received, $100,000; expenditures, $10,372; qualifying distributions, $9,000.
Limitations: Giving primarily in Durham, NC.
Application information: Application form not required.
Officers and Directors:* Rosa Corte,* Pres. and Secy.-Treas.; Loretta Corte,* V.P.
EIN: 541940655

55003
The Hottle Family Foundation
7230 Witson Dr.
Springfield, VA 22153
Contact: Sally S. Hottle, Dir.

Established in 2000 in VA.
Donor(s): Sally S. Hottle.
Financial data (yr. ended 06/30/01): Grants paid, $9,000; assets, $153,068 (M); gifts received, $167,207; expenditures, $9,144; qualifying distributions, $9,000.
Limitations: Giving primarily in MA, MD, PA, and VA.
Directors: Julie Hottle Day, Karen E. Hottle, Sally S. Hottle.
EIN: 541991307

55004
Duke Street Baptist Memorial Foundation
P.O. Box 22987
Alexandria, VA 22304

Established in 1997 in VA.
Financial data (yr. ended 12/31/99): Grants paid, $8,987; assets, $446,544 (M); expenditures, $27,254; qualifying distributions, $21,593.
Limitations: Giving primarily in VA, with priority given to northern VA.
Officers: Wanda S. Dowell, Pres.; Melrose B. Adams, V.P.; Frances B. Dean, Secy.; Shirley M. Stanis, Treas.
Directors: James F. Florence, Jo Ann Mosley, Rush G. Mosley, Sherry Potts, Hazeldean B. Stone, Leo S. Stonis, Madina Ward, Fred Wiggins, Jean Wiggins, Spencer Williams.
EIN: 541814318

55005
Keepers Preservation Education Fund
5 W. Luray Ave.
Alexandria, VA 22301

Donor(s): Barbara Timken.

Financial data (yr. ended 12/31/01): Grants paid, $8,900; assets, $195,166 (M); gifts received, $14,450; expenditures, $8,900; qualifying distributions, $8,900.
Limitations: Applications not accepted. Giving on a national basis.
Application information: Contributes only to pre-selected organizations.
Trustees: Eric Hertfelder, Dean F. Murtagh, William Seale, Barbara Timken.
EIN: 528292029

55006
Melvin C. Vernon & Jean H. Vernon Charitable Trust
105 River Oak Dr.
Danville, VA 24541

Established in 1985 in VA.
Financial data (yr. ended 12/31/01): Grants paid, $8,876; assets, $78,118 (M); expenditures, $9,057; qualifying distributions, $8,876.
Limitations: Applications not accepted. Giving primarily in Danville, VA.
Application information: Contributes only to pre-selected organizations.
Trustees: Owen T. Carter, C. Melvin Vernon III, R. Hutchings Vernon.
EIN: 546223509

55007
The Owen Family Foundation
2021 Dabney Rd.
Richmond, VA 23230

Established in 1999 in VA.
Donor(s): Jerry Owen.
Financial data (yr. ended 12/31/01): Grants paid, $8,865; assets, $35,188 (M); gifts received, $989; expenditures, $10,029; qualifying distributions, $8,865.
Officer: Jerry Owen, Pres.
EIN: 541946746

55008
Rostro Foundation
P.O. Box 71745
Richmond, VA 23255

Established in 1997 in VA.
Donor(s): John Pasco, Mary T. Pasco.
Financial data (yr. ended 12/31/01): Grants paid, $8,824; assets, $176,397 (M); expenditures, $9,446; qualifying distributions, $8,824.
Limitations: Applications not accepted.
Application information: Contributes only to pre-selected organizations.
Officers: Mary T. Pasco, Pres.; John Pasco, Secy.-Treas.
EIN: 541842038

55009
Denton Family Charitable Foundation, Ltd.
P.O. Box 632
Harrisonburg, VA 22803 (540) 434-6767
Contact: Edgar Warren Denton, Jr., Pres.

Established in 1985 in VA.
Donor(s): Edgar Warren Denton, Jr.
Financial data (yr. ended 11/30/01): Grants paid, $8,820; assets, $588,493 (M); gifts received, $110,035; expenditures, $27,604; qualifying distributions, $21,262.
Limitations: Giving primarily in Harrisonburg, VA.
Officers and Directors:* Edgar Warren Denton, Jr.,* Pres.; Terri D. Babcock,* Secy.; Thomas A. Wilson,* Treas; James McHone.
EIN: 541349360

55010 — VIRGINIA

55010
The Amstutz Foundation
c/o Daniel Amstutz
1301 N. Courthouse Rd., No. 1706
Arlington, VA 22201

Donor(s): Daniel G. Amstutz.
Financial data (yr. ended 01/31/02): Grants paid, $8,750; assets, $134,184 (M); expenditures, $9,801; qualifying distributions, $8,750.
Limitations: Applications not accepted. Giving on a national basis.
Application information: Contributes only to pre-selected organizations.
Trustees: Daniel G. Amstutz, Linda Rafael.
EIN: 133102848

55011
Davis Elkins Charitable Foundation
927 S. Walter Reed Dr.
Arlington, VA 22204 (703) 892-4966
Contact: William J. Reap, Tr.

Established in 1993 in FL.
Donor(s): Davis Elkins.
Financial data (yr. ended 12/31/01): Grants paid, $8,750; assets, $1,230 (M); gifts received, $9,000; expenditures, $9,200; qualifying distributions, $8,750.
Limitations: Giving primarily in Washington, DC and VA.
Application information: Application form not required.
Trustees: Robert D. Abbo, Col. David Blizzard, Davis Elkins, William J. Reap.
EIN: 650349764

55012
Napoleon Hill Foundation
P.O. Box 1277
Wise, VA 24293-1277 (847) 998-0408
Contact: Michael J. Ritt, Jr., V.P.

Established around 1966.
Financial data (yr. ended 12/31/00): Grants paid, $8,701; assets, $1,800,457 (M); gifts received, $160; expenditures, $409,482; qualifying distributions, $265,389; giving activities include $378,857 for programs.
Limitations: Giving on a national basis.
Application information: Application form not required.
Officers: W. Clement Stone, Chair.; Charles W. Johnson, Pres.; James L. Oleson, Exec. V.P.; Delford M. Smith, V.P.; Dr. James Yackel, V.P.; Philip K. Fuentes, V.P.-Secy.; Don M. Green, V.P.-Exec.-Dir.
EIN: 576029521

55013
Jaria Foundation
1100 Port Elissa Landing
Midlothian, VA 23113

Established in 2000 in VA.
Financial data (yr. ended 12/31/01): Grants paid, $8,700; assets, $47,061 (M); expenditures, $9,125; qualifying distributions, $8,700.
Officers and Directors:* Mohammed Imtiaz Husain,* Pres.; Zohara Husain,* Secy.
EIN: 541968373

55014
Joseph W. Bliley Memorial Fund
3801 Augusta Ave.
Richmond, VA 23230
Contact: Nancy M. Jones, Mgr.

Financial data (yr. ended 12/31/01): Grants paid, $8,550; assets, $5,482 (M); gifts received, $5,000; expenditures, $8,554; qualifying distributions, $8,550.
Limitations: Giving primarily in Richmond, VA.
Officers and Directors:* Nicholas M. Bliley,* Pres.; Norbert M. Bliley,* V.P.; Bobby R. Hall,* Mgr.; Nancy M. Jones,* Mgr.
EIN: 546053881

55015
The Ann T. Beane Charitable Foundation
c/o Mark A. Jones & Assocs., PC
8100 Three Chopt Rd., Ste. 220
Richmond, VA 23229-8601 (804) 285-5700

Established in 1997 in VA.
Donor(s): Ann T. Beane.
Financial data (yr. ended 12/31/01): Grants paid, $8,400; assets, $7,650 (M); gifts received, $12,000; expenditures, $10,167; qualifying distributions, $8,400.
Limitations: Giving primarily in NC and VA.
Trustee: Ann T. Beane.
EIN: 541854796

55016
The Joy Foundation for Ecological Education and Research
5402 Sunrise Dr.
P.O. Box 1104, 5402 Sunrise Dr.
Chincoteague Island, VA 23336
(757) 336-5688
Contact: Bertram S. Brown, Chair.; or Joy Gilman Brown, Pres.

Established in 1991 in VA.
Donor(s): Joy Gilman Brown, Bertram S. Brown.
Financial data (yr. ended 12/31/00): Grants paid, $8,400; assets, $1,445 (M); gifts received, $13,100; expenditures, $20,710; qualifying distributions, $8,400.
Limitations: Giving limited to the Chincoteague Island, VA, area.
Application information: Application form not required.
Officers and Directors:* Bertram S. Brown,* Chair.; Rena Goehl,* Vice-Chair.; Joy Gilman Brown,* Pres.; Dale Brown, Traci Brown, Wendy Brown-Blau, Kevin Browngoehl, Laurie Browngoehl, Art Spingarn.
EIN: 541575577

55017
Mary C. Henninger Haddad and Louis S. Haddad Foundation, Inc.
1435 Crossways Blvd.
Chesapeake, VA 23320

Established in 1998 in VA.
Donor(s): Mary C. Henninger-Haddad, Louis S. Haddad.
Financial data (yr. ended 10/31/01): Grants paid, $8,375; assets, $166,899 (M); gifts received, $50,060; expenditures, $9,085; qualifying distributions, $8,375.
Limitations: Applications not accepted.
Application information: Contributes only to pre-selected organizations.
Officers: Mary C. Henninger-Haddad, Pres.; Louis S. Haddad, V.P. and Secy.; Francis J. Henninger, V.P.
EIN: 541917341

55018
T. Nash and Gloria M. Broaddus Foundation
P.O. Box 205
Irvington, VA 22480-0205
Contact: T. Nash Broaddus, Pres.

Established in 1997 in VA.
Financial data (yr. ended 12/31/01): Grants paid, $8,230; assets, $1,195,843 (M); expenditures, $23,827; qualifying distributions, $11,652.
Limitations: Giving primarily in VA.
Officers: T. Nash Broaddus, Pres.; Gloria M. Broaddus, Secy.-Treas.
EIN: 541842036

55019
Bradley W. Jackson Foundation
207 Windwood Dr.
Bluefield, VA 24605 (540) 326-2246
Contact: Jerry W. Jackson, Tr.

Established in 1996 in VA.
Donor(s): Jerry W. Jackson.
Financial data (yr. ended 06/30/02): Grants paid, $8,200; assets, $113,325 (M); gifts received, $3,224; expenditures, $8,591; qualifying distributions, $8,200.
Application information: Application form not required.
Trustees: Jerry W. Jackson, Mary F. Jackson, Leanne J. Link.
EIN: 541807854

55020
John F. Kane Scholarship Fund, Inc.
12140 Eddystone Ct.
Woodbridge, VA 22192-2213

Established in 1997 in VA.
Financial data (yr. ended 12/31/01): Grants paid, $8,150; assets, $192,825 (M); expenditures, $9,722; qualifying distributions, $8,150.
Officers and Directors:* William T. Healey,* Pres.; Steve Moran,* V.P.; Alice Moore,* Secy.; J. Michael Tivnan,* Treas.; Barbara Tivnan.
EIN: 541811279

55021
The Anning & Doris Smith Family Foundation
652 S. Pickett St.
Alexandria, VA 22304-4620

Established in 1998 in VA.
Donor(s): Anning Smith Sr. Trust.
Financial data (yr. ended 12/31/99): Grants paid, $8,064; assets, $158,895 (M); gifts received, $960; expenditures, $9,471; qualifying distributions, $9,471.
Limitations: Applications not accepted. Giving primarily in NJ.
Application information: Contributes only to pre-selected organizations.
Officers: Doris Smith, Pres.; Anning Smith, Jr., Treas.
Director: Deborah Smith.
EIN: 311604018

55022
Thomas & Lolita Gayle Scholarship Trust
c/o Bank of America
P.O. Box 26606
Richmond, VA 23261-6606
Application address: c/o Thomas Dutton, Mathews High School, P.O. Box 38, Mathews, VA 23109, tel.: (804) 725-3702

Established in 1996 in VA.
Donor(s): Thomas W. Gayle.‡
Financial data (yr. ended 12/31/99): Grants paid, $8,000; assets, $181,875 (M); expenditures, $10,539; qualifying distributions, $9,060.
Application information: Application form required.
Trustee: Bank of America.
EIN: 546395347

55023
Harar Family Foundation, Ltd.
c/o Jerome Ostrov
9380 Mt. Vernon Cir.
Alexandria, VA 22309

Established in 1998 in VA.
Donor(s): Robert Harar, Elaine Harar.
Financial data (yr. ended 12/31/01): Grants paid, $8,000; assets, $27,394 (M); expenditures, $9,579; qualifying distributions, $8,000.
Limitations: Applications not accepted.
Application information: Contributes only to pre-selected organizations.
Officers: Robert E. Harar, Pres. and Treas.; Elaine M. Harar, V.P. and Secy.
EIN: 522101472

55024
R. M. & E. H. Ingram Charitable Trust
c/o SunTrust Banks, Inc.
P.O. Box 27385
Richmond, VA 23261-7385

Established in 1986 in VA.
Financial data (yr. ended 07/31/01): Grants paid, $8,000; assets, $167,470 (M); expenditures, $9,104; qualifying distributions, $8,087.
Limitations: Giving primarily in VA.
Trustee: SunTrust Banks, Inc.
EIN: 546234921

55025
Cora Gardner Jones Foundation
830 E. Main St., Ste. 1700
Richmond, VA 23219-2725 (804) 643-6886
Contact: Mary Buford Hitz, Pres.

Donor(s): Mary Buford Hitz.
Financial data (yr. ended 07/31/01): Grants paid, $8,000; assets, $176,995 (M); expenditures, $9,152; qualifying distributions, $8,000.
Limitations: Giving limited to VA.
Application information: Generally contributes to pre-selected organizations. Application form not required.
Officers and Directors:* Mary Buford Hitz,* Pres.; Bessie B. Carter,* Secy.; Frederic S. Bocock,* Treas.
EIN: 541289029

55026
Todd Family Foundation, Inc.
15 Emmett Ln.
Hampton, VA 23666

Established in 1999 in VA.
Donor(s): Calvin B. Todd.
Financial data (yr. ended 12/31/01): Grants paid, $8,000; assets, $1,043 (M); gifts received, $7,800; expenditures, $8,035; qualifying distributions, $8,000.
Limitations: Applications not accepted. Giving on a national basis.
Application information: Contributes only to pre-selected organizations.
Officers: Calvin B. Todd, Pres.; Donna L. Haynes, V.P.; Elaine C. Todd, V.P.; Jan L. Meredith, Secy.; Kimberly K. Mayo, Treas.
EIN: 541942058

55027
The Thomas and Barbara Walker Foundation
P.O. Box 26608
Richmond, VA 23261-6606

Established in 2000 in VA.
Donor(s): Barbara Jones Walker, Thomas A. Walker.
Financial data (yr. ended 12/31/00): Grants paid, $8,000; assets, $392,774 (M); gifts received, $503,669; expenditures, $17,533; qualifying distributions, $8,500.
Limitations: Applications not accepted. Giving on a national basis, with some emphasis on VA.
Application information: Contributes only to pre-selected organizations.
Officers and Directors:* Thomas A. Walker,* Pres.; Stephen Thomas Walker,* Secy.-Treas.; Virginia Leigh Walker Catillejo, Susan Lynn Walker Holliday, Barbara Jones Walker.
EIN: 541999825

55028
Charmarie Sims Foundation, Inc.
2621 Quality Ct.
Virginia Beach, VA 23454 (757) 340-1875
Contact: Christina Sims, V.P.

Established in 1998 in VA.
Financial data (yr. ended 12/31/00): Grants paid, $7,959; assets, $276,813 (M); gifts received, $46,525; expenditures, $46,396; qualifying distributions, $37,727.
Officers: Kenneth R. Sims, Pres.; Christina Sims, V.P.; Joan M. Sims, V.P.; Steve Sims, Secy.; Kevin Sims, Treas.
Directors: Mark D. Brynteson, Wendy Sims.
EIN: 541907946

55029
Kindt Christian Charitable Trust
2205 Brambleton Ave. S.W.
Roanoke, VA 24015
Contact: June Ann Gibson, Tr.

Established in 1990.
Donor(s): Warren Kindt, Lois Kindt.
Financial data (yr. ended 12/31/01): Grants paid, $7,800; assets, $62,038 (M); expenditures, $7,800; qualifying distributions, $7,800.
Limitations: Giving primarily in IL.
Application information: Application form not required.
Trustees: June Ann Gibson, John W. Kindt, Sr.
EIN: 546296044

55030
Charles Emory Bryant Foundation, Inc.
P.O. Box 219
Independence, VA 24348-0219
Contact: Alvin C. Proffit, Pres.

Established in 1990 in VA.
Financial data (yr. ended 12/31/99): Grants paid, $7,750; assets, $86,105 (M); expenditures, $8,269; qualifying distributions, $8,138.
Limitations: Giving limited to Grayson County, VA.
Application information: Application form required.
Officers and Directors:* Alvin C. Proffit, Pres.; Pete Campbell,* V.P.; Connie Farmer, Secy.-Treas.; Mike Phipps.
EIN: 541552742

55031
LMAC Foundation, Inc.
1345 Potomac School Rd.
McLean, VA 22101-2331

Established in 1999 in VA.
Donor(s): Sherley Koteen, Bernard Koteen.
Financial data (yr. ended 12/31/01): Grants paid, $7,750; assets, $133,940 (M); expenditures, $8,175; qualifying distributions, $7,750.
Application information: Application form required.
Officers and Directors: Lisa B. Koteen,* Pres.; Charles D. Koteen,* Secy.; Mark L. Gerchick,* Treas.
EIN: 541965097

55032
The Forehand foundation
1002 Fairway Dr.
Chesapeake, VA 23320 (757) 455-1800
Contact: V. Thomas Forehand, Jr., Pres.

Established in 1997 in VA.
Donor(s): V. Thomas Forehand, Jr.
Financial data (yr. ended 12/31/01): Grants paid, $7,688; assets, $109,600 (M); expenditures, $10,090; qualifying distributions, $7,688.
Limitations: Giving primarily in VA.
Officer: V. Thomas Forehand, Jr., Pres.
EIN: 541716853

55033
DuPont Guerry III Foundation
301 Flag Station Rd.
Richmond, VA 23220 (804) 784-5128
Contact: DuPont Guerry III, Tr.

Financial data (yr. ended 06/30/02): Grants paid, $7,574; assets, $303,390 (M); expenditures, $11,173; qualifying distributions, $7,574.
Limitations: Giving primarily in VA.
Application information: Application form not required.
Trustee: DuPont Guerry III.
EIN: 546052260

55034
Appomattox County Educational Foundation, Inc.
P.O. Box 548
Appomattox, VA 24522

Established in 1987 in VA.
Donor(s): Ellen P. Jamerson, W.E. Jamerson.
Financial data (yr. ended 12/31/00): Grants paid, $7,500; assets, $109,616 (M); gifts received, $1,532; expenditures, $8,095; qualifying distributions, $7,539.
Limitations: Applications not accepted. Giving limited to residents of Appomattox, VA.
Application information: Unsolicited requests for funds not accepted.
Officers and Directors:* Michael Willis,* Chair.; Ellen P. Jamerson,* Secy.-Treas.; Robert Carter, Walter Krug, Lannis Selz, Ruth Webb.
EIN: 541442864

55035
Lunger-Emory Family Foundation, Inc.
178 Dennis Dr.
Williamsburg, VA 23185

Established in 2000 in VA.
Donor(s): Eugene E. Lunger, Florence E. Lunger.
Financial data (yr. ended 12/31/01): Grants paid, $7,500; assets, $15 (M); gifts received, $6,699; expenditures, $8,274; qualifying distributions, $7,500.
Limitations: Applications not accepted. Giving on a national basis.
Application information: Contributes only to pre-selected organizations.
Officers: Eugene E. Lunger, Pres.; Florence E. Lunger, Secy.
EIN: 541961837

55036
Good Neighbor Foundation
(Formerly The Wilkins Foundation)
P.O. Box 958
Lynchburg, VA 24505-0958 (804) 846-9000
Contact: Robert C. Wood, III, Tr.

Financial data (yr. ended 12/31/99): Grants paid, $7,448; assets, $183,485 (M); gifts received, $14,472; expenditures, $16,434; qualifying distributions, $7,627.

55036—VIRGINIA

Limitations: Giving primarily in VA.
Application information: Application form not required.
Trustees: Kevin L. Cash, James O. Watts IV, Robert C. Wood III.
EIN: 541066542

55037
The Poster Foundation
c/o Arnel Investment Corp.
6 Pigeon Hill Dr., Ste. 270
Sterling, VA 20165

Financial data (yr. ended 12/31/01): Grants paid, $7,408; assets, $4,005 (M); expenditures, $7,552; qualifying distributions, $7,408.
Limitations: Applications not accepted. Giving primarily in VA.
Application information: Contributes only to pre-selected organizations.
Trustees: Rose P. Carr, Allan Poster.
EIN: 546070636

55038
CORT Foundation, Inc.
11250 Waples Mill Rd., Ste. 500
Fairfax, VA 22030-7400

Established in 1991 in VA.
Donor(s): Mohasco Foundation, Inc.
Financial data (yr. ended 12/31/01): Grants paid, $7,375; assets, $157,651 (M); expenditures, $7,702; qualifying distributions, $7,641.
Limitations: Applications not accepted. Giving primarily in Washington, DC, MD, and VA.
Application information: Contributes only to pre-selected organizations.
Officers and Directors:* Paul Arnold,* Pres.; Vicky Stiles,* V.P.; Maureen Thune.
EIN: 541566234
Codes: CS, CD

55039
Greenway Foundation
11800 Winterway Ln.
Fairfax Station, VA 22039-2107

Established in 1987 in VA.
Financial data (yr. ended 12/31/01): Grants paid, $7,325; assets, $20,805 (M); expenditures, $8,262; qualifying distributions, $7,325.
Limitations: Applications not accepted. Giving on a national basis, with some emphasis on VA.
Application information: Contributes only to pre-selected organizations.
Directors: Donald K. Allman, Mary Anne Allman.
EIN: 541398308

55040
The Irving and Jett Groves Charitable Foundation
1517 Mulberry Rd.
Martinsville, VA 24112-5713

Established in 1999 in VA.
Donor(s): Irving M. Groves, Jr., Jett C. Groves.
Financial data (yr. ended 09/30/01): Grants paid, $7,250; assets, $160,844 (M); expenditures, $7,838; qualifying distributions, $7,250.
Limitations: Applications not accepted.
Application information: Contributes only to pre-selected organizations.
Officer: Irving M. Groves, Jr., Pres.
Directors: Jett C. Groves, Mattie G. Sheppard.
EIN: 541961867

55041
The Williams-McClain Charitable Foundation
208 Lester St.
Martinsville, VA 24112-2821 (276) 632-5662
Contact: Allan McClain, Pres.

Established in 1996 in VA.
Financial data (yr. ended 12/31/01): Grants paid, $7,245; assets, $59,585 (M); gifts received, $8,078; expenditures, $7,292; qualifying distributions, $7,245.
Limitations: Giving primarily in Martinsville, VA.
Officers: Allan McClain, Pres.; Charlotte W. McClain, V.P.; Charles T. Williams, V.P.; David Mcl. Williams, Secy.; Ralph J. Pruitt, Treas.
EIN: 541810111

55042
Gerald and Paula McNichols Family Foundation
23349 Parsons Rd.
Middleburg, VA 20117-2817

Established in 2000 in VA.
Donor(s): Gerald R. McNichols.
Financial data (yr. ended 12/31/00): Grants paid, $7,238; assets, $5,642,256 (M); gifts received, $5,873,180; expenditures, $17,160; qualifying distributions, $17,661.
Limitations: Applications not accepted. Giving primarily in AL and VA.
Application information: Contributes only to pre-selected organizations.
Directors: Melissa S. Cardon, Katherine L. Loftis, Gerald R. McNichols, Gerald R. McNichols, Jr., Paula A. McNichols.
EIN: 541973996

55043
Doyle Foundation, Inc.
16520 Philpott Hwy.
Martinsville, VA 24112
Contact: Wilbur S. Doyle, Pres.

Established in 1952.
Donor(s): Doyle Lumber, Inc.
Financial data (yr. ended 12/31/01): Grants paid, $7,200; assets, $118,177 (M); expenditures, $8,571; qualifying distributions, $7,200.
Limitations: Giving primarily in Winston-Salem, NC, and Martinsville, VA.
Officers: Wilbur S. Doyle, Pres.; Lillie T. Doyle, V.P.
EIN: 546056454

55044
Marjorie Sutton Memorial Foundation
P.O. Box 3982
Martinsville, VA 24115-3982

Established in 1991 in VA.
Donor(s): J.P. Sutton.
Financial data (yr. ended 12/31/01): Grants paid, $7,197; assets, $128,531 (M); expenditures, $8,130; qualifying distributions, $7,197.
Limitations: Applications not accepted. Giving primarily in VA.
Application information: Contributes only to pre-selected organizations.
Officers: James P. Sutton, Pres. and Treas.; Jean S. Odachowski, V.P.; William F. Stone, Jr., Secy.
EIN: 541526922

55045
Lucille Barney Memorial Trust
3441 Commission Ct.
Lake Ridge, VA 22192-1753

Established in 1997 in VA.
Donor(s): Sidney Barney.

Financial data (yr. ended 12/31/01): Grants paid, $7,100; assets, $96,066 (M); expenditures, $23,417; qualifying distributions, $7,100.
Limitations: Applications not accepted.
Application information: Contributes only to pre-selected organizations.
Trustees: John E. Griswold, David B. Wilks.
EIN: 541864497

55046
The New River Valley Charitable Trust
(Formerly The New River Charitable Trust)
516 2nd St.
Radford, VA 24141-1404 (540) 731-1628
Contact: William Fry, Tr.

Established in 1984 in VA.
Donor(s): Peter Fletcher.
Financial data (yr. ended 12/31/01): Grants paid, $7,100; assets, $155,948 (M); expenditures, $7,677; qualifying distributions, $7,100.
Limitations: Giving primarily in VA.
Application information: Application form not required.
Trustees: Peter Fletcher, William Fry.
EIN: 546222894

55047
The Daniel G. Van Clief Friendly Fund
c/o McGuire Woods LLP
P.O. Box 397
Richmond, VA 23218-0397

Established in 1988 in VA.
Financial data (yr. ended 03/31/02): Grants paid, $7,100; assets, $145,924 (M); expenditures, $8,059; qualifying distributions, $7,100.
Limitations: Applications not accepted. Giving limited to VA.
Application information: Contributes only to pre-selected organizations.
Officers and Directors:* J. Courtlandt Van Clief,* Pres.; Alan S. Van Clief,* Secy.; Barry R. Van Clief, Daniel G. Van Clief, Jr.
EIN: 541454475

55048
The Brant Foundation, Inc.
1156 Nelson Dr.
Harrisonburg, VA 22801
Contact: Melvin B. Brant, Dir.

Established in 2000 in VA.
Donor(s): Elizabeth S. Brant.‡
Financial data (yr. ended 06/30/02): Grants paid, $7,000; assets, $427,471 (M); gifts received, $38,590; expenditures, $16,057; qualifying distributions, $7,000.
Limitations: Giving primarily in VA.
Directors: Annette H. Brant, Melvin B. Brant, Cynthia L. Giron, Melanie B. Lamb.
EIN: 542000681

55049
Pickard-Studley Foundation, Inc.
c/o James H. Maloney
104 N. Oak St.
Falls Church, VA 22046-3234

Established in 1996 in VA.
Donor(s): Wesley C. Pickard, Jeanette A. Studley.
Financial data (yr. ended 08/31/01): Grants paid, $7,000; assets, $252,329 (M); expenditures, $8,036; qualifying distributions, $7,000.
Limitations: Applications not accepted.
Application information: Contributes only to pre-selected organizations.
Officers and Directors:* Wesley C. Pickard,* Pres.; Jeanette A. Studley,* Secy.
EIN: 541827674

55050
F. & G. Woods Charitable Foundation, Inc.
c/o Cheely Burcham, et al.
7200 Glen Forest Dr., Ste. 203
Richmond, VA 23226

Established in 2000 in VA.
Financial data (yr. ended 12/31/01): Grants paid, $7,000; assets, $2,337 (M); gifts received, $589; expenditures, $7,566; qualifying distributions, $7,000.
Officers: Frederick P. Woods, Pres.; Gail Woods, Secy.
EIN: 541989644

55051
The CAPA Foundation
c/o Carlton Moffatt
1 Kingsway Ct.
Richmond, VA 23226

Established in 1999 in VA.
Donor(s): Camilla A. Hyde.
Financial data (yr. ended 03/31/02): Grants paid, $6,850; assets, $143,475 (M); expenditures, $8,483; qualifying distributions, $6,850.
Limitations: Applications not accepted.
Application information: Contributes only to pre-selected organizations.
Trustees: Camilla A. Hyde, C. Page Moffatt, Camilla H. Moffatt, Carlton P. Moffatt.
EIN: 546457602

55052
Virginia Foundation of Cooperation, Inc.
P.O. Box 25202
Richmond, VA 23260-5202
Application address: c/o Lester Meyers, Virginia Polytechnical Institute & State University, Blacksburg, VA 24601, tel.: (540) 231-6301

Financial data (yr. ended 12/31/01): Grants paid, $6,835; assets, $117,640 (M); gifts received, $100; expenditures, $7,207; qualifying distributions, $6,835.
Limitations: Applications not accepted. Giving limited to VA.
Application information: Contributes only to pre-selected organizations.
Officers: James Coyaues, Pres.; Greg White, V.P.; Donald Shillet, Recording Secy.
EIN: 510221281

55053
Edwin P. Conquest Memorial Trust
c/o Wachovia Bank, N.A.
1021 E. Cary St., 6th Fl.
Richmond, VA 23219-4000

Donor(s): Edwin P. Conquest, Jr.
Financial data (yr. ended 12/31/99): Grants paid, $6,822; assets, $73,174 (M); gifts received, $9,589; expenditures, $7,723; qualifying distributions, $6,822.
Limitations: Applications not accepted. Giving on a national basis.
Application information: Contributes only to pre-selected organizations.
Trustee: Edwin P. Conquest, Jr.
EIN: 546073824

55054
Birdsong Charitable Foundation
c/o Stephen L. Huber
P.O. Box 1400
Suffolk, VA 23439-1400

Established in 1991 in VA.
Donor(s): Birdsong Corp.
Financial data (yr. ended 12/31/01): Grants paid, $6,700; assets, $1,137,449 (M); gifts received, $201,000; expenditures, $11,482; qualifying distributions, $11,058.
Limitations: Applications not accepted. Giving primarily in VA.
Application information: Contributes only to pre-selected organizations. Unsolicited requests for funds not considered.
Directors: George Y. Birdsong, Thomas H. Birdsong III, Stephen L. Huber, W.J. Spain, Jr.
EIN: 541607210

55055
Bess R. Poff Scholarship Foundation
c/o Betty S. Nester
P.O. Box 122
Floyd, VA 24091
Application address: Rte. 2, Box 122, Floyd, VA 24091, tel.: (540) 745-2363
Contact: Robert G. Nester, Jr., Pres.

Established in 1997 in VA.
Donor(s): Bess R. Poff.‡
Financial data (yr. ended 12/31/00): Grants paid, $6,700; assets, $155,636 (M); expenditures, $7,108; qualifying distributions, $7,108.
Limitations: Giving primarily to residents of Floyd County, VA.
Application information: Applicant must include grade point average, college choice and extracurricular activities.
Officers and Directors:* Robert G. Nester, Jr.,* Pres.; Betty S. Nester,* Secy.-Treas.
EIN: 541867764

55056
Goodman & Company, CPA's Foundation Honoring Retired Partners, Inc.
1 Commercial Pl., Ste. 800
Norfolk, VA 23510

Established in 1997 in VA.
Donor(s): Goodman & Co., L.L.P.
Financial data (yr. ended 06/30/02): Grants paid, $6,550; assets, $122,481 (M); expenditures, $6,550; qualifying distributions, $6,550.
Limitations: Applications not accepted. Giving primarily in areas of company operations.
Application information: Contribute only to pre-selected organizations.
Officer: Donald M. Dale, Pres.
Directors: Julian Gutterman, Cris Toney, Steve Womack.
EIN: 541847474
Codes: CS, CD

55057
Virginia Payne Hunton Trust
c/o Bank of America
P.O. Box 26606
Richmond, VA 23261-6606 (804) 788-2963
Contact: Elizabeth D. Seaman, Trust Off., Bank of America

Financial data (yr. ended 06/30/99): Grants paid, $6,500; assets, $216,596 (M); expenditures, $9,063; qualifying distributions, $8,234.
Limitations: Giving limited to Richmond, VA.
Trustee: Bank of America.
EIN: 546030458

55058
R. Aumon & Mary Scott Bass Endowment Fund, Inc.
c/o First Virginia Bank, Trust Dept.
700 E. Main St.
Richmond, VA 23219
Application address: VSDB-Staunton, P.O. Box 2069, Staunton, VA 24401
Contact: Race Drake, Pres.

Established in 1985 in VA.
Donor(s): R. Aumon Bass,‡ Mary Scott Bass.‡
Financial data (yr. ended 09/30/00): Grants paid, $6,496; assets, $161,815 (M); expenditures, $9,043; qualifying distributions, $6,496.
Limitations: Giving limited to Staunton, VA.
Application information: Application form required.
Officers and Directors:* Race Drake, Pres.; Hugh C. Cunningham III,* Secy.; Vince A. Wood,* Treas.; John M. Lee, David C. Stables, Jr., Dawayne Werner.
EIN: 541296056
Codes: GTI

55059
Rowny Foundation, Inc.
c/o Rowny Capital
8500 Executive Park Ave., Ste. 200
Fairfax, VA 22031

Established in 1999 in MD and VA.
Donor(s): Michael J. Rowny.
Financial data (yr. ended 12/31/00): Grants paid, $6,462; assets, $928,190 (M); expenditures, $32,415; qualifying distributions, $5,467.
Limitations: Applications not accepted. Giving primarily in Washington, DC, MD, and NY.
Application information: Contributes only to pre-selected organizations.
Officers: Michael J. Rowny, Pres.; Peter E. Rowny, V.P.; Melissa B. Rowny, Secy.
EIN: 522190131

55060
The DMB Foundation
c/o David M. Breen
1600 N. Oak St., Ste. 715
Arlington, VA 22209 (703) 522-6094

Established in 1997 in VA.
Donor(s): Dermott M. Breen, Sue M. Breen.
Financial data (yr. ended 12/31/01): Grants paid, $6,315; assets, $131,703 (M); gifts received, $8,275; expenditures, $6,367; qualifying distributions, $6,315.
Limitations: Applications not accepted.
Application information: Contributes only to pre-selected organizations.
Trustees: David M. Breen, Dermott M. Breen, Nina B. Breen, Sue M. Breen.
EIN: 066434857

55061
The Parkerson Foundation
c/o Margaret L. Parkerson
3735 Knotts Creek Ln.
Suffolk, VA 23435

Established in 2000 in VA.
Donor(s): Charles H. Parkerson.
Financial data (yr. ended 12/31/01): Grants paid, $6,278; assets, $119,170 (M); expenditures, $7,925; qualifying distributions, $6,278.
Limitations: Applications not accepted.
Application information: Contributes only to pre-selected organizations.
Officer: Margaret L. Parkerson, Pres.
Directors: Arthur L. Parkerson, Laura S. Parkerson, Sarah L. Parkerson.
EIN: 542014686

55062
Judy W. Anderson Charitable Trust
1609 Pope Ave.
Richmond, VA 23227

Established in 1987 in VA.
Donor(s): Charles E. Wilkerson, Mrs. Charles E. Wilkerson.

Financial data (yr. ended 11/30/00): Grants paid, $6,275; assets, $95,138 (M); expenditures, $6,944; qualifying distributions, $6,899.
Limitations: Applications not accepted. Giving limited to VA.
Application information: Contributes only to pre-selected organizations.
Trustees: Paul E. Irwin, Jr., Ann W. Suber, Charles E. Wilkerson, Edward R. Wilkerson, Sallie B. Wilkerson.
EIN: 541472536

55063
Alice Reed & Hunter Holmes McGuire Endowment Trust
1218 Rothesay Cir.
Richmond, VA 23221

Donor(s): Alice Reed McGuire, Hunter Holmes McGuire, Jr.
Financial data (yr. ended 12/31/01): Grants paid, $6,271; assets, $306,091 (M); expenditures, $7,542; qualifying distributions, $6,271.
Limitations: Applications not accepted. Giving primarily in Fishers Island, NY and VA.
Application information: Contributes only to pre-selected organizations.
Trustees: Alice Reed McGuire, Hunter Holmes McGuire, Jr.
EIN: 546048453

55064
G. V. "Sonny" Montgomery Foundation
11 Canal Center Plz., Ste. 104
Alexandria, VA 22314

Established in 1999 in MS.
Donor(s): G. V. "Sonny" Montgomery.
Financial data (yr. ended 12/31/00): Grants paid, $6,250; assets, $71,974 (M); gifts received, $13,928; expenditures, $9,292; qualifying distributions, $6,250.
Limitations: Applications not accepted. Giving primarily in MS.
Application information: Contributes only to pre-selected organizations.
Officers and Directors:* G. V. "Sonny" Montgomery,* Pres.; Louise Medlin,* Treas.; Robert B. Deen, Jr., William P. Elliott.
EIN: 640911785

55065
John & Irene McIsaac Charitable Foundation
3452 Lyrac St.
Oakton, VA 22124-2213

Financial data (yr. ended 12/31/01): Grants paid, $6,216; assets, $57,778 (M); expenditures, $6,890; qualifying distributions, $6,216.
Limitations: Applications not accepted.
Application information: Contributes only to pre-selected organizations.
Officers: John McIsaac, Pres.; Irene McIsaac, Secy.
EIN: 222351679

55066
The Retta Leigh Perel Keil Foundation
112 Tempsford Ln.
Richmond, VA 23226

Established in 1993 in VA as partial successor to the Ruth & Milton Perel Foundation.
Financial data (yr. ended 12/31/01): Grants paid, $6,110; assets, $131,122 (M); expenditures, $7,135; qualifying distributions, $6,110.
Limitations: Applications not accepted. Giving primarily in VA.
Application information: Contributes only to pre-selected organizations.

Officer and Directors:* Retta Leigh Perel Keil,* Pres. and Secy.-Treas.; Douglas Perel Keil, Kirk David Keil.
EIN: 541612293

55067
The Blankman Foundation, Inc.
1149 Simmons Gap Rd.
Dyke, VA 22935

Established in 1982 in NY.
Financial data (yr. ended 06/30/01): Grants paid, $6,050; assets, $41,065 (M); expenditures, $7,769; qualifying distributions, $1,719.
Limitations: Applications not accepted. Giving primarily in NY.
Application information: Contributes only to pre-selected charitable organizations.
Officers: Norman E. Blankman, Pres.; Evelyn W. Blankman, Secy.
EIN: 136160881

55068
The Justine Nusbaum Family Foundation
P.O. Box 3460
Norfolk, VA 23514
Contact: Robert C. Nusbaum, Treas.

Established in 1985 in VA.
Financial data (yr. ended 04/30/02): Grants paid, $6,050; assets, $110,819 (M); gifts received, $650; expenditures, $7,861; qualifying distributions, $6,050.
Limitations: Applications not accepted.
Officers: Alan B. Nusbaum, Pres.; V.H. Nusbaum, Jr., V.P.; William L. Nusbaum, Secy.; Robert C. Nusbaum, Treas.
EIN: 541348553

55069
The Century Foundation
7416 Forest Hill Ave.
Richmond, VA 23225 (804) 330-4400
Contact: Z. Greene Hollowell, Jr., Dir.

Established in 1986 in VA.
Financial data (yr. ended 12/31/99): Grants paid, $6,000; assets, $59,532 (M); expenditures, $6,643; qualifying distributions, $6,409.
Limitations: Giving primarily in VA.
Directors: Z. Greene Hollowell, Jr., Stuart K. Morgan.
EIN: 541384796

55070
Jean B. Duerr Memorial Fund
c/o The National Bank of Blacksburg, Trust Dept.
P.O. Box 90002
Blacksburg, VA 24062-9002
Application address: c/o Chapter AU, Virginia - P.E.O. Sisterhood, P.O. Box 10415, Blacksburg, VA 24060

Established in 1992 in VA.
Donor(s): William Duerr.
Financial data (yr. ended 12/31/99): Grants paid, $6,000; assets, $204,386 (M); expenditures, $7,877; qualifying distributions, $6,000.
Limitations: Giving primarily in VA.
Application information: Application form required.
Trustee: The National Bank of Blacksburg.
EIN: 546317343

55071
Faber Foundation
(Formerly The Robert Carson Faber Foundation)
507 Roosevelt Blvd., Ste. C-201
Falls Church, VA 22044-3123

Donor(s): Robert Carson Faber, Joyce A. Faber.

Financial data (yr. ended 09/30/01): Grants paid, $6,000; assets, $13,432 (M); gifts received, $7,000; expenditures, $6,028; qualifying distributions, $6,000.
Limitations: Applications not accepted. Giving primarily in VA.
Application information: Contributes only to pre-selected organizations.
Trustees: Joyce A. Faber, Robert Carson Faber.
EIN: 686017848

55072
The Featherston Foundation, Inc.
3440 S. Jefferson St., Ste. 501
Falls Church, VA 22041

Established in 2000 in VA.
Donor(s): Sophia E. Featherston.
Financial data (yr. ended 12/31/01): Grants paid, $6,000; assets, $171,726 (M); gifts received, $200; expenditures, $8,973; qualifying distributions, $6,000.
Limitations: Applications not accepted. Giving primarily in Falls Church, VA.
Application information: Contributes only to pre-selected organizations.
Officers: Sophia E. Featherston, Pres.; Gerard S. Rugel, Secy.; George A. Fletcher, Treas.
EIN: 541985894

55073
Eppa Hunton IV Trust
c/o Bank of America
P.O. Box 26606
Richmond, VA 23261-6606 (804) 788-2963
Contact: Elizabeth D. Seaman, Trust Off., Bank of America

Financial data (yr. ended 06/30/00): Grants paid, $6,000; assets, $125,712 (M); expenditures, $8,218; qualifying distributions, $7,459.
Limitations: Giving limited to Richmond, VA.
Trustee: Bank of America.
EIN: 546166692

55074
James and Mary Nolan Foundation, Inc.
c/o James E. Nolan
P.O. Box 765
Mount Jackson, VA 22842

Established in 1995 in VA.
Donor(s): James E. Nolan, Mary B. Nolan.
Financial data (yr. ended 12/31/01): Grants paid, $6,000; assets, $79,835 (M); gifts received, $5,000; expenditures, $6,593; qualifying distributions, $6,000.
Limitations: Applications not accepted.
Application information: Contributes only to pre-selected organizations.
Officers and Directors:* James E. Nolan,* Pres.; Mary B. Nolan,* V.P.; Paul E. Hebert, Secy.-Treas.; John R. Barrett.
EIN: 541780662

55075
Morrow-Stevens Foundation
P.O. Box 3026
Oakton, VA 22124-3026 (703) 319-1527
Contact: Geraldine M. Graham, Dir.

Established in 1999 in VA.
Donor(s): Geraldine M. Graham, Alan S. Graham.
Financial data (yr. ended 12/31/01): Grants paid, $5,879; assets, $187,481 (M); gifts received, $44,431; expenditures, $7,735; qualifying distributions, $5,879.
Limitations: Giving limited to VA.
Application information: Application form required.

Directors: Alan S. Graham, Christopher M. Graham, Geraldine M. Graham, Matthew S. Graham.
EIN: 541949631

55076
Lucy Brown Bassett Foundation
c/o MainStreet Trust Co., N.A.
P.O. Box 5228
Martinsville, VA 24115-5228

Financial data (yr. ended 08/31/01): Grants paid, $5,800; assets, $53,684 (M); expenditures, $7,422; qualifying distributions, $5,800.
Limitations: Applications not accepted. Giving primarily in VA.
Application information: Contributes only to pre-selected organizations.
Officers: Mrs. J.D. Bassett, Jr., Pres.; Lucy B. Andrews, V.P.; Minnie Lane, V.P.; Jane Spilman, V.P.; John D. Bassett III, Secy.-Treas.
EIN: 237047152

55077
Bruce and Lois Forbes Charitable Foundation, Inc
P.O. Box 345
Basye, VA 22810-0345 (540) 432-0600
Contact: Lois J. Forbes, Pres., or Bruce Forbes, V.P.

Established in 1994.
Donor(s): Bruce Forbes, Lois Forbes.
Financial data (yr. ended 12/31/01): Grants paid, $5,800; assets, $1 (M); expenditures, $6,171; qualifying distributions, $5,800.
Limitations: Giving primarily in VA.
Officers: Lois J. Forbes, Pres.; Bruce Forbes, V.P; Jeffrey K. Forbes, Secy.-Treas.
EIN: 541632246

55078
The Family Trust, Inc.
c/o C. Cuddeback
1962 Milldale Rd.
Front Royal, VA 22630

Established in 1978 in MD.
Donor(s): Chris N. Cuddeback, Sons of the Immaculate Heart of Mary, Carol S. Cuddeback.
Financial data (yr. ended 06/30/01): Grants paid, $5,771; assets, $17,930 (M); gifts received, $18,030; expenditures, $5,771; qualifying distributions, $5,771.
Limitations: Applications not accepted. Giving primarily in MD and VA.
Application information: Contributes only to pre-selected organizations.
Officer: Chris N. Cuddeback, Pres. and Mgr.
Director: Carol S. Cuddeback.
EIN: 521130424

55079
Denoon Scholarship Fund
c/o Bank of America
P.O. Box 26606
Richmond, VA 23219-6606
Application address: c/o Scholarship Comm., Univ. of Virginia, Charlottesville, VA 22906

Financial data (yr. ended 12/31/99): Grants paid, $5,657; assets, $175,798 (M); expenditures, $6,830; qualifying distributions, $6,425.
Limitations: Giving limited to Charlottesville, VA.
Trustee: Bank of America.
EIN: 546051428

55080
Mary Ball Blackwell Foundation
P.O. Box 26606
Richmond, VA 23261 (804) 788-2143
Application address: P.O. Box 26903, Richmond, VA 23261, tel.: (804) 788-2295
Contact: Bob Richardson, Trust Off., Bank of America

Financial data (yr. ended 12/31/99): Grants paid, $5,600; assets, $114,177 (M); gifts received, $600; expenditures, $6,620; qualifying distributions, $6,186.
Limitations: Giving primarily in Richmond, VA.
Trustee: Bank of America.
EIN: 546059789

55081
International Theos Foundation, Inc.
7106 Park Terr. Dr.
Alexandria, VA 22307

Donor(s): Russell F. McKinnon, Deborah O. McKinnon.
Financial data (yr. ended 12/31/01): Grants paid, $5,600; assets, $43,355 (M); gifts received, $18,230; expenditures, $11,079; qualifying distributions, $5,600.
Limitations: Applications not accepted.
Application information: Contributes only to pre-selected organizations.
Officers: Russell F. McKinnon, Pres.; Deborah O. McKinnon, Secy.-Treas.
EIN: 541930052

55082
Larrymore Foundation
6477 College Park Sq., Ste. 306
Virginia Beach, VA 23464

Donor(s): I.W. Berger, Maxine Berger.
Financial data (yr. ended 12/31/01): Grants paid, $5,505; assets, $182,420 (M); gifts received, $15,000; expenditures, $7,316; qualifying distributions, $5,505.
Limitations: Applications not accepted. Giving primarily in VA.
Application information: Contributes only to pre-selected organizations.
Officers: Lawrence J. Goldrich, Chair.; I.W. Berger, Pres.; A.J. Goldrich, V.P.; V.E. Goldrich, Secy.-Treas.
EIN: 546052405

55083
Grace, Hope & Faith Foundation
3625 Beech Down Dr.
Chantilly, VA 20151 (703) 435-1440

Financial data (yr. ended 12/31/01): Grants paid, $5,500; assets, $64,895 (M); gifts received, $13,863; expenditures, $6,809; qualifying distributions, $5,500.
Directors: Kristine Beckwith, Richard A. Beckwith, Richard E. Beckwith, Sally P. Beckwith.
EIN: 541876919

55084
Kip Kephart Foundation
Cary Hill
11401 Eagles Nest Rd.
Charles City, VA 23030

Established in 1998 in VA.
Donor(s): Homer H. Kephart.
Financial data (yr. ended 06/30/01): Grants paid, $5,500; assets, $71,630 (M); gifts received, $2,320; expenditures, $5,804; qualifying distributions, $5,500.
Officer: Homer H. Kephart, Pres.
EIN: 541890463

55085
Edgar B. Rouse & Hunter Family Foundation, Inc.
c/o Healthcare Consulting
1928 Thomson Dr.
Lynchburg, VA 24501

Established in 1999 in VA.
Financial data (yr. ended 12/31/01): Grants paid, $5,500; assets, $167,006 (M); gifts received, $76,400; expenditures, $6,290; qualifying distributions, $5,500.
Limitations: Applications not accepted.
Application information: Contributes only to pre-selected organizations.
Directors: David Burch Hunter, James Gordon Hunter, Nancy Burch Hunter.
EIN: 541960123

55086
The Mary Josephine H. Allen Charitable Trust
c/o G. Nelson Mackey, Jr.
30 W. Franklin Rd., Ste. 300
Roanoke, VA 24014

Established in 1998 in VA.
Financial data (yr. ended 12/31/01): Grants paid, $5,483; assets, $143,436 (M); expenditures, $6,547; qualifying distributions, $5,483.
Limitations: Applications not accepted.
Application information: Contributes only to pre-selected organizations.
Trustee: Margaret H. Allen.
EIN: 546415239

55087
The Chachra Family Foundation
1701 Kraft Dr.
Blacksburg, VA 24060

Established in 1997 in VA.
Donor(s): Vinod Chachra.
Financial data (yr. ended 12/31/00): Grants paid, $5,350; assets, $124,150 (M); expenditures, $5,585; qualifying distributions, $5,350.
Limitations: Applications not accepted.
Application information: Contributes only to pre-selected organizations.
Officers and Director:* Vinod Chachra,* Pres.; Krisha Chachra, V.P.; Ranjana Chachra, Secy.-Treas.
EIN: 541877863

55088
The Imperial Charitable Trust
P.O. Box 638
Lynchburg, VA 24505-0638
Contact: C. Lynch Christian, III, Tr.

Financial data (yr. ended 09/30/01): Grants paid, $5,350; assets, $714,104 (M); gifts received, $100,000; expenditures, $5,660; qualifying distributions, $5,350.
Limitations: Giving primarily in VA and WV.
Application information: Application form not required.
Trustee: C. Lynch Christian III.
EIN: 510172334

55089
Newhouse Scholarship Trust Fund
c/o Virginia Commonwealth Trust Co.
P.O. Box 71
Culpeper, VA 22701

Established in 1991 in VA.
Financial data (yr. ended 12/31/99): Grants paid, $5,200; assets, $247,186 (M); expenditures, $8,346; qualifying distributions, $6,036.
Limitations: Applications not accepted. Giving primarily in VA.

Application information: Contributes only to pre-selected organizations.
Trustee: Virginia Commonwealth Trust Co.
EIN: 546260176

55090
The William & Annabel Perlik Family Foundation, Inc.
1249 Daleview Dr.
McLean, VA 22102

Established in 1996 in VA.
Donor(s): Annabel S. Perlik, William R. Perlik.
Financial data (yr. ended 07/31/01): Grants paid, $5,120; assets, $93,494 (M); gifts received, $5,100; expenditures, $7,423; qualifying distributions, $5,120.
Limitations: Applications not accepted.
Application information: Contributes only to pre-selected organizations.
Officers and Directors:* William R. Perlik,* Pres. and Treas.; Annabel S. Perlik,* V.P. and Secy.; Lynn Perlik, Ronald Perlik.
EIN: 541826304

55091
Eisenman Foundation
8901 Norwick Cir.
Richmond, VA 23229-8119

Donor(s): Marx Eisenman, Jr.
Financial data (yr. ended 12/31/01): Grants paid, $5,100; assets, $141,360 (M); expenditures, $6,027; qualifying distributions, $5,100.
Limitations: Applications not accepted. Giving primarily in Charlottesville, VA.
Application information: Contributes only to pre-selected organizations.
Officers: Marx Eisenman, Jr., Pres.; Bonnie Eisenman, V.P.; Brian E. Eisenman, V.P.
EIN: 546039652

55092
The Lennie and Bob Parker Foundation
101 Cyril Ln.
Richmond, VA 23229

Donor(s): Robert S. Parker, Jr., Lennie E. Parker.
Financial data (yr. ended 11/30/01): Grants paid, $5,100; assets, $187,810 (M); gifts received, $17,700; expenditures, $5,327; qualifying distributions, $5,100.
Limitations: Applications not accepted. Giving limited to Richmond, VA.
Application information: Contributes only to pre-selected organizations.
Officers: Lennie E. Parker, Pres.; Robert S. Parker, Jr., Secy.
EIN: 541398575

55093
The Jared Foundation, Inc.
c/o Wilson L. Rivers
1 Columbus Ctr., Ste. 1100
Virginia Beach, VA 23462-6765

Established in 1998 in VA.
Donor(s): Jerry Jared.
Financial data (yr. ended 12/31/01): Grants paid, $5,057; assets, $250,044 (M); gifts received, $1,942; expenditures, $11,757; qualifying distributions, $5,057.
Limitations: Applications not accepted.
Application information: Contributes only to pre-selected organizations.
Officers and Directors:* Jerry H. Jared, Chair. and Pres.; Timothy D. Jared,* V.P.; Wilson L. Rivers,* Secy.; Todd W. Jared,* Treas.
EIN: 541902472

55094
Fleming-Frenck Scholarship Foundation, Inc.
1805 Kempsville Rd.
Virginia Beach, VA 23464-6802

Financial data (yr. ended 09/30/01): Grants paid, $5,050; assets, $17,577 (M); expenditures, $5,290; qualifying distributions, $5,290.
Limitations: Applications not accepted. Giving primarily in VA.
Application information: Contributes only to pre-selected organizations.
Officers: W. Breck Wood, Pres.; Cassell D. Basnight, Secy.-Treas.
EIN: 521313020

55095
A Better Neighborhood Foundation
1453 Trombone Ct.
Vienna, VA 22182 (703) 847-0900
Contact: Warren Pretlow Riddick, Treas.

Established in 2000 in VA.
Donor(s): Warren Pretlow Riddick.
Financial data (yr. ended 12/31/00): Grants paid, $5,000; assets, $159,987 (M); gifts received, $155,000; expenditures, $8,422; qualifying distributions, $70,840.
Limitations: Giving primarily in VA.
Application information: Application form not required.
Officers and Directors:* Stacy Wharton Riddick,* Secy.; Warren Pretlow Riddick,* Treas.; William Pretlow Riddick.
EIN: 541976256

55096
Atkins Family Trust Foundation
4713 Rock Spring Rd.
Arlington, VA 22207-4241

Established in 1998 in VA.
Donor(s): Paul Atkins.
Financial data (yr. ended 07/31/01): Grants paid, $5,000; assets, $156,331 (M); gifts received, $19,000; expenditures, $8,641; qualifying distributions, $5,000.
Limitations: Applications not accepted. Giving primarily in SC.
Application information: Contributes only to pre-selected organizations.
Trustees: Paul Atkins, Sarah Atkins, Ethelmae Humphreys.
EIN: 546443344

55097
Backtrack, Inc.
c/o Randall S. Hawthorne
3901 Midlands Rd.
Williamsburg, VA 23188

Financial data (yr. ended 09/30/01): Grants paid, $5,000; assets, $7,038 (M); gifts received, $5,040; expenditures, $5,012; qualifying distributions, $0.
Limitations: Applications not accepted. Giving limited to Williamsburg, VA.
Application information: Contributes only to pre-selected organizations.
Officer: Randall S. Hawthorne, Pres.
EIN: 620871638

55098
The Marie A. Dornhecker Charitable Trust
308 Cedar Lakes Dr., 2nd Fl.
Chesapeake, VA 23322-8343

Established in 1997 in VA.
Donor(s): The Marie A. Dornhecker Revocable Trust.
Financial data (yr. ended 12/31/01): Grants paid, $5,000; assets, $389,536 (M); gifts received, $100,000; expenditures, $14,251; qualifying distributions, $5,000.
Limitations: Applications not accepted. Giving primarily in VA.
Application information: Contributes only to pre-selected organizations.
Trustees: Basnight, Kinser, et al., Tavss, Fletcher, Maiden & King, PC.
EIN: 541861674

55099
Sydene W. Kober Foundation, Inc.
7700 Georgetown Pike
McLean, VA 22102

Established in 2000 in VA.
Donor(s): Sydene W. Kober.
Financial data (yr. ended 12/31/01): Grants paid, $5,000; assets, $10,602 (M); gifts received, $17,032; expenditures, $6,435; qualifying distributions, $5,000.
Officers and Director:* Sydene W. Kober,* Pres.; Frederick A. Kober, Secy.-Treas.
EIN: 542013907

55100
The Mann Foundation
715 S. 22nd St.
Arlington, VA 22202

Established in 2000 in VA.
Donor(s): Nature Conservancy.
Financial data (yr. ended 06/30/01): Grants paid, $5,000; assets, $221,627 (M); gifts received, $250,000; expenditures, $7,208; qualifying distributions, $7,208.
Limitations: Applications not accepted.
Application information: Contributes only to pre-selected organizations.
Trustee: Christopher H. Mann.
EIN: 541995738

55101
McPartland Foundation, Inc.
P.O. Box 1495
Great Falls, VA 22066-8495

Established in 2000.
Financial data (yr. ended 03/31/02): Grants paid, $5,000; assets, $90,290 (M); expenditures, $7,936; qualifying distributions, $5,000.
Limitations: Applications not accepted. Giving primarily in Baltimore, MD.
Application information: Contributes only to pre-selected organizations.
Officers: Donna E.M. McPartland, Pres.; Francis M. McPartland, V.P.
EIN: 542020053

55102
Florence L. Page Visiting Nurse Association
c/o Roswell Page, III
1 James Ctr.
Richmond, VA 23219 (804) 775-1000
Contact: Deborah J. Agnor

Financial data (yr. ended 12/31/00): Grants paid, $5,000; assets, $300,212 (M); gifts received, $5,000; expenditures, $19,879; qualifying distributions, $5,000.
Limitations: Giving primarily in VA.
Application information: Application form not required.
Officers: Mrs. Fitzgerald Bemiss, Pres.; Rosewell Page III, Secy.-Treas.
EIN: 546053584

55103
J. L. & Helen B. Racey Foundation, Inc.
P.O. Box 864
Bassett, VA 24055-0864
Contact: Betty H. Wright, Dir.

Established in 1993 in VA.
Financial data (yr. ended 12/31/99): Grants paid, $5,000; assets, $124,928 (M); expenditures, $5,901; qualifying distributions, $5,000.
Limitations: Giving limited to residents of VA.
Application information: Application form required.
Directors: Roxann B. Dillon, A.L. Krumpski, Betsy Mattox, J. Creed Maxey, L. Dale McGhee, Betty H. Wright.
EIN: 541605493

55104
Stone Circle Foundation
7308 Calvert St.
Annandale, VA 22003

Established in 1999 in VA.
Donor(s): John Emery, Angela Emery.
Financial data (yr. ended 12/31/99): Grants paid, $5,000; assets, $6,783 (M); gifts received, $11,816; expenditures, $5,000; qualifying distributions, $5,000.
Limitations: Applications not accepted.
Application information: Contributes only to pre-selected organizations.
Officers: John Emery, Pres.; Angela Emery, V.P.
EIN: 541944117

55105
Rudy Treuenfels Educational Foundation
c/o Food Distributors Intl.
201 Park Washington Ct.
Falls Church, VA 22046-4519   (703) 532-9400
Contact: Mary Jorgenson, Tr.

Financial data (yr. ended 12/31/01): Grants paid, $5,000; assets, $51,225 (M); expenditures, $5,748; qualifying distributions, $5,000.
Trustees: John Block, Mary Griffin.
EIN: 136196286

55106
VuBay Foundation
c/o Cyrus A. Dolph, IV
P.O. Box 13109
Norfolk, VA 23506-3109

Established in 1997 in VA.
Donor(s): Gertrude S. Dixon.
Financial data (yr. ended 06/30/01): Grants paid, $5,000; assets, $3,461,811 (M); gifts received, $3,087,299; expenditures, $5,000; qualifying distributions, $5,000.
Officers: Ann D. Wallace, Pres.; Robert F. Shuford, V.P.; James R. Chisman, Treas.
EIN: 541840750

55107
The Dan Ottaviano Foundation, Inc.
4716 Orchard Ln.
Virginia Beach, VA 23464-5704

Established in 1997 in NC.
Financial data (yr. ended 03/31/02): Grants paid, $4,985; assets, $69,172 (M); expenditures, $5,750; qualifying distributions, $4,985.
Director: Dan Ottaviano.
EIN: 562026526

55108
Ruth Harris Joyce Foundation
c/o Ruth Harris Joyce
512 Taylor St.
Lexington, VA 24450

Established in 1998 in VA.
Donor(s): Ruth Harris Joyce.
Financial data (yr. ended 12/31/01): Grants paid, $4,968; assets, $96,405 (M); gifts received, $154; expenditures, $5,598; qualifying distributions, $4,968.
Limitations: Applications not accepted.
Application information: Contributes only to pre-selected organizations.
Officers and Directors:* Ruth Harris Joyce,* Pres.; Larry G. Harris,* Secy.; Rhea Eldridge Harris,* Treas.
EIN: 546434546

55109
The Hogg Foundation
409 River Rd.
Newport News, VA 23601   (757) 596-7451
Contact: John R. Hogg, Tr.

Donor(s): John R. Hogg.
Financial data (yr. ended 11/30/01): Grants paid, $4,960; assets, $104,811 (M); gifts received, $600; expenditures, $6,033; qualifying distributions, $4,960.
Limitations: Giving primarily in VA.
Trustee: John R. Hogg.
EIN: 541084092

55110
Fauquier County Law Enforcement Trust
c/o The Fauquier Bank
P.O. Box 561
Warrenton, VA 20188-0561

Financial data (yr. ended 06/30/01): Grants paid, $4,919; assets, $63,515 (M); expenditures, $6,312; qualifying distributions, $4,919.
Limitations: Applications not accepted. Giving primarily in Fauquier County, VA.
Application information: Contributes only to pre-selected organizations.
Trustee: The Fauquier Bank.
EIN: 546177934

55111
Cooper Wood Products Foundation, Inc.
P.O. Box 489
Rocky Mount, VA 24151-0489
Contact: Sue H. Chitwood, Treas.

Donor(s): Cooper Wood Products, Inc.
Financial data (yr. ended 10/31/01): Grants paid, $4,800; assets, $14,746 (L); expenditures, $4,839; qualifying distributions, $4,800.
Limitations: Giving limited to residents of VA.
Application information: Personal interview required.
Officer: Sue H. Chitwood, Treas.
EIN: 510234355
Codes: CS, CD, GTI

55112
The Rives Family Foundation, Inc.
4132 Thalia Dr.
Virginia Beach, VA 23452

Established in 1996 in GA.
Donor(s): George Rives.
Financial data (yr. ended 12/31/01): Grants paid, $4,675; assets, $2,097,606 (M); expenditures, $149,643; qualifying distributions, $4,675.
Limitations: Applications not accepted. Giving primarily in GA.
Application information: Contributes only to pre-selected organizations.
Officers and Directors:* Cornelia Rives Weis,* Pres.; George S. Rives, III,* V.P.; Kimbrough Lynn Reucassel, Robert J. Weis.
EIN: 582260514

55113
Howard F. Hale Charitable Trust
c/o The National Bank of Blackburg
P.O. Box 90002
Blacksburg, VA 24062-9002

Established in 1997 in VA.
Financial data (yr. ended 12/31/01): Grants paid, $4,620; assets, $126,931 (M); expenditures, $5,843; qualifying distributions, $4,620.
Limitations: Applications not accepted.
Application information: Contributes only to pre-selected organizations.
Trustee: The National Bank of Blacksburg.
EIN: 546422655

55114
Lucille Bonner Trust Fund
P.O. Box 28
Hot Springs, VA 24445
Application address: P.O. Box W, Hot Springs, VA 24445
Contact: Louise N. Carpenter, Tr., or Hugh S. Gwin, Tr.

Financial data (yr. ended 12/31/99): Grants paid, $4,500; assets, $53,501 (M); expenditures, $4,908; qualifying distributions, $4,670.
Limitations: Giving limited to residents of Hot Springs, VA.
Trustees: Louise N. Carpenter, Hugh S. Gwin.
EIN: 541219867

55115
The Beverly W. Grogan & Mabel Tudor Grogan Educational Fund, Inc.
c/o MainStreet Trust Co., N.A.
P.O. Box 5228
Martinsville, VA 24115-5228
Application address: c/o Priscilla Diggs, Patrick County High School, Stuart, VA 24171

Established in 1988 in VA.
Financial data (yr. ended 10/31/01): Grants paid, $4,500; assets, $788,513 (M); gifts received, $85; expenditures, $13,213; qualifying distributions, $51,189.
Limitations: Giving limited to residents of Patrick County, VA.
Application information: Application form required.
Officers and Directors: Howard C. Pilson, Pres.; Thomas C. Pratt, Cynthia A. Stovall.
EIN: 541511938

55116
Canaan House
P.O. Box 599
Lynchburg, VA 24505-0599

Established around 1993.
Financial data (yr. ended 08/31/01): Grants paid, $4,420; assets, $446 (M); gifts received, $5,104; expenditures, $4,697; qualifying distributions, $4,420; giving activities include $4,420 for programs.
Officer: Mary Cox, Pres.
EIN: 541602223

55117
Wellspring Charitable Foundation
999 Waterside Dr., Ste. 1515
Norfolk, VA 23510-3309

Donor(s): Virginia D. Berberian.

55117—VIRGINIA

Financial data (yr. ended 12/31/00): Grants paid, $4,400; assets, $132,790 (M); gifts received, $4,400; expenditures, $12,557; qualifying distributions, $6,036.
Officers: Virginia D. Berberian, Pres.; John Berberian, V.P.; Thomas D. Maddry, Secy.
EIN: 541921240

55118
Suffolk Community Hospital Foundation, Inc.
617 E. Washington St.
Suffolk, VA 23434

Financial data (yr. ended 12/31/01): Grants paid, $4,210; assets, $94,983 (M); expenditures, $6,894; qualifying distributions, $4,210.
Limitations: Applications not accepted. Giving limited to the Suffolk, VA, area.
Application information: Contributes only to pre-selected organizations.
Officers: W. Ross Boone, Pres.; Elaine D. Beaman, V.P.; Mildred M. Freeman, Secy.-Treas.
Director: Phillip B. Boone, O.W. Hoffler, Ruby Walden.
EIN: 541245182

55119
Hofmann Foundation Charitable Trust
6280 Dunaway Ct.
McLean, VA 22101-2204

Established in 1998 in VA.
Donor(s): George R. Hofmann, Judith L. Hofmann.
Financial data (yr. ended 12/31/01): Grants paid, $4,200; assets, $85,563 (M); gifts received, $10,421; expenditures, $6,269; qualifying distributions, $4,200.
Limitations: Applications not accepted.
Application information: Contributes only to pre-selected organizations.
Officers: Judith L. Hofmann, Pres. and Secy.; George R. Hofmann, V.P. and Treas.
EIN: 546440900

55120
The Lagnaippe Foundation
c/o Bay Trust
P.O. Box 1958
Kilmarnock, VA 22482
Application address: P.O. Box 1300, Kilmarnock, VA 22482, tel.: (804) 435-0373
Contact: William B. Moore, Jr., Chair.

Established in 1986 in VA.
Financial data (yr. ended 06/30/01): Grants paid, $4,080; assets, $71,467 (M); expenditures, $4,080; qualifying distributions, $4,080.
Limitations: Giving on a national basis, with emphasis on VA.
Application information: Application form not required.
Trustees: William B. Moore, Jr., Chair.; Lillian Wells Moore, William B. Moore III, Bethany Moore Richmond, Katherin Dannels.
EIN: 546241001

55121
Courtney Beryl Owens Memorial Scholarship Fund
P.O. Box 99
Rose Hill, VA 24281 (540) 445-5422
Contact: Beryl H. Owens, Chair.

Financial data (yr. ended 05/31/00): Grants paid, $4,000; assets, $40,555 (M); gifts received, $180; expenditures, $4,180; qualifying distributions, $124.
Limitations: Giving limited to VA.
Application information: Application form not required.

Trustees: Beryl H. Owens, Chair.; J.E. Owens, Mary Beth Owens, Capt. Whitney H. Owens.
EIN: 541252248

55122
Redwood Memorial Trust Fund
c/o SunTrust Banks, Inc.
P.O. Box 27385
Richmond, VA 23261-7385
Application address: c/o Div. Superintendent, Mathews County Public Schools, P.O. Box 368, Mathews, VA 23809

Established in 1986 in VA.
Financial data (yr. ended 10/31/00): Grants paid, $4,000; assets, $9,081 (M); expenditures, $4,967; qualifying distributions, $4,011.
Limitations: Giving limited to Mathews County, VA.
Application information: Application form required.
Trustee: SunTrust Banks, Inc.
EIN: 546108366

55123
Lily Webb Smith Trust
c/o Bank of America
P.O. Box 26606
Richmond, VA 23261
Application address: c/o Bank of America, P.O. Box 105495 SPS, Atlanta, GA 30348-5495

Financial data (yr. ended 12/31/99): Grants paid, $4,000; assets, $411,626 (M); expenditures, $7,640; qualifying distributions, $4,000.
Limitations: Giving limited to NC.
Trustee: Bank of America.
EIN: 546042385

55124
Joan M. Sowers Memorial Scholarship Fund
P.O. Box 436
Floyd, VA 24091

Donor(s): Dale Profitt.
Financial data (yr. ended 12/31/99): Grants paid, $4,000; assets, $32,980 (M); expenditures, $4,000; qualifying distributions, $4,000.
Limitations: Applications not accepted. Giving limited to VA.
Application information: Contributes only to pre-selected organizations.
Officers and Directors:* Dale Profitt,* Pres.; Omar N. Ross,* V.P. and Secy.; Judy G. Britt, Kathryn A. Van Tassell.
EIN: 541489643

55125
Ruth Lincoln Fisher Memorial Trust
c/o First Virginia Bank
6400 Arlington Blvd.
Falls Church, VA 22042-2399

Financial data (yr. ended 12/31/99): Grants paid, $3,974; assets, $173,456 (M); expenditures, $9,531; qualifying distributions, $3,974.
Limitations: Giving primarily in Washington, DC.
Trustee: Donald Skorupa.
EIN: 546435198

55126
Paul J. Hewgill Charitable Foundation
c/o Charles Clark
2942 Seminole Rd.
Woodbridge, VA 22192

Donor(s): Patricia J. Hewgill.
Financial data (yr. ended 12/31/01): Grants paid, $3,880; assets, $19,161 (M); expenditures, $4,010; qualifying distributions, $3,880.
Limitations: Applications not accepted. Giving on a national basis.

Application information: Contributes only to pre-selected organizations.
Officers and Directors:* Patricia M. Hewgill,* Pres.; Joseph E. Murphy,* V.P.; Mary E. Murphy,* Secy.; Charles C. Clark,* Treas.
EIN: 541796090

55127
The Smith-Martin Foundation, Inc.
c/o Rodney K. Martin
20941 Nightshade Pl.
Ashburn, VA 20147 (703) 736-3091

Established in 1998 in VA.
Donor(s): Rodney K. Martin, Belinda K. Smith-Martin.
Financial data (yr. ended 12/31/01): Grants paid, $3,867; assets, $74,470 (M); gifts received, $4,000; expenditures, $4,274; qualifying distributions, $3,867.
Limitations: Applications not accepted.
Application information: Contributes only to pre-selected organizations.
Officer: Rodney K. Martin, Pres.
EIN: 541921623

55128
The Mounzer Foundation for Service and Education
660 Tanager Dr.
Bluefield, VA 24605 (540) 322-5392
Contact: Assaad Mounzer, Pres.

Established in 1998 in VA.
Donor(s): Assaad Mounzer.
Financial data (yr. ended 06/30/02): Grants paid, $3,825; assets, $6,190 (M); gifts received, $2,285; expenditures, $3,825; qualifying distributions, $3,825.
Officers: Assaad Mounzer, Pres.; Carla Mounzer, V.P.; Khalil Mounzer, Secy.; Samira Mounzer, Treas.
EIN: 541921385

55129
The Andrew B. Weatherford Christian Scholarship Trust
c/o The Virginia Baptist Foundation
P.O. Box 17035
Richmond, VA 23226

Established in 1999 in VA.
Donor(s): A.B. Weatherford.‡
Financial data (yr. ended 12/31/01): Grants paid, $3,810; assets, $81,584 (M); expenditures, $4,626; qualifying distributions, $3,810.
Application information: Applicants must submit applications which set forth their qualifications, and must provide letters of reference.
Trustee: Virginia Baptist Foundation.
EIN: 546434492

55130
The NCI Foundation
c/o Judith L. Bjornaas
8260 Greensboro Dr., Ste. 400
McLean, VA 22102-3850

Financial data (yr. ended 06/30/01): Grants paid, $3,800; assets, $84,945 (M); expenditures, $3,817; qualifying distributions, $3,800.
Limitations: Applications not accepted. Giving on a national basis.
Application information: Contributes only to pre-selected organizations.
Trustees: Linda J. Allan, Judith L. Berg, Richard Filleh.
EIN: 541843091

55131
The Frank Foundation, Inc.
625 Potomac River Rd.
McLean, VA 22102

Established in 1995.
Donor(s): Howard Frank, Jane Frank.
Financial data (yr. ended 11/30/01): Grants paid, $3,750; assets, $52,517 (M); expenditures, $4,976; qualifying distributions, $3,750.
Limitations: Applications not accepted.
Application information: Contributes only to pre-selected organizations.
Director: Jane Frank.
EIN: 541782374

55132
The Sandra W. Murphy Family Foundation
c/o Mortensen & Mendonca, Ltd.
2787 Hartland Rd.
Falls Church, VA 22043

Established in 1998 in VA.
Donor(s): James P. Murphy, Sandra W. Murphy.
Financial data (yr. ended 12/31/01): Grants paid, $3,720; assets, $56,868 (M); expenditures, $4,784; qualifying distributions, $3,720.
Officer and Director:* Sandra W. Murphy,* Pres.
EIN: 541905071

55133
Edmondson Foundation, Inc.
4805 Lauderdale Ave.
Virginia Beach, VA 23455

Financial data (yr. ended 06/30/00): Grants paid, $3,650; assets, $100,294 (M); expenditures, $4,888; qualifying distributions, $3,915.
Limitations: Applications not accepted. Giving limited to VA.
Application information: Contributes only to pre-selected organizations.
Officers: W.P. Edmondson, Jr., Pres.; Mary Anne Grinnan, Treas.
EIN: 546046080

55134
The Rex I. and Mildred Wells Foundation
3930 Walnut St.
Fairfax, VA 22030

Donor(s): Mildred E. Wells.
Financial data (yr. ended 12/31/00): Grants paid, $3,630; assets, $112,464 (M); expenditures, $5,090; qualifying distributions, $4,808.
Limitations: Applications not accepted. Giving primarily in KS.
Application information: Contributes only to pre-selected organizations.
Officers: Mildred E. Wells, Chair.; Thomas E. Cox, Pres. and Treas.; Steven C. Preston, V.P. and Secy.
EIN: 541876329

55135
Spotswood Garden Foundation
165 Diamond Ct.
Harrisonburg, VA 22801

Established in 1998 in VA.
Financial data (yr. ended 06/30/01): Grants paid, $3,610; assets, $16,214 (M); gifts received, $200; expenditures, $3,659; qualifying distributions, $0.
Limitations: Giving limited to Harrisonburg and Rockingham County, VA.
Officer and Directors:* Rachel Holts,* Treas.; Glenn Graves, Mary Strickler, Rosemary Wallinger.
EIN: 311586313

55136
John K. Boardman, Jr. Foundation
P.O. Box 1167
Bedford, VA 24523-1167

Established in 2000 in VA.
Donor(s): J.K. Boardman, Jr.
Financial data (yr. ended 12/31/01): Grants paid, $3,500; assets, $40,296 (M); expenditures, $4,125; qualifying distributions, $3,500.
Directors: John Boardman, Frank Rodgers, Jr.
EIN: 541946363

55137
The Diane Donner Longest Memorial Foundation
1301 N. Hamilton St., Ste. 300
Richmond, VA 23230

Established in 1999 in VA.
Donor(s): R. Eldridge Longest.
Financial data (yr. ended 06/30/01): Grants paid, $3,500; assets, $99,515 (M); gifts received, $789; expenditures, $3,630; qualifying distributions, $3,500.
Limitations: Applications not accepted.
Application information: Contributes only to pre-selected organizations.
Trustee: Gerald L. Richardson.
EIN: 541928157

55138
Johnson-Edwards Family Foundation
11103 Prince Edward Ct.
Oakton, VA 22124
Contact: Thomas Johnson, Pres.

Established in 1999 in VA.
Donor(s): Thomas Johnson, Mary Johnson.
Financial data (yr. ended 06/30/01): Grants paid, $3,500; assets, $861,082 (M); expenditures, $7,998; qualifying distributions, $3,500.
Limitations: Applications not accepted.
Application information: Contributes only to pre-selected organizations.
Officers: Thomas Johnson, Pres.; Mary Johnson, Secy.-Treas.
EIN: 541977727

55139
The Longest Family Memorial Foundation
1301 N. Hamilton St., Ste. 300
Richmond, VA 23230

Established in 1999 in VA.
Donor(s): R. Eldridge Longest.‡
Financial data (yr. ended 06/30/01): Grants paid, $3,500; assets, $99,515 (M); gifts received, $789; expenditures, $3,630; qualifying distributions, $3,500.
Limitations: Applications not accepted.
Application information: Contributes only to pre-selected organizations.
Trustee: Gerald L. Richardson.
EIN: 541927731

55140
Wade Foundation
P.O. Box 329
Christiansburg, VA 24073-0329
Contact: H. Douglas Jones, Tr.

Financial data (yr. ended 12/31/01): Grants paid, $3,500; assets, $77,286 (M); expenditures, $3,707; qualifying distributions, $3,500.
Limitations: Giving primarily in VA.
Trustees: H. Douglas Jones, Bruce C. Stockburger, Dale W. Teel.
EIN: 546193839

55141
The Worrell Foundation
c/o McGuire, Woods, LLP
P.O. Box 397
Richmond, VA 23218

Established in 1987 in VA.
Financial data (yr. ended 12/31/01): Grants paid, $3,500; assets, $120,072 (M); expenditures, $4,505; qualifying distributions, $3,500.
Limitations: Applications not accepted. Giving limited to VA.
Application information: Contributes only to pre-selected organizations.
Officers and Directors:* Mary S. Worrell,* Pres.; David H. Worrell, Jr.,* Secy.
EIN: 541405778

55142
The Fine Foundation
(Formerly Morris & Mamie Fine Foundation)
2101 Parks Ave., Ste. 600
Virginia Beach, VA 23451 (757) 422-1678
Contact: Morris H. Fine, Pres.

Donor(s): Louis B. Fine.
Financial data (yr. ended 12/31/01): Grants paid, $3,400; assets, $1,377 (M); expenditures, $5,970; qualifying distributions, $3,400.
Application information: Application form not required.
Officers: Morris H. Fine, Pres.; Andrew S. Fine, Secy.
EIN: 546041777

55143
The Joseph Fund
c/o Gloucester Courthouse
P.O. Box 1878
Gloucester, VA 23061

Established in 1977 in VA.
Financial data (yr. ended 06/30/01): Grants paid, $3,381; assets, $337,109 (M); expenditures, $6,712; qualifying distributions, $3,381.
Limitations: Applications not accepted. Giving primarily in Hong Kong.
Application information: Contributes only to pre-selected organizations.
Officers: Edwin A. Joseph, Pres. and Treas.; Adrianne Ryder Cook, Secy.
Director: George B. Joseph.
EIN: 541081592

55144
Northern Virginia Council for Gifted & Talented Education
c/o Sue Jurey, Scholarship Comm.
P.O. Box 705
Falls Church, VA 22040-0705

Established around 1990.
Financial data (yr. ended 06/30/00): Grants paid, $3,357; assets, $13,748 (M); expenditures, $4,574; qualifying distributions, $3,357.
Limitations: Giving primarily in VA.
Officers: Alix Pearce Smith, Pres.; Cheryl Mangrum, V.P.; Ellen Wheeler, Secy.; Ruth Pavlik, Treas.
EIN: 510215332

55145
Raggers Unlimited, Inc.
2000 N. 14th St., Ste. 100
Arlington, VA 22201
Contact: James R. Schroll, Chair.

Financial data (yr. ended 12/31/00): Grants paid, $3,320; assets, $63,760 (M); gifts received, $6,664; expenditures, $3,372; qualifying distributions, $3,320.

55145—VIRGINIA

Officers: James R. Schroll, Chair.; John Golan, Vice-Chair.; Daniel C. Cramer, Secy.; Christopher Clark, Treas.
EIN: 541646842

55146
The Meade-Munster Foundation
P.O. Box 495
The Plains, VA 20198 (540) 253-5636

Established in 1998 in VA.
Donor(s): Walter N. Munster, Sr.
Financial data (yr. ended 12/31/00): Grants paid, $3,260; assets, $71,086 (M); gifts received, $30,500; expenditures, $3,494; qualifying distributions, $3,260.
Limitations: Applications not accepted.
Application information: Contributes only to pre-selected organizations.
Officer and Director:* Walter P. Munster, Sr.,* Pres.
EIN: 541905559

55147
Corduroy Charitable Trust
14103 Louisa Rd.
Louisa, VA 23093 (540) 967-1555

Established in 2001 in VA.
Donor(s): Mark D. Howland, Doniphan Howland.
Financial data (yr. ended 12/31/01): Grants paid, $3,250; assets, $31,480 (M); gifts received, $41,120; expenditures, $4,951; qualifying distributions, $3,250.
Trustees: Doniphan Howland, Mark D. Howland.
EIN: 546477842

55148
The Betty Ann & Ben Huger Family Foundation
1238 E. Bay Shore Dr.
Virginia Beach, VA 23451

Established in 2000 in VA.
Donor(s): Benjamin Huger II, Elizabeth C. Huger.
Financial data (yr. ended 12/31/01): Grants paid, $3,200; assets, $181,952 (M); gifts received, $100,000; expenditures, $6,822; qualifying distributions, $3,200.
Limitations: Applications not accepted.
Application information: Contributes only to pre-selected organizations.
Trustees: Benjamin Huger II, Elizabeth C. Huger.
EIN: 546480836

55149
Westmoreland County Public School Scholarship Fund
P.O. Box 639
Montross, VA 22520 (804) 493-8955
Contact: Larry D. Greene, Tr.

Financial data (yr. ended 06/30/01): Grants paid, $3,200; assets, $73,644 (M); gifts received, $5,000; expenditures, $3,370; qualifying distributions, $3,200.
Limitations: Giving limited to Westmoreland County, VA.
Application information: Application form required.
Trustees: Frank E. English, Larry D. Greene, Mary M. Ingram.
EIN: 541394300

55150
Serage Foundation
7419 Hogarth St.
Springfield, VA 22151
Contact: Barbara B. Serage, Pres.

Established in 1993.
Financial data (yr. ended 12/31/01): Grants paid, $3,125; assets, $10,545 (M); gifts received, $3,275; expenditures, $3,613; qualifying distributions, $3,125.
Application information: Application form required.
Officer: Barbara B. Serage, Pres.
EIN: 541666715

55151
The Chatata Trust
(Formerly The Hope Charitable Trust)
10717 Rosehaven St.
Fairfax, VA 22030

Established in 1989 in VA.
Donor(s): Samuel H. Hope, Judy Bucher Hope.
Financial data (yr. ended 12/31/01): Grants paid, $3,000; assets, $21,239 (M); gifts received, $7,250; expenditures, $3,878; qualifying distributions, $3,000.
Limitations: Applications not accepted. Giving on a national basis.
Application information: Contributes only to pre-selected organizations.
Trustees: Judy Bucher Hope, Samuel H. Hope.
EIN: 541513454

55152
DeWitt Family Foundation
12966 Highland Oaks Ct.
Fairfax, VA 22033-2030

Established in 2000 in VA.
Donor(s): International Investments, LLC.
Financial data (yr. ended 12/31/01): Grants paid, $3,000; assets, $457,909 (M); gifts received, $216,895; expenditures, $8,361; qualifying distributions, $3,000.
Limitations: Applications not accepted.
Application information: Contributes only to pre-selected organizations.
Directors: Bill B. DeWitt, Michell W. DeWitt.
EIN: 542016863

55153
The Ida C. & Morris Falk Foundation
1600 S. Eads St., Ste. 1033S
Arlington, VA 22202

Donor(s): David M. Falk.
Financial data (yr. ended 12/31/01): Grants paid, $3,000; assets, $105,335 (M); expenditures, $4,190; qualifying distributions, $3,000.
Limitations: Applications not accepted.
Application information: Contributes only to pre-selected organizations.
Officers: David M. Falk, Pres.; Stanley P. Snyder, Secy.-Treas.
EIN: 541828916

55154
Fauquier Scholarship Fund
c/o F & M Trust Co.
P.O. Box 93
Warrenton, VA 20188-0093
Application address: c/o Fauquier High School, 705 Waterloo Dr., Warrenton, VA 20186
Contact: John Pegues, Chair.

Established in 1997.
Financial data (yr. ended 12/31/01): Grants paid, $3,000; assets, $129,014 (M); expenditures, $5,140; qualifying distributions, $3,527.
Limitations: Giving limited to Fauquier County, VA.
Application information: Application form required.
Officers: John Pegues, Chair.; Ed Habrat, Admin.; Roger A. Sites, Admin.
Trustee: F & M Trust Co.
EIN: 546123242

55155
Alyce Z. and Edward A. Heidt, Jr. Charitable Foundation
c/o Edward A. Heidt, Jr.
1855 Duke of York Quay
Virginia Beach, VA 23454

Established in 1993 in VA.
Donor(s): Alyce Z. Heidt, Edward A. Heidt, Jr.
Financial data (yr. ended 12/31/01): Grants paid, $3,000; assets, $66,725 (M); gifts received, $10,000; expenditures, $5,110; qualifying distributions, $3,000.
Limitations: Applications not accepted. Giving primarily in VA.
Application information: Contributes only to pre-selected organizations.
Trustees: Alyce Z. Heidt, Edward A. Heidt, Jr.
EIN: 541659995

55156
Helen & Murray Main Foundation
c/o Helen K. Main
4022 Chesapeake Ave.
Hampton, VA 23669

Established in 1999 in VA.
Donor(s): Helen K. Main.
Financial data (yr. ended 09/30/00): Grants paid, $3,000; assets, $172,166 (M); gifts received, $200,000; expenditures, $3,025; qualifying distributions, $3,000.
Limitations: Applications not accepted.
Application information: Contributes only to pre-selected organizations.
Officer: Helen K. Main, Pres. and Secy.-Treas.
Directors: Steven Longenderfer, John Morello, Sr.
EIN: 541959919

55157
Nishanian Children's Foundation, Inc.
1880 Howard Ave., Ste. 204
Vienna, VA 22182-2611

Established in 1999 VA.
Financial data (yr. ended 12/31/01): Grants paid, $3,000; assets, $29,836 (M); gifts received, $26,000; expenditures, $3,025; qualifying distributions, $3,000.
Limitations: Applications not accepted.
Application information: Contributes only to pre-selected organizations.
Officers: Jerar Nishanian, Pres.; Anahid Nishanian, Secy.; Tagvor G. Nishanian, Treas.
EIN: 521850486

55158
Suzanne Poniatowski Quadt Memorial Foundation
c/o Robert P. Quadt
12024 Creekbend Dr.
Reston, VA 20194

Established in 1993 in VA.
Donor(s): Robert P. Quadt.
Financial data (yr. ended 02/28/02): Grants paid, $3,000; assets, $21,614 (M); gifts received, $650; expenditures, $3,075; qualifying distributions, $3,000.
Limitations: Giving primarily in Catonsville, MD.
Officers: Robert P. Quadt, Pres.; Rachel A. Quadt, V.P.; Eleanor McGillin, Secy.; David P. Quadt, Treas.
Directors: George Cummings, Maryanne Cummings.
EIN: 541675485

55159
Harry & Zackia Shaia Charitable Foundation
8550 Mayland Dr., Ste. 1
Richmond, VA 23294 (804) 747-0920
Contact: Harry Shaia, Jr., Pres.

Established in 2000 in VA.
Donor(s): Gregory J. Shaia, Mrs. Gregory J. Shaia, William H. Shaia, Mrs. William H. Shaia.
Financial data (yr. ended 12/31/01): Grants paid, $3,000; assets, $166,723 (M); gifts received, $29,541; expenditures, $4,225; qualifying distributions, $3,000.
Officers and Directors:* Harry Shaia, Jr.,* Pres.; William H. Shaia, Jr., Secy.; Michael A. Shaia,* Treas.; Richard H. Shaia.
EIN: 541991934

55160
Twin Oaks Fund
206 Santa Clara Dr.
Richmond, VA 23229-7122

Established in 1987 in VA.
Donor(s): H. Blair Smith.
Financial data (yr. ended 12/31/01): Grants paid, $3,000; assets, $21,599 (M); expenditures, $3,010; qualifying distributions, $3,000.
Limitations: Applications not accepted.
Application information: Contributes only to pre-selected organizations.
Trustee: H. Blair Smith.
EIN: 546261113

55161
W.H.L. Charities, Inc.
50 S. Cameron St.
Winchester, VA 22601-4726
Application address: 300 Walker St., Winchester, VA 22601, tel.: (540) 667-4556
Contact: Philip Bettenduff, Pres.

Financial data (yr. ended 12/31/01): Grants paid, $3,000; assets, $69,537 (M); gifts received, $1,527; expenditures, $3,286; qualifying distributions, $3,000.
Limitations: Giving limited to VA.
Application information: Application form required.
Officers: Philip Bettenduff, Pres.; Verne Collins, Secy.; Marshall J. Beverley, Treas.
EIN: 541577662

55162
John & Lillian Richmond Educational Trust Fund
P.O. Box 703
Jonesville, VA 24263
Contact: George F. Cridlin, Tr.

Financial data (yr. ended 06/30/99): Grants paid, $2,875; assets, $45,160 (M); expenditures, $3,402; qualifying distributions, $2,875.
Limitations: Giving limited to residents of Lee County, VA.
Application information: Application form required.
Trustee: George F. Cridlin.
EIN: 540248136

55163
The Stanbrook Foundation
c/o The Trust Co. of Virginia
9030 Stony Point Pkwy., Ste. 300
Richmond, VA 23235-1936

Established in 1996 in VA.
Donor(s): Stanley D. Smith, Jr.
Financial data (yr. ended 12/31/01): Grants paid, $2,815; assets, $91,398 (M); expenditures, $3,443; qualifying distributions, $2,815.
Limitations: Applications not accepted. Giving primarily in WV.
Application information: Contributes only to pre-selected organizations.
Officer: Stanley D. Smith, Jr., Pres.
Directors: Jeffrey S. Smith, Maryclay Smith.
EIN: 541794883

55164
Westmoreland Poor School Society
c/o Charles M. Sanford
P.O. Box 109
Hague, VA 22469

Financial data (yr. ended 05/31/00): Grants paid, $2,800; assets, $0 (M); gifts received, $4,008; expenditures, $2,845; qualifying distributions, $2,800.
Officer: F.F. Chandler, Pres.
EIN: 546159824

55165
David and Joan Berenson Foundation
879 Middle River Rd.
Staunton, VA 24401

Established in 2000 in VA.
Donor(s): Joan B. Berenson.
Financial data (yr. ended 12/31/01): Grants paid, $2,750; assets, $9,409 (M); gifts received, $6,075; expenditures, $2,925; qualifying distributions, $2,750.
Limitations: Applications not accepted.
Application information: Contributes only to pre-selected organizations.
Trustees: David A. Berenson, Joan B. Berenson.
EIN: 546479299

55166
The Ronald K. and Patricia Hannley Sable Charitable Foundation
1541 N. 22nd St.
Arlington, VA 22209

Established in 2000 in VA.
Donor(s): Ronald K. Sable, Patricia H. Sable.
Financial data (yr. ended 06/30/02): Grants paid, $2,740; assets, $10,591 (M); gifts received, $10,000; expenditures, $3,498; qualifying distributions, $2,740.
Limitations: Applications not accepted.
Application information: Contributes only to pre-selected organizations.
Trustees: Patricia H. Sable, Ronald K. Sable.
EIN: 541984901

55167
Eastern Shore Waterfowl Trust
P.O. Box 176
Capeville, VA 23313-0176

Financial data (yr. ended 06/30/00): Grants paid, $2,728; assets, $0 (M); expenditures, $3,050; qualifying distributions, $0.
Officers and Directors:* Grayson Chesser,* Pres.; Butch Lurty,* V.P.; Tylax Nickel,* V.P.; Tommy O'Connor,* Secy.-Treas.
EIN: 521419457

55168
Mark T. Meyer Charitable Foundation
5194 Celt Rd.
Stanardsville, VA 22973

Financial data (yr. ended 11/30/00): Grants paid, $2,525; assets, $31,900 (M); expenditures, $2,525; qualifying distributions, $2,525.
Limitations: Applications not accepted. Giving primarily in IL.
Application information: Contributes only to pre-selected organizations.
Officers: Mark T. Meyer, Pres.; Michael Meyer, Treas.
Director: Raymond T. Meyer.
EIN: 363554460

55169
Lincoln C. Bailey Memorial Scholarship Fund
c/o The Industrial Safety Equipment Assn.
1901 N. Moore St., Ste. 808
Arlington, VA 22209 (703) 525-1695

Established in 1989 in VA.
Donor(s): Industrial Safety Equipment Association.
Financial data (yr. ended 12/31/99): Grants paid, $2,500; assets, $56,282 (M); gifts received, $100; expenditures, $3,992; qualifying distributions, $3,864.
Limitations: Giving primarily in areas of company operations.
Application information: Application form required.
Trustee: Industrial Safety Equipment Association.
EIN: 546278949

55170
Rhona & Raymond Gottlieb Foundation
c/o R.L. Gottlieb
105 50th St.
Virginia Beach, VA 23451

Financial data (yr. ended 06/30/02): Grants paid, $2,500; assets, $514 (M); gifts received, $1,100; expenditures, $2,500; qualifying distributions, $2,500.
Limitations: Applications not accepted.
Application information: Contributes only to pre-selected organizations.
Trustees: N.R. Gottlieb, R.L. Gottlieb.
EIN: 237025064

55171
John Holliday Memorial Scholarship Fund, Inc.
c/o Marie Holliday
324 Pennsylvania Ave.
Salem, VA 24153-4307

Established in 1996 in VA.
Financial data (yr. ended 12/31/01): Grants paid, $2,500; assets, $11,546 (M); gifts received, $600; expenditures, $2,821; qualifying distributions, $2,821.
Application information: Application form required.
Officers and Directors:* Todd Holliday,* Pres.; Sharon Holliday,* V.P.; Lisa Grigg,* Secy.; Marie Holliday,* Treas.
EIN: 541784739

55172
Emily W. Kelly Foundation
775 Virginia Ave.
P.O. Box 885
Salem, VA 24153-5332 (540) 387-0217
Contact: Timothy A. Kelly, Dir.

Financial data (yr. ended 12/31/01): Grants paid, $2,500; assets, $2,451 (M); gifts received, $2,992; expenditures, $3,061; qualifying distributions, $2,500.
Limitations: Giving primarily in Roanoke, VA.
Director: Timothy A. Kelly.
EIN: 541384797

55173
The Farrand Foundation, Inc.
P.O. Box 718
Norfolk, VA 23501

Established in 2000 in VA.
Donor(s): Philip S. Farrand.
Financial data (yr. ended 08/31/01): Grants paid, $2,425; assets, $33,640 (M); gifts received,

55173—VIRGINIA

$1,800; expenditures, $3,921; qualifying distributions, $2,425.
Limitations: Applications not accepted. Giving primarily in VA.
Application information: Contributes only to pre-selected organizations.
Officers: Philip S. Farrand, Pres.; Todd S. Farrand, V.P. and Secy.; Jerry L. Bowman, V.P.; Michael W. Howlett, V.P.
EIN: 541958321

55174
The Mae Lee and T. Dalton Miller Charitable Foundation
P.O. Box 1165
Roanoke, VA 24006 (540) 985-0308
Contact: T. Dalton Miller, Pres.

Established in 1992 in VA.
Donor(s): T. Dalton Miller, Mae Lee Miller.
Financial data (yr. ended 12/31/01): Grants paid, $2,400; assets, $63,910 (M); gifts received, $1,000; expenditures, $2,981; qualifying distributions, $2,400.
Limitations: Giving primarily in VA.
Application information: Application form not required.
Officers: T. Dalton Miller, Pres.; Mae Lee Miller, Secy.-Treas.
EIN: 541646827

55175
Virginia Randolph Foundation
c/o Bank of America
P.O. Box 26606
Richmond, VA 23261
Application address: Rte. 1, Box 497, Glen Allen, VA 23060
Contact: Sadie Sears

Established in 1986 in VA.
Financial data (yr. ended 12/31/99): Grants paid, $2,400; assets, $76,850 (M); gifts received, $4,000; expenditures, $3,492; qualifying distributions, $2,919.
Limitations: Giving limited to Henrico County, VA.
Application information: Recipient recommended by high school staff.
Trustee: Bank of America.
EIN: 546046517

55176
Robert R. & Dean Fowler Cunningham Trust
c/o Old Point National Bank
P.O. Box 6270
Newport News, VA 23606
Application address: c/o Karen A. Compton, Trust Off., Old Point National Bank, P.O. Box 6270, Newport News, VA 23606

Financial data (yr. ended 03/31/00): Grants paid, $2,300; assets, $80,797 (M); expenditures, $4,325; qualifying distributions, $2,966.
Limitations: Giving limited to residents of Hampton and Phoebus, VA.
Trustee: Old Point National Bank.
EIN: 521224494

55177
The Jack W. and Kathleen J. Hugus Foundation
17165 Clarksridge Rd.
Leesburg, VA 20176

Established in 1998.
Donor(s): Jack W. Hugus, Kathleen J. Hugus.
Financial data (yr. ended 12/31/01): Grants paid, $2,250; assets, $49,943 (M); gifts received, $600; expenditures, $2,861; qualifying distributions, $2,250.
Limitations: Applications not accepted.

Application information: Contributes only to pre-selected organizations.
Trustee: Jack W. Hugus.
EIN: 541901339

55178
Cosby Charitable Trust
4405 Boonsboro Rd.
Lynchburg, VA 24503

Donor(s): Peter G. Crosby III.
Financial data (yr. ended 12/31/01): Grants paid, $2,078; assets, $41,456 (M); gifts received, $3,000; expenditures, $2,530; qualifying distributions, $2,065.
Limitations: Applications not accepted.
Application information: Contributes only to pre-selected organizations.
Trustees: Beverly R. Cosby, Mary C. Cosby, N. Gordon Cosby, Peter G. Cosby III.
EIN: 546416093

55179
Bleakhorn Foundation
c/o Signature Financial Mgmt., Inc.
999 Waterside Dr., Ste. 2220
Norfolk, VA 23510

Established in 2000 in VA.
Donor(s): Richard F. Barry III.
Financial data (yr. ended 12/31/01): Grants paid, $2,050; assets, $65,673 (M); gifts received, $62,120; expenditures, $2,860; qualifying distributions, $2,050.
Limitations: Applications not accepted.
Application information: Contributes only to pre-selected organizations.
Officers and Directors:* Richard F. Barry III,* Pres.; Mark R. Warden,* V.P. and Secy.-Treas.; Carolyn K. Barry,* V.P.; Michelle B. Warden, V.P.
EIN: 541987565

55180
International Health Foundation
(Formerly Northwest Medical Research Foundation)
6501 Bright Mountain Rd.
McLean, VA 22101-1701
Application address: 320 Chilean Ave., Palm Beach, FL 33480
Contact: R. L. Caleen, Tr.

Financial data (yr. ended 12/31/00): Grants paid, $2,042; assets, $1 (M); expenditures, $6,028; qualifying distributions, $2,042.
Officers: Kenneth D. Hansen, M.D., Pres.; Barbara C. Hansen, V.P.
Trustee: Raynold L. Caleen.
EIN: 237244805

55181
Sentry Services Charitable Foundation
1426 Holland Rd.
Suffolk, VA 23434 (757) 539-2358
Contact: Larry L. Felton, Secy.-Treas.

Financial data (yr. ended 12/31/01): Grants paid, $2,001; assets, $39,653 (M); expenditures, $2,001; qualifying distributions, $2,001.
Limitations: Giving primarily in Suffolk, VA.
Officers: Angus I. Hines, Jr., Pres.; Robert L. Story, V.P.; Larry L. Felton, Secy.-Treas.
Director: Timothy B. Hampton.
EIN: 541477775

55182
Lynell Oliver Baker Memorial Scholarship Fund
509 W. Washington St.
Suffolk, VA 23434
Application address: c/o Lakeland High School, 3373 Pruden Blvd., Suffolk VA 23434
Contact: Kay Kinsey, Counselor

Established in 1989 in VA.
Financial data (yr. ended 07/31/00): Grants paid, $2,000; assets, $30,147 (M); gifts received, $429; expenditures, $2,085; qualifying distributions, $2,000.
Limitations: Giving limited to Suffolk, VA.
Application information: Application form required.
Officers and Directors:* Martha K. Kinsey,* Pres.; Emily K. Andrews,* V.P.; Paige Hill,* Secy.; Frank A. Spady III,* Treas.; Lynn B. Baines, Kevin Beale, Lynne E. Cross, Blair Hines.
EIN: 541521506

55183
Bond Memorial Trust
c/o Thomas J. Bond
P.O. Box 629
Dunn Loring, VA 22027
Application address: P.O. Box 1301, Vienna, VA 22183, tel.: (703) 848-2663
Contact: Wilma M. Bond, Treas.

Financial data (yr. ended 12/31/99): Grants paid, $2,000; assets, $47,981 (M); expenditures, $2,151; qualifying distributions, $2,000.
Officers: Thomas J. Bond III, Pres.; Anne B. Smith, V.P.; Alma B. Bryant, Secy.; Wilma M. Bond, Treas.
EIN: 626273017

55184
Thomas E. Cofer Memorial Charitable Foundation
P.O. Box 658
Smithfield, VA 23431
Application address: c/o Principal, Smithfield High School, 1417 Turner Dr., Smithfield, VA 23430

Established in 1990 in VA.
Donor(s): Malcolm T. Cofer.
Financial data (yr. ended 06/30/99): Grants paid, $2,000; assets, $43,531 (M); gifts received, $2,585; expenditures, $2,451; qualifying distributions, $2,000.
Limitations: Giving limited to Smithfield, VA.
Application information: Application form required.
Trustees: Diana F. Beale, Edna P. Cofer, Malcolm T. Cofer, William F. Miller, Willa S. Powell.
EIN: 541548158

55185
Charles B. Cross, Jr. Citizenship Award
109-A Wimbledon Sq.
Chesapeake, VA 23320-4945

Established in 1989 in VA.
Donor(s): Mrs. Charles B. Cross.
Financial data (yr. ended 12/31/99): Grants paid, $2,000; assets, $45,139 (M); gifts received, $5,000; expenditures, $2,490; qualifying distributions, $2,469.
Trustees: Harry B. Blevins, James A. Roy.
EIN: 541484211

55186
Bill Dudley Scholarship Foundation of the Downtown Club of Richmond
901 E. Byrd St., Ste. 2000
Richmond, VA 23219

Established in 1998 in VA.

Financial data (yr. ended 12/31/00): Grants paid, $2,000; assets, $8,592 (M); gifts received, $2,196; expenditures, $2,953; qualifying distributions, $2,265.
Directors: Ramon E. Chalkley, Jr., Malcolm W. Christian, George D. Crosby, Jr., James T. Donley, Hon. James M. Lumpkin, David B. McNamara, John J. Muldowney, James T. Stewart, Robert W. Thalman, J.R. Wilburn.
EIN: 311596410

55187
Giving Forever Foundation
2004 E. Ocean View Ave.
Norfolk, VA 23503-2506

Established in 1997 in VA.
Donor(s): Leonard O. Oden.
Financial data (yr. ended 06/30/02): Grants paid, $2,000; assets, $211,766 (M); gifts received, $52,500; expenditures, $3,625; qualifying distributions, $2,000.
Limitations: Applications not accepted. Giving primarily in Norfolk, VA.
Application information: Contributes only to pre-selected organizations.
Officers and Directors:* Leonard O. Oden,* Pres.; Judith O. Swystun,* V.P. and Treas.; Virginia B. Oden,* Secy.; Robert Scharar.
EIN: 541874811

55188
Hawthorne Hottenstein Family Foundation, Inc.
6547 Kristina Ursula Ct.
Falls Church, VA 22044-1100

Established in 2000.
Donor(s): David J. Hottenstein Charitable Lead Annuity Trust.
Financial data (yr. ended 12/31/00): Grants paid, $2,000; assets, $39,743 (M); gifts received, $40,875; expenditures, $2,125; qualifying distributions, $2,000.
Officers: Pamela L. Hottenstein, Pres.; Parbury P. Schmidt, Secy.-Treas.
Director: Richard G. Wohltman.
EIN: 541971265

55189
Hunley Foundation
1353 Old Church Rd.
Mechanicsville, VA 23111-6001

Established in 1998 in VA.
Donor(s): Willie T. Hunley.
Financial data (yr. ended 11/30/01): Grants paid, $2,000; assets, $51,944 (M); expenditures, $2,069; qualifying distributions, $2,000.
Limitations: Applications not accepted.
Application information: Contributes only to pre-selected organizations.
Officers: Dallas J. Hunley, Pres.; David J. Hunley, V.P.; Elizabeth J. Hunley, Secy.; Willie T. Hunley, Treas.
EIN: 541922725

55190
Manchester Volunteer Fire Dept. Memorial Scholarship Fund
10108 Krause Rd., Ste. 101
Chesterfield, VA 23832
Application address: P.O. Box 843, Chesterfield, VA 23832
Contact: Donald A. Cocke, Tr.

Financial data (yr. ended 07/31/00): Grants paid, $1,988; assets, $44,193 (L); expenditures, $2,564; qualifying distributions, $44,291.
Limitations: Giving limited to Chesterfield County, VA.

Application information: Application form required.
Trustees: David E. Barfield, Donald A. Cocke, Michael R. Lohr, Jr.
EIN: 546270633

55191
The Peters Foundation
1529 Sunset Ln.
Richmond, VA 23221-3930

Established in 1986 in VA.
Donor(s): Clinton B. Peters.
Financial data (yr. ended 11/30/01): Grants paid, $1,900; assets, $30,451 (M); expenditures, $2,025; qualifying distributions, $1,900.
Limitations: Applications not accepted. Giving primarily in NC.
Application information: Contributes only to pre-selected organizations.
Officer and Director:* Clinton B. Peters,* Pres. and Secy.
EIN: 541395645

55192
The Baumbusch Foundation, Inc.
1436 Highwood Dr.
McLean, VA 22101

Donor(s): Peter L. Baumbusch, Cherry H. Baumbusch.
Financial data (yr. ended 11/30/99): Grants paid, $1,835; assets, $21,737 (M); expenditures, $18,416; qualifying distributions, $1,835.
Limitations: Applications not accepted. Giving primarily in the Washington, DC, area including VA.
Application information: Contributes only to pre-selected organizations.
Trustees: Cherry H. Baumbusch, Peter L. Baumbusch.
EIN: 541402811

55193
Virginia Botanical Associates, Inc.
5204 Riverside Dr.
Richmond, VA 23225
Contact: Robert A. S. Wright, Secy.-Treas.

Established in 1988 in VA.
Financial data (yr. ended 08/31/00): Grants paid, $1,827; assets, $50,030 (M); expenditures, $2,343; qualifying distributions, $2,322.
Limitations: Giving limited to VA.
Application information: Application form required.
Officers: Ted Bradley, Pres.; Robert A.S. Wright, Secy.-Treas.
EIN: 541483271

55194
Child Foundation
c/o Douglas B. Child
12021 Robinson Ferry Rd.
Brodnax, VA 23920-3215

Established in 1999.
Financial data (yr. ended 12/31/01): Grants paid, $1,809; assets, $0 (M); gifts received, $1,960; expenditures, $1,929; qualifying distributions, $1,809.
Limitations: Applications not accepted.
Application information: Contributes only to pre-selected organizations.
Officers and Trustees:* Douglas B. Child, Sr.,* Pres.; Helen S. Child,* Secy.
EIN: 621763721

55195
Tewes Charitable Foundation
c/o Eltromat Electronics, Inc.
P.O. Box 6977, 3819 Holland Blvd.
Chesapeake, VA 23323

Established in 1987 in VA.
Donor(s): Douglas Tewes.
Financial data (yr. ended 12/31/01): Grants paid, $1,800; assets, $2,332 (M); expenditures, $1,815; qualifying distributions, $1,810.
Limitations: Applications not accepted. Giving primarily in FL and VA.
Application information: Contributes only to pre-selected organizations.
Trustee: Douglas Tewes.
EIN: 541448787

55196
The Robert Stephen Weimann Endeavor Fund
509 Trents Ferry Rd.
Lynchburg, VA 24503-1115 (804) 386-3132
Contact: Carol Weimann, Tr.

Established in 1995.
Donor(s): Ruth Weimann,‡ Veronica Mills, Tannenbaum & Milask Realtors, Carol Weimann, Robert Weimann.
Financial data (yr. ended 12/31/01): Grants paid, $1,750; assets, $242,313 (M); gifts received, $3,440; expenditures, $15,668; qualifying distributions, $1,750.
Limitations: Giving primarily in WV.
Trustees: Stephen R. Cain, Frederick V. Meetre, Jeffrey W. Meetre, Carol Weimann, Lauren L. Weimann, Robert B. Weimann, Theodore H. Weimann.
EIN: 226654318

55197
The Woltz-Winchester Foundation
50 S. Cameron St.
Winchester, VA 22601
Contact: Jerry P. Kerr, Treas.

Established in 1999 in VA.
Donor(s): Robert K. Woltz.
Financial data (yr. ended 06/30/02): Grants paid, $1,700; assets, $27,129 (M); gifts received, $1,655; expenditures, $1,723; qualifying distributions, $1,700.
Application information: Application form not required.
Officers: John O. Marsh, Jr., Pres.; Rita R. Woltz, V.P.; Michael M. Foreman, Secy.; Jerry P. Kerr, Treas.
EIN: 541948947

55198
Miles & Ruth Horton Charitalbe Foundation, Inc.
c/o Joel Williams
1995 S. Main, Colony Park, Ste. 903
Blacksburg, VA 24060

Established in 1999 in VA.
Donor(s): Ruth C. Horton.
Financial data (yr. ended 12/31/01): Grants paid, $1,650; assets, $13,274 (M); expenditures, $2,902; qualifying distributions, $1,650.
Limitations: Giving primarily in the New River Valley area, VA.
Officers and Director:* Ruth C. Horton,* Pres.; Charles Cline, V.P.; Joel S. Williams, Secy.-Treas.
EIN: 541941095

55199—VIRGINIA

55199
E. S. Chappell Charitable Trust
9138 Barricade Ln.
Mechanicsville, VA 23111

Financial data (yr. ended 12/31/01): Grants paid, $1,500; assets, $29,292 (M); expenditures, $1,633; qualifying distributions, $1,500.
Limitations: Applications not accepted. Giving limited to VA.
Application information: Contributes only to pre-selected organizations.
Trustees: Holly C. Allen, E. Tyree Chappell.
EIN: 541234498

55200
Rose Kincaid Fund
P.O. Box 206
Warm Springs, VA 24484
Contact: Hugh S. Gwin, Tr.

Financial data (yr. ended 12/31/01): Grants paid, $1,414; assets, $129,087 (M); expenditures, $3,699; qualifying distributions, $2,526.
Limitations: Giving limited to Bath County, VA.
Trustees: Hugh S. Gwin, Mrs. F.L. Thompson, Mrs. J.M. Tremble.
EIN: 546044050

55201
The Perry Fund for Others
(Formerly The Sheelagh Perry Fund)
651 Miller School Rd.
Charlottesville, VA 22903

Donor(s): J. Christopher Perry, M.D.
Financial data (yr. ended 12/31/01): Grants paid, $1,300; assets, $28,883 (M); gifts received, $1,700; expenditures, $1,311; qualifying distributions, $1,300.
Limitations: Applications not accepted. Giving limited to Charlottesville, VA.
Application information: Contributes only to pre-selected organizations.
Trustee: J. Christopher Perry, M.D.
EIN: 546192630
Codes: TN

55202
The Young Musicians Summer Enrichment Fund
c/o Calvin L. Miller
19828 McCray Dr.
Abingdon, VA 24211-6916

Established in 1994 in VA.
Financial data (yr. ended 12/31/00): Grants paid, $1,285; assets, $23,931 (M); expenditures, $1,285; qualifying distributions, $1,285.
Limitations: Giving limited to Washington County, VA.
Application information: Applicant must include letter from music instructor and audition tape of performance. Application form required.
Trustees: Barbara K. Miller, Calvin L. Miller, Jean S. Miller.
EIN: 546352632

55203
Soldiers & Sailors Memorial and Community Endowment, Inc.
P.O. Box 588
Leesburg, VA 20178-0588

Financial data (yr. ended 12/31/01): Grants paid, $1,256; assets, $50,071 (M); expenditures, $1,612; qualifying distributions, $1,256.
Limitations: Applications not accepted. Giving limited to Leesburg, VA.
Application information: Contributes only to pre-selected organizations.

Officers and Directors:* J. Holmes Thomas,* Pres.; H. Wendell Kline,* V.P.; Perry Winston,* Secy.-Treas.; Hugh Grubb, Frederick R. Howard, Bruce McIntosh, George W. Titus, Edward T. Wright.
EIN: 546041528

55204
Lewis W. Webb/Edgewater Foundation
c/o Lewis W. Webb, III
P.O. Box 3037
Norfolk, VA 23514

Established in 1991 in VA.
Donor(s): Lewis W. Webb.
Financial data (yr. ended 12/31/01): Grants paid, $1,250; assets, $24,147 (M); gifts received, $1,250; expenditures, $1,296; qualifying distributions, $1,250.
Limitations: Applications not accepted. Giving primarily in VA.
Application information: Contributes only to pre-selected organizations.
Trustee: Lewis W. Webb.
EIN: 541574759

55205
John C. Wright Foundation
38083 Piggott Bottom Rd.
Purcellville, VA 20132

Financial data (yr. ended 12/31/01): Grants paid, $1,250; assets, $190,588 (M); expenditures, $2,632; qualifying distributions, $1,250.
Limitations: Giving primarily in VA.
Application information: Application form required.
Trustees: I. Marlene Wright, John R. Wright.
EIN: 546070811
Codes: GTI

55206
The Ararat Foundation
8909 Captains Row
Alexandria, VA 22308-2718

Established in 1986 in VA.
Donor(s): Dean V. Shahinian.
Financial data (yr. ended 12/31/99): Grants paid, $1,233; assets, $87,560 (M); gifts received, $13,556; expenditures, $15,763; qualifying distributions, $15,222; giving activities include $10,090 for programs.
Limitations: Applications not accepted. Giving on a national basis.
Application information: Contributes only to pre-selected organizations.
Officers: Paul Shahinian, Secy.; Grace J. Shahinian, Treas.; Dean V. Shahinian, Exec. Dir.
EIN: 521374405

55207
Hospice of Virginia Beach, Inc.
4663 Haygood Rd.
Virginia Beach, VA 23455

Established in 1997 in VA.
Financial data (yr. ended 12/31/99): Grants paid, $1,214; assets, $45,590 (M); gifts received, $56,950; expenditures, $55,419; qualifying distributions, $56,146; giving activities include $54,419 for programs.
Limitations: Applications not accepted.
Application information: Contributes only to pre-selected organizations.
Officers: Daniel S Dechert, Pres.; Judy Laster, V.P.; Mary Leeds, Corres. Secy.; Kathy Patterson, Rec. Secy.; Gilbert Young, Treas.; Katherine Herrmann, Exec. Dir.; Joyce Vandewater, Exec. Dir.; Naomi Warder, Exec. Dir.; Marcella Guillen, Mgr.
EIN: 541132733

55208
The Ratcliffe Foundation
P.O. Box 989
Grundy, VA 24614
Contact: A.M. Ratliff, Pres.

Established in 1970.
Donor(s): A.M. Ratliff.
Financial data (yr. ended 05/31/02): Grants paid, $1,204; assets, $3,592,783 (M); gifts received, $2,347,787; expenditures, $14,828; qualifying distributions, $1,204.
Limitations: Giving primarily in TN and VA.
Officers: A.M. Ratliff, Pres.; John Munsey, Secy.; Eugene Sutherland, Treas.
Director: Anne Bowman.
EIN: 237126937

55209
Kanitkar Foundation
13228 Stable Brook Way
Herndon, VA 20171-2925

Established in 1988 in NY.
Financial data (yr. ended 12/31/01): Grants paid, $1,150; assets, $22,647 (M); gifts received, $2,884; expenditures, $1,188; qualifying distributions, $1,150.
Limitations: Applications not accepted. Giving primarily in New York, NY.
Application information: Contributes only to pre-selected organizations.
Trustees: Abhijit Kanitkar, Rajan Kanitkar, Vijaya Kanitkar.
EIN: 161246730

55210
Skeen Family Foundation, Inc.
39850 Snickersville Turnpike
Middleburg, VA 20117 (703) 925-6000
Contact: Kerry Skeen, Pres.

Established in 1999 in VA.
Donor(s): Kerry B. Skeen.
Financial data (yr. ended 12/31/01): Grants paid, $1,150; assets, $973,911 (M); gifts received, $484,000; expenditures, $3,510; qualifying distributions, $1,150.
Application information: Application form not required.
Officers: Kerry B. Skeen, Pres. and Treas.; Kathleen Skeen, V.P. and Secy.
EIN: 311659995

55211
The Malone Family Foundation
P.O. Box 271
Buena Vista, VA 24416

Established in 1997 in CO.
Donor(s): John C. Malone.
Financial data (yr. ended 12/31/99): Grants paid, $1,100; assets, $112,903,034 (M); gifts received, $25,450; expenditures, $15,975; qualifying distributions, $1,300.
Limitations: Applications not accepted.
Application information: Contributes only to pre-selected organizations.
Officer: John C. Malone, Pres. and Treas.
EIN: 841408520

55212
Oakes-Williams Foundation
c/o Pamela S. Oakes
104 Benson Dr.
Hampton, VA 23664-1855

Financial data (yr. ended 12/31/01): Grants paid, $1,100; assets, $0 (M); gifts received, $1,104; expenditures, $1,104; qualifying distributions, $1,104.

Limitations: Applications not accepted.
Application information: Contributes only to pre-selected organizations.
Officers: Pamela Oakes, Exec. Dir.; Ruth Williams, Exec. Dir.
EIN: 541902057

55213
Pascale & Abbitt Memorial Foundation
98 Nelson Dr.
Newport News, VA 23601
Contact: Carolyn S. Abbitt, Tr.

Established in 1996 in VA.
Donor(s): Carolyn S. Abbitt, Richard F. Abbitt.
Financial data (yr. ended 12/31/01): Grants paid, $1,100; assets, $22,229 (M); gifts received, $7,000; expenditures, $1,157; qualifying distributions, $1,100.
Trustee: Carolyn S. Abbitt.
EIN: 546410300

55214
The Ambrose Foundation
3605 Tupelo Pl.
Alexandria, VA 22304-1844

Established in 1991 in VA.
Donor(s): Jane Flinn.
Financial data (yr. ended 09/30/99): Grants paid, $1,000; assets, $7,249 (M); expenditures, $1,205; qualifying distributions, $1,205.
Officers: Jane Flinn, Pres. and Treas.; Susan K. Flinn, V.P. and Secy.
EIN: 541610698

55215
Arrow Foundation of the NVAC of Pi Beta Phi, Inc.
1302 Gibson Pl.
Falls Church, VA 22046-3801
Application address: 12801 Misty Creek Ln., FAirfax, VA 22033, tel.: (703) 716-0135
Contact: Lisa Maloney

Financial data (yr. ended 06/30/00): Grants paid, $1,000; assets, $7,659 (M); gifts received, $260; expenditures, $16,684; qualifying distributions, $16,684.
Limitations: Giving limited to residents of VA.
Application information: Application form required.
Officers: Jan Jablonski, Pres.; Mary Tatum, Secy.; Louise Foreman, Treas.
Directors: Beth Arvan, Sheila Consaul, Amy Favor, Kim Perret, Karen Rasmussen.
EIN: 541888977

55216
Chisam Memorial Trust
P.O. Box 629
Dunn Loring, VA 22027 (703) 748-0092
Application address: P.O. Box 1301, Vienna, VA 22183, tel.: (703) 848-2663
Contact: Thomas J. Bond, III, Pres.

Financial data (yr. ended 12/31/99): Grants paid, $1,000; assets, $26,920 (M); gifts received, $1,000; expenditures, $1,151; qualifying distributions, $1,151.
Officers: Thomas J. Bond III, Pres.; Charles O. Chisam, V.P.; Judy H. Wyatt, Secy.; Wilma M. Bond, Treas.
EIN: 581978625

55217
DMPE Foundation, Inc.
5640 Heming Ave.
Springfield, VA 22151

Established in 1994 in VA.
Donor(s): Terrence R. Colvin.
Financial data (yr. ended 11/30/01): Grants paid, $1,000; assets, $359,863 (M); expenditures, $2,362; qualifying distributions, $1,000.
Limitations: Applications not accepted.
Application information: Contributes only to pre-selected organizations.
Officers and Director:* Terrence R. Colvin,* Pres.; Tamara D. Colvin, V.P.; Stephen M.A. Slough, Secy.
EIN: 541741113

55218
Alice M. & William E. Johnson Foundation
c/o F&M Trust Co.
P.O Box 93
Warrenton, VA 20188-0093
Contact: Thomas H. Kirk, Dir.

Established in 1997 in VA.
Financial data (yr. ended 12/31/00): Grants paid, $1,000; assets, $18,875 (M); gifts received, $2,000; expenditures, $1,887; qualifying distributions, $1,887.
Limitations: Giving limited to residents of Nokesville, VA.
Directors: Alice M. Johnson, William E. Johnson, Thomas H. Kirk.
EIN: 541733186

55219
The Mary Kathleen Kelley Scholarship Fund
7800 Foxhound Rd.
McLean, VA 22102
Contact: Michael T. Kelley, Dir.

Established in 1995 in VA.
Donor(s): Michael T. Kelley, Susan J. Kelley.
Financial data (yr. ended 12/31/01): Grants paid, $1,000; assets, $19,243 (M); gifts received, $85; expenditures, $1,089; qualifying distributions, $1,000.
Directors: Michael T. Kelley, Susan J. Kelley.
EIN: 541741776

55220
Nu Lambda Chapter of the Alpha Phi Alpha Fraternity Scholarship Fund, Inc.
P.O. Box 2711
Petersburg, VA 23804 (804) 526-7731
Contact: Walter Elias, Jr., Chair.

Financial data (yr. ended 12/31/00): Grants paid, $1,000; assets, $30,212 (M); gifts received, $1,100; expenditures, $1,054; qualifying distributions, $1,000.
Limitations: Giving limited to VA.
Application information: Application form required.
Officers: Walter Elias, Jr., Chair.; Jack C. Richardson, Pres.; Robert Hayes, Secy.; Conrad Gilliam, Treas.
EIN: 521348825

55221
Robinson, Farmer, Cox Associates Educational Foundation
P.O. Box 6580
Charlottesville, VA 22906-6580
(804) 973-8314
Contact: Robert M. Huff, Pres.

Established in 2000 in VA.
Donor(s): Robert M. Huff.
Financial data (yr. ended 12/31/00): Grants paid, $1,000; assets, $29,000 (M); gifts received, $30,000; expenditures, $1,523; qualifying distributions, $1,523.
Limitations: Giving primarily in VA.
Officers and Directors:* Robert M. Huff,* Pres.; Thomas P. Smith, Secy.-Treas.; James R. Berry, Robert W. Jackson.
EIN: 542016551

55222
Muriel Thomas Trust Fund
P.O. Box 28
Hot Springs, VA 24445
Contact: Louise N. Carpenter, Tr.

Financial data (yr. ended 12/31/99): Grants paid, $935; assets, $36,909 (M); expenditures, $1,367; qualifying distributions, $1,131.
Limitations: Giving limited to Bath County, VA.
Application information: Application form not required.
Trustees: Louise N. Carpenter, Hugh S. Gwin, Peter Judah.
EIN: 541420344

55223
Jeffrey G. Light, D.D.S. & Kendon Light, E.A. Charitable Foundation
4626 Kayhoe Rd.
Glen Allen, VA 23060-3531 (804) 965-6241
Additional addresses: c/o Mildred J. Light, 4445 Heather Rd., Long Beach, CA 90808; c/o Jeffrey G. Light, D.D.S., Sacramento Prosthodontist Group, 2650 21st St., Ste. 3, Sacramento, CA 95818
Contact: Kendon Light, E.A., Secy.-Treas.

Established in 1996.
Financial data (yr. ended 03/31/02): Grants paid, $900; assets, $3,968 (M); gifts received, $1,012; expenditures, $929; qualifying distributions, $900.
Application information: Application form required.
Officers and Directors:* Mildred J. Light,* Pres.; Jeffrey G. Light,* V.P.; Kendon Light, E.A.,* Secy.-Treas.
EIN: 541792931

55224
Heritage Hills Foundation
416 Kilmarnock Dr.
Richmond, VA 23229-7625

Established in 2000 in VA.
Donor(s): Charles D. Miller, Roberta L. Miller.
Financial data (yr. ended 12/31/01): Grants paid, $800; assets, $2,668 (M); gifts received, $3,633; expenditures, $1,208; qualifying distributions, $800.
Limitations: Giving primarily in Richmond, VA.
Officers: Charles D. Miller, Pres.; Roberta L. Miller, Secy.
EIN: 541977850

55225
Thomas R. and Barbara-lyn B. Morris Foundation, Inc.
P.O. Box 41
Emory, VA 24327
Contact: Thomas R. Morris, Pres.

Established in 1997 in VA.
Donor(s): Thomas R. Morris.
Financial data (yr. ended 12/31/00): Grants paid, $750; assets, $13,154 (M); gifts received, $39; expenditures, $1,803; qualifying distributions, $750.
Officers and Directors:* Thomas R. Morris,* Pres.; Barbara-lyn B. Morris,* Secy.; George R. Hinnant.
EIN: 541846703

55226—VIRGINIA

55226
James S. Darling Memorial Fund
c/o SunTrust Banks, Inc.
P.O. Box 27385
Richmond, VA 23261-7385
Application address: c/o Gloria Johnson, SunTrust Banks, Inc., Trust Dept., 5 Main Plz., Norfolk, VA 23510

Financial data (yr. ended 12/31/01): Grants paid, $680; assets, $35,680 (M); expenditures, $1,277; qualifying distributions, $723.
Limitations: Giving limited to residents of Hampton, VA.
Application information: Recommendation from the school's superintendent required. Application form required.
Trustee: SunTrust Banks, Inc.
EIN: 546060068

55227
Halstead Foundation
c/o Kent Halstead
1200 N. Nash St., Apt. 1112
Arlington, VA 22209-3612

Donor(s): Kent Halstead, Marjorie Halstead.
Financial data (yr. ended 12/31/01): Grants paid, $608; assets, $42,303 (M); gifts received, $300; expenditures, $657; qualifying distributions, $608.
Directors: A. Scott Halstead, D. Kent Halstead, Jason P. Halstead, Marjorie E. Halstead.
EIN: 541944688

55228
Bittinger Family Foundation
P.O. Box 23642
Alexandria, VA 22304 (703) 823-3625
Contact: Bradley L. Bittinger, Tr.

Established in 2000 in GA.
Donor(s): Dale A. Bittinger.
Financial data (yr. ended 12/31/00): Grants paid, $500; assets, $8,576 (M); gifts received, $13,566; expenditures, $2,746; qualifying distributions, $2,746.
Application information: Application form required.
Trustees: Bradley L. Bittinger, Dale A. Bittinger, Mark C. Bittinger, Mary L. Cantrell, Margaret B. Keith.
EIN: 582511130

55229
The Stephen R. Caplan Foundation
4505 Kelly Ct.
Virginia Beach, VA 23462-4518
Contact: Stephen R. Caplan, Pres.

Established in 1987 in VA.
Donor(s): Stephen R. Caplan.
Financial data (yr. ended 09/30/00): Grants paid, $500; assets, $30,832 (M); expenditures, $1,677; qualifying distributions, $500.
Limitations: Giving primarily in Norfolk, VA.
Officers and Directors:* Stephen R. Caplan,* Pres.; Renee S. Caplan,* V.P.; James M. Caplan,* Secy.-Treas.
EIN: 541298749

55230
The Chatham Family Charitable Trust
317 Turtle Rock Trail
Stanleytown, VA 24168 (540) 627-5005
Contact: Barbara Adams, Tr.;David C. Chatham, Tr.;and H.E. Haley, Jr., Tr.

Financial data (yr. ended 12/31/00): Grants paid, $500; assets, $94,349 (M); expenditures, $1,924; qualifying distributions, $452.
Limitations: Giving limited to residents of VA.
Trustees: Barbara Adams, David C. Chatham, H.E. Haley, Jr.
EIN: 224625841

55231
Craven Buddy Finch Foundation, Inc.
138 Freemor Dr.
Poquoson, VA 23662-1226 (757) 868-9082
Contact: Thomas Finch, Pres.

Donor(s): Wallace T. Finch, Bobby D. Finch, Thomas Finch.
Financial data (yr. ended 12/31/01): Grants paid, $500; assets, $54,232 (M); gifts received, $1,300; expenditures, $1,428; qualifying distributions, $500.
Trustees: Mary Finch Cooper, Bobby Dodd Finch, Rev. Jack Wayne Finch, Louise Finch, Phillip W. Finch, Thomas Finch, Rev. Zack S. Finch, Vicki L. Hopkins, Judy F. Wiggins, and 5 additional trustees.
EIN: 581406067

55232
The Carl J. Kreitler Foundation
c/o Dick Kreitler
15 Farmington Dr.
Charlottesville, VA 22901

Donor(s): Richard R. Kreitler.
Financial data (yr. ended 10/31/01): Grants paid, $500; assets, $411,341 (M); expenditures, $6,178; qualifying distributions, $500.
Limitations: Applications not accepted. Giving primarily in VA.
Application information: Contributes only to pre-selected organizations.
Officers: Richard R. Kreitler, Pres.; Joan Goodwin, Secy.-Treas.
EIN: 136137799

55233
Virginia Tompkins McLaughlin Scholarship Fund
P.O. Box 667
Halifax, VA 24558-0667 (804) 572-8123
Contact: William W. McLaughlin, Tr.

Financial data (yr. ended 12/31/99): Grants paid, $500; assets, $5,369 (M); expenditures, $506; qualifying distributions, $500.
Limitations: Giving limited to Halifax County, VA.
Trustees: Tucker W. McLaughlin, Sr., Tucker W. McLaughlin, Jr., William W. McLaughlin.
EIN: 546052815

55234
George C. & Ruth C. Ryffel Charitable Trust
2661 N. Upshur St.
Arlington, VA 22207
Contact: George C. Ryffel, Tr.

Established in 1996 in VA & MT.
Donor(s): George G. Ryffel, Ruth C. Ryffel.
Financial data (yr. ended 12/31/01): Grants paid, $500; assets, $30,545 (M); expenditures, $522; qualifying distributions, $500.
Limitations: Applications not accepted. Giving primarily in MT.
Application information: Contributes only to pre-selected organizations.
Trustees: Carolyn J. Ryffel, George G. Ryffel, Ruth C. Ryffel.
EIN: 816083524

55235
The Stouffer Family Charitable Trust
50 S. Cameron St.
Winchester, VA 22601 (540) 662-3417

Established in 1998 in VA.
Donor(s): Doris R. Stouffer.
Financial data (yr. ended 12/31/99): Grants paid, $500; assets, $105,498 (M); gifts received, $96,945; expenditures, $500; qualifying distributions, $500.
Trustee: Doris R. Stouffer.
EIN: 546442874

55236
Murray L. and Margaret C. Garson Foundation
426 River Bend
Great Falls, VA 22066
Contact: Larry B. Grimes, Tr.

Established in 1999 in VA.
Donor(s): Margaret Garson.
Financial data (yr. ended 12/31/01): Grants paid, $465; assets, $147,123 (M); gifts received, $46,390; expenditures, $30,647; qualifying distributions, $465.
Trustee: Larry B. Grimes.
EIN: 541964843

55237
The Home Mission Foundation
6098 Knotts Creek Ln.
Suffolk, VA 23435

Donor(s): Marion F. Vaughan, Jr.
Financial data (yr. ended 04/30/02): Grants paid, $450; assets, $10,452 (M); expenditures, $536; qualifying distributions, $450.
Limitations: Applications not accepted. Giving primarily in SC.
Application information: Contributes only to pre-selected organizations.
Officers: Marion F. Vaughan, Jr., Pres.; Francis V. Price, V.P.; Evelyn P. Vaughan, Secy.-Treas.
Director: Robert C. Price.
EIN: 541259280

55238
The Last Great Waters, Inc.
610 Moorefield Park Dr., Ste. 100
Richmond, VA 23236-3655 (804) 320-0380
Contact: Louis Clifford Schroeder, Pres.

Established in 1993 in VA.
Donor(s): Louis Clifford Schroeder.
Financial data (yr. ended 12/31/01): Grants paid, $450; assets, $399,281 (M); gifts received, $100,411; expenditures, $120,500; qualifying distributions, $450.
Limitations: Giving primarily in VA.
Application information: Application form required.
Officers and Directors:* Louis Clifford Schroeder,* Pres.; Lois T. Schroeder,* V.P.; Charles E. Hicks,* Secy.-Treas.
EIN: 541645994

55239
Stewart F. & Janet S. Reid Private Foundation
406 W. Franklin St.
Richmond, VA 23220
Contact: George R. Hinnant, Dir.

Established in 1996 in VA.
Financial data (yr. ended 12/31/01): Grants paid, $447; assets, $8,913 (M); expenditures, $454; qualifying distributions, $447.
Application information: Application form not required.
Officers and Directors:* Stewart F. Reid,* Pres.; Janet S. Reid,* Secy.; George R. Hinnant, Laura Reid.
EIN: 541820676

55240
William P. Guyton Foundation
c/o William P. Guyton
1944 N. Cleveland St.
Arlington, VA 22201

Established in 1999 in CO.
Financial data (yr. ended 12/31/01): Grants paid, $400; assets, $26,237 (M); gifts received, $13,978; expenditures, $1,746; qualifying distributions, $400.
Trustees: Samuel P. Guyton, William P. Guyton.
EIN: 841519669

55241
Poster Family Foundation
6 Pidgeon Hill Dr., Ste. 270
Sterling, VA 20165

Established in 1999 in VA.
Donor(s): Allan Poster, Rose Poster Carr.
Financial data (yr. ended 06/30/01): Grants paid, $300; assets, $16,674 (M); gifts received, $10,000; expenditures, $1,651; qualifying distributions, $1,635.
Limitations: Applications not accepted. Giving primarily in Charlottesville, VA.
Application information: Contributes only to pre-selected organizations.
Trustees: Allan Poster, Evan Poster, Lori Whitstock.
EIN: 546462986

55242
Thomas P. Duncan, Jr. Foundation
107 Botetourt Rd.
Newport News, VA 23601-3601
Contact: Charles M. Rutter III, Dir.

Donor(s): Thomas P. Duncan, Mildred P. Duncan.
Financial data (yr. ended 12/31/01): Grants paid, $280; assets, $1,562,605 (M); expenditures, $28,836; qualifying distributions, $280.
Limitations: Giving primarily in SC and VA.
Directors: Martha W. McMurran, Sue W. Redd, William J. Rue, Charles M. Rutter III, Thomas D. Rutter.
EIN: 540920302

55243
The Bolton Foundation
P.O. Box 579
Danville, VA 24543

Established in 2000 in VA.
Financial data (yr. ended 06/30/01): Grants paid, $261; assets, $189 (M); gifts received, $450; expenditures, $261; qualifying distributions, $261.
Directors: Howard W. Bolton, Jr., Howard W. Bolton III, Patricia T. Bolton.
EIN: 542009267

55244
The AMVEST Foundation
1 Boar's Head Pl.
Charlottesville, VA 22903
Application address: P.O. Box 5347, Charlottesville, VA 22905, tel.: (804) 977-3350
Contact: Carl W. Smith, Pres.

Established in 1991 in VA.
Donor(s): Carl W. Smith.
Financial data (yr. ended 11/30/01): Grants paid, $250; assets, $115,965 (M); expenditures, $361; qualifying distributions, $250.
Limitations: Giving primarily in Larchmont, NY.
Officers and Trustees:* Carl W. Smith,* Pres.; Hunter J. Smith,* Secy.; Richard G. Joynt.
EIN: 541612631

55245
R. E. and N. C. Dungan Foundation, Inc.
3914 Prosperity Ave.
Fairfax, VA 22031

Established in 1994.
Donor(s): Raymond E. Dungan.
Financial data (yr. ended 12/31/01): Grants paid, $250; assets, $5,598 (M); gifts received, $125; expenditures, $375; qualifying distributions, $250.
Limitations: Giving primarily in Fairfax, VA.
Officers: Raymond E. Dungan, Pres. and Secy.; Ronald E. Dungan, V.P. and Treas.; Cynthia Hatten, V.P.
EIN: 541429536

55246
Mahmoodian Educational, Medical and Cultural Organization, Inc.
Rte. 1, Box 55N
Fishersville, VA 22939
Contact: Saeed Mahmoodian, Pres.

Established in 1985 in WV.
Donor(s): Saeed Mahmoodian.
Financial data (yr. ended 04/30/99): Grants paid, $216; assets, $17,430 (M); gifts received, $10,000; expenditures, $6,010; qualifying distributions, $3,672; giving activities include $3,456 for programs.
Limitations: Giving primarily in Rapid City, SD.
Officers: Saeed Mahmoodian, Pres.; Virginia Mahmoodian, Secy.-Treas.
EIN: 311129124

55247
The Thomas E. Reynolds, Sr. Charitable Trust
c/o G. Nelson Mackey, Jr.
30 W. Franklin Rd., Ste. 300
Roanoke, VA 24011

Established in 1998 in VA.
Donor(s): Thomas E. Reynolds, Sr.
Financial data (yr. ended 12/31/01): Grants paid, $202; assets, $15,243 (M); expenditures, $1,370; qualifying distributions, $202.
Limitations: Applications not accepted.
Application information: Contributes only to pre-selected organizations.
Trustees: G. Nelson Mackey, Jr., Thomas E. Reynolds, Jr.
EIN: 546441386

55248
The Chartwell Foundation
46612 Hampshire Station Dr.
Sterling, VA 20165

Established in 1999 in VA.
Donor(s): David A. Klueter, Lissa C. Klueter.
Financial data (yr. ended 06/30/02): Grants paid, $200; assets, $185 (M); gifts received, $900; expenditures, $856; qualifying distributions, $200.
Limitations: Applications not accepted.
Application information: Contributes only to pre-selected organizations.
Trustees: David A. Klueter, Lissa C. Klueter.
EIN: 541961307

55249
The Huntly Foundation
909 E. Main St., Ste. 800
Richmond, VA 23219-3002

Established in 2000 in VA.
Financial data (yr. ended 04/30/02): Grants paid, $150; assets, $2,745 (M); expenditures, $756; qualifying distributions, $150.
Limitations: Applications not accepted.
Application information: Contributes only to pre-selected organizations.
Trustee: Fred J. Bernhardt, Jr.
EIN: 541988524

55250
The George Cohee, Jr. Foundation
c/o Katherine Cohee
107-B 78th St.
Virginia Beach, VA 23451

Financial data (yr. ended 12/31/01): Grants paid, $125; assets, $96,643 (M); gifts received, $33,876; expenditures, $313; qualifying distributions, $125.
Limitations: Applications not accepted.
Application information: Contributes only to pre-selected organizations.
Officers and Directors:* Katherine Cohee,* Pres. and Secy.; Mignon Gertrude Cohee Reynolds,* V.P.
EIN: 541945051

55251
Warren & Van Elliott Charitable Foundation, Inc.
1312 Hermitage Rd.
Manakin Sabot, VA 23103-2607

Established in 1999 in VA.
Donor(s): Van R. Elliott.
Financial data (yr. ended 12/31/01): Grants paid, $125; assets, $4,080 (M); gifts received, $2,971; expenditures, $1,075; qualifying distributions, $125.
Limitations: Applications not accepted.
Application information: Contributes only to pre-selected organizations.
Officer: Van R. Elliott, Pres.
EIN: 541969314

55252
H. B. & Ellen B. Wharton Scholarship Fund
c/o SunTrust Bank
P.O. Box 27385
Richmond, VA 23261-7385
Application address: P.O. Box 13888, Roanoke, VA 24038, tel.: (540) 982-3014
Contact: Perry Gorham, Trust Off., SunTrust Bank

Financial data (yr. ended 12/31/99): Grants paid, $107; assets, $104,204 (M); expenditures, $2,721; qualifying distributions, $939.
Limitations: Giving limited to VA.
Application information: Application form not required.
Trustee: SunTrust Bank.
EIN: 546059085

55253
Sarah E. Forbes Charitable Trust
12420 Warwick Blvd., Ste. 5-B
Newport News, VA 23606

Established in 1998 in VA.
Donor(s): Sarah E. Forbes.
Financial data (yr. ended 12/31/00): Grants paid, $72; assets, $951 (M); expenditures, $116; qualifying distributions, $72.
Trustee: Sarah E. Forbes.
EIN: 656274117

55254
The Irwin D. Kaplan Foundation, Inc.
(Formerly Irwin & Melanie Kaplan Foundation)
313 S. Gaskins Rd.
Richmond, VA 23233

Established in 1995 in VA.
Financial data (yr. ended 12/31/99): Grants paid, $60; assets, $15,651 (M); expenditures, $1,029; qualifying distributions, $60.
Limitations: Applications not accepted. Giving limited to Richmond, VA.

55254—VIRGINIA

Application information: Contributes only to pre-selected organizations.
Director: Irwin D. Kaplan.
EIN: 541525607

55255
Ann C. Smith and Raymond W. Smith Charitable Trust
1310 N. Courthouse Rd.
Arlington, VA 22201
Contact: Phyliss Bush

Established in 1986 in PA.
Donor(s): Ann C. Smith, Raymond W. Smith.
Financial data (yr. ended 12/31/01): Grants paid, $60; assets, $82,068 (M); expenditures, $214; qualifying distributions, $60.
Limitations: Giving on a national basis, with some emphasis on PA.
Application information: Application form not required.
Trustees: Ann C. Smith, Raymond W. Smith.
EIN: 236869486

55256
American Equine Foundation
8516 Culfor Crescent
Norfolk, VA 23503-4709

Donor(s): Herbert Cashvan,‡ Marvin Simon.
Financial data (yr. ended 12/31/01): Grants paid, $0; assets, $54,375 (M); expenditures, $221; qualifying distributions, $0.
Limitations: Applications not accepted. Giving primarily in VA.
Application information: Contributes only to pre-selected organizations.
Officers and Directors:* Jeffrey S. Cashvan,* Pres.; Deborah Cashvan,* V.P.; Brooke Ann Cashvan, John Jeffrey Cashvan.
EIN: 510250503

55257
Association for Unmanned Vehicle Systems Foundation, Inc.
3401 Columbia Pike, Ste. 400
Arlington, VA 22204

Established in 2000 in VA.
Donor(s): Association for Unmanned Vehicle Systems International, AUVSI Capital Chapter.
Financial data (yr. ended 12/31/01): Grants paid, $0; assets, $51,484 (M); gifts received, $25,857; expenditures, $1,896; qualifying distributions, $0.
Officers: Penn E. Mullowney, Pres.; William Bowes, Exec. V.P.; Kimberly Schwartz, V.P.; Dewar Donnithorne-Tait, Secy.; Robert D. Brown, Treas.
EIN: 521797483
Codes: CS, TN

55258
Barahona Foundation
7353 McWhorter Pl.
Annandale, VA 22003

Donor(s): Jose R. Barahona.
Financial data (yr. ended 09/30/01): Grants paid, $0; assets, $3,806 (M); expenditures, $545; qualifying distributions, $0.
Limitations: Applications not accepted.
Application information: Contributes only to pre-selected organizations.
Directors: Alicia Barahona, Jose R. Barahona, Kathy Barahona.
EIN: 541892428

55259
David and Nancy Bass Foundation
1864 Anchorage Farm
Charlottesville, VA 22903

Established in 1999 in VA.
Donor(s): David Bass, Nancy Bass.
Financial data (yr. ended 12/31/01): Grants paid, $0; assets, $36,966 (M); expenditures, $1,661; qualifying distributions, $0.
Limitations: Applications not accepted.
Application information: Contributes only to pre-selected organizations.
Officers: David Bass, Pres.; Nancy Bass, Secy.-Treas.
EIN: 541961238

55260
The Bibb Foundation, Inc.
P.O. Box 261
Danville, VA 24543
Application address: 2291 Memorial Dr., Danville, VA 24541, tel.: (804) 799-4912
Contact: Charles S. Bolt, Jr., Dir.

Incorporated in 1930 in GA.
Donor(s): The Bibb Co.
Financial data (yr. ended 07/31/01): Grants paid, $0; assets, $1,574,246 (M); expenditures, $12,504; qualifying distributions, $0.
Limitations: Giving primarily in GA, NC, SC, and VA.
Publications: Program policy statement, application guidelines.
Application information: Application form required.
Officers and Directors:* Joseph L. Lanier, Jr.,* Pres.; Richard L. Williams,* V.P.; Harry L. Goodrich, Secy.; Barry F. Shea,* Treas.; Charles S. Bolt, Jr., Larry W. Van de Visser, E. Linwood Wright.
EIN: 580566140
Codes: CS, TN

55261
Brachytherapy Research and Educational Foundation, Inc.
7643 Fullerton Rd.
Springfield, VA 22153-2862

Established around 1989.
Donor(s): Krishnan Suthanthiran.
Financial data (yr. ended 11/30/01): Grants paid, $0; assets, $4,082 (M); expenditures, $1,328; qualifying distributions, $0.
Limitations: Applications not accepted.
Application information: Contributes only to pre-selected organizations.
Officers: Basil Hilaris, Pres.; Dattatreyudu Nori, V.P.; Krishnan Suthanthiran, Secy.-Treas.
Directors: Charles W. Ballou, J.C. Howard, Jr.
EIN: 541440344

55262
The Nicolae Bretan Music Foundation
8542 Georgetown Pike
McLean, VA 22102-1206

Established in 1983.
Donor(s): Judit Bretan LeBovit.
Financial data (yr. ended 12/31/01): Grants paid, $0; assets, $242,332 (M); expenditures, $1,259; qualifying distributions, $0; giving activities include $1,259 for programs.
Limitations: Applications not accepted. Giving primarily in Hungary, Romania, and Switzerland.
Application information: Contributes only to pre-selected organizations.
Officer: Judit Bretan LeBovit, Pres.
EIN: 132935875

55263
N. R. Burroughs Educational Fund
c/o B.B. & T., Trust Dept.
P.O. Box 5228
Martinsville, VA 24115-5228 (276) 666-3198
Contact: Faye Hairston, Trust Off., B.B. & T.

Established in 1983 in VA.
Financial data (yr. ended 06/30/01): Grants paid, $0; assets, $7,600,634 (M); expenditures, $31,258; qualifying distributions, $546,248; giving activities include $550,000 for loans to individuals.
Limitations: Giving limited to residents of the Martinsville, VA, area.
Application information: Application form required.
Trustees: Lynanne H. Newman, Ricky L. Scott, Scott Taylor, David Yarter, B.B. & T.
EIN: 521303602
Codes: GTI

55264
William C. Cartinhour, Jr. Foundation
c/o Cardle L. Haynes
2832 Linden Ln.
Falls Church, VA 22042-2312

Established in 2001 in VA.
Donor(s): William C. Cartinhour, Jr.
Financial data (yr. ended 12/31/01): Grants paid, $0; assets, $910 (M); gifts received, $10,000; expenditures, $9,960; qualifying distributions, $9,960.
Limitations: Applications not accepted.
Application information: Contributes only to pre-selected organizations.
Officers and Directors:* Carol Haynes,* Pres. and Treas.; Mark Morrison,* Secy.; Patricia Bennett, William C. Cartinhour, Jr.
EIN: 311806008

55265
S. R. Clarke Foundation, Inc.
3554 Chain Bridge Rd., Ste. 201
Fairfax, VA 22030

Established in 2000.
Donor(s): S.R. Clarke, Inc.
Financial data (yr. ended 12/31/00): Grants paid, $0; assets, $61,990 (M); gifts received, $62,500; expenditures, $805; qualifying distributions, $0.
Officer: Spencer Clarke, Pres.
EIN: 542007606

55266
Routh Nash Coffman Charitable Trust
401 Wythe St.
Alexandria, VA 22314

Established in 2001 in VA.
Donor(s): Routh Nash Coffman.‡
Financial data (yr. ended 12/31/01): Grants paid, $0; assets, $614,616 (M); gifts received, $633,649; expenditures, $50; qualifying distributions, $0.
Limitations: Applications not accepted.
Application information: Contributes only to pre-selected organizations.
Trustee: N. Carr Stogner.
EIN: 546499550

55267
Mary Jane Combemale Memorial Foundation, Inc.
4431 Broad Run Church Rd.
Warrenton, VA 20187 (540) 347-9111
Contact: Jean-Loup R. Combemale, Dir.

Established in 1999 in VA.
Donor(s): Eric Billings, Colette A. Combemale.

Financial data (yr. ended 04/30/00): Grants paid, $0; assets, $33,514 (M); gifts received, $32,950; expenditures, $0; qualifying distributions, $0.
Directors: Jean-Loup R. Combemale, Mary Combemale, Sr. Cecilia Liberatore, David Wilkinson.
EIN: 541946261

55268
J. S. Cooley Educational Trust Fund
c/o Marshall National Bank & Trust Co.
P.O. Box 38
Marshall, VA 20116-0038

Donor(s): J.S. Cooley.‡
Financial data (yr. ended 08/31/01): Grants paid, $0; assets, $100,707 (M); expenditures, $260; qualifying distributions, $18,045; giving activities include $17,954 for loans to individuals.
Limitations: Applications not accepted. Giving limited to residents of Clarke, Culpepper, Fauquier, Frederick, Loudoun, Rappahanock, and Warren counties, VA.
Application information: Unsolicited requests for funds not accepted.
Trustee: Marshall National Bank & Trust Co.
EIN: 521274701
Codes: GTI

55269
W. G. Dearing Educational Trust Fund
c/o Marshall National Bank & Trust Co.
P.O. Box 38
Marshall, VA 20116-0038

Financial data (yr. ended 12/31/01): Grants paid, $0; assets, $289,831 (M); expenditures, $907; qualifying distributions, $6,226; giving activities include $6,000 for loans to individuals.
Limitations: Applications not accepted. Giving primarily in Marshall, VA.
Trustee: Marshall National Bank & Trust Co.
EIN: 546039319
Codes: GTI

55270
The Kenneth E. and Tena R. Delaski Foundation
100 Interpromontory Rd.
Great Falls, VA 22066

Donor(s): Kenneth E. Delaski, Tena R. Delaski.
Financial data (yr. ended 12/31/01): Grants paid, $0; assets, $788,352 (M); expenditures, $0; qualifying distributions, $0.
Limitations: Applications not accepted.
Application information: Contributes only to pre-selected organizations.
Officers: Kenneth E. Delaski, Pres.; Tena R. Delaski, Secy.-Treas.
EIN: 541902696

55271
Frank and Alma Delaura Foundation
9061 Blarney Stone Dr.
Springfield, VA 22152

Established in 2000.
Donor(s): Frances L. Delaura.
Financial data (yr. ended 12/31/00): Grants paid, $0; assets, $956 (M); gifts received, $39,214; expenditures, $38,258; qualifying distributions, $30,209; giving activities include $30,209 for programs.
Limitations: Applications not accepted.
Application information: Contributes only to pre-selected organizations.
Officers and Directors:* Frank A. Delaura, Sr.,* Chair.; Frances L. Delaura, Pres.; Alma L. Delaura, Lea McInally, Martin McInally, M.D.
EIN: 541987472

55272
The Constance Dundas Foundation
c/o Fred J. Bernhardt, Jr.
800 Mutual Bldg., 909 E. Main St.
Richmond, VA 23219

Established in 1997 in VA.
Donor(s): Constance Dundas.‡
Financial data (yr. ended 09/30/01): Grants paid, $0; assets, $3,928,976 (M); gifts received, $100,000; expenditures, $19,324; qualifying distributions, $300.
Limitations: Applications not accepted. Giving primarily in VA.
Application information: Contributes only to pre-selected organizations.
Trustee: Fred J. Bernhardt, Jr.
EIN: 541894989

55273
Reto Engler Memorial Trust
1225 Martha Custis Dr., Ste. 618
Alexandria, VA 22302-2019 (703) 671-7533
Contact: Lois A. Rossi, Tr.

Established in 1998 in VA; funded in 1999.
Donor(s): Lois A. Rossi.
Financial data (yr. ended 12/31/01): Grants paid, $0; assets, $9,863 (M); expenditures, $0; qualifying distributions, $0.
Limitations: Giving primarily in Blacksburg, VA.
Application information: Application form not required.
Trustees: Kevin Judge, Lois A. Rossi.
EIN: 526935646

55274
The Ferguson Family Foundation
315 S. Gaskins Rd.
Richmond, VA 23233

Established in 2000 in VA.
Donor(s): James Ferguson.
Financial data (yr. ended 12/31/00): Grants paid, $0; assets, $146,129 (M); gifts received, $146,129; expenditures, $0; qualifying distributions, $0.
Limitations: Applications not accepted.
Application information: Contributes only to pre-selected organizations.
Trustees: Dee B. Ferguson, James G. Ferguson, Jr.
EIN: 542014183

55275
Franklin Southampton Charities
P.O. Box 276
Franklin, VA 23851
Application address: P.O. Box 775, Franklin, VA 23851, tel.: (757) 562-5133
Contact: G. Elliott Cobb, Jr., Dir.

Established in 2000 in VA.
Donor(s): Old Hospital Corp., Southampton Memorial Hospital Endowment Fund.
Financial data (yr. ended 12/31/00): Grants paid, $0; assets, $14,947,829 (M); gifts received, $10,000; expenditures, $75,554; qualifying distributions, $12,413.
Directors: E. Warren Beale, Jr., Gene W. Beale, Jr., Glenn P. Bidwell, Jr., M.D., William M. Birdsong, Jr., G. Elliott Cobb, Jr., Asa B. Johnson, William A. Peak, Robert L. Putze, M.D., Sol W. Rawls, Jr., W. Elliott Whitfield, James J. Vasoti.
EIN: 311613116

55276
Fraser Family Foundation, Inc.
2513 N. Quantico St.
Arlington, VA 22207

Established in 2000 in NY.

Donor(s): Corey F. Huber, Katherine L. Huber.
Financial data (yr. ended 12/31/00): Grants paid, $0; assets, $143,818 (M); gifts received, $248,881; expenditures, $9,287; qualifying distributions, $0.
Limitations: Applications not accepted.
Application information: Contributes only to pre-selected organizations.
Officers: Corey F. Huber, C.E.O. and Pres.; Katherine L. Huber, V.P. and Treas.; Laurence G. Bousquet, Secy.
EIN: 161584090

55277
The George C. Freeman III Memorial Trust
213 Lakeshore Dr.
Fredericksburg, VA 22405-3118
Application address: c/o Paul S. Baker, Dir. of Financial Aid, P.O. Box 668, Hampden-Sydney, VA 23943, tel.: (804) 223-4381

Established around 1974.
Financial data (yr. ended 12/31/01): Grants paid, $0; assets, $75,844 (M); expenditures, $485; qualifying distributions, $0.
Limitations: Giving limited to Hampden-Sydney, VA.
Application information: Applicants must be enrolled at Hampden-Sydney College. Application form required.
Trustees: George C. Freeman, Jr., Patricia M. Freeman.
EIN: 237449735

55278
Richard S. Glasser Family Foundation
580 E. Main St., Ste. 600
Norfolk, VA 23510

Established in 2001 in VA.
Donor(s): Richard S. Glasser, Martha Mednick-Glasser.
Financial data (yr. ended 12/31/01): Grants paid, $0; assets, $87,983 (M); gifts received, $88,095; expenditures, $0; qualifying distributions, $0.
Limitations: Applications not accepted.
Application information: Contributes only to pre-selected organizations.
Officers: Richard S. Glasser, Pres.; Michael A. Glasser, Secy.; Martha Mednick-Glasser, Treas.
Director: Hara B. Glasser.
EIN: 542061975

55279
Good News Foundation
P.O. Box 12228
Newport News, VA 23612-2228
Contact: Caleb D. West, Jr., Pres.

Established in 1996.
Donor(s): Caleb D. West, Jr.
Financial data (yr. ended 12/31/01): Grants paid, $0; assets, $275 (M); expenditures, $550; qualifying distributions, $0.
Officer: Caleb D. West, Jr., Pres.
Directors: Robert W. Crowe, C. Dwight West, Jonathan C. West.
EIN: 541812414

55280
The Greenawalt Foundation, Inc.
518 Pocahantas Ave. N.W.
P.O. Box 12611
Roanoke, VA 24027-2611

Established in 1991 VA.
Donor(s): Kent S. Greenawalt, Monte H. Greenawalt.
Financial data (yr. ended 12/31/01): Grants paid, $0; assets, $12,906 (M); expenditures, $29; qualifying distributions, $0.

55280—VIRGINIA

Limitations: Applications not accepted.
Application information: Contributes only to pre-selected organizations.
Officers and Directors:* Kent S. Greenawalt,* Pres.; Monte H. Greenawalt,* V.P.; Max B. Lewis,* Secy.
EIN: 541605415

55281
Grills Family Foundation
P.O. Box 98
Rapidan, VA 22733-0098

Established in 2001 in VA.
Donor(s): Joe Grills, Margaret Grills.
Financial data (yr. ended 12/31/01): Grants paid, $0; assets, $192,384 (M); gifts received, $196,296; expenditures, $0; qualifying distributions, $0.
Limitations: Applications not accepted.
Application information: Contributes only to pre-selected organizations.
Trustees: Joe Grills, Margaret Grills.
EIN: 542056474

55282
Groves-Chaney Foundation
c/o B.B. & T., Trust Dept.
P.O. Box 5228
Martinsville, VA 24115

Established in 1984 in VA.
Financial data (yr. ended 10/31/01): Grants paid, $0; assets, $1,540,526 (M); expenditures, $15,890; qualifying distributions, $0.
Limitations: Applications not accepted. Giving limited to Martinsville, VA.
Application information: Contributes only to pre-selected organizations.
Officers and Directors:* Irving M. Groves, Jr.,* Pres.; Ruth G. Chaney,* V.P.; LynnAnne L. Newman, Secy.-Treas.
Trustee: B.B. & T.
EIN: 521403789

55283
The Ruth & Louis Harris Family Foundation
c/o Bank of America, N.A.
P.O. Box 26606
Richmond, VA 23261-6606
Application address: c/o Bank of America, N.A., P.O Box 26688, Richmond, VA 23261-6688
Contact: Louis Harris, Dir.; or Donald E. Koonce, Dir.

Established in 1999 in VA.
Donor(s): Louis Harris, Mrs. Louis Harris.
Financial data (yr. ended 07/31/00): Grants paid, $0; assets, $470,473 (M); gifts received, $506,958; expenditures, $2,808; qualifying distributions, $0.
Directors: Charles A. Harris, Louis Harris, Ruth S. Harris, Tobie Jeanne Meyer, Robyn Williams, Scott Williams.
EIN: 541961471

55284
The Charles I. Hiltzheimer Charitable Trust
P.O. Box 651
Ivy, VA 22945

Established in 1987 in NJ.
Donor(s): Charles I. Hiltzheimer.
Financial data (yr. ended 12/31/01): Grants paid, $0; assets, $561 (M); expenditures, $731; qualifying distributions, $0.
Limitations: Applications not accepted. Giving primarily in NJ.
Application information: Contributes only to pre-selected organizations.
Trustees: Charles I. Hiltzheimer, William P. Verdon.
EIN: 222785544

55285
Hirschkop Family Fund, Inc.
612B River Dr.
Lorton, VA 22079
Application address: 826 Emerald Dr., Alexandria, VA 22308, tel.: (703) 280-8266
Contact: Philip J. Hirschkop, Pres.

Established in 1997 in VA.
Donor(s): Philip J. Hirschkop.
Financial data (yr. ended 12/31/01): Grants paid, $0; assets, $8,365 (M); gifts received, $0; expenditures, $1,242; qualifying distributions, $0.
Application information: Application form not required.
Officer: Philip J. Hirschkop, Pres.
EIN: 311500829

55286
Hopper Family Foundation
206 Duke St.
Alexandria, VA 22314-3806

Established in 1999 in VA.
Donor(s): Harry F. Hopper III.
Financial data (yr. ended 12/31/00): Grants paid, $0; assets, $244,625 (M); gifts received, $240; expenditures, $240; qualifying distributions, $0.
Limitations: Applications not accepted.
Application information: Contributes only to pre-selected organizations.
Officers and Directors:* Maria V. Hopper,* Pres.; Harry F. Hopper III,* Secy.
EIN: 541968575

55287
The Hug Family Foundation
195 Catch Penny Ln.
P.O. Box 490
Lively, VA 22507

Established in 2001 in VA.
Donor(s): Philip Hug.
Financial data (yr. ended 12/31/01): Grants paid, $0; assets, $197,568 (M); gifts received, $198,150; expenditures, $0; qualifying distributions, $0.
Limitations: Applications not accepted.
Application information: Contributes only to pre-selected organizations.
Trustee: Philip Hug.
EIN: 260021231

55288
Hunter Family Foundation
11491 Sunset Hills Rd.
Reston, VA 20190

Established in 1990 in VA.
Donor(s): Elizabeth L. Hunter, Philip S. Hunter.
Financial data (yr. ended 12/31/01): Grants paid, $0; assets, $11,842 (M); expenditures, $815; qualifying distributions, $750.
Limitations: Applications not accepted. Giving primarily in NY.
Application information: Contributes only to pre-selected organizations.
Officer: Philip S. Hunter, Pres.
Directors: Elizabeth L. Hunter, Paul L. Hunter.
EIN: 541525152

55289
Jamerson Family Foundation
P.O. Box 27385
Richmond, VA 23261-7385

Established in 2000 in VA.
Donor(s): William E. Jamerson, Ellen P. Jamerson.
Financial data (yr. ended 12/31/01): Grants paid, $0; assets, $349,241 (M); gifts received, $340,000; expenditures, $572; qualifying distributions, $0.
Limitations: Applications not accepted.
Application information: Contributes only to pre-selected organizations.
Committee Members: Ellen P. Jamerson, Phillip C. Jamerson, William E. Jamerson.
Trustee: SunTrust Banks, Inc.
EIN: 546478829

55290
Jewish Philanthropic Foundation, Inc.
6266 Kingfisher Ln.
Alexandria, VA 22312

Established in 1985 in VA.
Donor(s): Stephen A. Bodzin, Tanya K. Bodzin.
Financial data (yr. ended 10/31/01): Grants paid, $0; assets, $21,362 (M); gifts received, $1,527; expenditures, $563; qualifying distributions, $0.
Limitations: Applications not accepted. Giving on a national basis, with emphasis on New York, NY and VA.
Application information: Contributes only to pre-selected organizations.
Officers: Lawrence H. Shuman, Pres.; Stephen A. Bodzin, V.P.; Tanya K. Bodzin, Secy.; Deanna M. Shuman, Treas.
EIN: 541372072

55291
JMJ & Tekel Foundation
7819 Lewinsville Rd.
McLean, VA 22102

Financial data (yr. ended 12/31/00): Grants paid, $0; assets, $3,094 (M); gifts received, $4,799; expenditures, $2,253; qualifying distributions, $2,253; giving activities include $1,890 for programs.
Officer: Stephen M. Weblian, Pres.
Directors: Matthew B. Weblian, Michael L. Weblian, Miriam A. Weblian.
EIN: 541778213

55292
The Kanawha Foundation
5219 W. Cary Street Rd.
Richmond, VA 23226

Established in 1986 in VA.
Donor(s): Fred T. Tattersall.
Financial data (yr. ended 04/30/01): Grants paid, $0; assets, $99,484 (M); expenditures, $1,330; qualifying distributions, $1,250.
Limitations: Applications not accepted. Giving primarily in Richmond, VA.
Application information: Contributes only to pre-selected organizations.
Officers: Rodney P. Tattersall, Pres.; Fred T. Tattersall, Treas.
EIN: 541407416

55293
Karlgaard Family Foundation
3019 Chichester Ln.
Fairfax, VA 22031

Established in 2001 in VA.
Donor(s): David C. Karlgaard, Marilyn E. Karlgaard.
Financial data (yr. ended 12/31/01): Grants paid, $0; assets, $2,633,453 (M); gifts received, $2,497,700; expenditures, $4,244; qualifying distributions, $0.
Limitations: Applications not accepted.
Application information: Contributes only to pre-selected organizations.
Officers and Directors:* David C. Karlgaard,* Pres.; Marilyn E. Karlgaard,* V.P. and Secy.
EIN: 311810538

55294
Kennard Educational Fund, Inc.
c/o Trust Dept., Planters Bank & Trust Co. of VA
P.O. Box 1309
Staunton, VA 24402-1309 (540) 885-1232

Financial data (yr. ended 09/30/01): Grants paid, $0; assets, $648,051 (M); expenditures, $7,554; qualifying distributions, $25,500; giving activities include $25,500 for loans to individuals.
Limitations: Giving limited to residents of the cities of Staunton or Waynesboro, or Augusta County, VA.
Application information: Application form required.
Officers: Thomas A. Davis, Pres.; Mollie K. Butler, Secy.-Treas.
EIN: 541157065
Codes: GTI

55295
John & Elizabeth Lane Foundation
4312-J Evergreen Ln.
Annandale, VA 22003-3274

Established in 1998 in DE and VA.
Donor(s): John Lane, Elizabeth Lane.
Financial data (yr. ended 12/31/01): Grants paid, $0; assets, $94,187 (M); expenditures, $1,386; qualifying distributions, $0.
Limitations: Applications not accepted.
Application information: Contributes only to pre-selected organizations.
Officer: John Lane, Pres.
EIN: 541921636

55296
William E. Larsen Charitable Trust for Wilderness Preservation
P.O. Box 3
Riner, VA 24149

Established in 2001 in VA.
Financial data (yr. ended 12/31/01): Grants paid, $0; assets, $101,909 (M); gifts received, $101,026; expenditures, $0; qualifying distributions, $0.
Trustee: Richard Lee Bailey II.
EIN: 546486066

55297
Jacque Edward Levy Trust
c/o Howard Lasser
5912 Camberly Ave.
Springfield, VA 22150

Established in 2000 in VA.
Financial data (yr. ended 12/31/01): Grants paid, $0; assets, $1,257,285 (M); expenditures, $21,814; qualifying distributions, $1,467.
Limitations: Applications not accepted.
Application information: Contributes only to pre-selected organizations.
Trustees: Howard Lasser, Robert Platt.
EIN: 546465629

55298
Loomis-Butts Charitable Trust, Inc.
c/o D. Wayne Loomis
176 Windmere Trail
Moneta, VA 24121 (540) 721-8037

Established in 1990 in VA.
Donor(s): D. Wayne Loomis.
Financial data (yr. ended 12/31/01): Grants paid, $0; assets, $7,320 (M); gifts received, $1,688; expenditures, $822; qualifying distributions, $0.
Limitations: Giving primarily in VA.
Officers and Directors:* D. Wayne Loomis,* Pres.; Brian D. Loomis,* V.P.; Beverly B. Loomis,* Secy.-Treas.

EIN: 541565560

55299
Magnolia Foundation
c/o Janet Miller
870 Owensville Rd.
Charlottesville, VA 22901

Established in 2001 in VA.
Donor(s): Knapp Foundation, Mrs. Russell F. Knapp.
Financial data (yr. ended 12/31/01): Grants paid, $0; assets, $42,789 (M); gifts received, $40,000; expenditures, $600; qualifying distributions, $0.
Trustee: Janet K. Miller.
EIN: 542049262

55300
The Maibach Foundation, Inc.
325 Queen St.
Alexandria, VA 22314

Established in 2001.
Donor(s): Michael C. Maibach.
Financial data (yr. ended 12/31/01): Grants paid, $0; assets, $97,518 (M); gifts received, $101,040; expenditures, $0; qualifying distributions, $0.
Limitations: Applications not accepted.
Application information: Contributes only to pre-selected organizations.
Officers: Michael C. Maibach, Pres. and Treas.; Henry Holling, Secy.
Directors: Charles Edward Maibach, George Scalise, Peter S. Watson.
EIN: 542061998

55301
Mcleod Family Foundation
410 1st St.
Roanoke, VA 24011

Established in 1999 in VA.
Donor(s): John G. Mcleod, Katherine L. Mcleod.
Financial data (yr. ended 12/31/01): Grants paid, $0; assets, $139,496 (M); gifts received, $30,220; expenditures, $4,511; qualifying distributions, $0.
Limitations: Applications not accepted.
Application information: Contributes only to pre-selected organizations.
Directors: John G. Mcleod, Katherine L. Mcleod.
EIN: 541967887

55302
Medical Foundation of Portsmouth Academy of Medicine, Inc.
P.O. Box 3365
Portsmouth, VA 23701-0365

Financial data (yr. ended 12/31/01): Grants paid, $0; assets, $136,923 (M); gifts received, $16,309; expenditures, $11,129; qualifying distributions, $0.
Limitations: Applications not accepted. Giving primarily in VA.
Application information: Contributes only to pre-selected organizations.
Officers and Directors:* Philip R. Thomason,* Pres.; John E. Kostinas,* V.P.; Paul J. Kovalcik, Secy.; Robert Baker, Wayne R. Devantier, Olivia Jones, Frances Seal, Vasken Tenekjian.
EIN: 540897409

55303
Martha Mabel Moore Charitable Trust
c/o Bank of America
P.O. Box 26606
Richmond, VA 23261-6606
Contact: Shannon Hopkins

Established in 1988 in VA.
Financial data (yr. ended 01/31/01): Grants paid, $0; assets, $829,550 (M); gifts received, $1,048;

expenditures, $13,271; qualifying distributions, $6,318.
Limitations: Giving primarily in VA.
Trustee: Bank of America.
EIN: 546262428

55304
National Folk Arts Foundation
1716 Wilson Blvd.
Arlington, VA 22209

Established in 1999 in VA.
Financial data (yr. ended 12/31/99): Grants paid, $0; assets, $3,401 (M); gifts received, $155; expenditures, $0; qualifying distributions, $0.
Directors: George Contis, M.D., Artemis Manos.
EIN: 541742377

55305
National Sports Educational Foundation, Inc.
6045 Wilson Blvd., Ste. 300
Arlington, VA 22205

Established in 2000 in VA.
Financial data (yr. ended 12/31/00): Grants paid, $0; assets, $5,050 (M); gifts received, $4,430; expenditures, $4,444; qualifying distributions, $0.
Officer: Frank Ceresi, Pres.
EIN: 541069765

55306
The James C. Overacre Foundation Charitable Trust
11550 Edenberry Dr.
Richmond, VA 23236

Established in 1999 in VA.
Financial data (yr. ended 12/31/00): Grants paid, $0; assets, $1,067 (M); expenditures, $1; qualifying distributions, $1.
Director: Elizabeth Overacre.
EIN: 546453643

55307
Dorothy M. Overcash Charitable Trust
c/o B.B. & T.
38 Rouss Ave.
Winchester, VA 22601 (540) 665-4200

Established in 2001 in VA.
Donor(s): Dorothy M. Overcash.
Financial data (yr. ended 12/31/01): Grants paid, $0; assets, $4,985 (M); gifts received, $5,016; expenditures, $0; qualifying distributions, $0.
Limitations: Giving primarily in VA.
Application information: Application form not required.
Trustee: B.B. & T.
EIN: 546498083

55308
R. Keith & Helen J. Parks Foundation Charitable Trust
406 W. Franklin St.
Richmond, VA 23220

Established in 1999.
Financial data (yr. ended 12/31/01): Grants paid, $0; assets, $2,224 (M); expenditures, $0; qualifying distributions, $0.
Officer: George R. Hinnant, Secy.
EIN: 546457287

55309
Phillips E. Patton Charitable Foundation
P.O. Box 35792
Richmond, VA 23235

Established in 1994 in PA.
Donor(s): Phillips E. Patton.

Financial data (yr. ended 12/31/01): Grants paid, $0; assets, $419,235 (M); expenditures, $3,603; qualifying distributions, $0.
Limitations: Applications not accepted. Giving primarily in FL and PA.
Application information: Contributes only to pre-selected organizations.
Officer: Phillips E. Patton, Pres.
EIN: 541715989

55310
The Pendray Family Charitable Foundation
11072 Thrush Ridge Rd.
Reston, VA 20191

Established in 1998 in VA.
Donor(s): John J. Pendray, Linda L. Pendray.
Financial data (yr. ended 06/30/02): Grants paid, $0; assets, $9,377 (M); expenditures, $683; qualifying distributions, $0.
Limitations: Applications not accepted.
Application information: Contributes only to pre-selected organizations.
Trustees: Andrew S. Pendray, Michael D. Pendray, Stephen L. Pendray.
EIN: 546441831

55311
The Kenneth and Bettie Corbin Perry Foundation
317 Clovelly Rd.
Richmond, VA 23221

Established in 1996 in VA.
Financial data (yr. ended 12/31/01): Grants paid, $0; assets, $62,490 (M); expenditures, $1,446; qualifying distributions, $0.
Limitations: Applications not accepted.
Application information: Contributes only to pre-selected organizations.
Officers and Directors:* Kenneth M. Perry,* Pres. and Treas.; Bettie Corbin Perry,* V.P.; John B. O'Grady, Secy.; Christopher M. Perry.
EIN: 541806557

55312
Dorothy Andrews Phillips and Edward E. Phillips, Sr. Foundation
3827 Old Gun Rd., W.
Midlothian, VA 23113

Established in 2000 in VA.
Donor(s): Linda P. Kaplan, Robert R. Kaplan, Edward E. Phillips, Jr., Elizabeth E. Phillips.
Financial data (yr. ended 12/31/01): Grants paid, $0; assets, $137,463 (M); gifts received, $17,826; expenditures, $23,411; qualifying distributions, $0.
Limitations: Applications not accepted.
Application information: Contributes only to pre-selected organizations.
Officer: Linda P. Kaplan, Mgr.
EIN: 542020441

55313
Margaret M. Pierce Scholarship Fund
c/o F&M Trust Co.
P.O. Box 93
Warrenton, VA 20188-0093

Established in 1997 in VA.
Financial data (yr. ended 12/31/01): Grants paid, $0; assets, $36,401 (M); gifts received, $500; expenditures, $1,175; qualifying distributions, $0.
Limitations: Giving limited to residents of VA.
Directors: Elizabeth Brittle, Robert N. Floyd, Thomas H. Kirk, Ann Cecil Renick.
EIN: 541527948

55314
The Pittaway Foundation, Inc.
3850 Pittaway Rd.
Richmond, VA 23235

Established in 1992 in VA.
Financial data (yr. ended 06/30/01): Grants paid, $0; assets, $3,964 (M); expenditures, $1,680; qualifying distributions, $0.
Limitations: Applications not accepted.
Application information: Contributes only to pre-selected organizations.
Officers and Directors:* William H. Sparrow,* Pres.; Thomas G. Aycock,* V.P.; David J. Bowling,* Secy.-Treas.; Lewis Boggs, Glenda A. Hilt, Joseph C. Kearfott, James M. Keeton, Jr., Sandra L. Mattes, John W. Sanderson, Richard T. Wilson.
EIN: 541670229

55315
The Nelson J. and Katherine Friant Post Foundation
c/o Russell, Evans & Thompson, PLLC
299 Herndon Pkwy.
Herndon, VA 20170

Donor(s): Nelson Post, Katherine Post.
Financial data (yr. ended 12/31/01): Grants paid, $0; assets, $589 (M); gifts received, $100; expenditures, $230; qualifying distributions, $0.
Officers: Grover B. Russell, Pres.; Jeffrey J. Fairfield, Secy.; W. Craig Thompson, Treas.
EIN: 541743148

55316
Lee Potter Family Charitable Foundation
5610 Southpoint Centre Blvd., Ste. 103
Fredericksburg, VA 22407 (540) 891-1234
Contact: Richard L. Potter, Pres.

Established in 2001 in VA.
Donor(s): Richard L. Potter, Potter Homes, Inc.
Financial data (yr. ended 12/31/01): Grants paid, $0; assets, $55,445 (M); gifts received, $55,500; expenditures, $500; qualifying distributions, $0.
Application information: Application form not required.
Officer: Richard L. Potter, Pres.
EIN: 311802133

55317
Real Estate Tax Institute Foundation, Inc.
3473 Mildred Dr.
Falls Church, VA 22042-3809

Financial data (yr. ended 05/31/02): Grants paid, $0; assets, $8,206 (M); expenditures, $90; qualifying distributions, $0.
Limitations: Applications not accepted.
Application information: Contributes only to pre-selected organizations.
Officers and Directors:* John Szymanski,* Chair.; James A. Sharp,* Secy.; Charles Harrison.
EIN: 521636696

55318
The Martha Davenport Reed Foundation
830 E. Main St., Ste. 1700
Richmond, VA 23219-2725

Donor(s): Martha Davenport Reed.
Financial data (yr. ended 12/31/01): Grants paid, $0; assets, $59,595 (M); expenditures, $795; qualifying distributions, $0.
Limitations: Applications not accepted. Giving primarily in Richmond, VA.
Application information: Contributes only to pre-selected organizations.
Trustee: Martha Davenport Reed.
EIN: 521351341

55319
Richard Family Charitable Foundation
17654 Canby Rd.
Leesburg, VA 20175-6906

Established in 2000 in VA.
Donor(s): Oliver G. Richard III, Donna Guzman Richard.
Financial data (yr. ended 12/31/00): Grants paid, $0; assets, $194,096 (M); gifts received, $194,096; expenditures, $0; qualifying distributions, $0.
Limitations: Applications not accepted.
Application information: Contributes only to pre-selected organizations.
Officers: Oliver G. Richard III, Pres.; Donna Guzman Richard, V.P.
EIN: 542020771

55320
The Annette Urso Rickel Foundation, Inc.
c/o Anne L. Stone & Associates, LLC
1749 Old Meadow Rd., Ste. 301
McLean, VA 22102

Established in 1999 in VA.
Donor(s): Annette U. Rickel.
Financial data (yr. ended 12/31/00): Grants paid, $0; assets, $214,684 (M); gifts received, $212,717; expenditures, $103; qualifying distributions, $0.
Officers: Annette U. Rickel, Pres.; John Ralph Urso, Secy.
Director: John R. Rickel.
EIN: 542185402

55321
The Michele K. and Marc S. Ross Family Foundation, Inc.
472 S. Union St.
Alexandria, VA 22314-3826

Established in 1999 in VA.
Donor(s): Michele K. Ross.
Financial data (yr. ended 06/30/02): Grants paid, $0; assets, $79,778 (M); gifts received, $100; expenditures, $1,272; qualifying distributions, $0.
Limitations: Applications not accepted.
Application information: Contributes only to pre-selected organizations.
Officers: Michele K. Ross, Pres.; Francine M. Ross, V.P.; Matthew S. Ross, Secy.-Treas.
EIN: 541963078

55322
Jack O. Scher Foundation, Inc.
4026 River Rd.
Faber, VA 22938

Donor(s): Jack O. Scher.
Financial data (yr. ended 09/30/01): Grants paid, $0; assets, $344,451 (M); expenditures, $2,006; qualifying distributions, $0.
Limitations: Applications not accepted. Giving on an international basis.
Application information: Contributes only to pre-selected organizations.
Officers and Directors:* Jack O. Scher,* Pres.; Judith Scher,* Secy.
EIN: 133250310

55323
Shenandoah Council of the Arts
103 S. Main St.
Harrisburg, VA 22801

Established in 2001 in VA.
Financial data (yr. ended 12/31/01): Grants paid, $0; assets, $2,000 (M); gifts received, $44,849; expenditures, $42,261; qualifying distributions, $0.

VIRGINIA—55337

Officers: Crystal Theodore, Pres.; Phillip James, V.P.; Polly Frue, Treas.
EIN: 541973610

55324
The Gertrude Perry Simpson Foundation
2802 Pine Hollow Rd.
Oakton, VA 22124

Established in 1998 in VA.
Donor(s): Julien G. Patterson.
Financial data (yr. ended 09/30/00): Grants paid, $0; assets, $104,280 (M); gifts received, $35,000; expenditures, $4,217; qualifying distributions, $4,058; giving activities include $4,058 for programs.
Limitations: Applications not accepted. Giving limited to VA.
Application information: Contributes only to pre-selected organizations.
Directors: Julien G. Patterson, Terri J. Wesselman.
EIN: 541922003

55325
Societas Homiletica
c/o Judith M. McDaniel
3737 Seminary Rd.
Alexandria, VA 22304-5202

Donor(s): Washington Theological Union, St. Paul's Endowment for Mission and Ministry, Seminary Consultation on Mission, Episcopal Church Center.
Financial data (yr. ended 12/31/01): Grants paid, $0; assets, $7,162 (M); expenditures, $4,062; qualifying distributions, $0.
Officers: Gerrit Immink, Pres.; Albrecht Groezinger, V.P.; Judith M. McDaniel, Treas.
EIN: 541912080

55326
Southampton County Historical Society
18137 Rosemont Rd.
Sedley, VA 23878
Contact: Anne W. Bryant, Treas.

Financial data (yr. ended 12/31/01): Grants paid, $0; assets, $760,217 (M); gifts received, $47,700; expenditures, $45,526; qualifying distributions, $0.
Officers: Lynda T. Updike, Pres.; Daniel T. Balfour, V.P.; Mrs. Glean Parker, Secy.; Mrs. Anne Bryant, Treas.
EIN: 546059028

55327
Spark Foundation
3600 Chain Bridge Rd.
Fairfax, VA 22030-3202

Established in 1998 in VA.
Donor(s): Jack Rothstein.
Financial data (yr. ended 05/31/00): Grants paid, $0; assets, $66,820 (M); gifts received, $81,455; expenditures, $255; qualifying distributions, $254.
Limitations: Applications not accepted.
Application information: Contributes only to pre-selected organizations.
Director: Jack Rothstein.
EIN: 311628398

55328
Stelfox Family Foundation
3286 Tilton Valley Dr.
Vienna, VA 22182

Established in 2000 in VA.
Donor(s): Jill Ann Stelfox, Steven Glenn Stelfox.
Financial data (yr. ended 12/31/00): Grants paid, $0; assets, $1,489,500 (M); gifts received, $1,500,000; expenditures, $10,500; qualifying distributions, $0.
Limitations: Applications not accepted.
Application information: Contributes only to pre-selected organizations.
Trustees: Stuart Leong, Michael Stain, Randall P. Smith, Jill Ann Stelfox, Steven Glenn Stelfox.
EIN: 546473509

55329
Marie Stopes International, Ltd.
c/o Michael Glomb
859 N. Jacksonville St.
Arlington, VA 22205

Financial data (yr. ended 12/31/00): Grants paid, $0; assets, $2,160 (M); expenditures, $112; qualifying distributions, $0.
Limitations: Applications not accepted.
Application information: Contributes only to pre-selected organizations.
Officers and Directors:* Timothy R.L. Black, M.D.,* Pres.; Michael B. Glomb,* Secy.; Philip D. Harvey,* Treas.
EIN: 133607969

55330
The Robert Hopkins Strickler & Lorraine Warren Strickler Foundation
1882 Keezletown Rd.
Harrisonburg, VA 22802-2707
(540) 434-3215
Contact: Robert Hopkins Strickler, Pres.

Established in 2001 in VA.
Donor(s): Robert Hopkins Strickland.
Financial data (yr. ended 12/31/01): Grants paid, $0; assets, $1,555,772 (M); gifts received, $1,575,227; expenditures, $0; qualifying distributions, $0.
Application information: Application form not required.
Officers and Directors:* Robert Hopkins Strickler,* Pres.; Lorraine Warren Strickler,* Secy.
EIN: 311815894

55331
SunTrust MidAtlantic Charitable Trust
(Formerly Crestar Bank Charitable Trust)
c/o SunTrust Bank, Inc.
P.O. Box 27385
Richmond, VA 23261-7385
Application address: 919 E. Main St., Richmond, VA 23219
Contact: J. Thomas Vaughan, Trust Off., SunTrust Banks, Inc.

Established in 1964 in VA.
Donor(s): Crestar Bank, SunTrust Bank.
Financial data (yr. ended 12/31/01): Grants paid, $0; assets, $1,815,622 (M); expenditures, $9,292; qualifying distributions, $43.
Limitations: Giving primarily in VA.
Publications: Informational brochure, program policy statement, application guidelines.
Application information: Application form not required.
Trustee: SunTrust Banks, Inc.
EIN: 546054608
Codes: CS, CD

55332
The Teleglobe Foundation
11480 Commerce Park Dr.
Reston, VA 20191

Established in 1998.
Financial data (yr. ended 12/31/01): Grants paid, $0; assets, $1 (M); expenditures, $0; qualifying distributions, $0.
Officers: Karen Reeves, Pres.; Donna Tanenbaum, V.P.; Danielle O. Saunders, Secy.
Director: Clifford Beek.
EIN: 541909929

55333
Carl and Emily Thompson Charitable Trust
c/o B.B. & T., Trust Dept.
P.O. Box 2800
Winchester, VA 22604

Established in 2001 in VA.
Donor(s): Carl Thompson Credit Shelter Trust.
Financial data (yr. ended 12/31/01): Grants paid, $0; assets, $1,198,419 (M); gifts received, $1,332,515; expenditures, $0; qualifying distributions, $0.
Limitations: Applications not accepted.
Application information: Contributes only to pre-selected organizations.
Trustee: B.B. & T.
EIN: 546493189

55334
George A. & Eleanor D. Thornton Foundation
24 Mystic Rd.
Richmond, VA 23233
Contact: J. Timothy Thornton, Pres.

Donor(s): J. Timothy Thornton, George A. Thornton III.
Financial data (yr. ended 12/31/01): Grants paid, $0; assets, $11,542 (M); expenditures, $2,088; qualifying distributions, $0.
Limitations: Giving primarily in NC and VA.
Officers: J. Timothy Thornton, Pres.; Mary E.T. Martin, V.P.; George A. Thornton III, Treas.
EIN: 237092738

55335
The Tilghman Family Foundation
c/o William L.S. Rowe, Hunton, & Williams
951 E. Byrd St.
Richmond, VA 23219

Established in 2001 in VA.
Donor(s): Richard Tilghman.
Financial data (yr. ended 12/31/01): Grants paid, $0; assets, $2,964,040 (M); gifts received, $3,017,191; expenditures, $48,991; qualifying distributions, $0.
Limitations: Applications not accepted.
Application information: Contributes only to pre-selected organizations.
Officer: Richard G. Tilgham, Pres.
EIN: 311799913

55336
20th Century Merchants Foundation
106-B E. Main St.
Charlottesville, VA 22902-5220

Established in 2000 in VA.
Financial data (yr. ended 12/31/00): Grants paid, $0; assets, $319,256 (M); gifts received, $329,372; expenditures, $1,650; qualifying distributions, $331,022.
Limitations: Applications not accepted.
Application information: Contributes only to pre-selected organizations.
Officers: E. Marshall Pryor, Pres.; Charles Baber, V.P.; William B. Downer, Secy.-Treas.
EIN: 541960041

55337
The Carol & Martha Wallenhorst Charitable Memorial Trust
3100 Maryland Ave.
Lynchburg, VA 24501-4626

Established in 2001 in VA.
Financial data (yr. ended 12/31/01): Grants paid, $0; assets, $3,837 (M); gifts received, $4,508; expenditures, $4,776; qualifying distributions, $176.

55337—VIRGINIA

Limitations: Applications not accepted.
Application information: Contributes only to pre-selected organizations.
Trustees: Martha W. Wallenhorst, Richard G. Wallenhorst.
EIN: 546486274

55338
John Buford Watson Trust
P.O. Box 17035
Richmond, VA 23226

Established in 2000 in VA.
Donor(s): John Watson.‡
Financial data (yr. ended 12/31/00): Grants paid, $0; assets, $514,519 (M); gifts received, $515,000; expenditures, $288; qualifying distributions, $0.
Limitations: Applications not accepted.
Application information: Contributes only to pre-selected organizations.
Trustee: Virginia Baptist Foundation.
EIN: 546476025

55339
Wellspring Foundation
2241 Tackett's Mill Dr., Ste. T
Woodbridge, VA 22192

Donor(s): Paulette J. Evans.
Financial data (yr. ended 06/30/01): Grants paid, $0; assets, $3,133 (M); gifts received, $3,000; expenditures, $374; qualifying distributions, $0.
Limitations: Applications not accepted.
Application information: Contributes only to pre-selected organizations.
Officer and Directors:* Nancy S. Kyme,* Secy.-Treas.; Claudia S. Johnsen, Paulette Sen'Gerni.
EIN: 521367056

55340
West End Foundation
12526 Summer Pl.
Oak Hill, VA 20171-2474

Established in 2000 in VA.
Donor(s): Nancie M. Barwick, Timothy P. Barwick.
Financial data (yr. ended 12/31/00): Grants paid, $0; assets, $198,850 (M); gifts received, $165,435; expenditures, $0; qualifying distributions, $0.
Limitations: Applications not accepted.

Application information: Contributes only to pre-selected organizations.
Officers: Nancie M. Barwick, Pres. and Secy.; Timothy P. Barwick, Pres. and Treas.; Johannah R. Barwick, V.P.; Samuel D. Barwick, V.P.
EIN: 542018505

55341
Mary Williamson Educational Loan Fund
P.O. Box 810
New Market, VA 22844-0810 (540) 740-3636
Contact: Allen D. Johnson, Tr.

Financial data (yr. ended 12/31/00): Grants paid, $0; assets, $796,021 (M); expenditures, $42,581; qualifying distributions, $0; giving activities include $28,372 for loans to individuals.
Limitations: Giving limited to residents of the New Market, VA, area.
Application information: Application form required.
Trustee: Allen D. Johnson.
EIN: 546043362
Codes: GTI

55342
The E. Tayloe Wise Charitable Foundation, Inc.
c/o White, Blackburn & Conte, PC
300 W. Main St.
Richmond, VA 23220-5630

Established in 2000 in VA.
Financial data (yr. ended 12/31/01): Grants paid, $0; assets, $1,185 (M); gifts received, $1,608; expenditures, $946; qualifying distributions, $946.
Officers and Directors:* E. Tayloe Wise,* Pres.; Janice Lee Privett Wise,* Secy.-Treas.; Charles W. Hundley.
EIN: 541984609

55343
Woodson Charitable Trust
c/o Bank of America
P.O. Box 26606
Richmond, VA 23261-6606
Application address: 115 Park St., Charlottesville, VA 22901, tel.: (804) 295-4637
Contact: William M. Currier, Tr.

Established in 1995 in VA.
Donor(s): Jannie P. Woodson.‡

Financial data (yr. ended 12/31/99): Grants paid, $0; assets, $1,374,519 (M); expenditures, $19,438; qualifying distributions, $3,633.
Limitations: Giving primarily in VA.
Trustee: William M. Currier.
EIN: 546309425

55344
Claude & Inez Woodward Foundation for the Needy & Homeless
116 Charnwood Rd.
Richmond, VA 23229
Contact: Edward Woodward, Tr.

Established in 1998 in VA.
Financial data (yr. ended 12/31/01): Grants paid, $0; assets, $170,798 (M); expenditures, $4,212; qualifying distributions, $0.
Limitations: Giving primarily in Richmond, VA.
Trustee: Edward R. Woodward.
EIN: 541896177

55345
World Society for Reconstructive Microsurgery
700 Onley Rd., Ste. 2055
Norfolk, VA 23510

Established in 2000.
Financial data (yr. ended 12/31/00): Grants paid, $0; assets, $24,267 (M); gifts received, $15,181; expenditures, $14,051; qualifying distributions, $14,051; giving activities include $4,200 for programs.
Officers: Viktor Meyer, M.D., Pres.; Julia K. Terzis, M.D., Secy.-Treas.
EIN: 541990358

55346
The Zhuang Foundation, Inc.
10911 Great Point Ct.
Great Falls, VA 22066 (703) 757-1885
Contact: Yimin Zhuang, Pres.

Established in 1999 in VA.
Donor(s): Yimin Zhuang.
Financial data (yr. ended 12/31/01): Grants paid, $0; assets, $2,532 (M); expenditures, $1,757; qualifying distributions, $0.
Officer: Yimin Zhuang, Pres.
Director: Fengxiao Zhang.
EIN: 541931569

WASHINGTON

55347
Bill & Melinda Gates Foundation
(Formerly William H. Gates Foundation)
P.O. Box 23350
Seattle, WA 98102 (206) 709-3140
FAX: (206) 709-3180; E-mail:
info@gatesfoundation.org; URL: http://
www.gatesfoundation.org
Contact: Grant Inquiry Coord.

Established in 1994 in WA; name changed in Aug. 1999. The Gates Learning Foundation merged into the foundation Jan. 1, 2000.
Donor(s): William H. Gates III, Melinda French Gates.
Financial data (yr. ended 12/31/01): Grants paid, $1,146,958,000; assets, $32,751,466,000 (M); gifts received, $2,107,500,000; expenditures, $1,233,278,000; qualifying distributions, $1,146,958,000; giving activities include $23,510,000 for programs.
Limitations: Giving on a national and international basis to support initiatives in health and learning; the foundation also supports community giving in the Pacific Northwest.
Publications: Annual report.
Application information: Review funding guidelines on foundation's Web site before initial contact with foundation; proposals should not be submitted without prior invitation by the foundation.
Officers: William H. Gates, Sr., Co-Chair. and C.E.O.; Patricia Q. Stonesifer, Co-Chair. and Pres.; Sylvia Mathews, C.O.O. and Exec. Dir., Libraries, Pacific N.W., an; Dr. Richard D. Klausma, M.D., Exec. Dir., Global Health; Tom Vander Ark, Exec. Dir., Ed.; Melinda F. Gates, Mgr.
Trustee: William H. Gates III.
EIN: 911663695
Codes: FD, FM

55348
The Seattle Foundation
425 Pike St., Ste. 510
Seattle, WA 98101 (206) 622-2294
FAX: (206) 622-7673; E-mail:
info@seattlefoundation.org; URL: http://
www.seattlefoundation.org
Contact: Anne V. Farrell, Pres.

Incorporated in 1946 in WA.
Financial data (yr. ended 12/30/01): Grants paid, $43,390,105; assets, $307,923,492 (M); gifts received, $63,254,677; expenditures, $48,573,054.
Limitations: Giving limited to the greater Puget Sound region, WA.
Publications: Annual report, informational brochure, program policy statement, application guidelines, grants list.
Application information: Application guidelines available on website. Application form not required.
Officers and Trustees:* Phyllis Campbell,* Chair.; Stewart Landefeld,* Vice-Chair.; Irwin Treiger,* Vice-Chair.; Anne V. Farrell, C.E.O. and Pres.; Carolyn J. Norton, V.P., Finance and Admin.; Steve Ulene,* V.P., Gift Planning; Molly Stearns, Sr. V.P., Progs. and DS; Susan G. Duffy, Secy.; Dan Regis, Treas.; and 26 additional trustees.
Corporate Trustees: Union Bank of California, N.A., Columbia Management Co., KeyBank, N.A., Miller Anderson Sherrad, PIMCO, T. Rowe Price Svc., Bank of America, Sirach Capital Management, Inc., U.S. Bank of Washington, N.A., Warburg, Pincus Cansellors, Inc., Washington Mutual Savings Bank, Wells Fargo Bank Northwest, N.A.
EIN: 916013536
Codes: CM, FD

55349
Community Foundation for Southwest Washington
(Formerly Clark County Community Foundation)
703 Broadway St., Ste. 610
Vancouver, WA 98660 (360) 694-2550
FAX: (360) 737-6335; E-mail:
director@cfsww.org; URL: http://www.cfsww.org/index.html
Contact: Nancy E. Sourek, Exec. Dir.

Incorporated in 1984 in WA.
Financial data (yr. ended 12/31/01): Grants paid, $30,871,334; assets, $40,309,365 (M); gifts received, $25,033,483; expenditures, $31,395,729.
Limitations: Giving limited to southwest WA.
Publications: Annual report, newsletter.
Application information: Application form required.
Officers and Directors:* Brot Bishop, Jr.,* Chair.; Leslie Durst,* Vice-Chair.; Lee Kearney,* Vice-Chair.; Nancy E. Sourek, C.E.O.; Jan Oliva,* Secy.; Bob Chace,* Treas.; Bruce Firstenburg, Don Fuesler, M.D., JoMarie Hansen, Sue Keil, Jim Ladley, Dolorosa Margulis, Jim McClaskey, Art Miles, Jim Parsley, Russ Tennant.
EIN: 911246778
Codes: CM, FD

55350
The Paul G. Allen Charitable Foundation
505 5th Ave., South, Ste. 900
Seattle, WA 98104
E-mail: INFO@PGAFOUNDATIONS.com; URL:
http://www.paulallen.com/foundations
Contact: Jo Allen Patton, Exec. Dir.

Established in 1987 in WA.
Donor(s): Paul G. Allen.
Financial data (yr. ended 12/31/01): Grants paid, $25,767,321; assets, $6,087,256 (M); gifts received, $31,750,000; expenditures, $25,774,225; qualifying distributions, $25,766,581.
Limitations: Giving primarily in AK, ID, MT, OR, and WA.
Publications: Informational brochure (including application guidelines).
Application information: If applying for Social Change Initiative applicant may submit letter of inquiry at least 30 days before application deadline for review by program staff. Application form required.
Officers and Directors:* Paul G. Allen,* Pres.; Richard E. Leigh, Jr., V.P. and Secy.; Nathaniel T. Brown, V.P.; Jo Allen Patton,* V.P.; William D. Savoy, Treas.
EIN: 943082532
Codes: FD, FM

55351
M. J. Murdock Charitable Trust
703 Broadway, Ste. 710
Vancouver, WA 98660 (360) 694-8415
Mailing address: P.O. Box 1618, Vancouver, WA 98668; Tel.: (503) 285-4086; FAX: (360) 694-1819; URL: http://www.murdock-trust.org
Contact: Dr. John Van Zytveld, Sr. Prog. Dir.

Trust established in 1975 in WA.
Donor(s): Melvin Jack Murdock.‡
Financial data (yr. ended 12/31/01): Grants paid, $22,814,880; assets, $561,814,435 (M); expenditures, $46,116,843; qualifying distributions, $24,874,912.
Limitations: Giving primarily in the Pacific Northwest (AK, ID, MT, OR, and WA).
Publications: Annual report (including application guidelines), informational brochure (including application guidelines), application guidelines.
Application information: Application form required.
Officers and Trustees:* James R. Martin, C.F.O.; Julie D. Cieloha, Cont.; Neal O. Thorpe, Ph.D,* Exec. Dir.; John W. Castles, Lynwood W. Swanson, Ph.D.
EIN: 237456468
Codes: FD, FM

55352
Washington Mutual Foundation
(Formerly Washington Mutual Savings Bank Foundation)
999 3rd Ave., FIS2913
Seattle, WA 98104 (800) 258-0543
URL: http://www.wamu.com/foundation
Contact: Marc Frazer, Mgr.

Established in 1979 in WA.
Donor(s): Washington Mutual Bank.
Financial data (yr. ended 12/31/01): Grants paid, $16,698,408; assets, $25,792,633 (M); gifts received, $41,255,080; expenditures, $15,062,173; qualifying distributions, $14,452,173.
Limitations: Giving primarily in areas of company operations in CA, FL, ID, IL, MA, NY, NV, OR, TX, UT, and WA.
Publications: Annual report, grants list, corporate giving report, informational brochure (including application guidelines).
Application information: Application form not required.
Officers and Directors:* Kerry Killinger,* Pres.; Craig Davis, V.P.; Deanna Oppenheimer,* V.P.; Cheryl Di Re,* Secy.; Rob Miles, Treas.; Craig Chapman, Daryl David, Brad Davis, Bill Ehrlich, Robert Flowers, Steve Freimuth, Marc Kittner, J. Benson Porter.
EIN: 911070920
Codes: CS, FD, CD, FM

55353
Apex Foundation
P.O. Box 1607
Bellevue, WA 98009

Established in 1999 in WA.
Donor(s): Bruce R. McCaw, The McCaw Foundation.
Financial data (yr. ended 12/31/00): Grants paid, $13,929,500; assets, $114,622,153 (M); gifts received, $2,532,079; expenditures, $13,929,500; qualifying distributions, $13,598,189.
Limitations: Applications not accepted. Giving primarily in Seattle, WA.
Application information: Contributes only to pre-selected organizations.
Officers: Bruce R. McCaw, Pres.; Jolene M. McCaw, V.P.; Craig W. Stewart, V.P.; Charles E. Hill, Secy.-Treas.
EIN: 911950397
Codes: FD

55354
The Craig and Susan McCaw Foundation
P.O. Box 2908
Kirkland, WA 98083

Established in 1998 in WA.

55354—WASHINGTON

Donor(s): Craig O. McCaw.
Financial data (yr. ended 12/31/00): Grants paid, $11,817,686; assets, $22,525,138 (M); gifts received, $10,244,000; expenditures, $11,902,363; qualifying distributions, $11,816,204.
Limitations: Applications not accepted. Giving primarily in Seattle, WA.
Application information: Contributes only to pre-selected organizations.
Officers and Directors:* Craig O. McCaw, Pres.; Susan R. McCaw,* Secy.
EIN: 911943269
Codes: FD

55355
The Boeing Company Charitable Trust
c/o The Boeing Co.
P.O. Box 3707, M.S. 14-04
Seattle, WA 98124-2207 (206) 655-6679
FAX: (206) 655-2133
Contact: Linda Testa, Sr. Mgr.

Trust established in 1964 in WA as successor to the Boeing Airplane Company Charitable Trust, established in 1952.
Donor(s): The Boeing Co.
Financial data (yr. ended 12/31/00): Grants paid, $9,085,254; assets, $23,385,212 (M); expenditures, $9,219,497; qualifying distributions, $9,089,970.
Limitations: Giving generally limited to areas of company operations.
Publications: Corporate giving report, annual report (including application guidelines).
Application information: Correspondence should be sent to the Boeing Company Contributions Program.
Trustee: Bank of America.
EIN: 916056738
Codes: CS, FD, CD

55356
Weyerhaeuser Company Foundation
EC2-2A8
P.O. Box 9777
Federal Way, WA 98063-9777 (253) 924-3159
FAX: (253) 924-3658; E-mail: foundation@weyerhaeuser.com; URL: http://www.weyerhaeuser.com/citizenship/philanthropy/weyerfoundation.asp
Contact: Elizabeth Crossman, Pres.

Incorporated in 1948 in WA.
Donor(s): Weyerhaeuser Co.
Financial data (yr. ended 12/31/01): Grants paid, $7,364,733; assets, $23,528,514 (M); gifts received, $9,668,980; expenditures, $8,668,020; qualifying distributions, $7,883,931.
Limitations: Giving limited to areas of company operations, especially AL, AR, MS, NC, southeastern OK, western OR, and western WA (including Tacoma, Seattle, and Federal Way); giving to national organizations in fields related to the forest products industry.
Publications: Biennial report (including application guidelines).
Application information: Requests received in the fall may be considered for the following year's budget. The foundation will acknowledge inquiries as soon as possible (normally within 30 days). If further consideration is warranted, additional information or a formal proposal may be requested. Personal meetings or site visits are normally arranged only for projects that have passed initial screening. Application form not required.
Officers and Trustees:* Mack L. Hogans,* Chair.; Elizabeth Crossman, Pres.; Karen L. Veitenhans, V.P. and Secy.; Dick Taggart, Treas.; Steve Hillyard,

Cont.; William R. Corbin, Dan Fulton, C.B. Gaynor, R.E. Hanson, Steven R. Hill, James R. Keller, Susan M. Mersereau, Mick Onustock, Steven R. Rogel, William C. Stivers, George Weyerhaeuser, Jr.
EIN: 916024225
Codes: CS, FD, CD, FM

55357
The Stewardship Foundation
Tacoma Financial Ctr., Ste. 1500
1145 Broadway Plz.
Tacoma, WA 98402 (253) 620-1340
Application address: P.O. Box 1278, Tacoma, WA 98401; FAX: (253) 572-2721; E-mail: info@stewardshipfdn.org; URL: http://www.stewardshipfdn.org
Contact: Cary Paine, Exec. Dir.

Trust established in 1962 in WA.
Donor(s): C. Davis Weyerhaeuser Irrevocable Trust.
Financial data (yr. ended 12/31/01): Grants paid, $6,925,980; assets, $115,058,278 (M); expenditures, $8,506,817; qualifying distributions, $7,323,160.
Limitations: Giving internationally, nationally and in western WA, especially in Tacoma and Pierce County and the Puget Sound Region.
Publications: Application guidelines.
Application information: Application limited to once a year. Application form required.
Officers and Directors:* William T. Weyerhaeuser,* Chair.; Annette B. Weyerhaeuser, Vice-Chair. and Treas.; Cary Paine, Exec. Dir.; Charles L. Anderson, Wesley J. Anderson, Carl T. Fynboe, Donald W. Mowat.
EIN: 916020515
Codes: FD, FM

55358
The Paul G. Allen Forest Protection Foundation
110 110th Ave. NE, Ste. 550
Bellevue, WA 98004
E-mail: foundations@paulallen.com; URL: http://www.paulallen.com/foundations
Contact: Jo Allen Patton, Exec. Dir.

Established in 1997 in WA.
Donor(s): Paul G. Allen.
Financial data (yr. ended 12/31/00): Grants paid, $6,835,800; assets, $590,828 (M); gifts received, $2,141,007; expenditures, $6,845,606; qualifying distributions, $7,345,488; giving activities include $545,000 for program-related investments.
Limitations: Giving limited to the Pacific Northwest.
Publications: Biennial report (including application guidelines).
Application information: Application form required.
Officers and Directors:* Paul G. Allen,* Chair.; Bert E. Kolde, Pres.; Richard E. Leigh, Jr., V.P. and Secy.; Jo Allen Patton,* V.P. and Exec. Dir.; Nathaniel T. Brown, V.P.
EIN: 911764177
Codes: FD, FM

55359
Glaser Progress Foundation
(Formerly The Glaser Foundation)
P.O. Box 91123
Seattle, WA 98111 (206) 728-1050
FAX: (206) 728-1123; E-mail: grants@glaserprogress.org; URL: http://www.glaserprogress.org
Contact: Leslie McDonald, Operations Dir.

Established in 1993 in WA.
Donor(s): Robert D. Glaser.

Financial data (yr. ended 12/31/01): Grants paid, $5,506,301; assets, $35,667,155 (M); expenditures, $5,713,949; qualifying distributions, $5,799,466.
Limitations: Giving on a national and international basis.
Publications: Application guidelines.
Application information: Guidelines available on website. Application form not required.
Officers: Martin Collier, Exec. Dir.; Robert D. Glaser, Mgr.; Sarah Glaser, Mgr.
EIN: 911626010
Codes: FD

55360
Allen Foundation for the Arts
110 110th Ave. N.E., Ste. 550
Bellevue, WA 98004
E-mail: foundations@paulallen.com; URL: http://www.paulallen.com/foundations
Contact: Jo Allen Patton, Exec. Dir.

Established in 1987 in WA.
Donor(s): Paul G. Allen.
Financial data (yr. ended 12/31/00): Grants paid, $5,411,167; assets, $13,954,598 (M); expenditures, $5,431,317; qualifying distributions, $5,412,527.
Limitations: Giving primarily in AK, ID, MT, OR, and WA.
Publications: Biennial report (including application guidelines).
Application information: Application form required.
Officers and Directors:* Paul G. Allen,* Pres.; Faye G. Allen,* V.P.; Jo Allen Patton,* Treas. and Exec. Dir.
EIN: 943082529
Codes: FD, FM

55361
Sequoia Foundation
820 A St., Ste. 345
Tacoma, WA 98402 (253) 627-1634
Contact: Frank D. Underwood, Exec. Dir.

Established in 1982 in WA.
Donor(s): W. John Driscoll, C. Davis Weyerhaeuser,‡ F.T. Weyerhaeuser, William T. Weyerhaeuser.
Financial data (yr. ended 10/31/01): Grants paid, $5,347,699; assets, $34,070,793 (M); gifts received, $2,809,845; expenditures, $5,843,448; qualifying distributions, $5,445,937.
Limitations: Applications not accepted. Giving primarily in the Pacific Northwest.
Application information: The foundation solicits proposals at its sole discretion. Unsolicited proposals are not considered.
Officers and Directors:* William T. Weyerhaeuser,* Pres. and Treas.; Gail T. Weyerhaeuser,* V.P.; Nicholas C. Spika, Secy.; Frank D. Underwood, Exec. Dir.; Annette B. Weyerhaeuser.
EIN: 911178052
Codes: FD, FM

55362
The Russell Family Foundation
P.O. Box 2567
Gig Harbor, WA 98335 (253) 858-5050
Toll Free tel: (888) 252-4331; FAX: (253) 851-0460; E-mail: steph@trff.org; URL: http://www.trff.org
Contact: Stephanie Anderson, Grants Mgr.

Established in 1994 in WA.
Donor(s): George F. Russell, Jr., Jane T. Russell.‡
Financial data (yr. ended 12/31/01): Grants paid, $5,194,545; assets, $121,183,000 (M);

expenditures, $6,726,200; qualifying distributions, $5,963,680.
Limitations: Giving primarily in the Puget Sound region of WA.
Application information: No unsolicited education grants in 2002. Application form required.
Officers and Directors:* Sarah R. Cavanaugh,* Pres.; George F. Russell, Jr.,* V.P.; Dion R. Rurik,* 2nd V.P.; Eric A. Russell,* Treas.; Richard Woo, Exec. Dir.; Tim Cavanaugh, Jileen Russell, Richard F. Russell.
EIN: 911663336
Codes: FD, FM

55363
The Bullitt Foundation
1212 Minor Ave.
Seattle, WA 98101-2825 (206) 343-0807
FAX: (206) 343-0822; E-mail: info@bullitt.org;
URL: http://www.bullitt.org
Contact: Denis Hayes, Pres.

Incorporated in 1952 in WA.
Donor(s): Members of the Bullitt family.
Financial data (yr. ended 12/31/01): Grants paid, $5,050,597; assets, $102,977,853 (M); expenditures, $6,423,743; qualifying distributions, $6,214,990; giving activities include $420,000 for loans.
Limitations: Giving exclusively in the Pacific Northwest.
Publications: Annual report, application guidelines.
Application information: Applications sent by FAX or other electronic applications are discouraged. Application form required.
Officers and Trustees:* B. Gerald Johnson,* Chair.; Katherine M. Bullitt,* Vice-Chair.; Denis Hayes,* Pres.; David Buck, Secy.; Tomoko Moriguchi-Matsuno,* Treas.; Jennifer Belcher, Harriet Bullitt, Estella Leopold, Hubert G. Locke, Ph.D., James Youngren.
EIN: 916027795
Codes: FD, FM

55364
Michael and Asya Kogan Foundation, Inc.
c/o George William Moseley
6540 Ebb Tide Ln.
Freeland, WA 98249

Established in 1996 in DE and WA.
Donor(s): Asya Kogan.
Financial data (yr. ended 12/31/01): Grants paid, $5,000,000; assets, $261,211 (M); gifts received, $4,992,342; expenditures, $5,013,665; qualifying distributions, $4,999,867.
Limitations: Applications not accepted. Giving on an international basis.
Application information: Contributes only to pre-selected organizations.
Officers: Asya Kogan, Pres. and Treas.; George Moseley, V.P. and Secy.
EIN: 521966485
Codes: FD

55365
The Norcliffe Foundation
(Formerly The Norcliffe Fund)
First Interstate Ctr.
999 3rd Ave., Ste. 1006
Seattle, WA 98104 (206) 682-4820
Contact: Dana Pigott, Pres.

Incorporated in 1952 in WA.
Donor(s): Theiline M. McCone.‡
Financial data (yr. ended 11/30/01): Grants paid, $4,924,581; assets, $97,170,905 (M); gifts received, $956,025; expenditures, $4,694,018; qualifying distributions, $4,802,457.
Limitations: Giving in the Puget Sound region of WA, with emphasis on Seattle.
Publications: Program policy statement, application guidelines.
Application information: Application form not required.
Officers and Trustees:* Dana Pigott,* Pres.; Ann Pigott Wyckoff,* V.P.; Arline Hefferline, Secy. and Fdn. Mgr.; Theiline P. Scheumann,* Treas.; Lisa Anderson, Mary Ellen Hughes, Charles M. Pigott, James C. Pigott, Susan Pohl.
EIN: 916029352
Codes: FD, FM

55366
Samis Foundation
208 James St., Ste. C
Seattle, WA 98104 (206) 623-0615
FAX: (206) 622-4918; E-mail: samis@samis.com
Contact: Eddie Hasson, Chair.

Established in 1979.
Donor(s): Samuel Israel.
Financial data (yr. ended 06/30/00): Grants paid, $4,373,616; assets, $104,740,655 (M); expenditures, $10,992,592; qualifying distributions, $4,720,221.
Limitations: Giving primarily in WA for Jewish organizations; some giving also in Israel.
Publications: Application guidelines, grants list, informational brochure (including application guidelines).
Application information: Application form required.
Officers and Trustees:* Eddie I. Hasson,* Chair. and Pres.; Albert S. Maimon,* V.P.; Irwin Treiger,* Secy.; Victor D. Alhadeff, Eli J. Almo, Jerome O. Cohen, Barry D. Ernstoff, David Friedenberg, Eli Genauer, Rabbi William Greenberg, Mike Israel, Morris Piha, Lucy Pruzan, Martin Selig, Ernest Sherman, Alex Sytman.
EIN: 911641746
Codes: FD

55367
The Wilburforce Foundation
3601 Fremont Ave. N., Ste. 304
Seattle, WA 98103 (206) 632-2325
Additional tel.: (800) 201-0148 (Seattle office), (800) 317-8180 (Montana office); FAX: (206) 632-2326; E-mail: grants@wilburforce.org; URL: http://www.wilburforce.org
Contact: Timothy Greyhavens, Exec. Dir.

Established in 1990 in WA.
Financial data (yr. ended 12/31/00): Grants paid, $4,011,850; assets, $20,362,891 (M); expenditures, $4,642,661; qualifying distributions, $4,647,416.
Limitations: Giving primarily in AK, AZ, MT, NM, NV, OR, UT, WA, British Columbia, and Yellowstone to Yukon corridor of U.S.-Canada.
Application information: Application form required.
Officers and Directors:* Rosanna Letwin,* Chair.; James G. Letwin,* Pres.; Tim Greyhavens, Exec. Dir.; Gary Austin, William S. Holder, Stephanie Nichols-Young.
EIN: 943137894
Codes: FD, FM

55368
Ben B. Cheney Foundation
1201 Pacific Ave., Ste. 1600
Tacoma, WA 98402 (253) 572-2442
E-mail: info@benbcheneyfoundation.org; URL: http://www.benbcheneyfoundation.org
Contact: Brad Cheney, Exec. Dir.

Incorporated in 1955 in WA.
Donor(s): Ben B. Cheney,‡ Marian Cheney Olrogg.‡
Financial data (yr. ended 12/31/00): Grants paid, $3,976,172; assets, $86,734,337 (M); expenditures, $4,810,430; qualifying distributions, $4,302,952.
Limitations: Giving limited to portions of Del Norte, Humboldt, Lassen, Shasta, Siskiyou, and Trinity counties in CA, southwest OR, particularly in the Medford area, Tacoma and Pierce County, and southwestern WA.
Publications: Informational brochure (including application guidelines).
Application information: Application deadline and final notification provided with application; may take six to nine months from the time a query letter arrives to the board's review of grant proposal. Application form required.
Officers and Directors:* Bradbury F. Cheney,* Pres.; Elgin E. Olrogg,* V.P.; John F. Hansler,* Secy.; Piper Cheney,* Treas.; Brad Cheney, Exec. Dir.; R. Gene Grant, Allan L. Undem.
EIN: 916053760
Codes: FD, FM

55369
E. K. and Lillian F. Bishop Foundation
c/o Bank of America
701 5th Ave., 47th Fl.
Seattle, WA 98104 (206) 358-0806
FAX: (520) 749-2990
Scholarship application address: Bishop Scholarship Comm., c/o Bank of America, Aberdeen Branch, P.O. Box 128, Aberdeen, WA 98520
Contact: Thomas J. Nevers, Grant Mgr.

Trust established in 1971 in WA.
Donor(s): E.K. Bishop,‡ Lillian F. Bishop.‡
Financial data (yr. ended 04/30/01): Grants paid, $3,963,917; assets, $24,298,929 (M); expenditures, $4,178,984; qualifying distributions, $4,019,927.
Limitations: Giving limited to WA, with emphasis on Grays Harbor County; scholarship applicants must be Grays Harbor County residents entering their 3rd year of college or beyond.
Publications: Program policy statement, application guidelines, informational brochure (including application guidelines).
Application information: Application form provided for scholarships. Telephone calls for scholarships not considered. Application form required.
Officer: Tom Nevers, Grant Mgr.
Directors: Isabelle Lamb, Jim Mason, Janet T. Skadon, Kate Webster.
Trustee Bank: Bank of America.
EIN: 916116724
Codes: FD, GTI

55370
PACCAR Foundation
c/o PACCAR Inc.
P.O. Box 1518
Bellevue, WA 98009 (425) 455-7400
Contact: Norm Proctor

Incorporated in 1951 in WA.
Donor(s): PACCAR Inc.

55370—WASHINGTON

Financial data (yr. ended 12/31/00): Grants paid, $3,586,245; assets, $14,596,432 (M); gifts received, $4,000,000; expenditures, $3,632,530; qualifying distributions, $3,612,530.
Limitations: Giving primarily in areas of company operations, with emphasis on King County, WA.
Application information: The foundation does not acknowledge receipt of proposals or grant interviews with applicants. Application form not required.
Officers and Directors:* Charles M. Pigott,* Pres.; Mark C. Pigott,* V.P.; Janice M. D'Amato,* Secy.-Treas.; William G. Reed, Jr.
EIN: 916030638
Codes: CS, FD, CD, FM

55371
The LJCP Foundation
(Formerly The LJC Foundation)
P.O. Box 21749
Seattle, WA 98111-3749 (425) 828-1815
Contact: Stanley B. McCammon, V.P. and Secy.

Established in 1993.
Donor(s): John E. McCaw, Jr., Donna McCaslin, Bruce R. McCaw.
Financial data (yr. ended 10/31/01): Grants paid, $3,161,431; assets, $182,324 (M); gifts received, $1,809,049; expenditures, $3,163,977; qualifying distributions, $3,151,986.
Limitations: Applications not accepted. Giving primarily in Atlanta, GA, New York, NY, and Seattle, WA.
Application information: Contributes only to pre-selected organizations.
Officers: John E. McCaw, Jr., Pres. and Treas.; Stanley B. McCammon, V.P. and Secy.
EIN: 953192332
Codes: FD

55372
Paul G. Allen Foundation for Medical Research
505 5th Ave., S., Ste. 900
Seattle, WA 98104
E-mail: foundations@paulallen.com; URL: http://www.paulallen.com/foundations
Contact: Jo Allen Patton, Exec. Dir.

Established in 1987 in WA; funded in 1989.
Donor(s): Paul G. Allen.
Financial data (yr. ended 12/31/00): Grants paid, $2,673,478; assets, $27,082,356 (M); expenditures, $2,706,300; qualifying distributions, $2,675,050.
Limitations: Giving on a national basis.
Publications: Informational brochure (including application guidelines).
Application information: The foundation is currently not accepting applications. Application form required.
Officers and Directors:* Paul G. Allen,* Pres.; Richard E. Leigh, Jr., V.P. and Secy.; Jo Allen Patton,* V.P. and Exec. Dir.; Nathaniel T. Brown, V.P.; William D. Savoy, Treas.
EIN: 943082530
Codes: FD

55373
Neukom Family Foundation
2120 Waverly Way E.
Seattle, WA 98112

Established in 1998 in WA.
Donor(s): William H. Neukom.
Financial data (yr. ended 03/31/01): Grants paid, $2,652,808; assets, $33,142,963 (M); gifts received, $1,301,347; expenditures, $2,656,955; qualifying distributions, $2,654,208.
Limitations: Applications not accepted.

Application information: Contributes only to pre-selected organizations.
Directors: Gillian Neukom, John McMakin Neukom, Josselyn Neukom, Samantha Neukom, William H. Neukom.
EIN: 911737888
Codes: FD

55374
The Brainerd Foundation
1601 2nd Ave., Ste. 610
Seattle, WA 98101 (206) 448-0676
FAX: (206) 448-7222; E-mail: info@brainerd.org; URL: http://www.brainerd.org
Contact: Ann Krumboltz, Exec. Dir.

Established in 1995 in WA.
Donor(s): Paul Brainerd.
Financial data (yr. ended 12/31/01): Grants paid, $2,515,516; assets, $41,398,000 (M); expenditures, $3,556,648; qualifying distributions, $3,556,648.
Limitations: Giving primarily in AK, ID, MT, OR, WA, and British Columbia and the Yukon territory.
Publications: Annual report (including application guidelines), financial statement, grants list.
Application information: Proposals are accepted by invitation only. Application form required.
Officers and Directors:* Paul Brainerd,* Pres. and Treas.; Sherry Brainerd,* V.P. and Secy.; Ann Krumboltz, V.P. and Exec. Dir., Comm. and Capacity Building.
EIN: 911675591
Codes: FD

55375
The Laurel Foundation
P.O. Box 77630
Seattle, WA 98177-0630
Contact: Jennifer D. Hannibal, Fdn. Admin.

Established in 1995 in WA.
Donor(s): Julia Calhoun.
Financial data (yr. ended 12/31/00): Grants paid, $2,501,292; assets, $21,815,679 (M); gifts received, $24,296,875; expenditures, $2,512,425; qualifying distributions, $2,503,476.
Limitations: Applications not accepted. Giving primarily in WA.
Application information: Contributes only to pre-selected organizations.
Officers: Julia Calhoun, Pres.; Christopher Larson, V.P.; Larry Bailey, Secy.
EIN: 911689238
Codes: FD, FM

55376
Medina Foundation
1300 Norton Bldg.
801 2nd Ave., 13th Fl.
Seattle, WA 98104 (206) 464-5231
URL: http://www.medinafoundation.org
Contact: Gregory P. Barlow, Exec. Dir.

Incorporated in 1948 in WA.
Financial data (yr. ended 12/31/99): Grants paid, $2,428,508; assets, $95,272,345 (M); expenditures, $3,366,551; qualifying distributions, $2,932,646.
Limitations: Giving limited to the greater Puget Sound, WA, area, with emphasis on Seattle.
Publications: Informational brochure, program policy statement, application guidelines.
Application information: Application form required.
Officers and Trustees:* Marion Hand,* Pres.; Davis O. Clapp,* V.P.; Rosalyn Owen, Secy.; Elizabeth Williams, Treas.; Gregory P. Barlow, Exec. Dir.; Samuel H. Brown, Jacqueline Clapp, James N. Clapp II, Kristina H. Clapp, Margaret

Clapp, Matthew N. Clapp, Jr., Tamsin Clapp, Gail Gant, Patricia Henry, Gary MacLeod, Anne Simons.
EIN: 910745225
Codes: FD

55377
Forest Foundation
820 A St., Ste. 345
Tacoma, WA 98402 (253) 627-1634
Contact: Frank D. Underwood, Exec. Dir.

Incorporated in 1962 in WA.
Donor(s): C. Davis Weyerhaeuser,‡ William T. Weyerhaeuser.
Financial data (yr. ended 10/31/01): Grants paid, $2,305,513; assets, $29,251,996 (M); expenditures, $2,834,215; qualifying distributions, $2,441,801.
Limitations: Giving primarily in southwestern WA, with emphasis on Pierce County. Grants given outside Pierce County are for capital projects only.
Publications: Application guidelines.
Application information: Application form required.
Officers and Directors:* Gail T. Weyerhaeuser,* Pres. and Treas.; Annette B. Weyerhaeuser,* V.P.; Nicholas C. Spika, Secy.; Frank D. Underwood, Exec. Dir.; William T. Weyerhaeuser.
EIN: 916020514
Codes: FD

55378
Washington Research Foundation
2815 Eastlake Ave., E., Ste. 300
Seattle, WA 98102 (206) 336-5600
FAX: (206) 336-5615; E-mail: amccormi@wrfseattle.org; URL: http://www.wrfseattle.org
Contact: Amy McCormick, Office Mgr.

Established in 1981 in WA.
Financial data (yr. ended 06/30/01): Grants paid, $2,009,900; assets, $49,463,330 (M); expenditures, $16,278,533; qualifying distributions, $2,535,259.
Limitations: Applications not accepted. Giving limited to research institutions in WA.
Publications: Annual report, informational brochure.
Application information: Contributes only to pre-selected organizations.
Officers and Directors:* Thomas J. Cable,* Chair.; Ronald S. Howell,* Pres.; C. Kent Carlson, Secy.; Paul Bialek, Barry Forman, Chuck Hirsch, Calvert Knudsen, W. Hunter Simpson, George I. Thomas, M.D.
EIN: 911160492
Codes: FD

55379
Foundation Northwest
(Formerly Spokane Inland Northwest Community Foundation)
Old City Hall
221 N. Wall St., Ste. 624
Spokane, WA 99201-0826 (509) 624-2606
FAX: (509) 624-2608; E-mail: info@foundationnw.org
Contact: C. Hanford, V.P.

Incorporated in 1974 in WA.
Financial data (yr. ended 06/30/02): Grants paid, $2,000,000; assets, $30,000,000 (M); expenditures, $585,554.
Limitations: Giving limited to the Inland Northwest: Benewah, Bonner, Boundary, Clearwater, Idaho, Kootenai, Latah, Lewis, Nez Perce, and Shoshone counties, ID, and Adams, Asotin, Columbia, Ferry, Garfield, Lincoln, Pend

Orielle, Spokane, Stevens, and Whitman counties, WA.
Publications: Annual report, biennial report, informational brochure (including application guidelines), newsletter, application guidelines.
Application information: Scholarship awards paid to educational institutions. Application form required.
Officers and Directors:* Bonnie Morrow, Chair.; Peter A. Jackson, Ph.D.,* Pres. and C.E.O.; Candy Hanford,* V.P.; and 10 additional directors.
EIN: 910941053
Codes: CM, FD

55380
The Foster Foundation
1929 43rd Ave.
Seattle, WA 98112
Contact: Jill Goodsell, Admin.

Established in 1984 in WA.
Donor(s): Evelyn W. Foster.
Financial data (yr. ended 12/31/00): Grants paid, $1,924,500; assets, $39,449,795 (M); expenditures, $2,060,109; qualifying distributions, $1,950,106.
Limitations: Giving primarily in the Pacific Northwest.
Officers and Trustees:* Michael G. Foster, Jr.,* Dir.; Jill Goodsell,* Admin.; Evelyn W. Foster, Michael G. Foster, Sr., Thomas B. Foster.
EIN: 911265474
Codes: FD

55381
Nesholm Family Foundation
P.O. Box 34345
Seattle, WA 98124-1345
Contact: Dian Kallmer

Established in 1987 in WA.
Donor(s): Elmer J. Nesholm.‡
Financial data (yr. ended 12/31/00): Grants paid, $1,789,680; assets, $67,357,029 (M); expenditures, $2,214,099; qualifying distributions, $1,993,297.
Limitations: Giving limited to Seattle, WA.
Publications: Program policy statement, application guidelines.
Application information: Application form required.
Officer and Directors:* Laurel Nesholm,* Exec. Dir.; Joseph M. Gaffney, Edgar K. Marcuse, M.D., John F. Nesholm.
Agent: Bank of America.
EIN: 943055422
Codes: FD

55382
The Jon and Mary Shirley Foundation
c/o Lawrence B. Bailey
701 5th Ave., No. 5000
Seattle, WA 98104-7078

Established in 1992 in WA.
Donor(s): Jon A. Shirley, E. Mary Shirley.
Financial data (yr. ended 09/30/01): Grants paid, $1,778,556; assets, $44,272,111 (M); gifts received, $22,995,631; expenditures, $2,187,377; qualifying distributions, $1,782,693.
Limitations: Applications not accepted. Giving primarily in WA.
Application information: Contributes only to pre-selected organizations.
Directors: E. Mary Shirley, Jon A. Shirley.
EIN: 943163120
Codes: FD

55383
Gottfried & Mary Fuchs Foundation
c/o Union Bank of California, N.A.
P.O. Box 84495
Seattle, WA 98124-5795 (253) 591-2082
Application address: 1011 Pacific Ave., Tacoma, WA 98402
Contact: Gayleene Berry

Trust established in 1960 in WA.
Donor(s): Gottfried Fuchs,‡ Mary Fuchs.‡
Financial data (yr. ended 12/31/00): Grants paid, $1,632,237; assets, $25,992,736 (M); expenditures, $1,798,212; qualifying distributions, $1,677,646.
Limitations: Giving limited to Pierce County, WA.
Publications: Application guidelines.
Application information: Applications from outside the Pierce county, WA area not accepted. Application form required.
Trustee: Union Bank of California, N.A.
EIN: 916022284
Codes: FD

55384
The Greater Tacoma Community Foundation
P.O. Box 1995
Tacoma, WA 98401-1995 (253) 383-5622
FAX: (253) 272-8099; *E-mail:* margy@gtcf.org; *URL:* http://www.tacomafoundation.org
Contact: Margy McGroarty, Pres.

Incorporated in 1977 in WA.
Financial data (yr. ended 06/30/01): Grants paid, $1,508,346; assets, $48,000 (M); gifts received, $6,444,370; expenditures, $17,172,029; giving activities include $23,464 for loans.
Limitations: Giving limited to Pierce County, WA.
Publications: Annual report, informational brochure (including application guidelines), newsletter, application guidelines.
Application information: Application form available on website. Application form required.
Officers and Directors:* Sally B. Leighton, Chair.; Tom Hosea,* Vice-Chair.; Margy McGroarty, Pres.; Gregory M. Tanbara,* Secy.; James P. Dawson,* Treas.; James Brown, Piper Cheney, Dick DeVine, Andrea S. Gernon, John Larsen, Barbara Skinner, Terry Stone, Pamela Transue, Michael Tucci, James Walton.
EIN: 911007459
Codes: CM, FD

55385
Sherwood Trust
P.O. Box 1855
Walla Walla, WA 99362 (509) 529-3362
Contact: George M. Edwards, Pres.

Established in 1991 in WA.
Donor(s): Donald Sherwood.
Financial data (yr. ended 12/31/00): Grants paid, $1,473,513; assets, $31,146,329 (M); expenditures, $1,772,418; qualifying distributions, $1,476,577.
Limitations: Giving limited to the Walla Walla, WA, area.
Application information: Application form not required.
Officers: James F. Aylward, Chair.; George M. Edwards, Pres.; L.W. Cummins, V.P.; Leona M. Clarno, Secy.-Treas.
Director: R.R. Reid.
EIN: 916337526
Codes: FD

55386
Wissner-Slivka Foundation
P.O. Box 3904
Bellevue, WA 98009-3904

Established in 1997 in WA.
Donor(s): Benjamin W. Slivka, Lisa Wissner-Slivka, Stella Wissner.
Financial data (yr. ended 12/31/00): Grants paid, $1,438,984; assets, $9,429,516 (M); expenditures, $1,509,630; qualifying distributions, $1,411,312.
Limitations: Applications not accepted. Giving on a national basis.
Application information: Contributes only to pre-selected organizations.
Trustees: Benjamin W. Slivka, Lisa Wissner-Slivka.
EIN: 916458451
Codes: FD

55387
The Compass Foundation, Inc.
711 Broadway E., No. 9
Seattle, WA 98102-4680

Established in 2000 in DE.
Donor(s): Stig Leschly.
Financial data (yr. ended 12/31/00): Grants paid, $1,411,625; assets, $160,346 (M); gifts received, $1,528,255; expenditures, $1,420,585; qualifying distributions, $1,418,996.
Limitations: Giving primarily in NJ; funding also in Boston, MA, and Seattle, WA.
Officers: Stig Leschly, Pres. and Secy.-Treas.; Sherry Riva, V.P.
EIN: 061581996
Codes: FD

55388
Crystal Springs Foundation
c/o Ahrens & DeAngelli
1001 4th Ave., Ste. 4333
Seattle, WA 98154-1142

Established in 1999 in WA.
Donor(s): Michael R. Murray, Joyce B. Murray.
Financial data (yr. ended 12/31/00): Grants paid, $1,400,632; assets, $44,556,150 (M); expenditures, $1,552,390; qualifying distributions, $1,416,170.
Limitations: Applications not accepted.
Application information: Contributes only to pre-selected organizations.
Officers and Directors:* Michael R. Murray,* Pres. and Treas.; Joyce B. Murray,* V.P. and Secy.
EIN: 912008832
Codes: FD

55389
Harder Foundation
401 Broadway
Tacoma, WA 98402 (253) 593-2121
Contact: Del Langbauer, Pres.

Incorporated in 1955 in MI.
Donor(s): Delmar S. Harder.‡
Financial data (yr. ended 12/31/00): Grants paid, $1,370,000; assets, $31,421,878 (M); gifts received, $202,500; expenditures, $2,009,616; qualifying distributions, $1,449,421.
Limitations: Giving limited to AK, CO, FL, ID, MT, NV, OR, UT, WA, and WY.
Publications: Annual report, application guidelines.
Application information: Proposals from LA and the Great Lake states not presently considered. Proposals from FL accepted by invitation only. Application form not required.
Officers and Trustees:* Del Langbauer,* Pres.; Robert Langbauer,* V.P.; Jay A. Herbst,* Secy.; John Driggers, William H. Langbauer.
EIN: 386048242

55389—WASHINGTON

Codes: FD

55390
Kaleidoscope Foundation
c/o Richard Leeds
1075 Bellevue Way, N.E., Ste. 366
Bellevue, WA 98004

Established in 1997 in WA.
Donor(s): Gerard Leeds, Liselotte Leeds, Richard Leeds.
Financial data (yr. ended 11/30/00): Grants paid, $1,358,200; assets, $20,734,784 (M); expenditures, $1,475,620; qualifying distributions, $1,425,673.
Limitations: Applications not accepted.
Application information: Unsolicited requests for funds not accepted.
Officers: Anne F. Kroeker, Co-Pres.; Richard Leeds, Co-Pres.; Robert H. Blais, Secy.
EIN: 911874926
Codes: FD

55391
The Hugh and Jane Ferguson Foundation
777 108th Ave. N.E., Ste. 1570
Bellevue, WA 98004 (206) 781-3472
E-mail: OgleFounds@aol.com; URL: http://fdncenter.org/grantmaker/ferguson
Contact: Hugh S. Ferguson

Established in 1986 in WA.
Donor(s): Hugh S. Ferguson, Jane Avery Ferguson.‡
Financial data (yr. ended 09/30/01): Grants paid, $1,295,800; assets, $2,364,494 (M); gifts received, $705,030; expenditures, $1,400,451; qualifying distributions, $1,323,425.
Limitations: Giving primarily in AK, ID, MT, OR, and WA, with emphasis on WA.
Publications: Grants list, application guidelines.
Application information: Application form not required.
Officers and Directors:* Hugh S. Ferguson,* Pres.; Ellen Lee Ferguson,* Secy.; Jane Avery Ferguson.
EIN: 911357603
Codes: FD

55392
Discuren Charitable Foundation
c/o Perkins Coie
1201 3rd Ave., 40th Fl.
Seattle, WA 98101-3099 (425) 828-3737
E-mail: gcoy@isomedia.com
Contact: F. Jean Watson, Admin. Asst.

Established in 1983 in WA.
Financial data (yr. ended 10/31/01): Grants paid, $1,265,274; assets, $1,527,336 (M); expenditures, $1,359,117; qualifying distributions, $1,349,018.
Limitations: Giving primarily in WA.
Publications: Informational brochure (including application guidelines), grants list, occasional report.
Application information: Application form required.
Trustee: Bank of America.
EIN: 916249597
Codes: FD

55393
Joshua Green Foundation, Inc.
P.O. Box 21829
Seattle, WA 98111-3829 (206) 622-2809
Contact: Margaret Fischer, Secy.

Trust established in 1956 in WA.
Donor(s): Joshua Green,‡ Mrs. Joshua Green.‡
Financial data (yr. ended 12/31/00): Grants paid, $1,226,326; assets, $19,780,102 (M); expenditures, $1,244,745; qualifying distributions, $1,226,326.
Limitations: Giving primarily in the King County, WA, area.
Publications: Application guidelines.
Application information: Application form required.
Officers and Trustees:* Joshua Green III,* Pres.; Charles P. Burnett III,* V.P.; Margaret Fischer, Secy.; Steven E. Carlson, Treas.; Charles E. Riley.
EIN: 916050748
Codes: FD

55394
Charlotte Y. Martin Foundation
c/o Bank of America
P.O. Box 34345
Seattle, WA 98124-1345 (206) 365-7892
Application address: 701 5th Ave., Ste. 4700, Seattle, WA 98104-7001; E-mail: info@charlottemartin.org; URL: http://www.charlottemartin.org
Contact: Andrea Grosso, V.P.

Established in 1988 in WA.
Donor(s): Charlotte Y. Martin.‡
Financial data (yr. ended 03/31/01): Grants paid, $1,204,165; assets, $24,402,115 (M); gifts received, $250; expenditures, $1,390,830; qualifying distributions, $1,285,454.
Limitations: Giving primarily in the Pacific Northwest.
Publications: Program policy statement, application guidelines.
Application information: Application information available on website. Application form not required.
Managers: Joan Gagliardi, Peter Galloway, Karl D. Guelich, Sheila Kelly, Kermit Rudolf.
Trustee: Bank of America.
EIN: 916294504
Codes: FD

55395
Blakemore Foundation
1201 3rd Ave., Ste. 4800
Seattle, WA 98101-3266 (206) 583-8778
FAX: (206) 583-8500; E-mail: blakemore@perkinscoie.com; URL: http://www.blakemorefoundation.org
Contact: Griffith Way, Tr.

Established in 1990 in WA.
Donor(s): Thomas L. Blakemore,‡ Frances L. Blakemore.‡
Financial data (yr. ended 12/31/01): Grants paid, $1,173,935; assets, $13,734,196 (M); gifts received, $511,814; expenditures, $1,396,969; qualifying distributions, $1,212,704.
Limitations: Giving limited to U.S. organizations for art grants; giving limited to U.S. citizens or permanent residents for language grants.
Application information: Application form required for language grants to individuals. No application form required for art grants.
Board Members: Dan Alexander, Marie C. Anchordoguy, Richard Barnhart, William Franklin, R. Kent Guy, Donald R. Marsh, Michiyo Morioka, Griffith Way.
EIN: 911505735
Codes: FD, GTI

55396
The Oki Foundation
(Formerly The Oki Charitable Foundation)
1416 112th Ave. N.E.
Bellevue, WA 98004 (425) 454-2800
FAX: (425) 455-3828
Contact: Laurie Oki, Pres.

Established in 1988 in WA.
Donor(s): Laurie Oki, Scott Oki.
Financial data (yr. ended 12/31/01): Grants paid, $1,139,107; assets, $58,014 (M); gifts received, $1,178,753; expenditures, $1,169,276; qualifying distributions, $1,156,428.
Limitations: Applications not accepted. Giving limited to King County, WA.
Application information: Unsolicited requests for funds not accepted.
Officers: Laurie Oki, Pres. and Treas.; Scott Oki, V.P. and Secy.
EIN: 911394156
Codes: FD

55397
James B. Pendleton Charitable Trust
P.O. Box 50005
Bellevue, WA 98015-0005
FAX: (425) 637-0272
Contact: David E. Ellison, Tr.

Established in 1992 in CA.
Donor(s): James B. Pendleton.‡
Financial data (yr. ended 12/31/01): Grants paid, $1,103,180; assets, $26,067,745 (M); expenditures, $1,589,621; qualifying distributions, $1,232,306.
Limitations: Giving on a national basis, with preference for the western United States.
Application information: Application form not required.
Trustee: David E. Ellison.
EIN: 956944277
Codes: FD

55398
Islands Fund
900 4th Ave., Ste. 2925
Seattle, WA 98164-1009

Established in 1995.
Donor(s): Sarah R. Werner.
Financial data (yr. ended 12/31/01): Grants paid, $1,070,000; assets, $19,036,257 (M); expenditures, $1,092,230; qualifying distributions, $1,063,754.
Limitations: Applications not accepted.
Application information: Contributes only to pre-selected organizations.
Directors: E. Leeds Gulick, George G. Gulick, John Munn, Rick S. Werner, Sarah R. Werner.
EIN: 911663838
Codes: FD

55399
New Horizon Foundation
820 A St., Ste. 345
Tacoma, WA 98402-5221 (253) 627-1634
Contact: Frank D. Underwood, Pres.

Established in 1983 in WA.
Donor(s): Sequoia Foundation.
Financial data (yr. ended 10/31/01): Grants paid, $1,062,082; assets, $334,885 (M); gifts received, $1,585,000; expenditures, $1,275,223; qualifying distributions, $1,275,223.
Limitations: Giving primarily in Pierce County, WA.
Publications: Application guidelines.
Application information: Proposal must include grant request summary sheet which the foundation distributes in its guidelines, and

statement of fiscal responsibility; only organizations located in Pierce County, WA, considered. Application form required.
Officers and Directors:* Frank D. Underwood,* Pres. and Treas.; John F. Sherwood,* V.P. and Secy.; Elvin J. Vandeberg.
EIN: 911228957
Codes: FD

55400
Winifred L. Stevens Foundation
c/o John V. Stevens, Sr.
1184 Schwartz Rd.
Nordland, WA 98358

Established in 1996 in CA.
Donor(s): Linda S. Spady.
Financial data (yr. ended 12/31/00): Grants paid, $1,050,100; assets, $18,020,156 (M); gifts received, $294,784; expenditures, $1,065,801; qualifying distributions, $1,035,563.
Limitations: Applications not accepted. Giving primarily in CA.
Application information: Contributes only to pre-selected organizations.
Officers and Directors:* John V. Stevens, Sr.,* Pres.; Linda S. Spady,* V.P.; John V. Stevens, Jr.,* Secy.
EIN: 954505998
Codes: FD

55401
Horizons Foundation
4020 E. Madison St., Ste. 322
Seattle, WA 98112 (206) 323-8061
E-mail: rhadac@aol.com
Contact: Ralph R. Hadac, Exec. Dir.

Established in 1990 in WA as partial successor to the McAshan Foundation, Inc.
Donor(s): The McAshan Foundation, Inc.
Financial data (yr. ended 12/31/01): Grants paid, $1,040,450; assets, $21,992,832 (M); expenditures, $1,151,341; qualifying distributions, $1,103,000.
Limitations: Giving primarily in WA.
Publications: Program policy statement, application guidelines.
Application information: Full proposal required if foundation accepts synopsis. Application form required.
Officers and Directors:* Lucy J. Hadac,* Pres.; Jerald Forster,* V.P.; Stephen Hadac,* Secy.; Ralph R. Hadac,* Treas. and Exec. Dir.
EIN: 911493424
Codes: FD

55402
Anderson Foundation
P.O. Box 24304
Seattle, WA 98124
Contact: Barbara A. Lawrence, Secy.-Treas.

Established in 1952.
Donor(s): Charles M. Anderson, Dorothy I. Anderson, William Anderson, Barbara A. Lawrence.
Financial data (yr. ended 06/30/01): Grants paid, $1,013,000; assets, $18,672,713 (M); gifts received, $15,000; expenditures, $1,159,882; qualifying distributions, $1,013,000.
Limitations: Applications not accepted. Giving primarily in WA, with emphasis on Seattle.
Application information: Unsolicited requests for funds not accepted.
Officers: Charles M. Anderson, Pres.; Helen Anderson, V.P.; Barbara A. Lawrence, Secy.-Treas.
Trustee: William Anderson.
EIN: 916031724
Codes: FD

55403
Ginger and Barry Ackerley Foundation
1301 5th Ave., Ste. 4000
Seattle, WA 98101-2634 (206) 624-2888
FAX: (206) 623-7853; E-mail: kcleworth@ackerley.com
Contact: Kimberly Cleworth, Exec. Dir.

Established in 1997 in WA.
Donor(s): Barry A. Ackerley, Gail A. Ackerley.
Financial data (yr. ended 12/31/01): Grants paid, $900,000; assets, $5,596,787 (M); expenditures, $1,001,714; qualifying distributions, $100,340.
Limitations: Giving primarily in the western WA.
Publications: Grants list, informational brochure (including application guidelines).
Application information: Application form required.
Officers: Kim Cleworth, Pres. and Exec. Dir.; Christopher Ackerley, V.P.; Edward Ackerley, V.P.
Directors: Barry A. Ackerley, Gail A. Ackerley.
EIN: 911800463
Codes: FD

55404
Benaroya Foundation
1001 4th Ave. Plz., Ste. 4700
Seattle, WA 98154
Contact: Jack A. Benaroya, Pres.

Established in 1984 in WA.
Donor(s): Jack A. Benaroya, Larry R. Benaroya.
Financial data (yr. ended 11/30/01): Grants paid, $900,000; assets, $11,058,875 (M); expenditures, $915,482; qualifying distributions, $900,000.
Limitations: Giving primarily in Seattle, WA.
Officers: Jack A. Benaroya, Pres.; Donna R. Benaroya, V.P.; Renee J. Naness, Secy.-Treas.
Directors: Alan G. Benaroya, Larry R. Benaroya, Rebecca B. Benaroya, Sherry-Lee Benaroya.
EIN: 911280516
Codes: FD

55405
Kongsgaard-Goldman Foundation
1932 1st Ave., Ste. 602
Seattle, WA 98101 (206) 448-1874
FAX: (206) 448-1973; E-mail: kgf@kongsgaard-goldman.org; URL: http://www.kongsgaard-goldman.org
Contact: Martha Kongsgaard, Pres.

Established in 1988 in WA.
Donor(s): Peter Goldman, Martha Kongsgaard.
Financial data (yr. ended 12/31/01): Grants paid, $885,698; assets, $86,291 (M); gifts received, $1,002,142; expenditures, $985,902; qualifying distributions, $981,701.
Limitations: Giving limited to AK, ID, MT, OR, and WA, with emphasis on Missoula, MT, Portland, OR, and Seattle, WA; giving also in British Columbia, Canada.
Publications: Informational brochure (including application guidelines).
Application information: Application form not required.
Officers and Directors:* Martha Kongsgaard,* Pres.; Peter Goldman,* V.P.
EIN: 943088217
Codes: FD

55406
444S Foundation
(also known as 444 Sierra Foundation)
P.O. Box 1128
Bellevue, WA 98008-1128
Contact: Peggy Ford, Fdn. Admin.

Established in 1998 in WA.
Donor(s): G. James Roush.
Financial data (yr. ended 12/31/01): Grants paid, $875,000; assets, $19,088,080 (M); expenditures, $1,001,322; qualifying distributions, $875,000.
Limitations: Applications not accepted. Giving primarily in the Pacific Northwest, including Western Canada.
Application information: Contributes only to pre-selected organizations. Foundation will solicit proposals. Unsolicited requests for funds not accepted.
Trustees: Del Langbauer, G. James Roush, William Morgan Roush, Cynthia Wayburn.
EIN: 916468421
Codes: FD

55407
Wadsworth Foundation
c/o Dawn Vinberg
1511 3rd Ave.
Seattle, WA 98101 (206) 749-5570

Established in 2001 in WA.
Donor(s): James Letwin.
Financial data (yr. ended 12/31/01): Grants paid, $852,500; assets, $127,157 (M); gifts received, $1,123,000; expenditures, $995,843; qualifying distributions, $995,843.
Officers and Directors:* James Letwin,* Pres. and Treas.; William Mathers, V.P. and Secy.
EIN: 912107331

55408
Leonard X. Bosack & Bette M. Kruger Foundation
8422 154th Ave., N.E.
Redmond, WA 98052-3800
Contact: Exec. Dir.

Established in 1990 in CA.
Donor(s): Leonard X. Bosack,‡ Sandra K. Lerner, Leonard Bosack.
Financial data (yr. ended 12/31/00): Grants paid, $836,748; assets, $33,750,353 (M); gifts received, $112,308; expenditures, $7,515,373; qualifying distributions, $3,153,508; giving activities include $607,487 for programs.
Limitations: Applications not accepted.
Publications: Informational brochure.
Application information: Contributes only to pre-selected organizations.
Officers and Directors:* Sandra K. Lerner,* Chair. and Pres.; Leonard Bosack,* V.P. and Secy.
EIN: 943128478
Codes: FD

55409
Satterberg Foundation
1932 1st Ave., No. 810
Seattle, WA 98101 (206) 441-3045
Contact: Peter F. Helsell, Treas.

Established in 1990 in WA.
Donor(s): Virginia S. Helsell, Judy P. Swenson, William A. Helsell.
Financial data (yr. ended 12/31/00): Grants paid, $779,437; assets, $4,363,828 (M); expenditures, $859,554; qualifying distributions, $793,762.
Limitations: Giving primarily in WA.
Application information: Application guidelines may be obtained by writing to the foundation. Application form required.
Officers and Directors:* Mary Pigott,* Pres.; Judy P. Swenson,* V.P.; Frank P. Helsell,* Secy.; Peter F. Helsell,* Treas.; Katherine Lazarus, Michael J. Pigott.
EIN: 911501066
Codes: FD

55410—WASHINGTON

55410
Frost and Margaret Snyder Foundation
c/o KeyBank, N.A., Trust Div.
P.O. Box 11500, M.S. WA 31-01-0310
Tacoma, WA 98411-5052 (253) 305-7203
Contact: Michael W. Steadman, Trust Off., KeyBank, N.A.

Trust established in 1957 in WA.
Donor(s): Frost Snyder,‡ Margaret Snyder.‡
Financial data (yr. ended 12/31/01): Grants paid, $751,250; assets, $12,712,077 (M); expenditures, $846,533; qualifying distributions, $768,073.
Limitations: Giving primarily in WA.
Application information: Application form not required.
Trustees: Margaret S. Cunningham, Andrea S. Gernon, KeyBank, N.A.
EIN: 916030549
Codes: FD

55411
Illsley B. Nordstrom Charitable Foundation
c/o Bank of America
P.O. Box 24565
Seattle, WA 98124-1345

Established in 1989 in WA.
Financial data (yr. ended 12/31/01): Grants paid, $750,000; assets, $6,276,162 (M); expenditures, $793,938; qualifying distributions, $770,515.
Limitations: Applications not accepted. Giving limited to Seattle, WA.
Application information: Contributes only to pre-selected organizations.
Trustee: Bank of America.
EIN: 916303747
Codes: FD

55412
The Dimmer Family Foundation
1019 Pacific Ave., Ste. 916
Tacoma, WA 98402-4492 (253) 572-4607
FAX: (253) 572-4647
Contact: Diane C. Dimmer, Exec. Dir.

Established in 1994.
Donor(s): John C. Dimmer.
Financial data (yr. ended 12/31/01): Grants paid, $743,464; assets, $11,634,249 (M); gifts received, $182,945; expenditures, $930,940; qualifying distributions, $772,795.
Limitations: Giving primarily in Tacoma, WA.
Publications: Grants list, informational brochure.
Application information: Application form not required.
Officers: John C. Dimmer, Pres.; Carolyn Dimmer, V.P.; Marilyn Dimmer, V.P.; Diane C. Dimmer, Secy. and Exec. Dir.; John B. Dimmer, Treas.
EIN: 911622059
Codes: FD

55413
PEMCO Foundation
325 Eastlake Ave. E.
Seattle, WA 98109
Contact: Stan W. McNaughton, Secy.-Treas.

Established in 1965 in WA.
Donor(s): Gladys McLaughlin,‡ PEMCO Corp., Washington School Employees Credit Union, Evergreen Bank, N.A., Evergreenbancorp, Inc., Teachers Foundation, PEMCO Technology Svcs., Inc.
Financial data (yr. ended 06/30/01): Grants paid, $735,055; assets, $35,941 (M); gifts received, $660,973; expenditures, $739,719; qualifying distributions, $739,618.
Limitations: Giving limited to WA residents for scholarships; organizational support in WA, with emphasis on Seattle.

Officers and Trustees:* Astrid I. Thompson,* Pres.; Sandra Kurack,* V.P.; Stan W. McNaughton,* Secy.-Treas.
EIN: 916072723
Codes: CS, FD, CD

55414
D. V. & Ida McEachern Charitable Trust
(Formerly Ida J. McEachern Charitable Trust)
c/o Union Bank of California, N.A.
P.O. Box 3123
Seattle, WA 98114 (206) 781-3472
E-mail: OgleFounds@aol.com; *URL:* http://fdncenter.org/grantmaker/mceachern
Contact: Therese Ogle, Grants Consultant

Trust established in 1966 in WA.
Donor(s): Ida J. McEachern,‡ D.V. McEachern.‡
Financial data (yr. ended 08/31/01): Grants paid, $715,500; assets, $18,836,230 (M); expenditures, $885,111; qualifying distributions, $778,529.
Limitations: Giving limited to the Puget Sound area of WA, particularly King, Pierce, and Snohomish counties.
Publications: Application guidelines.
Application information: See foundation's website for full application guidelines. Application form not required.
Trustee: Union Bank of California, N.A.
EIN: 916063710
Codes: FD

55415
Richard and Janet Geary Foundation, Inc.
c/o Bank of America
P.O. Box 34345, CSC-9
Seattle, WA 98124-1345

Established in 1996 in OR.
Donor(s): Richard Geary, Janet H. Geary.
Financial data (yr. ended 12/31/01): Grants paid, $693,756; assets, $7,726,469 (M); expenditures, $760,320; qualifying distributions, $702,476.
Limitations: Applications not accepted. Giving primarily in OR and WA.
Application information: Contributes only to pre-selected organizations.
Officers and Directors:* Janet H. Geary,* Chair.; Richard Geary,* Pres. and Treas.; Suzanne G. Paymar, Secy.
Trustee: Bank of America.
EIN: 911748475
Codes: FD

55416
PAH Foundation
c/o Parkland Mgmt. Co.
1705 132nd Ave., N.E.
Bellevue, WA 98005
Additional tel.: (216) 479-2200
Additional tel. for scholarships: (615) 292-4379
Contact: Thomas H. Oden, Treas.

Established in 1998 in WA as a follow-up to the Lois U. Horvitz Foundation.
Donor(s): Lois U. Horvitz Foundation.
Financial data (yr. ended 12/31/01): Grants paid, $683,779; assets, $8,311,217 (M); expenditures, $693,174; qualifying distributions, $686,716.
Limitations: Giving on a national basis with an emphasis on communities where foundation members reside.
Application information: Contact foundation for scholarship application. Application form not required.
Officers and Trustee:* Peter A. Horvitz,* Pres.; Margaret A. O'Meara, V.P.; Leo M. Krulitz, Secy. and Exec. Dir.; Thomas H. Oden, Treas.
EIN: 911866138
Codes: FD

55417
Glaser Foundation
P.O. Box 6548
Bellevue, WA 98008-0548

Incorporated in 1952 in WA.
Donor(s): Paul F. Glaser.‡
Financial data (yr. ended 11/30/01): Grants paid, $641,998; assets, $13,512,884 (M); expenditures, $807,818; qualifying distributions, $673,285.
Limitations: Giving primarily in King County, WA, and immediately adjoining areas.
Publications: Application guidelines.
Application information: Application form required.
Officers and Directors:* R. William Carlstrom, Pres.; R. Thomas Olson,* V.P.; Walter Smith,* Secy.; R.N. Brandenburg, Treas.; Janet L. Politeo.
EIN: 916028694
Codes: FD

55418
Kenneth and Marleen Alhadeff Charitable Foundation
c/o K. Alhadeff
615 2nd Ave., Ste. 100
Seattle, WA 98104 (206) 343-0080
Contact: Mike Manning

Established in 1996.
Donor(s): Kenneth Alhadeff.
Financial data (yr. ended 07/31/01): Grants paid, $637,752; assets, $292,524 (M); gifts received, $199,296; expenditures, $689,208; qualifying distributions, $673,199.
Limitations: Giving primarily in WA.
Application information: Application form not required.
Officers and Director:* Kenneth Alhadeff,* Pres. and Treas.; Marleen Alhadeff, Secy.
EIN: 911760871
Codes: FD

55419
Wood Family Foundation
10211 N.W. 59th St.
Kirkland, WA 98033
Application address: 5135 Ballard Ave., N.W., Seattle, WA 98107, tel.: (206) 781-3472; *E-mail:* oglefounds@aol.com; *URL:* http://www.fdncenter.org/grantmaker/wood
Contact: Theres Ogle, Grants Mgr.

Established in 1997 in WA.
Financial data (yr. ended 12/31/00): Grants paid, $632,010; assets, $13,319,260 (M); expenditures, $7,113,387; qualifying distributions, $639,880.
Limitations: Giving limited to King and Snohomish counties, WA, and the Olympic Peninsula.
Application information: Multi-year requests not considered. Application form not required.
Officers: Brenda K. Wood, Pres.; Donald R. Wood III, V.P.; Brandon C. Wood, Secy.
EIN: 911722889
Codes: FD

55420
The Allen Foundation for Music
505 5th Ave. S., Ste. 900
Seattle, WA 98104
E-mail: info@pgafoundations.com
Contact: Grants Admin., Paul G. Allen Foundations

Established in 1999 in WA.
Donor(s): Paul G. Allen.
Financial data (yr. ended 12/31/01): Grants paid, $622,500; assets, $301,329 (M); gifts received, $890,025; expenditures, $625,645; qualifying distributions, $622,500.

Limitations: Giving primarily in WA, with emphasis on Seattle.
Application information: Application form required.
Officers and Directors:* Paul G. Allen,* Chair.; Jo Allen Patton,* Pres.; Richard E. Leigh, Jr., V.P. and Secy.; Nathaniel T. Brown, V.P.; Joseph Franzi, V.P.
EIN: 911973980
Codes: FD

55421
RealNetworks Foundation
2601 Elliott Ave., Ste. 1000
Seattle, WA 98121 (206) 892-6644
Mailing address: P.O. Box 91123, Seattle, WA 98111-9223; FAX: (206) 956-8249; E-mail: info@realfoundation.org; URL: http://www.realfoundation.org

Established in 2000 in WA.
Donor(s): RealNetworks, Inc.
Financial data (yr. ended 12/31/01): Grants paid, $593,401; assets, $1,493,570 (M); gifts received, $350,600; expenditures, $687,095; qualifying distributions, $681,763.
Limitations: Applications not accepted. Giving on a national and international basis, with some emphasis on areas where company employees live and work.
Application information: Unsolicited requests for funds are not accepted at this time. The foundation will post grant application guidelines on its Web site when its next funding cycle opens. Prospective applicants can e-mail the foundation to be added to its mailing list to be notified of future funding opportunities.
Officers and Board Members:* Eileen Quigley,* Pres. and Treas.; Rob Glaser,* V.P.; Kelly Jo MacArthur,* Secy.; Susan Coskey.
EIN: 912033075
Codes: CS, FD, CD

55422
Norman Archibald Charitable Foundation
c/o Wells Fargo Bank Northwest, N.A.
P.O. Box 21927, 14th Fl.
Seattle, WA 98111 (206) 343-8367
Additional tel.: (206) 343-2217
Contact: Stuart H. Prestrud, Secy. of Board of Managers

Established in 1976 in WA.
Donor(s): Norman Archibald.‡
Financial data (yr. ended 09/30/01): Grants paid, $582,100; assets, $9,638,406 (M); expenditures, $690,841; qualifying distributions, $599,328.
Limitations: Giving primarily in the Puget Sound region of WA.
Publications: Annual report, application guidelines.
Application information: Application form not required.
Advisory Board: Robert L. Gerth, J. Shan Mullin, Stuart H. Prestrud.
Trustee: Wells Fargo Bank Northwest, N.A.
EIN: 911098014
Codes: FD

55423
North Pacific Marine Science Foundation
300 Elliot Ave. W., Ste. 360
Seattle, WA 98119-4138

Established in 1993 in WA.
Financial data (yr. ended 03/31/01): Grants paid, $564,174; assets, $154,588 (M); gifts received, $600,734; expenditures, $564,373; qualifying distributions, $564,373.
Limitations: Applications not accepted. Giving limited to WA.

Application information: Contributes only to pre-selected organizations.
Officers and Director:* Dave Hanson,* Pres.; Trevor McCabe, V.P.; Jim Brenner, Secy.-Treas.
EIN: 911582669

55424
Aven Foundation
P.O. Box 53508
Bellevue, WA 98015-3508 (425) 313-4410

Established in 1999 in WA.
Donor(s): John W. Stanton, Theresa E. Gillespie.
Financial data (yr. ended 12/31/01): Grants paid, $562,500; assets, $10,866,998 (M); expenditures, $699,283; qualifying distributions, $551,788.
Limitations: Giving primarily in Seattle, WA.
Application information: Application form not required.
Trustees: Theresa E. Gillespie, John W. Stanton.
EIN: 912009458
Codes: FD

55425
The John C. & Karyl Kay Hughes Foundation
2323 Eastlake Ave., E.
Seattle, WA 98102-3371
Contact: Gayle R. Bushnell, V.P. and Compt.

Established in 1984 in WA.
Donor(s): Karyl Kay Hughes.
Financial data (yr. ended 11/30/01): Grants paid, $556,600; assets, $9,277,382 (M); gifts received, $2,031,225; expenditures, $566,951; qualifying distributions, $557,642.
Limitations: Applications not accepted. Giving primarily in Seattle, WA.
Application information: Contributes only to pre-selected organizations. Unsolicited requests for funds not considered.
Trustee: Karyl Kay Hughes.
EIN: 911286019
Codes: FD

55426
The Herbert B. Jones Foundation
c/o Bank of America
P.O. Box 34345
Seattle, WA 98124-1345
Application address: c/o Seafirst Bank, P.O. Box 24565, Seattle, WA 98124, tel.: (206) 464-3043
Contact: Michael Bauer, Tr.

Established in 1989 in WA.
Donor(s): Herbert B. Jones.
Financial data (yr. ended 08/31/01): Grants paid, $553,260; assets, $12,249,293 (M); expenditures, $634,495; qualifying distributions, $579,146.
Limitations: Giving primarily in Seattle, WA.
Application information: Application form required.
Trustees: Michael P. Bauer, Bill Erwert, Gary Kumar, Nancy Lemke, Terry Smith, Janet Woods.
EIN: 943124801
Codes: FD

55427
Kreielsheimer Remainder Foundation
c/o Foundation Management Group, LLC
1000 Second Ave., Ste. 3400
Seattle, WA 98104-1022

Established in 2000 in WA.
Donor(s): Kreielsheimer Foundation.
Financial data (yr. ended 12/31/01): Grants paid, $553,232; assets, $15,156,962 (M); gifts received, $427,448; expenditures, $708,968; qualifying distributions, $547,331.
Limitations: Applications not accepted. Giving primarily in Seattle, WA.

Application information: Contributes only to pre-selected organizations.
Officers and Directors:* William P. Gerberding,* Chair.; Irwin L. Treiger,* Pres.; James F. Tune,* V.P. and Secy.; Susan B. Trapnell,* Treas.; Peter F. Donnelly.
EIN: 912064061
Codes: FD

55428
Moccasin Lake Foundation
1405 42nd Ave., E.
Seattle, WA 98112

Established in 1991 in WA.
Donor(s): James C. Pigott, Gaye T. Pigott, Mark Kranwinkle, Sara Kranwinkle.
Financial data (yr. ended 12/31/01): Grants paid, $544,186; assets, $867,133 (M); gifts received, $537,741; expenditures, $567,186; qualifying distributions, $545,631.
Limitations: Applications not accepted. Giving primarily in WA.
Application information: Contributes only to pre-selected organizations.
Officers and Directors:* Frederick Beau Gould,* Pres.; Mark Kranwinkle,* V.P.; Micheal Anderson,* Secy.; Gaye T. Pigott,* Co-Treas.; James C. Pigott,* Co-Treas.; Lisa Anderson, Julie Gould, Sara Kranwinkle, Maureen "Dina" Pigott, Paul Pigott.
EIN: 911545081
Codes: FD

55429
Robert G. Hemingway Foundation
c/o U.S. Bank
1420 5th Ave., 21st Fl.
Seattle, WA 98101
Contact: Lee-Norah Sanzo, V.P., U.S. Bank, or Lisa Carlson, Grants Coord.

Established in 1967 in UT.
Donor(s): Susan G. Hemingway.‡
Financial data (yr. ended 04/30/01): Grants paid, $541,833; assets, $8,501,261 (M); expenditures, $578,885; qualifying distributions, $565,006.
Limitations: Giving in the western U.S.
Application information: Phone requests will not be honored. Application form not required.
Officer: Susan G. Hemingway, Admin. Dir.
Trustee: U.S. Bank.
EIN: 876176774
Codes: FD

55430
Byron W. and Alice L. Lockwood Foundation
P.O. Box 4
Mercer Island, WA 98040 (206) 232-1881
Application address: 11033 N.E. 24th St., Ste. 200, Bellevue, WA 98004
Contact: Paul R. Cressman, Sr., Pres.

Established in 1968 in WA.
Financial data (yr. ended 12/31/99): Grants paid, $527,000; assets, $15,363,132 (M); expenditures, $879,330; qualifying distributions, $620,338.
Limitations: Giving primarily in Seattle and the Puget Sound area of WA.
Application information: Application form not required.
Officers and Trustees:* Paul R. Cressman, Sr.,* Pres.; James R. Palmer, Secy.-Treas.; Paul R. Cressman, Jr., Lee Kraft.
EIN: 910833426
Codes: FD

55431
The Community Foundation
(Formerly Greater Thurston County Community Foundation)
505 W. 4th Ave., Ste. A
Olympia, WA 98501 (360) 705-3340
FAX: (360) 705-2656; E-mail: gtccf@aol.com
Contact: Colleen Gillespie, Exec. Dir.

Established in 1989 in WA.
Financial data (yr. ended 12/31/00): Grants paid, $518,677; assets, $1,406,996 (L); gifts received, $775,218; expenditures, $677,621.
Limitations: Giving limited to Thurston, Mason and Lewis counties, WA.
Publications: Annual report, informational brochure.
Application information: Application form required.
Officers: Lynn Brunton, Pres.; Dennis Peterson, V.P.; Carolyn Lakewold, Secy.; Paul Strohmeier, Treas.; Colleen Gillespie, Exec. Dir.
Directors: Linnea Bremner, Brian Charneski, Kimberly Ellwanger, Brian Fluetsch, Jim Greene, Jay Johnson, Holly Mason, Phyllis McGavick, Frank J. Owens, Richard Phillips, Jr., Donald V. Rhodes, Gordon Shewfelt, Joyce Targus, Linda Wells.
EIN: 943121390
Codes: CM, FD

55432
Nestle Scholarship Foundation
(Formerly Carnation Company Scholarship Foundation)
c/o Bank of America
P.O. Box 34345
Seattle, WA 98124-1345
Application address: c/o Scholarship Mgmt. Svcs., 1505 Riverview Rd., P.O. Box 297, St. Peter, MN 56082, tel.: (507) 931-1682

Established in 1952 in CA; current name adopted after Carnation Co. was sold to Nestle.
Donor(s): Carnation Co., Nestle USA, Inc.
Financial data (yr. ended 12/31/01): Grants paid, $513,000; assets, $10,984,292 (M); expenditures, $590,732; qualifying distributions, $536,616.
Limitations: Giving on a national basis.
Application information: Personal references and academic transcripts required.
Advisory Committee: Peter D. Argentine, Kenneth W. Bentley, Mrs. Carn Starrett.
Scholarship Selection Committee: Scholarship Management Svc.
Trustee Bank: Bank of America.
EIN: 956118622
Codes: CS, FD, CD

55433
Schultz Family Foundation
108 S. Washington, Ste. 300
Seattle, WA 98104
Contact: Loren D. Hostek, Tr.

Established in 1996 in WA.
Donor(s): Howard D. Schultz, Sheri K. Schultz.
Financial data (yr. ended 06/30/01): Grants paid, $512,712; assets, $6,360,710 (M); expenditures, $514,408; qualifying distributions, $512,712.
Limitations: Giving primarily in Seattle, WA.
Trustees: Georgette Essad, Loren D. Hostek, Sheri Kersch-Schultz, Howard D. Schultz.
EIN: 911746414
Codes: FD

55434
Community Foundation of North Central Washington
(Formerly Greater Wenatchee Community Foundation)
7 N. Wenatchee Ave., Ste. 201
P.O. Box 3332
Wenatchee, WA 98807-3332 (509) 663-7716
FAX: (509) 667-2208; E-mail: gwcf@gwcfncw.org
Contact: G. Raymond Taylor, C.E.O. and Pres.

Incorporated in 1986 in WA.
Financial data (yr. ended 06/30/01): Grants paid, $504,638; assets, $14,095,068 (M); gifts received, $1,264,507; expenditures, $878,295; giving activities include $5,000 for loans.
Limitations: Giving limited to north central WA, especially Chelan, Douglas, Grant, and Okanogan counties.
Publications: Annual report, application guidelines, informational brochure, occasional report, grants list.
Application information: Contact foundation for application guidelines or use the PNGF Common Form. Application form not required.
Officers and Trustees:* John R. Applegate, M.D.,* Chair.; Leon McKinney,* Vice-Chair.; G. Raymond Taylor,* C.E.O. and Pres.; Terry Sorom,* Secy.-Treas.; Lloyd L. Berry, Mall Boyd, Roger Bumps, Gerald E. Gibbons, M.D., Douglas B. Harper, Dennis S. Johnson, Terrence M. McCawley, Christine Scull, John J. "Jack" Snyder, Jr., Christopher Stahler, Robert L. White.
EIN: 911349486
Codes: CM, FD, GTI

55435
Paul Lauzier Charitable Foundation
P.O. Box 1230
Ephrata, WA 98823
Contact: Michael Rex Tabler, Tr.

Established in 1997.
Financial data (yr. ended 12/31/00): Grants paid, $500,250; assets, $10,680,593 (M); expenditures, $863,771; qualifying distributions, $505,356.
Limitations: Giving primarily in WA, with emphasis on Ephrata, Moses Lake, and Pullman.
Application information: Application form not required.
Trustee: Michael Rex Tabler.
EIN: 911701539
Codes: FD

55436
J.S.S. Foundation
P.O. Box 866
Bellevue, WA 98009

Established in 1998 in WA.
Donor(s): Brad A. Silverberg, Jean S. Silverberg.
Financial data (yr. ended 12/31/01): Grants paid, $495,000; assets, $10,220,987 (M); expenditures, $551,029; qualifying distributions, $492,299.
Limitations: Applications not accepted. Giving on a national basis.
Application information: Contributes only to pre-selected organizations.
Trustees: Brad A. Silverberg, Jean S. Silverberg, Robert F. Trenner.
EIN: 364299373
Codes: FD

55437
Laird Norton Family Fund
801 Second Ave., Ste. 1600
Seattle, WA 98104
Contact: Barbara A. Potter

Established in 1963 in MN.
Financial data (yr. ended 12/31/00): Grants paid, $481,525; assets, $437,356 (M); gifts received, $450,059; expenditures, $492,797; qualifying distributions, $482,540.
Limitations: Applications not accepted. Giving on a national basis.
Publications: Annual report.
Application information: Contributes only to pre-selected organizations. Unsolicited requests for funds not accepted.
Officers and Directors:* Patrick de Freitas,* Pres.; Bruce Reed,* Secy.; James Kreamer,* Treas.; James N. Clapp II.
EIN: 916048373
Codes: FD

55438
Paul Lauzier Scholarship Foundation
P.O. Box 1230
Ephrata, WA 98823-1230
Contact: Michael Rex Tabler, Tr.

Established in 1997.
Financial data (yr. ended 12/31/00): Grants paid, $477,981; assets, $10,680,593 (M); expenditures, $841,502; qualifying distributions, $483,087.
Limitations: Giving limited to Grant County, WA.
Application information: Applicants can obtain an application through the Grant County high school that they have graduated from or are currently attending. Application form required.
Trustee: Michael Rex Tabler.
EIN: 911701545
Codes: FD, GTI

55439
Spirit Foundation
341 S. Garden St.
Bellingham, WA 98225

Financial data (yr. ended 12/31/01): Grants paid, $469,169; assets, $4,246 (M); gifts received, $1,198; expenditures, $480,354; qualifying distributions, $469,169.
Limitations: Applications not accepted.
Application information: Contributes only to pre-selected organizations.
Officer: Dennis T. Williams, Secy.
EIN: 911841376

55440
Poncin Scholarship Fund
c/o Bank of America
P.O. Box 24565
Seattle, WA 98124 (206) 358-3380
Contact: Mollie Determan, V.P., Bank of America

Trust established in 1966 in WA.
Donor(s): Cora May Poncin.‡
Financial data (yr. ended 12/31/00): Grants paid, $462,129; assets, $8,582,934 (M); expenditures, $517,121; qualifying distributions, $486,220.
Limitations: Giving limited to WA.
Publications: Application guidelines.
Application information: Application must be approved by head of applicant's institution. Application form required.
Trustee: Bank of America.
EIN: 916069573
Codes: FD, GTI

55441
Rhoady Lee, Jr. and Jeanne Marie Lee Foundation
c/o Rhoady Lee Jr.
P.O. Box 7
Bellevue, WA 98009-0007

Established in 1997 in WA.
Donor(s): Rhoady Lee, Jr., Jeanne Marie Lee.

Financial data (yr. ended 12/31/01): Grants paid, $460,000; assets, $0 (M); gifts received, $452,348; expenditures, $461,710; qualifying distributions, $459,999.
Limitations: Applications not accepted. Giving on a national basis.
Application information: Contributes only to pre-selected organizations.
Trustees: Jeanne Marie Lee, Rhoady Lee, Jr.
EIN: 916456085
Codes: FD

55442
Evertrust Foundation
(Formerly Everett Mutual Savings Bank Foundation)
2707 Colby Ave., Ste. 600
Everett, WA 98201-3510

Established in 1993.
Donor(s): Everett Mutual Savings Bank.
Financial data (yr. ended 12/31/01): Grants paid, $458,048; assets, $9,646,381 (M); expenditures, $514,490; qualifying distributions, $458,048.
Limitations: Applications not accepted. Giving limited to the Everett, WA, area.
Application information: Contributes only to pre-selected organizations.
Officers: Margaret Bavasi, Chair.; Mary B. Seavers, Exec. Dir.
Directors: Tom Collins, Michael Deller, Thomas J. Gaffney, George Newland, Ole Olson, Harry Stuchell.
EIN: 911510567
Codes: CS, FD, CD

55443
Sarkowsky Family Charitable Foundation
c/o Herman Sarkowsky
700 5th Ave., Ste. 6100
Seattle, WA 98104-5004

Established in 1991 in WA.
Donor(s): Herman Sarkowsky.
Financial data (yr. ended 12/31/01): Grants paid, $444,947; assets, $1,478,923 (M); gifts received, $115,150; expenditures, $447,147; qualifying distributions, $443,852.
Limitations: Applications not accepted. Giving primarily in WA.
Application information: Contributes only to pre-selected organizations.
Officers: Herman Sarkowsky, Pres. and Treas.; Faye Sarkowsky, V.P. and Secy.
EIN: 911479527
Codes: FD

55444
The Dudley Foundation
609A N. Shore Dr.
Bellingham, WA 98226-4414
E-mail: dudleyfdn@yahoo.com; URL: http://www.dudleyfoundation.org
Contact: Rick Dudley, Pres.

Established in 1990 in WA.
Donor(s): Tilford E. Dudley,‡ Gerric W. Dudley.
Financial data (yr. ended 12/31/02): Grants paid, $437,005; assets, $4,272,013 (M); expenditures, $519,063; qualifying distributions, $438,455.
Limitations: Applications not accepted. Giving on a national basis.
Application information: Contributes only to pre-selected organizations. Unsolicited requests for funds not accepted.
Officers and Board Members:* Gerric W. Dudley,* Pres.; Todd Jones,* V.P.; Eric Dudley,* Secy.-Treas.; Mike Feerer, Bob Keller, Colleen Verdon, Saul Weisberg.
EIN: 911474291

Codes: FD

55445
Henrik A. Valle Scholarship Trust
c/o Wells Fargo Bank Northwest, N.A.
P.O. Box 21927
Seattle, WA 98111-3927
Application address: The Valle Scandinavian Exchange Program, c/o College of Engineering, University of Washington, Seattle, WA 98195
Contact: Dale A. Carlson, Prog. Dir.

Financial data (yr. ended 09/30/01): Grants paid, $431,086; assets, $6,783,130 (M); expenditures, $523,616; qualifying distributions, $442,829.
Limitations: Giving limited to Seattle, WA.
Application information: Application form required.
Trustees: Paul R. Cressman, Sr., Wells Fargo Bank Northwest, N.A.
EIN: 916233353
Codes: FD

55446
Leslie Fund, Inc.
P.O. Box 17103
Seattle, WA 98107
Application address: 2400 N.W. 80th St., PMB154, Seattle, WA 98117
Contact: James W. Leslie, V.P.

Incorporated in 1956 in IL.
Donor(s): members of the Leslie family, Virginia A. Leslie Trust.
Financial data (yr. ended 03/31/01): Grants paid, $430,420; assets, $9,241,347 (M); expenditures, $505,576; qualifying distributions, $464,304.
Limitations: Giving primarily in Chicago, IL, and Seattle, WA.
Application information: Application form not required.
Officers: John H. Leslie, Pres.; James W. Leslie, V.P.; Victoria H. Leslie, Secy.-Treas.
Director: Judith W. McCue.
EIN: 366055800
Codes: FD

55447
James and Elsie Nolan Charitable Trust
c/o Wells Fargo Bank Alaska, N.A.
P.O. Box 21927, MAC P6540-141
Seattle, WA 98111
Application address: c/o Judith A. Baker, P.O. Box 927, Wrangell, AK 99929, tel.: (907) 874-2323

Established in 1992 in AK.
Financial data (yr. ended 12/31/01): Grants paid, $426,725; assets, $5,544,574 (M); expenditures, $488,979; qualifying distributions, $424,321.
Limitations: Giving primarily in southeastern AK.
Trustees: Maribeth Conway, David L. Dobbs.
EIN: 926021559
Codes: FD

55448
Runstad Foundation
c/o Judith M. Runstad
1111 3rd Ave., Ste. 3400
Seattle, WA 98101-3264

Established in 1999 in WA.
Donor(s): H. Jon Runstad, Judith Runstad.
Financial data (yr. ended 12/31/00): Grants paid, $424,391; assets, $500,500 (M); gifts received, $892,526; expenditures, $424,421; qualifying distributions, $424,421.
Limitations: Applications not accepted. Giving primarily in WA.
Application information: Contributes only to pre-selected organizations.

Directors: H. Jon Runstad, Judith M. Runstad.
EIN: 911873948
Codes: FD

55449
Potlatch Foundation for Higher Education
601 W. Riverside Ave., Ste. 1100
Spokane, WA 99201 (509) 835-1515
Contact: Joyce Laboure

Incorporated in 1952 in DE.
Donor(s): Potlatch Corp.
Financial data (yr. ended 12/31/00): Grants paid, $423,500; assets, $9,691 (M); gifts received, $438,955; expenditures, $456,331; qualifying distributions, $453,949.
Limitations: Giving limited to areas of company operations, primarily in AR, ID, and MN.
Publications: Annual report, program policy statement, application guidelines.
Application information: Application forms will be mailed to students seeking scholarships. Application form required.
Officers and Trustees:* L. Pendleton Siegel,* Pres.; Barbara M. Failing,* V.P.; Malcolm A. Ryerse,* Secy.-Treas.; A. L. Alford, Jr., Jack A. Buell, John B. Frazer, Jr., Robert W. Gamble, John L. Hogan, Sally J. Ihne, John M. Richards.
EIN: 826005250
Codes: CS, FD, CD, GTI

55450
Thurston Charitable Foundation
221 1st. Ave. W., Ste. 215
Seattle, WA 98119

Established in 1962 in WA.
Donor(s): Ellen E. Thurston.‡
Financial data (yr. ended 06/30/01): Grants paid, $418,997; assets, $5,294,121 (M); gifts received, $104,496; expenditures, $444,465; qualifying distributions, $419,045.
Limitations: Applications not accepted. Giving primarily in WA.
Application information: Contributes only to pre-selected organizations.
Officers: Robert H. Thurston, Pres.; Susan E. Thurston, V.P.; Sherrie Tossell, Secy.; Severt W. Thurston, Jr., Treas.
EIN: 916055032
Codes: FD

55451
Plum Creek Foundation
999 3rd Ave., Ste. 2300
Seattle, WA 98104
URL: http://www.plumcreek.com/company/foundation.cfm
Contact: Robert J. Jirsa, Pres.

Established in 1993 in WA.
Donor(s): Plum Creek Timber Co., L.P., Plum Creek Timber Co., Inc.
Financial data (yr. ended 12/31/00): Grants paid, $411,442; assets, $2,870 (M); gifts received, $155,000; expenditures, $411,640; qualifying distributions, $411,460.
Limitations: Giving primarily in ID, MT, and WA.
Application information: Application form required.
Officers: James A. Kraft, Chair.; Robert J. Jirsa, Pres.; Art H. Vail, V.P.; Barbara L. Crowe, Secy.; Scott N. Dell'Osso, Treas.
EIN: 911621028
Codes: CS, FD, CD

55452
Edmund F. Maxwell Foundation
P.O. Box 22537
Seattle, WA 98122-0537
E-mail: admin@maxwell.org; URL: http://www.maxwell.org
Contact: Jane Thomas, Admin.

Established in 1992 in WA.
Financial data (yr. ended 12/31/01): Grants paid, $407,979; assets, $8,567,874 (M); expenditures, $540,831; qualifying distributions, $438,613.
Limitations: Giving to organizations on a national basis; scholarship grants limited to students in western WA.
Publications: Informational brochure (including application guidelines).
Application information: Application forms available on website. Application form required.
Officer: Jane Thomas, Admin.
Trustees: David G. Johansen, David D. Lewis, Alan T. Robertson.
EIN: 916181008
Codes: FD, GTI

55453
Heritage Valley Foundation
c/o James Youngsman
18697 Hickox Rd.
Mount Vernon, WA 98273-9007

Donor(s): Jim Youngsman, Ruth Youngsman.
Financial data (yr. ended 12/31/01): Grants paid, $402,750; assets, $1,883,698 (M); expenditures, $409,177; qualifying distributions, $403,207.
Limitations: Applications not accepted. Giving primarily in WA.
Application information: Contributes only to pre-selected organizations.
Managers: Jim Youngsman, Ruth Youngsman.
EIN: 911784775
Codes: FD

55454
Harriet Cheney Cowles Foundation, Inc.
999 W. Riverside Ave., Rm. 626
Spokane, WA 99201

Incorporated in 1944 in WA.
Donor(s): Spokane Chronicle Co., Cowles Publishing Co., Inland Empire Paper Co.
Financial data (yr. ended 12/31/01): Grants paid, $402,000; assets, $16,263,019 (M); expenditures, $455,576; qualifying distributions, $389,802.
Limitations: Applications not accepted. Giving primarily in Spokane, WA.
Application information: Contributes only to pre-selected organizations.
Officers: J.P. Cowles, Pres.; M.K. Nielsen, Secy.
Trustees: E.A. Cowles, W.S. Cowles.
EIN: 910689268
Codes: FD

55455
William E. Bradley Family Foundation
P.O. Box 2127
Seattle, WA 98111

Established in 2001 in WA.
Donor(s): G. Mary Bradley.
Financial data (yr. ended 12/31/01): Grants paid, $401,000; assets, $9,388,517 (M); gifts received, $28,634; expenditures, $551,225; qualifying distributions, $479,327.
Limitations: Applications not accepted. Giving primarily in NJ, NY, and WA.
Application information: Contributes only to pre-selected organizations.
Trustee: G. Mary Bradley.
EIN: 916516130
Codes: FD

55456
William H. Cowles Foundation, Inc.
999 W. Riverside Ave., Rm. 626
Spokane, WA 99201

Incorporated in 1952 in WA.
Financial data (yr. ended 12/31/01): Grants paid, $400,000; assets, $5,245,081 (M); expenditures, $417,568; qualifying distributions, $400,000.
Limitations: Applications not accepted. Giving primarily in CA and CT.
Application information: Contributes only to pre-selected organizations.
Officers: J.P. Cowles, Pres.; M.K. Nielsen, Secy.
Trustees: E.A. Cowles, W.S. Cowles.
EIN: 916020496

55457
Quest for Truth Foundation
221 1st Ave. W., Ste. 405
Seattle, WA 98119-4238
Contact: DeLancey B. Lewis, Pres. and Treas.

Established in 1982 in WA.
Financial data (yr. ended 09/30/01): Grants paid, $400,000; assets, $7,287,753 (M); expenditures, $477,443; qualifying distributions, $394,894.
Limitations: Applications not accepted. Giving limited to ID, MT, OR, UT, and WA.
Application information: Unsolicited requests for funds not accepted.
Officers and Directors:* DeLancey B. Lewis,* Pres. and Treas.; Bradley F. Henke,* V.P. and Secy; Paul K. Scripps,* V.P.; Roxanne D. Greene, Marion W. Roozen.
EIN: 911190760
Codes: FD, GTI

55458
Howard S. Wright Family Foundation
(Formerly Howard S. Wright Foundation)
1264 Eastlake Ave. E.
Seattle, WA 98102
Contact: Sally S. Wright, Pres.

Established in 1984 in WA.
Donor(s): Howard S. Wright.‡
Financial data (yr. ended 12/31/01): Grants paid, $400,000; assets, $8,036,410 (M); expenditures, $507,358; qualifying distributions, $408,326.
Limitations: Applications not accepted. Giving primarily in the Pacific Northwest, with emphasis on Seattle, WA.
Application information: Unsolicited requests for funds not accepted.
Officers and Directors:* Sally S. Wright,* Pres.; Katherine A. Janeway,* Treas.; Theiline W. Rolfe, Korynne H. Wright.
EIN: 911276047
Codes: FD

55459
Elizabeth A. Lynn Foundation
PMB 6159-13300
Bothell Everett Hwy.
Mill Creek, WA 98012-5312 (425) 316-6842
Contact: Diane Titch

Established in 1981 in WA.
Donor(s): Elizabeth A. Lynn.‡
Financial data (yr. ended 11/30/01): Grants paid, $391,600; assets, $6,588,635 (M); expenditures, $431,644; qualifying distributions, $388,789.
Limitations: Giving primarily in WA, with emphasis on the Puget Sound area.
Publications: Application guidelines.
Application information: Application form required.
Trustees: Jeff Lynn, Traci Lynn, Jody Moss, Thomas J. Stephens.
EIN: 911156982

Codes: FD

55460
Elmer E. Rasmuson Endowment for The Boy Scouts of America in Alaska
c/o Wells Fargo Bank, N.A.
P.O. Box 21927
Seattle, WA 98111

Established in 2001 in AK.
Donor(s): Elmer Rasmuson.‡
Financial data (yr. ended 12/31/01): Grants paid, $391,235; assets, $9,987,467 (M); gifts received, $10,000,000; expenditures, $460,005; qualifying distributions, $407,871.
Limitations: Applications not accepted. Giving primarily in AK.
Application information: Contributes only to pre-selected organizations.
Trustee: Wells Fargo Bank, N.A.
EIN: 926031574
Codes: FD

55461
Wyman Youth Trust
510 Pioneer Bldg.
600 1st Ave.
Seattle, WA 98104 (206) 682-2256

Trust established in 1951 in WA.
Donor(s): Members of the Wyman family.
Financial data (yr. ended 12/31/99): Grants paid, $384,953; assets, $9,841,770 (M); expenditures, $443,486; qualifying distributions, $392,143.
Limitations: Giving primarily in York, Custer and Lancaster counties, NE, and King, Pierce, and Snohomish counties, WA, with emphasis on King County.
Publications: Program policy statement, application guidelines.
Application information: No telephone calls. Application form not required.
Trustees: David C. Wyman, David E. Wyman, Hal H. Wyman.
EIN: 916031590
Codes: FD

55462
Tillie and Alfred Shemanski Testamentary Trust
c/o Bank of America
P.O. Box 34345, No. CSC-9
Seattle, WA 98124-1345
Application address: P.O. Box 24565, Seattle, WA 98124, tel.: (206) 358-0806
Contact: Mollie Determan, V.P., Bank of America

Trust established in 1974 in WA.
Donor(s): Alfred Shemanski,‡ Tillie Shemanski.‡
Financial data (yr. ended 12/31/00): Grants paid, $381,695; assets, $9,455,519 (M); expenditures, $483,913; qualifying distributions, $408,212.
Limitations: Giving primarily in WA.
Trustee: Bank of America.
EIN: 916196855
Codes: FD

55463
Estate of Joseph L. Stubblefield
P.O. Box 1757
Walla Walla, WA 99362 (509) 527-3500
Contact: H.H. Hayner, Tr.

Trust established in 1902 in WA.
Donor(s): Joseph L. Stubblefield.‡
Financial data (yr. ended 12/31/00): Grants paid, $378,005; assets, $8,386,189 (M); expenditures, $485,299; qualifying distributions, $385,084.
Limitations: Giving limited to OR and WA.
Application information: Application form not required.
Trustees: H.H. Hayner, James K. Hayner.

EIN: 916031350
Codes: FD

55464
Saul and Dayee G. Haas Foundation, Inc.
701 5th Ave., Ste. 5000
Seattle, WA 98104-7078 (206) 467-2714
Contact: Frank S. Hanawalt, Exec. Dir.

Incorporated in 1971 in WA.
Donor(s): Saul Haas,‡ Dayee G. Haas.‡
Financial data (yr. ended 06/30/02): Grants paid, $377,877; assets, $8,109,585 (M); expenditures, $458,440; qualifying distributions, $377,877.
Limitations: Applications not accepted. Giving limited to WA.
Publications: Informational brochure, program policy statement.
Officers and Directors:* Charles Johnson,* Pres.; Jon Bowman,* 1st V.P.; Deesa Haas,* Secy.; Lee Miller,* Treas.; Frank S. Hanawalt, Exec. Dir.; Charles Chinn, Maurice R. Clark, Hon. Betty Fletcher, Carver Gayton, Gerald Grinstein, Duff Kennedy, Terry Macaluso, John L. McKenzie, Robert Nathane, Chris Peck, Roger Percy.
EIN: 237189670
Codes: FD

55465
Northwest Fund for the Environment
1904 3rd Ave., Ste. 615
Seattle, WA 98101 (206) 386-7220
FAX: (206) 386-7223; *E-mail:* staff@nwfund.org;
URL: http://www.nwfund.org
Contact: Pamela Fujita-Yuhas, Fund Admin. or Zoe Rothchild, Fund Admin.

Established in 1971 in WA.
Donor(s): Helen May Marcy Johnson.‡
Financial data (yr. ended 12/31/01): Grants paid, $373,425; assets, $7,211,797 (M); expenditures, $543,535; qualifying distributions, $459,599.
Limitations: Applications not accepted. Giving limited to WA.
Publications: Annual report.
Application information: Unsolicited requests for funds not accepted.
Officers and Trustees:* Derek Poon,* Pres.; Rodney Brown,* V.P.; Parrish Jones,* Treas.; Jef Baldi, Carol Bernthal, Dave Goeke, Chris Golde, Peter Golde, Kim Moore, Robert Rose, Tom Scribner, Judy Turpin.
EIN: 237134880
Codes: FD

55466
Foundation of Caring Fund
P.O. Box 2255
Wenatchee, WA 98807

Established in 1989 in WA.
Donor(s): Carl W. Campbell, Betty F. Campbell.
Financial data (yr. ended 12/31/01): Grants paid, $371,732; assets, $6,201,604 (M); gifts received, $500,000; expenditures, $388,174; qualifying distributions, $377,174.
Limitations: Applications not accepted. Giving primarily in Wenatchee, WA.
Application information: Contributes only to pre-selected organizations.
Officer: Thomas H. Dye, Pres.
EIN: 911461620
Codes: FD

55467
John A. and Helen M. Cartales Foundation
8710 N.E. Porter Cir.
Vancouver, WA 98664-2866

Established in 1998.
Donor(s): John A. Cartales, Helen M. Cartales.
Financial data (yr. ended 06/30/02): Grants paid, $370,000; assets, $7,191,859 (M); expenditures, $425,034; qualifying distributions, $370,000.
Limitations: Applications not accepted.
Application information: Contributes only to pre-selected organizations.
Trustees: Helen M. Cartales, John A. Cartales.
EIN: 911940389

55468
Richard & Lois Worthington Foundation
c/o U.S. Bank, Private Client Group
1420 5th Ave., PD-WA-T21P, Ste. 2100
Seattle, WA 98101
Contact: Lois M. Worthington, Dir.

Established in 1998 in WA.
Donor(s): Lois M. Worthington.
Financial data (yr. ended 09/30/01): Grants paid, $365,500; assets, $5,319,751 (M); expenditures, $406,511; qualifying distributions, $363,394.
Application information: Unsolicited requests for funds not accepted. Application form required.
Officers and Directors:* Lois M. Worthington,* Pres.; Barbara Matheson,* Treas.
EIN: 911909665
Codes: FD

55469
John and Wauna Harman Foundation
P.O. Box 10572
Yakima, WA 98909

Established in 1999 in WA.
Donor(s): Wauna Harman.
Financial data (yr. ended 12/31/01): Grants paid, $360,000; assets, $8,826,688 (M); expenditures, $382,773; qualifying distributions, $360,000.
Limitations: Applications not accepted. Giving on a national basis, with some emphasis on Yakima, WA.
Application information: Contributes only to pre-selected organizations.
Officers: Barry W. Harman, Pres.; Dawn Cook, V.P.; Elaine Harmon, Secy.
EIN: 911999241
Codes: FD

55470
The Magdalen Foundation
10655 N.E. 4th St., Ste. 611
Bellevue, WA 98004-5022

Established in 1980 in WA.
Donor(s): Nicholas J. Bez.
Financial data (yr. ended 08/31/01): Grants paid, $360,000; assets, $3,499,783 (M); expenditures, $367,237; qualifying distributions, $359,105.
Limitations: Applications not accepted. Giving primarily in CA, OR, and Seattle, WA.
Application information: Contributes only to pre-selected organizations.
Trustee: Nicholas J. Bez.
EIN: 911114068
Codes: FD

55471
Murray Foundation
1201 Pacific Ave., Ste. 1750
Tacoma, WA 98402 (253) 591-9892
Additional tel.: (253) 383-3261
Contact: Lowell Anne Butson, Pres.

Trust established in 1952 in WA.
Donor(s): L.T. Murray,‡ Mrs. L.T. Murray.‡
Financial data (yr. ended 12/31/01): Grants paid, $356,200; assets, $6,066,400 (M); expenditures, $462,755; qualifying distributions, $384,853.
Limitations: Giving limited to Tacoma and Pierce County, WA.
Publications: Informational brochure (including application guidelines), occasional report, application guidelines.
Application information: Application form not required.
Officers and Directors:* Lowell Anne Butson,* Pres.; Anne Murray Barbey,* V.P.; Steve Larson,* Secy.; L.T. Murray, Jr.,* Treas.; Amy Lou Eckstrom, L.T. Murray III.
EIN: 510163345
Codes: FD

55472
Janet Wright Ketcham Foundation
2711 E. Madison St., Ste. 211
Seattle, WA 98112-4749

Established in 1990 in WA.
Donor(s): Ellis H. Wright,‡ Janet W. Ketcham.
Financial data (yr. ended 12/31/00): Grants paid, $348,281; assets, $4,099,626 (M); gifts received, $402,600; expenditures, $381,143; qualifying distributions, $347,783.
Limitations: Applications not accepted.
Application information: Contributes only to pre-selected organizations.
Officer and Directors:* Janet W. Ketcham,* Pres., V.P., Treas., and Mgr.; Ellis Ketcham Johnson.
EIN: 911276055
Codes: FD

55473
John & Mary Wilson Foundation
c/o Univ. of Washington, Financial Aid Office, School of Medicine, T-557
P.O. Box 357430
Seattle, WA 98195-7430
Contact: Diane Noecker, Financial Aid Off.

Financial data (yr. ended 12/31/01): Grants paid, $345,500; assets, $7,577,214 (M); expenditures, $424,530; qualifying distributions, $354,924.
Limitations: Giving limited to Seattle, WA.
Application information: Application form required.
Trustee: Wells Fargo Bank Northwest, N.A.
EIN: 237425273
Codes: FD

55474
The Paul G. Allen Virtual Education Foundation
505 5th Ave. S.
Seattle, WA 98104
E-mail: info@pgafoundations.com; URL: http://www.pgafoundations.com
Contact: Grants Admin.

Established in 1997 in WA.
Donor(s): Paul G. Allen.
Financial data (yr. ended 12/31/01): Grants paid, $345,000; assets, $11,932,773 (M); expenditures, $348,907; qualifying distributions, $345,000.
Application information: Check Web site for revised funding guidelines. Application form required.
Officers and Director:* Paul G. Allen,* Chair.; Bert E. Kolde, Pres.; Richard E. Leigh, Jr., V.P. and Secy.; Nathaniel T. Brown, V.P.; Joseph D. Franzi, V.P.; Jo Allen Patton, V.P.
EIN: 911764165
Codes: FD

55475
De Falco Family Foundation
2205 55th St. Ct., N.W.
Gig Harbor, WA 98335
Contact: Santina De Falco, Pres.

Established in 1992 in CA.

55475—WASHINGTON

Financial data (yr. ended 09/30/01): Grants paid, $344,000; assets, $6,416,769 (M); expenditures, $477,388; qualifying distributions, $353,977.
Limitations: Applications not accepted. Giving primarily in San Diego, CA, and WA.
Application information: Contributes only to pre-selected organizations.
Officers and Trustees:* Santina De Falco,* Pres.; William Beamer,* V.P.; Sue Robertson,* Secy.-Treas.
EIN: 330526533
Codes: FD

55476
The Brettler Family Foundation
c/o Stephen R. Black
720 3rd Ave., Pacific Bldg., Ste. 2112
Seattle, WA 98104

Established in 1999 in WA.
Donor(s): Daniel E. Brettler, Cindy S. Brettler.
Financial data (yr. ended 12/31/01): Grants paid, $338,385; assets, $6,348,556 (M); gifts received, $25,240; expenditures, $396,133; qualifying distributions, $344,063.
Limitations: Applications not accepted.
Application information: Contributes only to pre-selected organizations.
Directors: Stephen R. Black, Cindy S. Brettler, Daniel E. Brettler.
EIN: 912014618
Codes: FD

55477
Kirlin Foundation
5350 Carillon Pt.
Kirkland, WA 98033-7384 (206) 381-2250
E-mail: ron@kirlinfoundation.org; URL: http://www.kirlinfoundation.org
Contact: Ron Rabin, Exec. Dir.

Established in 1999 in WA.
Donor(s): Daniel R. Kranzler, Sally J. Kranzler.
Financial data (yr. ended 12/31/01): Grants paid, $335,252; assets, $8,076,080 (M); expenditures, $558,806; qualifying distributions, $520,293.
Limitations: Applications not accepted. Giving limited to the Pacific Northwest.
Application information: Unsolicited requests for funds not accepted.
Trustees: Daniel R. Kranzler, Sally J. Kranzler, Ronald J. Rabin.
EIN: 916500102
Codes: FD

55478
Mark & Carolyn Guidry Foundation
P.O. Box 4482
Rollingbay, WA 98061

Established in 1994 in WA.
Donor(s): Carolyn Guidry.
Financial data (yr. ended 12/31/01): Grants paid, $335,000; assets, $5,314,220 (M); expenditures, $385,277; qualifying distributions, $335,950.
Limitations: Applications not accepted. Giving primarily in CA and WA.
Application information: Unsolicited requests for funds not accepted.
Officer: Carolyn Guidry, Mgr.
EIN: 943185161
Codes: FD

55479
Cameron Foundation
c/o Gerry Cameron
6902 N.E. Par Ln.
Vancouver, WA 98662

Established in 1997 in WA.
Donor(s): Gerry B. Cameron.

Financial data (yr. ended 12/31/01): Grants paid, $332,009; assets, $7,047,251 (M); gifts received, $714,935; expenditures, $360,213; qualifying distributions, $332,959.
Limitations: Applications not accepted. Giving primarily in Bend and Portland, OR.
Application information: Unsolicited requests for funds not accepted.
Trustees: Gerry B. Cameron, Marilyn C. Cameron.
EIN: 916437877
Codes: FD

55480
Lawrence True and Linda Brown Foundation
P.O. Box 45214
Seattle, WA 98145-2824 (206) 616-2449
Contact: Linda Brown, Tr.

Established in 1997 in VA.
Donor(s): Lawrence True, Linda Brown.
Financial data (yr. ended 12/31/00): Grants paid, $329,164; assets, $13,466,577 (M); gifts received, $6,217,699; expenditures, $347,742; qualifying distributions, $322,074.
Limitations: Giving primarily in Hyannis, MA.
Application information: Application form not required.
Trustees: Linda Brown, Lawrence True.
EIN: 911817055
Codes: FD

55481
The Lematta Foundation
900 Washington St., Ste. 800
Vancouver, WA 98660 (360) 750-0300
Contact: Nancy Lematta, Secy.-Treas.

Established in 1998 in WA.
Donor(s): Wes Lematta.
Financial data (yr. ended 12/31/99): Grants paid, $324,100; assets, $1,792,796 (M); gifts received, $200,000; expenditures, $339,945; qualifying distributions, $323,392.
Limitations: Giving primarily in Portland, OR and WA.
Officers and Directors:* Wes Lematta,* Pres.; Nancy Lematta,* Secy.-Treas.; Greg Damico, Bart Lematta, Betsy Lematta, Marcy Ann Lematta-Abel.
EIN: 911914392
Codes: FD

55482
T.E.W. Foundation
c/o 1001 Logan Bldg.
500 Union St.
Seattle, WA 98101

Established in 1997 in WA.
Donor(s): T. Evans Wyckoff.‡
Financial data (yr. ended 12/31/00): Grants paid, $316,739; assets, $10,838,109 (M); expenditures, $454,840; qualifying distributions, $326,233.
Limitations: Applications not accepted. Giving primarily in WA.
Application information: Contributes only to pre-selected organizations.
Officers: Alison Wyckoff Milliman, Co-Chair.; Paul L. Wyckoff, Co-Chair.
Trustees: Theiline Wyckoff Cramer, Susan Wyckoff Pohl, Ann P. Wyckoff, Martha Wyckoff-Byrne, Sheila Wyckoff-Dickey.
EIN: 911817398
Codes: FD

55483
Colf Family Foundation
c/o Bank of America
P.O. Box 34345
Seattle, WA 98124-1345

Established in 1997 in WA.

Donor(s): Richard W. Colf.
Financial data (yr. ended 12/31/01): Grants paid, $315,912; assets, $506,426 (M); expenditures, $330,308; qualifying distributions, $313,105.
Limitations: Applications not accepted. Giving limited to WA.
Application information: Contributes only to pre-selected organizations.
Officers and Directors:* Richard W. Colf,* Pres.; Margaret Hepola,* Secy.-Treas.; Robert L. Colf.
EIN: 911815575
Codes: FD

55484
Johnston-Fix Foundation
627 E. 17th Ave.
Spokane, WA 99203-2212 (509) 838-2108
Contact: Harriet J. Fix, Pres.

Established in 1948 as The Johnston Foundation; re-organized in 1988 under current name.
Donor(s): Eric Johnston.‡
Financial data (yr. ended 12/31/01): Grants paid, $312,070; assets, $5,662,844 (M); expenditures, $348,777; qualifying distributions, $320,731.
Limitations: Giving in general restricted to Spokane, WA; giving for independent education programs over a wider area.
Application information: Application form not required.
Officers and Trustees:* Harriet J. Fix,* Pres. and Treas.; William C. Fix,* V.P.; Scott B. Lukins,* Secy.; Allan C. Fix, Harold J. Fix, Maage E. LaCounte.
EIN: 943076779
Codes: FD

55485
The Osberg Family Trust
c/o Bank of America
P.O. Box 34345
Seattle, WA 98124-1345
Application address: c/o Bank of America, P.O. Box 24565, Seattle, WA 98124, tel.: (206) 358-1652
Contact: Kevin Fox

Established in 1988 in WA.
Donor(s): Hilma Osberg,‡ Axel Osberg.‡
Financial data (yr. ended 12/31/01): Grants paid, $308,805; assets, $5,886,401 (M); expenditures, $358,270; qualifying distributions, $336,539.
Limitations: Giving primarily in WA.
Application information: Application form not required.
Trustee: Bank of America.
EIN: 943067305
Codes: FD

55486
Fortune Family Foundation
P.O. Box 2847
Kirkland, WA 98083
URL: http://www.fortunefoundation.org
Contact: Kathleen Shaw

Established in 1998 in WA.
Donor(s): Cathryn R. Fortune.
Financial data (yr. ended 12/31/00): Grants paid, $308,603; assets, $3,986,725 (M); expenditures, $322,052; qualifying distributions, $316,487.
Limitations: Giving primarily in the Puget Sound, WA, area.
Application information: Application form required.
Officers and Directors:* Cathryn R. Fortune,* Pres.; John C. Shimer,* V.P.; Reginald S. Koehler III, Secy.; Robert A. Underhill,* Treas.; Scott R. Thomson.
EIN: 911913219

Codes: FD

55487
The Hyde Foundation
4715 133rd St. N.W.
Gig Harbor, WA 98332
Tel.: (253) 858-3278, ext. 7104
Contact: William B. Hyde, Pres.

Established in 1997.
Donor(s): William B. Hyde.
Financial data (yr. ended 12/31/01): Grants paid, $300,000; assets, $3,255,406 (M); expenditures, $306,632; qualifying distributions, $300,000.
Limitations: Giving limited to WA.
Application information: Application form not required.
Officers: William B. Hyde, Pres.; Elizabeth D. Hyde, V.P.; Pamela Hyde Smith, Treas.
EIN: 911797073
Codes: FD

55488
Marco J. Heidner Charitable Trust
c/o Union Bank of California, N.A.
P.O. Box 84495
Seattle, WA 98124-5795

Established in 1995 in WA.
Donor(s): Marco J. Heidner Trust B.
Financial data (yr. ended 12/31/01): Grants paid, $294,739; assets, $5,171,013 (M); expenditures, $328,281; qualifying distributions, $301,800.
Limitations: Applications not accepted. Giving primarily in Tacoma, WA.
Application information: Contributes only to pre-selected organizations.
Trustee: Union Bank of California, N.A.
EIN: 943219943
Codes: FD

55489
Albert Haller Foundation
P.O. Box 2739
Sequim, WA 98382 (360) 683-1119
Additional address: c/o Clallam County United Way, P.O. Box 937, Port Angeles, WA 98362
Contact: Alan Millet, Atty.

Established in 1992 in WA.
Donor(s): Albert G. Haller.‡
Financial data (yr. ended 06/30/01): Grants paid, $292,220; assets, $5,571,524 (M); gifts received, $255,799; expenditures, $360,618; qualifying distributions, $302,722.
Limitations: Giving limited to Clallam County, WA.
Publications: Informational brochure (including application guidelines).
Application information: Contact high school guidance counselor for scholarships. Application form required.
Officers and Directors:* Gary Smith,* Pres.; Dick Schneider, V.P.; Jan Holter,* Secy.-Treas.; Gary Cohn, Mike Joyner.
EIN: 911556810
Codes: FD, GTI

55490
Keller Foundation
c/o Keller Enterprises
1701 S.E. Columbia River Dr., Ste. 100
Vancouver, WA 98661

Established in 1997 in OR.
Financial data (yr. ended 12/31/01): Grants paid, $284,400; assets, $3,453,716 (M); expenditures, $317,813; qualifying distributions, $315,916.
Limitations: Applications not accepted. Giving primarily in Portland, OR.

Application information: Contributes only to pre-selected organizations.
Officers: Richard B. Keller, Chair. and Pres.; Ruth E. Keller, V.P.; Elizabeth K. McCaslim, V.P.
EIN: 911811697
Codes: FD

55491
Murr Family Foundation
1040 Southview Dr.
Walla Walla, WA 99362-9200 (509) 525-1555
Contact: Neil Follett, Pres.

Established in 1992 in WA.
Donor(s): Eva Murr, Michael Murr.
Financial data (yr. ended 06/30/01): Grants paid, $278,117; assets, $95,966 (M); gifts received, $132,372; expenditures, $279,150; qualifying distributions, $278,097.
Limitations: Giving primarily in Walla Walla, WA.
Officers: Neil Follett, Pres.; William Bieloh, V.P.; William Fleenor, Secy.-Treas.
EIN: 911568178
Codes: FD

55492
Ruth H. Brown Foundation
P.O. Box 1784
Friday Harbor, WA 98250
Contact: Charla Brown, Treas.

Established in 1959 in CO.
Donor(s): Ruth H. Brown.
Financial data (yr. ended 12/31/01): Grants paid, $276,500; assets, $5,039,883 (M); expenditures, $319,473; qualifying distributions, $277,098.
Limitations: Applications not accepted. Giving on a national basis.
Application information: Unsolicited requests for funds not considered.
Officers: Darcey Brown, Pres.; Albert Brown, V.P.; Laurene Cochran, Secy.; Charla Brown, Treas.
EIN: 846023395
Codes: FD

55493
Once Foundation
615 2nd Ave., Ste. 100
Seattle, WA 98104-2243

Established in 1998 in WA.
Donor(s): Michael Alhadeff, Marjorie Alhadeff.
Financial data (yr. ended 05/31/01): Grants paid, $275,000; assets, $263,309 (M); expenditures, $276,878; qualifying distributions, $275,000.
Limitations: Applications not accepted.
Application information: Contributes only to pre-selected organizations.
Officers and Directors:* Michael Alhadeff,* Pres.; Marjorie Alhadeff,* V.P. and Secy.-Treas.
EIN: 911894118
Codes: FD

55494
George T. Welch Testamentary Trust
c/o Baker Boyer National Bank
P.O. Box 1796
Walla Walla, WA 99362 (509) 525-2000
Contact: Ted W. Cohan, Trust Off., Baker Boyer National Bank

Established in 1938 in WA.
Financial data (yr. ended 09/30/01): Grants paid, $273,868; assets, $4,246,122 (M); expenditures, $313,301; qualifying distributions, $299,780.
Limitations: Giving limited to Walla Walla County, WA.
Publications: Program policy statement, application guidelines.
Application information: Application form required.

Trustee: Baker Boyer National Bank.
EIN: 916024318
Codes: FD, GTI

55495
Johnson Foundation
c/o Philip L. Johnson
4801 Harbor Ln.
Everett, WA 98203-1509
Application address: c/o Cascade Coffee, 1525 75th St, Everett, WA 98203
Contact: Philip L. Johnson, Tr.

Donor(s): Philip L. Johnson.
Financial data (yr. ended 12/31/01): Grants paid, $271,482; assets, $307,019 (M); expenditures, $305,424; qualifying distributions, $271,072.
Limitations: Giving primarily in Snohomish County, WA.
Application information: Application form required.
Trustee: Phil Johnson.
EIN: 916478049
Codes: FD

55496
Sinegal Family Foundation
P.O. Box 201
Medina, WA 98039

Established in 1998 in WA.
Donor(s): James D. Sinegal, Janet C. Sinegal.
Financial data (yr. ended 04/30/01): Grants paid, $267,100; assets, $6,618,996 (M); expenditures, $296,221; qualifying distributions, $267,100.
Limitations: Applications not accepted. Giving primarily in King County, WA.
Application information: Contributes only to pre-selected organizations.
Trustees: James D. Sinegal, Janet C. Sinegal.
EIN: 916466551
Codes: FD

55497
The Everard Family Foundation
15824 S.E. 296th St.
Kent, WA 98042 (253) 631-4737
Contact: Lloyd D. Everard, Tr.

Established in 2000 in WA.
Donor(s): Lloyd D. Everard, Glenda C. Everard.
Financial data (yr. ended 12/31/01): Grants paid, $262,661; assets, $932,026 (M); gifts received, $500; expenditures, $270,787; qualifying distributions, $258,851.
Application information: Application form not required.
Trustees: Donald Everard, Glenda C. Everard, Lloyd D. Everard, Alan Gray, Deanne Sandvold.
EIN: 911998779
Codes: FD

55498
Grays Harbor Community Foundation
630 Seafirst Bldg.
P.O. Box 63
Aberdeen, WA 98520 (360) 532-6873
FAX: (360) 532-6882
Contact: Frank H. Larner, Pres.

Established in 1994 in WA.
Financial data (yr. ended 12/31/01): Grants paid, $262,163; assets, $5,455,509 (M); gifts received, $860,000; expenditures, $280,439.
Limitations: Giving primarily in Grays Harbor County, and the Aberdeen, WA, area.
Publications: Annual report, informational brochure, application guidelines.
Application information: Application form required.

55498—WASHINGTON

Officers and Directors:* Stan Pinnick,* Chair.; Frank H. Larner, Pres.; Todd Lindley, V.P.; Tom Brennan,* Secy.; Bob Preble, Treas.
EIN: 911607005
Codes: CM

55499
The Breneman Jaech Foundation
(Formerly The Jaech Family Foundation)
c/o Quellos Financial Advisors, LLC
601 Union St., 56th Fl.
Seattle, WA 98101
Application address: 3020 Issaquah Pine Lake Rd., PMB No. 305, Sammamish, WA 98075; E-mail: kayleejaech@attbi.com
Contact: Kaylee Jaech

Established in 2000 in WA.
Donor(s): Jeremy A. Jaech, Linda R. Breneman.
Financial data (yr. ended 12/31/01): Grants paid, $259,304; assets, $5,168 (M); gifts received, $31,167; expenditures, $318,758; qualifying distributions, $256,381.
Limitations: Applications not accepted. Giving primarily in WA.
Application information: Contributes only to pre-selected organizations.
Officers and Directors:* Linda R. Breneman,* Pres., V.P., and Treas.; Frances McCue,* Secy.; Kaylee Jaech, Exec. Dir.
EIN: 912041065
Codes: FD

55500
The Spitzer Foundation
P.O. Box 2008
Kirkland, WA 98083-2008
Contact: Jack J. Spitzer, Pres.

Established in 1981 in WA.
Donor(s): Charlotte Spitzer, Jack J. Spitzer.
Financial data (yr. ended 12/31/99): Grants paid, $259,262; assets, $434,746 (M); expenditures, $262,560; qualifying distributions, $255,841.
Limitations: Applications not accepted. Giving primarily in WA.
Application information: Contributes only to pre-selected organizations.
Officers and Trustees:* Jack J. Spitzer,* Pres.; Charlotte Spitzer,* V.P.; Robert B. Spitzer,* Secy.; Davis B. Fox, Treas.; Kathleen Spitzer, Jill Spitzer-Fox.
EIN: 911160605
Codes: FD

55501
Irving A. Lassen Foundation
(Formerly The Irving A. Lassen Trust)
P.O. Box 1667
Olympia, WA 98507-1667 (360) 943-2820

Established in 1973 in WA.
Donor(s): Irving A. Lassen.‡
Financial data (yr. ended 12/31/01): Grants paid, $257,355; assets, $5,091,193 (M); gifts received, $12,226; expenditures, $375,407; qualifying distributions, $315,587.
Limitations: Giving limited to Thurston County, WA.
Publications: Informational brochure (including application guidelines), grants list.
Application information: Pacific Northwest Grantmakers Forum Common Grant Application Form accepted. Application form required.
Trustees: Arleigh T. Jones, Frank J. Owens, Julia E. Wiegman.
EIN: 916215691
Codes: FD

55502
Ordinary People Foundation
12810 N.E. 64th St.
Kirkland, WA 98033-8553

Established in 1999 in WA.
Donor(s): Daniel Welse, Laura Yedwab.
Financial data (yr. ended 12/31/01): Grants paid, $255,000; assets, $6,402,792 (M); gifts received, $4,200; expenditures, $261,787; qualifying distributions, $260,379.
Limitations: Applications not accepted. Giving primarily in NY and WA.
Application information: Contributes only to pre-selected organizations.
Officers: Laura Yedwab, Pres.; Daniel Welse, V.P.
EIN: 912014376
Codes: FD

55503
The Wellworth Foundation
11055-204th Ave. N.E.
Redmond, WA 98053

Established in 1997 in WA.
Donor(s): David J. Thacher, Nancy C. Thacher.
Financial data (yr. ended 12/31/00): Grants paid, $254,360; assets, $1,600,607 (M); gifts received, $351,262; expenditures, $257,147; qualifying distributions, $254,424.
Limitations: Applications not accepted.
Application information: Contributes only to pre-selected organizations.
Trustees: David J. Thacher, Nancy C. Thacher.
EIN: 916438273
Codes: FD

55504
Gordon D. Sondland and Katherine J. Durant Foundation
(Formerly Gordon D. Sondland Foundation)
1531 7th Ave., 20th Fl.
Seattle, WA 98101-1719
Contact: Gordon D. Sondland, Pres.

Established in 1991 in WA.
Donor(s): Gordon D. Sondland.
Financial data (yr. ended 12/31/01): Grants paid, $253,310; assets, $329,296 (M); gifts received, $200,000; expenditures, $254,643; qualifying distributions, $253,653.
Limitations: Applications not accepted. Giving primarily in OR and WA.
Application information: Contributes only to pre-selected organizations.
Officer: Gordon D. Sondland, Pres.
EIN: 911534721
Codes: FD

55505
drugstore.com Foundation
13920 S.E. Eastgate Way, Ste. 300
Bellevue, WA 98005
E-mail: foundation@drugstore.com

Established in 1999 in WA.
Donor(s): drugstore.com, inc.
Financial data (yr. ended 06/30/01): Grants paid, $252,500; assets, $3,038,569 (M); expenditures, $264,784; qualifying distributions, $255,580.
Limitations: Giving limited to organizations that have operations in western WA and/or southern NJ.
Application information: Proposals accepted upon invitation only following foundation review of letter of inquiry.
Officers and Directors:* Kal Raman,* Pres.; Alesia L. Pinney,* V.P. and Secy.; Bob Barton, Treas.
EIN: 943341248
Codes: CS, CD

55506
Paul L. King Charitable Foundation
P.O. Box 61669
Vancouver, WA 98666

Established in 1997 in WA.
Donor(s): Paul L. King.
Financial data (yr. ended 12/31/01): Grants paid, $251,820; assets, $3,700,645 (M); expenditures, $251,887; qualifying distributions, $251,188.
Limitations: Applications not accepted. Giving primarily in MA.
Application information: Contributes only to pre-selected organizations.
Trustee: Paul L. King.
EIN: 911811633
Codes: FD

55507
Mooney Charitable Trust
601 Union St., Ste. 3003
Seattle, WA 98101
Contact: Dean Amundson, Tr.

Established in 1997 in WA.
Financial data (yr. ended 12/31/00): Grants paid, $250,000; assets, $4,880,612 (M); expenditures, $272,394; qualifying distributions, $272,294.
Trustee: Dean Amundson.
EIN: 916411347
Codes: FD

55508
William Kilworth Charitable Foundation
c/o KeyBank, N.A.
1101 Pacific Ave., 3rd Fl., WA-31-01-0310
Tacoma, WA 98411-5052
Contact: Bollie C. Determan, V.P.

Trust established in 1968 in WA.
Financial data (yr. ended 12/31/01): Grants paid, $249,000; assets, $5,119,926 (M); expenditures, $288,077; qualifying distributions, $258,241.
Limitations: Giving limited to residents of Pierce County, WA.
Application information: Scholarship program administered by colleges; standard form available from each school.
Trustee: KeyBank, N.A.
EIN: 916072527
Codes: FD

55509
Opportunities for Education Foundation
P.O. Box 77630
Seattle, WA 98177-0630

Established in 2000 in WA.
Donor(s): Chris Larson.
Financial data (yr. ended 12/31/01): Grants paid, $246,006; assets, $10,171,930 (M); gifts received, $11,000; expenditures, $251,282; qualifying distributions, $246,006.
Limitations: Applications not accepted.
Application information: Contributes only to pre-selected organizations.
Officers: Chris Larson, Pres.; Julia Calhoun, V.P. and Treas.; Lawrence B. Bailey, Secy.
EIN: 912091348

55510
Teel Charitable Foundation
c/o Seattle Pacific Foundation
3307 3rd Ave. W.
Seattle, WA 98119-1940 (206) 281-2993
Contact: Gordan Nygard

Financial data (yr. ended 12/31/01): Grants paid, $246,000; assets, $5,166,621 (M); expenditures, $252,131; qualifying distributions, $236,282.

Limitations: Giving primarily in WA, with emphasis on Seattle.
Officers: E. Gerald Teel, Pres.; Chuck Teel, V.P.; Daryl Vander Pol, Secy.
EIN: 911083941
Codes: FD2

55511
Pendleton and Elisabeth Carey Miller Charitable Foundation
3147 Fairview Ave. E., Ste. 200
Seattle, WA 98102-3019 (206) 329-1019
FAX: (206) 329-8230; E-mail: Plangiv@aol.com
Contact: Frank Minton, Secy.-Treas.

Established in 1995 in WA.
Financial data (yr. ended 12/31/01): Grants paid, $245,308; assets, $12,044,278 (M); gifts received, $12,116,063; expenditures, $303,976; qualifying distributions, $259,522.
Limitations: Giving primarily in WA.
Publications: Application guidelines, occasional report, informational brochure (including application guidelines).
Application information: Application form not required.
Officers and Trustees:* Winlock W. Miller,* Pres.; Carey K. Miller,* V.P.; Frank D. Minton,* Secy.-Treas.; Elisabeth A. Bottler, Richard A. Brown, W. Howarth Meadowcroft, Malcolm Moore, Ralph Polumbo, Geoffrey G. Revelle.
EIN: 911671814
Codes: FD2

55512
W. Razore Family Foundation
3927 Lake Washington Blvd., N.E.
Kirkland, WA 98033-7867 (425) 822-1996
Contact: Jeffrey A. Williamson, V.P. and Treas.

Established in 1998.
Donor(s): Mary J. Razore.
Financial data (yr. ended 04/30/01): Grants paid, $245,000; assets, $3,389,248 (M); expenditures, $250,299; qualifying distributions, $245,000.
Limitations: Giving primarily in Denver, CO.
Officers: Mary J. Razore, Pres.; Robert S. Jaffe, V.P. and Secy.; Jeffrey A. Williamson, V.P. and Treas.
EIN: 911939131
Codes: FD2

55513
Johnston-Hanson Foundation
5118 S. Perry St.
Spokane, WA 99223 (509) 448-4708
Contact: Elizabeth J. Hanson, Chair.

Established in 1948 in WA as The Johnston Foundation; re-organized in 1988 under current name.
Donor(s): Eric Johnston.‡
Financial data (yr. ended 12/31/01): Grants paid, $242,650; assets, $4,739,031 (M); expenditures, $271,367; qualifying distributions, $255,911.
Limitations: Giving primarily in the Spokane, WA, area.
Application information: Application form not required.
Officers and Directors:* Elizabeth J. Hanson,* Chair. and Secy.-Treas.; Fred L. Hanson, Vice-Chair.; Herbert Johnston Butler, Victoria Carney, Eric Hanson, Maage E. LaCounte, Ann Hanson Scarborough, Gil Zwetsch.
EIN: 943077091
Codes: FD2

55514
George A. & Grace W. Barker Foundation
P.O. Box 34345
Seattle, WA 98124-1345

Established in 2000 in WA.
Donor(s): George A. Barker Trust.
Financial data (yr. ended 08/31/02): Grants paid, $240,000; assets, $4,425,659 (M); gifts received, $2,936,298; expenditures, $291,176; qualifying distributions, $240,000.
Limitations: Applications not accepted.
Application information: Contributes only to pre-selected organizations.
Trustee: Bank of America.
EIN: 957094103

55515
Robert C. and Nani S. Warren Foundation
82 Swigert Rd.
Washougal, WA 98671

Established in 1994 in WA and OR.
Donor(s): Nani S. Warren.
Financial data (yr. ended 12/31/00): Grants paid, $239,279; assets, $5,781,085 (M); gifts received, $45,701; expenditures, $266,186; qualifying distributions, $239,279.
Limitations: Applications not accepted.
Application information: Contributes only to pre-selected organizations.
Officer: Penny Guest, Treas.
Directors: Jack B. Schwartz, Elizabeth Warren, Nani S. Warren.
EIN: 931083078
Codes: FD2

55516
Carl M. Hansen Foundation, Inc.
1420 U.S. Bank Bldg.
Spokane, WA 99201-0395

Established in 1965.
Donor(s): Carl M. Hansen.‡
Financial data (yr. ended 12/31/01): Grants paid, $238,100; assets, $3,951,450 (M); expenditures, $269,619; qualifying distributions, $243,219.
Limitations: Applications not accepted. Giving primarily in WA, with some emphasis on Spokane.
Application information: Unsolicited requests for funds not accepted.
Trustees: Scott B. Lukins, Laurence D. Morse.
EIN: 916063191
Codes: FD2, GTI

55517
GLA Foundation
c/o Irwin L. Treiger
1420 5th Ave., No. 400
Seattle, WA 98101-1307
Application address: 949 S. Coast Dr., No. 600, Costa Mesa, CA 92626
Contact: Daniel Russo, V.P.

Established in 1990 in WA.
Donor(s): Hardball-I, LP, George L. Argyros.
Financial data (yr. ended 03/31/01): Grants paid, $233,100; assets, $6,382,877 (M); expenditures, $233,100; qualifying distributions, $233,100.
Limitations: Giving primarily in CA and Washington, DC.
Officers: George L. Argyros, Pres. and Treas.; Dan Russo, V.P. and Secy.
Director: Irwin L. Treiger.
EIN: 931029890
Codes: FD2

55518
Hugh S. Cannon Foundation
1420 5th Ave., Ste. 4100
Seattle, WA 98101-2338
Contact: James Robart, Tr.

Established in 1995 in WA.
Donor(s): Hugh S. Cannon.‡
Financial data (yr. ended 12/31/01): Grants paid, $230,000; assets, $4,758,861 (M); expenditures, $232,598; qualifying distributions, $225,963.
Limitations: Giving limited to the Pacific Northwest.
Trustees: James Robart, Winslow Wright.
EIN: 911691964
Codes: FD2

55519
The Floyd & Delores Jones Foundation
(Formerly The Jones Foundation)
16268 38th Ave., N.E.
Seattle, WA 98155

Established in 1986.
Donor(s): Delores H. Jones, Floyd U. Jones, Peasley Tugby & Co.
Financial data (yr. ended 12/31/01): Grants paid, $229,500; assets, $1,337,653 (M); gifts received, $15,630; expenditures, $236,198; qualifying distributions, $231,977.
Limitations: Applications not accepted. Giving primarily in Seattle, WA.
Application information: Contributes only to pre-selected organizations.
Trustees: Delores H. Jones, Floyd U. Jones.
EIN: 911356973
Codes: FD2

55520
The Burning Foundation
5135 Ballard Ave. N.W.
Seattle, WA 98107 (206) 781-8472
FAX: (206) 784-5987; E-mail: OgleFounds@aol.com; URL: http://fdncenter.org/grantmaker/burning
Contact: Therese Ogle, Grants Consultant

Established in 1997 in WA.
Donor(s): David Weise.
Financial data (yr. ended 12/31/99): Grants paid, $225,250; assets, $6,018,114 (M); expenditures, $230,987; qualifying distributions, $229,755.
Limitations: Giving limited to WA and OR for environmental requests, and the Puget Sound area for conservation programs for youth and teen pregnancy prevention programs.
Application information: See foundation Web site for complete application guidelines. Accepts Philanthropy Northwest Common Grant Application Form. Materials submitted by fax or e-mail not considered.
Officers: David Weise, Pres. and Secy.; Virginia Hadlett, V.P.; Ira Weise, Secy.
EIN: 911815335
Codes: FD2

55521
The Lindgren Foundation
P.O. Box 1681
Gig Harbor, WA 98335
Contact: Eric W. Lindgren, Secy.-Treas.

Established in 1992 in OR.
Donor(s): Ruby F. Lindgren Trust, Clarence R. Lindren.‡
Financial data (yr. ended 04/30/01): Grants paid, $225,000; assets, $3,959,972 (M); expenditures, $265,457; qualifying distributions, $229,251.
Limitations: Applications not accepted. Giving primarily in CA and WA.

55521—WASHINGTON

Officers: Paul E. Lindgren, Pres.; Eric W. Lindgren, Secy.-Treas.
Trustee: Theodore A. Nedderman.
EIN: 931090831
Codes: FD2

55522
Fales Foundation Trust
c/o Union Bank of California, N.A.
P.O. Box 84495
Seattle, WA 98114-3123 (206) 781-3472
Application address: c/o Union Bank of California, P.O. Box 3123, Seattle, WA 98114;
URL: http://fdncenter.org/grantmaker/fales
Contact: J. Thomas McCully

Established in 1985 in WA.
Donor(s): Gilbert R. Fales.‡
Financial data (yr. ended 01/31/02): Grants paid, $221,000; assets, $3,519,167 (M); expenditures, $306,150; qualifying distributions, $246,541.
Limitations: Giving limited to Seattle, WA.
Publications: Application guidelines.
Application information: Application form required.
Trustees: Ward L. Sax, Union Bank of California, N.A.
EIN: 916087669
Codes: FD2

55523
Peach Foundation
1017 Minor Ave., Ste. 1202
Seattle, WA 98104

Established in 2001 in WA.
Donor(s): Priscilla Collins.
Financial data (yr. ended 12/31/01): Grants paid, $219,000; assets, $5,000,033 (M); gifts received, $5,042,758; expenditures, $223,145; qualifying distributions, $219,751.
Limitations: Applications not accepted.
Application information: Contributes only to pre-selected organizations.
Officers and Directors:* Priscilla B. Collins,* Pres.; Delphine Haley,* Secy.; Crane Wright,* Treas.; Jean Gardner.
EIN: 912094325
Codes: FD2

55524
McKinstry Company Charitable Foundation
P.O. Box 24567
Seattle, WA 98124
Contact: J. William Teplicky, Jr., Tr.

Established in 1998 in WA.
Donor(s): McKinstry Co., Dean Allen.
Financial data (yr. ended 09/30/01): Grants paid, $214,100; assets, $403,115 (M); gifts received, $129,000; expenditures, $214,369; qualifying distributions, $213,919.
Limitations: Applications not accepted. Giving primarily in Seattle, WA.
Application information: Contributes only to pre-selected organizations.
Trustees: Dean Allen, George Allen, Vicki Allen, J. William Teplicky, Jr.
EIN: 911942024
Codes: CS, FD2

55525
The Tamaki Foundation
4739 University Way N.E., Ste. 1636
Seattle, WA 98105

Established in 1988 in WA.
Donor(s): Meriko Tamaki.
Financial data (yr. ended 12/31/01): Grants paid, $213,641; assets, $3,944,228 (M); expenditures, $245,639; qualifying distributions, $216,111.

Limitations: Giving on a national basis, with emphasis on CA.
Officers: Meriko Tamaki, Pres.; Fr. John Martin, V.P.; Kozo Yamamura, Secy.; John H. Hopkins, Treas.
EIN: 943099647
Codes: FD2

55526
The Schneebeck Foundation
1 Stadium Way N., Ste. 16
Tacoma, WA 98403

Established in 1998 in WA.
Donor(s): Bethel J. Schneebeck.
Financial data (yr. ended 12/31/00): Grants paid, $213,543; assets, $737,883 (M); expenditures, $231,899; qualifying distributions, $213,073.
Limitations: Applications not accepted.
Application information: Contributes only to pre-selected organizations.
Officers: Bethel J. Schneebeck, Pres.; Judith Bensinger, V.P.; David E. Schneebeck, V.P.; Robert G. Albertson, Secy.-Treas.
EIN: 912007229
Codes: FD2

55527
Dupar Foundation
P.O. Box 24488
Seattle, WA 98124-0488 (425) 831-1505
FAX: (425) 831-1505; E-mail: duparfoundation@attbi.com
Contact: Shirlee Hargett, Admin.

Incorporated in 1954 in WA.
Donor(s): Frank A. Dupar,‡ Ethel L. Dupar,‡ Palmer Supply Co.
Financial data (yr. ended 01/31/02): Grants paid, $213,475; assets, $3,058,898 (M); gifts received, $3,700; expenditures, $270,080; qualifying distributions, $221,723.
Limitations: Giving limited to King County, WA.
Publications: Program policy statement, application guidelines.
Application information: Application form required.
Officers and Trustees:* James W. Dupar,* Pres.; Adrienne Riley,* V.P.; Michelle Stuart,* Secy.; Thomas E. Dupar,* Treas.; Robert W. Dupar.
EIN: 916027389
Codes: FD2

55528
Stack Foundation
2201 6th Ave. S.
Seattle, WA 98134-2001 (206) 622-6288
Contact: Harold E. Stack, Pres.

Established in 1981 in WA.
Donor(s): Harold E. Stack, Gertrude W. Stack.
Financial data (yr. ended 12/31/01): Grants paid, $210,174; assets, $2,140,745 (M); gifts received, $362,231; expenditures, $211,126; qualifying distributions, $208,512.
Limitations: Applications not accepted. Giving primarily in Seattle, WA.
Application information: Contributes only to pre-selected organizations.
Officers: Harold E. Stack, Pres.; Gertrude W. Stack, V.P. and Treas.; Robert Purdue, Secy.
EIN: 911154782
Codes: FD2

55529
Connected Giving
c/o James Mallahan
7728 Fairway Dr. N.E.
Seattle, WA 98115

Established in 2000 in WA.

Donor(s): James Mallahan.
Financial data (yr. ended 12/31/01): Grants paid, $208,000; assets, $44,144 (M); expenditures, $210,734; qualifying distributions, $208,000.
Limitations: Applications not accepted. Giving primarily in NY.
Application information: Contributes only to pre-selected organizations.
Officer: Jeff Lum, Pres.
Directors: Steve Hicken, James Mallahan, Joseph Mallahan.
EIN: 912049019

55530
Kawabe Memorial Fund
(also known as Harry S. Kawabe Trust)
c/o Bank of America
P.O. Box 24565
Seattle, WA 98124-1345 (206) 358-3144
URL: http://fdncenter.org/grantmaker/kawabe
Contact: Margaret Liu

Trust established in 1972 in WA.
Donor(s): Tomo Kawabe,‡ Harry Kawabe.‡
Financial data (yr. ended 12/31/01): Grants paid, $208,000; assets, $4,140,101 (M); expenditures, $260,524; qualifying distributions, $240,129.
Limitations: Giving primarily in AK and the Seattle, WA, area; scholarships limited to graduating students in Seward, AK.
Publications: Application guidelines.
Application information: Application form not required.
Allocation Committee: Yasue Brevig, Rev. Donald Castro, Alan T. Hoshino, Aizo Kozai, Takashi Matsui, Tsuyoshi Nakano, Toru Sakahara, Fred Takayesu, Katsumi Tanino, Warren Yasutake.
Trustee: Bank of America.
EIN: 916116549
Codes: FD2

55531
The Baker Foundation
1201 Pacific Ave., Ste. 1475
Tacoma, WA 98402
Contact: Sydney Parker

Established in 1987 in WA.
Donor(s): Elbert H. Baker II, Martine Baker, Suzanne Bethke, Robert W. Bethke, Jay Prince.
Financial data (yr. ended 12/31/01): Grants paid, $206,950; assets, $7,029,467 (M); gifts received, $105,860; expenditures, $428,861; qualifying distributions, $291,897.
Limitations: Giving limited to WA.
Application information: Application form required.
Officer: Robert W. Bethke, Exec. Dir.
Directors: Suzanne Bethke, Jay Prince.
EIN: 943027892
Codes: FD2

55532
Kathryn & Otto H. Wagner Charitable Trust
c/o Bank of America
P.O. Box 34345
Seattle, WA 98124-1345
Application address: P.O. Box 128, Twisp, WA 99856-0128
Contact: Jodi Gardner, Tr.

Donor(s): Kathryn L. Wagner, Kathryn Wagner Trust.
Financial data (yr. ended 12/31/01): Grants paid, $206,824; assets, $866,732 (M); gifts received, $593,343; expenditures, $234,500; qualifying distributions, $229,043.
Application information: Recipients are selected by trustee. Application form required.
Trustees: Jodi Gardner, Bank of America.

EIN: 916103623
Codes: FD2, GTI

55533
Wilkins Charitable Foundation
(also known as Catherine Holmes Wilkins Foundation)
c/o Bank of America
P.O. Box 34345
Seattle, WA 98124-1345
Application address: P.O. Box 24565, Seattle, WA 98124, tel.: (206) 358-0806; URL: http://fdncenter.org/grantmaker/wilkins
Contact: Loy D. Smith, Secy.

Established in 1986.
Donor(s): Catherine Wilkins.‡
Financial data (yr. ended 08/31/01): Grants paid, $206,260; assets, $4,273,816 (M); expenditures, $265,417; qualifying distributions, $239,053.
Limitations: Giving limited to the greater Seattle, WA, area.
Publications: Application guidelines.
Application information: Application form required.
Officers: Brian Comstock, Chair.; Bob Bunting, Vice-Chair.; Loy D. Smith, Secy. and Mgr.
Trustee: Bank of America.
EIN: 916277933
Codes: FD2

55534
The Templin Foundation
P.O. Box 2190
Everett, WA 98203

Established in 1992 in WA.
Donor(s): Allys M. Templin,‡ Russell B. Templin.
Financial data (yr. ended 12/31/00): Grants paid, $202,402; assets, $4,484,477 (M); expenditures, $286,852; qualifying distributions, $202,402.
Limitations: Applications not accepted. Giving primarily in WA.
Application information: Contributes only to pre-selected organizations.
Officers: James Finlay, Pres.; Tracy Moore, Jr., V.P.; Ancil Davis, Secy.-Treas.
Directors: Patricia C. Nelson, Sidney R. Snyder.
EIN: 943166824
Codes: FD2

55535
Anderson Family Foundation
5000 Columbia Ctr., 701 5th Ave.
Seattle, WA 98104-7078 (206) 623-7580
Contact: Lisa Wasberg

Established in 1974 in WA.
Donor(s): Barbara May Anderson, Charles L. Anderson.
Financial data (yr. ended 09/30/01): Grants paid, $200,000; assets, $2,751,643 (M); gifts received, $65,000; expenditures, $228,802; qualifying distributions, $200,010.
Limitations: Giving on a national basis.
Application information: Application form not required.
Officers and Directors:* Charles L. Anderson,* Pres.; Barbara May Anderson,* V.P.; Richard B. Dodd, Secy.; Rebecca L. Barton,* Treas.; Paul J. Anderson, Linda D. Aruffo.
EIN: 510147901
Codes: FD2

55536
Samuel and Althea Stroum Philanthropic Foundation
(Formerly The Stroum Philanthropic Foundation)
1420 5th Ave., Ste. 3000
Seattle, WA 98101-2370

Established in 1987 in WA.
Donor(s): Samuel N. Stroum.
Financial data (yr. ended 12/31/01): Grants paid, $199,500; assets, $3,998,324 (M); expenditures, $254,135; qualifying distributions, $199,973.
Limitations: Applications not accepted. Giving primarily in WA.
Application information: Contributes only to pre-selected organizations.
Officers: Cynthia Stroum, Pres. and Treas.; Althea Stroum, Secy.
Directors: Adam Sloan, Courtney Sloan, Scott Sloan.
EIN: 911397126
Codes: FD2

55537
Morris, William, and Betty Rashkov Charitable Trust
c/o Bank of America, Tax Svcs.
P.O. Box 34345
Seattle, WA 98124-1345

Established in WA.
Financial data (yr. ended 12/31/01): Grants paid, $198,270; assets, $4,703,165 (M); gifts received, $326,365; expenditures, $260,728; qualifying distributions, $229,150.
Limitations: Applications not accepted. Giving primarily in New York, NY.
Application information: Contributes only to pre-selected organizations.
Trustees: C.E. Huppin, Bank of America.
EIN: 916479989
Codes: FD2

55538
Harold and Helen Shepherd Foundation
P.O. Box 1757
Walla Walla, WA 99362-0348
Contact: H.H. Hayner, Tr.

Established in 1996 in WA.
Financial data (yr. ended 12/31/00): Grants paid, $197,520; assets, $6,647,998 (M); expenditures, $280,366; qualifying distributions, $224,297.
Limitations: Giving primarily in Garried, Asotin, Columbia, and Walla Walla counties, WA.
Trustees: H.H. Hayner, Gary Houser.
EIN: 911708510
Codes: FD2

55539
Howarth Trust Fund
(Formerly Cawsey Trust Fund)
P.O. Box 5490
Everett, WA 98206-5490
Contact: Caryl Thorpe

Incorporated in 1960 in WA.
Donor(s): Mrs. Hugh R. Cawsey.‡
Financial data (yr. ended 12/31/01): Grants paid, $196,000; assets, $3,387,303 (M); gifts received, $550; expenditures, $203,188; qualifying distributions, $194,651.
Limitations: Giving primarily in Snohomish County, WA, with emphasis on the Everett area.
Publications: Application guidelines.
Officers and Trustees:* G. Paul Carpenter,* Pres.; H. Roy Yates,* V.P.; Elizabeth M. Campbell,* Secy.-Treas.; Mary Ellen Denman, W. Howarth Meadowcroft.
EIN: 916053815
Codes: FD2

55540
Razore Foundation
3927 Lake Washington Blvd. N.E.
Kirkland, WA 98033-7867 (425) 822-1996

Established in 1997 in WA.
Donor(s): Joan M. Razore, Josie Razore.
Financial data (yr. ended 04/30/01): Grants paid, $195,960; assets, $4,378,845 (M); gifts received, $19,200; expenditures, $199,206; qualifying distributions, $179,181.
Limitations: Giving primarily in WA, with emphasis on Seattle.
Application information: Application form not required.
Officer: Joan M. Razore, Pres. and Treas.
EIN: 911877166
Codes: FD2

55541
Whatcom Community Foundation
119 Grand Ave., Ste. A
Bellingham, WA 98225 (360) 671-6463
FAX: (360) 671-6437; E-mail: wcf@whatcomcf.org; URL: http://whatcomcf.org
Contact: Don Drake, Pres.

Established in 1996 in WA.
Financial data (yr. ended 06/30/02): Grants paid, $195,712; assets, $3,403,906 (M); gifts received, $508,354; expenditures, $423,845.
Limitations: Giving limited to Whatcom County, WA.
Publications: Annual report, grants list, informational brochure, application guidelines, newsletter.
Application information: Application form required.
Officers: Tom Hunter, Chair.; Mary Boire, Vice-Chair.; Don Drake, Pres.; Paul Tholfsen, Treas.
Directors: Randy Bode, Sue Cole, Paul B. Hanson, Marge Laidlow, D.C. Morse, Charles Self, Sue Sharpe, Tom Thornton, Sue Webber.
EIN: 911726410
Codes: CM, FD2

55542
Martin Family Foundation
3312 181st Pl. N.E.
Redmond, WA 98052

Established in 2000 in WA.
Donor(s): Darlene E. Martin, Roy W. Martin.
Financial data (yr. ended 12/31/01): Grants paid, $193,084; assets, $3,351,447 (M); expenditures, $194,441; qualifying distributions, $193,084.
Limitations: Giving primarily in Seattle, WA.
Trustees: Darlene E. Martin, Roy W. Martin.
EIN: 912089435

55543
Cooper & Levy Trust
c/o Union Bank of California, N.A.
P.O. Box 3123
Seattle, WA 98114 (206) 781-3472
E-mail: oglefounds@aol.com
Contact: Therese Ogle, Grants Consultant

Established in 1995 in WA.
Financial data (yr. ended 12/31/01): Grants paid, $192,361; assets, $3,340,799 (M); expenditures, $223,032; qualifying distributions, $201,656.
Limitations: Applications not accepted. Giving primarily in Seattle, WA.
Application information: Contributes only to pre-selected organizations.
Trustee: Union Bank of California, N.A.
EIN: 911726697
Codes: FD2

55544
The Larson Family Charitable Foundation
14224 168th Ave. N.E.
Woodinville, WA 98072

Established in 1997 in WA.
Donor(s): Dale Larson, Phyllis Larson.
Financial data (yr. ended 12/31/01): Grants paid, $190,921; assets, $2,746,985 (M); expenditures, $194,812; qualifying distributions, $189,635.
Limitations: Applications not accepted. Giving primarily in WA.
Application information: Contributes only to pre-selected organizations.
Officers: Dale Larson, Pres.; Phyllis Larson, Secy.
EIN: 911875867
Codes: FD2

55545
InfoSpace Foundation
601 108th Ave. N.E., Ste. 1200
Bellevue, WA 98004 (425) 201-8947
Contact: Angela Lee

Established in 2000.
Donor(s): InfoSpace, Inc.
Financial data (yr. ended 12/31/01): Grants paid, $186,000; assets, $173,584 (M); expenditures, $186,000; qualifying distributions, $187,380.
Limitations: Giving primarily in WA.
Application information: Application form required.
Officer: Anu Jain, Chair.
Directors: Gwya Baine, Corina Seale, Vargie Tarsey.
EIN: 912018349
Codes: CS, FD2, CD

55546
Whitaker Foundation
(Formerly Villa Care Foundation)
1505 N.W. Gilman Blvd., Ste. 1
Issaquah, WA 98027-5329 (425) 392-7583
Contact: Mary C. Whitaker, Pres.

Established in 1975 in WA.
Donor(s): John L. Whitaker, Mary C. Whitaker.
Financial data (yr. ended 12/31/01): Grants paid, $183,970; assets, $2,576,444 (M); gifts received, $101,775; expenditures, $191,091; qualifying distributions, $184,097.
Limitations: Giving primarily in WA.
Application information: Application form not required.
Officers: Mary C. Whitaker, Pres. and V.P.; Cheryl Matheny, Secy.
Director: William Whitaker.
EIN: 237301744
Codes: FD2

55547
The Patrice and Kevin Auld Foundation
1137 Harvard Ave. E.
Seattle, WA 98102 (206) 324-8817
Contact: Kevin Auld, Pres.

Established in 1997 in WA.
Donor(s): Kevin Auld, Patrice Auld, Bernard A. & Chris Marden Foundation.
Financial data (yr. ended 08/31/01): Grants paid, $183,755; assets, $1,965,089 (M); expenditures, $190,916; qualifying distributions, $187,379.
Limitations: Applications not accepted. Giving primarily in WA.
Application information: Contributes only to pre-selected organizations.
Officers: Kevin Auld, Pres.; Patrice Auld, V.P.
EIN: 911736747
Codes: FD2

55548
The F. Danz Foundation
P.O. Box 91723
Bellevue, WA 98009-1723

Established in 1998 in WA.
Donor(s): Frederic A. Danz.
Financial data (yr. ended 12/31/00): Grants paid, $183,250; assets, $592,644 (M); gifts received, $500,000; expenditures, $183,806; qualifying distributions, $183,390.
Limitations: Applications not accepted. Giving primarily in CA and WA.
Application information: Contributes only to pre-selected organizations.
Trustees: Alison Danz, Frederic A. Danz, William F. Danz.
EIN: 916477156
Codes: FD2

55549
Mattaini Family Foundation
91 Cascade Key
Bellevue, WA 98006
Application address: 5408 142nd Ave. S.E., Bellevue, WA 98006
Contact: Barry Mattaini, Pres.

Established in 1998 in WA.
Donor(s): Barry Mattaini, Nancy Mattaini.
Financial data (yr. ended 12/31/00): Grants paid, $181,460; assets, $2,635,546 (M); expenditures, $201,383; qualifying distributions, $179,314.
Limitations: Giving primarily in WA.
Application information: Application procedures being developed.
Officers and Directors:* Barry Mattaini,* Pres.; Nancy Mattaini,* V.P.
EIN: 911938648
Codes: FD2

55550
The Schoenfeld-Gardner Foundation
5701 Columbia Ctr., 701 5th Ave.
Seattle, WA 98104-7003
Contact: James Biagi

Established in 1956 in WA.
Financial data (yr. ended 04/30/02): Grants paid, $181,352; assets, $2,332,363 (M); expenditures, $210,567; qualifying distributions, $181,352.
Limitations: Giving primarily in WA.
Application information: Application form not required.
Officers and Trustees:* Herbert Schoenfeld, Jr.,* Pres.; Ralph A. Schoenfeld,* V.P.; Nancy S. Burnett, 2nd V.P.; Judy B. Schoenfeld, Secy.; Stanford M. Bernbaum, Jr., Treas.
EIN: 916055133

55551
Laird Norton Endowment Foundation
801 2nd Ave., Ste. 1300
Seattle, WA 98104 (206) 464-5242
FAX: (206) 464-5099; *E-mail:* defreitas@lairdnorton.org; *URL:* http://www.lairdnorton.org
Contact: Patrick de Freitas, Pres.

Incorporated in 1940 in MN.
Donor(s): Founding family members and related businesses.
Financial data (yr. ended 12/31/99): Grants paid, $180,420; assets, $5,547,278 (M); gifts received, $131,567; expenditures, $229,400; qualifying distributions, $208,197.
Limitations: Giving on a national basis, with emphasis on the Pacific Northwest.
Publications: Annual report, informational brochure (including application guidelines).
Application information: Letters of inquiry must be sent in two forms: via E-mail, and printed copy. Application form required.
Officers and Directors:* Patrick S. de Freitas,* Pres.; Mary C. Driver,* V.P.; Bruce Reed,* Secy.; William Baran-Mickle,* Treas.; Margaret F. Berger, Samuel Brown, Tori Brown, Linda Henry, Deborah S. Wicks.
EIN: 916339917
Codes: FD2

55552
Mabel Horrigan Foundation
c/o U.S. Bank of Washington, N.A., Trust Div.
P.O. Box 720
Seattle, WA 98111-0720
Additional address: c/o U.S. Bank Trust, 1420 5th Ave., Ste. 2100, Seattle, WA 98101
Contact: Leenorah Sanzo

Established in 1952 in WA.
Financial data (yr. ended 12/31/01): Grants paid, $178,052; assets, $2,357,387 (M); expenditures, $200,502; qualifying distributions, $181,533.
Limitations: Applications not accepted. Giving primarily in Seattle, WA.
Application information: Contributes only to pre-selected organizations.
Trustees: Mary S. Horrigan, U.S. Bank of Washington, N.A.
EIN: 866022633
Codes: FD2

55553
McMillan Family Foundation
500 Pine St., Ste. 500
Seattle, WA 98101

Established in 2000 in WA.
Donor(s): John A. McMillan.
Financial data (yr. ended 06/30/01): Grants paid, $177,800; assets, $3,746,909 (M); gifts received, $4,250,000; expenditures, $203,298; qualifying distributions, $178,683.
Limitations: Applications not accepted. Giving primarily in WA.
Application information: Contributes only to pre-selected organizations.
Trustee: John A. McMillan.
EIN: 916511722
Codes: FD2

55554
Paul Garrett Whitman College Foundation
345 Boyer Ave.
Walla Walla, WA 99362

Established in 1992 in WA.
Financial data (yr. ended 06/30/99): Grants paid, $177,484; assets, $3,615,787 (M); expenditures, $177,484; qualifying distributions, $173,324.
Limitations: Applications not accepted. Giving primarily in WA.
Application information: Contributes only to pre-selected organizations.
Officer: Peter W. Harvey, C.F.O.
Trustees: Charles E. Anderson, Robert S. Ball, James H. De Meules, William K. Deshler, Nancy Bell Evans, James K. Hayner, Richard E. Hunter, Michael C. More, Carl J. Schmitt, John W. Stanton, Elizabeth M. Welty, Colleen Willoughby.
EIN: 911648072
Codes: FD2

55555
Paul Pigott Scholarship Foundation
P.O. Box 1518
Bellevue, WA 98009 (425) 468-7909
Contact: Norm Proctor, Mgr.

Established in 1961 in WA.

Financial data (yr. ended 07/31/01): Grants paid, $175,000; assets, $1,522,052 (M); expenditures, $176,067; qualifying distributions, $175,000.
Application information: Application form required.
Manager: N.E. Proctor.
Directors: D.J. Hovind, G.G. Morie, M.C. Pigott, M.A. Tembreull.
EIN: 916030639
Codes: FD2, GTI

55556
Children Count Foundation
1414 31st Ave. S., Ste. 304
Seattle, WA 98144-3910 (206) 322-3690
Contact: Officers

Established in 1999 in WA.
Donor(s): Douglas Jackson.
Financial data (yr. ended 12/31/01): Grants paid, $173,775; assets, $4,412,367 (M); expenditures, $176,490; qualifying distributions, $173,746.
Limitations: Giving primarily in Washington, DC, and Seattle, WA.
Officers: Douglas Jackson, Pres.; Constance L. Proctor, V.P. and Secy.
EIN: 911703057
Codes: FD2

55557
Channel Foundation
P.O. Box 24524
Seattle, WA 98124-0524

Established in 1998 in WA.
Donor(s): Elaine M. Nonneman.
Financial data (yr. ended 12/31/01): Grants paid, $173,063; assets, $3,209,951 (M); gifts received, $624,899; expenditures, $206,284; qualifying distributions, $184,564.
Limitations: Applications not accepted.
Application information: Contributes only to pre-selected organizations.
Trustee: Elaine M. Nonneman.
EIN: 916478055
Codes: FD2

55558
Keyes Foundation
P.O. Box 50088
Bellevue, WA 98015
Contact: Doreen Keyes, Pres.

Established in 1998 in WA.
Donor(s): Doreen Keyes, David Keyes.
Financial data (yr. ended 12/31/01): Grants paid, $172,000; assets, $2,506,786 (M); expenditures, $174,593; qualifying distributions, $171,789.
Limitations: Applications not accepted.
Application information: Unsolicited requests for grants not accepted.
Officers: Doreen Keyes, Pres.; David Keyes, V.P.
EIN: 911939734
Codes: FD2

55559
Kelly Foundation of Washington
(Formerly KCPQ-TV/Kelly Foundation of Washington)
4212 Soundview Dr. W.
University Place, WA 98466
Contact: Keith Shipman

Established in 1995 in WA.
Financial data (yr. ended 09/30/01): Grants paid, $169,500; assets, $3,442,075 (M); gifts received, $56,334; expenditures, $211,271; qualifying distributions, $202,310.
Limitations: Giving primarily in Seattle, WA.
Application information: Application form required.

Officers: Robert E. Kelly, Pres.; Christopher R. Kelly, 1st V.P.; Roger C. Ottenback, 2nd V.P.; Marlene C. Gottfried, Secy.-Treas.; Maria Nicholas Kelly, Mgr.
EIN: 911620836
Codes: FD2

55560
New Priorities Foundation
c/o Community Bldg.
W. 35 Main, Ste. 310
Spokane, WA 99201 (509) 456-5977
FAX: (509) 835-3867; *E-mail:* npfoundation@aol.com
Contact: Patty Gates, Exec. Dir.

Established in 1996 in WA.
Donor(s): Nancy G. Schaub.
Financial data (yr. ended 12/31/01): Grants paid, $167,688; assets, $3,254,710 (M); expenditures, $208,186; qualifying distributions, $164,753.
Limitations: Giving primarily in the Pacific Northwest and East of the Cascades.
Application information: Application form required.
Officers and Trustees:* Nancy G. Schaub, Chair. and Treas.; Sally G. Douglas, Vice-Chair.; Patty Gates,* Exec. Dir.; Carole Rolando, Tim Schaub.
EIN: 911805939
Codes: FD2

55561
Curren Ludwig Foundation
c/o Cornerstone Advisors, Inc.
777-108th Ave. N.E., Ste. 2000
Bellevue, WA 98004
Contact: Ken Hart

Established in 1999 in WA.
Donor(s): Cristi Curren Ludwig, John H. Ludwig.
Financial data (yr. ended 12/31/01): Grants paid, $165,938; assets, $2,827,727 (M); expenditures, $185,030; qualifying distributions, $166,311.
Limitations: Applications not accepted.
Application information: Contributes only to pre-selected organizations.
Officers and Directors:* Cristi Curren Ludwig,* Pres.; John H. Ludwig,* Secy.-Treas.
EIN: 912015162
Codes: FD2

55562
The Sloan Foundation
1301 5th Ave., Ste. 3000
Seattle, WA 98101 (206) 340-1818

Established in 1997 in WA.
Donor(s): Stuart M. Sloan.
Financial data (yr. ended 12/31/00): Grants paid, $165,670; assets, $4,033,637 (M); expenditures, $178,132; qualifying distributions, $164,502.
Limitations: Applications not accepted. Giving primarily in CA and WA.
Application information: Contributes only to pre-selected organizations.
Officers: Stuart M. Sloan, Pres.; Adam D. Sloan, V.P.; Scott J. Sloan, Secy.
EIN: 911799087
Codes: FD2

55563
Herak Foundation
312 W. Sumner Ave.
Spokane, WA 99204-3653
Contact: Donald Herak, Tr.

Established in 1993 in WA.
Donor(s): Donald H. Herak, Carol L. Herak.
Financial data (yr. ended 12/31/01): Grants paid, $165,000; assets, $711,921 (M); expenditures, $171,652; qualifying distributions, $165,000.

Limitations: Giving primarily in Spokane, WA.
Trustee: Donald H. Herak.
EIN: 911621226
Codes: FD2

55564
Brookshire-Green Foundation
250 39th Ave. E.
Seattle, WA 98112

Established in 1997 in WA.
Financial data (yr. ended 12/31/01): Grants paid, $160,389; assets, $1,778,822 (M); expenditures, $183,550; qualifying distributions, $160,327.
Limitations: Applications not accepted.
Application information: Contributes only to pre-selected organizations.
Officers: Alexandra Brookshire, Pres.; Bert Green, V.P.
EIN: 911868189
Codes: FD2

55565
The Handsel Foundation
P.O. Box 1322
Freeland, WA 98249 (360) 331-7282
E-mail: handselfdn@aol.com
Contact: Diane Johnson, Pres.

Established in 1990 in CA.
Donor(s): Theodore R. Johnson, Sr.‡
Financial data (yr. ended 12/31/01): Grants paid, $160,350; assets, $3,529,053 (M); gifts received, $63,302; expenditures, $180,000; qualifying distributions, $163,706.
Limitations: Giving primarily in the western U.S.
Publications: Informational brochure (including application guidelines), informational brochure.
Application information: Application form not required.
Officers and Directors:* Diane N. Johnson,* Pres.; T.R. Johnson, Jr.,* Secy. and C.F.O.; Hilary Austen Johnson.
EIN: 943112006
Codes: FD2

55566
CGMK Foundation
(Formerly King Family Foundation)
c/o FMG, LLC
1000 2nd Ave., 34th Fl.
Seattle, WA 98104-1022
E-mail: cgmk@foundgroup.com

Established in 2000 in WA.
Donor(s): Martin T. King, Cheryl A. Grunbock.
Financial data (yr. ended 12/31/01): Grants paid, $158,500; assets, $5,380,379 (M); gifts received, $250,000; expenditures, $284,266; qualifying distributions, $158,500.
Limitations: Giving primarily in Seattle, WA.
Application information: Application form required.
Officer and Trustees:* Martin T. King,* Mgr.; Cheryl A. Grunbock.
EIN: 916500110

55567
Elizabeth Foundation
4629 W. View Dr.
Everett, WA 98203-2418 (425) 339-2372
Contact: Dawn Stieler, Mgr.

Established in 1998 in WA.
Donor(s): Mary Elizabeth Bernier.‡
Financial data (yr. ended 12/31/00): Grants paid, $155,694; assets, $3,661,120 (M); expenditures, $391,892; qualifying distributions, $309,316.
Limitations: Giving primarily in OR and WA.

55567—WASHINGTON

Application information: Contact foundation for application guidelines and Common Grant Application Form. Application form required.
Officers: Nathan Estis, Pres.; Jeri E. Estis, V.P. and Secy.; Dawn Stieler, Mgr.
EIN: 911890010
Codes: FD2

55568
The Arise Charitable Trust
P.O. Box 1014
Freeland, WA 98249-1014 (360) 331-5792
Contact: Charles W. Edwards, Mgr.

Established in 1986 in WA.
Donor(s): Judith P. Yeakel.
Financial data (yr. ended 09/30/01): Grants paid, $154,530; assets, $3,197,193 (M); expenditures, $199,094; qualifying distributions, $174,970.
Limitations: Giving limited to the South Whidbey, WA, area.
Publications: Informational brochure.
Application information: Application form required.
Officer and Trustees:* Charles W. Edwards,* Mgr.; John Watson, Judith P. Yeakel.
EIN: 911350780
Codes: FD2, GTI

55569
Charles See Foundation
1 Lake Bellevue Dr., Ste. 112
Bellevue, WA 98005 (425) 635-7250
Contact: Anne R. See, Pres.

Incorporated in 1960 in CA.
Donor(s): Charles B. See.
Financial data (yr. ended 12/31/01): Grants paid, $152,500; assets, $2,540,617 (M); expenditures, $204,719; qualifying distributions, $177,711.
Limitations: Giving primarily in CA and WA.
Application information: Application form not required.
Officers: Anne R. See, Pres. and Treas.; Harry A. See, V.P. and Secy.; Richard W. See, V.P.
Directors: Bruce M. Pym, Stephen D. Varon.
EIN: 956038358
Codes: FD2

55570
James D. and Sherry Raisbeck Foundation Trust
7536 Seward Park Ave. S.
Seattle, WA 98118-4247

Established in 1999 in WA.
Donor(s): James D. Raisbeck, Sherry Raisbeck.
Financial data (yr. ended 12/31/99): Grants paid, $150,988; assets, $9,960,968 (M); gifts received, $9,999,042; expenditures, $156,765; qualifying distributions, $149,790.
Limitations: Applications not accepted.
Application information: Contributes only to pre-selected organizations.
Trustees: James D. Raisbeck, Sherry Raisbeck.
EIN: 916478077
Codes: FD2

55571
Jungers Foundation
P.O. Box 3146
Battle Ground, WA 98604
Contact: Gary Jungers, Treas.

Established in 1999 in OR.
Donor(s): Francis Jungers, Gary Jungers, FJF, Inc.
Financial data (yr. ended 12/31/01): Grants paid, $150,951; assets, $2,328,977 (M); expenditures, $310,141; qualifying distributions, $152,847.
Limitations: Applications not accepted.
Application information: Contributes only to pre-selected organizations.

Officers and Directors:* Frank Jungers,* Chair.; Julia Jungers,* Secy.; Gary Jungers, Treas. and Exec. Dir.; Mary Ellen Jungers.
EIN: 931282864
Codes: FD2

55572
The Globe Foundation
P.O. Box 2274
Tacoma, WA 98401

Established in 1990 in WA.
Donor(s): Calvin D. Bamford, Jr.
Financial data (yr. ended 11/30/01): Grants paid, $150,800; assets, $1,981,009 (M); expenditures, $179,392; qualifying distributions, $150,800.
Limitations: Applications not accepted. Giving primarily in Tacoma, WA.
Application information: Contributes only to pre-selected organizations.
Officers and Directors:* Calvin D. Bamford, Jr.,* Pres. and Treas.; Joanne W. Bamford,* V.P.; Drew Bamford, Secy.; Heather Bamford, Holly Bamford.
EIN: 911504193

55573
Microsoft Charitable Trust
c/o Wells Fargo Bank Northwest, N.A.
P.O. Box 21927
Seattle, WA 98111
Additional address: c/o Microsoft Corp., 1 Microsoft Way, Bldg. 8, Redmond, WA 98052

Established in 1994 in WA.
Donor(s): Microsoft Corp.
Financial data (yr. ended 06/30/01): Grants paid, $150,000; assets, $1,472,255 (M); expenditures, $160,189; qualifying distributions, $152,156.
Limitations: Applications not accepted. Giving primarily in WA.
Application information: Contributes only to pre-selected organizations.
Trustee: Wells Fargo Bank Northwest, N.A.
EIN: 916374992
Codes: CS, FD2, CD

55574
George A. and Marion M. Wilson Foundation
6030 78th Ave. S.E.
Mercer Island, WA 98040-4823
Application address: c/o Amicus Law Group, 1325 4th Ave., Ste. 940, Seattle, WA 98101-2509
Contact: Laura W. Kilkelly, Secy.

Established in 1999 in WA.
Donor(s): George A. Wilson, Marion M. Wilson.
Financial data (yr. ended 12/31/01): Grants paid, $150,000; assets, $2,899,895 (M); expenditures, $183,840; qualifying distributions, $150,000.
Limitations: Giving primarily in Seattle, WA.
Officers and Directors:* George A. Wilson,* Pres.; Marian M. Wilson,* V.P.; Laura W. Kilkelly,* Secy.
EIN: 911952034
Codes: FD2

55575
The John Keister Family Foundation
2610 E. Helen St.
Seattle, WA 98112
E-mail: mmcgreevylewis@juno.com
Contact: Marcia McGreevy Lewis, Exec. Dir.

Established in 1999 in WA.
Donor(s): John Keister.
Financial data (yr. ended 12/31/01): Grants paid, $149,387; assets, $2,967 (M); gifts received, $151,600; expenditures, $201,537; qualifying distributions, $196,833.

Limitations: Applications not accepted. Giving limited to King and Snohomish counties, WA.
Application information: Unsolicited requests for funds not accepted.
Officers and Directors:* John Keister,* Pres.; Megan Keister,* V.P.; Marcia McGreevy Lewis, Exec. Dir.
EIN: 911980748
Codes: FD2

55576
Howard S. Whitney Foundation
P.O. Box 13342
Spokane, WA 99213-3342
Contact: Ross R. Whitney, Secy.-Treas.

Established in 1980 in WA.
Donor(s): Edith G. Whitney.
Financial data (yr. ended 12/31/01): Grants paid, $149,274; assets, $2,182,293 (M); gifts received, $163,621; expenditures, $201,685; qualifying distributions, $170,824.
Limitations: Giving primarily in Spokane, WA.
Application information: Application form required.
Officers: Howard B. Ness, Pres.; Robert A. Mott, V.P.; Ross R. Whitney, Secy.-Treas.
Director: David S. Whitney.
EIN: 916237884
Codes: FD2

55577
Walkling Memorial Trust
(Formerly Ben & Myrtle Walkling Memorial Trust)
P.O. Box 1588
Port Angeles, WA 98362
Application address: 1129 E. Front St., Port Angeles, WA 98362
Contact: Karen Yakovich

Established in 1993 in WA.
Donor(s): Virginia McFrederick, Clallam County Physicians Svc.
Financial data (yr. ended 12/31/00): Grants paid, $148,487; assets, $3,191,978 (M); expenditures, $202,590; qualifying distributions, $173,487.
Limitations: Giving limited to Clallam County, WA, and to graduates of Port Angeles High School, WA.
Application information: Scholarship applications for current students made through Port Angeles High School. Application form required.
Officers: Vicki Corson, Chair.; Charles R. Turner, Secy.
Directors: Joy Kase, Sandra Ruddell, Bob Wheeler.
EIN: 943166048
Codes: FD2

55578
Florence Lewis Carkeek Trust
c/o Union Bank of California, N.A.
P.O. Box 84495
Seattle, WA 98124-5795

Established in 1953 in WA.
Financial data (yr. ended 03/31/01): Grants paid, $146,920; assets, $3,080,117 (M); expenditures, $182,583; qualifying distributions, $154,780.
Limitations: Giving primarily in Seattle, WA.
Application information: Applications submitted directly to Trust not considered. Application information available from principals of public high schools in Seattle District No. 1.
Trustee: Union Bank of California, N.A.
EIN: 916022715
Codes: FD2, GTI

55579
The Ji Ji Foundation
2730 Westlake Ave. N.
Seattle, WA 98109-1916
Contact: Margo Reich, Treas.

Established in 1994 in WA.
Donor(s): Alan B. Harper.
Financial data (yr. ended 09/30/01): Grants paid, $145,630; assets, $708,812 (M); gifts received, $324; expenditures, $151,336; qualifying distributions, $143,425.
Limitations: Giving primarily in the western North American continent.
Publications: Grants list.
Application information: Application form not required.
Officers: Alan B. Harper, Pres.; Carol Baird, Secy.; Margo Reich, Treas.
EIN: 911664723
Codes: FD2

55580
Prairie Foundation
c/o Colin Moseley
P.O. Box 21866
Seattle, WA 98111-3866

Established in 1998 in WA.
Donor(s): Martha Moseley, Colin Moseley.
Financial data (yr. ended 12/31/01): Grants paid, $144,384; assets, $1,126,116 (M); expenditures, $145,345; qualifying distributions, $146,294.
Limitations: Applications not accepted. Giving primarily in Seattle, WA.
Application information: Contributes only to pre-selected organizations.
Officers: Martha P. Moseley, Pres. and Treas.; Colin Moseley, V.P. and Secy.
EIN: 911939662
Codes: FD2

55581
Paul M. Anderson Foundation
c/o Bank of America
P.O. Box 24565, No. CSC-23
Seattle, WA 98124
Contact: Rod Johnson

Established in 1994 in WA.
Donor(s): John Privat, Priscilla Privat.
Financial data (yr. ended 09/30/01): Grants paid, $144,000; assets, $3,083,032 (M); expenditures, $156,697; qualifying distributions, $140,081.
Limitations: Applications not accepted. Giving primarily in WA.
Application information: Contributes only to pre-selected organizations. Unsolicited requests for funds not accepted.
Officers: John Privat, Pres.; Priscilla Privat, V.P.
EIN: 911697666
Codes: FD2

55582
Bishop-Fleet Foundation
1420 5th Ave., Ste. 4400
Seattle, WA 98101-2602 (425) 453-8282
Contact: James Callaghan, Tr.

Established in 1941 in WA.
Donor(s): E.K. Bishop, Reuben Fleet.
Financial data (yr. ended 12/31/01): Grants paid, $143,477; assets, $2,697,498 (M); expenditures, $177,550; qualifying distributions, $149,814.
Limitations: Giving limited to the Seattle, WA, area.
Application information: Application form not required.
Trustees: Christian Birkeland, C. Leigh Callaghan, James R. Callaghan.
EIN: 916031057
Codes: FD2

55583
The Boeschen Family Foundation
2459 215th Ave. S.E.
Issaquah, WA 98029

Established in 1998 in WA.
Donor(s): Daniel A. Boescher, Susan W. Boescher.
Financial data (yr. ended 12/31/01): Grants paid, $143,000; assets, $2,268,003 (M); expenditures, $145,520; qualifying distributions, $144,825.
Limitations: Giving primarily in Napa County, CA, Deschutes County, OR, and King County, WA.
Officers: Susan W. Boescher, Pres. and Secy.; Daniel A. Boescher, V.P. and Treas.
EIN: 911913189
Codes: FD2

55584
Satya and Rao Remala Foundation
c/o Wellspring Group
10900 N.E. 4th, Ste. 920
Bellevue, WA 98004

Established in 1998 in WA.
Donor(s): Rao Remala, Satya Remala.
Financial data (yr. ended 12/31/01): Grants paid, $140,950; assets, $4,067,230 (M); gifts received, $1,142,039; expenditures, $159,408; qualifying distributions, $140,758.
Limitations: Applications not accepted. Giving primarily in WA.
Application information: Contributes only to pre-selected organizations.
Trustees: Rao V. Remala, Satya K. Remala.
EIN: 916477106
Codes: FD2

55585
Dunnigan Family Foundation
P.O. Box 75615
Seattle, WA 98125-0615

Established in 2001 in WA.
Donor(s): Jim Dunnigan, Francine Dunnigan.
Financial data (yr. ended 12/21/01): Grants paid, $140,828; assets, $14,965 (M); gifts received, $156,780; expenditures, $142,045; qualifying distributions, $142,045.
Limitations: Applications not accepted. Giving primarily in WA.
Application information: Contributes only to pre-selected organizations.
Trustees: Francine Dunnigan, Jim Dunnigan.
EIN: 912104666

55586
Marian E. Smith Foundation
8070 Grand Ave.
Bainbridge Island, WA 98110-2946

Established in 1996 in WA.
Donor(s): Marian E. Smith, Daniel G. Smith.
Financial data (yr. ended 12/31/01): Grants paid, $140,404; assets, $24,886 (M); gifts received, $152,000; expenditures, $140,440; qualifying distributions, $140,438.
Limitations: Applications not accepted. Giving primarily in WA.
Application information: Contributes only to pre-selected organizations.
Officers: Marian E. Smith, Pres.; Deborah S. Heg, Secy.; Daniel G. Smith, C.F.O.
EIN: 943252133
Codes: FD2

55587
W. F. & Blanche E. West Educational Fund
c/o Wells Fargo Bank
P.O. Box 21927
Seattle, WA 98111
Application address: c/o Scholarship Comm., P.O. Box 180, Chehalis, WA 98532

Established in 1969 in WA.
Financial data (yr. ended 12/31/01): Grants paid, $140,375; assets, $2,982,275 (M); expenditures, $177,666; qualifying distributions, $151,640.
Limitations: Giving limited to residents of Lewis County, WA.
Application information: Application forms available at school upon request. Application form required.
Trustee: Wells Fargo Bank Northwest, N.A.
EIN: 916101769
Codes: FD2, GTI

55588
Quitslund Foundation
c/o Dana Quitslund
13724 Sunrise Dr.
Bainbridge Island, WA 98110 (206) 780-9422
Contact: Nancy Quitslund, Pres.

Established in 1998 in WA.
Donor(s): Dana E. Quitslund, Nancy N. Quitslund.
Financial data (yr. ended 12/31/01): Grants paid, $140,000; assets, $1,583,326 (M); gifts received, $454,225; expenditures, $164,722; qualifying distributions, $136,741.
Limitations: Applications not accepted.
Application information: Unsolicited requests for funds not accepted.
Officers and Directors:* Nancy N. Quitslund,* Pres.; Dana E. Quitslund,* Secy.-Treas.; Beth M. Quitslund, Sarah N. Quitslund.
EIN: 911885633
Codes: FD2

55589
Mary S. Sigourney Award Trust
P.O. Box 10206
Bainbridge Island, WA 98110 (206) 842-1097
Contact: James D. Devine, Tr.

Established in 1989 in CA.
Financial data (yr. ended 12/31/01): Grants paid, $140,000; assets, $4,452,002 (M); expenditures, $242,774; qualifying distributions, $218,976.
Application information: Scholarship candidates are chosen by nomination; geographic focus varies from year to year.
Trustees: James D. Devine, Bernard L. Pacella, M.D.
EIN: 776054596
Codes: FD2, GTI

55590
Creating Critical Viewers
P.O. Box 58530
Seattle, WA 98138

Established in 1999 in WA.
Financial data (yr. ended 12/31/99): Grants paid, $139,540; assets, $4,969 (M); gifts received, $58,601; expenditures, $140,209; qualifying distributions, $108,224.
Limitations: Applications not accepted.
Application information: Contributes only to pre-selected organizations.
Officers: Catherine Carbone, Chair.; Steve Quant, Pres.; Jamie R. Williams, V.P.; Joanne M. Lisosky, Secy.; Sven White, Treas.
Trustee: Bill Stainton.
EIN: 311616828
Codes: FD2

55591
Geneva Foundation
8701 Madrona Ln.
Edmonds, WA 98026
Contact: Wanda Kamahele, Tr.

Established in 1964 in WA.
Donor(s): Genevieve Albers.‡
Financial data (yr. ended 06/30/01): Grants paid, $139,000; assets, $3,049,757 (M); gifts received, $50,000; expenditures, $140,458; qualifying distributions, $140,458.
Limitations: Applications not accepted. Giving primarily in Seattle, WA.
Publications: Annual report.
Application information: Contributes only to pre-selected organizations.
Trustee: Wanda Kamahele.
EIN: 916056767
Codes: FD2

55592
The Babare Foundation
2212 Day Island Blvd. W.
University Place, WA 98466-1810
(253) 566-1532
Contact: Robert S. Babare, Pres.

Established in 1989 in WA.
Donor(s): Mary Babare,‡ Robert S. Babare, George M. Babare.
Financial data (yr. ended 12/31/00): Grants paid, $138,050; assets, $1,612,944 (M); expenditures, $145,523; qualifying distributions, $138,859.
Limitations: Giving primarily in Tacoma, WA.
Officers: Robert S. Babare, Pres.; Cynthia Lou Babare, V.P.; Gwendolyn E. Babare, Secy.; Robert M. Babare, Treas.
EIN: 943099309
Codes: FD2

55593
June & Julian Foss Foundation
5510 Orchard St. W., Ste. B2-501
Tacoma, WA 98467 (877) 244-3677
FAX: (877) 244-3677; *E-mail:* administrator@fossfoundation.org; *URL:* http://www.fossfoundation.org
Contact: Emily Foss Harry, Admin.

Established in 1997 in WA.
Financial data (yr. ended 03/31/01): Grants paid, $137,000; assets, $7,410,849 (M); expenditures, $384,123; qualifying distributions, $296,542.
Limitations: Giving primarily in Phoenix, AZ, the San Francisco Bay Area, CA, Miami, FL, the Portland, OR area, and western WA.
Publications: Annual report (including application guidelines), informational brochure (including application guidelines).
Application information: Application form required.
Officers and Directors:* Julie Stuhr,* Pres.; Dawn Campbell,* V.P. and Secy.; Jerry M. Foss,* Treas.; Emily Harry, Admin.; James M. Foss, P. Joseph Foss, Mark Stuhr.
EIN: 911798171
Codes: FD2

55594
Lanham Foundation
c/o Bank of America
P.O. Box 34345, CSC-9
Seattle, WA 98124-1345
Application address: 617 Washington St., P.O. Box 2136, Wenatchee, WA 98807

Established in 1949 in WA.
Donor(s): Emma G. Gehr Foundation.
Financial data (yr. ended 12/31/01): Grants paid, $135,885; assets, $657,934 (M); gifts received, $128,794; expenditures, $151,294; qualifying distributions, $147,678.
Limitations: Giving limited to residents of Chelan County, WA.
Application information: Application form required.
Trustee: Bank of America.
EIN: 916020593
Codes: FD2, GTI

55595
Names Family Foundation
1019 Regents Blvd., Ste. 201
Fircrest, WA 98466 (253) 566-7000
Contact: Thomas S. Names, Jr.

Established in 1997 in WA.
Donor(s): T. Scott Names.
Financial data (yr. ended 12/31/01): Grants paid, $135,000; assets, $2,090,463 (M); gifts received, $42,245; expenditures, $156,042; qualifying distributions, $135,000.
Limitations: Giving primarily in Pierce County or western WA.
Directors: Paula Larkin, Evelyn Names, R. Clint Names, T. Scott Names, Thomas S. Names.
EIN: 943250195
Codes: FD2

55596
Thomas & Martina Horn Foundation
P.O. Box 3130
Bellingham, WA 98227
Contact: Donna MacDonald, Exec. Dir.

Established in 1996.
Donor(s): Thomas Horn.‡
Financial data (yr. ended 12/31/00): Grants paid, $133,250; assets, $3,430,256 (M); expenditures, $199,157; qualifying distributions, $146,457.
Limitations: Applications not accepted. Giving primarily in Bellingham and Whatcom County, WA.
Application information: Contributes only to pre-selected organizations.
Directors: Donna MacDonald, Exec. Dir.; Bruce Smith, Orphalee Smith.
EIN: 911701495
Codes: FD2

55597
Juniper Foundation
c/o Sheila Wyckoff-Dickey
144 Madrona Pl. E.
Seattle, WA 98112-5010

Established in 1998 in WA.
Donor(s): Sheila Wyckoff-Dickey, Charles D. Dickey III.
Financial data (yr. ended 12/31/01): Grants paid, $132,246; assets, $2,447,199 (M); expenditures, $148,199; qualifying distributions, $132,881.
Limitations: Applications not accepted.
Application information: Contributes only to pre-selected organizations.
Officers: Sheila Wyckoff-Dickey, Pres. and Secy.; Charles D. Dickey III, V.P. and Treas.
EIN: 911908199
Codes: FD2

55598
Sustainable Solutions Foundation
189 Coulter Rd.
Sequim, WA 98382-9362

Established in 1997 in WA.
Financial data (yr. ended 12/31/00): Grants paid, $130,000; assets, $2,560,358 (M); expenditures, $135,547; qualifying distributions, $129,483.
Limitations: Applications not accepted. Giving on a national basis.
Application information: Contributes only to pre-selected organizations.
Officers: Steve Clapp, Pres.; Robert L. Sander, Treas.
Trustees: Joe Bowen, Booth Gardner.
EIN: 911817420
Codes: FD2

55599
Mary Garner Esary Trust
P.O. Box 1757
Walla Walla, WA 99362
Contact: Kenneth Garner, Tr.

Established in 1998 in WA.
Financial data (yr. ended 12/31/01): Grants paid, $128,700; assets, $2,861,097 (M); expenditures, $182,455; qualifying distributions, $138,614.
Limitations: Applications not accepted. Giving limited to Walla Walla, WA.
Application information: Unsolicited requests for funds not accepted.
Trustee: Kenneth Garner.
EIN: 911901307
Codes: FD2

55600
The Dorothy and Fred Plath Charitable Foundation
3604 Howard Ave.
Yakima, WA 98902 (509) 452-9726
Contact: Fred M. Plath, Pres.

Established in 1999 in WA.
Donor(s): Fred M. Plath, Dorothy D. Plath.
Financial data (yr. ended 12/31/00): Grants paid, $128,050; assets, $830,257 (M); gifts received, $391,246; expenditures, $129,232; qualifying distributions, $127,666.
Limitations: Giving primarily in WA.
Officers: Fred M. Plath, Pres.; Dorothy D. Plath, Secy.-Treas.
Directors:: Clifford A. Plath, Peter D. Plath, Roderick C. Plath.
EIN: 911963474
Codes: FD2

55601
Mary Hoyt Stevenson Foundation, Inc.
c/o Laura Cheney
P.O. Box 1157
White Salmon, WA 98672

Established in 1986 in OR.
Donor(s): Mary H. Stevenson, Leslie Stevenson Campbell.
Financial data (yr. ended 09/30/01): Grants paid, $128,000; assets, $2,342,800 (M); gifts received, $100,000; expenditures, $136,278; qualifying distributions, $126,071.
Limitations: Applications not accepted. Giving primarily in OR and WA.
Application information: Contributes only to pre-selected organizations.
Officer: Laura Stevenson Cheney, Pres.
Directors: Leslie Stevenson Campbell, Anne Stevenson, Mary H. Stevenson.
EIN: 943028591
Codes: FD2

55602
Ralph & Elaine Sundquist Charitable & Educational Trust
c/o Bank of America
P.O. Box 34345
Seattle, WA 98124-1345

Established in 1954 in WA.
Donor(s): Marvin Sundquist.

Financial data (yr. ended 12/31/01): Grants paid, $127,100; assets, $2,597,996 (M); expenditures, $155,172; qualifying distributions, $140,286.
Limitations: Applications not accepted. Giving limited to WA.
Application information: Contributes only to pre-selected organizations.
Trustees: Marvin F. Sundquist, Bank of America.
EIN: 916025654
Codes: FD2

55603
Smiling Dog Foundation
6523 California Ave. S.W., PMB 346
Seattle, WA 98136
E-mail: june@beachstudio.com
Contact: June Martin, Secy.-Treas.

Established in 1999 in WA.
Donor(s): Richard F. Russell, Jileen Russell.
Financial data (yr. ended 12/31/00): Grants paid, $125,727; assets, $5,491 (M); gifts received, $135,000; expenditures, $130,938; qualifying distributions, $130,927.
Limitations: Applications not accepted. Giving primarily in Kohala, HI and Puget Sound, WA.
Application information: Contributes only to pre-selected organizations.
Officers: Richard F. Russell, Pres.; Jileen Russell, V.P.; June Martin, Secy.-Treas.
EIN: 911950165
Codes: FD2

55604
Joel E. Ferris Foundation
315 Paulsen Ctr.
Spokane, WA 99201
Contact: John Peterson, Secy.-Treas.

Established in 1955 in WA.
Financial data (yr. ended 12/31/01): Grants paid, $125,300; assets, $1,813,009 (M); expenditures, $137,525; qualifying distributions, $124,300.
Limitations: Giving primarily in Spokane, WA.
Officers: Cheney Cowles, Pres.; Phoebe McCoy, V.P.; John Peterson, Secy.-Treas.
Trustees: Joel E. Ferris III, Elizabeth Hanson.
EIN: 916048913
Codes: FD2

55605
O'Donnell Family Charitable Foundation
c/o Jim O'Donnell
1326 5th Ave., 703 Skinner Bldg.
Seattle, WA 98101

Established in 1996 in WA.
Donor(s): Harry J. O'Donnell, Mariette E. O'Donnell.
Financial data (yr. ended 12/31/01): Grants paid, $124,010; assets, $1,026 (M); gifts received, $120,925; expenditures, $124,020; qualifying distributions, $124,010.
Limitations: Giving primarily in Seattle, WA.
Officers: Harry J. O'Donnell, Jr., Pres.; Mariette E. O'Donnell, Secy.-Treas.
EIN: 911712175

55606
The Mannix Canby Foundation
1141 37th Ave. E.
Seattle, WA 98112 (206) 329-5859
FAX: (206) 329-7929
Contact: Caleb Canby, V.P.

Established in 1997 in WA.
Donor(s): Theresa Mannix, Caleb L. Canby.
Financial data (yr. ended 12/31/01): Grants paid, $123,800; assets, $1,612,188 (M); expenditures, $142,251; qualifying distributions, $125,274.

Limitations: Giving primarily in the Puget Sound region of WA.
Publications: Application guidelines, program policy statement.
Application information: Application form required.
Officers and Trustees:* Theresa Mannix,* Pres. and Treas.; Caleb L. Canby,* V.P. and Secy.
EIN: 911780178
Codes: FD2

55607
The Summit Family, a Washington Foundation
14100 S.E. 36th St., Ste. 201
Bellevue, WA 98006-1334
Contact: James A. Hirshfield, Jr., Tr.

Established in 1999 in WA.
Donor(s): James A. Hirshfield.
Financial data (yr. ended 12/31/00): Grants paid, $122,290; assets, $2,789,549 (M); gifts received, $5,000; expenditures, $153,630; qualifying distributions, $122,290.
Limitations: Giving primarily in Seattle, WA.
Trustees: James A. Hirshfield, Jr., Mary J. Hirshfield.
EIN: 916488392
Codes: FD2

55608
Leslie V. & Stella Raymond Foundation, Inc.
P.O. Box 423
Raymond, WA 98577-0423 (360) 942-3444
Contact: Karen M. Clements, Secy.

Established in 1962 in WA.
Donor(s): L.V. and S.J. Raymond Trust.
Financial data (yr. ended 12/31/01): Grants paid, $121,624; assets, $3,084 (M); gifts received, $113,972; expenditures, $125,307; qualifying distributions, $121,609.
Limitations: Giving limited to residents of the Raymond, WA, area.
Application information: Application form not required.
Officers: Ron Brummel, Pres.; Richard A. Mergens, V.P.; Karen M. Clements, Secy.
Directors: Sue Bale, Jeff Nevitt.
EIN: 916057558
Codes: FD2

55609
The Martin Family Foundation
c/o James Palmer
701 5th Ave., Ste. 3100
Seattle, WA 98104

Established in 1991 in WA.
Donor(s): Benn Martin.
Financial data (yr. ended 12/31/01): Grants paid, $121,027; assets, $3,405,966 (M); gifts received, $400,010; expenditures, $132,791; qualifying distributions, $122,317.
Limitations: Applications not accepted. Giving primarily in Seattle, WA.
Application information: Contributes only to pre-selected organizations.
Officers: James M. Palmer, Pres.; Marian M. Levy, V.P.; Robert Valentine, Secy.
Directors: Michael Alfstad, Howard Greenwald, Neal Hardin, Richard Lassman, Ray Lundeen, Barbara Root.
EIN: 911455940
Codes: FD2

55610
Frank B. and Virginia V. Fehsenfeld Charitable Foundation
1107 1st Ave., Ste. 1404
Seattle, WA 98101
Contact: H. Warren Smith, V.P.

Established in 1987 in MI.
Donor(s): Frank B. Fehsenfeld, Virginia V. Fehsenfeld.
Financial data (yr. ended 12/31/01): Grants paid, $119,500; assets, $1,789,320 (M); expenditures, $123,524; qualifying distributions, $118,396.
Limitations: Giving primarily in the Grand Rapids, MI and Seattle, WA, areas.
Officers: Frank B. Fehsenfeld, Pres. and Treas.; H. Warren Smith, V.P.; Nancy Fehsenfeld Smith, Secy.
Trustees: John A. Fehsenfeld, Thomas V. Fehsenfeld, William S. Fehsenfeld.
EIN: 382775201
Codes: FD2

55611
Moss Adams Foundation
1001 4th Ave., Ste. 2830
Seattle, WA 98154

Established in 1994 in WA.
Donor(s): Moss Adams, LLP, Robert Bunting, Roger Peterson.
Financial data (yr. ended 12/31/01): Grants paid, $118,525; assets, $43,462 (M); gifts received, $130,418; expenditures, $118,525; qualifying distributions, $118,525.
Limitations: Applications not accepted. Giving primarily in the Northwest.
Application information: Contributes only to pre-selected organizations.
Officers: Russ Wilson, Pres.; Paul Farkas, V.P.; Randy Fenich, Secy.; Tom Gaffney, Treas.
Directors: Gary Grimstad, Robert Ryker, Chris Schmidt.
EIN: 911496816
Codes: FD2

55612
Bernice A. B. Keyes Trust
c/o KeyBank, N.A.
P.O. Box 11500 MSWA 310-01-0310
Tacoma, WA 98411-5052 (253) 305-7203
Contact: Michael Steadman, V.P.

Established in 1978.
Donor(s): Bernice A.B. Keyes.‡
Financial data (yr. ended 12/31/01): Grants paid, $117,757; assets, $2,177,764 (M); expenditures, $150,105; qualifying distributions, $123,961.
Limitations: Applications not accepted. Giving limited to the Tacoma, WA, area.
Application information: Unsolicited requests for funds not accepted.
Trustees: Robert E. Ellison, KeyBank, N.A.
EIN: 916111944
Codes: FD2, GTI

55613
The Anders Foundation
c/o William A. Anders
P.O. Box 1630
Eastsound, WA 98245-1630

Established in 1993 in WA.
Donor(s): William A. Anders, Tom Hanks.
Financial data (yr. ended 12/31/99): Grants paid, $117,200; assets, $2,314,190 (M); expenditures, $117,650; qualifying distributions, $117,200.
Limitations: Applications not accepted. Giving on a national basis, with some emphasis on Seattle, WA.
Application information: Contributes only to pre-selected organizations.

55613—WASHINGTON

Directors: Valerie E. Anders, William A. Anders.
EIN: 911612850
Codes: FD2

55614
The Behnke Foundation
(Formerly Skinner Foundation)
520 Pike St., Ste. 2620
Seattle, WA 98101-4001 (206) 623-5449
Additional tel.: (206) 623-6106; FAX: (206) 623-6138; E-mail: BehnkeFoundation@aol.com

Trust established in 1956 in WA.
Donor(s): Skinner Corp., Alpac Corp., NC Machinery.
Financial data (yr. ended 12/31/01): Grants paid, $117,150; assets, $2,604,036 (M); expenditures, $152,880; qualifying distributions, $125,872.
Limitations: Giving primarily in the greater Seattle, WA, area.
Publications: Annual report, informational brochure (including application guidelines).
Application information: Application form required.
Officer: John Behnke, Chair.
Trustees: Carl Behnke, Marisa Behnke, Renee Behnke, Sally Skinner Behnke, Shari Behnke.
EIN: 916025144
Codes: CS, FD2, CD

55615
The Sanford Foundation
9248 S.E. 59th St.
Mercer Island, WA 98040
Contact: Patricia S. Turner, Secy.-Treas.

Donor(s): Alton L. Sanford, Elisabeth S. Sanford.
Financial data (yr. ended 08/31/01): Grants paid, $116,221; assets, $34,519 (M); gifts received, $116,627; expenditures, $117,152; qualifying distributions, $117,153.
Limitations: Applications not accepted. Giving limited to CA, NJ, and OR.
Application information: Contributions only to pre-selected organizations.
Officers: Alton L. Sanford, Co-Chair.; Elisabeth S. Sanford, Co-Chair.; Patricia S. Turner, Secy.-Treas.
EIN: 911194492
Codes: FD2

55616
David and Amy Fulton Foundation
c/o David Fulton
203 Bellevue Way N.E., Ste. 534
Bellevue, WA 98004

Established in 1997 in WA.
Donor(s): Amy Fulton, David Fulton.
Financial data (yr. ended 08/31/01): Grants paid, $116,165; assets, $3,020,072 (M); expenditures, $137,720; qualifying distributions, $116,165.
Limitations: Applications not accepted. Giving primarily in WA.
Application information: Contributes only to pre-selected organizations.
Officers: David Fulton, Pres.; Amy Fulton, Secy.-Treas.
EIN: 911811411
Codes: FD2

55617
Preston Memorial Trust Fund
c/o Bank of America
P.O. Box 34345
Seattle, WA 98124

Established in 1998 in WA.
Donor(s): Charles Preston Trust.
Financial data (yr. ended 10/31/01): Grants paid, $115,626; assets, $2,677,511 (M); expenditures, $147,123; qualifying distributions, $128,701.

Limitations: Applications not accepted.
Application information: Contributes only to pre-selected organizations.
Trustee: Bank of America.
EIN: 957078667
Codes: FD2

55618
The Eldon & Shirley Nysether Foundation
P.O. Box 1201
Everett, WA 98206

Established in 2000 in WA.
Donor(s): Eldon M. Nysether, Shirley Nysether.
Financial data (yr. ended 12/31/01): Grants paid, $114,304; assets, $625,284 (M); gifts received, $349,000; expenditures, $115,237; qualifying distributions, $114,103.
Limitations: Applications not accepted. Giving primarily in WA.
Application information: Contributes only to pre-selected organizations.
Officers: Eldon M. Nysether, Pres.; Shirley Nysether, V.P.; Bradley Nysether, Secy.; Mark A. Nysether, Treas.
EIN: 912084108
Codes: FD2

55619
Alfred & Tillie Shemanski Fund
c/o KeyBank, N.A., Trust Div.
P.O. Box 12907
Seattle, WA 98111-4907 (206) 684-6156

Established in 1953 in WA.
Donor(s): Alfred Shemanski,‡ Tillie Shemanski.‡
Financial data (yr. ended 08/31/01): Grants paid, $112,600; assets, $2,042,702 (M); expenditures, $138,467; qualifying distributions, $117,014.
Limitations: Giving limited to the Seattle, King County, WA, area.
Application information: Application form not required.
Trustee: KeyBank, N.A.
EIN: 916027124
Codes: FD2

55620
M. J. McIntyre and Shirley McIntyre Charitable Foundation
18609 15th Ave. N.W.
Seattle, WA 98177

Established in 2000 in WA.
Donor(s): Maurice J. McIntyre, Shirley A. McIntyre.
Financial data (yr. ended 06/30/01): Grants paid, $112,018; assets, $4,822,549 (M); gifts received, $5,980,658; expenditures, $141,874; qualifying distributions, $115,455.
Limitations: Applications not accepted. Giving primarily in WA.
Application information: Contributes only to pre-selected organizations.
Officers: Shirley Ann McIntyre, Pres.; Brian James McIntyre, V.P.; Sarah Ann McIntyre-Hess, Secy.-Treas.
EIN: 912073172
Codes: FD2

55621
Bannister Charitable Trust
1630 43rd E., Apt. 903
Seattle, WA 98112-3222
Contact: Lyman H. Black, Tr.

Financial data (yr. ended 12/31/99): Grants paid, $109,052; assets, $191,199 (M); gifts received, $6,624; expenditures, $118,104; qualifying distributions, $109,052.

Limitations: Giving limited to WA, with emphasis on Yakima and King counties.
Application information: Application form not required.
Trustee: Lyman H. Black.
EIN: 916106572
Codes: FD2

55622
Burke Foundation
3401 Evanston Ave. N., Ste. A
Seattle, WA 98103
Contact: Suzanne M. Burke, Pres.

Established in 1994 in WA.
Donor(s): Florence Burke, Fremont Dock Co., Suzanne M. Burke.
Financial data (yr. ended 12/31/01): Grants paid, $108,536; assets, $386,254 (M); gifts received, $10,000; expenditures, $111,352; qualifying distributions, $108,530.
Limitations: Giving limited to Seattle, WA.
Officers: Suzanne M. Burke, Pres.; Mike Osterfeld, V.P.; Kirby S. Lindsay, Secy.-Treas.
Directors: Gerry Burke, K. Gwen Kapuszoglu.
EIN: 911675495
Codes: FD2

55623
Thomas C. Wright Foundation
5400 Carillon Pt.
Kirkland, WA 98033-7356

Established in 1997 in WA.
Donor(s): Thomas C. Wright.
Financial data (yr. ended 12/31/01): Grants paid, $108,500; assets, $1,942,151 (M); expenditures, $163,855; qualifying distributions, $139,696.
Limitations: Giving on a national basis.
Trustees: Kathleen M. Brawn, Lisa A. Johnston, Thomas C. Wright, Thomas L. Wright.
Director: G. Kenneth Phillips, Exec. Dir.
EIN: 916457246
Codes: FD2

55624
Dr. H. A. Trippeer Charitable Foundation
701 5th Ave., Ste. 5000
Seattle, WA 98104-7078
Contact: John A. Gose, Tr.

Established in 1995 in WA.
Financial data (yr. ended 12/31/01): Grants paid, $107,695; assets, $1,367,278 (M); gifts received, $20,000; expenditures, $117,961; qualifying distributions, $116,902.
Limitations: Giving limited to graduates from Walla Walla County, WA, high schools.
Trustees: Peter F. Bechen, John A. Gose, Lynn M. Gose.
EIN: 916371911
Codes: FD2, GTI

55625
Raven Trust Fund
1000 2nd Ave., No. 3700
Seattle, WA 98104

Established in 1997 in WA.
Donor(s): John Standford Endowment, Tom A. Alberg.
Financial data (yr. ended 12/31/00): Grants paid, $106,570; assets, $15,292,646 (M); gifts received, $7,300,014; expenditures, $308,804; qualifying distributions, $112,447.
Limitations: Applications not accepted. Giving primarily in Seattle, WA.
Application information: Contributes only to pre-selected organizations.
Officers and Trustee:* Tom A. Alberg, Pres. and Treas.; Judith Beck,* V.P. and Secy.

EIN: 911816037
Codes: FD2

55626
Nellie Martin Carman Scholarship Trust
P.O. Box 60052
Seattle, WA 98160-0052
Contact: Sheri Ashleman, Exec. Secy.

Established in 1949 in WA.
Donor(s): Nellie M. Carman.‡
Financial data (yr. ended 05/31/01): Grants paid, $106,150; assets, $2,796,889 (M); gifts received, $5,150; expenditures, $154,111; qualifying distributions, $119,297.
Limitations: Giving limited to WA, with emphasis on King, Snohomish, and Pierce counties.
Publications: Annual report (including application guidelines).
Application information: Unsolicited requests for funds not accepted. Initial candidate selection made by high school counselor; application forms available only through high school and must be submitted by counselor. Nominees must be U.S. citizens and must attend college in WA. Application form required.
Trustee: KeyBank, N.A.
Officer and Scholarship Committee:* John T. John,* Chair.; Donna M. Monroe, Lynn Thorburn.
EIN: 916023774
Codes: FD2, GTI

55627
Pinkerton Foundation
514 N.E. 97th, Ste. 301
Seattle, WA 98115
Contact: Guy C. Pinkerton, Pres.

Established in 1994 in WA.
Donor(s): Guy C. Pinkerton, Nancy J. Pinkerton.
Financial data (yr. ended 04/30/01): Grants paid, $105,944; assets, $3,167,616 (M); expenditures, $107,970; qualifying distributions, $107,970.
Limitations: Giving primarily in WA.
Application information: Application form not required.
Officers: Guy C. Pinkerton, Pres. and Treas.; Nancy J. Pinkerton, V.P. and Secy.
EIN: 911665004
Codes: FD2

55628
Vidalakis Family Foundation
101 Stewart St., Ste.1111
Seattle, WA 98101

Established in 1999 in WA.
Donor(s): Nick S. Vidalakis, Nancy G. Vidalakis.
Financial data (yr. ended 12/31/00): Grants paid, $105,403; assets, $1,445,663 (M); gifts received, $600,000; expenditures, $118,329; qualifying distributions, $104,587.
Limitations: Applications not accepted.
Application information: Contributes only to pre-selected organizations.
Officers: Nick S. Vidalakis, Pres.; Perry N. Vidalakis, Exec. V.P. and Secy.; John N. Vidalakis, Exec. V.P. and Treas.; Nancy G. Vidalakis, Sr. Exec. V.P.; George N. Vidalakis, V.P.; Nicole N. Vidalakis, V.P.
EIN: 911997816
Codes: FD2

55629
Christopher R. Kelly Family Foundation
P.O. Box 99261
Seattle, WA 98199

Established in 1997 in WA.
Donor(s): Christopher R. Kelly, Maria C. Driano.
Financial data (yr. ended 12/31/00): Grants paid, $105,400; assets, $1,982,958 (M); gifts received, $1,500; expenditures, $132,682; qualifying distributions, $108,397.
Limitations: Applications not accepted.
Application information: Contributes only to pre-selected organizations.
Directors: Maria C. Driano, Christopher R. Kelly.
EIN: 911876347
Codes: FD2

55630
Neupert Family Foundation
1603 Evergreen Point Rd.
Medina, WA 98039

Established in 1996 in WA.
Donor(s): Peter M. Neupert, Sheryl Neupert.
Financial data (yr. ended 12/31/01): Grants paid, $105,000; assets, $849,663 (M); gifts received, $272,595; expenditures, $106,552; qualifying distributions, $105,949.
Limitations: Applications not accepted. Giving primarily in WA.
Application information: Contributes only to pre-selected organizations.
Officers and Directors:* Peter M. Neupert,* Pres.; Sheryl Neupert,* V.P.; John F. Neupert,* Secy.
EIN: 911748536
Codes: FD2

55631
Simperman Corette Foundation
5609 80th Ave. S.E.
Mercer Island, WA 98040-4831
E-mail: roy@semaphore.com
Contact: Roy F. Simperman, Pres.

Established in 1994 in WA.
Donor(s): Roy F. Simperman, Diane C. Simperman.‡
Financial data (yr. ended 12/31/01): Grants paid, $105,000; assets, $2,116,982 (M); gifts received, $90,010; expenditures, $105,828; qualifying distributions, $105,933.
Limitations: Applications not accepted. Giving primarily in HI, MT, and Seattle, WA.
Application information: Contributes only to pre-selected organizations.
Officers: Roy F. Simperman, Pres.; Roy W. Simperman, Jr., V.P.
Director: Jennifer Simperman.
EIN: 911656462
Codes: FD2

55632
Robert Mulvihill Scholarship Trust
c/o Wells Fargo Bank Northwest, N.A.
P.O. Box 21927
Seattle, WA 98111

Established in 1996 in WA.
Financial data (yr. ended 12/31/01): Grants paid, $104,988; assets, $1,686,478 (M); expenditures, $139,557; qualifying distributions, $111,568.
Limitations: Giving limited to WA.
Application information: Application form not required.
Trustee: Wells Fargo Bank Northwest, N.A.
EIN: 916025194
Codes: FD2

55633
Violet R. and Nada V. Bohnett Memorial Foundation
(Formerly Violet R. Bohnett Memorial Foundation)
7981 168th Ave. N.E., Ste. 220
Redmond, WA 98052
E-mail: jnbohnett@aol.com
Contact: Mr. Jamie Bohnett, Admin.

Established in 1968 in CA.
Donor(s): F. Newell Bohnett.
Financial data (yr. ended 12/31/00): Grants paid, $104,438; assets, $2,912,527 (M); gifts received, $5,756; expenditures, $204,444; qualifying distributions, $200,410; giving activities include $80,000 for programs.
Limitations: Giving primarily in western WA; some giving also in AZ, CA, CO, and HI.
Publications: Newsletter, informational brochure (including application guidelines).
Application information: Application form not required.
Officer and Trustees:* F. Newell Bohnett,* Chair.; Joe Bohnett III, Thomas D. Bohnett, William C. Bohnett III, Owen G. Johnston, James A. Nelson.
Director: James N. Bohnett.
EIN: 956225968
Codes: FD2, GTI

55634
The Bernard M. and Audrey Jaffe Foundation
P.O. Box 1151
Bellingham, WA 98227-1151

Established in 1988 in WA.
Donor(s): Bernard Jaffe,‡ Audrey Jaffe, BMJ Holdings, Inc.
Financial data (yr. ended 03/31/01): Grants paid, $104,300; assets, $1,799,824 (M); expenditures, $105,840; qualifying distributions, $104,300.
Limitations: Applications not accepted. Giving primarily in San Francisco, CA, New York, NY, and Bellingham, WA.
Application information: Contributes only to pre-selected organizations.
Trustees: Audrey Jaffe, Mark B. Packer.
EIN: 911409921
Codes: FD2

55635
Bobby's Fund Foundation
10655 N.E. 4th St., Ste. 611
Bellevue, WA 98004

Established in 1992 in WA.
Donor(s): Barbara B. Ward.
Financial data (yr. ended 12/31/00): Grants paid, $102,000; assets, $1,229,735 (M); gifts received, $4,382; expenditures, $107,962; qualifying distributions, $102,000.
Limitations: Applications not accepted. Giving limited to WA.
Application information: Contributes only to pre-selected organizations.
Trustees: Thomas C. Gores, Kriss A. Sjoblom, Barbara B. Ward.
EIN: 916354724
Codes: FD2

55636
The Gunnar and Ruth Lie Foundation
9309 Olympic View Dr.
Edmonds, WA 98020

Established in 2000 in WA.
Donor(s): Gunnar Lie, Ruth Lie.
Financial data (yr. ended 12/31/01): Grants paid, $101,500; assets, $1,989,317 (M); expenditures, $107,562; qualifying distributions, $100,672.

55636—WASHINGTON

Limitations: Applications not accepted. Giving primarily in FL and WA.
Application information: Contributes only to pre-selected organizations.
Directors: Elizabeth Lie, Gunnar Lie, Kirsten Lie, Ruth Lie.
EIN: 912090480
Codes: FD2

55637
Elliott Family Foundation
4826 105th Ave., N.W. Ct.
Gig Harbor, WA 98335
Contact: Gail W. Elliott, Pres.

Established in 1999 in NM.
Donor(s): Gail Williams Elliott.
Financial data (yr. ended 12/31/00): Grants paid, $101,329; assets, $2,091,917 (M); expenditures, $118,684; qualifying distributions, $113,353.
Application information: Application form not required.
Officer and Director:* Gail Williams Elliott,* Pres.
Board Members: Eva Garland Elliott, Ingrid Williams Elliott, Jonathan Neal Elliott.
EIN: 850457435
Codes: FD2

55638
George and Carlyn Steiner Family Foundation
811 34th Ave. E.
Seattle, WA 98112-4309

Established in 2000.
Donor(s): Carlyn Steiner, George Steiner.
Financial data (yr. ended 09/30/01): Grants paid, $100,375; assets, $20,395 (M); gifts received, $151,196; expenditures, $102,712; qualifying distributions, $101,543.
Limitations: Applications not accepted. Giving primarily in Seattle, WA.
Application information: Contributes only to pre-selected organizations.
Officers and Directors:* Carlyn Steiner,* Pres. and Treas.; George Steiner,* V.P. and Secy.
EIN: 912091417
Codes: FD2

55639
Taylor Bishop Foundation
P.O. Box 2317
Olympia, WA 98507-2317
Application address: c/o Fred Gentry, 320 N. Columbia, Olympia, WA 98501

Established in 1979 in WA.
Donor(s): Taylor Bishop.‡
Financial data (yr. ended 06/30/01): Grants paid, $100,000; assets, $480,042 (M); expenditures, $110,598; qualifying distributions, $100,000.
Limitations: Giving limited to WA.
Trustees: Roger Johansen, Marie Lathrop, Susan Milstein, James Parks.
EIN: 237174178
Codes: FD2

55640
The John Graham Foundation
c/o Bank of America
P.O. Box 34345, CSC-9
Seattle, WA 98124-1345

Established in 1992 in WA.
Donor(s): John Graham.‡
Financial data (yr. ended 12/31/01): Grants paid, $100,000; assets, $1,625,703 (M); gifts received, $80,000; expenditures, $121,758; qualifying distributions, $103,402.
Limitations: Applications not accepted. Giving primarily in WA.

Application information: Contributes only to pre-selected organizations.
Trustees: J. Kevin Callaghan, David Friedenberg, Thomas C. Gores, Bank of America.
EIN: 916339306
Codes: FD2

55641
The Elizabeth Herbert and Donald Guthrie Charitable Foundation
125 Maiden Ln. E.
Seattle, WA 98112 (206) 634-0758

Established in 1999 in WA.
Donor(s): Elizabeth Herbert, Donald Guthrie.
Financial data (yr. ended 12/31/01): Grants paid, $99,950; assets, $1,610,139 (M); expenditures, $136,171; qualifying distributions, $98,950.
Application information: Application form not required.
Directors: Donald Guthrie, Elizabeth Herbert.
EIN: 912010848
Codes: FD2

55642
Vancouver Methodist Foundation
401 E. 33rd St.
Vancouver, WA 98663-2203

Established in 1969.
Financial data (yr. ended 12/31/01): Grants paid, $99,671; assets, $921,284 (M); gifts received, $162,503; expenditures, $100,588; qualifying distributions, $99,671.
Limitations: Giving primarily in WA.
Application information: Include with application, 3 letters of reference from people other than family members. Application form required.
Officers: C. Ray Johnson, Pres.; Dean Lookingbill, V.P.; Irwin Landerholm, Secy.; Glenn LaFavre, Treas.
Trustees: Lucille Breunsbach, Joyce Carter, Florine Dufresne, Harold Firestone, Phillip McGuiness, Betty Perry.
EIN: 910850194
Codes: FD2, GTI

55643
Kulakala Point Foundation
1402 3rd Ave., Ste. 1318
Seattle, WA 98101

Established in 1997 in WA.
Donor(s): Victoria N. Reed, William G. Reed, Jr.
Financial data (yr. ended 12/31/01): Grants paid, $99,610; assets, $2,007,499 (M); expenditures, $100,240; qualifying distributions, $99,207.
Limitations: Applications not accepted. Giving on a national basis, with some emphasis on WA.
Application information: Contributes only to pre-selected organizations.
Officers: William G. Reed, Jr., Pres. and Treas.; Victoria N. Reed, V.P. and Secy.
EIN: 911816213
Codes: FD2

55644
Charles & Maxine Skaggs Foundation
c/o Neil S. McKay
P.O. Box 1269
Spokane, WA 99201

Established in 1995 in WA.
Financial data (yr. ended 12/31/01): Grants paid, $98,250; assets, $1,788,338 (M); expenditures, $145,358; qualifying distributions, $97,995.
Limitations: Applications not accepted.
Application information: Contributes only to pre-selected organizations.
Advisory Committee: Craig Korthase.

Trustee: Neil S. McKay.
EIN: 911645836
Codes: FD2

55645
Sherrard Charitable Trust
14378 Sandy Hook Rd.
Poulsbo, WA 98370

Financial data (yr. ended 09/30/01): Grants paid, $96,738; assets, $68,769 (M); gifts received, $69,819; expenditures, $101,885; qualifying distributions, $101,855.
Limitations: Giving primarily in WA.
Trustee: J.R. Sherrard.
EIN: 912007980
Codes: FD2

55646
Hamalainen Charitable Trust
1076 S. West Camano Dr.
Camano Island, WA 98292

Established in 1994 in WA.
Donor(s): Asko Hamalainen, Karen Hamalainen.
Financial data (yr. ended 12/31/01): Grants paid, $96,628; assets, $1,622,840 (M); expenditures, $97,687; qualifying distributions, $96,628.
Limitations: Applications not accepted. Giving primarily in WA.
Application information: Contributes only to pre-selected organizations.
Trustees: Asko Hamalainen, Karen Hamalainen.
EIN: 916376196

55647
Yancey P. Winans Trust
c/o Baker Boyer National Bank
P.O. Box 1796
Walla Walla, WA 99362 (509) 525-2000
Contact: Ted Cohan

Established in 1988 in WA.
Financial data (yr. ended 12/31/01): Grants paid, $96,615; assets, $1,623,343 (M); expenditures, $120,052; qualifying distributions, $102,584.
Limitations: Giving limited to Walla Walla, WA.
Application information: Application form required.
Trustee: Baker Boyer National Bank.
EIN: 916306164
Codes: FD2

55648
Newbold Family Foundation
423-86th Ave., N.E.
Medina, WA 98039-5341

Established in 1997 in WA.
Donor(s): Craig Newbold, Rose Newbold.
Financial data (yr. ended 04/30/01): Grants paid, $96,100; assets, $1,610,524 (M); expenditures, $120,879; qualifying distributions, $95,317.
Limitations: Applications not accepted. Giving limited to the Seattle, WA area.
Application information: Contributes only to pre-selected organizations.
Directors: Craig Newbold, Rose Newbold.
EIN: 911818747
Codes: FD2

55649
Van Waters & Rogers Foundation
(Formerly Univar Foundation)
P.O. Box 34325
Seattle, WA 98124-1325 (425) 889-3400
Contact: Nancy Johnson, Pres.

Established in 1967.
Donor(s): Van Waters & Rogers Inc., Vopak USA Inc.

Financial data (yr. ended 02/28/01): Grants paid, $96,000; assets, $33 (M); gifts received, $386; expenditures, $96,124; qualifying distributions, $96,000.
Limitations: Giving primarily in the Seattle, WA, area.
Application information: Application form not required.
Officer: Nancy Johnson, Pres.
Trustees: William A. Butler, Linda Holman, Gary Pruitt.
EIN: 910826180
Codes: CS, FD2, CD

55650
Janson Foundation
c/o Bank of America
701 5th Ave., Ste. 4700
Seattle, WA 98104   (206) 358-3381
Contact: Gus Cleveland, Rels. Mgr.

Established in 1982 in WA.
Financial data (yr. ended 11/30/01): Grants paid, $95,208; assets, $2,293,594 (M); expenditures, $124,560; qualifying distributions, $107,544.
Limitations: Giving limited to organizations and residents of Skagit County, WA.
Application information: Application form not available until Mar. 1. Grants to organizations for capital expenses only. Application form required.
Trustee: Bank of America.
EIN: 916251624
Codes: FD2, GTI

55651
John M. McClelland, Sr. Charitable Foundation
4020 E. Madison, No. 220
Seattle, WA 98112   (206) 323-8540
Contact: John M. McClelland, Jr., Pres.

Established in 1982.
Financial data (yr. ended 12/31/00): Grants paid, $94,000; assets, $1,299,785 (M); gifts received, $20,000; expenditures, $147,927; qualifying distributions, $106,679.
Limitations: Giving limited to WA.
Officers: John M. McClelland, Jr., Pres.; Burdette McClelland, V.P.; John M. McClelland III, Secy.-Treas.
EIN: 911169056
Codes: FD2

55652
ROMA Charitable Foundation
108 S. Washington St., Ste. 300
Seattle, WA 98104

Established in 1991 in WA.
Donor(s): Ray O'Leary.
Financial data (yr. ended 11/30/00): Grants paid, $91,000; assets, $1,511,063 (M); gifts received, $253,000; expenditures, $91,230; qualifying distributions, $91,000.
Limitations: Giving limited to WA.
Officers: Ray O'Leary, Pres.; Michael Angiuli, V.P.; John Crane, Secy.-Treas.
Directors: Carmen Angiuli-Wischman, Robert Berry, Kevin O'Learty, Lawrence Podnar.
EIN: 943142398
Codes: FD2

55653
David McKinlay Trust
(Formerly Orphans Home of Seattle, Inc.)
c/o Stanley Habib
1220 116th Ave., Ste. 201
Bellevue, WA 98004
Contact: Henry Iske, Treas.

Established in 1948 in WA.

Financial data (yr. ended 12/31/01): Grants paid, $90,000; assets, $2,989,584 (M); expenditures, $101,076; qualifying distributions, $96,030.
Limitations: Applications not accepted. Giving limited to King County, WA.
Application information: Contributes only to pre-selected organizations.
Officers and Directors:* C. William Rehm,* Pres.; Tom Constant,* V.P.; Arlene Miletich,* Secy.; Henry J. Iske,* Treas.; Diane Bain, Douglas Monaghan, Curtis A. West.
EIN: 910586921
Codes: FD2

55654
The Brechemin Family Foundation
1501 4th Ave., Ste. 2070
Seattle, WA 98101

Established in 1963 in WA.
Donor(s): Charlotte B. Brechemin, Mina B. Person.
Financial data (yr. ended 06/30/01): Grants paid, $89,500; assets, $590,075 (M); expenditures, $103,723; qualifying distributions, $94,617.
Limitations: Applications not accepted. Giving primarily in Seattle, WA.
Application information: Contributes only to pre-selected organizations.
Officers: Mina B. Person, Pres.; R. Bruce Swartz, V.P.; John F. Hall, Secy.; John P. Johnson, Treas.
EIN: 916050290
Codes: FD2

55655
Titcomb Foundation
P.O. Box 1278
Tacoma, WA 98401-1278   (253) 272-8336
FAX: (253) 572-2721; *E-mail:* bkr@fidcouns.com
Contact: Barbara K. Rousell

Established in 1960 in WA.
Financial data (yr. ended 12/31/00): Grants paid, $89,000; assets, $2,765,701 (M); gifts received, $2,000; expenditures, $103,143; qualifying distributions, $89,000.
Limitations: Giving primarily in MT, WA, and WY.
Publications: Application guidelines.
Application information: Application form not required.
Officers and Directors:* Stephen T. Titcomb,* Pres.; Peter C. Titcomb,* V.P.; David R. Titcomb, John W. Titcomb, Jr.
EIN: 916020513

55656
Edwards Mother Earth Foundation
7317 - 164th Pl., S.W.
Edmonds, WA 98026

Financial data (yr. ended 12/31/01): Grants paid, $88,975; assets, $24,967,332 (M); gifts received, $22,440,609; expenditures, $109,773; qualifying distributions, $88,975.
Limitations: Applications not accepted. Giving on a national basis.
Application information: Contributes only to pre-selected organizations.
Directors: Sonia Baker, Jonathan D. Edwards, Robert L. Edwards.
EIN: 911789783
Codes: FD2

55657
John Y. & Reiko E. Sato Foundation Trust
2707 N.E. 125th St.
Seattle, WA 98125

Established in 1997 in WA.
Financial data (yr. ended 12/31/00): Grants paid, $88,419; assets, $1,165,210 (M); expenditures, $110,335; qualifying distributions, $88,236.

Limitations: Applications not accepted. Giving primarily in WA, with some emphasis on Seattle and Bellevue.
Application information: Contributes only to pre-selected organizations.
Trustees: John Y. Sato, Reiko E. Sato.
EIN: 911873161
Codes: FD2

55658
Blue Mountain Community Foundation
(Formerly Blue Mountain Area Foundation)
8 S. 2nd, Ste. 618
P.O. Box 603
Walla Walla, WA 99362   (509) 529-4371
Contact: Lawson F. Knight, Exec. Dir.

Incorporated in 1984 in WA.
Financial data (yr. ended 06/30/00): Grants paid, $87,858; assets, $13,265,128 (M); gifts received, $1,028,104; expenditures, $184,542.
Limitations: Giving limited to Umatilla County, OR, and Walla Walla, Columbia, Garfield, Benton, and Franklin counties, WA.
Publications: Annual report, application guidelines, newsletter, informational brochure.
Application information: Application form not required.
Officers and Trustees:* John M. Reese,* Pres.; Jane Kreitzberg,* V.P.; Tom Baker,* Secy.; Jack L. Barga, Megan Clubb, Deborah Frol, Michael W. Gillespie, Peter Harvey, Jim Hayner, Jim Hobkirk, Tom Madsen, Judy Mulkerin, Terry Nealey, Bert Nelson, Ellen Wolf.
EIN: 911250104
Codes: CM, FD2, GTI

55659
John J. and Lois A. Tennant Foundation
(also known as John J. Tennant, Jr. Foundation)
754 Officers Row
Vancouver, WA 98661

Established in 1998 in WA.
Donor(s): John J. Tennant, Jr., Lois A. Tennant.
Financial data (yr. ended 12/31/00): Grants paid, $87,100; assets, $498,396 (M); gifts received, $2,000; expenditures, $92,368; qualifying distributions, $87,100.
Limitations: Applications not accepted. Giving primarily in Washington, DC, Portland, OR, and Vancouver, WA.
Application information: Contributes only to pre-selected organizations.
Officers: John J. Tennant, Jr., Pres.; Lois A. Tennant, Secy.
EIN: 911912105

55660
Daystar Northwest
P.O. Box 46261
Seattle, WA 98146

Donor(s): Hilda Anderson.
Financial data (yr. ended 12/31/01): Grants paid, $86,787; assets, $400,432 (M); gifts received, $7,892; expenditures, $89,195; qualifying distributions, $88,896.
Limitations: Applications not accepted. Giving primarily in Seattle, WA.
Application information: Unsolicited requests for funds not accepted.
Officers: Ethel Moore, Pres.; Jerome Smith, V.P.; Mary Dundon, Secy.-Treas.
Directors: Robert Braman, Roy Kannitzer, Merry Ann Peterson, Barbara Whittemore.
EIN: 910782369
Codes: FD2, GTI

55661—WASHINGTON

55661
Carrie Welch Trust
Rte. 5, Box 241
Walla Walla, WA 99362 (509) 526-8857
Contact: George Conkey, Tr.

Established in 1946 in WA.
Donor(s): Carrie Welch.‡
Financial data (yr. ended 10/31/99): Grants paid, $85,356; assets, $1,256,301 (M); expenditures, $125,323; qualifying distributions, $89,355.
Limitations: Applications not accepted. Giving limited to WA, with emphasis on the Walla Walla area.
Application information: No new grantmaking. Funds are fully committed.
Trustee: George Conkey.
EIN: 916030361
Codes: FD2, GTI

55662
Equality Network Foundation
6206 Woodlawn Ave. N.
Seattle, WA 98103-5717
E-mail: foundation@equality.net; URL: http://www.equality.net/Foundation/default.htm
Contact: Charles M. Gust, Pres.

Established in 1998 in WA.
Donor(s): Charles M. Gust, Maureen A. Thompson.
Financial data (yr. ended 05/31/01): Grants paid, $85,000; assets, $1,246,026 (M); expenditures, $109,818; qualifying distributions, $86,288.
Limitations: Giving primarily in Seattle, WA.
Application information: Check URL for application guidelines.
Officers: Charles M. Gust,* Pres. and Treas.; Maureen A. Thompson,* V.P. and Secy.
EIN: 911941336
Codes: FD2

55663
The Lissy Moore Foundation
1563 Parkside Dr., E.
Seattle, WA 98112-3719

Donor(s): Teresa A. Moore, Chad T. Moore.
Financial data (yr. ended 12/31/01): Grants paid, $84,525; assets $70,226 (M); gifts received, $69,293; expenditures, $86,809; qualifying distributions, $84,525.
Limitations: Applications not accepted. Giving primarily in Seattle, WA.
Application information: Contributes only to pre-selected organizations.
Officers: Teresa A. Moore, Pres.; Chad T. Moore, V.P.; Kendall Moore, Secy.; Riley Loftin, Treas.
EIN: 911911719
Codes: FD2

55664
Fries-Tait Foundation
2810 Cascadia Ave. S.
Seattle, WA 98144

Established in 1998 in WA.
Donor(s): William Rashkov,‡ Richard Tait, Karen Fries.
Financial data (yr. ended 12/31/99): Grants paid, $83,900; assets, $3,192,198 (M); expenditures, $96,071; qualifying distributions, $87,156.
Limitations: Applications not accepted. Giving on a national basis.
Application information: Contributes only to pre-selected organizations.
Trustees: Karen Fries, C.E. Huppin, Richard Tait.
EIN: 916458447
Codes: FD2

55665
Thomas D. Taylor Foundation
c/o Wells Fargo Bank Northwest, N.A.
P.O. Box 21927
Seattle, WA 98111
Application address: 900 Wilshire Rd., Ste. 230, Portland, OR 97225, tel.: (503) 292-3049
Contact: Arlene Lelanchon

Established in 1986 in OR.
Financial data (yr. ended 08/31/01): Grants paid, $83,500; assets, $1,649,824 (M); expenditures, $95,703; qualifying distributions, $85,997.
Limitations: Giving primarily in Portland, OR.
Application information: Application form not required.
Trustee: Wells Fargo Bank Northwest, N.A.
EIN: 936187704
Codes: FD2

55666
The Berwick Degel Family Foundation
c/o James A. Degel
705 Second Ave., Ste. 1111
Seattle, WA 98104

Established in 2000 in WA.
Donor(s): Jeanne E. Berwick, James A. Degel.
Financial data (yr. ended 12/31/01): Grants paid, $83,000; assets, $566,391 (M); gifts received, $218,756; expenditures, $83,946; qualifying distributions, $83,000.
Limitations: Applications not accepted.
Application information: Contributes only to pre-selected organizations.
Directors: Jeanne E. Berwick, James A. Degel.
EIN: 912083120

55667
The Sepic Family Foundation
6705 W. Mercer Way
Mercer Island, WA 98040

Established in 1998 in WA.
Donor(s): Jim Sepic, Carmen A. Sepic.
Financial data (yr. ended 12/31/01): Grants paid, $82,700; assets, $1,454,529 (M); expenditures, $85,651; qualifying distributions, $82,700.
Limitations: Giving primarily in WA.
Application information: Application form not required.
Officers: Carmen A. Sepic, Pres. and Treas.; Jim Sepic, V.P. and Secy.
EIN: 911938078
Codes: FD2

55668
Columbia Basin Foundation
P.O. Box 1623
Moses Lake, WA 98837 (509) 766-5808
FAX: (509) 766-5808; E-mail: colbasfd@atnet.net
Contact: Sherrye Wyatt, Exec. Dir.

Established in WA in 1996.
Financial data (yr. ended 12/31/00): Grants paid, $81,452; assets, $1,220,972 (M); gifts received, $322,507; expenditures, $103,027.
Limitations: Giving primarily in Grant and Adams counties, WA.
Publications: Newsletter, informational brochure, annual report.
Application information: Application form not required.
Officers and Directors:* Rick Rose,* Chair.; Dave Dollarhide,* Secy.; Matt Ely,* Treas.; Patty Sanford,* Mgr.; and 11 additional directors.
EIN: 911733104
Codes: CM

55669
The Massena Foundation
2505 3rd Ave., Ste. 200
Seattle, WA 98121

Established in 1999 in WA.
Donor(s): Shaula E.D. Massena, Darrin Massena.
Financial data (yr. ended 12/31/01): Grants paid, $81,000; assets, $1,272,548 (M); expenditures, $88,520; qualifying distributions, $87,490.
Limitations: Applications not accepted. Giving primarily in WA.
Application information: Contributes only to pre-selected organizations.
Officers: Shaula E.D. Massena, Pres. and Treas.; Darrin Massena, V.P.; Jennifer Keilin, Secy.
EIN: 931282847

55670
W. M. Shelton Educational Trust
c/o Bank of America
P.O. Box 34345
Seattle, WA 98124

Established in 1998 in WA.
Donor(s): W.M. Shelton.
Financial data (yr. ended 04/30/02): Grants paid, $80,705; assets, $806,526 (M); expenditures, $90,802; qualifying distributions, $80,705.
Limitations: Applications not accepted.
Application information: Contributes only to pre-selected organizations.
Trustee: Bank of America.
EIN: 916475182

55671
The Ash-Gudaitis Foundation
4180 134th Ave. N.E.
Bellevue, WA 98005-1121 (425) 885-1308
Contact: Robert W. Ash, Pres.

Established in 1993 in WA.
Donor(s): Robert W. Ash, Clodagh C. Ash, Richard J. Gudaitis, Sheryl A. Gudaitis.
Financial data (yr. ended 12/31/01): Grants paid, $80,520; assets, $613,622 (M); gifts received, $125; expenditures, $83,829; qualifying distributions, $80,520.
Limitations: Giving primarily in WA.
Officers and Directors:* Robert W. Ash,* Pres.; Sheryl A. Gudaitis,* V.P.; Richard J. Gudaitis,* Secy.; Clodagh C. Ash,* Treas.
EIN: 911578235
Codes: FD2

55672
Shrontz Family Foundation
10900 N.E. 4th St., Ste. 920
Bellevue, WA 98004
Contact: Frank Shrontz, Tr.

Established in 1994 in WA.
Donor(s): Frank Shrontz, Harriet A. Shrontz.
Financial data (yr. ended 12/31/01): Grants paid, $80,465; assets, $1,645,315 (M); expenditures, $90,365; qualifying distributions, $80,932.
Limitations: Giving primarily in Seattle, WA.
Officers: Harriet A. Shrontz, Chair.; Craig H. Shrontz, Pres.; Richard W. Shrontz, Secy.; David A. Shrontz, Treas.
Trustee: Frank Shrontz.
EIN: 916379530
Codes: FD2

55673
Worthington Foundation
4242 Sunset Beach Dr., N.W.
Olympia, WA 98502
Contact: W. Gary Worthington, Tr.

Established in 1994 in WA.
Donor(s): Gary Worthington, Sandra Worthington.
Financial data (yr. ended 12/31/01): Grants paid, $80,183; assets, $1,703,982 (M); expenditures, $81,885; qualifying distributions, $80,183.
Limitations: Applications not accepted. Giving primarily in Olympia, WA and India.
Application information: Contributes only to pre-selected organizations.
Trustees: Sandra Worthington, W. Gary Worthington.
EIN: 911645951

55674
The Kleo Foundation
P.O. Box 1272
Woodinville, WA 98072-1272
Contact: Grants Admin.

Established in 1999 in WA.
Donor(s): Leo Notenboom, Kathy Notenboom.
Financial data (yr. ended 12/31/00): Grants paid, $80,000; assets, $986,565 (M); gifts received, $70,000; expenditures, $84,846; qualifying distributions, $80,000.
Limitations: Giving primarily in WA.
Trustees: Kathy Notenboom, Leo Notenboom.
EIN: 912006733
Codes: FD2

55675
Orinoco Foundation, Inc.
5801 125th Ln. N.E.
Kirkland, WA 98033

Established in 1991 in AL.
Donor(s): Samuel T. Nash, Jr.
Financial data (yr. ended 12/31/01): Grants paid, $80,000; assets, $1,318,745 (M); expenditures, $89,148; qualifying distributions, $80,000.
Limitations: Giving on a national basis.
Officers and Directors:* Amelia J. Nash,* Pres.; Thomas A. Mitchell, Jr.,* Secy.; Mitsuko Mitchell.
EIN: 631055908
Codes: FD2

55676
Clara & Art Bald Trust
P.O. Box 1757
Walla Walla, WA 99362 (509) 527-3500
Contact: Tom Scribner, Tr.

Established in 1985 in WA.
Financial data (yr. ended 03/31/01): Grants paid, $79,500; assets, $2,111,171 (M); gifts received, $1,000; expenditures, $86,397; qualifying distributions, $79,500.
Limitations: Giving limited to Walla Walla, WA.
Application information: Application form not required.
Trustee: Tom Scribner.
EIN: 916275061
Codes: FD2

55677
Henry and Nancy Ketcham Foundation
2811 E. Madison St.
P.O. Box 22798
Seattle, WA 98122

Established in 1997 in WA.
Financial data (yr. ended 12/31/01): Grants paid, $79,200; assets, $30,612 (M); gifts received, $34,620; expenditures, $83,568; qualifying distributions, $80,200.
Limitations: Applications not accepted.
Application information: Contributes only to pre-selected organizations.
Officers: Nancy K. Ketcham, Chair.; Mary K. Kerr, Pres.; Henry H. Ketcham III, V.P.; Sally Ketcham, V.P.; Kathryn K. Strong, Secy.-Treas.
EIN: 911788920
Codes: FD2

55678
The Wells Charitable Trust
129 W. Main St.
Walla Walla, WA 99362 (509) 527-0477
Contact: Larry Siegel, Tr.

Established in 1992 in WA.
Financial data (yr. ended 12/31/01): Grants paid, $78,774; assets, $498,944 (M); expenditures, $90,381; qualifying distributions, $82,055.
Limitations: Giving limited to the Walla Walla, WA, area.
Trustee: Larry Siegel.
EIN: 916349205
Codes: FD2

55679
Morningside Foundation
8061 Lakemont Dr. N.E.
Seattle, WA 98115 (206) 729-0349
Contact: Thomas W. Phillips, Dir.

Established in 1999 in WA.
Donor(s): Thomas W. Phillips.
Financial data (yr. ended 12/31/01): Grants paid, $78,425; assets, $1,578,653 (M); expenditures, $92,160; qualifying distributions, $77,742.
Limitations: Giving primarily in WA.
Application information: Application form not required.
Directors: Thomas W. Phillips, Peggy Van Slice Phillips.
EIN: 912010842
Codes: FD2

55680
Hubbard Family Foundation
c/o Bank of America
P.O. Box 24565
Seattle, WA 98124-1345
Application address: c/o Leigh Bennett, 400 Dayton, Ste. A, Edmonds, WA 98020

Established in 1983 in WA.
Donor(s): Lawrence E. Hubbard.‡
Financial data (yr. ended 07/31/01): Grants paid, $78,185; assets, $2,242,672 (M); expenditures, $114,572; qualifying distributions, $90,592.
Limitations: Giving limited to Edmonds and Snohomish County, WA.
Trustee: Bank of America.
EIN: 916253897
Codes: FD2

55681
BECU Foundation
(also known as Boeing Employees Credit Union Foundation)
c/o Tara Cramer
12770 Gateway Dr.
Tukwila, WA 98168

Donor(s): Boeing Employees' Credit Union.
Financial data (yr. ended 12/31/01): Grants paid, $78,000; assets, $1,197,636 (M); gifts received, $75,971; expenditures, $109,973; qualifying distributions, $109,371.
Application information: Application forms available from Jan. 1 through Mar. 31. Application form required.
Officers: Barbara Johnson, Pres.; Jerry Calhoun, V.P.; Tara Cramer, Secy.; J. Michael Emerson, Treas.
EIN: 911703337

55682
The Martin Djos Family Foundation
2716 106th Pl., S.E.
Bellevue, WA 98004

Established in 1996 in WA.
Donor(s): Wayne Martin.
Financial data (yr. ended 12/31/01): Grants paid, $76,120; assets, $1,298,920 (M); expenditures, $98,785; qualifying distributions, $76,120.
Limitations: Applications not accepted.
Application information: Contributes only to pre-selected organizations.
Directors: Dylan D. Martin, Erikka A. Martin, Kristin D. Martin, Wayne D. Martin.
EIN: 911740305

55683
The Boeschoten Foundation
19403 N.E. 143rd Pl.
Woodinville, WA 98072-7838

Donor(s): Adrian P. Boeschoten.
Financial data (yr. ended 12/31/00): Grants paid, $76,000; assets, $1,326,938 (M); expenditures, $76,925; qualifying distributions, $75,575.
Limitations: Applications not accepted. Giving primarily in WA.
Application information: Contributes only to pre-selected organizations.
Trustees: Adrian P. Boeschoten, Ann M. Boeschoten, Paul A. Boeschoten, Monique G. Williams.
EIN: 470667399
Codes: FD2

55684
Sylvia Carmel Schlanger and I. Robert Schlanger Charitable Foundation
c/o David Carmel
9100 Battlepoint Dr. N.E.
Bainbridge Island, WA 98110

Established in 1996.
Financial data (yr. ended 12/31/01): Grants paid, $76,000; assets, $1,291,857 (L); expenditures, $101,166; qualifying distributions, $75,229.
Limitations: Applications not accepted. Giving on a national basis.
Application information: Contributes only to pre-selected organizations.
Successor Trustees: David B. Carmel, Gene K. Glasser.
EIN: 656201791
Codes: FD2

55685
Waggener Edstrom Charitable Foundation
225-108th Ave. N.E., Ste. 700
Bellevue, WA 98004
Contact: Michael Bigelow, Treas.

Established in 1998 in WA.
Financial data (yr. ended 12/31/00): Grants paid, $76,000; assets, $182,129 (M); gifts received, $84,981; expenditures, $76,571; qualifying distributions, $76,000.
Limitations: Applications not accepted. Giving primarily in Seattle, WA.
Application information: Contributes only to pre-selected organizations.
Officers: Deborah Hendrickson, Secy.; Michael Bigelow, Treas.
Directors: Pamela Edstrom, Mellissa Waggener Zorkin.
EIN: 911939988
Codes: FD2

55686
Keys Foundation
2811 E. Evergreen Blvd.
Vancouver, WA 98661
Application address: 1317 Stonehaven Dr., West Linn, OR 97068
Contact: Edwin J. Kawasaki, Dir.

Established in 1999 in OR.
Donor(s): Cynthia L. Dawson-Austin.
Financial data (yr. ended 12/31/01): Grants paid, $75,300; assets, $768,927 (M); expenditures, $87,020; qualifying distributions, $75,265.
Limitations: Giving primarily in CA, OR, and WA.
Officers and Directors:* Cynthia L. Dawson-Austin,* Pres.; Brandon M. Dawson,* Secy.; Cary B. Dawson, Edwin J. Kawasaki.
EIN: 931277432
Codes: FD2

55687
Beardsley Foundation Trust
(Formerly Beardsley Family Foundation Trust)
c/o Union Bank of California, N.A.
P.O. Box 84495
Seattle, WA 98124-5796 (206) 587-3627

Established in 1976 in WA.
Financial data (yr. ended 05/31/01): Grants paid, $75,100; assets, $2,144,363 (M); expenditures, $106,389; qualifying distributions, $82,526.
Limitations: Applications not accepted. Giving primarily in Seattle, WA.
Application information: Contributes only to pre-selected organizations.
Trustee: Union Bank of California, N.A.
EIN: 916214189
Codes: FD2

55688
The Hisey Foundation
6376 N.E. Tolo Rd.
Bainbridge Island, WA 98110

Established in 1998 in WA.
Donor(s): Hisey Construction.
Financial data (yr. ended 12/31/01): Grants paid, $74,183; assets, $46,402 (M); gifts received, $74,000; expenditures, $76,411; qualifying distributions, $76,355.
Limitations: Applications not accepted. Giving on a national basis.
Application information: Contributes only to pre-selected organizations.
Officers and Director:* John R. Hisey,* Pres., V.P. and Treas.; Brenda C. Hisey, Secy.
EIN: 911942803

55689
The Lester M. Smith Foundation
c/o Alexander M. Smith
P.O. Box 3010
Bellevue, WA 98009-3010

Established in 1981 in WA.
Donor(s): Lester M. Smith.
Financial data (yr. ended 10/31/01): Grants paid, $74,000; assets, $1,437,333 (M); expenditures, $77,592; qualifying distributions, $75,638.
Limitations: Applications not accepted. Giving primarily in WA.
Application information: Contributions only to pre-selected organizations.
Directors: Alexander M. Smith, Bernice R. Smith, Lester M. Smith.
EIN: 911156087

55690
The Kaiser, Borsari Educational Foundation
3765 Alpha Way
Bellingham, WA 98226-8302 (360) 647-2360

Established in 1997 in WA.
Donor(s): Grace L. Borsari, Fred Kaiser.
Financial data (yr. ended 12/31/01): Grants paid, $73,386; assets, $293,696 (M); gifts received, $250,000; expenditures, $74,386; qualifying distributions, $73,386.
Limitations: Applications not accepted.
Application information: Contributes only to a pre-selected organization.
Officer: G. Dennis Archer, Secy.
Directors: Grace L. Borsari, Fred Kaiser.
EIN: 911749100

55691
The Brad and Kathy Smith Foundation
9665 Lake Washington Blvd., N.E.
Bellevue, WA 98004

Established in 1999 in WA.
Donor(s): Bradford L. Smith, Kathryn Surace-Smith.
Financial data (yr. ended 12/31/01): Grants paid, $73,376; assets, $740,574 (M); gifts received, $101,048; expenditures, $83,432; qualifying distributions, $73,376.
Limitations: Applications not accepted.
Application information: Contributes only to pre-selected organizations.
Officers and Directors:* Bradford L. Smith,* Pres. and Treas.; Kathryn Surace-Smith,* V.P. and Secy.
EIN: 912013244

55692
The Taucher Family Foundation
4603 University Village Pl. N.E., Ste. 185
Seattle, WA 98105

Established in 1999 in WA.
Financial data (yr. ended 12/31/01): Grants paid, $73,131; assets, $937,585 (M); expenditures, $90,354; qualifying distributions, $77,450.
Limitations: Applications not accepted. Giving primarily in Seattle, WA.
Application information: Contributes only to pre-selected organizations.
Officers: Martin R. Taucher, Pres.; Colleen R. Taucher, V.P. and Secy.
EIN: 911998157

55693
The Ruth Anderson Wheeler and Henry O. Wheeler Charitable Trust
c/o Wells Fargo Bank Northwest, N.A., Trust Dept.
P.O. Box 21927
Seattle, WA 98111-0020
Application address: c/o Wells Fargo Bank Northwest, N.A., P.O. Box 1997, Tacoma, WA 98401

Established in 1982.
Financial data (yr. ended 09/30/01): Grants paid, $72,950; assets, $1,336,851 (M); expenditures, $101,317; qualifying distributions, $79,267.
Limitations: Giving primarily in Seattle and Tacoma, WA.
Application information: Application form not required.
Trustee: Wells Fargo Bank Northwest, N.A.
EIN: 916253678

55694
The REI Foundation
P.O. Box 1938
Sumner, WA 98390-0800 (253) 395-3780
Contact: Kathleen Beamer, Chair.

Established in 1993 in WA.
Donor(s): Recreational Equipment Inc.
Financial data (yr. ended 12/31/01): Grants paid, $72,740; assets, $245,456 (M); gifts received, $65,500; expenditures, $72,740; qualifying distributions, $72,740.
Limitations: Giving primarily in AK, CA, and NM.
Publications: Application guidelines.
Officers: Kathleen Beamer, Chair. and V.P.; Dennis Madsen, Pres.; David Jayo, Secy.; Rick Palmer, Treas.
EIN: 911577992
Codes: CS, CD

55695
Pace 8-591 Fallen Workers Memorial Scholarship
P.O. Box 483
Anacortes, WA 98221-0483
Contact: Directors

Established in 1999 in WA.
Financial data (yr. ended 06/30/01): Grants paid, $72,400; assets, $1,076,387 (L); expenditures, $78,814; qualifying distributions, $76,141.
Limitations: Giving primarily in WA.
Application information: Application form required.
Officers: Kim Nibarger, Pres.; Douglas Erlandson, Fin. Secy.; Rebecca Edson, Recording Secy.
Directors: Wayne Abbot, Steve Anderson, Liz Ford, Jeff Knudson, Tom Lind, Tom Montogomery, Brett Powers, Larry Reynolds, Dennis Roulson, Joe Solomon, Thor Solberg, George Welch.
EIN: 911986402

55696
Kirkpatrick Family Foundation
1916 Pike Pl., Ste. 245
Seattle, WA 98101-1013 (206) 781-7336
Contact: Kathleen M. Pierce, Tr.

Established in 1990 in WA.
Donor(s): Mildred E. Kirkpatrick, Kathleen M. Pierce.
Financial data (yr. ended 12/31/01): Grants paid, $72,050; assets, $868,745 (M); gifts received, $30,000; expenditures, $82,321; qualifying distributions, $72,050.
Limitations: Giving limited to King County, WA.
Publications: Application guidelines.
Application information: Application should be submitted on common grant form supplied by the foundation following approval of inquiry letter. Application form required.
Trustee: Kathleen M. Pierce.
Directors: Mildred E. Kirkpatrick, Kristina L. Maurer, Serena D. Maurer.
EIN: 916321948

55697
Eulalie Bloedel Schneider Foundation
1122 E. Pike St., No. 1080
Seattle, WA 98112 (206) 720-6116
Application address: c/o Therese Ogle, 5135 Ballard Ave. N.W., Seattle, WA 98107, tel.: (206) 781-3472; FAX: (206) 860-8406; E-mail: oglefounds@aol.com; URL: http://fdncenter.org/grantmaker/schneider
Contact: Eulalie M. Scandiuzzi, Tr.

Established in 1996 in WA.
Donor(s): Prentice Bloedel.‡
Financial data (yr. ended 12/31/00): Grants paid, $72,000; assets, $1,130,288 (M); gifts received,

$14,618; expenditures, $113,158; qualifying distributions, $85,720.
Limitations: Giving limited to the Puget Sound region of WA.
Publications: Application guidelines, grants list.
Application information: Accepts the Common Application Proposal format from Philanthropy Northwest. Requests submitted by FAX or E-mail not accepted.
Trustees: Carlo Scandiuzzi, Eulalie M. Scandiuzzi.
Advisor: Eulalie Bloedel Schneider.
EIN: 911719029

55698
George R. and Mildred E. Kingston Charitable Trust
c/o Bank of America
P.O. Box 34345
Seattle, WA 98124-1345

Established in 2000 in WA.
Financial data (yr. ended 06/30/01): Grants paid, $71,894; assets, $2,073,789 (M); gifts received, $7,392; expenditures, $95,861; qualifying distributions, $74,476.
Limitations: Applications not accepted.
Application information: Contributes only to pre-selected organizations.
Trustee: Bank Of America.
EIN: 957094110

55699
Noved Foundation
120 Lakeside Ave., Ste. 310
Seattle, WA 98122

Established in 2000 in WA.
Donor(s): Kathy L. Mares, Joseph N. Walter.
Financial data (yr. ended 12/31/01): Grants paid, $71,755; assets, $701,801 (M); expenditures, $74,044; qualifying distributions, $71,755.
Limitations: Applications not accepted.
Application information: Contributes only to pre-selected organizations.
Directors: Kathy L. Mares, Joseph N. Walter.
EIN: 912091158

55700
Hanlon Foundation
P.O. Box 25654
Seattle, WA 98125-1154

Established in 1999 in WA.
Donor(s): Michael Hanlon, Molly Hanlon.
Financial data (yr. ended 12/31/00): Grants paid, $70,750; assets, $1,570,827 (M); expenditures, $72,954; qualifying distributions, $69,538.
Limitations: Giving primarily in Seattle, WA.
Application information: Application form not required.
Directors: Michael Hanlon, Molly Hanlon, Joan M. McCoy.
EIN: 916485795

55701
Howard Kottler Testamentary Trust
c/o Dr. Bernard Goffe
1234 22nd Ave., E.
Seattle, WA 98112

Established in 1988 in WA.
Financial data (yr. ended 12/31/00): Grants paid, $70,092; assets, $597,385 (M); expenditures, $75,144; qualifying distributions, $74,738.
Limitations: Applications not accepted. Giving primarily in WA.
Application information: Unsolicited requests for funds not accepted.
Trustees: Bernard Goffe, Joyce Moty, Judith S. Schwartz.
EIN: 943090173

55702
G. M. Babare Foundation
2212 W. Day Island Blvd.
University Place, WA 98466 (253) 565-2479
Contact: George M. Babare, Pres.

Established in 1995 in WA.
Donor(s): The Babare Foundation.
Financial data (yr. ended 12/31/01): Grants paid, $70,071; assets, $1,533,001 (M); gifts received, $45,152; expenditures, $71,761; qualifying distributions, $69,137.
Limitations: Giving primarily in Tacoma, WA.
Officers: George M. Babare, Pres.; Evelyn G. Babare, V.P.; Martin D. Babare, Secy.-Treas.
EIN: 912065206

55703
The Edgar and Elizabeth Bottler Charitable Trust
3008 Webster Point Rd., N.E.
Seattle, WA 98105-5339
Contact: Elizabeth T. Bottler, Mgr.

Established in 1987 in WA.
Donor(s): Elizabeth T. Bottler.
Financial data (yr. ended 12/31/00): Grants paid, $70,032; assets, $1,199,450 (M); gifts received, $90,062; expenditures, $75,416; qualifying distributions, $69,481.
Limitations: Giving primarily in WA, with emphasis on Seattle.
Application information: Application form not required.
Officer: Elizabeth T. Bottler, Mgr.
Trustee: Edgar O. Bottler.
EIN: 916288481

55704
Bruce W. Gilpin Memorial Foundation
44 Silver Beach Dr.
Steilacoom, WA 98388
Contact: Arleigh T. Jones, Tr.

Established in 1996.
Donor(s): Jane G. Andrew.
Financial data (yr. ended 12/31/01): Grants paid, $70,000; assets, $1,707,360 (M); gifts received, $249,250; expenditures, $80,213; qualifying distributions, $74,113.
Limitations: Giving limited to Pierce County, WA.
Publications: Informational brochure (including application guidelines).
Application information: Accepts Pacific N.W. Grantmakers form. Application form required.
Trustees: Jane G. Andrew, Bruce W. Gilpin, Arleigh T. Jones.
EIN: 911745833

55705
The Lifeworks Foundation
2036-247th Pl. N.E.
Redmond, WA 98053
Contact: Brendan Dixon, Dir.

Established in 1998 in WA.
Donor(s): Brendan W. Dixon, Kim E. Dixon.
Financial data (yr. ended 12/31/00): Grants paid, $70,000; assets, $1,312,966 (M); expenditures, $86,949; qualifying distributions, $69,667.
Limitations: Giving primarily in Seattle, WA.
Directors: Brendan W. Dixon, Kim E. Dixon.
EIN: 911942043

55706
The PJA Foundation
999 3rd Ave., Ste. 2525
Seattle, WA 98104 (206) 382-2600
Contact: David E. Ketter, Pres.

Established in 1995 in WA.
Donor(s): Philip J. Aaron.‡

Financial data (yr. ended 12/31/01): Grants paid, $70,000; assets, $1,467,312 (M); expenditures, $114,485; qualifying distributions, $69,969.
Limitations: Applications not accepted. Giving primarily in Bellevue, WA.
Application information: Contributes only to pre-selected organizations.
Officers: David E. Ketter, Pres.; Alton O. Willoughby, V.P. and Treas.
Director: Marge L. Stevens.
EIN: 911679586

55707
The Levine Foundation
1535 9th Ave., W.
Seattle, WA 98119

Established in 2001 in WA.
Donor(s): Eric Levine, Suzane Levine.
Financial data (yr. ended 12/31/01): Grants paid, $68,800; assets, $10,147 (M); gifts received, $80,000; expenditures, $69,854; qualifying distributions, $69,854.
Limitations: Applications not accepted.
Application information: Contributes only to pre-selected organizations.
Officers: Suzane Levine, Pres.; Eric Levine, V.P. and Treas.; Phyllis Davidson, Secy.
EIN: 912143283

55708
The George Washington Foundation
403 E. E St.
Yakima, WA 98901 (509) 965-9265
Application address: 2581 Mapleway Rd., Yakima, WA 98908, tel.: (509) 965-0706
Contact: James R. Sharples, Secy.-Treas.

Established in 1921 in WA.
Financial data (yr. ended 06/30/01): Grants paid, $68,700; assets, $1,369,473 (M); gifts received, $500; expenditures, $81,590; qualifying distributions, $80,101.
Limitations: Giving primarily in WA.
Application information: Applications available through high school principal or counselor. Application form required.
Officers: John V. Staffan, Pres.; Benjamin McLean, V.P.; James R. Sharples, Secy.-Treas.
Trustees: Carl S. Geho, Michael Mackey, Paul Schafer, Bill Tolliver, E.F. Velikanje, Bryan Wells.
EIN: 916024141
Codes: GTI

55709
McDanel Land Foundation
12345 Lake City Way N.E.
Seattle, WA 98125-5490

Donor(s): Joanne M. Roberts.
Financial data (yr. ended 12/31/01): Grants paid, $68,000; assets, $1,272,423 (M); expenditures, $85,508; qualifying distributions, $68,490.
Limitations: Applications not accepted. Giving primarily in Seattle, WA.
Application information: Contributes only to pre-selected organizations.
Officers: Joanne Roberts, Pres.; Peter M. Roberts, V.P.; Jennifer Roberts, Secy.
EIN: 943121979

55710
Kenneth L. Kellar Foundation
435 Martin St., Rm. 4000
Blaine, WA 98230-4107 (360) 332-5239
Contact: Linda Summers, Secy.-Treas.

Established in 1990 in WA.
Donor(s): Kenneth L. Kellar, John Rockwell, Security State Bank.

55710—WASHINGTON

Financial data (yr. ended 09/30/01): Grants paid, $67,610; assets, $2,199,882 (M); gifts received, $20,429; expenditures, $235,349; qualifying distributions, $73,323.
Limitations: Giving primarily in Aitkin County, MN, Lawrence County, SD, and Whatcom County, WA.
Application information: Application form not required.
Officers and Director:* Kenneth L. Kellar,* Pres.; Linda Summers, Secy.-Treas.
EIN: 911425050

55711
The Lanterman Foundation
221 1st Ave. W., Ste. 108
Seattle, WA 98119-4223

Established in 1997 in WA.
Donor(s): A. Kirk Lanterman.
Financial data (yr. ended 12/31/01): Grants paid, $67,300; assets, $1,460,801 (M); expenditures, $69,260; qualifying distributions, $67,300.
Limitations: Applications not accepted. Giving on a national basis, with emphasis on WA, AK, and ND.
Application information: Contributes only to pre-selected organizations.
Officers: A. Kirk Lanterman, Pres.; Janet O. Lanterman, Secy.
Directors: Patricia Gable, Barbara Nixon.
EIN: 911789916

55712
The Burns McCabe Foundation
c/o Pamela B. McCabe
2226 Eastlake Ave. E., Ste. 108
Seattle, WA 98102

Established in 1998 in WA.
Financial data (yr. ended 12/31/01): Grants paid, $67,000; assets, $1,076,119 (M); expenditures, $69,313; qualifying distributions, $67,000.
Limitations: Applications not accepted.
Application information: Contributes only to pre-selected organizations.
Officers: Pamela B. McCabe, Pres.; Kristen Linn Burns, V.P.; Robert J. McCabe, Secy.-Treas.
EIN: 911935155

55713
Alex and Martin Tobias Foundation
3601 E. Union
Seattle, WA 98122

Established in 2000 in WA.
Donor(s): Alex A. Tobias, Martin G. Tobias.
Financial data (yr. ended 12/31/01): Grants paid, $66,650; assets, $229,197 (M); gifts received, $577,650; expenditures, $72,048; qualifying distributions, $66,650.
Limitations: Applications not accepted. Giving primarily in Seattle, WA.
Application information: Contributes only to pre-selected organizations.
Officers: Alex A. Tobias, Mgr.; Martin G. Tobias, Mgr.
EIN: 916506130

55714
Fernando and Dolores Leon Family Trust
c/o Bank Of America
P.O. Box 34345
Seattle, WA 98124   (503) 279-3592

Established in 1997 in OR.
Donor(s): Dolores Leon, Fernando Leon.
Financial data (yr. ended 12/31/01): Grants paid, $65,900; assets, $222,775 (M); expenditures, $68,700; qualifying distributions, $66,437.

Trustees: Dolores Leon, Fernando Leon, Bank Of America.
EIN: 916436088

55715
The Horowitz Foundation
1001 4th Ave.
Seattle, WA 98154

Established in 1999 in WA.
Donor(s): Russell Horowitz, David Horowitz.
Financial data (yr. ended 12/31/01): Grants paid, $65,716; assets, $5,201 (M); gifts received, $71,801; expenditures, $69,220; qualifying distributions, $65,716.
Limitations: Applications not accepted.
Application information: Contributes only to pre-selected organizations.
Officers: David Horowitz, Pres. and Treas.; Russell Horowitz, V.P. and Secy.
Director: Donald Horowitz.
EIN: 911982534

55716
The Frymoyer Foundation
P.O. Box 11715
Bainbridge Island, WA 98110   (206) 855-8298
Contact: Karen Rutherford

Established in 1999 in CA.
Donor(s): Edward M. Frymoyer.
Financial data (yr. ended 12/31/01): Grants paid, $65,000; assets, $0 (M); expenditures, $79,074; qualifying distributions, $65,000.
Limitations: Giving primarily in PA.
Officers: Edward M. Frymoyer, C.E.O; Diane L. Benson, C.F.O.
Directors: Krista Gilbert, Suresh Mahajan, Del Mindle.
EIN: 943379988

55717
Ray Hickey Foundation
1499 S.E. Tech Center Pl., Ste. 140
Vancouver, WA 98683-9575   (360) 604-4333
FAX: (360) 604-4343
Contact: Linda Hickey, Mgr.

Established in 1998 in WA.
Donor(s): Raymond Hickey, Hickey Family Co.
Financial data (yr. ended 12/31/01): Grants paid, $65,000; assets, $1,109,459 (M); gifts received, $311,000; expenditures, $72,686; qualifying distributions, $65,000.
Limitations: Giving primarily in OR and WA.
Officer and Trustees:* Linda Hickey,* Raymond Hickey.
EIN: 911887342

55718
The Peterson Family Foundation
16703 S.E. McGillvray Blvd., Ste. 210
Vancouver, WA 98683

Established in 1996 in WA.
Donor(s): Claudia Peterson, Ken Peterson.
Financial data (yr. ended 12/31/00): Grants paid, $64,550; assets, $2,872,101 (M); gifts received, $1,849,694; expenditures, $68,498; qualifying distributions, $66,482.
Limitations: Applications not accepted. Giving primarily in OR.
Application information: Contributes only to pre-selected organizations.
Officers: Kenneth D. Peterson, Jr., C.E.O. and Pres.; Claudia Peterson, Secy.-Treas.
EIN: 911746622

55719
Peter D. and Kathleen E. Dickinson Foundation
HCI Box 80
Eastsound, WA 98245
Application address: c/o Avansialo Melarkey Knobel McMullen, 165 W. Liberty St., Ste. 210, Reno, NV 89501
Contact: Kathleen Dickinson, Pres.

Established in 1995.
Donor(s): Kathleen Dickinson, Norman Dickinson, Jeanette Dickinson.
Financial data (yr. ended 12/31/99): Grants paid, $63,799; assets, $1,214,348 (M); gifts received, $30,782; expenditures, $65,773; qualifying distributions, $63,799.
Officers: Kathleen E. Dickinson, Pres.; Sue Baker, Secy.; John Klacking, Treas.
EIN: 880330188

55720
Robert Chase Erskine Foundation
c/o Bank of America
P.O. Box 34345
Seattle, WA 98124-1345

Established in 1998 in WA.
Donor(s): R.C. Erskine Trust.
Financial data (yr. ended 07/31/02): Grants paid, $63,000; assets, $463,862 (M); expenditures, $72,984; qualifying distributions, $63,000.
Trustee: Bank of America.
EIN: 916491855

55721
Cosette Foundation
1000 2nd Ave., Ste. 1200
Seattle, WA 98104

Established in 1999 in WA.
Donor(s): Keith D. Grinstein.
Financial data (yr. ended 12/31/00): Grants paid, $62,722; assets, $24,527 (M); expenditures, $67,383; qualifying distributions, $63,847.
Limitations: Applications not accepted. Giving primarily in Seattle, WA.
Application information: Contributes only to pre-selected organizations.
Officers and Director:* Keith D. Grinstein,* Pres. and Treas.; Silvia Estrada, Secy.
EIN: 911940911

55722
The Columbia Foundation
110 110th Ave. N.E., Ste. 445
Bellevue, WA 98004-5840

Financial data (yr. ended 09/30/01): Grants paid, $62,700; assets, $998,917 (M); expenditures, $71,812; qualifying distributions, $62,700.
Limitations: Applications not accepted.
Application information: Contributes only to pre-selected organizations.
Officers: Mary Youell Silk, Pres.; Susan Youell Jones, V.P.; Patricia A. Kinnaird, Secy.; Glen B. Youell, Treas.
EIN: 916028623

55723
Lynnwood Foundation MKE
P.O. Box 1
Lynnwood, WA 98046

Established in 2000 in WA.
Financial data (yr. ended 12/31/01): Grants paid, $62,500; assets, $1 (M); gifts received, $62,000; expenditures, $62,878; qualifying distributions, $62,500.
Trustees: Kathleen A. Echelbarger, Michael D. Echelbarger.
EIN: 912079404

55724
Raa & Helen Smith Charitable Foundation
1315 14th Ave.
Longview, WA 98632
Application address: 3125 N.W. 91st St., Seattle, WA 98117, tel.: (206) 782-0216
Contact: Morris Moen, Pres.

Established in 1997 in WA.
Donor(s): Helen B. Smith.
Financial data (yr. ended 12/31/00): Grants paid, $62,345; assets, $4,841 (M); gifts received, $65,000; expenditures, $65,312; qualifying distributions, $64,025.
Limitations: Giving primarily in WA.
Officers: Morris Moen, Pres.; Eric Smith, Secy.-Treas.
Directors: Dan McDonough, Dale R.I. Smith, Jean Thornsbury, Ron Thornsbury.
EIN: 911732068

55725
Block-Leavitt Foundation
3002 Cascadia Ave. S.
Seattle, WA 98144
Contact: William H. Block, Tr.

Established in 1996 in WA.
Donor(s): William H. Block.
Financial data (yr. ended 12/31/01): Grants paid, $62,210; assets, $975,590 (M); expenditures, $97,218; qualifying distributions, $62,210.
Limitations: Applications not accepted.
Application information: Unsolicited requests for funds not accepted.
Trustees: William H. Block, Susan J. Leavitt.
EIN: 367160637

55726
The Titus-Will Families Foundation
616 Broadway
Tacoma, WA 98402-3899
Contact: James W. Will, Pres.

Established in 1994 in WA.
Donor(s): James W. Will, Leon E. Titus, Jr., James M. Will.
Financial data (yr. ended 12/31/01): Grants paid, $62,150; assets, $1,325,444 (M); gifts received, $65,000; expenditures, $66,285; qualifying distributions, $62,150.
Limitations: Giving primarily in Pierce County, WA.
Officers and Trustees:* James W. Will,* Pres.; James M. Will,* Secy.; Leon E. Titus, Jr.,* Treas.; Carolyn A. Titus, Joanne S. Titus, Muriel J. Will.
EIN: 911659510

55727
Richard & Kathie Ann Jones Charitable Trust
c/o Union Bank of California, N.A.
P.O. Box 84495
Seattle, WA 98124-5795

Established in 1979 in WA.
Financial data (yr. ended 10/31/01): Grants paid, $61,826; assets, $1,173,531 (M); expenditures, $75,096; qualifying distributions, $61,826.
Limitations: Applications not accepted. Giving primarily in Seattle, WA.
Application information: Contributes only to pre-selected organizations.
Trustee: Union Bank of California, N.A.
EIN: 916223702

55728
AWL Charitable Foundation
275 Pine Forest Rd.
Goldendale, WA 98620-3307 (509) 773-6141
Contact: Robert E. Morrow, Tr.

Established in 1985 in WA.
Financial data (yr. ended 12/31/00): Grants paid, $61,760; assets, $18,075 (M); gifts received, $51,350; expenditures, $63,324; qualifying distributions, $61,794.
Limitations: Giving primarily in rural areas in eastern WA.
Trustees: Augusta W.L. Bishop, Bart Dalton, Robert E. Morrow.
EIN: 911275040

55729
Frank Rider Trust
2929 S. Waterford Dr.
Spokane, WA 99203 (509) 534-4005
Contact: William Kilpatrick, Chair.

Established in 1910 in WA.
Financial data (yr. ended 12/31/01): Grants paid, $61,750; assets, $1,389,210 (M); expenditures, $133,469; qualifying distributions, $67,113.
Limitations: Giving limited to Whitman, Lincoln, Adams, Franklin, and Grant counties, WA.
Application information: Application form required.
Officers and Trustees:* William Kilpatrick,* Chair.; Maurice Allert, Secy.-Treas.; Lonny Ellis, Robert Blank, Max Merritt.
EIN: 910641308
Codes: GTI

55730
The Schaub Foundation
9 S. Washington St., Ste. 500
Spokane, WA 99201

Donor(s): J. Stephen Schaub, Nancy G. Schaub.
Financial data (yr. ended 12/31/01): Grants paid, $61,400; assets, $1,415,100 (M); expenditures, $67,155; qualifying distributions, $61,451.
Limitations: Applications not accepted. Giving primarily in WA.
Application information: Contributes only to pre-selected organizations.
Officers and Directors:* J. Stephen Schaub,* Pres.; Nancy G. Schaub,* V.P.; Susan S. Cumming, Anne M. Schaub, David H. Schaub, Timothy S. Schaub.
EIN: 943069885

55731
Bonnie Braden Foundation
P.O. Box 1757
Walla Walla, WA 99362
Contact: H.H. Hayner, Tr.

Established in 1987 in WA.
Financial data (yr. ended 03/31/02): Grants paid, $61,085; assets, $1,167,610 (M); expenditures, $81,268; qualifying distributions, $61,085.
Limitations: Giving primarily in Walla Walla, WA.
Application information: Application form not required.
Trustees: H.H. Hayner, James K. Hayner.
EIN: 943030045

55732
Ireene S. Barnett Foundation
19156 66th Pl., N.E.
Seattle, WA 98155

Established in 1987 in WA.
Donor(s): Ireene S. Barnett.‡

Financial data (yr. ended 08/31/01): Grants paid, $60,500; assets, $152,635 (M); expenditures, $74,378; qualifying distributions, $60,461.
Limitations: Applications not accepted. Giving primarily in Seattle, WA.
Application information: Contributes only to pre-selected organizations.
Officer: Wallace R. Barnett, Mgr.
Trustees: Joyce Barnett, Louise Gallagher.
EIN: 911248214

55733
Robert Gleason and Mary Lou Skok Foundation
c/o Bank of America
P.O. Box 34345
Seattle, WA 98124-1345

Established in 2000 in WA.
Donor(s): Mary Lou Skok.
Financial data (yr. ended 12/31/01): Grants paid, $60,000; assets, $120,095 (M); expenditures, $61,721; qualifying distributions, $60,000.
Limitations: Applications not accepted.
Application information: Contributes only to pre-selected organizations.
Trustees: Karl D. Guelich, Mary Lou Skok, Bank of America.
EIN: 916508644

55734
The MacRae Foundation
2330 43rd Ave. E., Ste. 400-B
Seattle, WA 98112-2783

Established in 1999 in WA.
Donor(s): Jacqueline C. MacRae.
Financial data (yr. ended 12/31/01): Grants paid, $60,000; assets, $895,906 (M); expenditures, $59,613; qualifying distributions, $60,000.
Limitations: Applications not accepted. Giving primarily in IL and WA.
Application information: Contributes only to pre-selected organizations.
Officers and Directors: Jacqueline C. MacRae,* Pres. and Treas.; Caroline Jill Davis,* V.P. and Secy.
EIN: 912001720

55735
Riener Foundation
10002 Aurora Ave. N.
Seattle, WA 98133-9747

Established in 1986 in WA.
Donor(s): Francis G. Riener.
Financial data (yr. ended 11/30/01): Grants paid, $60,000; assets, $1,107,115 (M); gifts received, $25,000; expenditures, $68,455; qualifying distributions, $60,000.
Limitations: Applications not accepted. Giving primarily in Seattle, WA.
Application information: Contributes only to pre-selected organizations.
Director: Francis G. Riener.
EIN: 911362027

55736
Isador Simon Family Foundation
P.O. Box 9386
Seattle, WA 98109-0386

Established in 1988 in WA.
Donor(s): Edna Simon.
Financial data (yr. ended 12/31/01): Grants paid, $60,000; assets, $946,182 (M); gifts received, $103,422; expenditures, $73,143; qualifying distributions, $60,000.
Limitations: Applications not accepted. Giving primarily in Seattle, WA.
Application information: Contributes only to pre-selected organizations.

55736—WASHINGTON

Officers: Edna C. Simon, Mgr.; Samuel N. Stroum, Mgr.
Trustee: Herbert L. Pruzan.
EIN: 916308281

55737
Louis Ulrich Charitable Trust
5402 Ramona Rd.
Yakima, WA 98908

Established in 1996 in WA.
Donor(s): Louis Ulrich.‡
Financial data (yr. ended 12/31/01): Grants paid, $60,000; assets, $694,160 (M); expenditures, $71,506; qualifying distributions, $60,000.
Limitations: Applications not accepted. Giving limited to WA.
Application information: Contributes only to pre-selected organizations.
Trustees: Cragg Gilbert, Robert W. Mather.
EIN: 931226279

55738
Harvest Foundation
8315 Lake City Way N.E., PMB No. 214
Seattle, WA 98115-4411

Established in 2000 in WA.
Donor(s): Edward Ringness, Marjorie Ringness.
Financial data (yr. ended 12/31/01): Grants paid, $59,500; assets, $10,624,267 (M); gifts received, $120,674; expenditures, $196,613; qualifying distributions, $59,500.
Limitations: Applications not accepted.
Application information: Contributes only to pre-selected organizations.
Officers and Directors:* Edward Ringness,* Pres.; Marjorie Ringness,* Treas.
EIN: 912065635

55739
Craves Family Charitable Foundation
13023 167th Ave. N.E.
Redmond, WA 98052

Established in 1991 in WA.
Donor(s): Robert E. Craves, Geraldine Craves.
Financial data (yr. ended 12/31/01): Grants paid, $58,225; assets, $975,887 (M); expenditures, $87,165; qualifying distributions, $58,225.
Limitations: Applications not accepted. Giving primarily in Seattle, WA.
Application information: Contributes only to pre-selected organizations.
Officers and Directors:* Robert E. Craves,* Pres.; Geraldine Craves,* V.P.; Stacie Vaughn Craves.
EIN: 911539251

55740
Hidden Charitable Trust
2610 Kauffman Ave.
Vancouver, WA 98660 (360) 696-0579
Contact: Richard M. Hidden, Chair.

Financial data (yr. ended 12/31/99): Grants paid, $58,200; assets, $231,182 (M); gifts received, $249; expenditures, $80,571; qualifying distributions, $59,354; giving activities include $17,938 for programs.
Application information: Application form required.
Officers: Richard M. Hidden, Chair.; Oliver M. Hidden, Vice-Chair.; Naomi Hidden, Secy.
EIN: 916369053

55741
Angelo Foundation
14360 157th Ave. N.E.
Woodinville, WA 98072 (425) 867-5577
Contact: Marguerite T. Angelo, Pres.

Established in 2000 in WA.
Donor(s): Marguerite T. Angelo, Richard L. Angelo.
Financial data (yr. ended 12/31/00): Grants paid, $58,165; assets, $700 (M); gifts received, $59,717; expenditures, $59,043; qualifying distributions, $58,165.
Application information: Application form not required.
Officers: Marguerite T. Angelo, Pres. and Secy.; Richard L. Angelo, V.P. and Treas.
EIN: 911982569

55742
Milton-Freewater Area Foundation
c/o Baker Boyer Bank, Trust Div.
P.O. Box 1796
Walla Walla, WA 99362 (509) 525-2000

Established in 1962 in OR.
Financial data (yr. ended 12/31/00): Grants paid, $57,421; assets, $1,475,495 (M); gifts received, $4,050; expenditures, $77,107.
Limitations: Giving limited to residents of the Milton-Freewater, OR area.
Trustee: Baker Boyer National Bank.
EIN: 936025936
Codes: CM, GTI

55743
McEachern Foundation
c/o The Mellon Trust of Washington
1201 3rd Ave., Ste. 5010
Seattle, WA 98101-3029

Established in 1985.
Financial data (yr. ended 08/31/00): Grants paid, $57,030; assets, $1,324,164 (M); expenditures, $86,250; qualifying distributions, $70,433.
Limitations: Applications not accepted. Giving limited to Seattle, WA.
Application information: Contributes only to pre-selected organizations.
Trustees: Mary G. Ireland, Bonnie McEachern-Farrell, Janet Wozniak, Lynn Wuscher, The Trust Co. of Washington.
EIN: 916274269

55744
The Flour Bin Foundation
3103 Washington St.
Vancouver, WA 98660 (360) 694-4449
Contact: R. Jon Grover, Secy.

Established in 2000 in WA.
Donor(s): Mineva M. Grover.
Financial data (yr. ended 12/31/01): Grants paid, $57,000; assets, $937,552 (M); gifts received, $2,281; expenditures, $65,960; qualifying distributions, $57,000.
Officers and Directors: Mineva M. Grover,* Pres.; R. Jon Grover,* Secy.-Treas.
EIN: 912090501

55745
Alfred G. & Elma M. Milotte Scholarship Fund
c/o Bank of America, Tax Svcs.
P.O. Box 34345, FAB-22
Seattle, WA 98124-1345 (800) 526-7307
Application address: c/o Bank of America Private Bank Center, P.O. Box 34474, Seattle, WA 98124, tel.: (206) 358-7977; E-mail: info@milotte.org; URL: http://www.milotte.org

Established in 1989 in WA.
Donor(s): Alfred G. Milotte,‡ Elma M. Milotte.‡
Financial data (yr. ended 03/31/02): Grants paid, $56,244; assets, $992,043 (M); expenditures, $67,763; qualifying distributions, $64,196.
Limitations: Giving limited to WA.
Application information: Application form required.
Trustee: Bank of America.

EIN: 916307731
Codes: GTI

55746
The Orrico Foundation
c/o Dan Kettman
20565 N.E. 33rd Ct.
Redmond, WA 98053

Established in 1993 in WA.
Financial data (yr. ended 12/31/01): Grants paid, $56,200; assets, $1,225,417 (M); expenditures, $56,250; qualifying distributions, $56,200.
Limitations: Applications not accepted. Giving primarily in Seattle, WA.
Application information: Contributes only to pre-selected organizations.
Officers and Directors:* Brent A. Orrico,* Pres.; Mark V. Orrico,* V.P.; Paul E. Orrico,* Secy.; Daniel Kettman,* Treas.; Diane M. Kettman, Dean H. Orrico, F. Kevin Orrico, Phyllis Orrico.
EIN: 911597380

55747
Suskin Foundation
618 Priest Point Dr., N.W.
Marysville, WA 98271-6825

Established in 1999 in WA.
Donor(s): Margie Suskin.
Financial data (yr. ended 12/31/01): Grants paid, $56,000; assets, $2,853,617 (M); gifts received, $2,989,102; expenditures, $56,675; qualifying distributions, $56,000.
Limitations: Giving primarily in WA.
Trustees: Jon G. Bowman, James M. Hayes, Margie Suskin, Steven C. Suskin.
EIN: 912015382

55748
Peter Berkey Foundation
c/o Stockwell & Assocs.
19201 40th Ave. W.
Lynnwood, WA 98036
Additional address: P.O. Box 60104, Shoreline, WA 98160; E-mail: dberkey@cmc.net
Contact: David F. Berkey, Pres.

Incorporated in 1947 in IL.
Donor(s): Peter Berkey.‡
Financial data (yr. ended 12/31/00): Grants paid, $55,700; assets, $1,050,000 (M); expenditures, $55,700; qualifying distributions, $55,700.
Limitations: Applications not accepted. Giving primarily in CA, FL, and WA.
Publications: Annual report.
Application information: Unsolicited requests for funds not considered.
Officers: David F. Berkey, Pres.; June B. D'Arcy, V.P.; Bea Stockwell, Secy.
EIN: 362447326

55749
Leross Family Foundation
2000 Alaskan Way
Seattle, WA 98121

Established in 1999 in WA.
Donor(s): Lester M. Leross, Connie W. Leross.
Financial data (yr. ended 08/31/01): Grants paid, $55,500; assets, $864,743 (M); expenditures, $71,111; qualifying distributions, $55,500.
Limitations: Applications not accepted.
Application information: Contributes only to pre-selected organizations.
Directors: Connie W. Leross, Lester M. Leross.
EIN: 911935333

55750
Catherine Marie Elvins and Naomi Libby Elvins Scholarship Trust
11819 Marine View Dr. S.W.
Seattle, WA 98146-6323 (206) 242-6323
Contact: Barbara Herbst-Anderson, State Regent

Established in 1998 in WA.
Donor(s): Naomi Elvins.‡
Financial data (yr. ended 12/31/00): Grants paid, $55,000; assets, $2,411,440 (M); expenditures, $58,375; qualifying distributions, $56,595.
Limitations: Giving primarily in WA.
Application information: Application form required.
Officers: Barbara Herbst-Anderson, State Regent; Barbara Carlson, 1st Vice-Regent; Eileen Jameson, 2nd Vice-Regent; Cheryl Tallant, Recording Secy.; Sharon Neuswanger, Treas.
Trustees: Beverly Bills, Mary Breen, Karen Parsons.
EIN: 916470080

55751
The Hussey Foundation
1434 8th Ave., W.
Seattle, WA 98119

Established in 1999 in WA.
Donor(s): Jeffrey S. Hussey.
Financial data (yr. ended 12/31/00): Grants paid, $55,000; assets, $769,847 (M); gifts received, $807,138; expenditures, $60,459; qualifying distributions, $52,426.
Limitations: Applications not accepted.
Application information: Contributes only to pre-selected organizations.
Directors: Jeffrey S. Hussey, Traci J. Hussey.
EIN: 912013522

55752
John P. Angel Foundation, Inc.
1425 4th Ave., No. 420
Seattle, WA 98101-2218 (206) 622-0420
Contact: Steven Carlson, V.P.

Donor(s): John P. Angel.
Financial data (yr. ended 04/30/99): Grants paid, $54,700; assets, $820,959 (M); expenditures, $83,475; qualifying distributions, $83,475.
Limitations: Giving primarily in the Seattle, WA, area; giving also in Leros, Greece.
Officers and Trustees:* Demetrios Karanicolas,* Pres.; Steven Carlson,* V.P.; Alta Stewart,* Secy.; John John, George Pallis.
EIN: 916056571

55753
Jack F. and Zella Mae Nickel Foundation
203 W. Beach St.
Pateros, WA 98846

Established in 1999 in WA.
Financial data (yr. ended 12/31/01): Grants paid, $54,326; assets, $621,728 (M); expenditures, $59,192; qualifying distributions, $54,326.
Limitations: Applications not accepted.
Application information: Contributes only to pre-selected organizations.
Trustees: Jack F. Nickel, Zella Mae Nickel.
EIN: 911942447

55754
Helen Martha Schiff Foundation
c/o Union Bank of California, N.A.
P.O. Box 3123
Seattle, WA 98114
Contact: J. Thomas McCully

Established in 1971.
Donor(s): Helen Martha Schiff.‡
Financial data (yr. ended 12/31/00): Grants paid, $53,889; assets, $1,608,327 (M); expenditures, $77,596; qualifying distributions, $62,536.
Limitations: Giving primarily in WA.
Application information: Application form not required.
Trustee: Union Bank of California, N.A.
EIN: 237120813

55755
Polack Foundation
P.O. Box 3065
Seattle, WA 98114 (206) 323-4300
Contact: Valerie Polack, Dir.

Established in 1969 in WA.
Donor(s): Morris Polack, Dean Polik, and members of the Polack family.
Financial data (yr. ended 12/31/01): Grants paid, $53,720; assets, $1,412,357 (M); expenditures, $58,974; qualifying distributions, $52,857.
Limitations: Giving primarily in WA.
Application information: Application form not required.
Directors: Edith Polack, James Polack, Valerie Polack.
EIN: 910850767

55756
J. J. Lacefield & R. L. Richmond Foundation
c/o Active Voice
2901 3rd Ave., Ste. 500
Seattle, WA 98121 (206) 441-4700
Contact: Robert L. Richmond

Established in 1994 in WA.
Donor(s): Robert L. Richmond.
Financial data (yr. ended 12/31/01): Grants paid, $53,000; assets, $193,583 (M); gifts received, $1,705; expenditures, $54,705; qualifying distributions, $53,000.
Directors: Jill J. Lacefield, Robert L. Richmond.
EIN: 911685301

55757
J. Z. Knight Humanities Foundation
c/o J.Z. Knight
14507 Yelm Hwy., S.E.
Yelm, WA 98597 (360) 458-4492
Contact: J.Z. Knight, Pres.

Established in 1996 in WA.
Donor(s): J.Z. Knight.
Financial data (yr. ended 12/31/01): Grants paid, $52,544; assets, $662 (M); gifts received, $54,105; expenditures, $53,621; qualifying distributions, $52,544.
Limitations: Giving primarily in WA.
Officer: J.Z. Knight, Pres.
Directors: Linda Evans, Vicky Kady.
EIN: 911647430

55758
Alleniana Foundation
511 Lakeside Ave. S.
Seattle, WA 98144 (206) 860-6167
Contact: Linda and Thomas H. Allen, Trustees

Donor(s): Thomas Allen, Linda Allen.
Financial data (yr. ended 12/31/01): Grants paid, $52,531; assets, $12,388 (M); gifts received, $13,595; expenditures, $54,942; qualifying distributions, $54,272.
Limitations: Giving on a national basis.
Application information: Application form not required.
Trustees: Linda L. Allen, Thomas H. Allen.
EIN: 916488380

55759
Jean K. Lafromboise Foundation
c/o Leo Sheehan
3055 112th Ave., N.E., Ste. 210
Bellevue, WA 98004
Application address: 7725 Lakemont Ave., N.E., Seattle, WA
Contact: Jean K. Lafromboise, Pres.

Established in 1988 in WA.
Donor(s): Jean K. Lafromboise.
Financial data (yr. ended 12/31/01): Grants paid, $52,527; assets, $827,640 (M); expenditures, $57,821; qualifying distributions, $52,527.
Limitations: Giving primarily in Seattle, WA.
Officers: Jean K. Lafromboise, Pres.; Leo Sheehan, V.P.; John R. Allen, Secy.; Frank Coyle, Treas.
EIN: 911416209

55760
Clifford Braden Foundation
(Formerly Clifford and Bonnie Braden Trust)
P.O. Box 1757
Walla Walla, WA 99362 (509) 527-3500
Contact: H.H. Hayner, Tr.

Established in 1984 in WA.
Financial data (yr. ended 03/31/02): Grants paid, $52,265; assets, $1,091,984 (M); expenditures, $71,114; qualifying distributions, $52,265.
Limitations: Giving primarily in Walla Walla, WA.
Application information: Application form not required.
Trustees: H.H. Hayner, Douglas Heimgartner.
EIN: 916252951

55761
Hill Family Foundation
P.O. Box 700
Mercer Island, WA 98040-0700
Application address: 7900 S.E. 28th, Mercer Island, WA 98040, tel.: (206) 232-7500
Contact: Harold W. Hill, Pres., or Mary F. Hill, Secy.-Treas.

Established in 1991 in WA.
Donor(s): Harold W. Hill, Mary F. Hill.
Financial data (yr. ended 12/31/00): Grants paid, $52,200; assets, $527,957 (M); gifts received, $24,087; expenditures, $58,674; qualifying distributions, $58,674.
Limitations: Giving limited to Seattle, WA.
Application information: Application form not required.
Officers: Harold W. Hill, Pres.; Bonnie C. Hill, V.P.; Ellen A. Hill, V.P.; John G. Hill, V.P.; Stephen R. Hill, V.P.; Mary F. Hill, Secy.-Treas.
EIN: 911539805

55762
The I. S. & Emily Fetterman Foundation
4507 N. Elton Rd.
Spokane, WA 99212

Established in 1991 in WA.
Donor(s): Emily C. Fetterman.
Financial data (yr. ended 12/31/01): Grants paid, $52,000; assets, $1,432,344 (M); gifts received, $7,697; expenditures, $75,411; qualifying distributions, $52,000.
Limitations: Applications not accepted. Giving limited to Spokane, WA.
Application information: Contributes only to pre-selected organizations.
Officers and Directors:* Clark H. Gemmill,* Pres. and Treas.; Lawrence R. Small,* Secy.; Kristine L. Gemmill.
EIN: 911494181

55763
F. & D. Olson Foundation
c/o Donald A. Olson
6508 50th Ave., N.E.
Seattle, WA 98115 (206) 523-2907

Established in 1994.
Donor(s): Donald A. Olson, Francella E. Olson.
Financial data (yr. ended 12/31/01): Grants paid, $52,000; assets, $157,840 (M); expenditures, $58,080; qualifying distributions, $52,000.
Limitations: Applications not accepted.
Application information: Unsolicited requests for funds not accepted.
Officers and Directors:* Donald A. Olson,* Pres.; Francella E. Olson,* Secy.; Charlotte Olson Alkire, Gregory D. Olson, Peter B. Olson.
EIN: 911651996

55764
The Lucky Seven Foundation
2366 Eastlake Ave. E.
Seattle, WA 98102-3306

Established in 1996 in WA.
Donor(s): Edward A. Backus, Frances A. Backus.
Financial data (yr. ended 04/30/02): Grants paid, $51,765; assets, $1,185,173 (M); gifts received, $439,626; expenditures, $70,980; qualifying distributions, $51,765.
Officers: John T. Backus, Pres.; Edward A. Backus, V.P.; Susan B. Stoller, V.P. and Secy.-Treas.
Directors: Frances A. Backus, Manson F. Backus II.
EIN: 911722000

55765
The Loyal Bigelow and Jedediah Dewey Foundation
1815 E. McGraw St.
Seattle, WA 98112

Established in 2001 in WA.
Donor(s): Frederic A.C. Wardenburg IV.
Financial data (yr. ended 12/31/01): Grants paid, $50,400; assets, $1,160,989 (M); gifts received, $1,429,734; expenditures, $66,003; qualifying distributions, $50,400.
Limitations: Applications not accepted. Giving primarily in WA.
Application information: Contributes only to pre-selected organizations.
Officers: Frederic A.C. Wardenburg IV, Pres.; Sarah Frances Rutherford, V.P.
EIN: 912101719

55766
The Happy Kitten Charitable Trust
c/o Timothy Lykes
4505 University Way N.E., Ste. 269
Seattle, WA 98105

Established in 1997 in WA.
Donor(s): Timothy Lykes.
Financial data (yr. ended 12/31/00): Grants paid, $50,000; assets, $867,290 (M); expenditures, $50,626; qualifying distributions, $50,000.
Limitations: Applications not accepted. Giving primarily in NH.
Application information: Contributes only to pre-selected organizations.
Trustees: Lynda Rae Lykes, Timothy Lykes.
EIN: 911867996

55767
Hilen Foundation
4756 Univ. Village Pl. N.E., Ste. 382
Seattle, WA 98105
Contact: Andrew G. Hilen, Dir.

Established in 1994 in WA.
Donor(s): Frances Hilen.
Financial data (yr. ended 12/31/01): Grants paid, $50,000; assets, $735,369 (M); gifts received, $49,858; expenditures, $61,243; qualifying distributions, $50,000.
Limitations: Giving primarily in Seattle, WA.
Directors: Andrew G. Hilen, Frances L. Hilen, Kristen H. Orejuela, Ingrid H. Savage.
EIN: 911662466

55768
Frederick Stearns Foundation
408 Aurora Ave., N.
Seattle, WA 98109
Contact: Christopher L. Clark, Chair.

Established in 1998 in WA.
Financial data (yr. ended 06/30/02): Grants paid, $50,000; assets, $952,995 (M); expenditures, $51,040; qualifying distributions, $50,000.
Limitations: Giving primarily in WA.
Officer: Christopher L. Clark, Chair.
Board Members: Geoffrey M. Clark, Linda Clark.
EIN: 916449464

55769
Stoner Foundation
622 Holly Dr.
Shelton, WA 98584-3934

Established in 1990 in WA.
Donor(s): Donald L. Stoner, Lucy A. Stoner.
Financial data (yr. ended 12/31/00): Grants paid, $50,000; assets, $461,891 (M); expenditures, $54,296; qualifying distributions, $49,733.
Limitations: Applications not accepted. Giving limited to WA.
Application information: Contributes only to pre-selected organizations.
Officers and Trustee:* Marianne E. Heriford, Mgr.; Lucy A. Stoner,* Mgr.
EIN: 916325564

55770
Dorothy F. Thorne Foundation
c/o Bank of America
P.O. Box 34345
Seattle, WA 98124-1345

Established in 1997 in WA.
Donor(s): Dorothy F. Thorne.
Financial data (yr. ended 04/30/02): Grants paid, $50,000; assets, $487,932 (M); expenditures, $55,288; qualifying distributions, $50,000.
Limitations: Applications not accepted.
Application information: Contributes only to pre-selected organizations.
Directors: Gwen Akin, John Akin, Alison Righter, Nina R. Shambroom, Lisa Sloan, Dorothy F. Thorne.
EIN: 911817980

55771
The Zeneth F. Ward & Lanetta S. Ward Foundation, Inc.
12313 N.W. 43rd Ct.
Vancouver, WA 98685

Established in 2000 in OR.
Financial data (yr. ended 12/31/01): Grants paid, $49,600; assets, $1,547,851 (M); gifts received, $230,624; expenditures, $52,050; qualifying distributions, $49,600.
Limitations: Applications not accepted.
Application information: Contributes only to pre-selected organizations.
Officers and Directors:* Douglas G. Ward,* Pres.; Lanetta S. Ward,* Secy.; Mark L. Schoonmaker.
EIN: 931269745

55772
Fosseen Foundation
717 W. Sprague
Spokane, WA 99204
Application address: 2903 E. 25th St., Unit 701, Spokane, WA 99223
Contact: Neal R. Fosseen, Tr.

Established in 1994 in WA.
Financial data (yr. ended 12/31/01): Grants paid, $49,295; assets, $972,893 (M); expenditures, $54,479; qualifying distributions, $49,745.
Limitations: Giving primarily in Spokane, WA.
Application information: Application form required.
Trustees: Helen W. Fosseen, Neal R. Fosseen, Washington Trust Bank.
EIN: 911620966

55773
Woodrow Foundation
c/o U.S. Bank
P.O. Box 3588
Spokane, WA 99220

Established in 1990 in WA.
Financial data (yr. ended 06/30/00): Grants paid, $49,277; assets, $1,135,186 (M); expenditures, $58,580; qualifying distributions, $49,144.
Limitations: Applications not accepted. Giving primarily in Spokane, WA.
Application information: Contributes only to pre-selected organizations. Scholarships awarded only to students at Whitworth College, Spokane, WA.
Trustee: U.S. Bank.
EIN: 916326014
Codes: GTI

55774
The Larson Family Foundation
11120 N.E. 2nd St., Ste. 200
Bellevue, WA 98015
Application address: P.O. Box 53050, Bellevue, WA 98015, tel.: (425) 450-3300
Contact: John W. Larson, Dir. or Cynthia C. Larson, Dir.

Established in 1999 in WA.
Donor(s): John W. Larson, Cynthia C. Larson.
Financial data (yr. ended 12/31/01): Grants paid, $49,000; assets, $296,682 (M); gifts received, $40; expenditures, $50,900; qualifying distributions, $49,000.
Application information: Application form not required.
Directors: Ander K. Larson, Christi M. Larson, Cynthia C. Larson, John W. Larson.
EIN: 912011085

55775
Lindberg Foundation Charitable Trust
c/o Wells Fargo Bank Northwest, N.A.
P.O. Box 21927
Seattle, WA 98111

Financial data (yr. ended 12/31/01): Grants paid, $49,000; assets, $518,915 (M); expenditures, $60,979; qualifying distributions, $51,878.
Limitations: Giving limited to Tacoma, WA.
Trustee: Wells Fargo Bank Northwest, N.A.
EIN: 916023286

55776
Tellumind Foundation
525 Overlake Dr., E.
Medina, WA 98039-5326

Established in 1999 in WA.
Donor(s): Kevin Lee Phaup, Catherine Ann Wissink.

Financial data (yr. ended 12/31/01): Grants paid, $49,000; assets, $774,765 (M); expenditures, $58,439; qualifying distributions, $49,000.
Limitations: Applications not accepted. Giving primarily in Seattle, WA.
Application information: Contributes only to pre-selected organizations.
Trustees: Kevin Lee Phaup, Catherine Ann Wissink.
EIN: 916498738

55777
Richard W. and Karen J. Tschetter Foundation
1819 Evergreen Pt. Rd.
Medina, WA 98039 (425) 453-5160
Contact: Richard W. Tschetter, Pres., and Karen J. Tschetter, V.P.

Established in 2000 in WA.
Donor(s): Richard W. Tschetter, Karen J. Tschetter.
Financial data (yr. ended 12/31/01): Grants paid, $48,700; assets, $546,425 (M); expenditures, $48,713; qualifying distributions, $48,700.
Officers: Richard W. Tschetter, Pres.; Karen J. Tschetter, V.P.
EIN: 916519520

55778
Wolfe & Gita Churg Foundation
c/o Joan Morgan
1001 4th Ave., Ste. 3600
Seattle, WA 98154-1115

Donor(s): Jacob Churg, M.D., Andrew M. Churg.
Financial data (yr. ended 12/31/01): Grants paid, $48,500; assets, $1,940,303 (M); gifts received, $1,000,000; expenditures, $59,906; qualifying distributions, $48,500.
Limitations: Applications not accepted. Giving primarily in CA.
Application information: Contributes only to pre-selected organizations.
Trustees: Charles Chromow, Andrew M. Churg, Jacob Churg, M.D.
EIN: 237011455

55779
Robert and Lisa Bailey Foundation
5483 Canvasback Rd.
Blaine, WA 98230

Donor(s): Robert L. Bailey.
Financial data (yr. ended 12/31/01): Grants paid, $48,000; assets, $315,034 (M); expenditures, $53,844; qualifying distributions, $53,844.
Limitations: Applications not accepted.
Application information: Contributes only to pre-selected organizations.
Officers: Robert L. Bailey, Pres. and Treas.; M. Lisa Bailey, V.P. and Secy.
EIN: 912089219

55780
David & Dorothy Pierce Trust
c/o Washington Trust Bank, Trust Dept.
P.O. Box 2127
Spokane, WA 99210-2127

Financial data (yr. ended 12/31/01): Grants paid, $47,950; assets, $1,095,804 (M); expenditures, $60,284; qualifying distributions, $47,950.
Limitations: Giving limited to Spokane, WA.
Application information: Application form not required.
Trustee: Washington Trust Bank.
EIN: 916025848

55781
Johnson/Fortin Charitable Trust
110-110th Ave. N.E., Ste. 440
Bellevue, WA 98004

Financial data (yr. ended 12/31/00): Grants paid, $47,924; assets, $488,236 (M); expenditures, $52,602; qualifying distributions, $47,867.
Limitations: Applications not accepted. Giving primarily in Seattle, WA.
Application information: Contributes only to pre-selected organizations.
Trustee: Jennifer Fortin.
EIN: 911943011

55782
J. P. and Maude V. Schroeder Memorial Trust
P.O. Box 968
Ephrata, WA 98823 (509) 754-3586
Contact: Irmajean O. Moe, Tr.

Established in 1993 in WA.
Financial data (yr. ended 12/31/01): Grants paid, $47,866; assets, $1,057,969 (M); expenditures, $101,215; qualifying distributions, $47,860.
Limitations: Giving limited to Grant County, WA.
Trustee: Irmajean O. Moe.
EIN: 916306402
Codes: GTI

55783
CSM Foundation
1420 5th Ave., Ste. 3000
Seattle, WA 98101-2370

Established in 1986 in WA.
Donor(s): Cynthia Stroum.
Financial data (yr. ended 12/31/01): Grants paid, $47,750; assets, $277,838 (M); expenditures, $48,394; qualifying distributions, $47,750.
Limitations: Giving primarily in Seattle, WA.
Officers: Cynthia Stroum, Pres.; Irwin L. Treiger, Secy.
EIN: 911362111

55784
Robert L. Richmond Foundation
c/o Quellos Financial Adviosrs
601 Union St., 56th Fl.
Seattle, WA 98101
Contact: Robert L. Richmond, Dir.

Established in 1995 in WA.
Donor(s): Robert L. Richmond.
Financial data (yr. ended 12/31/01): Grants paid, $47,625; assets, $290,937 (M); gifts received, $874; expenditures, $69,914; qualifying distributions, $47,625.
Limitations: Giving primarily in NH and WA.
Director: Robert L. Richmond.
EIN: 911685302

55785
The Aslan Charitable Foundation
P.O. Box 1473
Tacoma, WA 98401

Established in 2000 in WA.
Donor(s): Eric A. Russell.
Financial data (yr. ended 12/31/01): Grants paid, $47,500; assets, $740,294 (M); expenditures, $62,259; qualifying distributions, $47,500.
Limitations: Applications not accepted.
Application information: Contributes only to pre-selected organizations.
Officer: Eric A. Russell, Pres.
Directors: Denny De Walt, Mark E. Holcomb, Marsha J. Russell.
EIN: 912090715

55786
Miller Foundation
P.O. Box 12680
Seattle, WA 98111-4680

Donor(s): Steven H. Miller.
Financial data (yr. ended 10/31/01): Grants paid, $47,500; assets, $815,174 (M); expenditures, $48,072; qualifying distributions, $47,500.
Limitations: Applications not accepted.
Application information: Contributes only to pre-selected organizations.
Directors: Irvin H. Karl, Kimberly K. Miller, Steven H. Miller.
EIN: 942538647

55787
Smith/Newport School District
c/o Bank of America
P.O. Box 34345
Seattle, WA 98124-1345

Established in 1996 in WA.
Financial data (yr. ended 08/31/01): Grants paid, $47,430; assets, $751,770 (M); expenditures, $59,152; qualifying distributions, $47,430.
Limitations: Applications not accepted.
Application information: Contributes only to pre-selected organizations.
Trustee: Bank of America.
EIN: 916365372

55788
The Chambers Rinks Foundation
4514-193rd Pl., S.E.
Issaquah, WA 98027

Established in 1997 in WA.
Donor(s): Thomas J. Chambers.
Financial data (yr. ended 12/31/01): Grants paid, $47,350; assets, $304,414 (M); gifts received, $500; expenditures, $54,983; qualifying distributions, $47,211.
Limitations: Applications not accepted.
Application information: Contributes only to pre-selected organizations.
Officers: Marianne Rinks-Pillsbury, Pres.; Thomas J. Chambers, Secy.
EIN: 911832158

55789
Ephesians 2:10 Foundation
13452 124th Ave., N.E.
Kirkland, WA 98034-5403 (425) 765-2773
Contact: Steven Fuchs, Pres.

Established in 1999 in WA.
Donor(s): Steven Fuchs, Marilyn Fuchs.
Financial data (yr. ended 04/30/01): Grants paid, $47,115; assets, $722,379 (M); gifts received, $994; expenditures, $49,945; qualifying distributions, $47,115.
Officers: Steven Fuchs, Pres.; Marilyn Fuchs, Secy.-Treas.
EIN: 912010850

55790
Robert V. Baker Foundation
P.O. Box 779
Tekoa, WA 99033-0779 (509) 284-2332
Contact: Theodore F.S. Rasmussen, Treas.

Established in 1990 in WA.
Donor(s): Robert V. Baker.
Financial data (yr. ended 12/31/01): Grants paid, $47,000; assets, $893,755 (M); expenditures, $84,662; qualifying distributions, $47,000.
Limitations: Giving primarily in Spokane, WA.
Officers: Robert V. Baker, Pres.; Ralph E. Gamon, Jr., V.P.; Gloria L. Rasmussen, Secy.; Theodore F.S. Rasmussen, Treas.

55790—WASHINGTON

EIN: 911437191

55791
Sequim Masonic Lodge Foundation
c/o Lewis W. Kastner
P.O. Box 1500
Sequim, WA 98382
Application address: 306 Reservoir Rd., Sequim, WA 98382
Contact: Glenn Greathouse, Secy.

Financial data (yr. ended 06/30/02): Grants paid, $47,000; assets, $390,900 (M); gifts received, $65; expenditures, $47,610; qualifying distributions, $47,305.
Limitations: Giving limited to Sequim, WA.
Officers: Robert Clark, Pres.; Glenn Greathouse, Secy.; Lewis W. Kastner, Treas.
EIN: 910987628
Codes: GTI

55792
Meadowdale Foundation
c/o Nicholas C. Spika
P.O. Box 1278
Tacoma, WA 98401-1278

Established in 1966.
Donor(s): W.H. Meadowcroft, G.H. Weyerhaeuser.
Financial data (yr. ended 12/31/01): Grants paid, $46,000; assets, $641,442 (M); expenditures, $48,481; qualifying distributions, $46,221.
Limitations: Giving primarily in WA.
Application information: Application form not required.
Trustees: W.H. Meadowcroft, G.H. Weyerhaeuser.
EIN: 916069287

55793
The Stockdale Family Foundation
1019 Pacific Ave., Ste. 1408
Tacoma, WA 98402-4492

Established in 1994 in WA.
Donor(s): Ronald A. Stockdale, Carol A. Stockdale.
Financial data (yr. ended 12/31/01): Grants paid, $45,700; assets, $989,429 (M); expenditures, $54,000; qualifying distributions, $45,700.
Limitations: Applications not accepted. Giving on a national basis.
Application information: Contributes only to pre-selected organizations.
Officer: Ronald A. Stockdale, Pres.; Carol A. Stockdale, Secy.-Treas.
Directors: Bryan R. Stockdale, Paul R. Stockdale, Russell A. Stockdale.
EIN: 911663715

55794
A. William and Eileen Pratt Foundation
101 Cascade Key
Bellevue, WA 98006

Established in 1986 in WA.
Donor(s): A. William Pratt, Eileen Pratt.
Financial data (yr. ended 12/31/01): Grants paid, $44,834; assets, $371,575 (M); expenditures, $48,143; qualifying distributions, $44,834.
Limitations: Applications not accepted. Giving primarily in WA.
Application information: Contributes only to pre-selected organizations.
Officers: A. William Pratt, Mgr.; Eileen Pratt, Mgr.
EIN: 911355633

55795
The Killpack Foundation
P.O. Box 4522
Rollingbay, WA 98061

Donor(s): J. Robert Killpack, Norma Killpack.

Financial data (yr. ended 12/31/00): Grants paid, $44,700; assets, $768,965 (M); expenditures, $44,809; qualifying distributions, $44,452.
Limitations: Applications not accepted. Giving primarily in Vero Beach, FL.
Application information: Contributes only to pre-selected organizations.
Officers: Norma H. Killpack, Pres.; John D. Killpack, V.P.; Jim Killpack, Secy.; Steven R. Killpack, Treas.
EIN: 341535697

55796
Sicklesteel Foundation
3610 Cedardale Dr., Ste. A
Mount Vernon, WA 98274

Financial data (yr. ended 12/31/01): Grants paid, $44,667; assets, $79,603 (M); expenditures, $45,892; qualifying distributions, $44,667.
Limitations: Applications not accepted.
Application information: Contributes only to pre-selected organizations.
Officers: Donald Sicklesteel, Pres.; Darla Sicklesteel, V.P.; Thom Sicklesteel, Secy.-Treas.
EIN: 912070155

55797
The W Foundation
P.O. Box 4679
Seattle, WA 98104-4679

Established in 1999 in WA.
Donor(s): Arthur L. Wahl, Eva S. Wahl.
Financial data (yr. ended 12/31/01): Grants paid, $44,160; assets, $549,017 (M); expenditures, $49,153; qualifying distributions, $44,160.
Limitations: Applications not accepted.
Application information: Contributes only to pre-selected organizations.
Directors: Arthur L. Wahl, Eva S. Wahl.
EIN: 912014762

55798
Eastern Star Charities Fund of Washington
P.O. Box 683
Silverdale, WA 98383

Financial data (yr. ended 12/31/01): Grants paid, $44,000; assets, $1,435,240 (M); gifts received, $330,877; expenditures, $59,634; qualifying distributions, $44,000.
Limitations: Applications not accepted. Giving primarily in WA.
Application information: Contributes only to pre-selected organizations.
Officers: Sandra Gay Cordell, Pres.; Mary Lou Addey, Secy.; Charles King, Treas.
Directors: Alice Ashley, Bill Hammontree, Mary Linker, Sandy Mcammond, Henry Radtke, Ted Rice, Leonard Seville, Gerry Shafer.
EIN: 916029876

55799
William O. Murphy Foundation
P.O. Box 2685
Spokane, WA 99220-2685

Donor(s): William O. Murphy, Naomi A. Murphy, M & M Investment Corporation, Murphy Bros., Inc., Shamrock Paving, William T. Murphy, Carol Ellis.
Financial data (yr. ended 12/31/01): Grants paid, $44,000; assets, $892,179 (M); gifts received, $60,000; expenditures, $44,388; qualifying distributions, $44,000.
Limitations: Applications not accepted. Giving limited to Spokane, WA.
Application information: Contributes only to pre-selected organizations.

Trustees: Carol Ellis, Naomi A. Murphy, William O. Murphy, William T. Murphy.
EIN: 911531342

55800
Brown Assistance Fund Trust
c/o Bank of America
P.O. Box 34345, No. CSC-9
Seattle, WA 98124-1345

Financial data (yr. ended 12/31/01): Grants paid, $43,005; assets, $753,382 (M); expenditures, $52,116; qualifying distributions, $43,005.
Limitations: Applications not accepted. Giving primarily in Spokane, WA.
Trustee: Bank of America.
EIN: 916029496

55801
John E. Manders Foundation
P.O. Box 5024
Bellevue, WA 98009-5024
Contact: John Woodley, Admin.

Established in 1978 in WA.
Financial data (yr. ended 12/31/00): Grants paid, $43,000; assets, $1,081,852 (M); expenditures, $57,363; qualifying distributions, $56,743.
Limitations: Giving primarily in WA.
Officer: John M. Woodley, Admin.
Trustees: Letha Wertheimer, Jane Woodley.
EIN: 911024201

55802
Dennis and Elizabeth Lane Family Foundation
1614 N.W. Gregory Dr.
Vancouver, WA 98665

Established in 2000.
Donor(s): Dennis W. Lane, Elizabeth H. Lane.
Financial data (yr. ended 12/31/01): Grants paid, $42,873; assets, $96,717 (M); gifts received, $75,070; expenditures, $49,456; qualifying distributions, $42,873.
Limitations: Applications not accepted. Giving primarily in Vancouver, WA.
Application information: Contributes only to pre-selected organizations.
Officers and Directors:* Dennis W. Lane,* Pres.; Elizabeth H. Lane,* Secy.-Treas.; Justine A. Lane.
EIN: 912052750

55803
The Winona Foundation
801 2nd Ave., Ste. 1600
Seattle, WA 98104

Donor(s): Frank Bumpus, Margaret Gunther, Elizabeth Helmholz.
Financial data (yr. ended 12/31/01): Grants paid, $42,798; assets, $683,176 (M); gifts received, $42,888; expenditures, $58,862; qualifying distributions, $42,798.
Limitations: Applications not accepted. Giving primarily in Winona, MN.
Application information: Contributes only to pre-selected organizations.
Officers and Directors:* Andreas Ueland,* Pres.; Laurie Musel,* V.P.; Rebecca Ueland,* Secy.; Rebecca Richardson, Treas.; Nathalie Brown, Margaret Gunther, Elizabeth Helmholz, Joan Lompart, Robert Mickle, Erica Ueland.
EIN: 911184043

55804
Leo & Katherine Gallagher Foundation
c/o KeyBank, N.A., Trust Div.
P.O. Box 11500, MS: WA31-01-0310
Tacoma, WA 98411-5052
Contact: Michael W. Steadman, Asst. V.P., KeyBank, N.A.

Financial data (yr. ended 12/31/01): Grants paid, $42,535; assets, $1,034,091 (M); expenditures, $45,270; qualifying distributions, $45,270.
Limitations: Giving primarily in WA.
Trustee: KeyBank, N.A.
EIN: 237131679

55805
Anthony/Maymudes Family Foundation
735 18th Ave. E.
Seattle, WA 98112

Established in 2000 in WA.
Donor(s): David Maymudes, Emily Anthony.
Financial data (yr. ended 12/31/01): Grants paid, $42,300; assets, $1,406,263 (M); gifts received, $99,856; expenditures, $44,939; qualifying distributions, $42,300.
Limitations: Applications not accepted. Giving primarily in Seattle, WA.
Application information: Contributes only to pre-selected organizations.
Officers: David Maymudes, Pres.; Emily Anthony, V.P.
EIN: 912014698

55806
The Picsha Foundation
PMB-485
700 N.W. Gilman Blvd. N.W., Ste. E-103
Issaquah, WA 98027
Contact: Juliann S. Phillips, Exec. V.P.

Established in 1986 in WA.
Donor(s): Julia P. Shaw, John F. Shaw.
Financial data (yr. ended 12/31/01): Grants paid, $42,100; assets, $1,142,747 (M); expenditures, $46,352; qualifying distributions, $42,100.
Limitations: Giving limited to the Pacific Northwest, with emphasis on the Seattle, WA, area.
Publications: Program policy statement, application guidelines.
Application information: Unsolicited requests for funds not considered. Application form required.
Officers and Trustees:* Julia P. Shaw,* Pres.; Juliann S. Phillips,* Exec. V.P.; John F. Shaw,* V.P. and Treas.
EIN: 911358995

55807
O. D. Fisher Charitable Foundation
600 University St., Ste. 1525
Seattle, WA 98101

Established in 1960 in WA.
Financial data (yr. ended 12/31/01): Grants paid, $42,000; assets, $1,705,248 (M); expenditures, $46,473; qualifying distributions, $44,658.
Limitations: Applications not accepted. Giving primarily in Seattle, WA.
Application information: Contributes only to pre-selected organizations.
Officers: Richard F. Graham,* Pres.; Evelyn I. Anderson, V.P. and Secy.; Donald G. Graham, Jr., V.P. and Treas.; Lida J. Buckner, V.P.; Ralph F. Dreitzler III, V.P.; Frederick A. Graham, V.P.; Robin J. Campbell Knepper, V.P.
EIN: 916024818

55808
Tumbleweed Foundation
c/o Katherine Arrington
P.O. Box 2541
Redmond, WA 98073

Established in 2000 in WA.
Donor(s): Katherine Arrington.
Financial data (yr. ended 12/31/01): Grants paid, $42,000; assets, $472,332 (M); expenditures, $47,888; qualifying distributions, $42,000.
Limitations: Applications not accepted.
Application information: Contributes only to pre-selected organizations.
Trustee: Katherine Arrington.
EIN: 912092280

55809
Riley & Nancy Pleas Family Foundation
2410 Boyer Ave. E., Ste. 1
Seattle, WA 98112-2157

Established in 1995 in WA.
Donor(s): Riley W. Pleas.
Financial data (yr. ended 12/31/01): Grants paid, $41,975; assets, $525,448 (M); gifts received, $505,000; expenditures, $45,100; qualifying distributions, $41,975.
Limitations: Applications not accepted. Giving primarily in WA.
Application information: Contributes only to pre-selected organizations.
Officers and Directors:* Riley W. Pleas, Pres.; Nancy A. Pleas,* V.P.; Theresa A. James,* Secy.; Joseph L. Brotherton,* Treas.
EIN: 911663829

55810
Herbert M. Zahl Foundation
c/o Bank of America
P.O. Box 34345, CSC-9
Seattle, WA 98124-1345
Application address: P.O. Box 129, Seaview, WA 98664
Contact: Kaye Mulvey

Financial data (yr. ended 12/31/01): Grants paid, $41,594; assets, $843,384 (M); expenditures, $52,892; qualifying distributions, $41,594.
Limitations: Giving primarily in WA.
Application information: Application form not required.
Directors: Kaye Mulvey, Charleen Southerland, Lt. Col. C.W. Stucki.
Trustee: Bank of America.
EIN: 910984570

55811
Floyd Foundation
c/o Bank of America
P.O. Box 34345
Seattle, WA 98124-1345

Established in 1997 in MT.
Donor(s): Raymon Thompson.
Financial data (yr. ended 12/31/01): Grants paid, $41,500; assets, $1,110,135 (M); expenditures, $42,381; qualifying distributions, $41,500.
Limitations: Applications not accepted.
Application information: Contributes only to pre-selected organizations.
Directors: Ladeine Thompson, Mike Thompson, Raymon Thompson.
EIN: 841406277

55812
Noe & Betty Higinbotham Fund
c/o Bank of America
P.O. Box 34345
Seattle, WA 98124-1345
Application address: c/o Dept. of Botany, Washington State Univ., Pullman, WA 99164-4328, tel.: (509) 335-3066

Established in 1992 in WA.
Donor(s): Betty W. Higinbotham.‡
Financial data (yr. ended 09/30/01): Grants paid, $41,441; assets, $876,641 (M); expenditures, $56,029; qualifying distributions, $41,441.
Limitations: Giving limited to WA.
Application information: Application form required.
Trustee: Bank of America.
EIN: 911612929

55813
Libra Fund
1075 Bellevue Way, N.E., Ste. 491
Bellevue, WA 98004 (425) 454-6463
Contact: Laurie Hamlin, Pres.

Established in 1998 in WA.
Donor(s): Laurie Hamlin.
Financial data (yr. ended 12/31/01): Grants paid, $41,425; assets, $595,641 (M); expenditures, $46,808; qualifying distributions, $41,425.
Officer: Laurie Hamlin, Pres.
EIN: 911911713

55814
The Cliff and Bee Swain Family Foundation
c/o Clifford G. Swain
602 E. 1st St.
Port Angeles, WA 98362-3304

Donor(s): Clifford G. Swain, Bernice V. Swain.
Financial data (yr. ended 12/31/01): Grants paid, $41,347; assets, $382,210 (M); gifts received, $202; expenditures, $42,503; qualifying distributions, $41,347.
Limitations: Applications not accepted. Giving primarily in Port Angeles, WA.
Application information: Contributes only to pre-selected organizations.
Officers: Glenda G. Cable, Pres.; Rebecca S. Gedlund, V.P.; James M. Cole, Secy.; Richard A. Cable, Treas.
EIN: 911504468

55815
John F. Coffman Scholarship Trust
c/o Wells Fargo Bank Northwest, N.A.
P.O. Box 21927
Seattle, WA 98111
Application address: c/o Student Counselor, W.F. West High School, Chehalis, WA 98532

Established around 1988 in WA.
Financial data (yr. ended 12/31/01): Grants paid, $40,556; assets, $772,511 (M); expenditures, $54,872; qualifying distributions, $44,860.
Limitations: Giving limited to residents of Chehalis, WA.
Application information: Application form required.
Trustee: Wells Fargo Bank Northwest, N.A.
EIN: 916274936
Codes: GTI

55816
William C. and Eleanor E. Butler Charitable Trust
(Formerly Eleanor B. Butler Charitable Trust)
c/o Wells Fargo Bank Northwest, N.A.
P.O. Box 21927
Seattle, WA 98111
Application address: c/o W. Murray Campbell, P.O. Box 69, Everett, WA 98206, tel.: (206) 258-3808

Financial data (yr. ended 04/30/01): Grants paid, $40,500; assets, $820,185 (M); expenditures, $47,716; qualifying distributions, $41,558.
Limitations: Giving limited to Snohomish, WA.
Trustee: Wells Fargo Bank Northwest, N.A.
EIN: 916025199

55817
Noel-Shoemaker Family Foundation
7934 Lake View Ln.
Mercer Island, WA 98040

Established in 1998 in WA.
Donor(s): Paul D. Shoemaker, Lori N. Shoemaker.
Financial data (yr. ended 12/31/01): Grants paid, $40,482; assets, $421,974 (M); expenditures, $41,240; qualifying distributions, $40,482.
Limitations: Applications not accepted.
Application information: Contributes only to pre-selected organizations.
Officers: Paul Shoemaker, Pres. and Treas.; Lori Shoemaker, V.P. and Secy.
EIN: 911935949

55818
Klaue Family Foundation
P.O. Box 14917
Spokane, WA 99214-4917 (509) 534-0266
Contact: August V. Klaue, Pres.

Established in 1990 in WA.
Donor(s): August V. Klaue.
Financial data (yr. ended 12/31/01): Grants paid, $40,100; assets, $447,008 (M); gifts received, $35; expenditures, $41,731; qualifying distributions, $40,819.
Limitations: Giving primarily in the Spokane, WA, area.
Application information: Application form not required.
Officers: August V. Klaue, Pres.; David A. Klaue, V.P.; Arlen B. Looney, Jr., Secy.-Treas.
Director: Dan F. Klaue.
EIN: 911503434

55819
Nicolov Foundation
2223 Alaskan Way, Ste. 220
Seattle, WA 98121 (206) 448-9200
Contact: Assen Nicolov, Tr.

Established in 2000 in WA.
Donor(s): Assen Nicolov.
Financial data (yr. ended 12/31/00): Grants paid, $40,005; assets, $613 (M); gifts received, $40,700; expenditures, $40,087; qualifying distributions, $40,087.
Limitations: Giving primarily in Portland, OR.
Trustees: Assen Nicolov, Christine Nicolov.
EIN: 916502652

55820
The Colymbus Foundation
1235 Eighth Ave. W.
Seattle, WA 98119

Established in 1998.
Donor(s): Charles M. Bagley, Jr., Nancy H. Bagley.
Financial data (yr. ended 12/31/01): Grants paid, $40,000; assets, $590,576 (M); gifts received, $73,504; expenditures, $42,915; qualifying distributions, $40,985.
Limitations: Applications not accepted.
Application information: Contributes only to pre-selected organizations.
Officers and Directors:* Charles M. Bagley, Jr.,* Pres. and Treas.; Nancy H. Bagley,* V.P. and Secy.
EIN: 911910041

55821
Edmonds Floral and Arts Foundation
408 Daley St.
Edmonds, WA 98020
Contact: Maude B. Hodgson, Tr.

Established in 1998 in WA.
Donor(s): Edgar J. Hodgson, Maude B. Hodgson.
Financial data (yr. ended 12/31/01): Grants paid, $40,000; assets, $1,531 (M); gifts received, $40,500; expenditures, $40,010; qualifying distributions, $40,000.
Limitations: Giving primarily in WA.
Trustees: Edgar J. Hodgson, Maude B. Hodgson.
EIN: 911695252

55822
First Baptist Church of Everett Foundation
1616 Pacific Ave.
Everett, WA 98201

Established in 1998 in WA.
Financial data (yr. ended 12/31/01): Grants paid, $40,000; assets, $783,566 (M); expenditures, $41,281; qualifying distributions, $40,000.
Limitations: Applications not accepted. Giving primarily in Everett, WA.
Application information: Contributes only to pre-selected organizations.
Officers: Doug Hadley, Pres.; Paul McKee, V.P.; Lois Tysseling, Secy.; Peter Sontra, Treas.
Directors: Stacey Ayers, William Deller, Roy Eastman, Brian Harpell, Ross Johnson, Cindi Linari, Roberta Miller, Keith Wilson.
EIN: 911313943

55823
The Shibata Benefits Fund
P.O. Box 4357
South Colby, WA 98384-0446

Established in 1999 in WA.
Financial data (yr. ended 12/31/01): Grants paid, $40,000; assets, $206,968 (M); gifts received, $694; expenditures, $42,123; qualifying distributions, $40,000.
Limitations: Applications not accepted. Giving primarily in MN.
Application information: Contributes only to pre-selected organizations.
Officers: Sandra H. Shibata, Pres.; David L. Shibata, V.P. and Treas.; Judith L. McQueen, Secy.
EIN: 912000905

55824
Sullivan Foundation
c/o Jack Sullivan
10 Roanoke St., Houseboat No. 1
Seattle, WA 98102

Donor(s): Members of the Sullivan family.
Financial data (yr. ended 11/30/99): Grants paid, $39,705; assets, $279,903 (M); expenditures, $42,986; qualifying distributions, $39,560.
Limitations: Applications not accepted.
Application information: Contributes only to pre-selected organizations.
Directors: Gerald J. Sullivan, John F. Sullivan, Jr.
EIN: 916318390

55825
Contorer Foundation
11023 N.E. 58th Pl.
Kirkland, WA 98033
Contact: Aaron Contorer, Dir.

Established in 2000 in WA.
Donor(s): Aaron Contorer, Rachael E.H. Contorer.
Financial data (yr. ended 09/30/01): Grants paid, $39,315; assets, $1,321,273 (M); gifts received, $1,588,548; expenditures, $52,405; qualifying distributions, $36,349.
Limitations: Giving primarily in WA.
Directors: Aaron Contorer, Rachael E.H. Contorer.
EIN: 912045646

55826
Bessie & Godfrey Thompson Charitable Foundation
c/o Bank of America
P.O. Box 34345
Seattle, WA 98124-1345

Established in 1998 in WA.
Donor(s): Bessie Thompson Trust.
Financial data (yr. ended 06/30/00): Grants paid, $38,963; assets, $1,482,595 (M); expenditures, $60,253; qualifying distributions, $47,907.
Limitations: Applications not accepted. Giving primarily in WA.
Trustee: Bank of America.
EIN: 957078668

55827
San Juan Island Community Foundation
P.O. Box 1352
Friday Harbor, WA 98250 (360) 378-6527
Contact: Joy H. Selak, Chair.

Donor(s): Barry Ackerley, David Bayley.
Financial data (yr. ended 12/31/99): Grants paid, $38,953; assets, $140,516 (M); gifts received, $67,672; expenditures, $44,045; qualifying distributions, $38,853.
Limitations: Giving limited to San Juan Island, WA.
Officers and Directors:* Joy H. Selak,* Chair.; James D. Skoog,* Secy.; Fred McCulloch,* Treas.; Alice Cook, Bill Greene, Carolyn Haugen, Liz Ills, Jim Maya, Kathleen McHarg, Carla Wright, Nancy Young, and 6 additional directors.
EIN: 911648730

55828
Rogers Memorial Fund
(Formerly W. O. and William O. Rogers Memorial Fund)
c/o Bank of America
P.O. Box 34345, CSC-10
Seattle, WA 98124-1345

Established in 1984 in WA.
Financial data (yr. ended 08/31/01): Grants paid, $38,646; assets, $756,042 (M); expenditures, $50,642; qualifying distributions, $38,646.
Limitations: Applications not accepted. Giving limited to the Seattle, WA, area.
Application information: Contributes only to pre-selected organizations.
Trustee: Bank of America.
EIN: 916283646

55829
Westran Foundation
P.O. Box 412
Custer, WA 98240-0412

Established in 1994.
Donor(s): Heward C. Little.
Financial data (yr. ended 12/31/01): Grants paid, $38,600; assets, $193,215 (M); expenditures, $39,537; qualifying distributions, $38,600.

Limitations: Applications not accepted. Giving primarily in Orlando, FL, IL and WA.
Application information: Contributes only to pre-selected organizations.
Directors: Heward C. Little, Sharon A. Little.
EIN: 911655551

55830
Josephine Stedem Scripps Foundation
221 1st Ave. W., Ste. 405
Seattle, WA 98119
Contact: Delancey B. Lewis, Treas.

Established in 1958 in WA.
Donor(s): Members of the Scripps family.
Financial data (yr. ended 11/30/01): Grants paid, $38,500; assets, $1,033,841 (M); expenditures, $50,357; qualifying distributions, $38,500.
Limitations: Applications not accepted. Giving primarily in CA and WA.
Application information: Contributes only to pre-selected organizations.
Officers and Trustees:* Roxanne D. Greene,* Pres.; Antonia Davis MacFarlane,* V.P.; Sally S. Weston,* V.P.; R. Erin Ball,* Secy.; Delancey B. Lewis, Treas.
EIN: 916053350

55831
The Skagit Community Foundation
407 Pine St.
Mount Vernon, WA 98273
FAX: (360) 299-0979; *E-mail:* gilkey@fidalgo.net
Contact: Leslie Gilkey, Exec. Dir.

Financial data (yr. ended 06/30/01): Grants paid, $38,400; assets, $815,119 (M); gifts received, $112,673; expenditures, $82,946.
Limitations: Giving limited to Skagit County, WA.
Application information: Application form not required.
Board Members: Jennifer Juckett, Dorothy Ives, Art Larvie, Jean Leib, Harry Lipp, John M. Meyer, Mike Minor, Steve Schutt, Bill Shuler, John Stewart, Brian Wolfe.
EIN: 911572414
Codes: CM

55832
Helen Miller Clancy Scholarship Foundation
P.O. Box 13476
Burton, WA 98013-0476 (206) 463-6655

Established in 1994 in WA.
Financial data (yr. ended 12/31/01): Grants paid, $38,250; assets, $473,272 (M); expenditures, $52,826; qualifying distributions, $43,548.
Limitations: Giving limited to residents of Vashon Island, WA.
Application information: Application form required.
Officers: David F. Cooper, Pres.; Beverly Beaumont, V.P.; Dominick Cvitanich, Secy.; Margaret Schoch, Treas.
Director: Nancy Zellerhoff.
EIN: 911658180
Codes: GTI

55833
Pelo Foundation
1859 Brevor Dr.
Walla Walla, WA 99362 (509) 525-2837
Contact: Richard R. Pelo, Pres.

Established in 1988 in WA.
Donor(s): Richard R. Pelo, Katherine Pelo, John E. Pelo, Donald C. Pelo, Richard L. Pelo.
Financial data (yr. ended 12/31/01): Grants paid, $37,750; assets, $720,198 (M); expenditures, $45,856; qualifying distributions, $37,750.
Limitations: Giving limited to Walla Walla, WA.

Application information: Application form not required.
Officers and Directors:* Richard R. Pelo,* Pres.; John E. Pelo,* V.P.; Katherine Pelo,* Secy.-Treas.; Jane Kreitzberg, James McCarthy, Melinda Pelo.
EIN: 911430570

55834
Schulze Family Foundation
7432 N. Mercer Way
Mercer Island, WA 98040

Established in 1998.
Donor(s): Gary F. Schulze, Marie J. Schulze.
Financial data (yr. ended 04/30/02): Grants paid, $37,500; assets, $712,544 (M); gifts received, $4,804; expenditures, $38,888; qualifying distributions, $37,500.
Limitations: Giving primarily in Seattle, WA.
Officers: Gary F. Schulze, Pres. and Treas.; Marie J. Schulze, V.P.
EIN: 911941658

55835
Ernest R. and Audrey M. Turner Foundation
c/o Jerry Sampont
2309 E. 3rd Ave.
Port Angeles, WA 98362-9011

Established in 1996 in WA.
Donor(s): Audrey Turner Trust.
Financial data (yr. ended 12/31/01): Grants paid, $37,500; assets, $1,274,149 (M); expenditures, $82,171; qualifying distributions, $37,500.
Limitations: Applications not accepted.
Application information: Contributes only to pre-selected organizations.
Trustee: Gerald Sampont.
EIN: 911740796

55836
HABCO Charitable Foundation
155 E. Wiser Lake Rd.
Lynden, WA 98264

Established in 1998 in WA.
Donor(s): Henk Berneds, Joanne T. Berends.
Financial data (yr. ended 12/31/01): Grants paid, $36,990; assets, $362,917 (M); expenditures, $42,003; qualifying distributions, $36,990.
Limitations: Applications not accepted.
Application information: Contributes only to pre-selected organizations.
Officers: Henk Berends, Pres.; Stephanie L. Bareman, 1st V.P.; G. Bernice Vreugdenhil, 2nd V.P.; Joanne T. Berends, Secy.; Janice Berends, Treas.
EIN: 911941799

55837
Mortar Board Alumni/Tolo Foundation
P.O. Box 53162
Bellevue, WA 98015

Financial data (yr. ended 05/31/99): Grants paid, $36,700; assets, $799,696 (M); gifts received, $3,605; expenditures, $46,779; qualifying distributions, $38,575.
Officers: Cleo Raulerson, Chair., Investments and Treas.; Meg Estep, Chair., Membership; Victoria Watson, Chair., Scholarships; Carol Scott-Kassner, Pres.; Mary Malins, V.P.; Lieslie Wurzburger, Secy.
Trustees: Michaelann Jundt, Margot Smith, Muriel Winterschied.
EIN: 916054386

55838
Dunn Foundation
727 Azalea Ave. N.E.
Bainbridge Island, WA 98110-2910

Established in 1999 in CA.

Financial data (yr. ended 12/31/00): Grants paid, $36,500; assets, $443,486 (M); expenditures, $71,364; qualifying distributions, $36,500.
Officers: Nancy Eiseman, Pres.; Michael Smith, V.P.; Cynthia Behrens, Secy.; Karla Smith, Treas.
Board Members: Doug Behrens, Don Ross.
EIN: 680425837

55839
The Hustler Family Foundation
11520 Quail Ln.
Edmonds, WA 98020 (206) 546-6483

Established in 1999 in WA.
Donor(s): Jean T. Hustler.
Financial data (yr. ended 12/31/01): Grants paid, $35,900; assets, $624,165 (M); expenditures, $41,835; qualifying distributions, $35,900.
Limitations: Applications not accepted.
Application information: Contributes only to pre-selected organizations.
Officers: Jean T. Hustler, Pres.; H. Dean Hustler, V.P.; Andrew J. Hustler, Secy.-Treas.
EIN: 912013526

55840
Clement Family Foundation
c/o Frank H. Clement
3701 E. Marion St.
Seattle, WA 98122

Established in 1994 in WA.
Donor(s): Frank H. Clement, Marilyn D. Clement.
Financial data (yr. ended 08/31/01): Grants paid, $35,465; assets, $294,233 (M); expenditures, $36,650; qualifying distributions, $35,465.
Limitations: Applications not accepted. Giving primarily in Seattle, WA.
Application information: Contributes only to pre-selected organizations.
Trustees: Andrew Clement, Elizabeth Clement, Frank H. Clement, Marilyn D. Clement.
EIN: 916381704

55841
Boyle Family Foundation
c/o Suzanne C. Hansen
2521 29th Ave. W.
Seattle, WA 98199-3323

Established in 1995 in WA.
Donor(s): Richard J. Boyle, Karen A. Boyle.
Financial data (yr. ended 12/31/01): Grants paid, $35,000; assets, $248,260 (M); expenditures, $52,689; qualifying distributions, $35,000.
Limitations: Applications not accepted. Giving primarily in WA.
Application information: Contributes only to pre-selected organizations.
Officer: Richard J. Boyle, Chair.
Directors: Christopher M. Boyle, Karen A. Boyle, Stephen R. Boyle, Suzanne C. Hansen, Linda K. Pallas.
EIN: 911663015

55842
The Lovett-McLuckie Family Trust
P.O. Box 4492
Seattle, WA 98104-0492 (206) 441-1558

Established in 1992 in WA.
Donor(s): Ruth McLuckie.
Financial data (yr. ended 12/31/01): Grants paid, $35,000; assets, $642,399 (M); expenditures, $44,630; qualifying distributions, $35,000.
Application information: Application form not required.
Trustees: Elisabeth McLuckie Keller, Ann Marie McLuckie, Benjamin Andrew McLuckie, Ruth McLuckie, Timothy Mark McLuckie.
EIN: 911570341

55843
Williams, Kastner & Gibbs Foundation in Memorial of J. K. McMullin & W. H. Robertson
1121 39th Ave. E.
Seattle, WA 98112-4401

Established in 1994.
Financial data (yr. ended 12/31/00): Grants paid, $35,000; assets, $366,417 (M); gifts received, $36,800; expenditures, $35,000; qualifying distributions, $35,000.
Limitations: Applications not accepted. Giving primarily in Seattle, WA.
Application information: Contributes only to pre-selected organizations.
Officers and Directors:* Teresa Bigelow,* Pres.; Robert Betts,* V.P.; Sara Robertson,* Secy.; Anne Kirk,* Treas.
EIN: 911461348

55844
The Boulanger Family Foundation
8117 N. 12th St.
Tacoma, WA 98406
Application Address: 1014 Crestwood Ln., Tacoma, WA 98466, tel. (253) 564-6377
Contact: Richard J. Boulanger, Pres.

Established in 1999 in WA.
Donor(s): Richard J. Boulanger, Maryann Boulanger.
Financial data (yr. ended 06/30/02): Grants paid, $34,575; assets, $167,497 (M); gifts received, $117,460; expenditures, $35,170; qualifying distributions, $34,575.
Limitations: Giving primarily in CA.
Officer: Richard J. Boulanger, Pres.
EIN: 912019510

55845
Good Fellows Foundation
(Formerly Good Fellows Charities, Inc.)
P.O. Box 459
Liberty Lake, WA 99019

Financial data (yr. ended 11/30/01): Grants paid, $34,250; assets, $694,570 (M); expenditures, $36,280; qualifying distributions, $34,174.
Limitations: Applications not accepted.
Application information: Contributes only to pre-selected organizations.
Officers: Arthur Putnam, Pres.; Ed Burtts, V.P.; Travis P. Fewel, Secy.-Treas.
Directors: Gilbert R. Allen, Ralph Axelson, Joe Sproul, Tom Spurgeon, Edwin E. Weber, Carl White.
EIN: 910654178

55846
Levine Family Foundation
P.O. Box 9300
Renton, WA 98057

Financial data (yr. ended 12/31/01): Grants paid, $34,175; assets, $41,458 (M); gifts received, $15,300; expenditures, $36,521; qualifying distributions, $34,175.
Limitations: Applications not accepted. Giving primarily in Seattle, WA.
Application information: Contributes only to pre-selected organizations.
Trustees: Dan Levine, Gayle Levine, Mark B. Levine.
EIN: 916064199

55847
The James R. and Donna H. Simanton Foundation
4816 S. Pender Ln.
Spokane, WA 99224

Established in 1988 in IL.
Donor(s): James R. Simanton, Donna H. Simanton.
Financial data (yr. ended 12/31/01): Grants paid, $34,155; assets, $655,183 (M); expenditures, $78,419; qualifying distributions, $34,155.
Limitations: Applications not accepted. Giving on a national basis.
Application information: Contributes only to pre-selected organizations.
Officers and Directors:* James R. Simanton,* Pres.; Donna H. Simanton,* V.P.; John Simanton,* Mgr.; James M. Simanton.
EIN: 363622388

55848
Pemberton Foundation
1722 N. Madson St.
Liberty Lake, WA 99019 (509) 891-9970
Contact: Evangeline Pemberton, Pres.

Established in 1986.
Financial data (yr. ended 12/31/01): Grants paid, $34,000; assets, $691,634 (M); expenditures, $35,225; qualifying distributions, $34,000.
Limitations: Giving primarily in WA.
Officers: Evangeline Pemberton, Pres.; Theodore C. Bantis, Secy.-Treas.
EIN: 237129940

55849
Stingl Family Foundation
7171 Hwy. 14
Lyle, WA 98635

Established in 1997.
Donor(s): Daniel M. Stingl.
Financial data (yr. ended 12/31/01): Grants paid, $33,816; assets, $303,732 (M); expenditures, $112,751; qualifying distributions, $33,816.
Officers and Directors:* Daniel M. Stingl,* Pres.; Jonica L. Stingl, V.P.; Lauren C. Stingl, Treas.; Katherine C. Stingl, Secy.; Cybil A. Stingl.
EIN: 911876151

55850
Heily Foundation
c/o Bank of America, Tax Svcs.
P.O. Box 34345, FAB-22
Seattle, WA 98124
Application address: John Heily, P.O. Box 88176, Seattle, WA 98138, tel.: (206) 358-1652

Established in 1987 in WA.
Donor(s): John M. Heily.
Financial data (yr. ended 12/31/00): Grants paid, $33,715; assets, $5,662 (M); gifts received, $28,000; expenditures, $34,092; qualifying distributions, $33,900.
Limitations: Giving primarily in WA.
Publications: Application guidelines.
Trustee: Bank of America.
EIN: 943041322

55851
Lindberg Charitable Trust
c/o Wells Fargo Bank Northwest, N.A.
P.O. Box 21927
Seattle, WA 98111

Established in 1996 in WA.
Financial data (yr. ended 12/31/01): Grants paid, $33,636; assets, $456,152 (M); expenditures, $46,170; qualifying distributions, $37,786.
Limitations: Applications not accepted. Giving primarily in Tacoma, WA.
Application information: Contributes only to pre-selected organizations.
Trustee: Wells Fargo Bank Northwest, N.A.
EIN: 916407305

55852
Marie H. Hamilton Scholarship Fund
c/o Bank of America
P.O. Box 34345, CSC-10
Seattle, WA 98124-1345
Application address: c/o Nancey Olson, Ocean Beach School District, P.O. Box I, No. 100, Iwalco, WA 98624
Contact: Lisa Nelson, Principal

Financial data (yr. ended 03/31/02): Grants paid, $33,500; assets, $886,375 (M); expenditures, $43,394; qualifying distributions, $38,863.
Limitations: Giving limited to residents of Iwalco, WA.
Application information: Application form required.
Trustee: Bank of America.
EIN: 916068558
Codes: GTI

55853
Martin W. Prins Charitable Trust
c/o Bank of America
P.O. Box 34345
Seattle, WA 98124-1345

Financial data (yr. ended 09/30/01): Grants paid, $33,320; assets, $716,636 (M); expenditures, $43,889; qualifying distributions, $33,320.
Limitations: Applications not accepted. Giving primarily in WA.
Application information: Contributes only to pre-selected organizations.
Trustee: Bank of America.
EIN: 916265187

55854
Dan and Pat Nelson Family Foundation
2921 Horsehead Bay Dr. N.W.
Gig Harbor, WA 98335 (253) 265-0088
Contact: Lori Ann Reeder, Secy.

Established in 1999 in WA.
Donor(s): Dan Nelson, Pat Nelson.
Financial data (yr. ended 12/31/01): Grants paid, $33,000; assets, $486,326 (M); expenditures, $41,001; qualifying distributions, $33,000.
Limitations: Giving limited to ID and WA.
Officers: Dan Nelson, Pres.; Lori Ann Reeder, Secy.; Pat Nelson, Treas.
EIN: 911939872

55855
The Snyder Foundation
14013 19th Ave. N.E.
Seattle, WA 98125-3213 (206) 362-3611
Contact: S. Charles Snyder, Pres.

Donor(s): S. Charles Snyder, Mike Moore.
Financial data (yr. ended 06/30/01): Grants paid, $32,870; assets, $121,103 (M); gifts received, $101,214; expenditures, $75,658; qualifying distributions, $53,341.
Limitations: Giving primarily in WA.
Application information: Application form required.
Officers and Directors:* S. Charles Snyder,* Pres. and Treas.; Barbara J. Snyder,* V.P.; Beverly Dechand,* Secy.; Debra Amble, Timothy M. Snyder.
EIN: 911143446

55856
Elizabeth McEachern Foundation
c/o Union Bank of California, N.A.
P.O. Box 84495
Seattle, WA 98124-5795

Established in 1999 in WA.
Donor(s): J.A. & Flavia McEachern Foundation.
Financial data (yr. ended 12/31/01): Grants paid, $32,850; assets, $449,627 (M); expenditures, $39,581; qualifying distributions, $32,850.
Limitations: Applications not accepted.
Application information: Contributes only to pre-selected organizations.
Trustee: Union Bank of California, N.A.
EIN: 911918532

55857
John and Nancy Sabol Foundation
3100 W. Commodore Way, Ste. 208
Seattle, WA 98199

Established in 2000 in WA.
Donor(s): John M. Sabol, Nancy A. Sabol.
Financial data (yr. ended 12/31/01): Grants paid, $32,600; assets, $2,005,238 (M); gifts received, $1,987,500; expenditures, $32,833; qualifying distributions, $32,600.
Limitations: Applications not accepted. Giving primarily in Seattle, WA.
Application information: Contributes only to pre-selected organizations.
Officers: John M. Sabol, Pres. and Treas.; Nancy A. Sabol, V.P. and Secy.
EIN: 912061780

55858
Kasin Family Foundation
9560 Moon Canyon Rd.
Leavenworth, WA 98826

Financial data (yr. ended 12/31/01): Grants paid, $32,500; assets, $501,504 (M); expenditures, $34,627; qualifying distributions, $32,500.
Limitations: Applications not accepted.
Application information: Contributes only to pre-selected organizations.
Officers: Cynthia D. Kasin, Pres.; Philip T. Kasin, V.P.; Jay H. Kasin, Treas.
EIN: 911875190

55859
Sidney Fund
999 3rd Ave., Ste. 2525
Seattle, WA 98104 (206) 382-2600
Contact: David E. Ketter, Pres.

Established in 1965 in WA.
Financial data (yr. ended 09/30/01): Grants paid, $32,500; assets, $1,906,559 (M); expenditures, $53,934; qualifying distributions, $32,500.
Limitations: Giving primarily in the greater Seattle, WA, area.
Application information: Application form not required.
Officers: David E. Ketter, Pres.; Kenneth A. Sheppard, Secy.-Treas.
EIN: 916062742

55860
Morgan Family Foundation
321 High School Rd. N.E., Ste. 381
Bainbridge Island, WA 98110

Donor(s): B.C. Morgan Charitable Lead Annuity Trust of 1997.
Financial data (yr. ended 12/31/01): Grants paid, $32,000; assets, $640,684 (M); gifts received, $145,000; expenditures, $34,080; qualifying distributions, $32,000.
Limitations: Applications not accepted.

Application information: Contributes only to pre-selected organizations.
Officers: Beverly C. Morgan, Pres. and Treas.; Thomas E. Morgan III, Secy.
EIN: 911815410

55861
Osteopathic Foundation of Yakima
P.O. Box 112
Yakima, WA 98907
Contact: Gary George, Exec. Dir.

Established around 1994.
Financial data (yr. ended 12/31/01): Grants paid, $32,000; assets, $1,592,470 (M); gifts received, $2,424; expenditures, $110,312; qualifying distributions, $98,859.
Limitations: Applications not accepted. Giving primarily in Yakima, WA.
Officers and Directors:* Malcolm Arnett, Pres.; Christopher Clark,* V.P.; Arthur Clevenger, Jr.,* Secy.; Melvin R. Lewis, Treas.; Gary George, Exec. Dir.; Arthur E. Borchardt, Lloyd H. Butler, Dennis Clark, William T. Cox, Leo Figgs, Guy Shinn, T. Kent Vye.
EIN: 911640626

55862
Johanna A. Rodman Foundation
5504 Pear Butte Dr.
Yakima, WA 98902

Established in 2000 in WA.
Donor(s): Johanna A. Rodman.‡
Financial data (yr. ended 12/31/01): Grants paid, $32,000; assets, $911,396 (M); expenditures, $60,369; qualifying distributions, $32,000.
Limitations: Applications not accepted. Giving limited to WA.
Application information: Contributes only to pre-selected organizations.
Directors: Linda Davis, Lauren W. Dobbs.
EIN: 912032417

55863
Drs. Hollingsworth and Bagdi Charitable Foundation
P.O. Box 653
Kirkland, WA 98083

Established in 2000 in WA.
Donor(s): Kennan Hollingsworth, Phyllis Bagdi Hollingsworth.
Financial data (yr. ended 12/31/01): Grants paid, $31,615; assets, $719,416 (M); gifts received, $5,700; expenditures, $45,386; qualifying distributions, $31,615.
Limitations: Applications not accepted.
Application information: Contributes only to pre-selected organizations.
Directors: Kennan Hollingsworth, Phyllis Bagdi Hollingsworth.
EIN: 912090705

55864
Mani Charitable Foundation
c/o Devindra S. Chainani
9922 181st Ave., N.E.
Redmond, WA 98052-6904

Established in 2001 in WA.
Donor(s): Devindra S. Chainani 5 year Charitable Trust.
Financial data (yr. ended 12/31/01): Grants paid, $31,615; assets, $173,454 (M); gifts received, $210,000; expenditures, $36,905; qualifying distributions, $36,905.
Limitations: Applications not accepted.
Application information: Contributes only to pre-selected organizations.

Trustees: Nalini B. Advani, Devindra S. Chainani, Manisha D. Chainani, Rukmini S. Chainani.
EIN: 916500144

55865
Millar Scholarship Fund
c/o Bank of America
P.O. Box 34345
Seattle, WA 98124-1345
Application address: c/o Reynolds High School, 1200 N.E. 201st. St., Troutdale, OR 97060

Financial data (yr. ended 06/30/01): Grants paid, $31,440; assets, $430,600 (M); expenditures, $44,660; qualifying distributions, $37,274.
Limitations: Giving limited to residents of OR.
Application information: Application form required.
Trustee: Bank of America.
EIN: 936054074
Codes: GTI

55866
The Kemper Freeman Foundation
10500 N.E. 8th St., Ste. 600
Bellevue, WA 98006

Financial data (yr. ended 11/30/01): Grants paid, $31,287; assets, $900 (M); gifts received, $33,785; expenditures, $33,672; qualifying distributions, $31,287.
Limitations: Applications not accepted. Giving primarily in Bellevue, WA.
Application information: Contributes only to pre-selected organizations.
Officers: F. Kemper Freeman, Jr., Pres.; Richard S. Sprague, V.P.
EIN: 911197306

55867
Leo J. Brockman Trust
c/o Bank of America
P.O. Box 34345
Seattle, WA 98124-1345
Loan application address: c/o Financial Aid Advisor, Gonzaga Univ., Spokane, WA 99207

Financial data (yr. ended 12/31/01): Grants paid, $31,000; assets, $430,072 (M); expenditures, $36,454; qualifying distributions, $34,502; giving activities include $31,000 for loans to individuals.
Limitations: Giving limited to Spokane, WA.
Application information: Application form required.
Trustee: Bank of America.
EIN: 916024372
Codes: GTI

55868
Kiwanis Club of South Bend, Inc.
c/o Richard Murakami
P.O. Box 435
South Bend, WA 98586

Financial data (yr. ended 12/31/00): Grants paid, $31,000; assets, $500,791 (M); gifts received, $4,000; expenditures, $32,437; qualifying distributions, $31,000.
Limitations: Applications not accepted. Giving limited to northern Pacific County, WA.
Officers and Directors:* Gary Hagen,* Pres.; Jean Shaudys, V.P.; Elizabeth Penoyar,* Secy.-Treas.; Charles Knudson, Lloyd Lougheed, Herbert Newton, Diantha Weilepp.
EIN: 910996428

55869
The Negrin Foundation
c/o Solomon and Robin Negrin
26 Columbia Key
Bellevue, WA 98006

Established in 2000 in WA.
Financial data (yr. ended 12/31/01): Grants paid, $30,766; assets, $1,720,723 (M); expenditures, $50,746; qualifying distributions, $30,766.
Limitations: Giving primarily in OH and WA.
Officer: Solomon A. Negrin.
EIN: 912026155

55870
W. H. Lindberg Charitable Trust
c/o Wells Fargo Bank Northwest, N.A.
P.O. Box 21927
Seattle, WA 98111

Established in 1997 in WA.
Donor(s): W.H. Lindberg.
Financial data (yr. ended 07/31/01): Grants paid, $30,525; assets, $642,583 (M); expenditures, $52,630; qualifying distributions, $34,532.
Limitations: Applications not accepted. Giving primarily in Tacoma, WA.
Application information: Contributes only to pre-selected organizations.
Trustee: Wells Fargo Bank Northwest, N.A.
EIN: 916456664

55871
James C. Dezendorf Charitable Trust
c/o Wells Fargo Bank Northwest, N.A.
P.O. Box 21927
Seattle, WA 98111

Financial data (yr. ended 12/31/01): Grants paid, $30,429; assets, $824,996 (M); expenditures, $49,270; qualifying distributions, $38,905.
Limitations: Applications not accepted. Giving primarily in LA and OR.
Application information: Contributes only to pre-selected organizations.
Trustee: Wells Fargo Bank Northwest, N.A.
EIN: 930735036

55872
Don L. Bradley Scholarship Trust Fund
301 N. Burlington Blvd.
Burlington, WA 98233
Application address: 927 E. Fairhaven Ave., Burlington, WA 98233, tel.: (360) 757-3311
Contact: Richard O. Jones, Tr.

Established in 1987 in WA.
Financial data (yr. ended 12/31/01): Grants paid, $30,225; assets, $266,947 (M); expenditures, $31,478; qualifying distributions, $30,132.
Limitations: Giving limited to residents of the Burlington, WA, area.
Application information: Application form required.
Trustees: John Aarstad, Jim Clem, Richard O. Jones.
EIN: 916291543
Codes: GTI

55873
The Robert J. Dickson and Carol J. Dickson Foundation
8517 Cascadia Ave.
Everett, WA 98208

Established in 1998 in WA.
Donor(s): Carol J. Dickson, Robert J. Dickson.
Financial data (yr. ended 12/31/01): Grants paid, $30,112; assets, $443,213 (M); gifts received, $79; expenditures, $31,705; qualifying distributions, $27,281.
Limitations: Applications not accepted.
Application information: Contributes only to pre-selected organizations.
Officers: Robert J. Dickson, Pres.; Carol J. Dickson, V.P. and Secy.
EIN: 911914799

55874
Freed Family Foundation
10503 Culpepper Ct. N.W.
Seattle, WA 98177-5317

Established in 1999 in WA.
Financial data (yr. ended 12/31/01): Grants paid, $30,000; assets, $562,615 (M); expenditures, $38,903; qualifying distributions, $30,000.
Limitations: Applications not accepted. Giving primarily in Billings, MT.
Application information: Contributes only to pre-selected organizations.
Officer: Jennifer Freed, Mgr.
EIN: 911935190

55875
Kitsap Community Foundation
P.O. Box 3670
Silverdale, WA 98383
URL: http://www.kitsapfoundation.org

Incorporated in 1993 in WA.
Financial data (yr. ended 12/31/01): Grants paid, $30,000; assets, $500,000 (M); gifts received, $100,000; expenditures, $45,000.
Limitations: Giving limited to Kitsap County, WA.
Publications: Informational brochure, biennial report.
Application information: Application form not required.
Officers: David Hedger, Chair.; Richard Tizzano, Vice-Chair.; Samuel Clarke, Secy.; Don M. Drury, Treas.
EIN: 943205217
Codes: CM

55876
Westmedia Charitable Foundation
P.O. Box 1194
Longview, WA 98632-7705
Application address: c/o John J. Natt, P.O. Box 1194, Longview, WA, 98632, tel.: (360) 423-4116
Contact: Ted M. Natt, V.P.

Established in 1987 in WA.
Donor(s): John M. McClelland, Jr., Martha Sue Natt Trust, John J. Natt, Ted M. Natt, Westmedia Corp.
Financial data (yr. ended 12/31/00): Grants paid, $30,000; assets, $533,741 (M); expenditures, $31,521; qualifying distributions, $30,000.
Officers: John J. Natt, Pres.; Ted M. Natt, V.P.; Diane S. Natt, Secy.; Cathy M. Natt, Treas.
EIN: 911361562
Codes: GTI

55877
Kevin & Linda Wold Family Foundation
411 Fairview Ave. N., Ste. 202
Seattle, WA 98109-5302
Contact: Kevin Wold, Tr.

Established in 1999 in WA.
Donor(s): Kevin Wold.
Financial data (yr. ended 12/31/00): Grants paid, $30,000; assets, $489,709 (M); expenditures, $31,418; qualifying distributions, $30,000.
Trustee: Kevin Wold.
EIN: 916499224

55878
The Stanny Foundation
c/o N. Callaghan Stanny
221 Middlepoint Rd.
Port Townsend, WA 98368

Established in 1991 in CA.
Donor(s): Norbert F. Stanny.
Financial data (yr. ended 10/31/01): Grants paid, $29,250; assets, $526,275 (M); expenditures, $30,177; qualifying distributions, $29,250.
Limitations: Applications not accepted. Giving primarily in CA and WA.
Application information: Contributes only to pre-selected organizations.
Trustees: B. Timothy Stanny, N. Callaghan Stanny.
EIN: 943166936

55879
Ehrlich-Donnan Foundation
c/o Marian D. Collier
2128 Broadmoor Dr. E.
Seattle, WA 98112

Financial data (yr. ended 12/31/00): Grants paid, $29,200; assets, $615,819 (M); expenditures, $33,842; qualifying distributions, $30,561.
Limitations: Applications not accepted. Giving primarily in WA.
Application information: Contributes only to pre-selected organizations.
Officers: Marian Donnan-Collier, Pres. and Treas.; Scott Balsam, V.P.; Jon G. Schneidler, Secy.
EIN: 916031055

55880
The Paul and Yvonne Hendricks Family Foundation
1420 5th Ave., Ste. 4100
Seattle, WA 98101-2338
Contact: Paul L. Hendricks, Pres.

Established in 1990 in WA.
Donor(s): Paul L. Hendricks, Yvonne B. Hendricks.
Financial data (yr. ended 12/31/01): Grants paid, $29,000; assets, $629,729 (M); gifts received, $26,556; expenditures, $36,902; qualifying distributions, $29,000.
Limitations: Giving primarily in Seattle, WA.
Application information: Application form not required.
Officers and Directors:* Paul L. Hendricks,* Pres.; Yvonne B. Hendricks,* V.P.; Leslie Hendricks Fall, M.D., Secy.; Julie Ann Hendricks, Treas.
EIN: 943136033

55881
Lowen Family Foundation
601 W. Mercer Pl., Ste. 502
Seattle, WA 98119-3890

Established in 1999 in WA.
Donor(s): Jeanette Lowen.
Financial data (yr. ended 12/31/01): Grants paid, $29,000; assets, $322,257 (M); gifts received, $29,228; expenditures, $29,512; qualifying distributions, $29,000.
Limitations: Applications not accepted.
Application information: Contributes only to pre-selected organizations.
Officers: Jeanette Lowen, Pres.; Howard Lowen, V.P.; Jan Lowen, Secy.
EIN: 911987399

55882
Kenneth Ardell Foundation
1851 Central Pl. S.
Kent, WA 98031 (253) 852-8500
Contact: William R. Chatham, Pres.

Financial data (yr. ended 02/28/02): Grants paid, $28,939; assets, $724,645 (M); expenditures, $39,646; qualifying distributions, $28,939.
Limitations: Giving primarily in WA.
Officer and Director:* William R. Chatham,* Pres.
EIN: 911891461

55883
Lyle P. Bartholomew Scholarship & Loan Fund
c/o Bank of America
P.O. Box 34345
Seattle, WA 98124-1345
Application address: c/o University of Oregon, School of Architecture, Lawrence Hall, Rm. 212, Eugene, OR 97403, tel.: (503) 686-3656

Financial data (yr. ended 04/30/02): Grants paid, $28,718; assets, $596,316 (M); expenditures, $36,746; qualifying distributions, $32,627.
Limitations: Giving limited to Eugene, OR.
Application information: Application form required.
Trustee: Bank of America.
EIN: 936091423
Codes: GTI

55884
The Richard Bangs Collier Pleneurethics Society
c/o The President's Office
6501 S. 19th St.
Tacoma, WA 98466-6100

Established in 1986 in WA.
Financial data (yr. ended 12/31/01): Grants paid, $28,075; assets, $1,392,797 (M); gifts received, $547,852; expenditures, $64,053; qualifying distributions, $28,075.
Limitations: Applications not accepted. Giving primarily in Tacoma, WA.
Application information: Contributes only to pre-selected organizations.
Officers and Directors:* James Dawson,* Chair.; Jim Carroll,* Pres. and V.P.; Pamela J. Transue,* Secy.; Julie Burton, Richard Moe, Becky Sproat, Gael Tower.
EIN: 911330526

55885
Claude R. and Sadie B. Jones Loan Fund
c/o Wells Fargo Bank Northwest, N.A.
P.O. Box 21927
Seattle, WA 98111
Application address: c/o James Armstrong, Branch Mgr., Wells Fargo Bank Northwest, N.A., P.O. Box 365, Oakridge, OR 97463

Financial data (yr. ended 09/30/01): Grants paid, $27,750; assets, $735,366 (M); expenditures, $35,345; qualifying distributions, $25,133.
Limitations: Giving limited to Lane County, OR.
Application information: Application form required.
Trustee: Wells Fargo Bank Northwest, N.A.
EIN: 936055774
Codes: GTI

55886
Beighle Family Foundation
4548 W. Sheridan St.
Seattle, WA 98199

Established in 2000 in WA.
Donor(s): Douglas Beighle.
Financial data (yr. ended 12/31/01): Grants paid, $27,500; assets, $244,164 (M); expenditures, $30,332; qualifying distributions, $27,500.
Limitations: Applications not accepted.
Application information: Contributes only to pre-selected organizations.
Officers: Douglas Beighle, Pres., V.P. and Treas.; Randall P. Beighle, Secy.
EIN: 912091096

55887
The Welty Foundation, Inc.
2231 S. Forest Estates Dr.
Spokane, WA 99223
Additional address: 601 W. Riverside Ave., Ste. 1800, Spokane, WA 99201

Established in 1995 in WA.
Donor(s): Elizabeth Welty.
Financial data (yr. ended 12/31/01): Grants paid, $27,500; assets, $441,503 (M); gifts received, $72,397; expenditures, $33,554; qualifying distributions, $27,500.
Limitations: Giving primarily in Spokane, WA.
Officer: Elizabeth Welty, Chair.
Directors: Berdine S. Bender, M.D., Christine Schnug, Robert D. Wigert, M.D.
EIN: 943210510

55888
Neudorfer Foundation
1326 42nd Ave. S.W.
Seattle, WA 98116

Donor(s): Margaret E. Neudorfer, William C. Neudorfer.
Financial data (yr. ended 12/31/01): Grants paid, $27,499; assets, $344,440 (M); gifts received, $4,900; expenditures, $36,804; qualifying distributions, $27,499.
Limitations: Applications not accepted.
Application information: Contributes only to pre-selected organizations.
Trustees: Margaret S. Neudorfer, William C. Neudorfer.
EIN: 911621459

55889
Harry Masto Foundation
c/o Norman Anderson
P.O. Box 401
Veradale, WA 99037-0401

Donor(s): Harry Masto,‡ Masie Masto.
Financial data (yr. ended 09/30/01): Grants paid, $27,400; assets, $695,083 (M); expenditures, $34,617; qualifying distributions, $27,400.
Limitations: Applications not accepted. Giving primarily in Seattle, WA.
Application information: Contributes only to pre-selected organizations.
Trustees: Masie Masto, Sherrie Sparks.
EIN: 911117863

55890
Hal Holmes Memorial Fund
c/o Bank of America
P.O. Box 34345, CSC-9
Seattle, WA 98124-1345

Financial data (yr. ended 10/31/01): Grants paid, $27,250; assets, $666,450 (M); expenditures, $39,213; qualifying distributions, $27,250.
Limitations: Applications not accepted. Giving primarily in Ellensburg, WA.
Application information: Contributes only to pre-selected organizations.
Trustee: Bank of America.
EIN: 916227746

55891
Judge C. C. Chavelle Foundation
P.O. Box 4742
Rollingbay, WA 98061-0474
Application address: 707 E. Harrison, Seattle, WA 98102
Contact: Karen C. Keefe, Tr.

Financial data (yr. ended 06/30/01): Grants paid, $27,000; assets, $555,069 (M); expenditures, $45,052; qualifying distributions, $41,788.
Limitations: Giving primarily in WA.
Application information: Scholarship awards are paid to the educational institution on behalf of the individual recipients. Application form required.
Trustee: Karen C. Keefe.
EIN: 911123055
Codes: GTI

55892
Motoda Foundation
P.O. Box 3424
Seattle, WA 98144 (206) 822-2701
Contact: Ken Nakano, Treas.

Established in 1982 in WA.
Donor(s): Kiyo Motoda.‡
Financial data (yr. ended 12/31/01): Grants paid, $27,000; assets, $1,091,677 (M); expenditures, $107,579; qualifying distributions, $27,000.
Limitations: Giving primarily in WA.
Officers: Matt Kohler, Pres.; Nobuyuki Koda, V.P.; Jim Akutsu, Secy.; Ken Nakano, Treas.
EIN: 911164679

55893
Gravel Family Foundation
2512 S.E. Norelius Dr.
Vancouver, WA 98683-8552

Established in 1999 in WA.
Donor(s): Eugene A. Gravel, Lorraine J. Gravel.
Financial data (yr. ended 12/31/01): Grants paid, $26,500; assets, $197,949 (M); expenditures, $28,055; qualifying distributions, $26,500.
Limitations: Applications not accepted.
Application information: Contributes only to pre-selected organizations.
Officers: Eugene A. Gravel, Pres. and Treas.; Lorraine J. Gravel, V.P. and Secy.
EIN: 912011016

55894
Hawkanson Family Foundation
5011 88th Ave. S.E.
Mercer Island, WA 98040

Established in 1999 in WA.
Donor(s): Jane H. Hawkanson, James C. Hawkanson.
Financial data (yr. ended 12/31/01): Grants paid, $26,500; assets, $480,925 (M); expenditures, $29,714; qualifying distributions, $26,500.
Limitations: Applications not accepted. Giving primarily in Seattle, WA.
Application information: Contributes only to pre-selected organizations.
Trustees: James C. Hawkanson, Jane H. Hawkanson.
EIN: 916498573

55895
Herman Oscar Schumacher Scholarship Fund for Men
717 W. Sprague Ave.
Spokane, WA 99201
Application address: c/o Washington Trust Bank, Private Banking, P.O. Box 2127, Spokane, WA 99210-2127

Financial data (yr. ended 06/30/01): Grants paid, $26,500; assets, $549,721 (M); expenditures, $40,728; qualifying distributions, $26,500.
Limitations: Giving limited to residents of Spokane County, WA.
Application information: Application form required.
Trustee: Washington Trust Bank.
EIN: 916237367
Codes: GTI

55896
Keck Foundation
c/o David Ketter
999 3rd. Ave., Ste. 2525
Seattle, WA 98104-4089

Established in 1996 in WA.
Donor(s): Robert A. Keck.‡
Financial data (yr. ended 12/31/01): Grants paid, $26,349; assets, $303,280 (M); expenditures, $27,866; qualifying distributions, $26,349.
Limitations: Applications not accepted.
Application information: Contributes only to pre-selected organizations.
Officers: Richard L. Epstein, Pres.; Ernest A. Humphrey, V.P. and Secy.; Peter Weiss, Treas.
EIN: 911734863

55897
B. Hamilton McDearmid Charitable Trust
2825 Colby Ave.
Everett, WA 98201

Established in 1997 in WA.
Financial data (yr. ended 06/30/00): Grants paid, $26,343; assets, $564,199 (M); expenditures, $30,950; qualifying distributions, $26,799.
Limitations: Applications not accepted.
Application information: Contributes only to pre-selected organizations.
Trustee: Frontier Bank.
EIN: 916378343

55898
Bartholomew Family Scholarship & Loan Fund
c/o Bank of America
P.O. Box 34345
Seattle, WA 98124-1345
Application address: 3017 Locust, S.E., Albany, OR 97321
Contact: Terry Murray, Chair.

Financial data (yr. ended 04/30/01): Grants paid, $26,250; assets, $597,768 (M); expenditures, $37,829; qualifying distributions, $30,919.
Limitations: Giving primarily in OR.
Application information: Application form required.
Trustee: Bank of America.
EIN: 936091422
Codes: GTI

55899
Six Foundation
7900 S.E. 28th St., Ste. 200
Mercer Island, WA 98040

Donor(s): Edgar B. Stern, Jr., Pauline S. Stern.
Financial data (yr. ended 12/31/01): Grants paid, $26,000; assets, $440,761 (M); gifts received, $5,306; expenditures, $29,783; qualifying distributions, $26,000.
Limitations: Applications not accepted. Giving primarily in CO, LA, and WA.
Application information: Contributes only to pre-selected organizations.
Officers and Directors:* Edgar B. Stern, Jr.,* Pres.; Pauline S. Stern,* V.P. and Secy.-Treas.; Lessing S. Stern,* V.P.
EIN: 742308489

55900
Horrigan Foundation, Inc.
12905 W. Court St.
Pasco, WA 99301-8942

Financial data (yr. ended 10/31/01): Grants paid, $25,850; assets, $256,380 (M); gifts received, $9,000; expenditures, $27,113; qualifying distributions, $25,850.
Limitations: Applications not accepted.
Application information: Contributes only to pre-selected organizations.
Officers: David A. Gallant, Pres.; David B. Gallant, V.P.; Hilke Gallant, Secy.-Treas.
Trustees: Theresa Gallant, Alana Horrigan, Leo Horrigan, Sigrun Horrigan.
EIN: 916058199

55901
McEachern Morrison Foundation
c/o Union Bank of California, N.A.
P.O. Box 84495
Seattle, WA 98124-5795

Established in 1999 in WA.
Donor(s): A.B. & Flavia McEachern Foundation.
Financial data (yr. ended 12/31/00): Grants paid, $25,750; assets, $559,761 (M); expenditures, $43,635; qualifying distributions, $25,750.
Limitations: Applications not accepted.
Application information: Contributes only to pre-selected organizations.
Trustee: Union Bank of California, N.A.
EIN: 870615664

55902
Loren H. Corder Foundation
P.O. Box 607
Long Beach, WA 98631-0607 (360) 665-4445
Contact: Charles A. Mikkola, Tr.

Established in 1990 in WA.
Financial data (yr. ended 12/31/01): Grants paid, $25,700; assets, $1,387,467 (M); expenditures, $50,568; qualifying distributions, $25,700.
Limitations: Giving limited to Pacific County, WA.
Trustees: Guy M. Glenn, Virginia Leach, Charles A. Mikkola, Gordon Schoewe.
EIN: 943168145

55903
Catherine & Hollis Plowman Memorial Scholarship Fund
(Formerly C. & H. Plowman Scholarship Fund)
c/o Wells Fargo Bank Northwest, N.A.
P.O. Box 21927
Seattle, WA 98111
Application address: c/o Oregon City High School, Counseling Center, 1306 12th St., Oregon City, OR 97045-2108

Established in 1991 in OR.
Donor(s): Hollis Plowman.‡
Financial data (yr. ended 08/31/01): Grants paid, $25,500; assets, $285,605 (M); expenditures, $31,870; qualifying distributions, $27,906.
Limitations: Giving limited to OR.
Application information: Application form required.
Trustee: Wells Fargo Bank Northwest, N.A.
EIN: 936247548
Codes: GTI

55904
Jean Risley Educational Trust
c/o Wells Fargo Bank Northwest, N.A.
P.O. Box 21927
Seattle, WA 98111

Established in 1989 in OR.
Donor(s): Jean Risley.‡
Financial data (yr. ended 11/30/01): Grants paid, $25,500; assets, $810,290 (M); expenditures, $39,132; qualifying distributions, $29,370; giving activities include $25,500 for loans to individuals.
Limitations: Giving limited to OR, with emphasis on Benton, Linn, and Marion counties.
Application information: Application form required.
Trustee: Wells Fargo Bank, N.A.
EIN: 943117918
Codes: GTI

55905
T. J. Tufts Charitable Foundation
P.O. Box 422
Wilbur, WA 99185-0422 (509) 647-5310
Contact: Charles Wyborney, Tr.

Financial data (yr. ended 12/31/01): Grants paid, $25,500; assets, $793,981 (M); expenditures, $45,260; qualifying distributions, $25,500.
Limitations: Giving limited to residents of the Wilbur, WA, area.
Application information: Application form required.
Trustee: Charles Wyborney.
EIN: 911489095
Codes: GTI

55906
Olive Kerry Trust
c/o Bank of America
P.O. Box 34345
Seattle, WA 98124-1345

Established in 1985 in WA.
Financial data (yr. ended 06/30/02): Grants paid, $25,292; assets, $464,695 (M); expenditures, $32,117; qualifying distributions, $25,292.
Limitations: Applications not accepted. Giving primarily in Seattle, WA.
Application information: Contributes only to pre-selected organizations.
Trustee: Bank of America.
EIN: 916113666

55907
MJF Foundation
1198 9th Ave.
Fox Island, WA 98333

Established in 1998 in WA.
Donor(s): Sandra J. Mowry.
Financial data (yr. ended 12/31/01): Grants paid, $25,200; assets, $489,373 (M); expenditures, $29,551; qualifying distributions, $25,200.
Limitations: Applications not accepted.
Application information: Contributes only to pre-selected organizations.
Officers: Sandra J. Mowry, Pres.; Nelson D. Jay III, V.P.; Hannah G. Jay, Secy.; Tiffany B. Jay, Treas.
EIN: 911912821

55908
Robert & Anna McCartney Foundation
P.O. Box 2007
Port Angeles, WA 98362

Donor(s): Anna McCartney, Robert McCartney.

Financial data (yr. ended 12/31/01): Grants paid, $25,100; assets, $185,494 (M); expenditures, $27,137; qualifying distributions, $25,100.
Limitations: Applications not accepted. Giving primarily in Port Angeles and Seattle, WA.
Application information: Contributes only to pre-selected organizations.
Directors: Thomas J. Gaffney, Anna D. McCartney, Christopher S. McCartney, Michael T. McCartney, Robert T. McCartney, Terrence J. McCartney.
EIN: 911115981

55909
Benjamin & Margaret Hall Foundation
c/o Benjamin D. Hall
110-110th Ave. N.E., Ste. 440
Bellevue, WA 98004-5860

Established in 1995 in WA.
Donor(s): Benjamin Hall, Margaret Hall.
Financial data (yr. ended 12/31/01): Grants paid, $25,000; assets, $1,696,176 (M); gifts received, $103,236; expenditures, $37,508; qualifying distributions, $25,000.
Limitations: Applications not accepted. Giving primarily in WA.
Application information: Contributes only to pre-selected organizations.
Officers: Benjamin Hall, Pres.; Margaret Hall, V.P. and Secy.-Treas.
EIN: 911705444

55910
J. A. McEachern Foundation
c/o Union Bank of California, N.A.
P.O. Box 84495
Seattle, WA 98124-5795

Established in 1999 in WA.
Donor(s): A.B. & Flavia McEachern Foundation.
Financial data (yr. ended 12/31/01): Grants paid, $24,900; assets, $424,733 (M); expenditures, $30,119; qualifying distributions, $24,900.
Limitations: Applications not accepted.
Application information: Contributes only to pre-selected organizations.
Trustee: Union Bank of California, N.A.
EIN: 911918533

55911
Vashon Island Coffee Foundation
c/o Seattle Coffee Co.
P.O. Box 964
Vashon Island, WA 98070

Established in 1996 in WA.
Donor(s): Seattle Coffee Co.
Financial data (yr. ended 12/31/01): Grants paid, $24,619; assets, $34,422 (M); gifts received, $38,209; expenditures, $25,053; qualifying distributions, $24,616.
Limitations: Applications not accepted. Giving primarily in Guatemala, El Salvador, and Costa Rica.
Application information: Contributes only to pre-selected organizations.
Officers: James Stewart, Pres.; Mary D. Cook, Secy.-Treas.
EIN: 911704071
Codes: CS, CD

55912
Bernard E. Shultz Eagle Scout Foundation
c/o Larry Bledsoe
200 W. 10th St.
Aberdeen, WA 98520-2423
Contact: Trustees

Donor(s): Bernard E. Shultz.
Financial data (yr. ended 12/31/01): Grants paid, $24,420; assets, $429,074 (M); expenditures, $24,813; qualifying distributions, $24,813.
Limitations: Giving primarily in Nampa, ID.
Application information: Application form required.
Officers: Marie Bledsoe, Secy.; Larry Bledsoe, Treas.
Trustees: Jeff Hill, Christopher McCaffrey, Raymond Ricks, Ron Ricks, Bernard E. Shultz.
EIN: 820446208
Codes: GTI

55913
Sahlin Foundation
6414 S. Helena St.
Spokane, WA 99223-8347
Contact: Lee J. Sahlin, Pres.

Donor(s): Lee J. Sahlin.
Financial data (yr. ended 08/31/01): Grants paid, $24,200; assets, $688,984 (M); gifts received, $38,175; expenditures, $26,843; qualifying distributions, $24,200.
Limitations: Giving primarily in Spokane, WA.
Application information: Application form required.
Officers: Lee J. Sahlin, Pres.; Joan Sahlin, Secy.; Janet L. Sahlin, Treas.
Trustees: Eric Sahlin, John Sahlin.
EIN: 911179315

55914
Andrew Pekema Memorial Scholarships
P.O. Box 937
Ferndale, WA 98248-0937
Contact: Carol Rush, Pres.

Established in 1986 in WA.
Donor(s): Elaine PeKema.
Financial data (yr. ended 12/31/01): Grants paid, $24,000; assets, $11,689 (M); gifts received, $27,179; expenditures, $24,000; qualifying distributions, $23,996.
Limitations: Giving limited to Ferndale, WA.
Application information: Application form required.
Officers and Directors:* Carol Rush,* Pres.; Elaine Pekema,* V.P.; Gary Duling,* Secy.
EIN: 911346995
Codes: GTI

55915
The Tong Family Foundation
685 Spring St., No. 210
Friday Harbor, WA 98250-8058

Established in WA in 1998.
Financial data (yr. ended 12/31/01): Grants paid, $23,887; assets, $654,070 (M); expenditures, $34,645; qualifying distributions, $23,887.
Limitations: Applications not accepted.
Application information: Contributes only to pre-selected organizations.
Directors: Sara Tong Sangmeister, David Tong, Janet Tong, Jennifer Tong, Jessica Tong, Peter Tong.
EIN: 916468627

55916
The Perrow Foundation
P.O. Box 245
Gig Harbor, WA 98332

Established in 1997 in WA.
Financial data (yr. ended 12/31/01): Grants paid, $23,055; assets, $591,745 (M); expenditures, $29,397; qualifying distributions, $23,055.
Limitations: Applications not accepted. Giving primarily in WA.
Application information: Contributes only to pre-selected organizations.
Officers: Elizabeth Perrow, Pres.; Jeffrey Perrow, V.P.; Wade Perrow, Secy.-Treas.
EIN: 911798883

55917
Edgar E. Whitehead Foundation
c/o Benton County Museum
P.O. Box 1407
Prosser, WA 99350
Application address: 955 Parkside Dr., Prosser, WA 99350
Contact: David Bayne, Pres.

Established in 1985 in WA.
Financial data (yr. ended 12/31/01): Grants paid, $22,597; assets, $2,248,712 (M); expenditures, $26,673; qualifying distributions, $22,597.
Limitations: Giving limited to the Prosser and Whitstran, WA, areas.
Application information: Application form not required.
Officers: David Bayne, Pres.; Inez Thompson, Secy.; Don Warmenhoven, Treas.
Directors: Dennis Pleasant, Robert White.
EIN: 911279093

55918
Ludlow Foundation
23004 E. Mocha Ln.
Liberty Lake, WA 99019

Financial data (yr. ended 12/31/01): Grants paid, $22,504; assets, $864,001 (M); expenditures, $84,327; qualifying distributions, $22,504.
Limitations: Giving limited to Thurston County, WA.
Application information: Application form required.
Officers: A. Ludlow Kramer, Pres.; Mary Higuchi, V.P.; Patricia Kramer, Secy.-Treas.
EIN: 910971634

55919
Lawyers Campaign for Hunger Relief
810 3rd Ave., Ste. 140-46
Seattle, WA 98104

Financial data (yr. ended 12/31/00): Grants paid, $22,500; assets, $11,186 (M); gifts received, $35,980; expenditures, $35,905; qualifying distributions, $22,500.
Limitations: Applications not accepted.
Application information: Contributes only to pre-selected organizations.
Officers: Barbara A. Mack, Chair.; Katherine J. Casey, Vice-Chair.; Maureen Mannix, Secy.; Kristi M. Kurata, Treas.
EIN: 911520942

55920
The Layton Foundation
2808 S.E. Bay Point Dr.
Vancouver, WA 98683

Established in 1998 in WA.
Donor(s): Ruth H. Layton.
Financial data (yr. ended 12/31/01): Grants paid, $22,500; assets, $458,134 (M); expenditures, $27,124; qualifying distributions, $22,500.
Application information: Application form not required.
Officers: C. Rex Layton, Pres. and Treas.; Ruth H. Layton, V.P. and Secy.
Director: Elizabeth Layton Forsythe, Jennifer Ruth Layton.
EIN: 911912141

IN THIS SECTION, WITHIN EACH STATE, FOUNDATIONS ARE LISTED IN DESCENDING ORDER BY TOTAL GRANTS PAID

55921
Ethel Davidson Charitable Trust
c/o Frontier Bank, Trust Dept.
2825 Colby Ave.
Everett, WA 98201

Established in 1997 in WA.
Donor(s): Ethel S. Davidson,‡ Leroy E. Davidson.‡
Financial data (yr. ended 12/31/01): Grants paid, $22,328; assets, $448,000 (M); expenditures, $28,263; qualifying distributions, $22,328.
Limitations: Applications not accepted. Giving limited to WA.
Application information: Contributes only to pre-selected organizations.
Trustee: Frontier Bank.
EIN: 911919314

55922
The Catch Foundation
c/o Cavender, Holleman & Donohue
1910 Fairview Ave. E., Ste. 101
Seattle, WA 98102-3620

Established in 1991 in WA.
Donor(s): David Valle, Alpac Corp.
Financial data (yr. ended 12/31/01): Grants paid, $22,300; assets, $92,727 (M); expenditures, $24,639; qualifying distributions, $22,300.
Limitations: Applications not accepted.
Application information: Contributes only to pre-selected organizations.
Trustees: David Valle, Victoria Valle.
EIN: 911510153

55923
Waldemar L. Stein Foundation
c/o Bank of America
P.O. Box 34345
Seattle, WA 98124-1345

Established in 1990 in WA.
Donor(s): W.L. Stein Wife's Unitrust, W.L. Stein Wife's Flexitrust.
Financial data (yr. ended 02/28/02): Grants paid, $21,958; assets, $619,027 (M); expenditures, $29,241; qualifying distributions, $21,958.
Limitations: Applications not accepted. Giving primarily in Seattle, WA.
Application information: Contributes only to pre-selected organizations.
Trustee: Bank of America.
EIN: 916317832

55924
ST Foundation
Bank of America, N.A.
P.O. Box 34345
Seattle, WA 98124-1345

Established in 1997 in MT.
Donor(s): Steven R. Thompson.
Financial data (yr. ended 12/31/01): Grants paid, $21,823; assets, $499,756 (M); expenditures, $26,425; qualifying distributions, $21,823.
Limitations: Applications not accepted. Giving primarily in MT.
Application information: Contributes only to pre-selected organizations.
Officers: Steven R. Thompson, Pres.; Sharon Thompson, Secy.-Treas.
Director: Michael R. Thompson.
EIN: 841406278

55925
Humanlinks
10900 N.E. 8th St. Ste. 900
Bellevue, WA 98004

Established in 1999 in WA.
Donor(s): Gretchen Garth.
Financial data (yr. ended 12/31/01): Grants paid, $21,800; assets, $3,286 (M); gifts received, $213,117; expenditures, $231,526; qualifying distributions, $21,800.
Limitations: Applications not accepted.
Application information: Contributes only to pre-selected organizations.
Officer: Gretchen Garth, Pres.
Directors: Judy Britton Courshon, Byron E. Garth, Catherine C. Garth.
EIN: 911980248

55926
The Marvin Foundation
c/o Marvin Reiner
3015 Country Club Rd. N.W.
Olympia, WA 98502

Established in 1988 in WA.
Financial data (yr. ended 12/31/01): Grants paid, $21,760; assets, $307,803 (M); expenditures, $21,867; qualifying distributions, $21,760.
Limitations: Applications not accepted. Giving limited to WA.
Application information: Contributes only to pre-selected organizations.
Officers and Directors:* Marvin Reiner,* Pres.; Mary-Lynne Reiner,* Secy.
EIN: 943084563
Codes: TN

55927
Beeler Foundation
7321 Hawkstone Ave., S.W.
Port Orchard, WA 98366 (360) 895-3454
Contact: H.W. Beeler, Mgr.

Financial data (yr. ended 05/31/02): Grants paid, $21,325; assets, $411,837 (M); expenditures, $22,337; qualifying distributions, $21,325.
Limitations: Giving primarily in CA and WA.
Officer: H.W. Beeler, Mgr.
Trustee: Marvin Shearer.
EIN: 237013247

55928
RHR Foundation
3213 W. Wheeler St., PMB 352
Seattle, WA 98199-3245 (206) 285-5198

Established in 2000 in WA.
Donor(s): Robert Rhodehamel.
Financial data (yr. ended 12/31/01): Grants paid, $21,250; assets, $78,992 (M); expenditures, $24,215; qualifying distributions, $21,250.
Limitations: Giving primarily in IN.
Application information: Application form required.
Officers and Directors:* Robert Rhodehamel,* Pres., V.P. and Treas.; Dana Snyder,* Secy.; Dean R. Sargent.
EIN: 912057386

55929
Treeclimber Foundation
545 5th Ave., West
Kirkland, WA 98033-4873

Established in 1999 in WA.
Donor(s): John W. Schwabacher, Joanne M. Shellan.
Financial data (yr. ended 12/31/01): Grants paid, $21,216; assets, $280,619 (M); gifts received, $350; expenditures, $29,732; qualifying distributions, $21,216.
Limitations: Applications not accepted.
Application information: Contributes only to pre-selected organizations.
Officers: John W. Schwabacher, Pres.; Joanne M. Shellan, Secy.-Treas.
Director: Irene S. Pasternack.
EIN: 911999061

55930
National Intercollegiate Rodeo Foundation, Inc.
2316 Eastgate St., Ste. 160
Walla Walla, WA 99362-1576 (509) 529-4402
Contact: Timothy L. Corfield, Pres.

Established in 1994 in WA.
Donor(s): National Intercollegiate Rodeo Assn.
Financial data (yr. ended 06/30/01): Grants paid, $21,010; assets, $83,728 (M); gifts received, $55,980; expenditures, $51,911; qualifying distributions, $33,465.
Limitations: Giving limited to the U.S., with emphasis on the West.
Application information: Application form required.
Officers: Timothy L. Corfield, Pres.; John Mahoney, V.P.; Steve Maki, Secy.; Wayne Smith, Treas.
EIN: 911659631

55931
Medical Education Scholarship Aid
(also known as M.E.S.A., Inc.)
6910 96th Ave., S.E.
Mercer Island, WA 98040

established in 1990 in WA.
Donor(s): David Lindstrom, Carl D. Lindstrom.
Financial data (yr. ended 12/31/01): Grants paid, $21,000; assets, $367,175 (M); expenditures, $21,736; qualifying distributions, $21,000.
Limitations: Applications not accepted. Giving primarily in Seattle, WA.
Application information: Contributes only to pre-selected organizations.
Officer: Carl D. Lindstrom, Pres.
EIN: 911471174

55932
Research and Scholarship Foundation of the Washington State Horticultural Association
P.O. Box 1308
Yakima, WA 98907-1308
Contact: Craig A. Sundquist, Secy.-Treas.

Financial data (yr. ended 12/31/01): Grants paid, $21,000; assets, $270,628 (M); gifts received, $12,430; expenditures, $22,535; qualifying distributions, $21,000.
Limitations: Giving primarily in WA.
Officer and Directors:* Craig A. Sundquist,* Secy.-Treas.; George Allan, Grady Auvil, Jack Bloxom, Gaylord Embom, Todd Hurlburt, Tom Mathison, Kent Mullinix.
EIN: 916057391

55933
Tennesen Family Foundation
4049 Erlands Point Rd., N.W.
Bremerton, WA 98312

Established in 1997 in WA.
Donor(s): Ethel Tennesen, Tennesen Family.
Financial data (yr. ended 12/31/01): Grants paid, $21,000; assets, $414,132 (M); expenditures, $22,832; qualifying distributions, $21,000.
Limitations: Applications not accepted. Giving primarily in WA.
Application information: Contributes only to pre-selected organizations.
Officers and Directors:* Beth K. Cornish,* Pres.; Philip C. Cornish, V.P. and Treas.; Ethel M. Tennesen,* Secy.; David C. Cornish, Terry M. Tennesen.
EIN: 911701428

55934
Anna L. Morgan Family Trust
c/o Bank of America
P.O. Box 34345
Seattle, WA 98124

Established in 1999 in WA.
Financial data (yr. ended 03/31/02): Grants paid, $20,921; assets, $567,661 (M); expenditures, $28,407; qualifying distributions, $20,921.
Limitations: Applications not accepted. Giving primarily in New York, NY and Seattle, WA.
Application information: Contributes only to pre-selected organizations.
Trustee: Bank of America.
EIN: 957078666

55935
P. A. & Marie B. Loar Student Loan Fund
c/o Wells Fargo Bank Northwest, N.A.
P.O. Box 21927
Seattle, WA 98111
Application address: c/o Greg Snyder, Silverton High School, 802 Schlador St., Silverton, OR 97381

Financial data (yr. ended 09/30/01): Grants paid, $20,741; assets, $506,435 (M); expenditures, $30,872; qualifying distributions, $24,277.
Limitations: Giving limited to the Silverton, OR, area.
Application information: Application form required.
Trustee: Wells Fargo Bank Northwest, N.A.
EIN: 936041499
Codes: GTI

55936
Foss Foundation
c/o Wells Fargo Bank Northwest, N.A.
P.O. Box 21927
Seattle, WA 98111
Application address: c/o Foss High School, Attn. Principal, 212 S. Tyler St., Tacoma, WA 98405

Financial data (yr. ended 12/31/01): Grants paid, $20,500; assets, $452,650 (M); expenditures, $27,848; qualifying distributions, $22,777.
Limitations: Giving limited to residents of Tacoma, WA.
Application information: Application form not required.
Trustee: Wells Fargo Bank Northwest, N.A.
EIN: 916075762

55937
Katherine Olson Foundation
2503 Nob Hill Ave. N.
Seattle, WA 98109 (206) 352-7306
Contact: Carol A. Olson, Pres.

Established in 1996 in WA.
Donor(s): K-2 Corp.
Financial data (yr. ended 12/31/01): Grants paid, $20,350; assets, $370,474 (M); expenditures, $21,977; qualifying distributions, $20,364.
Application information: Application form required.
Officers: Carol A. Olson, Pres.; R. Thomas Olson, Secy.-Treas.
EIN: 911703239

55938
The Family Foundation
2909 Laurel Rd.
Longview, WA 98632 (360) 423-1555
Contact: Lavina Jones, Dir.

Established in 1999 in WA.
Donor(s): Lavina Jones, Robert Jones.
Financial data (yr. ended 06/30/01): Grants paid, $20,000; assets, $132,447 (M); expenditures, $28,922; qualifying distributions, $20,000.
Limitations: Giving primarily in Cowltz County, WA.
Directors: Lavina Jones, Robert Jones, Sonya Jones, Christopher Jones, George Opsahl, Jr.
EIN: 912010505

55939
Fulghum Foundation
117 E. Louisa St., Ste. 225
Seattle, WA 98102
Contact: Kimberlee P. Brillhart, Treas.

Established in 1990 in WA.
Donor(s): Robert L. Fulghum.
Financial data (yr. ended 12/31/01): Grants paid, $20,000; assets, $55,461 (M); gifts received, $598; expenditures, $20,606; qualifying distributions, $20,000.
Application information: Application form not required.
Officers: Robert L. Fulghum, Pres.; David E. Ketter, Secy.; Kimberlee P. Brillhart, Treas.
Trustees: Lynn K. Edwards, W. Thomas Porter.
EIN: 911500225

55940
Howard Charitable Trust
c/o R. Newell
P.O. Box 3003
Longview, WA 98632

Established in 1999 in WA.
Donor(s): Robert S. Howard.
Financial data (yr. ended 12/31/01): Grants paid, $20,000; assets, $295,798 (M); expenditures, $20,314; qualifying distributions, $20,000.
Limitations: Applications not accepted. Giving primarily in San Diego, CA.
Application information: Contributes only to a pre-selected organization.
Officers: Robert S. Howard, Pres.; Richard D. Newell, Secy.-Treas.
EIN: 911952040

55941
E. & H. Humbly Bumbly Foundation
c/o Tonda Smith
2807 Lincoln Way
Lynnwood, WA 98037

Established in 1996.
Financial data (yr. ended 12/31/01): Grants paid, $20,000; assets, $933,712 (M); expenditures, $23,383; qualifying distributions, $22,888.
Limitations: Applications not accepted. Giving primarily in ID and WA.
Publications: Grants list.
Application information: Contributes only to pre-selected organizations.
Officers and Directors:* Elizabeth Poll,* Pres.; Harry Poll,* V.P.; Zachary D. Poll,* V.P.; Jason H. Poll,* Secy.; Ian J. Poll,* Treas.
EIN: 911747104

55942
Newman Family Foundation
13824 N.E. 87th St.
Redmond, WA 98052-1959

Established in 1999 in WA.
Donor(s): Jonathan S. Newman.
Financial data (yr. ended 12/31/01): Grants paid, $20,000; assets, $1,477,392 (M); expenditures, $23,775; qualifying distributions, $20,000.
Limitations: Applications not accepted. Giving primarily in Seattle, WA.
Application information: Contributes only to pre-selected organizations.
Director: Jonathan S. Newman.
EIN: 912003900

55943
The Wooster-Barcott Foundation
5029 27th Ave. W.
Everett, WA 98203

Established in 1996 in WA.
Donor(s): Dorothy Wallgren.
Financial data (yr. ended 12/31/01): Grants paid, $20,000; assets, $304,886 (M); gifts received, $241; expenditures, $24,284; qualifying distributions, $20,000.
Limitations: Applications not accepted. Giving primarily in WA.
Application information: Contributes only to pre-selected organizations.
Trustees: James W. Barcott, Richard A. Barcott, Donna Schwartz-Barcott, Dorothy Wallgren.
EIN: 911744796

55944
Fred O. Paulsell Foundation
1325 4th Ave., Ste. 1900
Seattle, WA 98101

Financial data (yr. ended 09/30/01): Grants paid, $19,990; assets, $4,511 (M); expenditures, $20,171; qualifying distributions, $19,990.
Limitations: Applications not accepted. Giving primarily in Seattle, WA.
Application information: Contributes only to pre-selected organizations.
Officers: Sherry Davidson Paulsell, Pres.; Frederick O. Paulsell, V.P. and Treas.; Joseph M. Gaffney, Secy.
EIN: 911441043

55945
W. L. Pegram Evangelistic Association
14709 E. 17th Ave.
Veradale, WA 99037-9499

Financial data (yr. ended 12/31/01): Grants paid, $19,725; assets, $33,868 (M); gifts received, $20,585; expenditures, $44,650; qualifying distributions, $42,696.
Limitations: Applications not accepted.
Officers: Rev. Thomas J. Williams, V.P.; Beverly Chapman, Secy.-Treas.
Directors: Greg Baldwin, Richard Barth, Rose Dunn.
EIN: 911424372
Codes: GTI

55946
The Palomaki Foundation
c/o John Palomaki
4509 Interlake Ave. N., Ste. 246
Seattle, WA 98103-6773

Established in 2000 in WA.
Donor(s): John M. Palomaki.
Financial data (yr. ended 12/31/00): Grants paid, $19,600; assets, $29,763 (M); gifts received, $50,000; expenditures, $20,895; qualifying distributions, $20,895.
Limitations: Applications not accepted.
Application information: Contributes only to pre-selected organizations.
Officers and Directors:* John M. Palomaki,* Pres. and Treas.; Patricia R. Palomaki,* Secy.
EIN: 912066516

55947
Louis Hennessy Foundation for Catholic Charities
P.O. Box 99429
Lakewood, WA 98499-0429
Application address: 109 Madrona Park Dr., Steilacoom, WA 98388-1423
Contact: Wayne C. Hogan, Treas.

Financial data (yr. ended 12/31/01): Grants paid, $19,500; assets, $464,099 (M); expenditures, $19,578; qualifying distributions, $19,500.
Limitations: Giving primarily in Tacoma, WA.
Officers and Directors:* Jose Veliz,* Pres.; Ernest L. Oliver, Sr.,* V.P.; Thomas P. Quinlan,* Secy.; Wayne C. Hogan,* Treas.; Ronald Hennessy.
EIN: 911818724

55948
The Premier Foundation
c/o Premier Industries, Inc.
1019 Pacific Ave., Ste. 1501
Tacoma, WA 98402-4483

Established in 1990 in WA.
Donor(s): Premier Industries, Inc.
Financial data (yr. ended 11/30/01): Grants paid, $19,295; assets, $10,117 (M); expenditures, $20,862; qualifying distributions, $19,295.
Limitations: Applications not accepted. Giving primarily in Tacoma, WA.
Application information: Contributes only to pre-selected organizations.
Officers: Michael R. Wall, Pres.; Calvin D. Bamford, V.P.; James Johnson, Treas.
EIN: 943141552
Codes: CS, CD

55949
The Brian and Traci Janssen Foundation
1000 Lakeside Ave. S.
Seattle, WA 98144
*Application address:*co/ Brian and Tracie Janssen, Quellos Financial Advisors; 601 Union St., 56th Fl., Seattle, WA 98101, tel.: (206) 613-6700

Established in 1999 in WA.
Donor(s): Brian Janssen, Traci Janssen.
Financial data (yr. ended 12/31/01): Grants paid, $19,225; assets, $127,494 (M); gifts received, $1,250; expenditures, $21,960; qualifying distributions, $19,225.
Limitations: Giving primarily in Seattle, WA.
Officers: Traci Janssen, Pres.; Brian Janssen, V.P.
EIN: 912011011

55950
Koh Lee Foundation
6669 N.E. Windermere Rd.
Seattle, WA 98115

Established in 1999.
Donor(s): ABCD Trust, James Koh, Maria Koh.
Financial data (yr. ended 12/31/01): Grants paid, $19,000; assets, $399,100 (M); expenditures, $20,140; qualifying distributions, $18,833.
Limitations: Applications not accepted. Giving primarily in WA.
Application information: Contributes only to pre-selected organizations.
Officers: James CY Koh, Pres. and Treas.; Audrey S. Koh, V.P.; Christopher J. Koh, Secy.
Director: Maria L. Koh.
EIN: 911922008

55951
Gladys Staufenbeil Student Loan Trust
c/o Bank of America
P.O. Box 34345, CSC-9
Seattle, WA 98124-1345
Application addresses: c/o School of Medicine, Univ. of Washington, Seattle, WA 98195, c/o School of Medicine, Univ. of Idaho, Moscow, ID 83843

Financial data (yr. ended 12/31/01): Grants paid, $19,000; assets, $300,132 (M); expenditures, $23,255; qualifying distributions, $22,003; giving activities include $19,000 for loans to individuals.
Limitations: Giving limited to ID and WA.
Application information: Application form required.
Trustee: Bank of America.
EIN: 916031720
Codes: GTI

55952
Kobe Foundation
P.O. Box 3771
Seattle, WA 98124
E-mail: mail@kobefoundation.org; *URL:* http://kobefoundation.org

Established in 2000 in WA.
Donor(s): Sunny Kobe Cook.
Financial data (yr. ended 12/31/01): Grants paid, $18,920; assets, $189,002 (M); gifts received, $1,575; expenditures, $24,016; qualifying distributions, $18,920.
Limitations: Giving primarily in the Pacific Northwest, with emphasis on WA, OR, and ID.
Application information: Application available on website. Application form required.
Officers: Sunny Kobe Cook, Pres.; Elizabeth Kobe Norris, V.P.; Deborah Kobe Norris, Secy.-Treas.
EIN: 912039274

55953
Victor & Neva Larson Charitable Trust
c/o Frontier Bank, Trust Dept.
2825 Colby Ave.
Everett, WA 98201

Established in 1997 in WA.
Financial data (yr. ended 12/31/00): Grants paid, $18,653; assets, $420,108 (M); expenditures, $23,411; qualifying distributions, $18,653.
Limitations: Applications not accepted. Giving primarily in WA.
Application information: Contributes only to pre-selected organizations.
Trustee: Frontier Bank.
EIN: 911928793

55954
The Straws Charitable Foundation
1526 Alki Ave., S.W., No. 402
Seattle, WA 98116-1890 (206) 937-1899
Contact: Carol Swarts, Pres.

Donor(s): Carol Swarts.
Financial data (yr. ended 12/31/01): Grants paid, $18,600; assets, $714,841 (M); gifts received, $100,346; expenditures, $23,780; qualifying distributions, $18,600.
Officer: Carol Swarts, Pres.
Directors: Grant Peters, Christopher K. Vick.
EIN: 911941211

55955
The Kirchner Foundation
1318 Kessler Blvd.
Longview, WA 98632
Contact: Pauline M. Kirchner, Pres.

Established in 1990 in WA.
Donor(s): Pauline M. Kirchner, Robert A. Kirchner.
Financial data (yr. ended 12/31/01): Grants paid, $18,350; assets, $322,208 (M); expenditures, $20,498; qualifying distributions, $18,350.
Limitations: Giving primarily in WA.
Application information: Application form not required.
Officers: Robert A. Kirchner, Chair.; Pauline M. Kirchner, Pres.; Robert P. Kirchner, V.P.; Diane M. Kirchner Nelson, Secy.; Kristin A. Fleischauer, Treas.
EIN: 911485456

55956
Peter J. Emt - Infant Jesus of Prague Trust Fund
c/o Bank of America
P.O. Box 34345, CSC-9
Seattle, WA 98124-1345 (206) 358-1652
Application address: c/o Bank of America, P.O. Box 24565, CSC-23, Seattle, WA 98124-1245

Established in 1980 in WA.
Financial data (yr. ended 06/30/02): Grants paid, $18,072; assets, $636,082 (M); expenditures, $27,768; qualifying distributions, $18,072.
Limitations: Giving primarily in Seattle, WA.
Trustee: Bank of America.
EIN: 916234094

55957
The E-Boys Club
11120 N.E. 2nd St., Ste. 200
Bellevue, WA 98004-5849 (425) 450-3300
Contact: Brian D. Emanuels, Dir.

Financial data (yr. ended 12/31/01): Grants paid, $18,050; assets, $494,203 (M); gifts received, $146,080; expenditures, $24,399; qualifying distributions, $18,050.
Limitations: Giving primarily in Little Rock, AR and Seattle, WA.
Directors: Anne S. Emanuels, Brian D. Emanuels.
EIN: 912013394

55958
DaVita Children's Foundation
c/o DaVita, Inc., Tax Dept.
1423 Pacific Ave.
Tacoma, WA 98402

Established in 2000 in CA and WA.
Donor(s): DaVita, Inc.
Financial data (yr. ended 12/31/01): Grants paid, $18,000; assets, $503,455 (M); gifts received, $2,000; expenditures, $18,332; qualifying distributions, $17,805.
Limitations: Giving limited to Tacoma, WA.
Application information: Unsolicited request for funds not accepted.
Officers and Directors:* Kent Thiry,* C.E.O. and Pres.; Richard K. Whitney, C.F.O.; Steve Udicious, Secy.; Ellie Fischbacher, John Goldman, Odetta Pura, Randall Pura.
EIN: 330932587
Codes: CS

55959
Echo Foundation
c/o Bank of America
P.O. Box 34345
Seattle, WA 98124-1345

Established in 1997 in MT.
Donor(s): Mike Thompson.
Financial data (yr. ended 12/31/01): Grants paid, $18,000; assets, $422,385 (M); gifts received, $60; expenditures, $22,699; qualifying distributions, $18,000.
Limitations: Applications not accepted.
Application information: Contributes only to a pre-selected organization.

Directors: Kenneth Ludzack, Julie Thompson, Mike Thompson.
EIN: 841406280

55960
Peter Ward Taylor Charitable Trust
801 2nd Ave., Ste. 1600
Seattle, WA 98104

Donor(s): Charlotte L. Taylor.
Financial data (yr. ended 12/31/01): Grants paid, $18,000; assets, $389,415 (M); expenditures, $25,887; qualifying distributions, $18,000.
Limitations: Applications not accepted. Giving on a national basis.
Application information: Contributes only to pre-selected organizations.
Directors: Elizabeth Bodien, Charlotte L. Taylor, Timothy N. Taylor.
Trustee: Laird Norton Trust Co.
EIN: 237383025

55961
Parnell Family Foundation
P.O. Box 1390
Eastsound, WA 98245

Established in 1990 in CA.
Donor(s): Melissa D. Parnell, Mike D. Parnell.
Financial data (yr. ended 12/31/99): Grants paid, $17,741; assets, $4,372,198 (M); gifts received, $300; expenditures, $215,236; qualifying distributions, $2,732,450; giving activities include $2,556,529 for loans and $136,654 for programs.
Limitations: Applications not accepted.
Application information: Contributes only to pre-selected organizations.
Officers: Mike D. Parnell, Pres.; Melissa D. Parnell, Secy.; Mike Taylor, C.F.O.
EIN: 330433123

55962
Guy and Nyda Prater Scholarship Fund
c/o Bank of America
P.O. Box 34345, FAB-22
Seattle, WA 98124-1345

Established in 1989 in WA.
Financial data (yr. ended 06/30/00): Grants paid, $17,700; assets, $440,578 (M); expenditures, $24,835; qualifying distributions, $18,365.
Limitations: Giving primarily in WA.
Application information: Application form required.
Selection Committee Members: Lynn Lupfer, Roland Schirman, Phyllis Straube.
Trustee: Bank of America.
EIN: 916305003
Codes: GTI

55963
Joseph M. & Martha L. Dunn Foundation
c/o Joseph M. Dunn
1620-43rd Ave. E., Ste. 15A
Seattle, WA 98112

Established in 1992 in WA.
Donor(s): Joseph M. Dunn, Martha L. Dunn.
Financial data (yr. ended 12/31/01): Grants paid, $17,500; assets, $227,049 (M); expenditures, $19,880; qualifying distributions, $17,433.
Limitations: Applications not accepted.
Application information: Contributes only to pre-selected organizations.
Officers and Directors:* Joseph M. Dunn,* Pres.; C.J. Dunn,* V.P.; Martha L. Dunn, Secy.-Treas.
EIN: 911557186

55964
The Maria John Nicholas Kelly Foundation
6918 75th St. S.W.
Lakewood, WA 98498
Contact: Maria John Nicholas Kelly, Pres.

Established in 1997 in WA.
Donor(s): Maria John Nicholas Kelly.
Financial data (yr. ended 12/31/01): Grants paid, $17,500; assets, $531,663 (M); gifts received, $32,900; expenditures, $19,681; qualifying distributions, $17,500.
Officers: Maria John Nicholas Kelly, Pres.; Robert E. Kelly, V.P.; James H. Morton, Secy.
EIN: 911784647

55965
James A. & Fannie E. Malarkey Foundation
c/o Portco Corp.
4200 Columbia Way
Vancouver, WA 98661-5596
Contact: Howard M. Wall, Jr., Pres.

Donor(s): Mary Wall.‡
Financial data (yr. ended 12/31/01): Grants paid, $17,200; assets, $316,397 (M); expenditures, $21,947; qualifying distributions, $17,200.
Limitations: Giving primarily in OR.
Application information: Application form not required.
Officers: Howard M. Wall, Jr., Pres.; Charles A. Adams, Secy.
Director: Bruce L. Byerly.
EIN: 936042088

55966
Francois Vinecore Scholarship Foundation
c/o Bank of America
P.O. Box 34345, 701 5th Ave.
Seattle, WA 98124-1345
Application address: P.O. Box 1230, Ephrata, WA 98823-1230
Contact: Michael Tabler

Established in 1989 in WA.
Financial data (yr. ended 03/31/01): Grants paid, $17,130; assets, $399,432 (M); expenditures, $23,568; qualifying distributions, $20,173.
Limitations: Giving limited to Douglas County, WA.
Application information: Application form required.
Trustee: Bank of America.
EIN: 916307756
Codes: GTI

55967
Louise Elliot Graves Testamentary Trust
P.O. Box 34345
Seattle, WA 98124-1345

Established in 1998 in WA.
Donor(s): Louise E. Graves.
Financial data (yr. ended 05/31/02): Grants paid, $17,019; assets, $606,708 (M); expenditures, $26,418; qualifying distributions, $17,019.
Limitations: Applications not accepted.
Application information: Contributes only to pre-selected organizations.
Trustee: Bank of America.
EIN: 916468626

55968
Genauer Foundation, Inc.
2005 8th Ave.
Seattle, WA 98121

Donor(s): Ben Genauer, Jack Genauer, Mendel Genauer, Sam Genauer,‡ M. Genauer & Co.
Financial data (yr. ended 09/30/01): Grants paid, $16,644; assets, $6,777 (M); gifts received, $19,500; expenditures, $18,257; qualifying distributions, $16,644.
Limitations: Applications not accepted.
Application information: Contributes only to pre-selected organizations.
Officers: Ben Genauer, Pres.; Sam Genauer, V.P.; Mendel Genauer, Secy.; Jack Genauer, Treas.
EIN: 910840366

55969
Allison Charitable Trust
1200 5th Ave., Ste. 1711
Seattle, WA 98101-1127

Donor(s): James E. Allison.
Financial data (yr. ended 12/31/01): Grants paid, $16,575; assets, $15,888 (M); gifts received, $144; expenditures, $17,450; qualifying distributions, $16,575.
Limitations: Applications not accepted. Giving primarily in WA.
Application information: Contributes only to pre-selected organizations.
Trustee: James E. Allison.
EIN: 916246156

55970
D. W. Morse Family Scholarship Fund
c/o Bank of America
P.O. Box 34345, CSC-9
Seattle, WA 98124-1345
Application address: c/o Vicki Anderson, Port Angeles Senior High, 304 E. Park Ave., Port Angeles, WA 98362, tel.: (360) 452-7602

Financial data (yr. ended 10/31/01): Grants paid, $16,500; assets, $609,782 (M); expenditures, $28,035; qualifying distributions, $20,732.
Limitations: Giving limited to Port Angeles and Olympic Peninsula, WA.
Application information: Application form not required.
Trustee: Bank of America.
EIN: 916218517
Codes: GTI

55971
LAGU Foundation
P.O. Box 216
Bellevue, WA 98009-0216

Donor(s): Claire S. Thomas.
Financial data (yr. ended 12/31/01): Grants paid, $16,450; assets, $287,897 (M); expenditures, $18,154; qualifying distributions, $16,450.
Trustees: Claire S. Thomas, Elaine M. Thomas, Eldred T. Thomas.
EIN: 911319639

55972
David Allan Robertson Memorial Scholarship Fund
c/o Wells Fargo Bank Northwest, N.A.
P.O. Box 21927
Seattle, WA 98111-3927
Application address: c/o Associated Chair., Dept. of English, Univ. of Washington, Seattle, WA 98111

Financial data (yr. ended 12/31/01): Grants paid, $16,387; assets, $301,944 (M); expenditures, $23,574; qualifying distributions, $19,480.
Limitations: Giving limited to Seattle, WA.
Application information: Application form required.
Trustee: Wells Fargo Bank Northwest, N.A.
EIN: 916033978

55973
Sena H. Wold Trust
c/o Bank of America
P.O. Box 34345
Seattle, WA 98124-1345
Application address: 701 5th Ave., Seattle, WA 98124, tel.: (206) 358-3380
Contact: Mollie Geterman, Trust Off., Bank of America

Established in 1984 in WA.
Financial data (yr. ended 06/30/02): Grants paid, $16,100; assets, $224,862 (M); expenditures, $19,652; qualifying distributions, $16,100.
Limitations: Giving limited to San Rafael, CA.
Trustee: Bank of America.
EIN: 916265217

55974
Alpine Education Foundation
(Formerly High Alpine Shelters Foundation)
100 W. Harrison St., Ste. 300
Seattle, WA 98119

Financial data (yr. ended 12/31/01): Grants paid, $16,000; assets, $300,997 (M); expenditures, $21,024; qualifying distributions, $16,000.
Limitations: Applications not accepted. Giving limited to Seattle, WA.
Application information: Contributes only to pre-selected organizations.
Officers: James Blessing, Pres.; Richard Wahlstrom, V.P.; David Lee, Secy.; Keith McGowan, Treas.
EIN: 237047907

55975
Percy & Gladys Burns Scholarship Fund
c/o Bank of America
P.O. Box 34345, CSC-9
Seattle, WA 98124-1345
Application address: c/o Financial Aid Office, Skagit Valley College, 2405 E. College Way, Mount Vernon, WA 98273, tel.: (360) 428-1140, Whidbey Campus, tel.: (360) 679-5320

Financial data (yr. ended 04/30/02): Grants paid, $16,000; assets, $244,639 (M); expenditures, $19,499; qualifying distributions, $16,000.
Limitations: Giving primarily in WA.
Application information: Application form required.
Trustee: Bank of America.
EIN: 911188794

55976
Vicki Moldovan Memorial Trust Fund
c/o JDK & DP&C
P.O. Box 1614
Tacoma, WA 98401-1614
Application address: c/o Bordentown Regional School, 78 Crosswick St., Bordentown, NJ 08505
Contact: Dennis Hurley

Financial data (yr. ended 12/31/01): Grants paid, $16,000; assets, $222,802 (M); expenditures, $17,260; qualifying distributions, $16,000.
Limitations: Giving primarily in AK.
Trustee: Georgene Moldovan.
EIN: 920069583

55977
The Dixon Family Foundation
c/o Brian R. Dixon
5825 111th St. S.W.
Mukilteo, WA 98275

Established in 1999 in WA.
Donor(s): Brian R. Dixon, Theresa A. Dixon.
Financial data (yr. ended 12/31/00): Grants paid, $15,940; assets, $233,335 (M); expenditures, $21,723; qualifying distributions, $15,856.
Limitations: Applications not accepted.
Application information: Contributes only to pre-selected organizations.
Officers and Director:* Brian R. Dixon, Chair.; Theresa A. Dixon,* Pres.
EIN: 912015108

55978
The Donald E. and Peggy Schaake Foundation
P.O. Box 450
Yakima, WA 98907

Donor(s): Donald E. Schaake, Peggy Schaake.
Financial data (yr. ended 12/31/01): Grants paid, $15,624; assets, $241,460 (M); expenditures, $16,634; qualifying distributions, $15,624.
Limitations: Applications not accepted.
Application information: Contributes only to pre-selected organizations.
Trustee: Donald E. Schaake.
EIN: 911360371

55979
Lopus Foundation Charitable Trust
6250 W. Mercer Way
Mercer Island, WA 98040

Established in 1986 in CO.
Donor(s): Alfred E. Lopus, Kathleen J. Lopus.
Financial data (yr. ended 12/31/01): Grants paid, $15,600; assets, $228,257 (M); gifts received, $27,700; expenditures, $16,846; qualifying distributions, $15,600.
Limitations: Applications not accepted.
Application information: Contributes only to pre-selected organizations.
Trustees: Alfred E. Lopus, Kathleen J. Lopus.
EIN: 756354675

55980
Loomis Foundation
P.O. Box 21926
Seattle, WA 98111-3926

Donor(s): Charles W. Loomis, Walter Loomis.
Financial data (yr. ended 12/31/01): Grants paid, $15,500; assets, $609,383 (M); expenditures, $21,791; qualifying distributions, $15,500.
Limitations: Applications not accepted. Giving primarily in Seattle, WA.
Application information: Contributes only to pre-selected organizations.
Officers: Walter Loomis, Pres. and Treas.; Ann A. Loomis, V.P.; Robert H. Lorentzen, Secy.
Director: Betty Loomis.
EIN: 911083208

55981
Olympia Brewing Company Employees Beneficial Trust
P.O. Box 4098
Olympia, WA 98501-0098

Established in 1950 in WA.
Financial data (yr. ended 12/31/01): Grants paid, $15,500; assets, $316,431 (M); expenditures, $18,844; qualifying distributions, $15,500.
Limitations: Applications not accepted. Giving limited to Olympia, WA.
Application information: Contributes only to pre-selected organizations.
Trustees: Stephen J. Bean, Lynn Brunton, Mimi S. Fielding, James A. Haight, Jennifer S. Ingham, James H. Jenner, Daniel C. O'Neill, Michael K. Schmidt, Peter G. Schmidt, Robert A. Schmidt, Susan S. Wilson.
EIN: 916031858

55982
S. B. Schaar & P. K. Whelpton Foundation
2606 116th Ave. N.E., Ste. 200
Bellevue, WA 98004-1422 (425) 629-1990
Contact: Dan Kovarik

Established in 1998 in WA.
Donor(s): Jabe Blumenthal.
Financial data (yr. ended 12/31/01): Grants paid, $15,500; assets, $1,793,470 (M); gifts received, $1,219,000; expenditures, $17,480; qualifying distributions, $15,500.
Limitations: Giving primarily in Seattle, WA.
Trustees: Jabe Blumenthal, Julie E. Edsforth.
EIN: 916468169

55983
Lila Miller Scholarship Trust
c/o Bank of America
P.O. Box 34345
Seattle, WA 98124-1345
Application address: c/o Marla Hood-Arbuckle, Asst. to Superintendent, Yakima Public Schools, 104 N. 4th Ave., Yakima, WA 98902, tel.: (509) 573-7001

Financial data (yr. ended 12/31/01): Grants paid, $15,472; assets, $254,689 (M); expenditures, $17,942; qualifying distributions, $16,641.
Limitations: Giving limited to Yakima, WA.
Application information: Application form required.
Trustee: Bank of America.
EIN: 916025597

55984
Charles and Nancy Oden Luce Trust
c/o Bank of America
P.O. Box 34345, CSC-10
Seattle, WA 98124-1345
Application address: c/o Financial Aid Off., Umatilla Indian Reservation, Pendleton, OR 97801

Financial data (yr. ended 12/31/01): Grants paid, $15,307; assets, $313,075 (M); expenditures, $20,320; qualifying distributions, $18,027.
Limitations: Giving limited to Pendleton, OR.
Application information: Application form not required.
Trustee: Bank of America.
EIN: 916026999
Codes: GTI

55985
Lige Eldridge Trust
c/o Washington Trust Bank, Trust Dept.
717 W. Sprague Ave.
Spokane, WA 99210-3922

Financial data (yr. ended 12/31/01): Grants paid, $15,126; assets, $304,945 (M); expenditures, $19,594; qualifying distributions, $15,126.
Limitations: Applications not accepted. Giving primarily in Marshall, WA.
Application information: Contributes only to pre-selected organizations.
Trustee: Washington Trust Bank.
EIN: 916101898

55986
Burt Snyder Educational Foundation
c/o Wells Fargo Bank Northwest, N.A.
P.O. Box 21927
Seattle, WA 98111
Application address: c/o Jim Lynch, 620 N. 1st St., Lake View, OR 97630-1506

Financial data (yr. ended 06/30/01): Grants paid, $15,021; assets, $574,336 (M); expenditures, $24,577; qualifying distributions, $18,316.

Limitations: Giving limited to Lake County, OR.
Application information: Application form required.
Trustee: Wells Fargo Bank Northwest, N.A.
EIN: 936033286

55987
The Dayspring Foundation
1000 2nd Ave., Ste. 3500
Seattle, WA 98104

Established in 1986 in WA.
Donor(s): Anne Schreiner Nelson Freitag.
Financial data (yr. ended 09/30/01): Grants paid, $15,000; assets, $318,187 (M); expenditures, $16,638; qualifying distributions, $15,000.
Limitations: Applications not accepted. Giving primarily in CT.
Application information: Contributes only to pre-selected organizations.
Directors: Anne Schreiner Nelson Freitag, John D. Freitag.
EIN: 911361308

55988
Environmental Enhancement Group
8705 N.E. 117th Ave.
Vancouver, WA 98662

Established in 1995 in WA.
Donor(s): Pacific Rock Products.
Financial data (yr. ended 12/31/01): Grants paid, $15,000; assets, $458,369 (M); gifts received, $55,000; expenditures, $56,763; qualifying distributions, $15,000.
Limitations: Applications not accepted.
Application information: Contributes only to pre-selected organizations.
Officers and Director:* Christopher J. Murphy,* Pres.; John J. Shaffer, V.P.; Jeffrey P. Wriston, Secy.-Treas.
EIN: 911632336

55989
Gary and Carol Milgard Family Foundation
P.O. Box 6825
Tacoma, WA 98406
Application address: c/o Woody Harris, 1010 54th Ave. E., Tacoma, WA 98401, tel.: (253) 922-4373

Established in 2000 in WA.
Donor(s): Gary E. Milgard, Carol B. Milgard.
Financial data (yr. ended 12/31/01): Grants paid, $15,000; assets, $82,259,561 (M); gifts received, $79,999,960; expenditures, $26,714; qualifying distributions, $15,000.
Application information: Application form required.
Officers and Directors:* Gary E. Milgard,* Pres.; Carol B. Milgard,* V.P. and Secy.-Treas.
EIN: 912074073

55990
The Don & Anne Stager Family Foundation
957 Wapato Way
Manson, WA 98831

Established in 1999 in WA.
Donor(s): Donald K. Stager, Anne H. Stager, Dillingham Construction.
Financial data (yr. ended 12/31/01): Grants paid, $15,000; assets, $473,040 (M); gifts received, $100,000; expenditures, $16,531; qualifying distributions, $15,000.
Limitations: Applications not accepted. Giving primarily in WA.
Application information: Contributes only to pre-selected organizations.
Trustees: Anne H. Stager, Donald K. Stager, Laura M. Stager.

EIN: 911943272

55991
W & G Scholarship Trust
c/o Karen Gates Hildt
P.O. Box 277
Port Townsend, WA 98368

Established in 1999 in WA.
Financial data (yr. ended 12/31/00): Grants paid, $15,000; assets, $485,047 (M); expenditures, $21,978; qualifying distributions, $15,000.
Limitations: Applications not accepted. Giving primarily in Port Townsend, WA.
Trustee: Karen Gates Hildt.
EIN: 911941288

55992
The Willow Foundation
8441 S.E. 68th St., Ste. 198
Mercer Island, WA 98040

Established in 1998 in WA.
Financial data (yr. ended 12/31/01): Grants paid, $15,000; assets, $406,067 (M); expenditures, $21,747; qualifying distributions, $15,000.
Officers: James W. Becker, Pres. and Treas.; Jane Furber Becker, V.P. and Secy.
Directors: Erin Lydon Becker, Stephen W. Becker, Thomas L. Becker.
EIN: 911907445

55993
Tai Foundation
8837 N.E. Juanita Ln.
Kirkland, WA 98034

Established in 2001 in WA.
Donor(s): Harold Tai, Joan Tai.
Financial data (yr. ended 12/31/01): Grants paid, $14,964; assets, $32,860 (M); gifts received, $50,000; expenditures, $17,615; qualifying distributions, $14,964.
Limitations: Applications not accepted. Giving primarily in Taiwan.
Application information: Contributes only to pre-selected organizations.
Trustee: Harold Tai.
EIN: 912135277

55994
Cruse of Oil
8515 192nd, S.W.
Edmonds, WA 98026-6125

Established in 1988 in WA.
Donor(s): Philip J. Werdal, Kris Werdal.
Financial data (yr. ended 12/31/01): Grants paid, $14,700; assets, $230 (M); gifts received, $16,002; expenditures, $16,040; qualifying distributions, $14,700.
Limitations: Applications not accepted. Giving primarily in WA; some giving also in Canada and Asia.
Application information: Contributes only to pre-selected organizations.
Officers and Directors:* Esther Werdal,* Pres.; Tim Whitman,* V.P.; Kris Werdal,* Secy.; Philip J. Werdal,* Secy.; Jubilee Whitman,* Treas.
EIN: 911414824

55995
The MRCW Foundation
1303 E. Lynn
Seattle, WA 98102
Application address: 1303 E. Lynn, Seattle, WA 98102, tel.: (206) 323-3079
Contact: Walter Walkinshaw, V.P.

Established in 1990 in WA.
Donor(s): Walter Walkinshaw, Jean S. Walkinshaw.

Financial data (yr. ended 12/31/01): Grants paid, $14,674; assets, $256,314 (M); gifts received, $14,039; expenditures, $19,382; qualifying distributions, $14,674.
Limitations: Giving primarily in Seattle, WA.
Officers and Trustees:* Jean S. Walkinshaw,* Pres.; Walter Walkinshaw,* V.P.; Charles A. Walkinshaw,* Secy.-Treas.; Margaret V. Farell, Robert B. Walkinshaw.
EIN: 911163454

55996
Everett O. Williams Foundation
P.O. Box 4283, Ste. 6
Bellingham, WA 98225

Established in 2000 in WA.
Donor(s): Everett O. Williams.‡
Financial data (yr. ended 12/31/00): Grants paid, $14,583; assets, $1,468,807 (M); gifts received, $1,399,324; expenditures, $19,917; qualifying distributions, $14,583.
Limitations: Applications not accepted. Giving primarily in Bellingham, WA.
Officers and Directors:* John Dullanty,* Pres. and Treas.; David Goddard,* V.P. and Secy.; Rev. David E. Murphy,* V.P.
EIN: 911988983

55997
Loeb Family Foundation
13808 N.E. 36th Pl.
Bellevue, WA 98005

Established in 2000 in WA.
Donor(s): Lawrence A. Loeb, M.D., Phyllis E. Loeb.
Financial data (yr. ended 12/31/01): Grants paid, $14,575; assets, $319,753 (M); gifts received, $58,060; expenditures, $23,169; qualifying distributions, $14,575.
Limitations: Applications not accepted. Giving on a national basis, with emphasis on Seattle, WA.
Application information: Contributes only to pre-selected organizations.
Officers: Lawrence A. Loeb, M.D., Pres.; Phyllis E. Loeb, V.P. and Secy.-Treas.; Corinne L. Kohrn, V.P.; Keith R. Loeb, M.D., V.P.; Alanna D. White, V.P.
EIN: 912010665

55998
Ulmschneider Educational Foundation
P.O. Box Q
Greenbank, WA 98253
Application address: 1107 31st Ave. S., Seattle, WA 98144, tel.: (206) 329-1084
Contact: Judy Ellis, Dir.

Established in 1998 in WA.
Financial data (yr. ended 12/31/01): Grants paid, $14,471; assets, $99,095 (M); expenditures, $15,456; qualifying distributions, $14,471.
Limitations: Giving primarily in NE and WA.
Application information: Application form not required.
Officers and Directors:* Carl Ulmschneider,* Pres.; M.J. Ellis,* Secy.; Jonathan P. Ellis.
EIN: 911886617

55999
The Forest C. & Ruth V. Kelsey Foundation
101 S. Main St.
Montesano, WA 98563
Application address: P.O. Box 111, Montesano, WA 98563
Contact: Charles Caldwell, Pres.

Established in 1999 in WA.
Donor(s): Forest Kelsey, Ruth Kelsey.
Financial data (yr. ended 12/31/00): Grants paid, $14,400; assets, $466,745 (M); gifts received,

$5,000; expenditures, $17,939; qualifying distributions, $14,226.
Limitations: Giving limited to Grays Harbor County, WA.
Application information: Application form required.
Officers: Charles Caldwell, Pres.; Larry James "Jim" Hliboki, V.P.; Linda Caldwell, Secy.; Joann Hliboki, Treas.
EIN: 912013369

56000
Perry/Yockey Family Foundation
1005 Harbor Ave. S.W., Ste. 601
Seattle, WA 98116

Established in 1999 in WA.
Donor(s): Philip Perry, Fredde Yockey-Perry.
Financial data (yr. ended 12/31/01): Grants paid, $14,335; assets, $87,907 (M); expenditures, $16,778; qualifying distributions, $14,335.
Limitations: Applications not accepted. Giving primarily in Seattle, WA.
Application information: Contributes only to pre-selected organizations.
Directors: Philip L. Perry, Fredde Yockey-Perry.
EIN: 912013378

56001
Richard B. & Barbara B. Odlin Foundation
507 N. 3rd St., Ste. 301
Tacoma, WA 98403

Established in 1996 in WA.
Donor(s): Barbara B. Odlin, Richard B. Odlin.
Financial data (yr. ended 12/31/01): Grants paid, $14,300; assets, $375,725 (M); gifts received, $835; expenditures, $15,905; qualifying distributions, $14,300.
Limitations: Applications not accepted. Giving primarily in CA and WA.
Application information: Contributes only to pre-selected organizations.
Trustees: Peter J. James, Barbara B. Odlin, Richard B. Odlin.
EIN: 911746644

56002
The Knoll Foundation
2303 88th Pl., N.E.
Bellevue, WA 98004-2463 (425) 454-6528

Established in 1988 in WA.
Donor(s): Diane E. Knoll, Jon Knoll.
Financial data (yr. ended 12/31/01): Grants paid, $14,109; assets, $1,264 (M); gifts received, $15,184; expenditures, $14,213; qualifying distributions, $14,109.
Application information: Application form required.
Trustee: Diane E. Knoll.
EIN: 911433381

56003
John P. Munson Scholarship Fund
c/o Bank of America
P.O. Box 34345, CSC-10
Seattle, WA 98124-1345
Application address: c/o Financial Counseling and Financial Aid, Central Washington State Univ., Barge Hall, Rm. 209, Ellensburg, WA 98926

Financial data (yr. ended 12/31/01): Grants paid, $14,064; assets, $313,429 (M); expenditures, $18,609; qualifying distributions, $14,064.
Limitations: Giving limited to Ellensburg, WA.
Application information: Students must submit a Central Washington University Financial Aid Application.
Trustee: Bank of America.
EIN: 916025613

56004
The Enersen Foundation
14410 S.E. Petrovitsky, Ste. 206
Renton, WA 98058

Established in 1998 in CA and WA.
Donor(s): Burnham Enersen, Nina W. Enersen.
Financial data (yr. ended 12/31/00): Grants paid, $14,000; assets, $1,209,165 (M); expenditures, $72,235; qualifying distributions, $28,752.
Limitations: Applications not accepted.
Application information: Contributes only to pre-selected organizations.
Officer: Richard W. Enersen, Pres.
EIN: 911913330

56005
Jessie O'Bryan McIntosh Fund
c/o Bank of America
P.O. Box 34345
Seattle, WA 98124-1345
Application address: c/o University of Alaska, Financial Aid Office, Fairbanks, AK, 99701

Financial data (yr. ended 12/31/01): Grants paid, $14,000; assets, $397,711 (M); expenditures, $19,965; qualifying distributions, $16,401.
Limitations: Giving limited to Fairbanks, AK.
Application information: Application form required.
Trustee: Bank of America.
EIN: 916026222

56006
Johnson, Farris Charitable Trust
P. O. Box 34345
Seattle, WA 98124-1345

Established in 1998 in WA.
Financial data (yr. ended 09/30/01): Grants paid, $13,999; assets, $266,815 (M); expenditures, $16,914; qualifying distributions, $13,999.
Limitations: Applications not accepted. Giving primarily in OR.
Application information: Contributes only to pre-selected organizations.
Trustee: Bank of America.
EIN: 916470425

56007
Living Hope Foundation
6354 N.E. Jones St.
Suquamish, WA 98392-9768
Contact: Mark L. Ross and Karen E. Ross

Established in 2000 in WA.
Financial data (yr. ended 12/31/00): Grants paid, $13,707; assets, $208,496 (M); gifts received, $206,481; expenditures, $14,266; qualifying distributions, $14,048.
Limitations: Giving primarily in CA, TX, and WA.
Trustees: Mark L. Ross, Karen E. Ross.
EIN: 916494217

56008
Margolis Foundation
4939 N.E. 65th St.
Seattle, WA 98115
Application address: 108 S. Washington, Ste. 300, Seattle, WA 98104
Contact: Loren D. Hostek

Established in 1999 in WA.
Financial data (yr. ended 06/30/01): Grants paid, $13,645; assets, $1,030,750 (M); expenditures, $16,979; qualifying distributions, $13,645.
Officers: Ronald Margolis, Pres.; Daniel Asher, Secy.-Treas.
EIN: 911995329

56009
Stuchell Family Foundation
2707 Colby Ave., Ste. 1208
Everett, WA 98201-3658

Established in 1995 in WA.
Donor(s): Harry W. Stuchell, Carol C. Stuchell.
Financial data (yr. ended 12/31/01): Grants paid, $13,600; assets, $270,070 (M); expenditures, $18,872; qualifying distributions, $13,600.
Limitations: Applications not accepted. Giving limited to WA.
Application information: Contributes only to pre-selected organizations.
Officers and Directors:* Carol C. Stuchell,* Pres.; Harry W. Stuchell, V.P.; Linda Chapman, Thomas J. Gaffney, Debra Roberts.
EIN: 911704020

56010
Frets Educational Trust
P.O. Box 1108
Mount Vernon, WA 98273-1109
Contact: David A. Welts, Tr.

Established around 1993.
Financial data (yr. ended 12/31/01): Grants paid, $13,526; assets, $171,349 (M); expenditures, $14,559; qualifying distributions, $13,733.
Limitations: Giving limited to residents of WA.
Application information: Applicant must include resume and three letters of recommendation. Application form not required.
Trustee: David A. Welts.
EIN: 916341455
Codes: GTI

56011
Furuta Lee Foundation
1110 12th Ave., N.E., Ste. 500
Bellevue, WA 98004

Established in 2000 in WA.
Donor(s): Jerry Q. Lee.
Financial data (yr. ended 09/30/01): Grants paid, $13,500; assets, $39,009 (M); gifts received, $52,500; expenditures, $13,506; qualifying distributions, $13,506.
Limitations: Applications not accepted. Giving primarily in Seattle, WA.
Application information: Contributes only to pre-selected organizations.
Officers: Jerry Q. Lee, Pres.; Charlene Lee, V.P.; Barbara A. Peters, Secy.-Treas.
EIN: 912088291

56012
Paul J. Wolf & Elizabeth A. Wolf Charitable Foundation
c/o Paul J. Wolf
15503 S.E. 39th Cir.
Vancouver, WA 98683

Established in 1999.
Financial data (yr. ended 12/31/00): Grants paid, $13,450; assets, $302,083 (M); gifts received, $57,000; expenditures, $13,450; qualifying distributions, $13,450.
Limitations: Applications not accepted.
Application information: Contributes only to pre-selected organizations.
Directors: Teresa Sykes, Brian Wolf, Elizabeth A. Wolf.
EIN: 931263727

56013
Austin V. and Beryl M. Edmonds Charitable Trust
215 W. 12th St.
P.O. Box 8904
Vancouver, WA 98660-8904

Established in 1999 in WA.
Financial data (yr. ended 12/31/01): Grants paid, $13,403; assets, $228,355 (M); expenditures, $18,902; qualifying distributions, $13,403.
Limitations: Applications not accepted.
Application information: Contributes only to pre-selected organizations.
Trustee: First Independent Bank.
EIN: 911942768

56014
Bobo Foundation
c/o Loren D. Hostek
970 N.W. Elford Dr.
Seattle, WA 98177
Application address: 108 S. Washington St., No. 300, Seattle, WA 98104

Established in 1999 in WA.
Financial data (yr. ended 06/30/01): Grants paid, $13,327; assets, $843,365 (M); expenditures, $22,321; qualifying distributions, $13,327.
Officers: Carol Bobo, Pres.; Daniel Asher, Secy.-Treas.
EIN: 911986745

56015
Denali Foundation
1160 Industry Dr.
Tukwila, WA 98188

Established in 2000 in WA.
Donor(s): Chuck Kim.
Financial data (yr. ended 12/31/01): Grants paid, $13,000; assets, $98,884 (M); gifts received, $50,000; expenditures, $14,330; qualifying distributions, $13,000.
Limitations: Applications not accepted.
Application information: Contributes only to pre-selected organizations.
Officer: Chuck Kim, C.E.O.
EIN: 912091447

56016
David C. Hawley Foundation
520 Pike St., Ste. 2250
Seattle, WA 98101-4013

Established in 2000 in MO.
Donor(s): Thorne G. Hawley.
Financial data (yr. ended 12/31/00): Grants paid, $13,000; assets, $198,145 (M); gifts received, $261,686; expenditures, $15,763; qualifying distributions, $13,000.
Limitations: Applications not accepted. Giving primarily in Kansas City, MO.
Application information: Contributes only to pre-selected organizations.
Officers: Thorne G. Hawley, Pres.; Charles G. Hawley, V.P.; Roger W. Hawley, Secy.; Harriett Morton, Treas.
EIN: 431868122

56017
Ray & Vesta Johnson Memorial Scholarship Fund
c/o Bank of America
P.O. Box 34345, 701 5th Ave
Seattle, WA 98124-1345
Application address: c/o Pastor, Almira Community Church, P.O. Box 55, Almira, WA 99103

Financial data (yr. ended 03/31/02): Grants paid, $12,999; assets, $292,197 (M); expenditures, $17,828; qualifying distributions, $15,332.
Limitations: Giving limited to female residents of Almira, WA.
Application information: Application form required.
Trustee: Bank of America.
EIN: 237375893
Codes: GTI

56018
Welch Foundation, Inc.
P.O. Box 8147
Spokane, WA 99203
Contact: Frederick Wilson, Jr., Pres.

Financial data (yr. ended 03/31/02): Grants paid, $12,878; assets, $411,379 (M); expenditures, $15,952; qualifying distributions, $12,878.
Limitations: Giving primarily in Spokane, WA.
Officers: Frederick Wilson, Jr., Pres.; Mrs. John R. Peterson, V.P.; Mrs. R.J. O'Neill, Secy.-Treas.
EIN: 916035155

56019
Zacker Ministries, Inc.
P.O. Box 181
Sequim, WA 98382-0181

Established in 2000.
Donor(s): Pat Zacker, Eva Zacker.
Financial data (yr. ended 12/31/00): Grants paid, $12,778; assets, $82 (L); gifts received, $22,894; expenditures, $22,812; qualifying distributions, $22,812.
Officers: Patrick L. Zacker, Pres.; Eva L. Zacker, V.P. and Secy.
EIN: 752769132

56020
Frederick S. & Emma Gartner Charitable Trust
P.O. Box 1151
Bellingham, WA 98227 (360) 671-1500
Contact: Mark B. Packer, Tr.

Established in 1996 in WA.
Donor(s): Emma Gartner.
Financial data (yr. ended 07/31/01): Grants paid, $12,600; assets, $68,428 (M); expenditures, $13,114; qualifying distributions, $12,541.
Limitations: Giving primarily to residents of Whatcom County, WA.
Trustees: Emma Gartner, Mark B. Packer.
EIN: 911733246

56021
The Rabbi Arthur A. Jacobovitz Institute
c/o Joseph Weinstein, Davis Wright Tremain
1501 4th Ave., Ste. 2600
Seattle, WA 98101-1688

Established in 2000 in WA.
Donor(s): Rabbi Arthur A. Jacobovitz.
Financial data (yr. ended 12/31/01): Grants paid, $12,500; assets, $1,103,138 (M); gifts received, $4,847; expenditures, $41,323; qualifying distributions, $12,500.
Limitations: Applications not accepted.
Application information: Contributes only to pre-selected organizations.
Officers and Directors:* Rabbi Arthur A. Jacobovitz,* Pres. and Treas.; Joseph D. Weinstein,* V.P. and Secy.
EIN: 912074198

56022
Hamilton Agricultural Youth Foundation
P.O. Box 1098
Okanogan, WA 98840 (509) 422-3030
Contact: Greg Hamilton, Chair.

Donor(s): Hamilton Farm Equipment Center, Greg Hamilton.
Financial data (yr. ended 12/31/01): Grants paid, $12,458; assets, $22,171 (M); gifts received, $11,347; expenditures, $12,856; qualifying distributions, $12,458.
Limitations: Giving primarily in WA.
Directors: Greg Hamilton, Chair.; Jerry Asmussen, Kevin Amsden, Georgia Goldmark, Jana Heindselman, Rod McCoy, Dennis Swanberg, Ed Townsend, Janice Wells.
EIN: 911586443

56023
Whitener Family Foundation
5955 Battle Point Dr. N.E.
Bainbridge Island, WA 98110

Donor(s): Philip C. Whitener.
Financial data (yr. ended 12/31/01): Grants paid, $12,450; assets, $201,482 (M); gifts received, $12,450; expenditures, $15,152; qualifying distributions, $12,450.
Limitations: Applications not accepted. Giving on a national basis.
Application information: Contributes only to pre-selected organizations.
Officers: Philip C. Whitener, Pres.; Joy Whitener, V.P.
Directors: Wendy Hirsch, Barbara Mesas, Dixie Moore, David Whitener.
EIN: 911079291

56024
Killian Baxter Memorial Scholarship Fund
c/o Bank of America
P.O. Box 34345
Seattle, WA 98124-1345
Application address: c/o Scholarship Committee Members, Centralia College, 600 W. Locust St., Centralia, WA 98531, tel.: (360) 736-9391

Financial data (yr. ended 03/31/02): Grants paid, $12,400; assets, $322,870 (M); expenditures, $17,897; qualifying distributions, $15,205.
Limitations: Giving limited to residents of Centralia, WA.
Application information: Recommendations and personal interview required. Application form required.
Scholarship Committee Members: Linda Antan, Mike Bryant, Greg Harris, Brenda Mock, Kathy Thornton.
Trustee: Bank of America.
EIN: 916101173

56025
The Duff & Dorothy Kennedy Foundation
(Formerly The Duff & Dorothy Kennedy Charitable Trust)
1200 Alki Ave. S.W., Unit 400
Seattle, WA 98116 (206) 624-9640
Contact: James Griffin

Established in 1986 in WA.
Donor(s): Dorothy Kennedy, Duff Kennedy.
Financial data (yr. ended 08/31/01): Grants paid, $12,385; assets, $0 (M); expenditures, $12,385; qualifying distributions, $12,385.
Limitations: Giving limited to WA.

56025—WASHINGTON

Trustees: Dorothy Kennedy, Duff Kennedy, John Bruce Kennedy, Mary Shuler.
EIN: 911350061

56026
Halverson Foundation
519 Shoreline Dr.
Liberty Lake, WA 99019 (509) 255-9215
Contact: Harley Halverson, Tr.

Established in 1992.
Donor(s): Harley Halverson, Lorraine Halverson.
Financial data (yr. ended 12/31/01): Grants paid, $12,365; assets, $3,985 (M); gifts received, $4,000; expenditures, $12,440; qualifying distributions, $12,440.
Limitations: Giving primarily in WA.
Application information: Application form not required.
Trustees: Harley Halverson, Lorraine Halverson.
EIN: 916348709

56027
Sorensen Foundation Trust
c/o Wells Fargo Bank Northwest, N.A.
P.O. Box 21927
Seattle, WA 98111-3927

Financial data (yr. ended 02/28/01): Grants paid, $12,113; assets, $420,224 (M); expenditures, $20,921; qualifying distributions, $14,982.
Limitations: Applications not accepted. Giving on an international basis, with emphasis on Copenhagen, Denmark.
Application information: Contributes only to pre-selected organizations.
Trustee: Wells Fargo Bank Northwest, N.A.
EIN: 916280010

56028
Mildred J. Weyenberg Scholarship Award
P.O. Box 655
Zillah, WA 98953

Established in 2000.
Donor(s): Mildred J. Weyenberg.‡
Financial data (yr. ended 02/28/02): Grants paid, $12,000; assets, $201,081 (L); expenditures, $12,186; qualifying distributions, $12,000.
Limitations: Giving primarily in Granger, WA.
Trustee: Tom Carpenter, Jr.
EIN: 912035833

56029
Blue Tarp Foundation, Inc.
12518 238th St. S.E.
Snohomish, WA 98296

Established in 1998 in TX and WA.
Donor(s): John C. Edwards, M. Geneva Edwards.
Financial data (yr. ended 12/31/00): Grants paid, $11,986; assets, $688,845 (M); gifts received, $20,887; expenditures, $41,822; qualifying distributions, $36,954; giving activities include $3,920 for programs.
Limitations: Applications not accepted. Giving primarily in WA.
Application information: Contributes only to pre-selected organizations.
Officers: John C. Edwards, Pres.; Jenny Edwards, V.P. and Secy.-Treas.
Director: John A. Edwards.
EIN: 742900180

56030
Richardson Musical Education Scholarship Fund
c/o Baker Boyer National Bank
7601 W. Clearwater Ave., Ste. 404
Kennewick, WA 99336-1677 (509) 783-6800
Contact: C. Wayne May, Trust Off., Baker Boyer National Bank

Established in 1990 in WA.
Donor(s): Robert W. Richardson.‡
Financial data (yr. ended 10/31/01): Grants paid, $11,628; assets, $338,397 (M); expenditures, $16,537; qualifying distributions, $13,510.
Limitations: Giving primarily to residents of Kennewick, Pasco, and Richland, WA.
Application information: Application form required.
Trustee: Baker Boyer National Bank.
EIN: 916326487
Codes: GTI

56031
Walter M. Charitable Trust
c/o Wells Fargo Bank Northwest, N.A.
P.O. Box 21927
Seattle, WA 98111

Established in 1996.
Financial data (yr. ended 12/31/01): Grants paid, $11,547; assets, $289,358 (M); expenditures, $19,535; qualifying distributions, $14,171.
Limitations: Applications not accepted. Giving primarily in OR.
Application information: Contributes only to pre-selected organizations.
Trustee: Wells Fargo Bank Northwest, N.A.
EIN: 936018244

56032
Leiter Family Foundation
101 Hawks Way
Sequim, WA 98382

Established in 1999 in WA.
Donor(s): Elliot Leiter.
Financial data (yr. ended 12/31/01): Grants paid, $11,399; assets, $170,930 (M); gifts received, $58,869; expenditures, $15,366; qualifying distributions, $11,399.
Application information: Application form required.
Officers: Elliot Leiter, Pres. and Treas.; Renee Leiter, V.P. and Secy.
Directors: Ariane Leiter, Michael Leiter.
EIN: 912010504

56033
TriFam Foundation
6187 Silverbeach Dr., N.W.
Bremerton, WA 98311-8907 (360) 377-5406
Contact: Raymond L. Soule, C.E.O.

Established in 1992 in WA.
Donor(s): Raymond L. Soule, Sharon Soule.
Financial data (yr. ended 12/31/01): Grants paid, $11,300; assets, $265,212 (M); gifts received, $1,979; expenditures, $13,279; qualifying distributions, $11,300.
Limitations: Giving primarily in WA.
Officers: Raymond L. Soule, C.E.O.; Scott R. Soule, Pres.; Sharon Soule, V.P. and Secy.; Kent Soule, Treas.
EIN: 911576502

56034
Spen Family Foundation
10530 S.E. 250th Pl., Ste. J-105
Kent, WA 98031-8232 (253) 520-6897
Contact: M. S. Rodeheffer, Pres. and Dir.

Financial data (yr. ended 12/31/99): Grants paid, $11,260; assets, $208,033 (M); expenditures, $12,303; qualifying distributions, $11,260.
Officers and Directors:* Madeleine S. Rodeheffer,* Pres.; Paul Goldberg,* V.P.; Samuel Barnum,* Secy.; William D. Herron,* Treas.
EIN: 592742185

56035
Joseph Brody Foundation
P.O. Box 11541
Bainbridge Island, WA 98110

Financial data (yr. ended 12/31/01): Grants paid, $11,250; assets, $192,378 (M); expenditures, $12,437; qualifying distributions, $11,250.
Limitations: Applications not accepted. Giving on a national basis, with emphasis on IL.
Application information: Contributes only to pre-selected organizations.
Officers: Merle J. Titus, Pres.; Mark L. Brody, V.P.; Karen F. Brody, Secy.-Treas.
EIN: 363017857

56036
Harrington Foundation, Inc.
23908 Timber Ln.
Edmonds, WA 98020-5232

Donor(s): Emmett S. Harrington.‡
Financial data (yr. ended 12/31/01): Grants paid, $11,100; assets, $479,780 (M); expenditures, $14,365; qualifying distributions, $11,100.
Limitations: Applications not accepted. Giving primarily in Seattle, WA.
Application information: Contributes only to pre-selected organizations.
Officer: Gladys M. Harrington, Secy.
EIN: 066073478

56037
Myrtle & John Gossett Charitable Foundation
15 Gossett Rd.
Port Angeles, WA 98363-9717

Established in 1998 in WA.
Donor(s): John Gossett, Myrtle Gossett.
Financial data (yr. ended 06/30/01): Grants paid, $11,025; assets, $279,216 (M); expenditures, $12,062; qualifying distributions, $11,025.
Limitations: Applications not accepted.
Application information: Contributes only to a pre-selected organization.
Directors: John Gossett, Myrtle Gossett, Charles McClain.
EIN: 911841995

56038
Marcia W. Zech Foundation
(Formerly Marcia Woodby Paulsell Foundation)
3041 60th Ave., S.E.
Mercer Island, WA 98040

Financial data (yr. ended 09/30/01): Grants paid, $11,000; assets, $412,990 (M); expenditures, $12,407; qualifying distributions, $11,000.
Limitations: Applications not accepted. Giving primarily in Seattle, WA.
Application information: Contributes only to pre-selected organizations.
Officers: Marcia W. Zech, Pres. and Treas.; Fred Paulsell III, V.P.
EIN: 911200096

56039
Henry E. Collier Law Student Fund
c/o Bank of America
P.O. Box 34345
Seattle, WA 98124-1345
Application address: c/o Richard Ludwick, Asst. Dean, Univ. of Oregon Law School, Eugene, OR 97403

Financial data (yr. ended 12/31/01): Grants paid, $10,751; assets, $116,516 (M); expenditures, $14,467; qualifying distributions, $10,751.
Limitations: Giving limited to Eugene, OR.
Application information: Application form not required.
Trustee: Bank of America.
EIN: 936018954

56040
Aydelotte Foundation
4113 N.E. Lookout Ln.
Poulsbo, WA 98370
Application address: 800 Bellevue Way, Ste. 300, Bellevue, WA 98009, tel.: (425) 637-3010
Contact: Richard Aydelotte, Pres.

Established in 1994 in WA.
Financial data (yr. ended 09/30/02): Grants paid, $10,625; assets, $242,081 (M); expenditures, $11,029; qualifying distributions, $10,625.
Limitations: Giving primarily in Kirkland, WA.
Officers: Richard Aydelotte, Pres.; Florence I. Aydelotte, Secy.
Director: James S. Aydelotte.
EIN: 911661424

56041
Ralph Benaroya Family Foundation
P.O. Box 2812
Kirkland, WA 98083-2812

Established in 1994 in WA.
Donor(s): Alfred R. Benaroya.
Financial data (yr. ended 12/31/01): Grants paid, $10,500; assets, $274,387 (M); expenditures, $15,684; qualifying distributions, $11,266.
Limitations: Applications not accepted. Giving primarily in Seattle, WA.
Application information: Contributes only to pre-selected organizations.
Officers: Alfred R. Benaroya, Pres. and Treas.; Kimberly Fisher, V.P.
EIN: 911630089

56042
Thiry Foundation
6619 Ripley Ln., N.
Renton, WA 98056-1530 (425) 271-1982
Contact: Pierre Thiry, Pres.

Financial data (yr. ended 12/31/01): Grants paid, $10,265; assets, $128,085 (M); expenditures, $11,187; qualifying distributions, $10,265.
Limitations: Giving primarily in WA.
Officers: Pierre Thiry, Pres.; Chris Thiry, Secy.
EIN: 237122653

56043
The Terrell Foundation
2314 S.E. Park Crest Ave.
Vancouver, WA 98683 (360) 896-2518

Established in 1997 in WA.
Donor(s): Richard M. Terrell, The Rick Terrell Family.
Financial data (yr. ended 12/31/01): Grants paid, $10,255; assets, $14,460 (M); expenditures, $10,285; qualifying distributions, $10,255.
Limitations: Applications not accepted. Giving primarily in OR and WA.
Application information: Contributes only to pre-selected organizations.
Officers: Richard M. Terrell, Pres.; Carol Terrell, Secy.
EIN: 911815091

56044
Mary Dilworth Nyce Trust
c/o Union Bank of California, N.A.
P.O. Box 84495
Seattle, WA 98124-5795

Financial data (yr. ended 12/31/01): Grants paid, $10,242; assets, $287,565 (M); expenditures, $14,771; qualifying distributions, $12,518.
Limitations: Applications not accepted. Giving primarily in Seattle, WA.
Application information: Contributes only to pre-selected organizations.
Trustee: Union Bank of California, N.A.
EIN: 916071590

56045
The E. S. Bergquist Foundation
717 W. Sprague Ave., Ste. 1200
Spokane, WA 99201

Established in 1994 in WA.
Financial data (yr. ended 12/31/01): Grants paid, $10,200; assets, $198,606 (M); gifts received, $10,000; expenditures, $11,214; qualifying distributions, $10,200.
Limitations: Applications not accepted. Giving primarily in Seattle, WA.
Application information: Contributes only to pre-selected organizations.
Officers and Directors:* Lawrence R. Small,* Pres.; Patsy M. Small,* Secy.
EIN: 911621484

56046
Ofstie Scholarship Fund Trust
c/o Wells Fargo Bank Northwest, N.A.
P.O. Box 21927
Seattle, WA 98111-3927
Application address: c/o Wells Fargo Bank Northwest, N.A., P.O. Box 69, Everett, WA 98206
Contact: Karen Hansen, Trust Off., Wells Fargo Bank Northwest, N.A.

Financial data (yr. ended 12/31/01): Grants paid, $10,200; assets, $182,159 (M); expenditures, $16,073; qualifying distributions, $12,135.
Limitations: Giving limited to residents of the Everett, WA, area.
Application information: Applications submitted by high school counselors.
Trustee: Wells Fargo Bank Northwest, N.A.
EIN: 916061649

56047
Emma & Julius Kleiner Foundation
1725 89th N.E.
Bellevue, WA 98004

Established in 1990 in WA.
Financial data (yr. ended 12/31/01): Grants paid, $10,150; assets, $235,249 (M); expenditures, $12,094; qualifying distributions, $10,150.
Limitations: Applications not accepted.
Application information: Contributes only to pre-selected organizations.
Officer: Walter H. Kleiner, Pres.
Director: David Kleiner.
EIN: 943112318

56048
Ten for Children
c/o Egger Betts Austin Treacy
11120 N.E. 2nd St., Ste. 200
Bellevue, WA 98004
Application address: 1107 1st Ave., Apt. 1904, Seattle, WA 98101, tel.: (206) 343-9940
Contact: Helen Stusser, Pres.

Established in 1990 in WA.
Financial data (yr. ended 12/31/00): Grants paid, $10,100; assets, $81 (M); gifts received, $9,981; expenditures, $10,112; qualifying distributions, $10,100.
Limitations: Giving limited to Seattle, WA.
Officers and Directors:* Helen Stusser,* Pres.; Mary Smith,* Secy.-Treas.; Roly Alhadeff, Phoebe Andrew, Sarah Ballard, Alice Calvert, Nan Crocker, Carole Pearl, Gaye Pigott, Patsy Sangster.
EIN: 911458942

56049
Loft Foundation
c/o Florin Lazar
122 State St. S., Apt 214
Kirkland, WA 98033-6607

Established in 1999 in WA.
Donor(s): Florin O. Lazar.
Financial data (yr. ended 12/31/01): Grants paid, $10,014; assets, $6,315 (M); gifts received, $4,608; expenditures, $12,217; qualifying distributions, $10,014.
Limitations: Applications not accepted.
Application information: Contributes only to pre-selected organizations.
Officers: Rose M. George, Secy.-Treas.; Florin O. Lazar, Exec. Dir.
EIN: 911940200

56050
Alternative Foundation
P.O. Box 22419
Seattle, WA 98122-0419 (206) 789-0263
Contact: Ann Lennartz, Pres.

Donor(s): Ann Lennartz.
Financial data (yr. ended 09/30/01): Grants paid, $10,000; assets, $103,465 (M); expenditures, $12,299; qualifying distributions, $11,805.
Limitations: Giving primarily in Seattle, WA.
Application information: Application form not required.
Officer: Ann Lennartz, Pres., V.P., and Secy.-Treas.
EIN: 911876804

56051
The Barrett Family Foundation
The Highlands
Seattle, WA 98177

Established in 1999 in WA.
Donor(s): Phil Barrett.
Financial data (yr. ended 12/31/00): Grants paid, $10,000; assets, $1,383,268 (M); gifts received, $1,031,250; expenditures, $21,062; qualifying distributions, $20,952.
Limitations: Applications not accepted. Giving primarily in Seattle, WA.
Application information: Contributes only to pre-selected organizations.
Officers: Tiia-mai Barrett, Pres.; Phil Barrett, V.P., Secy. and Treas.
EIN: 912021045

56052

Fisher Broadcasting Inc. Minority Scholarship Fund
(Formerly KOMO Radio and Television Minority Scholarship Fund)
c/o Fisher Broadcasting Inc., Minority Scholarship
2001 6th Ave., Ste. 3425
Seattle, WA 98121

Established in 1990 in WA.
Donor(s): Fisher Broadcasting Inc.
Financial data (yr. ended 12/31/99): Grants paid, $10,000; assets, $202,832 (M); expenditures, $10,000; qualifying distributions, $10,000.
Limitations: Giving limited to residents of CA, GA, ID, MT, OR, and WA.
Publications: Informational brochure.
Application information: Application form required.
Officers and Trustees:* Carlos Espinoza, Pres.; Sharon Sharer-Johnston,* Secy.-Treas.; Scott Boone, Lucy Ruiz, Patrick M. Scott, Shannon Sweatte, Ben Tucker, Pat VandenBrock, Dick Warsinske, Sharonda White.
EIN: 911500276
Codes: CS, CD, GTI

56053

Lyford Family Foundation
9529 Lake Washington Blvd.
Bellevue, WA 98004

Established in 2001 in WA.
Donor(s): Mary R. Zeeb.
Financial data (yr. ended 12/31/01): Grants paid, $10,000; assets, $993,107 (M); gifts received, $1,000,000; expenditures, $10,000; qualifying distributions, $10,000.
Limitations: Applications not accepted.
Application information: Contributes only to pre-selected organizations.
Officers: Charles A. Lyford, IV, Pres., V.P. and Treas.; Betty Dykstra, Secy.
EIN: 912162741

56054

Pink Lite Foundation
c/o Don Rasmussen
2485 N.E. McWilliams Rd.
Bremerton, WA 98311-8407

Established in 2000 in WA.
Donor(s): Don Rasmussen.
Financial data (yr. ended 09/30/01): Grants paid, $10,000; assets, $356,619 (M); gifts received, $375,264; expenditures, $11,800; qualifying distributions, $11,800.
Limitations: Giving primarily in Bremerton, WA.
Officers: Don Rasmussen, Pres. and Treas.; Kerma Peterson, Secy.
EIN: 912093277

56055

Walter Telfer & Everett Improvement Company Scholarship Trust
(Formerly Everett Improvement Company Scholarship Trust)
c/o Wells Fargo Bank Northwest, N.A.
P.O. Box 21927
Seattle, WA 98111
Application address: c/o Everett Community College, Financial Aid, 801 Wetmore Ave., Everett, WA 98201-1287

Financial data (yr. ended 06/30/01): Grants paid, $10,000; assets, $132,352 (M); expenditures, $13,657; qualifying distributions, $11,667.
Limitations: Giving limited to Everett, WA.
Application information: Application form required.

Trustee: Wells Fargo Bank Northwest, N.A.
EIN: 916231655

56056

Community Assistance Foundation
P.O. Box 9797
Bellingham, WA 98227 (360) 714-7700
Contact: Susan Cole, Pres.

Established in 1998 in WA.
Financial data (yr. ended 02/28/99): Grants paid, $9,992; assets, $389 (M); expenditures, $10,029; qualifying distributions, $9,990.
Officers: Susan Cole, Pres.; Craig W. Cole, V.P. and Secy.; James R. Anderson, Treas.
EIN: 911893257

56057

Alice Peirce Sylvester Trust
c/o Bank of America
P.O. Box 34345, CSC-9
Seattle, WA 98124-1345

Financial data (yr. ended 04/30/02): Grants paid, $9,941; assets, $339,036 (M); expenditures, $15,450; qualifying distributions, $9,941.
Limitations: Applications not accepted. Giving primarily in Seattle, WA.
Application information: Contributes only to pre-selected organizations.
Trustee: Bank of America.
EIN: 916229445

56058

The Howell Foundation
(Formerly The Stanley D. Howell Foundation)
2481 Anderson Lake Rd., No. 633
Chimacum, WA 98325

Financial data (yr. ended 12/31/01): Grants paid, $9,704; assets, $169,650 (M); expenditures, $15,145; qualifying distributions, $9,704.
Limitations: Applications not accepted. Giving primarily in WA.
Application information: Contributes only to pre-selected organizations.
Officer: Ruth Lewis, Pres.
EIN: 910786732

56059

Roberta Gose Trust
c/o Baker Boyer National Bank, Trust Div.
P.O. Box 1796
Walla Walla, WA 99362

Established in 1996 in WA.
Donor(s): Roberta Gose.‡
Financial data (yr. ended 12/31/99): Grants paid, $9,600; assets, $290,393 (M); expenditures, $20,548; qualifying distributions, $9,115.
Limitations: Applications not accepted.
Application information: Contributes only to pre-selected organizations.
Trustee: Baker Boyer National Bank.
EIN: 916406229

56060

Lovsted Family Charitable Foundation Trust
3879 W. Mercer Way
Mercer Island, WA 98040
Contact: Carl M. Lovested, Tr.

Established in 1995 in WA.
Donor(s): Carl M. Lovsted, Mrs. Carl M. Lovsted.
Financial data (yr. ended 12/31/01): Grants paid, $9,525; assets, $284,994 (M); gifts received, $8,248; expenditures, $10,179; qualifying distributions, $9,525.
Limitations: Giving primarily in Seattle, WA.
Trustee: Carl M. Lovsted.
EIN: 943216413

56061

Education & Russian Neuroscience Fund
1734 N.E. 55th Pl.
Seattle, WA 98105-2403 (206) 523-3496
Contact: Douglas M. Bowden, Dir.

Established in 1993.
Donor(s): Douglas M. Bowden, M.D.
Financial data (yr. ended 12/31/01): Grants paid, $9,500; assets, $1,128 (M); gifts received, $9,500; expenditures, $9,522; qualifying distributions, $9,500.
Directors: Douglas M. Bowden, M.D., Managing Dir.; Glen Hayden, M.D., Dir. for Scholarships; Michael Cole, Ph.D., Dir. for Grant Evaluation.
EIN: 911589082

56062

Lowell L. Vansoyoc Foundation
14203 183rd Ave.
Renton, WA 98059-7652
Application address: c/o Orting School District, P.O. Box 460, Orting, WA 98360
Contact: Leon Matz

Established in 1993 in WA.
Financial data (yr. ended 12/31/99): Grants paid, $9,500; assets, $193,377 (M); expenditures, $10,401; qualifying distributions, $12,529.
Limitations: Giving limited to the Orting Valley, WA, area.
Application information: Application form required.
Officers: Daniel Postoshnik, Pres.; Dennis Hess, 1st V.P.; Jim Schultz, 2nd V.P.; Marty Hilton, Secy.; Shirley Rhengren, Treas.
EIN: 911586880

56063

Washington Foundation for Long Term Care
2120 State Ave., N.E.
Olympia, WA 98506-6515

Financial data (yr. ended 05/31/01): Grants paid, $9,500; assets, $6,092 (M); gifts received, $3,481; expenditures, $9,953; qualifying distributions, $9,496.
Application information: Application form required.
Officers: Terry Mace, Pres.; Randy Hyatt, V.P.; Jeril Hansen, Secy.; Robert Washbond, Treas.
EIN: 911725655

56064

Clarence & Grace Lundberg Foundation
c/o Wells Fargo Bank Northwest, N.A.
P.O. Box 21927
Seattle, WA 98111

Established in 1996 in WA.
Financial data (yr. ended 12/31/01): Grants paid, $9,406; assets, $278,784 (M); expenditures, $18,632; qualifying distributions, $15,614.
Limitations: Applications not accepted. Giving primarily in Tacoma, WA.
Application information: Contributes only to pre-selected organizations.
Trustee: Wells Fargo Bank Northwest, N.A.
EIN: 916403214

56065

Clarence Colby Memorial Fund
c/o Washington Trust Bank, Trust Dept.
717 West Sprague
Spokane, WA 99204-3922

Financial data (yr. ended 12/31/00): Grants paid, $9,355; assets, $247,456 (M); expenditures, $12,997; qualifying distributions, $9,355.
Limitations: Applications not accepted. Giving primarily in Spokane, WA.

Application information: Contributes only to pre-selected organizations.
Trustee: Washington Trust Bank.
EIN: 916252781

56066
Sievers Foundation Trust
c/o Wells Fargo Bank Northwest, N.A.
P.O. Box 21927
Seattle, WA 98111-3927
Application address: c/o Wells Fargo Bank Northwest, N.A., 2801 Wetmore Ave., Everett, WA 98201
Contact: Karen Hansen, Trust Off., Wells Fargo Bank Northwest, N.A.

Financial data (yr. ended 12/31/01): Grants paid, $9,200; assets, $149,983 (M); expenditures, $13,909; qualifying distributions, $11,134.
Limitations: Giving primarily in WA.
Trustee: Wells Fargo Bank Northwest, N.A.
EIN: 916025344

56067
Kaelber Private Foundation
5317 Old Stump Dr., N.W.
Gig Harbor, WA 98332

Established in 1981 in AK.
Donor(s): Janeth N. Kaelber, Norman F. Kaelber.
Financial data (yr. ended 12/31/01): Grants paid, $9,000; assets, $205,327 (M); gifts received, $1,388; expenditures, $9,036; qualifying distributions, $9,000.
Limitations: Applications not accepted.
Application information: Contributes only to pre-selected organizations.
Officers: Norman F. Kaelber, Pres.; Janeth N. Kaelber, Secy.
Director: R.G. Benkart.
EIN: 920080738

56068
U. W. Nikkei Alumni Association
(Formerly University Students Club, Inc.)
1414 S. Weller St.
Seattle, WA 98144-2053
Application address: c/o Scholarship Comm., 2703-36th S.W., Seattle, WA 98126, tel.: (206) 932-8051

Established in 1965 in WA.
Financial data (yr. ended 06/30/01): Grants paid, $9,000; assets, $232,200 (M); gifts received, $2,145; expenditures, $10,375; qualifying distributions, $10,190.
Limitations: Giving limited to residents of WA.
Application information: Application form required.
Officers: K. Sato, Pres.; M. Fukuma, V.P.; D. Maekawa, Secy.; I. Mano, Treas.
EIN: 916035190
Codes: GTI

56069
Gertrude L. McRae Scholarship Fund
c/o Wells Fargo Bank Northwest, N.A.
P.O. Box 21927
Seattle, WA 98111
Application address: c/o Grant County Court House, Canyon City, OR 97820

Financial data (yr. ended 06/30/01): Grants paid, $8,900; assets, $272,730 (M); expenditures, $14,348; qualifying distributions, $11,333.
Limitations: Giving primarily to graduates from Grant County, OR, high schools; secondary perference to students from high schools in Wheeler, Morrow, or Wasco counties, OR.
Application information: Application form required.

Trustee: Wells Fargo Bank Northwest, N.A.
EIN: 936097780
Codes: GTI

56070
Pietrzycki School Trust Fund
c/o Bank of America
P.O. Box 34345, CSC-10
Seattle, WA 98124-1345

Financial data (yr. ended 12/31/01): Grants paid, $8,602; assets, $225,629 (M); expenditures, $12,449; qualifying distributions, $10,512.
Limitations: Applications not accepted. Giving limited to Dayton, WA.
Application information: Contributes only to pre-selected organizations.
Trustee: Bank of America.
EIN: 916025713

56071
Harold & Martha Barto Scholarship Trust
c/o Bank of America
P.O. Box 34345
Seattle, WA 98124-1345
Application address: c/o Central WA University Foundation, 400 E. 8th Ave., Ellensburg, WA 98926-7508, tel.: (509) 963-2111
Contact: Jen Gray, Dir. of Fdn. and Comm. Relations

Established in 1984 in WA.
Financial data (yr. ended 04/30/01): Grants paid, $8,514; assets, $406,654 (M); expenditures, $15,242; qualifying distributions, $11,752.
Limitations: Giving limited to Ellensburg, WA.
Application information: Application form required.
Trustee: Bank of America.
EIN: 916267640
Codes: GTI

56072
The Yaley Family Foundation
20029 Third Dr. SE
Bothell, WA 98012

Established in 1999 in WA.
Donor(s): Michael J. Yaley.
Financial data (yr. ended 12/31/01): Grants paid, $8,512; assets, $62,271 (M); expenditures, $14,997; qualifying distributions, $8,512.
Limitations: Applications not accepted. Giving primarily in WA.
Application information: Contributes only to pre-selected organizations.
Officers: Michael J. Yaley, Pres. and Treas.; Elizabeth Price Yaley, V.P. and Secy.
EIN: 912007314

56073
The Eugene L. and Ileen Shields Charitable Foundation
6321 Englewood Ave.
Yakima, WA 98908
Contact: Eugene L. Shields, Pres.

Established in 1995 in WA.
Donor(s): Eugene L. Shields, Ileen Shields.
Financial data (yr. ended 12/31/01): Grants paid, $8,500; assets, $220,131 (M); expenditures, $11,717; qualifying distributions, $8,500.
Limitations: Applications not accepted. Giving primarily in Yakima, WA.
Application information: Contributes only to pre-selected organizations.
Officers and Directors:* Eugene L. Shields,* Pres. and Treas.; William Shields,* Secy.; Lisa Shields Long, Patrick Shields.
EIN: 911657760

56074
Sophie L. Anderson Educational Trust
c/o Bank of America
P.O. Box 34345
Seattle, WA 98124-1345
Application address: c/o Private Bank Center, Bank of America, P.O. Box 34474, Seattle, WA 98124, tel.: 1-800-526-7307

Financial data (yr. ended 03/30/02): Grants paid, $8,498; assets, $234,696 (M); expenditures, $12,023; qualifying distributions, $10,273.
Limitations: Giving limited to WA.
Trustee: Bank of America.
EIN: 916076066
Codes: GTI

56075
Carl Hossman Family Foundation
12801 Standring Ln., S.W.
Seattle, WA 98146

Established in 1996 in WA.
Donor(s): Martha B. Hossman, Carl L. Hossman, Jr.
Financial data (yr. ended 12/31/01): Grants paid, $8,468; assets, $120,074 (M); gifts received, $26,000; expenditures, $8,804; qualifying distributions, $8,468.
Limitations: Applications not accepted.
Application information: Contributes only to pre-selected organizations.
Officers: Martha B. Hossman, Pres.; Alix A. McDonough-Heiple, V.P.; Carl L. Hossman, Jr., Secy.-Treas.
EIN: 911726290

56076
Goldberg Family Charitable Foundation
c/o Thomas A. Brown
P.O. Box 1806
Aberdeen, WA 98520 (360) 533-1600

Established in 1994 in WA.
Financial data (yr. ended 12/31/01): Grants paid, $8,443; assets, $331,403 (M); gifts received, $25; expenditures, $11,283; qualifying distributions, $8,443.
Limitations: Giving limited to the southwestern WA area.
Directors: Thomas A. Brown, Lynn Kessler.
EIN: 916382063

56077
Massengale Family Foundation
13316 28th Ave., S.E.
Bothell, WA 98012

Established in 1999 in WA.
Donor(s): Randy Massengale, Kathryn Lee Campbell Massengale.
Financial data (yr. ended 12/31/01): Grants paid, $8,430; assets, $78,175 (M); gifts received, $4,034; expenditures, $12,464; qualifying distributions, $8,430.
Limitations: Applications not accepted.
Application information: Contributes only to pre-selected organizations.
Officer and Directors:* Kathryn Lee Campbell Massengale,* Pres.; Randy Massengale.
EIN: 912013790

56078
Mildred Kanipe Charitable Trust
c/o Wells Fargo Bank Northwest, N.A.
P.O. Box 21927
Seattle, WA 98111

Established in 1996 in OR.

56078—WASHINGTON

Financial data (yr. ended 12/31/01): Grants paid, $8,352; assets, $91,143 (M); expenditures, $14,038; qualifying distributions, $9,840.
Limitations: Applications not accepted. Giving primarily in Oakland, OR.
Application information: Contributes only to pre-selected organizations.
Trustee: Wells Fargo Bank Northwest, N.A.
EIN: 936174305

56079
The Karl Foundation
1001 4th Ave. Plz., Ste. 2333
Seattle, WA 98154-1101

Established in 1986 in WA.
Donor(s): Irvin H. Karl.
Financial data (yr. ended 10/31/01): Grants paid, $8,179; assets, $131,046 (M); gifts received, $108,224; expenditures, $8,407; qualifying distributions, $8,179.
Limitations: Applications not accepted. Giving primarily in WA.
Application information: Contributes only to pre-selected organizations.
Directors: Irvin H. Karl, Laura I. Karl.
EIN: 911362028

56080
Grotto Foundation
P.O. Box 459
Liberty Lake, WA 99019

Financial data (yr. ended 11/30/01): Grants paid, $8,084; assets, $184,320 (M); gifts received, $2,038; expenditures, $9,523; qualifying distributions, $8,485.
Limitations: Applications not accepted. Giving limited to WA.
Application information: Contributes only to pre-selected organizations.
Officers: Tom Spurgeon, Pres.; Gilbert R. Allen, V.P.; Travis Prewitt, Secy.-Treas.
Directors: Gilbert R. Allen, Ralph Axelson, Ed Burtts, Arthur Putnam, Joe Sproul, Tom Spurgeon, Edwin E. Weber, Carl White.
EIN: 916031149

56081
Educational Loan Foundation of Spokane, Inc.
U.S. Bank Bldg.
Spokane, WA 99201 (509) 747-2158
Contact: Joan Bergdorf

Donor(s): Carl M. Hansen Foundation.
Financial data (yr. ended 05/31/00): Grants paid, $8,000; assets, $102,552 (M); gifts received, $4,000; expenditures, $8,804; qualifying distributions, $7,963; giving activities include $8,000 for loans to individuals.
Limitations: Giving primarily in Spokane, WA.
Application information: Application form required.
Officers: Daniel E. Finney, Pres.; Marion Peterson, Secy.; Laurence D. Morse, Treas.
Directors: Herbert H. Cardle, Frank Knott, Patsy McPhaden, Mary Moss, Margaret Ott, Stephen Page, Mildred Perry, Dorothy Powers, Holly Sonneland, Ruth Thompson, Darlene Weber.
EIN: 916031887
Codes: GTI

56082
Marilyn & Alan Johnson Memorial Trust
c/o Bank of America
P.O. Box 34345
Seattle, WA 98124-1345
Application address: 933 Bar 14 Rd., Ellensburg, WA 98926
Contact: Linda Lundy, Pres.

Financial data (yr. ended 12/31/01): Grants paid, $8,000; assets, $125,294 (M); expenditures, $11,793; qualifying distributions, $9,802.
Limitations: Giving primarily in Walla Walla, WA.
Officer: Linda Lundy, Pres.
Trustee: Bank of America.
EIN: 916095311

56083
Jerome L. Lewis Scholarship Fund
c/o Bank of America
P.O. Box 34345
Seattle, WA 98124-1345
Application address: Financial Aid Off., c/o Yakima Valley College, P.O. Box 1647, Yakima, WA 98907

Financial data (yr. ended 12/31/99): Grants paid, $8,000; assets, $254,015 (M); expenditures, $12,644; qualifying distributions, $10,315.
Limitations: Giving limited to Yakima, WA.
Application information: Application form required.
Trustee: Bank of America.
EIN: 916026991

56084
The Bill B. and Judith A. Williams Foundation
P.O. Box 147
Liberty Lake, WA 99019-0629

Donor(s): Bill B. Williams, Judith A. Williams.
Financial data (yr. ended 12/31/00): Grants paid, $7,973; assets, $243,719 (M); gifts received, $62,973; expenditures, $9,499; qualifying distributions, $7,973.
Limitations: Applications not accepted.
Application information: Contributes only to pre-selected organizations.
Officers: Bill B. Williams, Pres.; Judith A. Williams, Secy.-Treas.
Directors: Terina J. Williams, Donna L. Zier.
EIN: 911622534

56085
Maple Valley Community Club Charitable Trust
P.O. Box 12688
Seattle, WA 98111
Contact: Jo-Anne Jaech, Tr.

Established in 1994 in WA.
Financial data (yr. ended 12/31/01): Grants paid, $7,918; assets, $123,024 (M); expenditures, $10,404; qualifying distributions, $7,918.
Limitations: Giving limited to the greater Maple Valley, WA, area.
Officer: Gladys White, Secy.
Trustee: Jo-Anne Jaech.
EIN: 916368543

56086
Bill Family Foundation
1911 S.W. Campus Dr., PMB 319
Federal Way, WA 98023-6473

Established in 2000 in WA.
Donor(s): Harthon H. Bill.
Financial data (yr. ended 12/31/01): Grants paid, $7,731; assets, $112,982 (M); expenditures, $9,256; qualifying distributions, $7,731.
Limitations: Applications not accepted.

Application information: Contributes only to pre-selected organizations.
Trustee: Harthon H. Bill.
EIN: 912028676

56087
Margaret Lobdell Schack Memorial Scholarship Fund
c/o Union Bank of California, N.A., Trust Dept.
P.O. Box 84495
Seattle, WA 98124-5795
Application address: c/o Union Bank of California, N.A., P.O. Box 3123, Seattle, WA 98114
Contact: Kim Cacace, Trust Off., Union Bank of California, N.A.

Financial data (yr. ended 03/31/02): Grants paid, $7,700; assets, $153,762 (M); expenditures, $10,537; qualifying distributions, $9,328.
Limitations: Giving limited to residents of Seattle, WA.
Trustee: Union Bank of California, N.A.
EIN: 916240991
Codes: GTI

56088
The Donworth Family Foundation
1301 Spring St., No. 30-I
Seattle, WA 98104

Established in 1988 in WA.
Donor(s): Martha L. Donworth, C. Carey Donworth.
Financial data (yr. ended 12/31/01): Grants paid, $7,695; assets, $267,410 (M); expenditures, $12,821; qualifying distributions, $7,695.
Limitations: Applications not accepted. Giving primarily in Seattle, WA.
Application information: Contributes only to pre-selected organizations.
Trustee: Martha L. Donworth.
EIN: 916302440

56089
Frost Family Foundation
P.O. Box 7285
Kennewick, WA 99336-0617

Financial data (yr. ended 12/31/01): Grants paid, $7,670; assets, $45,548 (M); gifts received, $49,500; expenditures, $8,140; qualifying distributions, $7,670.
Limitations: Applications not accepted.
Application information: Contributes only to pre-selected organizations.
Officers: F. Daniel Frost, Pres. and Treas.; S. Fifer Frost, V.P. and Secy.
EIN: 911895273

56090
Martin Luther King School Dream Foundation
705 Spruce St.
Edmonds, WA 98020-4032

Established in 1994 in WA.
Donor(s): Vaughn A. Sherman.
Financial data (yr. ended 12/31/99): Grants paid, $7,600; assets, $156,417 (M); gifts received, $20,822; expenditures, $10,667; qualifying distributions, $7,493.
Application information: Application form required.
Officers and Directors:* Vaughn A. Sherman,* Chair.; Janice Lind-Sherman,* Vice-Chair.; Arthur D. Jackson, Jr.,* Secy.; Jim St. Germain,* Treas.; Phyllis Gutierrez Kenney, Ruby Smith Love, Louise McKinney, Karen Miller.
EIN: 911621291

56091
Beaty-Neary Family Foundation
401 Kirkland Ave., Apt. 303
Kirkland, WA 98033
Contact: Harry Beaty, Pres.

Established in 1998 in AZ.
Financial data (yr. ended 12/31/00): Grants paid, $7,500; assets, $155,162 (M); gifts received, $5,049; expenditures, $8,405; qualifying distributions, $7,500.
Officers and Directors:* Harry N. Beaty,* Pres.; Kara Beaty Neary,* V.P. and Secy.; Christopher D. Beaty,* V.P.; Georgia Kay Beaty, Kim Van Kueren Beaty, Thomas J. Neary.
EIN: 860938990

56092
The JKU Foundation
12674 Plateau Cir., N.W.
Silverdale, WA 98383

Established in 1995 in WA.
Donor(s): Mabel Joyner, Timothy Joyner.
Financial data (yr. ended 12/31/01): Grants paid, $7,500; assets, $179,042 (M); gifts received, $5,000; expenditures, $7,816; qualifying distributions, $7,500.
Limitations: Applications not accepted.
Application information: Contributes only to pre-selected organizations.
Officers and Directors:* Timothy Joyner,* Pres.; Mabel Joyner,* V.P. and Secy.; Dan H. Kusaka, Deborah M. Kusaka, Marianne Y. Uyeda.
EIN: 911702219

56093
Miriam Landy Charitable Corporation
c/o Watson & Assocs.
600 University St., Ste. 2828
Seattle, WA 98101

Donor(s): Miriam Landy.
Financial data (yr. ended 12/31/01): Grants paid, $7,500; assets, $142,472 (M); expenditures, $8,105; qualifying distributions, $7,500.
Limitations: Applications not accepted. Giving primarily in Washington, DC.
Application information: Contributes only to pre-selected organizations.
Directors: Miriam Landy, Robin L. Landy.
EIN: 521354123

56094
Marion Baldwin-Annie Wright Fund
c/o Bank of America
P.O. Box 34345, Ste. CSC-9
Seattle, WA 98124-1345

Financial data (yr. ended 12/31/01): Grants paid, $7,488; assets, $216,211 (M); expenditures, $12,303; qualifying distributions, $9,908.
Limitations: Applications not accepted. Giving primarily in Tacoma, WA.
Application information: Contributes only to pre-selected organizations.
Trustee: Bank of America.
EIN: 916389791

56095
Joshua Children's Foundation
P.O. Box 1885
Bellevue, WA 98009 (800) 376-7527
Contact: Nancy Williams, Dir.

Established in 2000 in WA.
Donor(s): Nancy Williams.
Financial data (yr. ended 12/31/00): Grants paid, $7,476; assets, $198,437 (M); gifts received, $202,176; expenditures, $7,797; qualifying distributions, $7,476; giving activities include $746 for programs.
Limitations: Giving primarily in Seattle, WA.
Application information: Application form not required.
Directors: Kathleen Searcy, Nancy Williams.
EIN: 912006086

56096
Toll & Wagner Family Foundation
13045 23rd Pl., N.E.
Seattle, WA 98125-4211

Established in 1993 in WA and OR.
Donor(s): Gretchen T. Wagner.
Financial data (yr. ended 12/31/01): Grants paid, $7,466; assets, $123,340 (M); gifts received, $11,000; expenditures, $8,627; qualifying distributions, $7,466.
Limitations: Applications not accepted. Giving primarily in OR.
Application information: Contributes only to pre-selected organizations.
Officers and Director:* Greta M. Toll,* Chair.; Howard C. Wagner, Pres.; Rena E. Wagner, V.P.; Heidi W. Dupuis, Secy.; Gretchen T. Wagner, Treas.
EIN: 911621467

56097
Qpoint Foundation Fund
c/o QPoint International
10900 N.E. 4th St., Ste. 1800
Bellevue, WA 98004

Established in 1998 in WA.
Donor(s): Qpoint International.
Financial data (yr. ended 12/31/00): Grants paid, $7,333; assets, $0 (M); gifts received, $8,013; expenditures, $9,146; qualifying distributions, $9,146.
Limitations: Giving primarily in WA.
Officers: Joe MaGee, Pres.; Mindy Greene, C.O.O.; Michael Petosa, V.P.; Gary Gigot, Secy.; Richard Von Riesen, Treas.
Directors: Geoff Boguch, Al Higginson, Skip Semon.
EIN: 911669241
Codes: CS, CD

56098
Michael Andrew Yukevich Foundation
8031 Meridian Ave. N.
Seattle, WA 98103-4526
Contact: Michael A. Yukevich, Tr.

Established in 1991 in PA.
Donor(s): Andrew R. Cochrane, Christine C. Yukevich, Michael A. Yukevich.
Financial data (yr. ended 12/31/01): Grants paid, $7,276; assets, $29,777 (M); gifts received, $13,862; expenditures, $7,356; qualifying distributions, $7,276.
Limitations: Giving on a national basis.
Application information: Application form not required.
Trustees: Andrew R. Cochrane, Christine C. Yukevich, Michael A. Yukevich.
EIN: 251649256

56099
C. J. and Esther Alexander Foundation
1055 Spokane St.
Prosser, WA 99350

Established in 1999 in WA.
Donor(s): Esther Alexander.
Financial data (yr. ended 12/31/01): Grants paid, $7,000; assets, $105,562 (M); expenditures, $8,468; qualifying distributions, $8,402.
Limitations: Applications not accepted.
Application information: Contributes only to pre-selected organizations.
Officers: Esther Alexander, Pres.; Mike Boone, V.P.; Stephen Winfrey, Secy.
Director: Paul Cotton.
EIN: 911927941

56100
The Sharing Foundation
P.O. Box 1633
Redmond, WA 98073-2633

Established in 1997 in WA.
Donor(s): Donald B. Rottler, D. Edson Clark.
Financial data (yr. ended 08/31/01): Grants paid, $7,000; assets, $100,351 (M); expenditures, $10,638; qualifying distributions, $7,000.
Limitations: Applications not accepted.
Application information: Contributes only to pre-selected organizations.
Directors: Barbara D. Angie-Rottler, John S. Angie-Rottler, D. Edson Clark, Andrew C. Rottler, Donald B. Rottler, Steven Rottler.
EIN: 911747663

56101
Sarina Slaid Memorial Scholarship Fund
4614 N.E. 45th Pl.
Vancouver, WA 98661-2873 (360) 253-6465
Contact: Greg Joy, Pres.

Established in 1993 in WA.
Donor(s): Reiko Nitta.‡
Financial data (yr. ended 12/31/99): Grants paid, $7,000; assets, $140,614 (M); expenditures, $8,990; qualifying distributions, $7,000.
Limitations: Giving limited to residents of WA.
Officer: Gregory M. Joy, Pres.
EIN: 943186332

56102
Voigt Charitable Foundation
3700 Pacific Hwy. E., Ste. 408
Tacoma, WA 98424-1163 (253) 922-3828
Contact: John G. Voigt, Mgr.

Financial data (yr. ended 12/31/01): Grants paid, $7,000; assets, $245,428 (M); expenditures, $10,280; qualifying distributions, $7,000.
Limitations: Giving primarily in WA.
Officer and Trustees:* John G. Voigt,* Mgr.; Mrs. Ralph Voigt.
EIN: 396049729

56103
Willinor Scholarship Fund
c/o Wells Fargo Bank Northwest, N.A.
P.O. Box 21927
Seattle, WA 98111
Application addresses: c/o Esther Workman, Everett High School, Everett, WA 98203, c/o Dan Jansen, Cascade High School, Everett, WA 98203

Donor(s): Irma Phillips.‡
Financial data (yr. ended 12/31/01): Grants paid, $6,750; assets, $108,374 (M); expenditures, $10,472; qualifying distributions, $8,583.
Limitations: Giving primarily in WA.
Application information: Application form required.
Trustee: Wells Fargo Bank Northwest, N.A.
EIN: 916263373

56104
Oleta Chu Scholarship Foundation
600 Stewart St., Ste. 305
Seattle, WA 98101
Contact: D. Lee Burdette, Tr.

Financial data (yr. ended 12/31/01): Grants paid, $6,674; assets, $64,992 (M); expenditures, $11,842; qualifying distributions, $9,454.
Limitations: Giving limited to residents of MO.
Trustee: D. Lee Burdette.
EIN: 431514131

56105
Donald & Edna Wheaton Foundation
c/o Paul Stritmatter
413 8th St.
Hoquiam, WA 98550

Financial data (yr. ended 12/31/01): Grants paid, $6,600; assets, $162,529 (M); expenditures, $6,966; qualifying distributions, $6,600.
Limitations: Giving primarily in Grays Harbor County, WA.
Application information: Application form required.
Directors: Jo Anne Barry, John Bauscher, John Mertz, Ann Monahan, Ralph Morris, Paul Strittmatter.
EIN: 911145955
Codes: GTI

56106
Odin & Gunhild Tjelde Foundation
3055 112th Ave., N.E., Ste. 210
Bellevue, WA 98004-2097 (425) 822-4080

Financial data (yr. ended 11/30/01): Grants paid, $6,500; assets, $69,223 (M); expenditures, $8,175; qualifying distributions, $6,500.
Limitations: Applications not accepted. Giving limited to WA.
Application information: Contributes to pre-selected organizations.
Trustees: David Craig, Larry Ostrom, Leo Sheehan, Deyonne Tegman.
EIN: 916050160

56107
Yakima Valley Memorial Fund for Medical Science Education
c/o Yakima County Medical Society
307 S. 12th Ave., Ste. 10
Yakima, WA 98902-3138

Financial data (yr. ended 12/31/00): Grants paid, $6,500; assets, $157,904 (M); gifts received, $1,585; expenditures, $7,491; qualifying distributions, $7,023.
Limitations: Giving primarily in Yakima, WA.
Application information: Application form required.
Trustees: James I. Abbenhaus, M.D., Robert K. Cooper, M.D., Jeffrey Kaplan, M.D., Nina Wiseley.
EIN: 916032497

56108
Betty J. Eberharter Foundation
c/o Betty J. Eberharter
2414 43rd Ave. E.
Seattle, WA 98112-2566

Donor(s): Betty J. Eberharter.
Financial data (yr. ended 12/31/01): Grants paid, $6,463; assets, $32 (M); expenditures, $6,898; qualifying distributions, $6,463.
Limitations: Applications not accepted. Giving primarily in WA.
Application information: Contributes only to pre-selected organizations.
Officer: Betty J. Eberharter, Mgr.
EIN: 943132198

56109
Garrison Foundation
c/o The Trust Co. of Washington
1201 3rd Ave., Ste. 5010
Seattle, WA 98101-3029

Financial data (yr. ended 05/31/01): Grants paid, $6,450; assets, $227,818 (M); gifts received, $7,000; expenditures, $11,398; qualifying distributions, $6,450.
Limitations: Applications not accepted.
Application information: Contributes only to pre-selected organizations.
Trustee: The Trust Co. of Washington.
EIN: 916235838

56110
Tillie & Alfred Shemanski Foundation
c/o Bank of America
P.O. Box 34345, CSC-9
Seattle, WA 98124-1345
Application address: P.O. Box 24565, Seattle, WA 98124, tel.: (206) 358-0806
Contact: Mollie Determan, Trust Off., Bank of America

Financial data (yr. ended 12/31/01): Grants paid, $6,450; assets, $307,641 (M); expenditures, $7,511; qualifying distributions, $6,450.
Limitations: Giving primarily in Seattle, WA.
Trustee: Bank of America.
EIN: 916026474

56111
Jolley Foundation
1011 Evergreen Dr.
Bellevue, WA 98004-4020

Donor(s): Jack J. Jolley.
Financial data (yr. ended 11/30/01): Grants paid, $6,334; assets, $0 (M); gifts received, $1,600; expenditures, $6,334; qualifying distributions, $6,334.
Limitations: Applications not accepted. Giving on a national basis, with emphasis on Portland, OR.
Application information: Contributes only to pre-selected organizations.
Directors: Bill Jolley, Jack J. Jolley, John J. Jolley, Joyce Jolley.
EIN: 911356811

56112
Langley Community Club
P.O. Box 32
Langley, WA 98260-0032 (320) 221-6590
Contact: Ethel Waters, Secy.

Financial data (yr. ended 12/31/00): Grants paid, $6,311; assets, $4,905 (M); expenditures, $6,521; qualifying distributions, $6,458.
Limitations: Giving limited to South Whidbey Island, WA.
Officers: Richard Proctor, Pres.; Ruth Turner, V.P.; Ethel Waters, Secy.; Ronald D. Childers, Treas.
Directors: Francis Brown, Emil Lindholt, David Swenson.
EIN: 237041588

56113
The Four-10 Foundation
1440 Madrona Dr.
Seattle, WA 98122

Established in 1998 in WA.
Donor(s): Robert S. Rogers, Gloria D. Rogers.
Financial data (yr. ended 05/31/00): Grants paid, $6,000; assets, $31,123 (M); gifts received, $3,279; expenditures, $7,097; qualifying distributions, $5,607.
Application information: Application form not required.
Directors: Lisa Bjerke, Pam Burnett, Sara Dawson, Gloria D. Rogers, Robert S. Rogers, Laura Victor.
EIN: 911912834

56114
Gius Foundation
P.O. Box 277
Quincy, WA 98848-0277 (509) 787-4513
Contact: David R. Lemon, Adv. Comm.

Donor(s): Leslie Ann Gius, Margaret M. Gius.
Financial data (yr. ended 12/31/01): Grants paid, $6,000; assets, $300,061 (M); gifts received, $1,000; expenditures, $12,048; qualifying distributions, $6,000.
Limitations: Giving primarily in Quincy, George, and Royal City, WA.
Application information: Application form required.
Advisory Committee: Margaret M. Gius, Marie Helen Gius, David R. Lemon.
Trustee: Leslie Ann Gius.
EIN: 911511475

56115
Lakeside Foundation
10333 N.E. 132nd St.
Kirkland, WA 98034

Established in 1991 in WA.
Financial data (yr. ended 06/30/01): Grants paid, $6,000; assets, $1,181 (M); expenditures, $6,050; qualifying distributions, $6,000.
Limitations: Applications not accepted. Giving limited to WA.
Application information: Contributes only to pre-selected organizations.
Officers: Charles H. Kester, Pres.; Charles D. Kester, V.P.; Helen Kester, Secy.
EIN: 911221016

56116
Frederic J. Blanchett Foundation
1011 E. Main, Ste. 452
Puyallup, WA 98372

Financial data (yr. ended 12/31/01): Grants paid, $5,920; assets, $73,025 (M); expenditures, $8,257; qualifying distributions, $5,920.
Limitations: Applications not accepted.
Application information: Contributes only to pre-selected organizations.
Officer and Directors:* Richard F. Rose,* Mgr.; Frederic W. Blanchett, Celeste J. Rose.
EIN: 916033811

56117
John P. Jundt Foundation
201 W. North River Dr., Ste. 305
Spokane, WA 99201-2262
Contact: John P. Lynch, Pres.

Established in 1991 in WA.
Donor(s): John P. Jundt.‡
Financial data (yr. ended 12/31/01): Grants paid, $5,850; assets, $926,325 (M); gifts received, $97,860; expenditures, $107,548; qualifying distributions, $14,846.
Limitations: Giving limited to WA.
Application information: Application form required.
Officers: John P. Lynch, Pres.; Vivian Lynch, V.P.; Debra Clary, Secy.
Director: Robert Moe.
EIN: 911482883

56118
Paul Schuler Foundation
3100 Evergreen Pt. Rd.
Bellevue, WA 98004
Contact: Dorin Schuler, Pres.

Donor(s): Dorin Schuler.
Financial data (yr. ended 12/31/01): Grants paid, $5,800; assets, $112,419 (M); expenditures, $8,102; qualifying distributions, $5,800.
Limitations: Applications not accepted. Giving limited to WA.
Application information: Contributes only to pre-selected organizations.
Officer: Dorin Schuler, Pres.
EIN: 911233537

56119
Edward M. Thurston Scholarship Fund
c/o Wells Fargo Bank Northwest, N.A.
P.O. Box 21927
Seattle, WA 98111
Application address: c/o University of Oregon Foundation, P.O. Box 3346, Eugene, OR 97403

Established in 1995 in OR.
Financial data (yr. ended 06/30/01): Grants paid, $5,675; assets, $215,487 (M); expenditures, $10,543; qualifying distributions, $7,918.
Limitations: Giving limited to Eugene, OR.
Application information: Application form required.
Trustee: Wells Fargo Bank Northwest, N.A.
EIN: 936298681

56120
William W. Powell Historical Society Trust
c/o Bank of America
P.O. Box 34345
Seattle, WA 98124-1345

Financial data (yr. ended 05/31/02): Grants paid, $5,670; assets, $116,208 (M); expenditures, $6,895; qualifying distributions, $5,670.
Limitations: Applications not accepted. Giving primarily in eastern WA.
Application information: Contributes only to pre-selected organizations.
Trustee: Bank of America.
EIN: 237301716

56121
Robert R. Waltz Scholarship Fund
P.O. Box 949
Snohomish, WA 98291-0949
Application address: c/o Snohomish Senior High School, 1316 5th St., Snohomish, WA 98290, tel.: (360) 563-4000

Established in 1990 in WA.
Donor(s): Mary R. Waltz.
Financial data (yr. ended 12/31/01): Grants paid, $5,600; assets, $57,432 (M); expenditures, $6,357; qualifying distributions, $5,570.
Limitations: Giving limited to residents of Snohomish, WA.
Officers: Robert R. Waltz, Jr., Pres.; Susan Nunes, V.P.; Mary R. Waltz, Secy.; David Nunes, Treas.
EIN: 911460844

56122
The Beck-Boa Foundation
P.O. Box 205
Redmond, WA 98073-0205
Contact: Grants Admin.

Established in 1999 in WA.
Donor(s): Doug Boa, Colleen Beck.
Financial data (yr. ended 12/31/99): Grants paid, $5,500; assets, $99,238 (M); gifts received, $104,100; expenditures, $5,500; qualifying distributions, $5,500.
Limitations: Giving primarily in Redmond, WA.
Trustees: Colleen Beck, Doug Boa.
EIN: 916495603

56123
Biella Foundation
P.O. Box 70385
Bellevue, WA 98007-0385

Established in 1988 in WA.
Donor(s): Mart Bert.
Financial data (yr. ended 09/30/01): Grants paid, $5,500; assets, $115,603 (L); expenditures, $7,140; qualifying distributions, $5,434.
Limitations: Applications not accepted. Giving primarily in WA.
Application information: Contributes only to pre-selected organizations.
Officers: Mart Bert, Pres.; Lorraine Hoff, V.P.; Gerald H. Shaw, Secy.
EIN: 911428508

56124
Doug Hanna Memorial Scholarship Foundation
E. 41 Island Lake Dr.
Shelton, WA 98584
Application address: c/o Via Holman, Shelton High School, Shelton Springs Rd., Shelton, WA 98584

Donor(s): B. Regnar Paulsen.
Financial data (yr. ended 06/30/99): Grants paid, $5,500; assets, $89,545 (M); expenditures, $5,844; qualifying distributions, $5,457.
Limitations: Giving limited to residents of Shelton, WA.
Application information: Applicants must include G.P.A., SAT scores, activities, and references. Application form required.
Trustees: David C. Balding, Sheryl L. Balding, Helen K. Goodletter-Miller, Lee Ann Hanna, Janet L. Janda, Peter R. Janda, Jerry L. Miller.
EIN: 911384689

56125
Steven Ball Memorial Scholarship Foundation
c/o Diane M. Best
4812 New Woods Pl., Ste. B
Mount Vernon, WA 98274 (360) 428-0265
Additional application address: c/o Jerry Ball, 2060 Skagit City Rd., Mt. Vernon, VA 98273, tel.: (360) 445-4128

Established in 1994 in WA.
Donor(s): Robt Lien, Diane Best.
Financial data (yr. ended 12/31/01): Grants paid, $5,495; assets, $990 (M); gifts received, $25; expenditures, $5,858; qualifying distributions, $5,473.
Limitations: Giving limited to residents of Mount Vernon, WA.
Officers: Jerry Ball, Pres.; Kathleen Theoe, V.P.
Directors: Richard Best, Bob Lien.
EIN: 911631544

56126
RIZAD Foundation
1325 14th Ave.
Longview, WA 98632
Application address: 6963 Old Pacific Hwy., S., Kalama, WA 98625, tel.: (360) 673-4641
Contact: Mike Nichols, Pres.

Established in 1987 in WA.
Financial data (yr. ended 12/31/01): Grants paid, $5,465; assets, $470,352 (M); expenditures, $13,264; qualifying distributions, $5,465.
Limitations: Giving limited to Cowlitz County, WA.
Application information: Grants disbursed on quarterly basis.
Officers and Directors:* Mike Nichols,* Pres.; Bill Mahoney,* V.P.; Art Jordan,* Treas.
EIN: 911368660

56127
Hope Mission Outreach
(Formerly Centennial Foundation)
c/o Hope Mission Outreach
P.O. Box 1394
Tacoma, WA 98401-1394

Donor(s): Thomas W. Healy, Kathleen A. Healy.
Financial data (yr. ended 12/31/01): Grants paid, $5,425; assets, $447 (M); expenditures, $6,207; qualifying distributions, $5,425.
Limitations: Applications not accepted. Giving primarily in WA.
Application information: Contributes only to pre-selected organizations.
Officers: Bro. Raymond F. Taylor, Pres.; Rev. John Wilkie, V.P.; Ray Surean, Secy.-Treas.
EIN: 911192930
Codes: TN

56128
Philip P. & Lucy Weber Scholarship Fund
c/o Bank of America
P.O. Box 34345
Seattle, WA 98124-1345
Application addresses: c/o Bob Grigg, Counselor, Kellogg Senior High School, Jacobs Gulch, Kellogg, ID 83837, tel.: (208) 784-1371, c/o James A. See, Counselor, Mullan High School, Mullan School Dist. No. 392, Mullan, ID 83846, tel.: (208) 744-1126, c/o David Oas, Counselor, Wallace Senior High School, Wallace, ID 83873, tel.: (208) 753-5315

Financial data (yr. ended 05/31/01): Grants paid, $5,400; assets, $112,724 (M); expenditures, $8,869; qualifying distributions, $7,300.
Limitations: Giving limited to Kellogg, Mullan, and Wallace, ID.
Application information: Recipients chosen by committee.
Trustee: Bank of America.
EIN: 916024706

56129
Clint Noel Trauma Foundation
P.O. Box 223
Cathlamet, WA 98612-0223 (360) 849-4002
Contact: Nancy E. Noel, Pres.

Donor(s): Nancy E. Noel, Robert M. Noel.
Financial data (yr. ended 12/31/01): Grants paid, $5,385; assets, $53,569 (M); expenditures, $6,250; qualifying distributions, $5,385.
Limitations: Giving primarily in Portland, OR.
Officers and Director:* Nancy E. Noel,* Pres.; Eric E. Noel, V.P.; Robert M. Noel, Secy.-Treas.
EIN: 943104402

56130
The Wizard of Oz Foundation
3010 77th Ave. S.E., Ste. 202
Mercer Island, WA 98040

Established in 1995 in WA.
Donor(s): John E. Morse, Janet M. Morse.
Financial data (yr. ended 12/31/01): Grants paid, $5,336; assets, $19,797 (M); gifts received, $33; expenditures, $6,621; qualifying distributions, $5,336.
Limitations: Applications not accepted. Giving primarily in Seattle, WA.
Application information: Contributes only to pre-selected organizations.

56130—WASHINGTON

Officers and Directors:* Janet M. Morse,* Pres.; John E. Morse,* Secy.; Marcia L. Ellis,* Treas.
EIN: 911704048

56131
Blue Baby Fund, Inc.
10125 N. Division
Spokane, WA 99218-1306
Contact: Kiwanis Club of N. Spokane

Financial data (yr. ended 09/30/01): Grants paid, $5,306; assets, $82,970 (M); expenditures, $5,415; qualifying distributions, $5,306.
Limitations: Giving primarily in WA.
Officers and Directors:* Gerald M. Hansen,* Pres.; Lois Legerski,* V.P.; Helen Townsend,* Secy.; Gerald M. Hansen,* Treas.; John Anspauch, A. Douglas Brossiot, Manuel De La Torre, Jan Redinger.
EIN: 916054668

56132
Lumir M. & Virginia Mares Trust
c/o Bank of America
P.O. Box 34345
Seattle, WA 98124-1345
Application address: c/o Wenatchee Valley College, 1300 5th St., Wenatchee, WA 98801

Financial data (yr. ended 03/31/02): Grants paid, $5,300; assets, $171,897 (M); expenditures, $8,825; qualifying distributions, $5,300.
Limitations: Giving limited to Wenatchee, WA.
Application information: Application form required.
Trustee: Bank of America.
EIN: 916114383

56133
Baron Foundation
323A Telegraph Rd.
Bellingham, WA 98226

Established in 1996.
Financial data (yr. ended 12/31/01): Grants paid, $5,267; assets, $164,588 (M); gifts received, $15,000; expenditures, $5,374; qualifying distributions, $5,267.
Limitations: Applications not accepted.
Application information: Contributes only to pre-selected organizations.
Officers: Sid Baron, Pres.; Margaret Baron, V.P. and Treas.; Arthur Tjoelker, Secy.
Trustees: M. James Baron, Ronald D. Baron, H.J. Baron, Ph.D., Kaye Lynd Baron, Ph.D.
EIN: 911726295

56134
Burlington-Edison School District Foundation
927 E. Fairhaven Ave.
Burlington, WA 98233-1918 (360) 757-4074
Contact: Lindsay Fiker, Dir.

Established in 1994 in WA.
Donor(s): Hurburt Gaskin, Betty Stump.
Financial data (yr. ended 12/31/00): Grants paid, $5,188; assets, $99,579 (M); gifts received, $19,730; expenditures, $6,425; qualifying distributions, $5,293.
Limitations: Giving primarily in WA.
Application information: Application form available at Career Placement Office at Burlington-Edison High School. Application form required.
Officers: Duane Stowe, Pres.; Dan Peth, V.P.; Geneva Sasnett, Secy.; Andrea Martin, Treas.
Directors: Colonel Betz, Cheryl Bishop, Ernie Dahl, Lindsay Fiker, Michael Fohn, Harvey Lipp, Kathi Williams.
EIN: 943199980

56135
Lions 19B Watters Charitable Trust
P.O. Box 1459
Lake Stevens, WA 98258

Established in 1997 in WA.
Donor(s): Harry Watters.‡
Financial data (yr. ended 06/30/01): Grants paid, $5,163; assets, $112,728 (M); expenditures, $7,649; qualifying distributions, $5,163.
Limitations: Applications not accepted.
Application information: Contributes only to pre-selected organizations.
Officers: James Knight, Pres.; Fred Hennig, Secy.-Treas.
Trustees: Peter Kline, Gary Lockert, Manolito Munar, Robert Schumer, Paul Wold, Robert Youngs, Chet Zobrist.
EIN: 911726281

56136
The Rose Foundation
7 Tree Top Rd.
Longview, WA 98632-5532 (360) 423-7640
Application tel.: (360) 423-0937
Contact: June L. Rose, Tr.

Donor(s): Stanley B. Rose, June L. Rose.
Financial data (yr. ended 12/31/01): Grants paid, $5,070; assets, $92,375 (M); gifts received, $110; expenditures, $6,245; qualifying distributions, $5,070.
Limitations: Giving primarily in Longview, WA.
Trustee: June L. Rose.
EIN: 510186327

56137
Allison Foundation
c/o Union Bank of California, N.A.
P.O. Box 84495, Trust Dept.
Seattle, WA 98124-5795

Established in 1999 in WA.
Donor(s): Florence Allison.
Financial data (yr. ended 12/31/00): Grants paid, $5,045; assets, $83,139 (M); expenditures, $8,259; qualifying distributions, $6,823.
Limitations: Applications not accepted. Giving primarily in WA.
Application information: Contributes only to pre-selected organizations.
Trustee: Union Bank of California, N.A.
EIN: 911996350

56138
Sally Heet Scholarship Fund of the Puget Sound Chapter, Public Relations Society of America
c/o Bank of America
P.O. Box 34345, 701 5th Ave.
Seattle, WA 98124-1345
Application address: c/o THINK FIRST Program, St. Joseph Medical Center, P.O. Box 2197, Tacoma, WA 98401-2197, tel.: (253) 591-6668;
E-mail: bmarket@nwrain.com
Contact: Beverly H. Tanis, APR.

Established in 1986 in WA.
Financial data (yr. ended 08/31/00): Grants paid, $5,000; assets, $122,862 (M); gifts received, $14,430; expenditures, $5,781; qualifying distributions, $5,219.
Limitations: Giving limited to WA.
Application information: Application form required.
Trustee: Bank of America.
EIN: 943038312

56139
The Lion Glass Foundation
c/o Wallis Kimble
8202 Sr. 104, Ste. 102
Kingston, WA 98346

Established in 2000 in WA.
Donor(s): Wallis R. Kimble, Marilyn V. Kimble.
Financial data (yr. ended 12/31/01): Grants paid, $5,000; assets, $84,627 (M); expenditures, $5,500; qualifying distributions, $5,000.
Directors: Marilyn V. Kimble, Wallis R. Kimble.
EIN: 912084407

56140
Naramore Foundation
111 S. Jackson St.
Seattle, WA 98104-2881 (206) 223-5555
Contact: William J. Bain, Jr., Pres.

Financial data (yr. ended 12/31/01): Grants paid, $5,000; assets, $123,098 (M); expenditures, $7,119; qualifying distributions, $5,000.
Officers: William J. Bain, Jr., Pres.; David C. Hoedemaker, V.P.; James O. Jonassen, Secy.-Treas.
EIN: 916063190

56141
Gordon Stuart Peek Foundation
4009 Burke Ave. N.
Seattle, WA 98103 (206) 632-7586
Contact: Gordon S. Peek, Tr.

Established in 1998.
Donor(s): Gordon S. Peek.
Financial data (yr. ended 12/31/01): Grants paid, $5,000; assets, $235,213 (M); expenditures, $6,893; qualifying distributions, $5,000.
Application information: Application form not required.
Trustee: Gordon S. Peek.
EIN: 916478062

56142
Pinion Foundation
20645 N.E. 28th Ct.
Sammamish, WA 98074

Established in 2000.
Donor(s): Victor P. Fung, Ellen G. Fung.
Financial data (yr. ended 12/31/01): Grants paid, $5,000; assets, $8,279 (M); gifts received, $6,800; expenditures, $6,280; qualifying distributions, $5,000.
Limitations: Applications not accepted. Giving primarily in San Francisco, CA.
Application information: Contributes only to pre-selected organizations.
Trustees: Victor P. Fung, Ellen G. Fung.
EIN: 912089656

56143
The Rinne Foundation
2648 Cascadia Ave. S.
Seattle, WA 98144

Established in 2001 in WA.
Donor(s): Peggy P. Rinne, Robert D. Rinne.
Financial data (yr. ended 12/31/01): Grants paid, $5,000; assets, $92,746 (M); gifts received, $96,987; expenditures, $6,224; qualifying distributions, $5,000.
Limitations: Applications not accepted.
Application information: Contributes only to pre-selected organizations.
Officers and Directors:* Peggy P. Rinne,* Pres. and Treas.; Kristin S. Rinne,* V.P. and Secy.; Nancy Rinne,* V.P. and Admin.; Robert D. Rinne,* V.P.
EIN: 912057678

56144
The Arthur C. and Eleanor Schreiber Family Charitable Foundation
600 108th Ave., N.E., Ste. 1030
Bellevue, WA 98004-5110 (425) 455-6600
Contact: Terry Smith, Tr.

Established in 1992 in WA.
Donor(s): Eleanor Schreiber.
Financial data (yr. ended 12/31/01): Grants paid, $5,000; assets, $63,972 (M); expenditures, $5,535; qualifying distributions, $5,000.
Limitations: Giving primarily in Seattle, WA.
Application information: Application form not required.
Trustees: Phillip E. Egger, David Keene, Eleanor Schreiber, Terry Smith.
EIN: 911577866

56145
Skerbeck Family Garden Foundation
c/o Leon Skerbeck
3225 E. Masters Rd.
Port Angeles, WA 98362-9051

Established in 1993 in WA.
Donor(s): Frank Skerbeck.
Financial data (yr. ended 12/31/01): Grants paid, $5,000; assets, $32,163 (M); gifts received, $1,476; expenditures, $7,288; qualifying distributions, $5,000.
Limitations: Applications not accepted.
Application information: Contributes only to pre-selected organizations.
Officers: K. Ben Skerbeck, Pres.; Andy Skerbeck, Treas.
EIN: 916357409

56146
S.O.S. Foundation
2410 Boyer Ave. E, No. 1
Seattle, WA 98112

Established in 1997 in WA.
Donor(s): Joseph L. Brotherton.
Financial data (yr. ended 12/31/01): Grants paid, $4,995; assets, $27,319 (M); gifts received, $10,000; expenditures, $5,075; qualifying distributions, $4,995.
Limitations: Applications not accepted. Giving limited to WA.
Application information: Contributes only to pre-selected organizations.
Officers: Maureen P. Brotherton, Pres.; Joseph L. Brotherton, Secy.-Treas.
EIN: 911774695

56147
Albert L. LaPierre Foundation
c/o Desa Conniff
615 Commerce, Ste. 150
Tacoma, WA 98402
Contact: Leo Gese, Pres.

Financial data (yr. ended 06/30/02): Grants paid, $4,798; assets, $83,737 (M); expenditures, $5,763; qualifying distributions, $4,798.
Officers: Leo Gese, Pres.; Ernie LaPierre, V.P.; Mary Lou LaPierre, Secy.
EIN: 910775571

56148
David & Melinda Gladstone Foundation
P.O. Box 803
Snohomish, WA 98291-0803

Established in 1998 in WA.
Donor(s): David Gladstone, Melinda Gladstone.
Financial data (yr. ended 05/31/01): Grants paid, $4,750; assets, $3,294,440 (M); gifts received, $760,940; expenditures, $41,209; qualifying distributions, $4,750.
Limitations: Applications not accepted.
Application information: Contributes only to pre-selected organizations.
Officers: David Gladstone, Pres.; Melinda Gladstone, V.P.
EIN: 911817049

56149
Carl J. Erickson Scholarship Educational Fund
c/o Bank of America
P.O. Box 34345
Seattle, WA 98124-1474
Application address: c/o Merilyn Baker, Superintendent, Educational Service District 123, 124 S. 4th Ave., Pasco, WA 99301

Financial data (yr. ended 12/31/01): Grants paid, $4,650; assets, $103,893 (M); expenditures, $8,230; qualifying distributions, $6,436.
Limitations: Giving limited to residents of Benton County, WA.
Application information: Application form required.
Trustee: Bank of America.
EIN: 916025631
Codes: GTI

56150
Harry B. Boyce Trust
c/o Bank of America
P.O. Box 34345
Seattle, WA 98124-1345 (206) 358-3380
Application address: P.O. Box 24565, Seattle, WA 98124, tel.: (206) 358-3380
Contact: Jennifer Sorensen, Trust Off., Bank of America

Financial data (yr. ended 12/31/01): Grants paid, $4,529; assets, $144,020 (M); expenditures, $8,054; qualifying distributions, $5,916.
Limitations: Giving primarily in WA.
Trustee: Bank of America.
EIN: 916025115

56151
Cornerstone Foundation for Christian Ministry
1730 S. Jackson Ave.
Tacoma, WA 98465

Established in 1999 in WA.
Donor(s): David Groff, Jeanne Groff.
Financial data (yr. ended 06/30/02): Grants paid, $4,512; assets, $77,544 (M); gifts received, $4,000; expenditures, $5,359; qualifying distributions, $4,512.
Limitations: Applications not accepted.
Application information: Contributes only to pre-selected organizations.
Officers: David Groff, Pres.; Jeanne Groff, Secy.
EIN: 911997803

56152
Beck-Rocchi Student Loan Fund
c/o Wells Fargo Bank Northwest, N.A.
P.O. Box 2971, MAC 6540-141
Seattle, WA 98111

Established in 1997 in OR.
Donor(s): Frances Rocchi.
Financial data (yr. ended 11/30/01): Grants paid, $4,500; assets, $137,163 (M); expenditures, $84,235; qualifying distributions, $6,548.
Limitations: Applications not accepted. Giving primarily in Eugene, OR.
Application information: Contributes only to pre-selected organizations.
Trustee: Wells Fargo Bank Northwest, N.A.
EIN: 916460095

56153
Marjorie K. Johnson Charitable Foundation
501 Peyton Bldg.
Spokane, WA 99201

Established in 1983 in WA.
Financial data (yr. ended 11/30/01): Grants paid, $4,500; assets, $70,838 (M); expenditures, $6,720; qualifying distributions, $4,500.
Officers and Directors:* James K. Johnson,* Pres.; Nancy J. Lindsay,* Secy.
EIN: 911233339

56154
Ray Wittman Scholarship Fund
c/o Glenn H. Watts
2320 Vista Ln.
Anacortes, WA 98221

Established in 2001 in WA.
Donor(s): Ray Wittman.‡
Financial data (yr. ended 12/31/01): Grants paid, $4,247; assets, $136,862 (M); gifts received, $125,207; expenditures, $4,787; qualifying distributions, $4,787.
Officers: Glenn Watts, Pres.; James Keating, Secy.; Donald Schmude, Treas.
EIN: 912093449

56155
Alta Foundation
c/o David R. Bishop
P.O. Box 58664
Renton, WA 98058

Established in 1999 in WA.
Donor(s): David R. Bishop, Lynda F. Bishop.
Financial data (yr. ended 12/31/01): Grants paid, $4,200; assets, $365,705 (M); gifts received, $2,431; expenditures, $6,631; qualifying distributions, $4,200.
Limitations: Applications not accepted.
Application information: Contributes only to pre-selected organizations.
Trustees: Amanda Bishop, David R. Bishop, Lynda F. Bishop, Ginger Schmersal.
EIN: 912014274

56156
W. Murray Campbell Charitable Foundation
(Formerly Campbell Charitable Foundation)
4319 N.E. 44th St.
Seattle, WA 98105

Established in 1991 in WA.
Donor(s): W. Murray Campbell, Elizabeth Moody Campbell.
Financial data (yr. ended 12/31/01): Grants paid, $4,200; assets, $32,340 (M); expenditures, $4,992; qualifying distributions, $4,200.
Limitations: Applications not accepted. Giving primarily in DE.
Application information: Contributes only to pre-selected organizations.
Officer: W. Murray Campbell, Pres. and Treas.
EIN: 911531188

56157
News Tribune Scholarship Foundation
c/o Morning News Tribune, H.R. Dept.
1950 S. State St.
Tacoma, WA 98405-2860
Contact: Jerald L. Allen, Pres.

Established in 1989 in WA.
Donor(s): Tacoma News Inc.
Financial data (yr. ended 12/31/01): Grants paid, $4,200; assets, $125,758 (M); expenditures, $4,960; qualifying distributions, $4,200.
Limitations: Giving limited to Tacoma, WA.

56157—WASHINGTON

Application information: Application form required.
Officers: Jerald L. Allen, Pres.; Jim Hickey, V.P.; Shelley Beroth, Treas.
Directors: Elizabeth Brenner, Mike McKeller, Harry Thacker.
EIN: 943082120
Codes: CS, CD

56158
Harlowe Hardinge Foundation
7270 W. Mercer Way
Mercer Island, WA 98040-5534
Contact: H. DeForest Hardinge, Pres.

Financial data (yr. ended 12/31/01): Grants paid, $4,100; assets, $61,132 (M); expenditures, $4,547; qualifying distributions, $4,100.
Limitations: Giving primarily in Seattle, WA.
Application information: Application form not required.
Officers: H. DeForest Hardinge, Pres. and Treas.; Susan B. Hardinge, V.P. and Secy.
EIN: 236298100

56159
Bennion Foundation
1150 22nd Ave. E.
Seattle, WA 98112
Contact: Roy I. Bennion, Tr.

Donor(s): Roy I. Bennion.
Financial data (yr. ended 12/31/01): Grants paid, $4,096; assets, $66,023 (M); expenditures, $5,187; qualifying distributions, $4,055.
Limitations: Giving primarily in Seattle, WA.
Application information: Application form not required.
Trustees: Molly M. Bennion, Roy I. Bennion, Barbara Cook Brownback.
EIN: 760190590

56160
John J. and Georgiana Theodore Foundation
c/o John J. Theodore
407 98th Ave. N.E.
Bellevue, WA 98004

Established in 2000 in WA.
Donor(s): John J. Theodore.
Financial data (yr. ended 12/31/01): Grants paid, $4,052; assets, $100,889 (M); expenditures, $8,806; qualifying distributions, $4,052.
Limitations: Applications not accepted.
Application information: Contributes only to pre-selected organizations.
Officers and Directors:* John J. Theodore,* Pres. and Treas.; Holly Theodore Finan,* V.P. and Secy.; Vernon M. Parrett.
EIN: 912090317

56161
Freeman and Emma Grow Memorial Scholarship Fund
P.O. Box 134
Goldendale, WA 98620 (509) 773-4646
Contact: Daryl G. Erdman, Secy.

Financial data (yr. ended 12/31/01): Grants paid, $4,000; assets, $79,769 (M); expenditures, $4,392; qualifying distributions, $4,000.
Limitations: Giving limited to Goldendale, WA.
Application information: Application form not required.
Officers: Daryl G. Erdman, Secy.; Herb Callan, Treas.
Trustees: Charles Bruce, Ed Carlson, Robert Cole, Dan Hopkins, Philip Klassen, Robert Niemela, Alvin Randall, Clarence Schroder.
EIN: 237123616
Codes: GTI

56162
KE of DKE Alumni Scholarship Foundation
c/o Doug Campbell
The Highlands
Seattle, WA 98177

Donor(s): Barbara Himmelman, Duncan Bronson.
Financial data (yr. ended 12/31/99): Grants paid, $4,000; assets, $31,561 (M); expenditures, $4,000; qualifying distributions, $4,000.
Limitations: Applications not accepted. Giving limited to residents of Seattle, WA.
Officers: Paul Meyer, Pres.; Webster Augustine, V.P.; John Killian, Secy.; Douglas Campbell, Treas.
EIN: 911640438

56163
Henry M. and Donna J. Robinett Foundation
5819 N. Ridge Dr.
Snohomish, WA 98290

Established in 1999 in WA.
Donor(s): Donna J. Robinett, Henry M. Robinett.
Financial data (yr. ended 12/31/01): Grants paid, $4,000; assets, $3,132 (M); expenditures, $4,227; qualifying distributions, $4,000.
Limitations: Applications not accepted. Giving primarily in Snohomish, WA.
Application information: Contributes only to pre-selected organizations.
Officers: Henry M. Robinett, Pres.; Donna J. Robinett, V.P.; Julie Ann Smith, Secy.; Joan Robinett Wilson, Treas.
EIN: 911886791

56164
The Tooth Fairy Foundation
P.O. Box 22486
Seattle, WA 98122-0486

Established in 1995 in WA.
Donor(s): Peter T. Morse, Marcia L. Ellis.
Financial data (yr. ended 12/31/01): Grants paid, $4,000; assets, $3,844 (M); expenditures, $5,335; qualifying distributions, $4,000.
Limitations: Applications not accepted. Giving primarily in Seattle, WA.
Application information: Contributes only to pre-selected organizations.
Officers and Directors:* Marcia L. Ellis,* Pres.; Peter T. Morse,* Secy.; Janet M. Morse,* Treas.
EIN: 911704052

56165
Lillian E. Whitmore Educational Foundation
2200 6th Ave., Ste. 535
Seattle, WA 98121 (206) 441-6900

Donor(s): Lillian E. Whitmore.
Financial data (yr. ended 12/31/00): Grants paid, $4,000; assets, $20,525 (M); expenditures, $4,360; qualifying distributions, $3,978.
Limitations: Giving limited to residents of western WA.
Application information: Application form required.
Trustees: Elizabeth K. Marks, Michael Thanem, Lillian E. Whitmore.
EIN: 911324769
Codes: GTI

56166
The Odell Foundation
c/o Jack Odell
7510 Foster Slough Rd.
Snohomish, WA 98290-5834

Established in 2001 in WA.
Donor(s): Jack L. Odell II.
Financial data (yr. ended 12/31/01): Grants paid, $3,983; assets, $21,704 (M); gifts received, $28,009; expenditures, $6,306; qualifying distributions, $3,983.
Limitations: Applications not accepted. Giving primarily in WA.
Application information: Contributes only to pre-selected organizations.
Officers and Directors:* Jack L. Odell II,* Pres.; Judy L. Odell,* V.P.; Joel L. Odell,* Secy.
EIN: 912083265

56167
Dean & Gladys Webster Charitable Trust
c/o Wells Fargo Bank Northwest, N.A.
P.O. Box 21927
Seattle, WA 98111

Financial data (yr. ended 09/30/01): Grants paid, $3,774; assets, $108,195 (M); expenditures, $8,618; qualifying distributions, $5,344.
Limitations: Applications not accepted. Giving limited to Portland, OR.
Application information: Contributes only to pre-selected organizations.
Trustee: Wells Fargo Bank Northwest, N.A.
EIN: 936017382

56168
Kuehnle Charitable Foundation
c/o Don Peters
1436 N. Summit Blvd.
Spokane, WA 99201
Application address: 1156 Leisure Dr., Hayden, ID 83835, tel.: (208) 772-9775
Contact: Georgia M. Kuehnle, Pres.

Established in 1996 WA.
Donor(s): Georgia M. Kuehnle.
Financial data (yr. ended 12/31/01): Grants paid, $3,695; assets, $71,883 (M); expenditures, $5,163; qualifying distributions, $3,695.
Limitations: Giving primarily in ID and WA.
Application information: Application form not required.
Officers and Directors:* Georgia M. Kuehnle,* Pres.; Don Peters,* V.P.; Jeanette L. Thomas,* Secy.-Treas.; Kristine J. Carey.
EIN: 911743156

56169
The Filer Foundation
c/o Don Filer
4201 Roosevelt Way N.E.
Seattle, WA 98105

Established in 1997 in WA.
Donor(s): Don Filer.
Financial data (yr. ended 12/31/01): Grants paid, $3,600; assets, $67,586 (M); gifts received, $20,000; expenditures, $4,276; qualifying distributions, $3,464.
Limitations: Applications not accepted.
Application information: Contributes only to pre-selected organizations.
Directors: Don Filer, Douglas Filer.
EIN: 911808108

56170
Clarence A. & Mary B. Maulding Foundation
P.O. Box 21927
Seattle, WA 98111 (800) 981-9063

Established in 1996 in OR.
Financial data (yr. ended 12/31/01): Grants paid, $3,525; assets, $119,698 (M); expenditures, $13,779; qualifying distributions, $5,152.
Limitations: Applications not accepted.
Application information: Contributes only to pre-selected organizations.
Trustee: Wells Fargo Bank Northwest, N.A.
EIN: 936082009

56171
Raymond A. & Lois J. Hanson Charitable Trust and Foundation
2031 S. Parkwood Cir.
Spokane, WA 99223-5037

Financial data (yr. ended 12/31/01): Grants paid, $3,500; assets, $58,817 (M); gifts received, $6,812; expenditures, $5,327; qualifying distributions, $3,500.
Limitations: Giving primarily in Spokane, WA.
Trustee: Raymond A. Hanson.
EIN: 911797889

56172
Jones Family Foundation
c/o W. Bruce Jones, Jr.
3110 130th Pl., N.E.
Bellevue, WA 98005-1739

Established in 1999.
Donor(s): W. Bruce Jones, Jr., Joanne Jones.
Financial data (yr. ended 12/31/01): Grants paid, $3,500; assets, $212,742 (M); expenditures, $5,056; qualifying distributions, $3,500.
Limitations: Applications not accepted.
Application information: Contributes only to pre-selected organizations.
Officers and Directors:* W. Bruce Jones, Jr.,* Pres. and Treas.; Grace Potter Jones,* V.P.; Joanne Jones,* Secy.
EIN: 912010155

56173
Foundation for Grace
4525 N. 26th St.
Tacoma, WA 98407-4603

Financial data (yr. ended 12/31/01): Grants paid, $3,455; assets, $1 (M); gifts received, $124,702; expenditures, $126,623; qualifying distributions, $3,455.
Officers: David G. Curry, Pres.; Becky Dela Cruz, Secy.
Directors: John Williamson, Karin Williamson.
EIN: 911957852

56174
Reed & Sarah Hunt Fund
c/o Gooding & Emken
242 Taylor St.
Port Townsend, WA 98368-5717
Application address: 20708 N.E. 142nd, Woodinville, WA 98072, tel.: (206) 883-6639
Contact: Reed O. Hunt, Jr., Pres.

Financial data (yr. ended 12/31/01): Grants paid, $3,422; assets, $82,909 (M); expenditures, $4,113; qualifying distributions, $3,422.
Officers: Reed O. Hunt, Jr., Pres.; Patricia Hunt Nixon, V.P.; Reed O. Hunt III, Secy.
EIN: 946069799

56175
Mary L. Peterson Memorial Fund
c/o Bank of America
P.O. Box 34345, CSC-10
Seattle, WA 98124-1345
Application address: Portland Art Assoc., 1219 S.W. Parks, Portland, OR 97205
Contact: Willodean Oswald

Financial data (yr. ended 11/30/01): Grants paid, $3,162; assets, $296,512 (M); expenditures, $8,791; qualifying distributions, $3,162.
Limitations: Giving limited to OR.
Application information: Applications available from Pacific Northwest College of Art. Application form required.
Trustee: Bank of America.
EIN: 936137926

56176
Margaret Dunn Scholarship Fund
c/o Bank of America
P.O. Box 34345
Seattle, WA 98124-1345

Established in 1993 in WA.
Donor(s): Margaret Dunn.‡
Financial data (yr. ended 08/31/01): Grants paid, $3,159; assets, $309,416 (M); expenditures, $8,968; qualifying distributions, $3,159.
Limitations: Giving limited to WA.
Application information: Application form required.
Trustee: Bank of America.
EIN: 916365396

56177
Mackenzie Charitable Living Trust
9222 Lake City Way, N.E.
Seattle, WA 98115-3268

Financial data (yr. ended 12/31/00): Grants paid, $3,145; assets, $46,659 (M); expenditures, $3,145; qualifying distributions, $6,253.
Limitations: Applications not accepted.
Application information: Contributes only to pre-selected organizations.
Trustee: Michael Oliver.
EIN: 911986950

56178
Ark Foundation
5217 21st Ave. N.E.
Seattle, WA 98105 (206) 523-4874
Contact: Margaret H. Parkinson, Tr.

Donor(s): Karen M. Creason, Daya M. Parkinson, Margaret H. Parkinson.
Financial data (yr. ended 12/31/01): Grants paid, $3,130; assets, $81,032 (M); gifts received, $700; expenditures, $4,063; qualifying distributions, $3,502.
Limitations: Giving primarily in WA.
Trustees: Karen M. Creason, Margaret H. Parkinson.
EIN: 911163445

56179
Defeyter Foundation
c/o Walter J. Haig
42399 Whitestone Dr., N.
Creston, WA 99117-9748

Established in 1999.
Financial data (yr. ended 12/31/00): Grants paid, $3,000; assets, $513,132 (M); expenditures, $3,012; qualifying distributions, $3,000.
Limitations: Applications not accepted.
Application information: Contributes only to pre-selected organizations.
Trustees: Philip J. Carstens, Donald Defeyter, Walter J. Haig II.
EIN: 911529803

56180
Forest Clinic Foundation
717 W. Sprague Ave., Ste. 801
Spokane, WA 99204
Application address: P.O. Box 6082, Spokane, WA 99207, tel.: (509) 483-8211
Contact: Ernest Wales, Chair.

Financial data (yr. ended 03/31/99): Grants paid, $3,000; assets, $50,106 (M); expenditures, $3,310; qualifying distributions, $3,085.
Limitations: Giving in the U.S. limited to the Pacific Northwest, primarily in WA and ID; some giving also in British Columbia, Canada.
Application information: Applicants must be interested in the field of forest utilization. Application form required.
Officers and Directors:* Ernest Wales,* Chair.; Albert A. Stadtmueller,* Secy.; Allen L. Hearst.
EIN: 916033026

56181
The Hay Family Charitable Foundation
4 Diamond S Ranch
Bellevue, WA 98004-2820

Established in 1998 in WA.
Donor(s): David M. Hay, Melinda M. Hay.
Financial data (yr. ended 12/31/00): Grants paid, $3,000; assets, $97,729 (M); expenditures, $5,510; qualifying distributions, $3,000.
Limitations: Applications not accepted.
Application information: Contributes only to pre-selected organizations.
Officers and Trustees:* David M. Hay,* Mgr.; Melinda M. Hay,* Mgr.
EIN: 911909057

56182
Kiwanis Club of Ellensburg Foundation
c/o Bob Johnson
951 Cowboy Ln.
Ellensburg, WA 98926
Application address: 270 Kavina Rd., Ellensburg, WA 98926, tel.: (509) 962-2412
Contact: Phyliss Ocker, Dir.

Established in 1998 in WA.
Financial data (yr. ended 09/30/00): Grants paid, $3,000; assets, $44,994 (M); expenditures, $3,052; qualifying distributions, $3,000.
Limitations: Giving limited to Ellensburg, WA.
Officers: Susan Madley, Pres.; Steve Hydorn-Young, V.P.; Bob Johnson, Secy.-Treas.
Directors: Jerry W. Grebb, Ginger Howard, Phyliss Ocker, Dolores Osborne.
EIN: 911744021

56183
Scott Rhoads Memorial Foundation
7525 Pioneer Way, Ste. 101
Gig Harbor, WA 98335
Application address: 4260 185th Pl. S.E., Issaquah, WA 98027
Contact: James Binder, V.P.

Established in 1997 in WA.
Financial data (yr. ended 12/31/00): Grants paid, $3,000; assets, $19,598 (M); expenditures, $12,571; qualifying distributions, $3,000.
Application information: Application form required.
Officers: Tiffany Rhoads-Olson, Pres.; James Binder, V.P.; Michael Misner, Secy.; Carlton Kester, Treas.
Directors: Charles Crickmore, Daniel Holden, Matthew Rhoads.
EIN: 911735897

56184
Stever Family Foundation
c/o Thomas Stever
4826 118th Ave. N.E.
Kirkland, WA 98033

Donor(s): James Stever, Katherine Stever, Timothy Stever, Sondra Stever.
Financial data (yr. ended 11/30/01): Grants paid, $2,900; assets, $89,704 (M); gifts received, $1,500; expenditures, $4,020; qualifying distributions, $2,900.
Limitations: Applications not accepted.
Application information: Contributes only to pre-selected organizations.

56184—WASHINGTON

Officers: James H. Stever, Pres.; Katherine K. Stever, V.P.; Timothy J. Stever, Secy.; Thomas J. Stever, Treas.
Directors: Heidi Y. Stever, Sondra K. Stever.
EIN: 841366584

56185
The James M. Carrico Scholarship Fund
c/o Lauren Hanson
10690 Vantage Hwy.
Ellensburg, WA 98926
Application address: c/o Lance Hyatt, Kittitas High School, P.O. Box 599, Kittitas, WA 98934

Established in 1990 in WA.
Donor(s): James A. Carrico.‡
Financial data (yr. ended 12/31/00): Grants paid, $2,896; assets, $97,384 (M); expenditures, $3,268; qualifying distributions, $3,134.
Limitations: Giving limited to residents of the Kittitas, WA, area.
Application information: Applicant must include transcript.
Directors: Lauren Hanson, Cliff Hubbard, Jo Ann Iverson, Connie Meier, Steve Yocom.
EIN: 943138292

56186
The Winant Fund
15908 N.E. 198th St.
Woodinville, WA 98072
Application address: 5740 Sofia Pl., Washington, DC 20521-5740
Contact: John H. Winant, Tr.

Established in 2000 in VA.
Donor(s): John H. Winant, Jane J. Winant.
Financial data (yr. ended 12/31/01): Grants paid, $2,857; assets, $14,993 (M); gifts received, $9,749; expenditures, $3,000; qualifying distributions, $2,857.
Trustees: Jane J. Winant, John H. Winant.
EIN: 527076191

56187
The Evalyn O. Flory Foundation
11901 176th St. Circle NE, Ste. 3708
Redmond, WA 98052
Contact: Ella Nuckolls, Dir.

Established in 1999 in WA.
Financial data (yr. ended 12/31/01): Grants paid, $2,752; assets, $178,489 (M); expenditures, $3,411; qualifying distributions, $2,752.
Limitations: Giving primarily in Seattle, WA.
Application information: Application form not required.
Directors: Donald H. Dawson, Eleanor E. Dawson, Ella Nuckolls.
EIN: 911978571

56188
Olympic Lions Foundation
227 W. 8th St.
Port Angeles, WA 98362-6014

Established in 1988 in WA.
Financial data (yr. ended 04/30/02): Grants paid, $2,750; assets, $56,953 (M); gifts received, $556; expenditures, $2,846; qualifying distributions, $2,750.
Limitations: Applications not accepted.
Application information: Contributes only to pre-selected organizations.
Officers: Gary Reidel, Pres.; Charles S. McClain, Treas.
EIN: 911334867

56189
Paul Joseph Blanchard Scholarship Trust
c/o Bank of America
P.O. Box 34345
Seattle, WA 98124-1345
Application address: c/o Guidance Office, R.A. Long High School, Longview, WA 98632, tel.: (360) 577-2731

Financial data (yr. ended 12/31/00): Grants paid, $2,700; assets, $64,324 (M); expenditures, $4,814; qualifying distributions, $3,744.
Limitations: Giving limited to residents of Longview, WA.
Application information: Application form required.
Trustee: Bank of America.
EIN: 916381751

56190
The Laurence and Naomi Anderson Family Foundation
705 Second Ave., Ste 1200
Seattle, WA 98104

Donor(s): Naomi Anderson.
Financial data (yr. ended 12/31/99): Grants paid, $2,655; assets, $28,224 (M); gifts received, $5,950; expenditures, $4,987; qualifying distributions, $4,307.
Limitations: Applications not accepted. Giving primarily in WA.
Application information: Contributes only to pre-selected organizations.
Officers: Naomi Anderson, Pres.; Diana Blakney, Exec. V.P.; Betty Hawk, V.P.; Richard J. Grunenfelder, Secy.; Laurence Anderson, Treas.
EIN: 911695689

56191
Lane Medical Memorial Fund
c/o Wells Fargo Bank Northwest, N.A.
P.O. Box 21927
Seattle, WA 98111

Financial data (yr. ended 09/30/01): Grants paid, $2,640; assets, $72,671 (M); expenditures, $5,460; qualifying distributions, $4,277.
Limitations: Applications not accepted. Giving limited to Eugene, OR.
Application information: Contributes only to pre-selected organizations.
Trustee: Wells Fargo Bank Northwest, N.A.
EIN: 936030001

56192
The Cora Foundation
1501 4th Ave., Ste. 2070
Seattle, WA 98101-1679

Financial data (yr. ended 12/31/01): Grants paid, $2,600; assets, $19,247 (M); expenditures, $3,365; qualifying distributions, $2,600.
Limitations: Applications not accepted. Giving primarily in Seattle, WA.
Application information: Contributes only to pre-selected organizations.
Officers and Trustees:* Paul R. Harper,* Pres.; C.C. Harper,* Secy.; Melinda A. Buckley,* Treas.
EIN: 943105496

56193
Martin T. and Rebecca A. Chaney Foundation
5802 298th Ave. N.E.
Carnation, WA 98014

Established in 1999 in WA.
Donor(s): Rebecca A. Chaney.
Financial data (yr. ended 12/31/01): Grants paid, $2,592; assets, $68,227 (M); gifts received, $820; expenditures, $4,007; qualifying distributions, $2,592.
Officers: Martin T. Chaney, Pres. and Treas.; Rebecca A. Chaney, V.P. and Secy.
Directors: Alma G. Chaney, Myra J. Chaney.
EIN: 911960796

56194
Temcov Foundation
c/o Michael Temcov
P.O. Box 1332
Issaquah, WA 98027-0054 (425) 392-5353

Donor(s): John M. Temcov.‡
Financial data (yr. ended 12/31/01): Grants paid, $2,570; assets, $964,870 (M); gifts received, $171,050; expenditures, $13,809; qualifying distributions, $3,938.
Officers: Michael Temcov, Pres.; Dean Jacobus, V.P.; Aslam Khan, V.P.; Joanne Temcov, Secy.
EIN: 943255515

56195
Riverstyx Foundation
1420 5th Ave., Ste. 4400
Seattle, WA 98101

Established in 2000 in WA.
Donor(s): James L. Swift, Lauren Swift.
Financial data (yr. ended 12/31/01): Grants paid, $2,556; assets, $1,663,253 (M); gifts received, $1,279,183; expenditures, $4,528; qualifying distributions, $2,556.
Limitations: Applications not accepted.
Application information: Contributes only to pre-selected organizations.
Officers: James L. Swift, Pres.; Lantson E. Eldred, V.P. and Secy.; Lauren Swift, Treas.
EIN: 943373712

56196
Andrew Bell Foundation
260 N.W. Birch Pl.
Issaquah, WA 98027

Established in 2000 in WA.
Financial data (yr. ended 12/31/00): Grants paid, $2,500; assets, $1,342 (M); gifts received, $7,500; expenditures, $6,158; qualifying distributions, $2,500.
Limitations: Giving primarily in Seattle, WA.
Officers: Andrew Bell, Pres.; Mary Swan, Secy.
EIN: 912043375

56197
Imagine Foundation
c/o Thomas F. Richardson
3443 E. Lake Sammamish Shore Ln., N.E.
Sammamish, WA 98074-4345

Established in 1999.
Financial data (yr. ended 12/31/00): Grants paid, $2,500; assets, $45,156 (M); gifts received, $8,000; expenditures, $6,235; qualifying distributions, $2,500.
Trustee: Thomas F. Richardson.
EIN: 916498745

56198
Fox Family Charitable Trust
50 W. Sentry Dr.
Shelton, WA 98584

Financial data (yr. ended 12/31/00): Grants paid, $2,450; assets, $104,515 (L); gifts received, $98,000; expenditures, $2,475; qualifying distributions, $2,450.
Limitations: Applications not accepted.
Application information: Contributes only to pre-selected organizations.
Director: Clarence J. Williams.
EIN: 911878648

56199
The Beckmann Foundation
14501 S.E. 51st St.
Bellevue, WA 98006-3509

Donor(s): Janet P. Beckmann.
Financial data (yr. ended 12/31/01): Grants paid, $2,432; assets, $49,058 (M); gifts received, $374; expenditures, $4,036; qualifying distributions, $2,432.
Limitations: Applications not accepted.
Application information: Contributes only to pre-selected organizations.
Trustees: Janet P. Beckmann, Dorothy D. Pitts.
EIN: 911819651

56200
Margueryte & Bern Mercer Scholarship & Loan Fund
c/o Marilu Smith
P.O. Box 809
Prosser, WA 99350-0809 (509) 786-2403

Financial data (yr. ended 12/31/01): Grants paid, $2,400; assets, $26,453 (M); expenditures, $2,596; qualifying distributions, $2,356.
Limitations: Applications not accepted. Giving limited to residents of Prosser, WA.
Officers: Marilu Smith, Pres.; Darrel K. Smith, V.P.; Sheryl Beck, Secy.
EIN: 911104215

56201
The Peacock Group
15521 N.E. 9th Circle
Vancouver, WA 98684

Donor(s): J. Bruce Peacock.
Financial data (yr. ended 12/31/01): Grants paid, $2,250; assets, $58,777 (M); gifts received, $10,500; expenditures, $2,687; qualifying distributions, $2,250.
Limitations: Applications not accepted.
Application information: Contributes only to pre-selected organizations.
Officers: Jeffrey C. Madsen, Pres.; David M. McGill, V.P.; Jeffrey B. Peacock, Secy.; J. Brad Peacock, Treas.
EIN: 911919144

56202
L & M Foundation
c/o I. Joan Berkowitz
P.O. Box 150
Olga, WA 98279

Financial data (yr. ended 12/31/01): Grants paid, $2,225; assets, $79,540 (M); expenditures, $2,797; qualifying distributions, $2,225.
Limitations: Applications not accepted.
Application information: Contributes only to pre-selected organizations.
Trustees: I. Joan Berkowitz, Glenn Matthews, Mark Matthews.
EIN: 046029209

56203
Glynn H. Bloomquist Scholarship Trust
c/o Security State Bank
P.O. Box 1050
Centralia, WA 98531

Financial data (yr. ended 12/31/00): Grants paid, $2,200; assets, $74,564 (M); gifts received, $276; expenditures, $4,403; qualifying distributions, $3,787.
Limitations: Applications not accepted. Giving limited to residents of WA.
Application information: Unsolicited requests for funds not accepted.
Trustee: Security State Bank.

EIN: 916264297

56204
Javid Foundation
c/o Farhang Javid
9916 Marine View Dr.
Mukilteo, WA 98275

Established in 2000 in WA.
Donor(s): Farhang Javid.
Financial data (yr. ended 12/31/01): Grants paid, $2,200; assets, $24,503 (M); gifts received, $7,425; expenditures, $2,227; qualifying distributions, $2,200.
Limitations: Applications not accepted.
Application information: Contributes only to pre-selected organizations.
Trustee: Farhang Javid.
EIN: 916506502

56205
Gienapp Family Foundation
12055 Lakeside Pl. N.E.
Seattle, WA 98125

Established in 2001.
Donor(s): John Gienapp.
Financial data (yr. ended 12/31/01): Grants paid, $2,155; assets, $46,180 (M); expenditures, $2,525; qualifying distributions, $2,155.
Limitations: Giving primarily in WA.
Officers: John C. Gienapp, Pres.; Katie A. Gienapp, V.P.; Anne A. Gienapp, Treas.
EIN: 912154805

56206
Red Electric Foundation
52 Thomas Rd.
Underwood, WA 98651

Established in 2000 in OR.
Donor(s): Cam Thomas.
Financial data (yr. ended 06/30/02): Grants paid, $2,150; assets, $147,468 (M); gifts received, $19,766; expenditures, $4,326; qualifying distributions, $2,150.
Limitations: Applications not accepted.
Application information: Contributes only to pre-selected organizations.
Board Members: Randy Knowles, Gene Ann Osterberg, Cam Thomas.
EIN: 912092459

56207
Jay Baumann Memorial Association
c/o Dennis Williams
119 N. Commercial, Rm. 1340
Bellingham, WA 98225-4458

Financial data (yr. ended 12/31/01): Grants paid, $2,100; assets, $17,886 (M); expenditures, $2,556; qualifying distributions, $2,100.
Limitations: Applications not accepted. Giving limited to WA.
Application information: Contributes only to pre-selected organizations.
Directors: Joyce Baumann, Dennis Williams.
EIN: 366142749

56208
The Shaun P. McCarthey Foundation
11120 N.E. 2nd St., No. 200
Bellevue, WA 98004

Financial data (yr. ended 12/31/01): Grants paid, $2,035; assets, $20,776 (M); gifts received, $400; expenditures, $2,435; qualifying distributions, $2,035.
Trustees: Maureen McCarthey, Shaun P. McCarthey, Terrence Stephens.
EIN: 911940913

56209
Ancilla Foundation
2205 169th Ave. N.E.
Bellevue, WA 98008

Established in 2000 in WA.
Donor(s): Silas Chai, Lucy Chao.
Financial data (yr. ended 04/30/02): Grants paid, $2,000; assets, $24,514 (M); gifts received, $13,597; expenditures, $3,287; qualifying distributions, $2,000.
Limitations: Applications not accepted. Giving primarily in New York, NY and Dallas, TX.
Application information: Contributes only to pre-selected organizations.
Officers: Silas Chai, Pres. and Treas.; Lucy Chao, V.P. and Secy.
Director: Ruth Lao.
EIN: 912038013

56210
Bishop Family Foundation
1419 42nd Ave. E.
Seattle, WA 98112

Established in 2001 in WA.
Donor(s): Mary R. Zeeb.
Financial data (yr. ended 12/31/01): Grants paid, $2,000; assets, $1,001,209 (M); gifts received, $1,000,000; expenditures, $2,011; qualifying distributions, $2,000.
Limitations: Applications not accepted.
Application information: Contributes only to pre-selected organizations.
Officers: Kim L. Bishop, Pres., V.P. and Treas.; Betty Dykstra, Secy.
EIN: 912162740

56211
The Robert A. Closson, M.D. Memorial Scholarship Trust
705 E. Upper A St.
Colfax, WA 99111-1626 (509) 397-2466
Contact: Donna Closson, Tr.

Financial data (yr. ended 12/31/01): Grants paid, $2,000; assets, $21,722 (M); expenditures, $2,004; qualifying distributions, $2,000.
Limitations: Giving primarily in Colfax, WA.
Application information: Application form required.
Trustee: Donna Closson.
EIN: 916390505

56212
The Didomi Foundation
1201 3rd. Ave., Ste. 3400
Seattle, WA 98101-3034
Application address: 2712 94th Ave. N.E., Bellevue, WA 98004, tel.: (425) 454-1136
Contact: Cabot J. Dow, Pres.

Financial data (yr. ended 12/31/01): Grants paid, $2,000; assets, $21,860 (M); gifts received, $1,500; expenditures, $2,442; qualifying distributions, $2,004.
Limitations: Giving limited to residents of WA.
Application information: Application form required.
Officers and Directors:* Cabot J. Dow,* Pres. and Treas.; Robert L. Gunter,* V.P. and Secy.
EIN: 911226492

56213
Arthur L. Foss Foundation
P.O. Box 1038
Gig Harbor, WA 98335

Established in 1999 in WA.
Donor(s): Holly E. D'Annunzio.

56213—WASHINGTON

Financial data (yr. ended 12/31/01): Grants paid, $2,000; assets, $18,228 (M); expenditures, $2,262; qualifying distributions, $2,000.
Limitations: Applications not accepted.
Application information: Contributes only to pre-selected organizations.
Officers and Directors:* Michael D'Annunzio,* Pres.; Holly F. D'Annunzio,* V.P. and Treas.; Sue Foss,* Secy.
EIN: 912002441

56214
The Fred W. Hill Foundation
c/o Sherard McGonagle & Green
P.O. Box 400
Poulsbo, WA 98370
Application address: c/o Senior Counselor, North Kitsap High School, 1780 NE Hostmark St., Poulsbo, WA 98370-7682

Established in 1995 in WA.
Donor(s): Peter J. Hill, Frederick D. Hill.
Financial data (yr. ended 12/31/01): Grants paid, $2,000; assets, $27,250 (M); gifts received, $1,000; expenditures, $2,628; qualifying distributions, $2,000.
Application information: Application form required.
Officers and Directors:* Frederick D. Hill,* Pres.; Peter J. Hill,* V.P.; Nancy Bryant, James F. Hill, John Hummel.
EIN: 911473434

56215
Lincoln Mutual Services, Inc. No. 1 Educational Trust, Inc.
c/o Lincoln Mutual Services, Inc., No. 1
P.O. Box 177
Almira, WA 99103-0177 (509) 639-2421

Donor(s): Lincoln Mutual Services, Inc. No. 1.
Financial data (yr. ended 11/30/01): Grants paid, $2,000; assets, $9,813 (M); expenditures, $2,000; qualifying distributions, $2,000.
Limitations: Giving limited to Almira, WA, and surrounding areas.
Application information: Application form required.
Directors: Todd Bodeau, Shawn Groh, Bill Higginbotham, John Hughes, Terry Poe, Bob Sieg.
EIN: 911294560
Codes: CS, CD

56216
Ralph and Sandra Richardson Miller Foundation
6900 S.E. Riverside Dr., Ste. 19
Vancouver, WA 98664

Established in 2001 in WA.
Donor(s): Community Foundation for Southwest Washington.
Financial data (yr. ended 12/31/01): Grants paid, $2,000; assets, $62,988 (M); gifts received, $63,888; expenditures, $2,150; qualifying distributions, $2,000.
Limitations: Applications not accepted. Giving primarily in OR and WA.
Application information: Contributes only to pre-selected organizations.
Officers: Sandra Richardson Miller, Pres.; Ralph Miller, Secy.-Treas.
EIN: 912144806

56217
VanDerbeek Foundation
155 108th Ave. N.E., Ste. 110
Bellevue, WA 98004-5928

Established in 1998 in WA.
Donor(s): John VanDerbeek.

Financial data (yr. ended 12/31/01): Grants paid, $2,000; assets, $15,807 (M); expenditures, $2,020; qualifying distributions, $2,000.
Limitations: Applications not accepted. Giving primarily in Aberdeen, WA.
Application information: Contributes only to pre-selected organizations.
Officers: John VanDerbeek, Pres.; Diane VanDerbeek, V.P.
EIN: 911898393

56218
Lane Walker Foundation
5111 Harbor Ln.
Everett, WA 98203-1556

Donor(s): Terry F. Walker, Sandra L. Walker.
Financial data (yr. ended 12/31/01): Grants paid, $2,000; assets, $24,717 (M); gifts received, $12,374; expenditures, $2,021; qualifying distributions, $2,000.
Limitations: Applications not accepted.
Application information: Contributes only to pre-selected organizations.
Officers: Sandra L. Walker, Pres.; Terry F. Walker, V.P.
EIN: 911948479

56219
Yakima Valley Dairy Scholarship Foundation
128 N. 2nd St.
Yakima, WA 98901-2814

Donor(s): Lynnel Rowan.
Financial data (yr. ended 12/31/00): Grants paid, $2,000; assets, $18,874 (M); expenditures, $2,103; qualifying distributions, $2,000.
Limitations: Giving limited to residents of WA.
Officer: Carol Van Slageren, Pres.
EIN: 911796898

56220
Christian Discipleship Foundation
11103 216th St. E.
Graham, WA 98338

Financial data (yr. ended 12/31/00): Grants paid, $1,950; assets, $35,620 (M); expenditures, $1,983; qualifying distributions, $1,950.
Limitations: Applications not accepted. Giving primarily in the Spokane, WA area.
Application information: Contributes only to pre-selected organizations.
Officers: Stanley Baker, Pres.; Dale L. Stol, Secy.
EIN: 510152651

56221
Jessie Pepper Padelford Scholarship Fund-Sigma Kappa Alumnae
1906 N.W. 97th
Federal Way, WA 98003 (253) 838-4978
Contact: Deverie Thompson

Classified as a private operating foundation in 1979.
Financial data (yr. ended 07/31/00): Grants paid, $1,850; assets, $34,589 (M); gifts received, $505; expenditures, $2,315; qualifying distributions, $1,885.
Limitations: Giving limited to Seattle, WA.
Application information: Contact the Univ. of WA Scholarship Office for information.
Officers: Grace Ogrosky, Pres.; Carol Leak, Secy.; Barbara Moore, Treas.
EIN: 911067412

56222
Christian Foundation of America
20613 6th Ave., S.W.
Seattle, WA 98166-4156
Application address: 2800 S. 192nd, Ste. 104, Seattle, WA 98166, tel.: (206) 246-8772
Contact: Phil Rehberg, Tr.

Established in 1997 in WA.
Donor(s): Jean Rehberg.
Financial data (yr. ended 12/31/01): Grants paid, $1,800; assets, $34,174 (M); gifts received, $2,772; expenditures, $2,659; qualifying distributions, $1,800.
Limitations: Giving primarily in WA.
Application information: Application form not required.
Trustees: Phil J. Rehberg, Ryan Rehberg, Robert Wheatly, Victor Wolfer.
EIN: 943048638

56223
Brent C. & Mary Katherine Nicholson Foundation
2333 Carillon Pt.
Kirkland, WA 98033
Application address: 1900-112th Ave. N.E., Bellevue, WA 98004, tel.: (425) 454-9950
Contact: Stephen J. Hopps, Tr.

Established in 1996 in WA.
Donor(s): Brent C. Nicholson, Mary K. Nicholson.
Financial data (yr. ended 12/31/99): Grants paid, $1,701; assets, $43,545 (M); gifts received, $10,363; expenditures, $2,246; qualifying distributions, $1,701.
Managers: Brent C. Nicholson, Mary K. Nicholson.
Trustee: Stephen J. Hopps.
EIN: 911747008

56224
The Williams Douthitt Lawrence Fund
(Formerly The Douthitt Fund)
3111 37th Pl. S.
Seattle, WA 98144-6207
Contact: Margaret Williams, Tr.

Financial data (yr. ended 12/31/01): Grants paid, $1,700; assets, $21,888 (M); expenditures, $2,035; qualifying distributions, $1,700.
Limitations: Giving limited to residents of Seattle, WA.
Trustees: Margaret Williams, Paul Williams, Raymond Williams.
EIN: 911205903

56225
Dedicated Service
2187 Crescent Beach Rd.
Port Angeles, WA 98363-8703

Financial data (yr. ended 10/31/00): Grants paid, $1,500; assets, $28,704 (M); expenditures, $1,686; qualifying distributions, $1,487; giving activities include $165 for programs.
Officers: Carol Ann Novak, Pres.; Joan Michaelson, V.P.; Marsha Kim Holbrook, Treas.
Director: Beth Felgate Srsen.
EIN: 237065990

56226
Florence S. Kitchen Education Scholarship Fund
P.O. Box 188
Arlington, WA 98223-0188 (360) 435-2168
Contact: David E. Duskin, Tr.

Financial data (yr. ended 09/30/00): Grants paid, $1,500; assets, $0 (M); expenditures, $1,500; qualifying distributions, $1,500.

Limitations: Giving limited to residents of Arlington, WA.
Application information: Application form required.
Trustees: David E. Duskin, Mabel S. McPherron, Alma Jean Tenbrink.
EIN: 911346502

56227
Charles E. Stuart Scholarship Fund
c/o Bank of America
P.O. Box 34345
Seattle, WA 98124-1345
Application address: c/o 1301 5th Ave., Ste. 2828., Seattle, WA 98101
Contact: Robert Behnke

Financial data (yr. ended 12/31/01): Grants paid, $1,500; assets, $161,105 (M); expenditures, $6,457; qualifying distributions, $4,341; giving activities include $1,500 for loans to individuals.
Limitations: Giving limited to WA.
Application information: Application form required.
Trustee: Bank of America.
EIN: 916026757
Codes: GTI

56228
David P. Taylor, Sr. Scholarship Foundation
5801 3rd Ave. S.
P.O. Box 80983
Seattle, WA 98108-3205 (206) 762-8585
Contact: Ronald S. Taylor, Tr.

Established in 1986 in WA.
Financial data (yr. ended 12/31/01): Grants paid, $1,500; assets, $17,857 (M); expenditures, $6,188; qualifying distributions, $1,494.
Limitations: Giving limited to residents of WA.
Application information: Application form required.
Trustees: David P. Taylor, Ronald S. Taylor.
EIN: 911346191

56229
Heins Global Foundation
100 2nd Ave., S.
Edmonds, WA 98020

Established in 2001 in WA.
Financial data (yr. ended 12/31/01): Grants paid, $1,300; assets, $3,820 (M); gifts received, $5,116; expenditures, $5,010; qualifying distributions, $1,300.
Officers: Cory Heins, Pres.; Helen Heins, V.P. and Secy.
Director: Doug Ruecker.
EIN: 912134967

56230
Ida M. Greer Scholarship Trust
100 W. 1st St.
Aberdeen, WA 98520-6202 (360) 533-3370
Contact: Harold L. Warren, Tr.

Financial data (yr. ended 12/31/01): Grants paid, $1,150; assets, $28,138 (M); gifts received, $2,000; expenditures, $1,375; qualifying distributions, $1,150.
Limitations: Giving limited to Aberdeen, WA.
Application information: Application form not required.
Trustees: Kenneth Erickson, Harold L. Warren.
EIN: 916085719

56231
Cahoon Memorial Scholarship Trust
517 10th Ave. W.
Kirkland, WA 98033
Application address: Twila Ostrander, Counselor, c/o Eisenhower High School, 702 S. 40th, Yakima, WA 98908

Financial data (yr. ended 12/31/99): Grants paid, $1,000; assets, $12,417 (M); expenditures, $1,000; qualifying distributions, $1,000.
Limitations: Giving limited to Yakima, WA.
Application information: Application form required.
Trustees: Bruce P. Lainter, Camille C. Winter, Principal, Eisenhower H.S.
EIN: 916248672

56232
The Dolsen Foundation I
301 N. 3rd St.
Yakima, WA 98901

Established in 2000 in WA.
Financial data (yr. ended 02/28/02): Grants paid, $1,000; assets, $209,444 (M); gifts received, $205,000; expenditures, $1,304; qualifying distributions, $1,000.
Limitations: Applications not accepted.
Application information: Contributes only to pre-selected organizations.
Trustees: Robert Dolsen, Ruth Dolsen.
EIN: 912084086

56233
Gasparovich Memorial Scholarship Award Fund
6701 160th St. S.W.
Edmonds, WA 98026
Application address: c/o Mary Coble, Ingraham High School, 1819 N. 135th St., Seattle, WA 98133, tel.: (206) 252-3880

Financial data (yr. ended 12/31/01): Grants paid, $1,000; assets, $27,428 (M); gifts received, $1,000; expenditures, $1,114; qualifying distributions, $1,114.
Limitations: Giving limited to Seattle, WA.
Application information: Students recommended through Ingraham High School Athletic Dept.
Officers: Michael B. Rohrbach, Pres. and Treas.; June Gasparovich, V.P.; May Namba, Secy.
Director: Jeff LeMaine.
EIN: 910986139

56234
Roger J. Gill Memorial Fund, Inc.
c/o J.W. Lamoureux
326 N. 137th St.
Seattle, WA 98133-7409 (206) 864-0328

Established in 1994 in WA.
Financial data (yr. ended 12/31/99): Grants paid, $1,000; assets, $25,873 (M); gifts received, $643; expenditures, $1,122; qualifying distributions, $1,122.
Officers: John Heider, Pres.; John Paul Dean, V.P.; Leslie L. Jankowski, Secy; J. William Lamoureux, Treas.
EIN: 911649689

56235
The Curtis P. Lindley and Mary B. Lindley Charitable Foundation
P.O. Box 53050
Bellevue, WA 98015 (425) 450-3300
Contact: Curtis P. Lindley, Dir.

Established in 1994 in WA.
Donor(s): Curtis P. Lindley, Mary B. Lindley.

Financial data (yr. ended 12/31/01): Grants paid, $1,000; assets, $11,033 (M); expenditures, $1,132; qualifying distributions, $1,000.
Limitations: Giving primarily in WA.
Application information: Application form not required.
Directors: Curtis P. Lindley, Mary B. Lindley.
EIN: 911661865

56236
Lotus Foundation
805 27th Ave.
Seattle, WA 98122

Established in 2000 in WA.
Donor(s): Georgiana Stevens, Philip Krohon, Michael Casey, Jeanie Casey.
Financial data (yr. ended 12/31/01): Grants paid, $1,000; assets, $33,736 (M); gifts received, $2,075; expenditures, $3,466; qualifying distributions, $1,000.
Limitations: Applications not accepted.
Application information: Contributes only to pre-selected organizations.
Trustees: Shannon B. Casey, Edward C. Welch.
EIN: 912054073

56237
Mary Rosser Pool Foundation
PMB 308 6523 California Ave. S.W.
Seattle, WA 98136

Donor(s): David L. Pool.
Financial data (yr. ended 12/31/01): Grants paid, $1,000; assets, $2,654 (M); gifts received, $2,201; expenditures, $2,611; qualifying distributions, $1,000.
Limitations: Applications not accepted.
Application information: Contributes only to pre-selected organizations.
Officers: David L. Pool, Pres.; Marna R. Woody, V.P.; Hubert Leavy Rosser, Secy.
EIN: 911935462

56238
San Juan County Parks Foundation
P.O. Box 106
Shaw Island, WA 98286

Financial data (yr. ended 12/31/99): Grants paid, $1,000; assets, $11,938 (M); gifts received, $12,200; expenditures, $1,000; qualifying distributions, $1,000.
Officers: Cathaleen T. Cavanoch, Pres.; Lynn Bahmick, Secy.-Treas.
Directors: Lola Deane, Maile Johnson.
EIN: 911953899

56239
Dean and Evelyn Sloppy Foundation
P.O. Box 429
Salkum, WA 98582-0429

Established in 1997 in WA.
Donor(s): Dean A. Sloppy, Evelyn Sloppy.
Financial data (yr. ended 12/31/01): Grants paid, $1,000; assets, $14,909 (M); expenditures, $2,016; qualifying distributions, $1,503.
Limitations: Applications not accepted.
Application information: Unsolicited requests for funds not accepted.
Officers: Dean A. Sloppy, Pres. and Treas.; Evelyn Sloppy, V.P. and Secy.
Director: P. Craig Walker.
EIN: 911800856

56240—WASHINGTON

56240
John C. Sourapas Educational Fund
c/o Bank of America, Tax Services
P.O. Box 34345
Seattle, WA 98124-1345

Established in 1989 in WA.
Financial data (yr. ended 12/31/99): Grants paid, $1,000; assets, $69,492 (M); expenditures, $4,997; qualifying distributions, $3,117.
Limitations: Applications not accepted. Giving limited to Astros, Greece.
Application information: Recipients are selected by Scholarship Comm.
Trustee: Bank of America.
EIN: 936018825

56241
Ziegler Family Scholarship Trust
717 W. Sprague
Spokane, WA 99204
Application address: c/o Admin. Office, John R. Rogers High School, 1622 E. Wellesley, Spokane, WA 99207

Established in 1990 in WA.
Donor(s): Vern E. Ziegler, Mary E. Ziegler.
Financial data (yr. ended 12/31/00): Grants paid, $1,000; assets, $41,526 (M); expenditures, $1,984; qualifying distributions, $1,000.
Limitations: Giving limited to Spokane, WA.
Application information: Application form required.
Trustee: Washington Trust Bank.
EIN: 916322757

56242
Seeley Foundation
P.O. Box 1123
Olympia, WA 98507

Financial data (yr. ended 12/31/01): Grants paid, $905; assets, $21,237 (M); expenditures, $1,131; qualifying distributions, $905.
Limitations: Giving primarily in WA.
Officers: Marian Seeley, Pres.; Gary Seeley, V.P.
EIN: 911072498

56243
Richard E. Fisch Memorial Scholarship Fund
c/o Janet Fisch
620 W. 9th St.
Port Angeles, WA 98362-7303

Established as a private operating foundation in 1995.
Financial data (yr. ended 10/31/01): Grants paid, $811; assets, $12,153 (M); expenditures, $811; qualifying distributions, $811.
Limitations: Applications not accepted. Giving primarily in WA.
Application information: Contributes only to pre-selected organizations.
Directors: Janet Fisch, Karl Fisch, Lisa Fisch, James Lunt.
EIN: 911517024

56244
The Young Foundation
c/o Carol E. Weismiller
305 Woodbridge Dr.
Port Ludlow, WA 98365

Financial data (yr. ended 12/31/01): Grants paid, $800; assets, $8,750 (M); gifts received, $5,000; expenditures, $1,952; qualifying distributions, $800.
Officer and Director:* Carol E. Weismiller,* C.E.O.
EIN: 943270349

56245
Magnolia Public Swimming Pool Corp.
c/o Tim Washburn
P.O. Box 99096
Seattle, WA 98199-8096

Financial data (yr. ended 12/31/01): Grants paid, $788; assets, $15,601 (M); expenditures, $788; qualifying distributions, $788.
Limitations: Applications not accepted.
Application information: Contributes only to pre-selected organizations.
Officers: T. Stewart, Pres.; Duncan Eader, V.P.; Will Show, Secy.; Tim Washburn, Treas.
EIN: 911561740

56246
Lillian M. Bailey Trust for Selkirk Consolidated School District
c/o Washington Trust Bank
P.O. Box 2127
Spokane, WA 99210-2127
Application address: c/o Selkirk School District, P.O. Box 129, Metaline Falls, WA 99153

Financial data (yr. ended 05/31/00): Grants paid, $750; assets, $16,668 (M); expenditures, $1,403; qualifying distributions, $750.
Limitations: Giving limited to Selkirk, WA residents.
Application information: Application form not required.
Trustee: Washington Trust Bank.
EIN: 916200172

56247
The Willox Foundation
c/o William McGonagle
241 Madison Ave.
Bainbridge Island, WA 98110

Established in 1998.
Financial data (yr. ended 12/31/01): Grants paid, $713; assets, $409,515 (M); gifts received, $3,000; expenditures, $6,253; qualifying distributions, $713.
Trustees: Robert Gray, Peter Hintziglou, William McGonagle.
EIN: 363669269

56248
Friends of the Loomis Forest
P.O. Box 36
Loomis, WA 98827-0036

Financial data (yr. ended 03/31/00): Grants paid, $705; assets, $5,174 (M); gifts received, $5,082; expenditures, $3,927; qualifying distributions, $705.
Limitations: Applications not accepted.
Application information: Contributes only to pre-selected organizations.
Directors: Linnea Riedel, Mark Skatud, Mark Vine.
EIN: 943162054

56249
Keith & Sonia Moore Foundation
14241 N.E. Woodinville-Duvall Rd.
Woodinville, WA 98072

Established in 1999 in WA.
Donor(s): C. Keith Moore, Sonia M. Moore.
Financial data (yr. ended 12/31/00): Grants paid, $648; assets, $182,988 (M); expenditures, $10,762; qualifying distributions, $8,257.
Limitations: Applications not accepted.
Application information: Contributes only to pre-selected organizations.
Trustees: C. Keith Moore, Sonia M. Moore.
EIN: 916498742

56250
James S. Black Memorial Scholarship Foundation
1924 N. Ash St.
Spokane, WA 99205-4206
Contact: David R. Black, V.P.

Financial data (yr. ended 12/31/99): Grants paid, $500; assets, $12,351 (M); expenditures, $563; qualifying distributions, $563.
Limitations: Giving primarily in Spokane, WA.
Application information: Application form required.
Officers: Robert M. Higgins, Pres.; David R. Black, V.P.; RuthAnn Zigler, Secy.
EIN: 911324117

56251
Crumb Memorial Foundation
236 E. 9th St.
Port Angeles, WA 98362

Established in 1986 in WA.
Donor(s): Rose Crumb.
Financial data (yr. ended 08/31/01): Grants paid, $500; assets, $11,511 (M); gifts received, $20; expenditures, $508; qualifying distributions, $500.
Limitations: Applications not accepted. Giving primarily in Port Angeles, WA.
Application information: Contributes only to pre-selected organizations.
Officers: Rose Crumb, Pres.; Gregory Crumb, V.P.
EIN: 911355705

56252
D.A.S.H. Charitable Foundation
c/o Stan Halle
4225 Sunrise Hts. N.W.
Olympia, WA 98502-9207

Established in 1986 in WA.
Donor(s): Stan Halle, Robin Shipman.
Financial data (yr. ended 10/31/00): Grants paid, $500; assets, $18,526 (M); expenditures, $775; qualifying distributions, $775; giving activities include $775 for programs.
Limitations: Applications not accepted. Giving primarily in WA.
Application information: Contributes only to pre-selected organizations.
Officers and Directors:* Robin B. Shipman,* Pres.; Stan Halle,* V.P. and Treas.; Ruth Shipman,* Secy.
EIN: 911383073

56253
MacDonald-Will Foundation
1517 S. Tacoma Way
Tacoma, WA 98409 (253) 472-4428
Contact: Bruce MacDonald, Mgr.

Financial data (yr. ended 12/31/01): Grants paid, $500; assets, $452,775 (M); gifts received, $6,000; expenditures, $11,261; qualifying distributions, $2,581.
Limitations: Giving primarily in Pierce County, WA.
Officer: Bruce MacDonald, Mgr.
EIN: 910789771

56254
The Miller Family Foundation
c/o Jeri C. Miller
209 E. 4th, Ste. 202
Olympia, WA 98501-6967
Application address: P.O. Box 263, Cut Bank, MT 59427
Contact: Evelyn Munsom

Established around 1993.

Financial data (yr. ended 12/31/01): Grants paid, $500; assets, $16,841 (M); expenditures, $0; qualifying distributions, $0.
Limitations: Giving limited to residents of Cut Bank, MT.
Application information: Application form not required.
Officers: Jeri C. Miller, Pres.; Wallace G. Miller, Secy.
EIN: 943182082

56255
Wendy K. Mittlestadt Memorial Foundation
25604 Pioneer Way
Poulsbo, WA 98370-9504

Donor(s): Roger Mittelstadt, Myra Mittelstadt.
Financial data (yr. ended 12/31/99): Grants paid, $500; assets, $0 (M); gifts received, $64; expenditures, $564; qualifying distributions, $0.
Limitations: Giving limited to Poulsbo, WA.
Officer: Myra Mittelstadt, Chair.
Trustees: Carol Ahlfs-Baker, Eric Dahl, Sherry Mittlestadt, Dave Sagdahl.
EIN: 911375326

56256
R. E. Nelson Family Foundation
P.O. Box 430
Spokane, WA 99210-0430 (509) 624-4296
Contact: R.E. Nelson, Pres.

Donor(s): R.E. Nelson, Leona S. Nelson.
Financial data (yr. ended 06/30/01): Grants paid, $500; assets, $1 (M); gifts received, $700; expenditures, $915; qualifying distributions, $500.
Limitations: Giving primarily in Spokane, WA.
Application information: Application form not required.
Officer and Trustees:* R.E. Nelson,* Pres.; Leona S. Nelson.
EIN: 916087403

56257
Nordstrom/Seifert Family Foundation
720 4th Ave., Ste. 102
Kirkland, WA 98033

Established in 2000 in WA.
Donor(s): Linda Nordstrom, Christian M. Seifert.
Financial data (yr. ended 12/31/01): Grants paid, $500; assets, $2,073,500 (M); expenditures, $2,437; qualifying distributions, $500.
Limitations: Applications not accepted.
Application information: Contributes only to pre-selected organizations.
Trustees: Linda Nordstrom, Christian M. Seifert.
EIN: 916516127

56258
The Steiner Foundation
7607 110th St. N.W.
Gig Harbor, WA 98332-6809

Established in 2000 in WA.
Financial data (yr. ended 12/31/01): Grants paid, $500; assets, $14,963 (M); gifts received, $10,000; expenditures, $500; qualifying distributions, $500.
Limitations: Applications not accepted.
Application information: Contributes only to pre-selected organizations.
Officers and Directors:* David R. Steiner,* Pres.; Gerald W. Harrington,* V.P.; Patricia L. Steiner,* Treas.; David Taylor, Craig Webster.
EIN: 911970828

56259
Luke G. Williams, Jr. Family Foundation
931 W. Comstock Ct.
Spokane, WA 99203-1407
Contact: Ethel M. Schuerman

Donor(s): Luke G. Williams.
Financial data (yr. ended 12/31/00): Grants paid, $500; assets, $15,866 (M); expenditures, $1,163; qualifying distributions, $1,135.
Limitations: Giving primarily in the northwestern U.S.
Application information: Application form required.
Officer: Luke G. Williams, Mgr.
EIN: 916088366

56260
Espeseth Foundation
P.O. Box 700
Sequim, WA 98382

Donor(s): Johannes Espeseth.
Financial data (yr. ended 12/31/99): Grants paid, $467; assets, $630,965 (M); gifts received, $17,339; expenditures, $17,339; qualifying distributions, $14,361; giving activities include $12,694 for programs.
Officers: Johannes Espeseth, Pres.; Bret Keehn, Secy.; Alan Davis, Treas.
EIN: 943266799

56261
Elma A. G. Boosters Foundation
c/o Tim Schneider
78 Fern Ln.
Montesano, WA 98563

Financial data (yr. ended 03/31/01): Grants paid, $400; assets, $44,111 (M); expenditures, $13,692; qualifying distributions, $861.
Limitations: Giving limited to residents of Elma, WA.
Officers: Jerry Bailey, Pres.; Bill Wickwire, V.P.; LaDonna Badgley, Secy.; Shirley Joplin, Treas.
EIN: 910792720

56262
Tinyblue Foundation
7810 N.E. 183rd St.
Kenmore, WA 98028

Established in 2001 in WA.
Donor(s): David Trowbridge.
Financial data (yr. ended 12/31/01): Grants paid, $360; assets, $564,605 (M); gifts received, $150,676; expenditures, $20,257; qualifying distributions, $135,635; giving activities include $20,257 for programs.
Limitations: Applications not accepted.
Application information: Contributes only to pre-selected organizations.
Officer: David Trowbridge, Pres.
EIN: 912089215

56263
The Thousand Hills Foundation
N. 17411 Dunn Rd.
Colbert, WA 99005-9577

Established in 1995 in WA.
Financial data (yr. ended 11/30/00): Grants paid, $276; assets, $0 (M); expenditures, $276; qualifying distributions, $276.
Limitations: Applications not accepted. Giving primarily in FL, OR, and WA.
Application information: Contributes only to pre-selected organizations.
Officer and Directors:* Roger B. Smith,* Pres. and Secy.-Treas.; Gail L. Smith, Peter B. Smith.
EIN: 911699111

56264
The Chang Family Foundation
7683 S.E. 27th, Ste. 217
Mercer Island, WA 98040

Established in 1998 in NV.
Donor(s): Michael T.P. Chang, Carl J.P. Chang.
Financial data (yr. ended 12/31/01): Grants paid, $250; assets, $2,527,155 (M); gifts received, $2,143,391; expenditures, $139,016; qualifying distributions, $250.
Limitations: Applications not accepted.
Application information: Contributes only to pre-selected organizations.
Officers and Directors:* Joe H.S. Chang,* Pres. and Treas.; Betty Chang, Secy.; Michael T.P. Chang, Carl J.P. Chang.
EIN: 880379688

56265
The Takayoshi Oshima Family Foundation
19800 N. Creek Pkwy., Ste. 200
Bothell, WA 98011

Established in 2000 in WA.
Donor(s): Takayoshi Oshima.
Financial data (yr. ended 12/31/01): Grants paid, $108; assets, $4,275 (M); expenditures, $899; qualifying distributions, $108.
Limitations: Applications not accepted.
Application information: Contributes only to pre-selected organizations.
Officers and Board Members:* Takayoshi Oshima,* Pres.; Phil Egger, Secy.; Michelle Burke, Sachi Oshima.
EIN: 912089917

56266
Ainsworth Blogg Memorial Fund, Inc.
c/o Ryan Montgomery
5020 102nd Ln., N.E.
Kirkland, WA 98033-7640
Application address: 1201 3rd Ave., Ste. 2500, Seattle, WA 98101-3044
Contact: James P. Mendenhall, Dir.

Financial data (yr. ended 09/30/99): Grants paid, $100; assets, $5,037 (M); gifts received, $815; expenditures, $175; qualifying distributions, $175.
Limitations: Giving primarily in Seattle, WA.
Directors: Bill Brastow, James P. Mendenhall, Ryan Montgomery.
EIN: 237253575

56267
The Lambiel Family Foundation
668 Olga Road
Eastsound, WA 98245 (360) 376-4544
Contact: Leo Lambiel, Tr.

Financial data (yr. ended 12/31/01): Grants paid, $100; assets, $1,569 (M); expenditures, $100; qualifying distributions, $100.
Limitations: Giving primarily in WA.
Trustee: Leo Lambiel.
EIN: 336130556

56268
Louella N. Lawrence Foundation
2295 Freshwater Bay
Port Angeles, WA 98363

Established in 1997 in WA.
Donor(s): Louella N. Lawrence.
Financial data (yr. ended 12/31/00): Grants paid, $50; assets, $341,259 (M); gifts received, $96,500; expenditures, $43,791; qualifying distributions, $51,547.
Limitations: Applications not accepted.
Application information: Contributes only to pre-selected organizations.

56268—WASHINGTON

Officer: Louella N. Lawrence, Pres.
EIN: 943190813

56269
Puget Sound Sumi Artists
c/o Pat Rogers
13303 S.E. 57th St.
Bellevue, WA 98006
URL: http://www.sumi.org

Financial data (yr. ended 12/31/00): Grants paid, $50; assets, $10,290 (M); gifts received, $3,098; expenditures, $2,218; qualifying distributions, $1,999; giving activities include $1,587 for programs.
Limitations: Applications not accepted.
Application information: Contributes only to pre-selected organizations.
Officers: Natalie Hendrickson, Pres.; Nola Tressler, Exec. V.P.; Gen Ashford, V.P.; Lois Yoshida, Secy.; Patricia D. Rogers, Treas.
EIN: 943120884

56270
The Atterbury Foundation
3045 E. Laurelhurst Dr., N.E.
Seattle, WA 98105

Established in 1994 in WA and NY.
Donor(s): Charles H. Atterbury.
Financial data (yr. ended 12/31/01): Grants paid, $0; assets, $1,512 (M); expenditures, $1,389; qualifying distributions, $0.
Limitations: Applications not accepted.
Application information: Contributes only to pre-selected organizations.
Officers: Charles H. Atterbury, Pres. and Treas.; Sherry M. Atterbury, V.P.; John G. Balzano, Secy.
EIN: 161462071

56271
The Baltimore Foundation
c/o King & Oliason
514 2nd Ave. W.
Seattle, WA 98119

Established in 1998 in WA.
Donor(s): Beatrice Davis.
Financial data (yr. ended 05/31/02): Grants paid, $0; assets, $333,473 (M); expenditures, $6,098; qualifying distributions, $0.
Limitations: Applications not accepted.
Application information: Contributes only to pre-selected organizations.
Officers: Caroline Davis, Pres.; Beatrice Davis, Secy.
EIN: 911913686

56272
The Bateman Foundation
c/o David A. Bateman
2120 State Ave. N.E., Ste. 101
Olympia, WA 98506

Established in 1998 in WA.
Donor(s): David A. Bateman.
Financial data (yr. ended 12/31/01): Grants paid, $0; assets, $15,796 (M); expenditures, $625; qualifying distributions, $0.
Limitations: Applications not accepted.
Application information: Contributes only to pre-selected organizations.
Officer: David A. Bateman, Pres.
EIN: 911882593

56273
Bayview Boys Home
(Formerly Bay View Youth Services)
P.O. Box 2013
Port Angeles, WA 98362-2013
Application address: 4310 Bean Rd., Port Angeles, WA 98363
Contact: Edwin L. Watson, Pres.

Established in 1987 in WA.
Financial data (yr. ended 12/31/00): Grants paid, $0; assets, $74,433 (M); expenditures, $1,254; qualifying distributions, $1,254.
Limitations: Giving limited to Clallam County, WA.
Officers: Edwin L. Watson, Pres.; William Gellor, V.P.; Lane Wolfley, Secy.; Stuart T. Smith, Treas.
EIN: 910851416

56274
Dave Beck, Sr. Foundation
999 3rd. Ave., Ste. 3000
Seattle, WA 98104-4001

Established in 1997 in WA.
Financial data (yr. ended 12/31/01): Grants paid, $0; assets, $6,675 (M); expenditures, $474; qualifying distributions, $0.
Limitations: Applications not accepted.
Application information: Contributes only to pre-selected organizations.
Officers and Trustees:* Paul R. Cressman, Sr.,* Pres.; Robert E. Heaton,* Secy.; Paul R. Cressman, Jr.
EIN: 911401746

56275
Bezos Family Foundation
c/o Lorri A. Dunsmore
1201 3rd Ave., Ste. 4800
Seattle, WA 98101-3266

Established in 2000 in WA.
Donor(s): Miguel A. Bezos, Jacklyn G. Bezos.
Financial data (yr. ended 12/31/00): Grants paid, $0; assets, $20,000 (M); gifts received, $20,000; expenditures, $0; qualifying distributions, $0.
Limitations: Applications not accepted.
Application information: Contributes only to pre-selected organizations.
Directors: Jacklyn G. Bezos, Miguel A. Bezos.
EIN: 912073258

56276
Brotman Family Foundation
999 Lake Dr., Ste. 300
Issaquah, WA 98027

Established in 2001 in WA.
Donor(s): Jeffrey H. Brotman, Susan T. Brotman.
Financial data (yr. ended 12/31/01): Grants paid, $0; assets, $3,988,840 (M); gifts received, $3,825,000; expenditures, $0; qualifying distributions, $0.
Limitations: Applications not accepted.
Application information: Contributes only to pre-selected organizations.
Officers: Susan T. Brotman, Pres. and Treas.; Jeffrey H. Brotman, V.P. and Secy.
EIN: 522364320

56277
Bushell Charitable Trust
1644 Sleather Kinney Rd., N.E.
Olympia, WA 98506

Established in 1990 in WA.
Donor(s): George Bushell.
Financial data (yr. ended 12/31/01): Grants paid, $0; assets, $574,499 (M); expenditures, $7,758; qualifying distributions, $0.
Limitations: Applications not accepted. Giving primarily in Olympia, WA.
Application information: Contributes only to pre-selected organizations.
Trustee: Larry W. Nelson.
EIN: 916323669

56278
Norman R. & Nellie J. Byrd Foundation
P.O. Box 158
Wapato, WA 98951
Contact: Jeannine Buntain, Tr.

Established in 1991 in WA.
Financial data (yr. ended 06/30/01): Grants paid, $0; assets, $194 (M); expenditures, $770; qualifying distributions, $0.
Limitations: Giving primarily in WA.
Trustee: J. Lawrence Wright.
EIN: 911549582

56279
Cahalan Foundation
c/o Bank of America
P.O. Box 34345, CSC-10
Seattle, WA 98124-1345
Application address: Scott Hay, c/o Western Bank, 211 E. Yakima Ave., Yakima, WA 98901, tel: (509) 577-7422

Established in 1986 in WA.
Financial data (yr. ended 09/30/01): Grants paid, $0; assets, $264,145 (M); expenditures, $14,196; qualifying distributions, $0.
Limitations: Giving limited to Yakima, WA.
Application information: Application form not required.
Trustee: Bank of America.
EIN: 916293964

56280
Laurie Clayton Foundation
390 W. Lake Sammamish Pkwy. N.E.
Bellevue, WA 98008-4223

Established in 2000 in WA.
Financial data (yr. ended 12/31/00): Grants paid, $0; assets, $10,119 (M); gifts received, $10,720; expenditures, $675; qualifying distributions, $0.
Limitations: Applications not accepted.
Application information: Contributes only to pre-selected organizations.
Trustees: David A. Clayton, Nadine Clayton, Todd Laney.
EIN: 912056271

56281
The Coleman Family Foundation
c/o Judy A. Mann
131 W. Bluff Dr.
Port Angeles, WA 98362 (360) 452-2367

Established in 2001 in WA.
Donor(s): James M. Coleman.
Financial data (yr. ended 12/31/01): Grants paid, $0; assets, $603,222 (M); gifts received, $603,222; expenditures, $0; qualifying distributions, $0.
Limitations: Applications not accepted.
Application information: Contributes only to pre-selected organizations.
Directors: James M. Coleman, Judy A. Mann.
EIN: 260014877

56282
Ripley S. Comegys Charitable Foundation
500 108th Ave. N.E., No. 800
Bellevue, WA 98004-5060
Contact: Ripley S. Comegys, Pres.

Established in 1998 in WA.

Financial data (yr. ended 12/31/01): Grants paid, $0; assets, $204,711 (M); expenditures, $5,297; qualifying distributions, $0.
Officers and Directors:* Ripley S. Comegys,* Pres. and V.P.; William M. Comegys III, Secy.; John Stafford Comegys.
EIN: 911913178

56283
Cooper-Newell Foundation
7710 31st Ave. N.W.
Seattle, WA 98117

Established in 2000 in WA.
Donor(s): Richard N. Cooper.
Financial data (yr. ended 12/31/00): Grants paid, $0; assets, $181,550 (M); gifts received, $166,497; expenditures, $0 qualifying distributions, $0.
Limitations: Applications not accepted.
Application information: Contributes only to pre-selected organizations.
Directors: Laura K. Cooper, Mark Cooper, Richard N. Cooper.
EIN: 912088813

56284
Cuyamaca Foundation
408 Aurora Ave. N.
Seattle, WA 98109 (206) 624-5244
Contact: Geoffrey M. Clark, Chair.

Established in 1998 in WA.
Financial data (yr. ended 06/30/01): Grants paid, $0; assets, $1,056,156 (M); expenditures, $1,040; qualifying distributions, $0.
Officer: Geoffrey M. Clark, Chair.
Board Members: Christopher L. Clark, Sara P. Clark.
EIN: 916449463

56285
Cybercamps Foundation
P.O. Box 85868
Seattle, WA 98145

Established in 2000 in WA.
Donor(s): Epson, Mattel, Inc., Symantec.
Financial data (yr. ended 12/31/00): Grants paid, $0; assets, $41,414 (M); gifts received, $48,240; expenditures, $6,826; qualifying distributions, $0.
Limitations: Applications not accepted.
Application information: Contributes only to pre-selected organizations.
Directors: Bill Grant, O. Shannon Hauser, John L. West.
EIN: 911990262
Codes: CS

56286
Daniel Family Charitable Trust
470 Wood Ave., Ste. 2B
Bainbridge Island, WA 98110

Established in 2000 in WA.
Donor(s): Richard H. Daniel.
Financial data (yr. ended 12/31/01): Grants paid, $0; assets, $169,310 (M); expenditures, $0; qualifying distributions, $0.
Limitations: Applications not accepted.
Application information: Contributes only to pre-selected organizations.
Trustees: Karen Louise Daniel, Richard H. Daniel, Kelly Ann Selva.
EIN: 916521071

56287
Eberharter Foundation
3231 Magnolia Blvd. W.
Seattle, WA 98199

Established in 1997 in WA.

Donor(s): Richard Eberharter.
Financial data (yr. ended 12/31/01): Grants paid, $0; assets, $490 (M); expenditures, $250; qualifying distributions, $250.
Limitations: Applications not accepted.
Application information: Contributes only to pre-selected organizations.
Officer: Richard Eberharter, Pres.
Directors: Stephanie Eberharter, Michael Hayden.
EIN: 911710311

56288
The Edgebrook Foundation
801 2nd. Ave., Ste. 1600
Seattle, WA 98104

Established in 1985 in WA.
Donor(s): Charlotte L. Taylor.
Financial data (yr. ended 12/31/01): Grants paid, $0; assets, $303,001 (M); expenditures, $5,012; qualifying distributions, $0.
Limitations: Applications not accepted. Giving primarily in San Francisco, CA.
Application information: Contributes only to pre-selected organizations.
Officers and Directors:* Charlotte L. Taylor,* Pres.; Elizabeth Bodien,* V.P.; Tamsin C. Taylor,* V.P.; Timothy N. Taylor,* Secy.
EIN: 911307405

56289
The Evans Family Foundation
5215 N.E. 45th St.
Seattle, WA 98105

Established in 2001 in WA.
Donor(s): Daniel J. Evans, Nancy B. Evans.
Financial data (yr. ended 12/31/01): Grants paid, $0; assets, $361,608 (M); gifts received, $359,980; expenditures, $0; qualifying distributions, $0.
Limitations: Applications not accepted.
Application information: Contributes only to pre-selected organizations.
Officers: Nancy B. Evans, Pres. and Treas.; Daniel J. Evans, V.P. and Secy.
EIN: 912173659

56290
The Foundation of Mercy
P.O. Box 323
Langley, WA 98260
Contact: Patrick F. Hussey, Pres.

Financial data (yr. ended 07/31/01): Grants paid, $0; assets, $526,093 (M); expenditures, $15,397; qualifying distributions, $0.
Officers: Patrick F. Hussey, Pres.; Fred Mercy, S.J., V.P. and Treas.; Patty Houts-Hussy.
EIN: 911616600

56291
Frazier Family Foundation
7703 S.E. 78th St.
Mercer Island, WA 98040

Established in 2001 in WA.
Donor(s): Alan D. Frazier, Mary D. Frazier.
Financial data (yr. ended 12/31/01): Grants paid, $0; assets, $50,012 (M); gifts received, $50,000; expenditures, $0; qualifying distributions, $0.
Directors: Alan D. Frazier, Mary D. Frazier.
EIN: 912171978

56292
Free School of Ballet for Boys and Girls
c/o Priscilla J. Hancock, M.D.
1501 S. Rockwood Blvd.
Spokane, WA 99203-3554

Established in 1994 in WA.

Financial data (yr. ended 12/31/01): Grants paid, $0; assets, $329 (M); gifts received, $4,889; expenditures, $5,617; qualifying distributions, $0.
Limitations: Applications not accepted.
Application information: Contributes only to pre-selected organizations.
Director: Priscilla J. Hancock, M.D.
EIN: 943231659

56293
Garner Family Foundation Trust
12900 S. Keyport Rd. N.E.
Poulsbo, WA 98370

Established in 2000 in WA.
Donor(s): Jerry Lee Garner.
Financial data (yr. ended 12/31/00): Grants paid, $0; assets, $9,042 (M); gifts received, $10,842; expenditures, $1,800; qualifying distributions, $0.
Trustees: Barbara Jo Garner, Jerry Lee Garner.
EIN: 912089618

56294
Global Partnerships Foundation
801 2nd Ave., Ste. 1300
Seattle, WA 98104

Established in 1993 in WA.
Donor(s): Bill Clapp, Jack Benaroya, Bernard Greer, Jack McMillan, Becky Benaroya, Paula Clapp, Jodi Greer, Loyal McMillan.
Financial data (yr. ended 06/30/01): Grants paid, $0; assets, $78,005 (M); gifts received, $89,708; expenditures, $509,381; qualifying distributions, $502,521; giving activities include $21,181 for programs.
Limitations: Applications not accepted. Giving limited to Alexandria, VA.
Application information: Contributes only to pre-selected organizations.
Officers: Paula Clapp, Co-Chair.; William Clapp, Co-Chair.; Peter Blomquist, Pres.; Ann Maria King, Secy.; Howard Brady, Treas.; Ellen Cole, Exec. Dir.
Board Members: Bud Greer, Judi Greer, Jay Hair, Leah Hair, Joanne Marrel, Jack McMillan, Gari Mulhair, Bonnie Robbins, Richard Robbins, Greg Stevenson.
EIN: 911602144

56295
Goosefoot Community Fund
P.O. Box 114
Langley, WA 98260

Established in 1999 in WA.
Donor(s): Nancy Nordhoff.
Financial data (yr. ended 12/31/00): Grants paid, $0; assets, $4,272,792 (M); gifts received, $961,741; expenditures, $490,230; qualifying distributions, $321,840; giving activities include $10,606 for programs.
Limitations: Applications not accepted.
Application information: Contributes only to pre-selected organizations.
Officers: Nancy Nordhoff, Pres.; Linda Moore, Secy.
EIN: 911960139

56296
Gordon Lovejoy Foundation
P.O. Box 12317
Seattle, WA 98111

Established in 1998 in WA.
Donor(s): Nicholas Lovejoy, Barbara Gordon.
Financial data (yr. ended 12/31/00): Grants paid, $0; assets, $2,887,683 (M); gifts received, $657,849; expenditures, $45,966; qualifying distributions, $996,084; giving activities include $1,000,000 for loans.

56296
Limitations: Applications not accepted. Giving primarily in CA.
Application information: Contributes only to pre-selected organizations.
Officers: Barbara Gordon, Pres.; Nicholas Lovejoy, Secy.-Treas.
EIN: 911941495

56297
International Players Alliance
905 Ferndale Cir., N.E.
Renton, WA 98056-3028

Established in 1999.
Financial data (yr. ended 12/31/00): Grants paid, $0; assets, $1,829 (L); expenditures, $3,093; qualifying distributions, $0.
Director: Bob Tillman.
EIN: 911947861

56298
The Irwin Foundation
P.O. Box 10668
Yakima, WA 98909 (509) 248-0194
Contact: Jere Irwin, Tr.

Established in 2000 in WA.
Donor(s): Jere Irwin.
Financial data (yr. ended 12/31/00): Grants paid, $0; assets, $100,000 (M); gifts received, $100,000; expenditures, $0; qualifying distributions, $0.
Application information: Application form not required.
Trustees: Steven L. Alegria, Jere Irwin, Charles A. Keith.
EIN: 912091416

56299
Dean A. Johnsen Foundation
12734 Plateau Cir. N.W.
Silverdale, WA 98383

Established in 2000 in WA.
Donor(s): Dean A. Johnsen.
Financial data (yr. ended 12/31/00): Grants paid, $0; assets, $4,338 (M); gifts received, $7,000; expenditures, $0; qualifying distributions, $0.
Limitations: Applications not accepted.
Application information: Contributes only to pre-selected organizations.
Officers and Director:* Dean A. Johnsen,* Pres.; Lisa L. Johnsen, Secy.
EIN: 912045707

56300
The Jordon Family Foundation
1122 E. Pike St., Ste. 692
Seattle, WA 98122-3916

Established in 2000 in WA.
Donor(s): John W. Jordan, Laura Welland, Stephen Hannock.
Financial data (yr. ended 12/31/00): Grants paid, $0; assets, $664,074 (M); gifts received, $743,094; expenditures, $0; qualifying distributions, $0.
Limitations: Applications not accepted.
Application information: Contributes only to pre-selected organizations.
Trustees: John W. Jordon, Laura Welland.
EIN: 916516005

56301
Kevin King Scholarship Trust Association
320 Stanley Blvd.
Yakima, WA 98902
Application address: c/o Principal, Garfield High School, Seattle, WA 98101

Financial data (yr. ended 12/31/01): Grants paid, $0; assets, $26,191 (M); expenditures, $228; qualifying distributions, $0.
Limitations: Giving limited to residents of Seattle, WA.
Application information: Application form required.
Trustee: Ron King.
EIN: 943074207

56302
The Knoblauch Shakespeare Trust
6129 140th Ct., N.E.
Redmond, WA 98052

Established in 2000 in WA.
Donor(s): Knoblauch Family Trust.
Financial data (yr. ended 12/31/01): Grants paid, $0; assets, $1 (M); expenditures, $15,878; qualifying distributions, $0.
Limitations: Giving primarily in Seattle, WA.
Officers: Susan Wilson, Chair.; Stephanie Larson, Treas.
Trustee: William Maschmeier.
EIN: 912032649

56303
Pansy K. W. Kong Foundation, Inc.
840 N.E. 125th St., Ste. 403
Seattle, WA 98125

Established in 1999 in WA.
Financial data (yr. ended 12/31/01): Grants paid, $0; assets, $5,698 (M); expenditures, $0; qualifying distributions, $0.
Limitations: Applications not accepted. Giving primarily in WA.
Officer: Kelvin P. Kong, Pres.
Directors: Katie Kong, Yuen Wing Kong.
EIN: 134071709

56304
Kvamme Christian Educational Foundation
3783 Hatley Rd.
Everson, WA 98247

Established in 1998 in WA.
Donor(s): Kevan Kvamme, Polly Kvamme.
Financial data (yr. ended 12/31/00): Grants paid, $0; assets, $900,000 (M); gifts received, $900,000; expenditures, $60; qualifying distributions, $0.
Limitations: Applications not accepted.
Application information: Contributes only to pre-selected organizations.
Officer: Polly Kvamme, Secy.
Director: Kevan Kvamme.
EIN: 911940264

56305
Learning Innovations Foundation
(Formerly Frontiers of Perception Institute)
P.O. Box 99151
Seattle, WA 98199
Application address: 3320 Magnolia Blvd. W., Seattle, WA 98199, tel.: (206) 282-2686
Contact: Bruce C. Mitchell

Established in 1996 in WA.
Donor(s): Bruce C. Mitchell.
Financial data (yr. ended 09/30/01): Grants paid, $0; assets, $15,500 (M); expenditures, $0; qualifying distributions, $0.
Officer and Director:* Bruce C. Mitchell,* Pres.

EIN: 943220588

56306
Alice Lee Lund Charitable Trust
13918 N.W. 9th Ave.
Vancouver, WA 98685

Established in 2001 in MD.
Donor(s): Alice Lee Lund Trust.
Financial data (yr. ended 12/31/01): Grants paid, $0; assets, $500,873 (M); gifts received, $480,434; expenditures, $0; qualifying distributions, $0.
Limitations: Applications not accepted.
Application information: Contributes only to pre-selected organizations.
Trustee: Wesley Keith Moholt.
EIN: 916530681

56307
Manke Memorial Fund
162 Government Rd.
Naselle, WA 98638-8605

Established in 1999 in OR.
Financial data (yr. ended 12/31/00): Grants paid, $0; assets, $0 (M); expenditures, $24; qualifying distributions, $0.
Officers and Directors:* James R. Manke,* Pres.; Cheryl D. Manke,* Secy.-Treas.; Linda Gramson, Betty Manke.
EIN: 911844321

56308
Master Gardener Foundation of Kitsap County
9633 Levin Rd., N.W., Ste. 204
Silverdale, WA 98383

Financial data (yr. ended 12/31/01): Grants paid, $0; assets, $11,477 (M); gifts received, $92; expenditures, $16,458; qualifying distributions, $0.
Officers: Karen Schoeppel, Pres.; Nikki Goodwin, V.P.; Donna Alber, Secy.; Vivian Durfee, Treas.
EIN: 943049072

56309
Edward and Lois McLeary Charitable Foundation
4008 Pioneer Way E.
Tacoma, WA 98443

Established in 1998 in WA.
Donor(s): Edward McLeary, Lois McLeary.
Financial data (yr. ended 12/31/01): Grants paid, $0; assets, $365,218 (M); gifts received, $681; expenditures, $2,521; qualifying distributions, $0.
Limitations: Applications not accepted.
Application information: Contributes only to pre-selected organizations.
Directors: Steven J. Brown, Edward McLeary, Lois McLeary, Randy McLeary, Russell McLeary.
EIN: 911932273

56310
Miailovich Family Foundation
218 Main St., No. 467
Kirkland, WA 98033 (425) 827-1109

Established in 2001 in WA.
Donor(s): Richard Miailovich, Patricia Miailovich.
Financial data (yr. ended 12/31/01): Grants paid, $0; assets, $146,070 (M); gifts received, $6,870; expenditures, $0; qualifying distributions, $0.
Trustees: Patricia Miailovich, Richard Miailovich.
EIN: 527240932

56311
Mid-Columbia Library Foundation
c/o Kennewick Library
405 S. Dayton St.
Kennewick, WA 99336-5690

Donor(s): Shirley Maxine Stroh.‡
Financial data (yr. ended 12/31/01): Grants paid, $0; assets, $268,384 (M); gifts received, $252,024; expenditures, $331; qualifying distributions, $0.
Limitations: Applications not accepted. Giving primarily in Kennewick, WA.
Application information: Contributes only to pre-selected organizations.
Officers: Phelps Shepard, Pres.; Bonnie Taylor, V.P.; Ruth Giese, Secy.
EIN: 911384278

56312
George And Betty Munro Foundation
1602 NW 87th Circle
Vancouver, WA 98665

Established in 2000 in WA.
Donor(s): David G. Munro, Ralph D. Munro, Ronlad T. Munro.
Financial data (yr. ended 12/31/01): Grants paid, $0; assets, $32,531 (M); gifts received, $638; expenditures, $1,017; qualifying distributions, $0.
Application information: Trustees solicit recommendations for potential scholarship recipients.
Trustees: David G. Munro, Ralph D. Munro, Ronald T. Munro.
EIN: 912010521

56313
Novak Family Scholarship Fund
14807 SE Rivershore
Vancouver, WA 98683
Contact: Walter Novak, Tr.

Established in 2000 in WA.
Donor(s): Walter Novak.
Financial data (yr. ended 12/31/01): Grants paid, $0; assets, $54,902 (M); expenditures, $765; qualifying distributions, $0.
Application information: Application form required.
Trustee: Walter Novak.
EIN: 912013375

56314
Oasis for Animals
P.O. Box 1304
Langley, WA 98260

Established in 2001 in WA.
Donor(s): Susan Walters.
Financial data (yr. ended 12/31/01): Grants paid, $0; assets, $9,915 (M); gifts received, $13,347; expenditures, $4,335; qualifying distributions, $4,317.
Limitations: Applications not accepted.
Application information: Contributes only to pre-selected organizations.
Officers: Jean Favini, Pres.; Susan Walters, Secy.-Treas.
EIN: 260022892

56315
Orcas Island Foundation
360 Indralaya Rd.
Eastsound, WA 98245-9272 (360) 376-4526
E-mail: oif@rockisland.com; *URL:* http://www.indralaya.org
Contact: Minor Lile, Mgr.

Established in 1931 in WA.
Financial data (yr. ended 12/31/01): Grants paid, $0; assets, $1,053,623 (L); gifts received, $394,317; expenditures, $153,031; giving activities include $103,910 for programs.
Limitations: Giving limited to Orcas Island, WA.
Officers: Neila Campbell, Chair.; Linda Jo Pym, Vice-Chair.; Sandy Detroit, Secy.; Kelly Bachman, Treas.
Directors: Austin Bee, Donna Erickson, Mitchell Herzog.
Managers: Minor Lile, Leonie Van Gelder.
EIN: 916076839
Codes: CM

56316
Mayor Lou Parberry's Foundation
P.O. Box R
Bellingham, WA 98227
Contact: Lou Parberry, Pres.

Financial data (yr. ended 03/31/02): Grants paid, $0; assets, $2,003 (M); expenditures, $471; qualifying distributions, $0.
Limitations: Giving limited to Whatcom County, WA.
Officers: Lou Parberry, Pres.; Sue Parberry, Secy.
EIN: 911258678

56317
Lorene M. Petrie Trust
c/o Bank of America
P.O. Box 34345, CSC-9
Seattle, WA 98124-1345
Application address: c/o Bank of America, 101 N. 2nd St., Yakima, WA 98901, tel.: (509) 575-6722

Established in 1983 in WA.
Donor(s): Lorene Petrie.‡
Financial data (yr. ended 07/31/02): Grants paid, $0; assets, $866,854 (M); expenditures, $12,145; qualifying distributions, $0.
Limitations: Giving limited to Yakima and Kittitas counties, WA.
Application information: Application form not required.
Trustee: Bank of America.
EIN: 916256555

56318
Pitts Sportmen's Foundation
2020 N. Shore Dr.
Bellingham, WA 98226

Established in 1995 in WA.
Financial data (yr. ended 12/31/01): Grants paid, $0; assets, $886,469 (M); gifts received, $96,605; expenditures, $56,096; qualifying distributions, $0.
Limitations: Applications not accepted.
Application information: Contributes only to pre-selected organizations.
Officers and Directors:* John Salstrom, Pres.; Don Young,* Secy.-Treas.; Ron Abbott, Elmer Doronso.
EIN: 911711542

56319
R & R Foundation
P.O. Box 657
Issaquah, WA 98027-0024

Established in 2000 in WA.
Donor(s): Katherine Elizabeth Riffle Roper, Troy Wayne Roper.
Financial data (yr. ended 12/31/01): Grants paid, $0; assets, $107,107 (M); expenditures, $149; qualifying distributions, $0.
Limitations: Applications not accepted.
Application information: Contributes only to pre-selected organizations.
Officer: Katherine Elizabeth Riffle Roper, Pres.
Director: Troy Wayne Roper.
EIN: 912010932

56320
Rath Family Foundation
c/o Kent Rath
178 San Juan Dr.
Friday Harbor, WA 98250

Established in 1999.
Donor(s): Kent Rath.
Financial data (yr. ended 06/30/01): Grants paid, $0; assets, $0 (M); gifts received, $829; expenditures, $4,029; qualifying distributions, $0.
Limitations: Applications not accepted.
Application information: Contributes only to pre-selected organizations.
Trustees: Deborah Falls, Karen Rath, Kent Rath.
EIN: 911996347

56321
Rucoda Foundation
P.O. Box 380
Mercer Island, WA 98040-0380
(206) 232-9292
Contact: Ron Cohn, Dir.

Donor(s): Ron Cohn.
Financial data (yr. ended 12/31/01): Grants paid, $0; assets, $559 (M); expenditures, $25; qualifying distributions, $0.
Limitations: Giving primarily in Bellevue, WA.
Application information: Application form not required.
Directors: Dave Cohn, Ron Cohn, Steve Cohn.
EIN: 911433240

56322
Seqium Town Partners
P.O. Box 269
Sequim, WA 98382
Contact: Michael S. Alton, Secy.-Treas.

Established in 2000 in WA.
Financial data (yr. ended 12/31/00): Grants paid, $0; assets, $13,257 (M); gifts received, $17,813; expenditures, $4,757; qualifying distributions, $0.
Limitations: Giving limited to Sequim, WA.
Officers and Directors:* Jean Haught,* Pres.; Sharin Metcalf,* V.P.; Michael S. Alton,* Secy.-Treas.; Darilyn Alton, Jeri Sanford, Thelma Sullock, Lynn Raysten.
EIN: 912025694

56323
Sleeping Lady Foundation
c/o Harriet S. Bullitt
P.O. Box 2025
Leavenworth, WA 98826

Established in 1999 in WA.
Donor(s): Harriet S. Bullitt.
Financial data (yr. ended 12/31/01): Grants paid, $0; assets, $870 (M); expenditures, $510; qualifying distributions, $0.
Officers and Directors:* Harriet S. Bullitt,* Pres.; Buford Howell,* Secy.; Werner Janssen,* Treas.; W. Scott Brewster, Wenda Brewster O'Reilly.
EIN: 911943121

56324
South Beach Foundation
9340 N.E. South Beach Dr.
Bainbridge Island, WA 98110

Established in 2000 in WA.
Donor(s): Janet McFarlane, Scott McFarlane.
Financial data (yr. ended 12/31/01): Grants paid, $0; assets, $50,232 (M); gifts received, $40,000; expenditures, $0; qualifying distributions, $0.
Limitations: Applications not accepted.

Application information: Contributes only to pre-selected organizations.
Trustees: Janet McFarlane, Scott McFarlane.
EIN: 916522312

56325
Spokane Medical Library
1101 W. College, Ste. 355
Spokane, WA 99201

Established in 2001.
Donor(s): Marvel Runkel Turst.
Financial data (yr. ended 12/31/01): Grants paid, $0; assets, $296,768 (M); gifts received, $296,579; expenditures, $0; qualifying distributions, $0.
Officer: Jan Monaco, Exec. Dir.
Trustees: Don Cubberley, M.D., Robert Harman, M.D., Deborah Harper, M.D., Gary Matsumoto, M.D., L. Elizabeth Peterson, M.D., Rod Trytko, M.D.
EIN: 910565012

56326
John & Kusumam Titus Foundation
c/o John Titus
23405 164th Ave. S.E.
Kent, WA 98042

Donor(s): John Titus, Kusumam Titus.
Financial data (yr. ended 12/31/01): Grants paid, $0; assets, $850 (M); expenditures, $34; qualifying distributions, $0.
Limitations: Giving primarily in Kerala, India.
Application information: Application form not required.
Officers: John Titus, Pres.; Kusumam Titus, Secy.-Treas.
EIN: 911508510

56327
Waldo Medical Foundation
(Formerly Fifth Avenue Medical Center/Waldo Medical Foundation)
9501 5th Ave. N.E.
Seattle, WA 98115-2108
Application address: 10564 5th Ave. N.E., Ste. 401, Seattle, WA 98125, tel.: (206) 362-6300
Contact: Stanley Herschberg, V.P.

Financial data (yr. ended 12/31/01): Grants paid, $0; assets, $1,367,533 (M); expenditures, $129,004; qualifying distributions, $0.
Limitations: Giving limited to the greater Seattle, WA, area.
Officers and Directors:* Rex Nilson,* Pres.; Stanley Herschberg,* V.P.; Opal Conner,* Secy.; Lance Hulbert,* Treas.; Byron Hutchinson.
EIN: 910590143

56328
Wildlife Support Charitable Trust
c/o Bank of America
P.O. Box 34345
Seattle, WA 98124-1345

Established in 2001 in WA.
Donor(s): Doris E. Jones.
Financial data (yr. ended 12/31/01): Grants paid, $0; assets, $100,000 (M); gifts received, $100,000; expenditures, $0; qualifying distributions, $0.
Limitations: Applications not accepted.
Application information: Contributes only to pre-selected organizations.
Trustees: Jeff Guidry, Myron G. Phillips, Bank of America.
EIN: 412029664

56329
Yakima Association for Community Living
421 S. 47th Ave.
Yakima, WA 98908-3237

Donor(s): Bobette Takiff.
Financial data (yr. ended 12/31/99): Grants paid, $0; assets, $657,340 (M); gifts received, $18,590; expenditures, $19,361; qualifying distributions, $53,213; giving activities include $72,933 for programs.
Limitations: Applications not accepted. Giving limited to Yakima, WA.
Officers: Dick Picatti, Pres.; Paul Strater, V.P.; Chuck Viele, Secy.-Treas.
Directors: Dan Baker, Don George, Wright Hawkes, Dave Joynt.
EIN: 911224878

56330
Fikret Yuksel Foundation
9709 S. 203rd St.
Kent, WA 98031-1470

Established in 1999 in WA.
Donor(s): Fikret Yuksel.
Financial data (yr. ended 12/31/01): Grants paid, $0; assets, $255 (M); expenditures, $0; qualifying distributions, $0.
Limitations: Applications not accepted. Giving in Turkey.
Application information: Contributes only to pre-selected organizations.
Officers and Directors:* Fikret Yuksel,* Pres.; Gary Burchard,* Secy.-Treas.; Susan Burchard.
EIN: 911918148

WEST VIRGINIA

56331
The Greater Kanawha Valley Foundation
Huntington Sq., Ste. 1600
900 Lee St. E.
Charleston, WV 25301   (304) 346-3620
FAX: (304) 346-3640; E-mail: tgkvf@tgkvf.org;
URL: http://www.tgkvf.org
Contact: Rebecca C. Cain

Established in 1962 in WV.
Financial data (yr. ended 12/31/01): Grants paid, $3,864,111; assets, $93,838,484 (M); gifts received, $3,491,514; expenditures, $5,515,340.
Limitations: Giving limited to the greater Kanawha Valley, WV, area, except scholarships which are limited to residents of WV.
Publications: Annual report (including application guidelines), informational brochure, application guidelines, financial statement, grants list, occasional report.
Application information: Application form required.
Officers and Trustees:* Stephan R. Crislip, Chair.; T. Randolph Cox,* Vice-Chair.; Lesley A. Russo, Secy.; Charles L. Capito, Jr., Daniel S. Foster, M.D., Rebecca B. Goldman, Judith N. McJunkin, Mary Anne Michael, Rick Morgan, Sandra Murphy, David Rollins, Barbara Rose.
Advisory Committee: Paul Arbogast, G. Thomas Battle, Frederick H. Belden, Jr., Elsie P. Carter, William D. Chambers, Elizabeth E. Chilton, William M. Davis, Deborah A. Faber, Charles R. McElwee, Thomas N. McJunkin, Harry Moore, William E. Mullett, Ph.D., Virginia Rugeley, Mark H. Schaul, Dolly Sherwood, K. Richard C. Sinclair, Olivia R. Singleton, Louis B. Southworth, Charles B. Stacy, L. Newton Thomas, Jr., Adeline J. Voorhees, Thomas C. Wetzel.
Trustee Banks: Bank One, West Virginia, N.A., City National Bank of Charleston, The Huntington National Bank West Virginia, United National Bank, WesBanco Bank, Inc., B.B. & T.
EIN: 556024430
Codes: CM, FD, GTI

56332
Bernard McDonough Foundation, Inc.
311 4th St.
Parkersburg, WV 26101   (304) 424-6280
FAX: (304) 424-6281
Contact: James T. Wakley, Pres.

Incorporated in 1961 in WV.
Donor(s): Bernard P. McDonough.‡
Financial data (yr. ended 12/31/99): Grants paid, $2,061,342; assets, $40,737,355 (M); expenditures, $2,394,070; qualifying distributions, $2,180,858.
Limitations: Giving primarily in WV.
Application information: Application form not required.
Officers and Directors:* James T. Wakley,* Pres.; Mary Riccobene,* V.P.; Katrina Valentine, Secy.; F.C. McCusker,* Treas.; Robert E. Evans, Dale A. Knight, Mark C. Kury, George F. Partridge, Jr., T.J. Wilson.
EIN: 556023693
Codes: FD

56333
Hugh I. Shott, Jr. Foundation
c/o First Century Bank, N.A.
500 Federal St., P.O. Box 1559
Bluefield, WV 24701
Contact: Richard W. Wilkinson, Pres.

Established in 1985 in WV.
Donor(s): Hugh I. Shott, Jr.‡
Financial data (yr. ended 12/31/00): Grants paid, $2,025,549; assets, $40,264,988 (M); expenditures, $2,434,722; qualifying distributions, $1,995,782.
Limitations: Giving limited to southwestern VA and southern WV.
Application information: Application form required.
Officers: R.W. Wilkinson, Pres.; Scott H. Shott, V.P.; John C. Shott, Secy.; B.K. Satterfield, Treas.
Directors: John H. Shott, W. Chandler Swope, Frank W. Wilkinson.
Trustee: First Century Bank, N.A.
EIN: 550650833
Codes: FD

56334
Clay Foundation, Inc.
1426 Kanawha Blvd. E.
Charleston, WV 25301   (304) 344-8656
FAX: (304) 344-3805
Contact: Charles M. Avampato, Pres.

Incorporated in 1986 in WV.
Donor(s): Charles M. Avampato, George Diab.
Financial data (yr. ended 10/31/01): Grants paid, $1,710,141; assets, $61,841,066 (M); expenditures, $2,579,387; qualifying distributions, $2,162,424.
Limitations: Giving limited to WV, with emphasis on the greater Kanawha Valley area.
Application information: Application form not required.
Officers and Directors:* Buckner W. Clay,* Co-Chair.; Lyell B. Clay,* Co-Chair.; Charles M. Avampato,* Pres.; Hamilton G. Clay,* V.P.; James K. Brown,* Secy.; Whitney Clay Diller,* Treas.
EIN: 550670193
Codes: FD

56335
The James H. and Alice Teubert Charitable Trust
P.O. Box 2131
Huntington, WV 25722-2131   (304) 525-6337
E-mail: teubert@access.mountain.net
Contact: Jimelle Bowen, Exec. Dir.

Established in 1987 in WV.
Financial data (yr. ended 09/30/01): Grants paid, $1,203,805; assets, $20,598,072 (M); expenditures, $1,312,588; qualifying distributions, $1,254,305.
Limitations: Giving primarily in Cabell and Wayne counties, WV.
Publications: Informational brochure, application guidelines.
Application information: Application form required.
Trustees: Grant McGuire, Chair.; Michael A. Fiery, Norma Irwin, David H. Lunsford, Michael Nuce, Sue Richardson, Matthew A. Rohrbach.
EIN: 556101813
Codes: FD

56336
The Daywood Foundation, Inc.
1600 Bank One Ctr.
Charleston, WV 25301   (304) 345-8900
Contact: William W. Booker, Secy.-Treas.

Incorporated in 1958 in WV.
Donor(s): Ruth Woods Dayton.‡
Financial data (yr. ended 12/31/99): Grants paid, $1,065,500; assets, $26,473,985 (M); expenditures, $1,146,975; qualifying distributions, $1,039,729.
Limitations: Giving limited to Barbour, Charleston, Greenbrier, Kanawha, and Lewisburg counties, WV.
Publications: Application guidelines.
Application information: Application form not required.
Officers and Directors:* L. Newton Thomas,* Pres.; Richard E. Ford,* V.P.; William W. Booker,* Secy.-Treas.; John O. Kizer.
EIN: 556018107
Codes: FD

56337
The H. P. and Anne S. Hunnicutt Foundation, Inc.
P.O. Box 309
Princeton, WV 24740
Contact: William Stafford II, Secy.

Established in 1987.
Donor(s): H.P. Hunnicutt, Anne S. Hunnicutt.‡
Financial data (yr. ended 06/30/01): Grants paid, $1,046,857; assets, $37,067,432 (M); expenditures, $1,168,149; qualifying distributions, $1,057,198.
Limitations: Giving limited to southern WV.
Officers: William P. Stafford, Pres.; James H. Sarver, V.P.; William Stafford II, Secy.; James H. Sarver II, Treas.
Trustee: First Community Bank, Inc.
EIN: 550670462
Codes: FD

56338
The Community Foundation for the Ohio Valley, Inc.
P.O. Box 1233
Wheeling, WV 26003   (304) 242-3144
E-mail: cfov@hgo.net, or mfisher@cfov.org;
URL: http://www.cfov.org
Contact: C.J. Kaiser, Jr., Pres. or Emily Schramm Fisher, Exec. Dir.

Established in 1972 in WV.
Financial data (yr. ended 05/31/00): Grants paid, $678,163; assets, $17,191,718 (M); gifts received, $696,580; expenditures, $739,606.
Limitations: Giving primarily in the Ohio Valley area.
Publications: Annual report (including application guidelines), application guidelines, newsletter, informational brochure, grants list.
Application information: Application form required.
Officers and Directors:* C. Kaiser, Jr.,* Pres.; Edward "Ted" Gompers,* V.P.; David B. Dalzell, Jr.,* Secy.; Jerome B. Schmitt,* Treas.; Emily Schramm Fisher, Exec. Dir.; Joseph W. Boutaugh, Ray A. Byrd, Sue Seibert Farnsworth, Mark C. Ferrell, James C. Gardill, John N. Kramer, C. Joe Mullen, Jean A. Mulroy, William O. Nutting, Rizal V. Pangilnan, Lee C. Paull III, Wilbur R. Roat, James G. Squibb, Jr., William J. Yaeger, Jr.
EIN: 310908698
Codes: CM, FD, GTI

56339
George A. Laughlin Trust
c/o WesBanco Bank, Inc., Trust Dept.
1 Bank Plz.
Wheeling, WV 26003   (304) 234-9428
Contact: Pattie Hoffman, Trust Off., WesBanco Bank, Inc.

Established in 1936 in WV.

Financial data (yr. ended 12/31/01): Grants paid, $640,655; assets, $13,525,561 (M); expenditures, $831,748; qualifying distributions, $738,585; giving activities include $640,655 for loans to individuals.
Limitations: Giving limited to Ohio County, WV, residents.
Application information: Application form required.
Trustee: WesBanco Bank, Inc.
EIN: 556016889
Codes: FD, GTI

56340
BB&T West Virginia Foundation
(Formerly One Valley Bank Foundation, Inc.)
c/o B.B. & T., Trust Dept.
P.O. Box 1793
Charleston, WV 25326-1793 (304) 348-7000
Contact: Michael W. Stajduhar, Dir.

Established in 1954 in WV.
Donor(s): One Valley Bank, N.A., Branch Banking & Trust Company.
Financial data (yr. ended 12/31/01): Grants paid, $581,600; assets, $10,728,155 (M); gifts received, $10,083,253; expenditures, $590,751; qualifying distributions, $581,600.
Limitations: Giving limited to WV, especially Charleston.
Application information: Application form not required.
Trustees: Phyllis H. Arnold, Nelle Ratrie Chilton, J. Holmes Morrison, John L.D. Payne, Brent Robinson, Steven M. Rubin, K. Richard C. Sinclair, Edwin H. Welch, Thomas D. Wilkerson, John Williams.
EIN: 556017269
Codes: CS, FD, CD

56341
Parkersburg Area Community Foundation
501 Avery St.
P.O. Box 1762
Parkersburg, WV 26102-1762 (304) 428-4438
Toll-free tel.: (304) 428-4438; *FAX:* (304) 428-1200; *E-mail:* info@pacfwv.com; *URL:* http://www.pacfwv.com
Contact: Judy Sjostedt, Exec. Dir.

Established in 1963 in WV.
Donor(s): Albert Wolfe,‡ The Keystone Foundation, members of the Wolfe family.‡
Financial data (yr. ended 06/30/01): Grants paid, $550,296; assets, $9,260,246 (M); gifts received, $1,175,753; expenditures, $755,816.
Limitations: Giving limited to the Mid-Ohio Valley of Calhoun, Doddridge, Gilmer, Wirt, Wood, Jackson, Pleasants, Ritchie, and Roane counties, WV, and Washington County, OH.
Publications: Annual report, informational brochure, newsletter, application guidelines.
Application information: Application form required.
Officers and Governors:* Thomas Weyer,* Chair.; Barbara N. Fish, Vice-Chair.; Judy Sjostedt,* Exec. Dir.; and 15 additional members.
Trustee Banks: B.B. & T., Banknorth Investment Management Group, N.A., United National Bank, WesBanco Bank, Inc.
EIN: 556027764
Codes: CM, FD, GTI

56342
Board of Trustees of the Prichard School
c/o Bank One, WV, N.A., Trust Dept.
P.O. Box 179
Huntington, WV 25706
Application address: c/o J. Seaton Taylor, 629 7th St., Huntington, WV 25701, tel.: (304) 697-4800

Established in 1923.
Financial data (yr. ended 12/31/00): Grants paid, $454,600; assets, $8,591,486 (M); expenditures, $485,863; qualifying distributions, $454,600.
Limitations: Giving primarily in VA and WV.
Application information: Application form not required.
Officers and Directors:* J. Seaton Taylor, Pres.; Marc W. Wild,* V.P.; Paul W. McCreight, Secy.; Margaret C. Breece, Treas.; Steven P. Hatten, Edward W. Morrison, John F. Speer, Ann Todd.
EIN: 550435910
Codes: FD

56343
Bernard H. and Blanche E. Jacobson Foundation
P.O. Box 1793
Charleston, WV 25326
Application address: 1210 B.B. & T. Sq., 300 Summers St., Charleston, WV 25301, tel.: (304) 342-1141
Contact: John L. Ray, Tr.

Established in 1954 in WV.
Donor(s): Bernard H. Jacobson, Blanche E. Jacobson.
Financial data (yr. ended 12/31/01): Grants paid, $448,500; assets, $7,427,208 (M); expenditures, $482,107; qualifying distributions, $454,042.
Limitations: Giving primarily in WV, with emphasis on the Kanawha Valley and Charleston areas.
Application information: Application form not required.
Trustees: John L. Ray, L. Newton Thomas, Christopher J. Winton, B.B. & T.
EIN: 556014902
Codes: FD

56344
The Huntington Foundation, Inc.
P.O. Box 2548
Huntington, WV 25726
Application address: 517 9th St., Ste. 203, Huntington, WV 25701, tel.: (304) 522-0611
Contact: Alyene Arthur, Exec. Secy.

Established around 1988 in WV.
Financial data (yr. ended 12/31/00): Grants paid, $426,806; assets, $6,847,384 (L); expenditures, $507,301; qualifying distributions, $428,716.
Limitations: Giving primarily in WV.
Application information: Application form required.
Officers: Cecil H. Underwood, Pres.; Frank E. Hanshaw, Jr., V.P.; Kermit E. McGinnis, Secy.-Treas.
Directors: John E. Jenkins, Jr., Joseph B. Touma.
EIN: 550370129
Codes: FD

56345
Ethel N. Bowen Foundation
c/o First Century Bank, N.A.
500 Federal St.
Bluefield, WV 24701 (304) 325-8181
Contact: R.W. Wilkinson, Pres.

Established about 1968 in WV.
Donor(s): Ethel N. Bowen.‡
Financial data (yr. ended 12/31/01): Grants paid, $406,861; assets, $10,439,178 (M); expenditures, $445,437; qualifying distributions, $412,278.
Limitations: Giving limited to southwestern VA and southern WV.
Application information: Application form not required.
Officers and Directors:* Richard W. Wilkinson,* Pres.; B.L. Jackson,* V.P.; Frank W. Wilkinson,* Secy.; B.K. Satterfield,* Treas.; Henry Bowen.
Trustee: First Century Bank, N.A.
EIN: 237010740
Codes: FD, GTI

56346
Evan G. Roberts Charitable Trust
P.O. Box 1793
Charleston, WV 25326
Application address: 496 High St., 3rd Fl., Morgantown, WV 26505, tel. (304) 285-2359
Contact: Frances M. Klink, V.P.

Established in 2001 in WV.
Donor(s): Evan G. Roberts Trust.
Financial data (yr. ended 12/31/01): Grants paid, $389,219; assets, $3,492,683 (M); gifts received, $1,891,259; expenditures, $418,593; qualifying distributions, $403,560.
Limitations: Giving limited to Marshall County, WV.
Trustees: Clinton Rogerson, B.B. & T.
EIN: 556016455

56347
Beckley Area Foundation, Inc.
129 Main St., Ste. 203
Beckley, WV 25801 (304) 253-3806
FAX: (304) 253-7304; *E-mail:* funds@beckleyareafoundation.com; *URL:* http://beckleyareafoundation.com
Contact: Chair., Grants Comm.

Established in 1985 in WV.
Donor(s): Dr. Thomas Walker Memorial Health Foundation.
Financial data (yr. ended 03/31/02): Grants paid, $388,264; assets, $12,374,087 (M); gifts received, $441,898; expenditures, $562,589.
Limitations: Giving limited to the Beckley and Raleigh County, WV, area.
Publications: Annual report, occasional report, informational brochure, grants list, newsletter, application guidelines.
Application information: See foundation Web site for application requirements and guidelines. Application form required.
Officers: Pete Torrico, Pres.; Sherry Cushman, V.P.; Nancy Kissinger, Secy.; Ned Eller, Treas.; Susan S. Landis, Exec. Dir.
EIN: 311125238
Codes: CM, FD

56348
James B. Chambers Memorial
P.O. Box 3047
Wheeling, WV 26003 (304) 243-9373
FAX: (304) 243-9373
Contact: Emily Schramm Fisher, Admin. Asst.

Established in 1924 in WV.
Financial data (yr. ended 12/31/01): Grants paid, $388,075; assets, $8,982,800 (M); expenditures, $449,028; qualifying distributions, $415,404.
Limitations: Giving limited to Washington County, PA, and Ohio County, WV.
Application information: Application form required.
Officers and Trustees:* Thomas L. Thomas,* Pres.; James E. Altmeyer,* V.P.; E. Lee Jones,* Treas.; Arthur Recht, C. Jack Savage.
EIN: 550360517
Codes: FD

56349
O. J. Stout Scholarship Fund
c/o United National Bank
P.O. Box 1508
Parkersburg, WV 26102 (304) 424-8800
Contact: Tracy Wharton, Trust Off., United National Bank

Established around 1973 in WV.
Financial data (yr. ended 12/31/01): Grants paid, $378,500; assets, $10,542,531 (M); expenditures, $537,967; qualifying distributions, $549,654; giving activities include $94,625 for loans to individuals.
Limitations: Giving limited to residents of WV from Wood and adjacent counties.
Application information: Application form required.
Trustee: United National Bank.
EIN: 556029015
Codes: FD, GTI

56350
Herschel C. Price Educational Foundation
P.O. Box 412
Huntington, WV 25708-0412 (304) 529-3852
Contact: Jonna L. Hughes, Dir.

Established in 1975 in WV.
Donor(s): Herschel C. Price.‡
Financial data (yr. ended 04/30/01): Grants paid, $353,925; assets, $6,263,005 (M); expenditures, $427,048; qualifying distributions, $398,852.
Limitations: Giving limited to WV residents and those attending WV colleges.
Application information: Limited number of applications are released to WV residents twice a year; out of state candidates are no longer offered applications unless they attend a WV college. Application form required.
Trustees: Jonna L. Hughes, Chandos H. Peak, Bank One, West Virginia, N.A.
EIN: 556076719
Codes: FD, GTI

56351
Sarah & Pauline Maier Foundation, Inc.
P.O. Box 6190
Charleston, WV 25362 (304) 343-2201
E-mail: edhmaier@genrlcorp.com
Contact: Edward H. Maier, Chair.

Established in 1958 in WV.
Donor(s): William J. Maier, Jr.,‡ Pauline Maier.
Financial data (yr. ended 10/31/01): Grants paid, $305,500; assets, $18,589,858 (M); expenditures, $781,431; qualifying distributions, $306,037.
Limitations: Giving limited to WV.
Publications: Application guidelines, program policy statement.
Application information: Application form required.
Officers and Board Members:* Edward H. Maier,* Chair. and Pres.; W.J. Maier III,* V.P.; Sara M. Rowe,* Secy.; Elizabeth M. Culwell,* Treas.; John T. Copenhaver, Pauline Maier, W. Warren Point, M.D., J. Randy Valentine.
EIN: 556023833
Codes: FD

56352
Vecellio Family Foundation, Inc.
(Formerly The Enrico Vecellio Family Foundation, Inc.)
P.O. Box 2438
Beckley, WV 25802

Established in 1972.
Donor(s): Leo A. Vecellio, Sr.,‡ Erma V. Grogan, Anna M. Vecellio,‡ Evelyn P. Vecellio.
Financial data (yr. ended 12/31/01): Grants paid, $290,750; assets, $5,554,977 (M); expenditures, $364,395; qualifying distributions, $391,044.
Limitations: Giving primarily in FL and WV.
Application information: Application form not required.
Officers and Trustees:* Leo A. Vecellio, Jr.,* Pres.; Dante E. Castrodale,* V.P.; John L. Taylor, Secy.-Treas.; Robert L. Castrodale, Evelyn P. Vecellio, Kathryn C. Vecellio, Patricia Vecellio.
EIN: 550538242
Codes: FD

56353
Hollowell Foundation, Inc.
(Formerly Hollowell-Ford Foundation, Inc.)
103 E. Washington St.
Lewisburg, WV 24901-1326 (304) 645-5414
Contact: Thomas G. Potterfield, Pres.

Established in 1975 in WV.
Donor(s): Margaret F. Hollowell,‡ Otto Hollowell Unitrust.
Financial data (yr. ended 06/30/01): Grants paid, $275,000; assets, $5,436,341 (M); gifts received, $10,708; expenditures, $358,375; qualifying distributions, $270,592.
Limitations: Giving limited to Greenbrier County, WV.
Application information: Application form required.
Officers: Thomas G. Potterfield, Pres.; Thomas G. McMillan, V.P.; Jesse O. Guills, Jr., Treas.
Director: Marshall Musser.
EIN: 510183517
Codes: FD

56354
George W. Bowers Family Charitable Trust
c/o WesBanco Bank, Inc.
1 Bank Plz.
Wheeling, WV 26003
Contact: R. Bruce Bandi

Established in 2001 in WV.
Donor(s): Frances B. Bowers.‡
Financial data (yr. ended 12/31/01): Grants paid, $269,340; assets, $7,001,928 (M); gifts received, $7,718,717; expenditures, $285,606; qualifying distributions, $276,004.
Limitations: Giving primarily in the city of Mannington and Marion County, WV.
Application information: Application form required.
Trustees: WesBanco Bank, Inc.
EIN: 556140783
Codes: FD

56355
Bloch Fund
c/o WesBanco Bank, Inc.
1 Bank Plz.
Wheeling, WV 26003-6548 (304) 234-9408
Contact: R. Shilling

Established in 1960.
Financial data (yr. ended 12/31/01): Grants paid, $256,673; assets, $815,176 (M); gifts received, $231,873; expenditures, $259,658; qualifying distributions, $255,434.
Limitations: Applications not accepted. Giving limited to cities where family members reside, with emphasis on WV.
Application information: Unsolicited requests for funds not accepted.
Trustee: WesBanco Bank, Inc.
EIN: 556014283
Codes: FD

56356
Robert W. McCormick Scholarship Fund
c/o Bank of Charles Town
P.O. Drawer 40
Charles Town, WV 25414-0040
(304) 728-2435

Established in 1994 in WV.
Donor(s): Robert W. McCormick.
Financial data (yr. ended 04/30/01): Grants paid, $234,487; assets, $4,874,198 (M); expenditures, $307,910; qualifying distributions, $234,487.
Limitations: Giving limited to residents of Jefferson County, WV.
Application information: Application form required.
Trustees: F. Samuel Byrer, Bank of Charles Town.
EIN: 550734149
Codes: FD2, GTI

56357
Lyell B. & Patricia K. Clay Foundation
1426 Kanawha Blvd. E.
Charleston, WV 25301 (304) 348-5129
Contact: Charles M. Avampato, Pres.

Established in 1993 in WV.
Donor(s): Lyell B. Clay.
Financial data (yr. ended 10/31/01): Grants paid, $215,000; assets, $4,101,594 (M); gifts received, $113; expenditures, $276,831; qualifying distributions, $212,036.
Limitations: Giving primarily in WV.
Application information: Application form not required.
Officers: Lyell B. Clay, Chair.; Charles M. Avampato, Pres.
Director: Louis S. Southworth II.
EIN: 550723844
Codes: FD2

56358
Hess Family Foundation
117 Edgington Ln.
Wheeling, WV 26003 (304) 242-9300
Contact: Joseph N. Gompers, Tr.

Established in 1997 in WV.
Donor(s): Andrew C. Hess, Mary Ann Hess.
Financial data (yr. ended 12/31/01): Grants paid, $196,925; assets, $4,029,798 (M); expenditures, $221,673; qualifying distributions, $201,347.
Limitations: Giving primarily in Wheeling, WV.
Trustees: Joseph A. Gompers, Joseph N. Gompers, Security National Trust.
EIN: 550751425
Codes: FD2

56359
The Peery/Cauthen Foundation
(Formerly Peery/Cauthen Charitable Trust)
c/o First Community Bank, Inc.
P.O. Box 950
Bluefield, WV 24701-0950
Contact: Selection Committee

Established in 1989 in WV.
Financial data (yr. ended 12/31/01): Grants paid, $192,650; assets, $2,605,939 (M); gifts received, $4,875; expenditures, $218,997; qualifying distributions, $192,650.
Limitations: Giving primarily in southwest VA, and southern WV.
Application information: Application form required.
Selection Committee: Charles E. Cauthen, Hazel Cauthen, and 8 additional members.
Trustee: First Community Bank, Inc.
EIN: 556065070
Codes: FD2

56360
John S. Thoner Charitable Family Trust
7 Point View Terr.
Wheeling, WV 26003

Established in 1998 in WV.
Donor(s): Louis F. Thoner.‡
Financial data (yr. ended 12/31/99): Grants paid, $191,927; assets, $7,545,687 (M); gifts received, $1,908,397; expenditures, $193,477; qualifying distributions, $191,927.
Limitations: Applications not accepted. Giving primarily in Wheeling, WV.
Application information: Contributes only to pre-selected organizations.
Trustees: Thomas G. Byrum, Rev. John R. Gallagher, Bishop Bernard W. Schmitt.
EIN: 556134268
Codes: FD2

56361
Gordon C. and Mildred R. Jackson Foundation
P.O. Box 273
Charleston, WV 25321-0273 (304) 340-3825
Contact: G. Thomas Battle, Pres.

Incorporated in 1993 in WV.
Financial data (yr. ended 12/31/01): Grants paid, $187,647; assets, $2,998,723 (M); expenditures, $211,615; qualifying distributions, $188,535.
Limitations: Giving primarily in the Mason County, WV, area.
Officers and Director:* G. Thomas Battle,* Pres. and Treas.; John F. Allevato, Secy.
EIN: 550729033
Codes: FD2

56362
One Foundation
550 N. Eisenhower Dr.
Beckley, WV 25801
Contact: Faramarz Attar, Tr.

Established in 1999 in WV.
Donor(s): Faramarz Attar, Ramananda "Tom" Attar, Mohan "Scott" Attar, Kalindi Attar.
Financial data (yr. ended 12/31/00): Grants paid, $181,980; assets, $1,566,574 (M); gifts received, $609,335; expenditures, $248,532; qualifying distributions, $240,948.
Trustees: Carrie Sanders Attar, Faramarz Attar, Ramananda "Tom" Attar.
Directors: David Mcclure, Florian Schleiff, Kathy Vance.
EIN: 316622764
Codes: FD2

56363
Stamp Charitable Fund
c/o WesBanco Bank, Inc.
1 Bank Plz.
Wheeling, WV 26003-3543
Contact: Frederick P. Stamp, Jr. or Joan C. Stamp

Established in 1997 in WV.
Financial data (yr. ended 12/31/01): Grants paid, $173,000; assets, $2,054,520 (M); expenditures, $187,812; qualifying distributions, $176,895.
Limitations: Giving primarily in Wheeling, WV.
Trustees: George S. Weaver, WesBanco Bank, Inc.
EIN: 311546068
Codes: FD2

56364
The McGee Foundation
c/o Stephen Kawash
707 Virginia St. E., Ste. 500
Charleston, WV 25301

Established in 1992 in WV.
Donor(s): John F. McGee, Ruth B. McGee.
Financial data (yr. ended 12/31/00): Grants paid, $167,918; assets, $4,787,751 (M); gifts received, $643,800; expenditures, $220,729; qualifying distributions, $178,132.
Limitations: Applications not accepted. Giving primarily in Charleston, WV; some support also for a journalism program in Austria.
Application information: Contributes only to pre-selected organizations.
Trustees: J. Michael Hines, Stephen E. Kawash, John Kuykendall, John F. McGee, Ruth B. McGee.
EIN: 550720406
Codes: FD2

56365
McDavid Foundation
1410 Woodmere Dr.
Charleston, WV 25314 (304) 347-1102
Contact: William R. McDavid, Pres.

Donor(s): William R. McDavid.
Financial data (yr. ended 12/31/00): Grants paid, $160,000; assets, $1,136,056 (M); gifts received, $9,643; expenditures, $180,835; qualifying distributions, $160,864.
Limitations: Giving primarily in Charleston, WV.
Officer and Directors:* William R. McDavid,* Pres. and Treas.; Anne R. McDavid, Bradford A. McDavid.
EIN: 550730152
Codes: FD2

56366
The Hamer Foundation
P.O. Box 418
Kenova, WV 25530 (304) 453-6381
Contact: J.C. Hamer, Tr.

Established in 1973.
Donor(s): J.C. Hamer, J.P. Hamer, Gladys F. Hamer, Lori D. Hamer.
Financial data (yr. ended 11/30/01): Grants paid, $152,144; assets, $3,102,771 (M); gifts received, $60,065; expenditures, $155,059; qualifying distributions, $151,053.
Limitations: Giving primarily in Atlanta, GA, Des Plains, IL, and Phillipi, WV.
Trustees: Gladys F. Hamer, J.C. Hamer, Lori Dale Hamer.
EIN: 237349926
Codes: FD2

56367
Starvaggi Charities, Inc.
401 Pennsylvania Ave.
Weirton, WV 26062-2322 (304) 748-1400
Contact: James A. O'Brien, Treas.

Established in 1953 in WV and MD.
Donor(s): Mike Starvaggi.
Financial data (yr. ended 01/31/02): Grants paid, $136,524; assets, $1,004,128 (M); gifts received, $51,132; expenditures, $153,558; qualifying distributions, $188,322.
Limitations: Giving primarily in WV.
Application information: Application form not required.
Officers: Donald R. Donell, Pres.; G. Michael Wehr, Secy.; James A. O'Brien, Treas.
EIN: 550602138
Codes: FD2

56368
Fenton Foundation, Inc.
310 W. 4th St.
Williamstown, WV 26187 (304) 375-6122
Contact: Frank M. Fenton, Treas.

Established in 1955 in WV.
Donor(s): Fenton Art Glass Co., Fenton Gift Shops, Inc.
Financial data (yr. ended 12/31/01): Grants paid, $132,566; assets, $3,291,658 (M); gifts received, $14,722; expenditures, $166,100; qualifying distributions, $132,566.
Limitations: Giving primarily in Washington County, OH, and Wood County, WV.
Application information: Application form not required.
Officers and Directors:* Wilmer C. Fenton,* Pres.; Thomas K. Fenton,* V.P.; Don A. Fenton,* Secy.; Frank M. Fenton,* Treas.
EIN: 556017260
Codes: CS, FD2, CD

56369
Segal-Davis Foundation, Inc.
810 Kanawha Blvd. E.
Charleston, WV 25301-2807
Contact: Scott S. Segal, Pres.

Established in 1998 in WV.
Donor(s): Scott S. Segal, Robin J. Davis.
Financial data (yr. ended 05/31/01): Grants paid, $132,550; assets, $185,414 (M); gifts received, $132,563; expenditures, $141,031; qualifying distributions, $139,166.
Limitations: Giving primarily in WV.
Officers: Scott S. Segal, Pres.; Robin J. Davis, Secy.; Mary Jane Kendall, Treas.
EIN: 550759703
Codes: FD2

56370
The West Virginia Foundation
608 Tennessee Ave.
Charleston, WV 25302 (304) 343-5511
Contact: Victor Grigoraci

Established in 1998 in WV.
Donor(s): Emmy Lou Tompkins.
Financial data (yr. ended 12/31/00): Grants paid, $130,000; assets, $2,576,788 (M); gifts received, $7,411; expenditures, $144,052; qualifying distributions, $129,276.
Limitations: Giving primarily in Charleston, WV.
Application information: Application form not required.
Trustees: Betsy C. Altizer, Joanna C. Dye, Boydie C. Girimont, Emmy Lou Tompkins.
EIN: 550759620
Codes: FD2

56371
Lynch Foundation, Inc.
P.O. Box 4268
Star City, WV 26504

Established in 1994 in WV.
Financial data (yr. ended 12/31/01): Grants paid, $119,650; assets, $2,951,630 (M); expenditures, $128,734; qualifying distributions, $119,650.
Limitations: Applications not accepted. Giving primarily in WV.
Application information: Contributes only to pre-selected organizations.
Officers: R. Emmett Lynch, Pres.; John D. Lynch, Jr., V.P.; Robert E. Lynch, Jr., V.P.; Ann L. Borchert, Secy.
EIN: 550737351
Codes: FD2

56372
Henry Logan Children's Home
415 Market St.
Parkersburg, WV 26101 (304) 424-0373
Contact: Randall Law, Dir.

Established in 1952 in WV.
Financial data (yr. ended 12/31/00): Grants paid, $118,962; assets, $4,004,005 (M); expenditures, $164,643; qualifying distributions, $141,093.

Limitations: Giving primarily in Wood County, WV.
Application information: Application form required.
Officers: Pat Carr, Pres.; Steve Reger, V.P.; Mary J. Zivkovich, Secy.; Dave Owen, Treas.
Directors: Randall Law, H. James Province.
EIN: 550365258
Codes: FD2

56373
The Warren and Betty Burnside Foundation, Inc.
300 W. Pike St.
Clarksburg, WV 26301
Application address: 360 Washington Ave., Clarksburg, WV 26301, tel.: (304) 624-5501
Contact: Dean C. Ramsey, Secy.

Established in 1991 in WV.
Donor(s): Warren Burnside, Betty Burnside.
Financial data (yr. ended 01/31/01): Grants paid, $111,375; assets, $2,482,443 (M); gifts received, $1,385; expenditures, $179,782; qualifying distributions, $140,564.
Limitations: Giving limited to residents of Harrison County, WV.
Application information: Application form required.
Officers: James C. West, Jr., Pres.; Daniel L. McCarthy, V.P.; John L. Westfall, V.P.; Dean C. Ramsey, Secy.; Kathryn K. Allen, Treas.
EIN: 550709158
Codes: FD2, GTI

56374
The Frank and Anna Bravchok Foundation
3200 Main St.
Weirton, WV 26062 (304) 748-3200
Contact: Jeffrey J. Rokisky, Tr.

Established in 1992 in OH and WV.
Donor(s): Anna Bravchok.
Financial data (yr. ended 12/31/01): Grants paid, $110,000; assets, $1,583,067 (M); expenditures, $160,101; qualifying distributions, $110,000.
Limitations: Giving primarily in OH.
Application information: Application form not required.
Trustee: Jeffrey J. Rokisky.
EIN: 556116674
Codes: FD2

56375
The Bernard C. & Pansy P. Wellington Foundation
214 North Blvd. W.
Huntington, WV 25701 (304) 522-8080
Contact: Robert Beymer, Tr.

Established in 1991 in WV.
Donor(s): Pansy P. Wellington.‡
Financial data (yr. ended 09/30/01): Grants paid, $109,500; assets, $1,331,572 (M); expenditures, $122,969; qualifying distributions, $109,167.
Limitations: Giving primarily in Huntington, WV.
Application information: Application form not required.
Trustee: Robert Beymer.
EIN: 550690968
Codes: FD2

56376
George M. Cruise Charitable Foundation
c/o First Community Bank, Inc.
P.O. Box 950
Bluefield, WV 24701
Contact: Selection Comm.

Established in 1988 in WV.
Donor(s): George M. Cruise.‡
Financial data (yr. ended 12/31/01): Grants paid, $107,345; assets, $3,264,111 (M); expenditures, $125,742; qualifying distributions, $109,017.
Limitations: Giving limited to southwestern VA and southern WV.
Application information: Application form required.
Committee Members: Diana Coulthard, Annette Osborne, Robert Schumacher.
Trustee: First Community Bank, Inc.
EIN: 626214545
Codes: FD2, GTI

56377
The Berkeley Minor and Susan Fontaine Minor Foundation
1210 One Valley Sq.
Charleston, WV 25301
Contact: John L. Ray, Tr.

Established in 1957 in WV.
Donor(s): Berkeley Minor, Jr.‡
Financial data (yr. ended 12/31/01): Grants paid, $104,000; assets, $2,730,617 (M); expenditures, $128,973; qualifying distributions, $116,645.
Limitations: Giving limited to residents of WV attending specified colleges and universities in VA and WV.
Application information: Only students attending West Virginia University should apply directly to the foundation; students applying to the other colleges must contact their school for application information. Application form not required.
Trustees: Charles W. Loeb, John L. Ray, Christopher J. Winston, One Valley Bank, N.A.
EIN: 556014946
Codes: FD2, GTI

56378
Seelinger Family Foundation
7150 State Rte. 34
Winfield, WV 25213 (304) 586-9891
Contact: Robert V. Ellis, Dir.

Established in 1994 in WV.
Donor(s): Frances Seelinger.
Financial data (yr. ended 12/31/01): Grants paid, $102,680; assets, $2,203,905 (M); expenditures, $109,708; qualifying distributions, $109,708; giving activities include $7,028 for programs.
Limitations: Giving limited to Nicholas County, WV.
Application information: Application form required.
Directors: Tom Dotson, Kay Duvall, Robert V. Ellis, Tom Freeman, Craig Kay, Frances Seelinger.
EIN: 550763222
Codes: FD2

56379
Adolph & Edith Harries & Eleanor Tippens Scholarship Trust
(also known as Tippens Charitable Trust)
c/o WesBanco Bank, Inc.
415 Market St.
Parkersburg, WV 26101

Established in 1992 in WV.
Financial data (yr. ended 12/31/01): Grants paid, $94,517; assets, $3,754,578 (M); expenditures, $116,959; qualifying distributions, $92,516.
Limitations: Giving limited to residents of Wood County, WV.
Application information: The principal and guidance counselor of each high school in Wood County, WV, select a maximum of 2 students to receive the award, unless sufficient funds allow for additional recipients.
Trustee: WesBanco Bank, Inc.
EIN: 556118733
Codes: FD2, GTI

56380
Herscher Foundation, Inc.
c/o 906 Kanawha Valley Bldg.
300 Capitol St.
Charleston, WV 25301 (304) 346-9630
FAX: (304) 346-9631; E-mail: jarrellcl@aol.com
Contact: Charles L. Jarrell, Pres.

Established in 1959 in WV.
Donor(s): J.W. Herscher.‡
Financial data (yr. ended 12/31/01): Grants paid, $93,000; assets, $1,887,583 (M); expenditures, $108,269; qualifying distributions, $93,000.
Limitations: Giving limited to WV, and adjacent areas of OH.
Application information: Application form not required.
Officers and Trustees:* Charles L. Jarrell,* Pres. and Treas.; Charles B. Stacy,* V.P.; G. Thomas Battle,* Secy.; Nelle R. Chilton, Betty Herscher, Russell L. Isaacs, Martha G. Wehrle.
EIN: 556018744
Codes: FD2

56381
Albert M. Price Trust
c/o United National Bank, Trust Dept.
P.O. Box 393
Charleston, WV 25392
Application address: c/o United National Bank, P.O. Box 1508, Parkersburg, WV 26101
Contact: Linda Richards, Trust Off., United National Bank

Established in 1989 in WV.
Financial data (yr. ended 12/31/01): Grants paid, $89,000; assets, $1,543,899 (M); expenditures, $105,604; qualifying distributions, $93,630.
Limitations: Giving primarily to residents of Boone County, WV.
Application information: Applications accepted from Dec. to Feb. Application form required.
Trustee: United National Bank.
EIN: 556081789
Codes: FD2, GTI

56382
The Mardi Gras Fund
P.O. Box 3622
Shepherdstown, WV 25443
FAX: (304) 876-8585; E-mail: qnorthrup@compuserve.com
Contact: Margaret L. Northrup, Pres.

Established in 1992 in RI.
Donor(s): Margaret L. Northrup.
Financial data (yr. ended 12/31/01): Grants paid, $86,785; assets, $1,242,976 (M); gifts received, $41,340; expenditures, $95,102; qualifying distributions, $86,443.
Limitations: Giving primarily in Washington, DC, the Chicago, IL, area, the Cleveland, OH, area, and WV.
Publications: Financial statement.
Application information: Application form required.
Officers: Margaret L. Northrup, Pres.; Anne L. Northrup, Secy.; Robert S. Northrup, Treas.
EIN: 050464995
Codes: FD2

56383
A. S. Thomas Memorial Fund, Inc.
P.O. Box 2073
Charleston, WV 25327-2073
Contact: Andrew S. Thomas, III, Pres.

Established in 1938.
Donor(s): Andrew S. Thomas, Jr.

56383—WEST VIRGINIA

Financial data (yr. ended 12/31/00): Grants paid, $83,001; assets, $1,608,869 (M); expenditures, $98,442; qualifying distributions, $98,281.
Limitations: Giving on a national basis, primarily in the South and the eastern U.S.
Officer: Andrew S. Thomas III, Pres.
EIN: 556017255
Codes: FD2

56384
Stelio and Betty Tracy Corte Charitable Foundation
c/o First Community Bank, Inc.
P.O. Box 950
Bluefield, WV 24701 (304) 325-7151

Established in 1992 in WV.
Donor(s): Stelio Corte, Betty Tracy Corte.
Financial data (yr. ended 06/30/01): Grants paid, $81,729; assets, $1,490,097 (M); gifts received, $50,000; expenditures, $88,286; qualifying distributions, $81,026.
Limitations: Giving primarily in southwestern VA and southern WV.
Application information: Application form not required.
Officers: Betty Tracy Corte, Mgr.; Stelio Corte, Mgr.
Trustee: First Community Bank, Inc.
EIN: 556119269
Codes: FD2

56385
Hinton Area Foundation
c/o Frances Crook
P.O. Box 220
Hinton, WV 25951
Application address: 110 James St., Hinton, WV 25951

Financial data (yr. ended 12/31/00): Grants paid, $81,574; assets, $1,292,108 (M); gifts received, $66,844; expenditures, $90,484.
Limitations: Giving primarily in the Hinton-Summers County, WV, area.
Application information: Scholarship applicants should request guidelines. Organizations should send 2 page letter describing the project with supporting attachments. Application form required.
Officers: Larry Meador, Pres.; Mike Tabor, V.P.; Dorothy Jean Boley, Secy.; Frances Crook, Treas.
Directors: Scott Briers, Regina Eckle, Larry Fox, Ann Gore, Richard Gunnoe, Dale McLaughlin, and 7 additional directors.
EIN: 550716276
Codes: CM

56386
Hope, Love and Charity Foundation
c/o John Cook
P.O. Box 492
Thomas, WV 26292

Established in 1994.
Financial data (yr. ended 12/31/01): Grants paid, $81,500; assets, $1,751,633 (M); expenditures, $83,577; qualifying distributions, $81,272.
Limitations: Applications not accepted.
Application information: Contributes only to pre-selected organizations.
Trustees: John J. Cook, Patrick A. Nichols, Donald G. Roth, Ellis Teets.
EIN: 550616253
Codes: FD2

56387
Carter Family Foundation
c/o United National Bank
129 Main St.
Beckley, WV 25801
Contact: Todd Robinson

Established in 1981 in WV.
Donor(s): Bernard E. Carter,‡ Georgia Carter,‡ Leslie R. Carter.‡
Financial data (yr. ended 06/30/01): Grants paid, $74,400; assets, $13,316,260 (M); expenditures, $132,577; qualifying distributions, $83,127.
Limitations: Giving limited to WV, with emphasis on Raleigh County residents for scholarships.
Application information: Application form not required.
Trustee: United National Bank.
EIN: 550606479
Codes: GTI

56388
Jefferson County Tuberculosis Association, Inc.
P.O. Box 610
Charles Town, WV 25414
Application address: 112 Court St., Charles Town, WV 25414, tel.: (304) 725-9616
Contact: Lacie Mumaw, Treas.

Financial data (yr. ended 12/31/00): Grants paid, $70,994; assets, $187,363 (M); gifts received, $44,245; expenditures, $77,053; qualifying distributions, $70,994.
Officers: John Blundell, Pres.; Gloria Wenger, V.P.; Betty Byrer, Secy.; Lacie Mumaw, Treas.
EIN: 550713040

56389
The Zip Foundation
(Formerly The Adventure Foundation, Inc.)
100 Bluefield Ave., Ste. 3
Bluefield, WV 24701 (304) 325-3514
Contact: Michael R. Shott, Dir.

Established in 1996 in WV.
Donor(s): Michael R. Shott.
Financial data (yr. ended 06/30/01): Grants paid, $70,650; assets, $941,131 (M); expenditures, $75,609; qualifying distributions, $70,650.
Application information: Application form not required.
Directors: John C. Shott, John H. Shott, Karen A. Shott, Michael R. Shott.
EIN: 540754735

56390
W. E. Stone Foundation
28 Byrd Ave.
Wheeling, WV 26003-2710 (304) 234-9296
Contact: Debra Garvin, Secy.-Treas.

Established in 1948 in WV.
Donor(s): Stone & Thomas.
Financial data (yr. ended 01/31/02): Grants paid, $62,769; assets, $1,514,843 (M); expenditures, $80,489; qualifying distributions, $71,218.
Limitations: Giving limited to WV.
Application information: Application form not required.
Officers: Wilbur S. Jones, Jr., Pres.; Debra Garvin, Secy.-Treas.
Trustees: Edward C. Armbrecht, Jr., Ben Exley IV, G. Ogden Nutting.
EIN: 556015330

56391
Charles L. and Anna N. Gault Memorial Scholarship Trust
c/o United National Bank
514 Market St.
Parkersburg, WV 26101-5144 (304) 424-8832
Application address: 514 Market St., Parkersburg, WV 26101
Contact: Tracy Wharton, Trust Off., United National Bank

Established in 1985 in WV.
Donor(s): Anna Gault.
Financial data (yr. ended 12/31/01): Grants paid, $60,160; assets, $1,006,544 (M); expenditures, $73,345; qualifying distributions, $61,038.
Limitations: Giving limited to Wood and Wirt counties, WV.
Application information: Application form required.
Trustee: United National Bank.
EIN: 556096793
Codes: GTI

56392
Gay R. Larsen Charitable Education Trust
P.O. Box 107
Wheeling, WV 26003 (304) 232-8900
Contact: Benjamin R. Honecker, Tr.

Established in 1997 in WV.
Financial data (yr. ended 12/31/00): Grants paid, $59,080; assets, $1,734,264 (M); gifts received, $5; expenditures, $78,589; qualifying distributions, $72,295.
Limitations: Giving limited to residents of Ohio County and counties in the Northern Panhandle, including Marshall, Hancock, and Brooke counties, WV.
Application information: Application form required.
Advisory Committee: Barbara Biglan, Lawrence Jones, Stuart Strait.
Trustee: Benjamin R. Honecker.
EIN: 556128918
Codes: GTI

56393
The Royal Scott Foundation
P.O. Box 550
Charles Town, WV 25414
Contact: Roy S. Steeley, Mgr.

Established in 1997 in WV.
Donor(s): Roy S. Steeley.
Financial data (yr. ended 12/31/01): Grants paid, $56,275; assets, $1,011,501 (M); expenditures, $59,518; qualifying distributions, $56,275.
Officer and Trustees:* Roy S. Steeley,* Mgr.; Stephen P. Goldman, Gwen Scott Steeley.
EIN: 316544542

56394
Jeannine Y. Francis Charitable Foundation Trust
P.O. Box 2846
Huntington, WV 25728-2846
Contact: Gary D. Baldwin, Tr.

Established in 1998 in WA.
Donor(s): Jeannie Y. Francis.
Financial data (yr. ended 12/31/01): Grants paid, $55,650; assets, $1,061,124 (M); expenditures, $65,649; qualifying distributions, $55,650.
Trustee: Gary D. Baldwin.
EIN: 550760949

56395
August J. & Thelma S. Hoffmann Foundation
83 Edgington Ln.
Wheeling, WV 26003-1541 (304) 242-2300
E-mail: JSOHN@HMHY.com
Contact: Jeremy Sohn, Secy.

Established in 2000 in WV.
Donor(s): Thelma S. Hoffman.‡
Financial data (yr. ended 12/31/01): Grants paid, $55,000; assets, $7,926,023 (M); gifts received, $7,722,880; expenditures, $83,828; qualifying distributions, $55,000.
Application information: Application form required.
Officer: Jeremy Sohn, Secy.
Trustees: Richard G. Herndon, Robert J. Krall, Harold J. Roth, William J. Yaeger.
EIN: 550769742

56396
Elizabeth Sarah Kraft Memorial Trust
c/o WesBanco Bank, Inc.
1 Bank Plz.
Wheeling, WV 26003 (304) 234-9400

Established in 1993 in WV.
Donor(s): Elizabeth Sarah Kraft.‡
Financial data (yr. ended 12/31/01): Grants paid, $54,247; assets, $1,722,516 (M); expenditures, $63,647; qualifying distributions, $56,618.
Limitations: Applications not accepted. Giving limited to WV.
Application information: Contributes only to pre-selected organizations.
Trustee: WesBanco Bank, Inc.
EIN: 556118512

56397
Elizabeth H. & H. B. Wehrle Foundation
P.O. Box 513
Charleston, WV 25322
Donor(s): H.B. Wehrle, Jr.
Financial data (yr. ended 12/31/01): Grants paid, $52,000; assets, $675,964 (M); expenditures, $53,930; qualifying distributions, $52,000.
Limitations: Giving primarily in WV.
Trustees: F.T. Graff, Jr., H.B. Wehrle, Jr., Martha G. Wehrle.
EIN: 556014416

56398
Eastern West Virginia Community Foundation
P.O. Box 645
Martinsburg, WV 25402 (304) 264-0353
URL: http://www.ewvcf.org
Contact: Amy E. Owen, Exec. Dir.

Established in 1995.
Financial data (yr. ended 06/30/02): Grants paid, $50,000; assets, $1,215,401 (M); gifts received, $94,031; expenditures, $72,725.
Limitations: Giving primarily in Berkeley, Jefferson, and Morgan counties, WV.
Publications: Annual report, informational brochure, newsletter.
Officers: Dorthea C. McMillan, Pres.; Diane Dailey, V.P.; Conrad Hammann, Secy.; William Sites, Treas.
EIN: 550742377
Codes: CM

56399
The Pace Family Foundation, Inc.
P.O. Box 950
Bluefield, WV 24701

Established in 2001 in WV.
Donor(s): Lawrence J. Pace 1999 Trust, Nettie Z. Pace 1999 Trust.
Financial data (yr. ended 12/31/01): Grants paid, $48,750; assets, $1,039,360 (M); gifts received, $828,004; expenditures, $50,631; qualifying distributions, $48,750.
Limitations: Giving primarily in WV.
Officers and Directors:* Margaret A. Pace,* Pres.; Charles W. Pace,* V.P.; Connie W. Pace,* Secy.; C.W. Pace, Jr.,* Treas.; Cindi Jones.
EIN: 550768136

56400
Huntington Clinical Foundation, Inc.
P.O. Box 117
Huntington, WV 25706

Established in 1986 in WV.
Donor(s): Rufus Switzer.‡
Financial data (yr. ended 12/31/01): Grants paid, $47,000; assets, $273,563 (M); gifts received, $75,825; expenditures, $48,518; qualifying distributions, $47,000.
Limitations: Giving limited to Huntington, WV.
Officers: J. David Daniels, Pres.; James H. Morgan, Jr., Secy.-Treas.
Directors: James Bailes, John P. Childers, Carroll E. Fry, Earl W. Heiner, Jr., John E. Jenkins, Jr., Carroll Justice, Menis E. Ketchum, James H. Morgan III, L. Frank Norton, J.B. Poindexter, Jr., Thomas F. Scott, Richard E. Thompson.
EIN: 310979390

56401
Touma Foundation, Inc.
1616 13th Ave., Ste. 100
Huntington, WV 25701 (304) 522-8800
E-mail: huntear@aol.com
Contact: Joseph B. Touma, M.D., Dir.

Established in 1993 in WV as successor to Touma Ear Foundation.
Donor(s): Touma Ear Foundation, Joseph B. Touma, M.D., Omayma T. Touma, M.D.
Financial data (yr. ended 12/31/01): Grants paid, $46,642; assets, $821,655 (M); expenditures, $54,372; qualifying distributions, $46,642.
Limitations: Giving primarily in WV.
Application information: Application form not required.
Directors: Joseph B. Touma, M.D., Omayma T. Touma, M.D.
EIN: 550718768

56402
Wyatt Charitable Trust
RR 10, Box 394A
Buckhannon, WV 26201-9470

Financial data (yr. ended 12/31/00): Grants paid, $45,998; assets, $0 (M); gifts received, $54,325; expenditures, $54,446; qualifying distributions, $53,262.
Trustee: Rick H. Wyatt.
EIN: 311551892

56403
Horne Family Charitable Foundation
P.O. Box 6397
Wheeling, WV 26003

Established in 1998 in WV.
Financial data (yr. ended 12/31/01): Grants paid, $44,913; assets, $698,829 (M); expenditures, $49,949; qualifying distributions, $44,913.
Trustee: Audrey S. Horne.
EIN: 550761702

56404
J. T. & C. B. Fish Foundation, Inc.
210 Dingess St.
Logan, WV 25601

Donor(s): J.T. Fish, Charlotte B. Fish, Jacqueline F. Lembeck.
Financial data (yr. ended 11/30/01): Grants paid, $44,299; assets, $1,112,211 (M); expenditures, $45,260; qualifying distributions, $44,299.
Officer: Charlotte B. Fish, Pres.
Directors: Jacqueline F. Lembeck, Frances F. Tompkins.
EIN: 556017410

56405
The Stanley M. Hostler Chartiable Trust
P.O. Box 4076
Charleston, WV 25304 (304) 342-3650
Contact: Stanley M. Hostler, Tr.

Established in 1996 in WV.
Donor(s): Stanley M. Hostler.
Financial data (yr. ended 12/31/01): Grants paid, $43,500; assets, $194,907 (M); gifts received, $50,000; expenditures, $43,600; qualifying distributions, $43,600.
Limitations: Applications not accepted. Giving primarily in WV.
Application information: Contributes only to pre-selected organizations.
Trustees: Carl E. Hostler, John A. Hostler, Stanley M. Hostler.
EIN: 550752550

56406
D'Annunzio Foundation, Inc.
P.O. Box 866
200 Ferry St.
Clarksburg, WV 26302-0866 (304) 624-9720
Contact: Vincent F. D'Annunzio, Dir.

Established in 1979.
Donor(s): Members of the D'Annunzio family.
Financial data (yr. ended 12/31/01): Grants paid, $43,000; assets, $393,920 (M); gifts received, $91,930; expenditures, $45,900; qualifying distributions, $43,000.
Limitations: Giving primarily in WV.
Directors: David D'Annunzio, Lucille J. D'Annunzio, Vincent F. D'Annunzio.
EIN: 550589828

56407
Thompson Chandler Memorial Trust
c/o United National Bank
P.O. Box 393
Charleston, WV 25322-0393

Established in 1997 in WV.
Financial data (yr. ended 12/31/01): Grants paid, $42,560; assets, $588,650 (M); expenditures, $51,088; qualifying distributions, $44,101.
Limitations: Applications not accepted. Giving primarily in WV.
Application information: Contributes only to pre-selected organizations.
Trustee: United National Bank.
EIN: 556111445

56408
Hill Stump Disaster Charitable Trust
c/o First Community Bank, Inc.
P.O. Box 5939, 1001 Mercer St.
Princeton, WV 24740
Application address: c/o Trust Dept., First Community Bank, Inc., P.O. Box 280, Buckhannon, WV 26201

Established in 1988 in WV.
Donor(s): Hill Stump.‡

56408—WEST VIRGINIA

Financial data (yr. ended 12/31/01): Grants paid, $42,472; assets, $750,411 (M); expenditures, $45,976; qualifying distributions, $42,591.
Limitations: Giving limited to residents of Upshur County, WV.
Application information: Application form required.
Trustee: First Community Bank, Inc.
EIN: 556104851
Codes: GTI

56409
Brier Patch Charitable Trust
c/o Alice Ann W. Mills
P.O. Box T
Shepherdstown, WV 25443-1113

Established in 1996 in IN.
Donor(s): Alice Ann W. Mills, Howard S. Mills, Jr.
Financial data (yr. ended 09/30/01): Grants paid, $42,400; assets, $617,316 (M); expenditures, $42,749; qualifying distributions, $42,818.
Limitations: Applications not accepted.
Application information: Contributes only to pre-selected organizations.
Trustees: Alice Ann W. Mills, Howard S. Mills.
EIN: 352000005

56410
Frank Litz Smoot Charitable Trust
c/o First Community Bank, Inc.
P.O. Box 950
Bluefield, WV 24701-0950 (304) 325-7151
Contact: Diana S. Coulthard, Trust Off., First Community Bank, Inc.

Established in 1992 in WV.
Donor(s): Frank Litz Smoot.‡
Financial data (yr. ended 12/31/99): Grants paid, $41,913; assets, $1,157,774 (M); expenditures, $49,881; qualifying distributions, $42,788.
Limitations: Giving limited to southwestern VA and southern WV.
Trustee: First Community Bank, Inc.
EIN: 550717997
Codes: GTI

56411
Bruce M. Van Wyk Charitable Educational Foundation
2470 Vineyard Dr.
Falling Waters, WV 25419 (304) 263-8993
Contact: Bruce M. Van Wyk, Tr.

Donor(s): Bruce M. Van Wyk.
Financial data (yr. ended 06/30/01): Grants paid, $41,912; assets, $210,720 (M); gifts received, $41,500; expenditures, $42,799; qualifying distributions, $41,912.
Trustee: Bruce M. Van Wyk.
EIN: 311047232

56412
Marjorie G. Chandler Memorial Trust
c/o United National Bank
P.O. Box 393
Charleston, WV 25322-0393

Established in 1997 in WV.
Donor(s): Marjorie G. Chandler.
Financial data (yr. ended 12/31/01): Grants paid, $41,841; assets, $740,057 (M); expenditures, $48,940; qualifying distributions, $42,921.
Limitations: Applications not accepted. Giving primarily in WV.
Application information: Contributes only to pre-selected organizations.
Trustee: United National Bank.
EIN: 556111446

56413
The Henaghan Sisters Foundation
P.O. Box 6406
Wheeling, WV 26003

Established in 1999 in WV.
Financial data (yr. ended 12/31/01): Grants paid, $39,500; assets, $543,024 (M); expenditures, $47,939; qualifying distributions, $39,500.
Limitations: Giving primarily in Wheeling, WV.
Application information: Application form required.
Officers: Suzanne Polen, Pres.; Sr. Marguerite O'Brien, V.P.; Paul Romano, Secy.-Treas.
Director: Tim Cogan.
EIN: 550763765

56414
Tucker Community Endowment Foundation
P.O. Box 491
Parsons, WV 26287 (304) 478-2930
Additional tel.: (304) 478-3533
Contact: Diane L. Hinkle, Pres., or Mariwyn M. Smith, Asst. Secy.

Established in 1988 in WV.
Financial data (yr. ended 12/31/01): Grants paid, $39,350; assets, $818,329 (M); gifts received, $134,634; expenditures, $68,126.
Limitations: Giving limited to Tucker County, WV and the surrounding areas (Preston and Randolph counties).
Publications: Annual report.
Application information: Application form required for scholarships.
Officers and Directors:* Diane L. Hinkle,* Pres.; Harry Boyce,* V.P.; David Cooper,* Secy.; James C. Cooper III, Treas.; Louetta Mason,* Treas.; James Arnold, Jane H. Barb, Diane T. Beall, Henry Roberts Biola, Ph.D., Dan Bucher, Pamela A. Chenoweth, David Collins, Carrie Cooper, Fritz Corey, Rachell R. Davis, Mark Doak, Nancy K. Dotson, Jodi Douglas, Amy Fiorini, Sam Goughnow, Adrea Hedrick, Janie Hedrick, Matthew Hinkle, Sherman Jarret, Patrick A. Nichols, Shawn Nichols, Milan Nypl, Marvin Parsons, Donna Patrick, Walt Ranalli, Randall R. Reed, Vidia Ross.
EIN: 550687098
Codes: CM

56415
Community Foundation of the Virginias, Inc.
(Formerly Bluefield Area Foundation, Inc.)
P.O. Box 4127
Bluefield, WV 24701
Tel./FAX: (304) 324-0222; E-mail: bla00684@mail.wvnet.edu
Contact: Katharine Light Sexton, Exec. Dir.

Established in 1993 in WV.
Financial data (yr. ended 12/31/01): Grants paid, $37,515; assets, $1,096,139 (M); gifts received, $76,013; expenditures, $82,930.
Limitations: Giving in Tazewell County, VA and Mercer County, WV.
Publications: Annual report, application guidelines, grants list, newsletter, financial statement, informational brochure (including application guidelines).
Application information: Contact foundation for applications available in Aug. Application form required.
Officers: Nick Ameli, Jr., Pres.; Annette Osborne, V.P.; Betty Bailey, Secy.; Ron Cambell, Treas.; Katherine Light Sexton, Exec. Dir.
Board Members: Mary Azzo, Paul Cole, Eugenia Hancock, Doris Sue Kantor, Marshell Miller, A.A. Modena, Charlie Peters, Larry Roe, June Shott.
EIN: 550724623

Codes: CM

56416
The Roy Chambers Foundation
1358 National Rd.
Wheeling, WV 26003 (304) 242-8410
Contact: Linda M. Bordas, Tr.

Established in 1993.
Financial data (yr. ended 12/31/01): Grants paid, $36,076; assets, $1,546,610 (M); expenditures, $42,863; qualifying distributions, $36,076.
Limitations: Giving limited to residents of Ohio County, WV.
Application information: Applications from outside of Ohio County, WV, will not be accepted. Application form required.
Trustees: James G. Bordas, Linda M. Bordas.
EIN: 556113902
Codes: GTI

56417
Mary F. Battle Memorial Educational Fund
c/o The Huntington National Bank
P.O. Box 895
Morgantown, WV 26507-0895

Established in 1990 in WV.
Donor(s): Mary F. Battle.‡
Financial data (yr. ended 12/31/99): Grants paid, $35,118; assets, $1,025,991 (M); expenditures, $48,606; qualifying distributions, $39,555.
Limitations: Giving limited to Taylor County, WV.
Application information: Application form required.
Selection Committee: Gregory H. Cartwright, Daniel E. Mankins, Marianne Meriefield, Rev. Prechtl, Wendell D. Teets.
Trustee: The Huntington National Bank.
EIN: 550699329

56418
Genevieve Starcher Educational Foundation
c/o United National Bank
P.O. Box 393
Charleston, WV 25322-0393
Application address: P.O. Box 266, Ripley, WV 25271
Contact: Kathryn Goodwin, Pres.

Donor(s): Genevieve Starcher.‡
Financial data (yr. ended 12/31/01): Grants paid, $33,250; assets, $561,516 (M); expenditures, $37,095; qualifying distributions, $34,835.
Limitations: Giving limited to residents of Jackson County, WV.
Application information: Application form required.
Officer and Directors:* Kathryn Goodwin,* Pres.; Bishop, Episcopal Diocese of WV, William E. Casto, Carroll Staats, Rev. Elizabeth Walker, Jack Wiseman.
Trustee: United National Bank.
EIN: 510159560
Codes: GTI

56419
Hancock County Savings Bank Charitable Foundation
351 Carolina Ave.
P.O. Box 245
Chester, WV 26034

Established in 1999 in WV.
Donor(s): Hancock County Savings Bank.
Financial data (yr. ended 12/31/01): Grants paid, $29,740; assets, $955,359 (M); gifts received, $6,500; expenditures, $36,912; qualifying distributions, $29,740.
Limitations: Giving limited to the market area of Hancock County Savings Bank.

Application information: Applications available at Hancock County Savings Banks. Application form required.
Officers: Harry Comm, Chair.; John Fitzjohn, Pres.; Shirley Barnhart, Secy.-Treas.
Trustees: Romie Castelli, Steven Cooper, Susan Smith, Catherine Watson.
EIN: 550767253

56420
Elizabeth Stifel Kline Foundation
c/o Wesbanco Trust & Investment Services
1 Bank Plz.
Wheeling, WV 26003

Established in 2000 in WV.
Financial data (yr. ended 12/31/01): Grants paid, $29,500; assets, $876,019 (M); gifts received, $34,675; expenditures, $38,809; qualifying distributions, $29,500.
Limitations: Applications not accepted.
Application information: Contributes only to pre-selected organizations.
Trustees: John C. Harmon, Wesbanco Trust & Investment Services.
EIN: 256714311

56421
The Fred Gilbert Charitable Foundation
c/o First Community Bank, Inc.
P.O. Box 950
Bluefield, WV 24701

Established in 1991 in WV.
Donor(s): Fred Gilbert.
Financial data (yr. ended 06/30/02): Grants paid, $29,000; assets, $118,758 (M); expenditures, $30,044; qualifying distributions, $29,000.
Limitations: Applications not accepted.
Application information: Contributes only to pre-selected organizations.
Trustees: Bernice Gilbert, LeRoy Mabe, First Community Bank, Inc.
EIN: 546114895

56422
Howard P. & Mary Needles McJunkin Family Foundation
(Formerly McJunkin Family Foundation)
c/o United National Bank
P.O. Box 393
Charleston, WV 25392 (304) 348-8450
Contact: Emilie Love, Trust Admin., United National Bank

Donor(s): Mary McJunkin Gray.
Financial data (yr. ended 12/31/01): Grants paid, $28,945; assets, $322,307 (M); gifts received, $9,659; expenditures, $34,554; qualifying distributions, $28,354.
Limitations: Giving primarily in Charleston, WV.
Trustees: Mary McJunkin Gray, United National Bank.
EIN: 556017085

56423
Arthur and Joan Weisberg Family Foundation, Inc.
2010 2nd Ave.
P.O. Box 5346
Huntington, WV 25703

Established in 1995 in WV.
Donor(s): Arthur Weisberg.
Financial data (yr. ended 08/31/01): Grants paid, $27,660; assets, $584,644 (M); gifts received, $120,000; expenditures, $27,719; qualifying distributions, $27,660.
Limitations: Applications not accepted. Giving limited to Huntington, WV.

Application information: Contributes only to pre-selected organizations.
Officers and Directors:* Arthur Weisberg,* Pres. and Treas.; Joan Weisberg,* V.P. and Secy.; Martha Weisberg Barvin, Charles Weisberg, Louis Weisberg, Pamela Weisberg, Seth Weisberg.
EIN: 550746517

56424
I.O.O.F. Grand Lodge Educational Fund, Inc.
c/o Walton D. Stowell
P.O. Box 603
Harpers Ferry, WV 25425-0603
Application address: Rte. 6, Box 295, Clarksburg, WV 26301
Contact: Carl C. Williams, Secy.

Financial data (yr. ended 12/31/01): Grants paid, $27,600; assets, $382,097 (M); gifts received, $4,095; expenditures, $30,912; qualifying distributions, $27,600.
Limitations: Giving limited to WV.
Application information: Application form required.
Officers: Edwin C. Runner, Pres.; D.J. Weekley, V.P.; Carl C. Williams, Secy.; W. D. Stowell, Treas.
EIN: 237003391
Codes: GTI

56425
The John and Lucia Pais Family Educational Foundation, Inc.
c/o First Century Bank, N.A.
500 Federal St.
Bluefield, WV 24701 (304) 325-8181

Established in 1997 in VA.
Donor(s): Lia Pais.
Financial data (yr. ended 06/30/01): Grants paid, $27,300; assets, $321,647 (M); gifts received, $5,064; expenditures, $30,772; qualifying distributions, $27,508.
Limitations: Giving limited to McDowell County, WV area.
Directors: Lia Pais, Elizabeth Pruett, B.K. Statterfield.
Trustee: First Century Bank, N.A.
EIN: 311561732
Codes: GTI

56426
Serra Foundation, Inc.
2525 Pennsylvania Ave.
Weirton, WV 26062

Established in 1991 in WV.
Donor(s): Louis Serra.
Financial data (yr. ended 12/31/99): Grants paid, $26,812; assets, $3,841 (M); gifts received, $160,739; expenditures, $28,618; qualifying distributions, $26,812.
Application information: Application form not required.
Trustees: Lucinda Alongi, Mary Ann Boyd, Mya Gill, Rhonda Quattrochi, Louis Serra.
EIN: 550696463

56427
S. Katherine Boxwell & Edwin P. Churchill WV Scholarship Fund
c/o Bank of Charles Town, Trust Dept.
P.O. Drawer 40
Charles Town, WV 25414-0040
(304) 728-2435

Established in 1999 in WV.
Donor(s): Edwin P. Churchill.‡
Financial data (yr. ended 06/30/02): Grants paid, $25,670; assets, $1,207,709 (M); gifts received, $820,000; expenditures, $35,784; qualifying distributions, $25,670.

Limitations: Giving limited to Berkeley, Grant, Hampshire, Hardy, Jefferson, Mineral, and Morgan counties, WV.
Application information: Application available at guidance departments of high schools in eligible counties. Application form required.
Trustee: Bank of Charles Town.
EIN: 556137104

56428
Helen J. Prince Foundation
c/o United National Bank
21 12th St.
Wheeling, WV 26003 (304) 231-1905
Contact: Mark Ferrell, V.P., United National Bank

Established in 2000 in WV.
Donor(s): Helen J. Prince.
Financial data (yr. ended 12/31/01): Grants paid, $24,530; assets, $436,817 (M); expenditures, $40,054; qualifying distributions, $24,530.
Limitations: Giving primarily in Wheeling, WV.
Application information: Application form required.
Trustees: Sue Seibert Farnsworth, United National Bank.
EIN: 256742423

56429
Tom C. Smith Charitable Trust
P.O. Box 1216
Huntington, WV 25714-1216 (304) 523-3424
Contact: George Sinkewitz, Tr.

Financial data (yr. ended 03/31/02): Grants paid, $23,168; assets, $184,693 (M); expenditures, $56,721; qualifying distributions, $56,721.
Limitations: Giving limited to Chesapeake, OH, and Huntington, WV.
Application information: Application form not required.
Trustees: Don Carnohan, Johnny C. Linkous, Chris A. McGoffen, George Sinkewitz, Clarence A. Snyder.
EIN: 550570334
Codes: GTI

56430
A. M. Scott Trust
c/o One Valley Bank, N.A.
P.O. Box 1793
Charleston, WV 25326-1793 (304) 348-7000
Contact: Susan S. Short, Trust Off., One Valley Bank, N.A.

Established in 1941 in WV.
Donor(s): A.M. Scott.‡
Financial data (yr. ended 12/31/01): Grants paid, $22,500; assets, $440,238 (M); expenditures, $31,065; qualifying distributions, $22,500.
Limitations: Giving limited to Kanawha County, WV.
Trustee: One Valley Bank, N.A.
EIN: 556025666

56431
The Dante Castrodale Scholarship Foundation
c/o First Community Bank, Inc.
P.O. Box 950
Bluefield, WV 24701
Application address: c/o Vecellio & Grogan, Drawer V, Beckley, WV 25801
Contact: Dante Enrico Castrodale, Selection Comm. Member

Established in 1987 in WV.
Donor(s): Dante Enrico Castrodale, Ida A. Castrodale.
Financial data (yr. ended 12/31/01): Grants paid, $20,000; assets, $521,659 (M); expenditures, $24,683; qualifying distributions, $20,875.

56431—WEST VIRGINIA

Limitations: Giving limited to southern WV, with emphasis on McDowell County.
Application information: Application form required.
Trustee: First Community Bank, Inc.
Selection Committee: Dante Enrico Castrodale, Robert Leo Castrodale.
EIN: 626198751
Codes: GTI

56432
The Paper Supply Company Charitable Foundation, Inc.
100 Bluefield Ave., Ste. 3
Bluefield, WV 24701
Application address: P.O. Box 130, Bluefield, WV 24701, tel.: (304) 325-3514
Contact: Michael R. Shott, Dir.

Established in 1996 in WV.
Donor(s): Paper Supply Co., Paper Supply Co. of Bristol, Paper Supply Co. of Winston-Salem, Inc., Greenville Paper Co.
Financial data (yr. ended 06/30/02): Grants paid, $17,750; assets, $250,200 (M); expenditures, $18,831; qualifying distributions, $17,750.
Limitations: Giving primarily in Bluefield, VA, and Bluefield, WV.
Application information: Application form not required.
Officer and Directors: Mark J. Sell,* C.F.O.; Roger Estep, John C. Shott, Michael R. Shott, Scott H. Shott.
EIN: 550754736
Codes: CS, CD

56433
Baker Educational Nursing Trust
c/o United National Bank
P.O. Box 1508
Parkersburg, WV 26102
Contact: Mrs. Tracy Wharton, Trust Off., United National Bank

Established in 1997 in WV.
Financial data (yr. ended 12/31/01): Grants paid, $17,565; assets, $197,824 (M); expenditures, $21,616; qualifying distributions, $17,565.
Limitations: Giving limited to residents of Washington County, OH and Wood County, WV.
Trustee: United National Bank.
EIN: 556132946

56434
The Tom & Virginia Seely Foundation
P.O. Box 616
Berkeley Springs, WV 25411

Established in 1997 in WV.
Donor(s): Harleigh E. "Tom" Seely, Virginia L. Seely.
Financial data (yr. ended 06/30/01): Grants paid, $15,000; assets, $272,807 (M); gifts received, $75,931; expenditures, $17,134; qualifying distributions, $15,000.
Limitations: Applications not accepted. Giving primarily in WV.
Application information: Contributes only to pre-selected organizations.
Officers: Harleigh E. "Tom" Seely, Pres.; Virginia L. Seely, V.P.; Barbara H. Pichot, Secy.; Philip P. Cox, Treas.
Directors: William Gaston Caperton IV, Monna Lea Hurst, J. Philip Kesecker, Jackie M. Morgan, Thomas F. Rokisky.
EIN: 550755475

56435
The David L. Strahan Educational Foundation, Inc.
926 20th St.
Vienna, WV 26105-1255
Application address: c/o Principal, Wirt County High School, Elizabeth, WV 26143, tel.: (304) 275-4241

Established in 1996 in WV.
Donor(s): David L. Strahan.
Financial data (yr. ended 06/30/00): Grants paid, $15,000; assets, $123,498 (M); gifts received, $55,004; expenditures, $15,809; qualifying distributions, $15,589.
Limitations: Giving limited to residents of WV.
Application information: Application form required.
Officers: David L. Strahan, Pres. and Secy.; Gary Altman, V.P.; John Greco, Treas.
EIN: 550752363
Codes: TN

56436
Ruby Enterprises Foundation, Inc.
P.O. Box 683
Morgantown, WV 26505

Donor(s): Hazel Ruby McQuain.
Financial data (yr. ended 12/31/01): Grants paid, $14,850; assets, $314,824 (M); expenditures, $16,686; qualifying distributions, $14,850.
Limitations: Giving primarily in Morgantown, WV.
Application information: Application form required.
Officers: Hazel Ruby McQuain, Pres.; J. Burl McQuain, V.P.; Sandra McCabe, Secy.; George R. Farmer, Jr., Treas.
EIN: 237035935

56437
Better Minerals & Aggregates Company Education Foundation
(Formerly U.S. Silica Company Education Foundation)
c/o John A. Ulizio
P.O. Box 187
Berkeley Springs, WV 25411-0187

Established in 1998.
Donor(s): U.S. Silica Co.
Financial data (yr. ended 12/31/01): Grants paid, $14,614; assets, $22,848 (M); gifts received, $14,614; expenditures, $14,614; qualifying distributions, $14,614.
Limitations: Giving primarily in areas of company operations.
Application information: Unsolicited requests for funds not accepted.
Officers and Directors: Richard A. Shearer,* Pres.; Walter C. Pellish, V.P.; John A. Ulizio,* Secy.; Michael L. Thompson, Treas.; Daniel N. Gerber.
EIN: 550760222
Codes: CS, CD

56438
Munawwar Jehan Education Foundation, Inc.
1 Portview Dr.
Charleston, WV 25311-9737

Established in 2000 in WV.
Donor(s): Jamal H. Khan.
Financial data (yr. ended 12/31/01): Grants paid, $14,000; assets, $91,040 (M); gifts received, $85,538; expenditures, $15,377; qualifying distributions, $14,000.
Limitations: Applications not accepted. Giving primarily in Pakistan.
Application information: Contributes only to pre-selected organizations.

Officer and Directors: Jamal H. Khan,* Pres.; Faisal H. Khan, Qamar J. Khan, Yusuf H. Khan, Lubna Shafi.
EIN: 550774156

56439
Farr Foundation, Inc.
200 Armstrong Ave.
Williamstown, WV 26187-1310

Established in 1989 in WV.
Donor(s): Farr Manufacturing & Engineering Co., Douglas R. Farr.
Financial data (yr. ended 12/31/01): Grants paid, $13,970; assets, $116,612 (M); gifts received, $30,000; expenditures, $14,027; qualifying distributions, $14,027.
Limitations: Giving limited to OH and WV.
Application information: Unsolicited requests for funds not accepted.
Officers and Trustees: Douglas R. Farr,* Pres.; Douglas R. Farr, Jr.,* V.P.; Marilyn E. Farr,* Secy.; Bradley E. Farr,* Treas.
EIN: 550694965
Codes: CS, CD

56440
Adaline C. Nugent Educational Fund
c/o United National Bank
514 Market St.
Parkersburg, WV 26101-5144

Financial data (yr. ended 12/31/00): Grants paid, $12,970; assets, $245,405 (M); expenditures, $16,240; qualifying distributions, $13,818.
Limitations: Applications not accepted. Giving limited to Parkersburg, WV.
Trustee: United National Bank.
EIN: 237425082
Codes: GTI

56441
Right Hand Charitable Trust
108 Hawksbury Trace
Beckley, WV 25801

Donor(s): N. Paige Ward.
Financial data (yr. ended 06/30/01): Grants paid, $12,125; assets, $253,425 (M); gifts received, $95,000; expenditures, $20,410; qualifying distributions, $12,125.
Limitations: Applications not accepted. Giving primarily in MI, PA, and WV.
Application information: Contributes only to pre-selected organizations.
Trustee: N. Paige Ward.
EIN: 556138402

56442
Emily Virginia Memorial Foundation, Inc.
P.O. Box 441
Matewan, WV 25678-0441

Established in 1976 in WV.
Donor(s): Frank M. Allara, Mrs. Frank M. Allara.
Financial data (yr. ended 12/31/00): Grants paid, $12,112; assets, $0 (M); gifts received, $12,501; expenditures, $12,501; qualifying distributions, $12,112.
Limitations: Applications not accepted.
Officers: Frank M. Allara, Pres.; Frank W. Allara, V.P.; George M. Blankenship, Secy.; Robert K. Allara, Treas.
EIN: 510173824

56443
Jamey Harless Foundation, Inc.
P.O. Box 1210
Gilbert, WV 25621 (304) 664-3227
Contact: Sharon Murphy, Secy.

Established in 1967 in WV.

Donor(s): James H. Harless.
Financial data (yr. ended 03/31/02): Grants paid, $11,650; assets, $583,534 (M); gifts received, $100; expenditures, $115,827; qualifying distributions, $11,650.
Limitations: Giving limited to WV, with emphasis on the southern communities of Mingo County.
Application information: Application form required.
Officers: James H. Harless, Pres.; Gary G. White, V.P.; Sharon Murphy, Secy.
EIN: 237093387
Codes: GTI

56444
Storck Family Foundation
c/o T. Weyer & J. STorck
501 Avery St., 9th FL.
Parkersburg, WV 26101-5123

Established in 1989 in WV.
Donor(s): V. James Mazzella, Sarah S. Mazzella.
Financial data (yr. ended 12/31/01): Grants paid, $11,000; assets, $156,698 (M); expenditures, $14,160; qualifying distributions, $11,000.
Limitations: Applications not accepted. Giving on a national basis.
Application information: Contributes only to pre-selected organizations.
Board Members: Joel Mazzella, Domenic Salamida, Ginger Salamida, Joan Storck.
EIN: 550691435

56445
Crandall, Pyles, Haviland & Turner Foundation, Inc.
(Formerly Crandall & Pyles Foundation)
P.O. Box 3465
122 Capitol St., Ste. 300
Charleston, WV 25334 (304) 345-3080
Contact: Todd A. Twyman, Pres.

Established in 1992 in WV.
Donor(s): Crandall, Pyles, Haviland & Turner, LLP.
Financial data (yr. ended 12/31/01): Grants paid, $10,800; assets, $228,835 (M); expenditures, $11,840; qualifying distributions, $10,800.
Limitations: Giving primarily in WV.
Officers: Todd A. Twyman, Pres.; William Turner, V.P.; Jim Haviland, Secy.-Treas.
Directors: Grant Crandall, Henry Hill, Brad Pyles.
EIN: 550717420
Codes: CS, CD

56446
Charles McCamic Foundation
c/o WesBanco Bank, Inc.
1 Bank Plz.
Wheeling, WV 26003-3543
Contact: R. Bruce Bandi, Trust Off., WesBanco Bank, Inc.

Donor(s): Charles McCamic.‡
Financial data (yr. ended 12/31/01): Grants paid, $10,500; assets, $182,744 (M); expenditures, $12,644; qualifying distributions, $10,924.
Limitations: Giving limited to Atlanta, GA, and WV.
Trustees: Thomas G. Byrum, John E.C. Taylor, William S. Whitaker.
EIN: 556015424

56447
Raymond B. Craig Scholarship Fund
c/o Robert P. Fitzsimmons
1609 Warwood Ave.
Wheeling, WV 26003-7110 (304) 277-1700

Established in 1997 in WV.
Financial data (yr. ended 12/31/99): Grants paid, $10,023; assets, $197,294 (M); gifts received, $31,000; expenditures, $10,023; qualifying distributions, $10,023.
Limitations: Giving limited to WV.
Trustee: Robert P. Fitzsimmons.
EIN: 550752656

56448
Arthur's Enterprises, Inc. Scholarship Foundation
P.O. Box 5654
Huntington, WV 25703-0654
Application address: P.O. Box 5346, Huntington, WV 25703
Contact: Joan Weisberg, Secy.

Established in 1991 in WV.
Donor(s): Arthur's Enterprises, Inc.
Financial data (yr. ended 06/30/01): Grants paid, $10,000; assets, $500 (M); gifts received, $9,000; expenditures, $10,000; qualifying distributions, $10,000.
Limitations: Giving limited to residents of WV.
Application information: Application form required.
Officers and Directors:* Arthur Weisberg,* Pres.; Clarence Martin,* V.P. and Treas.; Joan Weisberg, Secy.; John Spoor.
EIN: 550709058
Codes: CS, CD, GTI

56449
The Dunn Family Foundation, Inc.
Rt. 2, Box 143
Mineral Wells, WV 26150

Established in 1999 WV.
Donor(s): Wayne P. Dunn, Mamye Kay Dunn.
Financial data (yr. ended 12/31/01): Grants paid, $10,000; assets, $524,395 (M); gifts received, $435,700; expenditures, $16,471; qualifying distributions, $10,000.
Limitations: Applications not accepted.
Application information: Contributes only to pre-selected organizations.
Officer and Director:* Wayne P. Dunn,* Pres.
EIN: 550768879

56450
A. J. Guill Estate Trust
c/o B.B. & T., Trust Tax Dept.
P.O. Box 1793
Charleston, WV 25326

Financial data (yr. ended 12/31/01): Grants paid, $10,000; assets, $142,126 (M); expenditures, $12,293; qualifying distributions, $10,000.
Limitations: Applications not accepted. Giving limited to Charleston, WV.
Application information: Contributes only to pre-selected organizations.
Trustee: B.B. & T.
EIN: 556014885

56451
Stamp 2001 Charitable Fund
21 Bethany Pike
Wheeling, WV 26003
Contact: Joan C. Stamp, Tr.

Established in 2001 in WV.
Financial data (yr. ended 12/31/01): Grants paid, $10,000; assets, $153,624 (M); gifts received, $162,747; expenditures, $10,500; qualifying distributions, $10,250.
Trustees: Louis J. Costanzo III, Joan C. Stamp, George S. Weaver, Jr.
EIN: 256756834

56452
Woodbridge-Brown Fund
c/o One Valley Bank, N.A.
P.O. Box 1793
Charleston, WV 25326-1793
Contact: Bruce Leckie, Trust Off., One Valley Bank, N.A.

Financial data (yr. ended 12/31/01): Grants paid, $10,000; assets, $320,491 (M); expenditures, $16,260; qualifying distributions, $10,000.
Limitations: Giving primarily in Charleston, WV.
Trustees: James F. Brown, Glenn Crotty, G. Hamrick, Warren B. Point, One Valley Bank, N.A.
EIN: 556015016

56453
Donald W. & David J. Levenson Foundation, Inc.
1269 National Rd., No. 48
Wheeling, WV 26003 (304) 242-3848
Contact: Ethyl S. Levenson

Financial data (yr. ended 12/31/01): Grants paid, $9,865; assets, $35,552 (M); gifts received, $10,000; expenditures, $11,353; qualifying distributions, $9,865.
Limitations: Giving primarily in WV.
Officer: Donelda J. Godfrey, Mgr.
EIN: 556028445

56454
Carl Dee Stickley Educational Fund
c/o The Bank of Romney
P.O. Box 876
Romney, WV 26757
Contact: Lawrence Foley, Tr.

Financial data (yr. ended 03/31/02): Grants paid, $9,750; assets, $161,212 (M); expenditures, $10,663; qualifying distributions, $9,664.
Limitations: Giving limited to Hampshire County, WV.
Application information: Application form required.
Trustees: Lawrence Foley, Gerald Mathias, Jane McBride.
EIN: 550682624
Codes: GTI

56455
Princeton High School Class of 1926 Scholarship Fund
c/o First Community Bank, Inc., Trust Dept.
P.O. Box 5939
Princeton, WV 24740 (304) 487-9000
Contact: Ronda Lilly, Trust Off., First Community Bank, Inc.

Financial data (yr. ended 12/31/01): Grants paid, $9,500; assets, $123,565 (M); expenditures, $10,304; qualifying distributions, $9,500.
Limitations: Giving limited to Princeton, WV.
Application information: Application form required.
Trustee: First Community Bank, Inc.
EIN: 310889436
Codes: GTI

56456
Merwin C. Ludwig Educational Trust
P.O. Box 552
Wardensville, WV 26851
Application address: Rte. 3, Box 320, Wardensville, WV 26851, tel.: (304) 874-3633
Contact: Alfred J. Ludwig, Pres.

Established in 1990 in WV.
Financial data (yr. ended 06/30/99): Grants paid, $9,200; assets, $208,700 (M); expenditures, $9,798; qualifying distributions, $9,569.

56456—WEST VIRGINIA

Limitations: Giving limited to residents of Hardy County, WV.
Application information: Application form not required.
Officers: Alfred J. Ludwig, Pres.; Glen O. Bradfield, Secy.; William B. Sager, Treas.
EIN: 550699102

56457
Robert L. & Helen E. Levenson Family Charitable Trust
1 Archibald Ave.
Wheeling, WV 26003-6627 (304) 233-5630
Contact: Helen E. Levenson, Tr.

Established in 1981.
Donor(s): Robert L. Levenson,‡ Helen E. Levenson.
Financial data (yr. ended 12/31/01): Grants paid, $9,185; assets, $688,609 (M); gifts received, $10,000; expenditures, $11,455; qualifying distributions, $9,185.
Limitations: Giving primarily in Wheeling, WV; giving also to national organizations.
Trustee: Helen E. Levenson.
EIN: 556085920

56458
Leonard A. & Shirley E. Harvey Foundation
P.O. Box 184
Parkersburg, WV 26102

Established in 1988 in WV.
Donor(s): Leonard A. Harvey.
Financial data (yr. ended 12/31/01): Grants paid, $9,000; assets, $222,727 (M); gifts received, $40,500; expenditures, $9,069; qualifying distributions, $9,000.
Limitations: Applications not accepted. Giving primarily in WV.
Application information: Contributes only to pre-selected organizations.
Officer: Leonard A. Harvey, Mgr.
Trustees: Brian Harvey, Bruce Harvey, Christopher Harvey, Shirley E. Harvey.
EIN: 550688042

56459
Harrison H. Kennedy Award Trust
c/o WesBanco Bank, Inc.
1 Bank Plz.
Wheeling, WV 26003

Established in 1994 in WV.
Donor(s): Harrison H. Kennedy.‡
Financial data (yr. ended 12/31/01): Grants paid, $8,530; assets, $146,547 (M); expenditures, $9,136; qualifying distributions, $8,695.
Limitations: Applications not accepted. Giving primarily in Charleston and Wheeling, WV.
Application information: Contributes only to pre-selected organizations.
Trustee: WesBanco Bank, Inc.
EIN: 556125003

56460
Francis G. Horne Foundation
Rte. 1, Box 320
Fort Spring, WV 24936-9738

Established in 1957 in VA.
Donor(s): Francis G. Horne.
Financial data (yr. ended 08/31/01): Grants paid, $8,525; assets, $1,379 (M); gifts received, $6,000; expenditures, $8,713; qualifying distributions, $8,713.
Limitations: Applications not accepted. Giving primarily in WV.
Application information: Contributes only to pre-selected organizations. Unsolicited requests for funds not accepted.

Officers: Francis G. Horne, Pres. and Treas.; R.H. Phillips, V.P.; Sara P. Horne, Secy.
EIN: 546068007

56461
The Logan County Charitable and Educational Foundation, Inc.
213 Main St.
Logan, WV 25601 (304) 752-6850
E-mail: pcwin@bellatlantic.net

Financial data (yr. ended 12/31/99): Grants paid, $8,100; assets, $773,416 (M); gifts received, $248,330; expenditures, $8,779.
Limitations: Giving limited to Logan County, WV.
Application information: Application form not required.
Officers: Martha J. Becker, Pres.; Clinton Winter, V.P.; Reginald Osenton, Secy.; Jean Ray, Treas.
EIN: 311498923
Codes: CM

56462
K-G Trust
401 11th St., Ste. 1400
Huntington, WV 25701

Established in 1998.
Financial data (yr. ended 12/31/01): Grants paid, $7,468; assets, $8,374 (M); gifts received, $2,200; expenditures, $7,528; qualifying distributions, $7,468.
Limitations: Giving limited to WV.
Trustees: James Grant McGuire, Pik Kheng Yap McGuire.
EIN: 550755199

56463
Harvey Morgan Scholarship Fund
(Formerly Morgan-Robertson Memorial Scholarship and Welfare Fund)
c/o First Community Bank, Inc.
P.O. Box 950
Bluefield, WV 24701-0950

Financial data (yr. ended 07/31/99): Grants paid, $7,357; assets, $144,162 (M); expenditures, $8,951; qualifying distributions, $7,962.
Limitations: Applications not accepted. Giving limited to Morgantown, WV.
Trustees: A.I. Signiago, First Community Bank, Inc.
EIN: 556092124

56464
The Philip A. Haddad Scholarship Fund
c/o Herman & Cormany
1033 Quarrier St., Ste. 511
Charleston, WV 25301-2317
Application address: P.O. Box 4154, Charleston, WV 25364-4154, tel.: (304) 345-2320
Contact: Edward "Philip" A. Haddad, Tr.

Established in 1987 in WV.
Donor(s): Edward "Philip" A. Haddad.
Financial data (yr. ended 12/31/00): Grants paid, $6,200; assets, $96,575 (M); gifts received, $2,700; expenditures, $7,647; qualifying distributions, $6,200.
Limitations: Giving limited to Charleston, WV.
Application information: Application form required.
Trustee: Edward "Philip" A. Haddad.
EIN: 550668433

56465
The L-K Trust
1102 6th Ave.
P.O. Box 1330
Huntington, WV 25714-1330

Donor(s): L.E. Woods.

Financial data (yr. ended 12/31/01): Grants paid, $6,150; assets, $108,518 (M); expenditures, $6,807; qualifying distributions, $6,150.
Limitations: Applications not accepted. Giving primarily in WV.
Application information: Contributes only to pre-selected organizations.
Trustees: Kitty D. Woods, L.E. Woods, Sue D. Woods.
EIN: 510172476

56466
Stuart and Stephanie Bloch Family Foundation, Inc.
4000 Water St.
Wheeling, WV 26003 (304) 233-9223
Contact: Stuart F. Bloch, Pres.

Established in 1998 in WV.
Donor(s): Stuart F. Bloch, Stephanie H. Bloch.
Financial data (yr. ended 12/31/01): Grants paid, $6,108; assets, $84,278 (M); gifts received, $455; expenditures, $6,670; qualifying distributions, $6,108.
Officers: Stuart F. Bloch, Pres. and Treas.; Stephanie H. Bloch, V.P. and Secy.
EIN: 550760195

56467
Clyde W. Marshall and Leota B. Marshall Memorial Trust
P.O. Box 1525
Parkersburg, WV 26102

Established in 1993 in WV.
Donor(s): Joseph B. Farris.
Financial data (yr. ended 12/31/01): Grants paid, $6,000; assets, $415,752 (M); expenditures, $32,539; qualifying distributions, $6,000.
Limitations: Applications not accepted. Giving limited to Cairo, WV.
Application information: Contributes only to pre-selected organizations.
Trustees: Barbara Richards, Harold Wilson.
Directors: Joseph Garrett, Richard Jeffrey, Patricia Jenkins, Roydice Layfield.
EIN: 556120953

56468
The Williams Family Foundation, Inc.
(Formerly Buckhannon-Upshur Area Foundation, Inc.)
c/o Frank E. Williams, III
1 Larchmont St.
Buckhannon, WV 26201-2143

Established in 1989 in WV.
Financial data (yr. ended 12/31/01): Grants paid, $6,000; assets, $130,163 (M); gifts received, $55,422; expenditures, $6,160; qualifying distributions, $6,000.
Limitations: Applications not accepted. Giving primarily in Buckhannon, WV.
Application information: Contributes only to pre-selected organizations.
Officers: Frank E. Williams III, C.E.O.; Amy C. Williams, Pres. and Treas.; Jane E. Williams, Secy.
EIN: 550677420

56469
Randall H. McKinney Scholarship Fund
c/o One Valley Bank, N.A.
P.O. Box 698
Morgantown, WV 26507

Established in 1997 in WV.
Financial data (yr. ended 12/31/99): Grants paid, $5,844; assets, $0 (M); expenditures, $6,350; qualifying distributions, $5,844.
Trustee: One Valley Bank, N.A.
EIN: 556108302

56470
Dr. & Mrs. Charles O. Reynolds Medical Scholarship Fund
c/o City National Bank of WV
1900 3rd Ave.
Huntington, WV 25703
Contact: James Karnes, Trust Off., City National Bank of WV

Financial data (yr. ended 12/31/01): Grants paid, $5,000; assets, $107,015 (M); expenditures, $6,812; qualifying distributions, $5,000.
Limitations: Giving limited to WV.
Application information: Application form required.
Trustee: City National Bank of WV.
EIN: 556097807
Codes: GTI

56471
The Berkeley 2000 Foundation
P.O. Box 1537
Martinsburg, WV 25401 (304) 263-0836
Contact: Lacy I. Rice, Jr., Pres.

Established in 1991.
Donor(s): LCS Services, Inc.
Financial data (yr. ended 05/31/01): Grants paid, $4,910; assets, $263,312 (M); expenditures, $8,046; qualifying distributions, $4,910.
Limitations: Giving limited to Berkeley County, WV.
Application information: Application form required.
Officers and Directors:* Lacy I. Rice, Jr.,* Pres.; James M. Seibert,* V.P. and Secy.-Treas.; R. Stephen Catlett, Gilbert B. Miller, Jane Miller, Taylor J. Perry, Norma Lee Sutherland, Frank Williams.
EIN: 550712381
Codes: CS, CD

56472
Reuel K. Mehurin Trust
c/o B.B. & T.
P.O. Box 1793
Charleston, WV 25326 (304) 348-7000
Contact: Julia Jordan, Trust Off., B.B. & T.

Established in 1991 in WV.
Financial data (yr. ended 12/31/01): Grants paid, $4,672; assets, $42,312 (M); expenditures, $6,402; qualifying distributions, $4,798.
Limitations: Giving limited to Charleston and Kanawha County, WV.
Application information: Application form not required.
Trustee: B.B. & T.
EIN: 556016279

56473
Joseph R. Hatcher Scholarship Fund
c/o First Community Bank, Inc.
P.O. Box 5939
Princeton, WV 24740 (304) 487-9000
Contact: Ronda Bailey, Trust Off., First Community Bank, Inc.

Financial data (yr. ended 09/30/01): Grants paid, $4,529; assets, $112,403 (M); expenditures, $5,859; qualifying distributions, $4,529.
Limitations: Giving limited to Mercer County, WV.
Trustee: First Community Bank, Inc.
EIN: 310963961

56474
The Paul Cole Foundation, Inc.
2126 Reid Ave.
Bluefield, WV 24701 (304) 325-8116
Contact: William P. Cole, Jr., Dir.

Established in 1996 in WV.
Donor(s): William P. Cole, Jr.
Financial data (yr. ended 06/30/01): Grants paid, $4,109; assets, $70,999 (M); expenditures, $5,465; qualifying distributions, $4,109.
Directors: Carol M. Cole, Charles M. Cole, Thomas J. Cole, William P. Cole, Jr., William P. Cole III.
Trustee: First Century Bank, N.A.
EIN: 541830656

56475
The Valerie Canady Charitable Foundation Trust
c/o Leonard J. George
512 Princeton Ave.
Morgantown, WV 26505
Application address: c/o William J. Canady, 127 Jackson Ave., Morgantown, WV 26505, tel.: (304) 292-5171

Established in 1989 in WV.
Donor(s): William J. Canady, Loulie D. Canady.
Financial data (yr. ended 12/31/01): Grants paid, $4,000; assets, $45,402 (M); gifts received, $4,100; expenditures, $4,606; qualifying distributions, $3,978.
Limitations: Giving primarily in the Morgantown, WV, area.
Application information: Candidates for scholarships are usually selected by the principals of high schools in the Morgantown, WV, area. Application form required.
Trustees: Kent J. George, Leonard J. George, Robert P. George, Judith C. Hall, Eric Schorr.
EIN: 550692616

56476
Jeremy C. McCamic Family Foundation
c/o Jeremy C. McCamic
56 14th St.
Wheeling, WV 26003-3430

Donor(s): Jeremy C. McCamic.
Financial data (yr. ended 12/31/01): Grants paid, $4,000; assets, $330,456 (M); gifts received, $74,025; expenditures, $4,962; qualifying distributions, $4,000.
Limitations: Applications not accepted.
Application information: Contributes only to pre-selected organizations.
Officers: Jeremy C. McCamic, Pres.; Abigail M. Feinknopf, Secy.
EIN: 550757592

56477
A. D. Scaggs, Jr. Educational Trust
P.O. Box 836
Logan, WV 25601 (304) 752-3323
Contact: Owen L. Osenton, Tr.

Donor(s): Owen L. Osenton, Neal W. Scaggs.
Financial data (yr. ended 06/30/01): Grants paid, $4,000; assets, $50,305 (M); gifts received, $55; expenditures, $55; qualifying distributions, $55.
Limitations: Giving limited to residents of Logan County, WV.
Application information: Application form required.
Trustees: Owen L. Osenton, Phyllis M. Osenton, JoAnn B. Scaggs, Neal W. Scaggs.
EIN: 311056422

56478
Danhart Educational Trust
c/o United National Bank
514 Market St.
Parkersburg, WV 26101-5144

Financial data (yr. ended 12/31/01): Grants paid, $3,600; assets, $62,727 (M); expenditures, $6,116; qualifying distributions, $4,546.
Limitations: Applications not accepted. Giving limited to residents of Parkersburg, WV.
Application information: Recipients are selected by senior counselors at Parkersburg High School.
Trustee: United National Bank.
EIN: 556039494

56479
Kesan Inc. Foundation
c/o John S. Whelan
330 Town Mountain Rd.
Summersville, WV 26651

Financial data (yr. ended 12/31/01): Grants paid, $3,500; assets, $2,139 (M); gifts received, $2,000; expenditures, $3,534; qualifying distributions, $3,500.
Application information: Application form required.
Officers: Brian Johnson, Pres.; Bruce Dusch, V.P.; C.J. Hamilton, Treas.
Trustee: Gary Criste.
EIN: 550731836

56480
Mary Virginia Fairfax Memorial Scholarship
c/o WesBanco Bank, Inc.
1 Bank Plz.
Wheeling, WV 26003-3543 (304) 329-0572
Application address: 117 Albright Rd., Kingwood, WV 26537, tel.: (304) 329-2770
Contact: Claude McGhee, Chair.

Financial data (yr. ended 06/30/01): Grants paid, $3,158; assets, $40,797 (M); expenditures, $3,415; qualifying distributions, $3,129.
Limitations: Giving limited to Preston County, WV.
Application information: Application form required.
Officer and Trustees:* Claude McGhee,* Chair.; Nellie F. Hamstead, William Rosier.
EIN: 237451679

56481
Perry S. & Helen Wood Poffenbarger Foundation
c/o Wheat First
P.O. Box 2026
Charleston, WV 25327-2026 (304) 340-2926
Application address: 1200 United National Ctr., Charleston, WV 25301, tel.: (304) 340-2926
Contact: Carl Lehman, Tr.

Financial data (yr. ended 12/31/01): Grants paid, $3,155; assets, $201,634 (M); expenditures, $3,611; qualifying distributions, $3,155.
Limitations: Giving limited to Charleston, WV.
Trustees: Leonard Higgins, Carl Lehman, John Poffenbarger.
EIN: 550694974

56482
The Copen Family Foundation
c/o Noel Copen
P.O. Box 2185
Huntington, WV 25722

Established in 2001 in WV.
Donor(s): Berridge L. Copen.
Financial data (yr. ended 12/31/01): Grants paid, $3,000; assets, $631,565 (M); gifts received,

56482—WEST VIRGINIA

$122,064; expenditures, $3,723; qualifying distributions, $3,361.
Limitations: Giving primarily in GA.
Application information: Application form required.
Officers: Berridge L. Copen, Pres. and Treas.; Noel P. Copen, V.P. and Secy.
EIN: 550779472

56483
Levine Jacobson Foundation, Inc.
c/o L.K. Levine
1674 Cacapon Rd.
Berkeley Springs, WV 25411-9474

Established in 1999 in WV.
Financial data (yr. ended 12/31/01): Grants paid, $3,000; assets, $2,863 (M); gifts received, $4,018; expenditures, $3,052; qualifying distributions, $3,000.
Limitations: Applications not accepted.
Application information: Contributes only to pre-selected organizations.
Officers: L.K. Levine, Pres. and Secy.; Brian Shapiro, Treas.
Trustees: Abbey Josephson, M. Josephson, Mrs. M. Josephson, Kim Kevin, O. Levine, Mrs. O. Levine.
EIN: 550767262

56484
Tri-State Film Association of West Virginia, Kentucky & Ohio, Inc.
13 Prospect St.
Charleston, WV 25303-2022
Contact: Zenaida Anselmo, Treas.

Financial data (yr. ended 04/30/01): Grants paid, $3,000; assets, $10,762 (M); gifts received, $35,532; expenditures, $51,068; qualifying distributions, $3,000.
Limitations: Giving primarily in the Philippines.
Application information: Application form not required.
Officers and Directors:* Jose De Mesa,* Pres.; Maricel Bernardo,* Recording Secy.; Zenaida Anselmo,* Treas.; Helen V. Molano.
EIN: 550632536

56485
The John A. Sheppard Memorial Ecological Reservation, Inc.
P.O. Box 27
Naugatuck, WV 25685-0027

Financial data (yr. ended 06/30/01): Grants paid, $2,524; assets, $336,308 (M); gifts received, $125; expenditures, $11,857; qualifying distributions, $315,032.
Limitations: Giving primarily in Matewan, WV.
Officers and Director: Pauline Sturgill, Pres.; Sarah Sturgill, Secy.; Gretchen Sturgill, Treas.; Gretchen Shaffer.
EIN: 550667171

56486
Ray V. Harron Foundation
P.O. Box 400
Bridgeport, WV 26330-0400

Financial data (yr. ended 12/31/01): Grants paid, $2,500; assets, $34,221 (M); expenditures, $3,689; qualifying distributions, $2,472.
Limitations: Applications not accepted. Giving primarily in WV.
Application information: Contributes only to pre-selected organizations.
Officers: Ray A. Harron, Chair. and V.P.; Carolyn S. Harron, Pres.; Michael S. Harron, Secy.
EIN: 556037632

56487
Traders Bank Scholarship Foundation
c/o Traders Bank
P.O. Box 1009
Spencer, WV 25276-0040
Application addresses: c/o Guidance Counselor, Roane County High School, 702 Charleston Rd., Spencer, WV 25276; or c/o Guidance Counselor, Calhoun High School, RR1 Box 1H, Grantsville, WV 26147

Donor(s): Traders Bank.
Financial data (yr. ended 06/30/01): Grants paid, $2,500; assets, $39,915 (M); gifts received, $100; expenditures, $2,710; qualifying distributions, $2,660.
Limitations: Giving limited to residents of WV.
Trustees: Virgil Daugherty, Tom Hardman, John Kingery.
EIN: 311175049
Codes: CS, CD

56488
Jay T. McCamic Memorial Scholarship Trust
c/o Wheeling National Bank
1145 Market St.
Wheeling, WV 26003-2905 (304) 232-0110
Contact: Nancy J. Ritter, Trust Off., Wheeling National Bank

Donor(s): Jay T. McCamic, McCamic & McCamic.
Financial data (yr. ended 12/31/00): Grants paid, $1,725; assets, $32,155 (M); expenditures, $1,748; qualifying distributions, $1,725.
Limitations: Giving limited to residents of WA.
Application information: Application form required.
Trustee: Wheeling National Bank.
EIN: 237155794

56489
Barbour County Community Foundation, Inc.
304 Brown Ave.
Belington, WV 26250-9203

Financial data (yr. ended 12/31/00): Grants paid, $1,650; assets, $391,742 (M); gifts received, $162,850; expenditures, $8,040; qualifying distributions, $1,650.
Limitations: Giving limited to Barbour County, WV.
Officers: William Phillips, Pres.; John Phillips, V.P.; Leonard Lobello, Secy.; Eugene Righman, Treas.
Directors: Karen Hyde, Caroline Jett, Melody Jones, Joseph Mattaliano.
EIN: 311529922

56490
England Charitable Trust
R.R. 4, Box 490
Salem, WV 26426

Financial data (yr. ended 12/31/01): Grants paid, $1,500; assets, $3,506 (L); expenditures, $1,500; qualifying distributions, $1,500.
Limitations: Applications not accepted.
Application information: Contributes only to pre-selected organizations.
Trustees: Beatrice D. England, Wayne H. England.
EIN: 311551896

56491
The Dr. Frank and Mary Thomas Holroyd Foundation, Inc.
P.O. Box 147
Princeton, WV 24740 (304) 325-2644

Donor(s): Mary T. Holroyd.
Financial data (yr. ended 12/31/01): Grants paid, $1,500; assets, $1,069 (M); gifts received, $1,500; expenditures, $1,500; qualifying distributions, $1,500.
Limitations: Giving primarily in WV.
Application information: Application form required.
Officers: Mary T. Holroyd, Pres. and Treas.; Fred F. Holroyd, V.P. and Secy.
EIN: 541944882

56492
George A. Laughlin Scholastic Prizes Trust
c/o WesBanco Bank, Inc.
1 Bank Plz.
Wheeling, WV 26003

Donor(s): George A. Laughlin.‡
Financial data (yr. ended 12/31/01): Grants paid, $1,500; assets, $33,933 (M); expenditures, $1,952; qualifying distributions, $1,697.
Limitations: Applications not accepted. Giving limited to Wheeling, WV.
Application information: Unsolicited requests for funds not accepted.
Trustee: WesBanco Bank, Inc.
EIN: 556016882

56493
Gilson Charitable Trust
(Formerly The Hewws Charitable Trust)
29 Greentree Rd.
Wheeling, WV 26003

Established in 1998 in WV.
Financial data (yr. ended 12/31/00): Grants paid, $1,450; assets, $0 (M); gifts received, $2,310; expenditures, $1,780; qualifying distributions, $1,450.
Directors: Stephanie S. Gilson, Thomas A. Gilson.
EIN: 341852373

56494
The Erickson Foundation
400 Market St.
Parkersburg, WV 26101
Contact: Charles F. Erickson, Tr.

Established in 1993 in WV.
Donor(s): Charles F. Ericson.
Financial data (yr. ended 12/31/01): Grants paid, $1,000; assets, $5,761,156 (M); expenditures, $363,382; qualifying distributions, $1,000.
Limitations: Giving primarily in WV.
Application information: Application form not required.
Trustee: Charles F. Erickson.
EIN: 550722731

56495
North Parkersburg Kiwanis Foundation, Inc.
P.O. Box 4511
Parkersburg, WV 26104-4511

Financial data (yr. ended 12/31/99): Grants paid, $1,000; assets, $18,198 (M); expenditures, $1,000; qualifying distributions, $990.
Limitations: Applications not accepted. Giving primarily in Parkersburg and Williamstown, WV.
Officers: Paul Campbell, Pres.; Leon Bartlett, V.P.; Harvey Barger, Secy.; Richard Kalt, Treas.
EIN: 550619771

56496
The Brody-Hazen Foundation, Inc.
320 W. Main St.
White Sulphur Springs, WV 24986-2414
(304) 536-4870
Contact: Phillip Zxoldos

Established in 1992 in WV.
Donor(s): Joseph Hazen, Jamey Harless Foundation, Inc., John & Kelly Hartman Foundation, Inc.

Financial data (yr. ended 06/30/00): Grants paid, $969; assets, $129,965 (M); gifts received, $16,750; expenditures, $2,229; qualifying distributions, $969.
Limitations: Giving primarily in WV.
Application information: Application form required.
Officers: E.F. Baldwin, M.D., Pres.; Phyllis Bussard,* Secy.-Treas.; Douglas L. Jones, M.D., Thomas F. Mann, Rev. William G. Starkey.
EIN: 550715548

56497
Panhandle Ministries
c/o William R. Martin
P.O. Box 777
Kearneysville, WV 25430-0777

Established in 1995.
Financial data (yr. ended 12/31/01): Grants paid, $943; assets, $297 (M); gifts received, $970; expenditures, $1,015; qualifying distributions, $1,015.
Limitations: Giving primarily in VA and WV.
Officers: Rev. William R. Martin, Pres.; Louise C. Martin, Secy.
Trustees: Douglas H. Martin, Jay A. Martin.
EIN: 550743692

56498
The William T. Hancock Charitable Foundation
211 Federal St.
P.O. Box 950
Bluefield, WV 24701 (304) 325-7151
Contact: Jeffrey L. Farmer, Tr. Off., First Community Bank, Inc.

Established in 2000 in WV.
Donor(s): Willy Pierre Jacoebee.
Financial data (yr. ended 12/31/01): Grants paid, $800; assets, $162,024 (M); gifts received, $7,500; expenditures, $1,778; qualifying distributions, $800.
Limitations: Giving primarily in McDowell and Mercer counties, WV.
Trustee: First Community Bank, Inc.
EIN: 311746406

56499
Lowell Ball Scholarship Charitable Trust
P.O. Box 340
Philippi, WV 26416
Application address: c/o Principal, Philip Barbour High School, Philippi, WV 26416, tel.: (304) 457-1360
Contact: Ed Larry, Tr.

Financial data (yr. ended 03/31/99): Grants paid, $504; assets, $5,505 (L); expenditures, $511; qualifying distributions, $504.
Limitations: Giving limited to Morgantown, WV.
Application information: Application form required.
Trustees: Ed Larry, Roger Moats.
EIN: 556092143

56500
Clarence S. Lovitch Memorial Scholarship Foundation
601 Beech St.
Williamson, WV 25661

Established in 2000 in WV.
Financial data (yr. ended 12/31/00): Grants paid, $500; assets, $348 (M); gifts received, $1,035; expenditures, $687; qualifying distributions, $0.
Limitations: Giving primarily in WV.
Directors: Edward Lovitch, Fred Lovitch, Karen Lovitch.
EIN: 550771972

56501
The Fritz Prohl Charitable Trust
Rte. 4
P.O. Box 508
Salem, WV 26426

Donor(s): The Thea Prohl Organization.
Financial data (yr. ended 12/31/01): Grants paid, $350; assets, $2,781 (M); expenditures, $350; qualifying distributions, $350.
Limitations: Applications not accepted.
Application information: Contributes only to pre-selected organizations.
Director: Eva G. Van der Giessen.
EIN: 311555246

56502
Ethel M. Huggins Elliot Memorial Trust
20 Access Rd.
Williamstown, WV 26187
Contact: Patricia W. Pickens, Tr.

Established in 1993 in WV.
Financial data (yr. ended 12/31/01): Grants paid, $122; assets, $6,328 (M); expenditures, $145; qualifying distributions, $145.
Limitations: Giving limited to residents of Williamstown, WV.
Trustee: Patricia W. Pickens.
EIN: 550727799

56503
Warren Family, Inc.
1408 Bedford Rd.
Charleston, WV 25314

Established in 2000 in WV.
Donor(s): Stafford Warren.
Financial data (yr. ended 12/31/01): Grants paid, $40; assets, $97,929 (M); expenditures, $882; qualifying distributions, $40.
Directors: Carolyn S. Warren, Stafford Warren.
EIN: 550762359

56504
Ahmed 786 Charitable Trust
260 Starling St.
Princeton, WV 24740 (304) 425-9325
Contact: Afzal Ahmed, Tr.

Established in 1996 in WV.
Donor(s): Afzal Ahmed.
Financial data (yr. ended 06/30/02): Grants paid, $0; assets, $2,785 (M); expenditures, $0; qualifying distributions, $0.
Limitations: Giving on a national basis.
Application information: Application form not required.
Trustees: Afzal Ahmed, Asma Ahmed, Habeeb Ahmed, Aijaz Khan.
EIN: 550754758

56505
The John Patrick Albright Foundation
33 Woodland Park Dr.
Parkersburg, WV 26101

Established in 1991 in WV.
Donor(s): Joseph P. Albright, Mrs. Joseph P. Albright.
Financial data (yr. ended 12/31/01): Grants paid, $0; assets, $146,292 (M); gifts received, $5,879; expenditures, $937; qualifying distributions, $0.
Limitations: Applications not accepted. Giving primarily in Waco, TX.
Application information: Contributes only to pre-selected organizations.
Trustees: Joseph P. Albright, Joseph P. Albright, Jr., Loretta K. Albright, Peter J. Cavi, Theresa L. Cavi.
EIN: 550707906

56506
Kathleen Simmons Batalion Memorial Scholarship Trust
c/o Citizens National Bank
P.O. Box 1519
Elkins, WV 26241-1519

Financial data (yr. ended 12/31/01): Grants paid, $0; assets, $68,098 (M); expenditures, $1,273; qualifying distributions, $469.
Limitations: Applications not accepted. Giving limited to WV.
Trustee: Citizens National Bank.
EIN: 556091937

56507
Bill Carneal Charitable Trust
c/o One Valley Bank
1439 Main St.
Princeton, WV 24740

Established in 1999.
Financial data (yr. ended 12/31/99): Grants paid, $0; assets, $584,869 (M); expenditures, $1,117; qualifying distributions, $0.
Limitations: Applications not accepted.
Application information: Contributes only to pre-selected organizations.
Trustees: Warren N. Hunter, Robert D. Martin, Don Smathers.
EIN: 556453337

56508
The Credit Bureau of the Virginias Foundation, Inc.
P.O. Box 6380
Bluefield, WV 24701
Application address: Rt. 6, Box 38, Princeton, WV 24740
Contact: Jimmy W. Welch, Secy.

Established in 2001 in WV.
Donor(s): The Credit Bureau of the Vas, Inc.
Financial data (yr. ended 12/31/01): Grants paid, $0; assets, $53,252 (M); gifts received, $55,000; expenditures, $1,748; qualifying distributions, $0.
Limitations: Giving limited to residents of WV and VA.
Officers: James Sizemore, Pres.; Danny Coulthard, V.P.; Jimmy Welch, Secy. and Exec. Dir.; Dean Marshall, Treas.
EIN: 550781189

56509
Deitzler Foundation, Inc.
500 Tracy Way
Charleston, WV 25311

Established in 2001 in WV.
Donor(s): Harry G. Deitzler.
Financial data (yr. ended 12/31/01): Grants paid, $0; assets, $1,015,222 (M); gifts received, $1,004,115; expenditures, $6,541; qualifying distributions, $0.
Limitations: Applications not accepted.
Application information: Contributes only to pre-selected organizations.
Officers: Harry G. Deitzler, Pres.; Kathe E. Deitzler, Secy.-Treas.
EIN: 550783635

56510
The Emerich Scholarship Charitable Trust
c/o City National Bank Trust Division
P.O. Box 4868
Charleston, WV 25364-4168

Established in 2001 in WV.
Donor(s): John V. Emerich.‡
Financial data (yr. ended 12/31/01): Grants paid, $0; assets, $273,021 (M); gifts received,

56510—WEST VIRGINIA

$270,561; expenditures, $913; qualifying distributions, $0.
Trustee: City National Bank.
EIN: 311746382

56511
Esbenshade Foundation
c/o Harry Esbenshade III
15 60th St.
Vienna, WV 26105-8901

Established in 2001.
Financial data (yr. ended 12/31/01): Grants paid, $0; assets, $56,473 (M); gifts received, $56,811; expenditures, $500; qualifying distributions, $0.
Limitations: Applications not accepted.
Application information: Contributes only to pre-selected organizations.
Officers: Harry H. Esbenshade III, Pres.; Thomas R. Davies, V.P.; Michael D. Cain, Secy.-Treas.
EIN: 550779947

56512
Charles H. Feoppel Educational Loan Trust
c/o The Huntington National Bank
P.O. Box 2490
Clarksburg, WV 26302-2490 (304) 623-7460
FAX: (304) 291-7769; E-mail: bradenswaney@hwva.hbi.us
Contact: Braden Swaney III, Asst. V.P. and Tr. Off., The Huntington National Bank

Established in 1988 in WV.
Donor(s): Charles H. Feoppel,‡ Ruth Garrett Feoppel.‡
Financial data (yr. ended 12/31/00): Grants paid, $0; assets, $2,817,302 (M); expenditures, $44,242; qualifying distributions, $327,490; giving activities include $129,300 for loans to individuals.
Limitations: Giving limited to Harrison County, WV, residents.
Publications: Informational brochure (including application guidelines).
Application information: Contact foundation for loan information. Application form required.
Trustee: The Huntington National Bank.
EIN: 556107185
Codes: GTI

56513
Foundation for Children, Families, and Communities of West Virginia, Inc.
P.O. Box 1370
Clarksburg, WV 26301

Established in 2001 in WV.
Donor(s): Dominion Hope.
Financial data (yr. ended 12/31/01): Grants paid, $0; assets, $5,000 (M); gifts received, $5,000; expenditures, $0; qualifying distributions, $0.
Limitations: Applications not accepted. Giving primarily in WV.
Application information: Contributes only to pre-selected organizations.

Officers: Kelly R. Nelson, M.D., Pres.; Marcel C. Malfregeot, V.P.; Martha White, Secy.-Treas.
Directors: Annette Crislip, Thomas Durrett, Linda Holyfield, Michael R. Sieber, John Wilson.
EIN: 550717008

56514
Hampshire County Historical & Arts Museum
c/o Lawrence Foley, Bank of Romney
P.O. Box 876
Romney, WV 26757

Established in 1998 in WV.
Financial data (yr. ended 12/31/01): Grants paid, $0; assets, $896,531 (M); expenditures, $18,233; qualifying distributions, $0.
Limitations: Applications not accepted.
Application information: Contributes only to pre-selected organizations.
Officers: Maybelle L. Lipps, Secy.; Lawrence Foley, Treas.
Trustees: Robert A. Mayhew, David W. Pancake, Merceda Rowzee, Hoy G. Shingleton.
EIN: 311570205

56515
New Beginning World Outreach, Inc.
P.O. Box 1
War, WV 24892

Financial data (yr. ended 12/31/99): Grants paid, $0; assets, $621,204 (M); gifts received, $84,625; expenditures, $55,405; qualifying distributions, $0.
Officer: John Dash, Pres.
Director: Jimmy Dickens.
EIN: 550676703

56516
Louise Bowling Peters Scholarship Loan Fund
c/o First Community Bank, Inc.
P.O. Box 5939
Princeton, WV 24740 (304) 487-9000
Contact: Ronda K. Bailey, Trust Off., First Community Bank, Inc.

Financial data (yr. ended 12/31/01): Grants paid, $0; assets, $157,668 (M); expenditures, $1,374; qualifying distributions, $0.
Limitations: Giving limited to residents of WV.
Trustee: First Community Bank, Inc.
EIN: 556605200

56517
South Asia Cultural Society, Inc.
c/o S.L. Bembalkar
250 Stanford Rd.
Beckley, WV 25801

Established in 1994.
Donor(s): S.L. Bembalkar.
Financial data (yr. ended 03/31/01): Grants paid, $0; assets, $30,809 (M); gifts received, $10,066; expenditures, $6,622; qualifying distributions, $4,556; giving activities include $6,062 for programs.

Limitations: Applications not accepted.
Application information: Contributes only to pre-selected organizations.
Officers and Directors:* S.L. Bembalkar,* Pres.; Gireesh Bembalkar,* V.P.; Mary Gale Bembalkar,* Secy.-Treas.
EIN: 550718805

56518
The Strong-Treister Family Foundation, Inc.
503 Pennsylvania Ave.
Charleston, WV 25302

Established in 1997 in WV.
Financial data (yr. ended 06/30/01): Grants paid, $0; assets, $12,933 (M); expenditures, $10; qualifying distributions, $10.
Limitations: Applications not accepted. Giving primarily in Charleston, WV.
Application information: Contributes only to pre-selected organizations.
Officers: Diane W. Strong-Treister, Pres. and Treas.; Donley Strong, V.P. and Secy.
EIN: 550755503

56519
The Sun Lumber Company Education Foundation
P. O. Box 590
Weston, WV 26452-0590
Contact: Frank L. Brewster, Tr.

Established in 2000 in WV.
Donor(s): Sun Lumber Co., Frank L. Brewster.
Financial data (yr. ended 12/31/01): Grants paid, $0; assets, $9,119 (M); gifts received, $9,000; expenditures, $0; qualifying distributions, $0.
Limitations: Giving limited to residents of WV.
Trustees: Frank L. Brewster, June L. Brewster.
EIN: 550780820
Codes: CS

56520
Timms Family Foundation
801 Worthington Dr.
Bridgeport, WV 26330 (304) 842-4958
Contact: Leonard J. Timms, Jr., Tr.

Established in 2000 in WV.
Donor(s): Leonard J. Timms, Jr.
Financial data (yr. ended 12/31/00): Grants paid, $0; assets, $20,057 (M); gifts received, $20,100; expenditures, $100; qualifying distributions, $0.
Application information: Application form required.
Trustees: Rebecca T. Carlin, Sarah T. Chittaro, Cynthia T. Pulice, Annabel P. Timms, Leonard J. Timms, Jr.
EIN: 912052424

WISCONSIN

56521
The Lynde and Harry Bradley Foundation, Inc.
P.O. Box 510860
Milwaukee, WI 53203-0153 (414) 291-9915
FAX: (414) 291-9991; URL: http://www.bradleyfdn.org
Contact: Daniel P. Schmidt, Exec. V.P. and C.O.O.

Incorporated in 1942 in WI as the Allen-Bradley Foundation, Inc.; adopted present name in 1985.
Donor(s): Harry L. Bradley,‡ Caroline D. Bradley,‡ Margaret B. Bradley,‡ Margaret Loock Trust, Allen-Bradley Co.
Financial data (yr. ended 12/31/01): Grants paid, $35,304,281; assets, $579,739,000 (M); expenditures, $47,695,689; qualifying distributions, $41,991,868.
Limitations: Giving primarily in Milwaukee, WI; giving also on a national and international basis.
Publications: Application guidelines, occasional report (including application guidelines), annual report.
Application information: Application form not required.
Officers and Directors:* Thomas L. "Dusty" Rhodes,* Chair.; Michael W. Grebe,* Pres. and C.E.O.; Daniel P. Schmidt, Exec. V.P. and C.O.O.; Thomas L. Smallwood, Secy.; Robert N. Berkopec, Treas. and C.F.O.; Cynthia Friauf, Cont.; William Armstrong, Reed Coleman, Terry Considine, Pierre S. duPont IV, Br. Bob Smith, David V. Uihlein, Jr.
EIN: 396037928
Codes: FD, FM

56522
Greater Milwaukee Foundation
(Formerly Milwaukee Foundation)
1020 N. Broadway
Milwaukee, WI 53202 (414) 272-5805
FAX: (414) 272-6235; E-mail:info@mkefdn.org; URL: http://www.greatermilwaukeefoundation.org
Contact: Douglas M. Jansson, Exec. Dir.

Established in 1915 in WI by declaration of trust.
Financial data (yr. ended 12/31/01): Grants paid, $17,916,354; assets, $312,800,000 (M); gifts received, $16,135,735; expenditures, $24,986,251.
Limitations: Giving primarily in Milwaukee, Waukesha, Ozaukee, and Washington counties of WI.
Publications: Annual report (including application guidelines), grants list, newsletter, program policy statement, application guidelines, informational brochure (including application guidelines).
Application information: The foundation uses the Common Application Form used by many Milwaukee-area foundations. Capital requests are reviewed at Dec. board meeting. Application form required.
Officers: Douglas M. Jansson, Pres., Secy., and Exec. Dir.; James A. Marks, V.P.; Wendy Horton, C.F.O.
Directors: George Kaiser, Chair.; Linda T. Mellowes, Vice-Chair.; Ned W. Bechthold, William Fitzhugh Fox, Franklyn M. Gimbel, Stephen N. Graff, Stephen H. Marcus, Patricia McKeithan, Jose A. Olivieri, Joan Marie Prince, Ph.D., Blaine E. Rieke, Frederick P. Stratton, Jr.
Trustees: Bank One Investment Advisors Corporation, Firstar Investment Research and Management Company, Marshall & Ilsley Investment Management Corporation, The Northern Trust Co., U.S. Bank Private Financial Services.
EIN: 396036407
Codes: CM, FD, FM

56523
Northwestern Mutual Foundation
(Formerly Northwestern Mutual Life Foundation)
720 E. Wisconsin Ave.
Milwaukee, WI 53202 (414) 665-2200
Contact: Rebekah B. Barsch, V.P.

Established as a private foundation in 1992 in WI.
Donor(s): The Northwestern Mutual Life Insurance Co.
Financial data (yr. ended 06/30/01): Grants paid, $15,627,583; assets, $114,843,298 (M); expenditures, $17,476,663; qualifying distributions, $17,295,995.
Limitations: Giving primarily in the greater Milwaukee, WI, area.
Publications: Biennial report.
Application information: Application form required.
Officers and Directors:* Edward J. Zore,* Pres.; Frederic H. Sweet, Exec. V.P.; Rebekah B. Barsch, V.P.; Scott J. Morris, Secy.; Mark G. Doll, Treas.; Edward E. Barr, Patricia A. Graham, Stephen F. Keller, J. Thomas Lewis, Daniel F. McKeithan, Jr., Peter M. Sommerhauser.
EIN: 391728908
Codes: CS, FD, CD, FM

56524
Helen Bader Foundation, Inc.
233 N. Water St., 4th Fl.
Milwaukee, WI 53202 (414) 224-6464
FAX: (414) 224-1441; E-mail: info@hbf.org; URL: http://www.hbf.org
Contact: Daniel J. Bader, Pres.

Established in 1991 in WI.
Financial data (yr. ended 08/31/01): Grants paid, $11,762,550; assets, $2,402,968 (M); gifts received, $12,500,000; expenditures, $13,538,620; qualifying distributions, $13,445,204.
Limitations: Giving primarily in the greater Milwaukee, WI, area for education and economic development; giving locally and nationally for Alzheimer's disease and dementia; giving in Israel for early childhood development.
Publications: Annual report (including application guidelines), grants list, application guidelines.
Application information: If the foundation wishes to pursue a grant request, a full proposal and on-site visit are required. Preliminary application form must be submitted 10 weeks prior to board meeting dates; if accepted, a complete application must be submitted within 30 days of submission of preliminary application. Application form not required.
Officers and Directors:* Jere D. McGaffey,* Chair. and Secy.-Treas.; Daniel J. Bader,* Pres.; David M. Bader,* V.P.; Lisa Hiller, V.P., Admin.; Robin Bieger Mayrl, V.P., Prog. Devel.; Linda C. Bader, Michelle Henkin Bader, Deirdre H. Britt, Frances Wolff.
EIN: 391710914
Codes: FD, FM

56525
Jane Bradley Pettit Foundation
(Formerly Jane and Lloyd Pettit Foundation, Inc.)
660 E. Mason St.
Milwaukee, WI 53202 (414) 227-1266
URL: http://www.jbpf.org
Contact: Margaret T. Lund, Secy.-Treas.

Incorporated in 1986 in WI.
Donor(s): Jane Bradley Pettit.‡
Financial data (yr. ended 12/31/00): Grants paid, $10,256,626; assets, $3,169,249 (M); gifts received, $10,188,967; expenditures, $10,596,003; qualifying distributions, $10,519,749.
Limitations: Giving primarily in the greater Milwaukee, WI, area.
Publications: Application guidelines.
Application information: The foundation will not consider requests for additional support for the period in which an organization currently has a grant in effect.
Officers and Directors:* Francis R. Croak,* Pres.; Margaret T. Lund,* V.P.; JoAnn C. Youngman,* Secy.-Treas.
EIN: 391574123
Codes: FD, FM

56526
Community Foundation for the Fox Valley Region, Inc.
118 S. State St., F-2
P.O. Box 563
Appleton, WI 54912 (920) 830-1290
FAX: (920) 830-1293; E-mail: cffvr@cffoxvalley.org; URL: http://www.cffoxvalley.org
Contact: Larry L. Kath, C.E.O. and Pres., Barb Uehling, Fin. Dir., Tammy Williams, Comm. Dir., or Curt Detjen, V.P., Devel. and Donor Svcs.

Organized in 1986 in Appleton, WI.
Financial data (yr. ended 06/30/02): Grants paid, $9,584,952; assets, $91,926,001 (M); gifts received, $19,606,093; expenditures, $11,199,737.
Limitations: Giving limited to northern Winnebago, Outagamie, Calumet, and Waupaca counties, WI.
Publications: Annual report, informational brochure (including application guidelines), newsletter, grants list.
Application information: Application form required.
Officers and Directors:* Walter S. Rugland,* Chair.; Joe Bielinski, Vice-Chair.; William Griffith, Vice-Chair.; Barbara Schmidt, Vice-Chair.; Robert A. Underhill, Vice-Chair.; Curt Detjen,* C.E.O. and Pres.; Jeff Knezel, Secy.; Katherine Westover, Treas.; and 25 additional directors.
EIN: 391548450
Codes: CM, FD

56527
SC Johnson Fund, Inc.
(Formerly SC Johnson Wax Fund Inc.)
1525 Howe St.
Racine, WI 53403 (262) 260-4855
URL: http://www.scjohnson.com/community
Contact: Colleen Cribari, Prog. Admin.

Incorporated in 1959 in WI.
Donor(s): S.C. Johnson & Son, Inc.
Financial data (yr. ended 06/30/01): Grants paid, $8,140,025; assets, $6,523,783 (M); gifts received, $7,992,066; expenditures, $8,389,686; qualifying distributions, $8,363,184.
Limitations: Giving primarily in headquarters community of Racine, WI.
Publications: Annual report.

56527—WISCONSIN

Application information: Application form required.
Officers and Trustees:* Samuel C. Johnson,* Chair. and Pres.; William D. Perez,* Vice-Chair.; Jane M. Hutterly, Exec. V.P.; Jeffrey M. Waller,* Treas.; H. Fisk Johnson, S. Curtis Johnson, Helen P. Johnson-Leipold, J. Gary Raley.
EIN: 396052089
Codes: CS, FD, CD, FM

56528
Community Foundation of North Central Wisconsin, Inc.
(Formerly Wausau Area Community Foundation, Inc.)
500 3rd St., Ste. 310
Wausau, WI 54403-4857 (715) 845-9555
Additional tel.: (888) 845-9223; FAX: (715) 845-5423; E-mail: cfoncw@dwave.org; URL: http://www.wacf.org
Contact: Jean C. Tehan, Exec. Dir.

Incorporated in 1987 in WI.
Financial data (yr. ended 12/31/01): Grants paid, $7,642,974; assets, $16,502,063 (M); gifts received, $5,753,136; expenditures, $8,065,983.
Limitations: Giving limited to the greater Wausau, WI, area, including Marathon County.
Publications: Application guidelines, annual report, informational brochure (including application guidelines), newsletter.
Application information: Application form required.
Officers and Directors:* Sarah S. Miller,* Pres.; William M. Reif,* V.P.; G. Lane Ware, Secy.; John L. Skoug,* Treas.; Jean C. Tehan, Exec. Dir.; John W. Dunn, George A. Evenhouse, Paul J. Gassner, Nancy Hessert, Peggie Mallery, Michael E. Ravn, Harvey H. Scholfield, Ruth J. Schuette, Beverley Smith, James P. VanEyck.
EIN: 391577472
Codes: CM, FD

56529
Reiman Charitable Foundation, Inc.
115 S. 84th St., No. 221
Milwaukee, WI 53214

Established in 1986 in WI.
Donor(s): Roy J. Reiman, Roberta M. Reiman, Scott J. Reiman, Joni R. Winston, Cynthia A. Lambert, Julia M. Ellis, Terrin S. Riemer.
Financial data (yr. ended 12/31/00): Grants paid, $7,424,071; assets, $131,397,152 (M); gifts received, $8,970,000; expenditures, $8,723,870; qualifying distributions, $7,424,071.
Limitations: Applications not accepted.
Application information: Contributes only to pre-selected organizations.
Officers and Directors:* Scott J. Reiman,* Pres.; Michael J. Hipp,* Exec. V.P. and Secy.; Brian F. Fleischmann,* V.P.; Roberta M. Reiman,* V.P.; Roy J. Reiman,* V.P.
EIN: 391570264
Codes: FD, FM

56530
Pleasant T. Rowland Foundation, Inc.
3415 Gateway Rd., Ste. 200
Brookfield, WI 53045-5111
Application address: 1 S. Pinckney St., No. 810, Madison, WI 53703
Contact: Marti Sebree, Grants Mgr.

Established in 1997 in WI.
Donor(s): Pleasant T. Rowland.
Financial data (yr. ended 12/31/00): Grants paid, $6,494,141; assets, $160,890,352 (M); gifts received, $122,063; expenditures, $14,369,995; qualifying distributions, $12,241,937; giving activities include $5,839,670 for program-related investments.
Limitations: Giving primarily in, but not limited to, WI, with emphasis on Dane County.
Application information: Application form required.
Directors: Barbara Thiele Carr, Walter Jerome Frautschi, Valerie Tripp, Rhona E. Vogel.
EIN: 391868295
Codes: FD

56531
Johnson Controls Foundation
5757 N. Green Bay Ave.
P.O. Box 591, M.S. X-46
Milwaukee, WI 53201 (414) 524-2296
URL: http://www.johnsoncontrols.com/corpvalues/foundation.htm
Contact: Valerie Adisek, Fdn. Coord.

Trust established in 1952 in WI.
Donor(s): Johnson Controls, Inc.
Financial data (yr. ended 12/31/01): Grants paid, $5,958,094; assets, $39,043,033 (M); gifts received, $5,000,000; expenditures, $6,082,088; qualifying distributions, $5,946,878.
Publications: Application guidelines.
Application information: Employee-related scholarship awards are paid directly to institutions and not to individuals. Application form not required.
Trustee: U.S. Bank Corp.
EIN: 396036639
Codes: CS, FD, CD, FM, GTI

56532
Madison Community Foundation
2 Science Ct.
P.O. Box 5010
Madison, WI 53705-0010 (608) 232-1763
FAX: (608) 232-1772; E-mail: frontdesk@madisoncommunityfoundation.org; URL: http://www.madisoncommunityfoundation.org
Contact: Kathleen Woit, Pres.

Established in 1942 in WI.
Financial data (yr. ended 12/31/01): Grants paid, $5,830,467; assets, $59,602,990 (M); gifts received, $5,694,619; expenditures, $6,828,593.
Limitations: Applications not accepted. Giving limited to Dane County, WI.
Publications: Annual report.
Application information: Unsolicited requests for funds not accepted.
Officers and Board of Governors:* Melany Newby,* Chair.; James Burgess,* Vice-Chair.; Kathleen Woit,* Pres.; Ann Casey, V.P., Fin. and Admin.; Wendy Coe, V.P., Donor Rels.; Amy T. Overby, V.P., Prog.; George Nelson,* Treas.; and 12 additional members.
EIN: 396038248
Codes: CM, FD

56533
Pat and Jay Baker Foundation, Inc.
6350 N. Lake Dr.
Whitefish Bay, WI 53217

Established in 1993.
Financial data (yr. ended 12/31/01): Grants paid, $5,714,000; assets, $9,876,382 (M); expenditures, $5,800,717; qualifying distributions, $5,654,405.
Limitations: Applications not accepted. Giving primarily in Milwaukee, WI.
Application information: Contributes only to pre-selected organizations.
Officers and Directors:* Jay H. Baker,* Pres. and Treas.; Pat Good Baker,* V.P. and Secy.; Peter M. Sommerhauser.
EIN: 391776268
Codes: FD, FM

56534
Rockwell International Corporation Trust
c/o U.S. Bank
777 E. Wisconsin Ave., Ste. 1400
Milwaukee, WI 53202 (414) 212-5258
FAX: (414) 212-5279; E-mail: emwalter@corp.rockwell.com
Contact: Christine G. Rodriguez

Trust established in 1959 in PA.
Donor(s): Rockwell International Corp., Rockwell Automation, Inc.
Financial data (yr. ended 09/30/01): Grants paid, $5,560,644; assets, $15,386,346 (M); expenditures, $5,643,701; qualifying distributions, $5,597,175.
Limitations: Giving nationally in areas of corporate operations, except for selected national organizations and universities which are sources of recruits or whose research is of interest; giving internationally where the company has formal programs.
Publications: Annual report, informational brochure.
Application information: Local organizations should contact community relations/contributions administrators at local Rockwell facilities. Interviews with applicants may be granted. Application form required.
Officers and Trust Committee:* Don H. Davis,* Chair.; John D. Cohn,* Secy.; W. Michael Barnes, William J. Calise, Jr.
Trustee: U.S. Bank.
EIN: 251072431
Codes: CS, FD, CD, FM

56535
The Rath Foundation
P.O. Box 1990
Janesville, WI 53547 (608) 754-9090
Contact: James D. Dodson, Pres.

Established in 1989 in WI.
Donor(s): V. Duane Rath.
Financial data (yr. ended 12/31/00): Grants paid, $5,541,250; assets, $53,644,198 (M); expenditures, $5,911,500; qualifying distributions, $5,594,234.
Limitations: Giving on a national basis, with some emphasis on WI.
Officers: James D. Dodson, Pres.; James R. Sanger, V.P.; Frank J. Pelisek, Secy.
EIN: 391657654
Codes: FD, FM

56536
Overture Foundation
1 S. Pinckney St., Ste. 816
Madison, WI 53703
Contact: Rhona E. Vogel, Secy.

Established in 1996.
Donor(s): W. Jerome Frautschi.
Financial data (yr. ended 12/31/00): Grants paid, $4,656,181; assets, $97,639,174 (M); expenditures, $5,946,345; qualifying distributions, $4,580,189.
Limitations: Applications not accepted. Giving primarily in Madison, WI.
Officers: George E. Austin, Pres.; Rhona E. Vogel, Secy.
Directors: Grant J. Frautschi, W. Jerome Frautschi, Lance A. Frautschi.
EIN: 391855130
Codes: FD

56537
John J. Frautschi Family Foundation, Inc.
303 Lakewood Blvd.
Madison, WI 53704

Established in 1986 in WI.
Donor(s): John J. Frautschi, members of the Frautschi family.
Financial data (yr. ended 12/31/00): Grants paid, $4,568,016; assets, $4,580,072 (M); expenditures, $1,453,010; qualifying distributions, $4,603,274.
Limitations: Applications not accepted. Giving primarily in WI.
Application information: Contributes only to pre-selected organizations. Unsolicited requests for funds not considered.
Officers and Directors:* John J. Frautschi,* Pres.; Elizabeth J. Frautschi-Lingk,* V.P.; Christopher J. Frautschi,* Secy.-Treas.; Peter W. Frautschi,* Secy.-Treas.
EIN: 391561017
Codes: FD

56538
Kohler Foundation, Inc.
725 Woodlake Rd., Ste. X
Kohler, WI 53044 (920) 458-1972
FAX: (920) 458-4280
Contact: Terri Yoho

Incorporated in 1940 in WI.
Donor(s): Herbert V. Kohler,‡ Marie C. Kohler,‡ Evangeline Kohler,‡ Lillie B. Kohler,‡ O.A. Kroos.‡
Financial data (yr. ended 12/31/00): Grants paid, $4,355,716; assets, $135,742,465 (M); expenditures, $2,171,563; qualifying distributions, $5,562,829.
Limitations: Giving limited to WI.
Application information: Application guidelines available upon request. Application form not required.
Officers and Directors:* Ruth DeYoung Kohler II,* Pres.; Jeffrey P. Cheney,* V.P. and Treas.; Natalie A. Black,* V.P.; Paul Ten Pas,* Secy.
EIN: 390810536
Codes: FD

56539
Siebert Lutheran Foundation, Inc.
2600 N. Mayfair Rd., Ste. 390
Wauwatosa, WI 53226 (414) 257-2656
FAX: (414) 257-1387; E-mail: rdjslf@execpc.com; URL: http://www.siebertfoundation.org
Contact: Ronald D. Jones, Pres.

Incorporated in 1952 in WI.
Donor(s): A.F. Siebert,‡ Reginald L. Siebert.‡
Financial data (yr. ended 12/31/01): Grants paid, $4,285,568; assets, $95,868,070 (M); gifts received, $2,499,363; expenditures, $5,261,133; qualifying distributions, $4,451,282.
Limitations: Giving primarily in WI.
Publications: Program policy statement, application guidelines, informational brochure (including application guidelines), grants list, newsletter, annual report (including application guidelines).
Application information: Grantees are required to sign Grant Agreement Form. Application form not required.
Officers and Directors:* Ned Bechthold,* Chair.; Chris M. Bauer,* Vice-Chair.; Ronald D. Jones, Pres.; David W. Romoser, Secy.; John Zimdars, Treas.; Richard C. Barkow, Frederick H. Groth, Knute Jacobson, Raymond J. Perry, Julie Van Cleave.
EIN: 396050046
Codes: FD, FM

56540
Wisconsin Energy Corporation Foundation, Inc.
(Formerly Wisconsin Electric System Foundation, Inc.)
231 W. Michigan St.
Milwaukee, WI 53290 (414) 221-2106
Contact: Barbara J. Karow, Fdn. Coord.

Incorporated in 1982 in WI.
Donor(s): Wisconsin Energy Corp.
Financial data (yr. ended 12/31/00): Grants paid, $4,152,153; assets, $16,575,719 (M); gifts received, $3,000,000; expenditures, $4,309,940; qualifying distributions, $4,245,219.
Limitations: Giving primarily in service territories in the Upper Peninsula, MI, area and the southeastern and Fox Valley, WI, areas.
Application information: Application form not required.
Officers and Directors:* Richard A. Abdoo,* Pres.; Thomas H. Fehring, Secy.; Calvin H. Baker,* Treas.
EIN: 391433726
Codes: CS, FD, CD, FM

56541
The Oscar Rennebohm Foundation, Inc.
P.O. Box 5187
Madison, WI 53719 (608) 274-5991
Contact: Steven F. Skolaski, Pres. and Treas.

Incorporated in 1949 in WI.
Donor(s): Oscar Rennebohm.‡
Financial data (yr. ended 12/31/00): Grants paid, $3,425,000; assets, $66,987,820 (M); expenditures, $4,038,244; qualifying distributions, $3,267,277.
Limitations: Giving primarily in WI.
Application information: Application form not required.
Officers: Steven F. Skolaski, Pres. and Treas.; William H. Young, V.P.; Leona A. Sonderegger, Secy.
Directors: Patrick E. Coyle, Curtis F. Hastings, Robert B. Rennebohm.
EIN: 396039252
Codes: FD

56542
The Richard & Ethel Herzfeld Foundation, Inc.
219 N. Milwaukee St., 7th fl.
Milwaukee, WI 53202 (414) 727-1136
E-mail: herzfnd@execpc.com
Contact: Mark Warhus, Prog. Mgr.

Established around 1973 in WI.
Donor(s): Ethel D. Herzfeld,‡ Richard P. Herzfeld.‡
Financial data (yr. ended 12/31/01): Grants paid, $3,411,620; assets, $75,286,251 (M); gifts received, $500,000; expenditures, $4,584,176; qualifying distributions, $3,411,620.
Limitations: Giving primarily in WI, with emphasis on the greater Milwaukee area.
Publications: Application guidelines.
Application information: Application form required.
Officer: F. William Haberman, Pres. and Treas.
Directors: Edward Hinshaw, Roy C. LaBudde.
EIN: 237230686
Codes: FD, FM

56543
The Kern Family Foundation, Inc.
W305 S4239 Brookhill Rd.
Waukesha, WI 53189 (262) 968-6838
Ext: 2114
Contact: Paul A. Petitjean, Exec. Dir.

Established in 1998 in WI.
Donor(s): Robert D. Kern, Patricia E. Kern.
Financial data (yr. ended 06/30/00): Grants paid, $3,194,118; assets, $63,060,788 (M); expenditures, $3,410,850; qualifying distributions, $3,332,581.
Limitations: Giving primarily in WI.
Application information: Telephone for application form. Application form required.
Officers: Patricia E. Kern, Pres.; Robert D. Kern, V.P. and Treas.; Richard Van Deuren, Secy.; Paul A. Petitjean, Exec. Dir.
EIN: 391923558
Codes: FD

56544
Foundation of Faith, Inc.
(Formerly Ralph F. & Gertrude S. Findley Foundation, Inc.)
c/o The Legacy Group, Inc.
200 S. Executive Dr., Ste. 101
Brookfield, WI 53005
Contact: John Stanley

Established in 1991 in WI.
Donor(s): Ralph F. Findley, Gertrude S. Findley.‡
Financial data (yr. ended 12/31/01): Grants paid, $3,181,933; assets, $8,478,828 (M); expenditures, $3,375,756; qualifying distributions, $3,260,718.
Limitations: Applications not accepted. Giving primarily in Milwaukee, WI.
Application information: The foundation is no longer accepting requests for new funding.
Officers: Ralph F. Findley, Pres.; Don Bardonner, V.P.; John Findley, Secy.-Treas.
EIN: 391693993
Codes: FD

56545
Ted & Grace Bachhuber Foundation, Inc.
14 Tower Dr.
P.O. Box 228
Mayville, WI 53050

Established in 1982.
Donor(s): Theodore J. Bachhuber,‡ Mayville Engineering Co., Inc.
Financial data (yr. ended 12/31/01): Grants paid, $3,160,248; assets, $32,205,740 (M); gifts received, $130,000; expenditures, $3,569,126; qualifying distributions, $3,151,498.
Limitations: Applications not accepted. Giving limited to the Mayville, WI, area.
Application information: Contributes only to pre-selected organizations.
Officers and Directors:* JoAnn Bachhuber,* Pres. and Treas.; J. Dean Bartlett,* V.P.; Leo R. Fisher,* V.P.; Dan Edgarton,* Secy.; Carl N. Bachhuber, George Olsen, William Steinbach.
EIN: 391415821
Codes: FD

56546
Charlotte & Walter Kohler Charitable Trust
P.O. Box 1065
Sheboygan, WI 53082-1065 (920) 457-8616
Contact: Ruth Mckay, Grants Off.

Established in 1995 in WI.
Donor(s): Charlotte M. Kohler.‡
Financial data (yr. ended 12/31/00): Grants paid, $3,131,960; assets, $17,777,862 (M); expenditures, $3,292,762; qualifying distributions, $3,142,469.
Limitations: Applications not accepted. Giving on a national basis.
Application information: Contributes only to pre-selected organizations.
Trustees: Michael W. Grebe, Roland M. Neumann, Jr., U.S. Bank.
EIN: 391834766
Codes: FD

56547—WISCONSIN

56547
Robert T. Rolfs Foundation, Inc.
c/o U.S. Bank
P.O. Box 2043
Milwaukee, WI 53201-9116
Application address: 817 Crestview Dr., West Bend, WI 53095
Contact: Robert T. Rolfs, Pres.

Established in 1981 in WI.
Donor(s): Robert T. Rolfs, Amity Leather Products Co.
Financial data (yr. ended 09/30/01): Grants paid, $3,100,000; assets, $16,249,705 (M); expenditures, $3,147,819; qualifying distributions, $3,085,674.
Limitations: Giving primarily in WI.
Application information: Application form not required.
Officers: Robert T. Rolfs, Pres.; Marilyn Rolfs, V.P.; J. Lewis Perlson, Secy.-Treas.
Directors: Mark T. Rolfs, Robert T. Rolfs, Jr.
EIN: 391390015
Codes: FD

56548
The L. E. Phillips Family Foundation, Inc.
3925 N. Hastings Way
Eau Claire, WI 54703 (715) 839-2139
Additional address: P.O. Box 2105, Wilmington, DE 19899
Contact: Eileen Phillips Cohen, Dir.

Incorporated in 1943 in WI.
Donor(s): Members of the Phillips family and a family-related company.
Financial data (yr. ended 02/28/00): Grants paid, $2,959,880; assets, $50,069,050 (M); expenditures, $3,071,610; qualifying distributions, $2,942,861.
Limitations: Giving limited to northwestern WI, with emphasis on Eau Claire and Chippewa counties.
Application information: Application form not required.
Officers and Directors:* Melvin S. Cohen,* Pres.; Maryjo R. Cohen,* V.P. and Treas.; Edith Phillips,* V.P.; James F. Bartl,* Secy.; Eileen Phillips Cohen.
EIN: 396046126
Codes: FD

56549
Judd S. Alexander Foundation, Inc.
500 3rd St., Ste. 320
P.O. Box 2137
Wausau, WI 54402-2137 (715) 845-4556
FAX: (715) 848-9336
Contact: Gary W. Freels, Pres.

Incorporated in 1973 in WI.
Donor(s): Anne M. Alexander.‡
Financial data (yr. ended 06/30/01): Grants paid, $2,750,024; assets, $61,403,685 (M); expenditures, $3,032,656; qualifying distributions, $3,496,867; giving activities include $450,000 for program-related investments.
Limitations: Giving limited to Marathon County, WI, or to organizations directly benefiting the residents of Marathon County.
Application information: Application form not required.
Officers and Directors:* Stanley F. Staples, Jr.,* Chair.; Gary W. Freels,* Pres.; Richard D. Dudley,* V.P.; John F. Michler,* Secy.-Treas.; Dwight D. Davis, Harry N. Heinmann, Jr.
EIN: 237323721
Codes: FD

56550
Ruhar, Inc.
312 E. Wisconsin Ave., No. 210
Milwaukee, WI 53202-4305

Established in 1960.
Donor(s): Ruth B. Barker, Hartley B. Barker.
Financial data (yr. ended 12/31/00): Grants paid, $2,646,363; assets, $5,600,714 (M); gifts received, $1,844,063; expenditures, $2,655,639; qualifying distributions, $2,643,343.
Limitations: Applications not accepted. Giving primarily in WI, including Door County, Phoenix, AZ, and IL.
Application information: Contributes only to pre-selected organizations.
Officers: Hartley B. Barker, Pres.; Linda M. Jozefacki, V.P.; Ruth B. Barker, Secy.-Treas.
EIN: 396044471
Codes: FD

56551
The Nelson Family Foundation, Inc.
P.O. Box 447
Hudson, WI 54016-0447

Established in 1996 in WI.
Donor(s): Carol J. Nelson, Grant E. Nelson.
Financial data (yr. ended 12/31/00): Grants paid, $2,638,470; assets, $53,819,975 (M); expenditures, $3,312,172; qualifying distributions, $2,611,027.
Limitations: Applications not accepted.
Application information: Contributes only to pre-selected organizations.
Officers and Directors:* Grant E. Nelson,* Pres.; Carol J. Nelson,* Exec. V.P.; Sarah Nelson Hunter,* Secy.; Rodney G. Nelson,* Treas.; Burtch Hunter, Marybeth Nelson.
EIN: 391868979
Codes: FD

56552
Alliant Energy Foundation, Inc.
(Formerly Wisconsin Power and Light Foundation, Inc.)
222 W. Washington Ave.
Madison, WI 53703 (608) 252-5545
FAX: (608) 283-6991; E-mail: joannhealy@alliant-energy.com; URL: http://www.alliantenergy.com/community/charity.htm
Contact: Jo Ann Healy, Prog. Mgr.

Established in 1984 in WI.
Donor(s): Wisconsin Power and Light Co., Alliant Energy Corp.
Financial data (yr. ended 12/31/00): Grants paid, $2,625,339; assets, $33,612,218 (M); expenditures, $3,065,500; qualifying distributions, $2,458,479.
Limitations: Giving limited to areas of company operations in central and south central WI.
Publications: Annual report (including application guidelines), informational brochure (including application guidelines).
Application information: Application form required.
Officers: Pamela Wegner, Pres.; Diane Ramsey, V.P.; Edward Gleason, Secy.-Treas.
Directors: Erroll B. Davis, Jr., James E. Hoffman, Eliot G. Protsch, Barbara Swan.
EIN: 391444065
Codes: CS, FD, CD

56553
Community Foundation of Southern Wisconsin, Inc.
(Formerly United Community Foundation, Inc.)
111 N. Main St.
Janesville, WI 53545 (608) 758-0883
Additional tel.: (800) 995-CFSW; FAX: (608) 758-8551; E-mail: cfsw@jvlnet.com
Contact: Sue S. Conley, Exec. Dir.

Established in 1991 in WI.
Financial data (yr. ended 06/30/02): Grants paid, $2,620,614; assets, $16,608,521 (M); gifts received, $4,755,063; expenditures, $3,071,067.
Limitations: Giving limited to Rock, Grant, Green, Iowa, Lafayette, Walworth, and Jefferson counties, WI.
Publications: Annual report, informational brochure (including application guidelines), application guidelines, newsletter.
Application information: Scholarship applications accepted through recipient school districts only. Application form required.
Officers and Directors:* Robert Lisser,* Chair.; Margaret Hollenberger,* Vice-Chair.; Alan W. Dunwiddie,* Secy.; Frank Scott,* Treas.; Sue S. Conley, Exec. Dir.; John E. Condon, Barbara Daus, David G. Deininger, Alfred P. Diotte, Gregory Galvan, Patricia Guttenberg, James E. Hartwig, John Henderson, Timothy McGettingan, Ronald M. Spielman, James A. Stauff.
EIN: 391711388
Codes: CM, FD, GTI

56554
Patrick and Anna M. Cudahy Fund
P.O. Box 11978
Milwaukee, WI 53211 (414) 271-6020
IL address: 1007 Church St., Ste. 414, Evanston, IL, 60201; IL tel.: (847) 866-0760; FAX: (847) 475-0679; E-mail: jborcher@cudahyfund.org; URL: http://www.cudahyfund.org
Contact: Judith L. Borchers, Exec. Dir.

Incorporated in 1949 in WI.
Donor(s): Michael F. Cudahy.‡
Financial data (yr. ended 12/31/01): Grants paid, $2,420,433; assets, $23,552,805 (M); expenditures, $2,748,600; qualifying distributions, $2,546,731.
Limitations: Giving limited to Chicago, IL, and WI for local programs and for international (U.S.-based) programs.
Publications: Application guidelines, grants list.
Application information: See Web site for Summary of Request Form. Application form required.
Officers and Directors:* Richard D. Cudahy,* Chair.; Janet S. Cudahy,* Pres.; Dudley J. Godfrey, Jr.,* Secy.; Judith L. Borchers, Exec. Dir.; James Bailey, Daniel Cudahy, Michaela Cudahy, Jean Holtz, Wesley Scott, Annette Stoddard-Freeman.
EIN: 390991972
Codes: FD

56555
The Kellogg Family Foundation, Inc.
c/o Godfrey & Kahn
780 N. Water St.
Milwaukee, WI 53202

Established in 1993 in WI.
Donor(s): William Kellogg.
Financial data (yr. ended 12/31/01): Grants paid, $2,312,830; assets, $28,030,240 (M); gifts received, $1,041,525; expenditures, $2,342,466; qualifying distributions, $2,314,980.
Limitations: Applications not accepted. Giving primarily in Milwaukee, WI.

Application information: Contributes only to pre-selected organizations.
Officers and Directors:* William S. Kellogg,* Pres. and Treas.; Madelaine Kellogg,* V.P. and Secy.; Peter M. Sommerhauser.
EIN: 391775567
Codes: FD

56556
D. B. Reinhart Family Foundation
P.O. Box 2228
La Crosse, WI 54602-2228 (608) 782-4999

Established in 1987 in WI.
Donor(s): Marjorie A. Reinhart, D.B. Reinhart Enterprises, Reinhart Institutional Foods.
Financial data (yr. ended 08/31/00): Grants paid, $2,124,689; assets, $11,894,995 (M); expenditures, $2,138,244; qualifying distributions, $2,127,772.
Limitations: Applications not accepted. Giving primarily in WI, with emphasis on La Crosse.
Application information: Contributes only to pre-selected organizations.
Manager: Nancy Hengel.
Trustees: Gerald E. Connolly, Marjorie A. Reinhart.
EIN: 391564353
Codes: FD

56557
Fred J. Peterson Foundation, Inc.
41 N. 3rd Ave.
Sturgeon Bay, WI 54235-2413 (920) 743-5574
Contact: Marsha L. Kerley, Secy.

Incorporated in 1962 in WI.
Donor(s): Ellsworth L. Peterson, Fred J. Peterson,‡ Irene Peterson,‡ Peterson Builders, Inc.
Financial data (yr. ended 09/30/00): Grants paid, $2,118,570; assets, $4,539,801 (M); expenditures, $2,139,451; qualifying distributions, $2,126,856.
Limitations: Giving primarily in Door County, WI.
Application information: All scholarship decisions made by Rotary International or individual colleges. Application form not required.
Officers: Ellsworth Peterson, Pres.; Fred Peterson, V.P.; Marsha Kerley, Secy.
EIN: 396075901
Codes: FD

56558
David and Julia Uihlein Charitable Foundation, Inc.
735 N. Water St., Ste. 712
Milwaukee, WI 53202-4104

Established in 1995 in WI.
Donor(s): David V. Uihlein, Jr.
Financial data (yr. ended 12/31/01): Grants paid, $2,114,975; assets, $553 (M); gifts received, $2,120,665; expenditures, $2,122,123; qualifying distributions, $2,122,123.
Limitations: Applications not accepted. Giving primarily in Milwaukee, WI.
Application information: Contributes only to pre-selected organizations.
Officers and Directors:* David V. Uihlein, Jr.,* Pres. and Treas.; Julia A. Uihlein,* V.P. and Secy.
EIN: 391822364
Codes: FD

56559
The George Kress Foundation, Inc.
P.O. Box 408
Neenah, WI 54957-0408 (920) 433-3109
Application address: c/o Green Bay Packaging Co., 1700 N. Webster Ave., Green Bay, WI 54301
Contact: John F. Kress, Secy.

Incorporated in 1953 in WI.
Donor(s): Green Bay Packaging, Inc.
Financial data (yr. ended 12/31/01): Grants paid, $2,109,628; assets, $7,813,966 (M); gifts received, $2,000,000; expenditures, $2,154,861; qualifying distributions, $2,106,850.
Limitations: Giving primarily in Green Bay and Madison, WI.
Application information: Application form not required.
Officers: George F. Kress, Pres.; James F. Kress, V.P.; John Kress, Secy.
EIN: 396050768
Codes: FD

56560
Theodore W. Batterman Family Foundation, Inc.
625 Walnut Ridge Dr., Ste. 107
Hartland, WI 53029
FAX: (262) 241-0709
Contact: Carmen Witt, Exec. Dir.

Established in 1990 in WI.
Donor(s): Theodore W. Batterman, Spacesaver Corp.
Financial data (yr. ended 12/31/01): Grants paid, $2,103,475; assets, $45,956,294 (M); gifts received, $1,078,000; expenditures, $2,409,908; qualifying distributions, $2,163,659.
Limitations: Applications not accepted. Giving limited to WI.
Application information: Contributes only to pre-selected organizations.
Officers and Directors:* Theodore W. Batterman,* Pres. and Treas.; Marilyn H. Batterman,* V.P. and Secy.; Carmen Witt, Exec. Dir.; Christopher T. Batterman, Eric D. Batterman, Linda C. Batterman Johnson, Andrew R. Lauritzen, Laura G. Batterman Wilkins.
EIN: 391688812
Codes: FD

56561
Walter Schroeder Foundation, Inc.
1000 N. Water St., 13th Fl.
Milwaukee, WI 53202 (414) 287-7177
FAX: (414) 287-7025
Contact: William T. Gaus, V.P.

Incorporated in 1963 in WI.
Donor(s): Walter Schroeder Trust.
Financial data (yr. ended 06/30/01): Grants paid, $2,074,938; assets, $7,397,266 (M); expenditures, $2,196,111; qualifying distributions, $2,116,966.
Limitations: Giving primarily in Milwaukee County, WI.
Application information: Application form not required.
Officers and Directors:* James B. Wigdale,* Pres.; William T. Gaus,* V.P.; Marjorie A. Vallier,* Secy.; Robert M. Hoffer, Ruthmarie M. Lawrenz.
EIN: 396065789
Codes: FD

56562
Greater Green Bay Community Foundation
302 N. Adams St., Ste. 100
Green Bay, WI 54301 (920) 432-0800
FAX: (920) 432-5577; URL: http://www.ggbcf.org
Contact: Steve Schumeisser, Fin. Off.

Established in 1991 in WI.
Financial data (yr. ended 06/30/01): Grants paid, $1,851,569; assets, $15,704,029 (M); gifts received, $2,498,891; expenditures, $2,400,309.
Limitations: Giving limited to Brown, Door, Kewaunee and Oconto counties, WI.
Publications: Annual report, newsletter, informational brochure, application guidelines.
Application information: Scholarship application forms available through Northeast, WI high schools. Application form required for scholarships; scholarship recipients must be residents of Brown, Door, Kewaunee or Oconto counties, WI. Application form required.
Officers and Directors:* Charles Johnson,* Chair.; Kenneth D. Strmiska,* Pres.; Richard Beuerstein,* V.P.; Paul Meinke,* V.P.; Sheri Prosser,* V.P.; Jeff Ottum,* V.P.; Diane Conway,* Secy.; Tim Day,* Treas.
EIN: 391699966
Codes: CM, FD, GTI

56563
Harley-Davidson Foundation, Inc.
3700 W. Juneau Ave.
Milwaukee, WI 53208 (414) 343-4001
Contact: Mary Ann Martiny

Established in 1994 in WI.
Donor(s): Harley-Davidson, Inc.
Financial data (yr. ended 12/31/00): Grants paid, $1,841,864; assets, $7,007,915 (M); gifts received, $2,485,093; expenditures, $1,898,866; qualifying distributions, $1,841,864.
Limitations: Giving primarily in AL, MO, PA, and WI.
Application information: Accepts Milwaukee Area Funders Common Application Form. Application form required.
Officers: James L. Ziemer, Pres.; Gail A. Lione, Secy.; James M. Brostowitz, Treas.
Trustee: Firstar Trust Co.
EIN: 391769946
Codes: CS, FD, CD

56564
Beloit Foundation, Inc.
2870 Riverside Dr.
Beloit, WI 53511-1506
Contact: Gary G. Grabowski, Exec. Dir.

Incorporated in 1959 in WI.
Donor(s): Elbert H. Neese, Sr.‡
Financial data (yr. ended 12/31/00): Grants paid, $1,834,095; assets, $17,622,282 (M); expenditures, $2,147,822; qualifying distributions, $1,866,483.
Limitations: Giving limited to the local stateline area, including South Beloit, Rockton, Roscoe, IL and Beloit, WI.
Application information: Application form required.
Officers and Directors:* Elbert H. Neese,* Pres.; Kim M. Kotthaus, Secy.; Gary G. Grabowski,* Treas. and Exec. Dir.; Laura N. Malik, Harry C. Moore, Jr., Alonzo A. Neese, Jr., Gordon C. Neese, Jane Petit-Moore, Elizabeth Tardola.
EIN: 396068763
Codes: FD

56565
E.C. Styberg Foundation, Inc.
1600 Gould St.
P.O. Box 788
Racine, WI 53401-0788
Contact: E.C. Styberg, Jr., Pres.

Established in 1981 in WI.
Donor(s): E.C. Styberg, Jr., Bernice M. Styberg.
Financial data (yr. ended 06/30/01): Grants paid, $1,808,210; assets, $6,279,652 (M); gifts received, $1,087,297; expenditures, $605,639; qualifying distributions, $1,777,025.
Limitations: Giving primarily in southeastern WI; giving also in Evanston, IL.
Application information: Application form required.
Officers: E.C. Styberg, Jr., Pres.; Bernice M. Styberg, V.P. and Secy.; Paul L. Guenther, Treas.
EIN: 391410323

56565—WISCONSIN

Codes: FD

56566
Fleck Foundation
(Formerly Fleckenstein Family Foundation)
16655 W. Bluemound Rd., Ste. 290
Brookfield, WI 53005 (262) 860-1680
FAX: (262) 860-1683
Contact: Andrew J. Fleckenstein, Tr.

Established in 1996.
Donor(s): Andrew J. Fleckenstein.
Financial data (yr. ended 12/31/01): Grants paid, $1,800,000; assets, $16,750,000 (M); expenditures, $2,000,000; qualifying distributions, $1,800,000.
Limitations: Giving primarily in Milwaukee, WI.
Publications: Annual report.
Application information: Application form not required.
Officer and Trustees:* Jay Scott,* Exec. Dir.; Andrew J. Fleckenstein.
Board Members: Nate Cunniff, Carolyn Scott, Jim Stern.
EIN: 391832464
Codes: FD

56567
Cornerstone Foundation of Northeastern Wisconsin, Inc.
200 S. Washington St., Ste. 305
Green Bay, WI 54301 (920) 432-2045
FAX: (920) 432-5822
Contact: Sheri Prosser, V.P.

Incorporated in 1953 in WI.
Financial data (yr. ended 12/31/00): Grants paid, $1,783,585; assets, $29,369,108 (M); expenditures, $2,258,278; qualifying distributions, $1,845,905.
Limitations: Giving primarily in Brown County and northeastern WI.
Publications: Application guidelines.
Application information: Application form not required.
Officers and Directors:* Paul J. Schierl,* Pres.; Sheri Prosser, V.P. and Secy.; James J. Schoshinski,* V.P. and Treas.; John W. Hickey,* V.P.; Robert E. Manger,* V.P.; Carol A. Schierl,* V.P.; Michael J. Schierl,* V.P.; Thomas L. Shaffer,* V.P.; Diane D. Rees, Susan M. Touscany.
EIN: 362761910
Codes: FD

56568
Pollybill Foundation, Inc.
111 E. Kilbourn Ave., 19th Fl.
Milwaukee, WI 53202-6622

Incorporated in 1960 in WI.
Donor(s): William D. Van Dyke, Polly H. Van Dyke.
Financial data (yr. ended 12/31/00): Grants paid, $1,767,450; assets, $4,931,059 (M); gifts received, $1,947,820; expenditures, $1,795,028; qualifying distributions, $1,777,028.
Limitations: Applications not accepted. Giving primarily in Milwaukee, WI.
Application information: Contributes only to pre-selected organizations.
Officers and Directors:* Polly H. Van Dyke,* Pres. and Treas.; William D. Van Dyke III,* V.P.; Paul F. Meissner,* Secy.; Leonard C. Campbell.
EIN: 396078550
Codes: FD

56569
Herbert H. Kohl Charities, Inc.
825 N. Jefferson St., Ste. 250
Milwaukee, WI 53202

Established in 1977 in WI.
Donor(s): Herbert H. Kohl, Mary Kohl.
Financial data (yr. ended 06/30/00): Grants paid, $1,764,100; assets, $9,989,225 (M); expenditures, $1,822,306; qualifying distributions, $1,758,019.
Limitations: Applications not accepted. Giving primarily in Milwaukee, WI.
Application information: Contributes only to pre-selected organizations.
Officers and Directors:* Herbert H. Kohl,* Pres.; Allen D. Kohl,* V.P.; Sidney A. Kohl,* Secy.; Dolores K. Solovy,* Treas.
EIN: 391300476
Codes: FD

56570
Marshall & Ilsley Foundation, Inc.
(Formerly Marshall & Ilsley Bank Foundation, Inc.)
770 N. Water St.
Milwaukee, WI 53202 (414) 765-7835
Contact: Diane L. Sebion, Secy.

Incorporated in 1958 in WI.
Donor(s): Marshall & Ilsley Trust Co. N.A.
Financial data (yr. ended 12/31/00): Grants paid, $1,756,000; assets, $118,186 (M); gifts received, $1,800,000; expenditures, $1,759,740; qualifying distributions, $1,755,969.
Limitations: Giving primarily in WI.
Application information: Children of permanent, full-time employees of Marshall & Ilsley should contact foundation for scholarship guidelines. Application form not required.
Officers and Directors:* James B. Wigdale,* Pres.; Dennis J. Kuester,* V.P.; Margaret A. Zentner, Secy.-Treas.; Richard A. Abdoo, Wendell F. Bueche, Burleigh E. Jacobs, Jack F. Kellner, Stuart W. Tisdale, James A. Urdan, George E. Wardeberg, James O. Wright.
Trustee: Marshall & Ilsley Trust Company, N.A.
EIN: 396043185
Codes: CS, FD, CD, GTI

56571
Faye McBeath Foundation
1020 N. Broadway
Milwaukee, WI 53202 (414) 272-2626
FAX: (414) 272-6235; E-mail: info@fayemcbeath.org; URL: http://www.fayemcbeath.org
Contact: Sarah M. Dean, Exec. Dir.

Trust established in 1964 in WI.
Donor(s): Faye McBeath.‡
Financial data (yr. ended 12/31/01): Grants paid, $1,683,830; assets, $15,001,253 (M); gifts received, $2,000; expenditures, $1,889,016; qualifying distributions, $1,778,090.
Limitations: Giving limited to WI, with emphasis on the greater Milwaukee area.
Publications: Annual report, program policy statement, application guidelines, grants list.
Application information: Application form required.
Officers and Trustees:* William L. Randall,* Chair.; Charles A. Krause,* Vice-Chair.; Steven J. Smith,* Secy.; Sarah M. Dean, Exec. Dir.; Patsy Aster, Bonnie R. Weigell, U.S. Bank.
EIN: 396074450
Codes: FD

56572
The Evjue Foundation, Inc.
1901 Fish Hatchery Rd.
P.O. Box 8060
Madison, WI 53708 (608) 252-6401
Contact: Arlene Hornung

Incorporated in 1958 in WI.
Donor(s): William T. Evjue.‡
Financial data (yr. ended 02/28/01): Grants paid, $1,681,535; assets, $25,419,544 (M); expenditures, $1,809,692.
Limitations: Giving primarily in Dane County, WI.
Publications: Program policy statement, application guidelines, informational brochure (including application guidelines).
Application information: Application form required.
Officers and Directors:* John H. Lussier,* Pres.; Nancy Brooke Gage,* V.P.; Clayton Frink,* Secy.; Frederick W. Miller,* Treas.; Marion F. Brown, W. Jerome Frautschi, Virginia Henderson, James D. Lussier, Laura J. Lussier, Hal Mayer, Steve Mixtacki, Marianne D. Pollard, John S. Robison, John T. Robison, Andrew A. Wilcox, John Wiley.
EIN: 396073981
Codes: CM, FD

56573
Vine and Branches Foundation, Inc.
P.O. Box 627
Mukwonago, WI 53149 (262) 363-1570
FAX: (262) 363-1571; E-mail: pwoehrer@philanthropyatwork.com; URL: http://www.vineandbranchesfoundation.org
Contact: Pat Woehrer, Private Giving Mgr.

Established in 1995 in WI.
Financial data (yr. ended 12/31/01): Grants paid, $1,653,000; assets, $37,444,288 (M); expenditures, $2,479,226; qualifying distributions, $2,067,325.
Limitations: Giving primarily in southeast WI, with emphasis on Milwaukee and Waukesha counties.
Publications: Informational brochure (including application guidelines).
Application information: E-mail applications are not accepted. Application form not required.
Officer: Patricia Woehrer, Private Giving Mgr.
EIN: 391827808
Codes: FD

56574
Hedberg Foundation Inc.
P.O. Box 1422
Janesville, WI 53547-1422 (608) 756-1744
Contact: Robert C. Zahn, C.O.O.

Established in 1991 in WI.
Donor(s): Donald D. Hedberg, Geraldine Hedberg.‡
Financial data (yr. ended 12/31/00): Grants paid, $1,630,090; assets, $3,931,826 (M); gifts received, $567; expenditures, $1,666,460; qualifying distributions, $1,650,871.
Limitations: Giving primarily in WI.
Application information: Application form not required.
Officers and Directors:* Robert C. Zahn, C.O.O.; Donald D. Hedberg,* Pres.; Peggy H. Stich,* V.P.; Carla H. Westcott,* Secy.-Treas.
EIN: 391684914
Codes: FD

56575
Oshkosh Area Community Foundation
(Formerly OshKosh Foundation)
404 N. Main St.
P.O. Box 1726
Oshkosh, WI 54903 (920) 426-3993
FAX: (920) 426-6997
Contact: Eileen Connolly-Keesler, Exec. Dir.

Established in 1928 in WI by declaration of trust.
Donor(s): Pacific Income, Great Lakes.
Financial data (yr. ended 06/30/01): Grants paid, $1,623,880; assets, $28,063,322 (M); gifts received, $3,862,271; expenditures, $2,233,842.
Limitations: Giving limited to Winnebago, Green Lake, and Waukesha counties, WI.
Publications: Annual report, application guidelines, informational brochure, financial statement, newsletter.
Application information: Applications not accepted unless residency requirements are met. Application form required.
Officers and Foundation Committee:* Lorrie Heinemann,* Chair.; John Bermingham, Jr., Vice-Chair.; William Wyman, Secy.; Lawrence Bittner,* Treas.; Michael Castle, Marcy Coglianese, Tom Harenburg, Robert Hergert, Virginia Nelson, Bob Pung, Richard Rutledge, Pat Seubert, Sam Sundet.
Trustees: Associated Banc-Corp, Bank One, Oshkosh, N.A., U.S. Bank, Marshall & Ilsley Trust Company, N.A., Sound Capital Vanguard.
EIN: 396041638
Codes: CM, FD, GTI

56576
Ruth St. John & John Dunham West Foundation, Inc.
980 Maritime Dr., Suite 5
Manitowoc, WI 54221-1143
FAX: (920) 684-7381; E-mail: westfdt@lsol.net
Contact: Thomas J. Bare, Chair., Pres., and C.E.O.

Established in 1957.
Donor(s): Ruth St. John West,‡ John Dunham West.‡
Financial data (yr. ended 12/31/01): Grants paid, $1,604,072; assets, $47,649,500 (M); expenditures, $2,093,946; qualifying distributions, $2,071,057; giving activities include $257,739 for programs.
Limitations: Giving primarily in Manitowoc County, WI.
Publications: Annual report.
Application information: Application form not required.
Officers and Directors:* Thomas J. Bare,* Chair, Pres. and C.E.O.; August J. Schuette,* Vice-Chair. and V.P.; Evelyn Childs, Secy.; Phyllis Schippers, Treas.
EIN: 396056375
Codes: FD

56577
Racine Community Foundation, Inc.
(Formerly Racine County Area Foundation, Inc.)
818 6th St., Ste. 201
Racine, WI 53403 (262) 632-8474
FAX: (262) 632-3739; E-mail: info@racinecf.org; URL: http://www.racinecf.org
Contact: Margaret L. Kozina, Exec. Dir.

Incorporated in 1975 in WI.
Financial data (yr. ended 12/31/01): Grants paid, $1,550,346; assets, $25,477,599 (M); gifts received, $1,068,251; expenditures, $1,840,579.
Limitations: Giving limited to Racine County, WI.
Publications: Annual report, application guidelines, informational brochure, newsletter.
Application information: Application form required.
Officers and Directors:* Neal R. Nottleson,* Pres.; John S. Crimmings,* V.P., Donor Relations; Gabriella S. Klein,* V.P., Grants; Robert F. Taylor,* V.P., Marketing; David Ballweg,* Secy.; Michele A. Cody,* Treas. and Chair., Fin.; Virginia M. Buhler,* Chair., Board Affairs; David M. Perkins,* Chair., Investment; Jess S. Levin,* Chair., Personnel; Margaret L. Kozina, Exec. Dir.; Bruce A. Bernberg, James A. Eastman, Sharon J. Hamilton, Arthel L. Howell, Dorothy A. Metz, Sara E. Neubauer, Dwayne G. Olsen, James O. Parrish, William H. Stone, Bernice M. Styberg, Guadalupe G. Villarreal, Nancy E. Wheeler.
EIN: 510188377
Codes: CM, FD, GTI

56578
Milton and Lillian Peck Foundation, Inc.
c/o Komisar Brady & Co., LLP
633 W. Wisconsin Ave., Ste. 700
Milwaukee, WI 53203-1918

Established in 1958.
Donor(s): Peck Meat Packing Corp., Emmber Brands, Inc., Gibbon Packing, Inc., Moo-Battue, Inc.
Financial data (yr. ended 12/31/01): Grants paid, $1,525,833; assets, $11,621,667 (M); expenditures, $1,602,350; qualifying distributions, $1,492,847.
Limitations: Applications not accepted. Giving primarily in Milwaukee, WI.
Application information: Contributes only to pre-selected organizations.
Officers and Directors:* Bernard Peck,* Pres.; Miriam Peck,* V.P. and Treas.; William L. Komisar, Secy.; Miriam Lowe.
EIN: 396051782
Codes: FD

56579
Nancy Woodson Spire Foundation, Inc.
P.O. Box 65
Wausau, WI 54402-0065 (715) 845-9201
Contact: San W. Orr, Jr., Pres.

Financial data (yr. ended 06/30/02): Grants paid, $1,505,000; assets, $34,295,348 (M); gifts received, $16,210,356; expenditures, $1,590,427; qualifying distributions, $1,521,476.
Limitations: Giving primarily in Wausau, WI.
Application information: Application form not required.
Officers and Directors:* San W. Orr, Jr.,* Pres.; Ann M. Dubore,* Secy.; Julie A. Williams,* Treas.; Daryl E. Gebhart.
EIN: 391367383
Codes: FD

56580
Michael J. Cudahy Foundation
c/o Kevin L. Lindsey, Tr.
10850 W. Park Pl., Ste. 980
Milwaukee, WI 53224

Established in 1999 in WI.
Donor(s): Michael J. Cudahy.
Financial data (yr. ended 12/31/00): Grants paid, $1,489,675; assets, $77,824,920 (M); gifts received, $34,161,218; expenditures, $2,354,929; qualifying distributions, $1,899,518.
Limitations: Applications not accepted. Giving primarily in Milwaukee, WI.
Application information: Contributes only to pre-selected organizations.
Trustees: Joanna D. Hamadi, Kevin L. Lindsey, John W. Linnen.
EIN: 396720806
Codes: FD

56581
Mead Witter Foundation, Inc.
(Formerly Consolidated Papers Foundation, Inc.)
P.O. Box 39
Wisconsin Rapids, WI 54495-0039
(715) 424-3004
FAX: (715) 424-1314
Contact: Susan Feith, Pres.

Incorporated in 1951 in WI.
Donor(s): Consolidated Papers, Inc., and members of the George W. Mead family.
Financial data (yr. ended 12/31/00): Grants paid, $1,469,487; assets, $71,102,433 (M); gifts received, $48,000; expenditures, $2,296,301; qualifying distributions, $1,652,772.
Limitations: Giving primarily in WI, usually near areas of company operations.
Publications: Informational brochure (including application guidelines).
Application information: Application form not required.
Officers and Directors:* George W. Mead,* Chair.; Susan Feith,* Pres.; Emily B. McKay,* Secy.; J. Richard Matsch, Treas.
EIN: 396040071
Codes: FD

56582
Eugenie Mayer Bolz Family Foundation
P.O. Box 8100
Madison, WI 53708-8100 (608) 257-6761

Established in 1976 in WI and IL.
Donor(s): Eugenie M. Bolz, Eugenie M. Bolz Charitable Lead Trust.
Financial data (yr. ended 12/31/01): Grants paid, $1,384,100; assets, $6,257,018 (M); gifts received, $421,700; expenditures, $1,452,146; qualifying distributions, $1,385,547.
Limitations: Applications not accepted. Giving primarily in Madison, WI.
Application information: Contributes only to pre-selected organizations.
Officers: Robert M. Bolz, Pres.; Julia M. Bolz, V.P.; Sara L. Bolz, V.P.; John A. Bolz, Secy.-Treas.
EIN: 237428561
Codes: FD

56583
Puelicher Foundation, Inc.
1000 N. Water St.
Milwaukee, WI 53202 (414) 287-7184
Contact: James B. Wigdale, Pres.

Established in 1956.
Donor(s): John A. Puelicher.
Financial data (yr. ended 12/31/01): Grants paid, $1,345,500; assets, $10,953,035 (M); expenditures, $1,387,694; qualifying distributions, $1,341,865.
Limitations: Giving primarily in Milwaukee, WI.
Officers and Director:* James B. Wigdale, Pres.; Mary P. Uihlein,* V.P.; Diane L. Sebion, Secy.-Treas.
EIN: 396055461
Codes: FD

56584
Harvey Firestone, Jr. Foundation
c/o Bank One Trust Co., N.A.
P.O. Box 1308
Milwaukee, WI 53201
Application address: c/o Bank One Trust Co., N.A., 50 S. Main St., P.O. Box 3547, Akron, OH 44309, tel.: (330) 972-1872
Contact: Charles D'Arcy

Established in 1983 in OH.

56584—WISCONSIN

Financial data (yr. ended 12/31/00): Grants paid, $1,250,000; assets, $27,437,345 (M); expenditures, $1,488,747; qualifying distributions, $1,284,690.
Limitations: Giving primarily in the eastern U.S.
Application information: Application form not required.
Trustees: Anne F. Ball, Martha F. Ford.
EIN: 341388254
Codes: FD

56585
Ladish Company Foundation
P.O. Box 8902
Cudahy, WI 53110-8902
Contact: Ronald O. Wiese, Tr.

Trust established in 1952 in WI.
Donor(s): Ladish Co., Inc.
Financial data (yr. ended 11/30/01): Grants paid, $1,228,000; assets, $24,077,944 (M); expenditures, $1,240,058; qualifying distributions, $1,216,336.
Limitations: Applications not accepted. Giving primarily in WI.
Application information: Contributes only to pre-selected organizations.
Trustees: John H. Ladish, Wayne E. Larsen, Ronald O. Wiese.
EIN: 396040489
Codes: CS, FD, CD

56586
Melitta S. Pick Charitable Trust
c/o Foley & Lardner
777 E. Wisconsin Ave., Ste. 3800
Milwaukee, WI 53202 (414) 297-5748
Contact: Harrold J. McComas, Tr.

Established in 1972 in WI.
Donor(s): Melitta S. Pick.‡
Financial data (yr. ended 01/31/02): Grants paid, $1,224,500; assets, $27,801,968 (M); expenditures, $1,447,015; qualifying distributions, $1,274,960.
Limitations: Giving primarily in southeastern WI.
Application information: Application form not required.
Trustees: Harrold J. McComas, Joan M. Pick.
EIN: 237243490
Codes: FD

56587
Halbert & Alice Kadish Foundation
c/o Paul F. Meissner
111 E. Kilbourn Ave., 19th Fl.
Milwaukee, WI 53202

Established in 1994 in WI.
Donor(s): Alice B. Kadish.
Financial data (yr. ended 12/31/01): Grants paid, $1,209,400; assets, $7,844,554 (M); gifts received, $205,167; expenditures, $1,283,808; qualifying distributions, $1,279,131.
Limitations: Applications not accepted. Giving primarily in WI.
Application information: Contributes only to pre-selected organizations.
Officers: Adelbert L. Bertschy, Pres.; Dorothy Bertschy, V.P.; Nancy Lidecker, V.P.; Robert H. Lidecker, V.P.; Paul F. Meissner, Secy.
EIN: 391770402
Codes: FD

56588
Frank G. and Frieda K. Brotz Family Foundation, Inc.
(Formerly Frank G. Brotz Family Foundation, Inc.)
3518 Lakeshore Rd.
Sheboygan, WI 53083-2903 (920) 458-2121
Contact: Grants Comm.

Incorporated in 1953 in WI.
Donor(s): Plastics Engineering Co., Inc.
Financial data (yr. ended 09/30/01): Grants paid, $1,206,650; assets, $22,390,488 (M); expenditures, $1,260,650; qualifying distributions, $1,190,590.
Limitations: Giving primarily in WI.
Officers and Trustees:* Stuart W. Brotz,* Pres. and Treas.; Ralph R. Brotz,* V.P.; Adam T. Brotz,* Secy.; Roland M. Neumann.
EIN: 396060552
Codes: FD

56589
Greater Kenosha Foundation
(Formerly Kenosha Foundation)
P.O. Box 1829
Kenosha, WI 53141
Contact: Ann H. McDonough

Established in 1945.
Financial data (yr. ended 12/31/00): Grants paid, $1,204,603; assets, $2,990,305 (M); gifts received, $1,053,465; expenditures, $1,311,585.
Limitations: Giving limited to Kenosha County, WI.
Application information: Application form required.
Officers: Ann H. McDonough Loff, Exec. Dir.; Ralph J. Tenuta, Advisor.
EIN: 390826296
Codes: CM, FD

56590
Alexander Charitable Foundation, Inc.
1 Port Plz.
Port Edwards, WI 54469
Contact: John A. Casey, Pres.

Incorporated in 1955 in WI.
Donor(s): John E. Alexander.‡
Financial data (yr. ended 12/31/01): Grants paid, $1,193,173; assets, $15,886,272 (M); expenditures, $1,252,133; qualifying distributions, $1,248,212.
Limitations: Applications not accepted. Giving primarily in WI.
Application information: Contributes only to pre-selected organizations.
Officers and Directors:* John A. Casey,* Pres.; Leslie V. Arendt,* V.P.; Charles R. Lester,* V.P.; Joyce J. Rucinski, Secy.-Treas.; Thomas J. McCormick, Tim Wright.
EIN: 396045140
Codes: FD

56591
Briggs & Stratton Corporation Foundation, Inc.
12301 W. Wirth St.
Wauwatosa, WI 53222
Application address: P.O. Box 702, Milwaukee, WI 53201
Contact: Robert F. Health, Secy.-Treas., for grants; or Carolynn Tyloch, for scholarships

Incorporated in 1953 in WI.
Donor(s): Briggs & Stratton Corp.
Financial data (yr. ended 11/30/01): Grants paid, $1,178,500; assets, $12,580,520 (M); gifts received, $800,000; expenditures, $1,189,604; qualifying distributions, $1,179,350.
Limitations: Giving primarily in areas of company operations in Auburn, AL, Statesboro, GA, Murry, KY, Poplar Bluff and Rolla, MO, and Milwaukee, WI.
Application information: Application form not required.
Officers and Directors:* Frederick P. Stratton, Jr.,* Pres.; John S. Shiely,* V.P.; Robert F. Heath,* Secy.-Treas.; Michael D. Hamilton.
EIN: 396040377
Codes: CS, FD, CD, GTI

56592
Stewardship Trust
P.O. Box 3181
Eau Claire, WI 54702-3181

Established in 1997 in WI.
Donor(s): NBI, Inc.
Financial data (yr. ended 12/31/01): Grants paid, $1,177,000; assets, $143,310 (M); gifts received, $975,000; expenditures, $1,182,119; qualifying distributions, $1,177,000.
Limitations: Applications not accepted. Giving on a national and international basis.
Application information: Contributes only to pre-selected organizations.
Trustee: Roger Amundson.
EIN: 416429623
Codes: FD

56593
A. O. Smith Foundation, Inc.
P.O. Box 23971
Milwaukee, WI 53223-0971
Application address: P.O. Box 24508, Milwaukee, WI 53224-9508
Contact: Edward J. O'Connor, Secy.

Incorporated in 1955 in WI.
Donor(s): A.O. Smith Corp.
Financial data (yr. ended 12/31/01): Grants paid, $1,158,547; assets, $7,777,565 (M); expenditures, $1,177,098; qualifying distributions, $1,158,547.
Limitations: Giving primarily in areas of company operations in AR, IL, IN, KS, KY, NC, OH, SC, TN, TX, WA, and WI.
Publications: Annual report (including application guidelines).
Application information: Application form not required.
Officers and Directors:* A.O. Smith,* Pres.; R.J. O'Toole, V.P.; E.J. O'Connor,* Secy.
EIN: 396076924
Codes: CS, FD, CD

56594
The Lubar Family Foundation, Inc.
700 N. Water St., Ste. 1200
Milwaukee, WI 53202

Established in 1968 in WI.
Donor(s): Members of the Lubar family.
Financial data (yr. ended 12/31/01): Grants paid, $1,072,932; assets, $2,993,142 (M); expenditures, $1,073,082; qualifying distributions, $1,073,082.
Limitations: Applications not accepted. Giving primarily in WI.
Application information: Contributes only to pre-selected organizations.
Officers and Directors:* Marianne S. Lubar,* Pres.; Sheldon B. Lubar,* V.P. and Secy.; Mary Beth Wisniewski, Treas.
EIN: 391098690
Codes: FD

56595
Henry Uihlein II & Mildred A. Uihlein Foundation
c/o Leekley & Wotherspoon
231 W. Wisconsin Ave., Ste. 805
Milwaukee, WI 53203-2306

Established around 1979 in WI.
Donor(s): Henry Uihlein II.‡
Financial data (yr. ended 12/31/01): Grants paid, $1,036,633; assets, $21,948,651 (M); expenditures, $1,318,866; qualifying distributions, $1,030,324.
Limitations: Applications not accepted. Giving limited to NY, with emphasis on Lake Placid.
Application information: Contributes only to pre-selected organizations.
Trustees: John D. Leekley, Jr., John McKenna, William W. Wotherspoon.
EIN: 391322495
Codes: FD

56596
Robert W. Baird and Company Foundation, Inc.
c/o James D. Bell
777 E. Wisconsin Ave.
Milwaukee, WI 53202

Established in 1967 in WI.
Donor(s): Robert W. Baird and Co.
Financial data (yr. ended 12/31/01): Grants paid, $985,362; assets, $8,042,676 (M); gifts received, $593,704; expenditures, $889,602; qualifying distributions, $977,826.
Limitations: Applications not accepted. Giving primarily in WI.
Application information: Contributes only to pre-selected organizations.
Trustees: James D. Bell, G. Frederick Kasten, Jr.
EIN: 396107937
Codes: CS, FD, CD

56597
Wisconsin Public Service Foundation, Inc.
700 N. Adams St.
Green Bay, WI 54301 (920) 433-1457
Application address: P.O. Box 19001, Green Bay, WI 54307-9001
Scholarship application address: c/o Scholarship Prog., Scholarship Assessment Svc., P.O. Box 5189, Appleton, WI 54913-5189
Contact: P.J. Reinhard

Incorporated in 1964 in WI.
Donor(s): Wisconsin Public Service Corp.
Financial data (yr. ended 12/31/01): Grants paid, $967,499; assets, $17,718,356 (M); expenditures, $983,513; qualifying distributions, $983,513.
Limitations: Giving generally limited to upper MI and northeastern WI.
Publications: Informational brochure, application guidelines.
Application information: Application form required for grants and scholarships.
Officers: L.L. Weyers, Pres.; T.P. Meinz, V.P.; B.J. Wolf, Secy.; J.P. O'Leary, Treas.
EIN: 396075016
Codes: CS, FD, CD, GTI

56598
Evan and Marion Helfaer Foundation
P.O. Box 147
Elm Grove, WI 53122
Application address: 735 N. Water St., Milwaukee, WI 53202, tel.: (414) 276-3600
Contact: Thomas L. Smallwood, Admin.

Established in 1971 in WI.
Donor(s): Evan P. Helfaer.‡
Financial data (yr. ended 07/31/01): Grants paid, $949,060; assets, $26,851,186 (M); expenditures, $1,353,805; qualifying distributions, $1,099,418.
Limitations: Giving limited to WI.
Application information: Application form not required.
Trustees: Jack F. Kellner, Thomas L. Smallwood, Marshall & Ilsley Trust Company, N.A.
EIN: 396238856
Codes: FD

56599
Herman W. Ladish Family Foundation, Inc.
13255 W. Bluemound Rd., Ste. 201A
Brookfield, WI 53005 (262) 780-9640
Contact: William J. Ladish, Pres.

Incorporated in 1956 in WI.
Donor(s): Herman W. Ladish.‡
Financial data (yr. ended 06/30/01): Grants paid, $936,500; assets, $12,991,632 (M); expenditures, $1,033,954; qualifying distributions, $998,634.
Limitations: Giving primarily in WI, with strong emphasis on Milwaukee.
Application information: Application form not required.
Officers and Directors:* William J. Ladish,* Pres.; Laura L. Jacobson,* V.P.; Robert T. Stollenwerk,* Secy.-Treas.; Margaret L. Exner, Mary L. Selander, Elwin J. Zarwell.
EIN: 396063602
Codes: FD

56600
William and Catherine Bryce Memorial Fund
c/o Bank One Trust Co., N.A.
P.O. Box 1308
Milwaukee, WI 53201
Application address: c/o Bank One, Texas, N.A., P.O. Box 2050, Fort Worth, TX 76113, tel.: (817) 884-4151
Contact: Robert Lansford

Trust established in 1944 in TX.
Financial data (yr. ended 09/30/01): Grants paid, $935,240; assets, $16,702,019 (M); expenditures, $1,125,233; qualifying distributions, $965,106.
Limitations: Giving limited to TX, with emphasis on the Fort Worth area.
Trustee: Bank One Trust Co., N.A.
EIN: 756013845
Codes: FD

56601
Windhover Foundation, Inc.
c/o Quad/Graphics, Inc.
W224 N3322 Duplainville Rd.
Pewaukee, WI 53072
URL: http://www.qg.com/whoarewe/windhover.html
Contact: Michael Schroeder, Secy.

Established in 1983.
Donor(s): Quad/Graphics, Inc.
Financial data (yr. ended 12/31/99): Grants paid, $932,000; assets, $16,053,480 (M); expenditures, $1,107,354; qualifying distributions, $932,000.
Limitations: Giving primarily in WI.
Application information: Application form not required.
Officers: Elizabeth E. Quadracci, Pres.; Harry V. Quadracci, V.P.; Michael Schroeder, Secy.; John C. Fowler, Treas.
EIN: 391482470
Codes: CS, FD, CD, GTI

56602
Menasha Corporation Foundation
P.O. Box 367
Neenah, WI 54957-0367 (920) 751-1000
Contact: Steven S. Kromholz, Pres.

Established in 1953 in WI.
Donor(s): Menasha Corp.
Financial data (yr. ended 12/31/00): Grants paid, $894,030; assets, $821,435 (M); gifts received, $768,000; expenditures, $906,897; qualifying distributions, $899,803.
Limitations: Giving primarily in areas of company operations.
Publications: Application guidelines.
Application information: Application form required.
Officers: Oliver C. Smith, Chair.; Steven S. Kromholz, Pres.; Kristi Pavletich, V.P.; Heidi L. Coppock, Secy.; Kenneth J. Bonkoski, Treas.
EIN: 396047384
Codes: CS, FD, CD, GTI

56603
Bucyrus-Erie Foundation, Inc.
(Formerly Becor Western Foundation, Inc.)
c/o Greater Milwaukee Fdn.
1020 N. Broadway
Milwaukee, WI 53202 (414) 272-5805
Contact: Rita Flores

Incorporated in 1951 in WI.
Donor(s): Bucyrus-Erie Co.
Financial data (yr. ended 12/31/01): Grants paid, $889,765; assets, $15,977,418 (M); expenditures, $988,792; qualifying distributions, $925,673.
Limitations: Giving primarily in the metropolitan Milwaukee, WI, area.
Application information: Application form required for scholarships for children of employees.
Officers and Directors:* William B. Winter,* Pres.; Stephen N. Graff, V.P and Treas.; Fred R. Gutierrez, Secy. and Mgr.; Mary Ann La Bahn, Vincent L. Martin, Donald E. Porter, Brent H. Rupple, Sr.
EIN: 396075537
Codes: CS, FD, CD

56604
Byron L. Walter Family Trust
c/o Bank One Trust Co., N.A.
P.O. Box 1308
Milwaukee, WI 53201
Application address: P.O. Box 19020, Green Bay, WI 54307-9029, tel.: (920) 436-2610
Contact: Marilyn Wunrow

Trust established in 1981 in WI.
Donor(s): Arlene B. Walter.‡
Financial data (yr. ended 04/30/01): Grants paid, $857,288; assets, $15,343,957 (M); expenditures, $1,113,017; qualifying distributions, $1,084,640.
Limitations: Giving limited to Brown County, WI.
Publications: Application guidelines.
Application information: Application form not required.
Trustees: Richard J. Blahnik, Fred Will, Bank One Trust Co., N.A.
EIN: 396346563
Codes: FD

56605
Greater Kenosha Area Foundation, Inc.
P.O. Box 1829
Kenosha, WI 53141 (262) 654-2412
FAX: (262) 654-2615; *E-mail:* gkaf@acronet.net
Contact: Peter Walcott, Exec. Dir.

Established in 1926 in WI.

56605—WISCONSIN

Financial data (yr. ended 12/31/01): Grants paid, $844,012; assets, $3,264,086 (M); gifts received, $838,064; expenditures, $1,045,059.
Limitations: Giving primarily in Kenosha County, WI.
Application information: Application form required.
Officers: Alan R. Schaefer, Pres.; Kenneth L. Fellman, V.P.; Peter Walcott, Exec. Dir.
Directors: Constance M. Ferwerda, Neil F. Guttormsen, Jack S. Harris.
Board of Advisors: Mary Frost Ashley, George R. Connolly, Robert A. Cornog, Mary P. Euroth, Jerold P. France, A. Allan Jankus, Ralph J. Tenuta.
EIN: 396045289
Codes: CM, FD

56606
Tyson Fund
c/o Bank One Trust Co., N.A.
P.O. Box 1308
Milwaukee, WI 53201

Trust established in 1930 in IN.
Donor(s): James H. Tyson.
Financial data (yr. ended 12/31/01): Grants paid, $810,807; assets, $76,431,502 (M); expenditures, $1,010,539; qualifying distributions, $919,480.
Limitations: Applications not accepted. Giving limited to Versailles, IN.
Application information: Contributes only to pre-selected organizations.
Trustee: Bank One Trust Co., N.A.
EIN: 356009973
Codes: FD

56607
La Crosse Community Foundation
(Formerly La Crosse Foundation)
319 Main St., Ste. 300
La Crosse, WI 54601 (608) 782-3223
FAX: (608) 782-3222; E-mail: lacrosscommfound@centurytel.net; URL: http://www.laxcommfoundation.com
Contact: Sheila Garrity, Exec. Dir.

Established in 1930 in WI.
Financial data (yr. ended 12/31/01): Grants paid, $798,973; assets, $20,562,029 (M); gifts received, $232,475; expenditures, $1,037,718.
Limitations: Giving primarily in La Crosse County, WI, and surrounding area.
Publications: Annual report (including application guidelines).
Application information: Proposals are reviewed in cycles according to quarterly focus; contact foundation for initial application and more information. Application form required.
Officers and Directors:* Anita Froegel,* Chair.; Sheila Garrity,* Exec. Dir.; Joseph Connell, Sue Durtsche, Mike Hutson, Pauline Jackson, M.D., June Kjome, Roger LeGrand, Duane Ring, Jr., Brad Sturm, Norma Vinger.
Trustee: North Central Trust Co.
EIN: 396037996
Codes: CM, FD, GTI

56608
Stackner Family Foundation, Inc.
P.O. Box 597
Hartland, WI 53029 (262) 646-7040
FAX: (262) 646-5409; E-mail: Stackner@execpc.com
Contact: John A. Treiber, V.P. and Exec. Dir.

Incorporated in 1966 in WI.
Donor(s): John S. Stackner,‡ Irene M. Stackner.‡
Financial data (yr. ended 08/31/01): Grants paid, $797,425; assets, $15,665,391 (M); expenditures, $1,050,713; qualifying distributions, $908,131.

Limitations: Giving limited to Milwaukee and Waukesha counties, WI.
Application information: Application form not required.
Officers and Directors:* Patricia S. Treiber,* Pres.; John A. Treiber,* V.P.; David L. MacGregor,* Secy.-Treas.; Patrick W. Cotter, Paul Tilleman.
EIN: 396097597
Codes: FD

56609
David & Ruth Coleman Charitable Foundation, Inc.
1610 N. Prospect Ave.
Milwaukee, WI 53202 (414) 226-2209
Contact: Ruth Coleman, Pres.

Established in 1993 in WI.
Donor(s): Ruth Coleman, Ida Soref.
Financial data (yr. ended 12/31/01): Grants paid, $785,000; assets, $9,240,632 (M); expenditures, $887,341; qualifying distributions, $783,507.
Limitations: Giving primarily in Milwaukee, WI.
Application information: Application form not required.
Officers and Directors:* Ruth Coleman,* Pres.; Mark Sklar,* V.P.; Roberta Gornstein Caraway,* Secy.; Dennis L. Paul,* Treas.; Timothy R. Colombe.
EIN: 391772862
Codes: FD

56610
Sentry Insurance Foundation, Inc.
(Formerly Sentry Foundation, Inc.)
c/o Sentry Insurance
1800 N. Point Dr.
Stevens Point, WI 54481-1253
Contact: Sue Kurzynski, Exec. Dir.

Incorporated in 1963 in WI.
Donor(s): Sentry Insurance.
Financial data (yr. ended 12/31/00): Grants paid, $780,724; assets, $1,292,652 (M); expenditures, $781,431; qualifying distributions, $781,431.
Limitations: Giving primarily in WI.
Publications: Occasional report.
Application information: Application form not required.
Officers and Directors:* Gregory C. Mox,* Chair. and Pres.; Sue Kurzynski, V.P. and Exec. Dir.; William M. O'Reilly, Secy.; William J. Lohr,* Treas.; Dale R. Schuh, Carroll George Smith, James J. Weishan.
EIN: 391037370
Codes: CS, FD, CD

56611
William J. & Gertrude R. Casper Foundation
c/o U.S. Bank
P.O. Box 2043
Milwaukee, WI 53201-9116
Application address: c/o The Edward Rutledge Charity, Betty Manning, 404 N. Bridge St., Chippewa Falls, WI 54729
Contact: M. Berry

Established in 1988 in WI.
Donor(s): William J. Casper, Gertrude R. Casper.
Financial data (yr. ended 05/31/02): Grants paid, $775,700; assets, $17,386,802 (M); gifts received, $285,263; expenditures, $886,321; qualifying distributions, $831,845.
Limitations: Giving limited to residents of the Chippewa Falls, WI, area.
Application information: Application form required.
Trustee: U.S. Bank.
EIN: 396484669
Codes: FD, GTI

56612
Phoebe R. & John D. Lewis Foundation
9729 N. Lake Dr.
Milwaukee, WI 53217
Contact: John D. Lewis, Treas.

Established in 1995 in WI and OH.
Donor(s): Phoebe R. Lewis, John D. Lewis.
Financial data (yr. ended 12/31/01): Grants paid, $765,500; assets, $9,604,562 (M); expenditures, $872,771; qualifying distributions, $757,378.
Limitations: Applications not accepted. Giving on a national basis, with some emphasis on WI.
Application information: Contributes only to pre-selected organizations.
Officers: Phoebe R. Lewis, Pres.; Graham D. Lewis, V.P.; Lloyd L. Eagan, Secy.; John D. Lewis, Treas.
EIN: 311401478
Codes: FD

56613
Community Foundation of South Wood County, Inc.
P.O. Box 444
478 E. Grand Ave.
Wisconsin Rapids, WI 54495-0444
(715) 423-3863
FAX: (715) 423-3019; E-mail: cfswc@wctc.net
Contact: Kelly Lucas, Dir.

Established in 1994 in WI.
Financial data (yr. ended 06/30/01): Grants paid, $763,555; assets, $15,396,238 (M); gifts received, $9,783,998; expenditures, $1,056,774.
Limitations: Giving limited to South Wood County, WI.
Publications: Informational brochure, annual report, newsletter, application guidelines.
Officers and Directors:* Donald Stein,* Pres.; Carl Greeneway,* V.P.; Gerald Boyce,* Secy.; Joan McCarville,* Treas.; Leslie Arendt, Patrick Brennan, David Kumm, Nancy Lucas, Judith Paul.
EIN: 391772651
Codes: CM, FD

56614
The Todd Wehr Foundation, Inc.
111 E. Wisconsin Ave., Ste. 2100
Milwaukee, WI 53202-4894 (414) 273-2100
Contact: Ralph G. Schulz, Pres.

Incorporated in 1953 in WI.‡
Donor(s): C. Frederic Wehr.‡
Financial data (yr. ended 12/31/00): Grants paid, $760,000; assets, $15,336,987 (M); expenditures, $962,714; qualifying distributions, $795,389.
Limitations: Giving primarily in WI.
Application information: Application form not required.
Officers and Directors:* Ralph G. Schulz,* Pres.; Allan E. Iding,* V.P. and Secy.; M. James Termondt,* V.P. and Treas.; Richard J. Harland,* V.P.; Robert P. Harland,* V.P.
EIN: 396043962
Codes: FD

56615
Daniel E. Meehan Foundation, Inc.
(Formerly Meehan Seaway Service Scholarship Fund, Inc.)
1500 S. Lincoln Memorial Dr.
Milwaukee, WI 53207 (414) 481-7000
Contact: Theresa Meehan-Felknor, Pres.

Established in 1983 in WI.
Donor(s): Daniel E. Meehan.
Financial data (yr. ended 12/31/00): Grants paid, $753,671; assets, $4,689,912 (M); gifts received, $201,000; expenditures, $860,732; qualifying distributions, $840,792.

Publications: Application guidelines.
Application information: Individual scholarships are awarded only to children or grandchildren of employees of Meehan Seaway Service. Foundation is currently accepting applications from organizations. Application form required.
Officers and Directors:* Daniel E. Meehan, Chair.; Theresa Meehan-Felknor, Pres.; Carolyn E. Vogt,* Secy.; John T. Byrnes, Charles W. Foran, Henry Loos.
EIN: 391445333
Codes: FD, GTI

56616
CUNA Mutual Group Foundation, Inc.
(Formerly CUNA Mutual Insurance Group Charitable Foundation, Inc.)
5910 Mineral Point Rd.
Madison, WI 53705   (608) 231-7908
Application address: P.O. Box 391, Madison, WI 53701
Contact: Terri J. Fiez, Exec. Dir.

Incorporated in 1967 in WI.
Donor(s): CUNA Mutual Insurance Society.
Financial data (yr. ended 12/31/01): Grants paid, $751,691; assets, $497,162 (M); gifts received, $660,000; expenditures, $751,807; qualifying distributions, $751,691.
Limitations: Giving primarily in IA and WI.
Publications: Informational brochure (including application guidelines).
Application information: Application form required for requests over $500.
Officers: Neil A. Springer, Pres.; Michael B. Kitchen, Secy.-Treas. and Exec. Off.
EIN: 396105418
Codes: CS, FD, CD

56617
Managed Health Services, Inc.
890 Elm Grove Rd.
Elm Grove, WI 53122

Established in 1999 in WI.
Financial data (yr. ended 12/31/99): Grants paid, $749,911; assets, $25,865,551 (M); expenditures, $1,135,474; qualifying distributions, $1,067,888.
Limitations: Giving primarily in Milwaukee, WI.
Officers and Directors:* Richard Wiederhold,* Pres.; Claire Johnson,* V.P.; William Jollie,* V.P.; Samuel E. Bradt,* Secy.-Treas.
EIN: 391509757
Codes: FD

56618
Joy Global Foundation, Inc.
(Formerly Harnischfeger Industries Foundation)
P.O. Box 554
Milwaukee, WI 53201
Contact: Sandy McKenzie

Established in 1989 in WI.
Donor(s): Harnischfeger Industries, Inc., Joy Global Inc.
Financial data (yr. ended 10/31/01): Grants paid, $744,135; assets, $10,408,096 (M); expenditures, $819,438; qualifying distributions, $744,135.
Limitations: Giving primarily in areas of company operations in WI.
Publications: Application guidelines.
Application information: Application form not required.
Officers and Directors:* John N. Hanson, Pres.; James A. Chokey,* V.P.; Don Roof, V.P.; Dennis Winkleman, V.P.; Eric Fonstad, Secy.; Ken Stark,* Treas.
EIN: 391659070
Codes: CS, FD, CD

56619
Mercy Works Foundation
(Formerly The Follett Family Foundation)
P.O. Box 2518
Appleton, WI 54913
Contact: Robert C. Follett, Tr.

Established in 1992 in WI.
Donor(s): Anchor Food Products, Inc.
Financial data (yr. ended 12/31/00): Grants paid, $741,402; assets, $10,125,190 (M); gifts received, $1,813,297; expenditures, $935,464; qualifying distributions, $780,970.
Limitations: Applications not accepted. Giving primarily in Appleton, WI.
Application information: Contributes only to pre-selected organizations.
Trustees: Mark C. Follett, Robert C. Follett, Paula Malone.
EIN: 391717117
Codes: FD

56620
Elbridge and Evelyn Stuart Foundation
c/o Bank One Trust Co., N.A.
P.O. Box 1308
Milwaukee, WI 53201
Additional Address: c/o Bank One Trust Co., 70 W. Madison St., Chicago, IL, 60670
Contact: Anne Myers, Tr. Off.

Trust established in 1961 in CA.
Financial data (yr. ended 12/31/01): Grants paid, $740,000; assets, $13,636,455 (M); expenditures, $792,096; qualifying distributions, $747,408.
Limitations: Giving primarily in CA.
Application information: Application form not required.
Trustee: Bank One Trust Co., N.A.
EIN: 956014019
Codes: FD

56621
Jones Family Foundation
481 E. Division St., Ste. 800
P.O. Box 1167
Fond du Lac, WI 54936-1167

Established in 1989 in WI.
Donor(s): Donald Jones, Terri Jones.
Financial data (yr. ended 12/31/00): Grants paid, $735,989; assets, $2,118,017 (M); expenditures, $809,846; qualifying distributions, $745,218.
Limitations: Applications not accepted. Giving primarily in Fond du Lac, WI.
Application information: Contributes only to pre-selected organizations.
Trustees: Donald Jones, Terri Jones.
EIN: 396501525
Codes: FD

56622
Bleser Family Foundation, Inc.
P.O. Box 328
Shawano, WI 54166

Established in 1986 in WI.
Donor(s): Clarence P. Bleser.‡
Financial data (yr. ended 12/31/00): Grants paid, $717,000; assets, $27,217,877 (M); expenditures, $901,854; qualifying distributions, $726,588.
Limitations: Applications not accepted. Giving primarily in WI.
Application information: Contributes only to pre-selected organizations.
Officers and Directors:* Mary B. Hayes,* Pres.; Carol A. Bleser,* V.P.; Paul Bleser,* Secy.; James F. Bleser,* Treas.
EIN: 391585269
Codes: FD

56623
The Wagner Foundation, Ltd.
(Formerly R. H. Wagner Foundation, Ltd.)
P.O. Box 307
Lyons, WI 53148-0307

Established in 1981 in WI.
Donor(s): Richard H. Wagner, Roberta L. Wagner.
Financial data (yr. ended 06/30/01): Grants paid, $711,809; assets, $11,148,777 (M); gifts received, $55,800; expenditures, $738,184; qualifying distributions, $711,809.
Limitations: Applications not accepted. Giving in the U.S., primarily in IA and WI, and in Central America, South America, Africa, and the Philippines.
Application information: Contributes only to pre-selected organizations.
Officers: Richard H. Wagner, Pres.; Roberta L. Wagner, V.P.
Trustees: Paul B. Edwards, Marcy Essman, Julie O'Neill.
EIN: 391311452
Codes: FD

56624
The Aytchmonde Woodson Foundation, Inc.
P.O. Box 65
Wausau, WI 54402-0065   (715) 845-9201
Contact: San W. Orr, Jr., Treas.

Incorporated in 1947 in WI.
Donor(s): Members of the Woodson family.
Financial data (yr. ended 06/30/01): Grants paid, $709,309; assets, $13,539,107 (M); expenditures, $804,272; qualifying distributions, $708,630.
Limitations: Giving limited to Wausau, WI.
Application information: Application form not required.
Officers and Directors:* Alice W. Smith,* Pres.; Robert S. Hasse, Jr.,* V.P.; Stephen C. Spire,* V.P.; John E. Forester,* Secy.; San W. Orr, Jr.,* Treas.; Gale W. Fisher, Nancy-Leigh Fisher, A. Woodson Hagge.
EIN: 391017853
Codes: FD

56625
The Gentine Foundation, Inc.
P.O. Box 386
Plymouth, WI 53073
Application address: N6604 Riverview Rd., Plymouth, WI 53073; E-mail: esturzl@excel.net
Contact: Ann M. Sturzl, Pres.

Established in 1989 in WI.
Donor(s): Leonard A. Gentine, Sr.,‡ Dolores A. Gentine.
Financial data (yr. ended 06/30/01): Grants paid, $690,074; assets, $4,265,891 (M); gifts received, $3,000; expenditures, $706,402; qualifying distributions, $692,074; giving activities include $2,000 for loans.
Limitations: Giving primarily in the Midwest.
Application information: Application form required.
Officers: Ann Sturzl, Pres.; Lee M. Gentine, V.P. and Treas.; Kristin Gentine, Secy.
EIN: 391654230
Codes: FD

56626
The Brico Fund, Inc.
205 E. Wisconsin Ave., Ste. 200
Milwaukee, WI 53202   (414) 272-2747
FAX: (414) 272-2036; E-mail: bricofund@bricofund.org; URL: http://bricofund.org
Contact: Lynde B. Uihlein, Interim Exec. Dir.

Established in 1990 in WI.

56626—WISCONSIN

Donor(s): Lynde B. Uihlein.
Financial data (yr. ended 12/31/01): Grants paid, $683,220; assets, $3,713,518 (M); gifts received, $1,176,000; expenditures, $770,935; qualifying distributions, $683,220.
Limitations: Giving primarily in southeastern WI.
Publications: Application guidelines.
Application information: Application form not required.
Officers and Directors:* Lynde B. Uihlein,* Pres. and Treas.; Sue Hitler, V.P.; Miriam Reading, Secy.; Sarah O. Zimmerman.
EIN: 391656190
Codes: FD

56627
Raabe Foundation
c/o Kent Raabe
P.O. Box 1090
Menomonee Falls, WI 53052

Established in 1994 in WI.
Donor(s): Raabe Corp.
Financial data (yr. ended 12/31/01): Grants paid, $678,515; assets, $204,332 (M); gifts received, $203,722; expenditures, $702,785; qualifying distributions, $700,564.
Limitations: Applications not accepted. Giving primarily in WI.
Application information: Contributes only to pre-selected organizations.
Trustees: Daryl K. Raabe, Kent A. Raabe.
EIN: 396589876
Codes: CS, FD, CD

56628
A. G. Bishop Charitable Trust
c/o Bank One
P.O. Box 1308
Milwaukee, WI 53201
Application address: c/o Pamela Taeckens, Bank One, 111 E. Court St., Ste. 100, Flint MI, 48502

Trust established in 1944 in MI.
Donor(s): Arthur Giles Bishop.‡
Financial data (yr. ended 12/31/01): Grants paid, $671,016; assets, $12,794,893 (M); expenditures, $740,369; qualifying distributions, $671,016.
Limitations: Giving limited to the Flint and Genesee County, MI, community.
Publications: Application guidelines.
Application information: Application form not required.
Trustees: Robert J. Bellairs, Jr., Elizabeth B. Wentworth, Bank One.
EIN: 386040693
Codes: FD

56629
Charter Manufacturing Company Foundation, Inc.
411 E. Wisconsin Ave., Ste. 2040
Milwaukee, WI 53202-4497

Established in 1984 in WI.
Donor(s): Charter Manufacturing Co., Inc.
Financial data (yr. ended 12/31/01): Grants paid, $655,366; assets, $808,276 (M); gifts received, $800,000; expenditures, $656,049; qualifying distributions, $655,135.
Limitations: Applications not accepted. Giving primarily in Milwaukee, WI.
Application information: Contributes only to pre-selected organizations.
Officers and Directors:* Linda T. Mellowes,* Pres.; John A. Mellowes,* V.P. and Treas.; Henry J. Loos,* Secy.; Charles A. Mellowes, John W. Mellowes.
EIN: 391486363
Codes: CS, FD, CD

56630
Madison Gas and Electric Foundation, Inc.
P.O. Box 1231
Madison, WI 53701-1231 (608) 252-7024
Contact: Carol A. Wiskowski, Secy.

Established in 1966 in WI.
Donor(s): Madison Gas and Electric Co.
Financial data (yr. ended 12/31/01): Grants paid, $654,752; assets, $6,685,757 (M); gifts received, $1,250,000; expenditures, $706,280; qualifying distributions, $655,332.
Limitations: Giving limited to areas of company operations.
Application information: Application forms for scholarships are published in the company newsletter in Apr. or May each year.
Officers and Directors:* David C. Mebane,* Chair.; Frank C. Vondrasek,* Pres.; Mark C. Williamson,* V.P.; Gary J. Wolter,* V.P.; Carol A. Wiskowski,* Secy.; Terry A. Hanson,* Treas.; James C. Boll.
EIN: 396098118
Codes: CS, FD, CD

56631
United Wisconsin Services Foundation, Inc.
(Formerly Blue Cross and Blue Shield United of Wisconsin Foundation, Inc.)
401 W. Michigan St.
Milwaukee, WI 53203 (414) 226-5756

Established in 1984 in WI.
Donor(s): United Wisconsin Services, Inc., American Medical Security Group, Inc., Blue Cross & Blue Shield United of Wisconsin.
Financial data (yr. ended 12/31/01): Grants paid, $650,129; assets, $4,195,740 (M); expenditures, $660,774; qualifying distributions, $648,451.
Limitations: Giving limited to WI, with emphasis on Milwaukee.
Application information: Application form required.
Officers: Thomas R. Hefty, Chair. and Pres.; Stephen E. Bablitch, V.P. and Secy.; Penny J. Stewart, V.P. and Treas.; Mike Bernstein, V.P.; Timothy F. Cullen, V.P.; Gail Hanson, V.P.
EIN: 391514703
Codes: CS, FD, CD

56632
Chapman Foundation
312 E. Wisconsin Ave., Ste. 402
Milwaukee, WI 53202-4305

Established in 1944 in WI.
Donor(s): Laura Isabelle Miller,‡ G.M. Chester, W.M. Chester, Jr., M.C. Read, J.C. Chester.
Financial data (yr. ended 12/31/01): Grants paid, $649,979; assets, $5,109,034 (M); gifts received, $235,181; expenditures, $658,474; qualifying distributions, $643,596.
Limitations: Applications not accepted. Giving primarily in Milwaukee, WI.
Application information: Contributes only to pre-selected organizations.
Officers: George M. Chester, Pres.; John Chapman Chester, V.P.; Marion C. Read, V.P.; Verne R. Read, V.P.; William M. Chester, Jr., Secy.-Treas.
EIN: 396059569
Codes: FD

56633
Watertown Area Community Foundation
c/o Thomas Levi
117 N. 2nd St.
Watertown, WI 53094
Contact: Bruce Kasten, Treas.

Established in 1992 in WI.

Financial data (yr. ended 06/30/01): Grants paid, $631,422; assets, $3,032,560 (M); gifts received, $2,624,197; expenditures, $648,540.
Limitations: Giving limited to the Watertown, WI, area.
Officers: James Clifford, Pres.; Tom Schultz, V.P.; Dorothy Kasten, Recording Secy.; Bruce Kasten, Treas.
Directors: Dan Beltz, Joe Darcey, Thomas Levi, Ann Krystyniak, Bill O'Brien, Dave Pederson, Sue Rhodes.
EIN: 391708484
Codes: CM, FD

56634
Community Benefit Trust Fund
c/o Harold B. Jackson
260 W. Seeboth St.
Milwaukee, WI 53202

Established in 1995 in WI.
Financial data (yr. ended 12/31/99): Grants paid, $620,348; assets, $3,005,617 (M); gifts received, $1,100,000; expenditures, $712,233; qualifying distributions, $654,478.
Limitations: Applications not accepted. Giving limited to Milwaukee, WI.
Application information: Contributes only to pre-selected organizations.
Trustee: Harold B. Jackson.
EIN: 396630351
Codes: FD

56635
Davis Foundation
c/o Bank One Trust Co., N.A.
P.O. Box 1308
Milwaukee, WI 53201
Application address: 1155 Meadowbrook Ave., Youngstown, OH 44512, tel.: (216) 758-5626
Contact: David D. Davis or Velma D. Davis

Financial data (yr. ended 12/31/01): Grants paid, $617,000; assets, $19,257,157 (M); expenditures, $976,190; qualifying distributions, $627,135.
Limitations: Giving primarily in OH.
Advisory Committee: David D. Davis, Velma D. Davis.
Trustee: Bank One Trust Co., N.A.
EIN: 346566892
Codes: FD

56636
Brookbank Foundation, Inc.
P.O. Box 84
Grafton, WI 53024-0084

Established in 1984 in WI.
Donor(s): Orion Corp.
Financial data (yr. ended 10/31/01): Grants paid, $616,180; assets, $8,800,866 (M); expenditures, $651,828; qualifying distributions, $630,950.
Limitations: Applications not accepted. Giving primarily in WI.
Application information: Contributes only to pre-selected organizations.
Officers: Mary Ann La Bahn, Pres.; Charles P. La Bahn, Exec. V.P.; Ridge A. Braunschweig, V.P. and Treas.
EIN: 391516196
Codes: FD

56637
Stefanie H. Weill Charitable Fund, Inc.
636 Wisconsin Ave.
P.O. Box 171
Sheboygan, WI 53082-0171
Contact: Jon C. Keckonen, Treas.

Established in 1969.
Donor(s): Stefanie Weill,‡ Otto Byk.‡

Financial data (yr. ended 12/31/01): Grants paid, $610,347; assets, $3,744,285 (M); expenditures, $621,549; qualifying distributions, $610,718.
Limitations: Giving primarily in Sheboygan, WI.
Application information: Application form required.
Officers: Eldon Bohrofen, Pres.; K. Allen Voss, Secy.; Jon C. Keckonen, Treas.
Trustee: Wells Fargo Bank Wisconsin, N.A.
EIN: 930757054
Codes: FD

56638
A. G. Cox Charity Trust
c/o Bank One Trust Co., N.A.
P.O. Box 1308
Milwaukee, WI 53201
Contact: J. Pieper

Established in 1924 in IL.
Financial data (yr. ended 12/31/01): Grants paid, $602,333; assets, $13,650,809 (M); expenditures, $608,299; qualifying distributions, $592,127.
Limitations: Giving primarily in Chicago, IL.
Trustee: Bank One, Trust Co., N.A.
EIN: 366011498
Codes: FD

56639
Fond du Lac Area Foundation
384 N. Main St., Ste. 4
Fond du Lac, WI 54935 (920) 921-2215
FAX: (920) 921-1036; E-mail: info@fdlareafoundation.com; URL: http://www.fdlareafoundation.com
Contact: Sandi Braun Roehrig, Exec. Dir.

Established as a trust in 1975 in WI.
Financial data (yr. ended 04/30/02): Grants paid, $600,358; assets, $11,383,359 (M); gifts received, $2,210,896; expenditures, $721,271.
Limitations: Giving limited to the Fond du Lac, WI, area.
Publications: Annual report (including application guidelines), financial statement, grants list, informational brochure (including application guidelines), newsletter, application guidelines.
Application information: Application form required.
Officer and Directors:* Sandi Braun Roehrig,* Exec. Dir.; Thomas J Gross.
EIN: 510181570
Codes: CM, FD

56640
Jeffris Family Foundation, Ltd.
P.O. Box 650
Janesville, WI 53547-0650
Contact: Thomas Jeffris, Pres.

Established in 1977.
Donor(s): Thomas M. Jeffris.
Financial data (yr. ended 12/31/01): Grants paid, $595,896; assets, $22,083,870 (M); expenditures, $895,619; qualifying distributions, $1,149,827.
Limitations: Applications not accepted. Giving primarily in WI.
Application information: Contributes only to pre-selected organizations.
Officers and Directors:* Thomas M. Jeffris,* Pres.; Charles R. Rydberg,* V.P.; Marion M. Schumacher,* Secy.-Treas.; Henry E. Fuldner.
EIN: 391281879
Codes: FD

56641
Adeline and George McQueen Foundation of 1960
c/o Bank One Trust Co., N.A.
P.O. Box 1308
Milwaukee, WI 53201
Application address: c/o Bank One, Texas, N.A., P.O. Box 2050, Fort Worth, TX 76113, tel.: (817) 884-4448
Contact: Robert Lansford

Trust established in 1960 in TX.
Financial data (yr. ended 06/30/01): Grants paid, $589,000; assets, $14,577,712 (M); expenditures, $730,117; qualifying distributions, $714,192.
Limitations: Giving primarily in Fort Worth, TX.
Application information: Application form not required.
Trustee: Bank One Trust Co., N.A.
EIN: 756014459
Codes: FD

56642
Split Rail Foundation, Inc.
11109 N. Lakeshore Ln., 3E
Mequon, WI 53092
Contact: Peter R. Van Housen, Mng. Dir.

Established in 1985.
Donor(s): E.I. Van Housen,‡ Dorothy P. Van Housen.
Financial data (yr. ended 12/31/01): Grants paid, $576,950; assets, $1,828,899 (M); expenditures, $576,950; qualifying distributions, $576,950.
Limitations: Giving limited to areas of WI where directors have interest or involvement.
Application information: Does not respond to staff-signed of general mail requests. Application form not required.
Officers and Directors:* Dorothy P. Van Housen,* Pres.; Patricia Wendt,* V.P. and Secy.; Peter R. Van Housen,* Treas. and Managing Dir.
EIN: 391537158
Codes: FD

56643
The Neese Family Foundation, Inc.
2870 Riverside Dr.
Beloit, WI 53511 (608) 368-1300
Contact: Gary G. Grabowski, Exec. Dir.

Incorporated in 1986 in IL.
Donor(s): Members of the Neese family.
Financial data (yr. ended 06/30/01): Grants paid, $573,750; assets, $3,947,859 (M); gifts received, $25,552; expenditures, $582,715; qualifying distributions, $576,889.
Limitations: Giving primarily in the Beloit, WI, stateline area.
Officers: Margaret K. Neese, Pres.; Elbert H. Neese, V.P.; Gary G. Grabowski, Exec. Dir.
EIN: 363473918
Codes: FD

56644
The Ziegler Foundation, Inc.
215 N. Main St.
West Bend, WI 53095-3317
Contact: Bernard C. Ziegler, Pres.

Incorporated in 1944 in WI.
Donor(s): Members of the Ziegler family.
Financial data (yr. ended 12/31/00): Grants paid, $570,190; assets, $11,583,029 (M); expenditures, $628,325; qualifying distributions, $555,518.
Limitations: Giving primarily in the West Bend, WI, area.
Application information: Unsolicited requests not considered. Application information pertains only to organizations that have been invited to apply. Application form not required.
Officers and Directors:* Bernard C. Ziegler,* Pres.; R. Douglas Ziegler,* V.P. and Secy.-Treas.; Robert J. Bonner,* V.P.; Carolyn N. Schucht, Bernard C. Ziegler III, Carl H. Ziegler, Peter D. Ziegler.
EIN: 396044762
Codes: FD

56645
Banta Corporation Foundation, Inc.
P.O. Box 8003
Menasha, WI 54952-8003 (920) 751-7777
Contact: Gerald A. Henseler, Pres.

Incorporated in 1953 in WI.
Donor(s): Banta Corp.
Financial data (yr. ended 12/31/01): Grants paid, $569,237; assets, $29,821 (M); gifts received, $600,000; expenditures, $571,193; qualifying distributions, $571,193.
Limitations: Giving limited to areas of company operations, including CA, IL, MN, MO, NC, NY, VA, and WI.
Application information: Application form not required.
Officers: Gerald A. Henseler, Pres.; Rosalie N. Barbara, V.P.; Yvonne Lau, Secy.
Board Member: Ronald Kneezel.
EIN: 396050779
Codes: CS, FD, CD

56646
Clyde R. Evans Charitable Trust
c/o Bank One Trust Co., N.A., Tax Dept.
111 E. Wisconsin Ave., Ste. 940
Milwaukee, WI 53202

Established in 1997 in OK.
Financial data (yr. ended 06/30/01): Grants paid, $560,000; assets, $11,551,420 (M); expenditures, $627,641; qualifying distributions, $558,932.
Limitations: Applications not accepted. Giving primarily in Oklahoma City, OK.
Application information: Contributes only to pre-selected organizations.
Trustees: Roy W. Chandler, Gordon Henderson, David C. Johnston, Bank One Trust Co., N.A.
EIN: 736296082
Codes: FD

56647
Rose A. Monaghan Charitable Trust
c/o Walter F. Schmidt
17100 W. North Ave.
Brookfield, WI 53005

Established in 1980 in WI.
Donor(s): Rose Monaghan.‡
Financial data (yr. ended 06/30/01): Grants paid, $558,300; assets, $2,416,053 (M); expenditures, $590,856; qualifying distributions, $577,966.
Limitations: Applications not accepted. Giving primarily in Milwaukee, WI.
Application information: Contributes only to pre-selected organizations.
Trustee: Walter F. Schmidt.
EIN: 391363036
Codes: FD

56648
S. B. Waterman & E. Blade Charitable Foundation, Inc.
c/o Marshall & Ilsley Trust Co., N.A.
P.O. Box 2980, 12th Fl.
Milwaukee, WI 53201
Application address: Thomas C. Boettcher c/o Marshall & Ilsley Trust Co., N.A., 1000 N. Water St., Milwaukee, WI 53202, tel.: (414) 287-7228

Established in 1992 in WI.

56648—WISCONSIN

Financial data (yr. ended 12/31/01): Grants paid, $558,000; assets, $13,470,101 (M); expenditures, $586,393; qualifying distributions, $558,000.
Limitations: Giving primarily in Milwaukee, WI.
Application information: Application form not required.
Officers and Directors:* Roger L. Boerner,* Pres.; Lloyd D. Schermer,* V.P.; Arthur F. Lubke, Jr.,* Secy.-Treas.
EIN: 391645499
Codes: FD

56649
Ellsworth and Carla Peterson Charitable Foundation
55 Utopia Cir.
Sturgeon Bay, WI 54235
Contact: Ellsworth L. Peterson, or Carla J. Peterson, Trustees

Established in 1992 in WI.
Donor(s): Ellsworth L. Peterson, Carla J. Peterson.
Financial data (yr. ended 10/31/01): Grants paid, $556,490; assets, $3,188,441 (M); expenditures, $572,907; qualifying distributions, $559,720.
Limitations: Giving primarily in WI.
Trustees: Carla J. Peterson, Ellsworth L. Peterson.
EIN: 396566719
Codes: FD

56650
Bert L. and Patricia S. Steigleder Charitable Trust
c/o Quarles & Brady
411 E. Wisconsin Ave., Ste. 2040
Milwaukee, WI 53202-4497 (414) 277-5000
Contact: Henry J. Loos, Tr.

Established in 1991 in WI.
Donor(s): Bert L. Steigleder.‡
Financial data (yr. ended 06/30/02): Grants paid, $555,117; assets, $9,405,589 (M); expenditures, $645,309; qualifying distributions, $570,771.
Limitations: Giving primarily in the Milwaukee, WI, area.
Application information: Application form not required.
Trustees: Henry Loos, U.S. Bank.
EIN: 396541246
Codes: FD

56651
Nicholas Family Foundation
c/o Lynn Sharon Nicholas
10309 N. River Rd.
Mequon, WI 53092
FAX: (414) 242-0729

Established in 1993 in WI.
Financial data (yr. ended 12/31/00): Grants paid, $550,750; assets, $19,531,845 (M); gifts received, $5,020,000; expenditures, $541,075; qualifying distributions, $552,275.
Limitations: Giving primarily in Milwaukee, WI.
Trustees: Susan N. Fasciano, Albert O. Nicholas, David O. Nicholas, Lynn S. Nicholas, Nancy J. Nicholas.
EIN: 396589261
Codes: FD

56652
Marcus Corporation Foundation, Inc.
250 E. Wisconsin Ave., Ste. 1500
Milwaukee, WI 53202-4209
Contact: Stephan H. Marcus, Pres.

Established in 1961 in WI.
Donor(s): The Marcus Corp.
Financial data (yr. ended 12/31/00): Grants paid, $550,505; assets, $1,558,966 (M); gifts received, $326,668; expenditures, $575,125; qualifying distributions, $572,290.
Limitations: Giving limited to Milwaukee, WI.
Officers and Directors:* Stephen H. Marcus,* Pres. and Treas.; Thomas F. Kissinger,* Secy.; Diane Gershowitz.
EIN: 396046268
Codes: CS, FD, CD

56653
Otis A. Barnes & Margaret T. Barnes Trust
c/o Bank One Trust Co., N.A.
P.O. Box 1308
Milwaukee, WI 53201
Application address: c/o Chemistry Dept., The Colorado College, Colorado Springs, CO 80903

Established in 1952 in CO.
Financial data (yr. ended 06/30/01): Grants paid, $548,465; assets, $15,573,158 (M); expenditures, $613,396; qualifying distributions, $565,353.
Limitations: Giving limited to Colorado Springs, CO.
Application information: Application form required.
Trustee: Bank One, Arizona, N.A.
EIN: 846023466
Codes: TN

56654
McDonough Foundation, Inc.
c/o Richard Bliss
780 N. Water St.
Milwaukee, WI 53202-3590

Established in 1987 in WI.
Donor(s): John J. McDonough, Midwest Dental Products Corp.
Financial data (yr. ended 09/30/01): Grants paid, $546,311; assets, $390,898 (M); gifts received, $42,500; expenditures, $616,448; qualifying distributions, $608,592.
Limitations: Applications not accepted. Giving primarily in IL; some giving in NY and CA.
Application information: Contributes only to pre-selected organizations.
Officers and Directors:* Allison McDonough,* Pres.; John J. McDonough,* Treas.; Marilyn McDonough.
EIN: 391627844
Codes: FD

56655
Sensient Technologies Foundation, Inc.
777 E. Wisconsin Ave.
Milwaukee, WI 53202-5304 (414) 347-3727
FAX: (414) 347-4783
Contact: Doug Arnold

Incorporated in 1958 in WI.
Donor(s): Universal Foods Corp., Sensient Technologies Corp.
Financial data (yr. ended 09/30/01): Grants paid, $538,914; assets, $10,144,141 (M); expenditures, $591,938; qualifying distributions, $538,914.
Limitations: Giving primarily in CA, IN, MO, and WI.
Application information: Application form not required.
Officers: Kenneth P. Manning, Pres.; Richard Carney, V.P.; Richard F. Hobbs, V.P.; Steven J. Rolfs, Secy.-Treas.
EIN: 396044488
Codes: CS, FD, CD

56656
C. D. Smith Foundation, Inc.
889 E. Johnson St.
Fond Du Lac, WI 54935-2933

Established in 1999 in WI.
Donor(s): C.D. Smith Construction, Inc.
Financial data (yr. ended 12/31/00): Grants paid, $533,000; assets, $1,450,037 (M); gifts received, $1,000,000; expenditures, $533,213; qualifying distributions, $532,371.
Limitations: Applications not accepted. Giving primarily in IN and WI.
Application information: Contributes only to pre-selected organizations.
Officers: Gary M. Smith, Pres.; Thomas J. Baker, V.P.; Patrick S. Smith, Secy.; Robert Baker, Treas.
Directors: Thomas D. Baker, Mike P. Fortune, Mary Lou Smith.
EIN: 391972533
Codes: CS, FD

56657
Thousand Hills Foundation, Inc.
(Formerly Dennis J. and Sandra S. Kuester Foundation, Inc.)
c/o Dennis J. Kuester
770 N. Water St.
Milwaukee, WI 53202

Established in 1986 in WI.
Donor(s): Dennis J. Kuester, Sandra S. Kuester.
Financial data (yr. ended 12/31/01): Grants paid, $531,320; assets, $1,622,622 (M); gifts received, $975,848; expenditures, $531,410; qualifying distributions, $522,432.
Limitations: Applications not accepted. Giving primarily in Milwaukee, WI.
Application information: Contributes only to pre-selected organizations.
Officers and Directors:* Dennis J. Kuester,* Pres. and Treas.; Sandra S. Kuester,* V.P. and Secy.; Dennis R. Jones.
EIN: 391584969
Codes: FD

56658
Herman & Gwen Shapiro Foundation
c/o Foley & Lardner
P.O. Box 1497
Madison, WI 53701-1497
Contact: David G. Walsh, Tr.

Established in 1996 in WI.
Donor(s): Gwendolyn H. Shapiro.‡
Financial data (yr. ended 07/31/01): Grants paid, $529,601; assets, $9,719,276 (M); expenditures, $677,987; qualifying distributions, $594,711.
Limitations: Giving limited to Madison, WI.
Trustees: Dean Philip M. Farrell, Henry W. Ipsen, Dean Patricia A. Lasky, David W. Reinecke, John W. Thompson, David G. Walsh, John B. Walsh.
EIN: 391841051
Codes: FD

56659
GMO Charities, Inc.
8989 N. Port Washington Rd.
Milwaukee, WI 53217

Established in 1970.
Financial data (yr. ended 11/30/01): Grants paid, $515,568; assets, $5,838 (M); gifts received, $286,074; expenditures, $297,532; qualifying distributions, $518,167.
Limitations: Applications not accepted. Giving primarily in WI.
Application information: Contributes only to pre-selected organizations.
Directors: Francis Croak, James Kubinski, Robert Milbourne, Mark Reinemann, Keith Spore.
EIN: 237120884
Codes: FD

56660
Mae E. Demmer Charitable Trust
P.O. Box 1308
Milwaukee, WI 53201
Application address: c/o Bank One Trust Co., N.A., 111 E. Wisconsin Ave., Milwaukee, WI 53202
Contact: Dave Strelitz

Established in 1998 in WI.
Donor(s): Mae E. Demmer.‡
Financial data (yr. ended 12/31/01): Grants paid, $498,000; assets, $10,502,663 (M); expenditures, $640,894; qualifying distributions, $528,646.
Limitations: Giving primarily in Milwaukee, WI.
Trustees: Lawrence Demmer, Harrold McComas, Bank One Trust Co., N.A.
EIN: 311576907
Codes: FD

56661
Frances C. & William P. Smallwood Foundation
(also known as Smallwood Foundation)
c/o Bank One Trust Co., N.A.
P.O. Box 1308
Milwaukee, WI 53201
Application address: c/o Bank One, Texas, N.A., P.O. Box 2050, Fort Worth, TX 76113
Contact: Rick S. Piersall

Established in 1968.
Donor(s): William P. Smallwood Trust.
Financial data (yr. ended 12/31/01): Grants paid, $490,502; assets, $9,658,666 (M); expenditures, $564,344; qualifying distributions, $510,603.
Limitations: Giving primarily in Chapel Hill, NC, NV and Tarrant County, TX.
Application information: Requirements vary depending on type of grant requested.
Directors: Saul Baker, Harry Bartel, Sally Muller, Suzanne Stockdale.
Trustee: Bank One Trust Co., N.A.
EIN: 237000306
Codes: FD

56662
U.S. Oil/Schmidt Family Foundation, Inc.
425 Washington St.
P.O. Box 25
Combined Locks, WI 54113-1049
FAX: (920) 788-9909
Contact: Raymond Schmidt, Secy.

Established in 1984 in WI.
Donor(s): Raymond Schmidt, Arthur J. Schmidt, William Schmidt, Thomas A. Schmidt.
Financial data (yr. ended 07/31/01): Grants paid, $485,184; assets, $3,304,536 (M); gifts received, $400,000; expenditures, $509,939; qualifying distributions, $482,337.
Limitations: Applications not accepted. Giving primarily in WI.
Application information: Contributes only to pre-selected organizations.
Officers and Directors:* Thomas A. Schmidt,* Pres.; William Schmidt,* V.P.; Raymond Schmidt,* Secy.; Arthur J. Schmidt.
EIN: 391540933
Codes: FD

56663
Lunda Charitable Trust
620 Gebhardt Rd.
Black River Falls, WI 54615-0669
FAX: (715) 284-9146
Contact: Carl Holmquist, Tr.

Established in 1988 in WI.
Donor(s): Milton Lunda.
Financial data (yr. ended 12/31/01): Grants paid, $475,691; assets, $9,243,936 (M); expenditures, $514,424; qualifying distributions, $514,424.
Limitations: Giving primarily in Jackson County, WI.
Publications: Financial statement.
Application information: Application form required.
Trustees: Carl Holmquist, Larry Lunda, Lydia Lunda, Milton Lunda, Marlee Slifka, Mary van Gorden, Bill Waughtal.
EIN: 396491037
Codes: FD

56664
The Edwin E. and Janet L. Bryant Foundation, Inc.
(Formerly BGB Foundation)
P.O. Box 600
Stoughton, WI 53589-4114 (608) 877-3083

Established in 1993 in WI.
Financial data (yr. ended 12/31/01): Grants paid, $475,050; assets, $8,182,352 (M); expenditures, $1,150,699; qualifying distributions, $539,639.
Limitations: Giving primarily in Madison and Stoughton, WI.
Application information: Application form required.
Officers: Rockne G. Flowers, Pres.; David W. Bjerke, V.P.; June C. Bunting, Secy. and Exec. Dir.; Jerry A. Gryttenholm, Treas.
EIN: 391746858
Codes: FD

56665
Melvin F. and Ellen L. Wagner Foundation
(Formerly Melvin F. Wagner Foundation)
c/o U.S. Bank
P.O. Box 663
Sheboygan, WI 53081
Contact: Dennis Ohl, Secy.

Established in 1965.
Donor(s): Ellen L. Wagner.‡
Financial data (yr. ended 12/31/01): Grants paid, $470,000; assets, $8,472,942 (M); expenditures, $537,051; qualifying distributions, $473,148.
Limitations: Applications not accepted. Giving limited to Sheboygan, WI.
Application information: Contributes only to pre-selected organizations.
Officer: Dennis Ohl, Secy.
Trustees: James Raffel, Dolores Slesrick, Eugene D. Weber, U.S. Bank.
EIN: 396129125
Codes: FD

56666
John J. Burke Family Foundation, Inc.
622 N. Water St., Ste. 200
Milwaukee, WI 53202

Established in 1986 in WI.
Donor(s): John J. Burke, Jr., Kathryn M. Burke.
Financial data (yr. ended 12/31/01): Grants paid, $466,675; assets, $0 (M); gifts received, $256,570; expenditures, $540,238; qualifying distributions, $464,374.
Limitations: Applications not accepted. Giving primarily in Milwaukee, WI.
Application information: Contributes only to pre-selected organizations.
Officers and Directors:* John J. Burke, Jr.,* Pres. and Treas.; Kathryn M. Burke,* V.P. and Secy.; William F. Fox.
EIN: 391575325
Codes: FD

56667
The Modine Manufacturing Company Foundation, Inc.
1500 DeKoven Ave.
Racine, WI 53403
Contact: Alan D. Reid, V.P.

Established in 1995 in WI.
Donor(s): Modine Manufacturing Co.
Financial data (yr. ended 03/31/01): Grants paid, $464,535; assets, $19,911 (M); gifts received, $406,674; expenditures, $464,772; qualifying distributions, $464,569.
Limitations: Giving limited to headquarters city and major operating areas.
Application information: Application form not required.
Officers and Directors:* Donald R. Johnson,* Pres.; Roger L. Hetrick, V.P. and Secy.; Alan D. Reid,* V.P. and Treas.; David B. Rayburn.
EIN: 391818362
Codes: CS, FD, CD

56668
Oscar C. & Augusta Schlegel Foundation
c/o Marshall & Ilsley Bank
P.O. Box 2980
Milwaukee, WI 53201-2980

Established in 1987 in WI.
Financial data (yr. ended 03/31/02): Grants paid, $450,700; assets, $8,940,900 (M); expenditures, $478,875; qualifying distributions, $445,355.
Limitations: Applications not accepted. Giving limited to WI.
Application information: Contributes only to pre-selected organizations.
Officers: Marilyn L. Holmquist, Chair.; Roger T. Stephenson, Vice-Chair.; Steven J. Schumacher, Secy.
Director: Tom Lindell.
Trustee: Marshall & Ilsley Bank.
EIN: 391586544
Codes: FD

56669
Joe and Jessie Crump Fund
c/o Bank One Trust Co., N.A.
P.O. Box 1308
Milwaukee, WI 53201-1308

Trust established in 1965 in TX.
Financial data (yr. ended 09/30/01): Grants paid, $450,264; assets, $19,909,118 (M); expenditures, $823,875; qualifying distributions, $1,258,960; giving activities include $800,000 for loans to individuals.
Limitations: Applications not accepted. Giving primarily in TX.
Application information: Contributes only to pre-selected organizations.
Trustee: Bank One, Texas, N.A.
EIN: 756045044
Codes: FD

56670
Emory T. Clark Family Foundation
125 N. Executive Dr., Ste. 363
Brookfield, WI 53005 (262) 821-8610
FAX: (262) 821-1492
Contact: Linda J. Hansen, Dir.

Established in 1982 in WI.
Donor(s): Emory T. Clark.‡
Financial data (yr. ended 03/31/02): Grants paid, $445,150; assets, $9,524,910 (M); expenditures, $513,856; qualifying distributions, $477,357.
Limitations: Giving primarily in WI.
Publications: Informational brochure, application guidelines.

56670—WISCONSIN

Application information: Application form required.
Trustee: Firstar Trust Co.
EIN: 391410324
Codes: FD

56671
Goldbach Charitable Foundation, Inc.
304 East St.
Marathon, WI 54448

Established in 1997 in WI.
Donor(s): Marie S. Goldbach Life Trust, Marathon Cheese Corp., Packaging Tape, Inc.
Financial data (yr. ended 12/31/01): Grants paid, $439,800; assets, $1,146,671 (M); expenditures, $445,932; qualifying distributions, $439,360.
Limitations: Applications not accepted. Giving primarily in WI.
Officers: John L. Skoug, Pres. and Treas.; Marie S. Goldbach, V.P.
Director: Rev. Joseph G. Diermeier.
EIN: 391877824
Codes: FD

56672
The Fotsch Foundation
13965 W. Burleigh Rd., Ste. 101
Brookfield, WI 53005-3000

Established in 1967 in IL.
Donor(s): Abina D. Fotsch, William E. Fotsch, Baush Machine Tool Co., BMT Corp., JFC Enterprises.
Financial data (yr. ended 11/30/01): Grants paid, $434,900; assets, $9,031,916 (M); gifts received, $169,242; expenditures, $456,400; qualifying distributions, $432,145.
Limitations: Applications not accepted. Giving primarily in IL and WI.
Application information: Contributes only to pre-selected organizations.
Officer: William E. Fotsch, Pres.
EIN: 366190007
Codes: FD

56673
John and Engrid Meng, Inc.
P.O. Box 19010
Green Bay, WI 54307-9010

Established in 1982 in WI.
Donor(s): Engrid Meng, John C. Meng.
Financial data (yr. ended 11/30/01): Grants paid, $424,972; assets, $7,504,119 (M); gifts received, $1,000,000; expenditures, $520,139; qualifying distributions, $424,972.
Limitations: Applications not accepted. Giving limited to northeastern WI, with emphasis on Green Bay and Brown County.
Application information: Contributes only to pre-selected organizations.
Officers: Engrid Meng, Pres.; John C. Meng, V.P. and Treas.; Gerald C. Condon, Jr., Secy.
EIN: 391432568
Codes: FD

56674
Norman Bassett Foundation - Wisconsin
P.O. Box 3037
Madison, WI 53704 (608) 242-5265
FAX: (608) 242-5320; *E-mail:* jscott@madison-kipp.com
Contact: J. Reed Coleman, Pres.

Established in 1954 in WI.
Financial data (yr. ended 03/31/01): Grants paid, $418,800; assets, $2,891,131 (M); gifts received, $75,000; expenditures, $470,267; qualifying distributions, $420,580.

Limitations: Giving primarily in Madison and Dane County, WI.
Publications: Financial statement.
Application information: Application form not required.
Officers: J. Reed Coleman, Pres.; Thomas Ragatz, Secy.; Thomas R. Johnson, Treas.
Board Member: Milton McPike.
EIN: 396043890
Codes: FD

56675
Janesville Foundation, Inc.
121 N. Parker Dr.
P.O. Box 8123
Janesville, WI 53547-8123 (608) 752-1032
FAX: (608) 752-1952
Contact: Bonnie Lynne Robinson, Pres. and Exec. Dir.

Incorporated in 1944 in WI.
Donor(s): The Parker Pen Co.
Financial data (yr. ended 12/31/01): Grants paid, $417,710; assets, $9,261,173 (M); gifts received, $200; expenditures, $949,133; qualifying distributions, $484,946.
Limitations: Giving limited to the Janesville, WI, area; scholarships limited to Janesville high school students.
Publications: Informational brochure (including application guidelines).
Application information: Application form not required.
Officers and Directors:* George Parker,* Chair.; Alan W. Dunwiddie,* Vice-Chair.; Bonnie Lynne Robinson,* Pres. and Exec. Dir.; Roger E. Axtell,* V.P.; Alfred P. Diotte,* V.P.; Dolores M. Dilley, Secy.; Ronald K. Ochs,* Treas.; Rowland J. McClellan.
EIN: 396034645
Codes: FD, GTI

56676
John A. Elliott Foundation, Inc.
P.O. Box 2980
Milwaukee, WI 53201
Application address: 804 Cass St., Lacrosse, WI 54601
Contact: Marian R. Elliott, Pres.

Established in 1969.
Donor(s): Marian R. Elliott.
Financial data (yr. ended 07/31/01): Grants paid, $414,000; assets, $5,949,655 (M); expenditures, $450,154; qualifying distributions, $414,000.
Limitations: Giving primarily in La Crosse, WI.
Application information: Application form not required.
Officers: Marian R. Elliott, Pres.; Mark Chamberlian, Secy.-Treas.
EIN: 237108088
Codes: FD

56677
John H. Witte, Jr. Foundation
c/o U.S. Bank
P.O. Box 2043, Ste. LC4NE
Milwaukee, WI 53201-9116
Application address: c/o U.S. Bank, 201 Jefferson St., Burlington, IA 52601-5250
Contact: Terri Dowell

Established in 1979 in IA.
Donor(s): John H. Witte, Jr.‡
Financial data (yr. ended 08/31/01): Grants paid, $413,871; assets, $7,920,060 (M); expenditures, $483,233; qualifying distributions, $424,932.
Limitations: Giving primarily in the Burlington, IA, area.
Trustee: U.S. Bank.

EIN: 426297940
Codes: FD

56678
Dale R. & Ruth L. Michels Family Foundation
P.O. Box 414
Brownsville, WI 53006-0414

Established in 1999 in WI.
Donor(s): Ruth L. Michels.
Financial data (yr. ended 12/31/00): Grants paid, $413,000; assets, $2,164,638 (M); gifts received, $290,218; expenditures, $422,635; qualifying distributions, $409,927.
Limitations: Giving primarily in WI.
Trustees: Kevin P. Michels, Patrick D. Michels, Ruth L. Michels, Steven R. Michels, Timothy J. Michels.
EIN: 391949453
Codes: FD

56679
Badger Meter Foundation, Inc.
P.O. Box 245036
Milwaukee, WI 53224-9536
Application address: 4545 W. Brown Deer Rd., Milwaukee, WI 53223, tel.: (414) 371-5704
Contact: Beth McCallister, Secy.

Incorporated in 1952 in WI.
Donor(s): Badger Meter, Inc.
Financial data (yr. ended 12/31/01): Grants paid, $410,108; assets, $1,763,808 (M); gifts received, $106,000; expenditures, $248,957; qualifying distributions, $409,615.
Limitations: Giving limited to WI, with emphasis on the greater Milwaukee area.
Application information: Application form not required.
Officers and Directors:* James O. Wright,* Pres.; Ronald H. Dix,* V.P.; Beth M. McCallister, Secy.; John P. Biever, Treas.; Peter W. Bruce, Richard S. Gallagher, Barbara M. Wiley.
EIN: 396043635
Codes: CS, FD, CD

56680
Herb Kohl Educational Foundation
825 N. Jefferson St.
Milwaukee, WI 53202

Established in 1989 in WI.
Donor(s): Herbert H. Kohl, Herbert H. Kohl Charities, Inc.
Financial data (yr. ended 12/31/01): Grants paid, $409,900; assets, $3,356,431 (M); expenditures, $469,686; qualifying distributions, $421,758.
Limitations: Giving primarily in WI.
Application information: Teaching awards by nomination. Application form required.
Officers and Directors:* Herbert H. Kohl,* Pres.; Allen D. Kohl,* V.P.; Sidney A. Kohl,* Secy.; Dolores Kohl.
EIN: 391661743
Codes: FD, GTI

56681
F. K. Bemis Family Foundation, Inc.
c/o Bemis Manufacturing Co.
300 Mill St.
Sheboygan Falls, WI 53085 (920) 467-4621
Application address: P.O. Box 901, Sheboygan Falls, WI 53085-0901
Contact: Richard A. Bemis, Pres.

Established about 1953 in WI.
Donor(s): Bemis Manufacturing Co.
Financial data (yr. ended 12/31/01): Grants paid, $409,100; assets, $17 (M); gifts received, $409,100; expenditures, $409,100; qualifying distributions, $409,100.

Limitations: Giving primarily in Sheboygan County, WI.
Officers: Richard A. Bemis, Pres.; Peter F. Bemis, V.P.; Mary Parent, Secy.; Peter Lukaszewicz, Treas.
EIN: 396067930
Codes: CS, FD, CD

56682
Outagamie Charitable Foundation, Inc.
100 W. Lawrence St.
P.O. Box 727
Appleton, WI 54912-0727

Established in 1985 in WI.
Donor(s): Fox Valley Corp.
Financial data (yr. ended 03/31/01): Grants paid, $405,000; assets, $7,341,811 (M); expenditures, $468,982; qualifying distributions, $390,231.
Limitations: Applications not accepted. Giving on a national basis.
Application information: Contributes only to pre-selected organizations.
Officers and Directors:* Jean Vitalis,* Pres.; Jodey Fey,* V.P.; Nancy McLaughlin,* V.P.; Lyle H. Richter, Secy.-Treas.; Betsey Aalfs, David Buchanan, Wendy Buchanan, Linda Jacob, James Lenfestey, Jamie Lenfestey.
EIN: 391526589
Codes: FD

56683
Kurth Religious Trust
3780 N. 169th St.
Brookfield, WI 53005 (262) 790-9188
Contact: Katherine Kurth, Tr.

Trust established in 1946 in WI.
Donor(s): Kurth Malting Corp.
Financial data (yr. ended 12/31/00): Grants paid, $397,250; assets, $8,090,106 (M); expenditures, $456,133; qualifying distributions, $388,616.
Limitations: Applications not accepted. Giving primarily in NM and WI.
Application information: Contributes only to pre-selected organizations. Unsolicited requests for funds are not accepted.
Trustees: Katherine Kurth, Thomas Kurth, Tineka Kurth, Wendy Wrean.
EIN: 396048744
Codes: FD

56684
Oshkosh B'Gosh Foundation, Inc.
c/o U.S. Bank
P.O. Box 300
Oshkosh, WI 54902 (920) 231-8800
Contact: David Omachinski, V.P.

Established in 1985 in WI.
Donor(s): Oshkosh B'Gosh, Inc.
Financial data (yr. ended 12/31/00): Grants paid, $395,673; assets, $1,131,864 (M); gifts received, $500,000; expenditures, $408,285; qualifying distributions, $395,673.
Limitations: Giving primarily in WI.
Application information: Application form required for scholarships.
Officers and Directors:* Michael D. Wachtel,* Pres.; David Omachinski,* V.P.; William Wyman,* Secy.
EIN: 391525020
Codes: CS, FD, CD, GTI

56685
Terrance and Judith Paul Foundation, Inc.
P.O. Box 863
Wisconsin Rapids, WI 54495

Established in 1997 in WI.
Donor(s): Judith Paul, Terrance Paul.

Financial data (yr. ended 12/31/00): Grants paid, $392,119; assets, $652,682 (M); expenditures, $394,581; qualifying distributions, $387,531.
Limitations: Applications not accepted. Giving primarily in WI.
Application information: Contributes only to pre-selected organizations.
Officers: Judith Paul, Pres. and Treas.; Terrance Paul, V.P. and Secy.
Director: Mia Paul.
EIN: 391914369
Codes: FD

56686
Schoenleber Foundation, Inc.
c/o Janet Hoehnen
111 E. Wisconsin Ave., Ste. 1800
Milwaukee, WI 53202-4809
Contact: Peter C. Haensel, Pres.

Established in 1965 in WI.
Donor(s): Marie Schoenleber,‡ Louise Schoenleber,‡ Gretchen Schoenleber.‡
Financial data (yr. ended 12/31/01): Grants paid, $391,566; assets, $7,570,982 (M); expenditures, $503,489; qualifying distributions, $387,060.
Limitations: Giving primarily in WI, with emphasis on Milwaukee.
Publications: Informational brochure (including application guidelines).
Application information: Application form required.
Officers and Directors:* Peter C. Haensel,* Pres.; Frank W. Bastian,* Secy.; Walter Schorrak.
EIN: 391049364
Codes: FD

56687
AnnMarie Foundation
c/o Phillips Plastics Technology Ctr.
N4660 1165th St.
Prescott, WI 54021-7644
URL: http://www.phillipsplastics.com/corporateoverview/community/annmarie.html
Contact: Lori Feiten

Established in 1973 in WI.
Donor(s): Phillips Plastics Corp., Mike Litvinoff Memorial.
Financial data (yr. ended 04/30/02): Grants paid, $390,167; assets, $4,275,436 (M); gifts received, $412,865; expenditures, $415,200; qualifying distributions, $390,166.
Limitations: Giving primarily in WI.
Application information: Application form required.
Members: Jim Anderson, Doug Berends, Barb Chapman, Tom Gehrke, Sally Giese, Deborah Ballinger Hellerud, Karl Murch, Tami Satre.
EIN: 237301323
Codes: CS, FD, GTI

56688
Lucy & Emily Beasley Charitable Trust
c/o Bank One Trust Co., N.A.
P.O. Box 1308
Milwaukee, WI 53201
Application address: 50 S. Main St., Akron, OH 44308
Contact: Thomas D. Barsody

Established in 1981.
Donor(s): Robert P. Beasley Trust.
Financial data (yr. ended 09/30/01): Grants paid, $388,000; assets, $7,331,549 (M); gifts received, $28,776; expenditures, $461,392; qualifying distributions, $400,260.
Limitations: Giving primarily in OH.
Advisory Committee: Howard W. Cable, Jr., Robert E. Hissong, A. Russell Smith.

Trustee: Bank One Trust Co., N.A.
EIN: 341350747
Codes: FD

56689
Daniel and Linda Bader Foundation
(Formerly Daniel Bader 1993 Charitable Trust)
777 E. Wisconsin Ave., Ste. 3500
Milwaukee, WI 53202
Contact: Wayne R. Lueders, Tr.

Established in 1993 in WI.
Donor(s): Daniel Bader.
Financial data (yr. ended 12/31/01): Grants paid, $384,399; assets, $266,308 (M); gifts received, $14,474; expenditures, $388,388; qualifying distributions, $387,312.
Limitations: Applications not accepted. Giving primarily in WI.
Application information: Contributes only to pre-selected organizations.
Trustees: Daniel Bader, Linda Bader, Wayne R. Lueders, Jere D. McGaffey.
EIN: 396586346
Codes: FD

56690
St. Croix Valley Community Foundation
516 2nd St., Ste. 214
P.O. Box 39
Hudson, WI 54016 (715) 386-9490
FAX: (715) 386-1250; *E-mail:* info@scvcf.org;
URL: http://www.scvcf.org
Contact: David H. Griffith, Pres.

Established in 1995.
Financial data (yr. ended 06/30/02): Grants paid, $373,493; assets, $3,683,144 (L); gifts received, $2,450,078; expenditures, $600,241.
Limitations: Giving primarily in Chisago and Washington counties, MN and Pierce, Polk and St. Croix counties, WI.
Publications: Annual report, financial statement, informational brochure.
Application information: Applications required for art grants. Application form not required.
Officers and Directors: Sarah Andersen,* Chair.; Orville Johnson,* Vice-Chair.; David H. Griffith, Pres.; Rita Lawson,* Secy.; John M. Coughlin,* Treas.; John B. Baird, James H. Bradshaw, David H. Brandt, William E. Campbell, Heidi Smith Erspamer, C.R. Hackworthy, Karen Hansen, Larry Horsch, Peter Kilde, Marilyn McCarty, Erv Neff, Lynn Shafer, John R. Tunheim.
EIN: 411817315
Codes: CM, FD

56691
Lakeview Foundation, Inc.
c/o Kerber, Eck, and Braeckel, LLP
401 E. Kilbourn Ave., Ste. 400
Milwaukee, WI 53202-3212

Established in 1996 in WI.
Financial data (yr. ended 07/31/01): Grants paid, $372,000; assets, $4,844,181 (M); expenditures, $1,150,474; qualifying distributions, $372,266.
Limitations: Applications not accepted. Giving primarily in Milwaukee, WI.
Application information: Contributes only to pre-selected organizations.
Directors: Robert H. Brogan, William H. Foshag, David A. Grant, William J. Haese, Robert R. Magliocco, Charles J. Osborn, Vernon H. Swanson, John H. Woodin.
EIN: 391857646
Codes: FD

56692
Anon Charitable Trust
c/o U.S. Bank
P.O. Box 2059
Milwaukee, WI 53201
Contact: Donald S. Buzard, Tr.

Established in 1993 in WI.
Donor(s): Clarice Turer.
Financial data (yr. ended 12/31/01): Grants paid, $371,948; assets, $4,450,049 (M); expenditures, $448,423; qualifying distributions, $386,419.
Limitations: Giving primarily in Milwaukee, WI.
Trustees: Bert L. Bilsky, Donald S. Buzard, Wayne R. Lueders.
EIN: 391771579
Codes: FD

56693
Charles D. Jacobus Family Foundation
P.O. Box 13009
Milwaukee, WI 53213 (414) 577-0252
FAX: (414) 359-1357; E-mail: info@jacobusenergy.com; URL: http://www.cdjff.org
Contact: Missy Campion, Pres.

Established in 1986 in WI.
Donor(s): Charles D. Jacobus, Eugenia T. Jacobus, Jacobus Co.
Financial data (yr. ended 12/31/01): Grants paid, $370,368; assets, $4,978,144 (M); expenditures, $457,376; qualifying distributions, $419,130.
Limitations: Giving limited to southeastern WI.
Application information: Foundation will include grantseeking organizations on mailing list and will send letters of intent in the spring.
Officers: Missy Campion, Pres.; Eugenia T. Jacobus, V.P.; Victoria B. Jacobus, Secy.; Eugene T. Jacobus, Treas.
Directors: Russell R. Campion, Charles D. Jacobus, Colleen C. Jacobus.
EIN: 391559892
Codes: FD

56694
Fortis Healtth Foundation, Inc.
(Formerly Fortis Insurance Foundation, Inc.)
501 W. Michigan St.
Milwaukee, WI 53203
FAX: (414) 299-6749; E-mail: rob.guilbert@us.fortis.com; URL: http://www.etdbw.com/fh/fortishealth/index.jsp
Contact: Rob Guilbert, Pres.

Established in 1973 in WI.
Donor(s): Time Insurance Co., Fortis Insurance Co.
Financial data (yr. ended 12/31/01): Grants paid, $368,039; assets, $1,232,068 (M); expenditures, $382,898; qualifying distributions, $369,211.
Limitations: Giving primarily in southeastern WI.
Publications: Annual report, application guidelines, financial statement, informational brochure, grants list.
Application information: Unsolicited requests for funds not accepted. Requests for funds only accepted after the foundation sends out requests for proposals.
Officers: Rob Guilbert, Pres.; Carey Bongard, V.P.; Jennifer Kopps-Wagner, Secy.; Howard Miller, Treas.
Trustees: Bill Bergum, Tom Brophy, Mary Brown, Laree Daniel, Kim Pollard, Laura Hohing.
EIN: 237346436
Codes: CS, FD, CD

56695
Miriam & Bernard Peck Foundation, Ltd.
P.O. Box 441
Milwaukee, WI 53201-0441
Contact: Karen Katz, Dir.

Established in 1985 in WI.
Donor(s): Jodi Peck, Miriam Peck, Bernard Peck, Karen Katz.
Financial data (yr. ended 12/31/00): Grants paid, $365,895; assets, $3,424,438 (M); expenditures, $392,510; qualifying distributions, $361,473.
Limitations: Giving primarily in Fort Lauderdale, FL and Milwaukee, WI.
Application information: Application form not required.
Officers and Directors:* Miriam Peck,* Pres. and Treas.; Bernard Peck,* V.P. and Secy.; Karen Katz, William Komisar, Jodi Peck.
EIN: 391519687
Codes: FD

56696
The Robert J. Sullivan Family Foundation, Ltd.
1700 E. Juniper Way
Hartland, WI 53029-8669
Contact: Kay Sullivan, Dir.

Established in 1990 in WI.
Donor(s): Robert J. Sullivan.
Financial data (yr. ended 12/31/01): Grants paid, $363,688; assets, $3,373,990 (M); expenditures, $383,243; qualifying distributions, $363,688.
Limitations: Giving primarily in WI.
Officer and Directors:* Judith Sullivan,* V.P. and Secy.; Elizabeth Ann Cimler, Mary Kathleen Schwanke, Katherine Sullivan, Robert J. Sullivan, Jr., Timothy J. Sullivan.
EIN: 391686475
Codes: FD

56697
Willard E. & Ella P. Thompson Educational Fund
c/o U.S. Bank
P.O. Box 2043
Milwaukee, WI 53201-9116

Donor(s): Henrietta R. Thompson Annuity Trust, Willard E. Thompson Tust.
Financial data (yr. ended 12/31/00): Grants paid, $349,622; assets, $6,115,156 (M); expenditures, $398,035; qualifying distributions, $370,267.
Limitations: Giving limited to residents of Algona, IA.
Trustee: U.S. Bank.
EIN: 366028029
Codes: FD, GTI

56698
Alyward Family Foundation
(Formerly Neenah Foundry Foundation, Inc.)
P.O. Box 409
Neenah, WI 54957-0409 (920) 725-7000
Contact: E.W. Alyward, Pres.

Incorporated in 1953 in WI.
Donor(s): Neenah Foundry Co.
Financial data (yr. ended 12/31/01): Grants paid, $349,500; assets, $4,147,412 (M); expenditures, $370,347; qualifying distributions, $354,390.
Limitations: Giving primarily in Appleton, Menasha, Neenah, and New London, WI.
Officers: E.W. Alyward, Sr., Pres.; A.A. Alyward, Jr., V.P.; R.J. Alyward, Secy.-Treas.
EIN: 396042143
Codes: CS, FD, CD

56699
Wausau-Mosinee Paper Foundation, Inc.
(Formerly Wausau Paper Mills Foundation, Inc.)
1244 Kronenwetter Dr.
Mosinee, WI 54455-9099
Scholarship application address: c/o Principal, Mosinee High School, 1000 High St., Mosinee, WI 54455, tel.: (715) 693-2550

Established in 1958.
Donor(s): Wausau Paper Mills Co., Wausau-Mosinee Paper Corp., Rhinelander Paper Mills Co.
Financial data (yr. ended 08/31/01): Grants paid, $348,586; assets, $122,118 (M); gifts received, $340,000; expenditures, $348,586; qualifying distributions, $349,008.
Limitations: Giving primarily in Wausau, WI.
Officers: Thomas J. Howatt, C.E.O. and Pres.; Stuart R. Carlson, Exec. V.P., Fin. and Admin.; Gary P. Peterson, Sr. V.P., Fin. and Secy-Treas.
Directors: Walter Alexander, Harry R. Baker, Gary W. Freels, Richard G. Jacobus, San W. Orr, Jr., Richard L. Radt, David B. Smith, Jr.
EIN: 396080502
Codes: CS, FD, CD

56700
Cavaliere Foundation, Inc.
1716 Jefferson St.
Madison, WI 53711
Application address: 211 S. Patterson St., Madison, WI 53703, tel.: (608) 260-9500
Contact: James A. Knight, Dir.

Established in 1999 in WI.
Donor(s): James A. Knight, Jr.
Financial data (yr. ended 12/31/00): Grants paid, $348,563; assets, $6,150,398 (M); gifts received, $352,642; expenditures, $425,780; qualifying distributions, $348,563.
Directors: Lisa Ferin, Diana I. Ingraham, James A. Knight.
EIN: 391960035
Codes: FD

56701
The Coss Foundation
c/o Garry E. Nietz
42-160th St.
River Falls, WI 54022

Established in 1992 in MN.
Donor(s): Lawrence M. Coss.
Financial data (yr. ended 12/31/01): Grants paid, $346,619; assets, $3,040,585 (M); expenditures, $363,228; qualifying distributions, $353,419.
Limitations: Applications not accepted. Giving limited to MN.
Application information: Contributes only to pre-selected organizations.
Officer: Lawrence M. Coss, Pres. and Secy.-Treas.
EIN: 411726797
Codes: FD

56702
Will Ross Memorial Foundation, Inc.
P.O. Box 17814
Milwaukee, WI 53217
Contact: Mary Ann W. LaBahn, V.P. and Treas.

Established around 1963.
Donor(s): Cava Wilson Ross.‡
Financial data (yr. ended 12/31/01): Grants paid, $346,000; assets, $2,672,475 (M); expenditures, $398,731; qualifying distributions, $355,753.
Limitations: Giving limited to the metropolitan Milwaukee, WI, area.
Application information: Application form not required.

Officers and Directors:* John D. Bryson, Jr.,* Pres.; Mary Ann W. LaBahn,* V.P. and Treas.; David L. Kinnamon,* Secy.
EIN: 396044673
Codes: FD

56703
Cleary-Kumm Foundation, Inc.
(Formerly Cleary Foundation)
310 Sky Harbour Dr.
La Crosse, WI 54603 (608) 783-7500
FAX: (608) 781-6160
Contact: Gail K. Cleary, Pres.

Established in 1982 in WI; merged with the Kumm foundation in 2000.
Donor(s): Gail K. Cleary, Russell G. Cleary,‡ Lillian H. Kumm.‡
Financial data (yr. ended 11/30/01): Grants paid, $345,805; assets, $8,667,682 (M); expenditures, $371,517; qualifying distributions, $371,517.
Limitations: Giving primarily in the La Crosse, WI, area.
Application information: Application form not required.
Officer and Directors:* Gail K. Cleary,* Pres.; Kristine H. Cleary, Sandra G. Cleary.
EIN: 391426785
Codes: FD

56704
Kikkoman Foods Foundation, Inc.
P.O. Box 69
Walworth, WI 53184
Application address: 11 N. Wisconsin St., Elkhorn, WI 53121, tel.: (262) 723-3220
Contact: Robert V. Conover, Dir.

Established in 1993 in WI.
Donor(s): Kikkoman Foods, Inc.
Financial data (yr. ended 12/31/01): Grants paid, $343,920; assets, $5,104,117 (M); expenditures, $370,807; qualifying distributions, $340,705.
Limitations: Giving primarily in WI.
Application information: Application form not required.
Directors: Robert V. Conover, Hiroshi Futamura, Kuniki Hatayama, Yuzaburo Mogi, William E. Nelson, Milton E. Neshek, Malcolm Pennington, Mitsuo Someya, Shigeomi Ushijima.
EIN: 391763633
Codes: CS, FD, CD

56705
Krause Foundation, Inc.
700 E. Iola St.
Iola, WI 54945
Contact: Patricia Klug, V.P.

Established in 1987 in WI.
Donor(s): Krause Publications, Inc.
Financial data (yr. ended 12/31/99): Grants paid, $340,668; assets, $2,543,032 (M); gifts received, $100,280; expenditures, $351,989; qualifying distributions, $351,591.
Limitations: Giving primarily in central WI.
Officers: Chester L. Krause, Pres.; Patricia Klug, V.P.; Patricia Krause, V.P.; Bruce J. Meagher, Secy.-Treas.
EIN: 391571437
Codes: FD

56706
Hamilton Roddis Foundation, Inc.
c/o Augusta D. Roddis
1108 E. 4th St.
Marshfield, WI 54449-4539

Incorporated in 1953 in WI.
Donor(s): Hamilton Roddis,‡ Augusta D. Roddis, Catherine P. Roddis, Roddis Plywood Corp.
Financial data (yr. ended 12/31/00): Grants paid, $340,450; assets, $6,810,845 (M); gifts received, $10,129; expenditures, $380,283; qualifying distributions, $341,299.
Limitations: Applications not accepted. Giving on a national basis, with some emphasis on WI, particularly Marshfield.
Application information: Contributes only to pre-selected organizations.
Officers: William H. Roddis II, Pres.; Augusta D. Roddis, Secy.-Treas.
EIN: 396077001
Codes: FD

56707
Oshkosh Truck Foundation, Inc.
2307 Oregon St.
Oshkosh, WI 54902
Application address: P.O. Box 2566, Oshkosh, WI 54903-2566
Contact: Robert G. Bohn, Pres.

Incorporated in 1960 in WI.
Donor(s): Oshkosh Truck Corp.
Financial data (yr. ended 09/30/01): Grants paid, $338,045; assets, $43,270 (M); gifts received, $375,000; expenditures, $338,055; qualifying distributions, $338,055.
Limitations: Giving primarily in Oshkosh and the Winnebago County, WI, area. Generally, contributions are considered to organizations located close to Oshkosh Truck employees.
Application information: Application form not required.
Officers and Trustees:* Robert G. Bohn,* Pres.; Timothy M. Dempsey,* V.P. and Secy.; Charles Szews,* Treas.; Matthew J. Zolnowski.
EIN: 396062129
Codes: CS, FD, CD

56708
Pamida Foundation
P.O. Box 19060
Green Bay, WI 54307-9060
Application address: P.O. Box 3856, Omaha, NE 68103-0856, tel.: (402) 339-2400
Contact: Robert C. Hafner, V.P.

Established in 1983 in NE.
Donor(s): Pamida, Inc.
Financial data (yr. ended 02/03/01): Grants paid, $335,704; assets, $81,502 (M); gifts received, $300,000; expenditures, $337,286; qualifying distributions, $335,704.
Limitations: Giving limited to areas of company operations.
Application information: Application form required.
Officers and Trustees:* Michael J. Hopkins,* Pres.; Robert C. Hafner,* V.P.; Brian Bender,* Secy.-Treas.
EIN: 470656225
Codes: CS, FD, CD

56709
Thomas J. Rolfs Foundation, Inc.
P.O. Box 70
Nashotah, WI 53058
Contact: Theodore R. Rolfs, Secy.-Treas.

Established in 1959 in WI.
Donor(s): Amity Leather Products Co.
Financial data (yr. ended 09/30/01): Grants paid, $333,000; assets, $6,144,399 (M); gifts received, $1,000; expenditures, $385,430; qualifying distributions, $333,000.
Limitations: Giving primarily in IN and WI.
Officers: Thomas J. Rolfs, Pres.; Thomas J. Rolfs, Jr., V.P.; Theodore R. Rolfs, Secy.-Treas.
Directors: Claire L. Rolfs, Janet M. Rolfs.
EIN: 396043350
Codes: FD

56710
Jack & Joan Stein Foundation, Inc.
5400 S. 27th St.
Milwaukee, WI 53221

Established in 1994 in WI.
Donor(s): Jack Stein.
Financial data (yr. ended 12/31/00): Grants paid, $332,424; assets, $609,907 (M); gifts received, $122,086; expenditures, $335,452; qualifying distributions, $331,771.
Limitations: Applications not accepted. Giving on a national basis.
Application information: Contributes only to pre-selected organizations.
Officers: Jack Stein, Mgr.; Joan Stein, Mgr.
EIN: 391805213
Codes: FD

56711
R. D. and Linda Peters Foundation, Inc.
c/o Bank One Trust Co., N.A.
P.O. Box 1308
Milwaukee, WI 53201 (414) 765-2445
Contact: Richard G. Hugo, Dir.

Established in 1965.
Donor(s): R.D. Peters,‡ Linda Peters.‡
Financial data (yr. ended 12/31/01): Grants paid, $331,694; assets, $6,346,995 (M); expenditures, $438,634; qualifying distributions, $345,557.
Limitations: Giving primarily in the Brillion, WI, area.
Application information: Application form not required.
Directors: F. William Haberman, Richard G. Hugo, Lowell O. Reese, Harold Wolf.
Trustee: Bank One Trust Co., N.A.
EIN: 396097994
Codes: FD

56712
Victor and Mary D. Nelson Scholarship Fund
c/o Marshall & Ilsley Trust Company, N.A.
P.O. Box 2980
Milwaukee, WI 53201-2980
Application address: William Retinstrand, c/o Superior Senior High School, 2600 Catlin Ave., Superior, WI 54880, tel.: (715) 384-0271

Established in 1973 in WI.
Donor(s): Mary D. Nelson.‡
Financial data (yr. ended 06/30/01): Grants paid, $329,853; assets, $5,924,395 (M); expenditures, $372,408; qualifying distributions, $328,537.
Limitations: Giving limited to Superior, WI.
Application information: Applications available at school counseling offices. Application form required.
Trustee: Marshall & Ilsley Trust Company, N.A.
EIN: 396184729
Codes: FD, GTI

56713
Joseph & Sally Handleman Charitable Foundation Trust C
c/o Bank One Trust Co., N.A.
P.O. Box 1308
Milwaukee, WI 53201
Application address: c/o Bank One Trust Co., N.A., 3399 PGA Blvd., Ste. 100, Palm Beach Gardens, FL 33410, tel.: (561) 627-9400
Contact: Gary W. Gomoll, Mgr.

Financial data (yr. ended 12/31/00): Grants paid, $329,000; assets, $8,242,895 (M); expenditures, $545,196; qualifying distributions, $346,996.
Limitations: Giving primarily in FL and NY.

56713—WISCONSIN

Application information: Application form not required.
Officer: Gary W. Gomoll, Mgr.
Agent: Bank One Trust Co., N.A.
EIN: 656263328
Codes: FD

56714
Joseph & Sally Handleman Charitable Foundation Trust A
c/o Bank One Trust Co., N.A.
P.O. Box 1308
Milwaukee, WI 53201
Application address: c/o Bank One Trust Co., N.A., 3399 PGA Blvd., Palm Beach Gardens, FL 33410, tel.: (561) 627-9400
Contact: Gary W. Gomoll, Mgr.

Financial data (yr. ended 12/31/00): Grants paid, $328,500; assets, $8,218,883 (M); expenditures, $535,214; qualifying distributions, $342,280.
Limitations: Giving primarily in FL, NY and PA.
Officer: Gary W. Gomoll, Mgr.
Agent: Bank One Trust Co., N.A.
EIN: 656263326
Codes: FD

56715
Manpower Foundation, Inc.
5301 N. Ironwood Rd.
Milwaukee, WI 53217
Application address for scholarships: c/o Scholarship Prog. Coord., P.O. Box 2053, Milwaukee, WI 53201, tel.: (414) 961-1000

Established in 1953 in WI.
Donor(s): Manpower Inc.
Financial data (yr. ended 12/31/01): Grants paid, $326,750; assets, $587,322 (M); gifts received, $180,000; expenditures, $327,680; qualifying distributions, $327,111.
Limitations: Giving primarily in Milwaukee, WI.
Application information: For scholarship application information write to the Scholarship Program Coordinator.
Officers and Directors:* Jeffrey A. Joerres,* Pres.; Terry A. Hueneke,* V.P.; Michael Steinmetz,* V.P.; Michael J. Van Handel,* Secy.-Treas.
EIN: 396052810
Codes: CS, FD, CD, GTI

56716
Krause Family Foundation
(Formerly Charles A. Krause Foundation)
c/o Krause Consultants, Ltd.
700 N. Water St., Ste. 1246
Milwaukee, WI 53202-4206
Contact: Charles A. Krause III, Secy.-Treas.

Incorporated in 1952 in WI.
Financial data (yr. ended 12/31/01): Grants paid, $326,705; assets, $6,311,497 (M); expenditures, $395,499; qualifying distributions, $326,705.
Limitations: Giving limited to southeastern WI.
Application information: Employee-related scholarship program has been discontinued. Previous commitments honored; no new awards to individuals. Application form not required.
Officers and Directors:* Carol Krause Wythes,* Pres.; Eleanor T. Sullivan,* V.P.; Charles A. Krause III,* Secy.-Treas.; Victoria K. Mayer.
EIN: 396044820
Codes: FD

56717
Leo Potishman Foundation
c/o Bank One Trust Co., N.A.
P.O. Box 1308
Milwaukee, WI 53201
Application address: c/o Bank One, Texas, N.A., P.O. Box 2050, Fort Worth, TX 76113, tel.: (817) 884-4153
Contact: Lesley Atkinson

Established in 1983 in TX.
Financial data (yr. ended 06/30/01): Grants paid, $326,000; assets, $6,057,882 (M); expenditures, $360,625; qualifying distributions, $329,413.
Limitations: Giving primarily in TX.
Application information: Application form not required.
Trustee: Bank One Trust Co., N.A.
EIN: 756314202
Codes: FD

56718
Fort Atkinson Community Foundation
c/o Premier Bank
P.O. Box 218
Fort Atkinson, WI 53538

Established in 1974 in WI.
Financial data (yr. ended 06/30/01): Grants paid, $319,327; assets, $14,215,230 (M); gifts received, $8,528,314; expenditures, $381,892.
Limitations: Giving limited to the Fort Atkinson, WI, area.
Officers and Directors:* John McKenzie,* Pres.; James J. Vance, Secy.; Theodore Batterman, Leona Chadwick, Don V. Henning, Barbara Lorman.
Trustee: Premier Bank.
EIN: 396220899
Codes: CM, FD

56719
Weyers Family Foundation, Inc.
P.O. Box 12057
Green Bay, WI 54307

Established in 1997.
Donor(s): Ronald Weyers.
Financial data (yr. ended 12/31/99): Grants paid, $315,392; assets, $1,010,675 (M); gifts received, $259,625; expenditures, $333,023; qualifying distributions, $315,392.
Limitations: Applications not accepted.
Application information: Contributes only to pre-selected organizations.
Officer and Director:* Ronald Weyers,* Mgr.
EIN: 391901443

56720
Lutsey Family Foundation, Inc.
P.O. Box 22074
Green Bay, WI 54305-2074
Contact: T. Lutsey, Pres.

Established in 1989.
Donor(s): Thomas J. Lutsey.
Financial data (yr. ended 12/31/01): Grants paid, $314,098; assets, $4,359,141 (M); gifts received, $259,250; expenditures, $317,989; qualifying distributions, $316,404.
Limitations: Applications not accepted. Giving primarily in WI.
Application information: Unsolicited requests for funds not accepted.
Officer: Thomas J. Lutsey, Pres.
Directors: Charles N. Egan, Jr., Sharon L. Lutsey.
EIN: 391657029
Codes: FD

56721
Luther T. McCauley Charitable Trust
c/o Bank One Trust Co., N.A.
P.O. Box 1308
Milwaukee, WI 53201
Application address: Bank One, Colorado, N.A., Colorado Springs, CO 80942, tel.: (719) 227-6441

Established in 1978 in CO.
Financial data (yr. ended 04/30/01): Grants paid, $313,480; assets, $6,538,116 (M); expenditures, $343,368; qualifying distributions, $316,110.
Limitations: Giving limited to El Paso County, CO.
Publications: Application guidelines.
Application information: Application form not required.
Trustee: Bank One Trust Co., N.A.
EIN: 846152258
Codes: FD

56722
Gene & Ruth Posner Foundation, Inc.
152 W. Wisconsin Ave., Ste. 404
Milwaukee, WI 53203-2508 (414) 276-7440
FAX: (414) 276-8283
Contact: Gene Posner, Pres.

Established in 1963 in WI.
Donor(s): Gene Posner, Ruth Posner.
Financial data (yr. ended 12/31/00): Grants paid, $312,715; assets, $7,275,107 (M); expenditures, $387,019; qualifying distributions, $373,627.
Limitations: Giving primarily in Boca Raton, FL, and Milwaukee, WI.
Application information: Public charities receive 90 percent of disbursements, with remainder awarded to 501(c)(3) organizations. Application form not required.
Officer: Gene Posner, Pres. and Secy.
Directors: Fredric G. Posner, Barbara P. Ward.
EIN: 396050150
Codes: FD

56723
Frieda & William Hunt Memorial Trust
c/o Wayne Lueders
777 E. Wisconsin Ave., Ste. 3500
Milwaukee, WI 53202-5302 (414) 297-5786

Established in 1988 in WI.
Donor(s): Frieda E. Hunt.‡
Financial data (yr. ended 12/31/01): Grants paid, $311,100; assets, $6,647,543 (M); expenditures, $387,538; qualifying distributions, $353,967.
Limitations: Applications not accepted. Giving primarily in Milwaukee, WI.
Application information: Contributes only to pre-selected organizations.
Trustees: Wayne R. Lueders, John T. Seaman, Jr., John T. Seaman III, Patricia G. Seaman.
EIN: 391642918
Codes: FD

56724
Hattie Hannah Keeney Trust
c/o Bank One Trust Co., N.A.
P.O. Box 1308
Milwaukee, WI 53201

Established in 1950 in IL.
Donor(s): Hattie Hannah Keeney.‡
Financial data (yr. ended 12/31/01): Grants paid, $308,785; assets, $4,190,525 (M); expenditures, $393,633; qualifying distributions, $319,500.
Limitations: Applications not accepted. Giving primarily in the Traverse City, MI, area.
Application information: Contributes only to pre-selected organizations.
Trustee: Bank One Trust Co., N.A.
EIN: 366016171

Codes: FD

56725
Irvin L. Young Foundation, Inc.
15535 St. Therese Blvd.
Brookfield, WI 53005 (262) 495-2485
Contact: David S. Fisher, Pres.

Incorporated in 1949 in WI.
Donor(s): Irvin L. Young,‡ Fern D. Young,‡ David S. Fisher.
Financial data (yr. ended 12/31/01): Grants paid, $308,500; assets, $2,888,728 (M); expenditures, $347,449; qualifying distributions, $308,500.
Limitations: Giving primarily in Africa.
Application information: Application form not required.
Officers and Directors:* David S. Fisher,* Pres.; David Voetman,* V.P.; Robert W. Reninger,* Secy.; Bonnie E. Fisher,* Treas.; L. Arden Almquist, Mary Longbrake, Mitchell J. Simon.
EIN: 366077858
Codes: FD

56726
The Markos Foundation, Inc.
c/o Stephanie Mott, Reinhart, Boerner, Van Deuren
P.O. Box 2020, 22 E. Mifflin St., Ste. 600
Madison, WI 53701-2020

Established in 1995 in WI.
Donor(s): Dennis A. Markos.
Financial data (yr. ended 06/30/01): Grants paid, $306,750; assets, $3,099,017 (M); gifts received, $163,450; expenditures, $347,134; qualifying distributions, $315,677.
Limitations: Applications not accepted. Giving primarily in IL, IN, and WI.
Application information: Contributes only to pre-selected organizations.
Officers and Directors:* Dennis A. Markos,* Pres.; Carol J. Markos,* V.P. and Secy.-Treas.; William F. Conlon, James Lorimer, Kenneth Slattery.
Manager: Kay Erickson.
EIN: 391836400
Codes: FD

56727
Karl Junginger Foundation, Inc.
P.O. Box 127
Waterloo, WI 53594-0127 (920) 478-2101

Established in 1988 in WI.
Donor(s): Karl Junginger.‡
Financial data (yr. ended 12/31/01): Grants paid, $305,982; assets, $2,529,145 (M); expenditures, $324,921; qualifying distributions, $304,706.
Limitations: Giving primarily in Waterloo, WI.
Application information: Application form required.
Officers: Gus Harms, Pres. and Treas.; Bill Jensen, V.P.; Tim Jonas, V.P.
EIN: 391602319
Codes: FD

56728
K. C. Stock Foundation, Inc.
P.O. Box 19041
3110 Market St.
Green Bay, WI 54307-9041 (920) 337-1660
Contact: Steven Stock, Secy.-Treas.

Established in 1990 in WI.
Donor(s): Kenneth C. Stock, Georgia L. Stock.
Financial data (yr. ended 12/31/01): Grants paid, $305,649; assets, $6,168,477 (M); expenditures, $384,724; qualifying distributions, $301,762.
Limitations: Giving primarily in WI.
Application information: Application form not required.
Officers: Kenneth C. Stock, Pres.; Georgia L. Stock, V.P.; Steven Stock, Secy.-Treas.
EIN: 391688221
Codes: FD

56729
The Four-Four Foundation, Inc.
c/o Provident Investors
N27W23957 Paul Rd.
Pewaukee, WI 53072
Contact: Sally S. Manegold, Pres.

Established in 1994 in WI.
Financial data (yr. ended 12/31/01): Grants paid, $304,000; assets, $13,351,228 (M); gifts received, $6,074,130; expenditures, $351,898; qualifying distributions, $303,964.
Limitations: Applications not accepted. Giving primarily in Milwaukee, WI.
Application information: Contributes only to pre-selected organizations. Unsolicited requests for funds not accepted.
Officers and Directors:* Sally S. Manegold,* Pres.; Lynee M. Rix, Secy.; Robert L. Manegold,* Treas.; Katherine M. Biersach, Joan M. Dukes, Robert H. Manegold.
EIN: 391867243
Codes: FD

56730
Albert A. Christ Scholarships
c/o Bank One Trust Co., N.A.
PO. Box 1308
Milwaukee, WI 53201
Application address: c/o Bank One, West Virginia, N.A., 1114 Market St., Wheeling, WV 26003
Contact: Ed Johnson

Established in 1995 in WV.
Donor(s): Helen Christ.‡
Financial data (yr. ended 06/30/01): Grants paid, $299,470; assets, $5,468,906 (M); expenditures, $363,944; qualifying distributions, $314,676.
Limitations: Giving limited to residents of Wheeling, WV.
Application information: Application form not required.
Trustee: Bank One Trust Co., N.A.
EIN: 556129775
Codes: FD, GTI

56731
West Bend Mutal Charitable Trust
1900 S. 18th Ave.
West Bend, WI 53095
Contact: John R. Dedrick, Tr.

Established in 1995 in WI.
Financial data (yr. ended 12/31/00): Grants paid, $299,200; assets, $6,111,505 (M); expenditures, $314,682; qualifying distributions, $284,463.
Limitations: Giving primarily in WI, with emphasis on West Bend.
Application information: Application form not required.
Trustees: John R. Dedrick, John F. Duwell, James J. Pauly, Larry G. Roth, Sharon S. Ziegler.
EIN: 396591551
Codes: FD

56732
Purple Moon Foundation, Inc.
715 S. Few St.
Madison, WI 53703

Established in 1999 in WI.
Donor(s): Dale Leibowitz.
Financial data (yr. ended 12/31/00): Grants paid, $298,622; assets, $1,065,526 (M); gifts received, $146,798; expenditures, $217,679; qualifying distributions, $308,688.
Limitations: Applications not accepted. Giving primarily in WI.
Application information: Contributes only to pre-selected organizations.
Officers and Director:* Dale Leibowitz, Pres.; Gillian Blake,* V.P.; Sheri Kole, Secy.-Treas.
EIN: 391975376
Codes: FD

56733
Rexnord Foundation Inc.
P.O. Box 2191
Milwaukee, WI 53201-2191 (414) 643-3000
Application address: c/o Scholarship Admin., Rexnord Corp., 4701 W. Greenfield Ave., Milwaukee, WI 53214, tel.: (414) 643-2505

Incorporated in 1953 in WI.
Donor(s): Rexnord Corp.
Financial data (yr. ended 10/31/01): Grants paid, $297,720; assets, $3,983,863 (M); gifts received, $100,000; expenditures, $314,203; qualifying distributions, $298,751.
Limitations: Giving primarily in areas of company operations, with some emphasis on Milwaukee, WI.
Publications: Application guidelines.
Application information: Application form not required.
Officers and Directors:* C.R. Roy,* Pres. and Treas.; J.R. Swenson,* V.P. and Secy.; P.C. Wallace,* V.P.; R.M. MacQueen, W.E. Schauer, Donald Taylor, R.R. Wallis.
EIN: 396042029
Codes: CS, FD, CD, GTI

56734
Oliver W. Storer Scholarship Foundation
c/o Bank One Trust Co., N.A.
P.O. Box 130
Milwaukee, WI 53202
Application address: c/o Charles E. Retherford, Beasley, Glickison, Retherford & Buckles, 110 E. Charles St., Muncie, IN 47305, tel.: (765) 289-0661

Established in 1952 in IN.
Donor(s): Oliver W. Storer.‡
Financial data (yr. ended 02/28/01): Grants paid, $296,165; assets, $6,174,687 (M); expenditures, $371,015; qualifying distributions, $315,178.
Limitations: Giving limited to Delaware County, IN, residents.
Application information: Application form required.
Trustee: Bank One Trust Co., N.A.
EIN: 356012044
Codes: FD, GTI

56735
Ziemann Foundation, Inc.
830 Armour Rd., No. 8
Oconomowoc, WI 53066
Contact: Cindy Linnan, V.P.

Established in 1963 in WI.
Donor(s): Lillian Ziemann,‡ H.J. Ziemann,‡ Mrs. H.J. Ziemann.‡
Financial data (yr. ended 12/31/01): Grants paid, $293,725; assets, $3,074,533 (M); expenditures, $330,407; qualifying distributions, $303,782.
Limitations: Giving primarily in WI.
Publications: Program policy statement, application guidelines.
Application information: Accepts Milwaukee Area Common Grant Application Form (Donor's

56735—WISCONSIN

Forum). Applications received between Sept. 30 and Dec. 31 will not be reviewed. Application form required.
Officers and Directors:* Carolyn Wright,* Pres.; Cynthia Linnan,* V.P. and Treas.; Michael R. Smith,* Secy.; Elizabeth Boemer, Kristie R. Malone.
EIN: 396069677
Codes: FD

56736
Philip Rubenstein Foundation, Inc.
c/o Komisar Brady and Co., LLP
633 W. Wisconsin Ave., Ste. 700
Milwaukee, WI 53208-1918
Application address: 400 W. Boden St., Milwaukee, WI 53207
Contact: Herbert Rubenstein, Pres.

Established in 1978 in WI.
Donor(s): Philip Rubenstein,‡ Associated Sales & Bag Co., Inc.
Financial data (yr. ended 01/31/01): Grants paid, $292,234; assets, $3,071,775 (M); expenditures, $358,827; qualifying distributions, $299,196.
Limitations: Giving primarily in Milwaukee, WI.
Application information: Application form not required.
Officers and Directors:* Herbert Rubenstein,* Pres.; Beth Rubenstein,* V.P. and Secy.; William L. Komisar,* Treas.
EIN: 930757026
Codes: FD

56737
Hesta Stuart Christian Charitable Trust
c/o Bank One Trust Co., N.A.
P.O. Box 1308
Milwaukee, WI 53201
Application address: c/o Robert Lansford, Bank One, Texas, N.A., P.O. Box 2050, Fort Worth, TX 76113, tel. (817) 884-4151

Established in 1973 in TX.
Financial data (yr. ended 06/30/01): Grants paid, $285,968; assets, $5,707,868 (M); expenditures, $395,043; qualifying distributions, $315,470.
Limitations: Giving primarily in TX.
Application information: Application form not required.
Trustee: Bank One Trust Co., N.A.
EIN: 756177306
Codes: FD

56738
Frank L. Weyenberg Charitable Trust
c/o Quarles & Brady
411 E. Wisconsin Ave.
Milwaukee, WI 53202 (414) 277-5000
Contact: Henry J. Loos, Tr.

Established in 1983 in WI.
Financial data (yr. ended 07/31/02): Grants paid, $285,000; assets, $4,595,458 (M); expenditures, $312,524; qualifying distributions, $306,558.
Limitations: Applications not accepted. Giving on a national basis.
Application information: Contributes only to pre-selected organizations.
Trustees: Henry J. Loos, First National in Palm Beach.
EIN: 391461670
Codes: FD

56739
The Wanek-Vogel Foundation, Ltd.
c/o Ashley Furniture Industries, Inc.
1 Ashley Way
Arcadia, WI 54612-1218 (608) 323-6249
Contact: Paulette Rippley

Financial data (yr. ended 12/31/99): Grants paid, $281,683; assets, $17,143 (M); expenditures, $289,224; qualifying distributions, $281,658.
Limitations: Giving on a national basis.
Directors: Benjamin Charles Vogel, Charles H.E. Vogel, Ronald G. Wanek, Todd R. Wanek.
EIN: 391948289

56740
Archie & Viola Meinerz Family Foundation, Inc.
4525 W. Oakwood Rd.
Franklin, WI 53132

Established in 1992 in WI.
Donor(s): Viola Meinerz.
Financial data (yr. ended 12/31/00): Grants paid, $281,500; assets, $5,576,089 (M); expenditures, $302,713; qualifying distributions, $275,901.
Limitations: Applications not accepted. Giving primarily in WI.
Application information: Contributes only to pre-selected organizations.
Officers and Directors:* Viola Meinerz,* Pres. and Treas.; Leigh Peterson,* V.P.; William F. Fox,* Secy.
EIN: 391713840
Codes: FD

56741
Gertrude S. Gordon Foundation
c/o North Central Trust Co.
311 Main St.
La Crosse, WI 54601

Financial data (yr. ended 12/31/01): Grants paid, $279,059; assets, $9,721,332 (M); expenditures, $341,472; qualifying distributions, $279,559.
Limitations: Applications not accepted. Giving primarily in La Crosse, WI.
Application information: Contributes only to pre-selected organizations.
Trustee: North Central Trust Co.
EIN: 316672080
Codes: FD

56742
Stella H. Jones Foundation
c/o J. Lewis Perlson
100 E. Wisconsin Ave., Ste. 3300
Milwaukee, WI 53202-4108 (414) 271-6560

Established in 1997 in WI.
Donor(s): Jones Living Trust.
Financial data (yr. ended 12/31/01): Grants paid, $277,750; assets, $3,868,152 (M); expenditures, $373,791; qualifying distributions, $312,127.
Limitations: Applications not accepted. Giving primarily in Milwaukee, WI.
Application information: Contributes only to pre-selected organizations.
Trustees: Carol A. Bourne, Richard B. Bourne, Arthur F. Jeske, J. Lewis Perlson.
EIN: 396630656
Codes: FD

56743
Joseph J. and Vera Zilber Family Foundation, Inc.
(Formerly Joseph J. Zilber Family Foundation, Inc.)
710 N. Plankinton Ave., Ste. 1200
Milwaukee, WI 53203-2404
Contact: Stephan J. Chevalier, Treas.

Established in 1962.
Donor(s): Joseph J. Zilber, Vera J. Zilber.
Financial data (yr. ended 06/30/01): Grants paid, $272,724; assets, $7,177,076 (M); gifts received, $740,127; expenditures, $294,441; qualifying distributions, $272,724.
Limitations: Giving primarily in WI.
Officers and Directors:* Joseph J. Zilber,* Pres.; Vera J. Zilber,* V.P.; James F. Janz,* Secy.; Stephan J. Chevalier,* Treas.; Melissa S.A. Jackson, Shane M. Jackson, John W. Kersey, Gerald M. Stein, Marilyn Zilber, Marcy Zilber-Jackson.
EIN: 396077241
Codes: FD

56744
William M. Keller Trust
c/o Bank One Trust Co., N.A.
P.O. Box 1308
Milwaukee, WI 53201
Application address: c/o Jerry lathrop, 111 Monument Cir., IN1-0175, Indianapolis IN 46277

Established in 1995.
Financial data (yr. ended 12/31/01): Grants paid, $272,000; assets, $4,585,249 (M); expenditures, $321,893; qualifying distributions, $294,402.
Limitations: Giving limited to graduating high school students residing in Bartholomew County, IN.
Publications: Application guidelines.
Application information: Application form required.
Trustee: Bank One Trust Co., N.A.
EIN: 351035651
Codes: FD

56745
DeAtley Family Foundation, Inc.
c/o William B. DeAtley
1440 County Rd.
Mount Horeb, WI 53572

Established in 1997.
Donor(s): William B. DeAtley.
Financial data (yr. ended 12/31/01): Grants paid, $272,000; assets, $2,630,943 (M); expenditures, $275,540; qualifying distributions, $272,000.
Limitations: Applications not accepted. Giving on a national basis.
Application information: Contributes only to pre-selected organizations.
Officers: William B. DeAtley, Chair. and Treas.; Janine B. DeAtley, Secy.
Trustees: Brantner M. DeAtley, Leesa D. Schlimgen.
EIN: 061496358
Codes: FD

56746
Quixote Foundation, Inc.
c/o Erik M. Hanisch
5018 Milward Dr.
Madison, WI 53711-1109

Established in 1998 in WI.
Donor(s): Arthur S. Hanisch.
Financial data (yr. ended 12/31/01): Grants paid, $269,326; assets, $7,627,060 (M); gifts received, $2,532,482; expenditures, $427,437; qualifying distributions, $284,703.

Limitations: Applications not accepted. Giving primarily in WI.
Application information: Contributes only to pre-selected organizations.
Officers: Erik M. Hanisch, Chair. and Pres.; Richard J. Langer, V.P.; Martha Vukelich-Austin, Secy.-Treas.
Directors: Martha V. Austin, Richard J. Lauger, Paul R. Soglin.
EIN: 391916960
Codes: FD

56747
The JKO Foundation Charitable Trust
c/o Mr. & Mrs. Kenneth Ozinga
1858 Strawberry Point Dr.
Minocqua, WI 54548

Established in 1999 in IL.
Donor(s): Kenneth J. Zinga, Judith A. Zinga.
Financial data (yr. ended 12/31/01): Grants paid, $267,500; assets, $893,997 (M); gifts received, $186,570; expenditures, $323,646; qualifying distributions, $267,500.
Limitations: Applications not accepted. Giving primarily in Washington, DC and IL.
Application information: Contributes only to pre-selected organizations.
Trustees: Charles J. Ozinga, Judith A. Ozinga, Kenneth J. Ozinga.
EIN: 367293190
Codes: FD

56748
Karen J. Glanert Charitable Trust
c/o U.S. Bank
P.O. Box 3194
Milwaukee, WI 53201-3194
Contact: Karen J. Glanert, Tr.

Established in 1998 in WI.
Donor(s): Karen J. Glanert.
Financial data (yr. ended 12/31/01): Grants paid, $265,000; assets, $4,828,553 (M); expenditures, $275,069; qualifying distributions, $264,998.
Limitations: Giving primarily in FL and WI.
Application information: Application form not required.
Trustees: Jennifer G. Callahan, Karen J. Glanert, Paul R. Glanert.
EIN: 396695585
Codes: FD

56749
Marshfield Area Community Foundation
P.O. Box 456
Marshfield, WI 54449 (715) 384-9029
FAX: (715) 384-9029; *E-mail:* macf@tznet.com
Contact: Dean Markwardt, Exec. Dir.

Established in 1993 in WI.
Donor(s): Harry Chronquist,‡ Gladys Chronquist,‡ G. Stanley Custer,‡ Violet Custer,‡ Leonard L. Hartl,‡ Margaret Quirt Heck,‡ Melvin A. Hintz,‡ Laverne R. Kohs,‡ Patrice Legrand,‡ J.P. Leonard,‡ George Mackinnon,‡ and 15 additional donors.
Financial data (yr. ended 12/31/01): Grants paid, $262,628; assets, $1,801,612 (M); gifts received, $423,464; expenditures, $305,828.
Limitations: Giving limited to Marshfield, WI and surrounding areas.
Publications: Annual report, financial statement, grants list, informational brochure (including application guidelines).
Application information: Application form required.
Officers: Gregg Cleveland, Chair.; Carl Meissner, Chair., Allocations; John Bujalski, Chair., Development; James Bartelt, Chair., Investments;

Connie Willfahrt, Chair., Promotions; Dennis DeVetter, Vice-Chair.
Trustees: Anne Adler, Elizabeth Adler, Pat Anderson, Michelle Boernke, Georgette Frazer, Deborah Janz, Steve Johnson, Rev. Dean Pingle, Terri Richards, Aaron Staab, Jane Wagner.
EIN: 396578767
Codes: CM

56750
Sophie Yoerg Schroeder 1989 Charitable Trust
c/o Foley & Lardner
777 E. Wisconsin Ave.
Milwaukee, WI 53202 (414) 297-5786
Contact: Wayne Lueders

Established in 1989 in WI; funded in 1993.
Financial data (yr. ended 12/31/00): Grants paid, $262,500; assets, $3,493,326 (M); expenditures, $286,685; qualifying distributions, $265,509.
Limitations: Giving primarily in southeastern WI.
Application information: Application form not required.
Trustees: Robinson W. Bosworth III, Orin Purintun.
EIN: 396556548
Codes: FD

56751
The Steve J. Miller Foundation
1000 N. Water St., 13th Fl.
Milwaukee, WI 53202 (414) 287-7184
Contact: Thomas N. Tuttle, Jr., Secy.-Treas.

Trust established about 1946 in WI.
Donor(s): Steve J. Miller,‡ Central Cheese Co., Inc.
Financial data (yr. ended 12/31/01): Grants paid, $261,200; assets, $4,539,026 (M); expenditures, $306,563; qualifying distributions, $259,907.
Application information: Application form required.
Officers: Norman C. Miller, Pres.; Thomas N. Tuttle, Jr., Secy.-Treas.
Directors: Theodore W. Miller, Kurt Spreyer.
EIN: 396051879
Codes: FD

56752
Jack DeLoss Taylor Charitable Trust
c/o Buttonwood Partners, Inc.
8001 Excelsior Dr.
Madison, WI 53717-1956 (608) 827-6400
FAX: (608) 827-6407
Contact: Christopher Bugg, Tr.

Established in 1989 in WI.
Financial data (yr. ended 06/30/01): Grants paid, $261,000; assets, $6,380,290 (M); expenditures, $331,581; qualifying distributions, $284,928.
Limitations: Giving in the U.S., with some emphasis on WI, and in underdeveloped and developing countries.
Application information: Application form not required.
Trustees: Christopher Bugg, Lyle Larson, Catherine H. Taylor.
EIN: 396510710
Codes: FD

56753
The Gladys Ness-Brang Foundation
c/o Bank One Trust Co., N.A.
P.O. Box 1308
Milwaukee, WI 53201
Application address: c/o Walter Larson, 28857 Lake Lina Ln., Glenwood, MN 56334
Elementary School Incentive Awards: c/o Principal of Starbuck Elementary School, Starbuck, MN 56381; Dollars for Scholars: c/o Arne Pederson, Rt. 1, Box 113A, Starbuck, MN 56381

Established in 1998 in WI.
Donor(s): Gladys Ness-Brang.
Financial data (yr. ended 07/31/01): Grants paid, $259,528; assets, $2,326,679 (M); gifts received, $275; expenditures, $287,256; qualifying distributions, $270,346.
Limitations: Giving primarily in MN.
Trustees: Shirley Anderson, Ruth Brenden, F.D. Bucher, Thomas Bueckens, Walter Larson, David N. Ness, Arnold Pederson, Matthew Pederson, Mark Thompson, Bank One Trust Co., N.A.
EIN: 396696569
Codes: FD

56754
A. J. & M. D. Ruggiero Memorial Trust
c/o Bank One Trust Co.
P.O. Box 1308
Milwaukee, WI 53201

Established in 1995 in AZ.
Financial data (yr. ended 12/31/00): Grants paid, $258,069; assets, $7,142,988 (M); gifts received, $1,089,579; expenditures, $307,608; qualifying distributions, $270,257.
Limitations: Applications not accepted. Giving primarily in Tucson, AZ.
Application information: Contributes only to pre-selected organizations.
Trustee: Bank One, Trust Co.
EIN: 866240840
Codes: FD

56755
PPC Foundation
(Formerly Pieperpower Foundation, Inc.)
5070 N. 35th St.
Milwaukee, WI 53209-5302 (414) 462-7700
FAX: (414) 462-3589
Contact: Barb Jones, Exec. Asst.

Established in 1968.
Donor(s): Pieper Electric, Inc.
Financial data (yr. ended 12/31/01): Grants paid, $255,433; assets, $0 (M); gifts received, $151,204; expenditures, $255,525; qualifying distributions, $255,525.
Limitations: Giving primarily in Milwaukee, WI.
Application information: Application form not required.
Officers: Ronnie Hinson, Pres.; Richard Pieper, Sr., Secy.; Thomas Ohlgart, Treas.
EIN: 396124770
Codes: CS, FD, CD

56756
The Herma Family Foundation
1260 Overhill Rd.
Elm Grove, WI 53122

Established in 1993 in WI.
Financial data (yr. ended 12/31/01): Grants paid, $254,785; assets, $12,606,551 (M); expenditures, $272,480; qualifying distributions, $256,935.
Limitations: Applications not accepted.
Application information: Contributes only to pre-selected organizations.

56756—WISCONSIN

Officers and Directors:* John E. Herma,* Pres. and Treas.; Susan M. Herma,* V.P. and Secy.; Peter M. Sommerhauser.
EIN: 391776108
Codes: FD

56757
Ruth and Pat Crawford Family Foundation, Inc.
Old Keshena Rd., N5873
Shawano, WI 54166
Application address: 67 Thistle Down, Appleton, WI 54915
Contact: Kathryn Schuh, Tr.

Established in 1997 in WI.
Donor(s): Patrick J. Crawford, Ruth A. Crawford.
Financial data (yr. ended 12/31/00): Grants paid, $251,125; assets, $1,208,782 (M); gifts received, $909,814; expenditures, $261,361; qualifying distributions, $252,904.
Limitations: Giving limited to northeastern WI.
Trustees: Elizabeth M. Crawford, Kenneth J. Crawford, Michael J. Crawford, Patrick J. Crawford, Patrick L. Crawford, Ruth A. Crawford, Samuel J. Crawford, Cynthia A. Jesse, Katheryn D. Schuh, Mary E. Tree.
EIN: 391867905
Codes: FD

56758
Boerner Botanical Gardens and Arboretum Foundation
c/o Bank One Trust Co., N.A.
P.O. Box 1308
Milwaukee, WI 53201

Established in 1997 in WI.
Financial data (yr. ended 02/28/01): Grants paid, $250,000; assets, $694,182 (M); expenditures, $257,589; qualifying distributions, $251,800.
Limitations: Applications not accepted. Giving primarily in WI.
Application information: Contributes only to pre-selected organizations.
Trustees: Roger L. Boerner, Bank One Trust Co., N.A.
EIN: 396642435

56759
J. L. French Family Foundation, Inc.
P.O. Box 1291
Sheboygan, WI 53082-1291
Contact: Paula French Van Akkeren, Treas.

Established in 1986 in WI.
Donor(s): J.L. French Corp.
Financial data (yr. ended 07/31/01): Grants paid, $249,469; assets, $1,239,853 (M); gifts received, $726,000; expenditures, $260,219; qualifying distributions, $248,584.
Limitations: Giving primarily in Sheboygan County, WI.
Officers and Directors:* James L. French,* Pres.; Brian J. French,* V.P.; David French,* V.P.; Jeanna L. French,* Secy.; Paula French Van Akkeren,* Treas.
EIN: 391560736
Codes: FD

56760
J.P.C. Foundation
c/o William B. Vogt
P.O. Box 1148
Janesville, WI 53547-1148

Established in 1991 in WI.
Donor(s): J.P. Cullen & Sons, Inc., John P. Cullen.
Financial data (yr. ended 05/31/01): Grants paid, $248,938; assets, $1,940,209 (M); gifts received, $100,000; expenditures, $263,173; qualifying distributions, $247,445.

Limitations: Applications not accepted. Giving limited to Platteville, WI.
Application information: Contributes only to pre-selected organizations.
Trustees: John P. Cullen, Mark A. Cullen.
EIN: 391703739
Codes: CS, FD, CD

56761
Nelson G. and Vera C. Hicks Charitable Foundation
c/o Bank One Trust Co., N.A.
P.O. Box 1308
Milwaukee, WI 53201
Application address: 18 W. Jefferson St., Waupin, WI 53963-1939
Contact: John Karsten, V.P.

Financial data (yr. ended 12/31/00): Grants paid, $246,000; assets, $4,590,551 (M); gifts received, $13,888; expenditures, $298,373; qualifying distributions, $246,267.
Limitations: Giving primarily in Beaver Dam, WI.
Officers: Robert H. Keller, Pres.; John Karsten, V.P. and Secy.; W.E. Kinney, Treas.
EIN: 391582654
Codes: FD2

56762
Robert A. Uihlein Foundation
735 N. Water St., Ste. 712
Milwaukee, WI 53202-4104

Established in 1942 in WI.
Donor(s): Robert A. Uihlein III, James J. Uihlein.
Financial data (yr. ended 12/31/00): Grants paid, $244,300; assets, $4,346,795 (M); expenditures, $257,768; qualifying distributions, $243,227.
Limitations: Applications not accepted. Giving primarily in Milwaukee, WI.
Application information: Contributes only to pre-selected organizations.
Officers and Directors:* Lorraine G. Uihlein,* Pres.; Thomas F. Lechner,* V.P. and Secy.-Treas.
EIN: 396033236
Codes: FD2

56763
RDK Foundation
c/o U.S. Bank
P.O. Box 2043, LC 4NE
Milwaukee, WI 53201-9116
Application address: c/o U.S. Bank, P.O. Box 2054, Milwaukee, WI 53201, tel.: (414) 765-5044
Contact: Robert Archer

Established in 1984 in WI.
Donor(s): Ruth DeYoung Kohler.
Financial data (yr. ended 06/30/01): Grants paid, $243,187; assets, $5,674,494 (M); gifts received, $250,000; expenditures, $309,064; qualifying distributions, $268,555.
Limitations: Giving primarily in Sheboygan, WI.
Trustees: Ruth DeYoung Kohler, U.S. Bank.
EIN: 391524311
Codes: FD2

56764
Cops Foundation, Inc.
c/o Associated Banc-Corp
P.O. Box 408
Neenah, WI 54957-0408

Established in 1988 in WI.
Donor(s): Henry P. Cops,‡ James G. Cops,‡ Joyce Cops, Thomas P. Cops.‡
Financial data (yr. ended 12/31/01): Grants paid, $242,196; assets, $1,289,418 (M); gifts received, $418,748; expenditures, $254,708; qualifying distributions, $241,672.

Limitations: Applications not accepted.
Application information: Unsolicited requests for funds not accepted.
Trustee: Associated Banc-Corp.
EIN: 391633247
Codes: FD2

56765
Corley B. McFarland Trust
c/o Bank One Trust, N.A.
P.O. Box 1308
Milwaukee, WI 53201-1308
Contact: Cecile Sant Angelo, Trust Off., Bank One Trust Co., N.A.

Established in 1984 in IL.
Financial data (yr. ended 06/30/01): Grants paid, $241,890; assets, $4,912,494 (M); expenditures, $278,181; qualifying distributions, $249,246.
Limitations: Applications not accepted. Giving primarily in IN and ND.
Application information: Contributes only to pre-selected organizations.
Trustee: Bank One Trust Co., N.A.
EIN: 363311913
Codes: FD2

56766
Cremer Foundation, Inc.
P.O. Box 2980
Milwaukee, WI 53201
Application address: P.O. Box 1, Madison, WI 53701, tel.: (608) 837-5166
Contact: James Berkenstadt, Dir.

Established in 1965 in WI.
Financial data (yr. ended 12/31/01): Grants paid, $240,680; assets, $3,549,126 (M); expenditures, $265,433; qualifying distributions, $240,006.
Limitations: Giving primarily in the Madison, WI, area.
Publications: Application guidelines.
Application information: Application form not required.
Officers: Frances H. Cremer, Pres.; Robert R. Stroud, V.P.; Helen A. George, Secy.; Holly L. Cremer, Treas.
Directors: James A. Berkenstadt, James T. Sykes.
EIN: 396086822
Codes: FD2

56767
Ripples, Inc.
P.O. Box 128
Townsend, WI 54175-0128

Established in 1999.
Financial data (yr. ended 12/31/00): Grants paid, $240,000; assets, $4,416,147 (M); expenditures, $274,526; qualifying distributions, $238,486.
Limitations: Applications not accepted. Giving primarily in FL and WI.
Application information: Contributes only to pre-selected organizations.
Officers: Harold Petraske, Pres. and Treas.; Gretchen Petraske, V.P. and Secy.
Director: Debra Sadow Koenig.
EIN: 391938912
Codes: FD2

56768
Theda Clark Smith Family Foundation, Inc.
c/o Associated Banc-Corp
100 W. Wisconsin Ave.
Neenah, WI 54956 (920) 236-8175
Application address: c/o Associated Banc-Corp, P.O. Box 408, Neenah, WI 54957-0408
Contact: Tim Hazeltine

Established in 1968 in WI.
Donor(s): Clark R. Smith, Theda Clark Smith.‡

Financial data (yr. ended 12/31/01): Grants paid, $240,000; assets, $3,364,808 (M); gifts received, $10,000; expenditures, $310,000; qualifying distributions, $240,000.
Limitations: Giving primarily in WI.
Application information: Application form not required.
Officers: Clark R. Smith, Chair.; Sylvia Vaccaro, Pres.; Peter Radford, Sr. V.P.; Marc Vaccaro, Secy.; C. Carlton Smith, Treas.
Trustee: Associated Banc-Corp.
EIN: 396125329
Codes: FD2

56769
Baye Foundation, Inc.
4762 N. Cumberland Blvd.
Milwaukee, WI 53211
FAX: (414) 332-2915; *E-mail:* GLW@mixcom.com
Contact: Joan B. Peter, V.P.

Established about 1953.
Donor(s): Sam Stahl,‡ Nathan L. Berkowitz, Pearl S. Berkowitz, Muriel Stahl.
Financial data (yr. ended 12/31/99): Grants paid, $237,675; assets, $3,041,240 (M); gifts received, $530,694; expenditures, $249,792; qualifying distributions, $237,675.
Limitations: Applications not accepted. Giving primarily in Milwaukee, WI.
Application information: Contributes only to pre-selected organizations.
Officers: Nathan L. Berkowitz, Pres.; Joan B. Peter, V.P.; Susan B. Silverstein, Secy.; Pearl S. Berkowitz, Treas.
EIN: 396040573

56770
William G. and Myrtle E. Hess Charitable Trust
c/o Bank One Trust Co., N.A.
P.O. Box 1308
Milwaukee, WI 53201
Application address: 1116 W. Long Lake Rd., Bloomfield Hills, MI 48302, tel.: (248) 645-7360
Contact: Lydia Vaughan, Tr. Off., Bank One Trust Co., N.A.

Established in 1969 in MI.
Donor(s): William Hess,‡ Myrtle Hess.‡
Financial data (yr. ended 12/31/01): Grants paid, $233,332; assets, $3,735,605 (M); expenditures, $263,007; qualifying distributions, $233,345.
Limitations: Giving limited to Oakland County, MI.
Application information: Application form not required.
Trustee: Bank One Trust Co., N.A.
EIN: 386166831
Codes: FD2

56771
Edward Rutledge Charity
P.O. Box 758
Chippewa Falls, WI 54729 (715) 723-6618
Contact: Betty Manning

Incorporated in 1911 in WI.
Donor(s): Edward Rutledge.‡
Financial data (yr. ended 05/31/01): Grants paid, $231,698; assets, $5,615,842 (M); gifts received, $352; expenditures, $307,221; qualifying distributions, $284,066; giving activities include $5,259 for loans to individuals.
Limitations: Giving limited to Chippewa County, WI.
Application information: Application form required for scholarships and other grants to individuals.

Officers and Directors:* Gerald J. Naiberg,* Pres.; Richard H. Stafford,* V.P.; David Hancock,* Secy.-Treas.
EIN: 390806178
Codes: FD2, GTI

56772
Wesley Luehring Foundation
c/o Bank One Trust Co., N.A.
P.O. Box 1308
Milwaukee, WI 53201
Application address: c/o Bank One Trust Co., N.A., Bank One Plz., Chicago, IL 60670-2068

Established in 1989 in IL.
Donor(s): Marian D. Luehring Trust.
Financial data (yr. ended 12/31/01): Grants paid, $231,000; assets, $4,663,292 (M); gifts received, $121; expenditures, $269,300; qualifying distributions, $239,887.
Limitations: Giving primarily in IL.
Officers: Gary E. Crocus, Pres.; Janice G. Franzen, Secy.; Michael Celer, Treas.
Directors: Elsie Doering, Ruth E. Luehring, Janet H. Patterson.
Trustee: Bank One, N.A.
EIN: 363616086
Codes: FD2

56773
Victor F. Braun Foundation, Inc.
W. 1781 Washington Rd.
Oconomowoc, WI 53066

Established in 1956 in WI.
Donor(s): Victor F. Braun.‡
Financial data (yr. ended 11/30/01): Grants paid, $230,000; assets, $4,954,483 (M); expenditures, $234,488; qualifying distributions, $229,451.
Limitations: Applications not accepted. Giving primarily in TX and WI.
Application information: Contributes only to pre-selected organizations.
Officers and Directors:* Cole M. Braun, Pres.; Jeffrey V. Braun,* V.P.; Jennifer Braun,* Secy.; Diane Braun,* Treas.
EIN: 396043684
Codes: FD2

56774
Schneider National Foundation, Inc.
P.O. Box 2545
Green Bay, WI 54306-2545
Contact: Donald J. Schneider, Pres.

Established in 1983.
Donor(s): Schneider National, Inc.
Financial data (yr. ended 12/31/00): Grants paid, $229,450; assets, $82,004 (M); gifts received, $208,982; expenditures, $229,450; qualifying distributions, $229,450.
Limitations: Giving primarily in WI.
Application information: Application form not required.
Officers: Donald J. Schneider, Pres.; Thomas A. Gannon, Secy.-Treas.
EIN: 391457870
Codes: CS, FD2, CD

56775
Caroline S. Mark Foundation, Inc.
813 2nd St.
Wausau, WI 54401 (715) 845-9287
Contact: Sandra S. Robarge, Secy.-Treas.

Established in 1991 in WI.
Donor(s): Caroline S. Mark.
Financial data (yr. ended 03/31/02): Grants paid, $228,500; assets, $481,570 (M); expenditures, $229,626; qualifying distributions, $228,500.

Limitations: Giving primarily in Marathon County, WI.
Application information: Application form required.
Officers and Directors:* Caroline S. Mark,* Pres.; Sandra S. Robarge,* Secy.-Treas.
EIN: 391715367

56776
Wauwatosa Savings Bank Foundation
(Formerly Wauwatosa Savings and Loan Foundation)
2655 Woodhill Ct.
Brookfield, WI 53005
Application address: 7500 W. State St., Wallwatosa, WI 53214, tel.: (414) 258-5880
Contact: Raymond J. Perry, Tr.

Established in 1985 in WI.
Donor(s): Wauwatosa Savings Bank.
Financial data (yr. ended 12/31/00): Grants paid, $223,261; assets, $3,876,073 (M); gifts received, $250,000; expenditures, $231,538; qualifying distributions, $221,022.
Limitations: Giving primarily in the metropolitan Milwaukee, WI, area.
Application information: Employee-related scholarships are administered directly by guidance offices in schools receiving funds from the foundation. Application form not required.
Trustee: Charles A. Perry, Raymond J. Perry.
EIN: 391548588
Codes: CS, FD2, CD

56777
Endries Foundation, Ltd.
P.O. Box 111
Brillion, WI 54110

Established in 1988 in WI.
Donor(s): Endries, Inc., Endries International, Inc.
Financial data (yr. ended 07/31/01): Grants paid, $222,877; assets, $54,655 (M); gifts received, $115,625; expenditures, $225,247; qualifying distributions, $225,247.
Limitations: Applications not accepted. Giving primarily in WI.
Application information: Unsolicited requests for funds not accepted.
Officers and Directors:* Patricia M. Endries,* Pres. and Treas.; Tom Kees,* V.P.; Robert Mathiebe,* Secy.; Tom Endries, Doris Miller.
EIN: 391625689
Codes: CS, FD2, CD

56778
Fitzsimonds Charitable Trust
c/o Keith A. Christiansen
777 E. Wisconsin Ave., Ste. 3500
Milwaukee, WI 53202-5367

Established in 2000 in WI.
Donor(s): Leona I. Fitzsimonds, Roger L. Fitzsimonds.
Financial data (yr. ended 12/31/01): Grants paid, $222,000; assets, $2,769,225 (M); expenditures, $249,681; qualifying distributions, $234,243.
Limitations: Applications not accepted. Giving primarily in Chicago, IL.
Application information: Contributes only to pre-selected organizations.
Trustees: Leona I. Fitzsimonds, Mary Ellen Fitzsimonds, Roger L. Fitzsimonds, Stephen Fitzsimonds, Michael Hedrick, Susan L. Hedrick.
EIN: 311723311
Codes: FD2

56779
Harri Hoffmann Family Foundation, Inc.
125 N. Water St.
Milwaukee, WI 53202

Established in 1985 in WI.
Donor(s): Harri Hoffmann, Herta Hoffmann.
Financial data (yr. ended 12/31/01): Grants paid, $219,232; assets, $4,220,663 (M); gifts received, $369,143; expenditures, $223,126; qualifying distributions, $219,232.
Limitations: Giving primarily in Milwaukee, WI.
Officers and Directors:* Harri Hoffmann,* Pres.; Herta Hoffmann,* V.P.; Lorraine Hoffmann,* V.P.
EIN: 391537228

56780
MMG Foundation, Inc.
702 Eisenhower Dr., Ste. B
Kimberly, WI 54136

Established around 1994.
Donor(s): Cynthia F. Moeller Stiehl.
Financial data (yr. ended 12/31/00): Grants paid, $218,646; assets, $7,706,917 (M); expenditures, $298,801; qualifying distributions, $218,646.
Limitations: Applications not accepted. Giving primarily in WI.
Application information: Contributes only to pre-selected organizations.
Officers: Cynthia F. Moeller Stiehl, Pres.; Carl H. Stiehl, V.P. and Treas.; William D. Calkins, Secy.
EIN: 396571237
Codes: FD2

56781
The Elmer Leach Foundation, Inc.
c/o U.S. Bank
P.O. Box 2043
Milwaukee, WI 53201-9116
Application address: 2737 Harrison St., P.O. Box 2608, Oshkosh, WI 54903
Contact: Frederick E. Leach, Pres.

Established in 1965 in WI.
Donor(s): Leach Co.
Financial data (yr. ended 12/31/01): Grants paid, $218,200; assets, $3,010,962 (M); gifts received, $300; expenditures, $230,243; qualifying distributions, $219,335.
Limitations: Giving primarily in Oshkosh, WI.
Application information: Application form not required.
Officers: Frederick E. Leach, Pres.; David C. Leach II, Exec. V.P.; Phyllis L. Leach, Secy.; David Fischer, Treas.
EIN: 396093521
Codes: FD2

56782
Alvin and Marion Birnschein Foundation, Inc.
c/o Lichstinn & Haensel
111 E. Wisconsin Ave., Ste. 1800
Milwaukee, WI 53202-4813 (414) 276-3400
Contact: Peter C. Haensel, Pres.

Established in 1968 in WI.
Donor(s): Alvin Birnschein,‡ Marion Birnschein.‡
Financial data (yr. ended 12/31/01): Grants paid, $216,210; assets, $4,065,700 (M); expenditures, $306,774; qualifying distributions, $213,646.
Limitations: Giving primarily in the greater Milwaukee, WI area.
Publications: Informational brochure (including application guidelines).
Application information: Application form required.
Officers and Directors:* Peter C. Haensel,* Pres.; Janet M. Hoehnen,* Secy.; Ronald Jodat.
EIN: 396126798
Codes: FD2

56783
Earl & Eugenia Quirk Foundation, Inc.
314 W. Main St., Ste. 11
Watertown, WI 53094-7630 (920) 261-0223
Contact: Claude C. Held, II

Established in 1962 in WI.
Donor(s): Catherine J. Quirk,‡ Eugenia B. Quirk.‡
Financial data (yr. ended 04/30/01): Grants paid, $215,500; assets, $3,679,501 (M); expenditures, $270,254; qualifying distributions, $233,556.
Limitations: Applications not accepted. Giving limited to WI.
Application information: Contributes only to pre-selected organizations.
Officers and Directors:* Lillian Q. Conley,* Pres.; Ellen P. Conley,* V.P.; Wendy Q. Schuett,* Secy.; Darby R. Quirk,* Treas.; James E. Conley, M.D., James B. Quirk.
EIN: 396059626
Codes: FD2

56784
B. D. and Jane E. McIntyre Foundation
c/o Bank One Trust Co., N.A.
P.O. Box 1308
Milwaukee, WI 53201
Application address: c/o Bank One, 611 Woodward Ave., Ste. 8113, Detroit, MI 48226, tel.: (313) 225-3183, FAX: (313) 225-1574
Contact: Donald W. Korn

Trust established in 1961 in MI.
Donor(s): Members of the McIntyre family.
Financial data (yr. ended 11/30/01): Grants paid, $215,100; assets, $4,659,260 (M); expenditures, $252,148; qualifying distributions, $229,736.
Limitations: Giving primarily in MI, with some emphasis on Monroe and Midland.
Application information: Application form not required.
Trustee: Bank One Trust Co., N.A.
Advisory Committee: Don Korn, Rocque E. Lipford, C.S. McIntyre III.
EIN: 386046718
Codes: FD2

56785
Justine Sterkel Fund
(Formerly Justine Sterkel Trust)
c/o Bank One Trust Co., N.A.
P.O. Box 1308
Milwaukee, WI 53201
Application address: 28 Park Ave. W., Mansfield, OH 44701, tel.: (419) 525-5517
Contact: David Strub, Admin., Bank One Trust Co., N.A.

Trust established in 1966 in OH.
Donor(s): Justine Sterkel.‡
Financial data (yr. ended 12/31/01): Grants paid, $211,171; assets, $3,905,047 (M); expenditures, $236,608; qualifying distributions, $217,096.
Limitations: Giving primarily in the city of Mansfield and Richland County, OH.
Application information: Application form not required.
Trustees: H. Eugene Ryan, Bank One Trust Co., N.A.
EIN: 346576810
Codes: FD2

56786
The Stateline Community Foundation
(Formerly The Greater Beloit Community Foundation)
121 W. Grand Ave.
Beloit, WI 53511 (608) 362-4228
FAX: (608) 362-0056; *E-mail:* statelinecf@aol.com
Contact: Tara Tinder, Exec. Dir.

Established in 1986 in WI.
Financial data (yr. ended 12/31/01): Grants paid, $210,905; assets, $4,427,117 (M); expenditures, $362,846.
Limitations: Applications not accepted. Giving limited to the greater Stateline area encompassing Rock County, WI, and northern Winnebago County, IL.
Publications: Annual report.
Application information: Unsolicited requests for funds not accepted.
Officers and Directors:* John Erikson,* Chair.; D. Richard Barder, 1st Vice-Chair.; Charldene Schnier,* Secy.; Bruce Lans,* Treas.; Tara Tinder, Exec. Dir.; Joanne Acomb, Richard Bastian, Sally Burris, Tracy Dudkewicz, Diane Hendricks, Diane Henry, Samuel Paddock.
EIN: 391585271
Codes: CM, FD2, GTI

56787
Kailas J. & Becky L. Rao Foundation
5270 N. Lake Dr.
Milwaukee, WI 53217
Contact: Kailas J. Rao, Tr.

Established in 1993 in WI.
Donor(s): Carol V. Jackley.
Financial data (yr. ended 12/31/00): Grants paid, $208,794; assets, $1,060,183 (M); gifts received, $201,873; expenditures, $214,553; qualifying distributions, $210,991.
Limitations: Giving primarily in WI.
Application information: Application form not required.
Trustees: Becky L. Rao, Kailas J. Rao.
EIN: 396584791
Codes: FD2

56788
Martin Family Foundation
2601 W. Cedar Ln.
Milwaukee, WI 53217-1138

Established around 1994.
Donor(s): Janet Dowler Martin, Vincent L. Martin.
Financial data (yr. ended 07/31/01): Grants paid, $205,000; assets, $7,259,021 (M); gifts received, $6,000,000; expenditures, $226,978; qualifying distributions, $205,000.
Limitations: Applications not accepted. Giving primarily in WI.
Application information: Contributes only to pre-selected organizations.
Trustees: Janet Dowler Martin, Vincent L. Martin.
EIN: 396584789
Codes: FD2

56789
S. F. Shattuck Charitable Trust
c/o Bank One Trust. Co., N.A.
P.O. Box 1308
Milwaukee, WI 53201
Application address: 111 E. Wisconsin Ave., Neenah, WI 54957

Established in 1951 in WI.
Financial data (yr. ended 10/31/01): Grants paid, $203,800; assets, $3,508,150 (M); expenditures, $240,077; qualifying distributions, $201,402.

Limitations: Applications not accepted. Giving primarily in Neenah, WI.
Application information: Contributes only to pre-selected organizations.
Trustee: Bank One Trust Co., N.A.
EIN: 396048820
Codes: FD2

56790
Ralph Evinrude Foundation, Inc.
c/o Quarles & Brady
411 E. Wisconsin Ave.
Milwaukee, WI 53202-4497 (414) 277-5000
Contact: Henry J. Loos, Pres.

Incorporated in 1959 in WI.
Donor(s): Ralph Evinrude.‡
Financial data (yr. ended 07/31/02): Grants paid, $202,750; assets, $2,014,922 (M); expenditures, $219,523; qualifying distributions, $213,781.
Limitations: Giving primarily in Milwaukee, WI.
Application information: Application form not required.
Officers and Directors:* Henry J. Loos,* Pres.; John W. Daniels,* V.P.; Paul J. Tilleman,* Secy.-Treas.
EIN: 396040256
Codes: FD2

56791
Web Maddox Trust
c/o Bank One Trust Co., N.A.
P.O. Box 1308
Milwaukee, WI 53201
Application address: P.O. Box 2050, Fort Worth, TX 76113, tel.: (817) 884-4159
Contact: Jim Wright

Established in 1986 in TX.
Financial data (yr. ended 03/31/01): Grants paid, $202,500; assets, $4,529,818 (M); expenditures, $243,470; qualifying distributions, $243,470.
Limitations: Giving primarily in Tarrant County, TX.
Trustee: Bank One Trust Co., N.A.
EIN: 756347669
Codes: FD2

56792
Seeds of Faith, Inc.
P.O. Box 197
Hartland, WI 53029 (262) 367-1990
Contact: William Rose, Pres.

Established in 1999 in WI.
Financial data (yr. ended 12/31/01): Grants paid, $202,500; assets, $3,815,751 (M); expenditures, $252,642; qualifying distributions, $202,213.
Limitations: Giving primarily in WI.
Application information: Application form not required.
Officers: William Rose, Pres. and Treas.; Susan Rose, V.P. and Secy.
Director: Gretchen Petraske.
EIN: 391938697
Codes: FD2

56793
The Elmwood Foundation, Inc.
P.O. Box 2287
La Crosse, WI 54602-2287 (608) 781-0850
Contact: Peggy Birschbach, Secy.-Treas.

Incorporated in 1954 in WI.
Donor(s): Charles D. Gelatt, Northern Engraving and Manufacturing Co.
Financial data (yr. ended 06/30/01): Grants paid, $201,500; assets, $2,063,457 (M); gifts received, $68,639; expenditures, $201,834; qualifying distributions, $200,473.

Limitations: Giving primarily in WI, with emphasis on the La Crosse area.
Application information: Application form not required.
Officers: Daniel Gelatt, Pres.; Roberta K. Gelatt, V.P.; Peggy Birschbach, Secy.-Treas.
EIN: 396044165
Codes: FD2

56794
Frank Family Memorial Scholarship
(Formerly Simon Frank Scholarship Fund)
c/o Wells Fargo Bank Wisconsin, N.A.
P.O. Box 171, 636 Wisconsin Ave.
Sheboygan, WI 53082-0171
Application address: c/o Homestead High School, 5000 W. Mequon Rd., Mequon, WI 53092
Contact: Mary Jo Denk, Secy.

Financial data (yr. ended 12/31/00): Grants paid, $200,750; assets, $2,909,702 (M); gifts received, $875; expenditures, $228,764; qualifying distributions, $205,694.
Limitations: Giving limited to residents of Mequon, WI.
Application information: Application form required.
Officer: Mary Jo Denk, Secy.
Trustee: Wells Fargo Bank Wisconsin, N.A.
EIN: 396270979
Codes: FD2, GTI

56795
Leaf, Ltd.
125 S. 84th St., Ste. 100
Milwaukee, WI 53214-1498
Application address: 401 E. Kilbourn Ave., Ste. 400, Milwaukee, WI 53202, tel.: (414) 272-3146
Contact: Bruce A. Findley, Pres.

Established in 1999 in WI.
Donor(s): Foundation of Faith.
Financial data (yr. ended 12/31/01): Grants paid, $200,000; assets, $4,218,648 (M); expenditures, $278,609; qualifying distributions, $201,956.
Limitations: Giving primarily in WI.
Application information: Application form not required.
Officers and Directors:* Bruce A. Findley,* Pres. and Treas.; Ellen V. Findley,* V.P. and Secy.; Holly T. Brown.
EIN: 391938591
Codes: FD2

56796
Kelben Foundation, Inc.
5112 W. Highland Rd.
Mequon, WI 53092 (262) 242-4794
Additional tels.: Judy Shane (262) 241-4563; Janet Larscheid (262) 241-4086; Patty Schuyler (262) 354-7968; FAX: (262) 242-4760; E-mail: Kellner@execpc.com
Contact: Mary Kellner, Pres.

Established in 1983.
Donor(s): Ted D. Kellner.
Financial data (yr. ended 11/30/01): Grants paid, $198,465; assets, $1,831,366 (M); gifts received, $14,202; expenditures, $210,481; qualifying distributions, $210,481.
Limitations: Giving limited to WI.
Application information: Application form required.
Officers: Mary Kellner, Pres.; Ted D. Kellner, Treas.
EIN: 391494625
Codes: FD2, GTI

56797
Dorothy Inbusch Foundation, Inc.
(Formerly Charles E. & Dorothy Watkins Inbusch Foundation, Inc.)
660 E. Mason St.
Milwaukee, WI 53202
Contact: Thomas J. Drought, Secy.-Treas.

Established in 1964.
Financial data (yr. ended 12/31/01): Grants paid, $197,900; assets, $3,435,657 (M); expenditures, $255,776; qualifying distributions, $231,321.
Limitations: Giving primarily in the greater Milwaukee, WI, area.
Application information: Use Donor's Forum Common Grant Application. Application form required.
Officers and Directors:* Robert E. Cook,* Pres.; Harry F. Franke,* V.P.; Thomas J. Drought,* Secy.-Treas.
EIN: 396084238
Codes: FD2

56798
The Life Foundation
P.O. Box 1894
Appleton, WI 54913

Established in 1994 in WI.
Donor(s): Brian R. Follett.
Financial data (yr. ended 12/31/00): Grants paid, $197,860; assets, $1,634,487 (M); gifts received, $786,256; expenditures, $215,164; qualifying distributions, $202,076.
Limitations: Applications not accepted. Giving on a national and international basis.
Application information: Contributes only to pre-selected organizations.
Trustee: Brian R. Follett.
EIN: 396606399
Codes: FD2

56799
Don L. & Carol G. Taylor Foundation
c/o Wendy T. Florian
224 Muirfield Ct.
North Prairie, WI 53153

Established in 1994 in WI.
Donor(s): Carol G. Taylor Charitable Lead Annuity Trust, Don L. Taylor Charitable Lead Annuity Trust.
Financial data (yr. ended 12/31/01): Grants paid, $197,446; assets, $182,955 (M); gifts received, $196,926; expenditures, $198,893; qualifying distributions, $197,782.
Limitations: Applications not accepted. Giving primarily in the Waukesha, WI, area.
Application information: Contributes only to pre-selected organizations.
Officers and Directors:* Wendy T. Florian,* Pres.; Ty R. Taylor,* V.P.; Martin H. Frank,* Secy.; J. Bernard Fiedler,* Treas.
EIN: 391793545
Codes: FD2

56800
William G. and Betty Schuett Family Foundation, Inc.
2900 Hidden Lake Rd.
Mequon, WI 53092 (262) 240-0222
Contact: William G. Schuett, Jr., Pres.

Established in 1997 in WI.
Financial data (yr. ended 12/31/01): Grants paid, $197,375; assets, $3,686,718 (M); expenditures, $255,709; qualifying distributions, $196,459.
Application information: Application form not required.

56800—WISCONSIN

Officers and Directors:* William G. Schuett, Jr.,* Pres. and Treas.; Betty Jean Schuett,* V.P.; Katherine T. Schuett,* Secy.
EIN: 391892757
Codes: FD2

56801
SNC Foundation, Inc.
101 Waukau Ave.
Oshkosh, WI 54902
Contact: John L. Vette III, Pres.

Established in 1981 in WI.
Donor(s): SNC Manufacturing Co., Inc., Janet Vette.‡
Financial data (yr. ended 06/30/01): Grants paid, $197,358; assets, $1,634,532 (M); expenditures, $212,573; qualifying distributions, $207,005.
Limitations: Applications not accepted. Giving primarily in Oshkosh, WI.
Application information: Contributes only to pre-selected organizations.
Officer and Directors:* John L. Vette III,* Pres.; Burleigh Blust.
EIN: 391384595
Codes: CS, FD2, CD

56802
The Stone Foundation, Inc.
c/o National Exchange Bank, Trust Dept.
130 S. Main St.
Fond du Lac, WI 54935-4210

Financial data (yr. ended 12/31/00): Grants paid, $197,300; assets, $7,437,780 (M); expenditures, $240,254; qualifying distributions, $198,472.
Limitations: Applications not accepted. Giving primarily in Fond du Lac, WI.
Application information: Contributes only to pre-selected organizations.
Officers and Directors:* Peter E. Stone,* Pres. and Treas.; Dale G. Brooks,* V.P.; Eric P. Stone,* V.P.; S. Adam Stone,* V.P.; Barbara S. Stone,* Secy.; Michael L. Burch, James R. Chatterton.
EIN: 391597843
Codes: FD2

56803
Hayssen Family Foundation, Inc.
1714 Cambridge Ave.
Sheboygan, WI 53081-2640 (920) 457-5051
Contact: Daniel A. Merkel, Pres.

Established in 1944 in WI.
Financial data (yr. ended 12/31/01): Grants paid, $196,180; assets, $2,734,086 (M); expenditures, $216,835; qualifying distributions, $201,263.
Limitations: Giving limited to WI.
Application information: Application form not required.
Officers and Directors:* Daniel A. Merkel, Pres.; Marie Perry,* V.P.; Arlene Krauss, Secy.; Mary E. Hayssen,* Treas.; Eldon L. Bohrofen, Ronald L. Gottschalk, Arthur H. Hayssen, Arthur R. Imig, Konrad C. Testwuide III.
EIN: 396044222
Codes: FD2

56804
Wahlin Foundation
416 S. Academy St.
Stoughton, WI 53589

Financial data (yr. ended 12/31/01): Grants paid, $195,750; assets, $4,554,294 (M); expenditures, $228,692; qualifying distributions, $195,750.
Limitations: Applications not accepted.
Officers and Directors:* Donald D. Wahlin,* C.E.O.; Carol L. Wahlin,* Pres.; Robert A. Fleischacker, Secy.; Michael A. Fontaine, Treas.;

Margaret W. Blanchard, Elizabeth W. McClimon, Kathryn W. Schieldt.
EIN: 391948530
Codes: FD2

56805
Paul E. Stry Foundation, Inc.
311 Main St.
La Crosse, WI 54601

Established in 1988 in WI.
Donor(s): Paul E. Stry.‡
Financial data (yr. ended 12/31/01): Grants paid, $195,057; assets, $4,784,653 (M); expenditures, $266,890; qualifying distributions, $231,200.
Limitations: Applications not accepted. Giving primarily in WI.
Application information: Unsolicited requests for funds not accepted.
Officers: Robert Swartz, Pres.; Robert Skemp, V.P.; Erv Albrecht, Secy.-Treas.
EIN: 391598681
Codes: FD2

56806
Keller Foundation, Inc.
c/o Ronald M. Phillips
3003 W. Breezewood Ln.
Neenah, WI 54956

Established in 1990 in WI.
Donor(s): J.J. Keller & Assocs., Inc.
Financial data (yr. ended 12/31/01): Grants paid, $194,569; assets, $492,554 (M); expenditures, $195,074; qualifying distributions, $194,569.
Limitations: Applications not accepted.
Application information: Contributes only to pre-selected organizations.
Directors: Ethel D. Keller, James L. Keller, John J. Keller, Robert L. Keller, Marion Murvine, Frank Pelisek, Ronald Phillips.
EIN: 391683437
Codes: CS, FD2, CD

56807
CBM Credit Education Foundation, Inc.
c/o William Wilcox
2509 S. Stoughton Rd.
Madison, WI 53716

Established in 1999 in WI.
Donor(s): CBM of Madison, Inc.
Financial data (yr. ended 12/31/00): Grants paid, $194,040; assets, $7,422,614 (M); expenditures, $996,419; qualifying distributions, $194,040.
Limitations: Giving primarily in MD and WI.
Officers and Directors:* Douglas Timmerman,* Chair.; William Wilcox,* Pres. and Secy.-Treas.; Gary Switzky,* V.P.
EIN: 391974526
Codes: FD2

56808
Seramur Family Foundation, Inc.
c/o John C. Seramur
P.O. Box 104
Stevens Point, WI 54481-2959

Established in 1994 in WI.
Donor(s): John C. Seramur.
Financial data (yr. ended 09/30/01): Grants paid, $193,700; assets, $4,750,571 (M); expenditures, $203,173; qualifying distributions, $186,207.
Limitations: Applications not accepted. Giving primarily in WI.
Application information: Contributes only to pre-selected organizations.
Officers: John C. Seramur, Pres.; Gary T. Pucci, V.P.; Joan Seramur, Secy.-Treas.
EIN: 391806609
Codes: FD2

56809
Joseph & Sally Handleman Charitable Foundation Trust B
c/o Bank One Trust Co., N.A.
P.O. Box 1308
Milwaukee, WI 53201
Application address: 3399 PGA Blvd., Palm Beach Gardens, FL 33410, tel.: (561) 627-9400
Contact: Gary W. Gomoll, Mgr.

Financial data (yr. ended 12/31/00): Grants paid, $193,552; assets, $8,014,338 (M); expenditures, $395,426; qualifying distributions, $207,009.
Limitations: Giving primarily in CA, Washington DC, and FL.
Application information: Application form not required.
Officer: Gary W. Gomoll, Mgr.
Trustee: Bank One Trust Co., N.A.
EIN: 656263327

56810
Martina Mann Charitable Trust
c/o Foley & Lardner
777 E. Wisconsin Ave., Ste. 3500
Milwaukee, WI 53202-5302

Established in 1989 in WI.
Donor(s): Martina Mann, Christopher M. Mann.
Financial data (yr. ended 12/31/00): Grants paid, $193,500; assets, $10,804,289 (M); gifts received, $5,505,000; expenditures, $288,141; qualifying distributions, $200,608.
Limitations: Applications not accepted. Giving limited to New Berlin and Troy, WI.
Application information: Contributes only to pre-selected organizations.
Trustees: Sonja Mann Gorsch, Christopher M. Mann, Martina Mann.
EIN: 391635085
Codes: FD2

56811
Walter Alexander Foundation, Inc.
500 3rd St., Ste. 320
P.O. Box 2137
Wausau, WI 54402-2137 (715) 845-4556
FAX: (715) 848-9336
Contact: Stanley F. Staples, Jr., Secy.

Incorporated in 1952 in WI.
Donor(s): Ruth Alexander,‡ Anne M. Alexander.‡
Financial data (yr. ended 11/30/01): Grants paid, $191,404; assets, $3,577,250 (M); expenditures, $302,376; qualifying distributions, $213,896.
Limitations: Giving primarily in Marathon, Portage, Outagomie and Winnebago counties, WI.
Application information: Application form not required.
Officers and Directors:* Walter Koskinen,* Pres.; Alexander Reichl, V.P.; Stanley F. Staples, Jr.,* Secy.; John F. Michler,* Treas.; Nancy Anne Cordaro, Jean A. Koskinen.
EIN: 396044635
Codes: FD2

56812
Fromstein Foundation, Ltd.
1501 E. Fox Ln.
Fox Point, WI 53217

Established in 1977 in WI.
Donor(s): Mitchell S. Fromstein.
Financial data (yr. ended 06/30/01): Grants paid, $191,275; assets, $2,758,531 (M); expenditures, $203,455; qualifying distributions, $192,751.
Limitations: Applications not accepted. Giving primarily in Milwaukee, WI.
Application information: Contributes only to pre-selected organizations.

Officers: Mitchell S. Fromstein, Pres. and Treas.; Lita Fromstein, V.P. and Secy.
EIN: 391287508
Codes: FD2

56813
Marquette Electronics Foundation
c/o The Endeavors Grp.
9100 N. Swan Rd., Ste. 980
Milwaukee, WI 53224
Contact: William Browne, Mgr.

Established in 1987 in WI.
Donor(s): Marquette Electronics, Inc., Marquette Medical Systems, Inc.
Financial data (yr. ended 04/30/01): Grants paid, $190,462; assets, $714,830 (M); expenditures, $239,080; qualifying distributions, $235,080.
Limitations: Giving primarily in Milwaukee, WI.
Manager: W.D. Browne.
Trustees: M.J. Cudahy, F.G. Luber, M.S. Newman.
EIN: 391575554
Codes: CS, FD2

56814
Nelson Foundation, Inc.
(Formerly NMC Projects, Inc.)
P.O. Box 428
Stoughton, WI 53589

Established in 1959 in WI.
Donor(s): Nelson Industries, Inc.
Financial data (yr. ended 07/31/01): Grants paid, $189,095; assets, $568,116 (M); expenditures, $189,602; qualifying distributions, $180,969.
Limitations: Giving primarily in WI.
Publications: Annual report.
Application information: Decisions on scholarships made by high schools. Application form not required.
Officers: Stephen R. Slinde, Pres. and Secy.-Treas.; Michael C. Bemis, V.P.
EIN: 396043256
Codes: CS, FD2, CD, GTI

56815
Derse Family Foundation
14240 Heatherwood Ct.
Elm Grove, WI 53122
Contact: Judith E. Derse, V.P.

Established in 1986 in WI.
Financial data (yr. ended 12/31/00): Grants paid, $187,124; assets, $4,344,942 (M); expenditures, $346,044; qualifying distributions, $187,124.
Limitations: Giving limited to WI, with emphasis on Milwaukee and Waukesha counties.
Publications: Informational brochure (including application guidelines).
Application information: Application form required.
Officers: James F. Derse, Sr., Pres.; Judith E. Derse, V.P.
Directors: Richard T. Derse, Diane K. Dressler.
EIN: 391540822
Codes: FD2

56816
Heller Foundation, Inc.
1840 N. Farwell Ave., Ste. 407
Milwaukee, WI 53202-1789

Established in 1957 in WI.
Financial data (yr. ended 11/30/01): Grants paid, $187,000; assets, $3,594,429 (M); expenditures, $212,359; qualifying distributions, $184,335.
Limitations: Applications not accepted. Giving in the U.S., with emphasis on Milwaukee, WI.
Application information: Contributes only to pre-selected organizations.

Officers and Trustees:* William C. Heller, Jr.,* Pres. and Treas.; James K. Heller,* V.P. and Secy.; Avis M. Heller, William J. Heller.
EIN: 396045338
Codes: FD2

56817
The William B. Pollock II and Kathryn Challiss Pollock Foundation
c/o Bank One Trust Co., N.A.
P.O. Box 1308
Milwaukee, WI 53201
Application address: 106 E. Market St., Warren, OH 44481

Established in 1952 in OH.
Donor(s): William B. Pollock II, Kathryn Challiss Pollock.
Financial data (yr. ended 12/31/00): Grants paid, $186,800; assets, $4,055,082 (M); expenditures, $225,834; qualifying distributions, $194,465.
Limitations: Giving limited to the Youngstown, OH, area.
Application information: Application form not required.
Trustees: Franklin S. Bennett, Jr., Bank One Trust Co., N.A.
EIN: 346514079
Codes: FD2

56818
Steinhauer Charitable Foundation
P.O. Box 389
Madison, WI 53701

Established in 1987 in WI.
Donor(s): Frederick C. Steinhauer, Nancie Steinhauer, Frederick C. Steinhauer II, Madison Dairy Produce Co., Sherri Steinhauer, Gary Steinhauer, Randall Steinhauer.
Financial data (yr. ended 12/31/01): Grants paid, $182,600; assets, $2,013,041 (M); gifts received, $21,200; expenditures, $189,037; qualifying distributions, $183,093.
Limitations: Applications not accepted. Giving primarily in Madison, WI.
Application information: Contributes only to pre-selected organizations.
Trustees: Frederick C. Steinhauer, Frederick C. Steinhauer II, Gary Steinhauer, Nancie Steinhauer, Randall Steinhauer, Sherri Steinhauer, Thomas Steinhauer.
EIN: 391600091
Codes: FD2

56819
James & Joyce Kalscheur Foundation
c/o Marshall & Illsley Trust Co.
P.O. Box 2980
Madison, WI 53701

Established in 1997 in WI.
Donor(s): James H. Kalscheur, Joyce J. Kalscheur.
Financial data (yr. ended 12/31/01): Grants paid, $182,100; assets, $3,220,334 (M); gifts received, $1,876,065; expenditures, $209,153; qualifying distributions, $179,624.
Limitations: Applications not accepted. Giving primarily in WI.
Application information: Unsolicited requests for funds not accepted.
Trustees: U.S. Bank, Marshall & Illsley Trust Company, N.A.
EIN: 396681490
Codes: FD2

56820
Maxine Ann Staley Fund
c/o Bank One Trust Co., N.A.
P.O. Box 1308
Milwaukee, WI 53201

Established in 1994.
Financial data (yr. ended 12/31/01): Grants paid, $181,211; assets, $3,565,235 (M); expenditures, $226,465; qualifying distributions, $188,670.
Limitations: Applications not accepted. Giving primarily in OK.
Application information: Contributes only to pre-selected organizations.
Trustee: Bank One Trust Co., N.A.
EIN: 731455037
Codes: FD2

56821
Bank One, Illinois Charitable Trust
(Formerly First National Bank & Trust Company of Rockford Charitable Trust)
c/o BankOne Trust Co.
P.O. Box 1308
Milwaukee, WI 53201

Established in 1951 in IL.
Donor(s): Bank One, Illinois, N.A.
Financial data (yr. ended 12/31/01): Grants paid, $180,406; assets, $541,085 (M); expenditures, $185,060; qualifying distributions, $181,709.
Limitations: Applications not accepted. Giving primarily in Rockford, IL.
Application information: Contributes only to pre-selected organizations.
Trustee: Bank One Trust Co., N.A.
EIN: 366108107
Codes: CS, FD2, CD

56822
Webcrafters-Frautschi Foundation, Inc.
2211 Fordem Ave.
Madison, WI 53704
Application address: P.O. Box 7608, Madison, WI 53707; FAX: (608) 244-3174
Contact: John C. Weston, Pres.

Established in 1961.
Donor(s): Christopher Frautschi, John J. Frautschi, Jac Garner, Judy Peirick, John C. Weston.
Financial data (yr. ended 06/30/01): Grants paid, $178,500; assets, $6,769 (M); gifts received, $150,000; expenditures, $178,510; qualifying distributions, $178,493.
Limitations: Giving primarily in WI, with emphasis on the Madison area.
Officers and Directors:* John C. Weston,* Pres.; Christopher Frautschi,* Secy.; Robert Lay, Treas.; John J. Frautschi, Jac Garner, Judy Peirick.
EIN: 396045309
Codes: FD2

56823
Gretchen & Andrew Dawes Endowment, Inc.
c/o Foley & Lardner
777 E. Wisconsin Ave., Ste. 3500
Milwaukee, WI 53202-5367

Established in 1983 in WI.
Donor(s): Gretchen N. Dawes.
Financial data (yr. ended 12/31/00): Grants paid, $178,000; assets, $191,599 (M); gifts received, $100,000; expenditures, $180,589; qualifying distributions, $179,465.
Limitations: Applications not accepted. Giving primarily in Milwaukee, WI.
Application information: Contributes only to pre-selected organizations.
Officers and Directors:* Gretchen N. Dawes,* Pres.; Allen M. Taylor,* V.P.; Stephen M. Fisher,* Secy.-Treas.

56823—WISCONSIN

EIN: 391455825
Codes: FD2

56824
Frank C. Shattuck Charitable Trust
c/o Bank One Trust Co., N.A.
P.O. Box 1308
Milwaukee, WI 53201-1308

Established in 1950.
Financial data (yr. ended 06/30/01): Grants paid, $178,000; assets, $2,412,981 (M); expenditures, $200,777; qualifying distributions, $192,123.
Limitations: Applications not accepted. Giving primarily in WI.
Application information: Contributes only to pre-selected organizations.
Trustee: Bank One Trust Co., N.A.
EIN: 396048813
Codes: FD2

56825
Davey Scholarship Foundation
c/o Bank One Trust Co., N.A.
P.O. Box 1308
Milwaukee, WI 53201-1308
Application address: 1 E. Old State Capitol Plz., Springfield, IL 62701-1320, tel.: (217) 525-9747
Contact: JoAnn Ley, Trust Off., Trust Co., N.A.

Established in 1966.
Financial data (yr. ended 06/30/01): Grants paid, $177,711; assets, $2,350,024 (M); expenditures, $222,156; qualifying distributions, $195,621; giving activities include $177,711 for loans to individuals.
Limitations: Giving limited to the Springfield, IL, area.
Application information: Application form required.
Trustee: Bank One Trust Co., N.A.
Selection Committee: Preston Hott, Harvey Stephens, Gary Sullivan.
EIN: 376057502
Codes: FD2, GTI

56826
Walter and Mabel Fromm Scholarship Trust
c/o U.S. Bank
P.O. Box 2043, Ste. LC4NE
Milwaukee, WI 53201-9116
Application address: P.O. Box 3194, Milwaukee, WI 53201-3194, tel.: (414) 765-5047
Contact: Gil Lindemann

Established in 1975.
Donor(s): Mabel Fromm,‡ Walter Fromm.‡
Financial data (yr. ended 02/28/02): Grants paid, $176,500; assets, $3,232,495 (M); expenditures, $205,971; qualifying distributions, $190,377.
Limitations: Giving limited to Hamburg and Merrill, WI.
Publications: Application guidelines.
Application information: Scholarship application guidelines available; no other applications considered.
Trustee: U.S. Bank.
Committee Members: Erik Larsen, Ebra N. Olsen, John Sturm, Gary Lee Woller.
EIN: 396250027
Codes: FD2, GTI

56827
Bless Foundation, Inc.
5718 52nd St.
Kenosha, WI 53144-2237
Contact: Robert Block, Treas.

Established in 1987.
Donor(s): Laminated Products, Inc.
Financial data (yr. ended 12/31/00): Grants paid, $176,358; assets, $636,263 (M); gifts received, $100,000; expenditures, $181,494; qualifying distributions, $181,494.
Limitations: Giving on a national basis.
Officers: Mark Hess, Pres.; Robert Block, Treas.
EIN: 391574310
Codes: FD2

56828
Camille A. Lonstorf Trust
c/o Foley & Lardner
777 E. Wisconsin Ave.
Milwaukee, WI 53202 (414) 297-5748
Contact: Harrold J. McComas, Tr.

Established in 1985 in WI.
Donor(s): Marge Long.‡
Financial data (yr. ended 12/31/01): Grants paid, $176,000; assets, $3,562,495 (M); expenditures, $212,660; qualifying distributions, $188,054.
Limitations: Giving primarily in Milwaukee, WI.
Application information: Application form not required.
Trustee: Harrold J. McComas.
EIN: 391509343
Codes: FD2

56829
Ann E. & Joseph F. Heil, Jr. Charitable Trust
7560 N. River Rd.
River Hills, WI 53217-3323

Established in 1999 in WI.
Donor(s): Marjorie Heil.‡
Financial data (yr. ended 12/31/00): Grants paid, $175,250; assets, $3,680,168 (M); gifts received, $370,413; expenditures, $201,262; qualifying distributions, $177,771.
Limitations: Applications not accepted. Giving primarily in Milwaukee, WI.
Application information: Contributes only to pre-selected organizations.
Trustee: Ann E. Heil.
EIN: 396713764
Codes: FD2

56830
The One Foundation
(Formerly Premier Foundation of Sheveport/Bossier, Inc.)
c/o Bank One Trust Co.
P.O. Box 1308
Milwaukee, WI 53201
Application address: c/o Bank One Trust Co., P.O. Box 21116, Shreveport, LA 71154-1116, tel.: (318) 226-2382
Contact: Monette Holler

Incorporated in 1955 in LA.
Donor(s): Premier Bank, N.A.
Financial data (yr. ended 06/30/01): Grants paid, $174,000; assets, $2,174,674 (M); expenditures, $247,783; qualifying distributions, $197,440.
Limitations: Giving primarily in Shreveport, LA.
Application information: Application form not required.
Trustee: Bank One Trust Co., N.A.
EIN: 726022876
Codes: CS, FD2, CD

56831
St. Francis Bank Foundation, Inc.
13400 Bishops Ln., Ste. 350
Brookfield, WI 53005-6203 (262) 787-8722
Contact: Marianne T. Zappall, Secy.

Established in 1984 in WI.
Donor(s): St. Francis Bank, F.S.B.
Financial data (yr. ended 09/30/01): Grants paid, $173,031; assets, $750,361 (M); expenditures, $173,341; qualifying distributions, $172,832.
Limitations: Giving primarily in Milwaukee, WI.
Officers and Directors:* Thomas R. Perz,* Pres.; William R. Hotz, V.P.; Marianne T. Zappall, Secy.; Jon D. Sorenson, Treas.; Richard W. Double, David J. Drury, Rudolph T. Hoppe, Brian T. Kaye, Gerald A. Kiefer, John T. Lynch, Edward W. Mentzer, Jeffrey A. Reigle, Anthony O. Schmidt, Julia H. Taylor, Edmund O. Templeton.
EIN: 391535393
Codes: CS, FD2, CD

56832
Leon H. & Clymene M. Bond Foundation, Inc.
P.O. Box 299
Oconto, WI 54153 (920) 834-5585
Contact: Earl J. DeCloux, Pres.

Established in 1993 in WI.
Donor(s): Leon H. Bond.
Financial data (yr. ended 05/31/01): Grants paid, $171,493; assets, $6,933,380 (M); expenditures, $504,153; qualifying distributions, $354,705.
Limitations: Giving primarily in WI.
Officers: Earl J. DeCloux, Pres.; John Bostedt, V.P.
Directors: Paula Hanek, Eugene Wusterbarth.
EIN: 391762087
Codes: FD2

56833
Gering Family Foundation, Inc.
117 S. 3rd Ave.
Wausau, WI 54401
Contact: Paul Gassner, Secy.-Treas.

Established in 1997 in WI.
Donor(s): Rick Gering, Sue Gering.
Financial data (yr. ended 12/31/00): Grants paid, $170,965; assets, $3,875,807 (L); expenditures, $177,949; qualifying distributions, $177,629.
Limitations: Applications not accepted. Giving primarily in Wausau, WI.
Application information: Contributes only to pre-selected organizations.
Officers: Sue Gering, Pres.; Rick Gering, V.P.; Paul Gassner, Secy.-Treas.
EIN: 391874006
Codes: FD2

56834
Paul F. and Lois K. Heiss Family Foundation, Inc.
3412 W. Riviera Ct.
Mequon, WI 53092-5209
Contact: Paul F. Heiss, Pres.

Established in 1998 in WI.
Donor(s): Paul F. Heiss.
Financial data (yr. ended 12/31/01): Grants paid, $169,455; assets, $226,286 (M); gifts received, $74,700; expenditures, $181,138; qualifying distributions, $181,049.
Officer: Paul F. Heiss, Pres.
Directors: Lois K. Heiss, Norman Stolpe.
EIN: 391928659
Codes: FD2

56835
Grede Foundation, Inc.
P.O. Box 26499
Milwaukee, WI 53226-0494 (414) 256-9242
Contact: Burleigh E. Jacobs, Pres.

Incorporated in 1954 in WI.
Donor(s): Grede Foundries, Inc.
Financial data (yr. ended 12/31/01): Grants paid, $168,445; assets, $205,617 (M); expenditures, $169,755; qualifying distributions, $169,495.
Limitations: Giving primarily in WI.

Application information: Application form not required.
Officers and Directors:* Burleigh E. Jacobs, Pres.; Bruce E. Jacobs,* V.P.; W. Stewart Davis III,* Secy.; Susan L. Daigneau, Betty G. Davis, Mary J. York.
EIN: 396042977
Codes: CS, FD2, CD, GTI

56836
Johnson Family Foundation
4041 N. Main St.
Racine, WI 53402

Established in 1995 in WI.
Financial data (yr. ended 12/31/01): Grants paid, $168,000; assets, $4,523,877 (M); expenditures, $187,192; qualifying distributions, $168,000.
Limitations: Applications not accepted. Giving primarily in Racine, WI.
Application information: Contributes only to pre-selected organizations.
Officers and Trustees:* Samuel C. Johnson,* Chair.; Winifred J. Marquart,* Pres.; H. Fisk Johnson, Imogene P. Johnson, S. Curtis Johnson, Helen Johnson-Leipold.
EIN: 367092273
Codes: FD2

56837
Vilter Foundation, Inc.
5555 S. Packard Ave.
Cudahy, WI 53110-2623
Contact: Kris E. Wegner, Secy.-Treas.

Incorporated in 1961 in WI.
Donor(s): Vilter Manufacturing Corp.
Financial data (yr. ended 07/31/01): Grants paid, $168,000; assets, $3,636,758 (M); expenditures, $218,697; qualifying distributions, $192,470.
Limitations: Giving primarily in Milwaukee, WI.
Application information: Application form not required.
Officers and Directors:* R.A. Hall,* Pres.; K.E. Wegner,* Secy.-Treas.; G.F. Reinders.
EIN: 390678640
Codes: CS, FD2, CD

56838
Marjorie L. Christiansen Foundation
(Formerly Arthur J. & Cecelia L. Christiansen Foundation)
c/o Bank One Trust Co., N.A.
P.O. Box 1308
Milwaukee, WI 53201-1308

Established in 1960.
Financial data (yr. ended 05/31/01): Grants paid, $167,800; assets, $4,420,908 (M); expenditures, $208,305; qualifying distributions, $177,430.
Limitations: Giving limited to the Racine, WI, area.
Application information: Application form not required.
Trustees: Roy D. Stewart, Bank One Trust Co., N.A.
EIN: 396037585
Codes: FD2

56839
R. A. Stevens Family Foundation
S50 W30176 Seville Ln.
Mukwonago, WI 53149 (262) 303-7285
Contact: Paul Fleckenstein, Tr.

Established in 1999 in WI.
Donor(s): Andrew J. Fleckenstein, Rita A. Stevens.
Financial data (yr. ended 12/31/01): Grants paid, $167,773; assets, $5,264,346 (M); expenditures, $193,118; qualifying distributions, $169,708.
Limitations: Giving primarily in SC, and Milwaukee, WI.

Application information: Application form required.
Trustees: John Fleckenstein, Paul Fleckenstein, Rita A. Stevens.
EIN: 396711913
Codes: FD2

56840
Roehl Foundation, Inc.
P.O. Box 168
Oconomowoc, WI 53066-0168 (262) 569-3000
Contact: Peter G. Roehl, Pres.

Established in 1959.
Donor(s): Peter G. Roehl.
Financial data (yr. ended 06/30/02): Grants paid, $167,250; assets, $4,555,076 (M); expenditures, $197,308; qualifying distributions, $172,041.
Limitations: Giving primarily in WI.
Application information: Application form not required.
Officers and Directors:* Peter G. Roehl,* Pres.; Janet T. Roehl,* V.P.; Wendy A. Luengen,* Secy.; Nancy A. Roehl,* Treas.
EIN: 366048089
Codes: FD2

56841
786 Foundation
c/o Marshall & Ilsley Trust Company, N.A.
P.O. Box 2980
Milwaukee, WI 53201-2980
Application address: P.O. Box 8988, Madison, WI 53708, tel.: (608) 232-2056
Contact: Sharon Blank

Established in 1990 in WI.
Donor(s): Mary M. Lamar, Matthew W. Lamar, Michael Price, N. Stewart Stone III, Sarah Mead Stone, Timothy Stone.
Financial data (yr. ended 12/31/01): Grants paid, $166,000; assets, $4,199,887 (M); expenditures, $219,649; qualifying distributions, $166,000.
Limitations: Giving primarily in WI.
Application information: Application form not required.
Trustee: Marshall & Ilsley Trust Company, N.A.
EIN: 396515741

56842
Park Bank Foundation, Inc.
330 E. Kilbourn Ave., Ste. 150
Milwaukee, WI 53202-6619 (414) 270-3209
Contact: Carolyn Torcivia, Secy.

Established in 1980 in WI.
Donor(s): Park Bank.
Financial data (yr. ended 12/31/01): Grants paid, $163,570; assets, $889,012 (M); gifts received, $150,000; expenditures, $182,524; qualifying distributions, $178,615.
Limitations: Giving limited to the Milwaukee, WI, area.
Application information: Application form not required.
Officers and Directors:* P. Michael Mahoney,* Pres.; James W. Wright,* V.P. and Treas.; Lorraine A. Kelly,* V.P.; Michael J. Kelly,* V.P.; Carolyn Torcivia, Secy.
EIN: 391365837
Codes: CS, FD2, CD

56843
H. L. Epstein Family Foundation, Inc.
5215 N. Ironwood Ln., Ste. 114
Milwaukee, WI 53217

Established in 1954 in WI.
Donor(s): Harry L. Epstein.

Financial data (yr. ended 11/30/01): Grants paid, $162,250; assets, $2,236,612 (M); expenditures, $162,881; qualifying distributions, $160,848.
Limitations: Applications not accepted. Giving primarily in CA and Milwaukee, WI.
Application information: Contributes only to pre-selected organizations.
Officers: Harry L. Epstein, Pres.; Estelle Epstein, V.P.; Irene Casten, Secy.; Louise Kaminsky, Treas.
EIN: 396044168
Codes: FD2

56844
Philip M. Gelatt Foundation, Inc.
P.O. Box 17
Sparta, WI 54656-0017 (608) 269-6911
Contact: Rita A. Forbes, V.P.

Established in 1985 in WI.
Donor(s): PMG, Inc., Northern Engraving Corp.
Financial data (yr. ended 06/30/01): Grants paid, $160,500; assets, $2,326,801 (M); expenditures, $173,597; qualifying distributions, $165,231.
Limitations: Giving primarily in WI, with emphasis on the Sparta-La Crosse area.
Application information: Application form not required.
Officers and Directors:* Philip M. Gelatt, Pres. and Treas.; Rita A. Forbes,* V.P. and Secy.; Robert J. Wood.
EIN: 391568547
Codes: FD2

56845
The Jud and Mary Beth Fowler Foundation
1440 E. Forest Ave.
Neenah, WI 54956
Contact: Judson Fowler, Tr.

Financial data (yr. ended 12/31/01): Grants paid, $160,000; assets, $746,527 (M); expenditures, $168,363; qualifying distributions, $159,547.
Application information: Application form not required.
Trustees: Judson E. Fowler, Mary Beth Fowler.
EIN: 396691614
Codes: FD2

56846
Allan H. & Suzanne L. Selig Family Foundation, Inc.
c/o Foley & Lardner
777 E. Wisconsin Ave., Ste. 3500
Milwaukee, WI 53202-5367

Established in 2000 in WI.
Donor(s): Allan H. Selig.
Financial data (yr. ended 12/31/01): Grants paid, $159,000; assets, $11,444 (M); gifts received, $52,000; expenditures, $159,000; qualifying distributions, $159,000.
Limitations: Applications not accepted.
Application information: Contributes only to pre-selected organizations.
Officers and Directors:* Suzanne L. Selig,* Pres.; Allan H. Selig,* V.P.; Wayne R. Lueders,* Treas.
EIN: 311735982

56847
Mortenson Family Foundation
3113 W. Beltline Hwy., Ste. 300
Madison, WI 53708-8950

Established in 1997 in WI.
Donor(s): Loren D. Mortenson.
Financial data (yr. ended 12/31/01): Grants paid, $158,700; assets, $625,170 (M); gifts received, $22,217; expenditures, $177,862; qualifying distributions, $158,642.
Limitations: Applications not accepted.

56847—WISCONSIN

Application information: Contributes only to pre-selected organizations.
Trustees: Joelle Mortenson Hunter, Carole Ann Mortenson, Jay P. Mortenson, Loren D. Mortenson, Thomas G. Ragatz, William T. Young.
EIN: 396659441
Codes: FD2

56848
C. S. and Marion F. McIntyre Foundation
c/o Bank One Trust Co., N.A.
P.O. Box 1308
Milwaukee, WI 53201
Application address: c/o Bank One, 611 Woodward Ave., Ste. 8113, Detroit, MI 48226, tel.: (313) 225-3183, FAX: (313) 225-1574
Contact: Donald W. Korn

Trust established in 1961 in MI.
Donor(s): Members of the McIntyre family.
Financial data (yr. ended 11/30/01): Grants paid, $157,882; assets, $3,253,047 (M); expenditures, $187,743; qualifying distributions, $167,521.
Limitations: Giving primarily in MI, with emphasis on the Monroe area.
Application information: Application form not required.
Advisory Committee: Don Korn, Rocque L. Lipford, David L. McIntyre.
Trustee: Bank One Trust Co., N.A.
EIN: 386046733
Codes: FD2

56849
Linda Neville Trust
c/o Bank One Trust Co., N.A.
P.O. Box 1308
Milwaukee, WI 53201
Application address: c/o Bank One Trust Co.,N.A., 201 E. Main St., Lexington, KY 40502, tel.: (859) 231-2408
Contact: Ginger S. Dinsmore

Established in 1996 in KY.
Financial data (yr. ended 12/31/01): Grants paid, $157,170; assets, $2,940,438 (M); expenditures, $173,189; qualifying distributions, $160,555.
Limitations: Giving primarily in KY.
Trustee: Bank One Trust Co., N.A.
EIN: 616018696
Codes: FD2

56850
Courtier Foundation, Inc.
P.O. Box 1497
Madison, WI 53701-1497 (608) 258-4224
Contact: David W. Reinecke, Secy.-Treas.

Established in 1999 in WI.
Donor(s): Veryl F. Courtier Survivor's Trust, Wilma W. Courtier Residual Trust.
Financial data (yr. ended 12/31/00): Grants paid, $156,825; assets, $4,563,787 (M); gifts received, $313,101; expenditures, $241,900; qualifying distributions, $156,825.
Limitations: Giving limited to WI.
Application information: Application form required.
Officers and Directors:* Thomas G. Ragatz,* Pres.; Ronald M. Wanek,* V.P.; David W. Reinecke,* Secy.-Treas.
EIN: 391935038
Codes: FD2

56851
Jay Kay Foundation, Inc.
c/o Milwaukee Foundation
1020 N. Broadway, Ste. 112
Milwaukee, WI 53202-3157

Donor(s): Jane L. Kaiser, George C. Kaiser.
Financial data (yr. ended 12/31/01): Grants paid, $156,550; assets, $513,736 (M); expenditures, $162,883; qualifying distributions, $156,550.
Limitations: Applications not accepted. Giving primarily in Milwaukee, WI.
Application information: Contributes only to pre-selected organizations.
Officers and Directors:* Jane L. Kaiser,* Pres.; C. Daniel Gelatt, Jr.,* V.P.; Wendy Horton,* Secy.; George C. Kaiser,* Treas.; Roger Fitzsimonds, Douglas M. Jansson, Linda T. Mellowes, Frank Pellsek, Brent Rupple, Sr.
EIN: 391286422
Codes: TN

56852
Douglas and Eleanor Seaman Charitable Foundation
5205 N. Ironwood Rd., Ste. 101
Milwaukee, WI 53217 (414) 964-6310
Contact: Douglas Seaman, Tr.

Established in 1997 in WI.
Donor(s): Douglas Seaman.
Financial data (yr. ended 12/31/00): Grants paid, $156,001; assets, $2,664,237 (M); gifts received, $4,012; expenditures, $164,653; qualifying distributions, $156,001.
Limitations: Applications not accepted. Giving on a national basis.
Application information: Contributes only to pre-selected organizations.
Trustees: Harry V. Carlson, Gerald L. Hestekin, Douglas Seaman, Eleanor R. Seaman, Joseph B. Tyson, Jr.
EIN: 396636617
Codes: FD2

56853
Geiger Family Foundation, Inc.
111 E. Wisconsin Ave., Ste. 1800
Milwaukee, WI 53202

Established in 1997 in WI.
Donor(s): Anthony Geiger.
Financial data (yr. ended 12/31/01): Grants paid, $156,000; assets, $3,107,944 (M); gifts received, $107,873; expenditures, $204,785; qualifying distributions, $155,148.
Limitations: Applications not accepted. Giving primarily in Milwaukee, WI.
Application information: Contributes only to pre-selected organizations.
Officers and Directors:* Willard G. Neary,* Pres.; Theresa Kent,* Secy.; Donal Demet.
EIN: 391892888
Codes: FD2

56854
Tikkun Olam Foundation, Inc.
5225 N. Ironwood Rd., Ste. 117
Milwaukee, WI 53217 (414) 964-7400
Contact: Alexandra DeToro, Dir.

Established in 1994 in WI.
Donor(s): Eric Butlein, Jayne Butlein, Ejada Limited Partnership.
Financial data (yr. ended 12/31/00): Grants paid, $154,285; assets, $3,295,363 (M); gifts received, $507,869; expenditures, $247,936; qualifying distributions, $145,898.
Limitations: Giving primarily in WI, with emphasis on Milwaukee.
Officers: Eric Butlein, Pres.; Jayne Butlein, V.P.
Directors: Adam Butlein, David Butlein, Alexandra DeToro, Jerry H. Friedland.
EIN: 391806000
Codes: FD2

56855
Kingfisher Fund, Inc.
c/o Messner Tierney Fisher & Nichols
111 E. Kilbourn Ave., 19th Fl.
Milwaukee, WI 53202

Established in 1997 in WI.
Donor(s): Patricia Heidenreich, William Heidenreich.‡
Financial data (yr. ended 12/31/01): Grants paid, $153,000; assets, $363 (M); gifts received, $152,601; expenditures, $155,601; qualifying distributions, $155,601.
Limitations: Applications not accepted. Giving primarily in IA and NY.
Application information: Contributes only to pre-selected organizations.
Officers: Patricia F. Heidenreich, Pres. and Treas.; Pamela S. Heidenreich, Secy.
EIN: 391878090
Codes: FD2

56856
WCN Bancorp-Bell Charitable Foundation, Inc.
181 2nd St. S.
Wisconsin Rapids, WI 54494

Established in 1992 in WI.
Donor(s): Wood County National Bank, Steven Bell, Margaret Bell.
Financial data (yr. ended 11/30/01): Grants paid, $152,250; assets, $2,273,239 (M); gifts received, $100,000; expenditures, $159,788; qualifying distributions, $152,001.
Limitations: Applications not accepted. Giving primarily in WI.
Application information: Contributes only to pre-selected organizations.
Officers and Directors:* Chad D. Kane,* Pres.; Paula J. Bell,* V.P.; Margaret L. Bell,* Secy.; Steven C. Bell,* Treas.; David W. Kumm.
EIN: 396572208
Codes: CS, FD2, CD

56857
Phyllis A. Beneke Scholarship Fund
c/o Bank One Trust Co., N.A.
P.O. Box 1308
Milwaukee, WI 53202
Scholarship application address: R.D. No. 4, Box 1976, Wheeling, WV 26003, tel.: (304) 243-0400
Contact: George S. Krelis, Committee Member

Established in 1989 in WV.
Donor(s): Phyllis A. Beneke.‡
Financial data (yr. ended 02/28/01): Grants paid, $152,000; assets, $3,504,602 (M); expenditures, $194,885; qualifying distributions, $160,101.
Limitations: Giving limited to residents of Ohio County, WV.
Publications: Informational brochure (including application guidelines).
Application information: Application form required.
Committee Members: George S. Krelis, Arthur R. Mezerski, Frances Schoolcraft.
Trustee: Bank One Trust Co., N.A.
EIN: 556106147
Codes: FD2, GTI

56858
Robert T. Meyer Foundation
(Formerly Robert T. and Betty Rose Meyer Family Foundation)
469 Security Blvd.
Green Bay, WI 54313
Application address: P.O. Box 19006, Green Bay, WI 54307-9006, tel.: (920) 433-3102
Contact: Mark McMullen, Tr.

Established in 1985 in WI.
Donor(s): Janet E. Meyer.
Financial data (yr. ended 12/31/01): Grants paid, $151,500; assets, $3,118,727 (M); expenditures, $173,709; qualifying distributions, $150,415.
Limitations: Giving primarily in Green Bay, WI.
Application information: Application form not required.
Trustees: Mark McMullen, Janet E. Meyer, John M. Rose.
EIN: 396413619
Codes: FD2

56859
Clicquennoi Family Foundation
c/o Wells Fargo Bank Wisconsin, N.A.
636 Wisconsin Ave.
Sheboygan, WI 53081-4003

Established in 1994 in WI.
Donor(s): Joanne Clicquennoi.
Financial data (yr. ended 08/31/01): Grants paid, $151,200; assets, $1,287,564 (M); expenditures, $161,761; qualifying distributions, $152,609.
Limitations: Applications not accepted. Giving primarily in WI.
Application information: Contributes only to pre-selected organizations.
Directors: Eldon Bohrofen, Shelly Giesen, Teri Strub.
Trustee: Wells Fargo Bank Wisconsin, N.A.
EIN: 391771210
Codes: FD2

56860
John A. Johnson Foundation
709 Lakewood Blvd.
Madison, WI 53704
Contact: John C. Weston, Pres.

Incorporated in 1951 in WI.
Financial data (yr. ended 12/31/01): Grants paid, $150,500; assets, $2,508,232 (M); expenditures, $170,825; qualifying distributions, $152,550.
Limitations: Giving primarily in WI.
Application information: Application form not required.
Officers: John C. Weston, Pres.; Toby E. Sherry, V.P.; Ruth G. Weston, Secy.-Treas.
Directors: John A. Bolz, Richmond F. Johnson, Stanley A. Johnson, John R. Pike, Thomas D. Zilavy.
EIN: 396078592
Codes: FD2

56861
Lyon Foundation, Inc.
c/o Bank One Trust Co., N.A.
P.O. Box 1308
Milwaukee, WI 53201
Application address: c/o Therese M. Thorn, Bank One, Trust Div., 611 Woodward Ave., Detroit, MI 48226, tel.: (313) 225-3124

Incorporated in 1951 in MI.
Donor(s): G. Albert Lyon, Sr.
Financial data (yr. ended 12/31/01): Grants paid, $150,000; assets, $2,751,526 (M); expenditures, $168,220; qualifying distributions, $154,261.
Limitations: Giving primarily in Detroit, MI.
Application information: Application form not required.
Officers and Members:* A. Randolph Judd,* Pres. and Secy.; John Terrill Judd,* V.P.; Therese M. Thorn, Winn Lyon Wheeler.
Agent: Bank One Trust Co., N.A.
EIN: 386121075
Codes: FD2

56862
L. C. Christensen Charitable and Religious Foundation, Inc.
c/o Hostak, Henzl & Bichler, S.C.
P.O. Box 516
Racine, WI 53401
Additional address: c/o Harold K. Christensen, Jr., 403 Spruce St., Abbotsford, WI 54405; E-mail: ssmith@hhb.com
Contact: Stephen J. Smith, Secy.

Established in 1966 in WI.
Donor(s): Harold K. Christensen, Sr.‡
Financial data (yr. ended 12/31/01): Grants paid, $149,150; assets, $3,413,827 (M); expenditures, $183,629; qualifying distributions, $158,739.
Limitations: Giving primarily in the Racine and Abbotsford, WI, areas.
Application information: Application form not required.
Officers: Harold K. Christensen, Jr., Pres.; Russel L. Kortendick, Sr., V.P.; Stephen J. Smith, Secy.; John F. Thompson, Treas.
Directors: John E. Erskine, Jr., Dennis E. Schelling.
EIN: 396096022
Codes: FD2

56863
Allen-Edmonds Shoe Corporation Charitable Foundation
201 E. Seven Hills Rd.
Port Washington, WI 53074-2512

Financial data (yr. ended 12/31/00): Grants paid, $148,184; assets, $716 (M); expenditures, $148,686; qualifying distributions, $148,686.
Limitations: Applications not accepted. Giving primarily in WI.
Application information: Contributes only to pre-selected organizations.
Trustees: S. Stollenwerk Peltz, D. Schuenke, J. Stollenwerk, Jr., P. Stollenwerk.
EIN: 391949021
Codes: FD2

56864
B. A. Mason Trust
1251 1st Ave.
Chippewa Falls, WI 54729-1408
(715) 723-1871
Contact: William Scobie, Tr.

Trust established about 1953.
Donor(s): Mason Shoe Manufacturing Co.
Financial data (yr. ended 12/31/01): Grants paid, $148,000; assets, $378,873 (M); gifts received, $250,000; expenditures, $154,637; qualifying distributions, $148,000.
Limitations: Giving primarily in Chippewa Falls, WI.
Trustees: Jane Mason Lubs, Rosemary Scobie, William M. Scobie.
EIN: 396075816
Codes: FD2

56865
Weiss Family Foundation
1660 N. Prospect Ave., No. 1201
Milwaukee, WI 53202
Contact: Richard L. Weiss, Tr.

Established in 1998 in WI.
Donor(s): Richard L. Weiss, Barbara B. Weiss.
Financial data (yr. ended 12/31/01): Grants paid, $148,000; assets, $2,643,522 (M); expenditures, $169,276; qualifying distributions, $148,000.
Limitations: Giving primarily in Milwaukee, WI.
Trustees: Barbara B. Weiss, Richard L. Weiss.
EIN: 396687485
Codes: FD2

56866
Trabant North Knox County Trust
c/o Bank One, Tax Svcs.
P.O. Box 1308
Milwaukee, WI 53201

Established in 1989 in IN.
Financial data (yr. ended 12/31/01): Grants paid, $147,102; assets, $2,887,270 (M); expenditures, $178,476; qualifying distributions, $146,647.
Limitations: Applications not accepted. Giving limited to North Knox County, IN in townships of Vigo, Washington, Widner, and Busseron.
Application information: Contributes only to pre-selected organizations.
Trustee: Bank One, N.A.
EIN: 311247607
Codes: FD2

56867
Francis R. & Ruth E. Oberreich Foundation Corporation
33 N. Bridge St.
P.O. Box 400
Markesan, WI 53946-0400 (920) 398-2371
Contact: Richard Slate, Treas.

Established in 1999 in WI.
Financial data (yr. ended 12/31/01): Grants paid, $146,937; assets, $2,627,979 (M); gifts received, $120,000; expenditures, $155,744; qualifying distributions, $146,937.
Officers: Joan R. Slate, Pres.; Roger Zuleger, V.P.; Lynn Funk, Secy.; Richard Slate, Treas.
Director: William R. Slate.
EIN: 391941148
Codes: FD2

56868
Merkel Foundation, Inc.
3712 Bismarck Cir.
Sheboygan, WI 53083

Established in 1986 in WI.
Donor(s): Daniel A. Merkel, Betty Merkel, American Orthodontics Corp.
Financial data (yr. ended 07/31/01): Grants paid, $146,383; assets, $3,143,886 (M); gifts received, $100,000; expenditures, $149,848; qualifying distributions, $146,011.
Limitations: Applications not accepted. Giving primarily in WI.
Application information: Contributes only to pre-selected organizations.
Officers and Directors:* Betty Merkel,* Pres.; Daniel A. Merkel,* Secy.; Alvin R. Kloet.
EIN: 391582624
Codes: FD2

56869
Ruth H. Shattuck Charitable Trust
c/o Bank One Trust Co., N.A.
P.O. Box 1308
Milwaukee, WI 53201
Application address: 111 E. Wisconsin Ave., Neenah, WI 54956
Contact: Joseph E. McGrane, Sr. V.P., Bank One Trust Co., N.A.

Established about 1953 in WI.

56869—WISCONSIN

Financial data (yr. ended 10/31/01): Grants paid, $144,200; assets, $2,936,129 (M); expenditures, $177,362; qualifying distributions, $144,071.
Limitations: Giving on a national basis.
Trustee: Bank One Trust Co., N.A.
EIN: 396048821
Codes: FD2

56870
Anthony Petullo Foundation, Inc.
312 E. Buffalo St., Ste. 200
Milwaukee, WI 53202

Established in 1999 in WI.
Donor(s): Anthony Petullo.
Financial data (yr. ended 09/30/01): Grants paid, $143,510; assets, $2,361,344 (M); expenditures, $243,595; qualifying distributions, $199,299.
Limitations: Giving primarily in southeastern WI.
Application information: Donors Forum of Wisconsin Common Application Form must be used. Application form required.
Officers: Anthony Petullo, Pres.; Amy Cesarz, Exec. Dir.
Directors: Henry Loos, Meg Petullo, Scott Petullo, Steve Petullo.
EIN: 311656951
Codes: FD2

56871
James A. Dooley Foundation
c/o William F. Fox
622 N. Water St., No. 500
Milwaukee, WI 53202-4978

Established in 1956 in IL.
Donor(s): Anne Elston.‡
Financial data (yr. ended 09/30/01): Grants paid, $142,999; assets, $1,763,262 (M); expenditures, $174,423; qualifying distributions, $155,499.
Limitations: Applications not accepted. Giving on a national basis.
Application information: Contributes only to pre-selected organizations.
Officers and Director:* Virginia P. Dooley,* Pres.; William Fitzhugh Fox, Secy.
EIN: 366075580
Codes: FD2

56872
Suzanne & Richard Pieper Family Foundation
11602 N. Shorecliff Ln.
Mequon, WI 53092
Contact: Suzanne E. Pieper, Pres.

Established in 1991 in WI.
Donor(s): Suzanne E. Pieper, Richard R. Pieper.
Financial data (yr. ended 10/31/01): Grants paid, $142,500; assets, $2,236,368 (M); gifts received, $1,100,000; expenditures, $158,278; qualifying distributions, $146,860.
Limitations: Giving primarily in WI.
Officers and Directors:* Suzanne E. Pieper,* Pres.; Richard R. Pieper,* Secy.-Treas.; Ann Elizabeth Pieper, Bridget Pieper Sullivan.
EIN: 391715108
Codes: FD2

56873
Carrie Foundation
P.O. Box 348
Janesville, WI 53547-0348
Contact: George K. Steil, Sr., Mgr.

Established in 1984 in WI.
Donor(s): James F. Fitzgerald, Sr., Marilyn C. Fitzgerald.
Financial data (yr. ended 11/30/01): Grants paid, $142,250; assets, $202,757 (M); gifts received, $50,000; expenditures, $144,276; qualifying distributions, $143,330.

Limitations: Applications not accepted. Giving limited to WI, with emphasis on Janesville.
Application information: Funds limited; foundation rarely makes awards to non-local organizations. Non-local organizations are discouraged from applying. Unsolicited requests for funds not accepted.
Officer: George K. Steil, Sr., Mgr.
Trustees: James F. Fitzgerald, Sr., Marilyn C. Fitzgerald.
EIN: 391503227
Codes: FD2

56874
Walter L. Merten Charitable Trust
1960 N. Hwy. 67
Neosho, WI 53059-9723

Donor(s): Walter L. Merten.
Financial data (yr. ended 12/31/00): Grants paid, $141,150; assets, $990,860 (M); expenditures, $141,221; qualifying distributions, $141,150.
Limitations: Applications not accepted.
Application information: Contributes only to pre-selected organizations.
Trustees: Grace M. Merten, Walter L. Merten, Barbara M. Schneider.
EIN: 391976901
Codes: FD2

56875
Donald A. Gordon Foundation
c/o North Central Trust Co.
311 Main St.
La Crosse, WI 54601

Financial data (yr. ended 12/31/01): Grants paid, $140,937; assets, $4,873,990 (M); expenditures, $183,791; qualifying distributions, $141,437.
Limitations: Applications not accepted. Giving primarily in La Crosse, WI.
Application information: Contributes only to pre-selected organizations.
Trustee: North Central Trust Co.
EIN: 316672086
Codes: FD2

56876
A. Sturm & Sons Foundation, Inc.
P.O. Box 287
Manawa, WI 54949-0287 (920) 596-2511
Contact: Paul J. Sturm, Secy.-Treas.

Established in 1964 in WI.
Financial data (yr. ended 06/30/01): Grants paid, $140,400; assets, $2,742,390 (M); expenditures, $143,866; qualifying distributions, $138,295.
Limitations: Giving primarily in the Manawa, WI, area.
Officers: John A. Sturm, Pres.; DuWayne R. Carl, V.P.; James A. Sturm, V.P.; Paul J. Sturm, Secy.-Treas.
EIN: 396084283
Codes: FD2

56877
Stanley Kritzik Family Foundation, Inc.
1530 W. Cedar Ln.
Milwaukee, WI 53217-1101
Contact: Stanley Kritzik, Pres.

Established about 1959 in WI.
Donor(s): Stanley Kritzik.
Financial data (yr. ended 12/31/01): Grants paid, $137,150; assets, $6,895 (M); gifts received, $120,000; expenditures, $137,154; qualifying distributions, $137,146.
Limitations: Giving primarily in Milwaukee, WI.
Application information: Application form not required.
Officer: Stanley Kritzik, Pres.

EIN: 396044572
Codes: FD2

56878
Maihaugen Foundation, Inc.
311 Main St.
La Crosse, WI 54601
Application address: 16585 Deer Creek Pkwy., Brookfield, WI 53005
Contact: Julia B. Faulkner, Dir.

Established in 1996 in WI.
Donor(s): Frances May, Merrydelle May.‡
Financial data (yr. ended 12/31/01): Grants paid, $135,500; assets, $2,592,946 (M); expenditures, $154,262; qualifying distributions, $135,335.
Limitations: Giving primarily in Door County and Milwaukee, WI.
Application information: No international applications accepted. Application form not required.
Directors: Michael R. Burton, Paul R. Burton, Julia B. Faulkner, Frances May.
Investment Manager: North Central Trust Co.
EIN: 391857836
Codes: FD2

56879
The Holt Family Foundation, Ltd.
P.O. Box 88
Elm Grove, WI 53122
Contact: Wayne G. Holt, Pres.

Established in 1992.
Donor(s): Wayne G. Holt.
Financial data (yr. ended 12/31/01): Grants paid, $135,000; assets, $2,287,921 (L); expenditures, $168,271; qualifying distributions, $154,438.
Limitations: Giving primarily in FL and WI.
Application information: Application form not required.
Officers and Directors:* Wayne G. Holt,* Pres. and Treas.; Lynn Ann Hawkins,* V.P.; Ann Margaret Bannister, Susan Mary Bello, Patricia Ann Freyschlag, Paul Christopher Holt, Mary Beth T. Jansen.
EIN: 391714992
Codes: FD2

56880
Gilbert & J. Dorothy Palay Family Foundation, Ltd.
(Formerly G.P. Foundation, Ltd.)
7123 N. Barnett Ln.
Milwaukee, WI 53217-3608

Established in 1977.
Donor(s): Gilbert Palay, J. Dorothy Palay.
Financial data (yr. ended 06/30/01): Grants paid, $134,500; assets, $779,510 (M); expenditures, $137,720; qualifying distributions, $132,991.
Limitations: Applications not accepted. Giving primarily in Milwaukee, WI.
Application information: Contributes only to pre-selected organizations.
Officers and Directors:* Gilbert Palay,* Pres. and Treas.; J. Dorothy Palay,* V.P. and Secy.; Robert J. Palay, Thomas M. Palay.
EIN: 391287503
Codes: FD2

56881
Green Bay Packers Foundation
1265 Lombardi Ave.
Green Bay, WI 54304-3928 (920) 496-5700
URL: http://www.packers.com/community/packers_foundation
Contact: Phillip Pionek, Secy.

Established in 1986 in WI.
Donor(s): Green Bay Packers, Inc.

Financial data (yr. ended 03/31/02): Grants paid, $134,245; assets, $2,102,137 (M); gifts received, $22,522; expenditures, $158,471; qualifying distributions, $133,819.
Limitations: Applications not accepted. Giving limited to WI.
Publications: Annual report, financial statement.
Application information: Contributes only to pre-selected organizations.
Officers and Trustees:* Carl W. Kuehne,* Chair.; Phillip Pionek, Secy.; Donald F. Harden, C. Patricia LaViolette, Michael R. Reese, Gary M. Rotherham, James A. Temp, Associated Banc-Corp.
EIN: 391577137
Codes: CS, FD2, CD

56882
Anna W. Thornton & Alexander P. Thornton Charitable Trust
c/o Bank One Trust Co., N.A.
P.O. Box 1308
Milwaukee, WI 53201
Application address: P.O. Box 2050, Fort Worth, TX 76113, tel.: (817) 884-4442
Contact: Rick Piersall

Financial data (yr. ended 09/30/01): Grants paid, $134,000; assets, $2,393,236 (M); expenditures, $169,377; qualifying distributions, $140,803.
Limitations: Giving primarily in Tarrant County, TX.
Trustee: Bank One Trust Co., N.A.
EIN: 756496915
Codes: FD2

56883
George K. Tallman Trust
c/o Bank One Trust Co., N.A.
P.O. Box 1308
Milwaukee, WI 53201
Application address: c/o Joel Bailey, Bank One Trust Co., 100 W. Milwaukee St., Janesville, WI 53547, tel.: (608) 757-6247

Financial data (yr. ended 12/31/00): Grants paid, $133,700; assets, $2,997,133 (M); expenditures, $169,329; qualifying distributions, $137,847.
Limitations: Giving primarily in WI.
Application information: Application form not required.
Trustee: Bank One Trust Co., N.A.
EIN: 390800033
Codes: FD2

56884
Muma Family Foundation, Inc.
7960 N. River Rd.
River Hills, WI 53217

Established in 1998 in WI.
Donor(s): Leslie Muma.
Financial data (yr. ended 12/31/01): Grants paid, $133,600; assets, $1,671,691 (M); expenditures, $148,008; qualifying distributions, $143,838.
Limitations: Applications not accepted. Giving primarily in FL and WI.
Application information: Contributes only to pre-selected organizations.
Officers: Leslie M. Muma, Pres.; Pamela S. Muma, Secy.-Treas.
Director: Lisa D. Weitz.
EIN: 391933039
Codes: FD2

56885
Joan & Fred Brengel Family Foundation, Inc.
c/o Foley & Lardner
777 E. Wisconsin Ave.
Milwaukee, WI 53202-5367   (414) 297-5753

Established in 1994 in WI.
Donor(s): Fred L. Brengel.
Financial data (yr. ended 12/31/00): Grants paid, $132,500; assets, $2,661,038 (M); expenditures, $138,070; qualifying distributions, $136,482.
Limitations: Applications not accepted. Giving on a national basis.
Application information: Contributes only to pre-selected organizations.
Officers and Directors:* Fred L. Brengel,* Pres.; Joan E. Brengel,* V.P.; Stephen M. Fisher,* Secy.-Treas.
EIN: 391768859
Codes: FD2

56886
Barnitz Fund
c/o Bank One Trust Co., N.A.
P.O. Box 1308
Milwaukee, WI 53201
Application address: c/o Bank One Trust Co., N.A., 2 S. Main St., Middletown, OH 45042
Contact: Mark D. Welch

Established in 1951 in OH.
Financial data (yr. ended 12/31/01): Grants paid, $132,470; assets, $2,139,243 (M); expenditures, $150,703; qualifying distributions, $138,649.
Limitations: Giving primarily in Middletown, OH.
Trustee: Bank One Trust Co., N.A.
EIN: 316020687
Codes: FD2, GTI

56887
Fenton E. English Charitable Trust
c/o Bank One Trust Co., N.A.
P.O. Box 1308
Milwaukee, WI 53201

Established in 1977 in KY.
Financial data (yr. ended 12/31/00): Grants paid, $131,448; assets, $3,233,176 (M); expenditures, $159,295; qualifying distributions, $132,383.
Limitations: Applications not accepted. Giving primarily in IL and KY.
Application information: Contributes only to pre-selected organizations.
Trustee: Bank One Trust Co., N.A.
EIN: 376121328
Codes: FD2, GTI

56888
Max Fund, Inc.
1250 W. Dean Rd.
River Hills, WI 53217
Contact: R. Max Samson, Pres.

Established in 1986 in WI.
Donor(s): R. Max Samson.
Financial data (yr. ended 12/31/01): Grants paid, $131,111; assets, $123,543 (M); gifts received, $34,440; expenditures, $160,008; qualifying distributions, $133,211.
Limitations: Giving primarily in Milwaukee, WI.
Application information: Application form not required.
Officer: R. Max Samson, Pres.
EIN: 391563191
Codes: FD2

56889
Lenfestey Family Foundation, Inc.
P.O. Box 23200
Green Bay, WI 54305-3200

Established in 1992 in WI.
Donor(s): Josephine B. Lenfestey.
Financial data (yr. ended 06/30/01): Grants paid, $130,620; assets, $2,961,956 (M); expenditures, $159,698; qualifying distributions, $132,628.
Limitations: Applications not accepted. Giving primarily in Green Bay, WI.
Application information: Contributes only to pre-selected organizations.
Officers: Josephine B. Lenfestey, Pres.; Frederick Schmidt, V.P. and Secy.; James Lenfestey, Treas.
EIN: 391748548
Codes: FD2

56890
Anne and Fred Luber Foundation
777 N. Prospect Ave.
Milwaukee, WI 53202
Contact: Fred G. Luber, Pres.

Established in 1981.
Donor(s): Fred G. Luber.
Financial data (yr. ended 11/30/01): Grants paid, $130,151; assets, $1,607,990 (M); gifts received, $144,165; expenditures, $131,620; qualifying distributions, $131,351.
Limitations: Giving primarily in Milwaukee, WI.
Application information: Application form required.
Officers: Fred G. Luber, Pres.; Anne Luber, V.P.; Paul Luber, V.P.
EIN: 391426224
Codes: FD2

56891
Long Family Foundation Trust
P.O. Box 11008
Green Bay, WI 54307-1008

Established in 1989 in WI.
Donor(s): Donald J. Long, Sr.
Financial data (yr. ended 12/31/01): Grants paid, $129,634; assets, $89,427 (M); expenditures, $129,696; qualifying distributions, $129,696.
Limitations: Applications not accepted. Giving primarily in Green Bay, WI.
Application information: Contributes only to pre-selected organizations.
Trustees: Nancy G. Laubenstein, Darlene M. Long, Donald J. Long, Sr., Robert W. Schaefer.
EIN: 391615503
Codes: FD2

56892
Antoinette A. Keenan Trust
(also known as Matthew Keenan Endowment Fund)
c/o Marshall & Ilsley Bank
P.O. Box 2980
Milwaukee, WI 53201

Donor(s): Antoinette A. Keenan.‡
Financial data (yr. ended 06/30/02): Grants paid, $128,782; assets, $1,626,889 (M); expenditures, $153,809; qualifying distributions, $128,196.
Limitations: Applications not accepted. Giving limited to Milwaukee, WI.
Application information: Contributes only to pre-selected organizations.
Trustee: Marshall & Ilsley Bank.
EIN: 396042097
Codes: FD2

56893
Sub-Zero Foundation, Inc.
c/o Sub-Zero Freezer Co., Inc.
4717 Hammersley Rd.
Madison, WI 53711 (608) 270-3202
Contact: Laurie Sullivan

Established in 1998 in WI.
Donor(s): Sub-Zero Freezer Co., Inc.
Financial data (yr. ended 04/30/01): Grants paid, $128,600; assets, $844,436 (M); expenditures, $128,651; qualifying distributions, $127,399.
Limitations: Giving primarily in Madison, WI.
Trustees: Helen A. Bakke, James J. Bakke, Deborah A. Schwartz.
EIN: 391918462
Codes: CS, FD2, CD

56894
Anna C. Gamble Foundation
c/o Bank One Trust Co., N.A.
P.O. Box 1308
Milwaukee, WI 53201

Established in 1969 in IL.
Donor(s): Anna C. Gamble.‡
Financial data (yr. ended 02/28/02): Grants paid, $127,000; assets, $1,722,939 (M); expenditures, $173,254; qualifying distributions, $138,152.
Limitations: Applications not accepted.
Application information: Contributes only to pre-selected organizations.
Trustees: Thomas E. Devine, Bank One Trust Co., N.A.
EIN: 366429423
Codes: FD2

56895
Rudy and Louise Jakmas Charitable Trust
c/o Bank One Trust Co., N.A.
P.O. Box 1308
Milwaukee, WI 53201

Financial data (yr. ended 12/31/00): Grants paid, $127,000; assets, $812,610 (M); expenditures, $133,342; qualifying distributions, $127,612.
Limitations: Applications not accepted. Giving primarily in Lorain, OH.
Application information: Contributes only to pre-selected organizations.
Trustee: Bank One Trust Co., N.A.
EIN: 346922809
Codes: FD2

56896
The Leslie C. Robins Family Foundation
N9618 Winnebago Park Rd.
Fond du Lac, WI 54935
Contact: Richard Wehner, Tr.

Established around 1995 in WI.
Donor(s): Leslie C. Robins.
Financial data (yr. ended 07/31/01): Grants paid, $126,980; assets, $20,449 (M); gifts received, $400; expenditures, $129,948; qualifying distributions, $126,980.
Limitations: Giving primarily in WI.
Trustees: Charles F. Robins, Leslie C. Robins, Richard Wehner.
EIN: 391805982
Codes: FD2

56897
The Merrill Foundation, Inc.
312 E. Wisconsin Ave., Ste. 402
Milwaukee, WI 53202 (414) 765-5668
Contact: Marion C. Read, Pres.

Established in 1997 in WI.
Donor(s): Marion C. Read.
Financial data (yr. ended 12/31/01): Grants paid, $126,250; assets, $1,380,257 (M); gifts received, $129,219; expenditures, $130,516; qualifying distributions, $126,352.
Limitations: Giving primarily in Milwaukee, WI.
Application information: Application form not required.
Officers and Directors:* Marion Merrill Chester Read,* Pres.; Verne R. Read,* V.P.; Alice E. Read,* Secy.; V. Ross Read III,* Treas.; Alexander R. Read, Thomas Merrill Read.
Trustee: U.S. Bank.
EIN: 391892801
Codes: FD2

56898
Elizabeth B. & Philip J. Hendrickson Foundation, Ltd.
2538 Bittersweet Ave.
Green Bay, WI 54301-1843 (920) 435-0921
FAX: (920) 435-1027
Contact: Elizabeth B. Hendrickson, Pres.

Established in 1986 in WI.
Donor(s): Scott D. Hendrickson, Philip J. Hendrickson, Sara H. Fortune, Elizabeth B. Hendrickson.
Financial data (yr. ended 08/31/01): Grants paid, $125,396; assets, $1,869,760 (M); gifts received, $70,000; expenditures, $138,040; qualifying distributions, $124,725.
Limitations: Giving primarily in WI.
Application information: Application form not required.
Officers: Elizabeth B. Hendrickson, Pres. and Treas.; Sara H. Fortune, V.P.; Scott D. Hendrickson, V.P.; Philip J. Hendrickson, Secy.
EIN: 391395624
Codes: FD2

56899
Parker Foundation
c/o Marshall & Ilsley Trust Company, N.A.
P.O. Box 5000
Janesville, WI 53547 (608) 754-4700
Application address: c/o Robert E. Collins, V.P., 20 E. Milwaukee St., Ste. 300, Janesville, WI 53545

Established in 1953 in WI.
Financial data (yr. ended 12/31/01): Grants paid, $124,600; assets, $2,494,990 (M); expenditures, $151,598; qualifying distributions, $127,060.
Limitations: Giving on a national basis.
Officer and Director:* Robert E. Collins,* V.P. and Secy.-Treas.
EIN: 396074582
Codes: FD2

56900
The ROS Foundation
c/o Robert O. Schlytter
5111 S. 76th St.
Greendale, WI 53129-1115

Established in 1998 in WI.
Donor(s): Robert O. Schlytter, Marion C. Schlytter.
Financial data (yr. ended 12/31/00): Grants paid, $124,600; assets, $3,076,735 (M); gifts received, $249,875; expenditures, $133,586; qualifying distributions, $124,600.
Application information: Application form not required.
Trustees: Susan L. Riordan, Robert B. Schlytter, Robert O. Schlytter.
EIN: 391948463
Codes: FD2

56901
Jerome & Dorothy Holz Family Foundation
10400 Innovation Dr.
Milwaukee, WI 53226 (414) 774-1031
Contact: Don Tushaus

Established in 1996 in WI.
Donor(s): Dorothy Holz, Jerome J. Holz, Holz Motors, Inc., Hales Corners Acceptance, Inc.
Financial data (yr. ended 08/31/01): Grants paid, $124,500; assets, $4,130,663 (M); gifts received, $415,000; expenditures, $140,957; qualifying distributions, $132,459.
Limitations: Giving primarily in the greater Milwaukee, WI area.
Publications: Program policy statement, application guidelines.
Application information: Application form required.
Officers and Trustees:* Jerome J. Holz,* Pres.; Dorothy Holz,* Exec. V.P.; Loraine Schuffler,* V.P.; Barbara Holz Weis,* Secy.; Judith Holz Stathas,* Treas.
EIN: 391876121
Codes: FD2

56902
U.S. Paper Mills Foundation, Inc.
824 Fort Howard Ave.
De Pere, WI 54115-2313
Contact: Robert J. Cloud, Pres.

Established in 1984.
Donor(s): U.S. Paper Mills Corp.
Financial data (yr. ended 09/30/01): Grants paid, $123,000; assets, $2,748,639 (M); gifts received, $175,500; expenditures, $148,035; qualifying distributions, $123,000.
Limitations: Applications not accepted. Giving primarily in areas of plant locations in WI.
Application information: Contributes only to pre-selected organizations; funds severely limited.
Officers: Robert J. Cloud, Pres.; Nancy Gustavson, Secy.; Lisa Collar, Treas.
EIN: 391432753
Codes: CS, FD2, CD

56903
Isabel Van Horn Scholarship Trust
c/o Bank One Trust Co., N.A.
P.O. Box 1308
Milwaukee, WI 53201
Application address: c/o Central Christian Church, 587 Mount Vernon Rd., Newark, OH 43055
Contact: Rev. Mark Richardson

Established in 1993 in OH.
Financial data (yr. ended 12/31/01): Grants paid, $122,783; assets, $1,317,793 (M); expenditures, $138,467; qualifying distributions, $125,085.
Limitations: Giving primarily in IN, OH and KY.
Trustee: Bank One Trust Co., N.A.
EIN: 316464732
Codes: FD2, GTI

56904
Scott & Peggy Sampson Charitable Fund, Inc.
c/o J. Bernstein, Godfrey & Kahn, S.C.
780 N. Water St.
Milwaukee, WI 53202

Established in 1994 in WI.
Financial data (yr. ended 12/31/01): Grants paid, $121,200; assets, $3,170,795 (M); expenditures, $120,936; qualifying distributions, $121,200.
Limitations: Applications not accepted. Giving primarily in Milwaukee, WI.
Application information: Contributes only to pre-selected organizations.

Officers and Directors:* Scott A. Sampson,* Pres. and Treas.; Peggy Sampson,* V.P.; Joseph M. Bernstein,* Secy.; Richard H. Meyer.
EIN: 391796530
Codes: FD2

56905
Richard L. Boland, Love for Life Foundation, Inc.
c/o John A. Herbers
P.O. Box 514000
Milwaukee, WI 53203-3400

Established in 1992 in WI.
Donor(s): Elizabeth A. Boland.
Financial data (yr. ended 06/30/01): Grants paid, $120,000; assets, $37,826 (M); gifts received, $120,000; expenditures, $109,357; qualifying distributions, $109,357.
Limitations: Applications not accepted. Giving primarily in Milwaukee and Wauwatosa, WI.
Application information: Contributes only to pre-selected organizations.
Officers and Directors:* Elizabeth A. Boland,* Pres.; Dorothy E. Zanoni,* V.P.; John A. Herbers,* Secy.-Treas.
EIN: 391738990
Codes: FD2

56906
Chipstone Foundation
777 E. Wisconsin Ave., Ste. 3090
Milwaukee, WI 53202-5373
Contact: Allen M. Taylor, Chair.

Established in 1966.
Donor(s): Stanley Stone,‡ Ivor Noel Hume, Mrs. Ivor Noel Hume, I. Stanley Stone Charitable Trust.
Financial data (yr. ended 12/31/01): Grants paid, $120,000; assets, $56,600,000 (M); gifts received, $2,495,000; expenditures, $5,514,000; qualifying distributions, $5,000,000; giving activities include $4,500,000 for programs.
Limitations: Applications not accepted. Giving primarily in Madison and Milwaukee, WI.
Application information: Contributes only to pre-selected organizations. Unsolicited requests for funds not accepted.
Officers and Directors:* Allen M. Taylor,* Chair. and Secy.-Treas.; W. David Knox,* C.E.O. and Pres.; Dudley J. Godfrey, Jr.,* V.P.; Jonathan Prown, Exec. Dir.; Charles F. Hummel, Jere D. McGaffey, John S. McGregor, Philip L. Stone.
EIN: 396096593
Codes: FD2

56907
Juedes Family Foundation, Inc.
117 S. 3rd Ave.
Wausau, WI 54401

Established in 1997 in WI.
Donor(s): Arthur Juedes, Barbara Juedes.
Financial data (yr. ended 12/31/01): Grants paid, $120,000; assets, $2,220,096 (M); expenditures, $147,908; qualifying distributions, $119,769.
Limitations: Applications not accepted. Giving on a national basis.
Application information: Contributes only to pre-selected organizations.
Officers: Barbara Juedes, Pres.; Arthur Juedes, V.P.; Paul Gassner, Secy.-Treas.
EIN: 391873138
Codes: FD2

56908
Wildwood Foundation
3780 N. 169th St.
Brookfield, WI 53005-2198 (262) 790-9188
Contact: June Jager-Norman

Established in 1970 in WI.
Donor(s): Red Arrow Products Co., North American Corp.
Financial data (yr. ended 12/31/00): Grants paid, $120,000; assets, $2,423,363 (M); expenditures, $140,231; qualifying distributions, $117,464.
Limitations: Giving on a national basis.
Application information: Application form not required.
Trustees: Katherine Kurth, Thomas Kurth, Tineka Kurth, Elisabeth Wrean.
EIN: 237096923
Codes: FD2

56909
The F & A Trucking Foundation, Inc.
c/o Frederick P. Stratton, Jr.
777 E. Wisconsin Ave., Ste. 1400
Milwaukee, WI 53202-5302 (414) 347-1590

Established in 1994 in WI.
Donor(s): Anne Y. Stratton, Frederick P. Stratton, Jr.
Financial data (yr. ended 06/30/01): Grants paid, $119,950; assets, $117,071 (M); gifts received, $5,935; expenditures, $123,286; qualifying distributions, $121,030.
Limitations: Applications not accepted. Giving on a national basis, with emphasis on WI.
Application information: Contributes only to pre-selected organizations.
Officers and Directors:* Frederick P. Stratton, Jr.,* Pres.; Anne Y. Stratton,* V.P.; Henry J. Loos, Secy.-Treas.; Diane E. Stratton, Frederick P. Stratton III, Margaret E. Stratton.
EIN: 391783126
Codes: FD2

56910
Edward U. Demmer Foundation
c/o Bank One Trust Co., N.A.
P.O. Box 1308
Milwaukee, WI 53201 (414) 765-2800
Contact: David R. Strelitz

Established in 1963 in WI.
Donor(s): Edward U. Demmer.‡
Financial data (yr. ended 12/31/01): Grants paid, $119,000; assets, $1,155,570 (M); expenditures, $149,887; qualifying distributions, $125,132.
Limitations: Giving primarily in Milwaukee, WI.
Application information: Only accepting applications from organizations which have received funding in the past.
Trustees: Lawrence Demmer, Richard Goisman, Harold J. McComas, Bank One Trust Co., N.A.
EIN: 396064898
Codes: FD2

56911
Steven Sampson Charitable Fund, Inc.
c/o J. Bernstein, Godfrey & Kahn, S.C.
780 N. Water St.
Milwaukee, WI 53202

Established in 1994 in WI.
Financial data (yr. ended 12/31/00): Grants paid, $117,000; assets, $2,687,406 (M); expenditures, $139,472; qualifying distributions, $113,568.
Limitations: Applications not accepted. Giving primarily in Milwaukee, WI.
Application information: Contributes only to pre-selected organizations.
Officers and Directors:* Steven J. Sampson,* Pres. and Treas.; Joseph M. Bernstein,* V.P. and Secy.; Richard H. Meyer.
EIN: 391796526
Codes: FD2

56912
Arthur W. Strelow Trust
c/o Marshall & Ilsley Trust Company, N.A.
P.O. Box 2980
Milwaukee, WI 53201-2980
Application address: c/o Jeffrey Budzisz, P.O. Box 830, Madison, WI, 53701, tel.: (608) 232-2062

Established in 1980 in WI.
Donor(s): Arthur W. Strelow.‡
Financial data (yr. ended 03/31/02): Grants paid, $115,394; assets, $1,628,148 (M); expenditures, $136,920; qualifying distributions, $112,643.
Limitations: Giving primarily in WI, with emphasis on Madison.
Application information: Application form not required.
Trustees: Marcella Candlin, William Rosenbaum, Marshall & Ilsley Trust Company, N.A.
EIN: 396335082
Codes: FD2

56913
Carol and Richard Bayerlein Foundation, Ltd.
1810 Wedgewood Dr.
Elm Grove, WI 53122

Established in 1999 in WI.
Donor(s): Carol C. Bayerlein, Richard E. Bayerlein.
Financial data (yr. ended 12/31/01): Grants paid, $115,100; assets, $396,332 (M); gifts received, $116,925; expenditures, $118,055; qualifying distributions, $115,100.
Limitations: Applications not accepted. Giving primarily in Milwaukee, WI.
Application information: Contributes only to pre-selected organizations.
Directors: Carol C. Bayerlein, Douglas G. Bayerlein, Richard E. Bayerlein, Steven R. Bayerlein, Beth Wilson.
EIN: 391975173

56914
Sadoff Family Foundation
c/o Ronald Sadoff, Badger Liquor Co.
850 S. Morris St., P.O. Box 1137
Fond Du Lac, WI 54936-1137

Established in 1999 in WI.
Donor(s): Badger Liquor Company.
Financial data (yr. ended 12/31/01): Grants paid, $115,100; assets, $65,724 (M); gifts received, $25,000; expenditures, $115,103; qualifying distributions, $115,100.
Limitations: Applications not accepted. Giving primarily in Fond Du Lac, WI.
Application information: Contributes only to pre-selected organizations.
Trustees: Arthur Callistein, Gary Sadoff, Ronald Sadoff.
EIN: 396713550
Codes: FD2

56915
Ettinger Family Foundation, Inc.
2602 W. Lake Vista Ct.
Mequon, WI 53092
Contact: Suzy B. Ettinger, Mgr.

Donor(s): Anita Y. Ettinger, Anita Y. Ettinger Trust.
Financial data (yr. ended 07/31/01): Grants paid, $115,000; assets, $2,959,343 (M); gifts received, $1,546,071; expenditures, $171,722; qualifying distributions, $115,000.
Limitations: Giving primarily in Milwaukee, WI.
Application information: Application form not required.

Officer: Suzy B. Ettinger, Mgr.
Trustees: J. Lewis Perlson, Robert A. Yolles.
EIN: 396042926
Codes: FD2

56916
Robert W. & Josephine Pieper Foundation, Inc.
14425 Westover Rd.
Elm Grove, WI 53122

Established in 1963 in WI.
Donor(s): Isabel Schendel.‡
Financial data (yr. ended 12/31/01): Grants paid, $115,000; assets, $82,423 (M); gifts received, $120,564; expenditures, $115,610; qualifying distributions, $115,000.
Limitations: Applications not accepted. Giving primarily in WI.
Application information: Contributes only to pre-selected organizations.
Officer and Directors:* Richard A. Sachs,* Pres.; Harold Emch, Jr., William R. Law, Richard A. Sachs, Jr.
EIN: 396083875
Codes: FD2

56917
Richard G. Jacobus Family Foundation, Inc.
2323 N. Mayfair Rd.
Wauwatosa, WI 53226 (414) 475-6565
Contact: Barbara J. Wells, V.P.

Established in 1986 in WI.
Donor(s): Richard G. Jacobus.
Financial data (yr. ended 12/31/00): Grants paid, $114,769; assets, $2,446,238 (M); gifts received, $56,442; expenditures, $148,660; qualifying distributions, $115,165.
Limitations: Giving primarily in southeastern WI.
Officers and Directors:* Richard G. Jacobus,* Pres.; Barbara J. Wells,* V.P. and Secy.; William K. Jensen, V.P. and Treas.; Carolyn D. Jacobus, V.P.
EIN: 391555500
Codes: FD2

56918
Frank G. Andres Charitable Trust
c/o First Bank of Tomah
1001 Superior Ave., P.O. Box 753
Tomah, WI 54660-0753

Established in 1976 in WI.
Financial data (yr. ended 06/30/01): Grants paid, $113,846; assets, $2,973,381 (M); expenditures, $136,951; qualifying distributions, $117,474.
Limitations: Giving primarily in the Tomah, WI, area.
Application information: Application form required.
Officer and Trustees:* Roxana O'Conner,* Treas.; Richard Baumgarten, Jay Carmichael, Kevin Oliver, Raymond E. Paulis, Charles Schaeve.
EIN: 510172405
Codes: FD2

56919
Albert J. & Flora H. Ellinger Foundation, Inc.
1000 N. Water St., 13th Fl.
Milwaukee, WI 53202 (414) 287-7177
FAX: (414) 287-7025
Contact: William T. Gaus, Pres.

Established in 1956 in WI.
Donor(s): Albert J. Ellinger,‡ Flora H. Ellinger.‡
Financial data (yr. ended 07/31/01): Grants paid, $112,250; assets, $2,264,330 (M); expenditures, $134,500; qualifying distributions, $109,842.
Limitations: Giving primarily in Milwaukee, WI.
Application information: Application form not required.

Officers and Directors:* William T. Gaus,* Pres.; John U. Schmid, Jr.,* Secy.
EIN: 237098671
Codes: FD2

56920
Dorothy Kopmeier Vallier Foundation, Inc.
c/o Edwin P. Wiley
777 E. Wisconsin Ave.
Milwaukee, WI 53202-5373

Established in 1974.
Donor(s): Dorothy K. Vallier.
Financial data (yr. ended 06/30/01): Grants paid, $112,000; assets, $1,946,694 (M); expenditures, $130,118; qualifying distributions, $112,925.
Limitations: Applications not accepted. Giving primarily in WI.
Application information: Contributes only to pre-selected organizations.
Officers and Directors:* Dorothy K. Vallier,* Pres.; Edwin P. Wiley,* V.P.; Michael A. Gehl,* Secy.-Treas.; William G. Kummer.
EIN: 237417554
Codes: FD2

56921
Miles Kimball Foundation, Inc.
41 W. 8th St.
Oshkosh, WI 54901 (920) 231-3800
Contact: Mary Bathke, Exec. Asst.

Established in 1951 in WI.
Donor(s): Miles Kimball Co.
Financial data (yr. ended 12/31/01): Grants paid, $111,100; assets, $1,747,779 (M); gifts received, $1,300; expenditures, $123,476; qualifying distributions, $115,876.
Limitations: Applications not accepted. Giving limited to the Oshkosh, WI, area.
Application information: Contributes only to pre-selected organizations. Funds currently committed to local charities which have previously received foundation support.
Officers and Directors:* Mike Muoio,* Pres.; Cam Ross, Secy.-Treas.; John Rice.
EIN: 396075744
Codes: CS, FD2, CD

56922
Black River Falls Area Foundation
c/o Jackson County Bank
8 Main St.
Black River Falls, WI 54615 (715) 284-5341
Application address: P.O. Box 99, Black River Falls, WI 54615
Contact: Gilbert L. Homstad, Chair.

Established in 1985 in WI.
Financial data (yr. ended 12/31/00): Grants paid, $111,086; assets, $1,236,152 (M); gifts received, $177,899; expenditures, $127,631.
Limitations: Giving limited to Jackson County, WI, with emphasis on the city of Black River Falls.
Publications: Application guidelines, informational brochure, multi-year report.
Application information: Applications accepted between Apr. 1 and May 15. Application form required.
Officers and Trustees:* Gilbert L. Homstad,* Chair.; David Hoffman, Vice-Chair.; A.T. Lahmeyer, Secy.; John Lund,* Treas.; Todd Anderson, Ruth Buswell, Mike Dougherty, John Hogden, Mary O'Brien, Jerry Kitowski.
EIN: 391563654
Codes: CM, FD2

56923
Robert and Ida Nichol Educational Trust
c/o Bank One Trust Co., N.A.
P.O. Box 1308
Milwaukee, WI 53201
Application address: P.O. Box 635, Kenosha, WI 53141
Contact: Douglas G. Petermann

Established in 1993 in WI.
Financial data (yr. ended 12/31/01): Grants paid, $111,035; assets, $847,780 (M); gifts received, $16,635; expenditures, $120,823; qualifying distributions, $113,551.
Limitations: Giving limited to residents of Kenosha County, WI.
Application information: Application form required.
Trustee: Bank One Trust Co., N.A.
EIN: 396576895
Codes: FD2

56924
The Turner Foundation
c/o Bank One, Louisiana, N.A.
P.O. Box 1308
Milwaukee, WI 53201
Contact: Mike Robinson

Established in 1989 in LA.
Donor(s): Turner Industries, Inc., National Maintenance Corp., International Piping Systems, Nichols Construction, International Maintenance Corp., Burt S. Turner, Suzanne W. Turner.
Financial data (yr. ended 12/31/01): Grants paid, $110,500; assets, $1,595,114 (M); expenditures, $120,943; qualifying distributions, $113,453.
Limitations: Giving limited to LA.
Application information: Application form not required.
Trustee: Bank One, Louisiana, N.A.
EIN: 581875562
Codes: CS, FD2, CD

56925
Mid-States Aluminum Foundation, Inc.
132 Trowbridge Dr.
Fond Du Lac, WI 54937

Established in 2001 in WI.
Donor(s): Mid-States Aluminum, Inc.
Financial data (yr. ended 12/31/01): Grants paid, $110,000; assets, $506 (M); gifts received, $111,000; expenditures, $110,494; qualifying distributions, $110,480.
Limitations: Applications not accepted. Giving primarily in Fond Du Lac, WI.
Application information: Contributes only to pre-selected organizations.
Directors: Dawn Colwin, Betty Koenigs, Thomas E. Sewall.
EIN: 392014920
Codes: CS

56926
Harold C. Kallies Charitable Trust
c/o First National Bank of Manitowoc
P.O. Box 10
Manitowoc, WI 54221
Contact: Ronald G. Chinnock

Established in 1996 in WI.
Financial data (yr. ended 12/31/00): Grants paid, $109,000; assets, $2,194,178 (M); expenditures, $138,226; qualifying distributions, $109,000.
Limitations: Giving primarily in Manitowoc County, WI.
Application information: Student applicants should submit required scholarship application. Application form required.

Trustees: Arden A. Muchin, First National Bank of Manitowoc.
Allocations Committee: Thomas J. Bare, John W. Crubaugh, Robert Pietroski.
EIN: 396548517
Codes: FD2

56927
Phyllis & Walter Malzahn Charitable Trust
c/o Foley & Lardner
777 E. Wisconsin Ave.
Milwaukee, WI 53202 (414) 297-5748
Contact: Harrold J. McComas, Tr.

Established in 1989 in WI.
Financial data (yr. ended 12/31/01): Grants paid, $109,000; assets, $2,180,972 (M); expenditures, $126,559; qualifying distributions, $113,622.
Limitations: Giving primarily in Chehalis and Centalia, WA, and West Bend and Milwaukee, WI.
Application information: Application form not required.
Trustees: Richard R. Malzahn, Harrold J. McComas.
EIN: 396511776
Codes: FD2

56928
Eau Claire Area Foundation
P.O. Box 511
Eau Claire, WI 54702-0511 (715) 552-3801
Application address: 306 S. Barstow, Ste. 104, Eau Claire, WI 54701; FAX: (715) 552-3802; E-mail: info@ecareafoundation.org; URL: http://www.ecareafoundation.org
Contact: Sonya Tourville, Exec. Dir.

Established in 1997 in WI.
Financial data (yr. ended 12/31/01): Grants paid, $108,660; assets, $200,000 (M); gifts received, $315,000; expenditures, $206,000.
Limitations: Giving limited to the Eau Claire, WI school district.
Publications: Annual report, financial statement, grants list, newsletter, informational brochure (including application guidelines).
Application information: Application form required.
Directors: B.J. Farmer, Jon Homstad, Dick Larson, Jack Postlewaite, Sue Tietz, and 5 additional directors.
EIN: 391891064
Codes: CM, FD2

56929
Koss Foundation, Inc.
(Formerly John C. Koss Family Foundation, Inc.)
4129 N. Port Washington Rd.
Milwaukee, WI 53212-1029
Contact: John C. Koss, Pres.; or Nancy L. Koss, Secy.-Treas.

Established in 1968 in WI.
Donor(s): Koss Corp.
Financial data (yr. ended 12/31/01): Grants paid, $108,434; assets, $951,867 (M); gifts received, $138,092; expenditures, $109,152; qualifying distributions, $108,434.
Limitations: Giving primarily in the Milwaukee, WI, area.
Application information: Grants are allocated at fiscal year end based on company's profits. Application form not required.
Officers and Directors:* John C. Koss,* Pres.; Nancy L. Koss, Secy.-Treas.; Michael J. Koss.
EIN: 391098935
Codes: CS, FD2, CD

56930
Extendicare Foundation, Inc.
(Formerly Unicare Foundation, Inc.)
111 W. Michigan St.
Milwaukee, WI 53203-2903 (414) 908-8000
Additional tel.: (800) 395-5000; FAX: (414) 908-8507
Contact: Jim Wahner, Pres.

Established in 1985 in WI.
Donor(s): Extendicare Health Services, Inc.
Financial data (yr. ended 12/31/01): Grants paid, $108,367; assets, $546,959 (M); gifts received, $189,712; expenditures, $106,524; qualifying distributions, $122,767.
Limitations: Giving primarily in areas of company operations in AR, DE, FL, ID, IN, KY, MN, OH, OR, PA, TX, WA, WI, and WV.
Publications: Annual report (including application guidelines), informational brochure.
Application information: Contact a local Extendicare Health facility for further information. Application form required.
Officers and Directors:* Jim Wahner,* Pres.; Joy Calkin, V.P.; Lisa Hutchins,* Secy.; Steve Biondi,* Treas.; Cuba Adams, Lori Colwell, Holly Gould, Laura Hickey, Nancy Johnson, Christine Kovach, Ph.D., Kathy Locke, Jonathan Neagle, Anna Otigara, Chris Page, Jennifer Rittler, Mark A. Sager, M.D.
EIN: 391549381
Codes: CS, FD2, CD

56931
Lundman Family Foundation, Inc.
3631 W. Fredonia Kohler Rd.
Fredonia, WI 53021-9426 (262) 692-2416
Contact: Philip L. Lundman, Dir.

Established in 1981 in WI.
Donor(s): Philip L. Lundman, Petersen Resources, LLC.
Financial data (yr. ended 12/31/01): Grants paid, $107,900; assets, $1,244,225 (M); gifts received, $115,230; expenditures, $153,189; qualifying distributions, $125,692.
Limitations: Giving on a national basis.
Application information: Application form required.
Directors: Nancy L. Lundman, Philip L. Lundman.
EIN: 391401767
Codes: FD2

56932
Jean Thomas Lambert Foundation
c/o Bank One Trust Co., N.A.
P.O. Box 1308
Milwaukee, WI 53201

Established in 1999 in OH.
Financial data (yr. ended 12/31/01): Grants paid, $107,700; assets, $509,545 (M); gifts received, $400,000; expenditures, $118,924; qualifying distributions, $107,700.
Limitations: Applications not accepted. Giving on a national basis.
Application information: Contributes only to pre-selected organizations.
Trustees: Jean Thomas Lambert, Thomas Lambert, Nancy Reymann.
EIN: 341897221
Codes: FD2

56933
Michael L. and Nancy A. Hansen Family Foundation, Inc.
2033 Ludington Ave.
Wauwatosa, WI 53226-2715 (414) 453-5824
Contact: Michael L. Hansen, Pres.

Established in 1999 in WI.
Donor(s): Micheal L. Hansen, Nancy A. Hansen.
Financial data (yr. ended 12/31/01): Grants paid, $105,427; assets, $4,947 (M); gifts received, $100,500; expenditures, $107,650; qualifying distributions, $107,610.
Limitations: Giving primarily in WI.
Officers: Michael L. Hansen, Pres. and Treas.; Nancy A. Hansen, V.P. and Secy.
EIN: 391955791
Codes: FD2

56934
Joseph & Evaleen Neufeld Charitable Foundation Trust
c/o Bank One Trust Co., N.A.
P.O. Box 1308
Milwaukee, WI 53201
Application address: c/o Bank One Trust Co., N.A., 200 S. Adams St., P.O. Box 19029, Green Bay, WI 54307-9029, tel.: (262) 436-2610

Established in 1988 in WI.
Financial data (yr. ended 06/30/01): Grants paid, $105,000; assets, $2,599,270 (M); expenditures, $129,656; qualifying distributions, $122,517.
Limitations: Giving primarily in IN, MI, and WI.
Trustees: John E. Herald, Ingrid Hoffman Merkatoris, Bank One Trust Co., N.A.
EIN: 396480776
Codes: FD2

56935
Windway Foundation, Inc.
P.O. Box 897
Sheboygan, WI 53081
Application address: c/o Windway Capital Corp., 630 Riverfront Dr., Ste. 200, Sheboygan, WI 53081, tel.: (920) 457-8600
Contact: Terry J. Kohler, Pres.

Donor(s): The Vollrath Co., LLC, Windway Capital Corp.
Financial data (yr. ended 09/30/01): Grants paid, $104,647; assets, $145,763 (M); gifts received, $120,000; expenditures, $106,805; qualifying distributions, $106,805.
Limitations: Giving primarily in WI; some giving also in IL, MI, and nationally.
Officers and Directors:* Terry J. Kohler,* Pres.; Mary S. Kohler,* V.P.; Mary L. Tenhaken,* Secy.; Roland M. Neumann, Jr.,* Treas.
EIN: 396046987
Codes: CS, FD2

56936
Klauer Foundation Trust
c/o Bank One Trust Co., N.A.
P.O. Box 1308
Milwaukee, WI 53201
Application address: c/o Bank one Trust Co., N.A., 1 Bank One Plz., Chicago IL 60670-0697
Contact: Wendi Cotter

Established in 1952 in IL.
Financial data (yr. ended 12/31/01): Grants paid, $103,740; assets, $2,671,810 (M); expenditures, $135,272; qualifying distributions, $103,740.
Limitations: Giving primarily in Dubuque, IA.
Trustee: Bank One Trust Co., N.A.
EIN: 366013118

56937
Susan Cook House Educational Trust
c/o Bank One Trust Co., N.A.
P.O. Box 1308
Milwaukee, WI 53201-1308
Application address: c/o Lin Jones, Bank One Trust Co., N.A., 1 E. Old Capitol Plz., Springfield, IL 62701, tel.: (217) 525-9737

Trust established in 1969 in IL.

56937—WISCONSIN

Financial data (yr. ended 11/30/01): Grants paid, $103,600; assets, $2,904,418 (M); expenditures, $146,847; qualifying distributions, $106,861.
Limitations: Giving limited to Sangamon County, IL.
Trustee: Bank One Trust Co., N.A.
EIN: 376087675
Codes: GTI

56938
H. Chase Stone Trust
c/o Bank One Trust Co.
P.O. Box 1308
Milwaukee, WI 53201
Application address: c/o Bank One Colorado, N.A., 30 E. Pikes Peak, Colorado Springs, CO 80942

Established in 1974 in CO.
Financial data (yr. ended 12/31/01): Grants paid, $103,000; assets, $3,655,564 (M); expenditures, $130,769; qualifying distributions, $107,541.
Limitations: Giving limited to El Paso County, CO.
Publications: Application guidelines.
Application information: Application form not required.
Trustee: Bank One Trust Co., N.A.
EIN: 846066113
Codes: FD2

56939
Ellamae Siebert Foundation, Inc.
111 E. Wisconsin Ave., Ste. 1800
Milwaukee, WI 53202 (414) 276-3400
Contact: Frank W. Bastian, Pres.

Established in 1993 in WI.
Donor(s): Ellamae Siebert.‡
Financial data (yr. ended 12/31/00): Grants paid, $102,500; assets, $1,687,888 (M); expenditures, $122,756; qualifying distributions, $96,032.
Limitations: Giving primarily in the metropolitan Milwaukee, WI, area.
Application information: Application form required.
Officers and Directors:* Frank W. Bastian,* Pres.; Janet M. Hoehnen,* Secy.; Marjorie Aylen.
EIN: 391708686
Codes: FD2

56940
The Gardner Foundation
322 E. Michigan Ave., Ste. 250
Milwaukee, WI 53202 (414) 233-0308
Contact: Theodore Friedlander, Jr., Pres.

Incorporated in 1947 in NY.
Donor(s): Herman Gardner.‡
Financial data (yr. ended 12/31/01): Grants paid, $102,400; assets, $1,997,248 (M); expenditures, $112,077; qualifying distributions, $102,400.
Limitations: Giving primarily in the greater Milwaukee, WI, area.
Publications: Program policy statement, application guidelines.
Application information: Application form required.
Officers and Directors:* Theodore Friedlander, Jr.,* Pres.; Gardner L.R. Friedlander,* V.P.; Theodore Friedlander III,* V.P.; C. Frederick Geilfuss,* Secy.; Tony Asmuth, Cliff Astruta, Gardner L. Friedlander, Jean W. Friedlander, Louise Friedlander, Norman Paulsen, Lynde Uihlein.
EIN: 396076956
Codes: FD2

56941
Dora M. Hansen Charitable Trust
c/o Bank One Trust Co., N.A.
P.O. Box 1308
Milwaukee, WI 53201
Application address: 200 W. College Ave., Neenah, WI 54911, tel.: (414) 735-1322
Contact: Alan R. Blake, Trust Off., Bank One Trust Co., N.A.

Established in 1993 in WI.
Financial data (yr. ended 12/31/01): Grants paid, $101,721; assets, $1,137,191 (M); expenditures, $115,087; qualifying distributions, $105,320.
Limitations: Giving primarily in Neenah, WI.
Application information: Application form required.
Trustee: Bank One Trust Co., N.A.
EIN: 396570714
Codes: FD2

56942
Harold & Touraine Nash Foundation, Inc.
3618 N. Lake Dr.
Milwaukee, WI 53211-2644
Contact: Harold Nash, Pres.

Established in 1986 in WI.
Donor(s): Harold Nash.
Financial data (yr. ended 12/31/01): Grants paid, $101,500; assets, $283,417 (M); expenditures, $109,618; qualifying distributions, $101,048.
Limitations: Giving primarily in WI.
Application information: Application form not required.
Officer: Harold Nash, Pres.
Director: David Nash.
EIN: 391565807
Codes: FD2

56943
John N. & Kathleen S. MacDonough Foundation, Inc.
6208 Brumder Dr.
Hartland, WI 53029-9709

Established in 1998 in WI.
Donor(s): John N. MacDonough, Kathleen S. MacDonough.
Financial data (yr. ended 12/31/01): Grants paid, $101,462; assets, $200,954 (M); gifts received, $167,138; expenditures, $101,462; qualifying distributions, $101,462.
Limitations: Applications not accepted.
Application information: Contributes only to pre-selected organizations.
Trustees: Michael W. Grebe, John N. MacDonough, Kathleen S. MacDonough.
EIN: 391924028
Codes: FD2

56944
W. B. & Ellen Gordon Stuart Trust
c/o Bank One, Trust Co., N.A.
P.O. Box 1308
Milwaukee, WI 53201
Application address: P.O. Box 2050, Fort Worth, TX 76113, tel.: (817) 884-4151
Contact: Robert Lansford

Established in 1970.
Financial data (yr. ended 06/30/01): Grants paid, $100,807; assets, $3,601,923 (M); gifts received, $103,262; expenditures, $152,851; qualifying distributions, $142,910.
Limitations: Giving primarily in TX.
Trustee: Bank One Trust Co., N.A.
EIN: 756014224
Codes: FD2

56945
Elias & Hanna Regensburger Foundation
c/o Bank One Trust Co.,
P.O. Box 1308
Milwaukee, WI 53201
Application address: c/o John Sands, Bank One, Texas, N.A., Preston, P.O. Box 259000, Dallas, TX 75225

Established in 1985 in TX.
Donor(s): Morris A. Regensburger Family Trust, William L. Regensburger Family Trust.
Financial data (yr. ended 05/31/01): Grants paid, $100,683; assets, $2,189,236 (M); expenditures, $117,876; qualifying distributions, $104,521.
Limitations: Giving primarily in Denison and Sherman, TX.
Application information: Application form not required.
Trustee: Bank One, Texas, N.A.
EIN: 756322552
Codes: FD2

56946
Marcus Family Charitable Trust
250 E. Wisconsin Ave., No. 1700
Milwaukee, WI 53202-4209 (414) 905-1530
Contact: Stephen Marcus, Tr.

Established in 1997 in WI.
Donor(s): Ben Marcus, Celia Marcus, Joan Marcus, Stephen Marcus.
Financial data (yr. ended 12/31/01): Grants paid, $100,471; assets, $1,992,867 (M); gifts received, $435,000; expenditures, $101,630; qualifying distributions, $100,650.
Limitations: Giving primarily in Milwaukee, WI.
Trustees: Joan Marcus, Stephen Marcus.
EIN: 391891090
Codes: FD2

56947
The Dodson Foundation, Inc.
c/o Frank J. Pelisek
100 E. Wisconsin Ave., Ste. 3300
Milwaukee, WI 53202
Application address: 3140 Box Canyon Rd., Santa Ynez, CA 93460
Contact: James D. Dodson, Treas.

Established in 1991 in WI.
Donor(s): James D. Dodson.
Financial data (yr. ended 12/31/01): Grants paid, $100,166; assets, $718,021 (M); gifts received, $147,707; expenditures, $100,834; qualifying distributions, $100,166.
Limitations: Giving primarily in Santa Barbara, CA and Janesville, WI.
Application information: Application form not required.
Officers and Directors:* Jeanine L. Dodson,* Pres.; Frank J. Pelisek, Secy.; James D. Dodson,* Treas.; Michael J. Dodson, Cynthia L. Gardner.
EIN: 391694304

56948
Apple Family Foundation, Inc.
c/o U.S. Bank
P.O. Box MKLC4
Milwaukee, WI 53201-9116
Application address: 4684 N. Wilshire Rd., Milwaukee, WI 53211, tel.: (414) 258-0706
Contact: Jonathan P. Apple, Pres.

Established in 1965 in WI.
Donor(s): TPPO Holding Co., Inc.
Financial data (yr. ended 12/31/00): Grants paid, $100,150; assets, $1,102,130 (M); expenditures, $113,079; qualifying distributions, $100,760.
Limitations: Giving primarily in Milwaukee, WI.

Application information: Application form not required.
Officers: Jonathan P. Apple, Pres.; Patricia B. Apple, V.P. and Treas.; Mary Apple Boyer, Secy.
EIN: 391037948
Codes: FD2

56949
Frank and Mary Lamberson Foundation
c/o Bank One Trust Co.
P.O. Box 1308
Milwaukee, WI 53201
Application address: c/o Gary W. Gomoll, Bank One, 3399 PGA Blvd., Ste.100, Palm Beach, FL 33410, tel.: (561) 627-9400

Established in 1997.
Financial data (yr. ended 12/31/00): Grants paid, $100,000; assets, $1,655,445 (M); expenditures, $122,116; qualifying distributions, $99,692.
Limitations: Giving primarily in FL, MI, Asheville, NC, and Poughkeepsie, NY.
Application information: Application form required.
Trustees: Frank A. Lamberson, Mary T. Lamberson, Bank One, N.A.
EIN: 597096409
Codes: FD2

56950
The William B. Pollock Company Foundation
c/o Bank One Trust Co., N.A.
P.O. Box 1308
Milwaukee, WI 53201
Application address: c/o Bank One Trust Co.,N.A., 106 E. Market St., Warren, OH 44481

Established in 1952 in OH.
Financial data (yr. ended 12/31/00): Grants paid, $100,000; assets, $3,168,946 (M); expenditures, $130,843; qualifying distributions, $107,641.
Limitations: Giving primarily in the Youngstown, OH, area.
Trustees: Franklin Bennett, Bank One Trust Co., N.A.
EIN: 346514078
Codes: FD2

56951
The Pyle Foundation
c/o Pyle Group, LLC
3500 Corben Ct.
Madison, WI 53704-2571 (608) 245-3700
Contact: Thomas F. Pyle, Jr., Tr.

Established in 1997 in WI.
Donor(s): Judith D. Pyle, Thomas F. Pyle, Jr.
Financial data (yr. ended 12/31/00): Grants paid, $100,000; assets, $1,362,376 (M); expenditures, $101,051; qualifying distributions, $101,883.
Limitations: Giving primarily in Madison, WI.
Trustees: Benjamin Garmer III, Judith D. Pyle, Thomas F. Pyle, Jr., Glynn Rossa.
EIN: 391867322
Codes: FD2

56952
Stephen E. and Kathleen H. Seidel 1996 Charitable Trust
1306 E. Meinecke Ave.
Milwaukee, WI 53212

Established in 2001 in WI.
Donor(s): Stephen E. Seidel.
Financial data (yr. ended 12/31/01): Grants paid, $100,000; assets, $102,014 (M); gifts received, $197,125; expenditures, $100,000; qualifying distributions, $100,000.
Limitations: Applications not accepted.
Application information: Contributes only to pre-selected organizations.
Trustees: Kathleen H. Seidel, Stephen E. Seidel.
EIN: 396642602
Codes: FD2

56953
Teerlink Family Foundation, Ltd.
1765 Wedgewood Dr. W.
Elm Grove, WI 53122-1056

Established in 1993 in WI.
Donor(s): Richard F. Teerlink, Anna L. Teerlink.
Financial data (yr. ended 12/31/01): Grants paid, $100,000; assets, $2,392,476 (M); expenditures, $100,526; qualifying distributions, $100,000.
Limitations: Applications not accepted. Giving limited to WI.
Application information: Contributes only to pre-selected organizations.
Officers: Richard F. Teerlink, Pres. and Treas.; Anna L. Teerlink, V.P. and Secy.
Trustee: Henry E. Fuldner.
EIN: 391745090

56954
James and Virginia Wheeler Foundation, Inc.
c/o Bank One Wisconsin Trust Co.
P.O. Box 1308
Milwaukee, WI 53201
Contact: John F. Sennett

Established in 1994 in WI.
Donor(s): James H. Wheeler, Jr., Virginia M. Wheeler.
Financial data (yr. ended 12/31/01): Grants paid, $100,000; assets, $776,709 (M); expenditures, $110,478; qualifying distributions, $100,000.
Limitations: Giving on a national basis.
Officers and Directors:* James H. Wheeler, Jr.,* Chair. and Pres.; Virginia M. Wheeler,* V.P. and Secy.; Mary C. Mehan,* Treas.
EIN: 391818780

56955
Thompson Foundation, Inc.
3420 Sleepy Hollow Ln.
Brookfield, WI 53005-2860 (262) 781-3790
Contact: R.J. Glaser, Dir.

Established in 1992 in WI.
Donor(s): Judith M. Thompson.
Financial data (yr. ended 12/31/01): Grants paid, $99,900; assets, $724 (M); gifts received, $93,746; expenditures, $100,863; qualifying distributions, $98,900.
Limitations: Giving primarily in WI.
Directors: Richard J. Glaser, Thomas W. Hanson, Leigh A. Meier, Judith Thompson, Scott W. Thompson.
EIN: 391714988
Codes: FD2

56956
Alexandra Charitable Trust
210 Commerce St., Ste. 2B
Oshkosh, WI 54901-4802 (920) 231-1620
Contact: Edward F. Leyhe, Tr.

Established in 1986 in WI.
Donor(s): Edward F. Leyhe.
Financial data (yr. ended 12/31/01): Grants paid, $99,890; assets, $17,107 (M); gifts received, $105,000; expenditures, $103,173; qualifying distributions, $99,890.
Limitations: Giving primarily in WI.
Trustees: Edward F. Leyhe, James A. Urdan.
EIN: 391572878
Codes: FD2

56957
Clarence Talen Charitable Trust
c/o North Central Trust Co.
311 Main St.
La Crosse, WI 54602
Contact: Brenda Stuhr

Established in 1986.
Financial data (yr. ended 12/31/01): Grants paid, $99,500; assets, $1,450,184 (M); expenditures, $111,307; qualifying distributions, $100,389.
Limitations: Giving primarily in Menomonie, WI.
Application information: Application form not required.
Trustee: North Central Trust Co.
EIN: 396438509
Codes: FD2

56958
David B. & Katharine Stone Smith Foundation
(Formerly David B. Smith Family Foundation)
c/o Marshall & Ilsley Trust Company, N.A.
P.O. Box 2980
Milwaukee, WI 53201
Application address: P.O. Box 209, Wausau, WI 54402-0209, tel.: (715) 845-3121
Contact: David P. Guilliom, Tr., Marshall & Ilsley Trust Company, N.A.

Financial data (yr. ended 12/31/99): Grants paid, $99,495; assets, $6,737 (M); gifts received, $24,000; expenditures, $125,710; qualifying distributions, $98,596.
Limitations: Giving limited to WI, with emphasis on the Merrill area.
Trustee: Marshall & Ilsley Trust Company, N.A.
EIN: 396087997

56959
W. & H. Bender Memorial Fund
c/o Bank One Trust Co., N.A.
P.O. Box 1308
Milwaukee, WI 53201
Application address: c/o Bank One Trust Co., N.A., 6 Federal Plz. W., Youngstown, OH 44503, tel.: (216) 742-6822

Established in 1989 in OH.
Financial data (yr. ended 12/31/01): Grants paid, $99,300; assets, $2,015,782 (M); expenditures, $110,592; qualifying distributions, $101,534.
Limitations: Giving primarily in Youngstown, OH.
Trustee: Bank One Trust Co., N.A.
EIN: 346808983

56960
Shockley Foundation
401 Charmany Dr., Ste. 200
Madison, WI 53719 (608) 288-3040
Contact: Terry K. Shockley, Tr.

Established 2001 in WI.
Donor(s): Terry Shockley, Sandy Shockley.
Financial data (yr. ended 12/31/01): Grants paid, $99,000; assets, $1,006,558 (M); gifts received, $1,105,000; expenditures, $99,000; qualifying distributions, $98,994.
Limitations: Applications not accepted. Giving primarily in IL, KS, MN, and WI.
Application information: Contributes only to pre-selected organizations.
Trustees: Toni K. Peterson, Sandra K. Shockley, Terry K. Shockley, Todd L. Shockley.
EIN: 396764154
Codes: FD2

56961—WISCONSIN

56961
Waukesha County Community Foundation
2727 N. Grandview Blvd., Ste. 122
Waukesha, WI 53188   (262) 513-1861
E-mail: wccf@waukeshafoundation.org; URL: http://www.waukeshafoundation.org
Contact: Valerie J. Brown, Exec. Dir.

Established in 1999 in WI.
Financial data (yr. ended 12/31/01): Grants paid, $98,600; assets, $1,593,638 (M); gifts received, $525,000; expenditures, $173,038.
Limitations: Giving primarily in Waukesha County, WI.
Publications: Annual report, newsletter, informational brochure.
Application information: Application form required.
Officers and Directors:* Bryce P. Styza,* Pres.; Donald Fundingsland,* V.P.; Ronald L. Bertieri,* Secy.; Peter J. Lettenberger,* Treas.; Thomas E. Dalum, Russell J. Duris, E. John Raasch, Keith Rupple, T. Michael Schober, Donald J. Stephens.
EIN: 391969122
Codes: CM

56962
VPI Foundation, Inc.
c/o Richard L. Blamey
3123 S. 9th St.
Sheboygan, WI 53081
Application address: c/o Carol Grover, 635 School St., Kohler, WI 53044, tel.: (920) 458-8573

Established in 1993.
Donor(s): Vinyl Plastics, Inc., VPI, LLC.
Financial data (yr. ended 09/30/01): Grants paid, $98,125; assets, $386,864 (M); gifts received, $75,000; expenditures, $103,856; qualifying distributions, $97,967.
Limitations: Giving primarily in Salisbury, MD, and WI.
Application information: Application form not required.
Officers and Directors:* Carol Grover,* Pres.; John Crawford,* V.P.; R. Bruce Grover,* V.P.; Richard L. Blamey,* Secy.-Treas.; Robert H. Leverenz, Greg Mickelson, Karen Scott, Deborah Wente.
EIN: 391768404
Codes: CS, FD2, CD

56963
The William J. Curtin Charitable Trust
4800 Curtin Dr.
McFarland, WI 53558
Contact: Robert Dettman, Tr.

Established in 1999 in WI.
Donor(s): William J. Curtin, Sr.
Financial data (yr. ended 12/31/00): Grants paid, $97,800; assets, $114,041 (M); gifts received, $84,309; expenditures, $103,510; qualifying distributions, $98,128.
Limitations: Giving on a national basis.
Trustees: Eleanor R. Curtin, William J. Curtin, Jr., Robert M. Dettman.
EIN: 396703755
Codes: FD2

56964
The Hooper Foundation
2030 Pennsylvania Ave.
Madison, WI 53704-4783
Additional address: P.O. Box 7455, Madison, WI 53707-7455
Contact: Robert Schaller, Cont.

Donor(s): Hooper Construction Corp.
Financial data (yr. ended 12/31/01): Grants paid, $97,756; assets, $513,782 (M); gifts received, $100,000; expenditures, $98,616; qualifying distributions, $97,631.
Limitations: Applications not accepted. Giving primarily in WI.
Application information: Contributes only to pre-selected organizations.
Officer: Robert Schaller, Cont.
EIN: 396070368
Codes: FD2

56965
The Godfrey Foundation
1200 W. Sunset Dr.
Waukesha, WI 53189-8512   (262) 542-9311
Contact: Louis Stinebangh

Established in 1945 in WI.
Donor(s): Fleming Cos., Inc.
Financial data (yr. ended 12/31/00): Grants paid, $97,300; assets, $266,883 (M); expenditures, $97,518; qualifying distributions, $97,332.
Limitations: Giving primarily in Milwaukee and Waukesha, WI.
Officers and Directors:* Robert J. Fleming,* Pres.; Thomas J. Patzman,* V.P. and Secy.-Treas.; Dale D. Da.
EIN: 237423938
Codes: CS, FD2, CD

56966
Gilbert W. Siron Foundation
c/o James E. Hartwig
P.O. Box 1148
Janesville, WI 53547-1148

Established in 1992 in WI.
Donor(s): Gilbert Siron.‡
Financial data (yr. ended 06/30/99): Grants paid, $97,000; assets, $1,332,282 (M); expenditures, $121,460; qualifying distributions, $97,000.
Limitations: Applications not accepted. Giving primarily in Janesville, WI.
Application information: Contributes only to pre-selected organizations.
Trustee: Donald Sartell.
EIN: 396508464
Codes: FD2

56967
Kathleen & Frank Thometz Charitable Foundation, Inc.
8135 N. Range Line Rd.
Milwaukee, WI 53217
Contact: Frank Thometz, Pres.; or Kathleen Thometz, V.P.

Established in 1999 in WI.
Donor(s): Frank Thometz, Kathleen Thometz.
Financial data (yr. ended 12/31/01): Grants paid, $96,402; assets, $248,983 (M); gifts received, $52,405; expenditures, $101,860; qualifying distributions, $96,402.
Limitations: Giving primarily in Milwaukee, WI.
Officers: Frank Thometz, Pres. and Treas.; Kathleen Thometz, V.P. and Secy.
Director: Michael D. Thometz.
EIN: 391966766

56968
Braeger Foundation, Inc.
4100 S. 27th St.
Milwaukee, WI 53221-1830   (414) 281-5000
Contact: Robert W. Braeger, Pres.

Donor(s): Braeger Chevrolet, Inc., Bosca Realty, Inc.
Financial data (yr. ended 10/31/01): Grants paid, $95,581; assets, $21,768 (M); gifts received, $108,000; expenditures, $98,700; qualifying distributions, $98,700.
Limitations: Giving primarily in the Milwaukee, WI, area.
Officers: Robert W. Braeger, Pres. and Treas.; Deanna B. Braeger, V.P.; Mary A. Pritzlaff, Secy.
EIN: 396101438
Codes: CS, FD2, CD

56969
Agustin A. Ramirez, Jr. Family Foundation
411 E. Wisconsin Ave., Ste. 2040
Milwaukee, WI 53202-4497
Application address: c/o Scholarship Prog. Coord., P.O. Box 257, Waukesha, WI 53187-0257

Established in 1995 in WI.
Donor(s): Agustin A. Ramirez, Jr.
Financial data (yr. ended 12/31/00): Grants paid, $94,250; assets, $201,949 (M); gifts received, $100,000; expenditures, $98,264; qualifying distributions, $97,842.
Application information: Application form not required.
Trustees: Agustin A. Ramirez, Jr., Rebecca Page Ramirez, Eric J. Van Vugt.
EIN: 396626017
Codes: FD2, GTI

56970
Carl W. Nelson Charitable Trust
c/o Ray Feldman
P. O. Box 131
Mauston, WI 53948   (608) 847-6100
Application address: P.O. Box 119, Mauston WI, 53948

Established in 1997 in WI.
Donor(s): Carl W. Nelson.‡
Financial data (yr. ended 12/31/01): Grants paid, $94,000; assets, $290,235 (M); expenditures, $97,093; qualifying distributions, $93,813.
Limitations: Applications not accepted.
Application information: Contributes only to pre-selected organizations.
Trustees: Ray C. Feldman,* Thomas Jodarski, Linda Sue Miller.*
EIN: 391909929
Codes: FD2

56971
Plexus Corp. Charitable Foundation, Inc.
(Formerly Plexon Corp. Charitable Foundation, Inc.)
55 Jewelers Park Dr.
Neenah, WI 54956
Contact: Joseph D. Kaufman, Secy.

Established in 1995 in WI.
Donor(s): Plexus Corp., TGI Employee Fund.
Financial data (yr. ended 06/30/01): Grants paid, $93,552; assets, $38,914 (M); gifts received, $91,000; expenditures, $93,552; qualifying distributions, $93,550.
Limitations: Giving primarily in WI.
Officers: Joseph D. Kaufman, Pres.; Lori Hoersch, Secy.; William F. Denney, Treas.
EIN: 391828689
Codes: CS, FD2, CD

56972
Linda Gale Sampson Charitable Fund, Inc.
c/o J. Bernstein, Godfrey & Kahn
780 N. Water St.
Milwaukee, WI 53202

Established in 1994 in WI.
Financial data (yr. ended 12/31/01): Grants paid, $93,180; assets, $2,252,258 (M); expenditures, $121,483; qualifying distributions, $93,515.

Limitations: Applications not accepted. Giving primarily in WI.
Application information: Contributes only to pre-selected organizations.
Officers and Directors:* Linda Gale Sampson,* Pres. and Treas.; Joseph M. Bernstein,* V.P. and Secy.; Richard H. Meyer.
EIN: 391796554
Codes: FD2

56973
Joseph & Sarah Van Drisse Charitable Trust
c/o Bank One Trust Co., N.A.
P.O. Box 13
Milwaukee, WI 53201

Financial data (yr. ended 12/31/01): Grants paid, $93,000; assets, $5,443,713 (M); expenditures, $142,341; qualifying distributions, $101,002.
Limitations: Applications not accepted. Giving primarily in Green Bay, WI.
Application information: Contributes only to pre-selected organizations.
Trustee: Bank One Trust Co., N.A.
EIN: 396719617
Codes: FD2

56974
Lorraine & Morry Mitz Charitable Foundation
7161 N. Port Washington Rd.
Milwaukee, WI 53217
Contact: Sanford Mitz

Established in 1999 in WI.
Donor(s): Lorraine Mitz, Morry Mitz.
Financial data (yr. ended 12/31/00): Grants paid, $92,895; assets, $952,847 (M); gifts received, $350,000; expenditures, $106,724; qualifying distributions, $98,845.
Limitations: Giving primarily in Milwaukee, WI.
Trustees: Lorraine Mitz, Morry Mitz.
EIN: 391636941

56975
The William & Sandy Heitz Family Foundation
(Formerly The Heitz Family Foundation)
10800 N. Haddonstone Pl.
Mequon, WI 53092
FAX: (262) 241-3404; *E-mail:* sfleming@wi.rr.com
Contact: Stephanie L. Fleming, V.P.

Established in 1994 in WI.
Donor(s): Sandra Heitz, William Heitz.‡
Financial data (yr. ended 12/31/01): Grants paid, $92,790; assets, $1,784,404 (M); expenditures, $93,280; qualifying distributions, $92,790.
Limitations: Giving primarily in Milwaukee, WI.
Officers: Sandra D. Heitz, Pres.; Stephanie L. Fleming, V.P.; Gregory Heitz, Treas.
Directors: Peter Fleming, Kimberly Heitz.
EIN: 391799844

56976
John T. and Suzanne S. Jacobus Family Foundation
(Formerly John T. Jacobus Family Foundation)
2323 N. Mayfair Rd., Ste. 240
Wauwatosa, WI 53226 (414) 475-6565
Contact: Barbara J. Wells

Established in 1986 in WI.
Donor(s): John T. Jacobus, Suzanne S. Jacobus.
Financial data (yr. ended 12/31/00): Grants paid, $92,589; assets, $1,844,484 (M); expenditures, $117,873; qualifying distributions, $92,182.
Limitations: Giving primarily in southeastern WI.
Officers: John T. Jacobus, Pres. and Treas.; Suzanne S. Jacobus, V.P.; A. Peter McArthur, Secy.
EIN: 391560018
Codes: FD2

56977
Jones S. Davis Foundation
c/o Bank One Trust Co., N.A.
P.O. Box 1308
Milwaukee, WI 53201-1308

Established in 1961 in LA.
Financial data (yr. ended 08/31/01): Grants paid, $92,500; assets, $11,295,919 (M); expenditures, $127,274; qualifying distributions, $95,795.
Limitations: Giving primarily in Baton Rouge, LA.
Officers: David Mayeux, Pres.; Ann Miller, Secy.
Directors: Geneveive Bogan, Robert Greer, J. Luther Jordan, Jr., Winfred Miller.
Trustee: Bank One Trust Co., N.A.
EIN: 726023237

56978
H. J. Hagge Foundation, Inc.
500 3rd St., Ste. 506
Wausau, WI 54403-4896 (715) 845-1818
Contact: Carol M. Krieg

Established in 1956 in WI.
Donor(s): H.J. Hagge,‡ Helen S. Hagge.‡
Financial data (yr. ended 12/31/01): Grants paid, $92,015; assets, $2,108,724 (M); expenditures, $102,396; qualifying distributions, $97,517.
Limitations: Giving primarily in WI.
Application information: Application form not required.
Officers and Directors:* Robert S. Hagge, Jr.,* Pres. and Treas.; Kristin Single Hagge,* V.P.; Leigh Hagge Tuckey,* Secy.; A. Woodson Hagge, Daniel L. Hagge, Jr.
EIN: 396037112
Codes: FD2

56979
Trostel Foundation, Ltd.
800 N. Marshall St.
Milwaukee, WI 53202-3911 (414) 273-3421
Contact: Elizabeth H. Perry, Pres.

Established in 1986 in WI.
Donor(s): Albert Trostel and Sons Co.
Financial data (yr. ended 11/30/01): Grants paid, $91,100; assets, $13,803 (M); gifts received, $100,000; expenditures, $94,748; qualifying distributions, $94,748.
Limitations: Applications not accepted. Giving primarily in WI.
Officers and Directors:* Elizabeth H. Perry,* Pres. and Treas.; Anders Segerdahl,* V.P.; Ellen R. Ludwig,* Secy.; Kim Harter, Thomas Hauske, Jr., Charles D. Krull.
EIN: 391550227
Codes: FD2

56980
A. W. Asmuth Foundation
411 E. Wisconsin Ave., Ste. 2040
Milwaukee, WI 53202-4497

Established in 1977 in WI.
Donor(s): Anthony William Asmuth, Jr., Anton W. Asmuth.‡
Financial data (yr. ended 04/30/02): Grants paid, $91,000; assets, $1,865,776 (M); expenditures, $101,040; qualifying distributions, $97,180.
Limitations: Giving primarily in Milwaukee, WI.
Trustees: Anthony William Asmuth III, Clifford M. Asmuth.
EIN: 391280850
Codes: FD2

56981
Newby Memorial Students Loan Fund
c/o Bank One Trust Co., N.A.
P.O. Box 1308
Milwaukee, WI 53201
Application address: P.O. Box 2050, Fort Worth, TX 76113-2050, tel.: (817) 884-4151
Contact: Bob Lansford

Financial data (yr. ended 12/31/01): Grants paid, $91,000; assets, $1,796,129 (M); expenditures, $102,232; qualifying distributions, $93,442.
Limitations: Giving limited to TX.
Trustee: Bank One Trust Co., N.A.
EIN: 756013857
Codes: FD2

56982
Pelz Family Foundation
4600 N. Port Washington Rd.
Glendale, WI 53217 (414) 967-1800

Established in 1995 in WI.
Donor(s): Harry Pelz, Marilyn Pelz.
Financial data (yr. ended 12/31/01): Grants paid, $90,393; assets, $27,201 (M); gifts received, $14,599; expenditures, $91,468; qualifying distributions, $91,044.
Limitations: Applications not accepted. Giving primarily in WI.
Application information: Contributes only to pre-selected organizations.
Officers and Directors:* Harry Pelz,* Pres. and Treas.; Marilyn Pelz,* Secy.; Mara Lappin, Daniel Pelz, David Pelz, Jason Pelz.
EIN: 391837448
Codes: FD2

56983
Dickinson Scholarship Trust
c/o Marshall & Ilsley Trust Company, N.A.
P.O. Box 2980
Milwaukee, WI 53201 (414) 748-8108
Application address: c/o Admissions Office, Ripon College, P.O. Box 248, Ripon, WI 54971

Established in 1994 in WI.
Financial data (yr. ended 06/30/01): Grants paid, $90,000; assets, $2,175,114 (M); expenditures, $112,064; qualifying distributions, $89,483.
Limitations: Giving primarily in Ripon, WI.
Trustee: Marshall & Ilsley Trust Company, N.A.
EIN: 396599850
Codes: FD2

56984
The Muriel Rumsey Foundation
c/o Bank One Trust Co., N.A.
P.O. Box 1308
Milwaukee, WI 53201
Contact: Gary W. Gomoll, Trust Off., Bank One Trust Co., N.A.

Financial data (yr. ended 12/31/00): Grants paid, $90,000; assets, $739,995 (M); gifts received, $50,000; expenditures, $97,008; qualifying distributions, $91,279.
Limitations: Giving on a national basis.
Trustees: J.W. Wertenberger, Bank One, Florida, N.A.
EIN: 656047139

56985
St. Jude-Joe Pennings Foundation, Ltd.
W2602 Brookhaven Dr.
Appleton, WI 54915-8180

Established in 1986 in WI.
Donor(s): Joseph A. Pennings.
Financial data (yr. ended 05/31/01): Grants paid, $90,000; assets, $1,899,258 (M); gifts received,

56985—WISCONSIN

$265,750; expenditures, $112,963; qualifying distributions, $90,729.
Limitations: Applications not accepted. Giving limited to WI.
Application information: Contributes only to pre-selected organizations.
Officers: Joseph A. Pennings, Pres.; Cassie A. Pennings, V.P. and Secy.; Valerie A. Rohr, Treas.
Directors: Kerry J. Pennings, Pamela Pennings, Scott G. Pennings.
EIN: 391561582
Codes: FD2

56986
Howard and Nancy Frankenthal Foundation, Ltd.
9227 N. Tennyson Dr.
Bayside, WI 53217
Application address: 10535 N. Port Washington Rd., Mequon, WI 53092, tel.: (262) 241-7000
Contact: Howard M. Frankenthal, Pres.

Established in 1989 in WI.
Donor(s): Howard M. Frankenthal, Nancy Frankenthal.
Financial data (yr. ended 04/30/02): Grants paid, $89,310; assets, $1,257,680 (M); expenditures, $103,738; qualifying distributions, $89,310.
Limitations: Giving primarily in Milwaukee, WI.
Application information: Application form not required.
Officers and Directors:* Howard M. Frankenthal,* Pres. and Treas.; Nancy Frankenthal,* Secy.
EIN: 391642921
Codes: FD2

56987
Milber E. Kendall Trust
c/o Bank One Trust Co., N.A.
P.O. Box 1308
Milwaukee, WI 53201

Established in 1958 in IN.
Financial data (yr. ended 01/31/02): Grants paid, $89,269; assets, $1,673,668 (M); expenditures, $112,291; qualifying distributions, $93,370.
Limitations: Applications not accepted. Giving primarily in IN.
Application information: Contributes only to pre-selected organizations.
Trustee: Bank One Trust Co., N.A.
EIN: 356012143
Codes: FD2

56988
Community Trust
c/o Marshall & Ilsley Trust Company, N.A.
P.O. Box 1980
West Bend, WI 53095-7980
Contact: Stephen Zimmel

Established in 1953 in WI.
Donor(s): Norman A. Schowalter.‡
Financial data (yr. ended 12/31/00): Grants paid, $89,250; assets, $1,685,014 (M); expenditures, $101,246; qualifying distributions, $89,260.
Limitations: Giving primarily in Washington County, WI.
Application information: Contributes primarily to pre-selected organizations. Application form not required.
Trustees: Thomas R. Bast, Eldor Kannenberg, Thomas A. Schowalter.
EIN: 396040395
Codes: FD2

56989
Elinore L. Loveland Testamentary Trust
c/o First National Bank
170 W. Main St.
Platteville, WI 53818 (608) 348-7777

Established in 1998.
Financial data (yr. ended 12/31/00): Grants paid, $89,200; assets, $1,157,809 (M); expenditures, $105,880; qualifying distributions, $87,879.
Application information: Application form not required.
Trustee: First National Bank.
EIN: 396648986

56990
Rite-Hite Corporation Foundation, Inc.
8900 N. Arbon Dr.
Milwaukee, WI 53223-2437
Contact: Mark S. Kirkish, Treas.

Established in 1984.
Donor(s): RITE-HITE Corp.
Financial data (yr. ended 12/31/01): Grants paid, $88,600; assets, $3,737 (M); gifts received, $90,000; expenditures, $886,100; qualifying distributions, $88,600.
Limitations: Giving primarily in Milwaukee, WI.
Application information: Limited funds for unsolicited requests. Application form not required.
Officers and Directors:* Michael H. White,* Pres.; Clem F. Maslowski,* V.P.; Mark S. Kirkish, Treas.; Arthur K. White.
EIN: 391522057
Codes: CS, FD2, CD

56991
Moses and Caroline Shallow Scholarship Foundation, Inc.
P.O. Box 375
Wausaukee, WI 54177
Contact: William Pickett, Pres.

Established in 1979.
Financial data (yr. ended 12/31/01): Grants paid, $88,188; assets, $1,205,801 (M); expenditures, $104,085; qualifying distributions, $87,727.
Limitations: Giving limited to residents of Marinette County, WI.
Officers: William Pickett, Pres.; Mary Joslin, V.P.; Betty Betley, Secy.; John Dorner, Treas.
Directors: Sherry Ledvina, Paul Lewandowski.
EIN: 391336290
Codes: FD2, GTI

56992
Vaughn L. & Eleanore M. Beals Charitable Foundation
c/o U.S. Bank
P.O. Box 2043
Milwaukee, WI 53201-9116 (262) 241-7198
Application address: c/o U.S. Bank, 11111 N. Port Washington Rd., No. 13W, Mequon, WI 53092-5010
Contact: Thomas Kawasky

Established in 1989 in WI.
Donor(s): Eleanore M. Beals, Vaughn L. Beals.
Financial data (yr. ended 06/30/02): Grants paid, $87,900; assets, $3,916,431 (M); gifts received, $2,700,000; expenditures, $107,828; qualifying distributions, $87,900.
Limitations: Giving primarily in Carefree and Tempe, AZ.
Application information: Application form not required.
Trustees: Eleanore M. Beals, Vaughn L. Beals, Jr., U.S. Bank.
EIN: 391653407

56993
The Carl and Irma Swenson Foundation, Ltd.
6833 Cedar Creek Rd.
Cedarburg, WI 53012 (262) 376-9749
E-mail: tcjohnson@wi.rr.com
Contact: Todd C. Johnson, Pres.

Established in 1994 in WI.
Donor(s): Todd C. Johnson, Greg Larson, Avis L. Johnson, Douglas Johnson.
Financial data (yr. ended 08/31/01): Grants paid, $87,500; assets, $1,560,643 (M); gifts received, $5,000; expenditures, $98,519; qualifying distributions, $86,955.
Limitations: Giving primarily in Milwaukee, WI.
Officers: Todd C. Johnson, Pres. and Treas.; Jeff Swenson, V.P.; Douglas Johnson, Secy.
Directors: Avis L. Johnson, Carleen Larson, Greg Larson, Diane Regenfuss, Richard Swenson.
EIN: 363990754
Codes: FD2

56994
The Educational Foundation, Inc. at Ozaukee Bank
(Formerly Ozaukee Bank Educational Foundation, Inc.)
P.O. Box 3
Cedarburg, WI 53012 (262) 377-9000
E-mail: haas@ozaukeebank.com
Contact: Terri A. Haas, Mgr.

Established in 1992 in WI.
Donor(s): Ozaukee Bank, William J. Heitz.
Financial data (yr. ended 12/31/01): Grants paid, $87,312; assets, $1,191,411 (M); gifts received, $56,937; expenditures, $90,596; qualifying distributions, $87,313.
Limitations: Giving limited to Ozaukee County, WI, with occasional giving in the metropolitan Milwaukee, WI, area.
Application information: Application form required.
Officer: Terri A. Haas, Mgr.
Directors: William R. Arpe, Peter T. Barry, Larry R. Dalton, Dean Fitting, Daniel J. Haislmaier, M.D. Hepburn, George F. Roth.
EIN: 391745307
Codes: CS, FD2, CD, GTI

56995
Hartwig Family Foundation, Inc.
P.O. Box 733
Appleton, WI 54912-0733

Established in 1999 in WI.
Donor(s): Christopher Hartwig.
Financial data (yr. ended 06/30/02): Grants paid, $87,294; assets, $1,766,926 (M); gifts received, $300,220; expenditures, $88,961; qualifying distributions, $87,294.
Limitations: Applications not accepted. Giving primarily in Appleton, WI.
Application information: Contributes only to pre-selected organizations.
Officers and Directors:* Christopher Hartwig,* Pres. and Treas.; Evelyn Hartwig,* Secy.; Joseph Bielinski, Dennis Wojahn, Gary Wynveen.
EIN: 391977500

56996
Archibald Douglass, Jr. Charitable Trust
c/o Marshall & Ilsley Trust Company, N.A.
P.O. Box 2980
Milwaukee, WI 53201 (414) 287-7182
Application address: c/o Marshall & Ilsley Trust Company, N.A., P.O. Box 2427, Green Bay, WI 54306-2427, tel.: (920) 436-1905

Established in 1997 in WI.

Financial data (yr. ended 03/31/02): Grants paid, $87,061; assets, $1,664,709 (M); expenditures, $102,828; qualifying distributions, $86,778.
Limitations: Giving primarily in WI.
Trustee: Marshall & Ilsley Trust Company, N.A.
EIN: 396654547
Codes: FD2

56997
Gerald J. and Rosalie E. Kahn Family Foundation
c/o Godfrey & Kahn, S.C.
780 N. Water St.
Milwaukee, WI 53202-3590

Established in 1986 in WI.
Donor(s): Gerald J. Kahn, Rosalie E. Kahn.
Financial data (yr. ended 12/31/01): Grants paid, $87,010; assets, $832,699 (M); gifts received, $98,616; expenditures, $89,437; qualifying distributions, $87,984.
Limitations: Applications not accepted. Giving primarily in WI.
Application information: Contributes only to pre-selected organizations.
Officers and Directors:* Gerald J. Kahn,* Pres. and Treas.; Rosalie E. Kahn,* V.P. and Secy.; Nancy Grunfeld, Cynthia Kahn, Lori Kahn.
EIN: 391563071
Codes: FD2

56998
The Callicott Foundation
c/o Bank One Trust Co., N.A.
P.O. Box 1308
Milwaukee, WI 53201

Established in 1964.
Financial data (yr. ended 02/28/01): Grants paid, $87,000; assets, $1,354,242 (M); expenditures, $101,338; qualifying distributions, $89,867.
Limitations: Applications not accepted. Giving primarily in TX.
Application information: Contributes only to pre-selected organizations.
Trustee: Bank One Trust Co., N.A.
EIN: 726026675
Codes: FD2

56999
Bradlee H. Shattuck Charitable Foundation
c/o Bank One Trust Co., N.A.
P.O. Box 1308
Milwaukee, WI 53201

Established in 1994 in WI.
Donor(s): Bradlee H. Shattuck.
Financial data (yr. ended 12/31/01): Grants paid, $87,000; assets, $1,014,266 (M); expenditures, $98,510; qualifying distributions, $89,488.
Limitations: Applications not accepted.
Application information: Contributes only to pre-selected organizations.
Trustee: Bank One Trust Co., N.A.
EIN: 363991474
Codes: FD2

57000
General Charities, Inc.
c/o June Jager-Norman, C.P.A.
3780 N. 169th St.
Brookfield, WI 53005-2198 (262) 790-9188

Donor(s): Katherine Kurth.
Financial data (yr. ended 12/31/00): Grants paid, $86,095; assets, $859,912 (M); expenditures, $91,267; qualifying distributions, $86,095.
Limitations: Giving primarily in WI.
Directors: Katherine Kurth, Thomas Kurth, Tineka Kurth, Elisabeth Wrean.
EIN: 396048657
Codes: FD2

57001
Trainer Family Foundation, Inc.
735 N. Water St., Ste. 712
Milwaukee, WI 53202-4104
Contact: Thomas F. Lechner, Treas.

Established in 1981.
Donor(s): Members of the Trainer family.
Financial data (yr. ended 12/31/01): Grants paid, $85,650; assets, $1,919,844 (M); expenditures, $105,414; qualifying distributions, $85,650.
Limitations: Giving primarily in WI.
Officers and Directors:* Robert B. Trainer,* Pres.; Robert B. Trainer, Jr.,* V.P.; Mark A. Zaborske,* Secy.; Thomas F. Lechner,* Treas.; Charles I. Trainer, Steven U. Trainer.
EIN: 391366836

57002
Laskin Family Foundation, Inc.
(Formerly Arthur J. & Nancy Laskin Foundation, Inc.)
P.O. Box 510260
Milwaukee, WI 53203-0054
Contact: Arthur J. Laskin, Pres.

Established in 1967 in WI.
Financial data (yr. ended 12/31/01): Grants paid, $85,500; assets, $1,884,816 (M); expenditures, $98,309; qualifying distributions, $85,510.
Limitations: Applications not accepted. Giving primarily in Milwaukee, WI.
Officers and Directors:* Arthur J. Laskin,* Pres. and Treas.; Nancy L. Laskin,* V.P. and Secy.; Myron Laskin, Jr.
EIN: 396107521
Codes: FD2

57003
Mary Tabb & Clyde Berry Thompson Trust
c/o Bank One Trust Co., N.A.
P.O. Box 1308
Milwaukee, WI 53201
Application address: c/o Bank One, Texas, N.A., P.O. Box 2050, Fort Worth, TX 76113-2050, tel.: (817) 884-4151
Contact: Robert Lansford

Established in 1974 in TX.
Financial data (yr. ended 06/30/01): Grants paid, $85,000; assets, $1,796,118 (M); expenditures, $99,857; qualifying distributions, $88,412.
Limitations: Giving primarily in Fort Worth, TX.
Trustee: Bank One Trust Co., N.A.
EIN: 756186478
Codes: FD2

57004
The Egan Foundation, Inc.
P.O. Box 19031
1150 Springhunt Dr.
Green Bay, WI 54307-9031

Established in 1986 in WI.
Financial data (yr. ended 12/31/00): Grants paid, $84,300; assets, $913,698 (M); expenditures, $84,300; qualifying distributions, $85,039.
Limitations: Applications not accepted. Giving primarily in MN, NY and WI.
Application information: Contributes only to pre-selected organizations.
Officers and Directors:* M. Kathryn Egan Stout,* Pres.; Robert B. Olson,* V.P.; Thomas M. Egan,* Secy.; John A. Redick, Treas.; D. Kent Tippy.
EIN: 391570620
Codes: FD2

57005
The Stratton Foundation, Inc.
c/o Quarles & Brady
411 E. Wisconsin Ave., Ste. 2040
Milwaukee, WI 53202-4497

Established about 1958.
Donor(s): Frederick P. Stratton, Jr., Anne Youngclaus Stratton.
Financial data (yr. ended 07/31/01): Grants paid, $84,000; assets, $2,365,440 (M); expenditures, $88,868; qualifying distributions, $85,694.
Limitations: Applications not accepted. Giving primarily in Milwaukee, WI.
Publications: Annual report.
Application information: Contributes only to pre-selected organizations.
Officers and Directors:* John S. McGregor,* Pres.; Frederick P. Stratton, Jr.,* V.P.; Henry J. Loos,* Secy.-Treas.
EIN: 396042218
Codes: FD2

57006
Wisconsin Centrifugal Charitable Foundation, Inc.
905 E. St. Paul Ave.
Waukesha, WI 53188-3898

Established in 1987 in WI.
Donor(s): Wisconsin Centrifugal.
Financial data (yr. ended 06/30/01): Grants paid, $83,538; assets, $25,431 (M); gifts received, $80,355; expenditures, $84,064; qualifying distributions, $83,969.
Limitations: Applications not accepted. Giving primarily in WI.
Application information: Contributes only to pre-selected organizations.
Officer: Robert J. Smickley, Pres.
EIN: 391591534
Codes: CS, FD2, CD

57007
Youth Foundation, Inc.
c/o Metropolitan Assn. of Realtors
12300 W. Center St.
Milwaukee, WI 53222-4072 (414) 778-4929
E-mail: youth@metrorealtors.com; FAX: (414) 778-4920
Contact: Gary R. Petre, Pres.

Incorporated in 1951 in WI.
Donor(s): Arthur L. Richards.‡
Financial data (yr. ended 12/31/01): Grants paid, $83,397; assets, $1,708,093 (M); gifts received, $2,321; expenditures, $129,559; qualifying distributions, $83,397.
Limitations: Giving primarily in the metropolitan Milwaukee, WI, area.
Publications: Informational brochure (including application guidelines).
Application information: Application form required.
Officers: Gary R. Petre, Pres.; Robert Clark, V.P.; Scott Bush, Secy.-Treas.
Directors: Ronald Anders, Helen Sandor, Roy Scholtka, Thomas Witkowski, Cathleen Zeiler.
EIN: 390945311

57008
Elizabeth Elser Doolittle Charitable Trust No. 1
c/o Foley & Lardner
777 E. Wisconsin Ave.
Milwaukee, WI 53202
Contact: Richard S. Gallagher, Tr.

Established in 1988 in WI.
Financial data (yr. ended 12/31/01): Grants paid, $83,194; assets, $1,607,653 (M); expenditures, $113,419; qualifying distributions, $92,661.

Limitations: Giving primarily in the Milwaukee, WI, metropolitan area.
Trustees: Richard S. Gallagher, Richard H. Miller.
EIN: 391602180
Codes: FD2

57009
Joe Buley Trust for Holy Mother of God Monastery
c/o Bank One Trust Co., N.A.
P.O. Box 1308
Milwaukee, WI 53201

Financial data (yr. ended 12/31/00): Grants paid, $83,000; assets, $1,663,739 (M); expenditures, $104,993; qualifying distributions, $87,713.
Limitations: Applications not accepted. Giving primarily in Chicago, IL.
Application information: Contributes only to pre-selected organizations.
Trustee: Bank One Trust Co., N.A.
EIN: 356573650
Codes: FD2

57010
Lillian R. Coleman Scholarship Trust
(Formerly William S. and Lillian R. Coleman Scholarship Trust)
c/o Bank One Trust Co., N.A.
P.O. Box 1308
Milwaukee, WI 53201-1308
Application address: 111 Monument Cir., Ste. 1701, Indianapolis, IN 46277-0117, tel.: (317) 321-7544
Contact: Jacqueline Weitz, V.P. and Trust Off., Bank One Trust Co., N.A.

Established in 1974 in IN.
Financial data (yr. ended 06/30/01): Grants paid, $83,000; assets, $2,749,644 (M); gifts received, $106,285; expenditures, $104,291; qualifying distributions, $87,588.
Limitations: Giving limited to residents of Rush County, IN.
Application information: Application form required.
Directors: Ed Lyskowinski, David L. Mackey.
Trustee: Bank One Trust Co., N.A.
EIN: 356279390
Codes: FD2, GTI

57011
Ralph O. Franzen Charitable Foundation Trust
c/o Bank One Trust Co., N.A.
P.O. Box 1308
Milwaukee, WI 53201
Application address: c/o Gary E. Crocus, 218 E. Wesley, Ste. IL1-2054, Wheaton, IL 60187

Established in 1990 in IL.
Financial data (yr. ended 12/31/00): Grants paid, $83,000; assets, $1,968,336 (M); expenditures, $108,010; qualifying distributions, $87,265.
Limitations: Giving primarily in IL.
Trustee: Bank One Trust Co., N.A.
EIN: 366929982
Codes: FD2

57012
Silverman Family Foundation
P.O. Box 2980
Milwaukee, WI 53201

Established in 1993 in WI.
Donor(s): Albert A. Silverman, Francie H. Silverman.
Financial data (yr. ended 12/31/01): Grants paid, $83,000; assets, $1,534,222 (M); expenditures, $89,650; qualifying distributions, $82,145.
Limitations: Applications not accepted. Giving primarily in WI.

Application information: Contributes only to pre-selected organizations.
Trustees: William T. Gaus, Albert A. Silverman, Francie H. Silverman.
EIN: 396577946
Codes: FD2

57013
Bidwell Foundation
P.O. Box 873
Portage, WI 53901
Application address: W7334 Swan Cove Ln., Pardeeville, WI 53954, tel.: (608) 429-3818
Contact: Donald Witt, Tr.

Established in 1980 in WI.
Financial data (yr. ended 01/31/02): Grants paid, $82,500; assets, $1,623,404 (M); expenditures, $105,978; qualifying distributions, $82,500.
Limitations: Giving primarily in Columbia County, WI.
Application information: Application form not required.
Trustees: Robert D. Miller, Richard Rehm, Donald Witt.
EIN: 391340893
Codes: FD2

57014
James Wheeler Campbell Memorial Foundation, Inc.
c/o Leonard Campbell, Jr.
9016 N. Bayside Dr.
Milwaukee, WI 53217-1913

Established in 1992.
Donor(s): Leonard Campbell, Jr.
Financial data (yr. ended 12/31/01): Grants paid, $81,800; assets, $1,091,148 (M); gifts received, $100,000; expenditures, $84,890; qualifying distributions, $82,359.
Limitations: Applications not accepted. Giving primarily in Milwaukee, WI.
Application information: Contributes only to pre-selected organizations.
Officers: Leonard Campbell, Jr., Pres.; Carla C. Bartlett, V.P. and Secy.; Mary C. Brown, V.P.; Kay K. Campbell, Treas.
EIN: 391744652
Codes: FD2

57015
Claremont S. Jackman Foundation
P.O. Box 8636
Madison, WI 53708-8636
Application address: c/o Johnson Trust Co., 1 S. Main St., Janesville, WI 53545

Established in 1989 in WI.
Financial data (yr. ended 12/31/01): Grants paid, $81,636; assets, $2,167,558 (M); expenditures, $90,936; qualifying distributions, $82,036.
Limitations: Applications not accepted. Giving primarily in WI.
Application information: Contributes only to pre-selected organizations.
Trustee: Johnson Trust Co.
EIN: 391733837
Codes: FD2

57016
Powers-Wolfe Charitable Trust
c/o Thomas R. Wolfe
5110 Minocqua Crescent
Madison, WI 53705

Established in 1995 in WI.
Donor(s): Thomas R. Wolfe.
Financial data (yr. ended 11/30/00): Grants paid, $80,320; assets, $1,189,050 (M); expenditures, $80,889; qualifying distributions, $80,320.

Limitations: Applications not accepted. Giving primarily in WI.
Application information: Contributes only to pre-selected organizations.
Trustees: Patricia A. Powers, Thomas R. Wolfe.
EIN: 396609049
Codes: FD2

57017
John & Alice Forester Charitable Trust
P.O. Box 65
Wausau, WI 54402-0065 (715) 845-9201
Contact: San W. Orr, Jr., Tr.

Established in 1992 in WI.
Donor(s): John Forester.
Financial data (yr. ended 06/30/01): Grants paid, $79,900; assets, $1,676,765 (M); expenditures, $83,621; qualifying distributions, $79,998.
Limitations: Giving primarily in WI.
Application information: Application form not required.
Trustees: John E. Forester, San W. Orr, Jr., Leigh H. Tuckey.
EIN: 391741441
Codes: FD2

57018
Dalum Family Foundation
31917 Apple Ln.
Hartland, WI 53029

Established in WI in 1997.
Donor(s): Thomas E. Dalum, Mary P. Dalum.
Financial data (yr. ended 04/30/01): Grants paid, $79,150; assets, $458,692 (M); gifts received, $128,120; expenditures, $82,818; qualifying distributions, $19,104.
Limitations: Applications not accepted. Giving primarily in Milwaukee, WI.
Application information: Contributes only to pre-selected organizations.
Trustees: Mary P. Dalum, Thomas E. Dalum.
EIN: 396658948
Codes: FD2

57019
Joseph F. & Catherine M. Bennett Family Foundation, Inc.
111 E. Wisconsin Ave., Ste. 1800
Milwaukee, WI 53202-4809

Established in 1997 in WI.
Financial data (yr. ended 12/31/00): Grants paid, $79,000; assets, $1,163,343 (M); expenditures, $89,543; qualifying distributions, $78,392.
Limitations: Applications not accepted. Giving primarily in Milwaukee, WI.
Application information: Contributes only to pre-selected organizations.
Officers and Directors:* Joseph F. Bennett,* Pres.; Catherine M. Bennett,* V.P.; Mary C. Bennett,* Secy.; Michael J. Bennett,* Treas.; Ann Schoper.
EIN: 391879021

57020
William A. Siekman Foundation
c/o Marshall & Ilsley Trust Company, N.A.
1000 N. Water St., 12th Fl.
Milwaukee, WI 53202 (920) 738-3820
Contact: J. Robert Ellis

Established in 1991 in WI.
Donor(s): William A. Siekman.
Financial data (yr. ended 06/30/01): Grants paid, $78,000; assets, $1,670,791 (L); expenditures, $89,612; qualifying distributions, $77,400.
Limitations: Giving primarily in Appleton, WI.
Trustee: Marshall & Ilsley Trust Company, N.A.
EIN: 396539731
Codes: FD2

57021
Lillian D. Walker Scholarship Fund
c/o Bank One Trust Co., N.A.
P.O. Box 1308
Milwaukee, WI 53201
Application address: 24731 Michigan Ave.,
Dearborn, MI 48124
Contact: Bernice G. McCray, Tr.

Established in 1995 in MI.
Financial data (yr. ended 12/31/01): Grants paid, $78,000; assets, $139,143 (M); gifts received, $114; expenditures, $81,368; qualifying distributions, $78,943.
Limitations: Giving limited to MI.
Application information: Application form not required.
Trustees: Bernice G. McCray, Bank One Trust Co., N.A.
EIN: 386647558
Codes: GTI

57022
Maysteel Foundation, Ltd.
800 N. Marshall St.
Milwaukee, WI 53202-3911 (414) 273-3421
Contact: Elizabeth H. Perry, Pres.

Established in 1983.
Financial data (yr. ended 11/30/01): Grants paid, $77,949; assets, $734 (M); gifts received, $70,000; expenditures, $79,208; qualifying distributions, $79,208.
Limitations: Applications not accepted. Giving primarily in WI.
Application information: Contributes only to pre-selected organizations.
Officers and Directors:* Elizabeth H. Perry,* Pres. and Treas.; Kim Harter,* V.P.; Ellen Ludwig,* Secy.
EIN: 391480641
Codes: FD2

57023
R & M Foundation, Inc.
c/o Mary A. Splude
6320 Parkview Rd.
Greendale, WI 53129-2154 (262) 860-6411
Contact: John Splude, Dir.

Established in 1999 in WI.
Donor(s): John Splude.
Financial data (yr. ended 12/31/00): Grants paid, $77,905; assets, $139 (M); gifts received, $75,350; expenditures, $77,976; qualifying distributions, $77,976.
Officers: Mary Splude, Pres.; Michelle Splude, Secy.-Treas.
Directors: John Splude, Robert Splude.
EIN: 311612161
Codes: FD2

57024
NEV 2/11 Foundation
(Formerly Nevins Family Foundation)
P.O. Box 332
Genesee Depot, WI 53127
Contact: T. Nevins-Buchholtz, Secy.

Established in 1987 in FL.
Donor(s): M.E. Nevins, members of the Nevins family.
Financial data (yr. ended 12/31/01): Grants paid, $77,375; assets, $1,181,829 (M); expenditures, $83,013; qualifying distributions, $76,167.
Limitations: Applications not accepted. Giving primarily in FL, WA, and WI.
Application information: Contributes only to pre-selected organizations. Unsolicited requests for funds not considered.
Trustees: M. Nevins, M.E. Nevins, T. Nevins-Buchholtz.

EIN: 650020991
Codes: FD2

57025
David C. Scott Charitable Trust
777 E. Wisconsin Ave., Ste. 3800
Milwaukee, WI 53202
Contact: Blaine E. Rieke, Tr.

Established in 1990 in WI as successor to David C. Scott Foundation of FL.
Donor(s): David C. Scott.‡
Financial data (yr. ended 11/30/01): Grants paid, $77,293; assets, $1,446,724 (M); expenditures, $89,668; qualifying distributions, $80,302.
Limitations: Applications not accepted.
Application information: Contributes only to pre-selected organizations.
Trustees: Peter R. Baumler, Harry V. Carlson, Jr., Blaine E. Rieke, David C. Scott, Jr., Mary D. Scott.
EIN: 391689843
Codes: FD2

57026
William L. Law Foundation, Inc.
2420A Walnut Grove Ct.
Brookfield, WI 53005-4556 (262) 786-8336
Contact: Mary R. Law, Pres.

Established about 1964.
Financial data (yr. ended 12/31/01): Grants paid, $77,270; assets, $10,327 (M); gifts received, $77,000; expenditures, $77,287; qualifying distributions, $77,268.
Limitations: Giving primarily in WI.
Application information: Application form not required.
Officers: Mary R. Law, Pres.; William R. Law, V.P.; Jane L. Ashley, Secy.-Treas.
EIN: 396064046
Codes: FD2

57027
Colonel Robert H. Morse Foundation
c/o Marshall & Ilsley Trust Company, N.A.
P.O. Box 2980
Milwaukee, WI 53201-2980
Application address: 500 E. Grand Ave., Beloit, WI 53511, tel.: (608) 364-3829
Contact: Bonnie D. Wetter, Pres.

Established in 1942.
Financial data (yr. ended 12/31/01): Grants paid, $77,200; assets, $1,293,790 (M); expenditures, $93,996; qualifying distributions, $80,091.
Limitations: Giving primarily in Beloit, WI.
Officers and Directors:* Bonnie D. Wetter,* Pres.; John H. Franz,* V.P.; Richard Dashnaw, Gordon C. Neese, James Reuthling, Richard J. Rusch.
Trustee: Marshall & Ilsley Trust Company, N.A.
EIN: 396092711
Codes: FD2

57028
Eihorn Family Charitable Trust
8205 N. River Rd.
Milwaukee, WI 53217

Established in 1997.
Financial data (yr. ended 12/31/00): Grants paid, $76,500; assets, $483,232 (M); gifts received, $50,000; expenditures, $76,690; qualifying distributions, $76,500.
Limitations: Applications not accepted.
Application information: Contributes only to pre-selected organizations.
Trustees: Nancy Einhorn, Stephen Einhorn.
EIN: 396643717
Codes: FD2

57029
Donald M. Anderson Foundation
7940 Deer Run Rd.
Cross Plains, WI 53528 (608) 798-2319
Contact: Philip Hamilton, Tr.

Established in 1998 in WI.
Financial data (yr. ended 12/31/01): Grants paid, $76,358; assets, $1,096,873 (M); expenditures, $103,255; qualifying distributions, $76,358.
Limitations: Giving primarily in WI.
Trustees: James Escalante, Philip Hamilton, John Rieben.
EIN: 396614493
Codes: FD2

57030
Morey W. & Lillian L. Kasch Foundation, Inc.
2533 N. Wahl Ave.
Milwaukee, WI 53211
FAX: (414) 332-7163
Contact: Jeffrey C. Kasch, Pres.

Established in 1986 in WI.
Donor(s): Lillian L. Kasch, M.W. Kasch Co., Jeffrey C. Kasch.
Financial data (yr. ended 12/31/01): Grants paid, $76,200; assets, $278,759 (M); gifts received, $2,300; expenditures, $76,825; qualifying distributions, $76,493.
Limitations: Applications not accepted. Giving primarily in NY and WI.
Application information: Contributes only to pre-selected organizations.
Officers: Jeffrey C. Kasch, Pres.; Lillian L. Kasch, V.P.; James A. Kasch, Secy.-Treas.
EIN: 391530775
Codes: FD2

57031
Baer Foundation, Inc.
P.O. Box 1148
Janesville, WI 53547-1148

Established in 1994 in WI.
Donor(s): Michele R. Baer, Thomas R. Baer.
Financial data (yr. ended 12/31/00): Grants paid, $76,056; assets, $554,976 (M); gifts received, $20,626; expenditures, $77,066; qualifying distributions, $73,782.
Limitations: Applications not accepted. Giving limited to Janesville, WI.
Application information: Contributes only to pre-selected organizations.
Officers and Directors:* Michele R. Baer,* Pres.; William Baer,* V.P.; Thomas R. Baer,* Secy.-Treas.
EIN: 391800747
Codes: FD2

57032
Antioch Foundation
c/o North Central Trust Co.
311 Main St.
La Crosse, WI 54601
Contact: Darwin Isaacson, Trust Off., North Central Trust Co.

Established in 1998 in WI.
Donor(s): Jill Swanson, Scott Zietlow.
Financial data (yr. ended 12/31/00): Grants paid, $76,000; assets, $924,303 (M); gifts received, $39,664; expenditures, $93,830; qualifying distributions, $76,004.
Limitations: Giving primarily in the Rochester, MN, and La Crosse, WI, areas.
Trustee: North Central Trust Co.
EIN: 363779525
Codes: FD2

57033
Catherine E. Apple and Myrl S. Apple Family Foundation, Inc.
c/o Charles B. Apple
3203 Tuckaway Ct.
Green Bay, WI 54301

Established in 1991.
Financial data (yr. ended 12/31/01): Grants paid, $76,000; assets, $1,534,098 (M); gifts received, $160; expenditures, $77,203; qualifying distributions, $76,000.
Limitations: Applications not accepted. Giving primarily in WI.
Application information: Contributes only to pre-selected organizations.
Directors: Charles B. Apple, Robert T. Apple, Gerald M. Vande Loo, Mary S. Zwiefelhofer.
EIN: 391670356

57034
Chapin Foundation of Wisconsin
c/o Marshall & Ilsley Trust Company, N.A.
P.O. Box 2980
Milwaukee, WI 53201-2980
Application address: c/o Marshall & Ilsley Trust Company, N.A., 5935 7th Ave., Kenosha, WI 53140, tel.: (262) 658-5592
Contact: Sharon Kubica

Established in 1943 in WI.
Financial data (yr. ended 06/30/02): Grants paid, $76,000; assets, $1,236,556 (M); expenditures, $97,962; qualifying distributions, $76,000.
Limitations: Giving limited to WI.
Trustee: Marshall & Ilsley Trust Company, N.A.
EIN: 396033716
Codes: FD2

57035
Rene Von Schleinitz Foundation, Ltd.
5555 N. Port Washington Rd., Ste. 210
Milwaukee, WI 53217

Established in 1951 in WI.
Financial data (yr. ended 12/31/00): Grants paid, $76,000; assets, $1,328,993 (M); expenditures, $83,788; qualifying distributions, $76,704.
Limitations: Applications not accepted. Giving primarily in WI.
Application information: Contributes only to pre-selected organizations.
Officers: Geoffrey G. Maclay, Pres. and Treas.; Edith Maclay, V.P.; Junelle C. Geimer, Secy.
EIN: 396054122
Codes: FD2

57036
The Isadore Foundation, Inc.
700 N. Water St., Ste. 1100
Milwaukee, WI 53202-4206 (414) 273-0500
Contact: William J. Heilbronner, Pres.

Donor(s): William Feitlinger, Susan Hobart.
Financial data (yr. ended 12/31/01): Grants paid, $75,900; assets, $219,692 (M); expenditures, $77,604; qualifying distributions, $75,900.
Limitations: Giving on a national basis, with emphasis on WI.
Application information: Application form not required.
Officers: William J. Heilbronner, Pres. and Treas.; Neil L. Prupis, Secy.
EIN: 222911380

57037
Weyco Group Charitable Trust
P.O. Box 1188
Milwaukee, WI 53201 (414) 908-1600
Contact: John F. Wittkowske, Tr.

Established in 1996 in WI.
Donor(s): Weyco Group, Inc.
Financial data (yr. ended 12/31/01): Grants paid, $75,615; assets, $103,318 (M); gifts received, $3,992; expenditures, $75,808; qualifying distributions, $75,610.
Limitations: Giving primarily in WI.
Trustees: John W. Florsheim, Thomas W. Florsheim, Sr., Thomas W. Florsheim, Jr., John F. Wittkowske.
EIN: 396645370
Codes: CS, FD2, CD

57038
Gebhardt Foundation, Inc.
(Formerly Monarch Foundation, Inc.)
7123 W. Calumet Rd.
Milwaukee, WI 53223

Established in 1986 in WI.
Donor(s): Monarch Corp., Uihlein Electric Co., Inc., Ritus Rubber Corp., Kenny Electric Svcs.
Financial data (yr. ended 12/31/00): Grants paid, $75,523; assets, $1,393,032 (L); gifts received, $315,000; expenditures, $76,019; qualifying distributions, $76,019.
Limitations: Applications not accepted. Giving primarily in WI.
Application information: Contributes only to pre-selected organizations.
Officers: Richard D. Gebhardt, Pres.; Susan G. Gebhardt, V.P.; William P. Koehn, Secy.
EIN: 391574609
Codes: CS, FD2, CD

57039
Dr. R. G. & Sarah Raymond Foundation
c/o National Exchange Bank and Trust
130 S. Main St.
Fond du Lac, WI 54935-4210
Application address: P.O. Box 1003, Fond du Lac, WI 54931, tel.: (920) 922-0470
Contact: Robert V. Edgarton, Secy.

Established in 1957.
Financial data (yr. ended 12/31/00): Grants paid, $75,300; assets, $1,435,428 (M); expenditures, $89,472; qualifying distributions, $77,713.
Limitations: Giving primarily in Fond du Lac and Dodge counties, WI.
Officers and Directors:* Leland Friedrich,* Pres.; Michael W. Bachhuber, V.P.; Robert V. Edgarton,* Secy.; Peter Stone,* Treas.
EIN: 396051142
Codes: FD2

57040
St. Mary's High School Trust No. 3
c/o Bank One Trust Co., N.A.
P.O. Box 1308
Milwaukee, WI 53201
Application address: c/o Rev. J. Kline, 310 8th St., Lorain, OH 44052, tel.: (216) 245-5783

Established around 1981 in OH.
Financial data (yr. ended 12/31/01): Grants paid, $75,150; assets, $668,808 (M); gifts received, $1,500; expenditures, $84,787; qualifying distributions, $78,191.
Limitations: Giving limited to Lorain, OH.
Application information: Application form required.
Trustee: Bank One Trust Co., N.A.
EIN: 346631616
Codes: FD2, GTI

57041
William E. and Josephine B. Buchanan Family Foundation, Inc.
P.O. Box 727
Appleton, WI 54912

Established in 1987 in WI.
Donor(s): Josephine B. Buchanan.
Financial data (yr. ended 03/31/01): Grants paid, $75,000; assets, $1,416,921 (M); expenditures, $82,927; qualifying distributions, $73,912.
Limitations: Applications not accepted. Giving primarily in Appleton, WI.
Application information: Contributes only to pre-selected organizations.
Officers: Josephine B. Buchanan, Pres.; Charles B. Buchanan, V.P.; Jean B. Vitalis, V.P.; Robert C. Buchanan, Secy.-Treas.
EIN: 391598289

57042
Clyde F. Schlueter Foundation, Inc.
605 Scott St.
P.O. Box 867
Wausau, WI 54402-0867 (715) 845-6227
FAX: (715) 842-2515; *E-mail:* byll@hesslaw.com
Contact: William C. Hess

Established in 1981 in WI.
Donor(s): Clyde F. Schlueter.‡
Financial data (yr. ended 09/30/01): Grants paid, $74,791; assets, $1,595,981 (M); expenditures, $109,403; qualifying distributions, $72,414.
Limitations: Giving limited to the greater Wausau, WI, area.
Application information: Application form required.
Officers and Directors:* Richard D. Dudley,* Pres.; Gordon L. Backer, M.D.,* V.P.; Thomas A. Mack,* Secy.-Treas.; Harry Colcord, William D. Siebecker.
EIN: 391292262

57043
Kenneth G. Marsden Foundation
321 N. Main St.
Box 1980
West Bend, WI 53095-7980
Contact: Stephen Zemmel

Established in 1981.
Financial data (yr. ended 12/31/00): Grants paid, $74,700; assets, $1,705,487 (M); expenditures, $79,295; qualifying distributions, $74,030.
Limitations: Giving primarily in WI.
Application information: Application form not required.
Trustees: Gerald Marsden, James Marsden, R.T. Stephenson.
EIN: 391388865

57044
Telly Foundation, Ltd.
c/o James B. Wigdale
770 N. Water St.
Milwaukee, WI 53202

Established in 1986 in WI.
Donor(s): Elizabeth T. Wigdale, James B. Wigdale.
Financial data (yr. ended 12/31/01): Grants paid, $74,690; assets, $927,422 (M); expenditures, $74,721; qualifying distributions, $74,642.
Limitations: Applications not accepted. Giving primarily in Milwaukee, WI.
Application information: Contributes only to pre-selected organizations.
Officers and Directors:* Elizabeth T. Wigdale,* Pres.; James B. Wigdale, Jr.,* V.P.; James B. Wigdale,* Secy.-Treas.
EIN: 391570459

57045
Morley-Murphy Foundation
c/o Associated Banc-Corp
P.O. Box 408
Neenah, WI 54957-0408 (920) 433-3109
Additional address: c/o Associated Banc-Corp,
P.O. Box 19006, Green Bay, WI 54307-9006
Contact: Douglas J. Green, Tr.

Established about 1959.
Financial data (yr. ended 12/31/00): Grants paid, $73,500; assets, $1,447,228 (M); gifts received, $843; expenditures, $86,262; qualifying distributions, $73,515.
Limitations: Giving primarily in WI.
Officer: Stephen Stiles, Pres.
Trustee: Associated Banc-Corp.
EIN: 396051029

57046
Suder-Pick Foundation, Inc.
777 E. Wisconsin Ave.
Milwaukee, WI 53202 (414) 297-5748
Contact: Harrold J. McComas, V.P.

Donor(s): Melitta S. Pick,‡ Joan M. Pick.
Financial data (yr. ended 12/31/99): Grants paid, $73,500; assets, $36,281 (M); gifts received, $64,207; expenditures, $80,030; qualifying distributions, $78,057.
Limitations: Giving limited to West Bend, WI.
Officers and Directors:* Joan M. Pick,* Pres.; Harrold J. McComas,* V.P. and Secy.; Robert J. Bonner,* Treas.
EIN: 396048255
Codes: GTI

57047
Garton Family Foundation
P.O. Box 725
Sheboygan, WI 53082-0725
Application address: 39 Fox Point Dr., Appleton, WI 54911
Contact: Tony Garton, Pres.

Established about 1947.
Financial data (yr. ended 07/31/01): Grants paid, $72,200; assets, $938,047 (M); expenditures, $80,116; qualifying distributions, $76,565.
Limitations: Giving primarily in WI, with emphasis on Sheboygan.
Officers and Directors:* Tony Garton,* Pres.; Ann McIntyre,* V.P.; Gerald Loth,* Secy.-Treas.; Judy Baer, Diane Edie, Mary Garton, Michael Garton, Robert E. Garton, Tim Garton, Nan Siebert.
EIN: 396107459

57048
The Dyar Foundation
c/o Quarles & Brady
411 E. Wisconsin Ave., Ste. 2550
Milwaukee, WI 53202-4497 (414) 277-5000
Contact: Philip G. Brumder, Tr.; or Anthony W. Asmuth III, Tr.

Established in 1988 in WI.
Donor(s): Philip G. Brumder.
Financial data (yr. ended 12/31/01): Grants paid, $72,000; assets, $1,326,075 (M); expenditures, $78,305; qualifying distributions, $72,550.
Limitations: Giving primarily in Milwaukee, WI.
Application information: Application form not required.
Trustees: Anthony W. Asmuth III, Philip G. Brumder.
EIN: 391635082

57049
The JSW Adoption Foundation, Inc.
127 E. Main St., Ste. 5
Port Washington, WI 53074-1915
(262) 268-1386
URL: http://www.jsw-adoption.org
Contact: Eugene T. Wyka, Pres.

Established in 1996 in WI.
Donor(s): Eugene J. Wyka,‡ Eugene T. Wyka, Lucy M. Wyka.
Financial data (yr. ended 06/30/01): Grants paid, $71,743; assets, $892,923 (M); gifts received, $90,456; expenditures, $321,211; qualifying distributions, $71,743.
Limitations: Giving on a national basis.
Publications: Informational brochure (including application guidelines), newsletter, grants list.
Application information: Application form required.
Officers: Eugene T. Wyka, Pres. and Treas.; Lucy M. Wyka, V.P. and Secy.
EIN: 391863217

57050
Mary Pauly Lacy Foundation, Inc.
(Formerly William and Mary Lacy Foundation)
c/o Jere D. McGaffey
777 E. Wisconsin Ave., Ste. 3600
Milwaukee, WI 53202

Established in 1993 in WI.
Donor(s): William H. Lacy, Mary Lacy.
Financial data (yr. ended 12/31/00): Grants paid, $71,070; assets, $457,615 (M); expenditures, $88,364; qualifying distributions, $77,489.
Limitations: Applications not accepted. Giving primarily in Milwaukee, WI.
Application information: Contributes only to pre-selected organizations.
Officers and Directors:* Mary Lacy,* Pres.; Margaret Lacy,* V.P.; Sara Kate Lacy,* V.P.; Thomas Lacy,* Secy.; David Lacy,* Treas.
EIN: 391744801

57051
E. R. Wagner Manufacturing Company Foundation, Inc.
4611 N. 32nd St.
Milwaukee, WI 53209
Contact: Frank M. Sterner, Pres.

Established in 1955.
Donor(s): E.R. Wagner Manufacturing Co.
Financial data (yr. ended 12/31/01): Grants paid, $70,458; assets, $573,158 (M); gifts received, $50,000; expenditures, $75,379; qualifying distributions, $72,312.
Limitations: Giving primarily in Milwaukee, WI.
Application information: Application form not required.
Officers and Directors:* Frank M. Sterner,* Pres. and Treas.; Bernard S. Kubale,* V.P. and Secy.; Marna W. Fullerton, Cynthia W. Kahler.
EIN: 396037097
Codes: CS, CD

57052
Betty M. Stark Charitable Trust
c/o Bank One Trust Co., N.A.
P.O. Box 1308
Milwaukee, WI 53201

Established in 2001 in WI.
Donor(s): Betty M. Stark Charitable Lead Trust.
Financial data (yr. ended 12/31/01): Grants paid, $69,826; assets, $81,032 (M); gifts received, $150,866; expenditures, $69,887; qualifying distributions, $69,841.
Limitations: Applications not accepted. Giving primarily in WI.
Application information: Contributes only to pre-selected organizations.
Trustee: Bank One Trust Co., N.A.
EIN: 396729903

57053
William Eisner Foundation, Inc.
P.O. Box 28800
Milwaukee, WI 53220-0800

Established in 1969.
Donor(s): William A. Eisner, William Eisner & Assocs., Inc., Affiliated Consultants, Inc., Elaine B. Eisner, Debra Lynn Hackbarth.
Financial data (yr. ended 12/31/01): Grants paid, $69,500; assets, $295,898 (M); expenditures, $72,927; qualifying distributions, $69,500.
Limitations: Giving primarily in WI.
Application information: Application form not required.
Officers: Elaine B. Eisner, Pres.; William A. Eisner, V.P.; Debra Lynn Hackbarth, Secy.-Treas.
EIN: 237054795

57054
Zaun Memorial Foundation, Ltd.
P.O. Box 0663
Sheboygan, WI 53082-0663
Application address: 101 Falls Rd., Grafton, WI 53024-2612
Contact: Ralph Zaun, Pres.

Established around 1965 in WI.
Donor(s): Ralph Zaun.
Financial data (yr. ended 12/31/01): Grants paid, $68,354; assets, $1,578,804 (M); expenditures, $82,102; qualifying distributions, $68,354.
Limitations: Giving primarily in WI.
Officers and Directors:* Ralph Zaun,* Pres.; Frank Giuffre,* V.P.; Darlene Hausmann,* Secy.; Edith Zaun, Fred Zahn.
Trustee: U.S. Bank.
EIN: 396097805

57055
Immelt Family Foundation
411 E. Wisconsin Ave., Ste. 2040
Milwaukee, WI 53202-4497

Established in 1998 in WI.
Financial data (yr. ended 09/30/01): Grants paid, $68,344; assets, $0 (M); gifts received, $3,298; expenditures, $70,542; qualifying distributions, $68,341.
Limitations: Applications not accepted.
Application information: Contributes only to pre-selected organizations.
Trustees: Andrea A. Immelt, Jeffrey R. Immelt.
EIN: 396698330

57056
The Clarence Wallace and Dolores Lynch Wallace Family Foundation
1700 N. Viola St.
Appleton, WI 54911

Established in 1996 in WI.
Donor(s): Clarence E. Wallace, Dolores M. Wallace.
Financial data (yr. ended 12/31/01): Grants paid, $68,300; assets, $993,954 (M); expenditures, $72,716; qualifying distributions, $68,300.
Limitations: Applications not accepted. Giving primarily in WI.
Application information: Contributes only to pre-selected organizations.
Trustees: Brian Wallace, Clarence E. Wallace, Dolores M. Wallace.
EIN: 396624684

57057
RMSM Foundation
c/o Bank One Trust Co.
P.O. Box 1308
Milwaukee, WI 53201
Application address: 110 W. Berry, Ste. 2202, Fort Wayne, IN 46802
Contact: Susan M. Walbridge, Chair.

Established in 1997 in IN.
Financial data (yr. ended 09/30/01): Grants paid, $68,090; assets, $795,162 (M); expenditures, $80,555; qualifying distributions, $68,090.
Application information: Application form required.
Officer: Susan M. Walbridge, Chair.
Directors: John R. Giant, Harry W. Scott, Jane Surbeck, John Underwood.
Trustee: Bank One Trust Co., N.A.
EIN: 352034536

57058
Leila Kohl Scholarship Trust
c/o Marshall & Ilsley Trust Company, N.A.
P.O. Box 2980
Milwaukee, WI 53201-2980
Application address: c/o School District of Tomahawk, District Administration Office, 18 E. Washington Ave., Tomahawk, WI 54487, tel.: (715) 453-5551

Established in 1995 in WI.
Donor(s): Leila B. Kohl.‡
Financial data (yr. ended 03/31/02): Grants paid, $68,000; assets, $1,124,025 (M); expenditures, $81,345; qualifying distributions, $67,671.
Limitations: Giving limited to residents of Tomahawk, WI.
Application information: Application form required.
Trustee: Marshall & Ilsley Trust Company, N.A.
EIN: 396611696
Codes: GTI

57059
Ocular Research Trust
c/o Bank One Trust Co., N.A.
P.O. Box 13
Milwaukee, WI 53201

Established in 1995.
Financial data (yr. ended 12/31/01): Grants paid, $68,000; assets, $1,154,218 (M); expenditures, $76,147; qualifying distributions, $68,000.
Limitations: Applications not accepted. Giving primarily in Boston, MA.
Application information: Contributes only to pre-selected organizations.
Trustee: Bank One Trust Co., N.A.
EIN: 367131295

57060
Jane & Arthur Stangel Fund, Inc.
P.O. Box 2303
Manitowoc, WI 54221-2303 (920) 757-5008
Contact: Richard R. Jodarski, Pres.

Established in 1968.
Financial data (yr. ended 12/31/01): Grants paid, $68,000; assets, $1,564,909 (M); expenditures, $82,133; qualifying distributions, $68,000.
Limitations: Giving primarily in Manitowoc County, WI.
Officers: Richard R. Jodarski, Pres.; Nicholas B. Jagemann, V.P.; Kaye E. Johnson, Secy.-Treas.
EIN: 396120403

57061
Sand Dollar Foundation
(Formerly Marjorie & Robert Straus Endowment Fund)
c/o American National Bank & Trust Co.
P.O. Box 130
Milwaukee, WI 53201

Established in 1993 in IL.
Financial data (yr. ended 12/31/00): Grants paid, $67,500; assets, $1,232,759 (M); expenditures, $93,956; qualifying distributions, $70,239.
Limitations: Applications not accepted. Giving primarily in ME.
Application information: Contributes only to pre-selected organizations.
Trustees: Jeremy R. Wintersteen, Laurence M. Wintersteen, Margo S. Wintersteen, American National Bank & Trust Co.
EIN: 366035113

57062
Margaret Banta Humleker Charitable Foundation, Inc.
3415 Gateway Rd., Ste. 200
Brookfield, WI 53045-5111

Established in 1982 in WI.
Donor(s): Margaret Banta Humleker.
Financial data (yr. ended 11/30/01): Grants paid, $67,435; assets, $12,040 (M); gifts received, $50,706; expenditures, $67,435; qualifying distributions, $67,429.
Limitations: Applications not accepted. Giving primarily in WI.
Application information: Contributes only to pre-selected organizations.
Officers: Margaret Banta Humleker, Pres.; Anne Heintz, V.P.; George Humleker, V.P.; William Humleker, V.P.; Rhona E. Vogel, V.P.; John Hein, Treas.
EIN: 391427005

57063
Rosemann Family Foundation, Inc.
408 Arrowhead Dr.
Green Bay, WI 54301

Established in 1988 in WI.
Donor(s): Russell R. Rosemann, Virginia V. Rosemann.
Financial data (yr. ended 07/31/01): Grants paid, $67,325; assets, $1,354,374 (M); expenditures, $68,830; qualifying distributions, $69,164.
Limitations: Applications not accepted. Giving primarily in Green Bay, WI.
Application information: Contributes only to pre-selected organizations.
Officers: Russell R. Rosemann, Pres. and Treas.; Virginia V. Rosemann, V.P. and Secy.
EIN: 391621252

57064
Max and Bessie Bakal Foundation
c/o Quarles & Brady
411 E. Wisconsin Ave., Ste. 2550
Milwaukee, WI 53202-4497

Established in 1996 in WI.
Donor(s): Estelle Berman, Richard Bakal.
Financial data (yr. ended 12/31/01): Grants paid, $66,790; assets, $792,031 (M); expenditures, $76,330; qualifying distributions, $66,790.
Limitations: Applications not accepted.
Application information: Contributes only to pre-selected organizations.
Trustees: Richard Bakal, Estelle Berman, Dave Blanchard, June Long.
EIN: 396645353

57065
Thomas J. Bliffert Foundation, Inc.
111 E. Wisconsin Ave., Ste. 1800
Milwaukee, WI 53202

Established in 1992 in WI.
Financial data (yr. ended 12/31/01): Grants paid, $66,597; assets, $285,027 (M); expenditures, $68,630; qualifying distributions, $66,597.
Limitations: Applications not accepted.
Application information: Contributes only to pre-selected organizations.
Officers and Directors:* Thomas J. Bliffert,* Pres.; Jean Bliffert,* Secy.; Janet M. Hoehnen.
EIN: 391364810

57066
Plunkett Family Foundation
8500 N. River Rd.
Milwaukee, WI 53217
Application address: 317 E. Silver Spring Dr., Ste. 207, Milwaukee, WI 53217
Contact: Katherine Plunkett, Tr.

Donor(s): James G. Plunkett.
Financial data (yr. ended 12/31/01): Grants paid, $66,500; assets, $761,295 (M); gifts received, $109,500; expenditures, $92,957; qualifying distributions, $66,500.
Limitations: Giving primarily in WI.
Trustees: Karen Plunkett Muenster, James G. Plunkett, Katherine Plunkett, Laura Plunkett, Robert G. Plunkett.
EIN: 396681155

57067
Weather Shield Manufacturing Foundation, Inc.
P.O. Box 309
Medford, WI 54451-0309

Donor(s): Weather Shield Manufacturing, Inc.
Financial data (yr. ended 12/31/00): Grants paid, $66,500; assets, $439,724 (M); expenditures, $69,403; qualifying distributions, $65,500.
Limitations: Applications not accepted. Giving primarily in MN and WI.
Application information: Contributes only to pre-selected organizations.
Officers: Edward L. Schield, Pres.; John T. Marshall, V.P.; Steve J. Danen, Secy.; James A. Klinner, Treas.
EIN: 391362989
Codes: CS, CD

57068
Francis F. Carnes Education Charitable Trust
316 N. Main St.
Lake Mills, WI 53551 (920) 648-4456
Contact: Cherie L. Miller, Tr.

Established in 1999 in WI.
Financial data (yr. ended 01/31/01): Grants paid, $66,000; assets, $1,043,859 (M); expenditures, $69,027; qualifying distributions, $66,000.
Limitations: Giving primarily in Jefferson County, WI.
Application information: Applicants must have attained four years of high school at one of five Jefferson County high schools and have maintained a minimum GPA of 2.75. Application form required.
Trustees: Cherie L. Miller, Bradford Vail.
EIN: 391968680

57069
The Schoenauer Family Foundation, Inc.
1217A Milwaukee St.
Delafield, WI 53018-1630

Established in 1993 in WI.
Donor(s): Thomas E. Schoenauer.

Financial data (yr. ended 12/31/01): Grants paid, $65,765; assets, $441,268 (M); gifts received, $153,959; expenditures, $67,145; qualifying distributions, $65,765.
Limitations: Applications not accepted. Giving primarily in WI.
Application information: Contributes only to pre-selected organizations.
Officers and Directors:* Thomas E. Schoenauer,* Pres. and Treas.; Carolyn M. Schoenauer,* V.P. and Secy.; Jodi H. Schoenauer, Steven J. Shoenauer, Thomas E. Schoenauer, Jr.
EIN: 391775577

57070
Pauline W. Conover Scholarship Trust
c/o Bank One Trust Co., N.A.
P.O. Box 1308
Milwaukee, WI 53201
Application Address: 111 Monument Cir., IN1-0175, Indianapolis, IN 46277-0115
Contact: Lyle E. Fogel, V.P. & Trust Off., Bank One Trust Co.

Established in 1991 in IN.
Financial data (yr. ended 12/31/00): Grants paid, $65,685; assets, $584,090 (M); expenditures, $72,369; qualifying distributions, $68,610.
Limitations: Giving limited to residents of Montgomery County, IN.
Application information: Application form required.
Trustee: Bank One Trust Co., N.A.
EIN: 356512329
Codes: GTI

57071
Irving & Dorothy Levy Foundation, Inc.
P.O. Box 7725
Madison, WI 53707-7725

Established in 1961.
Donor(s): Irving Levy, Dorothy Levy.
Financial data (yr. ended 07/31/01): Grants paid, $65,535; assets, $1,658,224 (M); gifts received, $274,423; expenditures, $66,869; qualifying distributions, $65,077.
Limitations: Applications not accepted. Giving primarily in Madison, WI.
Application information: Contributes only to pre-selected organizations.
Officers and Directors:* Irving Levy,* Pres.; Dorothy Levy, V.P. and Secy.; Terry Von Haden, Treas.; Jeffrey Levy, Philip Levy.
EIN: 396045321

57072
Matrix Foundation
c/o Elaine D. Marshall
235 W. Thornapple Ln.
Mequon, WI 53092

Established in 2000 in WI.
Donor(s): Elaine D. Marshall.
Financial data (yr. ended 12/31/01): Grants paid, $65,500; assets, $286,204 (M); expenditures, $74,916; qualifying distributions, $65,500.
Limitations: Applications not accepted. Giving primarily in WI.
Application information: Contributes only to pre-selected organizations.
Trustee: Elaine D. Marshall.
EIN: 391999556

57073
Siron Foundation
c/o James E. Hartwig
P.O. Box 1148
Janesville, WI 53547-1148

Established in 1999 in WI.
Financial data (yr. ended 06/30/01): Grants paid, $64,500; assets, $1,254,751 (M); expenditures, $83,993; qualifying distributions, $64,500.
Limitations: Applications not accepted. Giving primarily in WI.
Application information: Contributes only to pre-selected organizations.
Trustee: Donald Sartell.
EIN: 396508465

57074
Christopher Neese Memorial Foundation
c/o Marshall & Ilsley Trust Company, N.A.
P.O. Box 2980
Milwaukee, WI 53201
Application address: 800 Laurel Oak Dr., Ste. 101, Naples, FL 33963, tel.: (941) 592-5461
Contact: Roger Mjoen

Financial data (yr. ended 10/31/01): Grants paid, $64,247; assets, $314,126 (M); expenditures, $70,019; qualifying distributions, $64,247.
Limitations: Giving primarily in Atlanta, GA.
Trustee: Marshall & Ilsley Trust Company, N.A.
EIN: 586326331

57075
Associated Banc-Corp Foundation
(Formerly First Financial Foundation, Inc.)
1200 Hansen Rd.
Green Bay, WI 54304
Application address: Jonathon Drayna, Trust Off., c/o Associated Banc-Corp, P.O. Box 13307, 112 N. Adams St., Green Bay, WI 54307-3307; E-mail: jon.drayna@associatedbank.com

Established in 1977 in WI.
Donor(s): First Financial Bank, Associated Banc-Corp.
Financial data (yr. ended 12/31/01): Grants paid, $64,000; assets, $763,893 (M); expenditures, $74,832; qualifying distributions, $64,000.
Limitations: Applications not accepted. Giving limited to areas of business in IL and WI.
Application information: Unsolicited requests for funds not accepted.
Officer and Directors:* Brian Bodager,* Pres.; Joanne P. Radeske.
EIN: 391277461
Codes: CS, CD

57076
Clifton E. Peterson, M.D. Family Foundation
7022 3rd Ave.
Kenosha, WI 53143

Donor(s): Clifton E. Peterson, M.D.
Financial data (yr. ended 12/31/01): Grants paid, $63,500; assets, $90,016 (M); expenditures, $63,500; qualifying distributions, $63,500.
Limitations: Applications not accepted.
Application information: Contributes only to pre-selected organizations.
Trustee: Clifton E. Peterson, M.D.
EIN: 396654435

57077
Robert G. Sharp Trust
2781 Queen Ann Ct.
Green Bay, WI 54304 (920) 494-8916

Established in 1963 in WI.
Donor(s): Robert G. Sharp.‡
Financial data (yr. ended 08/31/01): Grants paid, $63,500; assets, $871,336 (M); expenditures, $89,354; qualifying distributions, $69,461.
Limitations: Giving limited to residents of Oconto and Brown counties, WI.
Publications: Application guidelines.
Application information: Application forms, high school transcripts, FAF, and/or ACT analysis. Application form required.
Trustee: Edward M. Witczak.
EIN: 396084979
Codes: GTI

57078
Crystal Print Foundation, Inc.
c/o Paul Mahlberg
500 Hart Ct.
Little Chute, WI 54140

Established in 1993 in WI.
Donor(s): Crystal Print, Inc.
Financial data (yr. ended 12/31/01): Grants paid, $63,250; assets, $761,016 (M); gifts received, $100,000; expenditures, $66,675; qualifying distributions, $63,250.
Limitations: Applications not accepted. Giving primarily in the Fox Valley, WI, area.
Application information: Contributes only to pre-selected organizations.
Officers: Dan Gavronski, Pres.; James Miller, V.P.; Paul Mahlberg, Secy.-Treas.
Directors: Larry Banker, Bob Crosby, Jay Giordana, Thomas Hartenberger, Evelyn Hartwig, Joe Krull, Diane Reynolds, Jeff Rollo.
EIN: 391764046
Codes: CS, CD

57079
Muehrcke Family Foundation
7816 W. Island Rd.
Waterloo, WI 53594 (920) 478-3890
Contact: Robert C. Muehrcke, M.D., Treas.

Donor(s): JoAnn Muehrcke, Robert C. Muehrcke, M.D., Allan O. Muehrcke, M.D.
Financial data (yr. ended 12/31/01): Grants paid, $63,096; assets, $1,017,484 (M); expenditures, $75,715; qualifying distributions, $63,096.
Limitations: Giving primarily in IL.
Application information: Application form required.
Officers and Director:* JoAnn A. Muehrcke, Pres.; Allan O. Muehrcke, M.D., Secy.; Robert C. Muehrcke, M.D., Treas.; Conrad Muehrcke.
EIN: 363164934

57080
Mary P. Gill Foundation
c/o Bank One Trust Co., N.A.
P.O. Box 1308
Milwaukee, WI 53201

Established in 1985 in KY.
Financial data (yr. ended 12/31/99): Grants paid, $62,684; assets, $459,351 (M); expenditures, $66,807; qualifying distributions, $62,442.
Limitations: Applications not accepted. Giving primarily in Louisville, KY.
Application information: Contributes only to pre-selected organizations.
Trustee: Bank One Trust Co., N.A.
EIN: 616026688

57081
The Kolaga Family Charitable Trust
(Formerly The Joseph E. Kolaga Charitable Trust)
1621 N. 120th St.
Wauwatosa, WI 53226-2902
Contact: Joseph E. Kolaga, Tr.

Donor(s): Joseph E. Kolaga, Ruth Ann Kolaga.
Financial data (yr. ended 12/31/01): Grants paid, $62,445; assets, $161,643 (M); gifts received, $65,009; expenditures, $65,904; qualifying distributions, $62,445.
Limitations: Giving primarily in WI.

57081—WISCONSIN

Trustees: Joseph E. Kolaga, Paul Kolaga, Ruth Ann Kolaga.
EIN: 396281716

57082
Gerald & Dorothy Volm Foundation, Inc.
1804 N. Edison St.
P.O. Box 400
Antigo, WI 54409-2438

Donor(s): Gerald Volm.
Financial data (yr. ended 12/31/01): Grants paid, $62,415; assets, $1,772,156 (M); expenditures, $108,308; qualifying distributions, $65,360.
Limitations: Applications not accepted. Giving limited to Antigo, WI.
Application information: Contributes only to pre-selected organizations.
Officers: Gerald Volm, Pres.; Dorothy Volm, V.P.; Cynthia Hilger, Secy.; William Volm, Treas.
EIN: 391269616

57083
Helen Kelly Trust
c/o U.S. Bank
P.O. Box 2043
Milwaukee, WI 53201-9116

Established in 2000 in WI.
Financial data (yr. ended 12/31/01): Grants paid, $62,300; assets, $825,990 (M); expenditures, $70,432; qualifying distributions, $62,300.
Limitations: Applications not accepted.
Application information: Contributes only to pre-selected organizations.
Trustee: U.S. Bank.
EIN: 396648565

57084
The Masterson Foundation, Inc.
4023 W. National Ave.
Milwaukee, WI 53215-1000

Established in 1993 in WI.
Donor(s): The Masterson Co., Inc.
Financial data (yr. ended 12/31/01): Grants paid, $62,249; assets, $285,325 (M); gifts received, $5,000; expenditures, $62,249; qualifying distributions, $62,249.
Limitations: Applications not accepted. Giving primarily in Barrington, IL, and Milwaukee, WI.
Application information: Contributes only to pre-selected organizations.
Officers: Nancy J. Masterson, Pres.; Joe A. Masterson, V.P. and Treas.; Martin Zoberman, Secy.
EIN: 391758210

57085
Ervin & Suzann Colton Charitable Foundation
2419 E. Shorewood Blvd.
Shorewood, WI 53211

Established in 1997 in WI.
Donor(s): Ervin Colton.
Financial data (yr. ended 12/31/01): Grants paid, $61,750; assets, $932,449 (M); expenditures, $66,475; qualifying distributions, $61,750.
Limitations: Applications not accepted. Giving primarily in WI.
Application information: Contributes only to pre-selected organizations.
Trustees: Ervin Colton, Miriam Colton, David E. Schultz.
EIN: 396674253

57086
Grace F. Tschirgi Scholarship Fund
c/o U.S. Bank
P.O. Box 2043, LC4NE
Milwaukee, WI 53201-9116
Application address: c/o Tom Collins, Advisory Comm., Shuttleworth & Ingersoll, Firstar Bldg., 5th Fl., Cedar Rapids, IA 52401

Financial data (yr. ended 05/21/01): Grants paid, $61,000; assets, $1,005,343 (M); expenditures, $79,350; qualifying distributions, $64,540.
Limitations: Giving limited to Linn County, IA.
Application information: Application form not required.
Trustee: U.S. Bank.
EIN: 426054236
Codes: GTI

57087
Leon & Rena Frank Memorial Corporation
c/o Bank One Trust Co., N.A.
P.O. Box 1308
Milwaukee, WI 53201

Financial data (yr. ended 12/31/01): Grants paid, $60,990; assets, $284,143 (M); expenditures, $71,373; qualifying distributions, $60,990.
Limitations: Applications not accepted. Giving primarily in AZ, MI, and PA.
Application information: Contributes only to pre-selected organizations.
Officers: Daniel M. Frank, Pres.; Merrill Gordon, V.P.; Elizabeth Smith, Secy.
Trustee: Bank One Trust Co., N.A.
EIN: 386058044

57088
Pugh Foundation Scholarship Fund
(Formerly Hazel & Ben Pugh Foundation Scholarship Fund)
c/o Bank One Trust Co., N.A.
P.O. Box 1308
Milwaukee, WI 53201-1308
Application address: c/o Rick Colbo, School Counselor, Mukwonago High School, W. School Rd., Mukwonago, WI 53149

Financial data (yr. ended 09/30/01): Grants paid, $60,443; assets, $919,111 (M); expenditures, $74,116; qualifying distributions, $64,135.
Limitations: Giving limited to Mukwonago, WI.
Application information: Application form required.
Trustee: Bank One Trust Co., N.A.
EIN: 396452749
Codes: GTI

57089
Theodore & Catherine Schulte Foundation
c/o Bank One Trust Co., N.A.
P.O. Box 1308
Milwaukee, WI 53201-1308
Application address: c/o Robert Sharp, 610 Main St., Racine, WI 53403

Financial data (yr. ended 09/30/01): Grants paid, $60,443; assets, $919,111 (M); expenditures, $74,116; qualifying distributions, $64,135.
Limitations: Giving limited to Racine, WI.
Application information: Application form not required.
Trustee: Bank One Trust Co., N.A.
EIN: 396222864
Codes: GTI

57090
Jack and Penny Rohrbach Family Foundation, Inc.
339 Lake Rd.
Menasha, WI 54952
Contact: Nelson J. Rohrbach, V.P.

Established in 1993 in WI.
Donor(s): Nelson J. Rohrbach, Penny J. Rohrbach.
Financial data (yr. ended 12/31/02): Grants paid, $60,000; assets, $1,000,000 (M); expenditures, $60,000; qualifying distributions, $60,000.
Publications: Occasional report.
Officers: Holly Meeks, Pres.; Nelson J. Rohrbach, V.P.; Susan A. Rohrbach, Secy.; Nelson Rohrbach III, Treas.
Directors: Nancy Johnston, David Rohrbach, Penny J. Rohrbach.
EIN: 391778405

57091
Lester G. Wood Foundation, Inc.
3290 Vista Rd.
Green Bay, WI 54301-2632 (920) 336-1222
Contact: Patricia W. Baer, Pres.

Established in 1955.
Donor(s): members of the Baer and Lea families.
Financial data (yr. ended 12/31/01): Grants paid, $60,000; assets, $2,861,731 (M); expenditures, $64,492; qualifying distributions, $58,673.
Limitations: Giving primarily in Naples, FL and WI, with emphasis on Green Bay.
Application information: Application form not required.
Officers and Directors:* Patricia W. Baer,* Pres.; Charles S. Baer,* V.P.; Frederick E. Baer,* Secy.-Treas.; Frederick W. Baer, Richard R. Baer.
EIN: 396055567

57092
Hamparian Family Foundation
3051 Old Mill Dr.
Racine, WI 53405

Established in 2000 in WI.
Financial data (yr. ended 03/31/01): Grants paid, $59,745; assets, $3,698,259 (M); expenditures, $61,813; qualifying distributions, $58,019.
Limitations: Applications not accepted.
Application information: Contributes only to pre-selected organizations.
Officers: Gay Derderian, Pres.; Haig Derderian, V.P.; James Rose, Treas.
EIN: 391953042

57093
F. B. Parriott Educational Fund
c/o Bank One Trust Co., N.A.
P.O. Box 1308
Milwaukee, WI 53201
Application address: c/o Mike Bartel, V.P. & Trust Off., Bank One Trust Co., N.A., P.O. Box 1, Tulsa, OK 74193-0001

Donor(s): Jackson C. Parriott.
Financial data (yr. ended 06/30/01): Grants paid, $59,600; assets, $803,676 (M); expenditures, $69,304; qualifying distributions, $61,909.
Limitations: Giving limited to Tulsa, OK.
Trustee: Bank One Trust Co., N.A.
EIN: 736089907
Codes: GTI

57094
Robert W. Clark Charitable Foundation, Inc.
170 3rd St. N.
Wisconsin Rapids, WI 54494
Contact: Francis J. Podvin, Secy.

Established in 1994 in WI.

Donor(s): Robert W. Clark.
Financial data (yr. ended 08/31/01): Grants paid, $59,500; assets, $1,198,847 (M); expenditures, $70,936; qualifying distributions, $59,897.
Limitations: Giving primarily in HI and WI.
Application information: Application form not required.
Officers and Directors:* Robert W. Clark,* Pres. and Treas.; David W. Kumm,* V.P.; Francis J. Podvin,* Secy.
EIN: 391778665

57095
Loretta A. Wells Nursing Scholarship Trust
c/o Bank One Trust Co., N.A.
P.O. Box 1308
Milwaukee, WI 53201
FAX: (920) 735-1381
Application address: 200 W. College Ave., Appleton, WI 54911, tel.: (414) 735-1382
Contact: Marilyn Wunrow, Trust Off., Tammy Ross, Trust Off., Bank One Trust Co., N.A.

Established in 1983 in WI.
Donor(s): Loretta A. Wells.‡
Financial data (yr. ended 07/31/01): Grants paid, $59,473; assets, $1,981,760 (M); expenditures, $81,564; qualifying distributions, $65,567.
Limitations: Giving limited to Brown County, WI.
Application information: Application form not required.
Trustee: Bank One Trust Co., N.A.
EIN: 396364734
Codes: GTI

57096
Harriet Steel Charitable Trust
c/o Bank One Trust Co., N.A.
P.O. Box 1308
Milwaukee, WI 53201

Established in 1997 in WI.
Donor(s): Harriet Steel.‡
Financial data (yr. ended 12/31/01): Grants paid, $59,170; assets, $442,699 (M); expenditures, $63,966; qualifying distributions, $59,170.
Limitations: Applications not accepted. Giving primarily in WI.
Application information: Contributes only to pre-selected organizations.
Trustee: Bank One Trust Co., N.A.
EIN: 396496152

57097
Louis P. Diefenbach Trust
c/o Bank One Trust Co., N.A.
P.O. Box 1308
Milwaukee, WI 53201
Application address: 2 S. Main St., Middletown, OH 45042
Contact: Mark D. Welch, Trust Off., Bank One Trust Co., N.A.

Financial data (yr. ended 12/31/01): Grants paid, $59,066; assets, $1,000,743 (M); expenditures, $69,401; qualifying distributions, $61,857.
Limitations: Giving primarily in OH.
Application information: Application form required.
Trustee: Bank One Trust Co., N.A.
EIN: 316045149

57098
Henry W. Seger Memorial Trust Fund
c/o Bank One Trust Co., N.A.
P.O. Box 1308
Milwaukee, WI 53201
Application address: c/o John Williams, Pres., The Seger Comm., Vandalia Lions Club, 1359 Surrey Rd., Vandalia, OH 45377

Financial data (yr. ended 12/31/01): Grants paid, $59,032; assets, $565,397 (M); expenditures, $66,582; qualifying distributions, $59,032.
Limitations: Giving limited to Butler Township and Vandalia, OH.
Trustee: Bank One Trust Co., N.A.
EIN: 316193770

57099
St. Piran's Foundation
6536 Hillcrest Dr.
Wauwatosa, WI 53213

Established in 1997 in WI.
Donor(s): Elizabeth W. Boyce.
Financial data (yr. ended 06/30/01): Grants paid, $59,000; assets, $1,160,958 (M); expenditures, $63,674; qualifying distributions, $59,687.
Limitations: Applications not accepted. Giving primarily in IL and PA.
Application information: Contributes only to pre-selected organizations.
Trustees: Iunia L. Boyce, Thomas C. Boyce.
EIN: 396675978

57100
Lila Draper Burton Trust
c/o Bank One Trust Co., N.A.
P.O. Box 1308
Milwaukee, WI 53201
Application address: c/o Carol Ruekert, Coord., School District of Waukesha, 222 Maple Ave., Waukesha, WI 53186, tel.: (262) 521-5809

Established in 1992 in WI.
Financial data (yr. ended 12/31/00): Grants paid, $58,950; assets, $2,169,316 (M); expenditures, $88,089; qualifying distributions, $64,851.
Limitations: Giving primarily in Waukesha County, WI.
Application information: Application form required.
Scholarship Committee Members: John Inzeo, Hal Luedeman, David Schmidt.
Trustee: Bank One Trust Co., N.A.
EIN: 396146782
Codes: GTI

57101
W. D. & Prudence McIntyre Foundation
c/o Bank One
P.O. Box 1308
Milwaukee, WI 53201
Application address: c/o Bank One, 611 Woodward Ave., Ste. 8113, Detroit, MI 48226, tel.: (313) 225-3183, FAX: (313) 225-1574
Contact: Don Korn, Trust Off., Bank One

Established in 1960.
Financial data (yr. ended 11/30/01): Grants paid, $58,860; assets, $1,182,066 (M); expenditures, $73,687; qualifying distributions, $58,860.
Limitations: Giving primarily in MI, with emphasis on Monroe.
Application information: Application form required.
Advisory Committee: Don Korn, Rocque E. Lipford, William D. McIntyre, Jr.
Trustee: Bank One, N.A.
EIN: 386046659

57102
Elizabeth Upton Vawter Foundation
c/o Bank One Trust Co., N.A.
P.O. Box 1308
Milwaukee, WI 53201
Contact: Judith Pieper

Established in 1967 in IL.
Financial data (yr. ended 12/31/01): Grants paid, $58,500; assets, $762,586 (M); expenditures, $68,964; qualifying distributions, $61,692.
Limitations: Giving on a national basis.
Trustees: Henry S. Hoyt, Jr., Judith Upton Hoyt, Bank One Trust Co., N.A.
EIN: 366140878

57103
Harvey J. Nelson Charitable Trust
c/o Marshall & Ilsley Trust Company, N.A.
P.O. Box 2980
Milwaukee, WI 53201
Application address: P.O. Box 209, Wausau, WI 54402, tel.: (715) 845-3121
Contact: Colleen Gostisha, Trust Off., Marshall & Ilsley Trust Company, N.A.

Established in 1979.
Financial data (yr. ended 12/31/01): Grants paid, $58,150; assets, $1,319,137 (M); expenditures, $70,942; qualifying distributions, $58,150.
Limitations: Giving limited to the Wausau, WI, area.
Directors: James Lundberg, Duane Patterson.
Trustee: Marshall & Ilsley Trust Company, N.A.
EIN: 396307373

57104
Dr. William F. & Sandra L. Schneider Family Foundation, Inc.
4424 Oak Ridge Cir.
De Pere, WI 54115

Established in 1996 in WI.
Donor(s): Sandra L. Schneider, William F. Schneider.
Financial data (yr. ended 12/31/01): Grants paid, $57,377; assets, $332,756 (M); gifts received, $15,160; expenditures, $57,654; qualifying distributions, $57,377.
Limitations: Applications not accepted.
Application information: Contributes only to pre-selected organizations.
Directors: Sandra L. Schneider, William F. Schneider, William J. Schneider.
EIN: 391869772

57105
Charles N. Gorham Memorial Fund
c/o Bank One Trust Co., N.A.
P.O. Box 130
Milwaukee, WI 53201
Application address: c/o Brian Debenedetto, Bank One Trust Co., N.A., 6000 E. State St., IL 61108, tel.: (815) 394-4616

Financial data (yr. ended 12/31/01): Grants paid, $57,360; assets, $1,017,348 (M); expenditures, $71,207; qualifying distributions, $60,838.
Limitations: Giving limited to Winnebago County, IL.
Application information: Application form required.
Trustee: Bank One Trust Co., N.A.
EIN: 366032552
Codes: GTI

57106
Hoida Family Foundation, Inc.
c/o Hoida Lumber & Components
P.O. Box 5907, 3400 S. Ridge Rd.
De Pere, WI 54115-5907

Established in 1994 in WI.
Donor(s): Donald J. Hoida.
Financial data (yr. ended 09/30/01): Grants paid, $57,250; assets, $472,308 (M); expenditures, $65,851; qualifying distributions, $61,237.
Limitations: Applications not accepted. Giving primarily in Green Bay, WI.
Application information: Contributes only to pre-selected organizations.
Officers: Kay Dawson, Pres.; Donald F. Hoida, V.P.; James R. Hoida, Secy.-Treas.
EIN: 391774394

57107
Neal Sisters Foundation
c/o Bank One Trust Co., N.A.
P.O. Box 1308
Milwaukee, WI 53201
Application address: 1080 W. Northwood Dr., Caro, MI 48723
Contact: Carl Holmes, Treas.

Established in 1991 in MI.
Donor(s): Eleanor Neal.
Financial data (yr. ended 12/31/01): Grants paid, $57,000; assets, $1,583,932 (M); expenditures, $69,902; qualifying distributions, $60,571.
Limitations: Giving primarily in the Caro, MI, area.
Officers: Steve Fillion,* Pres.; Martha Thurston,* Secy.; Carl Holmes,* Treas.
Trustess: Dolores Rock Hutchinson, Bank One Trust Co., N.A.
EIN: 382942765

57108
Freda Nishan Scholarship Trust
c/o U.S. Bank
P.O. Box 7900
Madison, WI 53707-7900

Financial data (yr. ended 12/31/00): Grants paid, $57,000; assets, $1,255,458 (M); expenditures, $72,011; qualifying distributions, $57,495.
Limitations: Giving limited to WI.
Trustee: U.S. Bank.
EIN: 396038664
Codes: GTI

57109
Nicholson Foundation, Inc.
c/o Richard S. Gallagher
777 E. Wisconsin Ave., Ste. 3080
Milwaukee, WI 53202-5366

Established around 1974.
Donor(s): Elizabeth M. Nicholson.
Financial data (yr. ended 12/31/01): Grants paid, $56,950; assets, $226,864 (M); expenditures, $60,306; qualifying distributions, $57,536.
Limitations: Applications not accepted. Giving primarily in MA and Boothbay Harbor, ME.
Application information: Contributes only to pre-selected organizations.
Officers and Directors:* Elizabeth M. Nicholson,* Pres. and Treas.; Phillip T. Nicholson,* V.P.; Richard S. Gallagher,* Secy.
EIN: 237424390

57110
James R. Nicholl Memorial Foundation
c/o Bank One Trust Co., N.A.
P.O. Box 1308
Milwaukee, WI 53201
Application address: 1949 Broadway, Lorain, OH 44052
Contact: David Nocjar, V.P. and Sr. Trust Off., Bank One Trust Co., N.A.

Established in 1961.
Donor(s): Michael M. Milner, M.D., Brian A. Higgins, M.D., Cathy A. Krosky.
Financial data (yr. ended 12/31/99): Grants paid, $56,895; assets, $1,621,210 (M); gifts received, $225; expenditures, $78,308; qualifying distributions, $57,978.
Limitations: Giving limited to residents of Lorain County, OH.
Application information: Application form required.
Trustees: Joseph A. Cicerrella, M.D., Mike Joyce, Thomas Pillari, Bank One Trust Co., N.A.
EIN: 346574742
Codes: GTI

57111
W. H. Pugh, Inc.
200 Dodge St.
Racine, WI 53402

Financial data (yr. ended 06/30/01): Grants paid, $56,840; assets, $276,295 (M); expenditures, $59,263; qualifying distributions, $56,190.
Limitations: Applications not accepted. Giving primarily in Racine, WI.
Application information: Contributes only to pre-selected organizations.
Officer and Trustee:* William H. Pugh III,* Pres.
EIN: 391097280

57112
Edward J. Okray & Lucille S. Okray Foundation, Inc.
(Formerly Edward J. Okray Foundation, Inc.)
3808 Heffron St.
Stevens Point, WI 54481-5565

Established in 1984 in WI.
Donor(s): Edward J. Okray, Lucille S. Okray.
Financial data (yr. ended 09/30/01): Grants paid, $56,500; assets, $1,791,763 (M); expenditures, $64,393; qualifying distributions, $56,875.
Limitations: Applications not accepted. Giving primarily in SD, TN, and WI.
Application information: Contributes only to pre-selected organizations.
Officers: Edward J. Okray, Pres. and Treas.; Joseph J. Okray, Jr., V.P. and Secy.
Director: Michael J. Finnessy.
EIN: 391501333

57113
Holt Family Scholarship Foundation
c/o Marshall & Ilsley Trust Company, N.A.
P.O. Box 2980
Milwaukee, WI 53211-2980

Established in 1993 in WI.
Donor(s): Lillian Holt.‡
Financial data (yr. ended 07/31/01): Grants paid, $56,100; assets, $1,168,462 (M); gifts received, $1,142; expenditures, $64,269; qualifying distributions, $57,057.
Limitations: Giving limited to WI.
Application information: Application form required.
Trustees: Robert D. Holt, Jon P. Wilcox.
EIN: 391734323
Codes: GTI

57114
Edna Weigel Scholarship Fund
c/o Marshall & Ilsley Bank
P.O. Box 2980
Milwaukee, WI 53201
Application address: c/o Guidance Off., Watertown High School, 825 Endeavour Dr., Watertown, WI 53098, tel.: (414) 262-7500

Established in 1995 in WI.
Donor(s): Edna Weigel.‡
Financial data (yr. ended 05/31/01): Grants paid, $55,848; assets, $492,036 (M); expenditures, $65,846; qualifying distributions, $55,170.
Limitations: Giving limited to Watertown, WI, residents.
Application information: Application form required.
Trustee: Marshall & Ilsley Bank.
EIN: 396618926
Codes: GTI

57115
Catalyst Foundation
c/o Associated Banc-Corp
P.O. Box 408
Neenah, WI 54957-0408 (920) 727-5385

Established in 1986 in WI.
Donor(s): Anton G. Stepanek, Timothy A. Stepanek, Catherine Stepanek.
Financial data (yr. ended 12/31/01): Grants paid, $55,750; assets, $636,769 (M); expenditures, $69,503; qualifying distributions, $55,750.
Limitations: Giving primarily in FL.
Trustees: Anton G. Stepanek, Catherine Stepanek, Mary Jane Stepanek, Timothy A. Stepanek, Associated Banc-Corp.
EIN: 391574340

57116
G. Squared Foundation, Inc.
(Formerly The Sarah Gelatt Gephart Foundation, Inc.)
P.O. Box 1627
La Crosse, WI 54602-1627
Application address: 330 Barton Shore Dr., Ann Arbor, MI 54601
Contact: Sarah Jane Gephart, Pres.

Established in 1989 in WI.
Donor(s): Charles D. Gelatt.
Financial data (yr. ended 07/31/02): Grants paid, $55,500; assets, $981,583 (M); expenditures, $57,404; qualifying distributions, $55,500.
Limitations: Giving primarily in WI.
Application information: Application form not required.
Officers: Sarah Jane Gephart, Pres. and Treas.; Brent Gephart, Sr., V.P.; Robert P. Smyth, Secy.
Director: Charles D. Gelatt.
EIN: 391624154

57117
John Bosshard Charitable Trust
P.O. Box 966
La Crosse, WI 54601

Financial data (yr. ended 12/31/01): Grants paid, $55,413; assets, $1,024,249 (M); expenditures, $55,963; qualifying distributions, $55,413.
Limitations: Applications not accepted. Giving limited in WI.
Application information: Contributes only to pre-selected organizations.
Trustees: John Bosshard III, Kurt Bosshard, Sabina Bosshard, William H. Bosshard.
EIN: 391534028

57118
Von Schrader Foundation, Inc.
c/o Quarles & Brady
411 E. Wisconin Ave.
Milwaukee, WI 53202
Contact: Paul Tilleman, V.P.

Established in WI in 1997.
Financial data (yr. ended 06/30/02): Grants paid, $55,237; assets, $478,553 (M); expenditures, $62,263; qualifying distributions, $55,237.
Limitations: Applications not accepted. Giving primarily in WI.
Application information: Contributes only to pre-selected organizations.
Officers: Maria Von Schrader, Pres.; Paul Tilleman, V.P.; Brian J. McMahan, Treas.
Director: Herbert Meyer.
EIN: 391356827

57119
The Jenkins Family Foundation, Inc.
10645 N. Wood Crest Dr.
Mequon, WI 53092

Established in 1999 in WI.
Donor(s): Robert H. Jenkins Charitable Trust.
Financial data (yr. ended 12/31/01): Grants paid, $55,150; assets, $20,667 (M); gifts received, $50,000; expenditures, $55,314; qualifying distributions, $55,150.
Limitations: Applications not accepted.
Application information: Contributes only to pre-selected organizations.
Officers and Directors: Dianne L. Jenkins,* Pres. and Treas.; Michael H. Jenkins,* V.P. and Secy.; David F. Jenkins,* V.P.
EIN: 391984194

57120
Primun Bonum, Inc.
c/o J.L. VanEgeren
5374 Moonlite Dr.
De Pere, WI 54115-8794 (920) 432-6049
Contact: Paul D. Koch, Pres.

Established in 1992 in WI.
Donor(s): Paul D. Koch, Linda L. Koch.
Financial data (yr. ended 09/30/01): Grants paid, $55,039; assets, $1,366,293 (M); gifts received, $363,000; expenditures, $77,610; qualifying distributions, $54,430.
Limitations: Giving limited to residents of Green Bay, WI.
Officers and Directors:* Paul D. Koch,* Pres. and Treas.; Linda L. Koch,* V.P. and Secy.; Christine R. Koch.
EIN: 391742945

57121
The Nasgovitz Family Foundation, Inc.
4470 N. Lake Dr.
Shorewood, WI 53211
Contact: Marian R. Nasgovitz, V.P.

Established in 1997 in WI.
Donor(s): William J. Nasgovitz.
Financial data (yr. ended 12/31/01): Grants paid, $55,000; assets, $1,088,987 (M); expenditures, $59,031; qualifying distributions, $55,000.
Officers and Directors:* William J. Nasgovitz,* Pres.; Marian R. Nasgovitz,* V.P. and Treas.; Sarah Nasgovitz,* Secy.; Michael DeNicola, John Nasgovitz, Will Nasgovitz.
EIN: 391913334

57122
Charles D. and Elenore P. Ashley Foundation, Inc.
c/o U.S. Bank
P.O. Box 2043, LC4NE
Milwaukee, WI 53201-9116 (414) 765-5908
Application address: 223 E. Michigan St., Rm. 110, Milwaukee, WI 53202

Established in 1946 in WI.
Financial data (yr. ended 12/31/01): Grants paid, $54,925; assets, $955,026 (M); expenditures, $66,178; qualifying distributions, $58,653.
Limitations: Giving primarily in Milwaukee, WI.
Officers: Margot E. Ashley, Pres.; David W. Ashley, V.P.; David C. Batey, Jr., Secy.-Treas.
EIN: 396045395

57123
Founces M. Luley Scholarship & Educational Fund
c/o Bank One Trust Co., N.A.
P.O. Box 1308
Milwaukee, WI 53201

Established in 1972 in OH.
Donor(s): Founces M. Luley.‡
Financial data (yr. ended 12/31/00): Grants paid, $54,828; assets, $1,103,384 (M); expenditures, $58,341; qualifying distributions, $54,167.
Limitations: Giving limited to residents of Trumbull and Warren counties, OH.
Application information: Unsolicited request for funds not accepted.
Trustee: Bank One Trust Co., N.A.
EIN: 346672173
Codes: GTI

57124
Charles George Resch II Memorial Foundation, Inc.
1804 N. Edison St.
Antigo, WI 54409

Donor(s): Charles Resch.
Financial data (yr. ended 07/31/01): Grants paid, $54,800; assets, $67,091 (M); expenditures, $57,825; qualifying distributions, $54,800.
Limitations: Applications not accepted. Giving limited to Antigo, WI.
Application information: Contributes only to pre-selected organizations.
Officers: Charles Resch, Pres.; Geraldine Resch, Secy.
Directors: Michael Hunter, Gerald Volm.
EIN: 391333315

57125
Buck Foundation
3559 N. Summit Ave.
Milwaukee, WI 53211 (414) 964-8682
FAX: (414) 964-2002
Contact: David D. Buck, Pres.

Established in 1985 in CO.
Donor(s): Douglas H. Buck,‡ Mildred M. Buck, Douglas H. and Mildred M. Buck Charitable Lead Trust.
Financial data (yr. ended 12/31/01): Grants paid, $54,200; assets, $888,518 (M); gifts received, $7,000; expenditures, $67,817; qualifying distributions, $54,311.
Limitations: Giving primarily in CO.
Publications: Grants list, application guidelines.
Application information: Application form not required.
Officers and Directors:* David D. Buck,* Pres. and Treas.; Richard W. Yeo, V.P.; Douglas S. Buck, Secy.; Andrew D. Buck, Christopher W. Buck, Diane M. Buck, Leland Buck, Mildred Buck, Carol Dettmann, Jessica Dettmann, Nicholas Dettmann, Samuel Dettmann.
EIN: 742405298

57126
Cousins Submarines, Inc. Foundation
N83 W13400 Leon Rd.
Menomonee Falls, WI 53051

Established in 1999 in WI.
Financial data (yr. ended 12/31/01): Grants paid, $54,100; assets, $430,674 (M); gifts received, $100,000; expenditures, $55,809; qualifying distributions, $54,100.
Limitations: Applications not accepted.
Application information: Contributes only to pre-selected organizations.
Officers: William Specht, Pres.; Sandy Specht, V.P.; James Sheppard, Secy.; Jeffrey Nelson, Treas.
EIN: 391980576

57127
Wuethrich Foundation, Inc.
P.O. Box 160
Greenwood, WI 54437-0160
Contact: Dallas L. Wuethrich, Pres.

Donor(s): Dallas L. Wuethrich.
Financial data (yr. ended 12/31/01): Grants paid, $53,674; assets, $605,282 (M); expenditures, $60,154; qualifying distributions, $53,674.
Limitations: Giving primarily in Clark County, WI.
Officers: Dallas L. Wuethrich, Pres.; Lee A. Wuethrich, V.P.
EIN: 396045827

57128
Wild Resources Foundation
56 S. Brown St.
Rhinelander, WI 54501

Established in 1994 in WI.
Donor(s): Thomas Klein, Patricia Klein.
Financial data (yr. ended 12/31/01): Grants paid, $53,500; assets, $160,905 (M); expenditures, $56,657; qualifying distributions, $54,396.
Limitations: Applications not accepted. Giving limited to Ketchum, ID, and MT.
Application information: Contributes only to pre-selected organizations.
Trustees: Patricia Klein, Thomas Klein.
EIN: 396606088

57129
Elmer & Nannette Winter Family Foundation, Inc.
c/o Manpower, Inc.
P.O. Box 2053
Milwaukee, WI 53201 (414) 961-1000
Contact: Elmer L. Winter, Pres.

Established in 1958 in WI.
Donor(s): Winter Family Charitable Trust.
Financial data (yr. ended 12/31/01): Grants paid, $53,354; assets, $296,478 (M); gifts received, $14,524; expenditures, $87,171; qualifying distributions, $53,354.
Limitations: Giving primarily in New York, NY, and Milwaukee, WI.
Application information: Application form not required.
Officers and Directors:* Elmer L. Winter,* Pres.; Lynn W. Gross,* V.P.; Michael E. Freeman,* Secy.-Treas.; Marvin M. Gross, Martha W. Gross-Tracy, Robert L. Tracy.
EIN: 396052809

57130—WISCONSIN

57130
Arnold Van Den Wymelenberg Foundation
1570 Mesa Dr.
Green Bay, WI 54313-9366

Financial data (yr. ended 03/31/02): Grants paid, $52,900; assets, $1,303,198 (M); expenditures, $53,634; qualifying distributions, $52,900.
Limitations: Applications not accepted. Giving primarily in WI.
Application information: Contributes only to pre-selected organizations.
Trustees: Ruth Mercky, Gerald Van Den Wymelenberg, John Van Den Wymelenberg.
EIN: 396125548

57131
Mills Family Charitable Foundation
N. 22 W. 29050 Happy Hollow Rd.
Pewaukee, WI 53072

Established in 2000 in WI.
Donor(s): Douglas W. Mills, Virginia L. Mills.
Financial data (yr. ended 12/31/01): Grants paid, $52,700; assets, $1,018,310 (M); gifts received, $40,000; expenditures, $74,867; qualifying distributions, $52,700.
Limitations: Applications not accepted.
Application information: Contributes only to pre-selected organizations.
Trustees: Douglas W. Mills, Virginia L. Mills.
EIN: 367331361

57132
Paul O. & Carol H. Gehl Family Foundation, Inc.
203 S. 10th St.
P.O. Box 303
Hilbert, WI 54129

Established in 1995 in WI.
Donor(s): Carol H. Gehl, Paul O. Gehl.
Financial data (yr. ended 12/31/01): Grants paid, $52,562; assets, $968,934 (M); gifts received, $26,675; expenditures, $78,851; qualifying distributions, $52,562.
Limitations: Applications not accepted. Giving primarily in Hilbert, WI.
Application information: Contributes only to pre-selected organizations.
Officers: Paul O. Gehl, Pres.; Jane M. Gehl, V.P.; Carol H. Gehl, Secy.
EIN: 391839441

57133
Mayer Family Foundation, Inc.
622 N. Water St., No. 500
Milwaukee, WI 53202

Established in 1997 in WI.
Donor(s): Marian A. Mayer.
Financial data (yr. ended 12/31/01): Grants paid, $52,250; assets, $748,267 (M); expenditures, $62,927; qualifying distributions, $52,250.
Limitations: Applications not accepted.
Application information: Contributes only to pre-selected organizations.
Officers: Rick J. Schlehlein, Pres.; Holly J. Agner, V.P.; Michael S. Mayer, Secy.; Jodi A. Bichanich, Treas.
Directors: Rodney Agner, George Bichanich, Kathleen Mayer, Patricia A. Mayer, Kathleen Schlehlein.
EIN: 391912036

57134
Burmester Charitable Trust
c/o Bank One Trust Co., N.A.
P.O. Box 130
Milwaukee, WI 53201
Application address: P.O. Box 680, Janesville, WI 53545, tel.: (608) 757-6225
Contact: Joel Bailey

Established in 1999 in WI.
Financial data (yr. ended 07/31/01): Grants paid, $52,150; assets, $2,307,461 (M); expenditures, $68,179; qualifying distributions, $52,150.
Limitations: Giving primarily in Janesville, WI.
Trustee: Bank One Trust Co., N.A.
EIN: 396722474

57135
Shinaberry Public Scholarship Trust
c/o Bank One Trust Co., N.A.
P.O. Box 1308
Milwaukee, WI 53201
Application address: c/o Principal, Pocahontas County High School, Rte. 1, Box 133A, Dunmore, WV 24934; c/o Principal, Tygarts Valley High School, P.O. Box 68, Mill Creek, WV 26280

Established in 2000 in WV.
Financial data (yr. ended 02/28/02): Grants paid, $52,016; assets, $1,039,670 (M); expenditures, $62,415; qualifying distributions, $52,016.
Limitations: Giving primarily in WI.
Application information: Application form required.
Trustee: Bank One Trust Co., N.A.
EIN: 916528315

57136
MKL Foundation, Incorporated
P.O. Box 190
Lake Geneva, WI 53147

Established in 1998 in WI.
Donor(s): Joan E. Lammers.
Financial data (yr. ended 12/31/01): Grants paid, $52,000; assets, $1,031,127 (M); expenditures, $57,504; qualifying distributions, $52,000.
Limitations: Applications not accepted.
Application information: Contributes only to pre-selected organizations.
Officers and Directors:* Donald J. Parker, Jr., Pres. and Mgr.; George M. Lammers,* V.P.; Joan E. Lammers,* V.P.; Lisa A. Crispi,* Secy.; Katherine A. Cox,* Treas.
EIN: 391919848

57137
Joseph and Sharon Darcey Foundation, Inc.
(Formerly Joseph Darcey Foundation, Inc.)
314 W. Main St., Ste. 11
Watertown, WI 53094-7630 (920) 261-0223
Contact: Claude Held

Established in 1991 in WI.
Donor(s): Joseph W. Darcey.
Financial data (yr. ended 12/31/00): Grants paid, $51,841; assets, $1,241,760 (M); gifts received, $135,781; expenditures, $61,134; qualifying distributions, $56,162.
Limitations: Applications not accepted. Giving limited to Watertown, WI.
Application information: Contributes only to pre-selected organizations.
Officers and Directors:* Joseph W. Darcey,* Pres.; Charles Corbett,* V.P.; Sharon A. Darcey,* V.P.; Richard Conley,* Secy.; Jack Tobias,* Treas.
EIN: 391715481

57138
Richard J. Resch Foundation, Ltd.
P.O. Box 8100
Green Bay, WI 54308 (920) 468-2572
Contact: Richard J. Resch, Pres.

Established in 1989 in WI.
Donor(s): Richard J. Resch, Sharon J. Resch.
Financial data (yr. ended 12/31/01): Grants paid, $51,650; assets, $1,015,427 (M); expenditures, $60,393; qualifying distributions, $51,650.
Limitations: Applications not accepted. Giving primarily in Green Bay, WI and surrounding area.
Application information: Contributes only to pre-selected organizations.
Officers: Richard J. Resch, Pres. and Treas.; Sharon J. Resch, V.P.; Gerald C. Condon, Jr., Secy.
EIN: 391653788

57139
Bernard E. and Alyce G. Dahlin Foundation, Inc.
2670 Good Shepherd Ln.
Green Bay, WI 54313

Established in 1993 in WI.
Donor(s): Alyce G. Dahlin, Bernard E. Dahlin, Econo Paper Corp.
Financial data (yr. ended 12/31/01): Grants paid, $51,600; assets, $692,495 (M); expenditures, $62,671; qualifying distributions, $51,600.
Limitations: Applications not accepted. Giving primarily in Green Bay, WI.
Application information: Contributes only to pre-selected organizations.
Officers: Bernard E. Dahlin, Pres. and Treas.; Alyce G. Dahlin, V.P. and Secy.
Director: Bernard E. Dahlin III.
EIN: 391775171

57140
George E. Stifel Scholarship Fund
c/o Bank One Ohio Trust Co., N.A.
P.O. Box 1308
Milwaukee, WI 53201
Application address: 1114 Market St., Wheeling, WV 26003

Established in 1951 in WV.
Financial data (yr. ended 04/30/01): Grants paid, $51,500; assets, $1,886,013 (M); expenditures, $89,357; qualifying distributions, $73,400.
Limitations: Giving limited to residents of Ohio County, WV.
Application information: The 1-year scholarships are not awarded for more than 4 years per person. Application form required.
Trustee: Bank One Ohio Trust Co., N.A.
EIN: 556018248
Codes: GTI

57141
John A. & Evelyn Monahan Memorial Trust
c/o Bank One Trust Co., N.A.
P.O. Box 1308
Milwaukee, WI 53201 (414) 765-2800
Contact: Trust Off.

Financial data (yr. ended 04/30/02): Grants paid, $51,355; assets, $1,067,561 (M); expenditures, $59,005; qualifying distributions, $53,393.
Limitations: Applications not accepted. Giving limited to residents of Milwaukee County, WI.
Application information: Unsolicited requests for funds not accepted.
Trustee: Bank One Trust Co., N.A.
EIN: 391333780

57142
Barbara Meyer Elsner Foundation, Inc.
2420 N. Terrace Ave.
Milwaukee, WI 53211-4511

Established in 1991 in WI.
Financial data (yr. ended 12/31/01): Grants paid, $51,144; assets, $1,121,426 (M); expenditures, $55,612; qualifying distributions, $51,144.
Limitations: Applications not accepted. Giving primarily in WI.
Application information: Contributes only to pre-selected organizations.
Officers: Robert Elsner, Pres.; Barbara Elsner, Secy.-Treas.
EIN: 391710863

57143
The Goldammer Family Foundation, Inc.
9091 Gibraltar Bluff Rd.
P.O. Box 10
Fish Creek, WI 54212-0010

Established in 2000 in WI.
Donor(s): Colette Goldammer, William Goldammer, Sr.
Financial data (yr. ended 12/31/01): Grants paid, $51,143; assets, $405,313 (M); gifts received, $113,850; expenditures, $64,235; qualifying distributions, $51,143.
Limitations: Applications not accepted. Giving primarily in MN and WI.
Application information: Contributes only to pre-selected organizations.
Officers and Directors:* William Goldammer, Sr.,* Pres. and Treas.; Colette Goldammer,* V.P. and Secy.; William Goldammer, Jr.
EIN: 391987991

57144
Antonia Foundation, Inc.
4655 N. Port Washington Rd., Ste. 300
Glendale, WI 53212 (414) 964-4000
Contact: F. Michael Arnow, Treas.

Established in 1991 in WI.
Donor(s): Annette Marra, John M. Marra.
Financial data (yr. ended 03/31/02): Grants paid, $50,700; assets, $1,098,945 (M); gifts received, $188,068; expenditures, $65,238; qualifying distributions, $50,700.
Limitations: Giving primarily in WI.
Application information: Application form required.
Officers: Annette Marra, Pres.; John M. Marra, V.P.; Frederic G. Friedman, Secy.; F. Michael Arnow, Treas.
EIN: 391717099

57145
Rittenhouse Foundation
c/o Bank One Trust Co., N.A.
P.O. Box 13
Milwaukee, WI 53201
Application address: c/o Honeoye Falls-Lima Central School, 83 Easy St., Honeoye Falls, NY 14472, tel.: (716) 624-7051
Contact: Peter F. Cardamone

Established in 2000 in FL.
Financial data (yr. ended 12/31/01): Grants paid, $50,685; assets, $978,334 (M); expenditures, $89,536; qualifying distributions, $50,685.
Limitations: Giving primarily in Honeoye Falls, NY.
Trustee: Bank One Trust Co., N.A.
EIN: 311717147

57146
Frank E. & Salome B. Smith Scholarship Fund
Bank One Trust Co., N.A.
P.O. Box 1308
Milwaukee, WI 53201

Financial data (yr. ended 12/31/00): Grants paid, $50,291; assets, $813,336 (M); expenditures, $63,420; qualifying distributions, $54,137.
Limitations: Applications not accepted. Giving primarily in Manitou Springs, CO.
Application information: Contributes only to pre-selected organizations.
Trustee: Bank One Trust Co., N.A.
EIN: 846273155

57147
Edward L. Johnstone Memorial Trust
c/o Bank One Trust Co., N.A.
P.O. Box 13
Milwaukee, WI 53201
Application address: c/o Bank One Trust Co., N.A., 1125 17th St., Denver, CO 80202, tel.: (303) 244-3175

Established in 1998 in CO.
Donor(s): Carol E. Johnstone.‡
Financial data (yr. ended 07/31/01): Grants paid, $50,240; assets, $930,152 (M); expenditures, $57,998; qualifying distributions, $52,662.
Limitations: Giving primarily in Denver, CO.
Application information: Application form required.
Trustee: Bank One Trust Co., N.A.
EIN: 846324123

57148
Eloise Rueping Atkinson Foundation, Inc.
65 Sunset Cir.
Fond Du Lac, WI 54935 (920) 921-5159
Contact: Judy C. Pierner, Dir.

Established in 2000 in WI.
Financial data (yr. ended 12/31/01): Grants paid, $50,000; assets, $7,515 (M); gifts received, $50,000; expenditures, $51,735; qualifying distributions, $50,000.
Limitations: Giving limited to WI.
Application information: Application form not required.
Directors: Eloise Rueping Atkinson, Judy Pierner, Raymond Pierner.
EIN: 392001599

57149
Fritz A. Callies Foundation, Inc.
c/o Lichtsinn & Haensel, S.C.
111 E. Wisconsin Ave., Ste. 1800
Milwaukee, WI 53202

Established in 1999 in WI.
Donor(s): Fritz A. Callies.
Financial data (yr. ended 12/31/01): Grants paid, $50,000; assets, $159,574 (M); expenditures, $52,279; qualifying distributions, $50,000.
Limitations: Applications not accepted. Giving primarily in Milwaukee, WI.
Application information: Contributes only to pre-selected organizations.
Officers and Directors:* Fritz A. Callies,* Pres.; Dennis A. Kharitou, Secy.-Treas.; Thomas A. Buck.
EIN: 391968923

57150
Constance E. Dentzler Charitable Trust
c/o Elaine A. Shanebrook
120 N. Main St., Ste. 310
West Bend, WI 53095-3353

Established in 1996 in WI.
Donor(s): Constance E. Dentzler.
Financial data (yr. ended 12/31/01): Grants paid, $50,000; assets, $312,574 (M); expenditures, $52,995; qualifying distributions, $50,000.
Limitations: Applications not accepted. Giving primarily in WI.
Application information: Contributes only to pre-selected organizations.
Trustees: James H. Schloemer, Carl H. Ziegler.
EIN: 391827670

57151
The Lacek Foundation
28140 Brynilson Rd.
Danbury, WI 54830-8734

Established in 1999 in MN.
Financial data (yr. ended 12/31/00): Grants paid, $50,000; assets, $13,128 (M); gifts received, $50,913; expenditures, $52,541; qualifying distributions, $50,000.
Limitations: Applications not accepted.
Application information: Contributes only to pre-selected organizations.
Officer: Mark Lacek, Pres.
EIN: 391966677

57152
Malu, Ltd.
c/o Foley & Lardner
777 E. Wisconsin Ave., Ste. 4000
Milwaukee, WI 53202-5373 (414) 297-5115
Contact: Leah Brandt, V.P.

Established in 1969 in WI.
Donor(s): Harry L. Wallace.
Financial data (yr. ended 12/31/01): Grants paid, $50,000; assets, $758,521 (M); expenditures, $53,592; qualifying distributions, $50,000.
Application information: Application form not required.
Officers and Directors:* Harry L. Wallace,* Pres.; Mary Ann Frantz,* V.P. and Secy.-Treas.; Leah Brandt, V.P.
EIN: 237050162

57153
James A. Taylor Family Foundation, Inc.
1000 West Donges Bay Rd.
Mequon, WI 53092-5999 (262) 241-4321
Contact: James A. Taylor, Pres.

Established in 1959 in WI.
Donor(s): Taylor Electric Co., James A. Taylor.
Financial data (yr. ended 06/30/01): Grants paid, $49,280; assets, $684,699 (M); expenditures, $53,409; qualifying distributions, $49,782.
Limitations: Giving primarily in WI.
Application information: Giving to new applicants is very limited. Application form not required.
Officers and Directors:* James A. Taylor,* Pres.; James A. Taylor, Jr.,* V.P.; John W. Taylor,* Secy.-Treas.; Barbara T. Mans.
EIN: 396045247

57154
Habush Family Foundation, Inc.
777 E. Wisconsin Ave., Ste. 2300
Milwaukee, WI 53202 (414) 271-0900
Contact: Robert Habush, Dir.

Established in 1999 in WI.
Donor(s): Robert Habush.
Financial data (yr. ended 12/31/01): Grants paid, $49,177; assets, $1,889,622 (M); gifts received, $1,000,000; expenditures, $53,866; qualifying distributions, $49,177.
Application information: Application form not required.
Director: Robert Habush.
EIN: 391979841

57155
Hinrichs Foundation, Inc.
3927 48th Ave.
Kenosha, WI 53144

Financial data (yr. ended 09/30/01): Grants paid, $49,150; assets, $993,500 (M); expenditures, $53,933; qualifying distributions, $49,150.
Limitations: Applications not accepted. Giving primarily in Milwaukee, WI.
Application information: Contributes only to pre-selected organizations.
Officers: Anita Hinrichs Sculthorpe, Pres.; Christopher Hinrichs, V.P.; Roderick T. Dunne, Secy.-Treas.
Board Members: Darlene J. Brodjeski, Margaret Dunne, Mary Webster Levit.
EIN: 396048020

57156
Harvey and Carol Lange Family Foundation, Inc.
17540 Windmere Rd.
Brookfield, WI 53045

Established in 1993 in WI.
Donor(s): Harvey D. Lange, Carol A. Lange.
Financial data (yr. ended 12/31/01): Grants paid, $49,000; assets, $791,483 (M); expenditures, $50,979; qualifying distributions, $49,000.
Limitations: Applications not accepted.
Application information: Contributes only to pre-selected organizations.
Officers: Harvey D. Lange, Pres. and Treas.; Carol A. Lange, V.P. and Secy.
Director: David Lange.
EIN: 391765317

57157
Krantz Family Foundation
c/o U.S. Bank
P.O. Box 7900
Madison, WI 53707-7900 (608) 252-4172
Contact: Mark Vitense, Trust Off., U.S. Bank

Established in 1992 in WI.
Donor(s): Ronald Krantz, Lois Krantz.
Financial data (yr. ended 12/31/01): Grants paid, $48,961; assets, $925,638 (M); expenditures, $61,423; qualifying distributions, $48,961.
Limitations: Giving primarily in Madison, WI.
Trustees: Lois Krantz, Ronald Krantz, U.S. Bank.
EIN: 396565695

57158
Thomas H. Jacob Foundation, Inc.
P.O. Box 8010
Wausau, WI 54402-8010 (715) 845-3111
Contact: Clifford VanderWall, Pres.

Established in 1956.
Financial data (yr. ended 09/30/01): Grants paid, $48,179; assets, $377,043 (M); expenditures, $78,477; qualifying distributions, $48,179.
Limitations: Giving primarily in Wausau and northern WI.
Application information: Application form not required.
Officers: Clifford VanderWall, Pres.; V.J. Travis, V.P.
Director: Doris Ullrich.
EIN: 396044815

57159
Heid Family Foundation, Ltd.
c/o Bank One Trust Co., N.A.
P.O. Box 1308
Milwaukee, WI 53201
Application address: 2401 Cherokee Dr., Appleton, WI 54914
Contact: Peter M. Heid, Dir.

Established in 1985 in WI.
Donor(s): Peter M. Heid.
Financial data (yr. ended 03/31/01): Grants paid, $48,000; assets, $59,449 (M); expenditures, $50,690; qualifying distributions, $48,000.
Limitations: Giving primarily in Appleton, WI.
Director: Peter M. Heid.
Trustee: Bank One Trust Co., N.A.
EIN: 396412179

57160
Helen and Rudy Krejci Trust
110 W. Veteran's
P.O. Box 880
Tomah, WI 54660
Application address: 1905 Hollister Ave., Tomah, WI 54660
Contact: Robert Steele, Tr.

Financial data (yr. ended 12/31/99): Grants paid, $48,000; assets, $699,013 (M); expenditures, $50,094; qualifying distributions, $47,458.
Limitations: Giving limited to Monroe County, WI.
Application information: Application form required.
Trustees: Harold Gehrke, Leone Gehrke, Kevin McCoy, Arlys Steele, Robert Steele.
EIN: 396643512

57161
Lila Rinker Trust
(also known as Dr. E. B. Rinker Medical Scholarship Fund)
c/o Bank One Trust Co., N.A.
P.O. Box 1308
Milwaukee, WI 53201

Donor(s): Lila Rinker.‡
Financial data (yr. ended 06/30/01): Grants paid, $48,000; assets, $1,163,391 (M); expenditures, $64,094; qualifying distributions, $50,902.
Limitations: Giving limited to Indianapolis, IN.
Application information: Contact Indiana University School of Medicine for application. Application form required.
Trustee: Bank One Trust Co., N.A.
EIN: 356262657
Codes: GTI

57162
Carrie M. Harper Trust
c/o Bank One Trust Co., N.A.
P.O. Box 1308
Milwaukee, WI 53201

Established in 1989 in OH.
Financial data (yr. ended 12/31/00): Grants paid, $47,800; assets, $1,382,582 (M); expenditures, $59,337; qualifying distributions, $51,205.
Limitations: Giving limited to residents of Liverpool, OH.
Application information: Application form not required.
Trustee: Bank One Trust Co., N.A.
EIN: 346582259

57163
Jay M. & Joan K. Lieberman Charitable Fund
c/o Jay M. Lieberman
9300 N. Lake Dr.
Milwaukee, WI 53217

Established in 1990 in WI.
Donor(s): Jay M. Lieberman.
Financial data (yr. ended 12/31/01): Grants paid, $47,639; assets, $827,031 (M); expenditures, $48,639; qualifying distributions, $47,639.
Limitations: Applications not accepted. Giving primarily in WI.
Application information: Contributes only to pre-selected organizations.
Trustees: Jay M. Lieberman, Joan K. Lieberman.
EIN: 391686098

57164
John Oster Family Foundation, Inc.
P.O. Box 340035
Milwaukee, WI 53234 (414) 671-6800
Contact: John Oster III, V.P.

Financial data (yr. ended 12/31/01): Grants paid, $47,601; assets, $1,062,122 (M); expenditures, $59,011; qualifying distributions, $47,601.
Limitations: Giving primarily in Milwaukee, WI.
Officers: Robert Oster, Pres. and Treas.; John Oster III, V.P.
EIN: 396057530

57165
Charles D. Ortgiesen Foundation, Inc.
9609 N. Lake Dr.
Milwaukee, WI 53217
Contact: Margaret G. Reiter, Treas.

Incorporated in 1975 in WI.
Donor(s): Charles D. Ortgiesen.‡
Financial data (yr. ended 06/30/01): Grants paid, $47,000; assets, $1,013,830 (M); expenditures, $49,784; qualifying distributions, $47,651.
Limitations: Giving primarily in Milwaukee, WI.
Application information: Application form not required.
Officers and Directors:* Julia Petri,* Pres.; Mary Ann LaBahn, V.P.; Gloria Stanford,* Secy.; Margaret G. Reiter,* Treas.; Mary Pat Cunningham Hitchcock.
EIN: 391232384

57166
John R. Cameron Medical Physics Foundation, Inc.
c/o Marshall & Ilsely Bank of Middleton
7448 Hubbard Ave.
Middleton, WI 53562-3416
Application address: c/o Univ. of Wisconsin Hospital, 1300 University Ave., Madison, WI 53706
Contact: James Zagzebski, Pres.

Established in 1987 in WI.
Financial data (yr. ended 09/30/01): Grants paid, $46,940; assets, $320,917 (M); expenditures, $54,349; qualifying distributions, $46,940.
Limitations: Giving primarily in Madison, WI.
Publications: Application guidelines.
Officers and Directors:* James Zagzebski,* Pres.; Thomas M. Hinkes,* V.P.; William F. White,* Secy.; Terry Ackerman,* Treas.; Theodore F. Gunkel, T. Rockwell Mackie.
EIN: 391208707

57167
Waukesha Rotary Charitable Fund
P.O. Box 1876
Waukesha, WI 53187-1876
Application address: W229 N1433 Westwood Dr., Waukesha, WI 53186, tel.: (262) 513-9292
Contact: Martin T. Jannsen, Treas.

Established in 1964.
Financial data (yr. ended 06/30/01): Grants paid, $46,919; assets, $41,134 (M); gifts received, $563; expenditures, $505,532; qualifying distributions, $46,919.
Limitations: Giving limited to Waukesha County, WI.
Officers and Directors: Peter Van Horn,* Pres.; Ralph Redlin, V.P.; Arn Quakkelar, Secy.; Martin T. Jannsen, Treas.; Tom Constable, Thomas Custis, Lynda Dahlke, Mark Gempler, Wendy Kipperman, Richard Kobriger, Ann Nischke.
EIN: 396076427

57168
Elmore & Alyce Kraemer Charitable Trust
c/o Marshall & Ilsley Bank
P.O. Box 2980
Milwaukee, WI 53201

Established in 1990 in WI.
Donor(s): Alyce M. Kraemer.
Financial data (yr. ended 04/30/02): Grants paid, $46,512; assets, $1,486,091 (M); expenditures, $63,494; qualifying distributions, $46,512.
Limitations: Applications not accepted. Giving limited to WI.
Application information: Contributes only to pre-selected organizations.
Trustee: Marshall & Ilsley Bank.
EIN: 391666544

57169
Elizabeth Jones Chisholm Charitable Trust
c/o Foley & Lardner
777 E. Wisconsin Ave.
Milwaukee, WI 53202-5367

Established in 1999 in WI.
Donor(s): Elizabeth Jones Chisholm.‡
Financial data (yr. ended 12/31/01): Grants paid, $46,500; assets, $878,149 (M); expenditures, $51,950; qualifying distributions, $46,500.
Limitations: Applications not accepted. Giving primarily in WI.
Application information: Contributes only to pre-selected organizations.
Trustees: Stephen M. Fisher, Richard S. Gallagher, Edward C. Jones, Milo C. Jones.
EIN: 396696729

57170
Younger Family Foundation, Inc.
8129 N. Links Way
Milwaukee, WI 53217-2872 (414) 352-5484
Contact: William H. Younger, Pres.

Established in 1985 in WI.
Donor(s): William H. Younger.
Financial data (yr. ended 12/31/01): Grants paid, $46,500; assets, $1,032,914 (M); gifts received, $43,341; expenditures, $49,780; qualifying distributions, $46,500.
Limitations: Giving on a national basis.
Application information: Application form not required.
Officers: William H. Younger, Pres.; Phyllis L. Younger, V.P.
Directors: Sherry Y. Artemenko, William H. Younger, Jr.
EIN: 391097290

57171
American Appraisal Trust
411 E. Wisconsin Ave., Ste. 1900
Milwaukee, WI 53202

Established in 1952.
Donor(s): American Appraisal Assocs., Inc.
Financial data (yr. ended 06/30/01): Grants paid, $46,394; assets, $0 (M); gifts received, $46,399; expenditures, $46,399; qualifying distributions, $46,399.
Limitations: Applications not accepted. Giving primarily in Milwaukee, WI.
Application information: Contributes only to pre-selected organizations.
Officers: Joseph P. Zvesper, Chair.; Tracy Turowski, Secy.
EIN: 386048265

57172
Katharine B. Miner Charitable
c/o Bank One Trust Co.
P.O. Box 1308
Milwaukee, WI 53201
Application address: c/o Bank One, 111 E. Court St., Flint, MI 48502

Financial data (yr. ended 10/31/01): Grants paid, $46,000; assets, $744,928 (M); expenditures, $53,647; qualifying distributions, $48,319.
Limitations: Giving limited to MI, with emphasis on Flint.
Trustee: Bank One Trust Co., N.A.
EIN: 386419379

57173
Vernon G. Goelzer Trust
c/o Bank One Trust Co., N.A.
Box 1308
Milwaukee, WI 53201

Financial data (yr. ended 05/31/02): Grants paid, $45,862; assets, $790,102 (M); expenditures, $53,670; qualifying distributions, $45,862.
Limitations: Applications not accepted.
Application information: Contributes only to pre-selected organizations.
Trustee: Bank One Trust Co., N.A.
EIN: 396566242

57174
Kirt Fiegel Family Foundation, Inc.
c/o V. Kirt Fiegel
W5331 Hazel Ridge Rd.
Elkhorn, WI 53121

Established in 1995 in WI.
Donor(s): V. Kirt Fiegel.
Financial data (yr. ended 12/31/01): Grants paid, $45,618; assets, $903,439 (M); expenditures, $46,933; qualifying distributions, $45,618.
Limitations: Applications not accepted.
Application information: Contributes only to pre-selected organizations.
Officers: V. Kirt Fiegel, Pres. and Treas.; Dixie Fiegel, V.P. and Secy.
Directors: Andria Fiegel, Laurie Fiegel.
EIN: 391844265

57175
Lucile Wells Scholarship Fund
c/o Marshall & Ilsley Bank
1000 N. Water St.
Milwaukee, WI 53202
Application address: c/o Rev. George H. McKillington, 919 N. Wuthering Hills Dr., Janesville, WI 53546

Established in 1998 in WI.
Financial data (yr. ended 07/31/01): Grants paid, $45,500; assets, $1,164,892 (M); expenditures, $59,221; qualifying distributions, $45,120.
Limitations: Giving limited to residents of Janesville, WI.
Trustee: Marshall & Ilsley Bank.
EIN: 396694943

57176
Donald and Marie Belcher Charitable Foundation
17 Briarcliff Ct.
Appleton, WI 54915

Established in 1996 in WI.
Donor(s): Donald D. Belcher, M. Marie Belcher.
Financial data (yr. ended 12/31/01): Grants paid, $45,200; assets, $1,015,204 (M); expenditures, $47,355; qualifying distributions, $45,200.
Limitations: Applications not accepted. Giving primarily in WI; some giving also in OH, IN, IL, and MN.
Application information: Contributes only to pre-selected organizations.
Trustees: Donald D. Belcher, M. Marie Belcher.
EIN: 391868207

57177
Milton H. Callner Foundation
c/o Bank One Trust Co., N.A.
P.O. Box 1308
Milwaukee, WI 53201

Trust established in 1954 in IL.
Donor(s): Members of the Callner family.
Financial data (yr. ended 01/31/02): Grants paid, $45,000; assets, $1,339,188 (M); expenditures, $56,570; qualifying distributions, $48,283.
Limitations: Applications not accepted. Giving on a national basis.
Application information: Contributes only to pre-selected organizations.
Trustee: Bank One Trust Co., N.A.
EIN: 366034633

57178
Jeanette Elmer Trust
c/o U.S. Bank
P.O. Box 2043
Milwaukee, WI 53201-9116

Established in 1994 in WI.
Donor(s): Jeanette Elmer.‡
Financial data (yr. ended 05/31/01): Grants paid, $45,000; assets, $334,841 (M); expenditures, $50,687; qualifying distributions, $45,390.
Limitations: Applications not accepted. Giving primarily in Oshkosh, WI.
Application information: Contributes only to pre-selected organizations.
Trustee: U.S. Bank.
EIN: 396583906

57179
Joseph Gless Foundation
c/o Bank One Trust Co., N.A.
P.O. Box 1308
Milwaukee, WI 53201

Established in 1994 in MI.
Financial data (yr. ended 12/31/01): Grants paid, $45,000; assets, $716,984 (M); expenditures, $52,598; qualifying distributions, $46,919.
Limitations: Applications not accepted. Giving primarily in Grand Rapids, MI.
Application information: Contributes only to pre-selected organizations.
Trustees: Harold Gless, Bank One, N.A.
EIN: 383218718

57180
Walter M. Hughes Educational Trust
c/o Bank One Trust Co., N.A.
P.O. Box 1308
Milwaukee, WI 53201
Application address: c/o Jack Johnson, Trust Off., Bank One Ohio Trust Co., N.A., 100 E. Broad St., 9th Fl., Columbus, OH 43215-0192

Established in 1961 in OH.
Financial data (yr. ended 12/31/00): Grants paid, $45,000; assets, $1,314,262 (M); expenditures, $53,181; qualifying distributions, $48,064.
Limitations: Giving limited to Muskingum County, OH.
Application information: Application form required.
Trustee: Bank One Trust Co., N.A.
EIN: 316024847
Codes: GTI

57181—WISCONSIN

57181
Viola E. Lundeberg Trust
c/o R.V. Alexander
P.O. Box 46
River Falls, WI 54022-0046

Established in 1995 in WI.
Financial data (yr. ended 12/31/99): Grants paid, $45,000; assets, $752,998 (M); expenditures, $61,766; qualifying distributions, $45,000.
Limitations: Applications not accepted. Giving limited to MN and WI.
Application information: Contributes only to pre-selected organizations.
Trustees: R.V. Alexander, Roland Hammer.
EIN: 396503917

57182
Sangamon County Foundation
c/o Bank One Trust Co., N.A.
P.O. Box 13
Milwaukee, WI 53201
Application address: c/o 1 E. Old Capitol Plz., Springfield, IL 62701, tel.: (217) 525-9745

Financial data (yr. ended 12/31/01): Grants paid, $45,000; assets, $927,803 (M); expenditures, $53,231; qualifying distributions, $45,000.
Limitations: Giving limited to Sangamon County, IL.
Application information: Application form required.
Trustee: Bank One Trust Co., N.A.
EIN: 376170483

57183
The Messmer Foundation, Inc.
8741 W. National Ave.
West Allis, WI 53227-1609 (414) 321-4560
Contact: David A. Affeldt, Pres.

Established in 1965.
Financial data (yr. ended 12/31/01): Grants paid, $44,700; assets, $3,349,279 (M); expenditures, $56,327; qualifying distributions, $44,700.
Limitations: Giving primarily in Milwaukee, WI.
Application information: Application form not required.
Officers and Directors:* David A. Affeldt,* Pres. and Secy.; Thomas N. Tuttle,* V.P. and Treas.; William T. Gaus.
EIN: 366117571

57184
Ministrare, Inc.
777 E. Wisconsin Ave., Ste. 3800
Milwaukee, WI 53202

Financial data (yr. ended 12/31/01): Grants paid, $44,485; assets, $261,166 (M); gifts received, $39; expenditures, $49,906; qualifying distributions, $44,485.
Limitations: Applications not accepted. Giving limited to Chautauqua, NY.
Application information: Contributes only to pre-selected organizations.
Officers and Directors:* Richard H. Miller,* Pres. and Treas.; Miriam S. Reading,* V.P.; Richard S. Gallagher,* Secy.
EIN: 396099991

57185
Otzen Family Foundation, Inc.
P.O. Box 1056
Lake Geneva, WI 53147

Established in 1998 in WI.
Donor(s): Lucy T. Otzen.
Financial data (yr. ended 12/31/01): Grants paid, $44,112; assets, $1,037,550 (M); expenditures, $48,943; qualifying distributions, $44,112.
Limitations: Applications not accepted. Giving primarily in WI.
Application information: Contributes only to pre-selected organizations.
Officers and Directors:* Karl Otzen,* Pres.; Lucy T. Otzen,* V.P.; Carolyn J. Knop, Secy.; Donald J. Parker, Jr., Treas.; Liza E. Gavger, Leigh W. Otzen.
EIN: 391919852

57186
Marc and Michaele Butlein Family Foundation
c/o Diversified Mgmt., Inc.
5225 N. Ironwood Rd., No. 117
Milwaukee, WI 53217 (414) 964-7400
Contact: Mark Homan

Established in 1997 in WI.
Donor(s): Marc Butlein.
Financial data (yr. ended 12/31/01): Grants paid, $44,000; assets, $229,962 (M); expenditures, $45,588; qualifying distributions, $44,000.
Limitations: Giving primarily in Weston, CT.
Trustees: Marc Butlein, Michaele Butlein.
EIN: 396659912

57187
Debbink Family Foundation, Inc.
c/o MSI General Corp.
P.O. Box 7
Oconomowoc, WI 53066-0007

Established in 1997.
Donor(s): Dirk J. Debbink, Joan C. Debbink, John P. Debbink, Teresa L. Debbink.
Financial data (yr. ended 12/31/01): Grants paid, $44,000; assets, $1,209,813 (M); gifts received, $115,000; expenditures, $49,015; qualifying distributions, $44,000.
Limitations: Applications not accepted.
Application information: Contributes only to pre-selected organizations.
Officers: Teresa L. Debbink, Pres.; Joan C. Debbink, V.P.; Dirk J. Debbink, Secy.-Treas.
Director: John P. Debbink.
EIN: 391904743

57188
The Alice Aber Smith Scholarship
c/o First Banking Center
P.O. Box 658
Burlington, WI 53105
Application address: 455 S. Jefferson St., Waterford, WI 53185
Contact: Rev. Clarence Cheever, Comm. Chair.

Established in 1996 in WI.
Financial data (yr. ended 12/31/00): Grants paid, $44,000; assets, $959,768 (M); expenditures, $53,118; qualifying distributions, $44,000.
Limitations: Giving limited to residents of Racine County, WI, west of Interstate 94.
Application information: Application forms can be obtained from eligible high schools. Application form required.
Officers: Rev. Clarence Cheever, Comm. Chair.; Janet Cheever, Secy.
Trustee: First Banking Center.
EIN: 396628593
Codes: GTI

57189
Baylor Agerton Trust
c/o Bank One Trust Co., N.A.
P.O. Box 1308
Milwaukee, WI 53201
Application address: c/o Robert Lansford, Bank One, TX, N.A., P.O. Box 2050, Fort Worth, TX 76113, tel.: (817) 884-4151

Financial data (yr. ended 06/30/01): Grants paid, $43,500; assets, $1,090,516 (M); expenditures, $57,124; qualifying distributions, $54,996.
Limitations: Giving primarily in Fort Worth, TX.
Trustee: Bank One Trust Co., N.A.
EIN: 756020787

57190
Kohl Family Foundation
P.O. Box 354
Elkhart Lake, WI 53020-0354

Established in 1998 in WI.
Donor(s): William L. Kohl, Sadako U. Kohl.
Financial data (yr. ended 12/31/01): Grants paid, $43,348; assets, $588,343 (M); gifts received, $53,424; expenditures, $45,082; qualifying distributions, $43,348.
Limitations: Applications not accepted. Giving primarily in AZ.
Application information: Contributes only to pre-selected organizations.
Trustees: Sadako U. Kohl, William L. Kohl, Garry L. Matz, Lawrence L. Silton, Donald R. Sippel.
EIN: 391911092

57191
Greene Manufacturing Company Foundation
3900 Erie St., PMB 165
Racine, WI 53402
Contact: James M. Hamilton, Jr., Tr.

Donor(s): Green Manufacturing Company, James M. Hamilton, Sr., Louise Hamilton.
Financial data (yr. ended 07/31/01): Grants paid, $43,050; assets, $539,071 (M); gifts received, $39,101; expenditures, $43,759; qualifying distributions, $43,050.
Limitations: Giving primarily in WI.
Trustees: James M. Hamilton, Sr., James M. Hamilton, Jr., Louise Hamilton, Patricia L. Hamilton, Maryann Ricker.
EIN: 396074176
Codes: CS, CD

57192
Brakeman Scholarship Fund
c/o Bank One Trust Co., N.A.
P.O. Box 1308
Milwaukee, WI 53201

Financial data (yr. ended 10/31/01): Grants paid, $43,022; assets, $394,406 (M); expenditures, $50,434; qualifying distributions, $44,970.
Limitations: Applications not accepted. Giving primarily in Columbus, OH.
Application information: Contributes only to pre-selected organizations.
Trustee: Bank One Trust Co., N.A.
EIN: 316183157

57193
Brookwood Foundation
5611 6th Pl.
Kenosha, WI 53144-7232

Established in 2000 in WI.
Donor(s): Charles H. Heide.
Financial data (yr. ended 12/31/01): Grants paid, $43,000; assets, $1,226,464 (M); gifts received, $520,000; expenditures, $50,299; qualifying distributions, $43,000.

Limitations: Applications not accepted.
Application information: Contributes only to pre-selected organizations.
Trustees: Charles H. Heide, Charles H. Heide, Jr., Kathryn H. Heide, Paula J. Heide-Waller, Krista J. Reck, Kathryn H. Thompson.
EIN: 392012432

57194
The Thomas J. Reinhart Foundation
c/o John F. Emanuel
111 E. Wisconsin Ave., Ste. 2100
Milwaukee, WI 53202

Established in 1998 in WI.
Financial data (yr. ended 12/31/01): Grants paid, $43,000; assets, $697,819 (M); expenditures, $53,271; qualifying distributions, $43,000.
Limitations: Applications not accepted.
Application information: Contributes only to pre-selected organizations.
Trustee: John F. Emanuel.
EIN: 396685541

57195
Ethel Voris Scott Trust
c/o Bank One Trust Co., N.A.
P.O. Box 1308
Milwaukee, WI 53201
Application address: Bank One Trust Co., N.A., 111 Monument Circle, IN1-0169, Indianapolis, IN 46277, tel.: (317) 756-1362
Contact: Dennis Hickle, Trust Off., Bank One Trust Co., N.A.

Financial data (yr. ended 12/31/01): Grants paid, $42,900; assets, $1,042,197 (M); expenditures, $53,070; qualifying distributions, $44,276.
Limitations: Giving limited to residents of Montgomery County, IN.
Trustee: Bank One Trust Co., N.A.
EIN: 356011994
Codes: GTI

57196
Joseph & Evelyn Richardson Foundation, Inc.
P.O. Box 69
Sheboygan Falls, WI 53085-0069
Application address: 734 County Hwy. PP, Sheboygan Falls, WI 53085, tel.: (920) 467-4343
Contact: Evelyn Richardson, Pres.

Financial data (yr. ended 12/31/01): Grants paid, $42,760; assets, $729,767 (M); expenditures, $47,237; qualifying distributions, $42,760.
Limitations: Giving primarily in WI.
Application information: Application form not required.
Officers: Evelyn Richardson, Pres.; David W. Richardson, Sr., V.P.; Joseph E. Richardson II, V.P.; Gerald L. Loth, Secy.-Treas.
EIN: 391266696

57197
John and Barbara Nevins Foundation, Inc.
719 Oxford Rd.
Waukesha, WI 53186
Contact: John Nevins, Pres.

Established in 1989 in WI.
Donor(s): John Nevins.
Financial data (yr. ended 12/31/01): Grants paid, $42,700; assets, $963,780 (M); gifts received, $68,570; expenditures, $45,893; qualifying distributions, $42,700.
Limitations: Giving primarily in WI.
Officers: John Nevins, Pres. and Treas.; Thomas Nevins, V.P.; Barbara Nevins, Secy.
EIN: 391654907

57198
Schanock Family Foundation, Inc.
610 Brevoort Ln.
Green Bay, WI 54301

Established in 1996 in WI.
Donor(s): Mary Schanock, Romaine Schanock.
Financial data (yr. ended 12/31/01): Grants paid, $42,600; assets, $576,004 (M); expenditures, $53,485; qualifying distributions, $42,600.
Limitations: Applications not accepted.
Application information: Contributes only to pre-selected organizations.
Officers: Romaine Schanock, Pres.; Mary Schanock, V.P. and Treas.; Frederick L. Schmidt, Secy.
EIN: 391870066

57199
Helen Jeanne and Gus Zuehlke Family Foundation
c/o Marshall & Ilsley Bank
P.O. Box 1056
Appleton, WI 54912

Established in 1997 in WI.
Donor(s): Gus Zuehlke, Helen Jeanne Zuehlke.
Financial data (yr. ended 12/31/01): Grants paid, $42,350; assets, $962,239 (M); expenditures, $49,120; qualifying distributions, $40,222.
Limitations: Applications not accepted.
Application information: Contributes only to pre-selected organizations.
Trustee: Marshall & Ilsley Bank.
EIN: 391915805

57200
Forest H. Schafer Foundation, Inc.
199 7th St.
Clintonville, WI 54929-0209 (715) 823-4704
Contact: John P. Schafer, Pres.

Established in 1957 in WI.
Donor(s): Forest H. Schafer,‡ John P. Schafer.
Financial data (yr. ended 12/31/01): Grants paid, $42,340; assets, $603,203 (M); expenditures, $43,489; qualifying distributions, $42,340.
Limitations: Giving within a 50-mile radius of Clintonville, WI.
Application information: Application form not required.
Officers: John P. Schafer, Pres.; Ann M. Fuge, Secy.; Todd Schafer, Treas.
EIN: 396048425

57201
Fuvirese USA, Inc.
P.O. Box 350
Sister Bay, WI 54234-0350

Established in 1997 in WI.
Donor(s): Richard D. Egan.
Financial data (yr. ended 12/31/01): Grants paid, $42,300; assets, $35,677 (M); gifts received, $60,099; expenditures, $68,357; qualifying distributions, $42,300.
Officers and Directors:* Richard D. Egan,* Pres.; Anne W. Egan,* V.P. and Secy.; Hugh M. Eaton,* Treas.; Robert H. Boyer, Mary M. McGlone, Ronald P. McKenzie.
EIN: 391908976

57202
Proctor Charitable Trust
c/o Bank One Trust Co., N.A.
P.O. Box 1308
Milwaukee, WI 53201

Established in 1995 in OH.

Financial data (yr. ended 12/31/01): Grants paid, $42,200; assets, $1,222,342 (M); expenditures, $51,114; qualifying distributions, $45,050.
Limitations: Applications not accepted. Giving primarily in Warren, OH.
Application information: Contributes only to pre-selected organizations.
Trustee: Bank One Trust Co., N.A.
EIN: 316514773

57203
Isidore and Carol Kwaterski Family Foundation, Inc.
P.O. Box 11793
Green Bay, WI 54307-1793 (920) 494-7451
Contact: Sue Bellin, Secy.

Established in 1986 in WI.
Donor(s): Carol Kwaterski, Isidore Kwaterski.
Financial data (yr. ended 09/30/01): Grants paid, $41,990; assets, $770,566 (M); expenditures, $51,283; qualifying distributions, $46,729.
Limitations: Giving primarily in Green Bay, WI.
Officers and Directors:* Isidore Kwaterski,* Pres.; Carol Kwaterski,* V.P.; Sue Bellin, Secy.; Keith Kwaterski, Treas.
EIN: 391569225

57204
Gregory Menn Foundation
c/o Bank One Trust Co., N.A.
P.O. Box 1308
Milwaukee, WI 53201
Application address: c/o C. Radtke, Guidance Office, Appleton East High School, Appleton, WI 54911

Financial data (yr. ended 06/30/01): Grants paid, $41,798; assets, $919,677 (M); expenditures, $58,199; qualifying distributions, $51,255.
Limitations: Giving limited to Appleton, WI.
Application information: Application form not required.
Trustee: Bank One Trust Co., N.A.
EIN: 396143254
Codes: GTI

57205
Oilgear Ferris Foundation
P.O. Box 343924
Milwaukee, WI 53234-3924
Application address: 2300 S. 51st St., Milwaukee, WI 53219
Contact: Thomas Price, Treas.

Established in 1958 in WI.
Donor(s): The Oilgear Company.
Financial data (yr. ended 12/31/01): Grants paid, $41,695; assets, $646,477 (M); expenditures, $48,506; qualifying distributions, $42,295.
Limitations: Giving primarily in areas of company operations, with some emphasis on Milwaukee, WI, Longview, TX, and Fremont, NE.
Officers: David Zuege, Pres.; Gary Bahner, V.P.; Trudy LoFind, Secy.; Thomas J. Price, Treas.
EIN: 396050126
Codes: CS, CD, GTI

57206
Mathilde U. & Albert Elser Foundation, Inc.
c/o Richard S. Gallagher, Foley & Lardner
777 E. Wisconsin Ave., Ste. 3600
Milwaukee, WI 53202-5367 (414) 297-5734

Established in 1955 in WI.
Donor(s): Marianne Elser Markham, Gertrude Elser Schroeder, Nancy C. Snyder.
Financial data (yr. ended 12/31/01): Grants paid, $41,500; assets, $284,280 (M); gifts received, $7,525; expenditures, $43,378; qualifying distributions, $42,045.

57206—WISCONSIN

Limitations: Applications not accepted. Giving primarily in CA and WI.
Application information: Contributes only to pre-selected organizations.
Officers and Directors:* Nancy C. Snyder,* Pres.; Richard S. Gallagher, Secy.; Constance Coburn, Treas.; Lane W. Coburn, Peter E. Coburn.
EIN: 396044395

57207
John & Janet Van Den Wymelenberg Foundation, Inc.
1570 Mesa Dr.
Green Bay, WI 54313

Donor(s): John Van Den Wymelenberg.
Financial data (yr. ended 08/31/01): Grants paid, $41,400; assets, $1,432,044 (M); expenditures, $41,619; qualifying distributions, $41,400.
Limitations: Applications not accepted. Giving primarily in WI.
Application information: Contributes only to pre-selected organizations.
Officer and Directors:* Kathy McAllister,* Pres.; Linda Boss, Mary Ann Hunt, Susan Marten.
EIN: 391392405

57208
Quadracci Family Foundation, Inc.
W224, N3322 Duplainville Rd.
Pewaukee, WI 53072

Established in 1996 in WI.
Donor(s): Harry V. Quadracci, Elizabeth E. Quadracci.
Financial data (yr. ended 11/30/01): Grants paid, $41,000; assets, $316,333 (M); gifts received, $2,625; expenditures, $47,234; qualifying distributions, $43,634.
Limitations: Applications not accepted. Giving primarily in Milwaukee, WI.
Application information: Contributes only to pre-selected organizations.
Officers: Harry V. Quadracci, Pres.; John C. Fowler, Secy.-Treas.
EIN: 391879050

57209
Claude & Della Chilcutt Trust
c/o Bank One Trust Co., N.A.
P.O. Box 1308
Milwaukee, WI 53201-1308
Application address: c/o Jim Wright, P.O. Box 2050, Fort Worth TX 76113, tel.: (817) 884-4159

Financial data (yr. ended 09/30/01): Grants paid, $40,720; assets, $738,788 (M); expenditures, $49,042; qualifying distributions, $40,720.
Limitations: Giving limited to Parker County, TX.
Trustee: Bank One, Texas, N.A.
EIN: 756014433

57210
Paul A. Witty Trust
c/o Bank One Trust co., N.A.
P.O. Box 1308
Milwaukee, WI 53201

Financial data (yr. ended 01/31/02): Grants paid, $40,506; assets, $677,070 (M); expenditures, $47,137; qualifying distributions, $40,506.
Limitations: Applications not accepted. Giving primarily in IL and IN.
Application information: Contributes only to pre-selected organizations.
Trustee: Bank One Trust Co., N.A.
EIN: 366609448

57211
Helen B. & Robert H. Russell Scholarship Fund
c/o Bank One Trust Co., N.A.
P.O. Box 1308
Milwaukee, WI 53201
Application address: 1114 Market St., Wheeling, WV 26003, tel.: (304) 234-4123
Contact: H. Edward Johnson, Sr. Trust Off., Bank One Trust Co., N.A.

Established in 1993 in WV.
Donor(s): Robert H. Russell, Helen B. Russell.
Financial data (yr. ended 12/31/99): Grants paid, $40,500; assets, $892,825 (M); gifts received, $1,810; expenditures, $48,261; qualifying distributions, $40,888.
Limitations: Giving limited to residents of Belmont County, OH, and Ohio County, WV.
Application information: Application form required.
Trustees: Carol Hranko, Martha Jean Hsu, Robert H. Russell, Jr., Bank One Trust Co., N.A.
EIN: 556122686
Codes: GTI

57212
Associated Banc-Corp Founders Scholarship, Inc.
c/o Associated Bank Green Bay, N.A.
P.O. Box 408
Neenah, WI 54957-0408
Application address: c/o Jonathan Drayna, 112 N. Adams St, P.O. Box 13307, Green Bay, WI 54307-3307, tel.: (920) 491-7102

Established in 1984 in WI.
Donor(s): Associated Banc-Corp, Associated Trust Co.
Financial data (yr. ended 12/31/01): Grants paid, $40,250; assets, $598,318 (M); gifts received, $200; expenditures, $48,499; qualifying distributions, $40,050.
Limitations: Giving limited to WI.
Application information: Application form required.
Trustee: Associated Banc-Corp.
EIN: 391482448
Codes: CS, CD, GTI

57213
The Schregardus Family Foundation, Inc.
c/o Ralph Schregardus
1800 E. Fox Ln.
Fox Point, WI 53217

Established in 1996 in WI.
Donor(s): Ralph Schregardus.
Financial data (yr. ended 12/31/01): Grants paid, $40,175; assets, $1,054,262 (M); gifts received, $150,000; expenditures, $58,442; qualifying distributions, $39,500.
Limitations: Applications not accepted. Giving primarily in MI and WI.
Application information: Contributes only to pre-selected organizations.
Officers: Ralph Schregardus, Pres.; Randall Schregardus, V.P.; Andrea Votava, Secy.; Carla Wilson, Treas.
EIN: 391868672

57214
Dr. E. W. Adamson Scholarship Fund
c/o Bank One Trust Co., N.A.
P.O. Box 1308
Milwaukee, WI 53201
Application address: c/o Principal, Douglas High School, 1500 15th St., Douglas, AZ 85607, tel.: (520) 364-3462

Financial data (yr. ended 03/31/02): Grants paid, $40,000; assets, $495,644 (M); expenditures, $48,534; qualifying distributions, $42,964.
Limitations: Giving limited to Douglas, AZ.
Application information: Application form required.
Trustee: Bank One, Arizona, N.A.
EIN: 866042761
Codes: GTI

57215
Dorothy A. Ashcraft Charitable Trust
c/o Bank One Trust Co., N.A.
P.O. Box 1308
Milwaukee, WI 53201
Application address: c/o Kirsten McWilliams, Trust Off., Bank One Trust Co., N.A., 100 W. Milwaukee St., Janesville, WI 53545, tel.: (608) 752-6214

Established in 1987 in WI.
Financial data (yr. ended 07/31/01): Grants paid, $40,000; assets, $839,467 (M); expenditures, $46,873; qualifying distributions, $41,826.
Limitations: Giving limited to Janesville, WI.
Application information: Application form required.
Trustee: Bank One Trust Co., N.A.
EIN: 396461880

57216
Frances Sawyer Hefti Trust
c/o Bank One Trust Co., N.A.
P.O. Box 1308
Milwaukee, WI 53201
Application address: c/o Alan Blake, Bank One Trust Co., N.A., P.O. Box 789, Neenah, WI 54957-0789

Established in 1988 in WI.
Financial data (yr. ended 03/31/00): Grants paid, $40,000; assets, $1,046,975 (M); expenditures, $53,489; qualifying distributions, $43,995.
Limitations: Giving primarily in Neenah and Menasha, WI.
Application information: Applications also available at counselor's office. Application form not required.
Trustee: Bank One Trust Co., N.A.
EIN: 396474920
Codes: GTI

57217
Hufcor Foundation
c/o Marshall & Ilsley Bank
P.O. Box 5000
Janesville, WI 53547-5000

Established in 1988 in WI.
Donor(s): Hufcor, Inc.
Financial data (yr. ended 05/31/02): Grants paid, $40,000; assets, $702,729 (M); gifts received, $75,000; expenditures, $42,200; qualifying distributions, $39,943.
Limitations: Applications not accepted. Giving primarily in Janesville, WI.
Application information: Contributes only to pre-selected organizations.
Trustee: Marshall & Ilsley Bank.
EIN: 391574139

57218
James E. Hughes Scholarship Fund
c/o Bank One Trust Co., N.A.
P.O. Box 1308
Milwaukee, WI 53201

Financial data (yr. ended 05/31/01): Grants paid, $40,000; assets, $726,873 (M); expenditures, $42,120; qualifying distributions, $41,758.
Limitations: Applications not accepted. Giving limited to Marion County, IN.
Application information: Unsolicited requests for funds not considered or acknowledged.
Trustee: Bank One Trust Co., N.A.
EIN: 356009013
Codes: GTI

57219
Koeppen-Gerlach Foundation
c/o Marshall & Ilsley Bank
P.O. Box 2980
Milwaukee, WI 53201
Application address: 8741 W. National Ave., West Allis, WI 53227, tel.: (414) 321-4560
Contact: David A. Affelot

Established in 2000 in WI.
Financial data (yr. ended 06/30/01): Grants paid, $40,000; assets, $1,440,746 (M); gifts received, $1,445,575; expenditures, $44,596; qualifying distributions, $40,000.
Limitations: Giving primarily in Milwaukee, WI.
Trustee: Marshall & Ilsley Bank.
EIN: 392002931

57220
Kuehl Family Charitable Fund
c/o U.S. Bank
P.O. Box 3194, MK-WI-TWPT
Milwaukee, WI 53201-9116

Established in 1987 in WI.
Donor(s): Hal C. Kuehl, Joyce M. Kuehl.
Financial data (yr. ended 12/31/02): Grants paid, $40,000; assets, $838,420 (M); expenditures, $42,230; qualifying distributions, $40,000.
Limitations: Applications not accepted. Giving limited to Milwaukee, WI.
Application information: Contributes only to pre-selected organizations.
Trustees: Cynthia A. Figgatt, David C. Kuehl, Joyce M. Kuehl.
EIN: 391599548

57221
C. J. Williams Central Storage Foundation, Inc.
c/o Central Storage & Warehouse Co.
P.O. Box 7034
Madison, WI 53707 (608) 221-7600
Contact: Kenneth R. Williams, Pres.

Established in 1984 in WI.
Donor(s): Central Storage & Warehouse Company.
Financial data (yr. ended 12/31/01): Grants paid, $40,000; assets, $2,361 (M); gifts received, $40,000; expenditures, $40,000; qualifying distributions, $40,000.
Limitations: Giving primarily in FL and WI.
Officers: Kenneth R. Williams, Pres. and Treas.; Elroy Goetzke, Secy.
EIN: 391524830
Codes: CS, CD

57222
Artemus Bush - Helen Jones Trust
c/o U.S. Bank
P.O. Box 2043
Milwaukee, WI 53201-9116

Established in 1996 in IA.
Donor(s): Helen Jones.
Financial data (yr. ended 02/28/02): Grants paid, $39,873; assets, $793,346 (M); expenditures, $47,239; qualifying distributions, $39,873.
Limitations: Applications not accepted.
Application information: Contributes only to pre-selected organizations.
Trustee: U.S. Bank.
EIN: 426548371

57223
Albert H. Stahmer Foundation, Inc.
404 S. 3rd Ave.
Wausau, WI 54401-4639 (715) 845-7231
Contact: Albert H. Stahmer, Jr., Pres.

Established in 1966 in WI.
Financial data (yr. ended 12/31/01): Grants paid, $39,796; assets, $685,395 (M); expenditures, $54,708; qualifying distributions, $39,796.
Limitations: Giving on a national basis.
Officers and Directors:* Albert H. Stahmer, Jr.,* Pres.; Marilyn W. Stahmer Piehl,* V.P.; John W. Stahmer,* V.P.; Margaret L. Stahmer,* Secy.-Treas.; H. Charles Stahmer,* Secy.
EIN: 396100882

57224
Merganser Fund, Inc.
6925 Wildwood Point Rd.
Hartland, WI 53029-9411 (262) 966-7691
Contact: Samuel E. Bradt, Pres.

Established in 1997 in WI.
Donor(s): Samuel E. Bradt.
Financial data (yr. ended 12/31/00): Grants paid, $39,769; assets, $510,305 (M); expenditures, $78,073; qualifying distributions, $55,769; giving activities include $1,569 for programs.
Limitations: Giving primarily in WI.
Officer and Directors:* Samuel E. Bradt,* Pres.; Nancy B. Bradt, Robert L. Herro.
EIN: 391868940

57225
Thomas and Nancy Florsheim Family Foundation
P.O. Box 1188
Milwaukee, WI 53201
Contact: Thomas W. Florsheim, Tr.

Established in 2001 in WI.
Donor(s): Thomas W. Florsheim.
Financial data (yr. ended 12/31/01): Grants paid, $39,700; assets, $21,848 (M); gifts received, $61,750; expenditures, $39,700; qualifying distributions, $39,700.
Limitations: Giving primarily in Milwaukee, WI; some giving also in Washington, DC, NM, and NY.
Application information: Application form not required.
Trustees: Nancy P. Florsheim, Thomas W. Florsheim.
EIN: 392015101

57226
Ariens Foundation, Ltd.
655 W. Ryan
Brillion, WI 54110 (920) 756-2141
Contact: Mary M. Ariens, Pres.

Established in 1967 in WI.
Donor(s): Ariens Co.
Financial data (yr. ended 06/30/01): Grants paid, $39,355; assets, $25,003 (M); gifts received, $12,120; expenditures, $40,027; qualifying distributions, $39,355.
Limitations: Giving primarily in northeastern WI, with emphasis on Brillion.
Officers: Mary M. Ariens, Pres.; Clarence F. Wolf, V.P.; H. James Jensen, Treas.
EIN: 396102058

Codes: GTI

57227
The Sue & Roland G. Stephenson Family Foundation
N 7797 Lakeshore Ln.
Sherwood, WI 54169-9640

Established in 1998 in WI.
Donor(s): Sue Stephenson, Roland Stephenson.
Financial data (yr. ended 12/31/01): Grants paid, $39,145; assets, $217,107 (M); gifts received, $42,000; expenditures, $41,066; qualifying distributions, $39,145.
Limitations: Applications not accepted.
Application information: Contributes only to pre-selected organizations.
Trustees: Ronald Stephenson, Sue Stephenson.
EIN: 391933916

57228
George L. N. Meyer Family Foundation, Inc.
Elizabeth Meyer
6432 Upper Pkwy., N.
Wauwatosa, WI 53213

Established about 1958.
Financial data (yr. ended 12/31/01): Grants paid, $38,995; assets, $841,647 (M); expenditures, $50,916; qualifying distributions, $38,995.
Limitations: Giving primarily in Milwaukee, WI.
Application information: Application form not required.
Officers and Directors:* Elizabeth J. Meyer,* Pres.; George L.N. Meyer, Jr., V.P.; Mary Catherine Meyer,* Secy.; Barbara Joan Meyer.
EIN: 396043219

57229
Henry & Gladys Phillips Foundation, Inc.
P.O. Box 8050
Wausau, WI 54402-8050 (715) 845-4336
Contact: John F. Michler, Secy.

Financial data (yr. ended 11/30/01): Grants paid, $38,750; assets, $657,314 (M); expenditures, $55,440; qualifying distributions, $38,750.
Limitations: Giving primarily in WI.
Officers and Directors:* Nancy P. Frawley,* Pres. and Treas.; Elizabeth Peters,* V.P.; John F. Michler,* Secy.
EIN: 396068982

57230
The Exley Family Foundation, Inc.
(Formerly Exley/Ohio Valley-Clarksburg Community and Charitable Foundation, Inc.)
c/o Bank One Trust Co., N.A.
P.O. Box 1308
Milwaukee, WI 53202
Application address: 23 Aaron Woods, Wheeling, WV 26003
Contact: Ben Exley III, Pres.

Established in 1990 in WV.
Donor(s): Cardinal Distributing.
Financial data (yr. ended 12/31/01): Grants paid, $38,600; assets, $733,594 (M); expenditures, $41,659; qualifying distributions, $38,600.
Limitations: Giving primarily in Wheeling and Morgantown, WV.
Officers and Directors:* Ben Exley III,* Pres.; Ben Exley IV,* V.P. and Treas.; Paul W. Exley, R. Banford Exley.
Trustee: Bank One Trust Co., N.A.
EIN: 550702493

57231
Ray Koenig Charitable Foundation of WPS, Inc.
1717 W. Broadway
Madison, WI 53713-1834
Application address: P.O. Box 7786, Madison, WI 53707-7786, tel.: (608) 221-5117
Contact: William C. Beisenstein, Secy.-Treas.

Financial data (yr. ended 12/31/01): Grants paid, $38,550; assets, $598,562 (M); gifts received, $37,060; expenditures, $42,663; qualifying distributions, $40,033.
Limitations: Giving primarily in WI.
Application information: Application form not required.
Officers and Trustees:* James R. Riordan,* Chair.; Marvin C. Brickson,* Pres.; John S. Garman, M.D.,* V.P.; William C. Beisenstein,* Secy.-Treas.; William T. Bathke, Eugene J. Nordby, M.D., Martin V. Timmins.
EIN: 391568111

57232
Henry Bunn Memorial Fund
c/o Bank One Trust Co., N.A.
P.O. Box 1308
Milwaukee, WI 53201
Application address: 1 E. Old Capitol Plz., Springfield, IL 62701
Contact: JoAnn Ley, Trust Off., Bank One, N.A.

Established in 1953 in IL.
Financial data (yr. ended 12/31/01): Grants paid, $38,500; assets, $1,126,707 (M); expenditures, $52,107; qualifying distributions, $41,864.
Limitations: Giving limited to residents of Sangamon County, IL.
Application information: Application form required.
Trustees: Jacob Bunn IV, George Haven, Melinda Robinson.
EIN: 376041599
Codes: GTI

57233
Bruce & Mary Ann Erickson Foundation
c/o Stotz & Co.
P.O. Box 149
Grantsburg, WI 54840

Financial data (yr. ended 12/31/99): Grants paid, $38,500; assets, $260,065 (M); gifts received, $323; expenditures, $39,175; qualifying distributions, $38,295.
Limitations: Applications not accepted. Giving primarily in Grantsburg, WI.
Directors: Bruce E. Erickson, Mary Ann Erickson.
EIN: 391878571

57234
Midelfort Foundation, Inc.
733 W. Clairemont Ave.
P.O. Box 1510
Eau Claire, WI 54702-1510 (715) 838-5266
Contact: Gene Enders, M.D., Secy.

Established in 1988 in WI.
Donor(s): Midelfort Clinic Health Plan Coop.
Financial data (yr. ended 12/31/01): Grants paid, $38,492; assets, $762,304 (M); gifts received, $5,700; expenditures, $44,180; qualifying distributions, $38,492.
Limitations: Giving primarily in WI.
Officers and Directors:* Bruce C. Bayley, M.D.,* Pres.; Robert Downs, M.D.,* V.P.; Gene Enders, M.D.,* Secy.; David Van De Loo, M.D.,* Treas.
Trustee: U.S. Bank.
EIN: 391633407

57235
Thorne Family Foundation
640 School St.
Kohler, WI 53044

Established in 1996 in WI.
Donor(s): Gerald M. Thorne, Norrita O. Thorne.
Financial data (yr. ended 12/31/01): Grants paid, $38,373; assets, $811,266 (M); expenditures, $42,495; qualifying distributions, $38,373.
Limitations: Applications not accepted. Giving on a national basis.
Application information: Contributes only to pre-selected organizations.
Trustees: Gerald M. Thorne, Jeffrey L. Thorne, Michele H. Thorne, Norrita O. Thorne.
EIN: 391869184

57236
Freedom Plastics Foundation, Inc.
c/o Freedom Plastics, Inc.
P.O. Box 1488
Janesville, WI 53547

Established around 1994.
Donor(s): Freedom Plastics, Inc.
Financial data (yr. ended 03/31/02): Grants paid, $38,235; assets, $596,280 (M); expenditures, $40,442; qualifying distributions, $38,235.
Limitations: Applications not accepted. Giving primarily in area of company operations.
Application information: Contributes only to pre-selected organizations.
Trustee: Marshall & Ilsley Bank.
EIN: 391792307
Codes: CS, CD

57237
Francis Kerscher Foundation
1306 Fairmont Ln.
Manitowoc, WI 54220-2716
Contact: Francis W. Kerscher, Tr.

Established in 1966.
Donor(s): Francis W. Kerscher.
Financial data (yr. ended 12/31/01): Grants paid, $38,222; assets, $636,994 (M); expenditures, $62,300; qualifying distributions, $38,222.
Limitations: Giving primarily in WI.
Trustees: Frances M. Kerscher, Francis W. Kerscher.
Director: Ed Beno.
EIN: 396094544

57238
Thomas A. Fox Charitable Trust
100 E. Wisconsin Ave., Ste. 1020
Milwaukee, WI 53202 (414) 271-6364
FAX: (414) 271-6365; E-mail: Stan_Hack@hotmail.com
Contact: Stanley F. Hack, Tr.

Established in 1995.
Financial data (yr. ended 12/31/01): Grants paid, $38,150; assets, $1,310,521 (M); expenditures, $73,699; qualifying distributions, $38,150.
Limitations: Giving on a national basis.
Application information: Application form not required.
Trustee: Stanley F. Hack.
EIN: 396608889

57239
Ervin W. Johnson Scholarship Fund
434 N. Main St.
P.O. Box 209
Darlington, WI 53530-1428

Financial data (yr. ended 12/31/00): Grants paid, $37,785; assets, $802,696 (M); expenditures, $38,030; qualifying distributions, $37,785.
Limitations: Giving limited to Lafayette County, WI.
Application information: Application form required.
Trustees: David Chellevold, Steve Fitzsimons, Jim J. Johnson, Mary Lindell, Donald C. Osterday, Mayme L. Smith.
EIN: 391297197
Codes: GTI

57240
Helen A. McInnes Foundation
(Formerly Helen A. McInnes Charitable Foundation)
c/o Bank One Trust Co., N.A.
P.O. Box 1308
Milwaukee, WI 53201

Financial data (yr. ended 12/31/01): Grants paid, $37,745; assets, $731,560 (M); expenditures, $54,341; qualifying distributions, $37,745.
Limitations: Applications not accepted. Giving primarily in Canton, OH.
Application information: Contributes only to pre-selected organizations.
Trustee: Bank One Trust Co., N.A.
EIN: 346819879

57241
Richard & Kay Bibler Foundation, Inc.
c/o Rudolph Stone Assocs.
500 W. Brown Deer Rd., No. 104
Milwaukee, WI 53217
Contact: Richard S. Bibler, Pres.

Established in 1994.
Donor(s): Kay Bibler, Richard S. Bibler.
Financial data (yr. ended 11/30/01): Grants paid, $37,650; assets, $111,280 (M); expenditures, $37,902; qualifying distributions, $37,725.
Limitations: Giving primarily in Milwaukee, WI.
Application information: Application form not required.
Officers: Richard S. Bibler, Pres.; Kay Bibler, V.P.
EIN: 391807360

57242
L. B. Smith Family Foundation, Inc.
c/o Jere D. McGaffey
777 E. Wisconsin Ave.
Milwaukee, WI 53202-5300

Established in 1967 in WI.
Donor(s): Lloyd B. Smith.
Financial data (yr. ended 12/31/01): Grants paid, $37,625; assets, $39,153 (M); gifts received, $46,833; expenditures, $41,400; qualifying distributions, $37,625.
Limitations: Applications not accepted. Giving primarily in WI.
Application information: Contributes only to pre-selected organizations.
Officers and Directors:* Lloyd B. Smith,* Pres.; Lucy W. Smith,* V.P.; Arthur O. Smith,* Secy.-Treas.
EIN: 396106318

57243
Elizabeth Ferguson Foundation
(Formerly Elizabeth Ferguson Charitable Testamentary Trust)
c/o Bank One Trust Co., N.A.
P.O. Box 1308
Milwaukee, WI 53201-1308

Established in 1977 in IL.
Financial data (yr. ended 10/31/01): Grants paid, $37,500; assets, $159,315 (M); expenditures, $43,718; qualifying distributions, $39,373.
Limitations: Giving primarily in Chicago, IL.

WISCONSIN—57256

Trustees: Sam Elliott Pfeffer, Bank One Trust Co., N.A.
EIN: 366667227

57244
Momoney Foundation, Inc.
c/o John P. Richards
3934 Sumac Cir.
Middleton, WI 53562

Established in 1999 in WI.
Donor(s): John P. Richards, Elizabeth A. Richards.
Financial data (yr. ended 12/31/00): Grants paid, $37,500; assets, $898,016 (M); expenditures, $45,282; qualifying distributions, $38,282.
Limitations: Applications not accepted. Giving primarily in Springfield, IL and Madison, WI.
Application information: Contributes only to pre-selected organizations.
Officers: John P. Richards, Pres.; Jock Richards, V.P.; Elizabeth A. Richards, Secy.; Chris Richards, Treas.
EIN: 391980426

57245
Wilbert and Genevieve Schauer Foundation, Inc.
575 Park Cir.
Elm Grove, WI 53122

Established in 1987 in WI.
Donor(s): Wilbert Schauer, Genevieve Schauer.
Financial data (yr. ended 12/31/01): Grants paid, $37,413; assets, $677,910 (M); expenditures, $38,338; qualifying distributions, $38,223.
Limitations: Applications not accepted. Giving primarily in FL and WI.
Application information: Contributes only to pre-selected organizations.
Officers and Directors:* Wilbert E. Schauer,* Pres. and Treas.; Genevieve Schauer,* V.P. and Secy.; Martha S. Klinker, Constance S. Pire.
EIN: 363568775

57246
John and Blanche O'Hara Trust
c/o Marshall & Ilsley Bank
P.O. Box 2980
Milwaukee, WI 53201

Established in 1993 in CA.
Donor(s): John O'Hara,‡ Blanche O'Hara.
Financial data (yr. ended 12/31/01): Grants paid, $37,000; assets, $715,623 (M); expenditures, $43,132; qualifying distributions, $36,796.
Limitations: Applications not accepted. Giving primarily in MN and WI.
Trustee: Marshall & Ilsley Bank.
EIN: 946659540
Codes: GTI

57247
Jay Johnson Charitable Trust
c/o Bank One Trust Co., N.A.
P.O. Box 1308
Milwaukee, WI 53201

Established in 1995 in IL.
Financial data (yr. ended 12/31/01): Grants paid, $36,982; assets, $717,449 (M); expenditures, $44,323; qualifying distributions, $38,965.
Limitations: Applications not accepted.
Application information: Contributes only to pre-selected organizations.
Trustee: Bank One, N.A.
EIN: 366800001

57248
Samuel & Anne Rottman Charitable Trust
c/o North Central Trust Co.
311 Main St.
La Crosse, WI 54601

Established in 1992.
Financial data (yr. ended 12/31/99): Grants paid, $36,583; assets, $1,335,193 (M); expenditures, $46,471; qualifying distributions, $37,183.
Limitations: Applications not accepted. Giving primarily in Milwaukee, WI.
Application information: Contributes only to pre-selected organizations.
Trustee: North Central Trust Co.
EIN: 396537604

57249
Hugh & Ruth V. Ross Charitable Fund, Inc.
P.O. Box 171
636 Wisconsive Ave.
Sheboygan, WI 53082
Application address: 310 St. Clair Ave., Sheboygan, WI 53081
Contact: Hugh Andrew Ross, Treas.

Established in 1994 in WI.
Donor(s): Carl Ross.
Financial data (yr. ended 12/31/01): Grants paid, $36,500; assets, $591,031 (M); gifts received, $104; expenditures, $39,554; qualifying distributions, $36,500.
Limitations: Giving limited to Sheboygan, WI.
Officers: Janet Ross, Pres.; Carla Ross, V.P.; Robert L. Rohde, Secy.; Hugh Andrew Ross, Treas.
Trustee: Wells Fargo Bank Wisconsin, N.A.
EIN: 391807639

57250
David A. & Agatha T. Ulrich Foundation, Inc.
15300 W. Capital Dr., Ste. 202
Brookfield, WI 53005
Contact: Agatha T. Ulrich, Pres.

Established in 1990 in WI.
Donor(s): David A. Ulrich, Agatha T. Ulrich, Tri City National Bank.
Financial data (yr. ended 12/31/01): Grants paid, $36,480; assets, $13,299 (M); gifts received, $25,000; expenditures, $37,105; qualifying distributions, $36,480.
Officers and Directors:* Agatha T. Ulrich,* Pres.; David A. Ulrich,* V.P.; Marilyn Ulrich-Graves,* Secy.; Kathleen McGarry,* Treas.; Tom Ulrich.
EIN: 391688631

57251
C. H. Deem Scholarship Fund
c/o Bank One Trust Co., N.A.
P.O. Box 1308
Milwaukee, WI 53201
Application address: c/o Tom Honderich, Bank One, N.A., 111 Monument Cir., IN1-0169, Indianapolis, IN 46277-0115, tel.: (317) 321-1355

Financial data (yr. ended 02/28/02): Grants paid, $36,432; assets, $446,207 (M); expenditures, $42,615; qualifying distributions, $39,670.
Limitations: Giving limited to residents of Victoria, Australia.
Trustee: Bank One, N.A.
EIN: 356381311

57252
Hugh & Helena Brogan Foundation, Inc.
11308 Homestead Dr.
Ellison Bay, WI 54210 (920) 854-9883

Established in 1987 in WI.

Financial data (yr. ended 12/31/01): Grants paid, $36,300; assets, $591,891 (M); expenditures, $36,310; qualifying distributions, $36,006.
Limitations: Applications not accepted. Giving on a national basis, with emphasis on WI.
Application information: Contributes only to pre-selected organizations.
Officers and Directors:* Geraldine M. Brogan,* Pres.; Linda Timmel,* V.P.; Robert H. Brogan,* Secy.-Treas.
EIN: 391590025

57253
Olive M. Clark Trust
c/o Bank One Trust Co., N.A.
P.O. Box 1308
Milwaukee, WI 53201

Established in 2000 in IN.
Financial data (yr. ended 12/31/01): Grants paid, $36,000; assets, $1,675,082 (M); expenditures, $59,124; qualifying distributions, $41,042.
Limitations: Applications not accepted. Giving primarily in Winchester, IN.
Application information: Contributes only to pre-selected organizations.
Trustee: Bank One Trust Co., N.A.
EIN: 356057815

57254
The Gillette Family Foundation
c/o Jacobus Wealth Mgmt., Inc.
2323 Mayfair Rd., Ste. 240
Milwaukee, WI 53226-1506

Established in 1998 in WI.
Donor(s): Norman L. Gillette, Jr.
Financial data (yr. ended 12/31/00): Grants paid, $36,000; assets, $968,790 (M); gifts received, $372,714; expenditures, $46,118; qualifying distributions, $36,000.
Trustee: Marie E. Gillette-Thoe.
EIN: 396700437

57255
Vogel Foundation, Inc.
P.O. Box 7696
Madison, WI 53707 (608) 241-5454
Contact: David L. Vogel, Pres.

Established in 1989 in WI.
Donor(s): David L. Vogel, Vogel Bros. Bldg. Co.
Financial data (yr. ended 12/31/01): Grants paid, $35,650; assets, $567,519 (M); expenditures, $44,087; qualifying distributions, $35,650.
Limitations: Giving primarily in WI.
Officers: David L. Vogel, Pres.; Daniel C. Vogel, V.P.; Peter C. Vogel, Secy.
EIN: 391639595

57256
V. M. Slipher Testamentary Trust
c/o Bank One Trust Co.
P.O. Box 1308
Milwaukee, WI 53201
Application addresses: c/o Univeristy of Arizona, Head of Science Dept., Tucson, AZ 85721; Arizona State University, Head of Science Dept., Tempe, AZ 85287; or Northern Arizona University, Head of Science Dept., S. San Francisco St. Flagstaff, AZ 86011

Financial data (yr. ended 12/31/00): Grants paid, $35,250; assets, $742,606 (M); expenditures, $58,745; qualifying distributions, $50,058.
Limitations: Giving primarily in AZ.
Application information: Application form not required.
Trustee: Bank One Trust Co., N.A.
EIN: 866065266
Codes: GTI

57257—WISCONSIN

57257
Paul Joseph Foundation, Inc.
c/o Brennan, Steil, Basting, & MacDougal
P.O. Box 446, 512 E. Walworth St.
Delavan, WI 53115
Application address: W5447 US Hwy 12, Elkhorn, WI 53121-2428
Contact: Paul Joseph, Pres.

Established in 1997 in WI.
Donor(s): Paul Joseph.
Financial data (yr. ended 12/31/01): Grants paid, $35,170; assets, $340,511 (M); expenditures, $53,011; qualifying distributions, $35,170.
Limitations: Giving limited to WI.
Application information: Application form required.
Officers: Paul Joseph, Pres.; Brian Watson, Treas.
Director: Jana Joseph.
EIN: 391915905

57258
Clare Family Foundation
P.O. Box 267
Platteville, WI 53818-0267

Established in 1994 in WI.
Donor(s): E.R. Clare.
Financial data (yr. ended 06/30/01): Grants paid, $35,050; assets, $851,784 (M); gifts received, $7,700; expenditures, $35,150; qualifying distributions, $34,399.
Limitations: Applications not accepted.
Application information: Contributes only to pre-selected organizations.
Officer: E.R. Clare, Pres.
EIN: 396606086

57259
J & R Foundation, Inc.
William B. Vogt
1 E. Milwaukee St.
Janesville, WI 53545-3011 (608) 756-4141

Donor(s): William J. Ryan,‡ Joan J. Ryan.
Financial data (yr. ended 06/30/01): Grants paid, $35,000; assets, $195,882 (M); gifts received, $39,813; expenditures, $35,694; qualifying distributions, $34,901.
Limitations: Giving primarily in FL and WI.
Directors: Joan J. Ryan, William J. Ryan.
EIN: 391411975

57260
Kronlund Foundation Charitable Trust
c/o Bank One Trust Co., N.A.
P.O. Box 1308
Milwaukee, WI 53201
Application address: c/o Bank One, 611 Woodward Ave., Ste. 8113, Detroit, MI 48226, tel.: (313) 225-3183
Contact: Don Korn, Tr.

Donor(s): Louise B. Kronlund.‡
Financial data (yr. ended 12/31/01): Grants paid, $35,000; assets, $656,415 (M); expenditures, $41,595; qualifying distributions, $37,519.
Limitations: Giving primarily in MI.
Trustees: Don Korn, Thomas W. Payne, Bank One Trust Co., N.A.
EIN: 382117538

57261
Kuehn Family Foundation, Inc.
c/o Thomas Kuehn
1017 Park St.
Cross Plains, WI 53528 (608) 273-4167

Established in WI in 1998.
Donor(s): Thomas J. Kuehn.
Financial data (yr. ended 06/30/02): Grants paid, $35,000; assets, $732,712 (M); gifts received, $120,000; expenditures, $36,306; qualifying distributions, $35,000.
Limitations: Applications not accepted. Giving primarily in Madison, WI.
Application information: Contributes only to pre-selected organizations.
Officers: Patricia J. Kuehn, Pres.; Thomas J. Kuehn, V.P.
Director: Gail Nichols.
EIN: 391944186

57262
George & Julie Mosher Family Foundation
c/o Marshall & Ilsley Bank
P.O. Box 2980
Milwaukee, WI 53201

Established in 1995 in WI.
Donor(s): George Mosher, Julie Mosher.
Financial data (yr. ended 12/31/01): Grants paid, $35,000; assets, $746,159 (M); gifts received, $89,400; expenditures, $40,532; qualifying distributions, $34,850.
Limitations: Applications not accepted.
Application information: Contributes only to pre-selected organizations.
Trustees: George Mosher, Julie Mosher.
EIN: 396620969

57263
John & Peggy Zimdars Foundation
4168 Cherokee Dr.
Madison, WI 53711-3031

Established in 1985 in WI.
Donor(s): John C. Zimdars, Jr., Peggy D. Zimdars.
Financial data (yr. ended 07/31/01): Grants paid, $34,993; assets, $14,034 (M); gifts received, $30,500; expenditures, $35,942; qualifying distributions, $34,993.
Limitations: Applications not accepted. Giving primarily in Madison, WI.
Application information: Contributes only to pre-selected organizations.
Trustees: John C. Zimdars, Jr., Peggy D. Zimdars.
EIN: 391524362

57264
Mary Ellen & Goff Beach Family Foundation
c/o Thomas G. Beach
722 Wilder Dr.
Madison, WI 53704

Established in 1997 in WI.
Donor(s): Mary Ellen Beach Ela.
Financial data (yr. ended 04/30/02): Grants paid, $34,850; assets, $754,701 (M); expenditures, $42,048; qualifying distributions, $34,850.
Limitations: Applications not accepted. Giving on a national basis.
Application information: Contributes only to pre-selected organizations.
Trustees: Robert T. Beach, Thomas G. Beach, Mary Ellen Beach Ela, Nancy Walsh, Sally Whitner.
EIN: 391888573

57265
Trane Family Foundation, Inc.
c/o John Hilflicker, North Central Trust Co.
311 Main St.
La Crosse, WI 54601-3251
Contact: R. Nicholas Trane, II, Pres.

Financial data (yr. ended 12/31/01): Grants paid, $34,500; assets, $385,786 (M); expenditures, $41,509; qualifying distributions, $34,500.
Limitations: Giving primarily in La Crosse, WI.

Application information: Application form not required.
Officers: R. Nicholas Trane II, Pres.; Wayne Hood, Jr., V.P.; Cynthia Hood, Secy.-Treas.
EIN: 396048524

57266
Clifford A. Schuette Family Foundation
P.O. Box 1490
Wausau, WI 54402-1490 (715) 355-5611
Contact: Kathryn Schuette, V.P.

Established in 1996 in WI.
Financial data (yr. ended 12/31/01): Grants paid, $34,462; assets, $244,400 (M); expenditures, $35,709; qualifying distributions, $34,462.
Application information: Application form not required.
Officers: Clark Schuette, Pres.; Kathryn Schuette, V.P.; Ronald D. Pecha, Secy.-Treas.
EIN: 391816448

57267
Frank Bliss Enslow Foundation
c/o Bank One Trust Co., N.A.
P.O. Box 1308
Milwaukee, WI 53201

Financial data (yr. ended 12/31/01): Grants paid, $34,390; assets, $528,362 (M); expenditures, $38,068; qualifying distributions, $34,390.
Limitations: Applications not accepted. Giving primarily in WV.
Application information: Contributes only to pre-selected organizations.
Trustee: Bank One, N.A.
EIN: 556014659

57268
Marcella S. Pendall Charitable Remainder Annuity Trust
c/o John Butters
1328 Oakland Ave.
Janesville, WI 53545

Established in 1998.
Financial data (yr. ended 12/31/01): Grants paid, $34,382; assets, $685,589 (M); expenditures, $39,604; qualifying distributions, $34,382.
Limitations: Applications not accepted.
Application information: Contributes only to pre-selected organizations.
Trustees: John Butters, John Van Dinter, James Holmstrom, Diane Lalor, George Reinke, Margaret Tierney, Phil Willems.
EIN: 396501184

57269
Dorothy and Richard Burkhardt Family Foundation
c/o Foley & Lardner
777 E. Wisconsin Ave.
Milwaukee, WI 53202-5367

Established in 2000 in WI.
Donor(s): Dorothy J. Burkhardt, Richard W. Burkhardt.
Financial data (yr. ended 12/31/01): Grants paid, $34,000; assets, $415,579 (M); expenditures, $51,711; qualifying distributions, $39,042.
Limitations: Applications not accepted.
Application information: Contributes only to pre-selected organizations.
Trustees: Dorothy J. Burkhardt, Richard W. Burkhardt, Stephen M. Fisher, U.S. Bank.
EIN: 391998792

57270
Greenhill Foundation Charitable Trust
c/o Provident Trust
W23957 Paul Rd.
Pewaukee, WI 53072

Donor(s): Barbara Abert Tooman.
Financial data (yr. ended 12/31/01): Grants paid, $34,000; assets, $196 (M); gifts received, $35,000; expenditures, $35,000; qualifying distributions, $34,990.
Limitations: Applications not accepted.
Application information: Contributes only to pre-selected organizations.
Trustees: George A. Evans, Jr., Marianne K. Storin, Barbara Abert Tooman.
EIN: 391743438

57271
Louis L. Phillips Charities, Inc.
P.O. Box 202
Eau Claire, WI 54702-0202 (715) 839-7400
Contact: Mark F. Phillips, Pres.

Established in 1956.
Financial data (yr. ended 07/31/02): Grants paid, $33,925; assets, $534,026 (M); expenditures, $37,500; qualifying distributions, $33,925.
Limitations: Giving primarily in Eau Claire, WI.
Application information: Application form not required.
Officers and Directors:* Mark F. Phillips,* Pres.; Arlene Phillips,* V.P.; John F. Wilcox,* Secy.; Jan Hasart,* Treas.; Lisa Erickson.
EIN: 396086011

57272
Arnold Fisher Trust for the Homeless
c/o Bank One Trust Co., N.A.
P.O. Box 1308
Milwaukee, WI 53201
Application address: 200 S. Adams St. Green Bay, WI 54307-9029, tel.: (920) 436-2608

Established in 1994 in WI.
Financial data (yr. ended 08/31/01): Grants paid, $33,600; assets, $645,595 (M); expenditures, $50,169; qualifying distributions, $37,814.
Limitations: Giving primarily in Green Bay, WI.
Trustees: Robert W. Jonet, Bank One Trust Co., N.A.
EIN: 396578306

57273
Agsource DHI Foundation, Inc.
135 Enterprise Dr.
P.O. Box 930230
Verona, WI 53593-0230

Established in 1998.
Financial data (yr. ended 12/31/00): Grants paid, $33,559; assets, $638,046 (M); expenditures, $44,912; qualifying distributions, $33,270.
Application information: Application form required.
Officers: Craig Simon, Pres.; Dale Jensen, V.P.; Mark Kautzky, Secy.-Treas.
Directors: Pete Giacomini, Liz Hasburgh, Scott Heeg, Frank Jasurda, Doug Newman.
EIN: 391909207

57274
Don & Pat Spiegelhoff Charitable Foundation
6645 Prairie Rd.
Burlington, WI 53105

Established in 1986 in WI.
Donor(s): Don Spiegelhoff, Pat Spiegelhoff.
Financial data (yr. ended 12/31/01): Grants paid, $33,500; assets, $27,226 (M); gifts received, $20,475; expenditures, $33,957; qualifying distributions, $33,500.
Limitations: Applications not accepted. Giving primarily in Milwaukee, WI.
Application information: Contributes only to pre-selected organizations.
Trustee: Jon A. Spiegelhoff.
EIN: 391572045

57275
The Fairgive Foundation
R.R.1 , Box 373ML
Gillett, WI 54124

Established in 1994 in WI.
Donor(s): Sally Follett, Scott Follett.
Financial data (yr. ended 12/31/00): Grants paid, $33,476; assets, $44,522 (M); expenditures, $34,425; qualifying distributions, $34,425.
Limitations: Applications not accepted. Giving on a national basis.
Application information: Contributes only to pre-selected organizations.
Trustees: Sally Follett, Scott Follett.
EIN: 396606398

57276
Weber W. & Elmina McK. Sebald Fund
c/o Bank One Trust Co., N.A.
P.O. Box 1308
Milwaukee, WI 53201

Financial data (yr. ended 12/31/99): Grants paid, $33,395; assets, $411,234 (M); expenditures, $38,991; qualifying distributions, $34,459.
Limitations: Applications not accepted. Giving limited to Middletown, OH.
Application information: Contributes only to pre-selected organizations.
Trustee: Bank One Trust Co., N.A.
EIN: 316020731

57277
Frances & Laurence Weinstein Foundation, Inc.
P.O. Box 44326
Madison, WI 53744-4326 (608) 271-1234
Contact: Frances Weinstein, Pres.; or Laurence Weinstein

Established in 1980.
Donor(s): Laurence Weinstein, Frances Weinstein.
Financial data (yr. ended 12/31/01): Grants paid, $33,300; assets, $315,408 (M); expenditures, $34,375; qualifying distributions, $34,300.
Limitations: Giving primarily in Madison, WI.
Officers and Director:* Frances Weinstein, Pres. and Treas.; Daniel Weinstein,* V.P. and Secy.
EIN: 391377681

57278
CBR Foundation for Financial Education, Inc.
P.O. Box 081314
Racine, WI 53408 (262) 637-9580

Established in 2000 in WI.
Donor(s): Credit Bureau of Racine, Inc.
Financial data (yr. ended 02/28/02): Grants paid, $33,030; assets, $1,296,878 (M); gifts received, $585,817; expenditures, $109,644; qualifying distributions, $97,153.
Limitations: Giving limited to southeastern WI.
Officers and Directors:* Roy Meythaler,* Pres.; Gloria Mitchell, Exec. Dir.; Earle Christ, John Csapella, and 6 additional directors.
EIN: 391996496

57279
Maurine & Robert D. Goodrich Memorial Trust
c/o Bank One Trust Co., N.A.
P.O. Box 1308
Milwaukee, WI 53201
Application address: P.O. Box 2050, Fort Worth, TX 76113, tel.: (817) 884-4448
Contact: Donald Smith, Tr. Off., Bank One Trust Co., N.A.

Financial data (yr. ended 06/30/01): Grants paid, $33,000; assets, $666,143 (M); expenditures, $42,006; qualifying distributions, $41,629.
Limitations: Giving limited to TX.
Trustee: Bank One Trust Co., N.A.
EIN: 756014406

57280
Arnold P. Stamm Scholarship Trust
c/o Marshall & Ilsley Bank
P.O. Box 2980
Milwaukee, WI 53201
Application address: c/o Rick Altendorf, Weyauwega-Fremont High School, 500 E. Ann St., Weyauwega, WI 54983

Financial data (yr. ended 03/31/02): Grants paid, $32,927; assets, $625,983 (M); expenditures, $41,722; qualifying distributions, $32,832.
Limitations: Giving limited to residents of Weyauwega-Fremont, WI.
Trustee: Marshall & Ilsley Bank.
EIN: 396582045
Codes: GTI

57281
Chester Henrizi Scholarship Fund
P.O. Box 100
Sussex, WI 53089-0300 (262) 246-8500
Contact: Paul E. Schmidt, Tr.

Financial data (yr. ended 11/30/01): Grants paid, $32,906; assets, $296,375 (M); expenditures, $38,783; qualifying distributions, $38,590.
Limitations: Giving limited to Menomonee Falls, WI.
Application information: Application form required.
Trustee: Paul E. Schmidt.
EIN: 391501364
Codes: GTI

57282
Wigwam Mills Fund, Inc.
c/o Terry Ver Straate
P.O. Box 818
Sheboygan, WI 53082-0818

Donor(s): Wigwam Mills, Inc.
Financial data (yr. ended 11/30/01): Grants paid, $32,767; assets, $17,226 (M); gifts received, $35,000; expenditures, $32,777; qualifying distributions, $32,777.
Limitations: Applications not accepted. Giving primarily in Sheboygan, WI.
Application information: Contributes only to pre-selected organizations.
Officers: R.E. Chesebro, Jr., Pres.; J.G. Einhauser, V.P.; Terry Van Straate, Treas.
EIN: 396053425
Codes: CS, CD

57283
Martha L. A. Norris Foundation
c/o Bank One Trust Co.
P.O. Box 1308
Milwaukee, WI 53201
Application address: 148 Fairway Dr., Princeton, NJ 08540
Contact: Shawn W. Ellsworth, Tr.

Established in 1998 in NJ.
Donor(s): Martha L.A. Norris.
Financial data (yr. ended 12/31/01): Grants paid, $32,750; assets, $517,165 (M); expenditures, $40,789; qualifying distributions, $32,750.
Limitations: Giving on a national basis, with emphasis on Princeton, NJ, and Indianapolis, IN.
Trustees: Roberta N. Ellsworth, Shawn W. Ellsworth, Martha L.A. Norris.
Agent: Bank One Trust Co., N.A.
EIN: 226769266

57284
Van Hoof Family Foundation, Inc.
P.O. Box 7110
Appleton, WI 54912-7067

Established in 1996 in WI.
Financial data (yr. ended 12/31/01): Grants paid, $32,581; assets, $2,312 (M); gifts received, $33,604; expenditures, $33,191; qualifying distributions, $32,581.
Limitations: Applications not accepted. Giving primarily in WI.
Application information: Contributes only to pre-selected organizations.
Officers: Gerard H. Van Hoof, Pres.; Thomas O. Hurley, V.P. and Secy.; Daniel P. Vanden Heuvel, V.P. and Treas.
EIN: 391823933

57285
Betty Taylor Clarke Charitable Testamentary Trust
c/o Bank One Trust Co., N.A.
P.O. Box 130
Milwaukee, WI 53201
Application address: John Allerson, c/o Roosevelt University, 430 S. Michigan Ave., Chicago, IL 60605

Financial data (yr. ended 12/31/01): Grants paid, $32,539; assets, $613,494 (M); expenditures, $41,586; qualifying distributions, $32,539.
Limitations: Giving limited to Chicago, IL.
Trustees: Harvey A. Herman, Bank One, N.A.
EIN: 366667269

57286
Donald and Ruth P. Taylor Family Foundation, Inc.
c/o Foley & Lardner
777 E. Wisconsin Ave.
Milwaukee, WI 53202-5367

Established in 1987 in WI.
Donor(s): Donald Taylor, Ruth P. Taylor.
Financial data (yr. ended 12/31/01): Grants paid, $32,500; assets, $714,325 (M); expenditures, $33,536; qualifying distributions, $32,461.
Limitations: Applications not accepted. Giving primarily in Milwaukee, WI.
Application information: Contributes only to pre-selected organizations.
Officers and Directors:* Donald Taylor,* Pres. and Treas.; Ruth P. Taylor,* V.P.; Stephen M. Fisher,* Secy.
EIN: 391570608

57287
Maurice & Arlene Reese Foundation
c/o U.S. Bank
P.O. Box 7900
Madison, WI 53707
Application address: 302 E. Washington Ave., Madison, WI 53703
Contact: Maurice Reese, Chair.

Established in 1996 in WI.
Donor(s): Maurice Reese.
Financial data (yr. ended 12/31/01): Grants paid, $32,389; assets, $1,139,086 (M); gifts received, $33,111; expenditures, $39,440; qualifying distributions, $32,389.
Limitations: Giving primarily in Madison, WI.
Officers and Trustees:* Maurice Reese,* Chair.; Arlene Reese,* Vice-Chair.; Kathleen A. Reese, Richard M. Reese, Robert W. Reese, U.S. Bank.
EIN: 396635271

57288
Nell V. Bailey Charitable Trust
c/o Bank One Trust Co., N.A.
P.O. Box 1308
Milwaukee, WI 53201
Application address: c/o Bank One Texas, N.A., P.O. Box 2050, Fort Worth, TX 76113, tel.: (817) 884-4151
Contact: Robert Lansford, Trust Off., Bank One Trust Co., N.A.

Financial data (yr. ended 03/31/02): Grants paid, $32,300; assets, $633,706 (M); expenditures, $44,629; qualifying distributions, $35,723.
Limitations: Giving primarily in Fort Worth, TX.
Trustee: Bank One Trust Co., N.A.
EIN: 756013985

57289
Victor & Helen Geisel Foundation
500 3rd St., Ste. 700
P.O. Box 8050
Wausau, WI 54403-4857 (715) 845-4336
Contact: John F. Michler, V.P.

Established in 1988 in WI.
Donor(s): Helen S. Geisel.
Financial data (yr. ended 10/31/01): Grants paid, $32,100; assets, $520,883 (M); expenditures, $44,500; qualifying distributions, $32,100.
Limitations: Giving primarily in WI.
Officers and Directors:* Anne G. Fredlund,* Pres.; John F. Michler,* V.P. and Secy.; Robert Geisel,* Treas.
EIN: 391619399

57290
Clarence Keller Scholarship Trust
c/o U.S. Bank
P.O. Box 2043
Milwaukee, WI 53201-9116
Application address: P.O. Box 0663, Sheboygan, WI 53081
Contact: Paul Callan

Established in 1989 in WI.
Donor(s): Clarence Keller.‡
Financial data (yr. ended 07/31/01): Grants paid, $32,050; assets, $590,898 (M); expenditures, $40,059; qualifying distributions, $31,460.
Limitations: Giving primarily in Sheboygan, WI.
Application information: Application form required.
Trustee: U.S. Bank.
Scholarship Committee: Jennifer Brown, Suzanne Dennis, Judy Heinicke, Paul Hertel, Randy Holzer, Jay Johnson, Timothy B. Kaker, Ruth Lilly, Howard Vieth, Benjamin White.
EIN: 396500681
Codes: GTI

57291
Clarence & Olive Richards Scholarship Trust
c/o U.S. Bank
P.O. Box 2043
Milwaukee, WI 53201-9116

Established in 1997 in IA.
Donor(s): Olive Richards.‡
Financial data (yr. ended 12/31/00): Grants paid, $31,875; assets, $812,554 (M); expenditures, $40,977; qualifying distributions, $35,958.
Limitations: Giving limited to residents of Oregon Township, Washington County, IA.
Application information: Application form required.
Trustee: U.S. Bank.
EIN: 396672759

57292
Earl Lawrence Mullineaux Charitable Trust
c/o Bank One Trust Co., N.A.
P.O. Box 1308
Milwaukee, WI 53201

Established in 1996 in WV.
Financial data (yr. ended 12/31/01): Grants paid, $31,334; assets, $487,180 (M); expenditures, $34,250; qualifying distributions, $31,334.
Limitations: Applications not accepted. Giving primarily in WV.
Application information: Contributes only to pre-selected organizations.
Trustee: Bank One, Huntington, N.A.
EIN: 556051787

57293
Raymond & Loella Brown Foundation
c/o U.S. Bank
P.O. Box 7900
Madison, WI 53707-7900

Established in 1991 in WI.
Donor(s): Raymond G. Brown.
Financial data (yr. ended 12/31/00): Grants paid, $31,250; assets, $727,667 (M); expenditures, $37,965; qualifying distributions, $30,675.
Limitations: Giving limited to residents of WI.
Officer and Committee Members:* Raymond G. Brown,* Chair.; Earl Hawkins, Paul Koritzinsky.
Trustee: U.S. Bank.
EIN: 396530384
Codes: GTI

57294
Klopcic Family Foundation Trust
1131 Janesville Ave.
Fort Atkinson, WI 53538-2406

Established in 1990 in WI.
Donor(s): Richard F. Klopcic, Betty J. Klopcic.
Financial data (yr. ended 11/30/01): Grants paid, $31,212; assets, $655,455 (M); gifts received, $139,813; expenditures, $50,317; qualifying distributions, $44,669.
Limitations: Applications not accepted. Giving on a national basis.
Application information: Contributes only to pre-selected organizations.
Trustees: Betty J. Klopcic, Richard F. Klopcic.
EIN: 391691950

57295
Bauernfeind Family Foundation, Inc.
9704 N. Kelly Lake Rd.
Suring, WI 54174

Established in 1999 in WI.
Financial data (yr. ended 12/31/01): Grants paid, $31,160; assets, $23 (M); gifts received, $36,550; expenditures, $36,775; qualifying distributions, $31,160.

Directors: John Bauernfeind, M. Nicol Padway, William A. Padway.
EIN: 391951903

57296
Dorothy E. Werner Family Charitable Foundation Trust
215 X-Press Ln.
Sheboygan, WI 53081 (920) 458-3183
Contact: John M. Werner, Sr., Chair.

Financial data (yr. ended 12/31/01): Grants paid, $31,100; assets, $298,735 (M); expenditures, $49,054; qualifying distributions, $31,100.
Limitations: Giving primarily in WI.
Application information: Application form not required.
Trustees: John M. Werner, Sr., Chair.; Roland Neumann, Tim Werner.
EIN: 396039260

57297
Pukall Lumber Foundation, Inc.
AV 10894 Hwy. 70 E.
Woodruff, WI 54568
Contact: Susan Pukall

Donor(s): Pukall Lumber Co.
Financial data (yr. ended 06/30/01): Grants paid, $31,070; assets, $536,215 (M); gifts received, $15,000; expenditures, $31,839; qualifying distributions, $31,501.
Limitations: Giving limited to the northern central WI area.
Directors: Debra Pukall Christiansen, Mary Pukall, Roger L. Pukall.
EIN: 277396586
Codes: CS, CD

57298
Margaret L. Davis Trust Fund
c/o Bank One Trust Co., N.A.
P.O. Box 1308
Milwaukee, WI 53201-1308
Application addresses: c/o Principal, Perry Meridian High School, 410 W. Meridian School Rd., Indianapolis, IN 46217, or c/o Southport High School, 971 E. Banta Rd., Indianapolis, IN 46227

Established in 1994 in IN.
Donor(s): Margaret L. Davis.
Financial data (yr. ended 10/31/01): Grants paid, $31,000; assets, $546,485 (M); expenditures, $39,520; qualifying distributions, $33,050.
Limitations: Giving limited to residents of Marion County, IN.
Application information: Application form required.
Trustee: Bank One Trust Co., N.A.
EIN: 351973505
Codes: GTI

57299
Bernice Pickens Parsons Foundation
c/o Bank One Trust Co.
P.O. Box 1308
Milwaukee, WI 53201

Financial data (yr. ended 06/30/01): Grants paid, $30,925; assets, $707,803 (M); expenditures, $41,819; qualifying distributions, $32,450.
Limitations: Applications not accepted. Giving limited to WV.
Application information: Contributes only to pre-selected organizations.
Trustee: Bank One Trust Co., N.A.
EIN: 556026999

57300
Stuart R. Stair Charitable Trust
c/o Foley & Lardner
777 E. Wisconsin Ave., Ste. 3500
Milwaukee, WI 53202 (414) 297-5746
Contact: Keith A. Christiansen, Tr.

Donor(s): Lester D. Harkrider Charitable Trust.
Financial data (yr. ended 01/31/02): Grants paid, $30,867; assets, $29,864 (M); gifts received, $30,867; expenditures, $31,031; qualifying distributions, $30,867.
Limitations: Giving primarily in WI.
Trustees: Keith A. Christiansen, George A. Dionisopoulos.
EIN: 391539865

57301
Ralph M. Stair, Jr. Charitable Trust
c/o Foley & Lardner
777 E. Wisconsin Ave., Ste. 3500
Milwaukee, WI 53202 (414) 297-5746
Contact: Keith A. Christiansen, Tr.

Established in 1985 in WI.
Donor(s): Lester D. Harkrider Charitable Trust.
Financial data (yr. ended 01/31/02): Grants paid, $30,867; assets, $18,098 (M); gifts received, $30,867; expenditures, $31,104; qualifying distributions, $30,867.
Limitations: Giving primarily in WI.
Trustees: Keith A. Christiansen, George A. Dionisopoulos.
EIN: 391539868

57302
Kaytee Avian Foundation, Inc.
c/o David Krause
P.O. Box 230
Chilton, WI 53014

Established in 1995 in WI.
Donor(s): Kaytee Products, Inc.
Financial data (yr. ended 12/31/01): Grants paid, $30,836; assets, $62,778 (L); gifts received, $50,600; expenditures, $44,009; qualifying distributions, $42,561.
Limitations: Applications not accepted. Giving on a national basis, with some emphasis on IN, OR, and WI.
Application information: Contributes only to pre-selected organizations.
Officers and Directors:* Richard Best,* Pres. and Exec. Dir.; Randal Brue,* Secy.; Kevin Johnson, Treas.; Stacy Gedman, Myra Peffer, John Rost, James Wrobel.
EIN: 391810726
Codes: CS, CD

57303
Sommerhauser Foundation, Inc.
c/o Peter Sommerhauser
780 N. Water St.
Milwaukee, WI 53202

Established in 1994 in WI.
Financial data (yr. ended 12/31/01): Grants paid, $30,820; assets, $878,515 (M); expenditures, $33,514; qualifying distributions, $30,820.
Limitations: Applications not accepted.
Application information: Contributes only to pre-selected organizations.
Officers: Peter M. Sommerhauser, Pres.; Elizabeth H. Sommerhauser, V.P. and Treas.; Barbara J. Herbst, Secy.
EIN: 391805123

57304
Ocular Physiology Research & Education Foundation, Inc.
3006 Harvard Dr.
Madison, WI 53705

Established in 1989 in WI.
Financial data (yr. ended 06/30/02): Grants paid, $30,700; assets, $512,215 (M); gifts received, $73,000; expenditures, $37,918; qualifying distributions, $30,700.
Limitations: Applications not accepted.
Application information: Contributes only to pre-selected organizations.
Officers and Directors:* Paul L. Kaufman, M.D.,* Pres.; Howard S. Goldman, M.D.,* V.P.; Margaret Kaufman, Secy.-Treas.; Katherine B. Foehl.
EIN: 391661745

57305
Max H. Alberts Scholarship Trust
c/o Marshall & Ilsley Bank
P.O. Box 2980
Milwaukee, WI 53201-2980
Application address: c/o Johnson Creek High School, 111 South St., Johnson Creek, WI 53038

Established in 1989 in WI.
Financial data (yr. ended 04/30/01): Grants paid, $30,500; assets, $838,176 (M); expenditures, $40,669; qualifying distributions, $36,496.
Limitations: Giving limited to residents of Johnson Creek, WI.
Application information: Contact Johnson Creek High School for current application guidelines.
Trustee: Marshall & Ilsley Bank.
EIN: 396498404
Codes: GTI

57306
Louise S. & Henry G. Hart, Jr. Charitable Foundation
(Formerly Hubert & Wilma Silberman Charitable Foundation)
c/o Bank One Trust Co., N.A.
P.O. Box 1308
Milwaukee, WI 53201

Donor(s): Henry G. Hart, Jr.
Financial data (yr. ended 12/31/01): Grants paid, $30,390; assets, $607,146 (M); expenditures, $39,151; qualifying distributions, $31,138.
Limitations: Applications not accepted. Giving primarily in Chicago, IL.
Application information: Contributes only to pre-selected organizations.
Officers: Louise S. Hart, Pres.; James G. Hart, Secy.; John Hart, Treas.
EIN: 366055863

57307
Connor Foundation
c/o Becker & Kumm
214 W. Grand Ave., Ste. 18
Wisconsin Rapids, WI 54495-2782
Contact: Mary C. Pierce, Tr.

Donor(s): Members of the Connor family.
Financial data (yr. ended 06/30/02): Grants paid, $30,168; assets, $216,405 (M); expenditures, $32,743; qualifying distributions, $30,168.
Limitations: Giving primarily in WI.
Directors: Catherine C. Dellin, Melissa P. Demopoulos, Catherine P. Hurtgen.
Trustee: Mary C. Pierce.
EIN: 396126564

57308
The Weber W. Sebald Foundation
c/o Bank One Ohio Trust Co., N.A.
P.O. Box 1308
Milwaukee, WI 53201
Application address: P.O. Box 526, Middletown, OH 45042
Contact: Mark D. Welch, Trust Off., Bank One Trust Co., N.A.

Financial data (yr. ended 12/31/01): Grants paid, $30,010; assets, $418,899 (M); expenditures, $35,679; qualifying distributions, $30,010.
Limitations: Giving limited to the Middletown, OH, area.
Trustee: Bank One Ohio Trust Co., N.A.
EIN: 316020730

57309
Lucille Camp Trust
c/o Bank One Trust Co., N.A.
P.O. Box 1308
Milwaukee, WI 53201
Application address: c/o Wabash High School, 580 N. Miami St., Wabash, IN 46992
Contact: Steve Eikenberry

Established in 1997 in IN.
Donor(s): Lucille Camp.
Financial data (yr. ended 02/28/02): Grants paid, $30,000; assets, $451,803 (M); expenditures, $35,085; qualifying distributions, $31,589.
Limitations: Giving limited to residents of Wabash, IN.
Trustee: Bank One Trust Co., N.A.
EIN: 356648622

57310
Eugene J. Eder Charitable Foundation
c/o Zetley, Carneol & Stein
788 N. Jefferson St., Ste. 200
Milwaukee, WI 53202

Established in 1997 in WI.
Donor(s): Eugene J. Eder.
Financial data (yr. ended 12/31/01): Grants paid, $30,000; assets, $842,882 (M); gifts received, $259,338; expenditures, $30,855; qualifying distributions, $30,000.
Limitations: Applications not accepted.
Application information: Contributes only to pre-selected organizations.
Officers and Directors:* Eugene J. Eder,* Pres.; Craig H. Zetley,* V.P.; Allan J. Carneol,* Secy.-Treas.
EIN: 391870043

57311
Albert M. & Lyda M. Green Foundation
c/o Bank One Trust Co., N.A.
P.O. Box 1308
Milwaukee, WI 53201

Financial data (yr. ended 12/31/01): Grants paid, $30,000; assets, $848,928 (M); expenditures, $41,782; qualifying distributions, $33,656.
Limitations: Applications not accepted. Giving primarily in Washington, DC, and MI.
Application information: Contributes only to pre-selected organizations.
Officers and Directors:* David M. Rosenberger,* Pres.; Mark C. Larson,* 1st V.P.; James M. Elsworth,* V.P.; John K. Cannon,* Secy.; Gail A. Moro, Treas.
Trustee: Bank One Invest Mgmt. Co.
EIN: 382601744

57312
Mick A. Naulin Foundation, Ltd.
13455 Bobby Ln.
Elm Grove, WI 53122-1315 (262) 786-4454
Contact: Charles R. Clancy, Tr.

Established in 1973 in WI.
Donor(s): Mick A. Naulin.‡
Financial data (yr. ended 07/31/02): Grants paid, $30,000; assets, $515,291 (M); expenditures, $44,093; qualifying distributions, $30,000.
Limitations: Giving primarily in Gainesville, FL.
Application information: Application form not required.
Trustees: Roy G. Boland, Charles R. Clancy, Kenneth W. Schloerke.
EIN: 237350977

57313
John M. Olin Trust
c/o U.S. Bank
P.O. Box 7900
Madison, WI 53707-7900

Financial data (yr. ended 12/31/01): Grants paid, $30,000; assets, $581,034 (M); expenditures, $38,982; qualifying distributions, $30,000.
Limitations: Applications not accepted. Giving limited to Madison, WI.
Application information: Contributes only to pre-selected organizations.
Trustee: U.S. Bank.
EIN: 396038673

57314
The Dorothy and Margaretha Schmidtbauer Foundation, Inc.
13755 W. Tulane St.
Brookfield, WI 53005
Contact: Charles R. Stackpole, Pres.

Established in 1995 in WI.
Financial data (yr. ended 12/31/01): Grants paid, $30,000; assets, $603,932 (M); expenditures, $34,084; qualifying distributions, $30,000.
Officer and Director:* Charles R. Stackpole,* Pres.
EIN: 391784176

57315
Joseph P. & Ann Wenzler Family Foundation
10056 N. Range Line Rd.
Mequon, WI 53092

Established in 2000 in WI.
Donor(s): Ann Wenzler, Joseph P. Wenzler.
Financial data (yr. ended 12/31/01): Grants paid, $30,000; assets, $559,472 (M); expenditures, $48,897; qualifying distributions, $30,000.
Limitations: Applications not accepted. Giving primarily in Milwaukee, WI.
Application information: Contributes only to pre-selected organizations.
Trustees: Ann Wenzler, Joseph P. Wenzler.
EIN: 396732576

57316
Wardeberg Charitable Trust
9701 N. Columbia Dr.
Mequon, WI 53092-5644 (262) 241-3502
Contact: George E. Wardeberg, Tr.

Established in 2000 in WI.
Donor(s): George E. Wardeberg.
Financial data (yr. ended 12/31/00): Grants paid, $29,900; assets, $148,720 (M); expenditures, $30,400; qualifying distributions, $29,900.
Limitations: Giving primarily in Milwaukee, WI.
Trustees: David Wardeberg, Deanna J. Wardeberg, George E. Wardeberg, Gregory Wardeberg, Jeffrey Wardeberg.
EIN: 396732622

57317
Thomas S. Kemp Foundation, Inc.
c/o Thomas S. Kemp
W 8840 Hwy. CS
Poynette, WI 53955

Established in 1997 in WI.
Donor(s): Thomas S. Kemp.
Financial data (yr. ended 12/31/01): Grants paid, $29,840; assets, $251,887 (M); expenditures, $35,001; qualifying distributions, $29,840.
Limitations: Applications not accepted. Giving primarily in WI.
Application information: Contributes only to pre-selected organizations.
Officers: Thomas S. Kemp, Pres. and Treas.; Ann Ryan, V.P.; Jane Hockett, Secy.
EIN: 391888871

57318
Seippel Family Foundation, Inc.
P.O. Box 220
Beaver Dam, WI 53916-0220

Established in 1988 in WI.
Donor(s): Peter J. Seippel.
Financial data (yr. ended 12/31/01): Grants paid, $29,470; assets, $302,205 (M); expenditures, $42,097; qualifying distributions, $29,470.
Limitations: Applications not accepted. Giving primarily in Beaver Dam, WI.
Application information: Contributes only to pre-selected organizations.
Officers and Directors:* Peter J. Seippel,* Pres. and Treas.; Phillip R. Seippel,* V.P.; Virginia S. King,* Secy.; John Ralston.
EIN: 391633928

57319
Kaztex Foundation, Inc.
N15 W23217 Stone Ridge Dr.
Waukesha, WI 53188

Established in 1993 in WI.
Donor(s): John C. Kasdorf.
Financial data (yr. ended 12/31/01): Grants paid, $29,350; assets, $841,212 (M); gifts received, $326,543; expenditures, $29,586; qualifying distributions, $29,350.
Officers and Directors:* John C. Kasdorf,* Pres.; James F. Puchter,* V.P.; John Obermiller, Secy.-Treas.; Cheryl N. Kasdorf.
EIN: 391774373

57320
James E. and John A. Keyes Families Foundation, Inc.
788 N. Jefferson St., No. 900
Milwaukee, WI 53202

Established in 1999 in WI.
Financial data (yr. ended 12/31/01): Grants paid, $29,250; assets, $727,927 (M); expenditures, $35,384; qualifying distributions, $29,250.
Limitations: Applications not accepted. Giving primarily in IN and WI.
Application information: Contributes only to pre-selected organizations.
Officers: James E. Keyes, Pres.; John A. Keyes, V.P.; John P. Miller, Secy.
EIN: 391963274

57321
James E. Cleary Foundation, Inc.
c/o Thomas P. Cleary
70 N. Stevens St.
Rhinelander, WI 54501

Established in 1998 in WI.
Donor(s): Thomas P. Cleary.

Financial data (yr. ended 12/31/01): Grants paid, $29,210; assets, $182,248 (M); expenditures, $30,090; qualifying distributions, $29,210.
Limitations: Applications not accepted. Giving primarily in WI.
Application information: Contributes only to pre-selected organizations.
Officers: Thomas P. Cleary, Pres. and Treas.; Thomas Debyle, V.P.; Janet Debyle, Secy.
EIN: 391919108

57322
Cern Foundation, Inc.
c/o Robert C. Shaw
P. O. Box 259101
Madison, WI 53725

Financial data (yr. ended 11/30/01): Grants paid, $29,000; assets, $305,447 (M); expenditures, $51,712; qualifying distributions, $29,000.
Limitations: Applications not accepted. Giving primarily in Asheville, NC.
Application information: Contributes only to pre-selected organizations.
Officer: Robert C. Shaw, Mgr.
EIN: 312070315

57323
Virginia H. Glasson Charitable Trust
c/o Bank One Trust Co., N.A.
P.O. Box 1308
Milwaukee, WI 53201

Established in 1994 in WI.
Financial data (yr. ended 08/31/01): Grants paid, $29,000; assets, $629,471 (M); expenditures, $38,634; qualifying distributions, $34,991.
Limitations: Applications not accepted. Giving primarily in Asheville, NC.
Application information: Contributes only to pre-selected organizations.
Trustee: Bank One Trust Co., N.A.
EIN: 396605306

57324
Erna Marie Nehls Scholarship Trust
c/o U.S. Bank
P.O. Box 7900
Madison, WI 53707
Application address: c/o Trinity Lutheran Church, N60 W6047 Columbia Rd., Cedarburg, WI 53012

Financial data (yr. ended 12/31/99): Grants paid, $29,000; assets, $389,721 (M); expenditures, $33,474; qualifying distributions, $29,090.
Limitations: Giving limited to Cedarburg, WI.
Trustee: U.S. Bank.
EIN: 396320561

57325
Rolfs Educational Foundation, Ltd.
c/o Arthur Hoberg
P.O. Box 2043, Ste. LC 4NE
Milwaukee, WI 53201 (414) 287-5668

Established in 1990 in WI.
Financial data (yr. ended 12/31/01): Grants paid, $29,000; assets, $818,918 (M); expenditures, $34,249; qualifying distributions, $29,000.
Limitations: Applications not accepted. Giving limited to residents of WI.
Officers and Directors:* Steven J. Rolfs,* Pres.; Roger Neper,* V.P.; Theodore R. Rolfs,* Secy.-Treas.
EIN: 391651525

57326
The Panning Foundation, Inc.
P.O. Box 399
Thiensville, WI 53092

Established in 1986 in WI.
Donor(s): Martin H. Panning, Florence E. Panning.
Financial data (yr. ended 12/31/01): Grants paid, $28,900; assets, $743,308 (M); gifts received, $27,406; expenditures, $30,441; qualifying distributions, $28,900.
Limitations: Applications not accepted. Giving primarily in WI.
Application information: Contributes only to pre-selected organizations.
Officers and Directors:* Martin H. Panning,* Pres. and Treas.; Florence E. Panning,* V.P. and Secy.; William Fitzhugh Fox.
EIN: 391570442

57327
Dan Storey Foundation, Inc.
P.O. Box 8050
Wausau, WI 54402-8050 (715) 845-4336
Contact: John F. Michler, Secy.-Treas.

Established around 1967 in WI.
Financial data (yr. ended 06/30/02): Grants paid, $28,892; assets, $592,016 (M); expenditures, $55,913; qualifying distributions, $28,892.
Limitations: Giving primarily in the north central WI, area.
Officers: Robert K. Geisel, Pres.; John F. Michler, Secy.-Treas.
EIN: 396125496

57328
John R. & Beverly J. Larson Foundation
P.O. Box 404
Sparta, WI 54656-0404

Established in 1997 in WI.
Donor(s): Beverly J. Larson, John Larson.
Financial data (yr. ended 12/31/01): Grants paid, $28,750; assets, $422,152 (M); expenditures, $31,800; qualifying distributions, $30,059.
Limitations: Applications not accepted.
Application information: Contributes only to pre-selected organizations.
Trustees: Virginia M. Field, Beverly J. Larson, John R. Larson, Jacqueline A. Springer.
EIN: 396652338

57329
Asher and Susan Nichols Family Foundation, Inc.
401 E. Kilbourn Ave., Ste. 400
Milwaukee, WI 53202-3212 (414) 272-3146
Contact: Asher B. Nichols, Pres.

Established in 1997 in WI.
Donor(s): Asher B. Nichols, Susan S. Nichols.
Financial data (yr. ended 12/31/01): Grants paid, $28,700; assets, $307,819 (M); gifts received, $44,551; expenditures, $29,430; qualifying distributions, $28,700.
Limitations: Giving primarily in WI.
Application information: Application form required.
Officers: Asher B. Nichols, Pres.; Cynthia N. Stephenson, Secy.-Treas.
Directors: Catherine N. Maekson, Christopher A. Nichols, Scott A. Nichols, Susan S. Nichols.
EIN: 391892827

57330
Segel Family Foundation, Inc.
4700 N. 132nd St.
Butler, WI 53007
Application address: P.O. Box 913, Butler, WI 53007, tel.: (414) 645-6500
Contact: Justin N. Segel, Pres.

Established in 1955 in WI.
Donor(s): Wis-Pac Foods, Inc.
Financial data (yr. ended 11/30/01): Grants paid, $28,685; assets, $479,803 (M); expenditures, $39,360; qualifying distributions, $39,360.
Limitations: Giving primarily in Palm Beach, FL, and Milwaukee, WI.
Application information: Application form not required.
Officers: Justin N. Segel, Pres. and Treas.; Floyd A. Segel, V.P. and Secy.
EIN: 396040274

57331
Seymour Community School Scholarship Trust
P.O. Box 67
Seymour, WI 54165-0067 (920) 833-2356
Contact: Vernon Lubinski, Tr.

Donor(s): Francis Ruben.‡
Financial data (yr. ended 12/31/01): Grants paid, $28,662; assets, $628,417 (M); gifts received, $26,956; expenditures, $34,090; qualifying distributions, $28,331.
Limitations: Giving limited to residents of WI.
Trustees: John Cumicek, Michael Faundree, M.D., Vernon Lubinski, Jo Ann Redecki, John Selmer.
EIN: 391769065

57332
Sara H. Cowgill Trust
c/o Bank One Trust Co., N.A.
P.O. Box 1308
Milwaukee, WI 53201
Application address: c/o Citizens Scholarship Foundation of Guernsey County, P.O. Box 811, Cambridge, OH 43725

Financial data (yr. ended 06/30/01): Grants paid, $28,512; assets, $995,589 (M); expenditures, $39,169; qualifying distributions, $31,189.
Limitations: Giving limited to Cambridge, OH.
Application information: Application form required.
Trustee: Bank One Trust Co., N.A.
EIN: 316096015

57333
Robert W. & Caroline A. Fernstrum Scholarship Foundation Trust
P.O. Box 137
Marinette, WI 54143
Application address: c/o Randy Neelis, Advisory Comm., 1230 13th St., Menominee, MI 49858, tel.: (906) 863-9951

Established in 1996 in WI.
Donor(s): Caroline A. Fernstrum, Robert W. Fernstrum.
Financial data (yr. ended 12/31/01): Grants paid, $28,363; assets, $576,731 (M); expenditures, $33,227; qualifying distributions, $29,200.
Limitations: Giving limited to Menominee, MI.
Application information: Application form not required.
Trustees: Richard Doust, Sean Fernstrum, John Reinke.
EIN: 396625465
Codes: GTI

57334—WISCONSIN

57334
Williams Family Foundation, Inc.
P.O. Box 8100
Janesville, WI 53547
Application address: 8925 Stateline Rd., South Beloit, IL 61080
Contact: Steven D. Williams, Pres.

Established in 1996 in WI.
Donor(s): Linda M. Williams, Steven D. Williams.
Financial data (yr. ended 12/31/01): Grants paid, $28,256; assets, $376,184 (M); gifts received, $21,000; expenditures, $31,717; qualifying distributions, $28,256.
Officers: Steven D. Williams, Pres. and Treas.; Linda M. Williams, V.P. and Secy.
Director: Christine M. Williams.
EIN: 391865458

57335
Hazelyn and Harold McComas Charitable Trust
c/o Foley & Lardner
777 E. Wisconsin Ave., Ste. 3500
Milwaukee, WI 53202-5367
Contact: Harrold J. McComas, Tr.

Established in 1986 in WI.
Donor(s): Harrold J. McComas, Hazelyn McComas.
Financial data (yr. ended 12/31/01): Grants paid, $28,000; assets, $531,025 (M); expenditures, $29,828; qualifying distributions, $28,143.
Limitations: Giving primarily in Milwaukee, WI.
Trustees: Harrold J. McComas, Hazelyn McComas.
EIN: 391562476

57336
Roy Whistler Foundation, Inc.
c/o Bank One Trust Co., N.A.
P.O. Box 1308
Milwaukee, WI 53201

Established in 1997 in IN.
Financial data (yr. ended 12/31/01): Grants paid, $28,000; assets, $584,941 (M); expenditures, $32,855; qualifying distributions, $28,000.
Limitations: Applications not accepted.
Application information: Contributes only to pre-selected organizations.
Officers: William Harris Whistler, Pres.; James N. Bemiller, V.P.; Richard A. Boehning, Secy.; Kurt E. Wilson, Treas.
Director: Mary A. Moore.
EIN: 352007510

57337
Anne M. Ruemler Memorial Foundation, Inc.
c/o Thompson & Coates, Ltd.
840 Lake Ave.
Racine, WI 53403-1517

Donor(s): Natalie A. Ruemler.
Financial data (yr. ended 09/30/01): Grants paid, $27,711; assets, $464,244 (M); expenditures, $31,770; qualifying distributions, $27,711.
Limitations: Applications not accepted.
Application information: Contributes only to pre-selected organizations.
Officers: Natalie A. Ruemler, Pres.; Joseph R. Hilmer, V.P. and Treas.; Stephen J. Smith, Secy.
EIN: 391488771

57338
George Colletti Family Foundation
c/o Virchow Krause/Russ Wolff, C.P.A.
P.O. Box 7398
Madison, WI 53707-7398

Established in 1997 in WI.
Donor(s): George Colletti, Jr.
Financial data (yr. ended 06/30/02): Grants paid, $27,625; assets, $468,405 (M); expenditures, $27,717; qualifying distributions, $27,625.
Limitations: Giving primarily in ME.
Executive Committee: Cynthia A. Bunz, Melanie A. Carpenter, George Colletti, Jr., Maria Colletti, Kristen Mae Heller, Kimberly J. Colletti Robertson.
EIN: 396682650

57339
Daniel W. Hoan Foundation, Inc.
c/o Firstar Trust Co., LC 4NE
P.O. Box 2043
Milwaukee, WI 53201-9116
Application address: 3060 N. Marietta Ave., Milwaukee, WI 53211
Contact: Daniel J. Steininger, Pres.

Financial data (yr. ended 12/31/01): Grants paid, $27,600; assets, $573,643 (M); expenditures, $39,578; qualifying distributions, $27,600.
Limitations: Giving primarily in Milwaukee, WI.
Officers and Directors:* Daniel J. Steininger,* Pres. and Treas.; Clayton H. Steininger,* V.P.; Judy Steininger,* Secy.; Tom O'Brien.
EIN: 396075895

57340
Streich Family Foundation, Inc.
1423 W. Westport Cir.
Mequon, WI 53092

Established in 1986 in WI.
Donor(s): Charles F. Streich, Elton F. Streich III, Helen A. Streich.
Financial data (yr. ended 12/31/01): Grants paid, $27,600; assets, $360,767 (M); gifts received, $1,230; expenditures, $27,890; qualifying distributions, $27,600.
Limitations: Applications not accepted. Giving primarily in Milwaukee, WI.
Application information: Contributes only to pre-selected organizations.
Officers and Directors:* Charles F. Streich,* Pres.; Elton F. Streich,* V.P.; Helen A. Streich,* Secy.
EIN: 391574612

57341
Mielcarek Family Foundation, Inc.
3139 Vinburn Rd.
Sun Prairie, WI 53590

Established in 2000 in WI.
Donor(s): Timothy A. Mielcarek, Beth A. Mielcarek.
Financial data (yr. ended 12/31/01): Grants paid, $27,500; assets, $362,114 (M); gifts received, $200,000; expenditures, $27,782; qualifying distributions, $27,500.
Limitations: Applications not accepted. Giving primarily in WI.
Application information: Contributes only to pre-selected organizations.
Officers: Timothy A. Mielcarek, Pres.; Beth A. Mielcarek, V.P. and Treas.; Rebecca Nelson, Secy.
EIN: 392008964

57342
Marathon Savings Foundation, Inc.
P.O. Box 1666
Wausau, WI 54402-1666
Contact: Tom Terwilliger, Pres.

Established in 1994 in WI.
Donor(s): Marathon Savings Bank.
Financial data (yr. ended 06/30/02): Grants paid, $27,370; assets, $39,744 (M); gifts received, $30,000; expenditures, $27,400; qualifying distributions, $27,400.
Limitations: Giving primarily in Wausau, WI.

Officers: Tom Terwilliger, Pres.; Paul Shore, V.P.; Wanda Lyon, Secy.-Treas.
EIN: 391803453
Codes: CS

57343
Abbotsford Story, Inc.
401 E. Spruce St.
Abbotsford, WI 54405 (715) 223-2345
Contact: Patrick D. McCrackin, Pres.

Established in 1985 in WI.
Donor(s): Abbotsford State Bank.
Financial data (yr. ended 12/31/01): Grants paid, $27,344; assets, $430,245 (M); gifts received, $94,800; expenditures, $28,381; qualifying distributions, $27,344.
Limitations: Giving limited to the Abbotsford and Wausau, WI, areas.
Officers and Directors:* Patrick D. McCrackin,* Pres. and Treas.; Dennis Kramer,* V.P.; Harold K. Christensen, Jr., Karl Dehn, James Lamont, Donald A. Meyer.
EIN: 391540288
Codes: CS, CD

57344
Pfister & Vogel Tanning Company, Inc. Foundation
c/o U.S. Bank
P.O. Box 2043, LC4NE
Milwaukee, WI 53201-9116
Application address: c/o Pfister & Vogel Tanning Co., Inc., 1531 N. Water St., Milwaukee, WI 53202

Donor(s): Pfister & Vogel Tanning Co., Inc.
Financial data (yr. ended 05/31/01): Grants paid, $27,250; assets, $500,444 (M); expenditures, $37,105; qualifying distributions, $30,063.
Limitations: Giving primarily in the Milwaukee County, WI, area.
Committee Members: Terrell C. Horne, Daniel J. Yakel.
Trustee: U.S. Bank.
EIN: 396036556
Codes: CS, CD, GTI

57345
The McGuire Family Foundation, Inc.
c/o Thomas J. McGuire
P.O. Box 493
Oshkosh, WI 54903-0493 (920) 233-2430
Contact: Kristi J. McGuire, Dir.

Established in 2000 in WI.
Donor(s): Thomas J. McGuire, Kristi J. McGuire.
Financial data (yr. ended 12/31/01): Grants paid, $27,021; assets, $70,385 (M); expenditures, $29,902; qualifying distributions, $27,021.
Limitations: Giving primarily in Oshkosh, WI.
Application information: Application form not required.
Directors: Kevin T. McGuire, Kristi J. McGuire, Thomas J. McGuire.
EIN: 391996965

57346
Schumacher-Weiherman Family Foundation
c/o Bank One Trust Co., N.A.
P.O. Box 1308
Milwaukee, WI 53201

Established in 1996 in WI.
Financial data (yr. ended 12/31/01): Grants paid, $27,000; assets, $621,152 (M); gifts received, $26,642; expenditures, $31,507; qualifying distributions, $27,000.
Limitations: Applications not accepted. Giving primarily in Valparaiso, IN and WI.

Application information: Contributes only to pre-selected organizations.
Trustees: Jon R. Schumacher, Judy A. Schumacher.
EIN: 396644183

57347
Heffel Memorial Scholarship Trust
P.O. Box 15
Evansville, WI 53536 (608) 882-4679
Application address: c/o Evansville High School, 420 S. 3rd St., Evansville, WI 53536
Contact: Randy Keister, Tr.

Established in 1998.
Financial data (yr. ended 12/31/01): Grants paid, $26,900; assets, $217,787 (M); expenditures, $29,289; qualifying distributions, $26,900.
Trustees: L. Prentice Eager, Ken Fenrick, Natalie Golz, Randy Keister.
EIN: 746451982

57348
William Higgins Trust for Avelena Fund
c/o Bank One Trust Group
P.O. Box 1308
Milwaukee, WI 53201-1308
Application address: c/o National City Bank, Indiana, Lebanon, IN 46052, tel.: (317) 482-3300
Contact: Robert A. Duff

Financial data (yr. ended 10/31/01): Grants paid, $26,839; assets, $304,375 (M); expenditures, $31,243; qualifying distributions, $26,601.
Limitations: Giving limited to IN.
Trustee: Bank One Trust Group.
EIN: 356009209
Codes: GTI

57349
Price Foundation, Inc.
10910 W. Lapham St.
West Allis, WI 53214-3899 (414) 778-0300
Contact: Glenn L. Price, Pres.

Financial data (yr. ended 12/31/01): Grants paid, $26,700; assets, $82,512 (M); gifts received, $50,000; expenditures, $26,700; qualifying distributions, $26,700.
Limitations: Giving primarily in Milwaukee, WI.
Officers and Directors:* Glenn L. Price,* Pres. and Treas.; Mary E. Price,* V.P. and Secy.; Walter P. Rynkiewicz.
EIN: 391044368

57350
Wilson Family Foundation
(Formerly Donald and Sharon Wilson Family Foundation)
c/o Donald S. Wilson
19160 Still Point Trail
Brookfield, WI 53045

Donor(s): Donald S. Wilson.
Financial data (yr. ended 12/31/01): Grants paid, $26,650; assets, $2,796 (M); expenditures, $26,679; qualifying distributions, $26,650.
Limitations: Applications not accepted. Giving primarily in WI.
Application information: Contributes only to pre-selected organizations.
Trustees: Jennifer L. Healy, Katherine B. Otto, Bradley J. Wilson, Donald S. Wilson.
EIN: 391837871

57351
Harlan, Ruby & Phil E. Ott Scholarship Trust
(also known as Phil E. Ott Scholarships)
c/o Bank One Trust Co., N.A.
P.O. Box 1308
Milwaukee, WI 53201-1308
Application address: c/o George Stone, Supt., Central Noble, 200 E. Main St., Albion, IN 46701, tel.: (219) 636-2175

Established in 1988 in IN.
Donor(s): Ruby Ott.‡
Financial data (yr. ended 12/31/00): Grants paid, $26,556; assets, $598,825 (M); gifts received, $94,255; expenditures, $58,977; qualifying distributions, $27,972.
Limitations: Giving limited to IN.
Application information: Application form required.
Trustee: Bank One, N.A.
EIN: 356455490
Codes: GTI

57352
Jonathan D. Brege Memorial Foundation
c/o Bank One, Trust Tax
P.O. Box 1308
Milwaukee, WI 53201-1308
Application address: 5224 Byron Rd., Corunna, MI 48817
Contact: Donald R. Brege

Donor(s): Donald R. Brege.
Financial data (yr. ended 09/30/01): Grants paid, $26,500; assets, $439,875 (M); gifts received, $13,000; expenditures, $31,595; qualifying distributions, $28,075.
Limitations: Giving limited to MI.
Trustee: Bank One.
EIN: 386477703
Codes: GTI

57353
Charles Eckburg Foundation, Inc.
c/o Wells Fargo Bank Wisconsin, N.A.
P.O. Box 171, 636 Wisconsin Ave.
Sheboygan, WI 53082-0171
Application address: c/o University of Wisconsin, Madison, 600 Highland Ave., Madison, WI 53792
Contact: Vivian M. Littlefield, Pres.

Established in 1996 in WI.
Financial data (yr. ended 12/31/01): Grants paid, $26,366; assets, $970,476 (M); expenditures, $34,704; qualifying distributions, $28,786.
Limitations: Giving limited to WI.
Officers and Directors:* Vivian M. Littlefield,* Pres.; Douglas L. Rouse, V.P.; Ronald P. Dales,* Secy.; Jon C. Keckonen,* Treas.
Trustee: Wells Fargo Bank Wisconsin, N.A.
EIN: 391837809

57354
Jennifer Friedman Hillis Family Foundation, Inc.
951 E. Wye Ln.
Milwaukee, WI 53217
Contact: Jennifer Freidman Hillis, Dir.

Established in 1999 in WI.
Financial data (yr. ended 12/31/01): Grants paid, $26,314; assets, $1,001,854 (M); expenditures, $33,489; qualifying distributions, $26,314.
Limitations: Giving limited to Milwaukee, WI.
Directors: Jennifer Freidman Hillis, Robert Joseph Hillis, Elizabeth Friedman O'Connor.
EIN: 582464615

57355
Grootemaat Foundation, Inc.
9500 W. Hawthorne Rd.
Mequon, WI 53097
Contact: James E. Grootemaat, Pres.

Established in 1989.
Donor(s): James E. Grootemaat, Sally W. Grootemaat.‡
Financial data (yr. ended 12/31/01): Grants paid, $26,285; assets, $239,732 (M); expenditures, $29,418; qualifying distributions, $26,285.
Limitations: Applications not accepted. Giving limited to Milwaukee, WI.
Application information: Contributes only to pre-selected organizations.
Officers and Directors:* James E. Grootemaat,* Pres. and Treas.; Joan R. Grootemaat,* V.P. and Secy.-Treas.
EIN: 391051358

57356
Annabel Taylor Trust
c/o Bank One Trust Co., N.A.
P.O. Box 1308
Milwaukee, WI 53201-1308 (414) 765-2769

Financial data (yr. ended 12/31/01): Grants paid, $26,176; assets, $720,060 (M); expenditures, $32,862; qualifying distributions, $26,176.
Limitations: Applications not accepted. Giving limited to WI.
Application information: Contributes only to pre-selected organizations.
Trustee: Bank One Trust Co., N.A.
EIN: 396146785

57357
Deena Hatch Foundation
W5936 County Rd. F
Necedah, WI 54646

Established in 1998 in WI.
Donor(s): William Hatch, Sandra Hatch.
Financial data (yr. ended 06/30/02): Grants paid, $26,100; assets, $572,664 (M); gifts received, $70,500; expenditures, $31,942; qualifying distributions, $26,100.
Limitations: Applications not accepted. Giving primarily in WI.
Application information: Contributes only to pre-selected organizations.
Trustees: William T. Curran, Sandra L. Hatch, William G. Hatch.
EIN: 391943131

57358
William & Virginia E. Oosterhuis Charitable Trust
c/o U.S. Bank
P.O. Box 2043
Milwaukee, WI 53201-9116

Established in 1999 in FL.
Donor(s): Firstar Bank, N.A.
Financial data (yr. ended 05/31/01): Grants paid, $26,016; assets, $620,433 (M); gifts received, $546; expenditures, $33,360; qualifying distributions, $26,016.
Limitations: Applications not accepted.
Application information: Contributes only to pre-selected organizations.
Trustee: U.S. Bank.
EIN: 656304345

57359
Jean B. & E. T. Juday Gift Fund
6850 Anderson Ln.
Land O'Lakes, WI 54540
Application address: P.O. Box 597, Land O'Lakes, WI 54540
Contact: Patricia A. Juday, Tr.

Established in 1986 in IL.
Financial data (yr. ended 11/30/01): Grants paid, $26,000; assets, $482,785 (M); gifts received, $35,009; expenditures, $43,183; qualifying distributions, $26,000.
Limitations: Giving primarily in DeKalb County, IL.
Application information: Application form not required.
Trustees: Susan J. Golding, Patricia A. Juday, Sally A. Juday, Christine Larson Lamb.
EIN: 366850433

57360
David E. Thomas Trust
c/o Louise Policello
W7364 Creek Rd.
Wausaukee, WI 54177

Established in 1999 in WI.
Financial data (yr. ended 12/31/99): Grants paid, $26,000; assets, $1,084,167 (M); expenditures, $32,493; qualifying distributions, $26,000.
Limitations: Applications not accepted.
Trustee: Louise Policello.
EIN: 396156536

57361
The Vinger Family Foundation
c/o Jacobus Wealth Mgmt., Inc.
2323 N. Mayfair Rd., Ste. 240
Milwaukee, WI 53226-1506 (414) 475-6565

Established in 1998 in WI.
Donor(s): Norma J. Vinger.
Financial data (yr. ended 12/31/00): Grants paid, $26,000; assets, $896,018 (M); gifts received, $402,247; expenditures, $35,141; qualifying distributions, $22,073.
Limitations: Giving primarily in southwestern WI.
Trustees: Christopher A. Vinger, Donald Vinger, Eric A. Vinger, Norma J. Vinger.
EIN: 396700438

57362
Donald and Joyce Schuenke Charitable Fund
13600 Park Circle N.
Elm Grove, WI 53122

Established in 1986 in WI.
Donor(s): Donald J. Schuenke, Joyce A. Schuenke.
Financial data (yr. ended 12/31/01): Grants paid, $25,907; assets, $632,943 (M); expenditures, $48,887; qualifying distributions, $25,907.
Limitations: Applications not accepted. Giving primarily in Milwaukee, WI.
Application information: Contributes only to pre-selected organizations.
Trustees: Donald J. Schuenke, Joyce A. Schuenke.
EIN: 391576781

57363
Prohaska Scholarship Foundation
c/o Selection Comm.
132 W. State St.
Medford, WI 54451

Donor(s): Joseph Prohaska, Betty Prohaska.
Financial data (yr. ended 12/31/00): Grants paid, $25,750; assets, $364,094 (M); expenditures, $27,785; qualifying distributions, $25,498.
Limitations: Giving limited to residents of Medford, WI.
Selection Committee: Betty Prohaska, David Prohaska, Joseph Prohaska, Fred Schroeder, Principal, Medford High School.
Trustee: Mid-Wisconsin Trust.
EIN: 391712984
Codes: GTI

57364
Alverda Kegler Charitable Irrevocable Trust
c/o U.S. Bank
P.O. Box 2043, LC 4NE
Milwaukee, WI 53201-9116

Established in 1996 in IA.
Financial data (yr. ended 12/31/00): Grants paid, $25,654; assets, $723,832 (M); expenditures, $52,039; qualifying distributions, $28,886.
Limitations: Applications not accepted. Giving on a national basis.
Application information: Contributes only to pre-selected organizations.
Trustee: U.S. Bank.
EIN: 426410140

57365
Herbert & Fern Elliott Family Foundation, Inc.
c/o Lakeside Oil Co.
P.O. Box 240500
Milwaukee, WI 53224 (414) 540-4000
Contact: William Elliott, Dir.

Financial data (yr. ended 12/31/01): Grants paid, $25,480; assets, $432,447 (M); gifts received, $11,865; expenditures, $27,385; qualifying distributions, $25,480.
Limitations: Giving primarily in WI.
Application information: Application form not required.
Directors: Fern Elliott, Herbert H. Elliott, William Elliott.
EIN: 396042920

57366
Veronica Willo Scholarship Fund
c/o Bank One Trust Co., N.A.
P.O. Box 1308
Milwaukee, WI 53201-0013
Application address: c/o Relationship Mgr., P.O. Box 711075, Columbus, OH 43271-1075
Contact: Robert Clark, Admin., Bank One Ohio Trust Co., N.A.

Financial data (yr. ended 12/31/00): Grants paid, $25,354; assets, $230,776 (M); expenditures, $25,854; qualifying distributions, $24,469.
Limitations: Giving limited to Mahoning County, OH.
Application information: Students are recommended by principals of Mahoning County high schools.
Trustee: Bank One Trust Co., N.A.
EIN: 346577619
Codes: GTI

57367
Alois A. and Nina M. Fix Scholarship Fund
c/o John W. Drew
1730 Lakeview Dr.
Tomah, WI 54660-1016
Application address: c/o Ronald Geurkink, Counselor, Tomah Senior High School, Tomah, WI 54660, tel.: (608) 372-5986

Established in 1980 in WI.
Financial data (yr. ended 07/31/00): Grants paid, $25,300; assets, $385,976 (M); expenditures, $29,895; qualifying distributions, $26,805.
Limitations: Giving limited to residents of Tomah, WI.
Application information: Application form required.
Trustee: John W. Drew.
EIN: 396257879
Codes: GTI

57368
Otto Villwock Medical Educational Scholarship Fund
c/o Bank One Trust Co., N.A.
P.O. Box 1308
Milwaukee, WI 53201-1308
Application address: c/o Financial Aid Offices at Case Western Reserve University, University of Wisconsin Medical School, and University of Cincinnati Medical School

Financial data (yr. ended 05/31/00): Grants paid, $25,170; assets, $416,976 (M); expenditures, $29,968; qualifying distributions, $21,433.
Application information: Application form not required.
Trustee: Bank One Trust Co., N.A.
EIN: 510172011
Codes: GTI

57369
Schmidt Family Charitable Trust
P.O. Box 700034
Oostburg, WI 53070-0034

Established in 1997 in WI.
Donor(s): Richard L. Schmidt.
Financial data (yr. ended 12/31/01): Grants paid, $25,066; assets, $238,308 (M); expenditures, $25,066; qualifying distributions, $25,066.
Limitations: Applications not accepted.
Application information: Contributes only to pre-selected organizations.
Trustees: Richard A. Schmidt, Sandra L. Schmidt.
EIN: 396647942

57370
Evelyn M. Bach/Amil C. Bach Foundation, Ltd.
311 Main St.
La Crosse, WI 54601 (608) 782-1148
Contact: Gary M. Veldey, Treas.

Established in 1995 in WI.
Donor(s): Evelyn Bach.
Financial data (yr. ended 12/31/01): Grants paid, $25,000; assets, $593,595 (M); gifts received, $62,617; expenditures, $27,881; qualifying distributions, $21,091.
Limitations: Giving primarily in La Crosse, WI.
Officers and Directors:* Evelyn M. Bach,* Pres.; William J. Sauer,* Secy.; Gary M. Veldey,* Treas.
Trustee: North Central Trust Co.
EIN: 391830917

57371
The Gustav and Gladys Kindt Foundation
111 E. Wisconsin Ave., Ste. 2100
Milwaukee, WI 53202 (414) 273-2100
Contact: John B. Haydon, Tr.

Established in 1998 in WI.
Donor(s): Gladys R. Kindt.
Financial data (yr. ended 12/31/01): Grants paid, $25,000; assets, $2,407,681 (M); gifts received, $2,419,605; expenditures, $34,579; qualifying distributions, $29,927.
Limitations: Giving primarily in MA, MN, and WI.
Trustees: John B. Haydon, Alan C. Kindt, Donna Kindt.
EIN: 391971724

57372
Regal-Beloit Charitable Foundation
c/o Ken Kaplan
200 State St.
Beloit, WI 53511 (608) 364-8800

Established in 1995 in WI.

Donor(s): Regal-Beloit Corp.
Financial data (yr. ended 12/31/01): Grants paid, $25,000; assets, $268,157 (M); expenditures, $26,423; qualifying distributions, $25,000.
Limitations: Applications not accepted. Giving primarily in Janesville and Beloit, WI.
Application information: Contributes only to pre-selected organizations.
Officers: James L. Packard, Chair.; Kenneth F. Kaplan, Secy.-Treas.
Trustees: Frank E. Bauchiero, J. Reed Coleman, John M. Eldred, Stephen N. Graff, Paul W. Jones, G. Frederick Kasten, Jr., John A. McKay.
EIN: 391814812
Codes: CS, CD

57373
Frederick J. Hilgen Foundation, Ltd.
c/o Port Washington State Bank
206 N. Franklin St.
Port Washington, WI 53074
Application address: c/o Cedarburg Public School System, Cedarburg, WI 53012

Financial data (yr. ended 12/31/01): Grants paid, $24,750; assets, $251,106 (M); gifts received, $25; expenditures, $33,179; qualifying distributions, $25,650.
Limitations: Giving primarily in WI.
Application information: Application form required.
Officers and Directors:* Burnetta Y. Hilgen,* Pres.; John Vollmar,* V.P.; Roy C. LaBudde, Secy. and Mgr.; Frank M. Metz,* Treas.; Robert H. Dries, Jr.
EIN: 391287084

57374
Melanie V. Chmielewski Educational Foundation
2448 S. 102nd St., Ste. 170
West Allis, WI 53227
Contact: Alfred A. Drosen, Jr., Tr.

Financial data (yr. ended 12/31/01): Grants paid, $24,550; assets, $122,822 (M); expenditures, $29,413; qualifying distributions, $24,550.
Trustee: Alfred A. Drosen, Jr.
EIN: 396531505
Codes: GTI

57375
Endres Manufacturing Foundation, Inc.
c/o Endres Manufacturing Co.
2621 Park St.
Middleton, WI 53562-1756 (608) 836-1751
Contact: Diane Ballweg, Pres.

Established in 1995 in WI.
Donor(s): Endres Manufacturing Co.
Financial data (yr. ended 12/31/01): Grants paid, $24,300; assets, $652,472 (M); gifts received, $200,000; expenditures, $29,057; qualifying distributions, $24,300.
Limitations: Giving primarily in the southern WI area.
Application information: Application form required.
Officers: Diane Ballweg, Pres.; Ronald Endres, V.P.
Director: Alan Wolfe.
EIN: 391839327
Codes: CS, CD

57376
Loretta Herkenhoff Charitable Trust
c/o Bank One Trust Co., N.A.
P.O. Box 1308
Milwaukee, WI 53201
Application address: c/o Edward S. Noble, Montague and Moul, P.O. Box 331, 146 E. Spring St., St. Marys, OH, 45881, tel.: (419) 394-7441

Established in 1989 in OH.
Donor(s): Loretta Herkenhoff Trust.
Financial data (yr. ended 12/31/00): Grants paid, $24,200; assets, $911,483 (M); expenditures, $35,963; qualifying distributions, $24,200.
Limitations: Giving primarily in Minster, OH.
Trustee: Bank One Trust Co., N.A.
EIN: 316344461

57377
Reed Coleman Family Foundation
201 Waubesa St.
P.O. Box 3037
Madison, WI 53704

Established in 1997 in WI.
Donor(s): Jerome Reed Coleman.
Financial data (yr. ended 12/31/01): Grants paid, $24,000; assets, $356,884 (M); expenditures, $42,599; qualifying distributions, $24,000.
Limitations: Applications not accepted. Giving primarily in Seattle, WA and Madison, WI.
Application information: Contributes only to pre-selected organizations.
Officer: Audra Coleman Brown, Secy.
Directors: Jerome Reed Coleman, Ellen Coleman Riese.
Trustee: Susan Coleman Bennett.
EIN: 396651358

57378
Eugene H. Leslie Trust
c/o Bank One Trust Co., N.A.
P.O. Box 1308
Milwaukee, WI 53201

Financial data (yr. ended 12/31/00): Grants paid, $24,000; assets, $824,592 (M); expenditures, $30,928; qualifying distributions, $26,338.
Limitations: Applications not accepted. Giving primarily in Ann Arbor, MI.
Application information: Contributes only to pre-selected organizations.
Trustee: Bank One Trust Co., N.A.
EIN: 386377398

57379
Florence Lindsay Trust
c/o U.S. Bank
P.O. Box 2043
Milwaukee, WI 53201-2043
Application address: P.O. Box 3013, Cedar Rapids, IA, 52406
Contact: Carol Edwards, Trust Off., U.S. Bank

Financial data (yr. ended 03/31/02): Grants paid, $24,000; assets, $459,973 (M); expenditures, $29,427; qualifying distributions, $24,000.
Limitations: Giving primarily in IA.
Application information: Application form not required.
Trustee: U.S. Bank.
EIN: 237137537

57380
The Ehrlich Family Foundation, Inc.
c/o Clifton Gunderson, LLC
P.O. Box 1347
Racine, WI 53401-1347

Established in 1996 in WI.
Donor(s): Phydele G. Ehrlich.
Financial data (yr. ended 06/30/01): Grants paid, $23,950; assets, $571,847 (M); gifts received, $101,567; expenditures, $26,590; qualifying distributions, $23,559.
Limitations: Applications not accepted. Giving limited to WI.
Application information: Contributes only to pre-selected organizations.
Officers: Phydele G. Ehrlich, Chair. and Pres.; Susan E. Smith, V.P.; Robin J. Eastman, Secy.; James C. Small, Treas.
EIN: 391893203

57381
Harry J. Schofield Foundation, Ltd.
c/o Henry E. Fuldner, Godfrey & Kahn, SC
780 N. Water St.
Milwaukee, WI 53202

Financial data (yr. ended 12/31/01): Grants paid, $23,804; assets, $554,928 (M); expenditures, $26,871; qualifying distributions, $23,804.
Limitations: Applications not accepted. Giving limited to Milwaukee, WI.
Application information: Contributes only to pre-selected organizations.
Officers and Directors:* Helen E. Poehls,* Pres.; Harry Russell, V.P.; Andrew R. Lauritzen,* Secy.; Henry E. Fuldner,* Treas.; Donald J. Dries, Harvey A. Poehls, Kenneth E. Rich.
EIN: 391286691

57382
Hockerman Charitable Trust
c/o George A. Evans
735 N. Water St.
Milwaukee, WI 53202

Established in 1991 in WI.
Financial data (yr. ended 12/31/01): Grants paid, $23,732; assets, $125,763 (M); gifts received, $10,000; expenditures, $23,864; qualifying distributions, $23,732.
Limitations: Applications not accepted. Giving primarily in Milwaukee, WI.
Application information: Contributes only to pre-selected organizations.
Trustees: George A. Evans, Jr., Gary C. Hockerman, Glen A. Hockerman.
EIN: 396548548

57383
Gehl Foundation, Inc.
143 Water St.
West Bend, WI 53095-3415 (262) 334-9461
Contact: Kenneth P. Hahn, Treas.

Established in 1964 in WI.
Donor(s): Gehl Co.
Financial data (yr. ended 12/31/01): Grants paid, $23,584; assets, $766,060 (M); expenditures, $23,250; qualifying distributions, $23,250.
Limitations: Giving primarily in areas of company operations.
Application information: Application form not required.
Officers: William D. Gehl, Pres.; Michael J. Mulcahy, V.P. and Secy.; Kenneth P. Hahn, Treas.
EIN: 391039217
Codes: CS, CD, GTI

57384
Vogt Foundation
c/o Bank One Trust Co., N.A.
P.O. Box 1308
Milwaukee, WI 53210
Application address: c/o Vogt Industries, 4542 Roger B. Chaffee Blvd., S.E., Grand Rapids, MI 49548-7522
Contact: James B. Vogt, Pres.

Financial data (yr. ended 12/31/01): Grants paid, $23,500; assets, $626,787 (M); expenditures, $38,472; qualifying distributions, $29,005.
Limitations: Giving primarily in Grand Rapids, MI.
Officers: James B. Vogt, Pres.; Frederick J. Vogt, Jr., V.P.; Hillary F. Snell, Secy.; Joseph McCormick, Treas.
Trustee: Charlotte E. Vogt.
EIN: 386083816

57385
Norman Miller Family Foundation, Inc.
P.O. Box 3458
Green Bay, WI 54303-0458

Donor(s): Norman Miller.
Financial data (yr. ended 09/30/01): Grants paid, $23,475; assets, $863,639 (M); gifts received, $84,652; expenditures, $27,094; qualifying distributions, $24,380.
Limitations: Applications not accepted. Giving primarily in Green Bay, WI.
Application information: Contributes only to pre-selected organizations.
Officers: Norman Miller, Pres.; William Miller, V.P.; Susan Miller Neutzel, Secy.; Shirlyn Miller, Treas.
EIN: 396098847

57386
William J. Lorang Trust
c/o Bank One, N.A.
P.O. Box 1308
Milwaukee, WI 53201

Financial data (yr. ended 12/31/01): Grants paid, $23,022; assets, $564,482 (M); expenditures, $28,197; qualifying distributions, $24,697.
Limitations: Applications not accepted. Giving primarily in Elgin, IL.
Application information: Contributes only to pre-selected organizations.
Trustee: Bank One, N.A.
EIN: 366739565

57387
Charles H. Phipps Foundation
c/o Marshall & Ilsley Bank
1000 N. Water St.
Milwaukee, WI 53202
Application address: 6800 LBJ Fwy., Ste. 155, Dallas, TX 75240-6511
Contact: Charles H. Phipps, Pres.

Established in 1997.
Donor(s): Charles H. Phipps.
Financial data (yr. ended 04/30/02): Grants paid, $22,950; assets, $387,641 (M); expenditures, $24,580; qualifying distributions, $22,950.
Limitations: Giving primarily in Dallas, TX.
Officer and Trustee:* Charles H. Phipps,* Pres.
EIN: 752750645

57388
The Joan C. & Richard A. Van Deuren Family Foundation, Inc.
c/o R. Van Deuren
1000 N. Water St., Ste. 2100
Milwaukee, WI 53202-3197

Established in 1998 in WI.
Donor(s): Richard Van Deuren.
Financial data (yr. ended 06/30/01): Grants paid, $22,850; assets, $1,023,580 (M); expenditures, $23,619; qualifying distributions, $22,850.
Limitations: Applications not accepted. Giving primarily in MA and WI.
Application information: Contributes only to pre-selected organizations.
Officers: Richard Van Deuren, Pres. and Treas.; Susan V. Donovan, V.P.; Pamela K. Linke, Secy.
EIN: 391948321

57389
Emmet C. Grafton Trust
c/o Bank One Trust Co., N.A.
P.O. Box 1308
Milwaukee, WI 53201

Financial data (yr. ended 12/31/99): Grants paid, $22,702; assets, $226,917 (M); expenditures, $26,564; qualifying distributions, $22,823.
Limitations: Applications not accepted. Giving limited to Salineville, OH.
Application information: Contributes only to pre-selected organizations.
Trustee: Bank One Trust Co., N.A.
EIN: 346764768

57390
Susan & Leander Jennings Foundation, Inc.
230 E. MacArthur Rd.
Milwaukee, WI 53217 (414) 352-1791
Contact: Susan M. Jennings, V.P.

Established in 1996 in WI.
Donor(s): Leander Jennings, Susan Jennings.
Financial data (yr. ended 12/31/01): Grants paid, $22,500; assets, $216,097 (M); expenditures, $24,575; qualifying distributions, $22,500.
Limitations: Giving primarily in Milwaukee, WI.
Officers: Leander Jennings, Pres. and Treas.; Susan M. Jennings, V.P.; Patricia J. Ullrich, Secy.
EIN: 391868601

57391
Kaufan & Coffman Scholarship Fund
c/o Bank One Trust Co., N.A.
P.O. Box 13
Milwaukee, WI 53201
Application address: 416 W. Jefferson St., Louisville, KY 40202
Contact: Debra Kennedy

Established in 1999 in KY.
Financial data (yr. ended 12/31/00): Grants paid, $22,500; assets, $932,911 (M); expenditures, $30,807; qualifying distributions, $24,338.
Limitations: Giving primarily in Louisville, KY.
Application information: Applicants must be residents of the Louisville, KY area and attained the age of 30 prior to beginning of first school year of study towards a degree.
Trustee: Bank One Trust Co., N.A.
EIN: 616252774

57392
Lasater Family Charitable Trust
c/o Bank One Trust Co., N.A.
P.O. Box 1308
Milwaukee, WI 53201
Application address: c/o Christie L. Savage, 175 Sheridan Rd., Kenilworth, IL 60043

Established in 1988 in IL.
Donor(s): Robert L. Lasater.
Financial data (yr. ended 12/31/01): Grants paid, $22,500; assets, $468,496 (M); expenditures, $25,038; qualifying distributions, $23,101.
Limitations: Giving primarily in Chicago, IL.
Application information: Application form not required.
Trustees: Bradley L. Savage, Christie L. Savage.
EIN: 366848629

57393
Appleton Mills Foundation
c/o Bank One Trust Co., N.A.
P.O. Box 1308
Milwaukee, WI 53201
Application address: Thomas S. Scheetz, c/o Appleton Mills, P.O. Box 789, Neenah, WI 54956

Donor(s): Appleton Mills.
Financial data (yr. ended 09/30/01): Grants paid, $22,225; assets, $34,541 (M); expenditures, $23,704; qualifying distributions, $23,162.
Limitations: Giving limited to WI.
Trustee: Bank One Trust Co., N.A.
EIN: 396087213
Codes: CS, CD

57394
T & O Foundation, Inc.
6101 N. Shore Dr.
Eau Claire, WI 54703

Established in 1987 in WI.
Donor(s): David B. Westrate.
Financial data (yr. ended 11/30/01): Grants paid, $22,100; assets, $5,499,630 (M); expenditures, $63,468; qualifying distributions, $22,100.
Limitations: Applications not accepted. Giving on a national basis.
Application information: Contributes only to pre-selected organizations.
Officers: David B. Westrate, Pres.; Mike Westrate, V.P.; Brian Westrate, Secy.-Treas.
EIN: 391615711

57395
Borg Foundation, Inc.
c/o Frank W. Hammett
106 Eagle Pt. Dr.
Delavan, WI 53115-2100

Financial data (yr. ended 12/31/01): Grants paid, $22,000; assets, $505,023 (M); expenditures, $33,506; qualifying distributions, $22,000.
Limitations: Applications not accepted.
Application information: Contributes only to pre-selected organizations.
Officers: Frank W. Hammett, Pres.; Wilbur J. Scott, V.P.
Director: Eugene F. Groth.
EIN: 366047046

57396
The Lynne and Ben Exley IV Charitable Trust, Inc.
c/o Bank One Trust Co., N.A.
P.O. Box 1308
Milwaukee, WI 53201

Established in 1998 in WV.
Financial data (yr. ended 12/31/01): Grants paid, $22,000; assets, $220,520 (M); expenditures, $23,496; qualifying distributions, $22,951.
Limitations: Applications not accepted. Giving primarily in WV.
Application information: Contributes only to pre-selected organizations.
Officer: Ben Exley IV, Pres.
EIN: 550764386

57397
Garver Memorial Trust
c/o Marshall & Ilsley Bank
1000 N. Water St.
Milwaukee, WI 53202
Application address: 315 E. Main St., Stoughton, WI 53589
Contact: Anders Birkeland, Tr.

Financial data (yr. ended 12/31/01): Grants paid, $22,000; assets, $154,539 (M); expenditures, $28,351; qualifying distributions, $23,004.
Limitations: Giving primarily in the Madison, WI, area.
Trustees: Anders Birkeland, Marshall & Ilsley Bank.
EIN: 396084860

57398
Laird Youth Leadership Foundation, Inc.
411 Greenbriar Ave.
Stevens Point, WI 54481
Application address: c/o U.W.S.P. Foundation, 2100 Main St., Stevens Point, WI 54481

Donor(s): Melvin Laird, David Laird, M.D.
Financial data (yr. ended 12/31/01): Grants paid, $22,000; assets, $267,886 (M); gifts received, $12,000; expenditures, $23,258; qualifying distributions, $22,000.
Limitations: Giving primarily in WI.
Application information: Application form required.
Officers: John O. Laird, Pres.; Robert F. Froehlke, V.P.; John H. Dressendorfer, Secy.; David M. Laird, Treas.
Directors: Karen Engelhard, David Laird, M.D., Melvin R. Laird, Vanessa A. Laird, Alison Laird Large, Russell Lewis, George E. Magnin, Raymond D. Nass.
EIN: 396104415

57399
Pax Am Foundation
N591 County Pl.
Coon Valley, WI 54623

Established in 1997 in WI.
Donor(s): Dawn Smith Hundt, Vincent G. Hundt.
Financial data (yr. ended 12/31/01): Grants paid, $22,000; assets, $347,253 (M); expenditures, $22,764; qualifying distributions, $21,952.
Limitations: Applications not accepted.
Application information: Contributes only to pre-selected organizations.
Trustees: Dawn Smith Hundt, Vincent G. Hundt.
EIN: 396681135

57400
J. F. Ahern Company Foundation, Inc.
855 Morris St.
Fond du Lac, WI 54935 (920) 921-9020
Contact: Michael H. Krueger, Secy.

Established in 1989 in WI.
Donor(s): J.F. Ahern Co.
Financial data (yr. ended 06/30/01): Grants paid, $21,800; assets, $331,626 (M); gifts received, $30,000; expenditures, $22,008; qualifying distributions, $21,800.
Limitations: Giving primarily in IA, northern IL, eastern MO, eastern NE, and WI.
Application information: Application form not required.
Officers and Directors:* John E. Ahern III,* Pres.; Michael H. Krueger,* Secy.; Alan R. Fox,* Treas.
EIN: 391667434
Codes: CS, CD

57401
Henry H. Uihlein, Sr. and Marion (Polly) S. Uihlein Foundation, Inc.
(Formerly Herman A. Uihlein, Sr. & Claudia Holt Uihlein Foundation, Inc.)
c/o Claudia Holt Uihlein
P.O. Box 245040
Milwaukee, WI 53224-9540

Donor(s): Henry H. Uihlein, Sr.
Financial data (yr. ended 10/31/01): Grants paid, $21,750; assets, $117,254 (M); gifts received, $20,000; expenditures, $22,904; qualifying distributions, $21,750.
Limitations: Applications not accepted. Giving primarily in Milwaukee, WI.
Application information: Contributes only to pre-selected organizations.
Officers: Henry H. Uihlein, Jr., Pres.; Henry H. Uihlein, Sr., V.P.; Richard Uihlein, Secy.; Ralph C. Insbusch, Jr., Treas.
Directors: James C. Uihlein, Phillip Uihlein.
EIN: 396077488

57402
Kenneth & Mary Lee Jacobs Charitable Trust
c/o Foley & Lardner
777 E. Wisconsin Ave.
Milwaukee, WI 53202-5367

Established in 1994 in WI.
Donor(s): Mary Lee C. Jacobs.
Financial data (yr. ended 12/31/01): Grants paid, $21,570; assets, $57,513 (M); expenditures, $22,560; qualifying distributions, $22,036.
Limitations: Applications not accepted.
Application information: Contributes only to pre-selected organizations.
Trustees: Kenneth W. Jacobs, Jr., Mary Lee C. Jacobs.
EIN: 396564554

57403
Waverly Woods Charitable Foundation, Inc.
1781 E. Fence Lake Rd.
Minocqua, WI 54548

Established in 1999 in WI.
Financial data (yr. ended 12/31/01): Grants paid, $21,500; assets, $126,062 (M); expenditures, $21,640; qualifying distributions, $21,500.
Limitations: Applications not accepted. Giving primarily in WI.
Application information: Contributes only to pre-selected organizations.
Trustee: William Vickerstaff.
EIN: 391953334

57404
Miller Scholarship Trust
c/o Bank One, N.A.
P.O. Box 1308
Milwaukee, WI 53201

Established in 1989 in IL.
Financial data (yr. ended 12/31/01): Grants paid, $21,337; assets, $642,570 (M); expenditures, $27,262; qualifying distributions, $23,087.
Limitations: Giving limited to residents of Astoria, Canton, and Lewistown, IL.
Application information: Application form required.
Trustee: Bank One, N.A.
EIN: 376280528
Codes: GTI

57405
John Alvin Halverson Scholarship
c/o Marshall & Ilsley Bank
P.O. Box 2980
Milwaukee, WI 53201
Application address: c/o Marshall & Ilsley Bank, 401 N. Segoe Rd., Ste. 2N, Madison, WI 53708, tel.: (608) 232-2000
Contact: Sharon Blank, Trust Off.

Established in 1994.
Financial data (yr. ended 12/31/01): Grants paid, $21,333; assets, $19,251 (M); expenditures, $22,669; qualifying distributions, $21,305.
Limitations: Giving limited to residents of Iowa County, IA.
Trustee: Marshall & Ilsley Bank.
EIN: 391749711
Codes: GTI

57406
Hincke-Evans Charitable Foundation, Inc.
1201 Papoose Lake Rd.
Manitowish Waters, WI 54545

Financial data (yr. ended 12/31/01): Grants paid, $21,000; assets, $218,377 (M); expenditures, $21,868; qualifying distributions, $21,000.
Limitations: Applications not accepted. Giving primarily in IL.
Application information: Contributes only to pre-selected organizations.
Officers: Anne H. Evans, Pres.; H. Parker Sharpe, Secy.-Treas.
Director: Mildred C. Sharpe.
EIN: 363487230

57407
Al Hodes Charitable Trust
c/o Marshall & Ilsley Bank
P.O. Box 2980
Milwaukee, WI 53201

Established in 1988 in WI.
Donor(s): Al Hodes.‡
Financial data (yr. ended 06/30/02): Grants paid, $21,000; assets, $354,571 (M); expenditures, $26,320; qualifying distributions, $20,859.
Limitations: Applications not accepted. Giving limited to Wausau, WI.
Application information: Recipients selected by faculty.
Trustee: Marshall & Ilsley Bank.
EIN: 396480058
Codes: GTI

57408
The Lai Family Foundation
19660 Killarney Way
Brookfield, WI 53045 (262) 786-1053
Contact: Helen L. Lai, Dir.

Established in MI in 1997.
Donor(s): N.C. Joseph Lai, Helen L. Lai, Christopher Lai, Thomas Lai.
Financial data (yr. ended 10/31/01): Grants paid, $21,000; assets, $831,110 (M); expenditures, $26,155; qualifying distributions, $21,000.
Limitations: Giving primarily in Milwaukee, WI.
Application information: Application form required.
Directors: Christopher T. Lai, Helen L. Lai, N.C. Joseph Lai, Thomas T. Lai.
EIN: 391892636

57409
Robert K. and Joyce R. Cope Foundation
c/o Wisniewski Law Off.
812 E. State St.
Milwaukee, WI 53202
Contact: E. Jane Bekos, Tr.

Established in 1993 in WI.
Financial data (yr. ended 05/31/02): Grants paid, $20,800; assets, $936,430 (M); expenditures, $75,122; qualifying distributions, $20,800.
Limitations: Giving limited to WI.
Trustees: E. Jane Bekos, Franchion K. LeMere, Keith E. LeMere.
EIN: 391719598

57410
John M. Reed Trust
c/o Bank One Trust Co., N.A.
P.O. Box 1308
Milwaukee, WI 53201

Financial data (yr. ended 12/31/01): Grants paid, $20,741; assets, $305,799 (M); expenditures, $25,498; qualifying distributions, $20,741.
Limitations: Applications not accepted. Giving primarily in Lexington, KY.
Application information: Contributes only to pre-selected organizations.
Trustee: Bank One Trust Co., N.A.
EIN: 616121846

57411
Peter A. Fergus Foundation, Inc.
1727 Shawano Ave.
Green Bay, WI 54303
Application address: c/o Bellin College of Nursing, Financial Office, P.O. Box 23400, Green Bay, WI 54305-3400, tel.: (920) 433-3560

Donor(s): Peter A. Fergus.
Financial data (yr. ended 07/31/01): Grants paid, $20,712; assets, $93,119 (M); gifts received, $10,000; expenditures, $20,722; qualifying distributions, $20,711.
Limitations: Giving primarily in Green Bay, WI.
Application information: Application form required.
Officers and Directors:* Peter A. Fergus,* Pres. and Treas.; Rita Fergus,* V.P.; Catherine Fergus,* Secy.
EIN: 391717642

57412
Madison East Rotary Foundation, Inc.
372 Hoover St.
Sun Prairie, WI 53590-1527
Application address: c/o Virchow, Krause & Co., 4600 American Pkwy., Madison, WI, 53718-8333, tel.: (608) 249-6622
Contact: Richard Frohmader, V.P.

Financial data (yr. ended 12/31/01): Grants paid, $20,700; assets, $159,520 (M); gifts received, $16,041; expenditures, $22,017; qualifying distributions, $20,700.
Limitations: Giving primarily in Dane County, WI.
Officers: Jerry Henrich, Pres.; Richard Frohmader, V.P. and Secy.; Harold Ripp, Treas.
Trustees: Don Dega, Greg Dombrowski, John Steinhauer.
EIN: 237034141

57413
Charles and Eunice C. Tollander Foundation
7575 W. Hickory
Webster, WI 54893-8018

Established in 2000 in WI.
Donor(s): Charles Tollander, Eunice C. Tollander.
Financial data (yr. ended 12/31/01): Grants paid, $20,698; assets, $145,988 (M); gifts received, $32,500; expenditures, $21,712; qualifying distributions, $20,698.
Limitations: Applications not accepted.
Application information: Contributes only to pre-selected organizations.
Trustees: Charles Tollander, Eunice C. Tollander.
EIN: 392011009

57414
Cora W. Wood Scholarship Fund
c/o Bank One, N.A.
P.O. Box 1308
Milwaukee, WI 53201
Application address: 1125 17th St., Denver, CO 80202
Contact: Julie Birdwell, Trust Off., Bank One, N.A.

Financial data (yr. ended 12/31/01): Grants paid, $20,661; assets, $195,203 (M); expenditures, $26,390; qualifying distributions, $22,524.
Limitations: Giving limited to the Pikes Peak, CO, area.
Application information: Application form not required.
Trustees: Raymond E. Wilder, Bank One, N.A.
EIN: 237169976
Codes: GTI

57415
Elizabeth Breckinridge Scholarship Fund
c/o Bank One Trust Co., N.A.
P.O. Box 13
Milwaukee, WI 53201

Financial data (yr. ended 05/31/01): Grants paid, $20,610; assets, $303,891 (M); expenditures, $23,716; qualifying distributions, $21,527.
Limitations: Giving limited to Jefferson County, KY.
Application information: Recipients chosen by each high school's Scholastic Awards Committee. Application form not required.
Trustee: Bank One Trust Co., N.A.
EIN: 616019485
Codes: GTI

57416
Stanley Zebro Foundation
c/o Marshall & Ilsley Bank
P.O. Box 2980
Milwaukee, WI 53201
Application address: Carolie B. Kuehn c/o Marshall & Ilsley Bank, 500 3rd St., Wausau, WI 54402, tel.: (715) 845-3121

Established in 1986 in WI.
Donor(s): Stanley Zebro.
Financial data (yr. ended 12/31/01): Grants paid, $20,600; assets, $374,316 (M); expenditures, $26,675; qualifying distributions, $20,504.
Limitations: Giving primarily in WI.
Trustee: Marshall & Ilsley Bank.
EIN: 391540935

57417
Mid-Wisconsin Foundation, Inc.
132 W. State St.
Medford, WI 54451
Application address: 132 S. 8th St., Medford, WI 54451

Established in 1997 in WI.
Donor(s): Mid-Wisconsin Bank.
Financial data (yr. ended 12/31/01): Grants paid, $20,503; assets, $299,675 (M); gifts received, $10,000; expenditures, $21,755; qualifying distributions, $20,503.
Limitations: Giving primarily in WI.
Officers: Gene C. Knoll, Pres.; Jack Wild, V.P.; Sandra Lukas, Secy.-Treas.
Directors: Brian Hallgreen, Gay Marschke, Dawn Rog, Howard Sturtz II.
EIN: 391892577

57418
Renard Family Foundation, Inc.
931 Cedarview Ct.
Green Bay, WI 54311 (920) 468-0748
Contact: Sandra A. Renard, Pres.

Established in 1994 in WI.
Donor(s): Sandra A. Renard.
Financial data (yr. ended 09/30/01): Grants paid, $20,500; assets, $403,765 (M); expenditures, $20,779; qualifying distributions, $20,500.
Officers and Directors:* Sandra A. Renard,* Pres.; Andrea Renard Minar,* V.P.; William J. Meulbroek,* Secy.-Treas.
EIN: 391806623

57419
Florence E. Kasel Testamentary Trust
c/o Bank One Trust Co., N.A.
P.O. Box 1308
Milwaukee, WI 53201
Application address: 200 W. College Ave., Appleton, WI 54911, tel.: (920) 735-1444
Contact: Nancy Johnsoy, Trust Off., Bank One Trust Co., N.A.

Financial data (yr. ended 05/31/02): Grants paid, $20,491; assets, $216,851 (M); expenditures, $24,366; qualifying distributions, $20,491.
Limitations: Giving limited to Appleton, WI.
Trustee: Bank One Trust Co., N.A.
EIN: 396220043

57420
Friends of Domestic Animals Trust
c/o Bank One Trust Co., N.A.
P.O. Box 1308
Milwaukee, WI 53201

Established in 1996 in CO.
Financial data (yr. ended 12/31/01): Grants paid, $20,406; assets, $383,907 (M); expenditures, $25,098; qualifying distributions, $20,406.
Limitations: Applications not accepted. Giving primarily in CO.
Application information: Contributes only to pre-selected organizations.
Trustee: Bank One Trust Co., N.A.
EIN: 846213107

57421
Motor Castings Foundation, Inc.
1323 S. 65th St.
West Allis, WI 53214-3251
Contact: Joseph Kempen

Established in 1965 in WI.
Donor(s): Motor Castings Co.
Financial data (yr. ended 09/30/01): Grants paid, $20,370; assets, $625,776 (M); expenditures, $21,244; qualifying distributions, $20,381.
Limitations: Giving primarily in Milwaukee County, WI.
Application information: Application form not required.
Officer: Peter Sommerhauser, Pres.
EIN: 396086724
Codes: CS

57422
R and R Heritage Foundation, Inc.
c/o Lichtsinn and Haensel
111 E. Wisconsin Ave., Ste. 1800
Milwaukee, WI 53202

Established in 1999 in WI.

Donor(s): William A. Wernecke, Sue M. Wernecke.
Financial data (yr. ended 12/31/01): Grants paid, $20,350; assets, $182,296 (M); expenditures, $20,519; qualifying distributions, $20,350.
Limitations: Applications not accepted. Giving primarily in WI.
Application information: Contributes only to pre-selected organizations.
Officers and Directors:* William A. Wernecke,* Pres.; Sue M. Wernecke,* Secy.; Patricia Juranitch.
EIN: 391977961

57423
Lila D. Rankin Trust
c/o Bank One Trust Co., N.A.
P.O. Box 1308
Milwaukee, WI 53201

Financial data (yr. ended 12/31/01): Grants paid, $20,300; assets, $387,614 (M); expenditures, $25,424; qualifying distributions, $20,300.
Limitations: Applications not accepted. Giving primarily in Fort Madison, IA.
Application information: Contributes only to pre-selected organizations.
Trustee: Bank One Trust Co., N.A.
EIN: 396188959

57424
Caxambas Foundation, Inc.
780 N. Water St.
Milwaukee, WI 53202-3590

Established in 1995 in WI.
Donor(s): George S. Parker II.
Financial data (yr. ended 12/31/01): Grants paid, $20,073; assets, $14,855 (M); gifts received, $200,000; expenditures, $25,911; qualifying distributions, $22,618.
Limitations: Applications not accepted.
Application information: Contributes only to pre-selected organizations.
Officers: George S. Parker II, Pres. and Treas.; Henry E. Fuldner, V.P.; Dudley J. Godfrey, Jr., Secy.
EIN: 391826516

57425
Juri Lellep Trust
c/o Bank One Trust Co., N.A.
P.O. Box 1308
Milwaukee, WI 53201

Financial data (yr. ended 12/31/99): Grants paid, $20,030; assets, $529,446 (M); expenditures, $25,459; qualifying distributions, $22,462.
Limitations: Applications not accepted. Giving on a national basis.
Application information: Contributes only to pre-selected organizations.
Trustee: Bank One Trust Co., N.A.
EIN: 396103165

57426
Evans Beneditz Missionary Trust Fund
2025 Shore Dr.
Marinette, WI 54143 (715) 732-2877
Contact: Evans H. Beneditz, Pres.

Donor(s): Evans H. Beneditz.
Financial data (yr. ended 09/30/00): Grants paid, $20,004; assets, $443,186 (M); gifts received, $33,389; expenditures, $21,515; qualifying distributions, $20,166; giving activities include $162 for programs.
Limitations: Giving primarily in FL and WI.
Officers and Trustees:* Evans H. Beneditz,* Pres.; Josephine Beneditz,* V.P.; Nancy L. Beneditz.
EIN: 391290211

57427
Barnard Scholarship
c/o Marshall & Ilsley Bank
P.O. Box 2980
Milwaukee, WI 53201

Established in 1999 in WI.
Financial data (yr. ended 08/31/01): Grants paid, $20,000; assets, $335,096 (M); expenditures, $25,374; qualifying distributions, $19,849.
Limitations: Giving limited to WI.
Application information: Unsolicited request for funds not accepted.
Trustee: Marshall & Ilsley Bank.
EIN: 396719890

57428
Hislop Family Foundation
c/o U.S. Bank
P.O. Box 2043
Milwaukee, WI 53201-9116

Established in 2000 in WI.
Financial data (yr. ended 06/30/01): Grants paid, $20,000; assets, $453,042 (M); gifts received, $182,139; expenditures, $21,079; qualifying distributions, $20,539.
Limitations: Applications not accepted. Giving primarily in WI.
Application information: Contributes only to pre-selected organizations.
Trustees: Barbara Board, Joan L. Hislop, Marian H. Hislop, Margaret H. West.
EIN: 393735003

57429
Riverside Paper Foundation, Inc.
800 S. Lawe St.
Appleton, WI 54915-2242 (920) 991-2200
Contact: Michael Salvo, Tr.

Established around 1986.
Donor(s): Riverside Paper Corp., Amricon Corp., James K. Catlin.
Financial data (yr. ended 12/31/01): Grants paid, $20,000; assets, $1,694 (M); gifts received, $2,500; expenditures, $20,094; qualifying distributions, $20,094.
Limitations: Giving limited to the Appleton, WI, area.
Trustees: James Catlin, Joanne Catlin, Linda Heckel, Michael Salvo.
EIN: 391374319
Codes: CS, CD

57430
Anne Talen Foundation
c/o First Bank & Trust Co.
P.O. Box 100, 2405 Schneider Ave.
Menomonie, WI 54751-2541

Established in 1991 in WI.
Financial data (yr. ended 12/31/01): Grants paid, $20,000; assets, $388,614 (M); expenditures, $24,045; qualifying distributions, $20,000.
Limitations: Applications not accepted. Giving primarily in MI and WI.
Application information: Contributes only to pre-selected organizations.
Trustee: First Bank & Trust Co.
EIN: 396511259

57431
West Bend Clinic Foundation, Inc.
1700 W. Paradise Dr.
West Bend, WI 53095

Established in 1999.
Financial data (yr. ended 06/30/01): Grants paid, $20,000; assets, $278,924 (M); expenditures, $21,637; qualifying distributions, $21,605.

Limitations: Giving primarily in WI.
Application information: Unsolicited request for funds not accepted.
Officers and Directors:* Todd J. Hammer,* Pres.; Bruce Steinhardt,* V.P.; Denise Bonelander,* Secy.-Treas.; Beverly Griswold, Kathy Preisler.
EIN: 391833049

57432
Earl B. & Marie C. Whitecotton Scholarship Fund
c/o Bank One Trust Co., N.A.
P.O. Box 1308
Milwaukee, WI 53201
Application address: c/o Marjorie A. Record, Principal, Marion High School, 750 W. 26th St., Marion, IN 46953, tel.: (765) 664-9051; FAX: (765) 662-0383

Established in 1997 in IN.
Financial data (yr. ended 12/31/00): Grants paid, $20,000; assets, $510,123 (M); expenditures, $24,446; qualifying distributions, $21,275.
Limitations: Giving limited to residents of Marion, IN.
Application information: Application form required.
Trustee: Bank One Trust Co., N.A.
EIN: 356519667

57433
Robert E. Ringdahl Foundation, Inc.
P.O. Box 1627
La Crosse, WI 54602-1627
Contact: Robert E. Ringdahl, Pres.

Established in 1992 in WI.
Donor(s): Robert E. Ringdahl.
Financial data (yr. ended 12/31/01): Grants paid, $19,950; assets, $432,866 (M); expenditures, $26,194; qualifying distributions, $19,950.
Application information: Application form not required.
Officers and Directors:* Robert E. Ringdahl,* Pres.; Barbara C. Ringdahl,* V.P.; Thomas R. Ringdahl,* Secy.; Cheryl K. Fassbinder,* Treas.; Robert P. Smyth.
EIN: 391737656

57434
Roger W. & Mary C. Lyons Memorial Trust
c/o Bank One Trust Co., N.A.
P.O. Box 1308
Milwaukee, WI 53201
Application address: 200 W. College Ave., Appleton, WI 54911, tel.: (920) 735-1375
Contact: Bob Kemps, Trust Off., Bank One Trust Co., N.A.

Established in 1996 in WI.
Donor(s): Lyons Revocable Trust.
Financial data (yr. ended 06/30/01): Grants paid, $19,918; assets, $416,691 (M); expenditures, $24,786; qualifying distributions, $19,918.
Trustee: Bank One Trust Co., N.A.
EIN: 396642623

57435
Milwaukee Western Bank Foundation, Inc.
c/o Milwaukee Western Bank
6001 W. Capitol Dr.
Milwaukee, WI 53216-2196

Donor(s): Milwaukee Western Bank.
Financial data (yr. ended 12/31/01): Grants paid, $19,702; assets, $2,998 (M); gifts received, $20,000; expenditures, $19,715; qualifying distributions, $19,715.
Limitations: Applications not accepted. Giving primarily in the Milwaukee, WI, area.

57435—WISCONSIN

Application information: Contributes only to pre-selected organizations.
Officers and Directors:* Roger G. Dirksen,* Pres.; Michael P. Peters,* V.P. and Secy.-Treas.; David A. Davis.
EIN: 396067854
Codes: CS, CD

57436
Ironwood Foundation, Inc.
c/o Robert R. Kinde
250 W. River Rd.
Appleton, WI 54915 (920) 734-5759

Established in 1994 in WI.
Donor(s): Robert R. Kinde, Susan D. Kinde.
Financial data (yr. ended 12/31/01): Grants paid, $19,700; assets, $339,476 (M); gifts received, $5,000; expenditures, $21,121; qualifying distributions, $19,918.
Limitations: Applications not accepted. Giving primarily in WI.
Application information: Contributes only to pre-selected organizations.
Officers: Robert R. Kinde, Pres. and Treas.; Susan D. Kinde, V.P. and Secy.; Alison Elizabeth Attar, V.P.; Michael R. Kinde, V.P.
Director: Matthew Kinde.
EIN: 391806527

57437
Education Foundation of Wauwatosa, Inc.
12201 W. Burleigh St.
Wauwatosa, WI 53222-3102 (414) 476-5300
FAX: (414) 476-5302

Established in 1990 in WI.
Donor(s): Rotary Club of Wauwatosa.
Financial data (yr. ended 12/31/01): Grants paid, $19,630; assets, $289,617 (M); gifts received, $30,764; expenditures, $23,567; qualifying distributions, $19,630.
Limitations: Giving limited to Wauwatosa, WI.
Application information: Application form not required.
Officers and Directors:* Thomas L. Kirchen, Sr.,* Pres.; Melanie Aska Knox,* Secy.; William Komisar, Treas.; Audrey Baird, John Bauer, Jill Koch Hayford, Maureen J. Kenfield, Mary Pat Pfeil, Judith Q. Randall, Steve Romagna.
EIN: 391701838

57438
Brian D. Laviolette Scholarship Fund, Inc.
1135 Pleasant Valley Dr.
Oneida, WI 54155 (920) 405-9929
Contact: Renee Laviolette, V.P.

Established in 1995 in WI.
Financial data (yr. ended 12/31/01): Grants paid, $19,594; assets, $176,235 (M); gifts received, $20,000; expenditures, $85,542; qualifying distributions, $19,594.
Limitations: Giving primarily in De Pere, WI.
Application information: Application form required.
Officers: Douglas Laviolette, Pres. and Treas.; Renee Laviolette, V.P. and Secy.
Directors: Benjamin Laird, Kimberly Laviolette.
EIN: 391836591

57439
Emil Ewald Foundation, Inc.
P.O. Box 147
Oconomowoc, WI 53066-0147

Established in 1990 in WI.
Donor(s): Emil Ewald.
Financial data (yr. ended 12/31/01): Grants paid, $19,532; assets, $597,099 (M); gifts received, $125,000; expenditures, $20,566; qualifying distributions, $19,532.
Limitations: Applications not accepted. Giving limited to WI.
Application information: Contributes only to pre-selected organizations.
Officers and Directors:* Emil Ewald,* Pres. and Treas.; Craig A. Ewald,* V.P. and Secy.; Brian Ewald, Daniel T. Ewald.
EIN: 391687505

57440
Madigan Family Foundation
2627 Nicolet Dr.
Green Bay, WI 54311

Donor(s): James E. Madigan.
Financial data (yr. ended 06/30/02): Grants paid, $19,512; assets, $627,076 (M); expenditures, $27,231; qualifying distributions, $25,408; giving activities include $5,896 for programs.
Limitations: Applications not accepted.
Application information: Contributes only to pre-selected organizations.
Trustees: Cynthia Madigan Bell, Doris M. Madigan, James E. Madigan.
EIN: 237400242

57441
Nia Fund, Inc.
c/o Julilly W. Kohler
1674 N. Marshall St.
Milwaukee, WI 53202-2052

Established in 2000 in WI.
Donor(s): Julilly W. Kohler.
Financial data (yr. ended 12/31/01): Grants paid, $19,500; assets, $1,172,101 (M); expenditures, $21,112; qualifying distributions, $19,500.
Limitations: Applications not accepted.
Application information: Contributes only to pre-selected organizations.
Directors: Issa B. Kohler Hausmann, Julilly Kohler Hausmann, Julilly W. Kohler.
EIN: 392013649

57442
John N. Graber Irrevocable Scholarship Trust
c/o Marshall & Ilsley Bank
P.O. Box 2980
Milwaukee, WI 53201
Application address: Gary Galle c/o Mineral Point Unified School District, 705 Ross St., Mineral Point, WI 53565

Established in 1994 in WI.
Financial data (yr. ended 10/31/01): Grants paid, $19,388; assets, $743,105 (M); expenditures, $27,898; qualifying distributions, $19,388.
Limitations: Giving limited to residents of Mineral Point, WI.
Application information: Application form required.
Trustee: Marshall & Ilsley Bank.
EIN: 396603480

57443
Brookfield Rotary Foundation, Inc.
P.O. Box 293
Brookfield, WI 53008 (262) 796-0701
Application address: c/o Sandra M. Schultz, 10405 W. Manor Park, West Allis, WI 53227, tel.: (414) 545-5898

Established in 1986 in WI.
Financial data (yr. ended 06/30/01): Grants paid, $19,325; assets, $17,147 (M); expenditures, $37,808; qualifying distributions, $23,705; giving activities include $4,339 for programs.
Limitations: Giving primarily in WI.
Officers: Dean Casper, Pres.; Ron Chmil, V.P.; Mike Schultz, Secy.-Treas.
EIN: 391543536

57444
The Wallach Foundation, Inc.
P.O. Box 329
Wausau, WI 54402-0329
Application address: 1111 Highland Park Blvd., Wausau, WI 54401, tel.: (715) 845-1066
Contact: Peter B. Wallach, Pres.

Financial data (yr. ended 01/31/02): Grants paid, $19,323; assets, $216,194 (M); expenditures, $20,188; qualifying distributions, $19,323.
Limitations: Giving primarily in WI.
Officers: Peter B. Wallach, Pres. and Treas.; Toby L. Wallach, V.P. and Secy.
EIN: 237401477

57445
Lawrence A. & Clare A. Liebe Family Foundation, Inc.
3440 S. Monterey Dr.
New Berlin, WI 53151 (262) 786-0147
Contact: Clare A. Liebe, Pres.

Established in 1997 in WI.
Donor(s): Clare A. Liebe, Lawrence A. Liebe.
Financial data (yr. ended 12/31/01): Grants paid, $19,100; assets, $354,594 (M); gifts received, $150,000; expenditures, $23,384; qualifying distributions, $19,100.
Officers and Directors:* Clare A. Liebe,* Pres.; Lawrence A. Liebe,* V.P.; Jennifer A. Servias,* Secy.; Michael L. Liebe,* Treas.; Kara L. Liebe.
EIN: 391862248

57446
Owen G. Duncan Charitable Remainder Unitrust
c/o U.S. Bank
P.O. Box 2043
Milwaukee, WI 53201-9116

Established in 1993 in WI.
Financial data (yr. ended 12/31/01): Grants paid, $19,041; assets, $382,164 (M); expenditures, $26,630; qualifying distributions, $21,991.
Limitations: Applications not accepted. Giving primarily in Ashland, WI.
Application information: Contributes only to pre-selected organizations.
Trustee: U.S. Bank.
EIN: 396235682

57447
Julia Blake Munster & Adele Blake Scholarship Trust
c/o Port Washington State Bank
P.O. Box 176, 206 N. Franklin St.
Port Washington, WI 53074
Application address: c/o Scholarship Comm., Port Washington High School, 427 W. Jackson St., Port Washington, WI 53074, tel.: (262) 268-5500

Financial data (yr. ended 05/31/02): Grants paid, $19,000; assets, $696,737 (M); expenditures, $29,976; qualifying distributions, $25,567.
Limitations: Giving limited to Port Washington, WI.
Application information: Application form required.
Trustee: Port Washington State Bank.
EIN: 396178832
Codes: GTI

57448
Laurits R. and Dianne Cummings Christensen Foundation, Inc.
c/o Laurits and Dianne Christensen
1711 Kendall Ave.
Madison, WI 53705

Established in 2001 in WI.
Donor(s): Laurits R. Christensen, Dianne C. Christensen.
Financial data (yr. ended 12/31/01): Grants paid, $18,950; assets, $897,707 (M); gifts received, $954,659; expenditures, $19,577; qualifying distributions, $18,950.
Limitations: Giving primarily in WI.
Directors: Christopher Bugg, Dianne C. Christensen, Laurits R. Christensen.
EIN: 392041875

57449
George S. Weeks Trust
c/o Bank One Trust Co., N.A.
P.O. Box 1308
Milwaukee, WI 53201

Donor(s): George Weeks.‡
Financial data (yr. ended 12/31/01): Grants paid, $18,901; assets, $722,603 (M); expenditures, $26,024; qualifying distributions, $20,502.
Limitations: Applications not accepted. Giving limited to residents of Bourbon and Fayette counties, KY.
Trustee: Bank One Trust Co., N.A.
EIN: 616208193
Codes: GTI

57450
Arthur J. Donald Family Foundation, Inc.
c/o Foley & Lardner
777 E. Wisconsin Ave., Ste. 3500
Milwaukee, WI 53202-5367

Donor(s): Mary F. Donald.
Financial data (yr. ended 12/31/01): Grants paid, $18,900; assets, $248,746 (M); gifts received, $125; expenditures, $19,963; qualifying distributions, $18,900.
Limitations: Applications not accepted. Giving primarily in WI.
Application information: Contributes only to pre-selected organizations.
Officers and Directors:* Mary F. Donald,* Pres.; Benjamin F. Garmer III,* V.P.; Stephen M. Fisher,* Secy.-Treas.
EIN: 391480248

57451
Sally Adams Scholarship Fund
c/o Bank One Trust Co., N.A.
P.O. Box 1308
Milwaukee, WI 53201
Application address: c/o Bank One, West Virginia, Wheeling, N.A., 1114 Market St., Wheeling, WV 26003, tel.: (304) 234-4130
Contact: Ed Johnson

Financial data (yr. ended 12/31/01): Grants paid, $18,800; assets, $361,053 (M); expenditures, $24,460; qualifying distributions, $20,662.
Limitations: Giving limited to Wheeling, WV.
Application information: Application form required.
Trustees: J.R. Clark, J.T. McClure, J.C. Stamp, L.S. Whitaker, Bank One, West Virginia, N.A.
EIN: 556085702
Codes: GTI

57452
Catholic Club Association
2801 Schaefer Cir.
Appleton, WI 54915-6626
Application address: 218 E. Hoover Ave., Appleton, WI 54915, tel.: (920) 734-5140
Contact: Kenneth Springer, Dir.

Financial data (yr. ended 12/31/01): Grants paid, $18,750; assets, $419,067 (M); expenditures, $20,535; qualifying distributions, $18,750.
Limitations: Giving primarily in Appleton, WI.
Officers: Thomas Smudde, Pres.; Bernard Blob, V.P.; Lucinda Springer, Secy.; Martin Van Stippen, Treas.
Directors: Joseph Bodmer, Angus McIntyre, Robert Mulheron, Kenneth Springer, Michael Wachuta.
EIN: 391019718

57453
Christian J. Hubertz Family Foundation, Inc.
111 E. Wisconsin Ave., Ste. 1800
Milwaukee, WI 53202

Established in 1996 in WI.
Donor(s): Christian M. Hubertz, Sara J. Hubertz.
Financial data (yr. ended 12/31/00): Grants paid, $18,550; assets, $19,281 (M); expenditures, $20,640; qualifying distributions, $18,550.
Limitations: Applications not accepted.
Application information: Contributes only to pre-selected organizations.
Officers and Directors:* Curtis J. Hubertz,* Pres.; Rosemary R. Hubertz,* Secy.; Alissa J. Hubertz, Erin K. Hubertz, Kyle P. Hubertz, Leah K. Hubertz.
EIN: 391870993

57454
Kaap Charitable Trust
c/o Bank One Trust Co., N.A.
P.O. Box 1308
Milwaukee, WI 53201
Application address: c/o Jim Curran, Trust Off., Bank One Trust Co., N.A., P.O. Box 19029, Green Bay, WI 54307-9029, tel.: (920) 436-2601

Financial data (yr. ended 05/31/02): Grants paid, $18,523; assets, $382,540 (M); expenditures, $24,643; qualifying distributions, $18,523.
Limitations: Giving limited to Brown County, WI.
Trustee: Bank One Trust Co., N.A.
EIN: 391440159

57455
Braun Woodlands Foundation, Inc.
P.O. Box 290
Antigo, WI 54409-0388

Donor(s): Frederic W. Braun.
Financial data (yr. ended 07/31/02): Grants paid, $18,500; assets, $327,779 (M); expenditures, $19,100; qualifying distributions, $18,500.
Limitations: Applications not accepted. Giving primarily in Antigo, WI.
Application information: Contributes only to pre-selected organizations.
Officers: Leslie J. Frye, Pres.; Frederic H. Braun, V.P.; Joan D. Braun, Secy.
EIN: 391451324

57456
Outrider Foundation, Inc.
7686 Midtown Rd.
Verona, WI 53593
Contact: Frank E. Burgess, Pres.

Donor(s): Frank E. Burgess.
Financial data (yr. ended 12/31/01): Grants paid, $18,500; assets, $281,892 (M); gifts received, $20,000; expenditures, $21,179; qualifying distributions, $18,500.
Officers and Directors:* Frank E. Burgess,* Pres. and Treas.; Bonnie Munroe,* V.P. and Secy.; Sarah Stevens,* V.P.
EIN: 391947995

57457
George W. Askren Memorial Scholarship Trust
(Formerly Caroline L. Askren Trust)
c/o Bank One Trust Co., N.A.
P.O. Box 1308
Milwaukee, WI 53201-1308
Application address: c/o Principal, Warren Central High School, 9500 E. 16th St., Indianapolis, IN 46229, tel.: (317) 898-6133

Financial data (yr. ended 10/31/01): Grants paid, $18,400; assets, $350,969 (M); expenditures, $21,497; qualifying distributions, $19,581.
Limitations: Giving limited to residents of Indianapolis, IN.
Application information: Application forms are circulated to seniors at schools in Warren Township, IN. Application form required.
Trustee: Bank One Trust Co., N.A.
EIN: 356231596
Codes: GTI

57458
M. G. Bush - D. D. Nusbaum Foundation, Inc.
(Formerly Bush Nusbaum Charitable Foundation)
c/o Associated Banc-Corp.
P.O. Box 408
Neenah, WI 54957-0408

Donor(s): Schreiber Foods, Inc.
Financial data (yr. ended 12/31/01): Grants paid, $18,333; assets, $93,547 (M); gifts received, $10,000; expenditures, $20,121; qualifying distributions, $18,331.
Limitations: Applications not accepted. Giving primarily in areas of company operations.
Application information: Contributes only to pre-selected organizations.
Officers and Directors:* David D. Nusbaum,* Chair.; Robert G. Bush,* Pres.; Robert J. Pruess,* V.P. and Secy.-Treas.
Trustee: Associated Banc-Corp.
EIN: 391537768
Codes: CS, CD

57459
Appleton Rotary Foundation, Inc.
P.O. Box 703
Appleton, WI 54912-0703

Donor(s): Charles Heeter.
Financial data (yr. ended 06/30/00): Grants paid, $18,266; assets, $747,729 (M); gifts received, $15,053; expenditures, $42,539; qualifying distributions, $37,557; giving activities include $19,291 for programs.
Limitations: Applications not accepted. Giving limited to Appleton, WI.
Application information: Unsolicited requests for funds not accepted.
Officers and Directors:* William Hodgkiss,* Pres.; Bob Pedersen,* V.P.; Hurley Wilbourne,* V.P.; Donna Kidder,* Secy.; Warren Parsons,* Treas.; Roger Core, Louis McElrome, Ray Valitchka.
EIN: 396053036

57460
Gordon R. Connor Charitable Foundation, Inc.
c/o Becker & Kumm, C.P.A.
320 W. Grand Ave., Ste. 301
Wisconsin Rapids, WI 54495

Financial data (yr. ended 06/30/02): Grants paid, $18,000; assets, $355,640 (M); expenditures, $19,069; qualifying distributions, $18,000.
Limitations: Applications not accepted.
Application information: Contributes only to pre-selected organizations.
Officers: Catherine C. Dellin, Pres.; Catherine P. Hurtgen, V.P.; Mary C. Pierce, Secy.-Treas.
EIN: 391419612

57461
Fleshman Memorial Scholarship Fund
c/o Bank One Trust Co., N.A.
P.O. Box 130
Milwaukee, WI 53201
Application address: c/o Jeffersonville High School, Jeffersonville, IN 47130

Established in 1997 in IN.
Financial data (yr. ended 02/28/02): Grants paid, $17,860; assets, $461,711 (M); expenditures, $25,297; qualifying distributions, $20,794.
Limitations: Giving limited to Jeffersonville, IN.
Application information: Application form required.
Trustee: Bank One Trust Co., N.A.
EIN: 356639411
Codes: GTI

57462
Schuette Family Foundation, Inc.
c/o Associated Banc-Corp, Green Bay
P.O. Box 19006
Green Bay, WI 54307-9006

Financial data (yr. ended 12/31/01): Grants paid, $17,602; assets, $276,785 (M); expenditures, $24,520; qualifying distributions, $17,867.
Limitations: Giving limited to residents of Brown County, WI.
Trustee: Associated Banc-Corp.
EIN: 396103656

57463
P. J. Hedeen & Children Foundation, Inc.
4717 Martin Rd.
Sturgeon Bay, WI 54235

Established in 1997 in WI.
Donor(s): Patti Jo Hedeen.
Financial data (yr. ended 12/31/01): Grants paid, $17,600; assets, $379,459 (M); expenditures, $20,279; qualifying distributions, $17,600.
Limitations: Applications not accepted. Giving limited to Sturgeon Bay, WI.
Application information: Contributes only to pre-selected organizations.
Officers: Patti Jo Hedeen, Pres. and Treas.; Barret C. Hedeen, V.P. and Secy.
EIN: 391922280

57464
Taylor Family Charitable Irrevocable Trust of 1986
c/o Waukesha State Bank, Trust Dept.
P.O. Box 648
Waukesha, WI 53187-0648 (262) 549-8543

Established in 1986 in WI.
Financial data (yr. ended 12/31/01): Grants paid, $17,576; assets, $347,834 (M); expenditures, $20,850; qualifying distributions, $17,576.
Limitations: Applications not accepted. Giving primarily in Waukesha, WI.
Application information: Contributes only to pre-selected organizations.
Directors: Velma Geraldson, Don L. Taylor.
Trustee: Waukesha State Bank.
EIN: 396442284

57465
Abbot Machine Company Charitable Foundation, Inc.
519 Elm Spring Ave.
Wauwatosa, WI 53226-4659 (414) 258-3339
Contact: Stuart B. Eiche, Dir.

Donor(s): Abbot Machine Co.
Financial data (yr. ended 12/31/01): Grants paid, $17,550; assets, $271,767 (M); expenditures, $17,692; qualifying distributions, $17,452.
Limitations: Giving primarily in Milwaukee, WI.
Application information: Application form not required.
Directors: Jocelyn Eiche, Stuart B. Eiche, R.G. Urban.
EIN: 396125048
Codes: CS, CD

57466
Flowers Family Foundation, Inc.
1021 Cottonwood Dr.
Stoughton, WI 53589

Financial data (yr. ended 12/31/01): Grants paid, $17,500; assets, $407,865 (M); gifts received, $90,640; expenditures, $17,794; qualifying distributions, $17,500.
Officers: Stanley Reinholtz, Pres.; Rockne Flowers, V.P.; June Bunting, Secy.-Treas.
EIN: 391947789

57467
John Mueth, Jr. Trust
c/o Bank One Trust Co., N.A.
P.O. Box 1308
Milwaukee, WI 53201

Established in 1994 in WI.
Financial data (yr. ended 12/31/01): Grants paid, $17,500; assets, $733,620 (M); expenditures, $30,416; qualifying distributions, $17,500.
Limitations: Applications not accepted.
Application information: Contributes only to pre-selected organizations.
Trustees: Allan Reyhan, Priscilla Ann Reyhan, Bank One, Illinois, N.A.
EIN: 376061200

57468
Northwoods Foundation, Inc.
777 E. Wisconsin Ave., Ste. 1920
Milwaukee, WI 53202 (414) 276-0304
Contact: Robert P. Probst, Treas.

Donor(s): Joseph Uihlein, Jr.
Financial data (yr. ended 12/31/01): Grants paid, $17,500; assets, $340,289 (M); expenditures, $17,587; qualifying distributions, $17,500.
Limitations: Giving limited to WI.
Officers and Directors:* D.F. McKeithan, Jr.,* Pres.; Deborah M. Sullivan,* Secy.; Robert P. Probst,* Treas.
EIN: 396033247

57469
The Borisch Foundation, Inc.
c/o Foley & Lardner
777 E. Wisconsin Ave., Ste. 3500
Milwaukee, WI 53202

Established in 1996 in WI.
Donor(s): Borisch Family Foundation, Inc.
Financial data (yr. ended 12/31/01): Grants paid, $17,460; assets, $511,311 (M); expenditures, $26,480; qualifying distributions, $23,775.
Limitations: Applications not accepted. Giving primarily in WI.
Application information: Contributes only to pre-selected organizations.
Officers and Directors:* Joseph B. Tyson, Jr.,* Pres.; Bruce M. Peckerman,* V.P.; George A. Dionisopoulos,* Secy.-Treas.; Heather C. Borisch, Jennifer C. Borisch.
EIN: 396317013

57470
J. K. Caldwell Charitable Trust
c/o Bank One Trust Co., N.A.
P.O. Box 1308
Milwaukee, WI 53201

Established in 1995 in KY.
Financial data (yr. ended 12/31/01): Grants paid, $17,447; assets, $581,237 (M); expenditures, $21,723; qualifying distributions, $17,447.
Limitations: Applications not accepted. Giving primarily in Louisville, KY.
Application information: Contributes only to pre-selected organizations.
Trustee: Bank One Trust Co., N.A.
EIN: 616215681

57471
Joseph E. Beauchamp Charitable Trust
c/o Bank One Trust Co., N.A.
P.O. Box 1308
Milwaukee, WI 53201
Application address: c/o Bank One, N.A., Endowment and Foundation Div., 611 Woodward Ave., Detroit, MI 48226, tel.: (313) 225-1249; E-mail: michael_barry@em.fcnbd.com
Contact: Michael Barry, Mgr.

Established in 1976 in MI.
Financial data (yr. ended 12/31/01): Grants paid, $17,360; assets, $340,312 (M); expenditures, $25,036; qualifying distributions, $17,360.
Limitations: Giving limited to MI.
Application information: Application form not required.
Officer: Michael Barry, Mgr.
Trustee: Bank One Trust Co., N.A.
EIN: 382119454

57472
The Richard J. and Mary B. Chernick Family Foundation, Inc.
915 Kings Point Ct.
Oneida, WI 54155
Contact: Richard J. Chernick, Pres.

Established in 1998 in WI.
Donor(s): Richard J. Chernick, Norman Chernick.
Financial data (yr. ended 09/30/01): Grants paid, $17,350; assets, $391,692 (M); gifts received, $50,661; expenditures, $21,595; qualifying distributions, $17,350.
Limitations: Giving primarily in Green Bay, WI.
Officers and Directors:* Richard J. Chernick,* Pres.and Treas.; Norm Chernick, V.P.; Mary B. Chernick,* Secy.; Benjamin Chernick, Ryan Chernick, Richard Johnson.
EIN: 391969618

57473
Castlerock Foundation, Inc.
c/o Gary E. Schlosstein
W1586 County Rd. KK
Alma, WI 54610-8404

Established in 1998 in WI.
Donor(s): Gary E. Schlosstein.
Financial data (yr. ended 12/31/01): Grants paid, $17,349; assets, $1,011,508 (M); expenditures, $22,178; qualifying distributions, $17,349.

Limitations: Giving primarily in WI.
Officer: Gary B. Schlosstein, Pres.
Directors: Najib Schlosstein, Shelby J. Schlosstein.
EIN: 391942244

57474
Clarence H. Gribble Trust
c/o First National Bank of Platteville
170 W. Main St.
Platteville, WI 53818 (608) 348-7777
Contact: First National Bank

Financial data (yr. ended 12/31/01): Grants paid, $17,300; assets, $346,567 (M); expenditures, $20,989; qualifying distributions, $17,221.
Limitations: Giving limited to Platteville, WI.
Application information: Application form not required.
Trustee: First National Bank of Platteville.
EIN: 396083464

57475
Taylor Family Charitable Irrevocable Trust of 1977
c/o Waukesha State Bank, Trust Dept.
P.O. Box 648
Waukesha, WI 53187 (262) 549-8543

Established in 1977 in WI.
Financial data (yr. ended 12/31/01): Grants paid, $16,856; assets, $329,208 (M); expenditures, $20,577; qualifying distributions, $16,856.
Limitations: Applications not accepted. Giving primarily in Waukesha, WI.
Application information: Contributes only to pre-selected organizations.
Directors: Velma Geraldson, Don L. Taylor.
Trustee: Waukesha State Bank.
EIN: 396297286

57476
Ben Zadd Trust
c/o Bank One Trust Co., N.A.
P.O. Box 1308
Milwaukee, WI 53201-1308

Established in 1996 in WV.
Financial data (yr. ended 12/31/01): Grants paid, $16,548; assets, $287,139 (M); expenditures, $20,333; qualifying distributions, $16,548.
Limitations: Applications not accepted. Giving primarily in Huntington, WV.
Application information: Contributes only to pre-selected organizations.
Trustee: Bank One Trust Co., N.A.
EIN: 550566351

57477
William Bartlett Trust
c/o U.S. Bank
P.O. Box 7900
Madison, WI 53707-7900
Application address: c/o University of Wisoncsin-Eau Claire, Financial Aid Off., P.O. Box 4004, 115 Schofield, Eau Claire, WI 54702

Established in 1997 in WI.
Donor(s): William Bartlett.‡
Financial data (yr. ended 06/30/01): Grants paid, $16,500; assets, $405,887 (M); expenditures, $21,968; qualifying distributions, $15,945.
Limitations: Giving primarily in Eau Claire, WI.
Application information: Application through financial aid office. Application form required.
Trustee: U.S. Bank.
EIN: 396673414

57478
Benton & Louise Hale Memorial Scholarship Fund
c/o Marshall & Ilsley Bank
P.O. Box 2980
Milwaukee, WI 53201-2980

Financial data (yr. ended 12/31/01): Grants paid, $16,500; assets, $408,292 (M); expenditures, $20,744; qualifying distributions, $16,500.
Limitations: Giving limited to residents of Burlington, VT.
Application information: Application form required.
Trustee: Marshall & Ilsley Bank.
EIN: 396257040
Codes: GTI

57479
J. Leo Short Scholarship Fund
c/o Bank One Trust Co.
P.O. Box 1308
Milwaukee, WI 53201
Application address: 8111 Preston Rd., Dallas, TX 75255, tel.: (214) 360-4373
Contact: Dahl Marshall, Trust Off., Bank One Trust Co.

Established in 1987 in TX.
Financial data (yr. ended 12/31/01): Grants paid, $16,500; assets, $279,134 (M); expenditures, $20,108; qualifying distributions, $18,077.
Limitations: Giving limited to residents of Denison, TX.
Application information: Application form required.
Trustee: Bank One, Texas, N.A.
EIN: 756097737
Codes: GTI

57480
A. F. MacPherson Trust
(also known as Anonymous Fund)
c/o U.S. Bank
P.O. Box 7900
Madison, WI 53707-7900

Financial data (yr. ended 12/31/00): Grants paid, $16,412; assets, $616,304 (M); expenditures, $32,793; qualifying distributions, $23,435.
Limitations: Giving on a national basis; some giving to Canada.
Publications: Application guidelines.
Application information: Applicants must be recommended by professionals familiar with their need, such as a minister, social worker, doctor or dentist. Grants paid directly to the creditor (i.e. doctor, hospital, dentist, etc.). Application form not required.
Trustees: Roger Gierhart, U.S. Bank.
EIN: 396038607
Codes: GTI

57481
Elmer G. Biddick Charitable Foundation, Inc.
3810 Country Rd. Q.
Dodgeville, WI 53533-8540
Contact: Rachel L. Jordan, Secy.-Treas.

Established in 1984 in WI.
Financial data (yr. ended 12/31/01): Grants paid, $16,375; assets, $223,033 (M); expenditures, $19,000; qualifying distributions, $16,225.
Limitations: Giving limited to Iowa and Grant counties, WI.
Application information: Application form required.
Officers and Directors:* Roger D. Biddick,* Pres.; Rachel L. Jordan,* Secy.-Treas.; Robin Masters, James Neuendorf, William R. Warner.
EIN: 391502330

57482
Alma Doten Charitable Trust
c/o Marshall & Ilsley Bank
P.O. Box 5000
Janesville, WI 53547-5000

Financial data (yr. ended 12/31/01): Grants paid, $16,258; assets, $251,198 (M); expenditures, $22,843; qualifying distributions, $22,843.
Limitations: Applications not accepted. Giving limited to WI.
Application information: Contributes only to pre-selected organizations.
Trustee: Mary E. Wickhem.
EIN: 396282989

57483
Mabel E. Dupee Foundation, Inc.
c/o Union National Bank & Trust Co.
P.O. Box 249, 124 W. Oak St.
Sparta, WI 54656-1713
Contact: Shannon Perry

Established in 1980 in WI.
Financial data (yr. ended 12/31/01): Grants paid, $16,250; assets, $263,125 (M); expenditures, $17,123; qualifying distributions, $17,123.
Limitations: Giving limited to Sparta, WI.
Application information: Application form required.
Directors: Dave Bolstad, Jack Harr, Thomas Hemstock, Barb Schwartz, Ronald J. Wall.
EIN: 391383645
Codes: GTI

57484
Seaman-Goes Family Foundation, Inc.
5270 N. Maple Ln.
Nashotah, WI 53058 (262) 367-2729
Contact: Richard Seaman, Pres.

Donor(s): Richard Seaman.
Financial data (yr. ended 01/31/02): Grants paid, $16,245; assets, $494,304 (M); expenditures, $20,104; qualifying distributions, $16,245.
Limitations: Giving primarily in Milwaukee, WI.
Officers and Directors:* Richard Seaman,* Pres. and Treas.; June G. Seaman,* V.P. and Secy.; John F. Callan, Linda P. Seaman, Richard Seaman, Jr., Stephen F. Seaman.
EIN: 391487991

57485
Allgaier Foundation
2455 Buckingham Pl.
Brookfield, WI 53045

Established in 1999 in WI.
Financial data (yr. ended 12/31/01): Grants paid, $16,116; assets, $41,825 (M); expenditures, $16,609; qualifying distributions, $16,116.
Limitations: Applications not accepted. Giving primarily in Milwaukee, WI.
Application information: Contributes only to pre-selected organizations.
Trustees: Cynthia C. Allgaier, Glen R. Allgaier.
EIN: 396725201

57486
B & D Foundation, Inc.
P.O. Box 44966
Madison, WI 53744 (608) 831-8181

Established in 1997.
Donor(s): Duwayne Carl, Beverly Carl.
Financial data (yr. ended 12/31/01): Grants paid, $16,000; assets, $324,451 (M); expenditures, $18,338; qualifying distributions, $16,902.
Limitations: Applications not accepted.
Application information: Contributes only to pre-selected organizations.

57486—WISCONSIN

Directors: Beverly Carl, DuWayne Carl, John F. Suby.
EIN: 391915677

57487
Bell Foundation, Inc.
2650 N. Terrace Ave.
Milwaukee, WI 53211 (414) 964-5245
Contact: John S. Bell, Pres.

Financial data (yr. ended 08/31/01): Grants paid, $16,000; assets, $151,651 (M); expenditures, $17,465; qualifying distributions, $16,000.
Limitations: Giving primarily in Milwaukee, WI.
Officers: John S. Bell, Pres.; Joan D. Bell,* Secy.; Nancy E. Bell,* Treas.
EIN: 396042846

57488
Dick's Supermarket Foundation, Inc.
(Formerly Brodbeck Foundation, Inc.)
1035 E. Hwy. 151, Box 656
Platteville, WI 53818
Contact: Robert J. Brodbeck, Pres.

Established in 1987 in WI.
Donor(s): Brodbeck Enterprises, Inc.
Financial data (yr. ended 08/31/02): Grants paid, $16,000; assets, $175,812 (M); expenditures, $19,792; qualifying distributions, $16,000.
Limitations: Giving primarily in southwestern WI.
Officers and Directors:* Robert J. Brodbeck,* Pres. and Treas.; Barry J. Brodbeck,* V.P. and Secy.; Helen S. Brodbeck.
EIN: 391605932
Codes: CS, CD

57489
The Clifford G. and Grace A. Ferris Foundation
c/o Marshall & Ilsley Bank
1000 N. Water St.
Milwaukee, WI 53202
Application address: c/p David Guillion, Marshall & Ilsley Bank, 500 3rd St., P.O. Box 209, Wausau, WI 54402

Established in 1999 in WI.
Financial data (yr. ended 05/31/01): Grants paid, $16,000; assets, $283,733 (M); expenditures, $26,611; qualifying distributions, $15,860.
Limitations: Giving to residents of Wausau, WI.
Trustee: Marshall & Ilsley Bank.
EIN: 396716441

57490
Stephen D. Kander Scholarship Fund
c/o Bank One Trust Co., N.A.
P.O. Box 1308
Milwaukee, WI 53201-1308

Established in 1996 in WI.
Donor(s): Stephen D. Kander.‡
Financial data (yr. ended 07/31/01): Grants paid, $16,000; assets, $327,221 (M); expenditures, $20,848; qualifying distributions, $20,167.
Limitations: Giving primarily in WI.
Trustee: Bank One Trust Co., N.A.
EIN: 396631861

57491
The Neese-Malik Foundation
2870 Riverside Dr.
Beloit, WI 53511
Contact: Gary G. Grabowski, Tr.

Donor(s): Laura N. Malik.
Financial data (yr. ended 06/30/01): Grants paid, $16,000; assets, $284,251 (M); gifts received, $10,069; expenditures, $16,929; qualifying distributions, $16,000.
Limitations: Giving limited to the Berkeley, CA, area and Beloit, WI.

Trustees: Gary G. Grabowski, Laura N. Malik.
EIN: 363487447

57492
Wencel F. & Mabel M. Dufek Charitable Foundation
2424 Meadow Ln.
Manitowoc, WI 54220-3731
Application address: 900 S. 10th St., Manitowoc, WI 54220, tel.: (920) 682-6661
Contact: Theresa R. Burbey, Tr.

Established in 1996.
Donor(s): Mabel M. Dufek, Wencel F. Defek.
Financial data (yr. ended 06/30/02): Grants paid, $15,850; assets, $420 (M); gifts received, $16,000; expenditures, $16,058; qualifying distributions, $15,850.
Limitations: Giving primarily in Manitowoc County, WI.
Application information: Application form required.
Officer and Trustees:* Mabel M. Dufek,* Pres.; Theresa R. Burbey.
EIN: 396642714

57493
Richard F. Redfield Trust
4390 Hwy., 8 E.
Rhinelander, WI 54501

Established in 1998 in WI.
Donor(s): Richard Redfield.‡
Financial data (yr. ended 05/31/00): Grants paid, $15,848; assets, $1,129,266 (M); expenditures, $58,612; qualifying distributions, $37,951.
Limitations: Giving primarily in Rhinelander, WI.
Application information: Scholarship application form available at the foundation or from Rhinelander High School. Application form required.
Trustee: Thomas L. Knudsen.
EIN: 396694213

57494
MCP Charitable Foundation, Inc.
c/o Becker & Kumm, C.P.A.
320 W. Grand Ave., Ste. 301
Wisconsin Rapids, WI 54495

Donor(s): Mary C. Pierce, Dudley D. Pierce.
Financial data (yr. ended 06/30/02): Grants paid, $15,750; assets, $205,910 (M); expenditures, $16,738; qualifying distributions, $15,750.
Limitations: Applications not accepted. Giving primarily in WI.
Application information: Contributes only to pre-selected organizations.
Officers: Dudley W. Pierce, Pres.; Dudley D. Pierce, V.P.; Mary C. Pierce, Secy.-Treas.
EIN: 391419756

57495
Hazel Aslakson Scholarship Trust
c/o Associated Banc-Corp
P.O. Box 787
Manitowoc, WI 54221-0787
Application address: c/o First Lutheran Church, 521 N. 8th St., Manitowoc, WI 54220

Established in 1997.
Financial data (yr. ended 12/31/01): Grants paid, $15,500; assets, $128,061 (M); expenditures, $17,708; qualifying distributions, $17,681.
Trustee: Associated Banc-Corp.
EIN: 396638318

57496
Kibbutz Langdon Foundation, Inc.
5779 N. Witte Ln.
Glendale, WI 53209-4570 (414) 352-4817
Contact: David Lerman, V.P.

Financial data (yr. ended 12/31/00): Grants paid, $15,500; assets, $234,884 (M); gifts received, $200; expenditures, $16,591; qualifying distributions, $15,500.
Limitations: Giving primarily in WI.
Officers and Directors:* David Shavzin,* Pres.; David Lerman,* V.P.; Lynne Goldman,* Secy.; Mike Chudnoff,* Treas.; Laura Magid, Gigi Pomerantz, Karen Schur, Rabbi Ike Serotta.
EIN: 391515553

57497
Lang Family Foundation, Inc.
P.O. Box 085009
Racine, WI 53408-5009
Application address: P.O. Box 297, St. Peter, MN 56082

Established in 1997 in WI.
Donor(s): Helen Lang,‡ A & E Manufacturing.
Financial data (yr. ended 12/31/01): Grants paid, $15,460; assets, $338,302 (M); gifts received, $10,000; expenditures, $20,643; qualifying distributions, $15,460.
Application information: Application form required.
Officers: John R. Lang, Pres. and Treas.; Daniel Peterson, V.P.; Gregory A. Ruidl, Secy.
EIN: 391884671

57498
Robert and Jane Baker Foundation
c/o Bank One Trust Co., N.A.
P.O. Box 1308
Milwaukee, WI 53201

Established in 1998 in MI.
Financial data (yr. ended 12/31/01): Grants paid, $15,435; assets, $158,396 (M); expenditures, $18,307; qualifying distributions, $15,435.
Limitations: Giving limited to MI, with emphasis on Kalamazoo.
Officers: Robert S. Baker, Pres.; Jane Baker, V.P.
Trustee: Bank One Trust Co., N.A.
EIN: 383439074

57499
Walter Curtis Palmer Scholarship Trust
c/o Bank One Trust Co., N.A.
P.O. Box 1308
Milwaukee, WI 53201

Financial data (yr. ended 12/31/01): Grants paid, $15,417; assets, $210,060 (M); expenditures, $19,198; qualifying distributions, $16,606.
Limitations: Giving limited to residents of Racine, WI.
Application information: Application form not required.
Scholarship Committee Members: Major Armstead, Jr., Jan Ocker, James M. Smith.
Trustee: Bank One Trust Co., N.A.
EIN: 396037713

57500
Walters Technical Scholarship Fund
c/o Marshall & Ilsley Bank
P.O. Box 2980
Milwaukee, WI 53201

Established in 1989 in WI.
Donor(s): Francis O. Walters.
Financial data (yr. ended 09/30/01): Grants paid, $15,274; assets, $297,535 (M); expenditures, $19,302; qualifying distributions, $15,078.

Limitations: Giving limited to residents of north central WI.
Application information: Application form required.
Trustee: Marshall & Ilsley Bank.
EIN: 396509266

57501
Elwyn Remington Foundation, Inc.
c/o Charles Melzer
P.O. Box 290
Antigo, WI 54409-0290

Established in 1989 in WI.
Donor(s): Elwyn Remington.
Financial data (yr. ended 12/31/99): Grants paid, $15,159; assets, $348,169 (M); gifts received, $3,500; expenditures, $16,897; qualifying distributions, $16,897.
Limitations: Applications not accepted. Giving limited to Langlade County, WI.
Directors: Mark J. Bradley, Jeanne W. Lucht, Charles Melzer.
Trustee: Monson Investment Co.
EIN: 391633403

57502
Joseph P. Tate Foundation
c/o Carolyn A. Hegge
25 W. Main, Ste. 300
Madison, WI 53701
Application address: c/o Guidance Dept., Fort Atkinson High School, 310 E. SE 4, Fort Atkinson, WI 53538, tel.: (920) 563-7814

Established in 1995.
Donor(s): Superior Services, Joseph P. Tate.
Financial data (yr. ended 12/31/00): Grants paid, $15,085; assets, $614,939 (M); expenditures, $20,619; qualifying distributions, $15,085.
Limitations: Giving limited to residents of Whitewater, WI.
Application information: Application form required.
Officers: Joseph P. Tate, Pres.; Casandra Tate, V.P.; David Mack, Treas.
EIN: 391790720

57503
Moehring Charitable Trust
425 E. Parkway Blvd.
Appleton, WI 54911-2954
Application address: P.O. Box 1056, Appleton, WI 54912-0239, tel.: (920) 738-3820
Contact: M. Smith, Trust Off., Valley Trust Co.

Established in 1988 in WI.
Financial data (yr. ended 12/31/01): Grants paid, $15,000; assets, $228,536 (M); expenditures, $17,731; qualifying distributions, $15,000.
Limitations: Giving primarily in Appleton, WI.
Officers: Ethel I. Moehring, Mgr.; Ralph E. Moehring, Mgr.
Trustee: Valley Trust Co.
EIN: 391612461

57504
Thomas W. Mount Family Foundation
401 Pine Terr.
Oconomowoc, WI 53066

Donor(s): Thomas W. Mount.
Financial data (yr. ended 12/31/01): Grants paid, $15,000; assets, $193,282 (M); expenditures, $15,281; qualifying distributions, $15,000.
Limitations: Applications not accepted. Giving primarily in Oconomowoc, WI.
Application information: Contributes only to pre-selected organizations.
Trustees: Thomas C. Mount, Thomas W. Mount.
EIN: 396654434

57505
William J. & Myra L. Niederkorn Scholarship Trust
c/o Port Washington State Bank
206 N. Franklin St.
Port Washington, WI 53074
Application address: c/o Scholarship Comm., Port Washington High School, Port Washington, WI 53074, tel.: (262) 284-5569

Financial data (yr. ended 05/31/02): Grants paid, $15,000; assets, $376,434 (M); expenditures, $19,759; qualifying distributions, $18,842.
Limitations: Giving limited to residents of Port Washington, WI.
Application information: Application form not required.
Trustee: Port Washington State Bank.
EIN: 396297158
Codes: GTI

57506
Arthur J. Olsen Foundation, Ltd.
c/o Joan B. French
1515 Ridge Rd.
Sheboygan, WI 53083

Donor(s): Joan B. Olsen.
Financial data (yr. ended 12/31/01): Grants paid, $15,000; assets, $60,315 (M); gifts received, $15,000; expenditures, $15,805; qualifying distributions, $15,000.
Limitations: Applications not accepted. Giving primarily in WI.
Application information: Contributes only to pre-selected organizations.
Officers and Directors:* Joan B. French,* Pres.; Arthur John Olsen III,* V.P.; Jefren S. Olsen,* Secy.-Treas.
EIN: 391833337

57507
Jennie H. Olson Charitable Foundation, Inc.
c/o John C. Mitby
P.O. Box 1767
Madison, WI 53701-1767

Established in 1995 in WI.
Donor(s): Jennie H. Olson.
Financial data (yr. ended 12/31/01): Grants paid, $15,000; assets, $309,619 (M); gifts received, $101,316; expenditures, $18,557; qualifying distributions, $15,000.
Limitations: Applications not accepted. Giving primarily in WI.
Application information: Contributes only to pre-selected organizations.
Officers and Directors:* John C. Mitby,* Pres.; Edward M. Terry,* Secy.; Jennie H. Olson.
EIN: 391818653

57508
Trinity Charitable Trust
c/o Donald and Barbara Lynch
1230 E. Courtland Pl.
Milwaukee, WI 53211-1163

Established in 1998 in WI.
Donor(s): Donald Lynch, Barbara Lynch.
Financial data (yr. ended 12/31/01): Grants paid, $15,000; assets, $252,914 (M); expenditures, $18,391; qualifying distributions, $15,000.
Limitations: Applications not accepted.
Application information: Contributes only to pre-selected organizations.
Trustee: Barbara Lynch.
EIN: 396698787

57509
L. & W. Jorgensen Memorial Trust Fund
c/o Bank One Trust Co., N.A.
P.O. Box 130
Milwaukee, WI 53201

Established in 1997 in AZ.
Financial data (yr. ended 12/31/01): Grants paid, $14,876; assets, $359,426 (M); expenditures, $20,410; qualifying distributions, $16,857.
Limitations: Applications not accepted.
Application information: Contributes only to pre-selected organizations.
Trustee: Bank One Trust Co., N.A.
EIN: 866188175

57510
William J. Talty and Ethel O. Talty Charitable Fund
c/o Bank One Trust Co., N.A.
P.O. Box 1308
Milwaukee, WI 53201

Established in 1994 in IL.
Financial data (yr. ended 12/31/01): Grants paid, $14,825; assets, $547,354 (M); expenditures, $19,957; qualifying distributions, $14,825.
Limitations: Applications not accepted. Giving limited to IL.
Application information: Contributes only to pre-selected organizations.
Trustee: Bank One Trust Co., N.A.
EIN: 366060072

57511
Davidson & Harley Fund, Inc.
W306 N6620 Deer Trail Rd.
Hartland, WI 53029   (262) 966-7140
Contact: John A. Davidson, Pres.

Donor(s): Martha L. Davidson.
Financial data (yr. ended 09/30/01): Grants paid, $14,650; assets, $370,017 (M); gifts received, $30,000; expenditures, $15,200; qualifying distributions, $14,650.
Limitations: Giving limited to the greater Milwaukeee, WI, area.
Officers and Directors:* John A. Davidson,* Pres.; Arthur H. Davidson,* Secy.-Treas.; Elizabeth M. Lierk.
EIN: 396039228

57512
Schwartz Foundation
1701 Washington St.
Manitowoc, WI 54220-5049

Donor(s): Bernard Schwartz, Isadore Schwartz.
Financial data (yr. ended 12/31/01): Grants paid, $14,525; assets, $117,162 (M); expenditures, $16,040; qualifying distributions, $16,010.
Limitations: Applications not accepted. Giving primarily in Manitowoc, WI.
Application information: Contributes only to pre-selected organizations.
Officers and Directors:* Milton Schwartz, Pres. and Treas.; Isadore Schwartz, V.P.; Bess Schwartz, Secy.
EIN: 396054932

57513
Mary Alice Yakich Educational Foundation, Inc.
1640 East Elm Rd.
Oak Creek, WI 53154
Contact: Walter J. Yakich, Pres.

Donor(s): Walter J. Yakich.
Financial data (yr. ended 12/31/01): Grants paid, $14,515; assets, $293,898 (M); gifts received, $73,000; expenditures, $14,515; qualifying distributions, $14,515.

Limitations: Giving limited to Waco, TX, and Milwaukee, WI.
Application information: Application form required.
Officers: Walter J. Yakich, Pres.; John F. Maloney, V.P. and Secy.; John DuQuaine, Treas.
EIN: 391967691

57514
Raymond C. & Margaret S. Gee Foundation
c/o Bank One Trust Co., N.A.
P.O. Box 1308
Milwaukee, WI 53201

Financial data (yr. ended 03/31/02): Grants paid, $14,500; assets, $349,645 (M); expenditures, $19,953; qualifying distributions, $16,118.
Limitations: Applications not accepted. Giving primarily in TX.
Application information: Contributes only to pre-selected organizations.
Trustee: Bank One Trust Co., N.A.
EIN: 756068034

57515
C. Kevin Walker Foundation
P.O. Box 139
New Lisbon, WI 53950

Established in 1996 in WI.
Financial data (yr. ended 12/31/01): Grants paid, $14,500; assets, $208,336 (M); expenditures, $16,695; qualifying distributions, $14,500.
Limitations: Applications not accepted. Giving primarily in New Lisbon, WI.
Application information: Contributes only to pre-selected organizations.
Trustees: Donald Boudreau, Wes R. Christensen, Kevin C. Walker.
EIN: 391869238

57516
J. C. Meng Foundation, Inc.
c/o Schreiber Foods, Inc.
P.O. Box 19010
Green Bay, WI 54307-9010

Established in 1994 in WI.
Financial data (yr. ended 12/31/01): Grants paid, $14,450; assets, $334,013 (M); expenditures, $17,255; qualifying distributions, $14,450.
Limitations: Applications not accepted. Giving primarily in Green Bay, WI.
Application information: Contributes only to pre-selected organizations.
Officers and Directors:* John C. Meng,* Chair. and Pres.; Engrid H. Meng,* V.P.; Kathy J. Novickis,* Secy.-Treas.; Thomas F. Badciong.
EIN: 411768601

57517
Robert and Mary Jo Hartwig Family Foundation, Inc.
P.O. Box 149
Wausau, WI 54402-0149 (715) 842-3857
Contact: Robert Hartwig, Dir.

Established in 2000 in WI.
Donor(s): Robert R. Hartwig, Mary Jo Hartwig.
Financial data (yr. ended 12/31/01): Grants paid, $14,303; assets, $303,816 (M); expenditures, $18,363; qualifying distributions, $17,820.
Limitations: Giving primarily in WI.
Directors: Daniel G. Hartwig, James J. Hartwig, Linda J. Hartwig, Mary E. Hartwig, Mary Jo Hartwig, Robert R. Hartwig.
EIN: 421507930

57518
Koller Family Foundation
c/o Becker & Kumm
320 W. Grand Ave., Ste. 301
Wisconsin Rapids, WI 54495-2767

Donor(s): Betty J. Koller, Frank R. Koller.
Financial data (yr. ended 12/31/01): Grants paid, $14,300; assets, $151,000 (M); expenditures, $15,332; qualifying distributions, $14,300.
Limitations: Applications not accepted. Giving primarily in Manitowish Waters, WI.
Application information: Contributes only to pre-selected organizations.
Trustees: Betty J. Koller, Frank R. Koller.
EIN: 391530943

57519
Harry & Eleanor Vellmure Family Foundation
c/o Bank One Trust Co., N.A.
P.O. Box 1308
Milwaukee, WI 53201

Established in 2000 in MI.
Financial data (yr. ended 08/31/01): Grants paid, $14,200; assets, $659,906 (M); expenditures, $23,729; qualifying distributions, $14,200.
Limitations: Applications not accepted. Giving primarily in MI.
Application information: Contributes only to pre-selected organizations.
Director: Eleanor Vellmure.
Trustee: Bank One Trust Co., N.A.
EIN: 383496200

57520
David G. and Nancy B. Walsh Family Foundation
c/o Foley & Lardner
P.O. Box 1497
Madison, WI 53701-1497

Established in 1997 in WI.
Donor(s): David G. Walsh, Nancy B. Walsh.
Financial data (yr. ended 06/30/01): Grants paid, $14,200; assets, $1,117,314 (M); expenditures, $20,748; qualifying distributions, $14,200.
Limitations: Applications not accepted.
Application information: Contributes only to pre-selected organizations.
Officers and Directors:* David G. Walsh,* Pres. and Secy.; Nancy B. Walsh,* V.P. and Treas.; Harold Mayer, Thomas Stolper.
EIN: 391914595

57521
William Hoover Gamble Trust
c/o Bank One Trust Co., N.A.
P.O. Box 1308
Milwaukee, WI 53201

Established in 1989 in OH.
Financial data (yr. ended 12/31/99): Grants paid, $14,180; assets, $363,184 (M); expenditures, $19,241; qualifying distributions, $15,290.
Limitations: Applications not accepted. Giving primarily in OH.
Application information: Contributes only to pre-selected organizations.
Trustee: Bank One Trust Co., N.A.
EIN: 316026640

57522
The Karen Lee Schulenberg Memorial Trust, Inc.
2712 Keith St.
Eau Claire, WI 54701-6625 (715) 832-4217
Contact: Wallace A. Schulenberg, Tr.

Donor(s): Delores Schulenberg, Wallace A. Schulenberg.
Financial data (yr. ended 12/31/01): Grants paid, $14,114; assets, $41,814 (M); expenditures, $14,730; qualifying distributions, $14,061.
Limitations: Giving limited to Eau Claire, WI.
Trustees: Delores Schulenberg, Wallace A. Schulenberg, Sharon Stokes.
EIN: 391341845
Codes: GTI

57523
George and Monica Oess Foundation
c/o George Oess
5 Ironwood Ct.
Racine, WI 53402-2867

Established in 1992 in WI.
Donor(s): George P. Oess, Monica Oess.
Financial data (yr. ended 12/31/01): Grants paid, $14,053; assets, $85,761 (M); gifts received, $12,241; expenditures, $14,879; qualifying distributions, $14,053.
Limitations: Applications not accepted. Giving limited to Racine, WI.
Application information: Contributes only to pre-selected organizations.
Trustees: George Oess, Monica Oess.
EIN: 391746825

57524
H. H. Camp Foundation
c/o Wolf and Company, Milwaukee, S.C.
622 N. Water St.
Milwaukee, WI 53202
Application address: 1530 W. Market St., Mequon, WI 53092
Contact: Jack Van Dyke

Financial data (yr. ended 12/31/01): Grants paid, $14,000; assets, $326,282 (M); expenditures, $23,486; qualifying distributions, $14,000.
Limitations: Giving limited to the greater Milwaukee, WI, area.
Officers: J. Camp Van Dyke, Pres.; John S. Borges, V.P.; Nina K. Frantzen, Secy.; Nicholas C. Wilson, Treas.
Trustees: John M. Borges, Susan Mackie, John C. Van Dyke III, Thomas B. Wilson III.
EIN: 396045479

57525
Gialamas Family Foundation
c/o Virchow, Krause - Russ Wolff, C.P.A.
4600 American Pkwy.
Madison, WI 53718

Established in 1998 in WI.
Donor(s): George T. Gialamas, Candida L. Gialamas.
Financial data (yr. ended 03/31/02): Grants paid, $14,000; assets, $231,824 (M); expenditures, $14,227; qualifying distributions, $14,000.
Limitations: Applications not accepted.
Application information: Contributes only to pre-selected organizations.
Trustees: Candida L. Gialamas, George T. Gialamas.
Committee Members: Aris G. Gialamas, Demetria L. Gialamas, Gina M. Gialamas, Thomas G. Gialamas.
EIN: 396673858

57526
Hasselhofer-Wolf Scholarship Fund
c/o U.S. Bank
P.O. Box 2043
Milwaukee, WI 53201-9116
Application address: c/o St. Peter Claver Parish, 1444 S. 11 St., Sheboygan, WI 53081

Established in 1989 in WI.
Donor(s): David Hasselhofer.‡

Financial data (yr. ended 05/31/01): Grants paid, $14,000; assets, $275,236 (M); expenditures, $17,705; qualifying distributions, $14,500.
Limitations: Giving limited to Sheboygan, WI.
Directors: Barbara Adams, David Burkart, Fr. Brian Szyszko.
Trustee: U.S. Bank.
EIN: 396514224
Codes: GTI

57527
Malcolm F. Henning Foundation
c/o Bank One Trust Co., N.A.
P.O. Box 1308
Milwaukee, WI 53201
Contact: Susan Sycamore, Trust Off.

Financial data (yr. ended 12/31/01): Grants paid, $14,000; assets, $305,032 (M); expenditures, $20,242; qualifying distributions, $14,000.
Limitations: Giving primarily in Mount Vernon, IL.
Application information: Application form not required.
Director: David A. Bridewell.
Trustee: Bank One Trust Co., N.A.
EIN: 237030162

57528
Niccum Educational Trust Foundation
c/o Bank One Trust Co., N.A.
P.O. Box 1308
Milwaukee, WI 53201
Application address: c/o Mary Harder, 121 W. Franklin St., Elkhart, In 46516
Contact: Mary Harder

Financial data (yr. ended 12/31/01): Grants paid, $14,000; assets, $564,963 (M); gifts received, $80; expenditures, $19,795; qualifying distributions, $16,027.
Limitations: Giving limited to the Goshen, IN, area.
Publications: Application guidelines, program policy statement.
Application information: Application form required.
Trustee: Bank One Trust Co., N.A.
EIN: 356017515
Codes: GTI

57529
Wood Family Foundation, Inc.
c/o Marshall & Ilsley Bank
P.O. Box 2427
Green Bay, WI 54306-2427
Application address: c/o Frank Wood, P.O. Box 2467, Green Bay, WI 54306, tel.: (920) 432-2941

Financial data (yr. ended 11/30/02): Grants paid, $13,980; assets, $170,278 (M); gifts received, $1,000; expenditures, $15,585; qualifying distributions, $15,196.
Limitations: Giving primarily in Green Bay, WI.
Officer and Trustees:* Patricia Chase,* Secy.-Treas.; Marshall & Ilsley Bank.
EIN: 396171684

57530
Izna & Arden Longcroft Masonnic Trust
178 S. Pearl St.
P.O. Box 217
Berlin, WI 54923-0217 (920) 361-1555
Contact: Melvin Werch, Tr.

Financial data (yr. ended 12/31/01): Grants paid, $13,885; assets, $137,701 (M); expenditures, $15,306; qualifying distributions, $13,885.
Limitations: Giving limited to residents of Berlin, WI.

Trustees: David Barbola, Gerald Werch, Melvin Werch.
EIN: 396420214

57531
Romaine Gallmeier Seminarian Scholarship Fund
c/o Associated Banc-Corp
P.O. Box 408
Neenah, WI 54957-0408
Application address: c/o East Central Synod of Wisconsin, 33003 B N. Richmond St., Appleton, WI 54911, tel.: (920) 734-5381

Established in 1992 in WI.
Financial data (yr. ended 12/31/01): Grants paid, $13,865; assets, $282,471 (M); expenditures, $17,859; qualifying distributions, $13,714.
Limitations: Giving on a national basis.
Trustee: Associated Banc-Corp.
EIN: 396550978

57532
D. L. and L. F. Rikkers Family Foundation, Inc.
c/o W. David Knox, II
777 E. Wisconsin Ave., Ste. 3800
Milwaukee, WI 53202

Established in 1996.
Donor(s): Diane L. Rikkers, Layton F. Rikkers.
Financial data (yr. ended 12/31/01): Grants paid, $13,850; assets, $412,034 (M); expenditures, $20,268; qualifying distributions, $13,850.
Limitations: Applications not accepted.
Application information: Contributes only to pre-selected organizations.
Officers and Directors:* Layton F. Rikkers,* Pres.; Steven Layton Rikkers,* V.P.; Diane L. Rikkers,* Secy.; Kristin Rikkers Davis,* Treas.
EIN: 391870689

57533
Dennis & Cecilia Marcelle Trust
c/o U.S. Bank
P.O. Box 7900
Madison, WI 53707-7900

Established in 1999 in WI.
Financial data (yr. ended 06/30/02): Grants paid, $13,825; assets, $92,022 (M); expenditures, $16,589; qualifying distributions, $13,825.
Limitations: Applications not accepted.
Application information: Contributes only to pre-selected organizations.
Trustee: U.S. Bank.
EIN: 396719584

57534
Town & Country Community Foundation, Inc.
c/o Wells Fargo Bank Wisconsin, N.A.
P.O. Box 171, 636 Wisconsin Ave.
Sheboygan, WI 53082-0171
Application address: c/o Judy Konecki, Trust Off., Wells Fargo Bank IL, N.A., 121 W. First St., Geneseo, IL, 61254

Established in 1990 in IL.
Donor(s): Gretchen M. Ristau.‡
Financial data (yr. ended 12/31/00): Grants paid, $13,811; assets, $262,606 (M); expenditures, $15,726; qualifying distributions, $14,165.
Limitations: Giving limited to the greater Geneseo, IL, area.
Application information: Application form required.
Officers: Gaylon E. Martin, Pres.; E. Lynn Strum, Secy.-Treas.
Director: Christopher Thompson.
Trustee: Wells Fargo Bank Illinois, N.A.
EIN: 363696115
Codes: GTI

57535
The Keller Family Charitable Trust
448 W. Washington Ave.
Madison, WI 53703-2729
Contact: Robert H. Keller, Tr.

Established in 1987 in WI.
Donor(s): Robert H. Keller.
Financial data (yr. ended 12/31/01): Grants paid, $13,750; assets, $200,780 (M); gifts received, $45,000; expenditures, $16,651; qualifying distributions, $13,750.
Trustee: Robert H. Keller.
EIN: 391582385

57536
Ullery Charitable Trust
(Formerly Jimmie Ullery Charitable Trust)
c/o Bank One Trust Co., N.A.
P.O. Box 1308
Milwaukee, WI 53201
Application address: c/o Bank One, Oklahoma, N.A, 15 E. 5th St., Tulsa, OK 74103, tel.: (918) 586-5273
Contact: Bruce Currie, Trust Off.

Financial data (yr. ended 01/31/02): Grants paid, $13,750; assets, $510,636 (M); expenditures, $21,956; qualifying distributions, $16,298.
Limitations: Giving on a national basis.
Application information: Application form not required.
Trustee: Bank One Trust Co., N.A.
EIN: 736142334
Codes: GTI

57537
Lakeland Foundation, Inc.
2203 S. Memorial Pl.
Sheboygan, WI 53083-3715

Financial data (yr. ended 01/31/02): Grants paid, $13,675; assets, $63,117 (M); expenditures, $16,835; qualifying distributions, $13,675.
Limitations: Applications not accepted.
Application information: Contributes only to pre-selected organizations.
Officers: Robert Holman, Pres. and Treas.; William Holman, Secy.
Director: Jean Holman.
EIN: 396076078

57538
Florence Sullivan Larkin Trust
c/o Charles R. Berg
1704 Birch St.
Eau Claire, WI 54703-3270

Established in 1990 in WI.
Financial data (yr. ended 12/31/99): Grants paid, $13,672; assets, $361,001 (M); expenditures, $19,399; qualifying distributions, $13,672.
Limitations: Applications not accepted. Giving limited to WI.
Application information: Contributes only to pre-selected organizations.
Trustee: Charles R. Berg.
EIN: 396495212

57539
Kenosha Scholarship Foundation, Inc.
715 58th St.
Kenosha, WI 53140 (262) 657-1000
Contact: Arleen Wermeling

Financial data (yr. ended 12/31/00): Grants paid, $13,600; assets, $89,030 (M); gifts received, $699; expenditures, $14,526; qualifying distributions, $13,600.
Limitations: Giving limited to Kenosha, WI.
Publications: Application guidelines.

57539—WISCONSIN

Application information: Application form required.
Directors: Elizabeth K. Brown, Howard J. Brown, John Plous.
EIN: 391501320
Codes: GTI

57540
Paul and Ruth Schultz Foundation
c/o Marshall & Ilsley Bank
P.O. Box 2980
Milwaukee, WI 53201   (715) 845-6332

Financial data (yr. ended 08/31/01): Grants paid, $13,600; assets, $267,715 (M); expenditures, $17,440; qualifying distributions, $13,421.
Limitations: Giving primarily in Wausau, WI.
Trustee: Marshall & Ilsley Bank.
EIN: 391890044

57541
Felker Foundation, Inc.
c/o Associated Banc-Corp
P.O. Box 408
Neenah, WI 54957-0408
Contact: Patrick Felker, Pres.

Established around 1975 in WI.
Financial data (yr. ended 12/31/01): Grants paid, $13,583; assets, $110,528 (M); expenditures, $15,074; qualifying distributions, $13,538.
Limitations: Applications not accepted.
Application information: Contributes only to pre-selected organizations.
Officers: Patrick Felker, Pres.; Daniel Umhoefer, V.P.; Gretchen Felker, Secy.-Treas.
Trustee: Associated Banc-Corp.
EIN: 510188283

57542
J. Russell Ward and Margaret Ward Scholarship Fund
c/o Associated Banc-Corp
P.O. Box 408
Neenah, WI 54957-0408
Application addresses: c/o Neenah High School, Neenah, WI 54956; c/o St. Mary's Central Catholic High School, Menasha, WI 54952

Established in 1987 in WI.
Financial data (yr. ended 03/31/01): Grants paid, $13,568; assets, $280,758 (M); expenditures, $17,832; qualifying distributions, $13,320.
Limitations: Giving limited to Neenah and Menasha, WI.
Application information: Application form required.
Trustee: Associated Banc-Corp.
EIN: 396457338

57543
Muriel Thauer Scholarship Fund
c/o Marshall & Ilsley Bank
P.O. Box 2980
Milwaukee, WI 53201
Application address: c/o Watertown High School, 415 S. 8th St., Watertown, WI 53094

Established around 1963 in WI.
Donor(s): Wallace Thauer.‡
Financial data (yr. ended 12/31/01): Grants paid, $13,500; assets, $636,424 (M); expenditures, $21,653; qualifying distributions, $13,500.
Limitations: Giving limited to residents of Watertown, WI.
Trustee: Marshall & Ilsley Bank.
EIN: 396057804
Codes: GTI

57544
Richard B. Windsor Family Foundation
c/o Richard Windsor
426 Erie Ave.
Sheboygan, WI 53081-3508

Established in 1987 in WI.
Donor(s): Richard B. Windsor.
Financial data (yr. ended 11/30/01): Grants paid, $13,400; assets, $93,241 (M); gifts received, $10,837; expenditures, $13,887; qualifying distributions, $13,400.
Limitations: Applications not accepted. Giving on a national basis, with strong emphasis on WI.
Application information: Contributes only to pre-selected organizations.
Officers and Directors:* Richard B. Windsor,* Pres.; Charles B. Windsor,* V.P.; Mary Ann Windsor,* Secy.
EIN: 391576391

57545
Jessie Elfers Scholarship Trust No. 2
c/o U.S. Bank
P.O. Box 2043, LC4NE
Milwaukee, WI 53201-9116

Established in 1997 in IA.
Financial data (yr. ended 01/31/01): Grants paid, $13,224; assets, $269,318 (M); expenditures, $16,645; qualifying distributions, $14,957.
Limitations: Giving primarily in IA.
Application information: Unsolicited requests for funds not accepted.
Trustee: U.S. Bank.
EIN: 426546523

57546
Wisconsin Eastern Star Foundation, Inc.
4528 N. 72nd St.
Milwaukee, WI 53218-5422
Application address: W336 Golden Pk. Cir., Oconomowoc, WI 53066-9308, tel.: (262)593-2091
Contact: Mary Jane Kimber, Secy.

Financial data (yr. ended 12/31/00): Grants paid, $13,194; assets, $223,222 (M); gifts received, $3,510; expenditures, $17,089; qualifying distributions, $15,065.
Limitations: Giving limited to WI.
Application information: Application form required.
Officers: Wallace L. Lindholm, Pres.; Harley Bennett, V.P.; Mary Jane Kimber, Secy.; Leone R. Karow, Treas.
Trustees: Barbara J. Bollinger, Karen A. Carpenter, Phyllis O. Eklov, Jean James, Rae S. Ladd, W. David Olson, Phillip W. Schanke, Karen S. Stauffer.
EIN: 396059144
Codes: GTI

57547
Hedeen Foundation, Inc.
218 N. 14th Ave.
Sturgeon Bay, WI 54235-9709

Established in 1989 in WI.
Donor(s): Clemens V. Hedeen, Patti Jo S. Hedeen.
Financial data (yr. ended 12/31/01): Grants paid, $13,186; assets, $93,238 (M); expenditures, $14,397; qualifying distributions, $13,186.
Limitations: Applications not accepted. Giving limited to WI.
Application information: Contributes only to pre-selected organizations.
Officer: Clemens V. Hedeen, Pres. and Treas.
EIN: 391673742

57548
Lester H. Ihrig Memorial Scholarship Fund
c/o Bank One Trust Co., N.A.
P.O. Box 1308
Milwaukee, WI 53201   (414) 765-2769

Financial data (yr. ended 12/31/00): Grants paid, $13,000; assets, $428,152 (M); expenditures, $18,450; qualifying distributions, $14,447.
Limitations: Applications not accepted. Giving limited to residents of Oshkosh, WI.
Application information: Recipient selected by the principals of each high school. Unsolicited requests for funds not accepted.
Trustee: Bank One Trust Co., N.A.
EIN: 396049541
Codes: GTI

57549
Kearney Foundation, Inc.
(Formerly Kearney Negro Welfare Foundation, Inc.)
656 Evergreen Ct.
Milwaukee, WI 53217-1608
Contact: Carol A. Carpenter, Secy.-Treas.

Financial data (yr. ended 05/31/02): Grants paid, $13,000; assets, $246,158 (M); expenditures, $13,416; qualifying distributions, $13,000.
Limitations: Giving limited to Milwaukee, WI.
Officers and Directors:* William S. Carpenter,* Pres.; Carol A. Carpenter,* Secy.-Treas.; T. Michael Bolger, Matthew C. Carpenter, Nancy L. Carpenter, Ralph Ellis, Linda F. Stephenson, William D. Van Dyke III, Robert A. Wagner.
EIN: 390774273

57550
Langenfeld Pauly Foundation, Inc.
(Formerly Langenfeld Foundation, Inc.)
1711 Circle Dr.
New Holstein, WI 53061-1344
(920) 898-4842
Contact: Gregory E. Pauly, Pres.

Donor(s): Gregory E. Pauly.
Financial data (yr. ended 12/31/01): Grants paid, $13,000; assets, $103,510 (M); expenditures, $13,537; qualifying distributions, $13,000.
Limitations: Giving primarily in New Holstein, WI.
Officers: Gregory E. Pauly, Pres.; Susan D. Schmitz, V.P.; Dolores Pauly, Secy.-Treas.
EIN: 396076175

57551
D. J. Schneider Family Foundation, Inc.
c/o Foley & Lardner
777 E. Wisconsin Ave.
Milwaukee, WI 53202-5367

Financial data (yr. ended 12/31/01): Grants paid, $13,000; assets, $275,717 (M); expenditures, $17,804; qualifying distributions, $13,000.
Limitations: Applications not accepted. Giving primarily in AZ and CO.
Application information: Contributes only to pre-selected organizations.
Officers and Directors:* Marie A. Schneider,* Pres.; Christie A. Kienast,* V.P.; Timothy S. Schneider,* V.P.; Dana J. Schneider, Jr.,* Secy.-Treas.
EIN: 237023858

57552
David & Carol Anderson Family Foundation
c/o David R. Anderson
6193 Washington Cir.
Wauwatosa, WI 53213

Established in 2000 in WI.
Donor(s): David R. Anderson, Carol A. Anderson.

Financial data (yr. ended 12/31/01): Grants paid, $12,982; assets, $122,674 (M); expenditures, $23,558; qualifying distributions, $12,982.
Limitations: Applications not accepted. Giving primarily in WI.
Application information: Contributes only to pre-selected organizations.
Trustees: Carol A. Anderson, David R. Anderson.
EIN: 396728797

57553
Thomas R. Hennessy Family Charitable Trust
P.O. Box 489
La Crosse, WI 54602-0489

Donor(s): T.R. Hennessy, Cynthia J. Hennessy.
Financial data (yr. ended 08/31/01): Grants paid, $12,950; assets, $238,688 (M); expenditures, $14,030; qualifying distributions, $12,823.
Limitations: Applications not accepted. Giving primarily in Winona, MN.
Application information: Contributes only to pre-selected organizations.
Trustees: Lenora Boynton, Cynthia J. Hennessy, T.R. Hennessy, Robert Kanz, John McDonald, North Central Trust Co.
EIN: 237417558

57554
Walters Scholarship Fund
c/o Marshall & Ilsley Bank
P.O. Box 2980
Milwaukee, WI 53201-2980
Application address: Caroline B. Kuehn, c/o Marshall & Ilsley Bank, 500 3rd St., Wausau, WI 54402

Donor(s): Francis O. Walters, Mary O. Walters.
Financial data (yr. ended 09/30/01): Grants paid, $12,949; assets, $267,140 (M); gifts received, $5,000; expenditures, $16,653; qualifying distributions, $12,812.
Limitations: Giving limited to WI.
Trustee: Marshall & Ilsley Bank.
EIN: 930834256
Codes: GTI

57555
Elmer B. Ott Family Foundation, Inc.
c/o Nancy Ott Trainor
2619 Oakwood Ave.
Green Bay, WI 54301

Donor(s): Michael Ott Trainor, Nancy Ott Trainor.
Financial data (yr. ended 12/31/01): Grants paid, $12,917; assets, $238,412 (M); gifts received, $5,340; expenditures, $14,230; qualifying distributions, $12,917.
Limitations: Applications not accepted. Giving primarily in WI.
Application information: Contributes only to pre-selected organizations.
Officers and Directors:* Nancy Ott Trainor,* Pres.; Michael Ott Trainor,* V.P.; Kathleen Schumacher, Maureen Ott Trainor.
EIN: 391633778

57556
George F. & Virginia B. Markham Foundation, Inc.
(Formerly Marianne & George Markham Foundation, Inc.)
c/o Elser Family Offices
777 E. Wisconsin Ave., Ste. 3365
Milwaukee, WI 53202 (414) 225-2284

Donor(s): Marianne E. Markham.
Financial data (yr. ended 12/31/01): Grants paid, $12,850; assets, $322,331 (M); expenditures, $14,531; qualifying distributions, $12,850.
Limitations: Applications not accepted. Giving primarily in WI.
Application information: Contributes only to pre-selected organizations.
Officers and Directors:* George F. Markham, Jr.,* Pres. and Treas.; Virginia B. Markham,* V.P.; Richard S. Gallagher,* Secy.
EIN: 396044355

57557
Bostrom Foundation, Inc.
3107 Cedar Ridge Rd.
Oconomowoc, WI 53066-4905
(262) 646-2435
Contact: Harold W. Bostrom, Pres.

Established around 1967 in WI.
Donor(s): Harold W. Bostrom.
Financial data (yr. ended 09/30/02): Grants paid, $12,800; assets, $62,439 (M); gifts received, $10,000; expenditures, $12,800; qualifying distributions, $12,800.
Limitations: Giving primarily in Milwaukee, WI.
Officer: Harold W. Bostrom, Pres.
EIN: 396126790

57558
Stoelting Brothers Company Foundation, Inc.
502 State Hwy. 67
Kiel, WI 53042-1600
Application address: c/o Scholarship Admin., Kiel School District, P.O. Box 201, Kiel, WI 53042-0201

Donor(s): Stoelting, Inc.
Financial data (yr. ended 09/30/01): Grants paid, $12,800; assets, $272,485 (M); expenditures, $13,276; qualifying distributions, $13,101.
Limitations: Giving limted to Kiel, WI.
Application information: Application forms available at Kiel High School, WI. Application form required.
Officers: Frederick Stoelting, Pres.; John F. Stoelting, V.P.; Robert A. Voigt, Secy.-Treas.
EIN: 396123893
Codes: CS, CD

57559
J. Luty Family Charitable Foundation
7040 N. Port Washington Rd., Ste. 420
Milwaukee, WI 53217 (414) 540-1530
Contact: Alan H. Deutch, Tr.

Established in WI in 1998.
Donor(s): James Luty, Janet Luty.
Financial data (yr. ended 12/31/01): Grants paid, $12,750; assets, $603,185 (M); gifts received, $54,185; expenditures, $13,829; qualifying distributions, $12,750.
Trustees: Alan H. Deutch, James M. Luty, Janet L. Luty.
EIN: 396702652

57560
Warsaw Charitable Trust
c/o Bank One Trust Co., N.A.
P.O. Box 1308
Milwaukee, WI 53201

Established in 2000 in IL.
Donor(s): Harriette Warsaw.‡
Financial data (yr. ended 05/31/01): Grants paid, $12,712; assets, $819,804 (M); gifts received, $858,663; expenditures, $26,348; qualifying distributions, $15,599.
Limitations: Applications not accepted. Giving primarily in Chicago, IL and New York, NY.
Application information: Contributes only to pre-selected organizations.
Trustees: Charlotte Grimson, Bank One Trust Co., N.A.
EIN: 912158583

57561
Lesser Franklin Charitable Trust
(Formerly Lesser Franklin Family Memorial Charitable Trust)
c/o Bank One Trust Co., N.A.
P.O. Box 1308
Milwaukee, WI 53201

Financial data (yr. ended 12/31/01): Grants paid, $12,603; assets, $344,506 (M); expenditures, $17,134; qualifying distributions, $12,603.
Limitations: Applications not accepted. Giving primarily in Franklin Park, IL.
Application information: Contributes only to pre-selected organizations.
Trustee: Bank One Trust Co., N.A.
EIN: 366621337

57562
Daniel W. Erdman Foundation
1721 Hickory Dr.
Madison, WI 53705

Established in 2000 in WI.
Donor(s): Daniel W. Erdman.
Financial data (yr. ended 12/31/01): Grants paid, $12,500; assets, $2,364,503 (M); expenditures, $25,019; qualifying distributions, $12,500.
Limitations: Applications not accepted.
Application information: Contributes only to pre-selected organizations.
Directors: Darrell W. Behnke, Daniel W. Erdman, Deborah Erdman-Luder.
EIN: 392012234

57563
Senkbeil Family Foundation, Inc.
1114A Aspen Ct.
Kohler, WI 53044

Established in 2001 in WI.
Donor(s): Robert C. Senkbeil, Monica M. Senkbeil.
Financial data (yr. ended 12/31/01): Grants paid, $12,500; assets, $193,377 (M); gifts received, $207,162; expenditures, $14,265; qualifying distributions, $12,500.
Limitations: Applications not accepted. Giving primarily in CA, MO, and WI.
Application information: Contributes only to pre-selected organizations.
Officers: Robert C. Senkbeil, Pres.; Monica M. Senkbeil, V.P.; K. Allan Voss, Secy.; Michael J. Senkbeil, Treas.
EIN: 392010296

57564
John A. Slayton Charitable Trust
c/o Marshall & Ilsley Bank
P.O. Box 2980
Milwaukee, WI 53201

Financial data (yr. ended 08/31/01): Grants paid, $12,500; assets, $253,128 (M); gifts received, $41,675; expenditures, $16,483; qualifying distributions, $12,475.
Limitations: Giving primarily in WI.
Trustee: Marshall & Ilsley Bank.
EIN: 396671553

57565
Tapscott Charitable Trust
c/o Bank One Trust Co., N.A.
P.O. Box 1308
Milwaukee, WI 53201

Established in 1992 in KY.
Financial data (yr. ended 09/30/01): Grants paid, $12,448; assets, $334,498 (M); expenditures, $15,790; qualifying distributions, $12,448.

57565—WISCONSIN

Limitations: Applications not accepted. Giving limited to Owensboro, KY.
Application information: Contributes only to pre-selected organizations.
Trustee: Bank One Trust Co., N.A.
EIN: 616106179

57566
Alma Boernke Library Fund
c/o Bank One Trust Co., N.A.
P.O. Box 1308
Milwaukee, WI 53201-1308

Established in 1996 in WI.
Financial data (yr. ended 01/31/02): Grants paid, $12,284; assets, $294,810 (M); expenditures, $15,087; qualifying distributions, $12,284.
Limitations: Applications not accepted.
Application information: Contributes only to pre-selected organizations.
Trustee: Bank One Trust Co., N.A.
EIN: 396318801

57567
Ray & Gertrude M. Webb Scholarship Fund
c/o U.S. Bank
P.O. Box 2043, LC 4 N.E.
Milwaukee, WI 53201-9116

Financial data (yr. ended 06/30/99): Grants paid, $12,254; assets, $493,457 (M); expenditures, $17,738; qualifying distributions, $15,328.
Limitations: Applications not accepted. Giving primarily in IA.
Trustee: U.S. Bank.
EIN: 237434090

57568
Roswell N. and Leona B. Stearns Foundation, Inc.
(Formerly Stearns Foundation, Inc.)
c/o S.I.C.
11431 N. Port Washington Rd.
Mequon, WI 53092
Contact: L.B. Stearns, Pres.

Established in 1953.
Financial data (yr. ended 11/30/01): Grants paid, $12,250; assets, $12,070 (M); gifts received, $15,000; expenditures, $13,641; qualifying distributions, $12,250.
Limitations: Giving primarily in Milwaukee, WI.
Officers: L.B. Stearns, Pres.; J.R. Miller, Secy.; R.S. Krause, Treas.
EIN: 396055102

57569
Hart Design Foundation, Inc.
c/o Gerald T. Schaetz
1940 Radisson St.
Green Bay, WI 54302-2037

Established in 1993 in WI.
Donor(s): Hart Design, Inc., Gerald T. Schaetz, Marilyn Schaetz.
Financial data (yr. ended 09/30/01): Grants paid, $12,240; assets, $80,674 (M); gifts received, $10,000; expenditures, $12,435; qualifying distributions, $12,240.
Limitations: Applications not accepted.
Application information: Contributes only to pre-selected organizations.
Directors: Michelle A. Duval, Gerald T. Schaetz, Marilyn Schaetz, Richard B. Schaetz.
EIN: 391778333

57570
Institute for Advanced Christian Studies, Inc.
P.O. Box 44362
Madison, WI 53744-4362
Application address: 810 S. Wright St., Urbana, IL (217) 333-1549
Contact: Clifford G. Christians, Pres.

Financial data (yr. ended 06/30/01): Grants paid, $12,238; assets, $140,438 (M); gifts received, $2,665; expenditures, $25,951; qualifying distributions, $14,254.
Limitations: Giving primarily in IL.
Application information: Application form not required.
Officers and Directors:* Clifford Christians,* Pres.; V. Elving Anderson,* Treas.; C. Steven Evans, Robert Frykenberg, Carl F.H. Henry, Arthur Holmes, Kenneth Kantzer, Lamin Sanneh, Keith Yandell.
EIN: 237008040
Codes: GTI

57571
William D. Connor Educational Fund
1905 S. Roddis Ave.
Marshfield, WI 54449
Application address: 503 S. Cypress Ave., Marshfield, WI 54449, tel.: (715) 384-2778
Contact: Marietta Drach, Mgr.

Financial data (yr. ended 12/31/01): Grants paid, $12,151; assets, $172,201 (M); expenditures, $13,726; qualifying distributions, $12,151.
Limitations: Giving limited to the Marshfield, Auburndale and Stratford, WI, areas.
Application information: Application form not required.
Officer and Trustees:* Marietta Drach,* Mgr.; Kenneth E. Noble.
EIN: 396062183

57572
Usinger Foundation, Inc.
c/o Fred Usinger, Inc.
1030 N. Old World 3rd St.
Milwaukee, WI 53203-1302 (414) 276-9100
Contact: Debra L. Usinger, Pres.

Donor(s): Fred Usinger, Inc.
Financial data (yr. ended 12/31/01): Grants paid, $12,050; assets, $73,574 (M); gifts received, $19,500; expenditures, $12,316; qualifying distributions, $12,301.
Limitations: Giving primarily in the Milwaukee, WI, area.
Officers and Directors:* Debra L. Usinger,* Pres. and Mgr.; Frederick D. Usinger,* V.P.; Allen W. Weidler, Secy.-Treas.; Wilbur E. Holtz.
EIN: 396066333
Codes: CS, CD

57573
Randall J. & Judith F. Hake Family Foundation, Inc.
525 Pennsylvania Ave., Ste. 302
Sheboygan, WI 53081 (920) 803-8063
Contact: Randall J. Hake, Pres.

Established in 2001 in WI.
Donor(s): Randall J. Hake, Judith F. Hake.
Financial data (yr. ended 12/31/01): Grants paid, $12,030; assets, $5,991 (M); gifts received, $20,000; expenditures, $14,159; qualifying distributions, $12,028.
Limitations: Giving primarily in Sheboygan, WI.
Application information: Application form not required.
Officers: Randall J. Hake, Pres.; Judith F. Hake, Secy.
Director: Trentan F. Hake.

EIN: 392030307

57574
Ruth Coyer Scholarship Trust
c/o Bank One Trust Co., N.A.
P.O. Box 1308
Milwaukee, WI 53201
Application address: 200 W. College Ave., Appleton, WI 54911, tel.: (920) 735-1354
Contact: Don Jarek, Trust Off., Bank One Trust Co., N.A.

Financial data (yr. ended 06/30/01): Grants paid, $12,000; assets, $270,891 (M); expenditures, $15,646; qualifying distributions, $12,000.
Limitations: Giving primarily in WI.
Application information: Application form required.
Trustee: Bank One Trust Co., N.A.
EIN: 396582144

57575
James E. DeLong Foundation, Inc.
c/o Waukesha Engine
1000 W. St. Paul Ave.
Waukesha, WI 53188 (262) 549-2865
Application address: c/o Pres., Carrol College, 100 N. East Ave., Waukesha, WI 53186

Donor(s): Dresser Industries, Inc., Halliburton Co., Dresser, Inc.
Financial data (yr. ended 09/30/01): Grants paid, $12,000; assets, $123,239 (M); gifts received, $7,550; expenditures, $12,076; qualifying distributions, $12,010.
Limitations: Giving primarily in areas of company operations.
Application information: Application form required.
Officers: W.E. O'Connor, Pres.; G.D. Smith, V.P.; J.A. Staffeldt, Secy.-Treas.
EIN: 396050331
Codes: CS, CD, GTI

57576
Lydia Childs Eskridge Foundation, Inc.
6400 Brandywood Trail
Sun Prairie, WI 53590

Established in 2000 in WI.
Donor(s): Lydia B. Arden.
Financial data (yr. ended 12/31/01): Grants paid, $12,000; assets, $242,230 (M); gifts received, $18,128; expenditures, $16,344; qualifying distributions, $12,000.
Limitations: Applications not accepted.
Application information: Contributes only to pre-selected organizations.
Officers and Directors:* Lydia B. Arden,* Pres. and Treas.; Lydia Black,* V.P.; David Reinecke,* Secy.
EIN: 411966870

57577
The Gossen Corporation Foundation
2030 W. Bender Rd.
Milwaukee, WI 53209

Established in 1992 in WI.
Donor(s): The Gossen Corp.
Financial data (yr. ended 12/31/01): Grants paid, $12,000; assets, $1,803 (M); gifts received, $11,000; expenditures, $12,008; qualifying distributions, $12,000.
Limitations: Applications not accepted. Giving primarily in Milwaukee, WI.
Application information: Contributes only to pre-selected organizations.
Directors: F. Butterfield, Jr., Exec. Dir.; F. Butterfield, Sr.
EIN: 391745385

Codes: CS, CD

57578
Robert M. Hoffer Family Foundation
(Formerly Martha C. & Robert M. Hoffer Foundation)
4600 N. Lake Dr.
Whitefish Bay, WI 53211

Established in 1986 in WI.
Donor(s): Martha C. Hoffer, Robert M. Hoffer.
Financial data (yr. ended 12/31/01): Grants paid, $12,000; assets, $354,119 (M); expenditures, $13,488; qualifying distributions, $13,488.
Limitations: Applications not accepted. Giving primarily in Milwaukee, WI.
Application information: Contributes only to pre-selected organizations.
Trustees: Martha C. Hoffer, Robert M. Hoffer, Elizabeth Hoffer Maniaci.
EIN: 391575117

57579
New Life Foundation
c/o Foley & Lardner
777 E. Wisconsin Ave.
Milwaukee, WI 53202-5367

Established in 2000 in WI.
Donor(s): Margaret W. Frank, Douglas F. Frank.
Financial data (yr. ended 12/31/01): Grants paid, $12,000; assets, $294,192 (M); expenditures, $12,907; qualifying distributions, $12,000.
Limitations: Applications not accepted. Giving primarily in Portland, OR.
Application information: Contributes only to pre-selected organizations.
Trustees: Stephen M. Fisher, Douglas F. Frank, Margaret W. Frank, Michael W. Hatch.
EIN: 396728886

57580
Rindt Family Charitable Trust
(Formerly The Park N Shop Charitable Trust)
1317 N. 25th St.
Sheboygan, WI 53081-3168
Application address: 1629 Golf View E., Sheboygan, WI 53083, tel.: (920) 458-0404
Contact: Russell Rindt, Treas.

Established in 1979.
Financial data (yr. ended 10/31/01): Grants paid, $11,906; assets, $70,264 (M); expenditures, $12,345; qualifying distributions, $11,906.
Limitations: Giving primarily in Sheboygan, WI.
Officer: Russell Rindt, Treas.
EIN: 391346436

57581
Walter and Jessie Francisco Charitable Foundation
c/o Bank One Trust Co., N.A.
P.O. Box 1308
Milwaukee, WI 53201
Application address: 100 W. Milwaukee St., Janesville, WI 53545
Contact: Curt Parish, Trust Off., Bank One Trust Co.

Established in 1993 in WI.
Financial data (yr. ended 05/31/02): Grants paid, $11,900; assets, $485,850 (M); expenditures, $17,464; qualifying distributions, $11,900.
Limitations: Giving primarily in Rock County, WI.
Application information: Application form required.
Trustee: Bank One Trust Co., N.A.
EIN: 396566244

57582
Dane County Bicycle Association, Inc.
c/o Kathleen Villard, C.P.A.
2814 Center Ave.
Madison, WI 53704-5702 (608) 233-8569
Application address: 2720 Gregory St., Madison, WI 53711
Contact: Bill Putnam, Secy.

Financial data (yr. ended 12/31/01): Grants paid, $11,778; assets, $223,973 (M); expenditures, $12,671; qualifying distributions, $11,778.
Limitations: Giving limited to the Midwest.
Officers: Susan Kavulich, Pres.; Bill Havda, V.P.; Bill Putnam, Secy.; John H. DeVoro, Treas.
EIN: 391552516

57583
Flora Corpening Trust
c/o Bank One Trust Co., N.A.
P.O. Box 1308
Milwaukee, WI 53201
Application address: Principal, Bridgeport High School, Bridgeport WV

Financial data (yr. ended 12/31/01): Grants paid, $11,750; assets, $192,189 (M); expenditures, $16,929; qualifying distributions, $13,480.
Limitations: Giving limited to residents of Bridgeport, WV.
Application information: Application form required.
Trustee: Bank One, West Virginia, N.A.
EIN: 556035695
Codes: GTI

57584
Fern Brown Memorial Fund
c/o Bank One, N.A.
P.O. Box 1308
Milwaukee, WI 53201
Application address: P.O. Box 1, Tulsa, OK 74193
Contact: Mike Bartel, Trust Off., Bank One Trust Co., N.A.

Financial data (yr. ended 06/30/01): Grants paid, $11,700; assets, $221,827 (M); expenditures, $15,355; qualifying distributions, $12,896.
Limitations: Giving primarily in OK.
Application information: Application form not required.
Trustee: Bank One, N.A.
EIN: 736162573
Codes: GTI

57585
Christian Marius Lauritzen II Charitable Trust
c/o U.S. Bank
P.O. Box 2043, Ste. LC4NE
Milwaukee, WI 53201 (414) 765-6038
Application address: 777 E. Wisconsin Ave., Milwaukee, WI 53202-5300
Contact: Richard Bottoni, Trust Off., U.S. Bank

Established in 1997 in WI.
Donor(s): Christian Marius Lauritzen, Christian Marius Lauritzen II.
Financial data (yr. ended 12/31/01): Grants paid, $11,628; assets, $250,293 (M); expenditures, $15,837; qualifying distributions, $11,628.
Application information: Application form not required.
Trustee: U.S. Bank.
EIN: 396642995

57586
Varaby Foundation, Inc.
c/o Diversified Mgmt., Inc.
5225 N. Ironwood Rd., Ste. 117
Milwaukee, WI 53217 (414) 964-7400
Contact: Mark Homan

Established in 2000 in WI.
Donor(s): Drew Weber.
Financial data (yr. ended 12/31/01): Grants paid, $11,600; assets, $341,552 (M); expenditures, $17,259; qualifying distributions, $11,600.
Officer: Drew Weber, Pres.
Directors: Joann Weber, Katherine Weber, Michael Weber.
EIN: 392001775

57587
Curtis J. Hubertz Family Foundation
111 E. Wisconsin Ave., Ste. 1800
Milwaukee, WI 53202

Established in 1997 in WI.
Financial data (yr. ended 12/31/01): Grants paid, $11,545; assets, $42,204 (M); expenditures, $17,735; qualifying distributions, $11,545.
Limitations: Applications not accepted.
Application information: Contributes only to pre-selected organizations.
Officer: Curtis J. Hubertz, Mgr.
EIN: 391870992

57588
James D. Reigle Foundation
P.O. Box 67
Kewaskum, WI 53040

Donor(s): James D. Reigle.
Financial data (yr. ended 12/31/00): Grants paid, $11,517; assets, $76,616 (M); expenditures, $12,129; qualifying distributions, $11,517.
Limitations: Applications not accepted. Giving primarily in WI.
Application information: Contributes only to pre-selected organizations.
Trustees: Allen C. Koepke, James D. Reigle.
EIN: 391572035

57589
Badger Mining Scholarship Trust
c/o Markesan State Bank
84 N. Bridge St.
Markesan, WI 53946

Donor(s): Badger Mining Corp.
Financial data (yr. ended 12/31/01): Grants paid, $11,500; assets, $992 (M); gifts received, $11,500; expenditures, $11,792; qualifying distributions, $11,500.
Limitations: Giving limited to residents of WI.
Application information: Application form required.
Trustee: Markesan State Bank.
EIN: 396433973
Codes: CS, CD, GTI

57590
Tinsley Helton Charitable Trust
350 W. Green Tree Rd.
Milwaukee, WI 53217

Established in 2000 in WI.
Donor(s): Tinsley Helton.‡
Financial data (yr. ended 12/31/01): Grants paid, $11,499; assets, $735,740 (M); expenditures, $28,650; qualifying distributions, $11,499.
Limitations: Applications not accepted. Giving primarily in WI.
Application information: Contributes only to pre-selected organizations.
Trustee: Maryl Pittleman.

57590—WISCONSIN

EIN: 396728303

57591
Milne Family Foundation
N63 W29880 Woodfield Ct.
Hartland, WI 53029

Established in 2000 in WI.
Donor(s): W. Bruce Milne, Rebecca J. Milne.
Financial data (yr. ended 12/31/01): Grants paid, $11,250; assets, $336,793 (M); gifts received, $123,975; expenditures, $22,833; qualifying distributions, $11,250.
Limitations: Applications not accepted. Giving primarily in Colorado Springs, CO.
Application information: Contributes only to pre-selected organizations.
Trustees: Rebecca J. Milne, W. Bruce Milne.
EIN: 367317868

57592
W. T. Hansen Family Foundation, Inc.
6263 N. Teutonia Ave.
Milwaukee, WI 53209-3648
Contact: Donald W. Hansen, Secy.

Donor(s): Willard T. Hansen.
Financial data (yr. ended 08/31/01): Grants paid, $11,155; assets, $155,513 (M); expenditures, $18,922; qualifying distributions, $11,155.
Limitations: Giving primarily in WI.
Application information: Application form not required.
Officers: Willard T. Hansen, Pres.; Donald W. Hansen, Secy.
EIN: 396064799

57593
Siebecker Foundation, Inc.
(Formerly Wilson-Hurd Foundation, Inc.)
2323 N. Mayfair Rd., Ste. 240
Milwaukee, WI 53226

Donor(s): Wilson-Hurd Mfg. Co.
Financial data (yr. ended 08/31/01): Grants paid, $11,117; assets, $132,641 (M); gifts received, $15,000; expenditures, $14,135; qualifying distributions, $11,117.
Limitations: Applications not accepted. Giving primarily in Wausau, WI.
Application information: Contributes only to pre-selected organizations.
Officers: William D. Siebecker, Pres.; Nancy Siebecker, V.P.; Luke Sims, Secy.; Daniel Wieselman, Treas.
EIN: 237417555

57594
The Arrupe Foundation, Inc.
3415 Gateway Rd.
Brookfield, WI 53045-5111

Established in 2000 in WI.
Donor(s): Thomas Ewens.
Financial data (yr. ended 12/31/01): Grants paid, $11,000; assets, $26,067 (M); gifts received, $25,000; expenditures, $11,425; qualifying distributions, $11,000.
Limitations: Applications not accepted. Giving on a national and international basis.
Application information: Contributes only to pre-selected organizations.
Directors: James M. Ewens, Lara E. Ewens, Thomas Ewens.
EIN: 391973982

57595
William and Lena Fricke Foundation
127 Canterbury Rd
Eau Claire, WI 54701
Application address: c/o Robert E. Fricke, 217 Maple Tree Dr., Bristol, TN 37620, tel.: (423) 764-1260

Established in 1997.
Donor(s): Annadell Schump Noren.
Financial data (yr. ended 12/31/01): Grants paid, $11,000; assets, $278,483 (M); expenditures, $12,051; qualifying distributions, $11,000.
Trustees: Raymond C. Fricke, Helen F. Nordstrom, Annadell Schump Noren.
EIN: 396677792

57596
John B. McKinstry Charitable Foundation, Inc.
808 Lake Shore Dr.
Beaver Dam, WI 53916

Established in 1997 in WI.
Donor(s): Beatrice McKinstry.
Financial data (yr. ended 12/31/01): Grants paid, $11,000; assets, $398,864 (M); expenditures, $12,557; qualifying distributions, $11,000.
Limitations: Applications not accepted.
Application information: Contributes only to pre-selected organizations.
Officers: John B. McKinstry, Pres. and Treas.; Ricky H. Fiegel, V.P.; Annette Kamps, Secy.
EIN: 391888986

57597
Allen J. Shafer Trust
c/o U.S. Bank
P.O. Box 7900
Madison, WI 53707-7900

Financial data (yr. ended 12/31/01): Grants paid, $11,000; assets, $185,025 (M); expenditures, $13,958; qualifying distributions, $11,102.
Limitations: Giving limited to residents of WI.
Application information: Unsolicited request for funds not accepted.
Trustee: U.S. Bank.
EIN: 396140024
Codes: GTI

57598
The Third Founders Trust
c/o Bank One Trust Co., N.A.
P.O. Box 1308
Milwaukee, WI 53201
Application address: P.O. Box 2050, Fort Worth, TX 76113, tel.: (817) 884-4149
Contact: Randy Hale, Trust Off., Bank One Trust Co., N.A.

Financial data (yr. ended 12/31/01): Grants paid, $11,000; assets, $262,490 (M); expenditures, $13,778; qualifying distributions, $12,258.
Limitations: Giving primarily in Houston, TX.
Trustee: Bank One Trust Co., N.A.
EIN: 756014366

57599
Erwin J. Plesko Foundation, Inc.
c/o Erwin J. Plesko
27 Bayside Dr.
Madison, WI 53704

Established in 1998 in WI.
Donor(s): Erwin J. Plesko.
Financial data (yr. ended 12/31/01): Grants paid, $10,975; assets, $342,059 (M); gifts received, $191,370; expenditures, $12,045; qualifying distributions, $10,975.
Limitations: Applications not accepted. Giving primarily in Madison, WI.
Application information: Contributes only to pre-selected organizations.
Officers: Erwin J. Plesko, Pres.; Timothy W. Sherry, V.P.; Andrew E. Plesko, Secy.; Jennifer M. Richey, Treas.
EIN: 391961593

57600
Ida M. Sivyer Trust for Boys Trade Technical High School
c/o U.S. Bank
P.O. Box 2043
Milwaukee, WI 53201-2043

Financial data (yr. ended 06/30/00): Grants paid, $10,890; assets, $299,624 (M); expenditures, $14,880; qualifying distributions, $12,556.
Limitations: Applications not accepted. Giving limited to Milwaukee, WI.
Application information: Recipients are chosen by a committee of faculty members.
Trustee: U.S. Bank.
EIN: 396035625

57601
Mary Louise Hesse Trust
c/o Bank One Trust Co., N.A.
P.O. Box 1308
Milwaukee, WI 53201

Financial data (yr. ended 12/31/99): Grants paid, $10,810; assets, $472,140 (M); expenditures, $21,139; qualifying distributions, $11,857.
Limitations: Applications not accepted. Giving primarily in Steubenville, OH.
Application information: Contributes only to pre-selected organizations.
Trustee: Bank One Trust Co., N.A.
EIN: 316429794

57602
Ila M. Skelton Trust Fund
c/o Bank One Trust Co., N.A.
P.O. Box 1308
Milwaukee, WI 53201-1308

Established in 1992 in IL.
Financial data (yr. ended 07/31/01): Grants paid, $10,800; assets, $333,215 (M); expenditures, $16,198; qualifying distributions, $12,635.
Trustee: Bank One Trust Co., N.A.
EIN: 371297171

57603
Bart & Char Olson Foundation
337 Palisade St.
P.O. Box 40
Merrimac, WI 53561

Established in 1998 in WI.
Donor(s): Bartlett A. Olson, Charlotte Olson.
Financial data (yr. ended 12/31/01): Grants paid, $10,600; assets, $408,153 (M); expenditures, $15,388; qualifying distributions, $10,600.
Limitations: Applications not accepted. Giving primarily in WI.
Application information: Contributes only to pre-selected organizations.
Trustees: Bartlett A. Olson, Kirk Olson.
EIN: 396702648

57604
Sonnentag Foundation, Ltd.
900 East St.
Marathon, WI 54448-0100
Application address: P.O. Box 100, Marathon, WI 54448, tel.: (715) 443-2146
Contact: Carolyn Sonnentag, Secy.-Treas.

Financial data (yr. ended 09/30/00): Grants paid, $10,600; assets, $210,197 (M); gifts received,

$125,100; expenditures, $10,699; qualifying distributions, $10,531.
Limitations: Giving limited to residents of Marathon, WI.
Officers: John Sonnentag, Pres.; Carolyn Sonnentag, Secy.-Treas.
Director: Tim Sonnentag.
EIN: 391597420

57605
Michael & Susan Freeman Family Foundation, Inc.
5640 N. Shore Dr.
Milwaukee, WI 53217-4861

Donor(s): Susan W. Freeman, Michael E. Freeman.
Financial data (yr. ended 04/30/02): Grants paid, $10,531; assets, $4,335 (M); expenditures, $10,561; qualifying distributions, $10,531.
Limitations: Applications not accepted.
Application information: Contributes only to pre-selected organizations.
Officers and Directors:* Michael E. Freeman,* Pres. and Treas.; Susan W. Freeman,* V.P. and Secy.; Ellen F. Byrd.
EIN: 396090082

57606
Donald L. and Valerie D. Gottschalk Foundation
1465 Milwaukee St.
Delafield, WI 53018 (262) 392-9460
Contact: Donald L. Gottschalk, Tr.

Established in 1990 in WI.
Donor(s): Donald L. Gottschalk, Valerie D. Gottschalk.
Financial data (yr. ended 12/31/01): Grants paid, $10,505; assets, $70,007 (M); gifts received, $6,482; expenditures, $10,657; qualifying distributions, $10,505.
Limitations: Giving primarily in WI.
Trustees: Donald L. Gottschalk, Valerie D. Gottschalk.
EIN: 391686976

57607
T. Murrell Edmunds Testamentary Trust
c/o Bank One Trust Co., N.A.
P.O. Box 1308
Milwaukee, WI 53201
Application address: 201 St. Charles Ave., 29th Fl., New Orleans, LA 70170
Contact: John Lafargue

Established in 1999 in LA.
Financial data (yr. ended 12/31/00): Grants paid, $10,500; assets, $265,220 (M); expenditures, $24,283; qualifying distributions, $12,794.
Trustee: Bank One.
EIN: 756533776

57608
Charles Robert Evenson Foundation
c/o Bank One Trust Co., N.A.
P.O. Box 1308
Milwaukee, WI 53201-1308
Application address: c/o James D. Wright, 200 Ottawa Ave., N.W., Grand Rapids, MI 48503, tel.: (616) 771-7780

Financial data (yr. ended 10/31/01): Grants paid, $10,500; assets, $312,484 (M); expenditures, $20,733; qualifying distributions, $12,575.
Limitations: Giving limited to Grand Rapids, MI.
Officers: Robert Evenson, Jr., V.P.; Joan Newberry, V.P.
Trustee: Bank One Trust Co., N.A.
EIN: 386085626

57609
Self Reliance Foundation
5610 Gatewood Ln.
Greendale, WI 53129

Established in 2000.
Financial data (yr. ended 12/31/01): Grants paid, $10,500; assets, $352 (M); gifts received, $75; expenditures, $12,316; qualifying distributions, $10,500.
Limitations: Applications not accepted.
Application information: Contributes only to pre-selected organizations.
Officers: Dean Curtis, Pres.; Julie Curtis, V.P.; Larry Roepke, Treas.
EIN: 470815270

57610
Marth Foundation, Ltd.
c/o Scholarship Comm.
6752 S. Hwy. 107N
Marathon, WI 54448-9519

Financial data (yr. ended 05/31/02): Grants paid, $10,495; assets, $20,120 (M); gifts received, $7,500; expenditures, $10,847; qualifying distributions, $10,495.
Limitations: Giving limited to WI.
Officers: Paulette Natzke, Pres.; Jerome Natzke, V.P.; Kenneth Natzke, Secy.-Treas.
EIN: 391410550

57611
Edward A. Wilke Scholarship Trust
c/o Waukesha State Bank
P.O. Box 648
Waukesha, WI 53187-0648

Financial data (yr. ended 12/31/01): Grants paid, $10,339; assets, $229,078 (M); expenditures, $14,311; qualifying distributions, $10,339.
Limitations: Applications not accepted. Giving primarily in Wales, WI.
Application information: Contributes only to pre-selected organizations.
Trustee: Waukesha State Bank.
EIN: 396458482

57612
Dudley and Constance Godfrey Foundation, Inc.
780 N. Water St.
Milwaukee, WI 53202

Established in 1986 in WI.
Donor(s): Dudley J. Godfrey, Jr., Constance P. Godfrey.
Financial data (yr. ended 12/31/01): Grants paid, $10,200; assets, $251,317 (M); expenditures, $10,797; qualifying distributions, $10,797.
Limitations: Applications not accepted. Giving primarily in WI.
Application information: Contributes only to pre-selected organizations.
Officers and Directors:* Dudley J. Godfrey, Jr.,* Pres. and Treas.; Constance P. Godfrey,* V.P. and Secy.; Henry E. Fuldner.
EIN: 391562846

57613
Richard S. & Ann L. Gallagher Charitable Fund
1260 E. Dean Rd.
Milwaukee, WI 53217-2403

Established in 1986 in WI.
Donor(s): Richard S. Gallagher, Ann L. Gallagher.
Financial data (yr. ended 12/31/01): Grants paid, $10,150; assets, $85,447 (M); expenditures, $10,592; qualifying distributions, $10,150.
Limitations: Applications not accepted. Giving primarily in the Milwaukee, WI, area.

Application information: Contributes only to pre-selected organizations.
Trustees: Ann L. Gallagher, Richard S. Gallagher.
EIN: 391546740

57614
Hans & Anna Spartvedt Testamentary Trust
c/o Marshall & Ilsley Bank
P.O. Box 2980
Milwaukee, WI 53201
Application address: c/o Marshall & Ilsley Bank, 3330 University Ave., Madison, WI 53705

Financial data (yr. ended 12/31/01): Grants paid, $10,105; assets, $149,635 (M); expenditures, $13,690; qualifying distributions, $11,110.
Limitations: Giving limited to WI.
Trustee: Marshall & Ilsley Bank.
EIN: 396266732

57615
Ladky Associates Foundation, Inc.
7020 N. Green Bay Ave.
Milwaukee, WI 53209 (414) 351-2112
Contact: Frank J. Ladky, Chair.

Financial data (yr. ended 12/31/01): Grants paid, $10,030; assets, $135,164 (M); gifts received, $4,000; expenditures, $10,030; qualifying distributions, $10,030.
Application information: Application form not required.
Officers: Frank J. Ladky, Chair. and Mgr.; Thomas E. Ladky, Pres.
EIN: 396081103

57616
Benjamin David Bowling Trust f/b/o Charity
c/o Bank One Trust Co., N.A.
P.O. Box 1308
Milwaukee, WI 53201

Established in 1995.
Donor(s): Bowling Estate.
Financial data (yr. ended 12/31/01): Grants paid, $10,000; assets, $148,871 (M); expenditures, $11,629; qualifying distributions, $10,916.
Limitations: Applications not accepted. Giving primarily in Louisville, KY.
Application information: Contributes only to pre-selected organizations.
Trustee: Bank One Trust Co., N.A.
EIN: 616219708

57617
Joseph & Angela Bruneo Foundation
3505 30th Ave.
Kenosha, WI 53144 (262) 652-5050
Contact: Bruno M. Rizzo, Dir.

Financial data (yr. ended 12/31/00): Grants paid, $10,000; assets, $156,363 (L); expenditures, $11,510; qualifying distributions, $11,510.
Limitations: Giving primarily in WI.
Directors: Lucille Bruneo, Peter Bruneo, Sr., Bruno M. Rizzo.
EIN: 391917743

57618
Clyde R. Evans Scholarship Award Trust
c/o Bank One Trust Co., N.A.
111 E. Wisconsin Ave., Ste. 940
Milwaukee, WI 53202

Financial data (yr. ended 06/30/01): Grants paid, $10,000; assets, $260,826 (M); expenditures, $14,653; qualifying distributions, $10,180.
Limitations: Applications not accepted. Giving primarily in Mangum, OK.
Trustees: Roy W. Chandler, Gordon Henderson, David C. Johnston, Bank One Trust Co., N.A.
EIN: 736296081

57619
Margaret S. Keizer Testamentary Trust
c/o First National Bank of Platteville
170 W. Main St.
Platteville, WI 53818 (608) 348-7777

Financial data (yr. ended 12/31/01): Grants paid, $10,000; assets, $175,894 (M); expenditures, $11,963; qualifying distributions, $10,000.
Limitations: Giving limited to Platteville, WI.
Application information: Application form not required.
Trustee: First National Bank of Platteville.
EIN: 396659128

57620
Mildred R. Perry Scholarship Trust
c/o Baraboo National Bank
P.O. Box 50
Baraboo, WI 53913
Application address: c/o Principal, Webb High School, 707 N. Webb Ave., Reedsburg, WI 53959, tel.: (608) 524-4327

Established in 1984 in WI.
Financial data (yr. ended 12/31/01): Grants paid, $10,000; assets, $165,491 (M); expenditures, $13,357; qualifying distributions, $10,570.
Limitations: Giving limited to Reedsburg, WI.
Application information: Application form required.
Trustee: Charles T. Yeomans.
EIN: 391437634
Codes: GTI

57621
George E. Stifel Endowment Fund
c/o Bank One Trust Co., N.A.
P.O. Box 1308
Milwaukee, WI 53201
Application address: c/o Bank One, West Virginia, Wheeling, N.A., Wheeling, WV 26003, tel.: (304) 234-4130
Contact: Ed Johnson

Established in 1995 in WV.
Financial data (yr. ended 12/31/99): Grants paid, $10,000; assets, $3,974,184 (M); expenditures, $75,356; qualifying distributions, $13,271.
Limitations: Giving limited to residents of Wheeling, WV.
Application information: Application form required.
Trustee: Bank One Trust Co., N.A.
EIN: 556018247
Codes: GTI

57622
Stockton Charitable Foundation
(Formerly North J. and Florence Stockton Charitable Foundation)
c/o Bank One Trust Co., N.A.
P.O. Box 1308
Milwaukee, WI 53201

Established in 1995 in FL.
Donor(s): Florence Stockton.
Financial data (yr. ended 12/31/01): Grants paid, $10,000; assets, $176,962 (M); expenditures, $16,775; qualifying distributions, $10,000.
Limitations: Giving limited to Broward County, FL, and Wayne County, MI.
Trustees: Florence Stockton, Bank One Trust Co., N.A.
EIN: 386662894

57623
John D. & Mary E. Waterman Charitable Foundation, Inc.
c/o John C. Mitby
2 E. Mifflin St.
Madison, WI 53703-2889

Established in 1996 in WI.
Donor(s): John D. Waterman, Mary E. Waterman.
Financial data (yr. ended 12/31/01): Grants paid, $10,000; assets, $170,046 (M); expenditures, $11,379; qualifying distributions, $10,000.
Limitations: Applications not accepted.
Application information: Contributes only to pre-selected organizations.
Officers: John D. Waterman, Pres. and Treas.; Mary E. Waterman, V.P. and Secy.
Director: John C. Mitby.
EIN: 391869630

57624
Morris Family Foundation, Inc.
832 Country Club Ln.
Onalaska, WI 54650

Established in 1985 in WI.
Donor(s): David L. Morris, Sacia B. Morris.
Financial data (yr. ended 12/31/01): Grants paid, $9,995; assets, $842,652 (M); expenditures, $12,876; qualifying distributions, $10,199.
Limitations: Applications not accepted. Giving primarily in WI.
Application information: Contributes only to pre-selected organizations.
Officers: David L. Morris, Pres. and Treas.; Sacia B. Morris, V.P. and Secy.
Director: Timothy Morris.
EIN: 391527549

57625
Carol M. Wilmer Endowment, Inc.
344 Travellers Run
Burlington, WI 53105

Established in 1999.
Financial data (yr. ended 12/31/01): Grants paid, $9,900; assets, $209,765 (M); expenditures, $10,441; qualifying distributions, $9,900.
Limitations: Applications not accepted.
Application information: Contributes only to pre-selected organizations.
Officers: Patrick M. Lloyd, Pres.; Gerlad Richter, V.P.; David Edmundson, Secy.-Treas.
EIN: 391947746
Codes: TN

57626
Bob & Margaret DeBoise Foundation, Inc.
(Formerly Glenn R. Straub Foundation, Inc.)
P.O. Box 8010
Wausau, WI 54402-8010
Application address: 179 Cypress View Dr., Maples, FL 34113, tel.: (941) 417-2382
Contact: Margaret J. DeBoise, Pres.

Donor(s): Margaret J. DeBoise.
Financial data (yr. ended 12/31/01): Grants paid, $9,845; assets, $120,640 (M); expenditures, $10,705; qualifying distributions, $9,845.
Limitations: Giving limited to the Naples, FL, area, and northern WI.
Officers: Margaret J. DeBoise, Pres.; Richard J. Weber, V.P.; Robert A. DeBoise, Secy.-Treas.
Director: Clark D. Straub.
EIN: 396102370

57627
Wisconsin Troopers Association Scholarship Fund
2099 Ironwood Dr.
Green Bay, WI 54304
Application address: 600 S. Main St., Deerfield, WI 53531, tel.: (608) 764-8306
Contact: Gwen Schneider, Dir.

Established in 1987 in WI.
Financial data (yr. ended 12/31/01): Grants paid, $9,800; assets, $1,424 (M); expenditures, $10,120; qualifying distributions, $9,799.
Limitations: Giving limited to WI.
Director: Gwen Schneider.
Trustees: Kim Hurley, Candy Konz.
EIN: 391606135
Codes: GTI

57628
Schiferl Family Charitable Foundation, Inc.
P.O. Box 423
Abbotsford, WI 54405 (715) 223-4068
Contact: James Schiferl, Pres.

Established in 1995 in WI.
Donor(s): James Schiferl, Pauline A. Schiferl.
Financial data (yr. ended 12/31/01): Grants paid, $9,676; assets, $220,610 (M); gifts received, $38,800; expenditures, $10,256; qualifying distributions, $9,933.
Limitations: Giving primarily in the Abbotsford, WI, area.
Officers: James Schiferl, Pres.; Frank L. Nikolay, V.P.; Norman B. Kommer, Secy.-Treas.
Directors: James Maurina, James Nikolay, Carol O'Leary, Laurie Raatz, Martin Schultz, Jack Wild.
EIN: 391475094

57629
Richard and Ellen Glaisner Foundation, Ltd.
900 W. Bradley Rd.
River Hills, WI 53217 (414) 272-4707

Established in 1997 in WI.
Donor(s): Richard Glaisner, Ellen Glaisner.
Financial data (yr. ended 12/31/00): Grants paid, $9,650; assets, $143,706 (M); expenditures, $10,104; qualifying distributions, $9,650.
Limitations: Applications not accepted. Giving primarily in Milwaukee, WI.
Application information: Contributes only to pre-selected organizations.
Officers: Richard Glaisner, Pres. and Treas.; Ellen Glaisner, V.P. and Secy.
Director: Kurt Glaisner.
EIN: 391893384

57630
BayCare Clinic Foundation, Ltd.
2733 S. Ridge Rd.
Green Bay, WI 54304

Established in 2000 in WI.
Donor(s): BayCare Health Systems, LLC.
Financial data (yr. ended 12/31/01): Grants paid, $9,648; assets, $26,254 (M); gifts received, $21,575; expenditures, $44,467; qualifying distributions, $11,093.
Limitations: Applications not accepted. Giving primarily in Green Bay, WI.
Application information: Contributes only to pre-selected organizations.
Directors: Joseph Hodgson, Jeff Mason, Paul Summerside.
EIN: 392000503
Codes: CS

57631
Peter G. Flinn Trust
c/o Bank One Trust Co., N.A.
P.O. Box 1308
Milwaukee, WI 53201
Application address: 111 Monument Cir.,
IN1-0150, Indianapolis, IN 46277-0115
Contact: John D. Wilson, V.P. and Trust Off.,
Bank One Investment Mgmt. Group

Financial data (yr. ended 12/31/00): Grants paid,
$9,600; assets, $354,996 (M); expenditures,
$13,726; qualifying distributions, $11,472.
Limitations: Giving limited to Grant County, IN.
Application information: Applications are sent to
area schools from Bank One Trust Group.
Application form required.
Trustee: Bank One Trust Co., N.A.
EIN: 356016860
Codes: GTI

57632
Russell Phillips Trust
c/o Marshall & Ilsley Bank
P.O. Box 2980
Milwaukee, WI 53201
Application address: Robert F. Penn, c/o
Marshall & Ilsley Bank, Stevens Point, WI,
54481, tel.: (715) 342-3250

Financial data (yr. ended 12/31/01): Grants paid,
$9,540; assets, $125,453 (M); expenditures,
$15,667; qualifying distributions, $12,239.
Limitations: Giving limited to residents of Portage
County, WI.
Trustee: Marshall & Ilsley Bank.
EIN: 396276572
Codes: GTI

57633
Beutner Family Foundation, Inc.
2323 N. Mayfair Rd., Ste. 240
Milwaukee, WI 53226 (414) 475-6565

Established in 1997 in WI.
Donor(s): Grant C. Beutner, Rosemary A. Beutner.
Financial data (yr. ended 12/31/00): Grants paid,
$9,500; assets, $147,319 (M); expenditures,
$11,640; qualifying distributions, $10,462.
Application information: Application form
required.
Officers and Directors:* Grant C. Beutner,* Pres.
and Treas.; Rosemary A. Beutner,* V.P. and Secy.;
Thomas P. Ehr.
EIN: 391892337

57634
Burling-Potthast Scholarship Trust
(Formerly Beverly B. Burling-Potthast
Scholarship Fund)
c/o Bank One Trust Co., N.A.
P.O. Box 1308
Milwaukee, WI 53201 (414) 765-2769
Contact: Lisa A. Olson, Trust Off., Bank One
Trust Co., N.A.

Financial data (yr. ended 12/31/01): Grants paid,
$9,443; assets, $200,699 (M); expenditures,
$12,343; qualifying distributions, $10,695.
Limitations: Giving limited to Milwaukee County, WI.
Application information: Application form not
required.
Trustee: Bank One Trust Co., N.A.
EIN: 396182802

57635
Deland Foundation
c/o Wells Fargo Bank Wyoming, N.A.
P.O. Box 171
Sheboygan, WI 53082-0171
Application address: 607 N. 8th St., Plz. 8,
Sheboygan, WI 53081-4519, tel.: (920)
458-5501
Contact: K. Allen Voss, Secy.

Financial data (yr. ended 12/31/01): Grants paid,
$9,432; assets, $312,015 (M); expenditures,
$14,138; qualifying distributions, $9,432.
Limitations: Giving limited to Sheboygan County, WI.
Application information: Application form not
required.
Officers: Patricia Reiss, Pres.; William C.
Hollingsworth, V.P.; K. Allan Voss, Secy.; Hugh F.
Denison, Treas.
Trustee: Wells Fargo Bank Wisconsin, N.A.
EIN: 396045553

57636
Leff Family Foundation, Inc.
c/o Aaron N. Leff
6589 N. Crestwood Dr.
Glendale, WI 53209

Established in 1991 in WI.
Financial data (yr. ended 12/31/00): Grants paid,
$9,425; assets, $43,508 (M); gifts received,
$5,000; expenditures, $9,579; qualifying
distributions, $9,425.
Limitations: Applications not accepted.
Application information: Contributes only to
pre-selected organizations.
Officers: Ruth Leff, Pres. and Treas.; Barbara Leff,
V.P.; Aaron Leff, Secy.
EIN: 391676889

57637
Alfred Grindon, Jr. Private Foundation
c/o Bank One Trust Co., N.A.
P.O. Box 1308
Milwaukee, WI 53201

Financial data (yr. ended 06/30/01): Grants paid,
$9,400; assets, $403,361 (M); expenditures,
$25,233; qualifying distributions, $11,055.
Limitations: Applications not accepted. Giving
primarily in IL.
Application information: Contributes only to
pre-selected organizations.
Trustee: Bank One Trust Co., N.A.
EIN: 371267454

57638
Korupp & Waelti Scholarship Fund
c/o U.S. Bank
P.O. Box 7900
Madison, WI 53707

Financial data (yr. ended 12/31/00): Grants paid,
$9,400; assets, $199,416 (M); expenditures,
$12,757; qualifying distributions, $9,900.
Limitations: Giving limited to Blanchardville,
Hollandale, and Madison, WI.
Application information: Recipient selected by
Pecatonica High School staff.
Trustee: U.S. Bank.
EIN: 396291034

57639
Milton H. Kuether Foundation, Inc.
932 1st St.
Kiel, WI 53042-1208
Application address: c/o Guidance Counselor,
Kiel High School, Kiel, WI 53042, tel.: (920)
894-2263

Financial data (yr. ended 12/31/00): Grants paid,
$9,350; assets, $190,883 (M); expenditures,
$9,868; qualifying distributions, $9,772.
Limitations: Giving limited to Kiel, WI.
Application information: Application form
required.
Officers and Directors:* Marion Kuether,* Pres.
and Treas.; Jane Voigt,* V.P.; Nancy Gooding,
Secy.; Betty Gast, Judy Helms, Sally Phillips.
EIN: 391487379

57640
Sumnicht Family Foundation
2909 Fox Run
Appleton, WI 54914-8741

Established in 1985 in WI.
Donor(s): Vernon C. Sumnicht.
Financial data (yr. ended 12/31/01): Grants paid,
$9,310; assets, $4,215 (M); gifts received, $5,541;
expenditures, $10,312; qualifying distributions,
$9,310.
Limitations: Applications not accepted. Giving
primarily in WI.
Application information: Contributes only to
pre-selected organizations.
Officer: Vernon C. Sumnicht, Mgr.
Trustee: Debra A. Sumnicht.
EIN: 391537336

57641
Arthur C. Kootz Foundation
c/o William Clyde Surles
5060 N. Maple Ln.
Nashotah, WI 53058

Donor(s): Margrete K. Surles.
Financial data (yr. ended 12/31/01): Grants paid,
$9,200; assets, $199,280 (M); expenditures,
$9,378; qualifying distributions, $9,200.
Limitations: Applications not accepted. Giving
primarily in WI.
Application information: Contributes only to
pre-selected organizations.
Trustees: Margrete K. Surles, William Clyde Surles.
EIN: 237418817

57642
Alice E. Bunn for Community Chest
c/o Bank One Trust Co., N.A.
P.O. Box 1308
Milwaukee, WI 53201

Established in 1994 in IL.
Financial data (yr. ended 12/31/01): Grants paid,
$9,132; assets, $208,284 (M); expenditures,
$11,491; qualifying distributions, $10,214.
Limitations: Applications not accepted.
Application information: Contributes only to
pre-selected organizations.
Trustee: Bank One Trust Co., N.A.
EIN: 376025176

57643
Carl & Isabel Backlin Trust
c/o Marshall & Ilsley Bank
P.O. Box 2980
Milwaukee, WI 53201
Application address: c/o Marshall & Ilsley Bank,
Trust Co., 5835 7th Ave., Kenosha, WI 53140,
tel.: (262) 658-5580

Established in 1999 in WI.

57643—WISCONSIN

Financial data (yr. ended 07/31/01): Grants paid, $9,125; assets, $188,389 (M); expenditures, $12,411; qualifying distributions, $9,185.
Limitations: Giving limited to Burlington, Racine County, WI.
Trustee: Marshall & Ilsley Bank.
EIN: 396717250

57644
Annalea Stone Trust
c/o Bank One Trust Co., N.A.
P.O. Box 1308
Milwaukee, WI 53201

Established in 1997 in OH.
Financial data (yr. ended 12/31/99): Grants paid, $9,102; assets, $277,069 (M); expenditures, $13,427; qualifying distributions, $9,435.
Limitations: Applications not accepted. Giving primarily in Lorain, OH.
Application information: Contributes only to pre-selected organizations.
Trustee: Bank One Trust Co., N.A.
EIN: 911923693

57645
A. P. Jensen Foundation, Inc.
530 Farwell Dr.
Madison, WI 53704 (608) 249-4259
Contact: A. Paul Jensen, Dir.

Established in 1993 in WI.
Financial data (yr. ended 12/31/01): Grants paid, $9,070; assets, $172,547 (M); expenditures, $9,271; qualifying distributions, $9,070.
Limitations: Giving primarily in Madison, WI.
Directors: A. Paul Jensen, Abby Jensen, Aileen Jensen, Andrew Jensen.
EIN: 391744157

57646
Christmas Spirit Foundation
c/o M. Murphy
201 Pine Terr.
Oconomowoc, WI 53066

Established in 1999 in WI.
Financial data (yr. ended 12/31/01): Grants paid, $9,001; assets, $159,605 (M); gifts received, $1,043; expenditures, $10,183; qualifying distributions, $9,001.
Limitations: Applications not accepted. Giving primarily in WI.
Application information: Contributes only to pre-selected organizations.
Officers: Margaret I. Murphy, Pres.; Warren Steiner, V.P.; Leslie Broviak, Secy.; John Murphy, Treas.
EIN: 391960243

57647
Holler Charitable Foundation, Inc.
c/o Shane Lauterbach
N63W29822 Woodfield Ct.
Hartland, WI 53029

Established in 1997 in WI.
Donor(s): Jonathan Brent Lauterbach, Heath A. Lauterbach, W. Shane Lauterbach, Jeanne Lauterbach.
Financial data (yr. ended 12/31/00): Grants paid, $9,000; assets, $27,434 (M); gifts received, $6,125; expenditures, $9,502; qualifying distributions, $9,000.
Limitations: Applications not accepted.
Application information: Contributes only to pre-selected organizations.
Officers and Directors:* W. Shane Lauterbach,* Pres.; Brent Lauterbach,* V.P.; Heath A. Lauterbach, V.P.; John M. Remmers,* Secy.; Karen R. Lauterbach, Treas.; H. William Lauterbach.

EIN: 391879999

57648
Melvin S. Jozwiak Scholarship Trust
825 N. Jefferson St., Ste. 300
Milwaukee, WI 53202-3737 (414) 271-2718
Contact: Janet F. Resnick, Tr.

Established in 1999 in WI.
Financial data (yr. ended 12/31/00): Grants paid, $9,000; assets, $155,985 (M); expenditures, $17,910; qualifying distributions, $17,227.
Limitations: Giving primarily in WI.
Application information: Application form required.
Directors: Patricia Engbring, Laura J. Petrie.
Trustee: Janet F. Resnick.
EIN: 396696457

57649
Pagel Graphics Arts Scholarship Trust Fund
P.O. Box 34
Elm Grove, WI 53122-0034
Contact: Robert Carlson, Tr.

Financial data (yr. ended 06/30/01): Grants paid, $9,000; assets, $305,922 (M); gifts received, $8,956; expenditures, $42,007; qualifying distributions, $9,000.
Limitations: Giving primarily in WI.
Trustee: Robert Carlson.
EIN: 391674169

57650
St. John the Baptist Parish Parochial School Trust
N7231 County Rd. E.
River Falls, WI 54022-4038

Established in 1995.
Donor(s): Joseph Wieser.
Financial data (yr. ended 12/31/01): Grants paid, $9,000; assets, $176,245 (M); expenditures, $9,691; qualifying distributions, $9,000.
Limitations: Applications not accepted. Giving primarily in WI.
Application information: Contributes only to pre-selected organizations.
Trustees: Julie A. Behnke, Maria J. Lecheler, Daniel J. Wieser.
EIN: 396625622

57651
Venturedyne, Ltd. Foundation
(Formerly Wehr Corporation Foundation)
c/o Venturedyne, Ltd. Foundation
10201 W. Lincoln Ave., Ste. 400
Milwaukee, WI 53227
Contact: Brian L. Nahey, Pres.

Donor(s): Venturedyne, Ltd.
Financial data (yr. ended 12/31/01): Grants paid, $8,945; assets, $91,204 (M); expenditures, $8,945; qualifying distributions, $8,945.
Limitations: Giving primarily in MI and WI.
Application information: Application form not required.
Officers and Directors:* Brian L. Nahey,* Pres. and Treas.; Carole J. Nahey,* V.P. and Secy.; Nancy L. Johnson.
EIN: 396096050
Codes: CS, CD

57652
Badger Mining Associate Scholarship Trust
(Formerly BMC Associate Scholarship Trust)
c/o Markesan State Bank
84 N. Bridge St.
Markesan, WI 53946 (920) 361-2388

Donor(s): Badger Mining Corp.

Financial data (yr. ended 12/31/01): Grants paid, $8,866; assets, $6,542 (M); gifts received, $15,000; expenditures, $9,158; qualifying distributions, $8,866.
Limitations: Giving limited to WI.
Application information: Application form required.
Trustee: Markesan State Bank.
EIN: 396642667
Codes: CS, CD

57653
Lewis & Dorothy Kranick Foundation
(Formerly Dexter-Kranick Foundation, Inc.)
915 Otto Way
Elkhart Lake, WI 53020 (920) 876-2401
Contact: Lewis G. Kranick, Pres.

Financial data (yr. ended 12/31/01): Grants paid, $8,830; assets, $213,472 (M); expenditures, $9,391; qualifying distributions, $8,830.
Application information: Organizations that have been a volunteer or member in the past.
Officers: Lewis G. Kranick, Pres. and Treas.; Dorothy D. Kranick, V.P. and Secy.
EIN: 396075653

57654
Mary Ellen Peters Charitable Foundation, Inc.
c/o John Mitby
2 E. Mifflin St., Ste. 200
Madison, WI 53703

Established in 1996 in WI.
Donor(s): Mary Ellen Peters.
Financial data (yr. ended 12/31/01): Grants paid, $8,750; assets, $168,941 (M); gifts received, $40,000; expenditures, $9,867; qualifying distributions, $8,750.
Limitations: Applications not accepted.
Application information: Contributes only to pre-selected organizations.
Officer: Mary Ellen Peters, Pres.
EIN: 391869935

57655
Panax Foundation, Ltd.
2311 N. 96th Ave.
Wausau, WI 54401

Established in 1989 in WI.
Donor(s): Duane Vetter, Sara Vetter.
Financial data (yr. ended 10/31/01): Grants paid, $8,601; assets, $11,429 (M); expenditures, $9,030; qualifying distributions, $8,601.
Limitations: Applications not accepted. Giving limited to WI.
Application information: Contributes only to pre-selected organizations.
Officers: Duane Vetter, Pres.; Sara Vetter, V.P.; Alex Vetter, Secy.; Senia Vetter, Treas.
EIN: 391661741

57656
Charles and Shirley Pechous Family Foundation
7202 3rd Ave.
Kenosha, WI 53143-5561
Contact: Charles E. Pechous, Jr., Pres.

Established in 1994 in WI.
Donor(s): Charles E. Pechous, Jr., Shirley A. Pechous.
Financial data (yr. ended 12/31/01): Grants paid, $8,500; assets, $140,895 (M); expenditures, $10,547; qualifying distributions, $8,500.
Officers: Charles E. Pechous, Jr., Pres. and Treas.; Shirley A. Pechous, Secy.; Anne Holdsworth, V.P.; Charles E. Pechous III, V.P.; Elizabeth Pechous, V.P.; James Pechous, V.P.; Mary Pechous, V.P.; Thomas Pechous, V.P.
EIN: 391806532

57657
Edward F. Rathke Irrevocable Scholarship Trust
c/o Marshall & Isley Bank
P.O. Box 2427
Green Bay, WI 54306-2427 (920) 432-6361
Contact: Darlene Kuschel, V.P., Marshall & Isley Bank

Financial data (yr. ended 12/31/01): Grants paid, $8,500; assets, $116,634 (M); expenditures, $10,249; qualifying distributions, $8,649.
Limitations: Giving limited to Brown and Oconto counties, WI.
Trustee: Marshall & Ilsley Bank.
EIN: 510187617
Codes: GTI

57658
Victor Sumnicht Foundation
3313 N. 99th St.
Milwaukee, WI 53222-3415

Financial data (yr. ended 12/31/01): Grants paid, $8,500; assets, $170,818 (M); expenditures, $20,952; qualifying distributions, $8,500.
Limitations: Applications not accepted. Giving primarily in WI.
Application information: Contributes only to pre-selected organizations.
Trustees: Dan Sumnicht, Patricia Sumnicht.
EIN: 237108612

57659
Memmen Family Foundation, Inc.
4492 Choctaw Trail
Green Bay, WI 54313

Established in 2000 in WI.
Financial data (yr. ended 12/31/01): Grants paid, $8,400; assets, $213,639 (M); gifts received, $153,875; expenditures, $10,501; qualifying distributions, $8,400.
Limitations: Applications not accepted.
Application information: Contributes only to pre-selected organizations.
Officers: James Memmen, Pres.; Mary Memmen, V.P. and Secy.
Director: Alexander Memmen.
EIN: 391995802

57660
Schorer Foundation, Inc.
1495 Pineview Dr.
Reedsburg, WI 53959

Financial data (yr. ended 06/30/01): Grants paid, $8,400; assets, $350,215 (M); expenditures, $9,327; qualifying distributions, $8,400.
Limitations: Applications not accepted. Giving limited to WI.
Officers: William C. Schorer III, Pres.; M. LaVonna Schorer, V.P.; Charles B. Hamburg, Secy.-Treas.
EIN: 396085473

57661
Louise J. Desper Irrevocable Trust
c/o Wood County Trust Co.
P.O. Box 8000
Wisconsin Rapids, WI 54495-8000

Established in 2000 in WI.
Donor(s): Ronald Desper Administrative Trust.
Financial data (yr. ended 12/31/01): Grants paid, $8,353; assets, $302,380 (M); gifts received, $12,060; expenditures, $16,013; qualifying distributions, $8,353.
Limitations: Applications not accepted.
Application information: Contributes only to pre-selected organizations.
Trustee: Wood County Trust Co.
EIN: 396724543

57662
John Feith Foundation, Inc.
2839 Hwy. 33
Saukville, WI 53080

Established in 1986.
Donor(s): John Feith.
Financial data (yr. ended 01/31/02): Grants paid, $8,350; assets, $88,355 (M); expenditures, $9,145; qualifying distributions, $8,350.
Limitations: Applications not accepted. Giving primarily in Saukville, WI.
Application information: Contributes only to pre-selected organizations.
Officers: Elizabeth Feith, V.P.; John Feith, Mgr.
EIN: 391572031

57663
The Meyer M. Cohen Scholarship Fund
c/o Associated Banc-Corp
P.O. Box 408
Neenah, WI 54957-0408

Financial data (yr. ended 05/31/02): Grants paid, $8,332; assets, $60,328 (M); gifts received, $350; expenditures, $9,912; qualifying distributions, $8,332.
Limitations: Applications not accepted. Giving primarily in Green Bay, WI.
Application information: Contributes only to pre-selected organizations.
Trustee: Associated Banc-Corp.
EIN: 391414749

57664
Stevens Masonic Home Trust No. 7
c/o U.S. Bank
P.O. Box 2043
Milwaukee, WI 53201-9116

Financial data (yr. ended 12/31/01): Grants paid, $8,287; assets, $266,273 (M); expenditures, $12,210; qualifying distributions, $8,287.
Limitations: Applications not accepted. Giving limited to Cedar Rapids, IA.
Application information: Contributes only to pre-selected organizations.
Trustee: U.S. Bank.
EIN: 426054196

57665
Friends of the Royal Society of Chemistry, Inc.
c/o Richard Gallagher
777 E. Wisconsin Ave., Rm. 3600
Milwaukee, WI 53202

Established in 1988.
Financial data (yr. ended 11/30/99): Grants paid, $8,237; assets, $115,987 (M); gifts received, $100,000; expenditures, $20,850; qualifying distributions, $15,268.
Limitations: Applications not accepted. Giving on an international basis, with emphasis on England.
Officers and Directors:* K.W. Humphreys,* Pres.; Ned D. Heindel,* 1st V.P.; D.H.M. Bowen,* 2nd V.P.; T.D. Inch,* Secy.-Treas.
EIN: 391639596

57666
Acherman Memorial Trust
(Formerly Joseph & Alice Beller Acherman Memorial Fund Trust)
c/o Wisconsin Community Bank
P.O. Box 100
Monroe, WI 53566-0100 (608) 328-4042
Contact: Ron Spielman, Trust Off., Wisconsin Community Bank

Financial data (yr. ended 12/31/01): Grants paid, $8,150; assets, $178,015 (M); expenditures, $10,755; qualifying distributions, $8,150.
Limitations: Giving limited to Monroe, WI.
Trustee: Bank One Trust Co., N.A.
EIN: 396209178

57667
Gerald J. and Paula Jo Coffey, Inc.
c/o Gerald J. Coffey
824 County HWY K
Hartford, WI 53027-9069

Established in 1999 in WI.
Donor(s): Gerald J. Coffey, Paula Jo Coffey.
Financial data (yr. ended 12/31/01): Grants paid, $8,100; assets, $56,666 (M); gifts received, $21,250; expenditures, $8,603; qualifying distributions, $8,100.
Limitations: Applications not accepted. Giving primarily in WI.
Application information: Contributes only to pre-selected organizations.
Officers and Directors:* Gerald Coffey,* Pres. and Treas.; Paula Jo Coffey,* V.P. and Secy.; John Miller.
EIN: 391931409

57668
Ruud Family Foundation, Inc.
6800 Hoods Creek Rd.
Franksville, WI 53126

Donor(s): Christopher Ruud.
Financial data (yr. ended 12/31/01): Grants paid, $8,100; assets, $235,257 (M); expenditures, $10,562; qualifying distributions, $8,100.
Limitations: Applications not accepted.
Application information: Contributes only to pre-selected organizations.
Officers: Christopher A. Ruud, Pres. and Treas; Chantil F. Ruud, V.P.; Theodore O. Sokoly, Secy.
EIN: 391915760

57669
Konrad and Mary Jo Testwuide Foundation
1236 Riverview Dr.
P.O. Box 28
Sheboygan, WI 53083 (920) 458-4178
Contact: Mary Jo Testwuide, Dir.

Established in 1997 in WI.
Donor(s): Konrad C. Testwuide, Mary Jo Testwuide.
Financial data (yr. ended 12/31/00): Grants paid, $8,067; assets, $287,335 (M); gifts received, $200,000; expenditures, $9,529; qualifying distributions, $8,837.
Limitations: Giving primarily in Sheboygan, WI.
Directors: James A. Testwuide, Konrad C. Testwuide, Mary Jo Testwuide.
EIN: 391915639

57670
Castle Industries Foundation, Inc.
P.O. Box 357
Princeton, WI 54968-0357
Application address: 1544 W. County Hwy. J, Princeton, WI 54968, tel.: (920) 295-4208
Contact: Craig E. Castle, Jr., V.P.

Donor(s): Castle Industries.
Financial data (yr. ended 12/31/01): Grants paid, $8,045; assets, $133,545 (M); expenditures, $10,756; qualifying distributions, $8,045.
Limitations: Giving limited to Fond du Lac, WI, and surrounding counties.
Officers and Directors:* Craig E. Castle,* Pres. and Treas.; Craig E. Castle, Jr.,* V.P.; Kathryn F. Castle,* Secy.
EIN: 237161535

57671
Mari's Foundation
220 S. Morrison
Appleton, WI 54911-5739
Contact: Mari Taniguchi, Tr.

Established in 1997 in WI.
Donor(s): Mari Taniguchi.
Financial data (yr. ended 12/31/99): Grants paid, $8,043; assets, $233,583 (M); expenditures, $9,963; qualifying distributions, $11,334.
Trustees: Park M. Drescher, Barbara J. Hoffman, Mari Taniguchi.
EIN: 396647866

57672
Lee W. Metzner Memorial Fund
c/o Marshall & Ilsley Bank
P.O. Box 2980
Milwaukee, WI 53201
Application address: c/o Guidance Office, Algoma High School, 1715 Division St., Algoma, WI 54201

Established in 1996 in WI.
Financial data (yr. ended 12/31/01): Grants paid, $8,034; assets, $146,186 (M); expenditures, $11,202; qualifying distributions, $7,990.
Limitations: Giving limited to Kewaunee, WI.
Application information: Application form required.
Trustee: Marshall & Ilsley Bank.
EIN: 396428655

57673
Feingold Family Charitable Foundation
c/o U.S. Bank
P.O. Box 2043
Milwaukee, WI 53201-9116
Application address: P.O. Box 0663, Sheboygan, WI 53082
Contact: Camala Roberts, Trust Off., U.S. Bank

Donor(s): Harold D. Feingold.
Financial data (yr. ended 12/31/01): Grants paid, $8,000; assets, $271,839 (M); gifts received, $23,027; expenditures, $10,325; qualifying distributions, $8,000.
Limitations: Giving primarily in Sheboygan, WI.
Trustees: Harold D. Feingold, U.S. Bank.
EIN: 930756218

57674
Agusta Hamilton Foundation, Inc.
409 S. 29th St.
P.O. Box 1027
Manitowoc, WI 54221-1027
Application address: 1425 Gunnell Ln., Manitowoc, WI 54220, tel.: (920) 682-3655
Contact: Edson P. Foster, Jr., Secy.-Treas.

Financial data (yr. ended 12/31/01): Grants paid, $8,000; assets, $88,812 (M); expenditures, $11,253; qualifying distributions, $8,000.
Limitations: Giving limited to Manitowoc, WI.
Officers: Ann R. Mast, Pres.; Ella Longacre, V.P.; Edson P. Foster, Jr., Secy.-Treas.
Directors: Elizabeth Coffee, Margaret Hamilton, Ellen Mueller.
EIN: 396052912

57675
Saline Family Foundation
c/o North Central Trust Co.
311 Main St.
La Crosse, WI 54601

Established in 2001 in WI.
Donor(s): Lindon Saline, Jane Saline.
Financial data (yr. ended 12/31/01): Grants paid, $8,000; assets, $150,196 (M); gifts received, $150,600; expenditures, $9,882; qualifying distributions, $8,500.
Application information: Application form required.
Trustees: Susan J. Durtsche, Heron B. Saline, Jane Saline, Jeffrey L. Saline, Lindon Saline, Sandra Saline, North Central Trust Co.
EIN: 316649587

57676
W. R. and Floy A. Sauey Family Foundation
c/o Nordic Group
414 Broadway, Ste. 200
Baraboo, WI 53913
Contact: Alison Martin, Pres.

Established in 1998.
Donor(s): Flambeau Products, Flambeau Corp., Seats, Inc.
Financial data (yr. ended 12/31/00): Grants paid, $8,000; assets, $141,221 (M); gifts received, $94,198; expenditures, $14,184; qualifying distributions, $8,000.
Application information: Applicants must be children of employees of Nordic Group. Application form required.
Officers: Alison Martin, Pres.; Floy A. Sauey, V.P.; Bruce E. Taylor, Secy.; Dave M. Koch, Treas.
Directors: Todd L. Sauey, William R. Sauey.
EIN: 391934775

57677
Robert G. Chamberlain Foundation
W2728 Oakwood Beach Rd.
Markesan, WI 53946

Financial data (yr. ended 06/30/01): Grants paid, $7,965; assets, $53,269 (M); gifts received, $13,758; expenditures, $8,030; qualifying distributions, $7,965.
Limitations: Applications not accepted.
Application information: Contributes only to pre-selected organizations.
Officers: Robert G. Chamberlain, Pres. and Treas.; Jane H. Chamberlain, V.P.; James R. Chamberlain, Secy.
EIN: 391419134

57678
Pflugradt Foundation, Inc.
c/o Gerald J. Holz
6425 W. Norwich Ave., Apt. 121
Greenfield, WI 53220-2508
Application address: c/o Scott C. Roggenbauer, P.O. Box 263, Palmyra, WI 53156

Financial data (yr. ended 10/31/01): Grants paid, $7,937; assets, $154,693 (M); expenditures, $9,539; qualifying distributions, $7,937.
Limitations: Giving primarily in CA, IL, and WI.
Officer: Gerald J. Holz, Secy.-Treas.
EIN: 396047496

57679
The Shomos Family Foundation, Ltd.
c/o J. Bernstein, Godfrey & Kahn, SC
780 N. Water St.
Milwaukee, WI 53202-3512

Established in 1988 in WI.
Donor(s): Gustav V. Shomos, Veronica Shomos.
Financial data (yr. ended 12/31/01): Grants paid, $7,925; assets, $55,792 (M); expenditures, $11,643; qualifying distributions, $7,925.
Limitations: Applications not accepted. Giving primarily in WI.
Application information: Contributes only to pre-selected organizations.
Officers and Directors:* Gustav V. Shomos,* Pres. and Treas.; Veronica Shomos,* V.P. and Secy.
EIN: 391622902

57680
Walter J. Markham Private Foundation
c/o Walter J. Markham
P.O. Box 23819
Green Bay, WI 54305-3819

Established in 1991 in WI.
Donor(s): Walter J. Markham, Mary Jane Markham.
Financial data (yr. ended 06/30/01): Grants paid, $7,900; assets, $139,514 (M); expenditures, $9,254; qualifying distributions, $7,900.
Limitations: Applications not accepted. Giving primarily in Green Bay, WI.
Application information: Contributes only to pre-selected organizations.
Officers: Walter J. Markham, Pres.; Dorothy Temple, V.P.; Michael J. Shinners, Treas.
EIN: 383005646

57681
Salt and Light Foundation, Inc.
c/o Pellitteri's Container Haul Away
P.O. Box 259426
Madison, WI 53725-9426

Established in 1995 in WI.
Donor(s): Pellitteri's Container Haul Away.
Financial data (yr. ended 12/31/01): Grants paid, $7,822; assets, $5,733 (M); gifts received, $10,000; expenditures, $8,261; qualifying distributions, $8,261.
Limitations: Applications not accepted. Giving primarily in WI.
Application information: Contributes only to pre-selected organizations.
Officers: Thomas J. Pellitteri, Pres.; Michele J. Pellitteri, V.P.
Director: David A. Pellitteri.
EIN: 391810850
Codes: CS, CD

57682
Stanek Foundation, Inc.
c/o Stanek Tool Corp.
2500 S. Calhoun Rd.
New Berlin, WI 53151-2712
Contact: Thomas J. Stanek, Pres.

Donor(s): Stanek Tool Corp.
Financial data (yr. ended 06/30/02): Grants paid, $7,815; assets, $799 (M); gifts received, $1,000; expenditures, $7,845; qualifying distributions, $7,815.
Limitations: Giving primarily in WI.
Officers: Thomas J. Stanek, Pres.; Mary S. Wehrheim, V.P.; Barbara A. Kudriko, Secy.-Treas.
EIN: 396077475
Codes: CS, CD

57683
Lewitzke Foundation, Inc.
2259 Marbella Dr.
Mosinee, WI 54455

Financial data (yr. ended 12/31/01): Grants paid, $7,700; assets, $98,380 (M); expenditures, $7,700; qualifying distributions, $7,700.
Limitations: Applications not accepted.
Application information: Contributes only to pre-selected organizations.
Officers: Harlan Lewitzke, Pres.; Yvonne Lewitzke, V.P.
Directors: Alan Lewitzke, Bradley Lewitzke.
EIN: 391915849

57684
Garber Family Foundation
P.O. Box 170620
Milwaukee, WI 53217-8051

Donor(s): Julius Garber.
Financial data (yr. ended 10/31/00): Grants paid, $7,548; assets, $86,461 (M); gifts received, $17,800; expenditures, $8,761; qualifying distributions, $7,862.
Limitations: Applications not accepted. Giving primarily in Milwaukee, WI.
Application information: Contributes only to pre-selected organizations.
Trustees: Ann Garber, Julius Garber, Mark B. Garber.
EIN: 397058155

57685
Plymouth Advancement Association, Inc.
c/o Lee N. Gentine
P. O. Box 525
Plymouth, WI 53073-0525 (920) 892-2192

Established in 1995 in WI.
Financial data (yr. ended 12/31/99): Grants paid, $7,543; assets, $13,267 (M); expenditures, $22,485; qualifying distributions, $21,557.
Limitations: Giving primarily in Plymouth, WI.
Officers and Directors:* Lee Gentine,* Pres.; Barbara Lardon,* V.P.; Julie Sebranek, Secy.-Treas.; Jack Burkart, Terry Evans, Tom Faley, William Kiley, Don Sippel, Nancy Smith, Jim Stahlman.
EIN: 391778702

57686
John P. Mentzer Scholarship Trust
c/o U.S. Bank
P.O. Box 2043
Milwaukee, WI 53201-9116
Application address: c/o Guidance Counselor, Marion High School, Marion, IA 52302, tel.: (319) 377-9894

Established in 1962 in IA.
Financial data (yr. ended 09/30/01): Grants paid, $7,500; assets, $169,916 (M); expenditures, $10,443; qualifying distributions, $9,090.
Limitations: Giving limited to Marion, IA.
Application information: Application form required.
Trustee: U.S. Bank.
EIN: 426054056
Codes: GTI

57687
Karin J. & Peter L. Smith Foundation
N49 W28264 Maryann's Way
Pewaukee, WI 53072

Donor(s): Peter L. Smith.
Financial data (yr. ended 09/30/01): Grants paid, $7,500; assets, $5,495 (M); gifts received, $456; expenditures, $7,500; qualifying distributions, $7,500.
Limitations: Applications not accepted. Giving primarily in WI.
Application information: Contributes only to pre-selected organizations.
Trustees: Matthew D. Smith, Peter L. Smith.
EIN: 391805715

57688
Robert S. & Betsy Q. Hagge Foundation
500 3rd St., Ste. 506
Wausau, WI 54403-4857

Donor(s): Robert S. Hagge,‡ Betsy Q. Hagge,‡ Robert S. Hagge, Jr.
Financial data (yr. ended 09/30/01): Grants paid, $7,416; assets, $153,399 (M); gifts received, $7,300; expenditures, $7,758; qualifying distributions, $7,416.
Limitations: Applications not accepted. Giving limited to Wausau, WI.
Application information: Contributes only to pre-selected organizations.
Officers and Directors:* Carol M. Krieg,* Pres. and Treas.; Robert S. Hagge, Jr.,* V.P. and Secy.; A. Woodson Hagge, Daniel L. Hagge, Jr., David R. Scholfield, Leigh Hagge Tuckey.
EIN: 391446171

57689
Haupert Family Foundation, Inc.
3045 Rock Ln.
Cuba City, WI 53807

Established in 1998 in WI.
Donor(s): Carolyn S. Haupert, John C. Haupert.
Financial data (yr. ended 12/31/01): Grants paid, $7,400; assets, $214,067 (M); expenditures, $8,574; qualifying distributions, $7,400.
Limitations: Applications not accepted.
Application information: Contributes only to pre-selected organizations.
Officers: John C. Haupert, Pres. and Treas.; Carolyn S. Haupert, V.P. and Secy.
Director: Richard Elskamp.
EIN: 391948113

57690
New Glarus Masonic Lodge No. 310 Foundation, Inc.
207 6th Ave.
New Glarus, WI 53574 (608) 527-5068
Contact: David Baird, Pres.

Established in 2000 in WI.
Donor(s): New Glarus Masonic Lodge 310.
Financial data (yr. ended 12/31/01): Grants paid, $7,200; assets, $122,112 (M); expenditures, $7,200; qualifying distributions, $7,200.
Limitations: Giving primarily in New Glarus, WI.
Application information: Applicants must be graduates of New Glarus High School. Application form required.
Officers: David Baird, Pres.; Charles Schenkel, V.P.; Carey Schneider, Secy.
EIN: 391985798

57691
Ida Pacetti Charitable Trust
c/o Bank One Trust Co., NA
P.O. Box 13
Milwaukee, WI 53201

Established in 1998 in WI.
Donor(s): Ida Pacetti.‡
Financial data (yr. ended 12/31/01): Grants paid, $7,110; assets, $193,268 (M); expenditures, $9,349; qualifying distributions, $7,110.
Limitations: Applications not accepted. Giving primarily in Kenosha, WI.
Application information: Contributes only to pre-selected organizations.
Trustee: Bank One Trust Co., N.A.
EIN: 396700324

57692
Plotkin Foundation
4730 N. Lake Dr.
Milwaukee, WI 53211

Financial data (yr. ended 02/28/02): Grants paid, $7,100; assets, $112,634 (M); expenditures, $8,298; qualifying distributions, $7,100.
Limitations: Applications not accepted.
Application information: Contributes only to pre-selected organizations.
Officers: Lorraine Plotkin, Pres. and Treas.; Mark Plotkin, V.P.; Susan Gruenberg, Secy.
EIN: 396046144

57693
Earnest F. & Edna P. Aber Scholarship Fund
c/o First Banking Center
P.O. Box 660
Burlington, WI 53105-0660
Application address: 257 Kendall St., Burlington, WI 53105
Contact: Rev. Scott Carson, Chair.

Financial data (yr. ended 12/31/00): Grants paid, $7,004; assets, $127,502 (M); expenditures, $9,106; qualifying distributions, $7,004.
Limitations: Giving primarily in WI.
Application information: Application form required.
Trustee: First Banking Center.
Officer: Rev. Scott Carson, Chair.
EIN: 911817886

57694
George W. & Effie Borg Scholarship Fund
c/o U.S. Bank
P.O. Box 2043
Milwaukee, WI 53201-9116
Application address: P.O. Box 2054, Milwaukee, WI 53201-2054
Contact: Diem Nguyen, Trust Off., U.S. Bank

Financial data (yr. ended 10/31/01): Grants paid, $7,000; assets, $169,762 (M); expenditures, $10,331; qualifying distributions, $8,840.
Limitations: Giving limited to Delavan, WI.
Application information: Application form not required.
Trustee: U.S. Bank.
EIN: 396072993

57695
Bouwer Family Foundation
510 N. Appleton St.
Appleton, WI 54911-4724
Contact: Gilbert Bouwer, Tr.

Established in 1997.
Donor(s): Gilbert Bouwer.
Financial data (yr. ended 12/31/01): Grants paid, $7,000; assets, $154,168 (M); gifts received, $48,135; expenditures, $7,845; qualifying distributions, $6,939.
Trustees: Gilbert Bouwer, Joel Bouwer, Lisa Bouwer-Hansen, Marc Bouwer, Kathryn Peotter.
EIN: 391897340

57696
The Locher Family Foundation
121 S. 13th St.
La Crosse, WI 54601
Application address: c/o North Central Trust Co., 311 Main St., La Crosse, WI 54601
Contact: Sandra Locher, Tr.

Established in 1995 in WI.
Donor(s): Sandra Locher.
Financial data (yr. ended 12/31/01): Grants paid, $7,000; assets, $172,361 (M); expenditures, $8,727; qualifying distributions, $7,000.
Limitations: Giving primarily in La Crosse, WI.
Application information: Application form not required.
Trustees: Christian Locher, Eric Locher, Matthew Locher, Sandra Locher, Tonia Locher, Ytcher Locher, North Central Trust Co.
EIN: 391809106

57697
Margaret Wiegand Trust
c/o Bank One Trust Co., N.A.
P.O. Box 1308
Milwaukee, WI 53201
Application address: P.O. Box 866, Brookfield, WI 53008-0866, tel.: (262) 783-3934
Contact: Judith Holland, Trust Off., Bank One Trust Co., N.A.

Financial data (yr. ended 12/31/00): Grants paid, $6,992; assets, $224,336 (M); expenditures, $8,543; qualifying distributions, $7,432.
Limitations: Giving limited to Waukesha County, WI.
Application information: Recipients are referred from Waukesha Rehabilitation Office and other community service organizations, and through yearly notice in The Waukesha Freeman. Application form not required.
Trustee: Bank One Trust Co., N.A.
EIN: 391332458

57698
Jon and Mary Haas Family Foundation, Inc.
111 E. Wisconsin Ave., Ste. 1800
Milwaukee, WI 53202

Established in 1996 in WI.
Donor(s): Jon Haas, Mary Haas.
Financial data (yr. ended 12/31/01): Grants paid, $6,981; assets, $57,617 (M); expenditures, $9,303; qualifying distributions, $6,981.
Limitations: Applications not accepted.
Application information: Contributes only to pre-selected organizations.
Officers and Directors:* Jon Haas,* Pres.; Mary Haas,* Secy.; Frank W. Bastian.
EIN: 391842263

57699
Lillian V. Johnson Scholarship Trust
c/o Marshall & Ilsley Bank
P.O. Box 2980
Milwaukee, WI 53201-2980
Application address: c/o Kelly M. Gostisha, Marshall & Ilsley Trust Co., P.O. Box 209, Wausau, WI 54402-0209, tel.: (715) 845-6394

Established in 1987 in WI.
Financial data (yr. ended 06/30/01): Grants paid, $6,936; assets, $180,259 (M); expenditures, $10,452; qualifying distributions, $6,936.
Limitations: Giving limited to residents of Rhinelander, WI.
Trustee: Marshall & Ilsley Bank.
EIN: 396459811

57700
The Schilling Family Foundation, Inc.
c/o Allan Schilling
P.O. Box 369
La Crosse, WI 54602-0369

Established in 1991 in WI.
Financial data (yr. ended 12/31/01): Grants paid, $6,844; assets, $100,515 (M); gifts received, $10,000; expenditures, $7,944; qualifying distributions, $6,844.
Limitations: Applications not accepted.
Application information: Contributes only to pre-selected organizations.
Officer: Allan Schilling, Pres.
EIN: 391648299

57701
Neta & Edward Thompson Memorial Scholarship Fund
c/o Marshall & Ilsley Bank
1000 N. Water St.
Milwaukee, WI 53202
Application address: Patricia Chase c/o Marshall & Ilsley Bank, 500 3rd St., Wausau, WI 54402-0209

Established in 2000 in WI.
Financial data (yr. ended 03/31/02): Grants paid, $6,805; assets, $140,266 (M); expenditures, $10,446; qualifying distributions, $7,585.
Limitations: Giving limited to Outagamie, WI.
Application information: Application form required.
Trustee: Marshall & Ilsley Bank.
EIN: 396734119

57702
Edythe Hasler Vogelgesang Scholarship Fund
c/o Bank One Trust Co., N.A.
P.O. Box 1308
Milwaukee, WI 53201
Application address: 100 E. Broad St., Columbus, OH 43215
Contact: Phyllis Jeter

Financial data (yr. ended 12/31/99): Grants paid, $6,800; assets, $146,554 (M); expenditures, $9,400; qualifying distributions, $6,917.
Limitations: Giving limited to Canton, OH.
Trustee: Bank One Trust Co., N.A.
EIN: 346572320

57703
Kenneth L. and Betty R. Nelson Foundation
P.O. Box 149
Grantsburg, WI 54840

Established in 2000 in WI.
Donor(s): Kenneth L. Nelson, Betty R. Nelson.
Financial data (yr. ended 12/31/01): Grants paid, $6,780; assets, $18,537 (M); gifts received, $10,000; expenditures, $6,940; qualifying distributions, $6,780.
Limitations: Applications not accepted.
Application information: Contributes only to pre-selected organizations.
Directors: Betty R. Nelson, Kenneth L. Nelson.
EIN: 392011013

57704
Acorn Foundation, Inc.
P.O. Box 510348
Milwaukee, WI 53203-0061

Donor(s): Jon P. Barsanti, Terrie M. Barsanti.
Financial data (yr. ended 06/30/01): Grants paid, $6,546; assets, $100,302 (M); gifts received, $6,022; expenditures, $6,758; qualifying distributions, $6,438.
Limitations: Applications not accepted. Giving primarily in WI.
Application information: Contributes only to pre-selected organizations.
Officers: Jon P. Barsanti, Pres.; Jon P. Barsanti, Jr., V.P.; Terrie M. Barsanti, Secy.-Treas.
EIN: 391488174

57705
Kratzer Family Charitable Foundation, Ltd.
P.O. Box 1624
Appleton, WI 54913

Established in 1988 in WI.
Donor(s): Carl Kratzer, Helen Kratzer, Valley King, Inc.
Financial data (yr. ended 09/30/01): Grants paid, $6,500; assets, $189,489 (M); expenditures, $12,154; qualifying distributions, $6,500.
Limitations: Applications not accepted. Giving primarily in WI.
Application information: Contributes only to pre-selected organizations.
Officers: Kristine Hietpas, Pres. and Treas.; Helen Kratzer, V.P.; Katherine Reynolds, Secy.
Director: Carol Kratzer.
EIN: 391646268

57706
Russell L. Smith & Vera M. Smith Educational Medical & Charitable Foundation, Inc.
c/o North Central Trust
N. 2124 Valley Rd.
La Crosse, WI 54601   (608) 788-9581
Contact: Russell L. Smith, Pres.

Donor(s): Russell L. Smith.
Financial data (yr. ended 12/31/01): Grants paid, $6,500; assets, $196,612 (M); gifts received, $60,000; expenditures, $9,363; qualifying distributions, $6,500.
Officers and Directors:* Russell L. Smith,* Pres. and Treas.; Darwin Isaacson,* V.P.; George E. Smith,* V.P.
EIN: 391744162

57707
Marc and Marian Anderson Family Foundation, Inc.
4500 Scenic Way
De Pere, WI 54115

Established in 1998 in WI.
Donor(s): Marc Anderson, Marian Anderson.
Financial data (yr. ended 12/31/01): Grants paid, $6,420; assets, $5,573 (M); expenditures, $7,128; qualifying distributions, $6,420.
Limitations: Applications not accepted.
Application information: Contributes only to pre-selected organizations.
Officers and Directors:* Marian K. Anderson,* Pres.; Marc H. Anderson,* V.P. and Secy.; Teena Sue Reece,* Treas.
EIN: 391948557

57708
Nellie Jensen Charitable Trust
c/o U.S. Bank
P.O. Box 2043
Milwaukee, WI 53201-9116

Donor(s): Nellie Jensen Trust.
Financial data (yr. ended 12/31/01): Grants paid, $6,416; assets, $94,154 (M); expenditures, $8,716; qualifying distributions, $6,916.
Limitations: Applications not accepted.
Application information: Contributes only to pre-selected organizations.
Trustee: U.S. Bank.
EIN: 426582097

57709
Morris Family Foundation
411 E. Wisconsin Ave.
Milwaukee, WI 53202

Established in 1987 in WI.
Donor(s): Andrew K. Morris, Gail D. Morris.
Financial data (yr. ended 12/31/01): Grants paid, $6,405; assets, $90,578 (M); expenditures, $6,772; qualifying distributions, $6,405.
Limitations: Applications not accepted.
Application information: Contributes only to pre-selected organizations.
Directors: Andrew K. Morris, Gail D. Morris.
Trustees: Melissa H. Durot, Christopher A. Morris, J. Todd Morris, Jeffrey Morris.

EIN: 391606130

57710
John H. Goodwin Trust B
c/o Bank One Trust Co., N.A.
P.O. Box 1308
Milwaukee, WI 53201

Donor(s): John H. Goodwin.‡
Financial data (yr. ended 12/31/99): Grants paid, $6,259; assets, $190,577 (M); expenditures, $10,864; qualifying distributions, $6,583.
Limitations: Applications not accepted.
Application information: Contributes only to pre-selected organizations.
Trustee: Bank One Trust Co., N.A.
EIN: 316510727

57711
Wallace H. Jerome Foundation, Inc.
P.O. Box 255
Barron, WI 54812-0255

Established around 1965.
Donor(s): Jerome Foods, Inc., BASF Corp., Wallace H. Jerome, The Turkey Store Co.
Financial data (yr. ended 02/28/02): Grants paid, $6,250; assets, $28,975 (M); gifts received, $2,000; expenditures, $6,929; qualifying distributions, $6,908.
Limitations: Giving primarily in MN and WI.
Application information: Application form not required.
Officers: Wallace H. Jerome, Pres.; Mary Ella Jerome, V.P.; Tim Hafele, Secy.-Treas.
Director: Jerome K. Jerome.
EIN: 391040067
Codes: GTI

57712
Stella M. Kemble Trust
P.O. Box 1308
Milwaukee, WI 53201

Financial data (yr. ended 11/30/01): Grants paid, $6,214; assets, $197,874 (M); expenditures, $8,593; qualifying distributions, $6,214.
Limitations: Applications not accepted.
Application information: Contributes only to pre-selected organizations.
Trustee: Bank One, N.A.
EIN: 756041605

57713
Walter and Marion Jensen Foundation
c/o Larry Stotz, C.P.A.
210 S. Oak St.
Grantsburg, WI 54840-7857

Established around 1995.
Financial data (yr. ended 12/31/01): Grants paid, $6,160; assets, $291,557 (M); expenditures, $10,843; qualifying distributions, $6,160.
Limitations: Applications not accepted. Giving primarily in Grantsburg, WI.
Application information: Unsolicited requests for funds not accepted.
Directors: Renee Anderson, Bruce E. Erickson, W. Bryan Jensen.
EIN: 396585967

57714
Nicholas Giebel Scholarship Trust
c/o U.S. Bank
P.O. Box 2043
Milwaukee, WI 53201-9116
Application address: c/o Goodrich High School, 72 S. Portland St., Fond du Lac, WI 54935, or c/o St. Mary's Springs High School, 255 County Rd. K, Fond du Lac, WI 54935; or c/o Pastor, St. Mary's Parish, Fond du Lac, WI 54935

Donor(s): Nicholas Giebel.
Financial data (yr. ended 05/31/01): Grants paid, $6,100; assets, $66,141 (M); expenditures, $9,410; qualifying distributions, $6,591.
Limitations: Giving limited to Fond du Lac, WI.
Application information: Application form required.
Trustee: U.S. Bank.
EIN: 396120785

57715
The O. Edward Sparks Trust
c/o Bank One Trust Co., N.A.
P.O. Box 1308
Milwaukee, WI 53201-1308
Application address: 100 E. Broad St., Columbus, OH 43271-1075, tel.: (614) 248-2677
Contact: Phyllis Jeter, Trust Off., Bank One Trust Co., N.A.

Financial data (yr. ended 12/31/01): Grants paid, $6,100; assets, $95,460 (M); expenditures, $8,150; qualifying distributions, $6,100.
Limitations: Giving primarily in OH.
Application information: Application form required.
Trustee: Bank One Trust Co., N.A.
EIN: 316154601

57716
Heyrman Construction Co. Foundation
c/o Associated Banc-Corp
P.O. Box 408
Neenah, WI 54957-0408
Application address: c/o Heyrman Construction Co., Inc., 1030 Waube Ln., Green Bay, WI 54304
Contact: Audrey Feldhausen, Tr.

Established in 1995.
Donor(s): Heyrman Construction Co., Inc.
Financial data (yr. ended 12/31/01): Grants paid, $6,075; assets, $840,151 (M); expenditures, $7,877; qualifying distributions, $6,058.
Limitations: Giving primarily in areas of company operations.
Application information: Application form not required.
Trustees: Audrey Feldhausen, Earl Heyrman, Lawrence Heyrman, Vernon Heyrman, Associated Banc-Corp.
EIN: 396615213
Codes: CS, CD

57717
Helen V. and John M. Werner Charitable Foundation Trust
215 X-Press Ln.
Sheboygan, WI 53081   (920) 458-3183
Contact: John M. Werner, Sr., Tr.

Donor(s): Helen V. Werner, John M. Werner, Sr.
Financial data (yr. ended 12/31/01): Grants paid, $6,067; assets, $126,599 (M); expenditures, $6,471; qualifying distributions, $6,067.
Limitations: Giving primarily in Sheboygan, WI.
Application information: Application form not required.
Trustees: Helen V. Werner, John M. Werner, Sr.

EIN: 391572825

57718
Greenleaf Riders, Ltd. Charities Foundation
P.O. Box 61
Greenleaf, WI 54126

Financial data (yr. ended 08/31/00): Grants paid, $6,012; assets, $11,467 (M); gifts received, $6,000; expenditures, $6,012; qualifying distributions, $8,412.
Officers: Scott Schroeder, Pres.; Darrell Johns, V.P.; Bev Leick, Secy.; Teri Diny, Treas.
Directors: Dick Augustian, Jack Cornelissen, Mike Cornette, Mark Gilson, Dan Leick.
EIN: 391681578

57719
Fern Anderson & Verdell Arneson Trust
c/o James Kauffman
3312 Riverview Dr.
Eau Claire, WI 54703
Application address: c/o School District of Cadott Community, P.O. Box 310, Cadott, WI 54727; tel.: (715) 289-4211

Established in 1997.
Financial data (yr. ended 12/31/99): Grants paid, $6,000; assets, $113,220 (M); expenditures, $6,050; qualifying distributions, $6,000.
Limitations: Giving limited to Cadott, WI.
Application information: Application form not required.
Trustees: Harland Danielson, James Kauffman, Daniel Schmitt.
EIN: 396599642

57720
Discoverers Fund, Inc.
462 Clifden Dr.
Madison, WI 53711
Contact: John L. Desreanis

Financial data (yr. ended 09/30/00): Grants paid, $6,000; assets, $150,565 (M); expenditures, $6,075; qualifying distributions, $6,000.
Limitations: Giving primarily in WI.
Application information: Applicant must include transcripts. Application form not required.
Officer: Philip Harris, Pres.
EIN: 396048588

57721
Grafton Medical Foundation, Inc.
P.O. Box 104
Grafton, WI 53024-0104
Application address: c/o John E. Ketter, Grafton High School, Guidance Dept., 1900 Washington St., Grafton, WI 53024, tel.: (262) 377-6106

Financial data (yr. ended 12/31/01): Grants paid, $6,000; assets, $70,154 (M); expenditures, $6,806; qualifying distributions, $6,000.
Limitations: Giving limited to the Grafton, WI, area.
Officers and Directors:* Warren Mueller,* Pres.; Alfred Kohlwey,* V.P.; Carl Wegner,* Secy.-Treas.; Ray C. Sell, Jr., Michael Uhlein, Gene Werner.
EIN: 237054743

57722
Jung Family Foundation
708 Oneida St.
Beaver Dam, WI 53916

Donor(s): John C. Jung, Mary F. Jung.
Financial data (yr. ended 12/31/01): Grants paid, $6,000; assets, $165,318 (M); expenditures, $10,851; qualifying distributions, $6,000.
Limitations: Giving primarily in Beaver Dam, WI.
Trustees: John C. Jung, U.S. Bank.

EIN: 396669489

57723
The Kuntz Family Foundation
c/o Bank One Trust Co.
P.O. Box 1308
Milwaukee, WI 53201

Established in 1999 in WI.
Financial data (yr. ended 12/31/01): Grants paid, $6,000; assets, $320,964 (M); expenditures, $11,088; qualifying distributions, $6,000.
Limitations: Giving primarily in WI.
Officers: James Kuntz, Pres.; Helen Kuntz, V.P. and Treas.; David Reinecke, Secy.
EIN: 391962818

57724
Nagel Lumber Co. Foundation, Inc.
c/o Nagel Lumber Co., Inc.
P.O. Box 209
Land O'Lakes, WI 54540
Contact: Cathy Nordine, Secy.

Established in 1974 in WI.
Donor(s): Nagel Lumber Co., Inc.
Financial data (yr. ended 12/31/00): Grants paid, $6,000; assets, $161,959 (M); expenditures, $7,313; qualifying distributions, $6,630.
Limitations: Giving limited to Land O' Lakes, WI.
Officers: Edwin D. Nagel, Pres.; Marilyn Nagel, V.P. and Treas.; Cathy Nordine, Secy.
EIN: 237417699
Codes: CS, CD

57725
Lilyan Pfaender Trust
4535 N. 92nd. St., No. T401
Milwaukee, WI 53225-5419
Contact: Helen J. Van Vechten, Tr.

Established around 1993.
Financial data (yr. ended 12/31/99): Grants paid, $6,000; assets, $66,072 (M); expenditures, $6,387; qualifying distributions, $6,320; giving activities include $6,000 for loans to individuals.
Limitations: Giving primarily in WI.
Application information: Application form required.
Trustees: Harriet Pederson, Norman Rose, Helen J. Van Vechten.
EIN: 391648692

57726
Polly W. Roesch Vocal Scholarship Trust
c/o Bank One Trust Co., N.A.
P.O. Box 1308
Milwaukee, WI 53201
Application address: 1 E. Capital Plz., Springfield, IL 62701, tel.: (217) 525-9745
Contact: JoAnn Ley, Trust Off., Bank One Trust Co., N.A.

Established in 1985 in IL.
Financial data (yr. ended 12/31/01): Grants paid, $6,000; assets, $106,623 (M); expenditures, $9,107; qualifying distributions, $7,398.
Limitations: Giving limited to Sangamon County, IL.
Application information: Application form required.
Trustee: Bank One Trust Co., N.A.
EIN: 376234631
Codes: GTI

57727
The Jack L. Taylor Education Trust
c/o Bank One Trust Co., N.A.
P.O. Box 1308
Milwaukee, WI 53201
Application address: 111 Monument Cir., IN1-0150, Indianapolis, IN 46277-0115
Contact: Gail Randall

Established in 1991.
Donor(s): Jack L. Taylor.‡
Financial data (yr. ended 09/30/01): Grants paid, $6,000; assets, $83,310 (M); expenditures, $8,176; qualifying distributions, $7,100.
Limitations: Giving limited to residents of Whiting, IN.
Application information: Application form required.
Advisory Committee: Donald Adkins, Katherine Flaris, Dirk Flick, Robert Klosek, Paul Laub, Gail Lemon, Renee Mindas, William Reby, Jon Sarota, Beverly Sheldon.
Trustee: Bank One Trust Co., N.A.
EIN: 356549775
Codes: GTI

57728
Charles Joseph Wilber Educational Scholarship Trust
c/o Marshall & Ilsley Bank
P.O. Box 2980
Milwaukee, WI 53201-2980
Application address: c/o Superintendent of Schools, Tomahawk High School, 1048 E. Kings Rd., Tomahawk, WI 54487

Established in 1985 in WI.
Financial data (yr. ended 10/31/01): Grants paid, $6,000; assets, $132,549 (M); expenditures, $8,890; qualifying distributions, $5,938.
Limitations: Giving limited to residents of Tomahawk, WI.
Application information: Application form required.
Trustee: Marshall & Ilsley Bank.
EIN: 396371278
Codes: GTI

57729
Francis and Adele Sundberg Trust
P.O. Box 408
Neenah, WI 54957-0408

Established in 1991 in WI.
Financial data (yr. ended 12/31/01): Grants paid, $5,934; assets, $128,831 (M); expenditures, $8,056; qualifying distributions, $5,934.
Limitations: Applications not accepted. Giving primarily in Eagle River, WI.
Application information: Contributes only to pre-selected organizations.
Trustee: Associated Banc-Corp.
EIN: 396540988

57730
Maude Scranton Trust
c/o Bank One Trust Company, N.A.
P.O. Box 1308
Milwaukee, WI 53201

Financial data (yr. ended 12/31/01): Grants paid, $5,913; assets, $545,923 (M); expenditures, $17,169; qualifying distributions, $5,913.
Limitations: Applications not accepted. Giving primarily in IL.
Application information: Contributes only to pre-selected organizations.
Trustee: Bank One, Illinois, N.A.
EIN: 376040622

57731
Wilken-Harding Educational Foundation
1615 Notra Dame Blvd.
Elm Grove, WI 53122
Application address: c/o Thomas Oberwetter, 353 Miflin St., Madison, WI 53703

Financial data (yr. ended 12/31/01): Grants paid, $5,909; assets, $77,186 (M); expenditures, $5,999; qualifying distributions, $5,909.
Limitations: Giving limited to residents of Madison, WI.
Application information: Application form required.
Officers: Robert A. Feind, Pres.; Jeffrey S. Schanter, Treas.
EIN: 396054147
Codes: GTI

57732
Womonscape Foundation, Inc.
P.O. Box 2154
Madison, WI 53701-2154

Established in 2001 in WI.
Donor(s): Jane Leussler.
Financial data (yr. ended 12/31/01): Grants paid, $5,903; assets, $2,611 (M); gifts received, $10,037; expenditures, $7,573; qualifying distributions, $7,573.
Limitations: Applications not accepted. Giving primarily in Madison, WI.
Officers: Ricki Grunberg, Jane Leussler.
EIN: 392016745

57733
The Keith W. Tantlinger Foundation
c/o Bank One Trust Co., N.A.
P.O. Box 1308
Milwaukee, WI 53201
Application address: 611 Woodward Ave., Detroit, MI 48226, tel.: (313) 225-3454
Contact: Matthew H. Wasmund, Mgr., Bank One, Trust Div.

Financial data (yr. ended 12/31/01): Grants paid, $5,900; assets, $101,078 (M); expenditures, $7,055; qualifying distributions, $6,815.
Limitations: Giving on a national basis, with emphasis on CA.
Officer: Therese M. Thorn, Mgr.
Trustee: Bank One Trust Co., N.A.
EIN: 386046660

57734
Edward and Frieda Wagner Scholarship Fund
c/o Associated Banc-Corp
P.O. Box 408
Neenah, WI 54957-0408
Application address: c/o Scholarship Comm., Crandon High School, P.O. Box 310, Crandon, WI 54520-0310

Established in 1997 in WI.
Financial data (yr. ended 11/30/01): Grants paid, $5,868; assets, $97,184 (M); expenditures, $7,485; qualifying distributions, $5,846.
Limitations: Giving limited to residents of Crandon, WI.
Trustee: Associated Banc-Corp.
EIN: 396698990

57735
Therese Foundation, Inc.
1328 Vilas Ave.
Madison, WI 53715

Established in 2000 in WI.
Donor(s): Diane K. Farah, Peter Kelliher II, George S. Farah.

Financial data (yr. ended 12/31/01): Grants paid, $5,800; assets, $174,276 (M); gifts received, $70,100; expenditures, $14,049; qualifying distributions, $5,800.
Limitations: Applications not accepted. Giving primarily in Silver Spring, MD and Madison, WI.
Application information: Contributes only to pre-selected organizations.
Officer: George S. Farah, Exec. Dir.
Directors: Diane K. Farah, Simone V. Farah.
EIN: 391984065

57736
Carolyn M. & Leary E. Peterson Family Foundation, Inc.
110 E. Haydn
Prairie Du Chien, WI 53821

Established in 1999 in WI.
Donor(s): Peterson Family Lead Trust.
Financial data (yr. ended 05/31/01): Grants paid, $5,750; assets, $106,467 (M); gifts received, $52,760; expenditures, $7,080; qualifying distributions, $5,750.
Limitations: Applications not accepted. Giving limited to FL.
Application information: Contributes only to pre-selected organizations.
Directors: Jane Mullen, John L. Peterson, Thomas F. Peterson, Mary Jo Ruhl, Carole Sayer.
EIN: 391936484

57737
William Cherek Foundation, Inc.
199 S. County Rd. Y
Hatley, WI 54440-9358

Established in 1993 in WI.
Donor(s): William Cherek.
Financial data (yr. ended 05/31/02): Grants paid, $5,675; assets, $172,767 (M); expenditures, $7,048; qualifying distributions, $5,675.
Limitations: Applications not accepted. Giving primarily in WI.
Application information: Contributes only to pre-selected organizations.
Officers: William Cherek, Pres. and Treas.; Joan Kazmierczak, Secy.
EIN: 391802119

57738
Wascher Family Foundation
165 Pine Ct.
Appleton, WI 54915
Contact: Greg Wascher, Tr.

Established in 1997 in WI.
Donor(s): Thomas M. Wascher.
Financial data (yr. ended 12/31/01): Grants paid, $5,602; assets, $106,920 (M); expenditures, $9,058; qualifying distributions, $5,602.
Limitations: Giving primarily in WI.
Trustees: Greg Wascher, Thomas M. Wascher.
EIN: 396671421

57739
Robert A. & Lynn I. Doneff Foundation, Inc.
115 E. Waldo Blvd.
Manitowoc, WI 54220

Financial data (yr. ended 12/31/01): Grants paid, $5,600; assets, $102,858 (M); gifts received, $6,100; expenditures, $5,695; qualifying distributions, $5,600.
Limitations: Applications not accepted.
Application information: Contributes only to pre-selected organizations.
Trustee: Robert A. Doneff.
EIN: 391858063

57740
Simon Schwartz Fund, Inc.
1701 Washington St.
Manitowoc, WI 54220-5049 (920) 682-2434
Contact: Paul J. Grens, Secy.-Treas.

Financial data (yr. ended 12/31/99): Grants paid, $5,515; assets, $3,240 (M); expenditures, $6,801; qualifying distributions, $6,801.
Limitations: Giving limited to Manitowoc County, WI.
Application information: Application form required.
Officers and Directors:* Harlan Schwartz,* Pres.; James Schwartz,* V.P.; Paul J. Grens,* Secy.-Treas.; Diane Schwartz, Herbert Schmaltz.
EIN: 396072984

57741
Thomas A. Plein Foundation, Ltd.
3415 Commerce Ct.
Appleton, WI 54911 (920) 731-3190
Contact: Thomas A. Plein.

Donor(s): Thomas A. Plein.
Financial data (yr. ended 12/31/01): Grants paid, $5,500; assets, $319,251 (M); gifts received, $202,110; expenditures, $5,864; qualifying distributions, $5,500.
Limitations: Giving primarily in WI.
Application information: Application form not required.
Officer: Doris Plein, Secy.
Director: Thomas A. Plein.
EIN: 391558684

57742
Mary J. Proctor Trust
c/o Bank One Trust Co., N.A.
P.O. Box 1308
Milwaukee, WI 53201-1308
Application address: 111 Monument Cir., Ste. 1501, Indianapolis, IN 46277-0115, tel.: (317) 321-7544
Contact: Jacqueline W. Weitz, V.P. and Trust Off., Bank One Trust Co., N.A.

Financial data (yr. ended 10/31/01): Grants paid, $5,500; assets, $683,687 (M); expenditures, $12,608; qualifying distributions, $7,567.
Limitations: Giving primarily in Indianapolis, IN.
Trustee: Bank One Trust Co., N.A.
EIN: 356009070

57743
Edwin and Anne Roelli Charitable Trust
9511 Hwy. E.
Darlington, WI 53530-9801

Donor(s): Edwin Roelli, Anne Roelli.
Financial data (yr. ended 12/31/01): Grants paid, $5,500; assets, $88,698 (M); gifts received, $266; expenditures, $5,766; qualifying distributions, $5,500.
Limitations: Applications not accepted. Giving primarily in WI.
Application information: Contributes only to pre-selected organizations.
Trustees: Anne Roelli, Edwin Roelli, Richard Roelli.
EIN: 391465200

57744
Euna Brown Trust
c/o Bank One Trust Co., N.A.
P.O. Box 1308
Milwaukee, WI 53201
Application address: c/o Howard W. Strecher, 1 Court House Ln., Marietta, OH 45750

Financial data (yr. ended 12/31/99): Grants paid, $5,424; assets, $90,515 (M); expenditures, $7,732; qualifying distributions, $5,521.
Limitations: Giving limited to Washington County, OH.
Trustee: Bank One Trust Co., N.A.
EIN: 316050944

57745
Kenwood Lodge Masonic Foundation, Inc.
517 E. Beaumont Ave.
Whitefish Bay, WI 53217
Contact: William M. Huegel, Secy.

Financial data (yr. ended 12/31/99): Grants paid, $5,400; assets, $91,578 (M); gifts received, $74; expenditures, $5,993; qualifying distributions, $5,332.
Limitations: Giving primarily in WI.
Officers: Frank J. Reed, Jr., Pres.; John J. Olk, V.P.; William M. Huegel, Secy.; Bill B. Larson, Treas.
EIN: 391100641

57746
Julie and Daniel Meitus Foundation
914 Harbor House Dr., Ste. 7
Madison, WI 53719

Established in 1999.
Financial data (yr. ended 12/31/01): Grants paid, $5,395; assets, $244 (M); gifts received, $5,800; expenditures, $5,800; qualifying distributions, $5,395.
Officer: Scott Meitus, Pres.
Directors: James Meitus, Jon Meitus, Michael Meitus.
EIN: 364301091

57747
Grace Elizabeth Groner Foundation
c/o Bank One Trust Co., N.A.
P.O. Box 1308
Milwaukee, WI 53201
Application address: 1 Bank One Plz., Chicago, IL 60670
Contact: Charles W. Tramel

Established in 1999 in IL.
Financial data (yr. ended 12/31/01): Grants paid, $5,385; assets, $141,124 (M); expenditures, $7,331; qualifying distributions, $5,385.
Trustee: Bank One, Chicago, N.A.
EIN: 364335094

57748
Continental Grain-Westwego Educational Trust
c/o Bank One Trust Co., N.A.
P.O. Box 1308
Milwaukee, WI 53201
Application address: c/o Marcus Hock, Bank One, Lousiana, 201 St. Charles Ave., 29th Fl., New Orleans, LA 70170

Financial data (yr. ended 12/31/00): Grants paid, $5,353; assets, $54,677 (M); expenditures, $8,438; qualifying distributions, $6,779.
Limitations: Giving limited to residents in Atlanta, GA.
Trustee: Bank One Trust Co., N.A.
EIN: 720843735

57749—WISCONSIN

57749
Frances Cleo Frazier Trust f/b/o Emmerich Manual High School
c/o Bank One Trust Co., N.A.
P.O. Box 1308
Milwaukee, WI 53201-1308
Application address: c/o Dir. of Guidance, Emmerich Manual High School, 2405 Madison Ave., Indianapolis, IN 46225, tel.: (317) 266-6119

Financial data (yr. ended 09/30/01): Grants paid, $5,350; assets, $174,240 (M); expenditures, $8,451; qualifying distributions, $6,529.
Limitations: Giving limited to Indianapolis, IN.
Application information: Application form required.
Trustee: Bank One Trust Co., N.A.
EIN: 356319357

57750
George T. Meyer Foundation
9313 N. River Bend Ct.
Milwaukee, WI 53217
Contact: Kathleen M. Mueller, V.P.

Financial data (yr. ended 12/31/01): Grants paid, $5,300; assets, $101,900 (M); expenditures, $5,877; qualifying distributions, $5,300.
Limitations: Giving primarily in Milwaukee, WI.
Officers: Lucille E. Meyer, Pres.; Kathleen M. Mueller, V.P.
EIN: 396044377

57751
Robert & Marjorie Hartshorn Charitable Trust f/b/o Macular Degeneration
c/o First National Bank of Platteville
170 W. Main St.
Platteville, WI 53818

Established in 2000 in WI.
Financial data (yr. ended 12/31/01): Grants paid, $5,200; assets, $82,424 (M); expenditures, $10,366; qualifying distributions, $5,200.
Limitations: Applications not accepted.
Application information: Contributes only to pre-selected organizations.
Trustee: First National Bank of Platteville.
EIN: 396734176

57752
Claire and Marjorie Johnson, Inc.
c/o Claire W. Johnson
397 24 3/4 Ave.
Cumberland, WI 54829

Established in WI in 1998.
Donor(s): Claire Johnson, Marjorie Johnson.
Financial data (yr. ended 12/31/01): Grants paid, $5,133; assets, $173,189 (M); gifts received, $100,000; expenditures, $5,410; qualifying distributions, $5,133.
Limitations: Giving primarily in Cumberland, WI.
Officers: Claire Johnson, Pres.; Marjorie Johnson, V.P.
EIN: 391874405

57753
Freeman Family Foundation, Inc.
(Formerly L. L. & Cornelia G. Freeman Foundation)
175 W. Blackhawk Rd.
Milwaukee, WI 53217-3102

Donor(s): L.L. Freeman.
Financial data (yr. ended 12/31/01): Grants paid, $5,100; assets, $126,406 (M); expenditures, $5,952; qualifying distributions, $5,100.
Limitations: Applications not accepted. Giving primarily in Milwaukee, WI.

Application information: Contributes only to pre-selected organizations.
Trustee: Annette Stoddard Freeman.
EIN: 237000499

57754
Coles Family Foundation
2929 E. Hartford Ave.
Milwaukee, WI 53211 (414) 964-7088
Contact: Marcia Coles, Tr.

Established in 1986 in WI.
Donor(s): Elliot L. Coles.
Financial data (yr. ended 08/31/01): Grants paid, $5,050; assets, $84,703 (M); expenditures, $5,634; qualifying distributions, $5,536.
Limitations: Giving primarily in Milwaukee, WI.
Trustees: Elliot L. Coles, Marcia Coles, James A. Urdan.
EIN: 391572885

57755
Blake Family Foundation, Inc.
7561 Red Fox Trail
Madison, WI 53717

Established in 2001 in WI.
Donor(s): Philip Blake, Katherine Blake.
Financial data (yr. ended 12/31/01): Grants paid, $5,000; assets, $19,530 (M); gifts received, $24,513; expenditures, $5,718; qualifying distributions, $5,688.
Limitations: Applications not accepted.
Application information: Contributes only to pre-selected organizations.
Officer: Philip Blake, V.P.
EIN: 391999574

57756
Chronquist Scholarship Trust
c/o Associated Banc-Corp
P.O. Box 408
Neenah, WI 54957-0408
Application address: c/o Marshfield Senior High School, Guidance Dept., 1401 E. Becker Rd., Marshfield, WI 54449

Established in 1994 in WI.
Financial data (yr. ended 10/31/01): Grants paid, $5,000; assets, $83,680 (M); expenditures, $7,025; qualifying distributions, $4,973.
Limitations: Giving limited to residents of WI.
Application information: Application form required.
Trustee: Associated Banc-Corp.
EIN: 396589622

57757
The Devine Family Foundation, Inc.
c/o Raymond J. Devine
490 S. Midvale Blvd.
Madison, WI 53711

Established in 1999 in WI.
Donor(s): Raymond J. Devine.
Financial data (yr. ended 12/31/01): Grants paid, $5,000; assets, $109,844 (M); gifts received, $42; expenditures, $5,933; qualifying distributions, $5,000.
Limitations: Applications not accepted.
Application information: Contributes only to pre-selected organizations.
Officers: Raymond J. Devine, Pres.; Eunice C. Devine, V.P.
Directors: David Devine, Kevin M. Devine, Timothy R. Devine, William T. Devine.
EIN: 391966116

57758
Erdman Foundation
c/o Marshall & Ilsley Trust Co.
P.O. Box 2980
Milwaukee, WI 53201
Contact: Allen G. Hembel

Established in 1986.
Financial data (yr. ended 12/31/01): Grants paid, $5,000; assets, $287,905 (L); expenditures, $6,694; qualifying distributions, $5,000.
Limitations: Giving limited to greater Dane County, WI, with emphasis on the greater Madison area.
Directors: Joan Burke, Daniel William Erdman, M. Rustin Erdman, Timothy Butler Erdman, Deborah Erdman-Luder.
EIN: 396447538

57759
Greenley Charitable Trust
c/o U.S. Bank
P.O. Box 2043
Milwaukee, WI 53201-9116
Application address: Russ Curtis, V.P., c/o U.S. Bank Iowa, N.A., P.O. Box 39, Cedar Falls, IA, 50613-9940, tel.: (319) 277-1320

Financial data (yr. ended 06/30/02): Grants paid, $5,000; assets, $87,295 (M); expenditures, $7,103; qualifying distributions, $5,000.
Limitations: Giving primarily in IA.
Application information: Application form not required.
Trustee: U.S. Bank.
EIN: 426053950

57760
Cliff & Clara Herlache Foundation
c/o Baylake Bank
P.O. Box 9
Sturgeon Bay, WI 54235-0009

Financial data (yr. ended 12/31/00): Grants paid, $5,000; assets, $71,939 (M); expenditures, $5,167; qualifying distributions, $5,000.
Officer and Director:* Thomas L. Herlache,* Pres.
EIN: 391738459

57761
Hooper Foundation
429 N. 9th St.
Manitowoc, WI 54220
Application address: 1024 Meadow Dr., Bowling Green, KY 42104
Contact: Mary Hooper Hirst, Tr.

Donor(s): Lance Hooper.
Financial data (yr. ended 12/31/01): Grants paid, $5,000; assets, $250,644 (M); expenditures, $9,185; qualifying distributions, $5,000.
Limitations: Giving primarily in WI.
Trustees: Mary Hooper Hirst, Jacqueline Hooper, Sarah Hirst Scanlon.
EIN: 396047383

57762
Thomas L. & Mabel Grace Jones Scholarship Fund
c/o U.S. Bank
P.O. Box 2043
Milwaukee, WI 53201
Application address: c/o Superintendent, Williamsburg High School, Williamsburg, IA 52361

Financial data (yr. ended 04/30/00): Grants paid, $5,000; assets, $136,704 (M); expenditures, $7,959; qualifying distributions, $6,936.
Limitations: Giving limited to Williamsburg, IA.

Application information: Application form required.
Trustee: U.S. Bank.
EIN: 426144737

57763
Daniel A. Kohl Family Charitable Trust
c/o Foley & Lardner
777 E. Wisconsin Ave.
Milwaukee, WI 53202-5367

Established in 2001 in WI.
Donor(s): Allen D. Kohl Foundation, Inc., Daniel A. Kohl.
Financial data (yr. ended 12/31/01): Grants paid, $5,000; assets, $45,019 (M); gifts received, $52,259; expenditures, $7,259; qualifying distributions, $5,000.
Limitations: Applications not accepted.
Application information: Contributes only to pre-selected organizations.
Trustees: Daniel A. Kohl, Stacey Schiff Kohl.
EIN: 527243143

57764
Korb Family Foundation, Inc.
593 Ledgeview Blvd.
Fond Du Lac, WI 54935-3726 (920) 923-3300
Contact: John M. Korb, Pres.

Established in 1999 in WI.
Donor(s): Ann Korb, Catherine A. Korb, John M. Korb, Michael A. Korb.
Financial data (yr. ended 12/31/01): Grants paid, $5,000; assets, $124,384 (M); expenditures, $6,194; qualifying distributions, $5,000.
Application information: Application form not required.
Officers: John M. Korb, Pres.; Ann Korb, V.P.; Catherine A. Korb, V.P.; Michael A. Korb, Secy.
EIN: 391979649

57765
Robert & Rita Krauss Foundation
P.O. Box 295
Kewaunee, WI 54216-0295

Established in 1998 in WI.
Donor(s): Robert Krauss, Rita Krauss.
Financial data (yr. ended 12/31/99): Grants paid, $5,000; assets, $144,582 (M); gifts received, $1,000; expenditures, $5,462; qualifying distributions, $5,000.
Limitations: Giving limited to WI.
Officers: Rita Krauss, Pres.; Bonnie Schuller, V.P. and Treas.; Candy Malvitz, Secy.
EIN: 391598274

57766
R. V. Krikorian Foundation, Inc.
c/o Marshall & Ilsely Trust Co.
P.O. Box 2980
Milwaukee, WI 53201

Donor(s): Robert Krikorian.
Financial data (yr. ended 12/31/01): Grants paid, $5,000; assets, $82,764 (M); expenditures, $6,126; qualifying distributions, $5,000.
Limitations: Applications not accepted. Giving primarily in WI.
Application information: Contributes only to pre-selected organizations.
Directors: Dudley Godfrey, Jr., Virginia Krikorian.
EIN: 391506371

57767
The Lloyd and Patricia Maasch Family Foundation
208 W. Clark St.
Weyauwega, WI 54983

Established in 1996 in WI.
Donor(s): Lloyd Maasch, Patricia Maasch.
Financial data (yr. ended 12/31/01): Grants paid, $5,000; assets, $109,092 (M); expenditures, $5,930; qualifying distributions, $5,000.
Limitations: Applications not accepted.
Application information: Contributes only to pre-selected organizations.
Trustees: Lloyd Maasch, Patricia Maasch, Robert Maasch, Sue Ann Maasch Ryan.
EIN: 396624687

57768
Muetzel Educational Foundation
P.O. Box 409
Tomah, WI 54660-0409 (608) 372-2177
Application address: 1001 Superior Ave., Tomah, WI 54660
Contact: Terry Winchell, Trust Off., F&M Bank

Established around 1968 in WI.
Financial data (yr. ended 12/31/01): Grants paid, $5,000; assets, $67,520 (M); gifts received, $4,307; expenditures, $7,398; qualifying distributions, $5,000.
Limitations: Giving primarily in Tomah, WI.
Application information: Application form required.
Trustee: F & M Bank.
EIN: 396109753

57769
Elizabeth J. Tellier Foundation, Inc.
8230 N. Pelican Ln.
River Hills, WI 53209-1624 (414) 347-7089
Contact: Robert W. Chernow, Treas.

Established in 1995 in WI.
Donor(s): Elizabeth J. Tellier.
Financial data (yr. ended 03/31/02): Grants paid, $5,000; assets, $119,057 (M); gifts received, $30,004; expenditures, $6,478; qualifying distributions, $5,000.
Limitations: Giving primarily in WI.
Application information: Application form required.
Officers: Elizabeth J. Tellier, Pres.; John C. Dowd, Secy.; Robert W. Chernow, Treas.
EIN: 391777930

57770
Toby J. Tully Foundation
705 S. Main St.
Jefferson, WI 53549
Application address: P.O. Box 404, Jefferson, WI 53549
Contact: Toby J. Tully, Tr.

Donor(s): Toby J. Tully.
Financial data (yr. ended 12/31/99): Grants paid, $5,000; assets, $79,531 (M); expenditures, $5,940; qualifying distributions, $4,960.
Limitations: Giving primarily in WI.
Trustee: Toby J. Tully.
EIN: 391743495

57771
Doris M. Vennard Residual Trust
c/o Wells Fargo Bank Wisconsin N.A.
P.O. Box 288
Eau Claire, WI 54702-0288

Established in 1985 in WI.
Financial data (yr. ended 12/31/00): Grants paid, $5,000; assets, $88,318 (M); expenditures, $7,023; qualifying distributions, $5,700.
Limitations: Giving limited to residents of Chippewa County, WI.
Application information: Application form not required.
Trustee: Wells Fargo Bank Wisconsin, N.A.
EIN: 396376718

57772
Robert A. and Marjorie M. Hartshorn Charitable Trust
c/o First National Bank
170 W. Main St.
Platteville, WI 53818 (608) 348-7777

Established in 1999.
Financial data (yr. ended 12/31/01): Grants paid, $4,950; assets, $79,139 (M); expenditures, $8,074; qualifying distributions, $4,950.
Trustee: First National Bank.
EIN: 396718041

57773
William Higgins Trust for Buren Fund
c/o Bank One Trust Co., N.A.
P.O. Box 1308
Milwaukee, WI 53201-1308
Application address: c/o Robert A. Duff, National City Bank, P.O. Box 70, Lebanon, IN 46052

Donor(s): William L. Higgins.
Financial data (yr. ended 10/31/01): Grants paid, $4,914; assets, $121,519 (M); expenditures, $5,101; qualifying distributions, $4,914.
Limitations: Giving limited to residents of Boone County, IN.
Trustee: Bank One Trust Co., N.A.
EIN: 356009210
Codes: GTI

57774
W & M Schultz Scholastic Foundation
c/o Bank One Trust Co., N.A.
P.O. Box 1308
Milwaukee, WI 53201
Application address: c/o Clintonville Public High School District, 26 9th St., Clintonville, WI 54929-1595

Established in 1994 in WI.
Financial data (yr. ended 03/31/99): Grants paid, $4,800; assets, $125,897 (M); expenditures, $7,069; qualifying distributions, $5,892.
Limitations: Giving limited to residents of Clintonville, WI.
Application information: Application form required.
Trustee: Bank One Trust Co., N.A.
EIN: 396593363

57775
The Hampe Family Foundation
P.O. Box 248
Galesville, WI 54630-0248

Established in 1999 in WI.
Donor(s): Richard C. Hampe, William T. Hampe, Wilma C. Hampe.
Financial data (yr. ended 12/31/01): Grants paid, $4,750; assets, $121,188 (M); gifts received, $27,000; expenditures, $4,904; qualifying distributions, $4,750.
Limitations: Applications not accepted. Giving on a national basis.
Application information: Contributes only to pre-selected organizations.
Trustees: Richard C. Hampe, William T. Hampe, Wilma C. Hampe.
EIN: 391965828

57776
H. Woodsmall, Mary Homes Woodsmall Memorial Foundation for the Encouragement of the Arts Trust
c/o Bank One Trust Co., N.A.
P.O. Box 130
Milwaukee, WI 53201

Financial data (yr. ended 10/31/01): Grants paid, $4,709; assets, $102,515 (M); expenditures, $7,385; qualifying distributions, $4,709.
Limitations: Applications not accepted. Giving primarily in Indianapolis IN.
Application information: Contributes only to pre-selected organizations.
Trustee: Bank One, Indiana, N.A.
EIN: 356008883

57777
Columbiana County Public Health League Trust Fund
c/o Bank One Trust Co., N.A.
P.O. Box 1308
Milwaukee, WI 53201
Application address: c/o Bank One Trust Co., N.A., P.O. Box 1428, Steubenville, OH 43952
Contact: Sherry Schmied, Trust Off., Bank One Trust Co., N.A.

Financial data (yr. ended 04/30/01): Grants paid, $4,700; assets, $93,189 (M); expenditures, $6,392; qualifying distributions, $5,035.
Application information: Application form required.
Trustee: Bank One Trust Co., N.A.
EIN: 341313902
Codes: GTI

57778
La Crosse City Vision Foundation, Inc.
712 Main St.
La Crosse, WI 54601

Established in 1994.
Financial data (yr. ended 06/30/01): Grants paid, $4,695; assets, $1 (M); gifts received, $12,170; expenditures, $8,016; qualifying distributions, $4,695.
Officers: William Weber, Pres.; Jean Bassett, Secy.; Jack F. White, Treas.
Directors: Les Eversole, Tom Fider, Sue Gelatt, Sigurd Gundersen, Sr. Ladonna Kassmeyer, Tom Lynch, and 4 additional directors.
EIN: 391794887

57779
Optimist Youth & Charity Foundation of Appleton, Wisconsin, Inc.
c/o T.J. Oswald
P.O. Box 1831
Appleton, WI 54913-1831

Financial data (yr. ended 09/30/01): Grants paid, $4,642; assets, $9,789 (M); expenditures, $4,642; qualifying distributions, $4,642.
Limitations: Applications not accepted. Giving limited to Appleton, WI.
Application information: Contributes only to pre-selected organizations.
Officers and Directors:* Tom Riederer,* Pres.; Jim Fourness,* Secy.; Tom Oswald,* Treas.
EIN: 396088084

57780
Baehman Foundation, Inc.
2700 W. College Ave., PMB 333
Appleton, WI 54914-2918
Contact: Stanley W. Baehman, Dir.

Established in 1991 in WI.
Financial data (yr. ended 12/31/00): Grants paid, $4,610; assets, $45,713 (M); gifts received, $5,218; expenditures, $5,278; qualifying distributions, $5,264.
Limitations: Giving primarily in Appleton, WI.
Directors: Beau J. Baehman, Lucia J. Baehman, Stanley W. Baehman.
EIN: 391697610

57781
Phala Woods Loan Fund
c/o Bank One Trust Co., N.A.
P.O. Box 1308
Milwaukee, WI 53201

Established in 1996 in WV.
Financial data (yr. ended 12/31/01): Grants paid, $4,610; assets, $81,233 (M); expenditures, $5,649; qualifying distributions, $4,610.
Limitations: Applications not accepted. Giving primarily in WV.
Application information: Contributes only to pre-selected organizations.
Trustee: Bank One, West Virginia, N.A.
EIN: 556044337

57782
Elmer Scholarship Fund
c/o Marshall & Ilsley Bank
P.O. Box 2980
Milwaukee, WI 53201

Financial data (yr. ended 06/30/01): Grants paid, $4,600; assets, $146,112 (M); expenditures, $8,131; qualifying distributions, $4,600.
Limitations: Giving limited to residents of WI.
Application information: Unsolicited request for funds not accepted.
Trustee: Marshall & Ilsley Bank.
EIN: 396497710

57783
The Hennessy Family Foundation
2323 N. Mayfair Rd., Ste. 240
Milwaukee, WI 53226   (414) 475-6565
FAX: (414) 475-0317
Contact: Susan C. Steinkraus

Established in 1998 in IL.
Donor(s): Daniel J. Hennessy, J. Elizabeth Hennessy.
Financial data (yr. ended 12/31/99): Grants paid, $4,500; assets, $389,740 (M); expenditures, $235,032; qualifying distributions, $1,855.
Limitations: Giving primarily in IL.
Trustees: Daniel J. Hennessy, J. Elizabeth Hennessy.
EIN: 367255318

57784
Elsie Krueger Scholarship Fund, Inc.
N60 W16590 Kohler Ln.
Menomonee Falls, WI 53051
Contact: Stanley Krueger, V.P.

Financial data (yr. ended 12/31/99): Grants paid, $4,500; assets, $11,367 (M); expenditures, $4,739; qualifying distributions, $4,500.
Limitations: Giving limited to residents of Menomonee Falls, WI.
Application information: Application form not required.
Officers: Kathleen Krueger, Pres.; Karen Krueger, V.P.; Stanley Krueger, V.P.; Carman Krueger, Secy.; Steven Krueger, Treas.
EIN: 391656978

57785
Orvis Scholarship Fund
c/o Bank One Trust Co., N.A.
P.O. Box 1308
Milwaukee, WI 53201   (414) 765-2769
Application address: c/o Bank One Trust Co., N.A., 111 E. Wisonsin Ave., Milwaukee, WI 53202, tel.: (414) 765-2940; or North High School, 2222 Michigan Ave., Waukesha, WI 53188; or South High School, 401 E. Roberta Ave., Waukesha, WI, 53186; or West High School, 3301 Saylesville Rd., Waukesha, WI 53189

Established in 1991 in WI.
Financial data (yr. ended 12/31/01): Grants paid, $4,500; assets, $49,855 (M); expenditures, $6,550; qualifying distributions, $5,582.
Limitations: Giving limited to residents of WI.
Application information: Application form required.
Trustee: Bank One Trust Co., N.A.
EIN: 396041468

57786
Charles J. Ploetz Family Foundation, Inc.
10 White Oaks Lane
Madison, WI 53711   (608) 271-6361
Contact: Pamela Ploetz

Established in 1999 in WI.
Donor(s): Charles J. Ploetz.
Financial data (yr. ended 12/31/01): Grants paid, $4,500; assets, $224,719 (M); gifts received, $153,481; expenditures, $5,856; qualifying distributions, $4,500.
Limitations: Giving primarily in WI.
Application information: Application form not required.
Officers and Directors:* Pamela Ploetz,* Pres.; Charles J. Ploetz,* V.P.; Patricia Ploetz,* Secy.; Steve Ploetz,* Treas.
EIN: 391956306

57787
Schilling Covenant Foundation, Inc.
c/o John P. Schilling
W5734 Thistledown Dr.
La Crosse, WI 54601-2479   (608) 788-7165

Established in 1998 in WI.
Donor(s): Schilling Family Foundation.
Financial data (yr. ended 12/31/01): Grants paid, $4,500; assets, $80,314 (M); expenditures, $4,880; qualifying distributions, $4,500.
Limitations: Applications not accepted.
Application information: Contributes only to pre-selected organizations.
Officer: John Schilling, Pres.
EIN: 391912980

57788
John H. & Kathleen H. Schneider Family Foundation, Inc.
10620 N. Port Washington Rd.
Mequon, WI 53092
Application address: 401 E. Kilbourn Ave., Ste. 400, Milwaukee, WI 53202, tel.: (414) 272-3146
Contact: John H. Schneider, Pres.

Established in 2000 in WI.
Donor(s): John H. Schneider.
Financial data (yr. ended 12/31/01): Grants paid, $4,500; assets, $116,293 (M); gifts received, $56,000; expenditures, $4,778; qualifying distributions, $4,500.
Limitations: Giving on a national basis, with emphasis on WI.
Application information: Application form not required.

Officers: John H. Schneider, Pres. and Treas.; Janeen Doleschal, V.P.; Mary Jo McCormick, V.P.; Julie Ann Schlapbach, V.P.; H. Stephen Schneider, V.P.; Kathleen H. Schneider, V.P.; Gregory A. Ruidl, Secy.
EIN: 391988773

57789
Walter G. Sommer Family Charitable Foundation
P.O. Box 37
Mequon, WI 53092
Contact: Donald Sommer, Tr.

Established in 1999 in WI.
Donor(s): Donald G. Sommer, Erna E. Sommer, Walter B. Sommer.
Financial data (yr. ended 12/31/00): Grants paid, $4,500; assets, $43,287 (M); expenditures, $4,500; qualifying distributions, $4,472.
Application information: Application form not required.
Trustees: Donald G. Sommer, Erna E. Sommer, Walter B. Sommer.
EIN: 396724458

57790
Truscott Family Scholarship Fund
c/o Bank One Trust Co.
P.O. Box 1308
Milwaukee, WI 53201
Application address: c/o Bank One Trust Co., 1800 Broadway, Boulder, CO 80302, tel.: (303) 245-6703

Established in 1996.
Financial data (yr. ended 12/31/01): Grants paid, $4,500; assets, $60,706 (M); expenditures, $9,715; qualifying distributions, $6,388.
Limitations: Giving limited to residents of CO.
Trustee: Bank One Trust Co., N.A.
EIN: 846192161
Codes: GTI

57791
Reuben Kritzik Family Foundation, Inc.
2101 W. Good Hope Rd., No. 215
Milwaukee, WI 53209-2743 (414) 351-2254

Donor(s): Reuben Kritzik.
Financial data (yr. ended 12/31/01): Grants paid, $4,425; assets, $109,400 (M); expenditures, $5,038; qualifying distributions, $4,425.
Limitations: Applications not accepted. Giving primarily in Milwaukee, WI.
Application information: Contributes only to pre-selected organizations.
Officer: Muriel Kritzik, Mgr.
EIN: 396050684

57792
Gary Katz Foundation, Inc.
6780 N. Melissa Ct.
Milwaukee, WI 53209-3473

Financial data (yr. ended 12/31/01): Grants paid, $4,416; assets, $103,822 (M); gifts received, $925; expenditures, $5,244; qualifying distributions, $4,416.
Limitations: Applications not accepted. Giving primarily in Milwaukee, WI.
Application information: Contributes only to pre-selected organizations.
Officers: Leon H. Katz, Pres.; Jim Ostach, Secy.; Jacquelin Katz, Treas.
EIN: 396092881

57793
Wichmann-Horn Foundation, Inc.
(Formerly Wichmann Foundation, Inc.)
c/o Associated Banc-Corp
P.O. Box 408
Neenah, WI 54957-0408

Donor(s): Joan Horn Revocable Trust.
Financial data (yr. ended 12/31/01): Grants paid, $4,400; assets, $139,130 (M); expenditures, $6,419; qualifying distributions, $4,400.
Limitations: Applications not accepted. Giving primarily in Appleton, WI.
Application information: Contributes only to pre-selected organizations.
Officer: Louis Horn, Pres. and Secy.
Trustees: Joanne Horn, Associated Banc-Corp.
EIN: 396060815

57794
FEECO International Foundation, Inc.
3913 Algoma Rd.
Green Bay, WI 54311

Established in 1997 in WI.
Donor(s): FEECO International, Inc.
Financial data (yr. ended 06/30/02): Grants paid, $4,395; assets, $112,114 (M); gifts received, $500; expenditures, $4,455; qualifying distributions, $4,395.
Limitations: Applications not accepted. Giving limited to Green Bay, WI.
Application information: Contributes only to pre-selected organizations.
Officers and Directors:* Daniel P. Madigan,* Pres. and Treas.; Laura Madigan,* V.P. and Secy.; Justin Madigan.
EIN: 391916022
Codes: CS, CD

57795
Carrie H. Graham Trust
c/o Bank One Trust Co., N.A.
P.O. Box 1308
Milwaukee, WI 53201
Application address: c/o Glenda Mercer, Coord., Xenia High School, 303 Kinsey Rd., Xenia, OH 45385

Donor(s): Mabel Stevens.‡
Financial data (yr. ended 12/31/01): Grants paid, $4,350; assets, $66,276 (M); expenditures, $5,463; qualifying distributions, $5,257.
Limitations: Giving limited to Xenia, OH.
Application information: Application form required.
Trustee: Bank One Trust Co., N.A.
EIN: 316068310
Codes: GTI

57796
Gruett Scholarship Trust
c/o Trinity Lutheran Church
418 W. Main St.
Merrill, WI 54452-2223

Established in 1967 in WI.
Financial data (yr. ended 12/31/01): Grants paid, $4,250; assets, $111,299 (M); expenditures, $5,370; qualifying distributions, $4,250.
Limitations: Applications not accepted. Giving limited to Merrill, WI.
Officers: Richard Ruge, Chair.; Rev. Kenneth Albers, Pres.
Trustees: Glenn Frank, Herb Sermon.
EIN: 391093528

57797
John and Mary Ann Hartwig Family Foundation, Inc.
1415 McClellan
Wausau, WI 54403 (715) 845-1914
Contact: John Hartwig, Dir.

Established in 2000 in WI.
Donor(s): John Hartwig, Mary Ann Hartwig.
Financial data (yr. ended 12/31/01): Grants paid, $4,250; assets, $300,667 (M); expenditures, $6,962; qualifying distributions, $4,250.
Directors: Jason Hartwig, Jennifer Hartwig, John J. Hartwig, Mary Ann Hartwig.
EIN: 392001442

57798
Joyce Schwerm Memorial Foundation
7236 N. Crossway Rd.
Milwaukee, WI 53217-3519
Contact: Gerald Schwerm, Tr.

Donor(s): Gerald Schwerm, Judy Schwerm.
Financial data (yr. ended 12/31/00): Grants paid, $4,250; assets, $5,885 (M); gifts received, $1,500; expenditures, $4,260; qualifying distributions, $4,260.
Limitations: Giving primarily in WI.
Trustees: Mary J. Gray, Gerald Schwerm, Diane Sykes.
EIN: 396581160

57799
The Jeremy Hughes Engineering/Industrial Technology
450 Erie Rd.
Green Bay, WI 54311

Established in 1999 in WI.
Financial data (yr. ended 12/31/01): Grants paid, $4,236; assets, $410 (M); gifts received, $1,400; expenditures, $4,281; qualifying distributions, $4,236.
Trustees: Gregory L. Hughes, Shirley Triest Robertson.
EIN: 391976370

57800
Douglas Mental Health Foundation
306 W. State St.
Westby, WI 54667-1251
Contact: Aashild Douglas, Pres.

Financial data (yr. ended 12/31/99): Grants paid, $4,234; assets, $13,839 (M); gifts received, $3,181; expenditures, $4,239; qualifying distributions, $4,239.
Limitations: Giving limited to Vernon County, WI.
Officers: Aashild Douglas, Pres.; Donna Bean, V.P.; Patricia Stafslien, Secy.; Debra Sliomstad, Treas.
EIN: 391705197

57801
Gloria McAvoy Bremer Charitable Foundation
c/o Bank One Trust Co., N.A.
P.O. Box 1308
Milwaukee, WI 53201
Application address: c/o Bank One, Karen Mills, Trust Off., 218 E. Wesley St., Wheaton, IL 60187-0998

Established in 1996 in IL.
Donor(s): Gloria McAvoy Bremer.
Financial data (yr. ended 12/31/00): Grants paid, $4,220; assets, $142,569 (M); gifts received, $25,000; expenditures, $8,166; qualifying distributions, $5,758.
Trustee: Bank One Trust Co., N.A.
EIN: 367165500

57802
Jambor Family Foundation
111 E. Wisconsin Ave., Ste. 1800
Milwaukee, WI 53202

Established in 1998 in WI.
Financial data (yr. ended 12/31/01): Grants paid, $4,200; assets, $73,016 (M); expenditures, $5,156; qualifying distributions, $4,200.
Limitations: Applications not accepted. Giving primarily in IL and WI.
Application information: Contributes only to pre-selected organizations.
Directors: Anna Jambor, Robert Jambor, Terry Jambor.
EIN: 391933693

57803
Royce R. Thompson Scholarship Trust
c/o Port Washington State Bank
206 N. Franklin St.
Port Washington, WI 53074-1903
Application addresses: c/o Scholarship Comm., Port Washington High School, 427 W. Jackson St., Port Washington 53074, tel.: (262) 284-5569; c/o Scholarship Comm., Plainfield High School, P.O. Box 67, Plainfield 54966, tel.: (715) 335-6366; c/o Scholarship Comm., Ripon High School, P.O. Box 991, Ripon 54971, tel.: (920) 748-4616

Established in 1987 in WI.
Financial data (yr. ended 05/31/99): Grants paid, $4,200; assets, $102,707 (M); expenditures, $5,930; qualifying distributions, $5,670.
Limitations: Giving limited to residents of WI.
Application information: Application form required.
Trustee: Port Washington State Bank.
EIN: 396462343

57804
Emmett T. & Louise M. Ackerman Education Fund
c/o Richland County Bank
P.O. Box 677
Richland Center, WI 53581
Contact: Gail Surrem, Tr.

Financial data (yr. ended 12/31/01): Grants paid, $4,150; assets, $147,937 (M); expenditures, $9,438; qualifying distributions, $7,267.
Limitations: Giving limited to residents of WI.
Application information: Application form required.
Trustees: Judith Mackovec, Gail Surrem.
EIN: 396318690

57805
Everhard Fund
c/o Bank One Trust Co., N.A.
P.O. Box 1308
Milwaukee, WI 53201
Application address: Bill Feldmann, Bank One, Dayton, N.A., Kettering Tower, Dayton, OH 45401, tel.: (937) 449-8963

Financial data (yr. ended 12/31/99): Grants paid, $4,130; assets, $99,282 (M); expenditures, $5,472; qualifying distributions, $4,427.
Limitations: Giving limited to Dayton, OH.
Application information: Application form not required.
Trustee: Bank One Trust Co., N.A.
EIN: 316026761

57806
Jaleane Foundation, Inc.
1430 Memorial Dr.
Sturgeon Bay, WI 54235-1535

Donor(s): Jack Ginsberg.
Financial data (yr. ended 09/30/01): Grants paid, $4,100; assets, $37,796 (M); expenditures, $4,515; qualifying distributions, $4,516.
Limitations: Giving limited to residents of WI.
Directors: Jack Ginsberg, Lee Ginsberg, Diane Spizzirri.
EIN: 391350676

57807
Sara Vodrey Gardner Trust
c/o Bank One Trust Co., N.A.
P.O. Box 1308
Milwaukee, WI 53201

Established in 1989 in OH.
Financial data (yr. ended 12/31/99): Grants paid, $4,075; assets, $112,176 (M); gifts received, $23; expenditures, $5,810; qualifying distributions, $4,205.
Limitations: Giving limited to East Liverpool, OH.
Trustee: Bank One Trust Co., N.A.
EIN: 346514812

57808
Fred Fleshman Scholarship Fund
c/o Bank One Trust Co., N.A.
P.O. Box 1308
Milwaukee, WI 53202

Financial data (yr. ended 12/31/01): Grants paid, $4,062; assets, $82,623 (M); expenditures, $6,505; qualifying distributions, $5,198.
Limitations: Applications not accepted. Giving primarily in Huntington, WV.
Application information: Contributes only to pre-selected organizations.
Trustee: Bank One Trust Co., N.A.
EIN: 556014664

57809
Werner & Jermaine Buchel Foundation, Inc.
1712 Iroquois Ave.
Grafton, WI 53024 (262) 375-3513
Contact: James F. Haebig, Pres.

Donor(s): Agnes Martin, Lisa C. Houseman.
Financial data (yr. ended 07/31/01): Grants paid, $4,000; assets, $193,059 (M); expenditures, $4,645; qualifying distributions, $4,597.
Limitations: Giving limited to the greater Milwaukee, WI, area.
Application information: Application form not required.
Officers: James F. Haebig, Pres.; Eugene E. Weyer,* V.P.; Joseph Buchel, Secy.
EIN: 391421076

57810
Wendy Sue Cahoon Scholarship Trust
c/o The Baraboo National Bank
P.O. Box 50
Baraboo, WI 53913 (608) 356-8536
Application address: c/o Baraboo Community Scholarship Corp., P.O. Box 380, Baraboo, WI 53913

Established in 1989 in WI.
Donor(s): Members of the Cahoon family.
Financial data (yr. ended 12/31/01): Grants paid, $4,000; assets, $155,362 (M); gifts received, $3,200; expenditures, $7,177; qualifying distributions, $4,000.
Limitations: Giving limited to residents of Baraboo, WI.
Trustee: The Baraboo National Bank.

EIN: 391642009

57811
E. Dorothy Crain Scholarship Trust
c/o Associated Banc-Corp
P.O. Box 787
Manitowoc, WI 54221-0787
Application address: c/o Lincoln High School, Guidance Off., 1433 S. 8th St., Manitowoc, WI 54220

Established in 1997.
Financial data (yr. ended 12/31/01): Grants paid, $4,000; assets, $154,198 (M); expenditures, $6,357; qualifying distributions, $5,001.
Limitations: Giving limited to residents of Manitowoc, WI.
Trustee: Associated Banc-Corp.
EIN: 396667363

57812
Romaine William Dassow Trust
c/o U.S. Bank
P.O. Box 2043
Milwaukee, WI 53201-9116
Application address: c/o U.S. Bank, P.O. Box 0663, Sheboygan, WI 53082

Established in 1982 in WI.
Financial data (yr. ended 12/31/01): Grants paid, $4,000; assets, $48,328 (M); gifts received, $250; expenditures, $5,816; qualifying distributions, $4,000.
Limitations: Giving limited to Sheboygan, WI.
Application information: Application form required.
Trustee: U.S. Bank.
EIN: 391421846

57813
Foundation Organized for a Constitutional United States
3985 Paradise Dr.
West Bend, WI 53095-8776
Contact: Dolores V. Mills, Dir.

Established in 1990.
Donor(s): Ralph H. Schulz.
Financial data (yr. ended 06/30/01): Grants paid, $4,000; assets, $91,436 (M); expenditures, $4,000; qualifying distributions, $4,000.
Limitations: Giving primarily in IL.
Directors: Marie Fryatt, Dolores V. Mills, Edward N. Mills.
EIN: 363713043

57814
Michael Hunter & Jane Hunter, Inc.
P.O. Box 400
Antigo, WI 54409

Financial data (yr. ended 07/31/01): Grants paid, $4,000; assets, $14,529 (M); expenditures, $5,127; qualifying distributions, $4,012.
Limitations: Applications not accepted. Giving primarily in Antigo, WI.
Application information: Contributes only to pre-selected organizations.
Officers and Directors:* Michael Hunter,* Pres. and Treas.; Jane Hunter,* V.P. and Secy.; Michelle L. Hunter.
EIN: 391367380

57815
Keystone Charitable Foundation
c/o Roger & Marion Christoph
P.O. Box 1
Kansasville, WI 53139

Established in 2000 in WI.
Donor(s): Roger W. Christoph, Marion M. Christoph.

Financial data (yr. ended 12/31/00): Grants paid, $4,000; assets, $92,589 (M); gifts received, $117,313; expenditures, $6,069; qualifying distributions, $5,045.
Limitations: Applications not accepted.
Application information: Contributes only to pre-selected organizations.
Trustees: Marion M. Christoph, Roger W. Christoph.
EIN: 397980763

57816
KMTSJ Foundation, Inc.
c/o Claire W. Johnson
P.O. Box 3217
Eau Claire, WI 54702

Established in 1993 in WI.
Donor(s): KMTSJ, Inc., Group Health Cooperative of Eau Claire.
Financial data (yr. ended 12/31/01): Grants paid, $4,000; assets, $38,639 (M); expenditures, $5,120; qualifying distributions, $5,000.
Limitations: Applications not accepted. Giving primarily in Eau Claire, WI.
Officers and Directors:* Claire W. Johnson,* Pres.; Robert Wildenberg,* V.P.; Rob Bearrood,* Secy.; Stephen J. Hofkes,* Treas.
EIN: 391673898
Codes: CS, CD

57817
The Madison Advertising Federation Foundation
c/o Floyd Carlstrom
P.O. Box 5663
Madison, WI 53705   (608) 831-9242

Established in 1989.
Financial data (yr. ended 06/30/99): Grants paid, $4,000; assets, $101,719 (M); gifts received, $2,575; expenditures, $4,696; qualifying distributions, $4,596.
Limitations: Giving limited to residents of WI.
Application information: Application form required.
Trustees: Floyd Carlstrom, Annette Knapstein, Celest Regenberg.
EIN: 391630870

57818
Wendy J. Padden Memorial Foundation, Inc.
c/o Associated Banc-Corp
P.O. Box 408
Neenah, WI 54957-0408
Application address: 7432 N. Crossway Rd., Milwaukee, WI 53217
Contact: Nancy G. Padden, Pres.

Established in 1985 in WI.
Financial data (yr. ended 04/30/01): Grants paid, $4,000; assets, $100,114 (M); gifts received, $775; expenditures, $5,541; qualifying distributions, $4,000.
Limitations: Giving primarily in Milwaukee, WI.
Officer and Directors:* Nancy G. Padden,* Pres.; Jeff C. Padden, Jodi E. Padden, Rodd R. Padden.
Trustee: Associated Banc-Corp.
EIN: 396578774

57819
Yamagata Foundation
(Formerly Yamagata Foundation Agency)
c/o Bank One, Texas, N.A.
P.O. Box 1308
Milwaukee, WI 53201-1308

Established in 1990 in TX.
Donor(s): T. Yamagata, E.Y. Yamagata.
Financial data (yr. ended 09/30/01): Grants paid, $4,000; assets, $7,605 (M); gifts received, $10,000; expenditures, $5,300; qualifying distributions, $4,000.
Limitations: Applications not accepted. Giving primarily in TX.
Application information: Contributes only to pre-selected organizations.
Trustees: Harvey Yamagata, Mark Yamagata, Bank One Trust Co., N.A.
EIN: 752324175

57820
Arnold VanBogart Residuary Trust
c/o Associated Banc-Corp
P.O. Box 408
Neenah, WI 54957-0408

Established in 1993 in WI.
Financial data (yr. ended 12/31/01): Grants paid, $3,922; assets, $126,396 (M); expenditures, $6,301; qualifying distributions, $3,937.
Limitations: Applications not accepted. Giving primarily in WI.
Application information: Contributes only to pre-selected organizations.
Trustee: Associated Banc-Corp.
EIN: 396575378

57821
Hansen Family Foundation, Inc.
1022 19th St. S.
La Crosse, WI 54601-5811

Established in 2000 in WI.
Donor(s): Donna L. Hansen, John J. Hansen.
Financial data (yr. ended 12/31/01): Grants paid, $3,834; assets, $9,978,411 (M); expenditures, $76,122; qualifying distributions, $3,834.
Officers: Donna L. Hansen, Chair.; John J. Hansen, Pres.; Mary B. Brennan, 1st V.P.; Paul E. Hansen, 2nd V.P.; Amy L. Hansen-Strom, Secy.; Mark W. Hansen, Treas.
EIN: 392011330

57822
Robert Wodill Youth Fund
c/o Farmers & Merchants Union Bank
159 W. James St.
Columbus, WI 53925
Application address: c/o Fall River High School, P.O. Box 116, Fall River, WI 53932, tel.: (920) 484-3327
Contact: Steven Rubert, Treas.

Financial data (yr. ended 12/31/01): Grants paid, $3,820; assets, $27,959 (M); gifts received, $3,493; expenditures, $3,845; qualifying distributions, $3,820.
Limitations: Giving limited to Fall River, WI.
Application information: Application form not required.
Officers and Directors:* Michael Lubenau,* Pres.; Andrea Wodill,* Secy.; Steven Rubert,* Treas.; John Pratt, Jr.
EIN: 391706166

57823
Milton & Elsie Arnold Community Trust
P.O. Box 334
Menomonee Falls, WI 53052-0334
Application address: 200 Woodland Prime, Ste. 210, Menomonee Falls, WI 53051, tel.: (262) 359-9779
Contact: Michael C. Hurt, Tr.

Financial data (yr. ended 12/31/01): Grants paid, $3,800; assets, $190,100 (M); expenditures, $7,092; qualifying distributions, $3,800.
Limitations: Giving limited to Menomonee Falls, WI.
Application information: Application form not required.
Trustee: Michael C. Hurt.
EIN: 396581072

57824
Florence Marie Rossbach Fund
c/o Marshall & Ilsley Bank
P.O. Box 2980
Milwaukee, WI 53201

Financial data (yr. ended 03/31/02): Grants paid, $3,800; assets, $126,018 (M); expenditures, $6,928; qualifying distributions, $3,800.
Limitations: Giving primarily to residents of WI.
Application information: Unsolicited requests for funds not accepted.
Trustee: Marshall & Ilsley Bank.
EIN: 396363944

57825
George A. and Estle E. Weber Commerce and Banking Scholarship
c/o The Baraboo National Bank
P.O. Box 50
Baraboo, WI 53913
Application address: c/o Principal, Baraboo Senior High School, 1201 Draper, Baraboo, WI 53913, tel.: (608) 356-8536

Established in 1985 in WI.
Financial data (yr. ended 12/31/99): Grants paid, $3,750; assets, $52,487 (M); expenditures, $4,873; qualifying distributions, $3,735.
Limitations: Giving limited to the Baraboo, WI, area.
Application information: Application form required.
Trustee: The Baraboo National Bank.
EIN: 391512911

57826
The Vankep Family Foundation, Inc.
3455 Pilgrim Rd.
Brookfield, WI 53005

Donor(s): Stephen VanderBloemen, Christine VanderBloemen.
Financial data (yr. ended 12/31/00): Grants paid, $3,742; assets, $157 (M); expenditures, $3,960; qualifying distributions, $3,742.
Officers: C.M. VanderBloemen, Pres.; S.C. VanderBloemen, V.P.
Trustees: J.P. VanderBloemen, S.A. VanderBloemen.
EIN: 391629355

57827
E. G. Hoeppner Charities, Inc.
1767 Drummond St.
Eau Claire, WI 54701   (715) 835-6313
Contact: F. John Hoeppner, Mgr.

Donor(s): Judy Hoeppner, Maurine Hoeppner.
Financial data (yr. ended 03/31/02): Grants paid, $3,683; assets, $39,074 (M); expenditures, $4,466; qualifying distributions, $3,683.
Limitations: Giving primarily in WI.
Officer and Directors:* F. John Hoeppner,* Mgr.; Judy Hoeppner, Maurine Hoeppner.
EIN: 396044792

57828
Timothy J. Nebel Foundation
c/o Bank One Trust Co., N.A.
P.O. Box 1308
Milwaukee, WI 53201
Application address: c/o Bank One, Karen Mills, Trust Off., 1 Bank One Plz., Ste. IL1-2054, Chicago, Il 60670-2054

Established in 1999 in IL.

57828—WISCONSIN

Financial data (yr. ended 12/31/01): Grants paid, $3,679; assets, $230,006 (M); expenditures, $7,642; qualifying distributions, $3,679.
Limitations: Giving primarily in IL.
Trustees: Michael Nebel, Michelle Nebel, Bank One Trust Co., N.A.
EIN: 367312213

57829
Sanford Foundation
c/o Jeff Mitchell
1901 S. Webster, Ste. 3
Green Bay, WI 54304
Contact: Paul Wautier

Established in 1999 in WI.
Financial data (yr. ended 03/31/02): Grants paid, $3,671; assets, $52,294 (M); gifts received, $3,671; expenditures, $4,296; qualifying distributions, $3,671.
Limitations: Giving limited to East De Pere, WI, and Boston, Brockton, and Rockland, MA.
Application information: Application form required.
Officers: Frances Larson, Mgr.; Paul Wautier, Mgr.
EIN: 391973587

57830
Kathryn G. Luthi Memorial Trust
c/o Bank One Trust Co., N.A.
P.O. Box 1308
Milwaukee, WI 53201

Financial data (yr. ended 12/31/01): Grants paid, $3,622; assets, $149,746 (M); expenditures, $5,713; qualifying distributions, $3,622.
Limitations: Applications not accepted. Giving limited to Kenosha, WI.
Application information: Contributes only to pre-selected organizations.
Trustee: Bank One Trust Co., N.A.
EIN: 396253802

57831
John W. Daniels, Jr. & Valerie Daniels-Carter Charitable Trust
6933 W. Brown Deer Rd.
Milwaukee, WI 53223

Established in 1995.
Donor(s): John W. Daniels, Jr., V & J Foods, Inc., V & J Foods of Milwaukee, Inc.
Financial data (yr. ended 12/31/01): Grants paid, $3,500; assets, $149,142 (M); gifts received, $2,850; expenditures, $44,668; qualifying distributions, $3,500.
Limitations: Applications not accepted.
Application information: Contributes only to pre-selected organizations.
Officers: Valerie Daniels-Carter, Pres.; John W. Daniels, Jr., Secy.
EIN: 396615293

57832
Ernst Family Charitable Trust
c/o Foley & Lardner
777 E. Wisconsin Ave.
Milwaukee, WI 53202

Established in 1989 in WI.
Donor(s): Charles A. Ernst, Jr.
Financial data (yr. ended 12/31/01): Grants paid, $3,500; assets, $132 (M); gifts received, $3,500; expenditures, $3,500; qualifying distributions, $3,500.
Limitations: Applications not accepted. Giving limited to MA and PA.
Application information: Contributes only to pre-selected organizations.
Trustees: Charles A. Ernst, Jr., Jacqueline W. Ernst, Wayne R. Lueders, Julius A. Nicolai.

EIN: 391642922

57833
Clement C. Seibel Foundation Fund
c/o Bank One Trust Co., N.A.
P.O. Box 1308
Milwaukee, WI 53201

Established in 1987 in WI.
Financial data (yr. ended 06/30/01): Grants paid, $3,500; assets, $96,320 (M); expenditures, $5,309; qualifying distributions, $4,777.
Limitations: Applications not accepted. Giving primarily in Green Bay, WI.
Application information: Contributes only to pre-selected organizations.
Trustee: Bank One Trust Co., N.A.
EIN: 391591136

57834
Carol Lynne Stachnik Foundation, Inc.
W. 52 N220 Pierce Ave.
Cedarburg, WI 53012 (262) 377-1711
Contact: Donna Kramer, Pres.

Established in 1992 in WI.
Donor(s): Frank Stachnik, Ruth Stachnik.
Financial data (yr. ended 12/31/01): Grants paid, $3,500; assets, $63,893 (M); expenditures, $3,889; qualifying distributions, $3,500.
Limitations: Giving primarily in Milwaukee, WI.
Application information: Application form not required.
Officer and Director:* Donna Kramer,* Pres., V.P. and Secy.-Treas.
EIN: 391731435

57835
George W. Wilson Trust
c/o Bank One Trust Co., N.A.
P.O. Box 1308
Milwaukee, WI 53201

Financial data (yr. ended 12/31/99): Grants paid, $3,500; assets, $112,663 (M); gifts received, $5; expenditures, $5,702; qualifying distributions, $3,701.
Limitations: Applications not accepted. Giving limited to residents of OH.
Application information: Contributes only to pre-selected organizations.
Trustee: Bank One Ohio Trust Co., N.A.
EIN: 346768998

57836
Patrick and Anne McKenzie Family Foundation, Inc.
154 Detrie Dr.
Green Bay, WI 54301

Established in 1997 in WI.
Donor(s): Patrick J. McKenzie, Anne W. McKenzie.
Financial data (yr. ended 12/31/01): Grants paid, $3,430; assets, $215,437 (M); expenditures, $6,065; qualifying distributions, $3,430.
Limitations: Applications not accepted.
Application information: Contributes only to pre-selected organizations.
Officers and Directors: Patrick J. McKenzie,* Pres. and Treas.; Anne W. McKenzie,* V.P. and Secy.; John R. McKenzie.
EIN: 391893423

57837
Braun-Reiss Family Foundation, Inc.
1077-1A Creeks Cross Rd.
Kohler, WI 53044-1317

Established in 1996.
Donor(s): John D. Braun,‡ Patricia P. Reiss.

Financial data (yr. ended 12/31/01): Grants paid, $3,400; assets, $366,502 (M); gifts received, $10,000; expenditures, $6,431; qualifying distributions, $3,400.
Limitations: Applications not accepted. Giving primarily in WI.
Application information: Contributes only to pre-selected organizations.
Officers and Directors:* Patricia P. Reiss,* Pres. and Treas.; Rhoda R. Dales,* V.P.; K. Allan Voss,* Secy.; William A. Reiss.
EIN: 391864367

57838
Clarice E. Olson Scholarship Trust
c/o Dale Fern
2071 117th Ave.
Baldwin, WI 54002
Application address: c/o Guidance Counselor, B-W High School, Baldwin, WI 54002, tel.: (715) 684-3321

Established in 1988.
Financial data (yr. ended 12/31/01): Grants paid, $3,400; assets, $3,450 (M); expenditures, $3,551; qualifying distributions, $3,400.
Limitations: Giving limited to Baldwin, WI.
Trustee: Dale Fern.
EIN: 391616246

57839
Four Wheel Drive Foundation
105 E. 12th St.
Clintonville, WI 54929 (715) 823-2141
Contact: James M. Green, Pres.

Donor(s): FWD/Seagrave Fire Apparatus, Inc.
Financial data (yr. ended 09/30/01): Grants paid, $3,310; assets, $273,446 (M); gifts received, $425; expenditures, $7,957; qualifying distributions, $5,863.
Limitations: Giving limited to the Clintonville, WI, area.
Application information: Application form required.
Officers and Directors:* James M. Green,* Pres.; Joseph L. Kaufmann, V.P. and Treas.; John L. Rosenholm,* Secy.; Randolf W. Lenz.
EIN: 396059533
Codes: CS, CD

57840
Proctor W. Nichols Fund
c/o Bank One Trust Co., N.A.
P.O. Box 1308
Milwaukee, WI 53201
Application address: 1125 17th St., Denver, CO 80202, tel.: (303) 244-3175
Contact: Deborah Fuller, Trust Off., Bank One Trust Co., N.A.

Established in 1996.
Financial data (yr. ended 12/31/01): Grants paid, $3,308; assets, $79,683 (M); expenditures, $5,908; qualifying distributions, $3,308.
Limitations: Giving primarily in CO.
Trustee: Bank One, Colorado, N.A.
EIN: 846206849

57841
May Family Foundation, Inc.
500 3rd St., Ste. 700
Wausau, WI 54403
Contact: Mark J. Bradley, Board Member

Established in 2000 in WI.
Donor(s): Eleanor J. May.
Financial data (yr. ended 12/31/01): Grants paid, $3,306; assets, $512,962 (M); gifts received, $500; expenditures, $9,524; qualifying distributions, $3,306.

Application information: Application form required.
Board Members: Mark J. Bradley, Annette S. Marra, Edward W. May, Jr., Eleanor J. May, Robert P. Priest, Karen L. Sislo.
EIN: 392006747

57842
Ramiah Family Foundation
2450 Shelly Court
Brookfield, WI 53045
Contact: S.P. Ramiah, Tr.

Established in 1999 in WI.
Donor(s): S.P. Ramiah, Letha Joseph.
Financial data (yr. ended 12/31/00): Grants paid, $3,300; assets, $91,210 (M); gifts received, $67,210; expenditures, $4,290; qualifying distributions, $3,231.
Limitations: Giving primarily in WI.
Trustees: Letha Joseph, S.P. Ramiah.
EIN: 391980086

57843
Richland Medical Center, Ltd. Foundation
301 E. 2nd St.
Richland Center, WI 53581
Contact: Karl F. Hirsbruner

Established in 1994 in WI.
Financial data (yr. ended 12/31/00): Grants paid, $3,300; assets, $68,945 (M); expenditures, $3,390; qualifying distributions, $3,366.
Limitations: Giving limited to Richland, Iowa, Grant, and Sauk counties, WI.
Application information: Application form required.
Officers: L.M. Pippin, Pres.; Jack I. Spear, V.P.; Kay S. Wyman, Secy.
EIN: 391713810

57844
Richard M. Connor, Sr. & Florence B. Connor Memorial Foundation, Inc.
P.O. Box 95
Laona, WI 54541-0095

Established in 1987 in WI.
Financial data (yr. ended 08/31/01): Grants paid, $3,250; assets, $276 (M); gifts received, $3,500; expenditures, $3,260; qualifying distributions, $3,250.
Limitations: Applications not accepted.
Application information: Contributes only to pre-selected organizations.
Officers: Richard M. Connor, Jr., Pres.; Jeffrey Evans, Secy.-Treas.
EIN: 391601302

57845
PMI Community Foundation, Inc.
1901 S. Oneida St.
Green Bay, WI 54304

Established in 1997 in WI.
Donor(s): Promotional Management, Inc.
Financial data (yr. ended 12/31/01): Grants paid, $3,200; assets, $73,954 (M); gifts received, $10,000; expenditures, $3,314; qualifying distributions, $3,175.
Limitations: Applications not accepted. Giving primarily in areas of company operations.
Application information: Contributes only to pre-selected organizations.
Trustees: Peter Mancuso, David Rosenwasser, Ronald Weyers.
EIN: 391916843
Codes: CS, CD

57846
Richard H. Johnson Foundation
P.O. Box 171
636 Wisconsin Ave.
Sheboygan, WI 53082-0171

Established in 1999 in WI.
Financial data (yr. ended 12/31/01): Grants paid, $3,199; assets, $104,296 (M); expenditures, $4,689; qualifying distributions, $3,472.
Officer: Daniel Woehrar, Mgr.
EIN: 316628515

57847
Father Francis Heindl Assembly Religious Vocations Trust
202 E. Juneau St.
Tomah, WI 54660-2661

Established in 1998 in WI.
Financial data (yr. ended 12/31/01): Grants paid, $3,148; assets, $57,727 (M); gifts received, $700; expenditures, $3,912; qualifying distributions, $3,148.
Limitations: Applications not accepted.
Application information: Contributes only to pre-selected organizations.
Officers: Donald Aschenbrenner, Chair; James Feldmeier, Exec. Secy.
Trustees: Thomas Baumgarten, Anthony Felber, Kenneth Hoffman, Dennis Koranda, Paul Vlasek.
EIN: 396693532

57848
Louis and Anna Heuvelman Trust
c/o Associated Kellogg Trust
P.O. Box 19006
Green Bay, WI 54307-9006

Financial data (yr. ended 12/31/99): Grants paid, $3,146; assets, $213,393 (M); expenditures, $6,713; qualifying distributions, $3,420.
Limitations: Applications not accepted. Giving primarily in De Pere, WI.
Application information: Contributes only to pre-selected organizations.
Trustee: Nancy Balza.
EIN: 396424614

57849
Goldie Powiazer Foundation, Inc.
525 E. Wells St., No. 300
Milwaukee, WI 53202
Application address: 2902 W. Mequon Rd., Mequon, WI 53092
Contact: Rabbi Louis Swichkow, Pres.

Financial data (yr. ended 01/31/02): Grants paid, $3,100; assets, $53,515 (M); expenditures, $3,448; qualifying distributions, $3,100.
Limitations: Giving primarily in Milwaukee, WI.
Officers: Rabbi Louis Swichkow, Pres.; Martin Zuckerman, Secy.
EIN: 237048483

57850
John and Susan Swendrowski Charitable Foundation
c/o Lynette M. Zigman, Foley & Lardner
777 E. Wisconsin Ave., Ste. 3600
Milwaukee, WI 53202-5367

Established in 1996 in WI.
Donor(s): John Swendrowski.
Financial data (yr. ended 12/31/01): Grants paid, $3,100; assets, $4,883 (M); gifts received, $3,000; expenditures, $3,116; qualifying distributions, $3,100.
Limitations: Applications not accepted.
Application information: Contributes only to pre-selected organizations.
Trustees: John Swendrowski, Susan Swendrowski.
EIN: 391886109

57851
Broom Tree Foundation, Inc.
6993 Darnell Ln.
Greendale, WI 53129-2354
Contact: Enoch Carver, Pres.

Donor(s): Enoch Carver.
Financial data (yr. ended 12/31/99): Grants paid, $3,050; assets, $29,181 (M); gifts received, $16,228; expenditures, $4,886; qualifying distributions, $4,886.
Application information: Application form not required.
Officers: Enoch Carver, Pres.; Thomas Mahn, V.P. and Secy.; David Bier, Treas.
EIN: 391943846

57852
Marcella & Ambrose Gatton Nurses Training Scholarship Fund
c/o Bank One Trust Co., N.A.
P.O. Box 1308
Milwaukee, WI 53201   (414) 765-2769

Established in 1995 in IL.
Financial data (yr. ended 12/31/99): Grants paid, $3,030; assets, $84,492 (M); expenditures, $5,132; qualifying distributions, $4,082.
Limitations: Applications not accepted.
Trustee: Bank One Trust Co., N.A.
EIN: 376318836

57853
Joseph E. Lavine Foundation
c/o Bank One Trust Co., N.A.
P.O. 1308
Milwaukee, WI 53201
Application address: P.O. Box 231, Warren, OH 44482, tel.: (216) 841-7820
Contact: Jeanette McElhaney, Tr. Off., Bank One Youngstown, N.A.

Financial data (yr. ended 12/31/01): Grants paid, $3,025; assets, $104,413 (M); gifts received, $26,737; expenditures, $4,480; qualifying distributions, $3,025.
Limitations: Giving primarily in Warren, OH.
Directors: Jim Lavine, Leonard Lavine.
Trustee: Bank One Trust Co., N.A.
EIN: 346516724

57854
Marjorie Siebert Aylen Foundation, Inc.
111 E. Wisconsin Ave., Ste. 1800
Milwaukee, WI 53202

Established in 1998 in WI.
Donor(s): Marjorie Siebert Aylen.
Financial data (yr. ended 12/31/01): Grants paid, $3,000; assets, $107,069 (M); gifts received, $17,500; expenditures, $5,935; qualifying distributions, $3,000.
Limitations: Applications not accepted. Giving primarily in Milwaukee, WI.
Application information: Contributes only to pre-selected organizations.
Officers and Directors:* Frank W. Bastian,* Pres.; Janet M. Hoehnen,* Secy.; Marjorie Aylen.
EIN: 391707934

57855
The Baraboo High School Stock Market Club Scholarship Trust
P.O. Box 50
Baraboo, WI 53913
Application address: c/o Stock Market Club Advisor, The Baraboo High School, 1201 Draper St., Baraboo, WI 53913, tel.: (608) 355-3940

Established in 1999 in WI.
Financial data (yr. ended 12/31/01): Grants paid, $3,000; assets, $16,103 (M); expenditures, $3,854; qualifying distributions, $3,000.
Application information: Application form required.
Trustee: Greg L. Lurch.
EIN: 391974166

57856
Boldin Family Foundation, Inc.
c/o RAM Distribution, LLC
757 N. Broadway, Ste. 400
Milwaukee, WI 53202

Established in 2000 in WI.
Donor(s): RAM Software.
Financial data (yr. ended 12/31/01): Grants paid, $3,000; assets, $196,719 (M); expenditures, $9,062; qualifying distributions, $3,000.
Limitations: Applications not accepted.
Application information: Contributes only to pre-selected organizations.
Officers and Directors:* Anthony J. Boldin,* Pres.; Jodie M. Boldin,* V.P. and Secy.-Treas.; Chris K. Gawart.
EIN: 392013662

57857
Jack & Elizabeth Cody Memorial Foundation Trust
c/o Bank One Trust Co., N.A.
P.O. Box 1308
Milwaukee, WI 53201
Contact: Heather Brandt, Trust Off., Bank One Trust Co., N.A.

Established in 1987 in WI.
Financial data (yr. ended 07/31/01): Grants paid, $3,000; assets, $148,740 (M); expenditures, $5,022; qualifying distributions, $5,000.
Limitations: Giving limited to residents of the Elkhorn, WI, area.
Application information: Application form required.
Trustee: Bank One Trust Co., N.A.
EIN: 396459094

57858
D. C. Everest Foundation
c/o Marshall & Ilsley Bank
P.O. Box 2980
Milwaukee, WI 53201 (414) 287-7135
Application address: c/o David P. Guilliom, Marshall & Ilsley Trust Co., P.O. Box 209, Wausau, WI 54402, tel.: (715) 845-3121

Financial data (yr. ended 12/31/01): Grants paid, $3,000; assets, $52,676 (M); expenditures, $4,544; qualifying distributions, $3,000.
Limitations: Giving limited to northern WI, with emphasis on Wausau.
Trustee: Marshall & Ilsley Bank.
EIN: 396063922

57859
Martha & James Hawley Memorial Fund
(Formerly Martha & James Hawley Memorial Fund for Young Citizens of Wheeling)
c/o Bank One Trust Co., N.A.
P.O. Box 1308
Milwaukee, WI 53201
Application address: 56 14th St., Wheeling, NV 26003
Contact: Jay T. McCamic, Tr.

Established in 1986 in WV.
Donor(s): Lawrence A. Collins.
Financial data (yr. ended 12/31/01): Grants paid, $3,000; assets, $56,434 (M); expenditures, $5,022; qualifying distributions, $3,000.
Limitations: Giving limited to Ohio County, WV.
Trustees: Brent A. Bush, Jay T. McCamic, Paul M. McKay, Bank One, N.A.
EIN: 556102216

57860
International Foundation for Integrated Medicine, Ltd.
c/o James E. Guither
1157 Amherst Dr.
Madison, WI 53705

Established in 1999 in WI.
Donor(s): James E. Guither.
Financial data (yr. ended 12/31/01): Grants paid, $3,000; assets, $249,792 (M); expenditures, $17,699; qualifying distributions, $3,000.
Limitations: Applications not accepted.
Application information: Contributes only to pre-selected organizations.
Officer: James E. Guither, Pres.
EIN: 391982934

57861
K-M Legacy, Ltd.
c/o John P. Arakelian
959 N. Mayfair Rd.
Wauwatosa, WI 53226-3418

Financial data (yr. ended 12/31/01): Grants paid, $3,000; assets, $86,871 (M); expenditures, $3,420; qualifying distributions, $3,000.
Limitations: Applications not accepted. Giving primarily in Greenfield, WI.
Application information: Contributes only to pre-selected organizations.
Officer and Directors:* John P. Arakelian,* Mgr.; Eleanor K. Allen, Arthur Kashian.
EIN: 391745137

57862
Knights of Columbus Bishop Leo J. Brust Council No. 3702 Foundation, Inc.
(Formerly Wauwatosa Knights of Columbus Foundation, Inc.)
P.O. Box 1992
Brookfield, WI 53005-1992

Established in 1969 in WI.
Donor(s): Wauwatosa Knights of Columbus Council No. 3702.
Financial data (yr. ended 12/31/01): Grants paid, $3,000; assets, $83,761 (M); gifts received, $2,140; expenditures, $3,118; qualifying distributions, $3,000.
Limitations: Applications not accepted. Giving primarily in Milwaukee, WI.
Application information: Contributes only to pre-selected organizations.
Officer and Trustees:* John J. Wisniewski, Pres.; Peter Reilly, V.P.; Ken Christensen, Secy.; Thomas M. Powers,* Treas.; Jim Clark, Robert Dornoff, Jim Dragani, William Haas, Robert Kalscheur, Paul Reddin.
EIN: 237042261

57863
Patrons of PYC, Inc.
P.O. Box 558
Waukesha, WI 53187-0558

Financial data (yr. ended 12/31/01): Grants paid, $3,000; assets, $55,728 (M); expenditures, $4,479; qualifying distributions, $3,000.
Limitations: Giving primarily in WI.
Officers: Robert H. Burns, Pres.; Thomas Hyslop, V.P.; William Dale, Secy.
Directors: Thomas H. Frentzel, Peter O. Harken, H. Coleman Norris, William Perrigo, Cynthia A. Ziegler, Adolph C. Zinn.
EIN: 391973127

57864
William F. Praiss Memorial Scholarship Fund
c/o Associated Banc-Corp
P.O. Box 408
Neenah, WI 54957-0408
Application address: c/o Neenah High School, 1275 Tullar Rd., Neenah, WI 54956

Established in 1990 in WI.
Donor(s): Praiss Memorial Trust, Agnes Praiss.
Financial data (yr. ended 05/31/01): Grants paid, $3,000; assets, $73,815 (M); expenditures, $4,234; qualifying distributions, $3,000.
Limitations: Giving limited to residents of Neenah, WI.
Application information: Application form required.
Trustee: Associated Banc-Corp.
EIN: 396522494

57865
Roger and Nancy Ritzow Family Foundation
c/o Bank One Trust Co., N.A
P.O. Box 1308
Milwaukee, WI 53201

Established in 2000 in WI.
Donor(s): Nancy Ritzow, Roger Ritzow.
Financial data (yr. ended 12/31/01): Grants paid, $3,000; assets, $998,610 (M); expenditures, $8,293; qualifying distributions, $3,000.
Limitations: Applications not accepted.
Application information: Contributes only to pre-selected organizations.
Trustees: David Ritzow, Nancy Ritzow, Roger Ritzow, Bank One Trust Co., N.A.
EIN: 396744907

57866
Hugh & Marie Squires Scholarship Foundation, Ltd.
The 1887 Bldg.
Elkhorn, WI 53121 (414) 723-3160
Contact: William Trewyn, Treas.

Established around 1980 in WI.
Financial data (yr. ended 04/30/01): Grants paid, $3,000; assets, $68,139 (M); expenditures, $4,012; qualifying distributions, $2,951.
Limitations: Giving limited to Elkhorn, WI.
Application information: Application form required.
Officers and Directors:* Anthony R. Serpe, Pres.; Edward E. Carlson, M.D., V.P.; Gregory A. Wescott,* Secy.; William J. Trewyn,* Treas.; Mary Alder, Gary Baumann, Lisle Blackbourn, Larry Bray, Tim Brellenthin, Susan Davey, Paul Ormson, Mike Roberts, C.P.A.
EIN: 391354516

57867
Tomah PTA Scholarship Trust
c/o Clifton, Gunderson & Co., LLC
P.O. Box 547
Tomah, WI 54660-0547
Application address: c/o Tomah Senior High School, Tomah, WI 54660, tel.: (608) 372-5986

Financial data (yr. ended 12/31/99): Grants paid, $3,000; assets, $157,555 (M); expenditures, $4,241; qualifying distributions, $4,241.
Limitations: Giving primarily in WI.
Application information: Application form required.
Trustees: Fred G.J. Farris, Raymond Paulis, Terry Winchel.
EIN: 396078616

57868
The Ronald & Joyce Wanek Foundation, Ltd.
c/o Ashley Furniture Industries, Inc.
1 Ashley Way
Arcadia, WI 54612 (608) 323-6249
Contact: Paulette Rippley

Established in WI in 1998.
Donor(s): Ronald G. Wanek, Joyce A. Wanek.
Financial data (yr. ended 12/31/01): Grants paid, $3,000; assets, $56,910 (M); expenditures, $3,039; qualifying distributions, $3,000.
Limitations: Giving on a national basis.
Directors: Shari S. Wagner, Joyce A. Wanek, Ronald G. Wanek, Todd R. Wanek, Katie S. Wanek-Forsythe.
EIN: 391948292

57869
Harold H. Snively Foundation, Inc.
914 17th Ave.
Monroe, WI 53566-2003
Application address: c/o Karla Snively, 2720 6th St., Monroe, WI 53566, tel.: (608) 325-5333

Financial data (yr. ended 02/28/02): Grants paid, $2,982; assets, $80,975 (M); expenditures, $3,260; qualifying distributions, $2,982.
Limitations: Giving primarily in WI.
Officer: Harold H. Snively, Pres.
EIN: 396060343

57870
Mustard Seed Foundation of Delafield, Inc.
1219 Waterville Ct.
Oconomowoc, WI 53066
Contact: Thomas E. Aul, Tr.

Donor(s): Thomas E. Aul, Patricia C. Aul.
Financial data (yr. ended 12/31/01): Grants paid, $2,900; assets, $45,556 (M); gifts received, $5,500; expenditures, $2,900; qualifying distributions, $2,900.
Trustees: Charles R. Aul, Christopher W. Aul, Margaret A. Aul, Patricia C. Aul, Thomas E. Aul, Justin W. Winslow.
EIN: 391869007

57871
The Nicholson Charitable Trust
S24 W26893 Apache Pass
Waukesha, WI 53188-5405

Established around 1995.
Financial data (yr. ended 12/31/01): Grants paid, $2,880; assets, $13,925 (M); expenditures, $3,105; qualifying distributions, $2,880.
Limitations: Applications not accepted.
Application information: Contributes only to pre-selected organizations.
Trustees: Janet R. Nicholson, William L. Nicholson.
EIN: 396598335

57872
Alice Lindquist Family Trust
c/o R.V. Alexander Title & Trust Co.
P.O. Box 46
River Falls, WI 54022-0046

Financial data (yr. ended 12/31/01): Grants paid, $2,854; assets, $114,557 (M); expenditures, $4,256; qualifying distributions, $2,854.
Limitations: Applications not accepted. Giving primarily in River Falls, WI.
Application information: Contributes only to pre-selected organizations.
Trustee: R.V. Alexander Title & Trust Co., Inc.
EIN: 396435602

57873
Pelton Casteel Foundation, Inc.
c/o Lawrence S. Krueger
2929 S. Chase Ave.
Milwaukee, WI 53207-6406

Established around 1974.
Donor(s): Pelton Casteel, Inc.
Financial data (yr. ended 12/31/99): Grants paid, $2,812; assets, $178 (M); gifts received, $2,975; expenditures, $3,097; qualifying distributions, $2,812.
Limitations: Giving primarily in WI.
Officer and Director:* Lawrence S. Krueger,* Pres.
EIN: 237450938
Codes: CS, CD

57874
Allie J. Gibbs Trust
c/o Bank One Trust Co., N.A.
P.O. Box 1308
Milwaukee, WI 53201
Application address: c/o Steve Boughton, Trust Off., Bank One Trust Co., N.A., 200 E. Broad St., 9th Fl., Akron, OH 44308

Donor(s): Allie J. Gibbs.‡
Financial data (yr. ended 12/31/99): Grants paid, $2,794; assets, $113,908 (M); expenditures, $5,327; qualifying distributions, $3,025.
Limitations: Giving limited to Ravenna, OH.
Trustee: Bank One Trust Co., N.A.
EIN: 316213826

57875
G. A. Fritsche Memorial Scholarship Fund
c/o U.S. Bank
P.O. Box 2043, LC4NE
Milwaukee, WI 53201-9116
Application address: c/o Bay View High School, 2751 S. Lenox St., Milwaukee, WI 53207

Financial data (yr. ended 05/31/01): Grants paid, $2,750; assets, $32,018 (M); gifts received, $1,545; expenditures, $3,804; qualifying distributions, $3,468.
Limitations: Giving limited to WI.
Application information: Unsolicited request for funds not accepted.
Officers and Committee Members:* Robert Kraiss,* Chair.; Barbara Morbeck,* Secy.; Matthew Boswell, Karen Geiken, Gus Luetzow, Bruce Tammi, Peter Wolf.
Trustee: U.S. Bank.
EIN: 396037046

57876
Ione Turner Charitable Trust
c/o Bank One Trust Co., N.A.
P.O. Box 1308
Milwaukee, WI 53201-1308

Financial data (yr. ended 12/31/01): Grants paid, $2,729; assets, $34,769 (M); expenditures, $4,852; qualifying distributions, $2,729.
Limitations: Applications not accepted. Giving limited to Canton, OH.
Application information: Contributes only to pre-selected organizations.
Trustee: Bank One Trust Co., N.A.
EIN: 346534210

57877
Gregory C. Van Wie Charitable Foundation
c/o John Mitby
2 E. Mifflin St., Ste. 200
Madison, WI 53701-1767

Established in 1996 in WI.
Financial data (yr. ended 12/31/00): Grants paid, $2,710; assets, $144,083 (M); expenditures, $4,244; qualifying distributions, $3,095.
Limitations: Applications not accepted. Giving primarily in WI.
Application information: Contributes only to pre-selected organizations.
Officers: John C. Mitby, Pres. and Treas.; John Van Wie, V.P.; Bruce Rodger, Secy.
EIN: 391822927

57878
Harry & Irma Gray Scholarship Trust
c/o Marshall & Ilsley Bank
P.O. Box 2980
Milwaukee, WI 53201 (414) 287-7291
Application address: Sharon Blank, Trust Off., c/o Marshall & Ilsley Bank, 401 N. Segoe Rd., 2M, Madison, WI 53705, tel.: (608) 232-2000

Established in 1994.
Financial data (yr. ended 12/31/01): Grants paid, $2,700; assets, $67,771 (M); expenditures, $3,223; qualifying distributions, $2,700.
Limitations: Giving limited to residents of WI.
Trustee: Marshall & Ilsley Bank.
EIN: 391772033

57879
Veda Sweeney Trust Fund
c/o The Reedsburg Bank
P.O. Box 90
Reedsburg, WI 53959-0090 (608) 524-8251
Application address: c/o School District Administrator, 710 N. Walnut St., Reedsburg, WI 53959, tel.: (708) 524-2401

Financial data (yr. ended 12/31/01): Grants paid, $2,695; assets, $58,064 (M); expenditures, $3,231; qualifying distributions, $3,231.
Limitations: Giving limited to WI.
Application information: Application form required.
Scholarship Committee: Robert Allen, John Alt, Katherine E. Campbell.
Trustee: The Reedsburg Bank.
EIN: 396316399
Codes: GTI

57880
Agnes & Raleigh Sorge Administrative Trust
402 N 8th St.
P.O. Box 10
Manitowoc, WI 54221-0010
Contact: Ronald G. Chinnock

Financial data (yr. ended 12/31/01): Grants paid, $2,613; assets, $58,321 (M); expenditures, $3,830; qualifying distributions, $2,613.
Trustee: First National Bank of Manitowoc.
EIN: 396637709

57881
Edwin and Patricia Gabrielse Charitable Foundation, Inc.
2913 Evergreen Pkwy.
Sheboygan, WI 53083 (920) 459-7937

Established in 1996 in WI.
Financial data (yr. ended 12/31/99): Grants paid, $2,600; assets, $2,210 (M); expenditures, $2,619; qualifying distributions, $2,600.
Limitations: Applications not accepted.
Application information: Contributes only to pre-selected organizations.
Officers and Directors:* Edwin Gabrielse,* Pres. and Treas.; Patricia Gabrielse,* V.P. and Secy.; Kathi G. Brueggemann.
EIN: 391839772

57882
Maude T. Scott Memorial Scholarship Fund
c/o Bank One Trust Co., NA
P.O. Box 130
Milwaukee, WI 53201
Application addresses: c/o Franklin Community School Corp., Franklin, IN 46131, tel.: (317) 881-9326; c/o Bank One Trust Group, 111 Monument Cir., Ste. 1501, Indianapolis, IN 46204

Financial data (yr. ended 12/31/00): Grants paid, $2,600; assets, $94,033 (M); expenditures, $5,027; qualifying distributions, $3,963.
Limitations: Giving limited to Franklin, IN.
Application information: Application form required.
Trustee: Bank One, N.A.
EIN: 356271275

57883
Bachhuber Family Foundation, Inc.
1898 Old Valley Rd.
De Pere, WI 54115

Established in 1996 in WI.
Donor(s): Raymond Bachhuber.
Financial data (yr. ended 12/31/01): Grants paid, $2,500; assets, $47,211 (M); gifts received, $3,500; expenditures, $2,996; qualifying distributions, $2,500.
Limitations: Applications not accepted. Giving primarily in Green Bay, WI.
Application information: Contributes only to pre-selected organizations.
Officers: Joan Bachhuber, Pres.; David Bachhuber, V.P.; Raymond Bachhuber, Secy.-Treas.
EIN: 391869694

57884
Baldner Family Foundation
c/o North Central Trust
311 Main St.
La Crosse, WI 54601

Established in 1998 in WI.
Donor(s): Gerald Baldner, Betty Baldner.
Financial data (yr. ended 12/31/01): Grants paid, $2,500; assets, $88,496 (M); gifts received, $30,000; expenditures, $3,317; qualifying distributions, $2,837.
Trustees: Betty Baldner, Gerald Baldner, North Central Trust Co.
EIN: 311635806

57885
Ethel M. Brann Foundation, Inc.
2538 Bittersweet Ave.
Green Bay, WI 54301-1843
Contact: Elizabeth B. Hendrickson, Pres.

Donor(s): Elizabeth B. Hendrickson.
Financial data (yr. ended 12/31/01): Grants paid, $2,500; assets, $69,608 (M); gifts received, $5,000; expenditures, $2,960; qualifying distributions, $2,500.
Limitations: Giving primarily in WI.
Officers and Directors:* Elizabeth B. Hendrickson,* Pres. and Treas.; Philip J. Hendrickson,* V.P.; Scott Hendrickson,* Secy.; Sara H. Fortune.
EIN: 237083666

57886
Ray Carlson Testamentary Trust
c/o Bank One Trust Co., N.A.
P.O. Box 1308
Milwaukee, WI 53201

Established in 1994.
Financial data (yr. ended 07/31/01): Grants paid, $2,500; assets, $87,920 (M); expenditures, $6,224; qualifying distributions, $3,988.
Limitations: Applications not accepted. Giving limited to Appleton, WI.
Application information: Contributes only to pre-selected organizations.
Trustee: Bank One Trust Co., N.A.
EIN: 396465891

57887
Diversity Inventory Group, Inc.
c/o W. M. Alverson
1306 Morrison St.
Madison, WI 53703

Established in 1999.
Financial data (yr. ended 12/31/01): Grants paid, $2,500; assets, $60,750 (M); gifts received, $52; expenditures, $6,310; qualifying distributions, $2,500.
Limitations: Applications not accepted.
Application information: Contributes only to pre-selected organizations.
Officers and Director:* Donald Waller, Pres.; Paul Berry, V.P.; William S. Alverson,* Secy.; Lois Brako, Treas.
EIN: 391948519

57888
Robert G. Zach Family Foundation, Inc.
c/o Margaret L. Zach
1207 Eastview Dr.
Wausau, WI 54403-9220

Established in 1996 in WI.
Donor(s): Margaret L. Zach.
Financial data (yr. ended 12/31/01): Grants paid, $2,500; assets, $52,379 (M); gifts received, $5,000; expenditures, $3,273; qualifying distributions, $2,500.
Limitations: Applications not accepted. Giving primarily in WI.
Application information: Contributes only to pre-selected organizations.
Officer: David M. Zach, Pres.
Directors: James R. Zach, John P. Zach, Margaret L. Zach.
EIN: 391860482

57889
Earl & Irene Wiese Foundation
c/o F & M Bank
21 S. Nicolet Rd.
Appleton, WI 54914

Established in 2000 in WI.
Donor(s): Earl A. Wiese.
Financial data (yr. ended 12/31/01): Grants paid, $2,499; assets, $175,728 (M); gifts received, $305; expenditures, $7,290; qualifying distributions, $2,499.
Limitations: Applications not accepted.
Application information: Contributes only to pre-selected organizations.
Trustee: F & M Bank.
EIN: 396737448

57890
Atkinson-Ells Charitable Foundation
714 W. McIntosh Ln.
Mequon, WI 53092-6025
Application address: 703 E. Lexington Blvd., Milwaukee, WI 53217
Contact: Jennifer Ells Chou, Secy.

Established in 1999 in WI.
Donor(s): Mary Louise B. Atkinson, Ralph E. Ells, Madeline L. Ells, David Ells, Susan Ells, Mary M. Ells, Alex Chou, Jennifer Ells Chou.
Financial data (yr. ended 12/31/01): Grants paid, $2,400; assets, $59,245 (M); gifts received, $7,355; expenditures, $2,530; qualifying distributions, $2,400.
Limitations: Giving primarily in WI.
Application information: Application form not required.
Officers: David Ells, Pres.; Madeline Ells, V.P.; Jenny Ells Chou, Secy.; Ralph Ells, Treas.
EIN: 391966362

57891
The Hanson Family Foundation, Inc.
1318 Basswood Ave.
Spooner, WI 54801

Established in 2000 in WI.
Donor(s): Wayne Hanson, Mary Lee Hanson.
Financial data (yr. ended 12/31/01): Grants paid, $2,400; assets, $28,734 (M); expenditures, $2,900; qualifying distributions, $2,400.
Limitations: Applications not accepted.
Application information: Contributes only to pre-selected organizations.
Officers: Wayne Hanson, Pres. and Treas.; Mary Lee Hanson, V.P. and Secy.
EIN: 392013472

57892
Raleigh and Agnes Sorge Charitable Trust
c/o First National Bank of Manitowoc
P.O. Box 10, 402 N. 8th St.
Manitowoc, WI 54220
Contact: Richard R. Jordarski, Trust Off., First National Bank, Manitowoc

Established in 1997 in WI.
Financial data (yr. ended 12/31/01): Grants paid, $2,370; assets, $53,997 (M); expenditures, $3,763; qualifying distributions, $2,370.
Trustee: First National Bank of Manitowoc.
EIN: 396636699

57893
Gordon P. and Sigrid L. Connor Family Foundation, Inc.
100 Mill St.
Laona, WI 54541
Contact: Gordon P. Connor, Pres.

Established in 1999 in WI.
Donor(s): Gordon P. Connor.
Financial data (yr. ended 12/31/01): Grants paid, $2,350; assets, $11,314 (M); gifts received, $4,177; expenditures, $2,981; qualifying distributions, $2,350.
Officers and Directors:* Gordon P. Connor,* Pres.; Sigrid L. Connor,* V.P. and Secy.; Peter H. Connor,* Treas.
EIN: 391976199

57894
Gerald G. & Mary Jeanne Censky Charitable Foundation
c/o First National Bank of Manitowoc
P.O. Box 10
Manitowoc, WI 54221-0010
Application address: 1119 Lincoln Blvd., Manitowoc, WI 54220
Contact: Gerald Censky, Tr.

Donor(s): Gerald Censky, Mary Jeanne Censky.
Financial data (yr. ended 12/31/01): Grants paid, $2,300; assets, $55,590 (M); expenditures, $2,848; qualifying distributions, $2,300.
Limitations: Giving limited to the Manitowoc, WI, area.
Trustees: Gerald Censky, Mary Jeanne Censky, First National Bank of Manitowoc.
EIN: 396374855

57895
Myrla Block Educational Trust
c/o Bank One Trust Co., N.A.
P.O. Box 1308
Milwaukee, WI 53201 (414) 765-2017

Established in 1991 in IL.
Donor(s): Myrla Block.‡
Financial data (yr. ended 12/31/01): Grants paid, $2,250; assets, $130,126 (M); expenditures, $4,897; qualifying distributions, $2,250.
Limitations: Giving primarily in IL.
Trustee: Bank One Trust Co., N.A.
EIN: 366945387

57896
Wetlands Conservation League, Inc.
P.O. Box 307
Plover, WI 54467 (715) 344-8106

Established around 1983 in WI.
Financial data (yr. ended 12/31/01): Grants paid, $2,250; assets, $68,122 (M); gifts received, $27,209; expenditures, $26,706; qualifying distributions, $2,250.
Limitations: Giving limited to Portage County, WI.
Officers: Lyle Nauman, Pres.; Jerry Rozner, V.P.; Roy Rozner, Secy.; Allen Zorn, Treas.
Directors: Ron Berna, Dennis Hintz, Steve Ligman, Dale Navarre, R.J. Reidinger, Brian Simcakowski, Terry Spry, Dave Wanta.
EIN: 930833511

57897
Sheboygan Music Club Foundation
723 Tallgrass Ln.
Plymouth, WI 53073-4245
Application address for secondary schools: 1630 Sunnyside Ave., Sheboygan, WI 53081
Scholarship application address: c/o Joyce Conrardy, 3736 N. 12th Pl., Sheboygan, WI 53083; or c/o John Humbert, 809 Spring Ave., Sheboygan, WI 53081
Contact: Joyce Conrardy, John Humbert, & Mary Sommersburger

Financial data (yr. ended 06/30/01): Grants paid, $2,186; assets, $12,917 (M); gifts received, $50; expenditures, $2,691; qualifying distributions, $11,186.
Limitations: Giving limited to residents of Sheboygan County, WI.
Application information: Application form required.
Officers: Joyce Conrardy, Pres.; John Humbert, V.P.; Janice Ongna, Secy.; Barbara Ramm, Treas.
EIN: 391588809

57898
George & Ruth Raike Leadership Trust
c/o Bank One Trust Co., N.A.
P.O. Box 1308
Milwaukee, WI 53202

Established in 1998 in WV.
Donor(s): George Raike.
Financial data (yr. ended 12/31/00): Grants paid, $2,148; assets, $90,215 (M); expenditures, $5,602; qualifying distributions, $3,240.
Limitations: Applications not accepted. Giving primarily in WV.
Application information: Contributes only to pre-selected organizations.
Trustee: Bank One Trust Co., N.A.
EIN: 546423253

57899
Edith Bell O'Boyle Foundation, Inc.
c/o Leo E. Corr
6950 20th St.
Necedah, WI 54646 (608) 565-2721
Contact: April C. Corr, Pres.

Donor(s): April C. Corr.
Financial data (yr. ended 12/31/01): Grants paid, $2,140; assets, $45,831 (M); gifts received, $9,000; expenditures, $10,272; qualifying distributions, $2,140.
Officers: April C. Corr, Pres.; Christopher Corr, V.P.; Robert T. Freas, Secy.; Leo E. Corr, Treas.
EIN: 391774050

57900
Manitowoc County Crimestoppers, Inc.
P.O. Box 10
Manitowoc, WI 54221-0010 (920) 684-6611
Hotline tel.: (920) 683-4466
Contact: Thomas Bare, Treas.

Established in 1997 in WI.
Financial data (yr. ended 12/31/99): Grants paid, $2,101; assets, $6,986 (M); gifts received, $6,495; expenditures, $2,764; qualifying distributions, $2,743; giving activities include $2,745 for programs.
Limitations: Giving limited to residents of Manitowoc County, WI.
Officers and Directors:* Tom Witczak,* Chair.; Tom Kocourek,* Vice-Chair.; Kathy Leist,* Secy.; Thomas Bare,* Treas.; Gene Gates.
EIN: 391775129

57901
Kruyne Family Foundation, Inc.
111 E. Wisconsin Ave., Ste. 1800
Milwaukee, WI 53202

Established in 1999 in WI.
Donor(s): Barbara M. Kruyne, James P. Kruyne.
Financial data (yr. ended 12/31/01): Grants paid, $2,050; assets, $38,572 (M); expenditures, $4,923; qualifying distributions, $2,050.
Limitations: Applications not accepted.
Application information: Contributes only to pre-selected organizations.
Officers and Directors:* James P. Kruyne,* Pres.; James A. Kruyne,* V.P.; Julie Kruyne,* Secy.; Jennifer Kruyne,* Treas.; Barbara M. Kruyne.
EIN: 391974105

57902
Blanche Lepley Trust
c/o Bank One Trust Co., N.A.
P.O. Box 1308
Milwaukee, WI 53201

Established in 2000 in WI.

Financial data (yr. ended 12/31/00): Grants paid, $2,009; assets, $63,518 (M); expenditures, $4,123; qualifying distributions, $2,898.
Limitations: Applications not accepted. Giving primarily in OH.
Application information: Contributes only to pre-selected organizations.
Trustee: Bank One Trust Co., N.A.
EIN: 346735063

57903
Earl A. Aiken Scholarship Fund
c/o Bank One Trust Co., N.A.
P.O. Box 1308
Milwaukee, WI 53201
Application address: c/o Kayla Morrison, Bank One, Louisiana, N.A., Alexandria, LA 71301

Financial data (yr. ended 12/31/01): Grants paid, $2,000; assets, $54,312 (M); expenditures, $3,694; qualifying distributions, $2,986.
Limitations: Applications not accepted. Giving limited to the Tioga, LA, area.
Application information: Recipients are selected from senior class by Scholarship Committee.
Trustee: Bank One, Louisiana, N.A.
EIN: 726122855

57904
Copernicus Cultural Foundation of Stevens Point, Wisconsin, Inc.
5565 Riverview Ct.
Stevens Point, WI 54481-9213
Contact: John Kolinski, Treas.

Financial data (yr. ended 12/31/01): Grants paid, $2,000; assets, $61,458 (M); expenditures, $4,763; qualifying distributions, $2,000.
Limitations: Giving primarily in WI.
Officers: John Haka, Pres.; Chrismary Pacyna, V.P.; Nick Check, Secy.; John Kolinski, Treas.
Directors: Kathryn Bukolt, Donald Green, Gerald Skalaski.
EIN: 237190284

57905
Cynthia Graeber Memorial Scholarship Irrevocable Charitable Trust
c/o Menomonee Falls H.S.
W173, N4991 Chestnut Ct.
Menomonee Falls, WI 53051-6581

Donor(s): John A. Graeber.
Financial data (yr. ended 12/31/00): Grants paid, $2,000; assets, $19,604 (M); expenditures, $2,012; qualifying distributions, $2,000.
Limitations: Giving limited to residents of Menomonee Falls, WI.
Agent: John A. Graeber.
EIN: 391667752

57906
George E. & Katherine G. Hayward Trust
c/o Bank One Trust Co., N.A.
P.O. Box 1308
Milwaukee, WI 53201
Application address: c/o Steve Boughton, Trust Off., Bank One Ohio Trust Co., N.A., 33 N. 3rd St., Columbus, OH 43271-1075

Financial data (yr. ended 12/31/99): Grants paid, $2,000; assets, $108,266 (M); expenditures, $4,371; qualifying distributions, $2,222.
Limitations: Giving limited to Marietta, OH.
Trustee: Bank One Trust Co., N.A.
EIN: 316086621

57907
E. F. Jablonski Family Foundation, Inc.
1222 Single Ave.
Wausau, WI 54401-6551

Established in 1992 in WI.
Donor(s): Edwin Jablonski.
Financial data (yr. ended 12/31/99): Grants paid, $2,000; assets, $119,815 (M); gifts received, $62,653; expenditures, $6,475; qualifying distributions, $6,370; giving activities include $2,126 for programs.
Limitations: Applications not accepted.
Application information: Contributes only to pre-selected organizations.
Officers: Edwin Jablonski, Pres.; Barbara Wohlfahrt, V.P.; James Wrycha, Secy.-Treas.
EIN: 391718719

57908
The Paul and Harriet Lorenz Foundation, Inc.
c/o Bank One Trust Co., N.A.
P.O. Box 1308
Milwaukee, WI 53201
Application address: c/o William Hartman, Bank One, 38601 W. 12 Mile Rd, Farmington Hills, MI 48331

Established in 1993.
Donor(s): Paul F. Lorenz.
Financial data (yr. ended 12/31/01): Grants paid, $2,000; assets, $318,194 (M); expenditures, $5,135; qualifying distributions, $3,384.
Limitations: Giving primarily in MI and MO.
Officer: Paul F. Lorenz, Pres. and Treas.
Director: Robert P. Lorenz.
EIN: 388686900

57909
Mitchell Metal Products Inc. Foundation
c/o Marshall & Ilsley Bank
P.O. Box 209
Wausau, WI 54403-0209
Application address: 500 3rd St., Wausau, WI 54402, tel.: (715) 845-3121
Contact: Carolie B. Kuehn, Trust Off., Marshall & Ilsley Bank

Established in 1986 in WI.
Donor(s): Mitchell Metals Products, Gordon Mitchell, Arlette Mitchell.
Financial data (yr. ended 03/31/02): Grants paid, $2,000; assets, $47,508 (M); gifts received, $2,800; expenditures, $2,047; qualifying distributions, $2,000.
Limitations: Giving limited to Merrill, WI.
Application information: Application form required.
Trustee: Marshall & Ilsley Bank.
EIN: 396438696
Codes: CS, CD

57910
Oregon Rotary Foundation, Inc.
365 N. Perry Pkwy.
Oregon, WI 53575
Application address: c/o Guidance Dept., Oregon High School, 465 N. Perry, Oregon, WI 53575

Established in 1997 in WI.
Donor(s): Arlan Kay, Larry Mahr, Dave Gochberg, Jeff Larson, Linda Barrows.
Financial data (yr. ended 06/30/01): Grants paid, $2,000; assets, $56,000 (M); gifts received, $1,333; expenditures, $2,101; qualifying distributions, $2,000.
Limitations: Giving limited to Oregon, WI.
Officers: Arlan Kay, Pres.; Gail Brown, V.P.; Marshall Mennenga, Secy.-Treas.
EIN: 391563000

57911
Alvin A. Ott Scholarship Fund
(Formerly Alvin A. Ott Scholarship Trust)
c/o The Bank of New Glarus
P.O. Box 129
New Glarus, WI 53574-0129
Application address: 1420 2nd St., New Glarus, WI 53574
Contact: Robert Werner, Tr.

Financial data (yr. ended 12/31/01): Grants paid, $2,000; assets, $38,092 (M); gifts received, $11; expenditures, $2,041; qualifying distributions, $2,000.
Limitations: Giving limited to New Glarus, WI.
Trustees: Quinton Ott, Eugene Stuessy, John G. Thomson, Robert Werner.
EIN: 396351070

57912
Roger and Barbara Siegert Family Foundation
605 N. Highland Ave.
P.O. Box 523
Plymouth, WI 53073

Established in 2000 in MI.
Donor(s): Roger L. Siegert, Barbara A. Siegert.
Financial data (yr. ended 12/31/01): Grants paid, $2,000; assets, $42,676 (M); expenditures, $2,598; qualifying distributions, $2,000.
Limitations: Applications not accepted.
Application information: Contributes only to pre-selected organizations.
Trustees: Barbara A. Siegert, Roger L. Siegert.
EIN: 392010412

57913
J. Harold Townsend Trust
c/o Bank One Trust Co., N.A.
P.O. Box 13
Milwaukee, WI 53201
Application address: c/o Grant Young, 539 Main St., Findlay, OH 45840

Financial data (yr. ended 12/31/01): Grants paid, $2,000; assets, $11,077 (M); expenditures, $3,269; qualifying distributions, $2,910.
Limitations: Giving primarily in areas of company operations.
Trustee: Bank One Trust Co., N.A.
EIN: 356246218

57914
Whesco Scholarship Fund, Inc.
9046 N. 51st St.
Brown Deer, WI 53223

Established in 1997 in WI.
Donor(s): Whesco Group, Inc.
Financial data (yr. ended 12/31/01): Grants paid, $2,000; assets, $1,542 (M); expenditures, $2,261; qualifying distributions, $2,000.
Limitations: Applications not accepted.
Application information: Contributes only to pre-selected organizations.
Officer and Directors:* John Klusmeyer,* Pres.; Barbara Klusmeyer, Mike Memmel, Mark Parish.
EIN: 391873289

57915
Charles V. Jones Trust
c/o Bank One Trust Co., N.A.
P.O. Box 1308
Milwaukee, WI 53201

Established in 1991 in OH.
Financial data (yr. ended 12/31/99): Grants paid, $1,988; assets, $81,904 (M); expenditures, $5,082; qualifying distributions, $2,175.
Limitations: Applications not accepted. Giving limited to OH.
Application information: Contributes only to pre-selected organizations.
Trustee: Bank One Trust Co., N.A.
EIN: 316385718

57916
The Halbedel Trust
c/o Bank One Trust Co., N.A.
P. O. Box 1308
Milwaukee, WI 53201

Financial data (yr. ended 12/31/01): Grants paid, $1,928; assets, $48,087 (M); expenditures, $4,070; qualifying distributions, $3,034.
Limitations: Applications not accepted. Giving primarily in LA.
Application information: Contributes only to pre-selected organizations.
Trustee: Bank One Trust Co., N.A.
EIN: 726050244

57917
Nettie E. Karcher Memorial Scholarship Fund Trust
c/o Marshall & Ilsley Bank
P.O. Box 600
Burlington, WI 53105   (262) 763-9141

Financial data (yr. ended 07/31/01): Grants paid, $1,914; assets, $50,525 (M); expenditures, $2,800; qualifying distributions, $1,990.
Limitations: Giving limited to residents of Burlington, WI.
Application information: Application form required.
Trustee: Marshall & Ilsley Bank.
EIN: 396145740

57918
Elmbrook Youth Leadership Council
c/o Linda M. Kowalski
P.O. Box 1072
Brookfield, WI 53008-1072

Established in 1999 in WI.
Financial data (yr. ended 12/31/99): Grants paid, $1,831; assets, $1,192 (M); gifts received, $3,645; expenditures, $2,453; qualifying distributions, $2,279.
Officers: Mike Mamayek, Pres.; Kay Hartzell, Treas.
Directors: Bill Grasch, Gretchen Henry, Sharon Koenings, Ruth Regent-Smith, Gloria Renkert, Jonathan Roob, Mark Thurner, Marti Treutelaar.
EIN: 391688404

57919
Lund-Dahlberg Charitable Foundation Trust
1119 Merrill Springs Rd.
Madison, WI 53705

Established in 1998 in WI.
Donor(s): James Dahlberg, Elsebet Lund.
Financial data (yr. ended 12/31/01): Grants paid, $1,810; assets, $1,260 (M); gifts received, $2,000; expenditures, $2,185; qualifying distributions, $1,810.
Limitations: Applications not accepted.
Application information: Contributes only to pre-selected organizations.
Trustees: James Dahlberg, Elsebet Lund.
EIN: 396673842

57920
Duhr Family Foundation, Inc.
2636 W. Lake Forest Ct.
Mequon, WI 53092
Contact: Allen W. Duhr, Pres.

Established in 1997 in WI.
Donor(s): Allen W. Duhr.

Financial data (yr. ended 12/31/00): Grants paid, $1,750; assets, $156,447 (M); expenditures, $1,582; qualifying distributions, $2,197.
Officers: Allen W. Duhr, Pres. and Treas.; Peggy Duhr, V.P. and Secy.
EIN: 391892201

57921
Owen and Anne Gromme Scholarship Fund, Inc.
c/o Bank of Wisconsin Dells
P.O. Box 490
Wisconsin Dells, WI 53965

Established in 1986 in WI.
Donor(s): Ronald G. Bartel.
Financial data (yr. ended 12/31/99): Grants paid, $1,750; assets, $37,974 (M); gifts received, $43; expenditures, $2,185; qualifying distributions, $1,750.
Limitations: Applications not accepted. Giving primarily in WI.
Officers and Directors:* Ronald G. Bartel,* Pres.; Roy Gromme,* Secy.; Orrin K. Anderson,* Treas.
EIN: 391553615

57922
Donald and Jo Anne Krause Family Foundation
19635 Independance Ct.
Brookfield, WI 53045

Established in 2001 in WI.
Donor(s): Donald Krause, Jo Anne Krause.
Financial data (yr. ended 12/31/01): Grants paid, $1,750; assets, $135,981 (M); gifts received, $138,350; expenditures, $1,750; qualifying distributions, $1,750.
Limitations: Applications not accepted. Giving primarily in WI.
Application information: Contributes only to pre-selected organizations.
Trustees: Donald Krause, Jo Anne Krause.
EIN: 392035962

57923
Wisconsin Gamma Phi Beta Foundation, Inc.
c/o Quarles & Brady
1 S. Pinckney St., Ste. 600
Madison, WI 53701-2113
Application address: c/o Gamma Phi Beta Sorority, 270 Langdon St., Madison, WI 53703, tel.: (608) 256-8872
Contact: Ann Shea, Pres.

Financial data (yr. ended 12/31/99): Grants paid, $1,750; assets, $26,501 (M); gifts received, $3,958; expenditures, $4,943; qualifying distributions, $2,312.
Limitations: Giving limited to residents of Madison, WI.
Officers and Directors:* Ann Shea,* Pres.; Carol Giswold,* V.P.; Mary Padgham,* Secy.-Treas.
EIN: 237036126

57924
Florence A. Place Educational Testamentary Trust
c/o First National Bank
P.O. Box 270106
Hartford, WI 53027-0106

Financial data (yr. ended 12/31/99): Grants paid, $1,733; assets, $120,480 (M); expenditures, $3,217; qualifying distributions, $3,179.
Limitations: Applications not accepted.
Trustee: First National Bank of Hartford.
EIN: 396461369

57925
Broenen-Fogarty Charitable Foundation
c/o George Fogarty
N78W17250 Wildwood Dr.
Menomonee Falls, WI 53051

Established in 1986 in WI.
Donor(s): Darwin Broenen.
Financial data (yr. ended 05/31/01): Grants paid, $1,650; assets, $73,643 (M); gifts received, $1,500; expenditures, $1,720; qualifying distributions, $1,720.
Limitations: Applications not accepted. Giving limited to Milwaukee, WI.
Trustees: Darwin Broenen, George Fogarty.
EIN: 391574338

57926
The Jensen Charitable Trust
3525 E. O'Brien Rd.
Oak Creek, WI 53154-6044

Established in 1997 in WI.
Financial data (yr. ended 12/31/99): Grants paid, $1,650; assets, $52,660 (M); gifts received, $43,224; expenditures, $3,108; qualifying distributions, $3,108.
Limitations: Applications not accepted. Giving primarily in Milwaukee, WI.
Application information: Contributes only to pre-selected organizations.
Directors: Jack Y. Jensen, Mary Jensen.
EIN: 396642868

57927
Bill Kuehmsted Foundation
c/o Bank One Trust Co., N.A.
P.O. Box 1308
Milwaukee, WI 53201
Application address: c/o Claude Radtke, Guidance Office, Appleton East High School, Appleton, WI 54911, tel.: (920) 832-6200

Financial data (yr. ended 06/30/01): Grants paid, $1,600; assets, $64,593 (M); gifts received, $700; expenditures, $3,124; qualifying distributions, $2,949.
Limitations: Giving limited to Appleton, WI.
Application information: Application form not required.
Trustee: Bank One Trust Co., N.A.
EIN: 237108091

57928
Kenneth & Jani Wagner Charitable Trust
436 Fawn Dr.
Brillion, WI 54110

Established in 1997 in WI.
Donor(s): Kenneth E. Wagner, Jani Wagner.
Financial data (yr. ended 12/31/01): Grants paid, $1,564; assets, $40,801 (M); gifts received, $740; expenditures, $2,304; qualifying distributions, $1,564.
Limitations: Applications not accepted. Giving primarily in WI.
Application information: Contributes only to pre-selected organizations.
Trustees: Jani Wagner, Kenneth E. Wagner.
EIN: 391895005

57929
Melvin & Jean Adams Charitable Trust
c/o Bank One Trust Co., N.A.
P.O. Box 1308
Milwaukee, WI 53202

Established in 1997 in WV.
Financial data (yr. ended 12/31/01): Grants paid, $1,511; assets, $50,812 (M); expenditures, $3,550; qualifying distributions, $1,511.

Limitations: Applications not accepted. Giving primarily in Huntington, WV; some giving in OH.
Application information: Contributes only to pre-selected organizations.
Trustee: Bank One Trust Co., N.A.
EIN: 556081429

57930
The Emerald Foundation, Inc.
1400 E. Fox Ln.
Fox Point, WI 53217   (414) 352-8511
Contact: Nancy E. Eiseman, Pres.

Financial data (yr. ended 12/31/00): Grants paid, $1,500; assets, $13,461 (M); gifts received, $4,955; expenditures, $1,600; qualifying distributions, $1,600.
Limitations: Giving primarily in Fox Point, WI.
Officers: Nancy E. Eiseman, Pres.; William E. Eiseman, V.P.; Nora Platt, Secy.
EIN: 311600511

57931
Paul W. Langenfeld Foundation
P.O. Box 138
New Holstein, WI 53061-0138
Application address: 1701 Circle Dr., New Holstein, WI 53061
Contact: Mary Grace Langenfeld, Mgr.

Financial data (yr. ended 12/31/01): Grants paid, $1,500; assets, $63,852 (M); expenditures, $1,930; qualifying distributions, $1,500.
Limitations: Giving primarily in WI.
Officer: Mary Grace Langenfeld, Mgr.
Trustee: William E. Hertel.
EIN: 396076176

57932
St. Mary's High School Trust No. 2
c/o Bank One Trust Co., N.A.
P.O. Box 1308
Milwaukee, WI 53201
Application address: c/o Anthony V. Thomas, Advisory Comm. Member, 318 8th St., Lorain, OH 44052, tel.: (440) 245-5283

Financial data (yr. ended 12/31/99): Grants paid, $1,500; assets, $32,946 (M); gifts received, $10; expenditures, $2,790; qualifying distributions, $1,567.
Limitations: Giving limited to Lorain, OH.
Application information: Application form required.
Trustee: Bank One Trust Co., N.A.
EIN: 346662741

57933
Island Memorial Medical Fund, Inc.
c/o Virginia Thomas
P.O. Box 35
Washington Island, WI 54246

Financial data (yr. ended 12/31/99): Grants paid, $1,412; assets, $74,987 (M); gifts received, $31,851; expenditures, $6,279; qualifying distributions, $1,412.
Trustees: Karen Gunnlaugson, Arni Richter, Virginia Thomas.
EIN: 237303696

57934
Eric A. Wolfe Memorial Foundation
c/o Philip C. Stittleburg
P.O. Box 9
La Farge, WI 54639-0009

Established in 1999.
Financial data (yr. ended 12/31/99): Grants paid, $1,401; assets, $285 (M); gifts received, $1,125; expenditures, $1,401; qualifying distributions, $1,401.

57934—WISCONSIN

Officers: Gary A. Wolfe, Pres.; Adam F. Wolfe, V.P.; Sandra L. Wolfe, Secy.-Treas.
EIN: 311623649

57935
Julyle Foundation, Inc.
W6504 Klassy Rd.
New Glarus, WI 53574
Contact: Pongpom Dau Songpanya, Pres.

Established in 1998 in WI.
Donor(s): Pongpom Dau Songpanya, Julyle, Inc.
Financial data (yr. ended 12/31/00): Grants paid, $1,392; assets, $288 (M); gifts received, $7,581; expenditures, $2,127; qualifying distributions, $1,392.
Officers: Pongpom Dau Songpanya, Pres.; Julia Xistris, V.P.
Director: Matthew Storms.
EIN: 391921598

57936
Steven Knezevich Trust
100 E. Wisconsin Ave., Ste. 1020
Milwaukee, WI 53202-4107 (414) 271-6364
Contact: Stanley F. Hack, Tr.

Established around 1971 in WI.
Financial data (yr. ended 12/31/99): Grants paid, $1,350; assets, $43,108 (M); expenditures, $4,859; qualifying distributions, $4,859.
Application information: Application form required.
Trustee: Stanley F. Hack.
EIN: 396150899

57937
Jeffrey and Linda Salick Foundation
c/o Lichtsinn and Haensel, SC
111 E. Wisconsin Ave., Ste. 1800
Milwaukee, WI 53202

Donor(s): Jeffrey J. Salick, Linda Salick.
Financial data (yr. ended 12/31/01): Grants paid, $1,350; assets, $22,269 (M); expenditures, $2,082; qualifying distributions, $1,350.
Limitations: Applications not accepted.
Application information: Contributes only to pre-selected organizations.
Officers and Directors:* Jeffrey J. Salick,* Pres.; Linda Salick,* V.P.; Frank W. Bastian.
EIN: 391712023

57938
Phillip J. Fellner Foundation, Inc.
3818 Cheyenne Ct., Unit H
Racine, WI 53404-1456

Financial data (yr. ended 12/31/00): Grants paid, $1,280; assets, $29,411 (M); expenditures, $1,456; qualifying distributions, $1,280.
Limitations: Applications not accepted. Giving primarily in WI.
Application information: Contributes only to pre-selected organizations.
Officers: Mary Ann Fellner, Pres.; Carol Fox, V.P.; Andrew Fellner, Secy.
EIN: 396049793

57939
Gerhard Krieger Trust
c/o John F. Stoelting
502 Hwy. 67
Kiel, WI 53042-1650
Application address: c/o Guidance Counselor, Kiel High School, Kiel, WI 53042, tel.: (920) 894-2263

Established in 1986 in WI.
Financial data (yr. ended 12/31/00): Grants paid, $1,200; assets, $1,096 (M); expenditures, $1,296; qualifying distributions, $1,200.

Limitations: Giving limited to residents of WI.
Application information: Application form required.
Trustee: John F. Stoelting.
EIN: 396319555

57940
Lisa M. Nienhaus Charitable Trust
c/o Thomas N. Kirschbaum
7306 University Ave.
Middleton, WI 53562
Application address: c/o James Adams or Esther Kaufman, Catholic Central High School, 148 McHenry St., Burlington, WI 53105, tel.: (262) 763-1510

Established in 1997 in WI.
Donor(s): Dianna Nienhaus, Richard Nienhaus.
Financial data (yr. ended 04/30/01): Grants paid, $1,200; assets, $30,340 (M); gifts received, $600; expenditures, $1,285; qualifying distributions, $1,200.
Limitations: Giving limited to residents of WI.
Application information: Application form required.
Trustees: Kathleen Bush, Thomas Kirschbaum, Patricia Koenen, Karen MacKinnon, Dianna Nienhaus, Richard Nienhaus.
EIN: 396678316

57941
Nyholm Family Foundation, Inc.
2305 W. Applewood Ln.
Glendale, WI 53209-2109 (414) 352-4838
Contact: Scott A. Nyholm, Pres.

Established in 1996 in WI.
Donor(s): Scott A. Nyholm.
Financial data (yr. ended 06/30/01): Grants paid, $1,200; assets, $29,620 (M); expenditures, $1,230; qualifying distributions, $1,178.
Limitations: Giving primarily in WI.
Application information: Application form not required.
Officers and Directors:* Scott A. Nyholm,* Pres. and Treas.; Craig R. Nyholm,* V.P.; Joyce M. Nyholm,* Secy.
EIN: 391869651

57942
Osceola Historical Society, Inc.
P.O. Box 342
Osceola, WI 54020 (715) 268-2932
Contact: John Simenstad, Pres.

Financial data (yr. ended 12/31/01): Grants paid, $1,200; assets, $475,643 (M); gifts received, $1,736; expenditures, $24,269; qualifying distributions, $1,200.
Limitations: Giving limited to Osceola, WI.
Officers: John Simenstad, Pres.; Linda Gordon, Secy.; Sylvia K. Grant, Treas.
Directors: Mike Evans, Ron Johnson, Dale Morrill, Dan Reeves.
EIN: 391569065

57943
Jodie L. Scott Foundation, Inc.
714 Faryl Ave., Ste. 13
Delavan, WI 53115

Financial data (yr. ended 12/31/01): Grants paid, $1,200; assets, $38,489 (M); expenditures, $1,200; qualifying distributions, $1,200.
Application information: Unsolicited request for funds not accepted.
Officer and Director:* Wilbur J. Scott,* V.P.
EIN: 391420942

57944
Thoreson Family Foundation, Inc.
9123 N. 85th St.
Milwaukee, WI 53224-1803

Financial data (yr. ended 04/30/02): Grants paid, $1,200; assets, $24,242 (M); expenditures, $1,527; qualifying distributions, $1,200.
Limitations: Applications not accepted. Giving primarily in Thiensville, WI.
Application information: Contributes only to pre-selected organizations.
Officers: Betty Westphal, Pres. and V.P.; Donna Lemke, Secy.-Treas.
EIN: 391393535

57945
The John E. Kuenzl Foundation, Inc.
3031 Oregon St.
Oshkosh, WI 54902

Established in 2000 in WI.
Donor(s): Gambrinus Enterprises, Lee Beverage Co., Inc., John E. Kuenzl.
Financial data (yr. ended 12/31/01): Grants paid, $1,150; assets, $120,795 (M); gifts received, $118,651; expenditures, $2,608; qualifying distributions, $1,747.
Limitations: Applications not accepted.
Application information: Contributes only to pre-selected organizations.
Directors: Bruce D. Berndt, John E. Kuenzl, David Lindemann.
EIN: 391998578
Codes: CS

57946
Henry Predolin Foundation, Inc.
P.O. Box 2719
Madison, WI 53701-2719

Established in 1999 in WI.
Donor(s): Henry Predolin.
Financial data (yr. ended 12/31/01): Grants paid, $1,150; assets, $33,083 (M); expenditures, $3,236; qualifying distributions, $1,150.
Limitations: Applications not accepted.
Application information: Contributes only to pre-selected organizations.
Officers: Henry Predolin, Pres. and Treas.; Robert E. Chritton, V.P. and Secy.
Director: Anthony Medyn.
EIN: 391931309

57947
St. Luke the Healer, Ltd.
303 W. Lakeview Ave.
Madison, WI 53716

Donor(s): S. Luther Simonson.
Financial data (yr. ended 12/31/01): Grants paid, $1,088; assets, $2,766 (M); gifts received, $2,400; expenditures, $1,165; qualifying distributions, $1,088.
Officers: S. Luther Simonson, Pres.; Kathleen Anding, V.P.; Audrey P. Simonson, Secy.; Alfred E. Anding, Treas.
EIN: 391579525

57948
Carpe Diem Scholarship Fund, Inc.
c/o Mel Mickey
558 N. 68th St.
Wauwatosa, WI 53213-3955
Application address: c/o Wauwatosa East High School, 7500 Milwaukee Ave., Wanuatosa, WI 53213, tel.: (414) 773-2000
Contact: Joe Vitrano

Financial data (yr. ended 06/30/01): Grants paid, $1,080; assets, $35,559 (M); gifts received,

$2,030; expenditures, $1,356; qualifying distributions, $1,356.
Limitations: Giving limited to the residents of Wauwatosa, WI.
Application information: Application form required.
Officers: Mel A. Mickey, Pres.; Jill B. Mickey, V.P.; Lisa M. Hollander, Secy.
Directors: Michele M. Barnstable, Annette M. Henry, Lance A. Mickey.
EIN: 391880629

57949
Kevin & Christine Kelly Family Foundation
c/o Kevin & Christine Kelly
6329 Parkview Rd.
Greendale, WI 53129-2153

Established in 2000 in WI.
Donor(s): Kevin J. Kelly, Christine M. Walsh-Kelly.
Financial data (yr. ended 12/31/01): Grants paid, $1,024; assets, $25,724 (M); gifts received, $360; expenditures, $1,384; qualifying distributions, $1,024.
Limitations: Applications not accepted.
Application information: Contributes only to pre-selected organizations.
Trustees: Kevin J. Kelly, Christine M. Walsh-Kelly.
EIN: 396745161

57950
John & Beverly Anderson Charitable Trust
c/o U.S. Bank
P.O. Box 2043
Milwaukee, WI 53201

Financial data (yr. ended 12/31/01): Grants paid, $1,000; assets, $17,592 (M); expenditures, $1,631; qualifying distributions, $1,000.
Limitations: Applications not accepted. Giving limited to Vinton, IA.
Application information: Contributes only to pre-selected organizations.
Trustee: U.S. Bank.
EIN: 421286088

57951
Beta Upsilon Sigma Scholarship Investment Corporation
c/o Lucretia Mattson
Univ. of Wisconsin-Eau Claire
Eau Claire, WI 54702
Application address: c/o Lucretia Mattson, Dept. of Accounting, Univ. of Wisconsin-Eau Claire, Eau Claire, WI 54702-4004

Financial data (yr. ended 04/30/99): Grants paid, $1,000; assets, $34,088 (M); gifts received, $700; expenditures, $1,246; qualifying distributions, $1,340.
Limitations: Giving limited to Eau Claire, WI.
Application information: Application form not required.
Officers: Tom Olson, Pres.; Kristy Nystrom, V.P.; Sephanie Janson, Secy.; Derek Flottom, Treas.
EIN: 396102494

57952
Caliendo Family Foundation
N9618 Winnebago Park
Fond du Lac, WI 54935-6800

Established in 1997 in WI.
Donor(s): Colleen T. Caliendo.
Financial data (yr. ended 12/31/01): Grants paid, $1,000; assets, $204,238 (M); expenditures, $1,054; qualifying distributions, $1,000.
Limitations: Applications not accepted.
Application information: Contributes only to pre-selected organizations.

Directors: Chris Caliendo, Colleen T. Caliendo, Richard H. Wehner.
EIN: 391893007

57953
Jane Royer Carter Scholarship Foundation, Inc.
P.O. Box 268
116 S. Main St.
Mayville, WI 53050

Established in 1998 in WI.
Financial data (yr. ended 12/31/00): Grants paid, $1,000; assets, $20,022 (M); gifts received, $1,620; expenditures, $1,020; qualifying distributions, $1,000.
Limitations: Giving limited to residents of Mayville, WI.
Directors: Barbara J. Hagedorn, Daniel L. Rambo, Patrice B. Vossekuil.
EIN: 431800510

57954
Dells/Delton Area Community Foundation, Inc.
P.O. Box 8
Wisconsin Dells, WI 53965

Financial data (yr. ended 12/31/00): Grants paid, $1,000; assets, $6,670 (M); gifts received, $5,763; expenditures, $2,317.
Limitations: Giving limited to the Lake Delton and Wisconsin Dells area, WI.
Officers: Victor A. Ahlstrom, Pres.; Peter Tollaksen, V.P.; Catherine I. Sperl, Secy.-Treas.
Directors: Rita Ahlstrom, William Rudersdorf.
EIN: 391948575
Codes: CM

57955
Loren E. and Marian S. Hart Foundation
181 St. Mary's Blvd.
Green Bay, WI 54301-2601 (920) 336-8831
Contact: Loren E. Hart, M.D., Tr., or Marian S. Hart, Tr.

Established in 1988 in WI.
Donor(s): Marian S. Hart.
Financial data (yr. ended 12/31/01): Grants paid, $1,000; assets, $24,014 (M); expenditures, $1,644; qualifying distributions, $1,000.
Limitations: Giving primarily in Green Bay, WI.
Application information: Application form not required.
Trustees: Loren E. Hart, M.D., Marian S. Hart.
EIN: 391619579

57956
Edward W. Keyes Scholarship Trust
c/o Mound City Bank
25 E. Pine St.
Platteville, WI 53818 (608) 348-1685

Established in 1990 in WI.
Financial data (yr. ended 12/31/01): Grants paid, $1,000; assets, $13,750 (M); expenditures, $1,394; qualifying distributions, $1,000.
Limitations: Applications not accepted. Giving limited to residents of Cuba City, WI.
Application information: Contributes only to pre-selected organizations.
Trustee: Mound City Bank.
EIN: 396506830

57957
Arthur G. and Harriet Mehring Scholarship Trust
c/o Superintendant of Schools
100 W. Monroe St.
Port Washington, WI 53074-1217
Application address: c/o Scholarship Selection Comm., Port Washington High School, 427 W. Jackson St., Port Washington, WI 53074, tel.: (262) 268-5525

Financial data (yr. ended 12/31/01): Grants paid, $1,000; assets, $34,102 (M); expenditures, $1,030; qualifying distributions, $1,000.
Limitations: Giving limited to residents of Port Washington, WI.
Application information: Applicants must provide transcripts and a letter of recommendation. Application form required.
Officer and Trustees:* Steven R. Schowalter,* Pres.; Jo Anne N. Jacobson, Clemi Uselding.
EIN: 396418268
Codes: GTI

57958
Sandy Oaks Foundation, Inc.
c/o Douglas W. Caves
2250 Rugby Row
Madison, WI 53705

Established in 2001 in WI.
Donor(s): Douglas W. Caves.
Financial data (yr. ended 12/31/01): Grants paid, $1,000; assets, $289,816 (M); gifts received, $283,457; expenditures, $1,500; qualifying distributions, $1,000.
Officers and Directors:* Douglas W. Caves,* Pres.; Sherry Caves,* V.P.; Morris W. Caves.
EIN: 392043437

57959
Paul H. Schnenck Scholarship Trust
c/o Baraboo National Bank
P.O. Box 38
Rock Springs, WI 53961-0038 (608) 522-5266
Contact: Terry Geyman, Tr.

Established in 1989 in WI.
Financial data (yr. ended 12/31/99): Grants paid, $1,000; assets, $24,397 (M); expenditures, $1,273; qualifying distributions, $991.
Limitations: Giving limited to the Reedsburg, WI, area.
Application information: Application form required.
Trustees: Dorothy J. Gant, Terry Geyman, Dale Schultz.
EIN: 391594300

57960
Vincent Charles Sowinski Memorial Trust
5806 Fire Ln.
Rhinelander, WI 54501
Application address: 5901 Fire Ln., Rhinelander, WI 54501, tel.: (715) 272-1655
Contact: Paul Sowinski, Tr.

Financial data (yr. ended 12/31/01): Grants paid, $1,000; assets, $14,200 (M); gifts received, $457; expenditures, $1,007; qualifying distributions, $1,000.
Limitations: Giving limited to residents of Three Lakes, WI.
Trustee: Paul Sowinski.
EIN: 396477646

57961—WISCONSIN

57961
Woog Foundation, Inc.
c/o Willard G. Neary
111 E. Wisconsin Ave., Ste. 1800
Milwaukee, WI 53202-4809

Established in 1993 in WI.
Donor(s): Gunter G. Woog.
Financial data (yr. ended 12/31/01): Grants paid, $1,000; assets, $18,382 (M); gifts received, $1,250; expenditures, $1,000; qualifying distributions, $1,000.
Limitations: Applications not accepted.
Application information: Contributes only to pre-selected organizations.
Officers and Directors:* Gunter G. Woog,* Pres.; Barbara A. Woog,* Secy.; Willard G. Neary.
EIN: 391776118

57962
The James Yasko Scholarship Fund
(Formerly James Yasko Scholarship Trust Fund)
136 S. Whiton St.
Whitewater, WI 53190-1711
Contact: Richard Yasko, Tr.

Financial data (yr. ended 12/31/99): Grants paid, $1,000; assets, $170 (M); gifts received, $450; expenditures, $1,051; qualifying distributions, $60,208.
Limitations: Giving limited to residents of Whitewater, WI.
Trustees: Michael Brennan, Caryl Yasko, Richard Yasko.
EIN: 391634841

57963
August G. Barkow Family Foundation
2230 S. 43rd St.
Milwaukee, WI 53219-1689

Donor(s): Richard C. Barkow, Robert F. Barkow.
Financial data (yr. ended 06/30/01): Grants paid, $950; assets, $71,597 (M); expenditures, $1,660; qualifying distributions, $950.
Limitations: Applications not accepted. Giving primarily in IA.
Application information: Contributes only to pre-selected organizations.
Trustees: Richard Barkow, Robert Barkow.
EIN: 396120996

57964
Marchant Foundation, Inc.
225 E. Fairview Ave.
Green Bay, WI 54301
Contact: Jake L. Marchant, Pres.

Established in 1988 in WI.
Donor(s): Jake L. Marchant.
Financial data (yr. ended 12/31/01): Grants paid, $945; assets, $1,405 (M); expenditures, $1,092; qualifying distributions, $945.
Limitations: Giving limited to WI.
Officers and Directors:* Jake L. Marchant,* Pres. and Treas.; Mary Ann Marchant,* V.P. and Secy.; Brenda Marchant.
EIN: 391620557

57965
Don C. and Barbara B. Smith Foundation, Inc.
3450 W. Tillman St.
Appleton, WI 54914 (920) 731-3388
Contact: Don C. Smith, Pres.

Established in 1997 in WI.
Donor(s): Professional Park Inc., Barbara B. Smith, Don C. Smith.
Financial data (yr. ended 12/31/01): Grants paid, $919; assets, $7,324 (M); expenditures, $959; qualifying distributions, $919.

Officers: Don C. Smith, Pres. and Treas.; Barbara B. Smith, V.P. and Secy.
Director: Richard Stiles.
EIN: 391872046

57966
Merlin and Carol Johnson Charitable Trust
13229 State Rd. 70
Grantsburg, WI 54840

Established in 2001 in WI.
Donor(s): Merlin Johnson, Carol Johnson.
Financial data (yr. ended 12/31/01): Grants paid, $912; assets, $13,402 (M); gifts received, $15,000; expenditures, $1,759; qualifying distributions, $912.
Limitations: Applications not accepted.
Application information: Contributes only to pre-selected organizations.
Directors: Carol Johnson, Merlin Johnson.
EIN: 396751550

57967
St. Croix County Farm Bureau Scholarship Trust
1226 170th St.
Hammond, WI 54015 (715) 796-2712
Contact: Carl Oehlke, Tr.

Established in 1995 in WI.
Donor(s): Conrad Estate.
Financial data (yr. ended 12/31/99): Grants paid, $900; assets, $15,115 (M); expenditures, $1,108; qualifying distributions, $893.
Limitations: Giving limited to residents of St. Croix County, WI.
Trustees: Tim Bazille, David Druschke, Carl Oehlke.
EIN: 396606430

57968
John W. Varrell Trust
c/o Patricia Updike
1208 Elm St.
Boscobel, WI 53805

Financial data (yr. ended 12/31/00): Grants paid, $900; assets, $44,245 (M); expenditures, $1,418; qualifying distributions, $1,418.
Limitations: Giving primarily in Boscobel, WI.
Trustees: Jerry Staskal, Patricia Updike, Nancy Wagner.
EIN: 396052813

57969
Oliver B. Cunningham Memorial Fund
c/o Bank One Trust Co., N.A.
P.O. Box 1308
Milwaukee, WI 53201
Application address: c/o Gerald W. Leibforth, Evanston Twp. High School, 1600 Dodge Ave., Evanston, IL 60204

Financial data (yr. ended 12/31/99): Grants paid, $897; assets, $43,001 (M); expenditures, $2,854; qualifying distributions, $2,036.
Limitations: Giving limited to residents of Evanston, IL.
Application information: Recipients are chosen by Evanston Township High School Award Comm.
Trustee: Bank One Trust Co., N.A.
EIN: 526159228

57970
Hedwig Neitzel Trust Fund
c/o Bank One Trust Co., N.A.
P.O. Box 1308
Milwaukee, WI 53201 (414) 765-2769

Financial data (yr. ended 12/31/01): Grants paid, $874; assets, $95,099 (M); expenditures, $2,874; qualifying distributions, $874.
Limitations: Applications not accepted.

Application information: Contributes only to pre-selected organizations.
Trustee: Bank One Trust Co., N.A.
EIN: 396089958

57971
Robert A. Hilger & Cynthia L. Hilger Foundation, Inc.
P.O. Box 400
Antigo, WI 54409-0400

Donor(s): Robert A. Hilger, Cynthia L. Hilger.
Financial data (yr. ended 09/30/01): Grants paid, $850; assets, $39,570 (M); expenditures, $915; qualifying distributions, $850.
Limitations: Applications not accepted. Giving primarily in Antigo, WI.
Application information: Contributes only to pre-selected organizations.
Officers: Robert A. Hilger, Pres.; Gerald Volm, V.P.; Cynthia L. Hilger, Secy.-Treas.
EIN: 391421960

57972
Emily Brooks Foundation
15440 W. Woodview Dr.
New Berlin, WI 53151-1906

Established in 2000 in WI.
Donor(s): Jack Reichert, Corrine Reichert, The Reichert Foundation.
Financial data (yr. ended 12/31/01): Grants paid, $825; assets, $41,245 (M); gifts received, $5,133; expenditures, $1,113; qualifying distributions, $825.
Limitations: Applications not accepted.
Application information: Contributes only to pre-selected organizations.
Directors: Christy Brooks, Drew Brooks, Kathy Brooks, Susan Milanak.
EIN: 391992149

57973
Adolph Stoelting Scholarship Fund
c/o Jane Voigt
P.O. Box 127
Kiel, WI 53042-0127
Application address: c/o Administrative Office, Kiel High School, Kiel, WI 53042

Established around 1980 in WI.
Financial data (yr. ended 12/31/01): Grants paid, $800; assets, $21,579 (M); expenditures, $1,108; qualifying distributions, $800.
Limitations: Giving limited to Kiel, WI.
Application information: Application form required.
Trustees: John Stoelting, Robert Stoelting, Jane E. Voigt.
EIN: 391332668

57974
Lt. Ray Wehrlich & Mark Frewert Memorial Scholarship of the Sheboygan County Deputy Sheriff's Office
1748 Parkwood Blvd.
Sheboygan, WI 53081 (920) 458-6957
Contact: Wayne J. Wenske, Tr.

Established in 1968 in WI.
Financial data (yr. ended 12/31/01): Grants paid, $800; assets, $14,863 (M); gifts received, $250; expenditures, $958; qualifying distributions, $0.
Limitations: Giving limited to WI.
Application information: Recipients selected by respective guidance counselors from each high school.
Trustees: Vernon Boeckmann, Karl W. Perleberg, Wesley L. Prange, Wayne J. Wenske, John Grothe.
EIN: 237396259

57975
The Townsend Foundation, Inc.
N63 W15185 Pocahontas Dr.
Menomonee Falls, WI 53051

Established in 2000 in WI.
Financial data (yr. ended 12/31/01): Grants paid, $689; assets, $12,776 (M); gifts received, $6,520; expenditures, $2,738; qualifying distributions, $689.
Limitations: Applications not accepted. Giving primarily in Milwaukee, WI.
Application information: Contributes only to pre-selected organizations.
Officers and Directors:* Kenneth Semmann,* Pres.; Barbara Semmann,* Secy.; George Blommel.
EIN: 392000037

57976
Vogt Family Foundation, Inc.
2690 Hope Rd.
Cottage Grove, WI 53527-9574

Established in 1987 in WI.
Donor(s): George H. Vogt.
Financial data (yr. ended 12/31/01): Grants paid, $670; assets, $2 (M); expenditures, $948; qualifying distributions, $670.
Limitations: Applications not accepted.
Application information: Contributes only to pre-selected organizations.
Officers: George H. Vogt, Pres.; Carol L. Vogt, V.P.; Nancy R. Vogt, Secy.-Treas.
EIN: 391594747

57977
Busse Scholarship Foundation Trust
c/o Bank One Trust Co., N.A.
P.O. Box 1308
Milwaukee, WI 53201
Application address: c/o Scholarship Counselor, Chesterton High School, 2125 S. 11th St., Chesterton, IN 46304

Established in 1988 in IN.
Donor(s): Roy Melville Smith.‡
Financial data (yr. ended 12/31/00): Grants paid, $650; assets, $24,212 (M); expenditures, $3,303; qualifying distributions, $1,433.
Limitations: Giving limited to residents of Porter, IN.
Application information: Application form required.
Trustee: Bank One Trust Co., N.A.
EIN: 356039623

57978
Guy Stanton Ford Educational Foundation
P.O. Box 1644
Madison, WI 53701-1644 (608) 257-4812
Contact: Jack D. Walker, Treas.

Financial data (yr. ended 12/31/01): Grants paid, $641; assets, $68,339 (M); expenditures, $725; qualifying distributions, $725.
Limitations: Giving limited to WI.
Application information: Application form required.
Officers and Directors:* Steve Marshall,* Pres.; Robert Lieb,* V.P.; Thomas D. Eilers,* Secy.; Jack D. Walker,* Treas.; Robert Laeser, James Lindgren, James Lowe.
EIN: 396101946
Codes: GTI

57979
Birdie Hartsough Frey Memorial Fund
c/o Bank One Trust Co. N.A.
P.O. Box 1308
Milwaukee, WI 53201
Application address: c/o Bank One, Texas, N.A., P.O. Box 2050, Fort Worth, TX 76113, Tel.: (817) 884-4153
Contact: Lesley Atkinson, V.P. and Trust Off., Bank One Tr. Co., N.A.

Financial data (yr. ended 09/30/01): Grants paid, $600; assets, $378,189 (M); expenditures, $5,127; qualifying distributions, $600.
Limitations: Giving limited to Stephenville, TX.
Trustee: Bank One Trust Co., N.A.
EIN: 756038684

57980
Tomahawk Area Foundation for Youth
N11323 Stahmer Ln.
Tomahawk, WI 54487

Established in 2000.
Donor(s): Caroline Mark.
Financial data (yr. ended 06/30/01): Grants paid, $600; assets, $983,025 (M); gifts received, $1,008,111; expenditures, $1,749; qualifying distributions, $7,476.
Limitations: Giving limited to Tomahawk, WI.
Officers: William Mark, Pres.; Linda Mark, V.P. and Secy.; John Kopp, Treas.
Directors: Jeff Kahle, Mark Schouweiler, Terry Timm.
EIN: 392012451

57981
Walsh Family Foundation
P.O. Box 297
Elkhart Lake, WI 53020-0297
Contact: Patrick W. Walsh, Pres.

Established in 1987 in TN.
Financial data (yr. ended 06/30/02): Grants paid, $600; assets, $14,395 (M); expenditures, $620; qualifying distributions, $600.
Limitations: Giving primarily in WI.
Officers and Directors:* Patrick W. Walsh,* Pres. and Treas.; Jonathan Walsh,* V.P. and Secy.
EIN: 391586449

57982
Philip B. Mills Foundation, Inc.
W7485 CTH Z
Onalaska, WI 54650 (608) 781-6508
Contact: Daniel E. Mills, Pres.

Financial data (yr. ended 12/31/01): Grants paid, $575; assets, $70,421 (M); expenditures, $766; qualifying distributions, $575.
Limitations: Giving limited to Jackson County, WI.
Officers and Directors:* Daniel E. Mills,* Pres. and Treas.; Samuel P. Mills,* V.P.; Mary K. Falkner,* Secy.
EIN: 391369766

57983
Mary Eileen Ahern Foundation
c/o Bank One Trust Co., N.A.
P.O. Box 1308
Milwaukee, WI 53201-1308

Financial data (yr. ended 12/31/00): Grants paid, $551; assets, $12,496 (M); expenditures, $2,213; qualifying distributions, $1,576.
Limitations: Giving primarily in IN.
Application information: Unsolicited requests for funds not accepted.
Trustee: Bank One Trust Co., N.A.
EIN: 366015325

57984
August Foundation, Inc.
P.O. Box 5069
Madison, WI 53705

Established in 2000 in WI.
Donor(s): David Worzala, Julie Worzala.
Financial data (yr. ended 12/31/01): Grants paid, $500; assets, $51,753 (M); gifts received, $28,616; expenditures, $3,322; qualifying distributions, $500.
Limitations: Applications not accepted.
Application information: Contributes only to pre-selected organizations.
Officers: Julie Worzala, Pres. and Treas.; David Worzala, V.P. and Secy.; Michael Gruber, V.P.; Melissa Feldman, V.P.
EIN: 392010073

57985
Harold A. and Leone D. Brockman Scholarship Trust
1190 W. Hwy. 151
Platteville, WI 53818

Established in 2001.
Donor(s): Richard Brockman, Suzanne Neuser.
Financial data (yr. ended 12/31/01): Grants paid, $500; assets, $17,552 (M); gifts received, $17,870; expenditures, $840; qualifying distributions, $500.
Limitations: Applications not accepted.
Application information: Contributes only to pre-selected organizations.
Trustees: Richard Brockman, Suzanne Neuser.
EIN: 396747732

57986
Clasen Family Foundation
800 N. Marshall St.
Milwaukee, WI 53202-3911

Established in 1995 in WI.
Donor(s): Thomas F. Clasen.
Financial data (yr. ended 12/31/01): Grants paid, $500; assets, $57,706 (M); expenditures, $924; qualifying distributions, $500.
Limitations: Applications not accepted.
Application information: Contributes only to pre-selected organizations.
Trustees: Mary P. Clasen, Thomas F. Clasen.
EIN: 391807696

57987
Dugal Charitable Foundation, Inc.
c/o Hardev S. Dugal
N8315 N. Shore Rd.
Menasha, WI 54952

Established in 2000 in WI.
Donor(s): Hardev S. Dugal, Manmohini Dugal.
Financial data (yr. ended 12/31/01): Grants paid, $500; assets, $168,250 (M); gifts received, $68,000; expenditures, $7,882; qualifying distributions, $500.
Officers: Hardev S. Dugal, Pres.; Manmohini Dugal, Secy.
EIN: 392011980

57988
Larry G. Huss Scholarship Memorial Fund
1620 N. Clark St.
Appleton, WI 54911-3655
Application address: 1800 E. Wisconsin Ave., Appleton, WI 54911
Contact: Jim Seidl

Financial data (yr. ended 12/31/01): Grants paid, $500; assets, $4,820 (M); gifts received, $250; expenditures, $500; qualifying distributions, $500.
Limitations: Giving primarily in WI.

57988—WISCONSIN

Officers and Directors:* Sharon Huss,* Pres.; Ellen Hanlon, V.P.; Joan Hermsen,* Secy.; Diane Perillo,* Treas.; JoAnn Bowers, Tim Schuh, Norman Van Beek.
EIN: 391851191

57989
Initium Novum, Inc.
P.O. Box 8
Rosholt, WI 54473-0008

Donor(s): J.M. Real Estate.
Financial data (yr. ended 05/31/02): Grants paid, $500; assets, $536 (M); expenditures, $500; qualifying distributions, $500.
Limitations: Applications not accepted. Giving limited to WI.
Application information: Contributes only to pre-selected organizations.
Officers and Directors:* Jerome Bushman,* Pres. and Treas.; Barbara Bushman,* V.P.; Derrick Bushman,* Secy.; Mitchell Bushman, Tia Bushman.
EIN: 391497295

57990
Silvia and Otto Jung Family Foundation, Inc.
120 Superior Ave.
Sheboygan, WI 53081

Financial data (yr. ended 12/31/01): Grants paid, $500; assets, $28 (M); gifts received, $1,000; expenditures, $1,110; qualifying distributions, $500.
Limitations: Giving primarily in Sheboygan, WI.
Officers: Henry Jung, Pres.; Michael Jung, V.P.; Virginia Bench, Secy.; Elizabeth Talley, Treas.
EIN: 391950984

57991
K Foundation
(Formerly Kiekhaefer family Foundation)
7319 Dickinson Rd.
Greenleaf, WI 54126

Donor(s): James H. Kiekhaefer, Laurie A. Kiekhaefer.
Financial data (yr. ended 12/31/01): Grants paid, $500; assets, $194,426 (M); gifts received, $250; expenditures, $1,821; qualifying distributions, $500.
Limitations: Applications not accepted.
Application information: Contributes only to pre-selected organizations.
Trustees: James H. Kiekhaefer, Laurie A. Kiekhaefer.
EIN: 391747277

57992
Krainz Foundation, Inc.
4940 Steeple Dr.
Greendale, WI 53129-2011

Established in 1999 in WI.
Donor(s): Katherine E. Krainz, Robert E. Krainz.
Financial data (yr. ended 12/31/01): Grants paid, $500; assets, $61,461 (M); expenditures, $4,201; qualifying distributions, $500.
Limitations: Applications not accepted. Giving primarily in FL.
Application information: Contributes only to pre-selected organizations.
Officers and Directors: Robert E. Krainz,* Pres.; Katherine E. Krainz,* V.P.; Gertrude M. Martin,* Secy.; Dale G. Martin,* Treas.
EIN: 391979181

57993
Donald K. Martello Memorial Thespian Scholarship Fund, Inc.
5293 N. Norwood Ct. Rd.
Winter, WI 54896
Contact: Ethelwyn Martello, Tr.

Established in 1994 in OH.
Donor(s): Ethelwyn Martello.
Financial data (yr. ended 12/31/00): Grants paid, $500; assets, $7,356 (M); expenditures, $685; qualifying distributions, $500.
Limitations: Giving limited to residents of Park Ridge, IL.
Trustee: Ethelwyn Martello.
EIN: 311394108

57994
Punches Charitable Foundation, Inc.
20825 Swenson Dr., Ste. 150
Waukesha, WI 53186

Established in 2001 in WI.
Donor(s): Dennis G. Punches.
Financial data (yr. ended 12/31/01): Grants paid, $500; assets, $7,965 (M); gifts received, $10,000; expenditures, $2,070; qualifying distributions, $500.
Officers: Dennis G. Punches, Pres.; Beverly Wortman, Secy.
Director: Deborah Rogers.
EIN: 392014960

57995
Rowe Family Foundation, Inc.
c/o James C. Rowe
3510 N. Lake Dr.
Milwaukee, WI 53211

Established in 1989 in WI.
Donor(s): James C. Rowe, Cathy B. Rowe.
Financial data (yr. ended 12/31/01): Grants paid, $500; assets, $27,581 (M); expenditures, $510; qualifying distributions, $500.
Limitations: Applications not accepted. Giving limited to Milwaukee, WI.
Application information: Contributes only to pre-selected organizations.
Officers and Directors:* James C. Rowe,* Chair. and Secy.-Treas.; Cathy B. Rowe,* Pres.; Betty J. White.
EIN: 391645500

57996
Colin P. Smyth Memorial Scholarship Trust
c/o The Baraboo National Bank
P.O. Box 50
Baraboo, WI 53913
Application address: c/o Principal, Baraboo Senior High School, 1201 Draper St., Baraboo, WI 53913, tel.: (608) 355-3949

Established in 1989 in WI.
Financial data (yr. ended 12/31/99): Grants paid, $500; assets, $21,318 (M); gifts received, $1,648; expenditures, $767; qualifying distributions, $481; giving activities include $767 for programs.
Limitations: Giving limited to Baraboo, WI.
Publications: Application guidelines.
Application information: Recipients selected by Baraboo Senior High School faculty. Application form not required.
Selection Committee: Elgin Bulin, Elsie Gilmore, Rick Osgood, Robert Reid, Glen Richgels, Leonard Rott.
Trustee: The Baraboo National Bank.
EIN: 396493984

57997
Tall Grass Foundation, Inc.
7734 Bittersweet Ct.
Middleton, WI 53562-4054

Established in 2001 in WI.
Financial data (yr. ended 12/31/01): Grants paid, $500; assets, $2,500 (M); gifts received, $3,000; expenditures, $500; qualifying distributions, $500.
Limitations: Applications not accepted. Giving primarily in Washington, DC.
Application information: Contributes only to pre-selected organizations.
Officers: David Scott Fuller, Pres. and Treas.; Lynn Humbel Fuller, V.P. and Secy.
EIN: 392029149

57998
Hoffman York Foundation, Ltd.
c/o Vivian L. Moller
1000 N. Water St., Ste. 1600
Milwaukee, WI 53202-3197 (414) 289-9700
FAX: (414) 289-0417

Financial data (yr. ended 09/30/01): Grants paid, $450; assets, $63,826 (M); expenditures, $486; qualifying distributions, $450.
Limitations: Giving primarily in Milwaukee, WI.
Directors: David Brown, Nancy Deptolla, Vivian L. Moller.
EIN: 391454519

57999
John Holliday Trust No. 1
c/o Bank One Trust Co., N.A.
P.O. Box 1308
Milwaukee, WI 53201
Application address: c/o Dir. of Guidance, Emmerich Manual High School, 2405 Madison Ave., Indianapolis, IN 46225

Financial data (yr. ended 12/31/01): Grants paid, $402; assets, $31,588 (M); expenditures, $2,461; qualifying distributions, $1,491.
Limitations: Giving limited to Indianapolis, IN.
Application information: Application form required.
Trustee: Bank One Trust Co., N.A.
EIN: 356009910

58000
The Elizabeth Meyer Brewer Foundation
(Formerly Liz and Charles Kahn Foundation)
7037 N. Fairchild Cir.
Fox Point, WI 53217

Donor(s): Charles F. Kahn, Jr., Elizabeth Meyer Brewer.
Financial data (yr. ended 12/31/01): Grants paid, $400; assets, $11,045 (M); expenditures, $1,133; qualifying distributions, $400.
Limitations: Applications not accepted. Giving primarily in Milwaukee, WI.
Application information: Contributes only to pre-selected organizations.
Trustees: Elizabeth Meyer Brewer, Barbara H. Patterson.
EIN: 391587141

58001
Dudley Foundation, Inc.
500 3rd St., Ste. 208-16
Wausau, WI 54403-4857 (715) 849-5729
Contact: Ann Dudley Shannon, Pres.

Established in 2000 in WI.
Donor(s): Richard D. Dudley.
Financial data (yr. ended 12/31/01): Grants paid, $400; assets, $5,877,786 (M); expenditures, $37,590; qualifying distributions, $26,073.
Limitations: Giving primarily in Wausau, WI.

Application information: Application form not required.
Officers: Richard D. Dudley, Chair.; Ann Dudley Shannon, Pres.; John D. Dudley, V.P.; Paul C. Schlindwein II, Secy.; Gary W. Freels, Treas.
Directors: Mary C. Dudley, Robert J. Dudley II, Jeffrey W. Kowieski.
EIN: 392003427

58002
Rush C. Godfrey Medical Scholarship Trust
c/o F & M Trust Co.
321 S. Nicolet Rd.
Appleton, WI 54914
Contact: Peter Rogers, Pres.

Donor(s): Alma H. Godfrey.‡
Financial data (yr. ended 12/31/99): Grants paid, $400; assets, $23,244 (M); expenditures, $1,470; qualifying distributions, $671.
Limitations: Giving limited to residents of Lancaster, WI.
Officer: Peter Rogers, Pres.
EIN: 396061884

58003
Wisconsin SER - Jobs for Progress
1020-30 W. Mitchell St., 2nd Fl.
Milwaukee, WI 53204

Financial data (yr. ended 06/30/01): Grants paid, $363; assets, $270,655 (M); expenditures, $461,525; qualifying distributions, $461,525.
Officers: John Bernhardt, Chair.; Robert Welch, Vice-Chair.; Carl Dubin, Secy.; Ronald SanFelippo, Treas.
Directors: Jeff Byers, Vincent D. Milewski.
EIN: 391682983

58004
Margaret Bonn Scholarship Trust
c/o F & M Bank
321 S. Nicolet Rd.
Appleton, WI 54914 (920) 996-2131
Application address: P.O. Box 229, 4th St. Plz., Kaukauna, WI 54130-0229
Contact: Peter Rogers, Pres., F & M Bank

Financial data (yr. ended 12/31/00): Grants paid, $350; assets, $11,730 (M); expenditures, $1,698; qualifying distributions, $1,604.
Limitations: Giving limited to Bloomington, WI.
Application information: Application form required.
Trustee: F & M Bank.
EIN: 391446095

58005
The Jaeger-Mellerop Family Charitable Trust
c/o Michael John Jaeger
1052 E. Gorham St.
Madison, WI 53703

Established in 1996 in WI.
Donor(s): Michael John Jaeger.
Financial data (yr. ended 08/31/01): Grants paid, $350; assets, $7,767 (M); gifts received, $1,920; expenditures, $358; qualifying distributions, $350.
Trustees: Michael John Jaeger, Valerie C. Mellerop.
EIN: 391863498

58006
Peter and Minnie Hietpas Scholarship Trust
c/o Leroy J. Hietpas
1109 Hoover Ave.
Little Chute, WI 54140-2135
Application address: 1402 S. Freedom Rd., Little Chute, WI, tel.: (920) 788-7600
Contact: Kevin Pratt

Financial data (yr. ended 12/31/00): Grants paid, $325; assets, $11,750 (M); expenditures, $432; qualifying distributions, $325; giving activities include $11,560 for loans.
Limitations: Giving primarily in Little Chute, WI.
Trustees: Mike Hermsen, Leroy Hietpas.
EIN: 391831060

58007
Everson Memorial Scholarship, Inc.
808 1st Center Ave.
Brodhead, WI 53520-1382
Application addresses: c/o Steve Benton, County Hwy. GG, Brodhead, WI 53520, or c/o Steve McNeil, 106 W. Church St., Orfordville, WI 53576

Financial data (yr. ended 05/31/02): Grants paid, $300; assets, $10,300 (M); gifts received, $38,578; expenditures, $527; qualifying distributions, $300.
Limitations: Giving limited to residents of Brodhead and Orfordville, WI.
Application information: Application form required.
Officers: Bud Everson, Pres.; Betty Ann Everson, Secy.-Treas.
EIN: 391530801

58008
Reetz Foundation
c/o Wells Fargo Bank Wisconsin, N.A.
P.O. Box 171
Sheboygan, WI 53082-0171

Established in 1989 in WI.
Financial data (yr. ended 12/31/01): Grants paid, $258; assets, $12,771 (M); expenditures, $537; qualifying distributions, $258.
Limitations: Applications not accepted. Giving primarily in WI.
Application information: Contributes only to pre-selected organizations.
Trustee: Wells Fargo Bank Wisconsin, N.A.
EIN: 391643469

58009
Kube Family Foundation, Inc.
W27829 County Rd. A
Arcadia, WI 54612

Financial data (yr. ended 12/31/01): Grants paid, $250; assets, $2,442 (M); expenditures, $250; qualifying distributions, $250.
Officer and Directors:* Allen J. Kube,* Pres.; Michael W. Kube,* V.P.; Carol R. Kube,* Secy.-Treas.
EIN: 391911442

58010
Richard A. Pilak Memorial Trust
3807 W. Madison Blvd.
Franklin, WI 53132 (414) 288-7475
Contact: Thomas S. Pilak, Tr.

Financial data (yr. ended 12/31/00): Grants paid, $250; assets, $4,670 (M); expenditures, $250; qualifying distributions, $250.
Limitations: Giving primarily in WI.
Trustee: Thomas S. Pilak.
EIN: 391859490

58011
Perkins Family Foundation, Inc.
c/o Charles E. Perkins
6830 Brook Rd.
Franksville, WI 53126

Established in 2001.
Donor(s): Charles E. Perkins.
Financial data (yr. ended 12/31/01): Grants paid, $200; assets, $10,034 (M); gifts received, $10,000; expenditures, $200; qualifying distributions, $200.
Limitations: Applications not accepted.
Application information: Contributes only to pre-selected organizations.
Officers: Charles E. Perkins, Pres.; Barbara M. Perkins, David M. Perkins, Secy.
EIN: 392009882

58012
Frederick & Cornelia Kinsman Endowment Fund
c/o Bank One Trust Co.
P.O. Box 1308
Milwaukee, WI 53201

Established in 1991 in OH.
Financial data (yr. ended 12/31/99): Grants paid, $172; assets, $5,515 (M); expenditures, $1,095; qualifying distributions, $990.
Limitations: Applications not accepted. Giving limited to Warren, OH.
Application information: Contributes only to pre-selected organizations.
Trustee: Bank One Trust Co., N.A.
EIN: 346527597

58013
Bossard Foundation, Inc.
11561 N. Buntrock Ave.
Mequon, WI 53092-1846

Donor(s): James Bossard.
Financial data (yr. ended 12/31/01): Grants paid, $165; assets, $1,860 (M); expenditures, $417; qualifying distributions, $165.
Limitations: Applications not accepted.
Application information: Contributes only to pre-selected organizations.
Officers and Directors:* James W. Bossard,* Pres.; Paul Ziemer,* V.P.; Brian Muehl,* Secy.
EIN: 391514700

58014
James E. & Linda L. Falck Foundation, Inc.
P.O. Box 280
Lakewood, WI 54138

Established in 2000 in WI.
Financial data (yr. ended 12/31/01): Grants paid, $100; assets, $28,175 (M); gifts received, $12,903; expenditures, $100; qualifying distributions, $100.
Limitations: Applications not accepted.
Application information: Contributes only to pre-selected organizations.
Officers: James E. Falck, Pres.; Linda L. Falck, Secy.-Treas.
EIN: 392013850

58015
Global Vision and Missions, Inc.
c/o Victor O. Langen
3035 W. Wisconsin, Ste. 603
Milwaukee, WI 53208

Financial data (yr. ended 06/30/01): Grants paid, $100; assets, $22,713 (M); gifts received, $513; expenditures, $926; qualifying distributions, $140.
Limitations: Applications not accepted.
Application information: Contributes only to pre-selected organizations.
Officer and Directors:* Rev. Donald R. Clarke,* Treas.; N.J. Staunt Larson, Victor O. Langen, D. DeLeon Zier.
EIN: 391737004

58016
Magnificat Foundation, Inc.
c/o Diane Marsland
9 Bishops Hill Cir.
Madison, WI 53717

Established in 2000 in WI.

58016—WISCONSIN

Donor(s): Diane M. Marsland, Robert A. Marsland, Jr.
Financial data (yr. ended 12/31/01): Grants paid, $100; assets, $8,897 (M); expenditures, $844; qualifying distributions, $100.
Trustees: Diane M. Marsland, Robert A. Marsland, Jr., Robert E. Peplinski.
EIN: 392012589

58017
Milwaukee Cardiac Research Fund
2000 E. Layton Ave., Ste. 170
St. Francis, WI 53235-6255

Established in 1995.
Financial data (yr. ended 12/31/01): Grants paid, $57; assets, $1,045 (M); expenditures, $127; qualifying distributions, $57.
Limitations: Giving primarily in CO.
Directors: Michael D. Becker, W. Dudley Johnson, Saeo F. Saedi.
EIN: 391679347

58018
The Stark Foundation
c/o Nelson & Schmeling
P.O. Box 22130
Green Bay, WI 54305-2130

Established in 1999 in WI.
Financial data (yr. ended 12/31/01): Grants paid, $50; assets, $12,317 (M); gifts received, $6,870; expenditures, $50; qualifying distributions, $50.
Limitations: Giving primarily in New York, NY.
Trustees: Mary Ann Beemster Burke, Anne Stark Gallagher, Michael D. Willis.
EIN: 396724616

58019
Gerald O. Thorpe and Evelyn M. Thorpe Foundation
c/o Evelyn Thorpe
925 High St.
Chippewa Falls, WI 54729

Established in 1990.
Financial data (yr. ended 12/31/01): Grants paid, $10; assets, $110 (M); gifts received, $10; expenditures, $10; qualifying distributions, $10.
Limitations: Applications not accepted.
Application information: Contributes only to pre-selected organizations.
Trustees: Eugene Merrell, Evelyn M. Thorpe.
EIN: 391689403

58020
Billjo Foundation, Inc.
c/o William C. Heller, Jr.
1840 N. Farwell Ave., Ste. 407
Milwaukee, WI 53202-1716

Financial data (yr. ended 06/30/01): Grants paid, $1; assets, $6 (M); gifts received, $85; expenditures, $81; qualifying distributions, $81.
Limitations: Applications not accepted. Giving primarily in WI.
Application information: Contributes only to pre-selected organizations.
Officers: William C. Heller, Jr., Pres. and Treas.; Joan P. Heller, V.P.; William J. Heller, Secy.
EIN: 237161532

58021
John & Polly Alberts Family Foundation
P.O. Box 23819
Green Bay, WI 54305-3819

Established in 1998 in WI.
Donor(s): John G. Alberts, Polly Alberts.
Financial data (yr. ended 12/31/01): Grants paid, $0; assets, $23,572 (M); expenditures, $90; qualifying distributions, $0.
Limitations: Applications not accepted. Giving primarily in WI.
Application information: Contributes only to pre-selected organizations.
Officers: John G. Alberts, Pres.; Andrew Alberts, V.P.; Melissa Alberts, V.P.; Nathan Alberts, V.P.; Polly Alberts, Secy.-Treas.
EIN: 391948501

58022
Ansari Family Foundation, Inc.
c/o Quarles and Brady
411 E. Wisconsin Ave., Ste. 2040
Milwaukee, WI 53202-4497
Application address: 10537 N. Burning Bush Ln., Mequon, WI 53092
Contact: Mohsin Ansari, Pres.

Established in 2001 in WI.
Donor(s): Mohsin Ansari, Faizah Syed.
Financial data (yr. ended 12/31/01): Grants paid, $0; assets, $500,019 (M); gifts received, $500,000; expenditures, $8; qualifying distributions, $0.
Application information: Application form not required.
Officers: Mohsin Ansari, Pres.; Faizah Syed, V.P.
Director: Husam Ansari.
EIN: 800015664

58023
The Arden Foundation, Inc.
c/o Cook & Franke, S.C.
660 E. Mason St.
Milwaukee, WI 53202 (414) 271-5900
Contact: Margaret T. Lund

Established in 2000 in WI.
Donor(s): Marie H. Kohler.
Financial data (yr. ended 12/31/00): Grants paid, $0; assets, $1,478,523 (M); gifts received, $1,472,914; expenditures, $0; qualifying distributions, $0.
Application information: Application form not required.
Officers and Directors:* Marie H. Kohler,* Pres. and Treas.; Brian R. Mani,* V.P. and Secy.; Anne E. Cabot, Marie C. Cabot.
EIN: 392012512

58024
The Barney Family Foundation
c/o North Central Trust Co.
311 Main St.
La Crosse, WI 54601

Established in 2001 in WI.
Donor(s): William Barney, Ann Barney.
Financial data (yr. ended 12/31/01): Grants paid, $0; assets, $99,478 (M); gifts received, $4,467; expenditures, $582; qualifying distributions, $0.
Limitations: Giving limited to La Crosse, WI.
Trustees: Ann C. Barney, Charles R. Barney, Thomas T. Barney, William A. Barney, Lorinda B. Donaldson, Joan B. Jaeger, North Central Trust Co.
EIN: 391739101

58025
The William Bassett Foundation
N9437 County Rd. V
Holmen, WI 54636 (608) 857-3285
Contact: William Bassett, Dir.

Established in 2000 in WI.
Donor(s): William Bassett.
Financial data (yr. ended 12/31/01): Grants paid, $0; assets, $109,322 (M); expenditures, $0; qualifying distributions, $0.
Director: William Bassett.
EIN: 391989695

58026
The Bear Trap Trust
678 Bear Trap Ln.
Amery, WI 54001

Established in 1996 in WI.
Financial data (yr. ended 12/31/01): Grants paid, $0; assets, $14,417 (M); expenditures, $260; qualifying distributions, $0.
Limitations: Applications not accepted. Giving primarily in WI.
Application information: Contributes only to pre-selected organizations.
Trustee: Karl Steven Scriba.
EIN: 396642275

58027
Bierman Family Foundation, Inc.
1400 W. Taylor St.
P.O. Box 375
Merrill, WI 54452-8780

Established in 2000 in WI.
Donor(s): Carl Bierman, Jane C. Bierman.
Financial data (yr. ended 12/31/00): Grants paid, $0; assets, $46,398 (M); gifts received, $57,936; expenditures, $309; qualifying distributions, $0.
Officers: Jane C. Bierman, Pres.; Frederick Bliese, Secy.
EIN: 391673672

58028
Billings Foundation, Inc.
16985 W. Bluemound Rd., Ste. 207
Brookfield, WI 53005

Established in 1992 in WI.
Donor(s): Deborah Jane Billings.
Financial data (yr. ended 12/31/01): Grants paid, $0; assets, $1,670 (M); expenditures, $335; qualifying distributions, $0.
Limitations: Applications not accepted.
Application information: Contributes only to pre-selected organizations.
Directors: Deborah Jane Billings, Dennis J. Klein, Joseph B. Tyson, Jr.
EIN: 391733629

58029
Brand Family Foundation
2 E. Mifflin St., Ste. 900
Madison, WI 53703

Established in 2000 in WI.
Donor(s): Nathan F. Brand, Dora S. Brand.
Financial data (yr. ended 11/30/01): Grants paid, $0; assets, $1,002,490 (M); gifts received, $1,009,279; expenditures, $45; qualifying distributions, $45.
Limitations: Applications not accepted.
Application information: Contributes only to pre-selected organizations.
Trustees: Dora S. Brand, Nathan F. Brand, Nathan S. Brand, Dorothea B. Kennedy.
EIN: 392043572

58030
Charles & Margaret Buyck Charitable
c/o Wells Fargo Bank, N.A.
P.O. Box 171
Sheboygan, WI 53082-0171

Established in 1999.
Financial data (yr. ended 12/31/01): Grants paid, $0; assets, $557 (M); expenditures, $39; qualifying distributions, $0.
Trustee: Wells Fargo Bank, N.A.
EIN: 364105121

58031
Byers Foundation, Ltd.
c/o Robert Byers
3378 St. Augustine Rd.
Saukville, WI 53080

Financial data (yr. ended 12/31/00): Grants paid, $0; assets, $21,878 (M); expenditures, $70; qualifying distributions, $0.
Officers: Robert J. Byers, Pres.; Mary E. Byers, V.P.; Michael Byers, Secy.-Treas.
EIN: 391743977

58032
Michael Carlisle Charitable Trust
P.O. Box 509
Eau Claire, WI 54702-0509

Established in 2000 in WI.
Donor(s): Robert A. Kerbell.
Financial data (yr. ended 12/31/00): Grants paid, $0; assets, $1,002 (M); gifts received, $1,000; expenditures, $0; qualifying distributions, $0.
Trustee: Robert A. Kerbell.
EIN: 396741238

58033
Edward & Celia Cash Foundation
c/o Marshall & Ilsley Bank
P.O. Box 2980
Milwaukee, WI 53201
Application address: 710 N. Plankinton Ave., Milwaukee, WI 53203-2445, tel.: (414) 272-3661
Contact: Ira Bordow, Tr.

Established in 2000 in WI.
Donor(s): Delia A. Cash.‡
Financial data (yr. ended 08/31/01): Grants paid, $0; assets, $293,191 (M); gifts received, $290,000; expenditures, $2,684; qualifying distributions, $500.
Trustees: Ira Bordow, Marshall & Ilsley Bank.
EIN: 396742037

58034
The Children of Wisconsin Foundation, Inc.
c/o Frederic G. Friedman
P.O. Box 514000
Milwaukee, WI 53203-3400
Application address: 3038 S. California, MI 53207, tel.: (414) 773-2400
Contact: Matthew Keefe, Pres.

Established in 1999 in WI.
Donor(s): Children of Wisconsin Trust.
Financial data (yr. ended 12/31/00): Grants paid, $0; assets, $28,518 (M); gifts received, $25,000; expenditures, $0; qualifying distributions, $0.
Limitations: Giving primarily in Milwaukee, WI.
Application information: Applicants should submit Wisconsin Donor's Forum Uniform Grant Application. Application form required.
Officers: Matthew Keefe, Pres.; John DeRose, V.P. and Secy.; Martin Organ, Treas.
EIN: 391929571

58035
Leslie & Loretta Copeland Foundation
c/o Bank One Trust Co., N.A.
P.O. Box 1308
Milwaukee, WI 53211

Established in 1999 in IL.
Donor(s): Loretta M. Copeland.
Financial data (yr. ended 12/31/00): Grants paid, $0; assets, $97,262 (M); expenditures, $5,570; qualifying distributions, $1,123.
Limitations: Applications not accepted.
Application information: Contributes only to pre-selected organizations.
Trustee: Bank One Trust Co., N.A.
EIN: 367278445

58036
Carlie Cunningham Foundation
c/o Bank One Trust Co., N.A.
P.O. Box 1308
Milwaukee, WI 53201

Established in 1997 in IN.
Financial data (yr. ended 06/30/01): Grants paid, $0; assets, $2 (M); expenditures, $0; qualifying distributions, $0.
Limitations: Applications not accepted.
Application information: Contributes only to pre-selected organizations.
Trustee: Bank One Trust Co., N.A.
EIN: 352053212

58037
Daniels Partnership Foundation of Burlington, Inc.
241 Peters Pkwy.
Burlington, WI 53105

Financial data (yr. ended 12/31/99): Grants paid, $0; assets, $25,795 (M); expenditures, $0; qualifying distributions, $0.
Directors: Matthew Daniels, Paul B. Edwards, Richard Edwards.
EIN: 391085109

58038
Renuka & P. R. Dasgupta Foundation, Inc.
2628 Cochise Trail
Madison, WI 53711   (608) 263-6806
Contact: Bibhuti R. Dasgupta, Pres.

Established in 1998 in WI.
Donor(s): Bibhuti R. Dasgupta.
Financial data (yr. ended 06/30/01): Grants paid, $0; assets, $88,203 (M); gifts received, $37,350; expenditures, $883; qualifying distributions, $806.
Limitations: Giving primarily in WI.
Officers: Bibhuti R. Dasgupta, Pres.; Dipankar R. Dasgupta, V.P.; D'Arcy Kemnitz, Secy.; Barbara A. Cochrane, Treas.
EIN: 391939683

58039
Gladys Deuster Foundation
c/o Marshall & Ilsley Bank
P.O. Box 2980
Milwaukee, WI 53201
Application address: 1000 N. Water St., Milwaukee, WI 53202
Contact: Margaret Treadway, Trust Off., Marshall & Ilsley Bank

Financial data (yr. ended 12/31/01): Grants paid, $0; assets, $16,472 (M); expenditures, $742; qualifying distributions, $0.
Limitations: Giving primarily in Milwaukee, WI.
Trustee: Marshall & Ilsley Bank.
EIN: 396548014

58040
Herman M. Dicks Trust
c/o Bank One Trust Co., N.A.
P.O. Box 1308
Milwaukee, WI 53201
Application address: Debbie Miller, Relationship Mgr., c/o Bank One Trust Co., N.A., Indiana, 111 Monument Cir., Indianapolis, IN 46277

Donor(s): Herman Dicks.‡
Financial data (yr. ended 12/31/01): Grants paid, $0; assets, $51,834 (M); expenditures, $2,021; qualifying distributions, $0.
Limitations: Giving limited to the Crawfordsville, IN, area.
Trustee: Bank One Trust Co., N.A.
EIN: 356350401

58041
Bruno Diekmann Foundation, Inc.
1655 Hwy. V
Sturtevant, WI 53177

Established in 1996 in WI.
Financial data (yr. ended 06/30/02): Grants paid, $0; assets, $377 (M); expenditures, $0; qualifying distributions, $0.
Officers: Bruno Diekman, Pres.; Katherine M. Scheer, V.P.; Laura Rosenquist, Secy.-Treas.
EIN: 391862042

58042
Arnold and Lois Domer Foundation
1749 Rudolph Ct.
Eau Claire, WI 54701-4690

Donor(s): Arnold Domer, Lois Domer.
Financial data (yr. ended 12/31/01): Grants paid, $0; assets, $470,581 (M); gifts received, $37,384; expenditures, $16,135; qualifying distributions, $0.
Limitations: Giving limited to WI.
Trustees: Arnold Domer, Lois Domer.
EIN: 391966526

58043
Ebling Charitable Trust
c/o Gertrude Thiel
401 N. Eau Clairs Ave., Apt. 114
Madison, WI 53705-2835

Established in 1994 in WI.
Financial data (yr. ended 11/30/01): Grants paid, $0; assets, $956,032 (M); gifts received, $132,000; expenditures, $77; qualifying distributions, $0.
Limitations: Applications not accepted. Giving primarily in Shawano, WI.
Application information: Contributes only to pre-selected organizations.
Trustees: Walter R. Ebling, Mary J.E. Guhl, Gertrude A. Thiel.
EIN: 396590730

58044
Elaine B. Eisner Charitable Foundation
P.O. Box 28800
Milwaukee, WI 53220

Established in 1995 in WI.
Donor(s): Elaine B. Eisner.
Financial data (yr. ended 12/31/01): Grants paid, $0; assets, $66,685 (M); expenditures, $1,109; qualifying distributions, $0.
Limitations: Applications not accepted.
Application information: Contributes only to pre-selected organizations.
Trustee: Elaine B. Eisner.
EIN: 391834399

58045
Fenton E. English Scholarship Trust
c/o Bank One Trust Co., N.A.
P.O. Box 1308
Milwaukee, WI 53202

Financial data (yr. ended 12/31/01): Grants paid, $0; assets, $0 (M); expenditures, $840; qualifying distributions, $800.
Limitations: Applications not accepted. Giving primarily in Paris, IL.
Trustee: Bank One Trust Co., N.A.
EIN: 376121329
Codes: GTI

58046
EPS Solutions Foundation
111 E. Wisconsin Ave., Ste. 1800
Milwaukee, WI 53202

Established in 1999 in CA.
Financial data (yr. ended 12/31/01): Grants paid, $0; assets, $511,870 (M); expenditures, $0; qualifying distributions, $0.
Limitations: Applications not accepted. Giving on a national basis, with some emphasis on CA.
Application information: Contributes only to pre-selected organizations.
Officer: David Hoffman, Pres.
EIN: 330821213

58047
Faith Alive, Inc.
3201 S. 16th St., Rm. 600
Milwaukee, WI 53215-4532

Established in 1997.
Donor(s): E. Basil Jackson.
Financial data (yr. ended 12/31/01): Grants paid, $0; assets, $635 (M); expenditures, $0; qualifying distributions, $0.
Limitations: Applications not accepted.
Directors: Basil Jackson, Elizabeth Jackson, Lorraine Jackson.
EIN: 391488934

58048
Dr. Emily Farnum Charitable Trust
170 W. Main St.
Platteville, WI 53818

Established in 2000 in WI.
Financial data (yr. ended 12/31/01): Grants paid, $0; assets, $134,710 (M); gifts received, $60,428; expenditures, $1,790; qualifying distributions, $0.
Limitations: Giving primarily in Platteville, WI.
Application information: Application form not required.
Trustee: First National Bank of Platteville.
EIN: 396740904

58049
Forest Residue Research Foundation, Inc.
P.O. Box 33
Antigo, WI 54409

Financial data (yr. ended 08/31/99): Grants paid, $0; assets, $23,558 (M); expenditures, $36; qualifying distributions, $0.
Officers: Jack Rusch, Pres.; Greg M. Rusch, V.P.; Paula Spiegl, Secy.-Treas.
EIN: 237447359

58050
Dr. Robert J. Freedman, Sr. Scholarship Fund
c/o Bank One Trust Co., N.A.
P.O. Box 1308
Milwaukee, WI 53201
Application address: c/o LSUA Foundation, Attn: Ken Calhoun, 8100 Hwy. 71 S., Alexandria, LA 71302

Established in 1990 in LA.
Financial data (yr. ended 12/31/01): Grants paid, $0; assets, $86,410 (M); expenditures, $3,345; qualifying distributions, $1,175.
Trustee: Bank One Trust Co., N.A.
EIN: 721170481

58051
Millie & Jesse E. Fusfeld Charitable Trust
c/o Marshall & Ilsley Bank
1000 N. Water St.
Milwaukee, WI 53202

Established in 2000 in WI.
Financial data (yr. ended 10/31/01): Grants paid, $0; assets, $181,163 (M); gifts received, $192,000; expenditures, $2,295; qualifying distributions, $0.
Limitations: Applications not accepted.
Application information: Contributes only to pre-selected organizations.
Trustee: Marshall & Ilsley Bank.
EIN: 396742081

58052
Della B. Gardner Charitable Trust
c/o Bank One Trust Co., N.A.
P.O. Box 1308
Milwaukee, WI 53201
Application address: c/o Mark D. Welch, Trust Off., Bank One Trust Co., N.A., 2 S. Main St., Middletown, OH 45042, tel.: (513) 425-8430

Financial data (yr. ended 12/31/99): Grants paid, $0; assets, $383,966 (M); expenditures, $5,784; qualifying distributions, $1,044.
Limitations: Giving primarily in Middletown, OH.
Trustee: Bank One Trust Co., N.A.
EIN: 316020705

58053
Garig, Connell and Witter Family Foundation
c/o Bank One Trust Co., N.A.
P.O. Box 1308
Milwaukee, WI 53201

Financial data (yr. ended 10/31/01): Grants paid, $0; assets, $22,449 (M); expenditures, $1,604; qualifying distributions, $0.
Limitations: Giving primarily in Baton Rouge, LA.
Officers: Phillips Connell Witter, Pres.; J. Luther Jordan, Secy.-Treas.
Trustee: Bank One Trust Co., N.A.
EIN: 726021562

58054
Golf Foundation of Wisconsin, Inc.
8989 N. Port Washington Rd.
Milwaukee, WI 53217 (414) 540-3830

Financial data (yr. ended 12/31/99): Grants paid, $0; assets, $486,882 (M); gifts received, $462,521; expenditures, $322,224; qualifying distributions, $32,544.
Limitations: Applications not accepted.
Application information: Contributes only to pre-selected organizations.
Officer: Steve Quale, Exec. Dir.
Directors: Tony Coleman, Karla Deming, Tom Gilbertson, Eugene R. Haas, Bill Hughes, Tom Huset, and 20 additional directors.
EIN: 391296562
Codes: TN

58055
Goodman's, Inc.
P.O. Box 1436
Madison, WI 53701 (608) 257-6761
Contact: Irwin A. Goodman, Pres.

Established in 1961 in WI.
Donor(s): Irwin A. Goodman, Robert D. Goodman.
Financial data (yr. ended 08/31/01): Grants paid, $0; assets, $2,427,362 (M); gifts received, $50,000; expenditures, $13,127; qualifying distributions, $0.
Limitations: Giving primarily in Madison, WI.
Officers: Irwin A. Goodman, Pres.; Robert D. Goodman, V.P.
Director: Robert Pricer.
EIN: 396056619

58056
Habush, Habush, Davis & Rottier Charitable Foundation, Inc.
150 E. Gilman St., Ste. 2000
Madison, WI 53703 (608) 255-6663
Contact: Daniel A. Rottier, Dir.

Established in 1999 in WI.
Financial data (yr. ended 12/31/99): Grants paid, $0; assets, $1,929,639 (M); gifts received, $1,920,000; expenditures, $0; qualifying distributions, $0.
Application information: Application form not required.
Directors: Robert L. Habush, Richard Kabaker, Larry Kath, James Marks, William Reif, Daniel A. Rottier, Ralph J. Tease, Jr.
EIN: 391989358

58057
Gerald J. Haegele Family Foundation, Inc.
77 Steele St.
Algoma, WI 54201

Established in 2000 in WI.
Donor(s): Gerald J. Haegele.
Financial data (yr. ended 05/31/02): Grants paid, $0; assets, $53,482 (M); expenditures, $254; qualifying distributions, $0.
Limitations: Giving primarily in Algoma, WI.
Officers: Jane Sweasy, Pres.; William Goolsbey, Secy.-Treas.
EIN: 391938097

58058
Hamilton Family Foundation, Inc.
139 E. Chowning Cross
Mequon, WI 53092-6204

Established in 2000 in WI.
Donor(s): William H. Hamilton.
Financial data (yr. ended 12/31/01): Grants paid, $0; assets, $12,902 (M); expenditures, $390; qualifying distributions, $0.
Limitations: Applications not accepted.
Application information: Contributes only to pre-selected organizations.
Officers and Directors:* William H. Hamilton,* Pres.; Douglas H. Hamilton,* V.P.; Jane H. Musich,* Secy.; Sally H. Lensink,* Treas.
EIN: 391980599

58059
Robert & Marjorie Hartshorn Memorial Charitable Trust for Jesse W. White
c/o First National Bank
170 W. Main St.
Platteville, WI 53818 (608) 348-7777

Established in 2001.
Donor(s): Robert Hartshorn, Marjorie Hartshorn.
Financial data (yr. ended 12/31/01): Grants paid, $0; assets, $202,325 (M); gifts received, $221,925; expenditures, $834; qualifying distributions, $0.
Limitations: Giving primarily in Platteville, WI.
Trustee: First National Bank.
EIN: 396754553

58060
The Heck Family Foundation, Inc.
4219 Forest Dr.
Rhinelander, WI 54501

Established in 2001.
Financial data (yr. ended 12/31/01): Grants paid, $0; assets, $24,973 (M); expenditures, $0; qualifying distributions, $0.
Officers and Directors:* Robert G. Heck,* Pres.; June C. Heck,* V.P.; David M. Heck,* Secy.;

Kenneth R. Heck,* Treas.; Karen Bernsteen, Kathy McDonough, Julie Reinthaler.
EIN: 392014940

58061
High Cliff Forrest Park Association, Inc.
1 Bank Ave.
Kaukauna, WI 54130

Financial data (yr. ended 12/31/00): Grants paid, $0; assets, $48,813 (M); expenditures, $47; qualifying distributions, $0.
Limitations: Applications not accepted. Giving limited to WI.
Officers and Directors:* Wilmer Schulz,* Pres.; Patrick Egan,* V.P.; Jeffrey D. Riester,* Secy.; Gail E. Janssen,* Treas.; Gary E. Lakin, Melvin Rausch, Robert J. Roloff, Warren Schneider, Wilmer Schulz, and 6 additional directors.
EIN: 396063755

58062
Janet M. Hoehnen Foundation, Inc.
c/o Janet Hoehnen
111 E. Wisconsin Ave., Ste. 1800
Milwaukee, WI 53202-4809

Established in 2001 in WI.
Donor(s): Janet M. Hoehnen.
Financial data (yr. ended 12/31/01): Grants paid, $0; assets, $5,508 (M); gifts received, $5,508; expenditures, $0; qualifying distributions, $0.
Limitations: Applications not accepted.
Application information: Contributes only to pre-selected organizations.
Officers and Directors:* Janet M. Hoehnen,* Pres.; Frank W. Bastian,* Secy.; Kathleen R. Dahlgren.
EIN: 392014830

58063
Holiday Automotive Foundation, Inc.
321 N. Rolling Meadows Dr.
Fond Du Lac, WI 54935

Established in 2001 in WI.
Financial data (yr. ended 12/31/01): Grants paid, $0; assets, $100,983 (M); gifts received, $101,000; expenditures, $17; qualifying distributions, $0.
Limitations: Applications not accepted.
Application information: Contributes only to pre-selected organizations.
Officers: Michael R. Shannon, Pres.; James I. Flood, V.P.; Patrick McCullough, Secy.-Treas.
EIN: 392018969

58064
Holy Wounds Apostolate, Inc.
P. O. Box 98
Necedah, WI 54646

Established in 1991 in WI.
Financial data (yr. ended 12/31/01): Grants paid, $0; assets, $127,928 (M); gifts received, $65,619; expenditures, $90,791; qualifying distributions, $0.
Officers: Mary Terese Paul, Pres.; Steve J. Paul, V.P.; Gary McLellan, Treas.
EIN: 391628294

58065
Ed E. & Gladys Hurley Foundation
c/o Bank One Trust Co., N.A.
P.O. Box 1308
Milwaukee, WI 53201
Application address: c/o Monette Holler, Trust Off., Bank One, Louisiana, N.A., 200 Texas St., Shreveport, LA 71101, tel.: (318) 226-2020

Trust established in 1954 in LA.
Donor(s): Ed E. Hurley.‡

Financial data (yr. ended 12/31/00): Grants paid, $0; assets, $5,508,987 (M); expenditures, $94,993; qualifying distributions, $122,566; giving activities include $18,414 for loans to organizations and $109,000 for loans to individuals.
Limitations: Giving limited to residents of AR, LA, and TX.
Application information: Application form required.
Trustee: Bank One Trust Co., N.A.
EIN: 726018854

58066
International Medical Foundation
W303 N1673 Arbor Dr.
Delafield, WI 53018-2143

Financial data (yr. ended 12/31/01): Grants paid, $0; assets, $779,985 (M); expenditures, $10,805; qualifying distributions, $0.
Directors: Narendra M. Kini, M.D., Marc Marotta, Thomas J. Stanczyk, Jon E. Vice.
EIN: 112937410

58067
Iron River Area Foundation, Inc.
P.O. Box 683
Iron River, WI 54847-0683 (715) 372-8560
Contact: John LaGesse, Pres.

Established in 1994 in WI.
Financial data (yr. ended 12/31/99): Grants paid, $0; assets, $289,718 (M); gifts received, $54,115; expenditures, $23,619.
Limitations: Giving limited to Iron River, WI.
Officers: John LaGesse, Pres.; LeRoy Forslund, V.P.; Mary LaGesse, Secy.-Treas.
Board Members: John Joseph, Rudy Kavajecz, Dorothy Thompson, Don Zahler.
EIN: 391667325
Codes: CM

58068
Mary Ella Jerome Family Foundation, Inc.
759 S. Oak St.
Barron, WI 54812

Established in 2000 in WI; funded in 2001.
Donor(s): Mary Ella Jerome.
Financial data (yr. ended 12/31/01): Grants paid, $0; assets, $1,000,675 (M); gifts received, $1,003,985; expenditures, $3,985; qualifying distributions, $0.
Limitations: Applications not accepted.
Application information: Contributes only to pre-selected organizations.
Directors: Candace J. Arp, Julie M. Brown, Mary Ella Jerome.
EIN: 392001356

58069
Mary Hendrickson Johnson Foundation, Inc.
11039 N. River Trail
Mequon, WI 53092 (262) 238-9998
Contact: Paul R. Johnson, Pres.

Established in 1988 in WI.
Donor(s): Paul R. Johnson.
Financial data (yr. ended 12/31/99): Grants paid, $0; assets, $493,121 (M); expenditures, $20,110; qualifying distributions, $18,944; giving activities include $18,944 for programs.
Limitations: Giving primarily in Pewaukee, WI.
Officers: Paul R. Johnson, Pres. and Treas.; Richard L. Johnson, V.P.; Philip J. Hendrickson, Secy.
EIN: 391613991

58070
Jones Memorial Scholarship Fund
(Formerly Dennis R. and Nina B. Jones Memorial Scholarship Fund)
c/o Bank One Trust Co.
P.O. Box 1308
Milwaukee, WI 53201
Contact: Charles W. Tramel, Asst. V.P. and Trust Off., Bank One, Illinois, N.A.

Financial data (yr. ended 10/31/00): Grants paid, $0; assets, $494,230 (M); expenditures, $6,608; qualifying distributions, $2,767.
Limitations: Giving primarily in IL.
Application information: Application form not required.
Trustee: Bank One Trust Co., N.A.
EIN: 366760778

58071
Joy Foundation, Inc.
620 Main St.
La Crosse, WI 54601

Established in 2001 in WI.
Donor(s): Francis L. Rost, Hong X. Rost, Christopher T. Rost, Patricia S. Rost.
Financial data (yr. ended 12/31/01): Grants paid, $0; assets, $728,485 (M); gifts received, $585,100; expenditures, $3,746; qualifying distributions, $3,211.
Limitations: Applications not accepted.
Application information: Contributes only to pre-selected organizations.
Officers: Francis L. Rost, Pres. and Treas.; Hong X. Rost, V.P.; Christopher T. Rost, Secy.
EIN: 392039495

58072
The King's Daughters of Wisconsin Foundation, Inc.
c/o Mary Ann Wepfer
1444 Lakeshore Dr.
Menasha, WI 54952

Financial data (yr. ended 08/31/00): Grants paid, $0; assets, $3,154 (M); gifts received, $1,731; expenditures, $3,656; qualifying distributions, $0.
Limitations: Giving limited to WI.
Officers and Directors:* Nanci Micke,* Pres.; Laura Shinkan,* V.P. and Secy.; Mary Ann Wepfer,* Treas.
EIN: 510160730
Codes: GTI

58073
Melvin & Frances Kirby Foundation
c/o Marshall & Ilsley Bank
P.O. Box 2980
Milwaukee, WI 53201

Established in 1999 in WI.
Financial data (yr. ended 08/31/01): Grants paid, $0; assets, $40,310 (M); gifts received, $200; expenditures, $2,161; qualifying distributions, $0.
Limitations: Applications not accepted.
Application information: Contributes only to pre-selected organizations.
Trustee: Marshall & Ilsley Bank.
EIN: 396713131

58074
Dennis & Janice Klumb Family Foundation, Inc.
W571 County Rd. L
East Troy, WI 53120

Established in 2000 in WI.
Donor(s): Dennis G. Klumb, Janice Klumb.
Financial data (yr. ended 12/31/00): Grants paid, $0; assets, $321,875 (M); gifts received,

58074—WISCONSIN

$353,400; expenditures, $0; qualifying distributions, $0.
Limitations: Applications not accepted.
Application information: Contributes only to pre-selected organizations.
Officers and Directors:* Dennis G. Klumb,* Pres.; Janice Klumb,* V.P. and Treas.; Pamela Klumb, Secy.; Fred J. Fass, Dennis M. Klumb, Michael A. Klumb, Richard A. Klumb, Shawn D. Klumb, Thomas G. Schober.
EIN: 391996367

58075
Kohl Foundation, Inc.
825 N. Jefferson St., Ste. 250
Milwaukee, WI 53202

Established about 1955 in WI.
Donor(s): Mary Kohl 1982 Charitable Trust.
Financial data (yr. ended 09/30/01): Grants paid, $0; assets, $5,192 (M); expenditures, $24; qualifying distributions, $0.
Limitations: Applications not accepted. Giving primarily in Milwaukee, WI.
Application information: Contributes only to pre-selected organizations.
Officers and Directors:* Allen D. Kohl,* Pres.; Herbert Kohl,* V.P. and Treas.; Sidney Kohl,* Secy.; Dolores Kohl.
EIN: 396047415

58076
Milton A. Krom Scholarship Trust
c/o Associated Banc-Corp
P.O. Box 408
Neenah, WI 54957-0408

Established in 2000 in WI.
Donor(s): Milton A. Krom.‡
Financial data (yr. ended 09/30/01): Grants paid, $0; assets, $159,925 (M); gifts received, $169,686; expenditures, $3,132; qualifying distributions, $0.
Trustee: Associated Banc-Corp.
EIN: 396703209

58077
Gail F. Kursel Family Fund
c/o Foley & Lander
777 E. Wisconsin Ave.
Milwaukee, WI 53202-5367

Established in 2000 in WI.
Donor(s): Gail F. Kursel.
Financial data (yr. ended 12/31/01): Grants paid, $0; assets, $102,823 (M); gifts received, $48,059; expenditures, $377; qualifying distributions, $0.
Limitations: Applications not accepted. Giving primarily in WI.
Application information: Contributes only to pre-selected organizations.
Trustees: Stephen M. Fisher, Michael W. Hatch, Gail F. Kursel.
EIN: 391996109

58078
William Lacy Foundation, Inc.
c/o Jere D. McGaffey
777 E. Wisconsin Ave., Ste. 3600
Milwaukee, WI 53202

Established in 2000 in WI.
Donor(s): William H. Lacy.
Financial data (yr. ended 12/31/00): Grants paid, $0; assets, $452,964 (M); gifts received, $442,283; expenditures, $0; qualifying distributions, $0.
Limitations: Applications not accepted.
Application information: Contributes only to pre-selected organizations.

Officers and Directors:* William H. Lacy,* Pres. and Treas.; Olena Lacy,* V.P. and Secy.; Thomas Lacy.
EIN: 311742281

58079
Lakeland Air Safety Foundation, Inc.
11389 Airport Rd.
Arbor Vitae, WI 54568

Financial data (yr. ended 02/28/02): Grants paid, $0; assets, $13,751 (M); expenditures, $105; qualifying distributions, $0.
Limitations: Applications not accepted. Giving primarily in WI.
Application information: Contributes only to pre-selected organizations.
Officers: Tim Ashe, Pres.; Larry Hanna, Secy.; Thomas Schultz, Treas.
EIN: 237134933

58080
Larsen Family Foundation, Inc.
632 N. Broadway
De Pere, WI 54115

Established in 1997 in WI.
Donor(s): Bette Larsen.‡
Financial data (yr. ended 12/31/01): Grants paid, $0; assets, $70,638 (M); expenditures, $313; qualifying distributions, $0.
Limitations: Applications not accepted.
Application information: Contributes only to pre-selected organizations.
Officer: Eric Larsen Pres.
Director: Donald F. Larsen.
EIN: 391919058

58081
Madalynne F. Laux Memorial Trust
c/o Bank One Trust Co., N.A.
P.O. Box 1308, Tax Section
Milwaukee, WI 53201
Application addresses: c/o Glen LaFrombois, Counselor, Appleton West H.S., 610 N. Badger Ave., Appleton, WI 54911, tel.: (920) 832-6219; c/o Gary Ludwig or Maureen Killian, Counselors, Appleton East H.S., 2121 E. Emmers Dr., Appleton, WI 54915, tel.: (920) 832-6203

Established in 1992 in WI.
Donor(s): Beatrice Laux.‡
Financial data (yr. ended 05/31/01): Grants paid, $0; assets, $1,530,094 (M); expenditures, $14,836; qualifying distributions, $4,153.
Limitations: Giving limited to residents of Appleton, WI.
Application information: Application form required.
Trustee: Bank One Trust Co., N.A.
EIN: 396551972
Codes: GTI

58082
Terry Lemerond Family Foundation
825 Challenger Dr.
Green Bay, WI 54311

Established in 2000 in WI.
Donor(s): Terrence J. Lemerond.
Financial data (yr. ended 12/31/01): Grants paid, $0; assets, $387,864 (M); expenditures, $5,907; qualifying distributions, $0.
Officer: Terrence J. Lemerond, Pres.
EIN: 392012885

58083
Listle Family Private Foundation
P.O. Box 102
Antigo, WI 54409-0102

Established in 2000 in WI.

Financial data (yr. ended 12/31/01): Grants paid, $0; assets, $3,195 (M); expenditures, $163; qualifying distributions, $0.
Officers: Patricia Levis, Pres.; Catherine Iwen, V.P.; Lynn Mattek, Secy.; Mary Listle, Treas.
EIN: 391995090

58084
Mallory Foundation, Inc.
9994 Edgewood Shores
Edgerton, WI 53534-8964

Established in 1986.
Donor(s): Ethlynn Mallory.
Financial data (yr. ended 12/31/01): Grants paid, $0; assets, $46,805 (M); expenditures, $24; qualifying distributions, $0.
Limitations: Applications not accepted. Giving primarily in Salt Lake City, UT.
Application information: Contributes only to pre-selected organizations.
Officers: Alan K. Passey, Pres.; Lisa Blundell, V.P.; Ethlynn Mallory, Secy.-Treas.
EIN: 391566307

58085
Roger R. Mayer Foundation, Inc.
6520 67th St.
Kenosha, WI 53142
Contact: Roger R. Mayer, Dir.

Established in 2000 in WI.
Donor(s): Roger R. Mayer.
Financial data (yr. ended 07/31/01): Grants paid, $0; assets, $4,717 (M); gifts received, $5,000; expenditures, $300; qualifying distributions, $300.
Application information: Application form required.
Directors: Roger R. Mayer, Catherine Paupore, Cletus Willems.
EIN: 392013525

58086
Joan Woodman Orton McCullum Foundation, Inc.
28405 Woodman Rd.
Cazenovia, WI 53924

Established in 1999 in WI.
Donor(s): Joan Orton McCullum.
Financial data (yr. ended 12/31/01): Grants paid, $0; assets, $691 (M); expenditures, $131; qualifying distributions, $0.
Officers: Joan Orton McCullum, Pres.; James Chandler, V.P.; Jack E. White, Secy.-Treas.
EIN: 391955914

58087
McDonald Family Charitable Foundation
1283 Bayshore Dr.
Oshkosh, WI 54901

Established in 2001 in WI.
Donor(s): Donald H. McDonald.
Financial data (yr. ended 12/31/01): Grants paid, $0; assets, $12,490 (M); gifts received, $12,438; expenditures, $0; qualifying distributions, $0.
Limitations: Applications not accepted.
Application information: Contributes only to pre-selected organizations.
Advisory Committee Members: Meghan C. McDonald Harshman, Donald J. McDonald, Mary P. McDonald, Robert S. McDonald, Shaun P. McDonald, Heather H. McDonald Sleeman.
EIN: 396746083

58088
Matthew A. Meyer Fertility Fund, Inc.
721 American Ave.
Waukesha, WI 53188
Contact: Matthew A. Meyer, M.D., Pres.

Donor(s): Hermann W. Ladish Family Foundation, Inc.
Financial data (yr. ended 12/31/01): Grants paid, $0; assets, $39,763 (M); gifts received, $3,000; expenditures, $6,120; qualifying distributions, $0.
Limitations: Giving primarily in WI.
Application information: Application form not required.
Officers: Matthew A. Meyer, M.D., Pres.; Lenia Dacko, M.D., Secy.-Treas.
Directors: K. Paul Katayama, M.D., Roger Lalich, Carole Mural, M.D.
EIN: 391599648

58089
Mary Mikesell Charitable Trust
c/o Bank One Trust Co., N.A.
P.O. Box 1308
Milwaukee, WI 53201
Application address: 1700 Courthouse Plz., N.E., Dayton, OH 45402-1788
Contact: Belinda A. Burns

Established in 2000 in OH.
Donor(s): Mary Mae Mikesell.
Financial data (yr. ended 11/30/01): Grants paid, $0; assets, $794,763 (M); gifts received, $785,023; expenditures, $4,954; qualifying distributions, $1,614.
Application information: Application form required.
Trustees: Daniel W. Mapp, Martha Elizabeth Mapp, Bank One Trust Co., N.A.
EIN: 912091454

58090
Mueller Memorial Trust
502 Oak St.
Baraboo, WI 53913

Established in 2000 in WI.
Financial data (yr. ended 12/31/01): Grants paid, $0; assets, $1,677,386 (M); expenditures, $62,473; qualifying distributions, $34,147; giving activities include $34,147 for programs.
Limitations: Applications not accepted.
Application information: Contributes only to pre-selected organizations.
EIN: 396699866

58091
National Institute of Biogerontology
4610 University Ave.
P.O. Box 55231
Madison, WI 53705
Contact: Everett L. Smith, Pres.

Established in 1985 in WI.
Financial data (yr. ended 06/30/01): Grants paid, $0; assets, $6,700 (M); gifts received, $372; expenditures, $68; qualifying distributions, $0.
Limitations: Giving primarily in Germany.
Officers and Directors:* Everett L. Smith,* Pres.; Robert O. Ray,* V.P.; Patricia E. Smith,* Secy.-Treas.; Vernon N. Dodson, William G. Reddan.
EIN: 391484704
Codes: GTI

58092
New Rock Charities, Inc.
c/o Stephen A. Sinicropi
2979 N. Mayfair Rd.
Milwaukee, WI 53222

Established in 1996.
Donor(s): Cellar Door Concert Promotions.
Financial data (yr. ended 12/31/01): Grants paid, $0; assets, $1,020 (M); expenditures, $625; qualifying distributions, $0.
Officers: Stephen A. Sinicropi, Pres.; Willie D. Davis, V.P.; Vicki Krotts, Secy.-Treas.
EIN: 391856240

58093
Lawrence Norbert & Harry Schwabenlander Hilbert HS Memorial Scholarship Foundation
N5183 Hwy. 57
Chilton, WI 53014-9738 (920) 849-2790
Contact: Joyce M. Kopf, Pres.

Established in 2001 in WI.
Donor(s): Harry Schwabenlander.‡
Financial data (yr. ended 12/31/01): Grants paid, $0; assets, $257,925 (M); gifts received, $250,000; expenditures, $0; qualifying distributions, $0.
Limitations: Giving limited to residents of Hilbert, WI.
Application information: Application form required.
Officers and Directors:* Joyce M. Kopf,* Pres.; Arthur W. Kopf,* V.P.; Susan J. Ammerman,* Secy.-Treas.
EIN: 392012927

58094
Nutritional Resource Foundation
c/o Paul Stitt
P.O. Box 730, 4300 Cty. Trunk Cr.
Manitowoc, WI 54221-0730

Established in 1995 in WI.
Donor(s): Barbara Stitt, Paul Stitt, Natural Ovens of Manitowoc, Enreco.
Financial data (yr. ended 12/31/99): Grants paid, $0; assets, $326,348 (M); gifts received, $132,786; expenditures, $47,098; qualifying distributions, $40,882; giving activities include $53,853 for programs.
Limitations: Applications not accepted.
Application information: Contributes only to pre-selected organizations.
Trustees: Thomas Rusboldt, Barbara Stitt, Paul Stitt.
EIN: 391814121

58095
Frank L. Oakes Foundation
c/o Bank One, N.A.
P.O. Box 1308
Milwaukee, WI 53201
Application address: c/o Kathy Whitney, Bank One Trust Co., N.A., 111 Monument Cir., Indianapolis, IN 46277-0115, tel.: (317) 321-8189

Financial data (yr. ended 05/31/01): Grants paid, $0; assets, $600,300 (M); expenditures, $8,455; qualifying distributions, $4,801.
Limitations: Giving limited to Marion County, IN.
Application information: Formal nomination by school principal required. Application form required.
Trustee: Bank One, N.A.
EIN: 356015133
Codes: GTI

58096
The Paunack Foundation, Inc.
3006 Irvington Way
Madison, WI 53713-3414

Established in 2001 in WI.
Donor(s): Arlene R. Paunack.
Financial data (yr. ended 12/31/01): Grants paid, $0; assets, $14,698 (M); gifts received, $15,000; expenditures, $411; qualifying distributions, $411.
Limitations: Applications not accepted.
Application information: Contributes only to pre-selected organizations.
Officers: Arlene R. Paunack, Pres.; Mark D. Burish, V.P. and Secy.; Wilfred K. Kinney, Treas.
Directors: Richard E. Ela, William T. Graham.
EIN: 392014757

58097
R. Pautz and M. Pautz Life-Long Learning Foundation
5392 S. 46th St.
Milwaukee, WI 53220-5051

Established in 1996 in WI.
Donor(s): Mary Pautz.
Financial data (yr. ended 12/31/00): Grants paid, $0; assets, $101,845 (M); gifts received, $17,464; expenditures, $12,804; qualifying distributions, $11,810; giving activities include $11,810 for programs.
Trustee: Mary Pautz.
EIN: 391866937

58098
Pediatric Epidemiology Foundation, Inc.
9702 N. Valley Hill Dr.
Mequon, WI 53092

Established in 1997 in WI.
Financial data (yr. ended 12/31/01): Grants paid, $0; assets, $1 (M); gifts received, $2,500; expenditures, $1,976; qualifying distributions, $0.
Officers and Directors:* Peter L. Havens, M.D.,* Pres.; Abigail Singleton,* V.P.; Kathryn Klein Havens, M.D.,* Secy.-Treas.
EIN: 391835898

58099
Clare M. Peters Charitable Trust
c/o John F. Callan, Foley & Lardner
777 E. Wisconsin Ave., Ste. 3500
Milwaukee, WI 53202-5367
Contact: Harrold J. McComas, Tr.

Established in 2001 in WI.
Donor(s): Clare M. Peters 1996 Trust.
Financial data (yr. ended 12/31/01): Grants paid, $0; assets, $1,221,103 (M); gifts received, $1,269,186; expenditures, $12,380; qualifying distributions, $1,238.
Trustee: Harrold J. McComas.
EIN: 397356130

58100
Robert C. Peterson Memorial Foundation, Ltd.
c/o Lauretta Peterson
123 Edgewood Ct.
Barron, WI 54812

Established in 2001 in WI.
Financial data (yr. ended 12/31/01): Grants paid, $0; assets, $31,702 (M); gifts received, $32,545; expenditures, $855; qualifying distributions, $0.
Limitations: Giving primarily in northwest WI.
Officers: Lauretta Peterson, Pres.; Charles Nelson, V.P.; Joseph Johnston, Secy.
EIN: 392037583

58101—WISCONSIN

58101
Petherick Family Foundation, Inc.
P.O. Box 1008
Sheboygan, WI 53082-1008
Contact: Gary L. Williamson

Established in 1992 in WI.
Financial data (yr. ended 12/31/00): Grants paid, $0; assets, $68,488 (M); expenditures, $775; qualifying distributions, $0.
Limitations: Giving primarily in Sheboygan, WI.
Officers: Gordon W. Petherick, Pres. and Treas.; Susan M. Magnus, V.P.; Audrey Petherick, Secy.
EIN: 391691916

58102
Harry R. Quadracci Charitable Foundation, Inc.
512 Northview Rd.
Waukesha, WI 53188

Established in 1996 in WI.
Donor(s): Harry R. Quadracci, Angeline Quadracci.
Financial data (yr. ended 11/30/01): Grants paid, $0; assets, $28,797 (M); expenditures, $1,528; qualifying distributions, $328.
Limitations: Applications not accepted. Giving primarily in Milwaukee, WI.
Application information: Contributes only to pre-selected organizations.
Officers: Angeline Quadracci, Pres.; Harry V. Quadracci, V.P.; John C. Fowler, Secy.-Treas.
EIN: 391879051

58103
Rabbi's Dream Foundation, Inc.
1000 N. Water St., Ste. 2100
Milwaukee, WI 53202

Established in 1998 in WI.
Donor(s): Chaim Rogoff.
Financial data (yr. ended 12/31/01): Grants paid, $0; assets, $4,318 (M); expenditures, $3; qualifying distributions, $0.
Limitations: Applications not accepted.
Application information: Contributes only to pre-selected organizations.
Officers and Directors:* Chaim Rogoff,* Pres. and Treas.; Gail Flug,* V.P. and Secy.; Andrea Wolfer.
EIN: 391921641

58104
Donald and Diana Ryan Foundation, Ltd.
c/o Virchow, Krause & Co.
500 Midland Ct., P.O. Box 8130
Janesville, WI 53547-8130

Established in 2001 in WI.
Financial data (yr. ended 12/31/01): Grants paid, $0; assets, $1,597 (M); gifts received, $3,200; expenditures, $1,603; qualifying distributions, $0.
Limitations: Applications not accepted.
Application information: Contributes only to pre-selected organizations.
Directors: Susanna Ryan Bolster, Josephine J. Johnson, Adam S. Ryan, David P. Ryan, Nancy C. Ryan, Patrick W. Ryan, Polly W. Ryan, Rebecca C. Ryan.
EIN: 392007400

58105
Samuel D. & Virginia B. Saffro Charitable Trust
c/o Guaranty Bank
4000 W. Brown Deer Rd.
Milwaukee, WI 53209
Contact: Douglas S. Levy, Tr.

Established in 2001 in WI.
Donor(s): Safro Suvivor's Trust.
Financial data (yr. ended 12/31/01): Grants paid, $0; assets, $2,262,077 (M); gifts received, $1,889,156; expenditures, $4,983; qualifying distributions, $0.
Application information: Application form not required.
Trustees: Jill Levy Belconis, Douglas S. Levy, Ellin S. Levy, Carol S. Saffro.
EIN: 396755670

58106
Jerome & Caecilia Sarnowski Foundation
c/o John R. Nelson
111 E. Wisconsin Ave., Ste. 1500
Milwaukee, WI 53202

Established in 2000 in WI.
Financial data (yr. ended 12/31/01): Grants paid, $0; assets, $500,000 (M); gifts received, $500,000; expenditures, $0; qualifying distributions, $0.
Limitations: Applications not accepted.
Application information: Contributes only to pre-selected organizations.
Directors: John R. Nelson, Caecilia K. Sarnowski, Jerome T. Sarnowski.
EIN: 392012968

58107
The Savanna Oak Foundation, Inc.
1227 Dartmouth Rd.
Madison, WI 53705

Established in 2000 in WI.
Donor(s): Thomas D. Brock, Katherine M. Brock.
Financial data (yr. ended 12/31/01): Grants paid, $0; assets, $151,836 (M); gifts received, $42,000; expenditures, $37,171; qualifying distributions, $0.
Limitations: Applications not accepted.
Application information: Contributes only to pre-selected organizations.
Officers and Directors:* Thomas D. Brock,* Pres. and Treas.; Katherine M. Brock,* V.P. and Secy.; Brian Brock, Emily Brock.
EIN: 391980507

58108
Ja-Sa Schneck Foundation, Inc.
1249 W. Liebau Rd., Ste. 200
Mequon, WI 53092

Established in 2000 in WI.
Donor(s): James C. Schneck.
Financial data (yr. ended 12/31/01): Grants paid, $0; assets, $122,633 (M); gifts received, $4,800; expenditures, $6,004; qualifying distributions, $0.
Limitations: Applications not accepted.
Application information: Contributes only to pre-selected organizations.
Directors: James C. Schneck, Jason Schneck, Sarah Schneck.
EIN: 392010173

58109
Schreck Family Foundation
3433 Lake Mendota Dr.
Madison, WI 53705

Established in 1999 in IL.
Financial data (yr. ended 12/31/99): Grants paid, $0; assets, $92,096 (M); gifts received, $92,096; expenditures, $0; qualifying distributions, $0.
Limitations: Applications not accepted.
Application information: Contributes only to pre-selected organizations.
Officer: Myron Schreck, Pres.
EIN: 364312030

58110
Stark Family Foundation, Ltd.
6836 N. Barnett Ln.
Fox Point, WI 53217

Established in 2000 in WI.
Donor(s): Brian J. Stark.
Financial data (yr. ended 12/31/00): Grants paid, $0; assets, $1,500,000 (M); gifts received, $1,500,000; expenditures, $0; qualifying distributions, $0.
Limitations: Applications not accepted.
Application information: Contributes only to pre-selected organizations.
Directors: Colin Lancaster, Brian J. Stark, Debra Stark.
EIN: 392013796

58111
Andrew and Michael Stolper Foundation, Inc.
4001 Monona Dr., Ste. 402
Monona, WI 53716

Established in 1997 in WI.
Donor(s): Tom Stolper.
Financial data (yr. ended 06/30/01): Grants paid, $0; assets, $70,249 (M); expenditures, $132; qualifying distributions, $0.
Limitations: Applications not accepted.
Application information: Contributes only to pre-selected organizations.
Officers: Tom Stolper, Pres. and Treas.; David Walsh, V.P.; Virginia Deibel, Secy.
EIN: 391916231

58112
The Strom Family Foundation
151 Detrie Dr.
Green Bay, WI 54301

Established in 2001 in WI.
Donor(s): David A. Strom, Barbara Strom.
Financial data (yr. ended 12/31/01): Grants paid, $0; assets, $52,776 (M); gifts received, $49,109; expenditures, $1,384; qualifying distributions, $0.
Limitations: Applications not accepted.
Application information: Contributes only to pre-selected organizations.
Trustees: Randi B. Fay, Wendy A. Holland, Heidi K. Mercer, Sara R.S. Miller, Nancy S. Solhaug, Barbara M. Strom, David A. Strom.
EIN: 396739862

58113
Tanner Family Foundation, Inc.
8850 N. Port Washington Rd., Ste. 200
Milwaukee, WI 53217

Established in 1995 in WI.
Donor(s): Zenith Sintered Products.
Financial data (yr. ended 12/31/01): Grants paid, $0; assets, $97,146 (M); expenditures, $1,228; qualifying distributions, $0.
Limitations: Applications not accepted. Giving limited to WI.
Application information: Contributes only to pre-selected organizations.
Officers and Directors:* Jeanne S. Tanner,* Pres.; Deborah T. Hall,* V.P.; Judith T. Moon,* Secy.; Thomas H. Tanner, Jr.,* Treas.
EIN: 391800458

58114
Tharinger-Henter Family Foundation
19225 Lothmoor Dr. Lower
Brookfield, WI 53045

Established in 1999 in WI.
Financial data (yr. ended 12/31/99): Grants paid, $0; assets, $2,003 (M); gifts received, $2,000; expenditures, $0; qualifying distributions, $0.

Limitations: Applications not accepted.
Application information: Contributes only to pre-selected organizations.
Trustee: Erich H. Henter.
EIN: 391964062

58115
Tuchman Family Foundation, Inc.
c/o Peter Sommerhauser
780 N. Water St.
Milwaukee, WI 53202

Established in 2000 in WI.
Financial data (yr. ended 12/31/01): Grants paid, $0; assets, $103 (M); expenditures, $0; qualifying distributions, $0.
Limitations: Applications not accepted.
Application information: Contributes only to pre-selected organizations.
Officers and Directors:* Herman Tuchman,* Pres. and Treas.; Ailene Tuchman,* V.P. and Secy.; Jeremy Tuchman, Shila Tuchman.
EIN: 311758573

58116
Alice Vassau Scholarship Fund
c/o Bank One Trust Co., N.A.
P.O. Box 1308
Milwaukee, WI 53201
Application address: c/o Guidance Office, Antigo High School, 815 7th Ave., Antigo, WI 54409, tel.: (715) 623-7611

Established in 1992 in WI.
Financial data (yr. ended 08/31/01): Grants paid, $0; assets, $169,348 (M); expenditures, $3,643; qualifying distributions, $0.
Limitations: Giving primarily in WI.
Application information: Application form required.
Trustee: Bank One Trust Co., N.A.
EIN: 396554432

58117
The Vick Foundation
11429 N. Justin Dr.
Mequon, WI 53092 (262) 512-1138
Contact: Steven L. Vick, Pres.

Established in 1997 in KS.
Financial data (yr. ended 12/31/99): Grants paid, $0; assets, $64,496 (M); expenditures, $0; qualifying distributions, $0.
Officers: Steven L. Vick, Pres.; Susan C. Vick, V.P.
Directors: Dewane Ewert, Emily Jane Ewert.
EIN: 742834027

58118
Viglietti Family Foundation, Inc.
4125 Lakeshore Rd.
Sheboygan, WI 53083

Established in 2001 in WI.
Donor(s): John Viglietti.
Financial data (yr. ended 12/31/01): Grants paid, $0; assets, $301,725 (M); gifts received, $299,990; expenditures, $0; qualifying distributions, $0.
Directors: Christine Viglietti, John Viglietti, Mark Viglietti, Stefano Viglietti.
EIN: 912169553

58119
Edwin F. Vobeda Irrevocable Charitable Insurance Trust
c/o George L. Gissell
P.O. Box 1708
Racine, WI 53401-1708

Established in 1994 in WI.
Financial data (yr. ended 12/31/01): Grants paid, $0; assets, $61,570 (M); expenditures, $22,371; qualifying distributions, $0.
Limitations: Applications not accepted.
Application information: Contributes only to pre-selected organizations.
Trustee: George L. Gissell.
EIN: 396567517

58120
William Vodrey Trust
c/o Bank One Trust Co., N.A.
P.O. Box 1308
Milwaukee, WI 53201

Established in 1989 in OH.
Financial data (yr. ended 12/31/99): Grants paid, $0; assets, $53,532 (M); expenditures, $1,280; qualifying distributions, $130.
Limitations: Giving limited to East Liverpool, OH.
Trustee: Bank One Trust Co., N.A.
EIN: 346514869

58121
Robert J. and Eunice J. Wagner Foundation, Inc.
111 E. Wisconsin Ave., Ste. 1800
Milwaukee, WI 53202-4815
Contact: Janet M. Hoehnen, Secy.

Established in 1986.
Donor(s): Eunice J. Wagner.
Financial data (yr. ended 12/31/01): Grants paid, $0; assets, $58,187 (M); expenditures, $888; qualifying distributions, $0.
Limitations: Giving primarily in NC and WI.
Officers and Directors:* Eunice J. Wagner,* Pres.; Janet M. Hoehnen,* Secy.; Paul Wagner.
EIN: 391584983

58122
James D. & Jane P. Watermolen Foundation, Inc.
5364 Liegeois Rd.
Abrams, WI 54101

Established in 2000.
Donor(s): James D. Watermolen, Jane P. Watermolen.
Financial data (yr. ended 12/31/01): Grants paid, $0; assets, $1,063 (M); expenditures, $167; qualifying distributions, $167.
Trustees: James D. Watermolen, Jane P. Watermolen.
EIN: 392005195

58123
Mildred G. Westfall Trust
c/o U.S. Bank
P.O. Box 2043
Milwaukee, WI 53201-9116
Application address: c/o U.S. Bank, P.O. Box 1088, Burlington, IA 52601

Financial data (yr. ended 04/30/01): Grants paid, $0; assets, $110,431 (M); expenditures, $2,638; qualifying distributions, $8,803; giving activities include $8,803 for loans to individuals.
Limitations: Giving limited to residents of Burlington, IA.
Application information: Students must be recommended by the Pastor of the First Methodist Episcopal Church of Burlington, IA. Application form required.
Trustee: U.S. Bank.
EIN: 426321855

58124
Weston's Antique Apple Foundation, Inc.
19760 W. National Ave.
New Berlin, WI 53146

Established in 1999 in WI.
Financial data (yr. ended 12/31/99): Grants paid, $0; assets, $4,500 (M); gifts received, $4,500; expenditures, $0; qualifying distributions, $0.
Officer and Directors:* Kenneth Weston,* Pres.; Katie O'Brien Fournelle, Mary Hiebl, Tami Lax, Wally Marks, Joseph Sonza Novarra, Theresa Quednow, Genevieve W. Sekulovich, Genevieve Weston, William Weston, Thomas Woods.
EIN: 391942115

58125
Woodrow W. Woods Educational Trust
c/o Bank One Trust Co., N.A.
P.O. Box 1308
Milwaukee, WI 53201
Application address: c/o Bank One, West Virginia, Charleston, N.A., Clarksburg Trust Dept., P.O. Box 2330, 3rd & Main Sts., Clarksburg, WV 26302-2330

Established in 1996 in WV.
Donor(s): Woodrow W. Woods.‡
Financial data (yr. ended 12/31/00): Grants paid, $0; assets, $1,222,927 (M); expenditures, $10,630; qualifying distributions, $90,506; giving activities include $88,000 for loans to individuals.
Limitations: Giving limited to residents in WV.
Application information: Application form required.
Trustee: Bank One Trust Co., N.A.
EIN: 546409374
Codes: GTI

58126
Julie Ann Wrigley Foundation, Inc.
c/o James L. Mohr & Assocs. LLP
1233 N. Mayfair Rd., No. 304
Wauwatosa, WI 53226

Established in 2001 in WI.
Donor(s): Julie A. Wrigley.
Financial data (yr. ended 12/31/01): Grants paid, $0; assets, $8,268,475 (M); expenditures, $0; qualifying distributions, $0.
Limitations: Applications not accepted.
Application information: Contributes only to pre-selected organizations.
Officers: Julie A. Wrigley, Pres.; Wendy B. Collins, V.P.; Joan F. Kessler, Secy.; Patricia B. Gentry, Treas.
Director: Brian D. Collins.
EIN: 030395312

58127
Youth & Aviation, Inc.
4750 N. 42nd St.
Milwaukee, WI 53209-5830

Financial data (yr. ended 12/31/01): Grants paid, $0; assets, $66,817 (M); gifts received, $6,400; expenditures, $6,100; qualifying distributions, $0.
Limitations: Applications not accepted. Giving primarily in Milwaukee, WI.
Application information: Contributes only to pre-selected organizations.
Officers and Directors:* Marshall E. Lambrecht,* Pres.; Ralph Kroening,* V.P.; Eunice Lambrecht,* Secy.; James Heintskill,* Treas.; Raymond J. Fiorina, Frank J. Ruswick.
EIN: 396077777

WYOMING

58128
Community Foundation of Jackson Hole
180 Center St., No. 9
P.O. Box 574
Jackson, WY 83001 (307) 739-1026
FAX: (307) 734-2841; E-mail:
info@cfjacksonhole.org; URL: http://www.cfjacksonhole.org
Contact: Clare Payne Symmons, Exec. Dir.

Established in 1989 in WY as a component fund of Wyoming Community Foundation; in 1995 became a separate entity.
Financial data (yr. ended 12/31/01): Grants paid, $9,743,056; assets, $42,166,786 (M); gifts received, $38,116,659; expenditures, $10,304,750.
Limitations: Giving primarily in the Jackson Hole, WY, area.
Publications: Annual report (including application guidelines), informational brochure, application guidelines, newsletter, grants list.
Application information: Guidelines available on Web site. Application form required.
Officer: Clare Payne Symmons, Exec. Dir.
EIN: 830308856
Codes: CM, FD

58129
The George B. Storer Foundation, Inc.
P.O. Box 1270
Saratoga, WY 82331
Application address from Jan. 1 to May 15: P.O. Box 1907, Islamorada, FL 33036, tel.: (305) 664-4822
Contact: Peter Storer, Pres.

Incorporated in 1955 in FL.
Financial data (yr. ended 12/31/01): Grants paid, $4,255,000; assets, $90,270,513 (M); expenditures, $4,740,167; qualifying distributions, $4,209,247.
Limitations: Giving primarily in FL.
Publications: Grants list.
Application information: Application form not required.
Officers and Directors:* Peter Storer,* Pres. and Treas.; William Michaels,* V.P.; James P. Storer,* Secy.
EIN: 596136392
Codes: FD, FM

58130
S & G Foundation, Inc.
P.O. Box 20000, No. 25185
Jackson, WY 83001 (307) 733-7707

Established around 1995.
Donor(s): Gale L. Davis, Shelby M.C. Davis.
Financial data (yr. ended 06/30/01): Grants paid, $3,650,281; assets, $188,353,011 (M); gifts received, $64,707,495; expenditures, $5,029,080; qualifying distributions, $3,650,281.
Limitations: Applications not accepted. Giving primarily on the East Coast, with emphasis on FL, ME, NJ, and NY; some giving also in NM.
Application information: Contributes only to pre-selected organizations.
Officers: Shelby M.C. Davis, Pres.; Mary Ann McGrath, V.P.; Gale L. Davis, Secy.-Treas.
EIN: 364193183
Codes: FD

58131
Whitney Benefits, Inc.
P.O. Box 5085
Sheridan, WY 82801 (307) 674-7303
Contact: Patrick Henderson

Incorporated in 1927 in WY.
Donor(s): Edward A. Whitney,‡ Scott Foundation.
Financial data (yr. ended 12/31/01): Grants paid, $3,217,670; assets, $104,399,985 (M); gifts received, $25,000; expenditures, $4,294,529; qualifying distributions, $4,642,435; giving activities include $6,855 for loans to individuals.
Limitations: Giving limited to Sheridan County, WY.
Publications: Annual report.
Application information: Applications accepted for loan program only. Foundation does not fund grants. Application form required.
Officers and Directors:* Dorothy King,* Pres.; John P. Chase,* V.P.; David J. Withrow,* Secy.; Timothy R. Barnes,* Treas.; Robert W. Koester, Mgr.; Tom Belus, Roy Garber, Tom Kinnison, Gary Koltiska, Janet N. Ludwig, Nels A. Nelson, Jr., Sam Scott, Timothy Tarver, Tom Throne.
EIN: 830168511
Codes: FD, GTI

58132
Paul Stock Foundation
P.O. Box 2020
Cody, WY 82414-2020
Contact: Charles G. Kepler, Pres.

Incorporated in 1958 in WY.
Donor(s): Paul Stock,‡ Eloise J. Stock.
Financial data (yr. ended 12/31/01): Grants paid, $2,579,977; assets, $2,712,776 (M); expenditures, $2,634,097; qualifying distributions, $2,603,870.
Limitations: Giving primarily in Park County, WY; student aid limited to those who have resided in WY for one year or more.
Application information: Application form not required.
Officers: Charles G. Kepler, Pres.; Esther C. Brummage, V.P. and Secy.; Donald M. Robirds, V.P. and Treas.
EIN: 830185157
Codes: FD, GTI

58133
Cumming Foundation
165 Huckleberry Dr.
Jackson, WY 83001
Contact: Wendy Ware, Admin.

Established in 1986 in UT.
Donor(s): Ian M. Cumming.
Financial data (yr. ended 12/31/00): Grants paid, $1,781,092; assets, $31,754,866 (M); gifts received, $1,503,420; expenditures, $1,934,947; qualifying distributions, $1,830,821.
Limitations: Applications not accepted. Giving primarily in UT.
Application information: Contributes only to pre-selected organizations. Unsolicited requests for funds not considered.
Officers and Trustees:* Ian M. Cumming,* Pres.; Annette P. Cumming,* V.P.; Corinne Maki, Secy.-Treas.; David E. Cumming, John Darnaby Cumming, Stephen D. Swindle.
EIN: 870440091
Codes: FD

58134
The McMurry Foundation
P.O. Box 2016
Casper, WY 82602-2016 (307) 261-9953
FAX: (307) 234-4631; E-mail:
rachel@mcmurry.net
Contact: Rachel Chadderdon, Dir.

Established in 1998 in WY.
Donor(s): Neil A. McMurry, Mick McMurry, Susie McMurry.
Financial data (yr. ended 12/31/01): Grants paid, $1,273,664; assets, $65,232,355 (M); gifts received, $26,000,880; expenditures, $1,481,810; qualifying distributions, $1,260,486.
Limitations: Giving primarily in WY.
Publications: Application guidelines.
Application information: See application guidelines. Application form required.
Officers and Directors:* Mick McMurry,* Pres.; Susie McMurry,* Secy.; George Bryce,* Treas.; Rachel A. Chadderdon.
EIN: 830323982
Codes: FD

58135
The Robert S. and Grayce B. Kerr Foundation, Inc.
P.O. Box, 20000, PMB 25106
Jackson, WY 83001-7000
Contact: William G. Kerr, Pres., or Sarah J. Lacy, Admin. Asst.

Chartered in 1986 in OK.
Donor(s): Grayce B. Kerr Flynn.‡
Financial data (yr. ended 12/31/00): Grants paid, $1,240,458; assets, $36,748,229 (M); expenditures, $1,650,864; qualifying distributions, $1,758,938; giving activities include $331,339 for loans.
Limitations: Applications not accepted. Giving primarily in OK and WY; some giving also in OH.
Application information: Unsolicited proposals not considered.
Officers and Trustees:* William G. Kerr,* Chair. and Pres.; Joffa Kerr, Sr.,* V.P.; Mara Kerr,* Secy.; James G. Anderson,* Treas.
EIN: 731256123
Codes: FD

58136
Wyoming Community Foundation
221 Ivinson Ave., Ste. 202
Laramie, WY 82070-3038 (307) 721-8300
Additional tel.: toll free (866) 708-7878; FAX: (307) 721-8333; E-mail: wcf@wycf.org; URL: http://www.wycf.org
Contact: Michael J. Lindsey, Pres. and Exec. Dir.

Incorporated in 1989 in WY.
Financial data (yr. ended 12/31/01): Grants paid, $1,225,468; assets, $31,597,053 (M); gifts received, $4,601,677; expenditures, $1,806,094.
Limitations: Giving primarily in WY.
Publications: Annual report, newsletter, program policy statement, application guidelines.
Application information: Application form required.
Officers and Directors:* T. Mark Mickelson,* Chair.; Russell Zimmer,* Vice-Chair.; Michael J. Lindsey, Pres.; Lollie Benz Plank,* Secy.; Keith Hay,* Treas.; and 18 additional directors.
EIN: 830287513
Codes: CM, FD

58137
Homer A. Scott & Mildred S. Scott Foundation
P.O. Box 2007
Sheridan, WY 82801-2007 (307) 672-1448
FAX: (307) 672-1443
Contact: Lynn Mavrakis, Exec. Dir.

Established in 1982 in WY.
Donor(s): Homer A. Scott,‡ Mildred S. Scott.‡
Financial data (yr. ended 02/28/01): Grants paid, $1,118,973; assets, $25,188,519 (M); expenditures, $1,423,205; qualifying distributions, $1,164,791.
Limitations: Giving primarily within a 30-mile radius of Sheridan, WY.
Publications: Program policy statement, application guidelines.
Application information: Application form required.
Officers and Trustees:* James R. Scott,* Chair.; Lynn Mavrakis,* Exec. Dir.; Art Badgett, Susan Scott Heyneman, Jay M. McGinnis, Dan S. Scott, Homer A. Scott, Jr., Delphine Toner.
EIN: 742250381
Codes: FD

58138
Newell B. Sargent Foundation
P.O. Box 50581
Casper, WY 82605-0581
Contact: Charles W. Smith, Tr.

Established in 1984 in UT and WY.
Donor(s): Newell B. Sargent.
Financial data (yr. ended 10/31/01): Grants paid, $640,312; assets, $13,249,720 (M); gifts received, $1,762,099; expenditures, $817,810; qualifying distributions, $640,312.
Limitations: Giving primarily in WY, with emphasis on Worland.
Application information: Application form not required.
Trustees: Ron Hansen, Douglas W. Morrison, Charles W. Smith.
EIN: 830271536
Codes: FD

58139
Archie W. and Grace Berry Foundation
100 Rapid Creek Rd.
Sheridan, WY 82801

Established in 1988 in PA.
Donor(s): Archie W. Berry, Sr.
Financial data (yr. ended 06/30/01): Grants paid, $572,000; assets, $9,961,727 (M); expenditures, $648,261; qualifying distributions, $570,044.
Limitations: Applications not accepted. Giving primarily in PA and WY.
Application information: Contributes only to pre-selected organizations.
Trustees: Archie Berry, Jr., Robert B. Berry, Louis F. Rivituso.
EIN: 236951678
Codes: FD

58140
William E. Weiss Foundation, Inc.
P.O. Box 14270
Jackson, WY 83002 (307) 739-8330
FAX: (307) 733-7545; URL: http://www.weissfoundation.com
Contact: Liz D. Hutchinson

Incorporated in 1955 in NY.
Donor(s): William E. Weiss, Jr.,‡ Helene K. Brown.‡
Financial data (yr. ended 03/31/02): Grants paid, $512,750; assets, $10,761,879 (M); expenditures, $608,538; qualifying distributions, $509,120.
Limitations: Applications not accepted. Giving limited to CA, NY, TN, and WY.
Application information: Contributes only to pre-selected organizations. Unsolicited requests for funds not considered.
Officers and Directors:* Daryl B. Uber,* Pres.; Monte Brown,* V.P.; William D. Weiss, Secy.; Dwyer Brown, Treas.; Katrina D. Weiss, William U. Weiss.
EIN: 556016633
Codes: FD

58141
The Richardson Family Foundation
5025 Campstool Rd.
Cheyenne, WY 82007
Contact: Keith W. Richardson, Pres.

Established in 1994 in WY.
Donor(s): Sierra Trading Post.
Financial data (yr. ended 03/31/01): Grants paid, $500,385; assets, $23,412 (M); gifts received, $526,650; expenditures, $504,028; qualifying distributions, $500,385.
Limitations: Giving on a national basis, with emphasis on AZ, CA, CO, NV, TX, and WY.
Officers: Keith W. Richardson, Pres.; Roberta Richardson, V.P.; Norman J. Wyman, Secy.-Treas.
EIN: 830310875
Codes: FD

58142
The Goodstein Foundation
P.O. Box 2773
Casper, WY 82602 (307) 234-0821
Contact: Robert W. Miracle, Pres.

Incorporated in 1952 in CO.
Donor(s): J.M. Goodstein.‡
Financial data (yr. ended 06/30/01): Grants paid, $408,390; assets, $5,982,781 (M); expenditures, $466,838; qualifying distributions, $462,276.
Limitations: Giving primarily in the metropolitan Denver, CO area, and Natrona County, WY.
Publications: Annual report.
Officers and Directors:* Robert W. Miracle,* Pres.; Lucy M. Goodstein,* V.P. and Secy.; Morris R. Massey.
EIN: 836003815
Codes: FD

58143
Karalyn and Joseph Schuchert Foundation
(Formerly Schuchert Foundation)
1949 Sugarland Dr., Ste. 250
Sheridan, WY 82801 (307) 672-8700
Contact: Joseph Schuchert, Pres.

Established in 1996 in WY.
Donor(s): Joseph Schuchert, Karalyn Schuchert.
Financial data (yr. ended 12/31/01): Grants paid, $369,200; assets, $2,619,423 (M); gifts received, $112,000; expenditures, $376,100; qualifying distributions, $376,100.
Limitations: Applications not accepted. Giving primarily in Sheridan, WY.
Application information: Contributes only to pre-selected organizations.
Officers: Karalyn R. Schuchert, Pres.; Joseph S. Schuchert, V.P.; Carla J. Ash, Secy.-Treas.
Directors: Robert G. Berger, Blair Gustafson, Michele Halseide, Joseph S. Schuchert III.
EIN: 830319305
Codes: FD

58144
Matthew and Virgie O. Dragicevich Wyoming Foundation Trust No. 1
P.O. Box 385
Teton Village, WY 83025
Application address: P.O. Box 430, Teton Village, WY 83025
Contact: Calvin Mathieu, Tr.

Established in 1998 in NY.
Donor(s): Calvin Mathieu.
Financial data (yr. ended 09/30/01): Grants paid, $351,000; assets, $8,904,575 (M); expenditures, $469,929; qualifying distributions, $456,174.
Limitations: Giving primarily in Jackson, WY.
Trustees: Jolene C. Harmes, Lloyd Maryanov, Calvin Mathieu.
EIN: 836046045
Codes: FD

58145
Harry T. Thorson Foundation
26 S. Seneca Ave.
Newcastle, WY 82701

Donor(s): James D. Thorson.
Financial data (yr. ended 12/31/00): Grants paid, $328,871; assets, $556,105 (M); gifts received, $106,218; expenditures, $335,344; qualifying distributions, $328,558.
Limitations: Applications not accepted. Giving primarily in CO and WY.
Application information: Contributes only to pre-selected organizations.
Directors: Mary T. Gullikson, James D. Thorson, Thomas A. Thorson.
EIN: 830255344
Codes: FD

58146
Marna M. Kuehne Foundation
P.O. Box 6064
Sheridan, WY 82801
Contact: Bill Babcock

Established in 1997 in WY.
Donor(s): Marna M. Kuehne.‡
Financial data (yr. ended 10/31/01): Grants paid, $323,892; assets, $16,211,780 (M); expenditures, $811,632; qualifying distributions, $779,916.
Limitations: Applications not accepted. Giving primarily in WY.
Application information: Contributes only to pre-selected organizations.
Officers: Edward A. Hoffman, Pres.; Charles W. Babcock, V.P.; Dan B. Riggs, Secy.
Director: Claude Kissack.
EIN: 742276741
Codes: FD

58147
Wiancko Charitable Foundation, Inc.
P.O. Box 459
Teton Village, WY 83025

Established in 1989 in WY.
Donor(s): Thomas H. Wiancko, Sibyl S. Wiancko.
Financial data (yr. ended 12/31/01): Grants paid, $322,000; assets, $5,833,233 (M); expenditures, $383,199; qualifying distributions, $320,254.
Limitations: Applications not accepted. Giving on a national basis.
Application information: Contributes only to pre-selected organizations.
Officers: Thomas H. Wiancko, Pres.; Richard D. Wiancko, V.P.; Judith W. Parker, Secy.-Treas.
Trustees: Paul Chasman, Bradley Parker, Anna K. Wiancko-Chasman.
EIN: 830291490
Codes: FD

58148
The Arthur B. Schultz Foundation
620 Table Rock West Rd.
Alta, WY   83414   (307) 413-2273
FAX: (307) 353-2273; E-mail: info@absfoundation.org; URL: http://www.absfoundation.org
Contact: Erik B. Schultz, Exec. Dir.

Established in 1985 in CA.
Donor(s): Arthur B. Schultz.
Financial data (yr. ended 11/30/01): Grants paid, $320,290; assets, $4,894,643 (M); gifts received, $50,000; expenditures, $438,402; qualifying distributions, $438,402.
Limitations: Giving in Eastern Europe, Nepal, and Russia for economic development, and in western North America for environmental conservation. No geographic limitation on giving for disabled recreation and therapy.
Publications: Informational brochure (including application guidelines), application guidelines, financial statement.
Application information: No plastic folders or binders. Grants list, program policy statement and application on Web site. Application form not required.
Officer and Trustees:* Erik B. Schultz,* Exec. Dir.; Arthur B. Schultz.
EIN: 953980014
Codes: FD

58149
True Foundation
P.O. Drawer 2360
Casper, WY   82602
Contact: Cherie Miller

Established in 1958 in WY.
Donor(s): True Oil Co., H.A. True, Jr.‡
Financial data (yr. ended 11/30/01): Grants paid, $290,292; assets, $1,931,495 (M); expenditures, $293,576; qualifying distributions, $289,037.
Limitations: Applications not accepted. Giving primarily in WY and the Rocky Mountain area.
Application information: Funds severely curtailed; no new applications considered.
Trustee: Jean D. True.
EIN: 836004596
Codes: CS, FD, CD

58150
Lightner Sams Foundation of Wyoming
P.O. Box 429
Teton Village, WY   83025   (307) 733-9619
FAX: (307) 733-0843
Contact: Robin H. Lightner, Grants Admin.

Established in 1990 in WY.
Financial data (yr. ended 12/31/00): Grants paid, $279,630; assets, $7,640,971 (M); expenditures, $540,373; qualifying distributions, $409,735.
Limitations: Giving primarily in WY.
Directors and Trustees:* Earl Sams Lightner, Sr.,* Pres. and Treas.; Robin H. Lightner,* V.P. and Secy.; Camille M. Lightner, Earl Sams Lightner, Jr., Larry F. Lightner, Sue B. Lightner.
EIN: 830309453
Codes: FD

58151
Harry and Thelma Surrena Memorial Fund
P.O. Box 603
Sheridan, WY   82801-0603
Application address: P.O. Box 27, Buffalo, WY 82834-0027, tel.: (307) 684-5574

Established in 1973 in WY.
Financial data (yr. ended 10/31/01): Grants paid, $264,500; assets, $5,002,008 (M); expenditures, $301,257; qualifying distributions, $273,227.
Limitations: Giving primarily in WY.
Trustees: Stella Barker, John Pradere, Ralph C. Robinson.
EIN: 237435554
Codes: FD

58152
Walter Scott Foundation
2520 Deming Blvd., No. 1
Cheyenne, WY   82001   (307) 632-7278
E-mail: nickerthor@aol.com
Contact: Thorpe A. Nickerson, Pres.

Incorporated in 1903 in NY.
Financial data (yr. ended 09/30/01): Grants paid, $245,000; assets, $5,358,054 (M); gifts received, $22,500; expenditures, $311,706; qualifying distributions, $274,029.
Limitations: Giving primarily in WY.
Application information: Application form not required.
Officers and Directors:* Thorpe A. Nickerson,* Pres. and Secy.-Treas.; Jocelyn A. Nickerson, V.P. and Exec. Dir.; Brett R. Nickerson,* V.P.; Elizabeth Nickerson,* V.P.; George Van B. Cochran, M.D.
EIN: 135681161
Codes: FD2

58153
The Seeley Foundation
P.O. Box 513
Wilson, WY   83014
Contact: Ellen Fales Roberts, V.P. and Secy.

Incorporated in 1945 in MI.
Donor(s): Halsted H. Seeley,‡ Laurel H. Seeley.‡
Financial data (yr. ended 12/31/01): Grants paid, $208,000; assets, $2,897,893 (M); expenditures, $238,928; qualifying distributions, $218,918.
Limitations: Applications not accepted. Giving primarily in CO, CT, KS, MO, NM, VA, and WY.
Application information: The foundation engages in objective grantmaking. Unsolicited requests or proposals are not considered or acknowledged.
Officers and Trustees:* Judith S. Fales,* Co-Pres. and Treas.; Miles P. Seeley,* Co-Pres.; Ellen F. Roberts,* V.P. and Secy.; Eugene Fales, Dana M. Seeley, Laura M. Seeley.
EIN: 366049991
Codes: FD2

58154
Norman Hirschfield Foundation
P.O. Box 7443
Jackson, WY   83001

Established in 1957.
Donor(s): Alan J. Hirschfield, Bert E. Hirschfield.
Financial data (yr. ended 11/30/01): Grants paid, $196,183; assets, $3,791,412 (M); expenditures, $225,934; qualifying distributions, $211,880.
Limitations: Applications not accepted. Giving primarily in Jackson, WY.
Application information: Contributes only to pre-selected organizations.
Officers: Alan J. Hirschfield, Pres.; Bert E. Hirschfield, V.P. and Secy.-Treas.
EIN: 736092984
Codes: FD2

58155
C & N Foundation
P.O. Box 767
Wilson, WY   83014

Established in 1987 in MI.
Donor(s): Norman H. Hofley, Carole S. Hofley.
Financial data (yr. ended 05/31/01): Grants paid, $195,000; assets, $3,063,034 (M); gifts received, $3,000,000; expenditures, $200,900; qualifying distributions, $195,377.
Limitations: Applications not accepted. Giving primarily in WY.
Application information: Contributes only to pre-selected organizations.
Officers: Norman H. Hofley, Pres. and Treas.; Carole S. Hofley, V.P. and Secy.
EIN: 382746657
Codes: FD2

58156
Willard H. Moyer Foundation
P.O. Box 801
Powell, WY   82435
Application address: P.O. Box 763, Powell, WY 82435, tel.: (307) 754-2962
Contact: Joseph E. Darrah, Dir.

Established in 1988 in WY.
Financial data (yr. ended 12/31/01): Grants paid, $178,719; assets, $2,944,273 (M); expenditures, $201,537; qualifying distributions, $178,719.
Limitations: Giving limited to Powell, WY.
Publications: Application guidelines.
Application information: Application form required.
Directors: Joseph E. Darrah, Dexter Dearcorn, Nicholas W. Morris, Jr., David R. Reetz, John Max Stutzman.
EIN: 742480676
Codes: FD2

58157
Ken & Janette McNeal Foundation, Inc.
546 Vista E. Dr.
Thayne, WY   83127

Established in 1998.
Donor(s): Kenneth C. McNeal.
Financial data (yr. ended 12/31/00): Grants paid, $164,200; assets, $1,075,655 (M); expenditures, $214,423; qualifying distributions, $164,200.
Limitations: Applications not accepted. Giving primarily in ID.
Application information: Contributes only to pre-selected organizations.
Officers: Kenneth C. McNeal, Pres.; Janette A. McNeal, Secy.-Treas.
EIN: 830322609
Codes: FD2

58158
Karl M. Johnson Foundation
P.O. Box 7
Jackson, WY   83001
Contact: Karl M. Johnson, Chair.

Established in 1989 in WY.
Donor(s): Karl M. Johnson.
Financial data (yr. ended 12/31/99): Grants paid, $162,277; assets, $3,369,768 (M); expenditures, $597,396; qualifying distributions, $160,975.
Limitations: Giving primarily in the Teton Valley, WY area.
Application information: Application form not required.
Officer: Karl M. Johnson, Chair. and Pres.
Directors: Charles H. Foote, Floyd R. King.
EIN: 742554281
Codes: FD2

58159
Myra Fox Skelton Trust Foundation
c/o Wells Fargo Bank Wyoming, N.A., Trust Dept.
P.O. Box 2799
Casper, WY   82602   (307) 235-7739
Contact: Thomas D. Rohde

Established in 1987 in WY.

Financial data (yr. ended 12/31/01): Grants paid, $155,600; assets, $1,826,511 (M); expenditures, $214,207; qualifying distributions, $154,271.
Limitations: Giving primarily in Casper, WY.
Advisory Committee: Charles Chapin, Donald E. Chapin, John S. Miracle, R.W. Miracle, Wayne Weaver.
EIN: 836029858
Codes: FD2

58160
Nelson Family Foundation
3400 Arrowleaf Ln.
Wilson, WY 83014-9639

Established in 1985 in CA and WY.
Donor(s): Elizabeth S. Nelson.
Financial data (yr. ended 08/31/01): Grants paid, $147,000; assets, $2,945,531 (M); expenditures, $147,998; qualifying distributions, $146,304.
Limitations: Giving primarily in CA and WY.
Trustees: Clarke A. Nelson, Elizabeth S. Nelson.
EIN: 953945578
Codes: FD2

58161
The William F. Welch and Lorene W. Welch Foundation
P.O. Box 603
Sheridan, WY 82801 (307) 672-6494
Contact: William B. Ebzery, Tr.

Established in 1993 in WY.
Donor(s): Lorene W. Welch.
Financial data (yr. ended 08/31/01): Grants paid, $145,750; assets, $3,997,554 (M); expenditures, $225,808; qualifying distributions, $153,263.
Limitations: Giving primarily in WY.
Trustees: William B. Ebzery, Burgess & Davis.
EIN: 836033434
Codes: FD2

58162
Ruth R. Ellbogen Foundation
c/o Ruth R. Ellbogen
P.O. Box 3280
Casper, WY 82602-3280

Established in 1999 in WY.
Donor(s): Ruth R. Ellbogen.
Financial data (yr. ended 07/31/02): Grants paid, $130,166; assets, $1,417,577 (M); gifts received, $315,125; expenditures, $136,029; qualifying distributions, $130,166.
Limitations: Applications not accepted. Giving primarily in AZ and WY.
Application information: Contributes only to pre-selected organizations.
Officers: Thomas M. Ellbogen, Pres.; John P. Ellbogen II, V.P.; Mary L.E. Garland, Secy. and Treas.
Directors: Ruth R. Ellbogen, Theresa A. Ellbogen.
EIN: 830327143
Codes: FD2

58163
Homer A. Scott, Jr. & Janet E. Scott Family Foundation
c/o Wells Fargo Bank, N.A.
P.O. Box 2007
Sheridan, WY 82801 (307) 672-1498

Established in 1995 in WY.
Financial data (yr. ended 12/31/01): Grants paid, $125,335; assets, $93,953 (M); gifts received, $78,970; expenditures, $126,404; qualifying distributions, $125,335.
Trustees: Susan E. Scott Baker, Coralee Davis, Terril R. Moore, Homer R. Scott, James M. Scott, Janet E. Scott, Homer A. Scott, Jr., Sandra Scott Suzor, Wells Fargo Bank, N.A.

EIN: 911693889

58164
Joe F. and Roberta Napier Foundation
P.O. Box 6084
Sheridan, WY 82801 (307) 672-5805
Contact: John E. Tracy, Treas.

Established in 1988 in WY.
Financial data (yr. ended 12/31/01): Grants paid, $122,100; assets, $2,907,239 (M); expenditures, $176,932; qualifying distributions, $175,163; giving activities include $54,832 for programs.
Limitations: Giving limited to Sheridan County, WY.
Officers: Richard M. Davis, Jr., Pres.; John E. Tracy, Treas.
Director: Robert D. Fall.
EIN: 830266070
Codes: FD2

58165
Lund Foundation
(Formerly La Familia Foundation)
970 W. Broadway, PMB 946
Jackson, WY 83001-9475
Contact: Jeramy Lund, Treas.

Established in 1997 in WY.
Donor(s): Victor L. Lund, Linda Lund.
Financial data (yr. ended 04/30/01): Grants paid, $120,000; assets, $2,181,416 (M); gifts received, $457,832; expenditures, $136,524; qualifying distributions, $119,663.
Limitations: Giving primarily in WY and UT.
Officers: Linda Lund, Pres.; Chandler Lund, V.P.; Victor L. Lund, Secy.; Jeramy Lund, Treas.
EIN: 841417073
Codes: FD2

58166
Seven "C" Foundation
4292 S. Fork Rd.
Cody, WY 82414

Established in 1986 in WY.
Donor(s): Silas S. Cathcart.
Financial data (yr. ended 12/31/01): Grants paid, $117,200; assets, $158,156 (M); gifts received, $100,000; expenditures, $109,964; qualifying distributions, $117,165.
Limitations: Giving primarily in Cody, WY.
Application information: Application form not required.
Officers: Silas S. Cathcart, Pres.; Corlene A. Cathcart, V.P.; James A. Cathcart, Secy.
EIN: 830281196
Codes: FD2

58167
The Dunoir Fund Trust
c/o Stephen Gordon
P.O. Box 25009
Jackson, WY 83001

Established in 1991 in WY.
Financial data (yr. ended 12/31/00): Grants paid, $116,250; assets, $1,538,713 (M); expenditures, $136,443; qualifying distributions, $116,250.
Limitations: Applications not accepted. Giving on a national basis.
Application information: Contributes only to pre-selected organizations.
Trustee: Stephen Gordon.
EIN: 830294737
Codes: FD2

58168
Thomas M. Evans, Jr. Charitable Foundation
6805 W. Trail Creek County Rd., Box 259
Wilson, WY 83014

Established in 1998 in WY.
Financial data (yr. ended 12/31/00): Grants paid, $104,400; assets, $2,179,433 (M); expenditures, $111,540; qualifying distributions, $103,449.
Limitations: Applications not accepted.
Application information: Contributes only to pre-selected organizations.
Trustees: Thomas M. Evans, Jr., Tonia S. Evans.
EIN: 237949413
Codes: FD2

58169
Gertrude Kamps Memorial Foundation
P.O. Box 40
Casper, WY 82602 (307) 577-7755
Application address: P.O. Box 2274, Casper, WY 82602
Contact: Brad Bochmann, Chair.

Established in 1976 in WY.
Donor(s): Gertrude Kamps.‡
Financial data (yr. ended 07/31/01): Grants paid, $96,726; assets, $2,191,711 (M); expenditures, $124,558; qualifying distributions, $96,726.
Limitations: Giving limited to WY, with emphasis on Natrona County and the central WY region.
Application information: Application form not required.
Officer: Brad Bochmann, Chair.
Trustee: First Interstate Bank.
EIN: 836024918
Codes: FD2

58170
Maurice W. Brown Foundation
614 S. Greeley Hwy.
Cheyenne, WY 82007
Application address: 1426 E. Lincolnway, Cheyenne, WY 82001
Contact: Ed Carleo, Treas.

Donor(s): Maurice W. Brown.
Financial data (yr. ended 11/30/01): Grants paid, $96,000; assets, $890,066 (M); expenditures, $97,582; qualifying distributions, $97,582.
Limitations: Giving primarily in Cheyenne, WY.
Officers: Maurice W. Brown, Pres.; Wayne Brown, V.P.; Bonnie Brown, Secy.; Ed Carleo, Treas.
EIN: 742221742
Codes: FD2

58171
Tom and Helen Tonkin Foundation
c/o Wells Fargo Bank Wyoming, N.A.
P.O. Box 2799
Casper, WY 82602 (307) 235-7725

Trust established in 1956 in WY.
Donor(s): Helen B. Tonkin,‡ T.C. Tonkin.‡
Financial data (yr. ended 07/31/01): Grants paid, $95,248; assets, $3,057,007 (M); expenditures, $132,901; qualifying distributions, $106,069.
Limitations: Giving limited to WY, with emphasis on the Casper area.
Publications: Application guidelines.
Application information: Application form not required.
Members: Sheri Carlisle, Michelle Ferguson, Marvin Keller, R.M. Robertson, Ron Salveson.
Trustee Bank: Wells Fargo Bank Wyoming, N.A.
EIN: 836002200
Codes: FD2

58172
Cody Medical Foundation
721 Sheridan Ave.
Cody, WY 82414 (307) 587-9030
Contact: Marty Coe, Exec. Dir.

Established about 1940.
Financial data (yr. ended 06/30/01): Grants paid, $94,519; assets, $1,793,296 (M); gifts received, $38,504; expenditures, $282,338; qualifying distributions, $94,519.
Limitations: Giving limited to the West Park Hospital district, Park County, WY.
Officer: Marty Coe, Exec. Dir.
EIN: 836006491
Codes: FD2, GTI

58173
Giovanini Foundation
P.O. Box 160
Jackson, WY 83001
Application address: P.O. Box 607, Teton Village, WY 83205, tel.: (307) 739-1426

Established in 1994 in WY.
Donor(s): Joseph E. Giovanini, Clarice Jane Giovanini.
Financial data (yr. ended 01/31/02): Grants paid, $91,670; assets, $1,768,705 (M); expenditures, $125,143; qualifying distributions, $90,727.
Limitations: Giving primarily in WY, with some giving also in CO.
Application information: Application form required.
Officers and Directors:* Joseph E. Giovanini,* Pres.; Clarice Jane Giovanini,* Secy.; Amy U. Giovanini, Kathryn Sue Giovanini, Kernan R. Giovanini, Kerry T. Giovanini, Kristin B. Giovanini, Thomas J. Giovanini, Mary M.G. Keenan.
EIN: 830308568
Codes: FD2, GTI

58174
Draine Family Charitable Foundation, Inc.
P.O. Box 4158
Jackson, WY 83001-4158

Established in 1991 in WY.
Donor(s): Robert W. Draine, Steven T. Draine.
Financial data (yr. ended 12/31/01): Grants paid, $90,180; assets, $1,171,075 (M); expenditures, $95,541; qualifying distributions, $90,180.
Limitations: Applications not accepted. Giving primarily in CA and WY.
Application information: Contributes only to pre-selected organizations.
Officers and Trustees:* Patricia Lee Draine,* Pres.; Janet L. Odell,* Secy.-Treas.; Robert C. Draine, Robert W. Draine.
EIN: 830295696

58175
Socrates Foundation
(Formerly The Roy and Fay Foundation)
c/o R.R. Whitney
3441 Hwy. 34
Wheatland, WY 82201-8714
Contact: Ralph R. Whitney, Jr., Dir.

Established in 1985 in PA.
Donor(s): Ralph R. Whitney, Jr., Fay Whitney.
Financial data (yr. ended 12/31/00): Grants paid, $88,000; assets, $1,055,028 (M); expenditures, $110,220; qualifying distributions, $87,722.
Limitations: Giving primarily in NY.
Directors: Lynn Allen, Paula Skrotzki, Brian Whitney, Fay Whitney, Ralph R. Whitney, Jr., Robb Whitney.
EIN: 222620092
Codes: FD2

58176
The Kroeger Family Charitable Foundation
970 W. Broadway, Ste. 114
Jackson, WY 83001-0600
Application address: c/o Grace & Co., 3117 S. Big Bend Blvd., St. Louis, MO 63143
Contact: Mr. Stark

Established in 1996 in WY.
Financial data (yr. ended 12/31/00): Grants paid, $84,495; assets, $417,704 (M); expenditures, $99,132; qualifying distributions, $86,991.
Limitations: Giving on a national basis.
Officers and Directors:* Hol A. Kroeger,* Pres. and Treas.; George F. Kroeger,* V.P.; Harold R. Kroeger,* V.P.; Carole F. Kroeger,* Secy.
EIN: 830319291
Codes: FD2

58177
The Free Lunch Foundation
c/o David Walsh
P.O. Box 11450
Jackson, WY 83002

Established in 1997 in WY.
Donor(s): David Walsh, Jade Walsh.
Financial data (yr. ended 12/31/01): Grants paid, $82,526; assets, $532,005 (M); gifts received, $214,570; expenditures, $88,055; qualifying distributions, $83,023.
Limitations: Applications not accepted. Giving primarily in VT and WY.
Application information: Contributes only to pre-selected organizations.
Trustees: David Walsh, Jade Walsh.
EIN: 061482552
Codes: FD2

58178
James D. and Bess S. Polis Foundation
c/o Gloria W. Polis
P.O. Box 10909
Jackson, WY 83002-0909
Contact: James D. Polis, Tr.

Established in 1988 in FL.
Donor(s): James D. Polis, Bess S. Polis,‡ Gloria W. Polis.
Financial data (yr. ended 12/31/01): Grants paid, $67,920; assets, $1,240,168 (M); expenditures, $78,312; qualifying distributions, $67,920.
Limitations: Applications not accepted. Giving on a national basis.
Application information: Contributes only to pre-selected organizations.
Trustees: Gloria W. Polis, James D. Polis, James F. Polis.
EIN: 656016835

58179
Zimmerman Family Foundation
c/o Larry G. Bean
520 S. Walnut St., Ste., 102
Casper, WY 82601-2351

Established in 1998 in WY.
Donor(s): Gail D. Zimmerman, Anne D. Zimmerman.
Financial data (yr. ended 12/31/01): Grants paid, $64,244; assets, $660,910 (M); gifts received, $40,684; expenditures, $68,411; qualifying distributions, $64,244.
Limitations: Applications not accepted.
Application information: Contributes only to pre-selected organizations.
Officers and Directors:* Gail D. Zimmerman,* Pres.; Anne D. Zimmerman,* Secy.; Rhonda S. Zimmerman.
EIN: 830322568

58180
Kinskey Family Foundation
(Formerly Kinski Mini Mart Foundation)
P.O. Box 3259
Casper, WY 82602-3259
Application address: 3950 Cynthia Dr., Casper, WY 82609
Contact: Rodney Kinskey

Established in 1979 in WY.
Donor(s): Jeanne Kinskey, Rodney Kinskey.
Financial data (yr. ended 12/31/01): Grants paid, $62,297; assets, $744,094 (M); expenditures, $70,362; qualifying distributions, $62,297.
Limitations: Applications not accepted. Giving primarily in Casper, WY.
Application information: Contributes only to pre-selected organizations.
Officer and Directors:* Charles R. Kinskey,* Pres.; James R. Kinskey, Margaret J. Kinskey.
EIN: 830242355

58181
Hazel Patterson Memorial Trust
130 S. Main St.
Buffalo, WY 82834 (307) 684-2207
Contact: William D. Omohundro, Tr.

Established in 1989 in WY.
Financial data (yr. ended 09/30/01): Grants paid, $61,501; assets, $1,244,974 (M); expenditures, $85,210; qualifying distributions, $61,501.
Limitations: Giving limited to Johnson County, WY.
Application information: Application form required.
Trustees: Don Kraen, William D. Omohundro, Sandra Todd.
EIN: 742557301

58182
Wold Foundation
139 W. 2nd St., Ste. 200
Casper, WY 82601 (307) 265-7252
Contact: Peter I. Wold, Secy.-Treas.

Established in 1986 in WY.
Donor(s): John S. Wold.
Financial data (yr. ended 12/31/01): Grants paid, $60,959; assets, $1,149,886 (M); expenditures, $76,233; qualifying distributions, $60,959.
Limitations: Giving primarily in Casper, WY.
Application information: Application form required.
Officers and Trustees:* John P. Wold,* Pres.; Jane P. Wold,* V.P.; Peter I. Wold,* Secy.-Treas.; John S. Wold.
EIN: 742406069

58183
Elda Shoemaker Charitable Trust
P.O. Box 839
Powell, WY 82435-0839
Contact: Tracy Copenhaver, Tr.

Established in 1997 in WY.
Financial data (yr. ended 12/31/01): Grants paid, $60,640; assets, $709,908 (M); expenditures, $66,460; qualifying distributions, $60,640.
Limitations: Applications not accepted. Giving primarily in WY.
Application information: Contributes only to pre-selected organizations.
Trustee: Tracy Copenhaver.
EIN: 841392178

58184
The A. C. and Penney Hubbard Foundation, Inc.
P.O. Box 482
Wilson, WY 83014 (307) 734-0311
Contact: A.C. Hubbard, Pres.

Established around 1986 in MD.
Donor(s): A.C. Hubbard, Penney Hubbard.
Financial data (yr. ended 10/31/99): Grants paid, $59,600; assets, $769,191 (M); gifts received, $190,714; expenditures, $63,524; qualifying distributions, $57,499.
Limitations: Giving primarily in Baltimore, MD.
Application information: Application form not required.
Officers and Directors:* Albert C. Hubbard, Jr.,* Pres. and Treas.; Penney Hubbard,* V.P. and Secy.
EIN: 521486929

58185
B. F. & Rose H. Perkins Foundation
P.O. Box 1064
Sheridan, WY 82801 (307) 674-8871
FAX: (307) 674-8803
Contact: Donna B. Rawlings, Office Mgr.

Established in 1933 in WY.
Donor(s): Benjamin F. Perkins.‡
Financial data (yr. ended 12/31/01): Grants paid, $59,532; assets, $10,250,262 (M); gifts received, $70; expenditures, $201,298; qualifying distributions, $407,703; giving activities include $281,100 for loans to individuals.
Limitations: Giving limited to residents of Sheridan County, WY.
Application information: Application form required.
Trustees: Paddy Bard, Stephen D. Carroll, George P. Fletcher, Victor Garber, Michael Pilch.
EIN: 830138740
Codes: GTI

58186
The Mary K. Weiss Foundation
P.O. Box 1108
Jackson, WY 83001-1108
Contact: Mary K. Weiss, V.P.

Established in 1999 in WY.
Financial data (yr. ended 12/31/01): Grants paid, $58,515; assets, $868 (M); gifts received, $58,995; expenditures, $58,975; qualifying distributions, $58,515.
Officers: Arturo H. Peralta-Ramos, Pres.; Mary K. Weiss, V.P.; Lorian Peralta Ramos, Secy.-Treas.
EIN: 830325778

58187
Wheeler Family Foundation
5600 S. Poplar St.
Casper, WY 82601

Established in 2000 in WY.
Donor(s): Richard E. Wheeler, Linda S. Wheeler.
Financial data (yr. ended 12/31/01): Grants paid, $54,000; assets, $1,927,020 (M); gifts received, $1,074,133; expenditures, $63,079; qualifying distributions, $54,000.
Limitations: Applications not accepted.
Application information: Contributes only to pre-selected organizations.
Officers: Richard E. Wheeler, Pres. and Exec. Dir.; Linda S. Wheeler, Secy.-Treas.
Directors: Steven L. Fenton, Wendy W. Fenton, Cathrine J. Wheeler, David N. Wheeler, Paula M. Wheeler, Richard S. Wheeler.
EIN: 830331386

58188
Muriel & Seymour Thickman Family Charitable Foundation
c/o First Interstate Bank of Commerce
P.O. Box 2007
Sheridan, WY 82801-2007

Established in 1990 in WY.
Donor(s): Seymour Thickman, Muriel Thickman.
Financial data (yr. ended 12/31/01): Grants paid, $51,520; assets, $1,200,192 (M); gifts received, $115,896; expenditures, $69,810; qualifying distributions, $51,520.
Limitations: Applications not accepted. Giving primarily in Schenectady, NY, and WY.
Application information: Contributes only to pre-selected organizations.
Trustees: Seymour Thickman, First Interstate Bank of Commerce.
EIN: 830290571

58189
The Hilda and Raymond Milne Foundation
P.O. Box 1028
Gillette, WY 82717-1028 (307) 682-1313
Contact: Thomas E. Lubnau II, Dir.

Established in 1994 in WY.
Financial data (yr. ended 12/31/01): Grants paid, $51,000; assets, $896,954 (M); gifts received, $308,555; expenditures, $68,140; qualifying distributions, $51,000.
Limitations: Giving limited to residents of Campbell County, WY.
Application information: Application form not required.
Directors: Thomas E. Lubnau II, Steven H. Pecha, First Interstate Bank.
EIN: 830305556

58190
E. C. & Edith M. Gwillim Memorial Fund
c/o First Interstate Bank
P.O. Box 2007
Sheridan, WY 82801 (307) 674-7411
Contact: Jerome T. Pilch, Trust Off., First Interstate Bank

Donor(s): Edith Gwillim.‡
Financial data (yr. ended 07/31/01): Grants paid, $44,100; assets, $960,365 (M); expenditures, $54,625; qualifying distributions, $44,100.
Limitations: Giving limited to Sheridan, WY.
Trustee: First Interstate Bank.
EIN: 830254277

58191
The Herbert G. and Dorothy Zullig Foundation
P.O. Box 603
Sheridan, WY 82801
Application address: P.O. Box 5085, Sheridan, WY 82801
Contact: Robert W. Koester, Pres.

Established in 1987 in WY.
Financial data (yr. ended 12/31/01): Grants paid, $40,000; assets, $737,175 (M); expenditures, $56,201; qualifying distributions, $40,000.
Limitations: Giving limited to Sheridan County, WY.
Officers: Robert W. Koester, Pres.; Richard Kraft, V.P.; John Pradere, Secy.-Treas.
EIN: 830282365

58192
Johnson County High School Scholarship Fund Charitable Trust
P.O. Box 400
Buffalo, WY 82834 (307) 684-2211
Contact: Raymond Holt, Tr.

Financial data (yr. ended 12/31/01): Grants paid, $38,850; assets, $927,074 (M); gifts received, $2,500; expenditures, $39,570; qualifying distributions, $39,210.
Limitations: Giving limited to Johnson County, WY.
Application information: Applicant must include letters of reference, plans for higher education, name of intended school, intended course of study and dates of attendance.
Trustees: John Adams, Connie Goddard, George Grace, Raymond Holt, Richard Reimann.
EIN: 836003627
Codes: GTI

58193
Oletha C. Likins & Loren E. Likins Memorial Trust
P.O. Box 53
Torrington, WY 82240 (307) 532-7109
Contact: Donna Beth Downer

Established in 1994 in WY.
Donor(s): Oletha C. Likins.‡
Financial data (yr. ended 12/31/00): Grants paid, $38,700; assets, $980,568 (M); expenditures, $40,177; qualifying distributions, $37,931.
Limitations: Giving primarily in Goshen County, WY.
Application information: Application form required.
Officer and Trustees:* Kelly Vandel,* Chair.; Betty Anderson, James Fuller, Robert Heyl, Margaret Lee, Ellen Preston.
EIN: 836039257
Codes: GTI

58194
Business Advisory Council Foundation
P.O. Box 2673
Casper, WY 82602 (307) 266-0504
Application address: c/o Tina Elhart, Classroom Wyoming Project, P.O. Box 80, Casper, WY 82602; FAX: (307) 266-0501

Established in 1998 in WY.
Financial data (yr. ended 12/31/01): Grants paid, $38,015; assets, $41,663 (M); gifts received, $20,450; expenditures, $38,040; qualifying distributions, $37,986.
Limitations: Giving primarily in WY.
Officers: Margaret Benson, Chair.; T. Chris Muirhead, Secy.; John P. Jorgensen, Treas.
Directors: Ken Daraie, Tom Forslund, Rob Hurless, Jerry Moyle, Nick Murdock, Pat Nagel, Linda Nix, Gene Theriault.
EIN: 830304171
Codes: TN

58195
The Thomas A. & Diann G. Mann Foundation
P.O. Box 8129
Jackson, WY 83002 (307) 732-2121
Contact: Thomas A. Mann, Pres. or Diann G. Mann, V.P.

Established in 1996 in OH.
Donor(s): Diann G. Mann, Thomas A. Mann.
Financial data (yr. ended 12/31/01): Grants paid, $36,000; assets, $701,726 (M); expenditures, $40,239; qualifying distributions, $36,000.
Limitations: Giving on a national basis.

58195—WYOMING

Officers: Thomas A. Mann, Pres.; Diann G. Mann, V.P.; Richard Zellner, Secy.; Gerald Korngold, Treas.
Trustees: David Mann, William Mann, Julie Mann Simons.
EIN: 341847977

58196
Anderson Memorial Educational Trust
P.O. Box 519
Dubois, WY 82513-0519
Application address: c/o Scholarship Comm., P.O. Box 847, Dubois, WY 82513

Financial data (yr. ended 04/30/00): Grants paid, $32,750; assets, $642,806 (M); expenditures, $32,892; qualifying distributions, $32,892.
Limitations: Giving limited to Dubois, WY.
Trustees: Buck Butkovich, Jane Cheatham, Robert Cheatham, Barbara Shoemaker.
EIN: 836025176

58197
Woodson Family Foundation
c/o James Woodson
214 Lakeshore Dr.
Cheyenne, WY 82009

Donor(s): James Woodson.
Financial data (yr. ended 12/31/01): Grants paid, $32,450; assets, $278,529 (M); gifts received, $67,000; expenditures, $34,374; qualifying distributions, $32,450.
Limitations: Applications not accepted.
Application information: Contributes only to pre-selected organizations.
Officer: James Woodson, Mgr.
EIN: 830322634

58198
Anne & Scott Nickerson Family Foundation
56 Crown Dr.
P.O. Box 278
Big Horn, WY 82833

Established in 1997 in WY.
Donor(s): Scott Nickerson, Anne Nickerson.
Financial data (yr. ended 05/31/02): Grants paid, $29,750; assets, $797,455 (M); gifts received, $120,000; expenditures, $37,389; qualifying distributions, $29,750.
Limitations: Giving limited to Sheridan, WY.
Application information: Application form required.
Officers: Scott Nickerson, Pres.; Anne Nickerson, Secy.-Treas.
Directors: David Nickerson, Gregory Nickerson, Phillip Nickerson.
EIN: 841409098

58199
Glade M. Edwards Foundation, Inc.
c/o A.E. Hoffman
1030 Fremont St.
Thermopolis, WY 82443-2930
Application address: 1001 Araphoe, Thermopolis, WY 82443, tel.: (307) 864-5164
Contact: R.C. Johnson, V.P.

Established in 1985 in WY.
Financial data (yr. ended 06/30/00): Grants paid, $28,292; assets, $626,756 (M); gifts received, $375; expenditures, $30,069; qualifying distributions, $29,748.
Limitations: Giving limited to Thermopolis, WY.
Application information: Application form not required.
Officers and Directors:* Evelyn Welty,* Pres.; R.C. Johnson,* V.P. and Secy.; A.E. Hoffman,* Treas.
EIN: 830271524

Codes: GTI

58200
Tate Charitable Foundation
P.O. Box 2280
Casper, WY 82602
Application address: 200 S. Ctr., Casper, WY 82601, tel.: (307) 237-1400
Contact: William L. McDowell, Secy.

Established in 1994 in WY.
Donor(s): Inez M. Tate.
Financial data (yr. ended 11/30/01): Grants paid, $28,000; assets, $515,362 (M); expenditures, $29,991; qualifying distributions, $28,000.
Limitations: Giving limited to WY.
Application information: Application form required.
Officers: Inez M. Tate, Chair.; T. Chris Muirhead, Pres.; Donald E. Chapin, V.P.; William L. McDowell, Secy.; Dorothy A. Nichols, Treas.
Director: Eunice Griffin.
EIN: 830310832

58201
Likins-Masonic Memorial Trust
510 W. 27th Ave.
Torrington, WY 82240-1838
Contact: Gerald Connolly, Tr.

Established in 1994 in WY.
Donor(s): Oletha C. Likins.‡
Financial data (yr. ended 12/31/00): Grants paid, $27,216; assets, $1,102,075 (M); expenditures, $29,002; qualifying distributions, $28,168.
Application information: Application form required.
Trustees: Gerald Connolly, Larry Dodge, Mel Gabel, Dale Honstein.
EIN: 836041098
Codes: GTI

58202
Eileen M. Hunter Scholarship Fund
c/o Wells Fargo Bank Wyoming, N.A.
P.O. Box 2799
Casper, WY 82602
Application address: c/o Sharon J. Farrott, Teton County School Dist. No. 1, P.O. Box 568, Jackson, WY 83001

Donor(s): Eileen M. Hunter.‡
Financial data (yr. ended 12/31/00): Grants paid, $25,500; assets, $556,989 (M); expenditures, $29,754; qualifying distributions, $27,496.
Limitations: Giving limited to residents of Teton County School District No. 1, WY.
Application information: Application form required.
Trustee: Wells Fargo Bank Wyoming, N.A.
EIN: 836034396
Codes: GTI

58203
Ray and Kay Littler Trust
P.O. Box 922
Buffalo, WY 82834-0922 (307) 684-9595
Contact: G.L. Goddard, Tr.

Established in 1997.
Financial data (yr. ended 06/30/01): Grants paid, $25,289; assets, $962,298 (M); expenditures, $42,981; qualifying distributions, $26,887.
Limitations: Giving limited to residents of Johnson County, WY.
Application information: Application form required.
Trustees: G.L. Goddard, C.W. Johnson, D.D. Osborn.
EIN: 830320342

58204
Purdy Family Foundation
200 N. Wyoming Ave.
Buffalo, WY 82834

Established in 1995 in WY.
Donor(s): Virginia S. Purdy.
Financial data (yr. ended 12/31/01): Grants paid, $23,550; assets, $3,556,208 (M); gifts received, $5,032; expenditures, $26,709; qualifying distributions, $23,550.
Limitations: Applications not accepted.
Application information: Contributes only to pre-selected organizations.
Trustees: James R. Purdy, Virginia S. Purdy.
EIN: 830314774

58205
Arlene Wesswick Foundation
1624 Collins St.
Rock Springs, WY 82901 (307) 362-7462
Contact: Louis Wesswick, Pres.

Established in 1998 in WY.
Donor(s): Arlene Wesswick Revocable Living Trust.
Financial data (yr. ended 05/31/02): Grants paid, $22,000; assets, $430,155 (M); expenditures, $22,824; qualifying distributions, $22,000.
Officers: Louis Wesswick, Pres.; George Nelson, V.P.; Kerry W. Richards, Secy.
EIN: 841463861

58206
Sweet Life Foundation
P.O. Box 11540
Jackson, WY 83002

Established in 2000 in CA.
Donor(s): Thomas O. Muller, Anne A. Muller.
Financial data (yr. ended 12/31/01): Grants paid, $17,300; assets, $514,879 (M); gifts received, $7,525; expenditures, $25,599; qualifying distributions, $17,300.
Limitations: Applications not accepted.
Application information: Contributes only to pre-selected organizations.
Officers: Anne A. Muller, Pres.; Thomas O. Muller, Secy.-Treas.
EIN: 943382384

58207
Mary & Doc Robertson Handicapped Children's Trust
c/o Wells Fargo Bank Wyoming, N.A.
P.O. Box 2799
Casper, WY 82602-2799
Contact: S. Cobb

Financial data (yr. ended 03/31/02): Grants paid, $16,000; assets, $346,425 (M); expenditures, $18,794; qualifying distributions, $16,000.
Limitations: Giving primarily in Casper, WY.
Application information: Application form not required.
Trustee: Wells Fargo Bank Wyoming, N.A.
EIN: 510186287

58208
Etchepare Family Foundation
P.O. Box 848
Cheyenne, WY 82003
Application address: 1814 Warren Ave., Cheyenne, WY 82001, tel. (307) 634-1505

Established in 1991 in WY.
Donor(s): Paul G. Etchepare, Jr., Hellen Etchepare.
Financial data (yr. ended 12/31/01): Grants paid, $15,000; assets, $1,014,959 (M); gifts received, $15,217; expenditures, $17,041; qualifying distributions, $15,000.

Limitations: Giving primarily in Cheyenne, WY.
Application information: Application form not required.
Officers and Directors:* Paul G. Etchepare, Jr.,* Pres.; Rev. Carl A. Beavers, V.P.; LaVonna Beardsley,* Secy.; Antoinette E. Thomson,* Treas.; Rev. Carl A. Beavers, Angela E. Carter, John Etchepare.
EIN: 830297207

58209
Henry William Gillet Memorial, Inc.
P.O. Box 231
Pine Bluffs, WY 82082-0231 (307) 245-3504
Contact: J. William Parsons, V.P.

Financial data (yr. ended 06/30/00): Grants paid, $14,750; assets, $94,169 (M); expenditures, $16,428; qualifying distributions, $14,750; giving activities include $14,750 for loans to individuals.
Limitations: Giving limited to residents of Laramie County, WY.
Officers: Joyce Smock, Pres.; J. William Parsons, V.P.; Rudeen Malm, Secy.-Treas.
EIN: 237135637

58210
Stacy Marie True Memorial Trust
P.O. Box 2360
Casper, WY 82602
Contact: David L. True, Tr., or Melanie A. True, Tr.

Donor(s): H.A. True, Jr.
Financial data (yr. ended 06/30/01): Grants paid, $14,000; assets, $329,944 (M); gifts received, $10,561; expenditures, $15,375; qualifying distributions, $14,000.
Limitations: Giving primarily in Denver, CO.
Trustees: David L. True, Melanie A. True.
EIN: 830236856

58211
The Cheramy Foundation
970 W. Broadway, PMB 438
Jackson, WY 83001-9475
Contact: Shirley J. Cheramy, V.P.

Established in 1994 in WY.
Donor(s): Edward R. Cheramy, Shirley J. Cheramy.
Financial data (yr. ended 12/31/01): Grants paid, $12,400; assets, $1,629,935 (M); gifts received, $5,100; expenditures, $16,306; qualifying distributions, $12,400.
Limitations: Giving primarily in WY.
Officers: Edward R. Cheramy, Pres.; Shirley J. Cheramy, V.P. and Secy.-Treas.
Director: Susan A. Fisher.
EIN: 830310263

58212
Agape Foundation
(Formerly Warren and Martha Vangenderen Foundation)
P.O. Box 985
Jackson, WY 83001

Established in 1997 in WA & WY.
Donor(s): Martha Van Genderen, Warren Van Genderen.
Financial data (yr. ended 12/31/01): Grants paid, $12,000; assets, $246,452 (M); gifts received, $2,625; expenditures, $15,019; qualifying distributions, $12,000.
Limitations: Applications not accepted. Giving primarily in Pasadena, CA.
Application information: Contributes only to pre-selected organizations.
Officers: Warren Van Genderen, Pres. and Treas.; Martha Van Genderen, V.P. and Secy.
Directors: Todd Van Genderen, Courtney Woodside.

EIN: 830319884

58213
M. E. & Inez Tate Trust
c/o Wells Fargo Bank Wyoming, N.A.
P.O. Box 2799
Casper, WY 82602

Established in 2001 in WY.
Financial data (yr. ended 12/31/01): Grants paid, $11,298; assets, $1,300,503 (M); expenditures, $15,308; qualifying distributions, $11,298.
Limitations: Applications not accepted. Giving primarily in Casper, WY.
Application information: Contributes only to pre-selected organizations.
Trustee: Wells Fargo Bank Wyoming, N.A.
EIN: 836029197

58214
The Roberts Family Foundation
2 Soldier Creek Rd.
Sheridan, WY 82801

Donor(s): Sheri D. Teitjen, Donald H. Roberts, Roberts Family Fund.
Financial data (yr. ended 12/31/01): Grants paid, $10,600; assets, $513,750 (M); gifts received, $13,227; expenditures, $12,843; qualifying distributions, $10,600.
Limitations: Applications not accepted. Giving primarily in Sheridan, WY.
Application information: Contributes only to pre-selected organizations.
Officers: Donald B. Roberts, Pres.; Donald H. Roberts, Secy.-Treas.
Trustees: Ermal M. Roberts, Sheri D. Teitjen.
EIN: 742269660

58215
The Brooks Foundation
6810 N. Ellen Creek Rd.
P.O. Box 819
Teton Village, WY 83025-0819

Established in 2000 in WY.
Donor(s): T. Anthony Brooks.
Financial data (yr. ended 12/31/01): Grants paid, $10,330; assets, $1,488,716 (M); gifts received, $206,500; expenditures, $26,568; qualifying distributions, $10,330.
Limitations: Applications not accepted.
Application information: Contributes only to pre-selected organizations.
Trustees: T. Anthony Brooks, Linda Leith Brooks.
EIN: 223761279

58216
Dodd and Dorothy L. Bryan Foundation
c/o Rose Marie Madia
P.O. Box 6287
Sheridan, WY 82801 (307) 672-3535

Established in 1965 in WY.
Donor(s): Dorothy L. Bryan.‡
Financial data (yr. ended 12/31/01): Grants paid, $10,100; assets, $6,492,723 (M); expenditures, $91,448; qualifying distributions, $614,425; giving activities include $579,139 for loans to individuals.
Limitations: Giving limited to Powder River, Rosebud and Big Horn counties, MT, and Sheridan, Campbell and Johnson counties, WY.
Publications: Application guidelines.
Application information: Application form required.
Officers and Directors:* Arthur G. Felker, Pres.; Susan M. Van Allen, V.P.; Jack E. Pelissier,* Secy.; William B. Ebzery, Treas.; J. Leonard Graham.
EIN: 836006533
Codes: GTI

58217
Eldred Foundation, Inc.
c/o Robert E. Knight
429 W. 5th Ave.
Cheyenne, WY 82001

Financial data (yr. ended 12/31/01): Grants paid, $10,000; assets, $84,884 (M); expenditures, $10,025; qualifying distributions, $10,000.
Officers: Robert E. Knight, Chair.; E. Victor Eldred, Pres.; Martha K. Eldred, V.P. and Secy.-Treas.
Director: Carolyn S. Eldred.
EIN: 363444341

58218
The Frontiers Foundation, Inc.
P.O. Box 338
Moose, WY 83012-0095 (307) 733-7481
Contact: Michael Halpin, V.P. and Dir.

Established in 1998 in WY.
Donor(s): Gerald T. Halpin.
Financial data (yr. ended 12/31/01): Grants paid, $10,000; assets, $147,705 (M); gifts received, $1,500; expenditures, $13,539; qualifying distributions, $10,000.
Officers and Directors:* Gerald T. Halpin,* Pres. and Treas.; Michael T. Halpin,* V.P.; Peter T. Halpin,* V.P.; Christina L. Halpin,* Secy.; Helen H. Halpin.
EIN: 841407964

58219
Southeastern Wyoming Home Builders Scholarship Trust
P.O. Box 2066
Cheyenne, WY 82003 (307) 778-8222

Established in 1996 in WY.
Donor(s): Southeast Wyoming Home Builders Association.
Financial data (yr. ended 12/31/00): Grants paid, $8,750; assets, $218,466 (M); gifts received, $17,146; expenditures, $8,841; qualifying distributions, $8,661.
Limitations: Giving limited to residents of WY.
Officers and Trustee:* Maynard Richmeier,* Pres.; Sharon Radowicki, Treas.
EIN: 943161079

58220
Fehir Charitable Foundation
544 E. Bennett St.
Buffalo, WY 82834

Established in 1993.
Donor(s): John Fehir, Kim Fehir.
Financial data (yr. ended 12/31/00): Grants paid, $8,299; assets, $376,180 (M); gifts received, $7,000; expenditures, $16,642; qualifying distributions, $8,299.
Limitations: Applications not accepted. Giving primarily in Chicago, IL and Buffalo, WY.
Application information: Contributes only to pre-selected organizations.
Officers: John Fehir, Pres.; Kim Fehir, V.P.
Director: Mary Fehir.
EIN: 760426664

58221
The Tammy Hladky Foundation
c/o Tom Giblock
P.O. Box 908
Gillette, WY 82717-0908
Application address: 211 W. 7th, Gillette, WY 82718, tel.: (307) 682-9484
Contact: Susan L. Hladky, Dir.

Established in 1995 in WY.
Donor(s): James Hladky, Susan Hladky.

58221—WYOMING

Financial data (yr. ended 06/30/01): Grants paid, $7,600; assets, $184,397 (M); gifts received, $25,000; expenditures, $7,691; qualifying distributions, $7,585.
Limitations: Giving limited to residents of Campbell County, WY.
Application information: Application form required.
Directors: Tom Giblock, Susan L. Hladky, Ida Snead.
EIN: 830319044

58222
The George E. Ewan Family Foundation, Inc.
1112 Victoria St.
Sheridan, WY 82801 (307) 674-4255

Established in 1999 in WY.
Financial data (yr. ended 12/31/01): Grants paid, $7,500; assets, $202,824 (M); gifts received, $60,000; expenditures, $9,541; qualifying distributions, $7,500.
Application information: Application form not required.
Officers: George E. Ewan, Pres.; Robert Ewan, V.P.; Mrs. Robert Ewan, V.P.; Jeanne Ewan, Secy.-Treas.
Directors: Dana Arbaugh, Linda Arbaough, Loal Lorenzen, Mrs. Loal Lorenzen.
EIN: 830325285

58223
Glenard Johnson Charitable Trust
P.O. Box 148
Powell, WY 82435

Established in 1998.
Donor(s): Glenard Johnson.‡
Financial data (yr. ended 09/30/01): Grants paid, $7,500; assets, $1 (M); expenditures, $13,690; qualifying distributions, $7,500.
Limitations: Applications not accepted. Giving primarily in ID.
Application information: Contributes only to pre-selected organizations.
Trustee: David C. Ackley.
EIN: 820504793

58224
Eyas Foundation
P.O. Box 6769
Sheridan, WY 82801

Established in 1998 in WY.
Financial data (yr. ended 12/31/01): Grants paid, $7,230; assets, $1,575,061 (M); gifts received, $552,328; expenditures, $25,651; qualifying distributions, $16,394.
Limitations: Applications not accepted.
Application information: Contributes only to pre-selected organizations.
Trustees: Richard M. Davis, Jr., Edward A. Hoffman, P.A.B. Widener, Jr.
EIN: 830321698

58225
The Wilbur & Birdie Williams Trust
(Formerly Wilbur & Birdie Williams Scholarship Fund)
P.O. Box 400
Buffalo, WY 82834-0400
Contact: George Schafer, Tr.

Financial data (yr. ended 12/31/01): Grants paid, $7,000; assets, $130,930 (M); expenditures, $7,615; qualifying distributions, $7,200.
Limitations: Giving limited to residents of Johnson County, WY.
Trustees: Scott Gibbs, Timothy Kirven, George Schafer.
EIN: 830234332

58226
The Mary Frances Blackstone & Jack Dieterich Foundation
c/o Pauline Dunnuck
1273 N. 15th St., Ste. 121
Laramie, WY 82072

Established in 2000.
Donor(s): Mary Frances Blackstone.
Financial data (yr. ended 12/31/01): Grants paid, $6,900; assets, $120,716 (M); gifts received, $30,182; expenditures, $15,112; qualifying distributions, $6,900.
Limitations: Applications not accepted.
Application information: Contributes only to pre-selected organizations.
Officers: Mary Frances Blackstone, Pres.; Ann C. Williams, Secy.; Jean Christensen, C.F.O.
EIN: 830332574

58227
Luskey Family Foundation
14950 S. McCoy Rd.
Jackson, WY 83001-8884

Established in 2000 in WY.
Donor(s): Randolph K. Luskey, Nicole Christian Luskey.
Financial data (yr. ended 12/31/01): Grants paid, $6,835; assets, $828,540 (M); expenditures, $7,055; qualifying distributions, $6,835.
Limitations: Applications not accepted.
Application information: Contributes only to pre-selected organizations.
Trustees: Nicole Christian Luskey, Randolph K. Luskey.
EIN: 316652919

58228
John B. Speight Family Foundation
4021 Snyder Ave.
Cheyenne, WY 82001-1170 (307) 635-1239
Contact: John B. Speight, Pres.

Established in 1992 in WY.
Donor(s): John B. Speight.
Financial data (yr. ended 12/31/01): Grants paid, $6,775; assets, $116,210 (M); expenditures, $7,418; qualifying distributions, $6,775.
Limitations: Giving primarily in Cheyenne, WY.
Application information: Application form not required.
Officers: John B. Speight, Pres.; Carol Speight, Secy.
Director: Robert T. McCue.
EIN: 830302043

58229
Furrer Foundation
c/o John Furrer
P.O. Box 10849
Jackson, WY 83002

Established in 1986 in IL.
Donor(s): John Furrer.
Financial data (yr. ended 06/30/02): Grants paid, $6,500; assets, $63,614 (M); expenditures, $6,559; qualifying distributions, $6,500.
Limitations: Applications not accepted. Giving primarily in Vero Beach, FL, and Jackson Hole, WY.
Application information: Contributes only to pre-selected organizations.
Directors: Annie W. Furrer, Blake Furrer, John R. Furrer, Kimberly Van Nortwick.
EIN: 363496954

58230
W. K. Poulson Trust
c/o Community First National Bank
P.O. Box 9000
Sheridan, WY 82801

Financial data (yr. ended 05/31/02): Grants paid, $6,453; assets, $133,586 (M); expenditures, $8,633; qualifying distributions, $6,453.
Limitations: Applications not accepted. Giving limited to Sheridan, WY.
Application information: Contributes only to a pre-selected organization.
Trustee: Community First National Bank.
EIN: 836015044

58231
Buffalo High School Development Fund, Inc.
P.O. Box 324
Buffalo, WY 82834-1629
Application address: 601 W. Lott St., Buffalo, WY 82834
Contact: Rod Kessler, Dir.

Financial data (yr. ended 12/31/00): Grants paid, $6,186; assets, $139,517 (M); expenditures, $6,665; qualifying distributions, $6,505.
Limitations: Giving limited to residents of Buffalo, WY.
Directors: Marilyn Connolly, Kate Holt, Rod Kessler, Stan Lakin, Marilyn Novotny.
EIN: 830324160

58232
John B. & Dorothy D. Duncan Music for Sheridan Foundation
c/o First Interstate Bank of Commerce
P.O. Box 2007
Sheridan, WY 82801-2007 (307) 672-1490
Contact: Jerome T. Pilch

Established in 1994 in WY.
Financial data (yr. ended 12/31/01): Grants paid, $5,750; assets, $124,192 (M); expenditures, $7,102; qualifying distributions, $5,750.
Limitations: Giving primarily in WY.
Trustees: Robert James Wyatt, First Interstate Bank of Commerce.
EIN: 830309303

58233
Harold and Myrtle Hobson Educational Scholarship Fund
707 Circle Dr.
Wheatland, WY 82201 (307) 322-2882
Application address: Box 189, Wheatland, WY 82201
Contact: Bill Vines

Established in 1995 in WY.
Financial data (yr. ended 12/31/99): Grants paid, $5,572; assets, $170,140 (M); expenditures, $7,501; qualifying distributions, $5,572.
Limitations: Giving limited to residents of Wheatland, WY.
Application information: Application form required.
Trustee: Hugo Lenz.
EIN: 830310202

58234
James and Florence Depolo Foundation
P.O. Box 12469
Jackson, WY 83002-2469

Donor(s): Florence Depolo, James Depolo.
Financial data (yr. ended 12/31/00): Grants paid, $5,200; assets, $6,411 (M); gifts received, $6,000; expenditures, $5,987; qualifying distributions, $5,200.
Limitations: Applications not accepted.

Application information: Contributes only to pre-selected organizations.
Trustees: David Depolo, Florence Depolo, James Depolo.
EIN: 830320187

58235
Meadowlark Foundation
c/o Richard M. Davis, Jr.
P.O. Box 728
Sheridan, WY 82801

Financial data (yr. ended 12/31/01): Grants paid, $5,000; assets, $295,530 (M); gifts received, $134,672; expenditures, $15,302; qualifying distributions, $5,000.
Limitations: Giving primarily in Denver, CO.
Trustees: Pamela Davis Beardsley, Richard M. Davis, Jr., Bridget C. Fisher, Edward A. Hoffman, A. Gordon Rippey.
EIN: 830328313

58236
Leslie Foundation for Christian Ministries
c/o James E. Leslie
3060 S. Stirrup Dr.
Jackson, WY 83001-9123

Established in 1989 in WY.
Donor(s): James E. Leslie, Barbara E. Leslie.
Financial data (yr. ended 12/31/01): Grants paid, $4,686; assets, $86,580 (M); expenditures, $11,605; qualifying distributions, $4,686.
Limitations: Applications not accepted. Giving primarily in WY.
Application information: Contributes only to pre-selected organizations.
Officers: James E. Leslie, Pres.; Randy Foster, V.P.; Barbara E. Leslie, Secy.-Treas.
EIN: 830292703

58237
Ardon Foundation
(Formerly Eaton Scholarship)
c/o Eugene C. Eaton
P.O. Box 50157
Casper, WY 82605-0157 (307) 234-0201
Contact: Eugene C. Eaton, Tr.

Established in 1993 in WY.
Donor(s): Eugene C. Eaton, Ardith L. Eaton.
Financial data (yr. ended 12/31/99): Grants paid, $4,500; assets, $109,820 (M); gifts received, $5,357; expenditures, $5,057; qualifying distributions, $4,326.
Limitations: Giving limited to residents of WY.
Trustees: Ardith L. Eaton, Eugene C. Eaton, Inda A. Eaton, Richard A. Eaton.
EIN: 830305899

58238
Higby Trust
c/o Wells Fargo Bank Wyoming, N.A.
P.O. Box 2799
Casper, WY 82602-2799
Application address: Joe R. Kenney, P.O. Box 430, Lander, WY 82520, tel.: (307) 332-5683

Financial data (yr. ended 12/31/01): Grants paid, $4,250; assets, $96,578 (M); expenditures, $6,156; qualifying distributions, $4,250.
Limitations: Giving limited to WY high school graduates.
Trustee: Wells Fargo Bank Wyoming, N.A.
EIN: 237046350
Codes: GTI

58239
Edward J. Redle Memorial Foundation
c/o Peter C. Carroll
14 Estates Country Dr.
Sheridan, WY 82801

Financial data (yr. ended 12/31/01): Grants paid, $3,500; assets, $61,058 (M); gifts received, $595; expenditures, $3,950; qualifying distributions, $3,500.
Limitations: Applications not accepted. Giving limited to Sheridan, WY.
Application information: Contributes only to pre-selected organizations.
Officers and Directors:* Matthew F. Redle,* Pres.; E.A. Rotellini,* V.P.; Homer A. Scott, Jr.,* Secy.; Peter C. Carroll,* Treas.; Ed Brantz, Joe Dudrey, Patrick M. Meehan, David Mullinax, Floyd A. Songer, David J. Withrow.
EIN: 742115160

58240
The Veritas Foundation
P. O. Box 185
Wilson, WY 83014-0185
Contact: Charles I. Brown, Pres.

Established in 1995 in CO.
Donor(s): Charles I. Brown.
Financial data (yr. ended 12/31/00): Grants paid, $3,500; assets, $71,333 (M); expenditures, $3,506; qualifying distributions, $3,500.
Limitations: Giving primarily in Los Gatos, CA and Washington, DC.
Officers and Directors:* Charles I. Brown,* Pres. and Treas.; Kathleen M. Brown,* V.P. and Secy.; Dana S. Brown, Kelly M. Casterline, Tracy A. Lislac.
EIN: 841327469

58241
Ciel Foundation
P.O. Box 208
Moose, WY 83012 (307) 733-7995
Contact: Richard B. Black, Tr.

Established in 1994 in WY.
Donor(s): Richard B. Black.
Financial data (yr. ended 12/31/01): Grants paid, $3,000; assets, $436,907 (M); expenditures, $4,872; qualifying distributions, $3,500.
Limitations: Giving primarily in NY.
Trustees: Kathryn Ciel Black, Richard B. Black.
EIN: 830310522

58242
Lisle Lanier Scholarship Fund
c/o First National Bank of Buffalo
P.O. Box 400
Buffalo, WY 82834-0400
Contact: George J. Schafer, Trust Off., First National Bank of Buffalo

Established in 1985 in WY.
Financial data (yr. ended 06/30/00): Grants paid, $3,000; assets, $86,477 (M); expenditures, $4,210; qualifying distributions, $3,845.
Limitations: Giving limited to Johnson County, WY.
Trustees: James C. Guyton, Donald P. Kraen, George J. Schafer.
EIN: 742382401

58243
Lek Foundation
324 Wagon Box Rd.
Banner, WY 82832-9603

Established in 2000 in MN.
Donor(s): Louise B. Plank.

Financial data (yr. ended 12/31/01): Grants paid, $3,000; assets, $2,005,138 (M); gifts received, $81,000; expenditures, $15,668; qualifying distributions, $3,000.
Limitations: Applications not accepted.
Application information: Contributes only to pre-selected organizations.
Officer: Louise B. Plank, Pres.
EIN: 311725655

58244
Zona and Jack Loomis Platte County School District No. 1 Scholarship Trust
P.O. Drawer 189
Wheatland, WY 82201-0189 (307) 322-2882
Contact: W.H. Vines, Mgr.

Established in 1993.
Donor(s): Zona R. Loomis.‡
Financial data (yr. ended 01/31/00): Grants paid, $3,000; assets, $104,765 (M); expenditures, $4,419; qualifying distributions, $4,383.
Limitations: Giving limited to residents of Platte County, WY.
Application information: Application form required.
Officer and Directors:* W.H. Vines,* Mgr.; Don Brungelson, Meryl Lockwood, Mary Alice Stapelton.
EIN: 836036074

58245
Fitzgerald Foundation for Children
2108 Warren Ave.
Cheyenne, WY 82001-3740 (307) 634-4000
Contact: James Fitzgerald, Tr.

Established in 1998.
Donor(s): James E. Fitzgerald.
Financial data (yr. ended 03/31/00): Grants paid, $2,750; assets, $5,096 (M); gifts received, $1,500; expenditures, $10,023; qualifying distributions, $2,750; giving activities include $10,023 for programs.
Trustee: James E. Fitzgerald.
EIN: 830322737

58246
Davis-Roberts Scholarship Fund, Inc.
P. O. Box 20645
Cheyenne, WY 82003 (307) 632-0491
Application address: 342 Bocage Dr., Cheyenne, WY 82009-3524
Contact: Gary D. Skillern, Secy.

Donor(s): Glenn Swain.‡
Financial data (yr. ended 12/31/01): Grants paid, $2,500; assets, $73,142 (M); expenditures, $2,758; qualifying distributions, $2,758.
Limitations: Giving limited to WY.
Application information: Application form required.
Officers and Trustees:* Charles H. Moore,* Pres.; William H. Smith,* V.P.; Gary D. Skillern, Secy.-Treas.; Frank W. Angeli, Earl Christensen, Raymond H. Clark, James Daly, Charles W. Edwards, Michael L. James, Thomas N. Long, Jack E. Nixon, George C. Smith, Richard V. Thomas.
EIN: 836011403
Codes: GTI

58247
The Three T's Foundation
c/o Christopher Hawks, PC
P.O. Box 1495, 350 E. Bway.
Jackson, WY 83001

Established in 1997 in WY.
Donor(s): Michael H. Monier.
Financial data (yr. ended 12/31/00): Grants paid, $2,430; assets, $642,664 (M); gifts received,

58247—WYOMING

$120,675; expenditures, $2,802; qualifying distributions, $2,430.
Limitations: Applications not accepted.
Application information: Contributes only to pre-selected organizations.
Trustees: Brett Monier Giuliano, Michael H. Monier, Nicole Monier.
EIN: 137117633

58248
McDaniel Memorial Scholarship Fund
c/o Wayne Coates
2015 Baldwin Cr. Rd.
Lander, WY 82520
Application address: c/o Superintendent, Fremont County SD No. 1, Lander, WY 82520

Established in 1988 in WY.
Financial data (yr. ended 12/31/01): Grants paid, $1,650; assets, $71,104 (M); expenditures, $5,386; qualifying distributions, $1,664.
Limitations: Giving limited to residents of Lander, WY.
Application information: Application form required.
Trustee: Wayne Coates.
EIN: 830287371

58249
Gerald F. & Rose M. Kaul Foundation, Inc.
60 McCormick Rd.
Sheridan, WY 82801 (307) 672-7088
Contact: Gerald F. Kaul, Pres.

Established in 2000 in WY.
Donor(s): Gerald F. Kaul.
Financial data (yr. ended 12/31/01): Grants paid, $1,500; assets, $55,226 (M); expenditures, $5,500; qualifying distributions, $2,050.
Limitations: Giving limited to Sheridan, WY.
Application information: Application form required.
Officers: Gerald F. Kaul, Pres.; Tracy L. Eisele, V.P.; Teresa D. Kaul, Secy.; Cameron G. Kaul, Treas.
Directors: Rose M. Kaul, Rev. Ronald D. Nelson, Robert James Wyatt.
EIN: 830330570

58250
The Peter & Anna Gorgen Fund Charitable Trust
c/o First National Bank
P.O. Box 400
Buffalo, WY 82834
Alternate application address: Dennis Kirven, Tr., 104 Fort St., Buffalo, WY 82834
Contact: George Schafer, Tr.

Financial data (yr. ended 12/31/01): Grants paid, $1,057; assets, $103,575 (M); expenditures, $3,272; qualifying distributions, $2,511.
Limitations: Giving limited to residents of Johnson County, WY.
Trustees: Raymond A. Holt, Dennis Kirven, George Schafer.
EIN: 742250389

58251
Peter J. DePaul Memorial Foundation
P.O. Box 5039
Cheyenne, WY 82003-5039

Financial data (yr. ended 09/30/01): Grants paid, $1,000; assets, $17,700 (M); expenditures, $1,054; qualifying distributions, $1,000.
Limitations: Applications not accepted. Giving primarily in VT.
Application information: Contributes only to pre-selected organizations.
Officers: Jane D. Weskamp, Pres.; Jean Cochman, Treas.
Director: Russell J. Weskamp, Jr.

EIN: 830267047

58252
Niels P. Nielson Scholarship Fund
c/o First National Bank of Buffalo
P.O. Box 400
Buffalo, WY 82834-0400
Contact: George Schafer, Trust Off., First National Bank of Buffalo

Established in 1989 in WY.
Donor(s): Niels P. Nielson Trust.
Financial data (yr. ended 12/31/00): Grants paid, $900; assets, $19,984 (M); expenditures, $1,217; qualifying distributions, $1,093.
Limitations: Giving limited to Johnson County, WY.
Application information: Application form required.
Trustees: Della Johnson, First National Bank of Buffalo.
EIN: 836035370

58253
The Harold Cash Memorial Scholarship Fund Charitable Trust
P.O. Box 1044
Buffalo, WY 82834-1044 (307) 684-5198
Contact: Diana Borgialli, Tr.

Established in 1984 in WY.
Financial data (yr. ended 03/31/99): Grants paid, $800; assets, $4,730 (M); expenditures, $816; qualifying distributions, $814.
Limitations: Giving limited to residents of Johnson County, WY.
Application information: Application form required.
Trustees: Diana Borgialli, Gerry W. Miller, Steve Vercimak.
EIN: 742342848

58254
Wind River Valley Artists Guild
P.O. Box 26
Dubois, WY 82513-0026
Application address: P.O. Box 1099, Dubois, WY 82513
Contact: Charlotte Verhuel

Established in 1997 in WY.
Financial data (yr. ended 12/31/00): Grants paid, $500; assets, $186,186 (M); gifts received, $16,468; expenditures, $61,769; qualifying distributions, $29,085; giving activities include $32,910 for programs.
Limitations: Giving primarily in Dubois, WY.
Officers: Leota Didier, Pres.; Judy Christensen, Secy.; Alyse Bell, Treas.
Board Members: Greg Beecham, Laurie Ideker, Wanda Knowles, Leon Sanderson.
EIN: 510189034

58255
Friends of Our Lady of Guadalupe Youth Center, Inc.
1106 Front St.
Wheatland, WY 82201
Application address: 7247 Sausalito, Canoga Park, CA 91304, tel.: (818) 340-3123
Contact: Jose Duran, V.P.

Financial data (yr. ended 04/30/02): Grants paid, $400; assets, $1 (M); expenditures, $826; qualifying distributions, $400.
Limitations: Giving primarily in Canoga Park, CA.
Officers: Silvia Hernandez, Pres.; Jose Duran, V.P. and Treas.; Sarah Angulo, Recording Secy.; Shirley Jackson, Secy.
EIN: 956061083

58256
Patricia Hockett Memorial Scholarship Fund
c/o First National Bank of Buffalo
P.O. Box 400
Buffalo, WY 82834-0400

Financial data (yr. ended 06/30/99): Grants paid, $234; assets, $4,699 (M); gifts received, $100; expenditures, $234; qualifying distributions, $232.
Limitations: Giving limited to Buffalo, WY.
Application information: Application form required.
Trustees: John Hockett, Rick O. Newton, George Schafer.
EIN: 830268632

58257
Muriel E. Spacht Memorial Fund
1058 Duna Dr.
Laramie, WY 82072-5017
Application address: c/o Robert Pfister, Box 1077, Lusk, WY 82225
Contact: Donabelle Hollon, Tr., or Robert Pfister, Tr.

Financial data (yr. ended 08/31/99): Grants paid, $188; assets, $128,240 (M); expenditures, $1,807; qualifying distributions, $188.
Limitations: Giving limited to Niobrara County, WY.
Trustees: Donabelle Hollon, Robert Pfister.
EIN: 830245539

58258
Scarlett Family Foundation
P.O. Box 12139
Jackson, WY 83002-2139

Financial data (yr. ended 12/31/01): Grants paid, $55; assets, $5,197 (M); gifts received, $55; expenditures, $555; qualifying distributions, $55.
Limitations: Applications not accepted. Giving limited in Jackson, WY.
Application information: Contributes only to pre-selected organizations.
Officers: W. Richard Scarlett III, Pres.; Margaret Scarlett, Secy.-Treas.
EIN: 830323685

58259
Richard Black Foundation
P.O. Box 208
Moose, WY 83012 (307) 733-7995
Contact: Richard B. Black, Tr.

Established in 1995 in WY.
Donor(s): Richard B. Black.
Financial data (yr. ended 12/31/01): Grants paid, $0; assets, $1,629 (M); gifts received, $100; expenditures, $500; qualifying distributions, $500.
Limitations: Giving primarily in NY.
Trustees: Richard B. Black, Nara Cadorin.
EIN: 830310523

58260
Black-Periman Foundation
P.O. Box 208
Moose, WY 83012 (307) 733-7995
Contact: Richard B. Black, Tr.

Established in 1994 in WY.
Donor(s): Richard B. Black.
Financial data (yr. ended 12/31/01): Grants paid, $0; assets, $440,230 (M); expenditures, $1,872; qualifying distributions, $500.
Limitations: Giving primarily in NY.
Trustees: Erica Black-Periman, Richard B. Black, Nara Cadorin.
EIN: 830310521

58261
Alvin T. Clark Family Memorial Fund
c/o George Schafer
P.O. Box 400
Buffalo, WY 82834-0400

Established in 1989 in WY.
Financial data (yr. ended 12/31/00): Grants paid, $0; assets, $290,627 (M); expenditures, $2,220; qualifying distributions, $17,220; giving activities include $16,000 for loans to individuals.
Limitations: Giving limited to Buffalo, WY.
Application information: Application form required.
Trustees: Jim Guyton, Cleo W. Johnson, First National Bank.
EIN: 836025848
Codes: GTI

58262
Cross Charitable Foundation, Inc.
P.O. Box 849
Pinedale, WY 82941

Donor(s): C. Walker Cross.
Financial data (yr. ended 12/31/01): Grants paid, $0; assets, $83,536 (M); gifts received, $50,000; expenditures, $2,340; qualifying distributions, $0.
Limitations: Applications not accepted.
Application information: Contributes only to pre-selected organizations.
Officers: C. Walker Cross, Pres.; Charles Folland, V.P.; Terri Anderson, Secy.; John R. Clark, Treas.
Director: Rex Child.
EIN: 830331707

58263
The Frances Blayney Curtis Foundation
P.O. Box 405
Dayton, WY 82836
Application address: P.O. Box 176, Dayton, WY 82836, tel.: (307) 655-9260
Contact: Bonnie Marquiss, Secy.-Treas.

Established in 1992 in WY.
Donor(s): Frank B. Curtis.
Financial data (yr. ended 12/31/00): Grants paid, $0; assets, $524,295 (M); expenditures, $1,372; qualifying distributions, $38,671; giving activities include $38,215 for loans to individuals.
Limitations: Giving limited to residents of Sheridan County, WY.
Application information: Application form required.
Officers and Trustees:* Dorothy King,* Pres.; Clayton Curtis,* V.P.; Bonnie Marquiss,* Secy.-Treas.
EIN: 830300312
Codes: GTI

58264
Jon S. and Lyndon J. Ellefson Foundation, Inc.
(Formerly Jon S. Ellefson Foundation, Inc.)
P.O. Box 1028
Wilson, WY 83014-1028
Contact: Nyles Ellefson, Pres.

Donor(s): Nyles Ellefson.
Financial data (yr. ended 12/31/01): Grants paid, $0; assets, $61,085 (M); gifts received, $10,025; expenditures, $442; qualifying distributions, $0.
Limitations: Giving primarily in AL, WI, and WY.
Officers: Nyles Ellefson, Pres.; Jane Ellefson, V.P.; Ruth Ellefson, Secy.-Treas.
EIN: 510185472

58265
Fremont County Diabetes Education Foundation
(Formerly Bishop Randall Hospital Memorial Foundation)
185 S. 5th St.
Lander, WY 82520-3001

Financial data (yr. ended 12/31/00): Grants paid, $0; assets, $13,101 (M); expenditures, $1,746; qualifying distributions, $0.
Limitations: Applications not accepted. Giving primarily in WY.
Officers: Marty Ridenour, Pres.; Realla Gustafson, V.P.; Micky Schuster, Secy.; Dean McKee, Treas.
Directors: Frank Dusl, Sally Webster, Craig Wilkins.
EIN: 237375936
Codes: TN

58266
Guthrie Family Foundation
1800 Garfield
Laramie, WY 82070

Established in 2001.
Donor(s): Jack Guthrie, Pat Guthrie.
Financial data (yr. ended 12/31/01): Grants paid, $0; assets, $509,562 (M); gifts received, $505,450; expenditures, $0; qualifying distributions, $0.
Directors: Ellen J. Guthrie, John A. Guthrie, Jr., John A. Guthrie III.
EIN: 830314146

58267
Higgins Foundation
P.O. Box 6769
Sheridan, WY 82801

Financial data (yr. ended 12/31/01): Grants paid, $0; assets, $937,241 (M); gifts received, $374,801; expenditures, $16,908; qualifying distributions, $0.
Limitations: Applications not accepted.
Application information: Contributes only to pre-selected organizations.
Trustees: Richard M. Davis, Jr., Edward A. Hoffman, Joseph C. Widener.
EIN: 830321699

58268
McNeill Family Foundation
c/o Dorice S. McNeill
Box 8 Skyline Ranch, 525 N.W. Ridge Rd.
Jackson, WY 83001

Established in 2001 in WY.
Donor(s): Corbin A. McNeill, Jr.
Financial data (yr. ended 12/31/01): Grants paid, $0; assets, $446,146 (M); gifts received, $431,423; expenditures, $0; qualifying distributions, $0.
Limitations: Applications not accepted.
Application information: Contributes only to pre-selected organizations.
Officers: Corbin A. McNeill, Jr., V.P.; Dorice S. McNeill, Secy.
Directors: Alicia McNeill, Corbin McNeill IV, Kevin McNeill, Timothy McNeill, Michele Poirer-McNeill.
EIN: 364475641

58269
Mission of Mercy Foundation
799 S. 2nd St.
Lander, WY 82520-3703

Established in 1993 in WY.
Donor(s): Dale Peterson, Walt Girgen.
Financial data (yr. ended 04/30/01): Grants paid, $0; assets, $3,111 (M); gifts received, $21,664; expenditures, $24,374; qualifying distributions, $24,374; giving activities include $24,374 for programs.
Officers and Directors:* Irene Thomason,* Pres.; Mark Moxley,* V.P.; Melissa Brasel,* Secy.-Treas.; Nick Ecked.
EIN: 830288032

58270
Bess Muir Memorial Fund
326 S. Burritt Ave.
Buffalo, WY 82834-2139 (307) 684-2269

Financial data (yr. ended 12/31/99): Grants paid, $0; assets, $4,925 (M); expenditures, $14; qualifying distributions, $14.
Limitations: Giving limited to Buffalo, WY.
Application information: Application form required.
Trustee: Stan Lakin.
EIN: 836007488

58271
Sheridan County Fairgrounds Foundation
P.O. Box 6753
Sheridan, WY 82801-3260

Established in 1989.
Financial data (yr. ended 12/31/01): Grants paid, $0; assets, $6,584 (M); expenditures, $140; qualifying distributions, $0.
Limitations: Applications not accepted.
Application information: Contributes only to pre-selected organizations.
Officers: James House, Pres.; Matt Johnston, V.P.; Jean Strauser, Secy.; Susan Miller, Secy.
Director: Tim Brown.
EIN: 830289796

58272
The Sheridan Research Institute
(Formerly Sheridan Health Research Center)
1949 Sugarland Dr., Ste. 250
Sheridan, WY 82801

Established in 1999 in WY.
Donor(s): Joseph S. Schuchert, Karalyn R. Schuchert, Schuchert Foundation.
Financial data (yr. ended 12/31/00): Grants paid, $0; assets, $21,942 (M); gifts received, $475,617; expenditures, $457,060; qualifying distributions, $0; giving activities include $455,531 for programs.
Officers: Joseph S. Schuchert, Pres.; Karalyn R. Schuchert, V.P.; Timothy E. Brown, Secy.; Carla J. Ash, Treas.
EIN: 830326016

58273
Soka 'Piiwa Foundation
P.O. Box 6769
Sheridan, WY 82801

Financial data (yr. ended 12/31/01): Grants paid, $0; assets, $1,203,485 (M); gifts received, $440,555; expenditures, $16,961; qualifying distributions, $0.
Limitations: Applications not accepted. Giving primarily in MT.
Application information: Contributes only to pre-selected organizations.
Trustees: Richard M. Davis, Jr., Edward A. Hoffman, George D. Widener.
EIN: 830321664

58274
M. E. Tate Trust
c/o Donald E. Chapin
P.O. Box 2280
Casper, WY 82602

Established in 2001 in WY.

58274—WYOMING

Donor(s): M.E. Tate.
Financial data (yr. ended 12/31/01): Grants paid, $0; assets, $971,126 (M); expenditures, $10,154; qualifying distributions, $0.
Limitations: Applications not accepted. Giving primarily in Casper, WY.
Application information: Contributes only to pre-selected organizations.
Trustee: Donald E. Chapin.
EIN: 836014364

58275
Thomas the Apostle Center
34 Thomas the Aplostle Rd.
Cody, WY 82414

Established in 1994.

Financial data (yr. ended 12/31/00): Grants paid, $0; assets, $494,945 (M); gifts received, $58,706; expenditures, $68,952; qualifying distributions, $45,242; giving activities include $44,943 for programs.
Limitations: Applications not accepted. Giving primarily in WY.
Application information: Contributes only to pre-selected organizations.
Officers: Rev. Daphne Grimes, Pres.; Lili Turnell, Secy.; Rev. Warren Murphy, Treas.
Directors: Right Rev. Bruce Caldwell, Paul Gray, Jean McLean, L. Ann Wafer, Laurie Kedrich.
EIN: 830294212

58276
The Vega Foundation
P.O. Box 11458
Jackson, WY 83002

Established in 2000 in WY.
Donor(s): Gary K. Silberberg.
Financial data (yr. ended 11/30/01): Grants paid, $0; assets, $205,648 (M); gifts received, $41,038; expenditures, $500; qualifying distributions, $500.
Limitations: Applications not accepted.
Application information: Contributes only to pre-selected organizations.
Trustees: Veronica K. Ho, Gary K. Silberberg.
EIN: 223787992

OPERATING FOUNDATIONS
Within each state, foundations are listed in descending order by asset amount

OPERATING FOUNDATIONS

ALABAMA

58277
Lakeshore Foundation
3800 Ridgeway Dr.
Birmingham, AL 35209 (205) 868-2303
URL: http://www.trussville.net/lakeshore/baskball.html
Contact: Jeffrey T. Underwood, Pres.

Established in 1942 in AL.
Financial data (yr. ended 09/30/00): Assets, $108,323,740 (M); grants paid, $49,095; gifts received, $1,817,615; expenditures, $3,970,120; qualifying distributions, $8,218,644; giving activities include $1,774,589 for programs.
Limitations: Giving only in AL.
Publications: Newsletter, informational brochure.
Officers and Directors:* Michael E. Stephens,* Chair.; William P. Acker III,* Vice-Chair.; Jeffrey T. Underwood,* Pres.; Cathy S. Crenshaw,* Secy.; William J. Billingsley,* Treas.; Tom Angelillo, Walter M. Beale, Jr., Dell Brooke, Robert O. Burton, Jennifer K. Chandler, David Corbally, Robert M. Couch, Bill Crawford, Derrol Dawkins, M.D., James H. Emack, Sr., Antoinette Smith Epps, Herman Frazier, James P. Hayes, Jr., Larry D. Striplin, Jr., Thomas K. Yardley, and 10 additional directors.
EIN: 630288847

58278
Alpha Foundation, Inc.
159 Stoneway Trail
Madison, AL 35758
Contact: Lonnie S. McMillian

Donor(s): Lonnie S. McMillian.
Financial data (yr. ended 12/31/00): Assets, $22,185,545 (M); grants paid, $6,105,000; gifts received, $57,412,500; expenditures, $6,187,615; qualifying distributions, $6,157,453.
Limitations: Giving primarily in AL.
Directors: Barbara M. Fisk, Emily M. Key, Helen W. McMillian, Lonnie S. McMillian, Susan M. Whitehead, John R. Wynn.
EIN: 631188643
Codes: FD, FM

58279
Barber Vintage Motorsports Museum
27 Inverness Center Pkwy.
Birmingham, AL 35242

Established in 1993 in AL.
Donor(s): The Barber Companies, The George W. Barber, Jr. Foundation.
Financial data (yr. ended 12/31/00): Assets, $14,687,590 (M); grants paid, $0; gifts received, $5,703,820; expenditures, $7,928,113; qualifying distributions, $7,323,165; giving activities include $7,921,896 for programs.
Officers: George W. Barber, Jr., Pres.; Russell M. Cunningham III, V.P.; B. Austin Cunningham, Secy.; James N. Hicks, Treas.; Jeffrey A. Ray, Exec. Dir.
Director: Lynn L. Woehle.
EIN: 631125485

58280
The Benevolent Home of the Episcopal Diocese of the Central Gulf Coast
(Formerly Mobile Female Benevolent Society)
1257 Government St.
Mobile, AL 36604

Classified as a private operating foundation in 1989.
Financial data (yr. ended 12/31/99): Assets, $5,809,208 (M); grants paid, $0; gifts received, $23,258; expenditures, $1,042,664; qualifying distributions, $917,919; giving activities include $917,919 for programs.
Officers and Directors:* Lewis G. Odom, Jr.,* Pres.; Sally Greene,* V.P.; Carolyn Levensallor,* Secy.; Jack Solberger,* Treas.; Robert G. Baker, and 9 additional directors.
EIN: 630302149

58281
Roth Hook Foundation
P.O. Box 1169
Vernon, AL 35592-1169
Application address: c/o John Russell, Tr., P.O. Box 333, Aliceville, AL 35642, tel.: (205) 373-8714
Contact: Teresa Dunlap, Tr.

Established in 1988 in AL.
Financial data (yr. ended 07/31/01): Assets, $2,280,524 (M); grants paid, $123,397; expenditures, $136,031; qualifying distributions, $133,204.
Limitations: Giving primarily in Aliceville, AL.
Application information: Application form not required.
Trustees: Teresa Dunlap, John Russell.
EIN: 630985062
Codes: FD2

58282
Jasmine Hill Foundation
c/o Jim T. Inscoe
P.O. Box 6001
Montgomery, AL 36106

Established in 1996 in AL.
Donor(s): Elmore B. Inscoe, Jim T. Inscoe, Elmore I. Demott, Allison I. Chandler.
Financial data (yr. ended 11/30/99): Assets, $1,672,230 (M); grants paid, $0; gifts received, $11,995; expenditures, $421,859; qualifying distributions, $243,633; giving activities include $157,409 for programs.
Officers: Jim T. Inscoe, Pres.; Elmore B. Inscoe, V.P.; Helen C. Wells, Secy.
Directors: Allison I. Chandler, Elmore I. Demott.
EIN: 631133501

58283
The Child Health Foundation
c/o Sergio Stagno
P.O. Box 530964
Birmingham, AL 35253-0964
FAX: (205) 591-4581

Established in 1985 in AL.
Financial data (yr. ended 12/31/01): Assets, $1,547,887 (M); grants paid, $68,640; gifts received, $10,000; expenditures, $104,007; qualifying distributions, $79,018.
Limitations: Applications not accepted. Giving limited to South America.
Application information: Contributes only to pre-selected organizations.
Officers and Directors:* John Trafford,* Chair.; Sergio Stagno,* Exec. Dir.; Joseph D. Johnson, Mary Laura Stagno, Pablo Vial.
EIN: 621248169
Codes: GTI

58284
AHEPA 23, Inc.
1133 Rosedale Dr.
Montgomery, AL 36107

Established in 1988 in AL.
Financial data (yr. ended 06/30/00): Assets, $1,525,445 (M); grants paid, $0; expenditures, $388,837; qualifying distributions, $382,539; giving activities include $75,738 for programs.
Officers and Directors:* Mike Miaoulis,* Pres.; George Stathopoulos,* V.P.; John Cookorinis,* Secy.-Treas.; Nick Stratus.
EIN: 630877902

58285
The Pursell Foundation
c/o George Yeager
P.O. Box 382471
Birmingham, AL 35238

Established in 1996.
Financial data (yr. ended 12/31/00): Assets, $984,519 (M); grants paid, $23,000; gifts received, $500,000; expenditures, $28,965; qualifying distributions, $28,965.
Limitations: Giving primarily in AL.
Trustee: James T. Pursell.
EIN: 586321927

58286
Hargis Daffodil Hills Foundation
c/o Gerald D. Colvin, Jr.
1910 1st Ave. N.
Birmingham, AL 35203

Financial data (yr. ended 10/31/00): Assets, $862,415 (M); grants paid, $0; gifts received, $130,017; expenditures, $121,851; qualifying distributions, $115,307; giving activities include $90,230 for programs.
Trustees: Gerald D. Colvin, Jr., George Crawford, Taylor Littleton.
EIN: 630834782

58287
Nall-Whatley Foundation
(Formerly Nall Foundation)
119 Euclid Ave.
Birmingham, AL 35213-2906

Established in 1996 in AL.
Donor(s): Nall Partnership, Ltd., J.W. Nall, Sr., Catherine F. Nall.
Financial data (yr. ended 06/30/01): Assets, $807,907 (M); grants paid, $62,172; gifts received, $631,240; expenditures, $64,629; qualifying distributions, $64,087.
Limitations: Applications not accepted.
Application information: Contributes only to pre-selected organizations.
Officers: Nancy W. Nall, Pres.; James Wallace Nall III, V.P. and Treas.; James Wallace Nall, Jr., V.P.; Katherine N. Whatley, V.P.
Director: James Wallace Nall, Sr.
EIN: 631183109

58288
Blaylock Foundation, Inc.
1020 Indian Hills Dr.
Tuscaloosa, AL 35406-3046
Contact: Elizabeth B. Hollingsworth, Pres.

Established in 1987 in AL.
Donor(s): Elizabeth B. Hollingsworth.
Financial data (yr. ended 12/31/01): Assets, $742,689 (M); grants paid, $61,414; gifts received, $1,826; expenditures, $80,032; qualifying distributions, $61,414.
Limitations: Giving primarily in AL; some giving also in South America.
Officers: Elizabeth B. Hollingsworth, Pres.; James H. Hollingsworth III, V.P.; Lillian Hinton, Secy.; Jo Anne Robertson, Treas.
EIN: 630967721

58289
Sunburst Homes, Inc.
1100 7th Ave.
Jasper, AL 35501

Financial data (yr. ended 06/30/02): Assets, $712,954 (M); grants paid, $0; expenditures, $198,494; qualifying distributions, $0.
Officers: Eva H. Oates, Pres.; Joe Love, V.P.; Barbara Thorne, Secy.
EIN: 630955728
Codes: TN

58290
The Charles G. & Alice R. Mayson Scholarship Grant Fund
c/o First National Bank of Atmore, Trust Dept.
P.O. Box 27
Atmore, AL 36504

Financial data (yr. ended 12/31/00): Assets, $643,764 (M); grants paid, $40,862; expenditures, $51,828; qualifying distributions, $40,301.
Limitations: Giving primarily in Atmore, AL.
Application information: Recipients are nominated by 3 local area high schools.
Trustee: First National Bank.
EIN: 636161467
Codes: GTI

58291
Parker Family Foundation
c/o AmSouth Bank
P.O. Box 11426
Birmingham, AL 35202
Application address: c/o Jenks C. Parker, Rte. 3, Box 92A, Union Springs, AL 36089, tel.: (334) 224-5134

Established in 1997 in AL.
Donor(s): Jenks C. Parker.
Financial data (yr. ended 12/30/00): Assets, $590,066 (M); grants paid, $63,079; expenditures, $70,863; qualifying distributions, $64,005.
Limitations: Giving limited to Bullock County, AL.
Application information: Application form required.
Directors: Alice Parker, Jenks C. Parker, Jenks C. Parker, Jr., Michael R. Parker, Quincy M. Simon.
Trustee: AmSouth Bank.
EIN: 721358823

58292
The Richard D. Wells Foundation
1340 Sledge Dr.
Mobile, AL 36606

Financial data (yr. ended 12/31/00): Assets, $553,817 (M); grants paid, $16,520; expenditures, $17,378; qualifying distributions, $0.
Limitations: Applications not accepted.
Application information: Contributes only to pre-selected organizations.
Director: Paul Kalifeh.
EIN: 631212621

58293
Southern Progress Foundation
(Formerly Progressive Farmer Foundation)
2100 Lakeshore Dr.
Birmingham, AL 35209

Established in 1996 in AL.
Financial data (yr. ended 12/31/00): Assets, $496,954 (M); grants paid, $0; gifts received, $941,650; expenditures, $865,998; qualifying distributions, $683,758; giving activities include $619,963 for programs.
Limitations: Applications not accepted.
Application information: Contributes only to pre-selected organizations.
Officers and Directors:* Jack Odle,* Pres.; Susan Reynolds, V.P.; Billy Sims, V.P.; Sally S. Reilly, Secy.; Bruce W. Larson, Treas.; Doug Crichton, Ed Dickinson.
EIN: 631166618

58294
Al Hajj, Inc.
5755 Carmichael Pkwy.
Montgomery, AL 36117 (334) 272-7027
Contact: Nahiyah Seraaj, Secy.-Treas.

Financial data (yr. ended 12/31/01): Assets, $429,813 (M); grants paid, $32,940; gifts received, $229,177; expenditures, $197,599; qualifying distributions, $41,160; giving activities include $33,197 for programs.
Limitations: Giving primarily in Montgomery, AL.
Officers: Abdul Seraaj, Pres.; Nadiyah Seraaj, Secy.-Treas.
EIN: 363810269

58295
Sterne, Agee & Leach Charitable Foundation, Inc.
800 Shades Creek Pkwy., Ste. 700
Birmingham, AL 35209 (205) 949-3547
Contact: F. Eugene Woodham, Dir.

Established in 1999 in AL.
Financial data (yr. ended 12/31/00): Assets, $375,271 (M); grants paid, $16,400; gifts received, $200,000; expenditures, $19,320; qualifying distributions, $19,320.
Limitations: Giving primarily in Birmingham, AL.
Application information: Application form required.
Directors: Linda Daniel, James S. Holbrook, Jr., F. Eugene Woodham.
EIN: 631234814

58296
Danley Charitable Foundation
c/o Peggy Ellis
102 Briarcliff Rd.
Opp, AL 36467-1800

Established in 1985 in AL.
Financial data (yr. ended 12/31/01): Assets, $359,902 (M); grants paid, $0; expenditures, $2,385; qualifying distributions, $0.
Directors: David Ellis, John Ellis, Jr., Peggy D. Ellis.
EIN: 630913361

58297
Southern Hospice Foundation, Inc.
P.O. Box 1650
Livingston, AL 35470-1650

Financial data (yr. ended 12/31/00): Assets, $325,254 (M); grants paid, $41,000; expenditures, $42,070; qualifying distributions, $40,630.
Officer and Directors:* R. Bryan Crawford,* Chair.; Johnny Bell, Ed Manning, Hiram Patrenos.
EIN: 630994340

58298
The Woerner Foundation for World Missions, Inc.
(Formerly The Woerner Foundation)
805-A N. McKenzie St.
Foley, AL 36535-3544

Established in 1996 in FL.
Donor(s): Lester Woerner, Eddie Woerner, Woerner South, Inc., Woerner Management, Inc.
Financial data (yr. ended 06/30/01): Assets, $267,276 (M); grants paid, $120,225; gifts received, $31,900; expenditures, $141,998; qualifying distributions, $133,086; giving activities include $116,725 for programs.
Limitations: Applications not accepted. Giving on a national and international basis.
Application information: Contributes only to pre-selected organizations.
Officers and Director:* George A. Woerner, Chair.; Edward J. Woerner,* V.P.; Roger Woerner, Secy.; Edward E. Woerner, Treas.
EIN: 650687118
Codes: FD2

58299
HEALTHSOUTH Sports Medicine Council
c/o Richard Botts
1 Healthsouth Pkwy.
Birmingham, AL 35243-2358

Classified as a company-sponsored operating foundation in 1996 in AL.
Donor(s): HEALTHSOUTH Corp., The Coca-Cola Foundation, Inc., Travelers Group Inc., Salomon Smith Barney Holdings Inc.

Financial data (yr. ended 12/31/00): Assets, $212,919 (M); grants paid, $0; gifts received, $3,485,653; expenditures, $4,421,090; qualifying distributions, $4,419,401; giving activities include $4,429,401 for programs.
Officers and Directors:* Richard M. Scrushy,* Pres.; Anthony J. Tanner,* V.P.; Phillip Christian,* Secy.; Michael D. Martin,* Treas.
EIN: 631171520

58300
Mentone Communicatons Educational Association, Inc.
c/o Kathy C. Hollon
1750 Coleman Rd.
Anniston, AL 36207 (256) 832-0755

Established in 2000 in AL.
Donor(s): Richard T. Hardin, Jr., Christy P. Hardin.
Financial data (yr. ended 12/31/00): Assets, $155,000 (M); grants paid, $0; gifts received, $155,000; expenditures, $0; qualifying distributions, $0.
Officer and Directors:* Richard T. Hardin, Jr.,* Pres.; Benjamin S. Booth, Clay Williams.
EIN: 631267455

58301
Wesley Person Opportunity Program, Inc.
P.O. Box 481
Brantley, AL 36009

Established in 2000 in AL.
Donor(s): Wesley Person.
Financial data (yr. ended 12/31/00): Assets, $151,100 (M); grants paid, $3,737; gifts received, $176,438; expenditures, $25,338; qualifying distributions, $157,984.
Officers: Wesley Person, Pres.; Lillian Person, V.P.; A.Z. Burnett, Secy.; Johnny Young, Treas.
EIN: 631229758

58302
The Harry Brown Foundation, Inc.
(Formerly The Brown Foundation - A Corporation)
43 N. Broadway Ave.
Sylacauga, AL 35150

Classified as a private operating foundation in 1992.
Donor(s): Harry I. Brown, Jr.
Financial data (yr. ended 01/31/01): Assets, $146,815 (M); grants paid, $7,620; gifts received, $26,650; expenditures, $11,835; qualifying distributions, $7,620.
Limitations: Applications not accepted. Giving primarily in AL.
Application information: Contributes only to pre-selected organizations.
Officers: Harry I. Brown, Jr., Pres. and Treas.; Jamie C. Brown, V.P. and Secy.
EIN: 630830092

58303
Sumter County Nature Trust
P.O. Box 116
Livingston, AL 35470-0116
Application address: P.O. Box 1075, Livingston, AL 35470
Contact: Richard D. Holland, Chair.

Financial data (yr. ended 06/30/01): Assets, $120,990 (M); grants paid, $3,100; expenditures, $4,437; qualifying distributions, $3,100.
Limitations: Giving limited to Sumter County, AL.
Application information: Application form not required.
Officers: Richard D. Holland, Chair.; Sam Ledbetter, Secy.; Caryl H. Nixon, Treas.
Board Members: Aileen L. Nixon, Valtine Wright.

EIN: 630136980

58304
"Miss Elizabeth" Leckie Scholarship Fund
c/o Whitney National Bank
P.O. Box 508
Greenville, AL 36037
Contact: Melba Parker, Trust Off., Whitney National Bank

Classified as a private operating foundation in 1986.
Financial data (yr. ended 11/30/00): Assets, $113,454 (M); grants paid, $6,006; expenditures, $8,658; qualifying distributions, $6,470.
Limitations: Giving limited to Butler County, AL.
Application information: Application form required.
Directors: Ann B. Carter, Priscilla S. Davis, Frances Frakes, Roberta Gamble, Joanne McGowin.
Trustee: Whitney National Bank.
EIN: 630838764

58305
Franklin Foundation
194 Roy Dr.
Madison, AL 35758-8783
Contact: Olen Britnell, Dir.

Established in 1997.
Donor(s): Olen Britnell, Jane Britnell, S.O. Ward.
Financial data (yr. ended 12/31/00): Assets, $112,810 (M); grants paid, $6,200; expenditures, $6,827; qualifying distributions, $6,200.
Application information: Application form not required.
Directors: Barry Ward Britnell, Jane Britnell, Olen Britnell.
EIN: 721400061

58306
To Preach the Gospel
P.O. Box 3610
Hueytown, AL 35023 (205) 744-2230
Contact: Gene Calhoun, Treas.

Established in 1992 in AL.
Donor(s): William B. Cashion.
Financial data (yr. ended 12/31/01): Assets, $108,699 (M); grants paid, $225,000; expenditures, $225,059; qualifying distributions, $224,912.
Limitations: Giving primarily in AL, MS and TN.
Officers: William B. Cashion, Pres.; V.W. Baxley, Secy.; Gene Calhoun, Treas.
Trustee: Lester N. Wright.
EIN: 631001139
Codes: FD2

58307
American Council for Quebec Studies
6217 Burntwood Dr. S.
Mobile, AL 36609

Financial data (yr. ended 12/31/99): Assets, $108,670 (M); grants paid, $0; gifts received, $27,852; expenditures, $34,584; qualifying distributions, $34,584; giving activities include $11,774 for programs.
Officers: Robert K. Whelan, Pres.; Roseanna Dufault, V.P.; Milena Sontoro, Secy.; Samuel Fisher, Treas.
EIN: 020361150

58308
Jubilee Ministries, Inc.
4614 Carnegie Ave.
Fairfield, AL 35064

Established in 1997 in AL.

Financial data (yr. ended 12/31/00): Assets, $102,238 (M); grants paid, $0; expenditures, $9,591; qualifying distributions, $3,295; giving activities include $3,295 for programs.
Limitations: Applications not accepted.
Application information: Contributes only to pre-selected organizations.
Officers: Jon Putman, Chair.; Steven Antenello, Secy.; Vincent Smith, Treas.
Directors: Terry Gensemer, Anthony Gordon.
EIN: 630992036

58309
S. M. Reynolds and Jessie Dell Reynolds Scholarship Trust
2728 Fairmont Rd.
Montgomery, AL 36111 (334) 281-2179
Contact: Myrtle P. Ridolphi, Tr.

Financial data (yr. ended 12/31/99): Assets, $94,925 (M); grants paid, $5,000; expenditures, $6,631; qualifying distributions, $5,000.
Limitations: Giving limited to residents of Montgomery, AL.
Trustees: W.L. Flurry, Jane R. Goodson, Myrtle P. Ridolphi.
EIN: 635841040

58310
Anz Family Foundation
c/o Bertrand M. Anz, II, M.D.
3 Buckhead Ln.
Opelika, AL 36801-7645

Established in 1990 in AL.
Donor(s): Bertrand Anz II, M.D., Linda H. Anz, Bertrand Anz, Sr., M.D.
Financial data (yr. ended 12/31/99): Assets, $80,182 (M); grants paid, $29,360; gifts received, $35,800; expenditures, $29,760; qualifying distributions, $29,360.
Limitations: Applications not accepted. Giving primarily in AL.
Application information: Contributes only to pre-selected organizations.
Officers: Bertrand Anz II, M.D., Pres. and Treas.; Linda H. Anz, V.P. and Secy.
Director: Bertrand Anz, Sr., M.D.
EIN: 631018303

58311
The Laura Lee Pattillo Norquist Charitable Foundation
800 Shades Creek Pkwy., Ste. 125
Birmingham, AL 35209

Established in 1994 in AL.
Donor(s): Laura Lee Pattillo Norquist.
Financial data (yr. ended 12/31/99): Assets, $74,395 (M); grants paid, $600; expenditures, $1,966; qualifying distributions, $600.
Limitations: Applications not accepted.
Application information: Contributes only to pre-selected organizations.
Trustees: Frances A. Danly, Joel F. Danly, Jack W. Morgan, Sterne, Agee & Leach, Inc.
EIN: 636189797

58312
Leisa Chambless Endowment Scholarship Fund for the University of Alabama Medical School in Birmingham
P.O. Box 230759
Montgomery, AL 36123-0759 (334) 272-2230
Contact: Mark N. Chambless, Tr.

Classified as a private operating foundation in 1985.
Financial data (yr. ended 12/31/99): Assets, $68,140 (M); grants paid, $11,110; gifts received,

$635; expenditures, $11,410; qualifying distributions, $11,100.
Limitations: Giving limited to residents of AL.
Committee Members: Billie Ruth Chambless, William H. Chambless, Gayle Chambless Cool, Carol Chambless Wright.
Trustee: Mark N. Chambless.
EIN: 630865251
Codes: GTI

58313
Fellowship Ministries, Inc.
P.O. Box 1292
Mobile, AL 36633

Donor(s): Daniel A. Cowart, Scott McLeod, Danny Cowart.
Financial data (yr. ended 07/31/99): Assets, $34,287 (M); grants paid, $3,152; gifts received, $74,785; expenditures, $53,909; qualifying distributions, $43,696; giving activities include $43,696 for programs.
Limitations: Applications not accepted.
Application information: Contributes only to pre-selected organizations.
Officers: Daniel A. Cowart, Pres.; Scott McLeod, V.P.; Niece McLeod, Secy.; Tonya Cowart, Treas.
EIN: 630814637

58314
David Klein Memorial Scholarship
244 Mt. Carmel Rd.
Altoona, AL 35952

Established in 1998.
Financial data (yr. ended 12/31/00): Assets, $33,498 (M); grants paid, $1,000; expenditures, $1,050; qualifying distributions, $1,000.
Limitations: Applications not accepted. Giving primarily in AL.
Trustee: Ella Snead.
EIN: 721369301

58315
Vel-Nel Charitable Foundation
P.O. Box 562
East Tallassee, AL 36023
Contact: S. Vernon Spears, Chair.

Donor(s): S. Vernon Spears.
Financial data (yr. ended 12/31/00): Assets, $31,508 (M); grants paid, $5,300; gifts received, $37,000; expenditures, $6,829; qualifying distributions, $6,829.
Application information: Application form required.
Officer: S. Vernon Spears, Chair.
EIN: 631203030

58316
Albert Rieben Memorial Scholarship Fund, Inc.
11200 Albert Rieben Rd.
Bay Minette, AL 36507 (251) 937-7017

Established in 1998.
Donor(s): J. John Rieben, A. Ronnie Rieben.
Financial data (yr. ended 12/31/01): Assets, $27,818 (M); grants paid, $9,000; gifts received, $13,032; expenditures, $9,107; qualifying distributions, $9,107.
Limitations: Giving limited to residents of AL.
Officers: H. John Rieben, Pres.; A. Ronnie Rieben, Secy-Treas.
EIN: 630011787

58317
McPhearson Foundation, Inc.
P.O. Box 685
Butler, AL 36904-0685

Established in 1998 in AL.
Financial data (yr. ended 12/31/99): Assets, $27,571 (M); grants paid, $1,765; expenditures, $2,067; qualifying distributions, $0.
Limitations: Applications not accepted.
Application information: Contributes only to pre-selected organizations.
Officers and Directors:* Virginia L. McPhearson,* Pres.; J. Lee McPhearson,* Secy.-Treas.; Grace M. O'Grady.
EIN: 582168184

58318
Maddox Ministries Foundation
907 El Dorado Dr.
Dothan, AL 36303-2420

Financial data (yr. ended 12/31/01): Assets, $13,166 (M); grants paid, $0; gifts received, $12,940; expenditures, $14,947; qualifying distributions, $14,947; giving activities include $14,947 for programs.
Officer: Samuel E. Maddox, Pres.
EIN: 631095892

58319
Marks Family Foundation
509 Franklin St.
Huntsville, AL 35801

Established in 2000 in AL.
Donor(s): Joseph H. Marks, Ellen S. Marks.
Financial data (yr. ended 12/31/00): Assets, $11,339 (M); grants paid, $600; gifts received, $11,727; expenditures, $600; qualifying distributions, $600.
Limitations: Applications not accepted. Giving primarily in AL.
Application information: Contributes only to pre-selected organizations.
Officers and Trustees:* Joseph H. Marks,* Pres.; Ellen S. Marks,* Secy.-Treas.; Joseph H. Marks, Jr.
EIN: 631257308

58320
Nathan Taylor Scholarship Fund
c/o Martha Miles, The Citizens Bank of Winfield
P.O. Box 550
Winfield, AL 35594-0550

Financial data (yr. ended 08/31/01): Assets, $11,100 (M); grants paid, $1,000; expenditures, $1,000; qualifying distributions, $1,000.
Limitations: Applications not accepted. Giving limited to residents of the Winfield, AL, area.
Application information: Recipients are selected by faculty.
Trustee: The Citizens Bank of Winfield.
EIN: 630929395

58321
Louise Williams Foundation, Inc.
P.O. Box 446
Troy, AL 36081
Contact: Joel Lee Williams, Pres.

Established in 1994.
Financial data (yr. ended 12/31/00): Assets, $9,559 (M); grants paid, $315; expenditures, $315; qualifying distributions, $311.
Officer and Directors:* Joel Lee Williams,* Pres.; Alyene Lockler, Louise Williams.
EIN: 570907668

58322
Bill Pace World Mission Endeavor Foundation
658 Holland Rd.
Newton, AL 36352 (334) 692-3179
Contact: Joseph William Pace, Pres.

Established in 1993 in AL.
Financial data (yr. ended 12/31/99): Assets, $7,696 (M); grants paid, $550; gifts received, $14,150; expenditures, $13,054; qualifying distributions, $550.
Limitations: Giving primarily in AL.
Officer: Joseph William Pace, Pres.
EIN: 631094367

58323
Friends of Recreational Ice Activities, Inc.
2615 Vista Dr.
Huntsville, AL 35803

Established in 1994 in AL.
Donor(s): Keith H. Schonrock, Jr.
Financial data (yr. ended 12/31/00): Assets, $5,176 (M); grants paid, $1,334; gifts received, $15,849; expenditures, $15,177; qualifying distributions, $15,177; giving activities include $15,177 for programs.
Limitations: Giving primarily in Huntsville, AL.
Application information: Application form not required.
Officers: Fran Woodard, Pres.; Dennis Sierk, V.P.; Editha Dotson-Bowser, Treas.
EIN: 631078980

58324
The Spradling Family Foundation
P.O. Box 118
Trussville, AL 35173-0118

Established in 1998 in AL.
Donor(s): C. Gaither Spradling, Sr.
Financial data (yr. ended 07/31/01): Assets, $2,616 (M); grants paid, $200; gifts received, $500; expenditures, $337; qualifying distributions, $200.
Limitations: Applications not accepted.
Application information: Contributes only to pre-selected organizations.
Officers: C. Gaither Spradling, Sr., Pres.; Charles G. Spradling, Jr., V.P.; Barbara C. Spradling, Secy.-Treas.
Directors: Pamela S. McDowell, JoAnne S. Milam, Richard L. Spradling.
EIN: 631206699

58325
Garrett Foundation, Inc.
1015 Beaumont Rd.
Bessemer, AL 35020

Established in 1996.
Donor(s): Howard C. Garrett.
Financial data (yr. ended 12/31/01): Assets, $2,444 (M); grants paid, $0; gifts received, $28,306; expenditures, $27,111; qualifying distributions, $0.
Officers: Howard C. Garrett, Pres.; Thomas Keen, Sr., V.P.; Nancy G. Keen, Secy.; Carol Garrett, Treas.
EIN: 631178245

58326
The Forman Foundation
3000 Southtrust Tower
Birmingham, AL 35203-3204

Established in 1993 in AL.
Financial data (yr. ended 12/31/01): Assets, $1,586 (M); grants paid, $0; gifts received, $650; expenditures, $652; qualifying distributions, $0.
Directors: Dalton Forman Blankenship, J. Ross Forman III, Elizabeth Forman Norwood.
EIN: 582045009

58327
Send the Word Foundation
P.O. Box 531336
Birmingham, AL 35253

Established in 2000 in AL.

Financial data (yr. ended 12/31/00): Assets, $749 (M); grants paid, $5,846; gifts received, $5,766; expenditures, $5,846; qualifying distributions, $5,846.
Directors: Anthony Askew, Anthony D. Ayres, Edmund Bell, Doris Collins, Kenneth Dawson, Amanda Holmes, Rosalyn Willingham, Deborah Wood.
EIN: 631194320

58328
ACT, Inc.
146 Brooks Blvd.
Brewton, AL 36426
Contact: Cindy S. Waldrep, Dir.

Established in 1998 in AL.
Financial data (yr. ended 12/31/00): Assets, $535 (M); grants paid, $1,000; gifts received, $50; expenditures, $1,023; qualifying distributions, $1,000.
Directors: Margaret B. Cotten, Rebecca C. Jordan, Cindy S. Waldrep, Mitzi C. Whittle.
EIN: 631204106

58329
Pavmar, Inc.
P.O. Box 1536
Tuscaloosa, AL 35403

Established in 2000.
Financial data (yr. ended 12/31/00): Assets, $181 (M); grants paid, $0; gifts received, $122,642; expenditures, $126,109; qualifying distributions, $126,109; giving activities include $126,109 for programs.
Directors: Francine Marasco, Anthony M. Pavon, Sharon M. Pavon.
EIN: 631251391

58330
Dorothy Nichols Ministries, Inc.
310 Bryant Ct.
Saraland, AL 36571

Established in 2000.
Financial data (yr. ended 12/31/00): Assets, $22 (M); grants paid, $390; gifts received, $8,589; expenditures, $8,374; qualifying distributions, $390; giving activities include $7,984 for programs.
Officers: Dorothy Nichols, Pres.; Martha McRae, V.P.; Kathie Welsh, Secy.; Lois Cochran, Treas.
EIN: 631226369

58331
The Lasker Foundation
801 Princeton Ave. S.W., Ste. 424
P.O. Box 1
Birmingham, AL 35211
Contact: James C. Lasker, Pres.

Established in 1999 in AL.
Donor(s): James C. Lasker, M.D.
Financial data (yr. ended 02/28/01): Assets, $0 (M); grants paid, $5,000; gifts received, $5,533; expenditures, $5,533; qualifying distributions, $5,533.
Officers and Directors:* James C. Lasker, M.D.,* Pres. and Treas.; Carter Marsden,* V.P. and Secy.; Albert Brady, M.D.,* V.P.; Rev. John Claypool,* V.P.; Kim Johnson,* V.P.
EIN: 631196609

ALASKA

58332
Robert "Aqqaluk" Newlin, Sr. Memorial Trust
c/o NANA Regional Corp.
1001 E. Benson Blvd.
Anchorage, AK 99508-4256
Application address: P.O. Box 509, Kotzebue, AK 99752, tel.: (907) 442-2273, (800) 478-3301, FAX: (907) 442-2289
Contact: Sarah Scanlan

Financial data (yr. ended 12/31/99): Assets, $835,396 (M); grants paid, $20,100; gifts received, $643,870; expenditures, $344,911; qualifying distributions, $271,582; giving activities include $251,792 for programs.
Limitations: Giving limited to the Northwest Arctic Borough of AK.
Publications: Informational brochure (including application guidelines).
Application information: Application form required.
Officer: Dood Lincoln, Chair.
Trustees: Miles Cleveland, Charlie Curtis, Richard Lincoln, Becky Norton, Helvi Sandvix, Frank Stein.
EIN: 943116762
Codes: GTI

58333
Permafrost Technology Foundation
1531 Gillam Way
Fairbanks, AK 99701

Financial data (yr. ended 06/30/01): Assets, $291,895 (L); grants paid, $0; gifts received, $114,119; expenditures, $91,265; qualifying distributions, $88,815; giving activities include $36,643 for programs.
Officers: Terry McFadden, Ph.D., Pres.; Allen Vezey, 1st V.P.; Ruth McFadden, 2nd V.P.
Directors: Rad Carlson, Chris Guinn, A.G. Myers, David Somers.
EIN: 920135614

58334
Alutiiq Heritage Foundation
215 Mission Rd., Ste. 101
Kodiak, AK 99615-6327

Donor(s): Afognak Native Corporation.
Financial data (yr. ended 12/31/99): Assets, $288,745 (M); grants paid, $538; gifts received, $485,094; expenditures, $405,689; qualifying distributions, $343,262; giving activities include $356,949 for programs.
Limitations: Applications not accepted. Giving limited to Kodiak, AK.
Application information: Contributes only to pre-selected organizations.
Officers: Ruth Dawson, Pres.; Rita Stevens, V.P.; Clarence Selig, Secy.; Roger Malutin, Treas.
Directors: Fred Coyle, Tanya Inga, Teri Scheider, Donene Tweten.
EIN: 920150422

58335
Peter Rooney Wrangell Community Foundation
P.O. Box 1063
Wrangell, AK 99929 (907) 874-2074
Contact: Janelle Privett

Established in 1998 in AL.
Financial data (yr. ended 12/31/99): Assets, $219,856 (L); grants paid, $1,842; gifts received, $600; expenditures, $4,930; qualifying distributions, $4,451.
Limitations: Giving limited to southeast AK.
Application information: Application form required.
Directors: Kathleen Angerman, Judy Baker, Renata Davies, Roberta Floyd, Sondra Sexton Jones, Barbara Maenhout, Robert Rooney, Sharry L. Rooney, Robin Taylor, Kris Timothy.
EIN: 911834169

58336
Fairbanks Curling Club Foundation, Inc.
P.O. Box 73530
Fairbanks, AK 99707-3530
Application address: 330 Barnette St., Fairbanks, AK 99701
Contact: E.M. Cox, Pres.

Established in 1990 in AK.
Donor(s): E.M. Cox, Norman S. MacPhee.
Financial data (yr. ended 12/31/99): Assets, $181,891 (M); grants paid, $9,300; gifts received, $11,412; expenditures, $9,329; qualifying distributions, $9,329.
Officers: E.M. Cox, Pres.; David L. Swanson, V.P.; Margaret Cox Rich, Secy.-Treas.
EIN: 943111958

58337
The Foundation for the Protection of the Common People, Inc.
1706 Edgecumbe Dr.
Sitka, AK 99835-9663

Financial data (yr. ended 12/31/99): Assets, $80,562 (M); grants paid, $160; expenditures, $9,717; qualifying distributions, $3,568; giving activities include $9,717 for programs.
Limitations: Applications not accepted. Giving primarily in Sitka, AK.
Application information: Contributes only to pre-selected organizations.
Officers: Florian Sever, Pres.; Patricia L. Sever, V.P.
EIN: 943096971

58338
Halcro Family Foundation
P.O. Box 190028
Anchorage, AK 99519-0028 (907) 243-4300
Contact: Robert J. Halcro, Pres.

Established in 2000.
Donor(s): Robert J. Halcro, Barbara M. Halcro.
Financial data (yr. ended 12/31/00): Assets, $32,311 (M); grants paid, $22,200; gifts received, $55,000; expenditures, $22,888; qualifying distributions, $22,200.
Limitations: Giving primarily in Anchorage, AK.
Officers: Robert J. Halcro, Pres.; Barbara M. Halcro, V.P.; Mary E. Halcro, Secy.
EIN: 920170559

58339
Alaska Historical Publication
5836 E. 10th Cir.
Anchorage, AK 99504 (907) 337-2021
Contact: Steven C. Levi, Secy.

Established in 1999 in AK.
Financial data (yr. ended 12/31/99): Assets, $48 (M); grants paid, $4,500; gifts received, $5,110; expenditures, $5,062; qualifying distributions, $4,500.
Limitations: Giving primarily in AK.
Officers: Danny Daniels, Pres.; Sue White Levi, V.P.; Steven C. Levi, Secy.
EIN: 920167724

58340
Chenega Future, Inc.
4000 Old Seward Hwy., Ste. 101
Anchorage, AK 99503 (907) 561-0500
Contact: Patricia Totemoff Andrews, Dir.

Classified as a company-sponsored operating foundation in 1990.
Donor(s): Chenega Corporation.
Financial data (yr. ended 12/31/00): Assets, $0 (M); grants paid, $18,053; expenditures, $18,543; qualifying distributions, $18,543.
Limitations: Giving primarily in AK.
Application information: Application form required.
Officers: Patrick C. Selanof, Pres.; Phyllis Pipkin, V.P.; Joyce L. Kampkoff, Secy.
Directors: Patricia Totemoff Andrews, Lawrence M. Evanoff.
EIN: 943111730
Codes: CD

ARIZONA

58341
Research Corporation
101 N. Wilmot Rd., Ste. 250
Tucson, AZ 85711-3335 (520) 571-1111
FAX: (520) 571-1119; E-mail: awards@rescorp.org; URL: http://www.rescorp.org
Contact: Carmen Vitello, Editor

Incorporated in 1912 in NY.
Donor(s): Rachel Brown,‡ Frederick Gardner Cottrell,‡ Elizabeth Hazen,‡ Donald F. Jones,‡ Edward C. Kendall,‡ Paul C. Mangelsdorf, Charles H. Townes, Robert E. Waterman,‡ Robert R. Williams,‡ Robert B. Woodward.‡
Financial data (yr. ended 12/31/01): Assets, $147,729,096 (M); grants paid, $6,162,071; gifts received, $167,000; expenditures, $9,771,442; qualifying distributions, $9,471,353.
Limitations: Giving only in the U.S. and Canada.
Publications: Annual report, newsletter, occasional report.
Application information: Application form required.
Officers and Directors:* John P. Schaefer,* Chair.; Raymond Kellman, V.P.; Sherri R. Benedict, Secy.; Suzanne D. Jaffe,* Treas.; Herbert S. Adler, Stuart B. Crampton, Robert M. Gavin, Jr., Robert Holland, Jr., Joan Selverstone Valentine, G. King Walters, Laurel L. Wilkening.
EIN: 131963407
Codes: FD, FM, GTI

58342
DeGrazia Foundation, Inc.
(Formerly DeGrazia Art & Cultural Foundation, Inc.)
c/o Jon Fowler, Exec. Dir.
6300 N. Swan Rd.
Tucson, AZ 85718

Established in 1977 in AZ.
Donor(s): Marion DeGrazia.
Financial data (yr. ended 06/30/01): Assets, $24,522,443 (M); grants paid, $33,326; gifts received, $1,081; expenditures, $494,325; qualifying distributions, $370,783; giving activities include $358,463 for programs.
Limitations: Applications not accepted. Giving limited to AZ.

Publications: Informational brochure.
Application information: Contributes only to pre-selected organizations.
Officers: Lorraine Drachman, Pres.; Robert Vint, V.P. and Secy.; Jon Young, Treas.; Jon Fowler, Exec. Dir.
Directors: Kathy Bushroe, Abe Chanin, Marion DeGrazia, George Domino, Hal Grieve, David Hoefferle, James McNutty.
EIN: 860339837

58343
The Amerind Foundation, Inc.
P.O. Box 400
Dragoon, AZ 85609

Incorporated in 1937 in CT.
Donor(s): William Shirley Fulton,‡ Rose H. Fulton.‡
Financial data (yr. ended 12/31/01): Assets, $18,272,415 (M); grants paid, $0; gifts received, $8,618; expenditures, $430,296; qualifying distributions, $392,587; giving activities include $392,587 for programs.
Publications: Program policy statement, informational brochure.
Officers and Directors:* William Duncan Fulton,* Pres.; Peter L. Formo,* V.P.; Elizabeth F. Husband,* Secy.; Michael Hard,* Treas.; John A. Ware, Exec. Dir.; Marilyn F. Fulton, George J. Gumerman, Ph.D., Peter Johnson, J. William Moore, Sharline Reedy, Lawrence Schiever, Anne I. Woosley.
EIN: 860122680

58344
Tucson Osteopathic Medical Foundation
(Formerly Tucson Osteopathic Foundation)
4280 N. Campbell Ave., Ste. 200
Tucson, AZ 85718-6954 (520) 299-4545
Additional tel.: (800) 201-8663; FAX: (520) 299-4609; E-mail: opinion@tomf.org; URL: http://www.tomf.org/about.html; Additional URL: http://www.docenter.org/about.html
Contact: Lew Riggs, Exec. Dir.

Incorporated in 1986 in AZ; converted from sale of Tucson General Hospital.
Donor(s): Tucson Hospital Liquidating Corp.
Financial data (yr. ended 06/30/01): Assets, $12,407,599 (M); grants paid, $136,024; gifts received, $28,986; expenditures, $963,633; qualifying distributions, $744,425; giving activities include $749,443 for programs.
Limitations: Giving limited to AZ; loans primarily to residents of the seven southernmost counties of AZ: Cochise, Graham, Greenlee, Pima, Pinal, Santa Cruz, and Yuma.
Publications: Application guidelines.
Application information: Interview required for initial application for medical students. Application form required.
Officers: Nicholas Pazzi, D.O., Chair.; John Q. Harris, D.O., Vice-Chair.; Issa Y. Hallaq, D.O., Secy.-Treas.; Lew Riggs, Exec. Dir.
Trustees: Heidi Haight-Biehler, D.O., Jerry H. Hutchinson, Jr., D.O., William C. Inboden, D.O., John F. Manfredonia, D.O., Harmon L. Myers, D.O., R. Bart Powers, Oliver W. Shelksohn, D.O., Kenneth S. Snow, Jr., D.O.
EIN: 742449503
Codes: FD2, GTI

58345
Skystone Foundation, Inc.
114 N. San Francisco, No. 206
Flagstaff, AZ 86001

Financial data (yr. ended 06/30/01): Assets, $9,680,332 (M); grants paid, $0; gifts received, $622,205; expenditures, $343,521; qualifying distributions, $324,306; giving activities include $622,205 for programs.
Officers: Nancy Taylor, Pres.; Stephen Verkamp, Treas.
EIN: 942842873

58346
Transition Zone Horticultural Institute, Inc.
P.O. Box 670
Flagstaff, AZ 86002-0670

Classified as a private operating foundation in 1982.
Financial data (yr. ended 12/31/01): Assets, $8,588,842 (M); grants paid, $0; gifts received, $289,576; expenditures, $1,014,785; qualifying distributions, $0.
Officers and Directors:* David Vaselaar,* Pres.; John Warren,* V.P.; Robin Cameron,* Secy.; James Wick,* Treas.; William Doyle, and 13 additional directors.
EIN: 942788812

58347
Family Healthreach, Inc.
997 S. Pennington
Chandler, AZ 85224

Established in 1999 in AZ.
Financial data (yr. ended 08/31/01): Assets, $8,093,926 (M); grants paid, $0; expenditures, $2,757,958; qualifying distributions, $0.
Officers: Robert Brown, Pres.; Robert Campbell, Secy.-Treas.
Director: Steve Galasky, M.D.
EIN: 860776867

58348
Tohono Chul Park, Inc.
7366 N. Paseo del Norte
Tucson, AZ 85704

Classified as a private operating foundation in 1986.
Donor(s): Richard Wilson, J. Paul Getty Trust.
Financial data (yr. ended 06/30/00): Assets, $5,855,146 (M); grants paid, $0; gifts received, $717,879; expenditures, $998,957; qualifying distributions, $544,151; giving activities include $525,183 for programs.
Officers and Directors:* Gene Berry,* Pres.; Sarah Simmons,* V.P.; Richard Hoshaw, M.D.,* Secy.; Don Romano,* Treas.; Joan E. Donnelly, Exec. Dir.; J.T. Fey, Michael J. Harris, William H. Havens, Stephen Jewett, Lance MacVittie, Charles M. Pettis, Michael Racy, Britton Simmons, Nancy S. Wooding, and 4 additional directors.
EIN: 860438592
Codes: TN

58349
Lillian Lincoln Foundation
c/o Vika Corp.
1741 E. Morten Ave.
Phoenix, AZ 85020 (602) 944-7400
FAX: (602) 944-8930; E-mail: Robinsnest28@juno.com

Established in 1983 in CA.
Donor(s): Lillian L. Howell.
Financial data (yr. ended 02/28/02): Assets, $4,063,581 (M); grants paid, $12,500; expenditures, $102,740; qualifying distributions, $183,605.
Limitations: Applications not accepted. Giving primarily in the San Francisco Bay Area, CA.
Application information: Contributes only to pre-selected organizations.
Officers and Directors:* Lillian L. Howell,* C.E.O.; Lincoln C. Howell,* Secy.-Treas.; David C. Lincoln.

EIN: 942943599

58350
National Historical Fire Foundation
6730 N. Scottsdale Rd., Ste. 250
Scottsdale, AZ 85253-4424

Classified as a private operating foundation in 1973.
Donor(s): Bert A. Getz, George F. Getz, Jr.‡
Financial data (yr. ended 12/31/01): Assets, $3,964,125 (M); grants paid, $0; gifts received, $218,913; expenditures, $394,068; qualifying distributions, $0.
Officers and Directors:* George F. Getz,* Pres.; Bert A. Getz,* V.P.; Lynn Getz,* V.P.; James L. Johnson,* Secy.-Treas.; Peter M. Molloy, Exec. Dir.; James W. Ashley, Louis G. Jeckel, Bernard C. Lowe, Jr., C.L. Lux.
EIN: 366111510

58351
Frederick Gardner Cottrell Foundation
c/o Gary M. Munsinger, Pres.
101 N. Wilmot Rd., Ste. 600
Tucson, AZ 85711-3365

Established in 1998 in AZ.
Donor(s): Research Corporation Technologies, Inc.
Financial data (yr. ended 12/31/00): Assets, $3,892,873 (M); grants paid, $1,783,000; gifts received, $5,501,213; expenditures, $1,811,145; qualifying distributions, $1,798,663.
Limitations: Giving primarily in Woods Hole, MA, Hunt Valley, MD, Brunswick, ME, and Houston, TX.
Application information: Application form required.
Officers: Gary Munsinger, Pres.; Rebecca Buescher, Secy.; Linda Tansik, Treas.
Directors: John Schaefer, G. King Walters.
EIN: 860940147
Codes: FD

58352
The Thomas Hill Hubbard & H. H. Franklin Foundation
1405 E. Kleindale Rd.
Tucson, AZ 85719

Established in 1992 in AZ.
Donor(s): Thomas H. Hubbard.‡
Financial data (yr. ended 12/31/00): Assets, $3,520,893 (M); grants paid, $0; gifts received, $164,010; expenditures, $94,918; qualifying distributions, $91,799; giving activities include $92,565 for programs.
Limitations: Applications not accepted.
Application information: Contributes only to pre-selected organizations.
Officers: Dick Moffitt, Chair.; Scott Dwyer, Secy.; Frank B. Hantak, Treas.
Trustees: Louis W. Barassi, Edward Rollyson, Bourke Runton, Marlene G. Zimmerman.
EIN: 860702867

58353
The Agape Foundation
3603 N. 7th Ave., Ste. 14
Phoenix, AZ 85013-3638
Contact: Ruth Flack

Established in 1997 in AZ.
Donor(s): Barbara McClelland.
Financial data (yr. ended 12/31/00): Assets, $3,002,689 (M); grants paid, $347,243; gifts received, $320; expenditures, $368,866; qualifying distributions, $368,240.
Limitations: Giving on a national basis.

Officers and Directors:* Barbara S. McClelland,* Pres.; John C. Vryhof,* Secy.; Donna M. Vryhof,* Treas.
EIN: 860840802
Codes: FD, GTI

58354
The Nelson Family Foundation, Inc.
8711 E. Pinnacle Peak Rd., Ste. D-100
Scottsdale, AZ 85255

Established in 1999 in AZ.
Financial data (yr. ended 08/31/00): Assets, $2,897,291 (M); grants paid, $135,000; gifts received, $3,000,098; expenditures, $155,797; qualifying distributions, $155,797.
Limitations: Applications not accepted.
Officers: Jerry Nelson, Pres.; Jay Rader, V.P.; Marlan C. Walker, Secy.
EIN: 860971708
Codes: FD2

58355
William and Mary Ross Foundation
c/o Robert M. Struse
6750 N. Oracle Rd.
Tucson, AZ 85704-5618

Established in 1997 in AZ.
Donor(s): Mary Ross.
Financial data (yr. ended 12/31/01): Assets, $2,454,314 (M); grants paid, $91,250; gifts received, $1,033,278; expenditures, $127,183; qualifying distributions, $88,030.
Limitations: Applications not accepted.
Application information: Contributes only to pre-selected organizations.
Officers: Mary Ross, Pres.; Robert Struse, Secy.; Tim Garigan, Treas.
EIN: 860891827
Codes: FD2

58356
Dorothy Garske Center
7098 E. Cochise Rd., Ste. 100
Scottsdale, AZ 85253

Classified as a private operating foundation in 1988 in AZ.
Donor(s): Ganser Family Trust.
Financial data (yr. ended 12/31/01): Assets, $2,273,161 (M); grants paid, $0; gifts received, $246,664; expenditures, $263,463; qualifying distributions, $234,859; giving activities include $55,068 for programs.
Officers and Directors:* Dean A. Young,* Pres.; Thomas R. Hackett,* Secy.; Michael Baker, Exec. Dir.; Jerry Dixon, Ann Harris, Jeff Schneidman.
EIN: 860464987

58357
Our Lady of the Sierras Foundation
P.O. Box 269
Hereford, AZ 85615

Established in 1993 in AZ.
Donor(s): Gerald Chouinard, Patricia Chouinard.
Financial data (yr. ended 12/31/01): Assets, $2,034,032 (M); grants paid, $16,950; gifts received, $120,150; expenditures, $123,182; qualifying distributions, $92,585; giving activities include $40,938 for programs.
Limitations: Applications not accepted. Giving primarily in AZ.
Application information: Contributes only to pre-selected organizations.
Officers and Directors:* Gerald A. Chouinard,* Pres. and Treas.; Dolores Irwin,* V.P.; Patricia A. Chouinard,* Secy.
EIN: 860727824

58358
Asthma Foundation of Southern Arizona
P.O. Box 30069
Tucson, AZ 85751

Financial data (yr. ended 05/31/00): Assets, $1,613,547 (M); grants paid, $0; gifts received, $68,668; expenditures, $205,352; qualifying distributions, $193,456; giving activities include $192,445 for programs.
Officers and Directors:* Henry E. Dahlberg,* Pres.; Lowell E. Rothschild,* V.P.; William N. Poorton,* Secy.; William B. Addison, Jr.,* Treas.; Lynn Krust, Exec. Dir.; Marie Angeli C. Adamczyk, Eugene G. Isaac, Alan Willenbrock.
EIN: 860101712

58359
Robert H. Karatz and Naomi G. Karatz Foundation
6333 N. Scottsdale Rd., No. 10
Scottsdale, AZ 85250-5428

Established in 1988 in AZ.
Donor(s): Robert H. Karatz.
Financial data (yr. ended 12/31/01): Assets, $1,455,464 (M); grants paid, $152,899; expenditures, $173,863; qualifying distributions, $152,340.
Limitations: Applications not accepted. Giving primarily in AZ.
Application information: Contributes only to pre-selected organizations.
Officers and Directors:* Robert H. Karatz,* Pres.; Esther Sue Karatz,* Secy.
EIN: 742501011
Codes: FD2

58360
Novis M. Schmitz Foundation, Inc.
c/o Shimmel, Hill, Bishop & Gruender, P.C.
3700 N. 24th St.
Phoenix, AZ 85016-6511 (602) 224-9500
Contact: Daniel F. Gruender, Chair.

Established in 1987 in AZ.
Financial data (yr. ended 12/31/00): Assets, $1,006,833 (M); grants paid, $49,520; expenditures, $57,669; qualifying distributions, $50,742.
Limitations: Giving primarily in the Phoenix, AZ, area.
Officers: Daniel F. Gruender, Chair. and Secy.; Leonard Huck, Pres.; Mitzi Schechter, V.P.
EIN: 860534056

58361
Robert T. Wilson Foundation
P.O. Box 399
Flagstaff, AZ 86002-0399
Contact: Richard F. Wilson, Pres.

Trust established in 1954 in TX; incorporated in 1963.
Donor(s): Richard F. Wilson, Jean H. Wilson, Suzanne C. Wilson,‡ and other members of the Wilson family.
Financial data (yr. ended 12/31/01): Assets, $948,843 (M); grants paid, $414,413; gifts received, $580,704; expenditures, $829,122; qualifying distributions, $414,413.
Limitations: Giving primarily in AZ.
Publications: Application guidelines.
Application information: Application form not required.
Officers: Richard Wilson, Pres.; Jean Wilson, Secy.-Treas.
EIN: 860264036
Codes: FD

IN THIS SECTION, WITHIN EACH STATE, FOUNDATIONS ARE LISTED IN DESCENDING ORDER BY ASSET AMOUNT

58362
Phoenix Swim Club
(also known as Phoenix Swim & Sports Foundation)
2501 N. 32nd St.
Phoenix, AZ 85008

Financial data (yr. ended 12/31/00): Assets, $938,889 (M); grants paid, $21,000; expenditures, $177,387; qualifying distributions, $177,387; giving activities include $177,387 for programs.
Limitations: Applications not accepted. Giving primarily in Phoenix, AZ.
Application information: Contributes only to pre-selected organizations.
Officers and Directors:* Gary W. Hall,* Pres.; Jelena Koscak,* V.P.; Lori A. Quinn,* Secy.-Treas.; Andrew Crean, David Withington.
EIN: 742524291

58363
The Rev. Joseph F. Costanzo, S.J. Memorial Foundation
P.O. Box 12546
Tucson, AZ 85732-2546

Classified as a private operating foundation.
Donor(s): Mary Costanzo.‡
Financial data (yr. ended 12/31/01): Assets, $915,186 (M); grants paid, $0; expenditures, $51,594; qualifying distributions, $44,083; giving activities include $50,594 for programs.
Officers: Rev. Fabian W. Bruskewitz, Pres.; Sr. Mary Ruth Murphy, V.P. and Secy.-Treas.
Directors: Sr. Maure Ruane, Rev. Austin B. Vaughan.
EIN: 942942898

58364
Utah Elks Camp Wapiti, Inc.
c/o Jerry Dewey
2535 Talisman Ln.
Lake Havasu City, AZ 86406-8267

Donor(s): George Eccles Foundation, Utah Ladies of Elks Assn.
Financial data (yr. ended 12/31/00): Assets, $833,239 (M); grants paid, $0; gifts received, $40,688; expenditures, $92,687; qualifying distributions, $92,687; giving activities include $92,687 for programs.
Officers: Eldon Hill, Pres.; David Okubo, V.P.; Jodie Sims-Smith, Secy.; Jerry Dewey, Treas.
EIN: 870481146

58365
The Fairborn Observatory
P.O. Box 256 HC2
Patagonia, AZ 85624-9707

Classified as a private operating foundation in 1985.
Financial data (yr. ended 12/31/00): Assets, $796,221 (M); grants paid, $0; gifts received, $221,347; expenditures, $123,686; qualifying distributions, $123,686; giving activities include $123,686 for programs.
Officers and Trustees:* Donald Epand,* Secy.; Louis J. Boyd,* Treas.; Douglas S. Hall, Helen C. Lines, George C. Roberts, Douglas J. Sauer.
EIN: 311042912

58366
The Gloria F. Ross Center for Tapestry Studies
P.O. Box 3305
Tucson, AZ 85722-3305

Classified as a private operating foundation in 1998.
Donor(s): The Gloria F. Ross Foundation.
Financial data (yr. ended 06/30/00): Assets, $788,920 (M); grants paid, $0; gifts received, $156,759; expenditures, $179,521; qualifying distributions, $123,565; giving activities include $106,368 for programs.
Officers: Alice Zrebiec, Pres.; Ann Bookman, Secy.; Margi Poland Fox, Treas.
Board Members: Archie Brennan, Darienne L. Dennis, Mary Lane, Lotus Stack.
EIN: 860897710

58367
Top Vietnam Veterans
c/o Jesse Devaney
7400 N. Oracle Rd., Ste. 100W
Tucson, AZ 85704-6345

Established in 1998 in AZ and MO. Classified as a private operating foundation in 1999.
Donor(s): Jess Devaney.
Financial data (yr. ended 12/31/01): Assets, $773,402 (M); grants paid, $0; gifts received, $5,409; expenditures, $123,010; qualifying distributions, $110,202; giving activities include $88,351 for programs.
Officers and Directors:* Jesse Devaney,* Pres.; Hope Crabtree,* V.P.; Leo H. McDonald, Jr.,* Secy.
EIN: 431832781

58368
Seed Money for Growth Foundation, Inc.
(also known as SMFG Foundation, Inc.)
4716 N. Dromedary Rd.
Phoenix, AZ 85018-2939
Contact: Mary Upton, Grants Admin.

Classified as a private operating foundation in 1983.
Donor(s): Wallace A. Reed, Maria E. Reed, Kathryn L. Reed, M.D., Marylee Doud, Mary Crouch, Dorothy Finch, Surinder Kallar, M.D., Barbara Knize, M.D., Jack Levkowitz, D.D.S., Jan Marcou, Pat Meritt, Wendell Whitacre, M.D., Andrea Norman, Mary Upton, Medical Care America, Triclinica Communications.
Financial data (yr. ended 07/31/01): Assets, $762,782 (M); grants paid, $51,156; gifts received, $295,107; expenditures, $90,513; qualifying distributions, $88,228.
Limitations: Giving limited to AZ.
Publications: Informational brochure (including application guidelines).
Application information: Application form required.
Officers: Wallace A. Reed, M.D., Pres.; Vikki T. Reed, Secy.-Treas.
EIN: 942919372
Codes: GTI

58369
Henry Dahlberg Foundation
2946 Darca Dr.
Prescott, AZ 86301

Donor(s): Henry E. Dahlberg, Sr.
Financial data (yr. ended 12/31/99): Assets, $672,830 (M); grants paid, $0; gifts received, $10,627; expenditures, $146,506; qualifying distributions, $21,410; giving activities include $9,688 for programs.
Limitations: Applications not accepted. Giving primarily in Prescott, AZ.
Application information: Contributes only to pre-selected organizations.
Trustees: Henry E. Dahlberg, Sr., Henry E. Dahlberg, Jr., Gary Fry.
EIN: 237030927

58370
W.M.C.H. Development Corporation
(also known as White Mountain Communities Hospital Development Corporation)
2330 W. Mission Ln.
Phoenix, AZ 85021

Established in 1984 in AZ.
Financial data (yr. ended 12/31/01): Assets, $665,446 (M); grants paid, $0; expenditures, $256,078; qualifying distributions, $0; giving activities include $256,078 for programs.
Officers and Directors:* Darlene West,* Pres.; Criss Candelaria,* V.P.; Jim Brown,* Secy.-Treas.; Thomas Bennett, M.D., Barbara Laird, Anne Mengas, Carl A. Ollarton, Rebecca Trujillo, Marnie Uhl.
EIN: 742354546

58371
Leung Foundation
3550 N. 1st Ave., Ste. 150
Tucson, AZ 85719-1765 (520) 795-9800
Contact: Lawrence C. Leung, Pres.

Established in 1999 in AZ.
Donor(s): Lawrence C. Leung, Inc., New World Homes, Inc.
Financial data (yr. ended 12/31/00): Assets, $655,319 (M); grants paid, $3,870; gifts received, $4,000; expenditures, $3,890; qualifying distributions, $3,870.
Limitations: Giving primarily in AZ.
Officers: Lawrence C. Leung, Pres.; Nancy Leung, Secy.
EIN: 860944082

58372
Little Chapel of All Nations, Inc.
P.O. Box 40995
Tucson, AZ 85717-0995 (520) 623-1692
Contact: Mary Esther Clark, Pres.

Classified as a private operating foundation in 1981.
Financial data (yr. ended 08/31/99): Assets, $614,873 (M); grants paid, $4,446; gifts received, $74,296; expenditures, $104,529; qualifying distributions, $4,446.
Limitations: Giving limited to AZ.
Application information: Application form not required.
Officers: Mary Esther Clark, Pres.; Albert R. Mead, V.P.; Herbert K. Abrams, Secy.; Donald L. Deal, Treas.
Directors: Donald W. Carson, Abraham S. Chanin, John F. Molloy, Raquel Rubio-Goldsmith, Aldine Von Isser.
EIN: 860115546

58373
John K. and Aline L. Goodman Foundation
283 N. Stone Ave.
Tucson, AZ 85702

Established in 1993 in AZ.
Donor(s): John K. Goodman.
Financial data (yr. ended 12/31/00): Assets, $606,603 (M); grants paid, $34,075; expenditures, $39,325; qualifying distributions, $33,653.
Limitations: Applications not accepted. Giving primarily in Tucson, AZ, Lexington, KY, and Oklahoma City, OK.
Application information: Contributes only to pre-selected organizations.
Officers and Directors:* John K. Goodman,* Pres.; Aline L. Goodman,* Secy.-Treas.; John K. Goodman, Jr., Lucy Goodman Lee.
EIN: 860759710

58374
Fleischer Museum
c/o M.H. Fleischer
17207 N. Perimeter Dr.
Scottsdale, AZ 85255

Donor(s): Overland Gallery, FFCA Management Co.
Financial data (yr. ended 12/31/99): Assets, $571,370 (M); grants paid, $0; gifts received, $516,464; expenditures, $287,162; qualifying distributions, $256,431; giving activities include $266,431 for programs.
Officers and Directors:* Morton H. Fleischer, Chair. and Exec. V.P.; Donna H. Fleischer,* Pres. and Exec. Dir.; Christopher H. Volk,* V.P. and Secy.; John R. Barravecchia, V.P. and Treas.
EIN: 860637929

58375
The Whispering Hope Ranch Foundation
(Formerly The D.T.R. Charitable Foundation)
807 N. Graham Ranch Rd.
Payson, AZ 85541

Established in 1997 in AZ.
Donor(s): Diane T. Reid.
Financial data (yr. ended 12/01/99): Assets, $526,032 (M); grants paid, $0; gifts received, $304,996; expenditures, $462,411; qualifying distributions, $302,752.
Officers: Greg Grant, Chair.; Diane T. Reid,* Pres.; Denise D. Resnick, Pres.; Jonah Shacknai, Pres.; Mark A. Prygocki, V.P.; Michael Rosenthal, V.P.; Wendy Barnhart,* Secy.; Susan Anderson,* Treas.
Directors: William Lee Barnhart, Jr., Bill Benda, M.D., Robert G. Mayfield, Gilbert D. Mook, Daniel E. Nastro, John G. Pattullo, Mark Sklar, Gerritt Van Huisstede.
EIN: 860887696

58376
Liberty Wildlife Rehabilitation Foundation, Inc.
11825 N. 70th St.
Scottsdale, AZ 85254-4059

Classified as a private operating foundation in 1996.
Financial data (yr. ended 12/31/99): Assets, $411,084 (M); grants paid, $0; gifts received, $93,450; expenditures, $143,975; qualifying distributions, $101,236; giving activities include $101,236 for programs.
Directors: Darlene Fitchet, Megan Mosby, Robert Ohmart, Kathryn Orr.
EIN: 942738161

58377
Eloisa Diaz Educational Foundation
1439 W. Mendoza Ave.
Mesa, AZ 85202   (480) 345-8424
Contact: Jesus Lionel Diaz, Dir.

Established in 2000 in AZ.
Donor(s): Eloisa Diaz Parker.‡
Financial data (yr. ended 08/31/01): Assets, $384,650 (M); grants paid, $1,100; gifts received, $392,412; expenditures, $7,881; qualifying distributions, $1,100.
Limitations: Giving primarily in AZ.
Application information: Application form required.
Director: Jesus Lionel Diaz.
EIN: 861006606

58378
The Cornerstone Foundation
P.O. Box 5132
Sun City West, AZ 85376-5132
(623) 546-0702
Contact: Mildred C.R. Moore, Secy.-Treas.

Established in 1986 in MA.
Donor(s): Joseph H. Moore III, J. Christy Wilson, Jr.‡
Financial data (yr. ended 10/31/01): Assets, $350,520 (M); grants paid, $90,000; expenditures, $91,439; qualifying distributions, $90,000.
Limitations: Giving on a national basis.
Application information: Application form required.
Officers and Trustees:* Michael E. Littlefield,* Chair.; Mildred C.R. Moore,* Secy.-Treas.; Timothy C. Tennent.
EIN: 042940520
Codes: FD2

58379
The Pauline Preserve Inc.
c/o Martin Bakker
7550 S. Willow Dr.
Tempe, AZ 85283

Established in 1998.
Donor(s): Wilda I. Wilson.
Financial data (yr. ended 12/31/00): Assets, $316,904 (M); grants paid, $0; gifts received, $4,340; expenditures, $18,717; qualifying distributions, $4,340; giving activities include $4,340 for programs.
Officers and Directors:* Martin Bakker,* Pres.; Muriel Brott,* Secy.; H. Maxine Wilson,* Treas.
EIN: 311578343

58380
The Institute of Inner Growth and Development
c/o Kent Rossman
5443 E. Sahuaro Dr.
Scottsdale, AZ 85254-4766

Established in 1992 in AZ.
Donor(s): Kent Rossman.
Financial data (yr. ended 12/31/01): Assets, $246,984 (M); grants paid, $0; gifts received, $25; expenditures, $38,783; qualifying distributions, $0.
Officers and Directors:* Kent Rossman,* Pres.; Gloria Barnett,* Secy.; Barbara Rossman,* Treas.; George Adair, Les Plattner.
EIN: 860714121

58381
The McElhaney Charitable Trust
34673 E. County 9th St.
Wellton, AZ 85356

Donor(s): Vennie R. McElhaney.‡
Financial data (yr. ended 12/31/99): Assets, $221,815 (M); grants paid, $0; gifts received, $4,210; expenditures, $842; qualifying distributions, $0; giving activities include $842 for programs.
Trustee: Carol E. Oden.
EIN: 860806249

58382
Rim Institute
c/o Carter Norris and Joan B. Norris
6835 Pepper Tree Ln.
Paradise Valley, AZ 85253-3346

Financial data (yr. ended 12/31/00): Assets, $212,938 (M); grants paid, $4,000; gifts received, $30,031; expenditures, $20,282; qualifying distributions, $4,000.

Limitations: Applications not accepted.
Application information: Contributes only to pre-selected organizations.
Director: Joan B. Norris.
Trustee: Linda Bosse.
EIN: 866130706

58383
Grand Canyon Broadcasters, Inc.
5025 N. Hwy. 89
Prescott, AZ 86301

Financial data (yr. ended 12/31/00): Assets, $207,908 (M); grants paid, $200; gifts received, $297,379; expenditures, $391,483; qualifying distributions, $200.
Officer: Roger Camping, Pres.; Rex Collins, Secy.
Directors: Robert Thornberg, James Thweatt.
EIN: 860643356
Codes: TN

58384
The J. Watson Foundation, Inc.
c/o Alan J. Wood, C.P.A.
P.O. Box 80991
Phoenix, AZ 85060   (602) 955-0546
Contact: Joanne Watson, Treas.

Established in 1993.
Donor(s): John Watson, Joanne Watson, James Watson, Joseph Watson, Julia Watson.
Financial data (yr. ended 04/30/01): Assets, $186,186 (M); grants paid, $12,937; gifts received, $6,000; expenditures, $13,897; qualifying distributions, $13,509.
Application information: Application form required.
Officers: Tom Jennings, Pres.; Peggy Bunting, Secy.; Joanne Watson, Treas.
EIN: 860732335
Codes: GTI

58385
Braeside Observatory
P.O. Box 906
Flagstaff, AZ 86002-0906

Classified as a private operating foundation in 1976.
Donor(s): Robert Fried.
Financial data (yr. ended 06/30/99): Assets, $176,309 (M); grants paid, $0; gifts received, $5,930; expenditures, $16,948; qualifying distributions, $16,948; giving activities include $16,498 for programs.
Director: Robert Fried.
EIN: 510192048

58386
University of Phoenix Alumni Network
(Formerly University of Phoenix Network for Professional Development)
4615 E. Elwood St.
Phoenix, AZ 85040-1958   (800) 795-2586
Contact: Carrie Fries, Dir.

Established as Phoenix Institute of Education and Arts, Inc.
Financial data (yr. ended 08/31/01): Assets, $141,197 (M); grants paid, $194,884; gifts received, $207,544; expenditures, $460,317; qualifying distributions, $460,317; giving activities include $155,563 for programs.
Limitations: Applications not accepted. Giving limited to Phoenix, AZ.
Officers: Todd Nelson, Pres.; Bill Brebaugh, Secy.; Larry Fleischer, Treas.
Directors: Carrie Fries, Laura Palmer Noone, Shannon T. Wilson.
EIN: 953366652
Codes: FD2, GTI

58387
Grand Association - Arizona Youth Football Federation
(Formerly Grand Association - Pop Warner Football)
8642 N. 78th Ave., No. 3
Peoria, AZ 85345

Classified as a private operating foundation in 1976.
Financial data (yr. ended 12/31/01): Assets, $138,238 (M); grants paid, $0; gifts received, $208,841; expenditures, $237,741; qualifying distributions, $208,683; giving activities include $210,462 for programs.
Officers: Gilbert Munoz, Pres.; Tracey Williams, Secy.; Pam Smolinski, Treas.
EIN: 860317008

58388
Foundation for Cancer Research
300 W. Clarendon Ave., Ste. 350
Phoenix, AZ 85013

Financial data (yr. ended 12/31/01): Assets, $127,447 (M); grants paid, $0; gifts received, $105,865; expenditures, $308,419; qualifying distributions, $96,321; giving activities include $211,873 for programs.
Officers: Burton Speiser, M.D., Pres.; Kent J. Rossman, M.D., Secy.
EIN: 860645410

58389
Thomas J. Said Foundation
9849 N. 21st Ave.
Phoenix, AZ 85021

Established in 1996 in AZ.
Donor(s): Thomas J. Said.
Financial data (yr. ended 12/31/01): Assets, $122,838 (M); grants paid, $0; gifts received, $3,440; expenditures, $31,841; qualifying distributions, $0.
Officer: Thomas J. Said, Pres.
EIN: 860837157

58390
Campanella Family Foundation
6221 S. Maple Ave.
Tempe, AZ 85283

Established in 2000 in AZ.
Financial data (yr. ended 12/31/01): Assets, $116,143 (M); grants paid, $1,000; gifts received, $79,516; expenditures, $3,266; qualifying distributions, $1,000.
Officers: Karen Sechena, Pres.; Denise Borst, V.P.; Noreen Cravener, Secy.; Michele Calebaugh, Treas.
Directors: Brian Campanella, Renee Campanella.
EIN: 860999041

58391
La Paz Foundation
7100 W. El Camino Del Cerro
Tucson, AZ 85745

Established in 1999 in AR.
Donor(s): Sharon A. Malcolmson, Larry Malcolmson.
Financial data (yr. ended 09/30/00): Assets, $115,369 (M); grants paid, $46,750; gifts received, $221,592; expenditures, $82,400; qualifying distributions, $79,518.
Limitations: Applications not accepted. Giving on a national basis.
Application information: Contributes only to pre-selected organizations.
Directors: Craig Carnick, Larry B. Malcolmson, Sharon A. Malcolmson.

EIN: 860974691

58392
Gordan Cupiss Foundation
2001 E. Lexington Dr.
Sierra Vista, AZ 85635 (520) 458-4415
Contact: Patricia G. Reed

Established in 1997 in AZ.
Donor(s): Gordon Cupiss.‡
Financial data (yr. ended 12/31/00): Assets, $105,423 (M); grants paid, $8,875; gifts received, $386; expenditures, $9,488; qualifying distributions, $8,875.
Limitations: Giving limited to Cochise County, AZ.
Trustee: Edwin Reed, Jr.
EIN: 860864465

58393
Roth Family Foundation
7181 E. Ventana Canyon Dr.
Tucson, AZ 85750

Established in 1987 in AZ.
Donor(s): Joan Roth, Edwin Roth.
Financial data (yr. ended 12/31/99): Assets, $100,309 (M); grants paid, $7,933; gifts received, $10,000; expenditures, $10,093; qualifying distributions, $7,933.
Limitations: Giving primarily in Tucson, AZ.
Officers: Joan Roth, Pres.; Edwin Roth, Secy.
Directors: Barry Roth, Debbie Roth, Jeffrey Roth, Lori Roth Tompkins.
EIN: 860594042

58394
The Mary C. Schanz Foundation
301 W. Spring Valley Pl.
Tucson, AZ 85737

Established in 2000 in AZ.
Donor(s): Mary C. Schanz, Benjamin M. Watkins.
Financial data (yr. ended 12/31/01): Assets, $86,856 (M); grants paid, $1,898; gifts received, $22,051; expenditures, $21,998; qualifying distributions, $57,377.
Limitations: Applications not accepted. Giving primarily in AZ.
Application information: Contributes only to pre-selected organizations.
Officers: Mary C. Schanz, Pres.; Benjamin M. Watkins, Secy.
EIN: 860999483

58395
Marion Foundation, Inc.
10201 N. Scottsdale Rd.
Scottsdale, AZ 85253-1436
Contact: Marion S. Kauffman, Pres.

Established in 1993 in AZ and KS.
Donor(s): Marion S. Kauffman.
Financial data (yr. ended 12/31/99): Assets, $69,419 (M); grants paid, $55,175; gifts received, $16,631; expenditures, $282,140; qualifying distributions, $281,324.
Limitations: Giving primarily in AZ.
Officer: Marion S. Kauffman, Pres.
Director: James G. Butler.
EIN: 860744648

58396
The Research Ranch Foundation
c/o Mary Ellen Knisely
P.O. Box 301
Sonoita, AZ 85637-0301
Application address: 2850 N. Camino de Oeste, Tucson, AZ 85745, tel.: (520) 743-9707
Contact: Ruth Russell, Secy.

Classified as a private operating foundation in 1969.

Financial data (yr. ended 08/31/01): Assets, $59,195 (M); grants paid, $7,481; gifts received, $4,775; expenditures, $19,332; qualifying distributions, $7,481.
Limitations: Giving primarily in Elgin, AZ.
Officers and Trustees:* Owen McCaffrey,* Pres.; Nancy McCuistion,* V.P.; Ruth Russell,* Secy.; William H. Cook,* Treas.; Molly Anderson, Ariel B. Appleton, P. Bryce Appleton, Julie Ferdon, Bruce Goff, Eileen Goff, Petie Knisely, Arlene McCaffrey, and 13 additional trustees.
EIN: 860127922

58397
Asarco Conservation Foundation, Inc.
1150 N. 7th Ave.
Tucson, AZ 85705
Application address: 165 W. 56th St., Ste. 1902, New York, NY 10019, tel.: (212) 307-5360
Contact: Kevin J. McCaffrey, Secy.

Financial data (yr. ended 12/31/01): Assets, $47,670 (M); grants paid, $0; expenditures, $20; qualifying distributions, $0.
Application information: Application form not required.
Officer: Kevin J. McCaffrey, Secy.
EIN: 133932092

58398
Ernest W. McFarland Foundation
5555 N. 7th Ave., Rm. A-200
Phoenix, AZ 85013-1755

Established in 1994 in AZ.
Donor(s): Edna McFarland,‡ Kara L. Lewis.
Financial data (yr. ended 12/31/00): Assets, $41,926 (M); grants paid, $0; gifts received, $11,436; expenditures, $11,479; qualifying distributions, $0; giving activities include $10,204 for programs.
Officers: Kara L. Lewis, Pres.; William C. Lewis, V.P.; Leah L. Lewis, Secy.
Directors: Delbert R. Lewis, Jewell Lewis.
EIN: 860765366

58399
Arizona Association of Conservation Districts, Inc.
3003 N. Central Ave., Ste. 800
Phoenix, AZ 85012-2945

Established in 1999 in AZ.
Financial data (yr. ended 12/31/99): Assets, $34,070 (M); grants paid, $7,610; gifts received, $75,700; expenditures, $130,538; qualifying distributions, $7,610.
Limitations: Applications not accepted.
Application information: Contributes only to pre-selected organizations.
Officers: Sharon Reid, Pres.; Robert Ahkeah, V.P.
Director: Macario Herrera.
EIN: 860695025

58400
United Evangelism, Inc.
408 E. Michigan Dr.
Tucson, AZ 85714-2851

Financial data (yr. ended 09/30/01): Assets, $29,784 (M); grants paid, $0; gifts received, $7,657; expenditures, $13,059; qualifying distributions, $13,059.
Officer: Dorothy Lucero, Secy.
Director: Marcos V. Lucero.
EIN: 237442111

58401
San Manuel Library
108 5th Ave.
San Manuel, AZ 85631

Financial data (yr. ended 12/31/01): Assets, $15,469 (M); grants paid, $0; gifts received, $5,993; expenditures, $18,039; qualifying distributions, $0.
Officers: Don Read, Pres.; John Dean, V.P.; Sheri Skamser, Secy.; Judith Karle, Treas.
EIN: 860281109

58402
Christian Freedom Fund, Inc.
2607 S. Los Feliz Dr.
Tempe, AZ 85282 (480) 966-7003
Contact: Eugene C. Galant, Jr., Pres.

Classified as a private operating foundation in 1992.
Financial data (yr. ended 12/31/00): Assets, $13,460 (M); grants paid, $12,279; gifts received, $13,230; expenditures, $13,324; qualifying distributions, $13,191.
Officers and Directors:* Eugene C. Galant, Jr.,* Pres.; Karen S. Galant,* Secy.; Leroy Melby.
EIN: 742481219

58403
Arizona Institute for Breast Health, Inc.
300 W. Clarendon St., Ste. 350
Phoenix, AZ 85013

Established in 1998.
Financial data (yr. ended 06/30/01): Assets, $12,026 (M); grants paid, $0; gifts received, $13,158; expenditures, $31,401; qualifying distributions, $31,401; giving activities include $31,401 for programs.
Officer and Directors:* Coral Quiet, M.D.,* Mgr.; Belinda Barclay-White, Teresa Lee.
EIN: 860940150

58404
Casa Grande Union High School Foundation, Inc.
711 E. Cottonwood Ln.
Casa Grande, AZ 85222
Contact: Terry Billingsley, Pres.

Established in 1986 in AZ.
Donor(s): Willard Ingalls Trust.
Financial data (yr. ended 06/30/99): Assets, $11,776 (M); grants paid, $47,200; gifts received, $57,300; expenditures, $47,493; qualifying distributions, $47,200.
Limitations: Giving limited to residents of Casa Grande, AZ.
Application information: Contact foundation for application guidelines for the Willard Ingalls Scholarship. Application form required.
Officers: Terry Billingsley, Pres.; Don Witwell, V.P.; Tina Hudson, Secy.-Treas.; Nancy Pifer, Treas.
Directors: Barbara Cropper, Jim Cropper, Ira Green, Pat Griffen, Tina Hudson.
EIN: 860447142
Codes: GTI

58405
The Ramsey Community Services Foundation
2398 E. Camelback Rd., Ste. 340
Phoenix, AZ 85016-3455

Established in 1997 in AZ.
Financial data (yr. ended 12/31/00): Assets, $9,781 (M); grants paid, $22,425; gifts received, $240; expenditures, $26,295; qualifying distributions, $22,415.
Limitations: Applications not accepted.

Application information: Contributes only to pre-selected organizations.
Officers: Robert E. Ramsey, Pres.; Virginia L. Norton, V.P.; Patrick Cantelme, Secy.-Treas.
EIN: 860863929

58406
The Christopher Pomroy Memorial Fund
c/o Richard Pomroy
P.O. Box 1365
Hereford, AZ 85615

Classified as a private operating foundation in 1990.
Financial data (yr. ended 12/31/01): Assets, $9,591 (M); grants paid, $750; gifts received, $381; expenditures, $1,131; qualifying distributions, $745.
Limitations: Applications not accepted. Giving limited to residents of Pittsford, NY.
Application information: Recipients selected by Pittsford Sutherland High School.
Trustees: Cynthia Marcotte, Richard A. Pomroy, Carol L. Rogers.
EIN: 541551046

58407
The Rohame Foundation
3063 N. Camino de Oeste
Tucson, AZ 85745
Contact: Meryl Beck, Pres.

Established in 1994.
Donor(s): Meryl Beck.
Financial data (yr. ended 12/31/00): Assets, $7,555 (M); grants paid, $23,296; gifts received, $18,903; expenditures, $23,672; qualifying distributions, $23,672.
Limitations: Giving primarily in AZ.
Application information: Application form required.
Officers: Meryl Beck, Pres.; Alison Beck, V.P.; Henry Roth, Secy.
EIN: 341784736
Codes: GTI

58408
Radio Astronomy Institute
23011 N. 16th Ln.
Phoenix, AZ 85027-1331

Established in 2001 in AZ.
Donor(s): KDMA, Channel 25, Inc.
Financial data (yr. ended 12/31/01): Assets, $6,350 (M); grants paid, $0; gifts received, $14,800; expenditures, $8,527; qualifying distributions, $14,700; giving activities include $8,260 for programs.
Officers: Kenneth Casey, Pres.; Christopher Casey, V.P.; Charlene Casey, Secy.-Treas.
Director: Lee Stevenson.
EIN: 860970424

58409
Frances Moynihan Huger Foundation, Inc.
2777 E. Camelback Rd., Ste. 300
Phoenix, AZ 85016-4302

Established in 1994 in AZ.
Donor(s): Huger Family Trust.
Financial data (yr. ended 06/30/99): Assets, $6,104 (M); grants paid, $5,251; gifts received, $48,333; expenditures, $113,217; qualifying distributions, $110,363; giving activities include $110,363 for programs.
Officers and Directors:* Raymond Huger, M.D., Pres.; Karmen Lee,* V.P. and Exec. Dir.; Sarah O'Malley, Secy.; Dennis Landauer,* Treas.; Rev. W.W. Harnischfeger, Msgr. John McMahon, Hon. Thomas O'Toole, John Weldon.
EIN: 860763890

58410
The Bridge of Hope Foundation
P.O. Box 12818
Prescott, AZ 86304

Donor(s): Clarke Masters, Betty Masters.
Financial data (yr. ended 12/31/99): Assets, $5,871 (M); grants paid, $8,114; gifts received, $10,235; expenditures, $12,622; qualifying distributions, $12,622.
Officers: Clarke Masters, Pres.; Paula Matthew, V.P.; Melody Fisher, Secy.
EIN: 860787026

58411
Michael K. Shields Foundation
10800 E. Cactus Rd., Ste. 11
Scottsdale, AZ 85259

Established in 1999 in AZ.
Donor(s): Richard K. Shields.
Financial data (yr. ended 12/31/00): Assets, $4,377 (M); grants paid, $500; gifts received, $1,778; expenditures, $1,225; qualifying distributions, $500.
Limitations: Applications not accepted. Giving primarily in Phoenix, AZ.
Application information: Contributes only to pre-selected organizations.
Officer: Richard K. Shields, Pres.
EIN: 860966921

58412
Foundation for Optimal Planetary Survival
8776 E. Shea Blvd.
Scottsdale, AZ 85260-6629

Financial data (yr. ended 12/31/99): Assets, $4,315 (M); grants paid, $100; gifts received, $5,000; expenditures, $2,845; qualifying distributions, $100.
Officer: SuSu Levy, Pres.
EIN: 954109232

58413
The Register Community Foundation
1221 E. Osborn Rd., Ste. 105
Phoenix, AZ 85014-5540

Established in 1997 in AZ.
Donor(s): Keisha Register.
Financial data (yr. ended 12/31/99): Assets, $3,054 (M); grants paid, $3,000; gifts received, $5,962; expenditures, $3,634; qualifying distributions, $3,000.
Officer: John M. Register, Pres.
Director: Gayla Register.
EIN: 311554186

58414
The Dottie Boreyko Foundation
1920 E. Broadway Rd.
Tempe, AZ 85282-1702

Established in 1996 in AZ.
Donor(s): David L. Kwan, J. Richard Lee, Inc., New Vision International, Inc.
Financial data (yr. ended 12/31/00): Assets, $2,910 (M); grants paid, $365,250; gifts received, $6,500; expenditures, $388,139; qualifying distributions, $265,203.
Limitations: Applications not accepted.
Application information: Contributes only to pre-selected organizations.
Officers and Directors:* Jason P. Boreyko,* Pres. and Treas.; Benson K. Boreyko,* V.P. and Secy.; D. Lynne Boreyko, Karen L. Boreyko.
EIN: 860835220
Codes: TN

58415
Stoff Institute for Medical Research
2661 N. Camino de Oeste
Tucson, AZ 85745

Established in 1998.
Financial data (yr. ended 12/31/99): Assets, $1,641 (M); grants paid, $0; gifts received, $35,885; expenditures, $38,124; qualifying distributions, $38,124.
Officer: Jesse Stoff, Pres.
EIN: 222997354

58416
Assist
(Formerly Assist to Independence)
c/o Ann M. O'Connor
P.O. Box 4133
Tuba City, AZ 86045

Classified as a private operating foundation in 1998.
Financial data (yr. ended 12/31/99): Assets, $547 (M); grants paid, $0; gifts received, $196,099; expenditures, $124,283; qualifying distributions, $106,116; giving activities include $163,718 for programs.
Officers: Ann O'Connor, Pres.; Mike Blatchford, V.P.; Cleave Isaac, Secy.; Elizabeth Pifer, Treas.
EIN: 860881405

58417
World of Friends, Inc.
1739 E. Cinnabar Ave.
Phoenix, AZ 85020

Donor(s): Gary Lodmell.
Financial data (yr. ended 12/31/00): Assets, $339 (M); grants paid, $1,200; gifts received, $245; expenditures, $1,432; qualifying distributions, $1,432.
Officers: Nancy Norland, Pres.; Gary Ladnell, Treas.
EIN: 860696515

58418
McCoy-Robertson Heritage Association
16230 N. 70th Ave.
Peoria, AZ 85382-3901

Classified as a private operating foundation in 1991.
Donor(s): Leslie E. McCoy.
Financial data (yr. ended 12/31/01): Assets, $221 (M); grants paid, $0; gifts received, $367; expenditures, $339; qualifying distributions, $318; giving activities include $318 for programs.
Officers: Leslie E. McCoy, Pres.; Weslie M. McCoy, V.P.; Marjorie Derham, Secy.-Treas.
EIN: 742410986

58419
Student Builders AZ
2244 E. Indigo Bay Dr.
Gilbert, AZ 85234-2871

Classified as an operating foundation in 1998.
Financial data (yr. ended 11/30/01): Assets, $57 (M); grants paid, $213,012; gifts received, $210,000; expenditures, $213,012; qualifying distributions, $213,012.
Limitations: Applications not accepted.
Application information: Contributes only to pre-selected organizations.
Officer: D.E. Keats, Pres.
Directors: C.M. Keats, Thomas Leacn.
EIN: 860935689
Codes: FD2

58420
The Woodruff Foundation
635 E. 6th Pl.
Mesa, AZ 85203-6340

Classified as a private operating foundation in 1982.
Financial data (yr. ended 08/31/99): Assets, $34 (M); grants paid, $0; gifts received, $75; expenditures, $84; qualifying distributions, $0; giving activities include $84 for programs.
Trustees: Belinda Smith, Brent Swann, Phillip Van Fleet.
EIN: 942864988

58421
Foundation for Indigenous Arts
3921 E. Coronado Dr.
Tucson, AZ 85718

Established in 1999.
Donor(s): Richard Weiss, Nancy Weiss.
Financial data (yr. ended 06/30/01): Assets, $1 (M); grants paid, $1,100; gifts received, $2,000; expenditures, $1,100; qualifying distributions, $1,100.
Officer: Richard Weiss, Pres.
EIN: 860938560

ARKANSAS

58422
Harvey and Bernice Jones Center for Families
(Formerly MBM Charitable Foundation)
P.O. Box 2035
Springdale, AR 72765-2035

Established in 1992 in AR.
Donor(s): The Harvey and Bernice Jones Charitable Foundation.
Financial data (yr. ended 11/30/00): Assets, $68,563,454 (M); grants paid, $59,355; gifts received, $1,982,933; expenditures, $5,746,423; qualifying distributions, $4,077,916; giving activities include $4,067,868 for programs.
Limitations: Applications not accepted. Giving primarily in Springdale, AR.
Application information: Contributes only to pre-selected organizations.
Directors: Joel Carver, Dan Ferritor, Bernice Jones.
EIN: 710718507

58423
The HAR-BER Village Foundation
P.O. Box 2035
Springdale, AR 72765

Donor(s): Bernice Jones.
Financial data (yr. ended 11/30/99): Assets, $9,525,247 (M); grants paid, $500,000; gifts received, $21,251; expenditures, $1,035,058; qualifying distributions, $938,275.
Limitations: Applications not accepted. Giving primarily in AR.
Application information: Contributes only to pre-selected organizations.
Directors: Joel Carver, Bernice Jones.
Trustees: Ralph Crumpacker, Randy Dubois, Jim Johnson, Duke Logan, Jan Norman, Gary Smith.
EIN: 710541295
Codes: FD

58424
Harry O. Hamm Foundation
P.O. Box 469
Van Buren, AR 72957
Application address: c/o Senior Class Counselor, Van Buren High School, 1221 Pointer Trail, Van Buren, AR 72956, tel.: (501) 474-2621

Established in 1998 in AR.
Financial data (yr. ended 12/31/01): Assets, $4,220,554 (M); grants paid, $150,496; expenditures, $175,250; qualifying distributions, $175,250.
Limitations: Giving primarily to residents of Van Buren, AR.
Application information: Application form available through Senior Class Counselor, Van Buren High School. Application form required.
Trustee: Citizens Bank & Trust Co.
EIN: 710800702
Codes: FD2, GTI

58425
R. E. & Catherine Woodson Sampley Educational Foundation, Inc.
P.O. Box 1147
Mount Ida, AR 71957
Contact: Frances Dobbs, Secy.-Treas.

Established in 1994 in AR.
Financial data (yr. ended 12/31/01): Assets, $2,789,445 (M); grants paid, $106,500; expenditures, $123,909; qualifying distributions, $111,153.
Limitations: Giving limited to residents of Montgomery County, AR.
Application information: Application form required.
Officers and Directors:* Melvin Simpson,* Pres.; Ed Simmons,* V.P.; Frances Dobbs,* Secy.-Treas.; Barbara Fryar, Dan McCarter, Vonda Vines, L.J. Warneke.
EIN: 716156225
Codes: FD2

58426
Robert & Mary Taylor Foundation
400 Salem Rd., Ste. 3
Conway, AR 72034

Established in 2000 in AR.
Donor(s): Mary Margaret Taylor.‡
Financial data (yr. ended 12/31/00): Assets, $2,538,396 (M); grants paid, $0; gifts received, $2,679,424; expenditures, $31,320; qualifying distributions, $100,000; giving activities include $73,000 for programs.
Limitations: Applications not accepted.
Application information: Contributes only to pre-selected organizations.
Directors: John T. Bumpers, Elmer P. Freyalderhoven, Edgar J. Tyler.
EIN: 710839501

58427
Mana Charitable Foundation
P.O. Box 2418
Mountain View, AR 72560-2418

Established in 2001.
Financial data (yr. ended 12/31/01): Assets, $1,537,148 (M); grants paid, $45,000; expenditures, $46,524; qualifying distributions, $45,000.
Limitations: Applications not accepted. Giving primarily in AR.
Application information: Contributes only to pre-selected organizations.
Officers and Directors:* John Weaver,* Pres.; Elizabeth Reaves,* Secy.; Phyllis Poe.
EIN: 364376140

58428
Mildred B. Cooper Memorial Chapel
1801 Forest Hill Blvd.
Bella Vista, AR 72714

Classified as a private operating foundation in 1985.
Donor(s): George M. Billingsley, Boyce W. Billingsley, Mrs. John Cooper, Jr.
Financial data (yr. ended 12/31/99): Assets, $1,518,999 (M); grants paid, $0; gifts received, $9,719; expenditures, $81,374; qualifying distributions, $17,626; giving activities include $81,374 for programs.
Officers and Directors:* Ann Basore,* Pres.; Boyce W. Billingsley,* V.P.; Rebecca Whelan,* V.P.; John A. Cooper, Jr., Secy.-Treas.; J. Neff Basore, Jr., Pat W. Cooper.
EIN: 581606828

58429
Peel House Foundation
400 S. Walton Blvd.
Bentonville, AR 72712-5705

Established in 1992 in AR.
Donor(s): Wal-Mart Stores, Inc., W.H. Enfield.
Financial data (yr. ended 12/31/99): Assets, $1,414,910 (M); grants paid, $0; gifts received, $50,898; expenditures, $150,529; qualifying distributions, $121,285; giving activities include $121,285 for programs.
Limitations: Applications not accepted. Giving primarily in AR.
Application information: Contributes only to pre-selected organizations.
Officers: Ernest Lawrence, Pres.; Bob Harrison, V.P.; Ann Pestel, Secy.-Treas.
Directors: Kay Andresen, Karen Rollet-Crocker, Leah Whitehead.
EIN: 710713232

58430
Ruth Veasey Educational Foundation, Inc.
P.O. Box 326
Dermott, AR 71638
Application address: P.O. Box 3, Dermott, AR 71638, tel.: (870) 538-5342
Contact: David Holt, Dir.

Established in 1963.
Financial data (yr. ended 05/31/02): Assets, $1,148,515 (M); grants paid, $26,750; expenditures, $37,836; qualifying distributions, $37,348; giving activities include $26,750 for loans to individuals.
Limitations: Giving primarily in Dermott, AR.
Application information: 3 references are required, including one from a local business person if possible. Application form required.
Officers: Ralph L. McQueen, Pres.; Jimmy G. Parkerson, V.P.; A.F. Kinney, Secy.; H.W. Thomas, Treas.
Directors: Thomas Deen, David Holt, Mary K. Tucker.
EIN: 716051103
Codes: GTI

58431
Emmaus Foundation, Inc.
1650 Emmaus Rd.
Fayetteville, AR 72702

Donor(s): Stephen S. Adams, Teresa A. Adams, Betty M. Gaddy, James L. Gaddy.
Financial data (yr. ended 11/30/01): Assets, $754,673 (M); grants paid, $0; gifts received, $27,280; expenditures, $35,075; qualifying distributions, $0.
Limitations: Applications not accepted.

Application information: Contributes only to pre-selected organizations.
Officer: James L. Gaddy, Pres.
Directors: Stephen S. Adams, Teresa A. Adams, Betty M. Gaddy.
EIN: 710770828

58432
Glen Conklin Charitable Trust
111 N. Church Ave.
Fayetteville, AR 72701 (501) 442-8731
Contact: David E. Lashley, Pres.

Established in 1997.
Financial data (yr. ended 12/31/00): Assets, $532,679 (M); grants paid, $35,000; expenditures, $36,045; qualifying distributions, $35,000.
Limitations: Giving primarily in Fayetteville, AR.
Application information: Application form not required.
Officers: David E. Lashley, Pres.; Glen Conklin, V.P.; Lisa Higgins, Secy.-Treas.
EIN: 911911727

58433
J. Hawks Charitable Foundation, Inc.
240 Highway 65 N.
Conway, AR 72032

Donor(s): John H. Hawks.
Financial data (yr. ended 12/31/00): Assets, $443,562 (M); grants paid, $13,150; expenditures, $17,926; qualifying distributions, $13,150.
Limitations: Giving primarily in AR.
Officers: John H. Hawks, Pres.; Stephan Hawks, Secy.-Treas.
EIN: 710811273

58434
Clara Mary Schaefer Charitable Foundation
c/o Allen Brillhart
415 N. McKinley, Ste. 1030
Little Rock, AR 72205

Established in 1993 in AR.
Donor(s): Joseph Knoeber.
Financial data (yr. ended 12/31/01): Assets, $328,032 (M); grants paid, $41,281; expenditures, $45,996; qualifying distributions, $41,279.
Limitations: Applications not accepted.
Application information: Contributes only to pre-selected organizations.
Officer and Directors:* Allen T. Brillhart,* Secy.; Ernest Taeger.
EIN: 710717324

58435
New Futures for Little Rock Youth, Inc.
400 W. Markham St., Ste. 702
Little Rock, AR 72201 (501) 374-1011

Established in 1988 in AR.
Financial data (yr. ended 06/30/00): Assets, $260,356 (M); grants paid, $0; gifts received, $479,179; expenditures, $656,020; qualifying distributions, $642,134; giving activities include $598,896 for programs.
Officers and Directors:* Hon. Joyce William Warren,* Pres.; Nancy Kirsch,* V.P.; Albert Porter,* Treas.; Annie Abrams, Lou Claudell, and 19 additional directors.
EIN: 710664490
Codes: TN

58436
Vogel-Schwartz Foundation, Inc.
c/o Robert A. Vogel
11219 Financial Ctr. Pkwy., Ste. 300
Little Rock, AR 72211 (501) 225-6018

Donor(s): Robert A. Vogel, Sam M. Vogel, Jr., Landel, Inc.
Financial data (yr. ended 12/31/01): Assets, $252,438 (M); grants paid, $15,340; gifts received, $68,000; expenditures, $15,912; qualifying distributions, $15,302.
Limitations: Giving primarily in Little Rock, AR.
Directors: Dan Schwartz, Rose Vogel Schwartz, Robbie B. Vogel, Robert A. Vogel, Sam M. Vogel, Jr.
EIN: 710782093

58437
Arkansas Eastman Scholarship Trust
c/o Citizens Bank
P.O. Box 2156
Batesville, AR 72503
Application address: c/o Scholarship Comm., P.O. Box 2357, Batesville, AR 72503, tel.: (501) 698-5524

Financial data (yr. ended 12/31/00): Assets, $223,175 (M); grants paid, $8,500; gifts received, $675; expenditures, $10,702; qualifying distributions, $8,500.
Limitations: Giving limited to the north central AR area.
Application information: Application form not required.
Trustee: Citizens Bank.
EIN: 582024178
Codes: GTI

58438
K-Life of Ozark, Inc.
c/o Greg Miller
P.O. Box 808
Ozark, AR 72949 (501) 667-4388

Classified as a private operating foundation in 1993.
Donor(s): George Gleason, Linda Gleason, Dianne Ross, Mark Ross, Jesus Ozark, Inc.
Financial data (yr. ended 12/31/00): Assets, $205,753 (M); grants paid, $5,879; gifts received, $2,689; expenditures, $33,129; qualifying distributions, $29,426; giving activities include $11,258 for programs.
Application information: Application form not required.
Officers and Directors:* Becky McClain,* Co-Pres.; Randy McClain,* Co-Pres.; George Pfeifer,* 1st V.P.; Sherry Pfeifer,* 1st V.P.; Larhonda Melton,* 2nd V.P.; Randy Melton,* 2nd V.P.; Neal Wade,* Secy.; Tina Wade,* Secy.; Greg Miller,* Treas.; Kathy Miller,* Treas.; Bob Bennett, Cathy Bennett, Gail Bradshaw, Joe Bradshaw, Dawn Williams, Gary Williams.
EIN: 710739291

58439
Ernest R. Horton Student Loan Trust
c/o Union Planters Bank
P.O. Box 250
Marshall, AR 72650-0250 (870) 448-3341
Contact: Debbie Watts, Tr.

Classified as a private operating foundation in 1983.
Financial data (yr. ended 06/30/01): Assets, $165,994 (M); grants paid, $0; expenditures, $835; qualifying distributions, $3,999; giving activities include $3,164 for loans to individuals.
Limitations: Giving limited to residents of AR.

58439—ARKANSAS

Application information: Application form required.
Trustees: Ann K. Brown, Don Clifton, Danny Griffin, Danny Horton, Debbie Watts.
EIN: 716111979

58440
Katherine K. Stewart Foundation, Inc.
c/o Billie Cooper
2929 W. Walnut St.
Rogers, AR 72756-1113

Established in 1992.
Donor(s): James H. Stewart.
Financial data (yr. ended 12/31/01): Assets, $121,910 (M); grants paid, $7,300; expenditures, $7,785; qualifying distributions, $7,300.
Limitations: Applications not accepted. Giving primarily in AR.
Application information: Contributes only to pre-selected organizations.
Officer: Billie E. Cooper, Secy.
Board Members: Mary Mayfield, Bill Watkins.
EIN: 581986677

58441
David E. Puryear Center, Inc.
P.O. Box 2462
Jonesboro, AR 72402-2462

Established in 1989 in AR.
Financial data (yr. ended 06/30/00): Assets, $120,300 (M); grants paid, $0; gifts received, $560,076; expenditures, $542,655; qualifying distributions, $532,142; giving activities include $542,655 for programs.
Officers and Directors:* Linnette Pryor,* C.E.O.; Shannon Kaffka,* Pres.; Flo Jones,* V.P.; Lori Poston,* Secy.; Steve Alston,* Treas.; William Lee Rogers, Jr., Admin.; Paul Bookout, Rosamond Crawley, J.W. Mason, Guy Patteson, and 3 additional directors.
EIN: 710674576

58442
Arkansas Band Museum, Inc.
425 Main St.
Pine Bluff, AR 71601

Established in 1996 in AR.
Donor(s): Jerry Horne.
Financial data (yr. ended 12/31/00): Assets, $119,815 (M); grants paid, $104; gifts received, $34,074; expenditures, $34,587; qualifying distributions, $29,216; giving activities include $29,216 for programs.
Limitations: Applications not accepted.
Director: Jerry Horne.
EIN: 710752361

58443
Recovery, Inc.
1201 Gee St.
Jonesboro, AR 72401

Financial data (yr. ended 07/31/99): Assets, $119,758 (M); grants paid, $0; expenditures, $10,618; qualifying distributions, $0; giving activities include $10,618 for programs.
Trustees: Dick Clay, Carrol Feeser, Ann Laser, Terry Ramer, R.D. Stewart, Ron Willett, Todd Williams.
EIN: 710538173

58444
T.L. Foundation Trust
c/o Barbara A. Tyson
2210 W. Oaklawn Dr.
Springdale, AR 72762

Established in 1998 in AR.
Donor(s): Barbara A. Tyson.
Financial data (yr. ended 12/31/00): Assets, $103,586 (M); grants paid, $5,715; gifts received, $90,000; expenditures, $40,729; qualifying distributions, $40,711.
Limitations: Applications not accepted. Giving primarily in Springdale, AR.
Application information: Contributes only to pre-selected organizations.
Trustees: Les Baledge, Harry C. Erwin III, Barbara A. Tyson.
EIN: 311666013

58445
Mary Harmon Floral Garden, Inc.
P.O. Box 387
Hardy, AR 72542-0387
Application address: 60 Winnebago Dr., Cherokee Village, AR 72529, tel.: (870) 257-2314
Contact: Floyd D. Hannon, Pres.

Established in 1987 in AR.
Financial data (yr. ended 12/31/99): Assets, $93,703 (M); grants paid, $2,645; gifts received, $23,393; expenditures, $44,031; qualifying distributions, $58,549.
Limitations: Giving limited to Fulton and Sharp counties, AR.
Officers: Floyd D. Hannon, Pres.; Allen C. Dobberke, V.P.; Charles E. Wilson, Secy.-Treas.
Directors: Richard Gammie, Daniel McEntire.
EIN: 630946387

58446
The Janky Foundation
c/o Harry Janky
19 Lakeside Dr.
Holiday Island, AR 72631-4521

Established in 1993 in MN. Classified as a private operating foundation in 1994.
Donor(s): Harry Janky, Kay Janky.
Financial data (yr. ended 12/31/00): Assets, $84,156 (M); grants paid, $4,700; gifts received, $50,279; expenditures, $4,731; qualifying distributions, $4,704.
Limitations: Applications not accepted. Giving limited to MN.
Application information: Contributes only to pre-selected organizations.
Officers and Directors:* Harry Janky,* Pres. and Treas.; Kay Janky,* V.P. and Secy.; Steve Janky, Sr. Margaret Schweiss, Sarah Stowell.
EIN: 411766420

58447
Guru Nanak International Orphans Fund, Inc.
P.O. Box 1713
El Dorado, AR 71731-1713

Donor(s): Gurprem S. Kang.
Financial data (yr. ended 12/31/99): Assets, $82,939 (M); grants paid, $0; gifts received, $172; expenditures, $2,807; qualifying distributions, $2,338.
Officers: Gurprem S. Kang, Pres. and Treas.; Surinder S. Kang, Secy.
EIN: 341364638

58448
Fulton Family Charitable Foundation
P.O. Box 715
Rogers, AR 72757

Established in 1997 in AR.
Donor(s): Jeston Lynn Fulton, Phyllis M. Fulton.
Financial data (yr. ended 12/31/99): Assets, $78,336 (M); grants paid, $80,000; gifts received, $740; expenditures, $80,750; qualifying distributions, $80,750.
Limitations: Applications not accepted. Giving primarily in AR.
Application information: Contributes only to pre-selected organizations.
Trustees: Jeston Lynn Fulton, Phyllis M. Fulton.
EIN: 621692216
Codes: FD2

58449
Medallion Foods Competitive Edge Scholarship Trust
3636 Delta Ave.
Newport, AR 72112-9096
Application address: c/o Newport Campus Charitable Foundation, Box 189, Newport, AR 72112, tel.: (870) 523-3300

Established in 1995 in AR.
Financial data (yr. ended 12/31/99): Assets, $62,331 (M); grants paid, $55,747; gifts received, $53,474; expenditures, $56,047; qualifying distributions, $55,721.
Limitations: Giving limited to residents of and children of non-resident employees in Jackson County, AR.
Application information: Application form required.
Officers: Kaneaster Hodges, Jr., Pres.; Jim S. Gowen, Sr., V.P.; Ann Hout, Secy.-Treas. and Exec. Dir.
Trustees: Tommy Hargrove, Mike Imoue, George Kell, Sr., Hank Pierce, Lindley Smith, Brad Snider, Alice Walton, Union Planters Bank.
EIN: 710773955
Codes: GTI

58450
Foundation for Musculoskeletal Research and Education
600 S. Mckinley, Ste. 102
Little Rock, AR 72205

Financial data (yr. ended 12/31/00): Assets, $46,085 (M); grants paid, $0; gifts received, $72,641; expenditures, $64,817; qualifying distributions, $4,216; giving activities include $4,216 for programs.
Officers: C. Lowry Barnes, Pres.; Martha Bushmaier, Secy.
Director: Douglas Parker.
EIN: 710779306

58451
Gates/Rogers Foundation, Inc.
707 Main St.
North Little Rock, AR 72114

Established in 2001.
Donor(s): Victor C. Gates.
Financial data (yr. ended 12/31/01): Assets, $45,000 (M); grants paid, $0; gifts received, $45,000; expenditures, $0; qualifying distributions, $0.
Limitations: Applications not accepted.
Application information: Contributes only to pre-selected organizations.
Directors: Steve Caver, Victor C. Gates, Fred Knight, Ron Maxwell, George Mobbs.
EIN: 710859470

58452
John A. & Marsha L. Phillips Charitable Foundation Trust
5210 Village Pkwy.
Rogers, AR 72758

Established in 1997 in AR.
Donor(s): John A. Phillips, Marsha L. Phillips.
Financial data (yr. ended 12/31/00): Assets, $44,568 (M); grants paid, $67,722; gifts received,

$135,945; expenditures, $68,417; qualifying distributions, $68,413.
Limitations: Applications not accepted. Giving primarily in AR.
Application information: Contributes only to pre-selected organizations.
Trustees: John A. Phillips, Marsha L. Phillips.
EIN: 716170626

58453
April Brooks Memorial Foundation
P.O. Box 4145
Fort Smith, AR 72914

Established in 1997 in AR.
Financial data (yr. ended 12/31/99): Assets, $29,742 (M); grants paid, $1,200; expenditures, $1,290; qualifying distributions, $1,200.
Limitations: Applications not accepted.
Application information: Contributes only to pre-selected organizations.
Trustees: Eddie Brooks, Hugh Hardin, Roger Meek, Bob Ed Pevehouse, Tom Quinn.
EIN: 710804270

58454
Judge J. P. & Elizabeth Reed Foundation
P.O. Box 1305
Paragould, AR 72451-1305
Application address: c/o Elizabeth Reed, 1704 Carroll Rd., Paragould, AR 72450

Financial data (yr. ended 12/31/00): Assets, $20,698 (M); grants paid, $2,000; gifts received, $10,000; expenditures, $2,000; qualifying distributions, $2,000.
Limitations: Giving limited to residents of Greene County, AR.
Application information: Application form required.
Officers: Mike Ford, Pres.; Sharon Joy, V.P.; Kelly Wright, V.P.; Frances Mangrum, Secy.
EIN: 311603716

58455
Lu Nedrow Graduate Scholarship
1507 Frierson
Jonesboro, AR 72401
Contact: Carolyn Frierson, Chair.

Financial data (yr. ended 01/31/01): Assets, $19,220 (L); grants paid, $1,300; expenditures, $1,405; qualifying distributions, $1,300.
Application information: Application form required.
Officer: Carolyn Frierson, Chair.
Trustees: Lynn Bruner, Jimmie Sue Enchelmeyer, Kathy Farris, Shawna Starnes.
EIN: 716170687

58456
The Brett Minden Foundation, Inc.
24 E. Main St.
Paris, AR 72855-3322
Application address: c/o Counselor, Paris High School, Rte. 1, Paris, AR 72855
Contact: E.J. Penn, Dir.

Established in 1988 in AR.
Donor(s): James Smith.‡
Financial data (yr. ended 12/31/01): Assets, $12,388 (M); grants paid, $0; expenditures, $52; qualifying distributions, $9.
Limitations: Giving primarily in Paris, AR.
Application information: Application form required.
Officer: J.C. Smith, Pres.
Director: E.J. Penn.
EIN: 581763073

58457
Arkansas Business Council Foundation
P.O. Box 1860
Bentonville, AR 72712-1860

Established in 1987 in AR.
Donor(s): Walton Family Foundation, Inc.
Financial data (yr. ended 07/31/01): Assets, $2,876 (M); grants paid, $0; expenditures, $472; qualifying distributions, $0.
Officers and Directors:* Rob Walton,* Chair.; Charles Morgan,* Vice-Chair.; John Cooper, Jr.,* Treas.; R.S. "Rollie" Boreham, Jr., Bill Dillard II, Mike Flynn, Joe Ford, Frank Hickingbotham, J.B. Hunt, and 5 additional directors.
EIN: 710654043

58458
Mack Davis Scholarship Trust
c/o Betty Gale Davis
7101 Archwood Dr.
Little Rock, AR 72204-4706

Established in 1997.
Donor(s): Betty Gale Davis.
Financial data (yr. ended 12/31/99): Assets, $2,812 (M); grants paid, $1,000; gifts received, $600; expenditures, $1,040; qualifying distributions, $1,040.
Application information: Application form not required.
Trustees: Betty Gale Davis, Vonda Houchin.
EIN: 626325352

58459
Arkansas Preservation Foundation
4290 S. School St.
Fayetteville, AR 72703

Established in 1999 in AR.
Donor(s): Art Hollenback, Bill Stafford.
Financial data (yr. ended 12/31/99): Assets, $1,613 (M); grants paid, $0; gifts received, $1,600; expenditures, $0; qualifying distributions, $0.
Limitations: Applications not accepted.
Application information: Contributes only to pre-selected organizations.
Officers: Ben Lee, Pres.; Bill Callan, V.P.; Bill Stafford, Secy.-Treas.
EIN: 710816504

58460
Greater Happiness, Inc.
12420 Collins Rd.
Gentry, AR 72734-9375

Financial data (yr. ended 05/31/99): Assets, $1,251 (M); grants paid, $0; gifts received, $24,452; expenditures, $26,095; qualifying distributions, $25,753; giving activities include $25,648 for programs.
Officers and Directors:* Diana Hartfield,* Pres.; Dolores J. Adams,* V.P. and Treas.; Linda Williams,* Secy.; Erna Adams, Anthony Hartfield.
EIN: 710626158

58461
Lodestar Shelter, Inc.
P.O. Box 994
Mena, AR 71953-8270

Financial data (yr. ended 12/31/01): Assets, $662 (M); grants paid, $0; gifts received, $15,152; expenditures, $15,631; qualifying distributions, $0.
Limitations: Giving primarily in AR.
Officers: Victoria Andrews, Pres. and Treas.; Jennifer Lugenbend, V.P.
EIN: 592244310

58462
Beaver Lake Animal Shelter, Inc.
P.O. Box 174
Avoca, AR 72711

Financial data (yr. ended 03/31/99): Assets, $312 (M); grants paid, $0; gifts received, $22,626; expenditures, $23,208; qualifying distributions, $23,208; giving activities include $23,208 for programs.
Officer: Rosella Greenberg, Pres.
EIN: 710690846

58463
David Anderson Foundation
801 S. Benton St., Ste. 2301
Searcy, AR 72143-6956

Financial data (yr. ended 12/31/00): Assets, $77 (M); grants paid, $0; gifts received, $7,200; expenditures, $7,371; qualifying distributions, $7,371; giving activities include $7,371 for programs.
Officers: Muriel E. Beal, Pres.; Robert W. Anderson, V.P.; David W. Anderson, Secy.-Treas.
EIN: 710744596

58464
Allfund, Inc.
8201 Cantrell Rd.
Little Rock, AR 72227

Established in 1998 in AR.
Financial data (yr. ended 02/28/00): Assets, $0 (M); grants paid, $33,325; expenditures, $173,898; qualifying distributions, $33,324.
Limitations: Giving primarily in AR.
Trustees: Mary Ann Bell, Tom Garner, Stuart Hansen.
EIN: 710703133

CALIFORNIA

58465
J. Paul Getty Trust
1200 Getty Ctr. Dr., Ste. 800
Los Angeles, CA 90049-1685 (310) 440-7320
FAX: (310) 440-7703; *URL:* http://www.getty.edu
Contact: The Getty Grant Program

Operating trust established in 1953 in CA as J. Paul Getty Museum; Grant Program established in 1984.
Donor(s): J. Paul Getty.‡
Financial data (yr. ended 06/30/01): Assets, $8,793,485,757 (M); grants paid, $19,579,820; gifts received, $3,071,442; expenditures, $242,432,705; qualifying distributions, $267,956,299; giving activities include $242,135,723 for programs.
Limitations: Giving on an international basis.
Publications: Informational brochure, grants list, application guidelines, occasional report, annual report.
Application information: Detailed guidelines that outline eligibility requirements, deadlines, application procedures, the review process, and notification dates for most of the grant categories are available online at the foundation's Web site and from the Grant Program office. Before submitting an application, potential applicants should review the grant program's funding priorities and application procedure. If applicants are uncertain about how to proceed with their

submissions, they should contact the Grant Program office for assistance or review the grant program's website at www.getty.edu/grants.
Officers and Trustees:* David P. Gardner,* Chair.; Barry Munitz,* Pres. and C.E.O.; Stephen D. Rountree, Exec. V.P. and C.O.O.; Bradley W. Wells, V.P., Finance; Deborah Gribbon, V.P. and Dir., Museum; Peter C. Erichsen, V.P., and Genl. Counsel; Lewis W. Bernard, John H. Biggs, Louise H. Bryson, Ronald W. Burkle, Ramon C. Cortines, Barbara G. Fleischman, Agnes Gund, Helene L. Kaplan, Luis G. Nogales, Blenda J. Wilson, Ira E. Yellin.
EIN: 951790021
Codes: FD, GTI

58466
The Packard Humanities Institute
300 2nd St., Ste. 201
Los Altos, CA 94022

Established in 1987 in CA.
Donor(s): The David and Lucile Packard Foundation.
Financial data (yr. ended 12/31/00): Assets, $1,302,804,659 (M); grants paid, $20,655,346; expenditures, $33,496,700; qualifying distributions, $35,022,214.
Limitations: Applications not accepted. Giving primarily in CA.
Application information: Contributes only to pre-selected organizations.
Officers: David W. Packard, Chair. and Pres.; Susan Packard Orr, V.P.; Barbara P. Wright, Secy.; Edwin E. Van Bronkhorst, Treas.
Directors: G. Gervaise Davis III, Robert J. Glaser, M.D., George P. Goold, Walter B. Hewlett, William A. Johnson, Pamela Packard, Christopher Wolff.
EIN: 943038401
Codes: FD, FM

58467
The Henry J. Kaiser Family Foundation
2400 Sand Hill Rd.
Menlo Park, CA 94025 (650) 854-9400
Tel. for application guidelines: (800) 656-4533; FAX: (650) 854-4800; E-mail: rwells@kff.org; URL: http://www.kff.org
Contact: Renee Wells, Grants and Contracts Mgr.

Trust established in 1948 in CA; changed status to operating foundation in 1999.
Donor(s): Bess F. Kaiser,‡ Henry J. Kaiser,‡ Henry J. Kaiser, Jr.,‡ and others.
Financial data (yr. ended 12/31/01): Assets, $597,891,506 (M); grants paid, $1,358,843; gifts received, $1,139,433; expenditures, $68,333,150; qualifying distributions, $73,261,811; giving activities include $19,305,340 for programs.
Limitations: Giving limited to CA for the California Grants Program only; and South Africa for the international grants program; other grants nationwide.
Publications: Annual report, informational brochure (including application guidelines).
Application information: Most grants are initiated by the foundation. Very few unsolicited grants are funded. Application form not required.
Officers and Trustees:* Gerald M. Rosberg,* Chair.; Patricia A. King, J.D., Vice-Chair.; Drew E. Altman, Ph.D.,* Pres. and C.E.O.; Diane Rowland, Sc.D., Exec. V.P.; Bruce W. Madding, Sr. V.P. and C.F.O.; Matt James, Sr. V.P.; Michael R. Sinclair, Ph.D., Sr. V.P.; Mollyann Brodie, Ph.D., V.P.; Tina Hoff, V.P.; Larry Leuitt, V.P.; Marsha Lille-Blanton, V.P.; Barbara Lyons, Ph.D., V.P.; Tricia Neuman, Sc. D., V.P.; Vicky Rideout, V.P.; Alina Salganicoff, Ph.D., V.P.; Sheila P. Burke, RN, MPA, Amb. James Jones, Henry J. Kaiser III, Michael T. Kaiser, David A. Kessler, M.D., Charles I. Ogletree, Jr., Allan Rosenfield, M.D., Donna E. Shalala, Michael I. Sovern.
EIN: 946064808
Codes: FD, GTI

58468
Norton Simon Art Foundation
411 W. Colorado Blvd.
Pasadena, CA 91105-1825

Incorporated in 1954 in CA.
Donor(s): Norton Simon,‡ Norton Simon, Inc. and its subsidiaries and predecessors, and members of the Simon family.
Financial data (yr. ended 11/30/01): Assets, $586,420,006 (M); grants paid, $0; gifts received, $403,000; expenditures, $3,145,626; qualifying distributions, $2,386,452; giving activities include $2,386,452 for programs.
Officers and Trustees:* Walter W. Timoshuk,* Pres.; Ronald H. Dykhuizen, V.P. and Secy.-Treas.; Michael E. Phelps,* V.P.; Sara Campbell, Eppie Lederer, Edward F. Rover, Jennifer Jones Simon.
EIN: 956038921

58469
Public Policy Institute of California
500 Washington St., Ste. 800
San Francisco, CA 94111

Established in 1994 in CA.
Donor(s): William R. Hewlett.
Financial data (yr. ended 06/30/00): Assets, $267,017,200 (M); grants paid, $0; expenditures, $11,188,733; qualifying distributions, $10,083,096; giving activities include $10,911,394 for programs.
Officers: Raymond L. Watson, Chair.; David W. Lyon, Pres. and C.E.O.; Karen Grose, Secy.; Andrew Grose, C.F.O.
Directors: William K. Coblentz, David A. Coulter, Cheryl White Mason, A. Alan Post, Cynthia A. Telles, Raymond L. Watson, and 5 additional directors.
EIN: 943207299

58470
The Priem Family Foundation
4052 Kettering Terr.
Fremont, CA 94536

Established in 1999 in CA.
Donor(s): Curtis Priem.
Financial data (yr. ended 06/30/00): Assets, $262,282,603 (M); grants paid, $0; gifts received, $58,731,750; expenditures, $78,586; qualifying distributions, $6,036,998; giving activities include $60,000 for programs.
Officers and Directors:* Curtis Priem,* C.E.O. and Pres.; Edward Miles,* V.P.; Peter Dmytryk, Secy.; Veronica Priem,* C.F.O.
EIN: 943340371

58471
The Broad Art Foundation
10900 Wilshire Blvd., 12th Fl.
Los Angeles, CA 90024-6532
Contact: Eli Broad, Tr.

Established in 1984 in CA.
Donor(s): Eli Broad.
Financial data (yr. ended 06/30/02): Assets, $137,476,607 (M); grants paid, $477,500; gifts received, $11,513,552; expenditures, $2,291,289; qualifying distributions, $477,500.
Limitations: Applications not accepted. Giving primarily in CA and NY.
Publications: Informational brochure.
Application information: Contributes only to pre-selected organizations.
Trustee: Eli Broad.
EIN: 954664939
Codes: FD

58472
The Carnegie Foundation for the Advancement of Teaching
555 Middlefield Rd.
Menlo Park, CA 94025-3443

Established in 1905 under NY State charter; incorporated in 1906 under an Act of Congress.
Donor(s): Andrew Carnegie.‡
Financial data (yr. ended 06/30/01): Assets, $134,613,952 (M); grants paid, $201,350; gifts received, $7,896,200; expenditures, $9,487,499; qualifying distributions, $7,998,094; giving activities include $8,062,921 for programs.
Limitations: Applications not accepted.
Publications: Annual report, informational brochure.
Application information: Contributes only to pre-selected organizations.
Officers and Directors:* Lee Shulman,* Pres.; John H. Barcroft, V.P. and Treas.; Johanna Wilson,* Secy.
EIN: 131623924
Codes: FD2

58473
Monterey Bay Aquarium Research Institute
7700 Sandholdt Rd.
P.O. Box 628
Moss Landing, CA 95039-0628

Established in 1987 in CA.
Donor(s): The David and Lucile Packard Foundation, David Packard.
Financial data (yr. ended 12/31/99): Assets, $121,179,893 (M); grants paid, $15,043; gifts received, $49,917,539; expenditures, $29,831,975; qualifying distributions, $39,350,249; giving activities include $8,549,173 for programs.
Limitations: Applications not accepted.
Application information: Contributes only to pre-selected organizations.
Officers and Directors:* Julie Packard,* Chair.; Franklin Orr, Jr., Vice-Chair.; Marcia McNutt, C.E.O. and Pres.; Nancy Burnett,* Secy.-Treas.; Ross Heath,* Exec. Dir.; D. Allan Bromley, Robin Burnett, and 12 additional directors.
EIN: 770150580

58474
The Hogan Family Foundation, Inc.
2426 Townsgate Rd., Ste. 700
Westlake Village, CA 91361

Established in 1998 in CA and DE.
Donor(s): Edward J. Hogan, Marilyn J. Hogan.
Financial data (yr. ended 09/30/99): Assets, $104,159,509 (M); grants paid, $32,167; gifts received, $100,000,000; expenditures, $4,132,667; qualifying distributions, $5,027,486; giving activities include $4,824,194 for programs.
Limitations: Applications not accepted. Giving primarily in CA, HI, and NY.
Application information: Contributes only to pre-selected organizations.
Officers: Edward J. Hogan, Chair.; Marilyn J. Hogan, Vice Chair.; Patrick J. Birmingham, V.P.; A. Maurice Meyers, V.P.; Ronald M. Krueger, Secy.-Treas.
EIN: 364254944

58475
Smith-Kettlewell Eye Research Institute
2318 Fillmore St.
San Francisco, CA 94115-1821

Classified as a private operating foundation in 1985.
Financial data (yr. ended 12/31/01): Assets, $57,409,617 (M); grants paid, $0; gifts received, $7,395,031; expenditures, $9,971,363; qualifying distributions, $10,231,181; giving activities include $7,490,877 for programs.
Officers and Directors:* Alan Scott, M.D.,* C.E.O.; Bernard Petrie, Pres.; Alexander M. Wilson,* V.P.; Richard S. Grey,* Secy.; Brooks Walker, Jr.,* Treas.; Arthur Jampolsky, M.D., Exec. Dir.; Anthony J. Adams, Ph.D., Susan H. Day, M.D., C.T. Gamble, Preston Q. Hale, T.C. Hsu, Richard B. Madden, Henry S. Metz, M.D., Marilyn T. Miller, M.D., Ken Nakayama, Ph.D., Ruth S. Poole.
EIN: 946127237

58476
Santa Catalina Island Conservancy
P.O. Box 2739
Avalon, CA 90704-3749

Classified as a private operating foundation in 1973.
Financial data (yr. ended 12/31/00): Assets, $54,635,492 (M); grants paid, $0; gifts received, $1,393,379; expenditures, $4,934,113; qualifying distributions, $4,532,490; giving activities include $2,776,461 for programs.
Officers and Directors:* Rose Ellen Gardner,* C.E.O. and Pres.; William Bushing, V.P.; Lynn Burt, Secy.; J. Scott Wauben, Treas. and C.F.O.; James H. Ackerman, Bradley Phillip Bell, Keven R. Bellows, George Boone, Leon M. Cooper, Geoffrey C. Rusack, Robert Thorne, Julie A. Wrigley, and 5 additional directors.
EIN: 237228407

58477
Dancing Star Foundation
c/o Ballsun & Ledbetter, LLP
2029 Century Park E., 6th Fl.
Los Angeles, CA 90067 (310) 553-5750
Contact: Michael Tobias, Pres.

Donor(s): Sue M. Stiles.‡
Financial data (yr. ended 12/31/00): Assets, $51,140,935 (M); grants paid, $3,049; gifts received, $46,453,807; expenditures, $1,740,866; qualifying distributions, $2,045,930; giving activities include $1,624,897 for programs.
Limitations: Giving primarily in CA.
Officers and Directors:* Michael Tobias,* Pres.; Jane Morrison, Secy.-Treas.; Pat Fitzgerald, Geoffrey Holland, Robert Radin.
EIN: 770343380

58478
Iris & B. Gerald Cantor Foundation
(Formerly The B. G. Cantor Art Foundation)
P.O. Box 811
Beverly Hills, CA 90213 (310) 277-4600
E-mail: jsobol@ibgcf.org; *URL:* http://www.cantorfoundation.org
Contact: Judith Sobol, Exec. Dir.

Established in 1978 in CA.
Donor(s): B. Gerald Cantor,‡ Iris Cantor.
Financial data (yr. ended 04/30/01): Assets, $44,488,328 (M); grants paid, $2,378,467; gifts received, $425,350; expenditures, $2,786,928; qualifying distributions, $2,781,478.
Limitations: Applications not accepted. Giving primarily in CA and NY.

Application information: Contributes to pre-selected organizations.
Officers and Directors:* Iris Cantor,* Chair. and Pres.; Randi Ross Aitken,* Secy.; Joel Rothstein, Treas.; Judith Sobol, Exec. Dir.; Suzanne Fisher, Michele Geller, Monica Ross Muhart.
EIN: 136227347
Codes: FD, FM

58479
Everlasting Private Foundation
c/o Annie M.H. Chan
19770 Stevens Creek Blvd.
Cupertino, CA 95014 (408) 343-1088
Contact: Michelle Woo

Established in 1996 in CA.
Donor(s): Annie M.H. Chan.
Financial data (yr. ended 12/31/00): Assets, $41,405,425 (M); grants paid, $2,000,000; expenditures, $2,549,582; qualifying distributions, $9,049,572; giving activities include $6,873,405 for loans and $222,286 for programs.
Limitations: Applications not accepted. Giving on a national basis.
Application information: Contributes only to pre-selected organizations.
Officers: Annie M.H. Chan, Pres.; Myong Shin Woo, Secy. and C.F.O.
EIN: 770425562
Codes: FD

58480
Stupski Family Foundation
9 Via Paraiso E.
Tiburon, CA 94920

Established in 1996 in CA.
Donor(s): Lawrence J. Stupski.
Financial data (yr. ended 12/31/99): Assets, $39,581,980 (M); grants paid, $500,000; gifts received, $1,333,857; expenditures, $1,742,115; qualifying distributions, $764,027; giving activities include $621,260 for programs.
Limitations: Applications not accepted.
Application information: Contributes only to pre-selected organizations.
Officers: Lawrence J. Stupski, Chair.; Joyce L. Stupski, Pres.; Kathleen J. Burke, Exec. V.P.; Pamela R. Mantegani, Secy.; Kay Smith, Treas.
Director: Jim Losi.
EIN: 680397103
Codes: FD

58481
Frederick R. Weisman Art Foundation
(Formerly FRW/123 Art Foundation)
1875 Century Park E., Ste. 1790
Los Angeles, CA 90067 (310) 203-2233
Contact: Michael P. Chmura, V.P.

Established in 1993 in CA and DE.
Donor(s): Frederick R. Weisman Trust of 1991.
Financial data (yr. ended 01/31/01): Assets, $32,784,594 (M); grants paid, $34,127; gifts received, $118,200; expenditures, $1,019,505; qualifying distributions, $895,365; giving activities include $895,365 for programs.
Limitations: Giving primarily in Los Angeles, CA and Minneapolis, MN.
Officers and Directors:* Billie Milam Weisman,* Pres.; Michael P. Chmura,* V.P., Treas., and C.F.O.; Malcolm G. Smith,* Secy.; Steven L. Arnold, Ellen Morehead.
EIN: 954442307

58482
Shoot for the Stars, Inc.
2101 Pulgas Ave.
East Palo Alto, CA 94303

Established in 1993 in CA.
Donor(s): Donald Vermeil, Roger Winkle, Lynn Winkle.
Financial data (yr. ended 08/31/01): Assets, $30,124,677 (M); grants paid, $0; gifts received, $21,915,865; expenditures, $2,089,449; qualifying distributions, $2,089,449; giving activities include $2,089,449 for programs.
Officer: Christopher Bischof, Exec. Dir.
Directors: Nancy Anderson, Charla Baugh, John Baugh, Donald Vermeil, Lynn Winkle, and 7 additional directors.
EIN: 943187806

58483
Ganna Walska Lotusland Foundation
695 Ashley Rd.
Santa Barbara, CA 93108

Established in 1958 in CA.
Donor(s): Carol L. Valentine.
Financial data (yr. ended 12/31/00): Assets, $25,227,432 (M); grants paid, $0; gifts received, $1,108,580; expenditures, $1,973,262; qualifying distributions, $1,711,969; giving activities include $522,256 for programs.
Officers: Robert J. Emmons, Pres.; Anne W. Jones, V.P.; Arthur R. Gaudi, Secy.-Treas.
Trustees: Merryl Brown, Elizabeth W. Dake, William W. Drewry, Harry F. Kolb, Stanya Owen, Pamela B. Pesenti, David Potter, Michael Towbes, Carol L. Valentine, April N. Walstad.
EIN: 237082550

58484
The Kavli Institute
1801 Solar Dr., Ste. 250
Oxnard, CA 93030
Contact: Fred Kavli, Pres.

Established in 2000 in CA.
Donor(s): Fred Kavli.
Financial data (yr. ended 11/30/01): Assets, $24,032,782 (M); grants paid, $0; gifts received, $22,500,300; expenditures, $1,337,889; qualifying distributions, $131,629.
Officers: Fred Kavli, Pres.; Douglas Freeman, Secy.
Directors: Tom Everhart, Rockell Hankin, Jack Peltason.
EIN: 770560009

58485
Mechanics' Institute
57 Post St., Ste. 403
San Francisco, CA 94104

Classified as a private operating foundation in 1986.
Financial data (yr. ended 08/31/00): Assets, $23,264,433 (M); grants paid, $0; gifts received, $434,566; expenditures, $2,041,858; qualifying distributions, $1,149,277; giving activities include $1,528,706 for programs.
Officers and Trustees:* Vincent McCambridge,* Pres.; David B. Goodwin,* V.P.; David J. Madson,* V.P.; Mark Pinto, V.P.; Fumiye Quong, Secy.; Barbara Boucke,* C.F.O.; James W. Flack, Exec. Dir.; Jane Bryk, Georganne Conley, Neil E. Falconer, James W. Friedman, Hon. Tomar Mason, Richard Reinhardt, Magdalen Ross.
EIN: 941254644

58486
The Nethercutt Collection, Inc.
15180 Bledsoe St.
Sylmar, CA 91342-2709

Donor(s): J.B. Nethercutt.
Financial data (yr. ended 12/31/01): Assets, $19,424,825 (M); grants paid, $0; gifts received, $4,149,129; expenditures, $2,716,203; qualifying distributions, $2,920,195; giving activities include $2,287,863 for programs.
Officers and Directors:* J.B. Nethercutt,* Chair. and C.E.O.; Michael Regalia,* Pres.; Jack B. Nethercutt II,* Exec V.P.; Gordon Belt,* V.P.; Armin Lohbrunner, Secy.-Treas. and C.F.O.; Donna Tullis, Mgr.; Tony Heinsbergen, Phil Hill, Byron Matson, Dorothy S. Nethercutt, Tom Powell.
EIN: 954442622

58487
The Frank H. Bartholomew Foundation
c/o William M. Godward
1 Maritime Plz., Ste. 2000
San Francisco, CA 94111
Application address: c/o Jan V. Haraszthy, P.O. Box 311, Sonoma, CA 95176-0311

Classified as a private operating foundation in 1991.
Donor(s): Frank H. Bartholomew,‡ Antonia P. Bartholomew,‡ William W. Godward.
Financial data (yr. ended 12/31/00): Assets, $17,078,631 (M); grants paid, $31,670; expenditures, $934,347; qualifying distributions, $726,757; giving activities include $678,664 for programs.
Limitations: Giving primarily in Sonoma, CA.
Application information: Recommendation letter from Sonoma Valley High School, V.P. Application form required.
Officer: Jan V. Haraszthy, Mgr.
Trustee: William W. Godward.
EIN: 943129676

58488
Jacobs Center for Non-profit Innovation
P.O. Box 740650
San Diego, CA 92174-0650 (619) 527-6161
Contact: Jennifer Vanica, Exec. Dir.

Established in 1996 in CA.
Financial data (yr. ended 12/31/99): Assets, $14,687,421 (M); grants paid, $15,000; gifts received, $355,414; expenditures, $2,781,035; qualifying distributions, $2,606,131; giving activities include $1,590,194 for programs.
Limitations: Giving primarily in San Diego, CA.
Publications: Annual report, multi-year report, annual report (including application guidelines), informational brochure.
Officers: Valerie Hapke, Chair. and Pres.; Norman Hapke, V.P., Treas. and C.F.O.; Linda K. Jacobs, V.P.; Philip Mark Talbrook, V.P.; Margaret E. Jacobs, Secy.
Directors: Jennifer Vanica, Exec. Dir.; Joseph J. Jacobs, Violet J. Jacobs.
EIN: 330683658

58489
Robert Gumbiner Foundation
5456 The Toledo
Long Beach, CA 90803
Application address: c/o Mgmt. Activities, 638 Alamitos Ave., Long Beach, CA 90802
Contact: Mike Deovlet, Exec. Dir.

Established in 1987 in CA.
Donor(s): Robert Gumbiner.
Financial data (yr. ended 12/31/01): Assets, $13,647,925 (M); grants paid, $5,000; expenditures, $1,174,983; qualifying distributions, $882,070; giving activities include $559,091 for programs.
Limitations: Giving primarily in Long Beach and southern CA.
Publications: Annual report.
Officers: Robert Gumbiner, Chair.; Mike Deovlet, Exec. Dir.
Directors: Sandra Gibson, Alis Gumbiner, Burke Gumbiner, Robb Hankins, Fernando Trevino Lozano, Jr., Fernando Niebla.
EIN: 954167110

58490
The Environmental Trust
7879 El Cajon Blvd.
La Mesa, CA 91941-3623 (619) 461-8333
FAX: (619) 461-8313; E-mail: tet@cts.net; URL: http://www.tet.org
Contact: Don Hunsaker, II, Pres.

Established in 1994 in CA.
Donor(s): McMillin Co., City of Chula Vista Planning Dept., Waxie Corp., Vallecitos Water District.
Financial data (yr. ended 12/31/00): Assets, $12,668,129 (M); grants paid, $172; gifts received, $8,023; expenditures, $1,376,234; qualifying distributions, $1,312,313; giving activities include $810,053 for programs.
Limitations: Giving primarily in CA; some giving in Mexico and South America.
Publications: Occasional report, informational brochure (including application guidelines).
Officers: Don Hunsaker II, Ph.D., Pres.; David Barber, V.P.; David Gautereaux, Secy.-Treas.
Directors: Thomas Hahn, Brad Thornburgh.
EIN: 330436608
Codes: TN

58491
The Thomas W. Wathen Foundation
1525 E. Mountain Dr.
Santa Barbara, CA 93108

Established in 2000 in CA.
Donor(s): Thomas W. Wathen.
Financial data (yr. ended 12/31/00): Assets, $12,178,367 (M); grants paid, $0; gifts received, $12,042,746; expenditures, $237,931; qualifying distributions, $3,556,548; giving activities include $3,376,218 for programs.
Limitations: Applications not accepted.
Application information: Contributes only to pre-selected organizations.
Officers and Trustees: Thomas W. Wathen,* Pres.; John D. Lyon, Secy.; Kathleen D. Wathen.
EIN: 954752331

58492
The Whittier Educational Foundation
7316 Eureka Ave.
El Cerrito, CA 94530

Established in 1999 in CA.
Donor(s): Ronald J. Whittier.
Financial data (yr. ended 12/31/01): Assets, $10,887,116 (M); grants paid, $0; expenditures, $373,125; qualifying distributions, $329,370; giving activities include $332,026 for programs.
Officers: Ronald J. Whittier, Chair.; Ellen Fingerhut Whittier, Secy. and C.F.O.
EIN: 770525014

58493
Claremont House Incorporated
47 Quail Ct., Ste. 300
Walnut Creek, CA 94596

Donor(s): D. McManus, Mrs. D. McManus.

Financial data (yr. ended 12/31/00): Assets, $10,851,635 (M); grants paid, $0; expenditures, $4,360,400; qualifying distributions, $3,479,205.
Officers: Fritz Walgenbach, Pres.; Jeremy Howell, Secy.-Treas.
Directors: Thomas Brady, Derrell Kelch, Tom May.
EIN: 942394340

58494
The Rene & Veronica di Rosa Foundation
5200 Carneros Hwy.
Napa, CA 94559
URL: http://www.dirosapreserve.org

Established in 1983 in CA.
Donor(s): Rene di Rosa, Maude Conner.‡
Financial data (yr. ended 12/31/99): Assets, $10,425,733 (M); grants paid, $655; gifts received, $185,341; expenditures, $629,704; qualifying distributions, $573,864; giving activities include $501,981 for programs.
Publications: Informational brochure.
Officers and Directors:* Rene di Rosa,* C.E.O.; Alexandra K. Phillips,* Secy. and C.F.O.; Wanda Hansen Ashe, Henry Corning, James H. Elliot, Erika Hills, Sally Lilienthal, Cecile McCann, Richard Mendelson, Julie Desloge Newhall, Norma Schlesinger, Lorna Stevens, Virginia Van Asperen.
EIN: 942856000

58495
The George E. Hewitt Foundation for Medical Research
137 Jasmine Creek Dr.
Corona Del Mar, CA 92625-1422
(949) 760-0554
Contact: George E. Hewitt, Pres.

Established in 1982 in CA.
Donor(s): George E. Hewitt.
Financial data (yr. ended 12/31/00): Assets, $10,331,722 (M); grants paid, $247,422; expenditures, $300,882; qualifying distributions, $237,707.
Limitations: Applications not accepted. Giving primarily in CA.
Application information: Fellowship candidates must be recommended by principal researchers from major institutions in the southwest. Funding is currently fully committed; requests for future funding not considered.
Officers: George E. Hewitt, Pres. and C.F.O.; Roy B. Woolsey, Secy.
EIN: 953711123
Codes: FD, GTI

58496
The Dynamic Foundation
2185 Fortune Dr.
San Jose, CA 95131 (408) 262-2900
Contact: Theresa Pan, Pres.

Established in 1999 in CA.
Donor(s): Theresa Pan.
Financial data (yr. ended 12/31/00): Assets, $10,047,305 (M); grants paid, $5,000,000; expenditures, $5,319,596; qualifying distributions, $263,147; giving activities include $312,252 for programs.
Limitations: Giving on a national and international basis.
Application information: Application form not required.
Officers: Theresa Pan, Pres.; Jane Lau, C.F.O.
EIN: 770524369
Codes: FD

58497
Babilonia-Wilner Foundation
2733 Claremont Blvd.
Berkeley, CA 94705

Established in 1994 in CA.
Donor(s): David Wilner, Malou Babilonia-Wilner.
Financial data (yr. ended 12/31/00): Assets, $9,784,669 (M); grants paid, $0; gifts received, $28,724; expenditures, $256,974; qualifying distributions, $242,187; giving activities include $89,655 for programs.
Officers: Malou Babilonia-Wilner, Pres.; David Wilner, Secy.-Treas.
Director: David Pollard.
EIN: 943211139

58498
The Clark Center for Japanese Art
(Formerly The Clark Foundation for the Study of Art)
15770 10th Ave.
Hanford, CA 93230-9533

Established in 1995 in CA.
Donor(s): Willard Clark.
Financial data (yr. ended 12/31/01): Assets, $9,746,391 (M); grants paid, $0; gifts received, $962,186; expenditures, $460,814; qualifying distributions, $1,790,452; giving activities include $172,350 for programs.
Officers: Samuel Morse, Chair.; Stuart Clark, Vice-Chair.; Willard Clark, Pres. and Admin.; Amy Poster, Secy.; Wesley Clark, C.F.O.
Directors: Milo Beach, Catherine Clark, Tadashi Kabayashi, Anne Nishimura Morse, Katherine Lee Raid, John Rosenfield, James Ulak, and 7 additional directors.
EIN: 770402898

58499
The Irvine Museum
610 Newport Center Dr., Ste. 1220
Newport Beach, CA 92660

Established in 1992 in CA.
Donor(s): Athalie R. Clarke,‡ Joan Irvine Smith.
Financial data (yr. ended 04/30/02): Assets, $9,574,484 (M); grants paid, $0; gifts received, $1,105,515; expenditures, $698,446; qualifying distributions, $110,430.
Officers and Directors:* Joan Irvine Smith,* Pres.; James I. Swinden,* V.P. and Treas.; Russell S. Penniman IV,* V.P.; Russell G. Allen,* Secy.; Mark Ashworth, Paul Mosley, Morton I. Smith, Brett J. Williamson, Anita J. Ziebe.
EIN: 330501917

58500
The Bandai Foundation
5551 Katella Ave.
Cypress, CA 90630
Application address: c/o Alison Miller, The Carmen Group, 1299 Pennsylvania Ave. N.W., 8th Fl., Washington, D.C. 20004

Established in 1995 in CA.
Financial data (yr. ended 12/31/00): Assets, $9,519,931 (M); grants paid, $443,995; expenditures, $608,311; qualifying distributions, $537,595.
Limitations: Giving primarily in CA and NY.
Application information: Application form not required.
Officers: Masaaki Tsuji, Chair. and Pres.; Selichi Takauchi, Secy.-Treas.
EIN: 330655933
Codes: FD

58501
Doctor Lynch Foundation
180 S. Lake Ave., Ste. 425
Pasadena, CA 91101

Established in 1994 in CA.
Donor(s): James P. Lynch.
Financial data (yr. ended 02/28/99): Assets, $9,348,862 (M); grants paid, $43,900; expenditures, $1,908,163; qualifying distributions, $384,450; giving activities include $1,681,649 for programs.
Limitations: Applications not accepted.
Application information: Contributes only to pre-selected organizations.
Officers and Directors:* Trevor Grimm,* Chair.; William Wewer, Treas.; Peter Kaplanas, Aquinas McCormick, John Suttie.
EIN: 954414094
Codes: TN

58502
United World of the Universe Foundation
500 Broadway
Santa Monica, CA 90401-2406

Classified as a private operating foundation in 1981.
Donor(s): Frederick M. Segal, Ron Burkle.
Financial data (yr. ended 11/30/01): Assets, $7,892,258 (M); grants paid, $0; gifts received, $90,300; expenditures, $435,384; qualifying distributions, $0.
Limitations: Applications not accepted.
Officer and Trustees:* Michael Segal,* Secy.; Frederick M. Segal.
EIN: 953185105

58503
Hubbs Sea World Research Institute
2595 Ingraham St.
San Diego, CA 92109

Classified as a private operating foundation in 1980.
Donor(s): Sea World, Inc.
Financial data (yr. ended 06/30/00): Assets, $7,864,243 (M); grants paid, $0; gifts received, $3,556,507; expenditures, $3,943,332; qualifying distributions, $3,726,895; giving activities include $1,473,622 for programs.
Officers: Donald B. Kent, Pres.; Duane DeFreese, V.P.; Pamela K. Yochem, V.P.; Karie J. Wright, Secy. and C.F.O.
Trustees: Brad Andrews, Richard A. Burt, and 26 additional trustees.
EIN: 952304740

58504
Kali Pradip Chaudhuri Foundation
1225 E. Latham Ave., Ste. A
Hemet, CA 92543

Established in 1992 in CA.
Donor(s): Kali P. Chaudhuri, Sunanda Chaudhuri.
Financial data (yr. ended 12/31/00): Assets, $7,710,441 (M); grants paid, $62,500; expenditures, $172,885; qualifying distributions, $62,500.
Limitations: Applications not accepted.
Application information: Contributes only to pre-selected organizations.
Officers and Trustees:* Bishwajit Kar, Pres.; Sunanda Chaudhuri,* Secy.-Treas.; Subir Gupta, Naburn Rar.
EIN: 330441991

58505
The Kuhn Foundation
(Formerly The Kuhn Family Foundation, Inc.)
5 Park Plz., Ste. 1900
Irvine, CA 92614
Contact: Robert L. Kuhn, Chair. and Pres.

Established in 1997 in CA.
Donor(s): Robert L. Kuhn.
Financial data (yr. ended 12/31/00): Assets, $7,347,832 (M); grants paid, $103,829; gifts received, $550,000; expenditures, $112,749; qualifying distributions, $261,711; giving activities include $102,945 for programs.
Limitations: Applications not accepted. Giving primarily in the U.S. and Asia.
Application information: Contributes only to pre-selected organizations.
Officers: Robert L. Kuhn, Chair. and Pres.; Dora Kuhn, Vice-Chair.; Aaron Kuhn, V.P.; Daniella Kuhn, Secy.; Adam Kuhn, C.F.O.
EIN: 330783933
Codes: FD2

58506
Harbison Scholarship Trust
P.O. Box 3262
San Bernardino, CA 92413-3262
(909) 792-8919
FAX: (909) 335-6024
Contact: Dan Hatt, Atty.

Established in 1994 in CA.
Financial data (yr. ended 10/31/01): Assets, $7,233,084 (M); grants paid, $682,444; expenditures, $780,651; qualifying distributions, $678,673.
Limitations: Applications not accepted. Giving limited to high school students of San Bernardino County, CA.
Application information: Unsolicited requests for funds not accepted.
Trustee: Doreen Thornes.
EIN: 330621341
Codes: FD, GTI

58507
Charles M. & Linda J. Corbalis Family Foundation
P.O. Box 2426
Saratoga, CA 95070

Established in 1997 in CA.
Donor(s): Charles M. Corbalis, Linda J. Corbalis.
Financial data (yr. ended 12/31/01): Assets, $7,224,502 (M); grants paid, $50,000; expenditures, $594,176; qualifying distributions, $535,042; giving activities include $486,271 for programs.
Limitations: Applications not accepted. Giving on a national basis.
Application information: Contributes only to pre-selected organizations.
Directors: Charles M. Corbalis, Linda J. Corbalis.
EIN: 770456278

58508
Casa Del Herrero Foundation
1387 E. Valley Rd.
Santa Barbara, CA 93108-1202

Established in 1993 in CA.
Donor(s): Medora H. Bass, Ann Jackson Family, George S. Bass.
Financial data (yr. ended 12/31/01): Assets, $7,201,332 (M); grants paid, $0; gifts received, $72,934; expenditures, $370,013; qualifying distributions, $354,717; giving activities include $354,717 for programs.
Officers and Trustees:* Chapin Nolen,* Pres.; Donald Bensen,* V.P.; Alice Van De Water,* Secy.;

58508—CALIFORNIA

Susan McHale,* Treas.; George S. Bass, Ernest A. Bryant III, Peter Edwards, Dan Eidelson, Bruce Glesby, Kate Godfrey, Albert Hinckley, Jr., Joan Jackson, Thad MacMillan, Jill Nida, Joann Rodriguez, Nancy Salvucci.
EIN: 770340301

58509
Hans G. and Thordis W. Burkhardt Foundation
c/o Olincy & Karpel
10960 Wilshire Blvd., No. 1111
Los Angeles, CA 90024

Established in 1992 in CA.
Donor(s): Hans G. Burkhardt.
Financial data (yr. ended 04/30/00): Assets, $7,153,028 (M); grants paid, $1,000; expenditures, $101,863; qualifying distributions, $81,115; giving activities include $48,342 for programs.
Limitations: Applications not accepted. Giving primarily in CA.
Application information: Contributes only to pre-selected organizations.
Trustees: Gene Lesser, Dan Olincy.
EIN: 954392905

58510
The Stanford Theater Foundation
221 University Ave.
Palo Alto, CA 94301

Established in 1988.
Donor(s): David W. Packard, The Packard Humanities Institute.
Financial data (yr. ended 12/31/00): Assets, $7,089,557 (M); grants paid, $0; gifts received, $507,701; expenditures, $1,284,425; qualifying distributions, $190,054; giving activities include $1,284,425 for programs.
Officers and Directors:* David W. Packard,* Chair. and Pres.; Barbara P. Wright, Secy.; Colburn S. Wilbur,* Treas.; Walter B. Hewlett, Edith R. Kramer, Pamela M. Packard, Robert Rosen, Edward M. Stout.
EIN: 770197543

58511
Rudi Schulte Research Institute
(Formerly Schulte Research Institute)
P.O. Box 3130
Santa Barbara, CA 93130-3130

Established in 1975.
Donor(s): Rudolf R. Schulte, Harry Race.
Financial data (yr. ended 11/30/01): Assets, $7,083,445 (M); grants paid, $0; expenditures, $490,513; qualifying distributions, $408,231; giving activities include $409,437 for programs.
Officers and Directors:* Rudolf R. Schulte,* Pres.; Jean M. Devlin,* V.P.; Robert M. Barton,* Secy.; James H. Franzen, Treas.; Michael R. Franzen, Treas.; Gary P. East, J. Gordon McComb, Henry G. Schulte, Thomas H. Weiler, M.D.
EIN: 952919352

58512
Rest Haven Preventorium for Children, Inc.
(also known as Children's Health Fund)
P.O. Box 23389
San Diego, CA 92193-0389

Established in 1963 in CA.
Donor(s): Anna M. Spring Trust, Jessie Castle Roberts Trust.
Financial data (yr. ended 12/31/01): Assets, $6,799,414 (M); grants paid, $252,426; gifts received, $30,516; expenditures, $317,903; qualifying distributions, $278,755.
Limitations: Applications not accepted. Giving limited to residents of the San Diego, CA, area.

Officers: Raymond M. Peterson, M.D., Pres.; Jeanne L. Frost, V.P.; Jacqueline B. Wells, Secy.; Paul S. Condon, Treas.
EIN: 952128344
Codes: FD

58513
Robert C. & Lois C. Braddock Charitable Foundation
1221 Broadway, 21st Fl.
Oakland, CA 94612-1837 (510) 451-3300
Contact: Robert C. Braddock, Jr., Tr.

Classified as a private operating foundation in 1992.
Donor(s): Robert C. Braddock, Lois C. Braddock.
Financial data (yr. ended 06/30/01): Assets, $6,730,139 (M); grants paid, $447,256; gifts received, $255,000; expenditures, $484,788; qualifying distributions, $447,256.
Limitations: Giving primarily in CA.
Trustees: Lois C. Braddock, Robert C. Braddock, Jr., Cheryl Lee Keemar.
EIN: 680234966
Codes: FD

58514
The Sirpuhe & John Conte Foundation
42-900 Bob Hope Dr., Ste. 111
Rancho Mirage, CA 92270-7139

Established in 1999 in CA.
Financial data (yr. ended 12/31/00): Assets, $6,589,683 (M); grants paid, $327,000; expenditures, $456,688; qualifying distributions, $327,000.
Director: Sirpuhe Conte.
EIN: 330884049

58515
Soroptimist Gardens Housing Corporation
516 Burchett St.
Glendale, CA 91203

Financial data (yr. ended 09/30/01): Assets, $6,317,179 (M); grants paid, $0; gifts received, $143,635; expenditures, $503,134; qualifying distributions, $0.
Limitations: Applications not accepted.
Application information: Contributes only to pre-selected organizations.
Officers: Marlene Roth, Pres.; Thornton H. Hamilin, V.P.; Sue Brown, Secy.
Directors: Paul Hadley, Lisa McMurray, Fred C. Morrow, Lynne Raggio, Beth Stochl.
EIN: 953927250
Codes: TN

58516
Speros Basil Vryonis Center for the Study of Hellenism
3140 Gold Camp Dr., Ste. 50
Rancho Cordova, CA 95670

Established in 1987.
Donor(s): John S. Latsis, Angelo K. Tsakopoulos, George Vryonis, M.D.
Financial data (yr. ended 06/30/00): Assets, $5,953,814 (M); grants paid, $23,558; gifts received, $2,267,931; expenditures, $1,438,883; qualifying distributions, $1,393,515; giving activities include $304,532 for programs.
Limitations: Applications not accepted. Giving primarily in CA.
Application information: Contributes only to pre-selected organizations.
Officers and Board Members:* Andreas Kyrianides, Pres.; Sotiris Kolokotronis,* Secy.; Christos P. Ioannides,* Treas.; Speros Vryonis, Jr.,* Dir.; Vassillis Constantakopoulos, Styllanos Spyridakis, Angelo Tsakopoulos, Eleni Tsakopoulos, Demetrios Vryonis.
EIN: 954076622

58517
Mabelle McLeod Lewis Memorial Fund
c/o Wells Fargo Bank, N.A.
P.O. Box 63954
San Francisco, CA 94163
Application address: P.O. Box 3730, Stanford, CA 94305
Contact: Shirleyann Shyne

Trust established in 1968 in CA.
Donor(s): Donald McLeod Lewis.‡
Financial data (yr. ended 03/31/01): Assets, $5,729,543 (M); grants paid, $161,239; expenditures, $265,451; qualifying distributions, $208,510.
Limitations: Giving on a national basis to individuals affiliated with universities located in northern CA.
Publications: Application guidelines, program policy statement.
Application information: Submit application by mail only. Application form required.
Trustees: Robert M. Raymer, Wells Fargo Bank, N.A.
EIN: 237079585
Codes: FD2, GTI

58518
Frank R. Howard Foundation
44 Madrone St.
Willits, CA 95490-4249

Established in 1934 in CA.
Donor(s): Howard Hospital Auxiliary, Jayne Harrah.
Financial data (yr. ended 12/31/01): Assets, $5,598,093 (M); grants paid, $132,627; gifts received, $56,151; expenditures, $276,223; qualifying distributions, $189,739; giving activities include $271,539 for programs.
Limitations: Applications not accepted. Giving primarily in CA.
Application information: Unsolicited requests for funds not accepted.
Officers: Margie Handley, Pres.; William Bowen, M.D., V.P.; Arthur R. Harwood, V.P.; Jann Lamprich, Secy.
Director: Tom Hermon.
EIN: 941196197
Codes: FD2

58519
The Ronald Whittier Family Foundation
P.O. Box 1887
Los Altos, CA 94023-1887 (650) 529-0725
Contact: Jacqueline W. Kubicka, Secy.

Established in 1999 in CA.
Donor(s): Ronald J. Whittier.
Financial data (yr. ended 12/31/00): Assets, $5,585,595 (M); grants paid, $5,244; expenditures, $74,535; qualifying distributions, $295,882; giving activities include $306,984 for programs.
Limitations: Giving limited to the San Francisco Bay Area, CA.
Application information: Applicant must submit tax returns and medical records to support qualifications. Application form required.
Officers: Ronald J. Whittier, Chair.; Jacqueline Whittier Kubicka, C.O.O. and Secy.; Jennifer L. Miller, V.P.; John Huntington Whittier, V.P.
EIN: 770525013

58520
Open Doors International, Inc.
2953 S. Pullman St.
Santa Ana, CA 92705-5840

Established in 1993 in CA.
Financial data (yr. ended 12/31/00): Assets, $5,407,743 (M); grants paid, $8,665,007; gifts received, $9,253,836; expenditures, $10,748,826; qualifying distributions, $10,620,241; giving activities include $9,667,872 for programs.
Limitations: Applications not accepted. Giving on an international basis.
Application information: Contributes only to pre-selected organizations.
Officers and Directors:* Sealy Yates,* Chair.; Tokunboh Adeyemo,* Vice-Chair.; Johan Companjen, Pres.; Alan Hall, V.P., Devel.; David Hamilton, V.P., Finance; Evert Schut, V.P., Opers; Gunnhild Oftedal,* Secy.; Rev. Rey Johnson, Treas.; Brian McFarland, Roger Reed, Wayne Schock, Deryck Stone.
EIN: 330523832
Codes: FD, FM

58521
Kipp Foundation
1 Maritime Plz., Ste. 1400
San Francisco, CA 94111

Established in 2000 in CA.
Donor(s): Donald G. Fisher, Doris F. Fisher.
Financial data (yr. ended 06/30/01): Assets, $5,350,680 (M); grants paid, $0; gifts received, $5,250,017; expenditures, $1,221,468; qualifying distributions, $0.
Limitations: Applications not accepted.
Application information: Contributes only to pre-selected organizations.
Officers and Directors:* Donald G. Fisher,* Chair.; Scott Hamilton, Pres.; Michael Feinberg,* V.P.; David Levin, V.P.; Jane A. Spray, Secy. and C.F.O.; Doris F. Fisher.
EIN: 943362724

58522
San Felipe del Rio, Inc.
9666 Business Park Ave., Ste. 102
San Diego, CA 92131

Established in 1973 in CA.
Donor(s): Philip Y. Hahn Foundation, Katherine Wright.
Financial data (yr. ended 06/30/01): Assets, $5,212,593 (M); grants paid, $15,930; gifts received, $10,964; expenditures, $350,204; qualifying distributions, $283,620; giving activities include $69,688 for programs.
Limitations: Applications not accepted. Giving primarily in CA, OR, and MS.
Application information: Contributes only to pre-selected organizations.
Officers and Directors:* Dewayne Matthews,* Pres.; Charles Anderson,* 1st V.P.; Bonnie Baugh, 2nd V.P.; Mitchell Hornecker,* Secy.; Richard B. Donati, Treas.; Michele M. Del Conte,* Exec. Dir.; Andrew De Paolo, Eileen De Paolo, Charles M. Grace, June Marsh, Peter C. Marsh, Karen Russell-Roots, Howard Taylor, Mara Taylor, and 6 additional Directors.
EIN: 237276447
Codes: GTI

58523
Robert Gore Rifkind Foundation
10100 Santa Monica Blvd., Ste. 215
Los Angeles, CA 90067   (310) 552-0478
FAX: (310) 203-0311
Contact: Robert Gore Rifkind, Pres.

Established in 1979.
Financial data (yr. ended 03/31/99): Assets, $5,201,452 (M); grants paid, $23,530; gifts received, $86,500; expenditures, $86,876; qualifying distributions, $23,530; giving activities include $62,565 for programs.
Application information: Application form required.
Officer and Directors:* Robert Gore Rifkind,* Pres.; Ida Katherine Rigby, Harold Williams.
EIN: 953397350

58524
Harry & Ethel West Foundation
P.O. Box 1825
Bakersfield, CA 93303-1825
Contact: Richard G. McBurnie, Mgr.

Established in 1972.
Financial data (yr. ended 12/31/00): Assets, $5,015,508 (M); grants paid, $330,376; expenditures, $448,121; qualifying distributions, $330,376.
Limitations: Giving limited to Kern County, CA.
Officer: Richard G. McBurnie, Mgr.
Director: Silver D. Sack.
EIN: 237168492
Codes: FD

58525
Foundation for Psycho-Cultural Research
736 El Medio Ave.
Pacific Palisades, CA 90272-3451

Established in 2000 in CA.
Donor(s): Robert Lemelson, Susan Morse Lemelson.
Financial data (yr. ended 11/30/01): Assets, $4,860,168 (M); grants paid, $25,000; expenditures, $194,543; qualifying distributions, $162,696.
Limitations: Applications not accepted. Giving primarily in MA.
Application information: Contributes only to pre-selected organizations.
Officers and Directors:* Robert Lemelson, Ph.D.,* Pres.; Susan Morse Lemelson,* Secy.-Treas.; Douglas Hollan, Ph.D., Marvin Karno, M.D., Beate Ritz-Barr, M.D.
EIN: 954774901

58526
E-Z Spindizzies Foundation
1210 10th St.
Berkeley, CA 94710

Established in 2000 in CA.
Donor(s): Eric Zausner.
Financial data (yr. ended 12/31/00): Assets, $4,855,185 (M); grants paid, $0; gifts received, $4,861,721; expenditures, $8,153; qualifying distributions, $7,715; giving activities include $8,153 for programs.
Officers: Eric Zausner, Pres.; Dora Zausner, V.P.; Mary Coen, Secy.
Director: Andrew Zausner.
EIN: 943381342

58527
The Marmor Foundation
(Formerly The Cardea Foundation)
388 Market St., Ste. 400
San Francisco, CA 94111

Established in 1968; classified as a private operating foundation in 1987.
Donor(s): Judd Marmor, Katherine Marmor.
Financial data (yr. ended 12/31/01): Assets, $4,684,981 (M); grants paid, $73,437; gifts received, $14,943; expenditures, $114,900; qualifying distributions, $92,937.
Limitations: Applications not accepted. Giving primarily in CA.
Application information: Contributes only to pre-selected organizations.
Officers: Judd Marmor, Pres.; Michael Marmor, Secy.-Treas.
EIN: 237005963

58528
The Capital Group Foundation
333 S. Hope St., 55th Fl.
Los Angeles, CA 90071

Classified as a private operating foundation in 1982.
Donor(s): The Capital Group, Inc., Robert B. Egelston.
Financial data (yr. ended 06/30/00): Assets, $4,659,368 (M); grants paid, $0; gifts received, $248,000; expenditures, $59,642; qualifying distributions, $164,430; giving activities include $59,642 for programs.
Limitations: Applications not accepted.
Application information: Contributes only to pre-selected organizations.
Officers: Robert B. Egelston, Pres.; Roberta A. Conroy, Secy.; Edith H.L. Van Huss, C.F.O.
Directors: Nancy Englander, Solomon M. Kamm, Lillian Lovelace, Robert S. MacFarlane, Jr., Timothy W. Weiss, Martha W. Williams.
EIN: 953744134

58529
InterACT Foundation
P.O. Box 23189
San Jose, CA 95153-3189
Contact: David J. Cormia, Treas.

Established in 2000 in CA.
Donor(s): Mark A. Bryers, Jeanne Bryers.
Financial data (yr. ended 12/31/00): Assets, $4,606,764 (M); grants paid, $27,510; gifts received, $519; expenditures, $27,510; qualifying distributions, $27,510.
Officer: David J. Cormia, Treas.
EIN: 770548917

58530
Northern California Land Trust, Inc.
3126 Shattuck Ave.
Berkeley, CA 94705-1823

Classified as a private operating foundation in 1977.
Financial data (yr. ended 12/31/00): Assets, $4,595,134 (M); grants paid, $0; gifts received, $112,130; expenditures, $573,271; qualifying distributions, $0.
Officers and Directors:* Joanne Morrison, Pres.; Rick Jacobus,* V.P.; Justin Smith,* Secy.; Beth Dameron,* Treas.; David Jay-Bonn, Exec. Dir.; Teresa Clarke, Alison Hicks, Chris Urban, Ian Winters.
EIN: 237380534

58531
Loel Foundation
105 S. Washington St.
Lodi, CA 95240-2940

Classified as a private operating foundation in 1980.
Donor(s): Vino Farms.
Financial data (yr. ended 11/30/00): Assets, $4,229,738 (M); grants paid, $0; gifts received, $26,578; expenditures, $303,988; qualifying distributions, $254,893; giving activities include $206,285 for programs.
Officers and Directors:* Jack Leary,* Pres.; Ivan Suess,* V.P.; Frank Pegg,* Secy.; Debra Green,* Treas.; James V. DeMera III, Theresa Larson, Michael McCay, Ivan Suess, Caroline C. Wildman.
EIN: 942412399

58532
Meditation Groups, Inc.
P.O. Box 566
Ojai, CA 93023

Classified as a private operating foundation in 1972.
Financial data (yr. ended 06/30/00): Assets, $4,130,689 (M); grants paid, $36,185; gifts received, $58,350; expenditures, $520,215; qualifying distributions, $520,215.
Limitations: Applications not accepted.
Application information: Contributes only to pre-selected organizations.
Officers: Frances A. Moore, Secy.; Tom Carney, Treas.
Directors: Glenda Christian, Gordon Davidson, Eva Fugitt, Jack Hart, Michael Lindfield, Carol Robinson, Jeriel Smith.
EIN: 066054153

58533
Hathaway Ranch Museum
11901 E. Florence Ave.
Santa Fe Springs, CA 90670-4494

Established in 1986 in CA.
Donor(s): Nadine Hathaway.
Financial data (yr. ended 12/31/00): Assets, $4,104,716 (M); grants paid, $0; gifts received, $987; expenditures, $183,553; qualifying distributions, $81,207; giving activities include $84,249 for programs.
Officers: William A. Hathaway, Pres.; Jean E. Hathaway, V.P.; Jesse R. Hathaway, Secy.; Remy A. Hathaway, C.F.O.
Directors: Richard F. Hathaway, Jr., Betty Putnam.
EIN: 954071530

58534
United Samaritans Foundation
219 S. Broadway
Turlock, CA 95380

Established in 1994 in CA.
Financial data (yr. ended 08/31/99): Assets, $4,088,978 (M); grants paid, $0; gifts received, $1,717,903; expenditures, $689,124; qualifying distributions, $1,755,260; giving activities include $570,791 for programs.
Limitations: Applications not accepted.
Application information: Contributes only to pre-selected organizations.
Officers and Directors:* John S. Rogers,* Pres.; Mary Gallo, V.P.; Ernie Gemperle,* V.P.; Carol Bright Tougas,* V.P.; June A. Rogers,* Secy.; Cleveland Stockton,* Treas.; Rev. Bill McDonald, Cathee Vaugh.
EIN: 770393321

58535
Dorothea Tuney Foundation
c/o Leslie Batista
1959 Mendocino Blvd.
San Diego, CA 92107

Established in 2000 in CA.
Donor(s): Dorothea Tuney Trust.
Financial data (yr. ended 12/31/01): Assets, $4,065,219 (M); grants paid, $151,500; expenditures, $155,643; qualifying distributions, $155,643.
Limitations: Applications not accepted. Giving primarily in San Diego, CA.
Application information: Contributes only to pre-selected organizations.
Trustee: Leslie Batista.
EIN: 336277186
Codes: FD2

58536
The Barrios Trust
653 11th St.
Oakland, CA 94607

Established in 1999 in CA.
Donor(s): Warren Wilson, Joanne Casey.
Financial data (yr. ended 02/28/01): Assets, $3,866,088 (M); grants paid, $107,918; expenditures, $204,834; qualifying distributions, $143,283; giving activities include $123,147 for programs.
Limitations: Applications not accepted. Giving primarily in Oakland, CA.
Application information: Unsolicited requests for funds not accepted.
Officers: Warren Wilson, Pres.; Joanne Casey, V.P.
Directors: Natalie Delagnes, Margot Maurer, Todd Nathanson, Lori Perenon.
EIN: 943323331
Codes: FD2

58537
Thelma Doelger Animal & Wildlife Preserve Trust
950 John Daly Blvd., Ste. 300
Daly City, CA 94015-3004

Classified as a private operating foundation in 1986.
Financial data (yr. ended 06/30/00): Assets, $3,838,334 (M); grants paid, $0; expenditures, $186,770; qualifying distributions, $164,224; giving activities include $164,224 for programs.
Trustees: Edward M. King, Chester W. Lebsack, Howard E. Mason, Jr., D. Eugene Richard.
EIN: 946582690

58538
Nelson Maritime Arts Foundation
28441 Highridge Rd., Ste. 110
Rolling Hills Estates, CA 90274

Established in 1998 in CA.
Donor(s): Harry L. Nelson, Jr., Joyce Nelson.
Financial data (yr. ended 12/31/01): Assets, $3,807,270 (M); grants paid, $0; gifts received, $1,314,091; expenditures, $6,581; qualifying distributions, $563,041; giving activities include $6,581 for programs.
Officers and Directors:* Harry L. Nelson, Jr.,* Pres.; Joyce W. Nelson,* Secy.; Steve Hausman, Treas.; Mark Bacin.
EIN: 330833923

58539
Beverly Foundation
566 El Dorado St., Ste 100
Pasadena, CA 91101-2560

Established in 1978 in CA.

Financial data (yr. ended 12/31/01): Assets, $3,731,538 (M); grants paid, $0; gifts received, $135,100; expenditures, $473,490; qualifying distributions, $252,485; giving activities include $252,485 for programs.
Officers: Don M. Pearson, Chair.; Helen K. Kerschner, Pres.; Sarah Ingersoll, Secy.
Trustees: Ruth M. Covell, M.D., Jim Birren, Richard DeRock, William R. Kerler, Evelyn T. Kieffer, Ph.D., Bill Malthies, Mark Wortley.
EIN: 953382956

58540
The Lynch Operating Foundation
25660 La Lanne Ct.
Los Altos Hills, CA 94022

Established in 2000 in CA.
Donor(s): Lynch Family Foundation.
Financial data (yr. ended 12/31/00): Assets, $3,607,117 (M); grants paid, $0; gifts received, $3,822,119; expenditures, $317,700; qualifying distributions, $2,223,715; giving activities include $260,165 for programs.
Limitations: Applications not accepted.
Application information: Contributes only to pre-selected organizations.
Officers: Daniel C. Lynch, Pres.; Karen D. Lynch, Secy.
EIN: 770513617

58541
The Johnson Foundation
P.O. Box 351
Riverside, CA 92502

Established in 1986 in CA.
Donor(s): Johnson Machinery Corp.
Financial data (yr. ended 12/31/01): Assets, $3,560,673 (M); grants paid, $242,500; gifts received, $320,000; expenditures, $244,985; qualifying distributions, $243,388.
Limitations: Applications not accepted. Giving primarily in CA, with emphasis on Riverside.
Application information: Contributes only to pre-selected organizations.
Officers: William R. Johnson, Jr., C.E.O.; Brenda K. Clabough, Secy.; Kevin Kelly, C.F.O.
EIN: 330217264
Codes: FD2

58542
Keith and Pamela Fox Family Trust
c/o Keith and Pamela Fox
144 S. 3rd St., Ste. 131
San Jose, CA 95112

Established in 2000 in CA.
Donor(s): Keith Fox, Pamela Fox.
Financial data (yr. ended 12/31/01): Assets, $3,516,198 (M); grants paid, $81,000; gifts received, $21,940; expenditures, $108,462; qualifying distributions, $81,000.
Limitations: Applications not accepted.
Application information: Contributes only to pre-selected organizations.
Officers: Keith Fox, C.E.O. and Pres.; Pamela Fox, Secy.; Ken Ratcliffe, C.F.O.
EIN: 770560716

58543
Why Not, Community Housing Corporation
c/o Judy Almquist
9513 Flintridge Way
Orangevale, CA 95662
E-mail: whynotchc@hotmail.com

Financial data (yr. ended 12/31/00): Assets, $3,457,039 (M); grants paid, $0; gifts received, $71,067; expenditures, $277,486; qualifying distributions, $11,240.

Officers and Directors:* Eric Almquist,* Pres.; Jeff Johnson, Exec. Dir.; Alan Almquist, Andrei Simic.
EIN: 680373757

58544
Seascape Senior Housing, Inc.
c/o Christian Church Homes of Northern CA
303 Hegenberger Rd., Ste. 201
Oakland, CA 94621

Classified as a private operating foundation in 1987.
Financial data (yr. ended 03/31/02): Assets, $3,442,186 (M); grants paid, $0; expenditures, $834,837; qualifying distributions, $0.
Officer: Jim Suddeth, Pres.
Directors: Brooke Graff, Darrell Johnson, Richard Ulrey, Elisabeth Vogel, Velma White.
EIN: 942911626

58545
Fred C. Heidrick Museum
18284 County Rd., No. 97
Woodland, CA 95695-9359

Donor(s): Fred C. Heidrick, Sr.
Financial data (yr. ended 12/31/01): Assets, $3,383,078 (M); grants paid, $0; gifts received, $797,548; expenditures, $420,176; qualifying distributions, $180,502; giving activities include $420,177 for programs.
Officers and Directors: Fred C. Heidrick, Jr., Pres.; Robert Eoff, Treas.; Cyndi Blickle, Kristen Cracchiolo, Robert Giannoni, Keith Lawrie, Linda Lucchesi, D. Ross Parker.
Trustees: Carl A. Schneider, Curt Storz.
EIN: 944504986

58546
Military Vehicle Technology Foundation
c/o Jacques M. Littlefield
Pony Tracks Ranch
Portola Valley, CA 94028

Established in 1998 in CA.
Donor(s): Jacques M. Littlefield.
Financial data (yr. ended 12/31/00): Assets, $3,296,396 (M); grants paid, $0; gifts received, $1,707,000; expenditures, $227,369; qualifying distributions, $1,490,380; giving activities include $1,490,395 for programs.
Officers and Director:* Jacques M. Littlefield,* Pres.; Linda Parks, Secy. and C.F.O.
EIN: 943302363

58547
Arthur Zief, Jr. Foundation
150 Spear St., Ste. 1700
San Francisco, CA 94105

Classified as a private operating foundation in 1988.
Financial data (yr. ended 06/30/01): Assets, $3,288,259 (M); grants paid, $0; expenditures, $116,565; qualifying distributions, $0.
Officers: J.F. Gaillard, V.P.; Dorrainee Zief, Secy.
Director: Reinart Gelzayd.
EIN: 941676472

58548
Edward M. Smith Family Art Foundation
c/o Edward M. Smith
416 N. Hale Ave.
Escondido, CA 92029

Established as a private operating foundation in 1997 in CA.
Donor(s): Edward M. Smith.
Financial data (yr. ended 08/31/00): Assets, $3,270,987 (M); grants paid, $5,000; gifts received, $1,761,847; expenditures, $82,898; qualifying distributions, $129,913; giving activities include $25,000 for programs.
Limitations: Applications not accepted. Giving limited to CA.
Application information: Contributes only to pre-selected organizations.
Officers: Edward M. Smith, Pres.; Naomi Leensvaart, Secy.; Wilhelma Wilkie-Smith, C.F.O.
Director: Edward Smith, Jr.
EIN: 954605433

58549
The Capecchio Foundation
(Formerly The Cortopassi Family Foundation)
11292 N. Alpine Rd.
Stockton, CA 95212

Established in 1990 in CA.
Donor(s): Dean Cortopassi, Joan Cortopassi.
Financial data (yr. ended 12/31/01): Assets, $3,211,621 (M); grants paid, $606,470; expenditures, $633,464; qualifying distributions, $651,781.
Limitations: Applications not accepted. Giving primarily in Stockton, CA.
Application information: Contributes only to pre-selected organizations.
Officers: Dean Cortopassi, Pres.; Donald Lenz, Secy.-Treas.
Director: Joan Cortopassi.
EIN: 680232655
Codes: FD

58550
The Mark Ross Foundation
5 Dorman Ave.
San Francisco, CA 94124

Established in 1986.
Financial data (yr. ended 12/31/01): Assets, $3,176,204 (M); grants paid, $0; gifts received, $537,640; expenditures, $1,850; qualifying distributions, $0.
Limitations: Applications not accepted. Giving primarily in the San Francisco Bay Area, CA.
Application information: Contributes only to pre-selected organizations.
Directors: Thomas J. Miller, Mina Vitlin, Victor A. Vitlin.
EIN: 942990606

58551
Harvego Family Foundation
2356 Gold Meadow Way, Ste. 201
Gold River, CA 95670
Contact: Melinda Cassity

Established in 1998 in CA.
Financial data (yr. ended 12/31/01): Assets, $3,136,057 (M); grants paid, $150,001; expenditures, $197,958; qualifying distributions, $157,009.
Limitations: Giving primarily in Sacramento, CA.
Officer: Lloyd H. Harvego, Chair.
Trustees: Deborah S. Harvego, Sandra Harvego, Terrence Harvego, Larry E. Johnson, Tamara Johnson, James A. Whillock.
EIN: 680422816
Codes: FD2

58552
Italian-American Community Services Agency
(Formerly Italian Welfare Agency, Inc.)
678 Green St.
San Francisco, CA 94133-3896

Established in 1916 in CA; classified as a private operating foundation in 1972.
Donor(s): Marini Family Trust.
Financial data (yr. ended 12/31/01): Assets, $3,092,180 (M); grants paid, $15,690; gifts received, $256,848; expenditures, $331,652; qualifying distributions, $15,690; giving activities include $229,979 for programs.
Officers and Directors:* David Giannini,* Chair.; Stephen Leveroni,* Pres.; John Riccio, V.P.; Wayne Tomei, Secy.-Treas.
EIN: 941196199
Codes: GTI

58553
California Institute for Chinese Performing Arts
2677 N. Main St., Ste. 950
Santa Ana, CA 92705

Established in 1994 in CA. Classified as a private operating foundation in 1994.
Donor(s): Pei Chung Chao, Rosana Hsu Chao.
Financial data (yr. ended 06/30/00): Assets, $3,013,467 (M); grants paid, $0; gifts received, $1,142,500; expenditures, $289,670; qualifying distributions, $231,465; giving activities include $206,083 for programs.
Officers: Rosana Hsu Chao, Pres.; Raymond Chao, Secy.; Pei Chung Chao, C.F.O.
Directors: Rosalind Chao, Edward Miller, Julie Shen, Simon Templeman, Shu Rui Yang.
EIN: 330623380

58554
The Copen Family Foundation, Inc.
(Formerly Harry Copen Foundation, Inc.)
c/o Peter Copen
7228 Monte Vista Ave.
La Jolla, CA 92037

Established in 1988 in NY.
Donor(s): Pauline Copen, Copen Family CLAT, Karina Copen, Brent Copen.
Financial data (yr. ended 12/31/00): Assets, $2,888,245 (M); grants paid, $191,705; gifts received, $440,459; expenditures, $268,585; qualifying distributions, $251,005.
Limitations: Applications not accepted. Giving on a national and international basis.
Publications: Annual report.
Application information: Contributes only to pre-selected organizations.
Directors: Brent Copen, Karina Copen, Pauline Copen, Peter Copen.
EIN: 510196882
Codes: FD2

58555
Snyder Highland Foundation
c/o Wells Fargo Bank, N.A.
P.O. Box 63954
San Francisco, CA 94163
Contact: Virginia Updegrave

Classified as a private operating foundation in 1969.
Financial data (yr. ended 09/30/00): Assets, $2,886,267 (M); grants paid, $1,850; gifts received, $481; expenditures, $121,634; qualifying distributions, $56,816.
Limitations: Giving limited to CA.
Trustee: Wells Fargo Bank, N.A.
EIN: 941682757

58556
A.P. Reilly Foundation
Wilder Bldg.
5555 Melrose Ave., 2nd Fl.
Los Angeles, CA 90038

Established in 1999 in CA.
Donor(s): Mel Gibson.
Financial data (yr. ended 12/31/01): Assets, $2,867,442 (M); grants paid, $0; gifts received, $784,613; expenditures, $62,938; qualifying distributions, $0.

58556—CALIFORNIA

Limitations: Applications not accepted.
Application information: Contributes only to pre-selected organizations.
Officers and Director:* Mel Gibson,* C.E.O.; Robyn Gibson, V.P.; Vicki Christianson, Secy.-Treas.
EIN: 954768218

58557
J & V 2000 Foundation
4238 Suzanne Dr.
Palo Alto, CA 94306

Established in 1999 in CA.
Donor(s): Mr. Huang, Mrs. Huang.
Financial data (yr. ended 06/30/01): Assets, $2,862,920 (M); grants paid, $2,592; gifts received, $800,000; expenditures, $12,298; qualifying distributions, $2,592.
Limitations: Applications not accepted.
Application information: Contributes only to pre-selected organizations.
Trustee: Shao-Ling Chen.
EIN: 770543120

58558
RCL Foundation
(Formerly Richard S. Staley Foundation)
1805 Industrial St.
Los Angeles, CA 90021-1223 (213) 627-0972
Contact: Angela Tan, Secy.-Treas.

Established in 1978.
Donor(s): Regina Leimbach.
Financial data (yr. ended 04/30/01): Assets, $2,822,334 (M); grants paid, $71,166; gifts received, $49,580; expenditures, $116,898; qualifying distributions, $120,170.
Limitations: Giving primarily in CA.
Application information: Contact foundation for student loan application form. Application form required.
Officers and Directors:* Nancy Edelbrock,* Pres.; Regina Leimbach,* V.P.; Angela Tan,* Secy.-Treas.; Joan Schaffer.
EIN: 953387067
Codes: GTI

58559
Ray of Light Foundation
c/o PFM
P.O. Box 3367
Beverly Hills, CA 90212-3367
Contact: Caresse Norman, Tr.

Established in 1998 in CA.
Donor(s): Madonna Ciccone.
Financial data (yr. ended 12/31/01): Assets, $2,800,307 (M); grants paid, $1,240,000; gifts received, $1,200,000; expenditures, $1,256,023; qualifying distributions, $1,239,350.
Limitations: Giving primarily in CA.
Trustees: Madonna Ciccone, Caresse Norman.
EIN: 954716881
Codes: FD

58560
M.O.A. Foundation of Los Angeles, Inc.
8554 Melrose Ave.
West Hollywood, CA 90069-5196
Contact: Keizo Miyamoto

Established in 1987 in CA.
Donor(s): Sekai Kyusei Kyokai.
Financial data (yr. ended 03/31/99): Assets, $2,798,974 (M); grants paid, $47,307; gifts received, $302,283; expenditures, $445,474; qualifying distributions, $40,015.
Officers and Directors:* Toshiaki Kawai,* Pres.; Michihiro Kawasaki,* Secy.; Takemi Sato,* Treas.
EIN: 954125026

58561
02 for Life, a Rainforest Foundation
(Formerly Blumkin Foundation)
c/o Lawrence H. Cahn, C.P.A.
6440 Lusk Blvd., Ste. D103
San Diego, CA 92121

Established in 1999 in AR.
Donor(s): Steven Blumkin, Frances Blumkin.
Financial data (yr. ended 12/31/02): Assets, $2,707,318 (M); grants paid, $0; gifts received, $23,100; expenditures, $21,987; qualifying distributions, $21,987; giving activities include $21,987 for programs.
Officer and Directors:* Steven Blumkin,* Pres.; Frances Blumkin.
EIN: 860933652

58562
The CEC Foundation
c/o John R. Fuqua
P.O. Box 1324
Los Alamitos, CA 90720-2420

Established in 1999 in CA.
Donor(s): Carol Electric, Inc.
Financial data (yr. ended 12/31/01): Assets, $2,662,379 (M); grants paid, $435,784; gifts received, $1,350,000; expenditures, $447,347; qualifying distributions, $435,784.
Officers: John R. Fuqua, Pres.; Ronald J. Hathaway, Secy.; Allen W. Moffitt, Treas.
EIN: 330859870

58563
Robert Miller & Catherine Miller Charitable Foundation
679 University Ave.
Los Altos, CA 94022 (650) 948-3118
Contact: F. Robert Miller, Pres.

Established in 1998 in CA.
Donor(s): Catherine Miller, Robert Miller.
Financial data (yr. ended 12/31/99): Assets, $2,655,548 (M); grants paid, $52,350; expenditures, $119,131; qualifying distributions, $41,563.
Officers: F. Robert Miller, Pres. and Treas.; Catherine Miller, Secy.
Directors: Christopher Miller, Jennifer Miller.
EIN: 770499122

58564
Foundation for Enterprise Development
P.O. Box 2149
La Jolla, CA 92038-2149

Established in 1986 in CA.
Donor(s): John Robert Beyster.
Financial data (yr. ended 06/30/00): Assets, $2,637,661 (M); grants paid, $0; gifts received, $768,428; expenditures, $1,237,087; qualifying distributions, $753,824; giving activities include $202,929 for programs.
Officers: John Robert Beyster, Pres.; Lisa Hasler, V.P.; David Binns, Secy.; Ronald Bernstein, Treas.; E.C. Michael Higgins, Exec. Dir.; Stan Lundine, Exec. Dir.
Trustees: Joseph Blasi, Thomas Darcy, Michele Hunt, Laura Kilcrease, William E. Nelson, Robert Shapiro, Joseph P. Walkush, Mary Lindenstein Walshok, Jack Wilkins.
EIN: 330207662

58565
Paloheimo Charitable Trust
c/o Wells Fargo Bank, N.A.
P.O. Box 63954
San Francisco, CA 94163
Application address: c/o Larry Plumer, Wells Fargo Bank, N.A., 350 W. Colorado Blvd., Pasadena, CA 91105

Established in 1980 in CA.
Donor(s): Curtin Paloheimo Trust.
Financial data (yr. ended 06/30/01): Assets, $2,590,817 (M); grants paid, $0; gifts received, $1,000,000; expenditures, $63,252; qualifying distributions, $5,157.
Limitations: Giving limited to the Pasadena, CA, area.
Trustee: Wells Fargo Bank, N.A.
EIN: 953643948

58566
Oscar de la Hoya Foundation
633 W. 5th St., Ste. 6700
Los Angeles, CA 90071

Established in 1995 in CA.
Financial data (yr. ended 12/31/00): Assets, $2,524,746 (M); grants paid, $384,750; gifts received, $1,235,183; expenditures, $1,602,331; qualifying distributions, $1,050,481.
Limitations: Applications not accepted. Giving primarily in CA.
Application information: Contributes only to pre-selected organizations.
Officers: Oscar de la Hoya, Pres.; Richard Schaefer, Secy. and C.F.O.
Directors: Emanuel Brefin, Glenn Dryfoos.
EIN: 954586767
Codes: FD

58567
Alexander A. Jacobson and Ruth E. Jacobson Charitable Foundation
9454 Wilshire Blvd., PH-15
Beverly Hills, CA 90212

Established in 1999 in CA.
Financial data (yr. ended 12/31/01): Assets, $2,495,040 (M); grants paid, $107,750; expenditures, $174,885; qualifying distributions, $107,220.
Limitations: Applications not accepted.
Application information: Contributes only to pre-selected organizations.
Trustee: James A. Ostiller.
EIN: 957077548
Codes: FD2

58568
The Kyupin Philip and Gemma Hwang Foundation
(Formerly The Kyupin Philip and C. Gemma Hwang Foundation)
555 E. Washington
Sunnyvale, CA 94086

Donor(s): K. Philip Hwang, C. Gemma Hwang.
Financial data (yr. ended 12/31/00): Assets, $2,473,609 (M); grants paid, $17,700; gifts received, $2,000,000; expenditures, $23,831; qualifying distributions, $17,683.
Limitations: Giving primarily in Santa Clara County, CA.
Officers and Directors:* K. Philip Hwang,* Pres.; C. Gemma Hwang,* V.P.; Allan D. Smirni,* Secy.; James M. Eustice,* C.F.O.
EIN: 770029903

58569
The RORD Foundation
16130 Ventura Blvd., Ste. 320
Encino, CA 91436-2518

Established in 1987 in CT.
Donor(s): Richard O. Dowling,‡ Janet Dowling Sands.
Financial data (yr. ended 07/31/01): Assets, $2,468,676 (M); grants paid, $49,587; expenditures, $501,005; qualifying distributions, $414,280; giving activities include $250,000 for programs.
Limitations: Applications not accepted. Giving primarily in Greenwich, CT, and New York, NY.
Application information: Contributes only to pre-selected organizations.
Officer and Trustee:* Janet Dowling Sands,* Mgr.
EIN: 222848972

58570
Augustine Foundation
1031 Pine St.
Paso Robles, CA 93446

Classified as a private operating foundation in 1991.
Donor(s): William P. Clark, Joan Clark, Repatria, Inc.
Financial data (yr. ended 06/30/01): Assets, $2,426,381 (M); grants paid, $20,200; gifts received, $10,960; expenditures, $89,703; qualifying distributions, $60,800.
Limitations: Applications not accepted.
Application information: Contributes only to pre-selected organizations.
Officers and Directors:* Paul Clark,* Pres.; Jacquelyn Hill,* Secy.; Regina Clark, C.F.O.; Pete Clark.
EIN: 770265274

58571
The Paul I. Terasaki Foundation
12835 Parkyns St.
Los Angeles, CA 90049-2629

Donor(s): Paul I. Terasaki.
Financial data (yr. ended 12/31/99): Assets, $2,394,001 (M); grants paid, $500; gifts received, $1,985,558; expenditures, $16,825; qualifying distributions, $2,358.
Limitations: Giving primarily in CA.
Officers: Paul I. Terasaki, Pres.; Robert C. Kopple, Secy.; Hisako Terasaki, Treas.
EIN: 954249502

58572
Stacey Baba & James Vokac Charitable Foundation
13553 Old Oak Way
Saratoga, CA 95070 (408) 741-1471
Contact: James Vokac, Secy.

Established in 1998 in CA.
Financial data (yr. ended 12/31/01): Assets, $2,376,395 (M); grants paid, $500; gifts received, $105,787; expenditures, $151,548; qualifying distributions, $113,251; giving activities include $112,751 for programs.
Limitations: Applications not accepted.
Application information: Contributes only to pre-selected organizations.
Officers and Directors:* Stacey Baba,* Pres.; James Vokac,* Secy. and C.F.O.
EIN: 770497242

58573
The Stuart Foundation
P.O. Box 2268
Rancho Santa Fe, CA 92067-1966

Classified as a private operating foundation in 1979.
Donor(s): James DeSilva, Michael Krichman.
Financial data (yr. ended 11/30/00): Assets, $2,350,148 (M); grants paid, $200; gifts received, $18,507; expenditures, $4,609; qualifying distributions, $200.
Limitations: Applications not accepted.
Application information: Contributes only to pre-selected organizations.
Officer: Maryellen Koziol, C.F.O.
Directors: Richard Atkinson, Hugh Davies, James DeSilva, Peter DeSilva.
EIN: 953353820

58574
PADI Foundation
(also known as Professional Association of Diving Instructors Foundation)
9150 Wilshire Blvd., Ste. 300
Beverly Hills, CA 90212-3414
FAX: (310) 859-1430; *URL:* http://www.padifoundation.org
Contact: Charles P. Rettig, Pres.

Established in 1991 in CA.
Donor(s): Dept. of Justice, State of California, Capital Investments and Ventures Corp., and its subsidiaries.
Financial data (yr. ended 05/31/01): Assets, $2,328,996 (M); grants paid, $175,100; gifts received, $188,090; expenditures, $237,513; qualifying distributions, $221,920.
Limitations: Giving on a national and international basis.
Publications: Application guidelines, financial statement.
Application information: Application form not required.
Officers and Directors:* Charles P. Rettig,* Pres.; Andrew Saxon, M.D.,* Secy.; Paul K. Dayton, Ph.D., John Englander, Daniel M. Hanes, Ph.D.
EIN: 954326850
Codes: FD2, GTI

58575
Folk Art International
140 Maiden Ln.
San Francisco, CA 94108

Classified as a private operating foundation in 1984.
Donor(s): Louise M. Handley, Raymond G. Handley, Milla L. Handley.
Financial data (yr. ended 09/30/00): Assets, $2,273,463 (M); grants paid, $0; gifts received, $250,535; expenditures, $116,704; qualifying distributions, $109,929; giving activities include $116,704 for programs.
Officers: R.G. Handley, C.E.O.; Cheryl Goodwin, Secy.; Alice Holmes, C.F.O.
Directors: Yvonne Boretti, Sue Gartley, Denise Weinert.
EIN: 942716028

58576
Arnold Schoenberg Foundation
116 N. Rockingham Ave.
Los Angeles, CA 90049

Established as a private operating foundation in 1998 in CA.
Donor(s): Ronald R. Schoenberg, Lawrence A. Schoenberg, Nuria D. Nono.
Financial data (yr. ended 12/31/01): Assets, $2,273,408 (M); grants paid, $0; gifts received, $923,750; expenditures, $841; qualifying distributions, $0.
Limitations: Applications not accepted.
Application information: Contributes only to pre-selected organizations.
Officers: Ronald R. Schoenberg, Pres.; Nuria D. Nono, Secy.; Lawrence A. Schoenberg, Treas.
EIN: 954696266

58577
Mann Center for Education & Family Development
1801 Century Park E., Ste. 1930
Los Angeles, CA 90067-2321

Established in 1992 in CA.
Donor(s): Ted Mann Foundation.
Financial data (yr. ended 12/31/00): Assets, $2,268,261 (M); grants paid, $385,400; gifts received, $100,000; expenditures, $393,708; qualifying distributions, $385,400.
Limitations: Applications not accepted.
Application information: Contributes only to pre-selected organizations.
Officers: Victoria Mann Simms, Pres.; Ronald Simms, Secy.-Treas.
EIN: 954369610
Codes: FD

58578
The Whitman Institute
405 Davis Ct., Ste. 301
San Francisco, CA 94111-2405

Classified as a private operating foundation in 1985.
Donor(s): Frederick C. Whitman.
Financial data (yr. ended 06/30/01): Assets, $2,260,630 (M); grants paid, $10,000; expenditures, $256,698; qualifying distributions, $212,204; giving activities include $212,204 for programs.
Limitations: Giving primarily in VA.
Application information: Unsolicited requests for funds not accepted.
Officers: Frederick C. Whitman, Pres.; Carol Dugger-Lerer, V.P.; John Esterle, Secy.; Lloyd H. Skjerdal, Treas.
Directors: Robert Mackenzie, Joanna Pipes.
EIN: 942984079

58579
Living Free
P.O. Box 5
Mountain Center, CA 92561-0005

Established in 1993 in CA.
Donor(s): Living Free Charitable Trust.
Financial data (yr. ended 12/31/99): Assets, $2,258,740 (M); grants paid, $100; gifts received, $648,755; expenditures, $865,852; qualifying distributions, $685,289; giving activities include $745,975 for programs.
Limitations: Applications not accepted.
Application information: Contributes only to pre-selected organizations.
Officers and Directors:* Sunderland Everstill,* Pres.; Chris Watts,* Secy.-Treas.; John Qualtrough.
EIN: 953628770

58580
San Francisco Ewald Annual Talent Contest, Ltd.
9 Pennisula Rd.
Belvedere, CA 94920

Established in 1990 in CA.
Financial data (yr. ended 06/30/00): Assets, $2,250,190 (M); grants paid, $0; expenditures, $86,838; qualifying distributions, $78,441; giving activities include $74,941 for programs.
Limitations: Applications not accepted.

58580—CALIFORNIA

Application information: Contributes only to pre-selected organizations.
Officers and Trustees:* Lincoln Howell,* Chair. and Pres.; Njambi Mungai,* Vice-Chair. and V.P.; Alan Nichols,* Secy. and C.F.O.
EIN: 943099652

58581
The Whitney Foundation
323 W. Cromwell Ave., Ste. 103
Fresno, CA 93711 (559) 435-8072

Established in 2000 in CA.
Donor(s): Kathryn W. Stephens.
Financial data (yr. ended 12/31/00): Assets, $2,248,249 (M); grants paid, $25,000; gifts received, $2,131,244; expenditures, $99,944; qualifying distributions, $36,540.
Limitations: Giving primarily in Fresno, CA.
Officers: Kathryn W. Stephens, Pres.; Ellen Bush, Secy.-Treas.
Directors: Denise Daggett, Tom Durkin, Alan Gilmore, Ruth Graff, Roger Stephens.
EIN: 770534123

58582
Allgemeiner Deutscher Frauen-Hilfsverein
(also known as German Ladies General Benevolent Society)
P.O. Box 27101
San Francisco, CA 94127 (415) 391-9947
Contact: Jutta Kiel, Dir.

Established in 1881 in CA.
Financial data (yr. ended 12/31/01): Assets, $2,231,178 (M); grants paid, $75,157; gifts received, $14,630; expenditures, $131,801; qualifying distributions, $97,253.
Limitations: Giving limited to the residents of the San Francisco Bay Area, CA.
Publications: Annual report.
Application information: Application form required.
Officers and Directors:* Monika Deutsche,* Pres.; Ingrid Sponholz,* V.P.; Annerose Roemer,* Recording Secy.; Jutta Kiel, Treas.; Ute Nelson, Membership Dir.; Christel Anderson, Gisela Brugger, Inge Byrnes, Herta Hederich, Sigrid Heidenreich, Sigrid Jarrett, Doris Linnenbach, Gisela LLoyd, Brigitte Schwalbe, Heidi Tang.
EIN: 941528193
Codes: FD2, GTI

58583
O'Neal Family Foundation
c/o Charles Oneal, Jr.
540 St. Anns Dr.
Laguna Beach, CA 92651

Established in 2000 in CA.
Donor(s): Charles Oneal.
Financial data (yr. ended 12/31/01): Assets, $2,225,142 (M); grants paid, $105,000; gifts received, $1,400,000; expenditures, $105,030; qualifying distributions, $105,000.
Limitations: Applications not accepted.
Application information: Contributes only to pre-selected organizations.
Director: Charles Oneal, Jr.
EIN: 330940134

58584
Phillis Foundation
c/o Phillip G. Svalya
10455 Torre Ave.
Cupertino, CA 95014-3203

Established in 2001 in CA.
Donor(s): Philip G. Svalya, Lois F. Svalya.
Financial data (yr. ended 12/31/01): Assets, $2,213,743 (M); grants paid, $5,000; gifts received, $2,218,743; expenditures, $5,000; qualifying distributions, $5,000.
Limitations: Applications not accepted. Giving primarily in OK.
Application information: Contributes only to pre-selected organizations.
Officers: Phillip G. Svalya, Pres. and Treas.; Lois F. Svalya, V.P. and Secy.
Directors: Daniel G. Svalya, Karina R. Svalya.
EIN: 770578845

58585
Latham Foundation for the Promotion of Humane Education
1826 Clement Ave.
Alameda, CA 94501

Classified as a private operating foundation in 1973.
Donor(s): Edith Latham,‡ Hugh H. Tebault III.
Financial data (yr. ended 08/31/01): Assets, $2,134,458 (M); grants paid, $0; gifts received, $226,319; expenditures, $345,441; qualifying distributions, $0.
Publications: Newsletter.
Officers and Directors:* Hugh H. Tebault III,* Chair. and Pres.; Laura Thompson,* V.P.; Mary L. Tebault,* Secy.-Treas.; Denise Cahalan, Suzanne Crouch, Noel F. DeDora, Marion F. Holt, Dezsoe Nagy.
EIN: 941243662

58586
The Bruce & Patricia Hendrix Foundation
P.O. Box 130909
Carlsbad, CA 92013

Established in 2000 in CA.
Donor(s): Bruce Hendrix, Patricia Hendrix.
Financial data (yr. ended 02/28/01): Assets, $2,131,449 (M); grants paid, $0; gifts received, $2,497,922; expenditures, $126,140; qualifying distributions, $110,446; giving activities include $51,196 for programs.
Limitations: Applications not accepted.
Application information: Contributes only to pre-selected organizations.
Officers: Carol Myers, Pres.; Patricia Hendrix, Secy.; Bruce Hendrix, Treas.
EIN: 943359855

58587
The Jeanette Bertea Hennings Foundation
c/o Ed W. Hennings
831 Via Lido Soud
Newport Beach, CA 92663

Established in 1997 in CA.
Donor(s): Ed W. Hennings.
Financial data (yr. ended 12/31/00): Assets, $2,117,753 (M); grants paid, $169,000; gifts received, $1,356; expenditures, $178,537; qualifying distributions, $167,843.
Limitations: Applications not accepted.
Application information: Contributes only to pre-selected organizations.
Officers: Ed W. Hennings, Pres. and C.E.O.; Jeffrey J. Pagano, V.P.; Richard Bertea, Secy. and C.F.O.
EIN: 330774466
Codes: FD2

58588
J. H. Robbins Foundation
503 Princeton Rd.
San Mateo, CA 94402-3231 (650) 343-5300
Contact: Aron H. Hoffman, Treas.

Established in 1983; Classified as a private operating foundation in 1994.
Donor(s): Josephine H. Robbins.‡
Financial data (yr. ended 06/30/01): Assets, $2,101,375 (M); grants paid, $106,700; expenditures, $118,228; qualifying distributions, $118,228.
Limitations: Giving limited to San Mateo County, CA.
Officers: Russell A. Robbins, Pres.; Linda K. Hoffman, Secy.; Aron H. Hoffman, Treas.
EIN: 942911318
Codes: FD2

58589
Recare Foundation
1723 Karameos Dr.
Sunnyvale, CA 94087

Established in 2001 in CA.
Donor(s): Eunice T. Yan, Raymond S. Yan.
Financial data (yr. ended 12/31/01): Assets, $2,062,173 (M); grants paid, $0; gifts received, $2,024,585; expenditures, $12,846; qualifying distributions, $9,904; giving activities include $9,859 for programs.
Officers and Directors:* Eunice T. Yan,* Pres.; Raymond S. Yan,* V.P. and Secy.-Treas.
EIN: 912163535

58590
Michael Alan Rosen Foundation
c/o Geibelson, Young & Co.
16501 Ventura Blvd., Ste. 304
Encino, CA 91436-2067 (818) 971-7300

Established in 1986 in CA. Classified as a private operating foundation in 1991.
Donor(s): Tobi Haleen, Conrad Hilton Foundation, The AGR Trust.
Financial data (yr. ended 12/31/01): Assets, $2,044,412 (M); grants paid, $5,450; gifts received, $202,124; expenditures, $1,400,953; qualifying distributions, $553,580; giving activities include $195,347 for program-related investments and $781,575 for programs.
Limitations: Applications not accepted.
Application information: Contributes only to pre-selected organizations.
Officers: Arlene Rosen, Pres. and Treas.; Tobi Haleen, V.P. and Secy.
EIN: 943024736

58591
The John H. & Cynthia Lee Smet Foundation
2810 Tennyson Pl.
Hermosa Beach, CA 90254

Donor(s): John H. Smet, Cynthia Lee Smet.
Financial data (yr. ended 11/30/01): Assets, $2,018,825 (M); grants paid, $100,019; gifts received, $369,255; expenditures, $108,155; qualifying distributions, $100,019.
Limitations: Applications not accepted.
Application information: Contributes only to pre-selected organizations.
Officers: John H. Smet, Pres.; Cynthia Lee Smet, Secy.
EIN: 954399946
Codes: FD2

58592
Berneice U. Lynn Foundation
5973 Avenida Encinas, Ste. 200
Carlsbad, CA 92008-1615
Contact: Michael G. Perdue, Tr.

Established in 1993 in CA. Classified as a private operating foundation in 1994.
Financial data (yr. ended 12/31/99): Assets, $1,975,438 (M); grants paid, $36,748; expenditures, $176,398; qualifying distributions, $42,123.

Limitations: Giving limited to the high desert area of San Bernadino County, CA.
Trustee: Michael G. Perdue.
EIN: 330555611

58593
Lindley Institute for Conflict Resolution, Inc.
c/o Grayson Rogers
4530 Hendrickson Rd.
Ojai, CA 93023

Established in 1991 in CA.
Financial data (yr. ended 09/30/00): Assets, $1,960,841 (M); grants paid, $0; expenditures, $42,913; qualifying distributions, $28,872; giving activities include $38,506 for programs.
Officers and Directors:* Grayson Rogers,* Pres.; Annine Wycherley,* Secy.; James Wycherley,* C.F.O.
EIN: 770273705

58594
Entertainment Industry Referral & Assistance Center
15456 Ventura Blvd., Ste. 400
Sherman Oaks, CA 91403-3018

Financial data (yr. ended 06/30/00): Assets, $1,918,193 (M); grants paid, $0; gifts received, $918,806; expenditures, $705,071; qualifying distributions, $699,764; giving activities include $106,008 for programs.
Officers: Michael Wittern, Pres.; Deborah Christian, Secy.-Treas.
Directors: Sharon Feldman, Lynn Franzoi.
EIN: 953930725

58595
The Chestnut Foundation
5150 Overland Ave.
Culver City, CA 90230

Established in 2000 in CA.
Donor(s): Sol Kest.
Financial data (yr. ended 12/31/01): Assets, $1,913,389 (M); grants paid, $102,700; gifts received, $1,001,035; expenditures, $103,755; qualifying distributions, $102,700.
Limitations: Applications not accepted.
Application information: Contributes only to pre-selected organizations.
Officers: Benjamin Kest, Pres.; Anna Kest, Secy.
EIN: 954793268

58596
The Foundation for Honey's Children
P.O. Box 51801
Pacific Grove, CA 93950

Established in 2000 in CA.
Financial data (yr. ended 09/30/01): Assets, $1,883,271 (M); grants paid, $0; gifts received, $2,328,783; expenditures, $25,421; qualifying distributions, $17,794; giving activities include $17,794 for programs.
Limitations: Applications not accepted.
Application information: Contributes only to pre-selected organizations.
Officers: Gaye Russell-Bruce, C.E.O. and Pres.; Donald K. Bruce, Secy. and C.F.O.
EIN: 330939708

58597
The John Robinson Foundation
1956 Lombard St.
San Francisco, CA 94107

Established in 1989.
Donor(s): John Robinson.
Financial data (yr. ended 12/31/00): Assets, $1,866,839 (L); grants paid, $52,000; expenditures, $301,507; qualifying distributions, $52,000.
Limitations: Applications not accepted. Giving primarily in CA.
Application information: Contributes only to pre-selected organizations.
Officers: John Robinson, Pres.; Patricia L. Robinson, V.P.
EIN: 943103856

58598
Quarryhill Botanical Garden
P.O. Box 232
Glen Ellen, CA 95442

Established in 1991 in CA.
Donor(s): Jane Jansen, William Davenport, R.B. Davenport III.
Financial data (yr. ended 04/30/00): Assets, $1,805,445 (M); grants paid, $5,000; gifts received, $373,538; expenditures, $437,586; qualifying distributions, $401,412; giving activities include $388,185 for programs.
Limitations: Applications not accepted.
Application information: Contributes only to pre-selected organizations.
Officers and Directors:* Jane D. Jansen,* Pres.; Maynard Garrison,* Secy.; Floyd A. Moses,* C.F.O.; Donna Bowman, Daniel Campbell, Sally McBride, William McNamara, Eleanor D. Owen.
EIN: 680249110

58599
Gruter Institute for Law and Behavioral Research
158 Goya Rd.
Portola Valley, CA 94028 (650) 854-1191

Established in 1984. Classified as a private operating foundation in 1985.
Financial data (yr. ended 11/30/01): Assets, $1,758,351 (M); grants paid, $0; gifts received, $374,890; expenditures, $439,842; qualifying distributions, $325,934; giving activities include $146,880 for programs.
Officers: Margaret Gruter, Pres. and C.F.O.; Michael McGuire, V.P.; Helmut Poppa, V.P.; Monika G. Mormenn, Secy.
EIN: 942937951

58600
Spalding Family Foundation
100 Commonwealth Ave.
San Francisco, CA 94118

Established in 2000 in CA.
Donor(s): Helen M. Spalding, Richard C. Spalding.
Financial data (yr. ended 12/31/01): Assets, $1,749,896 (M); grants paid, $938,929; expenditures, $941,862; qualifying distributions, $938,929.
Limitations: Applications not accepted. Giving primarily in CA.
Application information: Contributes only to pre-selected organizations.
Directors: Helen M. Spalding, Richard C. Spalding.
EIN: 943369408
Codes: FD

58601
Alberta Hale Land Trust
c/o Kevin Bonneau
P.O. Box 57
Volcano, CA 95689

Established in 1995 in CA.
Donor(s): Alberta Hale.
Financial data (yr. ended 12/31/01): Assets, $1,736,713 (M); grants paid, $500; gifts received, $50,435; expenditures, $52,636; qualifying distributions, $500.
Officers: Brian Bonneau, Chair.; Kevin Bonneau, Pres.; Donna Braden, Secy.-Treas.
EIN: 680338376

58602
C n C Foundation
6 Blue Spruce
Irvine, CA 92620-1245

Established in 1999 in CA.
Donor(s): Yuhsieh F. Fu, Thuji S. Lin.
Financial data (yr. ended 12/31/00): Assets, $1,698,875 (M); grants paid, $50,000; gifts received, $1,119,188; expenditures, $56,261; qualifying distributions, $51,231.
Limitations: Applications not accepted. Giving primarily in Irvine, CA.
Application information: Contributes only to pre-selected organizations.
Officer and Directors:* Yuhsieh F. Fu,* Secy.; Thuji S. Lin.
EIN: 330883785

58603
The MAMA Foundation
555 E. Easy St.
Simi Valley, CA 93065

Established in 1986.
Donor(s): Eugene Czerwinski, Constance Czerwinski-Ostendorf, Stephen Czerwinski.
Financial data (yr. ended 06/30/01): Assets, $1,691,654 (M); grants paid, $0; gifts received, $75,434; expenditures, $189,990; qualifying distributions, $0; giving activities include $189,990 for programs.
Officers and Trustees:* Eugene Czerwinski,* Pres.; Constance Czerwinski-Ostendorf,* Exec. V.P.; Stephen Czerwinski,* Secy.; Carol Kaye.
EIN: 954054650

58604
Healthtrac Foundation
135 Farm Rd.
Woodside, CA 94062 (650) 529-9533
FAX: (650) 851-8995; E-mail: sarahfries@healthtrac.com; URL: http://www.healthtracfoundation.org
Contact: Sarah Tilton Fries, Pres. and Exec. Dir.

Established in 1991 in CA.
Donor(s): James F. Fries, Sarah Tilton Fries, Charles Parcell, and a small number of additional individuals and corporations.
Financial data (yr. ended 12/31/01): Assets, $1,691,172 (M); grants paid, $38,500; expenditures, $61,934; qualifying distributions, $38,500.
Limitations: Giving on a national basis.
Publications: Informational brochure (including application guidelines).
Application information: Individuals must be nominated by someone else to be considered for prize or award. Foundation brochure outlining nomination procedures available on request. Direct applications from individuals not considered. Application form required.
Officers and Directors:* James F. Fries, M.D.,* Chair.; Sarah Tilton Fries,* Pres. and Exec. Dir.; Kenneth E. Fries,* Secy.
EIN: 943131228
Codes: GTI

58605
The LIFT Foundation
1293 Lincoln Way., Ste. B
Auburn, CA 95603 (530) 887-9589
FAX: (530) 887-9599; E-mail: info@liftfoundation.org; URL: http://www.liftfoundation.org
Contact: Katherine M. Smith, Exec. Dir.

Established in 1998 in CA.
Donor(s): Katherine M. Miller, Richard C. Miller.
Financial data (yr. ended 12/31/00): Assets, $1,678,133 (M); grants paid, $124,820; gifts received, $20,814; expenditures, $241,560; qualifying distributions, $124,820.
Limitations: Giving on an international basis, primarily to benefit Romania.
Publications: Annual report, grants list, informational brochure, application guidelines.
Application information: Application form required.
Officers and Board Members:* Katherine M. Miller, Pres.; Paul Aronowitz,* Secy.; Katherine M. Smith, Exec. Dir.; Phil Booker, Donald Clutter, Maureen Gill, Karen O'Brien, Charles Smith.
EIN: 680404790
Codes: FD2

58606
Vailima Foundation
c/o William Von Metz
P.O. Box 409
St. Helena, CA 94574

Established in 1968; Classified as a private operating foundation in 1973.
Financial data (yr. ended 12/31/01): Assets, $1,672,475 (M); grants paid, $0; gifts received, $1,852; expenditures, $65,254; qualifying distributions, $92,112; giving activities include $61,071 for programs.
Limitations: Applications not accepted.
Application information: Contributes only to pre-selected organizations.
Officers and Trustees:* William Von Metz,* Chair.; Elizabeth Baer,* Chair Emeritus; Liz Martini, Chair Emeritus; Ann Kindred,* Secy.; Jack C. Morgan, Treas.; Jeanne Angell, Patricia Beresford, Anthony Bliss, Del G. Britton, Mrs. Jamie Davies, Larry Dinnean, Stanley Holt, John Ritchie, Hon. Scott Snowden.
EIN: 941673783

58607
The Howard G. and Samita B. Jacobs Foundation
23010 Lake Forest Dr., Ste. D
Laguna Hills, CA 92653-1351
Contact: H.G. Jacobs, Pres.

Established in 1998 in CA.
Donor(s): Howard G. Jacobs, Samita B. Jacobs.
Financial data (yr. ended 12/31/01): Assets, $1,658,854 (M); grants paid, $95,795; gifts received, $404,490; expenditures, $108,681; qualifying distributions, $95,771.
Limitations: Giving primarily in CA and NY.
Application information: Requests must be typed in large type format (12 points or higher).
Officers: Howard G. Jacobs, Pres.; Samuel Gulko, V.P.; Samita B. Jacobs, Secy.
EIN: 311657763
Codes: FD2

58608
Norplant Foundation
1 Market Plz.
Steuart St. Tower, Ste. 164
San Francisco, CA 94105
Contact: Karrie L. Bercik

Established in 1991 in CA as a company-sponsored operating foundation.
Donor(s): Wyeth-Ayerst Pharmaceuticals, Inc.
Financial data (yr. ended 12/31/00): Assets, $1,651,989 (M); grants paid, $1,007,110; gifts received, $2,311,265; expenditures, $1,764,762; qualifying distributions, $1,763,047; giving activities include $1,763,764 for programs.
Limitations: Applications not accepted. Giving on a national basis.
Application information: Contributes only to pre-selected organizations.
Officers: Stephen F. Heartwell, M.D., Chair.; Vanessa E. Cullins, M.D., Vice-Chair.; Bobbie A. Henderson, Ph.D., Secy.; Lybia Burgos, Treas.
Directors: Sandra P. Arnold, Andrew R. Davidson, Karla Witt Nalcon, Alfred N. Poindexter, Louise Tyrer, M.D.
EIN: 943155128
Codes: FD

58609
The Hurd Foundation, Inc.
c/o Pacific Western Productions, Inc.
270 N. Canon Dr., Ste. 1195
Beverly Hills, CA 90210
Contact: Julie Thomson, Secy.

Established in 1982 in CA.
Donor(s): Frank E. Hurd.
Financial data (yr. ended 11/30/99): Assets, $1,612,083 (M); grants paid, $52,950; gifts received, $4,650; expenditures, $58,832; qualifying distributions, $52,950.
Limitations: Giving primarily in CA.
Officers: Gale Anne Hurd, Pres.; Julie Thomson, Secy.
EIN: 953789957

58610
Dudley-Vehmeyer-Brown Memorial Foundation, Inc.
117 Walter Hays Dr.
Palo Alto, CA 94303-2924
Contact: Frank R. Hommowun, Treas.

Established in 1972 in CA.
Donor(s): Grace E. Vehmeyer Charitable Trust.
Financial data (yr. ended 12/31/01): Assets, $1,581,294 (M); grants paid, $86,000; expenditures, $121,019; qualifying distributions, $85,491.
Limitations: Giving limited to CA.
Application information: Scholarship recommendations are made to the foundation by four participating high schools; contact school for application guidelines.
Officers: Sandra Jo Spiegel, Pres.; Rebecca Wright, V.P.; Priscilla Mathis, Secy.; Frank R. Hommowun, Treas.
Board Members: Chet Frankenfield, Hinda Weber.
EIN: 237355824
Codes: FD2, GTI

58611
California Association of Criminalists
3777 Depot Rd., No. 409
Hayward, CA 94545

Established in 1995 in CA.
Financial data (yr. ended 06/30/00): Assets, $1,502,864 (M); grants paid, $500; expenditures, $175,305; qualifying distributions, $83,545; giving activities include $83,046 for programs.
Limitations: Applications not accepted.
Application information: Contributes only to pre-selected organizations.
Officers: Lisa Brewer, Co-Pres.; Daniel Gregonis, Co-Pres.; Brooke Barloewen, Secy.; Nancy McCombs, Education Secy.; Elissa Mayo-Thompson, Membership Secy.; Michelle Fox, Treas.
Directors: Ann Murphy, Jim Stam.
EIN: 953245268

58612
The Clyde and Mary Lou Porter Foundation
1737 Roscomare Rd.
Los Angeles, CA 90077

Established in 2000 in CA.
Financial data (yr. ended 12/31/01): Assets, $1,479,321 (M); grants paid, $0; gifts received, $1,320,162; expenditures, $129,371; qualifying distributions, $0.
Limitations: Applications not accepted.
Application information: Contributes only to pre-selected organizations.
Officers: Clyde Porter, Pres.; Pamela Porter, Secy.; Nancy Cook, C.F.O.
EIN: 954814385

58613
The Dorothy L. Griest Charitable Foundation
c/o Lodgies, Skirtich & Co.
1723 Karameos Dr.
Sunnyvale, CA 94087

Established in 1992 in CA.
Donor(s): The Dorothy L. Griest Charitable Lead Trust.
Financial data (yr. ended 12/31/00): Assets, $1,475,461 (M); grants paid, $0; gifts received, $345,600; expenditures, $388,332; qualifying distributions, $365,404; giving activities include $230,643 for programs.
Limitations: Applications not accepted.
Application information: Contributes only to a pre-selected organization.
Officer and Directors:* Shirley L. Hosfeldt,* Pres.; Joan Crowder, Denise L. Flammer, Lisa D. Henderson.
EIN: 770310778

58614
Hing Ng Charitable Trust
817 Canyon Del Rey
Monterey, CA 93940
Contact: Lit Ng, Tr.

Established in 1994 in CA.
Financial data (yr. ended 12/31/01): Assets, $1,440,034 (M); grants paid, $67,700; expenditures, $69,723; qualifying distributions, $66,707.
Limitations: Giving primarily in CA.
Trustees: Keong Ng, Lit Ng.
EIN: 776099760

58615
Paso Robles Youth Arts Foundation
5161 Vineyard Dr.
Paso Robles, CA 93446

Established in 1998 in CA.
Donor(s): Donna Berg.
Financial data (yr. ended 12/31/01): Assets, $1,410,882 (M); grants paid, $0; gifts received, $704,022; expenditures, $45,228; qualifying distributions, $982,383.
Officers and Directors:* Donna Berg, Pres.; Barbara Partridge, V.P.; James H. Knecht,* Secy.; Sandy Berg, C.F.O.; Kiki Anderson, Alison Denhuger, Suzanne Ervine, Phyllis Frank, Karen

Guth, Michael Mignone, Diana Miller, Janice Nelson, Deborah Thomsen.
EIN: 770488880

58616
The Foundation for College Christian Leaders
(Formerly Eckmann Foundation)
2658 Del Mar Heights Rd., Ste. 266
Del Mar, CA 92014
URL: http://www.collegechristianleader.com
Contact: Helen Eckmann, Dir.

Established in 1988.
Donor(s): James K. Eckmann.
Financial data (yr. ended 12/31/01): Assets, $1,407,352 (M); grants paid, $100,743; expenditures, $151,048; qualifying distributions, $151,048.
Limitations: Giving primarily to residents of southern CA.
Application information: Application form required for scholarship program. Application form required.
Directors: Helen L. Eckmann, James K. Eckmann.
EIN: 330323974
Codes: FD2, GTI

58617
Armand Hammer Foundation
2425 Olympic Blvd., Ste. 140-E
Santa Monica, CA 90404
Contact: Michael A. Hammer, Pres.

Established in 1968 in CA.
Donor(s): Armand Hammer.‡
Financial data (yr. ended 12/31/01): Assets, $1,403,658 (M); grants paid, $2,261,800; gifts received, $30,000; expenditures, $3,050,823; qualifying distributions, $2,299,354.
Limitations: Giving primarily in Dallas, TX.
Application information: Application form not required.
Officers and Directors:* Michael A. Hammer,* C.E.O. and Pres.; Scott Deitrick, V.P.; Dru A. Hammer, Secy. and C.F.O.; Rex Alexander, G. Dwight Claxton, W. Dayton Pittman.
EIN: 237010813
Codes: FD

58618
Margaret Beelard Community Foundation
P.O. Box 5254
Santa Rosa, CA 95402-5254 (707) 577-0481
Contact: Barbara Prebilich, Secy.

Established in 1999 in CA.
Donor(s): Margaret Beelard.
Financial data (yr. ended 12/31/01): Assets, $1,389,686 (M); grants paid, $80,050; expenditures, $118,978; qualifying distributions, $96,501.
Application information: Application form not required.
Officers and Directors:* Steve Jensen,* Pres.; Margaret Beelard,* V.P.; Barbara Prebilich,* Secy.; Jack Harper,* C.F.O.; William Brummond, Angie King, Karen O'Neill.
Trustee: Exchange Bank.
EIN: 680401810
Codes: FD2

58619
Stockton Fire Fighters Gladys Benerd Memorial Trust
P.O. Box 692201
Stockton, CA 95269-2201 (209) 937-8552
Contact: Larry Cooper, Treas.

Established in 1995 in CA.
Financial data (yr. ended 12/31/99): Assets, $1,374,701 (M); grants paid, $50,400; expenditures, $54,936; qualifying distributions, $49,996.
Limitations: Giving limited to Stockton, CA.
Application information: Scholarships awarded only to the children of active and retired Stockton, CA firefighters.
Officers: Andrew Shapiro, Pres.; Ron Hittle, V.P.; Jay Anema, Secy.; Larry Cooper, Treas.
Directors: Mitch Higgins, Mike Morrell, Dean Poullas.
EIN: 686117555
Codes: GTI

58620
Alta Vista Foundation
325 E. Figueroa St.
Santa Barbara, CA 93101

Classified as a private operating foundation in 1969.
Financial data (yr. ended 09/30/00): Assets, $1,360,833 (M); grants paid, $0; gifts received, $4,300; expenditures, $197,046; qualifying distributions, $119,911; giving activities include $169,939 for programs.
Officers and Directors:* George Obern,* Pres.; Margo Osherenko,* V.P.; Martha Shiffman, Secy.; Gene Smith,* Treas.; William Foster, Jo Haldeman.
EIN: 952576893

58621
The Barbara J. Rudder Foundation, Inc.
P.O. Box 1989
Big Bear Lake, CA 92315-1989

Established in 1997.
Donor(s): Barbara J. Rudder.
Financial data (yr. ended 12/31/00): Assets, $1,347,242 (M); grants paid, $3,229; expenditures, $306,251; qualifying distributions, $154,402; giving activities include $154,375 for programs.
Limitations: Applications not accepted.
Publications: Informational brochure, newsletter.
Application information: Contributes only to pre-selected organizations.
Officer: Fred Westcott, Pres.; John Elskovich, Secy.
Director: Terry Kovick.
EIN: 650751034

58622
The Caldwell-Fisher Charitable Foundation
3620 Clay St.
San Francisco, CA 94118
Application address: c/o Draper Fisher Assoc., 400 Seaport Ct., Ste. 250, Redwood, CA 94063, tel.: (650) 599-9000
Contact: John Fisher, C.E.O.

Established in 1999 in CA.
Donor(s): Jennifer Caldwell, John Fisher.
Financial data (yr. ended 12/31/00): Assets, $1,341,560 (M); grants paid, $70,000; gifts received, $669,804; expenditures, $75,678; qualifying distributions, $75,564.
Limitations: Giving primarily in San Francisco, CA.
Officers: John Fisher, C.E.O. and Secy.; Jennifer Caldwell, Pres. and V.P.
EIN: 770527966

58623
Crossroads Community Foundation, Inc.
1714 21st St.
Santa Monica, CA 90404

Donor(s): John Remeny, Richard Seigel.
Financial data (yr. ended 06/30/00): Assets, $1,335,546 (M); grants paid, $0; gifts received, $230,757; expenditures, $830,510; qualifying distributions, $545,078; giving activities include $545,078 for programs.

Officers and Trustees:* Anthony H. Browne, Co-Pres.; Gay Browne, Co-Pres.; Alison Crowell, V.P.; Kate Guinzburg, V.P.; Vivien Lesnik Weisman, V.P.; Debbie Myman,* Secy.; Michael Halpern,* Treas.; Richard Appel, Ruth Black, Todd Black, Carleen Cappelletti, and 10 additional trustees.
Directors: Paul Cummins, Alva Libuser.
EIN: 953931147
Codes: TN

58624
Sowing Circle
30151 Ave. De Las Banderas, Ste. B
Rancho Santa Margarita, CA 92688

Established in 1997 in CA.
Donor(s): Frank Rabinovitch.
Financial data (yr. ended 12/31/00): Assets, $1,308,730 (M); grants paid, $1,010,452; gifts received, $1,250,000; expenditures, $1,856,919; qualifying distributions, $1,816,049; giving activities include $711,309 for programs.
Limitations: Applications not accepted. Giving primarily in CA, with emphasis on Rancho Santa Margarita.
Application information: Contributes only to pre-selected organizations.
Officers: James P. Milligan, Chair. and Pres.; Stephen M. Greenberg, Secy. and C.F.O.
Board Members: Kenneth Buckley, Colin Christie, Robert Hoekstra, Frank B. Rabinovitch.
EIN: 330754078
Codes: FD

58625
Johnson and Louise H. Clark Charitable Foundation
6 Blackthorn Rd.
Lafayette, CA 94549

Established in 1998 in CA.
Donor(s): Johnson Clark, Louise H. Clark.
Financial data (yr. ended 11/30/01): Assets, $1,274,469 (M); grants paid, $83,500; expenditures, $83,500; qualifying distributions, $83,500.
Limitations: Applications not accepted. Giving primarily in CA.
Application information: Contributes only to pre-selected organizations.
Officer: Johnson Clark, Pres.
Directors: Charles Clark, Diddo Clark, Johnson Clark, Jr., Louise H. Clark, Peter Clark, Steven Clark, Candice Wozniak.
EIN: 680424794
Codes: FD2

58626
Son Care Foundation
c/o Jack H. Gould, Jr.
P.O. Box 457
Woodlake, CA 93286

Established in 1994 in TX.
Donor(s): Jack H. Gould, Karen H. Gould.
Financial data (yr. ended 12/31/00): Assets, $1,250,438 (M); grants paid, $0; gifts received, $11,499; expenditures, $333,002; qualifying distributions, $0.
Limitations: Applications not accepted.
Application information: Contributes only to pre-selected organizations.
Officers: Jack H. Gould, Pres.; Karen H. Gould, V.P. and Secy.-Treas.; Jennifer Gould, V.P.
EIN: 752547239

58627
Cedar Rapids RHF Housing, Inc.
(Formerly Westover Manor)
c/o RHF
911 N. Studebaker Rd.
Long Beach, CA 90815

Donor(s): U.S. Dept. of Housing & Urban Development.
Financial data (yr. ended 12/31/01): Assets, $1,247,741 (M); grants paid, $0; gifts received, $174,431; expenditures, $327,799; qualifying distributions, $223,238; giving activities include $320,631 for programs.
Officers: Rev. Glenn D. Hunt, Pres.; Laverne R. Joseph, V.P.; Rev. Fritz Mellberg, Recording Secy.; Linda Listoe, Secy.
Directors: Francis Camizzi, Charles Christensen, Mel Krause, Rev. Matthew Noffke.
EIN: 330240088

58628
The Marshall G. Cox Family Foundation
77892 Cottonwood Cove
Indian Wells, CA 92210
Contact: Marshall Cox, C.E.O.

Established in 1997 in CA.
Donor(s): Marshall Cox.
Financial data (yr. ended 12/31/00): Assets, $1,247,691 (M); grants paid, $64,709; expenditures, $76,921; qualifying distributions, $76,270.
Limitations: Giving primarily in CA.
Application information: Application form required.
Officers: Marshall Cox, C.E.O.; Donna Cox, Secy.
EIN: 770456887
Codes: GTI

58629
T By D Foundation
P.O. Box 1252
Morro Bay, CA 93443-1252

Financial data (yr. ended 12/31/99): Assets, $1,212,110 (M); grants paid, $38,062; expenditures, $38,062; qualifying distributions, $46,354; giving activities include $8,292 for loans.
Limitations: Applications not accepted. Giving primarily in CA.
Application information: Contributes only to pre-selected organizations.
Officers: Robert Lane, Pres.; Rose Lane, Secy.-Treas.
EIN: 942785097

58630
John & Karen Mathon Charitable Foundation
61 Lane Pl.
Atherton, CA 94027

Established in 2000 in CA.
Donor(s): John Mathon, Karen Mathon.
Financial data (yr. ended 12/31/00): Assets, $1,209,548 (M); grants paid, $269,750; gifts received, $2,205,000; expenditures, $270,882; qualifying distributions, $270,107.
Limitations: Applications not accepted. Giving primarily in CA and MA.
Application information: Contributes only to pre-selected organizations.
Officers and Director:* John Mathon,* Pres.; Karen Mathon, Secy.-Treas.
EIN: 943356179
Codes: FD

58631
Arlene Francis Foundation
c/o Peter J. Gabel
386 Elizabeth St.
San Francisco, CA 94114

Established in 1994 in CA. Classified as a private operating foundation in 1995.
Donor(s): Arlene Francis Gabel.
Financial data (yr. ended 10/31/01): Assets, $1,193,057 (M); grants paid, $0; gifts received, $33,787; expenditures, $87,512; qualifying distributions, $40,592.
Officers and Directors:* Peter J. Gabel,* Pres.; Lisa Jaicks,* Secy.; Martin Hamilton,* Treas.
EIN: 943216151

58632
Helen Ann Buckley Foundation
P.O. Box 2229
Sonoma, CA 95476
Application address: 425 First St., East Sonoma, CA 95476, tel.: (707) 938-2700
Contact: James Kemp, Tr.

Financial data (yr. ended 12/31/99): Assets, $1,173,266 (M); grants paid, $50,000; expenditures, $50,780; qualifying distributions, $50,780.
Limitations: Giving primarily in CA.
Trustees: Jean O. Foster, James Kemp.
EIN: 686183386

58633
Taormina Theosophical Manor House, Inc.
18 Taormina Ln.
Ojai, CA 93023

Financial data (yr. ended 06/30/01): Assets, $1,123,976 (M); grants paid, $0; expenditures, $79,464; qualifying distributions, $79,464; giving activities include $79,464 for programs.
Officers: Ruth Matthews, Pres.; Ellene Mullory, Secy.-Treas.
Directors: Eugene Bunner, Max Cumsille, Gertrude Laudahn.
EIN: 953357357

58634
Bruner Family Foundation
1144 Derbyshire Dr.
Cupertino, CA 95014
Contact: Mike Bruner, Pres.

Donor(s): Mike Bruner.
Financial data (yr. ended 12/31/99): Assets, $1,119,044 (M); grants paid, $14,550; gifts received, $500,000; expenditures, $21,371; qualifying distributions, $17,953.
Limitations: Giving primarily in CA.
Application information: Application form not required.
Officers and Directors:* Mike Bruner,* Pres.; Melanie Bruner,* Secy.; Steven Hallgrimson.
EIN: 440498665

58635
Center for Computer Assisted Research in the Humanities
c/o Stanford University
Braun Music Ctr., Rm. 129
Stanford, CA 94305

Established in 1987 in CA.
Donor(s): Walter B. Hewlett.
Financial data (yr. ended 09/30/00): Assets, $1,094,864 (M); grants paid, $0; gifts received, $798,162; expenditures, $416,609; qualifying distributions, $416,609; giving activities include $416,460 for programs.
Limitations: Applications not accepted.

Officer: Walter B. Hewlett, Pres.
Directors: J.C. Michael Guite, Dave Larwood, Stanley Peters, David C. Weber.
EIN: 943038594

58636
Frederic Whitaker and Eileen Monaghan Whitaker Foundation
5641 Beaumont Ave.
La Jolla, CA 92037

Classified as a private operating foundation in 1988.
Donor(s): Eileen Monaghan Whitaker.
Financial data (yr. ended 06/30/00): Assets, $1,074,861 (M); grants paid, $3,500; gifts received, $681; expenditures, $45,829; qualifying distributions, $45,126.
Officers and Directors:* Eileen Monaghan Whitaker,* Coord.; Frank Beiser,* Treas.; Tom Bush.
EIN: 330265872

58637
Lewis Kassis Family Charitable Foundation
1000 Vine St.
Sacramento, CA 95814 (916) 441-3001
Contact: Greg Kassis, Tr.

Established in 1988 in CA.
Financial data (yr. ended 12/31/01): Assets, $1,074,021 (M); grants paid, $62,975; expenditures, $65,688; qualifying distributions, $64,590.
Limitations: Applications not accepted.
Application information: Contributes only to pre-selected organizations.
Trustee: Greg Kassis.
EIN: 686008357

58638
The Maley-Thawley Family Foundation
931 W. Woodbridge Rd.
Lodi, CA 95242-9616 (209) 369-7434
Contact: Richard Thawley, Pres.

Established in 1999 in CA.
Donor(s): Richard Thawley, Cynthia Thawley.
Financial data (yr. ended 12/31/00): Assets, $1,039,310 (M); grants paid, $26,435; gifts received, $50,832; expenditures, $34,109; qualifying distributions, $26,435.
Officers and Directors:* Richard Thawley,* Pres.; Cynthia Thawley,* V.P. and Secy.-Treas.; Norman Maley, Willard Thawley.
EIN: 680442684

58639
Rio Hondo College Foundation
3600 Workman Mill Rd.
Whittier, CA 90608

Established in 1993.
Financial data (yr. ended 06/30/99): Assets, $1,031,089 (M); grants paid, $24,431; gifts received, $159,117; expenditures, $51,434; qualifying distributions, $24,431.
Limitations: Applications not accepted. Giving limited to Rio Hando College, Wittier, CA.
Application information: Contributes only to pre-selected organizations.
Officers: Rick McGill, Pres.; Mavis Hansen, V.P.; Sue Settlage, Secy.; Blanca Villasenor, Treas.
Directors: Elizabethanne Angevine, Ellie Bewley, Audrey Boyce, Don Jenkins, Christine Sutow, and 10 additional directors.
EIN: 954367487

58640
Victor Family Foundation
c/o Jonathan Victor
1605 Gilcrest Dr.
Beverly Hills, CA 90210

Established in 1999 in CA.
Financial data (yr. ended 12/31/01): Assets, $1,027,512 (M); grants paid, $145,955; expenditures, $146,035; qualifying distributions, $145,412.
Limitations: Applications not accepted. Giving primarily in CA.
Application information: Contributes only to pre-selected organizations.
Officer: Jonathan Victor, Pres.
EIN: 954717634
Codes: FD2

58641
The Ronald J. & Dianne B. Neuman Foundation
P.O. Box 1048
Boyes Hot Springs, CA 95416

Established in 2001.
Financial data (yr. ended 12/31/01): Assets, $1,027,384 (M); grants paid, $9,847; gifts received, $1,039,265; expenditures, $11,881; qualifying distributions, $9,847.
Trustee: Ronald J. Neuman.
EIN: 680464533

58642
The Linden Family Foundation
4041 MacArthur Blvd., Ste. 350
Newport Beach, CA 92660 (949) 223-5080
Contact: Thomas M. Linden, Secy.

Established in 1997 in CA.
Donor(s): Margaret I. Linden, Milton S. Linden.
Financial data (yr. ended 12/31/00): Assets, $1,022,412 (M); grants paid, $65,000; expenditures, $74,679; qualifying distributions, $64,910.
Limitations: Giving primarily in CA.
Application information: Application form required.
Officers: Milton S. Linden, Chair.; Margaret I. Linden, V.P.; Thomas M. Linden, Secy. and C.F.O.
EIN: 330737730

58643
Child Haven, Inc.
801 Empire St.
Fairfield, CA 94533

Established in 1983 in CA.
Financial data (yr. ended 06/30/01): Assets, $1,021,536 (M); grants paid, $0; gifts received, $645,612; expenditures, $1,501,356; qualifying distributions, $518,284; giving activities include $1,328,983 for programs.
Officers and Directors:* Marianne MacDonald, Chair.; Kevin Morley, Vice-Chair.; Madonna Spurlock, Secy.; Kathlan Latimer,* Treas.; Gaile Shea-Everidge, Exec. Dir.; Ellen Dutton, Pat Gross, Jan Hewitt, Kathleen Laplante, Lena Williams.
EIN: 942907687

58644
C. A. Wall Family Foundation
290 Santa Clara Ave.
San Francisco, CA 94127-1522

Established in 1988 in CA.
Donor(s): C. Allen Wall, Catherine Brooks, Elizabeth Hanson, David R. Wall.
Financial data (yr. ended 12/31/00): Assets, $1,018,258 (M); grants paid, $35,375; gifts received, $162,000; expenditures, $40,459; qualifying distributions, $35,375.

Limitations: Applications not accepted. Giving primarily in San Francisco, CA.
Application information: Contributes only to pre-selected organizations.
Officers: C. Allen Wall, Pres.; Elizabeth Hanson, Secy.-Treas.
Directors: Catherine Brooks, David R. Wall.
EIN: 943081338

58645
The Jon and Katherine Dart Charitable Foundation
1125 El Abra Way
San Jose, CA 95125

Established in 2000 in CA.
Donor(s): Jon Dart, Katherine Dart.
Financial data (yr. ended 12/31/00): Assets, $1,004,458 (M); grants paid, $9,900; gifts received, $1,050; expenditures, $28,235; qualifying distributions, $25,761.
Limitations: Applications not accepted. Giving primarily in CA and NM.
Application information: Contributes only to pre-selected organizations.
Officers and Directors:* Jon Dart,* Pres.; Katherine Dart,* Secy. and C.F.O.
EIN: 770536934

58646
Yu Charitable & Educational Foundation
4107 Oak Pointe Ct.
Hayward, CA 94542 (510) 582-7474
Contact: Larry K. Yu, Pres.

Financial data (yr. ended 12/31/00): Assets, $1,004,187 (M); grants paid, $7,575; expenditures, $52,450; qualifying distributions, $17,570.
Limitations: Giving primarily in CA; some giving also in China.
Officer: Larry K. Yu, Pres.
Directors: Benny E. Yu, Rosaline H. Yu.
EIN: 943347895

58647
Grace Foundation
P.O. Box 924
Menlo Park, CA 94026
Application address: 2406 Grand Ave., Ames, IA 50010. tel.: (515) 663-3118
Contact: Hari Adisasmito

Established in 1965 in IA.
Donor(s): Pak-Chue Chan.‡
Financial data (yr. ended 06/30/02): Assets, $991,829 (M); grants paid, $48,700; expenditures, $60,632; qualifying distributions, $48,700.
Limitations: Giving primarily in the U.S. and Southeast Asia.
Application information: Application form required.
Officers: W. May Chan, Chair.; Don R. Newbrough, Vice-Chair; David W. Koo, Secy.; Robert W. Stafford, Treas.
Trustees: Hari Adisasmito, William Blodgett, Ethel C. Chan, Rev. Donna Dong, Katherine Kleinke.
EIN: 237294779
Codes: GTI

58648
HFT Foundation
250 Oak Grove Ave., Ste. A
Menlo Park, CA 94025-3218

Classified as a private operating foundation in 1990.
Donor(s): Susan K. Lang, Robert H. Levenson.
Financial data (yr. ended 12/31/00): Assets, $980,598 (M); grants paid, $0; gifts received, $367,882; expenditures, $283,219; qualifying distributions, $279,279; giving activities include $201,766 for programs.
Officers and Directors:* Robert H. Levenson,* Pres.; Susan K. Lang,* Secy.; Sally Ann Talarico,* Treas.
EIN: 770201598

58649
The Feigenbaum-Nii Foundation
1017 Cathcart Way
Stanford, CA 94305

Established in 2000 in CA.
Donor(s): Edward A. Feigenbaum.
Financial data (yr. ended 12/31/01): Assets, $958,662 (M); grants paid, $21,625; expenditures, $49,013; qualifying distributions, $21,625.
Officers: Edward Feigenbaum, Pres.; H. Penny Nii, V.P.
EIN: 770560496

58650
Phillips-Morrison Institute of California
(Formerly Angel Island Institute of California)
P.O. Box 844
Tiburon, CA 94920

Established in 1997 in CA.
Donor(s): Keith N. Morrison, Christopher L. Morrison.
Financial data (yr. ended 12/31/00): Assets, $948,748 (M); grants paid, $0; expenditures, $73,176; qualifying distributions, $63,074; giving activities include $17,043 for programs.
Officers: Christopher L. Morrison, Pres.; Daren Engel, Secy.
EIN: 680065800

58651
Hays Antique Truck Museum
P.O. Box 2347
Woodland, CA 95695-2347

Donor(s): Alice Gibbons, Draying McLauglin, Gordon Shepherd.
Financial data (yr. ended 06/30/01): Assets, $944,825 (M); grants paid, $0; gifts received, $81,006; expenditures, $113,229; qualifying distributions, $0; giving activities include $98,869 for programs.
Limitations: Applications not accepted.
Application information: Contributes only to pre-selected organizations.
Officers: Terry Fortier, Chair.; Edward Rocha, Pres.; Terry Klenske, V.P.; Alice Gibbons, Secy.; Robert Lautze, Treas.
EIN: 942847227

58652
Gan Family Foundation
46347 Raindance Rd.
Fremont, CA 94539-6967

Established in 2000 in CA.
Donor(s): Der Hwa Gan.
Financial data (yr. ended 12/31/01): Assets, $942,618 (M); grants paid, $13,100; expenditures, $16,338; qualifying distributions, $13,100.
Directors: Der Hwa Gan, Ping C. Gan, Li Yuan Kong.
EIN: 943382934

58653
Prem Reddy Charitable Foundation
(Formerly Desert Valley Charitable Foundation)
16716 Bear Valley Rd.
Victorville, CA 92392 (760) 241-1200
E-mail: dvcf@aol.com
Contact: Peggy Franks

Established in 1993 in CA.
Donor(s): Prem N. Reddy, M.D.
Financial data (yr. ended 12/31/99): Assets, $938,239 (M); grants paid, $20,467; gifts received, $90,679; expenditures, $134,849; qualifying distributions, $68,595; giving activities include $45,105 for programs.
Limitations: Giving primarily in the High Desert, CA, area.
Publications: Informational brochure, application guidelines, financial statement.
Application information: Application form required.
Officer: Kavitha Reddy, Pres.
Directors: Val Armienti, Dov Rombro.
EIN: 330486173

58654
The Billy Blanks Foundation, Inc.
14708 Ventura Blvd.
Sherman Oaks, CA 91403

Established in 1999.
Donor(s): Billy Blanks, Gayle Blanks.
Financial data (yr. ended 12/31/99): Assets, $933,416 (M); grants paid, $103,614; gifts received, $1,091,063; expenditures, $160,809; qualifying distributions, $103,614.
Officers: Billy Blanks, Pres.; David Paller, Secy.; Gayle Blanks, Treas.
Director: Jan Yoss.
EIN: 954764513
Codes: FD2

58655
Wendell and Inez Robie Foundation
P.O. Box 714
Foresthill, CA 95631

Financial data (yr. ended 04/30/99): Assets, $928,779 (M); grants paid, $0; gifts received, $2,927; expenditures, $29,199; qualifying distributions, $23,379; giving activities include $15,358 for programs.
Officers and Directors:* Marrian Arnold,* Pres.; Jim D. Larimer, V.P. and Treas.; Richard Barsaleau, Corp. Secy.; Larry Deakyne,* Secy.; Wendell Arnold, Xo Larimer, Jack Veal.
Advisor: Curtis Sproul.
EIN: 942764542

58656
Marsden Starbuck Cason Foundation
3880 Washington St.
San Francisco, CA 94118
Application address: 2430 Broadway St., San Francisco, CA 94115
Contact: Marsden S. Cason, Pres.

Established in 1997 in CA.
Donor(s): Marsden S. Cason.
Financial data (yr. ended 12/31/00): Assets, $927,699 (M); grants paid, $62,564; expenditures, $95,213; qualifying distributions, $62,564.
Limitations: Giving primarily in San Francisco, CA.
Officers: Marsden S. Cason, Pres.; Roxanne Mankin Cason, Secy.
EIN: 943272274

58657
International Gospel Mission
15 Santa Rida
Irvine, CA 92606
Contact: Eugene J. Choy, Pres.

Classified as a private operating foundation in 1985. Established in 1983.
Donor(s): Eugene J. Choy.
Financial data (yr. ended 12/31/99): Assets, $920,038 (M); grants paid, $29,620; expenditures, $31,255; qualifying distributions, $31,255.
Limitations: Giving primarily in CA.
Officers: Eugene J. Choy, Pres.; Misang Choy, V.P.
EIN: 953842453

58658
Charles M. Weinberg Fund
c/o Stanley Hausner Accountancy Corp.
1416 6th St.
Santa Monica, CA 90401

Established in 1955 in CA.
Donor(s): Maynard and Charlotte Franklin Living Trust.
Financial data (yr. ended 11/30/01): Assets, $916,698 (M); grants paid, $83,700; expenditures, $91,256; qualifying distributions, $82,670.
Limitations: Applications not accepted. Giving primarily in southern CA.
Application information: Contributes only to pre-selected organizations.
Trustees: Charlotte Franklin, Gil Wayne.
EIN: 956029434
Codes: FD2

58659
Scientific Being Research Foundation, Inc.
8249 Meeks Bay Ave.
Meeks Bay, CA 96142

Established in 1999 in CA.
Donor(s): David E. Griswold.
Financial data (yr. ended 12/31/01): Assets, $915,073 (M); grants paid, $219; gifts received, $300,000; expenditures, $11,512; qualifying distributions, $219.
Limitations: Applications not accepted.
Application information: Contributes only to pre-selected organizations.
Officer: David E. Griswold, Pres.
Director: Marjorie S. Griswold.
EIN: 912026760

58660
Thomas & Donna Whitney Education Foundation
(also known as Whitney Education Foundation)
10410 Albertsworth Ln.
Los Altos Hills, CA 94024 (650) 949-3568
Contact: Donna Whitney, Pres.

Incorporated in 1981 in CA.
Donor(s): Thomas M. Whitney,‡ Donna Whitney.
Financial data (yr. ended 06/30/99): Assets, $905,125 (M); grants paid, $38,500; expenditures, $47,375; qualifying distributions, $43,595.
Limitations: Giving primarily in south San Mateo and Santa Clara counties, CA.
Publications: Application guidelines.
Officers: Donna Whitney, Pres.; Ann Crockett, V.P. and Secy.; Thomas A. Whitney, Treas.
EIN: 942775750

58661
Jon C. and Katherine L. Harvey Charitable Foundation
c/o Jon C. Harvey
3790 Smallwood Court
Pleasanton, CA 94566

Established in 1999 in CA.
Donor(s): Jon C. Harvey, Katherine L. Harvey.
Financial data (yr. ended 12/31/01): Assets, $889,486 (M); grants paid, $535; expenditures, $64,837; qualifying distributions, $46,021; giving activities include $7,000 for programs.
Officers and Directors:* Katherine L. Harvey,* Pres.; Jon C. Harvey,* C.F.O. and Secy.
EIN: 943334574

58662
Paul S. Veneklasen Research Foundation
1711 16th St.
Santa Monica, CA 90404-4401

Classified as a private operating foundation in 1981.
Financial data (yr. ended 11/30/01): Assets, $877,603 (M); grants paid, $35,609; expenditures, $65,915; qualifying distributions, $35,609.
Directors: Jerry Christoff, Donna Heyn, Joe Ortega, Lee Veneklasen.
EIN: 953555062

58663
The Negri Foundation
31244 Palos Verdes Dr. W., Ste. 234
Rancho Palos Verdes, CA 90275

Established in 1990 in CA.
Financial data (yr. ended 12/31/99): Assets, $877,046 (M); grants paid, $54,005; expenditures, $225,453; qualifying distributions, $54,005.
Limitations: Giving primarily in southern CA.
Officer: Max Negri, M.D., Pres. and Secy.-Treas.
EIN: 330432347

58664
Blue Bell Foundation for Cats
20982 Laguna Canyon Rd.
Laguna Beach, CA 92651-2408

Classified as a private operating foundation in 1988.
Financial data (yr. ended 01/31/02): Assets, $875,306 (M); grants paid, $0; gifts received, $173,660; expenditures, $114,685; qualifying distributions, $0.
Officers: Susan Hamil, Pres.; Dorothy M. Palmer, Treas.
Directors: Rose Gatzow, John Hamil.
EIN: 330246182

58665
Tennant Foundation
338 S. Glendora Ave.
West Covina, CA 91790-3043

Established in 1992 in CA.
Donor(s): Forest Tennant, Miriam Tennant.
Financial data (yr. ended 12/31/99): Assets, $865,400 (M); grants paid, $22,304; gifts received, $276,208; expenditures, $36,975; qualifying distributions, $22,304.
Limitations: Applications not accepted. Giving limited to CA.
Application information: Contributes only to pre-selected organizations.
Officers: Forest Tennant, Pres.; Miriam Tennant, V.P.; Robert Nordstrom, Secy.
EIN: 954353510

58666
The Marilyn and Irv Sobel Charitable Foundation
c/o Irv Sobel
10490 Wilshire Blvd., No. 1404
Los Angeles, CA 90024

Established in 1992 in CA.
Donor(s): Irv Sobel, Marilyn Sobel.
Financial data (yr. ended 12/31/00): Assets, $862,373 (M); grants paid, $7,105; expenditures, $79,105; qualifying distributions, $7,105.
Limitations: Applications not accepted. Giving primarily in the Los Angeles, CA, area.
Application information: Contributes only to pre-selected organizations.
Trustees: Irv Sobel, Marilyn Sobel.
EIN: 956941820

58667
Eris & Larry Field Family Foundation
433 N. Camden Dr., Ste. 820
Beverly Hills, CA 90210
Contact: Lawrence N. Field, Pres.

Established in 1983 in CA.
Donor(s): Lawrence N. Field, Eris M. Field.
Financial data (yr. ended 06/30/01): Assets, $855,504 (M); grants paid, $589,517; gifts received, $971,000; expenditures, $614,450; qualifying distributions, $589,517.
Limitations: Giving primarily in the Los Angeles, CA, area.
Application information: Application form not required.
Officers and Directors:* Lawrence N. Field,* Pres.; Eris M. Field,* V.P.; John Harrington, C.F.O.; Lisa S. Field, Robyn L. Field.
EIN: 953905829
Codes: FD

58668
Thomas R. and Constance C. Ferguson Foundation
1187 Coast Village Rd.
Montecito, CA 93108-2737

Established in 1998 in CA.
Donor(s): Constance C. Ferguson.
Financial data (yr. ended 12/31/01): Assets, $851,207 (M); grants paid, $0; gifts received, $42,000; expenditures, $46,290; qualifying distributions, $0.
Limitations: Applications not accepted.
Application information: Contributes only to pre-selected organizations.
Trustees: Constance C. Ferguson, Thomas Ferguson.
EIN: 770475247

58669
The Herrick Fund
3000 Sand Hill Rd., Bldg. 4, Ste. 170
Menlo Park, CA 94025-7113

Financial data (yr. ended 10/31/00): Assets, $850,071 (M); grants paid, $0; expenditures, $48,753; qualifying distributions, $43,279; giving activities include $42,000 for programs.
Officers: Sarah P. Herrick, Pres.; S. Gale Herrick, Secy.; Stephen B. Herrick, C.F.O.
EIN: 770098614

58670
Leathers Family Foundation
4 Norwood Ave.
Ross, CA 94957-1186

Established in 1993 as a company-sponsored operating foundation.
Donor(s): Pacific World Corporation.
Financial data (yr. ended 12/31/00): Assets, $849,709 (M); grants paid, $48,250; gifts received, $225,000; expenditures, $50,115; qualifying distributions, $47,827.
Limitations: Applications not accepted. Giving limited to headquarters city and major operating areas.
Application information: Contributes only to pre-selected organizations.
Officers: Robert Leathers, Pres.; Jennifer Leathers, V.P.
Director: Betty Jane Leathers.
EIN: 931135081
Codes: CD

58671
Tadeusz Ungar Foundation
770 Marshall St.
Redwood City, CA 94063 (650) 367-8940
Contact: Zdzislaw Zakrzewski, Pres.

Financial data (yr. ended 12/31/00): Assets, $839,008 (M); grants paid, $4,726; expenditures, $88,934; qualifying distributions, $4,726; giving activities include $4,726 for programs.
Limitations: Giving limited to Poland.
Officers: Zdzislaw Zakrzewski, Pres.; Peter Wrona, Secy.; Maciej Wrona, Treas.
EIN: 943213735

58672
Thatcher Foundation
16633 Ventura Blvd., Ste. 510
Encino, CA 91436-1807

Established in 1998 in CA.
Donor(s): George A. Thatcher, Georgia R. Thatcher.
Financial data (yr. ended 06/30/00): Assets, $838,018 (M); grants paid, $18,129; gifts received, $500,000; expenditures, $18,710; qualifying distributions, $35,855.
Limitations: Applications not accepted.
Application information: Contributes only to pre-selected organizations.
Officers and Directors:* George A. Thatcher,* Pres.; Georgia R. Thatcher,* V.P.; Phillip M. Bardack,* Secy. and C.F.O.; Diane Thatcher, Nancy Thatcher, Suzanne Thatcher, Thomas J. Thatcher.
EIN: 954697063

58673
The Basso/Healy Foundation
91 Bay Way
San Rafael, CA 94901

Established in 2000 in CA.
Donor(s): Robert Basso, Mary Basso.
Financial data (yr. ended 12/31/01): Assets, $828,941 (M); grants paid, $46,050; gifts received, $73,816; expenditures, $46,070; qualifying distributions, $43,192.
Limitations: Applications not accepted. Giving primarily in CA.
Application information: Unsolicited request for funds not accepted.
Officers and Directors:* Robert S. Basso,* Pres.; Mary H. Basso,* Secy.; Alan R. Grassano,* Treas.; Catherine Randall.
EIN: 680452102

58674
The Foundation
5751 Buckingham Pkwy., No. 105
Culver City, CA 90230

Established in 1997 in CA.
Financial data (yr. ended 06/30/00): Assets, $821,406 (M); grants paid, $0; gifts received, $286,000; expenditures, $35,791; qualifying distributions, $34,691; giving activities include $34,692 for programs.
Limitations: Applications not accepted.
Application information: Contributes only to pre-selected organizations.
Trustee: Frank Di Pasquale.
EIN: 944656856

58675
Museum of American Heritage
P.O. Box 1731
Palo Alto, CA 94302-1731

Established in 1990 in CA; Classified as a private operating foundation in 1998.
Financial data (yr. ended 12/31/00): Assets, $820,860 (M); grants paid, $0; gifts received, $94,027; expenditures, $193,847; qualifying distributions, $118,072; giving activities include $118,072 for programs.
Officers and Directors:* Allan Chin,* Chair.; W. George Zimmerman,* Vice-Chair.; Carl B. Moerdyke,* Pres.; Suzanne H. Beaver,* V.P.; Theodora Nelson,* V.P.; J. Robert Beck,* Secy.; Charles Pack, Treas.; Ellen B. Harrington, Exec. Dir.; Charles M. Gillis, and 13 additional directors.
EIN: 770106732

58676
Vivian F. Krodel Charitable Foundation
1696 Quail Ave.
Sunnyvale, CA 94087

Established in 1998 in CA.
Donor(s): Vivian F. Krodel.
Financial data (yr. ended 12/31/99): Assets, $818,603 (M); grants paid, $2,500; gifts received, $296,655; expenditures, $31,055; qualifying distributions, $2,500.
Officer: Gregory M. Krodel, Pres.
Director: Vivian F. Krodel.
EIN: 770499594

58677
Yasme Foundation, Inc.
1612 Via Escondido
San Lorenzo, CA 94580-2019
Application address: 651 Handley Trail, Redwood City, CA 94062, tel.: (650) 365-5918
Contact: Charles K. Epps, V.P.

Financial data (yr. ended 12/31/01): Assets, $808,009 (M); grants paid, $13,455; gifts received, $500; expenditures, $14,351; qualifying distributions, $14,351.
Limitations: Giving primarily in CA and Bloomfield, CT; some giving also in China.
Officers: Wayne A. Mills, Pres.; Charles K. Epps, V.P.; Robert B. Vallio, Secy.; Charles McHenry, Treas.
Directors: G. Kip Edwards, Martti Laine, Alfred A. Laun.
EIN: 941628934

58678
Hager Hanger Club Foundation
2511 Santa Clara Ave.
Alameda, CA 94501 (510) 337-9025
Contact: James Hager, Pres.

Established in 1996 in CA.
Donor(s): Margaret Hager.
Financial data (yr. ended 12/31/00): Assets, $788,793 (M); grants paid, $52,519; gifts received, $102,263; expenditures, $56,801; qualifying distributions, $54,659; giving activities include $54,034 for programs.
Limitations: Giving primarily in Alameda, CA.
Officers: James Hager, Pres.; Jackie C. Kirschner, V.P.; Steven P. Small, Secy.
EIN: 943245672

58679
HTR Vintage Motorsports Foundation
2425 Olympic Blvd., Ste. 140-E
Santa Monica, CA 90404
Contact: Michael A. Hammer, Pres.

Classified as a private operating foundation in 2001 in CA.
Donor(s): Hammer International Foundation.
Financial data (yr. ended 12/31/00): Assets, $768,573 (M); grants paid, $0; gifts received, $781,582; expenditures, $13,009; qualifying distributions, $447,694; giving activities include $435,878 for programs.
Application information: Application form not required.
Officer: Michael A. Hammer, Pres.
EIN: 954828821

58680
Cookson Ranch Foundation, Inc.
c/o Patti Miller
P.O. Box 973
Blue Lake, CA 95525-0973

Established in 1996 in CA.
Donor(s): Daryl Galusha, Gary Galusha.
Financial data (yr. ended 12/31/00): Assets, $758,916 (M); grants paid, $0; gifts received, $31,810; expenditures, $24,989; qualifying distributions, $11,491.
Officers: Dale Galusha, Chair.; Patti Miller, Secy.-Treas.
Directors: Don Buller, Brent Coeur-Barron, Dale Taylor.
EIN: 943237506

58681
Fahringer Foundation
c/o William Struve
P.O. Box 604
La Jolla, CA 92038-0604

Established in 1999 in CA.
Donor(s): Elizabeth Struve.
Financial data (yr. ended 12/31/00): Assets, $753,589 (M); grants paid, $6,000; gifts received, $100; expenditures, $12,433; qualifying distributions, $5,615.
Limitations: Applications not accepted.
Application information: Contributes only to pre-selected organizations.
Officers and Trustees:* Elizabeth Struve,* Pres.; William Struve,* Secy. and C.F.O.; Alexandra Mark, Charles H. Mullin, David P. Mullin, W. Jeffrey Mullin.
EIN: 330884548

58682
Ella K. Cummings Memorial Foundation
2801 Selby Ave.
Los Angeles, CA 90064-4226 (310) 838-9143
Contact: Timmie Lee Sperl Taylor, Tr.

Established in 1995 in CA.
Donor(s): Ella K. Cummings.‡
Financial data (yr. ended 12/31/99): Assets, $747,136 (M); grants paid, $3,215; expenditures, $99,336; qualifying distributions, $79,627; giving activities include $38,065 for programs.
Limitations: Giving primarily in Los Angeles, CA.
Trustee: Timmie Lee Sperl Taylor.
EIN: 956977716

58683
Hunter House Foundation
P.O. Box 150783
San Rafael, CA 94915

Financial data (yr. ended 12/31/01): Assets, $734,281 (M); grants paid, $0; expenditures, $29,922; qualifying distributions, $0.
Directors: George Ekwall, Frank George, Joseph Hogin, George Lagomarsino.
EIN: 680310367

58684
Synopsys Silicon Valley Science & Technology Outreach Foundation
c/o Synopsys, Inc. Western
700 E. Middlefield Rd.
Mountain View, CA 94043-4033
URL: http://www.outreach-foundation.org

Classified as a company-sponsored operating foundation in 1999.
Donor(s): Synopsys Technology Opportunity Scholarship Foundation, Industry Initiatives.
Financial data (yr. ended 12/31/00): Assets, $732,470 (M); grants paid, $315,926; gifts received, $807,294; expenditures, $760,957; qualifying distributions, $684,666.
Limitations: Applications not accepted. Giving primarily in CA.
Application information: Contributes only to pre-selected organizations.
Officers: Susan Hammer, C.E.O.; Gary Robinson, Pres.; Lorna Dejillo, Mgr.
EIN: 770520414
Codes: FD

58685
Lewis Brunswick and Rebecca Matoff Foundation, Inc.
10375 Wilshire Blvd., No. 4-H
Los Angeles, CA 90024

Established in 2000 in CA.
Donor(s): Lewis Brunswick.
Financial data (yr. ended 12/31/01): Assets, $728,839 (M); grants paid, $45,225; gifts received, $306,000; expenditures, $49,786; qualifying distributions, $45,225.
Limitations: Applications not accepted. Giving primarily in CA.
Application information: Contributes only to pre-selected organizations.
Trustees: Lewis Brunswick, Rebecca Matoff.
EIN: 954748693

58686
Estelle Funk Foundation
11077 E. Rush St.
South El Monte, CA 91733
Contact: Myron H. Funk, C.E.O.

Established in 1996 in CA.
Donor(s): Myron H. Funk.
Financial data (yr. ended 12/31/01): Assets, $727,999 (M); grants paid, $156,754; gifts received, $50,000; expenditures, $194,856; qualifying distributions, $155,724.
Limitations: Giving primarily in CA and NY.
Officers: Myron H. Funk, C.E.O.; Ray Zebrack, C.F.O.
Director: Herbert Schwartz.
EIN: 954599202
Codes: FD2

58687
Provident-Salierno Family Foundation
P.O. Box 3328
Visalia, CA 93278-3328 (209) 734-2071
Contact: Tony Salierno, Dir.

Established in 1991 in CA.
Donor(s): Tony Salierno, Mary Salierno.
Financial data (yr. ended 12/31/01): Assets, $727,519 (M); grants paid, $31,510; gifts received, $70,000; expenditures, $41,583; qualifying distributions, $41,317.
Limitations: Giving primarily in Visalia, CA.
Directors: Bruce Bickel, Dave Safina, Mary Salierno, Tony Salierno.
EIN: 770300193

58688
CB Wellness Foundation
108 Portola Rd., Ste. 103
Portola Valley, CA 94028

Established in 1999 in CA.
Donor(s): Bonnie Crater, Christopher Alan Buja.
Financial data (yr. ended 06/30/00): Assets, $721,649 (M); grants paid, $42,912; gifts received, $2,146,403; expenditures, $46,915; qualifying distributions, $46,915.
Limitations: Applications not accepted.
Application information: Contributes only to pre-selected organizations.
Trustees: Christopher Alan Buja, Bonnie Crater, Henry Anthony Jandl, Nancy Jandl, Christopher Penny.
EIN: 770528716

58689
Packard, Packard & Johnson Foundation
4 Main St., Ste. 200
Los Altos, CA 94022-2904 (650) 947-7300

Established in 2000 in CA as a company-sponsored operating foundation.
Donor(s): Packard, Packard, & Johnson, a Professional Corporation.
Financial data (yr. ended 12/31/00): Assets, $720,982 (M); grants paid, $50,281; gifts received, $775,100; expenditures, $61,516; qualifying distributions, $61,516.
Officers and Directors:* Craig H. Johnson,* Pres.; Von G. Packard,* V.P. and Secy.; Lon D. Packard,* V.P.; Ronald D. Packard,* C.F.O.
EIN: 770549749

58690
The Hirshberg Foundation for Pancreatic Cancer Research
(Formerly The Ronald S. Hirshberg Memorial Foundation)
375 Homewood Rd.
Los Angeles, CA 90049 (310) 472-6310
FAX: 310 471-1020; *URL:* http://www.pancreatic.org
Contact: Lisa Manheim

Established in 1997 in CA.
Donor(s): Agnes Berliner Hirshberg.
Financial data (yr. ended 12/31/01): Assets, $711,373 (M); grants paid, $263,000; gifts received, $423,742; expenditures, $379,681; qualifying distributions, $263,000.
Limitations: Applications not accepted.
Publications: Financial statement, newsletter, informational brochure.
Application information: Contributes only to pre-selected organizations.
Officer and Directors:* Agnes Berliner Hirshberg,* Pres.; Lisa Manheim.
Trustees: Jon Hirshberg, Lisa Hirshberg.
Advisory Board: Stephen Prince, Michael Scott.
EIN: 954640311

Codes: FD

58691
Matrix Institution on Addictions, Inc.
12304 Santa Monica Blvd., Ste. 108
Los Angeles, CA 90025-2586

Established in 1989 in CA.
Financial data (yr. ended 12/31/01): Assets, $694,954 (L); grants paid, $0; gifts received, $2,099,627; expenditures, $2,935,391; qualifying distributions, $2,512,046; giving activities include $431,624 for programs.
Officers and Directors:* Al Hasson,* Pres.; Michael McCann, Secy.; Dae Medman,* Treas.; Paul Brethen, Exec. Dir.; Patricia Marinelli Casey, Exec. Dir.; Jeanne Obert,* Exec. Dir.; Carol Archie, Grace Barrera, Alice Huber, Brian Murphy, Richard Rawson, Steve Shoptaw.
EIN: 954168619

58692
The George Lucas Educational Foundation
P.O. Box 3494
San Rafael, CA 94912-3494
URL: http://www.glef.org

Established in 1993 in CA.
Donor(s): Lucasfilm Ltd.
Financial data (yr. ended 12/31/01): Assets, $693,848 (M); grants paid, $0; gifts received, $12,390,897; expenditures, $2,460,626; qualifying distributions, $2,353,620; giving activities include $1,348,659 for programs.
Officers: George W. Lucas, Jr., Chair.; Stephen D. Arnold, Vice-Chair. and C.F.O.; Milton Chen, Secy. and Exec. Dir.
Directors: Kim Meredith, Kate Nyegaard, Marshall Turner, Osamu Yamada.
EIN: 680065687

58693
The Bamford-Lahey Children's Foundation
2995 Woodside Rd., Ste. 400
Woodside, CA 94062

Established in 2000 in CA.
Donor(s): Roger Bamford.
Financial data (yr. ended 12/31/01): Assets, $686,743 (M); grants paid, $44,163; gifts received, $136,000; expenditures, $135,790; qualifying distributions, $44,163.
Officers: Margaret Lahey, Pres.; Denise Lahey Bamford, Secy.; Roger Bamford, C.F.O.
Directors: David F. Boyle, Joel Moby.
EIN: 943368601

58694
Oceanographic & Marine Biology Trust
2600 Garden Rd., Ste. 320
Monterey, CA 93940
Contact: Stephen B. Ruth, Pres.

Classified as a private operating foundation in 1986.
Financial data (yr. ended 12/31/00): Assets, $678,867 (M); grants paid, $35,153; expenditures, $36,993; qualifying distributions, $35,153.
Limitations: Giving primarily in CA.
Application information: Application form not required.
Officers: Ferdinand S. Ruth, Pres.; Robert E. Williams, Secy.; Stephen B. Ruth, Treas.
EIN: 770094228
Codes: GTI

58695
The Minnie Perkins Foundation
1995 S. McDowell Blvd., Bldg. A
Petaluma, CA 94954 (707) 769-2700

Established in 1995 in CA.
Donor(s): Wallis D. Arnold.
Financial data (yr. ended 06/30/00): Assets, $676,177 (M); grants paid, $0; gifts received, $1,365; expenditures, $31,727; qualifying distributions, $31,724; giving activities include $24,359 for programs.
Officers: Wallis D. Arnold, Pres.; Robb Scott, Secy.
Director: Michael Sun.
EIN: 943231028

58696
The Slocum Puzzle Foundation
257 S. Palm Dr.
Beverly Hills, CA 90212 (310) 273-2270
Contact: Gerald K. Slocum, C.E.O.

Established in 1993 in CA.
Donor(s): Gerald K. Slocum.
Financial data (yr. ended 12/31/01): Assets, $669,871 (M); grants paid, $0; gifts received, $10,000; expenditures, $13,393; qualifying distributions, $16,096; giving activities include $14,902 for programs.
Officers: Gerald K. Slocum, C.E.O.; Allan K. Slocum, Secy.
EIN: 954446928

58697
The Revokip Foundation
625 Fair Oaks Ave., Ste. 360
South Pasadena, CA 91030

Established in 1999 in CA.
Donor(s): Yuri Pikover, Deana Pikover.
Financial data (yr. ended 12/31/00): Assets, $667,316 (M); grants paid, $4,441,665; expenditures, $4,613,956; qualifying distributions, $4,468,465.
Limitations: Applications not accepted. Giving primarily in Los Angeles, CA.
Application information: Contributes only to pre-selected organizations.
Officers: Yuri Pikover, Pres.; Deana Pikover, V.P.; Linda J. Blinkenberg, Secy.; Gaylin N. King, C.F.O.
EIN: 954724653
Codes: FD

58698
The Vons Companies Charitable Foundation, Inc.
c/o Safeway Inc., Tax Dept.
5918 Stoneridge Mall Rd.
Pleasanton, CA 94588-3229
Application address: c/o Sandra Calderon-Lidskin, P.O. Box 513338, Los Angeles, CA 90051-1338, tel.: (626) 821-7291

Established in 1995 in CA.
Financial data (yr. ended 12/31/01): Assets, $664,632 (M); grants paid, $391,919; gifts received, $705,039; expenditures, $415,167; qualifying distributions, $415,167.
Limitations: Giving limited to Vons service area within southern CA and NV.
Officers: Sandra S. Calderon-Lidskin, Pres.; Deborah Conrad, V.P. and Secy.; Tom Pankow, V.P. and Treas.
EIN: 954523801
Codes: FD

58699
Culver City Accessible Apartments Corp.
7630 Gloria Ave.
Van Nuys, CA 91406

Financial data (yr. ended 06/30/02): Assets, $650,437 (M); grants paid, $0; expenditures, $177,471; qualifying distributions, $0.
Officers: Richard Williams, Pres.; Yvetta Williams, V.P.; Charles Haughey, Secy.-Treas.
EIN: 954284777

58700
Karol Uryga-Nawaroski Foundation
c/o Jim Kryslak
18730 Crest Ave.
Castro Valley, CA 94546-2732
Contact: John C. Rusting, Treas.

Classified as a private operating foundation in 1985.
Donor(s): Charles Nawaroski,‡ Robert S. Krysick.
Financial data (yr. ended 12/31/99): Assets, $637,945 (M); grants paid, $16,774; expenditures, $88,995; qualifying distributions, $16,774.
Limitations: Giving primarily in CA.
Officers: James Krysiak, Pres.; Barry Klein, V.P.; John C. Rusting, Treas.
EIN: 680040630

58701
Peter Uccelli Foundation
1 Uccelli Blvd.
Redwood City, CA 94063 (650) 366-0922
Contact: Peter Uccelli, Dir.

Established in 1994 in CA.
Financial data (yr. ended 12/31/99): Assets, $624,662 (M); grants paid, $39,111; gifts received, $125,000; expenditures, $39,566; qualifying distributions, $39,111.
Officers and Directors:* Paula Uccelli,* Pres.; William Lanam, V.P.; Nancy Hack, Secy.; George Uccelli, C.F.O.; Peter Uccelli.
EIN: 943191524

58702
The Ademas Foundation
c/o Dana L. Bonda
4800 Bonvue Ave.
Los Angeles, CA 90027

Established in 1997 in CA.
Financial data (yr. ended 12/31/00): Assets, $618,466 (M); grants paid, $0; gifts received, $2,000; expenditures, $15,909; qualifying distributions, $18,565; giving activities include $12,818 for programs.
Officers and Directors:* Dana L. Bonda,* Pres.; Debbie Cope,* V.P.
EIN: 954634928

58703
Sarosi-Kanter Charitable Foundation
153 Ethel Ave.
Mill Valley, CA 94941

Established in 1999 in CA.
Donor(s): Charles M. Sarosi, Lillian K. Kanter.
Financial data (yr. ended 12/31/00): Assets, $609,941 (M); grants paid, $13,451; gifts received, $378,655; expenditures, $169,977; qualifying distributions, $69,835; giving activities include $56,384 for programs.
Officers and Directors:* Lillian K. Kanter,* Pres.; Charles M. Sarosi,* Secy.-Treas.
EIN: 943340445

58704—CALIFORNIA

58704
Advocacy Arts Foundation
c/o Levine & Assoc.
1040 S. Robertson Blvd., Ste. A.
Los Angeles, CA 90035-1505

Established in 1995 in CA.
Donor(s): Roger Grad, William Lund, The Lund Foundation.
Financial data (yr. ended 12/31/00): Assets, $606,283 (M); grants paid, $44,545; gifts received, $137,641; expenditures, $130,431; qualifying distributions, $100,781.
Limitations: Applications not accepted. Giving on a national basis.
Application information: Contributes only to pre-selected organizations.
Officers: Herb Belkin, Chair.; Robert G. Ketchum, Pres.
Directors: Roger Grad, Michelle Lund, Rhett Turner, John Uphold.
EIN: 954533243

58705
Gene & Elaine Allen Foundation
13654 Park St.
Whittier, CA 90601

Donor(s): Chester Allen, Elaine Allen.
Financial data (yr. ended 12/31/00): Assets, $603,688 (M); grants paid, $144,107; gifts received, $217,158; expenditures, $144,257; qualifying distributions, $144,107.
Limitations: Applications not accepted. Giving primarily in CA.
Application information: Contributes only to pre-selected organizations.
Trustee: Chester E. Allen.
EIN: 953886000
Codes: FD2

58706
Advanced Bioscience Resources, Inc.
1516 Oak St., Ste. 303
Alameda, CA 94501

Financial data (yr. ended 12/31/99): Assets, $600,293 (M); grants paid, $12,753; expenditures, $1,358,276; qualifying distributions, $1,332,895; giving activities include $1,320,336 for programs.
Limitations: Applications not accepted. Giving primarily in CA.
Application information: Contributes only to pre-selected organizations.
Officers and Directors:* Linda Tracy,* Pres.; James Logue,* V.P.; Daniel Kreiss,* Secy.
EIN: 943110160

58707
Anonymous Givers Charitable Foundation
1000 Hoffman Ln.
Byron, CA 94514-2516
Contact: Jo G. Tennant, Tr.

Donor(s): Edward A. Prewett.
Financial data (yr. ended 12/31/01): Assets, $598,291 (M); grants paid, $25,600; expenditures, $26,952; qualifying distributions, $26,952.
Limitations: Giving primarily in CA.
Trustees: Edward A. Prewett, Mary A. Prewett, Jo G. Tennant.
EIN: 680117271

58708
Gilbert Yamashiro Lund Foundation
1350 E. Lassen, Ste. 2
Chico, CA 95926

Donor(s): Gayle Y. Gilbert, John L. Burghardt.
Financial data (yr. ended 12/31/01): Assets, $594,691 (M); grants paid, $0; gifts received, $1,250; expenditures, $1,611; qualifying distributions, $0.
Application information: Application form not required.
Directors: John L. Burghardt, Herbert C. Cornuell, Gayle Y. Gilbert.
EIN: 680341048

58709
Institute for the Study of Human Resources
1017 Arlington Ave.
Los Angeles, CA 90019

Financial data (yr. ended 12/31/00): Assets, $588,725 (L); grants paid, $30,182; gifts received, $2,000; expenditures, $40,812; qualifying distributions, $30,182.
Limitations: Applications not accepted. Giving primarily in CA.
Application information: Contributes only to pre-selected organizations.
Officers: Thomas Hunter Russell, Pres.; David Mason Eichman, V.P.; Reid Rasmussen, Secy.; James Dunham, Treas.
EIN: 952369815

58710
Puente Hills Community Programming Corporation
16433 Wedgeworth Dr.
Hacienda Heights, CA 91745

Classified as a private operating foundation in 1986.
Financial data (yr. ended 12/31/00): Assets, $588,370 (M); grants paid, $0; expenditures, $105,774; qualifying distributions, $72,362; giving activities include $69,143 for programs.
Officers and Directors:* Wayne Huang,* Pres.; Richard Hobelsrud,* V.P.; Elodia Martinez,* Secy.; Charles Huff,* Treas.
EIN: 953936782

58711
Balochie Boone Charitable Foundation
1723 Karameos Dr.
Sunnyvale, CA 94087

Established in 1998 in CA.
Donor(s): Duvall C. Balochie, Deloris B. Balochie.
Financial data (yr. ended 12/31/00): Assets, $578,163 (M); grants paid, $3,400; expenditures, $49,119; qualifying distributions, $44,988; giving activities include $41,658 for programs.
Limitations: Applications not accepted.
Application information: Contributes only to pre-selected organizations.
Officers and Directors:* Duvall C. Balochie,* Pres.; Deloris B. Balochie,* V.P. and C.F.O; Eric D. Balochie,* Secy.
EIN: 770491509

58712
Andree Wagner Peace Trust
P.O. Box 1094
Arcata, CA 95518
Application address: P.O. Box 1127, Calistoga, CA 94515, tel.: (707) 942-4433
Contact: Robert Hitchcock, Tr.

Established in 1994 in CA.
Financial data (yr. ended 12/31/00): Assets, $572,543 (M); grants paid, $36,255; expenditures, $61,165; qualifying distributions, $41,665.
Trustees: Beverly Allen, Robert Hitchcock, Sue Lee Mossman.
EIN: 686053252

58713
Glenwood RHF Housing, Inc.
c/o Loess Hills Estates
911 N. Studebaker Rd.
Long Beach, CA 90815

Classified as a private operating foundation in 1987.
Financial data (yr. ended 06/30/00): Assets, $571,939 (M); grants paid, $0; gifts received, $84,217; expenditures, $129,752; qualifying distributions, $82,204; giving activities include $127,907 for programs.
Officers: Victor Engleman, Pres.; Linda Listoe, Secy.
Directors: Helen Boles, George Fraissinet, Connie Harms, Carrie Merritt, Terry Ross, Michael Rupe, Duane Stone.
EIN: 330240089

58714
The Harry Singer Foundation
c/o Margaret Bohannon-Kaplan
174 Spindrift Rd.
Carmel, CA 93923-9775

Established in 1988 in CA.
Donor(s): Members of the Kaplan family.
Financial data (yr. ended 12/31/00): Assets, $571,488 (M); grants paid, $0; gifts received, $153,185; expenditures, $14,084; qualifying distributions, $14,084; giving activities include $13,522 for programs.
Officers and Directors:* Melvin J. Kaplan,* Pres.; Margaret Bohannon-Kaplan,* Secy.-Treas.; Philip T. Curran, Donna Glacken.
EIN: 770176092

58715
MFU Training Plan Trust
240 2nd St.
San Francisco, CA 94105

Established in 1988 in CA.
Donor(s): American Ship Management, Ltd., Matson Navigation Co., Inc.
Financial data (yr. ended 12/31/00): Assets, $567,156 (M); grants paid, $66,427; gifts received, $204,009; expenditures, $96,786; qualifying distributions, $93,752; giving activities include $66,427 for programs.
Limitations: Applications not accepted. Giving primarily in CA.
Application information: Contributes only to pre-selected organizations.
Trustees: Henry Disley, Dennis Herrera, Robert Iwata, Daniel Johnson, Archibald Morgan, Thomas E. Percival.
EIN: 943058922
Codes: GTI

58716
The Rose Art Foundation
P.O. Box 2529
Avalon, CA 90704

Established in 1999 in CA.
Donor(s): Roy C. Rose.
Financial data (yr. ended 12/31/01): Assets, $565,000 (M); grants paid, $0; expenditures, $0; qualifying distributions, $0.
Officers: Roy C. Rose, C.E.O. and Pres.; Ray Redfern, V.P.; B. Martin Davis III, Secy.
EIN: 330863146

58717
Friendly Hills Foundation, Inc.
c/o Richard N. Ozenghar
7501 Palm Ave., No. 177
Yucca Valley, CA 92284-3657

Established in 1985 in CA.
Financial data (yr. ended 04/30/01): Assets, $562,196 (M); grants paid, $63,598; expenditures, $160,891; qualifying distributions, $63,598.
Limitations: Applications not accepted. Giving primarily in southern CA.
Application information: Contributes only to pre-selected organizations.
Officers: Richard N. Ozenghar, Pres.; Harold Faunt, Treas.
EIN: 237393087
Codes: GTI

58718
Kornberg Family Foundation
365 Golden Oak Dr.
Portola Valley, CA 94028
Application address: c/o Arthur Kornberg, Dept. of Biochemistry, Stanford University, Stanford, CA 94305, tel.: (650) 723-6988

Classified as a private operating foundation in 1996 in CA.
Donor(s): Arthur Kornberg.
Financial data (yr. ended 06/30/01): Assets, $555,496 (M); grants paid, $40,400; expenditures, $58,017; qualifying distributions, $49,853.
Limitations: Giving limited to San Francisco, CA.
Application information: Nominations are made by faculty at Stanford University and University of California at San Francisco. Application form required.
Officers: Kenneth Kornberg, Pres.; Arthur Kornberg, V.P.; Thomas Kornbert, Secy.; Roger Kornberg, Treas.
EIN: 943259687

58719
The McKelvey Foundation
86 La Cerra Dr.
Rancho Mirage, CA 92270

Established in 1989 in CA.
Donor(s): Paul D. McKelvey.
Financial data (yr. ended 12/31/00): Assets, $555,419 (M); grants paid, $36,123; gifts received, $20,000; expenditures, $39,589; qualifying distributions, $35,618.
Limitations: Applications not accepted. Giving primarily in CA.
Application information: Contributes only to pre-selected organizations.
Officers: Roberta M. Daugherty, Pres.; Paul D. McKelvey, V.P.; Alden D. McKelvey, Secy.-Treas.
EIN: 954210203

58720
The Edwards Family Foundation
317 Ramona Rd.
Portola Valley, CA 94028

Established in 1998.
Donor(s): Rosser B. Edwards.
Financial data (yr. ended 12/31/01): Assets, $545,206 (M); grants paid, $121,500; gifts received, $220,000; expenditures, $124,659; qualifying distributions, $121,500.
Limitations: Applications not accepted. Giving on a national basis.
Application information: Contributes only to pre-selected organizations.
Officer: Rosser B. Edwards, Jr., Pres.
EIN: 943302319

Codes: FD2

58721
The Gordon R. Irlam Charitable Foundation
326 A St.
Redwood City, CA 94063 (650) 364-6169
Contact: Gordon R. Irlam, Pres.

Established in 2000 in CA.
Donor(s): Gordon R. Irlam.
Financial data (yr. ended 12/31/01): Assets, $540,740 (M); grants paid, $0; expenditures, $26,863; qualifying distributions, $0.
Officer and Director:* Gordon R. Irlam,* Pres., V.P. and Secy.-Treas.
EIN: 943351212

58722
The Branes Foundation
9150 Santa Rita Rd.
Cayucos, CA 93430

Established in 1996 in CA.
Financial data (yr. ended 10/31/00): Assets, $534,301 (M); grants paid, $0; gifts received, $602,532; expenditures, $61,314; qualifying distributions, $43,782; giving activities include $20,356 for programs.
Officers and Director:* Jennifer Branes,* Pres.; Richard Arfa, V.P. and Secy.; Joyce C. Jordan.
EIN: 954609730

58723
Don F. and Rose Y. Tang Charitable Foundation
12542 Spring Blossom Court
Saratoga, CA 95070
Contact: Don F. Tang, Pres.

Established in 1998 in CA.
Financial data (yr. ended 12/31/99): Assets, $524,940 (M); grants paid, $1,000; expenditures, $36,477; qualifying distributions, $1,000.
Officers and Directors:* Don F. Tang,* Pres.; Rose Y. Tang,* Secy-Treas.
EIN: 770499215

58724
Charles B. Evans and Rose Marie Evans Family Foundation
16854 Little Tujunga Rd.
Santa Clarita, CA 91350

Established in 1998 in CA.
Donor(s): Charles B. Evans, Rose Marie Evans.
Financial data (yr. ended 12/31/00): Assets, $518,614 (M); grants paid, $26,000; expenditures, $41,822; qualifying distributions, $26,000.
Limitations: Applications not accepted.
Application information: Contributes only to pre-selected organizations.
Officers: Rose Marie Evans, Chair. and Pres.; Charles B. Evans, Secy.-Treas.
EIN: 954683338

58725
Hinz Family Charitable Foundation
c/o Hi Torque Publications
25233 Anza Dr.
Valencia, CA 91355
Contact: Roland Hinz, Tr.

Established in 1986 in CA.
Donor(s): Lila Hinz, Roland Hinz.
Financial data (yr. ended 06/30/01): Assets, $513,480 (M); grants paid, $718,380; gifts received, $1,100,000; expenditures, $719,880; qualifying distributions, $718,380.
Limitations: Giving primarily in CA and CO.
Application information: Application form not required.
Trustees: Lila Hinz, Roland Hinz.

EIN: 954121438
Codes: FD

58726
The Ravens Hill Foundation
P.O. Box 985
Point Arena, CA 95468

Established in 2000 in CA. Classified as a private operating foundation in 2001.
Donor(s): Gregory Jirak.
Financial data (yr. ended 12/31/01): Assets, $512,639 (M); grants paid, $100; gifts received, $400,100; expenditures, $10,800; qualifying distributions, $100.
Limitations: Applications not accepted.
Application information: Contributes only to pre-selected organizations.
Officers and Directors:* Gregory Jirak,* Pres.; Lori Hubbart,* Secy.; Ronald Casentini,* Treas.
EIN: 943379938

58727
Flatfields, Inc.
450 N. Rossmore Ave., Ste. 701
Los Angeles, CA 90004

Established in 1992 in CA.
Financial data (yr. ended 12/31/01): Assets, $507,048 (M); grants paid, $0; gifts received, $2,900; expenditures, $2,896; qualifying distributions, $2,896.
Officers: James Cox Chambers, C.E.O. and Pres.; Fred H. Beerman, Secy. and C.F.O.
EIN: 954378116

58728
Fitzhugh Trust
4910 Estrella Rd.
Paso Robles, CA 93446 (805) 238-2340

Established in 1987 in CA.
Financial data (yr. ended 07/31/01): Assets, $499,364 (M); grants paid, $0; gifts received, $2,713; expenditures, $19,997; qualifying distributions, $1,529; giving activities include $1,529 for programs.
Trustee: Lester Rougeot.
EIN: 770151723

58729
Frank Cross Foundation
10544 Wyton Dr.
Los Angeles, CA 90053
Additional tel.: (916) 296-6667
Contact: Walter Wotman

Established in 1990 in CA.
Donor(s): Frank Cross Trust.
Financial data (yr. ended 11/30/00): Assets, $496,010 (M); grants paid, $22,000; expenditures, $30,988; qualifying distributions, $22,000.
Limitations: Giving primarily in CA.
Officers: Robert S. Shahin, Pres.; Cecil Burgin, V.P. and Secy.
EIN: 954257181

58730
The Fremont Bank Foundation
39150 Fremont Blvd.
Fremont, CA 94538

Established in 1996 in CA as a company-sponsored operating foundation.
Donor(s): Fremont Bank.
Financial data (yr. ended 12/31/01): Assets, $490,360 (M); grants paid, $353,600; gifts received, $515,633; expenditures, $355,249; qualifying distributions, $353,456.
Limitations: Applications not accepted. Giving primarily in CA.

58730—CALIFORNIA

Application information: Contributes only to pre-selected organizations.
Officers and Directors:* Hattie Hughes,* Pres.; Alan Hyman,* V.P.; Michael Wallace,* Secy.; Howard Hyman.
EIN: 943170075
Codes: FD, CD

58731
The Anorcase Foundation
c/o Ronald Casentini
3702 Autumn Glen Ct.
Santa Rosa, CA 95403-0994

Established in 2000 in CA.
Donor(s): Ronald Casentini.
Financial data (yr. ended 12/31/01): Assets, $489,405 (M); grants paid, $0; gifts received, $233,841; expenditures, $24,715; qualifying distributions, $19,270; giving activities include $17,526 for programs.
Officers and Directors:* Ronald Casentini,* Pres.; Richard Reisman,* Secy.
EIN: 943379937

58732
Joseph Beggs Foundation for Kinematics
c/o Dawn A. Powers
4060 Chestnut St.
Riverside, CA 92501
Application address: 1423 Stillman Ave., Redlands, CA 92373, tel.: (909) 793-1604
Contact: Raymond S. Beggs, Pres.

Established in 1992 in CA.
Donor(s): Raymond S. Beggs, Laura V. Beggs.
Financial data (yr. ended 12/31/01): Assets, $483,115 (M); grants paid, $31,135; expenditures, $37,587; qualifying distributions, $34,631.
Limitations: Giving primarily in CA; some giving also in Canada.
Officers: Raymond S. Beggs, Pres.; Darlene Skelton, V.P.; Beatrice D. Beggs, Secy.; Dawn A. Powers, Treas.
EIN: 330508097

58733
Barbara H. McClellan Charitable Foundation
1331 Egret Dr.
Sunnyvale, CA 94087-3444
Contact: Barbara H. McClellan, Pres.

Established in 2000 in CA.
Donor(s): Barbara H. McClellan.
Financial data (yr. ended 12/31/00): Assets, $476,250 (M); grants paid, $308; gifts received, $435,094; expenditures, $30,772; qualifying distributions, $26,845.
Officer and Director:* Barbara H. McClellan,* Pres., Secy., and C.F.O.
EIN: 770527852

58734
Kalos Kagathos Foundation
P.O. Box 416
Laguna Beach, CA 92652

Donor(s): Bruce S. Hopping.
Financial data (yr. ended 12/31/00): Assets, $475,330 (M); grants paid, $0; gifts received, $89,641; expenditures, $133,356; qualifying distributions, $133,356; giving activities include $60,000 for programs.
Officer: Bruce S. Hopping, Pres.
EIN: 952555828

58735
Willis W. & Ethel M. Clark Foundation
P.O. Box 89
Pebble Beach, CA 93953 (831) 625-1175
Contact: Patricia E. Duran, Pres.

Classified as a private operating foundation in 1984.
Donor(s): June C. Duran.
Financial data (yr. ended 06/30/01): Assets, $472,557 (M); grants paid, $1,500; expenditures, $10,482; qualifying distributions, $5,891; giving activities include $738 for programs.
Limitations: Giving limited to CA.
Officers: Patricia E. Duran, Pres.; Timothy C. Duran, V.P.; June C. Duran, Secy.; David C. Wilsey, Treas.
Directors: Mary Capson, Paul M. Lee, Saul Weingarten.
EIN: 946104608

58736
Huguenin Rallapalli Foundation
3184 Linkfield Way
San Jose, CA 95135
Contact: Krishna Rallapalli, Pres.

Established in 2000 in CA.
Donor(s): Krishna Rallapalli, Philippine Rallapalli.
Financial data (yr. ended 12/31/00): Assets, $472,135 (M); grants paid, $0; gifts received, $41,052; expenditures, $26,903; qualifying distributions, $26,903; giving activities include $2,658 for programs.
Officers and Directors:* Krishna Rallapalli,* Pres.; Philippine Rallapalli,* Secy. and C.F.O.
EIN: 770553721

58737
New Endeavor Foundation
P.O. Box 180405
Coronado, CA 92178-0405

Established in 1997 in CA.
Donor(s): Rankine Van Anda.
Financial data (yr. ended 12/31/99): Assets, $471,847 (M); grants paid, $23,350; expenditures, $24,692; qualifying distributions, $24,692; giving activities include $23,350 for programs.
Limitations: Applications not accepted.
Application information: Contributes only to pre-selected organizations.
Officers and Directors:* Rankine Van Anda,* Chair. and Pres.; Mary Van Anda,* Secy.-Treas.; Diane Van Anda.
EIN: 330740545

58738
L. V. Island Preserve
6342 Bystrum Rd.
Ceres, CA 95307

Established in 1998 in CA.
Financial data (yr. ended 12/31/01): Assets, $471,252 (M); grants paid, $0; expenditures, $1,378; qualifying distributions, $0.
Officer: Fred T. Franzia, C.E.O.
EIN: 770481893

58739
Los Adobes de Los Rancheros
P.O. Box 1076
Santa Barbara, CA 93102

Donor(s): Amory J. Cooke, Santa Barbara Historical Society.
Financial data (yr. ended 12/31/01): Assets, $464,523 (M); grants paid, $0; gifts received, $1,435; expenditures, $3,649; qualifying distributions, $2,737.
Limitations: Applications not accepted.

Application information: Contributes only to pre-selected organizations.
Officers and Directors:* Ernest A. Bryant III, Pres.; Monroe Rutherford, 1st V.P.; Ralph A. Weston,* 2nd V.P.; Robert S. Herdman, Secy.-Treas.; John B. Balch, Edward C. Biaggini, Jr., Kristofer Kallman, Gragg J. Orton, Burke H. Simpson, and 5 additional directors.
EIN: 956053393

58740
M.E. Charitable Foundation
(also known as EJQ Charitable Foundation)
P.O. Box 2797
Saratoga, CA 95070

Established in 1998 in CA.
Donor(s): Estelita J. Que.
Financial data (yr. ended 12/31/99): Assets, $459,681 (M); grants paid, $10,000; gifts received, $10,000; expenditures, $90,059; qualifying distributions, $10,000.
Officer and Director:* Estelita J. Que,* Pres.
EIN: 770499218

58741
E. Honda Food Culture Museum & Communication/Education Center
1545 River Park Dr., Ste. 375
Sacramento, CA 95815

Established in 1999.
Donor(s): Eiji Honda.
Financial data (yr. ended 09/30/01): Assets, $453,612 (M); grants paid, $0; gifts received, $269,941; expenditures, $80,605; qualifying distributions, $0.
Officers: Eiji Honda, Chair.; Toru Matsushima, V.P. and Secy.
Directors: Hidemitsu Honda, Ichiro Honda.
EIN: 680427300

58742
Christian and Susan Hoebich Charitable Foundation
5770 Croy Rd.
Morgan Hill, CA 95037 (408) 778-6271
Contact: Christian Hoebich, Pres.

Established in 2000 in CA.
Donor(s): Christian Hoebich, Susan Hoebich.
Financial data (yr. ended 12/31/01): Assets, $447,107 (M); grants paid, $5,000; expenditures, $38,075; qualifying distributions, $5,000.
Officers and Directors:* Christian Hoebich,* Pres.; Susan Hoebich,* Secy. and C.F.O.
EIN: 770550344

58743
Hugh M. and Julie J. Pearce Foundation
14000 Miranda Rd.
Los Altos Hills, CA 94022
Tel.: (408) 530-1020, ext. 211
Contact: Hugh M. Pearce, Pres.

Established in 2000 in CA.
Donor(s): Hugh M. Pearce, Julie J. Pearce.
Financial data (yr. ended 12/31/01): Assets, $444,884 (M); grants paid, $0; expenditures, $26,060; qualifying distributions, $0.
Officers and Directors:* Hugh M. Pearce,* Pres.; Julie J. Pearce,* Secy. and C.F.O.
EIN: 770559719

58744
Lucid Art Foundation
P.O. Box 1199
Inverness, CA 94937-1199

Donor(s): Gordon Onslow Ford, Robert Anthoine.
Financial data (yr. ended 09/30/00): Assets, $444,591 (M); grants paid, $5,000; gifts received,

$327,200; expenditures, $44,856; qualifying distributions, $43,356; giving activities include $29,306 for programs.
Limitations: Applications not accepted. Giving primarily in Europe.
Application information: Contributes only to pre-selected organizations.
Officers: Gordon Onslow Ford, Chair. and Treas.; Franz von Braun, Vice-Chair.; Robert Anthoine, Pres.; Allen M. Singer, Secy.; Fariba Bogzaran, Exec. Dir.
Trustee: Elizabeth Rouslin.
EIN: 943316074

58745
The Wonder of Reading
120 N. Robertson Blvd.
Los Angeles, CA 90048-3102

Established in 1994 in CA.
Donor(s): Michael Forman, Christopher S. Forman.
Financial data (yr. ended 12/31/00): Assets, $435,511 (M); grants paid, $0; gifts received, $1,059,941; expenditures, $1,062,580; qualifying distributions, $1,062,580; giving activities include $856,953 for programs.
Officers and Directors:* Christopher S. Forman, Chair. and Pres.; James D. Vandever, V.P.; Michael R. Forman,* C.F.O.; Dorinda Lea Hairrell.
EIN: 954484325

58746
Sea Ranch Chapel Foundation
P.O. Box 424
The Sea Ranch, CA 95497-0424

Established in 1989 in CA.
Financial data (yr. ended 04/30/00): Assets, $426,140 (M); grants paid, $0; gifts received, $5,421; expenditures, $25,351; qualifying distributions, $25,351; giving activities include $25,351 for programs.
Officers: Betty U. Fouraud, Pres.; Patricia Ditzler, Secy.; Lyle Ditzler, Treas.
EIN: 330225425

58747
Streng Family Foundation, Inc.
176 White Oak Dr.
Arcadia, CA 91006

Established in 1998 in CA.
Donor(s): Joel Streng.
Financial data (yr. ended 12/31/99): Assets, $413,405 (M); grants paid, $20,000; gifts received, $200,000; expenditures, $24,765; qualifying distributions, $23,339.
Officers: Joel Streng, Pres.; Charlotte Streng, Secy.
EIN: 954667366

58748
William D. Lynch Foundation for Children
(Formerly William D. Lynch Foundation)
222 Camino del Rio, S., Ste. A
San Diego, CA 92108
Contact: Scott B. Himelstein, Exec. Dir.

Established in 1991 in CA.
Donor(s): William D. Lynch.
Financial data (yr. ended 06/30/01): Assets, $411,854 (M); grants paid, $110,798; gifts received, $320,170; expenditures, $252,644; qualifying distributions, $110,798; giving activities include $18,905 for programs.
Limitations: Giving primarily in San Diego County, CA.
Officers: Donna Lynch, Secy.; William D. Lynch, C.F.O.; Scott B. Himelstein, Exec. Dir.
EIN: 330516414

58749
Trust for Wildland Communities
5540 N. Hwy. 1
Littleriver, CA 95456-9501

Established in 1996 in CA.
Donor(s): Leslie Lebeau, Michael Lebeau.
Financial data (yr. ended 12/31/00): Assets, $406,167 (M); grants paid, $0; expenditures, $22,861; qualifying distributions, $22,361; giving activities include $22,862 for programs.
Officers and Directors:* Leslie Lebeau,* Pres.; Michael Lebeau,* Secy.-Treas.; William J. Harrison, Jr.
EIN: 680390062

58750
Pacific Advanced Center for Medical Education and Development
P.O. Box 1857
Pleasanton, CA 94566

Established as an operating foundation in 1997.
Donor(s): Karl Storz Endoscopy-America, Inc.
Financial data (yr. ended 12/31/99): Assets, $405,708 (M); grants paid, $0; gifts received, $342,526; expenditures, $171,418; qualifying distributions, $163,135; giving activities include $180,107 for programs.
Limitations: Applications not accepted.
Application information: Contributes only to pre-selected organizations.
Officers: Carlos R. Garcia, M.D., Pres.; Phil Gustafson, V.P.; Bill Upson, Secy.-Treas.
Directors: Mark Dresser, Yulan Wang, Ph.D.
EIN: 911763120

58751
The Peter R. and Victoria J. Johnson Foundation
333 Market St., No. 3300
San Francisco, CA 94105

Established in 1999 in CA.
Donor(s): Peter R. Johnson, Victoria J. Johnson.
Financial data (yr. ended 12/31/00): Assets, $398,652 (M); grants paid, $5,067; gifts received, $25,730; expenditures, $12,991; qualifying distributions, $5,067.
Officers: Victoria J. Johnson, C.E.O.; Russel K. Ouchida, Secy.; Peter R. Johnson, C.F.O.
EIN: 943347563

58752
Grace Family Vineyards Foundation
1210 Rockland Rd.
St. Helena, CA 94574

Established in 1994 in CA.
Financial data (yr. ended 12/31/00): Assets, $394,257 (M); grants paid, $194,678; gifts received, $575,163; expenditures, $313,973; qualifying distributions, $311,670.
Directors: Ann K. Grace, Richard H. Grace, Harriet Halliday.
EIN: 680331455
Codes: TN

58753
Y. Kwong and R. Fok Foundation
2920 F St., Ste. H-12
Bakersfield, CA 93301-1829

Established in 1996 in CA.
Donor(s): Randolph Fok.
Financial data (yr. ended 12/31/01): Assets, $393,769 (L); grants paid, $22,282; gifts received, $92,000; expenditures, $22,344; qualifying distributions, $22,231.
Limitations: Applications not accepted.
Application information: Contributes only to pre-selected organizations.
Officers: Randolph Fok, Secy.; Yuen Kwong, Treas.
EIN: 770411065

58754
Waldo Hunt Children's Museum
c/o Waldo Hunt
10900 Wilshire Blvd., Ste. 801
Los Angeles, CA 90024

Donor(s): Waldo Hunt.
Financial data (yr. ended 12/31/01): Assets, $387,061 (M); grants paid, $0; gifts received, $4,123; expenditures, $4,362; qualifying distributions, $0.
Limitations: Applications not accepted.
Officers: Waldo Hunt, Chair. and Pres.; Kimberly A. Hunt, V.P. and Secy.-Treas.
Directors: Elgin Davis, Jamie Hunt, Patricia Hunt, John Power.
EIN: 954463799

58755
The Northern California DX Foundation
4220 Chardonnay Ct.
Napa, CA 94558
Application address: 9705 Old Redwood Hwy., Penngrove, CA 94951
Contact: Len Geraldi, Pres.

Established in 1977.
Financial data (yr. ended 06/30/01): Assets, $380,531 (M); grants paid, $57,700; gifts received, $108,782; expenditures, $75,999; qualifying distributions, $75,774.
Limitations: Giving on a national and international basis.
Application information: Application form required.
Officers: Len Geraldi, Pres.; Al Burnhma, V.P.; Tom McShane, Secy.; Bruce Butler, Treas.
EIN: 942853576
Codes: GTI

58756
Fundacion Josef Y Gloria Gorelik
2920 Neilson Way, Ste. 401
Santa Monica, CA 90405-5369

Established in 1995 in CA.
Financial data (yr. ended 12/31/01): Assets, $374,722 (L); grants paid, $25,500; expenditures, $25,000; qualifying distributions, $25,236.
Limitations: Applications not accepted.
Application information: Contributes only to pre-selected organizations.
Directors: Gloria Gorelik, Guy Gorelik.
EIN: 954471057

58757
Arts and Sciences Foundation
1127 Wilshire Blvd., Ste. 1008
Los Angeles, CA 90017-4001

Established in 1967.
Donor(s): Eugene Shales, Chadwick F. Smith, M.D.
Financial data (yr. ended 05/31/00): Assets, $373,913 (M); grants paid, $123,450; gifts received, $123,390; expenditures, $126,568; qualifying distributions, $123,450.
Limitations: Applications not accepted. Giving primarily in CA.
Application information: Contributes only to pre-selected organizations.
Officers: Chadwick F. Smith, M.D., Pres.; Corinna Smith, V.P.
EIN: 952559826

58758
The Landecena Family Charitable Foundation
1791 N. 3rd Ave.
Upland, CA 91784

Financial data (yr. ended 12/31/00): Assets, $368,450 (M); grants paid, $23,825; expenditures, $25,826; qualifying distributions, $23,825.
Limitations: Giving primarily in Upland, CA.
Trustees: Dorothy M. Landecena, William V. Landecena, George L. Sellers, Katherine A. Sellers.
EIN: 336217645

58759
Bill & Nancy Leung Foundation, Inc.
44729 Lynx Dr.
Fremont, CA 94539 (510) 623-9328
Contact: Bill Leung, Dir.

Established in 2000 in CA.
Donor(s): Bill Leung, Nancy Choy.
Financial data (yr. ended 12/31/00): Assets, $362,658 (M); grants paid, $24,900; gifts received, $418,556; expenditures, $31,400; qualifying distributions, $24,900; giving activities include $6,500 for programs.
Limitations: Giving primarily in Milpitas, CA.
Directors: Lyndia Cheng, Nancy Choy, Bill Leung.
EIN: 943375205

58760
American Museum of Telephony
9169 Trails End
Mountain Ranch, CA 95246
Application address: P.O. Box 299, Mountain Ranch, CA 95246
Contact: John K. Larue, Pres.

Established in 2000 in CA.
Financial data (yr. ended 04/30/01): Assets, $354,906 (M); grants paid, $327; gifts received, $2,787; expenditures, $13,944; qualifying distributions, $165.
Officers: John K. Larue, Pres.; Dianne Larue, Secy. and C.F.O.; William Barrier, Secy.
EIN: 911979324

58761
Korean Senior Citizen's Association of San Fernando Valley
18531 Gresham St.
Northridge, CA 91324

Established in 1997.
Financial data (yr. ended 12/31/00): Assets, $354,311 (M); grants paid, $0; gifts received, $12,627; expenditures, $31,999; qualifying distributions, $9,601; giving activities include $6,474 for programs.
Officers: Joo Bong Lim, Pres.; Soo Kun Wang, V.P.; So Im Kim, Secy.; Chul Soon Lee, Treas.
EIN: 954032301

58762
H. & R. Peters Family Foundation
1723 Karameos Dr.
Sunnyvale, CA 94087 (408) 773-1387
Contact: Henry E. Peters, Secy.

Established in 1999 in CA.
Donor(s): Renee C. Peters, Henry E. Peters.
Financial data (yr. ended 12/31/00): Assets, $353,303 (M); grants paid, $7,108; gifts received, $32,562; expenditures, $39,412; qualifying distributions, $39,412.
Limitations: Giving on a national basis.
Officers and Directors:* Renee C. Peters,* Pres. and Treas.; Henry E. Peters,* Secy.; Steven P. Peters.
EIN: 770514959

58763
Izak and Cyla Bilers Charitable Foundation
c/o Erik Arnhem
4250 Wilshire Blvd., No. 213
Los Angeles, CA 90010

Established in 1989 in CA.
Financial data (yr. ended 12/31/00): Assets, $350,048 (M); grants paid, $3,386; expenditures, $7,682; qualifying distributions, $3,386.
Limitations: Applications not accepted.
Application information: Contributes only to pre-selected organizations.
Trustee: Erik Arnhem.
EIN: 954162954

58764
The Ritz & June Naygrow Foundation
c/o Ritz Naygrow
690 Coronado Blvd.
Sacramento, CA 95864 (916) 979-9769

Established in 1991 in CA.
Donor(s): June Naygrow, Ritz Naygrow.
Financial data (yr. ended 12/31/99): Assets, $347,174 (M); grants paid, $25,000; expenditures, $25,000; qualifying distributions, $25,000.
Limitations: Applications not accepted. Giving limited to Sacramento, CA.
Application information: Contributes only to pre-selected organizations.
Officers: Ritz Naygrow, Pres.; June Naygrow, Secy.-Treas.
EIN: 680220303

58765
Lux Art Institute
P.O. Box 9638
Rancho Santa Fe, CA 92067-9638

Established in 1998.
Financial data (yr. ended 12/31/00): Assets, $343,048 (M); grants paid, $0; gifts received, $357,465; expenditures, $164,175; qualifying distributions, $151,709; giving activities include $151,709 for programs.
Officers: Christopher Calkins, Pres.; Reesey Shaw, V.P.; Barbara Walbridge, V.P.; Ann Lievers, Secy.; Eileen Appleby, Treas.; Ramona Sahm, Mgr.
Trustees: Sandra Azcaraga, William Davidson, Mo Ecke, Anne Hoehn.
EIN: 330802336

58766
Barksdale Foundation
P.O. Box 187
Idyllwild, CA 92549-0187

Financial data (yr. ended 12/31/99): Assets, $341,914 (M); grants paid, $50; gifts received, $1,545; expenditures, $92,330; qualifying distributions, $76,793; giving activities include $76,895 for programs.
Limitations: Applications not accepted. Giving primarily in Idyllwild, CA.
Application information: Contributes only to pre-selected organizations.
Officers: Marlin C. Nelson, Pres.; John Lloyd, V.P.; Edward Zimmer, V.P.; Janice C. Burnett, Secy.; Richard Bednarik, Treas.
EIN: 956087367

58767
Nihewan Foundation
9595 Wilshire Blvd., Ste. 1020
Beverly Hills, CA 90212-2512

Financial data (yr. ended 12/31/00): Assets, $341,538 (M); grants paid, $3,673; gifts received, $299,487; expenditures, $312,302; qualifying distributions, $313,664; giving activities include $81,056 for programs.
Limitations: Applications not accepted.
Application information: Contributes only to pre-selected organizations.
Trustee: Buffy Saint-Marie.
EIN: 237047097

58768
Albert & Trudy Kallis Foundation, A California Public Benefit Corporation
(Formerly Albert & Trudy Kallis Foundation, Inc.)
2310 Canyonback Rd.
Los Angeles, CA 90049-6811 (310) 472-5898
Contact: Albert J. Kallis, Pres.

Classified as a private operating foundation in 1979.
Donor(s): Albert J. Kallis, Trudy Kallis.
Financial data (yr. ended 07/31/01): Assets, $334,388 (M); grants paid, $1,000; gifts received, $36,760; expenditures, $46,022; qualifying distributions, $11,819; giving activities include $21,082 for programs.
Limitations: Giving primarily in New York, NY.
Application information: Application form not required.
Officers: Albert J. Kallis, Pres. and C.F.O.; Matthew D. Kallis, V.P.; Trudy Kallis, Secy.
Directors: Daniel S. Kallis, Matthew D. Kallis, Marni A. Vaughan.
EIN: 953247394

58769
Patti McClain's Museum of Vintage Fashion, Inc.
1712 Chapparal Ln.
Lafayette, CA 94549-2138

Classified as a private operating foundation in 1992.
Donor(s): Richard McClain, Patricia McClain.
Financial data (yr. ended 05/31/01): Assets, $331,474 (M); grants paid, $250; gifts received, $34,424; expenditures, $37,041; qualifying distributions, $28,257; giving activities include $28,257 for programs.
Limitations: Applications not accepted.
Director: Patricia McClain.
EIN: 942616736

58770
California Home Energy Efficiency Rating System, Inc.
9400 Topanga Canyon Blvd., Ste. 220
Chatsworth, CA 91311

Established in 1990 in CA.
Financial data (yr. ended 12/31/01): Assets, $325,861 (M); grants paid, $0; gifts received, $435,305; expenditures, $1,078,384; qualifying distributions, $654,776; giving activities include $639,024 for programs.
Officers: Gene Rodrigues, Pres.; Charles Segerstorm, V.P.; David Goldstein, Secy.; Paul Jacobs, Treas.
Directors: Lance DeLaura, Michelle Thomas, Phil West.
EIN: 680233692

58771
Awaken Foundation
(Formerly God Love, Inc.)
c/o Edwin S. Douglas
P.O. Box 6
Three Rivers, CA 93271

Classified as a private operating foundation in 1991.
Donor(s): Edwin S. Doublas, Ruth H. Bastiani.
Financial data (yr. ended 12/31/01): Assets, $324,831 (M); grants paid, $0; gifts received,

$213,536; expenditures, $39,588; qualifying distributions, $0.
Officers: Edwin S. Douglas, Pres.; Lynn Orion, Secy.-Treas.
EIN: 954293288

58772
The Raies-Murr Educational Trust
315 Arden Ave., Ste. 18
Glendale, CA 91203

Established in 1992 in CA. Classified as a private operating foundation in 1993.
Donor(s): Evelyn Raies-Murr.
Financial data (yr. ended 12/31/00): Assets, $323,103 (M); grants paid, $18,500; gifts received, $3,505; expenditures, $22,843; qualifying distributions, $18,500.
Limitations: Applications not accepted. Giving primarily to residents of the Alhambra, CA, area.
Application information: Unsolicited requests for funds not accepted.
Trustees: John M. Gantus, Sondra Love, Joan Mamey, Phil Nassief, Evelyn Raies-Murr, John L. Sadd, Jr.
EIN: 956932192
Codes: GTI

58773
Evan McKenna Foundation
8 Blue Jay Way
Woodside, CA 94062-4306

Established in 1999 in CA.
Donor(s): Kay P. Emerson, Miles C. Walsh.
Financial data (yr. ended 11/30/01): Assets, $317,351 (M); grants paid, $0; gifts received, $194,661; expenditures, $158,106; qualifying distributions, $0.
Limitations: Applications not accepted.
Application information: Contributes only to pre-selected organizations.
Officers and Director:* Kay P. Emerson, Pres. and C.F.O.; Miles C. Walsh,* Secy.
EIN: 943347999

58774
Highway Foundation
1723 Karameos Dr.
Sunnyvale, CA 94087

Established in 2000 in CA.
Donor(s): R & E Scott Foundation.
Financial data (yr. ended 12/31/00): Assets, $316,901 (M); grants paid, $0; gifts received, $375,250; expenditures, $60,136; qualifying distributions, $296,000; giving activities include $296,000 for programs.
Limitations: Applications not accepted.
Application information: Contributes only to pre-selected organizations.
Officers and Directors:* Dean Smith,* Pres.; Martin A. Logies,* Secy.-Treas.; Randal Scott.
EIN: 770535704

58775
Jake J. Schreibman Foundation
208 Weymouth St.
Cambria, CA 93428
Contact: Marlene S. Bernstein, Pres.

Classified as a private operating foundation in 1996.
Financial data (yr. ended 12/31/99): Assets, $316,425 (M); grants paid, $36,633; expenditures, $43,426; qualifying distributions, $43,185.
Limitations: Giving on a national basis.
Application information: Application form required.

Officers: Marlene S. Bernstein, Pres. and Exec Dir.; Jerome L. Bernstein, V.P.
Director: Richard Bernstein.
EIN: 470790155

58776
The McCune Foundation
2979 Eucalyptus Hill Rd.
Montecito, CA 93108

Established in 1990 in CA.
Donor(s): Sara Miller McCune.
Financial data (yr. ended 02/28/00): Assets, $315,322 (M); grants paid, $33,737; gifts received, $37,196; expenditures, $40,556; qualifying distributions, $33,737.
Limitations: Applications not accepted. Giving primarily in the U.S., India, and the United Kingdom.
Application information: Contributes only to pre-selected organizations.
Officers: Sara Miller McCune, Chair., Pres., and C.F.O.; David McCune, V.P.; Sandra Ball-Rokeach, Secy.
Directors: Vicki Fisher, Marilyn Gittell, Cathy Sarvat, Susan McCune Sherman, Margaret Sirot-Hable.
EIN: 770242953

58777
Victory Road Rehabilitation Program, Inc.
3330 Churn Creek Rd.
Redding, CA 96002

Established in 1994 in CA.
Financial data (yr. ended 07/31/99): Assets, $314,869 (M); grants paid, $0; gifts received, $1,650; expenditures, $61,965; qualifying distributions, $56,918; giving activities include $48,380 for programs.
Officer: C. Donald Nelson, Pres.
Directors: Sam E. Nelson, Roy F. Peters.
EIN: 680304596

58778
Jorgensen Foundation
315 Briston St.
Cambria, CA 93428

Established in 1991 in CA.
Donor(s): Richard C. Jorgensen, Ethel L. Jorgensen.
Financial data (yr. ended 12/31/00): Assets, $314,491 (M); grants paid, $5,000; expenditures, $7,715; qualifying distributions, $5,000.
Limitations: Applications not accepted.
Application information: Contributes only to pre-selected organizations.
Trustees: Ardel Jorgensen, Ethel L. Jorgensen, Mark Jorgensen, Richard C. Jorgensen.
EIN: 770283757

58779
Jad Canning Foundation
P.O. Box 185
Firebaugh, CA 93622-9716 (559) 659-3391
Contact: Jill Marks

Established in 1986 in CA.
Donor(s): Henry M. Levy, Fred W. Canning, Jad Canning Trust Fund.
Financial data (yr. ended 12/31/99): Assets, $313,694 (M); grants paid, $1,000; gifts received, $85,702; expenditures, $73,680; qualifying distributions, $62,509; giving activities include $58,393 for programs.
Limitations: Giving limited to the San Joaquin Valley, CA, area.
Application information: Application form required.

Officer and Trustees:* Craig T. Ulrice,* V.P.; Fred W. Canning, William B. Coit, Donald A. Jackson, Henry M. Levy.
EIN: 770141528

58780
Tuscan, Incorporated
2655 Portage Bay E., No. 1
Davis, CA 95616

Financial data (yr. ended 12/31/01): Assets, $311,887 (M); grants paid, $0; expenditures, $29,396; qualifying distributions, $21,551; giving activities include $21,819 for programs.
Officers: David B. Kelley, Pres.; Linda D. Abrille, Secy.
EIN: 943180352

58781
Joanne Illig Foundation
c/o Wells Fargo Bank, N.A.
1221 Ocean Ave., Ste. 401
Santa Monica, CA 90401

Established in 1984 in NY.
Donor(s): Victor J. Illig.
Financial data (yr. ended 07/31/01): Assets, $310,253 (M); grants paid, $17,000; gifts received, $100,000; expenditures, $28,612; qualifying distributions, $16,933.
Limitations: Applications not accepted. Giving primarily in CA and VA.
Application information: Contributes only to pre-selected organizations.
Trustee: Wells Fargo Bank, N.A.
EIN: 956802175

58782
Walt Disney Family Foundation
c/o Motto Kryla & Fisher
899 Adams St., Ste. E
St. Helena, CA 94574

Established in 1997 in CA.
Donor(s): The Walt and Lilly Disney Foundation.
Financial data (yr. ended 12/31/99): Assets, $308,564 (M); grants paid, $381,083; gifts received, $765,000; expenditures, $476,031; qualifying distributions, $444,031; giving activities include $381,083 for programs.
Limitations: Applications not accepted.
Application information: Contributes only to pre-selected organizations.
Officers: Walter E.D. Miller, Pres.; Christopher D. Miller, V.P.; Diane D. Miller, Secy.-Treas.; Michael Fisher, C.F.O.
EIN: 954635927
Codes: FD

58783
Gregg Ranch Foundation
P.O. Box 1585
Callahan, CA 96014-1585
Application address: 214 Bessey Hall, Univ. of Nebraska, Lincoln, NE 68516, tel.: (402) 472-2629
Contact: Nancy Lindsley-Griffin, Pres.

Established in 1993.
Donor(s): John R. Griffin, Nancy Lindsley-Griffin.
Financial data (yr. ended 06/30/01): Assets, $304,491 (M); grants paid, $3,189; gifts received, $1,600; expenditures, $3,504; qualifying distributions, $3,189.
Limitations: Giving primarily in CA and OR.
Application information: Application form required.
Officers and Directors:* Nancy Lindsley-Griffin,* Pres. and Treas.; John R. Griffin,* V.P. and Secy.; Karen Jess Lindsley, E. Timothy Wallin.
EIN: 680225594

58784
Slater Family Foundation
1722 Marengo
South Pasadena, CA 91030-4819

Financial data (yr. ended 12/31/99): Assets, $299,338 (M); grants paid, $7,139; expenditures, $10,606; qualifying distributions, $7,139.
Director: Gene Slater.
EIN: 954685547

58785
Internet Science Education Project
1714 Stockton St., Ste. 100
San Francisco, CA 94133

Financial data (yr. ended 05/31/01): Assets, $293,506 (M); grants paid, $25,000; gifts received, $150,000; expenditures, $117,547; qualifying distributions, $25,000.
Officers and Trustees:* Jack Sarfatti,* Pres.; Dennis Wisanie,* Secy.; Bill Nurstensen, Henry Ward.
EIN: 943226270

58786
Laucks Foundation, Inc.
215 W. Figueroa St.
Santa Barbara, CA 93101

Financial data (yr. ended 12/31/01): Assets, $292,355 (M); grants paid, $0; expenditures, $9,728; qualifying distributions, $9,728; giving activities include $8,000 for programs.
Limitations: Applications not accepted.
Officers and Directors:* Eulah Laucks,* Chair. and Treas.; Mary Laucks,* C.E.O. and Pres.; Brian Swanson,* V.P.; Dennis Iden,* Secy.; Lorenzo Gon.
EIN: 952596850

58787
Jack In The Box Foundation
c/o Tax Dept.
9330 Balboa Ave.
San Diego, CA 92123-1516

Established in 1997 in CA.
Donor(s): Foodmaker, Inc., Jack in the Box, Inc.
Financial data (yr. ended 12/31/01): Assets, $282,206 (M); grants paid, $746,736; gifts received, $697,510; expenditures, $747,935; qualifying distributions, $746,736.
Limitations: Applications not accepted. Giving on a national basis.
Application information: Unsolicited requests for funds not accepted.
Officers and Directors:* Karen Bachman,* Pres.; James A. Spencer,* Secy.; Hal Sachs,* Treas.; Carlo Cetti, Linda Lang, Kathy Moorehouse.
EIN: 330776076
Codes: FD

58788
American Academy Foundation
(Formerly American Academy of Workers Compensation Specialists, Inc.)
19471 Peninsula Ln.
Huntington Beach, CA 92648

Established in 1988 in CA.
Donor(s): Richard Allen, Ronald Gilbert.
Financial data (yr. ended 12/31/00): Assets, $280,339 (M); grants paid, $17,738; expenditures, $781,993; qualifying distributions, $17,738.
Limitations: Applications not accepted. Giving primarily in CA and FL; some giving also in Mexico.
Publications: Annual report.
Application information: Contributes only to pre-selected organizations.

Officer and Directors:* Ronald Gilbert, M.D.,* Pres.; Craig Joseph, M.D., Adream Lawner.
EIN: 330311438

58789
Mr. & Mrs. Walter F. Leverenz Scholarship Trust
c/o Wells Fargo Private Banking Group
P.O. Box 63954
San Francisco, CA 94163-0001
Application address: c/o Wells Fargo Private Banking group, P.O. Box 20160, Long Beach, CA 90801
Contact: Linda Benton, Trust Admin., Wells Fargo Bank, N.A.

Classified as a private operating foundation in 1982.
Financial data (yr. ended 09/30/01): Assets, $277,083 (M); grants paid, $11,750; expenditures, $15,878; qualifying distributions, $11,473.
Limitations: Giving limited to residents of CA.
Application information: Applicants must submit transcript, letters of recommendation, and SAT/ACT scores. Application form required.
Trustees: Dale I. Gustin, Deborah Rodgers, Denise Tate, Wells Fargo Bank, N.A.
EIN: 956721631
Codes: GTI

58790
Harry W. Anderson and Mary Margaret Anderson Charitable Foundation
62 Faxon Rd.
Atherton, CA 94027
Application address: c/o Anderson Collection, 2440 Sand Hill Rd., Menlo Park, CA 94025
Contact: Harry W. Anderson, Tr.

Financial data (yr. ended 12/31/99): Assets, $273,367 (M); grants paid, $3,000; expenditures, $14,586; qualifying distributions, $13,254.
Limitations: Giving primarily in CA.
Trustee: Harry W. Anderson.
EIN: 943086311

58791
Institute for Herpetological Research
1682 E. Valley Rd.
Santa Barbara, CA 93108

Classified as an operating foundation since 1974.
Donor(s): Richard A. Ross, M.D., Brett Stearns.
Financial data (yr. ended 06/30/00): Assets, $273,090 (M); grants paid, $0; gifts received, $22,595; expenditures, $70,074; qualifying distributions, $57,152; giving activities include $68,817 for programs.
Limitations: Applications not accepted.
Application information: Contributes only to pre-selected organizations.
Directors: Richard A. Ross, M.D., Brett Stearns.
EIN: 237188772

58792
The David W. and Thais Lerner Family Foundation
(also known as Spark Foundation)
501 Benvenue Ave.
Los Altos, CA 94024
Additional tel.: (408) 453-2707
Contact: David W. Lerner, Pres.

Established in 1997 in CA.
Donor(s): David W. Lerner, Thais Lerner.
Financial data (yr. ended 11/30/00): Assets, $270,559 (M); grants paid, $32,392; gifts received, $42,480; expenditures, $99,989; qualifying distributions, $32,392.
Officers: David W. Lerner, Pres.; Thais Lerner, V.P.
EIN: 770470477

58793
China Culture Foundation
13149 Winstanley Way
San Diego, CA 92130
Contact: Lawrence Wong, Chair.

Established in 1988 in OH.
Financial data (yr. ended 10/31/99): Assets, $265,291 (M); grants paid, $0; expenditures, $16,282; qualifying distributions, $15,862; giving activities include $15,862 for programs.
Officers and Trustees:* Lawrence Wong,* Chair.; Chit Guan Goh,* Vice-Chair. and Secy.; Thomas J. Bonasera,* Vice-Chair.; Bobby Joe Payne,* Vice-Chair.; Margaret Wong, Treas.; Richard D. Uietzel.
EIN: 311233180

58794
The Bay Area Life Sciences Alliance
c/o UCSF Facilities Mgmt.
3130 20th St., Box 0894
San Francisco, CA 94143-0894

Established in 1996 in CA.
Financial data (yr. ended 12/31/01): Assets, $264,177 (M); grants paid, $0; gifts received, $3,060; expenditures, $1,711,814; qualifying distributions, $1,632,010; giving activities include $1,711,994 for programs.
Officers: Thomas B. Swift, Pres.; Jeannie M. Wong, Secy.
Directors: Gerson Baker, T. Robert Burke, Donald G. Fisher, John W. Larson, Rudolph Nothenberg, Sanford R. Robertson, William J. Rutter, Ph.D., Lloyd H. Smith, Jr., M.D.
EIN: 943258408

58795
Daniel L. & Judith Y. Auclair Charitable Foundation
438 Foxborough Dr.
Mountain View, CA 94040 (650) 964-9527
Contact: Danile L. Auclair, Dir.

Established in 1999 in CA.
Donor(s): Daniel L. Auclair, Judith Y. Auclair.
Financial data (yr. ended 12/31/00): Assets, $263,354 (M); grants paid, $1,125; expenditures, $44,895; qualifying distributions, $37,733; giving activities include $36,609 for programs.
Limitations: Giving primarily in Mountain View, CA.
Application information: Application form required.
Directors: Daniel L. Auclair, Judith Y. Auclair.
EIN: 770529004

58796
Canobie Films, Inc.
c/o Stair, Pedersen & Williams
7100 Redwood Blvd., Ste. 200
Novato, CA 94945-4110
Application address: 1621 Juanita Ln., Tiburon, CA 94920-2528, tel.: (415) 435-8002
Contact: Michael Davis, Treas.

Established in 1990 in MA.
Financial data (yr. ended 12/31/00): Assets, $262,808 (M); grants paid, $70,730; expenditures, $198,865; qualifying distributions, $198,865.
Officers: Janet Johnstone, Pres.; Michael Davis, Treas.
Director: Ken Pederson.
EIN: 043088675

58797
Deininger Foundation
621 W. Line St.
Bishop, CA 93514
Contact: Leslie L. Chapman, Tr.

Established in 1995 in CA.
Financial data (yr. ended 12/31/00): Assets, $260,113 (M); grants paid, $12,000; expenditures, $17,797; qualifying distributions, $14,863.
Limitations: Giving primarily in CA.
Application information: Application form required.
Directors: Mary Franke, Andrea Shallcross.
Trustee: Leslie L. Chapman.
EIN: 776112667

58798
Easton Sports Development Foundation
7855 Haskell Ave., Ste. 202
Van Nuys, CA 91406-1902

Classified as a company-sponsored operating foundation in 1982.
Donor(s): Easton Aluminum, Inc., National Archery Assn. Foundation.
Financial data (yr. ended 11/30/00): Assets, $257,688 (M); grants paid, $0; gifts received, $49,079; expenditures, $43,696; qualifying distributions, $43,696; giving activities include $57,771 for programs.
Officers and Directors:* James L. Easton,* Pres.; Erik Watts,* V.P.; John Cramer,* Secy.; Gregory J. Easton, Lynn E. Easton.
EIN: 953750153

58799
The M. Chris Dickson Foundation
1100 Via Callejon, Ste. 200
San Clemente, CA 92673-6230

Established in 1990 in CA.
Donor(s): M. Chris Dickson.
Financial data (yr. ended 12/31/99): Assets, $257,063 (M); grants paid, $14,775; gifts received, $40,000; expenditures, $15,696; qualifying distributions, $15,696.
Limitations: Applications not accepted. Giving primarily in southern CA.
Application information: Contributes only to pre-selected organizations.
Officers and Directors:* M. Chris Dickson,* Pres.; Nicholas J. Dickson,* Secy.-Treas.
EIN: 330421407

58800
Paul J. Santana and Laura M. Santana Charitable Foundation
14300 Longridge Rd.
Los Gatos, CA 95033 (408) 353-4129
Contact: Laura M. Santana, Secy.-Treas.

Established in 1999 in CA.
Donor(s): Paul Santana, Laura Santana.
Financial data (yr. ended 12/31/00): Assets, $254,546 (M); grants paid, $2,011; gifts received, $27,886; expenditures, $12,571; qualifying distributions, $2,011.
Application information: Application form not required.
Officers and Directors:* Paul J. Santana,* Pres.; Laura M. Santana,* Secy.-Treas.
EIN: 776182210

58801
Vadodara Education Technology Foundation
44240 Revere Pl.
Fremont, CA 94539

Established in 2000 in CA.

Donor(s): Amit Shah, Ameesh Divatia, Bhavesh Patel, Vimal Vidhya, Yatin Mandkur.
Financial data (yr. ended 12/31/01): Assets, $254,367 (M); grants paid, $375,000; gifts received, $557,601; expenditures, $375,214; qualifying distributions, $375,000.
Limitations: Applications not accepted.
Application information: Contributes only to pre-selected organizations.
Officers and Directors:* Amit Shah,* Pres.; Ajay Shah,* Secy.; Ameesh Divatia,* C.F.O.
EIN: 770548233

58802
Angel S. & Josephine M. Moran Charitable Foundation
c/o Angel S. Moran
2449 McLaughlin Ave.
San Jose, CA 95121

Established in 1998 in CA; Classified as a private operating foundation in 1999.
Donor(s): Angel S. Moran, Josephine M. Moran.
Financial data (yr. ended 12/31/01): Assets, $253,873 (M); grants paid, $0; gifts received, $4,800; expenditures, $18,867; qualifying distributions, $10,798; giving activities include $10,798 for programs.
Officers and Directors:* Angel S. Moran,* Pres.; Josephine M. Moran,* Secy.-Treas.
EIN: 770499698

58803
O'Connell Family Foundation
2872 Delaware St.
Oakland, CA 94602
Application address: 4964 Seaview Ave., Castro Valley, CA 94546, tel.: (510) 530-2516
Contact: Mary O'Connell Mattes, C.F.O.

Established in 2000 in CA.
Donor(s): Virginia O'Connell.
Financial data (yr. ended 12/31/00): Assets, $253,213 (M); grants paid, $0; gifts received, $253,213; expenditures, $0; qualifying distributions, $0.
Officers: Virginia O'Connell, Pres.; Colleen O'Connell Dezur, V.P.; James T. O'Connell, V.P.; William Joseph O'Connell, V.P.; Rosemary O'Connell Hagen, Secy.; Mary O'Connell Mattes, C.F.O.
EIN: 912065094

58804
Richmond Educational Foundation
P.O. Box 460129
Escondido, CA 92046-0129
Application address: 427 Washingtonia Dr., San Marcos, CA 92078-5033
Contact: James L. Richmond, Tr.

Financial data (yr. ended 12/31/01): Assets, $252,597 (M); grants paid, $14,801; gifts received, $16,050; expenditures, $38,017; qualifying distributions, $14,801.
Limitations: Giving primarily in CA.
Application information: Application form required.
Officers: Lois E. Richmond, C.E.O. and C.F.O.; Francis Warn, Secy.
Trustees: Darius Khayat, James L. Richmond.
EIN: 330638221

58805
Mabel M. Elliott Educational Foundation
P.O. Box 1930
San Marcos, CA 92079-1930 (760) 744-9101
Application address: 427 Washington Dr., San Marcos, CA 92078-5033
Contact: James L. Richmond, Pres.

Established in 1994 in CA.
Donor(s): Mabel Elliot Trust.
Financial data (yr. ended 12/31/01): Assets, $251,549 (M); grants paid, $16,242; expenditures, $18,565; qualifying distributions, $16,242.
Limitations: Giving primarily in CA.
Application information: Application form required.
Officers: James L. Richmond, Pres.; John Smylie, Secy.
Trustee: Darius Khayat.
EIN: 330617739
Codes: GTI

58806
Lake Family Foundation
c/o Cynthia G. Lake
3404 State Rd.
Bakersfield, CA 93308 (661) 399-9124

Classified as a private operating foundation in 1999 in CA.
Donor(s): Western Oilfields Supply Co.
Financial data (yr. ended 12/31/99): Assets, $248,184 (M); grants paid, $9,985; gifts received, $800; expenditures, $14,859; qualifying distributions, $9,985.
Officers: Cynthia G. Lake, Pres.; John W. Lake, Secy.; Robert C. Lake, C.F.O.
EIN: 770499114

58807
Rob & Joanne Smith Family Foundation
1308 S. Brand Blvd.
Glendale, CA 91204

Established in 1999.
Financial data (yr. ended 12/31/00): Assets, $244,935 (M); grants paid, $65,000; gifts received, $50,000; expenditures, $65,876; qualifying distributions, $65,000.
Limitations: Applications not accepted. Giving primarily in CA.
Application information: Contributes only to pre-selected organizations.
Officers: Joanne C. Smith, Pres.; Julie Alvarado, C.F.O.; Rob A. Smith, Secy.-Treas.
EIN: 954734887

58808
The Nuer Foundation
P.O. Box 150154
San Rafael, CA 94915-0154

Established in 2000 in CA as a company-sponsored operating foundation.
Donor(s): ACC International Institute, Jennifer Vainson, Paolo Vianson, Giorgio Vianson, Fairchild Semiconductor Corp.
Financial data (yr. ended 12/31/00): Assets, $241,659 (M); grants paid, $0; gifts received, $269,046; expenditures, $35,652; qualifying distributions, $24,519; giving activities include $23,560 for programs.
Officers: Lara Nuer, Pres.; Noah Nuer, V.P.; Shayne Hughes, C.F.O.
EIN: 943345263

58809
Andre Sobel River of Life Foundation
8899 Beverly Blvd., Ste. 111
Los Angeles, CA 90048 (310) 276-7111
Contact: Zoe Earl, Program Dir.

Donor(s): Alexander and Rose Gottdiener Foundation, Iacocca Foundation.
Financial data (yr. ended 06/30/01): Assets, $238,109 (M); grants paid, $100,000; gifts received, $533,822; expenditures, $754,254; qualifying distributions, $740,006; giving activities include $632,506 for programs.
Limitations: Giving primarily in CA and NY.
Application information: Application form required.
Officers: Valerie Sobel, Pres.; Barry Bruder, Secy.; Gary Bess, Treas.
EIN: 330671254
Codes: FD2

58810
Stance Foundation
4133 Orr Ranch Rd.
Santa Rosa, CA 95404

Established in 1999 in CA.
Donor(s): Gregory F. Sims, Catherine C. Sims.
Financial data (yr. ended 10/31/00): Assets, $234,659 (M); grants paid, $0; gifts received, $280,125; expenditures, $8,138; qualifying distributions, $7,943; giving activities include $1,614 for programs.
Limitations: Applications not accepted.
Application information: Contributes only to pre-selected organizations.
Officers: Gregory F. Sims, Pres. and C.F.O.; Catherine C. Sims, Secy.
EIN: 770530137

58811
Esther and Rudolph Lowy Charitable Foundation
4929 Wilshire Blvd., No. 690
Los Angeles, CA 90010-3820

Established in 1986 in CA.
Donor(s): Rudolph J. Lowy, Esther R. Lowy.
Financial data (yr. ended 09/30/00): Assets, $233,533 (M); grants paid, $14,285; expenditures, $15,177; qualifying distributions, $15,177.
Limitations: Applications not accepted. Giving primarily in Los Angeles, CA.
Application information: Contributes only to pre-selected organizations.
Officers: Esther R. Lowy, Secy.; Rudolph J. Lowy, Mgr.
EIN: 954071617

58812
A-T Medical Research Foundation
5241 Round Meadow Rd.
Hidden Hills, CA 91302-1163 (818) 704-8146
FAX: (818) 704-8310
Contact: Pamela Smith, V.P.

Established in 1983 in CA.
Donor(s): George A. Smith, Pamela J. Smith.
Financial data (yr. ended 09/30/01): Assets, $226,427 (M); grants paid, $362,600; gifts received, $579,802; expenditures, $639,117; qualifying distributions, $573,963.
Limitations: Giving on a national and international basis.
Publications: Annual report, newsletter, informational brochure.
Application information: Requests reviewed and approved by scientific director. Application form not required.
Officers: George A. Smith, Pres. and C.F.O.; Pamela J. Smith, V.P.

Directors: David Haskell, Lois Rosen.
EIN: 953882022
Codes: FD, GTI

58813
Don P. Nichols Foundation, Inc.
3184 Airway Ave. E
Costa Mesa, CA 92626

Established in 1996 in CA.
Donor(s): Donald P. Nichols.
Financial data (yr. ended 12/31/00): Assets, $224,761 (M); grants paid, $4,500; gifts received, $15,000; expenditures, $5,138; qualifying distributions, $4,500.
Limitations: Giving limited to residents of Orange County, CA.
Application information: Application form required.
Director: Donald P. Nichols.
EIN: 330734941

58814
Edgar J. and Ida G. Graun Family Fund, Inc.
(Formerly Chamber Music Fund)
907 Keeler Ave.
Berkeley, CA 94708-1419 (510) 526-3682
Contact: Edgar J. Braun, Pres.

Established in 1988 in CA.
Financial data (yr. ended 09/30/01): Assets, $224,601 (M); grants paid, $9,550; expenditures, $9,550; qualifying distributions, $9,550.
Limitations: Giving primarily in San Francisco, CA.
Officers: Edgar J. Braun,* C.E.O.; Ida Braun, V.P.
EIN: 946596698

58815
The Asian American Senior Citizen Association
9980 Bolsa Ave.
Westminster, CA 92683

Classified as a private operating foundation in 1999.
Financial data (yr. ended 12/31/01): Assets, $220,854 (M); grants paid, $0; gifts received, $240,860; expenditures, $226,909; qualifying distributions, $1,720; giving activities include $226,909 for programs.
Officers: Hien Nguyen, Pres.; Duc Nguyen, Treas.
EIN: 330487200

58816
Sepahmansour Family Foundation
14090 Shannon Rd.
Los Gatos, CA 95032
Contact: Faramarz Sepahmansour, Pres.

Established in 1999.
Donor(s): Faramarz Sepahmansour, Karen Sepahmansour.
Financial data (yr. ended 12/31/99): Assets, $214,250 (M); grants paid, $1,285; gifts received, $191,750; expenditures, $1,285; qualifying distributions, $1,285.
Application information: Application form not required.
Officers: Faramarz Sepahmansour, Pres. and Treas.; Karen Sepahmansour, Secy.
EIN: 770515617

58817
Sam Family Charitable Foundation, Inc.
10811 Barrington Bridge Ct.
Cupertino, CA 95014-6401

Established in 2000 in CA.
Donor(s): Richard Chung Sam, Mary Ho Sam.
Financial data (yr. ended 03/31/01): Assets, $212,699 (M); grants paid, $4,976; gifts received, $210,525; expenditures, $500; qualifying distributions, $4,976.

Directors: Andrew Ho, Richard Chung Sam, Mary Ho Sam.
EIN: 770558602

58818
Charlotte Smith Marston Foundation
16063 Oak Tree Crossing
Chino Hills, CA 91709

Established in 1998 in CA.
Financial data (yr. ended 12/31/99): Assets, $212,379 (M); grants paid, $500; gifts received, $800; expenditures, $939; qualifying distributions, $500.
Limitations: Applications not accepted.
Application information: Contributes only to pre-selected organizations.
Director: Margaret Marston.
EIN: 330803541

58819
Morro Bay Marine Rehabilitation Center
595 Embarcadero
Morro Bay, CA 93442-2217

Classified as a private operating foundation in 1983.
Financial data (yr. ended 09/30/01): Assets, $209,924 (M); grants paid, $12,555; gifts received, $222; expenditures, $226,285; qualifying distributions, $212,389; giving activities include $213,872 for programs.
Limitations: Applications not accepted. Giving primarily in CA.
Application information: Contributes only to pre-selected organizations.
Officers and Directors:* Dean R. Tyler,* Pres.; Bertha Tyler,* V.P.; Hon. J. Lloyd Neal.
EIN: 770032171

58820
Academy of Art College Library Fund, Inc.
79 New Montgomery St., 3rd Fl.
San Francisco, CA 94105

Classified as a private operating foundation in 1983.
Donor(s): Stephens Institute.
Financial data (yr. ended 12/31/00): Assets, $206,088 (M); grants paid, $0; expenditures, $33,437; qualifying distributions, $24,353; giving activities include $33,437 for programs.
Officers: Richard A. Stephens, C.E.O.; Elisa Stephens, Pres. and Secy.; Espi Sanjana, Treas.
Directors: Scott Rhude, Debra Zumwalt.
EIN: 942463376

58821
The Zathas Foundation
11905 Riverside Dr.
Lakeside, CA 92040 (619) 561-1061
Contact: Spero Tzathas, Pres.

Classified as a private operating foundation in 1992 in CA.
Donor(s): James Zathas.
Financial data (yr. ended 12/31/01): Assets, $204,274 (M); grants paid, $2,750; gifts received, $5,387; expenditures, $8,123; qualifying distributions, $5,272; giving activities include $2,522 for programs.
Limitations: Giving primarily in San Diego, CA.
Application information: Application form required.
Officers: Spero Tzathas, Pres.; Elias Katsoulas, Secy.-Treas.
Directors: Paul Anas, Helen Mellos, Patricia Moises, Mary Rodrigues, James Zathas.
EIN: 330495464

58822
Underwood Family Charitable Foundation
1553 Oramas Rd.
Santa Barbara, CA 93103-2064

Established in 1997 in CA.
Donor(s): William J. Underwood.
Financial data (yr. ended 12/31/01): Assets, $204,102 (M); grants paid, $15,840; expenditures, $16,973; qualifying distributions, $15,840.
Limitations: Applications not accepted. Giving primarily in Santa Barbara, CA.
Application information: Contributes only to pre-selected organizations.
Officer: Corinne Underwood, V.P.
EIN: 770456013

58823
The Lionel & Debra D'Luna Family Foundation
12 Ivy Glen
Irvine, CA 92620

Established in 2000 in CA.
Donor(s): Lionel D'Luna.
Financial data (yr. ended 12/31/01): Assets, $203,663 (M); grants paid, $25,000; expenditures, $25,000; qualifying distributions, $25,000.
Limitations: Applications not accepted.
Application information: Contributes only to pre-selected organizations.
Officers: Lionel D'Luna, Pres.; Debra D'Luna, Secy. and C.F.O.
EIN: 330931291

58824
International Health Research Foundation
2030 Pioneer Ct., No. 7
San Mateo, CA 94403

Established in 1998 in CA.
Financial data (yr. ended 12/31/00): Assets, $203,430 (M); grants paid, $215,700; gifts received, $200; expenditures, $223,821; qualifying distributions, $221,082.
Limitations: Applications not accepted. Giving primarily in CA.
Application information: Contributes only to pre-selected organizations.
Officers and Directors:* Clarise Blanchard,* Pres. and Exec. Dir.; Charles Blanchard,* V.P.
EIN: 943104083
Codes: FD2

58825
Dharma Cloud Charitable Foundation Trust
P.O. Box 1066
Mendocino, CA 95460

Donor(s): Vincent D. Taylor.
Financial data (yr. ended 12/31/99): Assets, $202,552 (M); grants paid, $1,379; gifts received, $15,857; expenditures, $34,492; qualifying distributions, $33,222; giving activities include $31,160 for programs.
Limitations: Giving primarily in CA.
Trustee: Vincent D. Taylor.
EIN: 030348679

58826
The Hing J. and Chow K. Lom Charitable Trust
433 Corral De Tierra
Salinas, CA 93908

Established in 1998 in CA.
Donor(s): Chow K. Lom, Michael Lom.
Financial data (yr. ended 05/31/01): Assets, $200,900 (M); grants paid, $12,500; gifts received, $10,000; expenditures, $15,605; qualifying distributions, $12,500.

Limitations: Applications not accepted.
Application information: Contributes only to pre-selected organizations.
Trustees: Chow K. Lom, Michael Lom, Lt Ng, Jr.
EIN: 776160326

58827
The E. & H. Chen Family Foundation
21009 Seven Springs Pkwy.
Cupertino, CA 95014 (408) 996-2670
Contact: Emily Yp Chen, Pres.

Established in 1999 in CA.
Donor(s): Emily Yp Chen, Hong Tao Chen.
Financial data (yr. ended 12/31/00): Assets, $197,987 (M); grants paid, $0; gifts received, $52,812; expenditures, $108,819; qualifying distributions, $107,458; giving activities include $107,615 for programs.
Officers and Directors:* Emily Yp Chen,* Pres. and Secy.; Hong Tao Chen,* V.P. and Treas.
EIN: 770528166

58828
Jerome M. and Marjorie B. Rosenberg Charitable Foundation
1570 Queensbury Ave.
Los Altos, CA 94024-5843 (650) 968-3800

Classified as a private operating foundation in CA.
Financial data (yr. ended 12/31/00): Assets, $194,606 (M); grants paid, $0; gifts received, $46,014; expenditures, $49,972; qualifying distributions, $42,860; giving activities include $42,665 for programs.
Officers and Directors:* Jerome M. Rosenberg,* Pres.; Marjorie B. Rosenberg,* Secy.-Treas.
EIN: 770497474

58829
Boyer House Foundation
900 Las Gallinas Dr.
San Rafael, CA 94903

Classified as a private operating foundation in 1989.
Donor(s): L. Bryce Boyer, M.D.
Financial data (yr. ended 12/31/01): Assets, $192,068 (M); grants paid, $0; gifts received, $33,525; expenditures, $864,874; qualifying distributions, $0.
Officers: Judy Sobieski, Ph.D., C.E.O.; Sue Von Baeyer, Ph.D., Secy.
Directors: Gloria Burk, Will Glaser, Crystal Johnson, Howard Pollack, Jevon Powell.
EIN: 942941622

58830
Gold Mountain Foundation, Inc.
P.O. Box 880
Graeagle, CA 96103

Financial data (yr. ended 07/31/00): Assets, $189,718 (M); grants paid, $0; gifts received, $399,382; expenditures, $301,760; qualifying distributions, $249,854; giving activities include $35,550 for programs.
Limitations: Applications not accepted.
Application information: Contributes only to pre-selected organizations.
Officers: Dariel Garner, Pres.; Margaret Garner, Secy.; Sark Antaramian, Treas.
EIN: 931223753

58831
The Andrew W. Evans Family Foundation
80 E. Sir Francis Drake Blvd., Ste. 3A
Larkspur, CA 94939

Established in 1999 in CA.
Donor(s): Elizabeth W. Evans, Brooks F. Evans, Michael A. Evans.

Financial data (yr. ended 12/31/00): Assets, $185,110 (M); grants paid, $7,500; gifts received, $225,851; expenditures, $9,469; qualifying distributions, $7,440.
Limitations: Applications not accepted. Giving primarily in CA and ID.
Application information: Contributes only to pre-selected organizations.
Officers and Directors:* Andrew W. Evans,* Pres.; Stephanie O. Evans,* Secy.; Michael A. Evans,* C.F.O.; Brooks F. Evans.
EIN: 680441810

58832
The Paul and Linda Kahn Foundation
1832 2nd St., Ste. M
Berkeley, CA 94710

Established in 1997.
Donor(s): Linda M. Kahn.
Financial data (yr. ended 12/31/00): Assets, $182,690 (M); grants paid, $0; gifts received, $71,591; expenditures, $9,489; qualifying distributions, $157,486; giving activities include $157,486 for programs.
Officers: Richard J. Arnason, Treas.; Linda M. Kahn, Mgr.
EIN: 946719673

58833
Spangler Charitable Foundation
2211 Westchester Dr.
San Jose, CA 95124

Established in 1998 in CA.
Donor(s): Linda S. Spangler, Paul A. Spangler.
Financial data (yr. ended 12/31/00): Assets, $178,759 (M); grants paid, $1,500; gifts received, $30,300; expenditures, $19,395; qualifying distributions, $13,538.
Limitations: Applications not accepted.
Application information: Contributes only to pre-selected organizations.
Officers and Directors:* Paul A. Spangler,* Pres.; Linda S. Spangler,* Secy. and C.F.O.; Jennifer A. Wallace.
EIN: 770491505

58834
Fresno Musical Club
2689 W. San Carlos
Fresno, CA 93711
Application address: 2672 E. Alluvial, Clovis, CA 93611
Contact: Saskia Dyer, Treas.

Established as a private operating foundation in 1988.
Financial data (yr. ended 06/30/00): Assets, $178,480 (M); grants paid, $9,150; gifts received, $3,512; expenditures, $12,170; qualifying distributions, $9,150.
Limitations: Giving limited to the Fresno, CA, area.
Officers: Jean Vavoulis, Pres.; Shirley Douty, V.P.; Audrey Kasparian, Recording Secy.; Linda Hamilton, Corresponding Secy.; Saskia Dyer, Treas.
EIN: 946075667
Codes: GTI

58835
Sovereign Fund
P.O. Box 49899
Los Angeles, CA 90049-0899
Application address: 1825 Westridge Rd., Los Angeles, CA 90049
Contact: Kurt W. Simon, Pres.

Classified as a private operating foundation in 1981.
Donor(s): Kurt W. Simon.

58835—CALIFORNIA

Financial data (yr. ended 12/31/01): Assets, $175,649 (M); grants paid, $20,000; gifts received, $25,000; expenditures, $37,656; qualifying distributions, $32,395.
Officer: Kurt W. Simon, Pres.
Board Members: Willard Chilcott, Thomas Ennis.
EIN: 953643952
Codes: GTI

58836
Modoc Scholarship Fund, Inc.
510 N. Main St.
Alturas, CA 96101
Contact: Dwight Beesom, Pres.

Established in 1989 in CA.
Donor(s): R. Kenneth Smith.‡
Financial data (yr. ended 12/31/00): Assets, $173,543 (M); grants paid, $4,500; gifts received, $235; expenditures, $4,803; qualifying distributions, $4,439.
Limitations: Giving limited to Alturas, CA.
Application information: Application form required.
Officers: Dwight Beesom, Pres.; Theodore Porter, Secy.; Ida Grace Armor, Treas.
EIN: 680143501

58837
Shunammite Foundation
2 Kite Hill Rd.
Santa Cruz, CA 95060-1418 (831) 423-6893
Contact: Linda S. Musselwhite, Pres.

Classified as a private operating foundation in 1989.
Donor(s): Linda S. Musselwhite, Edwin A. Musselwhite.
Financial data (yr. ended 06/30/01): Assets, $171,163 (L); grants paid, $62,173; expenditures, $66,180; qualifying distributions, $66,012.
Limitations: Giving limited to northern CA.
Application information: Application form required.
Officers: Linda S. Musselwhite, Pres.; Edwin A. Musselwhite, V.P.
EIN: 770224831
Codes: GTI

58838
The Glad Foundation
Channel Islands Harbor
2560 Peninsula Rd.
Oxnard, CA 93035

Classified as a private operating foundation in 1987.
Donor(s): Gary S. Carr, Patricia S. Carr.
Financial data (yr. ended 03/31/99): Assets, $169,988 (M); grants paid, $34,000; gifts received, $24,000; expenditures, $34,323; qualifying distributions, $34,000.
Limitations: Applications not accepted. Giving primarily in CA.
Application information: Contributes only to pre-selected organizations.
Officers: Gary S. Carr, Chair.; Jeff Oster, V.P.; Sharyn Y. Carr, Secy.; David Witt, Treas.
EIN: 954092927

58839
United Activists for Animal Rights
P.O. Box 2448
Riverside, CA 92516-2448

Classified as a private operating foundation in 1991.
Financial data (yr. ended 06/30/00): Assets, $169,804 (M); grants paid, $250; gifts received, $87,470; expenditures, $80,413; qualifying distributions, $76,908; giving activities include $80,412 for programs.
Limitations: Applications not accepted.
Application information: Contributes only to pre-selected organizations.
Officer and Directors:* Nancy Burnett,* C.E.O.; Betty Dillbeck, Carol Murphy, Paul Sax, Peggy Sax.
EIN: 330272670

58840
Intercenter Cancer Research Group, Inc.
(Formerly Comprehensive Cancer Research Group, Inc.)
1800 N. Indian Canyon Dr., Ste. E-320
Palm Springs, CA 92262

Established in 1987 in FL.
Donor(s): Bristol-Myers Squibb Co., Estee Lauder, Mrs. John Armonia, Charles Vogel, M.D.
Financial data (yr. ended 10/31/00): Assets, $169,625 (M); grants paid, $46,245; gifts received, $52,511; expenditures, $682,971; qualifying distributions, $164,276; giving activities include $518,647 for programs.
Limitations: Applications not accepted.
Application information: Contributes only to pre-selected organizations.
Officers and Directors:* John MacDonald,* Pres.; Susan Noble Kempin, R.N.,* Treas.
EIN: 650012760

58841
The Seymour R. and Odelia A. Cohen Charitable Foundation
c/o Seymour Cohen, M.D.
15456 Ventura Blvd., No. 408
Sherman Oaks, CA 91403-3022
Application address: 4301 Cromwell Ave. Los Angeles, CA 90027, tel.: (213) 662-4724

Classified as a private operating foundation in 1985.
Donor(s): Seymour Cohen, M.D.
Financial data (yr. ended 11/30/01): Assets, $168,664 (M); grants paid, $25; gifts received, $10,000; expenditures, $3,657; qualifying distributions, $2,435.
Officers: Seymour R. Cohen, M.D., Pres.; Odelia A. Cohen, V.P.
EIN: 954120586

58842
Wisdom Society
P.O. Box 2783
Escondido, CA 92033

Financial data (yr. ended 11/30/99): Assets, $167,770 (M); grants paid, $0; expenditures, $30,735; qualifying distributions, $28,245; giving activities include $3,051 for programs.
Limitations: Applications not accepted.
Application information: Contributes only to pre-selected organizations.
Officers and Directors:* Cheryll Blount,* Pres.; Gerald Reaster,* Secy.; Jodi Daly,* Treas.
EIN: 330396296

58843
Tower Hematology Oncology Cancer Research Foundation
8635 W. 3rd St., Ste. 665W
Los Angeles, CA 90048

Classified as a company-sponsored operating foundation in 1997 in CA.
Donor(s): Genzyme, Smithkline, Integrated Therapeutics, Glaxo Wellcome, Angen, Harriet Rouse.
Financial data (yr. ended 12/31/00): Assets, $166,519 (M); grants paid, $2,500; gifts received, $102,319; expenditures, $196,458; qualifying distributions, $2,500; giving activities include $72,550 for programs.
Directors: Leonard Blonder, Solomon Hamburg, Donald MacPherson, Philomena McAndrew, Ed McMahon, Larry Post, Fred Rosenfelt, Jacques Wertheimer.
EIN: 954596354

58844
Heiskell Bibliographical Foundation
1352 Apsley Rd.
Santa Ana, CA 92705-2330

Financial data (yr. ended 11/30/00): Assets, $166,144 (M); grants paid, $500; expenditures, $1,500; qualifying distributions, $500.
Limitations: Applications not accepted.
Application information: Contributes only to pre-selected organizations.
Officers and Directors:* Charles L. Heiskell,* Pres.; Thomas Wright,* V.P.; Elba N. Smith,* Secy.
EIN: 330037777

58845
Henry J. Mello Foundation
32 White Rd.
Watsonville, CA 95076 (831) 722-3280

Established in 1990 in CA.
Donor(s): Henry J. Mello.
Financial data (yr. ended 12/31/00): Assets, $163,949 (L); grants paid, $9,500; expenditures, $10,224; qualifying distributions, $9,500.
Limitations: Giving primarily in Watsonville, CA.
Officers and Directors:* Henry J. Mello,* Pres.; Helen A. Mello,* V.P.; John Mello, Michael Mello, Stephen Mello, Timothy Mello, Thomas Skillicorn.
EIN: 770238728

58846
San Diego Futures Foundation
P.O. Box 939011
San Diego, CA 92193-9011 (858) 784-5403
FAX: (858) 453-6047; *E-mail:* becky@sdfutures.org, lynn@sdfutures.org, jeff@sdfutures.org, kirk@sdfutures.org, maren@sdfutures.org, and wright@sdfutures.org; *URL:* http://www.sdfutures.org
Contact: Lynn A. Anderson

Established in 2000 in CA.
Donor(s): Computer Sciences Corporation, Science Applications International Corporation, Lucent Technologies Inc., SBC Communications, Pacific Bell North.
Financial data (yr. ended 12/31/01): Assets, $161,500 (M); grants paid, $261,232; gifts received, $926,653; expenditures, $892,293; qualifying distributions, $875,212.
Limitations: Giving limited to San Diego County, CA.
Application information: Application form required.
Officers: Mike Gross, Chair. and Pres.; William W. Wright, Secy. and C.F.O.; Rebecca Stawiski, Exec. Dir.
EIN: 330883460
Codes: FD

58847
Mothers Alone Foundation
15466 Las Gatos Blvd., Ste. 109-275
Los Gatos, CA 95032

Established in 1999 in CA.
Donor(s): Bernice Starrett.
Financial data (yr. ended 06/30/00): Assets, $161,297 (M); grants paid, $0; gifts received, $162,579; expenditures, $0; qualifying distributions, $0.

Limitations: Applications not accepted.
Application information: Contributes only to pre-selected organizations.
Trustee: Bernice Starrett.
EIN: 705180494

58848
Thompson Philanthropic Enterprises
(Formerly Thompson Charitable Enterprises)
c/o John S. McClintic
1350 Carlback Ave., Ste. 330
Walnut Creek, CA 94596

Established in 1991 in CA.
Donor(s): Milan Agency, Inc., Erik Thompson.
Financial data (yr. ended 06/30/00): Assets, $160,600 (M); grants paid, $0; expenditures, $6,717; qualifying distributions, $6,350; giving activities include $5,238 for programs.
Officer: Erik Thompson, Pres.
Directors: Maureen Carroll, Cecil Withrow.
EIN: 943152377

58849
Peggie R. Shedd Marine Education and Enchancement Trust
17351-B Murphy Ave.
Irvine, CA 92614-5919 (949) 660-8757
Contact: Milton C. Shedd, Tr.

Classified as a private operating foundation in 1996.
Financial data (yr. ended 12/31/99): Assets, $158,230 (M); grants paid, $17,000; gifts received, $34,937; expenditures, $17,780; qualifying distributions, $17,000.
Trustees: Milton C. Shedd, Steven A. Shedd, William D. Shedd.
EIN: 336192068

58850
Claude & Ada Low Foundation, Inc.
803 N. Cambridge St.
Orange, CA 92867
Application address: Rte. 1, Box 1060, Urbana MO 65767, tel.: (417) 993-5394
Contact: Robbie Low, Pres.

Donor(s): Robbie Low, Claudine Iwig, J.C. Low.
Financial data (yr. ended 12/31/00): Assets, $155,973 (M); grants paid, $4,000; gifts received, $15,000; expenditures, $4,347; qualifying distributions, $4,000.
Limitations: Giving limited to MO.
Application information: Application form required.
Officers: Robbie Low, Pres.; Claudine Iwig, V.P.; J.C. Low, Secy.-Treas.
EIN: 431628702

58851
The Rosita C. Victoria Foundation
c/o Rosita C. Victoria
21235 79th St.
California City, CA 93505-1812

Established in 1996 in CA.
Donor(s): Rosita C. Victoria.
Financial data (yr. ended 12/31/01): Assets, $153,194 (M); grants paid, $225; expenditures, $21,564; qualifying distributions, $225; giving activities include $1,020 for programs.
Limitations: Giving primarily in California City, CA.
Trustee: Rosita C. Victoria.
EIN: 770427450

58852
The Harry E. & Rachael M. Moeller Foundation
P.O. Box 300698
Escondido, CA 92030-0698

Classified as a private operating foundation in 1995.
Donor(s): Rachael M. Moeller.
Financial data (yr. ended 12/31/00): Assets, $152,314 (M); grants paid, $0; gifts received, $13,843; expenditures, $31,008; qualifying distributions, $29,435; giving activities include $12,474 for programs.
Officers and Directors:* Edward J. Zimmer,* Pres.; Marilyn Zimmer,* Secy.; Rachael M. Moeller,* Treas.
EIN: 330637163

58853
Rancho Immanuel
P.O. Box 1097
Ferndale, CA 95536

Classified as a private operating foundation in 1989.
Financial data (yr. ended 12/31/01): Assets, $152,096 (M); grants paid, $8,500; expenditures, $11,818; qualifying distributions, $8,566.
Limitations: Applications not accepted. Giving primarily in CA.
Application information: Unsolicited requests for funds not accepted.
Officer: Rev. Allan Bohner, Pres.
EIN: 952529168

58854
The Berchtold Foundation
2972 Motor Ave.
Los Angeles, CA 90064

Financial data (yr. ended 12/31/01): Assets, $151,996 (M); grants paid, $12,000; expenditures, $13,978; qualifying distributions, $13,978.
Limitations: Applications not accepted. Giving primarily in WA.
Application information: Contributes only to pre-selected organizations.
Officers: Mary Ann Berchtold, Pres.; Kenneth Berchtold, Secy.-Treas.
Director: Michael Harris.
EIN: 954663328

58855
The Nicholas Green Foundation
21495 Heron Dr.
Bodega Bay, CA 94923

Established in 1995 in CA.
Financial data (yr. ended 12/31/99): Assets, $151,703 (M); grants paid, $480; gifts received, $3,389; expenditures, $31,046; qualifying distributions, $30,946.
Limitations: Applications not accepted. Giving primarily in OR.
Application information: Contributes only to pre-selected organizations.
Directors: Reginald Green, Margaret Green.
EIN: 680349581

58856
Multicultural Foundation
1475 6th Ave., 4th Fl.
San Diego, CA 92101-3245

Established in 1997 in CA.
Donor(s): John Pifer.
Financial data (yr. ended 12/31/01): Assets, $149,232 (L); grants paid, $0; gifts received, $72,017; expenditures, $187,057; qualifying distributions, $0.

Officers: Richard O. Butcher, Pres.; Rodney G. Hood, Secy.
EIN: 330733292

58857
The Easter Island Foundation
(Formerly Inter-American Wildlife Foundation)
P.O. Box 6774
Los Osos, CA 93412

Classified as a private operating foundation in 1983.
Donor(s): Joan T. Seaver, M.D., William Liller, M.D.
Financial data (yr. ended 12/31/01): Assets, $146,770 (M); grants paid, $32,550; gifts received, $19,546; expenditures, $82,837; qualifying distributions, $49,705; giving activities include $17,164 for programs.
Limitations: Giving limited to Easter Island or the East Pacific.
Officers: Kay Kenady Sanger, Pres.; Thomas Christopher, V.P.; Christopher Stevenson, 2nd V.P.; Rose Marie Wallace, V.P., Chile; Catherine Orlac, Ph.D., V.P., Europe; Georgia Lee, Ph.D., Secy.; Barbara B. Hinton, Treas.
EIN: 953220730

58858
Thomas C. Carson and Nancy A. Carson Charitable Foundation
15542 Glen Una Dr.
Los Gatos, CA 95030 (408) 395-1571
Contact: Thomas C. Carson, Pres.

Donor(s): Thomas C. Carson.
Financial data (yr. ended 12/31/00): Assets, $146,432 (M); grants paid, $3,742; gifts received, $23,340; expenditures, $8,870; qualifying distributions, $3,742.
Application information: Application form not required.
Officers and Directors:* Thomas C. Carson,* Pres.; Nancy A. Carson,* Secy.-Treas.
EIN: 770528632

58859
Bruce E. Bruno and Vita P. Bruno Charitable Foundation
21970 Via Regina
Saratoga, CA 95070
Contact: Vita P. Bruno, Secy.-Treas.

Established in 1999.
Donor(s): Bruce E. Bruno, Vita P. Bruno.
Financial data (yr. ended 12/31/00): Assets, $146,115 (M); grants paid, $2,550; gifts received, $9,750; expenditures, $13,676; qualifying distributions, $13,676.
Limitations: Giving primarily in Saratoga, CA.
Application information: Application form not required.
Officers and Directors:* Bruce E. Bruno,* Pres.; Vita P. Bruno,* Secy.-Treas.
EIN: 770528039

58860
The Blanchard Foundation
c/o Marjorie M. Blanchard
125 State Pl.
Escondido, CA 92029

Established in 1990 in CA.
Donor(s): Kenneth H. Blanchard, Marjorie M. Blanchard, Blanchard Training & Development.
Financial data (yr. ended 02/28/01): Assets, $144,112 (M); grants paid, $348,180; gifts received, $427,872; expenditures, $434,702; qualifying distributions, $424,183; giving activities include $92,092 for programs.

Limitations: Applications not accepted. Giving primarily in CA.
Application information: Contributes only to pre-selected organizations.
Directors: Kenneth H. Blanchard, Marjorie Blanchard, James DeLapa, Frederic E. Finch, Eunice Parisi-Carew.
EIN: 956003017
Codes: FD

58861
Center for Integrative Health, Medicine and Research
2032-A Broadway
Santa Monica, CA 90404

Established in 1998 in CA.
Donor(s): Lucy Gonda Foundation.
Financial data (yr. ended 12/31/00): Assets, $142,422 (M); grants paid, $40,000; gifts received, $458,200; expenditures, $475,002; qualifying distributions, $442,707.
Limitations: Applications not accepted.
Application information: Contributes only to pre-selected organizations.
Officers: Lucy Gonda, Chair. and Pres.; Peter Mayer, Secy.-Treas.
Directors: Steven Litvak, Greg Osburn, Jean-Louise Rodriguez, Victoria Sutherland, Lonnie Zeltzer.
EIN: 954704599

58862
Fertig Freedom Foundation
927 Thayer Ave.
Los Angeles, CA 90024

Donor(s): David R. Fertig.
Financial data (yr. ended 12/31/00): Assets, $142,029 (M); grants paid, $6,000; gifts received, $13,768; expenditures, $9,394; qualifying distributions, $6,000.
Officer: Ralph H. Fertig, Pres.
EIN: 954691103

58863
Crimi-Roser Foundation
2650 W. 234th St.
Torrance, CA 90505

Established in 1997 in CA.
Donor(s): Marie C. Roser.
Financial data (yr. ended 12/31/00): Assets, $141,777 (M); grants paid, $28,875; gifts received, $80,000; expenditures, $32,584; qualifying distributions, $28,875.
Limitations: Giving primarily in CA.
Officer: Marie C. Roser, Pres.
Directors: Arnold W. Magasinn, Vicki F. Magasinn, Richard C. Spencer.
EIN: 954631851

58864
Cardinal Collection Educational Foundation
1723 Karameos Dr.
Sunnyvale, CA 94087

Established in 1999 in CA.
Donor(s): Martin A. Logies, John E. Skirtich.
Financial data (yr. ended 12/31/00): Assets, $140,000 (M); grants paid, $0; gifts received, $5,000; expenditures, $750; qualifying distributions, $5,750; giving activities include $5,750 for programs.
Officer and Director:* Martin A. Logies,* Pres. and Treas.
EIN: 770529783

58865
Colonial Research Center
1631 Crespo Dr.
La Jolla, CA 92037-3845

Established in 1999 in ME.
Donor(s): Rohrbach Foundation.
Financial data (yr. ended 12/31/01): Assets, $139,634 (M); grants paid, $0; expenditures, $16,001; qualifying distributions, $499.
Officers and Director:* Lewis Bunker Rohrbach, Pres.; Kumiko Ueki Buller,* V.P.; Carol Cressman Rohrbach, Secy.
EIN: 010530971

58866
Sage Canyon Animal Sanctuary
44444 Sage Rd.
Aguanga, CA 92536

Classified as a private operating foundation in 1994.
Donor(s): Homer Harris, Dolores Harris.
Financial data (yr. ended 12/31/01): Assets, $139,429 (M); grants paid, $0; gifts received, $11,265; expenditures, $32,684; qualifying distributions, $0.
Officers: Homer Harris, Chair.; Arlene Harris, Pres.; Dolores Harris, Secy.-Treas.
EIN: 330597510

58867
Wishing Well Ranch Charitable Trust
8737 Herring Rd.
Bakersfield, CA 93313-9638

Established in 1993 in CA.
Donor(s): Bonnie Bartell, Rose M. Roberts.
Financial data (yr. ended 03/31/01): Assets, $139,209 (M); grants paid, $0; gifts received, $420,050; expenditures, $463,978; qualifying distributions, $412,449; giving activities include $412,449 for programs.
Trustee: Bonnie Bartell.
EIN: 956953398

58868
H. M. Boyce and Sheila Christly Trust
2543 Cumtree Ln.
P.O. Box 1344
Fallbrook, CA 92088-1344

Classified as a private operating foundation in 1999 in CA.
Financial data (yr. ended 12/31/99): Assets, $138,167 (M); grants paid, $21,688; expenditures, $22,098; qualifying distributions, $19,607.
Application information: Application form not required.
Trustee: Sheila Christly.
EIN: 957051042

58869
Helping Us Help Ourselves Foundation
1825 S. New Hamshire Ave., Ste. 7
Los Angeles, CA 90006-4529

Established in 1999.
Donor(s): Levi Dangerfield.
Financial data (yr. ended 12/31/00): Assets, $137,901 (M); grants paid, $2,000; expenditures, $18,129; qualifying distributions, $2,000.
Officer: Levi Dangerfield, Pres.
EIN: 954695138

58870
Mia Lynn Corporation
325 Magnolia Ave.
Corona, CA 92879

Established in 2001 in CA.
Donor(s): Richard Frame.

Financial data (yr. ended 11/30/01): Assets, $137,669 (M); grants paid, $7,500; gifts received, $150,000; expenditures, $12,331; qualifying distributions, $7,500.
Limitations: Giving primarily in Pomona, CA.
Officers: Richard Frame, Pres.; Ian Richarson, Secy.; David Peters, C.F.O.
EIN: 330940504

58871
Endocrine Research and Education, Inc.
c/o Shlomo Melmed, M.D.
9437 Cresta Dr.
Los Angeles, CA 90035

Established in 1988 in CA.
Financial data (yr. ended 12/31/00): Assets, $136,769 (M); grants paid, $322,955; expenditures, $331,344; qualifying distributions, $322,955.
Officer: Shlomo Melmed, M.D., Pres.
Directors: Errol Fine, Errol I. Horwitz.
EIN: 954166085

58872
George Mateljan Foundation for Healthy Lifestyle
3239 N. Verdugo Rd.
Glendale, CA 91208-1633

Established in 1999 in CA; classified as a private operating foundation in 2000.
Donor(s): George Mateljan.
Financial data (yr. ended 12/31/01): Assets, $136,039 (M); grants paid, $0; expenditures, $503,731; qualifying distributions, $508,036; giving activities include $500,274 for programs.
Limitations: Applications not accepted.
Application information: Contributes only to pre-selected organizations.
Officer and Director:* George Mateljan,* Pres.
EIN: 954773757

58873
Henry T. Leyendecker Fund
501 W. Broadway, Ste. 900
San Diego, CA 92101 (619) 233-1155
Contact: John G. Davies, Tr.

Established in 1985.
Financial data (yr. ended 12/31/00): Assets, $134,651 (M); grants paid, $47,950; expenditures, $52,787; qualifying distributions, $49,017.
Limitations: Giving limited to residents of San Diego County, CA.
Application information: Application form required.
Trustee: John G. Davies.
EIN: 330102774
Codes: GTI

58874
Bon Air Cottage Foundation
P.O. Box 732
Kentfield, CA 94914

Established in 1980 in CA.
Donor(s): Harriet W. Richards.
Financial data (yr. ended 09/30/01): Assets, $131,354 (M); grants paid, $0; gifts received, $76,200; expenditures, $283,259; qualifying distributions, $0.
Officers: Doris Sutter, Pres.; Delpha Carpenter, Secy.; Harriet W. Richards, Treas.
Director: Richard Topkins.
EIN: 942598874

58875
Hungaria Nostra Foundation of Los Angeles, Inc.
c/o Peter Szabadi
1800 Century Park E., Ste. 505
Los Angeles, CA 90067

Established in 1999 in CA.
Financial data (yr. ended 12/31/99): Assets, $131,303 (M); grants paid, $8,000; gifts received, $141,100; expenditures, $16,153; qualifying distributions, $16,153.
Limitations: Applications not accepted.
Application information: Contributes only to pre-selected organizations.
Officers and Directors:* Eszter Vecsey,* Pres.; Brigita Lapenieks,* V.P.; Peter Szabadi,* Secy.; George Csicsery, Ricki Fourmier, Fredrick Hertz, Klara Mihaly, Eva Szorenyi, Eva Voisin, Molly Walker.
EIN: 522136473

58876
The Van der Geld Foundation
1343 S. Delay Ave.
Glendora, CA 91740

Established in 1997 in CA.
Donor(s): Alicia Vega-Van der Geld, Wladimir R. Van der Geld.
Financial data (yr. ended 12/31/99): Assets, $130,466 (M); grants paid, $6,756; gifts received, $4,230; expenditures, $7,624; qualifying distributions, $6,756.
Limitations: Applications not accepted.
Application information: Contributes only to pre-selected organizations.
Officers: Wladimir R. Van der Geld, Pres.; Alicia Vega-Van der Geld, Secy.-Treas.
EIN: 954610064

58877
Tai Won Suhr Foundation
3600 Wilshire Blvd., Ste. 1130
Los Angeles, CA 90010-2615 (213) 389-7356
Contact: Tong S. Suhr., Secy.

Donor(s): Tong S. Suhr.
Financial data (yr. ended 08/31/00): Assets, $130,179 (M); grants paid, $10,400; gifts received, $2,900; expenditures, $11,473; qualifying distributions, $10,400.
Limitations: Giving primarily in Los Angeles, CA.
Application information: Application form required.
Officers: T. Young Suhr, C.E.O.; Tong S. Suhr, Secy.; Tong M. Suhr, C.F.O.
EIN: 953976254

58878
B. B. and A. B. Bhagwat Trust
1769 Midwick Dr.
Altadena, CA 91001

Financial data (yr. ended 12/31/00): Assets, $127,126 (M); grants paid, $3,998; gifts received, $744; expenditures, $4,742; qualifying distributions, $4,742.
Limitations: Applications not accepted.
Application information: Contributes only to pre-selected organizations.
Trustees: Roy F. Grim, John Klotzle, Ben Mailbach, Jr.
EIN: 956791579

58879
Christian Business Ministries
24021 Lodge Pole Rd.
Diamond Bar, CA 91765
Contact: Alfred D. Hollingsworth, Pres.

Established in 1989 in CA.
Donor(s): Alfred D. Hollingsworth.
Financial data (yr. ended 12/31/99): Assets, $126,374 (M); grants paid, $14,610; gifts received, $376,087; expenditures, $281,346; qualifying distributions, $290,397; giving activities include $69,492 for programs.
Officers and Directors:* Alfred D. Hollingsworth,* Pres.; Hattie E. Hollingsworth,* Secy.; Gwethalyn Denise Talbert.
EIN: 954231341

58880
The Bodhi Sea Foundation
1840 Hurst Ave.
San Jose, CA 95125 (408) 723-8000
Contact: Albert Jen-Ta Lee, Pres.

Classified as a private operating foundation in 2000 in CA.
Donor(s): Albert Jen-Ta Lee.
Financial data (yr. ended 12/31/00): Assets, $119,057 (M); grants paid, $1,690; gifts received, $23,167; expenditures, $16,557; qualifying distributions, $16,043; giving activities include $14,427 for programs.
Officers and Director:* Albert Jen-Ta Lee,* Pres.; Ying Chen, V.P. and Secy.-Treas.
EIN: 770529339

58881
Vitamin D Workshop, Inc.
c/o Dept. of Bio-Chemistry
University of California, Webber Hall E.
Riverside, CA 92521-0129

Financial data (yr. ended 01/31/00): Assets, $118,694 (M); grants paid, $0; expenditures, $37,368; qualifying distributions, $35,316; giving activities include $15,654 for programs.
Officers: Anthony W. Norman, Ph.D., Pres.; Roger Bouillon, Secy.-Treas.
Director: Helen C. Henry, Ph.D.
EIN: 953173850

58882
The Guardian Angel Foundation
8320 Highway 99 E.
Los Molinos, CA 96055

Established in 1999 in CA.
Financial data (yr. ended 06/30/01): Assets, $118,631 (M); grants paid, $0; gifts received, $47,942; expenditures, $11,307; qualifying distributions, $0; giving activities include $9,309 for programs.
Limitations: Applications not accepted.
Application information: Contributes only to pre-selected organizations.
Trustees: Brenda Eitzen, Joe Eitzen.
EIN: 943341754

58883
David R. Trattner Foundation
c/o Joyce Leanse
1004 10th St.
Santa Monica, CA 90403-4105

Financial data (yr. ended 06/30/01): Assets, $115,209 (M); grants paid, $1,425; expenditures, $2,568; qualifying distributions, $1,425.
Limitations: Applications not accepted. Giving primarily in CA.
Application information: Contributes only to pre-selected organizations.
Officers: Barbara T. Bilson-Woodruff, C.E.O.; Joyce Leanse, Secy.-Treas.
Director: Jay Leanse.
EIN: 956085098

58884
Drucilla Barner Memorial Foundation
6640 Dahlberg Ct.
Foresthill, CA 95631-0714

Financial data (yr. ended 12/31/00): Assets, $113,062 (M); grants paid, $0; expenditures, $5,330; qualifying distributions, $4,081; giving activities include $3,208 for programs.
Officers: Jim Larimer,* Pres.; Marvin Jacinto,* V.P.; Larry Suddjian,* Secy.; Walt Tibbetts,* Treas.
Directors: Curt Sproul, Jack Veal.
EIN: 942271679

58885
The Shah Family Foundation
12104 Marilla Dr.
Saratoga, CA 95070

Donor(s): Bipin A. Shah, Rekha Shah.
Financial data (yr. ended 12/31/00): Assets, $110,135 (M); grants paid, $5,000; expenditures, $6,763; qualifying distributions, $5,000.
Limitations: Applications not accepted.
Application information: Contributes only to pre-selected organizations.
Trustees: Bipin A. Shah, Rekha Shah.
EIN: 770457575

58886
Charles M. Tracey Foundation
8825 Hollywood Blvd.
Los Angeles, CA 90069-1306

Classified as a private operating foundation in 1997.
Financial data (yr. ended 12/31/00): Assets, $109,280 (L); grants paid, $1,500; expenditures, $2,355; qualifying distributions, $1,500.
Director: Charles M. Tracey.
EIN: 954615980

58887
American Institute of Mathematics
360 Portage Ave.
Palo Alto, CA 94306 (650) 845-2071
FAX: (650) 845-2074
Contact: John Brian Conrey, Exec. Dir.

Established in 1994 in CA.
Donor(s): National Science Foundation, Fry's Electronics.
Financial data (yr. ended 12/31/00): Assets, $107,065 (M); grants paid, $318,127; gifts received, $304,897; expenditures, $859,523; qualifying distributions, $805,621; giving activities include $386,564 for programs.
Limitations: Giving on a national basis.
Publications: Biennial report.
Application information: Application should include a curriculum vita, 3 letters of reference, and a research plan. Application form not required.
Officers: Gerald L. Alexanderson, Chair.; Stephen Sorenson, Pres.; John Fry, Secy.; John Brian Conrey, Exec. Dir.
EIN: 943205114
Codes: FD

58888
Vision of Children
12730 High Bluff Dr., Ste. 250
San Diego, CA 92130 (858) 799-0810
URL: http://www.visionofchildren.org
Contact: Ron Nehring, Exec. Dir.

Financial data (yr. ended 12/31/01): Assets, $106,728 (M); grants paid, $125,748; gifts received, $27,782; expenditures, $226,042; qualifying distributions, $136,118.
Limitations: Applications not accepted.
Publications: Newsletter, informational brochure.
Application information: Contributes only to pre-selected organizations.
Officers and Directors:* Samuel A. Hardage,* Chair.; Darla Lopez, Secy.; Ron Nehring, Exec. Dir.; Craig Watson, C.F.O.; Debora B. Farber, Ph.D., Vivian L. Hardage, Jackie Johnson, Jan Tuttleman-Kriegler, Ken Widder.
EIN: 954271785
Codes: FD2

58889
LASO Foundation
(Formerly LASO Public/Private Partnership Foundation)
4700 Ramona Blvd.
Monterey Park, CA 91754

Established in 1987 in CA.
Financial data (yr. ended 06/30/01): Assets, $104,596 (M); grants paid, $2,741; gifts received, $121,000; expenditures, $22,767; qualifying distributions, $2,741.
Limitations: Applications not accepted.
Directors: Peter W. Dauterive, Herbert Hoover III, Louis A. Kwiker, Stephen J. Mulvany, Russell K. Snow, Jr., Mark Spraic, Carl Terzian, Gilbert R. Vasquez, John Winthrop.
EIN: 954151708

58890
Maddie's Spirit
2223 Santa Clara Ave., Ste. B
Alameda, CA 94501-4471

Established in 2000 in NV.
Donor(s): David A. Duffield.
Financial data (yr. ended 12/31/00): Assets, $103,470 (M); grants paid, $0; gifts received, $95,520; expenditures, $22,413; qualifying distributions, $22,413.
Limitations: Applications not accepted.
Application information: Contributes only to pre-selected organizations.
Officers: Amy D. Zeifang, Chair.; Richard Avanzino, Pres.; Laurie E. Peek, Secy.; Margaret L. Taylor, Treas.
Directors: Cheryl D. Duffield, David A. Duffield, Michael D. Duffield.
EIN: 943362163

58891
Jhass Foundation
P.O. Box 54081
San Jose, CA 95154-0081

Established in 2000 in CA.
Donor(s): Joseph Hassoun.
Financial data (yr. ended 10/31/01): Assets, $101,108 (M); grants paid, $10,000; gifts received, $212,438; expenditures, $59,048; qualifying distributions, $46,752; giving activities include $36,752 for programs.
Officers and Director:* Joseph Hassoun, Pres. and C.F.O.; May Alhariri,* Secy.
EIN: 770557845

58892
American Home Buyers Alliance Foundation
15585 Monterey Rd., Ste. E
Morgan Hill, CA 95037
Contact: Tina Triano, Exec. Dir.

Established in 2000 in CA.
Financial data (yr. ended 06/30/01): Assets, $100,764 (M); grants paid, $76,140; gifts received, $184,620; expenditures, $84,467; qualifying distributions, $84,467.
Limitations: Applications not accepted. Giving primarily in Alameda, San Benito, and Santa Clara counties, CA.
Application information: Contributes only to pre-selected organizations.
Trustees: Jeffrey Mentzos, Ted Triano.
EIN: 770544490
Codes: FD2

58893
Checkver Foundation, Inc.
c/o Simon Wyler
22225 Village 22
Camarillo, CA 93012

Financial data (yr. ended 02/28/99): Assets, $100,499 (M); grants paid, $5,476; expenditures, $6,003; qualifying distributions, $5,476.
Limitations: Applications not accepted. Giving primarily in CA.
Application information: Contributes only to pre-selected organizations.
Officer: Simon Wyler, Pres.
EIN: 136151479

58894
Rare & Wild Presentations, Inc.
18865 Santee Ln.
Valley Center, CA 92082-6807

Classified as a private operating foundation in 1990.
Financial data (yr. ended 12/31/01): Assets, $100,077 (M); grants paid, $0; expenditures, $255,873; qualifying distributions, $0.
Officers: David Nix, Pres.; Ron Hendriquez, V.P.; Renee Nix, Secy.; Bill Berill, Treas.
EIN: 330381109

58895
Robert J. Pond Foundation
c/o Robert J. Pond
64725 Acanto Dr.
Palm Springs, CA 92264

Established in 1995 in CA.
Donor(s): Robert J. Pond.
Financial data (yr. ended 12/31/01): Assets, $99,925 (M); grants paid, $0; gifts received, $4,973; expenditures, $3,933; qualifying distributions, $0.
Limitations: Applications not accepted. Giving primarily in CA.
Officers and Directors:* Robert J. Pond,* Pres.; Jo R. Pond, Secy.-Treas.; Bernard Aldrich, Polly Holley.
EIN: 330597788

58896
Mimbres Foundation
200 E. Del Mar, Ste. 250
Pasadena, CA 91105-2552

Classified as a private operating foundation in 1976.
Donor(s): Jay T. Last, Laura Stearns.
Financial data (yr. ended 12/31/01): Assets, $99,373 (M); grants paid, $0; gifts received, $5,000; expenditures, $4,981; qualifying distributions, $0.

Officers: Steven LeBlanc, Pres.; Laura Stearns, Secy.
Directors: Anthony Berlant, Jay T. Last.
EIN: 510186037

58897
Kern River Wildlife Sanctuary
360 Palos Verdes Dr. W.
Palos Verdes Estates, CA 90274-1212

Donor(s): Carl G. Allen.
Financial data (yr. ended 12/31/01): Assets, $98,993 (M); grants paid, $0; gifts received, $1,923; expenditures, $2,067; qualifying distributions, $0.
Officers and Directors:* Carl G. Allen,* Chair.; Daniel R. Christenson,* V.P.; Jennifer Babcock,* Secy.; Darcel Ramirez.
EIN: 953624496

58898
The Niels Wessel Bagge Art Foundation
c/o Fred Vandeveer
600 W. Broadway, Ste. 2600
San Diego, CA 92101
Application address: Sankt Anne Plads 28, 1250 Copenhagen, Denmark
Contact: Arne Engel, Tr.

Established in 1990 in CA; foundation not yet fully funded.
Donor(s): Niels Wessel Bagge.
Financial data (yr. ended 12/31/00): Assets, $98,720 (M); grants paid, $213,912; expenditures, $341,640; qualifying distributions, $341,379.
Limitations: Giving on an international basis, primarily Denmark.
Application information: Write for application information. Application form required.
Trustees: Arne Engel, Arthur Krasilnidoff, Anders Refn, Ebbe Wedell-Wedellsburg.
EIN: 954325239
Codes: FD2

58899
Ronald Coleman & Jill Coleman Charitable Foundation
99 Almaden Blvd., Ste. 500
San Jose, CA 95113
Contact: Jill P. Coleman, Secy.

Established in 1999 in CA.
Donor(s): Jill P. Coleman, Ronald G. Coleman.
Financial data (yr. ended 12/31/00): Assets, $98,294 (M); grants paid, $10,830; expenditures, $16,248; qualifying distributions, $11,519.
Officers and Directors:* Ronald G. Coleman,* Pres. and Treas.; Jill P. Coleman,* Secy.
EIN: 770499810

58900
Little C Athletic Club
1380 Galaxy Way
Concord, CA 94520-4912

Established in 1995 in CA.
Financial data (yr. ended 12/31/00): Assets, $98,027 (M); grants paid, $0; gifts received, $223,608; expenditures, $283,182; qualifying distributions, $215,985; giving activities include $283,182 for programs.
Officers: Ron Dawson, Pres.; Nick S. Rossi, Secy.; Dennis Drew, Treas.
EIN: 680358005

58901
Riverside County Physicians Memorial Foundation
3993 Jurupa Ave.
Riverside, CA 92506 (909) 686-3342

Financial data (yr. ended 12/31/00): Assets, $96,027 (M); grants paid, $0; gifts received, $71,848; expenditures, $106,088; qualifying distributions, $94,187; giving activities include $465,412 for programs.
Officers: William Cherry, Pres.; John Osborne, Secy.-Treas.; Dolores L. Green, Exec. Dir.
EIN: 956080778
Codes: TN

58902
Young People of Watts, Inc.
10712 Wilmington Ave.
Los Angeles, CA 90059

Financial data (yr. ended 12/31/00): Assets, $93,143 (M); grants paid, $0; gifts received, $88,260; expenditures, $188,267; qualifying distributions, $0.
Officers: Robert Saucedo, Pres.; Anthony Kerr, Secy.
EIN: 952765099

58903
The Parkos Family Foundation
420 Carroll Canal
Venice, CA 90291

Established in 1995 in CA.
Donor(s): Gregory T. Parkos.
Financial data (yr. ended 08/31/00): Assets, $91,809 (M); grants paid, $38,300; expenditures, $39,531; qualifying distributions, $38,240.
Officers: Gregory T. Parkos, C.E.O.; Nadine Leonsky, Secy. and C.F.O.
Directors: Elaine Holder, January M. Parkos.
EIN: 954546275

58904
Compassion for Animals Foundation, Inc.
3962 Landmark St.
Culver City, CA 90232-2315
Contact: Gilbert N. Michaels, Pres.

Established in 1986 in CA.
Donor(s): Gilbert N. Michaels.
Financial data (yr. ended 11/30/01): Assets, $91,474 (L); grants paid, $297,400; gifts received, $300,000; expenditures, $297,507; qualifying distributions, $297,507.
Limitations: Giving on a national basis.
Application information: Application form not required.
Officers: Gilbert N. Michaels, Pres.; Julie Javor, Secy.; Lonnie Horn, C.F.O.
EIN: 954082225
Codes: FD

58905
Manasseh's Children
1011 Shotwell St.
San Francisco, CA 94110-4015

Financial data (yr. ended 12/31/00): Assets, $91,325 (L); grants paid, $15,488; gifts received, $40,899; expenditures, $33,817; qualifying distributions, $31,583.
Limitations: Applications not accepted. Giving primarily in San Francisco, CA.
Application information: Contributes only to pre-selected organizations.
Officers: Michael Jacob Sinclair, Pres.; Merilee Rossi, Secy.; Paloma Carbonel, Treas.
EIN: 943226540

58906
LHP Educational Foundation, Inc.
469 18th St.
Santa Monica, CA 90402

Established in 1999 in CA.
Donor(s): Baye Foundation, Inc.
Financial data (yr. ended 12/31/99): Assets, $90,977 (M); grants paid, $0; gifts received, $116,240; expenditures, $26,067; qualifying distributions, $37,622; giving activities include $10,954 for programs.
Officer: Lizl Peter, Exec. Dir.
Directors: Kal Eisenberg, M.D., Penny Fogel.
EIN: 954748982

58907
Booth-Holt-Carlson Foundation
2616 Cove St.
Corona Del Mar, CA 92625

Donor(s): Karen Carlson.
Financial data (yr. ended 12/31/01): Assets, $90,910 (M); grants paid, $19,849; gifts received, $35,572; expenditures, $21,144; qualifying distributions, $21,129.
Limitations: Applications not accepted.
Application information: Contributes only to pre-selected organizations.
Officers: Karen K. Carlson, Pres.; Wendy Holt, Secy.; Bonnie Holt, Treas.
Director: Bonnie Carlson.
EIN: 237055571

58908
La Jolla Children's Foundation
7440 La Jolla Blvd
La Jolla, CA 92037-5029

Established in 1996 in CA; classified as a private operating foundation in 1999.
Financial data (yr. ended 12/31/01): Assets, $90,697 (M); grants paid, $0; expenditures, $35; qualifying distributions, $0.
Limitations: Applications not accepted. Giving primarily in Carmel, La Jolla, San Diego, CA.
Application information: Contributes only to pre-selected organizations.
Officers: Marc Chase, Pres.; Rueh Chase, Secy.; Jack Runke, Treas.
EIN: 330729725

58909
Foundation for the Preservation of the Mt. Helix Nature Theatre
P.O. Box 2733, Ste. 2220
La Mesa, CA 91944

Established in 1999 in CA.
Financial data (yr. ended 12/31/00): Assets, $89,557 (M); grants paid, $0; gifts received, $34,569; expenditures, $65,538; qualifying distributions, $0; giving activities include $65,462 for programs.
Limitations: Applications not accepted.
Application information: Contributes only to pre-selected organizations.
Officers: Robert A. Ball, Pres.; Mark B. Allan, V.P.; John D. Mead, V.P.; Sheryl A. Russell, V.P.; Alvin W. Platt, Secy.; Robert C. Cederdahl, Treas.
EIN: 330859352

58910
Operation One Warm Coat Plus/Children of Shelters
3560 Jackson St.
San Francisco, CA 94118

Financial data (yr. ended 12/31/00): Assets, $89,010 (M); grants paid, $0; gifts received, $67,816; expenditures, $45,918; qualifying distributions, $45,918; giving activities include $34,650 for programs.
Officers: Lois Pavlow, Pres.; Summer Tompkins-Walker, V.P.; Celia Barbaccia, Secy.; Sandra Wilder, Treas.
EIN: 943192608

58911
International World Peace Rose Gardens, Inc.
P.O. Box 15919
Sacramento, CA 95852-0919

Donor(s): T.J. David.
Financial data (yr. ended 12/31/00): Assets, $89,002 (M); grants paid, $0; gifts received, $19,113; expenditures, $8,460; qualifying distributions, $0.
Officer: T.J. David, Pres.
EIN: 680150998

58912
Fund for the Environment
522 N. Foothill Rd.
Beverly Hills, CA 90210-3402

Financial data (yr. ended 06/30/01): Assets, $88,595 (M); grants paid, $295; gifts received, $12,561; expenditures, $36,237; qualifying distributions, $36,237; giving activities include $46,394 for programs.
Officers: Ellen Stern Harris, Pres.; Betty H. Harris, V.P.; Sam Weisz, Secy.-Treas.
EIN: 953465332

58913
The Sherwood Foundation
2139 Century Woods Way
Los Angeles, CA 90067

Donor(s): Joseph Sherwood, Helene Sherwood.
Financial data (yr. ended 12/31/99): Assets, $88,461 (M); grants paid, $40,220; gifts received, $206,286; expenditures, $40,298; qualifying distributions, $40,220.
Limitations: Applications not accepted.
Application information: Contributes only to pre-selected organizations.
Officers: Joseph Sherwood, Pres.; Helene Sherwood, V.P.
EIN: 957042886

58914
The Esseff Foundation
351 Cortez Cir.
Camarillo, CA 93012 (805) 388-2138
FAX: (805) 987-6492

Donor(s): George Esseff, Sr., Supra Alloys, Inc.
Financial data (yr. ended 12/31/01): Assets, $88,109 (M); grants paid, $441,425; gifts received, $404,548; expenditures, $443,514; qualifying distributions, $441,425.
Limitations: Giving primarily in Arlington, VA, and CA, with emphasis on Thousand Oaks.
Officers: George J. Esseff, Pres.; Rosemary C. Esseff, Secy.
EIN: 953447950
Codes: FD

58915
Melvyn M. Okeon Charitable Foundation
2650 Sun Dr.
Hanford, CA 93230
Contact: Melvyn M. Okeon, Tr.

Established in 1998 in CA.
Donor(s): Melvyn M. Okeon, M.D.
Financial data (yr. ended 12/31/99): Assets, $87,308 (M); grants paid, $5,500; gifts received, $27,600; expenditures, $5,500; qualifying distributions, $5,500.
Limitations: Giving primarily in CA.

58915—CALIFORNIA

Trustee: Melvyn M. Okeon, M.D.
EIN: 770472673

58916
Southern California Track & Field Officials Endowment Fund
11300 Olympic Blvd., No. 870
Los Angeles, CA 90064   (310) 477-3612
Contact: Neil M. Baizer, Tr.

Donor(s): Neil M. Baizer.
Financial data (yr. ended 12/31/99): Assets, $87,205 (M); grants paid, $5,000; expenditures, $5,000; qualifying distributions, $5,000.
Limitations: Giving limited to southern CA.
Trustees: Neil M. Baizer, Sydney Kronenthal, George Poole.
EIN: 953792763

58917
Healthcare Partners Insititute for Applied Research & Education
19191 S. Vermont Ave.
Torrance, CA 90502

Established in 1996 in CA.
Financial data (yr. ended 12/31/99): Assets, $85,338 (M); grants paid, $4,722; gifts received, $129,371; expenditures, $174,365; qualifying distributions, $174,365; giving activities include $89,298 for programs.
Limitations: Applications not accepted.
Application information: Contributes only to pre-selected organizations.
Officers and Directors:* William Chin, M.D.,* Chair., C.E.O., and Pres.; John Johnson, M.D., Secy.; Ralph Mendez, M.D.,* Treas.; Matthew Mazdyasni, C.F.O.; Edward Zapanta, M.D.
EIN: 954591816

58918
Indo-American Foundation, Inc.
8254 E. Lorain Rd.
San Gabriel, CA 91775
Contact: Dr. Ramadas Abboy, Pres.

Established in 1988 in CA.
Donor(s): D.C. Dellinger,‡ Ramadas Abboy, S. Jagannathan, Naina Mohamed Rahman.
Financial data (yr. ended 12/31/01): Assets, $84,321 (M); grants paid, $63,339; gifts received, $161,775; expenditures, $80,159; qualifying distributions, $80,155.
Limitations: Giving primarily in India.
Officers: Ramadas Abboy, Pres.; Rajamannar Abboy, Secy.-Treas.
EIN: 954156556

58919
The Dirk Foundation
990 Bayside Cove W.
Newport Beach, CA 92660

Established in 1999 in CA.
Donor(s): Patrick Dirk, Mary Dirk.
Financial data (yr. ended 12/31/00): Assets, $81,316 (M); grants paid, $60,000; expenditures, $112,278; qualifying distributions, $108,191.
Officers: Mary Dirk, Pres.; Patrick J. Dirk, V.P. and Treas.; Brian Dirk, Secy.; Suzanna Dirk Anderson, C.F.O.
Board Members: Lorrie Dirk Brown, Kristine Dirk Gigerich.
EIN: 330887916

58920
Geraldine M. Derkum Panhellenic Scholarship Foundation
c/o Laurie Odlum
13582 Oak Hill Ct.
Yucaipa, CA 92399-9738
Application address: c/o Marcia Swanson, 215 Grandview, Redlands, CA 92373

Established in 1998 in CA.
Financial data (yr. ended 05/31/01): Assets, $81,303 (M); grants paid, $3,250; gifts received, $53,875; expenditures, $3,250; qualifying distributions, $3,250.
Limitations: Giving limited to residents in Redlands, CA.
Officers: Betty Jones, Pres.; Charline Kuntz, V.P.; Alice Daniels, Secy.-Treas.
Advisor: Laurie Odlum.
EIN: 330713399

58921
Canaries Foundation, Inc.
1930 Castillo Ct.
San Luis Obispo, CA 93405   (805) 547-1568

Established in 2000 in CA.
Donor(s): John A. Mc Elver.
Financial data (yr. ended 12/31/00): Assets, $81,288 (M); grants paid, $0; gifts received, $91,507; expenditures, $0; qualifying distributions, $0.
Application information: Application form not required.
Officers: Linda J. Mc Elver, Pres. and Treas.; John A. Mc Elver, V.P. and Secy.
EIN: 770559174

58922
Tim and Teresa Belcher Foundation
c/o Bill D. Ringer
1401 N. Hunter St.
Stockton, CA 95202

Donor(s): Timothy W. Belcher, Teresa H. Belcher.
Financial data (yr. ended 12/31/01): Assets, $81,192 (M); grants paid, $108,100; gifts received, $50,000; expenditures, $112,637; qualifying distributions, $108,100.
Limitations: Applications not accepted. Giving primarily in Fulton and Sparta, OH.
Application information: Contributes only to pre-selected organizations.
Directors: Teresa H. Belcher, Timothy W. Belcher, William D. Short.
EIN: 311486809
Codes: FD2

58923
Hierarchical Systerms Research Foundation
2826 Glen Dixon Ct.
San Jose, CA 95148

Established in 2001 in CA and DE.
Donor(s): David G. Doshay, Aviva Garrett.
Financial data (yr. ended 12/31/01): Assets, $79,854 (M); grants paid, $0; gifts received, $93,358; expenditures, $13,578; qualifying distributions, $13,578.
Officers and Director:* David G. Doshay, Pres.; Aviva Garrett,* Secy.
EIN: 943395824

58924
Country Woman's Club
P.O. Box 322
Campbell, CA 95009-0322

Financial data (yr. ended 06/30/99): Assets, $79,293 (M); grants paid, $11,740; gifts received, $5,541; expenditures, $16,972; qualifying distributions, $14,546.
Limitations: Giving primarily in Campbell and San Jose, CA.
Officers: Julie Kenney, Pres.; Barbara Campbell, 1st V.P.; Joan Reynolds, 2nd V.P.; Lois Ferro, Corresponding Secy.; Jane Madeiros, Recording Secy.; Pat Laufman, Treas.
Directors: Lorraine Gerin, Grace Shepard.
EIN: 941189432

58925
Touching Hands Foundation
550 W. C St., Ste. 1700
San Diego, CA 92101
Contact: Keenan W. McCardell, Dir.

Classified as a company-sponsored operating foundation.
Donor(s): CWC Sports, Jacksonville Chambers of Commerce, Quadra Productions, First Union National Bank, Battle by the Beach.
Financial data (yr. ended 08/31/01): Assets, $78,371 (M); grants paid, $1,812; gifts received, $18,506; expenditures, $66,894; qualifying distributions, $6,689.
Directors: Keenan W. McCardell, Nicole R. McCardell, Cleve Warren.
EIN: 593529626

58926
BK Medical Research Foundation
P.O. Box 6406
San Bernardino, CA 92412

Classified as a private operating foundation in 1978.
Donor(s): Brian S. Bull, M.D., Ralph A. Korpman, M.D.
Financial data (yr. ended 12/31/00): Assets, $76,043 (M); grants paid, $0; expenditures, $2,966; qualifying distributions, $2,566; giving activities include $2,462 for programs.
Officers: Brian S. Bull, M.D., Pres.; Ralph A. Korpman, M.D., V.P.
EIN: 953298222

58927
Croatian National Foundation
c/o Bernard Kotkin & Co.
520 S. Virgil Ave., Ste. 202
Los Angeles, CA 90020-1405

Established in 1991 in CA.
Financial data (yr. ended 12/31/99): Assets, $76,012 (M); grants paid, $136,415; gifts received, $102,553; expenditures, $138,574; qualifying distributions, $136,415.
Officers: Leo A. Majich, Pres.; Mike Volarich, V.P.; Peter Serdarusich, Financial Secy.; Heidi Granic, Treas.
Trustees: Zdravka Maruna, Mile J. Rasic.
EIN: 954065779
Codes: FD2

58928
Creative World, Inc.
9231 Gerald Ave.
Sepulveda, CA 91343

Financial data (yr. ended 06/30/00): Assets, $73,696 (M); grants paid, $0; gifts received, $228,107; expenditures, $228,242; qualifying distributions, $2,282,242; giving activities include $228,242 for programs.
Director: Lenny Levitz.
EIN: 954351317

58929
The Gerald and Sheila Jeffry Foundation
2730 Lone Tree Way., Ste. 1
Antioch, CA 94509
Contact: Gerald Jeffry, Pres.

Established in 1999 in CA.
Donor(s): Gerald Jeffry.
Financial data (yr. ended 12/31/00): Assets, $73,644 (M); grants paid, $4,800; expenditures, $4,800; qualifying distributions, $4,800.
Officers: Gerald Jeffry, Pres. and Secy.; Sheila Jeffry, V.P.
EIN: 943347146

58930
Lithuanian Freedom Through Education Fund, Inc.
c/o Liuda Avizonis
25802 Prairiestone Dr.
Laguna Hills, CA 92653

Established in 1992.
Donor(s): Brone M. Jucenas.
Financial data (yr. ended 12/31/01): Assets, $73,146 (M); grants paid, $16,616; gifts received, $26,330; expenditures, $17,948; qualifying distributions, $17,558.
Officers and Directors:* Liuda V. Avizonis,* Pres. and Treas.; Gaile E. Callo,* Secy.; Petras A. Avizonis, Vilija Avizonis, Anthony L. Jucenas, Brone M. Jucenas, Milda E. Liaukus, Sigitas Liaukus, Gregory B. McComas.
EIN: 650352349

58931
VPI Skeeter Foundation
3060 Saturn St.
Brea, CA 92822-2344 (714) 989-0555
Contact: Jack Stephens, Chair.

Established in 2001 in CA.
Donor(s): Jack Stephens, Vicki Stephens.
Financial data (yr. ended 12/31/01): Assets, $72,796 (M); grants paid, $81,001; gifts received, $161,916; expenditures, $97,284; qualifying distributions, $81,001.
Limitations: Giving on a national basis, including Washington, DC.
Officers and Directors:* Jack Stephens, Chair.; Robin Itzler,* Treas.; Rebecca Lewis, Vicki Stephens.
EIN: 330906193
Codes: FD2

58932
La Madre de los Pobres
2310 Meadowlark Dr.
Pleasanton, CA 94566-3116

Financial data (yr. ended 12/31/01): Assets, $72,302 (M); grants paid, $51,130; gifts received, $47,512; expenditures, $65,742; qualifying distributions, $51,130.
Limitations: Applications not accepted. Giving on a national and international basis.
Application information: Contributes only to pre-selected organizations.
Officers: Fr. Lawrence Lorenzoni, C.E.O.; Robert Fouts, Secy.; Gregory Gollnick, Treas.
EIN: 942838830

58933
J. M. Brown Charitable Foundation
c/o Stanton Accountancy Corp.
10474 Santa Monica Blvd., Ste. 306
Los Angeles, CA 90025

Financial data (yr. ended 12/31/00): Assets, $71,673 (M); grants paid, $66,950; expenditures, $67,189; qualifying distributions, $67,189.

Limitations: Applications not accepted.
Application information: Contributes only to pre-selected organizations.
Directors: Michael M. Eisenberg, Jon Charles Stanton.
EIN: 954773277

58934
The Center for Jewish Campus Life, Inc.
P.O. Box Y
Stanford, CA 94309-3775

Established in 1998 in CA.
Donor(s): Israel Englander, Leonard Shustek.
Financial data (yr. ended 06/30/99): Assets, $71,613 (M); grants paid, $0; gifts received, $114,464; expenditures, $53,468; qualifying distributions, $63,164; giving activities include $20,488 for loans and $46,589 for programs.
Limitations: Applications not accepted.
Application information: Contributes only to pre-selected organizations.
Officer: Bob Rosenzweig, Pres.
Directors: Sarah Bernstein-Jones, Michael Cowan, Shirley Feldman, Debra Feldstein, Rabbi Patricia Karlin-Neuman, Steve Zipperstein.
EIN: 770492512

58935
Making Waves Foundation, Inc.
591 Redwood Hwy., Ste. 3215
Mill Valley, CA 94941

Financial data (yr. ended 12/31/99): Assets, $70,609 (M); grants paid, $298,000; gifts received, $410,000; expenditures, $347,996; qualifying distributions, $347,801; giving activities include $49,804 for programs.
Limitations: Applications not accepted.
Application information: Contributes only to pre-selected organizations.
Officers: John Scully, Chair.; Portia Moore, Pres.; Donna Hubbard, V.P.; Donna Brown, Secy.; Sherry Smith, Treas.; Glenn W. Holsclaw, Exec. Dir.
EIN: 680204312

58936
The Thomopoulos Family Foundation
11726 San Vicente Blvd., Ste. 360
Los Angeles, CA 90049
Contact: Anthony D. Thomopoulos, V.P.

Financial data (yr. ended 12/31/00): Assets, $69,402 (M); grants paid, $63,113; gifts received, $8,300; expenditures, $63,143; qualifying distributions, $63,113.
Limitations: Giving primarily in CA.
Officers and Directors: Cristina Ferrare Thomopoulos,* Pres.; Anthony D. Thomopoulos,* V.P. and Secy.-Treas.; Sidney R. Tessler.
EIN: 945654619

58937
San Joaquin Valley Citizens For a Healthy Environment
P.O. Box 158
Kingsburg, CA 93631-0158 (559) 896-4420
Contact: David Michel, Pres.

Financial data (yr. ended 10/31/00): Assets, $69,044 (M); grants paid, $2,500; gifts received, $25,000; expenditures, $5,193; qualifying distributions, $5,193.
Limitations: Giving limited to Selma and Kingsburg, CA.
Officers: David Michel, Pres.; Ronald Beringer, V.P.; Ralph Garcia, Secy.-Treas.
EIN: 770289770

58938
Scottology Foundation
45 Nora Ct.
Walnut Creek, CA 94596

Established in 1999 in CA.
Financial data (yr. ended 12/31/01): Assets, $66,024 (M); grants paid, $0; gifts received, $65,163; expenditures, $80,921; qualifying distributions, $80,921.
Directors: Ann B. Scott, Lloyd F. Scott, Sally A. Scott, Susan S. Wiley.
EIN: 311470597

58939
California Age Research Institute, Inc.
1007 Live Oak Blvd., Ste. A-2
Yuba City, CA 95991-3454
Application address: P.O. Box 212, Yuba City, CA 95992
Contact: Leon M. Edelstein, M.D., Pres.

Donor(s): Leon M. Edelstein, M.D.
Financial data (yr. ended 12/31/99): Assets, $65,796 (M); grants paid, $5,000; gifts received, $6,584; expenditures, $8,216; qualifying distributions, $7,162.
Limitations: Giving primarily in Davis and Rio Oso, CA.
Officers: Leon M. Edelstein, M.D., Pres.; Lester Rose, M.D., V.P.; Karen Van Dyke, Secy.; Michael Gabhart, Treas.
Directors: Susan Bourland, Roger McDonald, Rachelle Ornelas.
EIN: 942676615

58940
Perseverence in Space & Mass Foundation
1950 1/2 Adeline St.
Oakland, CA 94607

Established in 1997; classified as a private operating foundation in 1998.
Donor(s): Joseph Farais.
Financial data (yr. ended 06/30/99): Assets, $64,610 (M); grants paid, $936; gifts received, $10,000; expenditures, $27,793; qualifying distributions, $27,150; giving activities include $1,745 for programs.
Officer and Trustees:* Joseph Farais,* Exec. Dir.; Jan Strong, Gail Wagner, Cedric Westworth.
EIN: 943289454

58941
Infectious Disease Research Institute
5601 Norris Canyon Rd., Ste. 220
San Ramon, CA 94583-5407

Established in 1989 in CA.
Financial data (yr. ended 06/30/01): Assets, $64,104 (M); grants paid, $0; gifts received, $17,500; expenditures, $6,386; qualifying distributions, $0; giving activities include $4,665 for programs.
Officers: Patrick Joseph, M.D., Pres.; June Joseph, V.P.
EIN: 943100486

58942
Victor and Wendy Coleman Family Foundation
11601 Wilshire Blvd., 4th Fl.
Los Angeles, CA 90025-1740
FAX: (310) 966-9494
Contact: Victor J. Coleman, Pres.

Established in 1997 in CA.
Financial data (yr. ended 12/31/01): Assets, $62,112 (M); grants paid, $68,500; gifts received, $75,000; expenditures, $68,556; qualifying distributions, $68,548.
Limitations: Applications not accepted.

58942—CALIFORNIA

Application information: Contributes only to pre-selected organizations.
Officers: Victor J. Coleman, Pres.; Wendy Coleman, Secy.
EIN: 954637142

58943
Women's International Center
6202 Friars Rd., No. 311
San Diego, CA 92108-1008 (619) 295-6446
Contact: Gloria Lane, Pres.

Classified as a private operating foundation in 1983.
Financial data (yr. ended 12/31/00): Assets, $61,890 (M); grants paid, $4,500; expenditures, $54,173; qualifying distributions, $4,500.
Limitations: Giving primarily in CA.
Officers and Directors:* Gloria Lane,* Pres.; Betty Nicholson,* V.P.; Mary Vaughn,* Secy.-Treas.; Janice Abbasov, Mary Ellen Hamilton, Marianne McDonald, Christy Billing Pasela, Robert Rector, Ph.D., Jody Simms, Sally B. Thorton.
EIN: 953806872

58944
Marshall Faulk Foundation
550 W. C St., Ste. 1700
San Diego, CA 92101-3568
Application address: 1116 E. Market St., Indianapolis, IN 46202
Contact: Jennifer Weber, Exec. Dir.

Donor(s): Marshall Faulk.
Financial data (yr. ended 12/31/01): Assets, $61,734 (M); grants paid, $131,018; gifts received, $336,346; expenditures, $313,414; qualifying distributions, $204,351; giving activities include $51,832 for programs.
Officers: Marshall Faulk, Chair.; Rocky Arceneaux, Pres.; Melissa Forrest, Secy.; Jennifer Weber, Exec.Dir.
General Counsel: Leslie Bond.
EIN: 721280424
Codes: FD2

58945
Radakovich Foundation
1038 Springfield Dr.
Walnut Creek, CA 94598-4359

Established in 1997 in CA.
Donor(s): Ronald Radakovich, Mildred Radakovich.
Financial data (yr. ended 12/31/99): Assets, $60,958 (M); grants paid, $30,434; expenditures, $35,681; qualifying distributions, $31,712.
Officers: Mildred Radakovich, Pres.; Ronald Radakovich, V.P.; Mike Radakovich, Secy.; Steve Radakovich, C.F.O.
EIN: 943271574

58946
The Brandenburg Historical Golf Museum
c/o Lee H. Brandenburg
333 W. Santa Clara St., Ste. 1212
San Jose, CA 95113-3103

Established in 1997 in CA.
Financial data (yr. ended 12/31/01): Assets, $60,936 (M); grants paid, $0; gifts received, $29,605; expenditures, $7,541; qualifying distributions, $0.
Officers: Lee H. Brandenburg, Pres.; Eric L. Brandenburg, V.P.; Ronald Zraick, Jr., Secretary-C.F.O.
Directors: William B. Baron, Diane M. Brandenburg.
EIN: 770463157

58947
Bellingham Porenta Foundation
485 Seaport Ct.
Redwood City, CA 94063
Application address: 1045 Deanna Ct., Menlo Park, CA 94025
Contact: William L. Warner, Pres.

Established in 1999 in CA.
Donor(s): William L. Warner.
Financial data (yr. ended 09/30/00): Assets, $60,295 (M); grants paid, $2,000; gifts received, $63,000; expenditures, $2,705; qualifying distributions, $2,000.
Limitations: Giving primarily in CA.
Officers: William L. Warner, Pres.; Juli E. Warner, Secy.-Treas.
EIN: 943349327

58948
Premier Hospitals Alliance Foundation
12225 El Camino Real
San Diego, CA 92130-2006

Established in 1992 in IL.
Donor(s): Beth Israel Boston, Beth Israel New York, Englewood Hospital, George Washington University, Georgia Baptist, Jewish Hospital-Louisville, Long Island Jewish Medical Ctr., Luthern of Indiana, Medical Ctr. of Central Mass, Monmouth Medical Ctr., Montefiore Medical Ctr., Newark Beth Israel, Providence Svcs., St. Vincent Medical Ctr., Summa Health System, University of Rochester/Strong Medical.
Financial data (yr. ended 12/31/00): Assets, $59,741 (M); grants paid, $5,000; expenditures, $13,963; qualifying distributions, $10,691.
Directors: Leo Brideau, Albert Gilbert, Ph.D., Allen Johnson, Phillip S. Schaengold, Robert J. Shakno, M. Kent Strum, Alan Weinstein.
EIN: 363381741

58949
Canyon Research
2052 Galveston St.
San Diego, CA 92110-1303 (858) 578-8411
URL: http://www.canyonresearch.org

Established in 1996 in CA.
Donor(s): J.C. Downing Foundation.
Financial data (yr. ended 09/30/00): Assets, $57,717 (M); grants paid, $0; gifts received, $135,000; expenditures, $163,722; qualifying distributions, $141,232; giving activities include $105,003 for programs.
Limitations: Giving on a national and international basis.
Application information: The foundation periodically issues a call for applications. See Web site for details. All applications must be submitted with a SASE. Applications sent by FAX, E-mail, or without a SASE will not be considered. Correspondence sent by certified mail will not be accepted.
Officers: John C. Downing, Pres.; Toni M. Leadingham, Secy.
Director: Stuart A. Winkelman.
EIN: 330643597

58950
The Hon Foundation
25200 La Paz Rd., Ste. 210
Laguna Hills, CA 92653 (949) 586-4400

Established in 1979.
Donor(s): Barry G. Hon, Valerie Hon.
Financial data (yr. ended 12/31/01): Assets, $57,477 (M); grants paid, $3,000; gifts received, $10,000; expenditures, $4,315; qualifying distributions, $3,000.

Limitations: Applications not accepted. Giving primarily in CA and HI.
Application information: Contributes only to pre-selected organizations.
Trustees: Barry G. Hon, Valerie Hon, Darrellyn Hon Melilli.
EIN: 953335452

58951
The Vivra Children's Foundation
533 Airport Blvd., Ste. 300
Burlingame, CA 94010
Contact: Rosalva Depillo

Classified as a company-sponsored operating foundation in 1992.
Donor(s): Vivra Inc.
Financial data (yr. ended 11/30/00): Assets, $57,187 (M); grants paid, $3,000; expenditures, $3,024; qualifying distributions, $2,985.
Limitations: Giving primarily in areas of company operations.
Application information: Application form required.
Officers: Kent J. Thiry, Pres.; Leanne Zumwalt, C.F.O.
EIN: 943167232
Codes: CD

58952
American Institute for Strategic Cooperation
2179 Mandeville Rd.
Los Angeles, CA 90049

Established in 1987 in CA.
Financial data (yr. ended 08/31/00): Assets, $56,021 (M); grants paid, $0; expenditures, $1,998; qualifying distributions, $1,845; giving activities include $1,845 for programs.
Officers and Directors:* Roberta Wohlstetter,* Pres. and C.F.O.; Fred Hoffman, Secy.; Brian Chow, Samuel P. Huntington, Jim Roche, Harry Rowen.
EIN: 954104627

58953
Far West Institute
236 W. Portal Ave.
P.O. Box 27901-113
San Francisco, CA 94127-1423

Classified as a private operating foundation in 1977.
Financial data (yr. ended 06/30/01): Assets, $55,370 (M); grants paid, $0; gifts received, $20,000; expenditures, $345; qualifying distributions, $0.
Officers: Ellen Zaslow, Pres.; Olivia Byrne, Secy.-Treas.
EIN: 237336130

58954
Erlene Troth Skeet Trust
c/o Anthony E. Erbacher
11110 Red Cedar Dr.
San Diego, CA 92131

Established in 1990 in CA.
Donor(s): Philip Troth.
Financial data (yr. ended 12/31/99): Assets, $55,330 (M); grants paid, $2,740; expenditures, $2,797; qualifying distributions, $2,740.
Limitations: Applications not accepted. Giving primarily in CA.
Trustee: Anthony E. Erbacher, Brian Holt.
EIN: 336083760

58955
Marysville Art Club
420 10th St.
Marysville, CA 95901

Classified as a private operating foundation in 1972.
Financial data (yr. ended 05/31/01): Assets, $54,985 (M); grants paid, $500; gifts received, $2,007; expenditures, $15,656; qualifying distributions, $2,125.
Officers: Magel Carter, Pres.; Janice Ozawa, V.P.; Anita Russell, Corresponding Secy.; Anita McWhirk, Recording Secy.; Vadna Epley, Treas.
Directors: Elois Ebey, Jean Smith, Margaret Pursch.
EIN: 946102760

58956
Fiat Voluntas Trust
214 Alvarado Way
Tracy, CA 95376 (209) 944-0740
Contact: Marylyn Hoffman, C.E.O.

Established in 1997 in CA.
Donor(s): Marylyn Hoffman.
Financial data (yr. ended 12/31/99): Assets, $54,905 (M); grants paid, $33,885; gifts received, $20,500; expenditures, $49,926; qualifying distributions, $33,869; giving activities include $25,585 for programs.
Officers: Marylyn Hoffman, C.E.O.; George Tinawi, Secy.; Paula Yroz, C.F.O.
Director: Fr. Robert Faricy, S.J.
EIN: 770462187

58957
The GET Foundation
(Formerly Gordon Tam & Elsie K. Tam Charitable Foundation)
46 Eugenia Way
Hillsborough, CA 94010
Contact: Gordon Tam, Pres.

Established in 1999 in CA.
Donor(s): Gordon Tam.
Financial data (yr. ended 12/31/01): Assets, $53,559 (M); grants paid, $0; gifts received, $960; expenditures, $19,456; qualifying distributions, $19,270; giving activities include $2,283 for programs.
Officers and Directors:* Gordon Tam,* Pres. and Treas.; Elsie K. Tam,* V.P. and Secy.
EIN: 946746714

58958
Colonel William J. & Helen Jackson Scholarship Fund
c/o William C. Krantz
1470 N. Main St.
Lakeport, CA 95453-3847 (707) 263-0242
Application address: c/o Joyce McGregor, 1319 20th St., Lakeport, CA 95453
Contact: Phil N. Crawford, Mgr.

Financial data (yr. ended 12/31/01): Assets, $52,817 (M); grants paid, $3,000; expenditures, $3,734; qualifying distributions, $3,734.
Limitations: Giving limited to residents of Lake County, CA.
Application information: Application form required.
Officer: Phil N. Crawford, Mgr.
Trustee: Freeman Haas.
EIN: 946287540
Codes: GTI

58959
The Spotlight Foundation
2374 Greenwich St.
San Francisco, CA 94123

Established in 1998 in CA.
Donor(s): Rajesh Atluru.
Financial data (yr. ended 12/31/99): Assets, $52,625 (M); grants paid, $15,000; gifts received, $65,291; expenditures, $15,315; qualifying distributions, $15,000.
Officer: Steven J. Sell, Pres.
EIN: 943288257

58960
Crescent City Rotary Scholarship Foundation
888 4th St.
Crescent City, CA 95531-4011

Classified as a private operating foundation in 1984.
Financial data (yr. ended 06/30/01): Assets, $52,331 (M); grants paid, $5,100; gifts received, $330; expenditures, $5,075; qualifying distributions, $5,100.
Limitations: Applications not accepted. Giving limited to residents of Del Norte County, CA.
Application information: Contributes only to pre-selected organizations.
Directors: Bob Berkowitz, Gerald Cochran, Robert F. Cochran, Sharon Dyer, John Menaugh.
EIN: 680008158

58961
Kosch-Westerman Foundation
c/o Pepper Westerman
897 Oak Park Blvd., Ste. 240
Pismo Beach, CA 93449

Established in 1999 in CO.
Donor(s): Brian Westerman, Pepper Westerman.
Financial data (yr. ended 12/31/00): Assets, $52,301 (M); grants paid, $5,000; gifts received, $50,000; expenditures, $7,699; qualifying distributions, $5,000.
Officers: Pepper Westerman, Pres. and Treas.; Brian Westerman, V.P. and Secy.
EIN: 912017147

58962
Rahim Family Foundation
20749 Russel Ln.
Saratoga, CA 95070 (408) 867-1495
Contact: Chowdhury F. Rahim, Pres.

Established in 2000 in CA.
Donor(s): Chowdhury F. Rahim.
Financial data (yr. ended 12/31/00): Assets, $51,525 (M); grants paid, $16,000; gifts received, $67,690; expenditures, $16,165; qualifying distributions, $16,000.
Officers: Chowdhury F. Rahim, Pres.; Selina Akhtar, Secy. and C.F.O.
EIN: 770544965

58963
Hillcrest Foundation
800 Wilshire Blvd., Ste. 1010
Los Angeles, CA 90017

Established in 1995.
Donor(s): Brack Duker, Elizabeth Duker.
Financial data (yr. ended 12/31/01): Assets, $51,126 (M); grants paid, $243,500; expenditures, $244,818; qualifying distributions, $243,500.
Limitations: Applications not accepted. Giving primarily in CA and PA.
Application information: Contributes only to pre-selected organizations.
Trustees: Brack Duker, Elizabeth Duker.

EIN: 954598366
Codes: FD2

58964
Greater San Diego Science & Engineering Fair, Inc.
P.O. Box 191
San Diego, CA 92112-4106

Financial data (yr. ended 12/31/01): Assets, $51,116 (M); grants paid, $3,150; gifts received, $31,507; expenditures, $49,587; qualifying distributions, $49,529; giving activities include $49,548 for programs.
Officers: Lynne Durkee, Pres. and C.F.O.; King Durkee, Pres. Emeritus; Phillip Gay, V.P.; Mary Mikkelson, V.P.; Howard Weisbrod, V.P.; Shirley Parrish, V.P.
EIN: 237332855

58965
Zoglin Family Foundation
2040 Franklin St.
San Francisco, CA 94109

Established in 1999 in CA.
Donor(s): John Zoglin.
Financial data (yr. ended 12/31/01): Assets, $50,948 (M); grants paid, $2,480; gifts received, $750; expenditures, $2,529; qualifying distributions, $2,520.
Limitations: Applications not accepted.
Application information: Contributes only to pre-selected organizations.
Officers: John Zoglin, Pres.; M.L. Zoglin, Secy.
EIN: 742931577

58966
Hinshaw Charitable Foundation
P.O. Box 255
San Anselmo, CA 94979 (415) 392-9200
Contact: Cameron Hinshaw, Secy.

Established in 1999 in CA. Classified as a private operating foundation in 2000.
Donor(s): Michael Hinshaw.
Financial data (yr. ended 11/30/00): Assets, $50,737 (M); grants paid, $0; gifts received, $950,000; expenditures, $1,148; qualifying distributions, $300.
Officers: Michael Hinshaw, Pres.; Cameron Hinshaw, Secy.
EIN: 943347889

58967
Wild Things, Inc.
P.O. Box 191
Weimar, CA 95736-0191

Financial data (yr. ended 12/31/99): Assets, $50,100 (M); grants paid, $0; gifts received, $87,400; expenditures, $86,239; qualifying distributions, $0.
Officer: Gabriel J. Kerschner, Mgr.
EIN: 680158667

58968
The Center for Policy Re-Design
P.O. Box 3236
Santa Barbara, CA 93130

Established in 2000 in CA.
Donor(s): Kenneth A. Goldsholl, Nancy Goldsholl.
Financial data (yr. ended 12/31/00): Assets, $50,000 (M); grants paid, $0; gifts received, $50,284; expenditures, $80; qualifying distributions, $0.
Limitations: Applications not accepted.
Application information: Contributes only to pre-selected organizations.

58968—CALIFORNIA

Officers: Kenneth A. Goldsholl, Pres.; Nancy Goldsholl, Secy.; Melinda Lee, C.F.O.; Randy Weiss, Exec. Dir.
EIN: 770556151

58969
Santa Monica Mountains Natural History Association
9000 W. Pacific Coast Hwy.
Malibu, CA 90265

Classified as a private operating foundation in 1985.
Financial data (yr. ended 12/31/01): Assets, $48,930 (M); grants paid, $0; gifts received, $2,219; expenditures, $28,948; qualifying distributions, $3,400; giving activities include $14,397 for programs.
Limitations: Applications not accepted.
Application information: Contributes only to pre-selected organizations.
Officers: Wayne Gilbert, Pres.; John Falk, Secy.; Wayne Ferber, Treas.
Director: Widge Galloway.
EIN: 953932372

58970
Fatima Welfare Foundation
84 Fairlake
Irvine, CA 92614-7553
Contact: Tariq Mahmood Chaudhary, Pres.

Established in 1994 in CA.
Donor(s): Interchange Standards Corp., Tariq Mahmood Chaudhary.
Financial data (yr. ended 11/30/01): Assets, $48,100 (M); grants paid, $19,885; gifts received, $5,000; expenditures, $22,002; qualifying distributions, $19,885; giving activities include $19,600 for programs.
Officers: Tariq Mahmood Chaudhary, Pres.; Uzma Chaudhary, V.P.
EIN: 330643401

58971
Irwindale Educational Foundation
(Formerly Irwindale Educational & Scholarship Foundation)
16102 Arrow Hwy.
P.O. Box 2307
Irwindale, CA 91706   (626) 960-6606
Contact: Carroll Oliver, Treas.

Established in 1979; classified as a private operating foundation in 1994.
Financial data (yr. ended 12/31/00): Assets, $47,927 (M); grants paid, $21,432; gifts received, $46,502; expenditures, $26,304; qualifying distributions, $21,432.
Limitations: Giving limited to residents of Irwindale, CA.
Publications: Informational brochure (including application guidelines).
Application information: Application form required.
Officers: Robert Diaz, Pres.; Terry Noriega, V.P.; Maria Romero, Secy.; Jacque Haines, Treas.
Directors: Lina Campa, Camille Diaz, Dave Hummel, and 5 additional directors.
EIN: 954274826
Codes: GTI

58972
Careway Charitable Foundation
c/o Stanton Accountancy Corp.
10474 Santa Monica Blvd., Ste. 306
Los Angeles, CA 90025

Classified as a private operating foundation in 2000 in CA.
Donor(s): Paula Caretto, Wayne Schaffnit.

Financial data (yr. ended 12/31/00): Assets, $47,519 (M); grants paid, $22,374; gifts received, $30,519; expenditures, $23,570; qualifying distributions, $22,374.
Limitations: Applications not accepted.
Application information: Contributes only to pre-selected organizations.
Director: Wayne Schaffnit.
EIN: 954773276

58973
Larry A. Modin Foundation
1748 Higgins Ave.
Santa Clara, CA 95051   (408) 985-7921
Contact: Larry A. Modin, Pres.

Established in 2000 in CA.
Donor(s): Larry A. Modin.
Financial data (yr. ended 12/31/01): Assets, $47,406 (M); grants paid, $0; gifts received, $80,000; expenditures, $33,135; qualifying distributions, $0.
Limitations: Giving limited to residents of Santa Clara, CA.
Officer and Director:* Larry A. Modin,* Pres., Secy. and C.F.O.
EIN: 770560164

58974
International Society for Trans-Oceanic Research, Inc.
(also known as ISTOR)
1500 Dana Pl.
Fullerton, CA 92831

Classified as a private operating foundation in 1988.
Financial data (yr. ended 12/31/99): Assets, $46,865 (M); grants paid, $0; gifts received, $543; expenditures, $6,542; qualifying distributions, $6,542.
Officers: Otto J. Von Sadouszky, Ph.D., Chair. and Pres.; Martin Schneyer, Secy.-Treas.
EIN: 330183726

58975
World Interdependence Fund, Inc.
3711 Dell Rd.
Carmichael, CA 95608-2605

Classified as a private operating foundation in 1989.
Financial data (yr. ended 03/31/02): Assets, $46,805 (M); grants paid, $0; gifts received, $42,224; expenditures, $86,687; qualifying distributions, $0.
Directors: Sid Akbar, Charles Ansbach, William G. Bronston, M.D., Joan Bryant, Gloria Evosevich, Daphne Gawthrop, Ken Knoll, Sal Russon, Bob Smart, Kurt Spataro, Sol Spector, Duane Thompson, Camille Vandenberg.
EIN: 680023611

58976
Nosutch Foundation of California
2401 Main St.
Santa Monica, CA 90405-3515

Established in 1965 in CA.
Donor(s): Paul L. Newman.
Financial data (yr. ended 05/31/99): Assets, $46,263 (M); grants paid, $2,160; expenditures, $2,205; qualifying distributions, $2,160.
Limitations: Applications not accepted.
Application information: Contributes only to pre-selected organizations.
Trustee: Irving Axelrad.
EIN: 510175314

58977
Mary-Ellen Gerber Foundation
13071 Ottoman St.
Arleta, CA 91331   (818) 767-8806

Classified as a private operating foundation in 1997 in CA.
Financial data (yr. ended 12/31/00): Assets, $46,069 (M); grants paid, $46,000; gifts received, $117,030; expenditures, $109,874; qualifying distributions, $109,874.
Limitations: Giving on a national and international basis.
Officers: Mary Ellen Gerber, Pres.; Christian Alexandre, V. P.; Mary Ellen Gerber, Secy.
Director: L. Gerber.
EIN: 954636343

58978
Athena Charitable Trust
5411 Bahia Ln.
La Jolla, CA 92037-7020

Established in 1997 in CA.
Donor(s): Donna Brooks, M.D., Catherine L. Conheim, Barbara Levy, M.D.
Financial data (yr. ended 06/30/01): Assets, $45,926 (M); grants paid, $48,700; gifts received, $134,580; expenditures, $144,395; qualifying distributions, $144,385.
Limitations: Applications not accepted. Giving primarily in MI.
Application information: Contributes only to pre-selected organizations.
Trustees: Donna Brooks, M.D., Catherine L. Conheim, Barbara Levy, M.D.
EIN: 336211470
Codes: GTI

58979
Mount Carmel Athletic Foundation
9550 Carmel Mountain Rd.
San Diego, CA 92129-2738   (858) 484-1180
Contact: Frank Andruski

Established in 1991.
Financial data (yr. ended 06/30/00): Assets, $44,442 (M); grants paid, $1,000; gifts received, $123,108; expenditures, $132,718; qualifying distributions, $1,000.
Officers: Willie Payne, Pres.; Cathy Payne, Secy.
EIN: 330142788

58980
San Jose Kendo Dojo
c/o Charles Tanaka
1156 Blackfield Dr.
Santa Clara, CA 95051

Financial data (yr. ended 12/31/99): Assets, $43,803 (M); grants paid, $0; gifts received, $779; expenditures, $13,058; qualifying distributions, $0; giving activities include $13,057 for programs.
Limitations: Applications not accepted.
Application information: Contributes only to pre-selected organizations.
Officers: Charles Tanaka, Pres.; Rev. Arnold Matsuda, Secy.; Mrs. Mikuni, Treas.
EIN: 770324315

58981
Westview Star Foundation
10522 Katella Ave.
Anaheim, CA 92804

Financial data (yr. ended 03/31/01): Assets, $43,231 (M); grants paid, $5,146; gifts received, $40,735; expenditures, $27,614; qualifying distributions, $7,715.
Limitations: Applications not accepted. Giving primarily in Anaheim, CA.

Application information: Contributes only to pre-selected organizations.
Officers: Mary Radecki, C.E.O.; Dorothy Williams, C.F.O.; Richard Radecki, Secy.
Directors: Marty Conlon, George Heed, Patti Kohn.
EIN: 330756094

58982
Ugly Duckling Foundation
1680 Mission Dr.
Solvang, CA 93463

Established in 1989 in CA; classified as a private operating foundation in 1990.
Donor(s): Gary Mullins, Kathy Mullins.
Financial data (yr. ended 12/31/01): Assets, $42,743 (M); grants paid, $0; gifts received, $395; expenditures, $1,575; qualifying distributions, $502; giving activities include $1,575 for programs.
Officers: Kathy Mullins, Pres. and Mgr.; Elaine Revelle, Secy.; Heather McCollum, Treas.
EIN: 770218813

58983
Koons-Brady Charitable Foundation
604 Calle Fierros
San Clemente, CA 92673

Established in 2000 in CA.
Donor(s): Ann Louise Barnard, Philip Brady, Joan Barnard Brady.
Financial data (yr. ended 12/31/01): Assets, $42,722 (M); grants paid, $0; gifts received, $4,000; expenditures, $39,071; qualifying distributions, $0.
Officers: Philip Brady, C.E.O. and Pres.; Joan Barnard Brady, Secy. and C.F.O.
EIN: 330862047

58984
Nishimoto Family Scholarship Trust
2280 Fleetwood Dr.
San Bruno, CA 94066 (650) 583-9652
Contact: Judy Nishimoto, Tr.

Financial data (yr. ended 02/28/01): Assets, $42,106 (M); grants paid, $4,000; gifts received, $4,740; expenditures, $4,589; qualifying distributions, $3,987.
Limitations: Giving limited to residents of Madera, CA.
Trustees: Judy Nishimoto, Mary Nishimoto, Joyce Wilkinson.
EIN: 770319721

58985
Epic Ministries
1954 Goodyear Ave.
Ventura, CA 93003-7322

Established in 1999 in CA.
Donor(s): Jeffrey L. Sponseller.
Financial data (yr. ended 12/31/00): Assets, $41,555 (M); grants paid, $10,000; gifts received, $50,000; expenditures, $13,219; qualifying distributions, $10,000.
Limitations: Applications not accepted. Giving primarily in MO.
Application information: Contributes only to pre-selected organizations.
Officers: Tim Garrety, C.E.O. and Pres.; Jeffrey L. Sponseller, Secy-Treas. and C.F.O.
Directors: Sandra Denise Sponseller, Roger Thompson.
EIN: 770516156

58986
Charles L. Morton & Lucile R. Morton Charitable Foundation
2434 Barkley Ave.
Santa Clara, CA 95051-2415

Established in 1998 in CA.
Financial data (yr. ended 12/31/99): Assets, $39,946 (M); grants paid, $1,481; gifts received, $14,523; expenditures, $1,541; qualifying distributions, $1,541.
Limitations: Applications not accepted.
Application information: Contributes only to pre-selected organizations.
Officers: Charles L. Morton, Pres.; Lucile R. Morton, Secy.
EIN: 770471496

58987
Grazute Sirutis Foundation
847 6th St., Ste. B
Santa Monica, CA 90403-1428

Established in 1998.
Donor(s): Grazute Sirutis.
Financial data (yr. ended 11/30/00): Assets, $39,217 (M); grants paid, $17,348; gifts received, $19,000; expenditures, $18,580; qualifying distributions, $18,580.
Limitations: Applications not accepted. Giving primarily in CA.
Application information: Contributes only to pre-selected organizations.
Officers: Grazute Sirutis, C.E.O.; Joseph Praske, Secy.; Albinas Markevicius, C.F.O.
EIN: 954660436

58988
Pathways Foundation
65 Hwy. 1
Carmel, CA 93923-9725

Classified as a private operating foundation in 2000 in CA.
Donor(s): Howard M. Evans.
Financial data (yr. ended 07/31/01): Assets, $38,056 (M); grants paid, $0; gifts received, $63,000; expenditures, $25,673; qualifying distributions, $25,673; giving activities include $25,673 for programs.
Officers: Jim Sullivan, Chair.; Howard M. Evans, C.E.O.; Ron Johnson, Secy. and C.F.O.
EIN: 770554062

58989
The Clark H. Wilbur Foundation
2156 Rock Glen
Escondido, CA 92026

Established in 1999 in CA.
Donor(s): Paula W. Traber, David C. Wilbur.
Financial data (yr. ended 12/31/00): Assets, $37,708 (M); grants paid, $0; gifts received, $900; expenditures, $618; qualifying distributions, $0; giving activities include $618 for programs.
Trustees: Paula W. Traber, David C. Wilbur, Julia A. Wilbur.
EIN: 954739857

58990
The Res Gestae Foundation, Inc.
521 Santa Rosa Ln.
Santa Barbara, CA 93108-2139

Established in 1989 in CA.
Donor(s): Philip J. Albaum.
Financial data (yr. ended 03/31/01): Assets, $37,557 (M); grants paid, $5,000; expenditures, $7,118; qualifying distributions, $5,000; giving activities include $540 for programs.
Limitations: Giving primarily in CA.
Trustees: David P. Albaum, Philip J. Albaum, Arthur S. Freedman.
EIN: 770226504

58991
Kiwanis Club of Palm Springs, California Foundation
P.O. Box 1524
Palm Springs, CA 92263

Classified as a private operating foundation in 1991.
Financial data (yr. ended 06/30/99): Assets, $37,067 (M); grants paid, $26,347; gifts received, $10,220; expenditures, $28,309; qualifying distributions, $26,347.
Limitations: Giving limited to Palm Springs, CA.
Officers: Ed Tefteller, Pres.; Harold Blumbull, V.P.; Eddie Choy, Secy.; Don Shaevel, Treas.
Directors: Judy Bronstein, Dianne Marantz.
EIN: 330217366

58992
Southern California Transplantation Institute Research Foundation
4000 14th St., Ste. 512
Riverside, CA 92501

Established in 1998 in NV.
Donor(s): Mary Morris Stein.
Financial data (yr. ended 12/31/01): Assets, $36,838 (M); grants paid, $0; gifts received, $49,225; expenditures, $60,998; qualifying distributions, $0; giving activities include $53,761 for programs.
Officers: Tarek Hassanein, M.D., Pres.; H. Erik Wahlstrom, M.D., C.F.O.
EIN: 330791935

58993
Asgard Foundation, Inc.
1326 Stage Coach Rd.
Trinidad, CA 95570

Established as a private operating foundation in 1998.
Financial data (yr. ended 03/31/99): Assets, $36,821 (M); grants paid, $500; gifts received, $1,638; expenditures, $3,748; qualifying distributions, $500.
Limitations: Applications not accepted.
Application information: Contributes only to pre-selected organizations.
Officers and Trustees:* Audrey Conant,* C.E.O.; George Strong, Secy.; Ralph Conant,* C.F.O.
EIN: 680402100

58994
The Blurock Foundation
c/o Edna M. Blurock
2300 Newport Blvd.
Newport Beach, CA 92663-3702

Established in 1993 in CA.
Donor(s): Edna Blurock, William Blurock.
Financial data (yr. ended 12/31/01): Assets, $35,907 (M); grants paid, $27,755; gifts received, $18,570; expenditures, $28,555; qualifying distributions, $28,551.
Limitations: Applications not accepted.
Application information: Contributes only to pre-selected organizations.
Officers: William E. Blurock, Pres.; Theresa Mitsueda, Secy.
Trustees: Robert Fulkerson, Terry Welsh.
EIN: 330553315

58995
Mary L. Fisher Foundation
13300 Holly Oak Cir.
Cerritos, CA 90703-1373

Established in 1994 in CA. Classified as a private operating foundation in 1995.
Donor(s): Gregory T. Fisher.
Financial data (yr. ended 12/31/01): Assets, $35,669 (M); grants paid, $0; expenditures, $11,480; qualifying distributions, $0.
Officer: Gregory T. Fisher, M.D., Pres. and Secy.-Treas.
Director: Willard Horwich.
EIN: 330558307

58996
James A. Milligan Foundation, Inc.
5371 E. Falls View Dr.
San Diego, CA 92115

Established in 1965 in CA.
Donor(s): Clinton D. Davis, Marc C. Davis.
Financial data (yr. ended 12/31/01): Assets, $35,319 (M); grants paid, $221; gifts received, $730; expenditures, $56,289; qualifying distributions, $221.
Limitations: Applications not accepted. Giving primarily in San Diego, CA.
Application information: Contributes only to pre-selected organizations.
Officers: Marc C. Davis, Pres.; Karen Mickelsen Davis, Secy.; Michael C. Dunn, Exec. Dir.
EIN: 952386618

58997
Our Lady of Guadalupe Radio, Inc.
c/o Robert Chinchiolo
3740 S. Monitor St.
Stockton, CA 95219

Established in 1999 in CA.
Donor(s): Robert Chinchiolo, Kathy Chinchiolo.
Financial data (yr. ended 12/31/99): Assets, $34,669 (M); grants paid, $0; gifts received, $0; expenditures, $5,418; qualifying distributions, $4,581; giving activities include $4,581 for programs.
Limitations: Applications not accepted.
Application information: Contributes only to pre-selected organizations.
Officers: Robert Chinchiolo, Pres.; Kathy Chinchiolo, V.P.; Mary Guardado, Secy.
EIN: 680439086

58998
Visual Testing & Therapy Trust Fund
c/o Hagenow
P.O. Box 1178
Grover Beach, CA 93483

Established in 1984 in CA.
Financial data (yr. ended 10/31/01): Assets, $34,553 (M); grants paid, $0; gifts received, $4,262; expenditures, $9,599; qualifying distributions, $0.
Limitations: Applications not accepted.
Trustees: Beth Ballinger, Dennis Spiro, Donald Studt, John Tassinari.
EIN: 953190726

58999
Ladies of the Grand Army of the Republic
(also known as George H. Thomas Circle No. 32, Ladies of the Grand Army of the Republic)
c/o Stephen J. Delahunty, C.P.A.
1500 Grant Ave., Ste. 200
Novato, CA 94945

Classified as a private operating foundation in 1974.
Donor(s): Arthur Brink Luther Trust.
Financial data (yr. ended 12/31/01): Assets, $34,105 (M); grants paid, $51,385; gifts received, $56,924; expenditures, $56,645; qualifying distributions, $56,645.
Limitations: Applications not accepted. Giving primarily in CA, with some giving also in Klamath Falls, OR.
Application information: Unsolicited requests for funds not accepted.
Officers: Marilyn Felland, Pres.; Mary Huson, Secy.; Mary Cole, Treas.
EIN: 946138985
Codes: GTI

59000
Hashivenu, Inc.
432 S. Beverly Dr.
Beverly Hills, CA 90212

Classified as a private operating foundation in 1998 in CA.
Donor(s): Martin Thuna.
Financial data (yr. ended 12/31/01): Assets, $33,650 (M); grants paid, $0; gifts received, $93,909; expenditures, $60,310; qualifying distributions, $0.
Limitations: Applications not accepted.
Application information: Contributes only to pre-selected organizations.
Officers: Mark Kinzer, Chair.; Stuart Dauermann, Pres.; Richard Nichol, V.P.; G. Robert Chenoweth, Secy.; Susan Chenoweth, Treas.
Directors: Ellen Quarry, Paul Saal, Michael Schiffman.
EIN: 954661494

59001
Clark-Ovitt Foundation, Inc.
P.O. Box 871
San Miguel, CA 93451-0871

Established in 1993 in CA.
Financial data (yr. ended 12/31/00): Assets, $33,603 (M); grants paid, $0; gifts received, $15,941; expenditures, $25,397; qualifying distributions, $0.
Directors: Susan Clark-Ovitt, Harry L. Ovitt III, Don Smith, Rowena Smith, Lyle Stevens, Patricia Stevens.
EIN: 770337117

59002
Marin Women's Foundation
851 Irwin St., Ste. 301
San Rafael, CA 94901
Contact: Kit M. Cole, Pres.

Financial data (yr. ended 12/31/01): Assets, $33,574 (M); grants paid, $2,400; expenditures, $4,034; qualifying distributions, $2,400.
Limitations: Giving primarily in Marin County, CA.
Officers: Kit M. Cole, Pres.; Kimberly Petrini, C.F.O.
EIN: 680166149

59003
Public Resource Foundation, Inc.
414 Mason St., Ste. 802
San Francisco, CA 94102 (415) 393-9000
Contact: Putnam Livermore, V.P.

Established in 1982 in CA.
Donor(s): John S. Livermore.
Financial data (yr. ended 11/30/00): Assets, $32,932 (M); grants paid, $37,000; gifts received, $55,000; expenditures, $38,534; qualifying distributions, $38,380.
Application information: Application form not required.
Officers and Directors:* John S. Livermore,* Pres.; Putnam Livermore,* V.P.; Susan B. Lynn,* Secy.; Donald L. Field,* Treas.
EIN: 942861353

59004
The Renee Slate Scholarship Fund
P.O. Box 1146
Lodi, CA 95241-1146
Application addresses: c/o Lodi High School Scholarship Comm., 1300 W. Lodi Ave., Lodi, CA 95242, tel.: (209) 331-7000; c/o St. Peter Lutheran School Scholarship Comm., 2400 Oxford Way, Lodi, CA 95242, tel.: (209) 333-2225

Established in 1989 in CA.
Financial data (yr. ended 12/31/00): Assets, $32,828 (M); grants paid, $1,486; expenditures, $1,511; qualifying distributions, $1,496.
Limitations: Giving limited to Lodi, CA.
Trustees: Robin D. Boriack, Ryan W. Slate.
EIN: 680158837

59005
H. Schaffer Foundation
10960 Wilshire Blvd., Ste. 1960
Los Angeles, CA 90024
Contact: Herbert Schaffer, Pres.

Established in 1986 in CA.
Donor(s): Herbert Schaffer.
Financial data (yr. ended 06/30/01): Assets, $32,215 (M); grants paid, $72,039; gifts received, $75,299; expenditures, $72,711; qualifying distributions, $72,039.
Limitations: Giving primarily in CA.
Application information: Application form not required.
Officers: Herbert Schaffer, Pres.; Robert Schaffer, V.P.
EIN: 954057558

59006
Children's Educational Opportunity Foundation
60 Bowling Dr.
Oakland, CA 94618
Scholarship address: P.O. Box 21456, Oakland, CA 94620, tel.: (510) 483-7971
Contact: Admin.

Established in 1997 in CA.
Donor(s): Chris Berg, Nancy Berg, Walter Meier, Mrs. Walter Meier, Ruth A. Berg Revocable Trust, Banbury Fund, The Clorox Company Foundation.
Financial data (yr. ended 06/30/01): Assets, $31,421 (M); grants paid, $412,880; gifts received, $422,000; expenditures, $418,692; qualifying distributions, $418,689.
Limitations: Giving limited to Oakland, CA.
Application information: Applications to be submitted with copies of current-year income tax returns. Award payments are made to student's choice of school. Application form required.
Officers: Ruth A. Berg, Pres.; Christopher H. Berg, Secy.; Nancy M. Berg, Treas.
Directors: Ces Butner, Kurt Herzog, Ann Manchester, Ed.D., Merrill Schwartz.
EIN: 943201181
Codes: FD, GTI

59007
John & Charlene Smylie Foundation
3643 Grand Ave.
San Marcos, CA 92069 (760) 727-0900
Contact: John Smylie, Pres.

Donor(s): Francis Warn, Lawrence Warn, Charlene Smylie, John Smylie.
Financial data (yr. ended 12/31/00): Assets, $31,389 (M); grants paid, $13,573; gifts received,

$10,746; expenditures, $16,210; qualifying distributions, $16,210.
Application information: Application form required.
Officer and Directors:* John Smylie,* Pres.; Darius Khayat, Francis Warn.
EIN: 943252120

59008
Spirit in Action
684 Vemocoa Dr., No.61
Santa Rosa, CA 95409

Established in 1998 in CA.
Donor(s): Frank Farr.
Financial data (yr. ended 05/31/00): Assets, $28,859 (M); grants paid, $12,585; gifts received, $22,739; expenditures, $29,229; qualifying distributions, $12,583.
Officers: Dennis Johnson, Pres.; Maggie Arner, V.P.; John Bayer, Secy.; Ervin Shipley, Treas.
EIN: 931207351

59009
The Family Communication Foundation
3232 Deer Hill Rd.
Lafayette, CA 94549

Established in 1992 in CA.
Donor(s): Anne Holding, Hunter Holding.
Financial data (yr. ended 06/30/99): Assets, $28,530 (M); grants paid, $1,595; gifts received, $10,015; expenditures, $5,821; qualifying distributions, $6,020.
Limitations: Applications not accepted. Giving primarily in CA.
Application information: Contributes only to pre-selected organizations.
Trustee: Anne Holding.
EIN: 680316049

59010
Bernard & Gloria Salick Foundation
(Formerly Bernard & Gloria Jeanne Salick Foundation)
c/o Alicia Anderson
8900 Wilshire Blvd., No. 100
Beverly Hills, CA 90211-1906
FAX: (310) 967-3377

Established in 1984 in CA.
Donor(s): Bernard Salick, M.D., Gloria Salick.
Financial data (yr. ended 12/31/01): Assets, $27,265 (M); grants paid, $22,600; expenditures, $24,889; qualifying distributions, $24,889.
Limitations: Applications not accepted. Giving primarily in CA, Gladstone, NJ, and New York, NY.
Application information: Contributes only to pre-selected organizations.
Trustees: Leslie F. Bell, Bernard Salick, M.D., Gloria Salick.
EIN: 953946003

59011
The Schilling Foundation
325 Coral Ave.
Newport Beach, CA 92662

Established in 1998 in CA.
Donor(s): Robert J. Schilling.
Financial data (yr. ended 12/31/00): Assets, $27,227 (M); grants paid, $0; gifts received, $93,525; expenditures, $79,835; qualifying distributions, $77,641; giving activities include $47,763 for programs.
Officers: Robert J. Schilling, Pres.; Christian L. Bakewell, V.P.; Steven W. Morris, Secy. and C.F.O.
EIN: 330816204

59012
The Stanwyck Family Foundation
9734 Wendover Dr.
Beverly Hills, CA 90210

Established in 1994 in CA.
Donor(s): Steven Stanwyck, Joan Stanwyck.
Financial data (yr. ended 10/31/99): Assets, $27,004 (M); grants paid, $27,737; gifts received, $27,737; expenditures, $53,008; qualifying distributions, $53,008.
Limitations: Applications not accepted.
Application information: Contributes only to pre-selected organizations.
Officers: Joan C. Stanwyck, Pres.; Steven Stanwyck, C.F.O.
EIN: 954498718

59013
City of Angels Ballet
2330 Ronda Vista Dr.
Los Angeles, CA 90027

Established in 1994 in CA.
Financial data (yr. ended 12/31/01): Assets, $26,717 (M); grants paid, $0; gifts received, $159,909; expenditures, $177,089; qualifying distributions, $175,649; giving activities include $177,089 for programs.
Limitations: Giving limited to Los Angeles, CA.
Officers: Bill Lincoln, Chair.; Mario Nugara, Pres.; Jerry Hill, Secy.; Sam Harris, Treas.
Directors: Anne Bartnett, Thomas Higgins, Melinda McIntyre-Koplin, Helen Sanchez.
EIN: 954251755

59014
InfoQuest Foundation
c/o Ron Maas
9432 Greenwich Dr.
Huntington Beach, CA 92646

Established in 1996 in CA. Classified as a private operating foundation in 1998.
Donor(s): Larry W. Dingus.
Financial data (yr. ended 06/30/01): Assets, $26,279 (M); grants paid, $12,500; gifts received, $70,501; expenditures, $62,877; qualifying distributions, $45,250.
Limitations: Applications not accepted.
Application information: Contributes only to pre-selected organizations.
Officers and Directors:* Larry W. Dingus,* Chair.; Lowell W. Dingus,* Pres.; Ronald R. Mass,* C.F.O.; Eugene S. Gaffney, Ph.D., John Russel, Meg Starr.
EIN: 330779508

59015
Steve and Ingrid Stout Foundation
14841 Blossom Hill Rd.
Los Gatos, CA 95032

Established in 2000 in CA.
Donor(s): Steve D. Stout, Ingrid A. Stout.
Financial data (yr. ended 07/31/01): Assets, $25,832 (M); grants paid, $0; gifts received, $374,003; expenditures, $22,723; qualifying distributions, $36,946; giving activities include $25,045 for programs.
Limitations: Applications not accepted.
Application information: Contributes only to pre-selected organizations.
Officers and Directors:* Steve D. Stout,* Pres.; Ingrid A. Stout,* V.P. and Secy.-Treas.
EIN: 770559474

59016
Aurora Foundation, Inc.
c/o D. Hettig
120A Santa Margarita Ave.
Menlo Park, CA 94025-2725

Classified as a private operating foundation in 1982.
Donor(s): Kimpton Investment Co., Katherine S. Jones,‡ Ginetta Sagan, Nancy Flowers, Mental Insight Foundation.
Financial data (yr. ended 03/31/00): Assets, $25,185 (M); grants paid, $13,000; gifts received, $58,000; expenditures, $33,003; qualifying distributions, $33,003; giving activities include $20,003 for programs.
Limitations: Applications not accepted. Giving on a national basis.
Publications: Occasional report.
Application information: Contributes only to pre-selected organizations.
Directors: Tom Claburn, Susan E. Rife Cort, Jane Crocker, Shirley D'Andrea, Nancy Flowers, Patricia Govan, David W. Hettig, Ginetta Sagan.
EIN: 942781617

59017
Ulan Bator Foundation
1666 1/2 Electric Ave.
Venice, CA 90291

Established in 1993 in CA.
Donor(s): Arnold Springer.
Financial data (yr. ended 09/30/99): Assets, $24,734 (M); grants paid, $40; gifts received, $16,516; expenditures, $7,901; qualifying distributions, $7,715.
Limitations: Giving primarily in Venice, CA.
Officer: Arnold Springer, Mgr.
EIN: 754301043

59018
River Island Collectors Museum
c/o Robert D. Wilson
32185 River Island Dr.
Springville, CA 93265-9664

Established in 1998.
Donor(s): Robert D. Wilson.
Financial data (yr. ended 06/30/02): Assets, $24,514 (M); grants paid, $0; gifts received, $34,572; expenditures, $1,096; qualifying distributions, $0.
Officer: Robert D. Wilson, Pres.
Trustees: Gary LaLanne, Jim Maples, Chris Ralph, Terry Treece, Betty Webb, Colette Wilson.
EIN: 954696171

59019
The Philip Lee Ellis and Elizabeth B. Ellis Foundation
8319 S. Greenleaf Ave.
Whittier, CA 90602 (562) 693-1191
Contact: Elizabeth B. Ellis, Mgr.

Established in 1998 in CA.
Donor(s): Philip Ellis, Elizabeth Ellis.
Financial data (yr. ended 12/31/99): Assets, $24,513 (M); grants paid, $1,825; gifts received, $15,000; expenditures, $3,605; qualifying distributions, $1,825.
Officers: Philip L. Ellis, C.E.O.; Elizabeth B. Ellis, Mgr.
EIN: 954686656

59020
Phillip and Nancy Schwiebert Charitable Foundation
c/o Questron
386 Railroad Ct.
Milpitas, CA 95035-4339

Established in 1999 in CA.
Donor(s): Phillip Schwiebert, Nancy Schwiebert.
Financial data (yr. ended 12/31/00): Assets, $24,468 (M); grants paid, $1,000; gifts received, $210,900; expenditures, $41,903; qualifying distributions, $37,697.
Limitations: Applications not accepted.
Application information: Contributes only to pre-selected organizations.
Officers and Directors:* Phillip Schwiebert,* Pres.; Nancy Schwiebert,* Secy. and C.F.O.
EIN: 770519627

59021
Herman Dooyeweerd Foundation
1915 Bahia Way
La Jolla, CA 92037-7024

Donor(s): Magnus Verbrugge.
Financial data (yr. ended 06/30/02): Assets, $23,258 (M); grants paid, $0; gifts received, $15,000; expenditures, $1,837; qualifying distributions, $0.
Officers: Herman Fokke Dooyeweerd, Pres.; Magnus Verbrugge, V.P.; Nateya Verbrugge, Secy.; W. Maria Verbrugge, Treas.
EIN: 953765512

59022
Duwayne J. Peterson and Nancy V. Peterson Family Foundation
2220 Orlando Rd.
San Marino, CA 91108

Established in 1998 in CA.
Donor(s): Duwayne J. Peterson, Jr.
Financial data (yr. ended 12/31/00): Assets, $23,084 (M); grants paid, $1,600; expenditures, $4,104; qualifying distributions, $1,600.
Directors: Duwayne J. Peterson, Jr., Nancy V. Peterson.
EIN: 954685788

59023
Fountain Theatre
(Formerly Barbara H. Culver Foundation)
5060 Fountain Ave.
Los Angeles, CA 90029-1422 (323) 663-2255
Application address: 8686 Lookout Mountain Ave., Los Angeles, CA 90046
Contact: Deborah C. Lawlor, Dir.

Classified as a private operating foundation in 1991.
Donor(s): Deborah C. Lawlor.
Financial data (yr. ended 12/31/99): Assets, $22,607 (M); grants paid, $10,149; gifts received, $394,703; expenditures, $543,082; qualifying distributions, $536,720.
Limitations: Giving primarily in CA.
Directors: A. Anthony Culver, Deborah C. Lawlor, Stephen Sachs.
EIN: 953119081

59024
Robert C. Pires Memorial Scholarship Fund
P.O. Box 6
Gustine, CA 95322
Application address: c/o Agriculture Instructor, Gustine High School, Gustine, CA 95322

Financial data (yr. ended 12/31/01): Assets, $22,149 (M); grants paid, $1,650; gifts received, $350; expenditures, $1,650; qualifying distributions, $1,650.
Limitations: Giving primarily in CA.
Trustees: Wilbur E. Gomes, John Nunes, Cecelia Pires, John Pires, Lloyd Vierra.
EIN: 770373188

59025
Annapolis Volunteer Fire Brigade
31909 Annapolis Rd.
Annapolis, CA 95412-9709

Financial data (yr. ended 12/31/00): Assets, $21,962 (M); grants paid, $0; gifts received, $3,427; expenditures, $19,768; qualifying distributions, $4,527; giving activities include $4,527 for programs.
Officers: Gary Craig, Pres.; Helga McDuffie, V.P.; Tanya Radkey, Secy.; Rita Miller, Treas.
Director: Chris Almind.
EIN: 942528596

59026
The Ask Jeeves Foundation
c/o Roger A. Strauch
918 Parker St., Ste. A-14
Berkeley, CA 94710-2583

Established in 1999 in CA.
Donor(s): Dan Miller, Roger Strauch, Garrett Gruener.
Financial data (yr. ended 12/31/01): Assets, $21,878 (M); grants paid, $221,541; expenditures, $226,299; qualifying distributions, $223,832.
Limitations: Applications not accepted. Giving primarily in CA, with emphasis on Oakland.
Application information: Contributes only to pre-selected organizations.
Officers and Directors:* Roger Strauch,* Chair.; Garrett Gruener,* Pres.; Dan Miller,* Secy.-Treas.; George Battle, Robert Wrubel.
EIN: 943346366
Codes: FD2

59027
The Sung-Kwok Foundation
651 Gateway Blvd., Ste. 880
South San Francisco, CA 94080
(650) 877-0780
Contact: C.B. Sung, Chair.

Established in 1984.
Donor(s): Sung Family Trust.
Financial data (yr. ended 06/30/99): Assets, $21,331 (M); grants paid, $4,500; gifts received, $4,000; expenditures, $4,562; qualifying distributions, $4,500.
Limitations: Giving limited to South San Francisco, CA.
Officers: C.B. Sung, Chair.; Beulah K. Sung, Pres.; Dean Sung, V.P.; Wingate Sung, V.P.
EIN: 942951655

59028
Stop Now, Inc.
c/o Fred G. Hudson, M.D.
3915 20th St.
San Francisco, CA 94114-2906

Financial data (yr. ended 12/31/00): Assets, $21,268 (M); grants paid, $10,000; gifts received, $425; expenditures, $10,626; qualifying distributions, $10,626.
Limitations: Applications not accepted. Giving primarily in San Francisco, CA.
Application information: Contributes only to pre-selected organizations.
Officers: Clifton L. Bell, Jr., Pres.; Jim Nixon, Secy.-Treas.; R. James Carlson, Exec. Dir.
Director: Fred G. Hudson, M.D.
EIN: 942370552

59029
Joshua Freeman Soccer Foundation
c/o Robert E. Freeman
427 Paco Dr.
Los Altos, CA 94024

Established in 1994 in CA.
Donor(s): Robert Freeman, Thomas Tripiano.
Financial data (yr. ended 09/30/99): Assets, $21,094 (M); grants paid, $0; gifts received, $5,058; expenditures, $127; qualifying distributions, $127.
Limitations: Applications not accepted.
Application information: Contributes only to pre-selected organizations.
Officer: Robert E. Freeman, Mgr.
EIN: 776110961

59030
Rising Arc Foundation
P.O. Box 411375
Los Angeles, CA 90041

Established in 1995 in CA.
Donor(s): Zareb Herman.
Financial data (yr. ended 12/31/01): Assets, $21,061 (M); grants paid, $0; gifts received, $4,844; expenditures, $4,395; qualifying distributions, $0.
Officers: Zareb Herman, Chair.; Mozzelle Juriga, Secy.
EIN: 954534379

59031
Pacific Rim College of Psychiatrists
760 Westwood Plz.
Los Angeles, CA 90024

Classified as a private operating foundation in 1982.
Financial data (yr. ended 12/31/00): Assets, $20,817 (M); grants paid, $0; expenditures, $31,868; qualifying distributions, $0.
Officers: Ching-Piao Chien, M.D., Co-Pres.; Kyu-Hang Lee, M.D., Co-Pres.; Francis G. Lu, M.D., Treas.
EIN: 953435923

59032
The Barry Bonds Family Foundation
(Formerly The Bonds Family Foundation)
c/o Seiler & Co., LLP
1100 Marshall St.
Redwood City, CA 94063

Donor(s): Barry Bonds.
Financial data (yr. ended 01/31/01): Assets, $20,516 (M); grants paid, $102,260; gifts received, $126,121; expenditures, $159,336; qualifying distributions, $155,008; giving activities include $47,372 for programs.
Limitations: Applications not accepted. Giving primarily in San Francisco, CA.
Application information: Contributes only to pre-selected organizations.
Officers: Barry Bonds, Pres.; Terrence Hall, Secy.; Steve Hoskins, C.F.O.
EIN: 954427535

59033
International Community Development Foundation
32 Lochness Ln.
San Rafael, CA 94901

Donor(s): Dean W. Cromwell, Barbara Euser.
Financial data (yr. ended 12/31/00): Assets, $20,474 (M); grants paid, $3,000; gifts received, $4,000; expenditures, $3,050; qualifying distributions, $5,364; giving activities include $2,364 for loans.

Limitations: Applications not accepted.
Application information: Contributes only to pre-selected organizations.
Officers: Dean W. Cromwell, Pres.; Jac Sperling, V.P.; Barbara Euser, Secy.-Treas.
EIN: 522050450

59034
National Station Car Association
c/o Martin J. Bernard III
963 Hillcroft Cir.
Oakland, CA 94610

Financial data (yr. ended 12/31/01): Assets, $19,649 (M); grants paid, $0; gifts received, $23,699; expenditures, $22,387; qualifying distributions, $0.
Officers: Victoria Nerenberg, Pres.; Don Borowski, V.P.; D.E. Francis II, Secy.-Treas.
Directors: Kent Harris, Kenneth M. McDonald.
EIN: 943195056

59035
RB Foundation
28761 Hilltop Dr.
Highland, CA 92346

Established in 1997.
Donor(s): Rebecca A. Ashworth, Raymond F. Ashworth.
Financial data (yr. ended 12/31/00): Assets, $19,619 (M); grants paid, $4,660; gifts received, $3,500; expenditures, $5,090; qualifying distributions, $5,240.
Limitations: Applications not accepted.
Application information: Contributes only to pre-selected organizations.
Officers: Rebecca A. Ashworth, Pres.; Raymond F. Ashworth, V.P. and Secy.-Treas.
EIN: 330760612

59036
Berakah Foundation
P.O. Box 636
Santa Maria, CA 93456-0636 (805) 925-9533

Classified as a private operating foundation in CA.
Donor(s): Robert P. Diani, James A. Diani, Michael J. Diani, Donald L. Ward.
Financial data (yr. ended 12/31/00): Assets, $19,381 (M); grants paid, $32,711; gifts received, $37,500; expenditures, $34,860; qualifying distributions, $34,670.
Application information: Application form required.
Officers: Michael J. Diani, Pres.; Donald L. Ward, V.P.; James A. Diani, Secy.; C.A. Quinn, Treas.
EIN: 770489106

59037
Nepal Educational Fund, Inc.
700 Front St., No. 2003
San Diego, CA 92101-6012
Application address: c/o Kedar G.C., Sajha Pasal Deva Pascal 1, Sajha Bhandar, KTM, Nepal

Established in 1992 in CA.
Donor(s): Mearl A. Naponic, M.D., Richard D. Della Penna, M.D.
Financial data (yr. ended 12/31/01): Assets, $19,023 (L); grants paid, $4,024; gifts received, $12,400; expenditures, $5,663; qualifying distributions, $5,663.
Limitations: Giving primarily in India and Nepal.
Officers: Richard D. Della Penna, M.D., Pres.; Guy Della Penna, Secy.; Mearl A. Naponic, M.D., C.F.O.
EIN: 330490545
Codes: GTI

59038
Merriam Irrigation Education Foundation, Inc.
235 Chaplin Ln.
San Luis Obispo, CA 93405-1932
Contact: John Merriam, Pres.

Established in 1998 in CA.
Donor(s): John Merriam.
Financial data (yr. ended 12/31/01): Assets, $18,931 (M); grants paid, $0; gifts received, $12,600; expenditures, $12,663; qualifying distributions, $0.
Officers and Directors:* John L. Merriam,* Pres.; Grant G. Davids,* V.P. and Secy.; Andrew G. Merriam,* C.F.O.; Stuart W. Styles, Edwin F. Sullivan.
EIN: 770491614

59039
Thomas & Pearl Martinez Foundation
344 E. Millan St.
Chula Vista, CA 91910-6314

Donor(s): Pearl Martinez, Thomas Martinez.
Financial data (yr. ended 12/31/01): Assets, $18,365 (M); grants paid, $2,500; gifts received, $2,770; expenditures, $2,795; qualifying distributions, $2,500.
Limitations: Applications not accepted.
Application information: Unsolicited requests for funds not accepted.
Officers: Thomas Martinez, Pres.; Pearl Martinez, Secy.-Treas.
EIN: 133497459

59040
Foundation for Mitochondrial and Metabolic Disease Research
(Formerly Foundation for Nutrition and Metabolism)
12818 Stebick Ct.
San Diego, CA 92130-2705

Established in 1992 in CA.
Financial data (yr. ended 12/31/00): Assets, $17,680 (M); grants paid, $1,250; gifts received, $13,549; expenditures, $21,896; qualifying distributions, $1,250.
Limitations: Giving limited to La Jolla, CA.
Officers: William L. Nyhan, M.D., Ph.D., Chair.; Angie Longenecker, Treas.
Director: Eileen Murphy-Zink.
EIN: 330530849

59041
Lost Highway Foundation
924 Anacapa St., No. 2B
Santa Barbara, CA 93101

Donor(s): Thomas M. Merkel.
Financial data (yr. ended 12/31/00): Assets, $17,397 (M); grants paid, $0; gifts received, $9,808; expenditures, $4,262; qualifying distributions, $0.
Officer: Thomas M. Merkel, Mgr.
Director: Mark Hoff.
EIN: 770434071

59042
Marian Stuart Memorial Scholarship Fund
11486 Huntington Village Ln.
Gold River, CA 95670-7544
Application address: 777 Terrapin Ct., Concord, CA 94518, tel.: (925) 798-0814
Contact: Margaret Powell

Financial data (yr. ended 05/31/00): Assets, $17,201 (M); grants paid, $1,200; gifts received, $300; expenditures, $1,200; qualifying distributions, $1,200.
Limitations: Giving primarily in CA.

Application information: Letters of recommendation from teachers or supervisors required. Application form required.
Officer: Harry G. Stuart, Admin.
EIN: 680142111

59043
Elliot, Marlo, Grant Gottfurcht Charitable Foundation
1018 Hartzell St.
Pacific Palisades, CA 90272
Contact: Elliot Gottfurcht, Tr.

Established in 1989 in CA.
Financial data (yr. ended 12/31/99): Assets, $16,712 (M); grants paid, $21,085; expenditures, $21,283; qualifying distributions, $21,085.
Limitations: Giving primarily in CA.
Trustees: Elliot Gottfurcht, Donald R. Lipton, Sheldon R. Stone.
EIN: 954238628

59044
Johnson Tri-Dom Foundation
1635 Candace Way
Los Altos, CA 94024-6243

Classified as a private operating foundation in 1988.
Financial data (yr. ended 12/31/99): Assets, $16,347 (M); grants paid, $5,750; expenditures, $5,853; qualifying distributions, $24,724; giving activities include $91 for programs.
Officers: Robert W. Johnson, C.E.O. and Pres.; Ezekiel L. Smith, V.P.; William E. Green, Secy.; Cecilie A. Vaughters-Johnson, Treas. and C.F.O.
EIN: 770145481

59045
Cherrie Foundation
5961 Bridgeview Dr.
Ventura, CA 93003

Established in 1992 in CA.
Donor(s): Gene A. Cherrie, Marty Cherrie.
Financial data (yr. ended 12/31/01): Assets, $16,286 (M); grants paid, $60,693; gifts received, $69,500; expenditures, $60,759; qualifying distributions, $69,501; giving activities include $8,741 for programs.
Limitations: Applications not accepted. Giving primarily in IN.
Application information: Contributes only to pre-selected organizations.
Officers and Directors:* Gene A. Cherrie,* Pres.; Janice Cherrie,* Secy.-Treas.; Marty Cherrie, Douglas Rundell.
EIN: 770308198

59046
Rational Decision Making Research Institute
1010 Turquoise St., Ste. 245
San Diego, CA 92109-1266

Established in 1999 in CA.
Donor(s): Harry Markowitz.
Financial data (yr. ended 12/31/00): Assets, $16,186 (M); grants paid, $0; gifts received, $20,000; expenditures, $17,373; qualifying distributions, $17,373; giving activities include $17,373 for programs.
Officers and Directors:* Harry Markowitz,* Pres.; Ruth Sirota, Secy.; Barbara Markowitz, Treas.; Gilbert Hammer, William F. Sharpe.
EIN: 330860950

59047
Friends of Curtin University, Inc.
c/o Egon Andersen
1687 Elverhoy Way
Solvang, CA 93463

Established in 1994 in MN.
Donor(s): H.J. Heinz Foundation, H.J. Heinz Co. Australia, Ltd., Dresser Industries, Inc.
Financial data (yr. ended 12/31/01): Assets, $16,142 (M); grants paid, $0; expenditures, $865; qualifying distributions, $0.
Officer and Directors:* Egon Andersen,* Treas.; Ian Fairnie, Hans Kristensen.
EIN: 411659550

59048
Joann Dobrin Foundation
c/o Robert C. Fellmeth
548 Adella Ln.
Coronado, CA 92118-1924

Established in 1996 in CA.
Financial data (yr. ended 12/31/99): Assets, $16,129 (M); grants paid, $0; gifts received, $10,916; expenditures, $191; qualifying distributions, $191; giving activities include $191 for programs.
Officers: Cliff Dobrin, Pres.; Don Armstrong, V.P.; Robert C. Fellmeth, Treas.
EIN: 330688043

59049
Ulan Bator Foundation
1666 1/2 Electric Ave.
Venice, CA 90291-4804
Contact: Jytte Springer, Treas.

Established in 1990 in CA.
Donor(s): Channel Gateway, J.H. Schneider Co., Arnold Springer.
Financial data (yr. ended 09/30/00): Assets, $16,090 (M); grants paid, $753; gifts received, $16,000; expenditures, $9,976; qualifying distributions, $9,976.
Limitations: Giving primarily in CA.
Officers: Arnold Springer, Pres.; Jytte Springer, Treas.
EIN: 954301043

59050
The Justin Wise Foundation
P.O. Box 41182
San Jose, CA 95160 (408) 283-8515
Contact: Elizabeth R. Costa, Pres.

Established in 1999 in CA.
Financial data (yr. ended 12/31/00): Assets, $15,830 (M); grants paid, $6,000; gifts received, $2,603; expenditures, $7,868; qualifying distributions, $6,000.
Officer: Elizabeth R. Costa, Pres.
EIN: 770507940

59051
Charles S. Denkert Family Foundation
115 Ketch Mall
Marina Del Rey, CA 90292

Established in 1999 in CA.
Donor(s): Darcie Denkert.
Financial data (yr. ended 12/31/00): Assets, $15,582 (M); grants paid, $5,000; gifts received, $10,000; expenditures, $5,060; qualifying distributions, $5,000.
Officers: Darcie Denkert, Pres.; Allen E. Susman, Secy.-Treas.
EIN: 954544552

59052
Team for International Eye Surgery, Inc.
(Formerly Vivente I, Inc.)
2324 Bath St.
Santa Barbara, CA 93105

Financial data (yr. ended 03/31/02): Assets, $15,368 (M); grants paid, $0; gifts received, $3,500; expenditures, $652; qualifying distributions, $0.
Officers and Directors:* Walter Hogan, M.D.,* Pres.; Lois Hogan,* Secy.
EIN: 770071269

59053
The Sigurd and Irene Peterson Family Foundation
c/o I. Peterson
304 Clearhaven Dr.
Azusa, CA 91702

Established in 2000 in CA.
Financial data (yr. ended 12/31/00): Assets, $15,140 (M); grants paid, $800; gifts received, $15,689; expenditures, $800; qualifying distributions, $800.
Limitations: Giving primarily in CA.
Officers: Irene Peterson, C.E.O.; C. Craig Paxton, C.F.O.
Director: Joseph Peterson.
EIN: 954794707

59054
Namaste Foundation
P.O. Box 336
Tecopa, CA 92389
Contact: Robert E. Graham, Secy.-Treas.

Established in 1988 in CA.
Donor(s): Wendy P. Graham, Robert E. Graham.
Financial data (yr. ended 12/31/99): Assets, $14,991 (M); grants paid, $69,579; gifts received, $68,000; expenditures, $78,984; qualifying distributions, $78,771.
Limitations: Giving primarily in CA.
Officers: Lara G. Truppelli, Pres.; Robert E. Graham, Secy.-Treas.
EIN: 680159559

59055
Ellis-Orpheus Club, Inc.
c/o Gene Ogle
3559 Michelle Dr.
Torrance, CA 90503-2545

Classified as a private operating foundation in 1976.
Financial data (yr. ended 05/31/01): Assets, $14,894 (M); grants paid, $76,843; gifts received, $6,488; expenditures, $79,345; qualifying distributions, $79,345.
Officers: Gene Ogle, Pres.; William Evans, Secy.; Fred Peitzman, Treas.
EIN: 510188758

59056
AHIMSA
(also known as Agency for Human Interconnectedness through Manifestation of Spiritual Awareness)
P.O. Box 8196
Berkeley, CA 94707

Donor(s): Kumar Mehta.
Financial data (yr. ended 12/31/00): Assets, $14,622 (M); grants paid, $0; gifts received, $13,526; expenditures, $3,032; qualifying distributions, $3,032; giving activities include $3,032 for programs.
Officers: Greg Richardson, Pres.; Nik Warren, V.P.; Kumar Mehta, Secy.; Henry Baer, Treas.
EIN: 943180384

59057
Mission Bay Educational Foundation
2640 Soderblom Ave.
San Diego, CA 92122

Established in 1998.
Financial data (yr. ended 06/30/99): Assets, $14,607 (M); grants paid, $0; gifts received, $6,046; expenditures, $3,934; qualifying distributions, $0.
Limitations: Applications not accepted.
Application information: Contributes only to pre-selected organizations.
Officers: George R. Phelps, Co-C.E.O.; Frank P. Uehle, Co-C.E.O.
EIN: 990472008

59058
T'Shuvah, Inc.
8831 Venice Blvd.
Los Angeles, CA 90034
Contact: Hariet Rosetto

Classified as a private operating foundation in 00 in CA.
Financial data (yr. ended 12/31/01): Assets, $14,559 (M); grants paid, $0; expenditures, $0; qualifying distributions, $0.
Officers: Warren Breslow, Pres.; David Azous, Secy.; Carole Glodney, C.F.O.
EIN: 954561785

59059
Merriam Sharp Foundation, Inc.
P.O. Box 1244
San Luis Obispo, CA 93406

Established in 1996.
Donor(s): Karen Merriam.
Financial data (yr. ended 12/31/99): Assets, $14,534 (M); grants paid, $2,000; gifts received, $5,000; expenditures, $2,915; qualifying distributions, $2,895.
Limitations: Applications not accepted. Giving primarily in CA.
Application information: Contributes only to pre-selected organizations.
Officers: Karen Merriam, Pres.; Robin Sharp, V.P.
Directors: Dean Armstrong, Lee Ann Armstrong, Scott Armstrong, Todd Armstrong.
EIN: 770432705

59060
Karpeles Manuscript Library
465 Hot Springs Rd.
Santa Barbara, CA 93108

Donor(s): David Karpeles, Marsha Karpeles.
Financial data (yr. ended 12/31/01): Assets, $14,454 (M); grants paid, $0; gifts received, $616,125; expenditures, $619,520; qualifying distributions, $0.
Directors: David Karpeles, Marsha Karpeles.
EIN: 593132767

59061
W. Edward Freuer & D. Lorene Freuer Family Foundation, A Charitable Corp.
4941 Kipling Dr.
Carmichael, CA 95608-6042

Classified as a private operating foundation in 1997 in CA.
Donor(s): D. Lorene Freuer, W. Edward Freuer.
Financial data (yr. ended 12/31/00): Assets, $14,336 (M); grants paid, $550; gifts received, $3,534; expenditures, $561; qualifying distributions, $546.
Limitations: Applications not accepted. Giving primarily in CA and OR.

Application information: Contributes only to pre-selected organizations.
Trustees: D. Lorene Freuer, W. Edward Freuer.
EIN: 911836647

59062
Elliott Angelo Doglione Memorial Baseball Scholarship Fund
647 La Mesa Dr.
Salinas, CA 93901-3816 (831) 424-9142
Contact: Donna Doglione, Dir.

Established in 1993.
Financial data (yr. ended 12/31/99): Assets, $14,252 (M); grants paid, $1,000; gifts received, $940; expenditures, $1,050; qualifying distributions, $1,000.
Limitations: Giving limited to Salinas, CA.
Directors: Donna Doglione, Gina M. Doglione, Michael J. Doglione, William Freeman.
EIN: 770353965

59063
Tulare County Dairy Women Scholarship Fund
P.O. Box 2097
Tulare, CA 93275-2097
Application address: c/o Denise Cahill, Bank of America, P.O. Box 551, Visalia, CA 93279

Classified as a private operating foundation in 1994.
Financial data (yr. ended 12/31/01): Assets, $14,114 (M); grants paid, $1,625; expenditures, $1,643; qualifying distributions, $1,625.
Limitations: Giving limited to residents of Tulare, CA.
Application information: Application form required.
Officers: Diane Sepeda, Pres.; Denise Cahill, V.P.; Kellie Kroes, Secy.; Amy Hoehn, Treas.
Director: Robin Souza.
EIN: 770226500

59064
One Hundred Acre Wood Foundation
c/o Michael P. Broida, C.P.A.
9454 Wilshire Blvd., Ste. 550
Beverly Hills, CA 90212

Established in 2000 in CA.
Donor(s): David W. Wyler.
Financial data (yr. ended 12/31/00): Assets, $14,000 (M); grants paid, $700; gifts received, $700,306; expenditures, $700; qualifying distributions, $700.
Limitations: Applications not accepted.
Application information: Contributes only to pre-selected organizations.
Officer: Jane Wyler, Pres.
EIN: 954774001

59065
AE Foundation
3965 Bonny Doon Rd.
Santa Cruz, CA 95060-9706
Contact: Gary Young, Treas.

Donor(s): Marcel Goodwin.‡
Financial data (yr. ended 12/31/01): Assets, $13,962 (M); grants paid, $0; gifts received, $6; expenditures, $1,162; qualifying distributions, $0.
Officers: Hollis de Lancey, Pres.; Avelet Almog, Secy.; Gary Young, Treas.
EIN: 942867836

59066
Mended Wings Foundation
195 Loma Alta
Los Gatos, CA 95032

Established in 1997 in CA. Classified as a private operating foundation in 1999.
Donor(s): Darrell Miller, M. Godare.
Financial data (yr. ended 08/31/99): Assets, $12,813 (M); grants paid, $0; gifts received, $3,723; expenditures, $17,935; qualifying distributions, $15,958; giving activities include $15,958 for programs.
Officers: Morgan Godare, Pres.; Darrell Miller, Secy.-Treas.
EIN: 770466596

59067
Cyberpeace, Inc.
857 Leonard Rd.
Los Angeles, CA 90049-1326

Established in 1995 in CA.
Financial data (yr. ended 06/30/01): Assets, $12,775 (M); grants paid, $0; expenditures, $229; qualifying distributions, $0.
Trustee: Sidney Friedman.
EIN: 954548048

59068
Friends of Ernest
920 41st Ave.
Santa Cruz, CA 95062

Established in 1997.
Donor(s): Alan F. Shugart.
Financial data (yr. ended 08/31/00): Assets, $12,642 (M); grants paid, $0; gifts received, $100,000; expenditures, $116,284; qualifying distributions, $112,962; giving activities include $112,962 for programs.
Officer: Alan F. Shugart, Chair.
Director: Teri Erickson.
EIN: 770465724

59069
Old Riverside Foundation
P.O. Box 601
Riverside, CA 92502-0601

Financial data (yr. ended 06/30/99): Assets, $12,188 (M); grants paid, $0; expenditures, $12,858; qualifying distributions, $3,609; giving activities include $3,609 for programs.
Directors: Ann Drown, Michael S. Emet, Robert Kneisel, Ph.D., Kathryn Maddox, Jack Reid, Diane Caltran Roth, Kenneth Stacey, Robert J. Vietrl, Jeannie Wesley.
EIN: 953407036

59070
Salzberg Equal Justice Foundation
(Formerly Equal Justice Institute, Inc.)
130 Ocean Park Blvd., Ste. 331
Santa Monica, CA 90405

Donor(s): Harry E. Salzberg.
Financial data (yr. ended 12/31/01): Assets, $11,593 (M); grants paid, $6,500; gifts received, $19,000; expenditures, $21,495; qualifying distributions, $19,194.
Limitations: Applications not accepted. Giving primarily in WI.
Application information: Contributes only to pre-selected organizations.
Officers and Directors:* Harry E. Salzberg,* Chair. and Treas.; Hedi M. Salzberg,* V.P.; David Schwab.
EIN: 042932036

59071
The Williams Foundation
3032 Market St.
Oakland, CA 94608
Contact: K.M. Williams, Pres.

Established in 1991.
Donor(s): Kenneth M. Williams.
Financial data (yr. ended 03/31/00): Assets, $11,013 (M); grants paid, $37,252; gifts received, $17,370; expenditures, $37,401; qualifying distributions, $37,252.
Officers: Kenneth M. Williams, Pres.; B.B. Williams, Secy.
EIN: 944318017

59072
Lawrence Library Foundation
7581 Delgado Pl.
Carlsbad, CA 92009-7705 (760) 436-6772
Contact: Virginia Moran, Tr.

Classified as a private operating foundation in 1990.
Donor(s): Virginia Moran.
Financial data (yr. ended 12/31/00): Assets, $10,349 (M); grants paid, $450; expenditures, $1,392; qualifying distributions, $1,392.
Limitations: Giving limited to CA.
Trustee: Virginia Moran.
EIN: 330405408

59073
Leadership Thru Books
14849 Firestone Blvd.
La Mirada, CA 90638-6009

Financial data (yr. ended 03/31/01): Assets, $10,243 (M); grants paid, $23,430; gifts received, $27,381; expenditures, $33,597; qualifying distributions, $23,430.
Limitations: Applications not accepted. Giving primarily in Patulul, Guatemala.
Application information: Contributes only to pre-selected organizations.
Officers: Dora Orellana, Pres.; Karen Fernandez, V.P.; Andrea Ruiz, Secy.; Miriam Axelrod, Treas.
EIN: 954593229

59074
Caroline June Miyake Memorial Foundation
c/o Tom Miyake
2885 Ashlan Ave.
Clovis, CA 93611

Established in 2001.
Donor(s): Tom Miyake.
Financial data (yr. ended 12/31/01): Assets, $10,174 (M); grants paid, $750; gifts received, $1,850; expenditures, $757; qualifying distributions, $990.
Limitations: Giving limited to residents of Fresno County, CA.
Application information: Application form required.
Officer: Tom Miyake, Admin.
Directors: Karen A. Miyake, Kirk A. Miyake, Lynnette A. Scherselaar.
EIN: 770552836

59075
Orange Park Acres Womens League
P.O. Box 2696
Orange, CA 92859

Established in 1994.
Financial data (yr. ended 06/30/00): Assets, $10,127 (M); grants paid, $9,470; gifts received, $268; expenditures, $12,186; qualifying distributions, $12,186.
Limitations: Applications not accepted. Giving limited to Orange County, CA.
Application information: Contributes only to pre-selected organizations.
Officers: Laura Thomas, Pres.; Barbara Martin, 1st V.P.; Elaine Olsen, 2nd V.P.; Suzanne Seegers, Treas.
EIN: 330522486

59076
Malcolm Evett Foundation
45 Shadyleaf Ct.
Santa Rosa, CA 95409-2740

Established in 1999 in CA. Classified as a private operating foundation in 2000.
Donor(s): Malcolm Evett.
Financial data (yr. ended 12/31/00): Assets, $9,960 (M); grants paid, $300; expenditures, $614; qualifying distributions, $614; giving activities include $89 for programs.
Limitations: Applications not accepted.
Application information: Contributes only to pre-selected organizations.
Officers and Directors:* H. James Price,* Chair.; Malcolm Evett,* Secy.-Treas.
EIN: 770527969

59077
The Panda Charitable Foundation
899 El Centro St.
South Pasadena, CA 91030
Contact: Julie Gunawan

Financial data (yr. ended 12/31/01): Assets, $9,919 (M); grants paid, $103,025; gifts received, $129,890; expenditures, $130,562; qualifying distributions, $130,562; giving activities include $27,527 for programs.
Limitations: Giving primarily in CA.
Trustees: Margaret Wong, Panda Mgmt. Co., Inc.
EIN: 954142346
Codes: FD2

59078
Battered Women's Assistance
P.O. Box 1119
Santa Cruz, CA 95061-1119

Classified as a private operating foundation in 1992 in CA.
Financial data (yr. ended 12/31/01): Assets, $9,890 (M); grants paid, $11,901; gifts received, $17,250; expenditures, $12,334; qualifying distributions, $12,334.
Limitations: Applications not accepted. Giving limited to residents of Santa Cruz County, CA.
Application information: Unsolicited requests for funds not accepted.
Officer and Directors:* Marsha B. Shanle,* Secy.-Treas.; Nell S. Cliff, Anne Levin, Gail Michaelis-Ow, Pat Rebele, Phyllis Simpkins, Mary Solari.
EIN: 770167239
Codes: GTI

59079
National Family Center, Inc.
321 S. Beverly Dr., Ste. K
Beverly Hills, CA 90212

Classified as a private operating foundation in 1995.
Financial data (yr. ended 06/30/01): Assets, $9,803 (M); grants paid, $0; expenditures, $3,663; qualifying distributions, $0.
Officer: Vivian A. Feintech, Pres.
EIN: 043120793

59080
The Rosalind M. Wang Family Foundation
c/o Rosalind Wang
321 E. Stocker St., No. 205
Glendale, CA 91207 (818) 240-8170

Established in 2001 in CA.
Donor(s): Rosalind Wang.
Financial data (yr. ended 12/31/01): Assets, $9,779 (M); grants paid, $0; gifts received, $10,000; expenditures, $2,000; qualifying distributions, $2,000.
Officers: Rosalind Wang, Pres.; Mimi Wang, Secy.; Eric Wang, Treas.
EIN: 954871855

59081
Underground Construction Company Charitable Trust
5145 Industrial Way
Benicia, CA 94510-0809 (707) 746-8800
Contact: James H. Curry, Tr.

Established in 1995. Classified as a company-sponsored operating foundation in 1996.
Donor(s): Underground Construction Co., Inc.
Financial data (yr. ended 10/31/00): Assets, $9,492 (M); grants paid, $17,514; gifts received, $25,000; expenditures, $18,086; qualifying distributions, $17,514.
Trustee: James H. Curry.
EIN: 680355002

59082
Hawaiian Gardens Food Bank, Inc.
21500 S. Pioneer Blvd., Ste. 103
Hawaiian Gardens, CA 90716

Donor(s): The Irving T. Moskowitz Foundation.
Financial data (yr. ended 12/31/00): Assets, $8,811 (M); grants paid, $0; gifts received, $393,864; expenditures, $395,515; qualifying distributions, $392,994; giving activities include $392,993 for programs.
Officers and Directors:* Irving Moskowitz,* Pres.; Cherna Moskowitz, V.P. and Secy.-Treas.; Joyce Canham.
EIN: 330676791

59083
Global Possibilities
1955 Mandeville Canyon Rd.
Los Angeles, CA 90049

Established in 1998 in CA.
Donor(s): Cassandra C. Danson.
Financial data (yr. ended 12/31/00): Assets, $8,742 (M); grants paid, $22,535; gifts received, $184,557; expenditures, $190,235; qualifying distributions, $186,820; giving activities include $29,425 for programs.
Limitations: Applications not accepted.
Application information: Contributes only to pre-selected organizations.
Director: Cassandra Coates Danson.
EIN: 954587068

59084
Western State University Law Review
1111 N. State College Blvd.
Fullerton, CA 92831-3014

Established in 1999 in CA.
Financial data (yr. ended 12/31/01): Assets, $8,737 (M); grants paid, $0; gifts received, $9,384; expenditures, $21,385; qualifying distributions, $0.
Directors: Richard W. Helms, Judy Hsu, Joseph Telezinski, Jon Wadsworth.
EIN: 510172561

59085
The Watts Family Foundation
63 Camino Por Los Arboles
Atherton, CA 94027-5940 (650) 326-7244
Contact: Teresa Watts, Tr.

Financial data (yr. ended 09/30/01): Assets, $8,671 (M); grants paid, $7,000; expenditures, $7,100; qualifying distributions, $7,000.

Officers and Trustees:* Jack L. Watts,* Pres.; Teresa Watts,* Secy.-Treas.
EIN: 770176038

59086
American Medical Charity Foundation, Inc.
912 S. 1st St.
Alhambra, CA 91801

Established in 1999.
Donor(s): Matthew Y.C. Lin.
Financial data (yr. ended 12/31/00): Assets, $7,907 (M); grants paid, $5,000; gifts received, $10,000; expenditures, $5,000; qualifying distributions, $5,000.
Limitations: Applications not accepted. Giving primarily in El Monte, CA.
Application information: Contributes only to pre-selected organizations.
Officer: Matthew Y.C. Lin, Pres.
EIN: 954747486

59087
Molecular Medicine Foundation
c/o Delsen & Caldwell, LLP
9740 Scranton Rd., Ste. 310
San Diego, CA 92121
Application address: 2362 Avenida de La Playa, La Jolla, CA 92037
Contact: K.J. Rogers, Pres.

Classified as a private operating foundation in 1983.
Donor(s): Joanne R. Edgington.
Financial data (yr. ended 06/30/00): Assets, $7,440 (M); grants paid, $6,000; gifts received, $5,000; expenditures, $7,018; qualifying distributions, $6,000.
Limitations: Giving primarily in La Jolla, CA.
Officers: K.J. Rogers, Pres.; T. Scott Edgington, Secy.
Trustees: Thomas S. Edgington, K.A. Perry, Phillip Perry.
EIN: 942900940

59088
American Association of University Oakdale-Riverbank Scholarship Fund
(Formerly Oakdale Riverbank Branch-American Association of University Women's Scholarship Fund)
1056 Maria Dr.
Oakdale, CA 95361 (209) 847-0408
Contact: Katherine Caster, Pres.

Established in 1991 in CA.
Financial data (yr. ended 06/30/99): Assets, $7,388 (M); grants paid, $250; gifts received, $883; expenditures, $281; qualifying distributions, $281.
Limitations: Giving limited to the Oakdale, CA, area.
Application information: Application form required.
Officers: Katherine Caster, Pres.; Kay Sarratt, V.P.; Evelyn Neubaum, Secy.; Betty Mondo, Treas.
EIN: 680248521

59089
Center for Social Epidemiology, Inc.
c/o Peter Schnall
1528 6th St., Ste. 202
Santa Monica, CA 90401

Established in 1987 in NY.
Donor(s): Peter Schnall, Sherry Schnall.
Financial data (yr. ended 08/31/99): Assets, $7,033 (M); grants paid, $0; gifts received, $193,000; expenditures, $191,736; qualifying distributions, $190,039; giving activities include $192,668 for programs.

Limitations: Applications not accepted.
Application information: Contributes only to pre-selected organizations.
Officer: Sherry Schnall, V.P.
Director: Peter Schnall.
EIN: 112878378

59090
D & J Kid's Foundation
7011 Sepulveda Blvd.
Los Angeles, CA 90045

Established in 1999 in CA.
Financial data (yr. ended 12/31/01): Assets, $7,000 (M); grants paid, $0; gifts received, $24,475; expenditures, $19,787; qualifying distributions, $0.
Officers: Russell D. Sheets, Pres.; June L. Sheets, V.P.
EIN: 954718418

59091
Al Malik Charitable Foundation
150 Pilgrim Loop
Fremont, CA 94539
Contact: Zafar Malik, Tr.

Donor(s): Zafar Malik.
Financial data (yr. ended 12/31/00): Assets, $6,925 (M); grants paid, $5,000; gifts received, $476,196; expenditures, $9,961; qualifying distributions, $5,000.
Limitations: Giving primarily in Pakistan.
Application information: Application form not required.
Director: Zafar Malik.
EIN: 943348105

59092
The Anne T. Hall Foundation
1835 Sullivan Ct.
Morgan Hill, CA 95037

Classified as a private operating foundation in 1997.
Donor(s): Diana Hall, George Hall.
Financial data (yr. ended 06/30/01): Assets, $6,725 (M); grants paid, $6,500; gifts received, $6,800; expenditures, $7,807; qualifying distributions, $7,807.
Limitations: Applications not accepted. Giving on a national basis, with emphasis on CA.
Application information: Contributes only to pre-selected organizations.
Trustees: Diana Hall, George Hall.
EIN: 770444117

59093
Sanderson Foundation for Senior Afro-Americans
2020 Stockton St.
San Francisco, CA 94133-2005

Financial data (yr. ended 05/31/99): Assets, $6,452 (M); grants paid, $0; expenditures, $0; qualifying distributions, $0.
Limitations: Applications not accepted.
Application information: Contributes only to pre-selected organizations.
Officers and Directors:* Sue Bailey Thurman,* Chair.; Glenn Nance,* V.P. and Treas.; Eloise McKinney Johnson,* Secy.; Felix Justice, Alice Royal.
EIN: 237426424

59094
The David William Upham Foundation
3550 Wilshire Blvd., Ste. 840
Los Angeles, CA 90010-2409

Established in 1997 in CA.
Donor(s): David William Upham.
Financial data (yr. ended 12/31/00): Assets, $6,384 (M); grants paid, $11,793; gifts received, $18,194; expenditures, $15,034; qualifying distributions, $13,598.
Limitations: Applications not accepted.
Application information: Contributes only to pre-selected organizations.
Directors: Robert Leonard, Willard M. Reisz, David William Upham.
EIN: 954652179

59095
Garnett Foundation
P.O. Box 25049
San Mateo, CA 94402

Established in 1998 in CA.
Donor(s): Terry Garnett, Katrina Garnett.
Financial data (yr. ended 12/31/00): Assets, $6,059 (M); grants paid, $3,332; gifts received, $18,359; expenditures, $33,104; qualifying distributions, $30,394.
Limitations: Applications not accepted. Giving primarily in San Jose, CA.
Application information: Contributes only to pre-selected organizations.
Officers: Katrina Garnett, Pres.; Howard Zeprun, Secy.; Terry Garnett, Treas.
EIN: 943267366

59096
Curt R. and Gerry Pindler Foundation
11910 Poindexter
Moorpark, CA 93021

Established in 1999 in CA.
Donor(s): Curt R. Pindler.
Financial data (yr. ended 12/31/00): Assets, $6,020 (M); grants paid, $19,770; gifts received, $20,000; expenditures, $19,780; qualifying distributions, $19,770.
Limitations: Applications not accepted. Giving primarily in CA.
Application information: Contributes only to pre-selected organizations.
Officers: Curt R. Pindler, Pres. and C.F.O.; Gerry Pindler, V.P. and Secy.
EIN: 770491644

59097
The Raymond Trybul Foundation
6504 Bridgeport Ln.
Bakersfield, CA 93309

Established in 1999 in CA.
Donor(s): Margaret Trybul.
Financial data (yr. ended 12/31/99): Assets, $6,000 (M); grants paid, $0; gifts received, $6,000; expenditures, $0; qualifying distributions, $0.
Limitations: Applications not accepted.
Application information: Contributes only to pre-selected organizations.
Trustees: Donald G. Trybul, Margaret Trybul.
EIN: 770529536

59098
Martin Operating Foundation
2569 Greenwich St.
San Francisco, CA 94123

Established in 2000 in CA.
Financial data (yr. ended 09/30/01): Assets, $5,961 (M); grants paid, $0; gifts received, $3,100; expenditures, $616; qualifying distributions, $100; giving activities include $100 for programs.
Limitations: Applications not accepted.
Application information: Contributes only to pre-selected organizations.
Officers and Directors:* Wendy Everett,* Chair.; Robert Levenson,* Secy.; Rick Berthold.
EIN: 943382431

59099
The Stacey Augmon Foundation
c/o TMHP
10866 Wilshire Blvd., 10th Fl.
Los Angeles, CA 90024

Established in 1999 in CA.
Donor(s): Stacey Augmon.
Financial data (yr. ended 12/31/00): Assets, $5,958 (M); grants paid, $0; gifts received, $32,160; expenditures, $30,713; qualifying distributions, $30,582; giving activities include $30,582 for programs.
Limitations: Applications not accepted.
Application information: Contributes only to pre-selected organizations.
Officer: Stacey Augmon, Pres.
EIN: 680475938

59100
Gibson Institute for Medical Research
P.O. Box 1914
Santa Rosa, CA 95402

Established in 1994 in CA.
Donor(s): John McCue, Alan Lucas.‡
Financial data (yr. ended 12/31/01): Assets, $5,758 (M); grants paid, $0; expenditures, $3,830; qualifying distributions, $2,893; giving activities include $3,566 for programs.
Officers: John McCue, Pres.; Mike McHugh, Secy.-Treas.
Directors: Chad Duravetz, Robert Stern.
EIN: 943196737

59101
Yuan Quan Foundation
21 Kerr Ave.
Kensington, CA 94707

Established as an operating foundation in 1981.
Donor(s): William Lowe.
Financial data (yr. ended 06/30/99): Assets, $5,737 (M); grants paid, $6,500; gifts received, $2,500; expenditures, $10,811; qualifying distributions, $6,500.
Limitations: Applications not accepted. Giving primarily in China.
Application information: Contributes only to pre-selected organizations.
Officer: William Lowe, Pres.
EIN: 942610438

59102
Meru Foundation
P.O. Box 1738
San Anselmo, CA 94979-1738

Classified as a private operating foundation in 1984.
Financial data (yr. ended 12/31/00): Assets, $5,473 (M); grants paid, $0; gifts received, $46,524; expenditures, $37,733; qualifying distributions, $30,152; giving activities include $29,239 for programs.
Officers: William Haber, Pres.; Cynthia Tenen, Secy.-Treas.
Directors: Grace Ackerman, Virginia Meyer, Stanley N. Tenen.
EIN: 680002931

59103
Laurence C. Gaebe Family Foundation, Inc.
132 1st St.
P.O. Box 268
Avila Beach, CA 93424-0268

Established in 1997 in CA.

59103—CALIFORNIA

Financial data (yr. ended 12/31/99): Assets, $5,470 (M); grants paid, $500; expenditures, $1,071; qualifying distributions, $500.
Limitations: Applications not accepted.
Application information: Contributes only to pre-selected organizations.
Officers: Laurence R. Gaebe, Pres.; John F. Sachs, Secy.; Paul D. Porter, Treas.
Director: Anne E. Gaebe Hall.
EIN: 770440553

59104
Korean Independence Historical Association, Inc.
1954 Redesdale Ave.
Los Angeles, CA 90039

Established in 1998 in CA.
Donor(s): David Hyun.
Financial data (yr. ended 12/31/00): Assets, $5,337 (M); grants paid, $1,600; gifts received, $80,636; expenditures, $80,754; qualifying distributions, $79,660; giving activities include $28,085 for programs.
Officer: David Hyun, Chair.
EIN: 954656228

59105
The Joyce & Paul Krasnow Charitable Foundation
11111 Santa Monica Blvd., Ste. 1050
Los Angeles, CA 90025-3344

Established in 2001 in CA.
Donor(s): Joyce Krasnow, Paul Krasnow.
Financial data (yr. ended 12/31/01): Assets, $5,337 (M); grants paid, $44,754; gifts received, $50,000; expenditures, $44,754; qualifying distributions, $44,754.
Limitations: Giving primarily in Los Angeles, CA.
Officers: Paul Krasnow, Pres.; Joyce Krasnow, C.F.O.
EIN: 311783169

59106
All Nations Benefits Ministry
c/o Charles Freeland
P.O. Box 2129
Berkeley, CA 94702-2129

Financial data (yr. ended 12/31/99): Assets, $5,256 (M); grants paid, $0; gifts received, $200; expenditures, $17,816; qualifying distributions, $0; giving activities include $17,816 for programs.
Officers: Fayre C. Moore, Secy.; Rev. Charles Freeland, Exec. Dir.
Director: Zada Flowers.
EIN: 521775514
Codes: TN

59107
Mighty Companions, Inc.
1500 Sunset Plaza Dr.
Los Angeles, CA 90069

Donor(s): Suzanne Taylor.
Financial data (yr. ended 12/31/99): Assets, $4,828 (M); grants paid, $0; gifts received, $31,964; expenditures, $32,830; qualifying distributions, $25,221; giving activities include $25,221 for programs.
Officer: Suzanne Taylor, Mgr.
EIN: 954255679

59108
Strome Youth Empowerment Foundation
(Formerly Big Bear Foundation)
100 Wilshire Blvd., Ste. 1500
Santa Monica, CA 90401

Established in 1998 in CA.

Financial data (yr. ended 03/31/00): Assets, $4,726 (M); grants paid, $0; gifts received, $66,211; expenditures, $62,211; qualifying distributions, $62,211; giving activities include $62,211 for programs.
Officers: Mark E. Strome, Pres.; Jeffrey Lambert, Treas.
EIN: 954632369

59109
Omega Center, Inc.
1651 N. Riverside Ave., No. 1013
Rialto, CA 92376-8038

Classified as a private operating foundation in 1991.
Financial data (yr. ended 12/31/00): Assets, $4,717 (M); grants paid, $0; expenditures, $12,032; qualifying distributions, $0.
Officers: Fritz C. Robinson, C.E.O.; Denice Peters, Secy.; Raymond Overstreet, Treas.
EIN: 330163066

59110
Human Eyes Help the Blind and Partially Sighted
(Formerly Human Eyes Help the Blind)
67 Patrick Way
Half Moon Bay, CA 94019-1772

Classified as a private operating foundation in 1993.
Financial data (yr. ended 12/31/01): Assets, $4,648 (M); grants paid, $1,170; expenditures, $3,191; qualifying distributions, $1,170.
Limitations: Giving primarily in CA.
Trustee: Bea Bel.
EIN: 943132188

59111
San Francisco Network of Mental Health Clients, Inc.
2940 16th St., Ste. B2
San Francisco, CA 94103-3664

Classified as a private operating foundation in 1992.
Financial data (yr. ended 06/30/00): Assets, $4,610 (M); grants paid, $0; gifts received, $37,622; expenditures, $33,012; qualifying distributions, $33,012; giving activities include $8,971 for programs.
Officers: Mickey Shirley, Pres.; Mark S. Adamec, V.P.; Michael Wise, V.P.; Susan Dweley, Secy.; Sonnie Colvid, Treas.
EIN: 943084340

59112
Howard & Helen House Family Foundation
2245 Melville Dr.
San Marino, CA 91108

Established in 1994 in CA.
Donor(s): Howard P. House.
Financial data (yr. ended 12/31/00): Assets, $4,602 (L); grants paid, $6,450; gifts received, $5,000; expenditures, $6,570; qualifying distributions, $6,570.
Limitations: Giving primarily in CA.
Officers: John W. House, Pres.; Kenneth M. House, V.P.; Carolyn Helmuth, Secy.-Treas.
EIN: 954441276

59113
Serrano Creek Conservancy
25201 Trabuco Rd.
Lake Forest, CA 92630

Established in 2000 in CA.
Financial data (yr. ended 12/31/00): Assets, $4,508 (M); grants paid, $0; gifts received, $6,885; expenditures, $11,659; qualifying

distributions, $10,674; giving activities include $2,957 for program-related investments and $5,500 for programs.
Limitations: Applications not accepted.
Application information: Contributes only to pre-selected organizations.
Officers: Matt Rayl, Pres.; Gary Beeler, V.P.; Jan Beeler, Secy.; Mark Ross, Treas.
EIN: 330899718

59114
Harold & Barbara Jones Foundation
10 Badger Ct.
Novato, CA 94949

Established in 2000 in CA.
Donor(s): Harold Jones, Barbara Jones.
Financial data (yr. ended 12/31/00): Assets, $4,472 (M); grants paid, $0; gifts received, $182,500; expenditures, $228,943; qualifying distributions, $228,943; giving activities include $21,905 for programs.
Limitations: Applications not accepted.
Application information: Contributes only to a pre-selected organization.
Directors: Barbara Jones, Harold Jones.
EIN: 943358394

59115
Valle Verde Scholarship Fund
900 Calle De Los Amigos
Santa Barbara, CA 93105-4435
Tel.: (805) 687-1571, Ext. 218
Contact: Susan McHale

Financial data (yr. ended 12/31/00): Assets, $4,266 (M); grants paid, $2,137; gifts received, $2,250; expenditures, $2,350; qualifying distributions, $2,137.
Committee Members: Mr. Bowers, Robynn Collins, Mrs. Hicks, Ditte Noack.
EIN: 770282472

59116
Club Lassen Volleyball
c/o Jack Catron
472-205 Debi Dr.
Susanville, CA 96130 (530) 257-3316

Established in 2000 in CA.
Financial data (yr. ended 12/31/00): Assets, $4,253 (M); grants paid, $0; gifts received, $11,992; expenditures, $7,739; qualifying distributions, $7,739; giving activities include $7,739 for programs.
Officer: Vicky Schmidt, Secy.
Director: Jack Catron.
EIN: 680401614

59117
San Francisco Tavern Guild Building Fund
2171 Junipero Serra Blvd., Ste. 500
Daly City, CA 94014

Established in 1997.
Financial data (yr. ended 12/31/00): Assets, $4,089 (L); grants paid, $38,985; gifts received, $4,388; expenditures, $41,437; qualifying distributions, $0.
Limitations: Applications not accepted.
Application information: Contributes only to pre-selected organizations.
Officers: Steven Rascher, Pres.; Linda Lopez, Secy.; Stanley Boyd, Treas.
Board Member: Jim Bliesner.
EIN: 943205042

59118
Prell-Sonenshine Foundation
2719 White Rd.
Irvine, CA 92614
Application address: 2437 Monaco Dr., Laguna Beach, CA 92651
Contact: Ygal Sonenshine

Classified as a private operating foundation in 1992.
Donor(s): Ygal Sonenshine.
Financial data (yr. ended 12/31/01): Assets, $3,948 (M); grants paid, $52,000; gifts received, $54,570; expenditures, $52,137; qualifying distributions, $52,134.
Limitations: Giving primarily in CA.
Officers: Ygal Sonenshine, Pres.; Jacob Prell Sonenshine, V.P.; Sheila Sonenshine, Secy.
EIN: 330515227

59119
John Saunders Foundation
(Formerly Sydney Foundation)
c/o Bryan Cave, LLP
120 Broadway, Ste. 500
Santa Monica, CA 90401-2386

Financial data (yr. ended 06/30/01): Assets, $3,929 (M); grants paid, $0; expenditures, $359; qualifying distributions, $0.
Limitations: Applications not accepted. Giving primarily in Sydney, Australia.
Application information: Contributes only to pre-selected organizations.
Officers: Lawrence Heller, Pres. and Treas.; Richard M. Eigner, Secy.
EIN: 954440135

59120
Mayer & Ezell Family Foundation
1552 Trumbower Ave.
Monterey Park, CA 91755

Classified as a private operating foundation in 1978.
Financial data (yr. ended 12/31/00): Assets, $3,468 (M); grants paid, $0; gifts received, $8,200; expenditures, $4,845; qualifying distributions, $4,845; giving activities include $4,099 for programs.
Officers: C. Lamar Mayer, Pres.; Tami Romero, V.P.; Jeannine Ezell Mayer, Secy.-Treas.
Director: VaLynn Melzer.
EIN: 953216414

59121
Sant Sarwan Dass Charitable Organization
44997 Pawnee Dr.
Fremont, CA 94539-6664 (510) 341-1800
Contact: Beldev Madahar, Dir.

Classified as a private operating foundation in 1993. Established in 1991 in CA.
Financial data (yr. ended 12/31/99): Assets, $3,421 (M); grants paid, $49,644; gifts received, $55,241; expenditures, $52,178; qualifying distributions, $49,644.
Limitations: Giving limited to Punjab, India.
Officer: Sushil Madahar, Secy. and C.F.O.
Director: Baldev Madahar.
EIN: 943148595

59122
Douglas Franklin Smith Memorial Foundation
P.O. Box 721613
San Diego, CA 92172

Established in 1999 in UT.
Financial data (yr. ended 12/31/99): Assets, $3,407 (M); grants paid, $48; gifts received, $10,304; expenditures, $7,983; qualifying distributions, $7,810.
Trustees: Matthew A. Golson, Mike Hassey, Bruce Riddle, Brooks H. Rohlen, Frederica Rohlen, Tamara H. Seiter, Mark Whitehead.
EIN: 870636433

59123
Public Interest Law and Legal Society
5075 Shoreham Pl.
San Diego, CA 92122-3966

Classified as a private operating foundation in 1992.
Financial data (yr. ended 09/30/00): Assets, $3,305 (M); grants paid, $0; gifts received, $600; expenditures, $594; qualifying distributions, $593; giving activities include $38 for programs.
Officers: Harvey Furgatch, Pres.; John B. Walsh, Secy.; Clyde Crockett, C.F.O.
EIN: 953696413

59124
Mountain Man Industries
802 El Redondo
Redondo Beach, CA 90277

Donor(s): James Wenker.
Financial data (yr. ended 12/31/01): Assets, $3,253 (M); grants paid, $0; expenditures, $20; qualifying distributions, $0.
Officers: James Wenker, Pres.; Marsha Whetham, Secy.; Betty Wenker, Treas.
Director: Marsha Stine.
EIN: 330320306

59125
The Fieldstead Charitable Trust
P.O. Box 18613
Irvine, CA 92623-8613

Established in 1985 in CA.
Donor(s): Howard F. Ahmanson, Roberta G. Ahmanson.
Financial data (yr. ended 12/31/01): Assets, $3,210 (M); grants paid, $0; gifts received, $40,000; expenditures, $65,165; qualifying distributions, $52,540; giving activities include $23,500 for programs.
Officers: Howard F. Ahmanson, Pres.; Roberta G. Ahmanson, Secy.
EIN: 330127363

59126
North American Christian Foundation
c/o Dan McKinnon
1125 Pacific Beach Ste. 101
San Diego, CA 92109

Established in 2000 in CA.
Donor(s): Dan Mckinnon.
Financial data (yr. ended 12/31/00): Assets, $3,102 (M); grants paid, $5,000; gifts received, $13,000; expenditures, $9,898; qualifying distributions, $5,000.
Limitations: Applications not accepted. Giving primarily in McLean, VA.
Application information: Contributes only to pre-selected organizations.
Officer: Dan Mckinnon, Pres.
EIN: 330922682

59127
Christian Rehabilitation Services, Inc.
24416 Peacock St.
El Toro, CA 92630-1864

Classified as a private operating foundation in 1992 in CA.
Financial data (yr. ended 12/31/00): Assets, $3,002 (M); grants paid, $0; gifts received, $300; expenditures, $374; qualifying distributions, $374; giving activities include $374 for programs.
Officer: Jack A. Wilder, Pres.
EIN: 330229540

59128
Ken and Shirley Van Sickle Scholarship Foundation
1030 College Ave.
Menlo Park, CA 94025-5210 (650) 473-0844

Established in 1988 in CA.
Financial data (yr. ended 12/31/01): Assets, $2,995 (M); grants paid, $4,625; gifts received, $6,222; expenditures, $4,716; qualifying distributions, $11,999.
Limitations: Giving limited to residents of Alameda, CA.
Application information: Application form required.
Officers and Directors:* Keith Van Sickle, Pres.; Shirley Van Sickle,* Secy.; Valerie Van Sickle, Treas.; Ken Van Sickle, Sherry Van Sickle.
EIN: 770163151

59129
The Levy Family Foundation
(Formerly The William and Melody Levy Foundation)
c/o Janice Adair
120 El Paseo
Santa Barbara, CA 93101-2118

Established in 1987 in CA.
Donor(s): William J. Levy, Melody J. Levy, Elizabeth C. Levy, Jill Lord.
Financial data (yr. ended 12/31/00): Assets, $2,972 (M); grants paid, $13,600; gifts received, $15,000; expenditures, $15,685; qualifying distributions, $15,477.
Limitations: Giving primarily in Santa Barbara, CA.
Officers and Directors:* Larry Crandell,* Chair.; William J. Levy,* Secy. and C.F.O.; Joseph Abkin, Jill Lord.
EIN: 770168400

59130
Bishop Lew Christian Culture Foundation
1813 Via Arriba
Palos Verdes Estates, CA 90274-1236

Financial data (yr. ended 12/31/00): Assets, $2,958 (M); grants paid, $900; expenditures, $5,628; qualifying distributions, $900.
Limitations: Giving primarily in CA.
Officers: Chul-Ho Kim, Secy.; Jean Lew Kim, Treas.
Directors: Raymond Kim, Sung-Hyun Kim.
EIN: 330383279

59131
Youth Touring Bands of North Tahoe
P.O. Box 905
Carnelian Bay, CA 96140-0905

Financial data (yr. ended 06/30/01): Assets, $2,898 (M); grants paid, $0; gifts received, $2,480; expenditures, $2,707; qualifying distributions, $0.
Directors: Debbie Keehn, Dean Nordy, Ken Yagura, Terry Yagura.
EIN: 680081513

59132
Narayan and Shvarajani Chilumula Foundation
c/o Chilumula R. Reddy, M.D.
2935 Holly Ridge
Los Angeles, CA 90068-1949

Established in 1998 in CA.
Donor(s): Chilumula R. Reddy, M.D.

59132—CALIFORNIA

Financial data (yr. ended 07/31/01): Assets, $2,895 (L); grants paid, $540; expenditures, $610; qualifying distributions, $610.
Officer: Chilumula R. Reddy, M.D., Pres.
EIN: 954658743

59133
International Technology Foundation
P.O. Box 23166
San Diego, CA 92193-3166

Classified as a private operating foundation in 1984.
Financial data (yr. ended 12/31/00): Assets, $2,860 (M); grants paid, $0; gifts received, $500; expenditures, $1,866; qualifying distributions, $1,866; giving activities include $1,070 for programs.
Officer and Trustees:* I.S. Tuba,* Exec. Dir.; Elizabeth Tuba.
EIN: 251313728

59134
Zuckerman International Eye Foundation
325 E. Sierra
Fresno, CA 93710

Classified as a private operating foundation in 1985.
Donor(s): Joel L. Zuckerman, M.D.
Financial data (yr. ended 09/30/99): Assets, $2,283 (M); grants paid, $0; expenditures, $18,315; qualifying distributions, $18,307; giving activities include $18,315 for programs.
Officer: Joel L. Zuckerman, M.D., Exec. Dir.
Directors: Rick Walker, Michael Waxman, M.D.
EIN: 770061461

59135
The Lucious Harris Youth Foundation
P.O. Box 2378
Manhattan Beach, CA 90267-2378

Established in 1999 in CA.
Financial data (yr. ended 12/31/00): Assets, $2,162 (M); grants paid, $0; expenditures, $0; qualifying distributions, $0.
Officer: Lucious Harris, Mgr.
EIN: 954745323

59136
Be Set Free, Inc.
4171 1st St.
Livermore, CA 94550

Established in 1995 in CA.
Donor(s): Edwin Hutka.
Financial data (yr. ended 12/31/00): Assets, $2,083 (L); grants paid, $0; gifts received, $1,200; expenditures, $605; qualifying distributions, $604.
Limitations: Applications not accepted.
Officers: Edwin Hutka, Pres.; Janice Hutka, Treas.
EIN: 942711086

59137
Center for Explorations in Consciousness
2080 Maricopa Hwy.
Ojai, CA 93023 (805) 886-5000
Contact: Martin Weiner, Pres.

Established in 1992 in CA.
Donor(s): Steven L. Bing.
Financial data (yr. ended 09/30/01): Assets, $2,073 (M); grants paid, $0; expenditures, $151,499; qualifying distributions, $0.
Application information: Application form not required.
Officers and Directors:* Martin Weiner,* Pres.; Gary Sherman,* V.P.; Marcia Weiner,* Secy.; Ellen Miller,* Treas.; Steven L. Bing.
EIN: 943167971

59138
Urban Art, Inc.
1436 Mt. Pleasant St.
Los Angeles, CA 90042

Established in 1995 in CA.
Financial data (yr. ended 06/30/02): Assets, $1,933 (M); grants paid, $92; expenditures, $184; qualifying distributions, $92.
Officers: Michael Several, Pres.; Ruth Several, Secy.-Treas.
Director: Julie Silliman.
EIN: 954004322
Codes: TN

59139
Digestive Diseases Foundation
8737 Beverly Blvd., Ste. 301 B
Los Angeles, CA 90048

Established in 1996 in CA.
Financial data (yr. ended 12/31/99): Assets, $1,889 (L); grants paid, $0; gifts received, $20,650; expenditures, $20,687; qualifying distributions, $20,687.
Officer: Herbert Rubin, Pres.
EIN: 954084508

59140
United Communal Services Foundation
7095 Hollywood Blvd., No. 692
Los Angeles, CA 90028

Established in 1999.
Financial data (yr. ended 12/31/00): Assets, $1,859 (L); grants paid, $0; expenditures, $685; qualifying distributions, $4,740.
Officers: Nathan Boatner, C.E.O.; Wayne Bien, Secy.; Ray Latveill, Treas.
EIN: 954530206

59141
Doors Foundation
9595 Wilshire Blvd., Ste. 1020
Beverly Hills, CA 90212

Established in 1998 in CA.
Financial data (yr. ended 12/31/00): Assets, $1,776 (M); grants paid, $0; expenditures, $70; qualifying distributions, $70; giving activities include $60 for programs.
Limitations: Applications not accepted.
Application information: Contributes only to pre-selected organizations.
Officers: John Densmore, C.E.O.; Robert Krieger, Secy.; Raymond Manzarek, C.F.O.
EIN: 954680391

59142
Cecille Gonzalez Gomez Library, Inc.
51 Uranus Terrace
San Francisco, CA 94114

Established in 2000 in CA.
Financial data (yr. ended 12/31/00): Assets, $1,738 (M); grants paid, $1,000; gifts received, $2,755; expenditures, $1,020; qualifying distributions, $1,000.
Officer: Evelyn Wang, Secy.-Treas.
Director: Gregg Butensky.
EIN: 943270250

59143
Poniecki Foundation
c/o Chet Grycz
8637 Arbor Dr.
El Cerrito, CA 94530

Classified as a private operating foundation in 1992 in CA.
Donor(s): Czeslaw Jan Grycz, Monica Dodds Grycz, Wandzia Grycz.

Financial data (yr. ended 12/31/00): Assets, $1,695 (M); grants paid, $0; gifts received, $15,343; expenditures, $16,643; qualifying distributions, $16,003; giving activities include $16,003 for programs.
Officers: Wandzia Grycz, Pres.; Ewa Witkowska, V.P.; Czeslaw Jan Grycz, Exec. Secy.
Directors: Artur Van Der Vant, Andrzej Witkowski.
EIN: 943139354

59144
Kadah Foundation
2 N. 1st St., 6th Fl.
San Jose, CA 95113

Established in 1996 as a company-sponsored operating foundation.
Donor(s): Solid State Optronics, Inc.
Financial data (yr. ended 12/31/00): Assets, $1,517 (M); grants paid, $42,600; gifts received, $44,000; expenditures, $42,782; qualifying distributions, $42,600.
Limitations: Applications not accepted. Giving primarily in CA; limited giving internationally.
Application information: Unsolicited requests for funds not accepted.
Officer: Zagoul Kadah, Mgr.
Directors: Juan Kadah, Sid Kadah.
EIN: 770426184
Codes: CD

59145
The Hari Krupa Seva Charitable Trust
2136 Applegate Dr.
Corona, CA 92882 (909) 737-8699
Contact: Kaneyalal B. Tejura, Tr.

Established in 2000 in CA.
Donor(s): Kaneyalal B. Tejura.
Financial data (yr. ended 12/31/00): Assets, $1,504 (M); grants paid, $28,492; gifts received, $30,000; expenditures, $28,500; qualifying distributions, $28,492.
Limitations: Giving primarily in India.
Application information: Application form not required.
Trustees: Hansa K. Tejura, Kaneyalal B. Tejura.
EIN: 336287312

59146
The Trust of the Associates for Religious Exercise
c/o Robert L. Webb, III
19640 Redberry Dr.
Los Gatos, CA 95030

Established in 1992 in CA.
Financial data (yr. ended 12/31/01): Assets, $1,457 (M); grants paid, $0; gifts received, $626; expenditures, $656; qualifying distributions, $759; giving activities include $147 for programs.
Trustee: Robert L. Webb III.
EIN: 770309144

59147
Sparrowworks Foundation
78365 Hwy. 111, PMB 346
La Quinta, CA 92253

Established in 1996 in CA.
Donor(s): Stanford M. Leland.
Financial data (yr. ended 12/31/00): Assets, $1,337 (M); grants paid, $2,517; gifts received, $200; expenditures, $3,342; qualifying distributions, $2,517.
Limitations: Applications not accepted. Giving on a national basis.
Application information: Contributes only to pre-selected organizations.
Trustee: Stanford M. Leland.
EIN: 330717073

59148
Ash Council on American Governance
1900 Ave. of the Stars, Ste. 1600
Los Angeles, CA 90067

Established in 1990 in CA.
Donor(s): Roy L. Ash.
Financial data (yr. ended 12/31/01): Assets, $1,311 (M); grants paid, $0; gifts received, $4,000; expenditures, $4,325; qualifying distributions, $0.
Officers and Trustees:* Roy L. Ash,* Pres.; Lila M. Ash,* V.P. and Secy.-Treas.; Charles Ash, James F. Ash, Robert C. Ash, Loretta Danko, Marilyn Hanna.
EIN: 954173147

59149
E-Tap, Inc.
1521 Caribbean Way
Laguna Beach, CA 92651

Established in 2000 in CA.
Donor(s): Blaise Subbiondo.
Financial data (yr. ended 12/31/00): Assets, $1,131 (M); grants paid, $0; expenditures, $26,169; qualifying distributions, $0.
Officer: Blaise Subbiondo, Pres.
EIN: 330897752

59150
Saban Children's Foundation
10960 Wilshire Blvd., Ste. 2233
Los Angeles, CA 90024

Established in 1999 in CA.
Donor(s): Haim Saban, Cheryl Saban.
Financial data (yr. ended 10/31/01): Assets, $1,129 (M); grants paid, $0; gifts received, $320,784; expenditures, $327,438; qualifying distributions, $0.
Officers: Cheryl Saban, Pres.; Jack O. Samuels, Secy.; Haim Saban, Treas.
EIN: 954714110

59151
Dreyer's Grand Ice Cream Charitable Foundation
5929 College Ave.
Oakland, CA 94618-1325 (510) 450-4586
URL: http://www.dreyersinc.com/dreyersfoundation/index.asp
Contact: Kelly Su'a, Secy.-Treas.

Established as a company-sponsored operating foundation.
Donor(s): Dreyer's Grand Ice Cream, Inc.
Financial data (yr. ended 12/31/01): Assets, $1,106 (M); grants paid, $337,031; gifts received, $518,750; expenditures, $556,449; qualifying distributions, $529,465.
Limitations: Giving primarily in the Oakland, CA, area.
Application information: Application form not required.
Officers: Diane McIntyre, Pres.; Jeffrey Porter, V.P.; Kelly Su'a, Secy.-Treas.
Directors: Margaret Harrington, Nancy Reed.
EIN: 943006987
Codes: FD, CD

59152
Knee and Laser Institute
c/o Michael M. Drucker, MD
360 San Miguel, Ste. 701
Newport Beach, CA 92660

Classified as a private operating foundation in 1995.
Donor(s): Michael Drucker.
Financial data (yr. ended 12/31/01): Assets, $1,091 (M); grants paid, $0; gifts received, $1,165; expenditures, $2,011; qualifying distributions, $0.
Officers: Michael Drucker, Pres.; Scot Forman, V.P.
Directors: Mike Roy, James Webb.
EIN: 330646855

59153
Alan Shapiro & Elizabeth Shapiro Charitable Foundation, Inc.
10642 Baton Rouge
Northridge, CA 91326-2906

Established in 1998 in CA.
Financial data (yr. ended 12/31/01): Assets, $1,053 (L); grants paid, $13,270; gifts received, $12,100; expenditures, $13,290; qualifying distributions, $13,270.
Limitations: Applications not accepted. Giving primarily in CA.
Application information: Contributes only to pre-selected organizations.
Officers: Elizabeth Shapiro, Pres.; Alan Shapiro, Secy.; Larry A. Gans, C.F.O.
EIN: 954708098

59154
Shoulder to Shoulder Ministries, Inc.
3013 Douglas Blvd., Ste. 160
Roseville, CA 95661

Established in 1999 in CA.
Donor(s): William Coibion.
Financial data (yr. ended 06/30/01): Assets, $999 (M); grants paid, $715; gifts received, $79,070; expenditures, $179,602; qualifying distributions, $0; giving activities include $64,845 for programs.
Officers: William Coibion, C.E.O. and Pres.; John Shiner, Exec. V.P.; Randy N. Neal, Secy.; William Holtz, C.F.O. and Treas.
EIN: 943343868

59155
The Steinert Family Foundation
3939 Bernard St., Ste. 1
Bakersfield, CA 93306

Established in 1988 in CA.
Donor(s): Marvin E. Steinert.
Financial data (yr. ended 12/31/01): Assets, $915 (M); grants paid, $0; gifts received, $500; expenditures, $1,081; qualifying distributions, $1,081; giving activities include $1,071 for programs.
Limitations: Applications not accepted. Giving primarily in CA.
Application information: Contributes only to pre-selected organizations.
Officers: Marvin E. Steinert, Pres.; Adala N. Steinert, Secy.; Randall Steinert, Treas.
Director: Max E. Steinert.
EIN: 770219732

59156
The Health & Energy Resources Foundation
4847 Hopyard Rd., No. 4-380
Pleasanton, CA 94588

Established in 1998 in CA.
Financial data (yr. ended 06/30/01): Assets, $854 (M); grants paid, $0; gifts received, $1,000; expenditures, $1,013; qualifying distributions, $0.
Limitations: Applications not accepted.
Application information: Contributes only to pre-selected organizations.
Trustees: Ruby Day, Tom Day.
EIN: 943306720

59157
Miracle Foundation
201-1 S. Golden State Blvd.
Turlock, CA 95380

Classified as a private operating foundation in 1975.
Donor(s): Members of the Christoffersen family.
Financial data (yr. ended 12/31/01): Assets, $840 (M); grants paid, $0; gifts received, $3,400; expenditures, $12,416; qualifying distributions, $0.
Officers: H.D. Christoffersen, Pres.; Stanley Sondeno, Secy.; Arlene Nosg, Treas.
EIN: 946102829

59158
Helena Modjeska Foundation
c/o Maria Debski
P.O. Box 9582
Newport Beach, CA 92660

Established in 1991 in CA.
Financial data (yr. ended 12/31/00): Assets, $741 (M); grants paid, $0; gifts received, $7,023; expenditures, $2,736; qualifying distributions, $550.
Officers: Pamela Harrell, Pres.; Bette Lindsey, V.P.; Shirley Gerst, Secy.; Ellen Lee, Treas.
EIN: 330458731

59159
Red Rock Foundation
27635 Red Rock Rd.
Los Altos Hills, CA 94022

Established in 1998 in CA.
Donor(s): Janice Cowen.
Financial data (yr. ended 12/31/99): Assets, $661 (M); grants paid, $400; gifts received, $45,717; expenditures, $46,183; qualifying distributions, $400; giving activities include $17,879 for programs.
Limitations: Applications not accepted.
Application information: Contributes only to pre-selected organizations.
Directors: Janice Cowen, Mary Falk, Dian Harrison, Lee Mahood, Patricia Williams.
EIN: 770468346

59160
ESE Foundation, Inc.
315 W. Adams Ave.
Los Angeles, CA 90007

Donor(s): Esse Clothing, LLC.
Financial data (yr. ended 12/31/00): Assets, $596 (M); grants paid, $31,100; gifts received, $31,700; expenditures, $32,813; qualifying distributions, $32,813.
Limitations: Applications not accepted.
Application information: Contributes only to pre-selected organizations.
Officer: Dong K. Joo, C.E.O.
EIN: 954667376

59161
Freeman, Freeman & Smiley Foundation for Philanthropy
3415 Sepulveda Blvd., No. 1200
Los Angeles, CA 90034-6060

Donor(s): Douglas K. Freeman, Richard D. Freeman, Bruce M. Smiley, Richard E. Gilbert, Fred J. Marcus, Jane Pebbles, Steve M. Kraus, Bruce L. Gelb, Laurence L. Hummer, Michael Blumenfeld, Glenn T. Sherman.
Financial data (yr. ended 12/31/01): Assets, $577 (M); grants paid, $0; gifts received, $4,000; expenditures, $5,413; qualifying distributions, $0.
Limitations: Applications not accepted.

59161—CALIFORNIA

Application information: Contributes only to pre-selected organizations.
Officers: Douglas K. Freeman, Pres.; Richard D. Freeman, V.P.; Richard E. Gilbert, V.P.; Glenn T. Sherman, V.P.; Bruce M. Smiley, V.P.; Fred J. Marcus, Secy.; Terri L. Wind, Treas.
Directors: Ross A. Arbiter, Michael Blumenfeld, Gregory M. Bordo, Laurence L. Hummer, Stephen M. Lowe, Jane Peebles, Gary M. Stern, Steven E. Young, Steven L. Ziven.
EIN: 954680836

59162
Charity International, Inc.
(Formerly Junior and Senior Association of Contra Costa, CA)
139 Fuchsia Ct.
Hercules, CA 94547

Funding in 2000 in CA.
Financial data (yr. ended 06/30/01): Assets, $573 (M); grants paid, $100; gifts received, $1,659; expenditures, $1,086; qualifying distributions, $1,053.
Limitations: Giving primarily in CA.
Officers: Rolly Manansala, Pres.; Gabriel Naguit, V.P.; Linda Panopio, Secy.-Treas.
EIN: 680219676

59163
New Energies Foundation
P.O. Box 385
Dulzura, CA 91917

Classified as a private operating foundation in 1983.
Donor(s): Gary K. Kring.
Financial data (yr. ended 12/31/01): Assets, $572 (M); grants paid, $0; gifts received, $301; expenditures, $301; qualifying distributions, $0.
Officers: Gary K. Kring, Pres.; Teodros Anley, Secy.; Patricia Anley, Treas.
EIN: 953490759

59164
The Friends of the Pittsburgh Institutions
117 S. Sycamore St.
Los Angeles, CA 90036

Established in 1998 in CA.
Donor(s): Henry Nogid, Esther Liebes, Judith Epstein, Robert Morris, Barbara Morris, Nochum Efroymson, Susan Efroymson, Samuel E. Morris.
Financial data (yr. ended 06/30/01): Assets, $549 (M); grants paid, $115,000; gifts received, $113,503; expenditures, $115,823; qualifying distributions, $115,813.
Limitations: Applications not accepted. Giving primarily in Israel.
Application information: Contributes only to pre-selected organizations.
Officer: Samuel E. Morris, Pres.
EIN: 954755776
Codes: FD2

59165
The Stage Family Organization Trust
12108 Bradford Pl.
Granada Hills, CA 91344 (818) 368-3988
Contact: H. Daniel Stage, Jr., Tr.

Classified as a private operating foundation in 1978.
Donor(s): A. Jean Stage, H. Daniel Stage.
Financial data (yr. ended 12/31/01): Assets, $524 (M); grants paid, $355; gifts received, $5,800; expenditures, $5,867; qualifying distributions, $9,837; giving activities include $5,512 for programs.
Limitations: Giving primarily in CA.
Trustees: A. Jean Stage, H. Daniel Stage, Jr.

EIN: 953245670

59166
Phoenix Educational Foundation
462 Stevens Ave., Ste. 202
Solana Beach, CA 92075-2065

Classified as a private operating foundation in 1992.
Financial data (yr. ended 12/31/01): Assets, $480 (M); grants paid, $0; expenditures, $30; qualifying distributions, $0.
Limitations: Applications not accepted.
Application information: Contributes only to pre-selected organizations.
Directors: Barbara Tracy, Brian Tracy.
EIN: 330225455

59167
Montebello Town Center Scholarship Fund
P.O. Box C-19525
Irvine, CA 92623

Donor(s): Aetna Life Insurance.
Financial data (yr. ended 12/31/99): Assets, $369 (M); grants paid, $7,500; gifts received, $8,000; expenditures, $8,100; qualifying distributions, $7,500.
Limitations: Giving limited to the Montebello, CA, area.
Application information: Application form required.
Directors: Deborah Blackford, Kathleen Burgi, Patrick Donahue, Steve Jarecki, Joy Moulton.
EIN: 954087696

59168
Janusz Korczak Cat Foundation
124 Casitas Ave.
San Francisco, CA 94127

Established in 1997 in CA.
Donor(s): Lance Kaufman, Barbara Curry Kaufman.
Financial data (yr. ended 09/30/99): Assets, $268 (M); grants paid, $0; gifts received, $51,159; expenditures, $53,230; qualifying distributions, $48,692; giving activities include $35,893 for programs.
Officers: Lance Kaufman, Pres.; Barbara Curry Kaufman, Treas.
EIN: 943282732

59169
Bradley & Stanley Duncan Memorial Scholarship Fund, Inc.
P.O. Box 750491
Petaluma, CA 94975-0491

Established as a private operating foundation in 1980.
Financial data (yr. ended 06/30/01): Assets, $248 (M); grants paid, $0; expenditures, $566; qualifying distributions, $10.
Limitations: Giving primarily in Tomales, CA.
Officers and Directors:* Wayne DuFond,* Pres.; Glen Tremari,* Treas.; Darrel Freitas, Thomas Kirkland, Ron Souza.
EIN: 942656026

59170
The West Los Angeles Orthopaedic Research and Education Foundation
11777 San Vicente Blvd., Ste. 777
Los Angeles, CA 90049-5052

Established in 1988 in CA.
Donor(s): Douglas Kilgus, Lunar Corp.
Financial data (yr. ended 11/30/99): Assets, $213 (M); grants paid, $0; expenditures, $462; qualifying distributions, $0.

Officers: Douglas Kilgus, M.D., Pres.; Steven Schreiber, M.D., V.P. and C.F.O.; Rick DeLamarter, M.D., Secy.
EIN: 954201826

59171
The Athena Foundation
11679 Mougle Ln.
Truckee, CA 96161

Classified as a private operating foundation in 1991.
Donor(s): Georgia Dini, Sheldon Johnson.
Financial data (yr. ended 12/31/01): Assets, $201 (M); grants paid, $0; gifts received, $750; expenditures, $755; qualifying distributions, $755; giving activities include $755 for programs.
Officers: Bernard Johnston, Pres.; William Wheatley, V.P.; Katherine Cofer, Secy.-Treas.
EIN: 946323073

59172
Sandton Lifestyles, Inc.
2731 Casiano Rd.
Los Angeles, CA 90077

Financial data (yr. ended 06/30/00): Assets, $170 (M); grants paid, $0; expenditures, $2,270; qualifying distributions, $0; giving activities include $1,406 for programs.
Officers: Lilian M. Tollman, Pres.; Gabriela Kim, Secy.; Ivan J. Tollman, C.F.O.
EIN: 954705917

59173
Harwood Foundation for Sustainable Forestry, Inc.
P.O. Box 224
Branscomb, CA 95417
Contact: Rebekah Harwood, Pres.

Established in 1997 in CA.
Donor(s): Harwood Products.
Financial data (yr. ended 12/31/00): Assets, $127 (M); grants paid, $53,254; gifts received, $79,559; expenditures, $81,213; qualifying distributions, $53,381.
Limitations: Giving primarily in CA.
Officers: Arthur C. Harwood, Chair.; Rebekah Harwood, Pres.; Christopher J. Neary, Secy.; Edward Horrick, Treas.
Directors: Jim Little, Marshall Rogers.
EIN: 911847605

59174
The Woods Family Foundation
11708 Melones Cir.
Gold River, CA 95670

Established in 2001 in CA.
Financial data (yr. ended 03/31/01): Assets, $56 (M); grants paid, $2,000; gifts received, $2,100; expenditures, $2,044; qualifying distributions, $2,000.
Officer: Robert D. Woods, Pres.
Director: Renee M. Anderson.
EIN: 680464584

59175
Twelve Eleven Press
P.O. Box 2816
Newport Beach, CA 92658-2816

Established in 1991 in CA. Classified as a private operating foundation in 1992.
Financial data (yr. ended 04/30/01): Assets, $52 (M); grants paid, $0; expenditures, $412; qualifying distributions, $412; giving activities include $412 for programs.
Officers and Directors:* Philip Allen Young,* Pres.; Cynthia A. Drennan, Secy.; David A. Brounstein, C.F.O.; James McClaren Dale, Larry

Michael McKay, Paula Sue McKay, Myron Samuel Steeves, Cathleen Pengra Young.
EIN: 330527279

59176
California Hungarian American Cultural Foundation, Inc.
9727 Corbin Ave.
Northridge, CA 91324

Classified as a private operating foundation in 1973.
Financial data (yr. ended 12/31/01): Assets, $1 (M); grants paid, $0; expenditures, $1; qualifying distributions, $0.
Officers: George Ashley, Pres.; Kurt von Braun, Secy.; Joseph S. Toth, Treas.
EIN: 237096986

59177
Children's Health Systems, Inc.
c/o Stanley Pappellbaum, M.D.
853 Ramona Ave.
Albany, CA 94706-1819

Established in 1998.
Financial data (yr. ended 03/31/02): Assets, $1 (M); grants paid, $0; expenditures, $906; qualifying distributions, $0.
Officers and Trustees:* Leonard A. Kutnik, M.D.,* Pres.; Kris Calvin,* Secy.; Robert Adler, M.D., Albert Gedissman, Anthony Hirsch, M.D., Joan Hodgman, M.D., Paul Ququndah, Burton Willis, M.D.
EIN: 330025512

59178
Amelio Curti Family Memorial Scholarship Fund
2228 W. Zumwalt
Tulare, CA 93274
Application address: c/o Tulare Union High School District, 426 N. Blackstone, Tulare, CA 93274, tel.: (559) 686-2021
Contact: Sandy Anderson

Established in 1995 in CA.
Financial data (yr. ended 12/31/01): Assets, $1 (M); grants paid, $3,000; expenditures, $2,978; qualifying distributions, $3,000.
Limitations: Giving primarily in Tulare, CA.
Application information: Application form required.
Officers: Benjamin Curti, Pres. and Secy.; Phillip Curti, V.P.; Kenneth Nunes, Treas.
EIN: 770404485

59179
The Five Plus Two Foundation
1215 Bixby Dr.
City of Industry, CA 91745

Established in 2000 in CA.
Donor(s): Frank W. Liu.
Financial data (yr. ended 12/31/01): Assets, $1 (M); grants paid, $11,000; expenditures, $26,246; qualifying distributions, $11,000.
Officers: Frank W. Liu, Pres.; Wendy Y.C. Liu, Secy.; Herbert H.B. Liu, Treas.
EIN: 954774464

59180
Francis E. Fowler, Jr. Foundation
41934 Main St., Ste. 204A
Temecula, CA 92590-2701

Classified as a private operating foundation in 1955.
Donor(s): Francis E. Fowler III.
Financial data (yr. ended 12/31/01): Assets, $1 (M); grants paid, $970; gifts received, $10; expenditures, $2,080; qualifying distributions, $2,080.

Officers and Directors:* Francis E. Fowler III,* Chair. and Pres.; Philip F. Fowler,* V.P.; Francis E. Fowler IV, Philip F. Fowler, Jr.
EIN: 956092412

59181
God's Work Foundation, Inc.
6665 Eastmont Dr.
Redding, CA 96002

Established in 2000 in CA.
Financial data (yr. ended 12/31/01): Assets, $1 (M); grants paid, $3,275; gifts received, $5,000; expenditures, $4,100; qualifying distributions, $3,275.
Officers and Directors:* Robert E. Milton, M.D.,* Pres.; Galina Milton, Secy.; Richard O. Evbuomwan.
EIN: 680448334

59182
International Institute for Curative Medicine and Inner Awareness
17240 Halsted
Northridge, CA 91325-1938

Classified as a private operating foundation in 1984.
Financial data (yr. ended 12/31/01): Assets, $1 (M); grants paid, $0; expenditures, $321; qualifying distributions, $0.
Officers: Beverly Navach, Pres.; Karen Mallory, Secy.
EIN: 953646688

59183
Keyan Foundation
318 S. Lincoln Blvd., Ste. 229
Venice, CA 90291

Established in 1987 in CA.
Donor(s): Ata O. Montazeri.
Financial data (yr. ended 11/30/00): Assets, $1 (M); grants paid, $0; gifts received, $18,702; expenditures, $44,244; qualifying distributions, $0.
Limitations: Giving primarily in MA.
Officers and Director:* Ata O. Montazeri,* Pres.; Mohammad H. Ranje, Secy.; Siamak Shajarian, C.F.O.
EIN: 954201683

59184
Harry L. and Joyce W. Nelson Maritime History Foundation
28441 Highridge Rd., Ste. 110
Rolling Hills Estates, CA 90274

Established in 1993 in CA.
Financial data (yr. ended 12/31/01): Assets, $1 (M); grants paid, $0; expenditures, $0; qualifying distributions, $0.
Officers and Directors:* Harry L. Nelson, Jr.,* Pres.; Dale Schoonhoven, V.P. and C.F.O.; Joyce W. Nelson,* Secy.; James Marenkos.
EIN: 330592919

59185
Mary Nicolai Charitable Trust
509 Whittier St.
Anaheim, CA 92806-3054

Classified as a private operating foundation in 1986.
Financial data (yr. ended 11/30/00): Assets, $1 (M); grants paid, $100,614; expenditures, $102,614; qualifying distributions, $100,614.
Trustees: William Heiden, Esther Herrera, Mary Nicolai, Doris Poole.
EIN: 330146207

59186
Santa Lucia Camps
c/o Mark Nye
14695 Seven Mile Rd.
Santa Margarita, CA 93453-9745

Financial data (yr. ended 12/31/01): Assets, $1 (M); grants paid, $0; gifts received, $100; expenditures, $237; qualifying distributions, $0.
Officers and Directors:* Mark Nye,* Pres.; Mike Kennedy,* Co-Treas.; Paul Kennedy,* Co-Treas.; Anne Lowenkoff, Edward Mintz.
EIN: 770066422

59187
The Y Foundation
(Formerly Daedalus Alliance for Environmental Education)
2260 Avenida de la Playa
La Jolla, CA 92037

Established in 1990 in CA.
Donor(s): M.B. Dalitz Foundation, Suzanne Brown.
Financial data (yr. ended 12/31/01): Assets, $1 (M); grants paid, $14,500; gifts received, $19,000; expenditures, $20,316; qualifying distributions, $20,316.
Limitations: Applications not accepted.
Application information: Contributes only to pre-selected organizations.
Officers and Directors:* Norman J. Eisenberg,* Chair. and Pres.; Toby J. Eisenberg,* Secy.; David L. Eisenberg,* Treas.
EIN: 330442122

59188
The Bernstein Foundation
11661 San Vicente Blvd., Ste. 707
Los Angeles, CA 90064

Donor(s): Leon B. Bernstein.
Financial data (yr. ended 09/30/01): Assets, $0 (M); grants paid, $0; expenditures, $2,475; qualifying distributions, $2,475.
Limitations: Applications not accepted. Giving primarily in Los Angeles, CA.
Application information: Contributes only to pre-selected organizations.
Officer: Robert M. Bernstein, Mgr.
EIN: 236449258

59189
Jo Ann Brassfield Charitable Giving Foundation
P.O. Box 1198
Los Gatos, CA 95030
Application address: 540 N. Santa Cruz, Ste. 101, Los Gatos, CA 95030-4347, tel.: (408) 354-2212
Contact: Jo Ann Brassfield, Mgr.

Donor(s): J.G. Brassfield.
Financial data (yr. ended 12/31/00): Assets, $0 (M); grants paid, $45,000; gifts received, $100,000; expenditures, $45,605; qualifying distributions, $45,000.
Limitations: Giving primarily in CA.
Officer: Jo Ann Brassfield, Mgr.
Directors: Julie Brassfield, Shann Brassfield, Joseph A. Sperske.
EIN: 943146881

59190
Roena Cornett Foundation
c/o Victor N. Cervantes
15501 S.P. Mission Blvd., Ste. 312
Mission Hills, CA 91345

Established in 1998 in CA.

59190—CALIFORNIA

Financial data (yr. ended 12/31/00): Assets, $0 (M); grants paid, $0; expenditures, $69,740; qualifying distributions, $0.
Officers: Johan Dixon, Pres.; Sharon Perida, V.P.
EIN: 957044437

59191
Feral Feline Feeders, Inc.
505 Alabama St.
Huntington Beach, CA 92648

Established in 1996 in CA.
Financial data (yr. ended 12/31/00): Assets, $0 (M); grants paid, $10; gifts received, $302; expenditures, $302; qualifying distributions, $302; giving activities include $292 for programs.
Officers and Directors:* Jim L. Banks,* Pres.; Marie St. Germain,* Secy.
EIN: 330718354

59192
Fern Cottage Foundation
P.O. Box 36
Ferndale, CA 95536-0036

Donor(s): Fern Cottage, Inc.
Financial data (yr. ended 06/30/01): Assets, $0 (M); grants paid, $0; gifts received, $10,300; expenditures, $21,402; qualifying distributions, $0.
Officers: Andrew McBride, Pres.; Joe Russ IV, V.P.; Patricia Hansen, Secy.; Virginia Dwight, Treas.
Director: Jerry Welch.
EIN: 943060700

59193
The Foundation for Pediatric and Laser Neurosurgery, Inc.
7930 Frost St., Ste. 103
San Diego, CA 92123

Classified as a private operating foundation in 1983.
Financial data (yr. ended 08/31/01): Assets, $0 (M); grants paid, $0; gifts received, $4,033; expenditures, $8,343; qualifying distributions, $5,225.
Officer: Hector E. James, M.D., Pres.
EIN: 953854309

59194
Free Bible Distribution to Those in Need
4641 N. Woodson
Fresno, CA 93705

Classified as a private operating foundation in 1990.
Donor(s): Alice Short.‡
Financial data (yr. ended 12/31/01): Assets, $0 (M); grants paid, $0; expenditures, $4,858; qualifying distributions, $4,858; giving activities include $4,246 for programs.
Officers: John Lawless, Chair. and Pres.; H.R. Lawless, V.P.; Dana Lawless, Secy.; Mark Witcher, Treas.
EIN: 770496026

59195
General James K. Herbert Foundation
575 E. Locust, No. 102
Fresno, CA 93720
Contact: Jim Herbert and Carol Herbert

Established in 1991 in CA.
Donor(s): James Herbert, Carol Sellers, Sharon Herbert.
Financial data (yr. ended 12/31/99): Assets, $0 (M); grants paid, $66,700; gifts received, $1,686; expenditures, $79,321; qualifying distributions, $68,923.
Limitations: Giving on a national basis.

Officers: James Herbert, Chair.; Carol Sellers, Pres.; Sharon Herbert, V.P.; Paul E. Quinn, Treas.
EIN: 770293968

59196
James K. & Carol Sellers Herbert Foundation
575 E. Locust, No. 102
Fresno, CA 93720

Donor(s): Genl. James K. Herbert Foundation.
Financial data (yr. ended 12/31/00): Assets, $0 (M); grants paid, $0; gifts received, $2,514; expenditures, $7,600; qualifying distributions, $0.
Officer: Carol Sellers Herbert, C.E.O.
EIN: 770460913

59197
The Hietbrink Foundation
567 San Nicolas Dr., Ste. 450
Newport Beach, CA 92660

Established in 2001 in CA.
Donor(s): Hietbrink Family Trust.
Financial data (yr. ended 12/31/01): Assets, $0 (M); grants paid, $2,000; expenditures, $2,000; qualifying distributions, $2,000.
Officer: James Hietbrink, Pres.
EIN: 330956825

59198
The A. Z. Kruse Foundation
P.O. Box 2587
Pasadena, CA 91102-2587

Established in 1992 in CA.
Financial data (yr. ended 12/31/01): Assets, $0 (M); grants paid, $500; gifts received, $3,560; expenditures, $2,491; qualifying distributions, $499.
Limitations: Applications not accepted. Giving primarily in CA.
Officer: Bettijune Kruse, C.E.O.
EIN: 954379852

59199
Su Lin Foundation for Education (U.S.A.)
7710 Balboa Ave., Ste. 327
San Diego, CA 92111

Established in 1996 in CA.
Donor(s): Lin Su.
Financial data (yr. ended 12/31/01): Assets, $0 (M); grants paid, $0; expenditures, $906; qualifying distributions, $0.
Officer: Lin Su, Pres.
EIN: 330688092

59200
Minerva Foundation
4849 Grizzly Peak Blvd.
Berkeley, CA 94705-1724 (510) 642-1076
Contact: Elwin Marg, V.P.

Established in 1983 in CA.
Donor(s): Elwin Marg, Helen Marg.
Financial data (yr. ended 12/31/00): Assets, $0 (M); grants paid, $69,999; gifts received, $201,500; expenditures, $99,816; qualifying distributions, $92,975; giving activities include $2,085 for programs.
Limitations: Giving primarily in CA.
Application information: Application form not required.
Officers: Helen Marg, Pres.; Elwin Marg, V.P.
Directors: Richard Buxbaum, Lawrence Stark.
EIN: 942940281

59201
Queens Row
1240 Norman Pl.
Los Angeles, CA 90049

Established in 1993 in CA.
Donor(s): Garfield Foundation, Motion Picture Assn. of America.
Financial data (yr. ended 04/30/01): Assets, $0 (M); grants paid, $0; expenditures, $343; qualifying distributions, $0.
Officers: Kathleen Garfield, Pres.; Irwin E. Garfield, V.P.
EIN: 954528044

59202
Shah Charitable Foundation
2300 N. Calle Meleno
Fullerton, CA 92833

Established in 2000.
Financial data (yr. ended 12/31/01): Assets, $0 (M); grants paid, $0; expenditures, $469; qualifying distributions, $0.
Trustee: A.M. Shah.
EIN: 954707593

59203
Shamballa Foundation
536 Westbourne Dr.
West Hollywood, CA 90048-1914

Established in 1998 in CA.
Donor(s): Shamballa-A Global Communication Co.
Financial data (yr. ended 12/31/00): Assets, $0 (M); grants paid, $0; gifts received, $873; expenditures, $861; qualifying distributions, $861.
Officers: Nana Maynard, Pres.; Aliah Majon, Secy.
EIN: 954264251

59204
Tatev Armenia
5112 Hollywood Blvd., Ste. 111
Los Angeles, CA 90027

Established in 2000 in CA.
Financial data (yr. ended 12/31/00): Assets, $0 (M); grants paid, $58,140; gifts received, $58,140; expenditures, $58,140; qualifying distributions, $58,140.
Director: V. Abaryan.
EIN: 954491048

59205
The C. M. Ward Ministerial Foundation
P.O. Box 7937
Stockton, CA 95267-0937
Contact: Ethelyne Wood Shannon, Pres.

Established in 1989 in CA.
Donor(s): C.M. Ward, Dorothy M. Ward.
Financial data (yr. ended 12/31/01): Assets, $0 (M); grants paid, $2,000; gifts received, $2,607; expenditures, $37,582; qualifying distributions, $37,394.
Officers and Directors:* William O. Vickery, V.P.; Heath Lowery, Secy.; Lill Anderson, Jim Shade, Robert Shannon.
EIN: 680197079

59206
Billy and Audrey L. Wilder Foundation
c/o Harold Nelson, CPA
6345 Balboa, Ste. 382
Encino, CA 91316

Established in 1996 in CA.
Financial data (yr. ended 12/31/01): Assets, $0 (M); grants paid, $138,200; gifts received, $150,000; expenditures, $138,674; qualifying distributions, $138,674.

Limitations: Applications not accepted. Giving on a national basis.
Application information: Contributes only to pre-selected organizations.
Officers: Billy Wilder, Pres.; Audrey Wilder, Secy.
EIN: 954569162
Codes: FD2

59207
Williamson Ranch Foundation, Inc.
4900 Lone Tree Way
Antioch, CA 94509

Classified as a private operating foundation in 1992.
Donor(s): Donald Williamson, Shirley Perry.
Financial data (yr. ended 12/31/01): Assets, $0 (M); grants paid, $0; gifts received, $8,941; expenditures, $20,055; qualifying distributions, $8,974; giving activities include $8,974 for programs.
Officer: Donald Williamson, Pres.
Directors: Jim Boccio, Jean Lauritzen, Vasili Millias, Robert J. Sehr, Jr., John Slatten, Barbara Van Buren.
EIN: 943101856

COLORADO

59208
Cook Communications Ministries Foundation
(Formerly David C. Cook Foundation)
4050 Lee Vance View
Colorado Springs, CO 80918

Classified as a private operating foundation in 1992.
Donor(s): Frances Kerr Cook Trust.
Financial data (yr. ended 05/31/00): Assets, $98,017,033 (M); grants paid, $0; gifts received, $618,403; expenditures, $47,523,130; qualifying distributions, $42,516,949; giving activities include $1,939,870 for programs.
Publications: Annual report, newsletter.
Officers and Trustees:* David L. Mehlis,* Pres.; Bruce Adair, Secy.; David R. Hachtel, Treas.; V. Gilbert Beers, Thomas J. Boodell, George Brushaber, Milton Cerny, Thomas H. Dunkerton, Benjamin F. Elson, James M. Houston, David M. Howard, Joseph T. Koch, Carl Lundstrom, Wilber Smith, Barry L. Swenson.
EIN: 366008100

59209
The Myron Stratton Home
555 Gold Pass Hts.
Colorado Springs, CO 80906 (719) 579-0930
FAX: (719) 579-0447
Contact: Mark Turk, Exec. Dir.

Classified as a private operating foundation in 1973.
Financial data (yr. ended 12/31/01): Assets, $84,016,905 (M); grants paid, $112,000; expenditures, $3,521,990; qualifying distributions, $3,352,948; giving activities include $2,308,535 for programs.
Limitations: Giving primarily in Colorado Springs, CO.
Application information: Application form required.
Officers: Gary O. Loo, Pres.; Barbara L. Yalich, V.P.; Robert G. Barker, Jr., Secy.-Treas.
Trustees: Jon J. Medved, Joseph C. Woodford.

EIN: 840404260
Codes: FD2

59210
Newkirk Engler & May, Inc.
P.O. Box 40096
Denver, CO 80204

Established in 2001.
Donor(s): Sara S. Foland, Cathleen L. May.
Financial data (yr. ended 12/31/01): Assets, $55,153,564 (M); grants paid, $150,000; gifts received, $55,593,880; expenditures, $440,970; qualifying distributions, $240,370; giving activities include $90,370 for programs.
Limitations: Applications not accepted. Giving on a national basis.
Application information: Contributes only to pre-selected organizations.
Officers: Cathleen L. May, Chair. and Pres.; Sara S. Foland, V.P.; Helen M. May, Secy.; Caroline M. Fauks, Treas.
Directors: Mary Ann Engler, Paul F. Engler, W. Steven Fauks, Laura Foland-Priver, Thomas W. May, Mark S. Priver.
EIN: 841591303
Codes: FD2

59211
Muriel L. MacGregor Charitable Trust
P.O. Box 4675
Estes Park, CO 80517 (970) 586-3749
E-mail: macgtrst@frii.com
Contact: Eric D. Adams, Exec. Dir.

Established in 1978 in CO.
Financial data (yr. ended 08/31/00): Assets, $18,463,254 (M); grants paid, $35,520; expenditures, $472,657; qualifying distributions, $556,381; giving activities include $198,979 for programs.
Limitations: Giving limited to Estes Park, CO.
Publications: Informational brochure.
Application information: Application form required.
Officer: Eric D. Adams, Exec. Dir.
Trustees: Eldon G. Freudenburg, James P. Johnson, Orpha Kendall.
EIN: 846154601
Codes: GTI

59212
Hach Scientific Foundation
2114 N. Lincoln Ave., Ste. 104
Loveland, CO 80538
Contact: Kathryn C. Hach-Darrow, Chair.

Established in 1982 in CO.
Donor(s): Kathryn C. Hach, C & K Enterprises, Ltd., Hach Co.
Financial data (yr. ended 09/30/01): Assets, $17,927,853 (M); grants paid, $390,700; gifts received, $6,000,250; expenditures, $923,951; qualifying distributions, $867,428; giving activities include $504,228 for programs.
Limitations: Giving limited to CO and IA.
Application information: Scholarship applications are no longer accepted. Application form required.
Officer: Kathryn C. Hach-Darrow, Chair.
Trustees: Bill Gunn, Bruce J. Hach, Loel Sirovy.
EIN: 840900668
Codes: FD, GTI

59213
The Richard Seth Staley Educational Foundation
(Formerly Richard Seth Staley Foundation for Psychological Development)
P.O. Box 4129
Aspen, CO 81612
Contact: Donald H. Keltner, Pres.

Established in 1980 as the Richard Seth Staley Foundation for Psychological Development.
Financial data (yr. ended 09/30/01): Assets, $12,156,354 (M); grants paid, $654,785; expenditures, $914,548; qualifying distributions, $706,718.
Limitations: Giving on a national basis.
Application information: Application form required for educational grants only.
Officers and Directors:* Donald H. Keltner,* Pres. and Treas.; S. Derrin Watson,* V.P.; Virginia Keltner,* Secy.; James F. Beley, Berkeley Johnston.
EIN: 953532336
Codes: FD

59214
Colorado Masons Benevolent Fund Association
7955 E. Arapahoe Ct., Ste. 1200
Englewood, CO 80112-1362
Contact: Robert L. Bartholic, Exec. Secy.

Established in 1899; incorporated in 1912 in CO.
Financial data (yr. ended 10/31/01): Assets, $11,613,613 (M); grants paid, $555,513; gifts received, $72,935; expenditures, $714,633; qualifying distributions, $596,033.
Limitations: Applications not accepted. Giving limited to CO.
Application information: Lodge officers seeking assistance on behalf of a member or widow must submit an Application for Assistance to the Fund. Scholarship application forms available in Nov. from CO public high school counselors; individual forms will not be mailed out by the association; letters requesting applications will not be answered. Requests accepted only through Colorado Masonic Lodge. Unsolicited requests for funds not accepted.
Officers and Trustees:* Joseph Hadad,* Chair. and C.E.O.; Milton Brandweis,* Pres.; Robert C. Bartholic, Jr.,* V.P.; Arthur J. Carlson, Exec. Secy.; David M. Naiman,* Secy.; Ben H. Bell,* Treas.; Rodney Jordan.
EIN: 840406813
Codes: FD, GTI

59215
The Museum of Outdoor Arts
1000 Englewood Pkwy., Ste. 2-230
Englewood, CO 80110

Classified as a private operating foundation in 1982.
Donor(s): John Madden Company, Cynthia Madden Leitner, John W. Madden.
Financial data (yr. ended 12/31/00): Assets, $7,710,792 (M); grants paid, $0; gifts received, $456,458; expenditures, $1,116,119; qualifying distributions, $657,983; giving activities include $535,709 for programs.
Officers: Cynthia Madden Leitner, Pres.; Marjorie P. Madden, Secy.; Joseph A. Babich, Treas.
Trustees: Bruce Deifik, Eric Siler, Ph.D., Todd Siler, Richard Steckel.
EIN: 742234944

59216
The Gill Operating Foundation
2215 Market St., Ste. 205
Denver, CO 80205 (303) 292-4455
Contact: Katherine Pease, Exec. Dir.

Established in 1999 in CO.

59216—COLORADO

Donor(s): Timothy Gill.
Financial data (yr. ended 12/31/99): Assets, $7,538,050 (M); grants paid, $0; gifts received, $48,083,411; expenditures, $116,926; qualifying distributions, $0; giving activities include $116,926 for programs.
Officers and Directors:* Tim Gill, Chair.; Jeanne E. Hathway,* Secy.; Greg Craig,* Treas.; Katherine Pease, Exec. Dir.; Jane Ragle, Chuck Supple.
EIN: 841520196

59217
The Binning Family Foundation
88 Glenmoor Pl.
Englewood, CO 80110

Established in 1999 in CO.
Donor(s): Thomas W. Binning.
Financial data (yr. ended 12/31/00): Assets, $5,024,197 (M); grants paid, $0; gifts received, $3,069; expenditures, $134,064; qualifying distributions, $0; giving activities include $109,239 for programs.
Limitations: Applications not accepted.
Application information: Contributes only to pre-selected organizations.
Officer and Director:* Thomas W. Binning,* Chair.
EIN: 841523987

59218
Love in Action
212 N. Wahsatch, Ste. 301
Colorado Springs, CO 80903-3476
Application address: 3730 Masters Dr., Colorado Springs, CO 80907, tel.: (719) 635-3200
Contact: Leroy Landhuis, Pres.

Donor(s): Leroy Landhuis.
Financial data (yr. ended 07/31/01): Assets, $4,514,083 (M); grants paid, $151,400; gifts received, $3,708,000; expenditures, $167,427; qualifying distributions, $158,446.
Limitations: Giving primarily in Colorado Springs, CO.
Officers: Leroy Landhuis, Pres.; Dave Cocolin, V.P.; Alan Vancil, Secy.-Treas.
Director: Eric T. Ryan, Gary Scheriman.
EIN: 841285975

59219
Frederick R. Mayer Foundation
1700 Lincoln St., Ste. 4750
Denver, CO 80217

Established in 1995 in CO.
Donor(s): Frederick R. Mayer.
Financial data (yr. ended 11/30/99): Assets, $3,937,431 (M); grants paid, $0; gifts received, $72,000; expenditures, $11,884; qualifying distributions, $10,011; giving activities include $493 for programs.
Officers: Frederick R. Mayer, Pres.; Jan Perry Mayer, V.P.; Gloria J. Higgins, Secy.
EIN: 841359652

59220
The Catamount Institute
1575 Sutherland Creek Rd.
Manitou Springs, CO 80829

Established as an operating foundation in 1998 in CO.
Donor(s): Muriel Francis, Paul Francis.
Financial data (yr. ended 12/31/00): Assets, $3,543,607 (M); grants paid, $8,500; gifts received, $1,033,701; expenditures, $124,300; qualifying distributions, $276,088; giving activities include $278,387 for programs.
Limitations: Applications not accepted.

Officers: Julie Francis, Pres.; Howard Drossman, V.P.; Muriel Francis, Secy.; Paul Francis, Treas.
Directors: Lee Francis, Michelle Gittler.
EIN: 841438996

59221
Gold Crown Foundation, Inc.
5675 DTC Blvd., Ste. 180
Englewood, CO 80111-3246

Established in 1986.
Donor(s): Ray Baker.
Financial data (yr. ended 09/30/01): Assets, $3,190,179 (M); grants paid, $10,015; gifts received, $289,232; expenditures, $1,336,681; qualifying distributions, $51,891; giving activities include $848,085 for programs.
Limitations: Applications not accepted. Giving primarily in the Denver, CO, area.
Application information: Contributes only to pre-selected organizations.
Officers: Raymond T. Baker, Pres.; William Hanzlik, V.P.; Sara C. Higdon, Secy.-Treas.
Board Members: Eric Carroll, Jay Clask, Joseph Coppola, Thomas Gleason, Ruth Rodriguez, Tim Romani, Vern Swanson, Mark Wiebe.
EIN: 742422126

59222
The Armstrong Family Foundation
1625 Broadway, Ste. 780
Denver, CO 80202

Established in 1994 in CO.
Donor(s): Dorothy R. Armstrong.
Financial data (yr. ended 12/31/01): Assets, $2,969,539 (M); grants paid, $171,000; expenditures, $173,970; qualifying distributions, $172,396.
Limitations: Giving primarily in CO.
Directors: Dorothy R. Armstrong, W.L. Armstrong, Dorothy A. Shanahan.
EIN: 841289655
Codes: FD2

59223
Caulkins Family Foundation
1600 Broadway, Ste. 1400
Denver, CO 80202

Established in 1993 in CO.
Donor(s): George P. Caulkins, Jr., John N. Caulkins, Mary I. Caulkins.
Financial data (yr. ended 12/31/01): Assets, $2,845,706 (M); grants paid, $209,000; gifts received, $196,000; expenditures, $222,512; qualifying distributions, $221,632.
Limitations: Applications not accepted. Giving primarily in CO.
Application information: Contributes only to pre-selected organizations.
Officers and Directors:* John N. Caulkins,* Pres.; Eleanor N. Caulkins,* V.P.; Maxwell O.B. Caulkins,* Secy.; Mary I. Caulkins, Treas.; David I. Caulkins, George P. Caulkins, Jr., George P. Caulkins III.
EIN: 841251441
Codes: FD2

59224
Jack and Marilyn MacAllister Foundation
69 Indigo Way
Castle Rock, CO 80104

Established in 1991 in CO.
Donor(s): Jack A. MacAllister, Marilyn MacAllister.
Financial data (yr. ended 12/31/00): Assets, $2,580,270 (M); grants paid, $260,000; expenditures, $280,420; qualifying distributions, $256,501.

Limitations: Applications not accepted. Giving primarily in CO.
Application information: Contributes only to pre-selected organizations.
Officers: Marilyn MacAllister, Pres.; Jack A. MacAllister, V.P. and Secy.
EIN: 742619186
Codes: FD

59225
Leona Stanford Vollintine Charitable Trust
c/o John R. Mehaffy
1655 Walnut St.
Boulder, CO 80302

Established in 1999 in CO.
Donor(s): Leona S. Vollintine.
Financial data (yr. ended 12/31/01): Assets, $2,411,818 (M); grants paid, $202,910; expenditures, $222,847; qualifying distributions, $200,766.
Limitations: Applications not accepted. Giving on a national basis, with emphasis on IL and CO.
Application information: Contributes only to pre-selected organizations.
Trustees: Richard U. Lansden, John R. Mehaffy.
EIN: 841524918
Codes: FD2

59226
The Kingdom Enlightenment Scholarship Foundation
12211 W. Chenango Dr.
Morrison, CO 80465
Application address: 2651 S. Wadsworth Cir., Lakewood, CO 80227, tel.: (303) 989-4348
Contact: Susan M. Duncan, Pres.

Established in 1991.
Donor(s): Stephen S. Fredericks,‡ Susan M. Duncan, Susan McGaw, Thomas McGaw.
Financial data (yr. ended 05/31/01): Assets, $2,391,921 (M); grants paid, $167,227; expenditures, $186,702; qualifying distributions, $167,227.
Limitations: Giving primarily in CO.
Application information: Application form required.
Officers: Susan M. Duncan, Pres.; Thomas McGaw, V.P.; Susan McGaw, Secy.-Treas.
EIN: 841174743
Codes: FD2

59227
Luck Family Foundation
5 Bald Eagle
Littleton, CO 80127-5766

Established in 2000 in CO.
Donor(s): Eric Luck, Cheryl Luck, Polly Luck.
Financial data (yr. ended 12/31/01): Assets, $2,225,761 (M); grants paid, $98,900; gifts received, $229,623; expenditures, $103,160; qualifying distributions, $98,900.
Limitations: Applications not accepted. Giving primarily in TX.
Application information: Contributes only to pre-selected organizations.
Officers and Directors:* David E. Luck,* Pres.; Cheryl M. Luck,* Secy.-Treas.; Kelly K. Dunn, W.K. Luck.
EIN: 841570129
Codes: FD2

59228
Institute for Children's Mental Disorders
c/o R. Freedman, M.D.
4200 E. 9th Ave., Ste. C268-71
Denver, CO 80220-3706

Established in 1999 in CO.

Donor(s): John Malone, M.D.
Financial data (yr. ended 12/31/00): Assets, $2,224,961 (M); grants paid, $50,000; gifts received, $1,177,180; expenditures, $55,733; qualifying distributions, $50,000.
Limitations: Giving primarily in Boulder, CO.
Officers: Robert Freedman, M.D., Pres.; Richard Saunders, V.P.; Jerome H. Keran, Treas.; Mary Rossick Kern, Secy.
Director: Robyn Loup.
EIN: 841491971

59229
The Piton Foundation
370 17th St., Ste. 5300
Denver, CO 80202-5653 (303) 825-6246
FAX: (303) 628-3839; URL: http://www.piton.org
Contact: Carol Bush, Cont.

Incorporated in 1976 in CO.
Donor(s): Samuel Gary, Gary Williams Energy Corp.
Financial data (yr. ended 11/30/01): Assets, $1,958,841 (M); grants paid, $996,571; gifts received, $2,721,101; expenditures, $3,293,867; qualifying distributions, $3,191,951; giving activities include $1,202,365 for programs.
Limitations: Applications not accepted. Giving limited to Denver, CO.
Publications: Biennial report, program policy statement.
Application information: Unsolicited requests for funds not considered.
Officers and Directors:* Samuel Gary,* Chair.; Ronald W. Williams,* Vice-Chair.; Mary Gittings Cronin,* Pres.; James E. Bye,* Secy.-Treas.; Kathryn Gary, Nancy Gary, Tom Gougeon, Jack A. MacAllister, Terry Minger, Adele Phelan, Robert Woolfolk, Dave Younggren.
EIN: 840719486
Codes: FD

59230
Sopris Foundation
c/o John P. McBride
303 E. AABC
Aspen, CO 81611-3539

Established in 1993 in CO.
Donor(s): John McBride.
Financial data (yr. ended 12/31/01): Assets, $1,958,050 (M); grants paid, $0; gifts received, $40,500; expenditures, $118,038; qualifying distributions, $101,747; giving activities include $71,494 for programs.
Directors: John McBride, Jr., John P. McBride, Kate McBride, Laurie McBride, Peter McBride, Lester Pedicord.
EIN: 841249444

59231
Canyon Colorado Equid Sanctuary
P.O. Box 60669
Colorado Springs, CO 80960

Classified as a private operating foundation in 1984.
Donor(s): William Gruenerwald.
Financial data (yr. ended 05/31/01): Assets, $1,634,995 (M); grants paid, $0; gifts received, $221,973; expenditures, $479,470; qualifying distributions, $364,742.
Officers: William Gruenerwald, Pres.; William J. Anton, V.P.; Dorothy J. Gruenerwald, Secy.
EIN: 742140294

59232
The Bread of Life Foundation, Inc.
c/o Paul Grant
4505 S. Yosemite St., Ste. 127
Denver, CO 80237-2519

Established in 1989 in DE.
Donor(s): Paul J. Grant.
Financial data (yr. ended 12/31/01): Assets, $1,304,384 (M); grants paid, $77,261; gifts received, $12,248; expenditures, $122,632; qualifying distributions, $115,176.
Limitations: Applications not accepted. Giving primarily in Denver, CO.
Application information: Unsolicited requests for funds not considered.
Officer: Paul J. Grant, Pres.
EIN: 136936495
Codes: FD2

59233
Alice N. Jenkins Foundation
343 Laurel Way
Lafayette, CO 80026-9390
FAX: (303) 664-9755

Established in 1979 in CO.
Donor(s): Alice N. Jenkins.‡
Financial data (yr. ended 09/30/00): Assets, $1,061,369 (M); grants paid, $43,180; expenditures, $82,614; qualifying distributions, $54,979.
Limitations: Giving limited to CO.
Publications: Application guidelines.
Application information: Qualification visit required to evaluate applicants. Application form required.
Trustees: Janis Frazier, Betty L. Lewis, Richard L. Lewis.
EIN: 840811678

59234
Dougherty Museum
8382 N. 107th St.
Longmont, CO 80501

Established in 1993 in CO.
Donor(s): Dorothy M. Dougherty, Marilyn R. Litzenberger, James M. Dougherty, Douglas R. Dougherty.
Financial data (yr. ended 12/31/01): Assets, $989,693 (M); grants paid, $0; gifts received, $20,931; expenditures, $4,562; qualifying distributions, $0.
Officer: Douglas R. Dougherty, Pres.
Directors: Dale Bernard, James M. Dougherty, Marilyn R. Litzenberger, Thomas Meier.
EIN: 841246854

59235
Jesusonian Foundation
P.O. Box 18764
Boulder, CO 80308

Established in 1984 in CO.
Financial data (yr. ended 12/31/99): Assets, $890,614 (M); grants paid, $4,800; gifts received, $261,824; expenditures, $215,816; qualifying distributions, $88,612; giving activities include $88,744 for programs.
Limitations: Giving primarily in Finland.
Officers: Paula Thompson, Pres.; Mo Siegel, V.P.
EIN: 840964867

59236
Atheneus Humanities Foundation
2303 E. Dartmouth Ave.
Englewood, CO 80110-3079
Application address: 5675 DTC Blvd., No. 210, Englewood, CO 80111, tel.: (303) 721-0700
Contact: Laurence J. Rich, Tr.

Donor(s): Enrique Feldman.
Financial data (yr. ended 12/31/99): Assets, $885,716 (M); grants paid, $352,350; gifts received, $1,045,785; expenditures, $362,704; qualifying distributions, $362,704.
Limitations: Giving primarily in Denver, CO, NJ, and New York, NY.
Application information: Application form required.
Trustees: Enrique Feldman, Laurence J. Rich.
EIN: 841357632
Codes: FD

59237
The Jack E. and Betty Jane Schuss 1999 Charitable Trust
P.O. Box 5179
Snowmass Village, CO 81615 (970) 923-6561
Contact: Kent Muller, Exec. Dir.

Established in 1999 in CO.
Donor(s): Schuss Family Foundation.
Financial data (yr. ended 12/31/00): Assets, $786,996 (M); grants paid, $48,754; gifts received, $349,317; expenditures, $83,797; qualifying distributions, $48,754; giving activities include $35,042 for programs.
Directors: Kent W. Mueller, Exec. Dir.; Jonathan A. Schuss, Saundra D. Swanson.
EIN: 841504921

59238
Wilson Foundation
P.O. Box 70
Monument, CO 80132
Contact: Kent Wilson, Pres.

Classified as a private operating foundation in 1972.
Financial data (yr. ended 12/31/01): Assets, $775,493 (M); grants paid, $182,112; gifts received, $4,326; expenditures, $186,353; qualifying distributions, $185,981; giving activities include $6,306 for programs.
Limitations: Applications not accepted.
Application information: Contributes only to pre-selected organizations.
Officer: Kent Wilson, Pres. and Mgr.
EIN: 846030627
Codes: FD2

59239
Hsu Family Foundation
605 Parfet St., Ste. 200
Lakewood, CO 80215

Established in 2001 in CO.
Donor(s): Pacific Western Technologies Ltd., Tai-Dan Hsu, Ding-Wen Hsu.
Financial data (yr. ended 12/31/01): Assets, $772,708 (M); grants paid, $5,500; gifts received, $193,000; expenditures, $39,790; qualifying distributions, $6,680.
Limitations: Applications not accepted. Giving primarily in CO.
Application information: Contributes only to pre-selected organizations.
Director: Karen Nakandakare.
EIN: 841592431

59240
Avenir Foundation, Inc.
P.O. Box 1749
Wheat Ridge, CO 80034

Established in 1993.
Donor(s): Berkshire Hathaway, Inc., Alice Dodge Wallace.
Financial data (yr. ended 06/30/01): Assets, $734,042 (M); grants paid, $13,692,800; gifts received, $13,675,252; expenditures, $13,832,974; qualifying distributions, $13,696,892.
Limitations: Applications not accepted. Giving in the U.S.; support also for an institute in Vienna, Austria.
Application information: Contributes only to pre-selected organizations.
Officers and Directors:* Alice Dodge Wallace,* Pres.; William Dodge Wallace,* V.P.; Margaret Boynton Wallace,* Secy.; Norman L. Wilson, Treas.
EIN: 841245939
Codes: FD

59241
Humane Society of Fremont County, Inc.
P.O. Box 748
Canon City, CO 81215-0748

Classified as a private operating foundation in 1989.
Financial data (yr. ended 12/31/01): Assets, $732,600 (M); grants paid, $0; gifts received, $342,646; expenditures, $369,195; qualifying distributions, $0.
Officers: Walter F. Jenks, Pres.; J.A. Carmack, V.P.; Ruth V. Stimack, Secy.-Treas.
EIN: 840434843

59242
Fred Harman Art Museum
P.O. Box 192
Pagosa Springs, CO 81147

Classified as a private operating foundation in 1985.
Donor(s): Fred Harman, Alan F. Kuykendall, Norma Harman.
Financial data (yr. ended 02/28/99): Assets, $640,059 (M); grants paid, $30; gifts received, $7,110; expenditures, $17,658; qualifying distributions, $30.
Officers: Fred Harman, Pres.; Alan F. Kuykendall, Secy.-Treas.
Directors: Virginia Bartlett, Medray H. Carpenter, Norma Harman, Earl E. Hoover, Bill Underhill.
EIN: 840845015

59243
King C. Hudson and Evelyn Leigh Hudson Foundation, Inc.
2888 W. Maplewood Ave.
Littleton, CO 80120-1807

Classified as a private operating foundation in 1987.
Donor(s): Evelyn Leigh Hudson.‡
Financial data (yr. ended 12/31/00): Assets, $612,185 (M); grants paid, $0; gifts received, $509,996; expenditures, $1,551,220; qualifying distributions, $790,401; giving activities include $790,401 for programs.
Officers: Rich Meredith, C.E.O.; Ron Martin, Pres.; Betty Lou Roberts, V.P.; Delorus "Dee" Gustafson, Secy.; Eric Johannisson, Treas.
Directors: Jean Carlberg, Sonya Ellingboe, Jody Randall, Doug Rockne, Marilyn Schalge, and 12 additional directors.
EIN: 841043276

59244
The Holland Foundation
1000 Castle Rock Dr.
Golden, CO 80401-1202
Application address: P.O. Box 603, Golden, CO 80402
Contact: Holland H. Coors, Pres.

Established in 1991 in CO.
Donor(s): Holland H. Coors.
Financial data (yr. ended 12/31/00): Assets, $611,405 (M); grants paid, $126,000; gifts received, $225,000; expenditures, $127,650; qualifying distributions, $125,922.
Limitations: Giving primarily in CO.
Application information: Contact foundation for application information and deadlines.
Officers and Directors:* Holland H. Coors,* Pres. and Treas.; Gail F. Coors,* Secy.; Lis L. Coors, Marilyn E. Coors, Sharna L. Coors, Sylvia N. Coors.
EIN: 841193723

59245
The Doris Denker Wheelchair Sports Foundation
c/o Lillian Brawer
1534B Crestview Way
Grand Junction, CO 81506-5210

Established in 1992 in CO.
Donor(s): Doris Denker.
Financial data (yr. ended 12/31/01): Assets, $558,901 (M); grants paid, $5,945; gifts received, $15,980; expenditures, $29,633; qualifying distributions, $23,688.
Limitations: Applications not accepted. Giving primarily in CO.
Application information: Contributes only to pre-selected organizations.
Officers: Lillian Brawer, Pres.; Wendy Marks, V.P.; Jerome Brawer, Secy.-Treas.
Directors: Dean Oba, Rick Wolfe.
EIN: 841216177

59246
Vance Kirkland Foundation
1700 Lincoln, Ste. 3950
Denver, CO 80203-4539
URL: http://www.vancekirkland.org
Contact: Letty Bass, Asst. Secy.

Established in 1996 in CO.
Donor(s): Merle C. Chambers, The Denver Foundation.
Financial data (yr. ended 12/31/01): Assets, $548,530 (M); grants paid, $131,787; gifts received, $507,515; expenditures, $1,216,709; qualifying distributions, $1,214,542; giving activities include $1,077,755 for programs.
Limitations: Applications not accepted. Giving primarily in CO.
Publications: Informational brochure.
Application information: Contributes only to pre-selected organizations.
Officers and Directors:* Hugh A. Grant,* Pres.; Merle C. Chambers,* V.P.; Sally W. Leibbrandt, Secy.; Ronald L. Kahler,* Treas.
EIN: 841360133
Codes: FD2

59247
The Ethridge Scholarship Foundation
c/o Milly Westphalen
P.O. Box 2087
Littleton, CO 80161-2087

Established in 1995.
Financial data (yr. ended 06/30/01): Assets, $524,988 (M); grants paid, $34,500; expenditures, $37,045; qualifying distributions, $36,644.
Limitations: Giving limited to residents of Denver, CO.
Application information: Application form required.
Officers and Directors:* Nancy L. Gentry,* Pres.; Frances Burbank,* V.P.; Gwendolyn H. Scott,* Secy.; Barbara L. Hughes,* Treas.; Frances Burbank, Karen Ellis, Brenda Olson, Carol Paisi.
EIN: 841270799
Codes: GTI

59248
Stanley Charitable Trust
c/o Mary Jane Shinn
200 W. Elm St.
Lamar, CO 81052

Established in 1997 in CO.
Financial data (yr. ended 12/31/01): Assets, $518,342 (M); grants paid, $0; expenditures, $31,304; qualifying distributions, $0.
Trustee: Mary Jane Shinn.
EIN: 841371971

59249
With a Child's Heart Foundation
900 W. Castleton Rd., Ste. 125
Castle Rock, CO 80104

Established in 1999 in CO.
Financial data (yr. ended 12/31/00): Assets, $477,787 (M); grants paid, $54,000; expenditures, $61,191; qualifying distributions, $53,748.
Limitations: Applications not accepted. Giving primarily in CO.
Application information: Contributes only to pre-selected organizations.
Officers: Jack A. Vickers III, Pres.; Alice Vickers, V.P.; Angela Elliott, Secy.-Treas.
EIN: 841521786

59250
The Shelby American Collection
5020 Chaparral Ct.
P.O. Box 19228
Boulder, CO 80308-2228

Established in 1996 in CO.
Donor(s): Steven B. Volk.
Financial data (yr. ended 12/31/00): Assets, $473,572 (M); grants paid, $250; gifts received, $40,769; expenditures, $55,837; qualifying distributions, $250.
Limitations: Applications not accepted.
Application information: Contributes only to pre-selected organizations.
Officers: Steven B. Volk, Pres.; David M. Furay, V.P.; Lisa M. Volk, Secy.
EIN: 841366547

59251
Serendipity Foundation
(Formerly Serendipity Associates, Inc.)
c/o Lyman Coleman
8100 Southpark Way, Ste. A-6
Littleton, CO 80120

Established in 1993 in CO.
Donor(s): H. Lyman Coleman.
Financial data (yr. ended 12/31/00): Assets, $464,724 (M); grants paid, $19,500; gifts received, $161,010; expenditures, $180,801; qualifying distributions, $19,500.
Limitations: Applications not accepted. Giving primarily in Dubuque, IL.
Application information: Contributes only to pre-selected organizations.
Officer: H. Lyman Coleman, Exec. Dir.
EIN: 363725406

59252
Random Acts of Kindness Foundation
1801 Broadway, Ste. 250
Denver, CO 80202

Established in 1999 in CO.
Donor(s): The Anschutz Foundation.
Financial data (yr. ended 11/30/00): Assets, $450,761 (M); grants paid, $6,000; gifts received, $1,060,000; expenditures, $619,039; qualifying distributions, $569,582; giving activities include $569,582 for programs.
Limitations: Applications not accepted. Giving in North America, primarily in Vancouver, British Columbia.
Application information: Contributes only to pre-selected organizations.
Officers: Philip F. Anschutz, Chair.; Will Glennon, Pres.; M. Lavoy Robison, V.P.; Craig D. Slater, V.P.
EIN: 841528369

59253
Sky Cliff Stroke Center
1200 South St.
Castle Rock, CO 80104

Established in 1987 in CO.
Donor(s): Helen Ludvigsen.
Financial data (yr. ended 08/31/00): Assets, $449,477 (M); grants paid, $0; gifts received, $253,230; expenditures, $75,129; qualifying distributions, $74,249; giving activities include $411,836 for programs.
Limitations: Applications not accepted.
Application information: Contributes only to pre-selected organizations.
Officers: Hon. Hilbert Schauer, Pres.; Norman Scheffel, V.P.; Allen Peck, Secy.; Ruth Molnar, Treas.
Trustees: Susan Walker Avis, Donald D'Amico, Daniel L. Novak, Robert Schauer, Mark Scheffel, Rev. Alan Whitelock.
EIN: 742342750

59254
Wings of the Morning Foundation
c/o Richard E. Williams
4189 Stone Canyon Ranch Rd.
Castle Rock, CO 80104

Established in 2000 in CO.
Donor(s): Richard E. Williams, Terry F. Williams.
Financial data (yr. ended 12/31/01): Assets, $431,708 (M); grants paid, $0; gifts received, $550; expenditures, $36,463; qualifying distributions, $0.
Limitations: Applications not accepted.
Application information: Contributes only to pre-selected organizations.
Officers: Terry F. Williams, Pres.; Richard E. Williams, Secy.-Treas.
EIN: 841554014

59255
Higbie Family Foundation
1600 Broadway
Denver, CO 80202

Established in 2000 in CO. Classified as a private operating foundation in 2001.
Donor(s): Harley G. Higbie, Jr.
Financial data (yr. ended 12/31/01): Assets, $395,603 (M); grants paid, $15,000; gifts received, $163,180; expenditures, $16,000; qualifying distributions, $15,000.
Directors: Harley G. Higbie, Jr., Lorraine N. Higbie.
EIN: 841569392

59256
Wild Oats Community Foundation
2602 Baseline Rd.
Boulder, CO 80303

Established in 1997 in CO.
Donor(s): Elizabeth C. Cook, Michael C. Gilliland.
Financial data (yr. ended 12/31/00): Assets, $380,873 (M); grants paid, $0; expenditures, $691,191; qualifying distributions, $218,306.
Officers: Elizabeth C. Cook, Pres.; David S. Brodie, V.P. and Secy.; Michael C. Gilliland, Treas.
EIN: 841440983

59257
Archstone Foundation
9200 E. Panorama Cir., Ste. 400
Englewood, CO 80112

Established in 2001 in CO.
Donor(s): Archstone-Smith Operating Trust.
Financial data (yr. ended 12/31/01): Assets, $341,536 (M); grants paid, $25,000; gifts received, $366,536; expenditures, $25,000; qualifying distributions, $25,000.
Limitations: Applications not accepted. Giving primarily in Washington, DC.
Application information: Contributes only to pre-selected organizations.
Officers and Directors:* R. Scot Sellers,* Chair. and C.E.O.; Caroline Brower,* Sr. V.P. and Secy.; Dana K. Hamilton,* Sr. V.P.; David Flory, V.P.; Charles E. Mueller, Jr., C.F.O.; Richard A. Banks, Managing Dir.; J. Lindsay Freeman, Managing Dir.
EIN: 364464966

59258
John and Elizabeth Hickey Family Foundation, Inc.
7700 W. 88th. Ave.
Arvada, CO 80005-1615

Established in 1998 in CO.
Donor(s): Elizabeth Hickey.‡
Financial data (yr. ended 12/31/00): Assets, $326,663 (M); grants paid, $14,750; expenditures, $51,549; qualifying distributions, $14,750.
Limitations: Giving primarily in CO and UT.
Officers: Elizabeth J. Keating, Pres.; Margaret P. Bullen, Treas.
EIN: 841460187

59259
Hertha Thomas-Zagari Giant Schnauzer Rescue, Inc.
1691 S. Arbutus Pl.
Lakewood, CO 80228-3730

Established in 1999 in CO.
Donor(s): Hertha Thomas-Zagari.‡
Financial data (yr. ended 12/31/01): Assets, $309,128 (M); grants paid, $800; gifts received, $246,538; expenditures, $18,672; qualifying distributions, $11,673.
Limitations: Applications not accepted. Giving on a national basis.
Application information: Contributes only to pre-selected organizations.
Officers: Carolyn J. Janak, Pres. and Treas.; Deborah Dayton, V.P.; Laurie Janak, Secy.
Directors: Marla Monahan, Miriam Rose.
EIN: 311680827

59260
Hill Family Foundation
P.O. Box 6118
Denver, CO 80206

Donor(s): Robert F. Hill, Laura L. Hill.

Financial data (yr. ended 12/31/99): Assets, $290,696 (M); grants paid, $47,883; expenditures, $55,708; qualifying distributions, $47,328.
Limitations: Applications not accepted. Giving primarily in CO.
Application information: Contributes only to pre-selected organizations.
Officers and Trustees:* Laura L. Hill,* Pres.; Robert F. Hill,* Secy.
EIN: 841289400

59261
The Flatirons Foundation
c/o Roaring Forks Scholarship Comm.
514 E. Hyman Ave.
Aspen, CO 81611
Contact: Robert Starodoj, Tr.

Financial data (yr. ended 12/31/01): Assets, $269,305 (M); grants paid, $11,950; expenditures, $15,319; qualifying distributions, $15,319.
Limitations: Giving primarily in Aspen, CO.
Application information: Application form required for scholarships.
Officers: Robert F. Starodoj, Pres.; Lynne Levinson, Secy.
Trustees: Rob Gile, David Guthrie, Lynne Levinson, Roger Marolt, Lorna Pedersen, Philip Wright.
EIN: 840563062
Codes: GTI

59262
Universal Education Foundation
P.O. Box 159
Cripple Creek, CO 80813-0159
(719) 689-0777

Established in 1986 in CO.
Financial data (yr. ended 12/31/01): Assets, $251,146 (M); grants paid, $0; gifts received, $4,732; expenditures, $12,771; qualifying distributions, $0.
Officers and Directors:* Rebecca Harrison,* Pres. and Treas.; Kent Kalb, V.P.; Marti Kalb,* Secy.; Hossca Harrison.
EIN: 742427145

59263
Petra Foundation
15 Cherry Lane Dr.
Englewood, CO 80110

Established in 1997 in CO.
Donor(s): Keene Z. Smith.
Financial data (yr. ended 12/31/00): Assets, $235,136 (M); grants paid, $1,000; gifts received, $19,150; expenditures, $2,128; qualifying distributions, $1,000.
Trustees: Cindy W. Beasley, Joan W. Smith, Keene Z. Smith, Keene Z. Smith, Jr.
EIN: 841398848

59264
Bonnie Langston Memorial Scholarship Trust
P.O. Box 327
Montrose, CO 81402-0327 (970) 249-4531
Contact: Victor T. Roushar, Tr.

Established in 1994 in CO.
Donor(s): Bonnie Langston.‡
Financial data (yr. ended 12/31/99): Assets, $224,598 (M); grants paid, $21,500; expenditures, $25,547; qualifying distributions, $21,500.
Limitations: Giving limited to residents of Montrose, CO.
Application information: Application form required.

Trustees: Shirley Ford, Victor T. Roushar, K.M. Townsend, Charles J. Vidmar.
EIN: 846268159

59265
William W. and Mollye B. Morrow Foundation
3718 N. County Rd. 27E
Bellvue, CO 80512-7105
Contact: William W. Morrow, Dir.

Established in 1995 in CO.
Donor(s): William W. Morrow, Mollye B. Morrow.
Financial data (yr. ended 12/31/99): Assets, $220,450 (M); grants paid, $7,350; gifts received, $15,000; expenditures, $8,260; qualifying distributions, $7,350.
Limitations: Giving primarily in Fort Collins, CO.
Directors: Ruth A. Casey, Mollye B. Morrow, William W. Morrow.
EIN: 841296738

59266
Caddo Lake Institute, Inc.
P.O. Box 2710
Aspen, CO 81612

Established in 1993; Classified as a private operating foundation in 1994.
Donor(s): Don Henley.
Financial data (yr. ended 06/30/00): Assets, $218,890 (M); grants paid, $3,700; gifts received, $414,477; expenditures, $381,259; qualifying distributions, $367,680; giving activities include $169,828 for programs.
Limitations: Applications not accepted.
Application information: Contributes only to pre-selected organizations.
Officers: Dwight Shellman, Pres.; Barbara Ornitz, Secy.-Treas.
EIN: 841249203

59267
Stoner Home, Inc.
c/o Alex C. Cook
P.O. Box 1958
Boulder, CO 80306-1958

Classified as a private operating foundation in 1986.
Financial data (yr. ended 12/31/01): Assets, $185,998 (M); grants paid, $0; gifts received, $332; expenditures, $406; qualifying distributions, $0; giving activities include $406 for programs.
Officers: George Bramhall, Pres.; Verna Hamm, V.P.; Gary Hampton, Secy.; Alex C. Cook, Treas.
EIN: 840536652

59268
The Brent and Connie Waldron Family Star Foundation
715 W. Main St., Ste. 201
Aspen, CO 81611
Application address: 720 E. Hyman Ave., Aspen, CO 81611
Contact: K. Brent Waldron, Pres.

Established in 1999 in CO.
Donor(s): K. Brent Waldron, Constance Waldron.
Financial data (yr. ended 12/31/00): Assets, $172,056 (M); grants paid, $0; gifts received, $10,000; expenditures, $1,739; qualifying distributions, $0.
Officers and Directors:* Keith B. Waldron,* Pres.; Noelle Waldron,* V.P.; Constance Waldron,* Secy.; Nathan Waldron,* Treas.
EIN: 841523196

59269
The Clan MacBean Foundation
c/o Raymond L. Heckethorn
441 Wadsworth Blvd., Ste. 213
Lakewood, CO 80226-1545

Classified as a private-operating foundation in 1989.
Donor(s): John B. Bean.
Financial data (yr. ended 12/31/01): Assets, $154,248 (M); grants paid, $12,500; gifts received, $20; expenditures, $21,385; qualifying distributions, $12,474.
Limitations: Giving on an international basis, with emphasis on Scotland.
Application information: Application form required.
Officers: Grant Crate, Chair. and V.P.; William Beane, Pres.; Jonathan P. Binnie, V.P.; George Wiseman, Secy.; Raymond Heckethorn, Treas.
EIN: 411445203
Codes: GTI

59270
Platinum Pro Foundation
2619 Canton Ct.
Fort Collins, CO 80525

Financial data (yr. ended 12/31/99): Assets, $141,665 (M); grants paid, $0; gifts received, $32,945; expenditures, $32,404; qualifying distributions, $32,404; giving activities include $5,425 for programs.
Trustees: Scott Carpenter, Robert Clark, Jean-Michel Cousteau, Sylvia Earle, Frank Fennel, Jere Hallenbeck, Frederick Lawson.
EIN: 841369641

59271
Kobayashi Family Foundation
1633 Fillmore St., Ste. 2100
Denver, CO 80206-1556

Established in 1995 in CO.
Donor(s): John M. Kobayashi.
Financial data (yr. ended 12/31/99): Assets, $135,265 (M); grants paid, $6,050; gifts received, $39,000; expenditures, $6,162; qualifying distributions, $6,162.
Limitations: Applications not accepted.
Application information: Contributes only to pre-selected organizations.
Trustee: John M. Kobayashi.
EIN: 841290227

59272
Eldon E. Veirs Scholarship Fund
c/o George L. Zoellner
12101 E. 2nd Ave., Ste. 207
Aurora, CO 80011
Application address: c/o Olathe High School, P.O. Box 280, Olathe, CO 81245
Contact: B.J. Brown, Dir.

Financial data (yr. ended 03/31/01): Assets, $130,971 (M); grants paid, $6,900; expenditures, $7,033; qualifying distributions, $7,033.
Limitations: Giving limited to residents of Olathe, CO.
Application information: Application form required.
Directors: B.J. Brown, Kathleen Sherman, George L. Zoellner.
EIN: 840935386

59273
Butterfield Foundation, Inc.
14595 Roller Coaster Rd.
Colorado Springs, CO 80921-2037

Established in 1988 in FL.
Donor(s): Craig W. Butterfield, Elaine N. Butterfield.
Financial data (yr. ended 09/30/01): Assets, $125,336 (M); grants paid, $6,500; expenditures, $6,835; qualifying distributions, $6,500.
Limitations: Applications not accepted.
Officers: Craig W. Butterfield, Pres.; Elaine N. Butterfield, V.P. and Secy.-Treas.
Directors: W. Thomas Brooks, William H. Cauthen.
EIN: 592972150

59274
Nuggets Stay in School Program
c/o Denver Nuggets
1000 Chopper Cir.
Denver, CO 80204

Established in 1995. Classified as a company-sponsored operating foundation.
Donor(s): Denver Nuggets L.P., Robert R. McCormick Tribune Foundation.
Financial data (yr. ended 07/31/00): Assets, $106,797 (M); grants paid, $0; gifts received, $208,000; expenditures, $131,330; qualifying distributions, $129,211; giving activities include $98,432 for programs.
Officers and Directors:* Ronald O. Sally,* Pres.; Bernadette Romero Seick,* V.P.; Mark Waggoner,* Treas.; Marge Tepper.
EIN: 841287212

59275
The Schuck Foundation
2 N. Cascade Ave., Ste. 1280
Colorado Springs, CO 80903

Established in 2000 in CO.
Donor(s): Stephen Schuck.
Financial data (yr. ended 12/31/00): Assets, $100,000 (M); grants paid, $0; gifts received, $100,000; expenditures, $0; qualifying distributions, $0.
Application information: Application form required.
Officers and Directors:* Stephen M. Schuck,* Pres.; Joyce H. Schuck,* V.P.; Steve L. Everson, Secy.-Treas.; Ann Schuck, Thomas Schuck, William D. Schuck.
EIN: 841569782

59276
Seward Foundation
P.O. Box 6
Eaton, CO 80615

Donor(s): R. Lee Seward, Rebecca M. Seward.
Financial data (yr. ended 12/31/00): Assets, $96,924 (M); grants paid, $6,870; expenditures, $7,404; qualifying distributions, $6,870.
Limitations: Applications not accepted. Giving primarily in Fort Collins, CO.
Application information: Contributes only to pre-selected organizations.
Officers: R. Lee Seward, Pres.; Rebecca M. Seward, V.P.
EIN: 311534855

59277
The Branches of Life Corporation
22748 Weld County Rd. 3
Berthoud, CO 80513 (970) 532-3477
Contact: Lisa M. Campbell, V.P.

Classified as a private operating foundation.
Donor(s): Dean T. Campbell, Lisa M. Campbell.
Financial data (yr. ended 12/31/00): Assets, $92,238 (M); grants paid, $9,100; gifts received, $84,112; expenditures, $84,636; qualifying distributions, $85,190; giving activities include $28,508 for programs.

Officers and Directors:* Dean T. Campbell,* Pres.; Lisa M. Campbell,* V.P. and Secy.-Treas.
EIN: 841410718

59278
Sally Conti Scholarship
13035 Willow Way
Golden, CO 80401 (303) 237-6685
Contact: Richard F. Conti, Pres.

Donor(s): Richard F. Conti.
Financial data (yr. ended 12/31/99): Assets, $91,258 (M); grants paid, $9,000; gifts received, $1,500; expenditures, $9,371; qualifying distributions, $8,700.
Application information: Application form required.
Officers: Richard F. Conti, Pres.; Barbara Swearingen, V.P.; Cheryl Robacker, Secy.; Deanna Alderman, Treas.
EIN: 841331801

59279
Lake Fork Community Foundation
P.O. Box 518
Lake City, CO 81235-0518 (970) 944-8111
Contact: Michelle Pierce, Secy.-Treas.

Classified as a private operating foundation in 1994.
Donor(s): Richard T. Hall, Ruthanna Hall, William Hall, Sandy Hardilek, Tom Hardilek.
Financial data (yr. ended 12/31/00): Assets, $88,283 (M); grants paid, $70,429; gifts received, $70,289; expenditures, $72,004; qualifying distributions, $70,401.
Limitations: Giving limited to Hinsdale, CO.
Officers: Tom Hardilek, Chair.; Bruce Vierheller, Vice-Chair.; Michelle Pierce, Secy.-Treas.
Directors: Jerry Gray, Marian Hollingsworth, Dan Milski, Kelli Murphy, Carolyn Virden.
EIN: 841254225

59280
Operation Game Thief, Inc.
6060 Broadway
Denver, CO 80216
Contact: David A. Croonquist, Coord.

Financial data (yr. ended 12/31/99): Assets, $88,172 (M); grants paid, $5,220; gifts received, $800; expenditures, $8,872; qualifying distributions, $8,061.
Limitations: Giving limited to CO.
Application information: Applicants must provide information pertinent to violations of CO wildlife statutes and regulations and information must result in a citation being issued for such violations.
Officers and Trustees:* Dick Hess,* Pres.; Gerhart L. Stengel,* V.P.; Bruce McDowell,* Secy.-Treas.; David A. Croonquist, Coord.; Pat Carlow, Jon Staples.
EIN: 742188212

59281
Wright Family Foundation
1440 High St.
Boulder, CO 80304-4116

Established in 1999 in CO.
Donor(s): Ken Wright, Ruth Wright.
Financial data (yr. ended 09/30/00): Assets, $87,453 (M); grants paid, $7,000; gifts received, $102,500; expenditures, $7,000; qualifying distributions, $7,000.
Limitations: Applications not accepted.
Application information: Contributes only to pre-selected organizations.
Officers and Directors:* Ruth M. Wright,* Pres. and Treas.; Kenneth R. Wright,* V.P. and Secy.
EIN: 841519941

59282
G & G Outreach Foundation
1105 Zuni St.
Denver, CO 80204 (303) 892-7003
Contact: Gary Armstrong, Pres.

Established in 1994 in CO as a company-sponsored operating foundation.
Donor(s): General Air Service & Supply Co.
Financial data (yr. ended 12/31/01): Assets, $79,078 (M); grants paid, $108,150; gifts received, $55,000; expenditures, $108,981; qualifying distributions, $108,150.
Limitations: Giving limited to headquarters city and major operating areas.
Officers: Gary Armstrong, Pres.; Gail Armstrong, Secy.
EIN: 841260656
Codes: FD2, CD

59283
Panorama Research & Education Foundation
660 Golden Ridge Rd., Ste. 250
Golden, CO 80401

Established in 2000 in CO. Classified as a company-sponsored operating foundation.
Donor(s): Zimmer, Smith & Nephew, EBI, Synthese Spine, ORP, Sanofi/Hyalgon, S.P.O.R.T., Aventis, BREG, Wyeth-Ayerst.
Financial data (yr. ended 12/31/01): Assets, $75,556 (M); grants paid, $0; gifts received, $336,340; expenditures, $351,853; qualifying distributions, $301,031; giving activities include $301,032 for programs.
Officer and Directors:* Thomas G. Friermood, M.D.,* Chair.; William Cowan, Allison Hawkes, M.D., Peter Lammens, M.D., Josef Schroeter, Rod Turner.
EIN: 841533376

59284
The Anna and John J. Sie Foundation
5445 DTC Pkwy., Ste. 600
Englewood, CO 80111

Established in 2000 in CO.
Donor(s): John J. Sie.
Financial data (yr. ended 12/31/01): Assets, $75,058 (M); grants paid, $87,500; gifts received, $103,915; expenditures, $113,958; qualifying distributions, $87,500.
Limitations: Applications not accepted.
Application information: Contributes only to pre-selected organizations.
Officers: Anna Sie, C.E.O.; John J. Sie, Pres. and Treas.; Michelle Sie Whitten, Secy.
EIN: 841548328

59285
Miriam Mitchell Memorial Scholarship Fund
c/o Wells Fargo Bank West, N.A.
1740 Broadway, MAC C7300-074
Denver, CO 80274-0001
Application address: c/o William D. Mitchell, Scholarship Coord., Univ. of Northern Colorado, Greeley, CO 80639, tel.: (970) 351-2502

Financial data (yr. ended 12/31/00): Assets, $72,097 (M); grants paid, $1,289; expenditures, $2,866; qualifying distributions, $1,289.
Limitations: Giving limited to Greeley, CO.
Trustee: Wells Fargo Bank West, N.A.
EIN: 846016637

59286
Ron Bombard Foundation
4566 Hwy. 114
Gunnison, CO 81230 (970) 641-2984
Contact: Ron Bombard, Pres.

Established in 2000 in CO.
Donor(s): Ron Bombard.
Financial data (yr. ended 12/31/00): Assets, $68,700 (M); grants paid, $0; gifts received, $68,700; expenditures, $0; qualifying distributions, $0.
Application information: Application form required.
Officers: Ron Bombard, Pres.; Dan McKenna, Secy.
Trustees: Gary Appleton, Mike Matthews, Vern Motor, Pete Proschold, Jesse Stone.
EIN: 841575122

59287
The Gordon Jackson Foundation
P.O. Box 220
Woodland Park, CO 80866 (719) 687-9351
Contact: Gordon Jackson, Pres.

Established in 2000 in CO.
Donor(s): Gordon D. Jackson.
Financial data (yr. ended 12/31/00): Assets, $56,820 (M); grants paid, $0; gifts received, $61,909; expenditures, $5,715; qualifying distributions, $5,715.
Officers: Gordon D. Jackson, Pres.; Julie J. Snyder, V.P.; Walter A. Jackson, Secy.-Treas.
EIN: 311687355

59288
The Five Centuries Foundation
775 Kalmia Ave.
Boulder, CO 80304

Established in 1999 in CO.
Donor(s): Theodore J. Mallon.
Financial data (yr. ended 12/31/00): Assets, $55,099 (M); grants paid, $1,500; gifts received, $345,000; expenditures, $293,095; qualifying distributions, $1,500.
Officer: Theodore Mallon, Pres. and Secy.-Treas.
EIN: 841499644

59289
The Shirley Anne Potestio Foundation
7374 E. Inspiration Dr.
Parker, CO 80138

Donor(s): Frank S. Potestio.
Financial data (yr. ended 12/31/00): Assets, $53,434 (M); grants paid, $4,000; gifts received, $22,073; expenditures, $4,000; qualifying distributions, $4,000.
Limitations: Giving primarily in CO.
Directors: Frank S. Potestio, M.D., Frank S. Potestio II.
EIN: 841485248

59290
Jeanne Land Foundation in Memory of Dean Gillespie and Walter Land
P.O. Box 36418
Denver, CO 80236-0418

Classified as a private operating foundation in 1988.
Donor(s): Jeanne Gillespie Land.
Financial data (yr. ended 11/30/99): Assets, $51,123 (M); grants paid, $10,000; expenditures, $10,000; qualifying distributions, $10,000.
Limitations: Giving limited to Denver, CO.
Officers and Directors:* Joseph Berebaum,* Pres.; John B. Dawson,* V.P.; Steven C. Hoth, Secy.; James B. Brackett,* Treas.

59290—COLORADO

EIN: 841064292

59291
The Noah Sirbu Meyers Fund
16414 Sandstone Dr.
Morrison, CO 80465

Established in 1999 in CO.
Donor(s): Peter Richard Sirbu.
Financial data (yr. ended 12/31/00): Assets, $50,500 (M); grants paid, $500; gifts received, $1,000; expenditures, $500; qualifying distributions, $500.
Limitations: Applications not accepted. Giving primarily in Denver, CO.
Application information: Contributes only to pre-selected organizations.
Officers: Peter Richard Sirbu, Jr., Chair. and C.E.O.; Karen Kearns Sirbu, Pres.; Kristin Sirbu Meyers, V.P. and Secy.-Treas.; Gary George Meyers, V.P.
EIN: 841525447

59292
Zentmeyer Family Foundation
14799 6130 Rd.
Montrose, CO 81401

Established in 1998 in CO.
Donor(s): Donald Zentmeyer, Montrose Ins. Service, Inc., Mylar's Auto Ref., Inc.
Financial data (yr. ended 12/31/00): Assets, $44,511 (M); grants paid, $500; gifts received, $12,893; expenditures, $6,360; qualifying distributions, $6,360; giving activities include $3,519 for programs.
Limitations: Applications not accepted.
Application information: Contributes only to pre-selected organizations.
Trustees: Donald L. Zentmeyer, John C. Zentmeyer, Suzanne B. Zentmeyer.
EIN: 841472937

59293
Jeffco Open Space Foundation
5855 Wadsworth Bypass, Bldg A., Ste. 100
Arvada, CO 80003

Established in 1998 in CO.
Financial data (yr. ended 12/31/01): Assets, $31,896 (M); grants paid, $55,452; gifts received, $112,499; expenditures, $58,125; qualifying distributions, $58,125.
Limitations: Applications not accepted. Giving primarily in CO.
Application information: Contributes only to pre-selected organizations.
Officers: Dan Kimball, Pres.; Joe Jehn, V.P.; Don Eikner, Secy.; John Litz, Treas.
EIN: 841471616

59294
SOGO WAY
c/o Shinsaku Sogo
3951 S. Hudson Way
Englewood, CO 80110-5135

Established in 1994 in CO.
Donor(s): Sinsaku Sogo.
Financial data (yr. ended 03/31/00): Assets, $28,482 (M); grants paid, $0; gifts received, $30,245; expenditures, $28,337; qualifying distributions, $15,543; giving activities include $28,337 for programs.
Officer and Directors:* Sinsaku Sogo,* Pres. and Treas.; William Hosokawa, Brian Pendalton.
EIN: 841251766

59295
Population Biology Foundation
Wubben Hall
1100 North Ave., Rm. 263
Grand Junction, CO 81501

Established in 1997 in OR.
Donor(s): Russell S. Lande.
Financial data (yr. ended 12/31/01): Assets, $23,302 (M); grants paid, $27,524; gifts received, $49,280; expenditures, $27,675; qualifying distributions, $27,524.
Officers: Russell S. Lande, Pres.; Philip J. Devries, Secy.
Director: Thomas R. Walla.
EIN: 911836116

59296
Foundation for a Better Life
1727 Tremont Pl.
Denver, CO 80202-4006

Established in 1999 in CO.
Donor(s): The Anschutz Foundation.
Financial data (yr. ended 11/30/00): Assets, $22,239 (M); grants paid, $0; gifts received, $2,049,125; expenditures, $2,026,886; qualifying distributions, $2,043,677; giving activities include $2,023,553 for programs.
Limitations: Applications not accepted.
Application information: Contributes only to pre-selected organizations.
Officers and Directors:* Philip F. Anschutz,* Chair.; Gary Dixon, Pres.; Nancy P. Anschutz,* V.P.; Craig D. Slater, Secy.-Treas.; M. Lavoy Robison, Exec. Dir.; Christian P. Anschutz, Elizabeth S. Brown, Sarah A. Hunt.
EIN: 841529209

59297
William Gorham Trust
c/o Colorado Bank & Trust Co.
P.O. Box 499
La Junta, CO 81050-0499

Established in 1999 in CO.
Financial data (yr. ended 12/31/01): Assets, $21,467 (M); grants paid, $0; expenditures, $559; qualifying distributions, $0.
Trustee: Colorado Bank & Trust Co.
EIN: 846174890

59298
Shane Kilgore Memorial Academic and Athletic Scholarship Fund
(Formerly Shane Kilgore Memorial)
1210 Scottswood Dr.
Monument, CO 80132-8446

Financial data (yr. ended 05/31/00): Assets, $20,434 (M); grants paid, $3,000; expenditures, $3,379; qualifying distributions, $3,363.
Limitations: Applications not accepted. Giving limited to Simi Valley, CA.
Directors: Harold L. Kilgore, Susan J. Kilgore.
EIN: 954284186

59299
Queen of Apostles Mission Association
2375 E. Arizona Ave.
Denver, CO 80210 (303) 733-1771
E-mail: qama@aol.com; *URL:* http://www.qama.org
Contact: A. Matt Werner, Pres.

Established in 1993 in CO.
Financial data (yr. ended 03/31/01): Assets, $18,028 (M); grants paid, $110,285; gifts received, $142,073; expenditures, $139,000; qualifying distributions, $110,285.
Limitations: Giving limited to benefit Russia, Ukraine, Belarus, and other former Soviet Union countries.
Officers: A. Matt Werner, Pres.; Kitty Kolody, Secy.; Joe McAleer, Treas.
Board Members: Jane Brennan, Rachel A. Breshahan.
EIN: 841212760
Codes: FD2

59300
Murphey Western Institute, Inc.
1120 Lincoln St, Ste. 1100
Denver, CO 80203

Established in 1999 in CO.
Financial data (yr. ended 12/31/00): Assets, $14,204 (M); grants paid, $4,300; gifts received, $78,984; expenditures, $95,565; qualifying distributions, $4,300.
Limitations: Applications not accepted. Giving primarily in CO.
Application information: Contributes only to pre-selected organizations.
Officers and Trustees:* Michael Martin Murphey,* Pres.; Pink L. Murphey,* Secy.-Treas.
EIN: 841490181

59301
Scott Treatment Scholarship Fund, Inc.
333 S. Allison Pkwy., Ste. 209
Lakewood, CO 80226

Classified as a private operating foundation in 1990.
Donor(s): Joseph A. Scott, Mary H. Scott.
Financial data (yr. ended 12/31/00): Assets, $13,860 (M); grants paid, $0; gifts received, $85,765; expenditures, $72,554; qualifying distributions, $72,319; giving activities include $72,319 for programs.
Officers and Directors:* Joseph A. Scott,* Pres.; Joan Peterson,* Secy.-Treas.
EIN: 742571404

59302
St. Thomas Hospice and Orphanage, Ltd.
c/o Matthew Zachariah
4120 S. Deframe St.
Morrison, CO 80465-1088

Established in 1996 in CO.
Donor(s): Fr. Matthew Zachariah.
Financial data (yr. ended 12/31/01): Assets, $11,259 (M); grants paid, $17,300; gifts received, $21,360; expenditures, $17,300; qualifying distributions, $17,300.
Limitations: Applications not accepted. Giving on an international basis, with emphasis on Kerala, India.
Application information: Unsolicited requests for funds not accepted.
Officers: Fr. Matthew Zachariah, Pres.; Ammini Zachariah, Secy.
Directors: Tom Doevk, Fr. Paul von Lobkowitz.
EIN: 841305239

59303
Sheridan Ross Charitable Foundation
1560 Broadway, Ste. 1200
Denver, CO 80202-5141

Established in 2000 in CO.
Financial data (yr. ended 12/31/00): Assets, $10,237 (M); grants paid, $15,350; gifts received, $25,550; expenditures, $15,381; qualifying distributions, $15,350.
Limitations: Applications not accepted. Giving primarily in CO.
Application information: Contributes only to pre-selected organizations.

Officers: Robert R. Brunelli, Pres.; Sabrina C. Stavish, V.P.; Richard L. Hughes, Secy.-Treas.
EIN: 841546781

59304
Margaret Vandenberg Education Trust
1533 Crestview Way, No. 13
Grand Junction, CO 81506-5204
(970) 241-7485
Contact: Mary Lou Vandenberg, Tr.

Established in 1994 in CO.
Financial data (yr. ended 12/31/00): Assets, $9,221 (M); grants paid, $600; expenditures, $632; qualifying distributions, $632.
Limitations: Giving primarily in CO.
Trustees: Peggy Mathis, Judy Scales, Jim Vandenberg, Mary Lou Vandenberg.
EIN: 746416366

59305
The JEM Foundation
4100 E. Mississippi Ave., Ste. 1515
Denver, CO 80222

Established in 1996 in CO.
Donor(s): Gerri Morahan, Joseph E. Morahan III.
Financial data (yr. ended 12/31/00): Assets, $5,128 (M); grants paid, $285,000; gifts received, $238,000; expenditures, $285,060; qualifying distributions, $285,000.
Limitations: Applications not accepted. Giving primarily in CO, IL, and IN.
Application information: Contributes only to pre-selected organizations.
Trustees: Gerri S. Morahan, Joseph E. Morahan III.
EIN: 841335384
Codes: FD

59306
Colorado Oncology Foundation, Inc.
12048 Blackhawk Dr.
Conifer, CO 80433

Donor(s): George E. Moore.
Financial data (yr. ended 10/31/00): Assets, $4,309 (M); grants paid, $0; gifts received, $8,064; expenditures, $7,496; qualifying distributions, $6,164; giving activities include $7,496 for programs.
Officers: George E. Moore, M.D., Pres.; Lorraine P. Moore, V.P.; Robert D. Garner, M.D., Secy.-Treas.
EIN: 742269654

59307
German Cultural Foundation
3900 E. 68th Ave.
Commerce City, CO 80022-2247

Financial data (yr. ended 12/31/01): Assets, $3,793 (M); grants paid, $1,500; expenditures, $2,016; qualifying distributions, $1,500.
Officers: Karl Schmidt, Pres.; Edith Gorner, V.P.; Jack Englert, V.P.; Bernhard Bleise, Treas.
EIN: 841288713

59308
Granite Ridge Nature Institute
13780 N. Saint Vrain Dr.
Lyons, CO 80540-9034

Established in 1999 in CO.
Financial data (yr. ended 10/31/00): Assets, $3,645 (M); grants paid, $0; gifts received, $7,147; expenditures, $8,448; qualifying distributions, $0; giving activities include $6,296 for programs.
Officers: Eugene A. Monroe, Pres.; Marilyn L. Monroe, Secy.-Treas.
EIN: 841498559

59309
The Harvey D. Oslund Foundation
(Formerly Harvey D. & Maybelle J. Oslund Charitable Foundation)
1501 Genesee Ridge Rd.
Golden, CO 80401

Donor(s): Harvey Oslund.
Financial data (yr. ended 11/30/01): Assets, $3,517 (M); grants paid, $12,771; gifts received, $4,313; expenditures, $13,525; qualifying distributions, $13,525.
Limitations: Applications not accepted.
Application information: Contributes only to pre-selected organizations.
Officer and Director:* Harvey Oslund,* Pres.
EIN: 521552860

59310
The Children's Treehouse Foundation
50 S. Steele St., No. 222
Denver, CO 80209

Established in 2001.
Donor(s): Peter R. Van Dernoot.
Financial data (yr. ended 09/30/01): Assets, $3,321 (M); grants paid, $0; gifts received, $14,000; expenditures, $10,679; qualifying distributions, $0.
Officers: Peter R. Van Dernoot, Chair. and Exec. Dir.; Ann K. Cooper, Treas.
EIN: 841575701

59311
Bible Stories for the Children of the World
12189 W. 64th Ave., Ste. 100
Arvada, CO 80004

Established in 1998.
Financial data (yr. ended 12/31/01): Assets, $2,619 (M); grants paid, $0; gifts received, $160; expenditures, $825; qualifying distributions, $0.
Limitations: Applications not accepted.
Officers: Roland L. Colbert, Pres. and Treas.; Cindi F. Colbert, V.P. and Secy.
EIN: 841190751

59312
Stambaugh Foundation
P.O. Box 346
Montrose, CO 81402-0346

Established in 1993 in CO.
Donor(s): John F.Y. Staumbaugh.
Financial data (yr. ended 06/30/01): Assets, $2,494 (M); grants paid, $550; expenditures, $0; qualifying distributions, $0.
Officers: John F.Y. Stambaugh, Jr., Pres. and Treas.; Sue Stambaugh, V.P. and Secy.
EIN: 841272214

59313
Living Waters Foundation
68884 Vicuna Dr.
Montrose, CO 81401

Established in 1999 in CO.
Financial data (yr. ended 12/31/01): Assets, $1,752 (M); grants paid, $200; expenditures, $523; qualifying distributions, $200.
Limitations: Applications not accepted.
Application information: Contributes only to pre-selected organizations.
Trustees: Elizabeth B. Burk, Robert A. Burk.
EIN: 841521460

59314
Quanz Family Charitable Foundation
110 W. Golf Pl.
Pagosa Springs, CO 81147
Contact: Richard J. Quanz, Tr.

Established in 1994 in CO.
Donor(s): Richard Quanz, Barbara Quanz.
Financial data (yr. ended 12/31/99): Assets, $1,554 (M); grants paid, $9,000; gifts received, $5,500; expenditures, $9,017; qualifying distributions, $8,999.
Limitations: Giving primarily to residents of La Mirada, CA.
Trustees: Barbara E. Quanz, Richard J. Quanz.
EIN: 856112422

59315
Nick Maloof Family Foundation
2982 S. Scranton St.
Aurora, CO 80014-3331

Established as a private operating foundation in 1997 in CO.
Financial data (yr. ended 12/31/00): Assets, $1,429 (M); grants paid, $3,988; gifts received, $4,500; expenditures, $4,164; qualifying distributions, $1,429.
Director: Nick C. Wilson.
EIN: 840136017

59316
The Anschutz Collection
555 17th St., Ste. 2400
Denver, CO 80202

Classified as a private operating foundation in 1982.
Financial data (yr. ended 11/30/00): Assets, $1,007 (M); grants paid, $0; expenditures, $20,049; qualifying distributions, $20,025.
Officers and Directors:* Philip F. Anschutz,* Pres.; Nancy P. Anschutz,* V.P.; Craig D. Slater, Secy.-Treas.; M. Lavoy Robinson, Exec. Dir.
EIN: 742213190

59317
Cherry Creek Medical Research Institute
1001 Adams Ave.
Louisville, CO 80027

Established in 1996 in CO.
Financial data (yr. ended 12/31/00): Assets, $954 (M); grants paid, $75; expenditures, $2,071; qualifying distributions, $1,366.
Directors: Daniel Bennett, James Hagen.
EIN: 841361866

59318
Wasyl & Joseph Memorial Foundation Trust
P.O. Box 36418
Denver, CO 80236-0418

Established in 1989 in MI.
Donor(s): Kenneth R. Kurple, Connie Kurple.
Financial data (yr. ended 11/30/99): Assets, $735 (M); grants paid, $1,090; expenditures, $1,106; qualifying distributions, $3,606.
Trustees: James B. Brackett, Connie Kurple, Rose Rivard.
EIN: 311323709

59319
Center for Senior Empowerment
6757 S. Ridge Ln.
Littleton, CO 80120

Financial data (yr. ended 12/31/99): Assets, $684 (M); grants paid, $0; expenditures, $291; qualifying distributions, $291; giving activities include $86 for programs.

59319—COLORADO

Officers: Enid Opal Cox, Pres.; Ina Kotich, Secy.; Virginia Fraser, Treas.
EIN: 742357390

59320
Hay Creek Rehabilitation Foundation
2855 Hay Creek Rd.
Colorado Springs, CO 80921

Established in 1999 in CO.
Financial data (yr. ended 12/31/01): Assets, $557 (M); grants paid, $0; expenditures, $395; qualifying distributions, $0.
Officer and Director:* Olga M. Fitzgerald,* Pres. and Treas.
EIN: 841494446

59321
Mezshu Foundation
c/o Gary M. Greenspan
11692 Kenosha Rd.
Longmont, CO 80501

Established in 1993 in CO.
Donor(s): Gary M. Greenspan, Jennifer Greenspan.
Financial data (yr. ended 12/31/01): Assets, $500 (M); grants paid, $0; gifts received, $16,221; expenditures, $16,221; qualifying distributions, $0.
Officer and Directors:* Gary M. Greenspan,* Exec. Dir.; Jennifer Greenspan.
EIN: 841177683

59322
Oz Foundation
(Formerly The Sky's the Limit)
555 17th St., Ste. 2400
Denver, CO 80202-3941

Classified as a private operating foundation in 1988.
Donor(s): The Anschutz Foundation, Big Sur Waterbeds, Inc.
Financial data (yr. ended 11/30/01): Assets, $418 (M); grants paid, $0; expenditures, $0; qualifying distributions, $0.
Officers: Sue Anschutz-Rodgers, Pres.; Robert S. Rich, V.P. and Secy.; Hugh C. Braly, Treas.
EIN: 742505793

59323
Wings of Eagles Ministries, Inc.
1400 Utah St., Ste. 121
Golden, CO 80401

Financial data (yr. ended 12/31/01): Assets, $2 (M); grants paid, $875; gifts received, $4,980; expenditures, $4,848; qualifying distributions, $4,848.
Officers: Jane Bucknot, C.E.O., Pres. and Treas.; Gary Busk, V.P.; Emily Francis, Secy.
EIN: 841247112

59324
Robert & Nancy Brooks Foundation, Inc.
c/o Karen Kotlarchyk
2920 County Rd., No. 233
Rifle, CO 81650-8737

Established in 1986 in NY.
Donor(s): Robert Brooks.
Financial data (yr. ended 09/30/01): Assets, $0 (L); grants paid, $15,000; expenditures, $20,705; qualifying distributions, $20,705.
Limitations: Applications not accepted.
Application information: Contributes only to pre-selected organizations.
Officers: Robert Brooks, Pres. and Treas.; Nancy Brooks, V.P.; David Warmflash, Secy.
EIN: 112847123

59325
Di Ciaccio Family Charitable Foundation
4700 Schoolfield Rd.
Westcliffe, CO 81252

Established in 2000.
Donor(s): John Di Ciaccio, Sonia Di Ciaccio.
Financial data (yr. ended 12/31/01): Assets, $0 (M); grants paid, $19,500; gifts received, $30,350; expenditures, $21,000; qualifying distributions, $19,500.
Limitations: Giving primarily in Pasadena, CA.
Trustees: John Di Ciaccio, Sonia Di Ciaccio.
EIN: 954829112

59326
Foundation for Israel
P.O Box 49487
Colorado Springs, CO 80949 (719) 590-1146

Established in 1996; classified as a private operating foundation in 1999.
Donor(s): Theodore Beckett.
Financial data (yr. ended 12/31/00): Assets, $0 (M); grants paid, $334,966; gifts received, $589,343; expenditures, $621,793; qualifying distributions, $334,966.
Limitations: Giving primarily in Israel.
Officers: Theodore T. Beckett, Pres.; Audrey Beckett, Secy.
Directors: Jerry Jensen, Dan Wooding.
EIN: 330313305

59327
Adam J. & Suzanne F. Freeman Irrevocable Trust
2345 Phillips Cir., Apt. A
Montrose, CO 81401-5635 (970) 249-1369
Contact: Adam J. Freeman, Mgr.

Donor(s): Adam J. Freeman, Suzanne F. Freeman.
Financial data (yr. ended 12/31/01): Assets, $0 (M); grants paid, $18,100; expenditures, $3,731; qualifying distributions, $18,106.
Limitations: Giving limited to residents in CO.
Application information: Application form required.
Officers and Trustees:* Adam J. Freeman,* Mgr.; Suzanne F. Freeman,* Mgr.
EIN: 954508493
Codes: GTI

59328
Safe Child, Inc.
725 Big Valley Dr.
Colorado Springs, CO 80919

Classified as a private operation foundation in 1987.
Financial data (yr. ended 03/31/99): Assets, $0 (M); grants paid, $4,055; gifts received, $25,268; expenditures, $18,456; qualifying distributions, $4,055.
Limitations: Applications not accepted.
Application information: Contributes only to pre-selected organizations.
Officer: Robert D. Telmosse Pres.
Directors: Dolly Throneberry, J.L. Tucker, Susan Tucker.
EIN: 742400981

CONNECTICUT

59329
The Bradley Home for the Aged
320 Colony St.
Meriden, CT 06451

Financial data (yr. ended 09/30/01): Assets, $42,449,057 (M); grants paid, $0; gifts received, $39,490; expenditures, $4,087,736; qualifying distributions, $2,955,340; giving activities include $4,724,483 for programs.
Officers and Directors:* Hon. John F. Papandrea,* Pres.; Patricia A. Patton,* 1st V.P.; Ann Giannetti, 2nd V.P.; Jean Wheaton,* Secy.; Paul H. Miller,* Treas.; Molly Savard, Admin.; John J. Gorman, and 14 additional directors.
EIN: 060646552

59330
Seven Bridges Foundation, Inc.
114 John St.
Greenwich, CT 06831

Established in 1997 in CT.
Donor(s): Richard C. McKenzie, The McKenzie Family Foundation.
Financial data (yr. ended 09/30/00): Assets, $37,636,561 (M); grants paid, $2,235; gifts received, $13,441,000; expenditures, $432,200; qualifying distributions, $1,385,424; giving activities include $1,402,092 for programs.
Limitations: Applications not accepted.
Application information: Contributes only to pre-selected organizations.
Officers and Directors:* Richard C. McKenzie,* Pres.; Margaret Byrne McKenzie,* Secy.-Treas.; Robert W. Byrne, Kelly Faulker Countoris, Paul M. Roy, Kathryn Smith.
EIN: 061498953

59331
Josef Albers Foundation, Inc.
88 Beacon Rd.
Bethany, CT 06524

Incorporated in 1971 in NY.
Donor(s): Josef Albers,‡ Anni Albers.‡
Financial data (yr. ended 12/31/99): Assets, $18,121,168 (M); grants paid, $779,345; gifts received, $261,400; expenditures, $2,363,611; qualifying distributions, $1,848,582; giving activities include $1,419,498 for programs.
Limitations: Applications not accepted. Giving primarily in CT.
Application information: Funds fully committed at present. Contributes only to pre-selected organizations.
Officer and Directors:* Nicholas F. Weber,* Exec. Dir.; John Eastman, Charles Kingsley.
EIN: 237104223
Codes: FD

59332
Stowe Day Foundation
(also known as Harriet Beecher Stowe Center)
77 Forest St.
Hartford, CT 06105-3243

Classified as a private operating foundation in 1986.
Financial data (yr. ended 12/31/01): Assets, $14,883,532 (M); grants paid, $0; gifts received, $109,153; expenditures, $1,321,929; qualifying distributions, $1,201,694; giving activities include $1,321,929 for programs.
Limitations: Applications not accepted.

Application information: Contributes only to pre-selected organizations.
Officers: Joan D. Hendrick, V.P.; Christine Farley, Secy.; Steve Erickson, Treas.; Katherine Kane, Exec. Dir.
Directors: Norma J. Cherry, Booker T. Devaughn, Susan B. Dunn, Gerladine Green, Carolyn L. Jennings, Linda A. Jorgensen, Paddi Leshane, Hans Miller, Kathleen Palm, Barbara Sicherman, Jane W. Wunder.
EIN: 066042822

59333
Southmayd Home, Inc.
250 Columbia Blvd.
Waterbury, CT 06710

Classified as a private operating foundation in 1989.
Donor(s): Sarah Chipman, Charles Harrub, Ida Henry, Harriet Kirk, Bertha Noble, Katherine Pomeroy.
Financial data (yr. ended 09/30/00): Assets, $13,448,594 (M); grants paid, $0; gifts received, $40,274; expenditures, $987,182; qualifying distributions, $839,206; giving activities include $839,206 for programs.
Officers and Trustees:* Mrs. Sanford Winters,* Pres.; Mrs. E. Donald Rogers,* V.P.; Patricia Emons,* Secy.; Nancy Camp,* Treas.; Dorothy Arnold, Susan Barber, Betty Belis, Jean Gentile, Patricia Levesque, Martha Padget, and 2 additional trustees.
EIN: 060646903

59334
Highstead Foundation, Inc.
c/o Richard G. Brodrick, Kelley Drye & Warren
P.O. Box 1097
Redding Center, CT 06875-1097

Established in 1985 in CT.
Donor(s): James C. Dudley,‡ Elisabeth C. Dudley.
Financial data (yr. ended 12/31/99): Assets, $8,897,877 (M); grants paid, $300; gifts received, $2,512,160; expenditures, $312,016; qualifying distributions, $243,536; giving activities include $243,536 for programs.
Limitations: Applications not accepted.
Application information: Contributes only to pre-selected organizations.
Officer and Directors:* Elisabeth C. Dudley,* Pres.; Paul R. Brenner, David C. Dudley, Henry C. Dudley, Sarah Dudley Plimpton, Jane Dudley Skinner.
EIN: 061108612

59335
The Anthony Trust Association
c/o Konowitz, Kahn, & Co., PC
110 Washington Ave.
North Haven, CT 06473
Application address: c/o The Chase Coggins Memorial Scholarship, 5471 Yale Station, New Haven, CT 06520

Established in 1941 in CT. Established as a private operating foundation in 1975.
Donor(s): Chase Coggins,‡ Robert G. Hawes Irrevocable Trust.
Financial data (yr. ended 06/30/01): Assets, $8,851,878 (M); grants paid, $4,275; gifts received, $37,252; expenditures, $260,137; qualifying distributions, $218,213; giving activities include $213,938 for programs.
Limitations: Giving limited to New Haven, CT.
Officers: James A. Lande, Pres.; Charles E. Roraback, V.P.; Katherine Lister, Secy.; Michael Davidian, Treas.
EIN: 060245162

59336
The New Haven Savings Bank Foundation, Inc.
c/o New Haven Savings Bank
195 Church St.
New Haven, CT 06510 (203) 784-5001
Contact: Paul McCraven, V.P.

Established in 1998 in CT. Classified as a company-sponsored operating foundation.
Financial data (yr. ended 03/31/01): Assets, $8,671,739 (M); grants paid, $379,880; gifts received, $2,700,000; expenditures, $426,630; qualifying distributions, $362,324.
Limitations: Giving primarily in CT.
Application information: Application form not required.
Officers and Trustees:* Cornell Scott,* Chair.; Julia McNamara,* Vice-Chair.; Kenneth P. Kaminsky,* Pres.; Paul McCraven,* V.P. and Secy.
EIN: 061506887
Codes: FD

59337
Couri Foundation, Inc.
63 Copps Hill Rd.
Ridgefield, CT 06877

Classified as a private operating foundation in 1989.
Donor(s): John A. Couri, Elaine C. Couri, Carl Reimerdes, Family Fitness Center.
Financial data (yr. ended 12/31/01): Assets, $8,018,291 (M); grants paid, $2,150; gifts received, $134,343; expenditures, $868,317; qualifying distributions, $706,860; giving activities include $426,694 for programs.
Limitations: Applications not accepted. Giving primarily in ME.
Publications: Newsletter.
Application information: Contributes only to pre-selected organizations.
Officers: John A. Couri, Pres.; Elaine C. Couri, V.P.
Directors: Alfred Carfora, Christopher J. Couri, Carl H. Reimerdes.
EIN: 010441043

59338
Topsfield Foundation, Inc.
Rte. 169
Pomfret, CT 06258
Contact: Paul J. Aicher, Co-Chair.

Established in 1982 in CT.
Donor(s): Paul J. Aicher, Paul J. Aicher Charitable Remainder Annuity Trust, Mott Foundation, Open Society, Proteus Fund.
Financial data (yr. ended 12/31/00): Assets, $7,692,747 (M); grants paid, $281,950; gifts received, $973,569; expenditures, $1,620,498; qualifying distributions, $1,577,704; giving activities include $1,610,609 for programs.
Limitations: Giving primarily in northeastern CT.
Publications: Annual report, newsletter, informational brochure.
Application information: Grantmaking is limited. Proposals are not solicited, and most grants are based on direct recommendation of board members.
Officers: Paul J. Aicher, Co-Chair.; Diana Johnson, Co-Chair.; V. Duncan Johnson, Treas.
Trustees: John Boland, Dennis Landis, Bruce L. Mallory, Jock McClellan, Suzanne W. Morse, Miles Rapaport, Selena Singletary, Susan Stroud.
EIN: 061074292
Codes: FD

59339
That's the Spirit Productions, Inc.
(also known as Clemons Productions, Inc.)
P.O. Box 7466
Greenwich, CT 06836-7466

Established around 1982.
Financial data (yr. ended 07/31/01): Assets, $5,990,894 (M); grants paid, $1,556; gifts received, $22,260; expenditures, $768,771; qualifying distributions, $411,915.
Limitations: Applications not accepted. Giving primarily in CT.
Application information: Contributes only to pre-selected organizations.
Officers and Directors:* Rev. Mark A. Connolly,* Pres.; John B. Lowe, Jr.,* Treas.; Loretta Bohinski, Cathleen Egan, John Ferguson, Jean E. Hughes, Thomas Huntington, Dorothy Riera, Mary Whalen.
EIN: 133025486

59340
Hill-Stead Museum
35 Mountain Rd.
Farmington, CT 06032

Classified as a private operating foundation in 1972.
Donor(s): Judith M. Mott, Lambert Mott, Theodate Pope Riddle, Mary T. Sargent, Joseph Sargent, Talcott Stanley, Melinda Martin Sullivan, Paul R.C. Sullivan, M.D., Arthur Ashley WMS Fund, Bissell Foundation, HTFD Foundation, Hoffman Foundation, Friends of Hillstead, Fleet Bank, N.A., Hartford Courant Foundation.
Financial data (yr. ended 06/30/00): Assets, $5,467,676 (M); grants paid, $0; gifts received, $1,454,504; expenditures, $923,621; qualifying distributions, $867,139; giving activities include $739,373 for programs.
Officers and Trustees:* Pamela Partridge West,* Pres.; Roger Klene,* V.P.; Ann Louise Price,* V.P.; James Fanelli,* Secy.-Treas.; Margaret B. Amstutz, Katharine B. Becker, and 23 additional trustees.
EIN: 060646673
Codes: TN

59341
Bacon and Hinkley Home, Inc.
(Formerly Bacon Memorial Home)
581 Pequot Ave.
New London, CT 06320-4338

Classified as a private operating foundation in 1973.
Financial data (yr. ended 09/30/00): Assets, $5,453,974 (M); grants paid, $0; gifts received, $2,316; expenditures, $356,031; qualifying distributions, $151,556; giving activities include $335,004 for programs.
Officers: Glenna M. Moalli, Pres.; Jane Bredeson, V.P.; Daniel E. Moalli, M.D., Secy.; Caroline Driscoll, Treas.
Directors: Donald Byles, Helen M. Daghlian, Elyse Detwiler, James C. McGuire, Richard E. Rowe, Robert H. Silverstein.
EIN: 060662103

59342
The Ron and Debra Harris Charitable Foundation, Inc.
340 Farms Rd.
Stamford, CT 06903

Established in 1994 in DE.
Donor(s): Ronald Harris, Debra Harris.
Financial data (yr. ended 10/31/01): Assets, $5,392,944 (M); grants paid, $279,000; expenditures, $334,158; qualifying distributions, $279,000.

59342—CONNECTICUT

Limitations: Applications not accepted. Giving primarily in RI.
Application information: Contributes only to pre-selected organizations.
Officers: Ronald Harris, Pres.; Debra Harris, V.P.
Director: Howard Presant.
EIN: 133793221
Codes: FD

59343
The Allan S. Gordon Foundation
50 N. Stanwich Rd.
Greenwich, CT 06831
Contact: Elan McAllister, Dir., Award Comm.

Established in 1997 in CT.
Donor(s): Laura Gordon.
Financial data (yr. ended 12/31/01): Assets, $4,345,915 (M); grants paid, $132,500; expenditures, $144,580; qualifying distributions, $144,580.
Application information: Contributes mostly to pre-selected organizations. Application form not required.
Directors: Allan S. Gordon, Edward S. Gordon, Timothy C. Gordon, Elan V. McAllister.
EIN: 137107377
Codes: FD2

59344
Library Association of Warehouse Point, Inc.
107 Main St.
East Windsor, CT 06088-9619

Classified as a private operating foundation in 1988.
Donor(s): Larry Tribble.
Financial data (yr. ended 06/30/00): Assets, $4,031,051 (M); grants paid, $0; gifts received, $161,610; expenditures, $350,561; qualifying distributions, $331,011; giving activities include $285,336 for programs.
Officers and Directors:* Albert Floyd, Chair.; Donna Grant,* Vice-Chair.; Cherie Watts, Secy.; Cynthia Miller, Treas.; Nancy Masters, David Pitney, Marion Webber, and 5 additional directors.
EIN: 060719521

59345
Action Wildlife Foundation, Inc.
43 Norfolk St.
Torrington, CT 06790

Established in 1994 in CT.
Donor(s): James Mazzarelli.
Financial data (yr. ended 06/30/00): Assets, $3,907,599 (M); grants paid, $0; gifts received, $537,185; expenditures, $569,967; qualifying distributions, $386,510; giving activities include $433,358 for programs.
Officers and Directors:* James Mazzarelli,* Pres.; Richard Walton, V.P.; Teresa Asklar, Secy.-Treas.
EIN: 061401697

59346
The Corinthian Foundation
155 Camps Flat Rd.
South Kent, CT 06785

Established in 1985 in CT.
Donor(s): Larry Miller, Aish Hatorah, Corinthian Media, Inc.
Financial data (yr. ended 12/31/00): Assets, $3,756,881 (M); grants paid, $221,440; gifts received, $1,001,452; expenditures, $223,151; qualifying distributions, $221,440.
Limitations: Applications not accepted. Giving primarily in CT and NY.
Application information: Contributes only to pre-selected organizations.
Trustee: Larry Miller.

EIN: 222701884
Codes: FD2

59347
Vintage Motorsport Educational Foundation, Inc.
60 Arch St.
Greenwich, CT 06830 (203) 625-0025

Established in 1993 in DE.
Donor(s): Syd Silverman.
Financial data (yr. ended 04/30/00): Assets, $3,502,633 (M); grants paid, $0; gifts received, $1,505,000; expenditures, $640,740; qualifying distributions, $633,065; giving activities include $640,740 for programs.
Officers and Directors:* Syd Silverman,* Pres.; Robert S. Critchell,* Secy.; Edmund C. Grainger,* Treas.; John E. Harden, Exec. Dir.; James Donick.
EIN: 223198273

59348
The Berkley Foundation, Inc.
165 Mason St.
Greenwich, CT 06830
Contact: William R. Berkley, Pres.

Established in 1997 in NY.
Donor(s): William R. Berkley.
Financial data (yr. ended 12/31/00): Assets, $2,678,838 (M); grants paid, $292,400; expenditures, $292,883; qualifying distributions, $291,767.
Limitations: Giving primarily in CT and NY.
Officers and Directors:* William R. Berkley,* Pres.; Jack H. Nusbaum,* Secy.; Peter W. Schmidt.
EIN: 133947554
Codes: FD

59349
The Ocean View Foundation, Inc.
171 Cat Rock Rd.
Cos Cob, CT 06807-1202

Established in 1999 in RI.
Donor(s): Josephine Merck.
Financial data (yr. ended 01/31/02): Assets, $2,632,580 (M); grants paid, $100; gifts received, $430,418; expenditures, $58,559; qualifying distributions, $100.
Limitations: Applications not accepted.
Application information: Contributes only to pre-selected organizations.
Officer: Josephine Merck, Pres.
Directors: Oona Coy, James Stevenson.
EIN: 223636378

59350
Torrington Historical Society, Inc.
192 Main St.
Torrington, CT 06790-5201

Classified as a private operating foundation in 1972.
Donor(s): Gertrude Hotchkiss.
Financial data (yr. ended 12/31/01): Assets, $2,294,402 (M); grants paid, $0; gifts received, $552,336; expenditures, $202,243; qualifying distributions, $191,556; giving activities include $188,556 for programs.
Officers: David R. Bennett, Pres.; Polly Doremus, V.P.; Lucia T. Fritz, Secy.; John Janco, Treas.; Mark McEachern, Exec. Dir.
Directors: Roberta August, Bruce Fox, Dwight Keeney, Marion Brooks Morosani, Charles W. Roraback, Gordon Todd, Tom Wall, Jr.
EIN: 060725798

59351
The Brant Foundation, Inc.
80 Field Point Rd., 3rd FL.
Greenwich, CT 06830

Established in 1996 in CT.
Donor(s): White Birch Farm, Inc., Peter M. Brant.
Financial data (yr. ended 12/31/99): Assets, $2,149,998 (M); grants paid, $0; gifts received, $127,229; expenditures, $115,067; qualifying distributions, $120,094; giving activities include $115,067 for programs.
Officers and Directors:* Peter M. Brant,* Pres.; Jean M. Bickley, Secy.-Treas.; Ryan A. Brant, Stephanie Seymour Brant.
EIN: 061470051

59352
The Johnson Home
100 Town St.
Norwich, CT 06360

Donor(s): Elsie Brown Fund.
Financial data (yr. ended 09/30/00): Assets, $2,031,577 (M); grants paid, $0; gifts received, $2,600; expenditures, $357,276; qualifying distributions, $348,756; giving activities include $350,058 for programs.
Officers and Directors:* Paul Chase,* Chair.; Edward Auger, Secy.-Treas.; Carolyn Gilbert, Charles Noyes, Richard Strouse.
EIN: 060646697

59353
George Flynn Classical Concerts, Inc.
P.O. Box 473
Clinton, CT 06413

Established in 1997 in CT.
Financial data (yr. ended 06/30/01): Assets, $1,942,539 (M); grants paid, $0; gifts received, $275; expenditures, $124,205; qualifying distributions, $0.
Officers: Ernest C. Burnham, Jr., Pres.; Jerome Silverstein, V.P.; Elaine F. Godowsky, Secy.; William R. Chaney, Treas.
Director: William David Brohn.
EIN: 061483931

59354
Wheeler School and Library of North Stonington
Main St.
P.O. Box 217
North Stonington, CT 06359-0217

Donor(s): Town of North Stonington.
Financial data (yr. ended 06/30/00): Assets, $1,777,377 (M); grants paid, $0; gifts received, $35,456; expenditures, $119,789; qualifying distributions, $86,916; giving activities include $119,789 for programs.
Officers: Thomas Eyles, Pres.; William Hiscock, V.P.; Nelda S. Nardone, Secy.; Thomas Downie, Treas.
Directors: Joyce Elias, Leda Stanley-Fiorch.
EIN: 060728869

59355
Card Home for the Aged, Inc.
154 Pleasant St.
Willimantic, CT 06226-3300

Donor(s): Charles A. Cagen Trust, Hanna T. Carol Trust.
Financial data (yr. ended 09/30/01): Assets, $1,400,789 (M); grants paid, $0; gifts received, $13,691; expenditures, $331,034; qualifying distributions, $314,419; giving activities include $201,608 for programs.

Officers: Johanne Philbrick, Pres.; Mary Lou DeVivo, V.P.; Wesley C. Johnson, V.P.; Lori-Anne Roy, Treas.; Ruth A. Toms, Admin.
Directors: David Fowler, George Fraser, Jr., Willard Stearns, Fred Surridge.
EIN: 060653041

59356
The Hascoe Foundation
c/o Hascoe Assocs., Inc.
24 Fieldpoint Rd.
Greenwich, CT 06830-5338

Established in 1984 in CT and DE.
Donor(s): Norman Hascoe.
Financial data (yr. ended 01/31/02): Assets, $1,384,033 (M); grants paid, $250,000; expenditures, $251,106; qualifying distributions, $250,000.
Officers and Directors:* Norman Hascoe,* Pres.; Suzanne Hascoe,* Secy.-Treas.; Lloyd Hascoe,* Treas.; Andrew Hascoe, Stephanie Hascoe Slotnick.
EIN: 222534970

59357
Hamilton Rare Breeds Foundation, Inc.
140 Sherman St., 4th Fl.
Fairfield, CT 06430

Financial data (yr. ended 06/30/99): Assets, $1,306,002 (M); grants paid, $0; gifts received, $1,243,838; expenditures, $241,473; qualifying distributions, $1,451,414; giving activities include $192,304 for programs.
Officers and Directors:* Deborah Hamilton,* Pres. and Treas.; Owen Hamilton,* Secy.; Penelope A. Depeyer.
EIN: 061497283

59358
Stamford Woman's Club, Inc.
P.O. Box 16793
Stamford, CT 06905
Contact: Roseanne Decamillo

Established in 1992 in CT.
Financial data (yr. ended 04/30/01): Assets, $1,240,913 (M); grants paid, $62,394; gifts received, $3,537; expenditures, $113,944; qualifying distributions, $61,183.
Limitations: Giving primarily in lower Fairfield County and Stamford, CT.
Application information: Application form required.
Officers: Margarete Georgi, Pres.; Lois Pontbriant, 1st V.P.; Lillian Filardo, 2nd V.P.; Lucille Flynn, Secy.; Dorothy Harris, Treas.
EIN: 060653184
Codes: GTI

59359
Griffis Art Center, Inc.
c/o Sharon Tripp Griffis
18 Bristol St.
New London, CT 06320-5916 (860) 447-3431

Established in 1974.
Donor(s): The Griffis Foundation, Marc Ginsberg, David Ginsberg.
Financial data (yr. ended 12/31/99): Assets, $1,235,630 (M); grants paid, $0; gifts received, $251,980; expenditures, $299,476; qualifying distributions, $255,280; giving activities include $255,280 for programs.
Officers and Trustees:* Sharon Tripp Griffis,* Pres. and Treas.; Hughes Griffis,* V.P. and Secy.; Niles Bond, Pamela Bond, Bettie Chu, Charles Chu, Timothy Foley, Jr., Rona Silver Rutchik, Patricia Shippee, Frances S. Tripp.
EIN: 061281243

59360
Colony Foundation
P.O. Box 89
New Haven, CT 06501-0089

Classified as a private operating foundation in 1973.
Financial data (yr. ended 06/30/00): Assets, $1,192,242 (M); grants paid, $0; gifts received, $131,994; expenditures, $129,783; qualifying distributions, $122,412; giving activities include $62,219 for programs.
Officers and Trustees:* Laura Baldwin, Pres.; Dick Shreiber, V.P.; Nikki S. Toole,* Secy.; Stanley Trotman,* Treas.; Kate Bazemore, Bob Blanchard, Ravi Goel, and 13 additional trustees.
EIN: 060261454

59361
Board of Management of Harrybrooke Park
P.O. Box 364
New Milford, CT 06776-0364

Financial data (yr. ended 06/30/00): Assets, $1,184,024 (M); grants paid, $0; gifts received, $66,000; expenditures, $83,530; qualifying distributions, $80,137; giving activities include $80,137 for programs.
Officers: Walter J. Conn, Chair.; Mark Wiston, Secy.-Treas.
Director: James Williams.
EIN: 237441860

59362
Institute for Research & Advancements in Public Service
2 Reynolds St.
Norwalk, CT 06855

Established around 1989.
Donor(s): Bernard Zimmern.
Financial data (yr. ended 12/31/99): Assets, $1,130,522 (M); grants paid, $0; expenditures, $390,427; qualifying distributions, $390,427; giving activities include $74,000 for programs.
Limitations: Applications not accepted.
Application information: Contributes only to pre-selected organizations.
Officers and Directors:* Bernard Zimmern,* Pres.; Marie Zimmern,* V.P.; William Lehrfeld.
EIN: 061246767

59363
Russel & Deborah Taylor Foundation
31 Indean Point Ln.
Riverside, CT 06878
Contact: Russel Taylor, Tr.

Established in 1997 in CT.
Donor(s): Russel Taylor.
Financial data (yr. ended 04/30/99): Assets, $1,117,930 (M); grants paid, $50,930; expenditures, $65,264; qualifying distributions, $1,137,539.
Limitations: Giving primarily in Fairfield County, CT and Westchester County, NY.
Application information: Application form required.
Trustees: Claire T. Kane Hall, Deborah Taylor, Russel Taylor.
EIN: 061483968

59364
Robert M. Schiffman Foundation, Inc.
6 Little Fox Ln.
Weston, CT 06883 (203) 222-9294

Established in 1989 in CT.
Donor(s): Richard Schiffman.
Financial data (yr. ended 12/31/99): Assets, $1,069,726 (M); grants paid, $52,000; expenditures, $55,699; qualifying distributions, $52,000.
Application information: Application form not required.
Officers: Ellen Schiffman, Pres.; Beatrice Schiffman, V.P.; Richard Schiffman, V.P.; Tyler Philpott, Secy.-Treas.
EIN: 061261222

59365
Fleck Family Foundation, Inc.
c/o AFA Management Partners
289 Greenwich Ave., 2nd Fl.
Greenwich, CT 06830
Contact: Kevin S. Aarons, C.F.O.

Established in 1997.
Donor(s): Aaron H. Fleck.
Financial data (yr. ended 12/31/01): Assets, $1,012,013 (M); grants paid, $163,720; expenditures, $166,750; qualifying distributions, $163,720.
Limitations: Applications not accepted.
Application information: Contributes only to pre-selected organizations.
Officers: Aaron H. Fleck, Pres. and Treas.; Barbara Fleck, V.P. and Secy.
EIN: 650729738
Codes: FD2

59366
Simsbury Free Library
P.O. Box 484
Simsbury, CT 06070

Classified as a private operating foundation in 1995.
Financial data (yr. ended 12/31/01): Assets, $999,771 (M); grants paid, $0; expenditures, $78,697; qualifying distributions, $46,410; giving activities include $46,410 for programs.
Officers and Trustees:* Mrs. Thomas J. Donohue,* Chair.; Richard D. Wagner,* Vice-Chair.; Robert H. Lindauer,* Secy.; Harvey Moger,* Treas.; Francis L. Guerry, Arthur House, Paul McAlenney, Emanuel Psarakis, Richard Schoenhardt, Mrs. Joseph W. Springman.
EIN: 060646898

59367
Paul Foundation, Inc.
c/o Justus W. Paul
1 Champlin Sq.
Essex, CT 06426

Established in 1993 in CT.
Donor(s): Geoffrey S. Paul.
Financial data (yr. ended 12/31/99): Assets, $978,612 (M); grants paid, $10,250; gifts received, $900; expenditures, $76,490; qualifying distributions, $16,903; giving activities include $5,720 for programs.
Limitations: Applications not accepted. Giving primarily in CT.
Application information: Contributes only to pre-selected organizations.
Officers and Directors:* Geoffrey S. Paul,* Pres.; Gregory M. Paul,* Secy.; Justus W. Paul,* Treas.
EIN: 061387521

59368
Grabe Family Foundation
1179 Pequot Ave.
Southport, CT 06490

Established in 1998 in CT.
Donor(s): William O. Grabe.
Financial data (yr. ended 12/31/01): Assets, $966,610 (M); grants paid, $117,075; gifts received, $49,227; expenditures, $149,527; qualifying distributions, $114,674.

59368—CONNECTICUT

Limitations: Applications not accepted.
Officers and Directors:* William O. Grabe,* Pres.; Caryn Grabe Robinson,* V.P.; Joan H. Grabe,* Secy.; Douglas Grabe, Treas.; Lisa Grabe, Laura Grabe.
EIN: 061532628
Codes: FD2

59369
The Wallingford Historical Society, Inc.
P.O. Box 73
Wallingford, CT 06492-0073

Financial data (yr. ended 09/30/00): Assets, $944,042 (M); grants paid, $0; gifts received, $14,166; expenditures, $10,776; qualifying distributions, $10,167.
Officers and Directors:* Robert N. Beaumont,* Pres.; Raymond Chappell,* 1st V.P.; Phyllis Lathrop,* 2nd V.P.; Barbara Sibley,* 3rd V.P.; Patricia A. Chappell,* Recording Secy.; Deborah Foley,* Financial Secy.; Nell Short,* Corresponding Secy.; Noma G. Beaumont,* Treas.; William E. Austin, James Leigh Barnes, Eunice Gilbert, Jean Holloway, Joyce Kowalczyk, Janet Meltabarger, and 3 additional directors.
EIN: 066035188

59370
The Lester Dequaine Foundation, Inc.
155 Brewster St.
Bridgeport, CT 06605

Established in 1994 in CT.
Donor(s): Lester Dequaine.
Financial data (yr. ended 12/31/99): Assets, $783,314 (M); grants paid, $650; gifts received, $25,897; expenditures, $105,352; qualifying distributions, $55,293; giving activities include $105,279 for programs.
Limitations: Applications not accepted.
Officers and Directors:* Lester Dequaine,* Pres.; Frank Chiarenza,* V.P.; Elsie Dequaine.
EIN: 061409314

59371
The Bartlett Tree Foundation, Inc.
P.O. Box 3067
Stamford, CT 06905-0067
Application address: P.O. Box 691, Chambersburg, PA 17201
Contact: John C. Good, Dir.

Donor(s): Robert A. Bartlett, The F.A. Bartlett Tree Expert Co.
Financial data (yr. ended 09/30/01): Assets, $685,049 (M); grants paid, $43,750; gifts received, $42,479; expenditures, $44,128; qualifying distributions, $43,750.
Limitations: Giving primarily in NY and VA.
Officers: Robert A. Bartlett, Jr., Pres.; John E. Sigonni, Secy.-Treas.
Directors: Gregory S. Daniels, John C. Good, Alan H. Jones, Frederick M. Tobin.
EIN: 222770557

59372
The Comer Family Foundation, Inc.
c/o James P. Comer
P.O. Box 207900
New Haven, CT 06520-7900

Established in 1997 in CT.
Donor(s): Heinz Family Foundation, Healthtrac Foundation.
Financial data (yr. ended 12/31/99): Assets, $566,490 (M); grants paid, $0; expenditures, $34,082; qualifying distributions, $23,972; giving activities include $20,500 for programs.
Officers and Directors:* James P. Comer,* Pres.; Dawn Comer,* Treas.; Brian Comer,* Secy.

EIN: 061469067

59373
Tai Soo Kim Architectural Fellowship Foundation, Inc.
41 Rear Concord St.
West Hartford, CT 06119 (860) 232-1719
Contact: Tai Soo Kim, Secy.-Treas. or Ryoung-Ja Kim, Dir.

Established in 1991 in CT.
Donor(s): Tai Soo Kim, Ryoung-Ja Kim.
Financial data (yr. ended 12/31/99): Assets, $547,553 (M); grants paid, $17,525; gifts received, $20,919; expenditures, $19,531; qualifying distributions, $19,531.
Limitations: Giving primarily to residents of South Korea.
Application information: Application form required.
Officers: Ryszard Szczypek, Pres.; Tai Soo Kim, Secy.-Treas.
Directors: T. Whitcomb Iglehart, Jung-Gon Kim, Ryoung-Ja Kim.
EIN: 223136019

59374
Godfrey Memorial Library
134 Newfield St.
Middletown, CT 06457-2526

Classified as a private operating foundation in 1973.
Financial data (yr. ended 12/31/01): Assets, $517,124 (M); grants paid, $0; gifts received, $15,110; expenditures, $137,514; qualifying distributions, $0.
Officers and Directors:* Anthony Marino, Chair.; Linda Banwarth, Vice-Chair.; Diane Rousseau,* Secy.; Joseph Lombardo, Treas.; Nancy J. Doane, and 8 additional directors.
EIN: 060655485

59375
Citizens Television, Inc.
873 State St.
New Haven, CT 06511

Financial data (yr. ended 03/31/00): Assets, $483,277 (M); grants paid, $0; gifts received, $455,848; expenditures, $485,048; qualifying distributions, $519,201; giving activities include $519,201 for programs.
Officers and Directors:* Robert Lampkin,* Pres.; Marc Palmieri,* V.P.; Lisa Monroe,* Secy.; Norman Forrester,* Treas.; James V. Martino, Exec. Dir.; Gary Felsted, Renay Ghant, Frank Logue, Sylvia Terk, Peter Vilano, Cheryl Volk.
EIN: 223148596
Codes: TN

59376
Guilford Smith Memorial Library Association, Inc.
17 Main St.
P.O. Box 81
South Windham, CT 06266

Financial data (yr. ended 12/31/01): Assets, $468,714 (M); grants paid, $0; gifts received, $11,800; expenditures, $63,979; qualifying distributions, $56,864; giving activities include $55,178 for programs.
Limitations: Applications not accepted.
Application information: Contributes only to pre-selected organizations.
Officers: Alta M. Berry, Pres.; Ted M. Colwell, V.P.; Dorothy Walworth, Secy.; Helen T. Card, Treas.
Trustees: Ruth Ann Archambault, Karen Calef, Ita Kanter, Sally Klitz, Betty Lowell.
EIN: 060776274

59377
Chuza Foundation
317 Hollow Tree Ridge Rd.
Darien, CT 06820

Established in 1997 in CT.
Donor(s): David M. Mace.
Financial data (yr. ended 12/31/00): Assets, $456,898 (M); grants paid, $75,860; expenditures, $77,333; qualifying distributions, $75,792.
Limitations: Applications not accepted.
Application information: Contributes only to pre-selected organizations.
Trustees: David M. Mace, Rosemary H. Mace.
EIN: 061517579
Codes: FD2

59378
The Lipton Foundation, Inc.
113 Roseville Rd.
Westport, CT 06880
Contact: Barbara Agar, Pres.

Classified as an operating foundation in 1976.
Financial data (yr. ended 12/31/01): Assets, $440,152 (M); grants paid, $18,373; expenditures, $19,431; qualifying distributions, $18,591.
Limitations: Giving primarily in CT and NY.
Officer: Barbara Agar, Pres.
EIN: 136143274

59379
The Glen R. Dash Charitable Foundation
P.O. Box 729
Woodstock, CT 06281

Established in 1997 in MA.
Donor(s): Glen R. Dash.
Financial data (yr. ended 12/31/01): Assets, $436,582 (M); grants paid, $0; expenditures, $33,719; qualifying distributions, $16,423; giving activities include $15,699 for programs.
Limitations: Applications not accepted.
Application information: Contributes only to pre-selected organizations.
Trustee: Glen R. Dash.
EIN: 043361601

59380
Mary L. Jobe Akeley Trust & Peace Sanctuary
c/o Denison Pequotsepos Nature Ctr.
P.O. Box 122
Mystic, CT 06355

Established in 1981.
Financial data (yr. ended 12/31/01): Assets, $432,268 (M); grants paid, $10,000; expenditures, $12,203; qualifying distributions, $11,292.
Limitations: Applications not accepted.
Application information: Contributes only to pre-selected organizations.
Trustees: Timothy D. Bates, Belton A. Copp, Eunice Sutphen.
EIN: 066089224

59381
Cobble Hill Farm Foundation, Inc.
40 Cobble Hill Rd.
West Cornwall, CT 06796

Established in 1997 in CT.
Financial data (yr. ended 03/31/00): Assets, $383,418 (M); grants paid, $0; gifts received, $250,089; expenditures, $230,323; qualifying distributions, $213,510; giving activities include $181,370 for programs.
Limitations: Applications not accepted.
Application information: Contributes only to pre-selected organizations.
Directors: Bruce Barron, Barbara Margolis, Brian Margolis, David I. Margolis, Robert Margolis.

EIN: 061486409

59382
J. J. Cooley Foundation, Inc.
c/o Chapel Investments
41 High St.
New Haven, CT 06511-4903

Financial data (yr. ended 03/31/02): Assets, $347,828 (M); grants paid, $17,000; expenditures, $21,293; qualifying distributions, $21,041.
Limitations: Applications not accepted. Giving primarily in New Haven, CT.
Application information: Contributes only to pre-selected organizations.
Trustee: Barbara C. Wareck.
EIN: 066049571

59383
Amity Art Foundation, Inc.
1 Bradley Rd., Ste. 202
Woodbridge, CT 06525 (203) 387-8380
Contact: John A. Stewart, Pres.

Classified as a private operating foundation in 2001 in CT.
Donor(s): John A. Stewart.
Financial data (yr. ended 12/31/01): Assets, $285,765 (M); grants paid, $0; gifts received, $285,928; expenditures, $1,557; qualifying distributions, $1,557.
Officers: John A. Stewart, Pres. and Treas.; Jennifer Moore, Secy.
EIN: 061591446

59384
The Nochera Family Foundation
201 N. Cove Rd.
Old Saybrook, CT 06475-2568
(860) 440-0224
Contact: Joseph Nochera, Tr.

Established in 1999 in CT.
Donor(s): Joseph Nochera, Virginia Nochera.
Financial data (yr. ended 12/31/00): Assets, $253,668 (M); grants paid, $16,000; expenditures, $16,000; qualifying distributions, $15,752.
Limitations: Giving primarily in CT, Washington, DC, and VA.
Trustees: Joseph Nochera, Virginia Nochera.
EIN: 066489312

59385
The Weiner Nusim Foundation, Inc.
c/o Roberta Jablonsky
155 Staples Rd.
Easton, CT 06612

Established in 1997 in CT.
Donor(s): Roberta Nusim Jablonsky.
Financial data (yr. ended 04/30/00): Assets, $232,320 (M); grants paid, $500; gifts received, $12,500; expenditures, $15,095; qualifying distributions, $15,009; giving activities include $12,734 for programs.
Limitations: Applications not accepted.
Application information: Contributes only to pre-selected organizations.
Officer: Roberta Nusim, Pres.
EIN: 061502654

59386
The Sturka Foundation
21 Knollwood Dr.
Greenwich, CT 06830

Established in 1996 in CT.
Donor(s): Dirk A. Stuurop, Donna Stuurop.
Financial data (yr. ended 12/31/00): Assets, $225,399 (M); grants paid, $122,100; gifts received, $51,738; expenditures, $124,266; qualifying distributions, $120,928.
Officer: Dirk A. Stuurop, Pres.
Directors: Frank Gilbride II, Donna Stuurop.
EIN: 061459567
Codes: FD2

59387
Rights, Education, Adoption & Protection for Animal Welfare
c/o Mark Sklarz, Cummings & Lockwood
P.O. Box 1960
New Haven, CT 06509-0651

Established in 1998 in CT.
Donor(s): Barbara A. Gingold.
Financial data (yr. ended 12/31/01): Assets, $220,703 (M); grants paid, $10,700; expenditures, $15,320; qualifying distributions, $10,687.
Limitations: Applications not accepted. Giving primarily in CT.
Application information: Contributes only to pre-selected organizations.
Officers and Directors:* Barbara A. Gingold,* Pres.; Mark G. Sklarz,* Secy.; Richard B. Buckley,* Treas.
EIN: 061498082

59388
The Real Estate Educational Foundation, Inc.
West Bldg., Lower level
127 Washington Ave.
North Haven, CT 06473-1715 (203) 234-7700

Donor(s): Real Estate, Inc.
Financial data (yr. ended 12/31/00): Assets, $217,723 (M); grants paid, $40,139; expenditures, $44,380; qualifying distributions, $41,016.
Limitations: Giving limited to residents of the New Haven, CT, area.
Officers: Henry S. Harrison, Pres.; Gregory J. Mulherin, 1st V.P.; Stephen Press, 2nd V.P.; Andrew Carbutti, Jr., Secy.; Joseph Waple, Treas.
Directors: Corinne Ambrose, William Bowles, Carl G. Russell, Teresa Sirico, Louise Zemina.
EIN: 061062962

59389
Shepherds Rest Ministries, Inc.
c/o G.M. Gabler
14 Musket Ridge Rd.
New Fairfield, CT 06812-5101

Financial data (yr. ended 12/31/00): Assets, $182,462 (M); grants paid, $0; gifts received, $83,161; expenditures, $66,099; qualifying distributions, $78,464; giving activities include $59,999 for programs.
Officers and Directors:* Harold Bryer,* C.E.O.; George M. Gabler,* Secy.; Thomas Wilson,* Treas.; Robert Hedlund, Medford McCoy, M.D., Tom Schulte, William Wilcox.
EIN: 621717371

59390
The Watkins Family Foundation
30 Crooked Mile Rd.
Darien, CT 06820

Established in 1995.
Donor(s): Ronald R. Watkins, Margaret M. Watkins.
Financial data (yr. ended 11/30/00): Assets, $178,668 (M); grants paid, $10,100; gifts received, $47,000; expenditures, $11,978; qualifying distributions, $11,878.
Limitations: Applications not accepted.
Application information: Contributes only to pre-selected organizations.
Trustees: Margaret M. Watkins, Ronald R. Watkins.
EIN: 061415279

59391
East Windsor Historical Society, Inc.
P.O. Box 363
East Windsor Hill, CT 06028

Established in 1996 in CT.
Financial data (yr. ended 12/31/00): Assets, $177,452 (M); grants paid, $0; gifts received, $32,027; expenditures, $9,866; qualifying distributions, $0; giving activities include $4,354 for programs.
Officers: Arend Jan Knuhel, Pres.; Barbara A. Mazurek, V.P.; Flicka Thrall, Secy.; Jean Lamezo, Treas.
EIN: 237077373

59392
Apostolate of the Mass, Inc.
467 Bloomfield Ave.
Bloomfield, CT 06002

Classified as a private operating foundation in 1992.
Donor(s): Rev. Anthony C. Ventura.
Financial data (yr. ended 12/31/01): Assets, $174,826 (M); grants paid, $500; gifts received, $13,551; expenditures, $21,390; qualifying distributions, $456.
Limitations: Applications not accepted.
Application information: Contributes only to pre-selected organizations.
Officers and Directors:* John Crowley,* Pres.; James Sansone,* V.P. and Treas.; Suzanna Crowley,* V.P.; Joseph P. Marenna,* Secy.; Rev. Anthony C. Ventura.
EIN: 061264858

59393
Automotive Museum, Inc.
c/o Donald E. Carlson
240 High Rd.
Berlin, CT 06037-9991

Financial data (yr. ended 03/31/02): Assets, $172,626 (M); grants paid, $0; gifts received, $3,500; expenditures, $3,387; qualifying distributions, $0.
Officer: Donald E. Carlson, Pres.
Directors: Gordon S. Alling, Charles J. Fisher, Walter A. Jaeger.
EIN: 066077938

59394
Brookfield/Burke Foundation, Inc.
22 Windrose Way, Mead Pt.
Greenwich, CT 06830

Established in 1997 in CT.
Donor(s): Nancy B. Burke.
Financial data (yr. ended 12/31/00): Assets, $163,957 (M); grants paid, $8,856; expenditures, $9,506; qualifying distributions, $8,856.
Limitations: Applications not accepted. Giving primarily in CT.
Application information: Contributes only to pre-selected organizations.
Officers: Nancy B. Burke, Pres.; Duncan G. Burke, V.P.; Samuel D.B. Millar, Jr., Secy.
EIN: 061484617

59395
Creative Connections, Inc.
412 Main St., Ste. D
Ridgefield, CT 06877

Established in 1992 in CT.
Donor(s): Alan R. Steckler, Lois R. Steckler Charitable Lead Trust.

59395—CONNECTICUT

Financial data (yr. ended 06/30/00): Assets, $156,357 (M); grants paid, $0; gifts received, $115,560; expenditures, $124,079; qualifying distributions, $124,079; giving activities include $37,852 for programs.
Officers and Directors:* Alan R. Steckler,* Pres.; Deborah S. Steckler,* Secy.; Robert J. Creamer, Walter F. Gips, Jr.,* Barry Miller.
EIN: 133697184

59396
Connecticut Waterfowl Trust
c/o J. Kemler Appell
2 Deer Run Rd.
Farmington, CT 06032

Established in 1998 in CT.
Donor(s): J. Kemler Appell.
Financial data (yr. ended 12/31/99): Assets, $145,093 (M); grants paid, $0; gifts received, $91,120; expenditures, $49,032; qualifying distributions, $77,669; giving activities include $77,669 for programs.
Trustees: J. Kemler Appell, Julia Appell, Michael Bean.
EIN: 066458694

59397
The Ridgefield Scholarship Group, Inc.
P.O. Box 823
Ridgefield, CT 06877
Application address: 118 Ramapoo Rd., Ridgefield, CT 06877
Contact: Linda Maggs, Treas.

Donor(s): Lewis Fund, Demrick Fund, E. Esser, Roche, Inc., F.F. Randolf, Manno Fund.
Financial data (yr. ended 12/31/01): Assets, $144,095 (M); grants paid, $23,700; gifts received, $32,977; expenditures, $28,509; qualifying distributions, $23,730.
Limitations: Giving limited to residents of Ridgefield, CT.
Application information: Application form required.
Officers: Jocelyn G. Fainer, Pres.; Harold E. Healy, V.P.; Margorie Campbell, Secy.; Linda Maggs, Treas.
EIN: 061010124
Codes: GTI

59398
Plainville Police Association, Inc.
P.O. Box 375
Plainville, CT 06062

Established in 1997 in CT.
Financial data (yr. ended 12/31/00): Assets, $143,589 (M); grants paid, $14,823; expenditures, $25,723; qualifying distributions, $14,742.
Limitations: Giving primarily in Plainville, CT.
Officers: Charles A. Smedick, Pres.; William F. Buden, V.P.; Jane Dickman Buden, Secy.-Treas.
Directors: Patrick J. Buden, Gabriele Paciotti.
EIN: 061139532

59399
Steven & Sharon Chrust Foundation, Inc.
107 Saddle Rock Rd.
Stamford, CT 06902

Established in 1998 in NY.
Financial data (yr. ended 12/31/99): Assets, $139,439 (M); grants paid, $12,480; gifts received, $124,371; expenditures, $12,480; qualifying distributions, $12,433.
Limitations: Applications not accepted.
Application information: Contributes only to pre-selected organizations.

Officers and Directors:* Steven G. Chrust,* Pres.; Sharon Chrust, V.P.; Florence Slimowitz, Secy.-Treas.
EIN: 223596127

59400
David and Kimberly Blank Charitable Trust
c/o David Blank
124 Brookside Dr.
Greenwich, CT 06831

Established in 2000 in CT.
Donor(s): David M. Blank.
Financial data (yr. ended 12/31/01): Assets, $137,252 (M); grants paid, $67,000; gifts received, $50,000; expenditures, $67,025; qualifying distributions, $67,000.
Limitations: Applications not accepted.
Application information: Contributes only to pre-selected organizations.
Trustee: David M. Blank.
EIN: 066504745

59401
The Kurt Forrest Foundation
c/o Thomas Cardello
22 Dellwood Ln.
Greenwich, CT 06830

Established in 1999 in CT.
Donor(s): Thomas Cardello, Renate Cardello.
Financial data (yr. ended 05/31/01): Assets, $130,144 (M); grants paid, $6,000; gifts received, $50; expenditures, $6,010; qualifying distributions, $6,000.
Officers and Directors:* Renate Kurowski-Cardello,* Pres. and Treas.; Thomas Cardello,* Secy.; Henry J. Cardello.
EIN: 061549428

59402
Brame Foundation, Inc.
201 Dolphin Rd.
Bristol, CT 06010-8000

Classified as a private operating foundation.
Established in 1995 in CT.
Donor(s): Whitman Controls Corp.
Financial data (yr. ended 12/31/01): Assets, $124,882 (M); grants paid, $10,000; expenditures, $10,375; qualifying distributions, $10,000.
Limitations: Applications not accepted.
Application information: Contributes only to pre-selected organizations.
Officers: J. Yancey Brame, Pres.; Jean E. Liskow, Secy.
EIN: 061433102

59403
Sarah G. Austin Foundation, Inc.
30 S. Beach Dr.
Rowayton, CT 06853

Established in 1995 in CT.
Donor(s): David Austin.
Financial data (yr. ended 06/30/00): Assets, $123,577 (M); grants paid, $0; gifts received, $6,623; expenditures, $48,541; qualifying distributions, $45,473; giving activities include $13,210 for programs.
Officers and Directors:* David E. Austin,* Pres.; Donald Monro Austin,* Secy.; Laura Austin Allyn, Eugene R. Gaddis.
EIN: 061442201

59404
The Joyce & Bernie Zimmerman Foundation
18 High Meadow Rd.
Weston, CT 06883

Established in 2000 in CT.
Donor(s): Bernard Zimmerman.

Financial data (yr. ended 09/30/01): Assets, $104,169 (M); grants paid, $3,341; gifts received, $98,500; expenditures, $6,256; qualifying distributions, $3,341.
Limitations: Applications not accepted. Giving primarily in CT and NY.
Application information: Contributes only to pre-selected organizations.
Officers: Joyce Zimmerman, Pres.; Bernard Zimmerman, V.P.
EIN: 061599625

59405
Ohiyesa Corporation
P.O. Box 11
Norwich, CT 06360-0011
Contact: Dean J. Seibert, Dir.

Donor(s): Mary Elizabeth Pearce.
Financial data (yr. ended 12/31/00): Assets, $102,932 (M); grants paid, $12,634; gifts received, $81,725; expenditures, $63,468; qualifying distributions, $61,536.
Directors: Lori Arviso Alvard, Carolyn Kehler, John H. Lyons, Dean J. Seibert.
EIN: 311586691

59406
The Bayer Institute for Health Care Communication
(Formerly The Miles Institute for Health Care Communication)
400 Morgan Ln.
West Haven, CT 06516 (800) 800-5907
FAX: (203) 812-5951; E-mail: bayer.institute@bayer.com; URL: http://www.bayerinstitute.org
Contact: Maysel Kemp White, M.D.

Established in 1993 in CT as a company-sponsored operating foundation.
Donor(s): Bayer Corp.
Financial data (yr. ended 12/31/99): Assets, $100,327 (M); grants paid, $86,890; gifts received, $145,000; expenditures, $679,905; qualifying distributions, $86,890.
Limitations: Giving on a national basis.
Publications: Informational brochure (including application guidelines), newsletter.
Application information: Application form required.
Officers and Directors:* Carl Calcagni, R.Ph.,* Chair., C.E.O., and V.P.; Richard K. Goodstein, M.D., Vice-Chair. and V.P.; Michael E. Herbert, Exec. V.P.; Donald A. Hodd,* V.P. and Secy.-Treas.; Joel Abelson, V.P.; John M. Amatruda, M.D., V.P.; J. Gregory Carroll, Ph.D.,* Exec. Dir.; Gerald B. Rosenberg, M.D., Mgr.; Thomas L. Campbell, M.D., Evan G. Pattishall, M.D., Ph.D., Carol Valois, M.D.
EIN: 223208010
Codes: FD2, CD, GTI

59407
The Magnaverde Foundation, Inc.
164 Mason St.
Greenwich, CT 06830-5531

Established in 1996 in CT.
Donor(s): Mary Anselmo.
Financial data (yr. ended 12/31/01): Assets, $75,305 (M); grants paid, $89,295; gifts received, $100,000; expenditures, $89,305; qualifying distributions, $89,295.
Officers: Karen Bedrosian Richardson, Pres.; Ursela Krackow Dunn, Treas.
Directors: Mary Anselmo, Reverge Anselmo, Berta Escurra.
EIN: 061442891

59408
Housatonic Charitable Trust
c/o Karl E. Schlachter
654-B Osage Ln.
Stratford, CT 06614-8345

Established in 1996.
Donor(s): Karl Schlachter.
Financial data (yr. ended 12/31/01): Assets, $71,876 (M); grants paid, $3,830; gifts received, $25,313; expenditures, $4,090; qualifying distributions, $3,830.
Limitations: Giving on a national basis.
Application information: Application form not required.
Trustees: Heidi Derlin, Karl E. Schlachter.
EIN: 061442597

59409
Loaves & Fishes Hospitality House, Inc.
40 Main St.
New Milford, CT 06776

Classified as a private operating foundation in 1991.
Financial data (yr. ended 12/31/99): Assets, $52,223 (M); grants paid, $0; gifts received, $19,823; expenditures, $16,349; qualifying distributions, $15,853; giving activities include $10,841 for programs.
Limitations: Applications not accepted.
Application information: Contributes only to pre-selected organizations.
Officers: John Roger, Pres.; Biddy Roger, V.P.
Director: Sherrie McAuliffe-Pilch.
EIN: 222544673

59410
Imagineering Foundation, Inc.
6 West St.
Newtown, CT 06470

Classified as a private operating foundation in 1986.
Donor(s): Harvey Hubbell IV.
Financial data (yr. ended 04/30/01): Assets, $44,130 (M); grants paid, $1,000; gifts received, $17,000; expenditures, $21,590; qualifying distributions, $21,590.
Limitations: Applications not accepted. Giving primarily in Windsor Locks, CT.
Application information: Contributes only to pre-selected organizations.
Officers: Harvey Hubbell IV, Pres.; Harvey Hubbell V, V.P.
Director: Anne Hubbell.
EIN: 061146475

59411
Guilford Community Television, Inc.
P.O. Box 275
Guilford, CT 06437

Established in 1992 in CT.
Financial data (yr. ended 06/30/00): Assets, $42,195 (M); grants paid, $0; gifts received, $29,535; expenditures, $39,792; qualifying distributions, $28,977; giving activities include $14,098 for programs.
Officers and Directors:* John Otto,* Pres.; Michael Graziano,* V.P.; Paul Thomas,* Secy.; Arthur Donkin,* Treas.; Joan Fowler, Donald Hurteau, James O'Keefe, Jeffrey Lincoln, Robert Vander Weide.
EIN: 061349846

59412
Mansfield Cooperative, Inc.
1 Silo Cir.
Storrs Mansfield, CT 06268

Classified as a private operating foundation in 1992.
Financial data (yr. ended 06/30/00): Assets, $41,660 (M); grants paid, $0; expenditures, $2,999; qualifying distributions, $0; giving activities include $15,660 for programs.
Limitations: Giving primarily in CT.
Officers: Betsy Reid, Pres.; George Ecker, V.P. and Treas.; John Rice, Secy.
Directors: Eva Eaton, Arthur Higgins, Charlotte Kennedy, Clinton Noble, Robert Peters, Ken Ulmer.
EIN: 061050335

59413
Thomas W. Williams 2nd Fund Trust
75 Messier Rd.
North Grosvenordale, CT 06255-2013
(860) 923-9052
Contact: Ida Ransom, Treas.

Established around 1993.
Financial data (yr. ended 10/31/01): Assets, $41,548 (M); grants paid, $2,561; expenditures, $2,700; qualifying distributions, $2,700.
Limitations: Giving limited to residents of the Groton and New London, CT, area.
Officer and Trustees:* Ida Ransom,* Treas.; Nancy Moffat.
EIN: 066368216

59414
The Stone Keenan Foundation
15 Lynch Brook Ln.
Ridgefield, CT 06877
Contact: Marilyn Stone Keenan, Pres.

Established in 1996 in CT.
Donor(s): Marilyn Stone Keenan.
Financial data (yr. ended 12/31/01): Assets, $40,657 (M); grants paid, $9,925; gifts received, $51,155; expenditures, $11,080; qualifying distributions, $9,925.
Limitations: Giving primarily in CT.
Officer: Marilyn Stone Keenan, Pres.
EIN: 061605162

59415
Blind Peoples Association of Connecticut, Inc.
c/o David Bates
44 Garden St.
Wethersfield, CT 06109

Financial data (yr. ended 12/31/99): Assets, $35,660 (M); grants paid, $2,400; gifts received, $5,000; expenditures, $6,290; qualifying distributions, $6,290; giving activities include $3,004 for programs.
Officers: Shirley Phelon, Pres.; Marie Beaulier, V.P.; Kathryn Hudson, Secy.; David Bates, Treas.
EIN: 066049860

59416
Fourth World Foundation, Inc.
138 Merrimac Dr.
Trumbull, CT 06611
Contact: Anne C. Seggerman, Pres.

Classified as a private operating foundation in 1979.
Donor(s): Harry G.A. Seggerman, Anne C. Seggerman.
Financial data (yr. ended 12/31/00): Assets, $33,158 (M); grants paid, $46,741; gifts received, $268,694; expenditures, $267,139; qualifying distributions, $258,801; giving activities include $258,809 for programs.
Limitations: Giving primarily in CT.
Officer: Anne C. Seggerman, Pres.
Directors: Virginia Fitzgerald, Francesca Braggloti Lodge, David Smith.
EIN: 060991636

59417
Leslie Jayne Meoni Trust
c/o Webster Trust Co., N.A.
P.O. Box 951
Meriden, CT 06450-0951
Application address: 26 Hillsboro Dr., West Hartford, CT 06107, tel.: (860) 561-2782
Contact: Alyce F. Hild

Classified as a private operating foundation in 1978.
Financial data (yr. ended 11/30/01): Assets, $31,697 (M); grants paid, $0; expenditures, $233; qualifying distributions, $0.
Trustees: Geraldine Meoni, Lucy Meoni, Rev. Allan H. O'Neil, Franklin Suzio, Webster Trust Co., N.A.
EIN: 060972510

59418
Maria Claudia Fabregas Foundation
c/o Joy Whitman
75 Wendy Rd.
Trumbull, CT 06611 (203) 374-4985

Established in 1996 in CT.
Donor(s): Louis Fabregas.
Financial data (yr. ended 12/31/00): Assets, $30,718 (M); grants paid, $2,500; expenditures, $2,725; qualifying distributions, $2,500.
Directors: Adriana Fabregas, Joy Whitman.
EIN: 061497303

59419
Jeffrey G. Casner Memorial Fund
c/o Gloria C. Casner
321 Robbins Rd.
Kensington, CT 06037

Established in 1991 in CT.
Financial data (yr. ended 12/31/00): Assets, $30,568 (M); grants paid, $6,000; expenditures, $6,360; qualifying distributions, $6,340.
Limitations: Applications not accepted. Giving primarily in Berlin, CT.
Application information: Contributes only to pre-selected organizations.
Trustees: Gloria C. Casner, Kathryn J. Casner, William R. Casner.
EIN: 061130011

59420
Broda O. Barnes, M.D., Research Foundation, Inc.
31 Prospect Ave.
Trumbull, CT 06611

Classified as a private operating foundation in 1990.
Financial data (yr. ended 12/31/01): Assets, $28,405 (M); grants paid, $0; gifts received, $51,626; expenditures, $101,568; qualifying distributions, $68,373; giving activities include $1,887 for programs.
Officers: Patricia A. Puglio, Pres.; Cindy M. Puglio, Secy.-Treas.
Directors: William Harding, Dorothea Linley, M.D.
EIN: 222587696

59421
Connecticut Physician Assistant Foundation, Inc.
c/o Keith Ritchie
8 Old Orchard Ln.
New Milford, CT 06776
Application address: 274 Church St., No. 5B, Guilford, CT 06437, tel.: (203) 789-4347
Contact: Cynthia Booth Lord, Pres.

Financial data (yr. ended 12/31/99): Assets, $27,870 (M); grants paid, $3,600; gifts received, $4,966; expenditures, $5,723; qualifying distributions, $5,698.
Limitations: Giving limited to residents of CT.
Application information: Application form required.
Officers: Cynthia Booth Lord, Pres.; Christiane Nockels, V.P.; John McNab, Secy.; Keith Ritchie, Treas.
Trustees: Joan M. Biskup, George Samuel Bottomley, Bruce Evans Bowman, Peggy DeGeus Elefteriades, Bruce Hansen, Frank M. Mackey, Nancy Najarian, Joseph Varano.
EIN: 223129015

59422
Thomas & Dorothy Lackman Charitable Foundation
14 Cushman Rd.
Ashford, CT 06278-1505

Established in 2000 in CT.
Donor(s): Thomas Lackman, Dorothy Lackman.
Financial data (yr. ended 12/31/00): Assets, $25,026 (M); grants paid, $9,420; gifts received, $29,684; expenditures, $9,420; qualifying distributions, $9,420.
Limitations: Applications not accepted. Giving primarily in CT.
Application information: Contributes only to pre-selected organizations.
Trustees: Dorothy Lackman, Thomas Lackman.
EIN: 061565397

59423
Paul Jepsen Scholarship Foundation
c/o Edward G. Jepsen
14 Gale Rd.
Bloomfield, CT 06002-1508

Established in 2001 in CT.
Donor(s): Edward Jepsen.
Financial data (yr. ended 12/31/01): Assets, $20,000 (M); grants paid, $0; gifts received, $25,472; expenditures, $5,472; qualifying distributions, $0.
Limitations: Applications not accepted.
Application information: Contributes only to pre-selected organizations.
Trustees: Holly Hoberman, Edward Jepsen, Jackie McKellan.
EIN: 061625705

59424
Potes & Poets Press, Inc.
181 Edgemont Ave.
West Hartford, CT 06110-1005

Established in 1988 in CT.
Financial data (yr. ended 12/31/00): Assets, $19,315 (M); grants paid, $0; expenditures, $6,174; qualifying distributions, $0.
Officer: Peter Ganick, Pres.
EIN: 041084669

59425
Norman Cousins Memorial Fund, Inc.
246 Post Rd. E.
Westport, CT 06880
Application address: 1910 Montana Ave., Santa Monica, CA 90403-1912, tel.: (310) 453-4255
Contact: Eleanor Cousins, Pres.

Classified as a private operating foundation in 1991.
Donor(s): Paul Newman.
Financial data (yr. ended 11/30/00): Assets, $19,266 (M); grants paid, $0; expenditures, $7; qualifying distributions, $0.
Officers and Directors:* Eleanor Cousins,* Pres.; Sherman Mellinkoff,* V.P.; Candis Cousins, Treas.; Leo Nevas.
EIN: 061310610

59426
The Ten Ten Foundation, Inc.
c/o Jennifer D. Port
170 Mason St.
Greenwich, CT 06830

Financial data (yr. ended 12/31/01): Assets, $19,044 (M); grants paid, $23,283; expenditures, $33,458; qualifying distributions, $32,433.
Limitations: Applications not accepted.
Application information: Contributes only to pre-selected organizations.
Officers: Judith S. Novak, Pres.; Jennifer D. Port, Secy.; Loraine Marquis, Treas.
EIN: 133897205

59427
Seth Gaynes Memorial Scholarship Fund
107 Davis Hill Rd.
Weston, CT 06883 (203) 226-5394

Established in 1989 in CT.
Financial data (yr. ended 12/31/00): Assets, $16,469 (M); grants paid, $500; gifts received, $350; expenditures, $500; qualifying distributions, $500.
Limitations: Applications not accepted. Giving limited to Weston, CT.
Trustees: Philip M. Gaynes, Suzan Gaynes.
EIN: 222970193

59428
Pat Blanco Scholarship
155 Burke St.
East Hartford, CT 06118-3409 (860) 568-7153
Contact: Meredith A. Barker, Dir.

Financial data (yr. ended 06/30/01): Assets, $16,140 (M); grants paid, $1,000; gifts received, $1,354; expenditures, $1,000; qualifying distributions, $1,000.
Limitations: Giving limited to residents of East Hartford, CT.
Application information: Application form required.
Directors: Meredith A. Barker, Charlene Ryan Fitzgerald, Rose Germano, Molly Macfarlane, Vaughn Sargisian, Jan Tirinzonie.
EIN: 222761122

59429
Lawrence & Natalie D. Portell Foundation
19 Orchard Rest Rd.
Sherman, CT 06784

Established in 1998 in CT.
Donor(s): Natalie D. Portell.
Financial data (yr. ended 09/30/01): Assets, $15,900 (M); grants paid, $5,000; gifts received, $5,590; expenditures, $5,589; qualifying distributions, $2,993.
Limitations: Applications not accepted.
Application information: Contributes only to pre-selected organizations.
Officer: Natalie D. Portell, Pres.
Directors: Paul B. Altermatt, Robert J. McDermott.
EIN: 061508183

59430
Southport Area Fund
P.O. Box 436
Southport, CT 06490
Contact: Harvey L. Gray, Pres.

Classified as a private operating foundation in 1985.
Financial data (yr. ended 05/31/01): Assets, $15,501 (M); grants paid, $55,000; gifts received, $70,076; expenditures, $56,570; qualifying distributions, $56,412.
Limitations: Applications not accepted. Giving primarily in Southport, CT.
Application information: Unsolicited requests for funds not accepted.
Officers and Directors:* Harvey L. Gray,* Pres.; Benjamin M. Baker III, V.P.; G. Whitney Biggs,* Secy.; Derby F. Anderson, Virginia K. Cargill, Charles B. Curtis, R. Bradford Evans, Julia W. Linsley, Archie F. MacAllaster, H. Barclay Morley, Hoyt O. Perry, Jr.
EIN: 222599664

59431
Echo Foundation, Inc.
P.O. Box 1098
Orange, CT 06477 (203) 795-5494
Contact: Deidre Topazian, Secy.

Donor(s): David S. Topazian.
Financial data (yr. ended 12/31/99): Assets, $11,831 (M); grants paid, $25,263; gifts received, $32,525; expenditures, $31,895; qualifying distributions, $31,645; giving activities include $6,632 for programs.
Application information: Application form not required.
Officers and Trustees:* Deidre Topazian,* Secy.; David S. Topazian,* Treas.
EIN: 066107764

59432
Alexander Julian Foundation for Aesthetic Understanding/Appreciation, Inc.
63 Copps Hill Rd.
Ridgefield, CT 06877

Established in 1984 in NY.
Donor(s): Alexander Julian.
Financial data (yr. ended 11/30/00): Assets, $11,220 (M); grants paid, $5,000; gifts received, $6,500; expenditures, $6,183; qualifying distributions, $5,351.
Limitations: Applications not accepted. Giving on a national basis.
Publications: Occasional report, informational brochure.
Application information: Contributes only to pre-selected organizations.
Officer and Trustee:* Alexander Julian,* Pres.
EIN: 133249236

59433
Douglas M. Romatzick Memorial Scholarship Trust Fund
331 Housatonic Dr.
Milford, CT 06460-4941
Application address: 32 Goodchild St., Milford, CT 06460, tel.: (203) 874-5297
Contact: David Romatzick, Jr., Tr.

Financial data (yr. ended 12/31/00): Assets, $10,635 (M); grants paid, $600; gifts received,

$27; expenditures, $627; qualifying distributions, $627.
Limitations: Giving primarily in Milford, CT.
Application information: Application form not required.
Trustees: Christine Romatzick, David Romatzick, Jr.
EIN: 061011995

59434
The J.L. Foundation, Inc.
Hemlock Ridge Farm
P.O. Box 104
Bridgewater, CT 06752 (860) 357-7772
Contact: Jean Farley Levy, Chair.

Donor(s): Jean Farley Levy.
Financial data (yr. ended 05/31/00): Assets, $9,527 (M); grants paid, $6,000; gifts received, $20,566; expenditures, $22,721; qualifying distributions, $20,690.
Limitations: Giving primarily in Washington, CT.
Officers and Trustee:* Jean Farley Levy,* Chair.; Marie Difilippantonio, Secy.; Miles Borzilleri, Treas.
EIN: 222647001

59435
Connecticut QBS Council, Inc.
2600 Dixwell Ave., Ste. 7
Hamden, CT 06514

Classified as a private operating foundation in 1994.
Financial data (yr. ended 12/31/01): Assets, $9,099 (M); grants paid, $0; gifts received, $6,300; expenditures, $6,331; qualifying distributions, $6,331; giving activities include $6,331 for programs.
Officers: John Dugan, Pres.; Thomas Hansen, Secy.; David Rode, Treas.
Directors: Eric Oliner, Fred Preiss, Michael Wilkes.
EIN: 061339409

59436
Marlyn W. Dugan Foundation, Inc.
21 Mollbrook Dr.
Wilton, CT 06897

Established in 1999 in CT.
Donor(s): Joseph R. Dugan, Marilyn W. Dugan.
Financial data (yr. ended 12/31/01): Assets, $8,147 (M); grants paid, $2,698; gifts received, $10,015; expenditures, $13,269; qualifying distributions, $9,782; giving activities include $10,571 for programs.
Limitations: Applications not accepted. Giving primarily in CT.
Application information: Contributes only to pre-selected organizations.
Officers: Marilyn W. Dugan, Pres.; Joseph R. Dugan, Secy.-Treas.
Director: Barbara Boyd.
EIN: 061503775

59437
The Hollander Foundation
1 Omega Dr.
Stamford, CT 06907 (203) 359-7634
Contact: Ralph S. Michel, Tr.

Established in 1988.
Donor(s): Milton B. Hollander, Betty Ruth Hollander.
Financial data (yr. ended 12/31/00): Assets, $7,624 (M); grants paid, $111,118; gifts received, $74,000; expenditures, $111,120; qualifying distributions, $111,118.
Limitations: Giving primarily in Stamford, CT.
Application information: Application form not required.

Trustees: Betty Ruth Hollander, Milton B. Hollander, Ralph S. Michel.
EIN: 222952194
Codes: FD2

59438
Theban Desert Road Survey
c/o John Coleman Darnell
34 Hawthorne Ave.
Hamden, CT 06517-1823

Established in 1999 in DE.
Financial data (yr. ended 12/31/00): Assets, $7,331 (M); grants paid, $0; gifts received, $2,000; expenditures, $733; qualifying distributions, $0; giving activities include $733 for programs.
Officers and Director:* John Coleman Darnell,* Pres.; Deborah Darnell, V.P. and Secy.-Treas.
EIN: 061540142

59439
Swedish Aid Society, Inc.
140 New Haven Ave.
Orange, CT 06477
Application address: 150 Cook Hill Rd., Apt. 4101, Cheshire, CT 06410, tel.: (203) 271-3145
Contact: Lennart Engstrom, Pres.

Financial data (yr. ended 12/31/99): Assets, $6,932 (M); grants paid, $21,850; gifts received, $20,182; expenditures, $22,214; qualifying distributions, $21,850.
Limitations: Giving limited to the New Haven, CT, area.
Officers: Lennart Engstrom, Pres.; Carl R. Carlson, V.P.; Kirstin Lindquist, Secy.; Raymond G. Carlson, Treas.
EIN: 510188188

59440
Friends of Young Musicians, Inc.
A.J. Klaff, C.P.A.
P.O. Box 491
Westport, CT 06881-0491

Donor(s): Arnold Deutsch.
Financial data (yr. ended 11/30/99): Assets, $6,849 (M); grants paid, $0; gifts received, $25,000; expenditures, $23,876; qualifying distributions, $23,876; giving activities include $10,293 for programs.
Officer and Directors:* Arnold Deutsch,* Mgr.; Lawrence Blumberg.
EIN: 133085960

59441
Norwalk Arts and Crafts Workshop
c/o Johanna Straczek & Co.
48 Railroad Pl.
Westport, CT 06880-5912

Classified as a private operating foundation in 1981.
Financial data (yr. ended 12/31/99): Assets, $6,845 (M); grants paid, $185; gifts received, $57,131; expenditures, $101,225; qualifying distributions, $101,225.
Officers and Directors:* Ian MacKenzie Sim,* Pres.; Margaret Rogers,* V.P.; Michael Cemiello,* Secy.; Johanna Straczek,* Treas.; Harold Dale Shaw,* Mgr.; and 3 additional directors.
EIN: 061018521

59442
Crusade, Inc.
36 Dan's Hwy.
New Canaan, CT 06840
Contact: Diana Wege, Chair.

Established in 1998 in CT.
Donor(s): Diana Wege.

Financial data (yr. ended 12/31/00): Assets, $5,684 (M); grants paid, $69,000; gifts received, $149,840; expenditures, $150,268; qualifying distributions, $69,000.
Limitations: Applications not accepted. Giving primarily in CT and NY.
Application information: Contributes only to pre-selected organizations.
Officer: Diana Wege, Chair.
Board Members: Peggi Chute, Simone Demou, Averell Manes.
EIN: 061534907

59443
Stand Tall, Inc., a Vin Baker Charitable Organization
P.O. Box 179
Old Saybrook, CT 06475 (860) 388-4627
Contact: Donald S. Brodeur, Dir.

Established in 1998 in CT.
Donor(s): Vincent Baker.
Financial data (yr. ended 12/31/99): Assets, $4,348 (M); grants paid, $11,639; gifts received, $317,527; expenditures, $425,867; qualifying distributions, $387,169; giving activities include $327,672 for programs.
Directors: Ella J. Baker, James E. Baker, Donald S. Brodeur.
EIN: 061506173

59444
The Slason Foundation, Inc.
67 Stuart Dr.
Southington, CT 06489

Financial data (yr. ended 12/31/00): Assets, $4,017 (M); grants paid, $150; gifts received, $1,000; expenditures, $150; qualifying distributions, $150.
Officers: Joan Deutson, Pres.; Evelyn Gubstein, V.P.; Eugene F. Slason, Jr., Secy.-Treas.
EIN: 222867554

59445
Anne E. Wall Educational Trust Fund
c/o Anne E. Wall
6 Marguerite Ave.
Bloomfield, CT 06002-3334

Established in 1998.
Donor(s): Anne E. Wall.
Financial data (yr. ended 12/31/01): Assets, $3,943 (M); grants paid, $0; gifts received, $1,256; expenditures, $301; qualifying distributions, $0.
Trustees: Marc Casslar, Rev. Joseph DiSciacca, Mayor P. Faith McMahon, Anne E. Wall.
EIN: 061509773

59446
Waldman Bass Foundation, Inc.
c/o David Adam Realty, Inc.
61 Wilton Rd.
Westport, CT 06880

Established in 1999 in CT.
Donor(s): Jessica Waldman, Stacy Waldman Bass, David A. Waldman.
Financial data (yr. ended 12/31/00): Assets, $3,475 (M); grants paid, $450; gifts received, $15,126; expenditures, $15,394; qualifying distributions, $14,603.
Officers: Jessica Waldman, Pres.; Stacy Waldman Bass, V.P.; David A. Waldman, V.P.; Yvette A. Waldman, Secy.; Howard K. Bass, Treas.
EIN: 061541335

59447—CONNECTICUT

59447
LaFarge Catalogue Raisonne, Inc.
721 N. Hilton Rd.
New Canaan, CT 06840-2420

Established in 1995 in CT.
Financial data (yr. ended 12/31/99): Assets, $3,311 (M); grants paid, $0; gifts received, $6,779; expenditures, $14,479; qualifying distributions, $14,479; giving activities include $14,400 for programs.
Officers and Directors:* James L. Yarnall,* Pres.; Mary A. LaFarge,* Secy.-Treas.
Trustees: Oliver L. Hamill, Albert LaFarge.
EIN: 061317960

59448
Burry Fredrik Foundation, Inc.
51 N. Hillside Rd.
Weston, CT 06883-1513

Classified as a private operating foundation in 1989.
Financial data (yr. ended 12/31/01): Assets, $3,116 (M); grants paid, $0; gifts received, $391; expenditures, $391; qualifying distributions, $0.
Director: Burry F. Gerber.
EIN: 061260274

59449
Class of 1968 Scholarship, Inc.
119 Putnam Park
Greenwich, CT 06830-6735 (203) 661-2161
Contact: Robert S.V. Platten, Pres.

Donor(s): Robert S.V. Platten.
Financial data (yr. ended 05/31/02): Assets, $3,064 (M); grants paid, $8,000; gifts received, $9,243; expenditures, $8,238; qualifying distributions, $8,000.
Limitations: Giving on a national basis, with emphasis on the East; giving also in Canada.
Application information: Application form required.
Officers: Robert S.V. Platten, Pres.; Peter E. Smith, V.P.; James A. Burness, Secy.
EIN: 222573776
Codes: GTI

59450
The Adelman Family Foundation, Inc.
P.O. Box 2420
Meriden, CT 06450-4336

Established in 1999 in CT. Classified as a private operating foundation in 2001.
Financial data (yr. ended 12/31/01): Assets, $2,433 (M); grants paid, $500; gifts received, $1,327; expenditures, $936; qualifying distributions, $870.
Limitations: Applications not accepted.
Officers: Georgia B. Adelmam, Pres.; Jessica S. Adelman, V.P.; Gerard I. Adelman, Secy.-Treas.
EIN: 061537647

59451
The Rear Admiral Henry E. Eccles Institute for Military and Logistics Analysis
123 York St., Apt. 11-C
New Haven, CT 06511

Established in 1988 in VT.
Financial data (yr. ended 09/30/01): Assets, $1,173 (M); grants paid, $0; gifts received, $5; expenditures, $0; qualifying distributions, $0.
Officer and Directors:* Scott A. Boorman,* Pres.; Mylinda R. Willsey.
EIN: 222983591

59452
David Russo Cancer Foundation
c/o Thomas Russo
3 Ridgewood Ave.
Stamford, CT 06907-2617

Financial data (yr. ended 12/31/01): Assets, $528 (M); grants paid, $13,118; gifts received, $26,136; expenditures, $27,332; qualifying distributions, $27,332.
Limitations: Applications not accepted.
Application information: Contributes only to pre-selected organizations.
Officers: Christine Russo, Pres.; Marc Russo, V.P.; Susan Zezima, Secy.; Thomas Russo, Treas.
EIN: 061438625

59453
Art Spirit Foundation, Inc.
c/o Dianne B. Bernhard
281 Pequot Ave.
Southport, CT 06490

Established in 1999.
Donor(s): Dianne B. Bernard.
Financial data (yr. ended 12/31/00): Assets, $27 (M); grants paid, $0; gifts received, $2,764; expenditures, $2,659; qualifying distributions, $0.
Officers and Directors:* Dianne B. Bernhard,* Pres.; Angela Thomas,* Secy.
EIN: 061571544

59454
TIMEXPO Foundation, Inc.
P.O. Box 310
Middlebury, CT 06762-0310

Established as a company-sponsored operating foundation in 1997 in CT.
Donor(s): Timex Corp.
Financial data (yr. ended 12/31/00): Assets, $1 (M); grants paid, $147,428; expenditures, $148,428; qualifying distributions, $147,428.
Limitations: Applications not accepted. Giving primarily in areas of company operations.
Application information: Contributes only to pre-selected organizations.
Officers and Directors:* Fredrik Olsen,* Chair.; Muhammad Saleh,* Pres.; Frank Sherer,* V.P. and Secy.; Madeline Lynn,* V.P.; Carl Rosa,* V.P.; Amir Rosenthal, Treas.; Kristine Olsen.
EIN: 061466342

59455
Hang Your Hat Foundation
213 Lyons Plain Rd.
Weston, CT 06883

Established in 2000 in NY.
Financial data (yr. ended 12/31/00): Assets, $0 (M); grants paid, $300,000; gifts received, $300,000; expenditures, $300,000; qualifying distributions, $0.
Officers and Directors:* Dawn Egan,* Pres.; John Egan,* V.P. and Treas.; Megan Loughney, V.P.; Richard M. Cayne,* Secy.
EIN: 061602834
Codes: FD

DELAWARE

59456
Delaware Museum of Natural History, Inc.
P.O. Box 3937
Greenville, DE 19807

Classified as a private operating foundation in 1973 in DE.
Financial data (yr. ended 12/31/01): Assets, $25,127,439 (M); grants paid, $0; gifts received, $2,544,831; expenditures, $1,936,806; qualifying distributions, $0.
Limitations: Giving primarily in DE.
Officers and Trustees:* Scott F. Nelson,* Pres.; Robert S. Kennedy,* V.P.; Carol M. Clement, Co-Secy.; Richard W. Thorington, Jr.,* Co-Secy.; Bruce W. Morrissey,* Treas.; Geoffrey Halfpenny, Exec. Dir.; Rudiger Bieler, Alison Bradford, Horace K. Dugdale, Richard I.B. Jones, Jr., Mrs. Robert C. Myers, and 5 additional trustees.
EIN: 510083535

59457
Community Service Building Corporation
100 W. 10th St., Ste. 201
Wilmington, DE 19801

Established in 1994.
Donor(s): Longwood Foundation, Inc.
Financial data (yr. ended 12/31/00): Assets, $25,083,525 (M); grants paid, $0; gifts received, $1,646,809; expenditures, $1,594,344; qualifying distributions, $964,371; giving activities include $964,371 for programs.
Officers: Peter Morrow, Pres.; Robert H. Bolling, Jr., V.P.; Stephen A. Martinenza, Secy.-Treas.
Directors: Thomas S. Shaw, Collis O. Townsend, David Wakefield.
EIN: 510362183

59458
Robert N. Downs Memorial Conservancy, Inc.
P.O. Box 3666
Wilmington, DE 19807 (302) 994-1614
Application address: 4700 Lancaster Pike, Wilmington, DE 19807
Contact: Pierre D. Hayward, Pres.

Established in 1989 in DE.
Donor(s): Alletta Laird Downs.
Financial data (yr. ended 03/31/02): Assets, $20,664,795 (M); grants paid, $5,000; gifts received, $325,000; expenditures, $304,739; qualifying distributions, $5,000.
Limitations: Giving primarily in Wilmington, DE; some giving in PA.
Officers: Pierre D. Hayward, Pres.; Paul D. Rossiter, Treas.
EIN: 510319062

59459
Children's Beach House, Inc.
100 W. 10th St., Ste. 411
Wilmington, DE 19801-1674

Established in 1937 in DE.
Financial data (yr. ended 09/30/00): Assets, $11,035,338 (M); grants paid, $0; gifts received, $4,699,363; expenditures, $585,282; qualifying distributions, $519,627; giving activities include $533,282 for programs.
Officers and Trustees:* Richard A. Dobbs,* Treas.; Harold L. Springer III, Exec. Dir.; Lillian M. Burris, Richard L. Dayton, Margot H. Kuniholm, Richard L. Laird, and 20 additional trustees.
EIN: 510070966

59460
Sophia G. Coxe Charitable Trust Fund
c/o Wilmington Trust Co.
1100 N. Market St., Ste. 505610
Wilmington, DE 19890-0001

Classified as a private operating trust in 1976.
Financial data (yr. ended 12/31/01): Assets, $5,599,904 (M); grants paid, $0; expenditures, $336,844; qualifying distributions, $0.
Trustee: Wilmington Trust Co.
EIN: 236001974

59461
Palmer Home, Inc.
P.O. Box 1751
Dover, DE 19903-1751
Contact: Jean T. DeLeo, Pres.

Established in 1930.
Financial data (yr. ended 02/28/01): Assets, $4,913,568 (M); grants paid, $230,000; gifts received, $31,772; expenditures, $244,474; qualifying distributions, $232,960.
Limitations: Giving limited to Kent County, DE.
Application information: Application form required.
Officers: Jean T. DeLeo, Pres.; Carol Braverman, V.P.; Lillian Hamm, Secy.-Treas.
EIN: 510066737
Codes: FD2

59462
The Barnett Newman Foundation
c/o JPMorgan Chase Bank
P.O. Box 6089
Newark, DE 19714-6089

Classified as a private operating foundation in 1980.
Donor(s): Annalee Newman.‡
Financial data (yr. ended 05/31/01): Assets, $1,349,875 (M); grants paid, $0; expenditures, $497,709; qualifying distributions, $485,507; giving activities include $485,782 for programs.
Trustee: Frank Stella.
EIN: 132989464

59463
Wunsch Americana Foundation, Inc.
c/o V.J. Kumar
53 The Strand
New Castle, DE 19720

Established in 1967 in DE.
Donor(s): Eric M. Wunsch, WEA Enterprises Co., Inc., Ninth Avenue Equities.
Financial data (yr. ended 12/31/99): Assets, $1,160,837 (M); grants paid, $104,210; gifts received, $20,500; expenditures, $104,809; qualifying distributions, $104,210.
Limitations: Applications not accepted. Giving primarily in NY.
Application information: Contributes only to pre-selected organizations.
Officer: Eric M. Wunsch, Pres.
EIN: 510106068
Codes: FD2

59464
The Bristle Cone Pine Foundation
c/o Wilmington Trust Co.
1100 N. Market St.
Wilmington, DE 19890-0001

Established in 1998 in DE.
Donor(s): Stephen Milliken.
Financial data (yr. ended 12/31/01): Assets, $1,023,183 (M); grants paid, $80,500; expenditures, $82,545; qualifying distributions, $79,905.

Limitations: Applications not accepted. Giving primarily in Washington, DC.
Application information: Contributes only to pre-selected organizations.
Advisors: Jesse C. Milliken, John W. Milliken, Rebecca C. Milliken, Stephen Milliken.
Trustee: Wilmington Trust Co.
EIN: 516508168
Codes: FD2

59465
Madison Trust
(Formerly Madison Trust & The Brittingham Fund)
5809 Kennett Pike
Wilmington, DE 19807-1194 (302) 655-9651
Contact: George D. Herrmann, Jr., Secy.-Treas.

Established in 1941 in DE.
Donor(s): Harold H. Brittingham.‡
Financial data (yr. ended 12/31/01): Assets, $709,765 (M); grants paid, $52,400; expenditures, $53,629; qualifying distributions, $43,230.
Limitations: Giving limited to Madison, WI.
Application information: Application form not required.
Officer: George D. Hermann, Jr., Secy.-Treas.
Trustee: Brittingham Fund, Inc.
EIN: 516017953

59466
The Lucas Family Charitable Foundation
c/o Wilmington Trust Co.
1100 N. Market St., Ste. 505610
Wilmington, DE 19890

Classified as an operating foundation in 1997.
Donor(s): Peter H. Lucas.
Financial data (yr. ended 12/31/99): Assets, $583,569 (M); grants paid, $6,160; gifts received, $64,926; expenditures, $14,704; qualifying distributions, $9,594.
Limitations: Applications not accepted.
Application information: Contributes only to pre-selected organizations.
Trustees: Peter Lucas, Wilmington Trust Co.
EIN: 526886506

59467
Popsies-Rencourt Foundation, Inc.
5714 Kennett Pike
Wilmington, DE 19807 (302) 652-3296
Contact: George A. Weymouth, Chair.

Established in 2000 in DE.
Donor(s): Rencourt Foundation.
Financial data (yr. ended 06/30/01): Assets, $473,908 (M); grants paid, $24,000; expenditures, $28,291; qualifying distributions, $24,000.
Limitations: Giving primarily in DE and PA.
Officers: George A. Weymouth, Chair.; Patricia W. Hobbs, Pres.; Cary A. Lambert, Secy.-Treas.
EIN: 510404250

59468
Sharabi Family Foundation
c/o JPMorgan Chase Bank
P.O. Box 6089
Newark, DE 19714-6089
Application address: c/o JPMorgan Chase Bank, 500 Stanton Christiana Rd., Newark, DE 19714, tel.: (302) 634-4319
Contact: Patricia E. Hall

Established in 1999.
Financial data (yr. ended 01/31/02): Assets, $416,291 (M); grants paid, $0; gifts received, $39; expenditures, $8,134; qualifying distributions, $6,812.

Limitations: Giving primarily in New York, NY.
Trustee: JPMorgan Chase Bank.
EIN: 516514248

59469
Mill Creek Foundation, Inc.
3713 Mill Creek Rd.
Hockessin, DE 19707-9725

Financial data (yr. ended 12/31/01): Assets, $361,540 (M); grants paid, $0; gifts received, $100; expenditures, $2,474; qualifying distributions, $0.
Officer: Michael B. Leach, Pres.
Directors: D. Crowley, M. Dowd, L. Maier.
EIN: 222848433

59470
Forum to Advance Minorities in Engineering, Inc.
DuPont Bldg.
1007 N. Market St., Ste. 8047
Wilmington, DE 19801 (302) 777-3254
FAX: (302) 777-0896

Established in 1986 in DE.
Financial data (yr. ended 12/31/99): Assets, $236,560 (M); grants paid, $0; gifts received, $478,049; expenditures, $325,556; qualifying distributions, $324,013; giving activities include $324,042 for programs.
Officers and Directors:* William Bazzelle,* Chair.; Claire LaMar Carey,* Vice-Chair.; Jean Tucker,* Secy.; Carey Sudler,* Treas.; Guizelous O. Molock, Exec. Dir.; and 40 additional directors.
EIN: 510210266

59471
Delaware State Golf Association Scholarship Fund, Inc.
(also known as DSGA Junior Golf Scholarship Fund, Inc.)
P.O. Box 101
Rehoboth Beach, DE 19971-0101
(302) 227-3616

Established in 1987 in DE.
Financial data (yr. ended 12/31/01): Assets, $180,899 (M); grants paid, $35,971; gifts received, $62,506; expenditures, $36,351; qualifying distributions, $35,971.
Limitations: Giving limited to residents of DE.
Application information: Application form required.
Officers and Directors:* Robert McCurry,* Pres.; Ronald L. Barrows,* V.P.; Eugene H. Bayard,* Secy.; Fred Dingle, Treas.
EIN: 510297378
Codes: GTI

59472
Henry Topel Foundation
1700 N. Rodney St.
Wilmington, DE 19806 (302) 656-3384
Contact: Henry Topel, Pres.

Established in 1987 in DE.
Donor(s): Henry Topel.
Financial data (yr. ended 06/30/01): Assets, $157,486 (M); grants paid, $36,548; expenditures, $37,723; qualifying distributions, $36,548.
Limitations: Giving primarily in Wilmington, DE.
Officer: Henry Topel, Pres.
EIN: 510305949

59473
Dog Writers Educational Trust
2508 Teal Rd.
Wilmington, DE 19805
Application address: c/o Mary Ellen Tarman, P.O. Box E, Hummelstown, PA 17036-0199

Established as a private operating foundation in 1962.
Financial data (yr. ended 12/31/01): Assets, $110,002 (M); grants paid, $5,000; gifts received, $9,795; expenditures, $8,791; qualifying distributions, $8,791.
Limitations: Giving on a national basis.
Application information: Applicant must include transcript with application form. Application form required.
Officers: Harold W. Sundstrom, Chair.; Allene McKewen, Secy.; Patricia F. Lehman, Treas.
EIN: 046088171
Codes: GTI

59474
The Northeast Community Development Corporation, Inc.
P.O. Box 9520
Wilmington, DE 19809

Established in DE in 1997.
Financial data (yr. ended 12/31/00): Assets, $69,053 (M); grants paid, $0; expenditures, $11,689; qualifying distributions, $0; giving activities include $58,793 for programs.
Officers: Theodore Spalding, Pres.; Edwin Lucas, Jr., V.P.; LaVida Owens-White, Secy.; Forrest Carter, Treas.
EIN: 510373584

59475
Plectra Music, Inc.
P.O. Box 730
Wilmington, DE 19899

Established in 2000 in DE.
Donor(s): Peter H. Flint.
Financial data (yr. ended 12/31/01): Assets, $31,296 (M); grants paid, $0; gifts received, $40,451; expenditures, $29,804; qualifying distributions, $0.
Limitations: Applications not accepted.
Application information: Contributes only to pre-selected organizations.
Officers: Peter H. Flint, Pres. and Treas.; Karen G. Flint, V.P. and Secy.
EIN: 510403569

59476
I Have a Dream Foundation of Delaware
1907 N. Van Buren St.
Wilmington, DE 19802

Established in 1988 in DE.
Donor(s): Sarah I. Gore, Robert W. Gore, Christopher Coons.
Financial data (yr. ended 06/30/01): Assets, $17,186 (M); grants paid, $5,111; gifts received, $5,000; expenditures, $6,271; qualifying distributions, $6,271.
Limitations: Applications not accepted. Giving limited to residents of DE.
Officers: Christopher Coons, Pres.; Stephen K. Coons, Secy.; Sally Gore, Treas.
Director: Sarah I. Gore.
EIN: 510313759

59477
AstraZeneca HealthCare Foundation
(Formerly Zeneca HealthCare Foundation)
c/o R.T. Kennedy
P.O. Box 15438, 1800 Concord Ave.
Wilmington, DE 19803-5438

Established in 1993 in DE. Classified as a company-sponsored operating foundation in 1995.
Donor(s): Zeneca Inc., AstraZeneca Pharmaceuticals LP.
Financial data (yr. ended 12/31/00): Assets, $12,649 (M); grants paid, $0; gifts received, $1,323,151; expenditures, $1,310,622; qualifying distributions, $1,310,622; giving activities include $1,310,622 for programs.
Officers: Alan J. Milbauer, Chair. and Pres.; Robert A. Rausch, V.P. and Treas.; Ann V. Booth-Barbarin, Secy.
EIN: 510349682

59478
McIntosh Ford Automotive Foundation
c/o The Company Corp.
1313 N. Market St.
Wilmington, DE 19801-1151

Established in 1997. Classified as a private operating foundation in 1999.
Financial data (yr. ended 12/31/00): Assets, $9,452 (M); grants paid, $820; gifts received, $11,160; expenditures, $1,708; qualifying distributions, $820.
Director: Robert McIntosh.
EIN: 161520539

59479
Research in Archaeology, Inc.
c/o Patrick M. Ashley
P.O. Box 730
Wilmington, DE 19899-730

Established in 2000 in DE.
Donor(s): Frederick H. West, Mrs. Frederick H. West.
Financial data (yr. ended 06/30/01): Assets, $4,310 (M); grants paid, $70,000; gifts received, $82,500; expenditures, $82,821; qualifying distributions, $70,000.
Limitations: Applications not accepted.
Application information: Contributes only to pre-selected organizations.
Officers and Directors:* Patrick M. Ashley,* Pres. and Treas.; Penny L. Tracey,* V.P. and Secy.
EIN: 510403437

59480
Feral and Friend Feline Foundation
c/o Arlette M. Lilly
137 Casimir Dr.
New Castle, DE 19720-4520

Established in 1998.
Donor(s): Arlette M. Lilly.
Financial data (yr. ended 12/31/01): Assets, $950 (M); grants paid, $0; gifts received, $11,458; expenditures, $11,458; qualifying distributions, $0.
Officers: Arlette M. Lilly, Pres.; Francene Larimore, V.P.; Paula Diemidio, Secy.
Trustee: Virginia Allen.
EIN: 510380737

59481
Mobius, The Poetry Magazine
c/o Jean Hull Herman
P.O. Box 7544
Talleyville, DE 19803-0544

Classified as a private operating foundation in 1994.

Financial data (yr. ended 12/31/01): Assets, $20 (M); grants paid, $0; gifts received, $3,216; expenditures, $3,943; qualifying distributions, $0.
Officers: Jean Hull Herman, Pres.; Allan Wendelberg, V.P.; Sandra Seaton Michael, Secy.; George Wendelberg, Jr., Treas.
EIN: 383126375

59482
Wellness By the Sea, Inc.
P.O. Box 651
Rehoboth Beach, DE 19971

Financial data (yr. ended 09/30/01): Assets, $1 (M); grants paid, $0; expenditures, $775; qualifying distributions, $0.
Officers: Ruth Carrol, Pres.; Jerry Davies, V.P.; Margaret Unuscavage, Secy.; Dorothy Neichter, Treas.
EIN: 510346238

59483
AstraZeneca Foundation
(Formerly Zeneca Pharmaceuticals Foundation)
1800 Concord Pike
P.O. Box 15437
Wilmington, DE 19850

Established in 1992 in DE.
Donor(s): Zeneca Inc., AstraZeneca Pharmaceuticals LP.
Financial data (yr. ended 12/26/99): Assets, $0 (M); grants paid, $0; gifts received, $43,645,941; expenditures, $43,645,941; qualifying distributions, $43,645,941; giving activities include $43,645,941 for programs.
Officers and Trustees:* Alan J. Milbauer,* Chair. and Pres.; Robert A. Rausch,* V.P. and Treas.; William C. Lucas,* Secy.
EIN: 510343305

DISTRICT OF COLUMBIA

59484
Carnegie Endowment for International Peace
1779 Massachusetts Ave. N.W.
Washington, DC 20036
URL: http://www.ceip.org

Founded in 1910 in DC; incorporated in 1929 in NY.
Donor(s): Andrew Carnegie.‡
Financial data (yr. ended 06/30/00): Assets, $273,654,304 (M); grants paid, $0; gifts received, $1,882,558; expenditures, $18,085,217; qualifying distributions, $13,007,943; giving activities include $6,723,377 for programs.
Publications: Occasional report, financial statement, informational brochure.
Officers and Trustees:* William H. Donaldson, Chair.; Gregory B. Craig, Vice-Chair.; Jessica Tuchman Mathews,* Pres.; Paul Balaran, Exec. V.P.; Michael V. O'Hare, Secy.; Robert Carswell, Richard A. Debs, Marion R. Fremont-Smith, Leslie H. Gelb, James A. Johnson, Donald Kennedy, Wilbert J. LeMelle, Stephen R. Lewis, Jr., and 10 additional trustees.
EIN: 130552040
Codes: TN

59485
The David Lloyd Kreeger Foundation
2401 Foxhall Rd. N.W.
Washington, DC 20007-1149

Established in 1961 in DC.
Donor(s): David Lloyd Kreeger,‡ Carmen M. Kreeger.
Financial data (yr. ended 12/31/99): Assets, $92,421,088 (M); grants paid, $0; gifts received, $62,162; expenditures, $507,496; qualifying distributions, $423,114; giving activities include $423,114 for programs.
Directors: Carol K. Ingall, Carmen M. Kreeger, Peter L. Kreeger.
EIN: 526037451

59486
Abraham and Laura Lisner Home for Aged Women
5425 Western Ave. N.W.
Washington, DC 20015

Classified as a private operating foundation in 1986.
Financial data (yr. ended 06/30/01): Assets, $39,245,645 (M); grants paid, $0; gifts received, $4,755; expenditures, $7,229,931; qualifying distributions, $1,033,487; giving activities include $5,612,830 for programs.
Limitations: Applications not accepted.
Application information: Contributes only to pre-selected organizations.
Officers and Directors:* Matthew Tobriner,* Pres.; David Povich,* V.P.; Eva Nash,* Secy.; B. Bernei Burgunder, Jr.,* Treas.; Juanita Archer, Rev. William Hague, Philip Israel, Jr., Bruce Kellison, Deirdre Parrot, Robert Walsh, and 12 additional directors.
EIN: 530228120

59487
Eno Transportation Foundation, Inc.
(Formerly Eno Foundation for Transportation, Inc.)
1634 I St.
Washington, DC 20006-4009

Classified as private operating foundation in 1985.
Donor(s): William Phelps Eno.‡
Financial data (yr. ended 12/31/99): Assets, $13,979,121 (M); grants paid, $9,500; gifts received, $831,922; expenditures, $1,838,167; qualifying distributions, $1,681,291; giving activities include $595,314 for programs.
Publications: Informational brochure.
Officers and Directors:* Lawrence D. Dahms,* Chair.; Damian J. Kulash,* Pres. and C.E.O.; Lillian C. Liburdi,* Secy.-Treas.; Tracie Andrie, Financial Mgr.; Joseph M. Clapp, Norman Mineta, Ted Tedesco.
EIN: 060662124

59488
Trustees of the Louise Home
c/o J. Bruce Kellison
5425 Western Ave. N.W.
Washington, DC 20015-2931

Established in 1875 in DC; classified as a private operating foundation in 1983.
Financial data (yr. ended 12/31/01): Assets, $7,267,618 (M); grants paid, $0; expenditures, $443,854; qualifying distributions, $400,776; giving activities include $289,200 for programs.
Limitations: Applications not accepted. Giving primarily in Washington, DC.
Application information: Contributes only to pre-selected organizations.

Officer and Trustees:* J. Bruce Kellison,* Pres.; Philip N. Israel, Jr., Philip P. O'Donoghue, Deirdre Parrot, Robert L. Walsh.
EIN: 530196601

59489
The Kelton Foundation
1642 R St. N.W.
Washington, DC 20009-6419

Established in 1993 in CA.
Donor(s): The Kelton Fund, Inc., Richard Kelton, Kelswan, Inc.
Financial data (yr. ended 12/31/00): Assets, $6,692,432 (M); grants paid, $1,049; gifts received, $1,080,875; expenditures, $350,069; qualifying distributions, $393,141; giving activities include $566,453 for programs.
Limitations: Applications not accepted.
Publications: Informational brochure.
Application information: Contributes only to pre-selected organizations.
Officers: Richard Kelton, Pres. and Treas.; Mark Kelton, V.P. and Secy.; Mary Nicholls, V.P.; Kerry Smallwood, V.P.
EIN: 521268434

59490
Alicia Patterson Foundation
1730 Pennsylvania Ave., N.W., Rm. 850
Washington, DC 20006 (202) 393-5995
Additional tel. and FAX: (301) 951-8512; *E-mail:* exec.director@aliciapatterson.org; *URL:* http://www.aliciapatterson.org
Contact: Margaret Engel, Exec. Dir.

Incorporated in 1960 in NY.
Donor(s): Alicia Patterson.‡
Financial data (yr. ended 12/31/01): Assets, $5,503,708 (M); grants paid, $373,563; expenditures, $539,694; qualifying distributions, $490,617.
Limitations: Giving on a national basis.
Publications: Annual report, informational brochure, newsletter, application guidelines, grants list.
Application information: Application form required.
Officers and Directors:* Joseph P. Albright,* Chair.; Alice Arlen, Pres.; Adam M. Albright,* V.P.; Blandina Albright,* V.P.; Margaret Engel, Secy. and Exec. Dir.; Cathy Trost, Treas.
EIN: 136092124
Codes: FD, GTI

59491
The Henry & Annie Hurt Home for the Blind
c/o Columbia Partners, LLP
1775 Pennsylvania Ave. N.W.
Washington, DC 20006

Established in 1987 in DC.
Donor(s): Pearson S. Meeks,‡ Emily G. Bready.
Financial data (yr. ended 06/30/01): Assets, $5,394,134 (M); grants paid, $109,000; gifts received, $7,000; expenditures, $392,626; qualifying distributions, $339,562.
Limitations: Applications not accepted. Giving primarily in Washington, DC.
Application information: Contributes only to pre-selected organizations.
Officers: Terence W. Collins, Pres.; Barbara L.F. Ingraham, Secy.
Trustees: William Hague, Helen Hoenig, Nancy Youden, First Union National Bank.
EIN: 526063279

59492
Elizabeth R. Shoemaker Home, Inc.
2701 Military Rd. N.W.
Washington, DC 20015

Classified as a private operating foundation in 1972.
Donor(s): Loughran Foundation.
Financial data (yr. ended 06/30/01): Assets, $4,586,105 (M); grants paid, $0; gifts received, $33,150; expenditures, $558,340; qualifying distributions, $501,376; giving activities include $501,376 for programs.
Officers: Terence W. Collins, Pres.; Barbara L.F. Ingraham, Secy.
Directors: Stephanie Desibour, Edward T. Dillon, Margaret Eastman, Judith Martin, Pam Murdock.
EIN: 530211708

59493
David R. MacDonald Foundation
c/o David R. MacDonald
815 Connecticut Ave. N.W.
Washington, DC 20006-4078

Established in 1996 in DE.
Donor(s): David R. MacDonald.
Financial data (yr. ended 12/31/99): Assets, $3,999,144 (M); grants paid, $3,550; gifts received, $1,445; expenditures, $55,073; qualifying distributions, $130,297.
Limitations: Applications not accepted.
Application information: Contributes only to pre-selected organizations.
Officers: David R. MacDonald, Pres. and Treas.; Verna Joy MacDonald, V.P. and Secy.
EIN: 521968656

59494
The Chopivsky Family Foundation
3215 Cathedral Ave., N.W.
Washington, DC 20008

Established in 1986 in DC.
Donor(s): George Chopivsky, Jr.
Financial data (yr. ended 11/30/00): Assets, $3,545,347 (M); grants paid, $26,250; expenditures, $78,617; qualifying distributions, $78,108; giving activities include $28,990 for programs.
Limitations: Applications not accepted. Giving primarily in the Ukraine.
Application information: Contributes only to pre-selected organizations.
Officers: George Chopivsky, Jr., Pres.; Lydia Benson, V.P.
EIN: 521493038

59495
Esperantic Studies Foundation, Inc.
3900 Northampton St., N.W.
Washington, DC 20015 (202) 362-3963
E-mail: EJL@Gwu.edu; *URL:* http://www.esperantic.org
Contact: Mark Fettes, Exec. Dir.

Established in 1968 in DC.
Donor(s): Catherine Schulze.
Financial data (yr. ended 12/31/00): Assets, $3,526,985 (M); grants paid, $56,598; gifts received, $26,957; expenditures, $155,887; qualifying distributions, $116,188; giving activities include $6,000 for programs.
Limitations: Giving on a national and international basis.
Application information: Application form required.
Officers: Humphrey Tonkin, Pres.; David K. Jordan, V.P.; Jonathan Pool, V.P.; Mark Fettes, Exec. Dir.
EIN: 520885287

59496
The William H. G. Fitzgerald Family Foundation
1730 Rhode Island Ave. N.W., Ste. 1105
Washington, DC 20036 (202) 659-8850
Contact: William H.G. Fitzgerald, Pres.

Established in 1999 in Washington, DC, and DE.
Donor(s): Annelise Fitzgerald, William H.G. Fitzgerald.
Financial data (yr. ended 04/30/01): Assets, $3,281,585 (M); grants paid, $149,376; expenditures, $177,367; qualifying distributions, $157,018.
Limitations: Applications not accepted. Giving on a national basis.
Application information: Contributes only to pre-selected organizations.
Officers: William H.G. Fitzgerald, Pres.; Annelise Fitzgerald, V.P.; Anne F. Slichter, Secy.; Desmond G. Fitzgerald, Treas.
EIN: 522097034
Codes: FD2

59497
Peter N. G. Schwartz Foundation
1350 Connecticut Ave. N.W., No. 1200
Washington, DC 20036

Established in 1992 in DC.
Donor(s): Peter N.G. Schwartz.
Financial data (yr. ended 09/30/01): Assets, $2,504,030 (M); grants paid, $15,250; gifts received, $2,501,000; expenditures, $114,018; qualifying distributions, $112,684; giving activities include $112,684 for programs.
Limitations: Applications not accepted. Giving limited to Washington, DC.
Publications: Grants list.
Application information: Unsolicited requests for funds not accepted.
Officers: Peter N.G. Schwartz, Pres. and Treas.; Patrick G. Dooher, V.P. and Secy.
EIN: 521797515
Codes: GTI

59498
Ada Harris Maley Memorial Fund
1818 N St., N.W., Ste. 700
Washington, DC 20036 (202) 331-7050
Contact: Michael J. Conlon, Tr.

Financial data (yr. ended 12/31/01): Assets, $2,470,595 (M); grants paid, $147,500; expenditures, $179,420; qualifying distributions, $149,800.
Limitations: Giving limited to the metropolitan Washington, DC area.
Application information: Application form not required.
Trustees: Michael J. Conlon, Brian P. Phelan.
EIN: 526035898
Codes: FD2

59499
The Finance Project
1000 Vermont Ave., N.W., No. 600
Washington, DC 20005

Classified as a private operating foundation in 1993.
Financial data (yr. ended 12/31/00): Assets, $2,213,325 (M); grants paid, $82,000; gifts received, $3,373,542; expenditures, $3,600,281; qualifying distributions, $3,605,626.
Limitations: Applications not accepted. Giving primarily in Washington, DC, and Chicago, IL.
Application information: Contributes only to pre-selected organizations.
Officers and Directors:* Ruth Massinga, Co-Chair.; Gary Stangler, Co-Chair.; Carol Cohen,* Secy. and Deputy Dir.; Barry Van Lare, Treas. and Exec. Dir.; Cheryl Hayes, Exec. Dir.; Ben Canada, Adolph Falcon, Randall Franke, Kathy Hoyt, and 8 additional directors.
EIN: 521841608
Codes: FD2

59500
The Caleb Foundation, Inc.
c/o Randy A. Weiss
1828 L St. N.W., Ste. 500
Washington, DC 20036

Established in 1989 in VA.
Donor(s): Vincent W. Sedmak.
Financial data (yr. ended 11/30/00): Assets, $2,022,210 (M); grants paid, $45,600; gifts received, $40,234; expenditures, $61,350; qualifying distributions, $45,550.
Limitations: Applications not accepted. Giving primarily in Arlington and Gainesville, VA.
Officers: Vincent W. Sedmak, Pres.; Janee Sedmak, V.P.
Director: Randy Alan Weiss.
EIN: 541527522

59501
The William G. Congdon Foundation
(Formerly Foundation for Improving Understanding of the Arts)
1050 17th St., N.W., Ste. 700
Washington, DC 20036

Established in 1986 in DC.
Financial data (yr. ended 12/31/00): Assets, $2,006,358 (M); grants paid, $0; gifts received, $15,078; expenditures, $219,085; qualifying distributions, $198,648; giving activities include $198,878 for programs.
Officers: Pablo G. Pisano, Pres.; Paolo Mangini, V.P.; Robert M. Reiner, Secy.
EIN: 521271472

59502
Foundation for Economic Liberty, Inc.
130 3rd St., S.E.
Washington, DC 20003

Financial data (yr. ended 12/31/99): Assets, $1,638,266 (M); grants paid, $0; gifts received, $86,441; expenditures, $315,904; qualifying distributions, $298,554; giving activities include $298,518 for programs.
Officers: Blayne Hutzel, Chair.; Michael Piper, Vice-Chair.; Mary Pflug, Secy.-Treas.
EIN: 521558272

59503
Federal Focus, Inc.
11 Dupont Cir. N.W., Ste. 700
Washington, DC 20036-1231

Established in 1987 in DC.
Financial data (yr. ended 12/31/00): Assets, $1,088,424 (M); grants paid, $7,250; expenditures, $148,942; qualifying distributions, $7,250.
Limitations: Applications not accepted.
Application information: Contributes only to pre-selected organizations.
Officers: James Tang, V.P.; William Kelly, Secy.; Barbara Tozzi, Treas.
Director: Jim J. Tozzi.
EIN: 521491985

59504
National Parental Alienation Foundation
816 Connecticut Ave. N.W., 9th Fl.
Washington, DC 20006

Established in 1999 in VA.
Donor(s): James F. Scott.
Financial data (yr. ended 12/31/99): Assets, $923,649 (M); grants paid, $0; gifts received, $1,034,018; expenditures, $150,877; qualifying distributions, $193,821; giving activities include $193,821 for programs.
Limitations: Applications not accepted.
Application information: Contributes only to pre-selected organizations.
Officers: James F. Scott, Chair.; Roderick S. Bolte, V.P.; April R. Fletcher, Secy.; Susan Hunter, Treas.; Pamela Stuart Mills, Exec. Dir.
EIN: 541945649

59505
Global Environmental Management Initiative, Inc.
1 Thomas Cir. N.W., 10th Fl.
Washington, DC 20005

Established in 1993 in DE.
Financial data (yr. ended 12/31/01): Assets, $644,105 (M); grants paid, $0; gifts received, $675,500; expenditures, $778,583; qualifying distributions, $759,620; giving activities include $494,430 for programs.
Officers and Directors:* Polly T. Strife,* Chair.; David Mayer,* Vice-Chair.; Steve Hellem, Exec. V.P.; Susan Moore, George Nagle, Vivian Pai, Bill Sugar, Darwin Wika.
EIN: 521845788

59506
The Per Jacobsson Foundation
700 19th St. N.W.
Washington, DC 20431

Established in 1964 in DC.
Financial data (yr. ended 04/30/00): Assets, $593,089 (M); grants paid, $0; expenditures, $34,927; qualifying distributions, $33,603; giving activities include $33,603 for programs.
Officers and Directors:* Jacques de Larosiere,* Chair.; Leo Van Houtven,* Pres.; Alexander Mountford,* V.P. and Secy.; G. Michael Fitzpatrick, Treas.; Michel Camdessus, Andrew Crockett, Toyoo Gyohten, Enrique Iglesias, Alexandre Lamfalussy, Jeremy Morse, Jacques J. Polak, Paul A. Volcker, Peter Wallenberg, H. Johannes Witteveen.
EIN: 526054065

59507
Economic and Social Research Institute
1015 18th St. N.W., Ste. 210
Washington, DC 20036-5203

Established in 1988 in VA.
Financial data (yr. ended 12/31/00): Assets, $374,416 (M); grants paid, $0; gifts received, $993,876; expenditures, $1,102,941; qualifying distributions, $1,058,243; giving activities include $782,662 for programs.
Officers and Directors:* Jack A. Meyer,* Pres.; Mark W. Legnini,* Sr. V.P.; Mickey Levy, William Lilley III, Kenneth McLennan, Beth Shulman, Sheila Zedlewski.
EIN: 541420476

59508
Standardswork, Inc.
(Formerly The Coalition for Goals 2000, Inc.)
c/o George Washington University
1001 Connecticut Ave. N.W., Ste. 901
Washington, DC 20036

Established in 1992 in DC and DE.
Donor(s): Richard King Mellon Foundation, Merrill Lynch & Co., Inc., Siemens Corp., The Walton Family Foundation.
Financial data (yr. ended 06/30/00): Assets, $272,278 (M); grants paid, $0; gifts received,

$345,880; expenditures, $693,480; qualifying distributions, $188,036; giving activities include $602,790 for programs.
Officers and Directors:* Dan Spalding,* Chair.; Leslye Arsht,* Pres.; Thomas L. Howard,* Secy.-Treas.; John Danielson, Edward Donley, Mary H. Futrell, John T. Kauffman, Sherra Kerns, Susan Pimental, Sheree Speakman, Jack Will.
EIN: 521785250

59509
Zauqi Charitable & Educational Trust
6458 32nd St. N.W.
Washington, DC 20015-2306

Established in 1993.
Donor(s): Azizali Mohammed.
Financial data (yr. ended 12/31/00): Assets, $267,742 (M); grants paid, $31,868; gifts received, $21,300; expenditures, $33,261; qualifying distributions, $33,166.
Limitations: Applications not accepted. Giving on an international basis.
Application information: Contributes only to pre-selected organizations.
Trustees: Afroze Mohammed, Arshad Mohammed, Azizali Mohammed, Sakina Mohammed, Zeba Rasmussen.
EIN: 521833177

59510
The National Commission on Entrepreneurship
444 N. Capitol St., Ste. 399
Washington, DC 20001

Established in 1998 in DC.
Donor(s): Kauffman Center.
Financial data (yr. ended 09/30/01): Assets, $257,316 (M); grants paid, $0; gifts received, $878,000; expenditures, $952,952; qualifying distributions, $946,347; giving activities include $946,382 for programs.
Limitations: Applications not accepted.
Application information: Contributes only to pre-selected organizations.
Directors: John Beyster, Pat Cloherty, Jon Ledecky, William Mays, Doug Mellinger, Mario Morino, Daniel Villanueva.
EIN: 431815206

59511
Lily Lambert McCarthy Foundation
c/o Donald Lewis Wright
1990 18th St. N.W.
Washington, DC 20009

Classified as a private operating foundation in 1980.
Donor(s): Lily Lambert McCarthy.
Financial data (yr. ended 12/31/01): Assets, $252,651 (M); grants paid, $0; gifts received, $433; expenditures, $433; qualifying distributions, $0.
Limitations: Applications not accepted.
Officers and Directors:* Lily Lambert McCarthy,* Pres.; Peter C. Fleming,* V.P.; Donald Lewis Wright,* Secy.-Treas.; John G. McCarthy, John G. McCarthy, Jr.
EIN: 521194544

59512
Eric J. Gewirz Foundation, Inc.
1730 K St. N.W., Ste. 317
Washington, DC 20006

Classified as a private operating foundation in 1997 in MD.
Donor(s): Carl Gewirz, Nancy Gewirz.
Financial data (yr. ended 12/31/00): Assets, $251,866 (M); grants paid, $0; gifts received, $6,500; expenditures, $1,260; qualifying distributions, $1,260.
Limitations: Applications not accepted.
Application information: Contributes only to pre-selected organizations.
Directors: Carl Gewirz, Eric Gewirz, Nancy Gewirz.
EIN: 522007639

59513
American Peace Society
1319 18th St. N.W.
Washington, DC 20036

Established in 1992.
Financial data (yr. ended 04/30/01): Assets, $205,576 (M); grants paid, $0; expenditures, $53,111; qualifying distributions, $53,013; giving activities include $52,771 for programs.
Officers and Directors:* Hon. Jeane J. Kirkpatrick,* Pres.; Garney L. Darrin,* V.P.; Hon. Charles Lichenstein,* V.P.; Joyce I. Horn,* Secy.; Walter E. Beach,* Treas.; J.W. Brabner-Smith, Hon. Anne E. Brunsdale, Karl H. Cerny, William Childs, Valerie A. Earle, L. Eugene Hedberg, Douglas Kirpatrick, Richard M. Scammon, and 5 additional directors.
EIN: 530204659

59514
The Vardaman Family Foundation
4411 Hadfield Ln. N.W.
Washington, DC 20007-2034 (202) 434-5081
Contact: Marianne F. Vardaman, Pres.

Established in 2000 in DC.
Donor(s): John W. Vardaman, Jr.
Financial data (yr. ended 12/31/00): Assets, $199,500 (M); grants paid, $0; gifts received, $170,700; expenditures, $0; qualifying distributions, $0.
Officer and Directors:* Marianne F. Vardaman,* Pres.; Shannon Faucette, Thomas E. Kane, H. Davis Varadman, John F. Vardaman, Jr., John W. Vardaman III.
EIN: 311740631

59515
R. & A. Goldfarb Art Law & Literary Fund
1501 M St., N.W., Ste. 1150
Washington, DC 20005

Financial data (yr. ended 12/31/99): Assets, $194,896 (M); grants paid, $12,500; expenditures, $14,982; qualifying distributions, $12,500.
Limitations: Applications not accepted. Giving primarily in the greater metropolitan Washington, DC, area.
Application information: Contributes only to pre-selected organizations.
Officer: Ronald L. Goldfarb, Pres.
Directors: Joanne Goldfarb, Jody Goldfarb, Nicholas Goldfarb.
EIN: 521987069

59516
The Crafts Center
1001 Connecticut Ave. N.W., Ste. 1138
Washington, DC 20036-5504

Established in 1996 in DC.
Donor(s): Caroline Ramsey Merriam, The Ford Foundation, The Robert J. Stransky Foundation.
Financial data (yr. ended 12/31/99): Assets, $149,166 (M); grants paid, $0; gifts received, $334,491; expenditures, $262,250; qualifying distributions, $259,149; giving activities include $63,541 for programs.
Officers and Directors:* Caroline Ramsey, Pres.; Leah Kaplan, Exec. Dir.; Thomas Birch, Paola Gianturco, Docey Lewis, Caroline Ramsey Merriam, Edward Millard, Andrea Sanford Schmertz, Nina Smith, Sandy Vogelgesang, Wilbur Wright.
EIN: 521489386

59517
District of Columbia American Guild of Organists Foundation
(also known as D.C.A.G.O.)
3325 Resevoir Rd. N.W.
Washington, DC 20007
Application address: 1105 N. Rockingham St., Arlington, VA 22205, tel: (703) 527-6800
Contact: Kyle Ritter, Pres.

Financial data (yr. ended 06/30/99): Assets, $129,542 (M); grants paid, $6,000; expenditures, $8,372; qualifying distributions, $5,946.
Limitations: Giving on a national basis.
Application information: Application form required.
Officers and Directors:* Kyle Ritter, Pres.; Albert Russell,* Treas.; Judith Ceclila Dodge, B. Michael Parrish, Jay Rader.
EIN: 521344942

59518
Nancy Ruyle Dodge Charitable Trust
c/o Nancy Ruyle Dodge
4451 29th St. N.W.
Washington, DC 20008

Established in 1996 in DC.
Donor(s): Nancy Ruyle Dodge, Sarah B. Ruyle.
Financial data (yr. ended 12/31/00): Assets, $128,983 (M); grants paid, $1,050; gifts received, $20,000; expenditures, $6,163; qualifying distributions, $6,080.
Limitations: Applications not accepted.
Application information: Contributes only to pre-selected organizations.
Trustees: Nancy Ruyle Dodge, Norton T. Dodge, Sarah B. Ruyle.
EIN: 526809987

59519
SAL Language and Arts Foundation
c/o Arnold H. Leibowitz
2801 McKinley Pl. N.W.
Washington, DC 20015

Established in 1995 in DC. Classified as a private operating foundation in 1996.
Donor(s): Arnold H. Leibowitz, Sandra A. Leibowitz.
Financial data (yr. ended 12/31/01): Assets, $111,168 (M); grants paid, $12,000; gifts received, $69,431; expenditures, $12,122; qualifying distributions, $12,115.
Limitations: Applications not accepted.
Application information: Contributes only to pre-selected organizations.
Directors: Arnold H. Leibowitz, Sandra A. Leibowitz, Wendy R. Leibowitz.
EIN: 521945368

59520
Near Eastern Art Research Center, Inc.
c/o William Pickering
3900 Cathedral Ave., No. 612A
Washington, DC 20016 (202) 965-9896

Financial data (yr. ended 12/31/99): Assets, $103,710 (M); grants paid, $2,700; expenditures, $3,930; qualifying distributions, $3,930.
Officers and Trustees:* William Russell Pickering,* Chair. and Treas.; Brooke Pickering,* V.P. and Secy.; Wayne D. Barton, Amedeo De Franchis, Hon. Harold M. Keshishian, James M. Keshishian, J. Barry O'Connell, Jr., William T.

Price, Ernest H. Roberts, Paul F. Ryan, Wendel Swan, Raoul E. Tschebull.
EIN: 136168757

59521
Kids, Inc.
4716 32nd St. N.W.
Washington, DC 20008-2224

Established in 1997 in DC.
Donor(s): J. Friedson, E. Friedson.
Financial data (yr. ended 12/31/99): Assets, $97,285 (M); grants paid, $1,145; gifts received, $2,600; expenditures, $2,038; qualifying distributions, $1,145.
Trustee: Edward Friedson.
EIN: 522037568

59522
The Alfred Friendly Foundation
1645 31st St., N.W.
Washington, DC 20007 (202) 416-1691
Application address: c/o Alfred Friendly Press Fellowships, 2000 L St., N.W., No. 200, Washington, DC 20036-4997; E-mail: AFPF@aol.com; URL: http://www.pressfellowships.org
Contact: Susan Albrecht, Exec. Dir.

Established in 1983 in DC.
Donor(s): Alfred Friendly.‡
Financial data (yr. ended 06/30/01): Assets, $91,530 (M); grants paid, $251,547; gifts received, $248,195; expenditures, $435,907; qualifying distributions, $425,039.
Limitations: Giving limited to journalists from Central or Eastern Europe, Africa, Asia, Latin America or the Caribbean.
Publications: Informational brochure (including application guidelines), newsletter.
Application information: Applicants must be fluent in English and have at least 3 years of professional experience. Application form required.
Officers and Directors:* Jean U. Friendly,* Pres. and Treas.; Lucinda F. Murphy,* 1st V.P.; John G. Murphy, Jr.,* 2nd V.P.; Jonathan Friendly,* Secy.; Alfred Friendly, Nicholas Friendly, Victoria F. Maby.
EIN: 521307387
Codes: FD, GTI

59523
Voyager Foundation, Inc.
1027 33rd St. N.W., 2nd Fl.
Washington, DC 20007

Established in 2000 in DC.
Donor(s): Robert Lehrman.
Financial data (yr. ended 12/31/00): Assets, $82,294 (M); grants paid, $0; gifts received, $266,812; expenditures, $184,894; qualifying distributions, $184,069; giving activities include $184,069 for programs.
Directors: Robert Lehrman, Jock Reynolds, Ned Rivkin.
EIN: 522224798

59524
O Street Museum Foundation
2020 O St. N.W.
Washington, DC 20036-5912

Established in 1998 in DC.
Financial data (yr. ended 12/31/01): Assets, $79,813 (M); grants paid, $0; expenditures, $62,980; qualifying distributions, $62,282; giving activities include $62,282 for programs.
Officers: H.H. Leonards, Pres.; Steve Goldman, Secy.; Jeffrey Neuman, Treas.
EIN: 311550078

59525
National Foundation for Alternative Medicine
c/o Berkley W. Bedell
1155 Connecticut Ave. N.W., Ste. 300
Washington, DC 20036-4327

Financial data (yr. ended 12/31/99): Assets, $72,403 (M); grants paid, $0; gifts received, $601,032; expenditures, $531,399; qualifying distributions, $531,399; giving activities include $371,999 for programs.
Officer: Berkley Bedell, Pres.
EIN: 421471957

59526
Kyorin Educational Foundation
2000 L St. N.W.
Washington, DC 20036-4907

Established in 1998.
Financial data (yr. ended 12/31/99): Assets, $57,300 (M); grants paid, $0; gifts received, $24,400; expenditures, $14,119; qualifying distributions, $0; giving activities include $14,119 for programs.
Officer: Katsuro Sakoh, Pres.
EIN: 521841833

59527
Victoria G. Gewirz Foundation, Inc.
1730 K St. N.W., Ste. 317
Washington, DC 20006

Established in 1998 in MD.
Donor(s): Victoria G. Gewirz.
Financial data (yr. ended 12/31/00): Assets, $38,362 (M); grants paid, $0; gifts received, $6,500; expenditures, $1,316; qualifying distributions, $0.
Directors: Carl Gewirz, Nancy Gewirz, Victoria G. Gewirz.
EIN: 311494319

59528
Global Commitment Foundation, Inc.
3544 Winfield Ln., N.W.
Washington, DC 20007

Financial data (yr. ended 12/31/00): Assets, $37,773 (M); grants paid, $0; gifts received, $75; expenditures, $9,838; qualifying distributions, $9,758; giving activities include $7,125 for programs.
Officers and Directors:* Sandra Alpert,* Pres.; Annette Friedman, Secy.; Arthur Jaffe,* Treas.
EIN: 521898911

59529
Friends of World Maritime University, Inc.
1331 Pennsylvania Ave. N.W., Ste. 560
Washington, DC 20004-1745

Established in 1984 in DC.
Donor(s): Bernard Zagorin.
Financial data (yr. ended 12/31/99): Assets, $32,726 (M); grants paid, $1,823; gifts received, $24,071; expenditures, $4,609; qualifying distributions, $4,324; giving activities include $4,324 for programs.
Limitations: Giving primarily in Malmo, Sweden.
Officers and Directors:* Sheldon H. Kinney,* Chair.; Gerald A. Malia,* Pres.; Henry Bell,* V.P.; Richard T. Soper,* V.P.; Robert L. Sullivan,* Secy.-Treas.; Charles R. Cushing, Sheila Dearybury, A.E. Henn, Caryn Houck, Marcus J. Johnson, James McNamara, Chuck Raymond, Kevin Woelflein.
EIN: 521320023

59530
National Association for Objectivity in Science
6856 Eastern Ave. N.W., Ste. 318
Washington, DC 20012-2165

Established in 1998 in DC.
Donor(s): Herman B. Bouma.
Financial data (yr. ended 12/31/01): Assets, $30,381 (M); grants paid, $0; gifts received, $23,050; expenditures, $19,344; qualifying distributions, $19,194; giving activities include $19,194 for programs.
Officer and Directors:* Herman B. Bouma,* Exec. Dir.; Angela M. Bouma.
EIN: 522146905

59531
The Institute for Technology in Health Care
1759 Q St. N.W.
Washington, DC 20009-2492 (202) 667-5041
Contact: Cesar A. Caceres, M.D.

Classified as a private operating foundation in 1985.
Donor(s): Cesar A. Caceres, M.D., Craig W. Wallace, W. Raymond Mize, Jr., Schering Sales Corp.
Financial data (yr. ended 12/31/99): Assets, $18,421 (M); grants paid, $2,148; gifts received, $1,500; expenditures, $2,439; qualifying distributions, $2,148.
Limitations: Giving primarily in Washington, DC.
Application information: Application form not required.
Officers and Directors:* W. Raymond Mize, Jr.,* Pres.; Stanley J. Kuliczkowski,* V.P. and Secy.; Craig W. Wallace,* Treas.
EIN: 521292049

59532
The Association of Computer & Information Science-Engineering in Minority Institutions
P.O. Box 30
Washington, DC 20059

Established in 1992 in DC. Classified as a private operating foundation in 1996.
Donor(s): National Science Foundation.
Financial data (yr. ended 08/31/00): Assets, $18,394 (M); grants paid, $0; expenditures, $20,231; qualifying distributions, $19,749; giving activities include $20,231 for programs.
Directors: Richard A. Alo, Exec. Dir.; Lester Jack Briggs, Vivian Fielder, Elva Jones, Andrea Lawrence, Forbes Lewis, Joseph Monroe, J.D. Oliver, Lawrence Oliver, John Trimble, Ramon Vasquez-Espinosa, Deidre Williams, Robert Willis.
EIN: 521779029

59533
Centre for Science and Environment
c/o Stuart Lemle
1775 Eye St. N.W., Ste. 950
Washington, DC 20006

Donor(s): Rita Duggal, Arun Duggal, Madhu John.
Financial data (yr. ended 12/31/00): Assets, $18,020 (M); grants paid, $5,500; gifts received, $5,500; expenditures, $31,400; qualifying distributions, $5,500.
Limitations: Applications not accepted. Giving limited to India.
Application information: Contributes only to pre-selected organizations.
Officers: Anil Agarwal, Chair.; Sunita Narain, Pres.; Gita Kavarama, V.P.; S. Sudha, Secy.
Board Members: Pierre Calame, Lincoln Chen, Sam Pitroda.
EIN: 521966278

59534
RUMOR Foundation
4627 Hilltop Terr. S.E.
Washington, DC 20019
Contact: Kevin Robbins, Pres.

Established in 1998.
Financial data (yr. ended 06/30/00): Assets, $16,835 (M); grants paid, $3,000; gifts received, $31,000; expenditures, $58,437; qualifying distributions, $57,413; giving activities include $48,900 for programs.
Officers: Kevin Robbins, Pres.; Janet Robbins, Secy.; Artusta Robbins, Treas.
EIN: 522123014

59535
D.C. Coaches Association, Inc.
c/o Frank Parks, Spingarn High School
26th & Benning Rd. N.E.
Washington, DC 20002 (202) 724-4964

Financial data (yr. ended 12/31/01): Assets, $16,094 (M); grants paid, $0; gifts received, $15,500; expenditures, $46,183; qualifying distributions, $0.
Officers: Bruce Bradford, Pres.; Bobby Richardson, 1st V.P.; Frank Young, 2nd V.P.; Willie Stewart, 3rd V.P.
EIN: 237067223

59536
Eleanor & George Kokiko, Sr. Foundation, Inc.
700 New Hampshire Ave. N.W., Ste. 718
Washington, DC 20037-2406
Application address: P.O. Box 5972, Bethesda, MD 20824
Contact: Elaine Kokiko, Pres.

Donor(s): Elaine Kokiko.
Financial data (yr. ended 12/31/01): Assets, $14,074 (M); grants paid, $0; gifts received, $243; expenditures, $294; qualifying distributions, $294.
Officers: Elaine Kokiko, Pres.; Jack Moshnian, V.P. and Treas.; Martin Shulman, Secy.
EIN: 522006451

59537
Mediterranean Affairs, Inc.
984 National Press Bldg.
14th & H Sts. N.W.
Washington, DC 20045

Donor(s): Minos X. Kyriakos.
Financial data (yr. ended 12/31/00): Assets, $11,559 (M); grants paid, $0; gifts received, $200,009; expenditures, $167,164; qualifying distributions, $167,164; giving activities include $129,569 for programs.
Officers: Minos X. Kyriakos, Pres.; Nikolaos A. Stavrou, V.P. and Treas.; Edward C. Dillery, Secy.
Trustees: Lucien N. Nedzi, Maria A. Stamoulas.
EIN: 521598843

59538
Research Associates of America, Inc.
1718 M St. N.W., No. 245
Washington, DC 20036

Established in 1988 in DC.
Donor(s): E.A.S.T. Dept.
Financial data (yr. ended 09/30/00): Assets, $11,343 (M); grants paid, $0; gifts received, $479,547; expenditures, $486,721; qualifying distributions, $499,982; giving activities include $499,982 for programs.
Officers: Richard C. Mayer, Pres.; Richard A. Plumb, Secy.-Treas.
EIN: 521541526

59539
Assassination Archives and Research Center, Inc.
1003 K St. N.W., Ste. 204
Washington, DC 20001

Financial data (yr. ended 12/31/00): Assets, $7,963 (M); grants paid, $0; gifts received, $13,294; expenditures, $13,094; qualifying distributions, $0.
Officer and Directors:* James H. Lesar,* Pres.; Daniel Alcorn, Mark Allen, Bernard Fensterwald III, Mary Ferrell, Katherine Kinsella, Chip Selby, David R. Wrone.
EIN: 521354369

59540
SGJIC Scholarship Fund Trust
c/o Grafton J. Daniels
P.O. Box 48387
Washington, DC 20002-0387
Application address: 14317 Perrywood Dr., Burtonsville, MD 20866, tel.: (301) 384-6063
Contact: Carmen D. Campbell, Chair.

Financial data (yr. ended 12/31/01): Assets, $6,352 (M); grants paid, $3,000; expenditures, $3,735; qualifying distributions, $3,000.
Limitations: Giving limited to Washington, DC.
Application information: Application form required.
Officers and Trustees:* Rev. Reginald G. Blaxton,* Chair.; Deborah D. Boddie,* Vice-Chair.; Martha C. Johnson,* Secy.; Grace H. Davis, Linda R. Deane, Rev. John C. Hayden, Rev. Richard C. Martin, Doris D. Quander, Frank L. Shuford, Jr., James Williams, La Monte G. Wyche, Sr.
Scholarship Committee Members: Carmen D. Campbell, Chair.; Vida Anderson, Vice-Chair.; Yvonne Miles-Scott, Treas.; Robert A. Brown, William Byrd, Rosemarie L. Duncan, Barbara Ford, Ethel Halsey, Judith S. Hutchinson, Col. John L. Jones, Margaret McDaniels, Lavinia Obedjimi, Alicia Olive, Doris Payne, Jackline Vickerie, Diane Wesley.
EIN: 522070666

59541
The Worklife Institute
2401 Tracy Pl. N.W.
Washington, DC 20008

Established in 1999 in IL.
Donor(s): John E. Robson, Margaret Z. Robson.
Financial data (yr. ended 12/31/01): Assets, $2,762 (M); grants paid, $0; expenditures, $1,346; qualifying distributions, $0.
Limitations: Applications not accepted.
Application information: Contributes only to pre-selected organizations.
Officers and Directors:* John E. Robson,* Pres. and Treas.; Margaret Z. Robson,* Secy.; Douglas O. Robson.
EIN: 943327783

59542
Washington Intern Foundation
c/o Kris Polly
111 2nd St. N.E.
Washington, DC 20002

Financial data (yr. ended 06/30/00): Assets, $620 (M); grants paid, $0; gifts received, $5,000; expenditures, $14,606; qualifying distributions, $12,786; giving activities include $8,533 for programs.
Officers: Kris Polly, Pres.; Laura Polly, Secy.
EIN: 541815538

59543
Mal Whitfield Foundation
1322 28th St. S.E.
Washington, DC 20020

Financial data (yr. ended 12/31/00): Assets, $0 (M); grants paid, $5,756; gifts received, $10,000; expenditures, $12,550; qualifying distributions, $0.
Officer: Malvin Whitfield, Pres.
EIN: 251623581

FLORIDA

59544
Harbor Branch Oceanographic Institution, Inc.
(Formerly Harbor Branch Foundation)
5600 U.S. 1 N.
Fort Pierce, FL 34946
URL: http://www.hboi.edu

Established in 1971; classified as a private operating foundation in 1974.
Financial data (yr. ended 12/31/99): Assets, $156,651,000 (M); grants paid, $12,193; gifts received, $25,915,408; expenditures, $32,930,658; qualifying distributions, $35,533,864; giving activities include $19,106,706 for programs.
Publications: Annual report, informational brochure (including application guidelines).
Officers and Trustees:* J. Seward Johnson, Jr.,* Chair. and C.E.O.; Richard J. Herman,* Pres. and Managing Dir.; Louis R. Hewitt, Secy.-Treas.; Stephen M. Farinacci, Cont.; Charles H. Bussmann, and 4 additional trustees.
Directors: Robert F. Carlson, Jennifer U. Johnson Duke, Charles Jefford, and 6 additional directors.
EIN: 591542017
Codes: GTI

59545
Charles Hosmer Morse Foundation, Inc.
P.O. Box 40
Winter Park, FL 32790

Donor(s): Hugh F. McKean.‡
Financial data (yr. ended 12/31/99): Assets, $50,737,765 (M); grants paid, $0; gifts received, $4,797,089; expenditures, $2,361,844; qualifying distributions, $2,935,486; giving activities include $1,970,941 for programs.
Officers and Trustees:* Harold A. Ward III,* Chair. and Pres.; Victor E. Woodman,* V.P.; Ann Gerken,* Secy.; Richard M. Strauss,* Treas.; Garcia Anderson, Winifred Clive, Susan Gibbs, Sandra Ogden, Ellen B. Pettitt, Ann Saurman, Lelia Trismen.
EIN: 591659392

59546
Bok Tower Gardens Foundation, Inc.
(Formerly The American Foundation, Inc.)
1151 Tower Blvd.
Lake Wales, FL 33853-3412

Incorporated in 1925 in DE.
Donor(s): Edward W. Bok,‡ Elsie Latimer, Shirley W. Fogg, Fulton Norris,‡ Frank M. Hubbard.
Financial data (yr. ended 06/30/01): Assets, $49,479,687 (M); grants paid, $8,000; gifts received, $420,486; expenditures, $4,527,216; qualifying distributions, $3,682,767; giving activities include $3,397,967 for programs.

59546—FLORIDA

Publications: Annual report, informational brochure.
Officers and Trustees:* A. Bronson Thayer, Chair.; Robert P. Sullivan, Pres.; M. Lewis Hall, Jr.,* Secy.; Joan W. Newton,* Treas.; Louise B. Adams, Hilary M. Bok, Suzanne L. Botts, Mary H. Cain, John Germany, Frank M. Hubbard, D. Burke Kibler III, and 9 additional trustees.
EIN: 231352009

59547
Archbold Expeditions, Inc.
330 Island Rd.
Palm Beach, FL 33480

Incorporated in 1971 in PA.
Financial data (yr. ended 12/31/01): Assets, $42,919,390 (M); grants paid, $0; gifts received, $2,536,201; expenditures, $3,629,464; qualifying distributions, $2,711,119; giving activities include $1,602,037 for programs.
Officers: Frances Archbold Hufty, Chair.; Mary Page Hufty, M.D., Pres.; Daniel S. Alegria, V.P.; Frances H. Leidy, V.P.; Lela P. Love, Secy.; Sebastian Atucha, Treas.
Trustees: Donna Hufty Lloyd George, Robert Lloyd George, Walter C. Sedgwick, Carter R. Leidy III.
EIN: 236400408

59548
The William J. von Liebig Foundation, Inc.
8889 Pelican Bay Blvd., Ste. 403
Naples, FL 34108 (239) 513-2229
E-mail: liebigfoundation@draxgroup.com; *URL:* http://www.vonliebigfoundation.com
Contact: Linda Hamilton, Pres.

Established in 1997 in FL.
Donor(s): William J. von Liebig.‡
Financial data (yr. ended 12/31/00): Assets, $42,542,640 (M); grants paid, $2,487,959; expenditures, $2,904,291; qualifying distributions, $2,449,860.
Limitations: Giving limited to the U.S.
Publications: Informational brochure (including application guidelines).
Application information: Application form not required.
Officers and Directors:* Suzanne von Liebig,* Chair.; Linda Hamilton,* Pres.; Jean A. Goggins, Ph.D.
EIN: 311470886
Codes: FD

59549
Montgomery Botanical Center
(Formerly The Montgomery Foundation, Inc.)
11901 Old Cutler Rd.
Miami, FL 33156-4242

Established in 1959 in DC.
Financial data (yr. ended 12/31/99): Assets, $38,791,908 (M); grants paid, $0; gifts received, $302,230; expenditures, $1,740,515; qualifying distributions, $1,601,458; giving activities include $1,601,458 for programs.
Officers and Directors:* Jeanne Bellamy,* Pres.; Arthur Montgomery,* V.P.; Nicholas Kelly, Peter Manz, Karl Smiley.
EIN: 136153649

59550
The Mineral Trust
P.O. Box 22190
Fort Lauderdale, FL 33335

Established in 1988 in FL.
Donor(s): Barry Yampol.
Financial data (yr. ended 12/31/99): Assets, $30,145,907 (M); grants paid, $0; gifts received, $412,320; expenditures, $15,338; qualifying distributions, $61,747; giving activities include $61,747 for programs.
Trustees: Alvin Martin, Barry Yampol, David Yampol.
EIN: 650086122

59551
Jay I. Kislak Foundation, Inc.
7900 Miami Lakes Dr., W.
Miami Lakes, FL 33016-5897

Established in 1984.
Donor(s): J.I. Kislak, Inc., Foundation of Jewish Philanthropies, Kislak Family Fund, Inc., The Greater Miami Jewish Gederation.
Financial data (yr. ended 12/31/01): Assets, $16,858,681 (M); grants paid, $30,250; gifts received, $855,495; expenditures, $137,359; qualifying distributions, $576,575.
Limitations: Applications not accepted. Giving primarily in NC.
Application information: Contributes only to pre-selected organizations.
Officers and Trustees:* Jay I. Kislak,* Pres.; Jonathan I. Kislak,* V.P.; Thomas Bartelmo,* Secy.-Treas.; Jean H. Kislak.
EIN: 592438331

59552
Wayne M. Densch Charities, Inc.
P.O. Box 536845
Orlando, FL 32853 (407) 896-3884
Contact: Application Committee

Established in 1992 in MI.
Financial data (yr. ended 12/31/01): Assets, $16,604,318 (M); grants paid, $252,408; gifts received, $10; expenditures, $901,079; qualifying distributions, $818,332.
Application information: Application form not required.
Officers and Director:* Leonard E. Williams,* Pres.; John A. Williams, V.P.
EIN: 582013696
Codes: FD

59553
Arthur and Holly Magill Foundation
c/o Steve Newman
2000 Glades Rd., Ste. 400
Boca Raton, FL 33431

Established in 1981 in SC.
Donor(s): Arthur F. Magill,‡ Alice H. Magill.
Financial data (yr. ended 06/30/00): Assets, $15,361,092 (M); grants paid, $456,120; expenditures, $794,858; qualifying distributions, $544,420.
Limitations: Applications not accepted. Giving primarily in Greenville, SC.
Application information: Contributes only to pre-selected organizations.
Officers and Trustees:* Holly H. Magill,* Chair.; Arturo Melosi,* Exec. Dir.; Gianfranco D'Augustino, Holly Melosi, Steve Newman.
EIN: 570713587
Codes: FD

59554
Martin Z. Margulies Foundation, Inc.
445 Grand Bay Dr., Ste. 210
Key Biscayne, FL 33149

Donor(s): Martin Z. Margulies.
Financial data (yr. ended 07/31/01): Assets, $15,300,888 (M); grants paid, $0; gifts received, $2,625,153; expenditures, $25,598; qualifying distributions, $0.
Officers and Director:* Martin Z. Margulies,* Pres.; Katherine Hinds, Secy.
EIN: 592130476

59555
Ida Mae Stevens Foundation, Inc.
4595 Lexington Ave., Ste.100
Jacksonville, FL 32210-2058 (904) 387-5400
Contact: Douglas J. Milne, Tr.

Established in 1967 in FL.
Donor(s): Virgil A. Stevens.‡
Financial data (yr. ended 12/31/00): Assets, $14,003,130 (M); grants paid, $730,369; expenditures, $1,780,280; qualifying distributions, $1,147,396; giving activities include $367,980 for programs.
Limitations: Giving limited to Jacksonville, FL.
Publications: Financial statement.
Application information: Application form required.
Trustees: G.L. Garnett Ashby, Ben W. Hightower, David Lemmel, Douglas J. Milne.
EIN: 591746148
Codes: FD

59556
Tampa Bay Retirement Center, Inc.
(also known as American Academy and Institute for Human Reason, Inc.)
1514 E. Chelsea St.
Tampa, FL 33610

Established in 1986 in CO.
Donor(s): Charles W. Lerch.‡
Financial data (yr. ended 07/21/01): Assets, $12,018,409 (M); grants paid, $0; expenditures, $11,426,858; qualifying distributions, $1,406,363; giving activities include $1,406,577 for programs.
Directors: Robert Leasum, Robert Mudge, Frank Rorvick.
EIN: 742382236

59557
Geraldine Livingston Foundation
P.O. Box 113, Rte. 2
Greenville, FL 32331

Established in 1997 in FL.
Financial data (yr. ended 12/31/99): Assets, $11,403,053 (M); grants paid, $16,000; gifts received, $21,750; expenditures, $127,008; qualifying distributions, $49,429; giving activities include $33,425 for programs.
Limitations: Applications not accepted.
Application information: Contributes only to pre-selected organizations.
Trustees: Christopher Addison, Sylvia Addison, John M. Finlayson, Dearl L. Hemphill, Julie R. Miller, Joseph O. Milligan, Jr., Summer A. Reed, Rosemary L. Ripley.
EIN: 593344093

59558
The Garner Foundation, Inc.
333 N.E. 23rd St.
Miami, FL 33137
Contact: Gerald W. Moore, John M. Garner, and James W. Moore

Established in 1987 in FL as a family foundation.
Financial data (yr. ended 03/31/01): Assets, $11,286,959 (M); grants paid, $690,650; expenditures, $706,310; qualifying distributions, $692,525.
Limitations: Giving primarily in FL and NC.
Application information: Application form not required.
Officers and Directors:* Alberta W. Garner,* Pres.; John Michael Garner,* V.P.; Beverly Garner Graves,* V.P.; James W. Moore,* Secy.; Kathryn

Anne Paulk,* Treas.; Gerald W. Moore, Janice Gayle Topping, Mary Garner Wright.
EIN: 311471961
Codes: FD

59559
Wilkes-Desmond Educational Foundation
c/o Downey and Downey
P.O. Box 2345
Palm Beach, FL 33480-2345

Donor(s): William C. Desmond.‡
Financial data (yr. ended 05/31/01): Assets, $9,221,707 (M); grants paid, $405,481; gifts received, $150,967; expenditures, $568,333; qualifying distributions, $405,481.
Limitations: Applications not accepted.
Application information: Contributes only to pre-selected organizations.
Trustee: David Beuttenmuller.
EIN: 650961676
Codes: FD

59560
Robert Rauschenberg Foundation
P.O. Box 54
Captiva, FL 33924

Established in 1990 in DE.
Donor(s): Robert Rauschenberg.
Financial data (yr. ended 05/31/00): Assets, $8,230,145 (M); grants paid, $0; gifts received, $1,933,500; expenditures, $183,305; qualifying distributions, $165,856; giving activities include $165,856 for programs.
Officers: Robert Rauschenberg, Chair.; Darryl Pottorf, V.P.; David White, V.P.; Bradley Jeffries, Secy.-Treas.
Trustees: William Goldston, Bennet H. Grutman, Donald J. Saff.
EIN: 650200989

59561
The Terra Foundation, Inc.
6101 Castaways Ln.
Sanibel, FL 33957

Established in 1988 in MA.
Donor(s): Jerry L. Holsinger.
Financial data (yr. ended 12/31/01): Assets, $7,748,259 (M); grants paid, $0; expenditures, $203,012; qualifying distributions, $121,568; giving activities include $46,460 for programs.
Limitations: Applications not accepted. Giving primarily in New York, NY.
Application information: Contributes only to pre-selected organizations.
Officers: Constance A. Holsinger, Pres.; Jerry L. Holsinger, Treas.
Director: Elizabeth Belle.
EIN: 222982226

59562
Orange Bowl Committee, Inc.
601 Brickell Key Dr., Ste. 206
Miami, FL 33131

Established as a private operating foundation in 1995.
Financial data (yr. ended 04/30/00): Assets, $7,441,497 (M); grants paid, $0; gifts received, $2,360,738; expenditures, $10,552,825; qualifying distributions, $10,485,716; giving activities include $9,703,357 for programs.
Limitations: Applications not accepted. Giving primarily in FL.
Application information: Contributes only to pre-selected organizations.
Officers: Edgar Jones, Pres.; Sherril W. Hudson, V.P.; Susan Norton, V.P.; Keith Tribble, Exec. Dir.
EIN: 590384382

59563
Marell Foundation, Inc.
P.O. Box 1291
Tarpon Springs, FL 34688-1291
Contact: John Pace, Secy.-Treas.

Established in 1997 in FL.
Donor(s): Carol E. Martin.
Financial data (yr. ended 04/30/01): Assets, $7,260,788 (M); grants paid, $0; gifts received, $0; expenditures, $248,349; qualifying distributions, $115,198; giving activities include $115,198 for programs.
Limitations: Giving primarily in Tarpon Springs, FL.
Officers: Carol E. Martin, Pres.; George Klimis, V.P.; Paul Martin, V.P.
EIN: 593451317

59564
The Marvin & Helene Gralnick Foundation, Inc.
2340 Perwinkle Way, No. M-1
Sanibel, FL 33957

Established in 1993 in FL.
Financial data (yr. ended 09/30/01): Assets, $7,073,431 (M); grants paid, $2,500; expenditures, $184,776; qualifying distributions, $405,500.
Limitations: Applications not accepted. Giving primarily in FL.
Application information: Contributes only to pre-selected organizations.
Officers and Directors:* Marvin J. Gralnick,* Pres.; Helene B. Gralnick,* Secy.-Treas.; Leslie C. Giordani.
EIN: 650445458

59565
Eleanor Patterson Reeves Foundation, Inc.
169 Seaview Ave.
Palm Beach, FL 33480

Established in 1998 in FL.
Financial data (yr. ended 12/31/01): Assets, $6,838,241 (M); grants paid, $333,641; expenditures, $452,190; qualifying distributions, $387,391.
Limitations: Applications not accepted. Giving primarily in FL.
Application information: Contributes only to pre-selected organizations.
Directors: Patricia A. Myura, Exec. Dir.; Anthony Myura.
EIN: 656230803
Codes: FD

59566
Watson Clinic Foundation, Inc.
1430 Lakeland Hills Blvd.
Lakeland, FL 33805 (863) 680-7113
Contact: Angelo P. Spoto, Jr., M.D., Pres.

Established in 1986 in FL.
Donor(s): William F. McKee, Jean Tanous, Intermedics, Watson Clinic, SciMed, Medtronic, Inc.
Financial data (yr. ended 12/31/00): Assets, $6,421,164 (M); grants paid, $6,600; gifts received, $5,710,281; expenditures, $852,550; qualifying distributions, $850,674; giving activities include $307,817 for programs.
Limitations: Giving limited to Latin America, the Caribbean, and Asia.
Application information: Awards by nomination only for third-year medical students attending the Univ. of FL College of Medicine or Duke Univ. School of Medicine.
Officers and Directors:* Glen A. Barden, M.D.,* Chair.; Steven T. Flax, M.D.,* Pres.; Robert H. Chapman, M.D.,* V.P.; Stanley L. Piotrowski,* Secy.-Treas.; Henry D. McIntosh, M.D., Dudley P. Towne, and 20 additional directors.
EIN: 591100876

59567
Historical Society of Martin County, Inc.
825 N.E. Ocean Blvd.
Stuart, FL 34996-1696

Classified as a private operating foundation in 1987.
Financial data (yr. ended 06/30/01): Assets, $5,688,149 (M); grants paid, $0; gifts received, $96,706; expenditures, $514,625; qualifying distributions, $330,345; giving activities include $410,590 for programs.
Limitations: Applications not accepted. Giving limited to FL.
Application information: Contributes only to pre-selected organizations.
Officers and Trustees:* Carol S. Waxler,* Pres.; Matthew L. Jones,* V.P.; Jane Dickerson,* Secy.; David A. Ralicki,* Treas.; Elizabeth Press, Exec. Dir.; Tom Prestagard, Exec. Dir.; Jane M. Buss, Alan P. Danforth, Bruce Hines, Edward Winpenny, and 7 additional trustees.
EIN: 590913326

59568
Weinberger Family Foundation, Inc.
4469 White Cedar Ln.
Delray Beach, FL 33445

Established in 1991 in FL.
Donor(s): Saul Weinberger.
Financial data (yr. ended 12/31/01): Assets, $4,557,213 (M); grants paid, $167,650; gifts received, $517,215; expenditures, $171,815; qualifying distributions, $170,609.
Limitations: Applications not accepted.
Application information: Contributes only to pre-selected organizations.
Officer: Saul Weinberger, Pres.
EIN: 650245748
Codes: FD2

59569
The Dharma Foundation III, Inc.
(Formerly Worrell Foundation, Inc.)
255 N.E. 6th Ave.
Delray Beach, FL 33483

Established in 1990 in DE and FL.
Donor(s): Thomas E. Worrell, Jr., Odette A. Worrell, The Shaffer Worrell Charitable Lead Trust, First Union National Bank.
Financial data (yr. ended 11/30/01): Assets, $4,534,252 (M); grants paid, $1,109,963; gifts received, $1,102,257; expenditures, $1,153,593; qualifying distributions, $1,109,963.
Limitations: Applications not accepted. Giving primarily in Delray Beach, FL, and Taos, NM; some funding also in New York, NY.
Application information: Contributes only to pre-selected organizations.
Officers and Directors:* Odette A. Worrell,* Pres.; Robert M. Smither, Jr.,* V.P. and Secy.-Treas.
EIN: 650239353
Codes: FD

59570
Hamlin Terrace Foundation
c/o Lawrence E. White
625 Waltham Ave.
Orlando, FL 32809

Established in 1997 in FL.
Donor(s): Patrick L. White, James W. Duncan, Joseph M. Dimino.
Financial data (yr. ended 03/31/01): Assets, $4,531,181 (M); grants paid, $300,000; gifts

received, $192,310; expenditures, $308,899; qualifying distributions, $1,619,952.
Limitations: Applications not accepted. Giving primarily in Orlando, FL.
Application information: Contributes only to pre-selected organizations.
Trustee: Lawrence E. White.
EIN: 593579317
Codes: FD

59571
C. E. Mendez Foundation, Inc.
601 S. Magnolia Ave.
Tampa, FL 33606-2725 (813) 251-3600
Contact: Charles E. Mendez, Jr., Pres.

Classified as a private operating foundation in 1982.
Donor(s): Hillsborough School Contract.
Financial data (yr. ended 06/30/01): Assets, $4,501,107 (M); grants paid, $19,125; gifts received, $1,261,886; expenditures, $2,032,430; qualifying distributions, $2,032,430; giving activities include $1,715,848 for programs.
Limitations: Giving primarily in Atlanta, GA.
Officers: Charles E. Mendez, Jr., Pres. and Treas.; Lawrence Mendez, V.P. and Secy.; Cynthia D. Coney, V.P.; Anita Mendez, V.P.; Yvonne Mendez, V.P.; Diana Mendez, Treas.
Directors: Michael Annis, Dr. Charles F. Mitchell.
EIN: 591086491

59572
Janet A. Carrington Foundation
140 Royal Palm Way, Ste. 205
Palm Beach, FL 33480

Financial data (yr. ended 12/31/99): Assets, $4,368,195 (M); grants paid, $1,500; gifts received, $3,601,000; expenditures, $27,765; qualifying distributions, $7,676.
Trustees: Robert L. Andrews, Janet A. Carrington, Robert G. Simses.
EIN: 061519819

59573
The Research Charitable Trust
P.O. Box 22190
Fort Lauderdale, FL 33335-2190

Donor(s): Barry Yampol.
Financial data (yr. ended 12/31/99): Assets, $4,057,438 (M); grants paid, $0; expenditures, $1,227; qualifying distributions, $4,364; giving activities include $294 for programs.
Trustees: Nathan Bellow, Frederick Galland, Barry Yampol.
EIN: 222249971

59574
American Friends of the Everest Foundation
(Formerly Kidmat Yerushalayim, Inc.)
1674 Meridian Ave., No. 408
Miami Beach, FL 33139

Donor(s): Irving T. Moskowitz, M.D.
Financial data (yr. ended 12/31/00): Assets, $4,044,096 (M); grants paid, $0; gifts received, $1,089; expenditures, $19,627; qualifying distributions, $0.
Directors: Oren Ben-Ezra, Cherna Moskowitz, Irving T. Moskowitz, M.D.
EIN: 113043242

59575
Woerner World Ministries, Inc.
777 S. Flagler Dr., Ste. 1100
West Palm Beach, FL 33401

Established in 1998 in FL.
Donor(s): Woerner Management, Inc., Woerner Foundation for World Missions, Inc.
Financial data (yr. ended 06/30/00): Assets, $3,939,696 (M); grants paid, $1,022,499; gifts received, $2,166,257; expenditures, $1,981,974; qualifying distributions, $1,871,501; giving activities include $1,378,248 for programs.
Limitations: Applications not accepted. Giving on a national and international basis.
Application information: Contributes only to pre-selected organizations.
Officers: Lester J. Woerner, Chair.; Larry J. Woerner, Pres.; Donald O. Young, V.P. and Secy.; Darren J. Woerner, V.P. and Treas.
EIN: 650907241
Codes: FD

59576
The Eunice Pitt Odom Semmes Foundation
4595 Lexington Ave.
Jacksonville, FL 32210
Contact: Edward McCarthy, Jr., Tr.

Established in 1989 in FL.
Donor(s): Eunice Pitt Odom Semmes.‡
Financial data (yr. ended 12/31/01): Assets, $3,914,671 (M); grants paid, $236,500; expenditures, $281,576; qualifying distributions, $280,161.
Limitations: Giving on a national basis.
Trustees: John W. Donahoo, Jr., Edward McCarthy, Jr., First Guaranty Bank & Trust Co.
EIN: 592940872
Codes: FD2

59577
Herman E. & Helen H. Turner Foundation Trust
5004 Riverview Blvd. W.
Bradenton, FL 34209

Established in 1998.
Donor(s): Herman E. Turner Trust.
Financial data (yr. ended 12/31/00): Assets, $3,878,371 (M); grants paid, $211,000; expenditures, $267,353; qualifying distributions, $229,422.
Limitations: Applications not accepted. Giving primarily in FL.
Application information: Contributes only to pre-selected organizations.
Trustees: Richard E. Turner, Sr., Richard E. Turner, Jr.
EIN: 656260563
Codes: FD2

59578
Society for the Prevention of Cruelty to Animals of Manatee County, Inc.
1301 6th Ave. W., Ste. 600
Bradenton, FL 34205

Financial data (yr. ended 12/31/01): Assets, $3,602,452 (M); grants paid, $0; gifts received, $674,842; expenditures, $749,069; qualifying distributions, $0.
Officers: W.E. Wentzel, Pres.; Mary E. Parker, V.P.; R.W. Pratt, Treas.
Directors: Paul Bartley, Robert Blalock, Woodrow Young.
EIN: 590826963

59579
Driscoll Foundation, Inc.
(Formerly Key Largo Foundation, Inc.)
12555 Orange Dr., Ste. 101
Davie, FL 33330
Application address: 332 Minnesota St., Ste. 2100, St. Paul, MN 55101-1308, tel.: (651) 228-0935
Contact: W. John Driscoll, Pres.

Established in 1998 in FL.
Financial data (yr. ended 12/31/01): Assets, $3,566,958 (M); grants paid, $189,000; expenditures, $192,372; qualifying distributions, $188,116.
Limitations: Giving largely in, but not exclusively to, the metropolitan areas of St. Paul and Minneapolis, MN.
Application information: Application form not required.
Officers and Directors:* W. John Driscoll,* Pres.; Frank E. Gardner,* V.P.; Michael J. Giefer, Secy.-Treas.; John B. Driscoll, Rudolph W. Driscoll.
EIN: 591142501
Codes: FD2

59580
The Foundation for Concepts in Education, Inc.
770 E. Atlantic Ave., Ste. 201
Delray Beach, FL 33483-5328

Established in 1996 in FL. Classified as a private operating foundation in 1997.
Donor(s): Diane F. Kessenich.
Financial data (yr. ended 02/28/00): Assets, $3,556,931 (M); grants paid, $725; expenditures, $3,306,747; qualifying distributions, $3,682,068; giving activities include $3,231,265 for programs.
Officer and Directors:* Diane F. Kessenich,* Pres.; John O'Brien, Sr. Mary Reap.
EIN: 650652535

59581
The Lou Church Educational Foundation, Inc.
1700 N.E. 26th St.
Wilton Manors, FL 33305

Established in 1986 in FL.
Financial data (yr. ended 12/31/00): Assets, $3,115,750 (M); grants paid, $40,000; gifts received, $19,212; expenditures, $135,049; qualifying distributions, $40,000.
Limitations: Applications not accepted. Giving primarily in AL, MI, NY and PA.
Application information: Contributes only to pre-selected organizations.
Officers and Directors:* Robert Helmholdt,* Pres.; Ike Eikevik,* Secy.; Brion Foulke,* Treas.; Mike Holt.
EIN: 592761512

59582
Florida Charities Foundation
c/o SunTrust Banks, Inc.
P.O. Box 3838
Orlando, FL 32802-3838
Application address: c/o John Tiedtke, Rollins College, Winter Park, FL 32789

Established in 1959 in FL.
Donor(s): John Tiedtke.
Financial data (yr. ended 07/31/01): Assets, $2,945,748 (M); grants paid, $621,562; gifts received, $65,000; expenditures, $642,772; qualifying distributions, $630,911.
Limitations: Giving primarily in central FL.
Trustee: SunTrust Banks, Inc.
EIN: 596125203
Codes: FD

59583
Joseph G. Markoly Foundation, Inc.
220 Arrowhead Ct.
Winter Springs, FL 32708

Established in 1998 in FL.
Financial data (yr. ended 12/31/01): Assets, $2,886,287 (M); grants paid, $155,000; gifts received, $4,516; expenditures, $218,781; qualifying distributions, $154,876.
Limitations: Giving primarily in Orlando and Winter Park, FL.

Application information: Unsolicited request for funds not accepted.
Trustee: Dorothy Benson.
EIN: 593506378
Codes: FD2

59584
The Johann Fust Community Library of Boca Grande, Florida, Inc.
c/o Lorena M. Mercier, C.P.A.
508 N. Indiana Ave.
Englewood, FL 34223

Financial data (yr. ended 12/31/01): Assets, $2,872,377 (M); grants paid, $0; gifts received, $58,596; expenditures, $143,295; qualifying distributions, $0.
Officers and Directors:* Thomas Burcham, Pres.; Mrs. William Hanley, V.P.; Pansy P. Cost,* Secy.; Charles Hill, Jr.,* Treas.; Mrs. Donald Hooker, Frank White, and 6 additional directors.
EIN: 590861994

59585
Louie R. and Gertrude Morgan Foundation
P.O. Box 550
Arcadia, FL 34265-0550 (941) 494-1551
Contact: Robert Summerall, Jr., V.P.

Established in 1960 in FL.
Donor(s): Louie R. Morgan,‡ Mildred Morgan,‡ Gertrude Morgan, Eleanor Morgan.
Financial data (yr. ended 12/31/01): Assets, $2,725,674 (M); grants paid, $145,000; expenditures, $170,687; qualifying distributions, $145,000.
Limitations: Giving primarily in FL.
Officers: Bobby C. Mixon, Pres.; Robert Summerall, Jr., V.P. and Treas.; James R. Wierichs, Secy.
Director: George E. Bellamy.
EIN: 596142359
Codes: FD2

59586
United Charitable Foundation, Inc.
(Formerly Norma Neal Ministries, Inc.)
c/o Angel & Assocs.
6709 Ridge Rd.
Port Richey, FL 34668

Classified as a private operating foundation in 1984.
Donor(s): R.P. Gause.
Financial data (yr. ended 12/31/01): Assets, $2,682,651 (M); grants paid, $0; gifts received, $994,924; expenditures, $208,601; qualifying distributions, $0.
Limitations: Applications not accepted.
Application information: Contributes only to pre-selected organizations.
Officers and Directors:* Jerrold Angel,* Pres.; Dave Parris,* V.P.; Thomas Bellante,* Treas.
EIN: 592278767
Codes: TN

59587
Heernett Environmental Foundation, Inc.
(Formerly Heernett Foundation, Inc.)
844 Anchor Rode Dr.
Naples, FL 34103

Established in 1997 in FL.
Donor(s): Gabriele N. Heertje, Manfred Nettek.
Financial data (yr. ended 12/31/00): Assets, $2,659,844 (M); grants paid, $0; gifts received, $1,123,397; expenditures, $148,316; qualifying distributions, $135,801.
Officers and Directors:* Manfred Nettek,* Pres.; Gabriele N. Heertje,* V.P.; Laura S. Upham,*

Secy.-Treas.; Phil Best, Brent Copin, Karina Copen, Jon E. Cushman, Thomas B. Garlick.
EIN: 593468448

59588
The Rayni Foundation, Inc.
300 S.W. 124 Ave.
Miami, FL 33184
Contact: Raul F. Rodriguez, Dir.

Established in 2000 in FL.
Donor(s): Raul F. Rodriguez.
Financial data (yr. ended 12/31/01): Assets, $2,628,412 (M); grants paid, $174,600; expenditures, $257,735; qualifying distributions, $237,133.
Limitations: Applications not accepted.
Application information: Unsolicited requests for funds not accepted.
Directors: Nidia Maldonado Rodriguez, Raul Francisco Rodriguez, Raul Rodriguez-Perez.
EIN: 650838191
Codes: FD2

59589
AMS Foundation for the Arts, Sciences and Humanities
c/o Chopin & Miller
505 S. Flagler Dr., Ste. 300
West Palm Beach, FL 33401
Application address: 660 Park Ave., New York, NY 10021
Contact: Gillian T. Sackler, Pres.

Established in 1980 in DC.
Donor(s): Gillian T. Sackler.
Financial data (yr. ended 12/31/01): Assets, $2,607,044 (M); grants paid, $43,500; gifts received, $105,000; expenditures, $95,515; qualifying distributions, $106,826; giving activities include $12,500 for programs.
Limitations: Giving on a national basis.
Officers: Gillian T. Sackler, Pres.; Doris Q. Tully, V.P.
Directors: Curtis Cutter, B.K. Tully.
EIN: 521188804

59590
William and Vernette More Family Foundation
c/o Stephen P. Chapman
855 S. Federal Hwy., Ste. 217-B
Boca Raton, FL 33432-6133

Established in 1997 in FL.
Donor(s): William More.
Financial data (yr. ended 06/30/02): Assets, $2,519,896 (M); grants paid, $79,500; gifts received, $24,801; expenditures, $110,472; qualifying distributions, $109,234.
Limitations: Applications not accepted. Giving primarily in FL and NJ.
Application information: Contributes only to pre-selected organizations.
Trustees: Barbara Bryan, Stephen P. Chapman, Barbara A. Sloan.
EIN: 650770654

59591
Dan C. Ferguson Charitable Trust
1300 3rd St. S., Ste. 300
Naples, FL 34102-7239
Contact: Daniel C. Ferguson, Tr.

Established in 1986 in FL.
Donor(s): Daniel C. Ferguson.
Financial data (yr. ended 11/30/01): Assets, $2,485,639 (M); grants paid, $12,500; expenditures, $39,138; qualifying distributions, $12,560.
Limitations: Giving on a national basis.
Trustee: Daniel C. Ferguson.

EIN: 366848627

59592
Verner Foundation, Inc.
P.O. Box 1118
Plant City, FL 33564-1118

Donor(s): John V. Verner Revocable Living Trust.
Financial data (yr. ended 12/31/01): Assets, $2,441,543 (M); grants paid, $114,567; gifts received, $205,000; expenditures, $119,601; qualifying distributions, $119,601.
Limitations: Applications not accepted. Giving primarily in FL.
Application information: Contributes only to pre-selected organizations.
Directors: Edward M. Verner, John V. Verner, S.P. Verner.
EIN: 593155858
Codes: FD2

59593
American Entomological Institute
3005 S.W. 56th Ave.
Gainesville, FL 32608

Established in 1994. Classified as a private operating foundation in 2000.
Financial data (yr. ended 12/31/01): Assets, $2,226,468 (M); grants paid, $0; gifts received, $31,230; expenditures, $139,159; qualifying distributions, $0.
Officers and Directors:* Dale Habeck,* Pres.; John Morse,* V.P.; David Wahl,* Secy.; James Lloyd,* Treas.; James S. Ashe, Clement Dascle, Ian Gauld, Lubomir Masner, Mary Jane West-Eberhard, Robert Wharton.
EIN: 381849251

59594
Richard Richardi Scholarship Trust
501 S. Ridgewood Ave.
Daytona Beach, FL 32114
Application address: c/o Walpole High School, 275 Common St., Walpole, MA 02081

Established in 1996 in FL.
Financial data (yr. ended 05/31/01): Assets, $2,134,198 (M); grants paid, $189,000; expenditures, $223,037; qualifying distributions, $206,706.
Limitations: Giving limited to MA.
Application information: Application form required.
Trustees: Donald E. Hawkins, First Union National Bank.
EIN: 597062049
Codes: FD2, GTI

59595
Esther Ragosin Charitable Foundation
317 71st St.
Miami Beach, FL 33141
Contact: Joel Piotrkowski, Tr.

Established in 1999 in FL.
Financial data (yr. ended 12/31/00): Assets, $1,958,433 (M); grants paid, $20,000; gifts received, $1,470,404; expenditures, $44,188; qualifying distributions, $20,000.
Trustees: Barret Blecker, Joel Piotrkowski.
EIN: 656319048

59596
Hein & Beverly Rusen Family Foundation, Inc.
25 S. Washington Dr.
Sarasota, FL 34236

Established in 1997 in FL.
Donor(s): Beverly Rusen, Hein Rusen.
Financial data (yr. ended 10/31/01): Assets, $1,935,931 (M); grants paid, $3,000;

expenditures, $98,412; qualifying distributions, $60,861; giving activities include $60,861 for programs.
Limitations: Applications not accepted.
Application information: Contributes only to pre-selected organizations.
Officers: Hein Rusen, Pres.; Beverly Rusen, Secy.-Treas.
EIN: 650538766

59597
Heartbeat International
(Formerly Heartbeat International of West Central Florida)
6800 N. Dale Mabry Hwy., No. 242
Tampa, FL 33614   (813) 243-8769
Contact: Liz Campos, Admin. Coord.

Established in 1984.
Donor(s): Medtronic, Inc., Pacesetter Systems, Inc., Intermedics, Inc., St. Joseph's Hospital, Watson Clinic Foundation, St. Jude Medical, CRM Div.
Financial data (yr. ended 06/30/01): Assets, $1,918,150 (M); grants paid, $1,840,990; gifts received, $1,654,085; expenditures, $1,933,795; qualifying distributions, $1,905,482.
Publications: Newsletter, informational brochure.
Officers: Peter Alagona, M.D., Pres.; Keith Power, Secy.-Treas.; Wil Mick, Exec. Dir.
EIN: 593236060
Codes: FD

59598
The Rose McFarland Finley Foundation
c/o First Union National Bank
200 S. Biscayne Blvd., 14th Fl.
Miami, FL 33131-5346
Scholarship application address: 1053 Palmetto Ave., Sebastian, FL 32958-4121, tel.: (561) 589-4502

Established in 1974 in FL.
Financial data (yr. ended 04/30/01): Assets, $1,879,333 (M); grants paid, $153,340; expenditures, $181,855; qualifying distributions, $164,825.
Limitations: Giving limited to residents of Indian River County, FL.
Application information: Application form required.
Directors: William J. McComack, Jr., M.D., Hon. Charles Smith, Gene Waddell.
EIN: 237414902
Codes: FD2, GTI

59599
LNR Foundation, Inc.
760 N.W. 107th Ave., Ste. 300
Miami, FL 33172
Contact: Stuart A. Miller, Pres.

Established in 1998.
Financial data (yr. ended 11/30/01): Assets, $1,875,755 (M); grants paid, $230,346; gifts received, $950,000; expenditures, $235,213; qualifying distributions, $230,346.
Limitations: Giving primarily in FL.
Officers: Stuart A. Miller, Pres.; Steven J. Saiontz, V.P. and Secy.; Jeffrey P. Krasnoff, Treas.
EIN: 650881678
Codes: FD2

59600
The Lee Foundation
P.O. Box 2113
Orlando, FL 32802   (407) 857-2835
Contact: Richard T. Lee, Tr.

Established about 1974.
Donor(s): Elizabeth M. Lee, T.G. Lee.‡
Financial data (yr. ended 12/31/01): Assets, $1,856,926 (M); grants paid, $109,200; expenditures, $110,560; qualifying distributions, $109,200.
Limitations: Giving primarily in central FL.
Application information: Application form not required.
Trustees: Kathleen S. Lee, Richard T. Lee.
EIN: 596148803
Codes: FD2

59601
The Glantz Family Foundation, Inc.
4674 Fountains Dr. S.
Lake Worth, FL 33467-5064
Contact: Edward R. Glantz, Pres.

Established in 1986 in FL.
Donor(s): Edward R. Glantz, Richard M. Glantz, Elaine Ostrin.
Financial data (yr. ended 12/31/01): Assets, $1,808,452 (M); grants paid, $115,300; gifts received, $115,000; expenditures, $118,748; qualifying distributions, $116,563.
Limitations: Applications not accepted. Giving primarily in FL.
Application information: Contributes only to pre-selected organizations.
Officers and Directors:* Edward R. Glantz,* Pres.; Elaine Ostrin,* V.P.; Thelma Glantz,* Secy.; Richard M. Glantz,* Treas.; Joseph LeFrank.
EIN: 592789071
Codes: FD2

59602
The American Sporting Arms and Art Museum, Inc.
1000 Brickell Ave., Ste. 1200
Miami, FL 33131

Established in 1991 in FL.
Donor(s): L. Allen Morris.
Financial data (yr. ended 12/31/01): Assets, $1,726,897 (M); grants paid, $0; gifts received, $10,000; expenditures, $9,885; qualifying distributions, $9,885; giving activities include $9,885 for programs.
Officers and Directors:* W. Allen Morris,* Pres.; James F. Bell, Jr.,* V.P.; M. Noel Connors, Secy.-Treas.; Gary L. Rupp.
EIN: 650238695

59603
The Mary Ann and Harold Perper Foundation, Inc.
c/o Mizer Lake Estate
331 S.E. 9th Ln.
Boca Raton, FL 33432

Donor(s): Harold E. Perper, Mary A. Perper.
Financial data (yr. ended 12/31/00): Assets, $1,617,765 (M); grants paid, $107,000; expenditures, $107,756; qualifying distributions, $106,018.
Limitations: Applications not accepted.
Application information: Contributes only to pre-selected organizations.
Officers: Harold E. Perper, Pres.; Catherine Mary Rafferty, V.P.; Mary A. Perper, Secy.-Treas.
EIN: 650370994
Codes: FD2

59604
Gloria Austin Foundation, Inc.
P.O. Box 318
Weirsdale, FL 32195

Established in 2000 in FL; Classified as a private operating foundation in 2001.
Donor(s): Gloria Austin.
Financial data (yr. ended 09/30/01): Assets, $1,606,717 (M); grants paid, $0; gifts received, $1,972,485; expenditures, $125,595; qualifying distributions, $168,159; giving activities include $168,159 for programs.
Officers and Directors:* Gloria Austin,* Pres.; Ned Schmidt,* Secy. and Mgr.; Vernon Eddy,* Treas.; Cecille K. Dunn.
EIN: 593683757

59605
Kane Family Foundation, Inc.
3825 Alhambra Ct.
Coral Gables, FL 33134

Established in 1999 in FL.
Donor(s): John Kane.
Financial data (yr. ended 12/31/99): Assets, $1,585,317 (M); grants paid, $4,299; gifts received, $1,470,000; expenditures, $11,936; qualifying distributions, $4,299.
Officers: John Kane, Pres.; Ileana Kane, Secy.
Director: Kelly Kane.
EIN: 650928906

59606
The J. S. & S. Michaan Foundation
220 Sunrise Ave.
Palm Beach, FL 33480

Established in 1995 in FL.
Donor(s): Joseph Michaan, Suzanne Michaan.
Financial data (yr. ended 06/30/01): Assets, $1,563,035 (M); grants paid, $1,085,460; gifts received, $1,000,000; expenditures, $1,089,762; qualifying distributions, $1,088,910.
Limitations: Applications not accepted. Giving primarily in FL and NY.
Application information: Contributes only to pre-selected organizations.
Trustees: Joseph Michaan, Suzanne Michaan.
EIN: 650635890
Codes: FD

59607
Lubee Foundation, Inc.
800 E. Broward Blvd., Ste. 601
Fort Lauderdale, FL 33301-2084

Established in 1989 in FL.
Donor(s): Luis Bacardi.‡
Financial data (yr. ended 08/31/01): Assets, $1,505,415 (M); grants paid, $0; gifts received, $680,210; expenditures, $666,765; qualifying distributions, $603,810; giving activities include $584,378 for programs.
Application information: Application form not required.
Officers: Facundo Bacardi, Pres.; Roger D. Haagenson, Exec. Dir.
Trustee: Sherry Haggenson.
EIN: 650145696

59608
Sonderling Spirit of Hope Fund, Inc.
c/o Carmichael
4501 Tamiami Trail N., Ste. 300
Naples, FL 34103

Established in 2000 in FL. Classified as a private operating foundation in 2001.
Financial data (yr. ended 12/31/00): Assets, $1,467,146 (M); grants paid, $30,000; expenditures, $30,000; qualifying distributions, $30,000.
Officers: Maria Michaels, Pres.; Nick Studds, V.P.; Tara J. Comuzzi, Treas.
EIN: 593662813

59609
Gardner Family Foundation
c/o Donald J. Gardner
3319 Anderson Rd.
Coral Gables, FL 33134

Established in 1997 in FL.
Donor(s): Donald J. Gardner.
Financial data (yr. ended 12/31/99): Assets, $1,463,491 (M); grants paid, $24,200; expenditures, $24,315; qualifying distributions, $24,200.
Limitations: Applications not accepted.
Application information: Contributes only to pre-selected organizations.
Officers: Donald J. Gardner, Pres.; Kathleen S. Gardner, Secy.-Treas.
Director: Claire Gardner.
EIN: 650748998

59610
Ann Norton Sculpture Gardens, Inc.
253 Barcelona Rd.
West Palm Beach, FL 33401-7707

Classified as a private operating foundation in 1983.
Financial data (yr. ended 12/31/01): Assets, $1,421,147 (M); grants paid, $0; gifts received, $105,560; expenditures, $193,182; qualifying distributions, $0.
Officers and Trustees:* Thomas Chastain,* Pres.; Veronica J. Boswell,* V.P.; Suzanne Mahoney, V.P.; Margaret L. Cooper,* Secy.; Craig U. Kahle,* Treas.; Cynthia Gibbons, Glenn P. Rawls, Wayne Villavaso, and 8 additional trustees.
EIN: 591874060

59611
Dorothy B. C. Steves Charitable Trust
c/o SunTrust Bank
P.O. Box 620005
Orlando, FL 32862-0005
Contact: Candace R. Marshall, V.P.

Financial data (yr. ended 06/30/01): Assets, $1,409,186 (M); grants paid, $109,000; expenditures, $121,964; qualifying distributions, $108,547.
Limitations: Giving primarily in FL.
Application information: Application form required.
Trustee: J. Robert Duggan.
EIN: 597134063
Codes: FD2

59612
Jack Silberberg Foundation
c/o Jack Silberberg
635 Lakewood Circle E.
Delray Beach, FL 33445

Established in 1971 in NJ.
Donor(s): Marion Silberberg.
Financial data (yr. ended 05/31/00): Assets, $1,369,583 (M); grants paid, $15,304; expenditures, $26,690; qualifying distributions, $15,304.
Limitations: Applications not accepted. Giving primarily in FL and NJ.
Application information: Contributes only to pre-selected organizations.
Officer: Marion Silberberg, Mgr.
EIN: 237112034

59613
Shane Family Foundation
c/o Ira Nusbaum
4101 Pinetree Dr., Ste. 1804
Miami Beach, FL 33140

Established in 1996 in FL.
Donor(s): Ronald Shane.
Financial data (yr. ended 12/31/00): Assets, $1,334,840 (M); grants paid, $30,315; gifts received, $68,175; expenditures, $162,024; qualifying distributions, $64,323.
Limitations: Applications not accepted. Giving primarily in FL.
Application information: Contributes only to pre-selected organizations.
Officers: Ira Nusbaum, Pres.; Stacey Shane-Nusbaum, V.P.; Balwant Cheema, Secy.-Treas.
EIN: 650715198

59614
The Cooper Institute for Advanced Studies in Medicine and the Humanities
600 5th Ave. S., Ste. 205
Naples, FL 34102
FAX: (941) 263-2338; E-mail: inform@cooperinstitute.org

Established about 1974 as the Naples Institute for Advanced Studies in Medicine and the Humanities.
Donor(s): Sissel H. Cooper, Irving S. Cooper.‡
Financial data (yr. ended 05/31/02): Assets, $1,322,803 (M); grants paid, $37,000; expenditures, $75,401; qualifying distributions, $56,063; giving activities include $75,401 for programs.
Limitations: Applications not accepted.
Publications: Informational brochure.
Application information: Contributes only to pre-selected organizations.
Officer: Sissel H. Cooper-Bos, Pres.
EIN: 232012011

59615
Sara and Ray Baden Charitable Trust
301 99th St. N.W.
Bradenton, FL 34209-9760

Established in 1992 in FL.
Donor(s): Sara B. Baden, H. Ray Baden.
Financial data (yr. ended 11/30/01): Assets, $1,259,869 (M); grants paid, $600; gifts received, $303,283; expenditures, $38,492; qualifying distributions, $839,816.
Limitations: Giving primarily in FL.
Application information: Application form not required.
Trustees: H. Ray Baden, Sara B. Baden.
Director: Virginia B. Knowles.
EIN: 656110415

59616
The Schacknow Museum of Fine Arts, Inc.
7080 N.W. 4th St.
Plantation, FL 33317

Established in 1999 in FL.
Financial data (yr. ended 12/31/00): Assets, $1,244,566 (M); grants paid, $550; gifts received, $1,312,733; expenditures, $177,993; qualifying distributions, $1,100.
Directors: Max Schacknow, Paul Schacknow, Sharma Schacknow.
EIN: 650936893

59617
Harold C. & Jacqueline F. Bladel Foundation, Inc.
1515 Ringling Blvd.
Sarasota, FL 34236

Established in 1997 in FL.
Financial data (yr. ended 12/31/00): Assets, $1,200,089 (M); grants paid, $65,000; expenditures, $76,568; qualifying distributions, $65,000.
Limitations: Applications not accepted. Giving primarily in Sarasota, FL.
Application information: Contributes only to pre-selected organizations.
Trustee: The Northern Trust Co.
EIN: 911910210

59618
Max & Evelyn Schacknow Foundation
10481 N.W. 17th St.
Plantation, FL 33322

Donor(s): Evelyn Schacknow, Max Schacknow.
Financial data (yr. ended 12/31/00): Assets, $1,199,798 (M); grants paid, $1,325,823; gifts received, $301,000; expenditures, $1,341,423; qualifying distributions, $1,334,923.
Limitations: Applications not accepted. Giving primarily in Plantation, FL.
Application information: Contributes only to pre-selected organizations.
Officer and Directors:* Max Schacknow,* Pres. and Treas.; Sharma Schacknow, Evelyn Schacknow, Paul Schacknow.
EIN: 650464694
Codes: FD

59619
William and Joan Brodsky Foundation, Inc.
2800 Ponce De Leon Blvd., Ste. 1125
Coral Gables, FL 33134

Established in 1997 in FL.
Donor(s): Joan Brodsky, William Brodsky.
Financial data (yr. ended 12/31/01): Assets, $1,195,891 (M); grants paid, $65,774; expenditures, $70,630; qualifying distributions, $69,971.
Limitations: Applications not accepted. Giving primarily in IL.
Application information: Contributes only to pre-selected organizations.
Officers: William Brodsky, Pres.; Joan Brodsky, Secy.-Treas.
Directors: Jonathan Brodsky, Michael Brodsky, Stephen Brodsky.
EIN: 650724452

59620
The Robert & Hoyle Rymer Foundation
124 N. Clara Ave.
DeLand, FL 32720

Established in 1988 in TN.
Donor(s): Plastine, Inc., Robert E. Rymer, Sr.
Financial data (yr. ended 12/31/00): Assets, $1,140,976 (M); grants paid, $79,016; expenditures, $81,254; qualifying distributions, $80,179.
Limitations: Applications not accepted. Giving primarily in Cleveland, TN.
Application information: Contributes only to pre-selected organizations.
Officers: J. Hoyle Rymer, Pres.; Sharon S. Rymer, Secy.
Director: Robert E. Rymer, Sr.
EIN: 621373262
Codes: FD2

59621
The Albert E. Feder Family Foundation
c/o Steven Feder
14 Isla Bahia Dr.
Fort Lauderdale, FL 33316
Contact: Steven Feder, Tr.

Established in 2000 in FL. Classified as a company-sponsored operating foundation.
Donor(s): West Communications, Inc., Steven Feder.
Financial data (yr. ended 12/31/00): Assets, $1,118,526 (M); grants paid, $0; gifts received, $1,182,887; expenditures, $0; qualifying distributions, $0.
Trustee: Steven Feder.
EIN: 656346215

59622
Albert E. and Esther G. Kaufman Foundation
c/o Shen Kogan
12515 W. Knedall Dr., Ste. 314
Miami, FL 33186

Donor(s): Esther G. Kaufman.
Financial data (yr. ended 12/31/00): Assets, $1,071,665 (M); grants paid, $20,150; gifts received, $1,056,089; expenditures, $21,328; qualifying distributions, $21,328.
Limitations: Applications not accepted.
Application information: Contributes only to pre-selected organizations.
Trustees: Michael Greenberg, Philip Shenkman, Murray Zohn.
EIN: 650763952

59623
Needles Family Foundation, Inc.
10178 Fresh Meadow Ln.
Boca Raton, FL 33498
Application address: c/o Randy Needles, 1414 Willow Ave., Elkins Park, PA 19027
Contact: Randy Needles, V.P.

Established 1997 in FL.
Financial data (yr. ended 12/31/99): Assets, $1,019,580 (M); grants paid, $56,112; expenditures, $66,496; qualifying distributions, $65,260.
Limitations: Giving on a national basis.
Application information: Application form required.
Officers and Trustees:* Stanley Needles,* Pres.; Jay Needles,* V.P.; Randy Needles,* V.P.; Beth Ost,* Secy.; Sallie Needles,* Treas.
EIN: 650754688

59624
Lura Bradfield Foundation, Inc.
5025 Collins Ave., Ste. 2107
Miami Beach, FL 33140

Established in 1997 in MD.
Financial data (yr. ended 12/31/01): Assets, $981,603 (M); grants paid, $122,500; gifts received, $3,017; expenditures, $184,184; qualifying distributions, $122,500.
Limitations: Applications not accepted.
Application information: Contributes only to pre-selected organizations.
Officer: Norma Opgrand, Pres.
EIN: 526799324
Codes: FD2

59625
Matthew 28:18-20 Charitable Trust
3708 S.E. 4th St.
Ocala, FL 34471-3002 (352) 694-3175
Contact: Stephen F. Saint, Pres.

Established around 1992.
Donor(s): Stephen F. Saint, Abraham C. Van Der Puy, Marjorie Van Der Puy.
Financial data (yr. ended 12/31/00): Assets, $979,560 (M); grants paid, $65,771; gifts received, $360,113; expenditures, $188,921; qualifying distributions, $209,729.
Limitations: Giving on a national basis; giving also in Ecuador.
Application information: Application form not required.
Officers: Jennie Saint, Co-Pres.; Stephen F. Saint, Co-Pres.
Trustees: Ross S. Drown, Abraham C. Van Der Puy, Marjorie Van Der Puy.
EIN: 593091298

59626
Robert K. Dixon Foundation, Inc.
c/o Nancy D. Haug
826 Glades Ct., N.E.
St. Petersburg, FL 33702-2780

Financial data (yr. ended 12/31/99): Assets, $966,550 (M); grants paid, $37,000; expenditures, $50,974; qualifying distributions, $38,356.
Limitations: Applications not accepted.
Application information: Contributes only to pre-selected organizations.
Officers and Directors:* Karen S. Touchton,* Pres. and Treas.; Nancy D. Haug,* V.P. and Secy.; Judith C. Akin, Susanna W. Schramek, Bret A. Touchton.
EIN: 592748301

59627
The Harvey L. Young Family Foundation, Inc.
1581 Brickell Ave., No. T-201
Miami, FL 33129-1243

Established in 1989 in FL.
Donor(s): Harvey L. Young.
Financial data (yr. ended 11/30/99): Assets, $951,763 (M); grants paid, $46,509; expenditures, $54,624; qualifying distributions, $46,509.
Limitations: Giving limited to Dade County, FL.
Application information: Application form required.
Officer and Directors:* Harvey L. Young,* Pres.; Clara Young.
EIN: 650171121

59628
Center for Middle East Peace & Economic Cooperation, Inc.
777 S. Flagler Dr., 14th Fl., W. Tower
West Palm Beach, FL 33401 (561) 820-1320
Contact: Brad Bleefeld

Donor(s): S. Daniel Abraham, Thompson Medical Co., Inc., Slim-Fast Foods Co., Inc.
Financial data (yr. ended 12/31/99): Assets, $940,690 (M); grants paid, $51,418; gifts received, $3,000,200; expenditures, $2,757,473; qualifying distributions, $2,708,935; giving activities include $2,708,935 for programs.
Officers: S. Daniel Abraham, Chair.; Wayne Owens, Pres.; Edward Steinberg, V.P.; Eliot Lauer, Treas.
EIN: 521621126

59629
Anne F. Forbes Family Foundation
P.O. Box 1349
Brandon, FL 33509-1349

Established in 2000 in FL.
Financial data (yr. ended 12/31/01): Assets, $913,078 (M); grants paid, $45,000; expenditures, $61,681; qualifying distributions, $45,000.
Limitations: Applications not accepted.
Application information: Contributes only to pre-selected organizations.
Trustees: Bernice H. Black, Anne F. Forbes, Lou Ann Lanier, Michael F. Nappa, Robert A. Nappa, Susan A. Nappa-Cocke, Elisa Nappa-Ralston.
EIN: 597195615

59630
The MacMillan Foundation, Inc.
(also known as Alicia Watchorn Snyder Foundation, Inc.)
305 Live Oak Rd.
Vero Beach, FL 32963-1432

Established in 1969.
Financial data (yr. ended 12/31/01): Assets, $906,093 (M); grants paid, $44,608; expenditures, $48,423; qualifying distributions, $44,472.
Limitations: Applications not accepted. Giving primarily in FL.
Application information: Contributes only to pre-selected organizations.
Officers: Ronald J. MacMillan, Pres.; David G. MacMillan, V.P.; Randolph MacMillan, Secy.-Treas.
EIN: 237049760

59631
Delta Sigma Delta Educational Foundation
301 Ebbtide Dr., Ste. F
North Palm Beach, FL 33408

Classified as a private operating foundation in 1974.
Donor(s): Russell Nyland.
Financial data (yr. ended 06/30/00): Assets, $902,607 (M); grants paid, $20,000; gifts received, $3,987; expenditures, $57,547; qualifying distributions, $20,000; giving activities include $20,000 for loans to individuals.
Limitations: Giving primarily in NY.
Application information: Contact deputy of Delta Sigma Delta at particular dental school. Application form required.
Officers: P. Charles Moyer, Pres.; Arthur Mourino, V.P.; William Kelly, Secy.-Treas.; Howard R. Lyboldt, Admin.
Trustees: Peter Neff, Paul Will.
EIN: 386089377
Codes: GTI

59632
Morris & Yetta Deckelbaum Family Foundation, Inc.
4430 Caspe Ct.
Hollywood, FL 33021-2416

Established in 2000.
Donor(s): Morris Deckelbaum, Yetta Deckelbaum.
Financial data (yr. ended 12/31/00): Assets, $890,071 (M); grants paid, $38,000; gifts received, $926,636; expenditures, $39,995; qualifying distributions, $39,995.
Officers: Morris Deckelbaum, Mgr.; Yetta Deckelbaum, Mgr.
EIN: 651049921

59633
The Foosaner Foundation
343 N. Tropical Trail, No. A208
Merritt Island, FL 32953
Contact: Dione L. Negroni, Pres.

Donor(s): Dione L. Negroni.
Financial data (yr. ended 12/31/99): Assets, $889,523 (M); grants paid, $41,175; gifts received, $57,725; expenditures, $41,245; qualifying distributions, $41,175.
Limitations: Giving primarily in FL.
Application information: Application form not required.
Officers and Directors:* Dione L. Negroni,* Pres.; Andrea Lee Negroni,* V.P.; Donald Hendrick,* Secy.; James L. Negroni, Jr.,* Treas.

EIN: 222308589

59634
John and Evelyn Trevor Charitable Foundation
c/o Brown Thornton
P.O. Box 12484
Pensacola, FL 32573

Established in 2000 in DE.
Donor(s): John B. Trevor, Jr., Evelyn Bruen Trevor.
Financial data (yr. ended 12/31/01): Assets, $885,110 (M); grants paid, $33,510; gifts received, $87,293; expenditures, $36,759; qualifying distributions, $33,510.
Officers: John B. Trevor, Jr., Pres.; Evelyn Bruen Trevor, V.P.; Alexander B. Trevor, Secy.-Treas.
EIN: 593688564

59635
The Nuzzo Family Foundation
800 Ocean Dr., Ste. 1101
Juno Beach, FL 33408-1724

Established in 1999 in FL.
Donor(s): Salvatore J. Nuzzo.
Financial data (yr. ended 12/31/00): Assets, $880,597 (M); grants paid, $21,381; gifts received, $450,000; expenditures, $28,094; qualifying distributions, $21,381.
Limitations: Applications not accepted.
Application information: Contributes only to pre-selected organizations.
Officers and Directors:* Salvatore J. Nuzzo,* Chair.; Lucille Nuzzo,* Pres.; D. Nuzzo,* V.P.; J. Nuzzo,* V.P.
EIN: 223700343

59636
Khumbula Thina, Inc.
P.O. Box 1166
Sanibel, FL 33957
DC tel.: (202) 333-0595
Contact: Fleur Wales-Baillie Cook, Pres.

Established in 1995 in WV.
Donor(s): Richard Cook, Robert Vago.
Financial data (yr. ended 12/31/99): Assets, $859,886 (M); grants paid, $15,250; gifts received, $7,823; expenditures, $41,979; qualifying distributions, $43,112; giving activities include $22,453 for programs.
Limitations: Giving primarily in South Africa.
Application information: Application form not required.
Officer and Directors:* Fleur Wales-Baillie Cook,* Pres. and Treas.; James Fowler, Col. Harry Zink.
EIN: 550740397

59637
United Cerebral Palsy of Palm Beach and Mid-Coast Counties, Inc.
c/o United Cerebral Palsy of Miami
1411 N.W. 14th Ave.
Miami, FL 33125

Established as an operating foundation in 1991.
Financial data (yr. ended 09/30/99): Assets, $832,749 (M); grants paid, $0; gifts received, $42,602; expenditures, $1,578,083; qualifying distributions, $50,102; giving activities include $1,497,888 for programs.
Officers: Regina Bianz, Pres.; Kathy Layman, V.P.; Jean Zimmerman, Secy.; James H. Mahoney, Jr., Treas.; Joseph A. Aniello, Exec. Dir.
Directors: Gene Boeninger, Norman Borchick, John E. Futch, Stephen Lord, Christian D. Searcy, Peter Slavis, Jon Smith.
EIN: 650229776
Codes: TN

59638
C. Frederick Thompson Foundation, Inc.
2831 N.W. 41st St.
Gainesville, FL 32606

Established in 1996 in FL.
Donor(s): Anse Thompson, C. Frederick Thompson.
Financial data (yr. ended 12/31/99): Assets, $812,656 (M); grants paid, $1,300; gifts received, $280,000; expenditures, $17,230; qualifying distributions, $17,112.
Limitations: Giving primarily in FL.
Officer and Directors:* C. Frederick Thompson,* Pres.; John Scott, Anse B. Thompson.
EIN: 593380217

59639
Feline Manor, Inc.
21251 Old State Rd., 4A
Cudjoe Key, FL 33042

Established in 1996 in FL.
Donor(s): Lenore Madeleine.
Financial data (yr. ended 12/31/99): Assets, $804,781 (M); grants paid, $0; gifts received, $3,461; expenditures, $68,013; qualifying distributions, $60,138; giving activities include $50,000 for programs.
Officers: Eileen Elkinson, Pres.; Lenore Madeleine, V.P. and Secy.-Treas.
Directors: Becky Barron, Jesse Harvey, Carroll Snow, Vicki Snow.
EIN: 650581581

59640
GMAA Grover Loening Scholarship Fund
c/o Charles Deeb
971 Plover Ave.
Miami Springs, FL 33166-4346
Application address: c/o Ursula M. Davidson, GMAA Scholarship Chair., 880 N.E. 69th St., Miami, FL 33138, tels.: (305) 963-3910 or (305) 757-2957

Established around 1992.
Financial data (yr. ended 12/31/00): Assets, $789,377 (M); grants paid, $45,000; gifts received, $76,975; expenditures, $86,146; qualifying distributions, $45,000.
Limitations: Giving limited to residents of FL.
Application information: Application form required.
Officers: Gil Gursky, Pres.; Jim Montie, V.P.; Bill Rivenbark, Secy.; Ed Calt, Treas.
EIN: 650270346
Codes: GTI

59641
Bryan W. & Minnie Judge Foundation
P.O. Box 6973
Vero Beach, FL 32961

Financial data (yr. ended 12/31/99): Assets, $787,161 (M); grants paid, $40,850; expenditures, $50,670; qualifying distributions, $43,065.
Application information: Application form required.
Directors: Jennifer Adamson, Jeffrey Cusson, Tom Owens.
EIN: 592691650

59642
Moody Manor, Inc.
7150 Holatee Trail
Fort Lauderdale, FL 33325

Donor(s): Strive Foundation, Deborah Olsen, Moody Electric, Inc.

Financial data (yr. ended 12/31/99): Assets, $767,368 (M); grants paid, $250; gifts received, $33,420; expenditures, $669,263; qualifying distributions, $604,023; giving activities include $604,023 for programs.
Limitations: Applications not accepted.
Application information: Contributes only to pre-selected organizations.
Officers and Directors:* Mary P. Briggs,* Pres.; Margaret Moody,* V.P.; Yvonne Moody,* Secy.; Eileen Benson, Dan Dolan, Richard Doyle, Jr., Joanne Harris, Arthur Heffernan, Thomas Knieriem, Joy Prescott.
EIN: 650162525

59643
Margaret E. Wilson Foundation
1600 Miccosukee Rd.
Tallahassee, FL 32308-5166

Established in 1989 in FL.
Financial data (yr. ended 12/31/00): Assets, $744,316 (M); grants paid, $3,779,460; gifts received, $10,525; expenditures, $3,807,405; qualifying distributions, $3,777,009.
Limitations: Giving primarily in FL.
Trustee: Capital City Trust Company.
EIN: 592918990
Codes: FD

59644
Moskowitz Charitable Trust
1674 Meridian Ave., Ste. 408
Miami Beach, FL 33139

Established in 1993 in CA.
Financial data (yr. ended 12/31/00): Assets, $729,484 (M); grants paid, $12,000; expenditures, $22,354; qualifying distributions, $22,354.
Limitations: Applications not accepted. Giving primarily in Brooklyn, NY.
Application information: Contributes only to pre-selected organizations.
Trustee: Ethel Richmond.
EIN: 336148445

59645
Taunton Family Children's Home, Inc.
P.O. Box 870
Wewahitchka, FL 32465-0870

Classified as a private operating foundation in 1984.
Donor(s): David L. Taunton, Abigail J. Taunton, Tom Taunton.
Financial data (yr. ended 12/31/99): Assets, $709,639 (M); grants paid, $2,180; gifts received, $253,706; expenditures, $204,167; qualifying distributions, $2,180.
Officers and Directors:* David L. Taunton,* Pres.; Charles R. Cleckley, V.P.; Abigail J. Taunton,* Secy.-Treas.; Rick Campbell, Mary Hartzog, Rev. Fred Melvin, Nathan Peters, Jr., and 7 additional directors.
EIN: 592335556

59646
The Evans-Cross Family Foundation
630 Ocean Rd.
Vero Beach, FL 32963

Established in 1998. Classified as a private operating foundation in 2000.
Financial data (yr. ended 12/31/99): Assets, $696,826 (M); grants paid, $3,850; expenditures, $24,377; qualifying distributions, $3,878.
Officers and Directors:* Nicholas M. Evans,* Pres.; Christine E. Evans,* V.P.; Nicholas M. Evans, Jr.,* V.P.; Christine T. Evans,* Secy.
EIN: 650843702

59647
P. R. Cunningham Family Foundation
1450 N.W. 1st Ave.
Boca Raton, FL 33432 (561) 368-8333
Contact: P. Rodney Cunningham, Pres.

Financial data (yr. ended 12/31/99): Assets, $688,452 (M); grants paid, $14,590; expenditures, $27,693; qualifying distributions, $14,590.
Officers: P. Rodney Cunningham, Pres.; Richard A. Murdoch, Secy.; Carolyn S. Cunningham, Treas.
Directors: P. Scott Cunningham, Sarah K. Cunningham.
EIN: 311597995

59648
United Cerebral Palsy Group Homes, Inc.
1411 N.W. 14th Ave.
Miami, FL 33125-1691

Classified as a private operating foundation in 1990.
Financial data (yr. ended 09/30/01): Assets, $673,398 (M); grants paid, $0; expenditures, $121,213; qualifying distributions, $30,544; giving activities include $121,213 for programs.
Officers: Ruth Spivak, Chair.; Jack Schillinger, Chair. Emeritus; Joseph A. Aniello, C.E.O. and Pres.; Majorie Schillinger, V.P.; Richard Rangel, Secy.; Harriet Stegman, Treas.
Board Members: Gene Boeninger, Fernando Cabrera, Domingo Escar, Lloyd E. Foley, Robert Levy, Roy Lustig, Maj. Robert Peryam, Roger Reece.
EIN: 592528117

59649
Green Charitable Trust
717 Manatee Ave. W., Ste. 200
Bradenton, FL 34205
Contact: Robert L. Miller, Tr.

Established in 2001 in FL.
Financial data (yr. ended 12/31/01): Assets, $672,363 (M); grants paid, $75,350; expenditures, $78,650; qualifying distributions, $75,350.
Limitations: Giving primarily in FL, IL, and OH.
Application information: Application accepted only through sponsoring organizations. Application form required.
Trustees: James L. Green, Robert L. Miller.
EIN: 656368603
Codes: FD2

59650
Naples Children and Education Foundation, Inc.
5811 Pelican Bay Blvd., Ste. 210
Naples, FL 34108

Established in 2000 in FL.
Donor(s): Dwight D. Opperman.
Financial data (yr. ended 06/30/01): Assets, $663,998 (M); grants paid, $2,067,250; gifts received, $1,120,267; expenditures, $2,663,565; qualifying distributions, $2,126,651.
Officers: Joyce Crossett, Exec. Dir.; Betsy Stranahan, Exec. Dir.
Directors: Pat Aluisi, J.D. Clinton, Mary Susan Clinton, Brian Cobb, Denise Cobb, Arlene D'Alessandro, Michael D'Alessandro, Bob Elkins, Shirlene Elkins, and 27 additional directors.
EIN: 651001650
Codes: FD

59651
Hamilton M. & Blanche C. Forman Christian Foundation
1526 coral Ridge Dr.
Fort Lauderdale, FL 33304
Contact: Hamilton C. Forman, Pres.

Established in 1955 in FL.
Donor(s): Members of the Forman family.
Financial data (yr. ended 10/31/00): Assets, $657,686 (M); grants paid, $11,062; expenditures, $60,953; qualifying distributions, $4,220.
Limitations: Giving primarily in FL.
Officers and Directors:* Hamilton C. Forman,* Pres.; Charles R. Forman,* V.P.
EIN: 596131560

59652
The Wild Family Foundation, Inc.
c/o Jeanne E. Sweeney
915 Emerald Row
Gulf Stream, FL 33483

Established in 1996 in FL.
Financial data (yr. ended 06/30/00): Assets, $647,636 (M); grants paid, $30,000; expenditures, $37,474; qualifying distributions, $30,000.
Limitations: Applications not accepted. Giving primarily in Delray Beach, FL.
Application information: Contributes only to pre-selected organizations.
Officers: John J. Wild, Pres.; Eileen H. Wild, V.P.; Jeanne E. Sweeney, Secy.
Director: John J. Wild, Jr.
EIN: 650709568

59653
The Christos Foundation, Inc.
1761 Cartina Way
Venice, FL 34292-4318

Classified as a private operating foundation in 1984.
Donor(s): Eugene G. Wach.
Financial data (yr. ended 12/31/00): Assets, $630,795 (M); grants paid, $38,100; gifts received, $200,000; expenditures, $39,278; qualifying distributions, $38,632.
Limitations: Applications not accepted. Giving primarily in the Buffalo, NY, area.
Application information: Contributes only to pre-selected organizations.
Officer: Eugene G. Wach, Pres.
EIN: 222519743

59654
W. T. Neal Civic Center, Inc.
P.O. Box 40
Blountstown, FL 32424-0040

Financial data (yr. ended 09/30/00): Assets, $568,885 (M); grants paid, $0; gifts received, $615,633; expenditures, $499,176; qualifying distributions, $499,176; giving activities include $499,176 for programs.
Directors: Finlay Corbin, Joe Ray Durham, Jeanette Johnson, Hentz H. McClellan, Phillip McMillan, Howell Montgomery.
EIN: 592140323

59655
The Recursionist Fund
c/o Scott M. Harris
4718 Villa Mare
Naples, FL 34103 (941) 430-0570
Contact: Scott M. Harris, Dir.

Established in 1998 in FL.
Financial data (yr. ended 08/31/00): Assets, $568,010 (M); grants paid, $55,000; expenditures, $60,244; qualifying distributions, $54,652.

Directors: Daniel F. Brophy, James R. Fox, Scott M. Harris.
EIN: 593535995

59656
John H. Sullivan & Robin E. Sullivan Charitable Foundation
c/o SunTrust Banks, Inc.
P.O. Bank 2018
Sarasota, FL 34230

Established in 1999 in CA.
Donor(s): John H. Sullivan, Robin E. Sullivan.
Financial data (yr. ended 12/31/01): Assets, $561,746 (M); grants paid, $14,676; expenditures, $36,994; qualifying distributions, $24,115.
Limitations: Applications not accepted.
Application information: Contributes only to pre-selected organizations.
Officers and Directors:* John H. Sullivan,* Pres.; Robin E. Sullivan,* Secy.-Treas.
EIN: 943341432

59657
Attata Foundation
c/o Iris B. Apfel
333 Sunset Ave.
Palm Beach, FL 33480-3829

Classified as a private operating foundation in 1986.
Donor(s): Iris B. Apfel.
Financial data (yr. ended 11/30/01): Assets, $537,724 (M); grants paid, $0; gifts received, $2,039; expenditures, $3,112; qualifying distributions, $0.
Officers: Iris B. Apfel, Pres.; Carl B. Apfel, Secy.
EIN: 133343096

59658
Religious Vacations, Inc.
524 N.E. 16th Ct.
Fort Lauderdale, FL 33305-3012

Donor(s): Hugh Hoffman.
Financial data (yr. ended 08/31/01): Assets, $522,912 (M); grants paid, $0; expenditures, $34,366; qualifying distributions, $34,366.
Officer: Hugh Hoffman, Pres. and Treas.
EIN: 596167637

59659
I Have a Dream Foundation of Delray Beach, Inc.
(Formerly I Have a Dream Foundation)
16870 Silver Oak Cir.
Delray Beach, FL 33445

Donor(s): Herman Green.
Financial data (yr. ended 12/31/00): Assets, $511,293 (M); grants paid, $0; gifts received, $122,333; expenditures, $81,389; qualifying distributions, $0.
Officers: Herman Green, Pres.; Jay Felner, V.P.; Arona Green, Secy.; Peter Kamins, Treas.
EIN: 650378506

59660
Bryant L. Coker Scholarship Loan Fund, Inc.
P.O. Box 545
Wauchula, FL 33873-0545
Application address: 302 Park Dr., Wauchula, FL 33873, tel.: (863) 773-4136
Contact: Jean Archambault, Secy.

Established in 1985 in FL.
Donor(s): Gladys Coker.
Financial data (yr. ended 02/28/01): Assets, $484,577 (M); grants paid, $0; gifts received, $20,070; expenditures, $1,154; qualifying distributions, $67,879.

Limitations: Giving limited to residents of Hardee County, FL.
Application information: Application form required.
Officers: Gladys Coker, Pres.; Jean Archambault, Secy.
Directors: Gerald Knight, Marcus Shackelford.
EIN: 592479238
Codes: GTI

59661
Ethel & Abraham Glass Charitable Foundation, Inc.
7325 La Reserve Cir.
Tamarac, FL 33321

Established in 2000.
Financial data (yr. ended 06/30/01): Assets, $481,545 (M); grants paid, $37,500; expenditures, $51,767; qualifying distributions, $37,500.
Limitations: Applications not accepted. Giving on a national basis, with emphasis on FL.
Directors: Bonnie L. Brumer, Marcy Haupt, Robert A. Haupt.
EIN: 651019738

59662
Heritage Oaks Foundation, Inc.
P.O. Box 7001
Wesley Chapel, FL 33543 (727) 536-4328
Contact: Larry Guilford, Pres.

Donor(s): Larry Guilford.
Financial data (yr. ended 09/30/00): Assets, $480,391 (M); grants paid, $1,500; gifts received, $10,000; expenditures, $2,384; qualifying distributions, $2,384; giving activities include $2,384 for programs.
Officer: Larry Guilford, Pres.
EIN: 880412086

59663
The Frank M. Wolfe Foundation, Inc.
505 N. Orlando Ave., Ste. 304
Cocoa Beach, FL 32931 (321) 783-2834
Contact: Frank M. Wolfe, Pres.

Donor(s): Frank M. Wolfe.
Financial data (yr. ended 12/31/99): Assets, $478,876 (M); grants paid, $6,429; expenditures, $8,102; qualifying distributions, $6,429.
Limitations: Giving primarily in FL.
Officers and Trustees:* Frank M. Wolfe,* Pres. and Treas.; Robert Baugher, Jennifer LeBlanc, Maria Medina.
EIN: 593482977

59664
The Robert and Aldona Beall Family Foundation, Inc.
(Formerly The Beall Family Foundation)
1806 38th Ave. E.
Bradenton, FL 34208
Application addresses: For scholarships: c/o Scholarship Committee Chair., Palmetto Youth Center, P.O. Box 608, Palmetto, FL 34220; For Law Enforcement and Teacher/Educator Grants: P.O. Box 25207, Bradenton, FL 34206-5207
Contact: Patricia Johnson, Admin.

Established in 1994 in FL.
Donor(s): Robert M. Beall II.
Financial data (yr. ended 11/30/01): Assets, $476,946 (M); grants paid, $22,667; gifts received, $500; expenditures, $25,178; qualifying distributions, $25,163.
Limitations: Giving limited to the Palmetto, FL, area.
Application information: Application form required.

Trustees: Aldona K. Beall, Egbert R. Beall, Robert M. Beall II, Stephen M. Knopik.
EIN: 650545213

59665
The Charles and Virginia Jacobsen Charitable Trust
c/o Bond Schoeneck & King
4001 Tamiami Trail N.
Naples, FL 34103

Established in 2001 in FL.
Donor(s): Virginia F. Jacobsen.‡
Financial data (yr. ended 12/31/01): Assets, $468,794 (M); grants paid, $5,000; gifts received, $505,000; expenditures, $12,064; qualifying distributions, $5,000.
Limitations: Giving limited to the greater Naples, FL, area.
Trustee: David N. Sexton.
EIN: 656368722

59666
The Gainesville Garden Club, Inc.
P.O. Box 357608
Gainesville, FL 32635-7608

Classified as a private operating foundation in 1982.
Financial data (yr. ended 06/30/00): Assets, $465,275 (M); grants paid, $0; gifts received, $3,475; expenditures, $49,256; qualifying distributions, $16,411; giving activities include $11,213 for programs.
Officers: Mrs. Hugh Turner, Pres.; Mrs. William Birket, 1st V.P.; Mrs. Wade Ring, 2nd V.P.; Mrs. Raymond Bender, Secy.; Mrs. Richard Buchanan, Corresponding Secy.; Mrs. C. Ross Sproul, Treas.
EIN: 596143160

59667
Howard T. Hirschy Foundation
2182 Tarpon Rd.
Naples, FL 34102 (941) 774-0733
Contact: Howard T. Hirschy, Tr.

Donor(s): Howard T. Hirschy.
Financial data (yr. ended 12/31/00): Assets, $456,122 (M); grants paid, $17,400; gifts received, $55,313; expenditures, $21,171; qualifying distributions, $17,400.
Limitations: Giving primarily in Naples, FL.
Trustee: Howard T. Hirschy.
EIN: 596875238

59668
Colonial Place Apartments, Inc.
c/o United Cerebral Palsy Assoc. of Miami
1411 N.W. 14th Ave.
Miami, FL 33125

Financial data (yr. ended 09/30/01): Assets, $454,523 (M); grants paid, $0; expenditures, $85,569; qualifying distributions, $23,868; giving activities include $85,569 for programs.
Officers: Jack Schillinger, Chair.; Joseph A. Aneillo, C.E.O. and Pres.; Majorie Schillinger, Vice-Chair.; Richard Rangel, Secy.; Harriet Stegman, Treas.
Directors: Gene Boeinger, Fernando Cabrera, Domingo Escar, Lloyd E. Foley, Robert Levy, Roy Lustig, Maj. Robert Peryam, Roger Reece.
EIN: 592775363

59669
Dean/Kluger Judaica Collection, Inc.
c/o Alan J. Kluger
201 S. Biscayne Blvd.
Miami, FL 33131

Classified as a private operating foundation in 1994 in FL.

Donor(s): Alan J. Kluger, Amy Dean.
Financial data (yr. ended 12/31/00): Assets, $444,075 (M); grants paid, $0; gifts received, $5,000; expenditures, $3,502; qualifying distributions, $0.
Directors: Amy Dean, Alan J. Kluger, Ronald Kohn.
EIN: 650470276

59670
Institute for Medical & Human Resources
c/o Kaufman, Rossin & Co.
2699 S. Bayshore Dr., Ste. 500
Miami, FL 33133

Established in 1994 in FL.
Donor(s): Carol R. Owen, Joseph Dorsey, M.D.
Financial data (yr. ended 04/30/00): Assets, $441,668 (M); grants paid, $0; expenditures, $58,433; qualifying distributions, $15,424; giving activities include $15,424 for programs.
Officers and Directors:* Joseph Dorsey, M.D.,* Pres.; Dorothea Goldstandt,* Secy.-Treas.; Marilyn Dorsey, Grant Perks.
EIN: 591574136

59671
For a Better World, Inc.
c/o Arthur Stein
5030 Champion Blvd., Ste. 6-303
Boca Raton, FL 33496-2473

Established in 1991 in NY.
Donor(s): Arthur Stein, Ph.D.
Financial data (yr. ended 12/31/01): Assets, $433,786 (M); grants paid, $1,000; gifts received, $100,000; expenditures, $21,909; qualifying distributions, $17,077; giving activities include $17,077 for programs.
Officers: Arthur Stein, Ph.D., Pres. and Treas.; Alex Feuer, V.P.; Priscilla Simmons, Secy.
EIN: 113081306

59672
The Jane & Stuart Watson Foundation, Inc.
P.O. Box 1483
Boca Grande, FL 33921-1483

Established in 1982.
Financial data (yr. ended 11/30/99): Assets, $428,381 (M); grants paid, $50,250; expenditures, $55,299; qualifying distributions, $54,799.
Limitations: Applications not accepted. Giving primarily in KY.
Application information: Contributes only to pre-selected organizations.
Officers: Jane Watson, Pres.; Sarah Ann DeCrew, V.P.; Beth Ellen Noujaim, V.P.; Stephen Harvey Watson, V.P.
EIN: 222479998

59673
Animal Welfare Foundation, Inc.
P.O. Box 5859, No. 545
Winter Garden, FL 34787

Established in 1987 in FL.
Donor(s): Lorrie Nassofer.
Financial data (yr. ended 09/30/00): Assets, $424,227 (L); grants paid, $10,000; gifts received, $126,378; expenditures, $155,763; qualifying distributions, $143,711; giving activities include $133,762 for programs.
Limitations: Applications not accepted.
Application information: Contributes only to pre-selected organizations.
Officer: Lorrie Nassofer, Mgr.
EIN: 592900296

59674
Charles E. & Jean H. Woodsby Private Foundation, Inc.
1260 Central Florida Pkwy.
Orlando, FL 32837

Donor(s): Charles E. Woodsby.
Financial data (yr. ended 05/31/01): Assets, $410,582 (M); grants paid, $67,035; gifts received, $101,526; expenditures, $78,132; qualifying distributions, $77,011.
Limitations: Applications not accepted. Giving on a national basis, with some emphasis on the South.
Application information: Contributes only to pre-selected organizations.
Officers and Directors:* Charles E. Woodsby,* Pres.; Dennis L. Monroe,* Secy.; Jean H. Woodsby,* Treas.
EIN: 593515126

59675
Musquito Cove Restorations, Inc.
c/o R. Adenbaum
177 Commadore Dr.
Jupiter, FL 33477-4007

Financial data (yr. ended 12/31/01): Assets, $404,117 (M); grants paid, $0; gifts received, $10,000; expenditures, $808; qualifying distributions, $0.
Director: Robert Adenbaum.
EIN: 112593497

59676
Longleaf Ecology and Forestry Society
c/o John C. Winn
12318 N.E., CR 1471
Waldo, FL 32694

Established in 1993 in FL.
Donor(s): John Winn, Mary Lou Winn.
Financial data (yr. ended 12/31/99): Assets, $401,503 (M); grants paid, $0; gifts received, $134,000; expenditures, $12,975; qualifying distributions, $80,964; giving activities include $12,975 for programs.
Trustees: John Winn, Mary Lou Winn.
EIN: 593209689

59677
B. Beall & R. Kemp Riechmann Foundation
1806 38th Ave., E.
Bradenton, FL 34208
Contact: Beverly Beall, Tr.

Established as a private operating foundation in 1998 in FL.
Donor(s): Beverly Beall, R. Kemp Reichman.
Financial data (yr. ended 11/30/00): Assets, $398,514 (M); grants paid, $10,900; gifts received, $11,700; expenditures, $11,534; qualifying distributions, $11,534; giving activities include $634 for programs.
Limitations: Giving primarily in FL.
Application information: Application form required.
Trustees: Beverly Beall, Robert M. Beall II, R. Kemp Reichmann.
EIN: 650808807

59678
The Paul Bush Family Foundation
12800 University Dr., Ste. 650
Fort Myers, FL 33907

Established in 1998 in DE, Fl and NY. Classified as a private operating foundation in 1999.
Donor(s): Paul S. Bush.
Financial data (yr. ended 12/31/00): Assets, $369,846 (M); grants paid, $36,100; expenditures, $47,698; qualifying distributions, $40,096.
Limitations: Applications not accepted.
Application information: Contributes only to pre-selected organizations.
Officers: Paul S. Bush, Pres.; Donna Doyle, Treas.
EIN: 161541439

59679
The Scmakete Foundation, Inc.
3647 Woodhill Dr.
Brandon, FL 33511

Established in 2000 in FL.
Donor(s): Marydine L. Lamb.
Financial data (yr. ended 12/31/00): Assets, $366,004 (M); grants paid, $0; gifts received, $423,815; expenditures, $8,090; qualifying distributions, $12,500; giving activities include $6,000 for loans and $6,500 for programs.
Officers: Marydine L. Lamb, Pres.; Scott Lamb, V.P.; Theodore E. Lamb, Secy.; Katherine L. Feinerman, Treas.
EIN: 593628296

59680
Bonomo Family Foundation, Inc.
c/o Jacobowitz & Ostroff
11900 Biscayine Blvd.
Miami, FL 33181

Established in 1997 in FL.
Donor(s): Victor Bonomo, Zephra Bonomo.
Financial data (yr. ended 12/31/99): Assets, $356,799 (M); grants paid, $50,800; gifts received, $263,520; expenditures, $55,505; qualifying distributions, $50,793.
Limitations: Applications not accepted.
Application information: Contributes only to pre-selected organizations.
Officers and Directors:* Tracy Arnold,* Pres.; Deborah Erenrich,* V.P.; Jordon B. Bonomo,* Secy.; Wayne Bonomo,* Treas.
EIN: 650743994

59681
Ezekiel Foundation, Inc.
150 S.E. 2nd Ave., Ste. 807
Miami, FL 33131

Established in 1996.
Donor(s): Alfred Ezekiel.
Financial data (yr. ended 12/31/01): Assets, $349,592 (M); grants paid, $29,287; gifts received, $2,600; expenditures, $30,302; qualifying distributions, $29,377.
Limitations: Applications not accepted. Giving primarily in Miami, Fl.
Application information: Contributes only to pre-selected organizations.
Directors: Alfred Ezekiel, Malcolm Ezekiel, Pearl Ezekiel.
EIN: 311468691

59682
Lyden Foundation, Inc.
P.O. Box 700
Winter Park, FL 32790

Established in 1998.
Financial data (yr. ended 05/31/00): Assets, $347,712 (M); grants paid, $13,000; gifts received, $960; expenditures, $13,091; qualifying distributions, $13,091.
Limitations: Applications not accepted.
Officers: James P. Lyden, Pres. and Treas.; Scott A. Lyden, V.P.; Kristia Allyden, Secy.
EIN: 593469366

59683
E. Blaine Schoolcraft Haiti Missions, Inc.
2001 Brinson Rd., Ste. 15
Lutz, FL 33549-5179

Financial data (yr. ended 12/31/00): Assets, $338,825 (M); grants paid, $1,500; gifts received, $1,650; expenditures, $35,359; qualifying distributions, $1,500.
Limitations: Applications not accepted.
Application information: Contributes only to pre-selected organizations.
Director: E. Blaine Schoolcraft.
EIN: 593536008

59684
Leonard & Mildred Igstaedter Foundation, Inc.
c/o Edward R. Carroll
4396 Bowsprit Ct., Ste. 1C
Fort Myers, FL 33919-4707 (941) 482-8558

Established in 1994 in DE and FL.
Donor(s): Mildred Igstaedter.
Financial data (yr. ended 12/31/00): Assets, $324,890 (M); grants paid, $26,542; expenditures, $28,232; qualifying distributions, $26,542.
Limitations: Applications not accepted. Giving primarily in DE.
Officers: Edward R. Carroll, Pres.; Ellen Shea, Treas.
EIN: 061399555
Codes: GTI

59685
Koops Family Foundation
14342A Harbour Landings Dr.
Fort Myers, FL 33908 (941) 267-2769
Contact: Earl C. Koops, Pres.

Classified as a private operating foundation in 1998 in MI.
Donor(s): Earl C. Koops.
Financial data (yr. ended 12/31/01): Assets, $292,583 (M); grants paid, $13,000; gifts received, $71,600; expenditures, $13,000; qualifying distributions, $13,862.
Officers: Earl C. Koops, Pres. and Treas.; Charlotte J. Koops, V.P. and Secy.
EIN: 383439120

59686
The John R. and Matilde F. Linders Foundation, Inc.
c/o Nutter & Nutter, PA
240 N. Washington Blvd., Ste. 430
Sarasota, FL 34236-5933

Established in 1989 in FL.
Donor(s): John R. Linders.
Financial data (yr. ended 12/31/99): Assets, $278,754 (M); grants paid, $0; gifts received, $76,427; expenditures, $67,167; qualifying distributions, $62,692; giving activities include $62,071 for programs.
Officers and Directors:* Jean R. Vogele,* Pres.; David Fancher,* Secy.; Peter Holmstedt, Dana K. Thompson.
EIN: 650136032

59687
Harmony Education Center, Inc.
111 N. Orange Ave., Ste. 1100
Orlando, FL 32801

Donor(s): Henrietta C. Bessemer.
Financial data (yr. ended 12/31/99): Assets, $275,710 (M); grants paid, $0; gifts received, $21,596; expenditures, $6,685; qualifying distributions, $119; giving activities include $119 for programs.

Officers and Directors:* Henrietta C. Bessemer, Pres.; Evelyn Hogan, V.P.; Glen Hubal,* Secy.; Anthoney Santangelo,* Treas.; B.J. Walton.
EIN: 591448961

59688
Overseas Chinese Christian Foundation
1221 E. Robinson St.
Orlando, FL 32801-2115
Application address: c/o Esther Yoh, 4219 Pascal Pl., Palos Verdes Peninsula, CA 90274

Established in 1981 in FL and NJ.
Financial data (yr. ended 01/31/01): Assets, $272,852 (M); grants paid, $154,921; gifts received, $130,218; expenditures, $156,445; qualifying distributions, $156,445.
Limitations: Giving on a national basis, with some giving in China and southeast Asia.
Officer: Esther Yoh, Pres.
EIN: 222357766
Codes: FD2

59689
Third Millennium Ministries, Inc.
PMB 15, 5840 Red Bug Lake Rd.
Winter Springs, FL 32708

Donor(s): Betty Edwards, Mike Guthrie, Billy Mounger, John Phillips, Doug Roossien.
Financial data (yr. ended 12/31/00): Assets, $270,772 (M); grants paid, $0; gifts received, $316,514; expenditures, $197,150; qualifying distributions, $0; giving activities include $191,536 for programs.
Limitations: Applications not accepted.
Application information: Contributes only to pre-selected organizations.
Officer and Directors:* Richard Lynwood Pratt, Jr.,* Pres.; Jane Parks Pillow, Jeanne Tomlinson Pratt, Richard Lynwood Pratt, Sr.
EIN: 311598585

59690
Peter & Andrew Lambos Foundation, Inc.
16101 9 Eagles Dr.
Odessa, FL 33556-2813
Contact: William A. Lambos, Exec. V.P.

Established as a private operating foundation in FL.
Donor(s): Constance P. Lambos.
Financial data (yr. ended 12/31/00): Assets, $270,746 (M); grants paid, $106,426; gifts received, $225,705; expenditures, $173,898; qualifying distributions, $106,301.
Limitations: Giving primarily in New York, NY.
Officers: Theodora Lambos, Pres.; William A. Lambos, Exec. V.P.; Carol Lambos, Treas.
EIN: 593477654
Codes: FD2

59691
The Grove Tree-Man Trust, Inc.
c/o Jim McMaster
2940 S.W. 30th Ct.
Coconut Grove, FL 33133

Established in 1997 in FL; Classified as a private operating foundation in 2001.
Financial data (yr. ended 03/31/01): Assets, $267,950 (M); grants paid, $400; gifts received, $100; expenditures, $28,933; qualifying distributions, $28,933.
Limitations: Giving primarily in Coconut Grove, FL.
Officers and Directors:* Jim McMaster,* Pres.; Anthony R. Parrish, Jr.,* V.P.; Ron Nelson,* V.P.; Nick Delmore,* Secy.; Nancy Cliff,* Treas.; Susan Billig, Miok Johnson, Joyce Nelson.
EIN: 650611127

59692
Northwest Florida Environmental Enhancement Foundation, Inc.
307 W. Gregory
Pensacola, FL 32501

Financial data (yr. ended 04/30/02): Assets, $265,645 (M); grants paid, $0; expenditures, $0; qualifying distributions, $0.
Officers: Thomas Godwin, Pres.; Jack Lowe, V.P.; John Coe, Secy.-Treas.
Trustee: Richard Godwin.
EIN: 591768739

59693
Conrad Family Foundation
9976 Brassie Bend
Naples, FL 34108

Established in 2000 in FL.
Donor(s): Stuart P. Conrad, Thomas D. Conrad.
Financial data (yr. ended 12/31/00): Assets, $265,152 (M); grants paid, $0; gifts received, $265,152; expenditures, $0; qualifying distributions, $0.
Trustees: Dale J. Conrad, Margaret Joan Conrad, Stuart P. Conrad, Thomas D. Conrad.
EIN: 656351362

59694
Anne K. Foundation, Inc.
P.O. Box 8987
Jacksonville, FL 32211
Contact: Anne Kufeldt, Treas.

Established in 2000 in FL.
Donor(s): Anne Kufeldt, James Kufeldt.
Financial data (yr. ended 12/31/01): Assets, $264,904 (M); grants paid, $49,500; expenditures, $53,915; qualifying distributions, $51,338.
Officers: Sara Anne Hall, Secy.; Anne Kufeldt, Treas.
EIN: 593677087

59695
Elizabeth Edgar Hall Corporation, Inc.
4427 Herschel St.
Jacksonville, FL 32210

Financial data (yr. ended 12/31/00): Assets, $251,539 (M); grants paid, $14,375; gifts received, $14,600; expenditures, $19,630; qualifying distributions, $14,375.
Limitations: Giving primarily in Jacksonville, FL.
Application information: Application form required.
Officers and Directors:* Karen B. Nuland,* Pres.; Geraldine Turbow,* Secy.; Davron Cardenas, Kathy Clower, Charlotte Hancock, Janet Johnson, Mrs. I.V. King, Deborah Knauer, Lucile R. McAuley, Adele Rothschild, Peggy Zell.
EIN: 592396975

59696
Clear Genesis, Inc.
3514 Sunrise Dr.
Key West, FL 33040

Established in 1997 in FL.
Donor(s): John T. Lincoln.
Financial data (yr. ended 06/30/00): Assets, $248,845 (M); grants paid, $0; gifts received, $1,237; expenditures, $87,377; qualifying distributions, $63,391; giving activities include $21,705 for programs.
Officer: John T. Lincoln, Pres.
Directors: Bradley Lincoln, Martha Lincoln.
EIN: 650777985

59697
William & Hannah Cohen Foundation
11519 Timberline Cir.
Fort Myers, FL 33912
Application address: 311 Strawtown Rd., West Nyack, NY 10994, tel.: (914) 358-2374
Contact: Mildred Karel, Secy.

Financial data (yr. ended 03/31/00): Assets, $242,525 (M); grants paid, $9,500; expenditures, $11,917; qualifying distributions, $95,001.
Limitations: Giving primarily in NJ and NY.
Officers and Directors:* Mildred Karel,* Secy.; Fred A. Cohen,* Treas.; Rochelle Adler, Philip Cohen, Dorothy Grimm, Anna Oken, Rose Poley-Weinstein, Mildred C. Rosenthal, Selma Slotnick.
EIN: 226085831

59698
Guy & Therese De La Valdene Family Foundation, Inc.
606 Robin Ln.
Havana, FL 32333

Established in 1999 in FL.
Donor(s): Guy De La Valdene, Therese De La Valdene.
Financial data (yr. ended 12/31/00): Assets, $240,945 (M); grants paid, $31,850; gifts received, $75,987; expenditures, $34,172; qualifying distributions, $31,850.
Limitations: Applications not accepted.
Application information: Contributes only to pre-selected organizations.
Officers: Guy De La Valdene, Pres.; Therese De La Valdene, Secy.-Treas.
Directors: Johnny De La Valdene, Valerie De La Valdene.
EIN: 597166295

59699
The Mabel & Ellsworth Simmons Charitable Foundation, Inc.
6718 Simmons Loop
Riverview, FL 33569

Financial data (yr. ended 12/31/00): Assets, $240,781 (M); grants paid, $13,000; expenditures, $13,000; qualifying distributions, $13,000.
Limitations: Giving primarily in Ruskin, FL.
Officers: Sandra Simmons, Pres.; James A. Jimenez, Secy.; Andrew Capello, Treas.
Directors: Jean Simmons Odell, George Simmons.
EIN: 593594418

59700
Gorilla Theatre, Inc.
4419 N. Manhattan Ave.
Tampa, FL 33614-7650

Donor(s): Aubrey Hampton, Susan Hussey, Aubrey Organics, Inc.
Financial data (yr. ended 12/31/99): Assets, $238,455 (M); grants paid, $0; gifts received, $445,504; expenditures, $433,517; qualifying distributions, $253,791; giving activities include $253,591 for programs.
Limitations: Applications not accepted.
Application information: Contributes only to pre-selected organizations.
Directors: Stephen Evans, Aubrey Hampton, Susan Hussey.
EIN: 593213527

59701
Joan Deckelbaum Foundation
c/o Morris Deckelbaum
4430 Casper Ct.
Hollywood, FL 33021-2416

Established in 2000.
Donor(s): Morris Deckelbaum.
Financial data (yr. ended 12/31/00): Assets, $226,105 (M); grants paid, $12,000; gifts received, $294,740; expenditures, $16,731; qualifying distributions, $12,500.
Officer: Morris Deckelbaum, Mgr.
EIN: 650969389

59702
Fry Foundation, Inc.
c/o William S. Fry
4919 Gardengate Ln.
Orlando, FL 32821-8251

Donor(s): William S. Fry.
Financial data (yr. ended 12/31/99): Assets, $222,823 (M); grants paid, $8,000; gifts received, $100,000; expenditures, $16,136; qualifying distributions, $15,893; giving activities include $1,411 for programs.
Limitations: Applications not accepted. Giving primarily in Orlando, FL.
Application information: Contributes only to pre-selected organizations.
Officers: William S. Fry, Pres.; Aleethe K. Fry, V.P.
EIN: 593547265

59703
Neural Engineering Clinic
330 Hammock Shore Dr.
Melbourne Beach, FL 32951-3963

Established in 1994 in ME.
Donor(s): Ross Davis.
Financial data (yr. ended 12/31/01): Assets, $217,596 (M); grants paid, $0; gifts received, $457,030; expenditures, $477,697; qualifying distributions, $477,629; giving activities include $477,697 for programs.
Officers: Ross Davis, M.D., Pres.; Sandy Emmons, Secy.-Treas.
Director: James McKendry.
EIN: 010494502

59704
Richardson Scholarship Foundation, Inc.
P.O. Box 370
Vero Beach, FL 32961
Application address: P.O. Box 339, Vero Beach, FL 32961-0339
Contact: Gary Lindsey, Exec. Dir.

Established in 1988 in FL.
Donor(s): Hopwood Charitable Trust, Richardson Foundation, Inc.
Financial data (yr. ended 12/31/01): Assets, $215,815 (M); grants paid, $104,960; gifts received, $100,000; expenditures, $114,267; qualifying distributions, $104,960.
Limitations: Giving primarily to Indian River County, FL, residents.
Application information: Scholarship recipients are selected based on recommendations from educational institutions and other parties. Application form required.
Officers: Danforth K. Richardson, Pres.; Marjorie H. Richardson, V.P.; Sandra R. Kahle, Secy.; Nancy R. Luther, Treas.; Gary W. Lindsey, Exec. Dir.
Directors: Samuel Block, Charles J. Bradshaw, Amanda Ford, Nancy Gisler, Carter W. Hopkins, George A. Kahle, Roy Lambert, John M. Luther, Sandra Walker.
EIN: 650064113

Codes: FD2, GTI

59705
John Miskoff Foundation
9605 N.W. 79th Ave., No. 16
Hialeah Gardens, FL 33016

Established in 1981 in FL.
Donor(s): John Miskoff,‡ Wilmoth Miskoff Irrevocable Trust.
Financial data (yr. ended 06/30/99): Assets, $202,701 (M); grants paid, $14,572; expenditures, $47,239; qualifying distributions, $45,047; giving activities include $14,572 for loans to individuals.
Limitations: Giving primarily in FL.
Application information: Preliminary screening is done by the college. Applicants are then interviewed by the foundation.
Trustees: Sylvia Cahan, Joyce Laker, George Palmer.
EIN: 592193608
Codes: GTI

59706
Educational Services Consortium, Inc.
P.O. Box 14776
Tallahassee, FL 32317-4776

Classified as a private operating foundation in 1976.
Donor(s): William K. Snyder.
Financial data (yr. ended 06/30/00): Assets, $198,584 (M); grants paid, $0; expenditures, $26,290; qualifying distributions, $22,797; giving activities include $12,337 for programs.
Officers: William K. Snyder, Pres.; Joel Dawson, V.P.; Peter Crowell, Treas.
EIN: 237318045

59707
Foundation for Cross Cultural Understanding, Inc.
478 Tequesta Dr., Apt.108
Tequesta, FL 33469

Classified as a private operating foundation in 1981.
Financial data (yr. ended 12/31/01): Assets, $198,435 (M); grants paid, $0; gifts received, $2,461; expenditures, $2,563; qualifying distributions, $0; giving activities include $2,563 for programs.
Officers: Kathryn S. Loughran, Chair.; John L. Loughran, Pres. and Treas.
EIN: 521166268

59708
The Littman Family Foundation, Inc.
18081 Biscayne Blvd., Ste. 601
Aventura, FL 33160

Established in 1996 in FL.
Donor(s): Benjamin B. Littman.
Financial data (yr. ended 12/31/00): Assets, $197,702 (M); grants paid, $10,592; expenditures, $11,600; qualifying distributions, $10,592.
Limitations: Applications not accepted.
Application information: Contributes only to pre-selected organizations.
Officers: Benjamin B. Littman, Pres.; Ruth R. Littman, Secy.
Director: Emily L. Eisen.
EIN: 650631633

59709
The Aloe Institute
3708 Maplewood Terr.
Bradenton, FL 34203
Application address: 19 Kitchum Rd., Westport, CT 06886, tel.: (203) 454-1919
Contact: Jess F. Clarke, Jr., Dir.

Established as a private operating foundation in 1996.
Financial data (yr. ended 12/31/01): Assets, $193,336 (M); grants paid, $7,500; gifts received, $86,986; expenditures, $41,190; qualifying distributions, $61,191.
Directors: Jess Clarke, Jr., Amanda Fried, Ellen Fried, Jane Grace.
EIN: 061463529

59710
The Jay and Becky Kaiserman Foundation
1955 N. Honore Ave., Apt. B415
Sarasota, FL 34235-9124

Established in 1986 in FL.
Donor(s): J.J. Kaiserman, Rebecca Kaiserman.
Financial data (yr. ended 12/31/01): Assets, $188,085 (M); grants paid, $30,655; gifts received, $44,284; expenditures, $31,180; qualifying distributions, $31,176.
Limitations: Applications not accepted. Giving primarily in FL.
Application information: Contributes only to pre-selected organizations.
Managers: J.J. Kaiserman, Rebecca Kaiserman.
EIN: 592549476

59711
Paul A. Nuzzo Memorial Scholarship Fund, Inc.
324 Plant Ave.
Tampa, FL 33606-2347
Contact: Scholarship Application Committee

Donor(s): James S. Nuzzo.
Financial data (yr. ended 02/28/99): Assets, $181,007 (M); grants paid, $10,000; gifts received, $25; expenditures, $11,712; qualifying distributions, $10,000.
Limitations: Giving limited to Hillsborough County, FL, area.
Application information: Application form required.
Directors: Thomas J. Crowe, Sam Giunta, James P. Hines, James S. Nuzzo, Malcolm G. Taffe.
EIN: 593058026

59712
Ann Sturgeon Memorial Rose Garden Fund, Inc.
13401 Indian Rocks Rd.
Largo, FL 33774-2017

Donor(s): George C. Sturgeon.
Financial data (yr. ended 12/31/01): Assets, $176,382 (M); grants paid, $0; gifts received, $120; expenditures, $16,247; qualifying distributions, $0.
Officers: Ben R. Wiley, Pres.; Dorothee Torpey, Secy.; Donna Connell, Treas.
Directors: Liz Buchanon, Thomas D. Feastor, Geoffrey Gray, Roger LaPlume, Ralph Scheidenhelm, George Storm, Jay Zinn.
EIN: 592108150

59713
G Foundation, Corp.
2255 Wilton Dr.
Wilton Manors, FL 33305

Established in 2000 in FL.
Donor(s): Fredrick Warten.
Financial data (yr. ended 12/31/00): Assets, $176,250 (M); grants paid, $0; gifts received,

$172,900; expenditures, $0; qualifying distributions, $0.
Limitations: Applications not accepted.
Application information: Contributes only to pre-selected organizations.
Directors: Dean Trantalis, Fredrick Warten.
EIN: 651062328

59714
Practical Christianity Foundation
2535 Success Dr.
Odessa, FL 33556

Financial data (yr. ended 06/30/02): Assets, $175,140 (M); grants paid, $0; gifts received, $471,148; expenditures, $396,021; qualifying distributions, $0.
Trustee: Richard W. Baker.
EIN: 593444993

59715
The Faass Foundation, Inc.
P.O. Box 839
LaBelle, FL 33975-0839
Contact: Hans O. Faass, Dir. and Tr.

Established in 1996 in FL.
Financial data (yr. ended 06/30/00): Assets, $170,010 (M); grants paid, $1,100; gifts received, $119,480; expenditures, $2,791; qualifying distributions, $2,503.
Limitations: Giving primarily in FL.
Directors and Trustees: Michael D. Faass, Hans O. Faass, Ruth A. Faass, James W. McFadden, F. J. Rief III, Richard H. Suddaby.
EIN: 650666083

59716
Sherman Foundation, Inc.
903 S.W. 93rd Terr.
Plantation, FL 33324

Donor(s): Rick Sherman.
Financial data (yr. ended 04/30/00): Assets, $165,886 (M); grants paid, $7,000; expenditures, $9,133; qualifying distributions, $10,743.
Limitations: Applications not accepted. Giving primarily in FL.
Application information: Contributes only to pre-selected organizations.
Officer: Rick Sherman, Pres.
EIN: 650484905

59717
Harold H. Cohen Foundation Charitable Trust
7098 Via Genova
Delray Beach, FL 33446
Contact: Harold H. Cohen, Mgr.

Financial data (yr. ended 12/31/01): Assets, $162,966 (M); grants paid, $7,581; expenditures, $8,426; qualifying distributions, $7,507.
Limitations: Giving on a national basis, with emphasis in Erie, PA.
Application information: Application form not required.
Officers: Adelle Cohen, Mgr.; Harold H. Cohen, Mgr.
EIN: 256084080

59718
Progress Village Foundation
4907 84th St. S.
Tampa, FL 33619 (813) 677-6438
Application address: 8306 Fir Dr., Tampa, FL 33619
Contact: Lois Bowers, Pres.

Established in 1986 in FL.
Donor(s): Robert E. Wooley, Gardinier, Inc.
Financial data (yr. ended 12/31/01): Assets, $160,872 (M); grants paid, $48,558; gifts received, $95,200; expenditures, $109,392; qualifying distributions, $107,976; giving activities include $108,013 for programs.
Limitations: Giving limited to residents of Progress Village in Tampa, FL.
Application information: Application form required.
Officers: Lois Bowers, Pres.; Alberta Shedrick, V.P; Mary Hobley, Rec. Secy.; Bertha Kemp, Treas.
Directors: Wallace Bowers, Juanita Cook, Gray Gordan, Mary Hobley, Dora Kellum, Bertha Kemp, Ben Smith, Rosalie Young.
EIN: 592807536
Codes: GTI

59719
Coastal Education & Research Foundation, Inc.
1656 Cypress Row Dr.
West Palm Beach, FL 33411-5108

Established around 1983 in VA.
Financial data (yr. ended 06/30/01): Assets, $152,905 (M); grants paid, $0; expenditures, $14,971; qualifying distributions, $0.
Officers: Charles W. Finkl, Jr., Pres.; Rhodes W. Fairbridge, V.P.; Barbara Fromberg, Secy.-Treas.
Directors: Per Bruun, Robert Dolan, Terry Healy, David Hopley, Robert M. Huff, Roland Paskoff, Maurice L. Schwartz, Ian Shennan, Andrew D. Short, Daniel J. Stanley.
EIN: 592302170

59720
The Arthur Sheir & Anne Sheir Foundation, Inc.
2801 N.E. 183rd St., Ste. 1402
Aventura, FL 33160-2131

Established in 1997.
Financial data (yr. ended 12/31/99): Assets, $152,830 (M); grants paid, $7,500; gifts received, $7,000; expenditures, $7,936; qualifying distributions, $7,936.
Directors: Arnold Sheir, Arthur Sheir, Robert Sheir.
EIN: 311547949

59721
The Christian Foundation
121 Lake Hollingsworth Dr.
Lakeland, FL 33801

Donor(s): Marie M. Miller, Truman W. Miller.
Financial data (yr. ended 02/28/02): Assets, $151,812 (M); grants paid, $14,125; expenditures, $21,799; qualifying distributions, $14,125.
Limitations: Giving on a national basis, with emphasis on the Southeast.
Officers: Truman W. Miller, Pres.; Marie M. Miller, Treas.
EIN: 566067052

59722
Bodine Family Foundation, Inc.
4351 Gulf Shore Blvd. N., Ste. 9S
Naples, FL 34103-2239 (941) 403-4034
Contact: Robert J. Bodine, Dir.

Established in 1999 in FL.
Donor(s): Robert J. Bodine.
Financial data (yr. ended 12/31/00): Assets, $141,205 (M); grants paid, $4,025; gifts received, $106,146; expenditures, $12,212; qualifying distributions, $12,212.
Application information: Application form required.
Directors: Robert J. Bodine, Joanne W. Bodine, Gayle Garrett, Carol Lloyd.
EIN: 650874850

59723
The LaMotte Family Foundation
5125 Joe Wood Dr.
Sanibel, FL 33957-7513
Contact: K. J. LaMotte, Dir.

Donor(s): Kenneth J. LaMotte.
Financial data (yr. ended 12/31/00): Assets, $140,287 (M); grants paid, $52,819; expenditures, $53,750; qualifying distributions, $58,750.
Directors: Kathleen LaMotte, Kenneth J. LaMotte, K. Russell LaMotte, Matthew LaMotte.
EIN: 383349383

59724
Lake Towers Good Samaritan Fund
101 Trinity Lakes Dr., Ste. 137
Sun City Center, FL 33573
Contact: Durwood J. Hedgecock

Established in 1999.
Financial data (yr. ended 12/31/00): Assets, $133,855 (M); grants paid, $4,669; expenditures, $4,669; qualifying distributions, $4,669.
Limitations: Giving limited to residents of Sun City, FL.
Officers: Durwood J. Hedgecock, Chair.; Berneice Herron, Secy.; Ruth Busbee, Treas.
EIN: 596777442

59725
The Lear Foundation, Inc.
13700 Roanoake St.
Davie, FL 33325

Established in 1999 in FL.
Financial data (yr. ended 12/31/00): Assets, $131,703 (M); grants paid, $0; gifts received, $320,000; expenditures, $286,442; qualifying distributions, $0; giving activities include $266,846 for programs.
Limitations: Applications not accepted.
Application information: Contributes only to pre-selected organizations.
Officer and Directors:* Timothy Richards,* V.P.; Denis Quinlan, Joel Secan.
EIN: 650929310

59726
Leroy and Alice Pate Family Foundation, Inc.
18246 Hancock Bluff Rd.
Dade City, FL 33523

Established in 2000 in FL.
Donor(s): Leroy L. Pate.
Financial data (yr. ended 12/31/00): Assets, $130,878 (M); grants paid, $875; gifts received, $140,875; expenditures, $875; qualifying distributions, $875.
Officer: Leroy L. Pate, Pres. and Secy.-Treas.
Directors: Beth A. Pate, Lynne P. Watson.
EIN: 593667465

59727
Lay Apostolate Foundation
801 S. Federal Hwy., Ste. 1106
Pompano Beach, FL 33062

Donor(s): John M. Haffert.
Financial data (yr. ended 01/31/00): Assets, $125,012 (M); grants paid, $71,005; gifts received, $156,769; expenditures, $184,434; qualifying distributions, $183,330.
Limitations: Applications not accepted.
Application information: Contributes only to pre-selected organizations.
Officers: John M. Haffert, Pres.; Patricia M. Haffert, V.P.; Stacia Denicola, Secy.
EIN: 630326413

59728
Christian Foundation of Florida, Inc.
5521 E. Hwy. 98
Panama City, FL 32404

Financial data (yr. ended 05/31/00): Assets, $123,899 (M); grants paid, $2,244; gifts received, $235; expenditures, $2,637; qualifying distributions, $2,637.
Limitations: Applications not accepted.
Application information: Contributes only to pre-selected organizations.
Officers: Holton R. Harders, Pres.; Nancy Harders, Secy.; Holton H. Harders, Treas.
EIN: 237153904

59729
Hermanns Family Foundation, Inc.
8600 Trotters Ln.
Parkland, FL 33067-1039

Donor(s): Richard Hermanns, Lisa Hermanns.
Financial data (yr. ended 12/31/99): Assets, $116,731 (M); grants paid, $17,500; expenditures, $18,006; qualifying distributions, $17,500.
Limitations: Giving primarily in TX.
Officers: R. Hermanns, Pres.; L. Hermanns, V.P.
EIN: 650760751

59730
The Bustraan Family Foundation, Inc.
1440 Handleman Dr.
Oviedo, FL 32765-8785 (407) 977-0285
Contact: James P. Bustraan, Pres.

Established in 1999 in FL.
Donor(s): James P. Bustraan, Dorothy A. Bustraan.
Financial data (yr. ended 11/30/00): Assets, $115,575 (M); grants paid, $14,000; gifts received, $149,000; expenditures, $16,904; qualifying distributions, $14,000.
Limitations: Giving primarily in GA and IN.
Officers: James P. Bustraan, Pres.; Dorothy A. Bustraan, Secy.
Directors: James P. Bustraan, Jr., Richard A. Bustraan, William A. Bustraan.
EIN: 593614638

59731
The Cultural Society, Inc.
200 W. 19th St.
Panama City, FL 32405
Contact: Yahya Abdul Rahim, Pres.

Established in 1974 in IN.
Donor(s): Mohammed Jaghlit, M.D., M.S. Hafiz, Abdul Rehman C. Amine, M.D., Bassam Osman.
Financial data (yr. ended 06/30/01): Assets, $114,434 (L); grants paid, $155,930; gifts received, $277; expenditures, $156,889; qualifying distributions, $0.
Limitations: Giving primarily in FL.
Application information: Application form not required.
Officers: Yahya Abdul Rahim, Pres. and Treas.; Rashda Al-Bibi, Secy.
EIN: 510183515
Codes: FD2

59732
For a New Social Science
c/o William B. Anderson
13379 Compton Rd.
Loxahatchee, FL 33470-4715

Established in 1988 in CA.
Donor(s): Samuel J. Leven.
Financial data (yr. ended 12/31/99): Assets, $113,655 (M); grants paid, $10,000; expenditures, $53,748; qualifying distributions, $47,005; giving activities include $37,082 for programs.
Limitations: Applications not accepted.
Directors: William E. Corley III, Samuel J. Leven, Lynne White.
EIN: 943089768
Codes: GTI

59733
Lonnie Bob Hurst Scholarship Trust
11465 75th Dr.
Live Oak, FL 32060-7118 (386) 364-5210
Contact: Donna C. Long, Tr.

Established in 1993 in FL.
Financial data (yr. ended 06/30/01): Assets, $111,662 (M); grants paid, $9,915; expenditures, $11,295; qualifying distributions, $11,026.
Limitations: Giving limited to residents of Suwannee County, FL.
Application information: Application form required.
Trustee: Donna C. Long.
EIN: 597011644

59734
Lemon Bay Boaters, Inc.
570 Bay Park Blvd.
Englewood, FL 34223

Established in 2001 in FL.
Financial data (yr. ended 12/31/01): Assets, $109,935 (M); grants paid, $1,000; gifts received, $3,190; expenditures, $6,155; qualifying distributions, $6,155.
Limitations: Applications not accepted.
Application information: Contributes only to pre-selected organizations.
Officer: Robert Schaaf.
EIN: 650049473

59735
Darrell Armstrong Foundation for Premature Babies, Inc.
6706 Magnolia Pointe Cir.
Orlando, FL 32810

Established in 2000 in FL.
Donor(s): Pepsi Cola Bottling Group, And 1 Basketball, BPI Global Asset Mgmt., LLP, Wayne Dench Charities.
Financial data (yr. ended 06/30/01): Assets, $109,452 (M); grants paid, $5,000; gifts received, $55,869; expenditures, $18,623; qualifying distributions, $7,185.
Limitations: Applications not accepted. Giving primarily in Orlando, FL.
Application information: Contributes only to pre-selected organizations.
Officers: Darrell Armstrong, Pres.; Thomas Rascoe, Jr., V.P.
Director: Paul Kuck.
EIN: 593620145

59736
Gross Family Foundation, Inc.
13647 Deering Bay Dr., Ste. 141
Miami, FL 33158 (305) 252-2436
Contact: Howard Gross, Pres.

Established in 1996 in FL.
Donor(s): American Paging, Dial Page.
Financial data (yr. ended 12/31/00): Assets, $107,662 (M); grants paid, $17,156; expenditures, $21,047; qualifying distributions, $17,156.
Application information: Application form not required.
Officers: Howard Gross, Pres. and Treas.; Renee Gross, V.P.
Directors: Andrew Gross, Peter Gross, Patricia Kalik.
EIN: 650644401

59737
Kids Learning Center of South Florida, Inc.
11366 Quail Roast Dr.
Miami, FL 33157

Financial data (yr. ended 12/31/00): Assets, $102,959 (M); grants paid, $2,987; expenditures, $583,567; qualifying distributions, $0.
Trustees: Antonio Garcia, Humberto Perez.
EIN: 650854434

59738
James and Deborah Piowaty Foundation, Inc.
8005 S. Indian River Dr.
Fort Pierce, FL 34982-7818
Contact: James Piowaty, Pres.

Established in 1986 in FL.
Donor(s): James Piowaty.
Financial data (yr. ended 10/31/01): Assets, $99,945 (M); grants paid, $157,705; expenditures, $158,446; qualifying distributions, $157,956.
Limitations: Giving primarily in IA.
Application information: Application form not required.
Director: James Piowaty.
EIN: 596875805

59739
Jordan Ministries, Inc.
5415 Shakespeare Dr.
Dover, FL 33527 (813) 787-6023
Contact: Mark Jordan, Pres.

Donor(s): Mark F. Jordan.
Financial data (yr. ended 12/31/01): Assets, $96,294 (M); grants paid, $775; gifts received, $2,500; expenditures, $1,082; qualifying distributions, $1,082.
Limitations: Giving primarily in Plant City, FL.
Application information: Application form required.
Officers: Mark Jordan, Pres.; Berta Jordan, Secy.
Director: Lynn J. Leino.
EIN: 593599085

59740
The Edwards Foundation
7383 Orangewood Ln.
Boca Raton, FL 33433-7460
Contact: Jackson A. Edwards, Mgr.

Established around 1968.
Donor(s): Jackson A. Edwards.
Financial data (yr. ended 12/31/01): Assets, $95,912 (M); grants paid, $9,270; expenditures, $9,549; qualifying distributions, $9,177.
Officer: Jackson A. Edwards, Mgr.
EIN: 136274441

59741
The John Lynch Foundation, Inc.
c/o Marcie Hall
P.O. Box 172247
Tampa, FL 33672 (813) 223-4447

Established in 2000 in FL.
Donor(s): John Lynch, Jr., Linda Lynch, Tampa Bay Interconnect, University Diagnostic Institute.
Financial data (yr. ended 12/31/00): Assets, $95,709 (M); grants paid, $0; gifts received, $165,000; expenditures, $69,428; qualifying distributions, $69,428; giving activities include $27,811 for programs.
Limitations: Giving limited to Tampa, FL.
Application information: Application form required.
Directors: Ann Allred, Doug Allred, John Allred, Dave Dunn, Pete Egoscue, Cathy Lynch, John Lynch, Sr., John Lynch, Jr., Linda Lynch.
EIN: 593665351

59742
Health Support Awareness, Inc.
2836 Fox Squirrel Dr.
Palm Harbor, FL 34684
Contact: Louis H. Mueller, Pres.

Established in 1999 in FL.
Donor(s): Louis H. Mueller.
Financial data (yr. ended 09/30/01): Assets, $85,838 (M); grants paid, $0; expenditures, $9,114; qualifying distributions, $0.
Officers: Louis H. Mueller, Pres.; Michael J. Mueller, V.P.; Estelle A. Mueller, Secy.
EIN: 593616245

59743
The Segal Family Foundation, Inc.
c/o Rose Segal
860 Lakeview Dr.
Miami Beach, FL 33140

Established in 1996 in FL.
Donor(s): Rose Segal.
Financial data (yr. ended 12/31/00): Assets, $82,958 (M); grants paid, $6,000; expenditures, $6,189; qualifying distributions, $6,110.
Limitations: Applications not accepted. Giving primarily in FL.
Application information: Contributes only to pre-selected organizations.
Officers and Directors:* Rose Segal,* Pres.; Martin E. Segal,* V.P., Secy.-Treas., and Mgr.; Skyward Barbara Segal Bernstein,* V.P.; Ruth S. Segal Goldman,* V.P.; Barry David Segal,* V.P.; Howard A. Segal,* V.P.
EIN: 650678828

59744
Michael Carmichael Family Foundation, Inc.
1511 S.W. 1st Ave.
Ocala, FL 34471

Donor(s): Michael J. Carmichael.
Financial data (yr. ended 12/31/99): Assets, $76,584 (M); grants paid, $166,275; gifts received, $143,053; expenditures, $186,900; qualifying distributions, $186,556.
Limitations: Applications not accepted. Giving on a national basis.
Application information: Contributes only to pre-selected organizations.
Officers and Directors:* Michael J. Carmichael,* Pres.; Becki E. Carmichael,* V.P.; Scott L. Whitaker,* Secy.-Treas.
EIN: 593205746
Codes: FD2

59745
Bosland Family Foundation
16 Sea Marsh Rd.
Amelia Island, FL 32034 (904) 277-4584
Contact: Paul C. Bosland, Tr.

Established in 2000 in FL.
Donor(s): Paul C. Bosland, Helen N. Bosland.‡
Financial data (yr. ended 05/31/01): Assets, $74,484 (M); grants paid, $0; gifts received, $108,934; expenditures, $5,844; qualifying distributions, $0.
Trustees: James Bosland, Julia Bosland, Paul C. Bosland, Richard Bosland, Susan Bosland.
EIN: 597176434

59746
James M. & Donna B. Santo Foundation, Inc.
3301 Bayshore Blvd., Ste. 906
Tampa, FL 33629 (813) 258-8545
Contact: Donna Santo, Dir.; or James Santo, Dir.

Established in 1994 in FL.
Donor(s): Donna B. Santo, James M. Santo.
Financial data (yr. ended 12/31/99): Assets, $74,432 (M); grants paid, $23,920; expenditures, $25,031; qualifying distributions, $24,696.
Limitations: Giving primarily in Tampa, FL.
Directors: Peter Kelly, Donna B. Santo, James M. Santo.
EIN: 593275370

59747
The Robey Charitable Trust
(Formerly The Edmund W. Robey Charitable Trust)
2986 Meadow Hill Dr.
Clearwater, FL 33761
Application address: 9 Brisbane Ct., Savannah, GA 31411, tel.: (912) 598-8202
Contact: Leon J. Robey, Tr.

Established in 1990 in FL.
Donor(s): E.W. Robey, Leon J. Robey.
Financial data (yr. ended 12/31/00): Assets, $73,913 (M); grants paid, $38,400; gifts received, $45,000; expenditures, $43,690; qualifying distributions, $43,690.
Limitations: Giving primarily in Merrimack, NH.
Trustees: A.M. Robey, Edmund W. Robey, Leon J. Robey.
EIN: 596961615

59748
JBJ Foundation, Inc.
640 Destacada Ave.
Coral Gables, FL 33156
Application address: 2665 S. Bayshore Dr., Ste. 301, Miami, FL 33133; tel.: (305) 341-3600
Contact: David Ertel, V.P.

Established in 2000 in FL.
Donor(s): David Ertel, Beth Ertel.
Financial data (yr. ended 12/31/00): Assets, $73,651 (M); grants paid, $6,584; gifts received, $135,182; expenditures, $65,985; qualifying distributions, $65,985; giving activities include $42,517 for programs.
Limitations: Giving primarily in southern FL.
Officers and Directors:* Beth Ertel,* Pres.; David Ertel,* V.P.; Lorna Sanchez,* Secy.-Treas.; Bertha Ertel, Salomon Ertel.
EIN: 651001949

59749
The Children's Foundation of Lake Wales, Florida, Inc.
c/o David E. Wilson
926 Dunkirk Pl.
Lake Wales, FL 33853-5008
Application address: c/o David M. Rockness, Chair., Schol. Comm., 16 N. 3rd St., Lake Wales, FL 33853

Financial data (yr. ended 05/31/00): Assets, $71,542 (M); grants paid, $3,300; expenditures, $3,345; qualifying distributions, $3,259.
Limitations: Giving limited to Lake Wales, FL.
Officers: David E. Wilson, Pres.; John S. Matteson, V.P.; Barbara S. Albritton, Secy.-Treas.
EIN: 596137951
Codes: GTI

59750
Center for Innovative Public Policies, Inc.
7913 N.W. 83rd St.
Tamarac, FL 33321

Established in 1999 in FL.
Donor(s): Kaiser Family Foundation.
Financial data (yr. ended 12/31/00): Assets, $70,995 (M); grants paid, $0; gifts received, $125,193; expenditures, $102,195; qualifying distributions, $102,195; giving activities include $15,548 for programs.
Directors: Beth Fallon, Michael McCampbell, Susan McCampbell.
EIN: 650898325

59751
Kirkella Charitable Foundation, Inc.
c/o Edwards & Angel
250 Royal Palm Way
Palm Beach, FL 33480-4309 (561) 833-7700
Contact: Dana Pickard, Tr.

Established in 1988 in FL.
Financial data (yr. ended 02/28/00): Assets, $66,807 (M); grants paid, $350; expenditures, $2,932; qualifying distributions, $350.
Limitations: Giving primarily in FL.
Trustees: Rebecca Black, Dana Pickard.
EIN: 650044965

59752
The Florida Health Occupations Students of America Foundation
c/o Dept. of Education
325 W. Gaines St., Rm. 344
Tallahassee, FL 32399-6533
Application address: c/o State Health Occupations Prog. Dir., Dept. of Education, 325 W. Gaines St., FEC Ste. 1224, Tallahassee, FL 32399-0400
Contact: Jerry L. Barnett, Treas.

Financial data (yr. ended 12/31/01): Assets, $66,457 (M); grants paid, $2,400; gifts received, $950; expenditures, $2,628; qualifying distributions, $2,592.
Limitations: Giving limited to residents of FL.
Application information: Application form required.
Officers and Trustees:* Etta McCulloch,* Chair.; Louise M. Davison,* Mgr.; Jerry L. Barnett,* Treas.; Betty Brisbin, Judy Conlin, Rachael Parcell, Janice Sandiford, and 10 additional directors.
EIN: 592638981

59753
Florida Hosa Foundation, Inc.
325 W. Gaines St., Rm. 344
Tallahassee, FL 32399-6533
Contact: Jerry L. Barnett, Treas.

Financial data (yr. ended 12/31/00): Assets, $66,317 (M); grants paid, $1,800; expenditures, $1,911; qualifying distributions, $1,868.
Limitations: Giving limited to FL.
Application information: Application form required.
Officers and Trustees:* Etta McCulloch,* Chair.; Jerry Barnett,* Treas.; Judy Conlin,* Mgr.; Betty Brisbin, Rachel Parcell, Janice Sandiford.
Advisors: Bobbi Fortner, Carol Hawk, Sandra A. Hendren, Dorothy Yost.
EIN: 590687423

59754
Global Mindlink Foundation, Inc.
160 S.W. 12th Ave., Ste. 103B
Deerfield Beach, FL 33442-3114

Established in 1996.
Financial data (yr. ended 08/31/00): Assets, $65,741 (M); grants paid, $9,132; gifts received, $39,460; expenditures, $596,477; qualifying distributions, $38,888; giving activities include $30,107 for programs.
Officers: Denise Colangelo, Pres.; Gary Vance, V.P.
Director: Daniel Battista.
EIN: 650630341

59755
The Augusta Dialysis Center Research Foundation, Inc.
c/o George Van Giesen, Jr.
12650 Treeline Ct.
Fort Myers, FL 33902-4728

Classified as a private operating foundation in 1983.
Donor(s): George E. VanGiesen, Jr., M.D.
Financial data (yr. ended 12/31/00): Assets, $63,918 (M); grants paid, $4,200; expenditures, $4,305; qualifying distributions, $4,305.
Limitations: Applications not accepted. Giving primarily in Augusta, GA.
Officers: George E. Van Giesen, Jr., M.D., Pres. and Treas.; Debra Anderson, Secy.
EIN: 581514612

59756
The Talcott Family Foundation, Inc.
2126 Plantinum Dr.
Sun City Center, FL 33573-6488

Established in 1995 in FL.
Donor(s): Catherine A. Talcott, Charles W. Talcott.
Financial data (yr. ended 12/31/01): Assets, $60,329 (M); grants paid, $100,550; gifts received, $95,167; expenditures, $101,988; qualifying distributions, $100,550.
Limitations: Applications not accepted.
Application information: Contributes only to pre-selected organizations.
Officers and Directors:* Charles W. Talcott, Pres. and Treas.; Catherine A. Talcott, Secy.; Jeffrey T. Talcott, Rebecca J. Talcott, William W. Talcott.
EIN: 593352732
Codes: FD2

59757
Get a Life! Foundation, Inc.
13367 N.W. 14th St.
Pembroke Pines, FL 33028

Established in 2000 in FL.
Donor(s): Roger Lucas, Teresa Lucas, Teresa's Country Homes, Inc.
Financial data (yr. ended 12/31/00): Assets, $59,750 (M); grants paid, $0; gifts received, $60,069; expenditures, $319; qualifying distributions, $319.
Officers: Roger Lucas, Pres.; Simon Witter, V.P.; Teresa Lucas, Secy.-Treas.
EIN: 651060817

59758
Fannie E. Taylor Home for the Aged-Taylor Foundation Services
6601 Chester Ave.
Jacksonville, FL 32217

Classified as a private operating foundation in 1987.
Financial data (yr. ended 12/31/01): Assets, $59,697 (M); grants paid, $0; gifts received, $197,571; expenditures, $652,678; qualifying distributions, $163,167.
Officers and Directors:* R. Irvin Christian,* Chair.; Robert J. Sizemore,* Vice-Chair.; C. Collier McGehee,* Secy.-Treas.; James Rice,* C.F.O. and Exec. Dir.; Wayne R. Compton, Herman M. Hendricks, Andrew Jackson, William B. Pence, Jr., Bert P. Poarch, Douglas L. Pullen.
EIN: 592681152

59759
The Dorothy Koch Family Foundation, Inc.
741 Emerald Harbor Dr.
Longboat Key, FL 34228

Established in 2000 in OH.
Financial data (yr. ended 12/31/01): Assets, $58,562 (M); grants paid, $2,250; gifts received, $49,183; expenditures, $2,350; qualifying distributions, $2,250.
Director: Dorothy Koch.
EIN: 311708123

59760
West Broward Club, Inc.
11486 State Rd. 84
Fort Lauderdale, FL 33325-4000

Classified as an operating foundation in 1977 in FL.
Financial data (yr. ended 12/31/01): Assets, $57,287 (M); grants paid, $0; gifts received, $93,344; expenditures, $120,454; qualifying distributions, $111,490; giving activities include $120,232 for programs.
Officers: John Edwards, Pres.; Richard Thomas, Secy.; Gerald Pelletier, Treas.
EIN: 591715486

59761
The Howard & Sharon Socol Family Foundation, Inc.
11 Tahiti Beach Island Rd.
Miami, FL 33143-6540

Established in 1999 in FL.
Donor(s): Howard Socol, Sharon Socol.
Financial data (yr. ended 12/31/00): Assets, $55,916 (M); grants paid, $29,000; gifts received, $1,538; expenditures, $34,001; qualifying distributions, $29,000.
Limitations: Applications not accepted. Giving primarily in Miami, FL.
Application information: Contributes only to pre-selected organizations.
Officers: Howard Socol, Exec. Dir.; Sharon Socol, Exec. Dir.
EIN: 650935728

59762
Effective Fathers Ministries, Inc.
1750 University Dr., Ste. 214
Coral Springs, FL 33071

Established in 2000 in FL.
Donor(s): John K. Ream, Rita M. Ream.
Financial data (yr. ended 12/31/00): Assets, $54,879 (M); grants paid, $0; gifts received, $74,243; expenditures, $19,869; qualifying distributions, $19,385; giving activities include $8,723 for programs.
Officers: John K. Ream, Pres.; Rita M. Ream, V.P.; Clinton R. Churchill, Secy.-Treas.
Directors: Robert Applegate, David Goduti, William Hanifan.
EIN: 651038783

59763
Ross & Diana Hubbard Foundation, Inc.
c/o McDonald & Osborne
3033 Riviera Dr., Ste. 105
Naples, FL 34103 (941) 263-4455
Contact: Ross Hubbard, Dir. or Diana Hubbard, Dir.

Established in 2000 in FL.
Donor(s): Ross Hubbard, Diana Hubbard.
Financial data (yr. ended 12/31/01): Assets, $53,349 (M); grants paid, $53,656; expenditures, $69,729; qualifying distributions, $53,656.
Limitations: Giving on a national basis.
Directors: Diana Hubbard, Ross Hubbard, Deborah Wiley.
EIN: 593613149

59764
Contney Family Charitable Trust
c/o John J. Contney
1428 N.E. 104th St.
Miami Shores, FL 33138-2663

Established in 1997.
Financial data (yr. ended 12/31/01): Assets, $53,260 (M); grants paid, $5,000; expenditures, $5,000; qualifying distributions, $5,000.
Limitations: Applications not accepted. Giving primarily in Boston, MA.
Application information: Contributes only to pre-selected organizations.
Trustees: Ross J. Contney, Wade A. Contney.
EIN: 311518673

59765
The American Foundation for the Arts, Inc.
c/o Richard Levine
3814 N.E. Miami Ct.
Miami, FL 33137-3636

Established around 1973.
Donor(s): Richard Levine.
Financial data (yr. ended 12/31/99): Assets, $50,995 (M); grants paid, $3,977; gifts received, $5,176; expenditures, $5,125; qualifying distributions, $3,977; giving activities include $1,577 for programs.
Limitations: Applications not accepted. Giving primarily in Miami, FL.
Application information: Contributes only to pre-selected organizations.
Officers and Directors:* Richard Levine,* Pres., Treas. and Mgr.; Mae Levine,* Secy.; Jose Calderin, Federico Guillen, Ronald Mallory.
EIN: 510166808

59766
The Florida Literary Foundation, Inc.
1391 6th St.
Sarasota, FL 34236 (941) 957-1281

Financial data (yr. ended 12/31/01): Assets, $49,658 (M); grants paid, $79; expenditures, $72,169; qualifying distributions, $79.
Officer: Jane McClintock, Secy.
Director: Anne Wellman.
EIN: 650113881

59767
The Foundation for Freedom and Responsibility
2230 J and C Blvd., Ste. 2
Naples, FL 34109-2040

Established in 2000.
Donor(s): Christopher T. Reed, American Health Capital.
Financial data (yr. ended 12/31/01): Assets, $47,096 (M); grants paid, $2,750; expenditures, $4,713; qualifying distributions, $4,713.
Limitations: Applications not accepted.
Application information: Contributes only to pre-selected organizations.
Trustees: Minda Donovan, Thomas W. Reed, Christopher T. Reed.
EIN: 656354416

59768
The San Miguel Foundation, Inc.
123 E. Enid Dr.
Key Biscayne, FL 33149-2205 (305) 361-6557
Contact: Jorge B. San Miguel, Pres. and Dir.

Established in 1999 in FL.
Donor(s): Jorge B. San Miguel.
Financial data (yr. ended 12/31/99): Assets, $46,881 (M); grants paid, $2,892; gifts received, $50,000; expenditures, $4,989; qualifying distributions, $4,989.

Limitations: Giving primarily in southern FL; some giving also for aid to Venezuela.
Officers and Directors:* Jorge B. San Miguel,* Pres.; Teresa G. San Miguel,* Secy.; Luis E. San Miguel.
EIN: 650939395

59769
The Salem Foundation, Inc.
4600 Kennedy Blvd., Ste. 100
Tampa, FL 33609-2520

Donor(s): Albert M. Salem, Jr., Teddy Salem.
Financial data (yr. ended 12/31/00): Assets, $45,593 (M); grants paid, $2,560; expenditures, $3,470; qualifying distributions, $2,560.
Limitations: Applications not accepted. Giving primarily in Tampa, FL.
Application information: Contributes only to pre-selected organizations.
Directors: Anne S. Hampton, Albert Salem III, Mary Salem, Nancy Salem.
EIN: 593445283

59770
The TGH Foundation for Post-Graduate Radiology & Nuclear Medicine, Inc.
511 W. Bay St., Ste. 301
Tampa, FL 33606

Financial data (yr. ended 12/31/99): Assets, $45,285 (M); grants paid, $2,198; gifts received, $1,500; expenditures, $6,536; qualifying distributions, $3,207.
Officer: Charles H. Fisher, Pres.
Directors: Thomas J. Black, James D. Cates, Carlos R. Martinez, Raul R. Otero.
EIN: 592883251

59771
Personal Ponies, Ltd.
c/o Marianne Alexander
890 A1A Beach Blvd., Unit 67
St. Augustine, FL 32080-6759

Donor(s): Marianne Alexander.
Financial data (yr. ended 12/31/01): Assets, $44,388 (M); grants paid, $0; gifts received, $27,840; expenditures, $27,015; qualifying distributions, $29,773; giving activities include $22,825 for programs.
Officer: Marianne Alexander, Exec. Dir.
Directors: Brian Alexander, Wade Alexander, Thomas Fuchs, Mrs. Thomas Fuchs, Hannah McCormick, Louis Porter, John Reynolds, William Woodams, Mrs. William Woodams.
EIN: 161485250

59772
Destiny Foundation, Inc.
P.O. Box 8582
Tampa, FL 33674-8582

Classified as a private operating foundation in 1998.
Donor(s): C.E. Prescott.
Financial data (yr. ended 12/31/01): Assets, $44,379 (M); grants paid, $68,534; expenditures, $69,898; qualifying distributions, $69,229.
Limitations: Applications not accepted.
Application information: Contributes only to pre-selected organizations.
Officer and Director:* Chester E. Prescott,* Pres.
EIN: 593535192

59773
Port Charlotte Lions Club Foundation, Inc.
P.O. Box 2007
Port Charlotte, FL 33949-2007

Financial data (yr. ended 06/30/00): Assets, $44,224 (M); grants paid, $2,828; gifts received, $6,000; expenditures, $3,136; qualifying distributions, $2,828.
Officers: William Jerrett, Pres.; Lyndon Pritchard, V.P.; Lucile Decosmo, Secy.; Richard Shade, Treas.
EIN: 650322478

59774
Michael John Lanahan Memorial Scholarship Trust Fund
2014 E. Adams St.
Jacksonville, FL 32202 (904) 356-0721
Contact: Michael Lanahan

Donor(s): Lanahan Lumber Co.
Financial data (yr. ended 12/31/01): Assets, $43,660 (M); grants paid, $13,250; gifts received, $2,000; expenditures, $13,310; qualifying distributions, $13,250.
Limitations: Giving limited to Jacksonville, FL.
Application information: Application form required.
Trustees: John W. Caven, Jr., Rev. Michael R. Houle, Mary Ann Vail Lanahan.
EIN: 596889157

59775
Rimrock Foundation, Inc.
3222 Casey Key Rd.
Nokomis, FL 34275

Established in 1992 in FL.
Financial data (yr. ended 12/31/99): Assets, $43,519 (M); grants paid, $6,000; gifts received, $26,700; expenditures, $31,292; qualifying distributions, $21,293.
Limitations: Applications not accepted.
Application information: Contributes only to pre-selected organizations.
Officers: Edith Dallas Ernst, Pres.; Amy L. Ernst, Secy.; Eric M. Ernst, Treas.
EIN: 650315875

59776
Gamma Eta Educational Foundation, Inc.
2246 Monaghan Dr.
Tallahassee, FL 32308
Application address: 2831 Yarmouth Ct., Tallahassee, FL 32308
Contact: John A. Yearty, Pres.

Financial data (yr. ended 12/31/00): Assets, $42,317 (M); grants paid, $1,500; expenditures, $1,500; qualifying distributions, $1,500.
Officers: John A. Yearty, Pres.; P. Michael Ruff, V.P.; E. Edward Murray, Jr., Secy.; Merritt E. Clements, Jr., Treas.
EIN: 593338740

59777
BJ's Foundation, Inc.
521 E. Las Olas Blvd.
Fort Lauderdale, FL 33301

Established in 1998.
Donor(s): Elizabeth H. Buntrock.
Financial data (yr. ended 12/31/99): Assets, $40,750 (M); grants paid, $89,750; gifts received, $22,158; expenditures, $91,827; qualifying distributions, $89,750.
Limitations: Giving primarily in FL.
Officer and Directors:* Elizabeth H. Buntrock,* Pres.; Cecily Buntrock, Dana Buntrock.
EIN: 650745280
Codes: FD2

59778
One World Foundation, Inc.
830-13 A1A N., No. 321
Ponte Vedra Beach, FL 32082
Contact: W. Scott McLucas, Pres.

Established in 1945.
Donor(s): W. Scott McLucas, Nancy McLucas.
Financial data (yr. ended 06/30/00): Assets, $37,309 (L); grants paid, $22,160; gifts received, $407,473; expenditures, $392,156; qualifying distributions, $392,011.
Officers and Directors:* W. Scott McLucas,* Pres.; Nancy McLucas,* V.P.; Philip D. Tingle,* Secy.; John M. McQuiggan, Samuel B. Tannahill.
EIN: 593326436

59779
Hirschhorn Foundation, Inc.
2600 Douglas Rd., PH 1
Coral Gables, FL 33134-6125
Contact: Joel Hirschhorn, Pres.

Financial data (yr. ended 12/31/00): Assets, $36,624 (M); grants paid, $3,050; gifts received, $3,153; expenditures, $3,584; qualifying distributions, $3,050.
Limitations: Giving primarily in FL.
Application information: Application form required.
Officers and Director:* Joel Hirschhorn,* Pres.; Douglas Hirschhorn, V.P.; Evelyn F. Hirschhorn, Treas.
EIN: 592159670

59780
Foundation for Science & Spirituality
(Formerly H. A. Perry Foundation, Inc.)
The Haas Bldg.
1001 N. U.S. Hwy. 1, Ste. 800
Jupiter, FL 33477-4407 (561) 659-3060

Established in 1987 in FL.
Donor(s): Henry A. Perry.
Financial data (yr. ended 12/31/99): Assets, $36,393 (M); grants paid, $0; gifts received, $134,236; expenditures, $111,065; qualifying distributions, $110,155; giving activities include $110,155 for programs.
Officers: Henry A. Perry, Pres.; Hunter Wilson, Secy.-Treas.
Director: Susan Young, Exec. Dir.
EIN: 592780096

59781
Harriett Lieberman Philanthropic Foundation
2775 Kipps Colony Dr.
Gulfport, FL 33707
Contact: Harriett Lieberman, Pres.

Donor(s): Harriett Lieberman.
Financial data (yr. ended 12/31/01): Assets, $35,504 (M); grants paid, $27,804; expenditures, $29,374; qualifying distributions, $29,374.
Limitations: Giving primarily in FL.
Officers and Directors:* Harriett Lieberman,* Pres.; Jaqueline M. Kanner,* V.P.; Bernard Kanner,* Treas.
EIN: 593323779

59782
James Granville Cunningham Foundation, Inc.
c/o James G. Cunningham, Inc.
P.O. Box 1012
Lake Alfred, FL 33850-1012

Financial data (yr. ended 05/31/01): Assets, $35,332 (M); grants paid, $4,215; expenditures, $5,706; qualifying distributions, $4,215.
Limitations: Giving limited to residents of FL, IL, and MN.
Application information: Applicant must include transcript.
Officers and Directors:* Thomas L. White,* Pres.; Pat R. Amato,* Secy.-Treas.; Owen Lee, Jr., Robert L. Leestamper.
EIN: 592224336

59783
Edith F. & Albert F. Carbonari Foundation
7812 Cloverfield Cir.
Boca Raton, FL 33433-3049

Donor(s): Albert Carbonari.
Financial data (yr. ended 12/31/01): Assets, $35,304 (M); grants paid, $1,315; expenditures, $1,498; qualifying distributions, $1,486.
Limitations: Applications not accepted.
Application information: Contributes only to pre-selected organizations.
Trustee: Albert Carbonari.
EIN: 066100712

59784
Michael G. Heiser Foundation
10 Live Oak Ln.
Palm Coast, FL 32137
Contact: Gary G. Heiser, Dir.

Donor(s): Frances H. Heiser, Gary G. Heiser.
Financial data (yr. ended 12/31/01): Assets, $34,168 (M); grants paid, $2,750; gifts received, $16,100; expenditures, $3,061; qualifying distributions, $3,061.
Directors: Frances H. Heiser, Gary G. Heiser.
EIN: 593670526

59785
The Burton and Harriet Palter Foundation, Inc.
c/o Robert G. Breier
1320 S. Dixie Hwy., Ste. 830
Coral Gables, FL 33146

Established in 1990 in FL.
Donor(s): Burton Palter, Harriet Palter.
Financial data (yr. ended 10/31/99): Assets, $33,759 (M); grants paid, $4,625; expenditures, $6,384; qualifying distributions, $4,625.
Limitations: Applications not accepted. Giving primarily in the Palm Beach, FL, area.
Application information: Contributes only to pre-selected organizations.
Officers: Burton Palter, Pres.; Harriet Palter, V.P.
Director: Daniel Palter.
Trustee: Robert G. Breier.
EIN: 650220930

59786
Rotary Club of Winter Park Charitable Foundation, Inc.
(also known as Rotary Club of Winter Park)
P.O. Box 1416
Winter Park, FL 32790-1416
Contact: Robert Coolidge, Secy.

Established in 1990 in FL.
Financial data (yr. ended 06/30/99): Assets, $32,816 (M); grants paid, $15,700; gifts received, $3,797; expenditures, $30,588; qualifying distributions, $15,685.
Limitations: Giving limited to Winter Park, FL, area.
Officers and Directors:* Terry Bangs,* Pres.; Jack Nelson,* V.P.; Thomas R. Donnelly,* Secy.; Nestor De Armas,* Treas.; Frank A. Salerno, and 8 additional directors.
EIN: 570923231

59787
Florida Eye Foundation, Inc.
1717 Woolbright Rd.
Boynton Beach, FL 33426
Contact: Jonathan Chua, M.D., Dir.

Financial data (yr. ended 12/31/00): Assets, $31,597 (M); grants paid, $1,500; gifts received, $300; expenditures, $4,144; qualifying distributions, $4,144.

Limitations: Giving primarily in Boynton Beach, FL.
Application information: Application form required.
Directors: Jonathan Chua, M.D., Lilly Lee, Edward A. Zuraw.
EIN: 582088997

59788
Lincoln and Elizabeth Frost Scholarship Fund
c/o Lincoln J. Frost, Sr.
P.O. Box 333
Everglades City, FL 34139-0333

Established in 1998 in FL.
Donor(s): Lincoln Frost, Elizabeth Frost.
Financial data (yr. ended 12/31/00): Assets, $31,405 (M); grants paid, $1,500; gifts received, $11,500; expenditures, $2,175; qualifying distributions, $2,175.
Limitations: Applications not accepted. Giving limited to Everglades, FL.
Application information: Unsolicited requests for funds not accepted.
Trustees: Elizabeth Frost, Lincoln Frost.
EIN: 593510429

59789
The National Foundation for Children, Inc.
3120 Center St.
Coconut Grove, FL 33133

Financial data (yr. ended 12/31/00): Assets, $30,841 (M); grants paid, $0; gifts received, $57,500; expenditures, $59,376; qualifying distributions, $54,901; giving activities include $55,839 for programs.
Officers: Joseph Braga, Pres.; Laurie Braga, Treas.
EIN: 592039890

59790
Fred J. Wellington Memorial Foundation for Child Development
2631-A N.W. 41st St.
Gainesville, FL 32606

Established in 2000.
Financial data (yr. ended 12/31/01): Assets, $30,565 (M); grants paid, $0; gifts received, $6,710; expenditures, $486; qualifying distributions, $0.
Officer and Directors:* Jane Lawyer,* Secy.-Treas.; Ann Alexander, Gene Frauenheim, Lynne Frauenheim, Bob Wellington, Bobby Wellington, Don Wellington.
EIN: 311648575

59791
Charles L. Wackerle Foundation, Inc.
c/o Duane Magnuson
3900 Clark Rd., Bldg. R
Sarasota, FL 34233

Established in 1997 in FL.
Donor(s): Charles Wackarle.
Financial data (yr. ended 12/31/99): Assets, $27,813 (M); grants paid, $1,000; expenditures, $1,580; qualifying distributions, $1,580.
Officers: Duane Magnuson, Pres.; Fred Schneider, Treas.
EIN: 650807329

59792
Emanuel Finkelstein Family Foundation
2295 S. Ocean Blvd., Apt. 304
Palm Beach, FL 33480

Established in 1990 in NY.
Donor(s): Emanuel Finkelstein, Ada Finkelstein.‡
Financial data (yr. ended 06/30/01): Assets, $27,101 (M); grants paid, $18,971; gifts received, $204; expenditures, $19,749; qualifying distributions, $18,970.
Limitations: Applications not accepted. Giving primarily in NY.
Application information: Contributes only to pre-selected organizations.
Officers and Directors:* Emanuel Finkelstein,* Pres.; Paul Finkelstein,* V.P.; Richard Finkelstein,* V.P.; Neil Finkelstein,* Secy.-Treas.
EIN: 135595557

59793
Shree Shiv Spiritual Foundation
1276 Little Oak Cir.
Titusville, FL 32780-7039
Contact: Vadilal Patel, Dir.

Established in 2000 in FL.
Donor(s): Jayesh V. Patel, Vadilal Patel.
Financial data (yr. ended 12/31/01): Assets, $26,106 (L); grants paid, $0; gifts received, $7,600; expenditures, $7,600; qualifying distributions, $21,327; giving activities include $21,327 for programs.
Directors: Jayesh V. Patel, Ramesh C. Patel, Vadilal Patel, William Tumblin.
EIN: 311773616

59794
Human Research Foundation, Inc.
2300 Intercoastal Dr.
Fort Lauderdale, FL 33305 (954) 776-7660
Contact: Gilbert P. Edwards, Pres.

Established in 1996 in FL.
Donor(s): Gilbert P. Edwards.
Financial data (yr. ended 12/31/00): Assets, $25,198 (M); grants paid, $150; expenditures, $900; qualifying distributions, $150.
Officers: Gilbert P. Edwards, Pres. and Treas.; Rose Marie Edwards, V.P. and Secy.
EIN: 591060507

59795
R. Chad Bogan Scholarship Foundation
2456 Via Sienna
Winter Park, FL 32789-1381
Contact: Ralph Van Bogan & Glenda Van Bogan

Financial data (yr. ended 12/31/01): Assets, $25,107 (M); grants paid, $8,000; gifts received, $3,189; expenditures, $8,062; qualifying distributions, $8,000.
Limitations: Giving primarily in FL.
Application information: Application form required.
Trustee: Ralph Van Bogan.
EIN: 311584418

59796
My Brother's/Sister's Keeper
675 Royal Palm Beach Blvd.
Royal Palm Beach, FL 33411
Contact: Jess R. Santamaria, Pres.

Established in 1997 in FL.
Financial data (yr. ended 03/31/00): Assets, $23,599 (M); grants paid, $510; gifts received, $15,350; expenditures, $515; qualifying distributions, $510.
Limitations: Giving limited to residents of the Western Palm Beach County, FL communities of Wellington, Royal Palm Beach, and the unincorporated areas of Loxahatchee and The Acreage, FL.
Officer and Directors:* Jess R. Santamaria,* Pres.; Robert Jones, Steven A. Templeton.
EIN: 650672664

59797
Palermiti Observatory, Inc.
16222 133rd North Dr.
Jupiter, FL 33478

Classified as a private operating foundation in 1980.
Financial data (yr. ended 12/31/00): Assets, $22,318 (M); grants paid, $0; gifts received, $8,382; expenditures, $5,733; qualifying distributions, $5,733; giving activities include $3,770 for programs.
Officers: Michael F. Palermiti, Pres.; Frank M. Palermiti, V.P.; Betty M. Palermiti, Secy.
EIN: 591978031

59798
LifeStream Behavorial Center Foundation, Inc.
P.O. Box 491000
Leesburg, FL 34749-1000

Financial data (yr. ended 06/30/00): Assets, $21,551 (M); grants paid, $1,059; expenditures, $3,334; qualifying distributions, $1,059; giving activities include $16,765 for programs.
Limitations: Applications not accepted.
Application information: Contributes only to pre-selected organizations.
Officers and Directors:* Jonathan M. Cherry,* C.E.O. and Pres.; John Mathews,* Pres.; Jo Simons-Maresca,* V.P.; Claire Hedgcock,* Secy.-Treas.; George O. Pringle, and 10 additional directors.
EIN: 592976392

59799
NA64 Yale Foundation, Inc.
31111 U.S. 19 N.
Palm Harbor, FL 34684
Contact: Peter Krauser, Pres.

Established in 2000 in FL.
Donor(s): Peter Krauser.
Financial data (yr. ended 12/31/00): Assets, $20,100 (M); grants paid, $0; gifts received, $20,100; expenditures, $0; qualifying distributions, $0.
Officers: Peter Krauser, Pres. and Treas.; Eileen Krauser, V.P.; E.J. Snyder, Secy.
EIN: 593689991

59800
Nafzger Family Foundation
6051 N. Ocean Dr., Ste. 1204
Hollywood, FL 33019

Established in 2001 in KY.
Donor(s): Carl Nafzger, Wanda Nafzger.
Financial data (yr. ended 12/31/01): Assets, $20,000 (M); grants paid, $0; gifts received, $20,000; expenditures, $0; qualifying distributions, $0.
Limitations: Applications not accepted.
Application information: Contributes only to pre-selected organizations.
Trustees: Carl Nafzger, Wanda Nafzger.
EIN: 306001287

59801
Natural Healing Foundation, Inc.
1429 Colonial Blvd., Ste. 101
Fort Myers, FL 33907

Established in 2000 in FL and MA.
Donor(s): Charles R. Shipley, Charles R. Shipley Foundation.
Financial data (yr. ended 12/31/00): Assets, $19,783 (M); grants paid, $0; gifts received, $245,000; expenditures, $234,731; qualifying distributions, $175,602; giving activities include $47,110 for programs.
Officers: Bradley W. Price, Pres.; Thomas P. Jalkut, Secy.; Carol Z. Price, Treas.
EIN: 043482564

59802
Realtor Association of Greater Fort Lauderdale Charitable Foundation, Inc.
(Formerly Fort Lauderdale Area Realtors Charitable Foundation, Inc.)
1765 N.E. 26th St.
Fort Lauderdale, FL 33305-1482
(954) 563-7261

Established in 1988 in FL.
Financial data (yr. ended 12/31/00): Assets, $17,754 (M); grants paid, $860; gifts received, $3,833; expenditures, $967; qualifying distributions, $860.
Limitations: Giving limited to Broward County, FL.
Application information: Application form required.
Officers: Claudette Bruck, Pres.; Myrtle T. Anderson, V.P.; Joseph R. Millsaps, Secy.-Treas.
Trustees: James Balisteri, James Nall.
EIN: 650003512

59803
Grace Foundation
3225 S. MacDill Ave.
Tampa, FL 33629-8171

Established in 2000 in FL.
Donor(s): Susan M. Rauenhorst.
Financial data (yr. ended 12/31/00): Assets, $17,468 (M); grants paid, $0; gifts received, $45,844; expenditures, $28,972; qualifying distributions, $28,708; giving activities include $28,708 for programs.
Officers: Susan M. Rauenhorst, Pres. and Secy.-Treas.; Nancy Brown, V.P.
Director: Roxann W. Moore.
EIN: 364335020

59804
Rosemere Foundation, Inc.
4532 W. Kennedy Blvd., Ste. 319
Tampa, FL 33609-2042 (813) 222-7500

Classified as a private operating foundation in FL.
Financial data (yr. ended 12/31/01): Assets, $15,843 (M); grants paid, $57,083; gifts received, $81,000; expenditures, $65,278; qualifying distributions, $57,083.
Limitations: Applications not accepted.
Application information: Contributes only to pre-selected organizations.
Officers: C. Klug, Pres.; B. Carter, Secy.-Treas.
EIN: 593545163

59805
Frank A. Reinhart Scholarship Fund
c/o Glenn Calhoun
P.O. Box 641083
Miami, FL 33164-1083
Application address: 500 W. Robinson St., Orlando, FL 32801
Contact: Deborah L. Fisher, Tr.

Established in 1994 in FL.
Financial data (yr. ended 12/31/99): Assets, $15,688 (M); grants paid, $500; gifts received, $680; expenditures, $634; qualifying distributions, $566.
Application information: Application form required.
Trustees: Karen Bryant, Glenn Calhoun, Deborah L. Fisher.
EIN: 650495979

59806
Arriba La Vida/Up With Life Foundation, Inc.
1521 Alton Rd., Ste. 347
Miami Beach, FL 33139-3301

Established in 1997 in FL.
Financial data (yr. ended 12/31/01): Assets, $15,504 (M); grants paid, $21,200; gifts received, $40,775; expenditures, $28,069; qualifying distributions, $28,069.
Limitations: Giving primarily in NY.
Officers: Juan M. Avila, Pres.; Cristina Saralegui, Secy.
EIN: 650724678

59807
Mirta Penelas Foundation, Inc.
6209 N.W. 171st St.
Hialeah, FL 33015

Established in 1999 in FL.
Financial data (yr. ended 12/31/99): Assets, $15,060 (M); grants paid, $55,467; gifts received, $168,617; expenditures, $152,655; qualifying distributions, $152,649.
Directors: Daisy Hernandez, Luis Penelas, Sr., Luis Penelas, Jr., Pedro Pablo Torres, Jr.
EIN: 650847710

59808
Lynch Family Foundation, Inc.
3 163rd Ave. E.
Redington Beach, FL 33708

Established in 1998 in FL.
Donor(s): Michael J. Lynch, Erika M. Lynch.
Financial data (yr. ended 09/30/00): Assets, $13,918 (M); grants paid, $2,000; gifts received, $10,000; expenditures, $5,575; qualifying distributions, $2,000.
Limitations: Applications not accepted.
Application information: Contributes only to pre-selected organizations.
Officers and Directors:* Michael J. Lynch,* Pres.; Erika M. Lynch,* Secy.-Treas.; Megan Lynch, Nora M. Smith.
EIN: 593504019

59809
Wheelchair Club of Shalom Temple No. 77, Inc.
c/o L. Shapiro
7700 Sunset Strip
Sunrise, FL 33322

Financial data (yr. ended 12/31/99): Assets, $13,850 (M); grants paid, $0; gifts received, $475; expenditures, $2,334; qualifying distributions, $0.
Officers: Arron Neuhause, Pres.; Allan Richard, V.P.; Steven Weiner, Secy.; Lester Shapiro, Treas.
EIN: 591807988

59810
The Owen Foundation, Inc.
1501 Corporate Dr., Ste. 120
Boynton Beach, FL 33426-6654

Established in 2000 in FL.
Donor(s): The Seinfeld Family Foundation.
Financial data (yr. ended 12/31/00): Assets, $13,047 (M); grants paid, $83; gifts received, $16,325; expenditures, $3,278; qualifying distributions, $3,278.
Limitations: Applications not accepted.
Application information: Contributes only to pre-selected organizations.
Officers: Martha S. Owen, Pres.; Frank Mulhall, Secy.
Directors: Virginia Loczover, Betty Seinfeld, Berniece Sturtz.
EIN: 650967648

59811
Jovius Foundation
699 E. 5th Ave.
Mount Dora, FL 32757-5625

Established in 1991 in FL and DE.
Donor(s): 431 Corp.
Financial data (yr. ended 07/31/00): Assets, $10,569 (M); grants paid, $0; expenditures, $470; qualifying distributions, $470; giving activities include $470 for programs.
Limitations: Giving limited to Winter Park, FL.
Officers and Directors:* Kenneth M. Mazik,* Pres. and Treas.; Donna H. Brown,* V.P.; Charles H. Burton,* Secy.; Judith Favell, Ph.D., Exec. Dir.; Thomas L. DeEmedio.
EIN: 593103892

59812
Frost Family Foundation Trust
721 Binnacle Point Dr.
Longboat Key, FL 34228

Established in 2001 in FL.
Donor(s): Weldon G. Frost.
Financial data (yr. ended 12/31/01): Assets, $9,514 (M); grants paid, $525; gifts received, $11,908; expenditures, $2,433; qualifying distributions, $525.
Limitations: Applications not accepted.
Application information: Contributes only to pre-selected organizations.
Trustees: Brenda T. Frost, James T. Frost, Terrence W. Frost, Weldon G. Frost.
EIN: 656378073

59813
Williams Family Foundation
P.O. Box 536845
Orlando, FL 32853-6846 (407) 896-6911
Contact: Leonard E. Williams, Pres.

Established in 2000 in FL.
Donor(s): Leonard E. Williams.
Financial data (yr. ended 12/31/00): Assets, $9,475 (M); grants paid, $525; gifts received, $10,000; expenditures, $525; qualifying distributions, $525.
Limitations: Giving primarily in FL.
Officers: Leonard E. Williams, Pres.; Marjorie H. Williams, V.P.
Directors: Douglas Williams, John A. Williams, Leonard E. Williams, Jr., Michael J. Williams.
EIN: 593688456

59814
Grace Fleming Reinhold Scholarship Trust
(Formerly Grace E. Reinhold Scholarship Trust)
c/o Carl D. Reinhold
629H Nerita St.
Sanibel, FL 33957-6808

Established in 1991 in WI.
Financial data (yr. ended 12/31/00): Assets, $8,635 (M); grants paid, $1,500; expenditures, $1,570; qualifying distributions, $1,500.
Limitations: Applications not accepted. Giving limited to residents of WI.
Trustees: Marie Fleming, Carl Reinhold, Robert Reinhold.
EIN: 391682031

59815
Karis Foundation
c/o Barney J. Barron
258 South Beach Dr.
Tarpon Springs, FL 34689

Established in 1990 in OK.
Donor(s): Barney J. Barron, Ann J. Barron Dicamillo, Joy Barron Traverse, William D. Barron, Sylvia Barron, John R. Barron.
Financial data (yr. ended 12/31/01): Assets, $8,089 (M); grants paid, $44,500; gifts received, $50,908; expenditures, $44,996; qualifying distributions, $44,996.
Limitations: Applications not accepted. Giving primarily in IL and OK.
Application information: Contributes only to pre-selected organizations.
Trustees: Barney J. Barron, Sylvia A. Barron.
EIN: 731372208

59816
Timoteo Family Foundation
c/o Reginald L. Timoteo
6109 Fountain Palm Dr.
Jupiter, FL 33458-3303

Established in 1999.
Financial data (yr. ended 12/31/99): Assets, $7,738 (M); grants paid, $4,172; gifts received, $13,337; expenditures, $5,599; qualifying distributions, $5,483.
Directors: Jim Samuels, Reginald L. Timoteo, Mitchell Timoteo, Janet B. Timoteo.
EIN: 650889581

59817
Sarasota Foundation for Health Care Alternatives, Inc.
1910 Robinwood St.
Sarasota, FL 34231

Established in 2000 in FL.
Donor(s): David Clark Swalm, Jr.
Financial data (yr. ended 12/31/00): Assets, $7,085 (M); grants paid, $0; gifts received, $34,274; expenditures, $28,261; qualifying distributions, $0.
Officers: D. Clark Swalm, Jr., Pres.; Nicole Swalm, V.P.; Steven Benson, Secy.-Treas.
EIN: 651007818

59818
Wildlife Sanctuary Fund, Inc.
45 Seton Trail
Ormond Beach, FL 32176

Financial data (yr. ended 12/31/00): Assets, $6,862 (M); grants paid, $44,000; gifts received, $5,250; expenditures, $44,267; qualifying distributions, $44,000.
Limitations: Applications not accepted. Giving on an international basis, primarily in Africa.
Application information: Contributes only to pre-selected organizations.
Officers and Directors:* J. Michael Eddy,* Pres.; F. Raymond Eddy,* V.P.; Jeffrey M. Pontious, Treas.; Brian Gaisford, Jonathan Kaney.
EIN: 593348526

59819
New Directions Employment and Training Services, Inc.
(Formerly New Directions for the Handicapped, Inc.)
5555 Biscayne Blvd.
Miami, FL 33137

Classified as a private operating foundation in 1980.
Financial data (yr. ended 06/30/00): Assets, $6,705 (M); grants paid, $0; gifts received, $411,432; expenditures, $447,815; qualifying distributions, $447,815; giving activities include $447,815 for programs.
Officers: Michael Upright, Pres.; Beverly Croslin, V.P.; Sylvia Sanchez, Secy.
Directors: Patricia Veine, Janet Wathaft.
EIN: 591989833

59820
J. Bell Moran, Jr. Foundation, Inc.
1897 Palm Beach Lakes, Blvd., Ste. 226
West Palm Beach, FL 33409
Application address: 630 Island Dr., Palm Beach, FL 33480, tel.: (561) 655-1951
Contact: J. Bell Moran, Jr., Dir.

Established in 1999 in FL.
Donor(s): J. Bell Moran, Jr.
Financial data (yr. ended 12/31/00): Assets, $5,865 (M); grants paid, $4,135; gifts received, $10,000; expenditures, $4,135; qualifying distributions, $4,135.
Limitations: Giving primarily in Palm Beach, FL.
Directors: Lore M. Dodge, J. Bell Moran, Jr., J. Bell Moran III, Lise G. Moran.
EIN: 650912849

59821
Stimpson Family Foundation, Inc.
3461 Creekview Dr.
Bonita Springs, FL 34134
Contact: John G. Stimpson, Pres.

Established in 1999 in FL.
Financial data (yr. ended 12/31/00): Assets, $5,848 (M); grants paid, $3,050; gifts received, $6,452; expenditures, $11,204; qualifying distributions, $3,050.
Officers and Directors:* John G. Stimpson,* Pres.; Kathleen E. Stimpson,* Secy.-Treas.; John M. Stimpson, Michael G. Stimpson, Robert D. Stimpson.
EIN: 650900897

59822
Zaman Charitable Trust
15141 Fintry Pl.
Miami Lakes, FL 33016

Established in 2000 in FL.
Donor(s): Kaiser Zaman, Wendy Zaman.
Financial data (yr. ended 12/31/00): Assets, $5,394 (M); grants paid, $204; gifts received, $15,600; expenditures, $2,604; qualifying distributions, $204.
Trustees: Kaiser Zaman, Wendy Zaman.
EIN: 656353294

59823
Melissa's Rescue Corporation
14035 125th Ave., N.
Palm Beach Gardens, FL 33418-7908

Financial data (yr. ended 06/30/01): Assets, $5,266 (M); grants paid, $0; gifts received, $34,627; expenditures, $29,754; qualifying distributions, $0.
Limitations: Applications not accepted.
Application information: Contributes only to pre-selected organizations.
Officers and Directors:* Mimi Wriedt,* Pres. and Treas.; William Lotzgo,* Secy.; Pamela Wriedt.
EIN: 650210049

59824
Three Notch Wildlife Research Foundation, Inc.
9580 S. Clear Spring Dr.
Floral City, FL 34436

Established in 2001 in FL.
Donor(s): Richard T. Carroll.
Financial data (yr. ended 12/31/01): Assets, $5,207 (M); grants paid, $0; gifts received, $135,840; expenditures, $130,633; qualifying distributions, $0.
Limitations: Applications not accepted.
Officers: Richard T. Carroll, Pres.; Marion S. Carroll, Secy.-Treas.

Director: William E. James.
EIN: 593658364

59825
Arango Design Foundation
7063 S.W. 53 Ln.
Miami, FL 33155-5632

Classified as a private operating foundation in 1982.
Financial data (yr. ended 12/31/01): Assets, $4,869 (M); grants paid, $0; expenditures, $20,668; qualifying distributions, $20,667; giving activities include $20,668 for programs.
Officers: Rene Gonzalez, Pres.; Diana Ursula Farmer, V.P.; Anthony Abbate, Secy.; Mark Hampton, Treas.
EIN: 592139450

59826
Northwestern Oral and Maxillofacial Surgery Foundation
c/o B. Pecaro
2390 Gulfshore Blvd., N.
Naples, FL 34103

Established in 1997 in IL.
Donor(s): Bernard C. Pecaro.
Financial data (yr. ended 10/31/00): Assets, $4,868 (M); grants paid, $0; expenditures, $2,796; qualifying distributions, $2,796; giving activities include $1,509 for programs.
Limitations: Applications not accepted.
Application information: Contributes only to pre-selected organizations.
Officers and Directors:* Bernard C. Pecaro,* Pres.; Alexis Olsson,* Secy.; Mark Erickson,* Treas.
EIN: 364104166

59827
Worldlife, Inc.
(Formerly Mana Foundation, Inc.)
1000 E. Broward Blvd., Ste. 100
Fort Lauderdale, FL 33301-2069

Donor(s): Carol J. Gardina.
Financial data (yr. ended 12/31/00): Assets, $4,808 (M); grants paid, $0; gifts received, $10,319; expenditures, $9,737; qualifying distributions, $7,356; giving activities include $7,356 for programs.
Limitations: Applications not accepted.
Application information: Contributes only to pre-selected organizations.
Officers and Directors:* George J. Gardina,* Pres.; Carol J. Gardina,* Secy.; Richard Moyroud.
EIN: 592343819

59828
Finally Home, Inc.
5623 Oleander Ave.
Fort Pierce, FL 34982

Donor(s): Jane Turmoil.
Financial data (yr. ended 01/01/00): Assets, $4,319 (M); grants paid, $0; gifts received, $24,700; expenditures, $24,383; qualifying distributions, $24,383; giving activities include $24,383 for programs.
Officers: Jane Turmoil, Pres.; Lee Turmoil, Secy.; Brian Turmoil, Treas.
EIN: 650904640

59829
The Rittersbach Foundation
2220 S.E. Stonehaven Rd.
Port St. Lucie, FL 34952

Established in 2001.
Donor(s): George H. Rittersbach, Helen H. Rittersbach.
Financial data (yr. ended 12/31/01): Assets, $3,771 (M); grants paid, $6,316; gifts received, $10,000; expenditures, $6,466; qualifying distributions, $6,316.
Officers and Trustee:* George H. Rittersbach,* Pres.; Helen H. Rittersbach, Secy.-Treas.
EIN: 651013565

59830
XAO Foundation
5101 S.E. 11th Ave.
Ocala, FL 34480

Donor(s): James E. Vander Mey.
Financial data (yr. ended 11/30/99): Assets, $3,678 (M); grants paid, $3,625; gifts received, $5,000; expenditures, $4,024; qualifying distributions, $4,024; giving activities include $3,625 for programs.
Limitations: Applications not accepted.
Application information: Contributes only to pre-selected organizations.
Trustee: James E. Vander Mey.
EIN: 222519725

59831
Frank Moya Charitable Foundation, Inc.
801 Arthur Godfrey Rd., Ste. 400
Miami Beach, FL 33140

Established in 1999.
Donor(s): Frank Moya.
Financial data (yr. ended 12/31/99): Assets, $3,500 (M); grants paid, $6,500; gifts received, $10,000; expenditures, $6,500; qualifying distributions, $6,500.
Limitations: Applications not accepted.
Application information: Contributes only to pre-selected organizations.
Directors: Elizabeth M. Moya, Frank Moya.
EIN: 586402421

59832
Symbiosis Foundation, Inc.
8210 N.W. 27th St.
Miami, FL 33122

Established in 1993 in FL.
Donor(s): Thomas O. Bales, Jr., Kevin W. Smith.
Financial data (yr. ended 12/31/00): Assets, $3,365 (M); grants paid, $35,728; gifts received, $21,990; expenditures, $36,508; qualifying distributions, $35,728.
Limitations: Applications not accepted. Giving primarily in FL.
Application information: Contributes only to pre-selected organizations.
Directors: Thomas O. Bales, Jr., J. William Box, Charles R. Slater, Kevin W. Smith.
EIN: 650414696

59833
The James T. & Joan Ann Cook Charitable Foundation
1601 S. Ocean Ln., Ste. 185
Fort Lauderdale, FL 33316

Donor(s): James T. Cook, Joan Ann Cook.
Financial data (yr. ended 12/31/00): Assets, $2,908 (M); grants paid, $10,912; gifts received, $25,368; expenditures, $24,157; qualifying distributions, $24,157.
Limitations: Applications not accepted.
Application information: Contributes only to pre-selected organizations.
Trustees: James T. Cook, Joan Ann Cook.
EIN: 650495249

59834
Michael Gerrits Foundation, Inc.
3501 N.W. 2nd Ave.
Miami, FL 33137

Established in 1996 in FL.
Donor(s): Michael Gerrits.
Financial data (yr. ended 12/31/00): Assets, $2,311 (M); grants paid, $16,733; gifts received, $18,200; expenditures, $16,869; qualifying distributions, $16,733.
Limitations: Giving primarily in FL.
Application information: Application must be accompanied with an official transcript and a letter of recommendation. Application form not required.
Officers: Michael Gerrits, Pres.; Meredith Broussard, V.P.; Jan S. Neiman, Secy.
EIN: 650637340

59835
The Miles Family Foundation
7 Sound Point Pl.
Amelia Island, FL 32034

Established in 2000.
Financial data (yr. ended 12/31/00): Assets, $2,002 (M); grants paid, $0; gifts received, $2,000; expenditures, $0; qualifying distributions, $0.
Trustees: Nancy S. Miles, Richard N. Miles.
EIN: 597170358

59836
Ruth Kenney Foundation
9067 Hilolo Ln.
Venice, FL 34293-7608

Established in 2001 in FL.
Financial data (yr. ended 12/31/01): Assets, $1,504 (M); grants paid, $0; gifts received, $1,500; expenditures, $0; qualifying distributions, $0.
Officers and Directors:* Allan R. Kenney,* Pres.; Keith R. Kenney,* V.P.; Kevin C. Kenney,* Secy.; Brian P. Kenney,* Treas.
EIN: 651055246

59837
Levine Family Foundation, Inc.
2608 N. Dixie Hwy., Ste. 100
West Palm Beach, FL 33407

Financial data (yr. ended 12/31/00): Assets, $1,367 (M); grants paid, $106,300; gifts received, $147,118; expenditures, $145,867; qualifying distributions, $144,281.
Limitations: Applications not accepted. Giving primarily in ME.
Application information: Contributes only to pre-selected organizations.
Officers: Robert A. Levine, Pres.; Lance Taggersell, V.P.; Vilean Taggersell, Secy.
EIN: 650834879
Codes: FD2

59838
The Dale Family Foundation
3257 Meadow Run Dr.
Venice, FL 34293-1428

Established in 2000 in MA.
Donor(s): Alan R. Dale, Margaret A. Dale.
Financial data (yr. ended 12/31/00): Assets, $1,000 (M); grants paid, $5,000; gifts received, $6,000; expenditures, $5,000; qualifying distributions, $5,000.
Limitations: Applications not accepted. Giving primarily in MA.
Application information: Contributes only to pre-selected organizations.

59838—FLORIDA

Trustees: Frank Bisset, Judy Bisset, Alan R. Dale, Margaret A. Dale.
EIN: 046931922

59839
Farley Family Foundation
1502 Haven Bend
Tampa, FL 33613-1153

Financial data (yr. ended 12/31/99): Assets, $968 (M); grants paid, $0; expenditures, $180; qualifying distributions, $180.
Officer and Directors:* Paul J. Farley,* Pres.; Margaret D. Farley, Stephen A. Farley.
EIN: 593187434

59840
Charles and Pat Dyson Charitable Foundation
3507 Cullen Lake Shore Dr.
Orlando, FL 32812

Established in 1988 in FL.
Donor(s): Charles A. Dyson, Patricia H. Dyson.
Financial data (yr. ended 12/31/99): Assets, $834 (M); grants paid, $200; expenditures, $200; qualifying distributions, $200.
Limitations: Applications not accepted.
Application information: Contributes only to pre-selected organizations.
Trustees: Charles A. Dyson, Patricia H. Dyson.
EIN: 592749421

59841
Nimrod Aircraft Museum, Inc.
22296 N.W. 75th Ave. Rd.
Micanopy, FL 32667-7405

Established in 1997.
Financial data (yr. ended 05/31/00): Assets, $810 (M); grants paid, $0; gifts received, $37,000; expenditures, $37,803; qualifying distributions, $37,803; giving activities include $13,499 for programs.
Officers: John Silberman, Pres.; George R. Moreau, Treas.
EIN: 593125872

59842
Michael Stevens Memorial Scholarship Fund
102 Stephen Dr.
Lake Placid, FL 33852

Established in 1988 in IN.
Donor(s): Robert Stevens.
Financial data (yr. ended 08/31/01): Assets, $669 (M); grants paid, $1,500; gifts received, $1,312; expenditures, $1,612; qualifying distributions, $1,612.
Limitations: Giving limited to La Porte, IN.
Application information: Application form required.
Officer and Directors:* Robert Stevens,* Chair.; James Garwood, Karen Lang.
EIN: 311070493

59843
We Care for Paws Foundation
6822 22nd Ave. N., Ste. 125
St. Petersburg, FL 33710

Established in 1999 in FL.
Donor(s): Carol Allard.
Financial data (yr. ended 03/31/02): Assets, $333 (M); grants paid, $0; gifts received, $11,094; expenditures, $10,897; qualifying distributions, $0.
Limitations: Applications not accepted.
Application information: Contributes only to pre-selected organizations.
Directors: Carol Allard, Betty J. Fletcher, Bonnie E. Fletcher.
EIN: 593502200

59844
J. E. Evans Foundation, Inc.
P.O. Box 2339
Dade City, FL 33526-2339

Financial data (yr. ended 12/31/99): Assets, $149 (M); grants paid, $2,500; gifts received, $2,600; expenditures, $2,566; qualifying distributions, $2,566.
Limitations: Applications not accepted.
Application information: Contributes only to pre-selected organizations.
Trustees: James E. Evans, Jr., Margaret E. Lowry.
EIN: 591146372

59845
Florida Wildlife and Livestock Foundation, Inc.
P.O. Box 12909
Fort Pierce, FL 34979-2909

Established in 1991 in FL.
Financial data (yr. ended 12/31/99): Assets, $120 (M); grants paid, $0; gifts received, $250; expenditures, $239; qualifying distributions, $0.
Officers and Directors:* Alto Adams, Jr.,* Pres.; Michael L. Adams,* Secy.; Walter Hill.
EIN: 650225460

59846
Swim for Life for Broward County, Inc.
3006 E. Commercial Blvd.
Fort Lauderdale, FL 33308-4312

Established in 1996 in FL.
Donor(s): W. C. Griffith Foundation Trust.
Financial data (yr. ended 12/31/01): Assets, $62 (M); grants paid, $0; gifts received, $4,158; expenditures, $3,450; qualifying distributions, $4,269; giving activities include $4,269 for programs.
Officers and Directors:* Robert Matheney,* Pres.; Richard Chelekis,* Treas.
EIN: 650630343

59847
National Save-A-Pet Foundation, Inc.
120 S. Olive Ave., Ste. 301
West Palm Beach, FL 33401-5532

Financial data (yr. ended 11/30/01): Assets, $10 (M); grants paid, $0; gifts received, $10; expenditures, $100; qualifying distributions, $0.
Officers and Directors:* Gertrude G. Maxwell,* Pres. and Treas.; Ina Sanooval, Secy.; Gene Drat, Timothy McAtre.
EIN: 650572604

59848
FRVTA Educational Foundation, Inc.
401 N. Parsons Ave., Ste. 107
Brandon, FL 33510-4538

Established in 1994 in FL.
Financial data (yr. ended 09/30/01): Assets, $1 (M); grants paid, $0; expenditures, $0; qualifying distributions, $0.
Officers: David Lance Wilson, Pres.; J. David Kelly, V.P.
Directors: Lyn Hart, Dell Sanders, Tom Tibbets.
EIN: 650585006

59849
All Outreaches, Inc.
23 Brookwood Dr.
Ormond Beach, FL 32174-9106

Established in 1991 in FL.
Donor(s): John Ackerman, Marlene Ackerman.
Financial data (yr. ended 12/31/01): Assets, $0 (M); grants paid, $23,874; gifts received, $26,121; expenditures, $27,742; qualifying distributions, $27,742.
Limitations: Applications not accepted. Giving primarily in Daytona Beach, FL.
Officer: Marlene Ackerman, Pres.
Director: John Ackerman.
EIN: 592961761

59850
Cornerstone Ministries
P.O. Box 2413
Valrico, FL 33595-2413

Classified as a private operating foundation in 1994.
Financial data (yr. ended 12/31/99): Assets, $0 (M); grants paid, $0; gifts received, $4,380; expenditures, $3,921; qualifying distributions, $3,921; giving activities include $2,163 for programs.
Director: Thomas N. Sampson II.
EIN: 541681686

59851
The Orange Bowl Foundation, Inc.
601 Brickell Key Dr., Ste. 206
Miami, FL 33131
Contact: Keith Tribble, Exec. Dir.

Established in 1998 in FL.
Donor(s): Sports for Life.
Financial data (yr. ended 04/30/00): Assets, $0 (M); grants paid, $179,385; gifts received, $155,972; expenditures, $192,757; qualifying distributions, $179,385.
Officers: Clark Cook, Co-Pres.; Leslie V. Pantin, Jr., Co-Pres.; Corey Johnson, V.P.; Keith Tribble, Exec. Dir.
EIN: 650853393
Codes: FD2

GEORGIA

59852
The University Financing Foundation, Inc.
(Formerly Georgia Scientific and Technical Research Foundation)
3333 Busbee Dr., Rm 150
Kennesaw, GA 30144 (770) 420-4300
Contact: C.M. Lampman, Mgr.

Classified as a private operating foundation in 1989.
Financial data (yr. ended 12/31/00): Assets, $89,088,164 (M); grants paid, $100,100; expenditures, $5,481,870; qualifying distributions, $7,198,769; giving activities include $886,862 for loans and $4,038,181 for programs.
Limitations: Giving primarily in Lakeland, FL and Atlanta, GA.
Application information: Very limited outright grants or gifts awarded. Application form not required.
Officers: J. Frank Smith, Pres.; John E. Aderhold, V.P.; James M. Sibley, Secy.; Thomas H. Hall III, Treas.; Charles M. Lampman, Mgr.
EIN: 581505902
Codes: FD2

59853
Pebble Hill Foundation, Inc.
P.O. Box 830
Thomasville, GA 31799
Contact: Wallace Goodman, Dir.

Incorporated in 1956 in GA.
Donor(s): Elisabeth Ireland Poe.‡
Financial data (yr. ended 09/30/01): Assets, $54,699,390 (M); grants paid, $75,439; expenditures, $2,169,665; qualifying distributions, $3,053,545; giving activities include $1,791,874 for programs.
Limitations: Applications not accepted.
Application information: Contributes only to pre-selected organizations.
Officers: Louise Ireland Humphrey, Pres.; George M. Humphrey II, Secy.-Treas.
Director: Wallace Goodman.
Trustee: Thomas H. Vann, Jr.
EIN: 346525857
Codes: FD2

59854
St. Catherine's Island Foundation, Inc.
Saint Catherine's Island
Midway, GA 31320

Classified as a private operating foundation in 1981.
Financial data (yr. ended 12/31/01): Assets, $21,914,905 (M); grants paid, $0; gifts received, $404,000; expenditures, $1,395,536; qualifying distributions, $0.
Officers and Directors:* June Noble Larkin,* Chair.; Frank Y. Larkin,* Pres.; Deborah Menton-Nightlinger, Secy.; E. Mary Hefferman,* Treas.; E.J. Noble Smith, Exec Dir.; William G. Conway, Ellen V. Futter, Howard Phipps, Jr., Frank P. Piskor, Bradford D. Smith, David S. Smith, Jeremy T. Smith, Carroll L. Wainwright, Jr.
EIN: 581449857

59855
Daughtry Foundation, Inc.
P.O. Box 1246
Jackson, GA 30233
Application address: College St., Jackson, GA 30233, tel.: (770) 775-7360
Contact: William M. Davis, Exec. Dir.

Established in 1943 in GA.
Donor(s): Hampton L. Daughtry.‡
Financial data (yr. ended 03/31/01): Assets, $21,207,323 (M); grants paid, $35,000; gifts received, $22,254; expenditures, $824,077; qualifying distributions, $701,038; giving activities include $620,411 for programs.
Limitations: Giving primarily in Jackson, GA.
Publications: Annual report, application guidelines, newsletter.
Application information: Application form required.
Officers and Trustees:* Lou W. Moelchert,* Chair.; Luke P. Weaver,* Vice-Chair.; Bailey M. Crockarell,* Secy.; Larry Morgan,* Treas.; William Mack Davis, Exec. Dir.; John L. Carter, David Haisten, Clyde Newman.
EIN: 580673985

59856
Morris Museum of Art
1 10th St.
Augusta, GA 30901-1139

Classified as a company-sponsored operating foundation in 1987 in GA.
Donor(s): Morris Communications Corp., Southeastern Newspapers Corp.
Financial data (yr. ended 09/30/00): Assets, $17,388,199 (M); grants paid, $0; gifts received, $1,887,818; expenditures, $1,809,407; qualifying distributions, $1,922,856; giving activities include $388,364 for programs.
Officer: L. Keith Claussen, Exec. Dir.
Directors: William H. Chew, Mrs. Joel Cohen, Mrs. George Crawford, Frank Dolan, Jr., Joseph D. Greene, and 13 additional directors.
Trustees: Lee Baker, W. Hale Barrett, David E. Hudson, J. Tyler Morris, William S. Morris III, William S. Morris IV, Mrs. Williams S. Morris III, Paul S. Simon.
EIN: 586189260

59857
Ichauway, Inc.
c/o Joseph W. Jones Ecological Research Ctr.
Rte. 2, Box 2324
Newton, GA 31770

Established in 1990 in GA.
Donor(s): Robert W. Woodruff Foundation.
Financial data (yr. ended 12/31/01): Assets, $9,112,364 (M); grants paid, $2,162; gifts received, $7,837,542; expenditures, $8,146,218; qualifying distributions, $7,153,828.
Limitations: Applications not accepted. Giving primarily in FL and GA.
Publications: Occasional report.
Application information: Contributes only to pre-selected organizations.
Officers and Trustees:* James B. Williams,* Chair.; James M. Sibley,* Vice-Chair; Charles H. McTier, Pres.; P. Russell Hardin, V.P. and Secy.; J. Lee Tribble, Treas.; Ivan Allen, Jr., J.W. Jones, Wilton Looney.
Director: Lindsay R. Boring.
EIN: 581824778

59858
Lockerly Arboretum Foundation
1534 Irwinton Rd.
Milledgeville, GA 31061

Classified as a private operating foundation in 1966.
Financial data (yr. ended 12/31/99): Assets, $8,564,391 (M); grants paid, $0; gifts received, $145,970; expenditures, $302,816; qualifying distributions, $284,540; giving activities include $234,540 for programs.
Officers and Trustees:* Albert F. Gandy,* Pres.; Alan B. Sibley, Jr.,* V.P.; William D. Millians, Jr.,* Secy.; Robert B. Wise,* Treas.; Henry D. Edwards, William L. Hartley, Randolph Puckett, Dudley Rowe, Harriett Whipple.
EIN: 581078686

59859
Ships of the Sea, Inc.
41 Martin Luther King Blvd.
Savannah, GA 31401-1223

Classified as a private operating foundation in 1972.
Donor(s): Mills B. Lane,‡ Anne W. Lane.
Financial data (yr. ended 12/31/00): Assets, $8,340,798 (M); grants paid, $0; gifts received, $597,260; expenditures, $915,349; qualifying distributions, $0.
Officers: Mills B. Lane IV, Chair.; J. Wiley Ellis, Vice-Chair.
Trustees: Gary Arthur, Jeff Fulton, John Hardman, Rick Newell, Emily Winburn.
EIN: 580959654

59860
Beehive Foundation, Inc.
321 Barnard St.
Savannah, GA 31401-4219

Established in 1995.
Financial data (yr. ended 12/31/00): Assets, $6,408,084 (M); grants paid, $851,813; gifts received, $28,475; expenditures, $1,090,853; qualifying distributions, $851,813.
Limitations: Applications not accepted. Giving primarily in GA.
Application information: Contributes only to pre-selected organizations.
Officers: Mills B. Lane IV, Pres.; Gary M. Arthur, V.P.; Dolly Chisholm, Secy.; Stewart Bromley, Treas.
Trustees: John Hardeman, Laura Hardeman, Betty Ann Lichner.
EIN: 581873376
Codes: FD

59861
James M. Williams, Jr. Family Foundation, Inc.
2076 W. Park Pl.
Stone Mountain, GA 30087-3533

Established in 1996 in GA.
Donor(s): James M. Williams, Jr.
Financial data (yr. ended 12/31/00): Assets, $6,163,621 (M); grants paid, $245,700; gifts received, $1,032,500; expenditures, $317,595; qualifying distributions, $244,401.
Limitations: Applications not accepted.
Application information: Contributes only to pre-selected organizations.
Officers: James M. Williams, Jr., Pres.; Barbara M. Matovina, Secy.-Treas.
Directors: Dondi Anne Bosson, Candace Cheri O'Neal, Linda Sue Williams.
EIN: 582275806
Codes: FD2

59862
Hughston Sports Medicine Foundation
P.O. Box 9517
Columbus, GA 31908-9517

Classified as a private operating foundation in 1983.
Financial data (yr. ended 03/31/01): Assets, $6,119,324 (M); grants paid, $0; gifts received, $1,424,525; expenditures, $1,474,450; qualifying distributions, $1,405,373; giving activities include $574,606 for programs.
Application information: Contributes only to pre-selected organizations.
Directors: Champ L. Baker, M.D., Frederick C. Flandry, M.D., Stephen C. Hunter, M.D., George M. McCluskey, Jr., Carlton G. Savory, M.D., and 8 additional directors.
EIN: 581354127

59863
Walton County Foundation, Inc.
P.O. Box 6758
Monroe, GA 30655-0232
Application address: 137 E. Hightower Trail, Social Circle, GA 30025, tel.: (770) 464-3330
Contact: Rebecca P. Dally, Secy.-Treas.

Established in 1958.
Donor(s): Emily B. Tichenor.‡
Financial data (yr. ended 09/30/00): Assets, $4,873,788 (M); grants paid, $47,445; expenditures, $90,101; qualifying distributions, $84,747.
Limitations: Giving limited to Walton County, GA.
Officers: Shirley W. Johnson, Chair.; Charles F. Sanders, Vice-Chair.; Rebecca P. Dally, Secy.-Treas.
Directors: Marsha T. Byrd, Randolph W. Camp, Sue H. Henson, Brenda L. Kitchens, Vickie Hearn Williamson.
EIN: 586034766

59864
The Farris Foundation, Inc.
P.O. Box 304
Lawrenceville, GA 30046

Established in 1995 in GA.
Donor(s): Timothy J. Farris.
Financial data (yr. ended 12/31/01): Assets, $4,554,094 (M); grants paid, $197,393; expenditures, $1,158,588; qualifying distributions, $1,245,599; giving activities include $640,391 for programs.
Limitations: Applications not accepted. Giving in the southern U.S., with emphasis on GA, KY, NC, TN, and TX.
Application information: Contributes only to pre-selected organizations.
Officers and Directors:* Timothy J. Farris,* Chair.; Otis P. Jones,* Pres.; Jeri A. Farris,* V.P.
EIN: 582204830
Codes: FD2

59865
Tuttle-Newton Home, Inc.
2196 Central Ave.
Augusta, GA 30904-4421 (706) 738-1472
Contact: Emily Boyles, Exec. Dir.

Financial data (yr. ended 06/30/01): Assets, $3,996,158 (M); grants paid, $110,615; gifts received, $45,245; expenditures, $212,093; qualifying distributions, $177,757.
Limitations: Giving primarily in the central Savannah, GA, area.
Application information: Referrals for awards are made by social workers and agencies.
Officers: Warren Daniel, Pres.; Mark Capers, 1st V.P.; Patrick H. Perry, 2nd V.P.; Susan Rice, Secy.; Emily Boyles, Exec. Dir.

Board Members: Paul Baxter Bailey, Jr., Martha H. Baxter, Grier Bovard, Raymond B. Bradley, Marshall Brown, Hugh Hamilton, David Hogg, Minta Nixon, Greg Scurlock, Jean B. Strickland.
EIN: 580566249
Codes: FD2

59866
The Paces Foundation, Inc.
P.O. Box 550492
Atlanta, GA 30355

Financial data (yr. ended 04/30/00): Assets, $3,397,578 (M); grants paid, $750; gifts received, $1,019,944; expenditures, $183,134; qualifying distributions, $601,881; giving activities include $181,937 for programs.
Limitations: Giving primarily in Atlanta, GA.
Officer: Mark M. du Mas, Pres.
Board Members: O. Carson Adams, Audrey Allen, Candice Bennett, Stephanie Bremner, Paul Cables, Suzanne Harriman, Carolyn Hatchett.
EIN: 581949667

59867
The Evelyn Vellguth Foundation, Inc.
3484 Carrick Cir.
Lithonia, GA 30058 (770) 978-9470
Contact: William E. Oliver, Pres.

Established in 1998 in GA.
Donor(s): Evelyn Vellguth.‡
Financial data (yr. ended 12/31/99): Assets, $2,740,800 (M); grants paid, $49,933; gifts received, $2,770,305; expenditures, $171,830; qualifying distributions, $49,933.
Limitations: Giving primarily in GA.
Application information: Applicant should include list of educational courses of study and the name of the educational institution.
Officers: William E. Oliver, Pres.; Bettye B. Snowden, V.P.; Penny B. Anderson, Secy.-Treas.
EIN: 582522659

59868
Leitalift Foundation, Inc.
1060 Canton St.
Roswell, GA 30075-5607

Established around 1956.
Financial data (yr. ended 12/31/00): Assets, $2,605,587 (M); grants paid, $16,001,300; expenditures, $334,679; qualifying distributions, $16,042,652.
Limitations: Applications not accepted.
Officer and Trustees: Sherri Harper,* Pres.; Clarice Bagwell, Thomas Campbell, Edith Ivey Johnson, Anthony C. Pappadakis.
EIN: 586048185
Codes: FD

59869
Spring Valley Nursing Home, Inc.
P.O. Box 957
Elberton, GA 30635

Established in 1996 in GA.
Financial data (yr. ended 12/31/01): Assets, $2,586,793 (M); grants paid, $0; expenditures, $521,058; qualifying distributions, $0.
Limitations: Applications not accepted.
Application information: Contributes only to pre-selected organizations.
Officers: Jack A. Wheeler, Chair.; Don R. Dye, Secy.-Treas.
Trustees: Sandra Fortson, Dan McAvoy, Pamelia Jo Phelps, Tom Robinson.
EIN: 586045561

59870
Kent Richard Hofmann Foundation, Inc.
337 Savannah Ave.
Statesboro, GA 30458
Application address: 1523 N. Highland Ave., Atlanta, GA 30306, tel.: (404) 874-0216
Contact: William B. Ellis, Pres.

Established in 1986 in GA.
Donor(s): Kent Richard Hofmann.‡
Financial data (yr. ended 01/31/02): Assets, $2,409,802 (M); grants paid, $75,875; expenditures, $152,882; qualifying distributions, $75,875.
Limitations: Giving primarily in the southeastern U.S.
Publications: Informational brochure.
Application information: 2 grant cycles during year. Application form not required.
Officers: William B. Ellis, Pres.; Andrew D. Parent, Secy.; J. Richard Price, Treas.
EIN: 581576454
Codes: FD2

59871
The Carpenter's Way Ranch, Inc.
P.O. Box 578
Columbus, GA 31908-0578

Established in 1990 in GA.
Financial data (yr. ended 09/30/01): Assets, $2,187,178 (M); grants paid, $0; gifts received, $374,736; expenditures, $884,721; qualifying distributions, $905,243; giving activities include $884,721 for programs.
Officers and Trustees:* Jack B. Key III,* Chair.; William B. Turner,* Vice-Chair.; Tracy Spencer, George C. Woodruff III, and 9 additional directors.
EIN: 581920222

59872
The Harrison Family Charitable Trust, Inc.
501 E. 44th St.
Savannah, GA 31405

Established in 1999 in GA and SC.
Donor(s): Louise Lynah Harrison.‡
Financial data (yr. ended 12/31/01): Assets, $2,142,483 (M); grants paid, $0; expenditures, $123,075; qualifying distributions, $0.
Limitations: Applications not accepted.
Application information: Contributes only to pre-selected organizations.
Officers and Trustees:* Robert L. Harrison,* Pres.; Joseph H. Harrison, Jr.,* V.P.; Elizabeth H. Austin, Secy.-Treas.
EIN: 582493567

59873
Georgia Rural Telephone Museum, Inc.
506 Bailey Ave.
Leslie, GA 31764

Classified an operating foundation in 1993.
Donor(s): Citizens Telephone Co., Inc., Tommy C. Smith.
Financial data (yr. ended 06/30/00): Assets, $1,920,347 (M); grants paid, $0; gifts received, $44,100; expenditures, $33,186; qualifying distributions, $0; giving activities include $33,186 for programs.
Officers and Directors:* Tommy C. Smith,* Pres.; Fran S. Deriso,* V.P.; Gail S. Ledger,* V.P.; Claire S. Simmerson,* V.P.; Ruth K. Smith,* Secy.; Ronald D. Chapman, Treas.; Archie B. Smith.
EIN: 582061294

59874
Ruth Hartley Mosley Memorial Women's Center
(Formerly Ruth Hartley Mosely Women's Center)
c/o SunTrust Banks, Inc.
P.O. Box 4248
Macon, GA 31208-4248

Classified as a private operating foundation in 1979.
Donor(s): Ruth Hartley Mosley Memorial Fund.
Financial data (yr. ended 05/31/01): Assets, $1,399,959 (M); grants paid, $0; gifts received, $150; expenditures, $121,444; qualifying distributions, $117,699; giving activities include $117,699 for programs.
Officers: Albert Billingslea, Chair.; Ella S. Carter, Secy.
Trustee: SunTrust Banks, Inc.
EIN: 586120821

59875
T. Harvey Mathis Eye Foundation, Inc.
3070 Windward Plz., Ste. F-105
Alpharetta, GA 30005

Established in 1992 in GA.
Donor(s): Harvey M. Cheatham, Elizabeth M. Cheatham, John M. Cheatham, M.D.
Financial data (yr. ended 12/31/01): Assets, $1,389,955 (M); grants paid, $68,790; gifts received, $12,006; expenditures, $307,058; qualifying distributions, $306,710; giving activities include $215,306 for programs.
Limitations: Applications not accepted. Giving on a national and international basis.
Application information: Contributes only to pre-selected organizations.
Officers: Harvey M. Cheatham, Pres.; Elizabeth M. Cheatham, V.P.; Ed Laughlin, Secy.
EIN: 581990162

59876
Savannah Widows Society
3025 Bull St.
Savannah, GA 31405-2016 (912) 232-6312
Contact: Rosetta Sellers, Pres.

Established in 1822 in GA.
Financial data (yr. ended 08/31/01): Assets, $1,373,524 (M); grants paid, $63,422; gifts received, $50; expenditures, $87,770; qualifying distributions, $63,422.
Limitations: Giving limited to Chatham County, GA.
Application information: Contact foundation for application guidelines. Application form required.
Officers and Board Members:* Rosetta Sellers,* Pres.; Margaret Callaway,* 1st V.P.; Ruthie Williams,* 2nd V.P.; Marjorie Coffey,* Corr. Secy.; Irene Michaels,* Rec. Secy.
EIN: 580603157
Codes: GTI

59877
The Bruce Weiner Microcar Museum, Inc.
515 Heards Ferry Rd.
Atlanta, GA 30328

Established in 2001 in GA.
Donor(s): Bruce Weiner.
Financial data (yr. ended 12/31/01): Assets, $1,333,457 (M); grants paid, $0; gifts received, $1,355,400; expenditures, $21,943; qualifying distributions, $21,943.
Directors: Nicholas Trist III, Bruce Weiner, Laura Jeanette Thomas Weiner.
EIN: 582643882

59878
Eugene and Martha Caldwell Foundation, Inc.
P.O. Box 53216
Atlanta, GA 30355-1216 (404) 239-0707
Contact: Eugene Caldwell, Pres.

Established in 1986 in GA.
Donor(s): Eugene Caldwell.
Financial data (yr. ended 12/31/01): Assets, $1,030,228 (M); grants paid, $106,188; gifts received, $55,389; expenditures, $106,659; qualifying distributions, $106,334.
Limitations: Applications not accepted. Giving primarily in GA.
Application information: Contributes only to pre-selected organizations.
Officers: Eugene Caldwell, Pres.; Martha N. Caldwell, V.P.
EIN: 581693151
Codes: FD2

59879
John & Emma Derst Foundation, Inc.
P.O. Box 22849
Savannah, GA 31403-2849 (912) 233-2235
Contact: Edward J. Derst, Jr., Chair.

Financial data (yr. ended 12/31/99): Assets, $1,022,335 (M); grants paid, $38,850; expenditures, $40,128; qualifying distributions, $38,932.
Officers: Edward J. Derst, Jr., Chair.; Edward J. Derst III, Vice-Chair.; Catherine Derst Miller, Vice-Chair.; D. Morgan Derst, Treas.
EIN: 586043441

59880
McNeight Family Foundation, Inc.
1525 Northwold Dr.
Atlanta, GA 30350-4106

Established in 2000 in GA.
Donor(s): Thomas Michael McNeight.
Financial data (yr. ended 12/31/00): Assets, $949,025 (L); grants paid, $51,000; expenditures, $51,000; qualifying distributions, $51,000.
Limitations: Giving primarily in GA.
Officers: Michael Thomas McNeight, Pres.; Joyce A. McNeight, Secy.
Directors: Christopher D. McNeight, Justin T. McNeight, Katie M. McNeight.
EIN: 311736314

59881
All Nations Bible Seminars, Inc.
922 McDonough Rd.
Jackson, GA 30233-1522

Established in 1983 in GA; classified as a private operating foundation in 1985.
Donor(s): Dorothy Westbury, S.J. Westbury Gospel Trust, Ron Westbury.
Financial data (yr. ended 03/31/00): Assets, $702,680 (L); grants paid, $15,211; gifts received, $193,898; expenditures, $148,175; qualifying distributions, $147,270; giving activities include $139,059 for programs.
Limitations: Applications not accepted. Giving primarily in Kenya; some giving also in GA.
Application information: Unsolicited requests for funds not considered.
Officers: Ron Westbury, Pres.; L. Mildred Addison, V.P.; Barry Erwin, Secy.-Treas.
Directors: W.A. Cook, Margie Hunt, Joy Larson, Rod Meadows, James Westbury, Phil Westbury.
EIN: 581544827

59882
Wesley G. Adair Scholarship Trust
c/o Synovus Trust Co.
P.O. Box 1747
Athens, GA 30603-1747 (706) 357-7115
Contact: Roy F. Shoemaker, Jr.

Established in 1999 in GA.
Financial data (yr. ended 12/31/00): Assets, $628,584 (M); grants paid, $35,000; gifts received, $13,417; expenditures, $43,886; qualifying distributions, $35,000.
Limitations: Giving limited to residents of Barrow County, GA.
Application information: Application form required.
Trustee: Synovus Trust Co.
Directors: L.A. Braselton, Syaral Bryant, Lindy Clack, Janie Jones, John Peterman, LaFar Sims.
EIN: 586376451

59883
Cobb Cares, Inc.
377 Henry Dr.
Marietta, GA 30064
Application address: c/o Cobb Senior Services, 32 N. Fairground St., Marietta, GA 30060-2160
Contact: Richard Meeks, Dir.

Established in 1998 in GA.
Donor(s): George Keeler,‡ Cobb County Medical Society.
Financial data (yr. ended 01/31/01): Assets, $628,161 (M); grants paid, $50,820; gifts received, $70,764; expenditures, $66,348; qualifying distributions, $50,433.
Limitations: Giving limited to Cobb County, GA.
Application information: Application form required.
Officers: Richard Meeks, Chair.; Jerri Barr, Treas.; Catherine C. Vandenberg, Recording Secy.
Directors: Sandra Boyce, Bonnie Cole, Jane Jones.
EIN: 582350131

59884
The Lindsay Houston Foundation, Inc.
249 Cobb Pkwy. S.
Marietta, GA 30062

Established in 2000 in GA.
Financial data (yr. ended 12/31/01): Assets, $627,476 (M); grants paid, $27,334; expenditures, $33,381; qualifying distributions, $27,334.
Limitations: Giving primarily in Marietta, GA.
Officers: James L. Houston, Chair.; James R. Houston, Pres.
EIN: 582454060

59885
Thomas T. and Bernice F. Irvin Foundation, Inc.
508 Toccoa Hwy.
Mount Airy, GA 30563

Established in 1998 in GA.
Donor(s): Thomas T. Irvin, Bernice Irvin.
Financial data (yr. ended 12/31/99): Assets, $567,280 (M); grants paid, $9,700; expenditures, $11,042; qualifying distributions, $9,700.
Limitations: Applications not accepted. Giving primarily in GA.
Application information: Contributes only to pre-selected organizations.
Officers: Thomas T. Irvin, Pres.; Bernice F. Irvin, V.P.
EIN: 582359763

59886
Turner Endangered Species Fund, Inc.
c/o M. A. Wilson
1 CNN Ctr., Ste. SW0932D
Atlanta, GA 30303

Established in 1997 in GA.
Donor(s): Turner Foundation, Inc., R. E. Turner, Jane S. Fonda.
Financial data (yr. ended 12/31/00): Assets, $559,313 (M); grants paid, $0; gifts received, $1,034,045; expenditures, $822,045; qualifying distributions, $822,045; giving activities include $528,863 for programs.
Limitations: Applications not accepted.
Application information: Unsolicited requests for funds not accepted.
Officers and Directors:* R. E. Turner,* Pres.; J. Rutherford Seydel II, Secy.; M. A. Wilson, Treas.; Mike Phillips, Exec. Dir.; Jane S. Fonda, Sarah Jean Turner Garlington, Laura Lee Turner Seydel, Robert Edward Turner IV, Rhett Lee Turner, Reed Beauregard Turner.
EIN: 582324975

59887
Dewar Wildlife Trust, Inc.
2031 Lowry Rd.
Morganton, GA 30560 (706) 374-2616

Classified as a private operating foundation in GA.
Donor(s): C.E. Steuart Dewar.
Financial data (yr. ended 12/31/99): Assets, $525,774 (M); grants paid, $0; gifts received, $371,040; expenditures, $46,613; qualifying distributions, $189,503; giving activities include $46,463 for programs.
Officers: C.E. Steuart Dewar, Chair. and Treas.; Jane T.R. Dewar, Pres. and Secy.
EIN: 582426535

59888
Douglas and Patricia McCurdy Foundation
1515 Silver Hill Rd.
Stone Mountain, GA 30087
Contact: Douglas McCurdy, Dir.

Established in 1997 in GA.
Donor(s): Douglas McCurdy.
Financial data (yr. ended 12/31/01): Assets, $524,619 (M); grants paid, $22,599; expenditures, $27,304; qualifying distributions, $22,397.
Limitations: Giving primarily in GA.
Directors: Douglas McCurdy, Patricia McCurdy.
EIN: 586338667

59889
J. M. & Suella Eaton Estate Charitable Foundation
P.O. Box 419
Blue Ridge, GA 30513
Contact: Steve Eaton, Pres.

Established in 1997 in GA.
Donor(s): Suella Eaton.‡
Financial data (yr. ended 05/31/01): Assets, $424,885 (M); grants paid, $10,500; expenditures, $16,461; qualifying distributions, $10,500.
Limitations: Giving primarily in Fannin County, GA.
Officer and Directors:* Steven Michael Eaton,* Pres.; Jan Hemphill Eaton.
EIN: 582341298

59890
Belle S. Marks Foundation
701 Greene St., Ste. 200
Augusta, GA 30901-2322

Established in 1959. Classified as a private operating foundation in 1960.
Donor(s): Augusta Sportswear, Marks Handkerchief, Abram J. Serotta.
Financial data (yr. ended 12/31/00): Assets, $388,053 (M); grants paid, $30,854; gifts received, $23,494; expenditures, $35,288; qualifying distributions, $388,053.
Limitations: Applications not accepted. Giving primarily in Augusta, GA.
Application information: Contributes only to pre-selected organizations.
Trustee: Abram J. Serotta.
EIN: 586037171

59891
Gertrude Herbert Memorial Institute of Art
506 Telfair St.
Augusta, GA 30901-2310

Financial data (yr. ended 06/30/00): Assets, $339,680 (M); grants paid, $0; gifts received, $425,161; expenditures, $419,292; qualifying distributions, $400,005; giving activities include $419,292 for programs.
Limitations: Applications not accepted.
Application information: Contributes only to pre-selected organizations.
Officers and Trustees:* Jackson Cheatham,* Chair.; Cheryl W. O'Keefe,* Vice-Chair.; Lucy Weigle,* Secy.; Clayton P. Boardman,* Treas.; Amy Meybohm,* Exec. Dir.; Martha Hall Baxter, Carol C. Boardman, Claud H. Booker, Jr., Patricia Bryant, Douglas D. Buchholz, and 14 additional trustees.
Advisory Board: Julia Barrett, Lynda Blanchard, Patrick G. Blanchard, and 8 additional advisory board members.
EIN: 586004465

59892
The Hamond Foundation
1129 Empire Rd.
Atlanta, GA 30329-3844

Established in 1986 in GA.
Donor(s): Saul B. Hamond.
Financial data (yr. ended 12/31/99): Assets, $311,153 (M); grants paid, $60,950; expenditures, $64,196; qualifying distributions, $63,756.
Limitations: Applications not accepted.
Application information: Contributes only to pre-selected organizations.
Directors: Nina R. Hafitz, Saul B. Hamond.
EIN: 581705602

59893
The Fadel Educational Foundation, Inc.
P.O. Box 211320
Martinez, GA 30907
E-mail: fef_grants@hotmail.com
Contact: Hossam E. Fadel, Dir.

Established in 1992 in GA.
Donor(s): Hossam E. Fadel, Skina H. Fadel.
Financial data (yr. ended 06/30/01): Assets, $305,018 (M); grants paid, $60,432; gifts received, $71,500; expenditures, $71,272; qualifying distributions, $60,407.
Limitations: Giving on a national basis.
Application information: Application form required.
Directors: Ayman H. Fadel, Hossam E. Fadel, Mohammad H. Fadel, Skina H. Fadel.
EIN: 582330050
Codes: GTI

59894
Hamilton Glen Foundation, Inc.
2727 Lynda Ln.
Columbus, GA 31906

Established in 1996 in GA.

Financial data (yr. ended 12/31/99): Assets, $263,692 (M); grants paid, $15,223; gifts received, $50; expenditures, $18,984; qualifying distributions, $18,976.
Limitations: Applications not accepted.
Application information: Contributes only to pre-selected organizations.
Officers: Charles W. Burgin, Pres. and Treas.; Larry A. King, V.P.; Geraldine S. King, V.P. and Secy.
EIN: 582220399

59895
Church of the Verity, Inc.
P.O. Box 1225
St. Mary's, GA 31558 (912) 882-9119
Contact: Ben Jenkins, M.D., Tr.

Classified as a private operating foundation in 1982.
Donor(s): C.B. Glover III, Ben Jenkins, M.D., Bruce Bullock.
Financial data (yr. ended 12/31/99): Assets, $256,099 (M); grants paid, $9,000; gifts received, $25,450; expenditures, $26,607; qualifying distributions, $35,607.
Limitations: Giving primarily in Grand Cayman, British West Indies.
Directors: Bruce Bullock, Joe Guy, Benjamin Jenkins, Jennifer Jenkins, Jack Overman.
EIN: 581334171

59896
The Camp Coca-Cola Foundation, Inc.
2500 Windy Ridge Pkwy., No. 1400
Atlanta, GA 30339

Classified as a company-sponsored operating foundation 2001.
Donor(s): Coca-Cola Enterprises Inc., Coca-Cola North America.
Financial data (yr. ended 12/31/01): Assets, $244,409 (M); grants paid, $0; gifts received, $425,500; expenditures, $183,277; qualifying distributions, $181,042; giving activities include $181,042 for programs.
Officers and Directors:* Norm Findley, Chair.; Paul Gunderson,* Pres. and Exec. Dir.; Sandy Douglas, Secy.; John Downs, Treas.; Steve Horn, Kevin Johnson, Ingrid Saunders Jones, Melody Justice, Vicki Palmer, Suzanne Robbins, David Van Houten.
EIN: 582647038

59897
Taylor Foundation for Georgia Farm Youth
1080 Donald L. Hollowell Pkwy.
Atlanta, GA 30318-6625

Classified as a private operating foundation in 1985.
Donor(s): Glenn Taylor, J.M. Tull Foundation.
Financial data (yr. ended 12/31/00): Assets, $205,011 (M); grants paid, $12,000; gifts received, $30,434; expenditures, $12,847; qualifying distributions, $12,000.
Limitations: Applications not accepted. Giving primarily in Cartersville, GA.
Application information: Contributes only to pre-selected organizations.
Trustees: E.R. Bates, Glenda T. Cole, Richard H. Cole, James C. Strickland, Jr.
EIN: 581638163

59898
Sword of Truth Ministries, Inc.
306 Cagle Rd. S.E.
Fairmount, GA 30139-2369

Established in 1989 in FL.
Donor(s): Robert O. Lowell.

Financial data (yr. ended 12/31/01): Assets, $192,747 (M); grants paid, $0; gifts received, $22,087; expenditures, $22,676; qualifying distributions, $21,387; giving activities include $21,387 for programs.
Officers: Robert O. Lowell, Chair.; Maxwell C. Burroughs, Pres.; Lieuella R. Burroughs, V.P.; Betty G. Pope, V.P.; Doris A. Lowell, Secy.-Treas.
EIN: 592981785

59899
The Ed McKenzie, Sr. Foundation
4104 Noblemon Pt.
Duluth, GA 30097 (770) 449-6658
Contact: Ed M. McKenzie, III, Pres.

Donor(s): Ed M. McKenzie III.
Financial data (yr. ended 12/31/00): Assets, $177,456 (M); grants paid, $7,000; gifts received, $141; expenditures, $7,141; qualifying distributions, $7,141.
Limitations: Giving limited to the Macon County, GA, area.
Officers: Ed M. McKenzie III, Pres.; Marguerite Gentry, Secy.; R.B. Gentry, Treas.
EIN: 586066013

59900
Macular Assistance Group, Inc.
Lenox Center Bldg.
3399 Peachtree Rd., Ste. 1750
Atlanta, GA 30326-1120

Established in 2000 in GA.
Financial data (yr. ended 12/31/00): Assets, $142,613 (M); grants paid, $15,062; gifts received, $251,600; expenditures, $119,770; qualifying distributions, $132,022.
Limitations: Giving primarily in GA.
Officer and Directors:* W. Mercer Dye, Jr.,* Pres. and Secy.; Winship E. Rees.
EIN: 582507543

59901
The Gangarosa International Health Foundation, Inc
5305 Greencastle Way
Stone Mountain, GA 30087-1427
(770) 491-0688
Contact: Eugene J. Gangarosa, M.D.

Established in 1996 in GA.
Donor(s): Eugene J. Gangarosa, Rose C. Gangarosa.
Financial data (yr. ended 12/31/99): Assets, $140,457 (M); grants paid, $4,930; gifts received, $11,275; expenditures, $7,643; qualifying distributions, $5,580.
Limitations: Giving on a national and international basis.
Officers: Eugene J. Gangarosa, Chair.; Raymond E. Gangarosa, Secy.; Rose C. Gangarosa, Treas.
Trustees: Eugene J. Gangarosa, Jr., M. Lynn Gangarosa, Margaret A. Gangarosa, Paul C. Gangarosa.
EIN: 582198167

59902
Lanier Parks, Inc.
P.O. Box 2241
Valdosta, GA 31604

Financial data (yr. ended 12/31/99): Assets, $121,457 (M); grants paid, $0; gifts received, $300; expenditures, $7,467; qualifying distributions, $7,467; giving activities include $7,467 for programs.
Officers: Nell Roquemore, Pres.; George Wynn, Secy.; J. Wendell Godbee, Treas.
EIN: 582055933

59903
The Gary & Vickie S. Leeman Foundation
5067 Old Mountain Trail
Powder Springs, GA 30127 (404) 626-1192
Contact: Gary Leeman, Tr.

Established in 1997 in GA.
Donor(s): Gary Leeman, Vickie S. Leeman.
Financial data (yr. ended 12/31/01): Assets, $110,379 (M); grants paid, $2,500; gifts received, $20,000; expenditures, $6,725; qualifying distributions, $0.
Limitations: Giving primarily in Fort Worth, TX.
Application information: Application form not required.
Trustees: Bradford Leeman, Gary Leeman, Vickie S. Leeman.
EIN: 582329250

59904
John Rigdon Foundation, Inc.
c/o Synovus Trust Co.
P.O. Box 120
Columbus, GA 31902-0120

Financial data (yr. ended 12/31/01): Assets, $108,491 (M); grants paid, $2,229; expenditures, $3,805; qualifying distributions, $2,229.
Limitations: Applications not accepted. Giving primarily in Columbus, GA.
Application information: Contributes only to pre-selected organizations.
Directors: Frances L. Adams, Charles M. Evert.
Trustee: Synovus Trust Co.
EIN: 586114823

59905
Thomson Foundation
c/o Frances Berry
P.O. Box 638
Thomson, GA 30824
Application address: W. Hill St., Thomson, GA 30824, tel.: (706) 595-5785
Contact: Robert E. Berry, Chair.

Financial data (yr. ended 12/31/01): Assets, $101,470 (M); grants paid, $3,400; expenditures, $4,011; qualifying distributions, $4,011.
Limitations: Giving primarily in Thomson, GA.
Officers and Trustees:* Robert E. Berry,* Chair.; Frances Berry, Treas.; Carroll Burton, Margarette Johnson, Rubye Schrader.
EIN: 586041078

59906
The Leet Foundation
3631 Lantern Dr.
Gainesville, GA 30504

Established in 2001 in GA.
Donor(s): Richard H. Leet.
Financial data (yr. ended 12/31/01): Assets, $100,872 (M); grants paid, $0; gifts received, $100,000; expenditures, $300; qualifying distributions, $0.
Limitations: Applications not accepted.
Application information: Contributes only to pre-selected organizations.
Directors: Dana L. Geiken, Alan C. Leet, Phyllis C. Leet, Richard H. Leet, Richard H. Leet II.
EIN: 586434982

59907
3D Ranger Battalion Memorial Fund
c/o 3D Battalion
75th Ranger Regiment
Fort Benning, GA 31905-5853

Established in 1998 in GA.

Financial data (yr. ended 06/30/00): Assets, $94,725 (M); grants paid, $600; expenditures, $6,609; qualifying distributions, $5,317.
Officers: Capt. Perino, Chair.; S.F.C. Eversman, Vice-Chair.; Lt. Crotty, Secy.-Treas.
EIN: 582179948

59908
Interface Environmental Foundation, Inc.
2859 Paces Ferry Rd., Ste. 2000
Atlanta, GA 30339

Established in 1998 in GA.
Donor(s): Dubai Municipality, Interface, Inc.
Financial data (yr. ended 12/31/00): Assets, $91,631 (M); grants paid, $6,000; gifts received, $28,100; expenditures, $6,021; qualifying distributions, $6,021; giving activities include $21 for programs.
Limitations: Applications not accepted. Giving primarily in NY and PA.
Application information: Contributes only to pre-selected organizations.
Officers and Trustees:* Ray C. Anderson,* Pres.; Keith J. Armstrong, V.P.; Michael D. Bertolucci,* V.P.; Raymond S. Willoch, Secy.; Daniel T. Hendrix,* Treas.
EIN: 582413898

59909
The Levin Center for the Development of Educational Potential, Inc.
1525 Richard Stokes Dr.
Decatur, GA 30033 (404) 634-4511
Contact: Wendy Levin Newby, Pres.

Established in 1999 in GA.
Donor(s): Martin P. Levin.
Financial data (yr. ended 12/31/00): Assets, $86,707 (M); grants paid, $7,000; gifts received, $9,200; expenditures, $10,258; qualifying distributions, $7,000.
Limitations: Giving limited to Decatur, GA.
Application information: Application form required.
Officers and Trustees:* Wendy Levin Newby,* Pres.; Jeremy Levin,* V.P.; Martin P. Levin,* Secy.-Treas.
EIN: 582475902

59910
P. B. & Margaret Watts Foundation
c/o Bank of America
P.O. Box 927
Augusta, GA 30903-0927

Established in 1995.
Financial data (yr. ended 12/31/01): Assets, $81,395 (M); grants paid, $0; gifts received, $1,200; expenditures, $375; qualifying distributions, $0.
Trustee: JoAnn Tyler.
EIN: 586252278

59911
The Frank Family Foundation
6 Downing Ln.
Decatur, GA 30033 (404) 321-6655
Contact: Ronald and Iris D. Frank, Directors

Established in 1999 in GA.
Donor(s): Ronald Frank, Iris Frank.
Financial data (yr. ended 12/31/00): Assets, $67,658 (M); grants paid, $2,000; gifts received, $300; expenditures, $3,775; qualifying distributions, $2,000.
Directors: Ronald E. Frank, Iris D. Frank.
EIN: 586405056

59912
BroadView Foundation
P.O. Box 43225
Atlanta, GA 30336
Contact: Joseph B. Carroll

Established in 1985 in CA.
Donor(s): Joseph B. Carroll.
Financial data (yr. ended 12/31/01): Assets, $66,259 (M); grants paid, $6,250; expenditures, $6,600; qualifying distributions, $6,219.
Limitations: Giving primarily in GA.
Director: Joseph B. Carroll.
EIN: 942998068

59913
The Shepherd's Hand, Inc.
P.O. Box 642
Hamilton, GA 31811

Established in 1997 in GA.
Financial data (yr. ended 12/31/01): Assets, $64,957 (M); grants paid, $98,606; gifts received, $74,547; expenditures, $111,449; qualifying distributions, $98,606.
Limitations: Applications not accepted.
Application information: Contributes only to pre-selected organizations.
Officers: Allen C. Levi, Pres. and Secy.-Treas.; A.C. Levi, V.P.
Board Members: Glenn Davis, Jack Hoey, Gary C. Levi, Jonothan Long.
EIN: 582369797
Codes: FD2

59914
J. Donald Childress Foundation, Inc.
c/o J. Donald Childress
300 Galleria Pkwy., N.E., Ste. 600
Atlanta, GA 30339

Established in 1998 in GA.
Donor(s): J. Donald Childress.
Financial data (yr. ended 12/31/99): Assets, $62,249 (M); grants paid, $321,000; expenditures, $321,376; qualifying distributions, $321,267.
Limitations: Applications not accepted.
Application information: Contributes only to pre-selected organizations.
Trustee: J. Donald Childress.
EIN: 582436179
Codes: FD

59915
DeSana Educational Fund, Inc.
320 Dahlonega St.
Cumming, GA 30040-2410
Application address: c/o Board of Directors, P.O. Box 601, Cumming, GA 30028-0601, tel.: (770) 887-7413

Established in 1998 in GA.
Donor(s): James DeSana, Jeanne DeSana.
Financial data (yr. ended 12/31/99): Assets, $54,921 (M); grants paid, $6,000; gifts received, $5,850; expenditures, $6,120; qualifying distributions, $6,120.
Limitations: Giving primarily in GA.
Application information: Application form required.
Officer: James A. DeSana, C.E.O.
Directors: Roger L. Crow, Jeanne DeSana, Russell McClelland, Ken Shugart, Judy Thornton.
EIN: 582353946

59916
Ludwig Family Foundation
1040 Cherokee Bluff
Greensboro, GA 30642-4983
Contact: John L. Ludwig, Sr., Tr.

Established in 1999 in GA.
Donor(s): John L. Ludwig, Sr., Nancy G. Ludwig.
Financial data (yr. ended 12/31/00): Assets, $53,273 (M); grants paid, $2,200; gifts received, $11,266; expenditures, $2,540; qualifying distributions, $2,200.
Trustees: Mary Ludwig James, John L. Ludwig, Sr., John L. Ludwig, Jr., Nancy G. Ludwig, Lynn Ludwig Warnock.
EIN: 586405802

59917
L. O. Benton Banking Foundation, Inc.
P.O. Box 4450
Eatonton, GA 31024

Established in 2000.
Donor(s): Putnam Greene Financial Corp.
Financial data (yr. ended 12/31/00): Assets, $42,885 (M); grants paid, $250,000; gifts received, $286,741; expenditures, $250,021; qualifying distributions, $250,000.
Limitations: Applications not accepted. Giving primarily in the Eatontown, Greensboro, and Pembroke, GA, areas.
Application information: Contributes only to pre-selected organizations.
Officer: L.O. Benton III, Pres.
EIN: 582568248
Codes: FD

59918
Clifford Kelly Ministries, Inc.
107 Independence Dr.
Martinez, GA 30907

Classified as a private operating foundation.
Financial data (yr. ended 12/31/99): Assets, $34,789 (M); grants paid, $1,415; expenditures, $1,550; qualifying distributions, $1,550.
Officers: Richard Kelley, Pres.; Jacqueline M. Kelley, Secy.
EIN: 581850310

59919
The Berry Foundation
2131 Dayron Cir.
Marietta, GA 30062

Donor(s): William R. Berry, Elaine L. Berry.
Financial data (yr. ended 11/30/99): Assets, $30,558 (L); grants paid, $3,003; gifts received, $3,503; expenditures, $3,610; qualifying distributions, $3,595.
Application information: Application form not required.
Officers: William R. Berry, Chair.; Elaine L. Berry, V.P. and Treas.; Neill B. Faucett, Secy.
EIN: 586074348

59920
The Joseph Foundation
P.O. Box 640
Comer, GA 30629
Application address: 8315 Hwy. 172, Comer, GA 30629
Contact: Karen D. Justinn, Mgr.

Established in 1997 in GA.
Donor(s): Karen D. Justin, Richard J. Justin.
Financial data (yr. ended 12/31/01): Assets, $29,724 (M); grants paid, $975; gifts received, $16,547; expenditures, $8,827; qualifying distributions, $32,341.
Limitations: Giving primarily to residents of Comer, GA.
Officer and Trustees:* Karen D. Justinn,* Mgr.; Richard J. Justinn, Delores Winder.
EIN: 582301582

59921
Callahan Educational Trust
2811 Ridgewood Rd., N.W.
Atlanta, GA 30327-1924

Financial data (yr. ended 12/31/99): Assets, $29,401 (M); grants paid, $1,800; expenditures, $2,134; qualifying distributions, $1,800.
Limitations: Giving primarily in GA.
Officer: Dorris C. Howell, Mgr.
EIN: 586168921

59922
Pumphouse Players, Inc.
P.O. Box 1261
Cartersville, GA 30120

Classified as a private operating foundation in GA.
Financial data (yr. ended 06/30/02): Assets, $28,464 (M); grants paid, $0; gifts received, $42,455; expenditures, $49,784; qualifying distributions, $0.
Officers: Marlene Blahut, Pres.; Jim Andrews, V.P.; Carole Roach, Secy.; Brenda Andradzki, Treas.
EIN: 581373279

59923
Loren and Kathleen Platzman Charitable Foundation
1359 Springdale Rd., N.E.
Atlanta, GA 30306-2416

Established in 1999 in GA.
Donor(s): Loren Platzman.
Financial data (yr. ended 12/31/01): Assets, $23,667 (M); grants paid, $6,000; expenditures, $6,810; qualifying distributions, $5,999.
Limitations: Applications not accepted. Giving primarily in Atlanta, GA.
Application information: Contributes only to pre-selected organizations.
Officers: Loren Platzman, Pres.; Kathleen Platzman, Secy.
EIN: 582317881

59924
Hart-Franklin Industries, Inc.
P.O. Box 823
Hartwell, GA 30643

Established in 1988 in GA.
Financial data (yr. ended 06/30/99): Assets, $12,224 (M); grants paid, $0; expenditures, $14,760; qualifying distributions, $4,575.
Officers: Michael J. Balbach, Pres.; Robert E. Ridgeway, Jr., Secy.-Treas.
EIN: 581520178

59925
Arthur G. Singer, Jr. Scholarship Foundation, Inc.
800 E. Doyle St.
Toccoa, GA 30577 (706) 886-7537

Established in 1999 in GA.
Financial data (yr. ended 12/31/99): Assets, $11,829 (M); grants paid, $0; gifts received, $11,100; expenditures, $0; qualifying distributions, $0.
Limitations: Applications not accepted.
Application information: Contributes only to pre-selected organizations.
Trustees: Robert H. Evans, L. P. Greer, Margaret Kopchick, M.D., Michael L. Maley, M.D., Robert B. Struble, R. E. Thompson, M.D.
EIN: 582452031

59926
The Landings Club Scholarship Foundation, Inc.
c/o Schol. Comm.
71 Green Island Rd.
Savannah, GA 31411

Established in 1991 in GA.
Financial data (yr. ended 12/31/99): Assets, $10,446 (M); grants paid, $33,100; gifts received, $39,077; expenditures, $33,130; qualifying distributions, $33,100.
Limitations: Giving limited to GA.
Application information: Application form required.
Officer: Phyllis Albertson, Chair.
Scholarship Committee Members: Martha Brown, Joyce Glenn, Robert Neumann.
EIN: 582584504

59927
Newman Foundation, Inc.
1410 10th St.
Columbus, GA 31906-3008

Established in 2000 in GA.
Donor(s): Cary C. Newman.
Financial data (yr. ended 12/31/01): Assets, $7,268 (M); grants paid, $3,500; gifts received, $6,283; expenditures, $4,078; qualifying distributions, $3,500.
Limitations: Applications not accepted.
Application information: Contributes only to pre-selected organizations.
Officer: Cary C. Newman, Pres.
EIN: 582564858

59928
Leanna Bray Park Memorial Scholarship Fund
P.O. Box 909
Zebulon, GA 30295
Application address: c/o Pike County High School, 268 Old Meansville Rd., Zebulon, GA 30295, tel.: (770) 567-3876
Contact: James Jackson

Established in 1999 in GA.
Financial data (yr. ended 12/31/00): Assets, $5,210 (M); grants paid, $2,000; gifts received, $500; expenditures, $2,000; qualifying distributions, $2,000.
Limitations: Giving primarily in Pike County, GA.
Application information: Application form required.
Officers: Jack L. Park, Pres. and Treas.; Charlsie B. Park, Secy.
Trustees: John P. Barker, Carrie Riggins.
EIN: 586396579

59929
Warren A. Bailey Foundation, Inc.
c/o Warren A. Bailey
P.O. Box 766
St. Mary's, GA 31558-0766

Established in 1997 in GA.
Donor(s): Warren A. Bailey.
Financial data (yr. ended 12/31/99): Assets, $5,072 (M); grants paid, $7,000; gifts received, $10,000; expenditures, $7,031; qualifying distributions, $7,031.
Limitations: Applications not accepted.
Application information: Contributes only to pre-selected organizations.
Officer and Directors:* Warren A. Bailey,* Mgr.; Charles C. Smith, Jr., Gary D. Willis.
EIN: 582344649

59930
Coastal Jewish Foundation, Inc.
400 Mall Blvd., Ste. M
Savannah, GA 31406-4820 (912) 355-1311
Contact: Charles Garfunkel

Financial data (yr. ended 09/30/01): Assets, $4,903 (L); grants paid, $16,926; gifts received, $17,126; expenditures, $16,986; qualifying distributions, $0.
Limitations: Giving primarily in Savannah, GA, and Spring Valley, NY.
Officers: Charlotte S. Garfunkel, Pres.; Nathan A. Garfunkel, V.P.; David Garfunkel, Secy.; Charles Garfunkel, Treas.
EIN: 581053510

59931
Sprayberry Band Parent Association
P.O. Box 671051
Marietta, GA 30066 (770) 509-6116
Contact: Dan Martin

Financial data (yr. ended 05/30/99): Assets, $4,588 (L); grants paid, $0; expenditures, $67,090; qualifying distributions, $0.
Officers: Don Barber, Pres.; Rick Waters, Pres.
EIN: 582001262

59932
Tula Foundation, Inc.
c/o Dancy C. Massey
61 Piedmont Point
Pine Mountain, GA 31822-3581

Financial data (yr. ended 07/31/01): Assets, $3,941 (M); grants paid, $2,170; expenditures, $2,170; qualifying distributions, $2,170.
Limitations: Applications not accepted. Giving primarily in Atlanta, GA.
Application information: Contributes only to pre-selected organizations.
Officers: Lil Friedlander, Pres.; Dancy C. Massey, Secy.-Treas.
EIN: 581933707

59933
Hometown Heroes Foundation, Inc.
3953 Balley Castle Ct.
Duluth, GA 30097

Financial data (yr. ended 12/31/99): Assets, $3,837 (L); grants paid, $2,000; gifts received, $7,232; expenditures, $4,395; qualifying distributions, $2,000.
Officers: Gary Downs, C.E.O.; Randy Fuller, C.F.O.
EIN: 582448818

59934
Chattahoochee Cold Water Tailrace Fishery Foundation, Inc.
710 Riverside Rd.
Roswell, GA 30075

Established in 1998 in GA.
Financial data (yr. ended 12/31/99): Assets, $3,539 (M); grants paid, $290; gifts received, $250; expenditures, $290; qualifying distributions, $210.
Officers: Chris Scalley, Pres. and Treas.; Lisa Klein, Secy.
Trustees: Bill Couch, Don Peitzer, John Vermont.
EIN: 582376381

59935
The Ray Ellis Foundation, Inc.
205 W. Congress St.
Savannah, GA 31410

Established in 1999 in GA.
Donor(s): Ray Ellis.

Financial data (yr. ended 04/30/00): Assets, $3,227 (M); grants paid, $500; gifts received, $6,000; expenditures, $2,773; qualifying distributions, $500.
Directors: Ray G. Ellis, Theodora Aktell Ellis, Treesa Germany.
EIN: 582470570

59936
James C. Grier Foundation
3525 Old Ivy Ln., N.E.
Atlanta, GA 30342-4513

Classified as a private operating foundation in 1978.
Financial data (yr. ended 12/31/00): Assets, $3,099 (M); grants paid, $229; expenditures, $248; qualifying distributions, $248.
Limitations: Applications not accepted.
Application information: Contributes only to pre-selected organizations.
Trustee: Robert W. Storey.
EIN: 581318652

59937
Eternal Kingdom Enterprises, Inc.
106 Corporate Dr.
Carrollton, GA 30117 (770) 834-9999
Contact: Anthony Dermo, Pres.

Established in 1997 in GA.
Donor(s): Anthony F. Dermo.
Financial data (yr. ended 12/31/99): Assets, $2,248 (M); grants paid, $29,833; gifts received, $33,230; expenditures, $31,371; qualifying distributions, $31,731.
Limitations: Giving primarily in GA.
Officers: Anthony F. Dermo, Pres.; Sonj L. Dermo, Secy.
Director: Alex Montgomery.
EIN: 581716080

59938
Cats in the Cradle, Inc.
2315 Saddlesprings Dr.
Alpharetta, GA 30004

Established in 2001 in GA.
Donor(s): Lynda Brinkley.
Financial data (yr. ended 12/31/01): Assets, $2,080 (M); grants paid, $0; gifts received, $19,660; expenditures, $17,680; qualifying distributions, $14,191; giving activities include $13,691 for programs.
Directors: Beverly Bank, Lynda Brinkley, Sue Kimberly.
EIN: 582653550

59939
R. Sidney Ross Foundation, Inc.
U.S. Hwy. 129 N.
P.O. Box 666
Ocilla, GA 31774 (229) 468-7472
Contact: R. Sidney Ross, Pres.

Established in 1998.
Donor(s): R. Sidney Ross.
Financial data (yr. ended 12/31/01): Assets, $1,663 (M); grants paid, $100; expenditures, $110; qualifying distributions, $100.
Officers: R. Sidney Ross, Pres.; W. Emory Walters, V.P.; Hugh W. Roberts, Secy.
EIN: 582273855

59940
Barry McNabb Memorial Fund
4411 Forest Valley Cir.
Valdosta, GA 31602

Established in 1999 in GA.
Financial data (yr. ended 12/31/99): Assets, $1,387 (M); grants paid, $4,000; gifts received,

59940—GEORGIA

$2,274; expenditures, $4,015; qualifying distributions, $4,015.
Agent: Mary V. McNabb.
EIN: 582391291

59941
Atlanta's Family, Inc.
235 Peachtree St. N.E., Ste. 300
Atlanta, GA 30303-1404

Established in 1997 in GA.
Financial data (yr. ended 09/30/99): Assets, $609 (M); grants paid, $1,883; gifts received, $2,050; expenditures, $2,039; qualifying distributions, $2,033.
Limitations: Giving limited to Atlanta, GA.
Officers and Directors:* Kay Loerch,* C.E.O.; David Trippe,* Secy.-Treas.; Gary Spurduto.
EIN: 582351556

59942
I 4110 Foundation, Inc.
c/o A. Michael McCracken
955 Tiverton Ln.
Alpharetta, GA 30022

Donor(s): A. Michael McCracken.
Financial data (yr. ended 12/31/01): Assets, $61 (L); grants paid, $0; gifts received, $369; expenditures, $344; qualifying distributions, $0.
Limitations: Applications not accepted.
Application information: Contributes only to pre-selected organizations.
Officers: A. Michael McCracken, Pres. and Secy.; Frances Teresa McCracken, V.P. and Treas.
EIN: 582275238

59943
J. H. Daniels, Sr./C. J. Hulsey Foundation, Inc.
9270 Waits Ferry Crossing
Duluth, GA 30097

Donor(s): Jan Daniels.
Financial data (yr. ended 12/31/01): Assets, $1 (M); grants paid, $0; expenditures, $0; qualifying distributions, $0.
Limitations: Applications not accepted.
Application information: Contributes only to pre-selected organizations.
Officers: Jim H. Daniels, Jr., Pres.; Jan H. Daniels, Jr., Secy.-Treas.
EIN: 582107845

59944
Housing People Economically, Inc.
133 Peachtree St., N.E.
Atlanta, GA 30303-1808

Established in 1988 in GA; funded in 1989.
Financial data (yr. ended 10/31/01): Assets, $1 (M); grants paid, $31,340; expenditures, $31,355; qualifying distributions, $31,340.
Limitations: Applications not accepted.
Application information: Contributes only to pre-selected organizations.
Officers: James E. Bostic, Jr., Chair., Pres., and C.E.O.; James F. Kelley, Sr. V.P.; Danny W. Huff, V.P. and Treas.; Curley M. Dossman, V.P.
Directors: A.D. Correll, John F. McGovern.
EIN: 581827303

59945
Rev. George Johnson Outreach
999 Sistrunk Ct.
Columbus, GA 31907 (706) 689-9604

Established in 1998.
Donor(s): Charlie W. Johnson.
Financial data (yr. ended 12/31/00): Assets, $0 (M); grants paid, $0; expenditures, $0; qualifying distributions, $12,638; giving activities include $12,638 for programs.

Limitations: Applications not accepted.
Officers: Edgar Purett, Pres.; J.P. Wilson, V.P.; Vickie Wilder, Secy.; Gwendolyn Williams, Treas.
EIN: 582254840

HAWAII

59946
Liliuokalani Trust
c/o First Hawaiian Bank, Trust Div.
P.O. Box 3708
Honolulu, HI 96811

Established in 1952 in HI.
Financial data (yr. ended 12/31/01): Assets, $365,085,954 (M); grants paid, $82,978; gifts received, $232,169; expenditures, $23,603,999; qualifying distributions, $15,557,500; giving activities include $14,821,453 for programs.
Limitations: Applications not accepted. Giving primarily in HI.
Application information: Contributes only to pre-selected organizations.
Trustees: Thomas Kaulukukui, David Peters, First Hawaiian Bank.
EIN: 990078890
Codes: FD2

59947
Consuelo Zobel Alger Foundation
110 N. Hotel St.
Honolulu, HI 96817

Established in 1988 in HI.
Donor(s): Consuelo Zobel Alger.
Financial data (yr. ended 12/31/00): Assets, $151,750,834 (M); grants paid, $3,053,250; expenditures, $10,533,494; qualifying distributions, $4,756,425; giving activities include $341 for loans and $2,983,220 for programs.
Limitations: Applications not accepted. Giving on an international basis, with emphasis on the Philippines; giving also in HI.
Application information: Contributes only to pre-selected organizations.
Officers: Jeffrey N. Watanabe, Chair.; Patti J. Lyons, C.E.O. and Pres.; Constance H. Lau, Secy.-Treas.
Directors: Rosemary B. Clarkin, Alejandro Z. Padilla, Robert S. Tsushima.
EIN: 990266163
Codes: FD

59948
Lunalilo Home
501 Kekauluohi St.
Honolulu, HI 96825

Classified as a private operating foundation in 1988.
Financial data (yr. ended 07/31/01): Assets, $16,211,817 (M); grants paid, $0; gifts received, $552,417; expenditures, $389,538; qualifying distributions, $0.
Trustees: James K. Ahloy, Jr., Keahi Allen, Eugene Tiwanak.
EIN: 990075244

59949
Na 'Aina Kai Botanical Gardens
4101 Wailapa Rd.
Kilauea, HI 96754

Classified as a private operating foundation in 2000 in HI.
Donor(s): Edwin V. Doty, Joyce H. Doty.
Financial data (yr. ended 12/31/00): Assets, $16,192,384 (M); grants paid, $0; gifts received, $16,320,529; expenditures, $152,365; qualifying distributions, $140,145; giving activities include $133,488 for programs.
Officers and Directors:* Joyce H. Doty,* Pres.; James C. Monroe,* V.P.; Jillian M. Helmer, Secy.-Treas.; Edwin V. Doty, Edward J. Gibson, Bruce Laymon, Steve T. Roush.
EIN: 990344486

59950
Kukuiolono Park Trust Estate
(Formerly Kukuiolono Park Endowment Fund)
c/o Pacific Century Trust
P.O. Box 3170
Honolulu, HI 96802-3170

Classified as a private operating foundation in 1973.
Financial data (yr. ended 12/31/00): Assets, $6,710,311 (M); grants paid, $0; gifts received, $214,431; expenditures, $688,254; qualifying distributions, $520,389; giving activities include $608,123 for programs.
Officer and Directors:* Don Phillip Scott,* Chair.; Wilfred J. Baldwin, Thomas P. Legacy, Thomas Y. Matsuoka, Jr., Joseph S. Tavares.
Trustee: Pacific Century Trust.
EIN: 996003335

59951
John A. Burns Foundation
P.O. Box 861149
Wahiawa, HI 96786 (808) 622-1637
Contact: Robert C. Oshiro, Pres.

Established in 1988.
Donor(s): Kenneth F. Brown, Keiji Kawakami, Matsuo Takabuki, Masaru Yokouchi.
Financial data (yr. ended 02/28/00): Assets, $2,925,916 (M); grants paid, $20,000; gifts received, $1,200; expenditures, $30,551; qualifying distributions, $20,000.
Limitations: Giving strictly limited to HI.
Application information: Unsolicited requests for funds not accepted.
Officers: Kenneth F. Brown, Chair.; Robert C. Oshiro, Pres.; Turk Tokita, V.P.; Shirley Kimoto, Secy.; Frank J. Hata, Treas.
EIN: 237391086
Codes: GTI

59952
Tennent Art Foundation
c/o Reg Baker, C.P.A.
P.O. Box 25640
Honolulu, HI 96825

Classified as a private operating foundation in 1972.
Financial data (yr. ended 09/30/01): Assets, $2,038,776 (M); grants paid, $0; gifts received, $20; expenditures, $26,726; qualifying distributions, $0.
Director: Elaine Tennent.
EIN: 990108484

59953
Hoku Lele Foundation
1001 Koohoo Pl.
Kailua, HI 96734

Classified as an operating foundation in 1997 in HI.
Donor(s): Gloria Slaughter.
Financial data (yr. ended 12/31/00): Assets, $898,352 (M); grants paid, $0; gifts received, $30,286; expenditures, $382,175; qualifying distributions, $0.
Officers: Gloria Slaughter, Pres.; M. Elizabeth Valente, V.P.; Kimberly Steinberg, Secy.-Treas.
EIN: 990330249

59954
American Association of University Women Honolulu Branch Educational Fund
1802 Keeaumoku St.
Honolulu, HI 96822

Financial data (yr. ended 06/30/00): Assets, $817,452 (M); grants paid, $28,500; gifts received, $2,442; expenditures, $37,319; qualifying distributions, $28,500.
Limitations: Giving on an international basis, with emphasis on Asia; giving also in HI.
Officers: Rebecca Senutovitch, Pres.; Bonnie Taomae, V.P., Prog. Mgmt.; Constance Ko, V.P., Prop. Mgmt.; Grace M. Tsutaoka, V.P., Prop. Mgmt.; Carol Parker, V.P., Finance; Linda Nishigaya, Corresponding Secy.; Anne Edmundson, Recording Secy.; Carol Parker, Treas.
EIN: 990117668
Codes: GTI

59955
Roy and Hilda Takeyama Foundation
Pacific Tower
1001 Bishop St., Ste. 2971
Honolulu, HI 96813 (808) 526-2416
Contact: Roy Y. Takeyama, Pres.

Established in 1999 in HI.
Donor(s): Hilda Y. Takeyama, Roy Y. Takeyama.
Financial data (yr. ended 12/31/00): Assets, $642,273 (M); grants paid, $600; gifts received, $350,000; expenditures, $2,543; qualifying distributions, $551.
Limitations: Giving primarily in HI.
Officers and Directors:* Roy Y. Takeyama,* Pres.; Hilda Y. Takeyama,* V.P.; Jan N. Sullivan,* Secy.; David Y. Takeyama,* Treas.
EIN: 990342196

59956
The Catalyst Foundation
(Formerly Earth Trust)
P.O. Box 90326
Honolulu, HI 96835-0326

Established in 1996.
Donor(s): John Michael O'Keefe.
Financial data (yr. ended 12/31/01): Assets, $450,000 (M); grants paid, $0; gifts received, $450,000; expenditures, $0; qualifying distributions, $0.
Officers: John Michael O'Keefe, Pres.; Gaulemalie Pam, Secy.-Treas.
EIN: 222769283

59957
The Deborah and Peter Martin Foundation
590 A Old Stable Rd.
Paia, HI 96779

Established in 1999 in HI.
Donor(s): Peter Martin, Deborah Martin.
Financial data (yr. ended 12/31/01): Assets, $272,785 (M); grants paid, $103,500; expenditures, $104,107; qualifying distributions, $103,500.
Limitations: Applications not accepted. Giving primarily in Lahaina and Wailuku, HI.
Application information: Contributes only to pre-selected organizations.
Officers: Peter Martin, Pres.; Thomas D. Welch, Jr., V.P.; Deborah L. Martin, Secy.-Treas.
EIN: 990345212
Codes: FD2

59958
Kevin Hughes Foundation
1088 Bishop St., Ste. 1224
Honolulu, HI 96813

Established in 2000 in HI.
Donor(s): Kevin M. Hughes.
Financial data (yr. ended 12/31/00): Assets, $234,991 (M); grants paid, $0; gifts received, $413,349; expenditures, $178,358; qualifying distributions, $209,349.
Limitations: Applications not accepted.
Application information: Contributes only to pre-selected organizations.
Officers: Kevin M. Hughes, Pres.; Michael Evan Tector, V.P.; Robert J. Esgro, Jr., Secy.-Treas.
EIN: 990352693

59959
Ohana Research Foundation
67 Hakui Loop
Lahaina, HI 96761-2203

Donor(s): Alfred M. Tenny.
Financial data (yr. ended 12/31/99): Assets, $233,945 (M); grants paid, $0; gifts received, $70,707; expenditures, $18,985; qualifying distributions, $0.
Limitations: Applications not accepted.
Application information: Contributes only to pre-selected organizations.
Officer and Director:* Alfred M. Tenny,* Pres.
EIN: 943240747

59960
The Patterson Family Foundation
2810 PAA St., Ste. 6
Honolulu, HI 96819

Established in 2000.
Financial data (yr. ended 12/31/00): Assets, $208,138 (M); grants paid, $600; gifts received, $210,000; expenditures, $1,862; qualifying distributions, $600.
Limitations: Giving primarily in Honolulu, HI.
Officers and Directors:* James A. Patterson,* Pres.; Kim D. Patterson,* V.P. and Secy.; Tammy L. Wolfe.
EIN: 990346079

59961
Hawaii Times Photo Archives Foundation
c/o Dennis Ogawa
567 S. King St., Ste. 110
Honolulu, HI 96813-3079

Established in 1997 in HI.
Financial data (yr. ended 10/31/01): Assets, $181,919 (M); grants paid, $0; gifts received, $3,100; expenditures, $4,591; qualifying distributions, $0.
Limitations: Applications not accepted.
Application information: Contributes only to pre-selected organizations.
Officers and Directors:* Russell K. Sato,* V.P. and Secy.; Matsuo Takabuki, Treas.; Rev. Yoshiaki Fujitani, Jane Komeji, Dr. Richard Kosaki, Dr. Dennis M. Ogawa, Dr. Andrea Rich.
EIN: 990332798

59962
Mid-Pacific Bonsai Foundation
P.O. Box 6000
Kurtistown, HI 96760-6000

Classified as a private operating foundation in 1987.
Financial data (yr. ended 12/31/01): Assets, $181,069 (M); grants paid, $0; gifts received, $100; expenditures, $153; qualifying distributions, $0.
Officers and Directors:* Michael S. Imaino,* Pres.; Robert Itamoto,* 1st. V.P.; Robert Moeller,* 2nd. V.P.; Bill Shriner,* Recording Secy.; Janice U. Biltoft,* Treas.
EIN: 990250843

59963
Hawaii Foundation for the Blind
1255 Nuuanu Ave., Ste. E1102
Honolulu, HI 96817

Established in 1996 in HI.
Financial data (yr. ended 12/31/00): Assets, $120,804 (M); grants paid, $25,000; gifts received, $44,100; expenditures, $28,093; qualifying distributions, $25,000.
Limitations: Applications not accepted.
Application information: Contributes only to pre-selected organizations.
Officers and Directors:* Warren Toyama,* Pres.; Filo Tu,* V.P.; Amelia T. Cetrone,* Secy.-Treas.; Thomas Morikami, Donald Thomson.
EIN: 998010224

59964
Elsie and Aluma Chun Family Foundation
1321 Alewa Dr.
Honolulu, HI 96817

Established in 1995 in HI.
Donor(s): Hung Lum Chun, Elsie T. Chun.
Financial data (yr. ended 03/31/99): Assets, $111,522 (M); grants paid, $4,170; expenditures, $5,995; qualifying distributions, $4,170.
Trustees: Cedric C. Chun, Elsie T. Chun, Hung Lum Chun, Caroline C. Wong.
EIN: 990324104

59965
Masayuki & Harue Tokioka Foundation
c/o Franklin M. Tokioka
1022 Bethel St., 4th Fl.
Honolulu, HI 96813

Established in 1995 in HI.
Donor(s): Lionel Y. Tokioka, Franklin M. Tokioka.
Financial data (yr. ended 12/31/01): Assets, $61,406 (M); grants paid, $0; expenditures, $848; qualifying distributions, $0.
Officers: Lionel Y. Tokioka, Pres.; Franklin M. Tokioka, V.P.; Colbert Matsumoto, Secy.; Steven Sakamaki, Treas.
Directors: Franklin M. Tokioka II, Tyler Tokioka.
EIN: 990322018

59966
Lanikuhonua Cultural Institute
1001 Kamokila Blvd.
Kapolei, HI 96707

Financial data (yr. ended 12/31/99): Assets, $30,264 (M); grants paid, $0; gifts received, $10,000; expenditures, $63,055; qualifying distributions, $5,970; giving activities include $5,970 for programs.
Officers and Directors:* David H. McCoy,* Pres.; Theresia C. McMurdo,* V.P.; D. Keola Lloyd,* Secy.-Treas.; A.K. Polly Grace, Dennis Kauahi.
EIN: 990252924

59967
East Hawaii IPA Foundation
333 Queen St.
Honolulu, HI 96813

Established in 1996 in HI.
Financial data (yr. ended 12/31/99): Assets, $16,915 (M); grants paid, $2,500; gifts received, $29,250; expenditures, $31,469; qualifying distributions, $26,068.
Limitations: Applications not accepted.
Application information: Contributes only to pre-selected organizations.
Officers: Richard Lee-Ching, Pres.; Craig Shikuma, V.P.; Kevin Kurohara, Secy.; Craig Kadooka, Treas.
EIN: 990325147

59968
Kauai 200
P.O. Box 200
Lihue, HI 96766

Established in 1997.
Financial data (yr. ended 06/30/99): Assets, $14,492 (M); grants paid, $1,558; expenditures, $3,077; qualifying distributions, $3,077.
Limitations: Applications not accepted. Giving primarily in HI.
Officers: Brian Fujiuchi, Pres.; Yoshiko Kano, Secy.; Samuel Pratt, Treas.
Directors: Wayne Ellis, Charles Kawakami, Saburo Yoshioka, Robert Yotsuda, Peter Yukimura.
EIN: 990243622

59969
Gibson Foundation
c/o Walakea Villa
400 Hualani St., Ste. 194
Hilo, HI 96720 (808) 961-2888

Established in 1987 in HI.
Donor(s): Naleen Andrade, M.D., William E. Gibson, Kahala-Ann Trask Gibson.
Financial data (yr. ended 11/30/01): Assets, $12,581 (M); grants paid, $42; gifts received, $67,150; expenditures, $63,347; qualifying distributions, $42.
Limitations: Giving limited to HI.
Officers and Directors:* William E. Gibson,* Pres.; Renata Foster-Au,* V.P.; Kahala-Ann Trask Gibson,* Secy.-Treas.; Mililani B. Trask, Exec. Dir.; Herb Kano.
EIN: 990259620

59970
The Barriocare Foundation, Inc.
c/o Fernando Ona
45-710 Keaahala Rd., No.7
Kaneohe, HI 96744

Established in 1997.
Financial data (yr. ended 12/31/00): Assets, $4,694 (M); grants paid, $0; gifts received, $10,885; expenditures, $15,057; qualifying distributions, $14,360; giving activities include $14,365 for programs.
Officers: Fernando V. Ona, Pres.; Jack Healy, V.P.; Tedoro R. Mariano, Secy.; Celia M. Ona, Treas.
EIN: 161538738

59971
Schrader Foundation
2909 Waialae Ave., No. 25
Honolulu, HI 96826-1838

Established in 1997.
Donor(s): Doris Lechner.
Financial data (yr. ended 12/31/00): Assets, $1,242 (M); grants paid, $2,700; expenditures, $3,862; qualifying distributions, $0.
Officer and Trustees:* Ralph A. Schrader,* Chair. and Pres.; Doris Lechner, Annette Schrader, Jean W. Schrader, Elise Schrader Scone.
EIN: 990299695

59972
Kau Historical Society
c/o Pele Hanoa
P.O. Box 606
Naalehu, HI 96772

Financial data (yr. ended 12/31/99): Assets, $189 (M); grants paid, $0; expenditures, $109; qualifying distributions, $0.
Officers: Dante Carpenter, Pres.; Preston Barnes, V.P.; Albert Nakane, Secy.; Edward E. Crook, Treas.
EIN: 990142670

IDAHO

59973
The Hardy Foundation, Inc.
1301 S. Vista Ave.
Boise, ID 83705

Established in 1997 in ID.
Donor(s): Earl M. Hardy, Lavane Hardy.
Financial data (yr. ended 10/31/01): Assets, $10,557,332 (M); grants paid, $1,100; expenditures, $274,628; qualifying distributions, $1,100.
Limitations: Applications not accepted.
Application information: Contributes only to pre-selected organizations.
Officers and Directors:* Earl M. Hardy,* Pres.; Anita K. Hardy,* V.P. and Secy.; Roger Martell,* Secy.
EIN: 820498583

59974
Washington Group Foundation
(Formerly Morrison Knudsen Corporation Foundation)
P.O. Box 73
Boise, ID 83729
Application address: 1 Morrison Knudsen Plz., Boise, ID 83729
Contact: Marlene Puckett, Admin.

Established in 1947 in ID as a company-sponsored operating foundation.
Donor(s): Morrison Knudsen Corp., Washington Group International, Inc.
Financial data (yr. ended 12/31/00): Assets, $6,827,999 (M); grants paid, $372,568; expenditures, $471,069; qualifying distributions, $403,092.
Limitations: Giving nationwide, exclusively in cities of company operations.
Application information: Application form required for individuals. Application form required.
Officers and Directors:* Stephen G. Hanks,* Pres.; Marlene M. Puckett, Secy.; John Zabala,* Treas.; Frank Finlayson, Betty Hurd, Dawn McCree.
EIN: 826005410
Codes: FD, CD, GTI

59975
Firstfruits Foundation
P.O. Box 510
Challis, ID 83226

Established in 1986 in FL.
Donor(s): Christopher W. James.
Financial data (yr. ended 12/31/00): Assets, $4,251,454 (M); grants paid, $25,500; gifts received, $139,000; expenditures, $243,643; qualifying distributions, $25,350.
Limitations: Applications not accepted.
Application information: Contributes only to pre-selected organizations.
Trustees: Christopher W. James, Debra E. James.
EIN: 596567913

59976
Cloudsledge Conservation Trust
P.O. Box 158
Hope, ID 83836

Established in 1998 in ID.
Financial data (yr. ended 12/31/01): Assets, $3,222,356 (M); grants paid, $0; gifts received, $83,161; expenditures, $127,845; qualifying distributions, $0.
Trustees: Arthur Greene, Harold H. Ohata, Claudia D. Stearns.
EIN: 820485545

59977
Women's Challenge, Inc.
P.O. Box 299
Boise, ID 83701

Financial data (yr. ended 12/31/00): Assets, $692,170 (M); grants paid, $0; gifts received, $98,085; expenditures, $799,387; qualifying distributions, $0; giving activities include $791,483 for programs.
Limitations: Applications not accepted.
Application information: Contributes only to pre-selected organizations.
Officers and Director:* Rick Williams, Pres.; Jim Rabdau,* V.P.; Lois Linday, Secy.-Treas.
EIN: 820459182

59978
Lee Schmidt Scholarship Trust Fund
c/o Mac Hatch, C.P.A.
834 Falls Ave., No. 1020D
Twin Falls, ID 83301
Application address: c/o Ray Strolberg, Tr., 1910 San LaRue Ave., Twin Falls, ID 83301

Classified as a private operating foundation.
Donor(s): Lee Schmidt Trust.
Financial data (yr. ended 12/31/00): Assets, $519,399 (M); grants paid, $26,400; expenditures, $29,532; qualifying distributions, $26,532.
Limitations: Giving limited to residents of Kimberly, ID.
Application information: Application form required.
Trustees: Janet Coonts, Peggy Kroll, Dan Shoemaker, Ray Strolberg, Saundra Strolberg.
EIN: 820497599

59979
New Covenant Farms, Inc.
1737 E. 1800 S.
Gooding, ID 83330

Established in 2000 in ID.
Donor(s): Lewis M. Davenport III.
Financial data (yr. ended 12/31/00): Assets, $197,903 (M); grants paid, $27,492; gifts received, $265,100; expenditures, $39,838; qualifying distributions, $39,838.

Limitations: Giving primarily in TX, with some giving in Mexico.
Application information: Application form required.
Officer: Lewis M. Davenport III, C.E.O. and Pres.
Directors: Nita Davenport, Lizette James.
EIN: 820519199

59980
Love Ranch Charitable Trust
c/o Tracy G. & Teresa L. Silver
3954 Track Rd.
Melba, ID 83641

Financial data (yr. ended 12/31/00): Assets, $162,929 (M); grants paid, $0; gifts received, $115,307; expenditures, $1,340; qualifying distributions, $0.
Trustees: Marvin France, Barbara Nelson, Teresa Silver, Tracy Silver, Leland Tiegs, Jerry Tlucek, Tom Westall.
EIN: 826075361

59981
Hess Heritage Musuem
Rte. 1
Ashton, ID 83420

Established in 1988 in ID.
Donor(s): Daniel S. Hess, Mary B. Hess.
Financial data (yr. ended 12/31/00): Assets, $145,882 (M); grants paid, $0; gifts received, $4,143; expenditures, $3,555; qualifying distributions, $3,555; giving activities include $3,555 for programs.
Officers: Daniel S. Hess,* Pres.; Mary B. Hess,* V.P.
EIN: 826066613

59982
Schermerhorn Family Trust
P.O. Box 1583
Boise, ID 83701-1583

Established in 1997 in ID.
Financial data (yr. ended 12/31/00): Assets, $100,065 (M); grants paid, $5,401; expenditures, $6,365; qualifying distributions, $5,350.
Limitations: Applications not accepted.
Application information: Contributes only to pre-selected organizations.
Trustee: Don Copple.
EIN: 841417105

59983
Lenore Community Activity Center, Inc.
c/o Randy Randal
P.O. Box 21
Lenore, ID 83541

Established in 1992.
Financial data (yr. ended 12/31/99): Assets, $60,448 (M); grants paid, $0; gifts received, $460; expenditures, $210; qualifying distributions, $0; giving activities include $550 for programs.
Officers: Emery Bateman, Pres.; Genevieve Luonge, Secy.; Carol Grag, Treas.
EIN: 820447968

59984
Wellspring Healing Retreat
Rte. 1, Box 43A
Kooskia, ID 83539-9733

Financial data (yr. ended 03/31/00): Assets, $31,055 (M); grants paid, $0; gifts received, $26,343; expenditures, $1,456; qualifying distributions, $2,049; giving activities include $1,456 for programs.
Limitations: Applications not accepted.
Application information: Contributes only to pre-selected organizations.

Officers: Natesa S. Sridharan, Pres.; Jim O'Connor, Treas.
Director: John Cordova.
EIN: 820497342

59985
The Homedale Trust
c/o Jim Duncan
P.O. Box 1026
Homedale, ID 83628-1026

Financial data (yr. ended 12/31/99): Assets, $30,900 (M); grants paid, $2,100; expenditures, $2,100; qualifying distributions, $2,687.
Limitations: Giving limited to the Homedale, ID, area.
Application information: Application form not required.
Officers and Trustees:* Herb Fritzley, Pres.; Jim Duncan,* Secy.; Paul Akichika, Ron Cammack, Fred Demshar, Philip George, Eric Kushlan, Shelley Shenk, Steve Zatica.
EIN: 826066474

59986
Advantage Management, Inc.
P.O. Box 50763
Idaho Falls, ID 83405

Established in 1994 in UT.
Donor(s): Frank L. Vandersloot.
Financial data (yr. ended 12/31/99): Assets, $23,071 (M); grants paid, $47,853; gifts received, $70,000; expenditures, $49,487; qualifying distributions, $49,487.
Limitations: Applications not accepted. Giving primarily in ID and UT.
Trustees: Cindy Armour, Marjean McConnell, Rod Nichols, Connie Stoneberg, Belinda Vandersloot.
EIN: 870531250

59987
Triumphant Kids Organization, Inc.
1299 N. Orchard, Ste. 201
Boise, ID 83706

Donor(s): Triumph, LLC.
Financial data (yr. ended 12/31/00): Assets, $20,843 (M); grants paid, $0; gifts received, $153,732; expenditures, $156,847; qualifying distributions, $154,884; giving activities include $8,219 for programs.
Limitations: Applications not accepted. Giving primarily in ID.
Directors: Dallis Fontenot, Darrell J. Fontenot, Shannon M. Fontenot.
EIN: 820508111

59988
Nishihara Sakota Family Foundation
c/o Douglas K. Sakota
P.O. Box 163
Rexburg, ID 83440-0163

Financial data (yr. ended 12/31/00): Assets, $20,074 (M); grants paid, $1,000; expenditures, $1,025; qualifying distributions, $1,000.
Limitations: Giving primarily in ID.
Officer: Douglas K. Sakota, Mgr.
Director: M. Nishihara.
EIN: 820445402

59989
William E. & Lulu Lunte Scholarship Trust Fund 2
3934 N. 1600 E.
Buhl, ID 83316
Contact: James W. Lunte, Tr.

Classified as a private operating foundation in 1974.

Financial data (yr. ended 12/31/01): Assets, $19,631 (M); grants paid, $1,500; expenditures, $1,891; qualifying distributions, $1,575.
Limitations: Giving primarily to residents of the Buhl, ID, area.
Trustee: James W. Lunte.
EIN: 237242576

59990
Ethan Jones Scholarship Fund
1495 Marshall Rd.
Viola, ID 83872-9713   (208) 882-8486
Contact: Joann C. Jones, Tr.

Financial data (yr. ended 12/31/01): Assets, $14,007 (M); grants paid, $1,100; gifts received, $500; expenditures, $1,120; qualifying distributions, $1,100.
Limitations: Giving limited to residents of the Moscow, ID, area.
Application information: Application form required.
Trustees: Richard B. Donati, Joann C. Jones, George Porter.
EIN: 943097059

59991
Foundation for Anthropological Research and Environmental Studies
400 N. 160 W.
Rupert, ID 83350

Established in 1997.
Financial data (yr. ended 12/31/99): Assets, $6,459 (M); grants paid, $0; gifts received, $47,679; expenditures, $142,342; qualifying distributions, $142,342; giving activities include $142,342 for programs.
Officers: Richard Hansen, Pres.; John Clark, V.P.; Jim Woods, V.P.; Jody Hansen, Secy.
EIN: 820486235

59992
Miller-Dewey, Inc.
743 Santa Paula Ct.
Boise, ID 83712

Classified as a private operating foundation in 1985.
Financial data (yr. ended 08/15/99): Assets, $1,969 (M); grants paid, $0; gifts received, $475; expenditures, $302; qualifying distributions, $302; giving activities include $302 for programs.
Officers: Georgia G. Malquist, Pres.; Jeffery M. Paul, V.P.; Cindy Lee Kelley, Secy.; Elaine G. Urban, Treas.
Directors: Teresa Dewey, Linda G. Dinsmoor, W. Dale Goodson, David D. Goodson, Gloria G. McCann.
EIN: 820394406

59993
eBits, Inc.
999 W. Main St., Ste. 1100
Boise, ID 83702
URL: http://www.ebits.org

Established in 2000.
Donor(s): Qwest.
Financial data (yr. ended 06/30/01): Assets, $0 (M); grants paid, $0; gifts received, $240,008; expenditures, $114,438; qualifying distributions, $114,438.
Officer: Matt Schoenfeldt, Pres.
EIN: 820523539

ILLINOIS

59994
The Mather Foundation
(Formerly AMFund)
1603 Orrington Ave., Ste. 1800
Evanston, IL 60201

Classified as a private operating foundation in 1986.
Financial data (yr. ended 12/31/00): Assets, $384,139,883 (M); grants paid, $1,000; gifts received, $1,792,947; expenditures, $327,890,620; qualifying distributions, $20,722,642; giving activities include $20,722,642 for programs.
Limitations: Applications not accepted. Giving primarily in Evanston and Chicago, IL.
Application information: Contributes only to pre-selected organizations.
Officers and Directors:* Edward F. Otto,* C.E.O. and Pres.; Joseph Haughney, Secy.; Carol Sussenbach, Treas.; Nancy Felton-Elkins, William J. Hagenah, Marilyn McCoy, Robert B. McDermott, Bernard F. Sergesketter, and 5 additional trustees.
EIN: 362233542
Codes: TN

59995
Cantigny Foundation
435 N. Michigan Ave., Ste. 770
Chicago, IL 60611
FAX: (630) 668-5332; E-mail: lmarsico@tribune.com
Contact: Lou Marsico, Treas.

Established in 1989 in IL as a company-sponsored operating foundation; funded in 1990.
Donor(s): Robert R. McCormick Charitable Trust, Robert R. McCormick Tribune Foundation.
Financial data (yr. ended 12/31/99): Assets, $272,616,943 (M); grants paid, $51,152; gifts received, $3,261,149; expenditures, $11,174,041; qualifying distributions, $11,055,035.
Limitations: Applications not accepted. Giving primarily in Chicago, IL.
Publications: Financial statement.
Application information: Contributes only to pre-selected organizations.
Officers and Directors:* J.W. Madigan, Chair.; R. Behrenhausen,* Pres. and C.E.O.; D. Grange,* Secy. and C.O.O.; Lou Marsico,* Treas.; J. Sutherland, Exec. Dir.; C.T. Brumback, S.R. Cook, J. Dowdle, D. Fitzsimons, J. Fuller.
EIN: 363689172

59996
Christian Buehler Memorial
3415 N. Sheridan Rd.
Peoria, IL 61604-1430

Classified as a private operating foundation in 1986.
Financial data (yr. ended 12/31/99): Assets, $83,292,435 (M); grants paid, $0; gifts received, $89,951; expenditures, $4,598,193; qualifying distributions, $4,043,502; giving activities include $3,800,826 for programs.
Officers and Directors:* Louis E. Amberg, Jr.,* Pres. and Treas.; Richard Amberg,* V.P. and Secy.; Clarence Ward,* V.P.
EIN: 370661194

59997
John C. Proctor Endowment
2724 W. Reservoir Blvd.
Peoria, IL 61615

Established in 1907 in IL.
Financial data (yr. ended 03/31/01): Assets, $54,886,921 (M); grants paid, $0; gifts received, $103,871; expenditures, $5,454,233; qualifying distributions, $2,086,590; giving activities include $1,941,429 for programs.
Officers: Harry C. Stone, M.D., Pres.; James F. Bubert, V.P.; William H. Christison IV, V.P.; David Higgs, V.P.; Arlyn Rubash, V.P.; Sara K. Stone, V.P.; John Sahn, Secy.; Thomas C. Biever, Treas.
EIN: 370662595

59998
King-Bruwaert House
6101 S. County Line Rd.
Burr Ridge, IL 60527

Classified as a private operating foundations in 1987.
Financial data (yr. ended 06/30/00): Assets, $51,809,876 (M); grants paid, $0; gifts received, $11,750; expenditures, $8,218,921; qualifying distributions, $6,494,035; giving activities include $6,518,765 for programs.
Officers: W.B. Martin Gross, Pres.; Barbara Jones, Secy.; John Kayser, Treas.; Carl F. Baker, Admin.
Directors: Katherine R. Birck, David Fox, Warren W. Furey, M.D., Robert E. Harbour, James Haugh, Mary S. Mortimer, Katherine Sylvester, William E. Whitney, Jr.
EIN: 362167769

59999
John R. and Eleanor R. Mitchell Foundation
P.O. Box 963
Mount Vernon, IL 62864-0963

Classified as a private operating foundation in 1983.
Financial data (yr. ended 09/30/00): Assets, $38,453,687 (M); grants paid, $2,000; gifts received, $121,970; expenditures, $994,566; qualifying distributions, $539,915; giving activities include $352,242 for programs.
Officers: Sarah Lou Bicknell, Secy.; Michael P. Stephenson, Exec. Dir.
Trustees: Karen Bayer, D. Bruce Geary, Dennis McEvaney, Jane H. Rader, and 5 additional trustees.
EIN: 376053100

60000
Centralia Foundation
115 E. 2nd St.
Centralia, IL 62801
Contact: Bill Sprehe, Tr.

Established in 1943.
Donor(s): Rollen Robinson, Lecta Rae Robinson.
Financial data (yr. ended 09/30/01): Assets, $21,945,937 (M); grants paid, $245,349; gifts received, $332,009; expenditures, $1,546,913; qualifying distributions, $1,295,006; giving activities include $966,351 for programs.
Limitations: Giving primarily in Centralia, Odin and Sandoval, IL.
Application information: Scholarship applicants must have attended a Centralia, IL area high school.
Officers and Trustees:* Wendell Lamblin,* Chair.; Verle Besant,* Vice-Chair.; Lloyd Allen, Bruce Geary, John Lackey, Dan Nichols, William Sprehe.
EIN: 376029269
Codes: FD2, GTI

60001
Max McGraw Wildlife Foundation
P.O. Box 9, Rte. 25
Dundee, IL 60118-0009 (847) 741-8000
Contact: Charles S. Polter, Jr.

Established in 1962.
Donor(s): McGraw Foundation.
Financial data (yr. ended 04/30/01): Assets, $20,591,658 (M); grants paid, $259,737; gifts received, $1,581,176; expenditures, $3,596,080; qualifying distributions, $1,992,080.
Limitations: Giving primarily in the Midwest.
Publications: Informational brochure.
Officers and Directors:* Frederick G. Acker,* Pres.; Scott M. Elrod,* V.P.; Richard T. Schroeder,* V.P.; Timothy N. Thoelecke,* Treas.; Stanley W. Koenig, Exec. Dir.; John J. Brittain, H. Grant Clark, Jr., William J. Cullerton, Robert G. Donnelley, Richard A. Giesen, Jack D. Noyes, Richard S. Pepper, Harold T. Perry, Charles R. Tonge, Allen M. Turner, Robert B. Wilson.
EIN: 362519612
Codes: FD

60002
The Colburn Collection
555 Skokie Blvd., Ste. 410
Northbrook, IL 60062

Established in 1986 in CA. Classified as a private operating foundation in 1998.
Donor(s): Carol Colburn Hogel, Richard D. Colburn, Northbrook Properties, Inc., Consolidated Electrical Distributors, Inc.
Financial data (yr. ended 12/31/00): Assets, $19,958,222 (M); grants paid, $0; expenditures, $57,150; qualifying distributions, $55,205.
Officer and Directors:* Richard W. Colburn,* Pres.; Keith W. Colburn, Richard D. Colburn, Carol Colburn Hogel.
EIN: 954021014

60003
Burpee Natural History Museum
(Formerly Burpee Museum Association)
813 N. Main St.
Rockford, IL 61103

Financial data (yr. ended 04/30/01): Assets, $11,945,242 (M); grants paid, $0; gifts received, $642,128; expenditures, $1,382,615; qualifying distributions, $891,164; giving activities include $892,690 for programs.
Officers and Directors:* Rolf Thienemann,* Chair.; D. Kraig Piercesons,* 1st Vice-Chair.; Adriana Villagomez,* 2nd Vice-Chair.; Lewis Crampton,* Pres.; Patricia Gomez,* Secy.; Hazen Tuck,* Treas.; Joe Arco, Allan Carlson, Henrietta Dotson-Williams, and 20 additional directors.
EIN: 362045414

60004
Julius W. Hegeler II Foundation
1521 N. Vermilion St.
Danville, IL 61832
Contact: Julius W. Hegeler, II, Dir.

Established in 1992 in IL.
Donor(s): Julius W. Hegeler II.
Financial data (yr. ended 06/30/01): Assets, $11,694,506 (M); grants paid, $301,365; expenditures, $490,681; qualifying distributions, $485,223; giving activities include $261,439 for programs.
Limitations: Giving primarily in IL.
Application information: Application form not required.
Officer and Directors:* Madelle G. Hegeler,* Mgr.; Alix S. Hegeler, Julius W. Hegeler II, Delores A. Roberts.

EIN: 371302455
Codes: FD

60005
Crab Tree Farm Foundation
P.O. Box 218
Lake Bluff, IL 60044

Established in 1995 in IL.
Donor(s): John H. Bryan, Neville Bryan.
Financial data (yr. ended 11/30/99): Assets, $11,665,391 (M); grants paid, $0; gifts received, $419,322; expenditures, $162,795; qualifying distributions, $1,572,192; giving activities include $1,572,192 for programs.
Officers and Directors:* John H. Bryan,* Pres. and Treas.; Neville Bryan,* V.P. and Secy.; John H. Bryan III, Margaret Bryan French, Michael Jarvi, Mrs. Jo Jormuth, Janice L. Tofrey.
EIN: 364052065

60006
Fred & Jean Allegretti Foundation, Inc.
53 W. Jackson Blvd., Ste. 905
Chicago, IL 60604-3607 (312) 360-0922
Contact: Thomas Bucaro, Secy.

Established in 1997.
Donor(s): Jean Allegretti.
Financial data (yr. ended 10/31/01): Assets, $10,195,642 (M); grants paid, $551,845; expenditures, $730,561; qualifying distributions, $553,798.
Officers: Jean Allegretti, Pres.; Thomas Bucaro, Secy.; Joseph Nolfi, Treas.
Directors: Thomas J. Czubak, Ann Pionke.
EIN: 364110761
Codes: FD

60007
The Robert E. Gallagher Charitable Trust
The Gallagher Centre
2 Pierce Pl.
Itasca, IL 60143-3141

Established in 1997 in IL.
Donor(s): Robert E. Gallagher.
Financial data (yr. ended 12/31/00): Assets, $7,029,524 (M); grants paid, $84,615; expenditures, $113,700; qualifying distributions, $103,662.
Limitations: Applications not accepted. Giving primarily in Chicago, IL.
Application information: Contributes only to pre-selected organizations.
Trustee: Robert E. Gallagher.
EIN: 367180671
Codes: FD2

60008
Douglas-Hart Foundation
1701 Lafayette Ave.
Mattoon, IL 61938

Classified as a private operating foundation in 1972.
Financial data (yr. ended 03/31/99): Assets, $6,910,772 (M); grants paid, $0; gifts received, $57,865; expenditures, $259,727; qualifying distributions, $348,620; giving activities include $172,978 for programs.
Officers: Greg Schaffer, Pres.; Glennadene Hamel, Secy.; Steve Wente, Treas.
Directors: Robert Blair, Roy Culp, Les Edwards, Barrie Hunt, Gary W. Jacobs.
EIN: 370840618

60009
Everly Home for the Aged Trust
c/o Citizens National Bank
127 S. Side Sq.
Macomb, IL 61455

Classified as a private operating foundation in 1987.
Financial data (yr. ended 06/30/01): Assets, $6,539,329 (M); grants paid, $0; gifts received, $955; expenditures, $798,693; qualifying distributions, $581,949; giving activities include $581,949 for programs.
Trustees: James Garner, Margaret Stites, Kirk Wesley.
EIN: 376047799

60010
The SLG Cohen Foundation, Inc.
416 Main St.
Peoria, IL 61602

Financial data (yr. ended 05/31/01): Assets, $6,227,246 (M); grants paid, $2,100; gifts received, $50,194; expenditures, $444,364; qualifying distributions, $595,149; giving activities include $305,149 for programs.
Limitations: Giving primarily in IL.
Officers and Directors:* David B. Mueller,* Pres.; John E. Cassidy,* Secy.; Kenneth L. Casper,* Treas.; Rhodell E. Owens, Exec. Dir.; Timothy J. Cassidy.
EIN: 363639861

60011
Krishna Foundation, Inc.
c/o Goerge J. Bahramis, C.P.A.
236 Waukegan Rd.
Glenview, IL 60025

Established in 1977 in IL.
Donor(s): Kishan Chand, Krishna Pahuja.
Financial data (yr. ended 10/31/00): Assets, $6,177,209 (M); grants paid, $217,821; expenditures, $318,094; qualifying distributions, $198,468.
Limitations: Applications not accepted.
Application information: Contributes only to pre-selected organizations.
Trustees: Kishan Chand, Krishna Pahuja Chand, Chandra Prakash.
EIN: 362945500
Codes: FD2

60012
The SNP Consortium, Ltd.
3 Parkway N. Ctr., Ste. 150 N
Deerfield, IL 60015

Established in 1999 in IL.
Donor(s): The Wellcome Trust.
Financial data (yr. ended 12/31/01): Assets, $6,070,507 (M); grants paid, $0; expenditures, $8,815,272; qualifying distributions, $4,533,528; giving activities include $8,809,272 for programs.
Limitations: Applications not accepted.
Application information: Contributes only to pre-selected organizations.
Officer: Arthur L. Holden, Chair., C.E.O., Pres. and Secy.-Treas.
Directors: Dalia Cohen, John A. Keller, Marcia Lewis, Klaus Lindapaintner, M.D., Daniel P. McCurdy, Michael Morgan, Nicholas J. Naclerio, Allen D. Roses, M.D., Sudhir Sahasrabudhe, Elliott Sigal, B. Michael Silber, Paul Spence, John F. Stageman.
EIN: 061541680

60013
The Van Kampen Foundation
(Formerly Verbum Vitae Foundation)
290 S. County Farm Rd., 3rd Fl.
Wheaton, IL 60187

Established in 1996.
Donor(s): Judith Van Kampen.
Financial data (yr. ended 12/31/00): Assets, $5,738,285 (M); grants paid, $0; gifts received, $206,040; expenditures, $173,611; qualifying distributions, $168,773; giving activities include $168,773 for programs.
Officers: David J. Allen, V.P. and Secy.; Jerald A. Trannel, Treas.; Scott R. Pierre, Exec. Dir.
Directors: Judith Van Kampen, Kristen Wisen.
EIN: 364019118

60014
Frank & Edith Catt Educational Fund
c/o The State Bank of Jerseyville, Trust Dept.
117 S. State St.
Jerseyville, IL 62052

Established in 1994.
Donor(s): Edith Catt.‡
Financial data (yr. ended 12/31/01): Assets, $5,394,330 (M); grants paid, $77,600; expenditures, $142,290; qualifying distributions, $258,219.
Limitations: Giving to residents of Jerseyville County, IL.
Application information: Interview required. Application form required.
Trustees: John Hefner, Cindi Rice, Bonnie Tunget.
EIN: 376352751
Codes: FD2

60015
The Elssy Fabela Foundation
501 E. College Ave., Ste. 308
Aurora, IL 60505 (630) 820-0400
FAX: (630) 820-0904; *E-mail:* salvaladez@aol.com
Contact: Sal Valadez, Exec. Dir.

Established in 1997 in IL. Classified as a private operating foundation in 1998.
Financial data (yr. ended 12/31/00): Assets, $5,160,264 (M); grants paid, $82,463; expenditures, $395,977; qualifying distributions, $359,464; giving activities include $250,802 for programs.
Limitations: Giving primarily in Aurora, IL.
Publications: Informational brochure.
Application information: Application form required.
Officers: Elssy Favbla, Chair. and V.P.; Augie K. Fabela, Sr., Pres.; Sofia Fabela Holcomb, Secy.-Treas.; Salvador Valadez, Exec. Dir.
EIN: 364144368
Codes: GTI

60016
Chicago Access Corporation
322 S. Green St.
Chicago, IL 60607

Classified as a company-sponsored operating foundation in 1984.
Donor(s): Chicago Access Corporation.
Financial data (yr. ended 12/31/00): Assets, $4,510,812 (M); grants paid, $0; gifts received, $51,814; expenditures, $1,978,189; qualifying distributions, $0; giving activities include $372,687 for programs.
Directors: Barbara Popovic, Exec. Dir.; Greg Boozell, Program Dir.; Lesley Johnson, Dir., Operations; Mary Stack, Financial Dir.; Pamela Little DeZutter, Melody Douglas-Tate, and 21 additional directors.

EIN: 363239826

60017
Alton Woman's Home Association
P.O. Box 552
Alton, IL 62002

Established in 1897 in IL.
Financial data (yr. ended 12/31/00): Assets, $3,857,359 (M); grants paid, $130,550; gifts received, $5,081; expenditures, $140,249; qualifying distributions, $132,004.
Limitations: Giving limited to Madison County, IL.
Publications: Financial statement.
Application information: Application form required.
Officers and Directors:* Gay Bryant,* Pres.; Erma Maloney,* V.P.; Patty Kralschmer,* Corr. Secy.; Irene McLaughlin,* Corr. Secy.; Carole Neudecker,* Recording Secy.; Beth Helm Kamp,* Treas.; Jean Gilkison, Dorothy Kelley, Judith Mottaz, and 11 additional directors.
EIN: 370799839
Codes: FD2

60018
The Fabela Family Foundation
2835 Aurora Ave., Ste. 115-383
Naperville, IL 60540 (630) 548-5766
FAX: (630) 548-5770
Contact: Marcela D. Jones, Prog. Dir.

Established in 1997 in IL.
Financial data (yr. ended 12/31/99): Assets, $3,752,048 (M); grants paid, $60,916; gifts received, $2,400; expenditures, $232,265; qualifying distributions, $207,704; giving activities include $144,726 for programs.
Limitations: Giving limited to King County and Aurora, IL.
Application information: Application form required.
Officers: Kathleen L. Fabela, Chair, V.P., and Exec. Dir.; Augie K. Fabela II, Pres.; David Oskandy, Secy.-Treas.
Trustee: U.S. Bank.
EIN: 364144423
Codes: GTI

60019
Richardson Wildlife Foundation
2316 Shaw Rd.
West Brooklyn, IL 61378-9603

Established in 1989 in IL.
Financial data (yr. ended 12/31/99): Assets, $3,748,304 (M); grants paid, $150; gifts received, $374,433; expenditures, $354,159; qualifying distributions, $297,779.
Officers: Edward J. Richardson, Pres.; Terry Moyer, V.P.; Scott Hodes, Secy.
EIN: 363718771

60020
Kurtis Conservation Foundation
25783 N. Saint Mary's Rd.
Libertyville, IL 60048

Established in 1997 in IL.
Donor(s): William H. Kurtis.
Financial data (yr. ended 12/31/00): Assets, $3,686,402 (M); grants paid, $0; gifts received, $724,500; expenditures, $255,412; qualifying distributions, $453,846; giving activities include $453,846 for programs.
Officers and Directors:* William H. Kurtis,* Pres.; Donna La Pietra,* V.P.; Jack Horton, Mary K. Kurtis.
EIN: 364172355

60021
Technical Assistance Corporation for Housing
180 N. LaSalle St., Ste. 2225
Chicago, IL 60601

Classified as a private operating foundation in 1972.
Financial data (yr. ended 06/30/01): Assets, $3,368,286 (M); grants paid, $0; gifts received, $89,000; expenditures, $285,200; qualifying distributions, $0.
Officers and Directors:* Ralph I. Brown,* Pres.; Fred L. Bonner, Sr. V.P.; Curtis Heaston,* V.P.; Donald Register,* V.P.; Eleanor Gross, V.P.; David Midgley,* Secy.; Eugene Ruark,* Treas.
EIN: 237058125

60022
Sophia and Elmer Oerter Charitable Foundation
121 W. Legion Ave.
Columbia, IL 62236
Application address: 321 E. Locust, Columbia, IL 62236
Contact: Norman Kutterer, Dir.

Established in 1987 in IL.
Donor(s): Sophia B. Oerter.
Financial data (yr. ended 06/30/01): Assets, $3,249,750 (M); grants paid, $171,189; gifts received, $164; expenditures, $199,170; qualifying distributions, $171,189.
Limitations: Giving limited to Columbia, IL.
Directors: Floyd E. Crowder, Norman Kutterer, Robert Schueler.
EIN: 371213789
Codes: FD2

60023
Maurice Walk Fine Arts Foundation
c/o R.L. Wiesenthal
70 W. Madison, Ste. 3200
Chicago, IL 60606

Established in 1999.
Financial data (yr. ended 12/31/01): Assets, $3,016,701 (M); grants paid, $204,350; gifts received, $2,500; expenditures, $229,227; qualifying distributions, $204,350.
Officers: Marguerite Walk, V.P.; Cynthia Walk, Secy.; Margarethe Walk, Treas.
EIN: 364327696
Codes: FD2

60024
The Michael A. Halikias and Frances Halikias Charitable Trust
15750 S. Harlem, Ste. 28
Orland Park, IL 60462

Established in 1998 in IL.
Donor(s): Michael A. Halikias.
Financial data (yr. ended 06/30/00): Assets, $2,926,635 (M); grants paid, $85,845; gifts received, $119,400; expenditures, $117,994; qualifying distributions, $84,088.
Limitations: Applications not accepted. Giving primarily in IL.
Application information: Contributes only to pre-selected organizations.
Trustee: Aristotle Halikias.
EIN: 367227832

60025
Florence F. Leifheit Foundation
1359 W. Garfield
Bartonville, IL 61607
Contact: William Raye Pillman, Pres.

Established in 1997 in IL.
Financial data (yr. ended 07/31/01): Assets, $2,850,910 (L); grants paid, $97,000; gifts received, $58,000; expenditures, $114,492; qualifying distributions, $94,784.
Limitations: Giving primarily in IL.
Application information: Application form not required.
Officers: William Raye Pillman, Pres.; Sally Pillman, V.P.; Donald Pillman, Secy.-Treas.
EIN: 364132886
Codes: FD2

60026
Blackfoot Valley Ranch Foundation
c/o Jay Proops
10 Long Meadow Rd.
Winnetka, IL 60093

Established in 1996.
Donor(s): M. Jay Proops, Dawn G. Meiners.
Financial data (yr. ended 12/31/99): Assets, $2,546,330 (M); grants paid, $2,015; gifts received, $113,500; expenditures, $174,363; qualifying distributions, $43,995.
Officers and Directors:* Jay Proops,* Pres. and Treas.; M. Kay Proops,* V.P. and Secy.; Jennifer Keenan, V.P.; Grant Proops, V.P.; Mary-Audrey Atteberry, V.P.; Paul Roos.
EIN: 364070274

60027
Smith Museum of Stained Glass Windows and American Art
321 N. Clark St., Ste. 3300
Chicago, IL 60610-4795

Classified as a private operating foundation in 1994 in IL.
Donor(s): Edward B. Smith, Jr.
Financial data (yr. ended 12/31/00): Assets, $2,453,042 (M); grants paid, $0; gifts received, $1,280,534; expenditures, $17,702; qualifying distributions, $1,480,969.
Limitations: Applications not accepted.
Application information: Contributes only to pre-selected organizations.
Officers and Directors:* Edward B. Smith, Jr.,* Chair. and Treas.; Maureen D. Smith,* Pres. and Secy.; Edward B. Smith III, Peter B. Smith.
EIN: 363947421

60028
Julia Pierson Trust
P.O. Box 29
Carrollton, IL 62016-1015 (217) 942-5244

Established in 1996.
Financial data (yr. ended 12/31/00): Assets, $2,339,699 (M); grants paid, $73,575; expenditures, $80,649; qualifying distributions, $80,649.
Limitations: Giving limited to residents of Carrollton, IL.
Trustees: E. Neal Gillingham, Stanley E. Roberts, Margaret A. Schnelt.
EIN: 376321165
Codes: GTI

60029
Wilderness Research Foundation
c/o F.B. Hubachek, Jr.
P.O. Box 2593
Chicago, IL 60690-2593 (312) 845-3008
Contact: F.B. Hubachek, Jr., Pres.

Established in 1957.
Donor(s): F.B. Hubachek, Jr., Marjorie H. Watkins.
Financial data (yr. ended 12/31/01): Assets, $2,320,826 (M); grants paid, $0; gifts received, $71,627; expenditures, $132,928; qualifying distributions, $122,277; giving activities include $122,277 for programs.

Limitations: Giving primarily in the wilderness area of northeastern MN.
Officers and Trustees:* F.B. Hubachek, Jr.,* Pres. and Secy.-Treas.; Charles A. Kelly,* V.P.; Steven Hubachek, Carl A. Mohn, Richard A. Skok, Alfred D. Sullivan.
EIN: 362355084

60030
Alden Ponds Foundation
14518 O'Brien Rd.
Harvard, IL 60033

Established in 1998 in IL.
Donor(s): James Blinder.
Financial data (yr. ended 04/30/01): Assets, $2,291,474 (M); grants paid, $0; gifts received, $175,350; expenditures, $243,178; qualifying distributions, $0; giving activities include $270,568 for programs.
Limitations: Applications not accepted.
Application information: Contributes only to pre-selected organizations.
Officers and Directors:* James Blinder,* Pres.; Mary Wilson,* V.P. and Treas.; Lisa Feinberg, Secy.; Mark Feinberg.
EIN: 364233412

60031
Cline-Lofftus Foundation
57 S.E. Public Sq.
Monmouth, IL 61462
Contact: Jane Hartley Pratt, Tr.

Established in 1987.
Financial data (yr. ended 12/31/00): Assets, $2,207,689 (M); grants paid, $100,000; expenditures, $160,699; qualifying distributions, $98,061.
Limitations: Giving primarily in IL.
Application information: Application form not required.
Officer and Trustees:* William Raye Pillman,* Pres.; Fred Novotny, Jane Hartley Pratt, Dorothy Ricketts.
EIN: 371216128
Codes: FD2

60032
Apostolic Christian Prairie Villa
231 N. Ostrom
P.O. Box 566
Princeville, IL 61559-0566

Established in 1999 in IL.
Financial data (yr. ended 12/31/99): Assets, $2,190,957 (M); grants paid, $0; gifts received, $6,375; expenditures, $146,346; qualifying distributions, $278,374; giving activities include $146,346 for programs.
Officers: Robert Scholl, Chair.; Art Baurer, Secy.; Steve Leuthold, Treas.
Directors: Lavern Berchtold, Jordan Feucht, Richard Graham, Gerald Kieser, Leonard Menold, Elwin Rumbold, Harold Steiner.
EIN: 371342113

60033
PALS Preschool and Kindergarten
7306 N. Allen Rd.
Peoria, IL 61614-1109

Financial data (yr. ended 12/31/00): Assets, $2,117,892 (M); grants paid, $0; expenditures, $2,433,461; qualifying distributions, $407,670; giving activities include $2,433,461 for programs.
Officers and Directors:* Carol A. Lund,* Pres.; Thomas C. Lund, V.P. and Secy.-Treas.; Kristin Lund Dobosh, Brittany Lund, Ryan Lund, T. Chad Lund.
EIN: 371154987

60034
Dolores Kohl Education Foundation
825 Green Bay Rd., Ste. 130
Wilmette, IL 60091

Established in 1972 in IL.
Donor(s): Dolores Kohl Solovy, Ruth Page Fisher, Leo Burnett, Jewish United Fund.
Financial data (yr. ended 06/30/01): Assets, $1,732,633 (M); grants paid, $130,000; gifts received, $507,323; expenditures, $870,303; qualifying distributions, $1,048,427; giving activities include $100,000 for programs.
Limitations: Applications not accepted. Giving on a national basis.
Application information: Unsolicited requests for funds not accepted.
Officers and Directors:* Dolores Kohl Solovy,* Pres.; Herbert Kohl,* Secy.; Allen Kohl.
EIN: 237206116
Codes: FD2, GTI

60035
Institute for the Study & Treatment of Endometriosis
2425 W. 22nd St., Ste. 102
Oak Brook, IL 60523

Established in 1989 in IL.
Donor(s): Winthrop Pharmaceuticals, Tap Pharmaceuticals, I.C.I. Pharmaceuticals.
Financial data (yr. ended 12/31/01): Assets, $1,595,494 (M); grants paid, $0; gifts received, $30,850; expenditures, $89,437; qualifying distributions, $82,027.
Officers: W. Paul Dmowski, M.D., Ph.D., Pres.; Nasiruddin Rana, M.D., Treas.
EIN: 363618839

60036
Symphony Orchestra Institute
14 Country Ln.
Northfield, IL 60093

Established in 1994 in IL.
Donor(s): Paul R. Judy.
Financial data (yr. ended 03/31/01): Assets, $1,538,902 (M); grants paid, $0; gifts received, $163,387; expenditures, $378,532; qualifying distributions, $0.
Officers and Directors:* Paul R. Judy,* Chair., Pres. and Treas.; Frederick Zenone, Vice-Chair.; Debra Levin, Secy.; H. Debra Levin, Mary Ann Judy.
EIN: 363955234

60037
Goldman Philanthropic Partnerships
(Formerly Judith and George Goldman Foundation for Fighting Catastrophic Diseases)
1500 Harlan Ln.
Lake Forest, IL 60045
Contact: Judith Goldman, Pres.

Established in 1998 in IL. Classified as a private operating foundation in 2000.
Donor(s): George Goldman, Mark Soriano.
Financial data (yr. ended 03/31/01): Assets, $1,515,576 (M); grants paid, $227,592; gifts received, $10,051; expenditures, $361,317; qualifying distributions, $356,445; giving activities include $129,761 for programs.
Limitations: Giving primarily in FL and MN.
Officers: Judith Goldman, Pres.; George N. Goldman, V.P.
Directors: Steve Goldman, Nanci Goldman-Soriano.
EIN: 364258390
Codes: FD2

60038
Collectors Club of Chicago
1029 N. Dearborn St.
Chicago, IL 60610-2803

Established in 1968.
Financial data (yr. ended 12/31/00): Assets, $1,504,167 (M); grants paid, $17,150; expenditures, $73,149; qualifying distributions, $17,150.
Officers and Directors:* Lester E. Winick,* Pres.; Harold M. Stral,* V.P.; James C. Czyl, Secy.; Raymond Vogel,* Treas.; Aubrey Berman, George Fabian, Bernard A. Hennig, Sr., James Mazepa.
EIN: 366169881

60039
Louis S. Oppenheim Trust
c/o National City Bank
301 S.W. Adams
Peoria, IL 61652 (309) 655-5385
Contact: JoAnn Harlan, V.P., National City Bank

Established around 1985 in IL.
Financial data (yr. ended 12/31/01): Assets, $1,444,812 (M); grants paid, $72,641; expenditures, $74,838; qualifying distributions, $74,054.
Limitations: Giving limited to residents of Peoria County, IL.
Application information: Application form not required.
Trustee: National City Bank.
EIN: 376030392
Codes: GTI

60040
Cantigny First Division Foundation
435 N. Michigan Ave., Ste. 770
Chicago, IL 60611

Classified as a private operating foundation in 1972.
Donor(s): Robert R. McCormick Tribune Foundation, Cantigny Foundation.
Financial data (yr. ended 12/31/01): Assets, $1,406,781 (L); grants paid, $0; gifts received, $1,547,098; expenditures, $1,442,314; qualifying distributions, $1,440,191; giving activities include $1,450,245 for programs.
Officers: D. Grange, C.O.O.; Richard A. Behrenhausen, Pres.; John F. Votaw, Secy. and Exec. Dir.; L. Marsico, Jr., Treas.
Directors: J. Dowdle, Jack Fuller, J. Madigan, D. FitzSimons.
EIN: 362379641
Codes: TN

60041
George C. Loveland Testamentary Trust
c/o Richard Brantner
513 W. 2nd St.
Dixon, IL 61021-2960

Classified as a private operating foundation in 1973.
Financial data (yr. ended 12/31/99): Assets, $1,360,384 (M); grants paid, $0; gifts received, $21,161; expenditures, $137,163; qualifying distributions, $137,163; giving activities include $137,163 for programs.
Trustees: Linda Brantley, Richard Brantner, Walter Lohse.
EIN: 361381197

60042
Burstein Family Foundation
6440 N. Central Ave.
Chicago, IL 60646-2935
Application address: 1775 Washington Ave., Miami, FL 33139-7538
Contact: Harvey Burstein, Pres.

Established in 1993 in IL.
Donor(s): Samuel A. Burstein.
Financial data (yr. ended 12/31/01): Assets, $1,346,819 (M); grants paid, $298,909; expenditures, $446,860; qualifying distributions, $297,943.
Limitations: Giving primarily in Chicago, IL.
Officer: Harvey Burstein, Pres.
Directors: Stuart Burstein, Robert Pernini.
EIN: 363923618
Codes: FD

60043
John R. Lucash Charitable Private Foundation Trust
(Formerly John R. Lucash Scholarship Trust)
c/o Union Planters Bank, Trust Div.
1 S. Church St., Ste. 500
Belleville, IL 62220

Established in 1996 in IL.
Financial data (yr. ended 12/31/01): Assets, $1,223,615 (M); grants paid, $46,817; expenditures, $62,702; qualifying distributions, $57,099.
Limitations: Giving limited to Freedburg, IL.
Application information: Application form required.
Trustee: Union Planters Bank.
EIN: 376342883

60044
Stack Family Foundation
c/o Edward J. McGillen
440 W. Randolph St., Ste. 500
Chicago, IL 60606

Established in 2000.
Financial data (yr. ended 12/31/01): Assets, $1,211,175 (M); grants paid, $2,500; gifts received, $1,193,317; expenditures, $7,680; qualifying distributions, $2,500.
Officer: Shirley Stack, Pres.
Directors: James R. Corrigan, Edward J. McGillen.
EIN: 364349733

60045
Maggie & Cotto Fanyo Foundation
c/o Samuel L. Martin
120 E. Walnut, Ste. 202
Watseka, IL 60970-1354

Financial data (yr. ended 10/31/00): Assets, $1,138,932 (M); grants paid, $43,196; gifts received, $1,051,621; expenditures, $48,804; qualifying distributions, $97,861.
Limitations: Applications not accepted. Giving primarily in Watseka, IL.
Application information: Contributes only to pre-selected organizations.
Trustees: Samuel L. Martin, Kathaleen Nagle, Russell Wessels.
EIN: 371311315

60046
Erwin H. Weder Family Decks Prairie Historical Educational and Research Foundation
1111 6th St.
Highland, IL 62249

Operating status granted in 1987.
Donor(s): Donald E. Weder, Louise G. Weder.
Financial data (yr. ended 12/31/01): Assets, $1,097,234 (M); grants paid, $0; gifts received, $120; expenditures, $45,174; qualifying distributions, $25,513; giving activities include $19,389 for programs.
Advisory Committee: Dona Lee Abbott, Mary K. Foley, Donald E. Weder, Janet M. Weder, Louis G. Weder, Wanda M. Weder.
Trustee: Frank L. Flanigan.
EIN: 376261717

60047
The Meyer Foundation
4 Leeds Ct.
Lake Forest, IL 60045-3432 (847) 234-3916

Established in 1992 in IL.
Donor(s): Eric T. Meyer, Barbara Neiman.
Financial data (yr. ended 12/31/00): Assets, $1,089,471 (M); grants paid, $0; gifts received, $5,000; expenditures, $3,652; qualifying distributions, $0; giving activities include $4,807 for programs.
Limitations: Applications not accepted.
Application information: Contributes only to pre-selected organizations.
Officers and Directors:* Eric T. Meyer,* Pres.; Barbara Neiman,* V.P.; George V. Neiman,* Secy.
EIN: 363817963

60048
United Center Community Economic Development Fund
1901 W. Madison St.
Chicago, IL 60612 (312) 445-4445
Contact: Howard C. Pizer, Dir.

Established in 1996 in IL.
Financial data (yr. ended 12/31/01): Assets, $1,019,217 (M); grants paid, $0; expenditures, $2,635; qualifying distributions, $0.
Officer and Directors:* Francesca Marciniak Maher,* Secy.; Walter Burnett, Peter C.B. Bynoe, Zerrie Campbell, Earnest Gates, Rev. John Hatchett, Sen. Rickey Hendon, Crandalyn McMath, Ms. Molly O'Connor, Donald R. Oder, Howard C. Pizer, John Rucker, Darrell A. Williams.
EIN: 364000614

60049
Stephenson County Crime Stop Foundation
15 N. Calena Ave.
P.O. Box 786
Freeport, IL 61032

Established in 1994 in IL.
Financial data (yr. ended 06/30/01): Assets, $1,014,176 (M); grants paid, $48,560; gifts received, $302; expenditures, $95,594; qualifying distributions, $87,648.
Limitations: Applications not accepted. Giving primarily in IL.
Application information: Contributes only to pre-selected organizations.
Officers: Brian L. Hamon, Pres.; James A. Dooley, V.P.; K.P. Hemesath, Secy.; N.L. Woitynek, Treas.
Directors: Robert L. Dommel, J. Karstedt, G.L. Kinney, J.F. Vehmeier, D. Youngblut.
EIN: 363127617

60050
A. L. Webster Foundation
(Formerly Webster Memorial Home)
c/o Old National Trust Co.
2 W. Main St.
Danville, IL 61832
Contact: Marilyn Burton, Trust Off., Old National Trust Co.

Established in 1950 in IL.
Financial data (yr. ended 12/31/01): Assets, $1,003,885 (M); grants paid, $52,184; expenditures, $60,084; qualifying distributions, $51,689.
Officers: Raj Karinattu, Pres.; Philip Muehl, V.P.; Marilyn Burton, Secy.-Treas.
Directors: Thomas Bott, Charles Hall, Rosie McDonel, Marilyn Mihm, Mike O'Brien, Jan O'Rourke.
EIN: 370682989

60051
Cat House Foundation, Inc.
10334 Fish Hatchery Rd.
Pecatonica, IL 61063

Donor(s): Clinton E. Maslen.
Financial data (yr. ended 02/28/01): Assets, $1,002,385 (M); grants paid, $0; gifts received, $75; expenditures, $97,824; qualifying distributions, $90,965; giving activities include $90,965 for programs.
Directors: William H. Barrick, Donald J. Gasparini.
EIN: 363773302

60052
Eardley Family Foundation
2008 Golf Course View Dr.
Edwardsville, IL 62025

Donor(s): Vernon Eardley, Kathy Eardley.
Financial data (yr. ended 12/31/00): Assets, $974,308 (M); grants paid, $64,700; expenditures, $75,781; qualifying distributions, $64,700.
Limitations: Applications not accepted.
Application information: Contributes only to pre-selected organizations.
Officer: Vernon Eardley, Pres.
EIN: 436830583

60053
Enterprise Development Foundation
1020 Church St.
Evanston, IL 60201-3623

Established in 1999 in IL.
Donor(s): Daniel Cheifetz.
Financial data (yr. ended 12/31/00): Assets, $971,614 (M); grants paid, $1,900; gifts received, $50,000; expenditures, $264,039; qualifying distributions, $223,963.
Limitations: Applications not accepted. Giving primarily in IL.
Application information: Unsolicited requests for funds are not accepted.
Officers: Daniel Cheifetz, Pres.; Kathine K. Cheifetz, V.P.; Mark Zaander, Secy.; Gabriel Cheifetz.
EIN: 364274227

60054
Max Kohl Charitable Trust No. SS2
(also known as The Stephen A. Solovy Charitable Trust)
1780 Green Bay Rd., Ste. 205
Highland Park, IL 60035

Classified as a private operating trust in 1984.
Financial data (yr. ended 09/30/00): Assets, $967,646 (M); grants paid, $1,500; expenditures, $15,719; qualifying distributions, $46,638.
Trustee: Stephen A. Solovy.
EIN: 930826225

60055
Siems Memorial Park, Inc.
P.O. Box 41
Union, IL 60180

Classified as a private operating foundation in 1992.

Financial data (yr. ended 12/31/00): Assets, $957,492 (M); grants paid, $0; gifts received, $150; expenditures, $33,789; qualifying distributions, $29,743; giving activities include $29,743 for programs.
Officers and Directors:* Alfred W. Guse,* Pres.; John Nienhuis,* Secy.-Treas.; Ronald G. Dollman, Albert P. Frohling, Gordon Wilke.
EIN: 363736220

60056
Liberty Prairie Foundation
c/o George A. Ranney, Jr.
32400 N. Harris Rd.
Grayslake, IL 60030-9403

Classified as a private operating foundation in 1994.
Financial data (yr. ended 12/31/99): Assets, $954,322 (M); grants paid, $0; gifts received, $930,568; expenditures, $655,269; qualifying distributions, $653,232; giving activities include $653,232 for programs.
Officers and Directors:* Victoria Post Ranney,* Pres.; George A. Ranney, Jr.,* Secy.; Paul R. Geiselhardt, Treas.; Mike Sands, Exec. Dir.; Gerald Adelmann.
EIN: 363888439

60057
Muhammad Islamic Foundation
(Formerly Muhammad Ali Foundation)
207 E. Ohio St., Ste. 343
Chicago, IL 60611 (312) 832-0406

Financial data (yr. ended 12/31/01): Assets, $939,482 (M); grants paid, $2,500; gifts received, $133,464; expenditures, $161,685; qualifying distributions, $84,787.
Limitations: Applications not accepted. Giving primarily in Chicago, IL.
Application information: Contributes only to pre-selected organizations.
Officers and Directors:* Muhammad M. Ramah,* Pres.; Safiyya Mohammed-Ramah,* Secy.-Treas.; Omar K. Mohammad.
EIN: 510195248

60058
I. & L. Shapiro Family Charitable Foundation
221 N. LaSalle St., Ste. 3200
Chicago, IL 60601 (312) 782-3636
Contact: Irvin M. Shapiro, Pres.

Established in 1997 in IL.
Donor(s): Irvin M. Shapiro, Lynn E. Shapiro.
Financial data (yr. ended 12/31/00): Assets, $931,201 (M); grants paid, $132,159; expenditures, $140,639; qualifying distributions, $131,398.
Limitations: Giving primarily in IL; some giving in Israel.
Officers: Irvin M. Shapiro, Pres.; Sherwin I. Pogrund, Secy.; Lynn E. Shapiro, Treas.
EIN: 367213112
Codes: FD2

60059
Rhodenbaugh Foundation
4115 Royal Troon Ct.
St. Charles, IL 60174

Established in 2000 in IL.
Donor(s): Jeffrey Rhodenbaugh.
Financial data (yr. ended 12/31/00): Assets, $915,515 (M); grants paid, $3,961; gifts received, $915,000; expenditures, $3,961; qualifying distributions, $3,961.
Limitations: Giving primarily in IL.
Officers: Jeffrey Rhodenbaugh, Pres.; Sharon Rhodenbaugh, Secy.; John Rhodenbaugh, Treas.

EIN: 364404572

60060
Grace E. Buchanan Memorial Fund, Inc.
P.O. Box 834
Monmouth, IL 61462 (309) 734-3033
Additional address: c/o Buchanan Center for the Arts, 66 Public Sq., Monmouth, IL 61462

Established in 1986 in IL.
Donor(s): Grace E. Buchanan.‡
Financial data (yr. ended 12/31/99): Assets, $897,312 (M); grants paid, $55,400; expenditures, $57,125; qualifying distributions, $55,400; giving activities include $838,000 for programs.
Limitations: Applications not accepted. Giving limited to Warren County, IL.
Officers and Directors:* Everitt F. Hardin,* Pres.; Bernice Critser,* V.P.; John D. Turnbull,* Secy.; William Smith,* Treas.; Julian Bruening, David Giles, Nancy Gossett, Janet Hunter, Judy Mahoney, Steve Murmann, John L. Ockert, Ralph Whitman, Richard Whitman, Gary Willhardt, Evelyn Work.
EIN: 371098842

60061
The Center for Economic Research and Social Change, Inc.
4015 N. Rockwell
Chicago, IL 60618

Established in 2000 in IL.
Donor(s): Bill Kimmel, Kevin Neel, Jesse Sharkey, Jason Yanowitz.
Financial data (yr. ended 08/31/01): Assets, $889,040 (M); grants paid, $0; gifts received, $1,431,844; expenditures, $363,355; qualifying distributions, $310,312.
Officers: Ahmed Sehray, Pres. and Secy.; Lance Selfa, V.P.; Sharon Smith, Treas.
EIN: 364400754

60062
Caroline Mark Home
222 E. Lincoln St.
Mount Carroll, IL 61053-9654

Financial data (yr. ended 05/31/02): Assets, $872,180 (M); grants paid, $0; gifts received, $6,725; expenditures, $120,608; qualifying distributions, $114,595; giving activities include $114,595 for programs.
Trustees: Elmer C. Gerlach, Judson F. Smith.
EIN: 362284287

60063
Daniel Levin Charitable Fund
1979 N. Mill St., No. 211
Naperville, IL 60563

Established in 1998 in IL.
Donor(s): Daniel E. Levin.
Financial data (yr. ended 12/31/01): Assets, $866,474 (M); grants paid, $1,900,000; gifts received, $1,000,000; expenditures, $1,903,016; qualifying distributions, $1,899,585.
Limitations: Applications not accepted. Giving primarily in IL and PA.
Application information: Contributes only to pre-selected organizations.
Directors: Mark D. Anderson, Daniel E. Levin, Fay Hartog Levin.
EIN: 364265104
Codes: FD

60064
Believers Broadcasting Corporation
P.O. Box 1198
Quincy, IL 62306-1189 (217) 228-1275
Contact: I. Carl Geisendorfer, Pres.

Classified as an operating foundation in 1981.
Donor(s): I. Carl Geisendorfer, Brenda Wellman, Ron Wellman, Frankford Assembly of God, Loraine Christian Church.
Financial data (yr. ended 12/31/99): Assets, $856,848 (M); grants paid, $18,534; gifts received, $370,861; expenditures, $539,767; qualifying distributions, $431,621; giving activities include $246,295 for programs.
Limitations: Giving primarily in India.
Officers: I. Carl Geisendorfer, Pres.; Kenneth Geisendorfer, V.P.; Jason Geisendorfer, Secy.-Treas.
EIN: 363052879

60065
SOS Rhino
(Formerly Dr. Nan Schaffer Foundation)
505 N. Lakeshore Dr., Ste. 4610
Chicago, IL 60611
URL: http://www.sosrhino.org

Financial data (yr. ended 12/31/00): Assets, $827,169 (M); grants paid, $0; expenditures, $186,222; qualifying distributions, $168,269; giving activities include $131,318 for programs.
Officers and Directors:* Nan Schaffer,* Pres.; Charles J. Egan, Jr.,* V.P. and Secy.; Dwight C. Arn.
EIN: 431790685

60066
Garwin Family Foundation
1102 W. Chautauqua St.
Carbondale, IL 62901-2453
Application address: 35 Hillcrest Dr., Carbondale, IL 62901-2444, tel.:(618)529-2005
Contact: Leo Garwin, Pres.

Established in 1994 in OK.
Donor(s): Leo Garwin, Marsha G. Ryan, Mark J. Garwin.
Financial data (yr. ended 12/31/00): Assets, $776,448 (M); grants paid, $44,562; gifts received, $6,232; expenditures, $94,898; qualifying distributions, $151,986.
Limitations: Giving primarily in IL.
Application information: Application form not required.
Officers: Leo Garwin, Pres. and Treas.; Mark J. Garwin, M.D., V.P.; Marsha G. Ryan, M.D., Secy.
EIN: 731440816

60067
Blackfoot River Conservation Foundation
10 Long Meadow Rd.
Winnetka, IL 60093

Established in 1998 in IL.
Donor(s): Jay Proops, Mrs. Jay Proops, Roberta K. Wingfield, Henry Wilson.
Financial data (yr. ended 12/31/99): Assets, $751,587 (M); grants paid, $0; gifts received, $45,280; expenditures, $46,247; qualifying distributions, $40,247; giving activities include $39,310 for programs.
Officer: Jay Proops, Pres. and Secy.
Directors: Henry Wilson, John L. Wilson.
EIN: 364209990

60068
The Richard H. Driehaus Museum
55 W. Monroe St., Ste. 3900
Chicago, IL 60603-2345

Established in 2000 in IL.
Donor(s): The Richard H. Driehaus Foundation.

60068—ILLINOIS

Financial data (yr. ended 12/31/01): Assets, $741,116 (M); grants paid, $0; gifts received, $680,000; expenditures, $30,971; qualifying distributions, $0.
Limitations: Applications not accepted.
Application information: Contributes only to pre-selected organizations.
Officers and Directors:* Richard Driehaus,* Pres.; Roger J. Guerin,* Secy.-Treas.; William R. Beck.
EIN: 364339951

60069
Hieronymus Mueller Family Foundation
c/o Jane Mueller
221 Southmoreland Pl.
Decatur, IL 62521-3740

Established in 1994 in IL.
Donor(s): Phillip Mueller.
Financial data (yr. ended 12/31/99): Assets, $727,803 (M); grants paid, $0; gifts received, $59,803; expenditures, $59,177; qualifying distributions, $35,403; giving activities include $14,041 for programs.
Limitations: Applications not accepted.
Application information: Contributes only to pre-selected organizations.
Officer: Jane Mueller, Pres.
EIN: 371328048

60070
William Clarkson Norris Irrevocable Trust
218 W. Main St.
Dundee, IL 60118-2093

Established in 1996 in IL.
Financial data (yr. ended 12/31/99): Assets, $702,391 (M); grants paid, $48,000; expenditures, $55,127; qualifying distributions, $48,000.
Limitations: Applications not accepted. Giving primarily in IL.
Application information: Contributes only to pre-selected organizations.
Trustee: First American Bank.
EIN: 366931565

60071
Dr. Barbara Mae Atwood Animal Foundation
(Formerly Animal Rehabilitation Foundation)
P.O. Box 7327
Rockford, IL 61126-3732

Financial data (yr. ended 02/28/02): Assets, $669,983 (M); grants paid, $0; gifts received, $31,055; expenditures, $39,245; qualifying distributions, $0.
Limitations: Applications not accepted.
Application information: Contributes only to pre-selected organizations.
Officers and Directors: Barbara Mae Atwood, Pres.; Sharon Fowler, Secy.; Marlowe Holstrum, Treas.
EIN: 237122747

60072
Harry J. Anderson Memorial Trust
c/o Trust Coord.
108 E. Central Blvd.
Kewanee, IL 61443-2246 (309) 853-4497

Established as a private operating foundation in 1979 in IL.
Financial data (yr. ended 12/31/99): Assets, $649,108 (M); grants paid, $29,130; expenditures, $32,567; qualifying distributions, $29,130.
Limitations: Giving limited to the Kewanee, IL, area.
Officers: Daniel Breedlove, Pres.; Beverly Spets, Secy.; Rodney Young, Treas.

Directors: Freieda Beaman, Kurt Crabtree, Bill Grice, Barb Mersman, Tom Pitzer, Robert Verheecke, Larry Wager.
EIN: 366549171

60073
Milton Horn Art Trust
c/o Peter and Paula Ellis
1932 N. Lincoln Ave.
Chicago, IL 60614

Established in 1995.
Donor(s): Milton Horn,‡ Hyman Horn.
Financial data (yr. ended 12/31/99): Assets, $606,386 (M); grants paid, $0; expenditures, $18,396; qualifying distributions, $0; giving activities include $18,396 for programs.
Limitations: Applications not accepted. Giving primarily in Chicago, IL.
Application information: Contributes only to pre-selected organizations.
Trustees: Paula G. Ellis, Peter G. Ellis.
EIN: 367118707

60074
The Cross Foundation
P.O. Box 808
Effingham, IL 62401

Donor(s): Jack Schultz, Betinha Schultz.
Financial data (yr. ended 12/31/00): Assets, $586,622 (M); grants paid, $0; gifts received, $251,389; expenditures, $19,744; qualifying distributions, $444,898; giving activities include $19,744 for programs.
Officers: James M. Schultz, Pres.; Robert F. Schultz, Secy.; Rev. Roger H. Marshall, Treas.
Directors: Rev. Robert Backhus, Craig Lindvahl, Tom Wright.
EIN: 364176913

60075
Rebuild Foundation, Inc.
2034 E. 79th St.
Chicago, IL 60649

Financial data (yr. ended 06/30/99): Assets, $573,746 (M); grants paid, $0; expenditures, $90,944; qualifying distributions, $90,944.
Officer: Ruby Eddie, Exec. Dir.
EIN: 363757668

60076
Lizzadro Museum of Lapidary Art
220 Cottage Hill
Elmhurst, IL 60126-3351

Classified as a private operating foundation in 1975.
Donor(s): Mary Lizzadro, John S. Lizzadro, Diana Nicholas, Joseph F. Lizzadro, Angela L. Anderson.
Financial data (yr. ended 12/31/01): Assets, $573,656 (M); grants paid, $0; gifts received, $245,817; expenditures, $286,268; qualifying distributions, $176,720; giving activities include $286,268 for programs.
Officers and Directors:* John S. Lizzadro, Sr.,* Pres.; Ivan E. Frick,* 1st V.P.; J. Chase Gilmore,* 2nd V.P.; Joseph F. Lizzadro,* Secy.-Treas.; Angela L. Anderson, David Carlquist, Russell M. Kemp, Mary Kies, Mary Lizzadro, Thomas Marcucci, Diana Nicholas.
EIN: 362487600

60077
The Tithing Foundation
(Formerly Layman Tithing Foundation)
79 W. Monroe St., No. 1021
Chicago, IL 60603-4907

Classified as a private operating foundation in 1977.

Financial data (yr. ended 12/31/01): Assets, $572,591 (M); grants paid, $0; expenditures, $42,430; qualifying distributions, $38,781; giving activities include $38,781 for programs.
Directors: Rev. Paul D. Berggren, Rev. Donald R. Brown, Darwin Cooper, Paul Johns, Lester O. Johnson, Robert T. Johnson, Priscilla A. Klail, John D. Rode.
EIN: 366008117

60078
The Joyce Harmon Foundation
19606 W. Shissler Rd.
Brimfield, IL 61517 (309) 446-3218

Established in 1993 in IL.
Donor(s): Harmon Medical Lab Svcs., C. Joyce Harmon.
Financial data (yr. ended 12/31/99): Assets, $571,102 (M); grants paid, $11,042; gifts received, $39,317; expenditures, $15,727; qualifying distributions, $11,042.
Limitations: Applications not accepted. Giving limited to Peoria, IL.
Application information: Contributes only to pre-selected organizations.
Trustee: C. Joyce Harmon.
EIN: 363859079

60079
Steve and Arlene Lazarus Foundation
620 Country Ln.
Glencoe, IL 60022-2017

Established in 1986 in IL.
Donor(s): Steven Lazarus, Arlene Lazarus.
Financial data (yr. ended 12/31/99): Assets, $559,271 (M); grants paid, $61,201; gifts received, $36,000; expenditures, $62,234; qualifying distributions, $60,915.
Limitations: Applications not accepted. Giving primarily in Chicago, IL.
Application information: Contributes only to pre-selected organizations.
Officers: Steven Lazarus, Pres.; Arlene Lazarus, V.P. and Secy.-Treas.
Directors: Paul Lazarus, Eugene F. Zelek, Jr.
EIN: 363479451

60080
Philip M. Klutznick Documentary Foundation
c/o James B. Klutznick
111 E. Wacker Dr., Ste. 2400
Chicago, IL 60601

Established in 1997 in IL.
Financial data (yr. ended 12/31/00): Assets, $558,285 (M); grants paid, $127,800; expenditures, $132,442; qualifying distributions, $131,375.
Limitations: Applications not accepted.
Application information: Contributes only to pre-selected organizations.
Officers: Samuel J. Klutznick, Pres. and Treas.; James B. Klutznick, V.P.; Bettylu Saltzman, Secy.
Directors: Robert C. Klutznick, Thomas J. Klutznick.
EIN: 364184585
Codes: FD2

60081
Gratiot Lake Conservancy
2215 York Rd., Ste. 304
Oak Brook, IL 60523 (630) 571-7200
Contact: Bonita L. Hay, V.P.

Established in 1999 in MI and IL.
Donor(s): Joseph F. Lizzadro, Bonita L. Hay, Angela L. Anderson, John S. Lizzadro, Sr.
Financial data (yr. ended 12/31/99): Assets, $557,910 (M); grants paid, $0; gifts received,

IN THIS SECTION, WITHIN EACH STATE, FOUNDATIONS ARE LISTED IN DESCENDING ORDER BY ASSET AMOUNT

$1,020,800; expenditures, $7,786; qualifying distributions, $5,669; giving activities include $750 for programs.
Limitations: Giving primarily in Oak Brook, IL.
Officers and Directors:* Joseph F. Lizzadro,* Pres.; Bonita L. Hay,* V.P.; Angela L. Anderson,* Secy.-Treas.; John S. Lizzadro, Sr.
EIN: 364242179

60082
Azzarelli Foundation Trust No. 1659
P.O. Box 767
Kankakee, IL 60901-0767

Donor(s): J.I. Azzarelli, Azzarelli Construction Co.
Financial data (yr. ended 12/31/01): Assets, $532,221 (M); grants paid, $34,169; gifts received, $1,000; expenditures, $34,776; qualifying distributions, $34,776.
Limitations: Applications not accepted. Giving primarily in Kankakee, IL.
Application information: Contributes only to pre-selected organizations.
Trustees: Bartle Azzarelli, John F. Azzarelli, Joseph I. Azzarelli, Samuel J. Azzarelli.
EIN: 366149976

60083
Union Station Foundation
c/o Richard E. Hart
1 N. Old State Capitol Plz., Ste. 501
Springfield, IL 62701

Classified as a private operating foundation in 1995.
Donor(s): Michael J. Scully.
Financial data (yr. ended 12/31/01): Assets, $526,242 (M); grants paid, $0; expenditures, $2,389; qualifying distributions, $1,714; giving activities include $2,389 for programs.
Directors: Earl W. Henderson, Jr., George J. Laubner, Michael Scully.
EIN: 371340127

60084
Joanne A. Coogan Charitable Trust
6443 N. Oakbrook Ct.
Peoria, IL 61614

Established in 1997.
Donor(s): Paul M. Coogan.
Financial data (yr. ended 12/31/00): Assets, $525,963 (M); grants paid, $20,390; gifts received, $206,800; expenditures, $20,787; qualifying distributions, $20,390.
Limitations: Applications not accepted. Giving primarily in Peoria, IL.
Application information: Contributes only to pre-selected organizations.
Trustees: Christopher S. Coogan, Daniel J. Coogan, Joanne A. Coogan, Kathleen J. Coogan, Paul J. Coogan, Paul M. Coogan, Bridget Coogan Manning.
EIN: 376347112

60085
John H. & Fran Schultz Foundation
(Formerly Liberty Foundation)
P.O. Box 218
Effingham, IL 62401
Scholarship application address: c/o Superintendent, Effingham County Schools, Effingham, IL 62401, tel.: (217) 342-1363

Established in 1967.
Donor(s): Akra Builders, Inc., Alberta C. Schultz, J.M. Schultz Investment Co., John H. Schultz.
Financial data (yr. ended 12/31/99): Assets, $516,996 (M); grants paid, $51,960; gifts received, $26,165; expenditures, $55,544; qualifying distributions, $51,960.
Limitations: Giving primarily in IL; scholarships limited to Effingham, St. Anthony, and Dieterich, IL.
Application information: Application form required for scholarships.
Officers: John H. Schultz, Chair. and Pres.; Jane Schultz Herman, V.P.; Nancy Schmidt, V.P.; Ann Schultz-Deters, V.P.; Mary Schultz-Lacksen, V.P.; Robert Schultz, Secy.; Frances C. Schultz, Treas.
EIN: 366160684

60086
John J. White Foundation
825 Pleasant Ln.
Glenview, IL 60025
Contact: John J. White, Pres.

Established in 1999 in IL.
Financial data (yr. ended 12/31/00): Assets, $513,725 (M); grants paid, $47,400; expenditures, $54,969; qualifying distributions, $54,544.
Officer: John J. White, Pres.
EIN: 367266862

60087
Gardner Museum of Architecture & Design
332 Maine St.
Quincy, IL 62301-3929

Financial data (yr. ended 12/31/99): Assets, $512,369 (M); grants paid, $0; gifts received, $104,170; expenditures, $132,290; qualifying distributions, $93,119; giving activities include $132,290 for programs.
Officers and Directors:* J. Willis Gardner III,* Pres.; Jack Boge,* V.P.; Doris Hoener,* V.P.; Kristin Shore, Secy.; Dennis Williams,* Treas.; Jeffrey Bruce, Susan Deege, Carla Gordon, Wayne Greenberg, Ruth Hultz, Jason Stone.
EIN: 237405244

60088
Whiting Home
320 S. Chestnut St.
Kewanee, IL 61443-2802

Financial data (yr. ended 12/31/00): Assets, $494,920 (M); grants paid, $0; expenditures, $118,451; qualifying distributions, $100,772; giving activities include $99,465 for programs.
Officers: William J. Good, Pres.; Marvin Charlet, V.P.; Dale Swanson, Secy.-Treas.
Trustees: Matha Carroll, Martin Hepner, Elwyn Karau, Marion Kubinsky, Virginia Nelson, Elizabeth Novak, Arnold L. Smith.
EIN: 361962705

60089
Nancy & Ann Kelley Home
c/o Janice Odorizzi
167 W. Elm St.
Canton, IL 61520-2513

Classified as a private operating foundation in 1972.
Financial data (yr. ended 12/31/01): Assets, $470,866 (M); grants paid, $0; expenditures, $96,400; qualifying distributions, $0.
Officer: Janice Odorizzi, Treas.
Trustees: Kenneth Etcheson, Joann L. Favorita, Patricia B. Linn, Charles L. Martin, Jr.
EIN: 370751543

60090
The Masters Fund, Inc.
695 Brierhill Rd.
Deerfield, IL 60015-4405
Contact: Virginia L. Ray, Pres.

Established in 1986 in IL.
Donor(s): C. Eugene Ray.
Financial data (yr. ended 12/31/01): Assets, $464,881 (M); grants paid, $115,000; gifts received, $2,556; expenditures, $122,629; qualifying distributions, $114,193.
Limitations: Giving primarily in CO and IL.
Application information: Application form not required.
Officers: Virginia L. Ray, Pres.; Melissa L. Ray, V.P.; Charles T. Ray, Secy.; C. Eugene Ray, Treas.
EIN: 363484151
Codes: FD2

60091
Oak Foundation
2N 501 Ancient Oaks Dr.
West Chicago, IL 60185

Established in 1997 in IL.
Donor(s): Edward A. Elliott.
Financial data (yr. ended 12/31/99): Assets, $464,178 (M); grants paid, $9,250; gifts received, $262,790; expenditures, $43,852; qualifying distributions, $35,039; giving activities include $25,937 for programs.
Limitations: Applications not accepted.
Application information: Contributes only to pre-selected organizations.
Directors: Edward A. Elliott, Matthew A. Elliott, Virginia A. Elliott.
EIN: 364200033

60092
Sardar Dalbir Singh Memorial Foundation
c/o Jasbir K. Singh
1575 Winberie Ct., N.
Naperville, IL 60564

Donor(s): Pavitar Singh, Jasbir K. Singh.
Financial data (yr. ended 12/31/99): Assets, $462,378 (M); grants paid, $1,726; gifts received, $4,050; expenditures, $13,962; qualifying distributions, $13,962; giving activities include $12,151 for programs.
Limitations: Applications not accepted.
Application information: Contributes only to pre-selected organizations.
Trustees: Jasbir K. Singh, Pavitar Singh.
EIN: 363669749

60093
Arlen Francis Klein Trust Fund
903 N. Dunlap
Savoy, IL 61874
Contact: Richard Woodworth, Treas.

Established around 1989 in IL.
Donor(s): Arlen Francis Klein.‡
Financial data (yr. ended 09/30/99): Assets, $460,141 (M); grants paid, $11,442; expenditures, $15,838; qualifying distributions, $15,838.
Limitations: Giving primarily in IL.
Application information: Application form required.
Officer: Richard Woodworth, Treas.
Trustee: J.R. Pankau.
EIN: 371284503

60094
Meek Memorial Trust of May 21, 1997
(also known as Beryl Meek Memorial Trust)
c/o Magna Trust Co.
P.O. Box 523
Belleville, IL 62222-0523

Classified as a private operating foundation in 1985.
Financial data (yr. ended 04/30/01): Assets, $452,685 (M); grants paid, $67,579; expenditures, $75,659; qualifying distributions, $67,579.
Limitations: Applications not accepted.

Application information: Contributes only to pre-selected organizations.
Trustees: Francis Boyle, Magna Trust Co.
EIN: 376237414

60095
Robert and Julie Montgomery Foundation
755 Lincoln Ave.
Winnetka, IL 60093

Established in 1998 in IL.
Donor(s): Robert M. Montgomery.
Financial data (yr. ended 12/31/99): Assets, $407,905 (M); grants paid, $18,187; gifts received, $103,462; expenditures, $20,054; qualifying distributions, $19,357.
Limitations: Applications not accepted.
Application information: Contributes only to pre-selected organizations.
Trustees: Julie Montgomery, Robert Montgomery.
EIN: 367210147

60096
Glickman Family Foundation
c/o M. Lipschultz
222 N. LaSalle St., Ste. 300
Chicago, IL 60601-1005
Contact: Edwin C. Glickman, Pres.

Established in 1990 in IL.
Donor(s): Edwin C. Glickman.
Financial data (yr. ended 12/31/00): Assets, $401,727 (M); grants paid, $35,918; expenditures, $37,290; qualifying distributions, $35,846.
Officer: Edwin C. Glickman, Pres.
EIN: 363720869

60097
Richard & Louise Abrahams Foundation
1725 Lily Ct.
Highland Park, IL 60035

Classified as a company-sponsored operating foundation in 1997.
Donor(s): Electro, Inc.
Financial data (yr. ended 12/31/01): Assets, $393,446 (M); grants paid, $58,646; expenditures, $65,328; qualifying distributions, $58,646.
Limitations: Applications not accepted. Giving primarily in IL.
Application information: Contributes only to pre-selected organizations.
Officers: Richard Abrahams, Pres.; Louise Abrahams, Treas.
Director: Ruth Terry.
EIN: 364161900

60098
The Center for Transcultural Studies
(Formerly Center for Psychosocial Studies)
2031 N. New England Ave.
Chicago, IL 60707

Classified as a private operating foundation in 1976.
Donor(s): Bernard Weissbourd.
Financial data (yr. ended 08/31/00): Assets, $389,200 (M); grants paid, $0; gifts received, $115,000; expenditures, $79,205; qualifying distributions, $67,971; giving activities include $67,971 for programs.
Officers: Harold M. Visotsky, Chair.; Charles Taylor, Pres.; James Wertch, V.P.; Greg Urban, Secy.-Treas.; Elvia Esparza, Treas.
Directors: Alberta Arthurs, Leonard Duhl, Reiko Hasuike, Leo Oufan Lee, Caroline L. Williams.
EIN: 237180280

60099
Good Old Burt Spain Trust
5119 S. Francisco Ave.
Chicago, IL 60632-2128
Donor(s): Burt Spain.‡
Financial data (yr. ended 06/30/00): Assets, $384,183 (M); grants paid, $28,000; expenditures, $29,597; qualifying distributions, $29,597.
Limitations: Applications not accepted.
Application information: Contributes only to pre-selected organizations.
Trustee: John G. Massura.
EIN: 367154959

60100
Edmund B. Thornton Foundation
P.O. Box 949
Ottawa, IL 61350 (815) 434-6664
Contact: Edmund B. Thornton, Pres.

Established in 1985 in IL.
Donor(s): Edmund B. Thornton.
Financial data (yr. ended 01/31/00): Assets, $366,021 (M); grants paid, $4,845; gifts received, $42,893; expenditures, $41,888; qualifying distributions, $39,943.
Limitations: Giving primarily in IL.
Application information: Application form required.
Officers and Directors:* Edmund B. Thornton,* Pres. and Treas.; Susan J. Thornton, Secy.; Kristina M. Fogarty.
EIN: 363538959

60101
Sheldon Glaser Trust
c/o 5/3 Investment Services
101 W. Stephenson St., P.O. Box 660
Freeport, IL 61032 (815) 233-6003
Contact: Troy Lessman, Tr.

Established in 2000 in IL.
Financial data (yr. ended 12/31/00): Assets, $350,073 (M); grants paid, $11,000; expenditures, $21,489; qualifying distributions, $17,818.
Limitations: Giving primarily in IL, MN, and TN.
Application information: Accepts applications for scholarships only. Application form required.
Trustee: Troy Lessman.
Advisory Committee: Karen Dammann, Don Grunder, Ray Mensendike.
EIN: 367074441

60102
SLK Foundation
1920 N. Clark St., Ste. 16C
Chicago, IL 60614-5401

Established in 1986 in IL.
Donor(s): Joseph D. Klemen.
Financial data (yr. ended 12/31/00): Assets, $344,714 (M); grants paid, $0; expenditures, $9,975; qualifying distributions, $9,975; giving activities include $9,205 for programs.
Officers: Simone L. Klemen, Pres.; Richard Peterson, Secy.
EIN: 363485924

60103
Brown Family Foundation
c/o Densil A. Brown
201 N. Schoenbeck Rd.
Prospect Heights, IL 60070 (847) 870-1600

Established in 1997 in IL.
Donor(s): Densil A. Brown, Peggy Brown.
Financial data (yr. ended 09/30/00): Assets, $342,246 (M); grants paid, $13,420; expenditures, $21,052; qualifying distributions, $16,655; giving activities include $16,155 for programs.
Limitations: Giving primarily in IL.
Officers: Densil A. Brown, Pres.; Peggy M. Brown, V.P.
EIN: 364198973

60104
Charles and Dorothy Brew Foundation
9 Regent Wood Rd.
Northfield, IL 60093-2728

Established in 1998 in IL.
Donor(s): Charles A. Brew, Dorothy Brew.
Financial data (yr. ended 12/31/00): Assets, $339,451 (M); grants paid, $16,600; expenditures, $18,163; qualifying distributions, $16,153.
Limitations: Applications not accepted. Giving primarily in St. Louis, MO.
Application information: Contributes only to pre-selected organizations.
Directors: Charles A. Brew, Charles A. Brew, Jr., Dorothy Brew.
EIN: 391933492

60105
The Colmar Foundation, Inc.
300 S. Wacker Dr., Ste. 1000
Chicago, IL 60606 (312) 922-1980

Established in 1996.
Donor(s): John L. Colmar.
Financial data (yr. ended 11/30/00): Assets, $326,880 (M); grants paid, $18,850; gifts received, $43,200; expenditures, $22,055; qualifying distributions, $21,855.
Officers and Directors:* John L. Colmar,* Pres.; Craig Colmar,* V.P.; Christine Colmar,* Secy.-Treas.; Steve Colmar.
EIN: 367166213

60106
Holson Family Foundation
c/o Michael M. Lockett, Ltd.
9933 N. Lawler, Ste. 202
Skokie, IL 60077

Established in 1999 in IL.
Donor(s): Holson Realty Charitable Lead Annuity Trust.
Financial data (yr. ended 12/31/00): Assets, $323,652 (M); grants paid, $7,000; gifts received, $4,000; expenditures, $7,105; qualifying distributions, $7,000.
Limitations: Applications not accepted.
Application information: Contributes only to pre-selected organizations.
Officers and Directors:* R.S. Holson, Jr.,* Pres.; James Holson,* V.P.; Peter Holson,* V.P.; R.S. Holson III,* V.P.; Hillary Holson Zimmerman,* V.P.; Joyce D. Holson,* Treas.
EIN: 364332846

60107
Ira A. Eichner & Barbara R. Eichner Foundation
1 AAR Pl.
1100 N. Wood Dale Rd.
Wood Dale, IL 60191-1159

Established in 1996 in IL.
Donor(s): Ira A. Eichner.
Financial data (yr. ended 01/31/02): Assets, $321,610 (M); grants paid, $111,134; expenditures, $111,185; qualifying distributions, $110,140.
Limitations: Applications not accepted. Giving primarily in IL.
Application information: Contributes only to pre-selected organizations.
Trustees: Barbara R. Eichner, Ira A. Eichner.
EIN: 367167187
Codes: FD2

60108
Pathways
3633 W. Lake St.
Glenview, IL 60025

Donor(s): Patrick G. Ryan, Shirley W. Ryan.
Financial data (yr. ended 11/30/00): Assets, $301,761 (M); grants paid, $0; gifts received, $472,054; expenditures, $1,657,949; qualifying distributions, $452,765; giving activities include $1,657,949 for programs.
Officer and Directors: Shirley W. Ryan,* Pres. and Secy.-Treas.; Patrick G. Ryan, Patrick G. Ryan, Jr.
EIN: 363337969

60109
David C. and Sarajean Ruttenberg Arts Foundation
(Formerly Ruttenberg Arts Foundation)
833 N. Orleans, Ste. 806
Chicago, IL 60610
Contact: David C. Ruttenberg, Pres.

Classified as a private operating foundation in 1983.
Donor(s): David C. Ruttenberg.
Financial data (yr. ended 07/31/00): Assets, $296,686 (M); grants paid, $2,600; gifts received, $2,075; expenditures, $13,679; qualifying distributions, $13,679.
Limitations: Giving primarily in Chicago, IL.
Officers: David C. Ruttenberg, Pres.; Sarajean Ruttenberg, V.P.; David W. Ruttenberg, Secy.; Roger F. Ruttenberg, Treas.
EIN: 363137264

60110
Ariel Education Initiative
307 N. Michigan Ave.
Chicago, IL 60601

Financial data (yr. ended 06/30/99): Assets, $285,303 (M); grants paid, $0; gifts received, $307,517; expenditures, $496,278; qualifying distributions, $490,949; giving activities include $359,879 for programs.
Officer: Roger Schmitt, Secy.
Directors: Diane Anderson, Stephanie Clark, Janie Davis, Arne Duncan, Sara Duncan, Sue Morton Duncan, Elizabeth Hurtig, Sophia Dorsey King, Kendall Hines Mallette, Dodie Norton, and 7 additional directors.
EIN: 364093845

60111
Robert W. Goltermann and Marcia M. Goltermann Charitable Trust
295 S. Prospect Ave.
Elmhurst, IL 60126-3309

Established in 1987 in IL.
Donor(s): Robert W. Goltermann, Marcia M. Goltermann.
Financial data (yr. ended 12/31/00): Assets, $284,732 (M); grants paid, $13,285; expenditures, $17,653; qualifying distributions, $13,285.
Limitations: Applications not accepted. Giving primarily in IL.
Application information: Contributes only to pre-selected organizations.
Trustees: Marcia M. Goltermann, Robert W. Goltermann.
EIN: 363533428

60112
Chicago Regional Organ and Tissue Bank
151 Sheridan Rd.
Kenilworth, IL 60043-1214

Financial data (yr. ended 12/31/01): Assets, $279,723 (M); grants paid, $0; expenditures, $15,163; qualifying distributions, $0.
Trustee: Frederick K. Merkel.
EIN: 363519112

60113
David & Lisette Eisendrath Foundation
100 Glade Rd.
Glencoe, IL 60022
Application address: c/o John E. Diemel, 1 Northfield Plz., Northfield, IL 60093

Financial data (yr. ended 12/31/01): Assets, $279,131 (M); grants paid, $15,000; expenditures, $16,835; qualifying distributions, $16,471.
Limitations: Applications not accepted. Giving primarily in IL.
Application information: Contributes only to pre-selected organizations.
Officers and Directors:* John E. Deimel,* Pres.; Doris Berman,* Secy.; Alice Deimel.
EIN: 366091728

60114
The Spirit of Chicago Education and Development Foundation for Children and Young Adults
c/o Howard Mardell, Ltd.
221 N. LaSalle St., Ste. 2040
Chicago, IL 60601

Established in 1996 in IL.
Donor(s): Mark Condic, Jr.
Financial data (yr. ended 12/31/99): Assets, $272,233 (M); grants paid, $100; gifts received, $36,000; expenditures, $24,229; qualifying distributions, $17,580.
Limitations: Applications not accepted.
Application information: Contributes only to pre-selected organizations.
Officers and Directors:* Mark A. Condic, Jr.,* Pres.; Richard B. Indyke,* Secy.-Treas.; John J. Condic, Sandra J. Condic, Susan M. Condic, Charles A. Lenart, William Somerville.
EIN: 364049037

60115
Herbert T. McLean Memorial Fund
503 W. Miller
Bloomington, IL 61701-6533
Contact: Allen Gibson, Secy.

Financial data (yr. ended 12/31/99): Assets, $269,554 (M); grants paid, $13,500; expenditures, $14,310; qualifying distributions, $13,380.
Application information: Application form not required.
Officer and Directors:* Allen Gibson,* Secy.; Hugh Evans, William Galloway, Gary Norman, Bary Weer.
EIN: 510176145
Codes: GTI

60116
Polsky Family Foundation
c/o M. Polsky
650 Dundee Rd.
Northbrook, IL 60062
Contact: Michael Polsky, Tr.

Established in 1999 in IL.
Financial data (yr. ended 12/31/99): Assets, $243,819 (M); grants paid, $37,200; gifts received, $200,225; expenditures, $39,136; qualifying distributions, $38,844.
Trustees: Alan Polsky, Gabe Polsky, Maya Polsky, Michael Polsky.
EIN: 364266016

60117
Twelve Otniel Foundation
1361 Champion Forest Ct.
Wheaton, IL 60187 (630) 681-0617
Contact: James M. Monson, Pres.

Established in 1999 in IL.
Donor(s): Emile Van Der Merwe, Susan Van Der, Merwe.
Financial data (yr. ended 12/31/01): Assets, $241,081 (M); grants paid, $5,000; gifts received, $220,000; expenditures, $5,566; qualifying distributions, $5,000.
Application information: Application form required.
Officers: James M. Monson, Pres.; John M. Monson, V.P.; Charles D. Schlueter, Secy.; Earl Hagar, Treas.
Directors: Polly M. Monson, Claris Nystron, Melvin L. Schlueter.
EIN: 364213139

60118
Thomas W. Griffin Foundation
3 Woodley Rd.
Winnetka, IL 60093

Established in 1997 in IL.
Donor(s): Roger S. Griffin.
Financial data (yr. ended 12/31/99): Assets, $223,951 (M); grants paid, $11,800; expenditures, $13,015; qualifying distributions, $12,883.
Limitations: Applications not accepted.
Application information: Contributes only to pre-selected organizations.
Trustees: Christine C. Griffin, Roger S. Griffin, Sherryl W. Griffin.
EIN: 367190592

60119
The Aldrich-Green College Scholarship Foundation
c/o Ralph D. Glenn
P.O. Box 146
Mattoon, IL 61938
Application address: Kathy L. Peters, P.O. Box 127, Toledo, IL 62468, tel.: (217) 849-2701

Established in 1995 in IL.
Donor(s): Helen Aldrich.‡
Financial data (yr. ended 12/31/00): Assets, $223,243 (M); grants paid, $6,500; expenditures, $6,655; qualifying distributions, $6,500.
Limitations: Giving limited to residents of Cumberland County, IL.
Application information: Special consideration will be given to students planning to return to Cumberland County to reside and/or seek employment. Application form required.
Officers: Ralph D. Glenn, Pres.; Keith Ashcraft, Secy.; Carol Jo Fritts, Treas.
EIN: 133705651

60120
The Trimble Foundation
105 S. Locust St.
Roberts, IL 60962-0188

Established in 1999 in IL.
Financial data (yr. ended 12/31/99): Assets, $214,621 (M); grants paid, $9,000; gifts received, $100; expenditures, $9,055; qualifying distributions, $9,000.
Limitations: Applications not accepted.

60120—ILLINOIS

Application information: Contributes only to pre-selected organizations.
Trustees: Pamela Schwarz, Charles R. Warlow, Shirley A. Warlow.
EIN: 371380272

60121
The Scriptorium
290 S. County Farm Rd., 3rd Fl.
Wheaton, IL 60187

Classified as a private operating foundation in 1999.
Financial data (yr. ended 12/31/00): Assets, $202,203 (M); grants paid, $0; gifts received, $206,040; expenditures, $184,447; qualifying distributions, $164,009; giving activities include $164,010 for programs.
Officers: Bastiaan Van Elderen, Pres.; David J. Allen, V.P. and Secy.; Scott Pierre, V.P.; Jerald A. Trannel, Treas.
Directors: Judith Van Kampen, David Wisen, Kristen Wisen.
EIN: 363991091

60122
Death Penalty Information Center
9333 N. Milwaukee Ave.
Niles, IL 60714

Classified as a private operating foundation in 1996.
Donor(s): J. Roderick MacArthur Foundation, John R. MacArthur, The Playboy (Hugh M. Hefner) Foundation, Richard Dieter.
Financial data (yr. ended 12/31/00): Assets, $197,258 (M); grants paid, $0; gifts received, $332,310; expenditures, $271,204; qualifying distributions, $268,733; giving activities include $268,733 for programs.
Officers and Directors:* Michael Millman,* Pres.; Richard Dieter, Secy. and Exec. Dir.; Marylou Bane, Treas.; Anthony Amsterdam, David Bradford, David I. Bruck, Steven Hawkins, George Kendall, John R. MacArthur.
EIN: 364056815

60123
The Kimberley Foundation, Inc.
c/o John Weise
2232 Central Pk.
Evanston, IL 60201

Established in 1997 in WI.
Donor(s): John T. Weise, Anne Weise.
Financial data (yr. ended 12/31/01): Assets, $194,426 (M); grants paid, $0; gifts received, $25,400; expenditures, $71,838; qualifying distributions, $67,292; giving activities include $67,316 for programs.
Officers and Directors:* John T. Weise,* Pres. and Treas.; Jessie Ann Weise,* V.P.; Julia Ann Weise,* Secy.
EIN: 391877467

60124
The Samaritan Foundation
33 W. Higgins Rd., Ste. 3010
South Barrington, IL 60010

Established in 1999 in IL.
Donor(s): Edward T. Owens.
Financial data (yr. ended 12/31/00): Assets, $192,801 (M); grants paid, $2,273,265; gifts received, $2,370,000; expenditures, $2,503,783; qualifying distributions, $2,502,386.
Limitations: Applications not accepted. Giving primarily in IL.
Application information: Contributes only to pre-selected organizations.

Officers and Directors:* Edward T. Owens,* Pres.; Daniel J. Lindquist,* Secy.-Treas.; Dimple Owens.
EIN: 364295983
Codes: FD

60125
Balzekas Family Foundation, Ltd.
4012 S. Archer Ave.
Chicago, IL 60632   (773) 847-1515
Contact: Stanley Balzekas, III, Secy.

Established around 1993.
Financial data (yr. ended 12/31/00): Assets, $192,641 (M); grants paid, $13,345; gifts received, $240; expenditures, $14,475; qualifying distributions, $13,345.
Limitations: Giving primarily in Chicago, IL.
Officers: Stanley Balzekas, Jr., Pres.; Stanley Balzekas III, Secy.; Robert Balzekas, Treas.
Director: Carole Miller.
EIN: 363898737

60126
JSJ Family Foundation
c/o Marvin Rotter
5 Revere Dr.
Northbrook, IL 60062-1570

Established in 1999 in IL.
Donor(s): Marvin Rotter.
Financial data (yr. ended 12/31/99): Assets, $192,571 (M); grants paid, $11,200; gifts received, $203,674; expenditures, $12,356; qualifying distributions, $11,200.
Limitations: Applications not accepted.
Application information: Contributes only to pre-selected organizations.
Officer: Marvin Rotter, Pres.
EIN: 364321978

60127
Caruso-Sperl Irrevocable Charitable Trust
721 N. Springfield St.
Virden, IL 62690
Contact: Rev. August J. Sperl, Pres.

Established in 1996 in IL.
Donor(s): Rev. August J. Sperl.
Financial data (yr. ended 12/31/99): Assets, $190,891 (M); grants paid, $7,694; gifts received, $43,850; expenditures, $9,046; qualifying distributions, $7,694.
Limitations: Giving limited to Virden, IL.
Financial Councils: George T. Murphy, Chair.; Rev. August J. Sperl, Pres.; Larry James, Secy.; Frank Maynerich.
EIN: 376336628

60128
Deltasig House Corporation
18 S. Loomis St.
Naperville, IL 60540-4937

Financial data (yr. ended 09/30/01): Assets, $189,500 (M); grants paid, $500; expenditures, $5,033; qualifying distributions, $500.
Limitations: Applications not accepted.
Application information: Contributes only to pre-selected organizations.
Officers: Virgil Needham, Pres.; Mark O'Daniell, V.P.; Jim Wills, Secy.-Treas.
Directors: Vincent Field, Donald Klein, Robert Lewis, Jack Metcalf, Robert Mocella, Jack Nikoleit, Robert Rebeck, Robert Swanson.
EIN: 362183254

60129
Tiffany Irwin Scholarship Foundation
522 Waikiki Dr.
Des Plaines, IL 60016

Established in 1997 in IL.
Donor(s): Linda Irwin, Mike Irwin.
Financial data (yr. ended 12/31/99): Assets, $184,786 (M); grants paid, $5,000; gifts received, $6,908; expenditures, $5,817; qualifying distributions, $4,912.
Limitations: Applications not accepted.
Application information: Contributes only to pre-selected organizations.
Officers and Directors:* Linda Irwin,* Pres.; Michael Bennett,* V.P.; Michael Latona,* Secy.; Michael Irwin,* Treas.
EIN: 364166962

60130
Holzer Family Foundation
c/o Alps International Mgmt., Inc.
600 Central Ave., Ste. 240
Highland Park, IL 60035

Established in 2000 in IL.
Donor(s): Ronald Holzer.
Financial data (yr. ended 12/31/01): Assets, $181,094 (M); grants paid, $17,180; gifts received, $98,000; expenditures, $22,663; qualifying distributions, $17,180.
Trustees: Erica Holzer, Marci Holzer, Ronald Holzer.
EIN: 367339861

60131
Robinson, Illinois Elks Crippled Children Charitable Commission
208 W. Walnut
Robinson, IL 62454
Application address: P.O. Box 824, Robinson, IL 62454
Contact: James Woodworth, Chair.

Financial data (yr. ended 03/31/99): Assets, $179,019 (M); grants paid, $4,600; gifts received, $695; expenditures, $6,050; qualifying distributions, $4,600.
Limitations: Giving primarily in Crawford County, IL.
Officers and Trustees:* Jim Woodworth,* Chair.; Tom Eden,* Secy.; Richard Ackman, Gary Carter, Mark Weber.
EIN: 371083369

60132
Charles & Kimberly Hemmer Foundation
c/o Greg Hunziker
416 Main St., Ste. 425
Peoria, IL 61602-1103

Established in 1999 in IL.
Donor(s): Charles Hemmer, Kimberly Hemmer.
Financial data (yr. ended 12/31/00): Assets, $163,851 (M); grants paid, $3,500; gifts received, $22,575; expenditures, $3,715; qualifying distributions, $3,500.
Limitations: Applications not accepted.
Application information: Contributes only to pre-selected organizations.
Directors: Bruce Graham, Ken Hoerr, Willis Hunzicker, Brent Teubel.
EIN: 371379077

60133
The Fine Line Prairie and Nature Area, Inc.
c/o C. Kazwick
4919 Whiffin Pl.
Downers Grove, IL 60515

Established in 1997 in IL.

Donor(s): Carol Mudloff Kazwick.
Financial data (yr. ended 12/31/01): Assets, $163,336 (M); grants paid, $0; gifts received, $3,285; expenditures, $6,730; qualifying distributions, $0.
Officers: Carol Mudloff Kazwick, Pres.; Bernard Kazwick, V.P.; Cynthia Halfar, Secy.; Jennifer Mudloff Pearson, Treas.
Director: Denise Kavanagh.
EIN: 364129696

60134
The Rothkopf Family Charitable Foundation
(Formerly The Jenner School Class 207 Educational Foundation)
311 W. Superior St., Ste., 600
Chicago, IL 60610

Established in 1989 in IL.
Donor(s): Richard E. Rothkopf.
Financial data (yr. ended 12/31/99): Assets, $155,676 (M); grants paid, $31,100; gifts received, $118,078; expenditures, $42,355; qualifying distributions, $40,938; giving activities include $9,433 for programs.
Limitations: Applications not accepted. Giving primarily in Chicago, IL.
Application information: Contributes only to pre-selected organizations.
Officers: Richard E. Rothkopf, Pres.; Barry Gersowsky, Secy.
Director: Ann F. Rothkopf.
EIN: 363639061

60135
Jennings-Lyon Day Home
(Formerly Jennings-Lyon Memorial Home)
P.O. Box 557
Sheridan, IL 60551-0557 (815) 496-2311

Classified as a private operating foundation in 1979.
Financial data (yr. ended 12/31/00): Assets, $151,176 (M); grants paid, $0; gifts received, $118,312; expenditures, $125,536; qualifying distributions, $80,481; giving activities include $80,877 for programs.
Officers and Directors:* David A. Pfoltner, Pres. and Treas.; Donna Vicars,* V.P.; Donna Pfoltner,* Secy.; Joyce Bernard, Virl Hallett, Linda Staton, Julie Timm.
EIN: 237450369

60136
Foundation for Leadership and Messianic Education
234 Surrey
Lake Forest, IL 60045-3474

Established in 1988 in IL.
Donor(s): Jeffrey E. Feinberg.
Financial data (yr. ended 12/31/00): Assets, $148,164 (M); grants paid, $0; gifts received, $7,739; expenditures, $36,907; qualifying distributions, $0.
Officers and Directors:* Jeffrey E. Feinberg,* Pres.; Ronald Pfefer,* V.P.; Patricia K. Feinberg,* Secy.-Treas.
EIN: 363589550

60137
Cameron Cunningham Foundation
380 Horizon
P.O. Box 520
Oakwood, IL 61858 (217) 431-4204
Contact: Leesa A. Cunningham Hubbard, Exec. Dir.

Established in 1995 in IL.
Financial data (yr. ended 12/31/00): Assets, $146,816 (M); grants paid, $3,350; gifts received, $452; expenditures, $10,038; qualifying distributions, $3,350.
Limitations: Giving limited to Vermilion County, IL.
Application information: Application forms available at each high school. Application form required.
Officers: Lyle Irvin, Vice-Chair.; Sue Dokey, Secy.; Karla Dukes, Treas.; Leesa A. Cunningham Hubbard, Exec. Dir.
Board Members: Chuck Cannaday, Lanette Cannaday, Crystal Chambers, Mike Chambers, Fred Dokey, Sandra Heffern, Tom Hubbard, Jane Huchel, Jim Huchel, Janet Irvin, Sherry Waggaman.
EIN: 371346422

60138
Michael Donnewald Foundation
115 Hartin Rd.
Centralia, IL 62801

Established in 1999 in IL.
Donor(s): Michael Donnewald, Robert Donnewald, Kurt Grandberg.
Financial data (yr. ended 12/31/00): Assets, $135,291 (M); grants paid, $2,141; gifts received, $47,438; expenditures, $3,844; qualifying distributions, $3,844.
Limitations: Giving primarily in IL.
Directors: Michael Donnewald, Robert Donnewald, Kurt Gradberg.
EIN: 371392792

60139
Midwest Heart Research Foundation
2340 Highland Ave., Ste. 310
Lombard, IL 60148

Classified as a private operating foundation in 1991.
Financial data (yr. ended 06/30/00): Assets, $134,292 (M); grants paid, $0; gifts received, $462,617; expenditures, $514,593; qualifying distributions, $503,928; giving activities include $397,533 for programs.
Officers: Vincent Bufalino, M.D., Chair.; Lawrence Barr, M.D., Medical Dir.; Elaine Enger, Clinical Dir.
Directors: John Cahill, M.D., Louis McKeever, M.D.
EIN: 363602197

60140
Charles Louis Davis, D.V.M. Foundation for Advancement of Veterinary Pathology Charitable Trust
6245 Formoor Ln.
Gurnee, IL 60031-4757 (847) 367-4359
Contact: Samuel W. Thompson, Chair.

Financial data (yr. ended 12/31/00): Assets, $132,873 (M); grants paid, $4,150; gifts received, $47,021; expenditures, $136,342; qualifying distributions, $410,422; giving activities include $57,978 for programs.
Limitations: Giving on a national basis; some giving also in Canada.
Officers and Directors:* Samuel W. Thompson,* Chair.; Bruce H. Williams,* Secy.; Cory F. Brayton, James O. Britt, Jr., Dimitry Danilenko, Stephen M. Dempsey, Annette P. Gendron, John Glaister, Howard A. Hartman, and 20 additional directors.
EIN: 626091432

60141
Chris L. Seth Foundation
1555 N. Astor St.
Chicago, IL 60610
Application address: 1055 Astor St., Chicago, IL 60626
Contact: Irene Seth, Secy.

Established in 1997 in IL.
Donor(s): Chris L. Seth.
Financial data (yr. ended 12/31/00): Assets, $131,877 (M); grants paid, $1,200; expenditures, $1,576; qualifying distributions, $7,069.
Officers: Chris L. Seth, Pres.; Barry Seth, V.P.; Irene Seth, Secy.
EIN: 364144869

60142
Norman Kutterer Family Foundation
321 E. Locust St.
Columbia, IL 62236-9300 (618) 281-4531
Contact: Norman D. Kutterer, Dir.

Established as a company-sponsored operating foundation.
Donor(s): Kathleen Kutterer, Stephanie Kutterer.
Financial data (yr. ended 06/30/01): Assets, $130,292 (M); grants paid, $5,624; gifts received, $10,000; expenditures, $6,808; qualifying distributions, $5,624.
Limitations: Giving primarily in Columbia, IL.
Directors: Kathleen Kutterer, Norman D. Kutterer, Stephanie Kutterer.
EIN: 371255881

60143
Mac Services, Inc. (IL)
c/o John D. and Catherine T. MacArthur Foundation
140 S. Dearborn St., Ste. 1100
Chicago, IL 60603-5285

Established in 1992 in IL.
Donor(s): John D. and Catherine T. MacArthur Foundation.
Financial data (yr. ended 12/31/99): Assets, $127,788 (M); grants paid, $0; gifts received, $1,045,501; expenditures, $935,653; qualifying distributions, $933,331; giving activities include $933,481 for programs.
Officers and Directors:* Joshua J. Mintz,* Pres.; David S. Chernoff, Secy.; Marc P. Yanchura,* Treas.; Lyn Hutton.
EIN: 363839388

60144
Maywood Fine Arts Association
25 N. 5th Ave.
Maywood, IL 60153

Established in 1997 in IL.
Financial data (yr. ended 12/31/99): Assets, $127,164 (L); grants paid, $550; gifts received, $27,095; expenditures, $99,290; qualifying distributions, $64,735; giving activities include $37,001 for programs.
Limitations: Giving limited to Maywood, IL.
Officers and Directors:* Lois Baumann,* Pres.; Alice Dowding, Secy.; David Simpson, Treas.; Audrey Brown, Catherine Brown, Steve Coughlin, Victoria Haas, Shirley Madlock-House, Kenneth Massa, Raymond Mottis, Sharon Plennert, Lenore Sanchez, Carrie Simpson, Richard Spurr.
EIN: 363822848

60145—ILLINOIS

60145
Charles Foundation
925 Stratford Ave.
Rockford, IL 61107 (815) 397-4787
Contact: Holly Lembkey, Tr.

Donor(s): Harriet R. Charles, Steven R. Charles, Barbara C. Hummel, Charles R. Hummel.
Financial data (yr. ended 12/31/99): Assets, $125,210 (M); grants paid, $42,910; gifts received, $20,000; expenditures, $43,918; qualifying distributions, $42,823.
Limitations: Giving primarily in Rockford, IL.
Application information: Application form not required.
Trustees: Andrew H. Charles, Steven R. Charles, Holly Lembkey.
EIN: 366103664

60146
Sherry-Lu Fund
1001 E. Lake Dr.
Springfield, IL 62707-8927

Donor(s): Louis Spiegel.
Financial data (yr. ended 12/31/01): Assets, $123,829 (M); grants paid, $6,582; expenditures, $7,120; qualifying distributions, $6,582.
Limitations: Applications not accepted. Giving primarily in Springfield, IL.
Application information: Contributes only to pre-selected organizations.
Trustee: Chesira Sherry Spiegel.
EIN: 376048394

60147
A. V. Sieglinger Memorial & Endowment Committee, Inc.
c/o Richard J. Stinson, Treas.
2102 Myrtle St.
Rock Falls, IL 61071-2043 (815) 625-8806

Financial data (yr. ended 12/31/01): Assets, $115,317 (M); grants paid, $0; expenditures, $861; qualifying distributions, $861.
Limitations: Giving primarily in Rock Falls, IL.
Application information: Interview required. Application form not required.
Officers: Irene Taylor, Secy.; Richard J. Stinson, Treas.
EIN: 363202136

60148
Edelson Foundation, Inc.
849 W. Fullerton
Chicago, IL 60614

Established in 1999 in IL.
Donor(s): Sheldon Edelson, Roberta Edelson.
Financial data (yr. ended 12/31/00): Assets, $114,980 (M); grants paid, $4,600; gifts received, $57,595; expenditures, $4,620; qualifying distributions, $4,556.
Limitations: Applications not accepted.
Application information: Contributes only to pre-selected organizations.
Officers and Directors:* Roberta Edelson,* Pres. and Treas.; Sheldon Edelson,* V.P. and Secy.; Marcia Festen.
EIN: 364328987

60149
Solomon Goldberg Family Foundation
164 Oakmont Dr.
Deerfield, IL 60015
Contact: Alvin L. Goldberg, Treas.

Established in 1993 in IL.
Financial data (yr. ended 12/31/99): Assets, $112,430 (M); grants paid, $7,375; expenditures, $7,805; qualifying distributions, $7,727.
Limitations: Giving primarily in IL.
Officers: Arthur Solomon, Pres.; Martha Goldberg, Secy.; Alvin L. Goldberg, Treas.
EIN: 364160879

60150
Charles & Rene Lipshitz Family Foundation
4536 W. Madison
Skokie, IL 60076-2667 (847) 679-0390
Contact: Rene Lipshitz, Pres.

Established in 1997 in IL.
Donor(s): Charles Lipshitz, Rene Lipshitz.
Financial data (yr. ended 12/31/00): Assets, $109,546 (M); grants paid, $5,387; gifts received, $31,938; expenditures, $5,444; qualifying distributions, $5,387.
Limitations: Giving primarily in Chicago, IL.
Application information: Application form required.
Officers: Rene Lipshitz, Pres.; Charles Lipshitz, Secy.; Leon Lipshitz, Treas.
EIN: 363729186

60151
Louis & Chermaine Bell Family Foundation
1500 Skokie Blvd., Ste. 420
Northbrook, IL 60062

Established in 2000 in IL.
Financial data (yr. ended 12/31/01): Assets, $105,593 (M); grants paid, $694; expenditures, $7,589; qualifying distributions, $694.
Officer: Chermaine Bell, Pres.
EIN: 364347159

60152
Harry and Beverly Bystricky Foundation
2208 R.F.D.
Long Grove, IL 60047

Financial data (yr. ended 12/31/99): Assets, $103,326 (M); grants paid, $10,000; gifts received, $20,000; expenditures, $12,226; qualifying distributions, $12,166.
Limitations: Applications not accepted.
Application information: Contributes only to pre-selected organizations.
Officers and Directors:* Beverly Bystricky,* Pres. and Treas.; Jill Flickinger,* Secy.; Sue Beatle.
EIN: 364053925

60153
Burton and Libby Hoffman Charitable Foundation
20 N. Clark St., Ste. 1700
Chicago, IL 60602

Established in 1996 in IL.
Donor(s): Burton L. Hoffman, Libby Hoffman.
Financial data (yr. ended 12/31/01): Assets, $103,282 (M); grants paid, $31,864; gifts received, $17,746; expenditures, $32,950; qualifying distributions, $31,796.
Limitations: Applications not accepted. Giving primarily in IL.
Application information: Contributes only to pre-selected organizations.
Directors: Anne Heltsley, Burton L. Hoffman, Libby Hoffman, Richard S. Hoffman.
EIN: 364094223

60154
Carnot & Luceile Allen Foundation
265 White Oak Ln.
Winnetka, IL 60093-3629

Classified as a private operating foundation in 1985.
Financial data (yr. ended 12/31/99): Assets, $100,640 (M); grants paid, $4,695; expenditures, $4,788; qualifying distributions, $4,695.
Limitations: Applications not accepted. Giving primarily in IL.
Application information: Contributes only to pre-selected organizations.
Officer and Directors:* Ronald L. Allen,* Pres.; Douglas E. Allen, James H. Allen, Stuart R. Allen, Susan A. Hughes, Cynthia J. Smith, Linda A. Walsh.
EIN: 363358749

60155
James D. Schlenker Foundation
6311 W. 95th St.
Oak Lawn, IL 60453 (708) 423-2258
Contact: James D. Schlenker, Mgr.

Established in 1997 in IL.
Financial data (yr. ended 12/31/00): Assets, $98,775 (M); grants paid, $5,000; expenditures, $6,433; qualifying distributions, $6,433.
Limitations: Giving primarily in IL.
Officer: James D. Schlenker, Mgr.
EIN: 364100891

60156
Stoneleigh Foundation, Inc.
454 E. Oxford Rd.
Barrington, IL 60010-2190

Established in 1997 in IL.
Donor(s): Richard F. Cavenaugh.
Financial data (yr. ended 11/30/99): Assets, $91,960 (M); grants paid, $3,000; expenditures, $5,363; qualifying distributions, $2,987.
Directors: Joan Carpenter, Elizabeth B. Cavenaugh, Richard F. Cavenaugh, Charles R. Hall, Rev. George Hull.
EIN: 364158545

60157
Kinship Foundation
400 Skokie Blvd., Ste. 300
Northbrook, IL 60062

Established in 1995 in IL.
Donor(s): Sudix Foundation, Salwil Foundation, D & D Foundation, Chicago Community Trust.
Financial data (yr. ended 09/30/00): Assets, $86,453 (M); grants paid, $0; gifts received, $230,000; expenditures, $490,368; qualifying distributions, $108,734; giving activities include $490,340 for programs.
Limitations: Applications not accepted.
Application information: Contributes only to pre-selected organizations.
Officers: Bryan R. Dunn, Pres.; Eric A. Schreiner, Secy.-Treas.
Directors: Julie B. Dixon, S. Gunnar Klarr, John R. Loacker, James D. Reichert, Daniel C. Searle, Nancy S. Searle.
EIN: 364056831

60158
Shinner Memorial Playground, Inc.
c/o Jack L. Witlin
3632 Torrey Pines
Northbrook, IL 60062

Financial data (yr. ended 12/31/01): Assets, $85,561 (M); grants paid, $0; gifts received, $309; expenditures, $489; qualifying distributions, $0.
Officers: Bob Petrus, Pres.; Jack Witlin, Treas.
EIN: 396078569

60159
Macwan Foundation
2337 W. Imperial Dr.
Peoria, IL 61614
Contact: Kamlesh Macwan, Pres.

Classified as a private operating foundation in 1996 in IL.

Donor(s): Kamlesh Macwan.
Financial data (yr. ended 12/31/01): Assets, $84,000 (M); grants paid, $900; gifts received, $99,700; expenditures, $71,160; qualifying distributions, $66,764; giving activities include $4,258 for loans to individuals and $71,160 for programs.
Limitations: Giving primarily in Chicago, IL.
Application information: Application form not required.
Officers: Kamlesh Macwan, Pres.; Samson Macwan, V.P.; Shantaben Macwan, Secy.
EIN: 364128132

60160
The Nick Carter Scholarship Fund
c/o First State Bank
120 State St.
Beardstown, IL 62618 (217) 323-4500
Contact: Barbara E. Merriman, Trust Off., First State Bank

Financial data (yr. ended 02/28/99): Assets, $80,515 (M); grants paid, $4,000; expenditures, $4,976; qualifying distributions, $4,976.
Limitations: Giving limited to residents of Beardstown, IL.
Application information: Applications available at Beardstown High School, IL. Application form required.
Trustee: First State Bank.
EIN: 371098809

60161
The Jeanette and John Cruikshank Memorial Foundation
1221 Heatherton Dr.
Naperville, IL 60563

Established in 1997 as an operating foundation.
Donor(s): Virginia C. Lacy.
Financial data (yr. ended 12/31/00): Assets, $79,562 (M); grants paid, $0; expenditures, $6,351; qualifying distributions, $2,926; giving activities include $2,926 for programs.
Officers: Virginia C. Lacy, Pres.; John Cruikshank, Secy.
EIN: 364136526

60162
The S-Cubed Foundation
535 E. Diehl, Ste. 333
Naperville, IL 60563

Established in 1999 in IL.
Financial data (yr. ended 09/30/01): Assets, $78,965 (M); grants paid, $66,392; gifts received, $66,722; expenditures, $66,443; qualifying distributions, $66,443.
Limitations: Applications not accepted.
Application information: Contributes only to pre-selected organizations.
Directors: Sheila Baig, Shalini Kumar, Udai Kumar.
EIN: 367254013

60163
Villa Park Bank Foundation
10 S. Villa Ave.
Villa Park, IL 60181 (630) 834-0800

Established around 1966. Classified as a company-sponsored operating foundation.
Donor(s): Villa Park Bank.
Financial data (yr. ended 12/31/01): Assets, $73,761 (M); grants paid, $17,550; gifts received, $20,000; expenditures, $17,570; qualifying distributions, $17,550.
Limitations: Giving limited to Villa Park, IL.
Application information: Application form required.

Officers: William C. Stege, Pres. and Treas.; Terry Nordensten, V.P. and Treas.; Margaret Topel, Secy.
Trustees: Genevieve Cortesi, Seymour Morris, Patricia P. Pace, Joseph Reedy, Carl Roth, Harold A. Stege, Robert Ziedler.
EIN: 366198333
Codes: CD, GTI

60164
Gantz Family Foundation
72 Indian Hill Rd.
Winnetka, IL 60093

Established in 1986 in IL.
Donor(s): Wilbur H. Gantz.
Financial data (yr. ended 12/31/99): Assets, $71,904 (M); grants paid, $29,185; expenditures, $30,160; qualifying distributions, $29,202.
Limitations: Applications not accepted. Giving primarily in Chicago, IL.
Application information: Contributes only to pre-selected organizations.
Officers and Directors:* Wilbur H. Gantz,* Pres.; Linda T. Gantz, V.P. and Secy.; Matthew J. Gantz.
EIN: 363484258

60165
Stephanie L. and Frederick E. Bishop Foundation
c/o Stephanie L. Bishop
525 Greenleaf Ave.
Glencoe, IL 60022-1705

Established in 1999 in IL.
Donor(s): Frederick E. Bishop.
Financial data (yr. ended 12/31/00): Assets, $71,858 (M); grants paid, $21,700; gifts received, $35,000; expenditures, $23,315; qualifying distributions, $21,700.
Limitations: Applications not accepted.
Application information: Contributes only to pre-selected organizations.
Trustees: Frederick E. Bishop, Stephanie L. Bishop.
EIN: 364281716

60166
Porterfield Family Foundation
1010 Jorie Blvd., Ste. 124
Oak Brook, IL 60521

Established in 1997 in IL.
Donor(s): Henry Porterfield.
Financial data (yr. ended 06/30/01): Assets, $67,679 (M); grants paid, $0; gifts received, $66,250; expenditures, $63,662; qualifying distributions, $0.
Officers and Directors:* Henry Porterfield,* Pres.; Michael Porterfield,* V.P.; Steven Porterfield,* V.P.; Christopher Porterfield,* V.P.; Beryl Readdy, Secy.-Treas.
EIN: 364199344

60167
Lithuanian Endowment Fund Ltd.
4012 S. Archer Ave.
Chicago, IL 60632-1140

Established in 1993.
Financial data (yr. ended 12/31/00): Assets, $59,417 (M); grants paid, $35,350; gifts received, $45,000; expenditures, $36,152; qualifying distributions, $35,350.
Limitations: Applications not accepted. Giving primarily in Chicago, IL.
Application information: Contributes only to pre-selected organizations.
Officers: Stanley Balzekas, Jr., Pres.; Stanley Balzekas III, Secy.; Robert Balzekas, Treas.
Directors: Joseph A. Katasukas, Jr., Carole Miller.
EIN: 363918313

60168
Fransen Family Mennonite Foundation
R.R. No. 8, Box 56A
Normal, IL 61761-9808

Established in 1994 in IL.
Donor(s): Werner K. Fransen.
Financial data (yr. ended 10/31/00): Assets, $56,971 (M); grants paid, $0; expenditures, $37,726; qualifying distributions, $37,726; giving activities include $36,126 for programs.
Officers and Directors:* Werner K. Fransen,* Pres. and Treas.; Kay Ann Fransen,* Secy.; Suzanne Marie Hitt, Sharon L. Landis.
EIN: 371335662

60169
Alliance for Collectible Education
P.O. Box 282
Bensenville, IL 60106 (630) 350-6789
Application address: 236 Mohawk, Bensenville, IL 60106
Contact: Sally Grace, Pres.

Established in 1995 in IL.
Donor(s): National Sports Collector's Convention, The Triple EEE Foundation, Leslie Rotman, Steven Rotman.
Financial data (yr. ended 12/31/00): Assets, $56,810 (M); grants paid, $28,340; gifts received, $42,512; expenditures, $32,860; qualifying distributions, $32,860.
Limitations: Giving limited to IL.
Application information: Application form not required.
Officers and Directors:* Sally Grace,* Pres.; Raymond Bright,* V.P.; Erwin Einhorn,* Secy.; John Broggi,* Treas.; Steven Rotman.
EIN: 364017263

60170
Gus Lohman Sports & Youth Activities Fund Foundation
N. Country Estates
Geneseo, IL 61254 (309) 944-6000
Contact: Verla Lohman, Dir.

Donor(s): Verla Lohman.
Financial data (yr. ended 12/31/00): Assets, $54,242 (M); grants paid, $2,211; gifts received, $2,500; expenditures, $2,579; qualifying distributions, $2,552.
Limitations: Giving limited to the Geneseo, IL, area.
Application information: Application form required.
Directors: David Lohman, Mark Lohman, Verla Lohman.
EIN: 363225788

60171
Verlon W. Braselton Memorial Foundation
P.O. Box 386
South Holland, IL 60473-0386
Additional address: 17000 South Park Ave.

Classified as a private operating foundation in 1984.
Financial data (yr. ended 08/31/01): Assets, $53,640 (M); grants paid, $4,300; expenditures, $4,670; qualifying distributions, $4,636.
Limitations: Giving primarily in Homewood, IL.
Application information: Application form required.
Directors: Kamala Buckner, John P. Kos, Russ W. Prekwas.
EIN: 363278398

60172
Luis Carlos Robinson-Newball Foundation
50 E. Bellevue Pl., Apt. 902
Chicago, IL 60611

Established in 1989.
Financial data (yr. ended 12/31/99): Assets, $51,467 (M); grants paid, $1,500; expenditures, $1,740; qualifying distributions, $1,740.
Limitations: Applications not accepted.
Application information: Contributes only to pre-selected organizations.
Officers: Irma Robinson, Pres.; Alfonso Pumarejo, V.P.; Lucia Suito, V.P.; Celso Catellanos, Secy.-Treas.
EIN: 363626421

60173
The Jules Millman Foundation, Inc.
c/o Jules Millman
132 E. Delaware, Ste. 6305
Chicago, IL 60611

Financial data (yr. ended 12/31/99): Assets, $51,183 (M); grants paid, $1,500; expenditures, $2,307; qualifying distributions, $1,500.
Limitations: Applications not accepted.
Application information: Contributes only to pre-selected organizations.
Directors: Jules Millman, Allen Schuh, Mark Tibbetts.
EIN: 364178000

60174
Midwest AIDS Foundation
(also known as The Engle Fund)
2202 N. Cleveland St.
Chicago, IL 60614   (312) 695-4994
Application address: P.O. Box 11320, Chicago, IL 60611; E-mail: r-murphy@northwestern.edu
Contact: Robert L. Murphy, M.D., Exec. Dir.

Established in 1990 in IL.
Financial data (yr. ended 04/30/99): Assets, $50,369 (M); grants paid, $161,238; gifts received, $19,500; expenditures, $161,291; qualifying distributions, $161,291.
Limitations: Giving limited to the Chicago, IL area.
Application information: Application form required.
Officer: Robert L. Murphy, M.D., Exec. Dir.
EIN: 363687399
Codes: FD2

60175
Hill-Plath Foundation
4 Clover Leaf Ct.
Savoy, IL 61874   (217) 351-2159

Established in 2001 in IL.
Donor(s): Jacquetta Hill, David Plath.
Financial data (yr. ended 12/31/01): Assets, $49,998 (M); grants paid, $0; gifts received, $50,000; expenditures, $447; qualifying distributions, $426.
Limitations: Giving primarily in Thailand.
Officers and Directors:* Jacquetta Hill,* Pres. and Secy.; David W. Plath,* Treas.; Piyanat Sukonthaman.
EIN: 371415365

60176
The Raj & Suman Sachdeva Foundation, Inc.
6456 Coach House Rd.
Lisle, IL 60532

Established in 2000 in IL.
Financial data (yr. ended 06/30/01): Assets, $49,975 (M); grants paid, $0; gifts received, $50,000; expenditures, $25; qualifying distributions, $0.
Officers: Rajender Sachdeva, Pres.; Suman Sachdeva, V.P.
Director: Sameer Sachdeva.
EIN: 364392738

60177
Majid Family Foundation
2325 Delaney Dr.
Ottawa, IL 61350

Established in 1997 in IL.
Donor(s): Abdul Majid, Mrs. Abdul Majid.
Financial data (yr. ended 12/31/01): Assets, $46,569 (M); grants paid, $38,193; gifts received, $50,750; expenditures, $38,227; qualifying distributions, $38,193.
Limitations: Applications not accepted. Giving on an international basis, with emphasis on Pakistan.
Application information: Unsolicited requests for funds not accepted.
Directors: Abdul Majid, Hassan Majid, Zarina Majid.
EIN: 364183120
Codes: GTI

60178
Mairin Christine Wallner Memorial Fund
c/o Greatbanc Trust Co.
105 E. Galena Blvd., Ste. 500
Aurora, IL 60505   (630) 844-7045

Classified as a private operating foundation in 1998. Established in 1997 in IL.
Financial data (yr. ended 12/31/99): Assets, $45,926 (M); grants paid, $3,000; expenditures, $4,442; qualifying distributions, $4,406.
Limitations: Giving primarily in Barrington Hills, IL.
Advisory Committee: Barbara Wallner, Dana Wallner, Edward Wallner, Lindsey Wallner.
Trustee: Greatbanc Trust Co.
EIN: 367202725

60179
Someone Cares Foundation
439 Cross Rd.
Gurnee, IL 60031-3248

Established in 1999 in IL.
Donor(s): James Wamsley, Kathie Wamsley.
Financial data (yr. ended 12/31/00): Assets, $44,403 (M); grants paid, $2,800; expenditures, $6,721; qualifying distributions, $2,800.
Limitations: Applications not accepted. Giving primarily in Waco, TX.
Application information: Contributes only to pre-selected organizations.
Directors: James Wamsley, Kathie Wamsley.
Trustee: Natalie Pimpo.
EIN: 364335687

60180
Kenneth & Gwendolyn Hoving Foundation
363 Trinity Ln.
Oak Brook, IL 60521

Established as a private operating foundation in 1995.
Donor(s): Kenneth Hoving.
Financial data (yr. ended 12/31/00): Assets, $42,193 (M); grants paid, $20,500; expenditures, $21,875; qualifying distributions, $21,875.
Limitations: Applications not accepted. Giving primarily in IL and MI.
Application information: Contributes only to pre-selected organizations.
Directors: Gwendolyn Hoving, Kenneth Hoving.
EIN: 363993239

60181
Donald K. and Yvonne M. Cardy Foundation
37224 Stanton Point Rd.
Ingleside, IL 60041
Contact: Donald J. Cardy, Tr.

Established in 1999 in IL.
Financial data (yr. ended 12/31/00): Assets, $41,968 (M); grants paid, $2,500; gifts received, $33,738; expenditures, $2,500; qualifying distributions, $2,161.
Limitations: Giving primarily in IL.
Trustees: Donald J. Cardy, Mary J. Cardy, Carol Cardy-Cuneo, Sally J. Mosko.
EIN: 367285645

60182
Illinois Broadcasters Association Minority Intern Program, Inc.
2621 Montega Dr.
Springfield, IL 62704-4189

Established in 1988 in IL.
Donor(s): Robert R. McCormick Foundation, Capital Cities/ABC, Inc.
Financial data (yr. ended 12/31/00): Assets, $41,843 (M); grants paid, $11,200; gifts received, $30,696; expenditures, $12,125; qualifying distributions, $11,200.
Limitations: Giving limited to IL.
Application information: Application forms available from the college's Dean of Communications at an Illinois institution of higher education. Application form required.
Officers: Emily Barr, Pres.; Steve Carver, V.P.; Drew Horowitz, Treas.
EIN: 371231448
Codes: GTI

60183
Kenneth Diehl Trust
c/o First Trust Bank
P.O. Box 500
Shelbyville, IL 62565   (217) 774-5515
Contact: Bob Pancoast, Trust Off., First Trust Bank

Donor(s): Bernadette McKittrick.
Financial data (yr. ended 12/31/01): Assets, $39,437 (M); grants paid, $500; gifts received, $25,000; expenditures, $986; qualifying distributions, $491.
Limitations: Giving limited to Shelby County, IL.
Application information: Application form required.
Trustee: First Trust Bank.
EIN: 376213964

60184
The Hirsch Family Foundation
(Formerly The Judith and Howard D. Hirsch Foundation)
8707 N. Skokie Blvd., Ste. 204
Skokie, IL 60077
Application address: c/o Howard D. Hirsch, 4602 N. Elsie St., Phoenix, AZ 85018-2015

Established in 1991 in IL.
Donor(s): Howard D. Hirsch.
Financial data (yr. ended 12/31/01): Assets, $38,788 (M); grants paid, $22,322; gifts received, $75,506; expenditures, $86,010; qualifying distributions, $86,010.
Limitations: Giving on a national basis, with emphasis on New York, NY.
Officers and Directors:* Howard D. Hirsch,* Pres.; Laurie Hirsch Winter,* Exec. Dir.; Ronald Hirsch.
EIN: 363703682

60185
American Friends of University of Buckingham
33 W. Monroe, Ste. 2000
Chicago, IL 60603

Established in 1999 in IL.
Financial data (yr. ended 12/31/99): Assets, $36,781 (M); grants paid, $33,000; gifts received, $18,525; expenditures, $33,010; qualifying distributions, $33,000; giving activities include $33,000 for programs.
Director: Marshall Lees.
EIN: 223315599

60186
Gloria Ministries, Inc.
P.O. Box 630
Lake Forest, IL 60045

Established in 1999.
Financial data (yr. ended 06/30/00): Assets, $34,337 (M); grants paid, $9,576; gifts received, $44,288; expenditures, $10,732; qualifying distributions, $10,732.
Limitations: Giving on a national basis.
Officers: Gloria C. Loukas, Pres. and Treas.; Katherine W. Schmitt, Secy.
Director: Laura Gerrish.
EIN: 364173034

60187
Braude Foundation
225 W. Washington St., Ste. 130
Chicago, IL 60606

Established in 2000 in IL.
Financial data (yr. ended 12/31/00): Assets, $33,992 (L); grants paid, $1,800; gifts received, $35,792; expenditures, $1,800; qualifying distributions, $1,800.
Limitations: Applications not accepted. Giving primarily in Rochester, MN.
Application information: Contributes only to pre-selected organizations.
Officers: Laurence Braude, Pres.; Solna Braude, Secy.; Eric Aker, Treas.
EIN: 364391568

60188
Edward Collins Family Foundation, Inc.
20 Boardwalk Pl.
Park Ridge, IL 60068-3472

Established in 1986 in IL.
Donor(s): Doris A. Collins, Edward W. Collins.
Financial data (yr. ended 12/31/01): Assets, $33,977 (M); grants paid, $7,650; expenditures, $7,650; qualifying distributions, $7,649.
Limitations: Applications not accepted. Giving primarily in IL.
Application information: Contributes only to pre-selected organizations.
Officers: Doris A. Collins, Pres.; Edward W. Collins, V.P.; Kimberly J. DiFranco, Secy.-Treas.
EIN: 363479573

60189
Garvin-Pierson Family Foundation
825 Forest Ct.
Bartlett, IL 60103

Donor(s): Ruth E. Pierson.
Financial data (yr. ended 12/31/00): Assets, $33,877 (M); grants paid, $2,500; gifts received, $3,000; expenditures, $6,582; qualifying distributions, $6,582.
Limitations: Applications not accepted. Giving primarily in IL.
Application information: Contributes only to pre-selected organizations.

Officers: Ruth E. Pierson, Pres.; Kay D. Garvin, Secy.-Treas.
Director: Millicent D. Garvin.
EIN: 364337047

60190
Solid Rock Foundation
311 Guthrie St.
Ottawa, IL 61350
Contact: Susan L. Wood, Tr.

Established in 2000 in AZ.
Donor(s): Cannon J. Wood, Susan L. Wood.
Financial data (yr. ended 12/31/00): Assets, $33,246 (M); grants paid, $500; gifts received, $33,246; expenditures, $500; qualifying distributions, $500.
Limitations: Giving limited to residents of Benson, St. David, Sierra Vista, and Tombstone, AZ; and to residents of Ottawa, IL.
Application information: Application form required.
Trustees: Cannon J. Wood, Susan L. Wood.
EIN: 364392269

60191
Merritt Family Foundation
419 Garden Rd.
DeKalb, IL 60115

Established around 1994.
Donor(s): James W. Merritt, Helen Henry Merritt.
Financial data (yr. ended 12/31/01): Assets, $31,789 (M); grants paid, $1,500; expenditures, $1,905; qualifying distributions, $1,500.
Officers: James W. Merritt, Pres.; Helen Henry Merritt, V.P.; Deborah Merritt Aldrich, Secy.-Treas.
Director: Stephen Aldrich.
EIN: 363959394

60192
Vincent Skowronski Music Foundation
(Formerly Vincent-Eleonore Skowronski Music Foundation)
1726 Sherman Ave., No. 2
Evanston, IL 60201-3713
Contact: Vincent Skowronski, Tr.

Donor(s): Eleonore Skowronski, Vincent Skowronski.
Financial data (yr. ended 12/31/99): Assets, $27,952 (L); grants paid, $1,250; expenditures, $1,476; qualifying distributions, $1,476.
Limitations: Giving primarily in Chicago, IL.
Trustees: June O'Nesti, Eleonore Skowronski, Vincent Skowronski.
EIN: 363117623

60193
Samuel J. Baskin Charitable Trust
222 N. LaSalle St., Ste. 1414
Chicago, IL 60601   (312) 726-0083
Contact: Sheldon Baskin, Tr.

Established in 1963.
Donor(s): Samuel J. Baskin,‡ Hadassah Baskin.
Financial data (yr. ended 08/30/01): Assets, $26,770 (M); grants paid, $46,648; gifts received, $50,000; expenditures, $48,688; qualifying distributions, $48,688.
Limitations: Giving on a national basis.
Application information: Application form not required.
Trustee: Sheldon Baskin.
EIN: 366118260

60194
The Kleinschmidt Charitable Foundation
c/o Jerry Pepping
105 7th St.
Silvis, IL 61282

Established in 2000 in IL.
Donor(s): William H. Kleinschmidt.
Financial data (yr. ended 12/31/01): Assets, $25,383 (L); grants paid, $0; gifts received, $10,000; expenditures, $3,375; qualifying distributions, $3,375; giving activities include $3,000 for programs.
Directors: Myra Kleinschmidt, William H. Kleinschmidt, John Nolan.
EIN: 371402293

60195
Libby Benjamin Foundation
c/o Bruce Benjamin
611 Landwehr Rd.
Northbrook, IL 60062

Donor(s): Albert Benjamin.
Financial data (yr. ended 12/31/00): Assets, $24,822 (M); grants paid, $200; gifts received, $592; expenditures, $792; qualifying distributions, $791.
Limitations: Applications not accepted. Giving primarily in FL.
Application information: Contributes only to pre-selected organizations.
Officers and Directors:* Albert Benjamin,* Pres.; Bruce Benjamin,* Secy.; Steven M. Benjamin,* Treas.
EIN: 363668525

60196
Joseph P. Koomar Scholarship Fund
c/o Duane Carder
P.O. Box 459
Peotone, IL 60468
Application address: c/o Guidance Counselor, Peotone High School, W. Garfield and N. Mill Rd., Peotone, IL 60468, tel.: (708) 258-3236

Classified as a private operating foundation in 1991.
Donor(s): Bernadine Koomar.
Financial data (yr. ended 12/31/01): Assets, $24,165 (M); grants paid, $1,000; expenditures, $1,203; qualifying distributions, $988.
Limitations: Giving limited to residents of Peotone, IL.
Application information: Application form required.
Trustees: Duane Carder, Bernadine Koomar.
EIN: 363713919

60197
Florence C. Fitzgerald Foundation
50 S. LaSalle St.
Chicago, IL 60675

Established in 1997 in IL.
Donor(s): Florence C. Fitzgerald.
Financial data (yr. ended 01/31/00): Assets, $24,162 (M); grants paid, $0; gifts received, $18,363; expenditures, $68,188; qualifying distributions, $66,219; giving activities include $56,852 for programs.
Limitations: Applications not accepted.
Application information: Contributes only to pre-selected organizations.
Officers and Directors:* Gail Papp,* Pres. and Secy.-Treas.; Gary L. Prior,* V.P.; Florence C. Fizgerald.
EIN: 364160855

60198
Morrie and Shirlee Mages Sports Foundation
1501 N. State Pkwy.
Chicago, IL 60610

Classified as a private operating foundation in 1988 in IL.
Financial data (yr. ended 05/31/00): Assets, $23,869 (M); grants paid, $9,552; expenditures, $11,741; qualifying distributions, $11,732.
Limitations: Applications not accepted.
Application information: Contributes only to pre-selected organizations.
Officers: Shirlee Mages, Pres. and Treas.; Lili Ann Zisook, V.P. and Secy.
Director: Lawrence Richman.
EIN: 363526692

60199
Diane Castillo Carver Memorial Scholarship Fund
c/o U.S. Bank
305 4th Ave.
Sterling, IL 61081
Contact: Wendy M. Blair, Tr. Off., U.S. Bank

Financial data (yr. ended 12/31/01): Assets, $21,813 (M); grants paid, $0; expenditures, $15; qualifying distributions, $0.
Limitations: Giving limited to residents of Sterling, IL.
Application information: Application form not required.
Trustee: U.S. Bank.
EIN: 366798875

60200
Izetta Cutrell-Mae Zimmerman Foundation
P.O. Box B
Herrin, IL 62948-0060
Application address: 203 N. Park Ave., Herrin, IL 62948
Contact: David R. Craig, Tr.

Financial data (yr. ended 12/31/00): Assets, $19,931 (M); grants paid, $4,000; expenditures, $4,152; qualifying distributions, $4,000.
Trustees: Bruce Childers, David R. Craig, Josh Fox, Bonnie Franklin, Sharon Walker.
EIN: 371284493

60201
The Joel and Laurel Bellows Foundation, Inc.
79 W. Monroe St., Ste. 800
Chicago, IL 60603
Contact: Joel J. Bellows, Tr.

Financial data (yr. ended 12/31/99): Assets, $19,490 (M); grants paid, $6,450; gifts received, $14,200; expenditures, $6,465; qualifying distributions, $6,450.
Trustees: Joel J. Bellows, Laurel G. Bellows, Lindsay B. Bellows.
EIN: 364120422

60202
James David Sedlack Memorial Fund
1155 Prospect Ln.
Des Plaines, IL 60018-2027

Established around 1987.
Donor(s): James D. Sedlack.
Financial data (yr. ended 06/30/01): Assets, $18,341 (M); grants paid, $2,500; gifts received, $871; expenditures, $2,500; qualifying distributions, $0.
Officer: James E. Sedlack, Mgr.
EIN: 363454677

60203
'Til Healing Comes Ministries
14360 Streamwood Dr.
P.O. Box 816
Orland Park, IL 60462-7101

Established in 1995.
Donor(s): Rev. Kenneth M. Dignan.
Financial data (yr. ended 12/31/01): Assets, $16,971 (M); grants paid, $600; gifts received, $58,265; expenditures, $72,225; qualifying distributions, $600.
Officers: Rev. Kenneth M. Dignan, Pres.; Rev. Joseph D. West, Secy.; Leo P. Dignan, Treas.
Director: Stephen P. Dignan.
EIN: 363778927

60204
Boyle Family Foundation
1133 W. 35th St.
Chicago, IL 60609

Donor(s): Patrick J. Boyle.
Financial data (yr. ended 12/31/00): Assets, $16,442 (M); grants paid, $5,000; gifts received, $20,000; expenditures, $5,409; qualifying distributions, $5,409.
Limitations: Applications not accepted.
Application information: Contributes only to pre-selected organizations.
Officers: Patrick J. Boyle, Pres.; Theresa M. Boyle, Secy.; Patricia E. Boyle, Treas.
Directors: Brian J. Boyle, Kevin M. Boyle, Michael D. Boyle, Karen Boyle Conboy, Caroline Boyle Salina.
EIN: 364057351

60205
Fox River Conservation Foundation
6 W. Downer Pl.
Aurora, IL 60506-5135

Classified as a private operating foundation in 1987.
Donor(s): Mrs. Chester Obma.
Financial data (yr. ended 06/30/00): Assets, $16,127 (M); grants paid, $0; gifts received, $10,000; expenditures, $7,145; qualifying distributions, $0.
Officers and Directors:* Raymond C. Kozloski,* Pres.; Holly Holtz-Paris, Secy.-Treas.; James Phillips, Admin.; Larry H. Miller.
EIN: 363504003

60206
Pickus Foundation
P.O. Box 710
Waukegan, IL 60079 (847) 336-5490
Contact: Edward I. Pickus, Pres.

Donor(s): Members of the Pickus family.
Financial data (yr. ended 12/31/01): Assets, $15,877 (M); grants paid, $18,660; gifts received, $13,426; expenditures, $18,699; qualifying distributions, $18,689.
Limitations: Giving primarily in IL.
Officers: Edward I. Pickus, Pres.; Nathan W. Pickus, Secy.
Director: Alan M. Pickus.
EIN: 366111384

60207
Darrow-Altgeld Foundation
3903 W. Dakin St.
Chicago, IL 60618-3101
Contact: Thomas H. Geoghegan

Classified as a private operating foundation.
Donor(s): Thomas H. Geoghegan.
Financial data (yr. ended 12/31/00): Assets, $15,624 (M); grants paid, $4,000; gifts received, $20,475; expenditures, $4,857; qualifying distributions, $17,500.
Limitations: Giving primarily in IN.
Officer: Gerald Anthony Judge, Pres.
EIN: 363812610

60208
Illinois Chapter Foundation
2122 Grove St.
Glenview, IL 60025-2820

Financial data (yr. ended 12/31/00): Assets, $14,988 (M); grants paid, $0; gifts received, $9,307; expenditures, $52; qualifying distributions, $0.
Officers: Joseph V. Messer, Pres.; James Talano, Secy.; L. Jack Carow III, Exec. Dir.
EIN: 364043969

60209
Kapgon Foundation, Inc.
19036 Jonathan Ln.
Homewood, IL 60430

Established in 2000 in IL.
Donor(s): Surinder Gondal.
Financial data (yr. ended 12/31/01): Assets, $14,452 (M); grants paid, $6,000; gifts received, $11,500; expenditures, $7,148; qualifying distributions, $7,148.
Limitations: Applications not accepted.
Application information: Contributes only to pre-selected organizations.
Officer: Surinder Gondal, Exec. Dir.
Directors: Jayant Gondal, Nitika Gondal.
EIN: 364358366

60210
The Leo Foundation
300 W. Washington St., 14th Fl.
Chicago, IL 60606

Established in 2001 in IL.
Financial data (yr. ended 12/31/01): Assets, $14,164 (M); grants paid, $11,750; gifts received, $27,550; expenditures, $13,386; qualifying distributions, $0.
Limitations: Giving primarily in IL.
Officers and Directors:* Carl Berveridge,* Pres.; Betty Beveridge,* Secy.; Don Beveridge,* Treas.
EIN: 364351570

60211
The Brady Foundation
c/o Lynda Brady
11 Scofield Ct.
Bloomington, IL 61704
Contact: Lynda Brady, Treas.

Established in 2000 in IL.
Donor(s): Pinehurst Development, Inc., APEX Properties, Inc., W.E.B. Construction Co., Inc.
Financial data (yr. ended 06/30/01): Assets, $13,410 (M); grants paid, $8,000; expenditures, $9,090; qualifying distributions, $8,000.
Officers: Nancy K. Brady, Pres.; Nancy T. Brady, V.P.; Michele L. Brady, Secy.; Lynda S. Brady, Treas.
EIN: 371401149

60212
The Creeden Foundation
425 Huehl Rd., Ste. 3B
Northbrook, IL 60062 (847) 291-4110
Contact: Robert J. Creeden, Chair.

Established in 1999.
Financial data (yr. ended 12/31/99): Assets, $12,792 (M); grants paid, $1,500; gifts received, $27,000; expenditures, $13,647; qualifying distributions, $1,500.
Officers: Robert J. Creeden, Chair.; Victoria Creeden, V.P.

Directors: Kevin J. Creeden, Thomas J. Creeden, William J. Creeden.
EIN: 364286498

60213
The Melvin and Susan Newman Foundation
5 Julie Ln.
Riverwoods, IL 60015
Application address: 222 S. Riverside Plz., Ste. 2100, Chicago, IL 60606, tel.: (312) 648-2300
Contact: Melvin S. Newman, Pres.

Established in 1997 in IL.
Donor(s): Melvin S. Newman.
Financial data (yr. ended 12/31/99): Assets, $12,529 (M); grants paid, $10,010; gifts received, $11,631; expenditures, $10,110; qualifying distributions, $10,110.
Application information: Application form not required.
Officers: Melvin S. Newman, Pres.; Susan Newman, V.P.
Trustee: Susan Newman.
EIN: 364149224

60214
Wayne Area Conservancy Foundation
c/o James Bramsen
North Ave. & Schmale
Wheaton, IL 60187

Established in 1994 in IL.
Financial data (yr. ended 12/31/01): Assets, $11,754 (M); grants paid, $0; expenditures, $503; qualifying distributions, $0.
Directors: James Bramsen, Carol Hancock.
EIN: 363917215

60215
Leonas-Kriauceliunas Foundation
2107 N. Magnolia Ave., Ste. 3A
Chicago, IL 60614-4016 (773) 880-0002
Contact: Jolita L. Arzbaecher, Pres.

Established in 1995 in IL.
Donor(s): Leon K. Leonas, Irene Leonas.
Financial data (yr. ended 12/31/01): Assets, $10,841 (M); grants paid, $14,999; gifts received, $19,765; expenditures, $15,708; qualifying distributions, $14,999.
Limitations: Giving primarily in Chicago, IL.
Officers: Jolita L. Arzbaecher, Pres.; Vida Jonusas, Secy.; Irene Leonas, Treas.
EIN: 363991540

60216
Jens Jensen Ravinia Area Preservation Association
405 Sheridan Rd.
Highland Park, IL 60035-5367

Classified as a private operating foundation in 1988.
Donor(s): Michael Segal.
Financial data (yr. ended 11/30/00): Assets, $10,718 (M); grants paid, $0; gifts received, $70,000; expenditures, $65,556; qualifying distributions, $65,556; giving activities include $54,847 for programs.
Directors: Stephen Christy, Michael Segal, Noel Wilner.
EIN: 363418417

60217
Albert and Joyce Rubenstein Family Foundation
219 E. Lake Shore Dr.
Chicago, IL 60611
Contact: Joyce Rubenstein, Pres.

Established in 1970.
Donor(s): Albert I. Rubenstein.

Financial data (yr. ended 12/31/01): Assets, $10,620 (M); grants paid, $1,270; expenditures, $1,275; qualifying distributions, $1,275.
Limitations: Giving primarily in IL.
Officer and Director:* Joyce Rubenstein,* Pres.
EIN: 237072103

60218
Clark/Bardes Foundation, Inc.
102 S. Wynstone Park Dr.
North Barrington, IL 60010

Established in 2000 in IL.
Financial data (yr. ended 12/31/01): Assets, $10,000 (M); grants paid, $0; expenditures, $0; qualifying distributions, $0.
Limitations: Applications not accepted.
Application information: Contributes only to pre-selected organizations.
Directors: Tera Mears, Thomas Pyra, W.T. Wamberg.
EIN: 364338725

60219
Central Wholesale Liquor Foundation
c/o Julian B. Venezky
301 S.W. Adams St., Ste. 700
Peoria, IL 61602-1564
Application address: 17577 Mockingbird Rd., Nashville, IL 62263, tel.: (618) 478-5556

Established in 1990 in IL as a company-sponsored operating foundation.
Donor(s): Central Wholesale Liquor Co.
Financial data (yr. ended 04/30/00): Assets, $9,698 (M); grants paid, $2,125; expenditures, $2,215; qualifying distributions, $2,125.
Limitations: Giving primarily in IL.
Application information: Application form not required.
Officers and Directors:* Julian B. Venezky,* Pres.; Ronald T. Rubin,* Secy.-Treas.
EIN: 371264351
Codes: CD

60220
Channel Cats
2007 Hillside Trail
Cary, IL 60013 (847) 639-5226
Contact: Mindy Acker, Dir.

Established in 1999.
Financial data (yr. ended 12/31/99): Assets, $7,891 (M); grants paid, $1,091; gifts received, $42,929; expenditures, $46,382; qualifying distributions, $1,091.
Limitations: Giving to residents of Root Springs County, IL.
Application information: Application form required.
Directors: Mindy Acker, Mike McCormick, Fred Rein, Roger Shelton, John Sirois.
EIN: 364266930

60221
Chaim Foundation
180 N. LaSalle St., Ste. 2805
Chicago, IL 60601

Classified as a private operating foundation in 1997.
Donor(s): Howard G. Kaplan.
Financial data (yr. ended 12/31/01): Assets, $7,496 (M); grants paid, $900; gifts received, $500; expenditures, $900; qualifying distributions, $897.
Limitations: Applications not accepted. Giving primarily in IL and NY.
Application information: Contributes only to pre-selected organizations.

Officers: Howard G. Kaplan, Pres.; Rhonda D. Kaplan-Katz, Secy.; Marlene J. Kaplan, Treas.
EIN: 363850004

60222
Francis Park Foundation, Inc.
9032 E. 2850 St.
Kewanee, IL 61443-8861

Classified as a private operating foundation in 1968.
Financial data (yr. ended 12/31/99): Assets, $6,992 (M); grants paid, $0; gifts received, $2,398; expenditures, $96; qualifying distributions, $0; giving activities include $3,907 for programs.
Officers: Donald P. Lundberg, Pres.; Frank Matuszyk, V.P.; Debbie Lundberg, Secy.; Mark R. Hepner, Treas.
EIN: 366162492

60223
Cardiovascular Institute of Chicago
c/o Terrell Isselhard
225 W. Washington St., Ste. 1300
Chicago, IL 60606

Established in 1995.
Donor(s): Robert M. Gasior, M.D.
Financial data (yr. ended 12/31/99): Assets, $6,760 (M); grants paid, $0; gifts received, $14,970; expenditures, $18,337; qualifying distributions, $18,187; giving activities include $5,607 for programs.
Officers and Directors:* Robert M. Gasior, M.D.,* Pres.; Tammo D. Hoeksema, M.D.,* Secy.; Terrell J. Isselhard,* Treas.; Dominick J. Alloco, M.D., Luke Pascale.
EIN: 237204587

60224
W. J. Bicket Foundation
920 Carmel Blvd.
Zion, IL 60099-3257

Classified as a private operating foundation in 1975.
Financial data (yr. ended 11/30/01): Assets, $6,518 (M); grants paid, $0; gifts received, $900; expenditures, $2,279; qualifying distributions, $2,279; giving activities include $2,279 for programs.
Publications: Annual report.
Officers: Jeffrey Bickett, Pres.; Patricia La Belle, Secy.; Donald La Belle, Treas.; Rev. W.E. Mayfield, Exec. Dir.
EIN: 237433961

60225
Schweinfurth Family Charitable Trust
20032 Tam O'Shanter Ct.
Olympia Fields, IL 60461

Financial data (yr. ended 09/30/00): Assets, $6,461 (M); grants paid, $400; gifts received, $400; expenditures, $739; qualifying distributions, $450.
Limitations: Applications not accepted.
Trustees: Nancy Farms, Wendy Green, Beverly A. Olson, Louise Schweinfurth, Roy Schweinfurth.
EIN: 366849207

60226
Evangel Mission
25-420 Burning Tr.
Wheaton, IL 60187-7906

Financial data (yr. ended 12/31/01): Assets, $6,104 (M); grants paid, $0; gifts received, $14,890; expenditures, $10,523; qualifying distributions, $10,334.

60226—ILLINOIS

Officers: Dwight Peterson, Pres.; Russell Bancroft, V.P.; Marvin Vogel, Secy.-Treas.; Carl Mortenson, Exec. Dir.
Director: Rev. Eugene Frost.
EIN: 366141718

60227
City-Wide Tax Assistance Program
350 N. Orleans, No. 851
Chicago, IL 60654

Established in 1996.
Donor(s): Robert M. Burke.
Financial data (yr. ended 04/15/00): Assets, $5,874 (M); grants paid, $0; gifts received, $1,110; expenditures, $10,467; qualifying distributions, $10,467; giving activities include $4,295 for programs.
Limitations: Applications not accepted.
Application information: Contributes only to pre-selected organizations.
Officers and Directors: Robert M. Burke,* C.E.O; Michael Donovan,* Co-Pres.; Antonio Schiappa,* Co-Pres.; Brad Brinegar, C.O.O.; David Bolger,* Exec. V.P.; Ellen Zfaney, V.P. and C.F.O; Barbara Klein,* C.F.O.; Rodger L. Boehm, Rev. Michael Boland, Thomas Hill, Frederick J. Krull, Michael Richards, Belkis Santos, Richard Strotman.
EIN: 364070692

60228
Niota Flood Control Council
c/o Melaney R. Piles
549 Meadow Ln.
Niota, IL 62358

Established in 1998 in IL.
Financial data (yr. ended 12/31/01): Assets, $5,674 (M); grants paid, $0; expenditures, $0; qualifying distributions, $0.
Limitations: Applications not accepted.
Application information: Contributes only to pre-selected organizations.
Officers: Butch Granneman, Pres.; Pete Boddeker, V.P.; Melaney Piles, Secy.-Treas.
EIN: 371228613

60229
Wood Hath Hope Prison Ministry, Inc.
2226 Newman Pkwy.
Peoria, IL 61604

Established in 1994 in TX.
Donor(s): Rodney M. Still, Jean M. Still.
Financial data (yr. ended 12/31/01): Assets, $5,551 (M); grants paid, $5,115; gifts received, $15,495; expenditures, $15,772; qualifying distributions, $15,772; giving activities include $10,657 for programs.
Limitations: Applications not accepted. Giving limited to TX.
Application information: Contributes only to pre-selected organizations.
Officers: Rodney M. Still, Pres.; Jean M. Still, Secy.
Director: Michael R. Tully.
EIN: 752566991

60230
Ausman-Isaacs Foundation
c/o Gary Ausman
400 E. Ohio St., Ste. 3803
Chicago, IL 60611

Established in 2000 in IL.
Financial data (yr. ended 12/31/00): Assets, $5,462 (M); grants paid, $284; gifts received, $6,472; expenditures, $1,025; qualifying distributions, $1,025.
Limitations: Applications not accepted.
Application information: Contributes only to pre-selected organizations.
Trustees: Gary Ausman, Jeffrey Sanchez, Jay Zabel.
EIN: 364373358

60231
Pedersen Family Foundation
c/o Robert A. Pedersen
1000 Lewis Rd.
Geneva, IL 60134

Established in 1999 in IL.
Donor(s): Carl S. Pedersen.
Financial data (yr. ended 12/31/00): Assets, $5,315 (M); grants paid, $1,493; gifts received, $1,400; expenditures, $15,042; qualifying distributions, $1,493.
Officers and Directors:* Robert A. Pedersen,* Pres.; Gail K. Pfister,* Secy.-Treas.; Kari Pedersen.
EIN: 364304424

60232
Hoffman Fishbein Charitable Foundation
174 Hazel Ave.
Highland Park, IL 60035

Financial data (yr. ended 12/31/99): Assets, $5,134 (M); grants paid, $20,000; expenditures, $20,890; qualifying distributions, $20,000.
Officers and Directors:* Barbara Hoffman,* Pres.; Todd Fishbein,* V.P. and Secy.; Brian Hoffman,* V.P. and Treas.; Lisa Fishbein,* V.P.; David Hoffman,* V.P.; Deborah Hoffman,* V.P.; Melanie Hoffman,* V.P.
EIN: 367248180

60233
La Esperanza, Inc.
c/o Allan J. Snape
200 Tower Pkwy.
Lincolnshire, IL 60069-3640

Established in 1991 in IL. Classified as a private operating foundation in 1992.
Donor(s): Desmond R. LaPlace, Douglas K. Chapman, Norman H. Wesley.
Financial data (yr. ended 03/31/99): Assets, $5,084 (M); grants paid, $21,110; gifts received, $4,150; expenditures, $21,205; qualifying distributions, $21,110; giving activities include $21,110 for programs.
Limitations: Applications not accepted. Giving limited to Nogales, Mexico.
Application information: Contributes only to pre-selected organizations.
Officers and Directors:* Douglas K. Chapman,* Pres.; Mark A. Roche, V.P.; Norman R. Wesley,* V.P.; Mark S. Lyon, Secy.; Allan J. Snape, Treas.; Kevin D. Chapman, Thomas R. Higgins, Desmond R. LaPlace.
EIN: 363782640

60234
Racial Justice Now
c/o Herbert N. Stevens
520 W. Patton St.
Paxton, IL 60957-1445

Established in 1998 in IL.
Donor(s): Herbert N. Stevens.
Financial data (yr. ended 12/31/01): Assets, $4,321 (M); grants paid, $5,016; gifts received, $48,853; expenditures, $65,928; qualifying distributions, $65,928; giving activities include $55,187 for programs.
Limitations: Applications not accepted.
Application information: Contributes only to pre-selected organizations.
Officers: Herbert N. Stevens, Pres.; Donald Register, V.P.; Judith Jepsen Popel, Treas.
Directors: Gail Brooks, Lorraine Brown, Willie B. Franklin, Catherine Hogue, John Lee Johnson, Ann Newbern.
EIN: 371375027

60235
The Stephen C. Adler and Anne H. Adler Charitable Foundation
3441 52nd St.
Moline, IL 61265

Established in 2000 in IL.
Donor(s): Stephen C. Adler.
Financial data (yr. ended 12/31/00): Assets, $3,978 (M); grants paid, $6,580; gifts received, $10,000; expenditures, $6,580; qualifying distributions, $6,580.
Limitations: Giving primarily in IL and NY.
Directors: Anne H. Adler, Eric D. Adler, Rebecca D. Adler, Stephen C. Adler.
EIN: 371401457

60236
Hintz Research Foundation
c/o Otto E. Hintz
2202-30 St.
Rock Island, IL 61201-5003

Established in 1994 in IL.
Donor(s): Otto E. Hintz.
Financial data (yr. ended 12/31/99): Assets, $3,578 (M); grants paid, $0; gifts received, $4,306; expenditures, $2,045; qualifying distributions, $2,083; giving activities include $2,015 for programs.
Limitations: Applications not accepted.
Application information: Contributes only to pre-selected organizations.
Trustees: Otto E. Hintz, Maryanna Valsar.
EIN: 371305860

60237
Suzanne Dreebin-Wilensky Foundation
2539 Stonebridge Ln.
Northbrook, IL 60062-8107

Established in 1997 in IL.
Donor(s): Reva Dreebin.
Financial data (yr. ended 12/31/00): Assets, $3,158 (M); grants paid, $1,500; expenditures, $1,501; qualifying distributions, $1,500.
Limitations: Applications not accepted.
Application information: Contributes only to pre-selected organizations.
Trustees: Harold Dreebin, Reva Dreebin.
EIN: 364134460

60238
Foundation for Ophthalmic Research and Development, Inc.
c/o Kraff Eye Institute
3115 N. Harlem Ave.
Chicago, IL 60634

Financial data (yr. ended 12/31/00): Assets, $3,010 (M); grants paid, $0; expenditures, $80; qualifying distributions, $80; giving activities include $80 for programs.
Officers: Manus C. Kraff, Pres.; Charles Perlman, Secy.
EIN: 363261628

60239
Chamber Opera of Chicago
1111 W. 35th St., 12th Fl.
Chicago, IL 60609

Classified as a private operating foundation in 1986.
Donor(s): Barre Seid.
Financial data (yr. ended 06/30/02): Assets, $1,929 (M); grants paid, $0; expenditures, $2,645; qualifying distributions, $0.
Officers and Directors:* Barre Seid,* Pres. and Treas.; Lawrence Rapchak,* Secy.; Carl Ratner.

EIN: 363247003

60240
Hawthorne Foundation
419 Sheridan Rd.
Winnetka, IL 60093

Established in 1993 in IL.
Donor(s): Keith M. Rudman.
Financial data (yr. ended 04/30/01): Assets, $1,425 (M); grants paid, $0; gifts received, $5,000; expenditures, $7,411; qualifying distributions, $0; giving activities include $7,411 for programs.
Limitations: Applications not accepted.
Application information: Contributes only to pre-selected organizations.
Officers and Directors:* Keith Rudman,* Pres.; Thomas F. Sax,* Secy.; William S. Singer,* Treas.; Peter Bensinger, Carol Blackwell Curry, Lillian Davis, Lawrence Dorf, Robert Furst, Neil Hartigan, William Smith, Jon Ukman, Jonathan Vegosen, Shari Vegosen.
EIN: 363892594

60241
The Robert Foundation
1512 Asbury Ave.
Evanston, IL 60201-4111

Financial data (yr. ended 12/31/00): Assets, $1,390 (M); grants paid, $0; expenditures, $705; qualifying distributions, $0; giving activities include $700 for programs.
Officers and Director:* Richard Carney,* Pres.; Victor Crowe, V.P.; Judith M. Carney, Secy.; Roberta Crowe, Treas.
EIN: 237013260

60242
Harry M. & Gertrude Y. Schwartz Foundation for Animals
827 Bob-O-Link Rd.
Highland Park, IL 60035

Established in 1998.
Financial data (yr. ended 05/31/01): Assets, $1,372 (M); grants paid, $0; expenditures, $0; qualifying distributions, $0.
Director: Sharon Seidler.
EIN: 367237810

60243
Harry M. & Gertrude Y. Schwartz Foundation for Education and the Arts
827 Bob-O-Link Rd.
Highland Park, IL 60035

Established in 1998.
Financial data (yr. ended 05/31/01): Assets, $1,372 (M); grants paid, $0; expenditures, $0; qualifying distributions, $0.
Director: Sharon Seidler.
EIN: 367237811

60244
Harry M. & Gertrude Y. Schwartz Foundation for Judaism
827 Bob-O-Link Rd.
Highland Park, IL 60035

Established in 1998.
Financial data (yr. ended 05/31/01): Assets, $1,372 (M); grants paid, $0; expenditures, $0; qualifying distributions, $0.
Director: Sharon Seidler.
EIN: 367237812

60245
Harry M. & Gertrude Y. Schwartz Foundation for Medical Research
827 Bob-O-Link Rd.
Highland Park, IL 60035

Established in 1998.
Financial data (yr. ended 05/31/01): Assets, $1,347 (M); grants paid, $0; expenditures, $0; qualifying distributions, $0.
Director: Sharon Seidler.
EIN: 367237813

60246
Kishan Patel Memorial Foundation, Inc.
P.O. Box 1371
Elk Grove Village, IL 60007

Established in 1995 in IL.
Donor(s): Vijay Patel.
Financial data (yr. ended 12/31/01): Assets, $949 (M); grants paid, $1,750; gifts received, $2,685; expenditures, $2,391; qualifying distributions, $1,750.
Limitations: Applications not accepted.
Officer: Vijay Patel, Pres. and Treas.
EIN: 363988026

60247
James E. Davis, M.D. Education & Research Foundation
2122 Grove St.
Glenview, IL 60025-2820

Classified as a private operating foundation in 1997 in IL.
Financial data (yr. ended 12/31/00): Assets, $639 (M); grants paid, $5; expenditures, $5; qualifying distributions, $5.
Officers: Donald H. Smith, Pres.; George E. McGee, M.D., V.P.; David Vanderpool, V.P.
Director: James E. Davis.
EIN: 364103325

60248
Samuel A. Cavallari & Margaret C. Cavallari Foundation
37492 Granada
Lake Villa, IL 60046

Established in 2001 in IL.
Financial data (yr. ended 12/31/01): Assets, $500 (M); grants paid, $0; expenditures, $0; qualifying distributions, $0.
Trustee: Margaret Cavallari.
EIN: 364410435

60249
Children's Heart Institute of Illinois, Inc.
c/o Dr. Dale M. Geiss
1624 N.E. Glen Oak Ave.
Peoria, IL 61603-3320
Application address: 515 N.E. Glen Oak Ave., Peoria, IL 61603-3320, tel.: (309) 674-2002
Contact: Robert C. Gomez, M.D.

Classified as a private operating foundation in 1984.
Financial data (yr. ended 08/31/01): Assets, $388 (M); grants paid, $350; gifts received, $4,345; expenditures, $5,095; qualifying distributions, $956.
Limitations: Giving primarily in Peoria, IL.
Officers and Directors:* Dale M. Geiss, M.D.,* Pres.; William H. Albers,* V.P.; Gail Eaton, Secy.; Robert C. Gomez, M.D.,* Treas.
EIN: 371161022

60250
Loy L. Barger Evangelistic Ministries, Inc.
130 Reynolds Cemetery Rd.
Harrisburg, IL 62946-5534

Established in 1998 in IL. Classified as a private operating foundation in 1990.
Financial data (yr. ended 12/31/00): Assets, $135 (M); grants paid, $0; gifts received, $4,384; expenditures, $6,393; qualifying distributions, $6,393; giving activities include $6,393 for programs.
Officers: Loy L. Barger, Pres.; Lena Barger, V.P.; Jean Duncan, Treas.
Trustees: Rhonda Berth, William Berth, Charles Duncan, Larry Johnson, Tammy Johnson.
EIN: 371186212

60251
Mid-North Animal Shelter Foundation
c/o H.W. Maxwell
427 S. Lincoln St.
Hinsdale, IL 60521-4009

Classified as a private operating foundation in 1980.
Donor(s): William S. Maxwell.
Financial data (yr. ended 06/30/00): Assets, $100 (M); grants paid, $0; gifts received, $24,537; expenditures, $24,537; qualifying distributions, $0; giving activities include $24,537 for programs.
Officer and Trustees:* William Sterling Maxwell,* Treas.; Anna Laura Kennedy, Z.S. Nobezenski.
EIN: 237136029

60252
Institute Museum, Inc.
2434 N. Greenview Ave.
Chicago, IL 60614-2093

Established in 1992 in IL.
Donor(s): Robert Goldman, Ronald Klatz, Lance Goldman.
Financial data (yr. ended 12/31/00): Assets, $1 (M); grants paid, $0; gifts received, $387,000; expenditures, $721; qualifying distributions, $0.
Directors: Kim Bardley, Eve Magnet, Steve Novil.
EIN: 363858489

60253
Razia Ashraf Foundation
210 W. 22nd St., No. 115
Oak Brook, IL 60523

Established in 1995 in IL.
Donor(s): Nasim Ashraf.
Financial data (yr. ended 12/31/99): Assets, $0 (M); grants paid, $40,500; gifts received, $11,000; expenditures, $40,633; qualifying distributions, $40,401.
Officers: Nasim Ashraf, Pres.; Mustafa A.J. Sherwani, Secy.
EIN: 364046542

60254
Cancerhelp Institute
1000 Skokie Blvd., Ste. 150
Wilmette, IL 60091
Contact: Celia Muench, Pres.

Established in 1991 in IL.
Donor(s): Peter Dyson.
Financial data (yr. ended 12/31/00): Assets, $0 (M); grants paid, $0; gifts received, $727,415; expenditures, $620,153; qualifying distributions, $0.
Officers: Celia Muench, Pres. and Treas.; Hugh Miller, V.P.; James Muench, Secy.; Edward Miller, C.I.O.
EIN: 363785778

60255
The Chicago Center for Ethnic/Minority Studies
1420 Sheridan Rd.
Wilmette, IL 60091-1850

Established in 1997 in IL.
Financial data (yr. ended 12/31/00): Assets, $0 (M); grants paid, $11,947; gifts received, $2,184; expenditures, $13,072; qualifying distributions, $13,072.
Limitations: Applications not accepted.
Application information: Contributes only to pre-selected organizations.
Trustees: Evelyn Salk, Allen Schwartz.
EIN: 364134960

60256
Buddy Guy Charities, Inc.
c/o R.C. Smith
2 E. 8th St., Ste. 100
Chicago, IL 60605

Established in 1998 in IL.
Financial data (yr. ended 12/31/99): Assets, $0 (M); grants paid, $26,182; gifts received, $30; expenditures, $26,251; qualifying distributions, $26,251.
Limitations: Applications not accepted. Giving primarily in IL.
Application information: Contributes only to pre-selected organizations.
Officers: George B. Guy, Pres.; Jennifer J. Guy, V.P.; Arthur W. Anderson, Secy.
Director: Scott A. Cameron.
EIN: 364178848

60257
Patrick Henry Community Arts Fund
3950 N. Lake Shore Dr., Ste. 1011
Chicago, IL 60613
Contact: Ann Barzel, Tr.

Established in 1990.
Financial data (yr. ended 12/31/99): Assets, $0 (M); grants paid, $3,650; expenditures, $3,685; qualifying distributions, $3,650.
Limitations: Giving primarily in Chicago, IL.
Trustees: Ann Barzel, Robert Callahan, Marie O'Connor.
EIN: 363696566

INDIANA

60258
Liberty Fund, Inc.
8335 Allison Pointe Trail, Ste. 300
Indianapolis, IN 46250-1684 (317) 842-0880
FAX: (317) 577-9067

Incorporated in 1960 in IN.
Donor(s): Pierre F. Goodrich,‡ Enid Goodrich,‡ John B. Goodrich.‡
Financial data (yr. ended 04/30/02): Assets, $366,404,060 (M); grants paid, $0; gifts received, $100; expenditures, $22,408,574; qualifying distributions, $19,980,755; giving activities include $696,169 for programs.
Publications: Informational brochure.
Officers and Directors:* T. Alan Russell,* Chair.; George Martin,* Pres.; Emilio J. Pacheco, Exec. V.P.; Sandra J. Schaller, V.P. and Cont.; Douglas J. Denllyl, V.P.; Patricia A. Gallagher, V.P.; Chris Talley,* Treas.; Manuel Ayau, George W. Carey, Roseda D. Decker, Richard W. Duesenburg, Ralph W. Husted, Joseph F. Johnston, George B. Martin, Edward B. McLean, Irwin H. Reiss, Richard A. Ware.
EIN: 351320021

60259
The Honeywell Foundation, Inc.
275 W. Market St.
Wabash, IN 46992 (219) 563-1102
FAX: (219) 563-0873
Contact: Philip L. Zimmerman, Secy.

Incorporated in 1941 in IN.
Donor(s): Howard Hagee,‡ Eugenia H. Honeywell,‡ Mark C. Honeywell,‡ Della D. Hubbard.‡
Financial data (yr. ended 09/30/01): Assets, $43,940,958 (M); grants paid, $76,460; gifts received, $1,227,335; expenditures, $4,066,065; qualifying distributions, $3,389,334; giving activities include $1,194,944 for programs.
Limitations: Giving limited to Wabash County, IN.
Publications: Newsletter, informational brochure, application guidelines.
Application information: Discretionary grants program is limited to $5,000-$10,000 per year. Application form required.
Officers and Directors:* Stephen Downs,* Pres.; Marilyn Ford,* V.P.; Philip L. Zimmerman, Secy. and Exec. Dir.; Larry Curless,* Treas.; Terry Agness, Kim Clark, Ken Grandstaff, Jan Halderman.
EIN: 350390706
Codes: FD2

60260
Dean V. Kruse Foundation
P.O. Box 1
Auburn, IN 46706

Established in 1999 in IN.
Donor(s): Mitchell Kruse, Dean V. Kruse.
Financial data (yr. ended 12/31/01): Assets, $30,474,326 (M); grants paid, $0; gifts received, $362,500; expenditures, $1,152,261; qualifying distributions, $8,226,096; giving activities include $823,735 for programs.
Limitations: Applications not accepted.
Application information: Contributes only to pre-selected organizations.
Officers and Directors:* Dean V. Kruse,* Pres.; Andrew Kruse,* Secy.; Diane Jernigan, Mitchell Kruse.
EIN: 352081163

60261
Fourth Freedom Forum, Inc.
803 N. Main St.
Goshen, IN 46526

Established in 1982; classified as a private operating foundation in 1988.
Donor(s): Howard S. Brembeck.
Financial data (yr. ended 12/31/01): Assets, $16,801,448 (M); grants paid, $0; gifts received, $307,382; expenditures, $1,264,652; qualifying distributions, $0.
Limitations: Applications not accepted.
Application information: Contributes only to pre-selected organizations.
Officers and Directors:* Howard S. Brembeck,* Chair.; David B. Cortright,* Pres.; Andrew L. Hardie,* V.P.; Miriam J. Redsecker,* Secy.; John C. Frieden,* Treas.; Charles W. Ainlay, J. Lawrence Burkholder, George Lee Butler, William P. Johnson, George A. Lopez, Frank K. Martin, LeRoy Troyer.
EIN: 351546655

60262
Indianapolis Retirement Home, Inc.
1731 N. Capitol Ave.
Indianapolis, IN 46202-1203

Classified as a private operating foundation in 1991.
Financial data (yr. ended 08/31/00): Assets, $16,102,458 (M); grants paid, $0; gifts received, $252,342; expenditures, $2,643,146; qualifying distributions, $2,516,829; giving activities include $2,627,959 for programs.
Officers: Emily Wren, Chair.; Vicki-Mech Hester, Pres.; Barbara Furlow, V.P.; Susan Guyett, Secy.; Betty Stilwell, Treas.; Mariellyn F. Hill, Exec. Dir.
Directors: Sylvia Hill, John Reynolds, Susan Shepherd, and 12 additional directors.
EIN: 350868098

60263
Coffee Creek Watershed Conservancy, Inc.
2198 S. Calumet Rd.
Chesterton, IN 46304

Established in 1999 in IN.
Donor(s): Lake Erie Land Co., Coffee Creek Center Congress.
Financial data (yr. ended 12/31/01): Assets, $13,906,547 (M); grants paid, $0; gifts received, $221,188; expenditures, $570,157; qualifying distributions, $0; giving activities include $228,707 for programs.
Officer: Thomas R. Anderson, Pres.
EIN: 352082745

60264
Solarbron Pointe, Inc.
c/o The National City Bank
1501 McDowell Rd.
Evansville, IN 47712

Classified as a private operating foundation in 1986.
Financial data (yr. ended 11/30/00): Assets, $13,513,316 (M); grants paid, $2,000; gifts received, $388,000; expenditures, $4,373,635; qualifying distributions, $3,379,820; giving activities include $3,379,820 for programs.
Officer: Terry Miller, Exec. Dir.
Directors: Bruce Baker, Robert Bronson, Charles Goldman, Wayne Trockman.
EIN: 351544098

60265
Robert Lee Blaffer Trust
P.O. Box 581
New Harmony, IN 47631 (812) 682-4431
Contact: Gary Gerard, Secy.

Established in 1986.
Donor(s): Barbara Franzheim, Jane B. Owen.
Financial data (yr. ended 02/28/01): Assets, $10,368,157 (M); grants paid, $139,775; gifts received, $5,380; expenditures, $608,202; qualifying distributions, $710,483.
Limitations: Giving primarily in IN.
Officers and Directors:* Gordon St. Angelo,* Chair.; Robert Guenther,* Vice-Chair.; Gary Gerard, Secy. and Mgr.; James Sanders, Treas.; Milo Coerper, Anne D. Owen, Jane D. Owen, Laurel Vaughn.
EIN: 746060871
Codes: FD2

60266
Indianapolis Motor Speedway Foundation, Inc.
4790 W. 16th St.
Indianapolis, IN 46222

Established in 1957 in IN.

Donor(s): General Motors Corporation, Indianapolis Motor Speedway.
Financial data (yr. ended 12/31/01): Assets, $9,371,745 (M); grants paid, $15,000; gifts received, $234,550; expenditures, $897,391; qualifying distributions, $472,972; giving activities include $490,726 for programs.
Limitations: Applications not accepted.
Application information: Contributes only to pre-selected organizations.
Officers: Anton H. George, Pres.; Mari H. George, Secy.; Jeffrey G. Belskus, Treas.
Directors: Donald E. Smith.
EIN: 356013771

60267
Charles Ford Memorial Home
(also known as Charles Ford Trust)
920 S. Main St.
New Harmony, IN 47631

Financial data (yr. ended 12/31/01): Assets, $8,987,253 (M); grants paid, $0; expenditures, $882,513; qualifying distributions, $781,612; giving activities include $882,513 for programs.
Limitations: Applications not accepted.
Application information: Contributes only to pre-selected organizations.
Trustees: Betty Gibbs, Charles Huck, Talmage Lee.
EIN: 350985961

60268
Quest for Excellence, Inc.
(Formerly Foltz Foundation, Inc.)
2051 N. College Ave.
Indianapolis, IN 46202-1741

Established in 1992 in IN.
Donor(s): Howard F. Foltz, Jr., St. Vincent Hospital Foundation, St. Francis Hospital Foundation, Indianapolis Foundation, City of Indianapolis, Indiana Dept. of Education.
Financial data (yr. ended 12/31/99): Assets, $8,723,715 (M); grants paid, $1,824; gifts received, $170,311; expenditures, $1,040,026; qualifying distributions, $681,134; giving activities include $620,472 for programs.
Officers: Howard F. Foltz, Jr., Pres.; Lisa L. Dellacqua, V.P.; Daniel E. Foltz, V.P.; Howard F. Foltz III, Secy.-Treas.; Nancy Crowder, Prog. Dir.; Michael D. Robinson, Dir.-Operations.
Directors: Patrick J. Brake, David R. Davis, Anita Gaillard, Fritz Gordner, Joanna Niehoff, Virginia L. O'Brien, Mary Rugh, Terry Scott, Stephen D. Smith.
EIN: 351860492

60269
The Beardsley Foundation
c/o KeyBank, Trust Dept.
301 S. Main St.
Elkhart, IN 46515-3119
Additional address: 302 E. Beardsley Ave., Elkhart, IN 46514

Trust established in 1955 in IN.
Donor(s): Walter R. Beardsley.‡
Financial data (yr. ended 12/31/00): Assets, $5,767,939 (M); grants paid, $4,200; expenditures, $403,413; qualifying distributions, $334,911; giving activities include $400,113 for programs.
Limitations: Giving primarily in Elkhart, IN.
Application information: Application form not required.
Officers: Robert B. Beardsley, Chair. and Pres.; Dorinda Miles Smith, Secy.; George Freese, Treas.; Kathleen Gray, Exec. Dir.
EIN: 351170807

60270
Welter Foundation, Inc.
301B S. Main St.
P.O. Box 1685
Elkhart, IN 46515 (219) 294-7491
Application address: 21027 Riverbrook Ln., Bristol, IN 46507
Contact: Edward P. Welter, Pres.

Established in 1997 in IN.
Donor(s): Edward P. Welter, Wilhelmina J. Welter.
Financial data (yr. ended 12/31/00): Assets, $4,759,417 (M); grants paid, $202,000; expenditures, $249,375; qualifying distributions, $199,612.
Limitations: Giving primarily in Elkart, IN.
Officers and Directors:* Edward P. Welter,* Pres.; Wilhelmina J. Welter,* V.P.; Cynthia S. Gilard,* Secy.
EIN: 352023590
Codes: FD2

60271
Jennie E. Caldwell Memorial Home Trust
5098 W. 550 N.
Earl Park, IN 47942

Classified as a private operating foundation in 1986.
Financial data (yr. ended 12/31/99): Assets, $4,514,665 (M); grants paid, $0; gifts received, $62,269; expenditures, $365,450; qualifying distributions, $224,176; giving activities include $224,176 for programs.
Trustees: Carol A. Butler, Ruth F. Rayle, Walter K. Smith, Jr., Rosemary Weist.
EIN: 350907305

60272
Anderson Fine Arts Foundation, Inc.
32 W. 10th St.
Anderson, IN 46016

Classified as a private operating foundation in 1987.
Financial data (yr. ended 04/30/00): Assets, $3,922,745 (M); grants paid, $0; gifts received, $117,696; expenditures, $304,946; qualifying distributions, $246,192; giving activities include $299,628 for programs.
Officers and Trustees:* Marilyn Ault,* Pres.; Dave Harbet,* V.P.; Darlene Miller,* Secy.; Jim Thompson,* Treas.; Deborah McBratney-Stapleton, Exec. Dir.; Joe Cook, Kevin Crawford, Dave DeHart, Harry Garretson, Kathy Howe, Leisa Julian, Jane A. Kendrick, Charles King, Thomas F. Lyons, Bill O'Neal, Tim Patishall, Diana Priser, Sharon Rich, Leisa Richardson, Robert W. Rock, Caroli Wolfe, Ken Zinzer.
EIN: 356058737

60273
The Yunker Foundation, Inc.
c/o The Madison Bank & Trust Co.
213-215 E. Main St.
Madison, IN 47250
Contact: John Muessel, Dir.

Established in 1952 in IN.
Donor(s): Ann Yunker.
Financial data (yr. ended 12/31/00): Assets, $3,779,189 (M); grants paid, $202,743; expenditures, $227,213; qualifying distributions, $227,213.
Limitations: Giving limited to Jefferson County, IN.
Application information: Application form not required.
Officers: Fr. John Meyer, Vice-Chair.; Dolores J. Spoonmore, Secy.-Treas.
Directors: Joe Hansley, John Muessel, Ralph Pratt.
EIN: 356041203

Codes: FD2

60274
Ruth C. Sabin Home
1603 Michigan Ave.
La Porte, IN 46350

Classified as a private operating foundation in 1973.
Financial data (yr. ended 03/31/01): Assets, $3,592,476 (M); grants paid, $0; expenditures, $557,202; qualifying distributions, $547,022; giving activities include $551,179 for programs.
Officers: Timothy Larson, Pres.; Thomas Larson, V.P.; Charlotte L. Jones, Secy.; Larry Rardin, Treas.
Trustees: John H. Bradley, Florence Carlson, Shirley Carlson, Dalimira Cmiel, Rebecca Larson, Elizabeth Oak, David D. Osborn, Irvin S. Swanson, Peg Swanson, Sandee Tonsoni, Rose Zahrt.
EIN: 350886845

60275
President Benjamin Harrison Foundation, Inc.
1230 N. Delaware St.
Indianapolis, IN 46202

Classified as a private operating foundation in 1979.
Donor(s): Arthur Jordan Foundation, Institute of Museum Svcs., NBD Bank, N.A., IPALCO Enterprises, Inc.
Financial data (yr. ended 12/31/00): Assets, $3,526,892 (M); grants paid, $0; gifts received, $429,597; expenditures, $595,866; qualifying distributions, $438,118; giving activities include $560,436 for programs.
Officers: Eugene M. Busche, Chair.; Richard A. Steele, V.P.; Gracia E. Meyer, Secy.; Dan R. DeMars, Treas.
Directors: William A. Browne, Richard D. Chegar, Thomas Cochrun, Thomas P. Ewbank, Phyllis D. Geeslin, Rev. Fr. Boniface Hardin, Paul Jontz, Julia L. Lacy, Mark Lubbers, Boris E. Meditch, Andrew J. Paine, Jr., Frank E. Russell, Susanne E. Sogard, J. Reid Williamson, Jr.
EIN: 351117501

60276
Stanley W. Hayes Research Foundation, Inc.
801 Elks Rd.
P.O. Box 1404
Richmond, IN 47374

Incorporated in 1959 in IN.
Donor(s): Stanley W. Hayes.‡
Financial data (yr. ended 06/30/02): Assets, $3,523,336 (M); grants paid, $0; gifts received, $17,102; expenditures, $517,620; qualifying distributions, $0.
Publications: Program policy statement, application guidelines.
Officers: Stephen H. Hayes, Pres. and Treas.; Edmund B. Hayes, V.P.; Robert E. McClure, Secy.
Directors: J. Brandon Griffis, Randall P. Kirk, Patricia A. Mayer, Ronald L. McDaniel, Rodney Waltz.
EIN: 351061111

60277
Lilly Cares Foundation, Inc.
c/o Eli Lilly and Co.
893 S. Delaware St., Lilly Corp. Ctr.
Indianapolis, IN 46285
Application address: P.O. Box 25768, Alexandra, VA 22313, tel.: (800) 545-6962

Established as a company-sponsored operating foundation in 1996 in IN.
Donor(s): Eli Lilly and Co.

60277—INDIANA

Financial data (yr. ended 12/31/00): Assets, $2,861,597 (M); grants paid, $86,650,335; gifts received, $69,747,680; expenditures, $87,803,940; qualifying distributions, $87,695,970; giving activities include $86,650,335 for programs.
Limitations: Giving on a worldwide basis.
Application information: Application form required.
Officers: Thomas A. King, Pres.; Michael R. Smith, Secy.; Jeffrey W. Henderson, Treas.
Directors: Charles E. Golden, Pedro Granadillo, Rebecca O. Kendall, John C. Lechleiter, Ph.D., Gerhard N. Mayr, Deborah Steelman, Sidney Taurel, August M. Watanabe, M.D.
EIN: 352027985
Codes: FD, CD

60278
Golay Community Center, Inc.
1007 E. Main St.
Cambridge City, IN 47327-1440

Established in 1981 in IN.
Donor(s): Marjorie M. Golay.
Financial data (yr. ended 10/31/00): Assets, $2,763,772 (M); grants paid, $31,725; gifts received, $821,813; expenditures, $600,268; qualifying distributions, $251,794; giving activities include $377,610 for programs.
Limitations: Applications not accepted. Giving primarily in the western Wayne County, IN area.
Publications: Annual report.
Application information: Contributes only to pre-selected organizations.
Officers: Marjorie M. Golay, Chair.; Jim King, Pres.; Brent Brinkley, V.P.; John Cutshaw, Secy.; Tony Gillam, Treas.; Shelly D. Brown, Exec. Dir.
EIN: 351518699

60279
Peter C. Kesling Foundation
P.O. Box 73
La Porte, IN 46350-0073

Established in 1981.
Donor(s): Peter C. Kesling.
Financial data (yr. ended 12/31/00): Assets, $2,087,363 (M); grants paid, $5,675; gifts received, $27,157; expenditures, $29,000; qualifying distributions, $53,690.
Limitations: Applications not accepted.
Application information: Contributes only to pre-selected organizations.
Trustees: Adam W. Kesling, Andrew C. Kesling, Charlene J. Kesling, Christopher K. Kesling, Emily Kesling, Peter C. Kesling, Daniel E. Lewis, Jr.
EIN: 356377932

60280
The Gabis Family Foundation, Inc.
71 N. County Rd., 500 W.
Valparaiso, IN 46385

Established in 1998 in IN.
Donor(s): Damien A. Gabis, Rita T. Gabis.
Financial data (yr. ended 12/31/01): Assets, $2,039,451 (M); grants paid, $0; gifts received, $350,376; expenditures, $249,580; qualifying distributions, $0.
Officers: Damien A. Gabis, Pres. and Treas.; Rita T. Gabis, V.P. and Secy.
Directors: Timothy Brust, Michael N. Dana, Arlene Dunn, Lauri Eberhardt, Ben A. Gabis, Mark A. Gabis, James Melton.
EIN: 352032442

60281
Apostolic Christian Village, Inc.
P.O. Box 797
Francesville, IN 47946-0797

Classified as a private operating foundation in 1996.
Donor(s): Frances Wuethrich, Marie Heinhold.
Financial data (yr. ended 12/31/01): Assets, $1,976,841 (M); grants paid, $0; expenditures, $87,050; qualifying distributions, $119,048.
Officers: Merle Bucher, Pres.; Wally Bucher, V.P.; Fred Wahl, Secy.; Eric Heinhold, Treas.
Directors: Bob Gerber, Sidney Lehman.
EIN: 351854153

60282
Wild Shore Foundation, Inc.
1950 E. Greyhound Pass, No. 18-364
Carmel, IN 46033-7730

Established in 1995 in IN.
Donor(s): Evan L. Noyes, Jr.
Financial data (yr. ended 12/31/01): Assets, $1,743,922 (M); grants paid, $0; expenditures, $59,977; qualifying distributions, $41,321; giving activities include $41,322 for programs.
Limitations: Applications not accepted.
Officers: Evan L. Noyes, Jr., Pres. and Treas.; Elizabeth Noyes, V.P. and Secy.
Directors: Robert Reynolds, Thomas M. Woiwode.
EIN: 351947845

60283
Wanda Dudzik Memorial Scholarship Foundation
c/o U.S. Bank
5243 Hohman Ave.
Hammond, IN 46320

Established in 1991 in IN.
Donor(s): Wanda Dudzik.
Financial data (yr. ended 12/31/01): Assets, $1,539,780 (M); grants paid, $45,000; expenditures, $54,225; qualifying distributions, $54,225.
Limitations: Giving limited to IN.
Trustee: U.S. Bank.
EIN: 351884585

60284
Brown County Art Guild, Inc.
P.O. Box 324
Nashville, IN 47448

Donor(s): Sally Kriner.
Financial data (yr. ended 12/31/99): Assets, $1,394,149 (M); grants paid, $0; gifts received, $39,560; expenditures, $98,566; qualifying distributions, $68,318; giving activities include $68,318 for programs.
Officers and Directors:* John Rudd,* Pres.; Louise Hansen,* V.P.; Donna Stouder,* Secy-Treas; Margaret Colglazier, Amanda Kirby, Sally Kriner, Joe Mayberry, Wilbur Meese, Rob O'Dell, Bill Updegraff, Jean Vietor.
EIN: 351035674

60285
Trump Indiana Foundation
6012 W. Industrial Hwy.
Gary, IN 46406

Financial data (yr. ended 12/31/00): Assets, $1,391,679 (M); grants paid, $85,039; expenditures, $100,665; qualifying distributions, $100,665.
Limitations: Giving limited to residents of IN.
Application information: Application form required.
Directors: John P. Burke, Donald J. Trump.

EIN: 351989786
Codes: FD2, GTI

60286
Porter Family Foundation, Inc.
2200 W. Monroe St.
Decatur, IN 46733-3028

Classified as a company-sponsored operating foundation in IN.
Donor(s): Porter, Inc.
Financial data (yr. ended 05/31/01): Assets, $1,270,829 (M); grants paid, $126,500; gifts received, $261,657; expenditures, $127,247; qualifying distributions, $125,907.
Limitations: Applications not accepted. Giving primarily in Decatur, IN.
Application information: Contributes only to pre-selected organizations.
Directors: Grant Porter, Kristine Porter, Victor Porter.
EIN: 311144513
Codes: FD2, CD

60287
Rose Ladies Aid Society
1925 Wabash Ave
P.O. Box 330
Terre Haute, IN 47807

Established in 1885.
Financial data (yr. ended 04/30/00): Assets, $1,216,470 (M); grants paid, $48,991; gifts received, $590; expenditures, $57,058; qualifying distributions, $48,991.
Limitations: Applications not accepted. Giving limited to Vigo County, IN.
Application information: Recipients are referred by welfare organizations in Vigo County, IN.
Officers: Nancy Haynes, Pres.; Susan Scott, V.P.; Linda Brighton, Secy.; Jennifer Thomas, Treas.
EIN: 350911948
Codes: GTI

60288
Olivet Foundation, Inc.
8949 Baker Rd.
Indianapolis, IN 46259

Financial data (yr. ended 12/31/01): Assets, $1,214,741 (M); grants paid, $0; gifts received, $6,065; expenditures, $50,691; qualifying distributions, $30,355; giving activities include $30,355 for programs.
Officers and Directors:* Roger Walter,* Pres.; Marcella Aikman, Pres. Emeritus; James W. Aikman,* V.P. and Treas.; Susan Larkey,* Secy.; Brian C. Hewitt, Raymond Kamstra, Ruth Ann Kamstra, Janice Rockey, John Rockey, Gary Starks, Ray Stein.
EIN: 237026852

60289
City of Firsts Automotive Heritage Museum, Inc.
1500 N. Reed Rd.
Kokomo, IN 46901

Established in 1996 in IN.
Donor(s): Pioneer Auto Club, Bob Gollner Construction, Kokomo Chrysler Plymouth, UAW Local 685, Button Motors.
Financial data (yr. ended 12/31/00): Assets, $1,171,829 (M); grants paid, $0; gifts received, $382,700; expenditures, $506,416; qualifying distributions, $0.
Officers: Dave Griffey, Pres.; Kirk Daniels, V.P.; Peggy Hobson, Secy.; Don Woolridge, Treas.; Paul Raver.
Directors: Bill Berabach, Jim Brannon, Dorinda Davis, Bob Gollner, Jack Harbaugh, Pam

Harbough, Dick Knight, Rick Saegert, Dwight Singer, Charlie Sparks, Jack Williams.
EIN: 351809830

60290
The Keiser Foundation, Inc.
4236 Reed Rd.
Fort Wayne, IN 46815-4942
Application address: 1400 One Summit Sq., Fort Wayne, IN 46802
Contact: Bruce O. Boxberger, Agent

Established in 1995 in IN.
Donor(s): Dale L. Keiser, Betty L. Keiser.
Financial data (yr. ended 12/31/01): Assets, $1,078,396 (M); grants paid, $133,750; expenditures, $152,972; qualifying distributions, $133,362.
Limitations: Giving primarily in Fort Wayne, IN.
Officers and Directors:* Dale L. Keiser,* Pres.; Betty L. Keiser,* V.P.; Joseph G. Ryan,* Secy.-Treas.
Agent: Bruce O. Boxberger.
EIN: 351968862
Codes: FD2

60291
Herbert and Gwendolyn Raab Educational Trust
428 E. National Ave.
Brazil, IN 47834-2632

Established in 1999 in IN.
Financial data (yr. ended 06/30/00): Assets, $1,034,627 (M); grants paid, $55,125; expenditures, $65,471; qualifying distributions, $65,471.
Limitations: Giving primarily in IN.
Trustees: John Baumunk, William M. Jones, Robert Lancaster, Gail Weaver.
EIN: 356645581

60292
Mosette Levin Trust
c/o Horizon Trust & Investment Mgmt.
P.O. Box 1125, 515 Franklin Sq.
Michigan City, IN 46360 (219) 873-2629
Contact: Brenda Smythe

Financial data (yr. ended 12/31/00): Assets, $979,598 (M); grants paid, $23,097; expenditures, $34,547; qualifying distributions, $28,917.
Limitations: Giving limited to La Porte County, IN.
Directors: Romona Hay, Lester Radke, John Sweeney.
Trustee: Horizon Trust & Investment Mgmt.
EIN: 356031456
Codes: GTI

60293
ELOC, Inc.
6207 Constitution Dr.
Fort Wayne, IN 46804

Established in 1987 in IN.
Financial data (yr. ended 03/31/00): Assets, $894,073 (M); grants paid, $0; expenditures, $580; qualifying distributions, $580; giving activities include $580 for programs.
Officers and Directors:* Emily E. Pichon,* Pres.; Maclyn Parker,* V.P. and Treas.; John N. Pichon, Jr.,* Secy.
EIN: 311059748

60294
Patrick Henry Sullivan Foundation, Inc.
225 W. Hawthorne St.
Zionsville, IN 46077-1620

Classified as a private operating foundation in 1974.
Financial data (yr. ended 12/31/00): Assets, $837,135 (M); grants paid, $0; gifts received, $46,591; expenditures, $162,430; qualifying distributions, $141,491; giving activities include $141,566 for programs.
Officers and Directors:* Betsy Harris,* Pres.; Meg Julien,* V.P.; Cynthia Yeo,* Secy.; Tom Kippelman,* Treas.; Eddie Mahaney, Exec. Dir.; Frances Anderson, Stan Evans, Irene Furman, Steve Furste, John Gephart, Jim Haines, Albert Harris, Drew Kogan, Al McKee, Jim Nehf.
EIN: 237080289

60295
Loogootee Community School Scholarship Trust
c/o Peoples National Bank
P.O. Box 560
Washington, IN 47501

Established in 1999 in IN.
Financial data (yr. ended 12/31/01): Assets, $829,500 (M); grants paid, $51,250; gifts received, $6,668; expenditures, $56,969; qualifying distributions, $50,866.
Limitations: Giving limited to residents of Loogootee, IN.
Officer: Robert W. Bell, Chair.
Committee Members: Roger Bailey, Anthony Beasley, Robert Green, Terry Hasler, George Templin, Charlotte Winkler.
EIN: 356399803

60296
Treaty-Line Pioneer Village, Inc.
(Formerly Treaty-Line Museum, Inc.)
765 E. Glade Montgomery Rd.
Liberty, IN 47353

Donor(s): Clyde Kassens.
Financial data (yr. ended 12/31/01): Assets, $817,727 (M); grants paid, $0; gifts received, $335; expenditures, $31,293; qualifying distributions, $25,429.
Officers: Oris Napier, Pres.; Clyde P. Kassens, Jr., Secy.; David O. Fields, Treas.
EIN: 356069108

60297
Albert & Grace Hahn Foundation of the Indiana Hospital Association
1 American Sq., Ste. 1900
P.O. Box 82063
Indianapolis, IN 46282-0004 (317) 633-4780

Established in 1990 in IN.
Donor(s): Indiana Hospital Assn.
Financial data (yr. ended 11/30/01): Assets, $787,713 (M); grants paid, $0; expenditures, $29,100; qualifying distributions, $29,100; giving activities include $16,683 for programs.
Directors: Roger J. Allman, William J. Loveday, Kenneth Stella, John R. Walling.
EIN: 356020062

60298
Cope Environmental Center/Parks Foundation, Inc.
4910 Shoemaker Rd.
Centerville, IN 47330
Contact: Bill Lewis, Exec. Dir.

Classified as a private operating foundation in 1992.
Donor(s): James B. Cope, Helen A. Cope, Francis Parks,‡ Sally Reahard, Peter Trueblood.
Financial data (yr. ended 12/31/00): Assets, $786,207 (M); grants paid, $981; gifts received, $118,808; expenditures, $214,026; qualifying distributions, $201,941; giving activities include $193,963 for programs.
Officers and Directors:* Susie Farrell, Chair.; Ellen Bennett,* Secy.; Peter M. Trueblood,* Treas.; Bill Lewis, Exec. Dir.; Edward A. Cope, Patricia C. Goss, Robert Green, Robert Hansen, Martha Hill, Charles Hobbs, Walter Jones, Helen King, Linda Miller, Marie C. Nicholson, Amy Spears.
EIN: 351856406

60299
Robert K. Greenleaf Center, Inc.
921 E. 86th St.
Indianapolis, IN 46240

Donor(s): John C. Bogle.
Financial data (yr. ended 12/31/00): Assets, $771,128 (M); grants paid, $0; gifts received, $17,045; expenditures, $924,214; qualifying distributions, $655,016.
Limitations: Giving limited to Indianapolis, IN.
Officers and Trustees:* Jack Lowe, Jr.,* Chair.; Hon. Linda Chezem,* Vice-Chair.; Larry Spears, Exec. Dir.; Juana Bordas, C.E. "Bill" Bottum, Diane Cory, Newcomb Greenleaf, William "Bill" Guillory, Jan Levy, Jeffrey McCollum, Andrew Morikawa, Ruth Mercedes Smith.
EIN: 046122305
Codes: TN

60300
Laverna Lodge, Inc.
1950 E. Greyhound Pass, Ste. 18
Carmel, IN 46033

Established in 1997 in IN.
Donor(s): Robert C. Smith, Joan H. Smith, Pax EF Bonum, Inc.
Financial data (yr. ended 12/31/00): Assets, $739,495 (L); grants paid, $0; gifts received, $274,770; expenditures, $550,285; qualifying distributions, $249,045; giving activities include $550,285 for programs.
Officers: Robert C. Smith, Pres.; L. Martin Berg, V.P.; Ted L. Worrell, Secy.; Robert S. Ford, Treas.
Directors: Sam T. Fonner, Kevin Kruse, Tony Mandarich, Thomas H. Pedersen, Meg Smith.
EIN: 352033179

60301
Ray L. Price Foundation, Inc.
P.O. Box 359
Plymouth, IN 46563

Established in 1999 in IN.
Financial data (yr. ended 12/31/99): Assets, $732,658 (M); grants paid, $0; expenditures, $43,926; qualifying distributions, $28,338; giving activities include $28,338 for programs.
Officers: Robert Price, Pres.; Ronald D. Gifford, Secy.; Robert O. Vore, Treas.
Directors: Harry W. Cripe, Milan Levett, William T. McQueen, Floyd Price.
EIN: 237115879

60302
David G. Buehler Charitable Trust
1100 W. 12th Ave.
Jasper, IN 47546

Established in 1996 in IN.
Donor(s): David G. Buehler.
Financial data (yr. ended 12/31/01): Assets, $677,765 (M); grants paid, $9,625; expenditures, $89,220; qualifying distributions, $9,380.
Limitations: Applications not accepted. Giving primarily in Jasper, IN.
Application information: Contributes only to pre-selected organizations.
Trustee: David G. Buehler.
EIN: 351967992

60303
Bertsch Family Charitable Foundation, Inc.
P.O. Box 1494
Warsaw, IN 46581-1494

Established in 1998.
Financial data (yr. ended 12/31/00): Assets, $658,133 (M); grants paid, $17,000; gifts received, $335,605; expenditures, $32,838; qualifying distributions, $17,000.
Application information: Application form not required.
Officers: Charles E. Bertsch, Pres.; Diane Bertsch, V.P.; June Bertsch, Secy.-Treas.
EIN: 352057621

60304
King's Ranch, Inc.
8173 Davison Rd.
Oldenburg, IN 47036

Established in 1999 in IN.
Donor(s): Vernon King, Phyllis King, Greg King.
Financial data (yr. ended 12/31/99): Assets, $643,706 (M); grants paid, $32,111; gifts received, $685,082; expenditures, $42,873; qualifying distributions, $61,458; giving activities include $29,347 for programs.
Limitations: Applications not accepted.
Application information: Contributes only to pre-selected organizations.
Trustees: Greg King, Phyllis King, Vernon King.
EIN: 352082821

60305
KAHM, Inc.
5735 N. U.S. Hwy. 31
Sharpsville, IN 46068

Classified as a private operating foundation in 1979.
Donor(s): E.W. Kelley.
Financial data (yr. ended 09/30/00): Assets, $619,046 (M); grants paid, $0; gifts received, $47,561; expenditures, $24,537; qualifying distributions, $48,951; giving activities include $9,508 for programs.
Officer: E.W. Kelley, Chair.
EIN: 310964804

60306
Linton Lodge No. 866 B.P.O.E. Foundation, Inc.
State Road 54-E
R.R. 1, Box 368
Linton, IN 47441

Established in 1995 in IN.
Financial data (yr. ended 12/31/99): Assets, $574,475 (M); grants paid, $23,000; expenditures, $23,019; qualifying distributions, $23,019.
Limitations: Giving primarily in Linton, IN.
Officers: Marion Bales, Pres.; Ralph Witty, V.P.; Mike Kelley, Secy.; Mark Robinson, Treas.
EIN: 351955193

60307
Potawatomi Park, Inc.
297 N. Main St.
Bourbon, IN 46504

Classified as a private operating foundation in 1984.
Financial data (yr. ended 06/30/99): Assets, $544,516 (M); grants paid, $1,100; gifts received, $12,104; expenditures, $41,840; qualifying distributions, $1,100.
Officers and Directors:* Barry Davis,* Pres.; Forrest Kantner,* V.P.; William Price,* Secy.; Larry Beeson,* Treas.; Wayne Bessinger.
EIN: 351547849

60308
Durham Home, Inc.
c/o David O'Neall
3506 S. 400 W.
Crawfordsville, IN 47933-1899
(765) 866-1498

Classified as a private operating foundation in 1975.
Financial data (yr. ended 12/31/01): Assets, $542,773 (M); grants paid, $0; gifts received, $120,000; expenditures, $197,961; qualifying distributions, $174,998; giving activities include $175,331 for programs.
Officers: Shirley O'Neall, Pres. and Treas.; Michael O'Neall, V.P.; Lucy Moody, Secy.
Directors: David O'Neall, Charles Phillips.
EIN: 350951864

60309
Foundation for Hand Research and Education
(Formerly Foundation for Surgical Hand Research)
P.O. Box 80434
Indianapolis, IN 46280-0434
Application address: 8501 Harcourt Rd., Indianapolis, IN 46280
Contact: Richard Idler

Established in 1993 in IN. Classified as a company-sponsored operating foundation.
Donor(s): Hand Surgery Associates of Indiana, Inc., James W. Strickland, M.D., James B. Steichen, M.D., William B. Kleinman, M.D., Thomas J. Fischer, M.D., Richard S. Idler, M.D., Robert M. Baltera, M.D.
Financial data (yr. ended 12/31/00): Assets, $540,586 (M); grants paid, $10,000; gifts received, $21,939; expenditures, $112,998; qualifying distributions, $92,303; giving activities include $13,927 for programs.
Limitations: Giving primarily in IN.
Officers: James W. Strickland, M.D., Pres.; Randolph P. Wilson, V.P.; Sandra Wuensch, Secy.; Hilary Salatich, Treas.; Elaine Skopelja, Mgr.
Directors: Allen T. Bishop, M.D., Jeffrey A. Greenberg, M.D., Hill Hastings II, M.D., Carleton A. Keck, Jr., M.D., Thomas R. Keifhaber, M.D., Gary M. Lourie, M.D., Kevin D. Plancher, M.D.
EIN: 351728352

60310
Children are Precious Foundation, Inc.
4253 Windsor Ln.
Columbus, IN 47201

Established in 2000 in IN.
Donor(s): W. Walter Able, Cynthia Ann Able, Susan Diane Able, Nancy Able Morrison, Able Ventures, Inc.
Financial data (yr. ended 11/30/01): Assets, $463,321 (M); grants paid, $12,843; gifts received, $488,400; expenditures, $25,102; qualifying distributions, $24,700.
Limitations: Applications not accepted.
Application information: Contributes only to pre-selected organizations.
Officers: W. Walter Able, Pres.; Joan G. Able, Secy.-Treas.
Directors: Cynthia Ann Able, Susan Diane Able, Nancy Able Morrison.
EIN: 352135341

60311
Norris Family Foundation, Inc.
1125 W. 6th St.
Jasper, IN 47546-2506

Established in 2000 in IN.
Donor(s): Randall Norris, Robin Norris.

Financial data (yr. ended 12/31/00): Assets, $455,934 (M); grants paid, $9,361; gifts received, $498,248; expenditures, $9,511; qualifying distributions, $9,361.
Limitations: Giving primarily in Jasper, IN.
Directors: Randall Norris, Robin Norris.
EIN: 352114824

60312
Richardson Wildlife Sanctuary, Inc.
c/o Dune Acres
64 West Rd.
Chesterton, IN 46304 (219) 787-8983
FAX: (219) 787-1341

Classified as a private operating foundation in 1986.
Donor(s): Flora S. Richardson Irrevocable Trust.
Financial data (yr. ended 12/31/01): Assets, $382,846 (M); grants paid, $0; gifts received, $69,720; expenditures, $60,517; qualifying distributions, $60,848; giving activities include $60,517 for programs.
Publications: Annual report, informational brochure, newsletter.
Officers: Robert F. Hartman, Pres.; Raymond Tindel, V.P.; Barbara Plampin, Treas.
Board Members: John Blew, Donald McVicker, Sue Smith, Doug Wilson.
Trustees: Emmie Ruffin, Michael Stoffregen.
EIN: 351076722

60313
Christian Stewardship Foundation
c/o Edward R. Skillin
P.O. Box 892
Angola, IN 46703-0892

Established in 1998 in IN.
Donor(s): Edward R. Skillin.
Financial data (yr. ended 12/31/00): Assets, $369,009 (M); grants paid, $52,400; gifts received, $70,562; expenditures, $52,870; qualifying distributions, $52,714.
Limitations: Applications not accepted.
Application information: Contributes only to pre-selected organizations.
Officers and Directors:* Edward R. Skillin,* Pres.; Ivan Godwin,* V.P.; Jolene Skillin,* Secy.; Ray Fager,* Treas.; Sheryl Fager, Kristina Godwin.
EIN: 352047703

60314
RPW Foundation, Inc.
(Formerly Wurster Foundation)
c/o Royal Pin Leisure Centers
8463 Castlewood Dr., 2nd Fl.
Indianapolis, IN 46250-1534 (317) 841-1002
Contact: Russell P. Wurster, Pres., or Ralph W. Carter, Secy.-Treas.

Established in 1989 in IN.
Financial data (yr. ended 12/31/01): Assets, $353,840 (M); grants paid, $89,779; gifts received, $123,961; expenditures, $90,536; qualifying distributions, $90,389.
Limitations: Giving limited to IN.
Application information: Application form required.
Officers: Russell P. Wurster, Pres.; Craig A. May, V.P.; Ralph W. Carter, Secy.-Treas.
EIN: 351778480
Codes: FD2, GTI

60315
Mary's King's Village Schoenstatt Center
(Formerly Our Lady of Schoenstatt Retreat)
c/o Fr. Elmer J. Burwinkel
3991 WCR 925-S
Madison, IN 47250

Financial data (yr. ended 12/31/00): Assets, $336,353 (M); grants paid, $900; gifts received, $72,000; expenditures, $4,950; qualifying distributions, $4,950.
Officers and Directors:* Fr. Elmer J. Burwinkel,* Pres.; Judith M. Strzelecki,* Secy.; R.J. Burwinkel.
EIN: 351824939

60316
Jerry E. Clegg Foundation
c/o James E. Peterson
1782 N. 400 E.
Lafayette, IN 47905

Classified as a private operating foundation in 1992.
Financial data (yr. ended 12/31/00): Assets, $330,389 (M); grants paid, $0; gifts received, $366; expenditures, $3,762; qualifying distributions, $0.
Officers: Ronald E. Melichar, Pres.; James E. Peterson, V.P., Treas. and Mgr.; Laura M. Bowker, Secy.
EIN: 356046360

60317
Patton Scholarship Trust
c/o Wells Fargo Bank Indiana, N.A.
P.O. Box 370
Peru, IN 46970
Application address: c/o Superintendent, Twin Lakes School Corp., 565 S. Main St., Monticello, IN 47960

Established in 1993 in IN.
Financial data (yr. ended 02/28/01): Assets, $322,066 (M); grants paid, $17,000; expenditures, $21,923; qualifying distributions, $20,938.
Limitations: Giving limited to residents of Monticello, IN.
Application information: Application form required.
Trustee: Wells Fargo Bank Indiana, N.A.
EIN: 356570391

60318
The Margaret Smith Home, Inc.
c/o U.S. Bank
P.O. Box 818
Richmond, IN 47375

Classified as a private operating foundation in 1972.
Financial data (yr. ended 04/30/01): Assets, $291,057 (M); grants paid, $0; expenditures, $76,641; qualifying distributions, $71,830; giving activities include $71,986 for programs.
Officer: John M. Sayre III, Pres.
EIN: 350957103

60319
Frank and Margaret Arvin Family Trust
c/o Peoples National Bank
P.O. Box 560
Washington, IN 47501

Classified as a private operating foundation in 1995 in IN.
Financial data (yr. ended 12/31/01): Assets, $275,981 (M); grants paid, $4,600; expenditures, $8,203; qualifying distributions, $4,485.
Limitations: Giving primarily in IN.
Trustee: Peoples National Bank.

Committee Members: Michael Andrews, Jean Corbin, Melodie Daily, Richard Lemmon, Donald J. Traylor, Robert Wilson, Joe Woods.
EIN: 356608360

60320
International Friendship Gardens Music Festival, Inc.
Pottowattomie Park
Michigan City, IN 46360

Classified as a private operating foundation in 1974.
Financial data (yr. ended 12/31/99): Assets, $274,580 (M); grants paid, $0; gifts received, $267,895; expenditures, $22,136; qualifying distributions, $22,136; giving activities include $5,905 for programs.
Officers: Barry Criswell, Pres.; George Neagu, V.P.; Shellee Wells, Secy.; Richard Houck, M.D., Treas.
EIN: 356044071

60321
Someone Cares International Fellowship, Inc.
P.O. Box 1199
Goshen, IN 46527-1199

Classified as a private operating foundation in 1981.
Financial data (yr. ended 12/31/01): Assets, $248,500 (M); grants paid, $0; gifts received, $35,422; expenditures, $34,203; qualifying distributions, $0.
Officers: Richard Jaeger, Pres.; David Snyder, V.P.; Jamiran Jaeger, Secy.-Treas.
EIN: 351372051

60322
Ray Oyler Scholarship Foundation, Inc.
70 E. 91st St., Ste. 200
Indianapolis, IN 46240-1550
Application address: c/o Scholarship Review Board, P.O. Box 40389, Indianapolis, IN 46240

Established in 1999 in IN.
Donor(s): Mark T. Duffin, Christopher A. Wirthwein.
Financial data (yr. ended 12/31/00): Assets, $241,927 (M); grants paid, $15,853; gifts received, $124,000; expenditures, $17,931; qualifying distributions, $15,853.
Limitations: Giving primarily in Indianapolis, IN.
Application information: Application form required.
Directors: Mark T. Duffin, Christopher A. Wirthwein.
EIN: 352058358

60323
Cloverdale Indiana Endowment Fund of the Rockwell & Cantwell Families, Inc.
10 N. Main St.
Cloverdale, IN 46120
Contact: Terry Puffer, Pres.

Established in 1965 in IN.
Financial data (yr. ended 12/31/00): Assets, $230,203 (M); grants paid, $9,262; expenditures, $27,052; qualifying distributions, $9,262.
Limitations: Giving limited to the Cloverdale, IN, area.
Officers: Terry Puffer, Pres; Dave Moore, Vice-Pres.; Sharon McNery, Secy.; Steve Walters, Treas.
EIN: 356036883

60324
Your Worship Hour, Inc.
P.O. Box 6094
South Bend, IN 46660

Financial data (yr. ended 04/30/99): Assets, $209,138 (M); grants paid, $0; expenditures, $10,323; qualifying distributions, $9,600; giving activities include $9,600 for programs.
Officers: Marvin E. Engbrecht, Chair.; Charles Miller, Vice-Chair.; Dale Pettifor, Secy.-Treas.
Directors: Gordon Bacon, Katie Sudlow.
EIN: 350960693

60325
Eagle Creek Nature Conservancy and Preservation, Inc.
135 N. Pennsylvania St., Ste. 1750
Indianapolis, IN 46204

Established in 1997 in IN. Classified as a private operating foundation in 1999.
Financial data (yr. ended 12/31/99): Assets, $201,420 (M); grants paid, $1,000; gifts received, $5,300; expenditures, $3,925; qualifying distributions, $3,425.
Limitations: Giving primarily in IN.
Directors: Jane Elder Kunz, Peter F. Kunz.
EIN: 352031657

60326
Big Creek Wildlife Foundation, Inc.
2425 Knob Hill Dr.
Evansville, IN 47711

Established in 1999 in IN.
Financial data (yr. ended 12/31/01): Assets, $195,615 (M); grants paid, $0; expenditures, $5,108; qualifying distributions, $0.
Limitations: Applications not accepted.
Application information: Contributes only to pre-selected organizations.
Officers: Michael L. Sandefur, Pres.; Richard L. Reising, Secy.
Director: Kent A. Brasseale II.
EIN: 352058406

60327
Wayside Foundation
c/o Julie R. Waterfield
12032 Kingsbridge Rd.
Fort Wayne, IN 46814-7555

Established in 2000 in IN.
Donor(s): Julie R. Waterfield.
Financial data (yr. ended 12/31/01): Assets, $170,261 (M); grants paid, $2,300; gifts received, $2,500; expenditures, $12,032; qualifying distributions, $2,300.
Trustees: J. Randall Waterfield, Jill L. Waterfield, Julie R. Waterfield, Richard R. Waterfield.
EIN: 356700048

60328
Thomas D. McGrain Cedar Glade Foundation for the Needy of Harrison County
1150 St. Michaels Rd., S.E.
Laconia, IN 47135-8308
Contact: Jill McGrain Biel, Admin.

Established in 1996 in IN.
Financial data (yr. ended 12/31/99): Assets, $169,436 (M); grants paid, $8,700; expenditures, $9,795; qualifying distributions, $9,237.
Limitations: Giving limited to residents of Harrison County, IN.
Officers: Jill McGrain Biel, Admin.; William H. Davis, Admin.; Rilla E. McGrain, Admin.; Thomas S. McGrain, Admin.; Charles T. Smith, Admin.; Frederick W. Snyder, Jr., Admin.
EIN: 351965505

60329
St. Clair Foundation, Inc.
525 N. Illinois St.
Indianapolis, IN 46204-0210

Established in 2000 in IN.
Donor(s): Grand Lodge Free and Accepted Masons of the State of Indiana.
Financial data (yr. ended 03/31/01): Assets, $163,270 (M); grants paid, $46,000; gifts received, $25,826; expenditures, $46,070; qualifying distributions, $46,000.
Limitations: Applications not accepted.
Application information: Contributes only to pre-selected organizations.
Officers: William S. Spyr, Pres.; Daniel J. Leonard, V.P.; Joseph H. Clark, Secy.; Alex L. Rogers, Treas.; George E. Proctor, Exec. Dir.
Trustees: Robert C. Anderson, William D. Blasingame, Stephen D. Chapman, James L. Chesney, George E. Galyean, Charles M. Hensler, Mark A. Higgins, Joyce Small.
EIN: 352087590

60330
Neff Family Foundation
3890 E. 79th St.
Indianapolis, IN 46240
Contact: Virginia M. Neff, Secy.

Established in 1997 in IN.
Financial data (yr. ended 12/31/00): Assets, $159,831 (M); grants paid, $7,600; gifts received, $38,000; expenditures, $9,032; qualifying distributions, $7,600.
Officers: Betty M. Neff, Pres. and Mgr.; Elizabeth W. Neff, V.P.; Julia D. Neff, V.P.; Virginia M. Neff, Secy.; I. Marie Neff, Treas.
EIN: 352008774

60331
Jeanette Lyons Surina Scholarship Fund, Inc.
c/o Birk, Gross, Bell & Coulter, PC
300 S. Madison Ave., Ste. 210
Greenwood, IN 46142-3124 (317) 299-0058
Contact: Kathleen Surina Grove, Pres.

Established in 1998 in IN.
Financial data (yr. ended 09/30/01): Assets, $146,349 (M); grants paid, $8,000; gifts received, $300; expenditures, $9,758; qualifying distributions, $9,568.
Officers: Kathleen Surina Grove, Pres. and Secy.; Jeffrey W. Birk, Treas.
Directors: Robert K. Brenton, Emily A. Dreyer, Charles C. Lake.
EIN: 351905548

60332
John W. Hillenbrand Memorial Fund, Inc.
c/o John A. Hillenbrand, II
324 Mitchell Ave.
Batesville, IN 47006-9015

Financial data (yr. ended 12/31/01): Assets, $144,554 (M); grants paid, $11,851; expenditures, $12,548; qualifying distributions, $12,548.
Limitations: Applications not accepted. Giving primarily in IN.
Officers: John A. Hillenbrand II, Pres. and Treas.; Ray J. Hillenbrand, V.P.; William G. Hillenbrand, V.P.
EIN: 310934822

60333
Joe and Mary Helen Bennett Scholarship Fund
c/o Donna R. Jones
607 N. C.R. 50 E.
Danville, IN 46122
Application address: c/o Danville Comm. High School, Principal's Office-Bennett Scholarship, 100 Westview Dr., Danville, IN 46122, tel.: (317) 475-2212

Established in 1995 in IN.
Donor(s): Mary Helen Bennett.‡
Financial data (yr. ended 12/31/00): Assets, $137,478 (M); grants paid, $17,100; expenditures, $21,422; qualifying distributions, $17,089.
Limitations: Giving primarily in IN.
Application information: Application form required.
Committee Members: Peter C. Davis, Rebecca Richard, Janet Stephenson, Luann Weed.
Trustee: Donna R. Jones.
EIN: 356605585
Codes: GTI

60334
The Bishop Joseph Chartrand Memorial Scholarship Trust Fund
c/o Harold H.M. Cloud
1046 Mohawk Hills Dr.
Carmel, IN 46032-2899 (317) 846-6787

Established in 1995 in IN.
Donor(s): Harold W. Cloud.
Financial data (yr. ended 12/31/99): Assets, $129,736 (M); grants paid, $7,750; gifts received, $48,004; expenditures, $11,370; qualifying distributions, $11,362.
Limitations: Giving primarily in IN.
Application information: Application form required.
Officers and Trustees:* Harold W. Cloud,* Chair.; John V. Accetturo,* Vice-Chair.; Christine M. Accetturo,* Secy.; James J. Divita, Andrew Stasic, Deborah C. Warner.
EIN: 351940230

60335
Indiana Equity Fund, Inc.
115 W. Washington St., Ste. 1350
Indianapolis, IN 46204-3413

Financial data (yr. ended 12/31/00): Assets, $115,418 (M); grants paid, $0; gifts received, $106,500; expenditures, $114,072; qualifying distributions, $114,072; giving activities include $106,677 for programs.
Officers and Directors:* Kimberly Green,* Chair.; Arlene Colvin,* Vice-Chair.; Dianna O'Rourke,* Secy.; Curtis Heflin, Ronald Katz, Michael Meagher.
EIN: 351905162

60336
Nevelyn Boszor Young Charitable Trust
116 W. Mitchell St.
Kendallville, IN 46755

Established in 2001 in IN.
Financial data (yr. ended 12/31/01): Assets, $110,464 (M); grants paid, $0; expenditures, $500; qualifying distributions, $500.
Limitations: Applications not accepted.
Application information: Contributes only to pre-selected organizations.
Director: John C. Thrapp.
EIN: 356721009

60337
History Dome and Art Park, Inc.
812 S. Washington St.
P.O. Box 1376
Marion, IN 46952
Application address: 38 Blueberry Ln., Alexander, ME 04694
Contact: Roland Paegle, Pres.

Classified as a private operating foundation in 2000. Established in 1999 in ME.
Donor(s): Roland Paegle.
Financial data (yr. ended 12/31/99): Assets, $101,528 (M); grants paid, $600; gifts received, $104,885; expenditures, $3,357; qualifying distributions, $102,208; giving activities include $101,608 for programs.
Officers: Roland Paegle, Pres.; Edward Paegle, Secy.; Grazina Paegle, Treas.
EIN: 311674092

60338
Rex and Alice A. Martin Foundation
1516 Middlebury St.
Elkhart, IN 46516-4740

Established in 2000 in IN.
Donor(s): Rex Martin, Alice A. Martin.
Financial data (yr. ended 06/30/01): Assets, $101,488 (M); grants paid, $0; gifts received, $100,024; expenditures, $0; qualifying distributions, $0.
Officer: Alice A. Martin, Pres.
EIN: 352117025

60339
Holland National Bank Foundation, Inc.
c/o David E. Price
P.O. Box 8
Holland, IN 47541 (812) 536-3131
Contact: Dale Altstadt, Secy.-Treas.

Established in 1991 in IN.
Financial data (yr. ended 12/31/00): Assets, $100,389 (M); grants paid, $5,000; gifts received, $225; expenditures, $5,135; qualifying distributions, $4,952.
Limitations: Giving limited to residents of IN.
Application information: Application form required.
Officers and Directors:* Lee Leinenbach,* Pres.; Deanna Eckert,* V.P.; Dale Altstadt,* Secy.-Treas.; Jerome Blesch, Jerry Hunefeld, Don Prusz.
EIN: 351824938

60340
East Noble Masonic Foundation, Inc.
c/o Kendallville Lodge
P.O. Box 122
Kendallville, IN 46755
Application address: c/o East Noble H.S., Guidance Dept., South Garden St., Kendallville, IN 46755

Established in 1995 in IN.
Financial data (yr. ended 12/31/00): Assets, $100,000 (M); grants paid, $6,750; expenditures, $7,096; qualifying distributions, $7,096.
Limitations: Giving limited to residents of IN.
Application information: Application form required.
Officers: Victor Nantz, Pres.; James Taylor, Secy.-Treas.
EIN: 351925627

60341
Walter O. Wells Foundation, Inc.
221 U.S. 20 West
Middlebury, IN 46540
Application address: c/o Citizens Scholarship Foundation of America (CSFA): P.O. Box 297, 1505 Riverview Rd., St. Peter, MN 56082, tel.: (507) 931-1682

Financial data (yr. ended 12/31/00): Assets, $95,624 (M); grants paid, $5,500; expenditures, $5,920; qualifying distributions, $344.
Application information: Application form required.
Officers: Walter E. Wells, Pres.; Kennard R. Weaver, Secy.
Directors: Robert J. Deputy, John P. Guequirre, Donald R. Pletcher.
EIN: 352007223

60342
S. Ray Miller Auto Museum, Inc.
2130 Middlebury St.
Elkhart, IN 46516

Established in 1996 in IN.
Donor(s): S. Ray Miller.
Financial data (yr. ended 04/30/02): Assets, $90,909 (M); grants paid, $0; gifts received, $57,859; expenditures, $139,272; qualifying distributions, $0.
Officers and Directors:* S. Ray Miller,* Pres.; Linda Miller,* V.P. and Treas.; John S. Frizzo,* Secy.; Eleanor Billey, Tim Weaver.
EIN: 351968620

60343
Ross Foundation, Inc.
P.O. Box 395
Dillsboro, IN 47018 (812) 432-1117
Contact: James Paul Deaton, Pres.

Established in 1989 in IN.
Donor(s): Dellas M. Ross, Dorothea M. Ross.
Financial data (yr. ended 06/30/01): Assets, $88,080 (M); grants paid, $13,500; gifts received, $6,000; expenditures, $14,476; qualifying distributions, $14,476.
Limitations: Giving primarily in Dillsboro, IN.
Officers: James Paul Deaton, Pres.; Harry Hoffman, Secy.; John L. Race, Treas.
Directors: Mike Heffelmire, Londalea Murray, Mary Lou Powers, Barbara Ruble.
EIN: 351796129

60344
DCB Foundation, Inc.
1 DCB Plz.
P.O. Box 550
Jasper, IN 47547-0550

Established in 1954 in IN as a company-sponsored operating foundation.
Donor(s): Dubois County Bank.
Financial data (yr. ended 12/31/00): Assets, $81,884 (M); grants paid, $17,095; expenditures, $17,095; qualifying distributions, $17,095.
Limitations: Applications not accepted. Giving primarily in IN.
Application information: Contributes only to pre-selected organizations.
Officers and Directors:* David E. Eckerle,* Pres.; Martha J. Wehr, Secy.-Treas.; Norbert C. Alles, John S. Chappell, Glenn H. Gramelspacher, Jerry C. Jackle, Andrew B. Krempp, Jack E. Newton, Paul R. Nolting, James J. Sonderman, Ed J. Stenftenagel.
EIN: 356041231
Codes: CD

60345
Kelly Prentiss Scholarship Fund
c/o Horizon Trust & Investment Mgmt.
515 Franklin Sq.
Michigan City, IN 46360
Application address: c/o Horizon Trust & Investment Mgmt., P.O. Box 1125, Michigan City, IN 46361, tel.: (219)873-2629

Financial data (yr. ended 12/31/01): Assets, $76,272 (M); grants paid, $0; expenditures, $1,455; qualifying distributions, $0.
Limitations: Giving limited to residents of La Porte County, IN.
Application information: Application form required.
Trustee: Horizon Trust & Investment Mgmt.
EIN: 356218582

60346
Shaikh Family Charitable Foundation Trust
51301 Shamrock Hill Dr.
Granger, IN 46530-7828

Established in 1999 in IN.
Donor(s): A.Z. Shaikh, Sarah Shaikh.
Financial data (yr. ended 12/31/00): Assets, $75,730 (M); grants paid, $12,030; gifts received, $20,391; expenditures, $17,889; qualifying distributions, $12,030.
Limitations: Applications not accepted.
Application information: Contributes only to pre-selected organizations.
Officers and Trustees:* A.Z. Shaikh,* Pres.; Sarah Shaikh,* Secy.-Treas.
EIN: 356691354

60347
Winkler Family Foundation, Inc.
924 Mill Pointe Ct.
Fort Wayne, IN 46845

Established in 2000.
Donor(s): Donald Winkler, Jane Winkler.
Financial data (yr. ended 12/31/01): Assets, $72,395 (M); grants paid, $0; gifts received, $6,000; expenditures, $58; qualifying distributions, $0.
Officers: Donald Winkler, Pres.; Jane Winkler, V.P.; Gary Winkler, Secy.; Gregory Winkler, Treas.
EIN: 352092914

60348
NiSource Inc. Environmental Challenge Fund
(Formerly NIPSCO Environmental Challenge Fund, Inc.)
c/o Karen McKean
801 E. 86th Ave.
Merrillville, IN 46410 (219) 647-5246

Classified as a company-sponsored operating foundation in 1995 in IN.
Donor(s): NIPSCO Industries, Inc., NiSource Inc.
Financial data (yr. ended 12/31/00): Assets, $61,765 (M); grants paid, $32,937; gifts received, $52,855; expenditures, $40,076; qualifying distributions, $32,958.
Limitations: Giving limited to northern IN.
Application information: Application form required.
Officers: Maria P. Hibbs, Pres.; Victor E. DeMeyer, Secy.; Arthur E. Smith, Treas. and Mgr.
EIN: 351937542
Codes: CD

60349
Nathan Taichert Education Trust
P.O. Box 550
Jasper, IN 47547
Application address: c/o Dubois County Bank, Trust Dept., 1 Dubois County Bank Plz., Jasper, IN 47546-0550

Financial data (yr. ended 02/28/01): Assets, $59,360 (M); grants paid, $0; gifts received, $500; expenditures, $1,585; qualifying distributions, $1,250.
Limitations: Giving limited to Jasper, IN.
Application information: Application form required.
Advisory Committee: Phillip Buecher, Jim Siebert, Joseph Steurer.
Trustee: Old National Trust Co.
EIN: 356025014

60350
Edward N. Kalamaros Family Charitable Foundation, Inc.
328 N. Michigan St., Ste. S-2
South Bend, IN 46601

Financial data (yr. ended 12/31/00): Assets, $48,846 (M); grants paid, $55,500; expenditures, $60,154; qualifying distributions, $59,605.
Limitations: Giving primarily in South Bend, IN.
Officers and Directors:* Philip E. Kalamaros,* Pres.; Timothy E. Kalamaros,* V.P. and Secy.-Treas.; Alexander E. Kalamaros, Harry Kevorkian, Anastasia A. Skalski.
EIN: 352031848

60351
I Have a Dream Foundation
201 W. 103rd St., Ste. 630
Indianapolis, IN 46290

Established in 1989 in IN.
Donor(s): Earl Harris, Carla Harris, Barton L. Kaufman.
Financial data (yr. ended 12/31/01): Assets, $46,088 (M); grants paid, $14,721; expenditures, $14,704; qualifying distributions, $14,686.
Limitations: Applications not accepted.
Application information: Contributes only to pre-selected organizations.
Officers and Directors:* Earl Harris,* Pres.; Carla Harris,* V.P.; Barton L. Kaufman,* Treas.; Robert Elzer.
EIN: 351769495

60352
Howard W. Lickerman Scholarship Fund
c/o Regal Rugs, Inc.
819 Buckeye St.
North Vernon, IN 47265
Contact: Angela Dart, Treas.

Established in 1994.
Financial data (yr. ended 03/31/01): Assets, $45,647 (M); grants paid, $3,750; expenditures, $4,064; qualifying distributions, $3,750.
Application information: Applicant must include SAT or ACT scores, class rank, transcript and a 200-word essay.
Officers: Chris Ertel, Pres.; Howard W. Lickerman, Secy.; Angela D. Dart, Treas.
EIN: 351877528

60353
W. A. Compton Oriental Arts Foundation
P.O. Box 4426
South Bend, IN 46634-4426

Financial data (yr. ended 06/30/00): Assets, $40,326 (M); grants paid, $0; expenditures, $397; qualifying distributions, $0.

Limitations: Applications not accepted.
Application information: Contributes only to pre-selected organizations.
Officer: Gordon E. Compton, Chair.
Trustees: Thomas Westfall, Tom Wutung.
EIN: 510177363

60354
Lingle Family Foundation
P.O. Box 1948
Richmond, IN 47375-1948

Established in 1994 in IN.
Donor(s): Paul W. Lingle, Meadow Park, Inc., Lingle Real Estate, Inc.
Financial data (yr. ended 12/31/01): Assets, $37,994 (M); grants paid, $40,775; gifts received, $55,000; expenditures, $41,397; qualifying distributions, $41,394.
Limitations: Applications not accepted.
Application information: Contributes only to pre-selected organizations.
Trustees: Julie Lingle Gardner, Laura Lee Lingle Luth.
EIN: 351927340

60355
Wildcat Recreation Association, Inc.
1302 E. Creighton Ave.
Fort Wayne, IN 46803-3502

Donor(s): McMillen Foundation, Wildcatters.
Financial data (yr. ended 12/31/01): Assets, $33,787 (M); grants paid, $0; gifts received, $376,564; expenditures, $357,337; qualifying distributions, $357,337; giving activities include $357,337 for programs.
Officers and Directors:* John F. McMillen, Chair.; John S. Grantham,* Pres.; Connie L Grantham, Secy.-Treas.; Payne Brown, Harold L. Donelson, Guenther K. Herzog, Daniel G. Howe.
EIN: 356007400

60356
Nand Krishna Ajay Charitable Fund, Inc.
6928 Yosemite Ct.
Indianapolis, IN 46217
Contact: Girdhar Lall Ahuja, M.D., Pres.

Donor(s): Girdhar Lal Ahuja, M.D., Mohini Ahuja.
Financial data (yr. ended 12/31/01): Assets, $33,692 (M); grants paid, $50,545; gifts received, $29,677; expenditures, $52,762; qualifying distributions, $50,887.
Limitations: Giving primarily in Indianapolis, IN.
Application information: Application form not required.
Officer and Directors:* Girdhar Lal Ahuja, M.D.,* Pres.; Ajay Ahuja, Amarjeet S. Luthra.
EIN: 351668129

60357
William & Fern Breinca Arboretum Foundation, Inc.
421 Blue Ridge Dr.
Bloomington, IN 47408

Established in 2000 in IN.
Donor(s): Janice C. Breinca Peterson.
Financial data (yr. ended 12/31/00): Assets, $29,607 (M); grants paid, $0; gifts received, $26,038; expenditures, $2,593; qualifying distributions, $38; giving activities include $100 for programs.
Limitations: Applications not accepted.
Application information: Contributes only to pre-selected organizations.
Officers and Trustees:* Janice C. Breinca Peterson,* Pres.; Marijhan Hunter,* V.P.; James A. Paterson,* Secy.-Treas.
EIN: 352063991

60358
Aremus Foundation, Inc.
111 Monument Cir., Ste. 900
Indianapolis, IN 46204-5125

Established in 2001 in IN.
Donor(s): Richard M. Stoeppelwerth.
Financial data (yr. ended 12/31/01): Assets, $28,447 (M); grants paid, $0; gifts received, $30,000; expenditures, $1,553; qualifying distributions, $0.
Officers: Brian C. Bosma, Pres.; Robert T. Mullin, Secy.; Stephen E. Hussey, Treas.
EIN: 352139947

60359
Ferman "Fuzzy" Rice Memorial Scholarship Fund
c/o White & White
P.O. Box 98
Covington, IN 47932-0098
Application addresses: 351 N. Shale Pit Rd., Veedersburg, IN 47987; c/o David Ziegler, Tr., 2076 E. 130 N., Veedersburg, IN 47987; c/o Linn Allen, Tr., 2956 E. Grain Bin Rd., Veedersburg, IN 47987
Contact: Lois Rice Ingalsbe, Tr.

Established in 1995 in IN.
Financial data (yr. ended 12/31/99): Assets, $23,044 (M); grants paid, $1,750; expenditures, $1,979; qualifying distributions, $1,956.
Trustees: Linn Allen, Lois Rice Ingalsbe, David Ziegler.
EIN: 356615248

60360
Royal Purcell Trust for Knowledge
c/o Royal Purcell
806 W. 2nd St.
Bloomington, IN 47403-2213

Classified as a private operating foundation in 1993.
Financial data (yr. ended 12/31/00): Assets, $20,867 (M); grants paid, $0; gifts received, $500; expenditures, $460; qualifying distributions, $0.
Director: Royal Purcell.
EIN: 351854808

60361
Friends of the Fort Foundation
5733 Cherry Hill Dr.
Newburgh, IN 47630-3294

Established in 1999 in IN.
Donor(s): Judy Kropfl.
Financial data (yr. ended 06/30/00): Assets, $19,871 (M); grants paid, $0; gifts received, $22,559; expenditures, $3,237; qualifying distributions, $3,099; giving activities include $3,099 for programs.
Trustee: Peter Cashel-Cordo.
Board Member: Lou Dennis.
EIN: 352083587

60362
Jacobi Family Foundation, Inc.
128 Valentine Ct.
Michigan City, IN 46360 (219) 879-7974
Contact: Mark D. Jacobi, Pres.

Classified as a private operating foundation in 1987.
Donor(s): Mark D. Jacobi, Hal L. Jacobi, Paula K. Jacobi.
Financial data (yr. ended 12/31/99): Assets, $19,575 (M); grants paid, $30,140; gifts received, $25,572; expenditures, $30,896; qualifying distributions, $30,140.

Officers: Mark D. Jacobi, Pres.; Paula K. Jacobi, V.P.; Judith Jacobi, Secy.
EIN: 351700105

60363
Chegar Foundation
3855 E. 106th St.
Carmel, IN 46033

Established in 1998 in IN.
Donor(s): Richard D. Chegar, Carol H. Chegar.
Financial data (yr. ended 09/30/00): Assets, $19,334 (M); grants paid, $500; gifts received, $10,150; expenditures, $826; qualifying distributions, $826.
Limitations: Applications not accepted.
Application information: Contributes only to pre-selected organizations.
Trustees: Carol H. Chegar, Richard D. Chegar.
EIN: 352063034

60364
Freeman-Spicer Charities, Inc.
316 S. Eddy St.
South Bend, IN 46617
Contact: Edward C. Levy, Pres.

Established in 1993 in IN.
Financial data (yr. ended 12/31/00): Assets, $19,075 (M); grants paid, $6,899; gifts received, $7,098; expenditures, $7,293; qualifying distributions, $7,133.
Limitations: Giving primarily in IN.
Officers: Edward C. Levy, Pres.; Eli Spicer, V.P.; Susan Levy, Secy.-Treas.
EIN: 351878608

60365
Insight Center, Inc.
4905 E. 56th St.
Indianapolis, IN 46220

Established in 1998 in IN.
Donor(s): Katharine L. Elliott.
Financial data (yr. ended 12/31/99): Assets, $18,107 (M); grants paid, $0; gifts received, $218,054; expenditures, $236,188; qualifying distributions, $216,523; giving activities include $141,199 for programs.
Officer and Director:* Katharine L. Elliott,* Pres.
EIN: 352047676

60366
St. Joseph County Medical Society Educational Foundation, Inc.
919 E. Jefferson Blvd., No. 105
South Bend, IN 46617-3115
Contact: James E. Reidy, M.D., Pres.

Donor(s): St. Joseph County Medical Society.
Financial data (yr. ended 09/30/01): Assets, $14,772 (M); grants paid, $7,000; gifts received, $3,979; expenditures, $7,460; qualifying distributions, $7,371.
Limitations: Giving primarily in IN.
Application information: Application form required.
Officer: James E. Reidy, M.D., Pres.
EIN: 310935856

60367
Yves R. Simon Institute, Inc.
508 Travers Cir.
Mishawaka, IN 46545

Classified as a private operating foundation in 1988.
Financial data (yr. ended 12/31/00): Assets, $12,456 (M); grants paid, $3,175; gifts received, $4,650; expenditures, $11,558; qualifying distributions, $5,949.

Officers and Director:* Dean Hudson, Chair.; Anthony O. Simon,* Pres.
EIN: 311248580

60368
Jericho Society for Pet Population Control, Inc.
c/o Henry Sakowitz
P.O. Box 187
Danville, IN 46122-0187

Established in 1988.
Donor(s): Henry Sakowitz.
Financial data (yr. ended 12/31/99): Assets, $6,979 (M); grants paid, $0; gifts received, $9,837; expenditures, $104,870; qualifying distributions, $104,407; giving activities include $39,684 for programs.
Directors: Brian Huot, Sherry Sakowitz.
EIN: 311193704

60369
Earles Family Charitable Foundation
P.O. Box 381
Ellettsville, IN 47429

Established in 1999 in IN.
Donor(s): William H. Earles.
Financial data (yr. ended 12/31/99): Assets, $4,994 (M); grants paid, $30,000; gifts received, $35,000; expenditures, $30,010; qualifying distributions, $30,000.
Limitations: Applications not accepted.
Application information: Contributes only to pre-selected organizations.
Trustee: William H. Earles.
EIN: 352083980

60370
Jefferson County Animal Welfare Fund, Inc.
c/o Mary G. Clashman
801 Filmore St.
Madison, IN 47250 (812) 265-2088

Classified as a private operating foundation in 1992.
Financial data (yr. ended 06/30/00): Assets, $4,548 (M); grants paid, $489; gifts received, $171; expenditures, $554; qualifying distributions, $437.
Limitations: Giving primarily in Jefferson County, IN and surrounding counties.
Directors: Merritt K. Alcorn, Mary G. Clashman, John Petscher, John Wurtz.
EIN: 351836388

60371
Hartman Arboretum, Inc.
5939 Spirit Trail
Evansville, IN 47720

Financial data (yr. ended 12/31/01): Assets, $3,060 (M); grants paid, $0; gifts received, $5,000; expenditures, $1,988; qualifying distributions, $0; giving activities include $1,988 for programs.
Officer: Grant H. Hartman, Jr., Pres.
EIN: 352140627

60372
Wheeler Christian Foundation
c/o Pickart, Weiss & Assoc.
911 Broadway, Ste. NN
Merrillville, IN 46410

Established in 1967.
Donor(s): Charles R. Wheeler.
Financial data (yr. ended 12/31/00): Assets, $2,981 (M); grants paid, $46,070; gifts received, $50,500; expenditures, $50,851; qualifying distributions, $46,070.
Limitations: Applications not accepted.
Application information: Contributes only to pre-selected organizations.
Officer: Charles R. Wheeler, Pres.
EIN: 356076275

60373
Jesus Christ Unlimited Evangelistic Association, Inc.
c/o Thomas B. Moore
1201 S. Elizabeth St.
Kokomo, IN 46902

Donor(s): Thomas Budd Moore, Marcillitta A. Moore.
Financial data (yr. ended 12/31/00): Assets, $2,670 (M); grants paid, $1,494; gifts received, $3,069; expenditures, $3,093; qualifying distributions, $32,076.
Limitations: Giving on a national basis.
Officers and Trustees:* Thomas Budd Moore,* Pres.; Marcillitta A. Moore,* V.P. and Treas.; Jon Sprinkle, Paula Sprinkle.
EIN: 351864749

60374
Team Indiana
7645 Cedarbrook Dr.
Indianapolis, IN 46227

Financial data (yr. ended 12/31/00): Assets, $1,614 (M); grants paid, $0; expenditures, $2,601; qualifying distributions, $0.
Officers: Wiley Embry, Pres.; Bert Tisserand, Secy.
EIN: 351870887

60375
Torabi Foundation, Inc.
2510 E. 37th Ave.
Lake Station, IN 46405

Established in 2000 in IN. Classified as a private operating foundation in 2001.
Donor(s): Tooraj Torabi.
Financial data (yr. ended 12/31/00): Assets, $97 (M); grants paid, $237; gifts received, $2,565; expenditures, $2,468; qualifying distributions, $2,468; giving activities include $2,468 for programs.
Officers: Tooraj Torabi, Pres.; Soraya Alavi Torabi, V.P.; Diana Barker, Secy.
EIN: 352092826

60376
Ispat Inland Foundation, Inc.
3210 Watling St.
East Chicago, IN 46312
Contact: J. Medelin, V.P.

Established in 2000 in IN.
Financial data (yr. ended 12/31/01): Assets, $0 (M); grants paid, $526,447; gifts received, $535,638; expenditures, $535,638; qualifying distributions, $530,282.
Limitations: Giving primarily in IN.
Officers and Directors:* William Mundell,* Pres. and Treas.; Joseph Medellin,* V.P.; John Nielsen,* V.P.; Marc Jeske,* Secy.
EIN: 352121803
Codes: FD

60377
D. R. Keltsch Family Foundation, Inc.
5009 Chaucer Dr.
Fort Wayne, IN 46835

Established in 1990 in IN.
Donor(s): Don Keltsch, Jane Keltsch.
Financial data (yr. ended 12/31/99): Assets, $0 (M); grants paid, $7,370; gifts received, $7,000; expenditures, $7,430; qualifying distributions, $7,430.
Limitations: Giving limited to Fort Wayne, IN.

Officer and Directors:* Jane Keltsch,* Pres.; Richard M. Keltsch, Wendy M. Wight.
EIN: 351783931

IOWA

60378
The Stanley Foundation
209 Iowa Ave.
Muscatine, IA 52761
FAX: (319) 264-0864; E-mail: Stanley@stanleyfdn.org.; URL: http://www.stanleyfdn.org

Incorporated in 1956 in IA; classified as an operating foundation in 1972.
Financial data (yr. ended 12/31/00): Assets, $103,534,998 (M); grants paid, $0; gifts received, $627,230; expenditures, $5,516,141; qualifying distributions, $4,217,030; giving activities include $4,111,760 for programs.
Limitations: Giving primarily in IA.
Publications: Occasional report, informational brochure.
Officers and Directors:* Richard H. Stanley,* Chair. and Pres.; Lynn Stanley,* Vice Chair.; Mary Jo Stanley,* Vice-Chair.; Jeffrey Martin, V.P., Comm.; Joan Winship, V.P., Outreach; Mark Sidel, V.P.; Dana Pittman, Secy.-Treas.; Brian Hanson, Jane Avery Stephenson.
Board Members: Donna Buckley, Alice Chasan, Lawrence Martz, Michael L. McNulty, Teri Schure, Elizabeth Shriver, Joseph P. Stanley, Nathan Woodlit Stanley, Sarah C. Stanley.
EIN: 426071036

60379
Clarissa C. Cooks Home for the Friendless
c/o Well Fargo Bank Iowa, N.A.
203 W. 3rd St.
Davenport, IA 52801

Financial data (yr. ended 05/31/01): Assets, $9,091,234 (M); grants paid, $0; gifts received, $1,041; expenditures, $401,584; qualifying distributions, $0.
Officers: Julia Thorsen, Pres.; June Hebber, V.P.; Olive Gallagher, Secy.; Rick Jennings, Treas.
Trustee: Wells Fargo Bank Iowa, N.A.
EIN: 420723017

60380
H. W. Grout Trust
503 South St.
Waterloo, IA 50701-1517

Classified as a private operating foundation in 1972.
Donor(s): Carl A. Bluedorn, Jean D. Parker, Cultural Enrichment Group.
Financial data (yr. ended 06/30/00): Assets, $8,776,267 (M); grants paid, $0; gifts received, $311,141; expenditures, $516,169; qualifying distributions, $504,339; giving activities include $504,339 for programs.
Officer and Trustees:* Edward Gallagher, Jr.,* Chair.; John J. Burns, Helen Guernsey, Jean D. Parker.
EIN: 237416881

60381
The John R. and Zelda Z. Grubb Charitable Foundation
2755 106th St.
Des Moines, IA 50322

Established in 1995 in IA.
Donor(s): John R. Grubb, John R. Grubb, Inc.
Financial data (yr. ended 12/31/00): Assets, $5,290,561 (M); grants paid, $629,714; expenditures, $4,489,821; qualifying distributions, $629,714; giving activities include $3,860,107 for programs.
Limitations: Applications not accepted. Giving primarily in IA.
Application information: Contributes only to pre-selected organizations.
Officer: John R. Grubb, Pres.
Trustees: John W. Grubb, Zelda Z. Grubb.
EIN: 426521745
Codes: FD

60382
Home for Aged Women
c/o Michael McDermott
115 3rd St. S.E.
Cedar Rapids, IA 52401-1222

Donor(s): Ella Johnson Miller.‡
Financial data (yr. ended 12/31/99): Assets, $5,069,612 (M); grants paid, $0; expenditures, $485,906; qualifying distributions, $254,777; giving activities include $446,182 for programs.
Officers and Directors:* Madge Phillips,* Pres.; Chuck Gardner,* V.P.; Michael O. McDermott,* Secy.; Hugo C. Burdt,* Treas.; Helen Arnold-Olsen, Robert Buckley, Pat Carstensen, Russell E. Curtis, Marvin Dais, Linda Drzycimski, Kay Jackson, R.D. Metcalf, Linda Smith.
EIN: 420681101

60383
F. William Beckwith & Leola I. Beckwith Charitable Foundation
P.O. Box 70
Boone, IA 50036-0070
Contact: F. William Beckwith, Pres.

Established in 1995.
Donor(s): F. William Beckwith, Leola I. Beckwith.
Financial data (yr. ended 12/31/01): Assets, $3,095,593 (M); grants paid, $266,025; gifts received, $483,040; expenditures, $267,015; qualifying distributions, $265,688.
Officers: F. William Beckwith, Pres. and Treas.; Leola I. Beckwith, Secy.
EIN: 421448419
Codes: FD

60384
John & Mary Pappajohn Art Foundation
2116 Financial Ctr.
Des Moines, IA 50309

Established in 1996.
Financial data (yr. ended 09/30/01): Assets, $2,360,594 (M); grants paid, $0; gifts received, $10,000; expenditures, $9,242; qualifying distributions, $9,231; giving activities include $9,231 for programs.
Directors: John Pappajohn, Mary Pappajohn, Ann Vassiliou.
EIN: 391870708

60385
Bickelhaupt Arboretum
340 S. 14th St.
Clinton, IA 52732-5432

Donor(s): Robert E. Bickelhaupt, Frances K. Bickelhaupt.
Financial data (yr. ended 12/31/00): Assets, $2,290,964 (M); grants paid, $0; gifts received, $364,670; expenditures, $227,407; qualifying distributions, $199,425; giving activities include $199,784 for programs.
Officers and Directors:* Robert E. Bickelhaupt,* Pres.; Frances K. Bickelhaupt,* 1st V.P. and Secy.; Linda A. Galanis,* 2nd V.P.; Alan Craig, A.H. Epstein, Justin C. Harper, Ed Hasselkus, Shawn Hill-Lamb, Kathryn Robbins, Pete Wessels.
EIN: 421020739

60386
King's Daughters Home for Old People
c/o Burlington Bank & Trust
222 N. Main St.
Burlington, IA 52601

Classified as a private operating foundation in 1992.
Financial data (yr. ended 03/31/00): Assets, $2,254,118 (M); grants paid, $9,775; gifts received, $20,525; expenditures, $148,408; qualifying distributions, $101,473; giving activities include $123,270 for programs.
Limitations: Applications not accepted. Giving primarily in IA.
Application information: Contributes only to pre-selected organizations.
Officers and Directors:* Lois Fort,* Pres.; Carol Dodge,* V.P.; Jeanette Fisher,* Secy.; Ruth Blackwood,* Treas.; Vivian Kellar, Patricia Latty, Ruth Rowley, and 12 additional directors.
Trustee: Burlington Bank & Trust.
EIN: 420627329

60387
Iowa Pharmacy Foundation
8515 Douglas Ave., Ste. 16
Urbandale, IA 50322-2900 (515) 270-0713
Contact: Thomas R. Temple, Secy.-Treas.

Established in 1988 in IA.
Donor(s): Marion Laboratories, Inc., The Upjohn Co., PNI, Inc., McKesson Foundation, Inc.
Financial data (yr. ended 12/31/99): Assets, $1,712,013 (M); grants paid, $30,500; gifts received, $219,052; expenditures, $536,982; qualifying distributions, $299,825; giving activities include $492,621 for programs.
Limitations: Giving limited to IA.
Application information: Application form not required.
Officers: Susan Frey, Pres.; Mark Richards, V.P.; Thomas R. Temple, Secy.-Treas.
EIN: 426075767
Codes: GTI

60388
The Christian & Lou Utz Zeidler Trust
622 N. 1st St.
Rockwell, IA 50469

Classified as a private operating foundation.
Financial data (yr. ended 12/31/00): Assets, $1,617,708 (M); grants paid, $0; expenditures, $39,603; qualifying distributions, $99,283; giving activities include $95,788 for programs.
Officers and Trustees:* Wendell Thomas, Pres.; Betty Huntbatch, V.P.; Sharon Kruckenberg,* Secy.-Treas.; Shirley Ballhagen, Dan Bram, Lester Dhondt, Steve Karabetsos, Kathy McGee, Lynn Weir, Kathy Wilson.
EIN: 426451771

60389
Grinnell Athletic and Recreation Center
P.O. Box 686
Grinnell, IA 50112-0686

Donor(s): Claude W. and Dolly Ahrens Foundation.
Financial data (yr. ended 09/30/00): Assets, $1,554,651 (M); grants paid, $0; gifts received, $511,317; expenditures, $204,538; qualifying distributions, $489,928; giving activities include $114,267 for programs.
Directors: Chad W. Ahrens, Julie Gosselink, Shannon Kintzinger, Mark Mawe, Jim Ramsey, Tracee Van Arkel, Susan E. Witt.
EIN: 421465766

60390
Wilder Memorial Museum, Inc.
c/o Jacquelyn Opperman
123 W. Mission St.
Strawberry Point, IA 52076

Established in 1996 in IA.
Donor(s): Marcey Alderson.‡
Financial data (yr. ended 12/31/01): Assets, $1,264,093 (M); grants paid, $0; gifts received, $310; expenditures, $29,569; qualifying distributions, $23,756.
Officers: Albert Hock, Pres.; Jon Banse, V.P.; Tara Baumgartner, Secy.; Jackie Opperman, Treas.
Directors: Margaret E. Bagby, Larry DeShaw, Laura Herrald, Haleisa Johnson, Linda Lenz, Helen Thomas.
EIN: 421463547

60391
Altoona Za-Ga-Zig Memorial Shrine Park
P.O. Box 35456
Des Moines, IA 50315

Established in 1997 in IA.
Donor(s): Kathleen G. Heiken, Richard D. Heiken.
Financial data (yr. ended 12/31/00): Assets, $1,244,335 (M); grants paid, $0; expenditures, $1,835; qualifying distributions, $0.
Limitations: Applications not accepted.
Officers: Richard D. Heiken, Pres.; Kathleen G. Heiken, Secy.-Treas.
Director: Jeff McDonald.
EIN: 421417484

60392
Morton J. and Maisie Kaplan Foundation
P.O. Box 627
Sioux City, IA 51102-0627

Established in 1991 in IA.
Donor(s): Morton J. Kaplan.
Financial data (yr. ended 09/30/01): Assets, $1,193,349 (M); grants paid, $60,312; expenditures, $60,989; qualifying distributions, $60,989.
Limitations: Applications not accepted. Giving primarily in Sioux City, IA.
Application information: Contributes only to pre-selected organizations.
Directors: Daniel F. Kaplan, David N. Kaplan.
EIN: 421377146

60393
Spencer Community School Foundation
23 E. 7th St.
Spencer, IA 51301 (712) 262-8950
Contact: Glen Lohman, Secy.

Classified as a private operating foundation in 1992.
Donor(s): Randall Trust, Mr. Hoeppner,‡ Marvin Kruse.

Financial data (yr. ended 12/31/00): Assets, $1,082,085 (M); grants paid, $64,297; gifts received, $57,976; expenditures, $74,165; qualifying distributions, $64,385.
Limitations: Giving limited to residents of Spencer, IA.
Officers: Chuck Pletke, Pres.; Glen Lohman, Secy.; David Woodcock, Treas.
EIN: 421306327

60394
H. Carl & William Lage Loan & Scholarship Trust Fund
2309B Chatburn Ave.
Harlan, IA 51537
Application address: c/o Harlan Community Schools, 2102 Durant St., Harlan, IA 51537
Contact: Robert J. Broomfield, Supt.

Financial data (yr. ended 10/31/00): Assets, $894,710 (M); grants paid, $35,154; expenditures, $38,177; qualifying distributions, $47,892; giving activities include $35,154 for loans to individuals.
Limitations: Giving limited to Harlan, IA.
Application information: Application form not required.
Officer and Directors:* Gaige Lytle,* Pres.; Karla Berndt, Suzy Larson Christensen, Larry Hopp, Steve Kenkel, Dennis Opheim, Donald Schomers.
Loan Committee: Roy Baker, Kent Klinkefus, J.C. Salvo.
EIN: 420369519
Codes: GTI

60395
The Britt Foundation
1840 S. Grandview Ave.
Dubuque, IA 52003-7919

Established in 1998.
Financial data (yr. ended 12/31/00): Assets, $885,279 (M); grants paid, $55,000; gifts received, $269,337; expenditures, $58,154; qualifying distributions, $55,000.
Limitations: Applications not accepted. Giving limited to Dubuque, IA.
Application information: Contributes only to pre-selected organizations.
Officer: Berlinda L. Britt, Mgr.
EIN: 421467630

60396
Paul S. Shepherd Charitable Trust
c/o U.S. Bank
123 E. 3rd St.
Ottumwa, IA 52501

Financial data (yr. ended 12/31/01): Assets, $869,915 (M); grants paid, $48,354; expenditures, $57,670; qualifying distributions, $48,400.
Limitations: Applications not accepted. Giving limited to Ottumwa, IA.
Application information: Contributes only to pre-selected organizations.
Trustee: U.S. Bank.
EIN: 426462993

60397
Fisher Governor Foundation
112 W. Church St.
Marshalltown, IA 50158-2863

Financial data (yr. ended 12/31/01): Assets, $852,147 (M); grants paid, $0; gifts received, $63,832; expenditures, $136,276; qualifying distributions, $0.
Officer: Rex J. Ryden, Treas.
Director: Ken Anderson.
EIN: 426068730

60398
Hobart A. and Alta V. Ross Family Foundation
P.O. Box AK
Spirit Lake, IA 51360
Contact: Keith A. Ross, Pres.

Established in 1985 in IA.
Financial data (yr. ended 12/31/00): Assets, $731,054 (M); grants paid, $114,500; expenditures, $116,431; qualifying distributions, $114,930.
Limitations: Giving primarily in Dickinson County, IA, and neighboring counties.
Application information: Form letter requests from outside geographic area not encouraged.
Officer and Directors:* Keith A. Ross,* Pres.; Larry Ross, Robert Ross, Michael Stineman.
EIN: 421242755
Codes: FD2

60399
Brenton Arboretum, Inc.
c/o J.C. Brenton
2600 Grand Ave., Ste. 218
Des Moines, IA 50312

Classified as a private operating foundation in 1998 in IA.
Donor(s): J.C. Brenton, Sue R. Brenton.
Financial data (yr. ended 12/31/00): Assets, $698,365 (M); grants paid, $0; gifts received, $155,445; expenditures, $82,490; qualifying distributions, $0; giving activities include $82,490 for programs.
Officers and Directors:* J.C. Brenton,* Pres.; Sue R. Brenton,* V.P.; Kenneth R. Brenton,* Secy.-Treas.; Julie Ann Brenton, Lockie Brenton Markusen.
EIN: 311578089

60400
Des Moines I Have a Dream Foundation
P.O. Box 805
Grinnell, IA 50112-0809

Classified as a private operating foundation in 1990.
Donor(s): Toni Jacobson, Joan Middleton, Lyle Middleton.
Financial data (yr. ended 06/30/99): Assets, $650,115 (M); grants paid, $13,938; gifts received, $38,249; expenditures, $69,918; qualifying distributions, $69,768; giving activities include $69,768 for programs.
Limitations: Applications not accepted.
Application information: Unsolicited requests for funds not accepted.
Directors: Carolyn Bucksbaum, Thomas J. Gaard, David Kruidenier, Robert E. Manheimer, James C. Work.
EIN: 421338832

60401
Amana Colonies Historical Sites Foundation
P.O. Box 189
Amana, IA 52203

Classified as a private operating foundation in 1995.
Financial data (yr. ended 12/31/01): Assets, $621,782 (M); grants paid, $0; gifts received, $62,389; expenditures, $93,519; qualifying distributions, $48,668; giving activities include $48,861 for programs.
Officers and Directors:* Reynold C. Moessner,* Pres.; Laura Hoover, Secy.; Lisa McGrath, Treas.; Lenny Haldy, Gordon Kellenberger, Roy Moser, Bruce Trumpold.
EIN: 421427266

60402
Ann & Mary Gilbert Charitable Trust
c/o Wells Fargo Bank Iowa, N.A.
P.O. Box 411
Mason City, IA 50402-0411

Established in 1993 in IA.
Financial data (yr. ended 06/30/01): Assets, $567,747 (M); grants paid, $69,129; expenditures, $75,864; qualifying distributions, $68,864.
Limitations: Applications not accepted. Giving primarily in IA.
Application information: Contributes only to pre-selected organizations.
Trustee: Wells Fargo Bank Iowa, N.A.
EIN: 426506489

60403
Molinaro Family Charitable Foundation
3545 Augusta Cir.
Waterloo, IA 50701
Application address: P.O. Box 420, Waterloo, IA 50704-0420, tel.: (319) 233-6113
Contact: Arthur Hellum, Secy.

Established in 1998 in IA.
Financial data (yr. ended 12/31/99): Assets, $495,998 (M); grants paid, $7,500; expenditures, $10,916; qualifying distributions, $10,844.
Officers: Robert Molinaro, Pres.; Mary Ellen Molinaro, V.P.; Arthur Hellum, Secy.; Tunis Den Hartog, Treas.
EIN: 421480506

60404
WTI Charitable Foundation
P.O. Box 420
Waterloo, IA 50704-0420
Contact: Arthur Hellum, Secy.

Established in 1998 in IA.
Financial data (yr. ended 12/31/99): Assets, $495,998 (M); grants paid, $22,500; gifts received, $110,000; expenditures, $28,253; qualifying distributions, $28,114.
Officers: Robert Molinaro, Pres.; Mary Ellen Molinaro, V.P.; Arthur Hellum, Secy.; Tunis Den Hartog, Treas.
EIN: 421480934

60405
Rippey Senior Citizens Apartments, Inc.
2954 144 Diagonal
Rippey, IA 50235-7001
Contact: M.M. Radebaugh, Pres.

Financial data (yr. ended 12/31/01): Assets, $490,937 (M); grants paid, $5,100; expenditures, $29,501; qualifying distributions, $13,606.
Officers: M.M. Radebaugh, Pres.; Myron Rinker, V.P.; Betty Young, Secy.; Doris Stewart, Treas.
Director: Ray Bardole.
EIN: 237083326

60406
The Cause No. CL3613 Foundation, Inc
705 Perdock Ct.
Washington, IA 52353 (319) 653-5716
Contact: Richard See, Treas.

Established in 1997 in IA.
Financial data (yr. ended 06/30/00): Assets, $490,596 (M); grants paid, $26,125; expenditures, $27,569; qualifying distributions, $25,847.
Limitations: Giving primarily in IA.
Application information: Application form required.

Officers: Robert J. McConnell, Pres.; Darlene Hecke, V.P.; Don Schmidt, Co-Secy.; Dorothy Schmidt, Co-Secy.; Richard See, Treas.
EIN: 421466768

60407
Mary Catherine Hagedorn Trust
c/o Thomas L. McCullough
P.O. Box 305
Lake View, IA 51450-0305
Contact: Msgr. James K. Lafferty, Tr.

Established in 1979 in IA.
Financial data (yr. ended 10/31/00): Assets, $428,208 (M); grants paid, $11,065; expenditures, $18,240; qualifying distributions, $18,083.
Limitations: Giving limited to IA.
Trustee: Msgr. James K. Lafferty.
EIN: 426291418

60408
The Freda B. & William H. Smith Trust
c/o First State Bank of Conrad
P.O. Box 10
Conrad, IA 50621-0010 (515) 366-2165

Established in 1992 in IA.
Financial data (yr. ended 12/31/01): Assets, $385,132 (M); grants paid, $24,600; expenditures, $32,323; qualifying distributions, $26,480.
Limitations: Giving limited to residents of Beaman, Conrad, and Liscomb, IA.
Application information: Application form required.
Trustee: First State Bank of Conrad.
EIN: 426478959
Codes: GTI

60409
Adora S. Jones Ministerial Trust
c/o Wells Fargo Bank Iowa, N.A.
101 3rd Ave. S.W.
Cedar Rapids, IA 52406-1967

Donor(s): Adora S. Jones.‡
Financial data (yr. ended 12/31/01): Assets, $356,616 (M); grants paid, $27,500; expenditures, $33,346; qualifying distributions, $27,500.
Limitations: Giving limited to residents of IA.
Trustee: Wells Fargo Bank Iowa, N.A.
EIN: 426506484

60410
The Leeper Scholarship Foundation
P.O. Box 180
Lineville, IA 50147-0180
Contact: Janet A. Mortimore, Secy.

Established in 1998.
Donor(s): Lowell Leeper, May Leeper.
Financial data (yr. ended 12/31/01): Assets, $297,042 (M); grants paid, $9,600; gifts received, $960; expenditures, $9,645; qualifying distributions, $9,379.
Limitations: Giving limited to Wayne County townships: Clinton, Grand River, Jefferson, and Warren; and the Decatur County townships: Eden, Hamilton, Morgan, and Woodland, IA.
Application information: Application form required.
Officers: James R. Cornet, Pres.; Robert M. Mortimore, V.P.; Janet A. Mortimore, Secy.; Jack Shields, Treas.
EIN: 470818991

60411
New Sharon Community Enterprises
c/o Jane L. Coffey
P.O. Box 113
New Sharon, IA 50207

Classified as a private operating foundation in 1977.
Financial data (yr. ended 07/31/00): Assets, $290,152 (M); grants paid, $0; gifts received, $31,439; expenditures, $14,114; qualifying distributions, $14,114; giving activities include $7,933 for programs.
Officers: Charles H. Lindhorst, Pres.; Larry Applegate, V.P.; Jane L. Coffey, Secy.-Treas.
Directors: Jean Davis, Wendell Knowler, Earl Schock, Arlene Stilwell, Bertha Ver Steegh.
EIN: 510148217

60412
Duane & Evelyn Munter Charitable Trust
c/o Union Bank & Trust Co.
P.O. Box 4
Strawberry Point, IA 52076

Financial data (yr. ended 07/31/01): Assets, $270,872 (M); grants paid, $13,183; expenditures, $15,039; qualifying distributions, $13,183.
Application information: Unsolicited request for funds not accepted.
Trustees: Alpha Evans, Mauree Roads, Union Bank & Trust Co.
EIN: 421286829

60413
Mabel Vacek Scholarship Trust
c/o Citizens State Bank
P.O. Box 198
Wyoming, IA 52362-0198

Financial data (yr. ended 12/31/00): Assets, $260,697 (L); grants paid, $2,505; gifts received, $799; expenditures, $4,769; qualifying distributions, $4,769.
Limitations: Applications not accepted. Giving primarily in Oxford Junction, IA.
Trustee: Citizens State Bank.
EIN: 426580517

60414
A. L. Lake Trust
c/o Wells Fargo Bank Iowa, N.A.
P.O. Box 411
Mason City, IA 50402-0411

Donor(s): Clara R.H. Lake.‡
Financial data (yr. ended 06/30/00): Assets, $220,684 (M); grants paid, $5,670; expenditures, $8,832; qualifying distributions, $6,572.
Limitations: Applications not accepted. Giving limited to Mason City, IA.
Application information: Contributes only to pre-selected organizations.
Trustee: Wells Fargo Bank Iowa, N.A.
EIN: 426101549

60415
Raccoon Valley Humane Society
2775 Fairgrounds Rd.
Adel, IA 50003

Financial data (yr. ended 12/31/01): Assets, $206,321 (M); grants paid, $0; gifts received, $140,426; expenditures, $129,086; qualifying distributions, $129,086; giving activities include $123,987 for programs.
Officers: Jean Bromert, Pres.; Doran Ryan, Treas.
Directors: Margaret Ann Ellis, Robert Ellis, Richard Cockrum, Donald Chestnutwood.
EIN: 421409512

60416
Father Daily Scholarship Foundation
c/o Boerner & Goldsmith Law Firm, P.C.
500 2nd St.
Ida Grove, IA 51445 (712) 364-2718
Contact: Fr. Gerald Fisch

Established in 1993 in IA.
Donor(s): Fr. Harry E. Dailey.‡
Financial data (yr. ended 12/31/00): Assets, $183,239 (M); grants paid, $17,450; gifts received, $5,000; expenditures, $18,740; qualifying distributions, $18,542.
Limitations: Giving limited to Ida Grove, IA.
Application information: Application form required.
Trustees: Cheryl Bresnahan, Fr. Gerald Fisch, Peter Goldsmith, Rich Renfro, Lenee Sinnott.
EIN: 421372214

60417
Paul S. & Mary Ellen L. Beckwith Charitable Foundation
c/o Robert Cramer
2600 E. 8th St.
Boone, IA 50036

Established in 1987 in IA.
Donor(s): F.W. Beckwith.
Financial data (yr. ended 12/31/00): Assets, $178,130 (M); grants paid, $10,000; gifts received, $21,010; expenditures, $10,607; qualifying distributions, $10,000.
Limitations: Applications not accepted. Giving primarily in Boone, IA.
Application information: Contributes only to pre-selected organizations.
Officers: Robert Cramer, Pres.; F.W. Beckwith, Secy.-Treas.
EIN: 421292408

60418
Harold L. Smith Memorial Scholarship Fund
223 E. Court Ave.
P.O. Box 67
Winterset, IA 50273-0067
Application address: c/o Winterset Community High School, 302 W. South St., Winterset, IA 50273, tel.: (515) 462-4912

Established in 1987 in IA.
Donor(s): Harriet L. Smith.‡
Financial data (yr. ended 12/31/00): Assets, $167,908 (M); grants paid, $8,250; expenditures, $10,568; qualifying distributions, $10,513.
Limitations: Giving limited to the Winterset, IA, area.
Application information: Application form required.
Trustee: Union State Bank.
EIN: 421282964

60419
The Prophetic Song of Songs, Inc.
1738 654th Ln.
Albia, IA 52531

Donor(s): John S. Resbeen.
Financial data (yr. ended 06/30/02): Assets, $165,810 (M); grants paid, $0; gifts received, $47,940; expenditures, $18,746; qualifying distributions, $18,581.
Officers: Marion G. Berry, Pres.; Kenneth J. Berry, V.P.
EIN: 421207984

60420
Laverty Foundation
c/o Wells Fargo Bank Iowa, N.A.
P.O. Box 837
Des Moines, IA 50304-0837

Established in 1999 in IA.
Financial data (yr. ended 12/31/00): Assets, $156,579 (M); grants paid, $500; gifts received, $75,000; expenditures, $1,291; qualifying distributions, $482.
Limitations: Applications not accepted.
Application information: Contributes only to pre-selected organizations.
Officers and Directors:* Steven E. Zumbach,* Pres.; Mark F. Zumbach,* V.P. and Secy.-Treas.
EIN: 421425617

60421
Osceola County Historical Society
c/o McCullum Museum
622 7th St.
Sibley, IA 51249

Financial data (yr. ended 12/31/01): Assets, $147,459 (M); grants paid, $0; gifts received, $8,658; expenditures, $6,058; qualifying distributions, $0.
Officers: Pauline Brink, Pres.; Norman Wheeler, V.P.; Donna Hantsma, Secy.; Pat Muitenberg, Treas.
EIN: 421212426

60422
The Caughell-Isaac Educational Trust
P.O. Box 405
Avoca, IA 51521-0405
Contact: Marcella Caughell, Tr.

Donor(s): Marcella Caughell.
Financial data (yr. ended 01/01/01): Assets, $141,635 (M); grants paid, $9,000; expenditures, $9,169; qualifying distributions, $9,169.
Limitations: Giving limited to residents of Avoca, Shelby, and Tennant, IA.
Application information: Application form required.
Trustees: Marcella Caughell, Milton L. Hanson, Darrell Jacobsen, Dean Kock.
EIN: 426479495

60423
Lohr Community Trust
c/o David E. Lohr & Christine Lohr
104 Oak Hill Dr.
Churdan, IA 50050

Established in 1999 in IA.
Financial data (yr. ended 12/31/00): Assets, $136,294 (M); grants paid, $4,950; expenditures, $4,950; qualifying distributions, $4,950.
Limitations: Applications not accepted.
Application information: Contributes only to pre-selected organizations.
Trustees: Christine E. Lohr, David C. Lohr.
EIN: 426587228

60424
Peace and Justice Foundation
(Formerly Peace and Justice Foundation of Eastern Iowa)
P.O. Box 566
Calmar, IA 52132-0566

Classified as a private operating foundation in 1988.
Financial data (yr. ended 12/31/00): Assets, $134,188 (M); grants paid, $18,000; expenditures, $18,982; qualifying distributions, $18,000.
Limitations: Applications not accepted. Giving limited to eastern IA.

Director: R.N. Hirsch.
EIN: 421233316

60425
Edgewood
c/o Gladys M. Sprugel
200 Moorhead Ave.
Iowa Falls, IA 50126-1945

Classified as a private operating foundation in 1973.
Financial data (yr. ended 06/30/02): Assets, $131,331 (M); grants paid, $0; gifts received, $24,083; expenditures, $25,084; qualifying distributions, $115.
Officers: Ruth G. Scallon, Pres.; Norma Pormmrehn, V.P.; Catherine C. McCord, Secy.; Gladys M. Sprugel, Treas.
Directors: Evelyn Beaman, Dorothy Campbell, Mary Lou Gasper, Arlene Hamilton, Kristi Harris, Velma W. Lord, Gladys Merklin, Mary E. Rommel, Colleen U. Tjaden.
EIN: 426060202

60426
Marie H. Ketelsen Learning Center for Children, Inc.
c/o William O'Donnell
1801 Swagosa Dr.
Maquoketa, IA 52060

Financial data (yr. ended 12/31/99): Assets, $130,392 (M); grants paid, $0; expenditures, $3,038; qualifying distributions, $2,811; giving activities include $3,038 for programs.
Officers: William O'Donnell, Pres.; Ronald Adrian, V.P.; Danny Kilburg, Secy.-Treas.
EIN: 421422915

60427
Credit Bureau of Fort Dodge Trust
312 11th Ave. N.
P.O. Box 722
Fort Dodge, IA 50501-0722
Application addresses: c/o Jack Grandgeorge, 244 11th Ave. N., Fort Dodge, IA 50501; c/o Bruck McCullough, 2749 21st Ave. N, Fort Dodge, IA 50501; c/o Tom Chalstrom, 825 Central Ave., Fort Dodge, IA 50501

Established in 1989 in IA.
Financial data (yr. ended 12/31/01): Assets, $114,308 (M); grants paid, $5,000; expenditures, $5,568; qualifying distributions, $4,999.
Limitations: Giving limited to Fort Dodge, IA.
Application information: Application form required.
Officers and Trustees:* Michael Scacci, Chair.; Keith Hillman,* Secy.; Tom Chalstrom, Jack Grandgeorge, Bruck McCullough.
EIN: 421319169
Codes: GTI

60428
William & Elsie Bandow Scholarship Fund
1231 Broadway. Ste. 300
Denison, IA 51442-1923 (712) 263-3159
Contact: D.R. Franck, Tr.

Financial data (yr. ended 12/31/01): Assets, $106,082 (M); grants paid, $3,901; expenditures, $4,654; qualifying distributions, $4,654.
Limitations: Giving limited to residents of IA.
Application information: Application form required.
Trustee: D.R. Franck.
EIN: 421209337

60429
Goodwin Sonstegard Scholarship Foundation
105 N. 4th St.
Estherville, IA 51334-2144
Application address: 321 2nd Ave. S.W., Sioux Center, IA 51250, tel.: (712) 722-1352
Contact: Harlan Harmelink, Pres.

Established in 1988 in IA.
Financial data (yr. ended 12/31/00): Assets, $104,780 (M); grants paid, $9,500; expenditures, $9,500; qualifying distributions, $9,434.
Limitations: Giving primarily in Estherville and Sioux City, IA.
Officers and Directors:* Harlan Harmelink,* Pres.; John Carlson, Sr.,* V.P.
EIN: 421335347

60430
Carrie and Oren Igou Scholarship Fund
c/o Craig Ensign
714 Central Ave.
Northwood, IA 50459-1518

Established in 1993.
Financial data (yr. ended 12/31/01): Assets, $96,079 (M); grants paid, $6,000; expenditures, $6,125; qualifying distributions, $6,000.
Limitations: Giving limited to residents of Northwood, IA.
Application information: Application form required.
Trustees: Craig Ensign, Ron Sietsma.
EIN: 421339046

60431
Burnett Community Development Association
666 Walnut St.
Des Moines, IA 50309 (515) 992-3755
Contact: Bruce L. Seymour, Pres.

Classified as a private operating foundation in 1984.
Financial data (yr. ended 12/31/00): Assets, $95,099 (M); grants paid, $7,000; expenditures, $11,734; qualifying distributions, $6,797.
Limitations: Giving limited to the Dallas Center, IA, area.
Application information: Application form required.
Officers and Directors:* Bruce L. Seymour,* Pres. and Treas.; John W. Thomas,* V.P.; Brian Wright,* Secy.
Trustee: Brenton Sank.
EIN: 421238252

60432
Marguerite Lord Education Trust
c/o United Bank of Iowa
P.O. Box 111, 501 2nd St.
Ida Grove, IA 51445 (712) 364-3393
Contact: Gerald Schmidt, Trust Off., United Bank of Iowa

Financial data (yr. ended 12/31/99): Assets, $85,258 (M); grants paid, $3,500; expenditures, $4,666; qualifying distributions, $4,666.
Limitations: Giving limited to residents of Ida Grove, IA.
Application information: Application form required.
Trustees: Joseph Graves, Norm Pfalzfraft, Elaine Thompson, United Bank of Iowa.
EIN: 421315585

60433
Margaret B. Barry Foundation
c/o Brenton Trust Dept.
P.O. Box 10478
Des Moines, IA 50306-0478
Contact: Jan Lindberg, Treas.

Donor(s): Margaret B. Barry.
Financial data (yr. ended 12/31/01): Assets, $79,667 (M); grants paid, $6,800; expenditures, $8,433; qualifying distributions, $6,800.
Officers: Margaret B. Barry, Pres.; Thomas Carpenter, Secy.; Jan Lindberg, Treas.
EIN: 426562404

60434
Heath Foundation, Inc.
c/o Keele Law Offices
P.O. Box 156
West Liberty, IA 52776-0156
Application address: P.O. Box 78, West Liberty, IA 52776, tel.: (319) 627-2191
Contact: Dennis Batty, Secy.-Treas.

Financial data (yr. ended 12/31/00): Assets, $43,228 (M); grants paid, $3,740; expenditures, $4,471; qualifying distributions, $4,480.
Limitations: Giving primarily in West Liberty, IA.
Officers: James Keele, Pres.; Thomas C. Brooke, V.P.; Dennis Batty, Secy.-Treas.
EIN: 421367113

60435
The Kessler Clinic, Inc.
1221 Myrtle St.
Davenport, IA 52804

Established in 1994 in IA.
Donor(s): Richard L. Vermeer, Kathleen E. Vermeer.
Financial data (yr. ended 12/31/99): Assets, $42,860 (M); grants paid, $0; gifts received, $46,642; expenditures, $47,213; qualifying distributions, $44,396; giving activities include $47,213 for programs.
Officers: Richard L. Vermeer, Pres.; Kathleen E. Vermeer, V.P. and Treas.; Karen A. Russell, Secy.
Directors: Ann Borders, Carol A. Howell, Nancy J. Nehlsen, Charlotte Pollock.
EIN: 421400246

60436
Norunn Stangland Foundation
P.O. Box 37, 207 N. 5th St.
Guthrie Center, IA 50115-0037
(641) 747-2218
Contact: Dennis Kunkle, Pres.

Financial data (yr. ended 12/31/01): Assets, $38,595 (M); grants paid, $4,500; expenditures, $4,880; qualifying distributions, $4,500.
Limitations: Giving limited to female residents of Guthrie Center, IA.
Application information: Application form required.
Officers: Dennis Kunkle, Pres.; Steve Smith, V.P.; Barbara Krakau, Secy.-Treas.
EIN: 421333089

60437
William G. Saunders Trust
c/o Elizabeth E. Garrels
2255 235th St.
Mount Pleasant, IA 52641-9801

Classified as a private operating foundation in 1972.
Financial data (yr. ended 11/30/00): Assets, $38,478 (M); grants paid, $1,086; expenditures, $2,390; qualifying distributions, $2,397.
Limitations: Giving limited to Henry County, IA.

Trustee: Elizabeth E. Garrels.
EIN: 426053395

60438
Credit Bureau of Ottumwa Inc. Trust
P.O. Box 533
Ottumwa, IA 52501-0533

Established in 1989 in IA.
Financial data (yr. ended 12/31/00): Assets, $34,394 (M); grants paid, $1,500; expenditures, $1,723; qualifying distributions, $1,500.
Limitations: Applications not accepted. Giving primarily in Ottumwa, IA.
Application information: Contributes only to pre-selected organizations.
Directors: Harry Carter, Carl Obermann, Hugh Pedrick, Leon Vaughn.
EIN: 420409970

60439
IA Realty Foundation
P.O. Box 657
666 Grand Ave.
Des Moines, IA 50303-0657
Application address: c/o Board of Directors, 3501 Westown Pkwy., West Des Moines, IA 50266

Established in 2000 in IA.
Financial data (yr. ended 12/31/00): Assets, $30,480 (M); grants paid, $50,536; gifts received, $81,010; expenditures, $50,559; qualifying distributions, $50,536.
Limitations: Giving primarily in IA.
Officers: Michael R. Knapp, Pres.; Daniel Cornelison, Secy.; James Koolhof, Treas.
EIN: 421502535

60440
Human Aid Society of Iowa
1601 W. Lakes Pkwy., Ste. 300
West Des Moines, IA 50266

Classified as a private operating foundation in 1978.
Donor(s): James Callanan.‡
Financial data (yr. ended 12/31/01): Assets, $30,447 (M); grants paid, $5,414; gifts received, $4,192; expenditures, $5,820; qualifying distributions, $5,779.
Limitations: Applications not accepted. Giving limited to residents of Polk County, IA.
Application information: Contributes only to pre-selected organizations.
Officers: Joseph S. Brick, Pres.; Charles O'Conner, Secy.-Treas.
EIN: 426075775
Codes: GTI

60441
Tama Public Library Foundation
133 W. 3rd St.
Tama, IA 52339

Established in 1999 in IA.
Financial data (yr. ended 12/31/00): Assets, $21,491 (M); grants paid, $0; gifts received, $8,705,238; expenditures, $0; qualifying distributions, $0.
Limitations: Applications not accepted.
Application information: Contributes only to pre-selected organizations.
Directors: Darla J. Cory, Edwin Draisey, Roger Hill.
EIN: 421481058

60442
White City Scholarship Association
410 Broad Ave.
Stanton, IA 51573   (712) 829-2111
Contact: Kevin Cabbage

Established in 1991 in IA.
Donor(s): Farmers Mutual Telephone Co. of Stanton, IA.
Financial data (yr. ended 12/31/99): Assets, $17,705 (M); grants paid, $1,000; expenditures, $1,509; qualifying distributions, $1,501.
Limitations: Giving limited to residents of Stanton, IA.
Application information: Application form required.
Officers and Directors:* Lee Sellergren,* Pres.; Max Peterson,* V.P.; Clayton Johnson,* Secy.-Treas.; Dan Lundgren, Leo Miller, Wayne Sederburg, Russell Sunderman.
EIN: 421343828

60443
Heft Educational Fund Charitable Trust
2574 Zinnia Ave.
Rockford, IA 50468-8169
Contact: Earle Heft, Tr.

Established in 1990.
Financial data (yr. ended 12/31/99): Assets, $16,524 (M); grants paid, $500; gifts received, $3,205; expenditures, $619; qualifying distributions, $619.
Limitations: Giving limited to residents of Rockford or Rockwell-Swaledale, IA.
Application information: Application form required.
Trustees: Earle Heft, Nora Heft.
EIN: 650159898

60444
Howard County Experimental Farms Association
P.O. Box 402
Cresco, IA 52136
Application address: c/o Howard County Extension Office, 132 1st Ave., Cresco, IA 52136, tel.: (319) 547-3001

Financial data (yr. ended 12/31/99): Assets, $16,352 (M); grants paid, $3,000; expenditures, $4,003; qualifying distributions, $4,003.
Limitations: Giving limited to residents of Howard County, IA.
Application information: Application form required.
Officers and Directors:* Greg Lichty,* Pres.; Dave Fritcher,* V.P.; Brent Brenner,* Treas.; Bart Brincks, Chris Christianson, Cory Christanson, Brian Goodman, Kurt Griver, Cory Hruska, Paul Loval, Greg Mahr, Allan Smith.
EIN: 421101260

60445
Crouch Education Foundation
c/o Mr. & Mrs. Harlan Crouch
2947 Sunset Cir.
Sioux City, IA 51104

Financial data (yr. ended 11/30/99): Assets, $14,357 (M); grants paid, $2,000; gifts received, $12,300; expenditures, $2,000; qualifying distributions, $2,000.
Officers and Directors:* Kim Crouch,* Pres.; Harlan Crouch,* Secy.-Treas.
EIN: 421467587

60446
Nishnabotna Valley Foundation
c/o Nishnabotna Valley REC
P.O. Box 714
Harlan, IA 51537-0714 (712) 755-2166
Contact: Mary Johnson

Classified as a company-sponsored operating foundation in 1998.
Donor(s): Western Ventures, Inc., Nishnabotna Valley REC.
Financial data (yr. ended 12/31/00): Assets, $14,051 (M); grants paid, $2,000; expenditures, $2,070; qualifying distributions, $2,000.
Limitations: Giving limited to residents of Audubon, Cass, Crawford, Harrison, Pottawatternie, and Shelby counties, IA.
Officers and Directors:* Gary B. Pool,* Pres.; Carmen P. Hosack,* V.P. and Secy.-Treas.; Lee McLauchlin.
EIN: 421467824

60447
Joshua One Eight Foundation
4220 Patricia Dr.
Des Moines, IA 50322

Donor(s): Charles D. Wenger.
Financial data (yr. ended 12/31/00): Assets, $13,450 (M); grants paid, $45,472; gifts received, $10,000; expenditures, $45,504; qualifying distributions, $45,502.
Limitations: Applications not accepted. Giving on a national basis.
Application information: Contributes only to pre-selected organizations.
Trustee: Charles Wenger.
EIN: 421285060

60448
Minitube of America Foundation, Inc.
P.O. Box 763
Ames, IA 50010

Established in 1998 in WI.
Financial data (yr. ended 12/31/99): Assets, $11,304 (M); grants paid, $11,478; gifts received, $12,000; expenditures, $11,478; qualifying distributions, $11,478.
Directors: Frederick T. Rikkers, Ludwig Simmet, Rebekah Simmet.
EIN: 391929515

60449
J. J. Wilke Trust
2716 Grand Ave.
Des Moines, IA 50312 (515) 243-5244
Contact: George E. Flagg, Tr.

Financial data (yr. ended 01/31/00): Assets, $7,001 (M); grants paid, $12,979; expenditures, $13,537; qualifying distributions, $13,023.
Limitations: Giving primarily in IA.
Application information: Application form required.
Trustee: George E. Flagg.
EIN: 426291892

60450
Ringgold County Community Foundation
201 E. Monroe St.
Mount Ayr, IA 50854

Financial data (yr. ended 12/31/00): Assets, $4,398 (M); grants paid, $3,121; gifts received, $3,121; expenditures, $3,123; qualifying distributions, $3,121.
Limitations: Applications not accepted. Giving primarily in IA.
Application information: Contributes only to pre-selected organizations.

Officers: Frank Richards, Pres.; Donna Pedersen, V.P. and Secy.; James L. Pederson, Treas.
EIN: 421431086

60451
ChristieAmor Foundation
P.O. Box 71394
Clive, IA 50325
Application address: 1808 N.W. 121st Cir., Clive, IA 50325, tel, : (515) 643-9699
Contact: Theodore Rooney, Secy.-Treas.

Established in 1997.
Donor(s): Theodore Rooney.
Financial data (yr. ended 12/31/01): Assets, $4,214 (M); grants paid, $14,500; gifts received, $10,000; expenditures, $14,669; qualifying distributions, $14,500.
Limitations: Giving limited to residents of IA.
Officers: Patricia Rooney, Pres.; Theodore Rooney, Secy.-Treas.
EIN: 421420913

60452
Medserv Foundation
P.O. Box 129
Cedar Falls, IA 50613-0129

Financial data (yr. ended 11/30/00): Assets, $3,571 (M); grants paid, $5,102; gifts received, $5,206; expenditures, $5,575; qualifying distributions, $5,575.
Officers: John W. Keiser, Pres.; Paul Houck, V.P.; Stephen C. Riggs, Secy.; Randall J. Bremner, Treas.
Directors: Richard L. Bremner, Robert N. Bremner, R. A. Frankhauser, John W. Keiser, James C. Peterson, Philip E. Rohrbaugh, Michael S. Squires, Steven W. Tarr, Carl Vanderkooi.
EIN: 421343463

60453
Walker Scholarship Grant
c/o U.S. Bank
P.O. Box 1880
Iowa City, IA 52244-1880
Application address: c/o School of Religion, Univ. of Iowa, Iowa City, IA 52242

Classified as a private operating foundation in 1974.
Financial data (yr. ended 08/31/01): Assets, $1,348 (M); grants paid, $4,100; gifts received, $5,633; expenditures, $4,381; qualifying distributions, $4,100.
Limitations: Giving limited to IA.
Application information: Application form required.
Trustee: U.S. Bank.
EIN: 237435737
Codes: GTI

60454
Augustine Foundation
2423 Duff Ave.
Ames, IA 50010-4852

Classified as a private operating foundation in 1999.
Financial data (yr. ended 12/31/01): Assets, $626 (M); grants paid, $0; gifts received, $400; expenditures, $367; qualifying distributions, $0.
Officers: Kenneth L. Augustine, Pres.; Karen L. Augustine, V.P.; Janice K. Augustine, Secy.
EIN: 421423878

60455
Future Entrepreneurs, Inc.
495 S. 51st. St., Apt. 23
West Des Moines, IA 50265

Established in 1996 in IA.

Financial data (yr. ended 12/31/00): Assets, $245 (M); grants paid, $0; gifts received, $1,500; expenditures, $1,738; qualifying distributions, $1,738; giving activities include $1,738 for programs.
Officer: Changyon Pak, Mgr.
EIN: 421449125

KANSAS

60456
Brown Memorial Foundation
409 N.W. 3rd St., Ste. G
P.O. Box 187
Abilene, KS 67410-0187
Application address: c/o Abilene High School, 1101 N. Mulberry St., Abilene, KS 67410-2044, tel.: (785) 263-1260

Established in 1926 in KS.
Donor(s): C.L. Brown,‡ Carrie Burton Trust, Allene Waddel Trust, Benadine Hoffman Trust.
Financial data (yr. ended 12/31/00): Assets, $17,604,717 (M); grants paid, $17,425; gifts received, $1,644; expenditures, $652,926; qualifying distributions, $664,766; giving activities include $610,659 for programs.
Limitations: Giving limited to Abilene, KS.
Application information: Scholarship application forms available from Abilene High School. Application form required.
Officers and Trustees:* Paul Veach,* Pres. and Mgr.; Al P. Jones,* V.P.; E.L. Fiedler,* Secy.-Treas.; Lila B. Clark, William A. Guilfoyle, Charles A. Norman.
EIN: 480573809
Codes: GTI

60457
V & H Charitable Foundation
P.O. Box 26128
Overland Park, KS 66225

Established in 1990 in KS.
Donor(s): Helen Regnier, Ranch Mart, Inc.
Financial data (yr. ended 03/31/01): Assets, $12,350,712 (M); grants paid, $196,260; gifts received, $11,876,370; expenditures, $216,747; qualifying distributions, $196,260.
Limitations: Applications not accepted. Giving primarily in Kansas City, MO.
Application information: Contributes only to pre-selected organizations.
Trustees: Catherine M. Regnier, Robert B. Regnier, Victor A. Regnier.
EIN: 436378149
Codes: FD2

60458
Kansas Health Institute
100 S.E. 9th Ave., 3rd Fl.
Topeka, KS 66612

Classified as a private operating foundation in 1995.
Donor(s): Kansas Health Trust.
Financial data (yr. ended 12/31/01): Assets, $6,851,002 (M); grants paid, $0; gifts received, $2,537,880; expenditures, $2,524,794; qualifying distributions, $2,390,079; giving activities include $2,547,911 for programs.
Officers: W. Kay Kent, Chair.; Hon. Karen M. Humphreys, Vice-Chair.; Robert F. St. Peter, Pres.; John Moore, Secy.-Treas.

60458—KANSAS

Directors: Estela Martinez, Thomas C. Simpson, M.D., John R. Zutavern.
EIN: 481148972

60459
Salgo Trust for Education
c/o Heritage Group, LC
300 W. Douglas Ave., Ste. 900
Wichita, KS 67202

Established in 1991 in KS.
Donor(s): Nicolas M. Salgo, Robert A. Page, Nicolas M. Salgo Revocable Trust.
Financial data (yr. ended 04/30/99): Assets, $6,388,211 (M); grants paid, $0; gifts received, $135,000; expenditures, $184,748; qualifying distributions, $215,620; giving activities include $380,150 for programs.
Trustees: Robert A. Page, Nicolas M. Salgo Revocable Trust.
EIN: 481101260

60460
Rolling Hills Ranch Wildlife Conservation Center, Inc.
500 Graves Blvd.
Salina, KS 67401

Established in 1994 in KS. Classified as a private operating foundation in 1996.
Donor(s): Charles W. Walker.
Financial data (yr. ended 12/31/99): Assets, $5,588,785 (M); grants paid, $0; gifts received, $2,903,465; expenditures, $1,804,493; qualifying distributions, $3,166,641; giving activities include $99,725 for programs.
Officers and Directors:* Charles W. Walker,* Chair.; Michael Walker,* Pres.; Trace Walker,* V.P.; Morris Soderberg,* Secy.-Treas.
EIN: 481153800

60461
Claude and Donalda Stauth Foundation
P.O. Box 396
Montezuma, KS 67867

Established in 1996 in KS.
Financial data (yr. ended 12/31/00): Assets, $4,272,418 (M); grants paid, $0; gifts received, $1,907; expenditures, $218,207; qualifying distributions, $107,668; giving activities include $108,800 for programs.
Limitations: Applications not accepted.
Directors: Clayton Ferguson, John B. Unruh, Debra Wall, Charles Wiley.
EIN: 486334425

60462
Morrison Foundation Trust
Ren Ingemanson
P.O. Box 737
Salina, KS 67402-0737 (785) 827-9331

Established in 1985 in KS.
Donor(s): Richard Morrison, Milton L. Morrison.
Financial data (yr. ended 05/31/01): Assets, $1,676,863 (M); grants paid, $197,678; expenditures, $214,736; qualifying distributions, $190,405.
Limitations: Giving primarily in Salina, KS.
Application information: Application form not required.
Trustees: Rebecca A. Morrison, Richard Morrison, Roger Morrison.
EIN: 486268660
Codes: FD2

60463
Delos V. Smith Senior Citizens Foundation
c/o Smith Ctr.
101 W. 1st Ave.
Hutchinson, KS 67501-5235
Contact: Delos V. Smith, Jr., Treas.

Established in 1977.
Donor(s): Delos V. Smith, Jr.
Financial data (yr. ended 06/30/99): Assets, $1,667,458 (M); grants paid, $1,195; gifts received, $560; expenditures, $122,247; qualifying distributions, $104,851; giving activities include $103,656 for programs.
Officers and Directors:* Porter K. Brown,* Pres.; John H. Shaffer,* Secy.; Delos V. Smith, Jr.,* Treas.
EIN: 480861681

60464
John K. and Jane N. Garvey Foundation
301 N. Main St., Ste. 1300
Wichita, KS 67202-4813

Financial data (yr. ended 12/31/01): Assets, $1,614,750 (M); grants paid, $0; expenditures, $0; qualifying distributions, $0.
Limitations: Applications not accepted.
Application information: Contributes only to pre-selected organizations.
Officer: John K. Garvey, Pres.
EIN: 742854540

60465
The Guise-Weber Foundation, Inc.
1303 Debbie Ln.
Marysville, KS 66508-1140 (785) 562-3082
Contact: Eulalia T. Guise, Pres.

Established around 1983.
Donor(s): Eulalia T. Guise.
Financial data (yr. ended 12/31/00): Assets, $1,176,760 (M); grants paid, $35,091; gifts received, $81,297; expenditures, $37,359; qualifying distributions, $35,485.
Limitations: Giving primarily in KS.
Officer: Eulalia T. Guise, Pres.
Directors: Allen L. Holeman, Norman Severns, Harold Wiler.
EIN: 480943695

60466
Western Professional Associates, Inc.
5020 W. 15th St., Ste. C
Lawrence, KS 66049-3884

Established in 1994 in CO, FL, IN, KS, MO, OK, and SD.
Donor(s): Kansas Legal Svcs., Inc.
Financial data (yr. ended 12/31/01): Assets, $1,137,700 (M); grants paid, $60,620; expenditures, $3,227,871; qualifying distributions, $69,027; giving activities include $3,167,251 for programs.
Limitations: Applications not accepted. Giving limited to Topeka, KS.
Application information: Contributes only to pre-selected organizations.
Officer and Board Members:* Brian Moline,* Pres.; Robert Harder, Anne Fehrenbacher Haught, Hon. Nancy Parrish, Hon. Charles E. Worden.
EIN: 431655154

60467
Ruth V. Gordanier Charitable Trust
c/o Ralph N. Germann
1404 Kingsburg Rd.
Garden City, KS 67846-3332
Application address: Box 439, Garden City, KS 67846
Contact: Jim D. Mills, Tr.

Established around 1991.
Financial data (yr. ended 12/31/01): Assets, $1,036,671 (M); grants paid, $57,000; expenditures, $84,800; qualifying distributions, $57,000.
Limitations: Giving primarily in Garden City, KS.
Trustees: Ralph N. Germann, Clifford R. Hope, Jr., Jim D. Mills.
EIN: 486308383

60468
Roma Holley Conroy Trust for Historic Preservation
c/o Jeaneane K.O. Black
410 Shawnee St.
Hiawatha, KS 66434-2130

Financial data (yr. ended 12/31/99): Assets, $922,232 (M); grants paid, $5,510; expenditures, $90,259; qualifying distributions, $90,259.
Trustees: Jeaneane K.O. Black, Dick Lanter, Donna Lanter, Jenny Morris, Van Morris.
EIN: 481202716

60469
President's College, Inc.
123 S. Market St.
Wichita, KS 67202-3701

Donor(s): Willard W. Garvey.
Financial data (yr. ended 05/31/00): Assets, $691,959 (M); grants paid, $0; gifts received, $530,800; expenditures, $362,308; qualifying distributions, $0.
Officers: Thomas P. Laurino, Pres.; Deborah A. Harper, Secy.-Treas.
Trustee: Willard W. Garvey.
EIN: 486128824
Codes: TN

60470
Sidwell Charitable Trust
P.O. Box 754
Winfield, KS 67156-0754 (620) 221-4600
Contact: Kay Roberts Light, Dir.

Established in 1989 in KS.
Donor(s): Martell Sidwell.
Financial data (yr. ended 12/31/01): Assets, $327,417 (M); grants paid, $23,326; gifts received, $800; expenditures, $28,620; qualifying distributions, $28,383.
Limitations: Giving limited to residents of Winfield, KS.
Application information: Application form required.
Directors: N. Dean Bradbury, J. Dennis Herlocker, Kay Roberts Light.
EIN: 486290978
Codes: GTI

60471
Benjamin Quapaw Foundation
P.O. Box 3758
Wichita, KS 67201 (316) 262-8371
Contact: Ernest Peterson, Tr.

Donor(s): Jean Ann Blue.
Financial data (yr. ended 12/31/01): Assets, $248,516 (M); grants paid, $15,750; expenditures, $16,880; qualifying distributions, $16,765.
Limitations: Giving primarily in Miami, OK.

Trustees: Jean Ann Blue, Ernest Peterson.
EIN: 736107218

60472
Gary R. & Victoria F. Smith Charitable Trust
10788 W. 247th St.
Bucyrus, KS 66013-9142

Established in 1991 in KS.
Donor(s): Victoria F. Smith.
Financial data (yr. ended 12/31/99): Assets, $244,959 (M); grants paid, $11,700; expenditures, $12,437; qualifying distributions, $11,598.
Limitations: Applications not accepted. Giving primarily in KS.
Application information: Contributes only to pre-selected organizations.
Officer: Janette C. Schumm, Mgr.
Trustee: Victoria F. Smith.
EIN: 486304756

60473
Citizens for Affordable Housing Association
2231 S.W. Wanamaker Rd.
Topeka, KS 66614-4275

Financial data (yr. ended 12/31/99): Assets, $175,489 (M); grants paid, $9,100; expenditures, $12,265; qualifying distributions, $12,265; giving activities include $12,265 for programs.
Limitations: Applications not accepted.
Application information: Contributes only to pre-selected organizations.
Officers and Directors:* Gregory E. Schwerdt,* Pres.; Bryon R. Schlosser,* Secy.-Treas.; Robert J. Bernica.
EIN: 481065932

60474
Richard John Kaiser and August G. Kaiser Charitable Trust
P.O. Box 546
Phillipsburg, KS 67661-0546
Contact: Dan Losey, Tr.

Financial data (yr. ended 12/31/01): Assets, $174,972 (M); grants paid, $12,000; expenditures, $13,067; qualifying distributions, $12,368.
Limitations: Giving primarily in KS.
Application information: Application form not required.
Trustees: Dan Losey, Gloria Nelson, Rodger Vanloenen.
EIN: 481201623

60475
Souders Historical Farm & Museum
c/o Norma H. Souders
P.O. Box 527
Cheney, KS 67025-0527

Classified as a private operating foundation in 1994.
Donor(s): Floyd R. Souders, Norma Souders.
Financial data (yr. ended 12/31/00): Assets, $168,104 (L); grants paid, $0; gifts received, $6,746; expenditures, $9,229; qualifying distributions, $9,229; giving activities include $6,865 for programs.
Officers and Directors:* Norma H. Souders,* Pres. and C.E.O.; Iva L. Baker, V.P.; Robert S. Wunsch,* Secy.; Raymond L. Kraus.
EIN: 481152824

60476
The Marvin White Foundation
1 N. Main Pl.
P.O. Box 913
Hutchinson, KS 67504-0913
Application address: Jeffrey W. Smith, Coord., White Scholarship Foundation, 717 4th Ave., Inman, KS 67546-8041

Established as a private operating foundation in 1987.
Donor(s): Marvin White, Gertrude White.
Financial data (yr. ended 12/31/01): Assets, $160,416 (M); grants paid, $8,700; expenditures, $9,834; qualifying distributions, $10,265.
Limitations: Giving limited to McPherson County, KS.
Application information: Application form required.
Officers: Ann Smith, Pres.; Wayne E. Smith, V.P.; Jeffrey W. Smith, Secy.; Michael S. Smith, Treas.
EIN: 486244419
Codes: GTI

60477
Cliff and Nina Fell Foundation
c/o First State Bank & Trust Co.
116 W. 6th St.
Larned, KS 67550
Application address: c/o Jerry Larson, 111 E. 8th St., Larned, KS 67550, tel.: (620) 285-3156

Established in 1994 in KS.
Financial data (yr. ended 12/31/01): Assets, $159,267 (M); grants paid, $6,000; expenditures, $9,719; qualifying distributions, $7,529.
Limitations: Giving limited to residents of KS.
Application information: Application form required.
Trustee: First State Bank & Trust Co.
EIN: 486332829

60478
Kilgore-Ramsey Scholarship Trust
P.O. Box 411
Kingman, KS 67068-0411
Contact: Dick Hall

Established in 1998 in KS.
Financial data (yr. ended 12/31/01): Assets, $135,485 (M); grants paid, $12,000; expenditures, $12,514; qualifying distributions, $12,000.
Limitations: Giving limited to residents of Chapman, KS.
Trustees: Richard Hall, Robert R. Roskens, Francis H. Taylor.
EIN: 486343752

60479
Mount Hope Foundation
c/o Joan Paris
10500 Barkley, Ste. 110
Overland Park, KS 66212

Classified as a private operating foundation in 1992.
Donor(s): Lloyd Brown, Carol Brown.
Financial data (yr. ended 12/31/01): Assets, $130,704 (M); grants paid, $0; expenditures, $9,092; qualifying distributions, $4,684; giving activities include $9,092 for programs.
Trustees: Carol Brown, Lloyd Brown.
EIN: 436418333

60480
Stagecoach Outpost
(Formerly Soldiers of Love)
P.O. Box 3
Prairie View, KS 67664-9601

Established in 1988 in CA.
Financial data (yr. ended 12/31/01): Assets, $111,590 (M); grants paid, $0; expenditures, $6,491; qualifying distributions, $4,455; giving activities include $2,095 for programs.
Officers and Directors:* David G. Marmon,* Pres.; Britt H. Muhlig,* Secy.-Treas.; Shirley Warner.
EIN: 330305430

60481
Margaret Brooks Testamentary Trust
P.O. Box 29
Larned, KS 67550

Financial data (yr. ended 12/31/00): Assets, $106,094 (M); grants paid, $9,125; expenditures, $10,224; qualifying distributions, $10,152.
Limitations: Giving limited to CO, KS, and PA.
Application information: Application form required.
Trustee: First National Bank & Trust Co.
EIN: 746443771

60482
Nielson Family Foundation
7007 College Blvd., Ste. 315
Overland Park, KS 662211

Established in 1999 in KS.
Financial data (yr. ended 12/31/00): Assets, $96,377 (M); grants paid, $5,500; expenditures, $7,757; qualifying distributions, $6,253.
Trustees: Rodney Nielson, Investors Services Trust Co.
EIN: 486838527

60483
The Rev. Charles Brink Scholarship Foundation, Inc.
c/o Brotherhood Bank & Trust
756 Minnesota Ave.
Kansas City, KS 66101-2704
Application address: c/o Susan Berry, 216 Allcutt, Bonner Springs, KS 66012

Financial data (yr. ended 12/31/01): Assets, $89,508 (M); grants paid, $9,400; expenditures, $9,874; qualifying distributions, $9,851.
Limitations: Giving limited to KS.
Application information: Application form required.
Advisory Committee Members: Allen Davis, Tony Dusal, Rev. Patrick Jerome, Ralph Mies, Robert Stephan, Leroy Toomes, Dave Van Mol.
Trustee: Brotherhood Bank & Trust.
EIN: 481105451

60484
George Hoy Family Scholarship Fund
201 South Mill
P.O. Box 607
Beloit, KS 67420
Application addresses: c/o Office of Principal, Beloit High School, 1711 N. Walnut, Beloit, KS 67420, tel.: (785) 738-3593; c/o Office of Principal, St. John's High School, 209 Cherry, Beloit, KS 67420, tel.: (913) 738-2942

Classified as a private operating foundation in 1983.
Financial data (yr. ended 12/31/00): Assets, $65,376 (M); grants paid, $4,000; expenditures, $4,651; qualifying distributions, $4,000.
Limitations: Giving limited to Beloit, KS.

60484—KANSAS

Trustees: Joseph Benson, Douglas R. Johnson, Charlotte Scheckel.
EIN: 486203636
Codes: GTI

60485
Vaughn E., Thesta A. and Fredric McColey Charitable Trust
c/o Smith County State Bank & Trust Co.
P.O. Box 307
Smith Center, KS 66967
Application address: c/o Unified School District No. 237, Smith Center, KS 66967, tel.: (785) 282-6600
Contact: William Blankenship

Established in 1994 in KS.
Financial data (yr. ended 03/31/00): Assets, $57,866 (M); grants paid, $2,937; expenditures, $3,771; qualifying distributions, $3,050.
Limitations: Giving limited to residents of Smith Center, KS.
Trustee: Smith County State Bank & Trust Co.
EIN: 486323688

60486
North Star Project, Inc.
P.O. Box 6881
Leawood, KS 66206

Established in 1995 in MO.
Donor(s): AMC.
Financial data (yr. ended 06/30/00): Assets, $52,638 (M); grants paid, $0; gifts received, $121,250; expenditures, $130,454; qualifying distributions, $128,191; giving activities include $130,454 for programs.
Limitations: Applications not accepted.
Application information: Contributes only to pre-selected organizations.
Director: Marcia McMullen.
EIN: 431716853

60487
Holmes-McDonald Foundation
2724 Verona Cir.
Shawnee Mission, KS 66208-1265
(913) 362-5556
Contact: Jean H. McDonald Deacy, Pres.

Financial data (yr. ended 12/31/01): Assets, $50,918 (M); grants paid, $5,040; expenditures, $5,515; qualifying distributions, $5,040.
Limitations: Giving primarily in Kansas City, MO.
Officers: Jean H. McDonald Deacy, Pres.; Virgina McDonald Miller, V.P. and Secy.; Jay H. McDonald, V.P.
EIN: 436056327

60488
Warren E. Bottenberg Memorial Scholarship Fund
13405 240th Ln.
Holton, KS 66436-8423
Contact: Warren D. Bottenberg, Pres.

Donor(s): Warren D. Bottenberg, Barbara Bottenberg.
Financial data (yr. ended 12/31/00): Assets, $34,928 (M); grants paid, $3,500; expenditures, $4,057; qualifying distributions, $4,057.
Limitations: Giving limited to Jackson County, KS.
Application information: Application form required.
Officers: Warren D. Bottenberg, Pres.; Barbara Bottenberg, Secy.; John C. Bottenberg, Treas.
EIN: 481055698

60489
Tom Grant Foundation
c/o Lab One, Inc.
10101 Renner Rd.
Lenexa, KS 66219

Established in 1992 in MO.
Donor(s): Tom Grant.
Financial data (yr. ended 12/31/00): Assets, $34,336 (M); grants paid, $8,922; gifts received, $202,856; expenditures, $191,125; qualifying distributions, $177,412.
Limitations: Applications not accepted. Giving primarily in KS and MO.
Officers: Tom Grant,* Pres.; Lafayette Norwood, V.P.
Director: Janie Grant.
EIN: 431623254
Codes: GTI

60490
Project H.O.P.E. & E., Inc.
(Formerly Project Hope, Inc)
P.O. Box 782050
Wichita, KS 67278-2050

Established in 1994 in KS.
Donor(s): Fran D. Jabara, Jabara Family Foundation, Inc.
Financial data (yr. ended 09/30/00): Assets, $29,849 (M); grants paid, $0; gifts received, $10,000; expenditures, $11,344; qualifying distributions, $11,344; giving activities include $11,344 for programs.
Officer and Directors:* Jeff Knoll,* Exec. Dir.; Fran Jabara, Geri Jabara, Harvey Jabara, Leesa Jabara, Lori Simmons.
EIN: 481160314

60491
Dustin M. Bradbury Foundation
807 Woodthrush Dr.
McPherson, KS 67460-9758
Contact: Marilyn S. Bradbury

Established in 1997 in KS.
Donor(s): Bradbury Co., Inc.
Financial data (yr. ended 04/30/00): Assets, $27,532 (M); grants paid, $4,500; gifts received, $30,000; expenditures, $5,019; qualifying distributions, $4,500.
Limitations: Giving limited to residents of McPherson, KS.
Application information: Application form required.
Officer and Director:* Philip E. Bradbury,* Pres.
EIN: 742832642

60492
Scholarship Worldwide Foundation
P.O. Box 4193
Topeka, KS 66604

Financial data (yr. ended 12/31/01): Assets, $17,785 (L); grants paid, $0; expenditures, $2,304; qualifying distributions, $2,304.
Officer: Gerald E. Wittmer, Pres. and Secy.-Treas.
EIN: 481220626

60493
George B. Tack Memorial Committee
2016 Joann St.
Wichita, KS 67203-1111
Application address: 1527 W. 20th St., Wichita, KS 67203
Contact: Kristen Keefer, Co-Chair.

Financial data (yr. ended 12/31/99): Assets, $13,876 (M); grants paid, $350; expenditures, $930; qualifying distributions, $862.

Limitations: Giving limited to the Sedgwick County, KS, area.
Application information: Application form required.
Officers: Amy Hoffman, Co-Chair.; Kristen Keefer, Co-Chair.; Marilyn Hitchcock, Treas.; Karen Harmon.
EIN: 480961008

60494
Chad Schwertfeger Memorial
c/o William Schwertfeger
505 N. Webb St.
Caldwell, KS 67022-1105

Classified as a private operating foundation in 1999.
Donor(s): William Schwertfeger.
Financial data (yr. ended 12/31/99): Assets, $12,656 (L); grants paid, $0; gifts received, $12,578; expenditures, $0; qualifying distributions, $0.
Limitations: Applications not accepted.
Application information: Contributes only to pre-selected organizations.
Trustees: Phil Perry, Tracey Schwertfeger, Vonya Schwertfeger, William R. Schwertfeger.
EIN: 486365974

60495
Frank W. Brinkman Memorial Scholarship
1820 Apollo Ave.
Great Bend, KS 67530-3008
Application address: c/o Guidance Dept., Great Bend High School, 2027 Morton St., Great Bend, KS 67530-2559

Financial data (yr. ended 12/31/01): Assets, $11,050 (M); grants paid, $800; expenditures, $854; qualifying distributions, $854.
Limitations: Giving limited to KS.
Officers and Directors:* Sharon Goss,* Chair.; Jennie Allford,* Secy.-Treas.; Clay Guthmiller.
EIN: 486119241

60496
R. Milford White Scholarship Fund
P.O. Box 628
Baldwin City, KS 66006-0628

Financial data (yr. ended 12/31/99): Assets, $10,368 (M); grants paid, $900; gifts received, $348; expenditures, $940; qualifying distributions, $940.
Limitations: Giving limited to the Baldwin City, KS, area.
Application information: Application form required.
Directors: Hannah R. White, Roger P. White.
EIN: 541409637

60497
Floyd T. Hepworth Testamentary Trust f/b/o the People of Osage City, Kansas & Community
704 Topeka Ave.
P.O. Box 487
Lyndon, KS 66451-0487

Financial data (yr. ended 09/30/00): Assets, $6,715 (M); grants paid, $1,362; expenditures, $2,266; qualifying distributions, $1,923.
Trustees: Clyde M. Burns, Patrick Lawless, Rev. James Stigall, and 3 additional trustees.
EIN: 486224920

60498
The Hershey Family Scholarship Foundation
120 W. 6th St.
P.O. Box 1089
Hugoton, KS 67951
Contact: Don O. Concannon, Tr.

Established in 1993 in KS.
Financial data (yr. ended 12/31/01): Assets, $0 (M); grants paid, $2,010; expenditures, $2,095; qualifying distributions, $2,075.
Limitations: Giving limited to residents of Hugoton, KS.
Trustees: Don O. Concannon, Mike Hershey, Jeff Hill, Vicki Hull, Mike Willis.
EIN: 486311429

KENTUCKY

60499
Kentucky Derby Museum Corporation
P.O. Box 3513
Louisville, KY 40201-3513

Established in 1981 in KY.
Financial data (yr. ended 09/30/01): Assets, $24,035,178 (M); grants paid, $0; gifts received, $905,841; expenditures, $3,286,164; qualifying distributions, $0.
Officers and Directors:* Carl F. Pollard,* Pres.; Graham B. Cooke,* V.P; Lynn Ashton,* Secy.; James D. Bohanon, Dave Carrico, H. Curtis Craig, Bill Samuels, Jr., Wayne T. Smith, and 8 additional directors.
EIN: 311023459

60500
Louisville Protestant Altenheim
936 Barret Ave.
Louisville, KY 40204

Financial data (yr. ended 12/31/99): Assets, $17,202,650 (M); grants paid, $0; gifts received, $260,062; expenditures, $1,817,280; qualifying distributions, $686,426.
Officers and Directors:* David Burkholder,* Pres.; David S. Stierle,* 1st V.P.; Dean Unthank,* 2nd V.P.; Robert Sims,* Secy.; Ronald Wright,* Treas.; Joan Walcutt, Admin.; Peter Burr, and 7 additional directors.
EIN: 610449634

60501
Marie R. & Ervine Turner Educational Foundation, Inc.
P.O. Box 620
Jackson, KY 41339 (606) 666-9366
Contact: Rebecca B. Henson, Exec. Dir.

Established in 1999 in KY.
Financial data (yr. ended 12/31/01): Assets, $13,957,734 (L); grants paid, $198,561; expenditures, $283,637; qualifying distributions, $278,912.
Limitations: Giving primarily in Breathitt County, KY.
Application information: Foundation office or schools in Breathitt County, KY. Application form required.
Officers and Directors:* Darrell A. Herald,* Chair.; Lesley Warrix-Allen,* Exec. Secy.; Lewis H. Warrix,* Secy.; Joy Rae Shelton,* Treas.; Rebecca B. Henson, Exec. Dir.; Leon L. Hollon, Donald Ison, Marcus Mullins.

EIN: 611333558
Codes: FD2

60502
Charles P. Moorman Home for Women
966 Cherokee Rd., Rm. E
Louisville, KY 40204

Classified as a private operating foundation in 1972.
Financial data (yr. ended 12/31/00): Assets, $9,280,117 (M); grants paid, $0; gifts received, $71,185; expenditures, $1,968,097; qualifying distributions, $1,921,719; giving activities include $1,854,442 for programs.
Limitations: Applications not accepted.
Application information: Contributes only to pre-selected organizations.
Officers and Director:* Joe T. Sudduth, Jr.,* Pres.; Ann Stewart-Anderson,* Secy.; Kennedy H. Clark, Jr.,* Treas.; Robert White.
EIN: 610444778

60503
Annie Gardner Foundation
620 S. 6th St.
Mayfield, KY 42066-2316
Contact: Nancy H. Sparks, Dir., Education

Established in 1941 in KY.
Donor(s): Ed Gardner Trust.
Financial data (yr. ended 05/31/01): Assets, $7,952,779 (M); grants paid, $629,038; gifts received, $813,530; expenditures, $834,930; qualifying distributions, $1,169,621; giving activities include $349,735 for loans to individuals and $674,032 for programs.
Limitations: Giving limited to residents of Graves County, KY.
Application information: Student loan application available from foundation. Application form required.
Director: Dalton Boyd.
Trustees: Greg Cook, Jack C. Fisher, Barry McDonald, George Pickens, Hugh Williams.
EIN: 610564889
Codes: FD, GTI

60504
Robert J. Lightner Foundation
11500 Victory School House Rd.
Union, KY 41091

Established in 1987 in KY.
Donor(s): Robert J. Lightner.
Financial data (yr. ended 09/30/01): Assets, $7,021,613 (M); grants paid, $0; gifts received, $1,007,761; expenditures, $757,175; qualifying distributions, $729,117; giving activities include $209,210 for programs.
Application information: Application form not required.
Officers and Directors:* Robert J. Lightner,* Pres. and Treas.; Mike Sipple,* Secy.; N. Jeffrey Blankenship,* Treas.; Jerry Delaney, Ernst Wilder.
EIN: 611130572

60505
Owsley Brown Frazier Historical Arms Museum Foundation, Inc.
4938 Brownsboro Rd., Ste. 200
Louisville, KY 40222

Established in 2000 in KY.
Donor(s): Owsley Brown Frazier.
Financial data (yr. ended 06/30/01): Assets, $6,770,256 (M); grants paid, $0; gifts received, $4,520,000; expenditures, $172,180; qualifying distributions, $0.
Limitations: Applications not accepted.

Application information: Contributes only to pre-selected organizations.
Officers: Owsley Brown Frazier, Chair.; Michael Salisbury, Pres.
EIN: 611378343

60506
The Lincoln Foundation, Inc.
233 W. Broadway, Ste. 120
Louisville, KY 40202 (502) 585-4733
Contact: Dr. Samuel Robinson, Pres.

Established in 1910.
Donor(s): Lee B. Thomas, Jr.
Financial data (yr. ended 04/30/99): Assets, $6,199,276 (M); grants paid, $768,977; gifts received, $854,153; expenditures, $1,074,527; qualifying distributions, $768,977; giving activities include $287,736 for programs.
Limitations: Giving primarily in KY.
Publications: Annual report, newsletter.
Application information: Application forms available for grants and loans from the Scholarship Committee. Application form required.
Officers: Theodore Rosky, Chair.; Larry McDonald, Vice-Chair.; Samuel Robinson, Pres.; Margaret Redmon, Secy.; David Hale, Treas.
Trustees: Eleanor Young Love, and 12 additional trustees.
EIN: 610449631
Codes: FD

60507
Schmidt Museum of Coca-Cola Memorabilia, Inc.
(Formerly Coca-Cola Memorabilia Museum of Elizabethtown, Inc.)
P.O. Box 848
Elizabethtown, KY 42702-0848

Classified as a private operating foundation in 1977.
Donor(s): Coca-Cola Bottling Co. of Elizabethtown, William B. Schmidt.
Financial data (yr. ended 12/31/00): Assets, $5,012,332 (M); grants paid, $0; gifts received, $4,544; expenditures, $36,745; qualifying distributions, $38; giving activities include $31,544 for programs.
Officers: William B. Schmidt, Pres.; Janet B. Schmidt, Secy.-Treas.
EIN: 610921414

60508
Creasey Mahan Nature Preserve, Inc.
(Formerly Oldham Civic Center & Game Preserve, Inc.)
12501 Harmony Landing Rd.
Goshen, KY 40026

Classified as a private operating foundation in 1981.
Financial data (yr. ended 12/31/01): Assets, $4,466,516 (M); grants paid, $0; gifts received, $5,058; expenditures, $201,409; qualifying distributions, $96,958; giving activities include $96,958 for programs.
Officers and Directors:* Dalton Oak,* Pres.; Ben Gardner,* V.P.; Annice Johnston, Secy.-Treas.; Glenn Yost, Exec. Dir.; Nana Lampton, Sally Landes, Rowland Miller, Buford Parrish, Glenn Watson.
EIN: 310908496

60509
Maysville & Mason County Library Historical and Scientific Association
215 Sutton St.
Maysville, KY 41056-1186

Classified as a private operating foundation in 1972.
Financial data (yr. ended 12/31/01): Assets, $2,376,152 (M); grants paid, $0; gifts received, $218,617; expenditures, $259,291; qualifying distributions, $201,141; giving activities include $236,501 for programs.
Officers and Directors:* Jay I. Andrews,* Pres.; John Hutchings,* V.P.; Stephanie V. McNeill,* Secy.; Robert D. Vance,* Treas.; Sue Ellen Grannis, Admin.; Dawn Browning, Robert Biddle, Jean W. Calvert, Mark Cares, Rebecca H. Cartmell, Mary V. Clarke, Jane Hendrickson, Anna Dale Pyles, Barbara C. Thornhill, Matza C. VanMeter, Donald L. Wood.
Trustees: Zoe Chamness, Sherman A. Glass, Stephen Jones, Louis N. Browning.
EIN: 610444776

60510
Vintage Warbirds Museum, Inc.
c/o Richard D. Thurman
10000 Shelbyville Rd., Ste. 210
Louisville, KY 40223

Established in 1995.
Donor(s): Richard D. Thurman.
Financial data (yr. ended 12/31/01): Assets, $2,312,811 (M); grants paid, $0; gifts received, $36,131; expenditures, $59,037; qualifying distributions, $16,823; giving activities include $16,823 for programs.
Officers: Richard D. Thurman, Chair. and Pres.; J.D. Nichols, Vice-Chair.; William E. Hitchcock, Secy.
EIN: 611275551

60511
Lions Arms II, Inc.
6000 Lions Arms Dr.
Louisville, KY 40216

Financial data (yr. ended 05/31/02): Assets, $1,812,296 (M); grants paid, $0; expenditures, $135,771; qualifying distributions, $0.
Officer: Albert Senn, Sr., Pres.
EIN: 611218438

60512
Vivian J. Barlow Foundation
c/o U.S. Bank
P.O. Box 2400
Paducah, KY 42002-2400

Established in 1990 in KY.
Financial data (yr. ended 06/30/01): Assets, $1,715,990 (M); grants paid, $0; expenditures, $62,343; qualifying distributions, $61,325; giving activities include $2,555 for programs.
Advisory Committee Members: David Barlow, Melissa Bradley, Henrietta Fridholm, Susan Sloan.
Trustee: U.S. Bank.
EIN: 616186289

60513
Mary E. Wharton Nature Sanctuary at Floracliff, Inc.
P.O. Box 4006
Lexington, KY 40544

Classified as a private operating foundation in 1989.
Donor(s): Mary E. Wharton.‡
Financial data (yr. ended 12/31/01): Assets, $1,656,894 (M); grants paid, $0; gifts received, $223; expenditures, $79,307; qualifying distributions, $68,370; giving activities include $68,370 for programs.
Officers and Directors:* Bob Wilson,* Pres.; Clara Es-Stel Wieland,* Secy.; Dag Ryan,* Treas.; Melissa Brown, Bill Bryant, Margaret Graves, Sara Gregg, Ed Hartowicz, Dag Ryen.
EIN: 611149642

60514
Owsley Brown Frazier Family Foundation, Inc.
4938 Brownsboro Rd., Ste. 200
Louisville, KY 40222

Established in 1997 in KY.
Donor(s): Owsley B. Frazier.
Financial data (yr. ended 12/31/01): Assets, $1,389,064 (M); grants paid, $1,060,977; gifts received, $1,054,000; expenditures, $1,069,207; qualifying distributions, $1,060,671.
Limitations: Applications not accepted. Giving primarily in KY.
Application information: Contributes only to pre-selected organizations.
Officers: Owsley B. Frazier, Pres.; Laura F. Huneke, Secy.
EIN: 311571175
Codes: FD

60515
Middle Creek National Battlefield Foundation, Inc.
197 S. Lake Dr., Ste. 200
Prestonsburg, KY 41653

Financial data (yr. ended 12/31/01): Assets, $880,345 (M); grants paid, $0; gifts received, $13,612; expenditures, $6,875; qualifying distributions, $0.
Limitations: Applications not accepted.
Application information: Contributes only to pre-selected organizations.
Officer and Directors:* Frank Fitzpatrick,* Pres.; Kathy A. Fitzpatrick, Linda R. Layne.
EIN: 611204708

60516
Mallory-Taylor Foundation, Inc.
115 W. Main St.
P.O. Box 229
La Grange, KY 40031-0229
Contact: Barry D. Moore, Chair.

Financial data (yr. ended 12/31/01): Assets, $646,674 (M); grants paid, $25,205; expenditures, $38,506; qualifying distributions, $38,506.
Limitations: Giving limited to residents of Oldham County, KY.
Application information: Application form required.
Officers: Barry D. Moore, Chair.; Jon Westbrook, Vice-Chair.; Tom Kramer, Secy.; Tom Clark, Treas.
EIN: 611187509
Codes: GTI

60517
Raymond & Mary D. Barnett Foundation, Inc.
223 Lake Rd.
Campbellsburg, KY 40011
Application address: P.O. Box 5, Campbellsburg, KY 40011, tel.: (502) 532-7350
Contact: Donald Heilman, Dir.

Established in 2001 in KY.
Financial data (yr. ended 12/31/01): Assets, $635,971 (M); grants paid, $7,000; expenditures, $7,970; qualifying distributions, $37,971.
Limitations: Giving limited to residents of KY.
Directors: Neil S. Bryan, Don Heilman, Zane Peyton.
EIN: 611371025

60518
The Hoskins Family Foundation, Inc.
1077 Eastland Dr.
Lexington, KY 40505-3801 (859) 254-8834
Contact: William Hoskins, Pres.

Established in 1985 in KY.
Donor(s): William Hoskins.
Financial data (yr. ended 12/31/99): Assets, $539,541 (M); grants paid, $32,966; gifts received, $59,000; expenditures, $33,496; qualifying distributions, $32,366.
Limitations: Giving primarily in central KY area.
Officers: William Hoskins, Pres.; George A. Hoskins, V.P.; Glenn A. Hoskins, Secy.; Audrey H. Booher, Treas.
EIN: 611043442

60519
Gene & John Ed McConnell Foundation
c/o Statenational Bank Trust Dept.
130 W. Main St.
Frankfort, KY 40601

Donor(s): John Ed McConnell.‡
Financial data (yr. ended 06/30/99): Assets, $527,711 (M); grants paid, $0; gifts received, $542,027; expenditures, $1,058; qualifying distributions, $0.
Trustees: John Baughman, William Crumbaugh, Ed Logan, Wallace McConnell, William G. McConnell, John Noel.
EIN: 311496038

60520
RLR Charitable Foundation, Inc.
5211 Tamerlane Rd.
Louisville, KY 40207
Application address: 9300 Shelbyville Rd., Ste. 100, Louisville, KY 40222
Contact: Armand Ostroff, Pres.

Established in 1998 in KY.
Financial data (yr. ended 12/31/00): Assets, $492,323 (M); grants paid, $26,200; expenditures, $28,736; qualifying distributions, $26,041.
Limitations: Giving primarily in Louisville, KY.
Officers: Armand Ostroff, Pres. and Secy.-Treas.; Miriam Ostroff, V.P.; Lori Roberts, V.P.
EIN: 311603634

60521
Operation Open Arms, Inc.
6410 Longview Ln.
Louisville, KY 40222-6174

Established in June 2001 in KY; Classified as a private operating foundation in Sept. 2001.
Donor(s): Metro United Way.
Financial data (yr. ended 12/31/01): Assets, $398,000 (M); grants paid, $500; gifts received, $401,000; expenditures, $3,000; qualifying distributions, $3,000.
Limitations: Applications not accepted.
Application information: Contributes only to pre-selected organizations.
Officers: Catherine Bailey, Pres.; Ellen Call, Secy.; Irving W. Bailey II, Treas.
EIN: 311787756

60522
Elenore Francisco Educational Trust
c/o Old National Trust Co. of KY
P.O. Box 390
Morganfield, KY 42437
Contact: David Buckman, V.P., Old National Trust Co. of KY

Established in 1987 in KY.
Financial data (yr. ended 12/31/00): Assets, $383,633 (M); grants paid, $0; expenditures,

$6,347; qualifying distributions, $119,434; giving activities include $119,404 for loans to individuals.
Limitations: Giving limited to Union County, KY.
Application information: Application form required.
Trustees: David Buckman, Old National Trust Co.
EIN: 616151610
Codes: GTI

60523
Stable of Memories, Inc.
1520 Lexington Rd.
Georgetown, KY 40324-9357

Financial data (yr. ended 08/31/00): Assets, $339,614 (M); grants paid, $0; gifts received, $1,280; expenditures, $6,592; qualifying distributions, $42,574; giving activities include $5,284 for programs.
Officers: Kathryn V. McKinley, Pres.; Martha Brown, V.P.; Katherine Sautter, Secy.; David Caldwell, Treas.; Mrs. David Caldwell, Treas.
Trustees: Jenny Dulworth Albert, Gladys Bell, Harold Monaghan, Corwin Nixon, Thomas W. White.
EIN: 616030889

60524
Sarabande Books, Inc.
2234 Dundee Rd., Ste. 200
Louisville, KY 40205 (502) 458-4028
Contact: Sarah Gorham-Skinner, Pres.

Classified as a private operating foundation in 1995. Established in 1994.
Donor(s): Sallie Bingham.
Financial data (yr. ended 12/31/99): Assets, $316,779 (M); grants paid, $4,000; gifts received, $385,473; expenditures, $272,055; qualifying distributions, $262,229.
Officers and Directors:* Sarah Gorham-Skinner,* Pres.; Douglas Sharps,* Secy.; Jeffrey Skinner,* Treas.; Laure-Anne Bosselaar, Kurt Brown, Susan Finnegan.
EIN: 611256352

60525
Henry's Ark, Inc.
P.O. Box 479
Prospect, KY 40059-0479

Established in 1992 in KY.
Donor(s): Henry Wallace.
Financial data (yr. ended 12/31/99): Assets, $297,151 (M); grants paid, $600; gifts received, $244,598; expenditures, $203,296; qualifying distributions, $260,286.
Officer: Henry Wallace, Pres.
EIN: 611223579
Codes: TN

60526
Rosenstein Family Charitable Foundation, Inc.
c/o Irving Rosenstein
343 Waller Ave., Ste. 100
Lexington, KY 40504

Established in 1997 in KY.
Donor(s): Irving Rosenstein, Robert Rosenstein.
Financial data (yr. ended 12/31/99): Assets, $256,529 (M); grants paid, $14,142; gifts received, $117,157; expenditures, $14,316; qualifying distributions, $14,188.
Limitations: Applications not accepted.
Application information: Contributes only to pre-selected organizations.
Officers: Irving Rosenstein, Pres.; Martin Welenken, Secy.
Directors: Ann Rosenstein, Irma Rosenstein, Robert Rosenstein.
EIN: 611316211

60527
Kate McClintock Home
P.O. Box 341
Paris, KY 40362-0341

Classified as a private operating foundation in 1971.
Donor(s): Kate McClintock.‡
Financial data (yr. ended 08/31/01): Assets, $243,032 (M); grants paid, $28,925; gifts received, $2,663; expenditures, $30,032; qualifying distributions, $26,539.
Limitations: Giving limited to Bourbon County, KY.
Application information: Application form required.
Officers: Henry Prewitt, Pres.; Steven W. Elam, Secy.; Lois Claypoole, Treas.
EIN: 610458372
Codes: GTI

60528
Knock Family Foundation, Inc.
10730 Omaha Trace
Union, KY 41091-9279
Contact: Richard R. Knock, Pres.

Established in 1994 in KY.
Donor(s): Richard R. Knock.
Financial data (yr. ended 11/30/99): Assets, $237,414 (M); grants paid, $56,750; gifts received, $106,722; expenditures, $58,303; qualifying distributions, $56,750.
Limitations: Giving primarily in KY.
Officers: Richard R. Knock, Pres.; Joann Knock, Treas.
EIN: 611251738

60529
Adair Family Charitable Foundation, Inc.
400 Farrell Dr., Ste. 246
Covington, KY 41011-5133

Financial data (yr. ended 12/31/01): Assets, $214,434 (M); grants paid, $9,800; expenditures, $9,804; qualifying distributions, $9,800.
Limitations: Giving primarily in CO and MO.
Officers: Martha B. Adair, Pres.; Sara A. Sperry, V.P.; Barbara A. Roach, Secy.; N. Douglas Adair, Treas.
EIN: 611358018

60530
The Eugene B. and Margery Ames Pflughaupt Charitable Foundation, Inc.
2115 Bruce Ave.
Louisville, KY 40218

Established in 1995 in KY.
Donor(s): Eugene B. Pflughaupt, Margery A. Pflughaupt.
Financial data (yr. ended 12/31/99): Assets, $198,453 (M); grants paid, $12,500; expenditures, $15,263; qualifying distributions, $12,500.
Limitations: Applications not accepted. Giving limited to residents of KY.
Officers: Eugene B. Pflughaupt, Chair.; Margery A. Pflughaupt, Vice-Chair.; Ernestine Jennings, Treas.
EIN: 611274891

60531
Vocational Education Construction Trades Association, Inc.
532 Broadway
Hazard, KY 41702

Financial data (yr. ended 08/31/00): Assets, $195,720 (M); grants paid, $0; expenditures, $1,769; qualifying distributions, $27,481; giving activities include $27,481 for programs.
Officers: Joe Goodlette, Pres.; Roy Pulliam, V.P.; Nancy Collind, Secy.-Treas.
Director: Steve Campbell.
EIN: 610976645

60532
Field House, Inc.
1826 Lexington Ave.
Owensboro, KY 42301

Classified as a private operating foundation in 1994.
Donor(s): The Joanne Field Foundation, Joanne M. Field-Weller.
Financial data (yr. ended 05/31/01): Assets, $149,913 (M); grants paid, $0; gifts received, $77,000; expenditures, $99,688; qualifying distributions, $84,054; giving activities include $84,054 for programs.
Officer and Directors: Joyce H. Edwards,* Exec. Dir.; Linda Rummage, Norman Rummage.
EIN: 611033636

60533
Kentucky Aviation Museum, Inc.
c/o Norman Lewis
1416 Willow Ave., Ste. 4B
Louisville, KY 40204

Donor(s): Norman V. Lewis.
Financial data (yr. ended 12/31/99): Assets, $142,288 (M); grants paid, $0; gifts received, $132,120; expenditures, $156,487; qualifying distributions, $148,760; giving activities include $148,760 for programs.
Limitations: Applications not accepted.
Application information: Contributes only to pre-selected organizations.
Officers: Norman Lewis, Pres.; Gilbert Becht, V.P.; Lee Davis, Secy.; David Baughman, Treas.
EIN: 611205440

60534
Clarkson Clinic Foundation, Inc.
3481 Elizabethtown Rd.
Clarkson, KY 42726

Established in 1992.
Donor(s): Patricia Beasley.
Financial data (yr. ended 02/28/02): Assets, $127,031 (M); grants paid, $0; gifts received, $4,963; expenditures, $2,281; qualifying distributions, $0.
Officers: Carolyn Graybell, Pres.; Stephanie Carroll, V.P.; Betty Ash, Secy.; Regina Alexander, Treas.
EIN: 611217885

60535
Ruby Stephenson Testamentary Trust
c/o Union Planters Bank
P.O. Box 1920
Paducah, KY 42002-1920
Application address: c/o Annie Gardner Foundation, S. 6th & College Sts., Mayfield, KY 42066

Established in 1998 in KY.
Donor(s): Anne Gardner Foundation, Inc.
Financial data (yr. ended 12/31/01): Assets, $82,585 (M); grants paid, $4,898; expenditures, $6,139; qualifying distributions, $5,047.
Limitations: Giving limited to residents of Graves County, KY.
Application information: Application form required.
Trustee: Union Planters Bank.
EIN: 316642084

60536
Cultural Insights, Inc.
10510 Buckeye Trace
Goshen, KY 40026-9756

Financial data (yr. ended 12/31/01): Assets, $75,000 (M); grants paid, $0; expenditures, $20,601; qualifying distributions, $0.
Limitations: Applications not accepted.
Application information: Contributes only to pre-selected organizations.
Officers: Michael C. Sack, Pres.; Susan E. Jinnet-Sair, V.P. and Secy.; Phyllis W. Smith, Treas.
EIN: 611295651

60537
The Kapinao Heiau Foundation
c/o Richard K. Williams
2211 Greene Way
Louisville, KY 40220

Established in 1996 in KY.
Financial data (yr. ended 12/31/99): Assets, $69,000 (M); grants paid, $0; expenditures, $552; qualifying distributions, $552; giving activities include $552 for programs.
Limitations: Applications not accepted.
Application information: Contributes only to pre-selected organizations.
Officer: Richard K. Williams, Pres.
Director: Jim Edmonds.
EIN: 611290610

60538
Missions Possible, Inc.
c/o Robert E. Wood
7726 Somerset Rd.
London, KY 40741-9621

Established in 1995 in KY.
Donor(s): Robert E. Wood, Mary Lou Wood.
Financial data (yr. ended 12/31/99): Assets, $62,746 (M); grants paid, $2,500; expenditures, $9,107; qualifying distributions, $2,500.
Limitations: Applications not accepted.
Application information: Contributes only to pre-selected organizations.
Officers: Robert W. Wood, Pres.; Timothy R. Wood, V.P.; Robert E. Wood, Secy.-Treas.
EIN: 621481171

60539
Owenton Rotary Student Loan Fund
c/o Gary T. Gibson
435 Georgetown Rd.
Owenton, KY 40359-9100 (502) 484-3471

Financial data (yr. ended 12/31/99): Assets, $60,764 (M); grants paid, $16,600; gifts received, $2,000; expenditures, $16,663; qualifying distributions, $16,663; giving activities include $16,600 for loans to individuals.
Limitations: Giving limited to Owen County, KY.
Officers: Richard Greene, Pres.; Carolyn Keith, V.P.; Gary Gibson, Treas.
EIN: 311533803

60540
R. Gene Smith Charitable Foundation
3600 National City Twr.
101 S. 5th St.
Louisville, KY 40202

Established in 1991 in KY.
Donor(s): R. Gene Smith.
Financial data (yr. ended 12/31/01): Assets, $59,045 (M); grants paid, $0; gifts received, $262,500; expenditures, $334,012; qualifying distributions, $322,144; giving activities include $215,320 for programs.

Officers and Director:* R. Gene Smith, Pres. and Secy.; Gina Smith, Treas.; Marilyn Foulke,* Mgr.
EIN: 611209797

60541
The Richardson Foundation, Inc.
501 Park Ave.
Louisville, KY 40208 (502) 637-2274
Contact: David N. Richardson, Chair.

Financial data (yr. ended 12/31/00): Assets, $46,561 (M); grants paid, $1,938; gifts received, $18,179; expenditures, $2,032; qualifying distributions, $1,938.
Application information: Application form not required.
Officers and Directors:* David N. Richardson,* Chair.; Pat M. Richardson,* Secy.-Treas.; Rita O. Williams.
EIN: 611109624

60542
Hopewell Gospel Ministries, Inc.
P.O. Box 130
Wilmore, KY 40390-0130

Donor(s): Rex A. McConnell, Luanita Music, Pamela Anderson, Loretta Wilson, Jack McCoy, Kristi McConnell.
Financial data (yr. ended 12/31/99): Assets, $42,840 (M); grants paid, $0; gifts received, $20,537; expenditures, $22,510; qualifying distributions, $17,574; giving activities include $17,574 for programs.
Officer: Rex A. McConnell, Pres.
Directors: Steve Sleeper, Rick Stone.
EIN: 611108000

60543
The Healing Word Corporation
P.O. Box 463
Mayfield, KY 42066

Classified as a private operating foundation in 1982.
Financial data (yr. ended 12/31/01): Assets, $28,301 (M); grants paid, $0; gifts received, $8,460; expenditures, $9,950; qualifying distributions, $9,950.
Officers: Frankie E. Robertson, Pres.; Paul E. Robertson, V.P.; Roland J. Hubbard, Secy.; Renee Robertson, Treas.
EIN: 310997467

60544
The Lincoln-Darst Foundation, Inc.
1534 Quadrant Ave.
Louisville, KY 40205

Established in 1998.
Donor(s): Timothy J. Darst.
Financial data (yr. ended 12/31/00): Assets, $27,097 (M); grants paid, $300; gifts received, $600; expenditures, $350; qualifying distributions, $300.
Limitations: Applications not accepted. Giving primarily in Louisville, KY.
Application information: Contributes only to pre-selected organizations.
Officers: Angela Lincoln, Pres.; Timothy J. Darst, Secy.-Treas.
EIN: 311564987

60545
Sarah E. Winn Home, Inc.
P.O. Box 449
Mount Sterling, KY 40353-1099

Financial data (yr. ended 03/31/99): Assets, $18,502 (M); grants paid, $0; gifts received, $34,778; expenditures, $45,859; qualifying distributions, $43,075; giving activities include $43,075 for programs.
Officers: Bill Lane, Pres.; Debbie Helton, Treas.
EIN: 610621997

60546
Elizabeth W. Garriott Charitable Trust
c/o Elizabeth S. Lambert
169 N. Arnold Ave.
Prestonsburg, KY 41653

Established as an operating foundation in 1997.
Financial data (yr. ended 12/31/99): Assets, $5,155 (M); grants paid, $155; expenditures, $165; qualifying distributions, $155.
Limitations: Applications not accepted.
Director: Elizabeth S. Lambert.
EIN: 611256171

60547
William Guy Springs Charitable Trust
P.O. Box 1139
Ashland, KY 41105-1139
Contact: William Guy Springs, Tr.

Established in 2001 in KY.
Donor(s): William Guy Springs.
Financial data (yr. ended 12/31/01): Assets, $4,188 (M); grants paid, $225,030; gifts received, $232,000; expenditures, $228,216; qualifying distributions, $225,030.
Limitations: Applications not accepted.
Application information: Contributes only to pre-selected organizations.
Trustee: William Guy Springs.
EIN: 611302589
Codes: FD2

60548
Kentucky Athletic Hall of Fame, Inc.
9300 Shelbyville Rd., Ste. 1100
Louisville, KY 40222

Donor(s): Kentucky Farm Bureau.
Financial data (yr. ended 12/31/00): Assets, $4,110 (M); grants paid, $0; gifts received, $17,800; expenditures, $36,057; qualifying distributions, $14,842; giving activities include $34,469 for programs.
Officers: Jim Ellis, Pres.; Gary Meeker, V.P.; Lyle Wright, Secy.; William P. Malone, Treas.
EIN: 616028840

60549
Sharing, Inc.
P.O. Box 1638
Owensboro, KY 42302-1638
Contact: Kenneth V. Lawson, Jr., Pres.

Financial data (yr. ended 06/30/99): Assets, $2,944 (M); grants paid, $925; gifts received, $1,000; expenditures, $937; qualifying distributions, $925.
Limitations: Giving limited to Daviess County, KY.
Application information: Application form not required.
Officers: Kenneth V. Lawson, Jr., Pres.; Kenneth V. Lawson, Sr., Secy.-Treas.
EIN: 510141931

60550
The Sidney W. Eline, Sr. Memorial Foundation, Inc.
4629 Beaver Rd.
Louisville, KY 40207-3513
Contact: Lynda G. Eline, V.P.

Financial data (yr. ended 09/30/01): Assets, $915 (M); grants paid, $10,756; gifts received, $11,675; expenditures, $10,756; qualifying distributions, $10,756.
Limitations: Giving primarily in Louisville, KY.

Officers: Sidney W. Eline, Jr., Pres.; Lynda G. Eline, V.P.; Sidney W. Eline III, Secy.-Treas.
EIN: 611125250
Codes: GTI

60551
Miracle on Caney Creek, Inc.
535 W. 2nd St., Ste. 200
Lexington, KY 40508

Established in 1989 in KY.
Financial data (yr. ended 12/31/99): Assets, $616 (M); grants paid, $10,000; gifts received, $12,725; expenditures, $12,224; qualifying distributions, $12,224.
Officers: Michael Johnathon, Pres.; Thomas Bowne, V.P.; Tammy Doyle Farley, Secy.-Treas.
EIN: 611101107

60552
Matt Haselton Charitable Foundation
c/o Waring Blake Haselton
106 Sunset Ave.
Lagrange, KY 400311021

Established in 2001 in KY.
Donor(s): Blake Haselton, Pam Haselton.
Financial data (yr. ended 12/31/01): Assets, $295 (M); grants paid, $4,730; gifts received, $5,000; expenditures, $4,730; qualifying distributions, $4,730.
Limitations: Applications not accepted. Giving primarily in KY.
Application information: Contributes only to pre-selected organizations.
Advisory Board: Andrew B. Haselton, Bradley F. Haselton, Daniel C. Haselton, Pam Haselton.
Trustee: Blake Haselton.
EIN: 611389040

60553
James & Cynthia Green Foundation, Inc.
P.O. Box 43135
Louisville, KY 40253-0135

Established in 1992 in KY.
Donor(s): James W. Green, Cynthia Green, David L. Smith, David Laughlin.
Financial data (yr. ended 12/31/00): Assets, $77 (M); grants paid, $19,014; gifts received, $50,000; expenditures, $19,440; qualifying distributions, $19,014.
Limitations: Applications not accepted.
Application information: Contributes only to pre-selected organizations.
Officers: David L. Smith, Pres.; David Laughlin, Secy.; James W. Green, Treas.
EIN: 611215733

60554
Teresa Hatton Foundation, Inc.
P.O. Box 4046
Frankfort, KY 40604

Classified as a private operating foundation in 1985.
Financial data (yr. ended 12/31/01): Assets, $1 (M); grants paid, $0; gifts received, $25,451; expenditures, $54,162; qualifying distributions, $0.
Officers and Directors:* Richard Tanner,* Pres.; Mike Neihaus,* V.P.; Mary Ann Geddes,* Secy.; Sue Hatton,* Treas.; Nancy Tanner, Exec. Dir.; and 9 additional directors.
EIN: 311137462

LOUISIANA

60555
Kemper and Leila Williams Foundation
521 Tchoupitoulas St.
New Orleans, LA 70130
Contact: Fred M. Smith, Mgr.

Incorporated in 1974 in LA.
Donor(s): L. Kemper Williams,‡ Leila M. Williams,‡ and others.
Financial data (yr. ended 03/31/02): Assets, $132,949,194 (M); grants paid, $65,486; gifts received, $671,237; expenditures, $5,503,576; qualifying distributions, $4,861,718; giving activities include $4,872,447 for programs.
Limitations: Applications not accepted. Giving primarily in Franklin, LA.
Application information: Contributes only to pre-selected organizations.
Officers and Directors:* Mary Lou M. Christovich,* Pres.; Fred M. Smith,* Mgr.; Drew Jardine, G. Henry Person, Jr., Charles A. Snyder, John E. Walker.
EIN: 237336090

60556
The R. W. Norton Art Foundation
c/o AmSouth Bank
333 Texas St., SH 2069
Shreveport, LA 71101

Classified as a private operating foundation in 1971.
Donor(s): Mrs. Richard W. Norton, Jr.
Financial data (yr. ended 12/31/01): Assets, $118,615,168 (M); grants paid, $5,000; gifts received, $49,274; expenditures, $1,361,480; qualifying distributions, $4,614,821; giving activities include $1,143,320 for programs.
Officers and Directors:* Mrs. Richard W. Norton, Jr.,* Pres.; A.W. Coon,* V.P.; Jerrold M. Bloomer, Secy.; Allen E. McGary, Treas.; Maxwell Lewis Norton, Richard W. Norton III, Richard Sale, Joseph A. Waddell, Jr.
Trustee: AmSouth Bank.
EIN: 720517182

60557
Society for the Relief of Destitute Orphan Boys
c/o Donald Darce
P.O. Box 13249
New Orleans, LA 70185

Established in 1986 in LA.
Financial data (yr. ended 12/31/01): Assets, $32,985,951 (M); grants paid, $0; expenditures, $1,135,401; qualifying distributions, $1,110,406; giving activities include $1,110,406 for programs.
Officers: Warren K. Watters, Pres.; J. Herbert Williams, V.P.; J. Thomas Lewis, Secy.; Thomas D. Westfeldt, Treas.
Directors: Barry M. Fox, Samuel Logan, F. Allen Roussel, Jr.
EIN: 720408986

60558
Sydney and Walda Besthoff Foundation
(Formerly Virlane Foundation)
1055 St. Charles Ave., Ste. 701
New Orleans, LA 70130-3942
FAX: (504) 586-8442
Contact: Sydney Besthoff III, Chair.

Incorporated in 1958 in LA.
Financial data (yr. ended 09/30/01): Assets, $13,309,548 (M); grants paid, $288,500; gifts received, $105,283; expenditures, $302,575; qualifying distributions, $288,500.
Limitations: Applications not accepted. Giving primarily in New Orleans, LA.
Application information: Unsolicited requests for funds not accepted.
Officers and Directors:* Sydney Besthoff III, Chair.; Walda Besthoff,* Pres.; Virginia F. Besthoff,* V.P.; Valerie Marcus,* V.P.; Jane Steiner,* V.P.; Ron Dyer, Secy.-Treas.
EIN: 726019440
Codes: FD

60559
The Matilda Geddings Gray Foundation
P.O. Box 40
Lake Charles, LA 70602
Application address: 714 Esplanade Ave., New Orleans, LA 70116
Contact: Matilda Gray Stream, Pres.

Established in 1969 in LA.
Donor(s): Matilda Geddings Gray,‡ Matilda Gray Stream.
Financial data (yr. ended 10/31/99): Assets, $9,036,048 (M); grants paid, $14,238; gifts received, $6,000; expenditures, $83,976; qualifying distributions, $62,082.
Limitations: Giving primarily in LA.
Application information: Application form not required.
Officers and Trustees:* Matilda Gray Stream,* Pres.; Harold H. Stream III,* Secy.; Bruce Kirkpatrick.
EIN: 237072892

60560
The Kathleen Elizabeth O'Brien Foundation
P.O. Box 1317
Mandeville, LA 70470-1317

Donor(s): Kathleen E. O'Brien.‡
Financial data (yr. ended 12/31/00): Assets, $6,567,960 (M); grants paid, $0; gifts received, $96,502; expenditures, $37,061; qualifying distributions, $34,616; giving activities include $34,616 for programs.
Officers and Directors:* John C. Christian,* Pres.; Edward Lowndes,* Mgr.; R. King Milling, G. Henry Pierson, Jr., Wilson S. Shirley, Jr., Charles A. Snyder.
EIN: 726025708

60561
Noel Foundation, Inc.
c/o Robert Leitz
1 University Pl.
Shreveport, LA 71115-2399

Classified as a private operating foundation in 1990.
Financial data (yr. ended 12/31/99): Assets, $5,529,156 (M); grants paid, $0; gifts received, $178,865; expenditures, $156,121; qualifying distributions, $145,697; giving activities include $32,512 for programs.
Officer and Trustees:* Robert Leitz,* Pres.; Merritt B. Chastain, Jr., Clarence Frierson, James Lake, Vincent Marsala, Lane Sartor, Gilbert R. Shanley, Jr., Shelby L. Smith, Laurene Zaporozhetz.
EIN: 237177629

60562
Biedenharn Museum and Gardens
(Formerly Emy-Lou Biedenharn Foundation)
2006 Riverside Dr.
Monroe, LA 71201 (318) 387-5281
E-mail: bmuseum@bayou.com
Contact: Christine Hilliard

Established in 1974 in LA.

60562—LOUISIANA

Financial data (yr. ended 12/31/99): Assets, $4,861,661 (M); grants paid, $51,748; gifts received, $2,017; expenditures, $692,722; qualifying distributions, $51,748.
Limitations: Giving primarily in the Ouachita Parish, LA, area, with emphasis on Monroe.
Officers: Murray Biedenharn, Pres. and Treas.; Jody Johnson, V.P.; Robert L. Curry, Secy.
Director: Ralph Calhoun.
EIN: 726040895

60563
D. L. Dykes, Jr. Foundation
415 Texas St., Ste. 105
Shreveport, LA 71101-3541
Tel.: (800) 882-7424; FAX: (318) 227-9275; E-mail: comments@dldykes.org

Established in 1985 in LA; Classified as a private operating foundation 1999.
Donor(s): R.Z. Biedenharn.‡
Financial data (yr. ended 06/30/01): Assets, $4,645,776 (M); grants paid, $0; gifts received, $77,218; expenditures, $350,179; qualifying distributions, $0.
Limitations: Applications not accepted.
Application information: Contributes only to pre-selected organizations.
Officers: Edwin T. Baldridge, Vice-Chair.; Sydney Biedenharn Walker, Secy.
Trustees: Sue Dykes, Edwin Greer, Paul Hagens, Al Vekovius.
EIN: 721085968

60564
Brandon Hall Foundation
P.O. Box 26087
New Orleans, LA 70186

Financial data (yr. ended 12/31/01): Assets, $4,034,271 (M); grants paid, $0; gifts received, $147,000; expenditures, $152,894; qualifying distributions, $0.
Officers and Directors:* James R. Diefenthal,* Chair.; Edward L. Diefenthal,* Pres.; Joseph R. Boyd, James E. Ryder, Jr.
EIN: 581691816

60565
Oak Alley Foundation
3645 LA 18
Vacherie, LA 70090

Financial data (yr. ended 12/31/99): Assets, $3,325,829 (M); grants paid, $0; expenditures, $1,697,076; qualifying distributions, $244,807; giving activities include $1,697,076 for programs.
Limitations: Applications not accepted.
Application information: Contributes only to pre-selected organizations.
Officers: Jonathon Mayhew, Chair.; Roy Dancy, Secy.
Director: Zeb Mayhew, Jr.
EIN: 726032652

60566
Hibernia Community Development Corporation, Inc.
313 Carondelet St.
New Orleans, LA 70131 (504) 533-5846
Contact: Willie L. Spears, Pres.

Classified as a private operating foundation in 1996.
Financial data (yr. ended 12/31/00): Assets, $3,314,947 (M); grants paid, $20,105; gifts received, $195,447; expenditures, $341,485; qualifying distributions, $20,105.
Officers and Directors:* Willie L. Spears,* Pres.; Cathy E. Chessin, Secy.; Alan M. Ganucheau, Treas.; J. Herbert Boydstun, Willie Gable, Jr.,

Susan Klein, Jan M. Macaluso, Gary L. Ryan, Ron E. Samford.
EIN: 721321970

60567
Vivian & Bill M. Teague Charitable Foundation
7524 Garnet St.
New Orleans, LA 70124

Established in 1999 in LA.
Financial data (yr. ended 12/31/99): Assets, $3,219,931 (M); grants paid, $199,686; gifts received, $2,296,269; expenditures, $199,686; qualifying distributions, $199,686.
Limitations: Applications not accepted. Giving primarily in LA.
Application information: Contributes only to pre-selected organizations.
Trustee: Vicky D. Bayley.
EIN: 721427504
Codes: FD2

60568
Kendall Vick Public Law Foundation
1100 Poydras St., Ste. 2200
New Orleans, LA 70163-2200

Established in 1998.
Donor(s): Kendall Vick.‡
Financial data (yr. ended 03/31/01): Assets, $3,121,650 (M); grants paid, $168,688; gifts received, $2,465,886; expenditures, $192,131; qualifying distributions, $168,688.
Limitations: Applications not accepted.
Application information: Contributes only to pre-selected organizations.
Officers: Jerome J. Reso, Jr., Pres.; Leon H. Rittenberg, Jr., Secy.
Director: Kathleen Moore Vick.
EIN: 721293729

60569
The Blanchard Foundation
2400 Jefferson Hwy., Ste. 600
Jefferson, LA 70121

Classified as a private operating foundation in 1988.
Donor(s): James U. Blanchard III.‡
Financial data (yr. ended 12/31/00): Assets, $3,082,560 (M); grants paid, $0; gifts received, $21,000; expenditures, $23,750; qualifying distributions, $23,673; giving activities include $23,673 for programs.
Officer: Paul T. Gariepy, Jr., Treas.
EIN: 721058156

60570
San Francisco Plantation
P.O. Box AC
Garyville, LA 70051

Financial data (yr. ended 12/31/01): Assets, $2,771,873 (M); grants paid, $0; expenditures, $344,822; qualifying distributions, $0.
Officers and Directors:* Manfred Spindler,* Chair.; Larry M. Echelberger,* Pres.; Joseph D. Pyner,* V.P.; Daniel L. Ehrhart,* Secy.-Treas.; John E. Fuselier.
EIN: 720789586

60571
The Giardina Family Foundation
1575 Hwy. 304
Thibodaux, LA 70301

Established in 1997 in LA.
Donor(s): Jacob A. Giardina, Maxine G. Giardina, Whitney Enterprises, Inc.
Financial data (yr. ended 08/31/01): Assets, $1,756,461 (M); grants paid, $57,555; expenditures, $215,305; qualifying distributions,

$200,357; giving activities include $142,943 for programs.
Limitations: Applications not accepted. Giving primarily in LA.
Application information: Contributes only to pre-selected organizations.
Trustees: Jacob A. Giardina, Maxine G. Giardina.
EIN: 726186958

60572
Audubon Lakes Foundation, Inc.
P.O. Box 1640
St. Francisville, LA 70775-1640

Donor(s): Arlin K. Dease.
Financial data (yr. ended 10/31/01): Assets, $1,480,997 (M); grants paid, $0; gifts received, $620; expenditures, $207,674; qualifying distributions, $0.
Limitations: Applications not accepted.
Application information: Contributes only to pre-selected organizations.
Officers: Arlin K. Dease, Pres.; Joseph A. Perrault, Secy.; William Mangham, Treas.
EIN: 581660684

60573
Longue Vue House and Gardens Corporation
7 Bamboo Rd.
New Orleans, LA 70124-1007

Financial data (yr. ended 12/31/99): Assets, $1,438,341 (M); grants paid, $0; gifts received, $623,477; expenditures, $159,470; qualifying distributions, $991,531; giving activities include $991,750 for programs.
Officers: Nan W. Galloway, Pres.; William R. Bell, Treas.
Directors: Hon. Joan B. Armstrong, Jay Aronson, Cary Bond, and 19 additional directors.
EIN: 581638039

60574
Charles & Elizabeth Wetmore Foundation
824 Elmwood Park Blvd. Ste. 210
New Orleans, LA 70123
Application address: 4700 Hessmer Ave., Metairie, LA 70002, tel.: (504) 779-1888; FAX: (504) 779-1830
Contact: Keta Lowe, Exec. Dir.

Established in 1969 in LA.
Financial data (yr. ended 12/31/99): Assets, $1,327,705 (M); grants paid, $507,669; gifts received, $173,361; expenditures, $574,907; qualifying distributions, $563,050.
Limitations: Giving limited to the metropolitan New Orleans, LA, area.
Application information: Referral from physician or treatment center required. Application form not required.
Officers: William Shaw, Jr., Pres.; Henry Jackson, M.D., V.P.; William C. Norris, Secy.; Jack Nichols, Treas.
EIN: 237120743
Codes: FD, GTI

60575
Zigler Museum Foundation
P.O. Box 986
Jennings, LA 70546

Classified as a private operating foundation in 1971.
Financial data (yr. ended 12/31/01): Assets, $1,138,797 (M); grants paid, $0; gifts received, $88,916; expenditures, $106,459; qualifying distributions, $113,519; giving activities include $91,064 for programs.

Officers: Gregory N. Marcantel, Pres.; Jim deCordova, V.P.; Jennifer L. Boudreaux, Secy.; Marie C. Romero, Treas.
Trustees: Julie Berry, Joe V. Black, Maxine Knelow, James P. Martin, Wendell Miller, Burt Tietje.
EIN: 726027971

60576
The Brownell Foundation
P.O. Box 949
Morgan City, LA 70381-0949

Classified as a private operating foundation in 1973.
Financial data (yr. ended 12/31/99): Assets, $1,016,614 (M); grants paid, $0; expenditures, $70,278; qualifying distributions, $42,098; giving activities include $16,699 for programs.
Officers and Directors:* Lorraine Brownell,* Pres.; Brenda Ayo,* Secy.; H.B. Chalstrom, Wilbur R. Cross, Mike Vanover.
EIN: 726041231

60577
H. E. Storer Charitable Foundation
P.O. Box 6761
Shreveport, LA 71106

Established in 1986 in LA.
Donor(s): Hubert Elmer Storer.
Financial data (yr. ended 12/31/01): Assets, $905,203 (M); grants paid, $25,000; gifts received, $201,040; expenditures, $25,000; qualifying distributions, $25,000.
Limitations: Applications not accepted. Giving primarily in Shreveport, LA.
Application information: Contributes only to pre-selected organizations.
Trustee: Hubert Elmer Storer.
EIN: 721089985

60578
Keyes Foundation
1113 Chartres St.
New Orleans, LA 70116-2504

Financial data (yr. ended 04/30/01): Assets, $851,184 (M); grants paid, $0; gifts received, $45,060; expenditures, $97,981; qualifying distributions, $17,637; giving activities include $97,981 for programs.
Officers: Clarke C. Hawley, Pres.; Gary R. Williams, V.P.; Jessie J. Poesch, Secy.; John Geiser III, Treas.
EIN: 042476116

60579
Gitter-Yelen Foundation
9 Bamboo Rd.
New Orleans, LA 70124

Established in 1998 in DE and LA.
Donor(s): Kurt A. Gitter, Alice Rae Yelen.
Financial data (yr. ended 12/31/00): Assets, $843,859 (M); grants paid, $17,950; expenditures, $87,503; qualifying distributions, $17,950.
Limitations: Applications not accepted. Giving primarily in LA.
Application information: Contributes only to pre-selected organizations.
Officers: Kurt A. Gitter, Pres.; Alice Rae Yellen, Secy.
EIN: 721340720

60580
Louisiana Disabled Persons Finance Corporation
4100 J. Bennett Johnston Ave.
Lake Charles, LA 70615

Classified as a private operating foundation in 1989.
Financial data (yr. ended 06/30/01): Assets, $418,085 (M); grants paid, $0; expenditures, $112,814; qualifying distributions, $96,349.
Officers: Dorothy Campbell, Pres.; Pansy Skipper, V.P.; Rebecca Hughes, Secy.-Treas.; Howard Stroud, Jr., Exec. Dir.; Albert H. Toombs, Fin. Dir.
Directors: Phillip Grass, R.A. Marriner, Sylvia Schwartzenberg.
EIN: 720979554
Codes: TN

60581
Donald Palmer Charitable Foundation
161 Hirboy Ave.
Harahan, LA 70123
Application address: 1319 Valence St., New Orleans, LA 70115
Contact: Donald A. Palmer, Pres.

Donor(s): Donald A. Palmer.
Financial data (yr. ended 12/31/99): Assets, $365,532 (M); grants paid, $12,475; gifts received, $52,093; expenditures, $13,059; qualifying distributions, $12,475.
Limitations: Giving primarily in New Orleans, LA.
Officers: Donald A. Palmer, Pres.; Simmon Savore, Jr., Secy.
EIN: 721329780

60582
Centerville Presbyterian Foundation
P.O. Box 343
Centerville, LA 70522

Classified as a private operating foundation in 1972.
Financial data (yr. ended 06/30/99): Assets, $245,289 (M); grants paid, $0; gifts received, $5,185; expenditures, $13,797; qualifying distributions, $13,607; giving activities include $8,173 for programs.
Officers: Hugh V. Dykes, Pres.; Beverly Phillips Adams, Secy.; Deidre O'Neill Strong, Treas.
EIN: 721199322

60583
Feliciana Property Owners Association
4644 Arrowhead St.
Baton Rouge, LA 70808

Established in 2000 in LA.
Financial data (yr. ended 12/31/01): Assets, $224,332 (M); grants paid, $100; gifts received, $128,252; expenditures, $876; qualifying distributions, $100.
Trustees: Chris Cartton, Dorothy Prowell.
EIN: 721288296

60584
The Corner Stone Foundation
P.O. Box 1129
St. Francisville, LA 70775-1129

Donor(s): Wilson Ray Mendow, Janet G. Mendow.
Financial data (yr. ended 06/30/01): Assets, $165,465 (M); grants paid, $665; expenditures, $7,480; qualifying distributions, $8,410.
Limitations: Applications not accepted. Giving on a national basis.
Application information: Contributes only to pre-selected organizations.
Officers: Wilson Ray Mendow, Pres.; Janet G. Mendow, Secy.-Treas.
EIN: 720926064

60585
Louisiana Poultry Industries Educational Foundation, Inc.
P.O. Box 931
Natchitoches, LA 71458-0931
Application address: 120 Ingram Hall, LSU, Baton Rouge, LA 70803
Contact: Theresia Laverge, Secy.

Classified as a private operating foundation in 1990.
Donor(s): Louisiana Poultry Federation.
Financial data (yr. ended 12/31/01): Assets, $108,711 (M); grants paid, $5,500; gifts received, $8,800; expenditures, $5,516; qualifying distributions, $120,351.
Limitations: Giving limited to LA.
Application information: Applicants must be enrolled in a Louisiana institution of higher learning. Application form required.
Officers: Billy Todd, Pres.; Paul Bridges, V.P.; Theresia Laverge, Secy.; Russ Danzy,* Treas.; Roger Teekel.
EIN: 721148406

60586
Institute of Politics
c/o Loyola Univ.
6363 St. Charles Ave., Box 119
New Orleans, LA 70118

Classified as a private operating foundation in 1968.
Financial data (yr. ended 06/30/00): Assets, $81,042 (M); grants paid, $0; gifts received, $22,150; expenditures, $33,031; qualifying distributions, $28,437; giving activities include $28,437 for programs.
Officers and Directors:* Fr. Thomas Clancy, S.J., Pres.; Edward F. Renwick,* V.P. and Treas.; C.B. Forgotston, Secy.; Ruthledge Clement, Maureen Detweiler, Griffin Harrell, Fr. Bernard Knoth, S.J., William A. Schultz.
EIN: 726041302

60587
Ellis and Elaine Mintz Foundation
3200 Energy Centre
1100 Poydras St.
New Orleans, LA 70163-3200

Established in 1998 in LA.
Donor(s): Ellis Mintz.
Financial data (yr. ended 12/31/99): Assets, $74,770 (M); grants paid, $26,000; expenditures, $27,266; qualifying distributions, $26,000.
Limitations: Applications not accepted.
Application information: Contributes only to pre-selected organizations.
Officer: Ellis Mintz, Pres.
EIN: 721431779

60588
Davis Family Fund
344 Ocean Ave.
Gretna, LA 70053

Established in 1963.
Financial data (yr. ended 12/31/99): Assets, $57,721 (M); grants paid, $0; expenditures, $292; qualifying distributions, $0; giving activities include $292 for programs.
Officers: Walter Davis III, Pres.; Marjorie Davis, V.P.
Director: Walter Davis, Jr.
EIN: 726029528

60589
John Kyle D'Amico Ransome Memorial Scholarship Foundation
37243 Weiss Rd.
Denham Springs, LA 70706 (225) 664-7268
Contact: Marie D. Ransome, V.P.

Financial data (yr. ended 12/31/99): Assets, $34,448 (M); grants paid, $1,500; expenditures, $1,661; qualifying distributions, $1,518.
Officers: Al J. Ransome, Pres.; Marie D. Ransome, V.P.; Justin P. Ransome, Secy.-Treas.
Director: Sam J. D'Amico.
EIN: 721130221

60590
The Good Shepherd Foundation, Inc.
Lambert Bldg.
1724 N. Burnside Ave.
Gonzales, LA 70707-1648
Application address: P.O. Box 1648, Gonzales, LA 70708-1648, tel.: (225) 673-8708
Contact: Louis J. Lambert, Pres.

Established in 1993 in LA.
Donor(s): Louis J. Lambert, Jr., South Central Bell, Atmos Energy Corp., Entergy Corp.
Financial data (yr. ended 12/31/99): Assets, $29,238 (M); grants paid, $7,234; expenditures, $8,219; qualifying distributions, $7,234.
Limitations: Giving limited to residents of LA.
Officer: Louis J. Lambert, Pres.
EIN: 721231453
Codes: GTI

60591
Greenwood Equine-Assisted Therapies, Inc.
333 Texas St., Ste. 1235
Shreveport, LA 71101

Established in 1997 in LA.
Financial data (yr. ended 12/31/01): Assets, $21,476 (M); grants paid, $0; gifts received, $9,345; expenditures, $26,680; qualifying distributions, $0.
Limitations: Applications not accepted.
Application information: Contributes only to pre-selected organizations.
Trustee: Dewey W. Corley.
EIN: 721377252

60592
Central Louisiana Pro Bono Project
P.O. Box 1324
Alexandria, LA 71309-1324

Classified as a private operating foundation in 1993.
Donor(s): Louisiana Bar Foundation.
Financial data (yr. ended 12/31/00): Assets, $19,384 (M); grants paid, $0; gifts received, $32,124; expenditures, $44,440; qualifying distributions, $42,908; giving activities include $42,908 for programs.
Officer and Directors:* William Polk, Chair.; Laura Sylvester, Vice-Chair.; Charles Elliott, Secy.-Treas.; Melissa Lary, Jennifer Munsterman, Danny Sylvester, Valerie Thompson.
EIN: 721198792

60593
Ruth Paz Foundation, Inc.
17 Waverly Pl.
Destrehan, LA 70047-2127 (504) 764-0395
Contact: J. Michael Paz, Pres.

Financial data (yr. ended 04/30/01): Assets, $13,807 (M); grants paid, $3,290; gifts received, $3,999; expenditures, $9,809; qualifying distributions, $3,290; giving activities include $4,609 for programs.

Limitations: Giving primarily in Honduras; some giving also in the U.S.
Officer: J. Michael Paz, Pres.
EIN: 721411723

60594
Henry and Pamela Bonura Foundation
7223 Ring St.
New Orleans, LA 70124

Established in 2000 in LA.
Donor(s): Pamela R. Bonura.
Financial data (yr. ended 12/31/01): Assets, $10,707 (M); grants paid, $40,000; gifts received, $23,340; expenditures, $43,340; qualifying distributions, $40,000.
Limitations: Applications not accepted.
Application information: Contributes only to pre-selected organizations.
Directors: Pamela R. Bonura, Jerome J. Reso, Jr., Darrah Schaefer.
EIN: 721486533

60595
Vida Nueva Counseling Foundation
17709 Lake Iris
Baton Rouge, LA 70817

Established around 1986.
Financial data (yr. ended 12/31/00): Assets, $6,868 (M); grants paid, $0; gifts received, $710; expenditures, $5,057; qualifying distributions, $0.
Directors: Betty Armstrong, Chris Curry, Cynthia Levy, Heida Shapiro.
EIN: 943035417

60596
Akula Foundation
c/o Shiva K. Akula
P.O. Box 850715
New Orleans, LA 70185-0715

Donor(s): Shiva K. Akula.
Financial data (yr. ended 12/31/00): Assets, $5,524 (M); grants paid, $2,795; gifts received, $4,921; expenditures, $2,947; qualifying distributions, $2,795.
Limitations: Applications not accepted. Giving primarily in LA.
Application information: Contributes only to pre-selected organizations.
Officer: J.R. Akula, Secy.-Treas.
Director: Shiva K. Akula.
EIN: 721258938

60597
The Ingrid Rhinehart Handicapped Children's Foundation, Inc.
416 Travis St., Ste. 715
Shreveport, LA 71101
Contact: Ingrid R. Campbell, Pres.

Established in 1997 in LA.
Financial data (yr. ended 12/31/00): Assets, $4,251 (M); grants paid, $54,413; gifts received, $36,300; expenditures, $55,391; qualifying distributions, $54,413.
Limitations: Applications not accepted.
Application information: Contributes only to pre-selected organizations.
Officers: Ingrid R. Rhinehart, Pres.; Cathy Campbell, V.P.; Kim Campbell, V.P.; Kathryn Campbell Hyde, V.P.; Darlene Drake, Secy.; Minnett Thornton, Treas.
EIN: 721399731

60598
South Louisiana Clinical Research Foundation, Inc.
4212 W. Congress St., No. 1200
Lafayette, LA 70506

Established in 1999 in LA.
Financial data (yr. ended 06/30/01): Assets, $3,333 (M); grants paid, $4,200; gifts received, $7,314; expenditures, $21,890; qualifying distributions, $4,200.
Officer: David Allie, Pres.
EIN: 721430540

60599
World Witness Evangelism Association, Inc.
441 Dew Ln.-Johnson Rd.
West Monroe, LA 71291-8664

Financial data (yr. ended 12/31/01): Assets, $1,559 (M); grants paid, $0; gifts received, $0; qualifying distributions, $0.
Limitations: Giving limited to LA.
Officers and Directors:* S. Jack Dew,* Pres.; Nan D. Dew,* Secy.; Cindy Williams, Johnny W. Williams.
EIN: 720837622

60600
St. John-Henthorne Foundation
P.O. Box 13485
Alexandria, LA 71315
Application address: 485 Downs Ln., Alexandria, LA 71303
Contact: Peggy D. St. John, Pres.

Established in 1999.
Financial data (yr. ended 12/31/01): Assets, $1,136 (M); grants paid, $6,265; gifts received, $1,256; expenditures, $7,861; qualifying distributions, $6,265.
Officers: Peggy D. St. John, Pres.; Carolyn J. Smilie, V.P.; Stephen E. Henthorne, Secy.-Treas.
EIN: 726181185

60601
Lee Haley Evangelistic Association, Inc.
P.O. Box 756
Denham Springs, LA 70727-0756

Classified as a private operating foundation in 1986.
Financial data (yr. ended 12/31/99): Assets, $1,068 (M); grants paid, $712; gifts received, $2,304; expenditures, $2,663; qualifying distributions, $2,663.
Limitations: Applications not accepted.
Application information: Contributes only to pre-selected organizations.
Officer: Lee Haley, Pres.
EIN: 720899932

60602
Joseph J. Frensilli Charitable
c/o Joseph J. Frensilli
392 Fairfield Ave.
Gretna, LA 70056-7003

Financial data (yr. ended 12/31/01): Assets, $900 (M); grants paid, $100; gifts received, $1,000; expenditures, $100; qualifying distributions, $100.
Director: Joseph J. Frensilli.
EIN: 726202600

60603
James P. Raymond, Jr. Charitable Foundation
1422 Marengo St.
New Orleans, LA 70115

Established in 1997 in LA.
Donor(s): James P. Raymond, Jr.

Financial data (yr. ended 12/31/01): Assets, $226 (M); grants paid, $500; gifts received, $1,000; expenditures, $1,144; qualifying distributions, $500.
Limitations: Applications not accepted. Giving primarily in New Orleans, LA.
Application information: Contributes only to pre-selected organizations.
Officer: James P. Raymond, Jr., Pres.
EIN: 311476555

60604
Acorn Television in Action for Communities, Inc.
1024 Elysian Fields Ave.
New Orleans, LA 70117 (504) 943-5954

Financial data (yr. ended 12/31/00): Assets, $21 (M); grants paid, $0; gifts received, $150; expenditures, $1,000; qualifying distributions, $0.
Officers and Directors:* Gayle Robbins,* Pres.; Ruby Webb,* V.P.; Ruby Booker,* Secy.; Fernando Lucero,* Treas.; Lena Burdette, Aaron Hartsfield, Annette Wilcoxsan.
EIN: 721054493

60605
International Foundation for Medical/Dental Research, Inc.
225 Highland Dr.
Many, LA 71449-3717

Financial data (yr. ended 12/31/01): Assets, $1 (M); grants paid, $0; expenditures, $0; qualifying distributions, $0.
Officers and Trustees:* Bobby Brocato,* Chair.; Samuel J. Callia,* Secy.-Treas.; Frank Brown, George McGowan.
EIN: 581750232

60606
God Rules Ministry, Inc.
1322 Lee Dr.
Baton Rouge, LA 70808

Classified as a private operating foundation in 1998.
Financial data (yr. ended 12/31/99): Assets, $0 (L); grants paid, $2,890; gifts received, $100; expenditures, $71,147; qualifying distributions, $71,147.
Officers and Trustees:* Bob Brunet,* Pres.; Tyler LaFauci,* V.P.; James Field,* Secy.; Gary Black,* Treas.; Todd Kinchen.
EIN: 582077591

60607
The Helping Hand of the World, Inc.
910 Sunshine Dr.
Baker, LA 70714

Donor(s): Gillie Clifton Crumholt.
Financial data (yr. ended 09/30/01): Assets, $0 (M); grants paid, $7,940; gifts received, $7,940; expenditures, $7,940; qualifying distributions, $7,940.
Limitations: Applications not accepted.
Director: Gillie Clifton Crumholt.
EIN: 721424051

MAINE

60608
Galen Cole Family Foundation, Inc.
510 Perry Rd.
Bangor, ME 04401 (207) 990-3600

Established in 1974 in ME.
Donor(s): Galen L. Cole, Garret E. Cole, Suzanne E. Cole.
Financial data (yr. ended 12/31/99): Assets, $20,414,124 (M); grants paid, $0; gifts received, $397,572; expenditures, $548,483; qualifying distributions, $602,828; giving activities include $462,582 for programs.
Officers: Galen L. Cole, Pres.; Suzanne E. Cole, V.P.; Garret E. Cole, Treas.
EIN: 237425774

60609
The Island Foundation
P.O. Box 208
Seal Harbor, ME 04675

Established in 1989 in NY.
Donor(s): David Rockefeller.
Financial data (yr. ended 12/31/01): Assets, $19,062,410 (M); grants paid, $0; gifts received, $6,909,507; expenditures, $707,865; qualifying distributions, $545,090; giving activities include $543,654 for programs.
Officers and Directors:* Neva R. Goodwin,* Pres.; Elizabeth Straus,* V.P.; S. Parkman Shaw, Treas.; R. Scott Asen, Brooke Astor, Patricia H. Blake, Don E. Coates, Sheldon Goldthwaite, Eileen Growald, Polly Guth, Penny Harris, Elise F. Hawtin, Denholm Jacobs, Robert P. Kogod, David MacDonald, David Rockefeller, Jr., James S. Sligar, Kathy Suminsby.
EIN: 237102758

60610
Rosscare, Inc.
489 State St.
P.O. Box 404
Bangor, ME 04402-0404

Established in 1985 in ME.
Donor(s): Sylvia E. Ross Trust.
Financial data (yr. ended 09/25/99): Assets, $12,856,507 (M); grants paid, $0; gifts received, $242,040; expenditures, $1,246,687; qualifying distributions, $188,046; giving activities include $1,243,639 for programs.
Officers and Directors:* George F. Eaton II,* Chair.; Kenneth A. Hews,* Pres.; William K. Sullivan, M.D.,* V.P.; Leonard Giambalvo,* Secy.; Daniel B. Coffey,* Treas.; Henry H. Atkins II, M.D., Douglas H. Brown, David M. Carlisle, Allan D. Currie, M.D., P. James Dowe, Jr., Norman A. Ledwin, Michael J. Melnnis, Deedy Schiro, Walter E. Travis, Richard J. Warren, John A. Woodcock, Jr.
EIN: 010391038

60611
Pine Tree Conservation Society, Inc.
c/o W. H. Hale
208 Concord St.
Portland, ME 04103-3102

Financial data (yr. ended 12/31/99): Assets, $12,160,905 (M); grants paid, $0; expenditures, $188,436; qualifying distributions, $368,552.
Officers and Trustees:* Kathleen McLaughlin Jeffords,* Pres.; George M. Jeffords,* V.P.; Wayne H. Hale,* Treas.; John D. Jeffords, Sara J. Jeffords.
EIN: 237158781

60612
Old Folks Home in Bath
1 Washington St.
Bath, ME 04530

Classified as a private operating foundation in 1973.
Financial data (yr. ended 12/31/00): Assets, $8,993,362 (M); grants paid, $0; gifts received, $432,914; expenditures, $1,108,464; qualifying distributions, $0.
Officers: Arthur F. Mayo III, Pres.; Patricia J. Ames, V.P.; Frank A. Donnell, Treas.
EIN: 010131950

60613
Old York Historical Society
P.O. Box 312
York, ME 03909

Classified as a private operating foundation in 1984.
Financial data (yr. ended 12/31/99): Assets, $8,722,540 (M); grants paid, $0; gifts received, $261,776; expenditures, $890,463; qualifying distributions, $710,237; giving activities include $649,243 for programs.
Officers: Russell A. Peterson, Pres.; James B. Bartlett, V.P.; Sarah Newick, Secy.; David T. Cousineau, Treas.; Scott Stevens, Exec. Dir.
Trustees: Karen Arsenault, Marion Fuller Brown, Joseph C. Donnelly, Jr., Daniel P. Epstein, James B. Gould, Philip L. Kimball, Jr., Mary MacLean, Hap Moore, Virginia Parson, Karen Ida Peterson, Paul Scudiere, Catherine B. Sherman, Henry Weeks Trimble III, S. Thompson Viele, William Wieting.
EIN: 222474846

60614
Kaler-Vaill Memorial Home
382 Black Point Rd.
Scarborough, ME 04074-9378

Classified as a private operating foundation in 1973.
Financial data (yr. ended 06/30/00): Assets, $8,584,088 (M); grants paid, $0; gifts received, $134,316; expenditures, $213,240; qualifying distributions, $215,651; giving activities include $181,467 for programs.
Officers: June Gillis, Pres.; Debbie Pierce, V.P.; Constance Martin, Secy.; John Messer, Treas.
EIN: 010261396

60615
McArthur Home for Aged People Association
292 Elm St.
Biddeford, ME 04005

Established in 1974.
Financial data (yr. ended 10/31/01): Assets, $7,571,534 (M); grants paid, $108,401; expenditures, $301,066; qualifying distributions, $274,877; giving activities include $108,401 for programs.
Officers: Francis T. Spencer, Pres.; Erica Doyon, V.P.; Kenton Norton, Treas.; Dean Wolfarnt, Treas.
EIN: 010212437
Codes: FD2

60616
Warren Memorial Foundation
P.O. Box 608
Boothbay, ME 04537 (207) 633-6044
URL: http://users.javanet.com/~warren/board.html
Contact: Judith L. Collins, Treas.

Incorporated in 1929 in ME.
Donor(s): Susan C. Warren.‡

Financial data (yr. ended 12/31/00): Assets, $7,252,019 (M); grants paid, $30,635; gifts received, $2,992; expenditures, $260,904; qualifying distributions, $304,438; giving activities include $208,803 for programs.
Limitations: Giving limited to ME, with emphasis on Westbrook.
Application information: Application form not required.
Officers and Directors:* Howard C. Reiche, Jr.,* Pres.; Judith Collins,* Treas. and Clerk; Luther B. Francis, Bruce Saunders.
EIN: 010220759

60617
Maine Education Services
1 City Ctr.
Portland, ME 04101

Established in 1993 in ME.
Financial data (yr. ended 12/31/99): Assets, $6,443,389 (M); grants paid, $14,350; expenditures, $4,858,338; qualifying distributions, $453,155; giving activities include $4,559,658 for programs.
Limitations: Applications not accepted.
Application information: Scholarships awarded based on entrance into various competitive events.
Officers: Richard H. Pierce, Pres. and C.E.O.; Richard D. Pushard, V.P.; Timothy A. Sabo, V.P.
Directors: Leroy J. Barry, Kenneth M. Curtis, Duane D. Fitzgerald, Bennett D. Katz, Blythe J. McGarvie, John R. McKernan, Jr., Patricia B. McNamara, Robert A. Moore, Walter H. Moulton, Peter J. Moynihan.
EIN: 010471533

60618
Wardwell Home for the Aging, Inc.
(Formerly Wardwell Home for Old Ladies of Saco & Biddeford)
43 Middle St.
Saco, ME 04072 (207) 284-7061
FAX: (207) 283-9642

Classified as a private operating foundation in 1986.
Financial data (yr. ended 06/30/01): Assets, $5,908,195 (M); grants paid, $385; gifts received, $17,850; expenditures, $668,771; qualifying distributions, $70,831; giving activities include $668,386 for programs.
Limitations: Applications not accepted. Giving primarily in ME.
Publications: Newsletter, informational brochure.
Application information: Contributes only to pre-selected organizations.
Officers and Trustees:* Roland Michaud,* Pres.; Larry Smith, Jr.,* V.P.; Charlene Donahue,* Secy.; Kevin Roberts, Secy.; Kevin Savage,* Treas.; Lorraine Bouchard, Eric Cole, Bernard Featherman, Agnes Flaherty, Vicki Gordan, John Hoyt, Barbara Renell.
EIN: 010213987

60619
Deborah Lincoln House
(Formerly Belfast Home for Aged Women)
60 Cedar St.
Belfast, ME 04915-1801

Classified as a private operating foundation in 1973.
Financial data (yr. ended 09/30/01): Assets, $5,195,419 (M); grants paid, $0; gifts received, $3,312; expenditures, $328,759; qualifying distributions, $0; giving activities include $294,481 for programs.
Limitations: Applications not accepted.

Application information: Contributes only to pre-selected organizations.
Officers and Directors:* Patricia Healey Thompson,* Pres.; Roger Blake,* V.P.; Anita Starrett, Recording Secy.; Raymond Nickerson,* Treas.
EIN: 010226346

60620
Redington Memorial Home
c/o Merrill, Hyde, Fortier & Youney
P.O. Box 3100
Skowhegan, ME 04976

Financial data (yr. ended 12/31/99): Assets, $4,891,256 (M); grants paid, $0; expenditures, $308,992; qualifying distributions, $276,946; giving activities include $278,189 for programs.
Officers and Directors:* Elton D. Powers,* Pres.; Dorothea LaCasse,* Secy.; Leslie Bray, Geoffrey F. Brown, Joan Cross, Gail H. Gibson, John D. Gibson, William J. Laney, Barbara E. Mullen, Alton B. Whittemore, Carol Withee.
EIN: 010211547

60621
The Farmington Home for Aged People
c/o Elizabeth Marks
P.O. Box 708
Farmington, ME 04938-0708

Classified as a private operating foundation in 1974.
Financial data (yr. ended 05/31/02): Assets, $2,914,260 (M); grants paid, $0; gifts received, $8,888; expenditures, $555,235; qualifying distributions, $0.
Officers and Trustees:* Elizabeth S. Marks,* Pres.; Craig Jordan,* V.P.; Beverly A. Besaw,* Treas.; Joseph Holman,* Clerk; Beverly Adams, Dan C. Adams, Elizabeth Bailey, Robert Bean III, John Bogar, Carol Bowne, Paul Brinkman, M.D., Carolyn Eaton, Richard Harvey, Mary Lovejoy, Joan Patterson, Jean Vachon, Mary Wing.
EIN: 010217212

60622
Eunice Frye Home
37 Capisic St.
Portland, ME 04102-2299

Classified as a private operating foundation in 1973.
Financial data (yr. ended 09/30/00): Assets, $2,682,758 (M); grants paid, $0; gifts received, $3,826; expenditures, $612,224; qualifying distributions, $552,311; giving activities include $97,864 for programs.
Officers and Directors:* Nancy Boyce,* Pres.; Gertrude Parker,* 1st V.P.; Andrea L. Varney,* 2nd V.P.; Florence Kelly,* Corresponding Secy.; Katherine Sullivan,* Recording Secy.; Vaun Born,* Treas.; Doris V. Chapman, Peg Clark, Lucile Cleaves, Helena Jensen, and 13 additional directors.
EIN: 010211504

60623
Good Samaritan Agency
(Formerly Good Samaritan Home Association)
100 Ridgewood Dr.
Bangor, ME 04401

Classified as a private operating foundation in 1971.
Donor(s): United Way.
Financial data (yr. ended 06/30/02): Assets, $2,632,830 (M); grants paid, $0; gifts received, $350,903; expenditures, $648,910; qualifying distributions, $0.

Officers and Directors:* James A. McLeod, Chair.; Theresa G. Bragg,* Pres.; Janet Milley,* 1st V.P.; Donna Wadleigh,* 2nd V.P.; Elizabeth A. Bard,* Secy.; Amanda Larson,* Treas.; and 23 additional directors.
EIN: 010211507

60624
Camden Home for Senior Citizens
c/o Adele Hopkins
66 Washington St.
Camden, ME 04843

Established in 1941; classified as a private operating foundation in 1972.
Financial data (yr. ended 05/31/01): Assets, $2,596,412 (M); grants paid, $77,354; expenditures, $97,686; qualifying distributions, $84,947.
Limitations: Giving limited to residents of Camden, Hope, Lincolnville, and Rockport, ME.
Officers: Sam Jones, Pres.; Marie Connell, V.P.; Adele Hopkins, Secy.-Treas.
EIN: 010248064
Codes: FD2, GTI

60625
Old Folks Home Association of Brunswick
52 Harpswell St.
Brunswick, ME 04011-2538

Financial data (yr. ended 03/31/01): Assets, $2,419,647 (M); grants paid, $0; gifts received, $8,150; expenditures, $517,226; qualifying distributions, $517,226; giving activities include $344,345 for programs.
Officers: John Hutchins, Pres.; Robert Nunn, V.P.; Nancy Morrill, Secy.; Maurice J. Boucher, Treas.
EIN: 010220389

60626
Cape Elizabeth Home
521 Ocean St.
South Portland, ME 04106-6697

Established in 1893.
Financial data (yr. ended 03/31/01): Assets, $2,413,023 (M); grants paid, $0; expenditures, $212,772; qualifying distributions, $180,854; giving activities include $179,039 for programs.
Officers and Directors:* Edward C. Dalton,* Pres.; Carolyn Carson,* V.P.; Elizabeth F. Honan,* Secy.; William J. Gilchrest,* Treas.; Heather Bowns, Wayne Brooking, John F. Gibbons, Marguerite Hallowell, William H. Jordan, Elaine L. Kersey, Edward J. McComb, Constance C. Murray, Florence Petrlik, Barbara Sanborn.
EIN: 010238086

60627
Araxine Wilkins Sawyer Foundation
P.O. Box 27
Greene, ME 04236-0027

Classified as a private operating foundation in 1973.
Financial data (yr. ended 10/31/01): Assets, $1,742,676 (M); grants paid, $0; gifts received, $2,543; expenditures, $65,806; qualifying distributions, $61,818; giving activities include $62,802 for programs.
Officers: Donald H. Rose, Pres.; Albert K. Murch, Treas.
Trustees: Roger A. Adams, Jere R. Clifford, and 3 additional trustees.
EIN: 010228468

60628
Senior Center at Lower Village, Inc.
175 Port Rd.
Kennebunk, ME 04043-5147

Established in 1990 in ME.
Donor(s): Ann Spaulding, Charles Spaulding.
Financial data (yr. ended 12/31/01): Assets, $1,723,010 (M); grants paid, $0; gifts received, $13,495; expenditures, $213,641; qualifying distributions, $125,372; giving activities include $41,720 for programs.
Officers: Steven Morris, Chair.; Douglas Stockbridge, Treas.
Directors: Diana Abbott, Richard Eaton, Martha Hussey, Florence Damon, Ann Spaulding, Hank Spaulding, and 7 additional directors.
EIN: 223075624

60629
The Talbot Home
(Formerly Knox Home for Aged)
73 Talbot Ave.
Rockland, ME 04841

Classified as a private operating foundation in 1984.
Donor(s): Harry M. Pratt.‡
Financial data (yr. ended 12/31/01): Assets, $1,646,817 (M); grants paid, $0; expenditures, $241,954; qualifying distributions, $137,434; giving activities include $233,133 for programs.
Officers: Mary Maddox, Pres.; Evelyn Eilers, Secy.; Winfield Chatto, Treas.
EIN: 010217325

60630
Seal Cove Auto Museum
P.O. Box 190
Camden, ME 04843-0189

Donor(s): Richard C. Paine, Jr.
Financial data (yr. ended 12/31/01): Assets, $1,326,197 (M); grants paid, $0; gifts received, $218,828; expenditures, $202,395; qualifying distributions, $195,712.
Officers: John J. Sanford, Pres. and Treas.; James G. Elliot, Clerk.
Directors: Mary Platt Cooper, Richard C. Paine, Jr.
EIN: 010277592

60631
Phoenix Foundation
P.O. Box 3531
Portland, ME 04101 (207) 774-5701
Contact: M. Patricia Corey, Pres.

Established in 1992 in ME.
Financial data (yr. ended 06/30/99): Assets, $1,124,578 (M); grants paid, $4,400; gifts received, $7,500; expenditures, $86,587; qualifying distributions, $77,893; giving activities include $78,821 for programs.
Limitations: Giving primarily in ME.
Officers and Directors:* M. Patricia Corey,* Pres.; Walter E. Corey,* V.P.; Parker Denoco,* Clerk; Constance Bingham, Heather Breed, Sarah Corey, Martha Maslan, Richard Romeo.
EIN: 223036674

60632
Ducktrap Wildlife Preserve
P.O. Box 166
Lincolnville Center, ME 04850

Established in 1998 in ME.
Donor(s): Hans Gautschi.
Financial data (yr. ended 12/31/01): Assets, $1,112,098 (M); grants paid, $0; expenditures, $19,744; qualifying distributions, $18,550; giving activities include $19,742 for programs.
Officers: Hans Gautschi, Pres.; Bridgette Gautschi, V.P.; Richard McKittrick, Secy.
Directors: Harry Hollins, Leslie Hyde.
EIN: 043366434

60633
Grand Banks Schooner Museum Trust
P.O. Box 123
Boothbay, ME 04537

Classified as a private operating foundation in 1981.
Donor(s): Mildred H. McEvoy Foundation.
Financial data (yr. ended 12/31/01): Assets, $933,658 (M); grants paid, $0; gifts received, $408,600; expenditures, $315,266; qualifying distributions, $304,706; giving activities include $304,706 for programs.
Limitations: Applications not accepted.
Trustees: George McEvoy, Paul Rossley, Robert Ryan, Roy Wheeler.
EIN: 010359164

60634
Bangor Fuel Society
Eaton Peabody
P.O. Box 1210
Bangor, ME 04402 (207) 945-0749
Contact: Alberta Little, Director/ Distributor

Financial data (yr. ended 10/31/01): Assets, $809,187 (M); grants paid, $15,095; gifts received, $2,475; expenditures, $19,685; qualifying distributions, $15,095.
Limitations: Giving limited to residents of Bangor, ME.
Application information: Application form required.
Officers and Trustees:* Calvin E. True,* Pres.; John Lord, Treas.; J. Bragg, K.T. Lothrop, R. Speirs.
EIN: 016010608
Codes: GTI

60635
Maine Charitable Mechanics Association
519 Congress St.
Portland, ME 04101
Contact: Robert W. Libby, Treas.

Financial data (yr. ended 03/31/00): Assets, $800,636 (M); grants paid, $250; expenditures, $81,849; qualifying distributions, $55,798; giving activities include $55,548 for programs.
Limitations: Giving primarily in Portland, ME.
Application information: Application form not required.
Officers: Bruce S. Tornquist, Secy.; Robert W. Libby, Treas.
EIN: 010248533

60636
Bar Harbor Village Improvement Association
c/o Sheldon F. Goldthwait, Jr.
22 Albert Meadow
Bar Harbor, ME 04609

Established in 1996 in ME.
Financial data (yr. ended 07/31/00): Assets, $749,341 (M); grants paid, $0; gifts received, $62,396; expenditures, $66,934; qualifying distributions, $50,777; giving activities include $50,777 for programs.
Limitations: Applications not accepted.
Application information: Contributes only to pre-selected organizations.
Officers: Leslie C. Brewer, Pres.; Philip Cunningham, Secy.; Sheldon F. Goldthwait, Jr., Treas.
Director: David Witham.
EIN: 010024907

60637
Abelard Foundation
c/o Wayne H. Hale
208 Concord St.
Portland, ME 04103

Classified as a private operating foundation in 1980.
Donor(s): Allen L. Miller.
Financial data (yr. ended 09/30/99): Assets, $537,176 (M); grants paid, $2,145; gifts received, $32,848; expenditures, $182,808; qualifying distributions, $176,920; giving activities include $176,920 for programs.
Limitations: Applications not accepted.
Application information: Contributes only to pre-selected organizations.
Officers and Trustees:* Allen L. Miller,* Pres.; Carl R. Barker,* V.P.; Wayne H. Hale,* Treas.
EIN: 010365685

60638
Steep Falls Library
P.O. Box 140
Steep Falls, ME 04085

Financial data (yr. ended 06/30/99): Assets, $471,011 (M); grants paid, $0; gifts received, $18,742; expenditures, $36,229; qualifying distributions, $32,119; giving activities include $15,744 for programs.
Officers: Joseph Paul, Pres.; David Robinson, V.P.; June Benner, Secy.; Ellen Walker, Treas.
Trustees: Cheri Allen, Martha Drew, James Elliott, Sue Johnson, William Schimmer.
EIN: 010441524

60639
Firebird Foundation for Anthropological Research
P.O. Box A
Phillips, ME 04966-1501

Donor(s): George N. Appell.
Financial data (yr. ended 03/31/02): Assets, $465,811 (M); grants paid, $0; gifts received, $82,288; expenditures, $81,433; qualifying distributions, $0.
Limitations: Applications not accepted.
Application information: Contributes only to pre-selected organizations.
Advisory Board Members: Louis J. Appell III, M.A., Helen N. Coon, T. N. Madan, Ph.D., Ida Nicolaisen, Jonathan C. M. Benthall, Daniella Sieff, Ph.D., Vinson H. Sutlive, Jr., Ph.D.
EIN: 010524375

60640
Maine Medical Assessment Foundation
P.O. Box 249
Manchester, ME 04351-0249 (207) 622-9342
FAX: (207) 622-5647; *E-mail:* rbkeller@acadia.net
Contact: Robert B. Keller, M.D., Exec. Dir.

Established in 1989 in ME.
Donor(s): Blue Cross and Blue Shield of Maine, Branta Foundation, Harvard Pilgrim Health Care, Healthsource Maine, Inc., Maine Dept. of Human Svcs., Maine Health Mgmt. Coalition, Tufts Health Plan, University of Washington, Commonwealth Fund, Maine Chiropractic Assn.
Financial data (yr. ended 12/31/99): Assets, $425,063 (M); grants paid, $275,983; gifts received, $986,503; expenditures, $1,027,137; qualifying distributions, $688,268.
Limitations: Giving primarily in ME.
Publications: Annual report, newsletter.
Application information: Primary funding is for foundation's own research.
Officer: Robert B. Keller, M.D., Exec. Dir.

EIN: 010440180
Codes: TN

60641
Anson Academy Association
R.F.D. 1, Box 4060
North Anson, ME 04958
Application address: c/o Guidance Counselor, Carrabec High School, MSAD No. 74, North Anson, ME 04958

Financial data (yr. ended 12/31/99): Assets, $417,577 (M); grants paid, $13,209; gifts received, $283; expenditures, $17,877; qualifying distributions, $14,725.
Limitations: Giving limited to North Anson, ME.
Officers and Trustees:* Arthur Morse,* Pres.; Robert Garland,* V.P.; Robert Dunphy, Jr.,* Secy.; Nancy Merrill,* Treas.; Alfred Everett, Ralph Manzer, Raynard Morrell, and 9 additional directors.
EIN: 016048483

60642
Kelmscott Rare Breeds Foundation
R.R. 2, Box 365
Lincolnville, ME 04849

Established in 1995 in ME.
Donor(s): Robert Metcalfe, Robyn Metcalfe.
Financial data (yr. ended 12/31/99): Assets, $300,991 (M); grants paid, $0; gifts received, $476,722; expenditures, $528,548; qualifying distributions, $482,867; giving activities include $482,867 for programs.
Officer and Directors:* Robyn S. Metcalfe,* Exec. Dir.; Lawrence Alderson, Donald Bixby, Braden Bohrmann, Russell W. Brace, Tom Cattell, Stephen Coit, Tom De Marco, C.R. "Cap" Derochemont, Robert Hawes, Nancy Caudle Johnson, Rick Kersbergen, Richard Lutwyche, Robert M. Metcalfe, David Morse, Keith Patten, Glenna Plaisted, Dick King-Smith.
EIN: 010501130

60643
The Martha J. Stevens Charitable Trust
P.O. Box 37
Athens, ME 04912

Established in 1996 in ME.
Financial data (yr. ended 12/31/00): Assets, $250,471 (M); grants paid, $5,855; expenditures, $10,083; qualifying distributions, $5,728.
Limitations: Applications not accepted.
Application information: Contributes only to pre-selected organizations.
Trustees: Vaughn Leblanc, Danny L. Warren.
EIN: 016127305

60644
The Dearborn Foundation
(Formerly The Real World Foundation)
P.O. Box 350
Fryeburg, ME 04037 (207) 935-2502
Contact: Howard Dearborn, Pres.

Financial data (yr. ended 12/31/01): Assets, $206,229 (M); grants paid, $93,440; gifts received, $100; expenditures, $129,416; qualifying distributions, $117,439.
Limitations: Applications not accepted. Giving primarily in Fryeburg, ME.
Application information: Contributes only to pre-selected organizations.
Officer: Howard Dearborn, Pres. and Treas.
Directors: William Almy, Millard Davis, Victor Hall.
EIN: 010477840
Codes: FD2, GTI

60645
Maine State Troopers Foundation
99 Western Ave.
Augusta, ME 04330
Contact: Larry Gross

Established in 1994 in ME.
Financial data (yr. ended 12/31/99): Assets, $137,485 (M); grants paid, $63,738; expenditures, $132,866; qualifying distributions, $63,738.
Limitations: Giving limited to ME.
Officers: Jon Doyle, Pres.; Jack Adamo, V.P.; Bryan Batchelder, Secy.-Treas.
EIN: 010490113

60646
Walsh Family Foundation
11 Belfield Rd.
Cape Elizabeth, ME 04107 (207) 767-7204
Contact: Gregory M. Walsh, Pres.

Established in 1999 in ME.
Donor(s): Gregory M. Walsh.
Financial data (yr. ended 12/31/99): Assets, $105,750 (M); grants paid, $2,000; expenditures, $2,428; qualifying distributions, $2,428.
Limitations: Giving primarily in ME.
Application information: Application form not required.
Officers: Gregory M. Walsh, Pres. and Secy.; Louise L. Valati, V.P. and Treas.
EIN: 010522485

60647
Dutch Neck Community Club
735 Dutch Neck Rd.
Waldoboro, ME 04572 (207) 832-4576
Contact: Connie J. Miller, Treas.

Classified as a private operating foundation in ME in 1985.
Financial data (yr. ended 08/31/01): Assets, $105,439 (M); grants paid, $875; gifts received, $66; expenditures, $3,594; qualifying distributions, $3,554; giving activities include $1,667 for programs.
Limitations: Giving primarily in ME.
Officers: Jill Richard, Pres.; Ronald Miller, V.P.; Jane Enman, Secy.; Connie J. Miller, Treas.
EIN: 010354717

60648
Bath Historical Society
33 Summer St.
Bath, ME 04530
Contact: Nathan Lipfert, Treas.

Established in 1989 in ME. Classified as a private operating foundation in 1990.
Financial data (yr. ended 12/31/00): Assets, $89,163 (M); grants paid, $6,000; gifts received, $7,543; expenditures, $9,661; qualifying distributions, $9,661; giving activities include $3,661 for programs.
Limitations: Giving limited to Bath, ME.
Officers: Marion E.J. Fear, Pres. and Secy.; Nathan Lipfert, Treas.
Trustees: Mary Conover, Margaret Edwards, Victoria Jackson, Kerry Nelson, Judith Schwenk, Victoria Simpson, Bartlett Van Note, Janice Wingate.
EIN: 222994036

60649
Bonney Woods Corporation
172 Stewart Ave.
Farmington, ME 04938-1613

Donor(s): James Flint.

Financial data (yr. ended 05/31/02): Assets, $75,132 (M); grants paid, $0; gifts received, $100; expenditures, $5,632; qualifying distributions, $0.
Officers: Verne Byers, Pres.; Arthur Perry, V.P.; Judith Bjorn, Clerk; Jill Perry, Treas.
EIN: 010360056

60650
Bio-Medical Institute
24 Coburn Ave.
Skowhegan, ME 04976-1206

Donor(s): W. Edward Jordan, Jr., M.D.
Financial data (yr. ended 12/31/01): Assets, $72,546 (M); grants paid, $0; expenditures, $1,245; qualifying distributions, $0.
Officers: W. Edward Jordan III, M.D., Pres.; Virginia E. Jordan, Secy.-Treas.
Director: John B. Jordan.
EIN: 237259889

60651
New England Museum of Telephony, Inc.
P.O. Box 1377
Ellsworth, ME 04605-1377

Classified as a private operating foundation in 1986.
Donor(s): Charles S. Dunne, Charles A. Galley.
Financial data (yr. ended 09/30/00): Assets, $71,414 (M); grants paid, $0; gifts received, $25,206; expenditures, $3,903; qualifying distributions, $1,232; giving activities include $1,157 for programs.
Officers and Directors:* Charles S. Dunne,* Pres.; Charles Galley,* V.P.; Sandra Russo Galley,* Secy.; Peggy Strong, Treas.; Jeffrey Webber, and 7 additional directors.
EIN: 042880394

60652
Company G Memorial Charitable Trust
103 Oak Hill Dr.
Oakland, ME 04963

Established in 2001 in ME.
Donor(s): Daniel J. Deroch.
Financial data (yr. ended 12/31/01): Assets, $34,917 (M); grants paid, $0; gifts received, $26,425; expenditures, $536; qualifying distributions, $0.
Director: Daniel J. Deroch.
EIN: 016165385

60653
Pleasant River Wildlife Foundation
c/o John K. Marshall
East Side Rd.
Addison, ME 04606

Established in 1999 in ME.
Financial data (yr. ended 12/31/99): Assets, $31,260 (M); grants paid, $0; gifts received, $31,999; expenditures, $981; qualifying distributions, $923; giving activities include $923 for programs.
Limitations: Applications not accepted.
Officers and Directors:* John K. Marshall,* Pres.; Michael R. Leonard,* Secy.; Anne E. Marshall,* Treas.; Robert Hinckley, David MacDonald.
EIN: 311631801

60654
Sheltered Employment Association, Inc.
(also known as Maine Association of Rehabilitation Services (M.A.R.S.))
c/o Group Home Foundation, Inc.
984 Sabattus St.
Lewiston, ME 04240

Financial data (yr. ended 10/31/00): Assets, $30,221 (M); grants paid, $0; expenditures,

$4,039; qualifying distributions, $4,039; giving activities include $4,039 for programs.
Officers: Greg Fraser, Pres.; Richard Farnsworth, V.P.; Linda Huntington, Secy.; Deborah Beam, Treas.
EIN: 010342628

60655
History House Association, Inc.
P.O. Box 832
Skowhegan, ME 04976-0832

Classified as a private operating foundation in 1978.
Financial data (yr. ended 12/31/00): Assets, $18,392 (M); grants paid, $0; gifts received, $3,282; expenditures, $3,308; qualifying distributions, $3,255; giving activities include $3,255 for programs.
Officers: Lee Z. Granville, Pres.; Lynn Perry, Secy.; James P. Hastings, Treas.
EIN: 010217324

60656
Student Communicant of St. Joseph's Church Trust
48 Perham St.
Farmington, ME 04938 (207) 778-2616
Contact: Richard M. Morton, Tr.

Established in 1965 in ME.
Donor(s): Helen A. True.‡
Financial data (yr. ended 06/30/00): Assets, $17,037 (M); grants paid, $850; expenditures, $1,200; qualifying distributions, $1,180.
Limitations: Giving limited to Farmington, ME.
Trustee: Richard M. Morton.
EIN: 016034642

60657
American Friends of Maru a Pula School, Inc.
c/o William T. Racine
859 Washington St.
Bath, ME 04530
Scholarship application address: 88, Clubhouse Rd., Tuxedo, NY 10987, tel.: (914) 351-2468
Contact: Nathaniel A. Jackson, Treas.

Established in 1974 in MA.
Financial data (yr. ended 12/31/99): Assets, $10,707 (M); grants paid, $22,459; gifts received, $27,430; expenditures, $25,466; qualifying distributions, $25,464.
Limitations: Giving limited to the Republic of Botswana, Africa.
Officers: Jane G. Briggs, Pres.; Mary Kay McGowen, Secy.; Nathaniel A. Jackson, Treas.
Directors: James Clark, Richard Kassissieh, Martha Lyman, Christopher Matthew.
EIN: 237449724

60658
Friends of the Wilhelm Reich Museum
P.O. Box 687
Rangeley, ME 04970 (207) 864-3443
Contact: Mary Henderson, Pres.

Classified as a private operating foundation in 1977.
Financial data (yr. ended 06/30/01): Assets, $9,917 (M); grants paid, $400; gifts received, $10,206; expenditures, $16,866; qualifying distributions, $0.
Officer and Directors:* Mary Henderson,* Pres.; Pilar Bates,* Secy.; Jill Allen, Rose Collins, Sharon Connally, Joan Cummings, Jean L. Forest, M.D., Ester George, Carmen Glidden, Lee Henderson, Hazel Hogan, Elizabeth Millbury, Patricia J. Middleton, M.D., Becky Rose, Ed Smith, Pete Smith, Alice Wilkinson.
EIN: 010359042

60659
Research Institute for Mathematics
383 College Ave.
Orono, ME 04473

Donor(s): Henry Pogorzelski.
Financial data (yr. ended 12/31/00): Assets, $4,263 (M); grants paid, $0; gifts received, $6,198; expenditures, $7,418; qualifying distributions, $0.
Officer: Henry Pogorzelski, Pres.
EIN: 222777124

60660
Aerie East Environmental Foundation
228 Holley Rd.
Farmington, ME 04938

Donor(s): Barbara Piel, The Woodward Fund, Emily Johnston.
Financial data (yr. ended 07/31/00): Assets, $1,475 (M); grants paid, $0; gifts received, $2,975; expenditures, $3,807; qualifying distributions, $3,807; giving activities include $3,808 for programs.
Officers and Directors:* James W. Parker, Ph.D.,* Pres and Treas.; Jane Parker,* Secy.
EIN: 010459515

60661
Silver Birch Foundation, Inc.
P.O. Box 457
Orono, ME 04473

Established in 1988 in ME.
Financial data (yr. ended 05/31/02): Assets, $360 (M); grants paid, $8,500; expenditures, $9,703; qualifying distributions, $8,500.
Limitations: Applications not accepted. Giving primarily in Orono, ME.
Application information: Contributes only to a pre-selected organization.
Officers: Jere Armstrong, Pres.; Richard Valentine, Treas.
Director: Richard Stolkner.
EIN: 010420172

60662
Betsy Barter Richardson Scholarship Fund
P.O. Box 38
Stonington, ME 04681-0038 (207) 367-2621
Contact: Sally R. Rice, Tr.

Financial data (yr. ended 06/30/01): Assets, $208 (M); grants paid, $2,850; gifts received, $3,000; expenditures, $2,850; qualifying distributions, $2,850.
Limitations: Giving limited to ME.
Trustees: Marshall Rice, Sally R. Rice.
EIN: 016013574

60663
The Cat's Corner, Inc.
(Formerly Cats Corner)
263-265 Brackett St.
Portland, ME 04102

Established in 1996 in ME.
Financial data (yr. ended 12/31/01): Assets, $7 (M); grants paid, $0; gifts received, $8,404; expenditures, $8,623; qualifying distributions, $8,623; giving activities include $8,623 for programs.
Directors: Bernard Wall Dum, Kari Lawrence, Sally J. Rollins.
EIN: 010496979

MARYLAND

60664
Commonweal Foundation, Inc.
10770 Columbia Pike, Ste. 100
Silver Spring, MD 20910 (301) 592-1316
FAX: (301) 592-1307; *URL:* http://www.commonweal-foundation.org
Contact: Barbara Bainum, Pres.

Established in 1968 in Washington, DC.
Donor(s): Stewart Bainum, Sr.
Financial data (yr. ended 12/31/01): Assets, $109,742,983 (M); grants paid, $9,835,666; gifts received, $101,289,816; expenditures, $13,685,100; qualifying distributions, $9,918,255; giving activities include $850,215 for programs.
Limitations: Giving primarily in Washington, DC, and MD.
Publications: Application guidelines, program policy statement.
Application information: WRAG common grant application form accepted. Application form required.
Officers and Directors:* Stewart Bainum, Sr.,* Chair.; Barbara Bainum,* Pres.; Bruce Bainum, Roberta Bainum, Garland P. Moore, Scott Renschler, Chris Shreve.
EIN: 237000192
Codes: FD

60665
The Erickson Foundation, Inc.
701 Maiden Choice Ln.
Baltimore, MD 21228-5968 (410) 737-8911
FAX: (410) 737-8856
Contact: John M. Parrish, Ph.D., Exec. Dir.

Established in 1998 in MD.
Donor(s): John C. Erickson, Nancy A. Erickson.
Financial data (yr. ended 12/31/00): Assets, $37,040,481 (M); grants paid, $318,850; expenditures, $2,759,187; qualifying distributions, $11,341,854; giving activities include $10,456,540 for programs.
Limitations: Giving primarily in Baltimore, MD.
Publications: Informational brochure, newsletter.
Officers and Trustees:* John C. Erickson,* Pres.; Nancy A. Erickson,* V.P. and Secy.; Jeffrey A. Jacobson, Treas.; John M. Parrish, Ph.D., Exec. Dir.; Craig A. Erickson, Mark P. Erickson, and 2 additional trustees.
EIN: 522112929
Codes: FD

60666
Doran Family Foundation, Inc.
3090 Mayberry Ave.
Huntingtown, MD 20639-3913
Application address: P.O. Box 238, Barstow, MD 20610, tel.: (410) 414-9300

Established in 1999 in MD.
Donor(s): John T. Doran.
Financial data (yr. ended 12/31/01): Assets, $22,272,938 (M); grants paid, $1,978,141; gifts received, $16,418,479; expenditures, $2,393,077; qualifying distributions, $1,824,566; giving activities include $527,497 for loans.
Limitations: Giving primarily in Calvert, St. Charles, St. Mary's, and Prince George's counties, MD.
Officers: John T. Doran, Pres.; Jean L. Doran, V.P.; Catherine J. Doran-Neal, Secy.-Treas.
EIN: 522136560

60666—MARYLAND

Codes: FD

60667
Trustees of the Home for the Aged of Frederick City
c/o Trustees
115 Record St.
Frederick, MD 21701

Classified as a private operating foundation in 1973.
Financial data (yr. ended 12/31/01): Assets, $18,487,065 (M); grants paid, $0; gifts received, $46,146; expenditures, $1,284,461; qualifying distributions, $1,374,742; giving activities include $1,284,461 for programs.
Limitations: Applications not accepted.
Application information: Contributes only to pre-selected organizations.
Officers and Trustees:* Joseph D. Baker,* Co-Pres.; Margaret Conley, Co-Pres.; Robert E. Gearinger,* V.P.; Diane Martz, 1st V.P.; Jane Byron, 2nd V.P.; M. Dunbar Ashbury,* Secy.-Treas.; Nancy Lesure, Corresponding Secy.; Betsy Randall, Recording Secy.; G. June Main, Treas.; James H. Clapp, Robert G. Hooper, Robert McCardell, George E. Randall, William R. Talley, Jr.
Directors: Linda Broadrup, Josephine Clapp, Louise Crevey, Catharine Crum, Peggy Denton, Edith Foland, Arlie Graham, Betty Hooper, Evelyn Manwiller, Barbara Rhoads, Eileen Rice, Ruth Schipper, Jeannette Shoemaker, Liza Stoner, Louise Talley, Judy L. Wolf, Margaret Young, Ann Ziegler.
EIN: 520591486

60668
Rothschild Art Foundation, Inc.
3408 Old Court Rd.
Baltimore, MD 21208

Established in 1986 in MD.
Donor(s): Stanford Z. Rothschild, Jr.
Financial data (yr. ended 12/31/01): Assets, $13,262,930 (M); grants paid, $0; gifts received, $12,000; expenditures, $24,684; qualifying distributions, $0.
Officers and Directors:* Stanford Z. Rothschild, Jr.,* Pres.; Manuel Dupkin,* V.P.; Frederick Steinmann,* Secy.
EIN: 521301060

60669
Harry Z. Isaacs Foundation, Inc.
c/o Alex, Brown Capital Advisory & Trust Co.
19 South St.
Baltimore, MD 21202

Classified as a private operating foundation in 1991.
Financial data (yr. ended 12/31/00): Assets, $11,987,152 (M); grants paid, $0; gifts received, $102,730; expenditures, $514,457; qualifying distributions, $409,467; giving activities include $409,467 for programs.
Trustees: Andre W. Brewster, Michael D. Hankin, Stanard T. Klinefelter.
EIN: 521706022

60670
Trustees of the Ladew Topiary Gardens, Inc.
3535 Jarrettsville Pike
Monkton, MD 21111

Classified as a private operating foundation in 1992.
Donor(s): John Boogher, Stiles Colwill, Susan Russell, Richard Von Hess, S. Bonsal White, Middendorf Foundation, The McKnight Foundation, Mercantile-Safe Deposit & Trust Co., Rouse Foundation.
Financial data (yr. ended 10/31/99): Assets, $11,152,640 (M); grants paid, $0; gifts received, $457,528; expenditures, $992,078; qualifying distributions, $509,642; giving activities include $717,593 for programs.
Officers and Directors:* Mrs. Thomas G. McCausland,* Pres.; Mrs. Richard A. Moore,* V.P. and Treas.; Mrs. L. Gittings Boyce,* Secy.; Jenny Shattuck, Exec. Dir.; Pat Albert, Marnie Berndt, Bunny Hathaway, Freddie Shaw, and 31 additional trustees.
EIN: 132782826

60671
Chase Home, Inc.
c/o Sharon Wimbish
900 Bestgate Rd., Ste. 200
Annapolis, MD 21401

Financial data (yr. ended 12/31/99): Assets, $8,886,570 (M); grants paid, $0; gifts received, $21,800; expenditures, $332,774; qualifying distributions, $252,675; giving activities include $254,359 for programs.
Limitations: Applications not accepted.
Application information: Contributes only to pre-selected organizations.
Officers: Rev. Robert Ihloff, Pres.; Molly B. Smith, V.P.; Mary M. Heald, Secy.; William Fasnacht, Treas.
Trustees: Bruce Beckner, Linda Council, Jennifer Goldsborough, Richard Lazenby, Ben Michaelson, Thomas Noble, Lois Pflugh, Peggy Darden Pickell, John R. Price, Peter Smith.
EIN: 520613676

60672
Alice Ferguson Foundation, Inc.
2001 Bryan Point Rd.
Accokeek, MD 20607

Classified as a private operating foundation in 1973.
Financial data (yr. ended 12/31/01): Assets, $8,369,749 (M); grants paid, $0; gifts received, $738,669; expenditures, $924,797; qualifying distributions, $1,008,673; giving activities include $1,008,673 for programs.
Officers: Jean Thompson, Pres.; Ann Chab, V.P.; Carol Graybill, Secy.; Marilyn Randall, Treas.; Tracy Brown, Exec. Dir.
Directors: Joe Andrews, Peggy DeStefanis, Kent Hibben, Bryan Logan, Shirly Nicolai.
EIN: 520694646

60673
Stronghold, Inc.
7901 Comus Rd.
Dickerson, MD 20842-9789

Donor(s): Gordon Strong.‡
Financial data (yr. ended 12/31/01): Assets, $5,711,013 (M); grants paid, $0; gifts received, $468,794; expenditures, $373,401; qualifying distributions, $200,475.
Officers: Elmer Pussey, Pres.; Marion Webster, V.P.; David F. Webster, Secy.-Treas.
Directors: Tom Mackintoch, Elmer Pussey, Joan Rice, Daniel Walser, John Webster, Leonard Williams.
EIN: 520560230

60674
Raymond I. Richardson Foundation, Inc.
P.O. Box 100
Keymar, MD 21757
FAX: (410) 876-0271; *E-mail:* bbps@cct.infi.net

Established in 1958.
Financial data (yr. ended 06/30/01): Assets, $4,746,661 (M); grants paid, $188,000; gifts received, $6,790; expenditures, $417,397; qualifying distributions, $188,000.
Limitations: Applications not accepted.
Application information: Contributes only to pre-selected organizations.
Officers and Trustees:* Jennifer Munch,* Pres.; Mary Harris,* V.P.; Michael K. Billingslea,* Treas.; Michael Sunday, Exec. Dir.; Philip Arbaugh, Louis V. Beard, Rev. Frederick P. Eckhardt, Greg Hare, J. Paul Herring, Susan Tabtsko.
EIN: 520685253

60675
The Dixon House, Inc.
108 N. Higgins St.
Easton, MD 21601

Established in 1993 in MD.
Donor(s): Carroll Elliott.‡
Financial data (yr. ended 06/30/01): Assets, $4,163,966 (M); grants paid, $200; gifts received, $186,318; expenditures, $436,282; qualifying distributions, $397,225; giving activities include $397,025 for programs.
Limitations: Applications not accepted. Giving primarily in Easton, MD.
Application information: Contributes only to pre-selected organizations.
Officers and Directors:* Sharon J. Ritter,* Pres.; Phyllis Widerkehr,* V.P.; Betty McC. Jones,* Secy.; Mrs. Edmund A. Cutts, Sr.,* Treas.; Joanne Prettyman,* Admin.; and 10 additional directors.
EIN: 520607903

60676
Ridge Residences, Inc.
c/o Housing and Health Svcs., Inc.
101 Timber Ridge Dr.
Westminster, MD 21157

Financial data (yr. ended 09/30/00): Assets, $3,890,483 (M); grants paid, $0; gifts received, $509,649; expenditures, $769,150; qualifying distributions, $623,598; giving activities include $769,150 for programs.
Officers and Directors:* Nancy Griesmyer Rock,* Pres.; Sandra Ferguson,* V.P.; Bertha B. Shriner,* Secy.; Frances Liggon, Treas.; Joyce C. Brown, Rev. Vernon Faid, Martin Gramlich, Sr., Barbara Groff, Frances Liggon, Thomas Whiteleather, and 9 additional directors.
EIN: 521363247
Codes: TN

60677
George W. McManus Foundation, Inc.
3703 Greenway
Baltimore, MD 21218

Established about 1959 in MD.
Donor(s): McManus Institute, Inc.
Financial data (yr. ended 12/31/01): Assets, $3,664,882 (M); grants paid, $94,254; expenditures, $335,236; qualifying distributions, $289,854.
Limitations: Applications not accepted. Giving primarily in the metropolitan Baltimore, MD, area.
Application information: Contributes only to pre-selected organizations.
Officers: George W. McManus, Jr., Pres.; T. Ann Miller, V.P. and Secy.; George W. McManus III, Treas.
Trustees: Mary Claire Boney, Sr. Patricia Ann Bossle, Patricia Kauffman, Margaret Ann Moag, Br. Kevin Strong.
EIN: 521884273
Codes: FD2

60678
Harrison & Conrad Memorial Trust
c/o Bank of America
10 Light St.
Baltimore, MD 21203-0995
Application address: c/o Loudoun Memorial Hospital, Office of the Admin., 70 W. Cornwall St., Leesburg, VA 22075, tel.: (703) 777-3300

Established in 1982 in VA.
Donor(s): Mary J. Conrad.‡
Financial data (yr. ended 01/31/01): Assets, $3,568,637 (M); grants paid, $90,704; expenditures, $156,062; qualifying distributions, $118,359.
Limitations: Giving limited to Leesburg or Loudoun County, VA.
Application information: Individual applicants are interviewed.
Trustees: Susan Singh, Bank of America.
EIN: 521300410
Codes: GTI

60679
Sotterley Foundation, Inc.
P.O. Box 67
Hollywood, MD 20636

Donor(s): Sandra I. Van Heerden, Mabel S. Ingalls, Hon. John Hanson Briscoe, Grace Anne Dorney Koppel.
Financial data (yr. ended 12/31/01): Assets, $3,505,881 (M); grants paid, $0; gifts received, $1,301,385; expenditures, $1,582,337; qualifying distributions, $0.
Officers and Trustees:* Hon. John Hanson Briscoe,* Pres.; Pat McKenney Horton,* V.P.; Michael J. Whitson,* Secy.-Treas.; Carolyn Laray, Exec. Dir.; Agnes Kane Callum, John H. Cumberland, Ph.D., Iris Carter Ford, Ph.D., Col. George G. Forrest, and 8 additional trustees.
EIN: 526037721

60680
Foundation for Torah Study, Inc.
1122 Kenilworth Dr., Ste. 215
Towson, MD 21204

Established in 1999 in MD.
Donor(s): Leroy E. Hoffberger.
Financial data (yr. ended 12/31/99): Assets, $3,196,924 (M); grants paid, $0; gifts received, $3,036,600; expenditures, $127,197; qualifying distributions, $111,414; giving activities include $91,292 for programs.
Limitations: Applications not accepted.
Application information: Contributes only to pre-selected organizations.
Officers and Directors:* Leroy E. Hoffberger,* Pres.; David Hoffberger,* V.P.; Lois Halpert, Secy.-Treas.
EIN: 522137496

60681
The Weiss Foundation
c/o Michael Gelman
4550 Montgomery Ave., Ste. 650 N.
Bethesda, MD 20814
Contact: Stanley Weiss, Pres.

Established in 1993 in DC.
Donor(s): Stanley Weiss.
Financial data (yr. ended 09/30/01): Assets, $2,335,130 (M); grants paid, $632,000; expenditures, $1,027,130; qualifying distributions, $916,288; giving activities include $415,000 for programs.
Limitations: Applications not accepted. Giving primarily in the greater metropolitan Washington, DC, area, and New York, NY.
Publications: Financial statement.
Application information: Contributes only to pre-selected organizations.
Officers: Stanley Weiss, Pres.; Lisa Weiss, V.P.; Anthony Weiss, Secy.
Director: Lori Christina Lurie.
EIN: 521848413
Codes: FD

60682
Lauer Philanthropic Foundation
11202 Woodland Dr., Ste. 100
Lutherville, MD 21093-3514

Established in 1998 in PA.
Donor(s): Carlyn Hubert.
Financial data (yr. ended 12/31/01): Assets, $2,299,710 (M); grants paid, $0; gifts received, $2,307,109; expenditures, $0; qualifying distributions, $0.
Trustee: Arnold Fleischmann.
EIN: 522036406

60683
Israel Bible Museum, Inc.
c/o Braunstein & Connor, CPAS LLP
1445 Research Blvd.
Rockville, MD 20850-3125

Donor(s): Dennis Ratner.
Financial data (yr. ended 08/31/00): Assets, $2,149,171 (M); grants paid, $0; gifts received, $494,177; expenditures, $148,723; qualifying distributions, $1,361,028; giving activities include $118,157 for programs.
Officers: Dennis Ratner, Pres.; Mark Weinberg, Secy.; Phillip Ratner, Treas.
EIN: 521374110

60684
Ethel & Emery Fast Scholarship Foundation, Inc.
12620 Rolling Rd.
Potomac, MD 20854 (301) 762-1102
Contact: Carol A. Minami, Secy.-Treas.

Established in 1993 in DC.
Financial data (yr. ended 12/31/00): Assets, $2,140,620 (M); grants paid, $43,333; expenditures, $101,611; qualifying distributions, $167,220.
Application information: Application form required.
Officers and Directors:* Bette Rothstein,* Pres.; Nathan M. Brown,* V.P.; Carol A. Minami,* Secy.-Treas. and Mgr.
EIN: 521817707
Codes: GTI

60685
Alfred Berman Foundation for Medical Research, Inc.
6205 Poindexter Ln.
Rockville, MD 20852 (301) 946-7089

Established in 1992 in MD.
Donor(s): Jonathan D. Berman, Alfred Berman.‡
Financial data (yr. ended 12/31/00): Assets, $2,140,133 (M); grants paid, $0; expenditures, $73,195; qualifying distributions, $71,108; giving activities include $54,000 for programs.
Officer and Directors:* Jonathan D. Berman,* Pres.; Judith Chertoff.
EIN: 521785514

60686
The Federated Charities Corporation of Frederick
22 S. Market St.
Frederick, MD 21701 (301) 662-1561

Established around 1994.
Financial data (yr. ended 12/31/99): Assets, $2,135,372 (M); grants paid, $0; gifts received, $69,650; expenditures, $99,780; qualifying distributions, $83,221; giving activities include $24,121 for programs.
Officers: Lloyd K. Hoover, Pres.; David L. Hoffman, V.P.; Donald Z. Koons, V.P.; Truby LaGarde, Secy.; Barbara A. Keeney, Treas.
Directors: Marvin Ausherman, Fred Broadrup, Charles W. Conley, William Ellison, Lecoast Mack, Bruce Mahlandt, Donald Staggers, and 8 additional directors.
EIN: 520608003

60687
The Jorgensen Family Foundation, Inc.
P.O. Box 237
Buckeystown, MD 21717

Established in 1996 in MD.
Donor(s): Roy E. Jorgensen, John S. Jorgensen, Barbara B. Jorgensen.
Financial data (yr. ended 12/31/01): Assets, $1,979,520 (M); grants paid, $0; expenditures, $135,397; qualifying distributions, $0.
Limitations: Applications not accepted.
Application information: Contributes only to pre-selected organizations.
Officers and Directors:* John S. Jorgensen,* Pres.; Roy E. Jorgensen,* V.P.; Barbara B. Jorgensen,* Secy.-Treas.
EIN: 521992602

60688
Harvey and Vera Patrick Family Foundation
11722 Foxspur Ct.
Ellicott City, MD 21042
Application address: 529 N.E. Plantation Rd., Unit 206, Stuart, FL 34996
Contact: H.O. Patrick, Pres.

Established in 1997 in MD.
Donor(s): Harvey Patrick, Holly York.
Financial data (yr. ended 12/31/01): Assets, $1,787,639 (M); grants paid, $25,435; gifts received, $187,500; expenditures, $2,544,207; qualifying distributions, $122,480; giving activities include $2,295,876 for programs.
Officers: Harvey Patrick, Pres.; Vera Patrick, V.P.; Edward York, V.P.; Holly York, V.P. and Treas.
EIN: 311489904

60689
Point of View Farm, Inc.
7620 Cabin Rd.
Cabin John, MD 20818

Established in 2000 in MD.
Donor(s): Joel D. Rosenthal.
Financial data (yr. ended 12/31/00): Assets, $1,742,495 (M); grants paid, $0; gifts received, $1,887,800; expenditures, $19,544; qualifying distributions, $623,267; giving activities include $6,060 for programs.
Director: Joel D. Rosenthal.
EIN: 522219449

60690
John M. & Sara R. Walton Foundation, Inc.
c/o Draper & McGinly
365 W. Patrick St.
Frederick, MD 21701

Classified as a private operating foundation in 1989.
Financial data (yr. ended 12/31/00): Assets, $1,249,998 (M); grants paid, $0; gifts received, $21,206; expenditures, $56,934; qualifying distributions, $53,093; giving activities include $52,939 for programs.
Limitations: Applications not accepted.
Application information: Contributes only to pre-selected organizations.

60690—MARYLAND

Officers: John M. Walton, Jr., Pres.; Elizabeth Ann Rupert, Treas.
Director: Eugene D. Mattison.
EIN: 521591823

60691
Cove Point Natural Heritage Trust, Inc.
P.O. Box 3466
Prince Frederick, MD 20678-1274

Established in 1995 in MD.
Donor(s): Columbia LNG Corp.
Financial data (yr. ended 12/31/99): Assets, $1,229,128 (M); grants paid, $0; gifts received, $120,000; expenditures, $55,879; qualifying distributions, $34,551; giving activities include $55,881 for programs.
Officers: Ruth Mathes, Pres.; Ewing Miller, Secy.; L. Michael Bridges, Treas.
EIN: 521910341

60692
International/Domestic Public Health Foundation
c/o Ann S. Vorys
208 E. Lake Ave.
Baltimore, MD 21212

Established in 1996 in OH.
Financial data (yr. ended 12/31/99): Assets, $1,145,380 (M); grants paid, $53,344; expenditures, $173,429; qualifying distributions, $137,967.
Limitations: Applications not accepted. Giving on a national and international basis.
Application information: Contributes only to pre-selected organizations.
Officers: Ann S. Vorys, M.D., Pres. and Treas.; Nancy Hull, V.P.; Mark Vannatta, Secy.
Trustees: Sandy Baran, William Crisp, Dorothy Brewster Lee, Ann Palmerton.
EIN: 311444007

60693
The William L. and Victorine Q. Adams Foundation, Inc.
306 Mondawmin Mall
Baltimore, MD 21215-8009
Scholarship application address: c/o Adams Future Business Leader Scholarship Fund, Associated Black Charities, 1114 Cathedral St., 2nd Fl., Baltimore, MD 21201, tel.: (410) 659-0000

Established in 1984.
Donor(s): William L. Adams.
Financial data (yr. ended 09/30/01): Assets, $1,130,587 (M); grants paid, $160,130; gifts received, $100,000; expenditures, $204,237; qualifying distributions, $198,756.
Limitations: Giving primarily in Baltimore, MD.
Application information: Application forms are available Nov. 1 through Apr. 1. Application form required.
Officers and Trustees:* William L. Adams,* Pres.; Theo C. Rodgers,* V.P. and Treas.; Victorine Q. Adams,* V.P.; Gertrude A. Venable,* Secy.
EIN: 521369556
Codes: GTI

60694
Baltimore Curriculum Project, Inc.
711 W. 40th St.
Baltimore, MD 21211-2120

Financial data (yr. ended 06/30/00): Assets, $1,086,554 (M); grants paid, $0; gifts received, $498,735; expenditures, $1,189,536; qualifying distributions, $1,177,413; giving activities include $1,177,413 for programs.
EIN: 521961406

Codes: TN

60695
The Sophron Foundation
4510 Mustering Drum
Ellicott City, MD 21042

Established in 1980; classified as a private operating foundation in 1981.
Donor(s): Estelle E. Rogers, Thomas F. Rogers.
Financial data (yr. ended 11/30/01): Assets, $1,041,685 (M); grants paid, $37,238; expenditures, $69,928; qualifying distributions, $56,935.
Limitations: Applications not accepted. Giving primarily in the metropolitan Washington, DC, area.
Application information: Contributes only to pre-selected organizations.
Officers and Directors:* Thomas F. Rogers,* Chair.; Estelle E. Rogers,* Vice-Chair.; Judith L. Reynolds, Pres.; Clare R. Rogers,* V.P.; Robert E. Grove, Secy.-Treas.; Daniel R. Grove, Hope E. Grove, Thomas Hibschmann, Hope V. Parks, Stephen A. Reynolds, Clare Rogers.
EIN: 521199140

60696
The Yahweh Yireh Foundation, Inc.
c/o Arthur W. Trump, Jr.
8503 Hill Spring Dr.
Lutherville, MD 21093
FAX: (410) 682-8921
Contact: Arthur Trump, Secy.-Treas.

Established in 1994 in MD.
Financial data (yr. ended 10/31/99): Assets, $976,330 (M); grants paid, $2,551,000; expenditures, $2,567,724; qualifying distributions, $2,666,001.
Limitations: Applications not accepted. Giving primarily in Baltimore, MD.
Application information: Contributes only to pre-selected organizations.
Officers: Heide Hungerford, Pres.; Arthur Trump, Secy.-Treas.
EIN: 521904761
Codes: FD

60697
Estonian-Revelia Academic Fund, Inc.
c/o Juri Taht
12901 Clearfield Dr.
Bowie, MD 20715-1106

Established in 1994 in MD.
Financial data (yr. ended 12/31/00): Assets, $953,254 (M); grants paid, $31,000; expenditures, $68,863; qualifying distributions, $58,324.
Limitations: Applications not accepted. Giving limited to Estonia.
Application information: Unsolicited requests for funds not accepted.
Directors: Juhan Jaakson, Juri Taht.
EIN: 521901554

60698
I Have a Dream Foundation of Washington, D.C.
(Formerly I Have a Dream Foundation)
416 Hungerford Dr., Ste. 223
Rockville, MD 20850

Established in 1987 in DC.
Donor(s): George F. Kettle.
Financial data (yr. ended 05/31/01): Assets, $951,219 (M); grants paid, $0; gifts received, $350,859; expenditures, $502,171; qualifying distributions, $498,171; giving activities include $498,171 for programs.
Limitations: Applications not accepted.

Application information: Contributes only to pre-selected organizations.
Officers: Chris White, Chair.; Mike Orends, Pres.; Ed Wilczynski, V.P.
EIN: 541421855

60699
Patrick J. Barcus Charitable Foundation, Inc.
c/o Joseph P. Bornstein
7101 Wisconsin Ave., Ste. 1200
Bethesda, MD 20814

Established in 2000 in MD.
Donor(s): Patrick J. Barcus.
Financial data (yr. ended 12/31/00): Assets, $867,930 (M); grants paid, $40,000; gifts received, $959,744; expenditures, $40,012; qualifying distributions, $40,000.
Limitations: Applications not accepted. Giving primarily in Clearwater, FL and Wheeling, WV.
Application information: Contributes only to pre-selected organizations.
Officers and Directors:* Patrick J. Barcus,* Pres.; J. Michael Barcus, Jr.,* V.P.; Amelia Barcus,* Secy.; Joseph P. Bornstein,* Treas.
EIN: 522276632

60700
Jaegal Foundation, Inc.
608 W. Northern Pkwy.
Baltimore, MD 21210-1422

Established in 1982 in MD.
Donor(s): George Alderman.
Financial data (yr. ended 12/31/01): Assets, $702,130 (M); grants paid, $0; gifts received, $1,808; expenditures, $826; qualifying distributions, $0.
Officers: Julianne Alderman, Pres.; George Alderman, V.P.; J. Edward Davis, Secy.; John Sayman, Treas.
EIN: 521273619

60701
Joan W. Jenkins Foundation, Inc.
P.O. Box 572
Ocean City, MD 21843-0572 (410) 289-9100
Contact: Charles R. Jenkins

Financial data (yr. ended 09/30/01): Assets, $653,315 (M); grants paid, $21,367; gifts received, $6,000; expenditures, $69,767; qualifying distributions, $21,367.
Application information: Application form not required.
Directors: Laura R. Jenkins, Michael Jones, Margie E. McBane, Bruce Moore.
EIN: 521486477

60702
The Phillipps-Murray Foundation
c/o Peter Yates, C.P.A.
3313 Floral Ct.
Silver Spring, MD 20902-1132
Application address: 3009 Birch St., N.W., Washington, DC 20012
Contact: Kali Grosvenor

Established in 1988 in DC.
Donor(s): George Murray, Stephanie Phillipps.
Financial data (yr. ended 12/31/01): Assets, $629,190 (M); grants paid, $64,763; expenditures, $74,915; qualifying distributions, $64,577.
Limitations: Giving on a national basis, with some emphasis on the greater Washington, DC, area.
Officers and Trustee:* George Murray, Pres. and Treas.; Stephanie Phillipps,* Secy.
Director: Richard Shannon.
EIN: 521624082

60703
Mpala Wildlife Foundation, Inc.
1800 Mercantile Bank & Trust Bldg.
2 Hopkins Plz.
Baltimore, MD 21201-2978
Contact: Jeffrey K. Gonya

Established in 1989 in MD; funded in fiscal 1990.
Donor(s): George L. Small, Princeton University.
Financial data (yr. ended 06/30/01): Assets, $570,951 (M); grants paid, $261,650; gifts received, $425,534; expenditures, $394,710; qualifying distributions, $394,710; giving activities include $48,749 for programs.
Limitations: Applications not accepted. Giving on an international basis, with emphasis on Nanyuki, Kenya.
Application information: Contributes only to pre-selected organizations.
Officers and Trustees:* Donald C. Graham, Chair.; Jeffrey K. Gonya,* Secy.-Treas.; Howard Ende, Dennis Keller, Michael H. Shaw, George L. Small, John Wreford-Smith.
EIN: 521656147
Codes: FD

60704
The Pathwork Foundation
13013 Collingwood Terr.
Silver Spring, MD 20904-1414

Established in 1990 in VA.
Financial data (yr. ended 08/31/01): Assets, $520,220 (M); grants paid, $0; gifts received, $28,348; expenditures, $111,449; qualifying distributions, $0.
Limitations: Applications not accepted.
Officers and Directors:* Johan Kos,* Pres.; Carey Conaway,* Secy.; Brian O'Donnell,* Treas.; Jack Clark, John Pierrakos.
EIN: 136544626

60705
Cecile D. Carpenter Foundation
10451 Mill Run Cir., Ste. 400
Owings Mills, MD 21117

Classified as a private operating foundation in 1999 in MD.
Financial data (yr. ended 12/31/00): Assets, $518,297 (M); grants paid, $19,235; expenditures, $22,137; qualifying distributions, $19,235.
Limitations: Applications not accepted.
Application information: Contributes only to pre-selected organizations.
Trustees: Carolyn White, Steven Yarn.
EIN: 526988224

60706
Phoenix Scholarship Foundation, Inc.
3261 Old Washington Rd., Ste. 3021
Waldorf, MD 20602
Contact: Parran Foster, Dir.

Classified as a company-sponsored operating foundation in 1996 in MD.
Donor(s): Phoenix Pharmaceuticals, Inc.
Financial data (yr. ended 09/30/01): Assets, $510,229 (M); grants paid, $201,000; gifts received, $464,679; expenditures, $210,911; qualifying distributions, $715,906.
Limitations: Giving limited to headquarters city and major operating areas.
Application information: Application form not required.
Director: Parran Foster.
Trustee: Charles Curry.
EIN: 311490141
Codes: FD2, GTI

60707
Historical Electronics Museum, Inc.
P.O. Box 746
Baltimore, MD 21203-1693

Classified as a private operating foundation in 1982.
Donor(s): Robert L. Dwight.
Financial data (yr. ended 12/31/01): Assets, $505,474 (M); grants paid, $1,500; gifts received, $100,502; expenditures, $123,406; qualifying distributions, $117,526; giving activities include $117,629 for programs.
Limitations: Applications not accepted.
Officers and Directors:* Allan L. Spencer,* Pres., Operations; Alfred A. Cooke,* V.P., Counsel; Robert L. McFarland,* V.P., Fin. and Treas.; Harold M. Watson,* Secy.; Russell T. Bahner, David J. Beck, William O. Brackney, Louis Brown, H. Warren Cooper, Jack Harris, Wallace J. Hoff, John H. Martin, Stephen W. Oliner, Steven N. Stitzer, Dennis M. Zembala.
EIN: 521226197

60708
The Foundation for Advanced Research in the Medical Sciences, Inc.
26890 Double Mills Rd.
Easton, MD 21601-7728 (410) 822-8973
Contact: Richard C. Fowler, Pres.

Classified as a private operating foundation in 1983.
Donor(s): Richard C. Fowler, M.D., Mavis D. Fowler.
Financial data (yr. ended 12/31/99): Assets, $503,966 (M); grants paid, $14,710; gifts received, $2,700; expenditures, $38,941; qualifying distributions, $14,710.
Officers: Richard C. Fowler, M.D., Pres.; Mavis D. Fowler, V.P.; Richard L. Veech, V.P.; Thomas K. Sawyer, Secy.; David E. Abercrombie, Treas.
Directors: Irene Crowe, Henry T. Leonard III.
EIN: 521198182

60709
Ross and Grace Pierpont Charitable Trust
215 Belmont Forest Ct., Ste. 408
Timonium, MD 21093
Application address: c/o Mercantile-Safe Deposit & Trust Co., 2 Hopkins Plz., Baltimore, MD 21201, tel.: (410) 237-5682
Contact: Lori Gehrig

Classified as an operating foundation in 1997.
Financial data (yr. ended 12/31/01): Assets, $412,336 (M); grants paid, $48,750; expenditures, $54,166; qualifying distributions, $48,750.
Limitations: Giving primarily in Baltimore, MD.
Trustees: Grace Pierpont, Ross Pierpont, Mercantile-Safe Deposit & Trust Co.
EIN: 526858237

60710
Grace Graves Huggins Foundation
P.O. Box 127
Chestertown, MD 21620 (410) 348-5408

Established in 1997 in MD.
Donor(s): Frank Huggins.
Financial data (yr. ended 05/31/00): Assets, $405,600 (M); grants paid, $29,380; gifts received, $12,521; expenditures, $55,746; qualifying distributions, $47,951.
Limitations: Giving on a national basis.
Application information: Application form required.
Officer and Trustees:* Frank Huggins,* Chair.; R. Scott Handel, Martha Werle.
EIN: 526854449

60711
Silver Spring Lions Club Foundation
1688 E. Gude Dr., Ste. 102
Rockville, MD 20850-5036
Applications address: 13217 Greenmount Ave., Beltsville, MD 20705
Contact: Gene Hoffmaster, Vice-Chair.

Established in 1993 in MD.
Donor(s): Madeline E. Allpress.‡
Financial data (yr. ended 06/30/01): Assets, $334,545 (M); grants paid, $53,740; gifts received, $215; expenditures, $59,874; qualifying distributions, $57,900.
Limitations: Giving limited to MD.
Application information: Application form required.
Officers: Richard W. Lawlor, Chair.; Gene Hoffmaster, Vice-Chair.; Arthur J. Paholski, Treas.
EIN: 521835867

60712
Fusion Power Associates
c/o Ruth Watkins
2 Professional Dr., Ste. 248
Gaithersburg, MD 20878 (301) 258-0545

Financial data (yr. ended 12/31/99): Assets, $286,865 (M); grants paid, $0; gifts received, $164,796; expenditures, $204,273; qualifying distributions, $200,359; giving activities include $200,359 for programs.
Officers and Directors:* Charles Baker, Chair.; Roger Bangerter, Vice-Chair.; Stephen O. Dean,* Pres.; Gerald Kulciniski, V.P.; Ruth A. Watkins,* V.P.; John F. Clarke, John Davis, and 12 additional directors.
EIN: 521162794

60713
Russell E. & Elizabeth W. Morgan Foundation
3916 Rosemary St.
Chevy Chase, MD 20815-5224

Established in 1991 in PA.
Donor(s): Russell E. Morgan, Elizabeth W. Morgan.
Financial data (yr. ended 12/31/99): Assets, $244,378 (M); grants paid, $6,100; expenditures, $6,248; qualifying distributions, $6,248.
Limitations: Applications not accepted. Giving primarily in the Bethlehem, PA, area.
Application information: Contributes only to pre-selected organizations.
Officers: Russell E. Morgan, Sr., M.D., Admin.; Russell E. Morgan, Jr., Admin.
EIN: 232627666

60714
Susan C. Fusco Memorial Scholarship Fund
8701 Ashcroft Dr.
Laurel, MD 20708 (301) 419-3848
Contact: Edward C. Diggs, V.P.

Established as a private operating foundation in 1992.
Financial data (yr. ended 06/30/01): Assets, $209,009 (M); grants paid, $18,000; expenditures, $21,783; qualifying distributions, $3,783.
Limitations: Giving limited to MD.
Application information: Applicant must include a high school transcript and proof of attendance at Beacon Heights Elementary School. Application form required.
Officers: David O. Mason, Pres.; Edward C. Diggs, V.P.; Janice Cook, Secy.; Marjorie Ntakounakis, Treas.
EIN: 521739989
Codes: GTI

60715
House of Hope Trust
17 Warren Rd., Ste. 3A
Baltimore, MD 21208

Established in 1998 in MD.
Financial data (yr. ended 12/31/00): Assets, $201,992 (M); grants paid, $0; gifts received, $59,493; expenditures, $91,012; qualifying distributions, $57,910; giving activities include $91,012 for programs.
Limitations: Applications not accepted.
Application information: Contributes only to pre-selected organizations.
Officers and Directors:* Jon B. Singer,* Pres.; Howard Cardin, V.P.; Dennis Trencher, Secy.; Marc Lichtenberg, Treas.; Stanton Ades, Barbara Einhorn, Roland Einhorn, Michelle Gilken, Chad Honkofsky, Philip Klein, Steve Lebowitz, Roger Michael, Morton Mower, Toby Mower, Howard Rosenbloom, Jeffrey Scherr, Ina Singer, Merideth Singer.
EIN: 521998445

60716
Applied Computer Security Associates, Inc.
c/o Marshall Abrams
2906 Covington Rd.
Silver Spring, MD 20910

Classified as a private operating foundation in 1988.
Financial data (yr. ended 12/31/01): Assets, $201,275 (M); grants paid, $0; expenditures, $232,527; qualifying distributions, $0.
Officers: Marshall Abrams, Pres.; Ronald A. Gove, V.P.; Diana Akers, Secy.; Ann B. Marmor-Squires, Treas.
EIN: 521575759

60717
Coile Foundation
c/o Christopher Coile
541-B Baltimore Annapolis Blvd.
Severna Park, MD 21146

Established in 2001 in MD.
Donor(s): Christopher C. Coile, Susan S. Coile.
Financial data (yr. ended 12/31/01): Assets, $200,071 (M); grants paid, $0; gifts received, $200,000; expenditures, $0; qualifying distributions, $0.
Limitations: Applications not accepted.
Application information: Contributes only to pre-selected organizations.
Trustees: Christopher C. Coile, Susan S. Coile.
EIN: 266001829

60718
Americans for Religious Liberty
P.O. Box 6656
Silver Spring, MD 20916-6656

Financial data (yr. ended 12/31/01): Assets, $190,032 (M); grants paid, $0; gifts received, $77,307; expenditures, $164,739; qualifying distributions, $163,967; giving activities include $154,180 for programs.
Officers and Directors:* Burton Caine,* Chair.; Michael Prival, Secy.; Edd Doerr,* Exec. Dir.; Herb Blinder, Carleton Coon, Jone Johnson-Lewis, George Kaplan.
EIN: 363118921

60719
Facchina Foundation
P.O. Box 186
La Plata, MD 20646

Established in 1993 in MD.
Donor(s): Paul Facchina, Sr.
Financial data (yr. ended 12/31/01): Assets, $185,237 (M); grants paid, $0; expenditures, $275; qualifying distributions, $0.
Officer: Charles McPherson, Treas.
Directors: Melissa Facchina, Paul Facchina, Sr., Paul Facchina, Jr.
EIN: 521853989

60720
The Miller Family Charitable Foundation, Inc.
P.O. Box 21545
Baltimore, MD 21208-1545 (410) 356-8097
Contact: Alvin Miller, Pres.

Established in 1991 in MD.
Donor(s): Alvin Miller.
Financial data (yr. ended 03/31/00): Assets, $185,044 (M); grants paid, $10,250; gifts received, $35,500; expenditures, $10,250; qualifying distributions, $10,207.
Limitations: Giving primarily in Baltimore, MD.
Application information: Application form not required.
Officers: Alvin Miller, Pres.; Adam Miller, V.P.; Ann Miller, V.P.; Mary Miller, V.P.; Sue Miller, V.P.
EIN: 521760308

60721
The George A. and Carmel D. Aman Memorial Trust
4703 Annapolis Rd.
Bladensburg, MD 20710-1201

Established in 1984 in MD.
Financial data (yr. ended 11/30/99): Assets, $183,508 (M); grants paid, $600; expenditures, $63,826; qualifying distributions, $31,940; giving activities include $31,397 for programs.
Trustees: W. Dickerson Charlton, Charles Day, Lee Doolittle, John Giannetti, David Murray, Sam Parker.
EIN: 521323637

60722
Safe Waterways in Maryland
10706 Beaver Dam Rd.
Cockeysville, MD 21030

Established in 2000 in MD.
Donor(s): Carolyn Smith.
Financial data (yr. ended 12/31/00): Assets, $181,144 (M); grants paid, $4,388; gifts received, $251,013; expenditures, $75,003; qualifying distributions, $73,386.
Limitations: Applications not accepted. Giving primarily in Baltimore, Md.
Application information: Contributes only to pre-selected organizations.
Trustees: Dyson Erhart, E S. Jackson, Daniel Keith, J. Duncan Smith, Frances E. Smith.
EIN: 522248482

60723
F. Struben Foundation, Inc.
3870 Jarrettsville Pike
Jarrettsville, MD 21084
Contact: Jean C. Struben, V.P.

Classified as a private operating foundation in 1970.
Financial data (yr. ended 09/30/00): Assets, $177,012 (M); grants paid, $9,000; gifts received, $3,500; expenditures, $10,115; qualifying distributions, $9,000.
Limitations: Giving on a national basis.
Officers: Francis L. Struben, Pres.; Jean C. Struben, V.P.; Linda S. Trott, Secy.; Carol S. Knickman, Treas.
EIN: 526050484

60724
18Below.com Foundation, Inc.
1777 Reisterstown Rd., Ste. B270
Baltimore, MD 21208-1344

Established in 2000 in MD.
Donor(s): Joseph Meyerhoff Fund, Inc.
Financial data (yr. ended 12/31/00): Assets, $172,730 (M); grants paid, $74,740; gifts received, $379,460; expenditures, $206,730; qualifying distributions, $202,437.
Limitations: Giving primarily in Baltimore and Owings, MD.
Officers and Directors:* Joseph Meyerhoff II,* Pres.; Laura Cutler,* V.P.; Bally Katz,* Secy.; Lee Hendler,* Treas.
EIN: 522268841

60725
Aklilu Lemma Foundation, Inc.
1007 Vineyard Hill Rd.
Catonsville, MD 21228
Contact: Zemedie Asfaw

Established in 1998 in MD.
Donor(s): Betzety B. Lemma.
Financial data (yr. ended 09/30/99): Assets, $168,692 (M); grants paid, $7,832; expenditures, $9,778; qualifying distributions, $7,832.
Officers: Betzety B. Lemma, C.E.O. and Pres.; Mulugeta Wodajo, V.P.
Directors: Mesfin A. Lemma, Tedros A. Lemma.
EIN: 521979501

60726
Joseph Sacco Scholarship Fund
(Formerly SIU Scholarship Foundation and Trust)
5201 Auth Way
Suitland, MD 20746 (301) 899-0675
Contact: John Fay, Tr.

Established in 1992 in MD. Classified as a company-sponsored operating foundation.
Donor(s): Seafarers International Union of North America, Lundeberg Maryland School of Seamanship.
Financial data (yr. ended 12/31/01): Assets, $161,008 (M); grants paid, $3,375; expenditures, $3,480; qualifying distributions, $3,480.
Limitations: Giving primarily in FL and MD.
Application information: Application form required.
Trustees: Margaret Bowen, John Fay, David Heindel, Leslie Tarantola.
EIN: 521642751
Codes: GTI

60727
The James E. Steuart Foundation, Inc.
6 Upland Rd., Apt. 55
Baltimore, MD 21211 (410) 366-0874
Contact: Germaine L. Sharretts, V.P.

Financial data (yr. ended 12/31/00): Assets, $147,599 (M); grants paid, $0; gifts received, $500; expenditures, $9,032; qualifying distributions, $0.
Officers and Trustees:* Jane W. Harlan,* Pres.; Germaine L. Sharretts,* V.P.; Wm. G. Woods, Jr., Treas.
EIN: 520817822

60728
Fullwood Foundation, Inc.
13 Country Mill Ct.
Baltimore, MD 21228 (410) 788-1313
Contact: Harlow Fullwood, Jr., Pres.

Established in 1990 in MD.
Donor(s): PepsiCo, Inc., Elpaha, Inc., RJR Nabisco Holdings Corp., Gillette Corp.

Financial data (yr. ended 12/31/01): Assets, $132,176 (M); grants paid, $114,311; gifts received, $200,618; expenditures, $234,168; qualifying distributions, $114,302.
Limitations: Giving primarily in Baltimore, MD.
Officers and Directors:* Harlow Fullwood, Jr.,* Pres.; Elnora Fullwood,* V.P.; J. Michael Recher, Allen M. Schiff.
EIN: 521701088
Codes: FD2

60729
Tis (Soumen) Lahiri Memorial Foundation, Inc.
c/o Asit K. Lahiri
14434 Twig Rd.
Silver Spring, MD 20905-7015

Established in 1991 in MD.
Donor(s): Asit K. Lahiri, Sabita Lahiri.
Financial data (yr. ended 12/31/99): Assets, $125,014 (M); grants paid, $1,500; gifts received, $3,000; expenditures, $2,075; qualifying distributions, $2,000.
Limitations: Applications not accepted. Giving primarily in PA, with giving also in TN.
Officers: Asit K. Lahiri, Pres.; Barry Edgar, V.P.; Sabita Lahiri, Secy.and Treas.
EIN: 521733405

60730
CUIC Foundation, Inc.
8501 LaSalle Rd., Ste. 318
Baltimore, MD 21286-5925
Contact: Maureen Walsh McAtee, Pres.

Established in 1992 in MD as a company-sponsored operating foundation.
Donor(s): Credit Union Insurance Corp.
Financial data (yr. ended 12/31/00): Assets, $122,449 (M); grants paid, $1,000; gifts received, $100,000; expenditures, $1,119; qualifying distributions, $1,119.
Limitations: Giving primarily in areas of company operations.
Application information: Application form required.
Officers and Director:* Kenneth Jones,* Chair.; Maureen Walsh McAtee, Pres.; Ed Languille, Secy.-Treas.; Otis Hendrix.
EIN: 521749045
Codes: CD

60731
Max and Jenny Katz Memorial Fund, Inc.
501 W. University Pkwy., Ste. C-1
Baltimore, MD 21210-3234
Contact: Fred Emil Katz, Pres.

Established in 2000 in MD.
Donor(s): Theodore Levitt.
Financial data (yr. ended 12/31/00): Assets, $121,652 (M); grants paid, $0; gifts received, $130,285; expenditures, $3,479; qualifying distributions, $1,638; giving activities include $1,638 for programs.
Officers and Directors:* Fred Emil Katz, Pres.; William H. Engleman,* V.P.; Gary W. Viener,* Secy.-Treas.; Rev. Carl Edwards, Renee Fuller, Prof. John Stone.
EIN: 522220529

60732
The Rose Salter Medical Research Foundation
517 St. Francis Rd.
Towson, MD 21286

Donor(s): Boron LePore, C.A. Beck, Inc., Intramedic, SmithKline Beecham, Unimed.
Financial data (yr. ended 12/31/01): Assets, $120,036 (M); grants paid, $0; gifts received, $30,616; expenditures, $2,696; qualifying distributions, $2,696; giving activities include $2,403 for programs.
Officer: Victoria Tittinger, Pres.
Directors: Jefferson Katims, M.D., Marc Rendell, Wynne Yoder, Joan Zarriello.
EIN: 522143781

60733
Rheumatoid Arthritis Assistance Foundation
9801 Washington Blvd., 9th Fl.
Gaithersburg, MD 20878

Established in 1999 in DC.
Financial data (yr. ended 12/31/99): Assets, $115,023 (M); grants paid, $0; gifts received, $600,675; expenditures, $663,995; qualifying distributions, $494,209; giving activities include $663,995 for programs.
Officers and Board Members:* Nancy Carteron, M.D.,* Pres.; Julie James, V.P. and Treas.; Jacqueline M. Dunbar-Jacob, Ph.D.,* Secy.; Valoree E. Dowell, M.A., Frederick L. Jones III, M.D.
EIN: 522143480

60734
Smart Family Foundation, Inc.
9805 Sunset Dr.
Rockville, MD 20850-3607

Established in 2000 in MD.
Donor(s): John N. Smart, Patricia E. Smart.
Financial data (yr. ended 12/31/00): Assets, $113,336 (M); grants paid, $6,934; gifts received, $127,000; expenditures, $13,664; qualifying distributions, $11,816.
Limitations: Applications not accepted.
Application information: Contributes only to pre-selected organizations.
Officers and Directors:* John N. Smart,* Pres.; Marie E. Zavisca,* Secy.; Patricia E. Smart,* Treas.; Michael J. Kelly, Patrick C. McKeever.
EIN: 522200241

60735
Kuethe Library, Inc.
P.O. Box 218
Glen Burnie, MD 21060

Classified as a private operating foundation in 1972.
Financial data (yr. ended 12/31/99): Assets, $111,807 (M); grants paid, $0; gifts received, $3,700; expenditures, $2,352; qualifying distributions, $2,352; giving activities include $2,352 for programs.
Officers: Mark N. Schatz, Pres.; Irene Newhouse, V.P.; F. William Kuethe, Jr., Secy.-Treas.
EIN: 520783089

60736
The Thelma March Scholarship Foundation
5719 York Rd.
Baltimore, MD 21212-3634
Application address: 928 E. North Ave., Baltimore, MD 21202, tel.: (410) 889-3987
Contact: Victor C. March, Tr.

Financial data (yr. ended 12/31/99): Assets, $110,460 (M); grants paid, $7,000; gifts received, $6,244; expenditures, $31,027; qualifying distributions, $7,000.
Limitations: Giving limited to MD.
Application information: Application form not required.
Trustees: Erich W. March, Julia R. March, Victor C. March, William C. March.
EIN: 521208748

60737
Low Vision Information Center
(Formerly Information for the Partially Sighted)
7701 Woodmont Ave., Ste. 302
Bethesda, MD 20814

Donor(s): The Freed Foundation, The Marjorie C. Adams Charitable Trust, JFK Pru Trust, Joan F. Kahn, B. Franklin Kahn, Edward Schmeltzer, Liz Schmeltzer, Blanche White.‡
Financial data (yr. ended 09/30/00): Assets, $107,794 (M); grants paid, $0; gifts received, $105,255; expenditures, $104,601; qualifying distributions, $104,994; giving activities include $84,514 for programs.
Limitations: Applications not accepted.
Application information: Contributes only to pre-selected organizations.
Officers: Pat Coupard, Pres. and Treas.; Sooz Stein, V.P.; Susan Wolman, Secy.; Andrew Chang, Treas.; Amy Gabala, Exec. Dir.
Directors: Melvin Alper, Stan Cohen, Karen Cooper, Bill Rolle.
EIN: 521155044

60738
Herman & Goldie Halpin Foundation, Inc.
3604 Inverness Dr.
Chevy Chase, MD 20815

Established in 1998 in MD.
Donor(s): Herman Halpin, Goldie Halpin.
Financial data (yr. ended 12/31/99): Assets, $105,101 (M); grants paid, $14,500; expenditures, $18,311; qualifying distributions, $14,500.
Limitations: Applications not accepted.
Application information: Contributes only to pre-selected organizations.
Directors: Beth Ann O'Hara, Martha Pleasure.
EIN: 522052715

60739
Anna and Charles Conigliaro Foundation, Inc.
c/o R.E. Wieder
3716 Court Pl.
Ellicott City, MD 21043

Financial data (yr. ended 12/31/99): Assets, $92,657 (M); grants paid, $5,000; expenditures, $5,168; qualifying distributions, $5,168.
Officer and Trustees:* Robert F. Wieder,* Mgr.; Anna Conigliaro, Sadie Orlando, Concetta J. Smith.
EIN: 521987868

60740
The Catalyst Foundation
c/o Michael J. Nagan
7809 Brickyard Rd.
Potomac, MD 20854-4820
Application address: c/o Andrew Fox, Sarasota County Technical Institute, Beneva & Proctor Rd., Sarasota, FL 34233

Financial data (yr. ended 12/31/99): Assets, $90,214 (M); grants paid, $8,481; gifts received, $38,867; expenditures, $14,367; qualifying distributions, $14,338.
Limitations: Giving primarily in Sarasota, FL.
Application information: Application form required.
Officers: Michael J. Nagan, Pres.; Laura N. Brown, V.P.; Claudia R. Nagan, Secy.; Stephen E. Brown, Treas.
EIN: 650488729

60741
Lester & Ruth Hiebert Scholarship Foundation
c/o Peter Hiebert
3207 Rolling Rd.
Chevy Chase, MD 20815

Established in 1994 in CA.
Financial data (yr. ended 12/31/00): Assets, $89,250 (M); grants paid, $4,000; expenditures, $4,300; qualifying distributions, $4,000.
Limitations: Applications not accepted. Giving limited to CA.
Application information: Contributes only to pre-selected organizations.
Directors: Helen Hiebert Grady, Heidi Hiebert, Peter N. Hiebert.
EIN: 770363012

60742
Montgomery County School Safety Committee, Inc.
9125 Gaither Rd.
Gaithersburg, MD 20877

Financial data (yr. ended 12/31/99): Assets, $86,806 (M); grants paid, $0; gifts received, $80,918; expenditures, $82,790; qualifying distributions, $82,790; giving activities include $92,690 for programs.
Officers: John M. Queen, Pres.; George A. Burroughs, Jr., V.P.; Robert A. Greenberg, Secy.; Sidney A. Katz, Treas.
EIN: 521839810

60743
Schwartz-Jurkovich Family Foundation, Inc.
4515 Willard Ave., Ste. 1203S
Chevy Chase, MD 20815-3617

Established in 1998 in MD.
Donor(s): Celesta S. Jurkovich, Lyle H. Schwartz.
Financial data (yr. ended 12/31/01): Assets, $79,940 (M); grants paid, $4,250; expenditures, $7,379; qualifying distributions, $4,250.
Limitations: Applications not accepted.
Application information: Contributes only to pre-selected organizations.
Director: Celesta S. Jurkovich, Lyle H. Schwartz.
EIN: 522136298

60744
Austin Gift Trust
8224 Lilly Stone Dr.
Bethesda, MD 20817
Contact: William P. Connolly, Tr.

Established in 1998 in MD.
Donor(s): Elizabeth L. Connolly, William P. Connolly.
Financial data (yr. ended 12/31/00): Assets, $79,274 (L); grants paid, $1,005; expenditures, $1,005; qualifying distributions, $1,005.
Trustees: Elizabeth L. Connolly, William P. Connolly.
EIN: 526974691

60745
Feeser Scholarship Fund, Inc.
c/o Claudia Harrington
280 Dill Ave.
Frederick, MD 21701-4936
Application address: 1281 Limit Ave., Baltimore, MD 21239, tel.: (410) 435-7345
Contact: Oriole Green, Pres.

Established in 1988 in MD.
Financial data (yr. ended 12/31/99): Assets, $77,121 (M); grants paid, $4,500; expenditures, $4,845; qualifying distributions, $4,845.
Limitations: Giving limited to DE and MD.

Application information: Application form required.
Officers and Directors:* Oriole Green,* Pres.; Marilyn Hembrock,* V.P.; Emma S. Dillow,* Secy.; Claudia Harrington,* Treas.; Valerie Eigner, Helen Englar, Diane Julian, Jeanette Loutenschlager, Lucille Schilling.
EIN: 521556229

60746
Max & Rebecca Rochkind Family Foundation
13903 N. Gate Ln.
Silver Spring, MD 20904
Application address: 1818 Beechwood Blvd., Pittsburgh, PA 15217, tel.: (412) 521-8561
Contact: Melissa L. Dubinsky, V.P.

Financial data (yr. ended 12/31/01): Assets, $66,481 (L); grants paid, $3,600; expenditures, $4,305; qualifying distributions, $3,600.
Limitations: Giving on a national basis.
Officers: Sandra R. Friedman, Pres.; Melissa L. Dubinsky, V.P. and Treas.; Joan E. Ressin, Secy.
EIN: 526060392

60747
The Cheswick Center
11140 Rockville Pike, Ste. 316
Rockville, MD 20852

Classified as a private operating foundation in 1971.
Financial data (yr. ended 06/30/02): Assets, $62,215 (M); grants paid, $0; expenditures, $1,252; qualifying distributions, $376.
Officers and Trustees:* Lawrence Butler,* Chair.; Barbara Taylor,* Pres. and Treas.; Francis J. Dineen, Eugene R. Smoley, Jr., Richard Umbdenstock.
EIN: 237131748

60748
Yvorra Leadership Development, Inc.
P.O. Box 408
Port Republic, MD 20676-0408
Application address: 2446 Azalea Ln., Port Republic, MD 20676

Financial data (yr. ended 06/30/99): Assets, $53,784 (M); grants paid, $6,000; gifts received, $4,447; expenditures, $10,678; qualifying distributions, $10,649.
Officers and Directors:* Michael S. Hildebrand,* Pres.; Gregory G. Noll,* V.P.; JoAnne F. Hildebrand,* Secy. and Treas.; Colin A. Campbell, Rose M. Cogan, George Dodson, John Hess.
EIN: 521560287

60749
The Veronica Bird Charitable Foundation
c/o Ahead with Autism
P.O. Box 599
Riva, MD 21140 (410) 956-5882
FAX: (410) 956-0306; *E-mail:* info@aheadwithautism.com; *URL:* http://www.aheadwithautism.com

Established in 2000 in MD.
Donor(s): Veronica Mahaffey, Redge Mahaffey.
Financial data (yr. ended 12/31/00): Assets, $47,866 (M); grants paid, $340; gifts received, $165,315; expenditures, $118,834; qualifying distributions, $115,113; giving activities include $80,683 for programs.
Officers: Veronica Bird Mahaffey, Pres.; Redge Mahaffey, Secy.-Treas.
EIN: 522174631

60750
SDA Literature Ministry, Inc.
6711 Old Branch Ave.
Temple Hills, MD 20748-6903

Established in 1995 in MD.
Donor(s): Bernard I. Hass.
Financial data (yr. ended 12/31/01): Assets, $46,958 (M); grants paid, $0; gifts received, $16,965; expenditures, $23,350; qualifying distributions, $0.
Directors: Bernard I. Hass, Karl May.
EIN: 521912935

60751
Lantern Ministry, Inc.
21 Montauk Ct.
Baltimore, MD 21234

Donor(s): Steve Zumbrun.
Financial data (yr. ended 12/31/00): Assets, $45,060 (M); grants paid, $0; gifts received, $18,325; expenditures, $2,555; qualifying distributions, $9,555; giving activities include $2,272 for programs.
Officer: Steve Zumbrun, Pres.
EIN: 522029192

60752
Metro Housing, Inc.
307 W. Allegheny Ave.
Towson, MD 21204

Classified as a private operating foundation in 1972.
Financial data (yr. ended 12/31/01): Assets, $43,695 (M); grants paid, $0; expenditures, $855; qualifying distributions, $0.
Officers: Eugene D. Byrd, Pres.; Francis Iglehart, Secy.-Treas.
EIN: 237130891

60753
Gita K. Shah Foundation
9209 Pegasus Ct.
Potomac, MD 20854-1661 (301) 983-9422
Contact: Gita K. Shah, M.D., Dir.

Financial data (yr. ended 12/31/00): Assets, $43,390 (M); grants paid, $7,468; expenditures, $7,911; qualifying distributions, $7,364.
Directors: Gita K. Shah, Kamlesh C. Shah.
EIN: 521864700

60754
Psychiatric Foundation, Inc.
4100 College Ave.
P.O. Box 396
Ellicott City, MD 21041-0396

Financial data (yr. ended 12/31/99): Assets, $43,170 (M); grants paid, $0; gifts received, $113; expenditures, $293; qualifying distributions, $293; giving activities include $185 for programs.
Limitations: Applications not accepted. Giving primarily in Baltimore, MD.
Application information: Contributes only to pre-selected organizations.
Officers: E.L. Taylor, Pres.; S. Taylor, V.P. and Treas.; Bruce Taylor, M.D., Secy.
EIN: 520895781

60755
Stahl Family Foundation
c/o David E. Stahl
100 Severn Ave., Ste. 607
Annapolis, MD 21403-2688

Donor(s): Dave Stahl, Carolyn Stahl.
Financial data (yr. ended 12/31/99): Assets, $43,135 (M); grants paid, $27,525; gifts received,

$30,000; expenditures, $27,500; qualifying distributions, $27,525.
Limitations: Applications not accepted.
Application information: Contributes only to pre-selected organizations.
Officers: David Stahl, Pres.; Carolyn Stahl, V.P. and Secy.; Barbara Stahl, Treas.
Directors: Anna Stahl, Claudia Stahl, Julie Stahl, Kurt Stahl, Michael Stahl, Steve Stahl, Tom Stahl.
EIN: 752605273

60756
Ameen Rihani Organization, Inc.
c/o Michael Regan
4915 Saint Elmo Ave., Ste. 503
Bethesda, MD 20814-6053

Donor(s): May Rihani.
Financial data (yr. ended 12/31/01): Assets, $39,323 (M); grants paid, $0; gifts received, $9,000; expenditures, $1,219; qualifying distributions, $0.
Officers: Sarmad Rihani, Pres.; May Rihani, Secy.; Ramzi Rihani, Treas.
EIN: 522144196

60757
Lancers Boys Club
c/o Hon. Robert Hammerman
100 E. Pratt St., Ste. 2440
Baltimore, MD 21201

Classified as a private operating foundation in 1969.
Donor(s): Hon. Robert I.H. Hammerman.
Financial data (yr. ended 12/31/99): Assets, $37,554 (M); grants paid, $0; gifts received, $39,349; expenditures, $53,096; qualifying distributions, $53,040; giving activities include $53,096 for programs.
Limitations: Applications not accepted.
Application information: Contributes only to pre-selected organizations.
Officers: Hon. Robert I.H. Hammerman, Pres.; Jerald Sachs, V.P.; Sam Handelman, Secy.-Treas.
EIN: 237003969

60758
Maryland-Delaware-D.C. Press Foundation, Inc.
2191 Defense Hwy., Ste. 300
Crofton, MD 21114

Classified as a company-sponsored operating foundation.
Donor(s): Maryland-Delaware-D.C. Press Service, Inc., Maryland-Delaware-D.C. Press Association, Inc.
Financial data (yr. ended 12/31/00): Assets, $35,717 (M); grants paid, $1,500; gifts received, $1,700; expenditures, $2,569; qualifying distributions, $2,038.
Limitations: Giving limited to headquarters city and major operating areas, including Washington DE, DE and MD.
Application information: Recommendation required from journalist, high school teacher or advisor. Application form required.
Officers: Peggy Schiff, Pres.; Legusta Floyd, V.P.; Alice Lucan, Secy.; Jean C. Halle, Treas.
Trustees: Jim Keat, John J. Oliver, Mike Powell.
EIN: 522135767

60759
National Council on Fireworks Safety, Inc.
4808 Moorland Ln., Ste. 109
Bethesda, MD 20814

Classified as a private operating foundation in 1989.
Donor(s): American Protechics Assn., Golden Gate Fireworks.

Financial data (yr. ended 12/31/01): Assets, $34,087 (M); grants paid, $0; gifts received, $75,885; expenditures, $124,371; qualifying distributions, $0.
Officers and Directors:* John Conkling,* Pres.; Dale Miller,* V.P.; Ann F. Crampton,* Secy.-Treas. and Exec. Dir.; Larry Brown, Donald McCaulley, Royce Trout.
EIN: 521630773

60760
Maryland Criminal Justice Administration Institute, Inc.
120 E. Baltimore St., Ste. 1250
Baltimore, MD 21202

Financial data (yr. ended 12/31/00): Assets, $28,267 (M); grants paid, $0; gifts received, $112,500; expenditures, $217,120; qualifying distributions, $217,097; giving activities include $217,120 for programs.
Officers: Jervis S. Finney, Pres.; Hon. Clarence E. Goetz, V.P.
Directors: Hon. Andre M. Davis, Michael J. Kelly, Doreen Rosenthal, Hon. Stephen H. Sachs.
EIN: 522171523

60761
The Dellon Foundation, Inc.
3333 N. Calvert St. 370
Baltimore, MD 21218
Contact: A. Lee Dellon, M.D., Pres.

Donor(s): A. Lee Dellon, M.D.
Financial data (yr. ended 12/31/00): Assets, $23,763 (M); grants paid, $1,100; gifts received, $4,900; expenditures, $11,542; qualifying distributions, $10,192.
Officer and Director:* A. Lee Dellon, M.D.,* Pres.
EIN: 521317729

60762
Banneker-Douglass Museum Foundation, Inc.
P.O. Box 751
Annapolis, MD 21401

Financial data (yr. ended 12/31/00): Assets, $23,248 (M); grants paid, $8,055; gifts received, $6,466; expenditures, $9,633; qualifying distributions, $9,633.
Officers and Directors:* Yevola S. Peters,* Pres.; James H. Johnson, V.P.; Brenda Lindsey, Secy.; Everett G. Pettigrew,* Treas.
EIN: 521095665

60763
Grammencs Adamantiades Scholarship Fund
c/o Achilles Adamaantiades
7 Bloomingdale Ct.
North Bethesda, MD 20852-5536

Established in 1995 in MD.
Financial data (yr. ended 12/31/99): Assets, $22,524 (M); grants paid, $1,000; gifts received, $650; expenditures, $1,000; qualifying distributions, $1,000.
Limitations: Applications not accepted. Giving primarily in MD.
Application information: Unsolicited requests for funds not accepted.
Officer: Maria C. Thomas, Pres.
Directors: Achilles Adamantiades, Marsha Adamantiades, Misha Adamantiades, John Moustakas.
EIN: 521947361

60764
Timbira Research and Education Foundation
c/o Dr. William H. Crocker
4 Chalfont Ct.
Bethesda, MD 20816-1805

Established in 1993 in VA.
Donor(s): William H. Crocker, Mrs. William H. Crocker.
Financial data (yr. ended 12/31/00): Assets, $19,571 (M); grants paid, $0; gifts received, $33,000; expenditures, $14,319; qualifying distributions, $0.
Officers: William H. Crocker, Pres.; Betty J. Meggers, V.P.; Jean G. Crocker, Secy.; Richard T. Nicodemus, Treas.; Gail E. Solomon, Exec. Dir.
EIN: 521829027

60765
Maryland State Lodge Sons of Italy Foundation, Inc.
602 E. Joppa Rd.
Baltimore, MD 21286

Financial data (yr. ended 12/31/99): Assets, $18,584 (M); grants paid, $23,000; gifts received, $15,974; expenditures, $28,100; qualifying distributions, $23,000.
Limitations: Applications not accepted. Giving limited to MD.
Application information: Contributes only to pre-selected organizations.
Officers: Dan Lango, Pres.; Frances Cipriotti, Treas.
EIN: 521366924

60766
Dara's Canine Foundation, Inc.
7507 Hampden Ln.
Bethesda, MD 20814

Donor(s): Lolo Sarnoff.
Financial data (yr. ended 12/31/99): Assets, $17,945 (L); grants paid, $13,414; gifts received, $30,043; expenditures, $33,183; qualifying distributions, $0.
Limitations: Applications not accepted.
Application information: Contributes only pre-selected organizations.
Officers: Lolo Sarnoff, Pres.; Donald T. Bliss, Jr., V.P.; Dorothy S. Whitehurst, Secy.-Treas.
Trustee: Gabriele Steers.
EIN: 522103633

60767
Mark T. Birns and Ann Krieger Birns Family Foundation
11413 Twining Ln.
Potomac, MD 20854

Established in 1994.
Financial data (yr. ended 12/31/99): Assets, $16,003 (M); grants paid, $12,500; expenditures, $12,603; qualifying distributions, $12,364.
Limitations: Applications not accepted.
Application information: Contributes only to pre-selected organizations.
Director: Mark T. Birns.
EIN: 526638866

60768
REALTORS Professional Designation & Educational Trust Fund
c/o GCAAR
1355 Piccard Dr.
Rockville, MD 20850-4328
Application address: P.O. Box 120, Upper Marlboro, MD 20772
Contact: Alvin Monshower, Tr.

Donor(s): Prince George's County Assn. of Realtors, Inc.

60768—MARYLAND

Financial data (yr. ended 08/31/00): Assets, $15,084 (M); grants paid, $625; expenditures, $625; qualifying distributions, $625.
Limitations: Giving limited to residents of MD.
Application information: Application form required.
Trustee: Alvin Monshower.
EIN: 526208995

60769
L.O.R.D. Corporation
3334 Charles St.
Fallston, MD 21047

Donor(s): Fred A. Kessler.
Financial data (yr. ended 12/31/99): Assets, $14,902 (M); grants paid, $0; gifts received, $2,206; expenditures, $1,515; qualifying distributions, $1,508; giving activities include $1,508 for programs.
Officers and Directors:* William M. Yarbrough,* Chair.; Darold K. Beard,* Secy.; Fred A. Kessler, Treas.
EIN: 521110628

60770
Anne Marie Loy Memorial Nursing Scholarship Trust Fund
5405 Stone Rd.
Frederick, MD 21703-6924
Application address: c/o John Handley High School Scholarship Comm., P.O. Box 910, Winchester, VA 22604

Classified as a private operating foundation in 1986.
Financial data (yr. ended 12/31/99): Assets, $13,939 (L); grants paid, $800; expenditures, $1,050; qualifying distributions, $1,050.
Limitations: Giving limited to residents of Winchester, VA.
Trustee: Carol Ballenger Loy.
EIN: 546225879

60771
One-Way Bible Fellowship, Inc.
8018 Carey Branch Dr.
Fort Washington, MD 20744 (301) 567-6795
Contact: James L. Cox, Dir.

Donor(s): James L. Cox.
Financial data (yr. ended 10/31/01): Assets, $12,900 (M); grants paid, $0; gifts received, $1,750; expenditures, $834; qualifying distributions, $834.
Director: James L. Cox.
EIN: 521238457

60772
Sands House Foundation, Inc.
c/o Ann Jensen
130 Prince George St.
Annapolis, MD 21401-1704

Established in 1999.
Financial data (yr. ended 12/31/01): Assets, $12,554 (M); grants paid, $0; gifts received, $7,000; expenditures, $5,000; qualifying distributions, $0.
Officer: Margaret R. Dowsett, Secy.-Treas.
EIN: 522130253

60773
Building Men for Others Foundation
5 Elmhurst Rd.
Baltimore, MD 21210

Established in 2000 in DE and MD.
Donor(s): Francis X. Poggi.
Financial data (yr. ended 12/31/00): Assets, $10,230 (M); grants paid, $23,380; gifts received, $213,105; expenditures, $207,686; qualifying distributions, $176,157.
Limitations: Giving primarily in Baltimore, MD.
Officers and Directors:* Rev. Joseph C. Ehrmann, Jr., Pres. and Exec. Dir.; Francis X. Poggi,* V.P.; Amy Poggi,* 2nd V.P.; Redmond C. S. Finney,* Secy.; Benjamin Griswold IV,* Treas.
EIN: 522226469

60774
The Shane Diggin Memorial Scholarship Charitable Trust
110 Kipling Ct.
Abingdon, MD 21009
Contact: Claudette R. Diggin, Tr.

Financial data (yr. ended 12/31/99): Assets, $10,221 (M); grants paid, $1,000; gifts received, $1,715; expenditures, $1,055; qualifying distributions, $1,055.
Limitations: Giving limited to Bel Air, MD.
Application information: Recipients are recommended by faculty.
Trustee: Claudette R. Diggin.
EIN: 521528429

60775
Joseph & Ada Mae Rudick Foundation
c/o KAWG&F
40 York Rd.
Baltimore, MD 21204

Established in 1995 in MD.
Financial data (yr. ended 12/31/99): Assets, $9,801 (M); grants paid, $0; expenditures, $440; qualifying distributions, $375; giving activities include $375 for programs.
Limitations: Applications not accepted.
Application information: Contributes only to pre-selected organizations.
Trustees: Mannes F. Greenberg, Alvin D. Katz, H. Reid Shaw, Jonathan B. Shaw.
EIN: 526725611

60776
Kirsten N. Russell Memorial Fund
c/o Leon B. Russell
41950 Swan's Ct.
Leonardtown, MD 20650-5715
Application address: c/o Lisa Tetlimer, School Registrar, Calvert High School, 600 Dares Beach Rd., Prince Frederick, MD 20678, tel.: (410) 535-7330

Financial data (yr. ended 07/31/01): Assets, $8,985 (M); grants paid, $1,000; expenditures, $1,000; qualifying distributions, $1,000.
Limitations: Giving limited to residents of MD.
Application information: Application form required.
Trustees: Karen E. Russell, Leon B. Russell.
EIN: 521722232

60777
The Institute for New Medicine, Inc.
10319 Glen Rd.
Potomac, MD 20854

Established in 1998 in VA.
Donor(s): Little River Foundation.
Financial data (yr. ended 12/31/99): Assets, $7,596 (M); grants paid, $0; gifts received, $25,734; expenditures, $22,882; qualifying distributions, $0; giving activities include $15,747 for programs.
Officers: Michael R. Ruff, Chair.; Dandace B. Pert, V.P.; Douglas E. Dieter, Secy.
EIN: 541912701

60778
C.H.T.J. Southard House Museum, Inc.
4701 Sangamore Rd., Ste. N. Plz. 40
Bethesda, MD 20816

Established in 1990 in ME.
Donor(s): Frederic F. Case.
Financial data (yr. ended 05/31/99): Assets, $6,592 (M); grants paid, $0; gifts received, $15,000; expenditures, $13,355; qualifying distributions, $13,005; giving activities include $13,005 for programs.
Officers: Carolyn Cocker Case, Pres. and Treas.; Frederic F. Case, V.P. and Treas.
Director: Wilbur Cooper.
EIN: 521686149

60779
Metropolitan Community Productions, Inc.
c/o Donna Randolph
16321 S. Westland Dr.
Gaithersburg, MD 20877-1511

Classified as a private operating foundation in 1992.
Financial data (yr. ended 12/31/00): Assets, $5,314 (M); grants paid, $0; gifts received, $4,075; expenditures, $23,154; qualifying distributions, $0; giving activities include $23,154 for programs.
Officers: Alice K. Helm, V.P.; Donna A. Randolph, Secy.; Lewis M. Helm, Treas.
EIN: 521662045

60780
The M.U.S.E. Foundation, Inc.
The Royston Bldg.
102 W. Pennsylvania Ave., Ste. 504
Towson, MD 21204-4542

Established in 1997 in MD.
Donor(s): Kenneth H. Roberts.
Financial data (yr. ended 06/30/02): Assets, $4,858 (M); grants paid, $1,175; gifts received, $281,708; expenditures, $289,537; qualifying distributions, $289,168; giving activities include $289,537 for programs.
Limitations: Applications not accepted.
Application information: Contributes only to 3 pre-selected organizations.
Officers: Kenneth H. Roberts, Pres.; Brian V. Roberts, Secy.; Kevin C. Roberts, Treas.; Lawrence E. Kushner, Exec. Dir.
EIN: 311563794

60781
The Patrick Hart Foundation, Inc.
c/o Steve Jackowitz
705 Bedford Rd.
Bel Air, MD 21014

Established in 1991 in MD.
Donor(s): N. Managua.
Financial data (yr. ended 12/31/99): Assets, $4,612 (M); grants paid, $20,070; expenditures, $33,933; qualifying distributions, $20,070.
Limitations: Applications not accepted. Giving primarily in Washington, DC.
Application information: Contributes only to pre-selected organizations.
Officers and Trustees:* Peggy Hart,* Pres.; Thomas Hart,* V.P.; Lorraine Nadden,* Secy.; Louis J. Trinchere,* Treas.; Phil Cramer, Tony DiPaula, Steve Jackovitz.
EIN: 521737811

60782
Lasky Family Foundation
c/o David L. Snyder
217 E. Redwood St.
Baltimore, MD 21202

Established in 1984 in MD.
Donor(s): Michael W. Lasky.
Financial data (yr. ended 12/31/00): Assets, $4,199 (M); grants paid, $1,000; expenditures, $2,875; qualifying distributions, $1,000.
Limitations: Applications not accepted. Giving primarily in Baltimore, MD.
Directors: Marilyn Bradford, Michael W. Lasky, David L. Snyder.
EIN: 521436960

60783
The Darlene F. Collins Charitable Foundation
9016 Hardesty Dr.
Clinton, MD 20735

Established in 2000 in MD.
Donor(s): Darlene F. Collins.
Financial data (yr. ended 12/31/00): Assets, $3,493 (M); grants paid, $6,500; gifts received, $10,000; expenditures, $6,546; qualifying distributions, $6,531.
Limitations: Applications not accepted. Giving primarily in Washington, DC.
Application information: Contributes only to pre-selected organizations.
Trustee: Darlene F. Collins.
EIN: 522243574

60784
Antonio Carmela & John Barbagallo Foundation
627 Gayle Dr.
Linthicum, MD 21090-2103
Contact: John Barbagallo, Tr.

Established in 1995 in MD.
Donor(s): John Barbagallo.
Financial data (yr. ended 12/31/99): Assets, $2,286 (M); grants paid, $300; gifts received, $311; expenditures, $334; qualifying distributions, $300.
Limitations: Giving limited to Baltimore, MD.
Trustees: John Barbagallo, Lucy Coco Bursco, Mary Coco.
EIN: 521887119

60785
Bernard D. Crooke, Jr. Foundation
4125 Queen Mary Dr.
Olney, MD 20832-2109

Classified as a private operating foundation in 1988.
Financial data (yr. ended 12/31/01): Assets, $1,487 (M); grants paid, $0; gifts received, $33; expenditures, $120; qualifying distributions, $0.
Limitations: Applications not accepted. Giving primarily in the Washington, DC, area, including MD.
Application information: Contributes only to pre-selected organizations.
Officers and Directors:* Elizabeth M. Roth,* Pres.; Joyce A. Crooke,* V.P.; John T. Roth,* Secy.-Treas.; Edward Crooke, Dianne M. Gooch.
EIN: 521570656

60786
Emmanuel Bansok Literature Mission, Inc.
1317-B E.W. Hwy.
Silver Spring, MD 20910

Classified as a private operating foundation in 1994.
Financial data (yr. ended 06/30/01): Assets, $988 (M); grants paid, $0; gifts received, $4,000; expenditures, $3,910; qualifying distributions, $0; giving activities include $3,910 for programs.
Trustee: Changho Choi.
EIN: 521849810

60787
Attman Family Foundation, Inc.
20 S. Charles St., 2nd Fl.
Baltimore, MD 21201

Donor(s): Leonard J. Attman, Edward Attman, Seymour Attman.
Financial data (yr. ended 12/31/99): Assets, $789 (M); grants paid, $4,862; gifts received, $4,749; expenditures, $4,970; qualifying distributions, $4,970.
Limitations: Applications not accepted. Giving primarily in Baltimore, MD.
Application information: Contributes only to pre-selected organizations.
Officers: Leonard J. Attman, Pres.; Edward Attman, V.P.; Seymour Attman, Secy.-Treas.
EIN: 520895930

60788
The Circle of One, Inc.
7945 MacArthur Blvd., Ste. 224
Cabin John, MD 20818

Established in 2000.
Financial data (yr. ended 12/31/00): Assets, $750 (M); grants paid, $0; gifts received, $3,620; expenditures, $7,928; qualifying distributions, $0.
Officer and Director:* Kourosh Kashani,* Pres.
EIN: 541976745

60789
Lipot and Irene Friedman Foundation, Inc.
4110 Old Washington Rd.
Waldorf, MD 20602

Established in 1993.
Donor(s): Irene Friedman.
Financial data (yr. ended 12/31/01): Assets, $566 (M); grants paid, $19,139; gifts received, $16,855; expenditures, $19,469; qualifying distributions, $19,139.
Limitations: Applications not accepted. Giving primarily in MD.
Application information: Contributes only to pre-selected organizations.
Officer: Irene Friedman, Pres.
EIN: 521836405

60790
J. Willard Marriott, Jr. Foundation
c/o Steve McNeil
10400 Fernwood Rd.
Bethesda, MD 20817
Application address: Box 925, Washington, DC 20058, tel.: (301) 380-1765

Established in 1992 in MD.
Financial data (yr. ended 12/31/00): Assets, $450 (M); grants paid, $9,500; gifts received, $10,078; expenditures, $9,683; qualifying distributions, $9,400.
Limitations: Giving limited to residents of NH.
Application information: Application form required.
Trustees: Sterling D. Colton, Donna Garff Marriott, J. Willard Marriott, Jr.
EIN: 526527249

60791
Porcaro Family Charitable Foundation
c/o John L. Porcaro
30 Lake Forest Dr.
Oakland, MD 21550

Established in 2000 in MD.

Financial data (yr. ended 12/31/01): Assets, $102 (M); grants paid, $0; gifts received, $375; expenditures, $375; qualifying distributions, $0.
Directors: Christine M. Porcaro, John L. Porcaro, M.D., Peter J. Porcaro.
EIN: 522226595

60792
Barcus Family Charitable Foundation, Inc.
20537 Anndyke Way
Germantown, MD 20874

Established in 2000 in MD.
Donor(s): J. Michael Barcus.
Financial data (yr. ended 12/31/01): Assets, $0 (M); grants paid, $281,500; expenditures, $281,500; qualifying distributions, $280,965.
Limitations: Applications not accepted. Giving primarily in MD.
Application information: Contributes only to pre-selected organizations.
Officers and Directors:* J. Michael Barcus,* Pres.; Amelia Barcus,* Secy.
EIN: 522239931
Codes: FD

60793
Adele Tyler Memorial Scholarship Trust
P.O. Box 757
Cambridge, MD 21613
Contact: Harold S. Robbins, Tr.

Financial data (yr. ended 12/31/01): Assets, $0 (M); grants paid, $8,000; expenditures, $10,300; qualifying distributions, $7,898.
Limitations: Giving primarily in Dorchester County, MD.
Trustee: Harold S. Robbins.
EIN: 526925623

MASSACHUSETTS

60794
The Rowland Institute for Science, Inc.
100 Edwin H. Land Blvd.
Cambridge, MA 02142

Donor(s): Rowland Foundation, Inc., Edwin H. Land.‡
Financial data (yr. ended 12/31/01): Assets, $84,976,346 (M); grants paid, $0; gifts received, $3,067,559; expenditures, $8,092,601; qualifying distributions, $7,775,529; giving activities include $7,436,566 for programs.
Officers and Directors:* Michael Burns, C.O.O.; Philip DuBois,* Pres.; Jennifer DuBois,* V.P.; Joseph W. Haley, Clerk; Guy Smallwood,* Treas.; Daniel W. Drake, Valerie Smallwood.
EIN: 042704639

60795
The Clay Mathematics Institute, Inc.
1770 Massachusetts Ave., No. 618
Cambridge, MA 02140

Established in 1998 in MA.
Donor(s): Landon T. Clay.
Financial data (yr. ended 09/30/00): Assets, $75,968,703 (M); grants paid, $0; gifts received, $20,000; expenditures, $3,553,519; qualifying distributions, $2,838,158; giving activities include $3,580,300 for programs.
Officers and Directors:* Arthur Jaffe,* Pres.; Landon T. Clay,* V.P. and Treas.; Lavinia D. Clay,*

Secy.; Finn M.W. Caspersen, William R. Hearst, David B. Stone.
EIN: 134025978

60796
Chestnut Knoll
(Formerly Chestnut Knoll Home for Aged Women)
24 Tabor Crossing
Longmeadow, MA 01116-9903

Classified as a private operating foundation in 1985.
Donor(s): Helen Harris Trust, Emerson Annuity Trust.
Financial data (yr. ended 09/30/01): Assets, $45,355,559 (M); grants paid, $0; gifts received, $904,759; expenditures, $5,085,576; qualifying distributions, $4,503,934; giving activities include $4,503,934 for programs.
Officers: Peter Vogian, Pres.; John Discenza, V.P.; Peter Pappas, Treas.; Weuda Restall, Clerk.
Directors: Deborah Basile, Larry Eagan, Ted Fleming, and 8 additional directors.
EIN: 042105937
Codes: TN

60797
Heritage Plantation of Sandwich, Inc.
67 Grove St.
Sandwich, MA 02563

Classified as a private operating foundation in 1980.
Donor(s): Josiah K. Lilly III,‡ Margaret M. Lilly, Orville D. Garland, Arnold Dyer.
Financial data (yr. ended 10/31/99): Assets, $32,043,978 (M); grants paid, $0; gifts received, $526,714; expenditures, $2,652,064; qualifying distributions, $1,791,227.
Officers and Trustees:* Gene A. Schott,* Pres.; Joel G. Cowell, Nancy Kendall, Robert S. Neese.
EIN: 042704457
Codes: TN

60798
Winchester Mount Vernon House
(Formerly Home for Aged People in Winchester)
110 Mount Vernon St.
Winchester, MA 01890

Financial data (yr. ended 12/31/01): Assets, $29,145,402 (M); grants paid, $0; gifts received, $2,200; expenditures, $1,184,119; qualifying distributions, $1,122,737; giving activities include $1,033,574 for programs.
Officers: Stephen Carr Anderson, Pres.; Lucille Leland Yuse, 1st V.P.; Roy A. Johnson, M.D., 2nd V.P.; F. Brooks Cowgill, M.D., 3rd V.P.; Gerald B. O'Grady III, Secy.; Truman S. Dayton, Treas.
Directors: William T. Bird, Neal J. Harte, Mrs. Ralph Seferian, Peter Segerstrom, and 8 additional directors.
Trustees: Daniel S. Ahearn, Harris S. Richardson, Jr., James R. Willing.
EIN: 042104317

60799
The Cambridge Homes
(Formerly Cambridge Home for Aged People)
360 Mount Auburn St.
Cambridge, MA 02138

Classified as a private operating foundation in 1972.
Donor(s): Adelaide K. Smith Trust, C. Wesley Smith,‡ Ruth Lindbloom Trust, Walter Learned Trust, Arthur H. Smith Trust, Marie L. Baohe.
Financial data (yr. ended 09/30/00): Assets, $28,466,646 (M); grants paid, $0; gifts received, $44,237; expenditures, $1,944,314; qualifying distributions, $1,574,067; giving activities include $1,550,652 for programs.
Officers and Directors:* John Macomber,* Pres.; Dirck Born,* Treas.; William Stone,* Clerk; Priscilla Elliot, and 6 additional directors.
EIN: 042103958

60800
Lynn Home for Elderly Persons
1 Atlantic Terr.
Lynn, MA 01902-3155

Classified as a private operating foundation in 1985.
Financial data (yr. ended 08/31/00): Assets, $24,319,265 (M); grants paid, $0; gifts received, $54,357; expenditures, $1,040,502; qualifying distributions, $885,957; giving activities include $885,957 for programs.
Officers and Trustees:* Suzanne Murray,* Pres.; Malcolm Heffelman,* V.P.; Gail Roberts,* V.P.; Mrs. Ralph Roberts,* Secy.; Richard F. Murray,* Treas.; Judy Bocock, Robert L. Bradley, Mrs. S. Whitney Bradley, Mrs. William Cruger, Lester B. Farwell, Mrs. Lester B. Farwell, and 20 additional trustees.
EIN: 042400070

60801
Davenport Memorial Foundation
c/o Herber Wells
70 Salem St.
Malden, MA 02148

Trust established in 1946 in MA; Classified as a private operating foundation in 1986.
Donor(s): Alice M. Davenport.‡
Financial data (yr. ended 05/31/00): Assets, $22,852,284 (M); grants paid, $43,750; expenditures, $876,694; qualifying distributions, $944,995; giving activities include $731,427 for programs.
Limitations: Applications not accepted. Giving limited to Malden, MA.
Officers and Trustees:* Edward Marston,* Pres.; Muriel H. Weldon, Clerk; Elizabeth Hirst,* Treas.; G. Dana Bill, C. Russell Blomerth, Barbara E. Brown, and 10 additional trustees.
EIN: 042104142

60802
New Horizons at Choate, Inc.
(Formerly Cummings Foundation New Horizons, Inc.)
200 W. Cummings Park
Woburn, MA 01801

Established in 1990 in MA.
Donor(s): Cummings Properties Foundation.
Financial data (yr. ended 12/31/00): Assets, $22,512,751 (M); grants paid, $0; gifts received, $7,131,585; expenditures, $2,679,780; qualifying distributions, $2,427,846; giving activities include $2,679,779 for programs.
Limitations: Applications not accepted.
Application information: Contributes only to a pre-selected organization.
Officers and Directors:* William S. Cummings,* Pres.; Susan F. Brand,* Clerk; Joyce M. Cummings,* Treas.; Barbara Whalen, Exec. Dir.; Marian E. Forsyth, James F. McDonough, M.D., Kenneth R. Summers, and 6 additional directors.
EIN: 043073023

60803
Josiah Willard Hayden Recreation Centre, Inc.
c/o Donald K. Mahoney
24 Lincoln St.
Lexington, MA 02421 (781) 862-8480

Established in 1937. Classified as a private operating foundation in 1991.
Donor(s): Josiah W. Hayden.‡
Financial data (yr. ended 08/31/01): Assets, $21,673,020 (M); grants paid, $36,050; gifts received, $2,255; expenditures, $3,755,259; qualifying distributions, $3,507,383.
Limitations: Giving limited to residents of Lexington, MA.
Application information: Application form required.
Officers and Directors:* Melville T. Hodder,* Pres.; Donald K. Mahoney,* V.P. and Exec. Dir.; John W. Maloney,* Treas.; Alan S. Fields, Robert M. Hutchinson, Jr., David G. Kirk, Anthony Mancini, Janice Whittemore.
EIN: 042203700
Codes: GTI

60804
Roxbury Home for Aged Women
1215 Centre St.
Roslindale, MA 02131

Classified as a private operating foundation in 1972.
Donor(s): Katherine E. Kenney.
Financial data (yr. ended 06/30/00): Assets, $19,750,507 (M); grants paid, $0; gifts received, $5,340; expenditures, $927,087; qualifying distributions, $832,243; giving activities include $832,243 for programs.
Officers and Directors:* Erling A. Hanson, Jr.,* Pres.; Lincoln W. Williams, V.P.; Priscilla A. Call,* Secy.; Richard B. Osterberg,* Treas.; Rev. Louis H.G. Bier, Elizabeth Hanson, Ralph H. Willard, Jr., and 20 additional directors.
EIN: 042104858

60805
Managers of Boston Port & Seamen's Aid Society
124 Main St., Thompson Sq.
Boston, MA 02129

Established in 1981 in MA.
Donor(s): Ashton Fund.
Financial data (yr. ended 12/31/00): Assets, $19,407,520 (M); grants paid, $49,000; gifts received, $58,000; expenditures, $764,550; qualifying distributions, $1,338,978; giving activities include $333,914 for programs.
Limitations: Applications not accepted. Giving primarily in MA.
Application information: Contributes only to pre-selected organizations.
Officers and Managers:* Elton McCausland, Pres.; Oliver A. Spalding, V.P.; Ralph R. Bagley,* Secy.-Treas.; William Doherty, Exec. Dir.; William L. Kingman, Harold F. Lynch, Richard Ostberg, and 18 additional managers.
EIN: 042104688

60806
World Peace Foundation
124 Mount Auburn St.
Cambridge, MA 02138

Classified as a private operating foundation in 1981.
Donor(s): Andrew W. Mellon Foundation, Agency for International Development, Edward Ginn Trust.
Financial data (yr. ended 06/30/00): Assets, $19,112,010 (M); grants paid, $0; gifts received, $525,820; expenditures, $555,459; qualifying

distributions, $488,676; giving activities include $358,148 for programs.
Officers and Trustees:* Richard H. Ullman,* Chair.; Robert I. Rotberg,* Pres.; Frederick G.P. Thorne,* Treas.; Peter D. Bell, Lincoln P. Bloomfield, Abram J. Chayes, Milton Katz, Judith K. Keenan, and 9 additional trustees.
EIN: 042105854

60807
Deutsches Altenheim, Inc.
2222 Centre St.
West Roxbury, MA 02132

Financial data (yr. ended 12/31/01): Assets, $18,100,035 (M); grants paid, $0; gifts received, $294,597; expenditures, $9,199,782; qualifying distributions, $0.
Limitations: Applications not accepted.
Application information: Contributes only to pre-selected organizations.
Officers: Henry Winkler, Pres.; Hans P. Birle, V.P.; Alan W. Eilertson, Secy.; Heinrich W. Brinkhaus, Treas.
Trustees: U. Barbara Bridge, Renate Engler, Michael Hager, George Munchbach, Rosemarie Jennings, Karin Leradi, Claire Munchbach, Agnes Pilot, and 3 additional trustees.
EIN: 042104144

60808
Association for the Relief of Aged Women of New Bedford
1140 State Rd.
P.O. Box 819
Westport, MA 02790

Established in 1866.
Financial data (yr. ended 03/31/01): Assets, $17,931,023 (M); grants paid, $668,967; gifts received, $3,600; expenditures, $800,127; qualifying distributions, $668,967.
Limitations: Applications not accepted. Giving limited to residents of New Bedford, Dartmouth, Fairhaven, and Acushnet, MA.
Application information: Unsolicited requests for funds not accepted.
Directors: Hope Atkinson, Mary Elinore Davies, Marion Richards, and 18 additional directors.
EIN: 046056367
Codes: FD, GTI

60809
Ames Free Library of Easton
53 Main St.
North Easton, MA 02356

Classified as a private operating foundation in 1999.
Financial data (yr. ended 12/31/00): Assets, $16,557,270 (M); grants paid, $0; gifts received, $442,896; expenditures, $660,436; qualifying distributions, $642,492; giving activities include $578,951 for programs.
Officers and Directors:* Donna Richman,* Pres.; Hazel L. Varella,* Secy.; Joseph F. Murphy, Treas.; Annalee Bundy,* Exec. Dir.; William M. Ames, Kathleen E. Boyle, Daniel W. Churchill, Gerard S. Marsan.
EIN: 237245953

60810
World Furniture Foundation, Inc.
(Formerly Charles River Square Antique Foundation, Inc.)
82 Devonshire St., No. S4A
Boston, MA 02109

Established in 1992 in MA.
Donor(s): Edward C. Johnson III.

Financial data (yr. ended 12/31/99): Assets, $16,183,953 (M); grants paid, $0; expenditures, $535,227; qualifying distributions, $3,257,540; giving activities include $2,236,675 for programs.
Officers and Directors:* Edward C. Johnson III,* Pres.; Peter G. Johannsen,* Clerk; Donald E. Alhart, Christopher C. Curtis.
EIN: 043165720

60811
Springfield Home for the Elderly
74 Walnut St.
Springfield, MA 01105

Classified as a private operating foundation in 1987.
Financial data (yr. ended 12/31/00): Assets, $15,903,444 (M); grants paid, $0; gifts received, $1,500; expenditures, $71,470; qualifying distributions, $0.
Officers and Trustees:* Whiting S. Houston, Jr.,* Pres. and Treas.; Robert W. Clarke,* V.P.; James H. Tourtelotte,* Clerk; Paul Kenyon, W. Robert McDonald, and 8 additional Trustees.
EIN: 042105936

60812
Brookfield Arts Foundation, Inc.
82 Devonshire St., Ste. F9A3
Boston, MA 02109-3605

Established in 1995 in MA.
Donor(s): Edward C. Johnson III, Edward C. Johnson Fund.
Financial data (yr. ended 12/31/00): Assets, $15,038,997 (M); grants paid, $211,107; gifts received, $1,000,000; expenditures, $778,706; qualifying distributions, $577,562; giving activities include $1,784,850 for programs.
Limitations: Applications not accepted. Giving primarily in Boston and Salem, MA.
Application information: Contributes only to pre-selected organizations.
Officers and Directors:* Edward C. Johnson III,* Pres.; Tara Cederholm, V.P.; Patricia R. Hurley, Secy.; Richard G. Weidmann, Treas.; Christopher C. Curtis.
EIN: 311681603
Codes: FD2

60813
Trustees of the Home for Aged Women in the City of Worcester
1183 Main St.
Worcester, MA 01603

Financial data (yr. ended 12/31/99): Assets, $14,683,793 (M); grants paid, $0; gifts received, $14,959; expenditures, $1,320,398; qualifying distributions, $1,226,439; giving activities include $1,263,325 for programs.
Officers: Edward Robbins, Pres.; Robin Spaulding, V.P.; John Hirbour, Secy.-Treas.
Trustees: John Budd, Michael Galica, John Hodgson, John Morgan.
EIN: 042108367

60814
The Stanley Park of Westfield, Inc.
P.O. Box 1191
Westfield, MA 01086

Classified as a private operating foundation in 1972.
Financial data (yr. ended 12/31/00): Assets, $13,390,062 (M); grants paid, $0; gifts received, $876,318; expenditures, $1,106,612; qualifying distributions, $684,941; giving activities include $410,646 for programs.
Officers and Directors:* Joseph B. Palmer,* Pres.; Latimer B. Eddy,* Treas.; John B. Caswell, Jr.,

Philip Caswell, Pamela Everets, Albert Ferst, Evelyn Janes, Harold C. Kraus, L. Douglas La Plante, Frank Pac, Ian C. Palmer, Homer G. Perkins, Richard K. Sullivan, and 2 additional directors.
EIN: 042131404

60815
The Art Complex, Inc.
189 Alden St.
P.O. Box 2814
Duxbury, MA 02331-2814

Donor(s): Carl Weyerhaeuser.
Financial data (yr. ended 12/31/01): Assets, $11,916,451 (M); grants paid, $0; gifts received, $943,034; expenditures, $689,976; qualifying distributions, $0.
Director: Carl Weyerhaeuser, Chair.
EIN: 046155696

60816
Shaw Fund for Mariners' Children
P.O. Box 403
Norwood, MA 02062-0403

Classified as a private operating foundation in 1972.
Donor(s): Robert Gould Shaw.‡
Financial data (yr. ended 12/31/00): Assets, $11,484,305 (M); grants paid, $0; gifts received, $195; expenditures, $310,559; qualifying distributions, $310,765; giving activities include $310,559 for programs.
Officers: S. Parkman Shaw, Jr.,* Pres.; Robert G. Shaw,* V.P. and Clerk; Norman C. Nicholson, Jr.,* Treas.; and 11 additional members.
Trustees and Finance Committee Members:* Jane Shaw Bizzi, Mrs. George B. Blake, Colin A. Canham, Jr., Edward D. Cook, Jr., Ingersoll Cunningham, L. Branch Harding, Mark Ingram, Robert B. Minture, Theodore E. Ober, William C. Shaw, Alexander Whiteside.
EIN: 042104861

60817
Burndy Library, Inc.
38 Memorial Dr., MIT E56-100
Cambridge, MA 02139

Donor(s): The Dibner Institute, Robert McKeon.
Financial data (yr. ended 06/30/00): Assets, $10,819,363 (M); grants paid, $0; gifts received, $2,245,032; expenditures, $537,541; qualifying distributions, $429,488; giving activities include $429,488 for programs.
Limitations: Applications not accepted.
Application information: Contributes only to a pre-selected organization.
Officers: David Dibner, Pres.; Frances K. Dibner, V.P.; Evelyn Simha, Exec. Dir. and Treas.
Directors: Sidney Altman, Dennis D. Berkey, Jed Z. Buchwald, Brent Dibner, Gary Feldman, Jerome Friedman, Stewart H. Greenfield, Hermann A. Haus, Franco Modigliani, A. Neil Papalardo, Gregory A. Petsko, Isadore M. Singer.
EIN: 060709286

60818
Hopedale Community House, Inc.
43 Hope St.
Hopedale, MA 01747

Classified as a private operating foundation in 1978.
Donor(s): Hopedale Foundation.
Financial data (yr. ended 07/31/00): Assets, $10,517,107 (M); grants paid, $0; gifts received, $25,000; expenditures, $338,401; qualifying distributions, $320,339; giving activities include $283,606 for programs.

60818—MASSACHUSETTS

Officers and Directors:* William B. Gannett,* Pres.; Merrily F. Sparling,* Secy.; Bernard J. Stock,* Treas.; William G. Burrill, Peter S. Ellis, Edward M. Horton.
EIN: 042133252

60819
The Berkeley Retirement Home
150 Berkeley St.
Lawrence, MA 01841-1224

Classified as a private operating foundation in 1992.
Donor(s): Arthur J. Dows,‡ Cornelia Battershill.
Financial data (yr. ended 12/31/99): Assets, $10,397,795 (M); grants paid, $0; gifts received, $57,685; expenditures, $2,534,233; qualifying distributions, $331,221; giving activities include $55,410 for programs.
Officers: Timothy Hatch, Pres.; Clifton Milne, V.P.; Jane Barlow, Secy.; Robert Perreault, Treas.
Trustees: Matthew A. Caffrey, John H. Campbell, Charles E. Crowninshield, Rev. Donald P. Dickinson, Anthony Giordano, Thomas C. MacLauchlan, Eleanor Porter, Angela Privitera, Ida Russell, Michael J. Sabbagh, Valerie Snigorski, Rev. Kenneth Swenson.
EIN: 042104374

60820
The Fitch Home, Inc.
75 Lake Ave.
Melrose, MA 02176

Classified as a private operating foundation in 1986.
Financial data (yr. ended 09/30/01): Assets, $9,915,849 (M); grants paid, $0; gifts received, $15,100; expenditures, $917,213; qualifying distributions, $0.
Officers: Lester H.N. Burnham, Pres.; L. Bradley Hutchinson, V.P.; C. Henry Kezer, Clerk; Lester Haddock, Treas.
Trustees: Emilie Burnham, Florence Hutchinson, Charles F. Kezer, and 2 additional trustees.
EIN: 042111388

60821
The Cloud Foundation
647 Boylston St.
Boston, MA 02116-2804 (617) 262-2949
FAX: (617) 262-2848; E-mail: info@cloudfoundation.org; URL: http://www.cloudfoundation.org
Contact: James W. Ryan, Exec Dir.

Established in 1999 in MA.
Donor(s): David A. Edwards, Aurelie Edwards.
Financial data (yr. ended 10/31/01): Assets, $9,462,728 (M); grants paid, $318,649; gifts received, $982,069; expenditures, $1,010,400; qualifying distributions, $751,496; giving activities include $401,528 for programs.
Limitations: Giving primarily in the greater Boston, MA, area.
Publications: Newsletter, informational brochure.
Application information: Associated Grantmaker's Common Proposal Form accepted. Application form required.
Trustees: Richard Batycky, Aurelie Edwards, David A. Edwards, Marc Jacquand.
EIN: 223681278
Codes: FD

60822
Merrimack River Valley House, Inc.
520 Fletcher St.
Lowell, MA 01854-3499

Financial data (yr. ended 09/30/01): Assets, $9,256,544 (M); grants paid, $0; expenditures, $1,043,814; qualifying distributions, $932,568; giving activities include $263,720 for programs.
Officers and Trustees:* Ernest G. Dixon, Jr.,* Pres.; Barry Pearson, 1st V.P.; Louise Derbyshire, 2nd V.P.; Ruth A. Sheahan, Secy.; Shirley E. Colmer, Treas.; Joanne Aldrich, Ingrid S. Bayliss, Louise Derbyshire, June Gunther, Wilfred Pearson, Paul B. Scribner, Daniel E. Walker, and 7 additional Trustees.
EIN: 042104808

60823
Dana Home of Lexington, Inc.
2027 Massachusetts Ave.
Lexington, MA 02421-4898

Classified as a private operating foundation in 1989.
Financial data (yr. ended 12/31/01): Assets, $9,024,611 (M); grants paid, $0; gifts received, $75; expenditures, $451,619; qualifying distributions, $0.
Officers and Directors:* Elaine Sullivan,* Pres.; Lester Savage,* 1st V.P.; Maryann Loveday,* 2nd V.P.; Sue Hurt, Secy.; Gerald W. Howell,* Treas.; Valerie Larsin, Daniel Whitney, and 6 additional directors.
EIN: 042111392

60824
Colonial Society of Massachusetts
c/o Loring, Wolcott & Coolidge
230 Congress St.
Boston, MA 02110

Classified as a private operating foundation in 1987.
Financial data (yr. ended 09/30/00): Assets, $8,797,375 (M); grants paid, $0; gifts received, $13,894; expenditures, $327,558; qualifying distributions, $247,907; giving activities include $230,095 for programs.
Officers and Trustees:* William M. Fowler, Jr.,* Pres.; Daniel R. Coquillette, V.P.; Celeste Walker, V.P.; Edward W. Hanson, Secy.; Leslie A. Morris, Secy.; Frederick D. Ballou, Treas.; Robert C. Anderson, Robert L. Hall, Ruth Morley.
EIN: 046110988

60825
The New England Home for the Deaf
154 Water St.
Danvers, MA 01923

Financial data (yr. ended 12/31/99): Assets, $8,165,937 (M); grants paid, $0; gifts received, $13,781; expenditures, $950,404; qualifying distributions, $53,734; giving activities include $4,840,090 for programs.
Officers and Trustees:* Ruth Moore,* Chair.; David Thomas, Vice-Chair.; Kathleen M. Vesey,* Vice-Chair.; Judith G. Good, C.E.O. and Pres.; Lee R. Kramer,* Pres.; Sharon P. Clark,* Secy.; Daniel J. Trombley,* Treas.; Thomas A. Boudrow, Mary Kelly, William H. Nye, Heidi L. Reed, and 6 additional trustees.
EIN: 042104760

60826
Kendall Whaling Museum Trust
27 Everett St.
P.O. Box 297
Sharon, MA 02067-0297

Financial data (yr. ended 12/31/99): Assets, $8,067,923 (M); grants paid, $0; gifts received, $930,950; expenditures, $867,195; qualifying distributions, $845,113; giving activities include $742,430 for programs.
Officer: Stuart M. Frank, Exec. Dir.
Trustees: Andrew W. Kendall, John P. Kendall.

EIN: 042294937

60827
Lathrop Home
215 South St.
Northampton, MA 01060

Classified as a private operating foundation in 1987.
Financial data (yr. ended 09/30/99): Assets, $7,900,130 (M); grants paid, $0; gifts received, $122,465; expenditures, $1,046,440; qualifying distributions, $972,115; giving activities include $945,621 for programs.
Officers and Directors:* Marjorie Cook,* Pres.; Dawn Carrier,* V.P.; Adaline Potter,* Secy.; Tom Sullivan,* Treas.; Stanford Blish, Joseph Brackett, Peter Hey, Shawki Kanazi, Thomas Kelley, Barbara Knittle, Lisa Mascaro, Marilyn Parsons, Helen Ross, William Stapleton, Donna Thurston, William Truswell, Constance Wilson.
EIN: 042104372

60828
Concord's Home for the Aged
110 Walden St.
Concord, MA 01742-2510

Established around 1957; Classified as a private operating foundation in 1989.
Financial data (yr. ended 11/30/01): Assets, $7,869,280 (M); grants paid, $270,650; expenditures, $523,317; qualifying distributions, $522,317.
Limitations: Applications not accepted. Giving limited to Concord, MA.
Application information: Contributes only to pre-selected organizations.
Officers: Jane Dahmen, Chair.; Mary A. Bramhau, Chair.; David Trask, Pres.; Thomas M. Ruggles, V.P.; Laura Ells, Secy.; Jane M. Brooks, Treas.
EIN: 042103762
Codes: FD

60829
The John Bertram House, Inc.
(Formerly Bertram Home for Aged Men in Salem)
29 Washington Sq.
Salem, MA 01970

Financial data (yr. ended 12/31/99): Assets, $7,777,488 (M); grants paid, $0; gifts received, $871; expenditures, $854,116; qualifying distributions, $123,060; giving activities include $727,508 for programs.
Officers: Jonathan Reardon, Pres.; Richard Hannah, V.P.; Betsy Rooks, Clerk; John F. Fisher, Treas.
Directors: Margaret Barmack, Shaun Clarke, Gareth Levy, Vincent Lique, and 4 additional directors.
EIN: 042103743

60830
Dibner Institute, Inc.
38 Memorial Dr., E56-100
Cambridge, MA 02139
Contact: Trudy Kontoff, Prog. Coord.

Established in 1990 in MA.
Donor(s): David Dibner, Frances K. Dibner.
Financial data (yr. ended 06/30/99): Assets, $7,633,022 (M); grants paid, $852,404; gifts received, $1,645,714; expenditures, $1,773,851; qualifying distributions, $1,658,641.
Application information: Application form required.
Officer: Evelyn Simha, Exec. Dir.
Board of Directors: Dennis D. Berkey, Jed Z. Buchwald, Brent Dibner, David Dibner, Frances K. Dibner, Mildred S. Dresselhaus, Gary Feldman,

Jerome Friedman, Stewart H. Greenfield, Herman A. Haus, Franco Modigliani, A. Neil Pappalardo, Gregory A. Petsko, Stephen Shapiro.
EIN: 043091094
Codes: TN

60831
Berkshire Retirement Home, Inc.
(Formerly Berkshire County Home for Aged Women)
89 South St.
Pittsfield, MA 01201

Classified as a private operating foundation in 1986.
Financial data (yr. ended 05/31/02): Assets, $7,251,999 (M); grants paid, $0; gifts received, $7,155; expenditures, $1,809,341; qualifying distributions, $0.
Officers and Directors:* David W. Murphy, Jr.,* Pres.; Joan E. Bancroft,* V.P.; Barbara Kie,* Secy.; W. Kelly Collins,* Treas.; Edward A. Forfa,* Admin.; Conrad Bernier, Annemarie Farrell, Mary Garofano, Thomas F. Plunkett, Jr., Ronald Rousseau, Donald Saint-Pierre, Gwen W. Sears, Shirley Whitehead.
EIN: 042103875

60832
C. Kevin Landry Charitable Foundation
c/o Ernest J. Grassey
50 Cole Pkwy., No. 27
Scituate, MA 02066
Application address: 125 High St., Ste. 2500, High St. Tower, Boston, MA 02110
Contact: C. Kevin Landry, Dir.

Established in 1986 in MA.
Donor(s): C. Kevin Landry.
Financial data (yr. ended 12/31/00): Assets, $7,195,680 (M); grants paid, $741,285; expenditures, $757,537; qualifying distributions, $757,477.
Limitations: Giving primarily in MA.
Directors: Ernest J. Grassey, C. Kevin Landry.
EIN: 042943405
Codes: FD

60833
The CARLISLE Foundation
P.O. Box 2464
Framingham, MA 01703 (508) 872-6377
FAX: (508) 872-6377; E-mail: rag@carlislefoundation.org; URL: http://www.carlislefoundation.org
Contact: Richard A. Goldblatt, Exec. Dir.

Established in 1991 in MA.
Donor(s): Helene T. Wilson, Grant M. Wilson.
Financial data (yr. ended 11/30/01): Assets, $7,122,923 (M); grants paid, $1,467,508; gifts received, $14,789; expenditures, $1,741,941; qualifying distributions, $2,489,441; giving activities include $747,500 for loans.
Limitations: Giving limited to New England, with emphasis on MA, including the greater Boston area.
Publications: Grants list, informational brochure (including application guidelines), multi-year report.
Application information: Application form required.
Officers: Helene T. Wilson, Pres.; Grant M. Wilson, Treas.; Richard A. Goldblatt, Exec. Dir.
Trustees: George B. Foote, Jr., Edward S. Heald, Kristen Wilson.
EIN: 046689264
Codes: FD

60834
The Dowmel Foundation
c/o H. Stuart
P.O. Box 719
Lenox, MA 01240-0719 (413) 637-1690

Established in 1995 in MA.
Donor(s): Catherine Mellon Dowd Revocable Living Trust.
Financial data (yr. ended 12/31/99): Assets, $6,627,087 (M); grants paid, $0; expenditures, $228,424; qualifying distributions, $221,350; giving activities include $212,802 for programs.
Trustee: Harry J. Stuart.
EIN: 046776623

60835
Center for Biomedical Science & Engineering Trust
30 Warren St.
Brookline, MA 02445

Established in 1996 in MA. Classified as a private operating foundation in 1997.
Financial data (yr. ended 12/31/01): Assets, $6,273,601 (M); grants paid, $2,312,835; gifts received, $4,035,272; expenditures, $2,821,482; qualifying distributions, $2,312,146.
Limitations: Applications not accepted. Giving primarily in MA.
Application information: Contributes only to pre-selected organizations.
Director and Trustees:* Elazer R. Edelman,* Dir.; Cheryl A. Edelman.
EIN: 043299490
Codes: FD

60836
Seth Mann II Home for Aged & Infirm Women, Inc.
349 N. Main St.
Randolph, MA 02368-4103

Classified as a private operating foundation in 1974.
Financial data (yr. ended 09/30/00): Assets, $6,210,160 (M); grants paid, $0; expenditures, $486,983; qualifying distributions, $454,116; giving activities include $403,975 for programs.
Limitations: Applications not accepted.
Application information: Contributes only to pre-selected organizations.
Officers and Directors:* Vernon W. Cannon,* Pres.; W. Bruce Lane,* V.P.; Ruby Long,* Secy.; Richard D. Marden,* Treas.; Ann M. Cederholm, Robert E. Getchell, Jacqueline Jernegan, Carol L. Wallace.
EIN: 042111410

60837
Quinque Foundation
c/o Philanthropic Advisors
400 Atlantic Ave., Ste. 401
Boston, MA 02110-3333

Established in 1999 in MA.
Donor(s): Helen D. Buchanan, The Royal Oak Foundation.
Financial data (yr. ended 12/31/00): Assets, $6,102,702 (M); grants paid, $17,850; gifts received, $2,302,000; expenditures, $313,014; qualifying distributions, $307,732.
Limitations: Applications not accepted.
Application information: Contributes only to pre-selected organizations.
Trustees: Fanchon M. Burnham, Helen D. Buchanan, Jane Watkins, Stephen D. Watkins.
EIN: 050508431

60838
Katharine C. Pierce Trust
c/o State Street Bank & Trust Co.
P.O. Box 351, MA010
Boston, MA 02101
Application address: 225 Franklin St., MA03, Boston, MA 02110
Contact: Amy F. Sahler

Classified as a private operating foundation in 1988.
Donor(s): Frank S. White.
Financial data (yr. ended 12/31/01): Assets, $6,030,881 (M); grants paid, $321,080; expenditures, $379,410; qualifying distributions, $344,217.
Limitations: Giving primarily in New England for organizations; giving limited to MA for individuals.
Application information: Application form required for individuals.
Trustees: William A. Truslow, State Street Bank & Trust Co.
EIN: 046095694
Codes: FD, GTI

60839
Achieve, Inc.
8 Story St., 1st Fl.
Cambridge, MA 02138

Donor(s): IBM, Eastman Kodak Co., Boeing, Inc, Proctor & Gamble, State Farm Insurance Co., Xerox Corp., The Pew Charitable Trusts.
Financial data (yr. ended 06/30/00): Assets, $5,562,662 (M); grants paid, $0; gifts received, $3,250,500; expenditures, $3,274,572; qualifying distributions, $3,247,234; giving activities include $2,392,193 for programs.
Officers: Robert Schwartz, Pres.; Frederick Balfour, V.P.; Matthew Gandal, V.P.
Directors: Keith Bailey, Philip Condit, Gray Davis, John Engler, George Fisher, Louis V. Gerstner, Jr., James B. Hunt, Jr., Mike Leavitt, Gary Locke, Edward Rust, Art Ryan, Tommy G. Thompson.
EIN: 522006429

60840
Home for Aged Men in the City of Brockton
c/o Silverstein & Creedon
71 Legion Pkwy., 3rd Fl.
Brockton, MA 02301
Contact: John F. Creedon, Pres.

Established in 1942 in MA.
Donor(s): Horace Howard,‡ Daniel W. Field Trust.
Financial data (yr. ended 03/31/01): Assets, $5,400,353 (M); grants paid, $300,000; gifts received, $6,848; expenditures, $376,265; qualifying distributions, $281,161.
Limitations: Giving limited to within 35 miles of Boston, MA.
Application information: Application form not required.
Officers: John F. Creedon, Pres.; Ida Caggiano, Clerk; Robert Prince, Treas.
EIN: 042103796
Codes: FD

60841
Stephen Phillips Memorial Charitable Trust For Historic Preservation
c/o LWC
230 Congress St.
Boston, MA 02110

Classified as a private operating foundation in 1998 in MA.
Financial data (yr. ended 12/31/00): Assets, $5,222,799 (M); grants paid, $0; expenditures, $286,970; qualifying distributions, $253,151; giving activities include $254,105 for programs.

60841—MASSACHUSETTS

Limitations: Applications not accepted.
Application information: Contributes only to pre-selected organizations.
Trustees: Lawrence Coolidge, Arthur H. Emery, John H. Finley IV, Richard Gross, Robert M. Randolph.
EIN: 046867291

60842
Eric Carle Foundation
38 Main St.
Northampton, MA 01061

Established in 1995 in MA.
Donor(s): Eric Carle, Barbara Carle.
Financial data (yr. ended 12/31/00): Assets, $4,939,490 (M); grants paid, $1,035; gifts received, $886,442; expenditures, $224,788; qualifying distributions, $192,615.
Limitations: Applications not accepted.
Application information: Contributes to pre-selected organizations.
Trustees: Barbara Carle, Eric Carle.
EIN: 043296725

60843
The Bay State Federal Savings Charitable Foundation
1299 Beacon St.
Brookline, MA 02446 (617) 739-9577
Contact: Pamela Tesler-Howitt

Established in 1997 in MA as a company-sponsored operating foundation.
Donor(s): Bay State Bancorp, Inc., Bay State Federal Savings Bank.
Financial data (yr. ended 03/31/01): Assets, $4,638,726 (M); grants paid, $211,523; expenditures, $407,770; qualifying distributions, $400,446.
Limitations: Giving primarily in MA.
Officers: John F. Murphy, Chair, C.E.O., and Pres.; Michael O. Gilles, Sr. V.P. and Treas.; Denise M. Renaghan, Exec. V.P.; Jill W. MacDougall, Corp. Secy.
Directors: Anthony F. Caruso, Phyllis M. Penta.
EIN: 043415547
Codes: FD2, CD

60844
The Colony Memorial
c/o Ropes & Gray
1 International Pl.
Boston, MA 02110-2624

Classified as a private operating foundation in 1988.
Financial data (yr. ended 12/31/99): Assets, $4,637,354 (M); grants paid, $0; expenditures, $81,854; qualifying distributions, $72,177; giving activities include $17,879 for programs.
Trustees: Stedman Buttrick, Jr., Francis L. Coolidge.
EIN: 042633276

60845
The Collings Foundation
River Hill Farm
Stow, MA 01775
Contact: Caroline Collings, Tr.

Established in 1977; classified as a private operating foundation in 1979.
Financial data (yr. ended 11/30/99): Assets, $4,499,923 (M); grants paid, $275,676; gifts received, $1,804,213; expenditures, $1,934,777; qualifying distributions, $2,263,154; giving activities include $605,834 for programs.
Limitations: Giving on a national basis.
Trustees: Caroline Collings, Thomas Garcia, Donald Rising.
EIN: 042658294

Codes: FD

60846
Fuller Trust, Inc.
c/o James J. McCusker
76 Canal St.
Boston, MA 02114

Classified as a private operating foundation in 1972.
Financial data (yr. ended 12/31/01): Assets, $4,450,526 (M); grants paid, $0; expenditures, $81,495; qualifying distributions, $1,191,068; giving activities include $53,068 for programs.
Trustees: James R. DeGiacomo, John P. Linehan, James J. McCusker.
EIN: 042104243

60847
Widows Society in Boston
581 Boylston St.
Boston, MA 02116 (617) 536-7951
FAX: (617) 536-7951
Contact: Jackie Husid, Exec. Dir.

Established in 1816 in MA. Incorporated in 1828.
Financial data (yr. ended 10/31/01): Assets, $4,383,220 (M); grants paid, $119,866; gifts received, $4,374; expenditures, $170,079; qualifying distributions, $161,771.
Limitations: Giving limited to applicants living within 25 miles of the State House in Boston, MA.
Publications: Annual report.
Application information: Application form required.
Officers: Peggy Hodder, Secy.; Richard V. Howe, Treas.; Jackie Husid, Exec. Dir.
Director: Mrs. Samuel E. Shaw II.
EIN: 042306840
Codes: FD2, GTI

60848
Old Colony Historical Society
66 Church Green
Taunton, MA 02780-3445

Established in 1986 in MA.
Financial data (yr. ended 12/31/99): Assets, $4,285,283 (M); grants paid, $350; gifts received, $82,547; expenditures, $163,148; qualifying distributions, $139,937; giving activities include $139,587 for programs.
Officers and Directors:* Marcus A. Rhodes, Jr.,* Pres.; David F. Gouveia, M.D., V.P.; Edward F. Kennedy, Jr.,* V.P.; Marjorie L. Largey,* V.P.; Herbert L. McClentic,* V.P.; William F. Hanna III,* Secy.; Philip R. LaFrance,* Treas.; Emma R. Andrade, Joseph C. Betz, Charles E. Crowley, Susanne Costa Duquette, Jordan H.F. Fiore, E. Dennis Kelly, Jr., Mark Litos, Maryan Nowak, Charles A. Thayer, M.D., Len Travers.
EIN: 042308455

60849
Griffin-White Home for Aged Men and Aged Couples, Inc.
170 Main St.
Haverhill, MA 01830

Financial data (yr. ended 12/31/99): Assets, $4,121,045 (M); grants paid, $0; expenditures, $231,440; qualifying distributions, $203,788; giving activities include $231,440 for programs.
Officers and Directors:* Richard F. Hubley,* Pres.; Kingsbury Davis,* V.P.; Virginia L. Guyot,* Secy.-Treas.; James P. Cleary III, Duncan C. Farmer, Thomas R. Faulkner, Frederick E. Malcolm, and 6 additional directors.
EIN: 042148009

60850
Irwin Chafetz Family Charitable Trust
300 1st Ave.
Needham, MA 02494

Established in 1995 in MA.
Donor(s): Irwin Chafetz.
Financial data (yr. ended 12/31/00): Assets, $4,080,241 (M); grants paid, $1,315,336; gifts received, $421,547; expenditures, $1,364,983; qualifying distributions, $1,315,336.
Limitations: Applications not accepted. Giving primarily in MA.
Application information: Contributes only to pre-selected organizations.
Trustees: Howard Chafetz, Irwin Chafetz, Laurence Chafetz, Roberta Chafetz.
EIN: 043282073
Codes: FD

60851
Piecework Partners Foundation
Todd Pond Rd.
P.O. Box 309
Lincoln, MA 01773 (781) 259-9626

Established in 1996 in MA.
Donor(s): Carolyn Birmingham, James G. Birmingham.
Financial data (yr. ended 11/30/00): Assets, $3,714,335 (M); grants paid, $0; gifts received, $1,202,422; expenditures, $147,175; qualifying distributions, $146,173; giving activities include $146,173 for programs.
Trustees: Carolyn Birmingham, James G. Birmingham.
EIN: 043340127

60852
Howard Benevolent Society
14 Beacon St., Rm. 804
Boston, MA 02108-3704 (617) 747-2952
FAX: (617) 723-8248; E-mail: hbsboston@aol.com
Contact: Marcia T. Burley

Established in 1812 in MA.
Donor(s): Elisha V. Ashton.‡
Financial data (yr. ended 09/30/01): Assets, $3,622,937 (M); grants paid, $132,276; gifts received, $124,979; expenditures, $249,922; qualifying distributions, $206,158.
Limitations: Giving limited to residents of the metropolitan Boston, MA, area.
Publications: Informational brochure.
Officers: Jonathan C. Randall, Pres.; Joseph Eaton, V.P.; Charles E. Rogerson, V.P.; Lucy W. West, Secy.; Richmond W. Bachelder, Treas.
EIN: 042129132
Codes: FD2, GTI

60853
Willard House and Clock Museum, Inc.
11 Willard St.
North Grafton, MA 01536-2011

Classified as a private operating foundation in 1979.
Financial data (yr. ended 03/31/01): Assets, $3,517,547 (M); grants paid, $0; gifts received, $43,452; expenditures, $170,085; qualifying distributions, $178,038; giving activities include $144,986 for programs.
Trustees: Joseph E. Brown, James H. Coulson, Richard Currier, Robert S. Edwards, Joseph R. Katra, Jr., George H. McEvoy, Bernice E. Norton, Richard H. Parker, Imogene Robinson, R. Lee Robinson, Roger W. Robinson, Douglas H. Shaffer, Sumner Tilton, Jr.
EIN: 042671799

60854
Clinton Home for Aged People
P.O. Box 218
Clinton, MA 01510-0218

Classified as a private operating foundation in 1985.
Financial data (yr. ended 09/30/01): Assets, $3,478,574 (M); grants paid, $50; expenditures, $367,376; qualifying distributions, $330,023.
Limitations: Applications not accepted. Giving primarily in Clinton, MA.
Application information: Contributes only to pre-selected organizations.
Officers and Directors:* John J. Graves,* Pres.; Lewis R. Paine,* V.P.; Walter T. Ryan,* Clerk; Betty A. Milewski,* Treas.; Gilbert D. Currier, Marjorie Lamy, Mark R. Laverdure, Catherine J. Murphy, Barbara Young.
EIN: 042131745

60855
Brookhouse Home
(Formerly Home for Aged Women in Salem)
180 Derby St.
Salem, MA 01970

Financial data (yr. ended 12/31/99): Assets, $3,423,516 (M); grants paid, $0; gifts received, $11,678; expenditures, $683,460; qualifying distributions, $676,329; giving activities include $683,460 for programs.
Officers: Robert Spychalski, Pres.; Susan O'Neill, V.P.; Marlene Hyde, Secy.; James B. Shatswell, Treas.
EIN: 042104318

60856
Fuller House of Stoneham
(Formerly Home for Aged People in Stoneham)
32 Franklin St.
Stoneham, MA 02180-1849

Classified as a private operating foundation in 1972.
Financial data (yr. ended 03/31/00): Assets, $3,331,575 (M); grants paid, $0; gifts received, $115,610; expenditures, $243,775; qualifying distributions, $538,898; giving activities include $243,775 for programs.
Officers: Elizabeth Well Denning, Pres.; Andrew M. Lizak, 1st V.P.; Kevin Brault, 2nd V.P.; Kathleen R. Carey, Secy.; Betty M. Welch, Treas.
Directors: William L. Burchard, John B. Cummings, Jr., Elizabeth B. Dawson, Robert Kitchen, Rev. Robert Lawrence, John McDonough, Constance C. Mendes, Walter J. Mitchell, Albertina Pacheco, Ira Rex, Jr., Philip T. Silvia, Jr.
EIN: 042121349

60857
Montgomery Home for Aged People, Inc.
64 S. Main St.
Middleboro, MA 02346

Classified as a private operating foundation in 1985.
Financial data (yr. ended 09/30/01): Assets, $3,197,829 (M); grants paid, $0; expenditures, $179,189; qualifying distributions, $0.
Officer and Directors:* Robert F. Howes,* Treas.; Jethro O. Ashley, Nancy E. Glidden, Richard L. Glidden, and 9 additional directors.
EIN: 042131757

60858
Historic Boston, Incorporated
3 School St.
Boston, MA 02108 (617) 227-4679
E-mail: HBI@historicboston.org; URL: http://www.HistoricBoston.org

Established in 1960; classified as a private operating foundation in 1984.
Donor(s): Henderson Foundation.
Financial data (yr. ended 12/31/01): Assets, $3,171,701 (M); grants paid, $119,726; gifts received, $234,670; expenditures, $164,076; qualifying distributions, $612,183.
Limitations: Applications not accepted. Giving limited to Boston, MA.
Application information: Unsolicited requests for funds not accepted.
Officers: Paul F. McDonough, Jr., Pres.; Edward P. Lawrence, V.P.; Carolyn M. Osteen, Clerk; Pauline Chase-Harrell, Treas.
Directors: Joan Goody-Faia, Matthew J. Kiefer, Marcia L. Myers, Maurice A. Reidy, Jr., and 8 additional directors.
EIN: 046111819
Codes: FD2

60859
Ella Clark Home for Aged People
P.O. Box 252
Easthampton, MA 01027-0252

Classified as a private operating foundation in 1987.
Financial data (yr. ended 10/31/01): Assets, $3,168,750 (M); grants paid, $0; expenditures, $168,095; qualifying distributions, $0.
Officers and Directors:* Charles Conner,* Pres.; Michael Szostak,* V.P.; Dorothy Perkins,* Secy.; Matthew A. Zawacki, Treas.; Albert I. Cartledge, Robert Ebert, Paul K. Gately, James G. Hayden, Thomas C. McCarthy, Michael V. O'Brien, Ann Parizo.
EIN: 046041104

60860
Stevens-Bennett Home, Inc.
337 Main St.
Haverhill, MA 01830-4054

Financial data (yr. ended 12/31/01): Assets, $3,077,372 (M); grants paid, $0; gifts received, $58,532; expenditures, $953,698; qualifying distributions, $526,326; giving activities include $1,098,548 for programs.
Officers and Directors:* Janet Boulanger, Emma Britton, Lisa Gardella,* Reva Judkins, Ruth Langlois, Mrs. Wilfred Mercer, Mariana Morse, Pearl Perry, and 21 additional directors.
EIN: 042104803

60861
Louis A. Frothingham Memorial Corporation
295 Main St.
P.O. Box 299
North Easton, MA 02356-1402

Established in 1930.
Financial data (yr. ended 09/30/00): Assets, $3,034,952 (L); grants paid, $800; expenditures, $110,821; qualifying distributions, $76,152; giving activities include $16,014 for programs.
Officers and Directors:* David Ames, Jr.,* Pres.; Wayne T. Evans,* V.P.; Douglas D. Porter, Clerk and Treas.; Robert J. Wooster, Exec. Dir.; William M. Ames, Patricia M. DeCoste, Carla A. Goodwin, Michael K. Manning, David E. Marsan.
EIN: 042103781

60862
Marblehead Female Humane Society, Inc.
P.O. Box 425
Marblehead, MA 01945-2927
Contact: Lee Weed, Pres.

Established in 1845.
Financial data (yr. ended 09/30/01): Assets, $2,974,021 (M); grants paid, $239,127; gifts received, $9,980; expenditures, $411,398; qualifying distributions, $308,031.
Limitations: Giving primarily in Marblehead, MA.
Officers: Lee Weed, Pres.; Barbara Ingalls, V.P.; Jane Faulkner, Secy.; Linda Cardile, Treas.
EIN: 042104694
Codes: FD2, GTI

60863
Words and Pictures, Inc.
136 West St., Ste. 107
Northampton, MA 01060

Established in 1990 in MA.
Donor(s): Kevin B. Eastman.
Financial data (yr. ended 11/30/99): Assets, $2,935,869 (M); grants paid, $130; gifts received, $130,220; expenditures, $665,399; qualifying distributions, $597,655; giving activities include $665,399 for programs.
Limitations: Applications not accepted. Giving primarily in MA.
Application information: Contributes only to pre-selected organizations.
Officer: Kevin B. Eastman, Pres. and Treas.
EIN: 043104763

60864
Brockton Community Cable Television, Inc.
P.O. Box 1057
Brockton, MA 02303-1057

Established in 1981 in MA as a company-sponsored operating foundation.
Donor(s): MediaOne of Brockton, Inc.
Financial data (yr. ended 12/31/00): Assets, $2,929,755 (M); grants paid, $0; gifts received, $500,000; expenditures, $502,010; qualifying distributions, $369,054; giving activities include $502,010 for programs.
Officers: Harold Weeks, Jr., Pres.; Marion Bonia, V.P.; Lois Schleffer, Treas.
Directors: Timothy Cruise, Steve Demos, Frances Pina, Adela Rodriquez, Moises Rodrigues, Nelson Suarez.
EIN: 042775817

60865
Amherst Home for Aged Women
1165 N. Pleasant St.
Amherst, MA 01002

Classified as a private operating foundation in 1988.
Financial data (yr. ended 12/31/00): Assets, $2,896,710 (M); grants paid, $1,138; expenditures, $366,868; qualifying distributions, $283,525; giving activities include $283,525 for programs.
Officers and Directors:* Steven W. Brode,* Pres.; Richard Beattie,* V.P.; Dennison Jones, V.P.; Solveig L. Clapp, Secy.; Thomas Carhart, Treas.; Frank Anderson, Mary Barkowski, Lillian Beattie, Daniel Clapp, M.D., Ruth Hobart, Dorothy Jenkins, Barbara Jones, Julie Kaneta, Andrew Larkin, Beverly Ziomek.
EIN: 042127021

60866
Farrington Memorial, Inc.
78 Ivy Rd.
Wellesley, MA 02482-4539

Classified as a private operating foundation in 1993.
Donor(s): The William J. Gould Associates, Inc.
Financial data (yr. ended 02/28/02): Assets, $2,847,045 (M); grants paid, $0; gifts received, $2,000; expenditures, $74,388; qualifying distributions, $0.
Officers and Trustees:* Austin Regolino,* Pres.; Harris G. Watts,* Treas.; Martha DeNormandie, Diane Haessler, Jennifer E. Hight, Terence McCourt, Charles McCrea, Theodore R. Parkins, Malcolm W. Stewart, Robert Wulff.
EIN: 042138907

60867
Seamen's Widow and Orphan Association
c/o George H. Villett
25 Lee St.
Salem, MA 01970

Financial data (yr. ended 12/31/99): Assets, $2,701,534 (M); grants paid, $12,200; expenditures, $111,768; qualifying distributions, $93,240.
Limitations: Applications not accepted. Giving limited to Salem, MA.
Application information: Contributes only to pre-selected organizations.
Officers and Managers:* Mrs. Ian F. Bigmore,* Pres.; C. Meade Camenga,* V.P.; Linzee Wallis, Secy.; George H. Villet,* Treas.
EIN: 046014352

60868
The Feigenbaum Foundation, Inc.
B. Riley
35 Pearl St.
Pittsfield, MA 01201

Established in 1988 in MA.
Donor(s): Armand V. Feigenbaum, Donald S. Feigenbaum.
Financial data (yr. ended 12/31/01): Assets, $2,650,240 (M); grants paid, $75,100; expenditures, $77,900; qualifying distributions, $75,100.
Limitations: Applications not accepted. Giving primarily in western MA.
Application information: Contributes only to pre-selected organizations.
Officers: Armand V. Feigenbaum, Pres.; Donald S. Feigenbaum, Clerk and Treas.
Director: Bernard E. Riley.
EIN: 043000345
Codes: FD2

60869
Cohasset Conservation Trust, Inc.
115 Border St.
Cohasset, MA 02025
Contact: John F. Hartshorne, Pres.

Financial data (yr. ended 12/31/01): Assets, $2,614,669 (M); grants paid, $0; gifts received, $6,625; expenditures, $12,475; qualifying distributions, $12,475; giving activities include $12,475 for programs.
Limitations: Giving primarily in MA.
Officers: Raymond G. Vanderweil, Jr., Pres.; Mark DeGiacomo, Secy.; Richard J. Avery, Treas.
Directors: Ellen M. Freda, John F. Harshorne, Richard D. Leggat, Edward B. Long, Nicholas W. Noon, Deborah A. Shadd, Jeffrey C. Waal.
EIN: 043270892

60870
Andover Historical Society
97 Main St.
Andover, MA 01810-3803

Classified as a private operating foundation in 1951.
Financial data (yr. ended 06/30/01): Assets, $2,596,749 (M); grants paid, $0; gifts received, $30,805; expenditures, $188,777; qualifying distributions, $88,725.
Officers and Trustees:* Cliff Markell,* Pres.; Wes Grace,* 1st V.P.; Norma Gammon, 2nd V.P.; Lola Sumberg, Corr. Secy.; Audrey Bedell, Recording Secy.; Donald Dobb, Treas.; Debbie Dubay, John Fragala, Jane Griswold, and 9 additional trustees.
EIN: 042312091

60871
Fannie Stebbins Memorial Wildlife Refuge, Inc.
c/o James Withgott
105 Church St.
Ware, MA 01082

Established in 1951.
Financial data (yr. ended 12/31/01): Assets, $2,586,869 (M); grants paid, $0; gifts received, $1,193; expenditures, $1,378; qualifying distributions, $0.
Officers: Edward Dzielenski, Pres.; Lucy Atkinson, V.P.; Sonia Burke, Secy.; James Withgott, Treas.
EIN: 046070364

60872
Childs Park Foundation, Inc.
c/o Dwyer & Sanderson
P.O. Box 658
Hadley, MA 01035-0658

Classified as a private operating foundation in 1973.
Financial data (yr. ended 12/31/01): Assets, $2,545,320 (M); grants paid, $0; gifts received, $106,499; expenditures, $102,365; qualifying distributions, $93,696; giving activities include $93,696 for programs.
Officers and Directors:* David A. Murphy,* Pres.; Gail Yacuzzo, V.P.; William E. Dwyer, Jr.,* Secy.-Treas.; Frank P. Conant, John F. Foley, Richard Garvey, Edward T. Heaphy, Jr., Hon. Mary Clare Higgins, Kimball Howes, Allison Lockwood.
EIN: 042143976

60873
Trustees of Hitchcock Free Academy
36 E. Hill Rd.
Brimfield, MA 01010
Application address: c/o Guidance Office, Tantasqua Regional High School, 319 Brookfield Rd., Sturbridge, MA 01566

Established in 1855 in MA.
Financial data (yr. ended 12/31/01): Assets, $2,540,723 (M); grants paid, $9,850; gifts received, $7,899; expenditures, $153,377; qualifying distributions, $86,250; giving activities include $50,903 for programs.
Limitations: Giving limited to residents of MA.
Application information: Application form required.
Officers and Trustees:* Kathleen Moloney,* Pres.; Carter Cooley,* V.P.; Lori Myers,* Clerk; Patricia Bamberger, Thomas Brown, and 10 additional trustees.
EIN: 042277210
Codes: GTI

60874
Sutton Home for Aged Women
7 Sewall St.
Peabody, MA 01960-3754

Financial data (yr. ended 12/31/01): Assets, $2,432,233 (M); grants paid, $950; expenditures, $40,565; qualifying distributions, $34,585; giving activities include $34,743 for programs.
Limitations: Applications not accepted. Giving primarily in MA.
Application information: Contributes only to pre-selected organizations.
Officers: Diane L. Durkee, Treas.; C. Edwin Needham, Treas.
EIN: 042105954

60875
Open Field Foundation, Inc.
c/o Gordon Thorne
150 Main St.
Northampton, MA 01060

Established in 1996 in MA.
Donor(s): Gordon Thorne.
Financial data (yr. ended 12/31/99): Assets, $2,431,282 (M); grants paid, $0; gifts received, $42,781; expenditures, $298,118; qualifying distributions, $197,567; giving activities include $2,750,000 for programs.
Officers and Directors:* Gordon Thorne,* Pres.; Thomas Asher, Secy; Anne Love Woodhull, Treas.; Robert Saul, Clerk.
EIN: 043313646

60876
Frog Pond Foundation, Inc.
82 Devonshire St., Ste. S3A
Boston, MA 02109

Established as a company-sponsored operating foundation in 2000 in MA.
Donor(s): FMR Corporation.
Financial data (yr. ended 12/31/01): Assets, $2,372,324 (M); grants paid, $250,000; gifts received, $2,500,000; expenditures, $1,145,016; qualifying distributions, $1,124,988.
Limitations: Applications not accepted.
Application information: Contributes only to pre-selected organizations.
Officers and Directors:* Peter E. Madsen,* Pres.; Lena G. Goldberg,* V.P.; Anne-Marie Soulliere,* V.P.; Patricia R. Hurley, Secy.; Richard G. Weidmann, Treas.
EIN: 043522036
Codes: FD

60877
Azazel Institute, Inc.
727 Massachusetts Ave.
Cambridge, MA 02139
Application address: 10 Rue Ourliac 11000 Carcassonne, France, tel.: 33-4-68-10-33-60
Contact: Jean Christophe Fuster

Established in 1992 in MA.
Donor(s): Jane Parfet.
Financial data (yr. ended 06/30/01): Assets, $2,339,451 (M); grants paid, $10,919; expenditures, $512,166; qualifying distributions, $401,732; giving activities include $184,815 for programs.
Limitations: Giving on a national and international basis, including the U.S., Britain, France, Japan, and South Africa.
Application information: Application form not required.
Officers: Hennie Boshoff, Pres.; Tobela Ramncwana, Secy.; Heike Hannerman Franklin, Treas.
EIN: 043158020

60878
Taunton Female Charitable Association
P.O. Box 704
Raynham Center, MA 02768

Established in 1816.
Financial data (yr. ended 12/31/01): Assets, $2,211,487 (M); grants paid, $205,025; expenditures, $233,271; qualifying distributions, $206,246.
Limitations: Applications not accepted. Giving primarily in Taunton, MA.
Application information: Contributes only to pre-selected organizations.
Officers: Mrs. Norman Lemaire, Pres.; Mrs. Herbert Borden, Secy.; David T. Noyes, Treas.
Directors: Mrs. Alton Hambly, Mrs. Paul Newman, Mrs. Marcus Rhodes.
EIN: 042105743
Codes: FD2

60879
South Mountain Association
P.O. Box 23
Pittsfield, MA 01202 (413) 442-2106
Contact: Lou R. Steigler, Exec. Dir.

Established around 1943.
Donor(s): Lou H. Willeke Trust.
Financial data (yr. ended 12/31/01): Assets, $2,207,864 (M); grants paid, $15,000; gifts received, $141,111; expenditures, $161,513; qualifying distributions, $158,422; giving activities include $75,330 for programs.
Limitations: Giving limited to residents of Berkshire County, MA.
Officer and Directors: Lou R. Steigler,* Exec. Dir.; Elizabeth Barbour, Thelma Bates, Kelton M. Burbank, Nancy Dolbeare, A. King Francis, Ann Galt, Ralph R. Johnson, Jr., Robert E. Koch, John A. Kreiger, Marcia Perry, Suzanne F. Nash, Jeannie Norris, Richard Perera, Adele Rodbell, Clifford Rudisill, Irwin Shainman, Joan Vazakas, Lawrence Wiklander.
EIN: 046049419
Codes: GTI

60880
Lynn Historical Society, Inc.
125 Green St.
Lynn, MA 01902

Classified as a private operating foundation in 1972.
Financial data (yr. ended 12/31/01): Assets, $2,190,818 (M); grants paid, $0; gifts received, $166,386; expenditures, $257,099; qualifying distributions, $0.
Officers and Directors:* Bill Conway,* Pres.; Tim Ring,* 1st V.P.; Stanley E. Cooke,* 2nd V.P.; Sue McFarlane,* Recording Secy.; Loren Rocker,* Treas.; Kenneth Turino.
Trustees: Douglass Allen, Aborn Breed, Thomas Costin.
EIN: 042269520

60881
Mountain Bay Foundation
34 Barton Dr.
Sudbury, MA 01776-2506

Established in 1997 in MA.
Donor(s): Lael M. Meixsell.
Financial data (yr. ended 12/31/00): Assets, $2,135,380 (M); grants paid, $0; expenditures, $38,455; qualifying distributions, $0.
Trustee: Anne B. Meixsell, Lael M. Meixsell.
EIN: 043369535

60882
I Have a Dream - Lawrence, MA, Inc.
34 Bobby Jones Dr.
Andover, MA 01810 (978) 475-0951
FAX: (978) 475-1215
Contact: R. Kingman Webster, Pres.

Established in 1991 in MA.
Donor(s): R. Kingman Webster.
Financial data (yr. ended 08/31/01): Assets, $2,057,203 (M); grants paid, $371,085; gifts received, $19,894; expenditures, $500,618; qualifying distributions, $451,353; giving activities include $97,307 for programs.
Limitations: Giving primarily in Lawrence, MA.
Application information: Application form not required.
Officers and Director:* R. Kingman Webster,* Pres. and Treas.; Dee M. Webster, Secy.
EIN: 043128494
Codes: FD

60883
Francis William's Park Trust
c/o Boston Safe Deposit & Trust Co.
1 Boston Pl.
Boston, MA 02108

Classified as a private operating foundation in 1975.
Financial data (yr. ended 08/31/00): Assets, $2,049,720 (M); grants paid, $0; expenditures, $17,148; qualifying distributions, $2,643; giving activities include $287 for programs.
Trustee: Boston Safe Deposit & Trust Co.
EIN: 046092035

60884
Rotch Travelling Scholarship, Inc.
c/o Fiduciary Trust Co.
P.O. Box 1647
Boston, MA 02105-1647
URL: http://www.rotchscholarship.org
Application address: c/o Boston Society of Architects, 52 Broad St., Boston, MA 02109
Contact: Hugh Shepley, V.P.

Established in 1883 in MA.
Financial data (yr. ended 12/31/01): Assets, $1,982,102 (M); grants paid, $33,000; expenditures, $105,204; qualifying distributions, $59,551.
Limitations: Giving limited to U.S. citizens with educational or professional experience in MA.
Publications: Informational brochure (including application guidelines).
Application information: Application form required.
Officers: Sarah A. Phillips, Pres.; Hugh Shepley, V.P.; Robert Holdway, Treas.
EIN: 046062249
Codes: GTI

60885
Wales Home, Inc.
(Formerly Wales Home for Aged Women, Inc.)
c/o Irene Reynolds
96 Lincoln St.
North Easton, MA 02356-1712

Donor(s): Daniel W. Fields Trust.
Financial data (yr. ended 04/30/02): Assets, $1,960,649 (M); grants paid, $105,000; gifts received, $12,251; expenditures, $156,058; qualifying distributions, $136,580; giving activities include $156,057 for programs.
Limitations: Applications not accepted. Giving primarily in MA.
Application information: Contributes only to pre-selected organizations.
Officers and Directors:* Thomas N. Sampson, Pres.; Priscilla Mueller, Clerk; Irene Reynolds,* Treas.; Ruth Capernaros, David Carleton, Maryanne Kelleher, Mark A. Lane, George Moberg.
EIN: 041940730
Codes: FD2

60886
Open Church Foundation
P.O. Box 81389
Wellesley Hills, MA 02481-0004

Classified as a private operating foundation in 1987.
Financial data (yr. ended 06/30/02): Assets, $1,765,378 (M); grants paid, $0; expenditures, $119,365; qualifying distributions, $0.
Officer and Trustees:* George Rideout, Jr.,* Pres. and Treas.; Joanne Emanuelson, David J. Horst, Alison Towler, Rev. Richard Weisenbach.
EIN: 042108377

60887
Pearson Family Charitable Foundation
c/o Peabody & Brown
101 Federal St.
Boston, MA 02110

Established in 1997 in MA.
Donor(s): Elizabeth E. Pearson, Hugh W. Pearson III.
Financial data (yr. ended 12/31/00): Assets, $1,725,525 (M); grants paid, $52,000; expenditures, $65,581; qualifying distributions, $52,267.
Limitations: Applications not accepted.
Application information: Contributes to pre-selected organizations.
Trustees: William C. Lance, Elizabeth E. Pearson, Hugh W. Pearson.
EIN: 043353589

60888
Eastham Conservation Foundation, Inc.
P.O. Box 183
Eastham, MA 02642

Donor(s): J. Coleman, H. Sibley, A. Avellar.
Financial data (yr. ended 06/30/00): Assets, $1,713,071 (M); grants paid, $0; gifts received, $59,840; expenditures, $2,314; qualifying distributions, $1,882; giving activities include $1,882 for programs.
Limitations: Applications not accepted.
Officers and Trustees:* Henry F. Lind,* Pres.; Joseph F. Moran,* V.P.; Hugh J. Daugherty,* Treas.; Richard W. Wallace, Clerk; Robert Seay.
EIN: 042668953

60889
Old Ladies Home Society
78 Lothrop St.
Beverly, MA 01915-5877

Classified as a private operating foundation in 1987.
Donor(s): Florence A. Muir Trust.
Financial data (yr. ended 06/30/01): Assets, $1,707,281 (M); grants paid, $0; gifts received, $21,695; expenditures, $304,623; qualifying distributions, $0; giving activities include $287,851 for programs.
Limitations: Applications not accepted.
Application information: Contributes only to pre-selected organizations.
Officers: Phyllis F. Clark, Pres., Treas. and Mgr.; Lucille Brindle, Mgr.; Sylvia Dana, Mgr.; Mary Donovan, Mgr.; Edith Estes, Mgr.; Eleanor Frazier, Mgr.; and 19 additional managers.
EIN: 042104810

60890
The Society of Colonial Wars in the Commonwealth of Massachusetts
c/o F. Gorham Brigham
101 Tremont St., Ste. 608
Boston, MA 02108-5004   (617) 357-1776

Established in 1935.
Financial data (yr. ended 09/30/00): Assets, $1,706,206 (M); grants paid, $12,900; gifts received, $6,846; expenditures, $105,207; qualifying distributions, $84,112.
Limitations: Applications not accepted. Giving primarily in MA.
Application information: Contributes only to pre-selected organizations.
Officers and Councilors:* Thomas H. Townsend,* Gov.; Thomas W. Thaler, Deputy Gov.; Charles A. Tarbell,* Lt. Gov.; Frederic A. Crafts III, Deputy Secy.; Scott D. Shiland,* Secy.; Philip T. Chaplin, Deputy Treas.; E. Russell Peach, Jr.,* Treas.; Walter S. Kerr, M.D., Surgeon General; Kenneth M. Hills, and 8 additional councilors.
EIN: 046049519

60891
Henry Lawton Blanchard Foundation
655 W. Main St.
Avon, MA 02322-1745

Financial data (yr. ended 09/30/01): Assets, $1,684,199 (M); grants paid, $0; expenditures, $71,229; qualifying distributions, $71,229.
Officers: Janet Aston Geiss, Pres.; Harold E. Smith, Secy.-Treas.
Trustees: Sharon L. Kelly, Bruce Lane, Richard J. Weiss.
EIN: 046054153

60892
Gravity Research Foundation
41 Kirkland Cir.
Wellesley Hills, MA 02481-4812
Application address: c/o Univeristy of Cincinnati, Cincinnati, OH 45221
Contact: Dr. Louis Witten

Established in 1949 in MA.
Financial data (yr. ended 06/30/01): Assets, $1,595,563 (M); grants paid, $9,000; gifts received, $250; expenditures, $113,085; qualifying distributions, $98,212.
Publications: Application guidelines.
Officers: George M. Rideout, Jr., Pres. and Treas.; Dr. Louis Witten, V.P.
Trustees: William W. Camp, Lee Cooper, David J. Horst.
EIN: 046002754
Codes: GTI

60893
Institute for Scientific Research in Music
c/o Melville Clark, Jr.
8 Richard Rd.
Wayland, MA 01778

Established in 1990 in MA.
Donor(s): Yamaha Corp., Melville Clark, Jr.
Financial data (yr. ended 11/30/00): Assets, $1,498,083 (M); grants paid, $0; expenditures, $38,438; qualifying distributions, $573,461; giving activities include $38,438 for programs.
Limitations: Applications not accepted.
Application information: Contributes only to pre-selected organizations.
Trustee: Melville Clark, Jr.
EIN: 043107517

60894
Animal Rescue League of Fall River
474 Durfee St.
Fall River, MA 02720

Classified as a private operating foundation in 1973.
Financial data (yr. ended 03/31/00): Assets, $1,488,861 (M); grants paid, $0; gifts received, $166,750; expenditures, $469,158; qualifying distributions, $219,194; giving activities include $322,809 for programs.
Officers and Directors:* Beth Fay,* Pres.; Sandra Barrow Feitelberg,* V.P.; Louise Gauthier,* Secy.; Susan K. Martineau,* Treas.; Michele L. Bailey, Exec. Dir.; Jeff Marques, Renee Tetrault, and 14 additional directors.
EIN: 042103711

60895
Ralph C. DeVitto Foundation
c/o A. Bram
43 Thorndike St.
Cambridge, MA 02141

Classified as a private operating foundation in 1993 in MA.
Financial data (yr. ended 12/31/00): Assets, $1,404,700 (L); grants paid, $0; expenditures, $38,269; qualifying distributions, $63,753.
Trustees: Andrew Bram, Ralph DeVitto, Jr.
EIN: 043141118

60896
Burnham Foundation, Inc.
P.O. Box 1400
Boston, MA 02205
Application address: c/o Nutter, McClennen & Fish, 1 International Pl., Boston, MA 02710, tel.: (617) 439-2000
Contact: Charles A. Rosebrock, Treas.

Established in 1989 in MA.
Donor(s): George R. Burnham.‡
Financial data (yr. ended 12/31/01): Assets, $1,393,956 (M); grants paid, $77,700; expenditures, $117,439; qualifying distributions, $90,231.
Limitations: Giving limited to MA.
Application information: Application form required for scholarships.
Officers and Directors:* Charles P. Burnham, Pres.; Charles A. Rosebrock, Treas. and Clerk; Lynn Lamar.
EIN: 222979498
Codes: FD2

60897
Fannie B. Pratt Trust
c/o Dane & Howe
45 School St., 4th Fl.
Boston, MA 02108-3204   (617) 227-3600
Contact: Marion K. Daley, Tr.

Financial data (yr. ended 12/31/01): Assets, $1,381,400 (M); grants paid, $16,120; expenditures, $26,363; qualifying distributions, $20,860; giving activities include $1,500 for programs.
Limitations: Giving limited to residents of Boston, MA.
Trustee: Marion K. Daley.
EIN: 046027727
Codes: GTI

60898
Fall River Historical Society
451 Rock St.
Fall River, MA 02720

Financial data (yr. ended 04/30/01): Assets, $1,347,660 (M); grants paid, $0; gifts received, $125,859; expenditures, $252,576; qualifying distributions, $168,636; giving activities include $252,576 for programs.
Officers: Michael Martins, Elizabeth Well Denning, Pres.; Andrew M. Lizak, 1st V.P.; Kevin Brault, 2nd V.P.; Kathleen R. Carey, Secy.; Betty M. Welch, Treas.
EIN: 042125012

60899
Creative Learning Exchange
c/o S. Stuntz
1 Keefe Rd.
Acton, MA 01720-5517

Classified as a private operating foundation in 1991.
Financial data (yr. ended 12/31/01): Assets, $1,299,693 (M); grants paid, $0; gifts received, $1,190; expenditures, $154,277; qualifying distributions, $105,666; giving activities include $154,277 for programs.
Officer and Trustee:* Lee M. Stuntz,* Exec. Dir.
EIN: 046672054

60900
The Seymour Kaplan Memorial Foundation
c/o Richard E. Kaplan
2345 Washington St.
Newton, MA 02462-1458

Donor(s): Constance E. Kaplan.
Financial data (yr. ended 11/30/00): Assets, $1,297,625 (M); grants paid, $15,000; gifts received, $32,300; expenditures, $24,072; qualifying distributions, $163,456; giving activities include $143,809 for programs.
Limitations: Applications not accepted. Giving primarily in CT.
Application information: Contributes only to pre-selected organizations.
Trustees: David E. Kaplan, Richard E. Kaplan, Judith K. Stansfield.
EIN: 222503795

60901
Cambridge Historical Society
159 Brattle St.
Cambridge, MA 02138-3303

Classified as a private operating foundation in 1998.
Financial data (yr. ended 12/31/99): Assets, $1,285,678 (M); grants paid, $0; gifts received, $28,138; expenditures, $122,007; qualifying distributions, $119,367; giving activities include $119,367 for programs.
Officers and Directors:* M. Wyllis Bibbins,* Pres.; Allison M. Crump,* 1st V.P.; Karen L. Davis,* 2nd V.P.; Karen F. Falb,* 3rd V.P.; W. David Klempin,* Secy.; Andrew Leighton,* Treas.; Anne M. Donaghy, and 6 additional directors.
EIN: 046032737

60902
Mary Kimball Hail Homestead
c/o Fleet National Bank
P.O. Box 1861
Boston, MA 02105

Classified as a private operating foundation in 1972.
Financial data (yr. ended 12/31/99): Assets, $1,284,323 (M); grants paid, $0; expenditures,

$48,936; qualifying distributions, $1,472; giving activities include $17,500 for programs.
Limitations: Applications not accepted.
Application information: Contributes only to pre-selected organizations.
Trustee: Fleet National Bank.
EIN: 510179744

60903
Concord Alternative Residence, Inc.
207 Main St.
Concord, MA 01742

Established in 1992 in MA.
Financial data (yr. ended 05/31/01): Assets, $1,275,214 (M); grants paid, $0; gifts received, $20,008; expenditures, $292,979; qualifying distributions, $36,334; giving activities include $292,979 for programs.
Officers: Judie Post, Pres.; Jeff Brown, V.P.; Jo Anne Kelch, Secy.; George L. Tisdale, Treas.
EIN: 042599779

60904
Durant Homestead Foundation, Inc.
1566A Washington St.
Holliston, MA 01746-2238

Financial data (yr. ended 12/31/00): Assets, $1,270,755 (M); grants paid, $0; gifts received, $45,421; expenditures, $25,227; qualifying distributions, $17,497; giving activities include $17,624 for programs.
Officers and Directors:* Roger C. Avery,* Pres.; Ruth D. Ewing,* V.P.; Rosemary S. Avery, Mgr.; Margaret A. Avery.
EIN: 222546214

60905
Wing's Neck Conservation Foundation, Inc.
c/o Kirkpatrick & Lockhart, LLP
75 State St.
Boston, MA 02109

Established in 1998 in MA.
Financial data (yr. ended 07/31/00): Assets, $1,266,992 (M); grants paid, $500; gifts received, $53,669; expenditures, $54,003; qualifying distributions, $359,843.
Limitations: Applications not accepted.
Application information: Contributes only to pre-selected organizations.
Officer and Directors:* Nicholas J. Baker,* Pres. and Treas.; Jennifer B. Pohlig.
EIN: 311614721

60906
Northampton Historical Society
46 Bridge St.
Del Parque, 403 Piso 3
Northampton, MA 01060

Financial data (yr. ended 09/30/00): Assets, $1,242,760 (M); grants paid, $0; gifts received, $10,661; expenditures, $149,604; qualifying distributions, $222,854; giving activities include $16,280 for programs.
Officers and Trustees:* Stanley Elkins,* Pres.; Pennington Geis,* V.P.; Amy Semerjian,* Treas.; Kenneth Bowen, Kerry Buckley, Lawrence A. Fink, Lisa Hahn, Martha J. Hoppin, Anne Digan Lanning, Richard Marquis, Tristram Metcalfe III, Richard Millington, William Muller, Marie Panik, Robert Paynter, Stephen Petegorsky, Herbert E. B. Ross III, Norman Winston, George A. Snook.
EIN: 046079243

60907
Elizabeth E. Boit Home for Women, Inc.
5 Bennett St.
Wakefield, MA 01880

Financial data (yr. ended 12/31/99): Assets, $1,236,991 (M); grants paid, $0; gifts received, $5,951; expenditures, $276,278; qualifying distributions, $275,001; giving activities include $276,278 for programs.
Officers: Joan King, Pres.; Nancy Watts, V.P. and Clerk; Ann Loughlin, Secy.; Barbara Carino, Treas.
Advisory Board: David Fieldhouse, Gorham Henshaw, Herb Leafquist, Edward Perreauth, Ed Schmidgall, Mario Simeola.
EIN: 042103890

60908
Boston Research Center for the 21st Century, Inc.
396 Harvard St.
Cambridge, MA 02138-3946

Established in 1997 in MA.
Donor(s): Soka Gakkai.
Financial data (yr. ended 03/31/01): Assets, $1,220,331 (M); grants paid, $0; gifts received, $928,505; expenditures, $693,213; qualifying distributions, $686,364; giving activities include $604,642 for programs.
Limitations: Applications not accepted.
Application information: Contributes only to pre-selected organizations.
Officer: Virginia Straus, Exec. Dir.
EIN: 043366125

60909
Home for the Aged People of Franklin County
24 Church St.
Greenfield, MA 01301-2999

Classified as a private operating foundation in 1975.
Financial data (yr. ended 12/31/99): Assets, $1,181,548 (M); grants paid, $0; gifts received, $73,928; expenditures, $107,200; qualifying distributions, $60,188; giving activities include $95,661 for programs.
Officers: Marsha Pratt, Pres.; Mary Lou Bueno, V.P.; Anne Connington, Clerk; Walter Sanders, Treas.
Directors: Amy Clarke, David P. Currey, Jr., Maggie LeBlanc, Mary Merriam, Carol Updike.
EIN: 237435548

60910
Neighbors for a Better Community, Inc.
216 Broadway
Cambridge, MA 02139

Established in 1998 in MA.
Financial data (yr. ended 06/30/01): Assets, $1,177,518 (M); grants paid, $4,500; gifts received, $38,289; expenditures, $237,592; qualifying distributions, $179,482; giving activities include $179,482 for programs.
Limitations: Giving primarily in MA.
Application information: Unsolicited request for funds not accepted.
Officers: Jacqueline Carroll, Pres.; Jonathan Carroll, V.P.; Lena Dobson, Secy.; Clifford Truesdell, Treas.; Janis Peterson, Exec. Dir.
Directors: Ron Benham, Michael Britt, Muriel Smith, Jacqueline Tynes.
EIN: 043437899

60911
The Battles Home
236 Fairmount St.
Lowell, MA 01852-3798

Classified as a private operating foundation in 1992.
Financial data (yr. ended 12/31/01): Assets, $1,149,181 (M); grants paid, $0; expenditures, $423,875; qualifying distributions, $0.
Officers: John H. Pearson, Jr., Pres.; David W. Caddell, V.P.; Arlene Miele, Treas.; Catherine F. Bastien, Admin.
Directors: Sheppard Bartlett, Jack Connors, Harry Gienandt, Daniel J. Mansur, David H. Mason, Nels Palm, Arthur Simensen, Brian Stafford, Mark Sullivan.
EIN: 042134817

60912
Forward, Inc.
1 Florence St.
Boston, MA 02131

Classified as a private operating foundation in 1985.
Financial data (yr. ended 06/30/01): Assets, $1,140,294 (M); grants paid, $0; gifts received, $75,000; expenditures, $183,785; qualifying distributions, $155,513.
Officers and Directors:* Ernest M. Boatswain,* Pres.; James Smith,* 1st V.P.; Dorothy Hunter,* 2nd V.P.; Dorothy Bell,* Secy.; Herbert Green,* Treas.; and 17 additional directors.
EIN: 042771148

60913
Byron Robinson Education Foundation, Inc.
2315 Washington St.
P.O. Box 900
Boston, MA 02119 (617) 445-9800
FAX: (617) 445-9109
Contact: Byron Robinson, Chair.

Established in 1991 in MA.
Donor(s): Byron Robinson, D.D.S., Dorothea Robinson, Mark A. Robinson, Stacey C. Robinson.
Financial data (yr. ended 12/31/99): Assets, $1,098,302 (M); grants paid, $51,561; expenditures, $422,922; qualifying distributions, $69,345.
Limitations: Giving primarily in the West Indies, West Africa, and Latin America.
Officers: Byron C. Robinson, Chair.; Mark A. Robinson, Pres.; Stacey C. Robinson, B.A., J.D., Treas.; Dorothea Robinson, R.N., M.A., Clerk.
EIN: 043119780

60914
Horn Home for Aged
98 Smith St.
Lowell, MA 01851-2699

Donor(s): Alma G. Hill.‡
Financial data (yr. ended 04/30/02): Assets, $1,084,273 (M); grants paid, $0; expenditures, $303,615; qualifying distributions, $0.
Officers and Directors:* Marshall L. Field,* Pres.; Stephen C. Olney,* Treas.; Barbara J. Skaar,* Clerk; George Dana, Susan Field, Harry F. Gienandt, Jean McCaffery, Evelyn McCartney, David E. Merrill, Richard H. Olney, Marjorie Richard, Tristaan N. Terveen, Rev. K. Gordon White.
EIN: 042103797

60915
Gordon Foundation
c/o Analogic Corp.
8 Centennial Dr.
Peabody, MA 01960-0790 (978) 977-3000
Contact: Julian Soshnick, Tr.

Established around 1983 in MA.
Donor(s): Frank B. Gordon, Bernard M. Gordon.
Financial data (yr. ended 12/31/01): Assets, $1,029,521 (M); grants paid, $394,947; gifts received, $228; expenditures, $396,291; qualifying distributions, $394,467.
Limitations: Giving primarily in MA.
Application information: Application form not required.
Trustees: Bernard M. Gordon, Sophia Gordon, Julian Soshnick.
EIN: 042794647
Codes: FD

60916
Vascular Laboratory, Inc.
1 Deaconess Rd.
Boston, MA 02215

Classified as a private operating foundation in 1975.
Donor(s): Erbamount.
Financial data (yr. ended 06/30/00): Assets, $982,470 (M); grants paid, $0; gifts received, $946,158; expenditures, $1,042,774; qualifying distributions, $1,006,888; giving activities include $872,729 for programs.
Officers and Directors:* Victor Gurevich, M.D.,* Pres.; Robert Ullian,* Clerk; Richard Fechtor, Jian-Ning Liu.
EIN: 237375422

60917
New Bedford Home for Aged
P.O. Box 2994
New Bedford, MA 02741-2994

Classified as a private operating foundation in 1974.
Financial data (yr. ended 04/30/00): Assets, $970,961 (M); grants paid, $0; expenditures, $42,640; qualifying distributions, $32,104; giving activities include $32,104 for programs.
Officers and Directors:* Frances Cuvilje,* Pres.; Annette Morton,* Clerk; Eleanor Morton,* Treas.; Gloria Hill.
EIN: 046050558

60918
Rowe Historical Society, Inc.
c/o Heidi Lehr
Zoar Rd., Box 455
Rowe, MA 01367

Classified as a private operating foundation in 1985.
Financial data (yr. ended 06/30/00): Assets, $942,671 (M); grants paid, $0; gifts received, $20; expenditures, $40,397; qualifying distributions, $34,170; giving activities include $40,397 for programs.
Officers and Trustees:* Marjorie Morse,* Pres.; Rob Williams,* V.P.; Billie Brown,* Secy.; Heidi Lehr,* Treas.; William Brown, Lenny Laffond, Al Morse, James Taylor, Martin Woodward.
EIN: 046049565

60919
Worcester Community Cable Access, Inc.
415 Main St.
Worcester, MA 01608

Established in 1986 in MA.
Financial data (yr. ended 06/30/99): Assets, $908,262 (M); grants paid, $0; gifts received, $6,708; expenditures, $272,892; qualifying distributions, $246,642; giving activities include $272,892 for programs.
Officers and Directors:* Rev. Michael Bafaro,* Pres.; Sitya Mitra,* Treas.; Joan D'Argenis, Mauro Depasquale, Ahmad Hosseininejad, Candace Jaegle, Laurie Letourneau, Keith McElhinney, Jose Perez, Walter C. Roach, Richard Roberts.
EIN: 042984716

60920
The Leland Home
21 Newton St.
Waltham, MA 02453

Classified as a private operating foundation in 1979.
Donor(s): Gladys Morton,‡ Mary Nichols.
Financial data (yr. ended 12/31/00): Assets, $905,535 (M); grants paid, $0; gifts received, $29,900; expenditures, $1,081,907; qualifying distributions, $57,337; giving activities include $1,024,570 for programs.
Officers: Louis Kirsch III, Pres.; W. Royce Taylor, V.P.; Gloria Pinkham, Secy.; David Hardy, Treas.; Alden Johnson, Exec. Dir; Linda Auld, Mgr.; George Coleman, Mgr.; Richard F. Dacey III, Mgr.; Joyce Hardy, Mgr.; Thomas Jewell, Mgr.; James E. Morgan, Jr., Mgr.; Virginia Platt, Mgr.; Raymond Vanderwyk, Mgr.; J. Alden Wentworth II, Mgr.; and 3 additional Managers.
EIN: 042104385

60921
New Salem Academy
28 Old County Rd.
New Salem, MA 01355-9611
Contact: Eleanor McGinnis, Treas.

Classified as a private operating foundation in 1974.
Financial data (yr. ended 06/30/01): Assets, $903,573 (M); grants paid, $11,410; expenditures, $40,264; qualifying distributions, $34,377; giving activities include $14,948 for programs.
Limitations: Giving limited to New Salem, MA.
Officers and Trustees:* Ward M. Hunting,* Pres.; Thomas S. Mann III, V.P.; Paul R. Wilbur,* Secy.; Eleanor McGinnis,* Treas.; Carlyle Field, Robert W. Gailey, and 6 additional trustees.
EIN: 046054087

60922
Corporation of the Ryder Home for Old People
c/o Genevieve Mayers
9 Brewster St.
Plymouth, MA 02360-3959

Financial data (yr. ended 02/28/02): Assets, $903,527 (M); grants paid, $0; expenditures, $141,517; qualifying distributions, $0.
Officers: Thomas F. Quinn, Pres.; Oliver S. Cole, V.P.; Janet Holmes, Secy.; Genevieve Mayers, Treas.
Directors: Marie Blessington, Emerson Burns, Alice Davis, Walter Fiander, John W. Lifrieri, Eleanor Maver, Ellen Parkis, Ronald A. Robinson, Richmond Talbot.
EIN: 042104418

60923
Monson Home for Aged People, Inc.
106 Main St.
P.O. Box 93
Monson, MA 01057

Classified as a private operating foundation in 1972.
Financial data (yr. ended 04/30/00): Assets, $895,500 (M); grants paid, $0; gifts received, $50; expenditures, $27,069; qualifying distributions, $31,739.
Officers and Directors:* David Haley,* Pres.; Robert Fay,* V.P.; Sue Ford,* Secy.; David Royce,* Treas.; Patricia Aliengena, Morgan Hodskins, Patricia McCarron, Elaine Nothe, Thomas Pratt.
EIN: 042127024

60924
Vernon House, Inc.
20 Vernon St.
Framingham, MA 01701-4760

Classified as a private operating foundation in 1973.
Donor(s): Margaret Kendell.‡
Financial data (yr. ended 12/31/01): Assets, $884,534 (M); grants paid, $0; gifts received, $11,806; expenditures, $554,313; qualifying distributions, $546,752; giving activities include $546,752 for programs.
Officers and Trustees:* Peter Tenbroeck,* Pres.; Richard Radar,* V.P.; Oskar Heininger,* Secy.; Richard Allen, Judy Dunham, Deborah McQuade, Claude Peabody, Sally S. Roda, and 12 additional trustees.
EIN: 042105895

60925
First Universalist Church of Hardwick Preservation Trust
9 Ruggles Hill Rd.
P.O. Box 72
Hardwick, MA 01037

Financial data (yr. ended 12/31/01): Assets, $870,031 (M); grants paid, $140; expenditures, $30,529; qualifying distributions, $140.
Limitations: Applications not accepted.
Application information: Contributes only to pre-selected organizations.
Officers: John Ritter, Pres.; Donald Hanson, V.P.; Ruth Ward, Secy.; Charlene Allen, Treas.
EIN: 046926212

60926
Downey-Farnsworth Family Charitable Foundation
73 Perkins St.
West Newton, MA 02465 (617) 244-2209
Contact: Thomas S. Downey, Tr.

Established in 1999 in MA.
Donor(s): Thomas S. Downey, Laurel Farnsworth.
Financial data (yr. ended 12/31/99): Assets, $867,917 (M); grants paid, $37,545; gifts received, $900,000; expenditures, $37,545; qualifying distributions, $37,545.
Trustees: Thomas S. Downey, Laurel Farnsworth.
EIN: 046888793

60927
New Bedford Day Nursery, Inc.
P.O. Box 344
Marion, MA 02738

Financial data (yr. ended 12/31/01): Assets, $848,207 (M); grants paid, $41,345; expenditures, $55,092; qualifying distributions, $51,106.
Limitations: Giving primarily in New Bedford, MA.
Officers: Kathleen Carter, Pres.; Kathleen Lang, 1st V.P.; Gig Lang, Secy.; Ruth Nicolaci, Treas.
EIN: 042103827

60928
Service League Foundation, Inc.
12 Converse Cir.
East Longmeadow, MA 01028 (413) 525-3684
Contact: Paul W. Kenyon, Treas.

Established in 1904 in MA.
Financial data (yr. ended 12/31/00): Assets, $828,102 (M); grants paid, $54,200; expenditures, $65,634; qualifying distributions, $54,015.
Limitations: Giving primarily in Holyoke and Springfield, MA.
Publications: Financial statement.
Application information: Application form not required.
Officers and Directors:* Whiting S. Houston, Jr.,* Pres.; Robert Humbertson,* V.P.; George Crum, Jr.,* Secy.; Paul W. Kenyon,* Treas.; Thomas Creed, Thea Katsounakis, Michael Oleksak.
EIN: 046006490

60929
Foundation for Nutritional Advancement
192 South St., Ste. 500
Boston, MA 02111-2708
Contact: Kathleen Shusta, Treas.

Established in 1976 in DC.
Financial data (yr. ended 12/31/00): Assets, $815,285 (M); grants paid, $135,840; expenditures, $174,805; qualifying distributions, $160,499.
Limitations: Giving on a national basis.
Publications: Informational brochure.
Officers: Louis Lasagna, M.D., Chair.; Michael R. Sonnenreich, Pres.; Richard J. Shusta, V.P.; Anthony J. Roccograndi, Secy.; Kathleen Shusta, Treas.
EIN: 521075437
Codes: FD2

60930
Arthur Griffin Center for Photographic Art Charitable Foundation
67 Shore Rd.
Winchester, MA 01890

Classified as a private operating foundation in 1991.
Donor(s): Arthur Griffin.
Financial data (yr. ended 05/31/00): Assets, $800,138 (M); grants paid, $0; gifts received, $60,594; expenditures, $159,296; qualifying distributions, $53,218; giving activities include $83,114 for programs.
Officers and Trustees:* Courtney Crandall,* Chair.; I.W. Dingwell,* Vice-Chair.; Sandra Rodgers,* Vice-Chair.; Glen Doyle, Exec. Dir.; Arthur Griffin, and 15 additional trustees.
EIN: 046653279

60931
Health and Development International, Inc.
23 Middle St.
Newburyport, MA 01950

Established in 1990 in MA.
Donor(s): Mrs. Nils O. Seim, The Conservation Food & Health Foundation.
Financial data (yr. ended 06/30/99): Assets, $770,570 (M); grants paid, $0; gifts received, $527,747; expenditures, $193,969; qualifying distributions, $192,856; giving activities include $193,971 for programs.
Limitations: Applications not accepted.
Application information: Contributes only to pre-selected organizations.
Officers and Directors:* Jacquie L. Kay,* Pres.; George Van Ausdall,* Treas.; George M. Hughes,* Clerk; David Addiss, Peter G. Bourne, Herbert B. Gleason, Ronald R. Hopkins, George M. Hughes, John J. Kao, Anders R. Seim, Harald Siem.
EIN: 043100270

60932
Albert N. Parlin House, Inc.
c/o Hemenway & Barnes
P.O. Box 6842
Boston, MA 02102

Financial data (yr. ended 12/31/01): Assets, $766,998 (M); grants paid, $0; gifts received, $100,000; expenditures, $135,429; qualifying distributions, $0.
Limitations: Applications not accepted.
Officers: Timothy F. Fidgeon, Pres.; Kurt F. Somerville, Treas. and Clerk.
EIN: 042106705

60933
Wright Charities Corp.
(Formerly Easthampton Home for Aged Women, Inc.)
78 Plain St.
Easthampton, MA 01027-2011

Classified as a private operating foundation in 1986.
Financial data (yr. ended 09/30/00): Assets, $761,026 (M); grants paid, $0; expenditures, $86,811; qualifying distributions, $61,406; giving activities include $61,406 for programs.
Officers and Trustees:* Phillip Matthews,* Pres.; Olive Dragon,* V.P.; Carolyn Lamoureux,* Secy.; Margaret J. Cernak,* Treas.; Bernice Conner, Dennis Dacunha, Maxine Hendrick, Gerry Lanen, Mavis McGowan, Jessie Sample, Esther Torberg, Herbert Torberg, and 10 additional trustees.
EIN: 042104166

60934
Tenney Educational Fund, Inc.
c/o Oakley, O'Sullivan, & Eaton, PC
89 Main St.
Andover, MA 01810 (978) 474-4447
Contact: John Oakley, Treas.

Financial data (yr. ended 04/30/01): Assets, $759,058 (M); grants paid, $33,250; expenditures, $35,921; qualifying distributions, $32,883.
Limitations: Giving limited to Methuen, MA.
Application information: Application form required.
Officer: John C. Oakley, Treas.
EIN: 046038700
Codes: GTI

60935
Robert and Iris Fanger Family Foundation
190 Dudley St.
Brookline, MA 02445 (617) 734-2735
Contact: Robert Fanger, Tr. and Iris Fanger, Tr.

Established in 1998 in MA.
Donor(s): Robert D. Fanger.
Financial data (yr. ended 12/31/01): Assets, $758,573 (M); grants paid, $66,947; expenditures, $78,637; qualifying distributions, $66,772.
Limitations: Giving primarily in Boston, MA.
Trustees: Iris Fanger, Robert D. Fanger.
EIN: 043425988

60936
Prescott Conservancy, Inc.
c/o Grant Management Assoc.
77 Summer St., 8th Fl.
Boston, MA 02110

Established in 1997 NH.
Donor(s): Samuel P. Pardoe, Charles H. Pardoe II, E. Spencer Pardoe Ballou, Prescott Bruce Pardoe, Charles H. Pardoe, Elizabeth P. Gray.
Financial data (yr. ended 06/30/00): Assets, $757,998 (M); grants paid, $0; gifts received, $50,000; expenditures, $82,359; qualifying distributions, $115,876; giving activities include $36,014 for loans and $79,862 for programs.
Limitations: Applications not accepted.
Application information: Contributes only to pre-selected organizations.
Officers: Prescott Bruce Pardoe, Pres.; Charles H. Parode II, V.P.; E. Spencer Pardoe Ballou, Secy.; Charles E. Parode, Treas.
EIN: 043387252

60937
Vineyard Youth Tennis, Inc.
c/o Choate, Hall & Stewart
53 State St. Bldg., 1 Exchange Pl.
Boston, MA 02109-2804

Established in 1999 in MA.
Donor(s): Gerald L. Deblois.
Financial data (yr. ended 12/31/01): Assets, $757,542 (M); grants paid, $0; gifts received, $790,000; expenditures, $88,648; qualifying distributions, $664,293; giving activities include $664,293 for programs.
Officers and Directors:* Gerald L. Deblois,* Pres.; Eric W. Wodlinger,* Clerk; Ronald Rappaport,* Treas.; Frank Biondi, Elizabeth Danziger, Harry Garvey, Stanley Hart, Ralph Stuart.
EIN: 043434874

60938
Walter R. & Helen P. Hennessey Charitable Foundation
c/o John G. Hennessey
P.O. Box 1723
North Falmouth, MA 02556-1723

Established in 1964.
Financial data (yr. ended 11/30/01): Assets, $737,175 (M); grants paid, $73,575; expenditures, $81,326; qualifying distributions, $81,326.
Limitations: Applications not accepted. Giving primarily in New England.
Application information: Contributes only to pre-selected organizations.
Trustees: John G. Hennessey, Stephen Kumian.
EIN: 046077295

60939
Obermayer Foundation, Inc.
239 Chestnut St.
West Newton, MA 02465 (617) 244-8990
Contact: Judith H. Obermayer, Clerk

Established in 1980.
Donor(s): Arthur S. Obermayer, Judith H. Obermayer.
Financial data (yr. ended 09/30/01): Assets, $730,121 (L); grants paid, $47,500; gifts received, $204,807; expenditures, $145,856; qualifying distributions, $145,856; giving activities include $41,425 for programs.
Limitations: Giving primarily in MA.
Officers and Directors:* Arthur S. Obermayer,* Pres.; Judith H. Obermayer,* Clerk.
EIN: 042711822

60940
Dorothy M. Tenney Charitable Trust
c/o Warren M. Yanoff
19 Cedar St.
Worcester, MA 01609-2530

Financial data (yr. ended 12/31/99): Assets, $702,572 (M); grants paid, $10,100; expenditures, $25,542; qualifying distributions, $24,542.
Limitations: Applications not accepted.
Application information: Contributes only to pre-selected organizations.
Trustee: Warren M. Yanoff.
EIN: 223022796

60941
Hunt Alternatives
(Formerly Swanee Hunt Operating Fund)
168 Brattle St.
Cambridge, MA 02138

Established in 1997 in CO and MA; classified as a private operating foundation in 1998.
Donor(s): Swanee Hunt.
Financial data (yr. ended 11/30/99): Assets, $697,263 (M); grants paid, $0; gifts received, $1,225,000; expenditures, $907,515; qualifying distributions, $897,796; giving activities include $485,901 for programs.
Officers and Directors:* Swanee Hunt,* Pres.; Henry Ansbacher,* V.P.; Marva Hammons,* Secy.; Charles Ansbacher,* Treas.; Katherine Archuleta, Lillian Hunt-Meeks, Jane Holl Lute.
EIN: 043397500

60942
John T. Collins Foundation
P.O. Box 675
Medway, MA 02053-0675

Established in 1998 in MA.
Donor(s): John T. Collins.
Financial data (yr. ended 09/30/01): Assets, $686,314 (M); grants paid, $11,500; expenditures, $16,884; qualifying distributions, $11,500.
Limitations: Applications not accepted.
Application information: Contributes only to pre-selected organizations.
Trustee: John T. Collins.
EIN: 043454186

60943
Southern Berkshire Visiting Nurse Foundation, Inc.
c/o C. Plungis
244 Main St.
Great Barrington, MA 01230-1605

Established in 1989 in MA.
Financial data (yr. ended 12/31/01): Assets, $667,150 (M); grants paid, $30,475; expenditures, $35,092; qualifying distributions, $31,575.
Limitations: Applications not accepted. Giving limited to western MA.
Application information: Contributes only to pre-selected organizations.
Officers and Trustees:* Rosemarie Siegel,* Chair. and Pres.; Irene Moskowitz,* Vice-Chair.; Sue Komanik,* Clerk; Charles Plungis,* Treas.; Sally Atwood, Ruth Beers, Gertrude Burdsall, and 14 additional trustees.
EIN: 042429871

60944
The Forbes Kirkside Foundation, Inc.
(Formerly The Kirkside, Inc.)
P.O. Box 855
Westborough, MA 01581-3346
Contact: Bruce Lopatin, Treas.

Classified as a private operating foundation in 1974.
Financial data (yr. ended 12/31/00): Assets, $651,086 (M); grants paid, $37,744; gifts received, $7,350; expenditures, $53,438; qualifying distributions, $52,642.
Limitations: Giving limited to Westboro, MA.
Officers: Lynn Henry, Pres.; Ricky Lopatin, V.P.; Elaine Sanborn, Clerk; Bruce Lopatin, Treas.
Trustee: Ruth Weisbauer.
EIN: 042311010
Codes: GTI

60945
The Joseph E. Corcoran Charitable Foundation
150 Mt. Vernon St., Ste. 500
Boston, MA 02125

Established in 1997 in MA.
Donor(s): Joseph E. Corcoran.
Financial data (yr. ended 12/31/01): Assets, $636,584 (M); grants paid, $30,000; expenditures, $45,161; qualifying distributions, $30,000.
Limitations: Giving primarily in Boston, MA.
Officer: Karen Migey, Mgr.
EIN: 043350462

60946
Belchertown Historical Association, Inc.
20 Maple St.
Belchertown, MA 01007

Classified as an operating foundation in 1974 in MA.
Financial data (yr. ended 04/30/01): Assets, $636,498 (M); grants paid, $0; gifts received, $700; expenditures, $42,747; qualifying distributions, $0.
Limitations: Applications not accepted.
Officers and Trustees:* Robert Handsbury,* Pres.; Suzanne Bay,* V.P.; Doris Dickinson,* V.P.; Nora Austin,* Secy.; June Henneman,* Treas.; Margot Austin, Shirley Bock, James Boyko, John Ferriter, John Futter, Mary Pratt, Randi Shenkman, Kenneth Snow, Kenneth Thayer, Donald Towne.
EIN: 046058218

60947
The Frank B. Mazer Foundation
10 Saville St.
Cambridge, MA 02138-1310
Contact: Frank B. Mazer, Tr.

Established in 1999 in MA.
Donor(s): Frank B. Mazer.
Financial data (yr. ended 09/30/01): Assets, $622,307 (M); grants paid, $27,788; expenditures, $34,532; qualifying distributions, $27,788.
Limitations: Giving primarily in MA.
Application information: Application form not required.
Trustee: Frank B. Mazer.
EIN: 046875253

60948
Hamilton Hall, Inc.
9 Chestnut St.
Salem, MA 01970

Financial data (yr. ended 02/28/02): Assets, $604,651 (M); grants paid, $0; gifts received, $18,111; expenditures, $136,269; qualifying distributions, $0.

Officers and Directors:* Donna Vinson,* Pres.; Richard Wyke,* 1st V.P.; Dean Lahikainen,* 2nd V.P.; Alyce Davis,* Secy.; Jeremiah Burns,* Treas.; Charles Allen, Abby Burns, Jean Dennis, Steven Forbes, Sherrie Goodhue, Joan Griffin, Richard Lindeman, Oscar Padjen, Rebecca Putnam, Tory Stevens, Gary Stirgwolt, Paul Viccica.
EIN: 222624536

60949
G. Barrie Landry Charitable Foundation
50 Cole Pkwy., Ste. 27
Scituate, MA 02066
Application address: 42 Round Hill Rd., Lincoln, MA 01742
Contact: G. Barrie Landry, Dir.

Established in 1997 in MA.
Financial data (yr. ended 12/31/99): Assets, $603,175 (M); grants paid, $113,500; expenditures, $118,723; qualifying distributions, $118,723.
Directors: Ernest J. Grassey, G. Barrie Landry.
EIN: 043350188
Codes: FD2

60950
Arlington Historical Society
c/o Patricia Harris
7 Jason St.
Arlington, MA 02476-6410 (781) 648-4300

Financial data (yr. ended 04/30/00): Assets, $602,752 (M); grants paid, $0; gifts received, $51,379; expenditures, $47,464; qualifying distributions, $47,464; giving activities include $37,700 for programs.
Officers: Richard Erickson, Pres.; Richard Duffy, V.P.; Diane Wells, V.P.; Oakes Plimpton, Secy.; Kendall Stewart, Treas.
Directors: Carleton Crockett, Richard Duffy, Donald Mathiessen, Pearl Morrison, Sally Rogers, Howard B. Winkler, John L. Worden III.
EIN: 046053994

60951
Ocean State Power Scholarship Foundation, Ltd.
62 Capron St.
Uxbridge, MA 01569 (508) 278-6943

Established in 1989 in MA.
Donor(s): Ocean State Power Co.
Financial data (yr. ended 12/31/01): Assets, $596,175 (M); grants paid, $41,350; gifts received, $70,000; expenditures, $48,804; qualifying distributions, $41,350.
Limitations: Giving limited to residents of Uxbridge, MA.
Application information: Application form required.
Officers: Barry P. McCloskey, Pres.; Jayne Hanscom, Treas.
Directors: John E. Creighton, Tracey Koprusak, Peter Lynch, J.G. Merriam, Michael Ronan.
EIN: 222908697
Codes: GTI

60952
Wurtman Foundation, Inc.
c/o Robert Finkel
233 Needham St., 5th Fl.
Newton, MA 02464

Established in 1998 in DE.
Donor(s): Elie C. Wurtman, Enid Wurtman, Stuart Wurtman.
Financial data (yr. ended 06/30/00): Assets, $584,137 (M); grants paid, $5,000; gifts received, $506,563; expenditures, $84,042; qualifying distributions, $9,600; giving activities include $36,264 for programs.

Limitations: Giving limited to Jerusalem, Israel.
Officers and Directors:* Elie C. Wurtman,* Pres.; Stuart Wurtman,* V.P.; Robert Finkel,* Secy.-Treas.; Enid Wutman.
EIN: 650881769

60953
Busy-Bee Transportation Services, Inc.
43 Nickerson Rd.
Ashland, MA 01721 (508) 881-2120

Financial data (yr. ended 09/30/01): Assets, $579,673 (M); grants paid, $0; expenditures, $2,361,168; qualifying distributions, $2,276,396; giving activities include $2,214,063 for programs.
Officers and Directors:* Linda Pinnelle,* C.E.O.; Helene de Ruiter,* Pres.; Joseph Todisco,* Secy.; Marty Udelson,* Treas.
EIN: 042770983

60954
Nichols House Museum, Inc.
55 Mount Vernon St.
Boston, MA 02108

Classified as a private operating foundation in 1978.
Financial data (yr. ended 01/31/02): Assets, $574,108 (M); grants paid, $0; gifts received, $39,686; expenditures, $98,434; qualifying distributions, $0.
Officer: Flavia Cigliano, Exec. Dir.
EIN: 046006789

60955
Trustees of the Ashley School & Charitable Fund
P.O. Box 438
West Springfield, MA 01090-0438

Established in 1989 in MA.
Financial data (yr. ended 12/31/00): Assets, $550,849 (M); grants paid, $19,750; expenditures, $23,598; qualifying distributions, $19,750.
Limitations: Giving limited to West Springfield, MA.
Trustees: Barbara Bozenhard, Robert Bozenhard, Alexander Hindmarsh, Frank Palmer, Robert Pratt.
EIN: 046050051

60956
Advancement Plus, Inc.
10 Rogers St.
Cambridge, MA 02142

Established in 2000 in MA.
Financial data (yr. ended 12/31/01): Assets, $543,369 (M); grants paid, $0; gifts received, $29,118; expenditures, $328,723; qualifying distributions, $306,851; giving activities include $307,257 for programs.
Officer and Directors:* A. Harold Howell,* Pres. and Treas.; L. Edward Lashman, Kevin J. Mullen.
EIN: 043323595

60957
General Charitable Fund, Inc.
c/o Family Bank
470 Main St.
Fitchburg, MA 01420

Financial data (yr. ended 12/31/99): Assets, $538,675 (M); grants paid, $6,000; expenditures, $12,898; qualifying distributions, $7,724.
Application information: Application form required.
Officers: William R. Freeman, Pres.; Peter C. Armbruster, Treas.
Trustee: Winthrop M. Mayo, Jr.
EIN: 046048360

60958
Albert H. Surprenant Charitable Trust
125 Summer St.
Boston, MA 02110-1616 (617) 664-4136
Contact: Frank T. Giannetta, Tr.

Financial data (yr. ended 12/31/00): Assets, $523,348 (M); grants paid, $12,210; expenditures, $16,994; qualifying distributions, $14,018.
Limitations: Giving primarily in MA.
Application information: Application form not required.
Trustees: Frank T. Giannetta, Charles D. Post.
EIN: 046040530

60959
Royall House Association
15 George St.
Medford, MA 02155

Financial data (yr. ended 03/31/02): Assets, $502,388 (M); grants paid, $0; gifts received, $46,975; expenditures, $60,897; qualifying distributions, $0.
Officers and Directors:* Peter Gittleman,* Pres.; Julia Royal,* Pres.; Francesca Lion,* 1st V.P.; Thomas Lincoln, 2nd V.P.; Jeanne Macgregor,* Secy. and Clerk; Allan K. Martorana, Treas.; Lillian Bombaci, and 12 additional directors.
EIN: 046046749

60960
Ames Foundation
c/o Palmer & Dodge, LLP
111 Huntington Ave.
Boston, MA 02199

Classified as a private operating foundation in 1970.
Donor(s): Spencer Foundation.
Financial data (yr. ended 05/31/01): Assets, $499,476 (M); grants paid, $95,550; gifts received, $138,000; expenditures, $124,303; qualifying distributions, $120,081.
Limitations: Giving primarily in MA.
Application information: Recipients selected by Harvard Law School faculty.
Officers and Directors:* Mary Ann Glendon,* Pres.; Daniel R. Coquillette,* Treas. and Clerk; William P. Alford, Reuven Avi-Jonah, Christine Dessan, Charles Donahue, Jr., William W. Fisher III, Louis J. Jaffe, Andrew L. Kaufman, Randall L. Kennedy, Harry S. Martin III.
EIN: 046061117
Codes: FD2

60961
The MacLean Charitable Foundation
585 Commercial St.
Boston, MA 02109-1024

Established in 1999 in MA.
Donor(s): William Q. MacLean.
Financial data (yr. ended 12/31/00): Assets, $484,291 (M); grants paid, $78,040; gifts received, $175,492; expenditures, $83,763; qualifying distributions, $78,040.
Trustees: Mary Jane MacLean, William Q. MacLean.
EIN: 043493004

60962
Sandra and Philip Gordon Family Foundation
300 Boylston St., No. 1201
Boston, MA 02116

Established in 1997 in MA.
Financial data (yr. ended 12/31/00): Assets, $480,760 (M); grants paid, $22,500; gifts received, $103,204; expenditures, $27,257; qualifying distributions, $22,500.
Limitations: Applications not accepted.
Application information: Contributes only to pre-selected organizations.
Trustees: Joanne Gordon Adams, Caryl Gordon Bishop, Jeffrey Gordon, Philip H. Gordon, Sandra P. Gordon, Barbara Gordon Levkowicz.
EIN: 046821284

60963
American Museum of Antique Toys, Inc.
(also known as The Schroeder Foundation, Inc.)
c/o Schroeder
35 Stoney Brook Rd.
Great Barrington, MA 01230-2100

Classified as a private operating foundation in 1978.
Donor(s): Aaron Schroeder, Abby Schroeder.
Financial data (yr. ended 04/30/01): Assets, $479,188 (M); grants paid, $0; gifts received, $19,246; expenditures, $21,928; qualifying distributions, $20,278; giving activities include $20,278 for programs.
Officers: Aaron Schroeder, Pres.; Abby Schroeder, Secy.
EIN: 222212289

60964
Western Massachusetts Energy Trust, Inc.
c/o John Renzi
104 Bailey Rd.
Lanesboro, MA 01237-1522

Established in 1998 in MA.
Financial data (yr. ended 06/30/00): Assets, $449,566 (M); grants paid, $0; expenditures, $19,785; qualifying distributions, $0; giving activities include $16,567 for programs.
Officer: John Renzi, Pres.
Director: Paul Tangredi.
EIN: 043339064

60965
Marjorie W. Sloper Charitable Foundation
c/o Caputo & Co., PC
100 Corporate Pl., Ste. 510
Peabody, MA 01960

Donor(s): Marjorie W. Sloper.
Financial data (yr. ended 12/31/00): Assets, $448,866 (M); grants paid, $25,000; expenditures, $25,948; qualifying distributions, $25,000.
Limitations: Applications not accepted. Giving primarily in MA.
Application information: Contributes only to pre-selected organizations.
Trustees: Louis M. Caputo, Jr., Marjorie W. Sloper.
EIN: 912142427

60966
Ladies Branch of the New Bedford Port Society
c/o Education Grant Chair.
15 Johnny Cake Hill
New Bedford, MA 02740 (508) 999-3295

Classified as a private operating foundation in 1987.
Financial data (yr. ended 12/31/01): Assets, $421,176 (M); grants paid, $13,250; gifts received, $424; expenditures, $19,094; qualifying distributions, $18,444.
Limitations: Giving limited to the greater New Bedford, MA, area.
Officers and Directors:* Joanna McQuillan Weeks,* Pres.; Mary Lou Garrett,* 1st V.P.; Sonja Sovik,* 2nd V.P.; Barbara Warburton,* Secy.; Brenda Dixon, Treas.; Joyce Borden, Kay Hayes,

60966—MASSACHUSETTS

Marian Mitchell, Martha Reed, Adele Smialek, and 22 additional directors.
EIN: 046079892
Codes: GTI

60967
Field Memorial Library
c/o Thelma French
P.O. Box 189
Conway, MA 01341

Donor(s): Marshall Field Trust.
Financial data (yr. ended 12/31/01): Assets, $417,009 (M); grants paid, $0; gifts received, $47,029; expenditures, $46,213; qualifying distributions, $0.
Officers: Deane Lee, Pres.; Thelma C. French, V.P.; Howard R. Boyden, Clerk; Ann H. Borton, Treas.
EIN: 042103768

60968
The Mansfield Historical Society, Inc.
150 Rumford Ave., Apt. 220
Mansfield, MA 02048-2149

Financial data (yr. ended 02/28/01): Assets, $405,729 (M); grants paid, $0; gifts received, $1,121; expenditures, $11,220; qualifying distributions, $11,220; giving activities include $11,220 for programs.
Officers: Kevin McNatt, Pres.; Andrew Todesco, V.P.; Marjorie Oldmixon, Secy.; Martha Flint, Treas.
EIN: 046056548

60969
Clinical Neuroscience Research Foundation, Inc.
c/o Joseph Lipinski, Jr.
89 College Rd.
Concord, MA 01742 (978) 369-6732
Contact: Joseph F. Lipinski, Jr, M.D., Pres.

Established in 1999 in MA and VA.
Donor(s): Richard Goldbach.
Financial data (yr. ended 12/31/99): Assets, $396,047 (M); grants paid, $25; gifts received, $51,200; expenditures, $50,695; qualifying distributions, $23,961.
Officer and Directors:* Joseph F. Lipinski, Jr., M.D.,* Pres. and Secy.-Treas.; Janet Goldbach, Richard Goldbach.
EIN: 522106068

60970
The Law-Reed-Huss Farm Foundation
c/o William Huss
2 Catherine's Farm Rd.
Wayland, MA 01778

Established in 2001 in OH.
Donor(s): Ella V. Huss.
Financial data (yr. ended 12/31/01): Assets, $391,754 (M); grants paid, $0; gifts received, $395,000; expenditures, $3,258; qualifying distributions, $0.
Limitations: Applications not accepted.
Application information: Contributes only to pre-selected organizations.
Officer: William Huss, Exec. Dir.
Trustees: Brad L. Hillyer, Ella V. Huss.
EIN: 341941030

60971
The Colburn Foundation
c/o Peter E. Bernardin, Ardiff & Morse
P.O. Box 59
Danvers, MA 01923

Established in 1982.
Financial data (yr. ended 12/31/00): Assets, $383,000 (M); grants paid, $0; expenditures, $0; qualifying distributions, $0; giving activities include $383,000 for programs.
Officers and Directors:* Frances H. Colburn,* Pres.; Oliver C. Colburn,* Clerk; Clarissa C. Hummewell,* Treas.; George C. Freeman, Jr., Mark Rubenstein.
EIN: 042748890

60972
Monson Historical Society, Inc.
c/o Shawmut Central Tax Unit
P.O. Box 114
Monson, MA 01057-0114

Classified as a private operating foundation in 1987.
Financial data (yr. ended 04/30/00): Assets, $382,009 (M); grants paid, $60; gifts received, $10,649; expenditures, $18,447; qualifying distributions, $14,515; giving activities include $7,905 for programs.
Officers: Frank Capsia, Pres.; Dennis Swierad, V.P.; Phila Vaill, Secy.; Evelyn Hodskins, Treas.
Directors: Tamara Cabey, William Dominick, John Mumford, and 2 additional directors.
EIN: 042595563

60973
F. Leo Murray & Irene D. Murray Scholarship Fund
P.O. Box 250
Winchendon, MA 01475
Application address: 1 Summer Dr., Winchendon, MA 01475, tel.: (973) 297-2042
Contact: Robert LaFortune, Tr.

Financial data (yr. ended 12/31/01): Assets, $366,248 (M); grants paid, $19,000; expenditures, $24,586; qualifying distributions, $19,000.
Limitations: Giving limited to residents of Winchendon, MA.
Application information: Application form required.
Trustees: Barry Jaffe, Robert LaFortune.
EIN: 046635075
Codes: GTI

60974
The Beta Kappa Phi Alpha Gamma Rho Scholarship Foundation
15 Mann St.
Hingham, MA 02043
Application address: P.O. Box 6145, Boston, MA 02109, tel.: (617) 261-9204
Contact: Tom Albert

Established in 1993 in MA.
Donor(s): Beta Kappa Phi Alpha Gamma Rho, Inc.
Financial data (yr. ended 12/31/99): Assets, $346,499 (M); grants paid, $21,250; expenditures, $22,374; qualifying distributions, $21,457.
Limitations: Giving primarily to MA residents.
Officers: James Pallota, Pres.; Brian Gaudet, Secy.; Thomas Albert, Treas.
Directors: J.C. Bejoin, Richard Gulman, Bruce Leaver, Dave Robison.
EIN: 043124308

60975
National Center for Nutrition & Fatty Acid Research, Inc.
P.O. Box 1387
Brookline, MA 02446

Classified as a private operating foundation in 1993.
Donor(s): Edward N. Siguel.
Financial data (yr. ended 12/31/00): Assets, $343,693 (M); grants paid, $0; gifts received, $100; expenditures, $28,899; qualifying distributions, $0.
Officer and Trustees:* Edward N. Siguel,* Pres.; Vera Siguel.
EIN: 043178432

60976
Ayer-Anderson Foundation, Inc.
(Formerly Frederick A. Ayer Foundation)
c/o Jon R. Conant
147 Wingaersheek Rd.
Gloucester, MA 01930-1454

Established in 1992.
Donor(s): Hilda Ayer.
Financial data (yr. ended 12/31/99): Assets, $338,824 (M); grants paid, $0; gifts received, $478,621; expenditures, $315,170; qualifying distributions, $311,841; giving activities include $315,170 for programs.
Officers: Hilda Ayer-Anderson, Pres. and Treas.; Jon R. Conant, Mgr. and Clerk.
EIN: 043153334

60977
The Jennison Charitable Foundation
150 Mt. Vernon St., Ste. 500
Boston, MA 02125

Financial data (yr. ended 12/31/01): Assets, $333,467 (M); grants paid, $12,500; expenditures, $12,500; qualifying distributions, $12,500.
Limitations: Applications not accepted. Giving primarily in MA.
Trustee: Karen F. Meyer.
EIN: 043332800

60978
Somerville Center House, Inc.
678 Massachusetts Ave., 10th Fl.
Cambridge, MA 02139

Classified as a private operating foundation in 1990.
Financial data (yr. ended 06/30/00): Assets, $331,692 (M); grants paid, $0; expenditures, $101,259; qualifying distributions, $98,980; giving activities include $92,280 for programs.
Officers and Directors:* Thomas Sadtler,* Pres.; Patricia Giulino,* V.P.; Nannette Glenny, Clerk; Douglas Muir,* Treas.; Betsey Eltonhead, Howard Friedman, and 2 additional directors.
EIN: 223048731
Codes: TN

60979
Educating Everyone, Inc.
140 Gould St., Ste. 200B
Needham, MA 02494 (781) 453-2388
FAX: (781) 453-2389; E-mail: information@educatinge.org

Established in FL.
Financial data (yr. ended 12/31/00): Assets, $328,783 (M); grants paid, $0; gifts received, $40,000; expenditures, $390,465; qualifying distributions, $317,000; giving activities include $341,227 for programs.
Officers: R. Scott Zimmer, Pres.; Paul A. Moran, Secy.; David Walsh, Treas.
Directors: Michael Elder, Dir.-Bus. Dev.; Monica Pilkey, Dir.-Ed. Serv.
EIN: 650821020

60980
The Edward O. Wilson Foundation
Palmer & Dodge, LLP
1 Beacon St.
Boston, MA 02108

Classified as a private operating foundation in 1995.
Donor(s): Edward O. Wilson.

Financial data (yr. ended 05/31/00): Assets, $312,147 (M); grants paid, $0; expenditures, $107,307; qualifying distributions, $102,658; giving activities include $98,574 for programs.
Trustees: James J. McCarthy, James M. Stone, Edward O. Wilson, R. Robert Woodburn, Jr.
EIN: 043278674

60981
Armenian Cultural Foundation
441 Mystic St.
Arlington, MA 02474-1108

Donor(s): John Miran Foundation.
Financial data (yr. ended 08/31/01): Assets, $312,119 (M); grants paid, $10,000; gifts received, $111,064; expenditures, $106,855; qualifying distributions, $10,000.
Trustees: Rev. Oshagan Minasian, John Mirak.
EIN: 046196015

60982
Edwin Prescott Scouthouse Charitable Trust
c/o E. Cancelliere
14 Woodbury St.
Arlington, MA 02476

Established in 2000 in MA.
Financial data (yr. ended 12/31/00): Assets, $300,269 (M); grants paid, $3,020; expenditures, $6,147; qualifying distributions, $6,147.
Limitations: Applications not accepted. Giving primarily in Arlington, MA.
Application information: Contributes only to pre-selected organizations.
Officer: Peter Silva, Chair.
Trustees: Gene Cancelliere, James Duddy, Henry Ferraro, Matt Ferraro, James Ferraro, John Frederick, Williams H. Groves, Sr., Joseph Marcone, Arnold Smith.
EIN: 223520792

60983
Warren L. Milliken & Alice Pratt Milliken Trust
c/o Hovey & Koenig
40 Broad St., Ste. 815
Boston, MA 02109

Classified as a private operating foundation in 1999 in MA.
Donor(s): Warren L. Millikien.
Financial data (yr. ended 12/31/01): Assets, $297,825 (M); grants paid, $0; gifts received, $49,621; expenditures, $25,559; qualifying distributions, $23,440; giving activities include $27,771 for programs.
Trustees: David J. Buckman, William Hovey, John L. Woods.
EIN: 046878528

60984
The Alphonse M. and Joyce L. Lucchese Charitable Foundation
16 Baxter Rd.
Marstons Mills, MA 02648-1811

Established in 1999 in MA.
Donor(s): Alphonse M. Lucchese.
Financial data (yr. ended 12/31/01): Assets, $290,463 (M); grants paid, $17,500; gifts received, $105,092; expenditures, $85,663; qualifying distributions, $17,500.
Limitations: Applications not accepted. Giving primarily in MA.
Application information: Contributes only to pre-selected organizations.
Trustees: Alphonse M. Lucchese, Alphonse M. Lucchese, Jr., James Lucchese, Joyce L. Lucchese, Paul R. Lucchese.
EIN: 043492751

60985
Enterprise Computing Institute, Inc.
226 Pond St.
Hopkinton, MA 01748

Established in 1994 in MA.
Donor(s): Worcester Polytechnic Institute.
Financial data (yr. ended 09/30/99): Assets, $280,063 (M); grants paid, $0; expenditures, $593,189; qualifying distributions, $57,437; giving activities include $593,189 for programs.
Officers: Thomas H. Probert, Pres.; Patricia R. Probert, Secy.-Treas.
Director: Edward Wagner.
EIN: 043251354

60986
Donald H. and Helen D. Peach Scholarship Fund
c/o Allan Martin
150 Washington St., Ste. 3
Marblehead, MA 01945-3338

Financial data (yr. ended 12/31/01): Assets, $278,093 (M); grants paid, $6,000; expenditures, $13,406; qualifying distributions, $6,000.
Limitations: Applications not accepted. Giving limited to Marblehead, MA.
Application information: Unsolicited requests for funds not accepted.
Trustee: Philanthropic Lodge F & AM.
EIN: 046721931

60987
Drew Bledsoe Foundation
5 Lincoln Rd.
Foxboro, MA 02035

Established in 1998 in WA and MA.
Donor(s): Drew M. Bledsoe.
Financial data (yr. ended 08/31/00): Assets, $259,257 (M); grants paid, $1,406; gifts received, $438,975; expenditures, $696,000; qualifying distributions, $659,064; giving activities include $321,025 for programs.
Officers: Joseph G. Lake, Chair.; Tom Heatherington, Vice-Chair.; Don Berube, C.E.O.; John Mac Bledsoe, Pres.; Barbara Bledsoe, Secy.; Mark C. Griege, Treas.
Directors: William N. Bulger, Jr., David Dunn, Karen Nerney, Brett Rodman, Karl White.
EIN: 911691382

60988
Fletcher Hospital Corporation
c/o Herbert F. Hunter, C.P.A.
137 School St.
Franklin, MA 02038-2015
Application address: c/o Operating Committee, P.O. Box K, Franklin, MA 02038

Financial data (yr. ended 09/30/01): Assets, $230,732 (M); grants paid, $14,000; expenditures, $15,325; qualifying distributions, $14,000.
Limitations: Giving limited to the Franklin, MA, area.
Officers: Peter Brunelli, Vice-Chair.; Theresa Robbins, Pres.; Roy Scipione, Jr., Secy.; Dona Mackintosh, Treas.
EIN: 046037899

60989
Upper Charles Conservation, Inc.
7 Norfolk Ln.
Holliston, MA 01746-2362

Established in 1992.
Financial data (yr. ended 12/31/01): Assets, $230,569 (M); grants paid, $0; gifts received, $39,927; expenditures, $11,248; qualifying distributions, $67,182; giving activities include $67,182 for programs.
Officers and Directors:* John E. Thomas,* Pres.; Sara Molyneaux, Clerk; Anne Rich, Treas.; Robert J. Buckley, George F. Fiske, Jr., David Hoag.
EIN: 223242438

60990
Therese A. & Maurice L. Sullivan Humanitarian Trust
c/o Frec. G. Herwig
8 Parsons St.
Peabody, MA 01960-6125

Classified as a private operating foundation in 1983.
Financial data (yr. ended 12/31/01): Assets, $226,076 (M); grants paid, $15,926; expenditures, $17,748; qualifying distributions, $17,748.
Limitations: Applications not accepted. Giving primarily in MA.
Application information: Contributes only to pre-selected organizations.
Officer and Trustees:* Fred G. Herwig,* Chair.; Robert A. Dow, Frank J Pellizzaro, Jr.
EIN: 042778084

60991
The Santayana Fund, Inc.
1 Bridge St., Ste. 101
Newton, MA 02458

Established in 1996 in MA.
Donor(s): Christopher Lutz, The Plumsock Fund, Sally Lutz.
Financial data (yr. ended 12/31/00): Assets, $223,096 (M); grants paid, $89,560; gifts received, $450,045; expenditures, $513,973; qualifying distributions, $547,369; giving activities include $547,374 for programs.
Limitations: Applications not accepted. Giving on a national and international basis, with an emphasis on Guatamala.
Application information: Contributes only to pre-selected organizations.
Officers and Directors:* Sally Lutz,* Pres.; Pam Solo, Clerk and Exec. Dir.; Ian Lutz,* Treas.; Christopher Lutz, Jennifer Lutz.
EIN: 043322480
Codes: FD2

60992
Shelburne Buckland Community Center, Inc.
P.O. Box 2
Shelburne Falls, MA 01370-0002

Classified as a private operating foundation in 1982.
Financial data (yr. ended 12/31/01): Assets, $220,926 (M); grants paid, $0; gifts received, $44,205; expenditures, $45,967; qualifying distributions, $46,787; giving activities include $41,988 for programs.
Limitations: Applications not accepted.
Officers: Harper T. Gerry, Pres.; Robert Legere, V.P.; Diane Cosby, Clerk; Marion Scott, Treas.
Directors: David Bishop, Frank Field, Robert Fischlein, Patricia Lowell, Wilbert Rainville, Jr., Douglas Turner.
EIN: 042552125

60993
Chelonian Research Foundation
168 Goodrich St.
Lunenburg, MA 01462 (978) 582-9668
Contact: Anders G.J. Rhodin, Dir.

Established in 1999 in MA.
Donor(s): Anders G.J. Rhodin.

Financial data (yr. ended 12/31/01): Assets, $204,488 (M); grants paid, $107,581; gifts received, $88,298; expenditures, $196,146; qualifying distributions, $107,572; giving activities include $179,694 for programs.
Directors: Russell A.M. Mittermeier, Peter C.H. Pritchard, Anders G.J. Rhodin.
EIN: 046705444
Codes: FD2, GTI

60994
Ahmed Foundation for Kurdish Studies, Inc.
447 Chapman St.
Canton, MA 02021-2077

Established in 1999.
Donor(s): Mohammed M.A. Ahmed, Shirley A. Ahmed.
Financial data (yr. ended 01/31/01): Assets, $204,042 (M); grants paid, $0; expenditures, $7,805; qualifying distributions, $7,805; giving activities include $6,629 for programs.
Directors: Mohammed M.A. Ahmed, Shirley A. Ahmed.
EIN: 541882708

60995
The Mirza Mehdi Charitable Trust
P.O. Box 1075, 30 Mill Pond Ln.
Duxbury, MA 02331
Contact: Jean M. Riley, Tr.

Established in 1989 in MA.
Donor(s): Mirza Z. Mehdi.
Financial data (yr. ended 11/30/00): Assets, $201,911 (M); grants paid, $1,250; expenditures, $3,161; qualifying distributions, $3,161.
Limitations: Giving on a national basis.
Trustee: Jean M. Riley.
EIN: 043071833

60996
Sarah H. Williams Treasure Hunt Farm Foundation
P.O. Box 696
Rutland, MA 01543-0696
Application address: 59 Wachusett St., Rutland, MA 01543
Contact: Sarah H. Williams, Tr.

Established in 2000 in MA.
Donor(s): Sarah H. Williams.
Financial data (yr. ended 12/31/01): Assets, $201,592 (M); grants paid, $0; gifts received, $97,477; expenditures, $139,388; qualifying distributions, $0.
Trustees: Stuart A. Hammer, Jefferson E. Williams, Sarah H. Williams.
EIN: 043463245

60997
The Donna R. & Douglas E. Barnard Charitable Foundation, Inc.
10 Beaver Pond Rd.
Beverly, MA 01915

Established in 2001 in MA.
Financial data (yr. ended 12/31/01): Assets, $200,473 (M); grants paid, $0; gifts received, $200,853; expenditures, $0; qualifying distributions, $0.
Limitations: Applications not accepted.
Application information: Contributes only to pre-selected organizations.
Officers: Douglas E. Barnard, Pres. and Treas.; Donna R. Barnard, Clerk.
EIN: 010563561

60998
Ruth A. Shultz Scholarship Fund
c/o The Trust Co. of the Berkshires, N.A.
99 North St.
Pittsfield, MA 01201
Application address: 54 North St., Pittsfield, MA 01201
Contact: Eugene D. Cornell, Sr. V.P., The Trust Co. of the Berkshires, N.A.

Donor(s): Ruth A. Shultz.‡
Financial data (yr. ended 12/31/00): Assets, $200,450 (M); grants paid, $5,550; expenditures, $8,651; qualifying distributions, $5,265.
Limitations: Giving limited to the Caanan, CT, area.
Application information: Application form required.
Officers: Paul B. Leavitt, Pres.; Eugene Cornell, V.P.
EIN: 066205123
Codes: GTI

60999
Theosophical Society in Massachusetts Trust
c/o Fernando de Torrijos
22 Midgley Ln.
Worcester, MA 01604-3562 (508) 792-4602

Financial data (yr. ended 12/31/01): Assets, $192,641 (M); grants paid, $0; gifts received, $415; expenditures, $21,653; qualifying distributions, $17,505; giving activities include $17,609 for programs.
Officers: Wanda Rodriguez, Pres.; Lorraine Starr, V.P.; Ruth Adams de Torrijos, Secy.; Fernando de Torrijos, Treas.
EIN: 046754568

61000
Wrentham Cable Access Corporation
c/o Wrentham Cable Access Corporation
P.O. Box 668
Wrentham, MA 02093 (508) 384-6275
Contact: Ravindra M. Nadkarni, Treas.

Established in 1991 in MA.
Donor(s): Wrentham Cable Access Corp.
Financial data (yr. ended 12/31/00): Assets, $179,014 (M); grants paid, $100; expenditures, $80,519; qualifying distributions, $100.
Limitations: Giving limited to Wrentham, MA.
Application information: Application form required.
Officers and Directors:* William King,* Pres.; William M. Arnold,* V.P.; Ravinda M. Nadkerni,* Secy.-Treas.; Helen Hefron, Marj Immonen, Frank Whitehead.
EIN: 043126509

61001
Frank C. Taylor & Helen M. Taylor Education Fund
c/o Welby Law Offices, PC
13 Ventura Dr.
North Dartmouth, MA 02747 (508) 998-6152

Financial data (yr. ended 12/31/01): Assets, $176,527 (M); grants paid, $7,000; expenditures, $8,725; qualifying distributions, $8,725.
Limitations: Giving primarily in MA.
Application information: Application form required.
Trustees: David Faria, James A. Flanagan, David Roderick.
EIN: 046071778
Codes: GTI

61002
Simran Woods Foundation
c/o Linda Cohen
P.O. Box 2298
Vineyard Haven, MA 02568

Classified as a private operating foundation in 1980.
Donor(s): Richard Wright.
Financial data (yr. ended 12/31/00): Assets, $165,673 (M); grants paid, $0; gifts received, $16,237; expenditures, $2,872; qualifying distributions, $2,086; giving activities include $2,086 for programs.
Limitations: Applications not accepted. Giving primarily in Vineyard Haven, MA.
Application information: Contributes only to pre-selected organizations.
Officers: Bruce MacNelly, Pres.; Linda Cohen, V.P.; Amy Zoll, Secy.; Patty French, Treas.
Directors: Ted Box, Patrick Brown, Margaret Knight.
EIN: 042707558
Codes: TN

61003
Greenfield Library Association
17 Bank Row
Greenfield, MA 01301

Established in 1968 in MA.
Financial data (yr. ended 05/31/99): Assets, $163,758 (M); grants paid, $0; expenditures, $16,111; qualifying distributions, $0.
Officers and Trustees:* Bernard Prescott,* Pres.; Carol Cloutier, V.P.; Ann Wilson,* Treas.
Directors: Bernice Cahill, Ethel Case, Dorothy Gagnon, Marian Kelleher, Karolyn Kemp, Ruth Paulsen.
EIN: 042263013

61004
Chester High School Alumni Association
Skyline Trail
Middlefield, MA 01243 (413) 623-5519
Contact: c/o Maurice H. Pease, Treas. of Scholarship Program

Financial data (yr. ended 06/30/01): Assets, $163,672 (M); grants paid, $3,800; gifts received, $45; expenditures, $8,699; qualifying distributions, $5,608.
Limitations: Giving limited to residents of Chester, MA.
Application information: Application form required.
Officers: William Koivisto, Pres.; Diane Demoss, V.P.; Janice Brown, Secy.; George A. Morey, Treas.
EIN: 046058373
Codes: GTI

61005
Institute of Traditional Science, Inc.
P.O. Box 380284
Cambridge, MA 02138-0284

Donor(s): Haven O'More.
Financial data (yr. ended 08/31/01): Assets, $159,400 (M); grants paid, $0; gifts received, $5,780; expenditures, $6,898; qualifying distributions, $0.
Officer and Directors:* Haven O'More,* Pres. and Treas.; Sue Ann Bankston, Rahel O'More.
EIN: 042577162

61006
Belmont Ranger Youth Hockey Association, Inc.
P.O. Box 154
Belmont, MA 02478-0002

Classified as a private operating foundation in 1989.
Financial data (yr. ended 06/30/01): Assets, $155,721 (M); grants paid, $3,475; expenditures, $167,888; qualifying distributions, $159,778; giving activities include $154,970 for programs.
Application information: Application form not required.
Officers and Directors:* Jack Foley,* Pres.; Charlie Uglietto,* V.P.; Donna Hubbard, Secy.; Candy Domos,* Treas.; Christine Hubbard, Donna Hubbard, Laurie Lentini, Connie Page, Chris Starr, Doug Sturz, Richie Wright.
EIN: 042948341
Codes: GTI

61007
Carol Mulloy Cuttle Foundation, Inc.
21 Brigham St.
Fitchburg, MA 01420 (978) 343-3072
Contact: Margaret Mulloy, Pres.

Donor(s): Margaret M. Mulloy, Mary Mulloy, Michael Mulloy, Paul X. Mulloy.
Financial data (yr. ended 03/31/01): Assets, $154,890 (M); grants paid, $32,250; expenditures, $34,758; qualifying distributions, $33,854.
Application information: Application form not required.
Officers: Paul X. Mulloy, C.E.O.; Margaret Mulloy, Pres.; Mary Mulloy, Clerk; Michael Mulloy, Exec. Dir.
EIN: 046811221

61008
Pettee-Chace Memorial Scholarship Fund
c/o E.E. Wiesner, Jr.
P.O. Box 694
Sandwich, MA 02563-0694
Application address: 309 Main St., Brockton, MA 02401, tel.: (508) 586-0399
Contact: Thomas Sampson, Pres.

Financial data (yr. ended 12/31/01): Assets, $147,371 (M); grants paid, $14,000; gifts received, $7,673; expenditures, $15,845; qualifying distributions, $14,000.
Limitations: Giving limited to residents of Brockton, MA.
Application information: Application form required.
Officers: Thomas Sampson, Pres.; E. Edwin Wiesner, Jr., Treas.; David W. Curtis, Clerk.
Trustees: David P. Frennette, Christos Giannaros, Maria LeFort, Mark E. Linde, Jonathan Parker.
EIN: 223051579
Codes: GTI

61009
Michael and Annette Miller Charitable Trust
199 Temple St.
Newton, MA 02465 (617) 332-8430
Contact: Michael Miller, Tr., or Annette Miller, Tr.

Established in 1998 in MA.
Donor(s): Michael A. Miller, Annette Miller.
Financial data (yr. ended 12/31/00): Assets, $143,986 (M); grants paid, $285,203; expenditures, $288,108; qualifying distributions, $285,000.
Limitations: Giving primarily in MA.
Application information: Application form not required.
Trustees: Annette Miller, Michael Miller.
EIN: 046868567

Codes: FD

61010
Robert J. Cantin and Pat Ryan Cantin Foundation
696 Quinobequin Rd.
Waban, MA 02468-2117

Established in 1997 in MA.
Donor(s): Robert J. Cantin.
Financial data (yr. ended 12/31/99): Assets, $142,573 (M); grants paid, $6,375; gifts received, $50,363; expenditures, $9,220; qualifying distributions, $6,375.
Limitations: Applications not accepted.
Application information: Contributes only to pre-selected organizations.
Trustees: Patricia Ryan Cantin, Robert J. Cantin.
EIN: 043402805

61011
Trust in Diversity
c/o Peckham, Lobel, Casey, Prince & Tye
150 Federal, 14th Fl.
Boston, MA 02110-1726

Established in 1994 in MA.
Donor(s): John R. Bemis, Charlotte H. Bemis.
Financial data (yr. ended 07/31/99): Assets, $139,861 (M); grants paid, $51,700; gifts received, $129,000; expenditures, $54,094; qualifying distributions, $51,715.
Trustees: Charlotte H. Bemis, John R. Bemis, Thomas E. Peckham, and 4 additional trustees.
EIN: 046747335

61012
Private Colleges and Universities Foundation
2 Lan Dr., Ste. 100
Westford, MA 01886
Contact: Paul D. Adams, Tr.

Established in 1989 in MA.
Donor(s): Private Colleges and Universities Magazine.
Financial data (yr. ended 12/31/99): Assets, $137,537 (M); grants paid, $6,000; expenditures, $6,000; qualifying distributions, $6,000.
Limitations: Giving on a national basis.
Application information: Application form required.
Trustees: Paul D. Adams, Owen E. Landon, Jr.
EIN: 061280421
Codes: GTI

61013
Somerset Club Charitable Trust
42 Beacon St.
Boston, MA 02108-3694 (617) 227-1731
Contact: Richard Boardman, Tr.

Classified as a private operating foundation in 1974.
Financial data (yr. ended 03/31/99): Assets, $134,761 (M); grants paid, $8,000; gifts received, $6,039; expenditures, $8,940; qualifying distributions, $7,899.
Limitations: Giving primarily in MA.
Trustees: Richard Boardman, Francis Lowell Coolidge, Richard Lee Tucker.
EIN: 046112332

61014
Matthew B. Friary Scholarship Fund
790 Norton Ave.
Taunton, MA 02780

Financial data (yr. ended 12/31/00): Assets, $133,500 (M); grants paid, $6,000; gifts received, $7,500; expenditures, $6,000; qualifying distributions, $6,000.

Limitations: Giving limited to residents of Taunton, MA.
Application information: Unsolicited request for funds not accepted.
Trustees: Brian Friary, Kevin Friary, Marlene Friary.
EIN: 043199847

61015
Goessel Family Foundation, Inc.
73 Hawthorne St.
Lenox, MA 01240
Contact: William W. Goessel, Pres.

Established in 1997 in MA.
Donor(s): Mr. Goessel, Mrs. Goessel.
Financial data (yr. ended 12/31/01): Assets, $132,342 (M); grants paid, $16,000; expenditures, $19,607; qualifying distributions, $18,005.
Limitations: Giving primarily in MD.
Application information: Application form not required.
Officers and Trustees:* William W. Goessel,* Pres. and Treas.; Nancy C. Goessel,* V.P. and Clerk; Traey K. Goessel, M.D., Christine G. Shore, Berkshire Bank.
EIN: 043369620

61016
The Anderson Foundation, Inc.
c/o Beverly Alexandre
149 Russell Ln.
Abington, MA 02351-1251

Classified as a private operating foundation in 1989.
Financial data (yr. ended 12/31/00): Assets, $129,712 (M); grants paid, $0; gifts received, $20,500; expenditures, $24,204; qualifying distributions, $24,119; giving activities include $22,963 for programs.
Officers and Directors:* Beverly Alexandre,* Pres. and Treas.; Karen Anderson,* Clerk.
EIN: 222368613

61017
Grace Makepeace Trust for Historic Preservation
P.O. Box 593
Monson, MA 01057

Established in 2000 in MA.
Financial data (yr. ended 12/31/01): Assets, $119,835 (M); grants paid, $4,369; gifts received, $3,338; expenditures, $7,190; qualifying distributions, $4,369.
Officers and Trustees:* Emmaladd Shepard,* Pres.; Susan S. Ford,* Treas.; Mary Louise Brewer, Edward S. Harrison, Dennis S. Swierad.
EIN: 043534914

61018
Nancy Patch Retirement Home, Inc.
(Formerly Leominster Home for Old Ladies, Inc.)
16 Pearl St.
Leominster, MA 01453-5684

Financial data (yr. ended 10/31/01): Assets, $119,186 (M); grants paid, $0; expenditures, $43,663; qualifying distributions, $0.
Officers and Directors:* Jane Doyle, Pres.; Patti Harris,* Treas.; Libby Philbin,* Clerk; Joseph Love, Richard Miles, and 16 additional directors.
EIN: 042104383

61019
Mathew H. Stauffer Foundation
154 Beacon St., Ste. 4
Boston, MA 02116

Classified as a private operating foundation in 2000.

Donor(s): Hoff Stauffer.
Financial data (yr. ended 12/31/01): Assets, $115,908 (M); grants paid, $14,775; expenditures, $14,775; qualifying distributions, $14,775.
Limitations: Applications not accepted.
Application information: Contributes only to pre-selected organizations.
Director: Hoff Stauffer.
EIN: 061563439

61020
Pluvia, Inc.
c/o Richard W. Stimets
23 Oakencroft Rd.
Wellesley, MA 02482   (781) 235-7621

Classified as a private operating foundation in 1995.
Donor(s): Richard W. Stimets.
Financial data (yr. ended 12/31/00): Assets, $108,915 (M); grants paid, $0; gifts received, $64,500; expenditures, $68,187; qualifying distributions, $67,035; giving activities include $67,096 for programs.
Officer: Richard W. Stimets, Ph.D., Pres. and Treas.
Directors: Frank Colby, Ph.D., Mark F. Murphy, Chuen Wong, Ph.D.
EIN: 043245998

61021
Hinsdale Volunteer Firemen's Association, Inc.
Maple St.
Hinsdale, MA 01235

Financial data (yr. ended 06/30/00): Assets, $105,547 (M); grants paid, $5,394; gifts received, $52,374; expenditures, $91,122; qualifying distributions, $34,893; giving activities include $34,893 for programs.
Officers: Larry E. Turner, Pres.; Ralph Cormier, 1st V.P.; David Olds, 2nd V.P.; Nancy Daniels, Secy.; William Pike, Treas.
EIN: 223116934

61022
David E. Smith Trust
P.O. Box 331
Rowley, MA 01969

Financial data (yr. ended 12/31/01): Assets, $100,054 (M); grants paid, $0; expenditures, $6,451; qualifying distributions, $0.
Limitations: Applications not accepted.
Officers: Nicholas George, Chair.; Aldene E. Gordon, Clerk; Geneva Melry, Treas.
EIN: 046410673

61023
James J. Cannon Scholarship Foundation
685 Main St.
Waltham, MA 02451
Application address: c/o Waltham High School, 617 Lexington St., Waltham, MA 02154, tel.: (781) 893-8050
Contact: Margatet Boyajian, Dir. of Pupil Services

Financial data (yr. ended 12/31/00): Assets, $92,781 (M); grants paid, $3,000; gifts received, $15,448; expenditures, $3,303; qualifying distributions, $3,142.
Limitations: Giving limited to Waltham, MA.
Application information: Application form required.
Trustees: Catherine A. Cannon, Laura Cannon-Ordile, John J. Daddona, Clare J. Hanley, Isabel Talanian.
EIN: 046529616

61024
Richard I. Johnson Family Foundation
c/o Richard Johnson
124 Chestnut Hill Rd.
Chestnut Hill, MA 02467-1310

Classified as a private operating foundation around 1962.
Donor(s): Richard I. Johnson.
Financial data (yr. ended 12/31/00): Assets, $91,999 (M); grants paid, $17,619; expenditures, $21,563; qualifying distributions, $17,534.
Limitations: Applications not accepted. Giving primarily in MA.
Application information: Contributes only to pre-selected organizations.
Trustees: Richard I. Johnson, Richard A. Kimball, Sally Weld Lurie.
EIN: 046043460

61025
David G. Mugar Foundation, Inc.
222 Berkeley St.
Boston, MA 02116-3763

Established in 1951.
Donor(s): David G. Mugar, Marian G. Mugar,‡ Stephen P. Mugar.‡
Financial data (yr. ended 09/30/99): Assets, $89,352 (M); grants paid, $60,222; expenditures, $60,589; qualifying distributions, $60,589.
Limitations: Applications not accepted. Giving primarily in Boston, MA.
Application information: Contributes only to pre-selected organizations.
Officers and Directors:* David G. Mugar,* Pres.; George Tuttle, Clerk; David T. Ting,* Treas.; Jennifer Mugar Flaherty, C.P. Jorgenson, Jonathan W.G. Mugar, Peter S. Mugar.
EIN: 042587530

61026
Perry N. Finley Foundation, Ltd.
10 Noyes Pl.
Boston, MA 02113

Financial data (yr. ended 12/31/01): Assets, $88,548 (M); grants paid, $0; expenditures, $9,128; qualifying distributions, $2,520; giving activities include $2,490 for programs.
Officers and Directors:* T.J.N. Finley,* Chair. and V.P.; Brian K. Zuzga,* Pres.; James J. Finley,* V.P. and Treas.; Keith Mackay,* V.P. and Clerk; Lyman C. Opie,* V.P.; Michael J. Regan,* V.P.; Amy Weaver-Johnson,* V.P.; Mansa A. Zuzga,* V.P.; Hannelore Finley,* Secy.
EIN: 043279823

61027
Chartres Institute, Inc.
4 Sewall St.
Marblehead, MA 01945

Established in 1998 in DE and MA.
Donor(s): Arthur Burns.
Financial data (yr. ended 12/31/01): Assets, $85,950 (M); grants paid, $0; gifts received, $5,000; expenditures, $20,737; qualifying distributions, $0.
Officers and Trustees:* Arthur Burns,* Pres.; Patricia Hoehn,* V.P.
EIN: 043395288

61028
HMR Health Foundation Charitable Trust
59 Temple Pl., Ste. 704
Boston, MA 02111   (617) 357-9876
Contact: Lawrence T.P. Stifler, Tr.

Established around 1990.

Financial data (yr. ended 12/31/99): Assets, $81,671 (M); grants paid, $6,328; expenditures, $6,406; qualifying distributions, $6,328.
Trustee: Lawrence T.P. Stifler.
EIN: 110029086

61029
Meg Brady/TJX Charitable Foundation
770 Cochituate Rd.
Framingham, MA 01701
Contact: Liz de Villafranca, Treas.

Established in 1998 in MA.
Donor(s): Steve Brady, Jane Brady.
Financial data (yr. ended 07/31/01): Assets, $81,384 (M); grants paid, $1,000; gifts received, $300; expenditures, $3,058; qualifying distributions, $1,000.
Officers and Directors:* Paul Lemire,* Pres.; Steve Brady,* Clerk; Liz De Villafranca,* Treas.; Jack Brady, Jane Brady, Paul Butka, Gary Davis, Barbara Tully.
EIN: 043440128

61030
National Youth Sports Safety Foundation, Inc.
(Formerly National Youth Sports Foundation for the Prevention of Athletic Injuries, Inc.)
1 Beacon St., Ste. 3333
Boston, MA 02108

Established in 1988 in MA.
Financial data (yr. ended 12/31/01): Assets, $78,720 (M); grants paid, $0; gifts received, $5,522; expenditures, $27,320; qualifying distributions, $17,111; giving activities include $24,320 for programs.
Limitations: Giving primarily in Boston, MA.
Officers: Michelle Klein, Pres.; Rita Glassman, Clerk; Jeffrey Glassman, Treas.
EIN: 043014030

61031
Ipswich Shellfish Foundation
8 Hayward St.
Ipswich, MA 01938   (978) 356-4371
Contact: Chrissi Pappas, Pres.

Established in 1998 in MA; Classified as a company-sponsored operating foundation in 1999.
Donor(s): Ipswich Shellfish Company, Inc., Ipswich Lobster Co., Inc., Maine Shellfish Co., Inc., United Shellfish Co., Inc.
Financial data (yr. ended 12/31/01): Assets, $75,856 (M); grants paid, $5,022; expenditures, $5,625; qualifying distributions, $5,022.
Limitations: Giving limited to residents of Ipswich, MA.
Application information: Application form required.
Directors: Chrissi Pappas,* Pres.; Peter G. Mandragouras, Edward Michon.
EIN: 043412318

61032
Kira Institute, Inc.
22 Orchard St.
Amherst, MA 01002-2516

Financial data (yr. ended 12/31/01): Assets, $74,123 (M); grants paid, $0; gifts received, $127,660; expenditures, $100,252; qualifying distributions, $98,623; giving activities include $25,872 for programs.
Officers and Directors:* Piet Hut,* Pres.; Steven Tainer,* Clerk; Arthur Zajonc,* Treas.
EIN: 043401660

61033
Cadenhead-Walters Charitable Foundation
846 Sudbury Rd.
Concord, MA 01742-2841

Established in 1994.
Donor(s): Lauren J. Walters.
Financial data (yr. ended 10/31/99): Assets, $73,588 (M); grants paid, $9,300; expenditures, $9,602; qualifying distributions, $9,300.
Limitations: Applications not accepted.
Trustees: Karen A. Cadenhead, Lauren J. Walters.
EIN: 436526278

61034
The Anita Howe-Waxman Foundation, Inc.
119 Undermountain Rd.
Lenox, MA 01240

Established in 1994 in MA.
Donor(s): Anita Howe-Waxman.
Financial data (yr. ended 09/30/00): Assets, $72,830 (M); grants paid, $45,500; gifts received, $5,032; expenditures, $122,075; qualifying distributions, $44,798.
Limitations: Applications not accepted. Giving primarily in MA.
Application information: Contributes only to pre-selected organizations.
Officers: Anita Howe-Waxman, Pres.; Joelle Anderson, V.P.; Jennifer Howe, V.P.; Alexis Waxman, V.P.; Samuel E. Bain, Jr., Clerk; Kathleen Ragusa, Treas.
Director: Andrew R. Menard.
EIN: 043255244

61035
Lancaster Social Service Association
c/o Henry Richter
36 Neck Rd.
Lancaster, MA 01523

Financial data (yr. ended 03/31/02): Assets, $72,187 (M); grants paid, $0; expenditures, $16,656; qualifying distributions, $0.
Officers: Anne Stadherr, V.P.; Sandra Vincent, Secy.; Henry Richter, Treas.
EIN: 042104376

61036
Phyllis G. Redstone Charitable Foundation
c/o Nutter, McClennen & Fish, LLP
P.O. Box 1400
Boston, MA 02205-1400

Established in 2000 in MA.
Donor(s): Phyllis G. Redstone.
Financial data (yr. ended 01/31/01): Assets, $70,073 (M); grants paid, $30,000; gifts received, $100,100; expenditures, $30,027; qualifying distributions, $30,027.
Limitations: Applications not accepted. Giving primarily in Boston, MA.
Application information: Contributes only to pre-selected organizations.
Trustee: Phyllis G. Redstone.
EIN: 043529807

61037
The Goldin Foundation for Excellence in Education
27 Petrini Cir.
Needham, MA 02492
Contact: Harriet K. Goldin, Pres.

Established in 1990 in MA.
Donor(s): Harriet K. Goldin, Marshall J. Goldin.
Financial data (yr. ended 12/31/99): Assets, $63,482 (M); grants paid, $3,000; gifts received, $4,200; expenditures, $3,258; qualifying distributions, $3,226.
Limitations: Giving primarily in Natick, MA.
Officers: Harriet K. Goldin, Pres.; Marshall J. Goldin, Treas.
EIN: 043090548

61038
Alzheimer Research Forum Foundation
82 Devonshire St.
Boston, MA 02109

Established in 1997 in MA.
Financial data (yr. ended 12/31/01): Assets, $62,862 (M); grants paid, $0; gifts received, $540,436; expenditures, $558,046; qualifying distributions, $540,864; giving activities include $543,919 for programs.
Officers and Directors:* Edward C. Johnson,* Pres.; Anne-Marie Soulliere,* V.P.; Patricia R. Hurley,* Secy.; Richard G. Weidmann,* Treas.
EIN: 043382717

61039
Worcester Institute for Student Exchange
159 Highland St.
Worcester, MA 01609
Contact: Charles D. Hanson

Donor(s): Charles D. Harson.
Financial data (yr. ended 09/30/00): Assets, $62,519 (L); grants paid, $100; gifts received, $37,090; expenditures, $34,587; qualifying distributions, $5,036; giving activities include $5,036 for programs.
Limitations: Giving for the benefit of Eastern Europeans studying in the U.S.
Trustees: Charles D. Hanson, M.D., Joseph Inglefinger, Sean Johnson, Paul Pradelyi, M.D.
EIN: 043139523

61040
The Danny Foundation for Autism
119 Glendale Rd.
Sharon, MA 02067 (781) 784-7022
Contact: Janet Abrahamson, Tr.

Established in 1999.
Financial data (yr. ended 12/31/01): Assets, $62,134 (M); grants paid, $3,030; expenditures, $3,530; qualifying distributions, $3,023.
Trustees: Janet Abrahamson, Valerie L. Abrahamson.
EIN: 043426612

61041
The Linda Loring Nature Foundation, Inc.
P.O. Box 1359, 90 Eel Point Rd.
Nantucket, MA 02554

Established in 1999 in MA.
Financial data (yr. ended 12/31/99): Assets, $60,000 (M); grants paid, $0; gifts received, $60,000; expenditures, $0; qualifying distributions, $0.
Limitations: Applications not accepted.
Application information: Contributes only to pre-selected organizations.
Officer and Directors:* Linda Loring,* Pres. and Treas.; Marsha Gardner Cook, Neil Sheridan.
EIN: 043496738

61042
National Coalition for Child Protection Reform, Inc.
1620 Massachusetts Ave.
Lexington, MA 02421

Established in 1997.
Donor(s): Open Society Institute, Edna McConnell Clark, Adco Foundation, Inc., Redleaf Foundation.
Financial data (yr. ended 12/31/99): Assets, $54,226 (M); grants paid, $0; gifts received, $79,500; expenditures, $88,258; qualifying distributions, $88,248; giving activities include $12,353 for programs.
Officers: Carolyn Kubitschek, Pres.; Joanne C. Fray, Clerk; Elizabeth W. Vorenberg, Treas.
Directors: Annette Ruth Appell, Ira Burnim, Martin Guggenhiem, Martha Matthews, Diane Redleaf.
EIN: 043156354

61043
Turimiquire Foundation, Inc.
c/o William W. Bloomstein
33 Richdale Ave., Ste. 213
Cambridge, MA 02140

Established in 1996 in PA.
Financial data (yr. ended 12/31/00): Assets, $53,929 (M); grants paid, $0; gifts received, $50,475; expenditures, $45,632; qualifying distributions, $0.
Officers and Trustees:* Steven Bloomstein,* Pres.; William W. Bloomstein, Secy.-Treas.; Robert Albert, Jr., Emilio Berrizbeitia, Margaret R. Bledsoe, Steven Morgan, Susan Reyna, Frances Vargas-Gibbons.
EIN: 043286660

61044
Junior Development Cycling Foundation, Inc.
24 Rutledge Rd.
Belmont, MA 02478
Application address: 1 Olympic Plz., Colorado Springs, CO 80909-5775, tel.: (719) 578-4856
Contact: Steven McCauley

Established in 1997 in CT.
Donor(s): Marco Hellman, Scott Montgomery.
Financial data (yr. ended 05/31/99): Assets, $53,847 (M); grants paid, $58,800; gifts received, $99,160; expenditures, $91,796; qualifying distributions, $53,847.
Limitations: Giving primarily in Colorado Springs, CO.
Application information: Application form required.
Officers: Scott Montgomery, Pres.; Marco Hellman, V.P.; Leslie Klein, Secy.; Dan Pullman, Treas.
EIN: 061484562

61045
Boston Chapter CPCU Trust
c/o Insurance Library Assn.
156 State St.
Boston, MA 02109
Application address: c/o Paul J. McGee Associates, Inc., 65 Franklin St., Boston, MA 02110
Contact: Paul J. McGee

Donor(s): Chartered Property Casualty Underwriters Society.
Financial data (yr. ended 12/31/00): Assets, $52,906 (M); grants paid, $3,000; expenditures, $3,780; qualifying distributions, $3,780.
Limitations: Giving primarily in areas of company operations in MA.
Application information: Application form required.
Officers: James J. McRan, Pres.; Charles R. Monaghan, 1st V.P.; Thomas C. Radziewicz, 2nd V.P.; William Milaschewski, Treas.
EIN: 046392433

61046
Tell Foundation
c/o Elton M. & Lu Linda Tucker
8 Oxbow Rd.
Medfield, MA 02052

Classified as a private operating foundation in 1990 in MA.
Donor(s): Elton M. Tucker, Lu Linda Tucker.
Financial data (yr. ended 11/30/01): Assets, $51,286 (M); grants paid, $2,500; expenditures, $2,592; qualifying distributions, $2,592.
Limitations: Applications not accepted. Giving on a national basis.
Application information: Contributes only to pre-selected organizations.
Trustees: Elton M. Tucker, Lu Linda Tucker.
EIN: 046558830

61047
Masiphumelele Corporation
c/o Robert B. Maloney
585 Commericial St.
Boston, MA 02109

Established in 1999 in MA.
Donor(s): John M. Thompson, Carol J. Thompson.
Financial data (yr. ended 12/31/01): Assets, $51,188 (M); grants paid, $52,762; gifts received, $133,193; expenditures, $107,300; qualifying distributions, $36,356.
Limitations: Applications not accepted.
Application information: Contributes only to pre-selected organizations.
Officers: John M. Thompson, Pres. and Treas.; Carol J. Thompson, V.P.; Robert P. Maloney, Clerk.
EIN: 020511758

61048
Female Benevolent Society at South Danvers, Inc.
(Formerly South Danvers Benevolent Society)
93 Central St.
Peabody, MA 01960
Contact: Sheila Kelley, Treas.

Established in 1987 in MA.
Financial data (yr. ended 04/30/00): Assets, $49,787 (M); grants paid, $4,056; gifts received, $20; expenditures, $4,464; qualifying distributions, $4,056.
Limitations: Giving limited to residents of Peabody, MA.
Officers and Directors:* Mary Stockwell,* Pres.; Nancy Holuck,* V.P.; Gladys Broughton,* Secy.; Sheila Kelley,* Treas.
EIN: 046041354

61049
North East Roofing Educational Foundation, Inc.
1400 Hancock St., 7th Fl.
Quincy, MA 02169-5203 (617) 472-5590
Contact: Kimberly Hurley

Classified as a company-sponsored operating foundation.
Donor(s): National Roofing Contractors Association.
Financial data (yr. ended 06/30/01): Assets, $48,875 (M); grants paid, $6,000; gifts received, $47,320; expenditures, $91,754; qualifying distributions, $84,246.
Limitations: Giving primarily on the East Coast.
Application information: Only NERCA applications accepted. Application form required.
Officers: Stephen McBrady, Chair.; Paul Cappello, Vice-Chair.; Robert W. Therrien, Jr., Treas.; Thomas Gunning, Exec. Dir.
EIN: 043466803

61050
The American City Coalition, Inc.
150 Mount Vernon St., Ste. 500
Boston, MA 02125

Established in 1994 in MA.
Donor(s): Joseph E. Corcoran.
Financial data (yr. ended 12/31/01): Assets, $48,115 (M); grants paid, $0; gifts received, $333,542; expenditures, $322,468; qualifying distributions, $322,468; giving activities include $322,468 for programs.
Officer: Vincent Paul Deare, Exec. Dir.
EIN: 043243095

61051
Serono Symposia USA, Inc.
100 Longwater Cir.
Norwell, MA 02061

Established in 1995 in MA as a company-sponsored operating foundation.
Donor(s): Serono Laboratories, Inc.
Financial data (yr. ended 12/31/99): Assets, $47,806 (M); grants paid, $55,000; gifts received, $836,500; expenditures, $1,328,025; qualifying distributions, $918,388; giving activities include $441,653 for programs.
Limitations: Applications not accepted.
Application information: Contributes only to pre-selected organizations.
Officers: Leslie Nies, Pres.; Ellen Rosenberg, Clerk; Martin Joyce, Treas.
Directors: Ernesto Bertarelli, Silvano Fumero, Hishram Samra.
EIN: 043258437
Codes: CD

61052
Life Studies Foundation, Inc.
382 Hammond St.
Chestnut Hill, MA 02467
Application address: 1581 Beacon St., Brookline, MA 02146, tel.: (617) 566-6555
Contact: Marjorie Daner

Established in 1984 in MA.
Financial data (yr. ended 08/31/99): Assets, $44,238 (M); grants paid, $0; gifts received, $4,000; expenditures, $84,227; qualifying distributions, $83,753; giving activities include $57,094 for programs.
Application information: Application form required.
Officers and Director:* Shera Samaraweera,* Pres.; Albert Samaraweera, Clerk; Joseph S. Micallef, Treas.
Trustees: Elliot L. Atamian, Eleanor M. Hackett.
EIN: 222546889

61053
Salvatore & Grace Rocco Charitable Trust
47 Webster St.
Everett, MA 02149-2821 (617) 387-9098
Contact: Virginia L. Fiske, Tr.

Financial data (yr. ended 12/31/01): Assets, $43,704 (M); grants paid, $1,625; expenditures, $3,258; qualifying distributions, $3,258.
Limitations: Giving primarily in Everett, MA.
Trustee: Virginia L. Fiske.
EIN: 237416890

61054
Kenneth A. Harding Foundation
c/o Richard J. Monahan
15 Church St.
Waltham, MA 02452-5501
Application address: c/o Waltham High School, Waltham, MA 02452
Contact: Margaret Boyajian, Tr.

Financial data (yr. ended 12/31/01): Assets, $43,212 (M); grants paid, $6,000; expenditures, $7,885; qualifying distributions, $6,000.
Limitations: Giving limited to Waltham, MA.
Application information: Application form required.
Trustees: Margaret Boyajian, Scott Bundy, William Foley, John Graceffa, Kenneth A. Harding, Richard J. Monahan.
EIN: 237347785

61055
Koster Insurance Scholarship Fund, Inc.
c/o Koster Insurance Agency, Inc.
1515 Hancock St.
Quincy, MA 02169
URL: http://www.kosterins.com/scholarship.htm

Established in 2000 in MA. Classified as a company-sponsored operating foundation in 2001.
Donor(s): Koster Insurance Agency, Inc.
Financial data (yr. ended 12/31/01): Assets, $42,282 (M); grants paid, $3,750; gifts received, $30,000; expenditures, $7,765; qualifying distributions, $7,766.
Limitations: Giving primarily to residents of MA.
Application information: Application form required.
Officer and Directors:* Teresa K. Koster,* Pres. and Secy.-Treas.; Michelle Bowdler, Clantha Carrigan-McCurdy, Richard Langerman, Roger Sullivan.
EIN: 043542547
Codes: CD

61056
Miracles and Magic Foundation, Inc.
100 Stockwell Dr.
Avon, MA 02322-1108

Established in 1999 in MA.
Financial data (yr. ended 12/31/01): Assets, $40,795 (M); grants paid, $0; gifts received, $107,577; expenditures, $72,207; qualifying distributions, $0.
Limitations: Applications not accepted.
Application information: Contributes only to pre-selected organizations.
Officers and Directors:* June Tatelman,* Pres.; Eliot Tatelman,* Clerk and Treas.
EIN: 043472643

61057
Jack and Eva Medzorian Foundation
8 Berkshire Dr.
Winchester, MA 01890

Established in 2000.
Donor(s): Jack Medzorian.
Financial data (yr. ended 12/31/00): Assets, $40,145 (M); grants paid, $1,350; gifts received, $38,291; expenditures, $1,350; qualifying distributions, $1,350.
Limitations: Applications not accepted.
Application information: Contributes only to pre-selected organizations.
Trustees: Jack Medzorian, Eva Medzorian, John Medzorian.
EIN: 046924174

61058
Blackey Family Foundation, Inc.
586 Depot Rd.
Boxboro, MA 01719
Contact: I. Katherine Blackey, Pres.

Established in 1999 in MA.
Donor(s): Harry H. Blackey.
Financial data (yr. ended 12/31/01): Assets, $40,105 (M); grants paid, $11,115; gifts received, $20,050; expenditures, $11,817; qualifying distributions, $11,115.
Limitations: Giving primarily in MA.
Officers and Directors:* I. Katherine Blackey,* Pres.; Harry H. Blackey,* Clerk and Treas.; Carrie A. Blackey, Carrie E. Blackey, Dean R. Blackey.
EIN: 043453516

61059
The Cheswatyr Foundation, Inc.
51 Jerusalem Rd.
Tyringham, MA 01264

Established in 1996 in MA.
Donor(s): Herbert Wasserman.‡
Financial data (yr. ended 12/31/01): Assets, $40,078 (M); grants paid, $15,858; gifts received, $41,843; expenditures, $16,314; qualifying distributions, $15,858.
Limitations: Giving primarily in MA.
Officers and Directors:* Cecille Wasserman,* Pres.; Emily Wasserman, Treas.; Charlotte Berkowitz, Michael Schiffer, Wendy Wasserman.
EIN: 043328552

61060
Fund for Civic Solutions, Inc.
76 Rowe St.
Auburndale, MA 02466-1530 (617) 969-4200
Contact: Richard L. Weinberg, Pres.

Established in 1999 in MA.
Donor(s): Richard L. Weinberg, Committee on Crimes Against Retailing Community.
Financial data (yr. ended 12/31/01): Assets, $40,027 (M); grants paid, $2,250; expenditures, $2,912; qualifying distributions, $2,250.
Limitations: Giving primarily in the Boston, MA, area.
Officers and Directors:* Richard L. Weinberg,* Pres.; Carol C. Weinberg,* Treas.; David L. Weinberg, Richard L. Weinberg, Jr.
EIN: 043469402

61061
The Thomas Berry Foundation
c/o Hale and Dorr, LLP
60 State St.
Boston, MA 02109

Established in 1999 in DC.
Donor(s): Margaret Berry.
Financial data (yr. ended 12/31/99): Assets, $37,667 (M); grants paid, $12,500; gifts received, $50,101; expenditures, $12,545; qualifying distributions, $12,423.
Limitations: Applications not accepted.
Application information: Contributes only to pre-selected organizations.
Trustees: Margaret Berry, Thomas Berry, John Grim, Mary Evelyn Tucker.
EIN: 522149696

61062
Julia Child Foundation for Gastronomy and the Culinary Arts
1 International Pl., 21st Fl.
Boston, MA 02110-2600

Established in 1996 in MA.
Donor(s): Julia Child.
Financial data (yr. ended 12/31/00): Assets, $37,586 (M); grants paid, $5,000; gifts received, $11,334; expenditures, $5,678; qualifying distributions, $5,022.
Limitations: Applications not accepted. Giving primarily in MA.
Application information: Contributes only to pre-selected organizations.
Trustees: Julia Child, William A. Truslow.
EIN: 043294783

61063
Native American Cultures & Crafts Trust
45 Hubbard St.
Concord, MA 01742

Established in 1978 in MA.
Donor(s): Septimus Foundation II.
Financial data (yr. ended 12/31/01): Assets, $36,751 (M); grants paid, $0; gifts received, $15,000; expenditures, $4,845; qualifying distributions, $4,811.
Trustees: John Todd Crocker, Henri H. Vaillencourt.
EIN: 042614067

61064
Marc Ernest Pallotta Foundation, Inc.
579 Millbury St.
Worcester, MA 01610 (508) 753-2115

Established in 1995 in DE and MA.
Donor(s): Ernest J. Pallotta.
Financial data (yr. ended 12/31/99): Assets, $36,478 (M); grants paid, $5,398; gifts received, $158; expenditures, $6,276; qualifying distributions, $6,205.
Limitations: Applications not accepted. Giving limited to residents of central MA.
Application information: Recipients are selected by secondary school principals and teachers.
Officers: Christopher D. Pallotta, Pres.; Marie K. Pallotta, Secy.; Adam Pelka, Treas.
EIN: 223351769

61065
Rocky Marciano Foundation, Inc.
8 Calypso Dr.
Brockton, MA 02301 (508) 587-1988
Contact: Joseph M. Picanzi, Treas.

Financial data (yr. ended 12/31/99): Assets, $34,744 (M); grants paid, $750; expenditures, $1,220; qualifying distributions, $1,220.
Limitations: Giving primarily in Brockton, MA.
Officers: Peter Marciano, Pres.; Ann DeMarco, V.P.; Betty Colombo, Secy.; Joseph M. Picanzi, Treas.
EIN: 042719968

61066
Ruth Brown Memorial Scholarship
(Formerly Ruth E. Brown Scholarship Fund)
108 W. Main St.
Georgetown, MA 01833-1523

Classified as a private operating foundation in 1990.
Financial data (yr. ended 12/31/01): Assets, $34,277 (M); grants paid, $2,000; gifts received, $572; expenditures, $2,035; qualifying distributions, $2,035.
Limitations: Giving limited to Georgetown, MA.
Officer and Trustees:* James H. Boynton, Jr.,* Secy.; Carolyn M. Boynton, Herbert T. MacDonald, Robert P. Rudolph, Ronald E. Spofford, Jr.
EIN: 042983704

61067
Value Mortgage Foundation
c/o Narendra Kapadia
11 Eldorado Rd.
Chelmsford, MA 01824-4410

Established in 1999 in MA.
Donor(s): Narendra Kapadia.
Financial data (yr. ended 12/31/00): Assets, $32,506 (M); grants paid, $10,600; gifts received, $10,000; expenditures, $10,720; qualifying distributions, $10,600.
Limitations: Giving primarily in India.
Director: Narendra Kapadia.
EIN: 043443031

61068
James A. Lobban Memorial Education Fund
c/o Yvette B. Cloutier
Bartlett High School
Webster, MA 01570-2401 (508) 943-8552
Contact: Yvette B. Cloutier, Treas.

Financial data (yr. ended 12/31/01): Assets, $32,085 (M); grants paid, $1,000; expenditures, $1,228; qualifying distributions, $1,000.
Application information: Application form required.
Officers: Ann Lada, Pres.; Richard Lobban, Jr., V.P.; Norman Deptula, Secy.; Yvette B. Cloutier, Treas.
EIN: 046115580

61069
Noah's Farm Educational Foundation, Inc.
23 Conant Rd.
Lincoln, MA 01773

Established in 1998 in MA.
Donor(s): Helen Milligan, Julia Summers.
Financial data (yr. ended 12/31/99): Assets, $30,000 (M); grants paid, $0; gifts received, $50,685; expenditures, $20,685; qualifying distributions, $0.
Officers and Directors:* Julia Summers,* Pres. and Treas.; James Summers, Jr.,* Secy.; Janet Milligan.
EIN: 043446267

61070
Lothropp Family Foundation, Inc.
c/o Elaine Baptlett
P.O. Box 462
Barnstable, MA 02630

Classified as a private operating foundation in 1992.
Financial data (yr. ended 12/31/00): Assets, $29,100 (M); grants paid, $1,010; expenditures, $3,849; qualifying distributions, $4,859.
Limitations: Applications not accepted. Giving on an international basis.
Application information: Contributes only to pre-selected organizations.
Officers and Directors:* Bruce D. Lathrop, Pres.; Sally MacVane, V.P.; Gary Enersen,* Secy.; Elaine Bartlett,* Treas.; Hope Baker Burley, Charles Lothropp, Rev. Donald Lothropp, George Lothropp, Helen Lothrop Taber.
EIN: 382904056

61071
Burke Mathes Family Foundation II
88 Pinckney St.
Boston, MA 02114-3308

Established in 1981.
Donor(s): Burke Mathes, Barbara Mathes.
Financial data (yr. ended 12/31/99): Assets, $27,427 (M); grants paid, $5,100; expenditures, $5,505; qualifying distributions, $5,100.

Limitations: Applications not accepted. Giving primarily in MA.
Application information: Contributes only to pre-selected organizations.
Trustees: Barbara Mathes, Burke Mathes, Kristen Mathes.
EIN: 751755473

61072
Ocean State Power Uxbridge Community Foundation, Ltd.
28 Snowling Rd.
Uxbridge, MA 01569 (508) 278-6250
Contact: Sandra Gazaille Lavoie, Secy.

Classified as a private operating foundation.
Donor(s): Ocean State Power Co.
Financial data (yr. ended 12/31/00): Assets, $26,422 (M); grants paid, $18,533; gifts received, $30,000; expenditures, $19,171; qualifying distributions, $18,533.
Limitations: Giving limited to the Uxbridge, MA, area.
Officers and Directors:* John McQuade,* Pres.; Sandra Gazaille Lavoie,* Secy.; Charles Brundage,* Treas.
EIN: 110123059

61073
Pat D'Arrigo Charitable Trust
c/o Canby, Maloney & Co., Inc.
161 Worcester Rd.
Framingham, MA 01701

Established in 1992 in MA.
Donor(s): Joseph D'Arrigo.
Financial data (yr. ended 12/31/99): Assets, $25,680 (M); grants paid, $34,312; gifts received, $34,545; expenditures, $36,875; qualifying distributions, $36,865.
Limitations: Applications not accepted. Giving primarily in Boston, MA.
Application information: Contributes only to pre-selected organizations.
Trustee: Joseph D'Arrigo.
EIN: 046691599

61074
Shaun P. Scully Scholarship Fund, Inc.
22 Locust Rd.
Chelmsford, MA 01824
Application address: c/o Guidance Dept., Chelmsford High School, Chelmsford, MA 01824

Classified as a private operating foundation in 1991.
Financial data (yr. ended 12/31/01): Assets, $24,695 (M); grants paid, $2,000; gifts received, $2,126; expenditures, $2,078; qualifying distributions, $2,000.
Limitations: Giving limited to residents of Chelmsford, MA.
Application information: Application form required.
Officers and Directors:* Michael J. Scully,* Pres. and Treas.; Michael C. Scully, Clerk; Dorothy Scully, Kevin Scully.
EIN: 042880378

61075
Joe Streadwick Quincy High School Scholarship Trust
94 Hogg Memorial Dr.
Whitman, MA 02382-1867
Application address: c/o Quincy High School/Vocational-Technical School Scholarship Committee, 52 Coddington St., Quincy, MA 02169, tel.: (617) 984-8754

Financial data (yr. ended 12/31/01): Assets, $23,114 (M); grants paid, $0; expenditures, $499; qualifying distributions, $0.
Limitations: Giving limited to residents of MA.
Trustee: Frank G. Finch.
EIN: 042985942

61076
The New Horizons Project, Inc.
Kendall Sq. Station
238 Main St., Ste. 401
Cambridge, MA 02142-0003
Contact: Donald R. Sohn, Pres.

Established in 1999 in MA.
Financial data (yr. ended 12/31/01): Assets, $22,365 (M); grants paid, $0; gifts received, $500,000; expenditures, $497,710; qualifying distributions, $0.
Officers and Directors:* Donald R. Sohn,* Pres.; William A. King,* Exec. V.P.; Elena Ivonova, Exec. Dir.
EIN: 043472503

61077
Foster Charitable Trust
270 Somerset St.
Belmont, MA 02478-2012
Contact: Ruth S. Foster, Tr.

Donor(s): Ruth S. Foster.
Financial data (yr. ended 12/31/00): Assets, $20,268 (M); grants paid, $2,145; expenditures, $2,145; qualifying distributions, $1,013.
Trustee: Ruth S. Foster.
EIN: 043074556

61078
Vera Richman Memorial Library, Inc.
1 Isabell Cir.
Randolph, MA 02368

Established around 1988.
Financial data (yr. ended 12/31/99): Assets, $17,842 (M); grants paid, $3,000; expenditures, $3,440; qualifying distributions, $3,000.
Officer: R.M. Richman, Pres.
EIN: 043007589

61079
Manuel Faria, Jr. and Bemvinda A. Faria Educational Fund, Inc.
492 Hillman St.
New Bedford, MA 02740-2724
Application address: c/o Welby Law Offices, PC, 13 Ventura Dr., North Dartmouth, MA 02747
Contact: Irene F. King, Pres.

Established in 2000 in MA.
Donor(s): Irene F. King.
Financial data (yr. ended 12/31/00): Assets, $16,612 (M); grants paid, $500; expenditures, $500; qualifying distributions, $500.
Limitations: Giving primarily in New Bedford, MA.
Application information: Application form required.
Officer: Irene F. King, Pres. and Treas.
EIN: 043429907

61080
The Rainville Family Foundation Trust
50 Swanson Ln.
Carlisle, MA 01741

Established in 2000 in MA.
Donor(s): Dennis Rainville.
Financial data (yr. ended 12/31/01): Assets, $15,119 (M); grants paid, $5,000; gifts received, $5,000; expenditures, $5,785; qualifying distributions, $5,000.
Limitations: Applications not accepted.
Application information: Contributes only to pre-selected organizations.
Trustees: Dennis Rainville, Joanne Rainville.
EIN: 043527276

61081
Puritan Lawn Memorial Park Education Foundation, Inc.
185 Lake St.
Peabody, MA 01960

Established in 1999 in MA.
Financial data (yr. ended 12/31/00): Assets, $14,616 (M); grants paid, $1,000; gifts received, $7,642; expenditures, $1,021; qualifying distributions, $1,000.
Limitations: Applications not accepted.
Application information: Contributes only to pre-selected organizations.
Officers and Directors:* Lawrence J. Glynn, Jr.,* Pres.; Peter B. McKay,* Treas.; Kim A. Matvichuk.
EIN: 043379671

61082
Robert W. Haynes Foundation
221 Clifton St.
Attleboro, MA 02703

Classified as a private operating foundation in 1990.
Financial data (yr. ended 12/31/00): Assets, $13,519 (M); grants paid, $0; gifts received, $2,000; expenditures, $745; qualifying distributions, $710; giving activities include $400 for programs.
Officer: Joyce Chatfield, Chair.; Eleanor Haynes, Pres.; Susan Curra, Secy.; Mary Pineo, Treas.
Trustees: Jean Archard, Harriet Bragg, Karen Chatfield, Virginia Leach, Julie Lena, Stephanie McGuane, Barbara Pesavento.
EIN: 046621675

61083
The Children's International Adoption Project, Inc.
15 Standish Ave.
Plymouth, MA 02360

Established in 1997 in MA.
Donor(s): Nancy Y. Conant.
Financial data (yr. ended 12/31/01): Assets, $13,516 (L); grants paid, $0; expenditures, $11,958; qualifying distributions, $0.
Officer: Nancy Y. Conant, Pres.
EIN: 043328394

61084
The Humanity Foundation, Inc.
P.O. Box 2488
Vineyard Haven, MA 02568

Established in 1994 in MA.
Donor(s): Deborah B. Balis, C.W. Balis III.
Financial data (yr. ended 12/31/00): Assets, $12,363 (M); grants paid, $0; gifts received, $1,266; expenditures, $83,921; qualifying distributions, $79,080; giving activities include $79,080 for programs.
Officer: C.W. Balis III, Pres.

EIN: 223084401

61085
The Nora Theatre Company, Inc.
P.O. Box 2764
Cambridge, MA 02238

Established in 1998 in MA.
Donor(s): Mary C. Huntington.
Financial data (yr. ended 06/30/00): Assets, $11,434 (M); grants paid, $0; gifts received, $105,356; expenditures, $140,195; qualifying distributions, $104,484; giving activities include $140,195 for programs.
Officers: Mary C. Huntington, Pres.; Stephanie Troisi, Secy.-Treas.
EIN: 042997440

61086
Jewish Cultural Center, Inc.
c/o Michael S. Perlman
96 Round Hill Rd.
Northampton, MA 01060 (413) 584-9060
Contact: Michael S. Perlman, Pres.

Financial data (yr. ended 12/31/99): Assets, $9,860 (M); grants paid, $500; expenditures, $555; qualifying distributions, $500.
Limitations: Giving primarily in MA.
Officer and Directors:* Michael S. Perlman,* Pres., Clerk, and Treas.; Mark Augarten, Esther Budgar, Robert Cilman, Doris Cohen, Barbara Goldin, Chaim Gunner, Amy Leos-Urbel, Adelle Oppenheim.
EIN: 046124941

61087
The Ivy Fund
c/o Courtney Ogg-Mancuso
33 Irving St.
Waltham, MA 02451-0758

Established in 1997 in MA.
Financial data (yr. ended 08/31/00): Assets, $8,053 (M); grants paid, $200; gifts received, $289; expenditures, $1,110; qualifying distributions, $1,110.
Limitations: Applications not accepted.
Application information: Contributes only to pre-selected organizations.
Trustees: Duncan Ogg, Courtney Ogg-Mancuso.
EIN: 043392239

61088
Fund for Psychiatry, Inc.
45 Clapboardtree St.
Westwood, MA 02090 (781) 762-7764
Contact: Gary Jacobson, Pres.

Financial data (yr. ended 12/31/99): Assets, $7,557 (M); grants paid, $1,850; gifts received, $44,632; expenditures, $44,234; qualifying distributions, $1,846.
Limitations: Giving primarily in MA.
Application information: Application form required.
Officer: Gary Jacobson, M.D., Pres.
EIN: 042843646

61089
Endeavour Foundation
c/o Neal Cornell
37 Shapquit Bars Rd.
Falmouth, MA 02540

Established in 1988 in DC. Classified as a private operating foundation in 1989.
Donor(s): Mary N. Cornell, Neal W. Cornell.
Financial data (yr. ended 05/31/01): Assets, $7,554 (M); grants paid, $34,512; expenditures, $35,708; qualifying distributions, $34,512.
Limitations: Applications not accepted. Giving primarily in PA.
Application information: Contributes only to pre-selected organizations.
Officer: Donald D. Korzusko, Secy.
Trustees: Mary N. Cornell, Neal W. Cornell.
EIN: 346891521

61090
National Memorial Trust
18 Lyman St.
Westborough, MA 01581

Financial data (yr. ended 06/30/00): Assets, $7,445 (M); grants paid, $0; gifts received, $1,640; expenditures, $2,097; qualifying distributions, $2,097; giving activities include $1,269 for programs.
Trustee: Philip G. Haddad, Jr.
EIN: 223078884

61091
Friends of the Pearle L. Crawford Memorial Library, Inc.
3 Village St.
P.O. Box 33
Dudley, MA 01571

Financial data (yr. ended 12/31/99): Assets, $7,337 (M); grants paid, $0; gifts received, $2,024; expenditures, $6,076; qualifying distributions, $0; giving activities include $5,261 for programs.
Officers: Cathy Racilot, Pres. and Clerk; Kathy Sandstrom, Treas.
EIN: 043279639

61092
The Paul and Helen Mitchell Scholarship Fund, Inc.
c/o James R. Morehead
26 Manning St.
Needham Heights, MA 02494-1510
FAX: (617) 444-5152
Contact: Russell Harrington, Dir.

Established in 1974.
Financial data (yr. ended 06/30/99): Assets, $6,734 (M); grants paid, $4,500; gifts received, $5,378; expenditures, $4,918; qualifying distributions, $4,500.
Limitations: Giving primarily in IL.
Application information: Application form required.
Officers and Directors:* James R. Morehead,* Pres.; Richard Simpson,* Treas.; Bradley Binder, Joellen Binder, Gena Carter, Andrew Crouch, Catherine Crouch, Donald Doucette, Nancy Doucette, Beth Harrington, Russell Harrington, Veronica Lanier, Debbie Morehead, Jean Morehead, Mark Morehead, Marie Simpson, Lola Smith, Norman Smith, Peggy Wilber.
EIN: 222777150

61093
William J. Eisen Family Charitable Foundation
64 Fairbanks Ave.
Wellesley, MA 02481

Donor(s): A. Raymond Tye, William J. Eisen.
Financial data (yr. ended 12/31/01): Assets, $6,402 (L); grants paid, $3,565; expenditures, $3,565; qualifying distributions, $3,565.
Limitations: Applications not accepted.
Application information: Contributes only to pre-selected organizations.
Trustee: William J. Eisen.
EIN: 046835054

61094
Armenian Review, Inc.
80 Bigelow Ave.
Watertown, MA 02472-2012

Financial data (yr. ended 12/31/01): Assets, $6,040 (M); grants paid, $0; gifts received, $9,295; expenditures, $13,274; qualifying distributions, $0.
Officers: Hayg Oshagan, Pres. and Treas.; Dikran M. Kaligian, Clerk.
EIN: 222515046

61095
The Frank L. Currier Charitable Foundation
22 True Rd.
Salisbury, MA 01952 (978) 462-5337
Contact: Janice C. Morse, Tr.

Established in 1999 in MA.
Donor(s): Frank L. Currier.
Financial data (yr. ended 12/31/99): Assets, $5,005 (M); grants paid, $125; gifts received, $5,000; expenditures, $175; qualifying distributions, $175.
Trustee: Janice C. Morse.
EIN: 046889522

61096
Microscope Associates, Inc.
c/o Elizabeth F. Martin
50 Village Ave.
Dedham, MA 02026-4209

Donor(s): Frederick W. Martin.
Financial data (yr. ended 06/30/00): Assets, $4,900 (M); grants paid, $0; gifts received, $2,300; expenditures, $1,969; qualifying distributions, $1,969; giving activities include $1,473 for programs.
Officers: Frederick W. Martin, Pres.; Elizabeth F. Martin, Treas.
Directors: Keith W. Jones, Frank A. Leith, Thomas Synott.
EIN: 042653536

61097
Sanders Christian Foundation, Inc.
33 Baker Ave.
South Hamilton, MA 01982

Financial data (yr. ended 12/31/01): Assets, $4,828 (M); grants paid, $170; gifts received, $921; expenditures, $17,562; qualifying distributions, $170.
Limitations: Applications not accepted.
Officers: John Sanders, Pres.; Richard Lovelace, V.P.
Director: John Sanders.
EIN: 041558830

61098
Bournewood Educational Foundation, Inc.
300 South St.
Chestnut Hill, MA 02467-3694

Established in 1998 in MA.
Financial data (yr. ended 12/31/01): Assets, $4,804 (M); grants paid, $7,500; gifts received, $9,700; expenditures, $7,550; qualifying distributions, $7,500.
Limitations: Applications not accepted. Giving primarily in MA, NH, OH, RI, and VA.
Trustees: Nasir A. Khan, Phillip A. Mason, Malcolm L. Rosenblatt, Edward L. Zarsley.
EIN: 043404422

61099
Vision Research Institute, Inc.
102 Maple St.
Lexington, MA 02420-2544

Established in 1998 in MA.
Financial data (yr. ended 12/31/01): Assets, $4,478 (M); grants paid, $0; gifts received, $4,900; expenditures, $4,183; qualifying distributions, $0.
Officers and Directors:* Ram L.P. Vimal,* Pres.; Rita Pandey,* V.P. and Treas.; C.K. Pandey, Krishna Pandey, Kunti Pandey, S.L. Pandey, K.D. Pandey Pendramp.
EIN: 043292597

61100
H. L. Farmer & Sons Aftercare Program, Inc.
106 Summer St.
Haverhill, MA 01830

Established in 1997.
Donor(s): H.L. Farmer & Sons, Inc.
Financial data (yr. ended 12/31/99): Assets, $3,497 (M); grants paid, $0; gifts received, $33,125; expenditures, $32,846; qualifying distributions, $7,382; giving activities include $32,846 for programs.
Officers and Directors:* Duncan C. Farmer,* Pres. and Treas.; Jason S. Cohen, Clerk; Richard A. Barry, Brenda Farmer, Nancy Thornton.
EIN: 043269493

61101
Clifford S. Bonney Charitable Trust
c/o Connolly & Connolly
P.O. Box 332
Newburyport, MA 01950 (978) 462-2251

Established in 2000 in MA.
Financial data (yr. ended 12/31/01): Assets, $3,172 (M); grants paid, $0; gifts received, $285; expenditures, $316; qualifying distributions, $0.
Limitations: Applications not accepted.
Application information: Contributes only to pre-selected organizations.
Trustees: Grace Gonzalez Connolly, James T. Connolly.
EIN: 046898001

61102
The Geopartners Foundation, Inc.
27 Larchwood Dr.
Cambridge, MA 02138

Established in 1998.
Donor(s): James F. Moore, Joanne C. Moore.
Financial data (yr. ended 09/30/01): Assets, $3,059 (M); grants paid, $0; gifts received, $1,000; expenditures, $141; qualifying distributions, $0.
Limitations: Applications not accepted.
Application information: Contributes only to pre-selected organizations.
Officers: James F. Moore, Co-Pres.; Joanne C. Moore, Co-Pres.
EIN: 043440279

61103
Jeffrey and Susan Hobbs-Steele Family Charitable Foundation
4 Ironwood Ln.
Millis, MA 02054-1344

Established in 2000 in MA.
Donor(s): Jeffrey Steele, Susan H. Steele.
Financial data (yr. ended 12/31/01): Assets, $2,584 (M); grants paid, $0; gifts received, $0; qualifying distributions, $0.
Trustees: Jeffrey Steele, Susan H. Steele.
EIN: 043500902

61104
Alvan F. and Beverly I. Rosenberg Family Foundation, Inc.
22 Rokeby Rd.
Waban, MA 02468

Established in 2000 in MA.
Donor(s): Alvan Rosenberg.
Financial data (yr. ended 12/31/00): Assets, $2,078 (M); grants paid, $25,000; gifts received, $28,000; expenditures, $26,101; qualifying distributions, $26,099.
Limitations: Applications not accepted.
Application information: Contributes only to pre-selected organizations.
Officers: Alvan Rosenberg, Pres.; Beverly Rosenberg, Treas.
EIN: 043230133

61105
Tattersall Farm Charitable Foundation Trust
476 Main St.
P.O. Box 708
Haverhill, MA 01831

Established in 2000 in MA.
Donor(s): Mary A. Tattersall.‡
Financial data (yr. ended 12/31/00): Assets, $1,092 (M); grants paid, $0; gifts received, $43,600; expenditures, $43,523; qualifying distributions, $42,523; giving activities include $42,523 for programs.
Trustees: Marilyn Allison, John G. Cleary, Emily Feigenbaum, Edward Mahoney, Luanne Meader, Mark Sheehan, Ron Stelline.
EIN: 046909192

61106
Charles J. and Nancy G. Brown Historical Military Figures Trust
c/o Charles J. Brown
141 Bay Ln.
Centerville, MA 02632-3303

Financial data (yr. ended 12/31/01): Assets, $518 (M); grants paid, $0; gifts received, $220; expenditures, $231; qualifying distributions, $231.
Trustee: Charles J. Brown.
EIN: 223148531

61107
Aaron Krock Foundation
300 Salisbury St.
Worcester, MA 01609

Donor(s): Aaron Krock Trust.
Financial data (yr. ended 03/31/01): Assets, $265 (M); grants paid, $1,000; expenditures, $1,735; qualifying distributions, $1,000.
Limitations: Applications not accepted. Giving primarily in MA.
Application information: Contributes only to pre-selected organizations.
Trustees: Beverly R. Goldman, Anna G. Krock, Barry Krock.
EIN: 046112429

61108
Pineal & Aging Research Institute
c/o Gregory Oxenkrug
100 Olde Field Rd.
Newton, MA 02459-2720

Financial data (yr. ended 12/31/00): Assets, $144 (M); grants paid, $0; expenditures, $911; qualifying distributions, $239.
Trustees: Gregory F. Oxenkrug, Anne Robbins, Josef Sternberg.
EIN: 046680996
Codes: TN

61109
The Boston Arts Festival, Inc.
c/o Mugar Enterprises
222 Berkeley St.
Boston, MA 02116-3763

Classified as a private operating foundation in 1986.
Financial data (yr. ended 09/30/00): Assets, $1 (M); grants paid, $104; gifts received, $104; expenditures, $104; qualifying distributions, $104.
Officers and Directors:* David G. Mugar,* Pres.; George W. Tuttle, Clerk; David T. Ting, Treas.; Nancy A. Randall.
EIN: 042862412

61110
Friends of the Esplanade, Inc.
c/o Mugar Enterprises
222 Berkeley St.
Boston, MA 02116-3763

Established in 1995 in MA.
Donor(s): David G. Mugar.
Financial data (yr. ended 09/30/01): Assets, $1 (M); grants paid, $0; gifts received, $50; expenditures, $50; qualifying distributions, $0.
Limitations: Applications not accepted.
Application information: Contributes only to pre-selected organizations.
Officers: David G. Mugar, Pres.; Stephen MacDonald, Clerk; David T. Ting, Treas.
Directors: William A. Cosel, C. Peter Jorgenson, Nancy A. Randall, Bradford Washburn.
EIN: 046490571

61111
Provincetown Positive-People with AIDS Coalition, Inc.
P.O. Box 1465
Provincetown, MA 02657

Financial data (yr. ended 09/30/01): Assets, $1 (M); grants paid, $0; gifts received, $28,550; expenditures, $37,093; qualifying distributions, $0.
Officers: Pasquale Natale, Pres.; Jim Bann, Clerk; John P. Ryan, V.P.
Directors: Steve Kovacev, Ken Russo, Sinan Unel.
EIN: 043039276

61112
Boston Human Rights Institute, Inc.
34 Edgerly Rd., Ste. 1
Boston, MA 02115

Established in 1995 in MA.
Financial data (yr. ended 12/31/00): Assets, $0 (M); grants paid, $0; gifts received, $382,502; expenditures, $197,885; qualifying distributions, $195,719; giving activities include $195,728 for programs.
Officers: David Scondras, Pres. and Exec. Dir.; Gary Dotterman, Treas.
Directors: Jon Ball, Shelagh Flynn, Dede Ketover, Jack Mills.
EIN: 223045883

61113
Genzyme Charitable Foundation, Inc.
c/o Ceredase Access Prog.
1 Kendall Sq.
Cambridge, MA 02139 (617) 252-7500

Established as a company-sponsored operating foundation in 1997 in MA.
Donor(s): Genzyme Corp.
Financial data (yr. ended 12/31/00): Assets, $0 (M); grants paid, $2,182,874; gifts received, $2,183,000; expenditures, $2,183,000; qualifying distributions, $0.

Application information: Application form required.
Officers and Directors:* Henri Termeer,* Pres.; Peter Wirth,* Clerk; Michael S. Wzyga,* Treas.
EIN: 043236375
Codes: FD, CD

MICHIGAN

61114
John E. Fetzer Institute, Inc.
(Formerly John E. Fetzer Foundation, Inc.)
9292 West KL Ave.
Kalamazoo, MI 49009-9398 (269) 375-2000
URL: http://www.fetzer.org
Contact: David J. Sluyter, Ed.D, Pres. and C.E.O.

Established in 1956.
Donor(s): John E. Fetzer.‡
Financial data (yr. ended 07/31/01): Assets, $338,166,353 (M); grants paid, $2,062,625; gifts received, $2,917,665; expenditures, $16,916,162; qualifying distributions, $15,686,430.
Limitations: Applications not accepted. Giving on a national basis.
Publications: Informational brochure, occasional report, program policy statement.
Application information: Contributes only to pre-selected organizations.
Officers and Trustees:* Jeremy P. Waletzky, M.D.,* Chair.; Janis A. Clafin,* Vice-Chair.; David J. Sluyter, Ed.D., Pres. and C.E.O.; Christina M. Adams, V.P., Fin.; Lynn G. Underwood, V.P., Health Research; Richard Frankel, Ph.D., V.P., Evaluation; Frances Vaughan,* Secy.; Bruce F. Fetzer,* Treas.; Bruce Carlson, Winston O. Franklin, Robert F. Lehman, Lynn Twist.
EIN: 386052788
Codes: FD

61115
The Edward Lowe Foundation
58220 Decatur Rd.
P.O. Box 8
Cassopolis, MI 49031-0008 (269) 445-4200
FAX: (269) 445-4350; E-mail: grants@lowe.org;
URL: http://www.EdwardLowe.org
Contact: Mark Lange, Exec. Dir.

Established in 1985 in MI.
Donor(s): Edward Lowe.‡
Financial data (yr. ended 12/31/00): Assets, $133,568,071 (M); grants paid, $770,648; expenditures, $7,639,951; qualifying distributions, $6,636,645; giving activities include $2,430,340 for programs.
Limitations: Applications not accepted. Giving on a national basis.
Publications: Informational brochure.
Application information: Contributes only to pre-selected organizations.
Officers and Trustees:* Darlene B. Lowe,* Chair. and C.E.O.; Kathy Schroder, Secy.; Don Bauters, Treas.; Daniel J. Wyant,* C.O.O.; Thomas F. Meagher, Peter Pairitz, Jack Pycik, Murray Swindell.
EIN: 382679673
Codes: FD

61116
McFarlan Home
700 E. Kearsley St.
Flint, MI 48503 (810) 235-3077

Established in 1926 in MI; classified as a private operating foundation in 1974.
Financial data (yr. ended 12/31/00): Assets, $27,043,781 (M); grants paid, $181,000; expenditures, $923,414; qualifying distributions, $822,582; giving activities include $620,473 for programs.
Limitations: Applications not accepted. Giving limited to Flint, MI.
Application information: Grants made at discretion of Board of Directors.
Officers and Trustees:* Robert A. Burchfield,* Pres.; Robert Bessert, V.P.; Wayne Knecht,* Secy.; Ellajane S. Rundles,* Treas.; Bob Carpenter, Mary Charlene Farella, Barbara Hayes, Mrs. Perry Love Lemelin, Louis Mcara, David J. Millhouse, Mary Snell.
EIN: 381390531
Codes: FD2

61117
Luella Hannan Memorial Foundation
(Formerly Luella Hannan Memorial Home)
4750 Woodward Ave.
Detroit, MI 48201 (313) 833-1300
FAX: (313) 833-1710
Contact: Tim Wintermute, Exec. Dir.

Classified as a private operating foundation in 1997.
Donor(s): William Hannan,‡ Luella Hannan.‡
Financial data (yr. ended 11/30/00): Assets, $23,899,952 (M); grants paid, $0; expenditures, $1,692,398; qualifying distributions, $1,463,377; giving activities include $1,463,377 for programs.
Limitations: Giving limited to Macomb, Oakland, and Wayne counties, MI.
Officers and Trustees:* Brent S. Treist,* Pres.; W.C. Osborn, Jr.,* V.P.; Joel D. Steinberg, M.D.,* Secy.; Harold Berry,* Treas.; Timothy Wintermute, Exec. Dir.; Brenda L. Ball, Zena Baum, Hon. Freddie Burton, Nicholas Hood, Sr., Michael A. Indenbaum.
EIN: 381358386

61118
Michigan Capital Fund for Housing Non-Profit Housing Corporation
530 W. Iona St., Ste. F
Lansing, MI 48933-1062

Financial data (yr. ended 12/31/00): Assets, $22,875,475 (M); grants paid, $414,547; gifts received, $100,000; expenditures, $2,917,427; qualifying distributions, $3,024,703; giving activities include $2,610,781 for program-related investments and $1,559,231 for programs.
Limitations: Applications not accepted. Giving primarily in MI.
Application information: Contributes only to pre-selected organizations.
Officers: Mark McDaniel, Pres.; Christopher Cox, V.P.
EIN: 383126310
Codes: FD

61119
The Kalamazoo Aviation History Museum
3101 E. Milham Rd.
Portage, MI 49002 (269) 382-6555

Classified as a private operating foundation in 1977.
Donor(s): Preston S. Parish, Suzanne D. Parish.
Financial data (yr. ended 12/31/00): Assets, $16,580,238 (M); grants paid, $0; gifts received, $11,324,013; expenditures, $4,058,546; qualifying distributions, $3,731,013; giving activities include $3,761,960 for programs.
Officers and Directors:* Preston S. Parish,* Chair.; Suzanne D. Parish,* Pres.; John M. Ellis III,* V.P.; Ronald N. Kilgore, Secy.-Treas.; Robert E. Ellis, and 8 additional directors.
EIN: 382144402

61120
Sola Scriptura
P.O. Box 770
Grand Haven, MI 49417
Application address: 290 S. County Farm Rd., 3rd Fl., Wheaton, IL 60187
Contact: David J. Allen, V.P.

Classified as a private operating foundation in 1995.
Donor(s): Judith Van Kampen.
Financial data (yr. ended 12/31/00): Assets, $15,429,525 (M); grants paid, $55,650; gifts received, $4,127,743; expenditures, $1,362,004; qualifying distributions, $1,362,004; giving activities include $1,362,004 for programs.
Limitations: Giving on a national basis.
Officers: Scott Pierre, Pres.; David J. Allen, V.P.; Jerald A. Trannel, Treas.
Director: Judith Van Kampen.
EIN: 363953755

61121
Genevieve and Donald Gilmore Foundation
6865 W. Hickory Rd.
Hickory Corners, MI 49060

Classified as a private operating foundation in 1981.
Donor(s): Cole Gilmore.
Financial data (yr. ended 12/31/00): Assets, $11,447,541 (M); grants paid, $0; gifts received, $89,778; expenditures, $496,127; qualifying distributions, $491,335; giving activities include $493,060 for programs.
Officers and Trustees:* William U. Parfet,* Pres.; Carol Coggan, V.P.; Martha B. Vandermolen, V.P.; Sherwood M. Boudeman,* Secy.; Ray T. Parfet, Jr.,* Treas.
EIN: 386154163

61122
Werner and Ruth Nartel Foundation
(Formerly Nartel Rare Bird Foundation)
4800 Fashion Sq. Blvd., Ste. 100
Saginaw, MI 48604-2612

Financial data (yr. ended 06/30/01): Assets, $5,829,916 (M); grants paid, $350,100; gifts received, $23,486; expenditures, $451,473; qualifying distributions, $374,944.
Limitations: Applications not accepted. Giving primarily in IL, MI, and NY.
Application information: Contributes only to pre-selected organizations.
Officers: Larry Nartel, Pres. and Treas.; Evelyn Nartelski, V.P. and Secy.
EIN: 382477768
Codes: FD

61123
Jesse Besser Museum
491 Johnson St.
Alpena, MI 49707-1496

Classified as a private operating foundation in 1972.
Donor(s): Besser Foundation.
Financial data (yr. ended 06/30/01): Assets, $5,746,006 (M); grants paid, $0; gifts received, $718,136; expenditures, $334,406; qualifying

distributions, $0; giving activities include $275,657 for programs.
Officers and Directors:* Mary E. Glawe,* Pres.; Jeffrey Rogg,* V.P.; Leona Wisniewski,* Secy.; Tammy Veasy,* Treas.; Barbara Adonelt, Robert Adonelt, Penny Bartnah, Barbara Bourdebris, Joanne Brandt, and 35 additional directors.
EIN: 386111671

61124
University Renal Research and Education Association
c/o Philip J. Held
315 W. Huron, Ste. 260
Ann Arbor, MI 48103

Established in 1996 in MI.
Financial data (yr. ended 12/31/00): Assets, $5,029,342 (M); grants paid, $0; gifts received, $5,090,584; expenditures, $4,922,929; qualifying distributions, $3,995,784; giving activities include $220,509 for programs.
Limitations: Applications not accepted.
Officers: Philip Held, Pres.; Patricia A. Fritz-Hobson, Secy.; Elizabeth Holzman, Treas.
Directors: Peter De Oreo, Lee Henderson, Allan Hull, Maureen Michael, John Nemann.
EIN: 383289521

61125
Gilbert & Lila Silverman Fluxus Collection Foundation
4054 Cranbrook Ct.
Bloomfield Hills, MI 48301

Classified as a private operating foundation in 1990.
Donor(s): Gilbert B. Silverman, Lila Silverman.
Financial data (yr. ended 12/31/01): Assets, $4,622,961 (M); grants paid, $1,500; gifts received, $100,000; expenditures, $177,029; qualifying distributions, $221,069; giving activities include $152,644 for programs.
Limitations: Applications not accepted.
Application information: Contributes only to pre-selected organizations.
Officers: Gilbert B. Silverman, Pres.; Jon Hendricks, V.P.; Lila Silverman, Secy.-Treas.
EIN: 382839549

61126
Ghassan M. Saab Foundation
3407 Torrey Rd.
Flint, MI 48507-0718

Established in 1998 in MI.
Donor(s): Ghassan M. Saab.
Financial data (yr. ended 12/31/01): Assets, $3,082,765 (M); grants paid, $86,000; expenditures, $93,438; qualifying distributions, $86,380.
Limitations: Applications not accepted. Giving primarily in MI and NY; some giving in Beirut.
Application information: Contributes only to pre-selected organizations.
Directors: Ghassan M. Saab, Khalil Saab, Nadim Saab.
EIN: 383416517
Codes: FD2

61127
The Les and Anne Biederman Foundation, Inc.
P.O. Box 564
Traverse City, MI 49685-0564
Contact: Chris Warren, Secy.

Established in 1986 in MI.
Donor(s): Lester M. Biederman,‡ Anna R. Biederman, Anne Biederman Trust.
Financial data (yr. ended 12/31/00): Assets, $3,071,517 (M); grants paid, $130,496; gifts received, $232,808; expenditures, $148,339; qualifying distributions, $136,797.
Limitations: Giving primarily in northern MI.
Publications: Application guidelines.
Application information: Application form required.
Officers and Trustees:* Ross Biederman,* Pres.; Lawrence E. Gorton, V.P.; Chris Warren, Secy.; Vojin Baic, Paul M. Biederman, Lee Russell.
EIN: 382449838
Codes: FD2

61128
The Redman Foundation
P.O. Box 630
Indian River, MI 49749

Established in 1999 in MI.
Donor(s): Robert Redman, Cynthia Redman.
Financial data (yr. ended 12/31/01): Assets, $3,034,729 (M); grants paid, $0; gifts received, $3,000; expenditures, $2,656; qualifying distributions, $0.
Limitations: Giving primarily in AR.
Officers: Robert Redman, Pres.; Cynthia Redman, V.P. and Secy.; Andrew Hoover, Treas.
EIN: 383517998

61129
Lowell Area Housing, Inc.
P.O. Box 186
Lowell, MI 49331-0186

Classified as a private operating foundation in 1991.
Financial data (yr. ended 12/31/00): Assets, $3,021,789 (M); grants paid, $0; gifts received, $105,000; expenditures, $327,232; qualifying distributions, $126,658; giving activities include $7,232 for programs.
Officers and Directors:* Phillip H. Schneider, Jr.,* Pres.; Stanley N. Gardner,* Secy.-Treas.; Samuel D. Wingeir.
EIN: 381945437

61130
Cascade Hemophilia Consortium
210 E. Huron St., Ste. C2
Ann Arbor, MI 48104
Contact: William T. Sparrow, Exec. Dir.

Established in 1996 in MI.
Financial data (yr. ended 12/31/00): Assets, $2,966,044 (M); grants paid, $224,974; gifts received, $1,350; expenditures, $481,965; qualifying distributions, $5,824,960; giving activities include $5,910,085 for programs.
Limitations: Giving primarily in MI and OH.
Application information: Contact foundation for requirements. Application form required.
Officer: William T. Sparrow, Exec. Dir.
Directors: Lynn Allen, Judith Andersen, M.D., William Berk, M.D., Randy Bradshaw, Jane Dinnen, R.N., Anne Eccles, Ivan Harner, David Meuleman, Ph.D., Stephen Munk, Amy Shapiro, M.D.
EIN: 383199649
Codes: FD2

61131
L & L Educational Foundation
160 McLean Dr.
Romeo, MI 48065 (586) 336-1608
FAX: (586) 336-1609
Contact: Patti Lange

Established in 1987 in MI.
Donor(s): W. Eugene Lane, Robert M. Ligon.
Financial data (yr. ended 12/31/01): Assets, $2,811,277 (M); grants paid, $155,279; gifts received, $399,847; expenditures, $190,403; qualifying distributions, $156,232.
Limitations: Giving limited to MI.
Application information: Application form required.
Officers and Trustees:* Margaret Domenick-Muscat, Pres.; Randolph Schaeffer Greene, V.P.; Peggy LaBelle, V.P.; Shelley Weiss, Secy.; Robert M. Ligon,* Treas.; Lesle Cole, Susan Mulke, Larry R. Schmidt.
EIN: 382785121
Codes: FD2, GTI

61132
Barros Research Foundation
2430 College Rd.
Holt, MI 48842-9704

Classified as a private operating foundation in 1981.
Donor(s): Barnett Rosenberg, Tina Rosenberg.
Financial data (yr. ended 12/31/01): Assets, $2,775,761 (M); grants paid, $0; gifts received, $508,910; expenditures, $455,675; qualifying distributions, $439,936; giving activities include $439,936 for programs.
Officers: Barnett Rosenberg, Pres.; Ritta Rosenberg, Secy.-Treas.
Directors: Paul A. Rosenberg, Tina Rosenberg.
EIN: 382380724

61133
Anna Botsford Bach Home of Ann Arbor, Michigan
(Formerly Old Ladies Home Association of Ann Arbor, Michigan)
1945 Pauline Blvd., Ste. 17
Ann Arbor, MI 48103

Classified as a private operating foundation in 1986.
Financial data (yr. ended 12/31/00): Assets, $2,228,153 (M); grants paid, $0; gifts received, $3,157; expenditures, $540,860; qualifying distributions, $221,608; giving activities include $524,436 for programs.
Officers and Directors:* Karen O'Neal,* Pres.; Elizabeth Payne,* V.P.; Connie Dunlap,* Secy.; C. Merle Crawford,* Treas.; Charles Cares, Nicholas Dever, Frances Holter, Robert Nichols, Ann Renfer, Ron Renfer, Jerry Weidenbach.
EIN: 381381276

61134
Howard & Ivah Hoffmeyer Charitable Trust
c/o Chemical Bank & Trust Co., Trust Dept.
P.O. Box 231
Midland, MI 48640 (989) 839-5404
FAX: (989) 839-5479
Contact: Norma J. Kendall, Asst. V.P. and Trust Off.

Established in 1992 in MI.
Donor(s): Ivah Hoffmeyer,‡ Howard Hoffmeyer.‡
Financial data (yr. ended 12/31/01): Assets, $2,126,317 (M); grants paid, $108,000; expenditures, $123,556; qualifying distributions, $108,000.
Limitations: Giving limited to Breckinridge, MI and St. Louis, MI.
Application information: Application form not required.
Trustee: Chemical Bank & Trust Co.
Advisory Committee: Brian Cross, George Kubin, James Laurenz, Andrew Root, Jr., Charles Seeley.
EIN: 383026124
Codes: FD2

61135
William Lyon Phelps Foundation
17 Kercheval Ave.
Grosse Pointe Farms, MI 48236
(313) 640-0123
FAX: (313) 640-0011; E-mail: kparcells@aol.com; URL: http://www.wlpf.org
Contact: Kathryn Parcells, Pres.

Established in 1947 in MI.
Donor(s): David S. Arms, Charles A. Parcells, Jr., Frank H. Parcells,‡ Frances H. Parcells,‡ Charles S. Arms, Mariana P. Wagoner, Anne Leete Parcells.
Financial data (yr. ended 12/31/00): Assets, $2,035,511 (M); grants paid, $301,665; gifts received, $36,955; expenditures, $480,296; qualifying distributions, $422,493; giving activities include $126,618 for programs.
Limitations: Applications not accepted. Giving primarily in MI.
Publications: Financial statement.
Application information: Contributes only to pre-selected organizations.
Officers and Trustees:* Charles A. Parcells, Jr.,* Chair.; Kathryn Parcells, Pres. and Treas.; Frances Ann Benoit,* V.P. and Secy.
EIN: 386006236
Codes: FD

61136
Conrad Schanz and Nellie Grant Schanz Family Memorial Trust
124 E. Fulton Ste. 100
Grand Rapids, MI 49503

Classified as a private operating foundation in 1992.
Financial data (yr. ended 12/31/00): Assets, $1,998,009 (M); grants paid, $37,500; gifts received, $93,817; expenditures, $84,467; qualifying distributions, $37,500.
Trustees: James B. Flickinger, Brian J. Plachta, Donald C. Schanz, Donald K. Schanz.
EIN: 383066991

61137
Dexter Intergenerational Center, Inc.
2801 Baker Rd.
Dexter, MI 48130

Established in 1996 in MI.
Financial data (yr. ended 09/30/00): Assets, $1,732,701 (M); grants paid, $0; gifts received, $1,048,107; expenditures, $978,108; qualifying distributions, $948,212; giving activities include $978,108 for programs.
Limitations: Applications not accepted. Giving primarily in MI.
Application information: Contributes only to pre-selected organizations.
Officers: Donald Socks, Pres.; Robert Doletsky, Secy.-Treas.; Lee Ann Tracey, Exec. Dir.
Directors: Karen Atko, Phil Jenkins, J.R. Tupper.
EIN: 383012573
Codes: TN

61138
W. S. Ballenger Trust f/b/o Ballenger Park
c/o Citizens Bank
328 S. Saginaw St.
Flint, MI 48502-2412

Classified as a private operating foundation in 1978.
Financial data (yr. ended 09/30/00): Assets, $1,651,333 (M); grants paid, $0; gifts received, $15,000; expenditures, $105,516; qualifying distributions, $102,943.
Trustee: Citizens Bank.
EIN: 381408046

61139
Northern Michigan Foundation
P.O. Box 932
Elk Rapids, MI 49629 (231) 938-4409
Application address: P.O. Box 1569, 5220 U.S. 31 N. Unit 2, Acme, MI 49610
Contact: Charles S. McDowell, Exec. V.P.

Established in 1996 in MI.
Financial data (yr. ended 12/31/99): Assets, $1,611,544 (M); grants paid, $6,632; gifts received, $7,842; expenditures, $395,664; qualifying distributions, $384,324; giving activities include $377,692 for loans.
Limitations: Giving limited to MI.
Application information: Application form required.
Officers: Joseph L. Ranzini, Pres.; Charles S. McDowell, Exec. V.P.; Stephen Lange Ranzini, Treas.
Directors: Stewart Brannen, Andrew Johnson, Louis B. Lukenda, Stuart Merillat, Sharon Teeple, Mary L. Trucks, James Trumbull.
EIN: 383136089

61140
Alden B. and Vada B. Dow Creativity Foundation
315 Post St.
Midland, MI 48640

Established in 1989 in MI; funded in 1991.
Donor(s): Vada B. Dow.‡
Financial data (yr. ended 12/31/01): Assets, $1,548,602 (M); grants paid, $0; gifts received, $560,568; expenditures, $582,451; qualifying distributions, $534,671; giving activities include $582,451 for programs.
Officers and Trustees:* Michael Lloyd Dow,* Pres.; Mary Lloyd Dow Mills,* Secy.; Bonnie K. Mills,* Treas.; Barbara D. Carras, Steven Carras, Diane Hullet.
EIN: 382852321

61141
Zimmer Foundation
350 Corrie Rd.
Ann Arbor, MI 48105-1033

Classified as a private operating foundation in 1982.
Donor(s): Edward F. Zimmer, Kathryn M. Straith.
Financial data (yr. ended 09/30/00): Assets, $1,537,269 (M); grants paid, $0; expenditures, $74,644; qualifying distributions, $71,341; giving activities include $57,877 for programs.
Officers: Edward Zimmer, Pres. and Treas.; Kathryn Zimmer, Secy.
Director: Amy Zimmer.
EIN: 382335996

61142
Hubbard Memorial Museum Foundation
317 Hanover St. Box 463
Concord, MI 49237

Classified as a private operating foundation in 1992.
Donor(s): Bruce Lindsay Co.
Financial data (yr. ended 12/31/01): Assets, $1,507,874 (M); grants paid, $350; gifts received, $9,530; expenditures, $49,077; qualifying distributions, $46,223; giving activities include $49,077 for programs.
Limitations: Applications not accepted. Giving primarily in Concord, MI.
Application information: Contributes only to pre-selected organizations.
Officers: Earl Schultz, Chair.; Elizabeth Schultz, Vice-Chair.; Joan Ropp, Secy.; Don Haughey, Treas.

Trustee: John Kinney.
EIN: 656084788

61143
Melvyn Maxwell & Sara Smith Foundation
32710 Franklin Rd.
Franklin, MI 48025

Established in 1997 in MI.
Donor(s): Robert N. Smith.
Financial data (yr. ended 12/31/99): Assets, $1,434,898 (M); grants paid, $200; gifts received, $141,305; expenditures, $120,635; qualifying distributions, $120,680; giving activities include $120,620 for programs.
Limitations: Applications not accepted.
Application information: Contributes only to pre-selected organizations.
Officer: Marvin S. Shwedel, Mgr.
EIN: 383335149

61144
Lloyd Ganton Auto Museum Foundation, Inc.
7925 Spring Arbor Rd.
Spring Arbor, MI 49283

Classified as a private operating foundation in 1989 in MI.
Donor(s): Lloyd G. Ganton, Joyce Ganton, Kevin Ganton, Scott Ganton.
Financial data (yr. ended 06/30/02): Assets, $1,340,284 (M); grants paid, $0; gifts received, $204,200; expenditures, $25,162; qualifying distributions, $0.
Officers and Directors:* Lloyd G. Ganton,* Pres.; Troy L. Ganton,* V.P. and Exec. Dir.; Kevin J. Ganton,* V.P.; Scott Ganton,* V.P.; Judith L. Ganton,* Secy.-Treas.
EIN: 382837086

61145
Charles & Alda Horgan Charitable Trust
c/o Citizens Bank
101 N. Washington Ave.
Saginaw, MI 48607 (989) 776-7368
Contact: Helen James, Trust Off., Citizens Bank

Established in 1996 in MI.
Financial data (yr. ended 09/30/01): Assets, $1,079,114 (M); grants paid, $63,552; expenditures, $80,114; qualifying distributions, $75,801.
Limitations: Giving limited to Saginaw, MI.
Application information: Applicants must have a G.P.A of at least 2.5 and display ambition and leadership skills. Application form required.
Trustee: Citizens Bank.
EIN: 386661683

61146
E. Root Fitch Foundation
107 Pennsylvania Ave.
Dowagiac, MI 49047-1748

Financial data (yr. ended 12/31/00): Assets, $1,067,769 (M); grants paid, $0; gifts received, $26,286; expenditures, $76,018; qualifying distributions, $68,236; giving activities include $68,616 for programs.
Officers: Paul Bakeman, Pres.; Denise Wierman, Secy.; John Magyar, Treas.
EIN: 386009605

61147
The Sonkin Family Foundation
3145 Bloomfield Shore Dr.
West Bloomfield, MI 48323-3505
Contact: Sheldon L. Sonkin, Pres.

Established in 1996 in MI.
Financial data (yr. ended 12/31/01): Assets, $1,008,276 (M); grants paid, $79,786;

61147—MICHIGAN

expenditures, $81,006; qualifying distributions, $79,325.
Limitations: Giving primarily in MI.
Officer: Sheldon L. Sonkin, Pres.
EIN: 383322771
Codes: FD2

61148
Deaconess Senior Citizens Housing Corp.
16300 Dix-Toledo Hwy.
Southgate, MI 48195-2941

Established around 1981.
Financial data (yr. ended 12/31/01): Assets, $967,682 (M); grants paid, $0; expenditures, $1,302,757; qualifying distributions, $1,302,757; giving activities include $1,302,757 for programs.
Officers: Peter Vougiouklakis, Pres.; Louis Kircos, V.P.; Evan Georvassilis, Secy.; Bobby Kollias,* Treas.
EIN: 382335658

61149
W. S. Ballenger Trust f/b/o Memorial Park
c/o Citizens Bank
328 S. Saginaw St.
Flint, MI 48502-2412

Classified as a private operating foundation in 1978.
Financial data (yr. ended 09/30/00): Assets, $933,508 (M); grants paid, $0; expenditures, $25,352; qualifying distributions, $23,805.
Trustee: Citizens Bank.
EIN: 381408160

61150
Lawrence & Violet Collins Music Foundation
2985 Scenic Dr.
Muskegon, MI 49445-9611 (231) 744-1511
Contact: Margaret M. DeLaurier, Mgr.

Classified as a private operating foundation in 1972.
Financial data (yr. ended 04/30/99): Assets, $930,696 (M); grants paid, $29,230; expenditures, $33,187; qualifying distributions, $31,557; giving activities include $31,057 for programs.
Limitations: Giving limited to Muskegon County, MI.
Officer and Director:* Margaret M. DeLaurier,* Mgr.
EIN: 386140533

61151
McDonald's Historic Automobile Foundation
3126 Davenport Ave.
Saginaw, MI 48602-3656
Application address: 1520 S. Thomas, Saginaw, MI 48609
Contact: Thomas W. McDonald, Sr., Pres.

Donor(s): Thomas W. McDonald, Sr., Ruth B. McDonald.
Financial data (yr. ended 12/31/99): Assets, $863,826 (M); grants paid, $500; gifts received, $51,078; expenditures, $61,086; qualifying distributions, $500.
Officers: Thomas W. McDonald, Sr., Pres.; Ruth B. McDonald, V.P.; Thomas W. McDonald, Jr., Secy.; William McDonald, Treas.
EIN: 382489799

61152
Greenwood Foundation
c/o George H. Jury
P.O. Box 190
Wolverine, MI 49799

Classified as a private operating foundation in 1979.
Donor(s): George H. Jury, Jo-Ann Jury.

Financial data (yr. ended 05/31/00): Assets, $792,320 (M); grants paid, $0; gifts received, $22,659; expenditures, $39,962; qualifying distributions, $52,670; giving activities include $14,184 for programs.
Officers and Trustees:* George H. Jury,* Pres. and Treas.; Claire A. Findlay, John R. Findlay, E. James Gamble, Mark W. Paddock, Paul R. Trigg.
EIN: 381775875

61153
Evergreene Foundation
19459 Thompson Ln.
Three Rivers, MI 49093-9039
Contact: Blaine A. Rabbers, Dir.

Financial data (yr. ended 12/31/01): Assets, $752,565 (M); grants paid, $43,000; expenditures, $44,609; qualifying distributions, $44,609.
Limitations: Giving primarily in MI.
Director: Blaine A. Rabbers.
EIN: 382737257

61154
Accelerated Learning Foundation
2114 Vinewood Blvd.
Ann Arbor, MI 48104 (734) 764-9339
Contact: Layman E. Allen, Pres.

Established in 1998 in MI.
Donor(s): Layman E. Allen.
Financial data (yr. ended 12/31/00): Assets, $746,812 (M); grants paid, $100; gifts received, $161,173; expenditures, $75,778; qualifying distributions, $51,629; giving activities include $51,529 for programs.
Application information: Application form not required.
Officers: Layman E. Allen, Pres.; Patricia R. Allen, Secy.; Layman G. Allen, Treas.
EIN: 383423350

61155
The Knowlton Foundation
1655 Yeager St.
Port Huron, MI 48060

Established in 1999 in MI.
Donor(s): Norman F. Knowlton.
Financial data (yr. ended 12/31/01): Assets, $683,062 (M); grants paid, $0; gifts received, $40,031; expenditures, $40,332; qualifying distributions, $0.
Limitations: Applications not accepted.
Application information: Contributes only to pre-selected organizations.
Officers and Directors:* Suzanne A. Knowlton,* Secy.; Judith A. Campbell,* Treas.; Agnes J. Knowlton, Charles J. Knowlton, Norman F. Knowlton.
EIN: 383506105

61156
Detroit Neurosurgical Foundation
8900 E. Jefferson Ave., Ste. 1117
Detroit, MI 48214-4180 (313) 259-0391
FAX: (313) 259-1841
Contact: Amy Berke, Exec. Dir.

Classified as a private operating foundation in 1977.
Donor(s): Joseph J. Berke, M.D., Ph.D.
Financial data (yr. ended 11/30/01): Assets, $641,681 (M); grants paid, $9,578; expenditures, $63,749; qualifying distributions, $54,185; giving activities include $45,402 for programs.
Limitations: Giving limited to the metropolitan Detroit, MI, area.
Publications: Informational brochure.
Application information: Application form not required.

Officers and Directors:* Joseph J. Berke, M.D., Ph.D.,* Pres.; Amy Berke, Exec. Dir.; Irving F. Keene, Herman Moehlman.
EIN: 382127946

61157
Mayim Foundation
c/o Century Bank and Trust
100 W. Chicago St.
Coldwater, MI 49036

Established in 1996 in MI.
Donor(s): More About Jesus Ministries.
Financial data (yr. ended 05/31/99): Assets, $640,571 (M); grants paid, $3,310; gifts received, $486; expenditures, $92,052; qualifying distributions, $85,637; giving activities include $57,677 for programs.
Limitations: Applications not accepted.
Application information: Contributes only to pre-selected organizations.
Officers: Patricia Sorko-Ram, Pres.; Peggy White, V.P. and Treas.
EIN: 383262768

61158
Evelyn & Fredrick Weissman Education and Charitable Foundation
31230 Ramble Rd.
Franklin, MI 48025

Established in 1994 in MI.
Financial data (yr. ended 12/31/99): Assets, $637,010 (L); grants paid, $51,091; gifts received, $10,258; expenditures, $58,254; qualifying distributions, $51,091.
Application information: Application form required.
Officers: Debra Shamoun Baltus, Secy.; Mary Lou Zangerele, Treas.
Directors: Steven G. Boggs, Margaret Futernick, Patricia Weissman, Rebecca Weissman.
EIN: 383196147

61159
Greater Niles Economic Development Full Employment Corporation
1105 N. Front St.
Niles, MI 49120-1673

Classified as a private operating foundation in 1983.
Financial data (yr. ended 12/31/99): Assets, $582,041 (M); grants paid, $35,000; gifts received, $35,000; expenditures, $183,413; qualifying distributions, $183,413; giving activities include $183,413 for programs.
Limitations: Applications not accepted.
Application information: Contributes only to pre-selected organizations.
Officers and Directors:* Timothy Wells,* Pres.; Robert Harrison,* V.P.; Tim Tyler,* Secy.; David Lawrence,* Treas.; Jerry French, Ted L. Halbritter III, James F. Keenan, Arthur McElwee.
EIN: 382477818

61160
Amway Environmental Foundation
2905 Lucerne
Grand Rapids, MI 49546

Established in 1989 in MI as a company-sponsored operating foundation.
Donor(s): Amway Corp.
Financial data (yr. ended 08/31/01): Assets, $557,520 (M); grants paid, $150,000; expenditures, $179,272; qualifying distributions, $177,050; giving activities include $28,116 for programs.
Limitations: Applications not accepted. Giving primarily in Grand Rapids, MI.

Application information: Contributes only to pre-selected organizations.
Officers and Directors:* Lynn Lyall,* Pres. and Treas.; Mark O. Bain,* V.P.; Kim S. Mitchell, Secy.; William G. Groth.
EIN: 382929328
Codes: FD2, CD

61161
The Gerard I. and Beverly L. Winkle Foundation
7116 W. Lake St.
Lake City, MI 49651-8795
Contact: Gerard I. Winkle, Tr., or Beverly L. Winkle, Tr.

Donor(s): Gerard I. Winkle, Beverly L. Winkle.
Financial data (yr. ended 12/31/00): Assets, $554,776 (M); grants paid, $30,808; gifts received, $75,890; expenditures, $57,294; qualifying distributions, $30,808.
Limitations: Giving primarily in western MI.
Application information: Application form not required.
Trustees: Beverly L. Winkle, Gerard I. Winkle.
EIN: 383212032

61162
Edith D. and E. William Heinrich Mineralogical Research Foundation Trust
43805 Paradise Rd.
Chassell, MI 49916-9200 (906) 523-6364
Contact: Beverly Salotti, Tr.

Established in 1992 in MT.
Financial data (yr. ended 12/31/00): Assets, $554,594 (M); grants paid, $41,893; expenditures, $46,983; qualifying distributions, $46,983.
Limitations: Giving primarily in MI.
Trustee: Beverly Salotti.
EIN: 386585026

61163
The Masri Foundation
26300 Telegraph Rd., 2nd Fl.
Southfield, MI 48034

Established in 1994 in MI.
Financial data (yr. ended 12/31/01): Assets, $525,217 (M); grants paid, $3,200; expenditures, $3,658; qualifying distributions, $3,200.
Application information: Unsolicited request for funds not accepted.
Officer: Haitham Masri, Pres.
EIN: 383188054

61164
Ruahmah J. Hutchings Fund Irrevocable Charitable Trust
c/o Howell Public Schools
411 N. Highlander Way
Howell, MI 48843
Contact: Richard Terres

Established in 2000 in MI.
Financial data (yr. ended 12/31/00): Assets, $515,285 (M); grants paid, $20,000; gifts received, $50,000; expenditures, $20,000; qualifying distributions, $0.
Limitations: Giving limited to Howell, MI.
Application information: Application form not required.
Trustee: Howell Public Schools.
EIN: 386743523

61165
Francis L. Wright and Bernice Harroff Wright Charitable Trust
c/o Terry L. Dalrymple
16728 Cleveland Ave.
Galien, MI 49113

Financial data (yr. ended 12/31/00): Assets, $514,142 (M); grants paid, $1,515; expenditures, $38,079; qualifying distributions, $0.
Limitations: Applications not accepted. Giving limited to Buchanan and Galien, MI.
Application information: Contributes only to pre-selected organizations.
Trustees: Carol L. Dalrymple, Terry L. Dalrymple.
EIN: 383081792

61166
A.I.R. Foundation
3181 Packard Rd.
Ann Arbor, MI 48108

Donor(s): George H. Muller, Brigitte D. Muller.
Financial data (yr. ended 12/31/00): Assets, $477,160 (M); grants paid, $0; gifts received, $13,473; expenditures, $21,051; qualifying distributions, $20,737; giving activities include $21,309 for programs.
Officers: George H. Muller, Pres.; Frank G. Muller, V.P. and Treas.; Brigitte D. Muller, V.P.
Trustees: Christine B. Ballard, Phillip G. Muller, Ph.D.
EIN: 386120750

61167
North Woodward Empowerment Center
17600 John Rd.
Detroit, MI 48203-2283 (313) 867-8348
Contact: Charles Tull, Pres.

Established in 1998 in MI.
Financial data (yr. ended 12/31/99): Assets, $470,933 (M); grants paid, $460; gifts received, $102,550; expenditures, $70,612; qualifying distributions, $36,045; giving activities include $36,065 for programs.
Officers: Charles Tull, Pres.; John Gruchala, V.P.; John S. White, Secy.
EIN: 383354331

61168
Highland-Waterford Center, Inc.
4501 Grange Hall Rd.
Holly, MI 48442

Classified as a private operating foundation in 1989.
Financial data (yr. ended 12/31/99): Assets, $458,214 (M); grants paid, $410; gifts received, $5,844; expenditures, $1,575,636; qualifying distributions, $410; giving activities include $1,575,636 for programs.
Officers and Directors:* Michael J. Filipek,* Exec. Dir.; Mark S. Anderson, Pamela A. Michel, Thomas J. Mitchell, Fred M. Peterson, Marilyn R. Russell, Frank Salucci, Ronald J. Zadora.
EIN: 382309544

61169
The Walter O. Evans Foundation for Art and Literature
4160 John R St., Ste. 702
Detroit, MI 48201

Established in 1997 in MI.
Donor(s): Walter O. Evans, Mrs. Walter O. Evans.
Financial data (yr. ended 12/31/00): Assets, $417,755 (M); grants paid, $0; gifts received, $23,500; expenditures, $25,708; qualifying distributions, $0.

Officers: Walter O. Evans, Pres.; Monica I. Evans, V.P.; Linda Evans, Secy.; Marsha Evans, Treas.
EIN: 383395424

61170
Leo and Betty Goldstein Family Foundation
28421 Eastbrook
Farmington, MI 48334

Established in 1997 in MI.
Donor(s): Betty Goldstein, Leo Goldstein.
Financial data (yr. ended 12/31/99): Assets, $382,277 (M); grants paid, $23,212; gifts received, $149,825; expenditures, $28,850; qualifying distributions, $23,186.
Officers: Leo Goldstein, Pres.; Betty Goldstein, V.P.; Lisa Goldstein, Secy.-Treas.
EIN: 383347294

61171
Wyandotte Public Schools Foundation
P.O. Box 412
Wyandotte, MI 48192-0012 (734) 246-1072
Application address: c/o High School Principal, 540 Eureka Rd., Wyandotte, MI 48192-5709, tel.: (734) 246-1000

Financial data (yr. ended 06/30/01): Assets, $375,623 (M); grants paid, $50,425; gifts received, $36,741; expenditures, $54,198; qualifying distributions, $54,198.
Limitations: Giving limited to residents of Wyandotte, MI.
Application information: Application forms available in high school office. Application form required.
Officers: Ron Gulyas,* Pres.; Dan Bielski,* V.P.; Patricia Cole,* Secy.; Jeff Kreger,* Treas.; Marcia Aller, Thomas Bertino, James Candela, William E. Kreger, Christine Mathews, Mary McFarlane, Kenneth Prygoski, Al Sliwinski, Patrick Sutka, James Wagner.
EIN: 382898957
Codes: GTI

61172
Michigan Railroad Historic Preservation Foundation, Inc.
1225 10th St.
Port Huron, MI 48060

Classified as a private operating foundation in 1983.
Donor(s): Alexander Ruthven II, M.D.
Financial data (yr. ended 06/30/01): Assets, $367,536 (M); grants paid, $0; gifts received, $1,010; expenditures, $28; qualifying distributions, $0.
Officer: Alexander Ruthven II, M.D., Pres.
EIN: 382477844

61173
The Coville Photographic Art Foundation
29100 Northwestern Hwy., Ste. 290
Southfield, MI 48034

Established in 1993 in MI.
Donor(s): Warren J. Coville, Margot E. Coville.
Financial data (yr. ended 06/30/01): Assets, $364,467 (M); grants paid, $36,630; gifts received, $36,020; expenditures, $79,704; qualifying distributions, $79,694; giving activities include $37,064 for programs.
Limitations: Applications not accepted. Giving on a national basis.
Application information: Contributes only to pre-selected organizations.
Officers and Director:* Warren J. Coville, Pres.; Margot E. Coville,* V.P.; Brent S. Triest, Secy.
EIN: 383153863

61174—MICHIGAN

61174
Dunnings Foundation, Inc.
530 S. Pine St.
Lansing, MI 48933 (517) 487-8222
Contact: Stuart J. Dunnings, Jr., Pres.

Financial data (yr. ended 09/30/00): Assets, $360,683 (M); grants paid, $15,230; gifts received, $100; expenditures, $20,533; qualifying distributions, $14,793.
Officers: Stuart J. Dunnings, Jr., Pres.; Janet Dunnings, Secy.-Treas.
Director: Susan Dunnings-Holman.
EIN: 382709388

61175
J. N. Nelson Family Foundation
9095 S. Saginaw Rd., Unit 13
Grand Blanc, MI 48439 (810) 238-4617
Contact: Jay N. Nelson, Pres.

Established in 1997 in MI.
Donor(s): Jay N. Nelson, Marilyn S. Nelson.
Financial data (yr. ended 12/31/00): Assets, $357,071 (M); grants paid, $16,500; gifts received, $55,719; expenditures, $27,391; qualifying distributions, $16,483.
Officers: Jay N. Nelson, Pres. and Treas.; Marilyn S. Nelson, V.P. and Secy.
Directors: Bonnie S. Nelson, David N. Nelson, Robin N. Nelson.
EIN: 383342652

61176
Fulwylie Motorsports, Inc.
c/o Delos P. Fulwylie, Jr.
13055 Grand River Ave.
Detroit, MI 48227-3503

Established in 1998 in MI.
Financial data (yr. ended 12/31/99): Assets, $348,700 (M); grants paid, $0; expenditures, $45,877; qualifying distributions, $100,256.
Officer: Samuel Craig, Pres.
EIN: 383356125

61177
Maxine and Stuart Frankel Foundation for Art
3221 W. Big Beaver Rd., Ste. 106
Troy, MI 48084

Established in 1996 in MI; funded in 1998.
Donor(s): Maxine Frankel, Stuart Frankel.
Financial data (yr. ended 12/31/99): Assets, $339,658 (M); grants paid, $0; gifts received, $335,000; expenditures, $8,766; qualifying distributions, $8,071; giving activities include $8,071 for programs.
Officers: Maxine Frankel, Pres.; Stuart Frankel, Secy.-Treas.
EIN: 383357965

61178
Douglas L. and Kathy J. Kool Charitable Foundation
2440 Glen Echo S.E.
Grand Rapids, MI 49546

Established in 1993 in MI.
Donor(s): Douglas L. Kool.
Financial data (yr. ended 12/31/99): Assets, $316,520 (M); grants paid, $24,500; expenditures, $25,522; qualifying distributions, $24,500.
Limitations: Applications not accepted. Giving primarily in MI.
Application information: Contributes only to pre-selected organizations.
Officers: Douglas L. Kool, Pres.; Harry De Jung, Secy.-Treas. and Mgr.
EIN: 383072060

61179
The Joseph & Suzanne Orley Foundation
201 W. Big Beaver Rd., Ste. 720
Troy, MI 48084

Established in 1997 in MI.
Donor(s): Joseph H. Orley, Suzanne E. Orley.
Financial data (yr. ended 12/31/99): Assets, $304,843 (M); grants paid, $17,100; gifts received, $50,000; expenditures, $22,795; qualifying distributions, $17,100.
Limitations: Applications not accepted. Giving primarily in MI.
Application information: Contributes only to pre-selected organizations.
Trustees: Joseph H. Orley, Suzanne E. Orley.
EIN: 383343679

61180
Greene View Foundation
3662 Tartan Cir.
Portage, MI 49024 (269) 329-7116
Contact: Lois A. Stuck, Pres.

Established in 1988.
Financial data (yr. ended 12/31/99): Assets, $294,855 (M); grants paid, $26,500; expenditures, $26,549; qualifying distributions, $26,544.
Limitations: Giving primarily in MI.
Officers and Director:* Lois A. Stuck,* Pres.; David T. Stuck, Secy.-Treas.
EIN: 382769679

61181
The Clayton Roberson Family Foundation, Inc.
3600 Enterprise Dr.
Allen Park, MI 48101

Established in 1996 in IN.
Donor(s): H. James Dial, Jr., Nidrah A. Dial.
Financial data (yr. ended 09/30/99): Assets, $261,005 (M); grants paid, $0; gifts received, $143,000; expenditures, $126,170; qualifying distributions, $131,287; giving activities include $126,089 for programs.
Limitations: Applications not accepted.
Officers and Directors:* H. James Dial, Jr.,* Pres. and Treas.; Nidrah A. Dial,* V.P. and Secy.; Jack Roberson.
EIN: 352002002

61182
Jackson Literary & Art Association
c/o Comerica Bank
P.O. Box 75000
Detroit, MI 48275
Application address: 1659 Kirby Rd., Jackson, MI 49203
Contact: Nancy Sparks, Pres.

Classified as a private operating foundation in 1984.
Financial data (yr. ended 12/31/99): Assets, $233,793 (M); grants paid, $8,320; expenditures, $9,959; qualifying distributions, $8,746.
Officers: Nancy Sparks, Pres.; Helen Greene, V.P.; Dorothy Levy, Secy.; Joyce Grace, Treas.
Trustees: Dorothy Kobs, Clara Noble, Beverly Walters, Comerica Bank.
EIN: 386089640

61183
The Myron P. Leven Foundation
29500 Telegraph Rd., 2nd Fl.
Southfield, MI 48034 (248) 358-4100
Contact: Myron P. Leven, Pres.

Established in 1998 in MI.
Donor(s): Myron P. Leven.
Financial data (yr. ended 12/31/99): Assets, $227,402 (M); grants paid, $25,000; gifts received, $190,411; expenditures, $25,000; qualifying distributions, $25,000.
Limitations: Giving primarily in MI.
Officers: Myron P. Leven, Pres.; Arnold P. Garber, Secy.
EIN: 383443921

61184
The Bill & Sally Wildner Foundation
4441 Clark Dr.
East China, MI 48054

Established in 2000 in MI.
Donor(s): William R. Wildner.
Financial data (yr. ended 12/31/01): Assets, $223,976 (M); grants paid, $13,820; expenditures, $15,497; qualifying distributions, $13,758.
Limitations: Applications not accepted. Giving primarily in MI.
Application information: Contributes only to pre-selected organizations.
Officers: William R. Wildner, Pres.; Sally Wildner, Secy.; W.M. Wildner, Treas.
Director: L.M. Jager.
EIN: 383513719

61185
Memorial Nature Preserve
1000 Michigan National Tower
Lansing, MI 48933

Classified as a private operating foundation in 1985.
Financial data (yr. ended 12/31/01): Assets, $218,673 (M); grants paid, $0; gifts received, $8,641; expenditures, $5,878; qualifying distributions, $0.
Officers and Directors:* Steve Armstrong, Pres.; Douglas Wing, V.P.; Mona A. Livingston, Secy.; J. Paul Thompson, Jr.,* Treas.; James Nicholas, William Schneider, Bruce Turnbull.
EIN: 382221489

61186
Michigan Wildlife & Forest Preservation Foundation
c/o Fred Van Alstine
1939 Briarcliff Blvd.
Owosso, MI 48867 (517) 725-6813

Classified as a private operating foundation in 1992.
Donor(s): Fred Van Alstine, Kathleen Van Alstine.
Financial data (yr. ended 12/31/01): Assets, $211,638 (M); grants paid, $0; gifts received, $10,575; expenditures, $43,112; qualifying distributions, $0.
Officer: Fred Van Alstine, Pres. and Treas.
Director: Kathleen Van Alstine.
EIN: 383005117

61187
Donald and Ethel Baughey Foundation
7620 W. U.S. 223
Adrian, MI 49221

Established in 2001.
Donor(s): Donald Baughey,‡ Ethel Baughey.‡
Financial data (yr. ended 12/31/01): Assets, $208,832 (M); grants paid, $0; gifts received, $204,888; expenditures, $2,433; qualifying distributions, $0.
Officers: Donald Baughey, Jr., Pres.; Dorcas Baughey, Secy.
EIN: 383562947

61188
The Al-Ameri Foundation
26300 Telegraph Rd.
Southfield, MI 48034-2436

Established in 1994 in MI.

Financial data (yr. ended 12/31/00): Assets, $200,468 (M); grants paid, $20,000; expenditures, $20,566; qualifying distributions, $20,000.
Officer: Mohammed W. Al-Ameri, Pres.
EIN: 383134935

61189
Pardee Cancer Treatment Fund of Bay County
213 Center Ave.
Bay City, MI 48708
Application address: 4817 Professional Dr., Bay City, MI 48706, tel.: (989) 894-5332
Contact: Patricia White, Fund Mgr.

Classified as a private operating foundation in 1991.
Financial data (yr. ended 12/31/00): Assets, $198,526 (M); grants paid, $50,323; gifts received, $77,855; expenditures, $60,834; qualifying distributions, $50,323.
Limitations: Giving limited to Bay County, MI.
Officers: Dominic Monastiere, Pres. and Treas.; George Heron, V.P.; Robert Sarow, Secy.
Trustees: Anthony Armstrong, Glenn Covaleski, Walter L. Howland, Gay McGee, Richard Steele, Rev. Andreas Tereh.
EIN: 382877951
Codes: GTI

61190
DeKock Family Foundation
861 Barkentine Dr.
Holland, MI 49424

Established in 2000 in MI.
Donor(s): Douglas DeKock, Sandra DeKock.
Financial data (yr. ended 12/31/01): Assets, $190,895 (M); grants paid, $23,000; gifts received, $33,682; expenditures, $34,657; qualifying distributions, $22,987.
Officers: Douglas DeKock, Pres. and Treas.; Sandra DeKock, Secy.
EIN: 383534244

61191
The Reid Family Foundation
2600 Auburn Ct.
Auburn Hills, MI 48326

Established in 2000 in MI.
Donor(s): Glenn J. Reid.
Financial data (yr. ended 12/31/01): Assets, $189,718 (M); grants paid, $50; gifts received, $175,704; expenditures, $1,328; qualifying distributions, $50.
Limitations: Applications not accepted.
Application information: Contributes only to pre-selected organizations.
Directors: Sharon R. Grant, David J. Reid, Douglas L. Reid, Glenn J. Reid, James G. Reid.
EIN: 912082304

61192
Nelson D. Rupp Foundation
P.O. Box 771
Marquette, MI 49855

Established in 2000.
Financial data (yr. ended 12/31/00): Assets, $185,502 (M); grants paid, $0; expenditures, $0; qualifying distributions, $0.
Trustee: Nelson D. Rupp.
EIN: 383563211

61193
Investment Education Institute
100 Renaissance Center, 34th Fl.
Detroit, MI 48243-1001

Established in 1998 in MI.
Financial data (yr. ended 09/30/00): Assets, $178,523 (M); grants paid, $0; gifts received, $7,182; expenditures, $5,976; qualifying distributions, $4,867; giving activities include $4,918 for programs.
Directors: Herbert K. Barnett, Donald E. Danko, Robert W. Hague, Richard A. Holthaus, Donald J. Houtakker, Kenneth S. Janke, Sr., Kenneth S. Janke, Jr., Robert A. O'Hara, Thomas E. O'Hara, Lewis A. Rockwell.
EIN: 383162028

61194
Institute for Religious Research
(Formerly Gospel Truths Ministries)
1340 Monroe Ave. N.W.
Grand Rapids, MI 49505 (616) 451-4562
Contact: Luke P. Wilson, Mgr.

Donor(s): Roger P. Hansen.
Financial data (yr. ended 02/28/99): Assets, $174,114 (M); grants paid, $4,850; gifts received, $49,263; expenditures, $35,480; qualifying distributions, $25,717; giving activities include $17,364 for programs.
Limitations: Giving primarily in San Juan Capistrano, CA.
Officers and Directors:* Roger P. Hansen,* Pres.; John H. Wilson,* Secy.-Treas.; Luke P. Wilson, Mgr.; James M. Grier, Wallace P. Johnson, Rev. Louis Konopka, Ruth Tucker.
EIN: 382678172

61195
Edmund Armstrong Foundation
(Formerly Edmund Armstrong Educational Corporation)
1011 Glenhurst Dr.
Birmingham, MI 48009 (248) 258-4977

Financial data (yr. ended 07/31/01): Assets, $145,546 (M); grants paid, $3,000; expenditures, $4,615; qualifying distributions, $4,517.
Directors: Jack Burket, Herbert Couf.
EIN: 351603618

61196
The Widow's Mite Foundation
5657 Glasgow Dr.
Troy, MI 48098-3156 (248) 879-7970
Contact: Executive Board

Established in 1994 in MI.
Donor(s): Stephen Marr, Mary Marr.
Financial data (yr. ended 12/31/01): Assets, $144,886 (M); grants paid, $0; gifts received, $209,770; expenditures, $123,573; qualifying distributions, $0.
Limitations: Giving primarily in Fort Huron, MI.
Application information: Application form required.
Officers: Stephen Marr, Pres.; Mary Marr, V.P. and Treas.; Merlynn Hanson, Secy.
Director: James Metlish.
EIN: 383190906

61197
Meridian Foundation
2356 Kings Cross N.
East Lansing, MI 48823

Established in 2000 in MI. Classified as an operating foundation in March 2001.
Donor(s): Roger W. Imeson, Mark D. Wahl, David L. Gingery.
Financial data (yr. ended 06/30/02): Assets, $139,528 (M); grants paid, $24,271; gifts received, $20,000; expenditures, $24,712; qualifying distributions, $24,271.
Limitations: Applications not accepted.
Application information: Contributes only to pre-selected organizations.
Officer: Roger W. Imeson, Pres.
EIN: 383572442

61198
Gleaner Life Insurance Society Scholarship Foundation
5200 W. U.S. Hwy. 223
Adrian, MI 49221
Contact: Frank Dick, Chair.

Established in 1992 in MI.
Donor(s): Gleaner Life Insurance Society.
Financial data (yr. ended 06/30/01): Assets, $118,233 (M); grants paid, $7,200; gifts received, $97,910; expenditures, $8,273; qualifying distributions, $8,050.
Limitations: Giving on a national basis.
Application information: Application form required.
Officers and Directors:* Frank Dick,* Chair.; Michael J. Wade,* Secy.; Richard Bennett, Suann D. Courtright, Dudley L. Douterman, David E. Sutton, Mark A. Willis.
EIN: 383006741
Codes: GTI

61199
Kaiser Family Charitable Trust
c/o First National Bank
88 N. Main St.
Three Rivers, MI 49093-1560

Established in 1997.
Financial data (yr. ended 12/31/00): Assets, $114,501 (M); grants paid, $7,661; expenditures, $9,625; qualifying distributions, $9,558.
Limitations: Applications not accepted. Giving limited to Three Rivers, MI.
Application information: Contributes only to pre-selected organizations.
Trustee: First National Bank.
EIN: 386685615

61200
Hillier Scholarship Fund of Evart
142 N. Main St.
Evart, MI 49631 (231) 734-5563
Application address: P.O. Box 608, Evart, MI 49631
Contact: Lynn Salinas, Tr.

Established in 1996.
Financial data (yr. ended 12/31/00): Assets, $111,731 (L); grants paid, $6,000; gifts received, $20,220; expenditures, $6,010; qualifying distributions, $0; giving activities include $6,000 for loans to individuals.
Limitations: Giving limited to Evart, MI.
Application information: Application form required.
Trustees: Alan Bengry, Bob Foster, Lynn Salinas, Lyle Seger.
EIN: 383299844

61201
The Hogue Family Foundation
c/o John H. Hogue
6051 Sierra Pass
Flint, MI 48532

Established in 2000 in MI.
Donor(s): John H. Hogue, Larry J. Hogue.
Financial data (yr. ended 12/31/01): Assets, $105,327 (M); grants paid, $0; gifts received, $50,450; expenditures, $600; qualifying distributions, $0.
Officers and Directors:* Larry J. Hogue,* Pres.; John H. Hogue,* Secy.-Treas.
EIN: 383511320

61202—MICHIGAN

61202
The Folk Foundation, Inc.
203 W. Main
Homer, MI 49245 (517) 568-4114
Contact: Richard D. Folk, Pres.

Established in 1998 in MI.
Donor(s): Richard D. Folk.
Financial data (yr. ended 12/31/99): Assets, $100,893 (M); grants paid, $1,075; gifts received, $9,242; expenditures, $2,593; qualifying distributions, $0.
Limitations: Giving limited to Homer, MI.
Officer: Richard D. Folk, Pres.
EIN: 383415747

61203
Hyman & Miriam Stein Foundation
32500 Telegraph Rd., Ste. 205
Bingham Farms, MI 48025

Established in 2000 in MI.
Financial data (yr. ended 12/31/00): Assets, $99,389 (M); grants paid, $0; gifts received, $82,148; expenditures, $2,143; qualifying distributions, $0.
Officer: Michael L. Stein, Pres.
EIN: 386760142

61204
Akbar Waqf Foundation, Inc.
(Formerly Aye-You Charitable Foundation, Inc.)
580 Golfview Dr.
Saginaw, MI 48603

Donor(s): Waheed Akbar.
Financial data (yr. ended 12/31/99): Assets, $99,281 (M); grants paid, $27,256; gifts received, $79,813; expenditures, $27,884; qualifying distributions, $27,113.
Limitations: Applications not accepted.
Application information: Unsolicited requests for funds not accepted.
Directors: Raana Akbar, Waheed Akbar, Nasim Ashraf.
EIN: 363917606

61205
The Kadry Foundation
26300 Telegraph Rd., 2nd Fl.
Southfield, MI 48034

Established in 2001 in MI.
Financial data (yr. ended 12/31/01): Assets, $97,938 (M); grants paid, $0; gifts received, $100,000; expenditures, $2,062; qualifying distributions, $0.
Trustee: Othman Kadry.
EIN: 383593641

61206
Let These Animals Live, Inc.
c/o Gerald Jenkins
13990 Fairmont Dr.
Rapid City, MI 49676

Financial data (yr. ended 05/31/99): Assets, $96,323 (M); grants paid, $0; gifts received, $3,999; expenditures, $5,831; qualifying distributions, $4,036; giving activities include $5,831 for programs.
Officers: Gerald J. Jenkins, Pres.; Mary Ann Bingham, Secy.-Treas.
Directors: Daniel Jenkins, Elizabeth Jenkins, Lerlie White.
EIN: 383301656

61207
The Henry B. & Carole M. Frank Memorial Foundation
1145 Greensted Way
Bloomfield Hills, MI 48302

Established in 1991 in MI.
Donor(s): Daniel M. Frank, Julie Frank Bostick, Susan Gordon.
Financial data (yr. ended 12/31/01): Assets, $89,156 (M); grants paid, $20,000; expenditures, $22,751; qualifying distributions, $21,747.
Limitations: Giving limited to Detroit, MI.
Trustees: Julie Frank Bostick, Daniel M. Frank, Susan Gordon.
EIN: 383024466

61208
Galesburg-Augusta Community Foundation
241 Blake St.
Galesburg, MI 49053 (269) 665-7088

Financial data (yr. ended 06/30/01): Assets, $82,069 (L); grants paid, $2,525; gifts received, $51,031; expenditures, $2,977; qualifying distributions, $2,971.
Limitations: Giving limited to residents of MI.
Officers: Miriam Shannon, Pres.; James Rayner, Secy.; Wanda Hartman, Treas.
Trustee: Glen Rhodes.
EIN: 383082334

61209
The Nawal & Jalal Shallal Foundation
30 Oak Hollow, Ste. 175
Southfield, MI 48034

Donor(s): Jalal Shallal, Nawal Shallal.
Financial data (yr. ended 12/31/99): Assets, $78,625 (M); grants paid, $8,700; expenditures, $9,393; qualifying distributions, $9,393.
Limitations: Applications not accepted. Giving primarily in MI.
Application information: Contributes only to pre-selected organizations.
Trustees: Jalal Shallal, Nawal Shallal.
EIN: 383352933

61210
The Rayes Foundation
26300 Telegraph Rd., 2nd Fl.
Southfield, MI 48034

Established in 1994 in MI.
Donor(s): Ayman Rayes.
Financial data (yr. ended 12/31/00): Assets, $67,337 (M); grants paid, $23,000; gifts received, $1,000; expenditures, $23,829; qualifying distributions, $23,000.
Limitations: Applications not accepted.
Application information: Contributes only to pre-selected organizations.
Officer: Ayman Rayes, Pres.
EIN: 383128284

61211
Nakadar Foundation
3707 Durham St.
Bloomfield, MI 48302 (248) 478-1100
Contact: Abdul Rahman Nakadar, Pres.

Financial data (yr. ended 12/31/00): Assets, $66,600 (M); grants paid, $19,153; gifts received, $15,209; expenditures, $20,942; qualifying distributions, $19,123.
Limitations: Giving primarily in MI.
Application information: Application form not required.
Officers: Abdul Rahman Nakadar, Pres.; Najma Nakadar, V.P.
EIN: 382541935

61212
Michigan Association of the Blind and Visually Impaired, Inc.
c/o Louis A. Morton
9422 Ivanhoe Dr.
Plymouth, MI 48170-3409

Classified as a private operating foundation in 1991.
Financial data (yr. ended 12/31/99): Assets, $56,097 (M); grants paid, $2,543; gifts received, $1,643; expenditures, $26,889; qualifying distributions, $26,889.
Limitations: Applications not accepted. Giving limited to MI.
Officers: Cornelius Dytmer, Pres.; Michael Geno, V.P.; Charis Austin, Secy.; Louis Morton, Treas.
EIN: 237365823

61213
Light Action Foundation
564 S. Main St.
Ann Arbor, MI 48104-2921

Financial data (yr. ended 06/30/01): Assets, $55,987 (M); grants paid, $1,100; gifts received, $675; expenditures, $1,134; qualifying distributions, $1,100.
Limitations: Applications not accepted. Giving primarily in Santa Monica, CA.
Application information: Contributes only to pre-selected organizations.
Officer: Henry J. Bednarz, Pres.
EIN: 382477755

61214
Navigations, Inc.
4820 Wayne Rd.
Battle Creek, MI 49015-1024

Financial data (yr. ended 12/31/99): Assets, $52,626 (M); grants paid, $43,500; expenditures, $304,976; qualifying distributions, $304,976; giving activities include $264,176 for programs.
Officers: Ed Rector, Chair.; Joseph Aitchison, Vice-Chair.; Philip Schiallaci, Vice-Chair.; Loretta Freeman, Secy.; Jan Perkins, Treas.
Directors: John Barrett, Sonny Bowens, Shirley Erskine, Kenneth Tabor, and 6 additional directors.
EIN: 383029800

61215
The Fleet Foundation
163 Windwood Pointe
St. Clair Shores, MI 48080
Contact: Virginia Burchett, Pres.

Financial data (yr. ended 12/31/00): Assets, $48,923 (M); grants paid, $3,350; gifts received, $500; expenditures, $3,954; qualifying distributions, $3,350.
Limitations: Giving primarily in MI.
Officers: Virginia Burchett, Pres.; Patricia Patterson, V.P.; John C. Burchett, Secy.-Treas.
EIN: 386072593

61216
Health Education Activities, Ltd.
178 E. Harmony
Spring Arbor, MI 49283-9703

Classified as a private operating foundation in 1988.
Financial data (yr. ended 11/30/01): Assets, $48,180 (M); grants paid, $35,000; expenditures, $72,522; qualifying distributions, $35,000.
Trustees: Beth A. Kuntzleman, Ronald L. Markowski.
EIN: 382287791

61217
DeShano Community Foundation
P.O. Box 539
Gladwin, MI 48624
Application address: 4339 Round Lake Rd., Gladwin, MI 48624, tel.: (989) 426-0670
Contact: Florence G. DeShano, Secy.

Donor(s): Florence G. DeShano, Gary L. DeShano.
Financial data (yr. ended 12/31/01): Assets, $47,772 (M); grants paid, $39,297; gifts received, $75,000; expenditures, $39,839; qualifying distributions, $39,297.
Limitations: Giving limited to MI.
Officers: Gary L. DeShano, Pres.; Florence G. DeShano, Secy.
Trustees: Scott G. DeShano, Douglas A. Jacobson, Douglas F. Larner.
EIN: 382902743

61218
Howard City Action Center for Senior Citizens
P.O. Box 399
Howard City, MI 49329

Financial data (yr. ended 12/31/99): Assets, $44,011 (M); grants paid, $240; gifts received, $4,000; expenditures, $16,345; qualifying distributions, $240.
Limitations: Applications not accepted.
Officers and Director:* Duane Voss, Chair.; Mike Burrows, Vice-Chair.; Dawny Kniffen,* Secy.; Nancy Turner, Treas.
EIN: 382427409

61219
The Farhan Foundation
26300 Telegraph Rd., 2nd Fl.
Southfield, MI 48034

Established in 2000 in MI.
Financial data (yr. ended 12/31/01): Assets, $43,127 (M); grants paid, $3,550; gifts received, $30,000; expenditures, $6,119; qualifying distributions, $3,550.
Officer: Jamal Farhan, Pres.
EIN: 383533248

61220
Sara L. Nieman Scholarship Fund
c/o Argus Corp.
12540 Beech Daly
Redford, MI 48239
Application address: 1012 Kensington, Grosse Pointe Park, MI 48230-1403, tel.: (313) 937-2900
Contact: Sandra K. Nieman, Pres.

Established in 2000 in MI.
Donor(s): Divine Child High School Scholarship Fund.
Financial data (yr. ended 12/31/00): Assets, $42,780 (M); grants paid, $1,000; expenditures, $1,000; qualifying distributions, $1,000.
Limitations: Giving primarily in MI.
Application information: Application form required.
Officers: Sandra K. Neiman, Pres. and Treas.; Fred J. Ransford, Secy.
EIN: 383570934

61221
Armenian Children's Relief Fund
c/o John Kchikian
31800 W. 8 Mile Rd.
Farmington Hills, MI 48336-5210

Established in 1992 in MI.
Donor(s): John Kchikian, K.P. Sogoigan.
Financial data (yr. ended 12/31/99): Assets, $42,350 (M); grants paid, $32,574; gifts received, $7,250; expenditures, $33,655; qualifying distributions, $32,574.
Limitations: Applications not accepted. Giving primarily in New York, NY.
Application information: Contributes only to pre-selected organizations.
Officers: John Kchikian, Pres.; Hovagim Manoogian, Treas.
EIN: 383024766

61222
Orlo H. Wright Scholarship Foundation
c/o Sharon Wenzel
10225 Whittaker Rd.
Ypsilanti, MI 48197-8915

Financial data (yr. ended 03/31/99): Assets, $32,032 (M); grants paid, $1,000; expenditures, $1,078; qualifying distributions, $1,078.
Limitations: Giving limited to residents of Ypsilanti, MI.
Application information: Applications available in Mar. from the Lincoln High School, MI, office. Application form required.
Trustees: David Androni, Ronald Mulka, Robert Orieskorn, Sharon Wenzel, Sidney Wright.
EIN: 386432958

61223
The Qamar Tawakul Siddiqui Charitable Foundation
428 S. Grove Rd.
Ypsilanti, MI 48198

Established in 1999 in MI.
Financial data (yr. ended 12/31/99): Assets, $28,687 (M); grants paid, $15,500; gifts received, $50,200; expenditures, $21,513; qualifying distributions, $21,513.
Limitations: Applications not accepted.
Application information: Contributes only to pre-selected organizations.
Officer: Athar Siddiqui, Pres.
EIN: 383429611

61224
Lyle and Diane Victor Foundation
6130 Wing Lake Rd.
Bloomfield Hills, MI 48301

Established in 2000 in MI.
Donor(s): Lyle D. Victor.
Financial data (yr. ended 07/31/00): Assets, $26,378 (M); grants paid, $1,500; gifts received, $27,949; expenditures, $1,500; qualifying distributions, $1,500.
Limitations: Giving primarily in MI.
Directors: Diane A. Victor, Lyle D. Victor, Nadine E. Victor, Natalie N. Victor.
EIN: 383497934

61225
American Friends of NARLA Research Institute and Library
30600 Telegraph Rd., Ste. 3350
Bingham Farms, MI 48025-4533

Established in 1986 in MI.
Financial data (yr. ended 06/30/00): Assets, $22,009 (M); grants paid, $20,000; expenditures, $21,060; qualifying distributions, $19,999.
Limitations: Giving primarily in MI.
Officers: D. Narla, Pres. and Treas.; J. Shatzman, Secy.
Directors: A. Narla, S. Subar.
EIN: 382687003

61226
The AFR Foundation
26300 Telegraph Rd.
Southfield, MI 48034

Established in 1994 in MI.
Financial data (yr. ended 12/31/99): Assets, $19,555 (M); grants paid, $26,429; gifts received, $40,000; expenditures, $27,789; qualifying distributions, $26,428.
Officer: Mustafa M. Afr, Pres.
EIN: 383123848

61227
Patricia Hickey Scholarship Fund
22563 Gill Rd.
Farmington Hills, MI 48335-4037
(248) 471-3048
Contact: Mary O. Hickey, Secy.

Financial data (yr. ended 06/30/00): Assets, $18,649 (M); grants paid, $2,880; expenditures, $3,006; qualifying distributions, $2,880.
Limitations: Giving limited to residents of Redford, MI.
Application information: Application form required.
Officers: Amy Roemer, Pres.; Mary O. Hickey, Secy.
EIN: 382927699

61228
Creative Health Institute
918 Union City Rd.
Union City, MI 49094-9753

Financial data (yr. ended 12/31/01): Assets, $17,804 (M); grants paid, $0; gifts received, $7,725; expenditures, $85,288; qualifying distributions, $0.
Trustees: Joe Basset, William Comer, Hiawatha Cromer, Mary J. Haughey.
EIN: 382557714

61229
Gratiot Physicians Foundation
300 E. Warwick Dr.
Alma, MI 48801-1014 (989) 681-3232
Contact: William Thiemkey, Secy.-Treas.

Established in 2001 in MI.
Financial data (yr. ended 12/31/01): Assets, $16,880 (M); grants paid, $885; gifts received, $17,600; expenditures, $904; qualifying distributions, $885.
Limitations: Giving limited to residents of Gratiot County, MI.
Application information: Application form required.
Officers: David K. Austin, Pres.; Gregg Stefanek, V.P.; William Thiemkey, Secy.-Treas.
EIN: 383571320

61230
World Outreach International
c/o Adalberto Vallejo
P.O. Box 10027
Detroit, MI 48210-0027

Established in 1999 in MI.
Financial data (yr. ended 12/31/01): Assets, $15,102 (M); grants paid, $0; gifts received, $10,163; expenditures, $6,543; qualifying distributions, $4,395; giving activities include $2,730 for programs.
Officers: Adalberto Vallejo, Pres.; Osvaldo Lasacunte, Secy.
Director: Pastor Luz Vallejo.
EIN: 383090684

61231
Derwood & Joyce Beck Foundation
221 S. Tompkins St.
Howell, MI 48843

Financial data (yr. ended 12/31/00): Assets, $15,056 (M); grants paid, $626; expenditures, $626; qualifying distributions, $626.
Limitations: Applications not accepted.
Application information: Contributes only to pre-selected organizations.
Officers: Roger Beck, Pres.; Richard Beck, V.P.; Catherine Elliott, Secy.; Roger Beck, Treas.
EIN: 383426242

61232
Rose Hamlin Tennis National Honor Society Scholarship Trust
7677 W. Sharpe Rd.
Fowlerville, MI 48836-8748
Contact: Ann Glover, Tr.

Classified as a private operating foundation in 1988.
Financial data (yr. ended 12/31/00): Assets, $13,909 (M); grants paid, $1,000; gifts received, $41; expenditures, $1,027; qualifying distributions, $1,027.
Limitations: Giving limited to residents of Fowlerville, MI.
Application information: Application form available at Fowlerville High School. Application form required.
Trustees: Edward Alverson, Ann Glover.
EIN: 382777453

61233
Zemke Scholarship Fund
4396 Coats Grove Rd.
Hastings, MI 49058-8425
Application address: c/o Ward Rook, Guidance Dir., Maple Valley Schools, Vermontville, MI 49096

Donor(s): Martha Zemke.
Financial data (yr. ended 12/31/01): Assets, $13,404 (M); grants paid, $1,000; gifts received, $177; expenditures, $1,013; qualifying distributions, $1,013.
Limitations: Giving limited to the Vermontville, MI, area.
Application information: Awards to students are for 1 year only. Application form required.
Trustees: Jeanne Bocher, Margaret Cook, Edith Grashuis, Martha Zemke, Mary Zemke.
EIN: 386515402

61234
Simplified Employment Services Charitable Foundation
2851 High Meadow Cir.
Auburn Hills, MI 48326 (800) 876-2749
Contact: Brian W. Lambka, Dir.

Established in 1994 in MI as a company-sponsored operating foundation.
Donor(s): Simplified Employment Services.
Financial data (yr. ended 12/31/00): Assets, $12,370 (M); grants paid, $8,000; gifts received, $40,605; expenditures, $34,537; qualifying distributions, $8,000.
Limitations: Giving primarily to residents of MI.
Application information: Application form required.
Directors: Ronald E. Bray, Brian W. Lambka, Dennis E. Lambka.
EIN: 383178385

61235
Fioroni Family Foundation
8972 Morning Mist Dr.
Clarkston, MI 48348-2870

Established in 2000 in MI.
Donor(s): John J. Fioroni, Lynette L. Fioroni.
Financial data (yr. ended 12/31/01): Assets, $11,935 (M); grants paid, $1,500; gifts received, $2,239; expenditures, $1,500; qualifying distributions, $1,500.
Limitations: Giving primarily in MI.
Officers: Lynette L. Fioroni, Pres.; John J. Fioroni, V.P.
EIN: 383558641

61236
The Steve and Elizabeth Tengler Educational Fund
P.O. Box 36656
Grosse Pointe Farms, MI 48236

Established in 1999 in MI.
Donor(s): Steve Tengler, Elizabeth Tengler, Jeff Cornell, Catherine Cornell, Joe Johnston, Susan Johnston.
Financial data (yr. ended 12/31/01): Assets, $10,865 (M); grants paid, $750; gifts received, $7,343; expenditures, $939; qualifying distributions, $939.
Limitations: Giving primarily in MI.
Application information: Application form required.
Trustees: Catherine Cornell, Jeff Cornell, Elizabeth C.J. Tengler, Steve Tengler.
EIN: 383432884

61237
Metro Macomb Productions
c/o MCGH Public Relations
1000 Harrington Blvd.
Mount Clemens, MI 48043

Established in 1994 in MI.
Financial data (yr. ended 12/31/00): Assets, $8,965 (M); grants paid, $0; gifts received, $29,700; expenditures, $27,472; qualifying distributions, $27,742; giving activities include $27,472 for programs.
Officers: David Girodat, Pres.; Doug Czajkowski, V.P.; Colleen O'Reilly, Secy.; Rita L. Cavatalo, Treas.
Directors: Delphine Becker, Rita Cavatio, David Girodat, Kent Kukuk, Nancy Seguin, Mark Vipperman, and 9 additional directors.
EIN: 383203456

61238
Andrew William Hartke Memorial Education Foundation
6060 Dixie Hwy., Ste. H
Clarkston, MI 48346-3476

Financial data (yr. ended 12/31/01): Assets, $8,824 (M); grants paid, $0; expenditures, $500; qualifying distributions, $0.
Officer: Rockwood W. Bullard III, Pres.
Directors: Edward S. Hartke, Margaret W. Hartke.
EIN: 383472247

61239
Paraklesis Ministries
1550 E. Beltline S.E., Ste. 340
Grand Rapids, MI 49506

Classified as a private operating foundation in 1988.
Donor(s): DLP, Inc., James H. DeVries, Judith L. DeVries.
Financial data (yr. ended 12/31/00): Assets, $6,628 (M); grants paid, $0; gifts received, $202,065; expenditures, $230,580; qualifying distributions, $208,832; giving activities include $208,832 for programs.
Officers: James H. DeVries, Pres.; Judith L. DeVries, Secy.-Treas.
EIN: 382805132

61240
The Taunt Foundation
700 E. Maple Rd., Lower Level
Birmingham, MI 48009-6357

Established in 1999 in MI.
Financial data (yr. ended 12/31/99): Assets, $5,959 (M); grants paid, $4,500; gifts received, $85,344; expenditures, $4,500; qualifying distributions, $4,500.
Limitations: Applications not accepted.
Application information: Contributes only to pre-selected organizations.
Officers: J. Lawrence Taunt, Pres. and Treas.; Charles J. Taunt, V.P.
Directors: Rosaleen T. Borton, Marjorie E. Carlisle, Jeannie L. Taunt, Michael L. Taunt.
EIN: 383403270

61241
International Wildlife Preservation Society
c/o J. Leonard Hyman
185 Oakland, Ste. 300
Birmingham, MI 48009-3473

Classified as a private operating foundation in 1993.
Financial data (yr. ended 12/31/00): Assets, $5,920 (M); grants paid, $0; gifts received, $3,274; expenditures, $3,274; qualifying distributions, $3,274; giving activities include $3,274 for programs.
Officers: William Gordon Hipp, Pres.; J. Leonard Hyman, V.P.; Jane Cambel, Secy.; David Rybicki, Treas.
EIN: 383113596

61242
Arjuna Institute
1507 Brooklyn Ave.
Ann Arbor, MI 48104

Established around 1982 in MI.
Financial data (yr. ended 12/31/00): Assets, $4,834 (M); grants paid, $0; gifts received, $19,453; expenditures, $19,453; qualifying distributions, $19,453; giving activities include $19,453 for programs.
Officers and Trustees:* Richard D. Mann,* Pres.; Edward N. Mann,* Secy.
EIN: 382110752

61243
Nehru-Lincoln Human Services
c/o Jitendra M. Mishra
1400 Michigan N.E.
Grand Rapids, MI 49503 (616) 454-5878

Established in 1991 in MI.
Donor(s): Jitendra Mishra, Mithilesh Mishra.
Financial data (yr. ended 12/31/00): Assets, $4,729 (M); grants paid, $0; gifts received, $23,626; expenditures, $22,289; qualifying distributions, $22,237; giving activities include $23,626 for programs.
Officers: Jitendra Mishra, Pres.; Mithilesh Mishra, V.P.
EIN: 382968976

61244
Buist Foundation
c/o Mark Wassink
8650 Byron Center Ave. S.W.
Byron Center, MI 49315-9201

Established in 1998 as a company-sponsored operating foundation.
Donor(s): Buist Electric, Inc.
Financial data (yr. ended 12/31/00): Assets, $4,589 (M); grants paid, $36,609; gifts received, $148,791; expenditures, $150,853; qualifying distributions, $150,853; giving activities include $95,807 for programs.
Limitations: Giving primarily in MI.
Officers and Directors:* Mark Buist,* Pres.; Cheryl Van Solkema,* Secy.-Treas.; Mike Cnossen, Ron Dykhouse, Cecil Harkema, Al Poupore, Roger Stern.
EIN: 383314509

61245
Share with the World Foundation
1417 Joliet Pl.
Detroit, MI 48207-2802

Established in 1997 in MI.
Financial data (yr. ended 12/31/99): Assets, $4,263 (M); grants paid, $4,000; gifts received, $5,409; expenditures, $4,047; qualifying distributions, $4,000; giving activities include $4,000 for programs.
Limitations: Giving primarily in India.
Officers: Kanji Khatana, Pres.; Shanta Khatana, Secy.
Trustees: Dinesh Mehta, Kirit Pandya, Marcella Silva, Yvan Silva, Nalin Vaidya.
EIN: 383277120

61246
Weinlander, Fitzhugh & Schairer Foundation, Inc.
P.O. Box 775
Bay City, MI 48707
Contact: Philip T. Southgate, Pres.

Established in 1997 in MI. Classified as a private operating foundation in 1999.
Financial data (yr. ended 09/30/01): Assets, $3,680 (M); grants paid, $10,547; gifts received, $11,000; expenditures, $10,588; qualifying distributions, $10,547.
Limitations: Giving primarily in Bay City, MI.
Officers: Philip T. Southgate, Pres.; Robert J. Duyck, Secy.
EIN: 383383676

61247
Dr. Uttam Chand Advani and Smt Narain Advani Charitable Trust
c/o Ram Advani
6815 Sunrise Ct. S.E.
Grand Rapids, MI 49546-6644

Financial data (yr. ended 12/31/99): Assets, $3,331 (M); grants paid, $23; expenditures, $23; qualifying distributions, $0.
Trustee: Ram Advani.
EIN: 383301349

61248
Fahd Foundation
15113 S. Dixie Hwy.
Monroe, MI 48161

Established in 2000 in MI.
Donor(s): Tanvir I. Quershi.
Financial data (yr. ended 12/31/00): Assets, $2,784 (M); grants paid, $31,500; gifts received, $15,000; expenditures, $31,500; qualifying distributions, $31,500.

Limitations: Giving primarily in Pakistan.
Officers: Tanvir I. Quershi, Pres. and Treas.; Amber T. Quershi, Secy.
Directors: Shala Riaz Ahmad, Muzzamil Malik.
EIN: 383229397

61249
E. Carlson Trust
330 E. Liberty St., Ste. 3D
Ann Arbor, MI 48104-2238 (734) 668-1523
Contact: Thomas B. Darnton, Tr.

Donor(s): Susan L. Glowski.
Financial data (yr. ended 12/31/99): Assets, $2,108 (M); grants paid, $8,529; gifts received, $8,400; expenditures, $9,946; qualifying distributions, $9,946.
Limitations: Giving limited to the Washtenaw County, MI, area.
Trustee: Thomas B. Darnton.
EIN: 386534551

61250
Ekrem Bardha Foundation, Inc.
3300 Lone Pine Rd.
West Bloomfield, MI 48323 (248) 851-7310
Contact: Ekrem Bardha, Pres.

Established in 1995 in MI.
Financial data (yr. ended 12/31/99): Assets, $1,779 (M); grants paid, $15,000; gifts received, $15,500; expenditures, $15,126; qualifying distributions, $15,000.
Officers: Ekrem Bardha, Pres.; Lumteri Bardha, Secy.
EIN: 383212623

61251
Double Talk, Inc.
P.O. Box 1322
Jackson, MI 49204

Classified as a private operating foundation in 1992.
Donor(s): Jacobson Stores, Inc.
Financial data (yr. ended 12/31/00): Assets, $1,043 (M); grants paid, $0; gifts received, $5,000; expenditures, $6,588; qualifying distributions, $418; giving activities include $6,588 for programs.
Officers and Directors:* David M. Fleming,* Chair.; David Marrion,* Vice-Chair.; Todd Gale,* Secy.; Sharon Fleming,* Treas.; Beth D'Haem, J. Julius Hoffman, Ruth Smith, Sara Thompson, Janine Winkler.
EIN: 382726570

61252
Abood Samaan Foundation
718 Cornell
Ypsilanti, MI 48197

Established in 2000 in MI.
Financial data (yr. ended 12/31/00): Assets, $1,000 (M); grants paid, $0; gifts received, $1,000; expenditures, $0; qualifying distributions, $0.
Officer: Abood Samaan, Pres.
EIN: 383524066

61253
Gloria Tactac Foundation
3995 Lakeland Ln.
Bloomfield Hills, MI 48302

Established in 2000 in MI.
Financial data (yr. ended 12/31/00): Assets, $1,000 (M); grants paid, $0; gifts received, $1,000; expenditures, $0; qualifying distributions, $0.
Officer: Gloria Tactac, Pres.
EIN: 383524065

61254
Ropp Foundation
1314 Long Lake Dr.
Brighton, MI 48114

Established in 2000 in MI.
Financial data (yr. ended 12/31/00): Assets, $871 (M); grants paid, $50; gifts received, $1,000; expenditures, $129; qualifying distributions, $129.
Limitations: Giving primarily in Akron, PA.
Officer: Leland Ropp, Pres.
EIN: 383542802

61255
Anu Bedi Charitable Society
c/o Parkash Bedi
2551 Rhodes Dr.
Troy, MI 48083-2440

Established in 1999 in MI.
Donor(s): Parkash Bedi.
Financial data (yr. ended 02/28/00): Assets, $848 (M); grants paid, $4,000; gifts received, $5,000; expenditures, $4,152; qualifying distributions, $4,000.
Limitations: Applications not accepted.
Application information: Contributes only to pre-selected organizations.
Directors: Aruna Bedi, Parkash Bedi.
EIN: 383475472

61256
The Mark C. and Carolyn A. McQuiggan Foundation
29653 Club House Ln.
Farmington Hills, MI 48334-2015

Established in 1998 in MI.
Donor(s): Mark C. McQuiggan, Carolyn A. McQuiggan.
Financial data (yr. ended 06/30/01): Assets, $599 (M); grants paid, $4,410; gifts received, $5,500; expenditures, $5,120; qualifying distributions, $4,410.
Limitations: Applications not accepted. Giving limited to MI.
Application information: Contributes only to pre-selected organizations.
Directors: Carolyn A. McQuiggan, Mark C. McQuiggan.
EIN: 383435181

61257
B & L Educational Foundation
c/o Robert M. Richmond
2111 Northridge Dr. N.E.
Grand Rapids, MI 49525-1282
Contact: Directors

Established in 1990 in MI.
Donor(s): Robert M. Richmond, Lois E. Richmond.
Financial data (yr. ended 12/31/99): Assets, $534 (M); grants paid, $46,350; gifts received, $47,530; expenditures, $47,007; qualifying distributions, $47,007.
Limitations: Giving limited to students and residents of AZ and MI.
Application information: Application form required.
Officers: Robert M. Richmond,* Pres.; Lois E. Richmond,* Secy.-Treas.
Directors: Ardis E. Phillips, Ronald Phillips.
EIN: 382909435
Codes: TN, GTI

61258
Blue Sky Foundation
430 N. Old Woodward
Birmingham, MI 48009

Established in 1997 in MI.

61258—MICHIGAN

Donor(s): Jeffrey Sloan, Richard Sloan.
Financial data (yr. ended 12/31/01): Assets, $355 (M); grants paid, $0; gifts received, $43,600; expenditures, $56,052; qualifying distributions, $0.
Officers: Jeffrey Sloan, Pres.; Richard Sloan, V.P.
EIN: 383320396

61259
The Aronoff Foundation, Inc.
38500 N. Woodward Ave., Ste. 310
Bloomfield Hills, MI 48304

Established in 1977 in MI.
Donor(s): Arnold Y. Aronoff, Edward C. Levy, Sr.‡
Financial data (yr. ended 05/31/00): Assets, $238 (M); grants paid, $36,175; gifts received, $37,575; expenditures, $37,348; qualifying distributions, $36,175.
Limitations: Applications not accepted. Giving primarily in MI.
Application information: Contributes only to pre-selected organizations.
Officers: Janet Aronoff, Pres.; Arnold Y. Aronoff, Secy.
Trustees: Daniel J. Aronoff, Jane Schulak.
EIN: 591865316

61260
Dr. Faite R-P. Mack Family Conservancy Foundation
c/o Dr. Faite R-P. Mack
466 Fountain St. N.E., Ste. 1
Grand Rapids, MI 49503-3335

Established in 2001.
Financial data (yr. ended 12/31/01): Assets, $110 (M); grants paid, $1,140; gifts received, $1,670; expenditures, $1,640; qualifying distributions, $1,640.
Limitations: Giving primarily in Thailand.
Officers: Faite R-P. Mack, Pres.; Voumany Norasing, V.P.; Katie Mack, Treas.
Trustee: Racheal Mack.
EIN: 383523916

61261
Henry E. & Annabel Larzelere Foundation
1944 Winchester Dr.
East Lansing, MI 48823

Established in 2000 in MI.
Financial data (yr. ended 12/31/00): Assets, $100 (M); grants paid, $0; expenditures, $0; qualifying distributions, $0.
Directors: Martha Larzelere Campbell, Mary Larzelere Dygert, Annabel S. Larzelere, Henry E. Larzelere, John H. Larzelere.
EIN: 383530833

61262
Mitchell Family Foundation
c/o William S. Mitchell
5746 Lake Ridge Dr.
Brighton, MI 48116

Established in 1997 in MI.
Donor(s): William S. Mitchell.
Financial data (yr. ended 12/31/01): Assets, $18 (M); grants paid, $9,793; expenditures, $10,152; qualifying distributions, $9,793.
Limitations: Applications not accepted.
Application information: Contributes only to pre-selected organizations.
Trustee: William S. Mitchell.
EIN: 383201358

61263
Karen Blackman Charitable Foundation
c/o Sidney D. Blackman
6297 Ramwyck Ct.
West Bloomfield, MI 48322-2252

Classified as a private operating foundation in 1998 in MI.
Financial data (yr. ended 12/31/00): Assets, $1 (M); grants paid, $500; gifts received, $500; expenditures, $550; qualifying distributions, $500.
Limitations: Giving primarily in MI.
Officers: Sidney D. Blackman, Pres.; Debra R. Blackman, V.P.; Marc S. Blackman, Secy.; Jeffrey S. Blackman, Treas.
EIN: 383381251

61264
Elsona Foster Care, Inc.
1402 Jackson Ave.
Flint, MI 48504

Established around 1986.
Financial data (yr. ended 12/31/01): Assets, $1 (M); grants paid, $0; expenditures, $44,324; qualifying distributions, $0.
Officer: Sonia Walker, Pres.
EIN: 382661888

61265
HAI Medical and Research Institute Foundation
47077 Bing Dr.
Canton, MI 48187-4681

Established in 2000.
Financial data (yr. ended 06/30/02): Assets, $1 (M); grants paid, $0; gifts received, $8,263; expenditures, $13,929; qualifying distributions, $0.
Officer: Mahimood A. Hai.
EIN: 383462033

61266
Lifespan Resources, Inc.
(Formerly New Age)
1212 Roosevelt Ct.
Ann Arbor, MI 48104-3905

Classified as a private operating foundation in 1981.
Donor(s): Carol H. Tice.
Financial data (yr. ended 12/31/01): Assets, $1 (M); grants paid, $0; gifts received, $24,980; expenditures, $23,072; qualifying distributions, $0.
Officers: Carol H. Tice, Pres.; Karen E. Tice, V.P.; Stephanie Newman, Secy.
EIN: 382353743

61267
UAW-GM Human Resource Center
2630 Featherstone Rd.
Auburn Hills, MI 48326-2814

Donor(s): United Automobile Workers International Union, General Motors Corp.
Financial data (yr. ended 12/31/00): Assets, $1 (M); grants paid, $0; expenditures, $0; qualifying distributions, $0.
Officers and Directors:* Larry E. Knox,* Secy.; Thomas P. Hill,* C.F.O.; Richard J. Monczka,* Treas.; James Beardsley, Frederick R. Curd, Jr., Gerald A. Knechtel, Richard Shoemaker, Henderson Slaughter.
EIN: 382533493

61268
Little Caesar's Love Kitchen, Inc.
2211 Woodward Ave.
Detroit, MI 48201-3461

Established as a company-sponsored operating foundation.
Donor(s): Little Caesar Enterprises, Inc.
Financial data (yr. ended 12/31/00): Assets, $0 (M); grants paid, $0; gifts received, $60,511; expenditures, $60,511; qualifying distributions, $60,511.
Officers: Michael Ilitch, Pres.; Marian Ilitch, Secy.-Treas.
EIN: 382676572

MINNESOTA

61269
Mary and Jackson Burke Foundation
1400 Norwest Ctr.
55 E. 5th St.
St. Paul, MN 55101

Classified as a private operating foundation in 1972.
Donor(s): Mary Griggs Burke.
Financial data (yr. ended 12/31/00): Assets, $23,242,197 (M); grants paid, $0; gifts received, $1,271,333; expenditures, $154,774; qualifying distributions, $1,117,820; giving activities include $154,774 for programs.
Officers: Mary G. Burke, Pres.; Eleanor Briggs, V.P.; Marvin J. Pertzik, Secy.-Treas.
Director: C.E. Bayliss Griggs.
EIN: 237209330

61270
The Camargo Foundation
125 Park Sq. Ct.
400 Sibley St., Ste. 125
St. Paul, MN 55101-1928

Established in 1967 in NY.
Donor(s): Jerome Hill.
Financial data (yr. ended 12/31/01): Assets, $22,897,825 (M); grants paid, $0; gifts received, $291; expenditures, $760,984; qualifying distributions, $0.
Publications: Biennial report.
Officers and Trustees:* Michael J. Pretina, Jr.,* Exec. Dir.; Mari Hill Harpur,* Admin.; Cynthia A. Gehrig,* Mgr.; Ann ffolliott, Paul C. Sheeline, George C. White.
EIN: 132622714

61271
Belwin Foundation
1660 S. Hwy.
100 Parkdale Plz., Ste. 426
St. Louis Park, MN 55416

Classified as a private operating foundation in 1971.
Donor(s): Charles H. Bell, Lucy Winton Bell, James F. Bell Foundation, Lucy Bell Hartwell.
Financial data (yr. ended 12/31/99): Assets, $15,633,806 (M); grants paid, $0; gifts received, $417,212; expenditures, $281,354; qualifying distributions, $228,489; giving activities include $82,218 for programs.
Officers and Directors:* Charles H. Bell,* Chair.; David Bell Hartwell,* Pres.; Lucy Bell Hartwell,* V.P.; Brenda Jones, Secy.; Randall Sukovich, Treas.;

Lucy Winton Bell, Mrs. A.D. Hulings, Douglas L. Johnson, Stanley Shepard.
EIN: 410967891

61272
The Bakken
(Formerly Bakken Library of Electricity in Life)
3537 Zenith Ave., S.
Minneapolis, MN 55416-4623
Contact: David J. Rhees, Exec. Dir.

Established in 1975.
Donor(s): Earl E. Bakken.
Financial data (yr. ended 12/31/00): Assets, $12,093,001 (M); grants paid, $0; gifts received, $1,108,968; expenditures, $1,605,944; qualifying distributions, $0.
Limitations: Giving primarily in Italy.
Officers and Directors:* Earl E. Bakken,* Chair.; Marjorie F. Andersen,* Pres.; Ronald T. Hagenson,* V.P.; John L. Powers,* Secy.; Georgine L. Busch,* Treas.; David J. Rhees, Exec. Dir.; William G. Asp, Brad Bakken, Lawrence Boll, John Cook, Russell K. Hobbie, and 5 additional directors.
EIN: 510175508
Codes: TN

61273
Thomas E. and Edna D. Carpenter Foundation
12805 St. Croix Trail S.
Hastings, MN 55033

Classified as a private operating foundation in 1987.
Financial data (yr. ended 12/31/99): Assets, $8,531,833 (M); grants paid, $0; gifts received, $591,661; expenditures, $585,596; qualifying distributions, $681,035; giving activities include $380,000 for programs.
Officers: Dan Greenwald, Pres.; Dan Baasen, V.P.; Gordon Bailey, Jr., Secy.; Jay Griggs, Treas.
Trustees: Sue Alleva, Joe Arndt, Don Fluegel, George Hoel, Marybeth Lorbiecki, Pinky Peck, Lynn Shafer, Ann Stout, Wendy Wustenberg.
Director: James Fitzpatrick.
EIN: 237275337

61274
WACOSA
320 Sundial Dr.
P.O. Box 757
Waite Park, MN 56387-0757

Financial data (yr. ended 12/31/01): Assets, $4,347,408 (M); grants paid, $0; gifts received, $3,367,585; expenditures, $3,723,278; qualifying distributions, $2,976,024; giving activities include $3,268,946 for programs.
Officers: Richard Seitz, Pres.; Melinda Sanders, V.P.; Jill Bauer, Secy.; Bill LeClaire, Treas.; Kristine Pflepsen, Exec. Dir.
Directors: Cheryl Allaire, Tammy Anhalt-Warner, Judy Jacobson Berg, Dave Borgert, Kathleen Friedrich, Sheila Krogman, Don Otte, Sue Schlicht.
EIN: 410871466

61275
Lakeland Foundation, Inc.
(Formerly Minnesota Family Television Foundation, Inc.)
c/o Lakeland Group TV, Inc.
1700 W. Hwy. 96, Ste. 100
Arden Hills, MN 55112-5734 (651) 636-9631
Contact: Larry Brook, Dir.

Classified as a private operating foundation in 1984. Established as Twin Cities Christian Television, Inc. and changed its name to Minnesota Family Foundation, Inc. in 1993; current name adopted in 1995.
Donor(s): Karen Wong.
Financial data (yr. ended 12/31/00): Assets, $4,278,888 (M); grants received, $73,018; expenditures, $475,089; qualifying distributions, $179,700; giving activities include $84,534 for programs.
Limitations: Giving primarily in MN.
Officers: Morris Vaagenes, Chair.; Rev. Alan Langstaff, V.P.; Richard J. Runbeck, Corp. Secy.; Linda Rios Brook, Exec. Dir.
Directors: Larry Brook, Norman Haagfors, Gerald R. Peltier.
EIN: 363304708

61276
Life Science Foundation
P.O. Box 369
Excelsior, MN 55331

Established as a private operating foundation in 1995 in MN.
Donor(s): Lynn L. Charlson.
Financial data (yr. ended 12/31/00): Assets, $4,216,171 (M); grants paid, $115; gifts received, $2,400,000; expenditures, $528,671; qualifying distributions, $519,326; giving activities include $82,844 for programs.
Limitations: Applications not accepted. Giving primarily in CA, and Springfield, MO.
Application information: Contributes only to pre-selected organizations.
Officer: Darlene Chiles, V.P.
EIN: 411797804

61277
Sacred Portion Foundation
6085 Pagenkopf Rd.
Maple Plain, MN 55359
Application address: 8150 20th St. S.E., Buffalo, MN 55313, tel.: (763) 477-6777
Contact: David A. Clark, Secy.-Treas.

Established in 1996 in MN.
Donor(s): John L. Clark, Nancy E. Clark, David A. Clark.
Financial data (yr. ended 12/31/00): Assets, $2,892,128 (M); grants paid, $239,496; gifts received, $287,000; expenditures, $351,160; qualifying distributions, $317,527; giving activities include $89,250 for programs.
Limitations: Giving primarily in MN.
Application information: Application form required.
Officers: John L. Clark, Pres.; David A. Clark, Secy.-Treas.; Nancy E. Clark, Exec. Dir.
EIN: 411825330
Codes: FD2

61278
Schwans Corporate Giving Foundation
115 W. College Dr.
Marshall, MN 56258
Contact: David Paskach, Vice-Chair.

Established in 2000 in MN.
Donor(s): Schwan's Sales Enterprises, Inc.
Financial data (yr. ended 12/31/01): Assets, $2,771,082 (M); grants paid, $1,666,667; gifts received, $1,750,000; expenditures, $1,667,381; qualifying distributions, $1,665,811.
Limitations: Giving primarily in Marshall, MN.
Officers: M. Lenny Pippin, Chair.; David M. Paskach, Vice-Chair.; Randy Gaffney, Treas.
EIN: 411990835
Codes: FD

61279
Cook Waterfowl Foundation
7850 Metro Pkwy., Ste. 121
Minneapolis, MN 55425

Classified as a private operating foundation in 1984.
Donor(s): James R. Cook, Diane Cook, Joseph Tonnelli.
Financial data (yr. ended 11/30/01): Assets, $1,693,298 (M); grants paid, $0; gifts received, $16,500; expenditures, $43,711; qualifying distributions, $0.
Officers: Joseph Tonnelli, Pres.; Diane Cook, Secy.; James R. Cook, Treas.
EIN: 363327050

61280
McGlynn Family Foundation
226 S. Grotto St.
St. Paul, MN 55105
Contact: Molly McGlynn Varley, Pres.

Established in 1994 in MN.
Donor(s): Burton J. McGlynn, Patricia J. McGlynn.
Financial data (yr. ended 12/31/01): Assets, $1,581,062 (M); grants paid, $105,000; expenditures, $112,392; qualifying distributions, $107,045.
Limitations: Applications not accepted. Giving primarily in MN.
Application information: Contributes only to pre-selected organizations.
Officer and Directors:* Molly McGlynn Varley,* Pres. and Secy.-Treas.; Burton J. McGlynn, Daniel J. McGlynn, Michael J. McGlynn, Patricia J. McGlynn, Thomas P. McGlynn.
EIN: 411784157
Codes: FD2

61281
Jacob E. Goldenberg Foundation
7900 Chicago Ave. S.
Bloomington, MN 55420-1324
(952) 854-8600

Donor(s): Jack Goldenberg, Arnold Lipson, Kalman S. Goldenberg.
Financial data (yr. ended 12/31/01): Assets, $1,507,298 (M); grants paid, $300,000; expenditures, $321,553; qualifying distributions, $304,375.
Limitations: Applications not accepted. Giving primarily in New York, NY.
Application information: Contributes only to pre-selected organizations.
Officers: Kalman S. Goldenberg, Pres.; Paul Curley, V.P.; William S. Goldenberg, Treas.
Directors: Jack Goldenberg, Elizabeth Haimson.
EIN: 416019275
Codes: FD

61282
Sheibler Family Foundation
12219 Wood Lake Dr.
Burnsville, MN 55337
Contact: William P. Perron, Tr.

Established in 1999 in MN.
Donor(s): William Shiebler, Joanne Shiebler.
Financial data (yr. ended 12/31/00): Assets, $1,452,067 (M); grants paid, $24,500; expenditures, $24,580; qualifying distributions, $24,500.
Limitations: Giving primarily in UT.
Application information: Application form not required.
Trustees: William P. Perron, Christina M. Shiebler, Jason M. Shiebler, Joanne F. Shiebler, William N. Shiebler.
EIN: 411960074

61283
Godes String Instruments Library Trust, Inc.
1220 Sylvandale Rd.
Mendota Heights, MN 55118

Established in 1986 in MN.
Donor(s): Thomas Godes, Lakeland Envelope Co.
Financial data (yr. ended 12/31/99): Assets, $1,189,705 (M); grants paid, $0; gifts received, $256,100; expenditures, $2,093; qualifying distributions, $2,085.
Director: Thomas Godes.
EIN: 363431218

61284
Shalom Hill Farm, Inc.
R.R. 3, Box 222
Windom, MN 56101

Established in 1992 in MN.
Donor(s): Rev. Mark Yackel-Juleen, Margaret Yackel-Juleen.
Financial data (yr. ended 05/31/99): Assets, $1,132,529 (M); grants paid, $0; gifts received, $294,518; expenditures, $129,155; qualifying distributions, $798,372; giving activities include $129,155 for programs.
Officers and Directors:* Rev. Larry Wohlrabe,* Pres.; Margaret Yackel-Juleen,* V.P. and Secy.; Rev. Mark Yackel-Juleen.
EIN: 411734003

61285
Charles Thompson Memorial Hall
1824 Marshall Ave.
St. Paul, MN 55104-6009

Classified as a private operating foundation in 1991.
Financial data (yr. ended 12/31/00): Assets, $1,107,724 (M); grants paid, $0; gifts received, $3,910; expenditures, $47,626; qualifying distributions, $47,626; giving activities include $47,626 for programs.
Limitations: Applications not accepted.
Application information: Contributes only to pre-selected organizations.
Officers: James Jones, Pres.; Bertha Scofield, V.P.; Ralph Fuechtmann, Secy.-Treas.
Trustees: Ruby Vine, Doug Bahl.
EIN: 410575949

61286
Veit Automotive Foundation
14000 Veit Pl.
Rogers, MN 55374

Established in 1999 in MN.
Donor(s): Vaughn A. Veit.
Financial data (yr. ended 12/31/00): Assets, $1,071,004 (M); grants paid, $0; gifts received, $1,041,595; expenditures, $1,591; qualifying distributions, $127,601; giving activities include $127,028 for loans.
Limitations: Applications not accepted.
Application information: Contributes only to pre-selected organizations.
Officers and Directors:* Vaughn A. Veit,* Pres. and Secy.-Treas.; Darryle C. Anderson,* V.P.; Dave F. Senger, Chadwick V. Veit.
EIN: 411948093

61287
Morris Hockey Association, Inc.
P.O. Box 303
Morris, MN 56267

Financial data (yr. ended 12/31/99): Assets, $1,041,669 (M); grants paid, $250; gifts received, $8,995; expenditures, $192,260; qualifying distributions, $73,501; giving activities include $73,251 for programs.
Limitations: Applications not accepted. Giving primarily in Morris, MN.
Application information: Contributes only to pre-selected organizations.
Officers: Jeff Mahoney, Pres.; John Schultz, V.P.; Verna Zeiher, Secy.; Carol Beyer, Treas.
EIN: 411515723

61288
Thom Charitable Foundation
c/o Wells Fargo Bank Minnesota, N.A.
230 W. Superior, Ste. 4400
Duluth, MN 55802

Donor(s): Jeff A. Thom, Cynthia L. Thom.
Financial data (yr. ended 12/31/00): Assets, $865,501 (M); grants paid, $46,416; expenditures, $76,416; qualifying distributions, $45,102.
Limitations: Applications not accepted. Giving on a national basis.
Application information: Contributes only to pre-selected organizations.
Trustee: Wells Fargo Bank Minnesota, N.A.
EIN: 416363881

61289
The Breeding Foundation
c/o Blanski Peter Kronlage & Zoch
7500 Olson Memorial Hwy., Ste. 200
Golden Valley, MN 55427
Contact: John Edson

Established in 1994 in MN.
Donor(s): John G. Breeding, Diane L. Breeding.
Financial data (yr. ended 12/31/00): Assets, $776,577 (M); grants paid, $26,808; expenditures, $28,807; qualifying distributions, $26,800.
Limitations: Giving primarily in MN.
Application information: Application form required.
Directors: Diane L. Breeding, John G. Breeding.
EIN: 411808408

61290
Goldsteen-Cohodes Family Foundation
4885 E. Lake Harriet Pkwy.
Minneapolis, MN 55409

Financial data (yr. ended 12/31/00): Assets, $724,349 (M); grants paid, $35,723; expenditures, $37,951; qualifying distributions, $37,951.
Limitations: Giving primarily in Minneapolis, MN.
Officers: David Goldsteen, Pres.; Jeff Zalasky, Secy.; Marcia Cohodes, Treas.
EIN: 411950439

61291
Rosemary Foundation Home, Inc.
22223 190th St.
Hutchinson, MN 55350-4235

Financial data (yr. ended 12/31/01): Assets, $702,206 (M); grants paid, $0; expenditures, $36,785; qualifying distributions, $0.
Officers: Norma Berke, Pres.; Pat Thomas, Secy.; John H. Havemeier, Treas.
Directors: Jan Hopper, Vi Klindt.
EIN: 237130093

61292
St. Paul Educational Foundation, Inc.
1355 Geneva Ave., No. 201
Oakdale, MN 55128-5706

Classified as a private operating foundation in 1974.
Financial data (yr. ended 08/31/01): Assets, $609,936 (M); grants paid, $2,638; gifts received, $50; expenditures, $433,604; qualifying distributions, $26,719; giving activities include $26,719 for programs.
Limitations: Applications not accepted. Giving primarily in St. Paul, MN.
Application information: Contributes only to pre-selected organizations.
Officers: Thomas L. Harrington, Pres.; Willam Mahre, V.P.; William E. Ryan, Treas.
EIN: 416077965

61293
Dr. W. C. Stillwell Foundation
c/o Philip Wold
25 Browns Ct.
Mankato, MN 56001
Application address: 1630 Adams St., Mankato, MN 56001, tel.: (507) 345-6151
Contact: John Hoines, M.D., Secy.

Financial data (yr. ended 12/31/01): Assets, $571,461 (M); grants paid, $30,000; gifts received, $1,000; expenditures, $31,615; qualifying distributions, $30,013.
Limitations: Giving limited to south central and southwestern MN.
Application information: Application form required.
Officers: Anthony Jaspers, M.D., Pres.; John Hoines, M.D., Secy.; Philip Wold, M.D., Treas.
EIN: 411423785
Codes: GTI

61294
Ellen Korpy Foundation, Inc.
1104 9th Ave. S.
Virginia, MN 55792

Established in 1998 in MN.
Donor(s): Ellen Korpy.
Financial data (yr. ended 12/31/99): Assets, $535,162 (M); grants paid, $36,629; expenditures, $45,776; qualifying distributions, $36,592.
Application information: Application form required.
Officers: Helvi Mertel, Pres.; Helen M. Pakola, V.P.; Joseph W. Mertel, Secy.; Mary Lou Feroni, Treas.
EIN: 411908484

61295
The Rachel Liba Cardozo Children's Foundation
1007 Pine Tree Trail
Stillwater, MN 55082-5918

Financial data (yr. ended 12/31/00): Assets, $516,933 (M); grants paid, $27,750; expenditures, $29,191; qualifying distributions, $27,750.
Limitations: Applications not accepted.
Application information: Contributes only to pre-selected organizations.
Officers and Directors:* Arlene Cardozo,* Pres.; Richard N. Cardozo, Secy.; Miriam Cardozo, Rebecca Cardozo.
EIN: 411740746

61296
The Sedona Foundation
8775 Darnel Rd.
Eden Prairie, MN 55344 (952) 946-9500
Contact: Richard L. Bain, Pres.

Established in 2000 in MN.
Donor(s): Richard L. Bain.
Financial data (yr. ended 12/31/00): Assets, $500,000 (M); grants paid, $0; gifts received, $500,000; expenditures, $0; qualifying distributions, $0.
Application information: Application form not required.
Officers: Richard L. Bain, Pres.; Gregory A. Jennings, Treas.

EIN: 412005511

61297
Willow Lake Nature Preserve Foundation
P.O. Box 64683
St. Paul, MN 55164-0683

Financial data (yr. ended 11/30/00): Assets, $451,333 (M); grants paid, $0; gifts received, $10,600; expenditures, $51,911; qualifying distributions, $1,868; giving activities include $1,868 for programs.
Officers: Leo Johnson, Pres. and Treas.; Tony Bennett, V.P. and Secy.
Directors: Anita Boldt, Greg Mack.
EIN: 411477457

61298
Vernon & Leoma Jenniges Education Trust
c/o Farmers & Merchants Bank
P.O. Box 126
Springfield, MN 56087
Contact: Paul Pieschel, Trust Off., Farmers & Merchants Bank

Financial data (yr. ended 12/31/01): Assets, $449,349 (M); grants paid, $17,500; expenditures, $18,952; qualifying distributions, $17,500.
Limitations: Giving limited to residents of Springfield, MN.
Application information: Application form required.
Trustees: Luther Heller, Fr. Labat, Paul Pieschel, Pastor Dave Putz, Doris Weber.
EIN: 416325986
Codes: GTI

61299
John O. & Barbara N. Hanson Family Foundation
14116 Frontier Ln.
Burnsville, MN 55337

Donor(s): John O. Hanson, Barbara N. Hanson.
Financial data (yr. ended 12/31/00): Assets, $439,907 (M); grants paid, $5,000; gifts received, $173,455; expenditures, $9,658; qualifying distributions, $9,658.
Limitations: Applications not accepted. Giving primarily in Burnsville, MN.
Application information: Contributes only to pre-selected organizations.
Directors: Barbara N. Hanson, John O. Hanson.
EIN: 411957108

61300
Majestic Hills Ranch Foundation
24580 Dakota Ave.
Lakeville, MN 55044

Established in 1997 in MN.
Donor(s): Karen K. Howard.
Financial data (yr. ended 12/31/99): Assets, $439,845 (M); grants paid, $0; gifts received, $104,852; expenditures, $93,234; qualifying distributions, $104,201; giving activities include $104,201 for programs.
Limitations: Applications not accepted.
Application information: Contributes only to pre-selected organizations.
Officers: Karen K. Howard, C.E.O. and Pres.; Jodi Howard, V.P.; Mary J. Richter, Secy.-Treas.
Director: Bonita Brauninger.
EIN: 911839509

61301
Schmitt Biomimetic Charitable Foundation
c/o David Butler
6625 Lyndale Ave. S.
Richfield, MN 55423 (618) 826-5012

Established in 1999 in MN.
Financial data (yr. ended 12/31/01): Assets, $427,055 (M); grants paid, $29,000; gifts received, $1,033; expenditures, $59,414; qualifying distributions, $28,839.
Limitations: Giving primarily in IL.
Officer: Kenneth Young, Mgr.; David Butler, Secy.-Treas.
Directors: Donald Craighead, Bill Delaittre, Thomas Moorhouse, Bob P. Patterson, David J. Rhees, PhD.
EIN: 410376570

61302
Charles Babbage Foundation
c/o Anderson Library
University of Minnesota, Ste. 211
Minneapolis, MN 55455
Contact: Arthur L. Norberg, Dir.

Established in 1978 in CA.
Donor(s): Erwin Tomash.
Financial data (yr. ended 06/30/01): Assets, $377,058 (M); grants paid, $50,597; gifts received, $95,117; expenditures, $103,576; qualifying distributions, $50,597.
Limitations: Giving primarily in MN.
Application information: Application form not required.
Officers: James Cortada, Chair.; George Glaser, Pres.; Paul Baran, Secy.; Arthur L. Norberg, Treas.
EIN: 953177229

61303
Frances Bane Crockett and H. Paul Crockett Scholarship Trust
(Formerly Frances Crockett Trust)
5224 17th Ave. S.
Minneapolis, MN 55417

Established in 1999 in IA.
Donor(s): H. Paul Crockett, Frances Bane Crockett.
Financial data (yr. ended 12/31/00): Assets, $358,114 (M); grants paid, $18,000; expenditures, $21,059; qualifying distributions, $20,789.
Limitations: Giving limited to residents of Britt, MN.
Trustees: Paul B. Crockett, Nancy F. Wallen.
EIN: 416446873

61304
Bernard & Betty Sweet Family Foundation
3300 Wells Fargo Ctr.
90 S. 7th St.
Minneapolis, MN 55402-4140

Established in 2000 in MN.
Donor(s): Bernard Sweet.
Financial data (yr. ended 12/31/01): Assets, $352,702 (M); grants paid, $5,450; expenditures, $9,185; qualifying distributions, $5,450.
Limitations: Applications not accepted.
Application information: Contributes only to pre-selected organizations.
Officers and Directors:* Bernard Sweet,* C.E.O. and Pres.; Neil I. Sell,* V.P.; Laurie N. Smith,* Secy.; Betty Sweet,* C.F.O. and Treas.
EIN: 411965931

61305
Then Family Charitable Foundation
c/o Jerome A. Then
4660 County Rd. 134
St. Cloud, MN 56303-9546

Established in 1999.
Donor(s): Jerome A. Then, Esther Then.
Financial data (yr. ended 12/31/01): Assets, $348,052 (M); grants paid, $7,200; expenditures, $14,583; qualifying distributions, $14,583.
Limitations: Applications not accepted.
Application information: Contributes only to pre-selected organizations.
Officer: Jerome A. Then, C.E.O.
EIN: 411943976

61306
Spicola Family Foundation
6405 Indian Hills Rd.
Edina, MN 55439-1133

Classified as a private operating foundation in 1991.
Donor(s): Eleanor H. Spicola.
Financial data (yr. ended 12/31/00): Assets, $325,368 (M); grants paid, $14,900; expenditures, $20,996; qualifying distributions, $14,900.
Limitations: Applications not accepted. Giving primarily in MN.
Application information: Contributes only to pre-selected organizations.
Directors: Ann Jerhoff, Steven Jerhoff, Brigid Spicola, Catherine Spicola, Eleanor H. Spicola, John Spicola, Thomas Spicola.
EIN: 411696272

61307
Pacific Foundation
P.O. Box 408
Hibbing, MN 55746-2242

Established in 1957 in MN.
Donor(s): E.T. Binger, J.D. Boentje, Jr.
Financial data (yr. ended 03/31/02): Assets, $308,894 (M); grants paid, $110,055; gifts received, $151,650; expenditures, $113,086; qualifying distributions, $112,487.
Limitations: Applications not accepted. Giving primarily in northeastern MN.
Application information: Contributes only to pre-selected organizations.
Officer and Directors:* Donald V. Larson,* Pres.; E.T. Binger.
EIN: 416033767
Codes: FD2

61308
Hans & Thora Petraborg Educational Trust Fund
c/o Paul R. Beyreuther
38 Minnesota Ave. S.
Aitkin, MN 56431-1621 (218) 927-2115
Contact: Edward Anderson, Tr.

Financial data (yr. ended 12/31/00): Assets, $305,939 (M); grants paid, $28,500; gifts received, $60,124; expenditures, $28,691; qualifying distributions, $28,566; giving activities include $26,500 for loans to individuals.
Limitations: Giving limited to residents of Aitkin, MN.
Application information: Application form required.
Trustees: Edward Anderson, Paul R. Beyreuther, Security State Bank & Trust Co.
EIN: 411360435
Codes: GTI

61309
Rios Brook Foundation, Inc.
6120 Earle Brown Dr., Ste. 450
Brooklyn Center, MN 55430

Classified as a private operating foundation in 2000 in MN.
Donor(s): Larry O. Brook, Linda Brook, Lakeland Foundation.
Financial data (yr. ended 12/31/00): Assets, $290,035 (M); grants paid, $4,070; gifts received, $17,000; expenditures, $60,437; qualifying distributions, $48,595.
Limitations: Applications not accepted. Giving primarily in MN.
Application information: Contributes only to pre-selected organizations.
Officer: Larry Brook, Exec. Dir.
Directors: Linda Rios Brook, Christopher M. Rios.
EIN: 411925899

61310
The Donald R. Wahlund Foundation
6010 Earle Brown Dr.
Brooklyn Center, MN 55430-2506
Contact: Donald R. Wahlund, Pres.

Classified as a private operating foundation in 1999.
Financial data (yr. ended 12/31/01): Assets, $277,515 (M); grants paid, $26,750; gifts received, $15,000; expenditures, $27,318; qualifying distributions, $26,624.
Limitations: Giving primarily in MN.
Officers: Donald R. Wahlund, Pres.; Ed Brummet, V.P.; Pat O'Connor, Secy.-Treas.
Directors: Geraldine Jaunty, E. Ron Magnuson, Dean Nelson, Sara Wahl.
EIN: 411929671

61311
B. H. Chesley Foundation
P.O. Box 130370
Roseville, MN 55113-0004

Established in 1990.
Financial data (yr. ended 12/31/01): Assets, $245,822 (M); grants paid, $9,000; expenditures, $9,000; qualifying distributions, $9,000.
Limitations: Giving limited to residents living within 100 miles of Roseville, MN.
Application information: Application form required.
Trustees: Steve Chesley.
EIN: 411674753
Codes: GTI

61312
Elmer M. Johnson Conservation Trust
705 18th St. S.E.
Owatonna, MN 55060

Classified as a private operating foundation in 1997.
Donor(s): Elmer M. Johnson.
Financial data (yr. ended 12/31/99): Assets, $239,133 (M); grants paid, $2,500; expenditures, $25,550; qualifying distributions, $2,500.
Trustees: Lias Kalleneyn, Paul Rognes.
EIN: 416418164

61313
Thorbeck Foundation
Rte. 1, Box 30
Gonvick, MN 56644

Established in 1986 in MN.
Donor(s): Oscar E. Thorbeck.
Financial data (yr. ended 12/31/01): Assets, $203,897 (M); grants paid, $31,000; gifts received, $7,000; expenditures, $31,356; qualifying distributions, $30,971.
Limitations: Applications not accepted. Giving limited to residents of northern Clearwater County, MN.
Application information: Unsolicited requests for funds not accepted.
Officers: George Thorbeck, Pres.; Katherine Imle, Secy.-Treas.
Directors: Douglas Johnson, Ray Thorbeck.
EIN: 363487775
Codes: GTI

61314
The Dougherty Foundation, Inc.
6120 Earle Brown Dr., Ste. 450
Brooklyn Center, MN 55430
Application address: 912 Sarah Ln., Endicott, NY 13760
Contact: Erica McQuade, Exec. Dir.

Established in 1997 in MN. Classified as a private operating foundation in 1999.
Donor(s): Thomas W. Dougherty.
Financial data (yr. ended 06/30/01): Assets, $203,492 (M); grants paid, $1,000; gifts received, $30,600; expenditures, $16,091; qualifying distributions, $12,303.
Limitations: Giving primarily in Endicott, NY.
Officer: Erica McQuade, Exec. Dir.
Directors: Thomas Dougherty, Richard J. Runbeck.
EIN: 411894046

61315
Harold C. Anderson Educational Trust
Box 98
Comfrey, MN 56019 (507) 877-2511
Contact: Ronald Winch, Tr.

Financial data (yr. ended 12/31/01): Assets, $192,852 (M); grants paid, $11,025; expenditures, $11,769; qualifying distributions, $10,906.
Limitations: Giving primarily in Comfrey, MN.
Application information: Application form required.
Trustees: Pastor Timothy Baglien, Joan Brummund, R.P. Carlson, Pastor Thomas Christopher, Robert Meyer, John Moritz, Gary Poortvliet, Ronald Winch.
EIN: 416325121
Codes: GTI

61316
The Cammack Marshall Fund for Children
(Formerly Gertrude E. Cammack Fund for Children)
100 N. Oxford St.
St. Paul, MN 55104-6540

Established in 1987 in MN.
Financial data (yr. ended 03/31/01): Assets, $191,769 (M); grants paid, $14,565; gifts received, $20,407; expenditures, $15,562; qualifying distributions, $14,565.
Limitations: Applications not accepted.
Officers and Directors:* Bill Cammack,* Chair.; Deborah Muller,* Pres.; Anne Hodgson,* Secy.; Rev. Paul Tidemann,* Treas.; Richard Gwynne, Roy Lafayette, Susan Mathews, Susan Sanborn, Karen Schreiner.
Advisors: Martha Cammack, William Cammack, Gregory Closmore, Claudia Weins.
EIN: 237444450

61317
Gray Wildlife Habitat Foundation, Inc.
20140 Geneva Ct.
Faribault, MN 55021

Established in 1992 in MN.
Donor(s): Paul S. Gray.
Financial data (yr. ended 06/30/02): Assets, $190,255 (M); grants paid, $0; gifts received, $10,500; expenditures, $10,030; qualifying distributions, $10,030; giving activities include $10,030 for programs.
Officer: Paul S. Gray, Pres.
EIN: 411708599

61318
Garden Valley Education Foundation
201 Ross Ave.
Erskine, MN 56535

Established in 1991 as a company-sponsored operating foundation.
Donor(s): Garden Valley Telephone Co.
Financial data (yr. ended 12/31/01): Assets, $185,643 (M); grants paid, $0; gifts received, $10,871; expenditures, $49; qualifying distributions, $49.
Limitations: Applications not accepted. Giving limited to headquarters city and major operating areas.
Officers: Vernon Hamnes, Pres.; Byron V. Ness, V.P.; Warren C. Larson, Secy.; Jerry Freitag, Treas.; George W. Fish, Mgr.
Directors: Ronald E. Engelsted, Edgar L. Olson, Joe O. Sandberg, Armond G. Sannes.
EIN: 411682056
Codes: CD

61319
Western Minnesota Masonic Foundation
101 S. 1st St.
P.O. Box 658
Montevideo, MN 56265
Application address: 121 N. 6th St., Montevideo, MN 56265
Contact: Ralph Lunde, Secy.

Classified as a private operating foundation in 1988.
Financial data (yr. ended 12/31/00): Assets, $178,229 (M); grants paid, $6,875; expenditures, $7,083; qualifying distributions, $0.
Limitations: Giving limited to residents of Montevideo, MN.
Application information: Application form required.
Officers: John P. Givan, Pres.; Ralph Lunde, Secy.; Myron Hansen, Treas.
EIN: 411570211

61320
Sister Thea Bowman Black Catholic Educational Foundation
627 E. 39th St.
Hibbing, MN 55746

Established in 1989 in VT.
Donor(s): Mary Lou Jennings, Leonard Jennings.
Financial data (yr. ended 06/30/00): Assets, $170,094 (M); grants paid, $96,278; gifts received, $105,785; expenditures, $104,092; qualifying distributions, $96,278.
Limitations: Applications not accepted. Giving primarily in Pittsburgh, PA.
Application information: Contributes only to pre-selected organizations.
Officers and Directors:* Bishop George V. Murry,* Pres.; Bishop John Ricard,* V.P.; John R. Morrison, Secy.; Leonard Jennings, Treas.; Mary Lou Jennings,* Exec. Dir.; Calvin Allen, Bishop Kenneth Angel, Mrs. Alan Bordeau, Gov. John Engler, Fr. John Harfmann, and 9 additional directors.
EIN: 030322037

61321
Crosslake/Ideal Scholarship Fund, Inc.
38889 S. Landing
Crosslake, MN 56442-9804

Established in MN in 1997.
Financial data (yr. ended 03/31/99): Assets, $150,041 (M); grants paid, $7,000; gifts received, $600; expenditures, $8,275; qualifying distributions, $7,000.
Limitations: Giving limited to graduates of Pequot Lakes and Pine River, MN, school districts.
Application information: Application form required.
Officers: Scott Galloway, Pres.; Richard Schalow, Secy.-Treas.
Directors: Dane A. Carney, Ross Foss, Rev. David Harvey, Thomas Lochler, Thomas Ottoson.
EIN: 411636618

61322
Geraldine N. Lemieux Charitable Testimentary Trust
c/o Jack B. Velzen
31114 Bluff Ridge Trail
Grand Rapids, MN 55744
Application address: c/o Risen Christ Catholic School, Lemieux Scholarship, 3800 Pleasant Ave. S., Minneaplis, MN 55409
Contact: Sally Velzen

Established in 1999 in MN. Classified as a private operating foundation in 2000.
Financial data (yr. ended 12/31/00): Assets, $135,256 (M); grants paid, $3,000; expenditures, $3,412; qualifying distributions, $3,315.
Limitations: Giving primarily in MN.
Application information: Application form required.
Trustees: Richard Scherman, Jack B. Velzen.
EIN: 416461599

61323
McLeod Trail Development Foundation
495 Shady Ridge Rd.
Hutchinson, MN 55350-1431

Established in 1994 in MN.
Donor(s): Spruce Ridge, Inc.
Financial data (yr. ended 12/31/99): Assets, $129,918 (M); grants paid, $14,231; gifts received, $700; expenditures, $16,014; qualifying distributions, $15,898.
Officer: Philip Schweizer, Chair.
Directors: Edwin Doring, Douglas Flaa, Vernon Hahn.
EIN: 411790850

61324
Crosslands, Inc.
c/o Investment Rarities, Inc.
7850 Metro Pkwy., Ste. 121
Minneapolis, MN 55425-1539

Classified as a private operating foundation in 1985.
Donor(s): James R. Cook, Diane Cook.
Financial data (yr. ended 11/30/01): Assets, $117,740 (M); grants paid, $0; expenditures, $3,952; qualifying distributions, $3,952.
Limitations: Giving primarily in MN.
Officer: James R. Cook, Pres.
EIN: 363386172

61325
The Mullen Flynn Foundation
c/o Brian Mullen
1122 Orchard Cir.
St. Paul, MN 55118-4146

Financial data (yr. ended 12/31/99): Assets, $115,740 (M); grants paid, $11,597; expenditures, $12,524; qualifying distributions, $11,597.
Limitations: Applications not accepted.
Application information: Contributes only to pre-selected organizations.
Directors: Kevin G. Fahey, Brian E. Mullen, Michael E. Mullen.
EIN: 364171920

61326
Clem Jaunich Education Trust
7801 E. Bush Lake Rd., Ste. 260
Bloomington, MN 55439-3109
Contact: Joseph L. Abrahamson, Tr.

Financial data (yr. ended 12/31/99): Assets, $114,494 (M); grants paid, $4,000; expenditures, $7,366; qualifying distributions, $7,304.
Limitations: Giving limited to the Delano and Wright County, MN, areas.
Trustees: Joseph L. Abrahamson, The Church of St. Joseph.
EIN: 416118376

61327
Don & Jean Lein Family Foundation
16428 Ellerdale Ln.
Eden Prairie, MN 55346

Established in 1991 in MN.
Donor(s): Don C. Lein.
Financial data (yr. ended 12/31/99): Assets, $105,541 (M); grants paid, $26,690; gifts received, $66,500; expenditures, $26,690; qualifying distributions, $26,690.
Limitations: Applications not accepted. Giving primarily in FL.
Application information: Contributes only to pre-selected organizations.
Officer and Directors:* Don C. Lein,* Pres.; Jean C. Lein, Susan E. Lein.
EIN: 411684023

61328
William D. Radichel Foundation
1175 Park Rd.
Madison Lake, MN 56063-9701

Established in 2000 in MN.
Financial data (yr. ended 06/30/00): Assets, $103,932 (M); grants paid, $44,000; gifts received, $122,250; expenditures, $44,199; qualifying distributions, $19,983.
Limitations: Applications not accepted. Giving primarily in MN.
Application information: Contributes only to pre-selected organizations.
Directors: Christina Radichel Caulkins, Brenda Radichel Quaye, Brad Radichel, W. D. Radichel.
EIN: 411944317

61329
The OrphanAge Foundation
2450 Pleasant Ave. S., 3rd Fl.
Minneapolis, MN 55404
Contact: Jonathan N. Wright, Pres.

Established in 2000 in MN.
Donor(s): Jonathan N. Wright, Julie K. Wright.
Financial data (yr. ended 12/31/00): Assets, $101,647 (M); grants paid, $220; gifts received, $101,820; expenditures, $220; qualifying distributions, $220.
Officers: Jonathan N. Wright, Pres.; Julie K. Wright, Secy.-Treas.
Director: Laura J. Smythe.
EIN: 411991155

61330
The Barks Family Foundation
2600 Jewel Ln.
Plymouth, MN 55447

Established in 1999 in MN.
Donor(s): Bradley E. Barks, Melissa S. Barks.
Financial data (yr. ended 12/31/00): Assets, $99,205 (M); grants paid, $4,300; expenditures, $9,607; qualifying distributions, $4,300.
Limitations: Applications not accepted.
Application information: Contributes only to pre-selected organizations.
Officer and Directors:* Bradley E. Barks,* C.E.O.; Melissa S. Barks.
EIN: 411950594

61331
St. Croix Valley Health & Care Research Foundation
921 S. Greeley St.
Stillwater, MN 55082

Established in 1998 in MN.
Financial data (yr. ended 09/30/00): Assets, $93,961 (M); grants paid, $12,500; gifts received, $27,300; expenditures, $37,622; qualifying distributions, $12,500.
Limitations: Applications not accepted.
Application information: Contributes only to pre-selected organizations.
Officers: Charles Bransford, Chair.; Mark S. Fisher, Exec. V.P.; Andrew Dorwart, V.P.; Timothy Balder, Secy.; Thomas Weber, Treas.
Directors: Brian Cress, Craig Howard, Martha Sanford, Donald Wessel.
EIN: 411923524

61332
Flynn Family Foundation
5409 River Bluff Dr.
Bloomington, MN 55437
Contact: Kathleen Flynn Fox, Mgr.

Established around 1993.
Financial data (yr. ended 12/31/00): Assets, $87,867 (M); grants paid, $18,680; gifts received, $32,652; expenditures, $19,333; qualifying distributions, $18,780.
Officer: Kathleen Flynn Fox, Mgr.
Directors: Joseph Boener, Mary Boener, Barbara Flynn, Laura Flynn, Michael Flynn, Patrick J. Flynn, Jr.
EIN: 411705760

61333
Psychoanalytic Foundation of Minnesota
c/o Elisabeth W. Horton
3141 Dean Ct., C1101
Minneapolis, MN 55416

Financial data (yr. ended 12/31/99): Assets, $84,284 (M); grants paid, $3,707; expenditures, $12,139; qualifying distributions, $3,707.
Limitations: Applications not accepted. Giving primarily in MN.
Application information: Contributes only to a pre-selected organization.
Directors: Gail Hartman, Elizabeth W. Horton, Ruth Lauritzen, Patricia O'Brien, Rita Weiss, and 5 additional directors.
EIN: 237206561

61334
Knitcraft - St. Croix Foundation, Inc.
4020 W. 6th St.
Winona, MN 55987 (507) 454-1163
Contact: Jan L. Ryan, Treas.

Established in 1994 in MN. Classified as a company-sponsored operating foundation.
Donor(s): Brenco Limited Partnership, Knitcraft Corp.
Financial data (yr. ended 06/30/01): Assets, $80,249 (M); grants paid, $47,500; gifts received, $47,702; expenditures, $47,869; qualifying distributions, $47,500.
Limitations: Giving primarily in MN.
Application information: Application form required.
Officers and Directors:* Bernhard J. Brenner,* Pres.; Colleen Brenner, 1st V.P.; Samuel P. Shea, 2nd V.P.; Robert C. Shoup, Secy.; Jan L. Ryan, Treas.; Mary J. Bergin, Wilfred J. Hahn.
EIN: 411794859

61335
Metropolitan Sociometrics Research Institute
c/o James N. Haidos
P.O. Box 2459, Loop Sta.
Minneapolis, MN 55402-0459

Classified as a private operating foundation in 1975.
Donor(s): James N. Haidos.
Financial data (yr. ended 12/31/01): Assets, $77,646 (M); grants paid, $0; gifts received, $45,130; expenditures, $44,538; qualifying distributions, $45,526; giving activities include $31,922 for programs.
Officers: James N. Haidos, Pres.; James E. Graham, V.P. and Secy.; David J. Thomas, Treas.
EIN: 510150352

61336
The Heenan Foundation, Inc.
2786 McKinley Dr.
Woodbury, MN 55125
Contact: Susan Skinner, V.P.

Established in 1991 in MN.
Donor(s): George Heenan.
Financial data (yr. ended 05/31/99): Assets, $75,703 (M); grants paid, $10,103; gifts received, $132; expenditures, $11,455; qualifying distributions, $11,224.
Limitations: Giving primarily in MN.
Application information: Generally contributes to 3 pre-selected organizations. Application form required.
Officers: George Heenan, Chair.; Lucille Heenan, Pres. and Treas.; Susan Skinner, V.P. and Secy.; Lynda Alvashere, V.P.; Michael Heenan, V.P.
EIN: 411718396

61337
South Washington County Scholarship Committee
944 Portland Ave.
St. Paul Park, MN 55071

Established in 1986 in MN.
Financial data (yr. ended 12/31/01): Assets, $74,219 (M); grants paid, $18,000; gifts received, $16,100; expenditures, $18,484; qualifying distributions, $17,964.
Limitations: Giving limited to South Washington County, WI.
Application information: Applications are issued by counselors at Woodbury and Park High Schools. Application form required.
Officers: Norm H. Larsen, Chair.; Shirley Burbank, Secy.; Elaine Schlemmer, Treas.

Directors: Thomas Bartl, Al Boche, Robert C. Briggs, Tony Schommer, Alan Wilkie.
EIN: 411433314
Codes: GTI

61338
Tabgha Foundation
c/o John E. Schwarz
6913 Gleason Rd.
Edina, MN 55439-1604

Donor(s): John E. Schwarz.
Financial data (yr. ended 12/31/99): Assets, $72,677 (M); grants paid, $2,000; gifts received, $238,942; expenditures, $171,351; qualifying distributions, $171,351.
Officers and Directors:* John E. Schwarz,* Pres. and Secy.-Treas.; Barbara E. Schwarz,* V.P.; Jay B. Schwarz.
EIN: 411718007

61339
Retel Foundation Charitable Trust
291 Lakeview Terrace Blvd.
Waconia, MN 55387-9691

Established in 1998.
Financial data (yr. ended 12/31/00): Assets, $71,300 (M); grants paid, $3,225; gifts received, $13,949; expenditures, $3,800; qualifying distributions, $6,315.
Limitations: Applications not accepted.
Application information: Contributes only to pre-selected organizations.
Trustees: Charles L. Dueber, Regena J. Dueber.
EIN: 416443943

61340
Vosh-Minn, Inc.
(also known as V.O.S.H., Inc.)
225 Mississippi Dr.
Monticello, MN 55362

Financial data (yr. ended 03/31/00): Assets, $67,448 (M); grants paid, $0; gifts received, $8,877; expenditures, $11,472; qualifying distributions, $74,424; giving activities include $1,907 for programs.
Officers: James J. Hess, Pres.; Kirk R. Thomas, V.P.; Lori Kirschenmann, Secy.; Robert Rolling, Treas.
EIN: 411298649
Codes: TN

61341
The Harrington Foundation
4248 Park Glen Rd.
Minneapolis, MN 55416-4775
Contact: Edward A. Harrington, Pres.

Classified as a private operating foundation in 1998. Established in 1997 in MN.
Donor(s): Edward Harrington.
Financial data (yr. ended 12/31/01): Assets, $63,566 (M); grants paid, $19,597; gifts received, $10,170; expenditures, $28,860; qualifying distributions, $19,582.
Limitations: Giving primarily in MN.
Officer: Edward A. Harrington, Pres.
EIN: 411894989

61342
Marquit-Grieser Fund
3512 W. 22nd St.
Minneapolis, MN 55416-3635

Established in 1996 in MN.
Donor(s): Erwin Marquit.
Financial data (yr. ended 12/31/99): Assets, $59,431 (M); grants paid, $23,050; gifts received, $36,839; expenditures, $23,124; qualifying distributions, $23,109.
Limitations: Applications not accepted.

Application information: Contributes only to pre-selected organizations.
Officers and Directors:* Doris G. Marquit,* Pres. and Secy.; Erwin Marquit,* V.P. and Treas.; Janet Quaife.
EIN: 411827841

61343
Trimont Area Youth Foundation
P.O. Box 388
Trimont, MN 56176 (507) 639-9921
Contact: Michael A. Mulder, Secy.-Treas.

Established in 1990 in MN.
Financial data (yr. ended 12/31/99): Assets, $53,411 (M); grants paid, $1,500; expenditures, $1,626; qualifying distributions, $3,026.
Limitations: Giving limited to residents of the Trimont, MN, area.
Application information: Applications available in counselor's office of the Trimont High School District. Application form required.
Officers: Leslie W. Peterson, Pres.; Beverly J. Anthony, V.P.; Michael A. Mulder, Secy.-Treas.
EIN: 411653403

61344
Johnny B. Good Foundation
c/o John B. Goodman
1107 Hazeltine Blvd., Ste. 200
Chaska, MN 55318

Established in 1990.
Donor(s): John B. Goodman.
Financial data (yr. ended 12/31/01): Assets, $51,995 (M); grants paid, $0; gifts received, $3,000; expenditures, $10,123; qualifying distributions, $0.
Officers and Directors:* John B. Goodman,* Pres.; Daniel R. Peterka, Treas.; Sidney A. Goodman.
EIN: 411693703

61345
The Global Healing Community Foundation
1818 Oliver Ave. S., Ste. 2
Minneapolis, MN 55405

Established in 2001 in MN.
Donor(s): National Philanthropic Trust, Mitch Gaynor, Catherine Gaynor.
Financial data (yr. ended 12/31/01): Assets, $49,964 (M); grants paid, $14,345; gifts received, $775,000; expenditures, $725,571; qualifying distributions, $725,471; giving activities include $700,030 for programs.
Limitations: Applications not accepted.
Application information: Contributes only to pre-selected organizations.
Officers: M. Bridget Duffy, Pres.; Fiona Druckenmiller, V.P.; Kathryn McCarthy, Secy.-Treas.
EIN: 412006456

61346
Red Wing Environmental Learning Center, Inc.
3594 Tower View Dr.
Red Wing, MN 55066-1134

Classified as a private operating foundation in 1972.
Donor(s): Red Wing Shoe Co. Inc. Foundation.
Financial data (yr. ended 06/30/00): Assets, $48,494 (M); grants paid, $0; gifts received, $235,040; expenditures, $263,364; qualifying distributions, $263,364; giving activities include $263,364 for programs.
Director: Bruce Ause, Exec. Dir.
EIN: 410967058

61347
Moose Willow Sportsman Club
P. O. Box 206
Hill City, MN 55748-0206
Contact: Pam Pierce

Established in 1998 in MN.
Financial data (yr. ended 06/30/00): Assets, $48,378 (M); grants paid, $0; gifts received, $2,435; expenditures, $2,801; qualifying distributions, $7,252; giving activities include $2,801 for programs.
Trustees: Dorothy Biskey, John Biskey, Dale Landrus.
EIN: 411681476

61348
Nandale Foundation
c/o Dale Anderson
17319 Olinda Tr.
Marine On St. Croix, MN 55047

Donor(s): Dale R. Anderson, Nancy J. Anderson.
Financial data (yr. ended 12/31/99): Assets, $42,567 (M); grants paid, $3,230; gifts received, $6,731; expenditures, $3,989; qualifying distributions, $3,230.
Limitations: Applications not accepted.
Application information: Contributes only to pre-selected organizations.
Officers and Directors:* Dale R. Anderson,* C.E.O.; Nancy J. Anderson,* Treas.
EIN: 411814184

61349
Marso Foundation
c/o Mary Schmitz
350 N. Robert St., Ste. 100
St. Paul, MN 55101-1502

Established around 1992.
Donor(s): Donald Schmitz, Mary Schmitz.
Financial data (yr. ended 12/31/99): Assets, $34,598 (M); grants paid, $19,067; gifts received, $41,000; expenditures, $19,937; qualifying distributions, $19,067.
Limitations: Applications not accepted. Giving limited to St. Paul, MN.
Application information: Contributes only to pre-selected organizations.
Director: Mary Schmitz.
EIN: 411717043

61350
Lupins Garden, Inc.
814 Grand Ave.
St. Paul, MN 55105

Financial data (yr. ended 03/31/02): Assets, $33,796 (M); grants paid, $0; gifts received, $57,128; expenditures, $61,691; qualifying distributions, $0.
Officers: Laura Stone, Pres.; Patricia Walsh, V.P.; Patrick Williams, Secy.; Catherine Szyman, Treas.
EIN: 411786207

61351
John Warren Johnson and Marion Louise Johnson Family Foundation
5101 Irving Ave. S.
Minneapolis, MN 55419

Established in 1998 in MN.
Donor(s): John Warren Johnson, Marion Louise Johnson.
Financial data (yr. ended 12/31/00): Assets, $32,682 (M); grants paid, $30,050; gifts received, $35,000; expenditures, $30,050; qualifying distributions, $30,050.
Limitations: Applications not accepted.
Application information: Contributes only to pre-selected organizations.
Trustees: John Warren Johnson, Marion Louise Johnson.
EIN: 411915363

61352
Harvest Workers Foundation
6305 Upper 44th St., Ct. N.
Oakdale, MN 55128-2522

Established in 1997 in MN.
Financial data (yr. ended 04/30/00): Assets, $26,453 (M); grants paid, $2,300; expenditures, $4,683; qualifying distributions, $2,831.
Limitations: Applications not accepted.
Application information: Contributes only to pre-selected organizations.
Officers and Directors:* Daniel Muckula,* V.P.; Marla Muckala, Secy.; Ray Muckala,* Treas. and Exec. Dir.
EIN: 411876892

61353
India Association of Minnesota, Inc.
(Formerly India Club, Inc.)
P.O. Box 130158
St. Paul, MN 55113-0158

Financial data (yr. ended 12/31/99): Assets, $24,561 (M); grants paid, $0; expenditures, $23,559; qualifying distributions, $0; giving activities include $23,558 for programs.
Officers and Directors:* Bhupat Desai,* Pres.; Ananth Shanker,* V.P.; Vioin Gopal,* Secy.; Sunondo Ghosh,* Treas.; Dharam Bobra, Devesh Chandra, Deepshika Gupia, Mary Gupia, Shashi Gupia, Ginny Jacobson, and 11 additional directors:.
EIN: 237364647

61354
Minnesota Decoy Foundation
c/o R.W. Brust
2172 Ferris Ln.
Roseville, MN 55113

Financial data (yr. ended 12/31/99): Assets, $24,152 (M); grants paid, $590; gifts received, $8,250; expenditures, $889; qualifying distributions, $590.
Officers: Howard V. Anderson, Pres. and Treas.; Frank Canfield, V.P. and Secy.
Directors: Marty Hansen, Larry Thomforde, Dick Tyrell.
EIN: 411699514

61355
Park Press, Inc.
P.O. Box 8106
St. Paul, MN 55108

Classified as a private operating foundation in 1979.
Financial data (yr. ended 06/30/00): Assets, $23,441 (M); grants paid, $0; gifts received, $16,613; expenditures, $105,152; qualifying distributions, $105,152; giving activities include $83,463 for programs.
Officer and Directors:* Bill Lorimer, Pres.; Thor Kammedahl, Rachel Larson, Carolyn Nestingen, Bettye Olson, Mark Olson, Steve Plagens, Alisa Potter, Regula Russelle, Jeanne Schacht, Marietta Spencer.
EIN: 510178125

61356
Sampson Foundation, Inc.
6612 Gleason Terr., Ste. 404
Edina, MN 55439-1131

Established in 1996.
Donor(s): John E. Sampson.
Financial data (yr. ended 12/31/01): Assets, $18,380 (M); grants paid, $21,025; gifts received, $10,050; expenditures, $22,629; qualifying distributions, $22,629.
Limitations: Applications not accepted. Giving on a national basis, with some emphasis on MN.
Application information: Contributes only to pre-selected organizations.
Directors: J. Mark Sampson, John E. Sampson, Mary M. Sampson, Sharon M. Sampson.
EIN: 411886805

61357
Henry K. and Mildred M. Grawe Charitable Foundation
678 Sioux St.
Winona, MN 55987
Contact: Robin Grawe, Committee Member

Established in 2000 in MN.
Donor(s): Paul Grawe.
Financial data (yr. ended 12/31/00): Assets, $7,555 (M); grants paid, $11,550; gifts received, $11,600; expenditures, $11,550; qualifying distributions, $11,550.
Limitations: Giving primarily in MN.
Officer: Nathan Grawe, Chair.
Committee Members: Elizabeth Grawe, Paul Grawe, Robin Grawe.
Trustee: Charles Grawe.
EIN: 416446187

61358
Willmar Crime Prevention Center
P.O. Box 533
Willmar, MN 56201-0533

Financial data (yr. ended 12/31/00): Assets, $5,624 (M); grants paid, $200; gifts received, $1,600; expenditures, $1,107; qualifying distributions, $200.
Limitations: Applications not accepted.
Directors: Walt Gislason, Carl E. Jones, Leland Nelson, Stanley Ray, John Tradup.
EIN: 411364757

61359
Nolan Family Foundation
7020 Willow Creek Rd.
Eden Prairie, MN 55344-3224 (612) 829-8295
Contact: Pamela K. Nolan, Dir.

Established in 1998 in MN.
Donor(s): Stuart H. Nolan.
Financial data (yr. ended 12/31/00): Assets, $920 (M); grants paid, $10,767; gifts received, $10,000; expenditures, $10,885; qualifying distributions, $0.
Directors: Courtney B. Nolan, Michael B. Nolan, Pamela K. Nolan, Stuart H. Nolan.
EIN: 411910972

61360
The Association of Marriage Builders, Inc.
12568 Ethan Ave. N.
White Bear Lake, MN 55110

Established in 2001 in MN.
Donor(s): Willard F. Harley.
Financial data (yr. ended 12/31/01): Assets, $791 (M); grants paid, $0; gifts received, $10,625; expenditures, $9,834; qualifying distributions, $9,834; giving activities include $4,300 for programs.
Limitations: Applications not accepted.
Application information: Contributes only to pre-selected organizations.
Director: Willard F. Harley.
EIN: 411962538

61361
Children of the World Foundation
5160 Hemlock Lane N.
Plymouth, MN 55442-2118

Established in 1999 in MN.
Financial data (yr. ended 12/31/99): Assets, $0 (L); grants paid, $1,350; gifts received, $2,587; expenditures, $1,677; qualifying distributions, $2,587.
Limitations: Giving primarily in OH.
Officers: Brigid L. Bechtold, Chair.; Dale O. Wick, Secy.; Jim Krattenmaker, Treas.
EIN: 411941687

MISSISSIPPI

61362
Eastman Memorial Foundation
P.O. Box 1108
Laurel, MS 39441-1108

Classified as a private operating foundation in 1985.
Financial data (yr. ended 05/31/00): Assets, $15,165,606 (M); grants paid, $0; gifts received, $268,673; expenditures, $809,403; qualifying distributions, $7,188,843; giving activities include $563,079 for programs.
Director: George Bassi.
EIN: 640308406

61363
L. D. Hancock Foundation, Inc.
P.O. Box 2203
Tupelo, MS 38803-2203 (662) 844-4080
Contact: Billy Haygood

Established in 1988 in MS.
Donor(s): L.D. Hancock.
Financial data (yr. ended 12/31/01): Assets, $9,318,589 (M); grants paid, $284,000; expenditures, $298,541; qualifying distributions, $284,000.
Limitations: Giving primarily in MS.
Officers and Directors:* Elaine G. Hancock,* Pres.; Janice H. Allen,* V.P.; Doyce H. Deas,* V.P.; Larry Hancock,* V.P.; Lauren H. Patterson,* Secy.
EIN: 640582491
Codes: FD

61364
The O'Keefe Foundation
P.O. Box 430
Ocean Springs, MS 39566
Application address: 611 Jackson Ave., Ocean Springs, MS 39564, tel.: (228) 872-2939
Contact: J.J. O'Keefe, Jr., Chair.

Established in 1996 in MS.
Financial data (yr. ended 06/30/01): Assets, $4,705,792 (M); grants paid, $63,325; gifts received, $10,124; expenditures, $684,384; qualifying distributions, $539,235; giving activities include $389,148 for programs.
Limitations: Giving primarily in MS.
Officers: J.J. O'Keefe, Jr., Chair. and Pres.; M.R.J. Howze, Vice-Chair.; Joseph O'Keefe, Secy.; Maureen O'Keefe, Treas.; Susan O'Keefe, Treas.
EIN: 640881459

61365
Phillips Foundation
P.O. Box 471
Columbus, MS 39703-0471
Application address: 116 5th St. N., Columbus, MS 39701, tel.: (662) 327-8401
Contact: Atwell Andrews

Established in 1941.
Donor(s): Phillips Foundation Trust.
Financial data (yr. ended 12/31/01): Assets, $4,391,933 (M); grants paid, $134,708; gifts received, $5,800; expenditures, $166,021; qualifying distributions, $150,913.
Limitations: Giving primarily to residents of Lowndes County, MS.
Application information: Application form required.
Officers and Trustees:* Frank J. Baird, Pres.; Hunter Gholson,* Secy.; T.E. Lott, Jr.,* Treas.
EIN: 646020136
Codes: FD2

61366
John James Audubon Foundation
4541 Ridgeway Dr.
Belden, MS 38826

Classified as a private operating foundation in 1971.
Donor(s): Sara Gladney.‡
Financial data (yr. ended 12/31/00): Assets, $2,322,303 (M); grants paid, $350; expenditures, $35,752; qualifying distributions, $350.
Officers: Neil Odenwald, Pres.; Harold Hogan, V.P.; Hope Norman, Secy.; Joseph W. Gary, Treas.
EIN: 726028699

61367
East Mississippi Development Corporation
c/o Meridian Community College
910 Hwy. 19 N.
Meridian, MS 39307

Established in 1991 in MS.
Financial data (yr. ended 12/31/00): Assets, $1,885,039 (M); grants paid, $0; gifts received, $10,195; expenditures, $107,631; qualifying distributions, $196,653; giving activities include $185,063 for program-related investments.
Officers and Directors:* Scott D. Elliott,* Pres.; Archie McDonnell,* V.P.; William S. Crawford,* Secy.-Treas.; Susan Coats, Frank Farley, Myles Frank, Kim Gianakos, George Hampton, Sam Henry, Larry Johnson, John B. Jones, Jeff McCoy, Natalie Purvis, Allen Stewart, and 4 additional directors.
EIN: 640773932

61368
John M. & Elizabeth Beeman Bleuer Scholarship Fund
P.O. Box 289
Biloxi, MS 39533-0289 (228) 374-2100
Contact: Lyle M. Page, Tr.

Established in 1991 in MS.
Donor(s): Elizabeth Beeman Bleuer.‡
Financial data (yr. ended 12/31/99): Assets, $1,829,360 (M); grants paid, $58,700; expenditures, $68,648; qualifying distributions, $58,700.
Limitations: Giving limited to residents of Biloxi, MS.
Publications: Informational brochure (including application guidelines).
Application information: Application guidelines available at local area schools and colleges. Application form required.
Trustees: Lyle M. Page, Mildred B. Page.
EIN: 646197850

Codes: GTI

61369
Soli Deo Gloria Foundation
400 E. Capitol St., Ste. 201
Jackson, MS 39201-2610
Contact: Stuart C. Irby, Jr., Pres.

Established in 1995 in MS.
Donor(s): Stuart C. Irby, Jr.
Financial data (yr. ended 12/31/01): Assets, $1,628,542 (M); grants paid, $145,570; expenditures, $158,163; qualifying distributions, $154,760.
Limitations: Applications not accepted. Giving on a national basis, with emphasis on Washington, DC, and MS.
Application information: Contributes only to pre-selected organizations.
Officers: Stuart C. Irby, Jr., Pres.; Carson Hughes, V.P.; Debbie Sue West Irby, Secy.-Treas.
Trustees: David Beard, Gilbert V. Kelling.
EIN: 640864685
Codes: FD2

61370
The Dalrymple Family Foundation, Inc.
P.O. Box 210
Amory, MS 38821-0210

Established in 1998 in MS.
Financial data (yr. ended 04/30/01): Assets, $613,896 (M); grants paid, $32,542; expenditures, $35,833; qualifying distributions, $33,476.
Limitations: Applications not accepted.
Application information: Contributes only to pre-selected organizations.
Officers: Arch Dalrymple, Pres.; Adine Dalrymple, V.P.; Rita H. Caldwell, Secy.
Director: Martha Dalrymple.
EIN: 721373976

61371
Leigh Foundation, Inc.
824 7th St. N.
Columbus, MS 39705

Established in 2000 in MS.
Donor(s): Frank M. Leigh, Martha Polk Leigh.
Financial data (yr. ended 12/31/00): Assets, $135,000 (M); grants paid, $0; gifts received, $135,000; expenditures, $0; qualifying distributions, $0.
Officers and Director:* Frank M. Leigh, Chair. and Pres.; Martha Polk Leigh,* Secy.
EIN: 640920175

61372
Carothers Construction Charitable Foundation
c/o Sean B. Carothers
P.O. Box 687
Water Valley, MS 38965-0687

Established in 1998.
Donor(s): Sean B. Carothers.
Financial data (yr. ended 12/31/01): Assets, $126,701 (M); grants paid, $4,310; gifts received, $27,000; expenditures, $4,319; qualifying distributions, $4,319.
Limitations: Applications not accepted.
Application information: Contributes only to pre-selected organizations.
Officers: Sean B. Carothers, Pres.; Cathy A. Guarr, Secy.; Sherry Johnson, Treas.
EIN: 640892836

61373
Hughes Memorial Foundation
P.O. Box 43
Bailey, MS 39320-0043

Established in 1989 in MS.

Donor(s): Harry N. Lackey.
Financial data (yr. ended 06/30/00): Assets, $105,991 (M); grants paid, $0; gifts received, $12,110; expenditures, $7,067; qualifying distributions, $3,934; giving activities include $2,148 for programs.
Officers and Directors:* Berta Lee Hughes White,* Pres.; Jack Hayless Smith,* V.P.; Yerby Lee Hughes, Jr.,* Secy.; Will Smith Lackey, Jr.,* Treas.; Berta Joan White Evans, James Franklin Hughes, George Edward Lackey, Harry Noel Lackey, Barbara Anne Hughes Landry, Betty Jane Hughes Lavergne, and 5 additional directors.
EIN: 640781670

61374
Paul T. Benton Charitable Trust
P.O. Box 1341
Biloxi, MS 39533-1341

Established in 2000 in MS.
Donor(s): Paul T. Benton.
Financial data (yr. ended 12/31/00): Assets, $100,121 (M); grants paid, $0; gifts received, $100,000; expenditures, $0; qualifying distributions, $0.
Limitations: Applications not accepted.
Application information: Contributes only to pre-selected organizations.
Trustee: Paul T. Benton.
EIN: 646222377

61375
Dale R. & Judith A. Anderson Endowment Foundation
2497 S. Greensburg Rd.
Liberty, MS 39645 (601) 654-3236

Financial data (yr. ended 12/31/01): Assets, $94,465 (L); grants paid, $5,175; expenditures, $5,175; qualifying distributions, $5,175.
Trustees: Marie Matlosz, Dennis Willson.
EIN: 646212107

61376
Southland Ministries, Inc.
c/o Terrell Yonkers
P.O. Box 246
Clinton, MS 39060

Donor(s): J. Malcolm Yonkers.
Financial data (yr. ended 12/31/01): Assets, $47,766 (M); grants paid, $0; gifts received, $42,191; expenditures, $33,045; qualifying distributions, $0.
Officers and Directors:* John Moore,* Pres.; Marie Fisher,* V.P.; James Yonker,* Secy.; Terrell Yonkers, Administrator; Lois Fisher, William Flickinger, and 10 additional directors.
EIN: 640823350

61377
Mississippi Dental Association
(also known as Mississippi Dental Relief Fund)
2630 Ridgewood Rd.
Jackson, MS 39216-4290

Classified as a private operating foundation in 1975.
Financial data (yr. ended 06/30/00): Assets, $36,708 (M); grants paid, $2,550; gifts received, $7,804; expenditures, $2,550; qualifying distributions, $2,550.
Limitations: Applications not accepted. Giving primarily in MS.
Officers: Robert Rives, Pres.; Melvyn Stromeyer, V.P.; Pat Welsh, Secy.-Treas.
EIN: 510175942

61378
The Holly Foundation
P.O. Box 9483
Jackson, MS 39206-9483 (601) 353-5423

Classified as a private operating foundation in 1984.
Donor(s): Sandra F. Holly.
Financial data (yr. ended 12/31/01): Assets, $18,828 (M); grants paid, $616; gifts received, $2,000; expenditures, $1,505; qualifying distributions, $1,506.
Officers: Sandra F. Holly, Chair.; Lavern J. Holly, Secy.; Lavonia A. Holly, Treas.
EIN: 640685537

61379
Tollison Charitable Fund
100 Courthouse Sq.
Oxford, MS 38655

Financial data (yr. ended 12/31/01): Assets, $3,971 (M); grants paid, $4,000; gifts received, $4,320; expenditures, $4,210; qualifying distributions, $4,319.
Limitations: Applications not accepted. Giving limited to residents of MS.
Director: Grady F. Tollison III.
EIN: 640893097

61380
Smiles Learning Center, Inc.
P. O. Box 352
Starkville, MS 39759

Financial data (yr. ended 12/31/01): Assets, $3,745 (M); grants paid, $0; gifts received, $173,452; expenditures, $173,452; qualifying distributions, $0.
Officers: W.L. Smith, Pres.; Eva Smith, Exec. Dir.
EIN: 640785793

MISSOURI

61381
Linda A. Hall Library Trusts
c/o Paul D. Bartlett, et al.
5109 Cherry St.
Kansas City, MO 64110-2425

Classified as a private operating foundation in 1988.
Financial data (yr. ended 12/31/00): Assets, $235,802,331 (M); grants paid, $0; gifts received, $96,935; expenditures, $7,841,780; qualifying distributions, $10,078,465; giving activities include $6,283,159 for programs.
Officers: C. Lee Jones, Dir.; Marcia Fennesy, Bus. Off.; Paula L. Volk, Inv. Off.
Trustees: Marilyn Bartlett Hebenstreit, David H. Hughes, Landon H. Rowland, Dwight D. Sutherland, Robert H. West.
EIN: 440527122

61382
Masonic Home of Missouri
13990 Olive Rd., Ste. 100
Chesterfield, MO 63017

Classified as a private operating foundation in 1987.
Financial data (yr. ended 06/30/00): Assets, $85,275,267 (M); grants paid, $0; gifts received, $2,772,004; expenditures, $3,400,866; qualifying distributions, $2,547,386; giving activities include $3,400,866 for programs.
Limitations: Applications not accepted.
Officers: Freddie D. Adams, Pres.; Glenn E. Means, V.P.; John W. Mayo, Treas.; Thomas H. Nations, Secy.
Directors: Don Cox, James D. Gibson, Robert E. Hardester, John W. Hess, Jimmie D. Lee, Richard H. Montgomery, Wilfred G. Soutiea, Jr., Stanley M. Thompson, Gail S. Turner.
EIN: 430653370

61383
Dennis M. Jones Family Foundation
(Formerly Dennis & Judith Jones Charitable Foundation Trust)
1700 S. Warson Rd.
St. Louis, MO 63124 (314) 576-6100
Contact: Dennis M. Jones, Jr., Tr.

Established in 1998 in MO.
Donor(s): Dennis M. Jones.
Financial data (yr. ended 12/31/00): Assets, $51,839,301 (M); grants paid, $2,187,766; gifts received, $51,409,300; expenditures, $2,187,766; qualifying distributions, $2,187,766.
Limitations: Giving primarily in MO, with emphasis on St. Louis.
Trustees: J. Denise Franz, Dennis M. Jones, Jr.
EIN: 436786094
Codes: FD

61384
Pulitzer Foundation for the Arts
900 N. Tucker Blvd.
St. Louis, MO 63101

Established in 1996 in MO.
Donor(s): Emily Rauh Pulitzer.
Financial data (yr. ended 12/31/01): Assets, $22,764,737 (M); grants paid, $0; gifts received, $97,000; expenditures, $1,127,401; qualifying distributions, $0.
Officers and Directors:* Emily Rauh Pulitzer,* Pres.; William Bush,* V.P.; Walter L. Metcalfe, Jr.,* Secy.; James V. Maloney, Treas.
EIN: 431752949

61385
The Charless Home
4431 S. Broadway
St. Louis, MO 63111

Classified as a private operating foundation in 1986.
Financial data (yr. ended 10/31/00): Assets, $18,408,620 (M); grants paid, $0; gifts received, $32,477; expenditures, $2,997,056; qualifying distributions, $3,060,053; giving activities include $2,997,056 for programs.
Directors: Alice Appel, Janet Hatton, William Howery, Belinda Janos, Gary V. Sluyter, Lori Tipton, Shirley Valley.
Advisory Committee: Charles C. Allen, Jr., Lucien R. Fouke, Jr., Donald H. Streett.
Trustees: William Barnes, P. Taylor Bryan III, Nicholas B. Clifford, Earl Dille, George S. Goding, Samuel F. Gordon III, and 12 additional trustees.
EIN: 430666753

61386
Kemper Museum Operating Foundation
4420 Warwick Blvd.
Kansas City, MO 64111

Established in 1996 in MO.
Financial data (yr. ended 12/31/01): Assets, $13,913,069 (M); grants paid, $0; gifts received, $2,253,990; expenditures, $3,153,933; qualifying distributions, $3,531,180; giving activities include $2,616,473 for programs.

Officers and Trustees:* R. Crosby Kemper,* Chair.; Louis Joshua Sosland,* Vice-Chair.; David Miller, Secy.; Walter Dietrich, Mgr.; Thomas Morton Bloch, Marilyn Bartlett Hebenstreit, Dan Keegan, Bebe Kemper, Jerome Stanley Nerman, Sharon Wood Orr.
EIN: 431715390

61387
Powell Gardens, Inc.
1609 N.W. U.S. Hwy. 50
Kingsville, MO 64061-9000

Established in 1988 in MO.
Donor(s): The Powell Family Foundation, The Friends of Powell Gardens, Inc.
Financial data (yr. ended 12/31/01): Assets, $13,845,154 (M); grants paid, $0; gifts received, $1,892,420; expenditures, $2,902,038; qualifying distributions, $2,948,931.
Officers: Wendy J. Powell, Jr., Chair.; Marilyn P. Rinker, Vice-Chair.; Eric N. Tschanz, Pres.; Nicholas K. Powell, Secy.; Linda Gill Taylor, Treas.
Directors: Gregory B. Allen, Richard B. Cray, George R. Russell, Norma Sutherland, and 5 additional directors.
EIN: 431483357

61388
Eric P. Newman Numismatic Education Society
6450 Cecil Ave.
St. Louis, MO 63105

Established in 1958 in MO.
Donor(s): Eric P. Newman, Evelyn E. Newman.
Financial data (yr. ended 11/30/01): Assets, $11,575,253 (M); grants paid, $350; gifts received, $929,298; expenditures, $61,341; qualifying distributions, $350.
Officers: Eric P. Newman, Pres.; Andrew E. Newman, V.P.; Evelyn E. Newman, V.P.; Linda N. Schapiro, V.P.
EIN: 436048614

61389
Gateway Center of Metropolitan St. Louis, Inc.
720 Olive St., 24th Fl.
St. Louis, MO 63101

Donor(s): Malcolm W. Martin.
Financial data (yr. ended 12/31/01): Assets, $10,614,593 (M); grants paid, $0; gifts received, $18,095; expenditures, $340,692; qualifying distributions, $0.
Officer and Director:* Malcolm W. Martin,* Pres.
EIN: 237004665

61390
Andrew Drumm Institute
3210 Lee's Summit Rd.
Independence, MO 64055

Financial data (yr. ended 08/31/01): Assets, $10,348,140 (M); grants paid, $0; gifts received, $40,655; expenditures, $702,509; qualifying distributions, $621,417; giving activities include $621,417 for programs.
Trustees: Raymond A. Braswell, Cindy Cable Cavanah, Stanley Crumbaugh, Paul Allen Foster, Hap Graff, Sr., V. Carl Jelley, Kathleen D. Kiilip, Richard A. King, Kenneth B. McClain, Elizabeth A. McClure, Michele C. McIntosh, Bjorn E. Olsson, Richard Rhodes, David A. Rock, Sandy Rolf, Judy M. Simonitsch.
EIN: 440569643

61391
Mary Culver Home, Inc.
(also known as Blind Girls' Home, Inc.)
221 W. Washington Ave.
Kirkwood, MO 63122

Classified as a private operating foundation in 1974 in MO.
Donor(s): Adele G. Faloon Trust.
Financial data (yr. ended 12/31/01): Assets, $10,188,258 (M); grants paid, $0; gifts received, $59,466; expenditures, $1,315,117; qualifying distributions, $1,134,215; giving activities include $1,134,215 for programs.
Officers: Lorraine Schuk, Pres.; Karen Smith, V.P.; Irene Menos, Treas.
Directors: Zdena Aschinger, Margaret Axtell, Carol Bachman, Eleanor Curran, Betty Heiman, Doris Klos, Mary Jane McCarty, Diane Scanga, Beth Shreffler, Clare Turner.
EIN: 430662450

61392
Toy & Miniature Museum of Kansas City Foundation
(Formerly Miniature Museum of Kansas City Foundation)
5235 Oak St.
Kansas City, MO 64112-2877

Classified as a private operating foundation in 1980.
Donor(s): James Kemper, Jr., John Francis, Mary Harris Francis, Barbara H. Marshall.
Financial data (yr. ended 12/31/01): Assets, $7,404,312 (M); grants paid, $80; gifts received, $302,813; expenditures, $397,684; qualifying distributions, $80.
Officers: Barbara H. Marshall, Pres. and Treas.; Mary Harris Francis, V.P.; James Bernard, Sr., Secy.; John Francis, Treas.
Directors: Scott Francis, Miriam Formanek-Brunell, Peggy Silva, Eleanor Swartz.
EIN: 431187852

61393
McBeth Foundation Trust
P.O. Box 66734
St. Louis, MO 63166

Established in 1989 in CA.
Donor(s): Barbara Woodruff.
Financial data (yr. ended 09/30/01): Assets, $5,931,736 (M); grants paid, $170,000; expenditures, $339,547; qualifying distributions, $196,200.
Limitations: Giving primarily in CA.
Trustees: Barbara Woodruff, A.G. Edwards Trust Co.
EIN: 330399736
Codes: FD2

61394
Charles & Ethel Hughes Foundation, Inc.
460 W. 5th St.
Lebanon, MO 65536-2815
Contact: Kareh Cook, Secy.-Treas.

Established in 1978 in MO.
Donor(s): Charles Hughes.‡
Financial data (yr. ended 12/31/00): Assets, $5,159,590 (M); grants paid, $47,000; expenditures, $188,102; qualifying distributions, $183,791; giving activities include $144,088 for programs.
Limitations: Giving primarily in Laclede County, MO.
Application information: Application form not required.
Officers: H. Dale Hooker, Chair.; Karen Myers Cook, Secy.

Directors: Donnelly Baldwin, Margaret Burtin, Howard Carrington.
EIN: 431134135

61395
Sylvia G. Thompson Charitable Trust
P.O. Box 1546
Sedalia, MO 65302-1546

Established in 1990.
Financial data (yr. ended 12/31/01): Assets, $3,965,169 (M); grants paid, $0; expenditures, $207,533; qualifying distributions, $800,134; giving activities include $783,327 for program-related investments.
Limitations: Applications not accepted. Giving limited to Sedalia, MO.
Application information: Contributes only to a pre-selected organization.
Trustees: Adam B. Fischer, Henry Lamm, James Mathewson, William Shumake.
EIN: 436368333

61396
Helen and Sam Kaplan Charitable Foundation
c/o R. Caspermeyer
414 Nichols Rd.
Kansas City, MO 64112

Established in 2000 in MO.
Financial data (yr. ended 12/31/01): Assets, $2,201,795 (M); grants paid, $629,250; gifts received, $1,537,437; expenditures, $667,145; qualifying distributions, $628,218.
Trustee: Country Club Bank.
EIN: 431862067
Codes: FD

61397
Grand Arts
(Formerly Margaret Hall Silva Foundation)
1819 Grand Ave.
Kansas City, MO 64108
FAX: (816) 421-1561; *E-mail:* grandart@gvi.net

Classified as a private operating foundation in 1995 in MO.
Donor(s): Margaret Hall Silva.
Financial data (yr. ended 12/31/01): Assets, $2,096,540 (M); grants paid, $0; gifts received, $580,058; expenditures, $779,440; qualifying distributions, $683,763; giving activities include $340,884 for programs.
Officers and Directors:* Margaret Hall Silva,* Pres. and Treas.; Charles J. Egan, Jr.,* V.P.; Richard Haydon,* V.P.; Sean Kelley.
EIN: 431698172

61398
L-A-D Foundation, Inc.
c/o Claudia Spener
7260 Stanford Ave.
St. Louis, MO 63130

Established in 1962 in MO.
Donor(s): Leo A. Drey.
Financial data (yr. ended 06/30/01): Assets, $1,958,752 (M); grants paid, $5,250; expenditures, $6,920; qualifying distributions, $6,920.
Limitations: Applications not accepted. Giving primarily in MO.
Application information: Contributes only to pre-selected organizations.
Officers and Directors:* Leo A. Drey, Chair.; John Karel, Pres.; Eleanor A. Drey,* V.P.; Laura K. Drey,* V.P.; Leonard L. Drey,* V.P.; Kay K. Drey, Secy.; Claudia Spener, Treas.; Leon Cambre, Dorothy Ellis, Susan Flader, P. Wayne Goode, Jerry Vinyard.
EIN: 436036974

61399
Norman K. Probstein Charitable Foundation, Inc.
c/o Madeseo Investment Corp.
4630 Lindell Blvd.
St. Louis, MO 63108

Established in 1994 in MO.
Donor(s): Norman K. Probstein.
Financial data (yr. ended 12/31/01): Assets, $1,621,825 (M); grants paid, $0; expenditures, $1,777; qualifying distributions, $0.
Officers: Norman K. Probstein, Pres. and Treas.; James N. Probstein, V.P.; Margaret Avers, Secy.
EIN: 431676961

61400
Thomas Dunn Memorials Trust
c/o U.S. Bank
3113 Gasconade St.
St. Louis, MO 63118-4346
Application address: 1 Firstar Plz., St. Louis, MO 63166-0387
Contact: Jim Nelson, Trust Off., U.S. Bank

Established as a private operating foundation in 1978.
Donor(s): Thomas Dunn Trust.
Financial data (yr. ended 12/31/00): Assets, $1,575,118 (M); grants paid, $215; gifts received, $249,786; expenditures, $331,975; qualifying distributions, $292,921; giving activities include $263,409 for programs.
Application information: Application form not required.
Officers: Gary Grammer, Pres.; Kathy Bangert, V.P. and Exec. Dir.; Stephen H. Lewis, Secy.-Treas.
Directors: Robert J. Baer, Henry D. Shannon, Ph.D.
Trustee: U.S. Bank.
EIN: 436020367

61401
Paul & Regina Meyer Scholarship Trust
P.O. Box 1830
Sikeston, MO 63801 (573) 471-2424
Contact: Richard Adams, Tr.

Established as a private operating foundation in MO.
Financial data (yr. ended 03/31/02): Assets, $1,488,607 (M); grants paid, $87,923; expenditures, $97,233; qualifying distributions, $87,923.
Limitations: Giving limited to Sikeston High School graduates attending college in MO.
Trustee: Richard Adams.
EIN: 436721837
Codes: FD2

61402
First Hand Foundation
2800 Rockcreek Pkwy.
Kansas City, MO 64117 (816) 201-1024
Contact: Jeanne Lillig-Patterson, Mgr.

Classified as a company-sponsored operating foundation.
Donor(s): Cerner Corp.
Financial data (yr. ended 12/31/00): Assets, $1,376,653 (M); grants paid, $0; gifts received, $676,437; expenditures, $372,835; qualifying distributions, $330,404; giving activities include $330,404 for programs.
Limitations: Giving primarily in KS and MO.
Application information: Application form required.
Officers and Directors:* Neal L. Patterson,* Pres.; Marc G. Naughton,* V.P. and Treas.; Randy E. Sims, Secy.; Jeanne Lillig-Patterson, Mgr.; Clifford W. Illig.
EIN: 431725294

61403
Margaret G. Buckner Scholarship Trust
P.O. Box 721
Marshall, MO 65340-0721
Application address: 4435 Main St., Ste. 840, Kansas City, MO 64111, tel.: (816) 756-0030
Contact: John Wassberg

Established in 1996 in MO.
Financial data (yr. ended 12/31/01): Assets, $1,070,649 (M); grants paid, $36,276; gifts received, $201,438; expenditures, $37,765; qualifying distributions, $36,276.
Limitations: Giving limited to benefit Saline County, MO.
Application information: Application form required.
Directors: Leslie Coslet, Thomas B. Hall III, M.D., William B. Kessinger, Robert B. Rose.
Trustee: Wm. Gordon Buckner.
EIN: 431735027

61404
REC Music Foundation
c/o Robert E. Crawford, Jr.
61 Crestwood Dr.
Clayton, MO 63105

Established in 1992 in MO.
Donor(s): Robert E. Crawford, Jr.
Financial data (yr. ended 12/31/01): Assets, $1,069,081 (M); grants paid, $29,400; expenditures, $55,569; qualifying distributions, $29,400.
Limitations: Giving on a worldwide basis.
Officers and Directors:* Robert E. Crawford, Jr.,* Pres. and Secy.-Treas.; William G. Crawford,* V.P.; John S. Scandabit.
EIN: 431607598

61405
Walter Herbert Bonnell Trust
c/o Frank B. Green
P.O. Box 238
Weston, MO 64098

Classified as a private operating foundation around 1987.
Financial data (yr. ended 11/30/00): Assets, $1,042,331 (M); grants paid, $0; gifts received, $136; expenditures, $42,688; qualifying distributions, $38,014; giving activities include $32,180 for programs.
Trustee: Frank B. Green.
EIN: 431353465

61406
Winfred L. & Elizabeth C. Post Foundation, Inc.
300 S. Main St.
Joplin, MO 64801-2384

Classified as a private operating foundation in 1977.
Donor(s): Elizabeth C. Post, Winifred L. Post.
Financial data (yr. ended 12/31/01): Assets, $1,018,903 (M); grants paid, $0; expenditures, $67,750; qualifying distributions, $54,595.
Officers: Virginia Laas, Pres.; Chuck Brown, V.P.; Gail Smith, Secy.; Sharyn Lee, Treas.
EIN: 431105701

61407
The Lovett Pinetum Charitable Foundation
2850 Versailles
Springfield, MO 65804

Established in 1996 in MO, TX, and CA.
Donor(s): Robert L. Lovett.
Financial data (yr. ended 11/30/00): Assets, $989,631 (M); grants paid, $0; expenditures, $17,822; qualifying distributions, $12,803; giving activities include $12,161 for programs.
Officer and Directors:* Robert L. Lovett,* Chair.; Susan Burks, Charles E. Gray, Paul E. Lovett, Steven R. Lovett, Susanna M. Lovett, Michael Roling.
EIN: 431770714

61408
Mr. & Mrs. Barney A. Ebsworth Foundation, Inc.
7733 Forsyth Blvd., Ste. 1675
St. Louis, MO 63105

Classified as a private operating foundation in 1986.
Financial data (yr. ended 12/31/00): Assets, $890,000 (M); grants paid, $8,000,000; gifts received, $1,415; expenditures, $8,001,415; qualifying distributions, $8,001,415.
Limitations: Applications not accepted. Giving primarily in Washington, DC.
Application information: Contributes only to pre-selected organizations.
Officer and Directors:* Barney A. Ebsworth,* Pres.; Christiane Ebsworth, Pamela L. Ebsworth.
EIN: 431397651
Codes: FD

61409
Austin Memorial Home for the Aged, Inc.
102 Smith St.
Carrollton, MO 64633-1244

Established in 1985 in MO.
Financial data (yr. ended 12/31/01): Assets, $889,232 (L); grants paid, $0; gifts received, $55,278; expenditures, $39,481; qualifying distributions, $37,044; giving activities include $37,285 for programs.
Officers: Ann Leimkuhler, Pres.; Pat McAtee, Secy.; Jack Franken, Treas.
EIN: 431308882

61410
Lowe Family Foundation
228 E. Primrose St.
Springfield, MO 65807-5206

Established in 1997 in MO.
Donor(s): Carl A. Lowe, Dianna D. Lowe, V. Brent Lowe, Derrick C. Lowe.
Financial data (yr. ended 09/30/01): Assets, $878,267 (M); grants paid, $116,840; expenditures, $146,611; qualifying distributions, $116,840.
Limitations: Applications not accepted. Giving primarily in MO.
Application information: Contributes only to pre-selected organizations.
Officers: Carl A. Lowe, Pres.; Derrick C. Lowe, V.P.; V. Brent Lowe, V.P.; Kimberly Lowe Root, Secy.; Dianna D. Lowe, Treas.
EIN: 431799494
Codes: FD2

61411
The Schaeffer Foundation
118 Diekamp Ln.
St. Charles, MO 63303-5137 (636) 947-0555
Contact: Harold Schaeffer, Dir.

Established in 1992 in MO.
Donor(s): Harold Schaeffer, Joan Schaeffer.
Financial data (yr. ended 12/31/01): Assets, $851,729 (M); grants paid, $70,289; gifts received, $3,573; expenditures, $71,966; qualifying distributions, $71,966.
Limitations: Giving primarily in MO.
Application information: Application form required.

Officer and Directors:* Bess Maxwell,* Exec. Dir.; Rudy Beck, Lawrence Beilsmith, James M. Cochran, Jerry Hollingsworth, Paul Humberg, Judi Kapeller, Bess Maxwell, Joan Nigh, David Rohlfing, Harold Schaeffer, Jean Schaeffer, Joan Schaeffer, Sue Schaeffer, Walter Schaeffer.
EIN: 431597983

61412
The Alexander Majors Historical Foundation
8201 State Line Rd.
Kansas City, MO 64114

Donor(s): Terry W. Chapman.
Financial data (yr. ended 12/31/00): Assets, $749,186 (M); grants paid, $0; gifts received, $6,369; expenditures, $23,816; qualifying distributions, $11,857; giving activities include $11,857 for programs.
Officers and Directors:* Terry W. Chapman,* Pres. and Treas.; Art E. Asel,* V.P.; Pauline Dunn,* V.P.; Rodney V. Hipp,* Secy.
EIN: 480943475
Codes: TN

61413
Wood Place Public Library of California
c/o Paul Bloch
P.O. Box 127
California, MO 65018-0127

Classified as a private operating foundation in 1998 in MO.
Donor(s): Buddy W. Bolinger, Nancy Bolinger, Phyllis Heyssell,‡ Letha Papen Trust.
Financial data (yr. ended 12/31/01): Assets, $741,641 (M); grants paid, $0; gifts received, $65,711; expenditures, $64,132; qualifying distributions, $107,368; giving activities include $54,986 for programs.
Officers: Robert A. Hoff, Pres.; Nancy Lewis, V.P.; Terry Brown, Secy.; Paul Bloch, Treas.
EIN: 431810781

61414
Dan Broida/Sigma-Aldrich Scholarship Fund, Inc.
3050 Spruce St.
St. Louis, MO 63103-2530
Contact: Dan Broida

Established in 1982 in MO as a company-sponsored operating fund.
Donor(s): Sigma-Aldrich Corp.
Financial data (yr. ended 03/31/01): Assets, $711,034 (M); grants paid, $51,000; expenditures, $56,415; qualifying distributions, $50,468.
Limitations: Giving primarily in the St. Louis, MO, area.
Application information: Application form required.
Officers: Joseph Ackerman, Pres.; Richard Fenske, V.P.; Barbara Branchfield, Secy.-Treas.; Ben Sandler, Secy.-Treas.
Directors: June Dahl, Faith Sandler.
EIN: 431253095
Codes: CD, GTI

61415
Martha Lafite Thompson Nature Sanctuary
407 N. LaFrenz Rd.
Liberty, MO 64068

Classified as a private operating foundation in 1977.
Financial data (yr. ended 09/30/01): Assets, $655,823 (M); grants paid, $0; gifts received, $225,554; expenditures, $185,016; qualifying distributions, $0.
Officers and Directors:* Laurie Brown,* Pres.; Nancy Eberhart,* V.P.; Debra Ahem,* Secy.; Louis Bussjaeger,* Treas.; Ralph Brant, Duane Martin, Dee Rosekrans, Nancy Shy, Sylvia Willoughby, and 6 additional directors.
EIN: 431094434

61416
Gorman Foundation
7777 Bonhomme Ave., Ste. 2300
Clayton, MO 63105 (314) 431-4282
Application addresses: c/o Student Financial Aid Off., Univ. of Missouri-Rolla, 106 Parker Hall, Rolla, MO 65401; c/o Student Financial Aid Off., Massachusetts Institute of Technology, 77 Massachusetts Ave., Rm. 5-119, Cambridge, MA 02139

Established in 1986 in MO.
Donor(s): Stephan P. Gorman.‡
Financial data (yr. ended 06/30/01): Assets, $628,212 (M); grants paid, $28,750; expenditures, $40,337; qualifying distributions, $31,450.
Limitations: Giving limited to residents of St. Louis, MO.
Publications: Annual report, informational brochure, application guidelines.
Application information: Application form required.
Trustees: Rosemarie Fitzsimmons, Karon Matlock.
EIN: 431377593
Codes: GTI

61417
The Horizons Foundation
106 Bogey Estates Dr.
St. Charles, MO 63303-5000

Established in 1996 in MO.
Financial data (yr. ended 12/31/00): Assets, $520,113 (M); grants paid, $60,020; gifts received, $150,999; expenditures, $73,943; qualifying distributions, $0.
Limitations: Applications not accepted. Giving on a national basis.
Application information: Contributes only to pre-selected organizations.
Trustees: Charlotte K. Lockhart, Elery A. Lockhart.
EIN: 436663523

61418
Dickinson Community Investment Corporation
c/o City Center Sq.
1100 Main St., Ste. 350
Kansas City, MO 64105

Established in 1997 in MO.
Financial data (yr. ended 02/28/01): Assets, $501,953 (M); grants paid, $0; expenditures, $7,565; qualifying distributions, $316,516; giving activities include $243,082 for program-related investments and $7,565 for programs.
Officers: Bob Hall, Chair.; Ed Buckley, Pres.; Sheri Ramirez, Secy.; Diane Bales, Treas.
Directors: Martha Clark, Glen Giboney, Turner Pettaway, Gregory Reichert, Paula Willett.
EIN: 431780252

61419
Foundation for Idiodynamics & the Creative Process
8029 Washington Ave.
St. Louis, MO 63114

Classified as a private operating foundation in 1979.
Donor(s): Saul Rosenzweig.
Financial data (yr. ended 06/30/00): Assets, $446,519 (M); grants paid, $550; expenditures, $20,481; qualifying distributions, $550.
Limitations: Applications not accepted. Giving primarily in St. Louis, MO.

Application information: Contributes only to pre-selected organizations.
Officers: Louise Rosenzweig, Secy.; Saul Rosenzweig, Mgr.
Trustees: Joel Gopen, Julie M. Hahn, Kenneth L. Nabors.
EIN: 237193774

61420
Midwest Spine Foundation
2750 Clay Edwards Dr., Ste. 600
North Kansas City, MO 64116

Established in 1991 in MO.
Donor(s): Roger P. Jackson, M.D.
Financial data (yr. ended 05/31/00): Assets, $443,605 (M); grants paid, $0; expenditures, $5,935; qualifying distributions, $5,902; giving activities include $5,936 for programs.
Limitations: Applications not accepted.
Application information: Contributes only to pre-selected organizations.
Officers and Directors:* Roger P. Jackson, M.D.,* Pres.; Sandy Jackson, Treas.; Christopher Hales, Anne McManus.
EIN: 431615796

61421
Chiefs Children's Fund
1 Arrowhead Dr.
Kansas City, MO 64129
Contact: Dale M. Young

Established in 1983 in MO as a company-sponsored operating fund.
Donor(s): Kansas City Chiefs Football Club Inc.
Financial data (yr. ended 01/31/02): Assets, $439,501 (M); grants paid, $96,295; gifts received, $138,550; expenditures, $350,820; qualifying distributions, $211,595.
Limitations: Giving primarily in the greater Kansas City, MO, area.
Officers: Jack W. Steadman, Chair.; Carl D. Peterson, Pres.; James T. Seigfried, Secy.
EIN: 431299453
Codes: FD2, CD, GTI

61422
Friends of Hem Sheela Model School
2102 E. Wayland St.
Springfield, MO 65804

Classified as a private operating foundation in 1997.
Donor(s): Rabindra Nath Roy, Protima Roy.
Financial data (yr. ended 12/31/01): Assets, $435,825 (L); grants paid, $0; gifts received, $80,515; expenditures, $64,220; qualifying distributions, $0; giving activities include $75,603 for programs.
Officers: Rabinda Nath Roy, Pres.; Protima Roy, V.P.; Lakshmi Roy, Secy.
EIN: 431638217

61423
The Rainbow Network, Inc.
(Formerly The Keith and Karen Jaspers Charitable Foundation)
3844 S. South Ave.
Springfield, MO 65807

Established in 1995 in MO and Nicaragua.
Classified as a private operating foundation in 1997.
Donor(s): Keith Jaspers, Karen Jaspers.
Financial data (yr. ended 05/31/01): Assets, $398,025 (M); grants paid, $0; gifts received, $584,420; expenditures, $509,549; qualifying distributions, $491,732; giving activities include $252,766 for loans to individuals.
Limitations: Giving limited to Nicaragua.

Officers and Directors:* Rocky Levell, Chair.; Keith A. Jaspers, Pres.; Karen L. Jaspers,* Treas.; Betty Baldner, Klem Belt, Dave Blackmer, Tom Cardin, Rev. Bruce Davis, Tim Geisse, Patricia Leonard, Charlene Meyer, Edward Schanda, Rev. Mel West.
EIN: 431720451

61424
Nance Museum & Library of Antiquity
7717 Grand Ave.
Kansas City, MO 64114-1931

Donor(s): Paul J. Nance.
Financial data (yr. ended 12/31/01): Assets, $376,274 (M); grants paid, $0; gifts received, $17,647; expenditures, $22,755; qualifying distributions, $0.
Officers and Trustees:* Colleen L. Nance,* Vice-Chair. and Secy.-Treas.; Paul J. Nance,* Pres.; Robert Mickey, Jr., Edwin Nance.
Directors: James T. Nance, Mark P. Nance, Rasma Al Turki.
EIN: 431234830

61425
Sheridan E. Kindle Foundation, Inc.
P.O. Box 601
Camdenton, MO 65020

Donor(s): Sheridan E. Kindle.
Financial data (yr. ended 12/31/01): Assets, $351,712 (M); grants paid, $1,000; gifts received, $134; expenditures, $9,693; qualifying distributions, $0.
Limitations: Giving limited to Climax Springs, MO.
Application information: Application form required.
Officer and Directors:* Sherri H. Babbitt,* Pres.; Essie I. Babbitt, Kristi Bobbitt, Dale Steiner.
EIN: 431030117

61426
Ernest and Lillian Swanson Memorial Scholarship Trust
c/o U.S. Bank
1504 Ave. A
St. Louis, MO 63119 (314) 962-9421
Contact: Joann Hood, 1st V.P.

Established in 1995 in MO.
Financial data (yr. ended 12/31/01): Assets, $295,677 (M); grants paid, $10,800; expenditures, $15,301; qualifying distributions, $10,800.
Limitations: Giving limited to residents of MO.
Application information: Application forms available from accredited community colleges or universities. Application form required.
Officers: Kassie Smiley, Pres.; Joann Hood, 1st V.P.; Mary Ann Meador, 2nd V.P.
EIN: 431713377
Codes: GTI

61427
United Cerebal Palsy Association of Missouri
8645 Old Bonhomme Rd.
St. Louis, MO 63132-3901

Financial data (yr. ended 09/30/01): Assets, $294,925 (M); grants paid, $1,820; gifts received, $6,538; expenditures, $19,200; qualifying distributions, $19,200.
Limitations: Applications not accepted.
Application information: Contributes only to pre-selected organizations.
Officers and Directors:* Steve Mahler,* Pres.; David Tushaus,* V.P.; Ken Schaeffer,* Secy.; Robert Robinson,* Treas.; Richard Forkosh, Exec. Dir.; Janice Brunstrom, M.D., Jerry McKenney, Bruce Scott, Barbara Wilkerson.

EIN: 440579903

61428
Time Being Press
10411 Clayton Rd., Ste. 201-203
St. Louis, MO 63131

Donor(s): Saul Brodsky.
Financial data (yr. ended 12/31/01): Assets, $253,063 (M); grants paid, $0; gifts received, $155,894; expenditures, $196,929; qualifying distributions, $188,897; giving activities include $188,897 for programs.
Officers: L.D. Brodsky, Pres.; Jane Goldberg, V.P.; Jerry Call, Secy.-Treas.
EIN: 431685801

61429
Trimble House, Inc. of Louisiana, Missouri
200 S. Main St.
Louisiana, MO 63353

Classified as a private operating foundation in 1977.
Financial data (yr. ended 03/31/02): Assets, $240,444 (M); grants paid, $5,000; gifts received, $51,675; expenditures, $83,435; qualifying distributions, $5,000.
Officers: John Pitzer, Pres.; John Sitton, V.P.; John Shade, Secy.; Robert Kilby, Treas.
Directors: Harry Clark, John Fitzer.
EIN: 431016468

61430
Sinclair Wildlife Preserve, Inc.
3901 S. Fremont Ave.
Springfield, MO 65804

Established in 1998 in MO.
Financial data (yr. ended 12/31/99): Assets, $227,010 (M); grants paid, $0; gifts received, $333,017; expenditures, $110,045; qualifying distributions, $0; giving activities include $110,043 for programs.
Officer: Damian Sinclair, Pres.
EIN: 911930031

61431
Animal Education, Protection & Information Foundation
21 Crestview Ln.
Fordland, MO 65652

Classified as a private operating foundation in 1992.
Donor(s): Arlan Seidon.
Financial data (yr. ended 12/31/00): Assets, $226,531 (M); grants paid, $0; gifts received, $1,669; expenditures, $18,429; qualifying distributions, $18,429; giving activities include $18,429 for programs.
Officer: Murray Hill, Pres.
EIN: 232418679

61432
I Have a Dream Foundation - St. Louis
P.O. Box 16940
St. Louis, MO 63105-1340

Donor(s): Andrew Newman.
Financial data (yr. ended 09/30/00): Assets, $223,850 (M); grants paid, $0; expenditures, $31,395; qualifying distributions, $30,820; giving activities include $30,820 for programs.
Officers: Peggy Newman, Pres. and Secy.; Andrew Newman, V.P.
Director: Charles A. Lowenhaupt.
EIN: 431428740

61433
Leadership Education and Development Foundation
287 N. Lindbergh, Ste. 207
St. Louis, MO 63141

Financial data (yr. ended 04/30/00): Assets, $211,839 (M); grants paid, $5,200; expenditures, $191,893; qualifying distributions, $191,893; giving activities include $186,693 for programs.
Limitations: Applications not accepted.
Application information: Contributes only to pre-selected organizations.
Officers: Michael Reiner, Pres.; Elana Spitzberg, V.P.; David Smith, Secy.-Treas.
EIN: 431412968

61434
Harrington Holloway Education Foundation, Inc.
27 H N. Shore Dr.
Lake Lotawana, MO 64086
Contact: B.J. Hinkle, Pres.

Financial data (yr. ended 12/31/01): Assets, $176,724 (M); grants paid, $3,500; gifts received, $64,120; expenditures, $38,497; qualifying distributions, $3,500.
Limitations: Giving primarily to residents of KS.
Officer and Trustees:* B.J. Hinkle,* Pres.; George Baldwin, William Cohn, Mike Elwell, Charles Hyer, R.D. Rose.
EIN: 480721253

61435
Rabbi Samuel Thurman Educational Foundation
15332 Braefield Dr.
Chesterfield, MO 63017 (314) 290-5720

Established around 1965.
Financial data (yr. ended 05/31/02): Assets, $152,083 (M); grants paid, $16,000; gifts received, $1,710; expenditures, $16,306; qualifying distributions, $15,923.
Limitations: Giving limited to residents of St. Louis, MO.
Application information: Application form required.
Officer: Martin E. Oberman, Pres.
EIN: 431063744
Codes: GTI

61436
Board of Directors of the South Harrison R-II School District as Trustees of the Dick & Helen VanHoozer Scholarship Funds
c/o South Harrison R-II School District
P.O. Box 445
Bethany, MO 64424 (660) 425-8044

Donor(s): Cloyce H. VanHoozer.‡
Financial data (yr. ended 06/30/02): Assets, $142,562 (M); grants paid, $7,328; expenditures, $7,702; qualifying distributions, $7,702.
Limitations: Giving limited to graduates of South Harrison School District, MO.
Application information: Application form required.
Officer: Charles McKinny,* Pres.
EIN: 431679256

61437
Downtown St. Louis Management, Inc.
906 Olive St., Ste. 200
St. Louis, MO 63101

Classified as a private operating foundation.
Financial data (yr. ended 06/30/01): Assets, $141,472 (M); grants paid, $0; expenditures, $956,520; qualifying distributions, $0.

Directors: Andrea Allen, Vincent J. Bommarito, Karen Carroll, Franklin D. Kimbrough, Dorothy White-Coleman, and 12 additional directors.
EIN: 431797878

61438
Robert Victor Sager & Beatrice Mintz Sager Foundation
P.O. Box 2046
Rolla, MO 65402-2046
Application address: 8 Laird Ave., Rolla, MO 65401, tel.: (573) 368-5551
Contact: Thomas J. Sager, Tr.

Donor(s): Thomas J. Sager.
Financial data (yr. ended 12/31/01): Assets, $127,034 (M); grants paid, $2,300; gifts received, $108,657; expenditures, $42,438; qualifying distributions, $42,438; giving activities include $35,388 for programs.
Limitations: Giving on a national and international basis, with emphasis on Central America.
Trustees: Kimberly Beth Dill, Mark Haim, Thomas J. Sager.
EIN: 436711652

61439
Verna Wulfekammer Memorial Trust
c/o Jean M. Williams
108 Dundee Dr.
Columbia, MO 65203
Application address: 1909 Blueridge, Columbia, MO 65202, tel.: (573) 474-6906
Contact: Debbie Schluckebier, Pres.

Donor(s): Verna Wulfekammer.‡
Financial data (yr. ended 12/31/01): Assets, $122,021 (M); grants paid, $8,109; expenditures, $8,682; qualifying distributions, $7,266.
Limitations: Giving limited to MO organizations and residents.
Application information: Application form required.
Officers: Debbie Schluckebier, Pres.; Jenny Niekrasz, Secy.; Jean M. Williams, Treas.
EIN: 431722077

61440
Louis D. Beaumont Employees Trust Fund
c/o The May Department Stores Co., Corp. Tax Dept.
611 Olive St.
St. Louis, MO 63101-1721 (314) 342-6403
Additional tel.: (314) 342-6374; FAX: (314) 432-6588

Established as a company-sponsored operating foundation.
Donor(s): The May Department Stores Co.
Financial data (yr. ended 12/31/01): Assets, $119,967 (M); grants paid, $68,500; expenditures, $70,800; qualifying distributions, $68,500.
Limitations: Applications not accepted. Giving primarily in areas of company operations to employees and former employees of the May Department Stores Co. across the nation.
Application information: Applicants must be employees or former employees of the May Department Stores Co.
Trustees: Donald N. Baxter, Richard A. Brickson, John L. Dunham, Douglas J. Giles, Jan R. Kniffen, John A. Sztukowski.
EIN: 436027539
Codes: CD, GTI

61441
William S. & Billie K. Ross Charitable Foundation
3800 Greengrass Dr.
Florissant, MO 63033 (314) 921-3365
Contact: William Ross, Dir.

Established in 2001 in MO.
Donor(s): William Ross.
Financial data (yr. ended 12/31/01): Assets, $107,709 (M); grants paid, $7,711; gifts received, $151,600; expenditures, $11,711; qualifying distributions, $11,711.
Limitations: Giving primarily in Florissant, MO.
Directors: Janet L. Cole, William Ross, William S. Ross.
EIN: 431912330

61442
Leon M. Jordan Scholarship & Monument Fund, Inc.
5540 Wayne Ave.
Kansas City, MO 64110
Application address: c/o Advisory Committee, P.O. Box 15544, Kansas City, MO 64106
Contact: Alexander Ellison, Treas.

Classified as a private operating foundation in 1993.
Financial data (yr. ended 06/30/01): Assets, $96,384 (M); grants paid, $9,000; expenditures, $11,307; qualifying distributions, $9,126.
Limitations: Giving primarily in MO.
Application information: Authorization for release of financial information submitted to the college or university financial aid officer. Application form required.
Officers: Curtis Rogers, Pres.; Will McCarther, V.P.; Franklin Walker, Secy.; Alexander Ellison, Treas.
EIN: 431248204
Codes: GTI

61443
Charles Dick Educational Foundation, Inc.
Rt. 1, Box 23
Ionia, MO 65335
Application address: Rt. 4, Box 171, Warsaw, MO 65355, tel.: (660) 438-7493
Contact: Charles Dick, Dir.

Donor(s): Charles Dick.
Financial data (yr. ended 12/31/01): Assets, $93,982 (M); grants paid, $5,700; expenditures, $6,028; qualifying distributions, $5,700.
Limitations: Giving limited to residents of Lincoln, MO.
Application information: Application form required.
Directors: Charles Dick, John Dick, Carolyn Kreissler, Kenneth Sartin.
EIN: 431772301

61444
St. Louis Tax Assistance Program
12909 Lampadaire Dr.
St. Louis, MO 63141-7361

Established in 1998. Classified as a private operating foundation in 1999.
Donor(s): City-Wide Tax Assistance Program, Citi-Corp Mortgage, Inc., Mercantile Bank.
Financial data (yr. ended 04/30/01): Assets, $73,343 (M); grants paid, $0; gifts received, $39,887; expenditures, $9,206; qualifying distributions, $9,206; giving activities include $9,206 for programs.
Officers: Ronald J. Szweda, Pres.; Carol W. Szweda, Secy.
Director: John McCartney.
EIN: 431828350

61445
Humanities Instructional Television
P.O. Box 78307
St. Louis, MO 63178

Established in 1998 in MO.
Financial data (yr. ended 12/31/01): Assets, $67,581 (M); grants paid, $0; expenditures, $17,973; qualifying distributions, $0; giving activities include $17,972 for programs.
Limitations: Giving primarily in St. Louis, MO.
Officers: Fred Bleeke, Pres.; Gerald Arbini, V.P.; Paul Guzzardo, Secy.-Treas.
EIN: 431689900

61446
Virginia & Forrest Murphy Charitable Trust
1401 S. Brentwood, Ste. 550
St. Louis, MO 63144
Application address: P.O. Box 8088, St. Louis, MO 63156
Contact: Jerry J. Murphy, Tr.

Established in 1985 in MO.
Financial data (yr. ended 12/31/01): Assets, $67,095 (M); grants paid, $3,500; expenditures, $4,106; qualifying distributions, $4,106.
Limitations: Giving primarily in St. Louis, MO.
Trustees: Forrest J. Murphy, Jerry J. Murphy.
EIN: 237057050

61447
Dent County Livestock Educational Association, Inc.
P.O. Box 226, Rte. 1
Salem, MO 65560 (573) 729-7239
Contact: Darrell Skiles, Treas.

Financial data (yr. ended 12/31/99): Assets, $67,089 (L); grants paid, $1,850; gifts received, $207; expenditures, $2,182; qualifying distributions, $1,850.
Limitations: Giving limited to MO.
Officers: Paul Thompson, Pres.; George Barnitz, V.P.; Darrell Skiles, Treas.
Director: Charles Triplett.
EIN: 431608213

61448
The North Platte Foundation
P.O. Box 68
Dearborn, MO 64439-0068
Application address: c/o Ms. Babcock, North Platte High School, 212 W. 6th St., Dearborn, MO 64439, tel.: (816) 450-3344

Established in 1996 in MO.
Financial data (yr. ended 06/30/00): Assets, $65,436 (M); grants paid, $5,200; gifts received, $26,263; expenditures, $5,622; qualifying distributions, $5,148.
Officers: Bernard Thomas, Pres.; Jane Hagg, Secy.; Jerry Hagg, Treas.
EIN: 431725048

61449
Michelle Hayes Memorial Scholarship Fund
21212 S. Ore Rd.
Pleasant Hill, MO 64080 (816) 540-5620
Contact: Carol H. Hayes, Pres.

Classified as a private operating foundation. Established in 1995 in MO.
Donor(s): Jerrall L. Hayes, Nancy L. Hayes.
Financial data (yr. ended 08/31/01): Assets, $57,459 (M); grants paid, $2,001; gifts received, $450; expenditures, $2,036; qualifying distributions, $2,001.
Limitations: Giving primarily in HI and MO.

Application information: Contact the University of Hawaii at Hilo and Pleasant Hill High School guidance offices for details.
Officers: Carol H. Hayes, Pres.; Greg D. Hayes, V.P.
EIN: 431749620

61450
John & Maxine Belger Family Foundation
2100 Walnut St.
Kansas City, MO 64108 (816) 474-3250
Contact: C. Richard Belger, Secy.

Established in 1995 in MO.
Donor(s): Edna M. Belger.
Financial data (yr. ended 12/31/00): Assets, $55,636 (M); grants paid, $25,000; gifts received, $37,500; expenditures, $30,036; qualifying distributions, $25,000.
Officers and Directors:* John W. Belger II,* Pres.; C. Richard Belger,* Secy.; Fred J. Valentine,* Treas.
EIN: 431713818

61451
UniGroup, Incorporated Scholarship Foundation
1 United Dr.
Fenton, MO 63026 (636) 349-3947

Established in 1998 in MO as a company-sponsored operating foundation.
Donor(s): UniGroup, Incorporated.
Financial data (yr. ended 12/31/01): Assets, $55,624 (M); grants paid, $60,000; gifts received, $67,508; expenditures, $86,405; qualifying distributions, $86,405.
Limitations: Giving primarily in MO.
Application information: Application form required.
Directors: Keith Dailey, Patrick Larch, George Mitsch, John Temporiti.
EIN: 431806966
Codes: GTI

61452
Upsilon Chapter of Delta Sigma Delta International Dental Fraternity Memorial Foundation
c/o Charles D. Fuzner
505 Couch Ave.
Kirkwood, MO 63122

Financial data (yr. ended 12/31/00): Assets, $55,438 (M); grants paid, $0; expenditures, $4,586; qualifying distributions, $3,590; giving activities include $3,590 for programs.
Trustees: Charles D. Fuszner, Roger L. Parrott, Gordon C. Thompson.
EIN: 436783462

61453
J. K. Burney Scholarship Fund
700 W. Pleasant St.
Aurora, MO 65605-1453 (417) 678-2314
Contact: Carol Ann Pilkenton, Pres.

Financial data (yr. ended 11/30/01): Assets, $51,312 (M); grants paid, $2,500; expenditures, $2,579; qualifying distributions, $2,500.
Limitations: Giving limited to Aurora, MO residents.
Application information: Application form required.
Officers: Carol Ann Pilkenton, Pres.; Linda Carr, V.P.; Alana Phariss, Secy.
Director: Johnna Russell.
EIN: 431284372

61454
Harvey Kornblum Foundation
55 Conway Close Rd.
St. Louis, MO 63124-1633 (314) 991-0877
Contact: Harvey Kornblum, Tr.

Donor(s): Harvey Kornblum.
Financial data (yr. ended 12/31/01): Assets, $50,022 (M); grants paid, $26,380; expenditures, $26,970; qualifying distributions, $26,311.
Limitations: Giving primarily in St. Louis, MO.
Trustee: Harvey Kornblum.
EIN: 431697637

61455
Polk County Fire Rescue and Training Association
1563 E. 517th Rd.
Brighton, MO 65617

Financial data (yr. ended 12/31/01): Assets, $39,116 (M); grants paid, $0; gifts received, $11,827; expenditures, $6,139; qualifying distributions, $0.
Officers: David Agee, Chair.; Charles Polodna, Vice-Chair.; Katy Franka, Secy.; Shawn Rowley, Treas.
EIN: 436096893

61456
Hope for Animals, Inc.
1600 S. Brentwood, Ste. 600
St. Louis, MO 63144

Classified as a private operating foundation in 1993.
Donor(s): Hope H. Burghardt.
Financial data (yr. ended 06/30/02): Assets, $37,451 (M); grants paid, $0; gifts received, $339,531; expenditures, $344,658; qualifying distributions, $334,355; giving activities include $334,355 for programs.
Limitations: Applications not accepted.
Officers and Directors:* Hope H. Burghardt,* Pres.; Paul Burghardt,* V.P.
EIN: 431594883

61457
The Whitehill Graham Foundation
101 S. Hanley Rd., Ste. 1280
St. Louis, MO 63105-3406

Classified as a private operating foundation in 1977.
Donor(s): R. Graham Myers.
Financial data (yr. ended 11/30/01): Assets, $31,416 (M); grants paid, $0; gifts received, $12; expenditures, $1,069; qualifying distributions, $1,069; giving activities include $1,069 for programs.
Officers: F. Lewis Carlisle, Pres.; R. Graham Myers, V.P. and Treas.; David H. Russell, Secy.
EIN: 431106011

61458
Oceans for Youth Foundation
5215 N.W. Crooked Rd.
Parkville, MO 64152

Established in 1999 in DE.
Financial data (yr. ended 12/31/01): Assets, $29,914 (M); grants paid, $0; gifts received, $3,450; expenditures, $22,351; qualifying distributions, $4,468; giving activities include $1,484 for programs.
Officers: Wayne Hasson, Pres.; Edward Mark Young, V.P.; Jerry Beaty, Secy.; Gary Worden, Treas.
EIN: 431851505

61459
Linn County R-1 Educational Foundation
P.O. Box 130
Purdin, MO 64674-0130 (660) 244-5045
Contact: John Brinkley, Secy.-Treas.

Established in 1997.
Financial data (yr. ended 12/31/01): Assets, $27,527 (M); grants paid, $1,000; gifts received, $235; expenditures, $1,187; qualifying distributions, $1,000.
Limitations: Giving primarily in Purdin, MO.
Application information: Application form required.
Officers: Eldons Tietsort, Pres.; Virginia Barrows, V.P.; John Brinkley, Secy.-Treas.
EIN: 431734483

61460
AED/Roy Vickrey Memorial Scholarship Fund
c/o The Western Assn.
638 W. 39th St.
Kansas City, MO 64111
Contact: Robert Foreman, Chair.

Established in 1994 in MO.
Financial data (yr. ended 12/31/99): Assets, $26,548 (M); grants paid, $2,000; gifts received, $3,200; expenditures, $2,774; qualifying distributions, $2,000.
Application information: Application supplied upon request. Application form required.
Officer and Trustees:* Robert Foreman,* Chair.; James Foreman, Ed Hammond, Judy Hippe, David Knopke, James Rudolph.
EIN: 431723584

61461
West Nodaway Educational Foundation
P.O. Box 660
Maryville, MO 64468
Application address: 1720 N. Clayton, Unit 113, Maryville, MO 64468-1169, tel.: (660) 562-3996
Contact: Eileen A. Dow, Pres.

Donor(s): Eileen A. Dow.
Financial data (yr. ended 12/31/01): Assets, $21,085 (M); grants paid, $2,000; expenditures, $2,015; qualifying distributions, $2,015.
Limitations: Giving limited to residents of Burlington Junction, MO.
Application information: Application form required.
Officers: Eileen A. Dow, Pres.; Robert E. Sundell, Secy.-Treas.
EIN: 431848515

61462
Leila Normandie Permanent Perpetual Custodial Education Fund
c/o Frank B. Surber
1036 N.W. High Point Dr.
Lee's Summit, MO 64081

Established in 1989 in MO.
Financial data (yr. ended 08/31/00): Assets, $18,333 (M); grants paid, $1,094; expenditures, $1,177; qualifying distributions, $1,177.
Officers: Patricia Surber, Pres.; Virginia Burberich, Secy.; Viola Crabtree, Treas.
EIN: 431523100

61463
Xenia Booth Testamentary Trust
1405 High Dr.
Lexington, MO 64067 (660) 259-3582
Contact: Karen Ensor, Tr.

Established around 1976.

Financial data (yr. ended 12/31/01): Assets, $15,215 (M); grants paid, $8,250; expenditures, $9,757; qualifying distributions, $8,777.
Limitations: Giving limited to residents of Lafayette County, MO.
Trustees: Karen Ensor, Joyce Neville, James Shannon, Arnold Viebrock.
EIN: 436206072
Codes: TN

61464
Missouri Girls State Program
1704 W. Broadway
Columbia, MO 65203

Financial data (yr. ended 12/31/01): Assets, $14,173 (M); grants paid, $0; gifts received, $6,241; expenditures, $10; qualifying distributions, $0.
Officers: Martha Yancey, Pres.; Virginia Schnurbusch, V.P.; Joann Cronin, Secy.; Lois Brown, Treas.
EIN: 311671606

61465
Montgomery Foundation Trust
11264 Northview Dr.
Dexter, MO 63841-8960 (573) 624-4608
Contact: Breman L. Montgomery, Tr.

Classified as a private operating foundation in 1985.
Financial data (yr. ended 12/31/99): Assets, $12,977 (M); grants paid, $2,000; gifts received, $1,000; expenditures, $2,009; qualifying distributions, $2,009.
Limitations: Giving limited to residents of Dexter, MO.
Application information: Application form required.
Trustees: Breman L. Montgomery, Carolyn J. Montgomery, Neva N. Settles, William R. Settles.
EIN: 436280031

61466
Birthright of West Plains
P.O. Box 377
West Plains, MO 65775-0377

Financial data (yr. ended 12/31/01): Assets, $11,597 (M); grants paid, $130; gifts received, $9,386; expenditures, $13,780; qualifying distributions, $13,780; giving activities include $13,780 for programs.
Officers: Tricia Hight, Secy.; Beth Lynch, Treas.
Directors: Linda Collins, Sylvia McCormack.
EIN: 431347523

61467
Davis L. Smith Foundation
13801 Riverport Dr., Ste. 301
Maryland Heights, MO 63043

Classified as a private operating foundation in 1992.
Donor(s): Brice R. Smith III, Holly P. Smith.
Financial data (yr. ended 12/31/01): Assets, $11,088 (M); grants paid, $13,717; gifts received, $3,383; expenditures, $14,941; qualifying distributions, $13,717.
Limitations: Applications not accepted. Giving primarily in St. Louis, MO.
Application information: Contributes only to pre-selected organizations.
Directors: Brice R. Smith III, Dorothy Davis Smith, Holly P. Smith.
EIN: 431602112

61468
John M. Coleman Scholarship Fund
9730 E. Watson Rd., Ste. 100
St. Louis, MO 63126

Established in 2001. Classified as a company-sponsored operating foundation.
Donor(s): Engineered Fire Protection, Inc.
Financial data (yr. ended 12/31/01): Assets, $10,727 (M); grants paid, $0; gifts received, $10,680; expenditures, $0; qualifying distributions, $0.
Officers: Dennis C. Coleman, Pres. and Secy.; David Robert Johnson, V.P.; Brian G. Toennies, Secy.-Treas.
EIN: 431939854

61469
Dorothy Lustgarten Riekes and John M. Riekes Foundation, Inc.
48 Kingsbury Pl.
St. Louis, MO 63112-1859

Established in 1967.
Donor(s): Max Riekes.
Financial data (yr. ended 12/31/01): Assets, $10,647 (M); grants paid, $0; gifts received, $400; expenditures, $1,211; qualifying distributions, $0.
Limitations: Giving on a national basis.
Application information: Unsolicited requests for funds not accepted.
Officers and Directors:* Max Riekes,* Pres.; Linda Riekes,* V.P. and Secy.; Gary S. Riekes,* Treas.; Yale Richards.
EIN: 476046034

61470
C-Snap
c/o Elizabeth D. Pauly
314 Euclid Blvd.
Carthage, MO 64836

Financial data (yr. ended 12/31/99): Assets, $7,339 (M); grants paid, $350; gifts received, $800; expenditures, $350; qualifying distributions, $350.
Officers: Elizabeth D. Pauly, Pres.; C. Pauly, Treas.
Director: John Williams.
EIN: 431803071

61471
Clay Harris Memorial Scholarship Foundation
c/o Janet K. Harris
13267 B Hwy.
Boonville, MO 65233-0372
Application address: c/o Guidance Counselor, Boonville High School, 1690 W. Ashley Rd., Boonville, MO 65233, tel.: (660) 882-7426

Classified as a private operating foundation in 1993.
Financial data (yr. ended 12/31/01): Assets, $6,123 (L); grants paid, $300; expenditures, $329; qualifying distributions, $296.
Limitations: Giving limited to residents of Boonville, MO.
Application information: Application form required.
Director: Janet K. Harris.
EIN: 431554934

61472
Vanovia Animal Sanctuary, Inc.
8247 Hwy. 47
St. Clair, MO 63077

Donor(s): Laura Sutter.
Financial data (yr. ended 06/30/01): Assets, $5,205 (M); grants paid, $0; gifts received, $48,025; expenditures, $50,111; qualifying distributions, $0.
Limitations: Giving limited to MO.
Officer: Gloria Sutter, Pres.
EIN: 431179209

61473
Jerry D. Rowland Memorial Scholarship
403 Prospect St.
Tipton, MO 65081-8521 (660) 433-5637
Contact: Joe Rowland, Tr.

Established in 1989 in MO.
Donor(s): Amelia Rowland, Anita Rowland.
Financial data (yr. ended 06/30/02): Assets, $3,768 (M); grants paid, $200; expenditures, $200; qualifying distributions, $200.
Limitations: Giving primarily in Tipton, MO.
Application information: Application form not required.
Trustees: Cheryl Knipp, Fred Norman, Joe Rowland.
EIN: 431488080

61474
The Woodcock Foundation for the Appreciation of the Arts
509 Olive St., Ste. 300
St. Louis, MO 63101-1852

Established in 2000 in MO.
Donor(s): Lorrin S. Watson, Aileen E. Woodcock.
Financial data (yr. ended 12/31/00): Assets, $3,285 (M); grants paid, $0; gifts received, $510,519; expenditures, $514,557; qualifying distributions, $514,557; giving activities include $514,557 for programs.
Trustees: Lynne M. Gale, Lorrin S. Watson, Aileen E. Woodcock.
EIN: 431890141

61475
Martin Family Foundation
5335 Lancelot Dr.
St. Charles, MO 63304-5742

Established in 1995 in MO.
Donor(s): Edward B. Martin, Sharon A. Martin.
Financial data (yr. ended 12/31/00): Assets, $1,010 (M); grants paid, $1,200; gifts received, $975; expenditures, $1,200; qualifying distributions, $1,200.
Officers: Sharon A. Martin, Pres.; Misty Martin, V.P.; Edward B. Martin, Secy.; Ricky L. Martin, Treas.
EIN: 431665864

61476
Mali Education Foundation
54-B 69 Hwy. N.E.
P.O. Box 11153
Kansas City, MO 64119

Established in 2000 in MO.
Financial data (yr. ended 12/31/01): Assets, $302 (M); grants paid, $25; gifts received, $73; expenditures, $40; qualifying distributions, $25.
Limitations: Giving primarily in WI.
Officers: Melford V. McCormick, Pres.; Harvey L. McCormick, Secy.; Anita J. McCormick, Treas.
EIN: 431729540

61477
The Phoenix Fund
1034 S. Brentwood Blvd., Ste. 1492
St. Louis, MO 63117-1214

Donor(s): M. Peter Fischer.
Financial data (yr. ended 11/30/01): Assets, $128 (M); grants paid, $0; expenditures, $242; qualifying distributions, $0.
Trustees: M. Peter Fischer, Mary S. Hawker, Margaret Bush Wilson.
EIN: 237230870

61478
McCarthy Family Emergency Assistance Fund
1341 N. Rock Hill Rd.
St. Louis, MO 63124-1498

Classified as a private operating foundation in 1981.
Financial data (yr. ended 10/31/01): Assets, $58 (M); grants paid, $24,172; gifts received, $10,169; expenditures, $24,218; qualifying distributions, $24,218.
Limitations: Applications not accepted.
Trustees: Michael M. McCarthy, George F. Scherer.
EIN: 431221550

61479
Anthony W. Joynt, Jr. Charitable Foundation
c/o Randall A. Martin
911 Washington Ave., 7th Fl.
St. Louis, MO 63101

Established in 2001 in IL.
Donor(s): Anthony W. Joynt, Jr.
Financial data (yr. ended 12/31/01): Assets, $10 (M); grants paid, $0; gifts received, $10; expenditures, $0; qualifying distributions, $0.
Limitations: Applications not accepted.
Application information: Contributes only to pre-selected organizations.
Trustee: Anthony W. Joynt, Jr.
EIN: 316651844

MONTANA

61480
Olive Rice Reierson Foundation
c/o Wells Fargo Bank Montana, N.A.
P.O. Box 597
Helena, MT 59624 (406) 447-2050
Contact: Martin J. Lewis

Donor(s): Joann Shelley, Milton Shelley.
Financial data (yr. ended 09/30/01): Assets, $1,279,022 (M); grants paid, $60,500; gifts received, $6,000; expenditures, $75,454; qualifying distributions, $64,052.
Limitations: Giving limited to residents of Powell County, MT.
Publications: Application guidelines.
Application information: Application form required.
Trustee: Wells Fargo Bankk Montana, N.A.
EIN: 363463190
Codes: GTI

61481
Sweetgrass Lodge, Inc.
Box 710
Chester, MT 59522-0710

Classified as a private operating foundation in 1978.
Financial data (yr. ended 12/31/01): Assets, $1,165,219 (M); grants paid, $0; expenditures, $201,552; qualifying distributions, $0.
Officers: Steve Brown, Pres.; Rose Ish, V.P.; Krys Cole, Secy.; Shirley Peck, Mgr.
Directors: Chris Kolstad, Terry Lavelly, Gordon Nelsen, Chuck Saxton, Marion Wanken, Janell Wardell.
EIN: 810383156

61482
Paul Clark Home
c/o Suzanne Hull
926 S. Arizona St.
Butte, MT 59701-4808 (406) 723-3266

Classified as a private operating foundation in 1974.
Donor(s): S. Gretchen Leipheimer.
Financial data (yr. ended 12/31/01): Assets, $837,926 (M); grants paid, $5,150; expenditures, $13,800; qualifying distributions, $13,800; giving activities include $10,678 for programs.
Application information: Application form not required.
Officers: Don Hutchinson, Pres.; S. Gretchen Leipheimer, 1st V.P.; Catherine McIntosh, 2nd V.P.; Philip G. Aguir, Treas.
EIN: 810233496

61483
E. A. Hinderman Scholarship Memorial, Inc.
P.O. Box 236
Whitefish, MT 59937
Application address: c/o Guidance Counselor, Whitefish High School, 600 E. 2nd St., Whitefish, MT 59937

Financial data (yr. ended 12/31/01): Assets, $669,141 (M); grants paid, $32,000; gifts received, $780; expenditures, $32,222; qualifying distributions, $31,466.
Limitations: Giving limited to residents of Whitefish, MT.
Application information: Application form required.
Officers: Bob Lawson, Pres.; Steve Howke, V.P.; Mary Yants, Secy.; Vivian Hull, Treas.
EIN: 810392053
Codes: GTI

61484
God's Love, Inc.
533 N. Main St.
Helena, MT 59601-3346 (406) 442-7000
Contact: Ann E. Miller, Mgr.

Established in 1981 in MT; Classified as a private operating foundation in 1982.
Donor(s): Wayne H. Miller, George Geissler, and others.
Financial data (yr. ended 12/31/99): Assets, $654,469 (M); grants paid, $85,623; gifts received, $485,346; expenditures, $423,289; qualifying distributions, $379,170.
Limitations: Giving limited to residents of MT.
Officer: Ann E. Miller, Mgr.
Trustee: Wayne H. Miller.
EIN: 810400234
Codes: FD2

61485
Conrad Mansion Directors, Inc.
P.O. Box 8600
Kalispell, MT 59904-1600

Financial data (yr. ended 06/30/99): Assets, $299,188 (M); grants paid, $0; gifts received, $6,690; expenditures, $80,172; qualifying distributions, $78,612; giving activities include $73,912 for programs.
Officers: Louis Bibler, Pres.; Norbert Donahue, V.P.; E.A. Sliter, Treas.
Directors: Richard Champoux, Norma Happ, Lorene Johnson, Betty Norem, C.S. Robinson, Gayle Vidal.
EIN: 510166540

61486
Cut Bank Elks Lodge Charitable Corp.
38B S. Central Ave.
Cut Bank, MT 59427
Application address: P.O. Box 2117, Cut Bank, MT 59427
Contact: Robert Smith, Secy.

Established in 1999 in MT.
Financial data (yr. ended 12/31/00): Assets, $285,372 (M); grants paid, $12,400; gifts received, $200; expenditures, $16,002; qualifying distributions, $15,879.
Limitations: Giving primarily in Cut Bank, MT.
Application information: Application form required.
Officers: Robert A. Smith, Pres.; Robert Smith, Secy.; Dave Bell, Treas.
Directors: David Henderson, Ford Houdej, Danny Murphy.
EIN: 810495546

61487
Warren J. Hancock Bird Resources, Inc.
P.O. Box 1555
Billings, MT 59103

Donor(s): Thomas B. Hancock, William J. Hancock, Sheila H. McKay.
Financial data (yr. ended 12/31/01): Assets, $245,459 (M); grants paid, $0; gifts received, $80,000; expenditures, $85,860; qualifying distributions, $0.
Officers and Directors:* William J. Hancock,* Pres.; Thomas B. Hancock,* V.P.; Sheila H. McKay,* V.P.; Glenn W. Weidler, Secy.-Treas.
EIN: 810413918

61488
L Heart Foundation, Inc.
234 N. Ennis Lake Rd.
McAllister, MT 59740 (406) 682-4424

Classified as a private operating foundation in 1999 in MT.
Donor(s): Linn W. Krieg Charitable Lead Unitrust.
Financial data (yr. ended 12/31/99): Assets, $236,647 (M); grants paid, $3,500; gifts received, $214,660; expenditures, $8,039; qualifying distributions, $3,500.
Limitations: Applications not accepted.
Application information: Contributes only to pre-selected organizations.
Directors: Penelope M. Henning, Kevin Krieg, Linn W. Krieg.
EIN: 810522506

61489
Callant Family Foundation
P.O. Box 305
Harlowton, MT 59036 (406) 632-4798
Additional tel.: (406) 632-5846
Contact: M.A. Callant, Pres.

Established in 1992 in MT.
Donor(s): M.A. Callant.
Financial data (yr. ended 12/31/00): Assets, $127,063 (M); grants paid, $7,600; expenditures, $8,087; qualifying distributions, $7,427.
Limitations: Giving primarily in MT.
Officers and Directors:* M.A. Callant,* Pres.; Alfred Martello, V.P.; Joseph J. Fahn,* Secy.-Treas.; Laurence G. Callant, Mary A. Callant, James R. Hunter, Francis O. Rosenberg.
EIN: 363851512

61490—MONTANA

61490
The Mountain West Track & Field Club, Inc.
P.O. Box 8081
Missoula, MT 59807
Contact: Mark William Timmons, Pres.

Classified as a private operating foundation in 1993. Established in 1990 in MT.
Donor(s): Mark William Timmons.
Financial data (yr. ended 09/30/01): Assets, $107,530 (M); grants paid, $76,646; gifts received, $225,755; expenditures, $273,077; qualifying distributions, $273,035.
Limitations: Giving primarily in MT.
Application information: Applicants for program assistance must have NCAA eligibility, by invitation only.
Officers and Directors:* Mark William Timmons,* Pres.; Mike McKay,* V.P.; Anne Timmons, Secy.; Jennifer Draughon,* Treas.; Courtney Babcock, Linda McCarthy.
EIN: 810459511
Codes: FD2, GTI

61491
Pioneer Federal Community Foundation, Inc.
102 N. Washington St.
Dillon, MT 59725

Established in 1998.
Donor(s): Pioneer Federal Savings & Loan.
Financial data (yr. ended 12/31/00): Assets, $84,123 (M); grants paid, $1,200; gifts received, $30,600; expenditures, $1,224; qualifying distributions, $1,163.
Limitations: Applications not accepted.
Application information: Contributes only to pre-selected organizations.
Directors: Tom Beck, Theodore B. Hazelbaker, Spece Hegstad, Hugh Moore, Thomas Welch.
EIN: 810522327

61492
The Katie Michael Moran Foundation
c/o Michael Moran
4041 Palisades Park Dr.
Billings, MT 59106-1431

Established in 1999 in MT.
Donor(s): Michael J. Moran.
Financial data (yr. ended 12/31/00): Assets, $64,041 (M); grants paid, $4,000; gifts received, $3,170; expenditures, $7,771; qualifying distributions, $4,000.
Officers: Marlene M. Moran, Co-Pres. and Secy.; Michael J. Moran, Co-Pres. and Treas.
Director: Chad M. Moran.
EIN: 810529515

61493
Rolling Dog Ranch Animal Sanctuary Foundation
331 Dry Gulch Rd.
Ovando, MT 59854

Classified as a private operating foundation in 2001 in MT.
Donor(s): Steven P. Smith, Alayne M. Marker.
Financial data (yr. ended 11/30/01): Assets, $45,165 (M); grants paid, $100; gifts received, $65,075; expenditures, $19,910; qualifying distributions, $61,145; giving activities include $60,530 for programs.
Limitations: Applications not accepted.
Application information: Contributes only to pre-selected organizations.
Directors: Alayne M. Marker, Susan Michaels, Steven P. Smith.
EIN: 810537598

61494
Dan Labonte Memorial Scholarship Fund
R.R. 1, Box 1401
Fairview, MT 59221
Application address: 7460 McCray Rd., Fairview, PA 16415, tel.: (406) 747-5351
Contact: Loren Young, Pres.

Financial data (yr. ended 12/31/00): Assets, $27,748 (M); grants paid, $1,000; expenditures, $1,267; qualifying distributions, $1,267.
Limitations: Giving limited to residents of Fairview, PA.
Application information: Application form required.
Officers: Loren Young, Pres.; Mike Webber, Secy.
Trustees: Don Hillman, Monte Martin.
EIN: 363670972

61495
Jim & Doris Daley Scholarship Foundation
P.O. Box 343
Somers, MT 59932
Application address: c/o Career Center, Flathead High School, Kalispell, MT 59901
Contact: Ashley Mason

Established in 2001 in MT.
Donor(s): Jim Daley.
Financial data (yr. ended 12/31/01): Assets, $25,867 (M); grants paid, $15,000; gifts received, $36,286; expenditures, $15,869; qualifying distributions, $15,869.
Limitations: Giving primarily in Kalispell, MT.
Application information: Application form required.
Officer: Jim Daley, Pres.
EIN: 810533021

61496
Families First
P.O. Box 8095
Missoula, MT 59807

Established in 1996 in MT.
Donor(s): The Charles Englehard Foundation.
Financial data (yr. ended 12/31/99): Assets, $14,539 (M); grants paid, $0; gifts received, $128,101; expenditures, $171,671; qualifying distributions, $157,026; giving activities include $171,671 for programs.
Limitations: Applications not accepted.
Application information: Contributes only to pre-selected organizations.
Officers: Judy Scott, Chair.; Robert B. Hausmann, Secy.; Kim Gordon, Treas.
Trustees: Larry Howell, Sally Francis Kehayes.
EIN: 810490719

61497
John Osborne Foundation
767 E. Bench Rd.
Twin Bridges, MT 59754 (406) 684-9994
Contact: John Osborne, Pres.

Established in 1992 in CA.
Donor(s): John Osborne.
Financial data (yr. ended 10/31/01): Assets, $10,954 (M); grants paid, $750; gifts received, $33; expenditures, $1,096; qualifying distributions, $1,096; giving activities include $65 for programs.
Limitations: Giving limited to residents of MT.
Officers: John Osborne, Pres.; Bill Formby, Secy.
EIN: 770293002

61498
Howling Wolf Ranch Foundation
P.O. Box 190
Whitefish, MT 59937-0190

Established in 2000 in MT.
Donor(s): William Cohen, Michael Yranas.
Financial data (yr. ended 12/31/00): Assets, $9,058 (M); grants paid, $0; gifts received, $24,699; expenditures, $15,641; qualifying distributions, $0; giving activities include $15,641 for programs.
Officer: William Cohen, Mgr.
EIN: 810524817

61499
Extend! Foundation, Inc.
15 River Dr.
Livingston, MT 59047

Donor(s): Pathway Systems, Inc.
Financial data (yr. ended 12/31/01): Assets, $1,986 (M); grants paid, $65,643; gifts received, $16,576; expenditures, $72,355; qualifying distributions, $65,643.
Limitations: Applications not accepted.
Application information: Contributes only to pre-selected organizations.
Officers: Raymond C. Pierson, Pres.; Bruce Pierson, Secy.
Governors: Bruce Hein, Steve Mathewson, Godfrey O'Rear, Eric Pierson, Winifred Pierson.
EIN: 810527528

NEBRASKA

61500
The Susan A. Buffett Foundation
3555 Farnam St., Ste. 209
Omaha, NE 68131

Established in 1999 in NE.
Financial data (yr. ended 12/31/01): Assets, $33,768,814 (M); grants paid, $1,299,065; expenditures, $1,394,601; qualifying distributions, $1,299,065.
Officer: Susan A. Buffett, Pres. and Treas.
Directors: Susan T. Buffett, Warren E. Buffett, Allen Greenberg.
EIN: 470824755

61501
Harold Warp Pioneer Village Foundation
1248 O St., Ste. 200
Lincoln, NE 68501-1806

Classified as a private operating foundation in 1983.
Donor(s): Harold G. Warp, Construction and Agricultural Film Manufacturers Assn.
Financial data (yr. ended 12/31/01): Assets, $11,169,331 (M); grants paid, $0; gifts received, $42,449; expenditures, $1,410,353; qualifying distributions, $0; giving activities include $1,410,353 for programs.
Officer and Directors:* Harold G. Warp,* Pres.; Delbert L. Christensen, Jack R. Hlustik, Alfred R. Hunsicker, Ray Van Norman.
EIN: 363136921

61502
Coffman-Levi Charitable Trust, Inc.
(Formerly Gold Crest Retirement Center)
c/o Adams State Bank
200 Levi Ln.
Adams, NE 68301-0106

Financial data (yr. ended 06/30/02): Assets, $4,808,209 (M); grants paid, $0; gifts received, $5,499; expenditures, $2,846,782; qualifying distributions, $2,679,071; giving activities include $2,679,071 for programs.
Directors: Karl Gramann, Jr., Max Gramann, Everett Larson, Albert Siefkes, Ronald Sutter.
EIN: 470690851

61503
The Smith Collection
300 Speedway Cir.
Lincoln, NE 68502

Classified as a private operating foundation in 1994.
Donor(s): Speedway Motors, Inc.
Financial data (yr. ended 12/31/01): Assets, $3,403,353 (M); grants paid, $0; gifts received, $268,240; expenditures, $1,842; qualifying distributions, $0.
Officers: D. William Smith, Pres.; Carson W. Smith, V.P.; A. Joyce Smith, Secy.-Treas.
Trustees: Clay F. Smith, Craig A. Smith, Jason D. Smith.
EIN: 470761420

61504
The Jim and Elaine Wolf Foundation
(Formerly Wolf Foundation)
P.O. Box 548
Albion, NE 68620-0548

Established in 1982 in NE.
Donor(s): Elaine S. Wolf, James M. Wolf.
Financial data (yr. ended 09/30/00): Assets, $2,664,953 (M); grants paid, $60,733; gifts received, $124,475; expenditures, $93,080; qualifying distributions, $62,113.
Limitations: Applications not accepted. Giving primarily in NE.
Application information: Contributes only to pre-selected organizations.
Officers: James M. Wolf, Pres.; Elaine S. Wolf, V.P.; Pat Neidhardt, Secy.
EIN: 470611456

61505
Doug Riley Family Foundation
(Formerly The H. Doug Riley Foundation)
P.O. Box 241207
Omaha, NE 68124 (402) 390-0853
Contact: H. Douglas Riley, Pres.

Established in 1986 in NE.
Donor(s): Riley Advertising Co., H. Douglas Riley, Berkshire Hathaway, Inc.
Financial data (yr. ended 12/31/01): Assets, $1,513,974 (M); grants paid, $132,758; gifts received, $1,626; expenditures, $134,290; qualifying distributions, $132,758.
Limitations: Giving primarily in Omaha, NE.
Officers: H. Douglas Riley, Pres.; Karen M. Riley, V.P.
Director: Fred. Haekins, Jr.
EIN: 470700057
Codes: FD2

61506
National Heart Savers Association, Inc.
9140 W. Dodge Rd.
Omaha, NE 68114-3317

Established in 1978 in NE.
Donor(s): Philip Sokolof.
Financial data (yr. ended 12/31/99): Assets, $1,335,395 (M); grants paid, $0; gifts received, $144,220; expenditures, $159,302; qualifying distributions, $126,987; giving activities include $43,859 for programs.
Trustees: Gary Javitch, Karen Javitch, Philip Sokolof.
EIN: 470609751

61507
The Center for Human Nutrition, Inc.
(Formerly Swanson Center for Nutrition)
502 S. 44th St., Rm. 3007
Omaha, NE 68105-1065

Classified as a private operating foundation in 1980.
Donor(s): Gretchen Swanson Velde.
Financial data (yr. ended 12/31/01): Assets, $1,280,028 (M); grants paid, $0; gifts received, $5,418; expenditures, $718,276; qualifying distributions, $512,980; giving activities include $718,276 for programs.
Officers and Directors:* William F. Welsh II,* Chair.; Charles R. Eisele,* V.P.; C.R. "Bob" Bell,* Secy.; Dan Gardner,* Treas.; Frederick Bueholz, Louis Burgher, Ann C. Grandjean, Mary S. Landen, Martin A. Massengale, Ph.D., Mary Rahal, Gretchen Swanson Velde, Del Weber, Tom Whelan, Gail Walling Yanney.
EIN: 237175802

61508
The Federated Church of Columbus Foundation, Inc.
2704 15th St.
Columbus, NE 68601
Application address: c/o Scholarship Committee, P.O. Box 564, Columbus, NE 68602-0564

Established in 1999 in NE.
Donor(s): Arthur Philip Wilson, Jr.‡
Financial data (yr. ended 12/31/00): Assets, $792,711 (M); grants paid, $22,000; gifts received, $273,350; expenditures, $23,493; qualifying distributions, $21,849.
Limitations: Giving primarily in Columbus, NE.
Application information: Application form required.
Officers: Clark Lehr, Pres.; Steve Hoops, 1st V.P.; Johr Lohr, 2nd V.P.; Roger Angspuraer, 3rd V.P.
EIN: 470818736

61509
CBOL, Inc.
(Formerly Kum Ba Yah, Inc.)
233 S. 13th St., Ste. 1900
Lincoln, NE 68508-2094 (402) 474-6900
Contact: Daniel R. Stogsdill, Pres.

Established in 1987 in NE.
Donor(s): Daniel R. Stogsdill, Melinda J. Stogsdill.
Financial data (yr. ended 12/31/99): Assets, $761,365 (M); grants paid, $0; gifts received, $33,573; expenditures, $67,775; qualifying distributions, $67,625; giving activities include $67,625 for programs.
Limitations: Giving limited to IN, NE, and TX.
Application information: Application form not required.
Officers: Daniel R. Stogsdill, Pres.; Michael D. Young, V.P.; Melinda J. Stogsdill, Treas.
Directors: Anthony M. Rager, Joyce A. VanOsdol.
EIN: 470707083

61510
Cornhusker Christian Children's Foundation
1606 W. 3rd St.
McCook, NE 69001

Financial data (yr. ended 06/30/99): Assets, $641,263 (M); grants paid, $50,586; gifts received, $23,465; expenditures, $62,156; qualifying distributions, $50,586.
Officer: Keith Arterburn, Chair.
EIN: 237127011

61511
Benjamin A. Black Charitable Trust for Children
c/o Wells Fargo Bank Nebraska, N.A.
10010 Regency Cir., Ste. 300
Omaha, NE 68114

Established in 1991 in NE.
Donor(s): Benjamin A. Black.‡
Financial data (yr. ended 07/31/00): Assets, $575,481 (M); grants paid, $25,650; expenditures, $29,469; qualifying distributions, $27,335.
Limitations: Applications not accepted. Giving limited to Grand Island, NE.
Application information: Contributes only to pre-selected organizations.
Trustee: Wells Fargo Bank Nebraska, N.A.
EIN: 476179439

61512
Nels and Lucille Winther Foundation
P.O. Box 110
Minden, NE 68959
Application address: P.O. Box 179, Minden, NE 68959
Contact: Ray Van Norman, Pres.

Established in 1990 in NE.
Donor(s): Nels Winther.‡
Financial data (yr. ended 12/31/01): Assets, $523,397 (M); grants paid, $72,750; expenditures, $73,953; qualifying distributions, $73,993.
Limitations: Giving limited to the Blue Hill, Kearny County, and Minden, NE, areas.
Application information: Application form required.
Officer and Directors:* Ray Van Norman,* Pres. and Treas.; Gerald K. Koepke, Scott Maline, Fr. James O'Conner, George Plester, Rev. Manick Samuel, Wes Shannon.
EIN: 363727675
Codes: GTI

61513
Hormel Family Foundation
c/o Terry G. Ellinger, C.P.A.
P.O. Box 918
McCook, NE 69001

Established in 2000 in NE.
Donor(s): Ben F. Hormel.
Financial data (yr. ended 12/31/01): Assets, $509,493 (M); grants paid, $0; gifts received, $250,380; expenditures, $0; qualifying distributions, $0.
Limitations: Applications not accepted.
Application information: Contributes only to pre-selected organizations.
Officers and Directors:* Anabeth Frazier Cox,* Pres.; Marysue Hormel Harris,* V.P.; Ben Hormel Harris, Stephanie Frazier Stacy.
EIN: 470837935

61514
The Graff Charitable Foundation, Inc.
c/o Peter M. Graff
220 Norris Ave.
McCook, NE 69001

Established in 1998 in NE.
Donor(s): Peter M. Graff.
Financial data (yr. ended 12/31/99): Assets, $305,164 (M); grants paid, $5,164; gifts received, $125,000; expenditures, $7,070; qualifying distributions, $5,164.
Limitations: Applications not accepted.
Application information: Contributes only to pre-selected organizations.
Officers and Directors:* Peter M. Graff,* Pres.; Dolores O. Graff,* Secy.; P. Mark Graff,* Treas.; Mary Christine Graff.
EIN: 470816806

61515
Warren and Velda Wilson Foundation
P.O. Box 121
Clay Center, NE 68933
Contact: Jennifer Fleischer, Dir.

Established in 1993 in NE.
Financial data (yr. ended 12/31/01): Assets, $285,468 (M); grants paid, $11,000; expenditures, $14,960; qualifying distributions, $14,960.
Limitations: Giving limited to NE.
Application information: Application form required.
Officers and Directors:* John F. Farrell,* Pres.; Janet A. Hajny, Secy.; Kent Miller,* Treas.; Jennifer Fleischer.
EIN: 470741012

61516
Bran, Inc.
10730 Pacific St., Ste. 218
Omaha, NE 68114-4761 (402) 397-9785
Contact: Ray Weinberg, Pres.

Established as a private operating foundation in 1987.
Financial data (yr. ended 06/30/01): Assets, $257,492 (M); grants paid, $15,500; expenditures, $68,075; qualifying distributions, $15,500; giving activities include $47,760 for programs.
Limitations: Giving limited to NE.
Officers: Ray Weinberg, Pres.; Fred Jalass, V.P.; John Marcil, Secy.; Patrick LaVelle, Treas.
EIN: 363449742
Codes: GTI

61517
Butch Berman Charitable Music Foundation Trust
c/o Daniel R. Stogsdill
233 S. 13th St., No. 1900
Lincoln, NE 68508-2095
Contact: Byron L. Berman, Tr.

Established in 1995.
Donor(s): Harriet Berman Revocable Trust, Lucille C. Rappaport Irrevocable Trust.
Financial data (yr. ended 12/31/99): Assets, $211,382 (M); grants paid, $6,646; gifts received, $175,628; expenditures, $210,285; qualifying distributions, $210,285.
Limitations: Giving primarily in Lincoln, NE.
Trustee: Byron L. Berman.
EIN: 476199958

61518
College of Psychiatric and Neurologic Pharmacists (CPNP)
1303 S. 181 Plz.
Omaha, NE 68130

Established in 1998 in NE.
Donor(s): Eli Lilly, Inc., Zeneca Inc., Pfizer Inc.
Financial data (yr. ended 06/30/00): Assets, $207,040 (M); grants paid, $1,000; gifts received, $285,140; expenditures, $134,313; qualifying distributions, $125,450.
Limitations: Applications not accepted.
Application information: Contributes only to pre-selected organizations.
Officers: Alex Cardoni, Co-Pres.; Roger Sommi, Co-Pres.; Cherry Jackson, Secy.; James E. Wilson, Treas.
Directors: Larry Cohen, Sally Guthrie.
EIN: 470808612

61519
Ervin E. and Ruth A. Gellermano Foundation
c/o First National Bank & Trust Co.
5th and Midland Sts.
Syracuse, NE 68446

Established in 1998 in NE.
Financial data (yr. ended 12/31/99): Assets, $201,514 (M); grants paid, $33,700; expenditures, $36,740; qualifying distributions, $11,038.
Trustee: First National Bank & Trust Co.
EIN: 470806349

61520
Jacob J. and Anne B. Walter Educational Charitable Trust
171 Vincent Ave.
P.O. Box 345
Chappell, NE 69129

Financial data (yr. ended 12/31/01): Assets, $185,348 (M); grants paid, $9,500; expenditures, $9,689; qualifying distributions, $36,832.
Limitations: Applications not accepted. Giving primarily in CO and NE.
Application information: Contributes only to pre-selected organizations.
Trustee: John D. Wertz.
EIN: 476188317

61521
Arthur & Dora Bingel Foundation, Inc.
12829 W. Dodge Rd., Ste. 100
Omaha, NE 68134-2155

Classified as a private operating foundation in 1990.
Financial data (yr. ended 06/30/02): Assets, $115,875 (M); grants paid, $0; expenditures, $10,000; qualifying distributions, $0.
Officers: James R. Coe, Pres.; Ronald Hale, Secy.; Carroll E. Fredrickson, Treas.
EIN: 476032558

61522
The Dochas Foundation
c/o Thomas F. Dowd
3809 Hawk Woods Cir.
Omaha, NE 68112

Established in 1999 in NE.
Donor(s): Thomas Dowd, Barbara Dowd.
Financial data (yr. ended 12/31/00): Assets, $104,413 (M); grants paid, $59,975; expenditures, $61,017; qualifying distributions, $59,975.
Limitations: Applications not accepted.
Application information: Contributes only to pre-selected organizations.
Trustees: Barbara Dowd, Thomas Dowd.
EIN: 470816773

61523
The Krieger Family Foundation
6421 S. 66th St.
Lincoln, NE 68516
Contact: James Krieger, Pres.

Classified as a private operating foundation in 2002 in NE.
Donor(s): James Krieger.
Financial data (yr. ended 11/30/01): Assets, $96,775 (M); grants paid, $4,775; gifts received, $101,980; expenditures, $7,387; qualifying distributions, $4,775.
Limitations: Giving primarily in Lincoln, NE.
Application information: Application form required.
Officers and Director:* James Krieger, Pres. and Treas.; Penny Krieger, V.P. and Secy.; Matthew Krieger,* V.P.
EIN: 470839962

61524
Wallace and Panzer Trust
c/o James F. Panzer
807 N. Ash St.
Gordon, NE 69343

Established in 1988 in NE.
Financial data (yr. ended 12/31/00): Assets, $80,753 (M); grants paid, $4,358; expenditures, $4,435; qualifying distributions, $4,391.
Limitations: Applications not accepted. Giving primarily in Gordon, NE.
Application information: Contributes only to pre-selected organizations.
Trustee: James F. Panzer.
EIN: 476162473

61525
HELP Foundation of Omaha, Inc.
c/o Robert D. Becker
626 N. 164th St.
Omaha, NE 68118 (402) 493-6864
Contact: Anil K. Agarwal, M.D., Pres.

Established in 1986 in NE.
Donor(s): Anil K. Agarwal, M.D.
Financial data (yr. ended 06/30/01): Assets, $78,966 (M); grants paid, $0; gifts received, $31,546; expenditures, $28,897; qualifying distributions, $0.
Limitations: Giving in India.
Officer and Trustees:* Anil K. Agarwal, M.D.,* Pres. and Mgr.; Vijay Agarwal, M.D., Mohiud Din, M.D., A.U. Kahn, M.D.
EIN: 363428793

61526
Nordlund Family Charitable Foundation
1302 S. 101st St., Ste. 110
Omaha, NE 68124
Contact: Gordon Nordlund, Pres.

Donor(s): Gordon Nordlund, Sally Nordlund.
Financial data (yr. ended 12/31/01): Assets, $76,289 (M); grants paid, $20,000; expenditures, $20,000; qualifying distributions, $19,991.
Limitations: Giving in Douglas and Lancaster counties, NE.
Officers: Gordon Nordlund, Pres.; Sally Nordlund, V.P.
EIN: 470816677

61527
JAMS Foundation
c/o Jann A. Harrington
9130 Decatur Cir.
Omaha, NE 68114-1334

Established in 1999 in NE.

Financial data (yr. ended 12/31/99): Assets, $43,795 (M); grants paid, $10,000; expenditures, $10,000; qualifying distributions, $10,000.
Limitations: Applications not accepted. Giving primarily in Omaha, NE.
Application information: Contributes only to pre-selected organizations.
Officers: Anita Swanson, Chair and Pres.; Jann Harrington, Vice-Chair, V.P. and Secy.-Treas.; Michael J. Harrington, V.P.
EIN: 470819276

61528
Leonard & Lewise Foreman Kimball County Scholarship Fund
115 W. 2nd St.
Kimball, NE 69145-1240 (308) 235-4861
Application address: c/o Kimball County High School, 901 S. Nadine, Kimball, NE 69145, tel.: (308) 235-4861

Financial data (yr. ended 12/31/99): Assets, $35,394 (M); grants paid, $1,677; expenditures, $1,677; qualifying distributions, $1,655.
Officers: Terry Bourlier, Treas.; DeLoy Bremer, Admin.; Jerry Williams, Admin.
EIN: 470661404

61529
Loretta Mickle & Dorothy E. Bush Neuter/Spay Foundation
P.O. Box 5707
Lincoln, NE 68505
Contact: Dorothy E. Bush, Pres.

Classified as a private operating foundation in 1984.
Financial data (yr. ended 05/31/00): Assets, $27,145 (M); grants paid, $14,419; gifts received, $15,738; expenditures, $22,215; qualifying distributions, $21,865.
Limitations: Giving primarily in NE.
Application information: Application form required.
Officers: Dorothy E. Bush, Pres.; David E. Cygan, V.P.; Cecelia Servedio, Treas.
Directors: Ruth Ann Macolini, Wally Martin, Carolyn Petty, Audun Ravnan, Barbara Ravnan, Kelli Stanley-Smith, Jean Stroud.
Advisor: Becky Arnold.
EIN: 363276762

61530
Ockeghem Foundation
c/o Quentin Faulkner
1505 A St.
Lincoln, NE 68502 (402) 475-2927

Established in 2000 in NE.
Donor(s): Mary Murrell Faulkner, Quentin Faulkner.
Financial data (yr. ended 12/31/01): Assets, $26,374 (M); grants paid, $0; gifts received, $11,100; expenditures, $1,206; qualifying distributions, $1,045; giving activities include $1,278 for programs.
Trustees: Mary Murrell Faulkner, Quentin Faulkner.
EIN: 470827810

61531
Hengstler Scholarship Loan Fund
P.O. Box 102
Creighton, NE 68729 (402) 358-5616
Application address: W. Rice St., Creighton, NE 68729
Contact: Robert L. Snyder, Chair.

Financial data (yr. ended 12/31/99): Assets, $23,028 (M); grants paid, $375; expenditures, $100; qualifying distributions, $475; giving activities include $375 for loans to individuals.
Limitations: Giving primarily in Creighton, NE.
Officers: Robert L. Snyder, Chair.; William R. Hengstler, Treas.
EIN: 476032700

61532
Mildred & Dee Valder Scholarship Trust
c/o State Bank & Trust Co.
P.O. Box 8, 234 S. 13th St.
Tekamah, NE 68061 (402) 374-1476
Contact: Ralph M. Anderson, Jr., Tr.

Financial data (yr. ended 12/31/01): Assets, $22,291 (M); grants paid, $800; expenditures, $805; qualifying distributions, $866.
Limitations: Giving limited to NE.
Application information: Application form not required.
Trustees: Ralph M. Anderson, Jr., Lowell DeVasure, Donna Mock.
EIN: 476157769

61533
Walter L. & Nancy E. Griffith Foundation, Inc.
719 S. 75th St.
Omaha, NE 68114 (402) 391-8474
Contact: Walter L. Griffith, Jr., Pres.

Established in 2000 in NE.
Donor(s): Walter L. Griffith.
Financial data (yr. ended 12/31/01): Assets, $18,928 (M); grants paid, $1,500; expenditures, $2,011; qualifying distributions, $1,500.
Application information: Application form not required.
Officers: Walter L. Griffith, Jr., Pres.; Nancy E. Griffith, V.P.; Donald H. Schultz, Secy.-Treas.
EIN: 470834272

61534
Nebraska Midwest Fish and Wildlife Conference Foundation
c/o Patrick Cole
2200 N. 33rd St.
Lincoln, NE 68503

Classified as a private operating foundation in 1989.
Financial data (yr. ended 12/31/01): Assets, $11,106 (M); grants paid, $0; expenditures, $275; qualifying distributions, $0.
Officers: Darrell Feit, Pres.; Gary Hergenrader, V.P.; Patrick H. Cole, Secy.-Treas.
Directors: Bill Baxter, Ted Blume, Jim Douglas, Darrell Feit, Kirk Nelson.
EIN: 363657995

61535
New Christendom Foundation
c/o Rev. Joseph M. Walsh
8101 O St., Ste., 5111
Lincoln, NE 68510

Established in 1999 in NE.
Financial data (yr. ended 12/31/00): Assets, $5,973 (M); grants paid, $0; gifts received, $2,609; expenditures, $6,042; qualifying distributions, $2,496; giving activities include $5,553 for programs.
Officers: Joseph Walsh, Pres.; Christopher M. Walsh, Secy.; John Rajewski, Treas.
EIN: 470809892

61536
First and Goal Foundation
116 Ginger Cove Rd.
Valley, NE 68064

Classified as a private operation foundation in 1999 in NE.
Donor(s): David Cisar.
Financial data (yr. ended 12/31/00): Assets, $5,147 (M); grants paid, $610; gifts received, $32,451; expenditures, $30,692; qualifying distributions, $30,658; giving activities include $30,081 for programs.
Limitations: Applications not accepted.
Application information: Contributes only to pre-selected organizations.
Directors: David Cisar, W. T. Gilbert, Jay Smith, Rev. Robert Timberlake.
EIN: 470811021

61537
The Minnechaduza Foundation
902 E. 8th St.
Valentine, NE 69201

Established in 1999 in NE.
Donor(s): Timothy W. Ryschon, Kay Lynn Ryschon.
Financial data (yr. ended 12/31/00): Assets, $3,000 (M); grants paid, $0; gifts received, $8,000; expenditures, $5,000; qualifying distributions, $5,000; giving activities include $5,000 for programs.
Limitations: Applications not accepted.
Application information: Contributes only to pre-selected organizations.
Officer and Director:* Kay Lynn Ryschon,* Pres.
EIN: 470826851

61538
The Laurine Volkmer Foundation
c/o Robert M. Schafer
114 N. 6th St.
Beatrice, NE 68310

Established in 2000 in NE.
Financial data (yr. ended 12/31/01): Assets, $2,772 (M); grants paid, $0; expenditures, $420; qualifying distributions, $0.
Officers: Keith J. Volkmer, Pres.; Laurine Volkmer, V.P.; Lee Volkmer, Secy.-Treas.
EIN: 470833156

61539
Nebraska Tax Research Foundation, Inc.
1701 K St.
Lincoln, NE 68508-2662

Established in 1989 in NE.
Donor(s): Union Pacific Corp.
Financial data (yr. ended 12/31/00): Assets, $2,289 (M); grants paid, $0; gifts received, $7,000; expenditures, $7,040; qualifying distributions, $0.
Directors: Steven Ferris, John Jordison, Donald Swanson.
EIN: 363663707

61540
Odd Fellows South Oak Building Corporation
1100 S. Oak
North Platte, NE 69101

Established around 1979.
Financial data (yr. ended 12/31/01): Assets, $1 (M); grants paid, $0; expenditures, $509,604; qualifying distributions, $0.
Officers: Don Lakey, Pres.; Richard Lilly, V.P.; Ken Hill, Secy.; Jim Pence, Treas.
Trustees: Steve Armescher, Hollis Branting, Victor Kovanda, Albert Nielsen.
EIN: 470624421

NEVADA

61541
Tuscany Research Institute
4495 S. Polaris Ave.
Las Vegas, NV 89103
FAX: (702) 739-9897
Contact: Robert C. Anderson, Tr.

Established in 1986 in NV.
Donor(s): CCRC Farms, Anthony A. Marnell II.
Financial data (yr. ended 09/30/99): Assets, $14,852,020 (M); grants paid, $0; gifts received, $10,925; expenditures, $372,026; qualifying distributions, $37,411; giving activities include $37,411 for programs.
Limitations: Giving primarily in CA.
Application information: Application form required.
Trustees: Robert C. Anderson, James A. Barrett, Jr., Christopher L. Kaempfer, Alisa A. Marnell, Anthony A. Marnell II, Anthony A. Marnell III, John Stuart.
EIN: 943025713

61542
Las Vegas Jaycees Senior Citizens Mobil Home Corporation
5805 W. Harmon Ave.
Las Vegas, NV 89103

Classified as a private operating foundation in 1989.
Financial data (yr. ended 06/30/02): Assets, $5,056,984 (M); grants paid, $0; expenditures, $1,316,409; qualifying distributions, $0.
Officers: Jeff Margolin, Pres.; Jean Lidgett, Treas.
EIN: 942553808

61543
The Boyd Foundation
2950 S. Industrial Rd.
Las Vegas, NV 89109-1100
Contact: William S. Boyd, Pres.

Established in 1986 in NV.
Donor(s): Sam A. Boyd, William S. Boyd.
Financial data (yr. ended 12/31/01): Assets, $4,127,166 (M); grants paid, $92,250; expenditures, $163,053; qualifying distributions, $121,115.
Limitations: Giving primarily in Las Vegas, NV.
Application information: Application form required.
Officer: William S. Boyd, Pres.
Trustees: Samuel J. Boyd, William R. Boyd, Marianne E. Boyd Johnson, Bruno Mark.
EIN: 880220082
Codes: FD2

61544
Joshua Foundation
P.O. Box 42698
Las Vegas, NV 89116 (702) 897-0449
Contact: Forrest Purdy, Mgr. or Jan M. Purdy, Mgr.

Established in 1996 in NV.
Financial data (yr. ended 12/31/99): Assets, $4,067,375 (M); grants paid, $4,800; gifts received, $696,038; expenditures, $130,190; qualifying distributions, $115,411.
Limitations: Giving on a national basis.
Application information: Application form not required.
Officers: Forrest Purdy, Jr., Mgr.; Jan Marie Purdy, Mgr.
EIN: 880368741

61545
Baumann Foundation
P.O. Box 34402
Las Vegas, NV 89133-4402
Contact: Josef Baumann, Dir.

Established in 1999 in NV.
Donor(s): Josef Baumann.
Financial data (yr. ended 06/30/00): Assets, $3,520,482 (M); grants paid, $21,000; gifts received, $2,484,719; expenditures, $25,983; qualifying distributions, $17,797.
Limitations: Giving on a national basis.
Director: Josef Baumann.
EIN: 880439595

61546
Lydia E. Pinkham Memorial, Inc.
801 S. Rancho Dr., Ste. E6
Las Vegas, NV 89106

Financial data (yr. ended 12/31/99): Assets, $2,525,011 (M); grants paid, $0; expenditures, $136,969; qualifying distributions, $117,665; giving activities include $114,265 for programs.
Officers: Stephen N. Doty, Pres. and Treas.; Paul Doty, V.P.; Richard L. Camann, Secy.
EIN: 042104836

61547
Grace Dangberg Foundation, Inc.
P.O. Box 696
Carson City, NV 89702-1627
Application address: P.O. Box 1627, Carson City, NV 89702-1627, tel.: (775) 882-4466
Contact: James H. Bean, Secy.-Treas.

Financial data (yr. ended 06/30/01): Assets, $1,740,302 (M); grants paid, $7,283; expenditures, $170,778; qualifying distributions, $197,137; giving activities include $190,391 for programs.
Limitations: Giving primarily in NV.
Officers: David Thompson, Pres.; Denise Dangberg, V.P.; James H. Bean, Secy.-Treas.
EIN: 880185985

61548
Marie Crowley Foundation
11675 Osage Rd.
Reno, NV 89506 (775) 972-0618
Contact: Mary Ann Arnold, Tr.

Established in 1997 in NV.
Donor(s): Crowley Charitable Lead Trust.
Financial data (yr. ended 12/31/01): Assets, $1,523,080 (M); grants paid, $63,527; gifts received, $301,269; expenditures, $73,469; qualifying distributions, $67,861.
Limitations: Giving on a national basis.
Trustee: Mary Ann Arnold.
EIN: 880362044

61549
Nevada Science Foundation
206 S. Division St.
Carson City, NV 89703
Application address: 2031 Hamilton Ave., Carson City, NV 89706, tel.: (775) 883-5182
Contact: Josef Waxler, Tr.

Established in 1990 in NV. Classified as a private operating foundation in 1992.
Donor(s): Josef Waxler.
Financial data (yr. ended 03/31/01): Assets, $1,422,597 (M); grants paid, $12,277; gifts received, $29,000; expenditures, $47,468; qualifying distributions, $12,277.
Limitations: Giving on an international basis, with emphasis on Chile.
Officers: Lavina A. Atkinson, Pres.; Debbie Bovard, Secy.-Treas.
Trustee: Josef Waxler.
EIN: 880259800

61550
Charles & Ruth Hopping Charitable Foundation
c/o Steve S. Johnson
1485 Coronet Dr.
Reno, NV 89509

Established in 1999 in NV.
Financial data (yr. ended 12/31/01): Assets, $1,173,589 (M); grants paid, $229,013; expenditures, $246,603; qualifying distributions, $230,203.
Limitations: Applications not accepted. Giving primarily in NV.
Application information: Contributes only to pre-selected organizations.
Trustee: Steve S. Johnson.
EIN: 880417390
Codes: FD2

61551
Gilcrease Bird Sanctuary
8103 Racel St.
Las Vegas, NV 89131

Donor(s): William Gilcrease.
Financial data (yr. ended 12/31/99): Assets, $928,535 (M); grants paid, $0; gifts received, $148,568; expenditures, $145,245; qualifying distributions, $142,384; giving activities include $128,166 for programs.
Officers and Directors:* William Gilcrease,* Pres.; Ted Gilcrease,* V.P.; Mary Ellen Racel,* Secy.-Treas.
EIN: 880263602

61552
John and Grace Nauman Foundation
c/o Todd Russell
402 N. Division St.
Carson City, NV 89703-4168

Established in 1997 in NV.
Financial data (yr. ended 06/30/02): Assets, $890,223 (M); grants paid, $39,500; expenditures, $40,367; qualifying distributions, $40,015.
Limitations: Applications not accepted. Giving primarily in NV.
Application information: Contributes only to pre-selected organizations.
Trustees: Howard Anderson, Violet Burley, Loretta Grace Nauman, Todd Russell.
EIN: 880399323

61553
Don Hudson Foundation, Inc.
2375 E. Tropicana Ave.
Las Vegas, NV 89119-6564

Established as an operating foundation in OH.
Donor(s): Donald W. Hudson.
Financial data (yr. ended 12/31/01): Assets, $816,347 (M); grants paid, $60,850; gifts received, $100,000; expenditures, $66,365; qualifying distributions, $63,116.
Limitations: Applications not accepted.
Application information: Contributes only to pre-selected organizations.
Officers and Trustees:* Donald W. Hudson,* Pres. and Treas.; Kimberly R. Poppe,* Secy.; Jamie S. Griffif, Donald A. Hudson, Edwin Hollis Hudson, Jr., Jodie L. Vogel.
EIN: 341852232

61554
Paula Knickerbocker Foundation, Inc.
(Formerly Paula Knickerbocker Kremer Foundation, Inc.)
700 Willington Dr.
Spring Creek, NV 89815-7078
Application adddress: c/o Idaho Trust, 608 Northwest Blvd., Coeur D'Alene, ID 83814
Contact: Paula Knickerbocker

Classified as a private operating foundation in 1996 in ID.
Donor(s): Paula Knickerbocker.
Financial data (yr. ended 12/31/01): Assets, $705,527 (M); grants paid, $33,384; gifts received, $286,433; expenditures, $267,823; qualifying distributions, $281,602; giving activities include $182,288 for loans.
Limitations: Giving primarily in ID.
Application information: Application form not required.
Officers and Directors:* Paula Knickerbocker,* Pres.; Daniel Prohaska,* V.P.
EIN: 820482954

61555
Thomas D. Lynch Family Foundation
1011 Armadillo Ct.
Henderson, NV 89015

Established in 1994 in CA.
Donor(s): Thomas D. Lynch.
Financial data (yr. ended 12/31/00): Assets, $562,203 (M); grants paid, $19,409; gifts received, $200,440; expenditures, $20,181; qualifying distributions, $19,409.
Limitations: Applications not accepted. Giving primarily in CA.
Application information: Contributes only to pre-selected organizations.
Officers: Thomas D. Lynch, Pres.; Sheryl Lynch, Secy.; Edward D. Lynch, C.F.O.
EIN: 330636270

61556
The Fred and Judy Alexander Foundation
P.O. Box 6746
Stateline, NV 89449-6746

Established in 1996.
Donor(s): Judy Alexander, Ken Alexander.
Financial data (yr. ended 12/31/99): Assets, $536,520 (M); grants paid, $0; gifts received, $154,925; expenditures, $197,053; qualifying distributions, $129,076; giving activities include $59,322 for programs.
Officers: Judy Alexander, Pres.; Chris Bailey, V.P.; Shelly Godken-Wright, Exec. Dir.
Directors: Ken Alexander, Darbi Gilbert, Daniel G. Kabat.
EIN: 880351454

61557
W. & E. Smith Foundation, Inc.
591 Mt. Hunter Way
Boulder City, NV 89005-1021

Donor(s): William M. Smith.
Financial data (yr. ended 06/30/01): Assets, $503,200 (M); grants paid, $0; gifts received, $22,000; expenditures, $17,815; qualifying distributions, $17,815; giving activities include $55,684 for programs.
Officers: William M. Smith, Pres. and Treas.; Elaine K. Smith, V.P.
Directors: Ruth Clark, Marilyn K. Kraft, Gloria Pidgeon.
EIN: 880322504

61558
Annebelle E. Dennis Education Foundation
P.O. Box 11571
Zephyr Cove, NV 89448-3571

Classified as a private operating foundation in 2000 in NV.
Financial data (yr. ended 08/31/01): Assets, $490,127 (L); grants paid, $0; expenditures, $35,166; qualifying distributions, $0.
Officers: Leonard Jones, Pres.; Walter Ponty, V.P.
Director: Oliver Q. Forst.
EIN: 880469639

61559
Robert Lynn Horne Foundation
44 Quail Run Rd.
Henderson, NV 89014

Financial data (yr. ended 12/31/00): Assets, $452,715 (M); grants paid, $0; gifts received, $208,991; expenditures, $24,819; qualifying distributions, $200,620; giving activities include $13,249 for programs.
Limitations: Applications not accepted.
Application information: Contributes only to pre-selected organizations.
Officer: Robert Lynn Horne, Pres.
Trustees: Robert Bolick, Michael Lantz, David Leubitz, Jerry Lewis, Mark Salls.
EIN: 943263761

61560
Morris Family Fund
1100 E. William St., Ste. 207
Carson City, NV 89701

Established in 1997.
Donor(s): Anjali Morris, M.D., Unni Narayanan, M.D.
Financial data (yr. ended 09/30/99): Assets, $419,838 (M); grants paid, $20,040; gifts received, $329,000; expenditures, $28,228; qualifying distributions, $28,228.
Limitations: Applications not accepted.
Application information: Contributes only to pre-selected organizations.
Officer: Donald Morris, Pres.
Directors: Anjali Morris, M.D., Unni Narayanan, M.D., Adrienne Smith.
EIN: 880379711

61561
The Trigiano Foundation
1421 Casa Del Rey Ct.
Las Vegas, NV 89117-1538

Established in 1998.
Donor(s): Lucien Trigiano.
Financial data (yr. ended 12/31/99): Assets, $411,461 (M); grants paid, $14,500; gifts received, $176,299; expenditures, $22,855; qualifying distributions, $16,464.
Limitations: Applications not accepted.
Application information: Contributes only to pre-selected organizations.
Officer: Lucien Trigiano, Pres.
Directors: Glenn L. Trigiano, Robert N. Trigiano.
EIN: 860889932

61562
Edna Rose Crane Educational Foundation
3910 Pecos-McLeod, Ste. A-100
Las Vegas, NV 89121

Classified as a private operating foundation in 1995 in NV.
Donor(s): Edna Rose Crane, Dorothy Kidd, Gary E. Mohler, Eldon A. Mohler.
Financial data (yr. ended 12/31/99): Assets, $409,475 (M); grants paid, $27,872; gifts received, $110,000; expenditures, $28,190; qualifying distributions, $28,190.
Limitations: Applications not accepted. Giving limited to Las Vegas, NV.
Application information: Contributes only to pre-selected organizations.
Officers: Edna Rose Crane, Pres.; Beckey Buckley, V.P.; Judy Frank, V.P.; Dorothy Kidd, V.P.; Karen Layne, Secy.; Eldon Mohler, Treas.
EIN: 880302464

61563
Colby Operating Foundation
9715 Passa Tempo Dr.
Reno, NV 89511

Established in 2000 in NV.
Donor(s): John J. Cassani, Starla A. Cassani.
Financial data (yr. ended 12/31/01): Assets, $396,982 (M); grants paid, $500; gifts received, $10,000; expenditures, $13,156; qualifying distributions, $500.
Limitations: Applications not accepted.
Application information: Contributes only to pre-selected organizations.
Trustees: John J. Cassani, Starla A. Cassani.
EIN: 880445730

61564
Tiberti Family Foundation
c/o J.A. Tiberti
1806 Industrial Rd.
Las Vegas, NV 89102

Classified as a private operating foundation in 1992.
Financial data (yr. ended 12/31/99): Assets, $390,510 (M); grants paid, $17,600; gifts received, $140,000; expenditures, $17,879; qualifying distributions, $17,600.
Limitations: Applications not accepted. Giving primarily in NV.
Application information: Contributes only to pre-selected organizations.
Trustees: Mary A. Maffey, J.A. Tiberti, J. Tito Tiberti, Jelindo A. Tiberti II, Laura Lisa Tiberti, Mario A. Tiberti, Renaldo M. Tiberti.
EIN: 880253491

61565
The Braunstein Foundation
1705 Calle de Espana
Las Vegas, NV 89102-4003

Classified as a private operating foundation in 1993.
Donor(s): Michael C. Braunstein, Manetta Braunstein.
Financial data (yr. ended 11/30/00): Assets, $387,991 (M); grants paid, $0; gifts received, $240; expenditures, $370; qualifying distributions, $110; giving activities include $268 for programs.
Officers and Trustees:* Michael C. Braunstein, M.D.,* Pres. and Treas.; Manetta Braunstein,* Secy.; Lawrence S. Branton, Robert J. Gottlieb, Ph.D.
EIN: 880279482

61566
Braerwood Charitable Trust
3660 Townsend St.
Las Vegas, NV 89121

Established in 1997.
Donor(s): Robert J. Harelson, Anna M. Harelson.
Financial data (yr. ended 12/31/00): Assets, $365,207 (M); grants paid, $6,500; gifts received, $115,000; expenditures, $76,707; qualifying distributions, $6,500.
Trustee: Katherine Derusso.

61566—NEVADA

EIN: 911808246

61567
Elvirita Lewis Forum for Intergenerational Resources
(Formerly Elvirita Lewis Foundation for Geriatric Health and Nutrition)
P.O. Box 4110
Sparks, NV 89431 (775) 358-2768

Established about 1974 in CA and NV.
Donor(s): Elvirita L. Stafford.‡
Financial data (yr. ended 06/30/99): Assets, $337,998 (M); grants paid, $530; gifts received, $621,851; expenditures, $464,994; qualifying distributions, $530.
Officers and Directors:* Lillie Bourriague,* Chair.; Steven W. Brummel, Pres.; Carolynn Pickard, V.P.; Janette O'Hair, Secy.
EIN: 942344734

61568
Robert Belliveau Foundation
5850 N. Park St.
Las Vegas, NV 89129

Established in 1985 in NV.
Donor(s): Robert R. Belliveau, M.D.
Financial data (yr. ended 12/31/00): Assets, $297,930 (M); grants paid, $7,600; gifts received, $40,900; expenditures, $27,604; qualifying distributions, $25,841.
Limitations: Applications not accepted. Giving primarily in Las Vegas, NV.
Application information: Contributes only to pre-selected organizations.
Officers: Robert R. Belliveau, M.D., Pres.; Rita D. Abbey, Secy.-Treas.
EIN: 942973284

61569
Western Nevada Youth Foundation
c/o Freeman and Williams, LLP
3470 GS Richards Blvd.
Carson City, NV 89703-8373
Application address: P.O. Box 20404, Carson City, NV 89721
Contact: James S. Bradshaw, Secy.-Treas.

Classified as an operating foundation in 1996.
Financial data (yr. ended 12/31/01): Assets, $269,457; grants paid, $17,200; expenditures, $68,488; qualifying distributions, $64,908.
Limitations: Giving limited to Carson and Lyon counties, NV.
Officers and Trustees:* Thomas Bruce,* Pres.; Newton Freeman,* V.P.; James S. Bradshaw,* Secy.-Treas.; Evan Bruce, Virginia Bruce.
EIN: 880341420

61570
I Have a Dream Foundation - Las Vegas, Inc.
3773 Howard Hughes Pkwy., 3rd Fl. S.
Las Vegas, NV 89109-0949

Established in 1994 in NV.
Donor(s): Harrah's Las Vegas.
Financial data (yr. ended 12/31/01): Assets, $241,405 (M); grants paid, $0; gifts received, $174,972; expenditures, $126,510; qualifying distributions, $0; giving activities include $124,325 for programs.
Limitations: Applications not accepted.
Application information: Contributes only to pre-selected organizations.
Officers and Directors:* Kevin Stolworthy,* Pres.; Julie A. Foley,* V.P.; Louise Helton,* Secy.; Teri Stolworthy,* Treas.; Bill Bayno, Diana Bennett, Joseph W. Brown, Paula Dulak, Sidney Franklin, Jerry Keller, Scott Nielson, Ed Skonicki, Betty Turner.

EIN: 880312222

61571
The Polis Charitable Foundation
980 American Pacific Dr., Ste. 111
Henderson, NV 89014

Established in 1999 in NV.
Financial data (yr. ended 12/31/99): Assets, $176,777 (M); grants paid, $48,290; gifts received, $218,390; expenditures, $50,190; qualifying distributions, $48,290.
Limitations: Applications not accepted. Giving primarily in NV.
Application information: Contributes only to pre-selected organizations.
Officers: Jerry E. Polis, Pres.; Eric Polis, Secy.; David Polis, Treas.
EIN: 880418257

61572
The Tito and Sandra Tiberti Foundation
1806 Industrial Rd.
Las Vegas, NV 89102-2681

Established in 1986 in NV.
Financial data (yr. ended 12/31/00): Assets, $166,157 (M); grants paid, $8,500; expenditures, $8,602; qualifying distributions, $8,602.
Limitations: Applications not accepted. Giving limited to Las Vegas, NV.
Application information: Contributes only to pre-selected organizations.
Trustees: Michael Leavitt, J. Tito Tiberti, Sandra Boots Tiberti.
EIN: 880224337

61573
DiRienzo Foundation, Inc.
4735 Saddlehorn Dr.
Reno, NV 89511-6756 (775) 853-8962
Contact: Margaret A. DiRienzo, Exec. Dir.

Established in 1994.
Donor(s): Frederick H. DiRienzo, Margaret A. DiRienzo.
Financial data (yr. ended 12/31/99): Assets, $132,160 (M); grants paid, $10,000; gifts received, $161; expenditures, $12,117; qualifying distributions, $12,001.
Limitations: Giving primarily in NV and OH.
Application information: Application form required.
Officers and Trustees:* Frederick H. DiRienzo,* Treas.; Margaret A. DiRienzo,* Exec. Dir.; Amara L. DiRienzo, Alyssa C. DiRienzo.
EIN: 311393435

61574
Church of Jesus Power
4321 Cobblehill Way
North Las Vegas, NV 89032

Established in 1999 in NV.
Financial data (yr. ended 12/31/01): Assets, $126,584 (M); grants paid, $5,000; expenditures, $48,200; qualifying distributions, $40,391; giving activities include $40,411 for programs.
Limitations: Applications not accepted. Giving primarily in Las Vegas, NV.
Application information: Contributes only to pre-selected organizations.
Officers: Douglas J. Cooke, Pres.; Patricia L. Cooke, Secy.
EIN: 880193399

61575
TD4HIM Foundation, Inc.
60 Shoreline Cir.
Incline Village, NV 89451

Donor(s): Trent F. Dilfer.

Financial data (yr. ended 12/31/01): Assets, $110,191 (M); grants paid, $142,850; gifts received, $250,055; expenditures, $142,873; qualifying distributions, $142,850.
Limitations: Applications not accepted. Giving on a national basis.
Application information: Contributes only to pre-selected organizations.
Officer: Trent F. Dilfer, Pres.
EIN: 311689460
Codes: FD2

61576
Forum for a Common Agenda
10981 Dryden Dr.
Reno, NV 89511

Donor(s): L.S. Allen, Bob Burn, Don Carano, Dave Clark, Sue Clark-Jackson, Michael C. Dermody, Clark J. Guild, Jr., Walter Higgins, William J. Keepers, M.E. King, Louis J. Phillips, Jim Rogers, John J. Russell, Joey Scolari, Larry Tuntland, Bill Dickerson, Alan Means, Tom Baker, Tom Outland, Ferenc Szony.
Financial data (yr. ended 10/31/00): Assets, $90,598 (M); grants paid, $0; gifts received, $210,975; expenditures, $161,780; qualifying distributions, $161,713; giving activities include $102,434 for programs.
Officers: Jim Devolld, Chair.; Alan Means, Secy.; Tom Outland, Treas.; Canadace Evart, Exec. Dir.
Trustees: Tom Baker, Phil Bryan, Don Carano, Joe Crowley, Michael C. Dermody, Ross Golding, M.D., Brian Kennedy, Ron Krump, Stephanie Kruse, Marsha Lindsay, Rhett Long, Malyn Malquist, Jim Miller, Mike Murdock, Phil Satre, Ferenc Szony, and 9 additional trustees.
EIN: 880279054

61577
Warren & Ethyln Reed-Carson Valley Lions Scholarship Foundation
P.O. Box 1
Minden, NV 89423

Donor(s): Alan Reed, Michael Reed.
Financial data (yr. ended 12/31/00): Assets, $68,782 (M); grants paid, $5,000; gifts received, $30,600; expenditures, $7,974; qualifying distributions, $77,055; giving activities include $68,835 for program-related investments.
Limitations: Giving primarily in Gardnerville, NV.
Application information: Application form required.
Directors: Mike Coleman, Sandra Coverly, James Loughrey, Jim Norton, Alan Reed.
EIN: 880441355

61578
The Agee Memorial Wildlife Fund
3032 Ste. Tropez
Las Vegas, NV 89128 (702) 228-1324
Contact: Cindy Minghelli, Pres.

Established in 1999 in NV.
Donor(s): Cindy Minghelli, Ed Minghelli.
Financial data (yr. ended 09/30/00): Assets, $46,926 (M); grants paid, $1,000; gifts received, $63,149; expenditures, $68,223; qualifying distributions, $68,223; giving activities include $28,506 for programs.
Officers: Cindy Minghelli, Pres.; Ed Minghelli, Secy.
EIN: 880435331

61579
John E. Sells Foundation
P.O. Box 7597
Incline Village, NV 89452-7579

Donor(s): John E. Sells.

Financial data (yr. ended 12/31/00): Assets, $30,025 (M); grants paid, $2,500; gifts received, $20,275; expenditures, $2,775; qualifying distributions, $2,500.
Limitations: Applications not accepted. Giving primarily in Incline Village, NV.
Application information: Contributes only to pre-selected organizations.
Officer: John E. Sells, Pres. and Secy.-Treas.
Trustees: Betty Sells Robertson, Charles O. Sells, Christine Scharff Sells.
EIN: 880319741

61580
Schulman Family Foundation
6600 W. Charleston Blvd., Ste. 124
Las Vegas, NV 89146 (702) 737-6091
Contact: Robert H. Schulman, Pres.

Established in 1999 in NV.
Financial data (yr. ended 07/31/00): Assets, $27,534 (M); grants paid, $2,265; gifts received, $30,000; expenditures, $2,757; qualifying distributions, $2,265.
Officer: Robert H. Schulman, Pres.
EIN: 880401555

61581
Gymnastics Nevada Booster Club
6170-B Ridgeview Ct.
Reno, NV 89509

Classified as a private operating foundation in 1987.
Financial data (yr. ended 05/31/00): Assets, $22,194 (M); grants paid, $0; gifts received, $9,307; expenditures, $104,405; qualifying distributions, $104,205; giving activities include $64,342 for programs.
Officers: Terry J. Redmon, Pres.; Judy Stewart, V.P.; Kay Culp, Secy.; Chuck Koehler, Treas.
Directors: Linda Cesnik, Linda Hayes, Beth Heggeness, Joanne Herzog, Curtis Lampert, Kathy Schroeder, Lorraine Toole.
EIN: 943043542

61582
The Hettie Van Sickle Library, Inc.
304 S. Minnesota St.
Carson City, NV 89703-4270

Established in 1997 in NV.
Donor(s): Hettie Van Sickle.
Financial data (yr. ended 12/31/01): Assets, $21,426 (M); grants paid, $0; expenditures, $0; qualifying distributions, $0.
Limitations: Applications not accepted.
Application information: Contributes only to pre-selected organizations.
Trustee: Jack Van Sickle.
EIN: 880323019

61583
Wilson Family Foundation
7201 W. Lake Mead Blvd., Ste. 400
Las Vegas, NV 89128

Established in 1999 in PA.
Donor(s): Lawrence R. Wilson.
Financial data (yr. ended 06/30/00): Assets, $10,798 (M); grants paid, $24,390; gifts received, $35,188; expenditures, $24,390; qualifying distributions, $24,390.
Limitations: Applications not accepted.
Application information: Contributes only to pre-selected organizations.
Officers: Lawrence R. Wilson, Pres.; Claire Wilson, Secy.
EIN: 911874341

61584
The George Mano Mantis Foundation, Inc.
4170 W. Harmon Ave.
Las Vegas, NV 89103

Established in 1999.
Donor(s): Fasteners Inc. SW Supply.
Financial data (yr. ended 12/31/00): Assets, $9,708 (L); grants paid, $8,200; gifts received, $8,692; expenditures, $9,498; qualifying distributions, $8,200.
Limitations: Applications not accepted.
Application information: Contributes only to pre-selected organizations.
Officer and Directors:* Keith W. Mantis, Exec. Dir.; Kristine Dannen, Mark A. Jimenez, Kevin Kelsay, Tom Zay.
EIN: 880417989

61585
Bethesda Foundation
3753 Howard Hughes Pkwy., No. 200
Las Vegas, NV 89109-0938

Established in 1998 in CA and NV.
Donor(s): Blaine Cook, Becky Cook.
Financial data (yr. ended 12/31/99): Assets, $8,761 (M); grants paid, $32,357; gifts received, $75,763; expenditures, $91,747; qualifying distributions, $65,857.
Directors: Becky Cook, Blaine Cook.
EIN: 880397485

61586
William L. Gohres and Mildred Hohmann Gohres Foundation
6150 W. Palmyra Ave.
Las Vegas, NV 89102

Established in 1993.
Donor(s): First Republic Savings Bank.
Financial data (yr. ended 09/30/00): Assets, $8,060 (M); grants paid, $59; gifts received, $15,724; expenditures, $8,833; qualifying distributions, $8,510.
Officers: Mildred Hohmann Gohres, Pres. and Treas.; William L. Gohres, V.P. and Secy.
EIN: 880308528

61587
Law Enforcement Racers Against Drugs
6530 Bradley Rd.
Las Vegas, NV 89131-2913

Established in 1997 in NV.
Donor(s): Fletcher Jones, 5 Star Group, Doc Holidays, Hoosier Tires, Squack Racing.
Financial data (yr. ended 12/31/00): Assets, $8,002 (M); grants paid, $50; gifts received, $18,415; expenditures, $17,950; qualifying distributions, $12,453; giving activities include $12,454 for programs.
Officers: Steve Steckel, Pres.; Thomas Mildren, Secy.-Treas.
Director: Alan Wall.
EIN: 913141955

61588
The Laura L. Tiberti Charitable Foundation
1806 Industrial Rd.
Las Vegas, NV 89102

Established in 1999.
Donor(s): Laura L. Tiberti.
Financial data (yr. ended 12/31/01): Assets, $6,132 (M); grants paid, $7,900; gifts received, $10,000; expenditures, $8,430; qualifying distributions, $8,430.
Limitations: Applications not accepted.
Application information: Contributes only to pre-selected organizations.
Trustees: Robert E. Clark, Hazzard Brannon Roney, Laura L. Tiberti.
EIN: 880417025

61589
Elizabeth Ackerman Family Foundation
2877 Paradise Rd., Ste. 2073
Las Vegas, NV 89109

Classified as a company-sponsored operating foundation in 1999.
Donor(s): FH Holding Ltd.
Financial data (yr. ended 06/30/01): Assets, $3,287 (M); grants paid, $1,365; expenditures, $1,530; qualifying distributions, $1,365.
Limitations: Applications not accepted.
Application information: Contributes only to pre-selected organizations.
Officer: Elizabeth Ackerman, Pres.
EIN: 880432991

61590
CAU Foundation
P.O. Box 1781
Carson City, NV 89702

Classified as a private operating foundation in 1986.
Financial data (yr. ended 12/31/01): Assets, $3,169 (M); grants paid, $12,250; gifts received, $15,000; expenditures, $12,671; qualifying distributions, $12,250.
Limitations: Applications not accepted. Giving limited to Carson City, NV.
Application information: Contributes only to pre-selected organizations.
Trustee: Roger Shaheen.
EIN: 880208180

61591
Foundation for Performing Arts Education
10008 Rolling Glen Ct.
Las Vegas, NV 89117

Established in 2000 in NV.
Financial data (yr. ended 12/31/00): Assets, $525 (M); grants paid, $1,600; gifts received, $2,140; expenditures, $1,749; qualifying distributions, $1,734.
Directors: Charles E. Cleveland II, Ellerie L. Cleveland, John Ficarrotta.
EIN: 880463202

61592
Wild Horse Foundation
625 Akard Cir.
Reno, NV 89503 (775) 747-7914
Contact: Tincia Seginski, Pres.

Established in 2000 in NV.
Financial data (yr. ended 12/31/00): Assets, $200 (M); grants paid, $210; gifts received, $210; expenditures, $624; qualifying distributions, $210.
Limitations: Giving primarily in Reno, NV.
Officers: Tincia Seginski, Pres.; Carolyn Lynn Furnis, V.P.; Mary Larson, Secy.
EIN: 311654895

61593
Lander County Humane Society
2236 Pinto Rd.
Battle Mountain, NV 89820

Classified as a private operating foundation in 1989.
Donor(s): Gladys Bartz Trust.
Financial data (yr. ended 12/31/00): Assets, $112 (M); grants paid, $0; gifts received, $9,100; expenditures, $9,085; qualifying distributions, $9,085; giving activities include $9,085 for programs.

61593—NEVADA

Officers: Joanne Weeks, Pres.; Andrea Gamble, Treas.
EIN: 880245086

61594
Dr. Miriam & Sheldon G. Adelson Charitable Trust
c/o Sheldon G. Adelson
201 E. Sands Ave.
Las Vegas, NV 89109
Application address: 2950 Augusta Dr., Las Vegas, NV 89109
Contact: Miriam O. Adelson, Tr.

Established in 1994 in NV.
Financial data (yr. ended 12/31/00): Assets, $0 (M); grants paid, $643,279; gifts received, $638,940; expenditures, $643,372; qualifying distributions, $643,277.
Limitations: Giving on a national basis.
Application information: Application form not required.
Trustees: Miriam O. Adelson, Sheldon G. Adelson.
EIN: 886063073
Codes: FD

61595
Committee for a National Pension Plan
4525 W. Twain Ave., No. 24
Las Vegas, NV 89103

Classified as a private operating foundation in 1988.
Financial data (yr. ended 12/31/01): Assets, $0 (M); grants paid, $0; gifts received, $15; expenditures, $474; qualifying distributions, $474.
Officers: Peter J. Montagnoli, Pres.; Richard Owen, Secy.
Directors: Christina Clemente, Blanche Montagnoli.
EIN: 880159980

NEW HAMPSHIRE

61596
The Taylor Home
435 Union Ave.
Laconia, NH 03246

Classified as a private operating foundation in 1985.
Donor(s): Frank Stanley Trust, Nila Magidoff, Frank Busiel Trust, Oscar George Trust, Helen Busiel Trust, Douglas Stone.
Financial data (yr. ended 04/30/01): Assets, $40,856,070 (M); grants paid, $2,851; gifts received, $580,840; expenditures, $6,759,515; qualifying distributions, $8,593,613; giving activities include $9,718,256 for programs.
Limitations: Applications not accepted. Giving primarily in NH.
Application information: Contributes only to pre-selected organizations.
Officers: Janet Mitchell, Chair.; Brenda Long, 1st Vice-Chair.; Philip Daigneault, 2nd Vice-Chair. and Treas.; Wesley J. Colby, C.O.O.; Howard Chandler, Secy. and Exec. Dir.; James O. Anderson, C.F.O.
Trustees: Martha Clement, Dennis Denoncourt, Rodney Dyer, Mark Koerner, Henry Lipman, Mendon MacDonald, Otto Olson, Susan Smith, William Smith, Lydia Torr, Richard Trombly, H. Thomas Volpe.
EIN: 020222149

61597
Hunt Community, Inc.
10 Allds St.
Nashua, NH 03060

Classified as a private operating foundation in 1987.
Donor(s): Bertha Clark,‡ David Adams.
Financial data (yr. ended 04/30/00): Assets, $36,826,394 (M); grants paid, $0; gifts received, $49,751; expenditures, $7,324,534; qualifying distributions, $6,639,407; giving activities include $6,639,407 for programs.
Officers: Jody S. Wilbert, Pres.; Jack R. Law, 1st V.P.; Normand A. LaPlante, 2nd V.P.; Frederick S. Lyford, Secy.; William Gorham, Treas.
Trustees: Maurice L. Arel, J. Richard Burns, Nancy Eldredge, Nancy Ford, Margaret Gilmour, John Parolin, David Pastor, William Thompson.
EIN: 020369906

61598
The Gale Home
133 Ash St.
Manchester, NH 03104

Classified as a private operating foundation in 1942.
Donor(s): Fannie Moulton McLane.
Financial data (yr. ended 02/28/00): Assets, $15,460,095 (M); grants paid, $0; gifts received, $2,913; expenditures, $1,340,723; qualifying distributions, $1,253,945; giving activities include $1,253,945 for programs.
Officers and Trustees:* Therese Benoit,* Pres.; Kathleen Sullivan,* V.P.; Theodore Wadleigh,* Secy.; Jeffrey Hickok,* Treas.; Genevieve T. Merrill, Barbara Trucellito, and 7 additional trustees.
EIN: 020223444

61599
Mark H. Wentworth Home for Chronic Invalids
346 Pleasant St.
Portsmouth, NH 03801-4587

Classified as a private operating foundation in 1987.
Financial data (yr. ended 12/31/01): Assets, $13,718,038 (M); grants paid, $0; gifts received, $32,821; expenditures, $5,367,348; qualifying distributions, $5,196,736; giving activities include $5,331,613 for programs.
Officers: John Hebert, Pres.; Dale Smith, V.P.; Morton Schmidt, V.P.; Jay Gibson, Treas.
Trustees: Rev. Gordon Allen, Cynthia Blood, Maurice Buttrick, William Henson, Dan Hoefle, Joan P. Nickell, Morton Schmidt, Dale Smith, Richard Yeaton.
EIN: 020222243

61600
Chase Home for Children
698 Middle Rd.
Portsmouth, NH 03801

Classified as a private operating foundation in 1983.
Financial data (yr. ended 12/31/00): Assets, $10,914,501 (M); grants paid, $0; gifts received, $10,608; expenditures, $794,856; qualifying distributions, $768,397; giving activities include $725,471 for programs.
Officers and Trustees:* Richard Ward,* Pres.; Bertha Rocray,* V.P.; Joan Woodworth,* Secy.; Michael Chubrich, John E. Durkin, Salvatore Grasso, Carolyn Harvey, Landya McCafferty, Priscilla Mullen, John Pratt.
EIN: 022229190

61601
The Carl Siemon Family Charitable Trust
c/o Cynthia Wyatt
307 Applebee Rd.
Milton Mills, NH 03852

Classified as an operating foundation in 1995.
Donor(s): Carl Siemon.
Financial data (yr. ended 12/31/00): Assets, $9,353,649 (M); grants paid, $195; gifts received, $2,256,806; expenditures, $358,832; qualifying distributions, $313,073.
Limitations: Applications not accepted. Giving primarily in Milton, NH.
Application information: Contributes only to pre-selected organizations.
Trustees: Roger Leighton, Beverly Siemon, Carl Siemon, Cynthia S. Wyatt.
EIN: 226670093

61602
The Scott-Farrar Home
11 Elm St.
Peterborough, NH 03458-1031

Financial data (yr. ended 10/31/01): Assets, $8,319,237 (M); grants paid, $1,170; gifts received, $191,945; expenditures, $499,821; qualifying distributions, $446,556; giving activities include $426,651 for programs.
Officers and Trustees:* Joanne Chamberlain, Chairman; Nancy Gorr, Vice-Chair.; Helen McCarthy,* Clerk; Gordon Hale,* Treas.; Bruce Armer, Robert Cormack, Mert Dyer, Louise Fredericks, Norman H. Makechnie, Ruth Nace, Robert Ray, George Sterling.
EIN: 020241739

61603
Women's Aid Home
(also known as Pearl Manor)
1228 Elm St.
Manchester, NH 03101

Classified as a private operating foundation in 1987.
Financial data (yr. ended 06/30/01): Assets, $8,157,744 (M); grants paid, $0; gifts received, $2,333; expenditures, $3,115,291; qualifying distributions, $338,566; giving activities include $3,115,291 for programs.
Officers: Douglas Dean, Pres.; Richard Elwell, Secy.
Directors: Karen Bryant, M.D., Mary Chambers, Peter T. Cheung, M.D., Sheila Evjy, R.N., Beth Hughes, Rochelle H. Lindner, D.M.D., Mary Monagan, Selma Naccach-Hoff, Jwalant R. Vadalia, M.D.
EIN: 020222249

61604
Mary A. Sweeney Home
50 E. Pearl St.
Nashua, NH 03060-3439

Classified as a private operating foundation in 1975.
Donor(s): Isabelle R. Dionne.‡
Financial data (yr. ended 01/31/02): Assets, $8,021,616 (M); grants paid, $0; gifts received, $30,000; expenditures, $226,240; qualifying distributions, $0.
Officers: Martha E. O'Neill, Pres.; Joseph Paladino, V.P.; A. Scott Behman, Treas.
Trustees: Maureen Canny, John H. Collins, Donal Dignan, Ray Dumont, Bobbie French, Louise Kelly, Fr. Martin Kelly, Mary Levine, Fred Mayer, Fr. Joseph T. McDonough, Steve Wojcik.
EIN: 020312307

61605
Centennial Senior Center, Inc.
c/o Lorraine Carter
P.O. Box 4149
Concord, NH 03302-4149

Established in 2000 in NH. Classified as a private operating foundation in 2001.
Donor(s): New Hampshire Centennial Home for the Aged.
Financial data (yr. ended 06/30/01): Assets, $7,738,991 (M); grants paid, $0; gifts received, $7,897,744; expenditures, $159,121; qualifying distributions, $169,733; giving activities include $4,380 for programs.
Officers: Dale K. Klatzker, Chair.; Hon. Gloria Seldin, Vice-Chair.; Kenneth Chenette, 2nd Vice-Chair.; Rev. Anna C. Beach, Secy.; Natalie R. Smith, Treas.
Directors: Freda Drown, Michael Palmien, Phyllis Poulin, Douglas Richards.
EIN: 020519812

61606
Rolfe & Rumford Home, Inc.
23 Rundlett St.
Concord, NH 03301

Classified as a private operating foundation in 1990.
Financial data (yr. ended 06/30/00): Assets, $6,408,445 (M); grants paid, $0; gifts received, $6,350; expenditures, $432,086; qualifying distributions, $401,163; giving activities include $385,619 for programs.
Limitations: Applications not accepted.
Application information: Contributes only to pre-selected organizations.
Officers: Richard B. Couser, Pres.; Frederic R. Pilch, V.P.; Timothy W. Woodman, Secy.-Treas.; Jacqueline Pope, Exec. Dir.
Trustee: State Street Bank & Trust Co.
EIN: 020223340

61607
Rannie Webster Foundation
795 Washington Rd.
Rye, NH 03870-0262

Classified as a private operating foundation in 1977.
Financial data (yr. ended 08/31/00): Assets, $6,362,262 (M); grants paid, $0; expenditures, $3,332,181; qualifying distributions, $215,535; giving activities include $3,332,181 for programs.
Officers and Trustees:* J. Leo Appel,* Pres.; John W. Patrick,* V.P.; Marilyn Marchant,* Secy.; Calvin Canney,* Treas.; George E. Carpenter, Judith M. Kish, Robert Papp, Naomi Scott, Irving S. Skinner.
EIN: 020331198

61608
Wentworth Home for the Aged
795 Central Ave.
Dover, NH 03820

Classified as a private operating foundation in 1987.
Donor(s): Walter Franklin,‡ Etta Shaw Trust.
Financial data (yr. ended 12/31/01): Assets, $5,665,417 (M); grants paid, $0; gifts received, $440,995; expenditures, $775,819; qualifying distributions, $969,086; giving activities include $378,446 for programs.
Officer and Trustees:* Darlene Smith,* Admin.; Noreen Biehl, Paul Boucher, Donald R. Bryant, Francis Cassidy, John Delude, David C. Dopp, Joseph Evans, Lloyd Jordan, Carol J. Leonard, Willis E. Littlefield, Jr., Beatrice Page, Marion Pelletier, Sidney Peterman, Jay Whitehouse.
EIN: 020223354

61609
The Nashua Historical Society
5 Abbott St.
Nashua, NH 03064-2119
Contact: Yolanda Santerre, Treas.

Established in 1870 in NH.
Financial data (yr. ended 04/30/00): Assets, $4,920,392 (M); grants paid, $2,000; gifts received, $22,466; expenditures, $177,703; qualifying distributions, $138,078.
Publications: Annual report, newsletter.
Officers: William Ross, Pres.; Taylor Cole, 1st V.P.; A. Nancy Wood, 2nd V.P.; Yolanda Santerre, Treas.; Jeanne Scheer, Clerk.
Directors: Faith Flythe, William Frost, Terry Romano, Rudy Slosek, Jodi Lowery Tilbury.
EIN: 020246187

61610
Dover Children's Home
207 Locust St.
Dover, NH 03820-4097

Classified as a private operating foundation in 1973.
Financial data (yr. ended 05/31/02): Assets, $4,068,162 (M); grants paid, $0; gifts received, $63,406; expenditures, $732,570; qualifying distributions, $699,630; giving activities include $732,570 for programs.
Officers: Marjorie Fisher, Pres.; Pam Simpson, 1st V.P.; Ron Clymer, 2nd V.P.; Frank Biehl, 3rd V.P.; Nancy Roemer, Corresponding Secy.; Paul Boucher, Recording Secy.; Lloyd Jordan, Treas.
Managers: Kathy Casey, Norm Champagne, Tom Clark, Judi Creteau, Jim McShane, Rita Robbins, Dave Terlemezian.
Trustees: Paul Arthur, David C. Dopp, W. Kent Marling.
Advisors: D. James McAtavey, Walworth Johnson, Jr.
EIN: 022233230

61611
Stonewall Farm
242 Chesterfield Rd.
Keene, NH 03431

Established in 1994 in NH.
Donor(s): Michael Kidder.
Financial data (yr. ended 06/30/00): Assets, $3,751,407 (M); grants paid, $0; gifts received, $1,088,699; expenditures, $869,765; qualifying distributions, $525,100; giving activities include $869,765 for programs.
Officers: Edward Kingsbury, Jr., Pres.; Mary Ann Kristiansen, V.P.; Dana O'Brien, Secy.-Treas.
Directors: Mike Blaisdell, Donna Flanagan, Clara Galante, Frank Mazzola, and 6 additional directors.
EIN: 020474456

61612
Blue Hills Foundation, Inc.
c/o C. Russell Shillaber
P.O. Box 1200
Rochester, NH 03866-1200

Classified as a private operating foundation in 1982.
Donor(s): George M. Lovejoy, Jr., Hortense L. Cahill, Henry Wheeler.
Financial data (yr. ended 12/31/01): Assets, $3,584,128 (M); grants paid, $0; gifts received, $545,223; expenditures, $43,558; qualifying distributions, $43,413; giving activities include $40,753 for programs.
Officers: George M. Lovejoy, Jr., Pres.; C. Russell Shillaber, Secy.; Paul S. Goodof, Treas.
Directors: John Bozak, Roger Leighton, G. Montgomery Lovejoy III, Henry W. Lovejoy, Henry Wheeler.
EIN: 020366576

61613
Institute of Current World Affairs, Inc.
(also known as The Crane-Rogers Foundation)
4 W. Wheelock St.
Hanover, NH 03755 (603) 643-5548
FAX: (603) 643-9599; *E-mail:* icwa@valley.net;
URL: http://www.icwa.org
Contact: Peter Bird Martin, Exec. Dir.

Incorporated in 1925 in NY as a private operating foundation.
Donor(s): Charles R. Crane.
Financial data (yr. ended 12/31/00): Assets, $3,541,979 (M); grants paid, $350,646; gifts received, $599,283; expenditures, $816,225; qualifying distributions, $769,603.
Limitations: Giving limited to fellowships conducted outside the U.S.
Publications: Informational brochure, application guidelines.
Application information: Write for brochure listing current areas of interest.
Officers: Paul A. Rahe, Chair.; Carol Rose, Vice-Chair.; Ann Mische, Secy.; Edmund Sutton, Treas.; Peter Bird Martin, Exec. Dir.
Trustees: Carol Beaulieu, Mary Lynne Bird, Steve Butler, William F. Foote, Pramila Jayapal, Dorothy S. Patterson, Chad Rosenberger, John Spencer, Diederik J. Vandewalle, Sally Wriggins.
EIN: 131621044
Codes: FD, GTI

61614
Howfirma Trust
45 Hilldale Ave.
South Hampton, NH 03827-3513
(603) 394-7832
Contact: James Van Bokkelen, Tr.

Established in 1994 in NH.
Donor(s): James B. Van Bokkelen, Jocelyn N. Van Bokkelen.
Financial data (yr. ended 11/30/01): Assets, $3,038,532 (M); grants paid, $0; gifts received, $20,000; expenditures, $27,044; qualifying distributions, $7,922.
Trustees: James B. Van Bokkelen, Jocelyn N. Van Bokkelen, Katrina R. Van Bokkelen.
EIN: 026102175

61615
The Edwin C. Remick Foundation
c/o Paul L. Normandin
P.O. Box 575
Laconia, NH 03247-0575

Classified as a private operating foundation in 1994.
Financial data (yr. ended 12/31/01): Assets, $2,651,623 (M); grants paid, $0; gifts received, $574,814; expenditures, $676,384; qualifying distributions, $0.
Limitations: Applications not accepted.
Trustees: William McCarthy, Paul L. Normandin, Carroll W. Stafford, Jr., Earline S. Wright.
EIN: 020469603

61616
The Woodward Home, Inc.
194 Court St.
Keene, NH 03431-3412

Classified as a private operating foundation in 1986.
Financial data (yr. ended 12/31/01): Assets, $2,561,740 (M); grants paid, $0; gifts received,

$8,481; expenditures, $608,416; qualifying distributions, $134,057; giving activities include $608,416 for programs.
Officers and Directors:* Alfred Lerandeau,* Pres.; Christine Searles Ballou,* Secy.; William S. Abbott,* Treas.; Neil Berkson, L. Dean Bernius, Arthur Cohen, Florence Cristiano, Martha Curtis, Louise DiNuovo, Susan B. Grine, Charles Schofield, Timothy Wolfe.
EIN: 020224025

61617
Annie E. Woodman Institute
P.O. Box 146
Dover, NH 03820-0146

Classified as a private operating foundation in 1972.
Financial data (yr. ended 12/31/01): Assets, $2,200,745 (M); grants paid, $0; gifts received, $26,667; expenditures, $65,190; qualifying distributions, $63,391; giving activities include $57,517 for programs.
Trustees: Thom Hindle, Raymond R. Ouellette, David G. Torr.
EIN: 020223356

61618
Timothy & Abigail B. Walker Lecture Fund
41 Centre St.
Concord, NH 03301-1256 (603) 225-6627
Contact: David E. Tardif, Tr.

Financial data (yr. ended 03/31/00): Assets, $2,172,142 (M); grants paid, $7,700; expenditures, $92,591; qualifying distributions, $80,088; giving activities include $19,201 for programs.
Limitations: Giving limited to the Concord, NH, area.
Trustees: David E. Tardif, Ernest J. Tsourds, Harriet M. Ward.
EIN: 026004661

61619
Franklin Home for the Aged Association
24 Peabody Pl.
Franklin, NH 03235-1607

Classified as a private operating foundation in 1981.
Financial data (yr. ended 12/31/99): Assets, $2,146,044 (L); grants paid, $0; expenditures, $1,283,475; qualifying distributions, $1,221,550; giving activities include $1,221,550 for programs.
Limitations: Giving primarily in NH.
Officers and Trustees:* Walter G. Hall, Jr.,* Pres.; John L. Lard,* V.P.; Kenneth Ackerson,* Treas.; Robert Gilbreth,* Clerk; Marsha A. Charron, Mary Goodwin, Carolyn Hurst, Beverly Kidder, Tom Matzke.
EIN: 020202330

61620
Eventide Home, Inc.
81 High St.
Exeter, NH 03833

Financial data (yr. ended 12/31/99): Assets, $1,848,205 (M); grants paid, $0; gifts received, $180,543; expenditures, $748,221; qualifying distributions, $252,372; giving activities include $252,372 for programs.
Officers: Sam Daniels, Pres.; Brian Lortie, V.P.; Edwin C. Baker, Treas.; Brian McCaffrey, Clerk.
EIN: 020228137

61621
Kimball Jenkins Historic and Community Center
(Formerly Carolyn L. Jenkins Trust)
266 N. Main St.
Concord, NH 03301

Established in 1982 in NH.
Financial data (yr. ended 12/31/00): Assets, $1,819,914 (M); grants paid, $0; gifts received, $4,817; expenditures, $345,913; qualifying distributions, $404,077; giving activities include $73,233 for programs.
Officer and Directors:* Leigh Miller-Green,* Exec. Dir.; Mark Coen, Dennis Hager, Pamela Kenison, William C. Saturley, Jill Wilson.
EIN: 026055621

61622
Home for the Aged of Grafton County
c/o James E. Graham
P.O. Box 11
Woodsville, NH 03785-0011

Classified as a private operating foundation in 1985.
Financial data (yr. ended 12/31/01): Assets, $1,733,249 (M); grants paid, $0; gifts received, $40; expenditures, $58,259; qualifying distributions, $49,313.
Officers: James E. Graham, Pres.; Harold O. Taylor, V.P.; Shirley McAllister, Secy.; Paula R. House, Treas.
Directors: Ina Anderson, Poppy Clark, Ethel Cooper, Caroline Gale, Grace Hoefs, Judy Lupien.
Trustees: John Cobb, Larry Fournier, Frank O'Malley.
EIN: 020227598

61623
Daughters of the American Revolution, Molly Starks Chapter, Inc.
P.O. Box 246
Manchester, NH 03105-0246

Financial data (yr. ended 04/30/00): Assets, $1,639,867 (M); grants paid, $41,996; gifts received, $2,470; expenditures, $56,814; qualifying distributions, $53,350; giving activities include $41,996 for programs.
Officer: Mrs. Arthur Ruszenas, Treas.
Director: Dorothy Antis.
EIN: 026009448

61624
Animal Rescue League of New Hampshire
545 Rte. 101
Bedford, NH 03110

Established as an operating foundation as of 11/1/82.
Financial data (yr. ended 12/31/01): Assets, $1,600,243 (M); grants paid, $0; gifts received, $187,248; expenditures, $320,425; qualifying distributions, $0.
Officers: John Maglia, Pres.; Bill Thomas, V.P.; Sheryl Hammond, Secy.
Directors: Linda Hamada, Mark Isenberg, Mitzie Kocsis.
EIN: 020222790

61625
Pillsbury Home
(also known as Milford Home for Aged Women)
95 High St.
Milford, NH 03055-1412

Classified as a private operating foundation in 1988.
Financial data (yr. ended 03/31/01): Assets, $1,592,476 (M); grants paid, $0; gifts received, $425; expenditures, $292,592; qualifying distributions, $0; giving activities include $292,592 for programs.
Officers and Directors:* Harold Beaubien,* Pres.; Betsy Fisk,* V.P.; Claire Reever,* Secy.; Cecile Steele,* Treas.; William Dyer, Linda Ferguson, Bernard Harding, Kathy Heald, and 3 additional directors.
EIN: 020223604

61626
New Hampshire Bible Society
P.O. Box 1087
Concord, NH 03302-1087

Classified as a private operating foundation in 1972.
Financial data (yr. ended 06/30/01): Assets, $1,359,971 (M); grants paid, $0; gifts received, $10,511; expenditures, $71,077; qualifying distributions, $0.
Officers: Bro. Paul Demers, Pres.; Rt. Rev. Douglas Theuner, V.P.; Rev. Elizabeth Davis, Clerk; Rev. Carolyn Keilig, Treas.
Directors: Philip Cunningham, and 6 additional directors.
EIN: 020223913

61627
Institute and Center for Human Development and Environmental Services
2 Long Hill Rd.
Stratham, NH 03885

Established in 1997 in NH.
Donor(s): U.S. Environmental Protection Agency, Greater Piscataqua Community Foundation.
Financial data (yr. ended 12/31/01): Assets, $1,072,567 (M); grants paid, $0; gifts received, $468,853; expenditures, $173,631; qualifying distributions, $160,461; giving activities include $160,539 for programs.
Officers: Robert K. McLellan, M.D., Pres.; Kathleen M. Schusler, Secy.; Gary Testa, Treas.
Directors: John Di Gesu, Brook Dupee, Brian Moroze, Nelson Buck Robinson, Jeffrey Coleman Salloway, Ph.D., Kevin M. Webb.
EIN: 020483398

61628
Wentworth-Gardner and Tobias Lear Houses Association
P.O. Box 563
Portsmouth, NH 03802

Financial data (yr. ended 09/30/99): Assets, $925,086 (M); grants paid, $0; gifts received, $23,488; expenditures, $10,291; qualifying distributions, $17,111; giving activities include $17,111 for programs.
Officers: William Manfull, Pres.; John Baybutt, V.P.; Timothy Durkin, Treas.
EIN: 026011454

61629
Livermore Community Association, Inc.
c/o Earnest L. Barrett
4 Walnut St.
Milford, NH 03055-4426

Financial data (yr. ended 06/30/00): Assets, $757,626 (M); grants paid, $0; gifts received, $1,000; expenditures, $20,875; qualifying distributions, $11,378; giving activities include $11,378 for programs.
Officers: Rodney C. Woodman, Jr., Pres.; Betsy Deasy, Secy.; Ernest L. Barrett, Treas.
EIN: 020222854

61630
Leonard Boyd Chapman Wildbird Sanctuary
Box 96
North Sandwich, NH 03259

Classified as a private operating foundation in 1972.
Donor(s): John V. Visney.‡
Financial data (yr. ended 12/31/01): Assets, $720,743 (M); grants paid, $0; gifts received, $19,156; expenditures, $20,081; qualifying distributions, $18,107; giving activities include $18,107 for programs.
Officers and Trustees:* Suzanne Rowan,* Pres.; Leslie S. Christodoulopoulos,* Secy.; Ronald G. Lawler, Treas.; Randolph Brown, and 5 additional trustees.
EIN: 042210786

61631
Portsmouth Historical Society
P.O. Box 728
Portsmouth, NH 03802-0728

Financial data (yr. ended 12/31/00): Assets, $625,022 (M); grants paid, $0; gifts received, $8,867; expenditures, $49,378; qualifying distributions, $29,179; giving activities include $30,128 for programs.
Officers: Bradley M. Lown, Pres.; Jock Brodie, V.P.; Arthur M. Heard, Treas.
Trustees: Stephen R. Alie, John G. Brodie, Mary Ellen Burke, Thomas R. Watson, and 7 additional trustees.
EIN: 020240383

61632
Fuller Foundation of New Hampshire, Inc.
P.O. Box 479
Rye Beach, NH 03871

Financial data (yr. ended 12/31/99): Assets, $560,977 (M); grants paid, $0; gifts received, $186,699; expenditures, $210,087; qualifying distributions, $152,776; giving activities include $219,047 for programs.
Application information: Does not make gifts, grants or awards.
Trustees: Miranda Fuller Bocko, John T. Bottomley, Ann Fuller Donovan, James D. Henderson, Peter Fuller, Peter Fuller, Jr., Suzanne Fuller MacDonald, Melinda Fuller Vanden Heuvel, John C. Pierce, Blair Donovan.
EIN: 020248142

61633
Thompson-Ames Historical Society
P.O. Box 7404
Laconia, NH 03247-7404

Donor(s): Grace King.
Financial data (yr. ended 12/31/01): Assets, $551,240 (M); grants paid, $0; gifts received, $43,395; expenditures, $31,212; qualifying distributions, $31,212; giving activities include $28,000 for programs.
Officers: Judith Buswell, Pres.; Joan Nelson, V.P.; Marjorie Muelke, Secy.; Carole H. Johnson, Treas.
EIN: 026013076

61634
The Mae Casali Bonvicini Charitable Foundation
146 Main St.
Nashua, NH 03060 (603) 883-5501
Contact: Dino Casali, Tr.

Established in 2000 in NH.
Financial data (yr. ended 12/31/00): Assets, $513,415 (M); grants paid, $0; gifts received, $34,534; expenditures, $0; qualifying distributions, $0.

Application information: Application form not required.
Trustees: Corinne Casali, Dino Casali, Paul Casali, Joseph W. Kenny.
EIN: 026124449

61635
New Ipswich Library
P.O. Box 320
New Ipswich, NH 03071-0320

Financial data (yr. ended 07/31/00): Assets, $438,874 (M); grants paid, $0; gifts received, $22,450; expenditures, $32,479; qualifying distributions, $32,138; giving activities include $30,706 for programs.
Officers: Jack Klein, Pres.; Greg Hanselman, V.P.; Ann Marie Forest, Treas.
Trustees: Harvey Green, Richard Hall, Geoffrey Rhodes, Sharon Rosenfelder, Carol Stein, John Sterrett, Kitty Waite.
EIN: 020262059

61636
Eastern Slope Animal Welfare League
P.O. Box 18
North Conway, NH 03860

Financial data (yr. ended 05/31/99): Assets, $414,615 (M); grants paid, $0; gifts received, $4,950; expenditures, $23,777; qualifying distributions, $20,660; giving activities include $20,660 for programs.
Officers: Eugene R. Hussey, Pres.; David Walker, M.D., V.P.; Dolyn Dunning, Secy.
EIN: 026010400

61637
James E. Whalley Museum and Library
351 Middle St.
Portsmouth, NH 03801-5009

Classified as a private operating foundation in 1981.
Financial data (yr. ended 12/31/01): Assets, $365,377 (M); grants paid, $0; gifts received, $10; expenditures, $7,875; qualifying distributions, $7,148; giving activities include $7,148 for programs.
Officers and Trustees:* Edgar W. Anderson,* Pres.; Lawrence W. Kent,* V.P.; Warren Ward,* Clerk; Richard C. Staples,* Treas.; Robert E. Buffum, Joseph W.P. Frost, Knute H. Lundgren, Charles A. Tarbell.
EIN: 026011431

61638
Young Ladies Library Association of Plymouth
1 Russell St.
Plymouth, NH 03264

Classified as a private operating foundation in 1984 in NH.
Donor(s): Charlotte Wakefield Charitable Rem. Trust.
Financial data (yr. ended 04/30/02): Assets, $360,734 (M); grants paid, $0; gifts received, $56,257; expenditures, $12,794; qualifying distributions, $9,688.
Officers: Blake H. Allen, Pres.; Nancy Dyer, V.P.; Elaine Melquist, Secy.; Marilyn Ashley, Treas.
Directors: Elizabeth Batchelder, Winifred Hohlt, Suzanne Montour, Elsa Turmelle.
EIN: 026005307

61639
The Gilman Home, Inc.
c/o Laconia Savings Bank Trust
62 Pleasant St.
Laconia, NH 03246

Classified as a private operating foundation in 1974.
Financial data (yr. ended 03/31/01): Assets, $236,143 (M); grants paid, $0; gifts received, $53,907; expenditures, $64,485; qualifying distributions, $64,485; giving activities include $64,485 for programs.
Officers and Trustees:* Arthur Dyck,* Chair.; Phyllis Draper,* Secy.; Gladys Howe,* Treas.; Russell Jones, Jon Nivus, James Pellowe, Jr., Shirley Young.
EIN: 020310404

61640
Fond Rev. Edmond Gelinas, Inc.
39 Carpenter St.
Manchester, NH 03104-2206 (603) 623-6979
Contact: Donald N. Fournier, Pres.

Financial data (yr. ended 12/31/01): Assets, $212,501 (M); grants paid, $15,000; expenditures, $16,565; qualifying distributions, $15,000.
Limitations: Giving limited to NH.
Application information: Application form required.
Officers: Donald N. Fournier, Pres. and Treas.; Maurice Pilotte, Secy.
Directors: N. Gerald Beaulieu, Guy Couture.
EIN: 020262914
Codes: GTI

61641
Kensington Social Library
126 Amesbury Rd.
Kensington, NH 03833

Established in 1895 in NH; classified as a private operating foundation in 1973.
Financial data (yr. ended 04/30/02): Assets, $205,189 (M); grants paid, $0; gifts received, $5,065; expenditures, $10,243; qualifying distributions, $0.
Officers: Dorothy B. Felch, Pres.; Peter Greer, Secy.; Carlton F. Rezendes, Treas.
EIN: 026009096

61642
Linwood Educational Trust Fund, Inc.
c/o Jimmie McLaughlin
P.O. Box 1391
Lincoln, NH 03251

Established in 1999 in NH.
Financial data (yr. ended 06/30/01): Assets, $167,678 (M); grants paid, $10,000; gifts received, $10,400; expenditures, $10,799; qualifying distributions, $10,239.
Officers: Duncan W. Riley, Pres.; Bob Nelson, Secy.; Jeanie McLaughlin, Treas.
EIN: 020474928

61643
Lebanon Outing Club, Inc.
P.O. Box 295
Lebanon, NH 03766-0295

Established in 1986 in NH.
Financial data (yr. ended 06/30/99): Assets, $154,350 (M); grants paid, $0; gifts received, $60,225; expenditures, $99,339; qualifying distributions, $0; giving activities include $99,339 for programs.
Limitations: Giving limited to the Lebanon Valley, PA area.

61643—NEW HAMPSHIRE

Officers: John Emery, Pres.; Kevin Follenobee, V.P.; Jennifer Kerl, V.P.; Wanda Daniels, Secy.; Claudia Grant, Treas.
Directors: Diane Grant, Andy Langley, Gary Parent, Bob Ricker, Bill Torville, Nathan Wood.
EIN: 222839786

61644
The Criminal Justice Policy Foundation
39 Wentworth Rd.
New Castle, NH 03854-0192

Financial data (yr. ended 12/31/99): Assets, $43,797 (M); grants paid, $0; gifts received, $427,508; expenditures, $410,342; qualifying distributions, $393,182; giving activities include $393,182 for programs.
Limitations: Applications not accepted.
Application information: Contributes only to pre-selected organizations.
Trustees: Russell N. Cox, Robert J. Richards, Robert C. Silver.
EIN: 222946139

61645
Southeast Asia Art Foundation
71 Stone House Rd.
Hill, NH 03243

Donor(s): John A. Thierry.
Financial data (yr. ended 12/31/01): Assets, $38,004 (M); grants paid, $27,221; gifts received, $1,500; expenditures, $28,368; qualifying distributions, $28,429.
Limitations: Applications not accepted. Giving on a national basis, with emphasis on MD, MI, and NH.
Application information: Contributes only to pre-selected organizations.
Officer and Trustees:* John A. Thierry,* Mgr.; Hiram W. Woodward, Jr.
EIN: 391285590

61646
Exeter Swimming Association
P.O. Box 766
Exeter, NH 03833-0766

Financial data (yr. ended 08/31/01): Assets, $31,434 (M); grants paid, $0; gifts received, $201,101; expenditures, $183,934; qualifying distributions, $0.
Officers: Lisa Chandler, Pres.; Martha Lemire, V.P.; Diane Stump, Secy.; Karen Baetzel, Treas.
EIN: 020353417

61647
Ken Piatt Memorial Fund
(Formerly Ken Piatt Memorial Children's Athletic Association)
1221 Briar Hill Rd.
Contoocook, NH 03229

Established in 1987 in NH.
Financial data (yr. ended 12/31/00): Assets, $26,163 (M); grants paid, $1,500; gifts received, $1,372; expenditures, $1,500; qualifying distributions, $0.
Limitations: Giving primarily in NH.
Officers: Donald K. Lane, Chair.; Donald K. Piatt, Pres. and Admin.
Advisory Committee: Jim Cook, Paul Semple.
EIN: 020398294

61648
New England Circle
230 Commerce Way, Rm. 300
Portsmouth, NH 03801

Established in 1974. Classified as a private operating foundation in 1988.

Donor(s): John P. Dunfey, Robert J. Dunfey, Gerald Dunfey.
Financial data (yr. ended 12/31/01): Assets, $21,673 (M); grants paid, $0; gifts received, $154,640; expenditures, $176,684; qualifying distributions, $176,683.
Officers: John P. Dunfey, Co-Chair.; Eleanor Dunfey Freiburger, Co-Chair; Jerry Dunfey, Pres.; Robert J. Dunfey, Sr.,* Treas.; Margaret Connolly, Prog. Dir.; Theo Spanos Dunfey, Managing Dir.
Directors: William Batson, Sophia Collier, Richard J. Dunfey, Robert J. Dunfey, Jr., Rodney Ellis, Lew Feldstein, Freida Gracia, William S. Green, William B. Hart, Jr., Meg Hirshberg, Herbert L. Holtz, Nicole Hynes, Frederick M. Jervis, Ph.D., William J. McNally, Carolyn Mugar, Bik Fung Ng, Geralyn White-Dreyfous, Joanne Wilburn, Percy Wilson.
EIN: 222655540

61649
The Wolf Family Charitable Trust
(Formerly Wolf Communications and Transportation Museum Trust)
369 Boston Post Rd.
Amherst, NH 03031-2727   (603) 579-0556
Contact: Steven T. Wolf, Tr.

Established in 1984 in NH. Classified as a private operating foundation in 2000.
Financial data (yr. ended 12/31/00): Assets, $20,801 (M); grants paid, $50,500; gifts received, $71,314; expenditures, $50,613; qualifying distributions, $50,500.
Trustees: Julie A. Wolf, Scott Wolf, Steven T. Wolf.
EIN: 222509486

61650
Carye Family Charitable Foundation
c/o Raymond and Barbara Carye
P.O. Box 7327
Laconia, NH 03246

Donor(s): Raymond A. Carye, Barbara F. Carye.
Financial data (yr. ended 12/31/01): Assets, $7,457 (M); grants paid, $2,500; expenditures, $3,100; qualifying distributions, $2,500.
Limitations: Applications not accepted.
Application information: Contributes only to pre-selected organizations.
Trustees: Barbara F. Carye, Raymond A. Carye.
EIN: 046866306

61651
The Tommy Walker Sports Fund Charitable Trust
c/o Dorothy W. Belmore
27 Bryan St.
Littleton, NH 03561   (603) 444-5925
Application address: c/o Scholarship Comm., Littleton High School, Littleton, NH 03561, tel.: (603) 444-3402

Financial data (yr. ended 12/31/00): Assets, $4,617 (M); grants paid, $400; expenditures, $400; qualifying distributions, $400.
Limitations: Giving limited to Littleton, NH.
Application information: Application form required.
Trustees: Dorothy W. Belmore, C. Thomas Walker III, David Walker, Edna Walker.
EIN: 020393948

61652
Aware: A Citizens' Group for Bethlehem's Future, Inc.
P.O. Box 842
Bethlehem, NH 03574-0842
Contact: George Manupelli, Pres.

Established in 1999 in NH.

Financial data (yr. ended 12/31/00): Assets, $2,395 (M); grants paid, $0; gifts received, $5,086; expenditures, $5,095; qualifying distributions, $0; giving activities include $5,095 for programs.
Limitations: Giving primarily in Bethlehem, NH.
Officers: George Manupelli, Pres.; Natalie Woodroofe, V.P.; Anita Gelman, Secy.
EIN: 020404570

61653
Annard Foundation
25 Sylvan Dr.
Salem, NH 03079

Established in 1999.
Financial data (yr. ended 12/31/00): Assets, $31 (M); grants paid, $100; gifts received, $100; expenditures, $118; qualifying distributions, $100.
Limitations: Applications not accepted.
Application information: Contributes only to pre-selected organizations.
Trustees: Bernard O. Geaghan, Judith A. Geaghan.
EIN: 020477072

61654
Humane Society of New England
(Formerly Humane Society of Southern Hillsborough County)
24 Ferry Rd.
Nashua, NH 03060-1131

Classified as a private operating foundation in 1973.
Financial data (yr. ended 12/31/00): Assets, $1 (M); grants paid, $0; expenditures, $0; qualifying distributions, $0.
Officers: Linda Argenti, Pres.; Nancy Kopec, Secy.; Marion Cross, Treas.
Trustees: Barbara Alves, Cynthia Lloyd.
EIN: 020277701

61655
The Krempels Foundation
(Formerly 2001 Brain Injury Support Fund, Inc.)
Box 4388
Portsmouth, NH 03802   (603) 659-2001
Contact: Lisa Hanson

Donor(s): David M. Krempels.
Financial data (yr. ended 12/31/00): Assets, $0 (M); grants paid, $129,144; gifts received, $249,950; expenditures, $228,255; qualifying distributions, $231,047.
Limitations: Giving primarily in NH.
Officers: David M. Krempels, Pres.; John Ahlgren, Secy.
Board Members: Gale G. Brown, Jr., M.D., Jackie Felix, Jim Fisher, Newton Kershaw, Effie Malley, Larry R. Raiche.
EIN: 020499997
Codes: FD2

NEW JERSEY

61656
The Corella & Bertram Bonner Foundation, Inc.
10 Mercer St.
Princeton, NJ 08540   (609) 924-6663
FAX: (609) 683-4626; *E-mail:* Info@Bonner.org; *URL:* http://www.Bonner.org
Contact: Wayne Meisel, Pres.

Established in 1981 in NJ; reactivated in 1989.

Donor(s): Bertram F. Bonner,‡ Corella A. Bonner.‡
Financial data (yr. ended 06/30/01): Assets, $71,863,781 (M); grants paid, $4,436,495; gifts received, $625,737; expenditures, $5,618,367; qualifying distributions, $4,436,495; giving activities include $447,604 for programs.
Limitations: Giving limited to domestic programs in the U.S.
Publications: Informational brochure.
Application information: Application form required.
Officers and Trustees:* Wayne Meisel, Pres.; Robert Hackett, V.P.; William Bush, Carol Clark, Edward Farley, Jr., Charles Goodfellow, Kenneth F. Kunzman.
EIN: 222316452
Codes: FD, FM, GTI

61657
Job Haines Home for Aged People
250 Bloomfield Ave.
Bloomfield, NJ 07003-4818

Classified as a private operating foundation in 1974.
Donor(s): Marjorie D. Taylor, Dorothy Duke.
Financial data (yr. ended 12/31/99): Assets, $38,196,560 (M); grants paid, $0; expenditures, $3,208,393; qualifying distributions, $7,671,339; giving activities include $854,970 for programs.
Officers: William R. Beardslee, Jr., Pres.; Gemma Sullivan, 1st V.P.; John A. Brenneis, 2nd V.P.; Ellen Oldham, Secy.; Michael W. Bristol, Treas.; Susan Clapp, Counsel.
EIN: 220972180

61658
D & K Charitable Foundation
485 Sylvan Ave.
Englewood, NJ 07632

Established in 1997 in NJ.
Donor(s): Daniel Borislow, George P. Farley.
Financial data (yr. ended 12/31/99): Assets, $17,100,616 (M); grants paid, $1,233,211; expenditures, $2,980,093; qualifying distributions, $1,286,404.
Limitations: Applications not accepted. Giving primarily in New York, NY, and Philadelphia, PA.
Application information: Contributes only to pre-selected organizations.
Officers and Directors:* Daniel Borislow,* Pres.; George P. Farley,* Treas.; Michele Borislow.
EIN: 232928907
Codes: FD

61659
Arab Student Aid International Corp.
P.O. Box 10
Fanwood, NJ 07023 (908) 654-5511
Contact: Joseph Qutub, Pres.

Established in 1998 in NJ.
Donor(s): Prince Turkin Bin Abdul Aziz.
Financial data (yr. ended 06/30/00): Assets, $13,442,413 (M); grants paid, $1,562,706; expenditures, $1,927,899; qualifying distributions, $1,742,312; giving activities include $365,193 for programs.
Application information: Institutions must be accredited and students must maintain a "B" average. Application form required.
Officers: Joseph Qutub, Pres.; Mustafa D. Shamy, V.P. and Treas.; Robert W. Thabit, Secy.
EIN: 223519297
Codes: FD

61660
The Sculpture Foundation, Inc
14 Fairgrounds Rd.
Hamilton, NJ 08619

Established in 2001 in NJ.
Financial data (yr. ended 06/30/01): Assets, $12,756,254 (M); grants paid, $0; gifts received, $8,497,480; expenditures, $1,424,980; qualifying distributions, $1,124,671; giving activities include $1,338,611 for programs.
Limitations: Applications not accepted.
Application information: Contributes only to pre-selected organizations.
Officers: J Seward Johnson, Jr., Pres.; Louis R. Hewitt Secy., John S. Johnson.
EIN: 223694372

61661
Josh & Judy Weston Family Foundation
217 Christopher St.
Montclair, NJ 07042 (973) 744-0902

Established in 1992 in NJ.
Donor(s): Josh S. Weston.
Financial data (yr. ended 12/31/01): Assets, $12,555,834 (M); grants paid, $899,017; gifts received, $1,248,775; expenditures, $916,646; qualifying distributions, $916,646.
Limitations: Applications not accepted. Giving primarily in NJ and New York, NY.
Application information: Contributes only to pre-selected organizations.
Officers: Josh S. Weston, Pres.; Heather Weston, V.P.; Judy Weston, Treas.
Director: Eric Weston.
EIN: 521798616
Codes: FD

61662
Mannheimer Foundation, Inc.
(Formerly Mannheimer Primatological Foundation)
c/o Donato, Hayes & Co.
201 Main St., Ste. 1B
Allenhurst, NJ 07711-1140

Classified as a private operating foundation in 1969.
Financial data (yr. ended 12/31/00): Assets, $11,606,529 (M); grants paid, $0; gifts received, $304,000; expenditures, $1,775,565; qualifying distributions, $2,191,055.
Officers and Trustees:* Warren Lloyd Lewis,* Pres.; Theodore I. Malinin,* V.P.; John C. Leeds,* Secy.-Treas.
EIN: 221851590

61663
Gund Collection of Western Art
P.O. Box 449
Princeton, NJ 08542

Classified as a private operating foundation in 1972.
Financial data (yr. ended 12/31/01): Assets, $11,558,994 (M); grants paid, $0; expenditures, $2,465; qualifying distributions, $0.
Trustees: Gordon Gund, Graham Gund.
EIN: 346623289

61664
The Fred C. Rummel Foundation
c/o Summit Bank
316 Lenox Ave., Ste. 2C
Westfield, NJ 07090 (908) 317-8600
Contact: Cynthia Norton Cockren, Exec. Dir.

Established in 1997 in NJ.
Financial data (yr. ended 12/31/01): Assets, $10,915,044 (M); grants paid, $474,684; gifts received, $5; expenditures, $588,948; qualifying distributions, $528,091.
Limitations: Giving primarily in NJ.
Application information: Application form required.
Officer: Cynthia Norton Cockren, Exec. Dir.
Trustees: Robert W. Cockren, Summit Bank.
EIN: 226703253
Codes: FD

61665
Liberty Hall Foundation
1003 Morris Ave.
Union, NJ 07083
FAX: (908) 352-8915; E-mail: liberty-hall@juno.com

Classified as a private operating foundation in 1983.
Donor(s): John Kean, Sr., Stewart B. Kean, Mary Alice Barney Kean,‡ May Raynolds, Pamela Kean, John Kean, Jr.
Financial data (yr. ended 12/31/99): Assets, $10,833,336 (M); grants paid, $0; gifts received, $843,966; expenditures, $650,334; qualifying distributions, $997,194; giving activities include $485,331 for programs.
Officers and Trustees:* Stewart B. Kean,* Pres. and Treas.; Robert Gregory Raynolds, V.P.; Lita Kean Haack,* Secy.; Katherine Kean Czarnecki, John Kean, Jr., Pamela Kean, David Raynolds, May Alice Kean Raynolds, Joel D. Siegel.
EIN: 226109813

61666
The Joe and Teresa L. Long Foundation for the Arts
c/o Merrill Lynch Trust Co.
P.O. Box 30531, Tax 2W
New Brunswick, NJ 08989-0531

Classified as a private operating foundation in 2000.
Donor(s): Joe R. Long.
Financial data (yr. ended 04/30/00): Assets, $10,064,389 (M); grants paid, $0; gifts received, $624,561; expenditures, $73,053; qualifying distributions, $920,000; giving activities include $920,000 for programs.
Officers: Teresa L. Long, Secy.; Joe R. Long, Treas.; Mitchell Long, Exec. Dir.
EIN: 742916682

61667
WKBJ Partnership Foundation
(Formerly The Made in Dover Foundation)
15 W. Fairview Ave.
Dover, NJ 07801 (973) 328-0303
FAX: (973) 328-0388
Contact: Bob Howitt, Exec. Dir.

Established in 1990 in NJ.
Donor(s): Joan S. Howitt, Robert M. Howitt.
Financial data (yr. ended 12/31/01): Assets, $7,503,352 (M); grants paid, $1,021,021; gifts received, $1,444,321; expenditures, $1,187,128; qualifying distributions, $1,153,135; giving activities include $132,114 for programs.
Limitations: Applications not accepted. Giving limited to the northeastern U.S.
Application information: Funds for grants to individuals are fully committed until 2000; at that time, the foundation will cease making awards to individuals. Unsolicited requests for these funds will not be accepted or acknowledged.
Officer and Trustees:* Robert M. Howitt,* Exec. Dir.; Norman Atkins, Dan Corley, Brett Peiser, Dacia Toll.
EIN: 223000244
Codes: FD

61668
The Beekman Memorial Home Charitable Trust
c/o The Trust Co. of New Jersey, Trust Dept.
35 Journal Sq.
Jersey City, NJ 07306

Established in 1988 in NJ.
Financial data (yr. ended 06/30/02): Assets, $6,343,234 (M); grants paid, $0; expenditures, $345,632; qualifying distributions, $231,664; giving activities include $232,694 for programs.
Limitations: Applications not accepted.
Application information: Contributes only to pre-selected organizations.
Trustee: The Trust Co. of New Jersey.
EIN: 222744215

61669
The Phyllis & George Rothman Foundation
c/o Merrill Lynch Trust Co.
P.O. Box 30531
New Brunswick, NJ 08989-0531

Established in 1984 in FL.
Donor(s): George Rothman, Phyllis Rothman.
Financial data (yr. ended 06/30/01): Assets, $5,215,303 (M); grants paid, $0; expenditures, $67,100; qualifying distributions, $0.
Limitations: Applications not accepted. Giving primarily in FL.
Application information: Contributes only to pre-selected organizations.
Trustee: Merrill Lynch Trust Co.
EIN: 592474404

61670
Searle Patients in Need Foundation
c/o Pharmacia Corp.
100 Rte. 206 N.
Peapack, NJ 07977
Application address: P.O. Box 52059, Phoenix, AZ 85072, tel: (800) 242-7014

Established in 1990 in IL as a company-sponsored operating foundation.
Donor(s): G.D. Searle & Co., Pharmacia Corp., Tablesweet, Inc.
Financial data (yr. ended 12/31/01): Assets, $4,647,673 (M); grants paid, $62,658,691; gifts received, $66,206,726; expenditures, $63,714,171; qualifying distributions, $63,676,149; giving activities include $62,206,726 for programs.
Application information: A special postcard has been developed for physicians to request program participation certificates, as well as a toll free telephone number. Attending physicians should request program participation certificates for patients who require Pharmacia products, are not covered by insurance, and fall within certain income standards. Application form required.
Officers: Mark Spiers, Pres.; Franz Waibel, V.P.; Judy Reinsdorf, Secy.; Brian Batchelder, Treas.
EIN: 363718488
Codes: FD, CD

61671
W. Parsons Todd Foundation, Inc.
c/o Drinker Biddle & Shanley LLP
500 Campus Dr.
Florham Park, NJ 07932

Incorporated in 1949 in NJ.
Donor(s): W. Parsons Todd.
Financial data (yr. ended 12/31/01): Assets, $4,643,573 (M); grants paid, $192,922; expenditures, $201,206; qualifying distributions, $197,206.
Limitations: Applications not accepted. Giving primarily in NJ.
Application information: Contributes only to pre-selected organizations.
Trustees: Melvin S. Heller, Douglas A. Propp, Ephraim Propp, Mortimer J. Propp.
EIN: 136116488
Codes: FD2

61672
The Cesatam Foundation, Inc.
P.O. Box 690
New Vernon, NJ 07976

Established in 1999 in NJ.
Financial data (yr. ended 12/31/00): Assets, $4,592,525 (M); grants paid, $410,500; gifts received, $1,241,819; expenditures, $419,628; qualifying distributions, $410,500.
Officers: Raul E. Cesan, Pres. and Treas.; Liliana C. Cesan, V.P.; Thomas C. Lauda, Secy.
EIN: 223692117

61673
Memorial Home of Upper Montclair for Aged People
185 Fernwood Ave.
Montclair, NJ 07043

Financial data (yr. ended 09/30/01): Assets, $4,591,359 (M); grants paid, $0; gifts received, $828; expenditures, $519,449; qualifying distributions, $473,031; giving activities include $474,343 for programs.
Officers and Trustees:* Mavis Smith,* Pres.; Madeline Johnson,* Secy.; Wayne Johnson,* Treas.; Leslie Z. Celentano, Martha Neal Day, Dorothy Ellis, Harry B. Fisher, Jr., Emma Stanivukovich, Agness Steenland, Herta Sternbach, Maryl Walker, Francis A. Wood.
EIN: 221487239

61674
Margate Terrace Corporation
610 N. Fredericksburg Ave.
Margate City, NJ 08402

Financial data (yr. ended 06/30/01): Assets, $3,804,271 (M); grants paid, $0; expenditures, $1,012,142; qualifying distributions, $0.
Officers: Jay Cooke, Pres.; Shirley Bernstein, V.P.; Joan Johnson, Secy.; Harry Brown, Treas.
Trustees: William B. Aarons, Sr., Lois Baker, Martin Klein, Doris Lippencott, Dennis Piccone, James Robson, Dean Scarpa.
EIN: 222706023

61675
Charity Navigator
1200 MacArthur Blvd.
Mahwah, NJ 07430

Established in 2000 in DE.
Donor(s): John P. Dugan.
Financial data (yr. ended 11/30/01): Assets, $3,468,742 (M); grants paid, $0; gifts received, $13,688,000; expenditures, $353,460; qualifying distributions, $453,983; giving activities include $127,095 for programs.
Officers: John P. Dugan, Pres.; Marion C. Dugan, Secy.-Treas.; Trent Stamp, Exec. Dir.
Directors: Peter J. Dugan, Matthew Giegerich, Charles Saldarini, Eric Swerdlin.
EIN: 134148824

61676
Buehler Challenger & Science Center Foundation, Inc.
305 N. State Rte. 17 S.
Paramus, NJ 07652

Classified as a private operating foundation in 1993.

Financial data (yr. ended 11/30/00): Assets, $3,181,355 (M); grants paid, $0; gifts received, $268,859; expenditures, $982,271; qualifying distributions, $981,161; giving activities include $428,756 for programs.
Officers: Stephen T. Boswell, Ph.D., Pres.; Ellen Mary Bor, Secy.-Treas.
EIN: 223180605

61677
E. S. P. Das Educational Foundation, Inc.
10 Edgewood Dr.
Summit, NJ 07901
Contact: K. Das, Secy.

Established in 1994 in NJ.
Donor(s): E.S.P. Das.
Financial data (yr. ended 12/31/01): Assets, $2,976,347 (M); grants paid, $287,000; expenditures, $2,929,555; qualifying distributions, $285,941.
Limitations: Applications not accepted. Giving on a national basis.
Application information: Contributes only to pre-selected organizations.
Officers: E.S.P. Das, Pres. and Treas.; Kuntala Das, Secy.
EIN: 223346203
Codes: FD

61678
The Brown Foundation
71 W. Park Ave.
Vineland, NJ 08360

Established in 1966 in NJ.
Donor(s): Bernard A. Brown, Shirley Brown.
Financial data (yr. ended 04/30/01): Assets, $2,798,744 (M); grants paid, $171,684; expenditures, $177,858; qualifying distributions, $172,504.
Limitations: Applications not accepted. Giving primarily in NJ, with emphasis on Vineland.
Application information: Contributes only to pre-selected organizations.
Officer and Trustees:* Bernard A. Brown,* Pres.; Irvin J. Brown, Jeffrey S. Brown, Shirley Brown, Sidney R. Brown.
EIN: 226083927
Codes: FD2

61679
Civitas Foundation
(Formerly Quigley Family Foundation)
P.O. Box 1525
Pennington, NJ 08534-1525

Established in 1998 in NJ.
Financial data (yr. ended 12/31/01): Assets, $2,389,438 (M); grants paid, $228,500; gifts received, $722; expenditures, $288,204; qualifying distributions, $228,981.
Limitations: Applications not accepted. Giving primarily in Washington, DC, NJ, and NY.
Application information: Contributes only to pre-selected organizations.
Officers: John G. Quigley, Pres. and Treas.; Kathryn Quigley, V.P. and Secy.
EIN: 223594586
Codes: FD2

61680
Everly Scholarship Fund, Inc.
Fairway Corp. Ctr., Ste. 311
4300 Haddonfield Rd.
Pennsauken, NJ 08109 (856) 661-2094
FAX: (856) 662-0165; E-mail: jlolio@sskrplaw.com
Contact: John R. Lolio, Jr., Pres.

Established in 1992 in NJ.

Donor(s): Richard S. Gardinier.‡
Financial data (yr. ended 03/31/02): Assets, $2,362,171 (M); grants paid, $33,750; expenditures, $51,202; qualifying distributions, $37,176.
Limitations: Giving limited to residents of Burlington, Camden, and Gloucester counties, NJ.
Publications: Application guidelines.
Application information: Application form required.
Officers: John R. Lolio, Jr., Pres. and Treas.; Russ Haun, V.P.; Kathy Haun, Secy.
EIN: 223161410
Codes: GTI

61681
Children's Foundation for the Arts, Inc.
(Formerly Ira B. Brown Foundation, Inc.)
500 Rte. 17 S.
Hasbrouck Heights, NJ 07604 (201) 288-5301
FAX: (201) 288-5305; E-mail: cfa.nj@verizon.net
Contact: Maria Beerman, Mgr. Dir.

Established in 1994 in NJ.
Donor(s): Ira B. Brown.
Financial data (yr. ended 08/31/01): Assets, $2,285,201 (M); grants paid, $104,679; gifts received, $1,550; expenditures, $334,566; qualifying distributions, $318,682; giving activities include $53,691 for programs.
Limitations: Giving primarily in the metropolitan New York, NY, and Houston, TX.
Publications: Annual report, newsletter, informational brochure.
Application information: Application form required.
Officers: Ira B. Brown, Pres.; Myra Brown, Secy.
EIN: 223329717
Codes: FD2, GTI

61682
Patricia J. & Edward W. Zeh Charitable Foundation
c/o First Union National Bank
190 River Rd., 2nd Fl.
Summit, NJ 07901

Donor(s): Edward W. Zeh, Patricia J. Zeh.
Financial data (yr. ended 12/31/99): Assets, $2,055,182 (M); grants paid, $18,950; gifts received, $324,251; expenditures, $33,483; qualifying distributions, $18,950.
Application information: Application form required.
Officers and Trustees:* Edward W. Zeh,* Pres.; Patricia J. Zeh,* V.P.; Wendy Wann Whiting,* Secy.; Stuart E. Zeh,* Treas.; Andrew G. Davis, Mgr.
EIN: 223554864

61683
Foundations, Inc.
821 E. Gate Dr.
Mount Laurel, NJ 08054-1208

Established in 1992 in DE, NJ, and PA.
Financial data (yr. ended 08/31/00): Assets, $1,993,152 (M); grants paid, $4,545; gifts received, $3,226,100; expenditures, $6,068,485; qualifying distributions, $4,061,842; giving activities include $5,230,699 for programs.
Limitations: Applications not accepted. Giving limited to PA.
Application information: Contributes only to pre-selected organizations.
Officer and Directors*: Rhonda Lauer,* C.E.O.; Carol Auerbach, David Bressler, Robert Schwartz, Paul Silberberg.
EIN: 521801849
Codes: TN

61684
Nancy and Herbert Burns Foundation
c/o Dorothy Eccleston
2 Golf Ave.
Maywood, NJ 07607
Application address: 3 Bridle Way, Saddle River, NJ 07458, tel.: (201) 327-0396
Contact: Nancy Burns, Pres.

Established in 1998 in NJ.
Donor(s): Nancy Burns.
Financial data (yr. ended 12/31/01): Assets, $1,964,808 (M); grants paid, $157,000; expenditures, $160,838; qualifying distributions, $157,000.
Limitations: Giving on a national basis.
Officers: Nancy Burns, Pres.; Dorothy Eccleston, Secy.
EIN: 223583333
Codes: FD2

61685
Ashbrook D. Snelbaker Home
50 S. Main St.
Woodstown, NJ 08098-0248

Classified as a private operating foundation in 1948.
Financial data (yr. ended 03/31/00): Assets, $1,908,911 (M); grants paid, $5,402; gifts received, $161,837; expenditures, $195,600; qualifying distributions, $188,430; giving activities include $188,430 for programs.
Officers and Directors:* Horace Siebert,* Pres.; Helen Sickler,* V.P.; Earle L. Walker,* Secy.; Kathryn Evans, Treas.; William Cobb, Sharon Eastlack, Elizabeth Richmond.
EIN: 210687933

61686
The Bristol-Myers Squibb Patient Assistance Foundation, Inc.
777 Scudders Mill Rd.
Plainsboro, NJ 08536 (800) 736-0003

Established in 1999 in NJ as a company-sponsored operating foundation.
Donor(s): E.R. Squibb & Sons, Inc., E.R. Squibb & Sons, LLC.
Financial data (yr. ended 12/31/01): Assets, $1,898,348 (M); grants paid, $176,437,675; gifts received, $184,498,580; expenditures, $184,498,580; qualifying distributions, $182,600,230.
Application information: Application form required.
Officers and Trustees:* John L. Damonti,* Pres.; John A. Nordberg,* V.P.; James Prazak, V.P.; Margaret Yonco-Haines,* V.P.; Sandra Leung,* Secy.; Harrison M. Bains, Jr.,* Treas.
EIN: 223622487
Codes: FD, CD

61687
The Residence, Inc.
(Formerly Indigent Widows and Single Women's Home Society of Trenton)
320 Spring St.
Trenton, NJ 08618

Financial data (yr. ended 04/30/02): Assets, $1,864,954 (M); grants paid, $0; gifts received, $207,815; expenditures, $550,503; qualifying distributions, $550,076; giving activities include $168,869 for programs.
Officers and Directors:* Joanna Jenkins,* Pres.; Ruth Bills,* V.P.; Serena Ashmen, Jeannette Bellisfield, Dorothy Cochran, Nancy Coleman, Janet Corbin, Mary Duffy, Edythe Duke, and 8 additional directors.
EIN: 210639869

61688
CWJ Classic Automobile Museum, Inc.
c/o Alfred C. Eckert, III
500 Campus Dr., Ste. 220
Florham Park, NJ 07932

Established in 1999 in NJ.
Donor(s): Alfred C. Eckert III.
Financial data (yr. ended 06/30/01): Assets, $1,778,491 (M); grants paid, $800; gifts received, $325,000; expenditures, $237,773; qualifying distributions, $212,133.
Limitations: Applications not accepted. Giving primarily in NJ.
Application information: Contributes only to pre-selected organizations.
Board Members: Alfred C. Eckert III, Claire C. Eckert, Cynthia Kempleton.
EIN: 223668584

61689
Yvette J. and Herbert G. Stolzer Foundation, Inc.
c/o Richard E. Ingram
410 George St.
New Brunswick, NJ 08901

Established in 1997 in NJ.
Donor(s): Herbert G. Stolzer.
Financial data (yr. ended 08/31/01): Assets, $1,542,096 (M); grants paid, $80,500; expenditures, $82,520; qualifying distributions, $81,126.
Limitations: Applications not accepted.
Application information: Contributes only to pre-selected organizations. Unsolicited requests for funds not accepted.
Officers and Trustees:* Herbert G. Stolzer,* Pres.; Ira G. Stolzer,* Secy.-Treas.; Ronnie H. Forrest, Leslie J. Logal.
EIN: 311479510
Codes: FD2

61690
Barrier Aung Foundation
506 E. Ridgewood Ave.
Ridgewood, NJ 07450

Established in 1996 in NJ.
Financial data (yr. ended 12/31/01): Assets, $1,476,714 (M); grants paid, $11,500; gifts received, $500; expenditures, $127,931; qualifying distributions, $118,943.
Limitations: Applications not accepted. Giving primarily in MA.
Application information: Unsolicited requests for funds not accepted.
Officers: Leon Shipper, Chair.; Dean Cardasis, Pres.; Elizabeth Thompson, Secy.
EIN: 237185798

61691
The Noyes Museum
3430 Atlantic Ave.
Atlantic City, NJ 08401

Established in 1988 in NJ.
Donor(s): Noyes Foundation, NJSCA GOS Grant, NJSCA Fellowship.
Financial data (yr. ended 06/30/00): Assets, $1,401,399 (M); grants paid, $0; gifts received, $372,806; expenditures, $506,319; qualifying distributions, $259,802; giving activities include $459,489 for programs.
Officers: Michael Hyett, Pres.; Anthony Coppola, V.P.; Lois Wallen, Secy.; Jerrold L. Jacobs, Treas.
Trustees: Peter Caporilli, Dorothy Goldstein, Gary Hill, Alan E. Kligerman, Rhoda Steinberg Malamut, Robert McCormick, Diane Tucker-McKoy, Richard P. Vogl, and 3 additional trustees.

EIN: 222858713
Codes: TN

61692
The Goodwin Foundation
c/o Goodwin Enterprises
420 Church Rd.
Mount Laurel, NJ 08054

Established in 1987 in NJ.
Donor(s): Richard C. Goodwin.
Financial data (yr. ended 12/31/00): Assets, $1,221,851 (M); grants paid, $57,216; gifts received, $1,400; expenditures, $68,532; qualifying distributions, $57,216.
Limitations: Applications not accepted. Giving primarily in NJ.
Application information: Contributes only to pre-selected organizations.
Trustees: John Goodwin, Richard C. Goodwin, Robert Goodwin, Joanne Goodwin-Edleman, Denise Vasco.
EIN: 222882244

61693
Parnassus Foundation
25 N. Murray Ave.
Ridgewood, NJ 07450

Established in 1986 in DE.
Donor(s): Raphael Bernstein.
Financial data (yr. ended 11/30/01): Assets, $1,075,595 (M); grants paid, $498,374; gifts received, $82,532; expenditures, $722,051; qualifying distributions, $708,398; giving activities include $200,000 for programs.
Limitations: Applications not accepted. Giving on a national and international basis, with emphasis on Hanover, NH, New York, NY, Canada, and London, England.
Application information: Contributes only to pre-selected organizations.
Officers: Raphael Bernstein, Pres. and Treas.; Jane Bernstein, V.P.; Carol Boulanger, Secy.
Trustees: Daniel S. Bernstein, John M. Bernstein.
EIN: 521491214
Codes: FD

61694
Janssen Ortho Patient Assistance Foundation, Inc.
1 Johnson & Johnson Plz.
New Brunswick, NJ 08933 (908) 722-4092

Established as a company-sponsored operating foundation in 1998 in NJ.
Donor(s): Janssen Pharmaceutica Inc., Johnson & Johnson, Ortho Biotech Inc., Ortho-McNeil Pharmaceutical, Inc.
Financial data (yr. ended 12/31/01): Assets, $1,050,353 (M); grants paid, $96,086,495; gifts received, $109,343,310; expenditures, $109,343,310; qualifying distributions, $96,086,495.
Limitations: Giving on a national basis.
Application information: Patients must have Proof of Income by providing their most recent Federal Tax Return. Application form required.
Officers: Carol A. Webb, Pres.; Denise Sitarik, V.P.; Lisa G. Jenkins, Secy.; Richard J. Moran, Treas.
Directors: Zandra Fennell, Carol Goodrich, Rebecca Hayes, Conrad Person, Thomas H. Schwend, Louise Weingrod, Michael Ziskind.
EIN: 311520982
Codes: FD, CD, FM, GTI

61695
Harold Yellen Charitable Foundation
c/o Merrill Lynch Trust Co.
P.O. Box 30531, Tax 2W
New Brunswick, NJ 08989-0531

Donor(s): Harold Yellen.
Financial data (yr. ended 12/31/01): Assets, $1,041,635 (M); grants paid, $19,500; gifts received, $28,662; expenditures, $58,862; qualifying distributions, $19,500.
Limitations: Applications not accepted.
Application information: Contributes only to pre-selected organizations.
Trustee: Merrill Lynch Trust Co.
EIN: 954724231

61696
Charles Grunfeld Foundation, Inc.
326 1st St.
Lakewood, NJ 08701-3321 (732) 905-7799
Contact: Stanley Pechenick, Tr.

Established in 1999 in NJ.
Financial data (yr. ended 12/31/00): Assets, $1,011,144 (M); grants paid, $45,000; gifts received, $75,000; expenditures, $80,919; qualifying distributions, $45,000.
Limitations: Giving primarily in Lakewood, NJ.
Trustees: Stanley Pechenick, Eleanor Peters, Mark Sininsky.
EIN: 223649095

61697
The Reuven and Zlate Foundation, Inc.
403 6th St.
Lakewood, NJ 08701-2705
Contact: Stanley Katz

Established in 1998.
Donor(s): Paul Z. Levovitz.
Financial data (yr. ended 12/31/01): Assets, $940,817 (M); grants paid, $15,000; expenditures, $15,301; qualifying distributions, $15,000.
Officer: Paul Z. Levovitz.
EIN: 223569807

61698
Elizabethtown Historical Foundation
c/o Stewart B. Kean
P.O. Box 1
Elizabeth, NJ 07207

Classified as a private operating foundation in 1971.
Donor(s): Mary Alice Barney Kean.‡
Financial data (yr. ended 02/28/01): Assets, $938,450 (M); grants paid, $0; expenditures, $45,356; qualifying distributions, $28,093; giving activities include $28,238 for programs.
Officer: Stewart B. Kean, Treas.
Trustees: Robert B. Gibby, Donald C. Sims.
EIN: 226055641

61699
Charles E. Marshall and Shirley S. Marshall Charitable Trust
c/o Lois S. Armstead
P.O. Box 54
Lawnside, NJ 08045

Established in 2000 in NJ.
Financial data (yr. ended 06/30/02): Assets, $902,313 (M); grants paid, $0; gifts received, $901,313; expenditures, $0; qualifying distributions, $0.
Trustees: Lois S. Armstead, Thomas H. Watkins, Jr.
EIN: 256697119

61700
Cannstatter Foundation, Inc.
282 Barnstable Dr.
Wyckoff, NJ 07481
Contact: Joseph Pfeifer, V.P.

Established in 1996 in NY.
Financial data (yr. ended 12/31/01): Assets, $852,737 (M); grants paid, $42,000; gifts received, $1,250; expenditures, $43,201; qualifying distributions, $41,427.
Officers and Trustees:* Werner Hiller, Pres.; Joseph Pfeifer,* V.P. and Treas.; Guenther Klein,* Secy.
EIN: 133874613

61701
The Mark and Jannie Wu Foundation
c/o Merrill Lynch Trust Co.
P.O. Box 1525
Pennington, NJ 08534

Established in 2000 in CA.
Donor(s): Jannie T. Wu.
Financial data (yr. ended 10/31/01): Assets, $830,391 (M); grants paid, $15,500; expenditures, $48,272; qualifying distributions, $9,739.
Limitations: Applications not accepted. Giving primarily in CA and IL.
Application information: Contributes only to pre-selected organizations.
Officer: Jannie T. Wu, Chair.
EIN: 770555799

61702
Charles A. Meyers Private Foundation
c/o Jacalyn M. Sullivan
48 Beachhurst Dr.
North Cape May, NJ 08204

Established in 1998.
Financial data (yr. ended 12/31/00): Assets, $779,360 (M); grants paid, $41,064; expenditures, $41,064; qualifying distributions, $41,064.
Trustee: Jacalyn M. Sullivan.
EIN: 621745120

61703
A. A. Previti Family Charitable Foundation, Inc.
23 Vreeland Rd., Ste. 120
Florham Park, NJ 07932
Application address: 908 Shore Rd., Somers Point, NJ 08244, tel.: (609) 927-2759
Contact: Lucille P. Lupton, V.P.

Established in 1999 in NJ.
Financial data (yr. ended 12/31/99): Assets, $757,290 (M); grants paid, $1,000; gifts received, $740,000; expenditures, $1,000; qualifying distributions, $1,000.
Officers: Andrew Previti, Pres.; Lucille P. Lupton, V.P. and Secy.
Trustee: L. Gene Gatter.
EIN: 223633945

61704
Monroe and Florence Nash Foundation, Inc.
108 Highwood Ave.
Tenafly, NJ 07670-1122 (201) 567-7012
Application address: 7 Pine Ridge Rd., Woodbridge, CT 06525
Contact: Irwin Nash, M.D., Dir.

Established as a private operating foundation in 1988.
Donor(s): Monroe Nash,‡ Florence Nash.
Financial data (yr. ended 12/31/99): Assets, $734,172 (M); grants paid, $31,414; expenditures, $41,735; qualifying distributions, $31,414.
Directors: Florence Nash, Irwin Nash.
EIN: 136888050

61705
The Joseph & Helen Weisberger Home for the Elderly
c/o Gingras, Colllister, Babinski & Co.
333 Fairfield Rd.
Fairfield, NJ 07004

Financial data (yr. ended 12/31/01): Assets, $682,123 (M); grants paid, $300; gifts received, $7,500; expenditures, $35,389; qualifying distributions, $16,195; giving activities include $35,389 for programs.
Officers: Gary Weiss, Pres.; Ruth Weiss, V.P.
EIN: 221173799

61706
The Scudiery Family Foundation
19 Brentwood Dr.
North Caldwell, NJ 07006

Established in 1999 in NJ.
Donor(s): Mark W. Scudiery.
Financial data (yr. ended 12/31/99): Assets, $665,071 (M); grants paid, $35,000; gifts received, $501,000; expenditures, $35,000; qualifying distributions, $35,000.
Limitations: Applications not accepted.
Officers: Mark W. Scudiery, Pres. and Treas.; Carol Ann Scudiery, V.P. and Secy.; Gina M. Scudiery, V.P.; Lisa M. Scudiery, V.P.
EIN: 223648325

61707
The National Foundation on Counseling
P.O. Box 2380
Princeton, NJ 08543

Classified as a private operating foundation in 1985.
Donor(s): Bernard G. Segal.
Financial data (yr. ended 07/31/01): Assets, $664,348 (M); grants paid, $0; gifts received, $354,680; expenditures, $123,289; qualifying distributions, $0; giving activities include $123,262 for programs.
Officers and Trustees:* Harris L. Wofford,* Chair.; Richard M. Segal,* Pres.; John A. Edie,* Secy.-Treas.; Richard G. Bowers, Lawrence T. Ellis, Lawrence Lucchino.
EIN: 232313241

61708
The Society for Organizing Charity of the City of Salem, New Jersey, Inc.
c/o Annabelle D. Williams
118 Washington St.
Woodstown, NJ 08098

Established in 1993.
Financial data (yr. ended 09/30/01): Assets, $645,031 (M); grants paid, $27,697; gifts received, $75; expenditures, $30,023; qualifying distributions, $27,697.
Limitations: Giving limited to residents of Salem, NJ.
Officers: Mary C. Arnold, Pres.; Lourene S. Plasket, V.P.; Barbara A. Fithian, Secy.; Annabelle D. Williams, Treas.
EIN: 216015103
Codes: GTI

61709
Sarkis & Ruth Bedevian Foundation
887 Kinderkamack Rd.
River Edge, NJ 07661

Established in 1998 in NJ.
Donor(s): Sarkis Bedevian.
Financial data (yr. ended 12/31/00): Assets, $643,304 (M); grants paid, $16,000; gifts received, $205,630; expenditures, $19,624; qualifying distributions, $16,000.
Limitations: Applications not accepted.
Application information: Contributes only to pre-selected organizations.
Officers: Sarkis Bedevian, Pres.; Ruth Bedevian, V.P.; Debra Bedevian, Secy.; Margaret Geragos, Treas.
EIN: 223619205

61710
Doris & Stanley Berenzweig Charitable Foundation, Inc.
111 Wagaraw Rd.
Hawthorne, NJ 07506-2720
Contact: Stanley Berenzweig, Pres; or Doris Berenzweig, V.P.

Established in 1991 in NJ.
Donor(s): Doris Berenzweig, Stanley Berenzweig.
Financial data (yr. ended 09/30/01): Assets, $642,300 (M); grants paid, $44,440; gifts received, $200,000; expenditures, $47,340; qualifying distributions, $44,440.
Limitations: Giving primarily in northern NJ.
Officers and Trustees:* Stanley Berenzweig,* Pres.; Doris Berenzweig,* V.P. and Secy.; Mona Adelson,* Treas.
EIN: 223135104

61711
Cilento Family Foundation, Inc.
(Formerly Cilento Foundation, Inc.)
121 Pelican Dr.
Avalon, NJ 08202 (609) 967-7962
Contact: Constance A. Cilento, M.D., Pres.

Established in 1995.
Donor(s): Constance A. Cilento, M.D.
Financial data (yr. ended 12/31/99): Assets, $630,018 (M); grants paid, $24,000; gifts received, $129,096; expenditures, $24,000; qualifying distributions, $24,000.
Limitations: Giving primarily in NJ.
Officers: Constance A. Cilento, M.D., Pres.; Rosemary B. Cilento, V.P.; Milena Reckseit, Secy.; Dominic J. Cilento, Treas.
EIN: 521829637

61712
Marie and Edward Wilkerson Animal Welfare Trust Fund
P.O. Box 185
Lavallette, NJ 08735

Financial data (yr. ended 12/31/99): Assets, $623,167 (M); grants paid, $24,315; expenditures, $29,057; qualifying distributions, $24,315.
Limitations: Applications not accepted.
Application information: Contributes only to pre-selected organizations.
Trustees: Garnet L. Tilton, Kirk W. Tilton.
EIN: 521626006

61713
Richard W. Melosh Family Foundation, Inc.
c/o Dugan, Colthart & Zoch
P.O. Box 576
Closter, NJ 07624

Established in 1993 in NJ.
Donor(s): Richard W. Melosh.
Financial data (yr. ended 12/31/00): Assets, $604,946 (M); grants paid, $26,550; expenditures, $32,383; qualifying distributions, $27,693.
Limitations: Applications not accepted. Giving primarily in NJ.
Application information: Contributes only to pre-selected organizations.
Officers: Richard W. Melosh, Pres.; Richard Lee Melosh, V.P.; Edna Lee Melosh, Secy.-Treas.
EIN: 223252484

61714
Westminster Foundation at Princeton
61 Nassau St.
Princeton, NJ 08542

Classified as a private operating foundation in 1980.
Financial data (yr. ended 06/30/99): Assets, $601,812 (M); grants paid, $350; gifts received, $47,626; expenditures, $67,472; qualifying distributions, $143,072.
Limitations: Applications not accepted.
Application information: Contributes only to pre-selected organizations.
Officers and Trustees:* William Scheide,* Pres.; Barbara Chappel,* V.P.; Alfred Kaemmerlan,* Treas.; and 13 additional trustees.
EIN: 210672776

61715
Edward A. Jesser Foundation, Inc.
196 Wind Hollow Ct.
Mahwah, NJ 07430

Classified as a private operating foundation in 1997 in NJ.
Donor(s): Edward A. Jesser.
Financial data (yr. ended 12/31/00): Assets, $592,868 (M); grants paid, $31,000; gifts received, $100,000; expenditures, $31,688; qualifying distributions, $30,704.
Limitations: Applications not accepted. Giving primarily in Easton, PA.
Application information: Contributes only to pre-selected organizations.
Officers: Edward A. Jesser, Pres.; Ruth A. Jesser, V.P.; Wynne J. McGrew, Secy.-Treas.
Trustee: Edward A. Jesser, Jr.
EIN: 223516245

61716
The Ben Appelbaum Foundation, Inc.
P.O. Box 600
Hawthorne, NJ 07507
Additional address: 204 Middle Neck Rd., Port Washington, NY 11050, tel. and FAX: (516) 883-0488; E-mail:
info@benappelbaumfoundation.org; URL: http://www.benappelbaumfoundation.org

Established in 1998. Classified as a private operating foundation in 1999.
Donor(s): Samuel Vichness, Joseph Appelbaum, Fern Cohen, Richard E. Malizia, Henry Skier.
Financial data (yr. ended 12/31/01): Assets, $585,241 (M); grants paid, $0; gifts received, $16,332; expenditures, $38,053; qualifying distributions, $0.
Application information: Application form can be downloaded from foundation Web site or submitted online. Application form required.
Officers: Samuel Vichness, Pres.; Joseph Appelbaum, V.P.; Fern Cohen, Secy.; Richard E. Malizia, Treas.
Directors: Jeffrey Ackerman, Alan Appelbaum, Barbara Appelbaum, Sheila Brody, Hersch Cohen, Stephen Fields, Henry Skier, and 4 additional directors.
EIN: 223575114

61717—NEW JERSEY

61717
Resurgens Foundation, Inc.
304 Brookmere Ct.
Ridgewood, NJ 07450-2604 (201) 445-8026
Contact: Joseph T. Lynaugh, Chair.

Established in 1997 in NJ. Classified as a private operating foundation in 1998.
Donor(s): Joseph T. Lynaugh.
Financial data (yr. ended 12/31/01): Assets, $566,702 (M); grants paid, $350; gifts received, $125,000; expenditures, $93,732; qualifying distributions, $170,703; giving activities include $77,000 for loans.
Limitations: Giving primarily in NJ.
Officers: Joseph T. Lynaugh, Chair. and Pres.; Charles Mulligan, V.P.; John Lynaugh, Secy.; Margaret M. Lynaugh, Treas.
EIN: 223525011

61718
Our House Foundation, Inc.
599 Springfield Ave.
Berkeley Heights, NJ 07922-1012
Tel.: (908) 464-8008, ext. 122; FAX: (909) 464-8263
Contact: Karen Feinblatt, Exec. Dir.

Classified as a private operating foundation in 1989.
Financial data (yr. ended 12/31/01): Assets, $549,315 (M); grants paid, $209,235; gifts received, $303,232; expenditures, $454,185; qualifying distributions, $234,553.
Limitations: Giving primarily in NJ.
Publications: Newsletter, financial statement.
Application information: Application form required.
Officers: Kathy James, Pres.; Linda Peck, V.P.; Sarah Christensen, Secy.; Michael Gambro, Treas.
Directors: Karen Feinblatt, Exec. Dir.; Lizbeth Adams, Barbara Lee, Jack Lyness, Leonard Solondz.
EIN: 222856145
Codes: FD2

61719
Jane and Tom Tang Foundation for Education, Inc.
c/o Tom Tang
800 Palisades Ave., Ste. 23C
Fort Lee, NJ 07024

Established in 2000 in NJ.
Donor(s): Tom Y.C. Tang.
Financial data (yr. ended 12/31/00): Assets, $520,506 (M); grants paid, $18,620; gifts received, $39,443; expenditures, $19,120; qualifying distributions, $19,120.
Limitations: Applications not accepted.
Application information: Contributes only to pre-selected organizations.
Trustees: Edwin C. Landis, Jr., Carl Schwartz, Jane Y. Tang, Tom Y.C. Tang.
EIN: 223693816

61720
J.W.G. Foundation, Inc.
c/o Cranes Mill
459 Passaic Ave., No. 319
West Caldwell, NJ 07006

Established in 1996 in NJ.
Donor(s): Jane W. Griffith.
Financial data (yr. ended 12/31/99): Assets, $516,749 (M); grants paid, $26,000; expenditures, $30,668; qualifying distributions, $27,457.
Limitations: Applications not accepted. Giving primarily in NJ.
Application information: Contributes only to pre-selected organizations.

Officer: Jane W. Griffith, Pres.
EIN: 223130629

61721
Moorestown Education Foundation
c/o Robert J. Oldt, Jr.
803 N. Stanwick Rd.
Moorestown, NJ 08057-2147
Application address: c/o Veronica Hughes, 350 Bridgeboro Rd., Moorestown, NJ 08057, tel.: (856) 778-6610

Financial data (yr. ended 12/31/99): Assets, $505,046 (M); grants paid, $119,334; gifts received, $122,022; expenditures, $140,129; qualifying distributions, $119,334.
Limitations: Giving limited to Moorestown, NJ.
Application information: Application form required.
Officers: Frank Keith, Pres.; Vito Germinario, V.P.; Robert J. Oldt, Secy.-Treas.
EIN: 222699954
Codes: FD2, GTI

61722
Raynault Foundation
(Formerly Paul Raynault Research Foundation)
214 N. Woodland St.
Englewood, NJ 07631

Classified as a private operating foundation in 1993 in NJ.
Donor(s): Paul Raynault.
Financial data (yr. ended 12/31/01): Assets, $468,601 (M); grants paid, $0; expenditures, $11,319; qualifying distributions, $11,319; giving activities include $11,319 for programs.
Trustee: Paul Raynault.
EIN: 223109295

61723
Jesus Said
132 Fairview Dr.
Neshanic Station, NJ 08853 (908) 369-4339
Contact: J. Peter Vermeulen, Tr.

Financial data (yr. ended 06/30/99): Assets, $448,391 (M); grants paid, $19,935; expenditures, $22,928; qualifying distributions, $19,779.
Limitations: Giving in the U.S.
Trustees: W.R. Everett, E.D. Melachinos, J. Peter Vermeulen.
EIN: 222405660

61724
Billian Family Charitable Foundation
128 E. High St.
Bound Brook, NJ 08805

Established in 1997 in NJ.
Donor(s): Robert W. Billian.
Financial data (yr. ended 12/31/99): Assets, $421,039 (M); grants paid, $4,808; gifts received, $56,000; expenditures, $9,559; qualifying distributions, $5,037.
Limitations: Applications not accepted.
Application information: Contributes only to pre-selected organizations.
Trustees: Alfred A. Billian, Douglas C. Billian, Robert W. Billian, Wayne R. Billian.
EIN: 586338666

61725
Michelle R. Weiss Charitable Foundation, Inc.
c/o International Granite & Marble Co.
2038 83rd St.
North Bergen, NJ 07047

Established in 1997.
Donor(s): John Weiss, Sonia Weiss.
Financial data (yr. ended 07/31/00): Assets, $412,418 (M); grants paid, $49,100; gifts received, $35,500; expenditures, $49,217; qualifying distributions, $49,100.
Limitations: Giving primarily in NJ.
Officers: John Weiss, Pres.; Sonia Weiss, V.P.
Trustees: Robert Weiss, Steven Weiss.
EIN: 223538607

61726
Jatain Charitable Foundation
8 Norfolk Dr.
Princeton Junction, NJ 08550 (609) 409-1720
Contact: Bob Cheng, Dir.

Established in 2000 as a company-sponsored operating foundation in NJ.
Donor(s): Fema Electronics Corp.
Financial data (yr. ended 12/31/00): Assets, $378,674 (M); grants paid, $23,350; gifts received, $600,000; expenditures, $24,403; qualifying distributions, $24,403.
Limitations: Giving primarily in CA and NJ.
Directors: Bob Cheng, Jean Cheng.
EIN: 226824275

61727
Leonard J. & Gloria Phillips Foundation, Inc.
310 Allwood Rd.
Clifton, NJ 07012-1701 (973) 473-5300
Contact: Leonard J. Phillips, Mgr.

Established in 1984 in NJ.
Donor(s): Gloria Phillips, Leonard J. Phillips.
Financial data (yr. ended 03/31/00): Assets, $374,852 (M); grants paid, $35,515; expenditures, $36,449; qualifying distributions, $35,515.
Limitations: Giving primarily in FL.
Application information: Application form not required.
Officers: Gloria Phillips, Mgr.; Leonard J. Phillips, Mgr.
EIN: 222561173

61728
Thomas and Helen Davis Memorial Foundation
c/o Fulton Financial Advisors, N.A.
Rte. 45 and Elm Ave.
Woodbury Heights, NJ 08097
Application address: c/o Mable Johnson, Guidance Off., Woodstown High School, East Ave., Woodstown, NJ 08098, tel.: (856) 769-0144

Classified as a private operating foundation in 1986.
Financial data (yr. ended 02/28/00): Assets, $361,449 (M); grants paid, $18,000; expenditures, $22,597; qualifying distributions, $22,597.
Limitations: Giving limited to NJ.
Publications: Application guidelines.
Application information: Application form required.
Trustee: Fulton Financial Advisors, N.A.
EIN: 222764049
Codes: GTI

61729
Wendee Foundation
P.O. Box 1482
Princeton, NJ 08542-1482

Donor(s): Sau-Hai Lam.
Financial data (yr. ended 11/30/01): Assets, $360,349 (M); grants paid, $0; expenditures, $4,532; qualifying distributions, $390.
Officers: Sau-Hai Lam, Pres.; Louana Howling, Secy.; Patsy C. Lam, Treas.
Directors: Karen Lam, Nelson Lam.
EIN: 222381582

61730
MacCulloch Hall Historical Museum
45 MacCulloch Ave.
Morristown, NJ 07960-5228

Classified as a private operating foundation in 1980.
Financial data (yr. ended 12/31/99): Assets, $343,091 (M); grants paid, $0; gifts received, $256,098; expenditures, $275,924; qualifying distributions, $275,923 for programs.
Officers: Rosaland Fischell, Pres.; Walter Savage, 1st V.P.; Carol Bere, 2nd V.P.; Janet Simon, Secy.; Joy Mercer, Treas.
Trustees: Charles Bippart, Alice Cutler, Mrs. George Emory, Richard C. Simon, and 16 additional trustees.
EIN: 226109895

61731
Sylvia and Edward H. Zucker Foundation, Inc.
604 Cleveland Ln.
Rockaway, NJ 07866

Established in 1986 in NJ.
Donor(s): Sylvia Zucker.
Financial data (yr. ended 12/31/00): Assets, $314,914 (M); grants paid, $30,775; gifts received, $22,000; expenditures, $51,861; qualifying distributions, $30,775.
Limitations: Applications not accepted. Giving primarily in NJ and NY.
Application information: Contributes only to pre-selected organizations.
Officer: Sylvia Zucker, Pres.
EIN: 222663037

61732
The Lowenthal Family Foundation
13 Ackerman Rd.
Saddle River, NJ 07458

Established in 1997 in NJ.
Donor(s): Edward Lowenthal.
Financial data (yr. ended 02/28/00): Assets, $314,535 (M); grants paid, $5,500; expenditures, $5,853; qualifying distributions, $5,500.
Limitations: Applications not accepted.
Application information: Contributes only to pre-selected organizations.
Trustees: Edward Lowenthal, Ilene Lowenthal.
EIN: 137110502

61733
The Rajaratnam Family Foundation, Inc.
57 Cobblestone Crossing
Norwood, NJ 07648

Established in 2000 in NJ.
Donor(s): J.M. Rajaratnam.
Financial data (yr. ended 12/31/01): Assets, $308,167 (M); grants paid, $12,500; gifts received, $100,000; expenditures, $13,290; qualifying distributions, $12,500.
Officer: J.M. Rajaratnam.
EIN: 226866723

61734
Dick and Jackie Deskovick Foundation
166 Ridgedale Ave.
Morristown, NJ 07962-2007

Established in 2001 in NJ.
Donor(s): Dick Deskovick, Jackie Deskovick.
Financial data (yr. ended 12/31/01): Assets, $306,744 (M); grants paid, $10,000; gifts received, $366,150; expenditures, $10,707; qualifying distributions, $10,000.
Limitations: Applications not accepted.
Application information: Contributes only to pre-selected organizations.
Trustees: Louise Deskovick, Robert R. Deskovick.
EIN: 223762653

61735
The Edward F. & Lois J. Ryan Foundation, Inc.
c/o Edward F. Ryan
177 Highland Ave.
Short Hills, NJ 07078

Established in 1998 in NJ.
Donor(s): Edward F. Ryan.
Financial data (yr. ended 12/31/00): Assets, $291,944 (M); grants paid, $12,675; expenditures, $13,504; qualifying distributions, $13,050.
Limitations: Applications not accepted.
Application information: Contributes only to pre-selected organizations.
Officers: Edward F. Ryan, Pres.; Lois J. Ryan, V.P.
EIN: 223594000

61736
Arthur Venneri Foundation
1340 Outlook Dr.
Mountainside, NJ 07092

Financial data (yr. ended 12/31/00): Assets, $290,159 (M); grants paid, $15,271; expenditures, $18,086; qualifying distributions, $16,771.
Limitations: Applications not accepted. Giving primarily in NJ; some giving to Italy.
Application information: Contributes only to pre-selected organizations.
Trustees: Esther Iarvssi, Marilyn Lawson, Arlene Post, Arthur Venneri.
EIN: 226047469

61737
Kinosian Armenian Educational Foundation, Inc.
c/o Bedros Tashjian
198 Main St.
Little Ferry, NJ 07643

Donor(s): Garabed Kinosian.‡
Financial data (yr. ended 03/31/02): Assets, $278,002 (L); grants paid, $19,500; expenditures, $20,982; qualifying distributions, $19,352.
Limitations: Applications not accepted. Giving primarily in NJ and NY.
Application information: Contributes only to pre-selected organizations.
Officers: Martin Nalbandian, Chair.; Vahakn Hovnanian, Secy.; Bedros Tashjian, Treas.
EIN: 222579046

61738
The Pinkham Charitable Foundation
423 Long Hill Dr.
Short Hills, NJ 07078-1207

Established in 1986 in NJ.
Donor(s): Sybil Pinkham.
Financial data (yr. ended 12/31/00): Assets, $274,013 (M); grants paid, $20,000; gifts received, $376; expenditures, $20,000; qualifying distributions, $20,000.
Limitations: Applications not accepted. Giving primarily in MA, NH, and NJ.
Application information: Contributes only to pre-selected organizations.
Trustees: Cynthia S. Pinkham, Susan M. Pinkham, Sybil Pinkham, William D. Pinkham III.
EIN: 222779172

61739
B'nai B'rith Food Industry Lodge Foundation, Inc.
c/o Steven Piller
12 Canterbury Ct.
Warren, NJ 07059

Financial data (yr. ended 12/31/99): Assets, $268,358 (M); grants paid, $9,500; expenditures, $10,011; qualifying distributions, $9,433.
Officer: Steve Pillar, Pres.
Trustees: Francis Hagler, Michael Hersh, Larry Oberman, Barry Zinns.
EIN: 223223678

61740
Jane Dorothy Perlmutter Foundation
183 High St.
Newton, NJ 07860
Contact: Harold S. Perlmutter, Tr.

Classified as a private operating foundation in 1997.
Donor(s): Harold S. Perlmutter.
Financial data (yr. ended 12/31/00): Assets, $256,754 (L); grants paid, $27,775; expenditures, $29,518; qualifying distributions, $27,775.
Limitations: Giving primarily in New York, NY.
Trustee: Harold S. Perlmutter.
EIN: 223508081

61741
Inter-County Council on Drug & Alcohol Abuse
480 Kearny Ave.
Kearny, NJ 07032

Classified as a private operating foundation in 1971.
Financial data (yr. ended 06/30/01): Assets, $236,605 (M); grants paid, $0; gifts received, $408,394; expenditures, $605,045; qualifying distributions, $398,463; giving activities include $398,463 for programs.
Officer and Director:* Harry Bachler,* Pres.
EIN: 237094253

61742
The Caroline Doherty Foundation
5302 1/2 Lake Rd.
Wildwood, NJ 08260

Established in 1999 in NJ.
Donor(s): Caroline Doherty.
Financial data (yr. ended 12/31/00): Assets, $230,954 (M); grants paid, $69,333; gifts received, $210,000; expenditures, $97,210; qualifying distributions, $69,333.
Trustees: Caroline Doherty, R. Whyne Rafferty, Vernon C. Walker.
EIN: 223692658

61743
The Isko Foundation, Inc.
Prentice Ln.
P.O. Box 24
Mendham, NJ 07945 (973) 540-8845
Contact: Irving D. Isko, Pres.

Donor(s): Irving D. Isko, Kathe Isko.
Financial data (yr. ended 12/31/99): Assets, $228,530 (M); grants paid, $14,600; expenditures, $15,234; qualifying distributions, $14,600.
Limitations: Giving primarily in Chester and South Orange, NJ.
Officers and Directors:* Irving D. Isko,* Pres.; Kathe Isko,* V.P.; Immanuel Kohn, Michael Macris, John D. Young.
EIN: 222463337

61744
The Morello Foundation
3036 Central Ave.
Ocean City, NJ 08226
Contact: John B. Morello, Tr.

Donor(s): John B. Morello.
Financial data (yr. ended 12/31/99): Assets, $205,461 (M); grants paid, $3,550; gifts received, $4,060; expenditures, $3,860; qualifying distributions, $3,564.
Limitations: Giving primarily in Vineland, NJ.
Application information: Application form required.
Trustees: Judith A. Browne, Geraldine A. Gabage, John B. Morello.
EIN: 237051152

61745
BGM Kumar Foundation, Inc.
58 Tatum Dr.
Middletown, NJ 07748-3126

Established in 1999 in NJ.
Donor(s): Birendra Kumar, Madhu Kanta.
Financial data (yr. ended 12/31/00): Assets, $196,274 (M); grants paid, $1,750; gifts received, $124,820; expenditures, $13,846; qualifying distributions, $1,750.
Officers: Birendra Kumar, Pres.; Madhu Kanta, Secy.
Director: Prem Lata.
EIN: 223696329

61746
Oster Family Foundation, Inc.
429 Sylvan Ave.
Englewood Cliffs, NJ 07632

Established in 1992 in NJ.
Financial data (yr. ended 04/30/01): Assets, $192,548 (M); grants paid, $270,630; gifts received, $200,000; expenditures, $270,645; qualifying distributions, $270,630.
Limitations: Applications not accepted. Giving primarily in NJ and NY.
Application information: Contributes only to pre-selected organizations.
Officers: Miriam Oster, Pres.; Abraham Oster, V.P. and Secy.; Daniel Oster, V.P. and Treas.; Ann Oster, V.P.
EIN: 223188305
Codes: FD

61747
Fisher Family Foundation, Inc.
994 Wildwood Rd.
Oradell, NJ 07649

Financial data (yr. ended 12/31/00): Assets, $190,662 (M); grants paid, $50,000; expenditures, $50,000; qualifying distributions, $50,000.
Limitations: Applications not accepted.
Application information: Contributes only to pre-selected organizations.
Officers: Florence Fisher, Pres.; Meredith Fisher, V.P.; Judith Furer, Secy.; Leslie Greenblatt, Treas.
EIN: 223684160

61748
Andrew Friedland Memorial Fund
385 S. Maple Ave.
Ridgewood, NJ 07450
Application address: 329 Canterbury Ln., Wyckoff, NJ 07481
Contact: Edward Friedland, Tr.

Established in 1998 in NJ.
Donor(s): Dollar Land Syndicate.
Financial data (yr. ended 12/31/00): Assets, $184,826 (M); grants paid, $42,535; gifts received, $14,975; expenditures, $42,636; qualifying distributions, $42,535.
Trustees: Edward Friedland, Kathryn Friedland.
EIN: 222155603

61749
The New Brunswick Columbian Club Foundation, Inc.
P.O. Box 47
New Brunswick, NJ 08903
Contact: John J. Hoagland, Jr., Pres.

Financial data (yr. ended 06/30/99): Assets, $184,552 (M); grants paid, $13,408; gifts received, $40; expenditures, $17,265; qualifying distributions, $13,408.
Officers: John J. Hoagland, Jr., Pres.; John A. Anderson, V.P.; Theodore G. Acchione, Secy.; John A. Varga, Treas.
Trustee: Edwin J. Keefe, Jr.
EIN: 223652871

61750
Kusum-Jayesh Aseem Seva Charitable Foundation
7 Jennie Ct.
Cedar Grove, NJ 07009
Contact: Jayesh Shah, Pres.

Established in 1999.
Donor(s): Jayesh Shah.
Financial data (yr. ended 12/31/00): Assets, $179,220 (M); grants paid, $2,601; gifts received, $5,000; expenditures, $3,955; qualifying distributions, $2,601.
Officers: Jayesh Shah, Pres.; Kusum Shah, V.P.
EIN: 223696326

61751
Salem Old House Foundation, Inc.
P.O. Box 454
Salem, NJ 08079-0454

Established in 2000.
Financial data (yr. ended 12/31/01): Assets, $173,289 (M); grants paid, $0; gifts received, $102,050; expenditures, $23,057; qualifying distributions, $0.
Officers: Ronald E. Magill, Pres.; Carol Y. Reese, V.P.; John P. McCarthy, Secy.
EIN: 223733610

61752
Tobelmann Foundation
1199 Raritan Rd.
Clark, NJ 07066

Financial data (yr. ended 12/31/01): Assets, $169,713 (M); grants paid, $23,917; gifts received, $12,859; expenditures, $27,229; qualifying distributions, $25,745.
Limitations: Applications not accepted. Giving on a national basis.
Application information: Contributes only to pre-selected organizations.
Officers: Ruth T. Grant, Pres.; Elaine Tobelmann Grose, Secy.
EIN: 221711668

61753
Cannon Family Foundation, Inc.
112 Forest Way
Essex Fells, NJ 07021-1602

Established in 1997 in NJ.
Donor(s): Thomas Cannon.
Financial data (yr. ended 12/31/99): Assets, $160,667 (M); grants paid, $11,948; expenditures, $38,030; qualifying distributions, $11,948.
Officer: Thomas Cannon.
EIN: 223505286

61754
Allman Medical Scholarship Foundation
2 Ocean Way, Ste. 1000
Atlantic City, NJ 08401 (609) 345-7571
Application address: c/o Sharon J. Becker, Miss America Organization, P.O. Box 119, Atlantic City, NJ 08404; URL: http://www.missamerica.org/scholarships/allmanmedical.asp

Established in 1974 in NJ.
Donor(s): Mrs. David B. Allman.‡
Financial data (yr. ended 07/31/01): Assets, $155,285 (M); grants paid, $10,000; expenditures, $10,000; qualifying distributions, $0.
Limitations: Giving on a national basis.
Publications: Application guidelines.
Application information: Application form required.
Trustees: Toni Fauntleroy, C. Patrick McKoy, Robert Renneisen.
EIN: 237414385
Codes: GTI

61755
The Benninghoff Foundation, Inc.
605 Hilltop Rd.
Cinnaminson, NJ 08077
Contact: Herman Benninghoff, Dir.

Established in 2000 in NJ.
Donor(s): Herman Benninghoff, Sara Joan Benninghoff.
Financial data (yr. ended 12/31/00): Assets, $144,541 (M); grants paid, $0; gifts received, $154,025; expenditures, $9,484; qualifying distributions, $9,484; giving activities include $9,484 for programs.
Directors: Herman Benninghoff, Joan Benninghoff, Keith Benninghoff.
EIN: 223756203

61756
The Englard Family Foundation, Inc.
400 Kelby St., 11th Fl.
Fort Lee, NJ 07024

Established in 1995 in NY.
Financial data (yr. ended 12/31/00): Assets, $142,101 (L); grants paid, $11,178; expenditures, $11,388; qualifying distributions, $11,178.
Limitations: Applications not accepted. Giving primarily in NY.
Application information: Contributes only to pre-selected organizations.
Director: Bernard Englard.
EIN: 133857792

61757
Usss Shah Family Foundation, Inc.
16 Gathering Rd.
Pine Brook, NJ 07058

Established in 1999 in NJ.
Donor(s): Sunil Shah.
Financial data (yr. ended 12/31/99): Assets, $139,795 (L); grants paid, $27,001; gifts received, $137,000; expenditures, $27,115; qualifying distributions, $27,001.
Director: Sunil Shah.
EIN: 223589593

61758
Louis Williams Foundation
c/o Benenson & Scher
159 Millburn Ave.
Millburn, NJ 07041-1825 (973) 467-9750
Contact: Elliot Scher, Pres.

Financial data (yr. ended 12/31/00): Assets, $137,728 (M); grants paid, $1,212; expenditures, $2,549; qualifying distributions, $1,330.
Limitations: Giving primarily in New York, NY.
Officers and Trustees:* Elliott Scher,* Pres.; Jean Baron,* Treas.; Jay Benenson.
EIN: 222596060

61759
Foster Wheeler Foundation
Perryville Corporate Park
53 Frontage Rd.
Clinton, NJ 08809-4000

Financial data (yr. ended 12/31/00): Assets, $134,084 (M); grants paid, $10,000; expenditures, $11,399; qualifying distributions, $10,000.
Limitations: Applications not accepted.
Application information: Contributes only to pre-selected organizations.
Officers and Directors:* Richard J. Swift,* Pres.; Lisa Fries Gardner, Secy.; Robert D. Iseman, Treas.; Henry E. Bartoli, John C. Blythe, Thomas R. O'Brien, James E. Schessler.
EIN: 223446229

61760
Dr. Herbert R. Axelrod Foundation
c/o Music Selection Comm.
308 Main St.
Allenhurst, NJ 07711 (732) 531-1995

Established in 1991 in NJ.
Donor(s): TFH Publications.
Financial data (yr. ended 12/31/01): Assets, $131,267 (M); grants paid, $0; gifts received, $7,000; expenditures, $1,652; qualifying distributions, $0.
Limitations: Giving primarily in Philadelphia, PA.
Application information: Application form required.
Officers: Herbert R. Axelrod, Pres.; Evelyn Axelrod, V.P. and Secy.; Rosalind A. Cuccurullo, V.P. and Treas.; Bernard Duke, V.P.
Trustees: Todd Michael Axelrod, Douglas M. Calhoun.
EIN: 521739492

61761
The James B. Boskey Memorial Foundation, Inc.
c/o Adele Boskey
4 Winding Way
North Caldwell, NJ 07006

Established in 2001 in NJ.
Donor(s): Adele Boskey, Elizabeth Boskey, Ahmed Bubulia.
Financial data (yr. ended 12/31/01): Assets, $130,755 (M); grants paid, $0; gifts received, $130,000; expenditures, $18; qualifying distributions, $0.
Officers and Directors:* Adele L. Boskey,* Pres.; Elizabeth R. Boskey,* V.P.; Bardin Levavy,* Secy.; Eileen Dombrowsky, J. Gregory Kinnett.
EIN: 223787050

61762
Mildred & Rudy Reis Foundation
c/o DiMarco Hecht
16-00 Route 20B
Fair Lawn, NJ 07410-2503
Application address: 435 W. 57th St., New York, NY 10019, tel.: (212) 246-4450
Contact: Rudy Reis, Pres.

Donor(s): Rudy Reis, Mildred Reis.‡
Financial data (yr. ended 12/31/99): Assets, $123,590 (M); grants paid, $2,325; expenditures, $2,547; qualifying distributions, $2,325.
Limitations: Giving limited to the neighboring counties in NJ, including Long Island and the New York, NY area.
Application information: Application form required.
Officers: Rudy Reis, Pres. and Treas.; Susan Lyons, V.P.
EIN: 133018214

61763
The Dorsky Foundation
c/o Frances Dorsky
70 Skylark Rd.
Springfield, NJ 07081

Establish in 1998.
Financial data (yr. ended 12/31/99): Assets, $122,354 (M); grants paid, $5,000; gifts received, $693; expenditures, $5,010; qualifying distributions, $4,459.
Officers: Frances Dorsky,* Pres. and Treas.; Steven Dorsky, Secy.
Trustee: Howard Sontag.
EIN: 223591681

61764
Reina Family Foundation, Inc.
c/o Illva Saronno Corp.
80 Cottontail Ln.
Somerset, NJ 08873

Established in 1997 in NY.
Donor(s): Angelo Reina.
Financial data (yr. ended 06/30/99): Assets, $121,427 (M); grants paid, $3,000; gifts received, $157,538; expenditures, $121,342; qualifying distributions, $121,329.
Limitations: Applications not accepted.
Application information: Contributes only to pre-selected organizations.
Officers: Angelo Reina, Pres.; David Kelso, V.P.; Tina Pedrazzani, Treas.
Director: Augusto Reina.
EIN: 223432426

61765
The Carol and Robert J. Palle', Jr. Charitable Trust
21 Desai Ct.
Freehold, NJ 07728
Contact: Robert Palle', Dir.

Established in 1999 in NJ.
Financial data (yr. ended 12/31/00): Assets, $118,029 (M); grants paid, $6,750; expenditures, $6,750; qualifying distributions, $6,645.
Application information: Application form required.
Directors: Carol Palle', Robert Palle'.
EIN: 237993619

61766
Tregoe Education Forum, Inc.
34 Heather Ln.
Princeton, NJ 08540

Establishied in 1997 in NJ.
Donor(s): Benjamin B. Tregoe.
Financial data (yr. ended 12/31/99): Assets, $109,815 (M); grants paid, $2,000; gifts received, $144,860; expenditures, $306,365; qualifying distributions, $295,097; giving activities include $306,365 for programs.
Limitations: Applications not accepted. Giving primarily in NJ.
Application information: Contributes only to pre-selected organizations.
Trustees: Charles L. Jaffin, Benjamin B. Tregoe, Jan Tregoe.
EIN: 133740564

61767
The WBS Charitable Trust
55 Green St.
Hackensack, NJ 07601-4003

Donor(s): Wayne Kiltz.
Financial data (yr. ended 12/31/00): Assets, $108,413 (M); grants paid, $5,400; expenditures, $5,400; qualifying distributions, $5,400.
Limitations: Applications not accepted.
Application information: Contributes only to pre-selected organizations.
Trustee: Wayne Kiltz.
EIN: 916430458

61768
Matrix Foundation, Inc.
400 Forsgate Dr., CN4000
Cranbury, NJ 08512

Established in 1994 in NJ.
Donor(s): Matrix Special Events, Matrix Realty.
Financial data (yr. ended 12/31/01): Assets, $102,229 (M); grants paid, $33,300; gifts received, $133,600; expenditures, $36,110; qualifying distributions, $36,110.
Limitations: Applications not accepted.
Application information: Contributes only to pre-selected organizations.
Trustees: Donald M. Epstein, Gerald W. Hull, Jr., Joseph S. Taylor, Robert J. Twomey.
EIN: 223231774

61769
Goldstein Charity Fund, Inc.
1423 Cedar Row
Lakewood, NJ 08701 (732) 370-1141
Contact: Joshua Goldstein, Tr.

Established in 2000 in NJ.
Donor(s): Joshua Goldstein.
Financial data (yr. ended 12/31/01): Assets, $102,007 (M); grants paid, $0; gifts received, $100,500; expenditures, $4; qualifying distributions, $0.
Trustees: Joshua Goldstein, Morris Silberberg, Joseph Singer.
EIN; 223711451

61770
The Joseph Mazzarella & Grace Mazzarella Educational Foundation Trust
501 Trenton Ave.
Point Pleasant Beach, NJ 08742

Established in 1999; classified as a private operating foundation in 2000.
Donor(s): Joseph Mazzarella, Grace Mazzarella.
Financial data (yr. ended 12/31/00): Assets, $100,594 (M); grants paid, $3,000; gifts received, $3,000; expenditures, $3,239; qualifying distributions, $3,000.
Trustees: Carl R. Lepis, Sr., Grace Mazzarella, Joseph Mazzarella.
EIN: 223696654

61771
The People Technology Foundation, Inc.
25 Chatham Rd.
Summit, NJ 07901-1399 (908) 277-6100
Contact: Frank J. Ponzio, Dir.

Established in 1994 in NY and DE.
Donor(s): Frank J. Ponzio, Cymbolic Systems & Co.
Financial data (yr. ended 12/31/00): Assets, $96,288 (M); grants paid, $0; gifts received, $50,000; expenditures, $4,774; qualifying distributions, $4,774.
Limitations: Giving limited to Eastern Europe, with emphasis in Romania.
Application information: Application form not required.
Director: Frank J. Ponzio.
EIN: 223273424

61772
The Polonsky Brothers Foundation
151 Harding Rd.
P.O. Box 821
Red Bank, NJ 07701 (732) 741-8438
Contact: Ivan Polonsky, Secy.

Classified as a private operating foundation in 1990.
Donor(s): Jay Polonsky, Ivan Polonsky, Leonard Polonsky.
Financial data (yr. ended 12/31/01): Assets, $95,515 (M); grants paid, $94,916; expenditures, $114,253; qualifying distributions, $114,076.
Limitations: Giving on a national basis.
Application information: Application form required.
Officers and Directors:* Leonard Polonsky,* Pres.; Ivan Polonsky,* Secy.; Jay Polonsky,* Treas.
EIN: 136169593
Codes: FD2, GTI

61773
Petri Family Foundation
Thanksgiving Rd.
Morristown, NJ 07960

Established in 1997 in NJ.
Donor(s): Joseph Petri.
Financial data (yr. ended 12/31/01): Assets, $90,055 (M); grants paid, $175,600; gifts received, $49,500; expenditures, $175,633; qualifying distributions, $175,153.
Limitations: Applications not accepted. Giving primarily in NJ and NY.
Application information: Contributes only to pre-selected organizations.
Director and Trustees:* Stephen R. Maffei,* Joseph Petri,* Patricia G. Petri.
EIN: 223490738
Codes: FD2

61774
Foundation for Aviation World War I
c/o Murphy & Hoffer, PA
P.O. Box 30, 15 Roszel Rd.
Princeton, NJ 08542

Established in 1981 in NJ.
Donor(s): Neal W. O'Connor.
Financial data (yr. ended 09/30/00): Assets, $83,479 (M); grants paid, $0; gifts received, $15,000; expenditures, $17,935; qualifying distributions, $33,513; giving activities include $17,674 for programs.
Officers: Neal W. O'Connor, Pres.; Jerry J. Siano, V.P.; William Klaus, Secy.; Samuel R. Hoffer, Treas.
Trustees: Peter Grosz, Eric Ludvigsen.
EIN: 222374860

61775
The Fisher Family Foundation
203 Chews Landing Rd.
Haddonfield, NJ 08033-3837 (609) 922-5252
Contact: George Ross Fisher, M.D., Tr.

Established in 1998 in NJ.
Donor(s): George Ross Fisher, M.D.
Financial data (yr. ended 08/31/00): Assets, $82,030 (M); grants paid, $2,400; gifts received, $21,724; expenditures, $3,695; qualifying distributions, $2,325.
Limitations: Giving primarily in NJ.
Trustees: George Ross Fisher, M.D., Mary S. Fisher, M.D.
EIN: 237991527

61776
Inflamation Research Association, Inc.
c/o Dennis M. Roland
20 Heather Ln.
Basking Ridge, NJ 07920

Established in 1997 in CT.
Financial data (yr. ended 12/31/00): Assets, $81,700 (M); grants paid, $0; gifts received, $24,000; expenditures, $210,492; qualifying distributions, $2,488; giving activities include $197,719 for programs.
Officers: Lisa A. Marshall, Ph.D., Pres.; Richard D. Dyer, Ph.D., V.P.; Stephen Stimpson, Ph.D., Secy.; Dennis M. Roland, Ph.D., Treas.
EIN: 222697282

61777
The Hartford Family Foundation
6 Dogwood Ln.
Rumson, NJ 07760-1412

Established in 1983 in NJ.
Donor(s): Olivia Wrightson Switz.
Financial data (yr. ended 10/31/01): Assets, $81,686 (M); grants paid, $0; gifts received, $38,940; expenditures, $22,235; qualifying distributions, $22,170; giving activities include $22,170 for programs.
Officers and Trustees:* Jeffrey G. Wrightson,* Pres.; Maria Hartford Switz Halman,* V.P.; Grace Wrightson,* Secy.; Stephen Hartford Besch, Lorraine Besch Gibson, William L. Gibson, Olivia Wrightson Switz, William J. Vitulli, Martha Ramsing Zoubek.
EIN: 222545227

61778
Anchor of Hope Foundation, Inc.
101 Tilton St.
Hammonton, NJ 08037
Contact: Frank S. Donio, Pres.

Established in 2000 in NJ.
Donor(s): Frank G. Donio.
Financial data (yr. ended 12/31/01): Assets, $80,576 (M); grants paid, $47,000; gifts received, $55,838; expenditures, $47,050; qualifying distributions, $47,000.
Limitations: Giving primarily in NJ.
Officers and Trustees:* Frank S. Donio,* Pres.; Frank G. Donio,* V.P.; Angela L. Donio,* Secy.-Treas.
EIN: 223721425

61779
The Westville Foundation, Inc.
c/o SJM & Assoc. PC
14 Ridgedale Ave., Ste. 255
Cedar Knolls, NJ 07927

Established in 1997 in NJ.

Financial data (yr. ended 12/31/99): Assets, $77,895 (M); grants paid, $28,841; expenditures, $29,281; qualifying distributions, $28,791.
Limitations: Applications not accepted.
Application information: Contributes only to pre-selected organizations.
Officers and Trustees: Ann Minton,* Pres.; Sean M. Aylward,* Secy.; Cynthia Aylward,* Treas.; Andrew Aylward, Christine Aylward, Kara Aylward.
EIN: 223516051

61780
Ganguly Family Foundation
96 Cooper Ave.
Upper Montclair, NJ 07043-2219
(973) 746-7245
Contact: Ashit K. Ganguly, Pres.

Established in 2000 in NJ.
Donor(s): Ashit K. Ganguly, Jean C. Ganguly.
Financial data (yr. ended 12/31/01): Assets, $76,982 (M); grants paid, $3,390; gifts received, $2,812; expenditures, $3,540; qualifying distributions, $3,390.
Officers: Ashit K. Ganguly, Pres.; Jean C. Ganguly, V.P.; Nomita Ganguly, Secy.-Treas.
EIN: 223769532

61781
M. & D. Loewenthal Foundation, Inc.
744 Orchard Ln.
Franklin Lakes, NJ 07417

Established in 1997 in NJ.
Donor(s): Dorothy Loewenthal, Michael Loewenthal.
Financial data (yr. ended 12/31/99): Assets, $71,803 (M); grants paid, $4,780; gifts received, $3,430; expenditures, $5,510; qualifying distributions, $5,510.
Officers: Michael Loewenthal, Pres.; Dorothy Loewenthal, Secy.-Treas.
EIN: 223513423

61782
The Ruane Family Foundation, Inc.
c/o SJM & Assoc.
14 Ridgedale Ave., Ste. 255
Cedar Knolls, NJ 07927

Established in 1997 in NJ.
Financial data (yr. ended 12/31/99): Assets, $70,435 (M); grants paid, $8,000; gifts received, $411; expenditures, $8,410; qualifying distributions, $8,000.
Limitations: Applications not accepted. Giving primarily in NJ.
Application information: Contributes only to pre-selected organizations.
Officers and Trustees: Gerald P. Ruane, Pres.; Ann Minton, Secy.; Marie F. Tookey, Treas.
EIN: 223516143

61783
Scott Van Doren Memorial Scholarship Fund
60 Deerhill Rd.
Lebanon, NJ 08833

Donor(s): John A. Van Doren, Judy E. Van Doren.
Financial data (yr. ended 06/30/00): Assets, $69,200 (M); grants paid, $7,000; gifts received, $5,025; expenditures, $7,055; qualifying distributions, $6,968.
Limitations: Applications not accepted. Giving limited to residents of Annandale, NJ.
Application information: Unsolicited requests for funds not accepted.
Directors: Cindy L. Van Doren, John A. Van Doren, Judy E. Van Doren, Michael A. Van Doren.
EIN: 223117696

Codes: GTI

61784
The Elizabeth O. Shear Foundation
P.O. Box 205
Tuckerton, NJ 08087

Established in 2000.
Donor(s): Elizabeth O. Shear.
Financial data (yr. ended 12/31/01): Assets, $68,363 (M); grants paid, $0; expenditures, $1,543; qualifying distributions, $0.
Trustee: Alan S. Gerber.
EIN: 226803705

61785
Russian Research Foundation, Inc.
770 Anderson Ave., Apt. 20F
Cliffside Park, NJ 07010

Established in 1981 in NJ.
Donor(s): Boris Pushkarev.
Financial data (yr. ended 12/31/99): Assets, $67,417 (M); grants paid, $15,040; gifts received, $21,951; expenditures, $21,626; qualifying distributions, $21,626.
Limitations: Applications not accepted. Giving primarily in Russia.
Application information: Contributes only to pre-selected organizations.
Officers: Boris Pushkarev, Chair.; Vladimir Burkevitch, Vice-Chair.; Ekaterina Breitbart, Treas.
Trustee: Iradia Vandeillos.
EIN: 222378898

61786
The Steven E. and Phyllis Gross Family Foundation
49 Farley Rd.
Short Hills, NJ 07078

Established in 2000 in NJ.
Donor(s): Steven E. Gross.
Financial data (yr. ended 12/31/00): Assets, $67,125 (M); grants paid, $6,100; gifts received, $66,022; expenditures, $6,690; qualifying distributions, $6,100.
Limitations: Applications not accepted.
Application information: Contributes only to pre-selected organizations.
Officers: Steven E. Gross, Pres.; Phyllis Gross, V.P.
EIN: 223762454

61787
William & Marilyn Kalellis Foundation, Inc.
P.O. Box 754
Haddonfield, NJ 08033-0506

Established in 1999 in NJ.
Donor(s): William Kalellis.
Financial data (yr. ended 12/31/01): Assets, $66,872 (M); grants paid, $4,500; expenditures, $7,473; qualifying distributions, $7,473; giving activities include $4,500 for programs.
Limitations: Applications not accepted.
Application information: Contributes only to pre-selected organizations.
Trustees: Marilyn Kalellis, William Kalellis, Barbara McCourt.
EIN: 223679380

61788
Center for Action Research
20 Nassau St., Rm. 200
Princeton, NJ 08542

Classified as a private operating foundation in 1975.
Donor(s): David H. McAlpin, Jr.
Financial data (yr. ended 12/31/00): Assets, $64,595 (M); grants paid, $6,200; gifts received, $11,777; expenditures, $15,669; qualifying distributions, $14,724.
Limitations: Applications not accepted.
Application information: Contributes only to pre-selected organizations.
Officers: David H. McAlpin, Jr., Pres. and Treas.; R. William Porter, V.P.; Marvin R. Reed, Secy.
EIN: 221936493

61789
American Counsel Scholarship Foundation, Inc.
c/o Roger L. Toner
5 Becker Farm Rd.
Roseland, NJ 07068

Financial data (yr. ended 12/31/01): Assets, $64,345 (M); grants paid, $7,500; gifts received, $5,500; expenditures, $8,675; qualifying distributions, $7,500.
Limitations: Applications not accepted. Giving limited to IL, IN, and WI.
Application information: Candidates for scholarship submitted by law school.
Officers: Bruce C. Ramsey, Pres.; Roger L. Toner, Secy.-Treas.
EIN: 521720223

61790
Theodore Maier Scholarship Foundation
c/o Milgrom, Galuskin, Rosner & Co.
2025 Lincoln Hwy., Rm. 210
Edison, NJ 08817
Contact: Paul Milgrom, Tr.

Classified as an operating foundation in 1972.
Financial data (yr. ended 08/31/99): Assets, $59,865 (M); grants paid, $1,500; expenditures, $1,661; qualifying distributions, $1,661.
Limitations: Giving limited to Metuchen, NJ.
Application information: Applicant must provide proof of enrollment at Metuchen High School.
Trustees: Ronald J. Berger, Eva Burck, Paul D. Milgrom.
EIN: 227111563

61791
Catholic Information Center on Internet
150-B Wierimus Ln.
Hillsdale, NJ 07642-1223

Financial data (yr. ended 08/31/01): Assets, $59,485 (M); grants paid, $25,200; gifts received, $150,000; expenditures, $149,032; qualifying distributions, $133,942.
Limitations: Applications not accepted. Giving primarily in Cheshire, CT.
Application information: Contributes only to pre-selected organizations.
Directors: Msgr. Eugene Clark, George Johnston, James Mulholland, Jr.
EIN: 223402967

61792
Stephen Holdampf & Company, Inc.
38 Park Ave.
Pompton Plains, NJ 07444

Donor(s): Stephen Holdampf.
Financial data (yr. ended 12/31/00): Assets, $56,680 (M); grants paid, $1,920; gifts received, $250; expenditures, $3,403; qualifying distributions, $1,420; giving activities include $270 for programs.
Limitations: Applications not accepted.
Application information: Contributes only to pre-selected organizations.
Officers: Stephen Holdampf, Pres.; Catherine Holdampf, V.P.
Trustees: Allen Meyerun, Jeanne Wirtz.
EIN: 222743511

61793
Solomon Foundation
38 Duke Dr.
Paramus, NJ 07652
Contact: Anita Grossman, Pres.

Donor(s): Horace H. Solomon.
Financial data (yr. ended 09/30/01): Assets, $56,475 (M); grants paid, $0; gifts received, $300; expenditures, $268; qualifying distributions, $0.
Officer: Anita Grossman, Pres.
EIN: 226029626

61794
Dollinger Foundation
1773 Queen Anne Rd.
Cherry Hill, NJ 08003

Classified as a private operating foundation in 1990.
Donor(s): H. Richard Dollinger, Marsha Z. Dollinger.
Financial data (yr. ended 12/31/99): Assets, $56,443 (M); grants paid, $48,560; expenditures, $48,652; qualifying distributions, $48,652.
Limitations: Applications not accepted. Giving primarily in Cherry Hill, NJ.
Application information: Contributes only to pre-selected organizations.
Trustee: H. Richard Dollinger.
EIN: 226506170

61795
The Cuta-Papa Foundation, Inc.
c/o C.J. Heuser
54 Shrewsbury Ave.
Red Bank, NJ 07701

Established in 1998 in NJ.
Financial data (yr. ended 12/31/99): Assets, $54,837 (M); grants paid, $4,000; gifts received, $4,428; expenditures, $4,355; qualifying distributions, $4,134.
Limitations: Applications not accepted. Giving primarily in New York, NY, some funding also in Phoenixville, PA.
Application information: Contributes only to pre-selected organizations.
Trustees: Dennis Concannon, Regina Cuta, Charles J. Heuser, Jr., Christopher Papa.
EIN: 223536657

61796
Hunter Douglas Foundation, Inc.
c/o Hunter Douglas, Inc.
2 Park Way & Rt. 17 S.
Upper Saddle River, NJ 07458
Tel. for applications: (201) 327-8200, ext. 4256
Contact: Kathy O'Keefe, Scholarship Awards Admin.

Established as a Company-sponsored operating foundation in 1999 in NJ.
Donor(s): Hunter Douglas, Inc.
Financial data (yr. ended 12/31/00): Assets, $54,395 (M); grants paid, $47,750; expenditures, $95,580; qualifying distributions, $47,830.
Limitations: Giving limited to residents of Upper Saddle River, NJ.
Application information: Application form required.
Officers and Directors:* Thom Hill, V.P. and Secy.; Gordon Khan,* V.P.; Arthur Lorenz,* Treas.; Marvin Hopkins.
EIN: 223694713

61797
Straube Foundation, Inc.
c/o Winfried H. Straube
106 W. Franklin Ave.
Pennington, NJ 08534-1422 (609) 737-3322

Classified as a private operating foundation in 1995.
Financial data (yr. ended 12/31/01): Assets, $53,983 (M); grants paid, $1,500; gifts received, $27,000; expenditures, $2,070; qualifying distributions, $1,500.
Trustees: David D. Straube, Hildegard K. Straube, Winfried H. Straube, Victor Walcoff.
EIN: 223381978

61798
The Kleinman Foundation, Inc.
153 Charlotte Pl.
Englewood Cliffs, NJ 07632-1616

Established in 1997 in NJ.
Donor(s): Albert Kleinman.
Financial data (yr. ended 12/31/99): Assets, $51,856 (M); grants paid, $4,821; expenditures, $5,801; qualifying distributions, $5,718.
Limitations: Applications not accepted.
Application information: Contributes only to pre-selected organizations.
Trustees: Beatrice Kleinman, Gilbert Weisbart, Randy Weisbart.
EIN: 223489180

61799
Achat, Inc.
418 4th St.
Lakewood, NJ 08701
Contact: Abraham Taubus, Tr.

Established in 1998 in NJ.
Donor(s): Abraham Taubus.
Financial data (yr. ended 12/31/99): Assets, $51,505 (M); grants paid, $20,747; gifts received, $22,275; expenditures, $21,284; qualifying distributions, $21,284.
Trustees: Barry Rothschild, Abraham Taubus, Chaya Taubus.
EIN: 223558447

61800
Adelaide Hollander Scholarship Foundation, Inc.
61 W. Jimmie Leeds Rd., Box 723
Pomona, NJ 08240-0723

Financial data (yr. ended 12/31/99): Assets, $51,061 (M); grants paid, $4,000; gifts received, $25; expenditures, $4,082; qualifying distributions, $4,082.
Officers and Trustees:* Leonard M. Hollander,* Chair.; Bernard W. Capaldi, Sr.,* Vice-Chair.; Richard J. Kathrins,* Secy.-Treas.
EIN: 223217578

61801
Anton R. Stobb Memorial Scholarship Trust
c/o Ronald M. Marks
185 Bridge Plz. N., Ste. 205
Fort Lee, NJ 07024-5997 (201) 947-8772
Contact: Walter J. Stobb, Tr.

Established in 1984 in NJ.
Donor(s): Elizabeth H. Stobb.
Financial data (yr. ended 12/31/00): Assets, $48,822 (M); grants paid, $4,000; expenditures, $5,721; qualifying distributions, $5,160.
Limitations: Giving primarily to residents of NJ.
Trustee: Anthony M. Stobb, Walter J. Stobb.
EIN: 526253731

61802
Procrit Foundation, Inc.
1 Johnson & Johnson Plz.
New Brunswick, NJ 08933

Established in 2001 in NJ.
Financial data (yr. ended 12/31/01): Assets, $47,532 (M); grants paid, $213,634; gifts received, $390,556; expenditures, $390,556; qualifying distributions, $213,634.
Application information: Application form required.
Officers and Directors:* Carol A. Webb,* Pres.; Cathleen Dooley,* V.P.; Peter Keating,* Secy.; Richard J. Moran,* Treas.; Michael McCulley, Conrad Person.
EIN: 311756693

61803
The Monica T. Buckley Memorial Foundation
807 Millbridge Ct.
P.O. Box 149
Leeds Point, NJ 08220

Established in 1999.
Financial data (yr. ended 12/31/00): Assets, $42,941 (M); grants paid, $8,000; gifts received, $30,358; expenditures, $20,311; qualifying distributions, $7,999.
Limitations: Giving primarily in Atlantic County, NJ.
Officers and Board Members:* John L. Buckley, Jr.,* Chair. and Pres.; Marilyn C. Buckley, V.P. and Secy.; Peter N. Bonitatibus, Treas.; Lt. E. Matthew Buckley, John L. Buckley III, Mary Catherine Buckley, Daniel T. Campbell, Thomas A. Duffy, Cornelia Connelly Marakovitz, Robert Marakovitz, Sr. Grace Marie, Rev. George Riley.
EIN: 223617616

61804
Ruth Bass Memorial Foundation, Inc.
P.O. Box 392
Maplewood, NJ 07040-0392

Financial data (yr. ended 12/31/99): Assets, $42,504 (M); grants paid, $50,404; gifts received, $23,797; expenditures, $150,692; qualifying distributions, $77,626.
Limitations: Applications not accepted.
Application information: Contributes only to pre-selected organizations.
Officers: Thomas Bass, Pres.; Peter Gelwarg, Treas.; Peggy Gelwarg, Admin.
Directors: Judy Diehl, Wolfgang Diehl, Ken Heyman, Mimi Heymen.
EIN: 223207547

61805
Electrophysiology Research Foundation
33 Fairway Dr.
Green Brook, NJ 08812

Classified as a private operating foundation in 1984.
Financial data (yr. ended 08/31/99): Assets, $42,256 (M); grants paid, $0; gifts received, $50,225; expenditures, $107,656; qualifying distributions, $92,610; giving activities include $6,138 for programs.
Trustees: Dennis J. Bruschi, Sanjeev Saksena.
EIN: 222415051

61806
Edward B. Zahn FFA Scholarship Trust at the Iola High School
c/o Richard W. Zahn
P.O. Box 388
Oldwick, NJ 08858
Application address: c/o David South, Principal, Iola High School, 300 E. Jackson Ave., Iola, KS 66749

Established in 1993 in KS.
Donor(s): Richard Zahn, Schering Plough Foundation.
Financial data (yr. ended 12/31/99): Assets, $41,830 (M); grants paid, $8,000; gifts received, $8,500; expenditures, $8,313; qualifying distributions, $7,974.
Limitations: Giving limited to residents of Iola, KS.
Application information: Application form required.
Trustee: Richard W. Zahn.
EIN: 486327729

61807
H & B Charitable Family Foundation
313 Sayre Dr.
Princeton, NJ 08540

Established in 1999 in NJ.
Donor(s): Harvey Friedman.
Financial data (yr. ended 12/31/00): Assets, $41,217 (M); grants paid, $7,000; expenditures, $10,529; qualifying distributions, $7,000.
Limitations: Applications not accepted.
Application information: Contributes only to pre-selected organizations.
Trustee: Harvey Friedman.
EIN: 223700673

61808
Anyone Can Fly Foundation, Inc.
127 Jones Rd.
Englewood, NJ 07631
CA tel.: (858) 534-4597
Contact: Grace Welty Mathews, Secy.

Established in 2000 in NJ.
Donor(s): Faith Ringgold.
Financial data (yr. ended 07/31/01): Assets, $39,630 (M); grants paid, $0; gifts received, $46,858; expenditures, $8,239; qualifying distributions, $0.
Officers: Faith Ringgold, Pres.; Michelle Wallace, V.P.; Grace Welty Matthews, Secy.; Marjorie Durden, Treas.
Directors: Lisa Farrington, Burdette Ringgold, Moira Roth.
EIN: 223762980

61809
Marian Burke Collins Foundation for Music, Education and the Arts, Inc.
c/o Marian Burke Collins
3 Byron Rd.
Short Hills, NJ 07078-1809

Established in 1997 in NJ.
Financial data (yr. ended 12/31/01): Assets, $35,216 (M); grants paid, $0; expenditures, $700; qualifying distributions, $0.
Officers and Trustees:* Marian Burke,* Pres. and Mgr.; Edmond Adrian Collins,* V.P.; Elizabeth Anne Collins,* Secy.; Adrian Anthony Collins,* Treas.
EIN: 223477852

61810
The Beitler Family Foundation, Inc.
c/o Lorraine Beitler
1225 River Rd., Ste. 4C
Edgewater, NJ 07020

Donor(s): Martin Beitler, Lorraine Beitler.
Financial data (yr. ended 12/31/99): Assets, $35,063 (M); grants paid, $0; gifts received, $148,885; expenditures, $118,993; qualifying distributions, $118,993; giving activities include $71,293 for programs.
Officers: Lorraine Beitler, Pres.; Martin Beitler, Secy.
EIN: 133917282

61811
Justice Lodge No. 285 F. & A. M., Educational Trust
420 N. Douglass Ave.
Margate City, NJ 08402-1929

Established in 1988 in NJ.
Donor(s): Justice Lodge No. 285 F. & A. M.
Financial data (yr. ended 12/31/01): Assets, $35,063 (M); grants paid, $35,063; gifts received, $4,326; expenditures, $35,870; qualifying distributions, $34,747.
Limitations: Giving primarily in NJ.
Application information: Application form required.
Officers and Trustees:* Norris S. Biron, Chair.; Bruce L. Peskoe, Vice-Chair.; Marvin N. Rimm,* Secy.; Marvin Davidson, Charles W. Kramer, Nathan Lecuyer, Kenneth Novakoff, Albert B. Packman, Michael Pressman, Douglas S. Stanger, David J. Woodland.
EIN: 222857778
Codes: GTI

61812
The Nutcracker Irene Fokine Ballet, Inc.
c/o John F. Chiodi
251 Rock Rd.
Glen Rock, NJ 07452 (201) 652-7653
Application address: 33 Chestnut St., Ridgewood, NJ 07450, tel.: (201) 652-9653
Contact: Irene Fokine, Pres.

Established in 1992 in NJ.
Financial data (yr. ended 12/31/99): Assets, $34,926 (M); grants paid, $0; expenditures, $57,124; qualifying distributions, $57,124; giving activities include $57,124 for programs.
Officer: Irene Fokine, Pres.
EIN: 222815816
Codes: TN

61813
The Avi Yosef Foundation, Inc.
140 Chadwick Rd.
Teaneck, NJ 07666 (201) 836-3613
Contact: Mark Karasick, Pres.

Established in 2000 in NJ.
Donor(s): Mark Karasick.
Financial data (yr. ended 12/31/01): Assets, $34,555 (M); grants paid, $62,725; expenditures, $66,427; qualifying distributions, $62,725.
Officer: Mark Karasick, Pres.
EIN: 223772451

61814
National Poetry Series, Inc.
100 W. Broad St.
Hopewell, NJ 08525-1919

Classified as a private operating foundation in 1985.
Financial data (yr. ended 10/31/99): Assets, $34,496 (M); grants paid, $5,000; gifts received, $155,103; expenditures, $119,402; qualifying distributions, $118,577.
Director: Daniel Halpern.
EIN: 132964957

61815
Bryce Curry Memorial Trust Fund
c/o NJ Savings League
411 North Ave. E.
Cranford, NJ 07016-2444

Established in 1996.
Financial data (yr. ended 02/28/02): Assets, $33,241 (M); grants paid, $0; expenditures, $32; qualifying distributions, $0.
Trustees: Walter Celuch, Joseph Kliminski, John P. Mulkerin, James R. Silkensen.
EIN: 226411777

61816
The Gershon Benjamin Foundation, Inc.
c/o Zelda Benjamin
P.O. Box 310
Scotch Plains, NJ 07076-0310

Financial data (yr. ended 12/31/01): Assets, $32,359 (M); grants paid, $0; expenditures, $7,259; qualifying distributions, $0.
Limitations: Applications not accepted.
Trustees: Zelda Benjamin, Joan H. Facey, Jean Henry.
EIN: 222672246

61817
Kiwanis Club of Cape May Foundation
P.O. Box 124
Cape May, NJ 08204

Classified as a private operating foundation in 2000 in NJ.
Financial data (yr. ended 12/31/01): Assets, $31,465 (M); grants paid, $4,216; gifts received, $7,100; expenditures, $4,216; qualifying distributions, $24,216.
Limitations: Giving primarily to residents of Cape May, NJ.
Officers: Paul Lundholm, Pres.; James R. Washington, Secy.; David Danaher, Treas.
EIN: 223734672

61818
Clive S. Cummis and Ann D. Cummis Family Foundation, Inc.
1 Riverfront Plz.
Newark, NJ 07102

Established in 1998 in NJ. Classified as a private operating foundation in 1999.
Financial data (yr. ended 12/31/00): Assets, $29,436 (M); grants paid, $250; gifts received, $25,000; expenditures, $488; qualifying distributions, $250.
Limitations: Applications not accepted.
Application information: Contributes only to pre-selected organizations.
Directors: Ann D. Cummis, Clive S. Cummis, Steven S. Radin.
EIN: 223589707

61819
H & F Fund, Inc.
313 Autumn Rd.
Lakewood, NJ 08701
Application address: 2122 Quentin Rd., Brooklyn, NY 11229, tel.: (718) 382-6731
Contact: Howard Sanders, Pres.

Financial data (yr. ended 12/31/99): Assets, $27,493 (M); grants paid, $29,271; gifts received, $29,725; expenditures, $29,970; qualifying distributions, $29,970.
Officer: Howard Sanders, Pres.
EIN: 113352901

61820
Andrew George De Grado Memorial Foundation, Inc.
P.O. Box 1064
Springfield, NJ 07081-3545

Established in 1999 in NJ.
Donor(s): Libby De Grado-Condo, Deborah Cariddi.
Financial data (yr. ended 12/31/00): Assets, $23,287 (M); grants paid, $0; gifts received, $10,035; expenditures, $17,860; qualifying distributions, $17,860; giving activities include $15,386 for programs.
Officers: Libby De Grado-Condo, Pres.; Leonard Condo, Secy.
Trustees: Deborah Cariddi, Gustave Ferri.
EIN: 223589122

61821
Joseph Pep Novotny Scholarship Fund, Inc.
31 Phalanx Rd.
Lincroft, NJ 07738

Established in 1999.
Financial data (yr. ended 12/31/00): Assets, $22,414 (M); grants paid, $3,000; expenditures, $3,720; qualifying distributions, $3,000.
Limitations: Giving limited to resident of Union City, NJ.
Application information: Application form required.
Trustees: Robert Fazio, Harry Novotny, Daniel Rizzi, Marty Seglio, Emerson Varsity Football Coach.
EIN: 223621378

61822
Manville Reformed Church Building and Maintenance Foundation
c/o James Kline
25 Chamberlain Way
Martinsville, NJ 08836-2259

Established in 1997 in NJ.
Donor(s): James Kline, Marian Kline.
Financial data (yr. ended 01/31/02): Assets, $21,738 (M); grants paid, $0; expenditures, $600; qualifying distributions, $0.
Trustees: James Kline, Marian Kline, William Kovacs, Steven Strickler.
EIN: 311545290

61823
Sunup Foundation, Inc.
c/o J.H. Cohn, LLP
997 Lenox Dr., Bldg. 3
Lawrenceville, NJ 08648

Established in 1999.
Donor(s): Edward C. Taylor, Virginia C. Taylor.
Financial data (yr. ended 12/31/01): Assets, $20,549 (M); grants paid, $1,200; expenditures, $2,677; qualifying distributions, $1,200.
Officers: Edward C. Taylor, Pres.; Virginia C. Taylor, Secy.-Treas.
Directors: Richard Spielman, Susan Spielman, Connie Taylor, Edward N. Taylor.
EIN: 223693832

61824
The Esther Felsen Foundation, Inc.
1530 Palisades Ave., Ste. 26H
Fort Lee, NJ 07024

Established in 1999 in NJ.
Donor(s): David Felson.
Financial data (yr. ended 12/31/99): Assets, $19,480 (M); grants paid, $10,918; gifts received,

61824—NEW JERSEY

$24,270; expenditures, $10,918; qualifying distributions, $10,918.
Limitations: Applications not accepted. Giving primarily in Washington, DC and New York, NY.
Application information: Contributes only to pre-selected organizations.
Trustees: Alan Felsen, David Felsen, Diane Felsen.
EIN: 223625786

61825
Dekbon Housing Development Corp.
439 Roosevelt Ave.
Northfield, NJ 08225

Established in 1999 in NJ.
Financial data (yr. ended 12/31/01): Assets, $19,427 (M); grants paid, $50; expenditures, $21,234; qualifying distributions, $12,118.
Officers: Otero Jones, Pres.; Vanessa Gerald, Secy.; Norman Edmead, Treas.
EIN: 223172593

61826
Noor Foundation, Inc.
847-A2 Pompton Ave.
Cedar Grove, NJ 07009 (973) 857-6667
Contact: Akram and Khalida Choudhry, Trustees

Established in 1993 in NJ.
Donor(s): Akram Choudhry, Khalida Choudhry.
Financial data (yr. ended 07/31/01): Assets, $18,723 (M); grants paid, $84,083; gifts received, $120,900; expenditures, $108,107; qualifying distributions, $108,107.
Limitations: Giving primarily in NJ and NY.
Trustees: Akram Choudhry, Khalida Choudhry.
EIN: 222908817
Codes: FD2

61827
The Irving Falk Foundation, Inc.
552 High Mountain Rd.
North Haledon, NJ 07508
Contact: Benjamin M.G. Stein, Tr.

Established in 1994 in NJ.
Donor(s): Florence Falk.
Financial data (yr. ended 12/31/99): Assets, $18,303 (M); grants paid, $0; expenditures, $44; qualifying distributions, $39.
Trustees: Florence Falk, David A. Jacobs, Benjamin M.G. Stein, Dominick T. Stingone.
EIN: 223340946

61828
L'Chayim Foundation, Inc.
25 Clifton Ave., Apt. 1814
Newark, NJ 07104-1822
Contact: Aaron Kirzner, Tr.

Donor(s): Aaron Kirzner.
Financial data (yr. ended 12/31/00): Assets, $17,768 (M); grants paid, $48,000; gifts received, $40,000; expenditures, $48,325; qualifying distributions, $48,000.
Trustees: Andrew Fradkin, Rita Kirner, Aaron Kirzner.
EIN: 223551010

61829
Jayant & Yogini Shroff Family Foundation
32 Crest Dr.
South Orange, NJ 07079

Established in 1999 in NJ.
Donor(s): Jayant Shroff.
Financial data (yr. ended 12/31/00): Assets, $16,719 (M); grants paid, $4,673; expenditures, $5,173; qualifying distributions, $4,673.
Limitations: Applications not accepted.
Application information: Contributes only to pre-selected organizations.

Trustees: Jayant Shroff, Yogini Shroff.
EIN: 223696649

61830
Early Childhood Communication Center
(also known as The Sengstack Foundation for Early Childhood)
P.O. Box 707
Princeton, NJ 08542

Established in 1991 in NJ.
Donor(s): David K. Sengstack.
Financial data (yr. ended 12/31/00): Assets, $12,322 (M); grants paid, $0; gifts received, $41,000; expenditures, $42,530; qualifying distributions, $0.
Officer: David K. Sengstack, Pres.
EIN: 226533476

61831
Point Owoods Historical Society
c/o James M. Bennett
38 Fairview Ave.
Summit, NJ 07901-1728

Established in 1996.
Financial data (yr. ended 12/31/00): Assets, $11,973 (M); grants paid, $0; gifts received, $281; expenditures, $489; qualifying distributions, $0.
Officers: R. Bruce Silver, Pres.; James J. Marshall, V.P.; Babs Sloan, Secy.; James M. Bennett, Treas.
Directors: Jennie Austin, Thomas Flagg, Nancy Hanaway, Madeline C. Johnson, William V. Johnson, John Montgomery, Alexander Podmaniczky, Julie Taussig, Jean Weir.
EIN: 133581619

61832
Gerard Peter Weinmann Memorial Scholarship Fund
c/o Robert Tarantolo
500 Monmouth Rd.
West Long Branch, NJ 07764-1227

Financial data (yr. ended 12/31/01): Assets, $11,021 (M); grants paid, $2,607; gifts received, $1,047; expenditures, $2,654; qualifying distributions, $2,654.
Limitations: Applications not accepted. Giving limited to West Long Branch, NJ.
Application information: Unsolicited requests for funds not accepted.
Trustees: Salvatore J. Busacca, Robert Tarantolo.
EIN: 237455814

61833
The Dottie Giesler Foundation, Inc.
636 Township Line Rd.
Belle Mead, NJ 08502-4214
Contact: Gerald T. Giesler, V.P.

Established as a private operating foundation in 1995.
Donor(s): Dottie Giesler, Gerry Giesler, Chubb and Son, Inc.
Financial data (yr. ended 12/31/99): Assets, $10,734 (M); grants paid, $1,750; gifts received, $4,196; expenditures, $2,394; qualifying distributions, $8,394; giving activities include $519 for programs.
Application information: Individuals must be nominated by P.G.A. or L.P.G.A. professional or golf coach. Application form required.
Officers: Dorothy A. Giesler, Pres.; Gerald T. Giesler, V.P. and Secy.; Donna Giesler, V.P.; Doug Giesler, V.P.; Peter Johnson, Treas.
EIN: 223336861

61834
The Cornerstone Foundation
270 Sylvan Ave., Ste. 200
Englewood Cliffs, NJ 07632
Contact: Eunie H. Sheen, Secy.

Established in 1999 in NJ.
Donor(s): Alpine Capital Management.
Financial data (yr. ended 12/31/99): Assets, $9,999 (M); grants paid, $9,195; gifts received, $20,000; expenditures, $10,320; qualifying distributions, $10,320.
Officers and Trustee:* Sung Chin Kim,* Pres. and Treas.; James C. Nugent, V.P.; Eunie H. Sheen, Secy.
EIN: 223640459

61835
The Gribbin Fund, Inc.
c/o Donald Reich
40 W. Ridgewood Ave.
Ridgewood, NJ 07450-3131

Classified as a private operating foundation in 1995.
Donor(s): Robal H. Johnson.
Financial data (yr. ended 12/31/01): Assets, $9,841 (M); grants paid, $10,000; gifts received, $19,276; expenditures, $10,608; qualifying distributions, $10,000.
Officers and Trustees:* Robal H. Johnson,* Pres.; Donald Reich, Secy. and C.F.O.; Lynn Johnson, John Raisley.
EIN: 223347371

61836
Di Goldene Keyt (The Golden Chain), Ltd.
P.O. Box 578
Roosevelt, NJ 08555-0578
Contact: Mark Zuckerman, Pres.

Established in 1995 in NY.
Donor(s): Rosalyn and Joseph Newman Foundation, Inc.
Financial data (yr. ended 06/30/00): Assets, $9,086 (M); grants paid, $3,160; gifts received, $16,810; expenditures, $15,011; qualifying distributions, $13,023; giving activities include $14,940 for programs.
Officers: Rosalyn Newman, Chair.; Mark Zuckerman, Pres.; Frank Stella, Jr., Secy.-Treas.
EIN: 133849152

61837
Morton H. Derchin Charitable Foundation
c/o Michael W. Derchin
P.O. Box 200
Fair Haven, NJ 07704

Established in 1999 in PA.
Financial data (yr. ended 12/31/00): Assets, $7,059 (M); grants paid, $859; expenditures, $859; qualifying distributions, $859.
Limitations: Applications not accepted.
Application information: Contributes only to pre-selected organizations.
Trustee: Michael W. Derchin.
EIN: 256610594

61838
Maurice and Helen Shalam Charitable Foundation, Inc.
c/o Freeze
51 Saw Mill Pond Rd.
Edison, NJ 08817-6025

Established in 1998 in NJ.
Donor(s): Maurice Shalam.
Financial data (yr. ended 12/31/00): Assets, $6,544 (M); grants paid, $2,380; gifts received,

$3; expenditures, $2,383; qualifying distributions, $2,380.
Limitations: Applications not accepted.
Application information: Contributes only to pre-selected organizations.
Trustees: Helen Shalam, Maurice Shalam, Julia Sherr.
EIN: 223552419

61839
The Hopetree Foundation
127 Main St.
Chatham, NJ 07928 (973) 635-6300
Contact: Andrew E. Anselmi, Tr.

Established in 2000 in NJ.
Financial data (yr. ended 12/31/01): Assets, $6,072 (M); grants paid, $500; gifts received, $2,230; expenditures, $1,711; qualifying distributions, $1,711.
Limitations: Giving primarily in NJ.
Trustees: Andrew E. Anselmi, Joseph R. Bezzone, Jr.
EIN: 223733893

61840
Zichron Rivkah Charitable Foundation
c/o Elliot Gewitz
228 Aycrigg Ave.
Passaic, NJ 07055-4704

Established in 1998 in NJ.
Financial data (yr. ended 12/31/01): Assets, $6,039 (M); grants paid, $19,593; gifts received, $4,500; expenditures, $19,849; qualifying distributions, $19,590.
Limitations: Applications not accepted.
Application information: Contributes only to pre-selected organizations.
Officers and Trustee: Elliot Gewirtz,* Pres.; Anne R. Gewirtz, V.P. and Secy.-Treas.
EIN: 223597808

61841
Old Orchard Trust
P.O. Box 523
Mendham, NJ 07945-0523
Application address: 35 Old Orchard Rd., Morristown, NJ 07960
Contact: Thomas Callahan, Pres.

Established in 2001 in NJ.
Donor(s): Thomas Callahan, Eileen Callahan.
Financial data (yr. ended 12/31/01): Assets, $5,170 (M); grants paid, $1,365; gifts received, $6,542; expenditures, $1,365; qualifying distributions, $1,365.
Officers: Thomas Callahan, Pres.; Eileen Callahan, V.P.; Eileen Festa, Mgr.; Jean Jackson, Mgr.
EIN: 223772709

61842
Sarnak Family Foundation, Inc.
P.O. Box 524
Tenafly, NJ 07670

Established in 2000 in NJ.
Donor(s): Neil Sarnak.
Financial data (yr. ended 12/31/00): Assets, $5,115 (M); grants paid, $0; gifts received, $5,115; expenditures, $0; qualifying distributions, $0.
Officers: Sheryl Sarnak, Pres.; Peter Sarnak, V.P.; Mark Sarnak, Secy.
EIN: 223772573

61843
Helen and Bob Levine Family Foundation, Inc
c/o Robert B. Levine
509 Northumberland Rd.
Teaneck, NJ 07666-1922

Established in 2001 in NJ.
Donor(s): Robert B. Levine, Helen B. Levine.
Financial data (yr. ended 12/31/01): Assets, $5,000 (M); grants paid, $0; gifts received, $5,000; expenditures, $0; qualifying distributions, $0.
Limitations: Applications not accepted.
Application information: Contributes only to pre-selected organizations.
Trustees: Helen B. Levine, Robert B. Levine.
EIN: 223803911

61844
Mohuchy Philanthropic Foundation, Inc.
184 Vreeland Ave.
Nutley, NJ 07110-1621

Established in 1999 in NJ.
Financial data (yr. ended 12/31/01): Assets, $3,783 (M); grants paid, $5,428; gifts received, $5,331; expenditures, $5,792; qualifying distributions, $5,428.
Trustee: Walter Mohuchy.
EIN: 223642356

61845
The Richard Kevin Rockoff Foundation
56 Horizon Terr.
Hillsdale, NJ 07642
Contact: Norman Rockoff, Tr.

Established in 1998 in NJ.
Donor(s): Norman Rockoff.
Financial data (yr. ended 12/31/01): Assets, $3,250 (M); grants paid, $0; gifts received, $9,100; expenditures, $1,165; qualifying distributions, $0.
Trustees: Janis Rockoff, Nancy Rockoff, Norman Rockoff, Thomas Rockoff.
EIN: 137113019

61846
Max and Lillian Rappaport Foundation
c/o Sondra Rappaport
110 Charlotte Pl.
Englewood Cliffs, NJ 07632

Established in 1997.
Financial data (yr. ended 11/30/99): Assets, $3,117 (M); grants paid, $650; gifts received, $1,050; expenditures, $783; qualifying distributions, $783.
Directors: Milton Bliss, Sondra Rappaport.
EIN: 223410986

61847
Laura and Alan Wechsler Charitable Foundation
1200 Haddonfield Rd.
Cherry Hill, NJ 08002-2750
Contact: Alan Wechsler, Mgr.

Established in 1987 in NJ.
Donor(s): Alan Wechsler, Laura Wechsler.
Financial data (yr. ended 12/31/01): Assets, $2,970 (M); grants paid, $19,830; gifts received, $181; expenditures, $20,634; qualifying distributions, $20,609.
Limitations: Giving primarily in NJ and PA.
Officers: Alan Wechsler, Mgr.; Laura Wechsler, Mgr.
EIN: 222664317

61848
Small Dog Rescue, Inc.
(Formerly Small Animal Rescue, Inc.)
943 Canal Rd.
Princeton, NJ 08540

Established in 1998.
Donor(s): Emmett Wilson, Jr.
Financial data (yr. ended 12/31/00): Assets, $2,790 (M); grants paid, $0; gifts received, $127,785; expenditures, $125,457; qualifying distributions, $125,457; giving activities include $125,890 for programs.
Trustees: Carolyn Kuhlman, Donna Nardini, Emmett Wilson, Jr.
EIN: 223572645

61849
BLSJ Charitable Foundation
114 Haddontowne Ct.
Cherry Hill, NJ 08034-3699

Established in 2000 in NJ.
Financial data (yr. ended 12/31/00): Assets, $2,516 (M); grants paid, $3,000; gifts received, $10,390; expenditures, $7,876; qualifying distributions, $7,876.
Directors: Mary Anderson, Pete Haran, Sal Messina, Jerri Silvi, John Tuscano, Perri Wachter, David Waronker.
EIN: 223752549

61850
The Dialysis Foundation, Inc.
1925 Hwy. 35
Wall, NJ 07719

Established in 1999 in NJ.
Donor(s): Sushil K. Mehandru, M.D.
Financial data (yr. ended 12/31/99): Assets, $2,129 (M); grants paid, $8,662; gifts received, $12,000; expenditures, $9,888; qualifying distributions, $8,662.
Limitations: Applications not accepted.
Application information: Contributes only to pre-selected organizations.
Officer: Sushil K. Mehandru, M.D., Pres.
Trustees: Ruth Crease, Urmila Mehandru.
EIN: 223626032

61851
C. Mildred Petaccio Memorial Fund Charitable Trust
95 Churchill Dr.
Clifton, NJ 07013-3830
Contact: Robin Petaccio Buchan, Tr.

Financial data (yr. ended 12/31/00): Assets, $1,997 (M); grants paid, $500; expenditures, $585; qualifying distributions, $500.
Limitations: Giving limited to residents of NJ.
Trustees: Robin Petaccio Buchan, Wayne Buchan.
EIN: 222548494

61852
Glen Rock High School Unified Scholarship Council, Inc.
c/o Guidance Counselor, Glen Rock High School
400 Hamilton Ave.
Glen Rock, NJ 07452-2399 (201) 445-7700

Financial data (yr. ended 06/30/01): Assets, $1,766 (M); grants paid, $15,400; gifts received, $50; expenditures, $17,476; qualifying distributions, $17,476.
Limitations: Giving limited to Glen Rock, NJ.
Officers: Jim Quinlan, Pres.; Harold D. Corney, Jr., V.P.; Peggy Quinlan, Secy.; A.K. Meier, Treas.
EIN: 226053789
Codes: GTI

61853
Tenafly Eruv Association, Inc.
c/o Cindy Osen
136 Engle St.
Tenafly, NJ 07670-2702

Established in 1999 in NJ.
Financial data (yr. ended 12/31/00): Assets, $1,633 (M); grants paid, $0; gifts received, $14,808; expenditures, $19,590; qualifying distributions, $0.
Directors: Chaim Book, Erez Gotlieb, Cindy T. Osen.
EIN: 223671167

61854
L. & T. Salameno Foundation
200 E. Allendale Ave.
Allendale, NJ 07401

Established in 1999 in NJ.
Donor(s): Lawrence Salameno.
Financial data (yr. ended 12/31/01): Assets, $1,559 (M); grants paid, $90,781; gifts received, $91,745; expenditures, $91,781; qualifying distributions, $91,781.
Limitations: Applications not accepted. Giving primarily in Saddle River, NJ and Stonehill, VT.
Application information: Contributes only to pre-selected organizations.
Directors: Lawrence Salameno, Theresa Salameno.
EIN: 223641157
Codes: FD2

61855
Saraiya Foundation
c/o Upendra Saraiya
31 Jenni Ln.
Norwood, NJ 07648-1828

Established in 1998.
Financial data (yr. ended 08/31/00): Assets, $1,535 (M); grants paid, $804; gifts received, $1,000; expenditures, $804; qualifying distributions, $804.
Limitations: Giving limited to NJ.
Trustee: Upendra Saraiya.
EIN: 223189833

61856
Hoyt Doll Museum
283 Beechwood Ave.
Middlesex, NJ 08846

Established in 2000 in NJ.
Financial data (yr. ended 12/31/00): Assets, $1,521 (M); grants paid, $0; gifts received, $2,000; expenditures, $500; qualifying distributions, $0.
Officers and Trustees:* Guy Hoyt,* Pres.; G. Paul Hoyt,* V.P.; Carol Hoyt,* Secy.; Jay A. Mevorah,* Treas.; Ed Johnson, John True, John Verb.
EIN: 223690520

61857
Elizabeth Meier & Ronny Meier Foundation, Inc.
1343 Trafalgar St.
Teaneck, NJ 07666

Established in 1995 in NJ.
Donor(s): Ronny Meier.
Financial data (yr. ended 12/31/00): Assets, $1,484 (M); grants paid, $24,100; gifts received, $25,000; expenditures, $24,140; qualifying distributions, $24,140.
Limitations: Applications not accepted.
Application information: Contributes only to pre-selected organizations.
Trustees: Efrat Meier, Elizabeth Meier, Ronny Meier.
EIN: 223410629

61858
The Lend-A-Hand Society, Inc.
P.O. Box 2139
Fort Lee, NJ 07024

Donor(s): Gary J. Gabriel.
Financial data (yr. ended 08/31/00): Assets, $1,320 (M); grants paid, $6,990; gifts received, $62,300; expenditures, $68,443; qualifying distributions, $61,453.
Directors: Clayelle Dalfenas, Gary J. Gabriel, Gloria Gallinlame.
EIN: 223327691

61859
Narvaez Family Foundation
21 Theyken Pl.
Ridgewood, NJ 07450
Contact: Guillermo Narvaez and Norminta Narvaez

Established in 2001 in NJ.
Financial data (yr. ended 12/31/01): Assets, $1,307 (M); grants paid, $2,043; gifts received, $3,500; expenditures, $2,193; qualifying distributions, $0.
Trustees: Guillermo Narvaez, Normita Narvaez.
EIN: 223773655

61860
B. & M. Friedlander Charitable Foundation, Inc.
25 Forest Dr.
Short Hills, NJ 07078

Established in 2001 in NJ.
Donor(s): B. Friedlander.
Financial data (yr. ended 12/31/01): Assets, $977 (M); grants paid, $4,025; gifts received, $5,000; expenditures, $4,025; qualifying distributions, $4,025.
Limitations: Applications not accepted.
Application information: Contributes only to pre-selected organizations.
Trustees: B. Friedlander, M. Friedlander, Jerome M. Leifer.
EIN: 223780129

61861
Joseph E. Enright Foundation
120 Summit Ave.
Summit, NJ 07901

Established in 1999 in NJ.
Financial data (yr. ended 12/31/01): Assets, $909 (M); grants paid, $2,913; gifts received, $22,635; expenditures, $64,193; qualifying distributions, $2,913; giving activities include $36,674 for programs.
Officers: Mark Zimmerman, M.D., Chair.; Marianne Jacobson, Secy.; Michael J. O'Hea, Treas.
Trustees: Andrew R. Mintz, Richard Nelson, M.D.
EIN: 223680835

61862
WorldWorks Foundation, Inc.
9 Easy St.
P.O. Box 149
Bound Brook, NJ 08805-0149
Contact: Marguerite Chandler, Pres.

Established in 1986 in NJ.
Donor(s): Richmond B. Shreve, Marguerite Chandler.
Financial data (yr. ended 12/31/99): Assets, $757 (M); grants paid, $21,240; gifts received, $25,200; expenditures, $24,680; qualifying distributions, $21,240.
Officers and Trustees:* Marguerite Chandler,* Pres.; Richmond B. Shreve, V.P. and Treas.; Edward Seliga,* Secy.
EIN: 222790422

61863
The Aviv Family Foundation
1417 Cedar Row
Lakewood, NJ 08701
Contact: Jace Aviv, Pres.

Established in 1995 in NJ.
Financial data (yr. ended 12/31/99): Assets, $430 (M); grants paid, $17,060; gifts received, $17,310; expenditures, $17,651; qualifying distributions, $17,651.
Officer and Trustees:* Jace Aviv,* Pres.; David Anafi, Kenneth Breslauer.
EIN: 223323810

61864
The Haremza Foundation, Inc.
122 W. 21st St.
Bayonne, NJ 07002

Established in 1999 in NJ.
Financial data (yr. ended 12/31/00): Assets, $409 (M); grants paid, $0; gifts received, $250; expenditures, $14,099; qualifying distributions, $0.
Officers: Edward Haremza, Pres.; Wayne Schultz, V.P.; Christine Haremza, Secy.-Treas.
EIN: 223590796

61865
Thomas J. DeFelice, Sr. Memorial Scholarship Fund, Inc.
641 Shrewsbury Ave.
Shrewsbury, NJ 07702

Established as a private operating foundation in 1995 in NJ.
Financial data (yr. ended 12/31/01): Assets, $353 (M); grants paid, $5,000; gifts received, $5,000; expenditures, $5,353; qualifying distributions, $5,000.
Trustees: Dolores DeFelice, Paul DeFelice, Thomas J. DeFelice, Jr.
EIN: 223337823

61866
My Sister's Keeper Foundation, Inc.
109 Gregory Ave.
West Orange, NJ 07052

Financial data (yr. ended 12/31/99): Assets, $348 (M); grants paid, $4,911; gifts received, $5,919; expenditures, $5,684; qualifying distributions, $4,911; giving activities include $2,421 for programs.
Trustees: Jacqueline Cusack, Johnetta Dix Cusack, Juanita Faulkner.
EIN: 223241680

61867
Richard G. Nowalk Scholarship Memorial Fund
2650 Rte. 130 N.
Cranbury, NJ 08512

Established in 2000 in NJ.
Financial data (yr. ended 12/31/00): Assets, $319 (M); grants paid, $25,000; gifts received, $24,685; expenditures, $25,000; qualifying distributions, $25,000.
Limitations: Giving primarily in Bethlehem, PA.
Directors: Tricia Billy, Elizabeth Nowalk.
EIN: 223722324

61868
The Pinnacle Foundation, Inc.
c/o Pinnacle Communities, Ltd.
225 Millburn Ave.
Millburn, NJ 07041

Established in 2000 in NJ. Classified as a company-sponsored operating foundation.
Donor(s): Pinnacle Communities, Ltd., Brian M. Stollar.
Financial data (yr. ended 12/31/00): Assets, $136 (M); grants paid, $20,196; gifts received, $23,400; expenditures, $20,974; qualifying distributions, $20,196.
Limitations: Giving primarily in NJ.
Officers: Michael Cantor, Pres.; Howard Irwin, Treas.
EIN: 223377688

61869
The Vanessa Gonzalez Dream 27 Hope for the Children Foundation, Inc.
22 Lake Wallkill Rd.
Sussex, NJ 07461 (973) 875-1012
Contact: Esperanza Gonzalez, Pres.

Established in 2000 in NJ.
Donor(s): Esperanza Gonzalez.
Financial data (yr. ended 12/31/00): Assets, $107 (M); grants paid, $25,800; gifts received, $30,974; expenditures, $30,867; qualifying distributions, $30,867.
Officer and Trustee:* Esperanza Gonzalez,* Pres.
EIN: 223739919

61870
Meadowlands Human Resource Development Corp.
516 Valley Brook Ave.
Lyndhurst, NJ 07071

Established around 1990.
Financial data (yr. ended 06/30/01): Assets, $100 (M); grants paid, $0; expenditures, $0; qualifying distributions, $0.
Officers: Richard J. DeLuca, Pres.; David Cathcart, 1st V.P.; Frederick Curro, 2nd V.P.; Philip Bogle, Secy.; William O'Hea, Treas.; Peter Scorbo, Exec. Dir.
Trustees: Ralph Cerrito, Leonard de Palma, Linda C. Fenyar, Catherine Mills, Michael G. Prestia, and 8 additional trustees.
EIN: 222689975

NEW MEXICO

61871
The Spencer Theatre for the Performing Arts, Inc.
P.O. Box 140
Alto, NM 88312

Established in 1992 in NM.
Donor(s): Jacqueline E. Spencer, The Hugh Bancroft, Jr. Foundation.
Financial data (yr. ended 12/31/00): Assets, $26,821,844 (M); grants paid, $0; gifts received, $2,587,731; expenditures, $2,935,398; qualifying distributions, $1,505,647; giving activities include $1,473,019 for programs.
Officers: Jacqueline E. Spencer, Pres.; Lloyd Davis, V.P.; Jane E. McGuire, Secy.; Tom Battin, Treas.; Charles Centilli, Exec. Dir.
Trustees: Jackie Corbin, Ann Dunlap, Terry Dunlap, Dorothy Faye Holt, Troy Mason, Robert Pace.
EIN: 850403693

61872
The Georgia O'Keeffe Foundation
P.O. Box 40
Abiquiu, NM 87510-0040 (505) 685-4539
FAX: (505) 685-4428

Established in 1989 in NM.
Donor(s): Georgia O'Keeffe.‡
Financial data (yr. ended 12/31/01): Assets, $15,474,647 (M); grants paid, $10,000; gifts received, $75; expenditures, $745,555; qualifying distributions, $622,527; giving activities include $112,027 for programs.
Limitations: Applications not accepted. Giving on a national and international basis.
Application information: Contributes only to pre-selected organizations. Unsolicited requests for funds not considered.
Officers: Elizabeth Glassman, Pres.; Agapita Judy Lopez, Secy.-Treas.
Directors: Vincent Cazzozza, Juan Hamilton, Bill Katz, Raymond R. Krueger, June O'Keeffe Sebring.
EIN: 850375930

61873
The Helene Wurlitzer Foundation of New Mexico
P.O. Box 1891
Taos, NM 87571 (505) 758-2413
FAX: (505) 758-2559; E-mail: hwf@taosnet.com
Contact: Michael A. Knight, Exec. Dir.

Incorporated in 1956 in NM.
Donor(s): Mrs. Howard E. Wurlitzer.‡
Financial data (yr. ended 03/31/01): Assets, $9,800,641 (M); grants paid, $39,265; gifts received, $2,640; expenditures, $235,254; qualifying distributions, $131,896; giving activities include $131,581 for programs.
Limitations: Giving on a national and international basis.
Application information: Application form required.
Officers and Trustees:* Tahlia Rainbolt,* Pres.; Michael A. Knight,* Exec. Dir.; Mary Alexander, William D. Ebie, Harold Hahn, Tito Naranjo, Rena Rosequist, Howard Sherman.
EIN: 850128634
Codes: GTI

61874
Tijeras Foundation
P.O. Box 1397
Cedar Crest, NM 87008

Established in 1998 in NM and TX.
Donor(s): Kenneth E. Johns, Cynthia Johns.
Financial data (yr. ended 09/30/00): Assets, $9,056,833 (M); grants paid, $0; gifts received, $10,100; expenditures, $473,696; qualifying distributions, $379,541; giving activities include $379,541 for programs.
Publications: Newsletter, informational brochure.
Officers and Directors:* Kenneth E. Jones, Chair. and V.P.; Virgil S. Dugan,* Pres.; Cynthia Johns,* V.P.; Don Miller, Secy.-Treas.; Jeffrey Johns, Julie Johns-Taylor, George Sanchez.
EIN: 850456831

61875
Aquaris Foundation
410 Graham Ave.
Santa Fe, NM 87501
Contact: Jackie L. Barnes, Dir.

Established in 1998.
Financial data (yr. ended 12/31/01): Assets, $7,192,567 (M); grants paid, $44,850; gifts received, $2,060,000; expenditures, $111,326; qualifying distributions, $44,850.
Limitations: Giving on a national basis.
Director: Jackie L. Barnes.
EIN: 746464347

61876
Santa Fe Art Foundation
P.O. Box 2437
Santa Fe, NM 87504
Contact: Lisa Bronowicz, Exec. Dir.

Classified as a private operating foundation in 1982.
Donor(s): Gerald P. Peters, Kathleen K. Peters.
Financial data (yr. ended 11/30/99): Assets, $5,201,619 (M); grants paid, $22,350; gifts received, $102,850; expenditures, $27,724; qualifying distributions, $26,919.
Limitations: Giving primarily in Santa Fe, NM.
Officers: Robert Worcester, Pres.; Donald Gonzales, Secy.; Bradley M. Odegard, Treas.; Lisa Bronowicz, Exec. Dir.
EIN: 850300616

61877
Bolack Museum Foundation
3901 Bloomfield Hwy.
Farmington, NM 87401

Classified as a company-sponsored operating foundation in 2001 in NM.
Donor(s): Bolack Minerals Company.
Financial data (yr. ended 02/28/01): Assets, $4,961,657 (M); grants paid, $0; gifts received, $5,136,135; expenditures, $174,478; qualifying distributions, $176,260.
Officers and Directors:* Duane T. Bolack,* Pres. and Treas.; Terry E. Bolack,* V.P. and Secy.; James C. Henderson.
EIN: 850456388

61878
The Gihon Foundation
c/o Marsha Roberts
Rte. 1, Box 110-F
Santa Fe, NM 87501 (505) 455-3848

Classified as a private operating foundation in 1982.
Donor(s): Bette C. Graham.‡
Financial data (yr. ended 12/31/00): Assets, $3,509,611 (M); grants paid, $0; expenditures, $409,725; qualifying distributions, $334,790; giving activities include $339,535 for programs.
Limitations: Giving primarily in NM.
Application information: Application form not required.
Officers and Directors:* Patricia Hill,* V.P.; Victoria Kennedy, Secy.; Michael Nesmith,* Treas.; Mary Ann Henneberger, Jessica Nesmith.
EIN: 751612234

61879
Code of the West Foundation
37 Rancho Allegre
Santa Fe, NM 87508

Donor(s): R. Michael Kammerer.
Financial data (yr. ended 12/31/00): Assets, $3,088,817 (M); grants paid, $322,124; gifts received, $760,622; expenditures, $629,627; qualifying distributions, $576,239.
Limitations: Applications not accepted.
Application information: Contributes only to pre-selected organizations.
Officer: Joann Lynn Balzer, Exec. Dir.
EIN: 850468005
Codes: FD

61880
Van Vechten-Lineberry Taos Art Museum
P.O. Box 1948
Taos, NM 87571

Established in 1992 in NM.
Donor(s): Edwin C. Lineberry.
Financial data (yr. ended 12/31/00): Assets, $3,049,735 (M); grants paid, $200; gifts received, $271,732; expenditures, $140,605; qualifying distributions, $140,569.
Limitations: Applications not accepted.
Application information: Contributes only to pre-selected organizations.
Officers and Trustee:* Reed Weimer,* Pres.; Erion Simpson,* Secy.; Terry Pennington,* Treas.; Nat Troy.
Directors: Roy Coffee, Jr., Sandra Hulse, Robert E. McKee III, Dean A. Porter.
EIN: 850400684

61881
Paul McCutchen Foundation
P.O. Box 1955
Roswell, NM 88202-1955

Established in 1963 in NM.
Donor(s): Paul McCutchen.‡
Financial data (yr. ended 12/31/00): Assets, $2,936,388 (M); grants paid, $94,000; expenditures, $157,417; qualifying distributions, $92,546.
Limitations: Applications not accepted. Giving primarily in NM.
Application information: Contributes only to pre-selected organizations.
Officers and Directors:* David M. Parsons,* Pres.; Brian W. Copple,* V.P. and Secy.; Bruce D. Ritter,* V.P. and Treas.
EIN: 736104369
Codes: FD2

61882
Cibola Foundation, Inc.
P.O. Box 669
Grants, NM 87020

Classified as a private operating foundation in 1992.
Financial data (yr. ended 06/30/02): Assets, $1,120,775 (M); grants paid, $0; expenditures, $8,705; qualifying distributions, $0.
Officers and Trustees:* Charles K. Gunderson,* Pres.; Antonio C. Esparza,* V.P.; W. Ken Martinez,* Secy.-Treas.; Ken Pauling, G.D. Ramsey.
EIN: 850354399

61883
Ochel Tree Foundation, Inc.
P.O. Box 159
Gila, NM 88038-0159

Classified as a private operating foundation in 1997 in NM.
Financial data (yr. ended 12/31/99): Assets, $979,325 (M); grants paid, $0; expenditures, $62,474; qualifying distributions, $60,654; giving activities include $20,880 for programs.
Officers: Bonnie Ocheltree, Pres.; Arthur Ocheltree, V.P.; Alex Ocheltree, Secy.-Treas.
Director: Robin Ocheltree.
EIN: 850324142

61884
Pink Church Art Center, Inc.
1516 Pacheco St.
Santa Fe, NM 87505-3912

Financial data (yr. ended 12/31/99): Assets, $978,852 (M); grants paid, $0; expenditures, $49,174; qualifying distributions, $0.

Limitations: Applications not accepted.
Application information: Contributes only to pre-selected organizations.
Officers and Directors:* Eugene V. Thaw, Pres.; Clare E. Thaw,* V.P.; Sherry Thompson,* V.P.
EIN: 850454221

61885
The Allan Houser Foundation
P.O. Box 5217
Santa Fe, NM 87502

Established in 1998 in NM.
Donor(s): Anna M. Houser.
Financial data (yr. ended 12/31/99): Assets, $797,861 (M); grants paid, $0; gifts received, $477,668; expenditures, $95,440; qualifying distributions, $106,449; giving activities include $95,159 for programs.
Officers: Anna M. Houser, Pres. and Treas.; Donald A. Gonzales, V.P.; Robert Worcester, Secy.; Bob Haozous, Exec. Dir.
EIN: 850449009

61886
Project Crossroads
96 Barberia Rd.
Santa Fe, NM 87505

Established in 1985 in NM.
Donor(s): Elise Turner, Caudel Rymer Foundation.
Financial data (yr. ended 06/30/00): Assets, $561,224 (M); grants paid, $0; gifts received, $44,500; expenditures, $187,723; qualifying distributions, $182,637; giving activities include $11,684 for programs.
Officers and Directors:* Elise Turner,* Pres. and Treas.; Donell D. Moor,* V.P.; Jane Bates,* Secy.; Peter D. Dyke,* Secy.; Joe Baca, Griffin N. Dodge, Holly Jones, Lucy Moore, Brad Rymer.
EIN: 850339963

61887
Bethlehem Foundation of New Mexico
5000 Ladera Ct., N.E.
Albuquerque, NM 87111

Established in 1988 in NM.
Donor(s): Steve Benoit, Jolene Beniot.
Financial data (yr. ended 11/30/00): Assets, $403,743 (M); grants paid, $22,000; expenditures, $22,111; qualifying distributions, $22,111.
Limitations: Applications not accepted. Giving primarily in Albuquerque, NM.
Application information: Contributes only to pre-selected organizations.
Officers and Trustees:* Steve Benoit,* Pres. and Treas.; Jolene Benoit,* V.P. and Secy.; Alexiss Benoit, Jennifer Benoit, Kristen Benoit, Dennis R. James.
EIN: 850370521

61888
Sherman Family Charitable Foundation
(also known as Luna County Charitable Foundation)
P.O. Box 850
Deming, NM 88031-0850 (505) 546-8846
Contact: Frederick H. Sherman, Pres.

Established in 1990 in NM.
Donor(s): Frederick H. Sherman.
Financial data (yr. ended 12/31/00): Assets, $292,785 (M); grants paid, $0; expenditures, $674; qualifying distributions, $674.
Officer: Frederick H. Sherman, Pres.
Directors: Linda Brown, Emanuel Davis, Diane Donaldson.
EIN: 856083870

61889
OLBAR Foundation, Inc.
841 Vista Canada Ln.
Santa Fe, NM 87501-8714

Classified as a private operating foundation in 1983.
Donor(s): Edward C. Barth.
Financial data (yr. ended 11/30/00): Assets, $272,237 (M); grants paid, $0; expenditures, $21,916; qualifying distributions, $21,365; giving activities include $21,600 for programs.
Officers and Directors:* Alan R. Weston,* Pres.; Edward C. Barth,* Secy.-Treas.
EIN: 953679542

61890
Technology Ventures Corporation
c/o Randy Wilson
1155 University Blvd. S.E.
Albuquerque, NM 87106-4320
Contact: Sherman McCorkle, C.E.O.

Classified as a Company-sponsored operating foundation in 1996.
Donor(s): Technology Ventures Corporation, Lockheed Martin Corp.
Financial data (yr. ended 12/31/00): Assets, $245,621 (M); grants paid, $25,000; gifts received, $1,755,904; expenditures, $1,889,674; qualifying distributions, $1,695,433; giving activities include $5,789,674 for programs.
Limitations: Giving primarily in Albuquerque, NM.
Officers and Directors:* William Haight, Chair.; Sherman McCorkle,* C.E.O. and Pres.; Dana L. Bennett, Secy.; Janet McGregor,* Treas.; Henry Debnam, J. Leonard Martinez, Neal J. Murray, A. Romig, Dale H. Von Haase.
EIN: 521844455

61891
Helix Foundation
6820 Raasaf Cir.
Las Cruces, NM 88005

Classified as a private operating foundation in 1982.
Donor(s): Charles Andrews, Ellen Andrews.
Financial data (yr. ended 04/30/01): Assets, $177,848 (M); grants paid, $8,424; expenditures, $22,004; qualifying distributions, $12,590; giving activities include $4,200 for programs.
Limitations: Applications not accepted. Giving primarily in Las Cruces, NM.
Application information: Contributes only to pre-selected organizations.
Directors: Charles Andrews, Karen Andrews.
EIN: 850304740

61892
Fab-Steel Products Foundation, Inc.
4600 Mabry Dr.
Clovis, NM 88101 (505) 763-4414
Contact: Nannette B. Winton, Secy.-Treas.

Established in 1986 in NM as a company-sponsored operating foundation.
Donor(s): Fab-Steel Products Co., Inc.
Financial data (yr. ended 12/31/00): Assets, $161,666 (M); grants paid, $11,200; gifts received, $9,634; expenditures, $11,220; qualifying distributions, $11,200.
Limitations: Giving primarily in Albuquerque and Clovis, NM.
Officers and Directors:* Ted Van Soelen,* Pres.; Nannette B. Winton,* Secy.-Treas.; M. Virginia Glenn.
EIN: 850339249
Codes: CD

61893
Colket Family Foundation
1523 Eagle Ridge N.E.
Albuquerque, NM 87122-1156
Contact: Charles H. Colket, Pres.

Established in 1999 in NM.
Donor(s): Charles H. Colket, Patricia A. Colket.
Financial data (yr. ended 12/31/01): Assets, $124,546 (M); grants paid, $20,945; gifts received, $60,000; expenditures, $23,305; qualifying distributions, $23,190.
Limitations: Giving on a national basis.
Officers: Charles H. Colket, Pres.; Lisa C. Schrimsher, V.P.; Lauri C. Youngblood, V.P.; Patricia A. Colket, Secy.; Leslie C. Jackson,* Treas.
EIN: 850457199

61894
Mary Tresco Foundation for the Aged, Inc.
c/o Community First National Bank, Trust Dept.
P.O. Box 457
Las Cruces, NM 88004-0457

Financial data (yr. ended 12/31/00): Assets, $93,553 (M); grants paid, $5,543; expenditures, $6,542; qualifying distributions, $5,530.
Limitations: Giving limited to NM.
Directors: Kenneth James, C. Alvin Rohne, Jack O. Scott.
Trustee: Community First National Bank.
EIN: 850241940

61895
Clovis Community College Foundation, Inc.
417 Schepps Blvd.
Clovis, NM 88101 (505) 769-4994
Contact: Tom Drake, Mgr.

Donor(s): Mable Hawkins, Bobby Newman.
Financial data (yr. ended 06/30/00): Assets, $67,775 (M); grants paid, $32,817; gifts received, $78,445; expenditures, $32,817; qualifying distributions, $14,817.
Officers and Directors:* Jeff Jacobs,* Pres.; Connie Landry,* Secy.-Treas.; Tom Drake, Mgr.; Lynn Blair, Don Bonner, Clay Bracken, Jim Hart, George Krattiger, Jerry Lott, and 13 additional directors.
EIN: 742849118

61896
Paul Leland Blankenship Memorial Foundation
P.O. Box 1463
Cedar Crest, NM 87008-1463
Application address: Sandia High School, 7001 Candelavia, N.E., Albuquerque, NM 87110, tel.: (505) 294-1511, ext. 225
Contact: Elke Zinnert

Established in 1997.
Donor(s): Ralph Blankenship, Sharon Blankenship.
Financial data (yr. ended 12/31/00): Assets, $50,613 (M); grants paid, $2,500; gifts received, $6,230; expenditures, $2,634; qualifying distributions, $2,634.
Application information: Application form not required.
Trustee: George Kennedy.
EIN: 850403776

61897
Charles A. Winans Memorial Trust
c/o Carlsbad National Bank
P.O. Box 1359
Carlsbad, NM 88220
Application address: c/o Beaumont High School, Student Counseling Off., 1519 N. Cherry, Beaumont, CA 92223

Classified as a private operating foundation in NM.
Financial data (yr. ended 12/31/01): Assets, $46,815 (M); grants paid, $0; expenditures, $1,114; qualifying distributions, $0.
Limitations: Giving limited to Beaumont, CA.
Application information: Application form required.
Trustee: Carlsbad National Bank.
EIN: 836011160
Codes: GTI

61898
New Mexico Foundation for Human Rights and Achievement
(Formerly Manzano Foundation for International Accomplishment)
12324 Pine Ridge, N.E.
Albuquerque, NM 87112
Application address: P.O. Box 248, Montezuma, NM 87731, tel.: (505) 454-4255
Contact: Theodore Reincke, Tr.

Classified as a private operating foundation in 1989.
Financial data (yr. ended 12/31/01): Assets, $46,726 (M); grants paid, $0; gifts received, $10,470; expenditures, $36,541; qualifying distributions, $0.
Trustees: C.A. Coonce, Theodore Reincke.
EIN: 850367901

61899
Los Ninos, Inc.
c/o Mike Mechenbier
4400 Alameda Blvd. N.E., Ste. E
Albuquerque, NM 87113-1520

Established in 1993 in NM.
Financial data (yr. ended 12/31/99): Assets, $20,234 (M); grants paid, $36,063; gifts received, $35,200; expenditures, $37,095; qualifying distributions, $37,092.
Limitations: Applications not accepted.
Application information: Contributes only to pre-selected organizations.
Officers: Mike Mechenbier, Pres.; J. Kerwin Hollowwa, V.P.; Laura M. Farris, Secy.-Treas.
EIN: 850404695

61900
Christman Foundation
36 Plaza San Blas, N.E.
Albuquerque, NM 87109

Donor(s): Patricia E. Christian.
Financial data (yr. ended 12/31/00): Assets, $15,395 (M); grants paid, $3,000; expenditures, $3,010; qualifying distributions, $3,010.
Limitations: Applications not accepted.
Application information: Contributes only to pre-selected organizations.
Officers: Patricia E. Christman, Pres.; Jack H. Gakstatter, V.P.; Jeffrey J. Gakstatter, Secy.-Treas.
EIN: 850452835

61901
Community Assistance Foundation
610 Gold Ave. S.W., Ste. 111
Albuquerque, NM 87102-3146

Established in 1999 in NM.
Donor(s): Freedman Foundation, CEO America.
Financial data (yr. ended 12/31/99): Assets, $1,122 (M); grants paid, $5,000; gifts received, $151,500; expenditures, $156,623; qualifying distributions, $5,000; giving activities include $151,623 for programs.
Limitations: Giving primarily in NM.
Trustee: William Turner.
EIN: 850422783

61902
The Sandy Murray Memorial Fund, Inc.
HCR 74 Box 24702
El Prado, NM 87529

Established in 2000.
Financial data (yr. ended 12/31/00): Assets, $588 (M); grants paid, $2,500; gifts received, $4,304; expenditures, $4,983; qualifying distributions, $4,983.
Limitations: Applications not accepted.
Application information: Contributes only to pre-selected organizations.
Officers: Barri Sanders, Pres.; Roger Sanders, Secy.-Treas.
EIN: 522215171

61903
Asian Humanitarian Aid
c/o James Gober
1408 Wells Dr., N.E.
Albuquerque, NM 87112-6382
(505) 294-4428

Donor(s): Dick Gober.
Financial data (yr. ended 12/31/01): Assets, $93 (M); grants paid, $11,403; gifts received, $12,900; expenditures, $13,091; qualifying distributions, $11,403.
Limitations: Giving primarily in Vietnam.
Officers: James R. Gober, Pres.; Tan Thai, Secy.; Tuyet Gober, Treas.
EIN: 850472858

NEW YORK

61904
The Frick Collection
1 E. 70th St.
New York, NY 10021

Classified as a private operating foundation in 1971.
Donor(s): Helen Clay Frick Foundation.
Financial data (yr. ended 12/31/00): Assets, $250,207,891 (M); grants paid, $0; gifts received, $2,463,995; expenditures, $14,408,432; qualifying distributions, $11,311,048; giving activities include $8,089,034 for programs.
Officers and Trustees:* Henry Clay Frick II,* Chair.; Helen Clay Chace,* Pres.; Howard Phipps, Jr.,* V.P.; Paul G. Pennoyer, Jr.,* Secy.; L.F. Boker Doyle,* Treas.; Peter P. Blanchard III, Margot C. Bogert, I. Townsend Burden III, Walter J.P. Curley, Jr., Emily T. Frick, Nicholas H.J. Hall, Melvin R. Seiden.
Directors: Robert Goldsmith, Samuel Sachs II.
EIN: 131624012
Codes: TN

61905
Russell Sage Foundation
112 E. 64th St.
New York, NY 10021 (212) 750-6000
FAX: (212) 371-4761; *URL:* http://www.russellsage.org
Contact: Christopher Brogna, C.F.O.

Incorporated in 1907 in NY.
Donor(s): Mrs. Russell Sage.‡
Financial data (yr. ended 08/31/01): Assets, $245,524,614 (M); grants paid, $6,434,951; gifts received, $755,484; expenditures, $13,998,784; qualifying distributions, $18,256,836; giving activities include $12,132,199 for programs.
Limitations: Giving on a national basis.
Publications: Application guidelines, biennial report, informational brochure (including application guidelines), newsletter, financial statement.
Application information: Awards are given to post-Ph.D.s only. Application form not required.
Officers and Trustees:* Ira Katznelson,* Chair.; Phoebe C. Ellsworth,* Vice-Chair.; Eric Wanner,* Pres.; Madeline Spitaleri, V.P., Admin., and Secy.; Timothy Hultquist, Treas.; Alan Blinder, Christine K. Cassel, Thomas Cook, Robert E. Denham, Jennifer L. Hochschild, Ellen Condliffe Lagemann, Cora B. Marrett, Neil J. Smelser, Eugene Smolensky, Marta Tienda.
EIN: 131635303

61906
Miriam Osborn Memorial Home Association
101 Theall Rd.
Rye, NY 10580

Classified as a private operating foundation in 1986.
Financial data (yr. ended 12/31/00): Assets, $179,497,966 (M); grants paid, $0; gifts received, $54,028; expenditures, $20,881,025; qualifying distributions, $2,555,126; giving activities include $18,688,384 for programs.
Officers: Jack Bowen, Chair.; Mark R. Zwerger, C.E.O.; William W. Mauritz, Pres.; Daniel C. DeMenocal, V.P.; Nathan Soffio, C.F.O. and Treas.
Trustees: Jesse Carrol, Terry Fulmer, Edmund C. Grainger, Herbert L. Jamison, Harvey Kelsey, John R. Miller, Bob Pratt, George G. Reader, Mason Rees, and 4 additional trustees.
EIN: 135562312

61907
Open Society Institute
400 W. 59th St., 4th Fl.
New York, NY 10019 (212) 548-0600
FAX: (212) 548-4605; *URL:* http://www.soros.org
Contact: Inquiry Mgr.

Established in 1993 in NY.
Donor(s): George Soros.
Financial data (yr. ended 12/31/01): Assets, $176,900,034 (M); grants paid, $131,930,520; gifts received, $220,378,692; expenditures, $165,767,095; qualifying distributions, $166,731,723; giving activities include $1,500,000 for program-related investments and $22,847,579 for programs.
Limitations: Giving on a national and international basis.
Publications: Annual report.
Application information: For program application guidelines and deadlines see the foundation's Web site. The site includes a wizard to help determine eligibility and submit an inquiry electronically.
Officers and Trustees:* George Soros,* Chair.; Aryeh Neier,* C.E.O. and Pres.; Stewart Paperin, Exec. V.P.; Gara LaMarche, V.P.; Morton Abramowitz, Leon Botstein, Geoffrey Canada, Joan B. Dunlop, Lani Guinier, Bill D. Moyers, David J. Rothman, Thomas M. Scanlan, Jr., John G. Simon, Herbert Sturz.
EIN: 137029285
Codes: FD, FM, GTI

61908
The American Contemporary Art Foundation, Inc.
(also known as The American Art Foundation, Inc.)
c/o Meredith Edwards
767 5th Ave., 40th Fl.
New York, NY 10153

Established in 1999 in DE and NY.
Donor(s): Leonard A. Lauder.
Financial data (yr. ended 06/30/01): Assets, $156,312,659 (M); grants paid, $0; gifts received, $60,463,621; expenditures, $2,680,821; qualifying distributions, $71,444,041; giving activities include $782,156 for programs.
Limitations: Applications not accepted. Giving primarily in New York, NY.
Application information: Contributes only to pre-selected organizations.
Officers: Leonard A. Lauder, Pres.; Carol Boulanger, V.P.; Meredith Edwards, Secy.; Joan Krupskas, Treas.
Trustees: William Lauder, Marshall Rose.
EIN: 134069969

61909
Gerry Foundation, Inc.
P.O. Box 311
Liberty, NY 12754 (845) 295-2400
Contact: Darrell Supak

Established in 1997 in NY.
Donor(s): Alan Gerry.
Financial data (yr. ended 10/31/01): Assets, $140,129,286 (M); grants paid, $1,665,100; expenditures, $4,662,940; qualifying distributions, $8,809,315; giving activities include $433,764 for programs.
Limitations: Giving primarily in Sullivan County, NY.
Officers and Directors:* Alan Gerry,* Pres.; Louis J. Boyd, Secy.-Treas.; Adam Gerry, Annelise Gerry, Robyn Gerry, Sandra Gerry.
EIN: 141798234
Codes: FD

61910
Margaret Woodbury Strong Museum
1 Manhattan Sq.
Rochester, NY 14607-3941

Classified as a private operating foundation in 1974.
Donor(s): John W. Castle, George Sommers.
Financial data (yr. ended 12/31/01): Assets, $127,039,075 (M); grants paid, $0; gifts received, $5,050,732; expenditures, $822,863; qualifying distributions, $7,854,182.
Officers and Trustees:* Robert E. Moore, Chair.; Margaret M. Freeman,* Vice-Chair.; Donald J. Riley,* Vice-Chair.; G. Rollie Adams, C.E.O. and Pres.; Judy A. Toyer,* Secy.; Burton S. August, Rita Augustine, and 18 additional trustees.
EIN: 160954168

61911
Wenner-Gren Foundation for Anthropological Research, Inc.
220 5th Ave., 16th Fl.
New York, NY 10001-7708 (212) 683-5000
FAX: (212) 683-9151; *E-mail:* info@wennergren.org; *URL:* http://www.wennergren.org
Contact: Dr. Richard Fox, Pres.

Incorporated in 1941 in DE.
Donor(s): Axel L. Wenner-Gren.‡
Financial data (yr. ended 12/31/00): Assets, $115,667,172 (M); grants paid, $3,327,506; expenditures, $6,849,898; qualifying distributions, $5,330,801; giving activities include $1,048,229 for programs.
Limitations: Giving on a national and international basis.
Publications: Program policy statement, application guidelines, biennial report (including application guidelines).
Application information: Contact foundation for application guidelines. Application form not required.
Officers and Trustees:* Hiram F. Moody, Jr.,* Chair.; Richard C. Hackney, Jr.,* Co-Vice-Chair. and Treas.; Frank W. Wadsworth,* Co-Vice-Chair.; Richard G. Fox, Pres. and Secy.; David Alexander, Beverly F. Chase, William L. Cobb, Jr., Ruth Kennedy, George D. Langdon, Jr., Seth J. Masters, Ellen Mickiewicz, David Patterson, Dorothy K. Robinson, Curtis A. Williams.
EIN: 131813827
Codes: FD, FM, GTI

61912
Milbank Memorial Fund
645 Madison Ave., 15th Fl.
New York, NY 10022-1095 (212) 355-8400
E-mail: mmf@milbank.org; *URL:* http://www.milbank.org
Contact: Daniel M. Fox, Ph.D., Pres.

Incorporated in 1905 in NY.
Donor(s): Elizabeth Milbank Anderson.‡
Financial data (yr. ended 12/31/00): Assets, $81,320,400 (M); grants paid, $0; expenditures, $4,575,296; qualifying distributions, $3,862,688; giving activities include $3,682,688 for programs.
Publications: Informational brochure (including application guidelines).
Officers and Directors:* Samuel L. Milbank,* Chair.; Peter M. Gottsegen,* Vice-Chair.; Daniel M. Fox, Ph.D.,* Pres.; Kathleen S. Andersen, V.P. and Secy.; Byron L. Kneif,* Treas.; John R. Ball, Carmen Hooker Buell, Carolyn C. Clark, Thomas E. Harvey, Carolyn Boone Lewis, Louisa J. Palmer, Carl J. Schramm, Jr., Rosemary A. Stevens, John D. Stoeckle, Joseph M. Sullivan, Carll Tucker.
EIN: 135562282

61913
The Harry Frank Guggenheim Foundation
527 Madison Ave., 15th Fl.
New York, NY 10022-4304 (212) 644-4907
FAX: (212) 644-5110; *E-mail:* hfgacf@aol.com; *URL:* http://www.hfg.org
Contact: Staff

Incorporated in 1929 in NY.
Donor(s): Harry Frank Guggenheim.‡
Financial data (yr. ended 12/31/00): Assets, $78,695,003 (M); grants paid, $1,342,037; expenditures, $2,692,674; qualifying distributions, $2,407,260.
Limitations: Giving on a national and international basis.
Publications: Biennial report, application guidelines, occasional report.

Application information: Career Development Awards program has been discontinued. New program: Dissertation Fellowship. Application form required.
Officers and Directors:* Peter O. Lawson-Johnston,* Chair.; James M. Hester,* Pres.; Mary-Alice Yates, Secy.; Joseph A. Koenigsberger, Treas.; Karen Colvard, Sr. Prog. Off.; Madeline Albright, Josiah Bunting III, Peyton Cochran, Jr., Dana Draper, James B. Edwards, Don Hood, Carol Langstaff, Peter Lawson-Johnston II, Gillian Lindt, Theodore D. Lockwood, J.M. Millbank III, Tania L.J. McCleery, Alan Pifer, Lois Dixon Rice.
EIN: 136043471
Codes: FD, GTI

61914
Canajoharie Library & Art Gallery
2 Erie Blvd.
Canajoharie, NY 13317

Classified as a private operating foundation in 1984.
Financial data (yr. ended 12/31/00): Assets, $76,929,975 (M); grants paid, $0; gifts received, $120,961; expenditures, $293,021; qualifying distributions, $266,532; giving activities include $266,532 for programs.
Officers and Trustees:* Oliver Simonsen,* Pres.; Charlotte Schlotzhauer,* V.P.; Faith Griffiths,* Secy.; Joseph A. Santangelo,* Treas.; Willis Barshied, Jr., Donald L. Bowden, Jean S. Dern, Grace Fenno, Judith McMillan, Charles Tallent.
EIN: 141398373

61915
Soros Economic Development Fund
c/o Stephen Gutmann
400 W. 59th St.
New York, NY 10019 (212) 548-0630

Classified as an operating foundation in 1997 in NY.
Donor(s): Open Society Institute.
Financial data (yr. ended 12/31/00): Assets, $68,823,901 (M); grants paid, $0; expenditures, $1,023,720; qualifying distributions, $0.
Officers: Herbert Sturz, Chair.; Stewart Paperin, C.E.O. and Pres.; Ricardo A. Castro, Secy.; Daniel R. Eule, Treas.
Directors: Peter Bartha, Ira Lieberman, and 3 additional directors.
EIN: 133965896

61916
The Century Foundation
(Formerly Twentieth Century Fund, Inc.)
c/o The Leonard Silk Journalism Fellowship
41 E. 70th St.
New York, NY 10021 (212) 535-4441
URL: http://www.tcf.org
Contact: Jason Renker

Incorporated in 1919 in MA.
Donor(s): Edward A. Filene.‡
Financial data (yr. ended 06/30/01): Assets, $64,761,960 (M); grants paid, $55,000; gifts received, $829,289; expenditures, $5,747,154; qualifying distributions, $5,560,163; giving activities include $5,505,163 for programs.
Limitations: Giving on a national and international basis.
Publications: Annual report, program policy statement, application guidelines, newsletter, financial statement.
Application information: Generally, no grants to institutions or individuals, but foundation will review independent project proposals within program guidelines as well as soliciting its own. Application form not required.
Officers: Alan Brinkley, Chair.; James A. Leach, Vice-Chair.; Richard C. Leone, Pres.; Charles V. Hamilton, Secy.; Matina S. Horner, Clerk; Richard Ravitch, Treas.
Trustees: Morris B. Abram, H. Brandt Ayers, Peter A.A. Berle, Jose A. Cabranes, Joseph A. Califano, Jr., Alexander Morgan Capron, Hodding Carter III, Edward E. David, Jr., Brewster C. Denny, Lewis B. Kaden, Alicia H. Munell, P. Michael Pitfield, Arthur M. Schlesinger, Jr., Harvey I. Sloane, M.D., Theodore C. Sorensen, Kathleen Sullivan, James Tobin, David B. Truman, Shirley Williams, William Julius Wilson.
EIN: 131624235

61917
The Solow Art & Architecture Foundation
9 W. 57th St., Ste. 4500
New York, NY 10019 (212) 751-1100
Contact: Rosalie S. Wolff, V.P.

Established in 1991 in DE.
Donor(s): The Solow Foundation, Sheldon H. Solow Foundation, Sheldon H. Solow.
Financial data (yr. ended 11/30/01): Assets, $61,436,953 (M); grants paid, $165,850; gifts received, $15,086,000; expenditures, $193,555; qualifying distributions, $165,850.
Limitations: Giving on a national basis.
Application information: Application form not required.
Officers: Sheldon H. Solow, Pres.; Rosalie S. Wolff, V.P.; Steven M. Cherniak, Treas.
EIN: 133614971

61918
American Academy of Arts and Letters
(Formerly American Academy & Institute of Arts and Letters)
633 W. 155th St.
New York, NY 10032-7599 (212) 368-5900
Contact: Virginia Dajani, Exec. Dir.

Established in 1898 as the National Institute of Arts and Letters. The American Academy of Arts and Letters was founded in 1904. In 1976 the two merged into The American Academy and Institute of Arts and Letters. In 1993, name changed to American Academy of Arts and Letters.
Donor(s): Mildred B. Strauss,‡ Channing Pollock,‡ Archer M. Huntington,‡ Charles Ives,‡ Katharine Lane Weems.‡
Financial data (yr. ended 12/31/01): Assets, $51,289,795 (M); grants paid, $934,575; gifts received, $616,992; expenditures, $2,852,390; qualifying distributions, $2,658,065.
Limitations: Giving on a national basis.
Publications: Informational brochure.
Application information: Applications accepted only for the Richard Rodgers Awards for the Musical Theater. Applications for other prizes not accepted under any circumstances. Award nominations made by membership recommendations only. The Academy will not respond to unsolicited requests for nomination consideration from individuals or organizations. Application form required.
Officers and Directors:* Ned Rorem,* Pres.; Will Barnet,* V.P., Art; Varujan Boghosian,* V.P., Art; Jane Wilson,* V.P., Art; Shirley Hazzard, V.P., Literature; Anthony Hecht,* V.P., Literature; Alison Lurie,* V.P., Literature; Leon Kirchner,* V.P., Music; Ezra Laderman,* V.P., Music; John Hollander,* Secy.; Henry N. Cobb,* Treas.; Virginia Dajani, Exec. Dir.
EIN: 130429640
Codes: FD, GTI

61919
Duke Farms Foundation
650 5th Ave., 19th Fl.
New York, NY 10019

Established in 1999 in NY.
Financial data (yr. ended 12/31/99): Assets, $50,281,442 (M); grants paid, $40,000; gifts received, $8,522,157; expenditures, $6,381,759; qualifying distributions, $6,800,465; giving activities include $5,795,386 for programs.
Officers: Joan E. Spero, Pres.; Betsy Fader, Secy.; Alan Altschuler, C.F.O.
Trustees: J. Carter Brown, Marion Oates Charles, Harry B. Demopoulos, Anthony S. Fauci, James F. Gill, Nannerl O. Keohane, John J. Mack.
EIN: 134008720

61920
Greenacre Foundation
30 Rockefeller Plz., Rm. 5600
New York, NY 10112-0001

Established in 1968 in NY.
Donor(s): Abby M. O'Neill, Abby Rockefeller Mauze.‡
Financial data (yr. ended 12/31/99): Assets, $49,841,099 (M); grants paid, $30,000; gifts received, $6,102; expenditures, $1,018,002; qualifying distributions, $964,493; giving activities include $775,132 for programs.
Officers and Trustees:* Gail O'Neill Caulkins,* Pres.; Donal C. O'Brien,* V.P.; James Sligar,* Secy.; George J. Pipino,* Treas.; Ruth Kuhlman,* Exec. Dir.; Abby M. O'Neill, and 6 additional trustees.
EIN: 132621502

61921
Dedalus Foundation, Inc.
(Formerly Motherwell Foundation, Inc.)
c/o Hecht & Co., PC
111 W. 40th St.
New York, NY 10018
Senior Fellowship Program address: 555 W. 57th St., Ste. 1222, New York, NY 10019
Contact: Richard Rubin, Pres.

Established in 1981.
Donor(s): Robert Motherwell.‡
Financial data (yr. ended 12/31/01): Assets, $49,215,921 (M); grants paid, $1,069,122; gifts received, $107,500; expenditures, $2,467,404; qualifying distributions, $2,124,108; giving activities include $1,054,986 for programs.
Limitations: Giving on a national basis.
Publications: Informational brochure (including application guidelines).
Application information: Contributes to mostly to pre-selected organizations, but has 3 separate grant programs offered to individuals: Senior Fellowship Program (application must be submitted by Oct. 1), Ph.D. Dissertation Fellowship, and M.F.A. Fellowship. Application form required.
Officers and Directors:* Richard Rubin,* Pres. and Treas.; Joan Banach,* V.P. and Secy.; Dore Ashton, John Elderfield, Jack Flam, Lynn Kearney, David Rosand.
EIN: 133091704
Codes: FD, GTI

61922
Frelinghuysen Morris Foundation
c/o Perelson Weiner
1 Dag Hammarskjold Plz., 42nd Fl.
New York, NY 10017

Established in 1992 in NY and MA.
Donor(s): Estelle F. Morris.‡
Financial data (yr. ended 12/31/99): Assets, $48,301,761 (M); grants paid, $0; gifts received,

$1,000; expenditures, $525,294; qualifying distributions, $399,213; giving activities include $326,316 for programs.
Trustees: Christine Beshar, Thomas K. Frelinghuysen.
EIN: 133471554

61923
Orentreich Foundation for the Advancement of Science, Inc.
910 5th Ave.
New York, NY 10021   (212) 606-0877

Classified as a private operating foundation in 1972.
Donor(s): Norman Orentreich, M.D.
Financial data (yr. ended 12/31/00): Assets, $47,239,608 (M); grants paid, $3,000; gifts received, $920,943; expenditures, $2,358,781; qualifying distributions, $1,974,775; giving activities include $1,607,255 for programs.
Officers and Directors:* Norman Orentreich, M.D.,* Pres.; Edward I. Klar,* V.P.; Sari Mass,* V.P.; Catherine Orentreich, M.D.,* V.P.; David Orentreich, M.D.,* V.P.; Fay Pines,* Treas.
EIN: 136154215

61924
The Howard Karagheusian Commemorative Corporation
386 Park Ave. S., Ste. 1601
New York, NY 10016

Incorporated in 1921 in NY.
Donor(s): Miran Karagheusian,‡ Zabelle Karagheusian,‡ Leila Karagheusian,‡ Vartan H. Jinishian.‡
Financial data (yr. ended 12/31/99): Assets, $43,843,862 (M); grants paid, $22,200; expenditures, $1,622,199; qualifying distributions, $1,349,756; giving activities include $1,109,620 for programs.
Limitations: Applications not accepted. Giving primarily in the Middle East; some giving also in New York, NY.
Publications: Annual report.
Application information: Contributes only to pre-selected organizations.
Directors: Harry A. Dorian, Helene Irma Der Stepanian, Michael Haratunian, Edward Janjigian, Louis M. Najarian, Pergrouhi Svajian, Richard J. Varadian, Bedros Yavru-Sakuk.
EIN: 136149578

61925
The Shelley and Donald Rubin Cultural Trust
115 5th Ave., 7th Fl.
New York, NY 10003

Established in 1999 in NY.
Donor(s): Donald Rubin, Shelley Rubin.
Financial data (yr. ended 04/30/00): Assets, $39,340,631 (M); grants paid, $0; gifts received, $29,131,888; expenditures, $867,226; qualifying distributions, $681,823; giving activities include $1,208,003 for programs.
Limitations: Applications not accepted.
Application information: Contributes only to pre-selected organizations.
Trustees: Rev. James Morton, Jonathan Rose, Donald Rubin, Shelley Rubin.
EIN: 226799567

61926
Dahesh Museum, Inc.
601 5th Ave., 5th Fl.
New York, NY 10017

Classified as a private operating foundation.
Donor(s): Mervat Zahid, Amira Zahid.
Financial data (yr. ended 05/31/00): Assets, $39,274,048 (M); grants paid, $0; gifts received, $274,064; expenditures, $1,996,774; qualifying distributions, $2,132,766; giving activities include $2,037,833 for programs.
Officers: Mervat Zahid, Pres.; Amr Zahid, V.P.; Amira Zahid, Secy.-Treas.
Trustees: Hoda Zahid, Mahmoud Zahid.
EIN: 133458208

61927
Boscobel Restoration, Inc.
1601 Rte. 9D
Garrison, NY 10524

Classified as a private operating foundation in 1974.
Financial data (yr. ended 12/31/99): Assets, $35,758,882 (M); grants paid, $300; gifts received, $20,883; expenditures, $1,554,804; qualifying distributions, $1,514,756; giving activities include $8,512,188 for programs.
Officers: Carolin Serino, Treas.; Charles Lyle, Exec. Dir.
Directors: Robert O. Binnewies, Gilman S. Burke, Kathleen Cullen, T. Jefferson Cunningham, III, Robert G. Goelet, Col. Williams L. Harrison, Richard J. Kelly, Bernard Levy, Mrs. Richard Manney, Barnabas McHenry, Arnold S. Moss, Frederick H. Osborn III, Elizabeth B. Pugh, Mrs. Willis Reese, Richard J. Schwartz, Frederick W. Stanyer.
EIN: 141458845

61928
The Judith Rothschild Foundation
1110 Park Ave.
New York, NY 10128   (212) 831-4114
FAX: (212) 831-6222; *URL:* http://fdncenter.org/grantmaker/rothschild
Contact: Elizabeth Simonson Slater, V.P., Grant Program

Established in 1993 in NY.
Donor(s): Judith Rothschild.‡
Financial data (yr. ended 12/31/00): Assets, $34,286,854 (M); grants paid, $465,984; gifts received, $165,750; expenditures, $1,853,416; qualifying distributions, $1,803,606; giving activities include $1,097,709 for programs.
Limitations: Giving on a national basis.
Publications: Application guidelines, grants list.
Application information: Request grant program guidelines. Application form required.
Officer: Wilder Green, Chair.
Trustee: Harvey S. Shipley Miller.
EIN: 133736320
Codes: FD

61929
Doris Duke Foundation for Islamic Art
650 5th Ave., 19th Fl.
New York, NY 10019

Established in 1999 in NY and HI.
Financial data (yr. ended 12/31/99): Assets, $34,239,424 (M); grants paid, $1,000; gifts received, $1,440,000; expenditures, $1,477,372; qualifying distributions, $1,425,846; giving activities include $1,407,949 for programs.
Officers and Trustees:* James F. Gill,* Chair.; Joan E. Spero, Pres.; Betsy Fader, Secy.; Alan Altschuler, C.F.O.; J. Carter Brown, Marion Oates Charles, Harry B. Demopoulos, Anthony S. Fauci, Nannerl O. Keohane, John J. Mack.
EIN: 134008719

61930
The Corning Museum of Glass
1 Museum Way
Corning, NY 14830-2253

Classified as a private operating foundation in 1952.
Financial data (yr. ended 12/31/01): Assets, $32,815,786 (M); grants paid, $0; gifts received, $15,128,927; expenditures, $22,937,562; qualifying distributions, $19,113,281; giving activities include $22,926,074 for programs.
Officers and Directors:* E. Mane McKee,* Pres.; Amory Houghton, Jr.,* V.P.; James R. Houghton,* V.P.; Denise A. Hauselt,* Secy.; David Whitehouse, Exec. Dir.; Robert K. Cassetti, Nancy J. Earley, Robert J. Grassi, and 24 additional directors.
EIN: 160764349

61931
The Culinarians' Home Foundation, Inc.
400 Madison Ave., Rm. 505
New York, NY 10107-1531

Established in 1942 in NY.
Financial data (yr. ended 06/30/01): Assets, $24,405,694 (M); grants paid, $41,375; gifts received, $100; expenditures, $897,740; qualifying distributions, $731,656; giving activities include $251,561 for programs.
Limitations: Applications not accepted. Giving primarily in New Paltz, NY.
Application information: Contributes only to pre-selected organizations.
Officers: Roger Le Bosser, Pres.; Jean LeRouzic, V.P.; Patrick Smet-Chevron, Treas.
EIN: 131635296

61932
Sutton Place Foundation
(Formerly St. John's Foundation)
c/o Peller
55 Oyster Shores Rd.
East Hampton, NY 11937

Established in 1984 in NY.
Donor(s): Frederick R. Koch.
Financial data (yr. ended 12/31/00): Assets, $23,574,352 (M); grants paid, $0; expenditures, $589,958; qualifying distributions, $589,824; giving activities include $574,623 for programs.
Officers and Director:* Frederick R. Koch, Pres.; Carl J. Stinchcomb,* Secy.-Treas.
EIN: 980070731

61933
The Havens Relief Fund Society
475 Riverside Dr.
New York, NY 10115
Contact: Joyce Wolbarst Willis, Exec. Dir.

Incorporated in 1870 in NY.
Financial data (yr. ended 12/31/01): Assets, $22,178,906 (M); grants paid, $1,052,261; expenditures, $1,310,881; qualifying distributions, $1,284,558.
Limitations: Applications not accepted. Giving limited to New York, NY.
Application information: Contributes only to pre-selected individuals; unsolicited requests for funds not accepted.
Officers: Arthur V. Savage, Pres.; Frances F. Davis, V.P.; Michael Loening, V.P.; Cynthia C. Lefferts, Secy.; Paul J. Brignola, Treas.; Joyce Wolbarst Willis, Exec. Dir.
EIN: 135562382
Codes: FD, GTI

61934
Hod Foundation
c/o American Stock Transfer
59 Maiden Ln., Plaza Level
New York, NY 10038
Contact: Henry Reinhold, Tr.

Established in 2000 in NY.
Donor(s): Michael Karfunkel, Karfunkel Family Foundation.
Financial data (yr. ended 06/30/01): Assets, $22,129,738 (M); grants paid, $1,639,452; gifts received, $4,010,000; expenditures, $1,769,111; qualifying distributions, $1,616,232.
Application information: Application form not required.
Officers: Michael Karfunkel, Pres.; George Karfunkel, V.P.
Trustee: Henry Reinhold.
EIN: 133922069
Codes: FD

61935
Henry & Rose Pearlman Foundation, Inc.
c/o Gettry, Marcus, Stern & Lehrer
220 5th Ave., 4th Fl.
New York, NY 10001 (212) 684-3399

Incorporated in 1953 in NY.
Donor(s): Henry Pearlman,‡ Rose Pearlman,‡ Eastern Cold Storage Insulation Co., Inc.
Financial data (yr. ended 11/30/01): Assets, $22,068,103 (M); grants paid, $1,800; expenditures, $55,750; qualifying distributions, $1,800.
Officers and Directors:* Marge Scheuer,* Pres.; Alex W. Pearlman,* V.P.; Dorothy Edelman,* Secy.-Treas.; David Scheuer, Jeffrey Scheuer.
EIN: 136159092

61936
Louis August Jonas Foundation, Inc.
c/o Phyliss Dunne
2 Rhinebeck Savings Village Plz.
Rhinebeck, NY 12572

Established in 1971 in NY.
Financial data (yr. ended 03/31/00): Assets, $18,449,095 (M); grants paid, $0; gifts received, $233,648; expenditures, $1,079,502; qualifying distributions, $1,012,722; giving activities include $613,476 for programs.
Officer and Directors:* David Ives,* Exec. Dir.; George Ames, Helen Baldwin, Andre Campbell, Leonard Duhl, and 26 additional directors.
EIN: 141387863
Codes: TN

61937
Civitella Ranieri Foundation
c/o Carter Rupp & Roberts
10 E. 40th St., Ste.3807
New York, NY 10014

Classified as a private operating foundation in 1993.
Donor(s): Ursula Corning.
Financial data (yr. ended 12/31/00): Assets, $18,371,591 (M); grants paid, $0; gifts received, $3,001,021; expenditures, $1,217,180; qualifying distributions, $931,139; giving activities include $99,674 for programs.
Trustees: Alexander D. Crary, John A. Downey, M.D., Helen C. Evartz, John Roberts, JPMorgan Chase Bank.
EIN: 133674360

61938
Young Morse Historic Site, Inc.
2683 South Rd.
Poughkeepsie, NY 12601

Classified as a private operating foundation in 1980.
Donor(s): Frances S. Reese, Environmental Protection Fund, NYS Library, Preservation League of New York.
Financial data (yr. ended 12/31/01): Assets, $17,578,886 (M); grants paid, $0; gifts received, $82,222; expenditures, $1,314,088; qualifying distributions, $789,582; giving activities include $993,622 for programs.
Officers: Frances S. Reese, Pres.; Everett M. Rood, V.P.; David H. Cullen, V.P. and Secy.; Anthony V. Campilii, Treas.; Raymond J. Armater, Exec. Dir.
Trustees: Stephen W. Cole, Carleton Mabee, Julia C. Rosenblatt.
EIN: 141619998

61939
Lucerna Fund
85 Channel Dr.
Port Washington, NY 11050

Incorporated in 1965 in NY.
Donor(s): LuEsther T. Mertz.‡
Financial data (yr. ended 12/31/00): Assets, $17,516,257 (M); grants paid, $0; gifts received, $385; expenditures, $787,131; qualifying distributions, $673,851; giving activities include $159,098 for programs.
Officers and Directors:* William B. O'Connor,* Pres. and Treas.; Georgia Delano, V.P. and Secy.; Paul D. Richards, V.P.; Lloyd Burlinghame, Larry E. Condon, Robert W. Russell.
EIN: 116044099

61940
Kurt Weill Foundation for Music, Inc.
7 E. 20th St.
New York, NY 10003 (212) 505-5240
FAX: (212) 353-9663; E-mail: cweber@kwf.org;
URL: http://www.kwf.org
Contact: Carolyn Weber, Dir.

Established in 1962.
Donor(s): Lotte Lenya.‡
Financial data (yr. ended 12/31/00): Assets, $16,029,301 (M); grants paid, $255,250; gifts received, $44,605; expenditures, $1,232,889; qualifying distributions, $889,979.
Limitations: Giving on an international basis.
Publications: Informational brochure, application guidelines, newsletter.
Application information: Application form required.
Officers and Trustees:* Kim Kowalke,* Pres.; Philip Getter,* V.P.; Lys Symonette,* V.P.; Guy Stern,* Secy.; Milton Coleman,* Treas.; Paul Epstein, Walter Hinderer, Harold Prince, Julius Rudel.
Director: Carolyn Weber.
EIN: 136139518
Codes: FD, GTI

61941
Lead International, Inc.
(also known as Leadership for Environment & Development International, Inc.)
425 Lexington Ave.
New York, NY 10017-3954

Classified as a private operating foundation in 1998.
Financial data (yr. ended 12/31/00): Assets, $15,106,608 (M); grants paid, $0; gifts received, $8,017,594; expenditures, $7,950,394; qualifying distributions, $7,979,375; giving activities include $5,693,876 for programs.
Officers: Jose Maria Figureres, Pres.; Teya Ryan, V.P.; Julia Marton-Lefevre, Secy. and Exec. Dir.
Directors: Samuel Abiola Adenekan, Akin Oludele Adesola, Julia Carabias, C.J. Chetsanga, Anjuly Chib Duggal, Fabio Feldmann, Parvez Hassan, Song Jian, Saburo Kawai, Geoffrey Lean, Reginald A. Mengi, Marie Angelique Savane, Maurice Strong.
EIN: 133723995

61942
The Frederick R. Koch Foundation
c/o Peller
55 Oyster Shores Rd.
East Hampton, NY 11937

Classified as a private operating foundation in 1982.
Donor(s): Frederick R. Koch.
Financial data (yr. ended 12/31/01): Assets, $14,899,644 (M); grants paid, $0; gifts received, $3,000; expenditures, $2,830; qualifying distributions, $0.
Limitations: Applications not accepted.
Application information: Contributes only to pre-selected organizations.
Officer and Directors:* Frederick R. Koch,* Mgr.; L.F. Boker Coyle, James Goodfellow, Charles Reiscamp, John Sare, J. Rigby Turner.
EIN: 133088563

61943
Hoffman Center
55 Piping Rock Rd.
Glen Head, NY 11545

Donor(s): The M.O. & M.E. Hoffman Foundation, Inc.
Financial data (yr. ended 06/30/02): Assets, $14,347,308 (M); grants paid, $0; gifts received, $950,650; expenditures, $630,855; qualifying distributions, $0.
Officers: Ursula Niarakis, Pres.; William Niarakis, V.P. and Treas.
Director: Nicholas Niarakis.
EIN: 223413122

61944
Albany Guardian Society
553 Clinton Ave.
Albany, NY 12203-2738

Classified as a private foundation in 1988.
Financial data (yr. ended 11/30/99): Assets, $14,020,025 (M); grants paid, $0; expenditures, $1,032,705; qualifying distributions, $931,791; giving activities include $1,032,705 for programs.
Officers and Directors:* Jane E. Ordway,* Co-Chair. and Pres.; Barbara Carovano,* Co-Chair. and V.P.; Pat Eggenschiller,* Co-Chair. and Secy.; Wendy Brandow,* Co-Chair.; Prudence Ciaccio,* Co-Chair.; Mary Hughes,* Co-Chair.; Terry Kalohn,* Co-Chair.; Ethel Lamar,* Co-Chair.; Alice Murphy,* Co-Chair.; Richard S. Ambuhl,* Treas.; Marjory Chesney, Anne E. Fitzgerald, Janet Hengerer, Jean Joel, Terry Kalohn, Kate McLaughlin, Peter Newkirk, Gertrude Olcott, Sally Poole, Dorothy Reed, Mrs. John R. Titus, Dora Vine, Audrey Woolsey.
EIN: 141363010

61945
Clara Welch Thanksgiving Home, Inc.
48 Grove St.
Cooperstown, NY 13326-1427

Classified as a private operating foundation in 1972.

Financial data (yr. ended 12/31/01): Assets, $13,974,094 (M); grants paid, $0; gifts received, $105,415; expenditures, $1,229,405; qualifying distributions, $1,160,715; giving activities include $1,075,857 for programs.
Officers and Directors:* James Forbes Clark,* Pres.; Edward Gozigan,* V.P.; William T. Burkick,* Secy.; Glen A. Perrone,* Secy.; Richard C. Vanison,* Treas.; James Bordley IV, M.D., Stephen M. Duff, William H. Hermann, Mrs. John G. Logan, Barbara I. Mook, Kevin S. Moore, Marian Mullet, Gordon B. Roberts, Edward W. Stack, Karen Streck.
EIN: 150543655

61946
The Dorothy Russell Havemeyer Foundation, Inc.
c/o Gene Pranzo
230 Park Ave., 26th Fl.
New York, NY 10169 (212) 682-3700

Donor(s): Dorothy Havermeyer McConville.‡
Financial data (yr. ended 10/31/00): Assets, $13,028,067 (M); grants paid, $0; expenditures, $899,123; qualifying distributions, $724,206; giving activities include $249,491 for programs.
Officer: Gene M. Pranzo, Pres.
Directors: David Schaengold, Melanie G. Tenney.
EIN: 133022482

61947
Karfunkel Family Foundation
59 Maiden Ln., Plaza Level
New York, NY 10038
Contact: Henry Reinhold

Established in 1991 in NY.
Donor(s): Michael Karfunkel, George Karfunkel.
Financial data (yr. ended 06/30/01): Assets, $12,984,208 (M); grants paid, $9,046,380; gifts received, $9,102,906; expenditures, $12,945,669; qualifying distributions, $8,978,687.
Limitations: Giving primarily in NY.
Officer and Trustees:* Michael Karfunkel,* Pres.; George Karfunkel, Henry Reinhold.
EIN: 116405368
Codes: FD

61948
Nancy Graves Foundation, Inc.
c/o Hecht and Company, PC
111 W. 40th St.
New York, NY 10018

Established in 1996 in NY.
Financial data (yr. ended 09/30/00): Assets, $12,874,867 (M); grants paid, $0; gifts received, $458,346; expenditures, $347,788; qualifying distributions, $324,397; giving activities include $324,397 for programs.
Officers and Directors:* Sanford Hirsch,* Chair.; Janie C. Lee,* Pres.; William K. Joseph,* V.P.; Eugene V. Kokot,* Secy.; Michael Hecht, Treas.; Linda K. Kramer, Exec. Dir.; Trisha Brown.
EIN: 133885307

61949
John E. Andrus Memorial, Inc.
185 Old Broadway
Hastings-on-Hudson, NY 10706-3899

Financial data (yr. ended 12/31/00): Assets, $12,649,745 (M); grants paid, $0; expenditures, $9,951,520; qualifying distributions, $1,838,922; giving activities include $9,951,520 for programs.
Limitations: Applications not accepted.
Application information: Contributes only to a pre-selected organization.
Officer: Lauren Reinersten, Admin.

Directors: Peter B. Benedict, Michael M. Bialek, Vitina A. Biondo, Amy Cohn, Christopher F. Davenport, Marc De Venoge, Kate Downs, Jack Fallon, Lynne S. Katzmann, Henriette Kole, Robert Levine, Josephine B. Lowman, John Lynagh, Frederick F. Moon III, Michael R. Potack, Edward Skloot, Mary Sloane, Suzanne K. Smith, Edwin H. Stern III, Samuel S. Thorpe III.
EIN: 135596795

61950
Raymond and Beverly Sackler Foundation, Inc.
17 E. 62nd St.
New York, NY 10021-7204

Established in 1967 in NY.
Donor(s): Raymond R. Sackler, R.S. Sackler, J.D. Sackler, Beverly Sackler.
Financial data (yr. ended 12/31/99): Assets, $12,580,374 (M); grants paid, $25,000; expenditures, $739,314; qualifying distributions, $689,008; giving activities include $664,008 for programs.
Limitations: Applications not accepted.
Application information: Contributes only to pre-selected organizations.
Officers and Directors:* Raymond R. Sackler,* Pres.; Jonathan D. Sackler,* V.P.; Richard S. Sackler,* V.P.; Beverly Sackler,* Secy.-Treas.
EIN: 237022467

61951
The Lehrman Institute
42 North Ave., No. L
New Rochelle, NY 10805-3506
Contact: Richard J. Behn, Dir.

Donor(s): Lewis E. Lehrman, Five Way Partners, LLP, F.P. Trotta.
Financial data (yr. ended 07/31/01): Assets, $12,352,445 (M); grants paid, $987,964; gifts received, $1,630,782; expenditures, $1,391,852; qualifying distributions, $1,333,838.
Limitations: Giving primarily in CT and NY.
Publications: Application guidelines.
Application information: Contact foundation for complete guidelines.
Officers and Directors:* Thomas Lehrman,* Chair.; Frank Trotta, Pres.; Steve Szymanski, Treas.; Richard J. Behn, Mario Di Fiore, D. Gilbert Lehrman, Lewis E. Lehrman, Louise Lehrman, Christopher K. Potter.
EIN: 237218534
Codes: FD

61952
Chenango Valley Home for Aged People
c/o NBT Bank, N.A.
24 Canasawacta St.
Norwich, NY 13815

Classified as a private operating foundation in 1974.
Financial data (yr. ended 09/30/00): Assets, $12,298,595 (M); grants paid, $0; gifts received, $398,406; expenditures, $1,106,478; qualifying distributions, $1,062,540; giving activities include $1,106,478 for programs.
Officers: Frank Benenati, Pres.; Mary Emerson, V.P.; Donna Dunne, Secy.; Doris Dudley, Treas.
Trustee: NBT Bank, N.A.
EIN: 150543650

61953
The Clark Manor House
318 Fort Hill Ave.
Canandaigua, NY 14424

Financial data (yr. ended 10/31/01): Assets, $12,291,197 (M); grants paid, $0; expenditures, $647,422; qualifying distributions, $0.

Officers: Mary Ann Bell, Pres.; James Avery, V.P.; Carol Murphy, Secy.; Gregory MacKay, Treas.; William Adams, Mgr.; Dorothy Blanck, Mgr.; Lucy Case, Mgr.; Robert Gage, Mgr.; Dorothy Harkness, Mgr.; Roy Johnston, Mgr.; Bruce Kennedy, Mgr.; Barbara Murphy, Mgr.; Jane Ogden, Mgr.; Richard Rayburn, Mgr.; Martha Wilbur, Mgr.
EIN: 160755755

61954
Robert Schalkenbach Foundation, Inc.
149 Madison Ave., Ste. 601
New York, NY 10016-6713 (212) 683-6424
FAX: (212) 683-6454; E-mail: staff@schalkenbach.org, or cwilliams@schalkenbach.org; URL: http://www.schalkenbach.org
Contact: Christopher R. Williams, Secy. and Exec. Dir.

Incorporated in 1925 in NY.
Donor(s): Robert Schalkenbach.‡
Financial data (yr. ended 06/30/01): Assets, $12,012,255 (M); grants paid, $208,300; gifts received, $87,988; expenditures, $980,388; qualifying distributions, $586,327.
Limitations: Giving on a national basis.
Publications: Annual report, application guidelines, grants list.
Application information: Application form required.
Officers and Directors:* Francis Peddle, Pres.; Nicolaus Tideman, V.P.; Christopher R. Williams, Secy. and Exec. Dir.; Larry Abele,* Treas.; Robert V. Andelson, Herbert Barry III, Mary M. Cleveland, Clifford Cobb, Clifford W. Cobb, J. Anthony Coughlan, Gregg Erickson, Kris Feder, M. Mason Gaffney, Ted Gwartney, Drew Harris, Albert Hartheimer, Ben Howells, Garry Nixon, Richard Noyes, Heather Remoff, Warren Samuels, Tom Smith.
EIN: 131656331
Codes: FD2

61955
Comunita Giovanile San Michele, Inc.
c/o Arthur Fox, C.P.A.
126 E. 56th St., 12th Fl.
New York, NY 10022-3613

Donor(s): Anne Franchetti.
Financial data (yr. ended 12/31/01): Assets, $11,942,963 (M); grants paid, $0; gifts received, $25,000; expenditures, $382,545; qualifying distributions, $0.
Officers and Directors:* Anne M. Franchetti,* Pres. and Treas.; Maria Giulia Senni,* V.P.; John H. Mason,* Secy.; Carlo Stefano Franchetti, Cody Eduardo Franchetti, Giorgio Andrea Franchetti.
EIN: 136102743

61956
Mona Bismarck Foundation, Inc.
1133 Ave. of the Americas
New York, NY 10036-6710

Donor(s): Mona Bismarck Charitable Trust.
Financial data (yr. ended 12/31/00): Assets, $11,891,877 (M); grants paid, $0; gifts received, $625,143; expenditures, $1,190,053; qualifying distributions, $1,080,808; giving activities include $1,104,725 for programs.
Officers and Trustees:* Russell M. Porter,* Pres.; Herbert H. Chaice,* V.P. and Secy.; Guy H. Dunham,* V.P.; Maria-Gaetana Matisse, Caroline A. Porter, C. Rajakaruna, Pierre Schneider.
EIN: 133073031

61957
The Medway Institute
(Formerly Medway Environmental Trust)
c/o Behan, Ling & Ruta
358 5th Ave., 9th Fl.
New York, NY 10001

Classified as a private operating foundation in 1993 in SC.
Financial data (yr. ended 12/31/00): Assets, $11,790,574 (M); grants paid, $0; gifts received, $11,230,649; expenditures, $140,570; qualifying distributions, $83,055; giving activities include $55,314 for programs.
Trustee: Bokara Legendre.
EIN: 576151065

61958
The Leir Foundation, Inc.
641 Lexington Ave.
New York, NY 10022-4503

Established in 1996 in CT.
Donor(s): Henry J. Leir,‡ Louis Lipton, The Ridgefield Foundation.
Financial data (yr. ended 02/28/01): Assets, $11,771,229 (M); grants paid, $265,400; gifts received, $1,500; expenditures, $1,176,331; qualifying distributions, $1,037,810; giving activities include $298,448 for programs.
Limitations: Applications not accepted. Giving primarily in Ridgefield, CT.
Application information: Contributes only to pre-selected organizations.
Officers: Arthur S. Hoffman, Pres. and Treas.; Fred M. Lowenfels, Secy.
Directors: Mary-Ann Fribourg, Margot Gibis.
EIN: 061466481
Codes: FD

61959
Classical American Homes Preservation Trust
c/o WSW
466 Lexington Ave.
New York, NY 10017

Classified as a private operating foundation in 1994.
Donor(s): Richard H. Jenrette.
Financial data (yr. ended 11/30/00): Assets, $11,626,050 (M); grants paid, $330; gifts received, $362,514; expenditures, $402,530; qualifying distributions, $172,576.
Officers and Directors:* Richard H. Jenrette,* Pres.; Joseph M. Jenrette,* V.P.; Marjorie S. White, Secy.-Treas.; Scott Bessent, Michael A. Boyd, Charles H.P. Duell, John W. Smith, William L. Thompson.
EIN: 133747036

61960
Foundation for a Course in Miracles, Inc.
1275 Tennanah Lake Rd.
Roscoe, NY 12776
Contact: Kenneth Wapnick, Pres.

Financial data (yr. ended 12/31/99): Assets, $11,618,370 (M); grants paid, $1,250; gifts received, $279,873; expenditures, $1,141,595; qualifying distributions, $125,739; giving activities include $1,142,845 for programs.
Officers: Kenneth Wapnick, Pres.; Gloria Wapnick, V.P.
EIN: 133168245
Codes: TN

61961
Arthur M. Sackler Foundation
461 E. 57th St.
New York, NY 10022
E-mail: artmsackfd@aol.com
Contact: Elizabeth A. Sackler, Pres.

Established in 1965 in NY; classified as a private operating foundation in 1977.
Donor(s): Arthur F. Sackler, Else Sackler.
Financial data (yr. ended 12/31/00): Assets, $11,077,664 (M); grants paid, $192,000; expenditures, $976,210; qualifying distributions, $846,321; giving activities include $846,321 for programs.
Officers and Directors:* Elizabeth A. Sackler,* C.E.O. and Pres.; Arthur F. Sackler,* Secy.; Carol Master,* Treas.
EIN: 521074954
Codes: FD2

61962
Post-Morrow Foundation, Inc.
c/o Bruce T. Walllace
P.O. Box 204
Brookhaven, NY 11719-9741

Established in 1969 in NY.
Donor(s): Elisabeth Post Morrow.‡
Financial data (yr. ended 12/31/01): Assets, $10,836,773 (M); grants paid, $45,350; gifts received, $101,271; expenditures, $431,806; qualifying distributions, $542,865.
Limitations: Applications not accepted. Giving limited to Bellport and Brookhaven, NY.
Publications: Financial statement, newsletter.
Application information: Contributes only to pre-selected organizations.
Officers: Bruce T. Wallace, Pres.; Thomas Williams, V.P. and Treas.; Thomas Ludlam, 2nd V.P.; Faith C. McCutcheon, Secy.
Director: Norman Nelson.
EIN: 237028533

61963
Advertising Educational Foundation, Inc.
220 E. 42nd St., Ste. 3300
New York, NY 10017

Established in 1983 in NY.
Donor(s): RJR Nabisco Holdings Corp., Capital Cities Foundation, Warner-Lambert Foundation, and others.
Financial data (yr. ended 12/31/01): Assets, $10,741,473 (M); grants paid, $0; gifts received, $55,250; expenditures, $1,084,017; qualifying distributions, $1,027,648; giving activities include $903,774 for programs.
Officers and Directors:* Herbert M. Baum,* Chair. and C.E.O.; David Bell,* Vice-Chair.; Joseph A. Ripp,* Exec. V.P.; Douglass L. Alligood,* Sr. V.P.; Paula A. Alex, Janet E. Klug, Wally Snyder, Edward L. Wax, and 32 additional directors.
EIN: 133228986

61964
Candace King Weir Foundation
c/o C.L. King & Assocs., Inc.
9 Elk St.
Albany, NY 12207
Contact: Candace K. Weir, Tr.

Established in 1994 in NY.
Donor(s): Candace K. Weir.
Financial data (yr. ended 12/31/01): Assets, $10,720,741 (M); grants paid, $512,950; gifts received, $999,750; expenditures, $522,499; qualifying distributions, $518,505.
Limitations: Giving primarily in NY.
Trustees: Meredith Prime, Amelia F. Weir, Candace K. Weir, David A. Weir.
EIN: 133797919
Codes: FD

61965
The Tufenkian Foundation, Inc.
902 Broadway, 2nd Fl.
New York, NY 10010

Donor(s): James Tufenkian.
Financial data (yr. ended 11/30/01): Assets, $10,526,868 (M); grants paid, $325,404; gifts received, $3,000,000; expenditures, $397,337; qualifying distributions, $396,428.
Limitations: Applications not accepted.
Application information: Contributes only to pre-selected organizations.
Officer and Directors:* James Tufenkian,* Pres.; Diane L. Hodges, David F. Tufenkian.
EIN: 133976159
Codes: FD

61966
The Anchor Foundation, Inc.
410 West St.
New York, NY 10014

Classified as a private operating foundation in 1972.
Donor(s): Mary Alice Waters, Jack Barnes.
Financial data (yr. ended 12/31/00): Assets, $10,180,691 (M); grants paid, $0; gifts received, $8,160,156; expenditures, $154,523; qualifying distributions, $122,666; giving activities include $100,791 for programs.
Officers and Directors:* Norton Sandler,* Pres.; Steve Clark,* Secy.-Treas.; Jack Barnes, Mary Alice Waters.
EIN: 132706215

61967
Blue Mountain Center
c/o Yohalem Gillman & Co.
477 Madison Ave.
New York, NY 10022

Established in 1983.
Donor(s): Adam Hochschild, Cedar Fund.
Financial data (yr. ended 12/31/99): Assets, $9,901,761 (M); grants paid, $27,120; gifts received, $595,471; expenditures, $736,286; qualifying distributions, $592,951; giving activities include $687,926 for programs.
Limitations: Applications not accepted. Giving on a national basis.
Application information: Contributes only to pre-selected organizations.
Director: Harriet Barlow.
Trustee: Adam Hochschild.
EIN: 222370485

61968
Cabbage Hill Farm Foundation, Inc.
c/o KISCO Mgmt. Corp.
111 Radio Cir.
Mount Kisco, NY 10549

Established in 1997 in NY.
Donor(s): Jerome Kohlberg.
Financial data (yr. ended 12/31/00): Assets, $9,844,133 (M); grants paid, $240,692; gifts received, $225,000; expenditures, $1,126,184; qualifying distributions, $896,685; giving activities include $730,350 for programs.
Limitations: Applications not accepted. Giving primarily in MA, NY, and PA.
Application information: Contributes only to pre-selected organizations.
Officers and Directors:* Nancy S. Kohlberg,* Pres.; Walter W. Farley,* V.P. and Secy.; Eileen M. Capone,* Treas.; Jerome Kohlberg, Pamela

Kohlberg, Nancy Mccabe, Wilkes Mcclave, III, Anne Farrell.
EIN: 133914519
Codes: FD2

61969
Brayson Foundation, Ltd.
P.O. Box 786
Medford, NY 11763-0786   (631) 585-8779

Established in 1997 in NY.
Donor(s): Lake Grove School.
Financial data (yr. ended 12/31/00): Assets, $9,640,896 (M); grants paid, $0; gifts received, $7,728; expenditures, $8,744; qualifying distributions, $0; giving activities include $2,288,904 for program-related investments.
Application information: Application form required.
Officers: Donald G. Pearce, Pres.; Donald M. Miller, V.P.; John C. Bahrenburg, Secy.-Treas.
Directors: Matthew J. Merritt, Jr., Andrew Schenkel.
EIN: 113231782

61970
Lake Delaware Boys Camp, Inc.
P.O. Box 31, Lake Delaware
Delhi, NY 13753   (607) 832-4451
FAX: (607) 832-4841
Contact: Catherine Hewitt, Secy.

Established in 1909 in NY.
Donor(s): Gladys and Roland Harriman Foundation, Elbridge T. Gerry, Sr., Elbridge T. Gerry, Jr.
Financial data (yr. ended 12/31/01): Assets, $9,637,914 (M); grants paid, $141,938; gifts received, $144,918; expenditures, $201,107; qualifying distributions, $169,050.
Limitations: Giving primarily in Delhi, NY.
Publications: Financial statement, informational brochure (including application guidelines).
Application information: Application form required.
Officers: Marjorie Gerry-Ryland, Pres.; Wilber S. Oles, Jr., V.P. and Secy.; Edward H. Gerry, V.P. and Treas.; Ronald L. Reopel, V.P.
Directors: Elbridge T. Gerry, Jr., Peter G. Gerry.
EIN: 150563429
Codes: FD2

61971
Franklin Windsor Housing Development
c/o Community Housing
5 W. Main St.
Elmsford, NY 10523

Financial data (yr. ended 10/31/00): Assets, $9,574,779 (M); grants paid, $0; expenditures, $1,438,878; qualifying distributions, $214,229.
Officer: Rev. Frederick Schumacher, Pres.
EIN: 133357760

61972
The National Academy of Education
c/o New York University, School of Education
726 Broadway, 5th Fl.
New York, NY 10003-9580   (212) 998-9035
FAX: (212) 995-4435; *E-mail:* nae.info@nyu.edu; *URL:* http://www.nae.nyu.edu

Established in 1965 in NY; classified as a private operating foundation in 1973.
Donor(s): Spencer Foundation, U.S. Dept. of Education.
Financial data (yr. ended 12/31/00): Assets, $9,466,720 (M); grants paid, $1,440,000; expenditures, $2,086,696; qualifying distributions, $1,440,000.
Limitations: Giving on an international basis.
Publications: Informational brochure, application guidelines, newsletter.
Application information: Request application before Nov. 17. Applications must be in English. Application form required.
Officers: Nel Noddings, Pres.; Maureen Hallinan, V.P.; Alan Schoenfeld, V.P.; Tony Bryk, Secy.-Treas.; Kerith Gardner, Exec. Dir.
EIN: 770415802
Codes: FD, GTI

61973
The Four Oaks Foundation, Inc.
635 Madison Ave.
New York, NY 10022

Established in 1984 in NY.
Donor(s): Walter Scheuer.
Financial data (yr. ended 10/31/99): Assets, $9,278,736 (M); grants paid, $22,000; gifts received, $243,838; expenditures, $1,934,772; qualifying distributions, $19,283.
Limitations: Applications not accepted. Giving primarily in NY.
Application information: Contributes only to pre-selected organizations.
Officers and Directors:* Walter Scheuer, Pres.; David A. Scheuer,* V.P.; Judith E. Scheuer,* V.P.; Marge Scheuer,* V.P.; Susan C. Scheuer,* V.P.
EIN: 133225336

61974
The Paul Simons Foundation, Inc.
200 Harbor Rd.
Stony Brook, NY 11790

Classified as a private operating foundation in 1997.
Financial data (yr. ended 02/28/01): Assets, $8,640,620 (M); grants paid, $0; gifts received, $2,008,000; expenditures, $486,536; qualifying distributions, $0.
Directors: Kathy Griffiths, James H. Simons.
EIN: 133937693

61975
Egon & Hildegard Neustadt Museum of Tiffany Art
2166 Broadway, Apt. 23C
New York, NY 10024

Classified as a private operating foundation in 1974.
Financial data (yr. ended 09/30/00): Assets, $8,566,390 (M); grants paid, $0; expenditures, $434,466; qualifying distributions, $179,587; giving activities include $2,255 for loans and $185,695 for programs.
Officers: Milton D. Hassol,* Pres. and Treas.; Richard Hanna,* Secy.
Trustees: Mary Alice MacKay, David K. Specter, Sheila K. Tabakoff.
EIN: 237361022

61976
The Institute for Aegean Prehistory
c/o The Millburn Corp.
1270 Ave. of the Americas
New York, NY 10020
E-mail: all@styx.ios.com
Contact: Adelaide Lewis

Established in 1983 in NY.
Donor(s): Malcolm H. Wiener.
Financial data (yr. ended 06/30/01): Assets, $8,462,056 (M); grants paid, $2,696,601; gifts received, $15,958; expenditures, $3,844,047; qualifying distributions, $3,386,365.
Limitations: Giving on a national and international basis, with emphasis on Greece.
Officers and Directors:* Malcolm H. Wiener, Pres. and Treas.; Phillip Betancourt, V.P. and Secy.; Harvey Beker,* V.P.; George E. Crapple,* V.P.; Martin J. Whitman, Carolyn S. Wiener.
EIN: 133137391
Codes: FD, GTI

61977
The Saul Steinberg Foundation
c/o John Silberman Assoc., PC
145 E. 57th St.
New York, NY 10022

Established in 2000 in DE and NY.
Financial data (yr. ended 03/31/01): Assets, $8,432,101 (M); grants paid, $0; gifts received, $8,811,007; expenditures, $90,437; qualifying distributions, $69,926; giving activities include $90,437 for programs.
Limitations: Applications not accepted.
Application information: Contributes only to pre-selected organizations.
Officers: John Hollander, Pres.; Prudence Crowther, V.P.; Ian Frazier, Secy.; John Silberman, Treas.
EIN: 134115047

61978
The Jerome Belson Foundation
(Formerly Joseph Belsky Foundation)
495 Broadway, 6th Fl.
New York, NY 10012   (212) 941-9500
Contact: Jerome Belson, Pres.

Established in 1976.
Donor(s): Jerome Belson.
Financial data (yr. ended 12/31/00): Assets, $8,375,667 (L); grants paid, $2,183,812; gifts received, $25,493; expenditures, $2,237,855; qualifying distributions, $2,183,812.
Limitations: Giving primarily in NY.
Application information: Application form not required.
Officers: Jerome Belson, Pres.; I. Victor Belson, V.P.; Ruth Kessler, Secy.; Maxine Belson, Treas.
EIN: 510195570
Codes: FD

61979
The Leon Polk Smith Foundation
31 Union Sq. W.
New York, NY 10003

Established in 1998 in NY.
Donor(s): Robert M. Jamieson.
Financial data (yr. ended 12/31/00): Assets, $8,356,271 (M); grants paid, $50,000; gifts received, $5,000; expenditures, $137,741; qualifying distributions, $63,871.
Limitations: Applications not accepted. Giving primarily in Dallas, TX.
Application information: Contributes only to pre-selected organizations.
Trustees: John Bergman, Robert T. Buck, Robert Mead Jamieson, Gordon H. Marsh, Carter Ratcliffe.
EIN: 137147740

61980
Woodbrook Adult Home, Inc.
(also known as The Home for the Aged)
1250 Maple Ave.
Elmira, NY 14904

Established in 1874 in NY.
Financial data (yr. ended 03/31/01): Assets, $8,321,930 (M); grants paid, $0; gifts received, $4,420; expenditures, $1,734,690; qualifying distributions, $1,368,288; giving activities include $1,536,682 for programs.

Officers and Directors:* Betsy Dalrymple,* Pres.; Mindy Elzufon,* V.P.; Sheila Giovannini,* Secy.; Vincent R. Valicenti,* Treas.; Laurie Brann, Exec. Dir.; David Biviano, Kathy Carozza, Fran Crew, Dennis Fagan, Michael Hosey, Jim Perrotta, Mary Booth Roberts.
EIN: 160766337

61981
The Alice Desmond and Hamilton Fish Library
P.O. Box 265
Garrison, NY 10524

Classified as a private operating foundation in 1978.
Donor(s): Alice Desmond,‡ Hamilton Fish, Sr.‡
Financial data (yr. ended 12/31/01): Assets, $7,880,941 (M); grants paid, $0; gifts received, $114,404; expenditures, $572,214; qualifying distributions, $413,776; giving activities include $415,117 for programs.
Limitations: Applications not accepted. Giving primarily in NY.
Application information: Contributes only to pre-selected organizations.
Officers and Trustees:* Hamilton Fish,* Pres.; Arthur Ross,* V.P.; Katherine O. Roberts,* 2nd V.P.; Susan Bates,* Secy.; Catherine Patton,* Treas.; Patricia Adams, John Winthrop Aldrich, Lynn Carano, and 15 additional trustees.
EIN: 132933774

61982
St. George's Society of New York
175 9th Ave.
New York, NY 10011-4977 (212) 924-1434
FAX: (212) 727-1566; E-mail: info@stgeorgessociety.org; URL: http://www.stgeorgessociety.org
Contact: John Shannon, Exec. Dir.

Established in 1770 in NY.
Financial data (yr. ended 12/31/01): Assets, $7,860,375 (M); grants paid, $345,878; gifts received, $48,413; expenditures, $561,364; qualifying distributions, $412,003.
Limitations: Giving limited to the metropolitan New York, NY, area.
Publications: Annual report, newsletter, application guidelines, informational brochure.
Application information: Personal interviews and visits from the Society's social worker. Application form required.
Officers: Peter L. Raven, Pres.; William R. Miller, 1st V.P.; Rodney N. Johnson, 2nd V.P.; Michael A. Boyd, Secy.; Arthur J. Rawl, Treas.
EIN: 237426425
Codes: FD, GTI

61983
The Elkes Foundation
12 Trails End
Rye, NY 10580 (914) 381-5350
Contact: Terrence A. Elkes, Tr.

Established in 1989 in NY.
Financial data (yr. ended 11/30/99): Assets, $7,513,104 (M); grants paid, $344,626; gifts received, $996,000; expenditures, $344,926; qualifying distributions, $341,986.
Trustees: Ruth F. Elkes, Terrence A. Elkes.
EIN: 133497016
Codes: FD

61984
The Randall & Barbara Smith Foundation
c/o Smith Management LLC
885 3rd Ave., 34th Fl.
New York, NY 10022 (212) 888-5500
Contact: John W. Adams, Secy.

Established in 1993 in NY.
Donor(s): Randall D. Smith.
Financial data (yr. ended 12/31/00): Assets, $7,239,966 (M); grants paid, $20,000; expenditures, $20,371; qualifying distributions, $20,000.
Officers: Barbara S. Smith, Pres.; John W. Adams, Secy.; Jeffrey A. Smith, Treas.
EIN: 133748695

61985
The Stepping Stones Foundation
P.O. Box 452
Bedford Hills, NY 10507 (914) 232-4822
URL: http://www.steppingstones.org
Contact: Eileen Giuliani, Exec. Dir.

Established in 1980 in NY.
Donor(s): Lois B. Wilson.‡
Financial data (yr. ended 12/31/01): Assets, $7,007,541 (M); grants paid, $2,500; gifts received, $12,579; expenditures, $258,746; qualifying distributions, $200,890.
Officers: Peter O. Rosenberg, M.D., Pres.; William Borchert, V.P.; Jack Keegan, Secy.; Robert Hoguet, Treas.; Eileen Giuliani, Exec. Dir.
Trustees: John Allen, George Bloom, Julie Clark Boak, Joanna Cohlan, Owen Quattlebaum, Maureen Sullivan, Paul Wood, Lawrence Yermack.
EIN: 133031164

61986
Research Institute for the Study of Man
162 E. 78th St.
New York, NY 10021-0406 (212) 678-4040
Application address: Teachers College, Columbia University, TC Box 045, 525 W. 120th St., New York, NY 10027; URL: http://www.rism.org/sft.html
Contact: Lambros Comitas, Pres.

Established in 1955.
Financial data (yr. ended 12/31/99): Assets, $6,978,252 (M); grants paid, $7,000; gifts received, $250,000; expenditures, $293,861; qualifying distributions, $283,674.
Limitations: Giving on a national basis.
Application information: Application form not required.
Officers and Directors:* Lambros Comitas,* Pres.; Reed Rubin,* V.P. and Treas.; June Anderson,* Secy.
EIN: 131874676
Codes: GTI

61987
The GreenPark Foundation, Inc.
1 E. 53rd St., Rm. 1400
New York, NY 10022-4200 (212) 888-2520

Classified as a private operating foundation in 1971.
Financial data (yr. ended 12/31/01): Assets, $6,753,280 (M); grants paid, $0; gifts received, $225,270; expenditures, $291,209; qualifying distributions, $253,275; giving activities include $245,875 for programs.
Officers and Directors:* William C. Paley,* Pres.; Daniel L. Mosley,* V.P. and Secy.; Sidney W. Harl,* V.P.; Patrick S. Gallagher,* Treas.; Phillip A. Raspe, Jr.
EIN: 136155738

61988
Van Alen Institute
30 W. 22 St.
New York, NY 10010

Established in 1938.
Financial data (yr. ended 12/31/99): Assets, $6,680,007 (M); grants paid, $29,592; gifts received, $64,342; expenditures, $747,600; qualifying distributions, $420,035.
Limitations: Applications not accepted.
Application information: Contributes only to pre-selected organizations.
Director: Raymond Gastil, Exec. Dir.
EIN: 131655152
Codes: TN

61989
Alice T. Miner Colonial Collection
P.O. Box 90
Chazy, NY 12921-0090

Classified as a private operating foundation in 1986.
Financial data (yr. ended 12/31/00): Assets, $6,645,799 (M); grants paid, $0; gifts received, $4,046; expenditures, $201,299; qualifying distributions, $150,723; giving activities include $150,723 for programs.
Officers and Trustees:* Joan Burke,* Chair. and Pres.; Miriam Wiley,* V.P.; Judy B. Pombrio, Secy.; Paul J. Beattie, Jr.,* Treas.; Judith F. Heintz, Mary Riley.
EIN: 141405827

61990
Glens Falls Home, Inc.
178 Warren St.
Glens Falls, NY 12801-3764

Financial data (yr. ended 12/31/00): Assets, $6,369,578 (M); grants paid, $0; gifts received, $1,530; expenditures, $578,951; qualifying distributions, $161,078; giving activities include $6,193 for programs.
Officers: Frank O'Keefe, Pres.; Pat Boyle, Sr. V.P.; William Cutler, 1st V.P.; Mary Lou Noone, 2nd V.P.; Kay Barton, Secy.; Roy Steves, Treas.
Directors: Lesley Charlebois, Peggy Forbes, Mary Gijanto, and 10 additional directors.
EIN: 141340067

61991
T. Backer Fund, Inc.
P.O. Box 364
Chatham, NY 12037-0364

Donor(s): Judith B. Grunberg, Daniel Grunberg.
Financial data (yr. ended 12/31/01): Assets, $6,300,926 (M); grants paid, $343,050; gifts received, $231,314; expenditures, $416,701; qualifying distributions, $354,790.
Limitations: Applications not accepted. Giving primarily in NY.
Application information: Contributes only to pre-selected organizations.
Officers: Judith Grunberg, Pres.; Daniel Grunberg, V.P.
Director: David Grunberg.
EIN: 141640994
Codes: FD

61992
Westmoreland Davis Memorial Foundation, Inc.
c/o U.S. Trust
114 W. 47th St.
New York, NY 10036
FAX: (212) 852-3377

Financial data (yr. ended 12/31/00): Assets, $6,253,207 (M); grants paid, $107,964; gifts

61992—NEW YORK

received, $1,637,235; expenditures, $1,714,457; qualifying distributions, $1,478,138.
Limitations: Applications not accepted. Giving limited to Leesburg, VA.
Publications: Financial statement.
Application information: Contributes only to pre-selected organizations.
Trustees: Thomas Ashbridge III, Erskine L. Bedford, Frederic Carter, Edith A. Cassidy, Margaret Good, B. Powell Harrison, Michael Hoffman, Pamela Ohrstrum, Joseph M. Rogers, M.D., Margarita N. Serrell, Harold P. Wilmerding, Col. Paul Wimert, Mark Winmill.
EIN: 136170029

61993
The Troob Family Foundation
c/o David H. Troob
425 Park Ave.
New York, NY 10022

Established in 1999 in NY.
Donor(s): David H. Troob.
Financial data (yr. ended 11/30/00): Assets, $6,165,360 (M); grants paid, $28,408; gifts received, $0; expenditures, $29,988; qualifying distributions, $254,988; giving activities include $225,000 for programs.
Limitations: Applications not accepted.
Application information: Contributes only to pre-selected organizations.
Directors: Douglas M. Troob, Marjorie D. Troob, Peter J. Troob, Robyn W. Troob, Tara K. Troob.
Trustee: David H. Troob.
EIN: 367252941

61994
The Hau'Oli Mau Loa Foundation
c/o Debevoise & Plimpton
919 3rd Ave., 31st Fl.
New York, NY 10022-3902 (212) 909-6000

Established in 1990 in NY.
Donor(s): Helga Glaesel-Hollenback.‡
Financial data (yr. ended 04/30/01): Assets, $6,078,712 (M); grants paid, $280,000; expenditures, $375,694; qualifying distributions, $280,000.
Limitations: Applications not accepted. Giving primarily in HI.
Application information: Contributes only to pre-selected organizations.
Officers and Directors:* Hans Bertram-Nothnagel,* Pres.; Wayne M. Pitluck,* V.P.; Gary M. Friedman, Secy.-Treas.
EIN: 133588071
Codes: FD

61995
Christodora, Inc.
1 E. 53rd St., 14th Fl.
New York, NY 10022

Classified as a private operating foundation in 1997; Reorganized in 1992; Operated as a grantmaker since 1981; Established in 1897 as Christodora House.
Financial data (yr. ended 09/30/99): Assets, $6,019,327 (M); grants paid, $0; gifts received, $91,034; expenditures, $410,711; qualifying distributions, $365,642; giving activities include $143,774 for programs.
Officers and Trustees:* Pamela Manice,* Chair.; Thomas N. McCarter III, Chair Emeritus; Katrina F.C. Cary,* Pres.; Edward S. Elliman, Pres. Emeritus; James Rose,* V.P.; George W. Gowan,* Secy.; R. Scott Johnston,* Treas.
Directors: Edward H. Elliman, Matthew J. Lloyd, Arvid Nelson, Hugh D. Robertson, Stephen Slobadin, H. Gibb Taylor, Russell C. Wilkinson.

EIN: 135562192

61996
Home for the Aged
(Formerly Hudson New York Home for the Aged)
620 Union St.
Hudson, NY 12534-2812

Classified as a private operating foundation in 1984.
Financial data (yr. ended 09/30/01): Assets, $5,933,838 (M); grants paid, $0; gifts received, $46,286; expenditures, $605,487; qualifying distributions, $510,316; giving activities include $355,763 for programs.
Officers: Edward P. Ginouves, Pres.; Hildegard Thompson, V.P.; Susan Koskey, Secy.; Carl G. Whitbeck, Treas.
EIN: 141436628

61997
Phipps Community Development Corporation
43 W. 23rd St.
New York, NY 10010

Classified as a private operating foundation in 1988.
Donor(s): Howard Phipps Trust.
Financial data (yr. ended 12/31/00): Assets, $5,919,228 (M); grants paid, $0; gifts received, $5,275,183; expenditures, $4,058,794; qualifying distributions, $3,984,884; giving activities include $2,055,774 for programs.
Officers: Ronay Menschel, Chair.; Robert Pincus, Secy.; Owen Stemmer, Treas.; Stephen Tosh, Exec. Dir.
Directors: William Aguado, Dita Amory, Roscoe C. Brown, Jr., Ph.D., David Chao, and 9 additional directors.
EIN: 132707665

61998
Doris Duke Management Foundation
650 Fifth Avenue, 19th Fl.
New York, NY 10019

Established in 1999 in NY.
Financial data (yr. ended 12/31/99): Assets, $5,762,009 (M); grants paid, $0; gifts received, $6,640,000; expenditures, $7,287,833; qualifying distributions, $954,049; giving activities include $6,592,960 for programs.
Officers: Joan Spero, Pres.; Betsy Fader, Secy.; Alan Alschuler, C.F.O.
Trustees: J. Carter Brown, Marion Oates Charles, Harry B. Demopoulos, Anthony S. Fauci, James F. Gill, Nannerl O. Keohane, John J. Mack.
EIN: 134008718

61999
Park Charitable Trust
(Formerly Park Foundation)
5223 15th Ave.
Brooklyn, NY 11219 (718) 851-4811
Contact: Efraim Landau, Dir.

Donor(s): Efraim Landau, A. Landau Trust, Triangle Trust.
Financial data (yr. ended 12/31/00): Assets, $5,455,794 (M); grants paid, $356,400; gifts received, $1,255,000; expenditures, $395,385; qualifying distributions, $356,400.
Directors: Chaim Landau, David Landau, Efraim Landau.
EIN: 116450788
Codes: FD

62000
National Sculpture Society, Inc.
237 Park Ave.
New York, NY 10017 (212) 764-5645
FAX: (212) 764-5651
Contact: Gwen Putzig Pier, Exec. Dir.

Established in 1893 in NY; classified as a private operating foundation in 1972.
Donor(s): Charlotte Geffken.‡
Financial data (yr. ended 09/30/01): Assets, $5,270,257 (M); grants paid, $19,400; gifts received, $468,365; expenditures, $669,809; qualifying distributions, $287,050; giving activities include $468,648 for programs.
Limitations: Giving on a national basis.
Publications: Financial statement, informational brochure (including application guidelines).
Application information: Application form required.
Officers and Directors:* Elliot Offner,* Pres.; Dan Ostermiller, 1st V.P.; Stanley Horowitz, 2nd V.P.; Debra Campbell, Treas.; Gwen Putzig Pier, Exec. Dir.; Nina Akamu, Giancarlo Biagi, Sergey Eylanbekov, Christopher Gow, Ray Kaskey, Kirsten Kokkin, Tuck Langland, Richard MacDonald, Margaret K. Nicholson, Joseph Veach Noble, Charles Parks, Robin Salmon, Jonathan Shahn, Alan Stahl, Tylden W. Street, Robert Weinman, Harvey Weiss.
EIN: 131656673
Codes: GTI

62001
Westmoreland Sanctuary, Inc.
Chestnut Ridge Rd.
Mount Kisco, NY 10549

Financial data (yr. ended 03/31/02): Assets, $5,208,855 (M); grants paid, $0; gifts received, $75,906; expenditures, $199,126; qualifying distributions, $0.
Officers and Directors:* Minturn V. Chace,* Pres.; S. Mackintosh Pulsifer,* V.P.; C. Nicholas Spofford,* V.P.; William M. Throop, Jr.,* Secy.; Jeremiah M. Bogart,* Treas.; Judith Paletta, Ann H. Polk, Edward R. Weidlein, Jr., and 6 additional directors.
EIN: 131855977

62002
The Watts Family Foundation
c/o Bessemer Trust Co., N.A.
630 5th Ave.
New York, NY 10111

Established in 1997 in MA.
Donor(s): Beverly Watts, David B. Watts.
Financial data (yr. ended 06/30/01): Assets, $5,202,849 (M); grants paid, $279,794; expenditures, $337,049; qualifying distributions, $276,450.
Limitations: Applications not accepted. Giving primarily in MA.
Application information: Contributes only to pre-selected organizations.
Trustees: Beverly Watts, David B. Watts.
EIN: 043402936
Codes: FD

62003
The Arnold Simon Family Foundation, Inc.
c/o Schneider, Schecter and Yoss, PC
1979 Marcus Ave., Ste. 232
New Hyde Park, NY 11042-1002

Established in 1996 in NJ.
Donor(s): Arnold Simon.
Financial data (yr. ended 12/31/99): Assets, $5,156,604 (M); grants paid, $1,557,368; gifts

received, $581,100; expenditures, $1,675,757; qualifying distributions, $1,553,901.
Limitations: Applications not accepted.
Application information: Contributes only to pre-selected organizations.
Trustees: Howard Schneider, Arnold Simon, Debra Simon.
EIN: 223480373
Codes: FD

62004
Mamaroneck Senior Citizen's Apartment Housing Development Fund Corporation, Inc.
c/o Community Housing Mgmt. Corp.
5 W. Main St., Ste. 214
Elmsford, NY 10523

Established in 1991 in NY.
Financial data (yr. ended 06/30/02): Assets, $5,111,024 (M); grants paid, $0; expenditures, $1,194,971; qualifying distributions, $0.
Officers and Directors:* Beverly Brewer-Villa,* Pres.; Gerhard Spies, V.P.; Ellen Levy, Exec. Dir.; Lorraine Castagna, Marzella Garland, Charles Grosjean, Laura Holbrook, Barbara King, Jefferson D. Meighan, Clark Neuringer, Kay Richards, Shirley Romney, Jefferson Shearman.
EIN: 133213293

62005
Pan-American MOA Foundation, Inc.
235 E. 40th St., Ste. 10-E
New York, NY 10016-1744

Established in 1997 in FL, CA, and HI.
Donor(s): Sekai Kyusei Kyo, Takemi Sato, Bless Ebesugawa, Reiko Nagata, Joseph Naruishi, Roy Shiraki, Edna Shiraki, Ronald Nakata, Jessie Nakata, Centro Cultural MOA De Toluca, AC, Toho No Hikari, Moa Int'l Mokichi Okada Foundation, Inc., Moa Foundation New York, Inc.
Financial data (yr. ended 03/31/01): Assets, $5,091,068 (M); grants paid, $61,897; gifts received, $1,852,764; expenditures, $2,145,795; qualifying distributions, $1,559,194; giving activities include $1,410,386 for programs.
Limitations: Applications not accepted. Giving on a national and international basis.
Application information: Contributes only to pre-selected organizations.
Officers and Directors:* Teruaki Kawai,* Chair.; Toshiaki Kawai,* Pres.; Masahiko Hiraizumi, Secy.; Eizo Tanaka, Treas.; Hideo Sonobe, Kazuya Udagawa.
EIN: 650733515

62006
Rye Manor Senior Citizens Apartment Housing Development Fund Corporation, Inc.
c/o Community Housing Mgmt.
5 W. Main St., Ste. 214
Elmsford, NY 10523

Established in 1985 in NY.
Financial data (yr. ended 10/31/01): Assets, $4,912,166 (M); grants paid, $0; expenditures, $1,172,283; qualifying distributions, $0.
Limitations: Giving limited to Rye, NY.
Officers and Directors:* Gilbert Weinstein,* Pres.; Carolyn Cunningham,* V.P.; Anne Pastor,* Secy.; Edward J. Collins,* Treas.; Betty Schneider, and 9 additional directors.
EIN: 133112042
Codes: TN

62007
Agnes Martin Foundation
c/o John J. Kearney
11 Sunrise Plz.
Valley Stream, NY 11580

Established in 2000 in NM.
Donor(s): Agnes Martin.
Financial data (yr. ended 12/31/00): Assets, $4,858,033 (M); grants paid, $150,000; gifts received, $5,000,000; expenditures, $150,074; qualifying distributions, $150,000.
Limitations: Applications not accepted. Giving primarily in Taos, NM; giving also in New York, NY.
Application information: Contributes only to pre-selected organizations.
Officer: Marc Glimcher, Pres.
Trustees: John J. Kearney, Agnes Martin.
EIN: 311724644
Codes: FD2

62008
Ira and Beth Leventhal Foundation
10 Bessel Ln.
Chappaqua, NY 10514

Donor(s): Ira Leventhal, Beth Leventhal.
Financial data (yr. ended 12/31/00): Assets, $4,783,580 (M); grants paid, $75,570; gifts received, $1,999,321; expenditures, $91,599; qualifying distributions, $75,570.
Limitations: Giving primarily in NY.
Officers and Trustee:* Beth Leventhal, Pres.; Ira Leventhal, V.P.; Richard Cayne,* Secy.
EIN: 134092955
Codes: FD2

62009
Dove Givings Foundation
c/o OTA, LP
1 Manhattanville Rd.
Purchase, NY 10577 (516) 889-3530
Application addresses: c/o John A. Heneghan, 125 Freeport Ave., Point Lookout, NY 11569, c/o Kevin Heneghan, 177 Bayside Dr., Point Lookout, NY 11569, and c/o Bartly Heneghan, 417 Manning Blvd., Albany, NY 12206

Established in 1995.
Donor(s): Kevin J. Heneghan.
Financial data (yr. ended 12/31/00): Assets, $4,741,520 (M); grants paid, $1,269,820; gifts received, $3,072,500; expenditures, $1,277,577; qualifying distributions, $1,268,618.
Application information: Application form not required.
Officers: John A. Heneghan, Pres.; Bartly Heneghan, V.P.; Kevin J. Heneghan, Secy.-Treas.
EIN: 133795957
Codes: FD

62010
Kiki Kogelnik Foundation
330 Lafayette St., No. 7
New York, NY 10012

Established in 1997 in NY.
Financial data (yr. ended 12/31/01): Assets, $4,565,389 (M); grants paid, $0; gifts received, $635,126; expenditures, $67,237; qualifying distributions, $0.
Limitations: Applications not accepted.
Application information: Contributes only to pre-selected organizations.
Officer: George Schwarz, Pres.
EIN: 137101223

62011
The BL Squared Foundation
10 E. 40th St., 22nd Fl.
New York, NY 10016-0201

Established in 1997.
Donor(s): Stanley Bernstein, Sandy Liebhard, Mel Lifshitz, Sandy Bernstein, Vivian Bernstein.
Financial data (yr. ended 12/31/00): Assets, $4,534,563 (M); grants paid, $0; gifts received, $857,935; expenditures, $7,468; qualifying distributions, $7,468.
Limitations: Applications not accepted.
Application information: Contributes only to pre-selected organizations.
Trustees: Stanley Bernstein, Sandy Liebhard, Mel Lifshitz.
EIN: 137104062

62012
Ingersoll Memorial for Aged Men, Inc.
3421 State St.
Schenectady, NY 12304

Classified as a private operating foundation in 1988.
Financial data (yr. ended 09/30/00): Assets, $4,523,126 (M); grants paid, $0; gifts received, $25,266; expenditures, $647,824; qualifying distributions, $526,696; giving activities include $562,595 for programs.
Officers and Trustees:* Robert M. Armbrust,* Pres.; James H. Erceg,* V.P.; Van C. Mekeel,* Secy.; Thomas Prawdzik,* Treas.; Lenore Bethka, and 11 additional trustees.
EIN: 141364550

62013
Pearson Art Foundation, Inc.
(Formerly Spencer Art Foundation)
c/o Wollin Assocs.
350 5th Ave., Ste. 2822
New York, NY 10118

Established around 1986.
Donor(s): Gerald Pearson, Beverly Pearson.
Financial data (yr. ended 09/30/00): Assets, $4,449,669 (M); grants paid, $82,389; gifts received, $14,341; expenditures, $312,414; qualifying distributions, $218,018.
Limitations: Applications not accepted. Giving primarily in IA.
Application information: Contributes only to pre-selected organizations.
Officers: Gerald Pearson, Pres.; Beverly Pearson, V.P.; Lonnie E. Wollin, Secy.; Perry Pearson, Treas.
EIN: 237087276
Codes: FD2

62014
Elizabeth Brewster House
41 S. Main St.
Homer, NY 13077-1323

Donor(s): R. Wilkins.
Financial data (yr. ended 12/31/01): Assets, $4,171,259 (M); grants paid, $0; gifts received, $1,305; expenditures, $753,738; qualifying distributions, $0.
Officers and Trustees:* Peter Potter,* Pres.; Gwynne Crosley, Pres.; Marion Calale, V.P.; Evelyn Crofoot, V.P.; Laura Johnson, Secy.; Jean Cadwallader, Treas.; Carl Edlund,* Treas.
EIN: 150533548
Codes: TN

62015
The BFF Foundation, Inc.
5612 18th Ave.
Brooklyn, NY 11204-1955

Established in 1996 in NY.
Donor(s): Joseph Bistritzky.
Financial data (yr. ended 12/31/00): Assets, $4,086,007 (M); grants paid, $122,106; gifts received, $1,632,911; expenditures, $122,347; qualifying distributions, $122,281.
Limitations: Giving primarily in NJ and Brooklyn, NY.
Officers: Joseph Bistritzky, Pres.; Yehudis Gold, Secy.; Sheila Bistritzky, Treas.
EIN: 113261912
Codes: FD2

62016
The Rockwell Museum
Cedar St. at Denison Pkwy.
Corning, NY 14830-2253

Classified as a private operating foundation in 1984.
Financial data (yr. ended 12/31/01): Assets, $4,034,697 (M); grants paid, $0; gifts received, $2,644,096; expenditures, $2,306,725; qualifying distributions, $2,211,835; giving activities include $2,223,108 for programs.
Director: Stuart Chase.
Trustees: Richard B. Bessey, Thomas S. Buechner, George F. Connors, Donald J. Egan, Gerald J. Fine, James B. Flaws, and 17 additional trustees.
EIN: 222468604

62017
Bohemian Gymnastic Association (Sokol) of the City of New York
420-424 E. 71st St.
New York, NY 10021-4802

Classified as a private operating foundation in 1989, established in NY.
Financial data (yr. ended 12/31/01): Assets, $3,948,789 (M); grants paid, $1,015; gifts received, $9,080; expenditures, $233,419; qualifying distributions, $106,285; giving activities include $214,707 for programs.
Limitations: Applications not accepted.
Officers: Norma Zabka, Pres.; Stanley Mergl, 1st V.P.; William Cermak, 2nd V.P.; Beatrice Cihak, Fin. Secy.; Antonie Mahoney, Recording Secy.; Jean Stefkovic, Treas.
Directors: Joseph Balogh, Donna Sbriglia.
EIN: 130508060

62018
Performing Arts Foundation, Inc.
c/o Spitz & Greenstein
21 E. 40th St., Rm. 1006
New York, NY 10016-0501
Application address: 115 Central Park W., New York, NY 10023
Contact: Herman Rottenberg, Pres.

Established in 1963.
Donor(s): Herman Rottenberg.
Financial data (yr. ended 08/31/00): Assets, $3,946,417 (M); grants paid, $40,000; gifts received, $200; expenditures, $329,054; qualifying distributions, $268,150.
Limitations: Giving primarily in NY.
Application information: Application form not required.
Officer: Herman Rottenberg, Pres.
EIN: 136149781

62019
Human Potential Foundation
548 Broadhollow Rd.
Melville, NY 11747

Classified as a private operating foundation in 1985.
Donor(s): Gerald Kessler.
Financial data (yr. ended 11/30/01): Assets, $3,935,580 (M); grants paid, $0; gifts received, $44,903; expenditures, $93,617; qualifying distributions, $0.
Trustee: Gerald Kessler.
EIN: 112670749

62020
Acriel Foundation
c/o U.S. Trust
P.O. Box 2004
New York, NY 10109-1910

Established in 1994 in NY.
Financial data (yr. ended 11/30/00): Assets, $3,865,195 (M); grants paid, $105,000; gifts received, $981,967; expenditures, $163,292; qualifying distributions, $125,861.
Limitations: Applications not accepted.
Application information: Contributes only to pre-selected organizations.
Trustee: U.S. Trust.
EIN: 133802863
Codes: FD2

62021
D. C. Miller Trust
c/o Vittoria, Forsythe, & Purdy, LLP
630 5th Ave.
New York, NY 10111-0100 (212) 489-8104
Contact: Theodore J. Vittoria, Jr.

Classified as a private operating trust in 1992.
Donor(s): Dorothy Miller Bloeser Trust, William Henry Miller Trust.
Financial data (yr. ended 12/31/01): Assets, $3,816,011 (M); grants paid, $5,000; expenditures, $102,213; qualifying distributions, $56,964; giving activities include $56,964 for programs.
Limitations: Giving primarily in New York, NY.
Application information: Application form not required.
Trustee: Theodore J. Vittoria, Jr.
EIN: 133629880

62022
The Rojtman Foundation, Inc.
22 E. 64th St.
New York, NY 10021 (212) 752-5532

Classified as a private operating foundation in 1972.
Financial data (yr. ended 12/31/01): Assets, $3,797,207 (M); grants paid, $0; expenditures, $30,261; qualifying distributions, $30,261; giving activities include $26,153 for programs.
Officers: Myles Berkman, Pres. and Treas.; Barbara Hagani, Pres. and Treas.; Jonathan Koslow, Pres. and Treas.; Harold Winters, Pres. and Treas.; Janice Whitmore Sahlstrand, V.P.
Director: Lisa Hagani.
EIN: 396050193

62023
Parapsychology Foundation, Inc.
228 E. 71st St.
New York, NY 10021 (212) 628-1550
FAX: (212) 628-1559; URL: http://www.parapsychology.org
Contact: Eileen Coly, Pres.

Incorporated in 1951 in DE; classified as a private operating foundation in 1983.
Financial data (yr. ended 12/31/01): Assets, $3,709,561 (M); grants paid, $14,557; expenditures, $925,637; qualifying distributions, $762,904.
Limitations: Giving on a national and international basis.
Publications: Annual report (including application guidelines), informational brochure (including application guidelines).
Application information: Application form required.
Officers and Trustees:* Eileen Coly,* Pres.; Lisette Coly,* V.P.; Stephen Powers, Secy.-Treas; Sandra R. Miller, Rose Moloney, Edward Swensen.
EIN: 131677742
Codes: GTI

62024
Frank Melville Memorial Foundation
P.O. Box 2967
Setauket, NY 11733

Donor(s): Ruth Berlin,‡ Frank Melville III.
Financial data (yr. ended 12/31/01): Assets, $3,674,590 (M); grants paid, $0; gifts received, $9,400; expenditures, $104,891; qualifying distributions, $68,991; giving activities include $68,991 for programs.
Limitations: Applications not accepted.
Officers: Beverly Tyler, Pres.; Frank Melville III, Secy.; Albert Meyer, Treas.
EIN: 116036411

62025
The Johnny Mercer Foundation
c/o Prager and Fenton
675 3rd Ave.
New York, NY 10017 (212) 382-2790
Application address: 234 W. 44th St., New York, NY 10036
Contact: George C. White, Exec. Dir.

Established in 1982 in CA.
Donor(s): Elizabeth M. Mercer.
Financial data (yr. ended 07/31/01): Assets, $3,673,678 (M); grants paid, $781,800; gifts received, $4,945; expenditures, $1,163,077; qualifying distributions, $834,728.
Limitations: Giving on a national basis.
Publications: Annual report.
Application information: Applicants for Songwriters Award for American popular music should consult application guidelines. Application form required.
Officers and Directors:* Margaret Whiting,* Pres.; Lewis M. Bachman,* V.P.; Michael A. Kerker, V.P.; Charles S. Tigerman,* V.P.; George C. White, Exec. Dir.; Ray Evans, William M. Suttles, Jack Wrangler, and 10 additional directors.
EIN: 953728115
Codes: FD

62026
Kermit Gitenstein Foundation, Inc.
51 Montgomery Blvd.
Atlantic Beach, NY 11509-1412

Established in 1969.
Financial data (yr. ended 12/31/01): Assets, $3,652,521 (M); grants paid, $104,400; gifts

received, $1,403,961; expenditures, $105,460; qualifying distributions, $104,199.
Limitations: Applications not accepted. Giving primarily in NY.
Application information: Contributes only to pre-selected organizations.
Officer: Shirley Gitenstein, Pres. and V.P.
EIN: 237032219
Codes: FD2

62027
Poetry Society of America
15 Gramercy Park
New York, NY 10003-1705 (212) 254-9628

Classified as a private operating foundation in 1976.
Donor(s): Lila Wallace-Readers Digest Fund.
Financial data (yr. ended 09/30/99): Assets, $3,568,405 (M); grants paid, $0; gifts received, $314,899; expenditures, $537,952; qualifying distributions, $433,131; giving activities include $327,575 for programs.
Limitations: Giving on a national basis.
Application information: Award winners selected by Society. Application form required.
Officers and Directors:* William Louis-Dreyfus,* Pres.; Anna Rabinowitz,* V.P.; Mary Jo Salter,* V.P.; Ellen Rachlin, Treas.; John Barr, Lucille Clifton, Dana Gioia, Molly Peacock, Jack Stadler, and 13 additional directors.
EIN: 136019220
Codes: TN

62028
Plan for Social Excellence, Inc.
c/o Kisco Management Corp.
111 Radio Cir.
Mount Kisco, NY 10549
URL: http://www.pfse.org
Contact: Mario J. Pena, Exec. Dir.

Established in 1989 in NY.
Donor(s): James A. Kohlberg, Nancy S. Kohlberg.
Financial data (yr. ended 07/31/01): Assets, $3,549,331 (M); grants paid, $978,440; gifts received, $5,118,792; expenditures, $1,560,871; qualifying distributions, $1,480,432; giving activities include $1,002 for programs.
Limitations: Applications not accepted.
Publications: Newsletter.
Application information: Unsolicited requests for funds not considered.
Officers: James A. Kohlberg, Pres.; Walter W. Farley, Secy.-Treas.; Mario J. Pena, Exec. Dir.
Directors: Eileen Capone, James P. Honan, Suzanne Kohlberg, Hloy Pena.
Trustee: Kisco Management Corp.
EIN: 066082681
Codes: FD

62029
Price Institute for Entrepreneurial Studies, Inc.
450 Park Ave., Ste. 1102
New York, NY 10022 (212) 752-9335
FAX: (212) 752-9338; *E-mail:* rguidone@priceinstitute.org
Contact: Rosemary Guidone, Pres.

Established in 1979 in NY.
Donor(s): The Louis & Harold Price Foundation, Inc.
Financial data (yr. ended 12/31/00): Assets, $3,513,326 (M); grants paid, $1,651,821; gifts received, $970,807; expenditures, $2,193,125; qualifying distributions, $2,170,063.
Application information: See Price Foundation Web site for grantmaking process, URL: http://www.pricefoundation.org. Application form not required.

Officers: Rosemary Guidone, Pres.; Tim A. Jones, Exec. V.P.; James J. Loeb, Treas.
Trustees: Milton Eulan, Robert F. Hatch, Oliver M. Mendell, Morris Offit, Alfred Osborne, Jr.
EIN: 133008173
Codes: FD, GTI

62030
Dreyfus Charitable Foundation
(Formerly Dreyfus Medical Foundation)
4 W. 58th St.
New York, NY 10019

Established in 1961 in NY as a private operating foundation.
Donor(s): Jack J. Dreyfus, Jr., John Dreyfus, Joan D. Blout.
Financial data (yr. ended 12/31/99): Assets, $3,466,431 (M); grants paid, $0; gifts received, $65; expenditures, $5,233,196; qualifying distributions, $5,230,242; giving activities include $5,232,427 for programs.
Officers and Directors:* Jack J. Dreyfus,* Pres.; John Dreyfus,* V.P.; Dean Gould,* Secy.; Arnold D. Friedman,* Treas.
EIN: 136086089

62031
Power of Attorney, Inc.
330 7th Ave.
New York, NY 10001
URL: http://www.powerofattorney.org

Established in 1999 in NY.
Financial data (yr. ended 06/30/01): Assets, $3,378,028 (M); grants paid, $362,500; gifts received, $129,301; expenditures, $1,589,830; qualifying distributions, $1,025,204; giving activities include $900,260 for programs.
Limitations: Giving on a national basis.
Officers: Cynthis R. Shoss, Chair.; Allen R. Bromberger, Pres.; Shari Dunn Buron, V.P.; Stephen D. Cooke, Secy.; Michael K. Hertz, Treas.
EIN: 134063066
Codes: FD

62032
Old Westbury Gardens, Inc.
P.O. Box 430
Old Westbury, NY 11568

Donor(s): Howard Phipps, Jr., Mrs. Howard Phipps, Jr., Deidre Costa-Major, Robert Eichelberger, Mrs. Robert Eichelberger, Julian H. Robertson, Jr., Mrs. Julian H. Robertson, Jr., Frank Castagna, Mrs. Frank Castagna, Colton P. Wagner, Mrs. Colton P. Wagner, Henry C. Frick II, Mrs. Henry C. Frick II, Patrick Gerschel, Mrs. Patrick Gerschel.
Financial data (yr. ended 12/31/00): Assets, $3,347,450 (M); grants paid, $0; gifts received, $2,138,617; expenditures, $2,492,872; qualifying distributions, $0.
Officers and Trustees:* Mrs. Howard Phipps, Jr.,* Chair.; Mrs. James M. Large, Jr., Pres.; Frank Castagna,* V.P.; J. Oliver Crom,* V.P.; Mrs. Colton P. Wagner,* V.P.; Mrs. Richard Gachot,* Secy.; Laureen Stanton Knutsen,* Treas.; Susan Lathrop, Exec. Dir.; and 18 additional trustees.
Directors: Wendy Belser, Kenneth Gass, Nelson Sterneer, Diane Turner.
EIN: 111902968

62033
Siran & Anoush Mathevosian Charitable Foundation, Inc.
30 Candy Ln.
Great Neck, NY 11023

Donor(s): Siran Mathevosian.

Financial data (yr. ended 12/31/00): Assets, $3,332,381 (L); grants paid, $3,517,750; gifts received, $7,152,798; expenditures, $3,518,425; qualifying distributions, $0.
Trustee: Siran Mathevosian.
EIN: 113379318
Codes: FD

62034
Society of Kastorians "Omonoia", Inc.
150-28 14th Ave.
Whitestone, NY 11357 (718) 746-4505

Established in 1989 in NY.
Financial data (yr. ended 12/31/01): Assets, $3,304,158 (M); grants paid, $74,475; gifts received, $18,178; expenditures, $460,141; qualifying distributions, $223,229; giving activities include $35,225 for programs.
Limitations: Giving primarily in NY.
Application information: Application form required.
Officers: Arsenis Kostopoulos, Pres.; Stefanos Amanatides, V.P.; Steven Boutis, Secy.; John Kyrou, Treas.
Directors: Vasilios Athanasopoulos, George Jimas, Anastasios Kokalenios, Evangelos Kotsidis, Nick Mavrovitis, George Mesaikos, Damianos Pekmezaris, Panos Politides, Dimitros Tassopoulos, Damis Yancopoulos.
EIN: 133000517
Codes: GTI

62035
The Norwegian Children's Home Association of NY, Inc.
P.O. Box 280104
Brooklyn, NY 11228-0104 (718) 238-4326
Contact: John Nersten, Pres.

Established in 2000 in NY.
Financial data (yr. ended 12/31/01): Assets, $3,298,795 (M); grants paid, $100,300; gifts received, $411; expenditures, $124,866; qualifying distributions, $110,873.
Application information: Applicants must be at least of 25 percent Norwegian ancestry or have a significant Norwegian affiliation.
Officers: John Nersent, Pres.; Ruth Santoro, V.P.; Lynn Mannino, Corr. Secy.; Kjell Kittnsen, Financial Secy.; Lillian Fidhammer, Rec. Secy.; George Outzin, Treas.
EIN: 111666853
Codes: FD2

62036
Schweinfurth Memorial Art Center, Inc.
205 Genesee St.
P.O. Box 916
Auburn, NY 13021-0916

Established in 1978 in NY.
Financial data (yr. ended 12/31/01): Assets, $3,289,483 (M); grants paid, $0; gifts received, $126,394; expenditures, $229,088; qualifying distributions, $0.
Officers: Wesley Clymer, Pres.; Tom Champion, V.P.; Guy Cosentino, Secy.; John Latanyshyn, Treas.; Donna Lamb, Exec. Dir.
Trustees: Roy Bench, Pat Blackwell, and 7 additional trustees.
EIN: 161097876

62037
Sedgwick & North Halls HDFC, Inc.
c/o Metro Mgmt. Development, Inc.
42-25 21st St.
Long Island City, NY 11101

Financial data (yr. ended 12/31/00): Assets, $3,231,001 (M); grants paid, $0; expenditures,

$1,280,203; qualifying distributions, $1,130,191; giving activities include $1,280,203 for programs.
Officers: J. Kenneth Pagano, Pres.; George Golovchenko, V.P.; Dolores Magnotta, Secy.; Ella Stewart, Treas.
EIN: 133098855

62038
The Russell Maguire Foundation, Inc.
c/o Hecht and Assoc., LLP
10 E. 40th St., Rm. 710
New York, NY 10016

Incorporated in 1941 in NY.
Donor(s): Russell Maguire.‡
Financial data (yr. ended 12/31/01): Assets, $3,219,506 (M); grants paid, $157,500; expenditures, $244,769; qualifying distributions, $189,031.
Limitations: Applications not accepted. Giving primarily in CT and NY.
Application information: Contributes only to pre-selected organizations.
Directors: F. Richards Ford III, Natasha B. Ford, Tina Grayson.
EIN: 136162698
Codes: FD2

62039
Harvey R. Lewis Foundation, Inc.
275 Main St.
P.O. Box 711
Port Washington, NY 11050-0201

Established in 1985.
Donor(s): Harvey R. Lewis.
Financial data (yr. ended 06/30/01): Assets, $3,191,674 (M); grants paid, $110,500; gifts received, $646,682; expenditures, $158,857; qualifying distributions, $110,500.
Application information: Submit academic transcripts, extracurricular activities and financial need statement. Application form not required.
Directors: Robert A. Brady, Charles H. Walker, Jr.
EIN: 112630467
Codes: FD2, GTI

62040
Warner Home for the Aged
1103 W. 3rd St.
Jamestown, NY 14701-4699

Classified as a private operating foundation in 1972.
Financial data (yr. ended 12/31/01): Assets, $3,180,675 (M); grants paid, $0; expenditures, $322,389; qualifying distributions, $288,069; giving activities include $289,030 for programs.
Officers and Trustees:* Sue Foley,* Pres.; Diane Wellman, 1st V.P.; Carol Nord,* 2nd V.P.; Connie Flowers,* Recording Secy.; Kollie Bargar,* Corresponding Secy.; Judy Lockwood,* Treas.; Ozzie Johnson, Carole Sellstrom, and 17 additional trustees.
EIN: 160743217

62041
Salute to the Seasons Fund, Inc.
110 E. 42nd St., Ste. 1300
New York, NY 10017

Classified as a private operating foundation in 1971.
Donor(s): Mary W. Lasker.‡
Financial data (yr. ended 12/31/99): Assets, $3,126,856 (M); grants paid, $22,125; gifts received, $508,459; expenditures, $812,304; qualifying distributions, $731,847; giving activities include $752,359 for programs.
Limitations: Applications not accepted. Giving primarily in New York, NY.

Publications: Newsletter.
Application information: Contributes only to pre-selected organizations.
Officers and Directors:* James W. Fordyce,* Pres. and Treas.; Anne Boardman Fordyce, V.P.; James E. Hughes, Jr., Secy.; Margaret Ternes, Exec. Dir.
EIN: 136162773

62042
Ossorio Foundation
164 Mariner Dr.
Southampton, NY 11968

Classified as a private operating foundation in 1996.
Donor(s): Edward F. Dragon Young.
Financial data (yr. ended 12/31/00): Assets, $3,015,789 (M); grants paid, $0; gifts received, $110,041; expenditures, $198,958; qualifying distributions, $196,656; giving activities include $198,287 for programs.
Officers: Edward F. Dragon Young, Pres.; Sally R. Vanasse, Secy.; Michael Solomon, Treas.
EIN: 113270671

62043
Olga Fleisher Ornithological Foundation, Inc.
161 Avondale Rd.
Rochester, NY 14622-1915

Established around 1981.
Financial data (yr. ended 12/31/00): Assets, $2,958,257 (M); grants paid, $0; expenditures, $131,139; qualifying distributions, $169,539; giving activities include $14,397 for programs.
Officers: Margarita Neumann, Pres.; Christopher Neumann, V.P.; Elizabeth Van Acker, Secy.-Treas.
EIN: 591952648

62044
Eugenie A. T. Smith Testamentary Trust
c/o Rehman & Knoetig
10 S. Ocean Ave.
Patchogue, NY 11772

Donor(s): George C. Furman.‡
Financial data (yr. ended 02/28/01): Assets, $2,937,360 (M); grants paid, $0; expenditures, $89,490; qualifying distributions, $89,490; giving activities include $89,490 for programs.
Trustees: George H. Furman, Judith Furman.
EIN: 111731972

62045
Parents in Charge
c/o Forstmann Little & Co.
767 5th Ave., 44th Fl.
New York, NY 10153

Established in 2000 in NY.
Donor(s): Theodore J. Forstmann, Paul Tudor Jones.
Financial data (yr. ended 12/31/00): Assets, $2,925,113 (M); grants paid, $0; gifts received, $10,670,512; expenditures, $7,832,173; qualifying distributions, $7,826,798; giving activities include $7,628,486 for programs.
Officers and Directors:* Theodore J. Forstmann,* Chair. and Pres.; Margot McGinness,* V.P.; Stephen Fraidin.
EIN: 134124186

62046
Lucille Lortel Theatre Foundation, Inc.
c/o Hecht & Co.
111 W. 40th St.
New York, NY 10018

Established as a private operating foundation in 1998 in NY.
Donor(s): Lucille Lortel Foundation, Inc., Lortel, Inc.

Financial data (yr. ended 06/30/01): Assets, $2,920,379 (M); grants paid, $0; gifts received, $324,628; expenditures, $588,995; qualifying distributions, $360,711; giving activities include $88,247 for programs.
Officers: James J. Ross, Pres.; George Forbes, V.P. and Finance Admin.; George Shaskin, V.P.; Richard M. Ticklin, Secy.; Michael Hecht, Treas.
EIN: 133995881

62047
The Annie Tinker Association for Women, Inc.
(Formerly Annie Rensselaer Tinker Memorial Fund)
1393 York Ave.
New York, NY 10021 (212) 628-4022
Contact: Nancy Houghton, Tr.

Established in 1924 in NY.
Donor(s): Annie Rensselaer Tinker.‡
Financial data (yr. ended 06/30/01): Assets, $2,885,855 (M); grants paid, $66,293; gifts received, $48,799; expenditures, $165,108; qualifying distributions, $136,077.
Limitations: Giving primarily in the greater metropolitan New York, NY area.
Publications: Newsletter.
Application information: Application form required.
Officers and Trustees:* R. Dyke Benjamin,* Pres.; Mary Rogers,* V.P.; Carolyn Smith,* Secy.; Frederic Howard,* Treas.; Sue Chandler, Nancy Houghton, Phyliss Ross Schless.
EIN: 136405671
Codes: GTI

62048
Virgil Thomson Foundation, Ltd.
c/o Brown Raysman, LLP
900 3rd Ave.
New York, NY 10022 (212) 895-2367
URL: http://www.virgilthomson.org
Contact: James M. Kendrik, Secy.

Established around 1982.
Donor(s): Virgil Thomson.‡
Financial data (yr. ended 12/31/01): Assets, $2,857,089 (M); grants paid, $238,350; expenditures, $325,303; qualifying distributions, $277,023.
Limitations: Giving primarily in New York, NY.
Publications: Informational brochure (including application guidelines).
Application information: Application form required.
Officers: Richard Flender, Pres. and Treas.; Charles Fussell, V.P.; James M. Kendrik, Secy.
Directors: Ellis Freedman, H. Wiley Hitchcock, Anne-Marie Soulliere.
EIN: 133070053
Codes: FD2

62049
Mainwaring Archive Foundation
c/o Brown Brothers Harriman Trust Co.
63 Wall St., 26th Fl.
New York, NY 10005-3001

Established in 2000 in PA.
Donor(s): A. Bruce Mainwaring.
Financial data (yr. ended 12/31/01): Assets, $2,812,445 (M); grants paid, $0; expenditures, $322,054; qualifying distributions, $308,323; giving activities include $85,070 for programs.
Trustees: A. Bruce Mainwaring, Brown Brothers Harriman Trust Co.
EIN: 527106931

62050
The Quinn Family Foundation
6 Pond View Dr.
Oyster Bay, NY 11771

Established in 1999.
Donor(s): William Quinn, Joanne Quinn.
Financial data (yr. ended 06/30/01): Assets, $2,811,781 (M); grants paid, $50,000; gifts received, $1,352,369; expenditures, $70,610; qualifying distributions, $50,000.
Limitations: Applications not accepted.
Application information: Contributes only to pre-selected organizations.
Trustees: James Barling, Rosemary Eisenberg, Patricia Myzwinski, Courtney Ann Quinn, Joanne Quinn, William John Quinn, William John Quinn III.
EIN: 113520444

62051
The Bogliasco Foundation, Inc.
885 2nd Ave., Rm. 3100
New York, NY 10017 (212) 940-8204
E-Mail: MAU@bfny.org; URL: http://www.liguriastudycenter.org.

Established in 1994 in NY.
Donor(s): Cristina Biaggi, Marina Harrison, Giovanni B. Biaggi De Blasys.
Financial data (yr. ended 12/31/01): Assets, $2,788,690 (M); grants paid, $0; gifts received, $468,833; expenditures, $703,582; qualifying distributions, $628,742; giving activities include $442,315 for programs.
Officers and Directors:* James Harrison,* Pres.; Anna Maria Quaiat,* V.P.; R. Andrew Boose, Secy.; Michael Hecht, Treas.; Lucinda Rosenfeld, Exec. Dir.; Giovanni B. Biaggi De Blasys, Marina B. Harrison.
EIN: 133632296
Codes: GTI

62052
The Ward Melville Heritage Organization
P.O. Box 572
Stony Brook, NY 11790

Classified as a private operating foundation in 1986.
Financial data (yr. ended 06/30/99): Assets, $2,756,028 (M); grants paid, $0; gifts received, $148,485; expenditures, $628,576; qualifying distributions, $628,576; giving activities include $432,768 for programs.
Officers: Richard Rugen, Chair.; Charles Pieroth, Vice-Chair; Gloria D. Rocchio, Pres.; Joseph Rebolt, Secy.; Edward J. Gutleber, Treas.
Trustees: Mary Elizabeth Coughlan, Duane Davis, Erwin Ernst, Marion Gaigal, Anna M. Kerekes, Nora Lynn, Charles Napoli.
EIN: 112440592

62053
Keren Teferet Yaacov
10 Ralph Blvd.
Monsey, NY 10952

Financial data (yr. ended 04/30/01): Assets, $2,733,552 (M); grants paid, $112,527; expenditures, $162,814; qualifying distributions, $112,527.
Limitations: Applications not accepted. Giving primarily in NY.
Application information: Contributes only to pre-selected organizations.
Officers: Kenneth Marsh, Secy.; Julius Klein, Treas.
EIN: 133824844
Codes: FD2

62054
Tov V Chesed Foundation
4515 18th Ave.
Brooklyn, NY 11204

Donor(s): Itzhak Toub.
Financial data (yr. ended 12/31/00): Assets, $2,715,000 (M); grants paid, $182,530; gifts received, $660,000; expenditures, $191,166; qualifying distributions, $179,930.
Limitations: Applications not accepted.
Application information: Contributes only to pre-selected organizations.
Officers: Jacob Stern, Pres.; Abraham Stern, V.P.
EIN: 113407656
Codes: FD2

62055
Innisfree Foundation, Inc.
c/o D'Arcangelo & Co.
P.O. Box D
Millbrook, NY 12545

Financial data (yr. ended 05/31/00): Assets, $2,682,654 (M); grants paid, $100; gifts received, $75,109; expenditures, $224,570; qualifying distributions, $140,058; giving activities include $68,857 for programs.
Officers and Directors:* Petronella Collins,* Pres.; E. Peter Krulewitch, V.P.; Louis H. Blair,* Secy.; Spencer Davidson,* Treas.; Oliver Collins, William Metcalf, Jr., George S. Wislocki.
EIN: 131972195

62056
Old York Foundation
1155 Ave. of the Americas
New York, NY 10036-2711

Classified as a private operating foundation in 1987.
Donor(s): Seymour Durst.
Financial data (yr. ended 12/31/01): Assets, $2,615,712 (M); grants paid, $63,000; expenditures, $217,463; qualifying distributions, $217,463.
Limitations: Applications not accepted. Giving primarily in NY.
Application information: Contributes only to pre-selected organizations.
Officer and Director:* Douglas Durst,* Pres.
EIN: 133387401

62057
The Stone Trust Corporation
c/o James Greer
101 Central Park W., Ste. 3E
New York, NY 10023

Donor(s): James Greer, Dana Martin, John Hullar, James A. Greer II.
Financial data (yr. ended 08/31/00): Assets, $2,584,864 (M); grants paid, $6,500; gifts received, $84,365; expenditures, $150,040; qualifying distributions, $169,721; giving activities include $116,775 for programs.
Limitations: Applications not accepted.
Application information: Contributes only to pre-selected organizations.
Officers and Directors:* James Greer,* Pres.; Camille-Helen Chwalek,* V.P. and Secy.; Dana Martin,* Treas.; Edward L. Barlow, John Brubaker, Edward Scully Burke, Alison Fenn, Penelope Laurans, Willard Overlook, Bruce Roberts, Daniel Rosenthal, James Thompson, W. Perry Welch.
EIN: 060552923

62058
Brooklyn Section, Community Senior Citizen Center
1001 Quentin Rd., 3rd Fl.
Brooklyn, NY 11223

Financial data (yr. ended 09/30/00): Assets, $2,531,235 (M); grants paid, $0; expenditures, $56,669; qualifying distributions, $60,080; giving activities include $56,669 for programs.
Officers: Arden Slavin, Pres.; Edith Gothelf, Secy.; Rosalind Ornstein, Treas.
EIN: 237389126

62059
Mary L. Fitch Trust
c/o JPMorgan Chase Bank
P.O. Box 31412
Rochester, NY 14603-1412

Financial data (yr. ended 12/31/01): Assets, $2,457,958 (M); grants paid, $0; gifts received, $2,375; expenditures, $88,826; qualifying distributions, $59,401.
Trustees: Marjorie B. Krubiner, Ronald B. Noren, Virginia M. Read, Irwin Tucker, JPMorgan Chase Bank.
EIN: 060646546

62060
International Brit Milah Association, Inc.
c/o Metropolitan Ambulance
5811 Foster Ave.
Brooklyn, NY 11234

Established in 1991 in NY.
Donor(s): Mark I. Davidman, Steve Zakheim.
Financial data (yr. ended 12/31/99): Assets, $2,419,004 (M); grants paid, $0; gifts received, $2,540,124; expenditures, $169,152; qualifying distributions, $115,999; giving activities include $115,999 for programs.
Officers: Steve Zakheim, Pres.; Mark I. Davidman, V.P.; Chaim Fessel, Secy.-Treas.
EIN: 113047483

62061
Fiscal Philatelic Foundation, Inc.
155 1st St.
Mineola, NY 11501-4099

Classified as a private operating foundation in 1980.
Donor(s): Adolph Koeppel.
Financial data (yr. ended 03/31/02): Assets, $2,415,384 (M); grants paid, $0; gifts received, $9,000; expenditures, $13,441; qualifying distributions, $0.
Officer: Adolph Koeppel, Pres.
Trustees: Raymond Manners, Michael Martone, Alvin S. Schartz.
EIN: 112506077

62062
Directors Guild of America Producers Training Trust
1697 Broadway, Ste. 600
New York, NY 10019

Financial data (yr. ended 12/31/01): Assets, $2,370,979 (M); grants paid, $0; gifts received, $493,821; expenditures, $365,472; qualifying distributions, $0.
Officer and Trustees:* Sandra Forman,* Admin.; Lucille Andreozzi, Al Califano, Barbara DeFina, Thomas DeWolfe, Bob Fisher, Gina Leonetti, Nancy Littlefield, Joseph Ray, Glen Trotiner.
EIN: 132946883

62063
Institute for Socioeconomic Studies, Inc.
20 New King St.
White Plains, NY 10604-1206 (914) 428-0400
Contact: Leonard M. Greene, Pres.

Established in 1972.
Donor(s): Leonard M. Greene, Safe Flight Investment Corp.
Financial data (yr. ended 07/31/01): Assets, $2,358,387 (M); grants paid, $36,500; expenditures, $556,423; qualifying distributions, $548,330; giving activities include $40,894 for programs.
Limitations: Giving primarily in NY.
Officers and Trustees:* Leonard M. Greene,* Pres.; Donald F. Greene,* V.P.; Arnold Shaw, Secy.-Treas.; Joyce Greene, Arthur E. Ludwig, Jr.
EIN: 237167096
Codes: GTI

62064
Foundation Historical Association, Inc.
5654 South St. Rd.
P.O. Box 276
Auburn, NY 13021-0276

Classified as a private operating foundation in 1972.
Donor(s): Fred L. Emerson, Samuel and Bertha Schwartz Foundation, The Allyn Foundation.
Financial data (yr. ended 12/31/01): Assets, $2,317,296 (M); grants paid, $0; gifts received, $1,414,510; expenditures, $293,826; qualifying distributions, $290,552; giving activities include $290,552 for programs.
Officers and Directors:* David L. Emerson,* Pres.; Daniel C. Labeille,* V.P.; Jill E. Franceschelli,* Secy.; Ronald D. West,* Treas.; Henry Jay Pearson III, and 4 additional directors.
EIN: 150551238

62065
Lillian M. Slater Trust
14 Birch Ln.
Scotia, NY 12302-5517
Contact: Donald W. Krauter, Tr.

Established in 1997 in NY.
Financial data (yr. ended 12/31/02): Assets, $2,302,009 (M); grants paid, $92,121; expenditures, $108,591; qualifying distributions, $92,121.
Limitations: Giving primarily in Schenectady, NY.
Application information: Application form not required.
Trustees: Donald W. Krauter, William W. Price, Frances M. Summerville.
EIN: 146179935
Codes: FD2

62066
Museum of American Financial History
26 Broadway, Bowling Green
New York, NY 10004-1763

Classified as a private operating foundation in 1983.
Donor(s): John E. Herzog.
Financial data (yr. ended 12/31/00): Assets, $2,287,127 (M); grants paid, $3,613; gifts received, $99,324; expenditures, $253,645; qualifying distributions, $247,150; giving activities include $247,188 for programs.
Officers and Trustees:* John E. Herzog,* Chair.; John L. Watson III,* V.P.; William E. Prinzler,* Secy.; and 13 additional trustees.
EIN: 133540880
Codes: TN

62067
Ladies Union Benevolent Society
701 McGraw House
Ithaca, NY 14850

Established around 1941.
Financial data (yr. ended 09/30/01): Assets, $2,253,063 (M); grants paid, $11,650; expenditures, $167,614; qualifying distributions, $135,184; giving activities include $123,534 for programs.
Limitations: Applications not accepted. Giving primarily in Ithaca, NY.
Application information: Contributes only to pre-selected organizations.
Officers and Directors:* Carol Franklin,* Pres.; Jean Dunlavey,* V.P.; Katie Forker,* V.P.; Libby Patton,* V.P.; Lucille Ruthig,* Corresponding Secy.; Helen Wardeberg,* Recording Secy.; Patricia Johnson, Treas.; and 19 additional directors.
EIN: 150539106

62068
Hispanic Information and Telecommunications Network
449 Broadway, 3rd Fl.
New York, NY 10013-2549

Financial data (yr. ended 12/31/00): Assets, $2,178,530 (M); grants paid, $0; expenditures, $5,887,912; qualifying distributions, $0.
Officers: Peter T. Lewis, Chair.; Jose Luis Rodriguez, Pres.; George Herrera, V.P.
Director: Louis Bransford.
EIN: 133112110

62069
Abram and Ray Kaplan Foundation
1401 Rte. 35
South Salem, NY 10590-1627 (914) 764-8149

Established in 1995 in NY.
Donor(s): Ezra Kaplan.
Financial data (yr. ended 12/31/00): Assets, $2,139,436 (M); grants paid, $31,000; gifts received, $1,655,527; expenditures, $31,784; qualifying distributions, $31,000.
Limitations: Applications not accepted. Giving primarily in NY.
Application information: Contributes only to pre-selected organizations.
Trustee: Ezra Kaplan.
EIN: 133798875

62070
Women's Christian Association of Fredonia, New York
134 Temple St.
Fredonia, NY 14063

Financial data (yr. ended 05/31/00): Assets, $2,077,110 (M); grants paid, $0; gifts received, $54,885; expenditures, $487,698; qualifying distributions, $507,256; giving activities include $488,198 for programs.
Officers: Dana Wheelock, Pres.; Ruth Hart, V.P.; Mary Kay Szwebjka, Secy.; David Doino, Treas.
Trustees: Jean Marsillo, Exec. Dir.; William Baker, Shirley Erbsmehl, Lou Ann Laurito-Bahgat, Mac McCoy, Sallie Pullano, Audra Renswick, Barbara Servatius.
EIN: 160771085

62071
Athanasiades Cultural Foundation, Inc.
30-96 42nd St.
Astoria, NY 11103-3031 (718) 278-3014

Established in 1991.
Donor(s): Costas Anthanasiades, Maria Athanasiades.
Financial data (yr. ended 12/31/01): Assets, $2,013,612 (M); grants paid, $15,110; gifts received, $200; expenditures, $58,773; qualifying distributions, $432,266.
Limitations: Giving primarily in New York, NY.
Application information: Application form not required.
Officers and Directors:* Costas Athanasiades,* Pres.; Christos G. Tzelios,* Secy.; Maria Athanasiades,* Treas.
EIN: 133614414
Codes: GTI

62072
Hasbrouck Family Association, Inc
P.O. Box 176
New Paltz, NY 12561

Financial data (yr. ended 12/31/01): Assets, $1,995,987 (M); grants paid, $4,300; gifts received, $2,363; expenditures, $209,335; qualifying distributions, $191,562; giving activities include $180,825 for programs.
Limitations: Applications not accepted.
Application information: Contributes only to pre-selected organizations.
Officers and Directors:* Robert W. Hasbrouck, Jr.,* Pres.; Eleanor C. Sears,* V.P. and Secy.; John O. Delamater,* V.P.; Robert C. Hasbrouck, Jr.,* V.P.; Thad M. Hasbrouck,* Treas.
EIN: 141786723

62073
John and Janet Kornreich Charitable Foundation, Ltd.
78 Yale St.
Roslyn Heights, NY 11577

Established in 1999 in NY.
Donor(s): John Kornreich, Mrs. John Kornreich.
Financial data (yr. ended 12/31/01): Assets, $1,992,932 (M); grants paid, $374,765; expenditures, $395,338; qualifying distributions, $373,978.
Officer: John Kornreich, Mgr.
Directors: Myron Bloom, Janet Kornreich.
EIN: 133974159
Codes: FD

62074
The Hallingby Family Foundation, Inc.
c/o Paul Hallingby
530 E. 86th St.
New York, NY 10028

Established in 1998 in CT.
Donor(s): Paul L. Hallingby.
Financial data (yr. ended 04/30/01): Assets, $1,946,816 (M); grants paid, $100,400; expenditures, $102,545; qualifying distributions, $101,574.
Limitations: Applications not accepted.
Application information: Contributes only to pre-selected organizations.
Officers: Paul L. Hallingby, Pres.; Julia H. Hallingby, V.P.; Thomas P. Spellane, Secy.-Treas.
EIN: 061516271
Codes: FD2

62075
The Brodsky Family Foundation
400 W. 59th St.
New York, NY 10019 (212) 315-5555
Contact: Nathan Brodsky, Tr.

Established in 1984 in NY.
Donor(s): Nathan Brodsky.
Financial data (yr. ended 12/31/01): Assets, $1,929,130 (M); grants paid, $99,000; gifts

received, $300,000; expenditures, $100,444; qualifying distributions, $100,444.
Limitations: Giving primarily in NY.
Application information: Application form not required.
Trustees: Hady Amr, Daniel Brodsky, Katherine Brodsky, Nathan Brodsky, Shirley Brodsky.
EIN: 133236064
Codes: FD2

62076
Albert and Mary Lasker Foundation, Inc.
110 E. 42nd St., Ste. 1300
New York, NY 10017   (212) 286-0222
FAX: (212) 286-0924; E-mail: nhunt@laskerfoundation.org; Additional E-mail for applications: dkeegan@laskerfoundation.org; URL: http://www.laskerfoundation.org
Contact: David Keegan, Lasker Medical Research Awards Prog. Admin.

Incorporated in 1942 in NY.
Donor(s): Albert D. Lasker,‡ Mary W. Lasker.‡
Financial data (yr. ended 12/31/00): Assets, $1,832,350 (M); grants paid, $126,000; gifts received, $630,000; expenditures, $778,341; qualifying distributions, $749,104.
Limitations: Giving on a national basis.
Publications: Application guidelines.
Application information: Application form required.
Officers: James W. Fordyce, Chair.; Neen Hunt, Ed.D., Pres.; Mrs. William McCormick Blair, Jr., V.P.; Anne B. Fordyce, V.P.; James E. Hughes, Secy.; Christopher W. Brody, Treas.
Directors: Purnell W. Choppin, M.D., Robert J. Glaser, M.D, Jordan U. Gutterman, M.D., Hon. Mark O. Hatfield, Daniel E. Koshland, Jr., Ph.D.
EIN: 131680062
Codes: FD2, GTI

62077
Nonsequitur, Inc.
c/o Hecht and Co., PC
111 W. 40th St.
New York, NY 10018

Classified as a private operating foundation in 1990 in NY.
Donor(s): Jonathan Scheuer, Daniel Scheuer.
Financial data (yr. ended 12/31/01): Assets, $1,759,325 (M); grants paid, $92,000; expenditures, $173,519; qualifying distributions, $147,738; giving activities include $63,946 for programs.
Limitations: Applications not accepted. Giving on a national basis.
Application information: Contributes only to pre-selected organizations.
Officers: Jonathan Scheuer, Pres. and Treas.; Tom Guralnick, V.P.; Ean White, Secy.
Directors: Mimi Johnson, Steven Peters.
EIN: 133526327
Codes: FD2

62078
The Gilder Lehrman Institute of American History
c/o Anchin, Block & Anchin
1375 Broadway
New York, NY 10018

Classified as a private operating foundation in 1995.
Donor(s): Gilder Foundation, John M. Olen Foundation, The Lynde and Harry Bradley Foundation, Inc.
Financial data (yr. ended 06/30/01): Assets, $1,742,078 (M); grants paid, $629,712; gifts received, $7,986,660; expenditures, $9,305,820; qualifying distributions, $9,289,600; giving activities include $5,522,637 for programs.
Limitations: Applications not accepted.
Application information: Contributes only to pre-selected organizations.
Officers and Trustees:* James Basker, Pres.; Lewis E. Lehrman,* Exec. V.P.; Howard Rothman,* Secy.; Richard S. Gilder, Treas.; Richard Schneidman.
Director: Lesley S. Herrmann.
EIN: 133795391
Codes: FD

62079
Hudson Valley Artists Foundation, Inc.
111 E. 14th St., Ste. 350
New York, NY 10003

Established in 1997.
Financial data (yr. ended 12/31/00): Assets, $1,732,497 (M); grants paid, $0; gifts received, $260,093; expenditures, $175,426; qualifying distributions, $253,574; giving activities include $253,574 for programs.
Officers: Julie Ann Hodson, Pres.; Charles Edward Ward III, V.P. and Secy.; Donna Irwin, Treas.
EIN: 133945713

62080
Constantinos C. Polychronis Foundation
51 Cardinal St.
Pearl River, NY 10965
Application address: c/o Schiller, Saueo and Hartnett, P.A., 6 Chapel Ave., Jersey City, NJ 07305, tel.: (201) 521-1000
Contact: Marc C. Polychronis, Pres.

Established in 1966.
Financial data (yr. ended 12/31/00): Assets, $1,727,993 (M); grants paid, $90,000; expenditures, $311,116; qualifying distributions, $302,863.
Limitations: Giving primarily in NJ and NY.
Officers: Marc C. Polychronis, Pres.; Helen C. Polychronis, V.P. and Treas.; Kathleen Polychronis, Secy.
Director: Gus Chafos.
EIN: 237172254
Codes: FD2

62081
Wellfleet Foundation, Inc.
c/o Cowan, Debaets & Abrahams
40 W. 57th St.
New York, NY 10019

Established in 1984.
Financial data (yr. ended 03/31/01): Assets, $1,690,530 (M); grants paid, $40,100; gifts received, $130,650; expenditures, $42,569; qualifying distributions, $44,125.
Limitations: Applications not accepted. Giving primarily in MA, NJ, and NY.
Application information: Contributes only to pre-selected organizations. Unsolicited requests for funds not accepted.
Directors: Gerald Feil, Hila Feil, Stanley Roth.
EIN: 133170169

62082
The Mountain Top Arboretum, Inc.
(Formerly Onteora Arboretum, Inc.)
c/o Christine Story
P.O. Box 379
Tannersville, NY 12485

Classified as a private operating foundation in 1979.
Donor(s): Edward H. Ahrens, Jr.
Financial data (yr. ended 12/31/01): Assets, $1,664,783 (M); grants paid, $0; gifts received, $104,201; expenditures, $129,632; qualifying distributions, $144,717; giving activities include $129,632 for programs.
Officers: Philip Palmer, Chair.; Bruce K. Riggs, Pres.; Bonnie E. Ahrens, V.P.; Dede Terns-Thorpe, Secy.; Michael Magdol, Treas.; Christine Story, Exec. Dir.
EIN: 222240075

62083
Dorothy K. Commanday Foundation
420 Lexington Ave., Ste. 2150
New York, NY 10170
Contact: Edward Yelon, Pres.

Established in 1996 in NY.
Donor(s): Dorothy Commanday.‡
Financial data (yr. ended 12/31/00): Assets, $1,644,433 (M); grants paid, $66,000; expenditures, $88,392; qualifying distributions, $63,141.
Limitations: Giving on a national basis.
Officers: Edward Yelon, Pres.; Peter Commanday, V.P.; Susan Tanzer, Secy.
EIN: 133851188

62084
The Anita Shapolsky Art Foundation, Inc.
c/o Anita Shapolsky
152 E. 65th St.
New York, NY 10021

Established in 1999 in PA.
Donor(s): Anita Shapolsky.
Financial data (yr. ended 03/31/01): Assets, $1,631,471 (M); grants paid, $127; gifts received, $28,000; expenditures, $32,586; qualifying distributions, $127.
Limitations: Applications not accepted.
Application information: Contributes only to pre-selected organizations.
Officers: Anita Shapolsky, Pres.; Ian Shapolsky, V.P.; Lisa Goldberg, Secy.-Treas.
EIN: 223698386

62085
Axis Theatre Co., Inc.
c/o Peter Sharp & Co., Inc.
545 Madison Ave., 11th Fl.
New York, NY 10022

Donor(s): Randall A. Sharp.
Financial data (yr. ended 12/31/00): Assets, $1,631,065 (M); grants paid, $200; gifts received, $1,325,000; expenditures, $1,199,532; qualifying distributions, $1,176,180; giving activities include $1,009,430 for programs.
Officers: Randall A. Sharp, Pres.; Jeffrey Resnick, V.P. and Secy.; Barry Tobias, Treas.
EIN: 133667916

62086
William H. Bush Memorial Library
P.O. Box 141
Martinsburg, NY 13404

Classified as a private operating foundation in 1978.
Donor(s): William H. Bush.‡
Financial data (yr. ended 12/31/01): Assets, $1,611,838 (M); grants paid, $1,050; gifts received, $1,099,024; expenditures, $46,573; qualifying distributions, $40,218; giving activities include $40,218 for programs.
Limitations: Applications not accepted.
Officers: Martin Hirschy, Jr., Pres.; Sally Ingersoll, V.P.; Eileen Greenwood, Secy.; Nelson Schwartzentruber, Treas.
Directors: Sandra Arthur, Jean Demko, Lawrence Woodhouse.
EIN: 150581771

62087
Urban Home Ownership Corporation
494 8th Ave., 19th Fl.
New York, NY 10001

Classified as a private operating foundation in 1973.
Financial data (yr. ended 12/31/01): Assets, $1,602,184 (M); grants paid, $0; expenditures, $1,267,118; qualifying distributions, $1,286,400; giving activities include $215,199 for programs.
Officers and Directors:* Alexander James,* Chair.; Preston C. Moore,* Pres.; Dorothy Hill Moscov,* Secy.; Nathaniel James, Damon Kinebrew, Hawatha Selby, George Silcott.
EIN: 132611472

62088
Abraham J. & Phyllis Katz Foundation
107-40 Queens Blvd., Ste. 206
Forest Hills, NY 11375
Contact: Monica Pier

Established in 1994 in NY.
Donor(s): Abraham J. Katz, Phyllis Katz, Kason Industries, Inc.
Financial data (yr. ended 12/31/01): Assets, $1,594,490 (M); grants paid, $285,921; gifts received, $349,505; expenditures, $294,906; qualifying distributions, $292,481.
Limitations: Giving on a national basis.
Application information: Application form required.
Trustees: Abraham J. Katz, Phyllis Katz.
EIN: 116442077
Codes: FD

62089
The Hirschhorn Foundation, Inc.
(Formerly Pioneer Valley Art Foundation, Inc.)
c/o L. Wollin
350 5th Ave., Rm. 2822
New York, NY 10118

Classified as a private operating foundation in 1985.
Financial data (yr. ended 06/30/01): Assets, $1,570,728 (M); grants paid, $0; expenditures, $146,147; qualifying distributions, $0; giving activities include $104,915 for programs.
Limitations: Applications not accepted.
Application information: Contributes only to pre-selected organizations.
Officers: Robert Hirschhorn, Pres.; Marjorie Hirschhorn, V.P.; Lonnie Wollin, Secy.; Carolyn Hirschhorn Schenker, Treas.
EIN: 133002070

62090
Bahuleyan Charitable Foundation, Inc.
900 Delaware Ave., Ste. 302
Buffalo, NY 14209
Application address: c/o Brain & spine Center, Chemmanakary, Viakom 686-143 Kerala, India
Contact: Kumar Bahuleyan, Pres.

Established in 1989 in NY.
Donor(s): Kumaran Bahuleyan.
Financial data (yr. ended 12/31/00): Assets, $1,540,507 (M); grants paid, $0; gifts received, $22,351; expenditures, $806,287; qualifying distributions, $377,077; giving activities include $347,361 for programs.
Limitations: Giving limited to residents of Viakom and Cochin, India.
Application information: Application form required.
Officers: Kumar Bahuleyan, Pres. and Treas.; Indira Bahuleyan, V.P.; Saju Bahuleyan, Secy.
EIN: 223015430

62091
Foundation for Southeast Asian Art & Culture
650 5th Ave., 19th Fl.
New York, NY 10019

Classified as a private operating foundation in 1972.
Donor(s): Doris Duke.‡
Financial data (yr. ended 12/31/01): Assets, $1,509,665 (M); grants paid, $0; expenditures, $74,264; qualifying distributions, $7,352; giving activities include $74,264 for programs.
Officers: Joan E. Spero, Pres.; Betsy Fader, Secy.; Alan Altshuler, C.F.O.
Trustees: J. Carter Brown, Marion Oates Charles, Harry Demopoulos, Anthony S. Fauci, James F. Gill, Nannerl O. Keohane, John J. Mack, John T. Wilson.
EIN: 990109198

62092
John and Linda Bohlsen Family Foundation
c/o North Fork Bank
275 Broadhollow Rd., 4th Fl.
Melville, NY 11747

Financial data (yr. ended 12/31/01): Assets, $1,496,514 (M); grants paid, $61,901; gifts received, $25,000; expenditures, $66,124; qualifying distributions, $61,901.
Limitations: Applications not accepted. Giving primarily in CT and NY.
Application information: Contributes only to pre-selected organizations.
Officers: John Bohlsen, Pres.; Linda Bohlsen, Secy.
Directors: Kurt Bohlsen, Michael Bohlsen.
EIN: 113440712

62093
The Peter F. Drucker Foundation for Nonprofit Management
320 Park Ave., 3rd Fl.
New York, NY 10022-6839 (212) 224-1174
FAX: (212) 224-2508; E-mail: info@pfdf.org;
URL: http://www.drucker.org

Established in 1990 in NY.
Financial data (yr. ended 12/31/99): Assets, $1,479,468 (M); grants paid, $25,000; gifts received, $863,478; expenditures, $1,194,141; qualifying distributions, $1,184,314; giving activities include $995,609 for programs.
Limitations: Giving on a national basis.
Publications: Annual report, newsletter, financial statement, informational brochure.
Application information: Enclose an electronic copy of the application on a 3.5 inch floppy disk. Application form required.
Officers and Governors:* Frances Hesselbein,* Chair. and Pres.; Peter F. Drucker, Chair.; David R. Beatty,* Vice-Chair.; Richard F. Schubert,* Vice-Chair.; John E. Jacob, V.P.; Thomas J. Moran,* Secy.; Geneva B. Johnson, Treas.; Robert Buford, Richard E. Cavanagh, Doris Drucker, Marshall Goldsmith, Sidney E. Harris, John A. McNeice, Jr., C. William Pollard, Iain Somerville.
EIN: 133591396
Codes: TN

62094
The Ellen E. Howe Foundation
c/o Executive Monetary Mgmt.
220 E. 42nd St., 32nd Fl.
New York, NY 10017

Established in 1998 in DE and NY.
Financial data (yr. ended 11/30/01): Assets, $1,479,419 (M); grants paid, $94,510; gifts received, $8,409; expenditures, $123,321; qualifying distributions, $97,032.
Limitations: Applications not accepted.
Application information: Contributes only to pre-selected organizations.
Officer: Ellen E. Howe, Pres.
EIN: 134010542
Codes: FD2

62095
JMS Foundation, Inc.
180 Montague St., Ste. 22C
Brooklyn, NY 11201-3607

Established in 1998 in NY.
Financial data (yr. ended 12/31/01): Assets, $1,478,637 (M); grants paid, $38,293; expenditures, $66,159; qualifying distributions, $50,632.
Limitations: Applications not accepted. Giving primarily in NY.
Application information: Contributes only to pre-selected organizations.
Officers: Robert Smith, Pres.; Richard Pelosi, Secy.-Treas.
EIN: 061507500

62096
Samuel F. Vilas Home, Inc.
61 Beekman St.
Plattsburgh, NY 12901-2701

Donor(s): New York State Office for the Aging.
Financial data (yr. ended 12/31/01): Assets, $1,459,772 (M); grants paid, $0; gifts received, $17,306; expenditures, $799,995; qualifying distributions, $0.
Officers: William Deloria, Pres.; Herbert Ryder, V.P.; John Bartoszek, Secy.; Rodney Ralston, Treas.
Directors: Marie Beemer, John A. Coolidge, Monica Day, James Keable.
EIN: 141373023

62097
Children's Aid Association of Amsterdam, NY
P.O. Box 327
Amsterdam, NY 12010-0327

Established around 1914 in NY.
Donor(s): Donald T. Bixby.
Financial data (yr. ended 05/31/01): Assets, $1,453,552 (M); grants paid, $64,453; gifts received, $5,496; expenditures, $70,486; qualifying distributions, $70,815.
Limitations: Giving limited to residents of Montgomery County, NY.
Application information: Telephone calls not accepted. Application form required.
Officers: Jacque Bresonis, Pres.; Barbara Morini, 1st V.P.; Diane Casano, 2nd V.P.; Margo Hotaling, Corresponding Secy.; Robin Sise, Recording Secy.; Shirley Iodice, Treas.
EIN: 141340035
Codes: GTI

62098
Riverside Episcopal Housing Development Fund Co., Inc.
24 Rhode Island St.
Buffalo, NY 14213-2142

Classified as a private operating foundation.
Financial data (yr. ended 06/30/99): Assets, $1,425,021 (M); grants paid, $0; expenditures, $285,167; qualifying distributions, $22,518; giving activities include $285,167 for programs.
Officers and Directors:* Allen W. Judd,* Chair.; Jacquelyn Coolbaugh,* Vice-Chair.; Edward C. Weeks, C.E.O. and Pres.; Alfred H. Pullbrook,* Secy.; James W. Vossier,* Treas.
EIN: 222607664
Codes: TN

62099
The Toni Morrison Foundation
c/o Donald S. Taaly
317 Little Tar Rd. S.
New City, NY 10956

Established in 1999 in NY.
Donor(s): Toni Morrison.
Financial data (yr. ended 07/31/01): Assets, $1,413,823 (M); grants paid, $0; gifts received, $1,229,824; expenditures, $119,362; qualifying distributions, $0.
Officers: Toni Morrison, Pres.; H. Ford Morrison, V.P. and Exec. Dir.; Donald S. Taaly, Secy.-Treas.
EIN: 134076448

62100
Institute for Cooperation of Art and Research, Inc.
c/o M. Plotnitsky
77 Bleeker St.
New York, NY 10012

Donor(s): Marsha Plotnitsky.
Financial data (yr. ended 11/30/00): Assets, $1,406,817 (M); grants paid, $10,000; gifts received, $534,188; expenditures, $162,557; qualifying distributions, $159,767; giving activities include $54,615 for programs.
Limitations: Applications not accepted.
Application information: Contributes only to pre-selected organizations.
Officers and Directors:* Arkady Plotnitsky,* Pres.; Rens Lipsius, V.P.; Marsha Plotnitsky,* Secy.; Nina Nazarova.
EIN: 133747781

62101
Serge Sabarsky Foundation
58 E. 79th St.
New York, NY 10021

Donor(s): Serge Sabarsky.
Financial data (yr. ended 09/30/00): Assets, $1,360,323 (M); grants paid, $25,000; expenditures, $574,031; qualifying distributions, $57,403.
Limitations: Applications not accepted. Giving limited to the Czech Republic.
Application information: Contributes only to pre-selected organizations.
Officers: Vally Sabarsky, Pres.; Michael D. Lesh, V.P.; Christa E. Hartmann, Secy.
EIN: 510350495

62102
Elizabeth Patrick Foundation
490 West End Ave., Apt. 11B
New York, NY 10024

Established in 1968.
Donor(s): Elizabeth Patrick.
Financial data (yr. ended 08/31/99): Assets, $1,301,503 (M); grants paid, $60,000; expenditures, $61,815; qualifying distributions, $61,815.
Limitations: Applications not accepted.
Officer: Elizabeth Patrick, Pres.
EIN: 136277883
Codes: TN

62103
National Video Resources, Inc.
73 Spring St., Ste. 606
New York, NY 10012   (212) 274-8080
FAX: (212) 274-8081; URL: http://www.nvr.org

Incorporated in 1990 in NY and DE.
Donor(s): The Rockefeller Foundation, The MacArthur Foundation, Corporation for Public Broadcasting, W. Kellogg Foundation, AT&T Foundation, The Ford Foundation.
Financial data (yr. ended 12/31/00): Assets, $1,274,426 (M); grants paid, $0; gifts received, $1,363,330; expenditures, $1,276,602; qualifying distributions, $1,246,660; giving activities include $1,091,316 for programs.
Officers and Directors:* Alberta B. Arthurs,* Chair.; Timothy H. Gunn, Pres. and Exec. Dir.; Tania Blanich,* Secy.; Steve Savage,* Treas.; Peggy Charren, Eli Evans, Martin Gomez, Sheldon Hackney, Phil Hallen, Gary Knell, Sam Pollard, John Roche, Suzanne Sato, Stuart Sucherman.
EIN: 133572353

62104
Abbe Berman Foundation Trust
(Formerly Abbe Family Foundation Trust)
c/o Colman Abbe
26 Lawrence Rd.
Scarsdale, NY 10583-7209

Established in 1995 in NY.
Donor(s): Colman Abbe, Leo Abbe.
Financial data (yr. ended 12/31/00): Assets, $1,253,915 (M); grants paid, $57,190; expenditures, $68,810; qualifying distributions, $62,982.
Limitations: Applications not accepted. Giving primarily in NY.
Application information: Contributes only to pre-selected organizations.
Trustees: Colman Abbe, Nancy Abbe.
EIN: 137054887

62105
Julian Reiss Foundation
140 Saranac Ave.
Lake Placid, NY 12946
Contact: Paul J. Reiss, Chair.

Established in 1955 in NY; classified as a private operating foundation in 1971.
Donor(s): Paul J. Reiss, Rosemary Reiss.
Financial data (yr. ended 12/31/00): Assets, $1,240,709 (M); grants paid, $50,229; gifts received, $58,621; expenditures, $52,184; qualifying distributions, $52,184; giving activities include $50,229 for programs.
Limitations: Applications not accepted. Giving primarily in Lake Placid, NY.
Publications: Annual report.
Application information: Contributes only to pre-selected organizations.
Officers and Directors:* Paul J. Reiss,* Chair.; Gregory G. Reiss,* Secy.; Julia DeSantis, Steven Reiss, Miriam Watson.
EIN: 146012292

62106
Edmund Niles Huyck Preserve, Inc.
P.O. Box 188
Rensselaerville, NY 12147

Established in 1931 in NY.
Donor(s): Huyck Foundation.
Financial data (yr. ended 12/31/00): Assets, $1,239,779 (M); grants paid, $0; gifts received, $237,599; expenditures, $312,041; qualifying distributions, $230,802; giving activities include $288,941 for programs.
Officers and Directors:* Carol Ash-Friedman,* Pres.; Laura Carter,* V.P.; Marge Rooney,* Secy.; Daniel McNamee,* Treas.; Richard Wyman, Exec. Dir.; Paul Baitsholts, Barbara Blum, Martin Brand, William P. Carey, Camille Douglas, James Foster, Albert Hessberg, Michael Huxley, Peter McChesney, Jerome G. Rozen, Jr., Virginia Carter Steadman.
EIN: 141338387

Codes: GTI

62107
The Robert David Lion Gardiner Foundation, Inc.
c/o CFCD
10 Roosevelt Ave.
Port Jefferson Station, NY 11776

Classified as a private operating foundation in 1987.
Donor(s): Robert David Lion Gardiner.
Financial data (yr. ended 11/30/00): Assets, $1,225,613 (M); grants paid, $0; gifts received, $94,914; expenditures, $96,715; qualifying distributions, $96,715; giving activities include $29,926 for programs.
Officers and Directors:* Robert David Lion Gardiner,* Pres. and Treas.; Eunice Gardiner,* V.P.; Muriel Benning,* Secy.
EIN: 133354308

62108
Institute for Advanced Studies of World Religions
Rd. No. 2, Rte. 3001
Carmel, NY 10512

Classified as a private operating foundation in 1999.
Donor(s): David C.T. Shen, Thomas H. Mordow, C.T. Shen, Margaret Shen.
Financial data (yr. ended 09/30/01): Assets, $1,215,206 (M); grants paid, $0; gifts received, $11,228; expenditures, $213,924; qualifying distributions, $0.
Limitations: Applications not accepted.
Application information: Contributes only to pre-selected organizations.
Officers: C.T. Shen, Pres.; Margaret Chen, V.P. and Treas.; David C.T. Shen, V.P.; N.S. Shen, V.P.; Thomas H. Morrow, Secy.
EIN: 237085108

62109
The Schlichter Foundation
885 3rd Ave.
New York, NY 10022

Established in 2000 in NY and DE.
Donor(s): Bernard Madoff.
Financial data (yr. ended 12/31/01): Assets, $1,208,699 (M); grants paid, $33,000; expenditures, $43,855; qualifying distributions, $33,000.
Limitations: Applications not accepted.
Application information: Contributes only to pre-selected organizations.
Officers: Bernard Madoff, Pres.; Peter Madoff, Secy.
EIN: 134077536

62110
George W. & Dacie Clements Agriculture Research Institute, Inc.
P.O. Box 255
Morristown, NY 13664

Established in 1998 in NY.
Financial data (yr. ended 12/31/01): Assets, $1,208,357 (M); grants paid, $0; gifts received, $211,624; expenditures, $468,577; qualifying distributions, $0.
Limitations: Applications not accepted.
Application information: Contributes only to pre-selected organizations.
Officers and Directors:* Mahlon T. Clements,* Pres. and Treas.; Thomas Gray Clements, V.P. and Secy.; Douglas Lee Clements, Elizabeth Clements.
EIN: 161557571

62111
Van Itallie Foundation, Inc.
Cooper Station, P.O. Box 1573
New York, NY 10008-1573
Contact: Rosemary Quinn, Secy.

Established in 1963 in NY.
Donor(s): H.F. Van Itallie.
Financial data (yr. ended 11/30/01): Assets, $1,195,911 (M); grants paid, $72,450; expenditures, $81,018; qualifying distributions, $79,361.
Limitations: Applications not accepted. Giving primarily in NY.
Application information: Contributes only to pre-selected organizations.
Officers: Jean-Claude Van Itallie, Pres.; Rosemary Quinn, Secy.; Michael Van Itallie, Treas.
EIN: 136065514

62112
The Krusos Foundation, Inc.
250 Lawrence Hill Rd.
Cold Spring Harbor, NY 11724

Established in 1994 in NY.
Donor(s): Denis A. Krusos.
Financial data (yr. ended 11/30/01): Assets, $1,177,099 (M); grants paid, $0; gifts received, $252,750; expenditures, $165,555; qualifying distributions, $135,274; giving activities include $135,274 for programs.
Limitations: Applications not accepted. Giving primarily in MA and Long Island, NY.
Application information: Contributes only to pre-selected organizations.
Officers: Peri Krusos Wenz, Pres.; Martin C. Wenz, V.P. and Treas.; Denis Z. Krusos, Secy.
Director: Denis A. Krusos.
EIN: 113241704

62113
David Foundation, Inc.
45 Broadway
New York, NY 10006 (212) 859-9293
Contact: Lawrence David, Pres.

Established around 1949 in NY.
Donor(s): Joan David, Lawrence David.
Financial data (yr. ended 06/30/01): Assets, $1,164,247 (M); grants paid, $109,735; gifts received, $41,876; expenditures, $110,340; qualifying distributions, $110,340.
Application information: Application form not required.
Officer: Lawrence David, Pres.
EIN: 136125004
Codes: FD2

62114
The Gerard Souzay Vocal Arts Foundation
161 W. 61st St., Ste. 18C
New York, NY 10023

Established in 1997 in NY. Classified as a private operating foundation in 1998.
Donor(s): Gerard Souzay.
Financial data (yr. ended 07/31/00): Assets, $1,162,934 (M); grants paid, $1,000; gifts received, $446,170; expenditures, $81,072; qualifying distributions, $49,602.
Limitations: Applications not accepted.
Application information: Contributes only to pre-selected organizations.
Officers and Trustees:* Louis L. Broudy,* Chair.; C. Randolph Holladay, V.P.; Stacey Cameron, Secy.; M.K. Cheung, Treas.; P. Marchand.
EIN: 133965025

62115
The Grodetsky Family Foundation
360 E. 72nd St., Ste. 1803
New York, NY 10021-4765 (212) 772-3930
Contact: Meyer Grodetsky, Pres.

Established in 1989 in NY.
Financial data (yr. ended 06/30/01): Assets, $1,158,600 (M); grants paid, $62,468; expenditures, $64,533; qualifying distributions, $64,533.
Limitations: Giving primarily in NY.
Officers: Meyer Grodetsky, Pres.; Merrill Grodetsky, V.P.; Rachelle Grodetsky, Secy.; Sandra Grodetsky, Treas.
EIN: 133417399

62116
Sara Roby Foundation
c/o Asbjorn R. Lunde
525 W. 238 St., Apt. 3B
Bronx, NY 10463-1819

Financial data (yr. ended 12/31/00): Assets, $1,154,629 (M); grants paid, $55,000; expenditures, $60,544; qualifying distributions, $60,001.
Limitations: Applications not accepted. Giving primarily in Washington, DC.
Application information: Contributes only to pre-selected organizations.
Officers and Directors:* Joseph Roby III,* Pres. and Treas.; Asbjorn R. Lunde, V.P.; Candida Gold,* Secy.; Virginia Hecklenburg.
EIN: 136020675

62117
Elizabeth Klein Foundation, Inc.
P.O. Box 549
Baldwinsville, NY 13027-0549

Established in 1998 in NY.
Donor(s): Arlene Yager.
Financial data (yr. ended 12/31/00): Assets, $1,134,339 (M); grants paid, $48,216; gifts received, $203,752; expenditures, $974,098; qualifying distributions, $48,216.
Limitations: Applications not accepted.
Application information: Contributes only to pre-selected organizations.
Officers: Gary Yager, Pres.; Robert C. Failmezger, V.P.
EIN: 161497511

62118
The Burlington Magazine Foundation, Inc.
c/o Sullivan & Cromwell
125 Broad St., Ste. 2945
New York, NY 10004-2498

Established in 1986 in NY.
Financial data (yr. ended 12/31/99): Assets, $1,128,456 (M); grants paid, $0; gifts received, $11,814; expenditures, $14,189; qualifying distributions, $13,959; giving activities include $10,959 for programs.
Officers and Directors:* Christopher White,* Pres.; Marilyn Perry,* V.P.; Caroline Elam,* Secy.; Kate Trevelyan,* Treas.; Joseph Conners, F.J. Haskell, Nicholas B. Penny, M.D., Seymour Slive, Craig Hugh Smyth, John Walsh, M.D.
EIN: 133347776

62119
Tudor City Greens, Inc.
c/o Tudor Realty
5 Tudor Pl.
New York, NY 10017-6853

Established in 1987 in NY.
Financial data (yr. ended 12/31/00): Assets, $1,119,008 (M); grants paid, $0; gifts received, $34,299; expenditures, $94,451; qualifying distributions, $40,121.
Officers and Directors:* William Baltz,* V.P.; Marcia Thompson, Treas.; Charles Beardsley, Francis Greenburger, Sherry Halpern,* Harry Laughlin, Tony Quill, David Reiff, Elna Seabrooks.
EIN: 133418536

62120
Global Works, Inc.
37 W. 65th St., 5th Fl.
New York, NY 10023

Donor(s): Peter Max.
Financial data (yr. ended 03/31/01): Assets, $1,115,480 (M); grants paid, $55,631; expenditures, $93,766; qualifying distributions, $55,631.
Limitations: Giving limited to Buckingham, VA.
Application information: Application form not required.
Officer and Directors:* Peter Max,* Pres.; Adam Sokolow.
EIN: 133525323

62121
The Eakins Press Foundation
c/o June Mayhall Katz
15 W. 67th St.
New York, NY 10023

Classified as a private operating foundation in 1974.
Donor(s): Leslie G. Katz,‡ Jane Mayhall Katz.
Financial data (yr. ended 06/30/00): Assets, $1,091,270 (M); grants paid, $0; gifts received, $100,000; expenditures, $129,441; qualifying distributions, $129,441; giving activities include $45,606 for programs.
Officers and Directors:* Jane Mayhall Katz,* Pres.; Peter Kayafas, Co-Secy.; Dorothy Mont,* Co-Secy.
EIN: 132760185

62122
Yates Art Foundation, Inc.
c/o Lonnie Wollin
350 5th Ave., Ste. 2822
New York, NY 10118

Financial data (yr. ended 06/30/01): Assets, $1,083,418 (M); grants paid, $0; gifts received, $562,907; expenditures, $9,350; qualifying distributions, $0.
Officers: Charlotte Yates, Pres.; Lonnie Wollin, Secy.
EIN: 223527668

62123
Crescentera
c/o Richard A. Eisner & Co., LLP
750 3rd Ave.
New York, NY 10017

Established in 1993 in NY.
Donor(s): Carina Courtright.
Financial data (yr. ended 06/30/01): Assets, $1,078,575 (M); grants paid, $77,046; gifts received, $5,000; expenditures, $172,606; qualifying distributions, $123,590; giving activities include $46,544 for programs.
Limitations: Applications not accepted. Giving primarily in New York, NY.
Application information: Contributes only to pre-selected organizations.
Officers and Directors:* Carina Courtright,* Pres.; Connie Chen,* V.P.; Dean Silvers,* V.P.
EIN: 133736294
Codes: FD2

62124
Augustus L. & Jennie D. Hoffman Foundation
c/o JPMorgan Chase Bank
P.O. Box 31412
Rochester, NY 14603-1412
Application address: Marjorie Perez for Scholarships or James Brady for grants, c/o Wayne County Historical Society, 22 Butternut St., Lyon, NY 14489, tel.: (315) 946-6191

Financial data (yr. ended 12/31/01): Assets, $1,076,700 (M); grants paid, $11,075; expenditures, $36,841; qualifying distributions, $27,816.
Limitations: Giving limited to residents of Wayne County, NY.
Publications: Application guidelines.
Trustee: JPMorgan Chase Bank.
EIN: 166014973
Codes: GTI

62125
George Lichter Family Foundation
c/o Miller, Levine & Co.
419 Park Ave., Ste. 506
New York, NY 10016-8410

Donor(s): George Lichter.
Financial data (yr. ended 12/31/00): Assets, $1,059,043 (M); grants paid, $18,250; expenditures, $20,015; qualifying distributions, $20,015.
Limitations: Applications not accepted. Giving on a national basis.
Application information: Contributes only to pre-selected organizations.
Officer: George Lichter, Pres.
Trustees: Albert Miller, Saul Strauss.
EIN: 136807703

62126
Theodore N. Voss Charitable Foundation
c/o Morris Pliskow, PC
641 Lexington Ave., Ste. 1400
New York, NY 10022 (212) 421-6211
Contact: Theodore N. Voss, Pres.

Established in 1997 in NY.
Financial data (yr. ended 12/31/00): Assets, $1,056,302 (M); grants paid, $40,300; expenditures, $41,339; qualifying distributions, $40,580.
Limitations: Giving primarily in NY.
Application information: Application form required.
Officers and Directors:* Theodore N. Voss,* Pres. and Treas.; Leland Smith,* Secy.; Sophia Voss.
EIN: 133978579

62127
Bridging the Ocean Foundation, Inc.
c/o Tucker & Latifi
160 E. 84th St.
New York, NY 10028

Established in 1997 in DE and NY. Classified as a private operating foundation in 1998.
Donor(s): Pinkas E. Lebovits.
Financial data (yr. ended 12/31/01): Assets, $1,049,165 (M); grants paid, $25; gifts received, $10,000; expenditures, $40,337; qualifying distributions, $28,796; giving activities include $27,771 for programs.
Limitations: Applications not accepted.
Application information: Contributes only to pre-selected organizations.
Officers and Directors:* Judith Lebovits,* Pres.; Robert Tucker, Secy.-Treas.; Gabriel Erem, Robert Tornambe.
EIN: 522082852

62128
The Fred and Edith Horowitz Fund for Jewish Survival, Inc.
c/o BDO Seidman, LLP
401 Broadhollow Rd., 2nd Fl.
Melville, NY 11747

Established in 1983.
Donor(s): Fred Horowitz, Lewis Brass and Copper Co., Inc., Edith Horowitz.
Financial data (yr. ended 12/31/01): Assets, $1,018,645 (M); grants paid, $35,000; gifts received, $15,000; expenditures, $65,179; qualifying distributions, $35,000.
Limitations: Applications not accepted. Giving primarily in NY.
Application information: Contributes only to pre-selected organizations.
Officers and Directors:* Edith Horowitz,* Pres. and Treas.; Jay Horowitz,* V.P.; Marla Horowitz, Secy.; Elliot Horowitz, Exec. Dir.; Fred Horowitz.
EIN: 061073698

62129
The Herrick Theatre Foundation, Inc.
c/o Rhoda R. Herrick
605 Park Ave., No. 7A
New York, NY 10021

Established around 1983; classified as a private operating foundation in 1985.
Donor(s): David Rosenthal,‡ Rhoda R. Herrick.
Financial data (yr. ended 05/31/01): Assets, $1,014,058 (M); grants paid, $124,900; gifts received, $25,000; expenditures, $343,084; qualifying distributions, $294,739; giving activities include $35,000 for loans.
Limitations: Applications not accepted. Giving primarily in New York, NY.
Application information: Contributes only to pre-selected organizations.
Officers and Directors:* Rhoda R. Herrick,* Pres.; Thomas E. Gough,* Secy.; Robert M. Rosenthal.
EIN: 133171936
Codes: FD2

62130
Morton Memorial Library and Community House
P.O. Box 220
Rhinecliff, NY 12574-0220

Classified as a private operating foundation in 1990.
Financial data (yr. ended 12/31/00): Assets, $1,013,343 (M); grants paid, $0; gifts received, $7,391; expenditures, $86,800; qualifying distributions, $70,423; giving activities include $70,755 for programs.
Officers: Mildred Z. Young, Pres.; Benson R. Frost, V.P.; William Cotting, Secy.; Richard Kopyscianski, Treas.
EIN: 141425035

62131
American Airpower Museum, Inc.
(Formerly American Museum for the Preservation of Historic Aircraft)
c/o Avirex Ltd.
33-00 47th Ave.
Long Island City, NY 11101

Established in 1993.
Donor(s): Avirex, Ltd., NYS Urban Development Corp.
Financial data (yr. ended 12/31/00): Assets, $1,003,579 (M); grants paid, $0; gifts received, $693,611; expenditures, $643,742; qualifying distributions, $627,093; giving activities include $264,301 for programs.
Limitations: Applications not accepted.

Application information: Contributes only to pre-selected organizations.
Trustees: Helen J.R. Clyman, Jeffrey Clyman, Scott A. Clyman, E. Cooke Rand, Therese Robin.
EIN: 113162087

62132
Raoul Hague Foundation, Inc.
Box 579, Prince St. Station
New York, NY 10012

Established in 1995 in NY. Classified as a private operating foundation in 1999.
Financial data (yr. ended 12/31/00): Assets, $998,328 (M); grants paid, $0; expenditures, $19,478; qualifying distributions, $17,008; giving activities include $17,008 for programs.
Officers: Holly Hughes, Pres.; Peter Larkin, V.P.; Michael Rubinstein, Secy.-Treas.
Directors: Debra Balken, Christopher Schwabacher, Naomi Spector.
EIN: 133759863

62133
Finkelstein Family Foundation
c/o Katz & Bloom, LLC
200 South Service Rd., Ste. 208
Roslyn Heights, NY 11577

Established in 1998 in NY.
Donor(s): Estelle Finkelstein, Jerome Finkelstein.
Financial data (yr. ended 04/30/01): Assets, $994,403 (M); grants paid, $22,250; gifts received, $16,000; expenditures, $23,850; qualifying distributions, $23,267.
Limitations: Applications not accepted.
Application information: Contributes only to pre-selected organizations.
Officers: Estelle Finkelstein, Pres.; Eve Silver, Secy.
Directors: Deborah Entel, Jerome Finkelstein, Michael Finkelstein.
EIN: 113438221

62134
Good News Foundation of Central New York
10475 Cosby Manor Rd.
Utica, NY 13502

Financial data (yr. ended 04/30/01): Assets, $978,422 (M); grants paid, $88,454; gifts received, $249,271; expenditures, $296,955; qualifying distributions, $86,992.
Limitations: Applications not accepted. Giving primarily in NY.
Application information: Contributes only to pre-selected organizations.
Officers: Edward Paparella, Pres.; Raymond Schultz, V.P.; Elizabeth Droz, Secy. and Exec. Dir.; John Dillon, Treas.
EIN: 161421215

62135
The Trumansburg Charitable Trust
P.O. Box 368
Trumansburg, NY 14886-0368

Established in 1994 in NY.
Financial data (yr. ended 12/31/00): Assets, $960,482 (M); grants paid, $45,000; expenditures, $57,193; qualifying distributions, $46,300.
Limitations: Giving limited to the Trumansburg, NY, area.
Application information: Application form required.
Trustees: Marsha L. Georgia, Osmo Heila, Alex Rachun, Roger Rector, G. Wolf.
EIN: 161422770
Codes: GTI

62136
The Esther and Robert Born Foundation, Inc.
871 7th Ave.
New York, NY 10019

Donor(s): Robert Born,‡ Esther Born.
Financial data (yr. ended 12/31/01): Assets, $956,196 (M); grants paid, $50,627; expenditures, $54,778; qualifying distributions, $50,627.
Limitations: Giving primarily in New York, NY.
Officers: Esther Born, Pres.; Richard Born, Secy.; Rita Distenfeld, Treas.
EIN: 133797585

62137
American Friends of Mosdos Hakerem, Inc.
4 Treetop Ln.
Monsey, NY 10952 (845) 425-1952
Contact: Jacob Kreitman, Dir.

Established in 1994 in NY.
Financial data (yr. ended 08/31/01): Assets, $945,841 (L); grants paid, $44,000; gifts received, $75,779; expenditures, $44,761; qualifying distributions, $43,608.
Limitations: Giving limited to Israel.
Directors: Jacob Kreitman, Rivkah Kreitman.
EIN: 133047558

62138
John Conley Foundation for Ethics and Philosophy in Medicine, Inc.
211 Central Park W.
New York, NY 10024-6020

Established in 1991 in NY.
Donor(s): John Conley.
Financial data (yr. ended 12/31/01): Assets, $909,052 (M); grants paid, $156,000; expenditures, $222,815; qualifying distributions, $211,985.
Limitations: Applications not accepted. Giving primarily in New York, NY.
Officers: Monika Conley, V.P.; Harry T. Forlenza, Secy.-Treas.
EIN: 133626727
Codes: FD2

62139
The Smithy-Pioneer Gallery, Inc.
53 Pioneer St.
Cooperstown, NY 13326

Classified as a private operating foundation in 1985.
Financial data (yr. ended 12/31/01): Assets, $899,430 (M); grants paid, $0; gifts received, $20,536; expenditures, $89,925; qualifying distributions, $78,640; giving activities include $78,640 for programs.
Officers and Directors:* Susan F.C. Weil,* Pres.; James F. Cooper,* V.P.; Katherine L.F.C. Cary,* Secy.; Henry S.F. Cooper,* Treas.; Katrina Cary, and 4 additional directors.
EIN: 222585458

62140
Pfeiffer Nature Center and Foundation, Inc.
c/o Community Bank, N.A.
201 N. Union St.
Olean, NY 14760

Established in 1998 in NY.
Financial data (yr. ended 06/30/00): Assets, $890,925 (M); grants paid, $0; gifts received, $5,495; expenditures, $56,825; qualifying distributions, $37,357; giving activities include $56,825 for programs.
Officers: Nicholas Dicerbo, Pres.; Stephen Eaton, V.P.; Michael Myers, Secy.; Michael Patton, Treas.

Directors: Joe Bohan, Roy Griffin, Cathy Koebelin, Judy Palton, Doug Price, Mary Ellen Shaughnessy, Nicholas Vaczek.
EIN: 161557741

62141
The Oliver and Elizabeth Laster Foundation
(Formerly The Laster Foundation)
52 Prospect Ave.
Hewlett, NY 11557 (516) 599-8066
Contact: Oliver Laster, Mgr.

Donor(s): Oliver Laster, Elizabeth Laster.
Financial data (yr. ended 06/30/01): Assets, $880,919 (M); grants paid, $29,123; gifts received, $32,745; expenditures, $29,901; qualifying distributions, $29,297.
Officers: Elizabeth Laster, Secy.-Treas.; Oliver Laster, Mgr.
EIN: 112804171

62142
John F. O'Brien Foundation
P.O. Box 11296
Loudonville, NY 12211-0296
Contact: Roseanna Biondo, Tr.

Established in 1989 in NY.
Donor(s): John F. O'Brien.
Financial data (yr. ended 12/31/01): Assets, $878,306 (M); grants paid, $110,000; expenditures, $124,734; qualifying distributions, $110,000.
Limitations: Giving primarily in the Albany, NY, area.
Publications: Annual report.
Application information: Application form not required.
Trustee: Roseanna Biondo.
EIN: 223061594
Codes: FD2

62143
Schleifer Family Foundation
49 Carolyn Pl.
Chappaqua, NY 10514
Contact: Harriet P. Schleifer, Pres.

Donor(s): Harriet P. Schleifer.
Financial data (yr. ended 10/31/00): Assets, $866,788 (M); grants paid, $25,014; expenditures, $47,930; qualifying distributions, $25,014.
Officers: Harriet P. Schleifer, Pres.; Leonard S. Schleifer, Secy.
Director: Lawrence M. Schleifer.
EIN: 133925934

62144
American Conservation Association, Inc.
30 Rockefeller Plz., Rm. 5600
New York, NY 10112
Contact: Charles M. Clusen, Exec. Dir.

Incorporated in 1958 in NY.
Donor(s): Laurance S. Rockefeller, Laurance Rockefeller, Rockefeller Brothers Fund, Jackson Hole Preserve, Inc.
Financial data (yr. ended 12/31/00): Assets, $863,426 (M); grants paid, $237,500; gifts received, $500,000; expenditures, $577,031; qualifying distributions, $569,388; giving activities include $97,391 for programs.
Limitations: Giving on a national basis, with emphasis on Washington, DC.
Application information: Application form not required.
Officers and Trustees:* Laurance Rockefeller,* Pres.; R. Scott Greathead,* Secy.; Carmen Reyes, Treas.; Charles M. Clusen, Exec. Dir.; John H. Adams, Frances G. Beinecke, Nash Castro, William G. Conway, Henry L. Diamond, Fred I. Kent III, W. Barnabas McHenry, Patrick F. Noonan, Story Clark Resor, David S. Sampson, Cathleen Douglas Stone, Russell E. Train, William H. Whyte, Jr.
EIN: 131874023
Codes: FD2

62145
Louis F. Payn Foundation for Aged People
c/o Rosa P. Cummings
Coleman St.
Chatham, NY 12037-1304

Established in 1923.
Financial data (yr. ended 03/31/01): Assets, $843,678 (M); grants paid, $0; gifts received, $54,529; expenditures, $271,421; qualifying distributions, $0.
Officers: Richard Leggett, Pres.; Elizabeth Rundell, V.P.; Elizabeth Iaconetti, Secy.-Treas.
Directors: Rosa Cummings, Keith Flint, Paul Fuller, Susannah Marks.
EIN: 141364559

62146
The Griffin Family Foundation
51 Pondfield Rd.
Bronxville, NY 10708

Established in 1999 in NY.
Donor(s): William E. Griffin.
Financial data (yr. ended 12/31/01): Assets, $841,151 (M); grants paid, $45,225; gifts received, $187,200; expenditures, $45,439; qualifying distributions, $44,852.
Limitations: Applications not accepted. Giving primarily in NY.
Application information: Contributes only to pre-selected organizations.
Officers: William E. Griffin, Pres.; Margaret O. Griffin, Secy.
EIN: 134090207

62147
Merinoff Charitable Trust
c/o E.D. Loewenwarter
10 E. 40th St., Ste. 2105
New York, NY 10016-0200
Application address: 19-50 48th St., Astoria, NY 11105, tel.: (718) 726-2500
Contact: Charles Merinoff, Tr.

Classified as a private operating foundation in 1996.
Donor(s): Herman Merinoff.
Financial data (yr. ended 12/31/00): Assets, $816,495 (M); grants paid, $59,050; gifts received, $369,116; expenditures, $67,224; qualifying distributions, $59,028.
Limitations: Giving primarily in NY.
Trustees: Barbara Merinoff, Charles Merinoff, Linda Merinoff, Spencer Merinoff, Cathy Onufrychuk.
EIN: 137068846

62148
Female Charitable Society of Baldwinsville, Inc.
10 River St.
Baldwinsville, NY 13027-2510
Application address: 15 Elizabeth St., Baldwinsville, NY 13027, tel.: (315) 635-7614
Contact: Mrs. Gordon Slye, Pres.

Classified as a private operating foundation in 1957.
Financial data (yr. ended 06/30/00): Assets, $809,552 (M); grants paid, $28,337; gifts received, $1,534; expenditures, $43,486; qualifying distributions, $30,283.
Limitations: Giving limited to the Baldwinsville, NY, area.

Officers: Mrs. Gordon Slye, Pres.; Mrs. Richard Hovey, 1st V.P.; Mrs. William Hosey, 2nd V.P.; Mrs. Edward J. McManus, Jr., Secy.; Mrs. Nelson Huntley, Treas.
EIN: 156019000

62149
Collins Charitable Foundation, Inc.
(Formerly Albany Saratoga Charitable Foundation, Inc.)
P.O. Box 4550
Saratoga Springs, NY 12866-8028
(518) 584-8745
Application address: 703 Grand Ave., Saratoga Springs, NY 12666
Contact: Donald Alan Collins, Pres.

Financial data (yr. ended 09/30/01): Assets, $804,592 (M); grants paid, $41,000; gifts received, $25,000; expenditures, $42,626; qualifying distributions, $42,626.
Limitations: Giving on a national basis.
Officers: Donald Alan Collins, Pres.; Barbara C. Longe, V.P.; Lawrence R. Hamilton, Secy.; Patrick J. Fitzgerald, Jr., Treas.
EIN: 141623884

62150
Palisades Geophysical Institute, Inc.
P.O. Box 642, 60 Dutch Hill Rd.
Orangeburg, NY 10962-0642

Established in 1970 in NY; classified as a private operating foundation in 1974.
Financial data (yr. ended 12/31/01): Assets, $791,669 (M); grants paid, $0; expenditures, $1,838,051; qualifying distributions, $1,877,245; giving activities include $1,877,245 for programs.
Officers and Directors:* John Lamar Worzel, M.D.,* Chair. and Pres.; Dean B. Seifried,* V.P.; Magdalene M. Fennessy, Secy.; Catherine M. Powers, Treas.; Frank Mongelli,* Admin.; H. James Dorman, M.D., W. Arnold Finck, Thomas A. Graves, Gary V. Latham, M.D., Arthur E. Maxwell, M.D., Robert E. Wall, M.D.
EIN: 237069955

62151
Bruce A. Gimbel Foundation, Inc.
c/o Barbara P. Gimbel
66 E. 79th St.
New York, NY 10021-0233

Established in the 1940s in NY.
Donor(s): Bruce A. Gimbel.‡
Financial data (yr. ended 01/31/00): Assets, $788,220 (M); grants paid, $19,300; expenditures, $22,623; qualifying distributions, $22,623.
Limitations: Applications not accepted. Giving primarily in New York, NY.
Application information: Contributes only to pre-selected organizations.
Officers: Barbara P. Gimbel, Pres.; John B. Gimbel, V.P.; Judith Mendelsund, V.P.
EIN: 136198296

62152
Jay M. Aidikoff Foundation, Inc.
95 Horatio St., Ste. 301
New York, NY 10014-1520
Application address: 95 Horatio St., Ste. 301, New York, NY 10014, tel.: (212) 243-1133
Contact: Jay Aidikoff, Pres.

Established in 1994.
Donor(s): Jay M. Aidikoff.
Financial data (yr. ended 12/31/01): Assets, $779,522 (M); grants paid, $40,750; expenditures, $44,308; qualifying distributions, $40,438.
Limitations: Giving primarily in New York, NY.
Officer: Jay M. Aidikoff, Pres.
EIN: 133799857

62153
Alter Isaac & Charlotte Gross Irrevocable Charitable Trust
c/o Shanholt, Glassman, Klein, Kramer
488 Madison Ave., 10th Fl.
New York, NY 10022

Established in 1992 in NY.
Donor(s): Alter Isaac Gross, Charlotte Gross.
Financial data (yr. ended 12/31/00): Assets, $777,239 (M); grants paid, $113,310; gifts received, $52,416; expenditures, $116,787; qualifying distributions, $114,832.
Limitations: Applications not accepted.
Trustees: Henry Gross, Mark Gross.
EIN: 133694308
Codes: FD2

62154
New York City Association for the Help of Retarded Children Housing Development Company, Inc.
200 Park Ave. S.
New York, NY 10003-1503

Classified as a private operating foundation in 1979.
Financial data (yr. ended 06/30/01): Assets, $775,991 (M); grants paid, $0; expenditures, $104,939; qualifying distributions, $77,031; giving activities include $104,939 for programs.
Officers: Al Agovino, Pres.; James P. Murphy, 1st V.P.; Blanche Fierstein, 2nd V.P.; George G. Hirsh, Fin. Secy.; I. William Stone, Treas.
EIN: 133131470

62155
Lorraine M. & Eugene P. Brady Memorial Scholarship Trust
P.O. Box 456
Lockport, NY 14095-0456   (716) 439-6422
Contact: Paul Foster, Chair.

Established in 1994 in NY.
Donor(s): Lorraine M. Brady.
Financial data (yr. ended 12/31/00): Assets, $773,097 (M); grants paid, $22,390; expenditures, $48,082; qualifying distributions, $26,376.
Limitations: Giving limited to Lockport, NY.
Application information: Application form not required.
Officers and Trustees:* Paul Foster, Chair.; Kathleen Granchelli,* Treas.; Mark Albiez, Bruce Frazier, Sr. Carol Ann Kleindinst.
EIN: 166411714

62156
Jules and Barbara Nordlicht Foundation
255 W. Beech St.
Long Beach, NY 11561-3201   (516) 432-4621
Contact: Jules Nordlicht, Pres.

Established in 1991 in NY.
Donor(s): Barbara Nordlicht, Jules Nordlicht.
Financial data (yr. ended 12/31/01): Assets, $755,669 (M); grants paid, $69,388; expenditures, $69,934; qualifying distributions, $69,388.
Limitations: Giving primarily in NY.
Officers: Jules Nordlicht, Pres.; Barbara Nordlicht, Treas.
EIN: 113074444

62157
The Stanley & Vivian Bernstein Foundation
300 Trenor Dr.
New Rochelle, NY 10804

Established in 1997 in NY.
Donor(s): Stanley Bernstein, Vivian Bernstein.
Financial data (yr. ended 12/31/00): Assets, $738,015 (M); grants paid, $80,400; gifts received, $23,077; expenditures, $81,088; qualifying distributions, $80,400.
Limitations: Applications not accepted. Giving primarily in New York, NY.
Application information: Contributes only to pre-selected organizations.
Trustees: Stanley Bernstein, Vivian Bernstein.
EIN: 137104060
Codes: FD2

62158
M. J. De Lucia Foundation
1199 Park Ave.
New York, NY 10128-1711

Donor(s): Marie J. De Lucia.
Financial data (yr. ended 01/31/01): Assets, $735,611 (M); grants paid, $24,846; gifts received, $10,382; expenditures, $29,003; qualifying distributions, $24,712.
Limitations: Applications not accepted.
Application information: Contributes only to pre-selected organizations.
Officers: Marie J. De Lucia, Pres. and Treas.; Edwin L. Solot, Secy.
EIN: 133794509

62159
Isaiah 61 Foundation
c/o Andrew Schonbek
61 Industrial Blvd.
Plattsburgh, NY 12901

Established in 2000 in NY.
Donor(s): Andrew J. Schonbek.
Financial data (yr. ended 12/31/00): Assets, $734,249 (M); grants paid, $17,500; gifts received, $750,000; expenditures, $25,070; qualifying distributions, $17,500.
Limitations: Applications not accepted.
Application information: Contributes only to pre-selected organizations.
Trustees: Eileen Schonbeck Beer, Michael Beer, Alice J. Schonbek, Andrew J. Schonbek.
EIN: 141827942

62160
Harold F. & Hanna A. Brooks Charitable Trust
c/o The Central National Bank
24 Church St.
Canajoharie, NY 13317
Tel.: (518) 673-3243 ext. 1212
Contact: Scott Vaughan, Sr.V.P., Central National Bank

Established in 2001 in NY.
Donor(s): Hanna A. Brooks.
Financial data (yr. ended 12/31/01): Assets, $701,880 (M); grants paid, $10,000; gifts received, $700,000; expenditures, $13,645; qualifying distributions, $10,000.
Limitations: Giving primarily in Edmeston, NY.
Trustees: Dorothy Blackman, The Central National Bank.
EIN: 166520061

62161
Thomas F. and Laura L. Moogan Family Foundation, Ltd.
191 Rauber St.
Wellsville, NY 14895 (716) 593-1984
Contact: Herbert G. Sherman, Treas.

Established in 1994 in NY.
Donor(s): Thomas F. Moogan.
Financial data (yr. ended 12/31/00): Assets, $697,721 (M); grants paid, $2,925; gifts received, $595,217; expenditures, $5,955; qualifying distributions, $5,955.
Application information: Application form required.
Officers and Directors:* L. Christine Moogan, Pres.; Erkie Kailbourne, V.P.; Beth Farwell,* Secy.; Herbert G. Sherman, Treas.; Eugene Nye, John Walchli.
EIN: 161463956

62162
John A. Reddington Scholarship Fund & Trust
c/o Genesee Valley Trust Co.
5 Tobey Village Office Park
Pittsford, NY 14534-1741 (716) 586-6900

Established in 1998 in NY.
Financial data (yr. ended 08/31/00): Assets, $695,051 (M); grants paid, $33,287; expenditures, $43,493; qualifying distributions, $33,212.
Trustee: Genesee Valley Trust Co.
EIN: 161555796

62163
The Schiff Family Foundation
1060 5th Ave.
New York, NY 10128

Donor(s): Nelson Schiff.
Financial data (yr. ended 12/31/99): Assets, $672,193 (M); grants paid, $25,000; gifts received, $52,987; expenditures, $26,513; qualifying distributions, $24,291.
Limitations: Applications not accepted.
Application information: Contributes only to pre-selected organizations.
Officers: Andrew Schiff, Pres.; Corinne Schiff, Secy.; Karen Schiff, Treas.
Directors: Allison Schiff, Barbara Schiff, John Schiff, Nelson Schiff.
EIN: 133920396

62164
The Farbenblum Foundation
(Formerly The Martin Farbenblum Foundation)
495 Finehurst Ct.
Roslyn, NY 11576

Classified as a private operating foundation in 1999; Established in 1997 in NY.
Donor(s): Martin Farbenblum.
Financial data (yr. ended 12/31/00): Assets, $665,861 (M); grants paid, $60,384; gifts received, $63,000; expenditures, $62,759; qualifying distributions, $60,384.
Limitations: Giving on a national basis.
Application information: Application form required.
Trustee: Martin Farbenblum.
EIN: 137120066

62165
Merl Art Foundation, Inc.
c/o Lonnie Wollin
350 5th Ave., No. 2822
New York, NY 10118

Donor(s): Bede Levinson, Steve Levinson.

Financial data (yr. ended 06/30/00): Assets, $655,378 (M); grants paid, $0; expenditures, $6,280; qualifying distributions, $38,616.
Officers: Steve Levinson, Pres.; Beatrice Levinson, V.P.; Lonnie Wollin, Secy.
EIN: 223525125

62166
Hudson Valley Technology Development Center, Inc.
300 Westage Business Ctr., Ste. 130
Fishkill, NY 12524

Classified as a private operating foundation in 1988.
Financial data (yr. ended 09/30/00): Assets, $655,369 (M); grants paid, $0; gifts received, $1,671,356; expenditures, $2,291,060; qualifying distributions, $1,618,836; giving activities include $2,189,651 for programs.
Officers and Directors:* Kenneth Kaufman, Chair.; Robert J. Incerto,* Vice-Chair.; Phyllis F. Levine, Secy.; John Prusmack,* Treas.; Thomas Phillips, Exec. Dir.; Donna Cornell, and 8 additional directors.
EIN: 141698513

62167
Atomic Research, Inc.
28 2nd Ave.
Central Islip, NY 11722-3012

Donor(s): Harold McGowan.
Financial data (yr. ended 12/31/01): Assets, $653,228 (M); grants paid, $0; gifts received, $123,027; expenditures, $86,120; qualifying distributions, $0.
Officer: Harold McGowan, Pres.
EIN: 116015086

62168
Ernest Lowenstein Foundation, Inc.
P.O. Box 236
Lawrence, NY 11559-0236

Established in 1957.
Donor(s): Tom Lowenstein, Marvin Wildenberg, Margit Lowenstein, Robert Lowenstein, Hanna Wildenberg, Martin Lowernstein.
Financial data (yr. ended 11/30/01): Assets, $646,376 (M); grants paid, $90,091; gifts received, $68,857; expenditures, $94,302; qualifying distributions, $90,091.
Limitations: Applications not accepted. Giving on a national basis.
Application information: Contributes only to pre-selected organizations.
Officers: Marvin Wildenberg, Pres.; Hanna Wildenberg, V.P and Secy.; Martin Lowenstein, V.P.; Andrew Wildenberg, Treas.
EIN: 136085585
Codes: FD2

62169
Dungannon Foundation, Inc.
c/o CPI Assocs., Inc.
32 E. 57th St., 14th Fl.
New York, NY 10022-2513

Established in 1985 in NY.
Donor(s): Mrs. Henry Chalfant, Cynthia C. Giles, Harlan R. Giles, Michael Moorhead Rea,‡ Rives R. Yost, Homer J. Rose, Rossco of Palm Beach, Inc.
Financial data (yr. ended 12/31/00): Assets, $643,894 (M); grants paid, $50,000; expenditures, $81,408; qualifying distributions, $79,460.
Officers and Directors:* Elizabeth Richebourg Rea,* Pres.; Arthur Potts, Jr.,* Secy.
EIN: 133312300
Codes: GTI

62170
Douglas S. Cramer Foundation
c/o Mason & Co., LLP
400 Park Ave., Ste. 1200
New York, NY 10022

Established in 1985 in CA.
Donor(s): Douglas S. Cramer.
Financial data (yr. ended 04/30/01): Assets, $626,840 (M); grants paid, $379,895; expenditures, $396,949; qualifying distributions, $387,181.
Limitations: Applications not accepted. Giving primarily in, but not limited to New York, NY.
Application information: Contributes only to pre-selected organizations.
Officer: Douglas S. Cramer, Pres.
EIN: 954079366
Codes: FD

62171
Harlem Educational Activities Fund
200 Madison Ave., 5th Fl.
New York, NY 10016
Contact: Daniel Rose, Pres.

Established in 1990 in DE.
Donor(s): Daniel and Joanna S. Rose Fund, Inc.
Financial data (yr. ended 12/31/99): Assets, $620,861 (M); grants paid, $989,753; gifts received, $1,660,175; expenditures, $1,599,809; qualifying distributions, $1,549,375.
Limitations: Applications not accepted. Giving limited to New York, NY.
Publications: Annual report.
Application information: Contributes only to pre-selected organizations.
Officers and Directors:* Daniel Rose,* Pres. and Secy.; Maria J. Rodriguez, V.P.; Courtney Welsh, Exec. Dir.; Gen. Colin L. Powell, Hon. Dir.; Sheri Berman, Henry Louis Gates, Frank Levy, Brig. Gen. George B. Price, Adam Robinson, Joanna S. Rose, Nell Kincaid Semel, Maurice Sonnenberg, Isabel Carter Stewart, Hon. James L. Watson.
EIN: 133568672
Codes: FD

62172
The Easton Foundation, Inc.
c/o David J. Silverman & Co.
866 United Nations Plz., No. S-415
New York, NY 10017-3597

Donor(s): Louise Bourgeois.
Financial data (yr. ended 10/31/01): Assets, $614,992 (M); grants paid, $146,000; gifts received, $125,000; expenditures, $163,701; qualifying distributions, $159,586.
Limitations: Applications not accepted. Giving primarily in New York, NY.
Application information: Contributes only to pre-selected organizations.
Trustees: Alain Bourgeois, Jean-Louis Bourgeois, Louise Bourgeois.
EIN: 133190220
Codes: FD2

62173
Tee & Charles Addams Foundation
P.O. Box 248
Wainscott, NY 11975-0248

Established in 2000 in NY.
Donor(s): Marilyn Addams.
Financial data (yr. ended 12/31/01): Assets, $614,352 (M); grants paid, $0; gifts received, $192,798; expenditures, $46,842; qualifying distributions, $0.
Limitations: Applications not accepted.
Application information: Contributes only to pre-selected organizations.

Directors: Marilyn Addams, H. Kevin Miserocchi.
EIN: 113506582

62174
Pilzer Foundation, Inc.
53 Walden Rd.
Tarrytown, NY 10591 (914) 631-4766
Contact: Herbert Pilzer, Dir.

Established in 1997 in NY.
Donor(s): Herbert R. Pilzer.
Financial data (yr. ended 09/30/00): Assets, $607,456 (M); grants paid, $23,000; gifts received, $90,278; expenditures, $23,369; qualifying distributions, $22,732.
Directors: Herbert R. Pilzer, Neal R. Pilzer, Lynn A. Sobel.
EIN: 133973639

62175
The Sabin Conservation Fund, Inc.
P.O. Box 968
Amagansett, NY 11930-0968

Established in 1992 in NY.
Donor(s): Evelyn M. Kahn, Annette Sabin, Andrew Sabin.
Financial data (yr. ended 05/31/01): Assets, $606,742 (M); grants paid, $0; gifts received, $58,250; expenditures, $58,050; qualifying distributions, $0.
Limitations: Applications not accepted.
Application information: Contributes only to pre-selected organizations.
Officers: Andrew Sabin, Pres.; Robert Sabin, V.P.; Annette Sabin, Secy.; Jonathan Sabin, Treas.
Directors: Jeffrey Keil, Kari Lyn Sabin, Shawn Sabin.
EIN: 112809232

62176
Center for Alternative Media and Culture
c/o Starr & Co.
350 Park Ave.
New York, NY 10022-6022
Application address: c/o Veronica Moore, 3725 Caminito E. Bluff, Apt. 204, La Jolla, CA 92037

Financial data (yr. ended 12/31/00): Assets, $602,612 (M); grants paid, $42,798; expenditures, $55,007; qualifying distributions, $51,418.
Limitations: Giving on a national basis.
Officers: Michael Moore, Pres.; Al Hirvela, Secy.; Kathleen Glynn, Treas.
EIN: 382415253
Codes: GTI

62177
The RJM Charitable Trust
15 E. 10th St., Ste. 5F
New York, NY 10003-5939

Donor(s): Stephen J. Ziffer.
Financial data (yr. ended 12/31/99): Assets, $602,302 (M); grants paid, $429; gifts received, $5,000; expenditures, $41,327; qualifying distributions, $41,327; giving activities include $37,831 for programs.
Limitations: Applications not accepted.
Application information: Contributes only to pre-selected organizations.
Trustees: William H. Allman, Jr., Andrew Humm, Stephen J. Ziffer.
EIN: 597069460

62178
Greenfield Foundation
c/o Stephen P. Reynolds
215 E. 72nd St.
New York, NY 10021

Established in 2000 in NY.
Donor(s): Stephen P. Reynold.
Financial data (yr. ended 12/31/00): Assets, $600,144 (M); grants paid, $95,094; gifts received, $798,540; expenditures, $112,552; qualifying distributions, $105,429.
Limitations: Applications not accepted.
Application information: Contributes only to pre-selected organizations.
Officer: Stephen P. Reynolds, Pres.
EIN: 134103999
Codes: FD2

62179
Charles Ives Society, Inc.
c/o Eichler, Bergsman, and Co., LLP
404 Park Ave. S., Ste. 700
New York, NY 10016 (212) 827-9502

Donor(s): American Academy & Institute of Art & Letters.
Financial data (yr. ended 09/30/00): Assets, $595,000 (M); grants paid, $0; gifts received, $168,640; expenditures, $32,843; qualifying distributions, $31,778; giving activities include $31,778 for programs.
Officer and Directors:* Arnold Broido,* Pres.; William Bolcom, J. Peter Burkholder, Susan Feder, Ronald Freed, Charles Ives Tyler, Todd Vunderink, and 18 additional directors.
EIN: 132751129

62180
Roberts Foundation, Inc.
(Formerly Louis & Edith Roberts Foundation)
c/o Louis Katz
20 Old Turnpike Rd.
Nanuet, NY 10954
Contact: Richard Roberts, Dir.

Established in 1985 in NY.
Financial data (yr. ended 12/31/99): Assets, $585,751 (M); grants paid, $3,524; expenditures, $5,843; qualifying distributions, $3,524.
Limitations: Giving primarily in New York, NY.
Director: Richard Roberts.
EIN: 237416892

62181
Center Manor, Inc.
(also known as Menands Manor)
272 Broadway
Menands, NY 12204-2781

Donor(s): Center for the Disabled Foundation, Inc.
Financial data (yr. ended 12/31/01): Assets, $566,928 (M); grants paid, $0; gifts received, $67,756; expenditures, $164,720; qualifying distributions, $0.
Officers and Directors:* James P. Coleman,* Chair.; Patrick J. Bulgaro,* Pres. and Exec. Dir.; Robert D. Clore,* V.P.; Joanne Kress,* Secy.; Donald Hayward,* Treas.; and 21 additional directors.
EIN: 141365185

62182
Demeter Fund, Inc.
c/o Rock & Co., Inc.
30 Rockefeller Plz., Rm. 5600
New York, NY 10020

Established in 1991 in NY.
Donor(s): Steven C. Rockefeller.

Financial data (yr. ended 12/31/01): Assets, $564,458 (M); grants paid, $3,212; expenditures, $26,180; qualifying distributions, $13,606.
Limitations: Applications not accepted. Giving primarily in ME and VT.
Application information: Contributes only to pre-selected organizations.
Officers: Steven C. Rockefeller, Pres.; James S. Sligar, Secy.; Dennis J. Ryan, Treas.
EIN: 133575487

62183
Western Monroe Historical Society, Inc.
151 S. Main St.
Brockport, NY 14420

Financial data (yr. ended 06/30/00): Assets, $540,703 (M); grants paid, $0; gifts received, $10,223; expenditures, $81,393; qualifying distributions, $46,107; giving activities include $30,642 for programs.
Officers: Merritt Ackles, Pres.; Mary Lynn Welch, Secy.; Rudy Aceto, Treas.
EIN: 166059055

62184
Amos F. & Sarah L. Holden Home for Aged Women
(Formerly Amos F. & Sarah L. Holden Home)
73 Grand St.
Newburgh, NY 12550

Donor(s): William Kaplan, Elaine Kaplan.
Financial data (yr. ended 12/31/01): Assets, $535,040 (M); grants paid, $0; gifts received, $100,425; expenditures, $533,419; qualifying distributions, $511,898; giving activities include $418,411 for programs.
Officers: Cathy McCarty, Pres.; John R. Hutton, 1st V.P.; William Vacca, 2nd V.P.; Nancy McBride, Secy.; R. Frederick Najork, Treas.
Directors: Stewart P. Glenn, Susan Maloney, Sandra Mazzie, Robert McKenna, Michael A. Smith, Nicholas Valentine.
EIN: 141365995

62185
Art Science Research Laboratory, Inc.
c/o Rhonda Roland Shearer
62 Greene St.
New York, NY 10013

Established in 1998 in NY.
Donor(s): Paul Mellon, Rhonda Roland Shearer.
Financial data (yr. ended 12/31/00): Assets, $523,622 (M); grants paid, $0; gifts received, $200,000; expenditures, $452,102; qualifying distributions, $429,783; giving activities include $429,812 for programs.
Limitations: Applications not accepted.
Application information: Contributes only to pre-selected organizations.
Officers: Rhonda Roland Shearer, Pres.; Stephen J. Gould, V.P.; Robert B. Gould, Secy.
EIN: 134012474

62186
Kenneth and Phyllis Canary Family Foundation
c/o Mario Papa
6 Fremont St.
Gloversville, NY 12078

Established in 2000.
Donor(s): Kenneth C. Canary, Phyllis E. Canary.
Financial data (yr. ended 12/31/01): Assets, $507,062 (M); grants paid, $10,000; expenditures, $13,050; qualifying distributions, $10,000.
Trustees: Keith C. Canary, Kenneth C. Canary, Phyllis E. Canary, The Central National Bank.
EIN: 146199366

62187
Alan Morton Foundation
73 Crescent St.
Sag Harbor, NY 11963-2533

Established in 1985 in NY.
Donor(s): W. Alan Morton.
Financial data (yr. ended 08/31/00): Assets, $504,385 (M); grants paid, $86,683; gifts received, $7,036; expenditures, $106,730; qualifying distributions, $96,658.
Limitations: Applications not accepted. Giving primarily in New York, NY.
Application information: Contributes only to pre-selected organizations.
Officer: W. Alan Morton, Pres.
Directors: Michelle Connelly, Arthur R. Little, Donna Milazzo, Elaine Morton, Neil Morton.
EIN: 133295743

62188
Roslyn Preservation Corporation
P.O. Box 167
Roslyn, NY 11576-0167

Classified as a private operating foundation in 1983.
Donor(s): Roger G. Gerry,‡ Floyd Lyon, Ruth M. Seaman Estate.‡
Financial data (yr. ended 08/31/01): Assets, $501,077 (M); grants paid, $0; expenditures, $4,904; qualifying distributions, $0.
Officers: Donald Kayanagh, V.P.; John Collins, Secy.
EIN: 237170075

62189
Marion Brill Scholarship Foundation, Inc.
P.O. Box 420
Ilion, NY 13357-0420 (315) 895-7771
Application address: c/o Guidance Office, Ilion Central School District High School, P.O. Box 480, Ilion, NY 13357

Financial data (yr. ended 06/30/01): Assets, $499,246 (M); grants paid, $35,000; expenditures, $39,583; qualifying distributions, $38,836.
Limitations: Giving limited to residents of Ilion Central School District, NY.
Application information: Application form required.
Officers and Directors:* Robert Jones,* Pres.; Gary A. Tutty,* V.P.; Jack Manley, Donna Steele.
Scholarship Selection Committee: Lawrence Bousquet, Leola Reynolds, Harold Whittemore.
EIN: 222373170
Codes: GTI

62190
I Have a Dream Foundation - New York
330 7th Ave., 20th Fl.
New York, NY 10001 (212) 293-5480
FAX: (212) 293-5478; *URL:* http://www.ihad.org
Contact: Kara Forte, Exec. Dir.

Established in 1986 in NY.
Donor(s): Eugene M. Lang, and various other donors.
Financial data (yr. ended 08/31/01): Assets, $488,862 (M); grants paid, $311,783; gifts received, $860,198; expenditures, $786,470; qualifying distributions, $780,886.
Limitations: Applications not accepted.
Publications: Financial statement, informational brochure.
Application information: Giving only for pre-determined educational projects organized by the foundation's sponsors.
Officers: Jeff Gural, Chair.; Stanley Picheny, Co-Chair.; Barbara Eisold, Secy.; Brian Hiedtke, Treas.

Directors: Rick Aidekman, Page Ashley, Warren Eisenberg, Harold Friedman, Donald Hatcher, William James, Sharon Kaufman, Howard Kaye, Chris McNickle, Susan Pinco, Bernie Robinson, Howard Wendy.
EIN: 133370648
Codes: FD

62191
Psychoanalytic Research & Development Fund, Inc.
515 E. 72nd St., Ste. 110
New York, NY 10021

Financial data (yr. ended 08/31/99): Assets, $486,642 (M); grants paid, $0; gifts received, $104,807; expenditures, $87,125; qualifying distributions, $60,160; giving activities include $211,084 for programs.
Director: Sidney Furst, M.D.
EIN: 131990917

62192
The Fund for Children of the Americas
c/o Yohalem Gillman & Co., LLP
477 Madison Ave.
New York, NY 10022-5802

Financial data (yr. ended 06/30/99): Assets, $484,527 (M); grants paid, $0; gifts received, $328,595; expenditures, $161,135; qualifying distributions, $131,952; giving activities include $39,429 for programs.
Officers: Roy M. Adams, Pres.; William S. Villafranco, Secy.-Treas.
EIN: 363993358

62193
Musicians Emergency Relief Fund-Local 802
322 W. 48th St.
New York, NY 10036 (212) 245-4802
Contact: William Moriarity, Tr.

Established in 1967 in NY.
Financial data (yr. ended 12/31/01): Assets, $483,858 (M); grants paid, $98,021; gifts received, $11,121; expenditures, $117,204; qualifying distributions, $117,029.
Limitations: Giving primarily to residents of New York, NY.
Publications: Program policy statement.
Application information: Application form required.
Trustees: Katherine Hafemeister, William Moriarity, Erwin Price.
EIN: 136222619
Codes: FD2, GTI

62194
Beaver Dam Sanctuary, Inc.
c/o William Cody
P.O. Box 377
Katonah, NY 10536-0377

Financial data (yr. ended 03/31/00): Assets, $476,195 (M); grants paid, $0; gifts received, $10,450; expenditures, $4,142; qualifying distributions, $4,142; giving activities include $4,142 for programs.
Officers and Directors:* Robert B. Hodes,* Pres.; Jeffrey T. Carpenter, Treas.; Mary Berol, John Fry, Ann McDuffie, Thomas H. Meyer, Jan Montgomery, Laura Thorn, Jean P. Tilt, and 7 additional directors.
EIN: 237021288

62195
Ruth and Itzhak Fisher Foundation, Inc.
545 5th Ave.
New York, NY 10017

Established in 1999 in DE and NY.

Financial data (yr. ended 12/31/01): Assets, $472,799 (M); grants paid, $0; expenditures, $98,150; qualifying distributions, $93,833; giving activities include $82,500 for programs.
Officers: Ruth Fisher, Pres.; Itzhak Fisher, Secy.-Treas.
Director: Celia Kaminer.
EIN: 134036796

62196
Crowing Rooster Arts, Inc.
180 W. Broadway, Ste. 302
New York, NY 10013

Established in 1997 in NY.
Donor(s): Katherine Kean.
Financial data (yr. ended 06/30/01): Assets, $468,355 (L); grants paid, $0; gifts received, $600,222; expenditures, $136,055; qualifying distributions, $102,319; giving activities include $499,074 for programs.
Directors: David Belle, Katherine Kean, Albert Maysles.
EIN: 133693565

62197
Arthur & Hilda Wenig Foundation
445 S. Mountain Rd.
New City, NY 10956
Contact: Arthur Wenig, Dir.

Donor(s): Arthur Wenig, Hilda Wenig.
Financial data (yr. ended 12/31/01): Assets, $464,957 (M); grants paid, $37,265; gifts received, $49,069; expenditures, $37,365; qualifying distributions, $36,800.
Limitations: Giving primarily in NY.
Directors: Arthur Wenig, Hilda Wenig.
EIN: 113189670

62198
Rudman Family Foundation
114 Joseph Ave.
Staten Island, NY 10314

Established in 1999 in NY.
Donor(s): Robert Rudman.
Financial data (yr. ended 12/31/00): Assets, $464,568 (M); grants paid, $26,660; gifts received, $427,126; expenditures, $29,377; qualifying distributions, $26,660.
Trustees: Jack Rudman, Robert Rudman.
EIN: 134093676

62199
Friends of Jong Bonaire Foundation
c/o Sexter & Warmflash
115 Broadway, 15th Fl.
New York, NY 10006

Established in 1999 in DE.
Donor(s): Michael Wilson.
Financial data (yr. ended 11/30/01): Assets, $463,896 (M); grants paid, $0; gifts received, $26,071; expenditures, $13,848; qualifying distributions, $0.
Directors: Michael Gorman, Alan Gross, Jane Townsend, David Warmflash.
EIN: 134090990

62200
The Alvin Friedman-Kien Foundation, Inc.
1 Lexington Ave., Ste. 2A
New York, NY 10010

Established in 1997 in NY.
Donor(s): Alvin Friedman-Kien.
Financial data (yr. ended 12/31/00): Assets, $462,162 (M); grants paid, $26,300; gifts received, $149,362; expenditures, $26,641; qualifying distributions, $26,300.
Limitations: Applications not accepted.

Application information: Contributes only to pre-selected organizations.
Officers: Alvin E. Friedman-Kien, Pres.; Robert H. Horowitz, Secy.
Director: Theodora Edelman.
EIN: 133929462

62201
Esmond Nissim Foundation, Inc.
c/o Bosworth, Gray & Fuller
116 Kraft Ave.
Bronxville, NY 10708-4185
Contact: J. Rockhill Gray, Secy.

Established in 2000.
Financial data (yr. ended 12/31/00): Assets, $461,675 (M); grants paid, $50,000; gifts received, $463,549; expenditures, $62,909; qualifying distributions, $50,000.
Limitations: Giving primarily in New York, NY.
Officers: J. Rockhill Gray, Secy.; Krystyna B. Forst, Treas.
EIN: 134086914

62202
Roy M. and Francis K. Anderson Fund, Inc.
P.O. Box 151
22 Mill St.
Rhinebeck, NY 12572

Established in 1997.
Financial data (yr. ended 12/31/00): Assets, $457,121 (M); grants paid, $40,000; expenditures, $55,684; qualifying distributions, $39,875.
Limitations: Applications not accepted. Giving primarily in NY.
Application information: Contributes only to pre-selected organizations.
Officers and Director:* Robert J. Marvin,* Chair.; Adeline P. Malone, Secy.-Treas.
EIN: 141801851

62203
The Jerome and Sondra Bloomberg Family Foundation, Inc.
16 Bramble Ln.
Melville, NY 11747

Classified as a private operating foundation in 1996 in NY.
Donor(s): Jerome Bloomberg.
Financial data (yr. ended 12/31/01): Assets, $455,295 (M); grants paid, $7,800; gifts received, $38,720; expenditures, $33,622; qualifying distributions, $7,667.
Limitations: Applications not accepted. Giving primarily in NY.
Application information: Contributes only to pre-selected organizations.
Officers and Directors:* Sondra Bloomberg,* Pres.; Michael Bloomberg,* V.P.; Ronald Bloomberg,* V.P.; Jerome Bloomberg,* Secy.; Lee Bloomberg,* Treas.
EIN: 113350909

62204
Kvistad Foundation
167 DuBois Rd.
Shokan, NY 12481
E-mail: fund@chimes.com
Contact: Diane Herrick Kvistad, Pres.

Established in 1988.
Donor(s): Garry Kvistad, Diane Herrick Kvistad, Woodstock Percussion, Inc.
Financial data (yr. ended 12/31/01): Assets, $452,446 (M); grants paid, $57,541; gifts received, $50,000; expenditures, $63,709; qualifying distributions, $63,709.
Limitations: Giving primarily in Ulster County, NY.

Application information: Application form not required.
Officers: Diane Herrick Kvistad, Pres.; Garry Kvistad, Secy.
EIN: 141702791

62205
Ballard Park Foundation, Ltd.
P.O. Box 381
Westport, NY 12993

Established in 1990 in NY.
Donor(s): Anne B. Cerf.
Financial data (yr. ended 12/31/00): Assets, $452,318 (M); grants paid, $0; gifts received, $43,348; expenditures, $17,121; qualifying distributions, $46,340; giving activities include $16,316 for programs.
Officers and Directors:* Elizabeth D. Jones,* Chair.; Tony Ware,* V.P.; Carol Buchanan,* Secy.; William Johnston,* Treas.; Russell Ames, Donna Beal, Don Thompson.
EIN: 222999434

62206
Foundation for Film Preservation
c/o Starr & Co.
350 Park Ave.
New York, NY 10022

Established in 1997.
Donor(s): Keith Barish, Nicolas Cage.
Financial data (yr. ended 12/31/99): Assets, $444,659 (M); grants paid, $5,000; gifts received, $101,250; expenditures, $6,841; qualifying distributions, $126,430; giving activities include $121,400 for programs.
Limitations: Applications not accepted.
Application information: Contributes only to pre-selected organizations.
Directors: Martin Scorsese, Kenneth I. Starr.
EIN: 133968595

62207
Nurses House, Inc.
2113 Western Ave., Ste. 2
Guilderland, NY 12084-9501 (518) 456-7858
Contact: Catheryne Welch

Established in 1925 in NY.
Donor(s): Willie May Bradley,‡ Samuel and May Rudin Foundation, New York State Nurses Assn., Springhouse Corp., AON Foundation.
Financial data (yr. ended 12/31/01): Assets, $429,522 (M); grants paid, $157,432; gifts received, $127,389; expenditures, $361,299; qualifying distributions, $339,108.
Limitations: Giving only to registered nurses licensed in the U.S., including its possessions.
Publications: Newsletter, informational brochure, application guidelines.
Application information: Applicant must be a registered nurse, licensed in at least one state. Application form required.
Officers: Gail Kuhn Weissman, Pres.; Carolee Fauth-Brooks, 1st V.P.; Karen A. Ballard, 2nd V.P.; Dorothy H. Rohrmiller, Secy.; Claire F. Murray, Treas.
Directors: Miriam Aaron, Sylvia M. Barker, William R. Donovan, and 9 additional directors.
EIN: 131927913
Codes: FD2, GTI

62208
George McNeil Charitable Trust
195 Waverly Ave.
Brooklyn, NY 11205

Financial data (yr. ended 05/31/01): Assets, $428,441 (M); grants paid, $9,045; expenditures, $14,659; qualifying distributions, $14,659.
Limitations: Giving primarily in NY.
Officer: Helen McNeil, Pres.
Trustee: James McNeil.
EIN: 137063382

62209
The Grace McLean Abbate Foundation, Inc.
c/o Martin Bregman
641 Lexington Ave., Ste. 1400
New York, NY 10022-4503 (212) 421-6161
Contact: Martin Bregman, Pres.

Classified as a private operating foundation in 1983.
Donor(s): Grace McLean Abbate.‡
Financial data (yr. ended 08/31/01): Assets, $426,757 (M); grants paid, $30,130; expenditures, $36,437; qualifying distributions, $35,963.
Limitations: Giving primarily in NY.
Officers and Director:* Martin Bregman, Chair. and Pres.; Cornelia S. Bregman,* Secy.
EIN: 133136587

62210
R. Futures Charitable Foundation, Ltd.
1324 Lake Shore Dr.
Massapequa Park, NY 11762

Established in 1999.
Donor(s): Rosemary Mittelmark.
Financial data (yr. ended 12/31/00): Assets, $425,590 (M); grants paid, $12,355; expenditures, $24,610; qualifying distributions, $12,355.
Limitations: Applications not accepted.
Application information: Contributes only to pre-selected organizations.
Officer: Rosemary Mittelmark.
Directors: Sherri Hughes, Howard Mittelmark.
EIN: 134083486

62211
Center for Integrative Studies, Inc.
526 W. 113th St., Ste. 61
New York, NY 10025

Established in 1998 in NY.
Financial data (yr. ended 12/31/99): Assets, $424,580 (M); grants paid, $8,750; expenditures, $15,534; qualifying distributions, $15,477.
Officer: David Mellins, Pres.
EIN: 582396644

62212
Diebold Institute for Public Policy Studies, Inc.
P.O. Box 515
Bedford Hills, NY 10507-0515

Classified as a private operating foundation in 1975.
Donor(s): Thomas R. DiBenedetto, John B. Diebold.
Financial data (yr. ended 12/31/99): Assets, $418,725 (M); grants paid, $125; gifts received, $300,000; expenditures, $225,296; qualifying distributions, $217,810.
Officer and Director:* John Diebold,* Mgr.
EIN: 237218998

62213
William G. Hieber and Jean F. Hieber Charitable Foundation
314 Cambridge Ave.
Garden City, NY 11530-5419

Established in 1997 in NY.
Donor(s): William G. Hieber, Jean Hieber.
Financial data (yr. ended 12/31/01): Assets, $418,116 (M); grants paid, $14,200; gifts received, $26,620; expenditures, $15,107; qualifying distributions, $13,591.
Limitations: Applications not accepted. Giving primarily in NH.
Application information: Contributes only to pre-selected organizations.
Trustees: Christina Hieber, Jean Hieber, Jennifer Hieber.
EIN: 113358337

62214
George Bird Grinnell American Indian Children's Education Fund
(Formerly George Bird Grinnell American Indian Children's Education Foundation)
c/o Kirshon, Shron & Chernick
311 Mills St.
Poughkeepsie, NY 12601
Application address: 11602 Montegue Ct., Potomac, MD 20854
Contact: Paula Mintzies, Pres.

Established in 1988 in NY.
Donor(s): Schuyler M. Meyer, Jr.‡
Financial data (yr. ended 12/31/99): Assets, $412,337 (M); grants paid, $15,775; gifts received, $11,276; expenditures, $36,684; qualifying distributions, $15,775.
Limitations: Giving primarily in Sioux City, IA.
Officers and Directors:* Paula Mintzies,* Pres.; Scott Meyer,* V.P.; Eileen Charbonneau, Secy.; Joseph Bruchac, Patricia Tridell Gordon.
EIN: 141713061

62215
Morris Memorial
17 Park Row
Chatham, NY 12037-1209

Classified as a private operating foundation in 1970.
Donor(s): Morris Trust.
Financial data (yr. ended 09/30/99): Assets, $409,791 (M); grants paid, $0; gifts received, $125,803; expenditures, $62,997; qualifying distributions, $29,879; giving activities include $29,879 for programs.
Officers: Marcus Scott Wood, Jr., Pres. and Treas.; Dean West, Secy.
EIN: 146028969

62216
The Mincolla Foundation
110 Home Ave.
Binghamton, NY 13903-2469

Established as a private operating foundation in 1999.
Donor(s): Anthony V. Mincolla.‡
Financial data (yr. ended 12/31/99): Assets, $405,960 (M); grants paid, $20,000; expenditures, $29,759; qualifying distributions, $20,000.
Limitations: Applications not accepted. Giving primarily in NY.
Application information: Contributes only to pre-selected organizations.
Trustees: Anthony V. Mincolla III, Catherine E. Wolfe.
EIN: 166476836

62217
Kent-Delord House Corporation
17 Cumberland Ave.
Plattsburgh, NY 12901

Financial data (yr. ended 06/30/00): Assets, $402,826 (M); grants paid, $0; gifts received, $18,817; expenditures, $72,732; qualifying distributions, $58,070; giving activities include $58,070 for programs.
Officers and Trustees:* Judy Heaton,* Pres.; Greg Ledges,* V.P.; Marlene Waite,* Secy.; Lisa Roberts,* Treas.; Christopher Booth, Gary Hackett, Evelyn Heins, Zaidee Laughlin, Martha Lockwood, Eileen Egan Mack, Philip Mason, Michael McCormick, Robert Newton, John Tanner.
EIN: 141368176

62218
Art 21, Inc.
c/o Mac Corkindale
137 Broadway, Ste. H
Amityville, NY 11701

Established in 1996 in NY.
Financial data (yr. ended 09/30/00): Assets, $402,726 (M); grants paid, $0; gifts received, $1,044,864; expenditures, $829,873; qualifying distributions, $0; giving activities include $695,924 for programs.
Trustees: Beryl Korot, Richard Lisle.
EIN: 133920288

62219
Mark D. Spitzer Family Foundation, Inc.
791 Park Ave., Apt. 8B
New York, NY 10021

Established in 1997 in DE.
Donor(s): Mark Spitzer.
Financial data (yr. ended 11/30/01): Assets, $397,068 (M); grants paid, $32,500; gifts received, $305; expenditures, $32,588; qualifying distributions, $32,588.
Limitations: Applications not accepted. Giving primarily in New York, NY, and Philadelphia, PA.
Application information: Contributes only to pre-selected organizations.
Officer and Director:* Mark Spitzer,* Pres.
EIN: 133980907

62220
David and Gisela King Foundation
500 Old Country Rd., Ste. 304
Garden City, NY 11530

Established in 1998 in NY.
Donor(s): David V. King.
Financial data (yr. ended 12/31/01): Assets, $391,138 (M); grants paid, $0; gifts received, $2,500; expenditures, $62,138; qualifying distributions, $23,125; giving activities include $25,647 for programs.
Directors: Bradley King, David V. King, Gisela King.
EIN: 113410706

62221
Bronx Medical Research Foundation, Inc.
(Formerly Nassau County Cardiovascular Institute Research Foundation, Inc.)
c/o Edward J. Brown, M.D., Cardiology Div., NCMC
1650 Grand Concourse
Bronx, NY 10457-7606

Established in 1992 in NY.
Financial data (yr. ended 12/31/01): Assets, $388,978 (M); grants paid, $0; gifts received, $800; expenditures, $78,256; qualifying distributions, $75,686; giving activities include $75,686 for programs.
Officers: Edward J. Brown, M.D., Pres.; Theodore Henstenberg, V.P.; Raj Patcha, Secy.
EIN: 113125823

62222
Pollack Art Foundation, Inc.
c/o L. Wollin
350 5th Ave., Ste. 2822
New York, NY 10118

Established in 2000 in DE.
Financial data (yr. ended 06/30/01): Assets, $382,420 (M); grants paid, $0; gifts received, $234,500; expenditures, $7,330; qualifying distributions, $22,500.
Limitations: Applications not accepted.
Application information: Contributes only to pre-selected organizations.
Officers: Alexander Pollack, Pres. and V.P.; Lonnie Wollin, Secy.
EIN: 134136043

62223
John, Mary & Bernard A. Jacobs Foundation, Inc.
c/o Robert S. Warshaw
51 E. 42nd St., Ste. 1601
New York, NY 10017-5404

Financial data (yr. ended 07/31/00): Assets, $379,298 (M); grants paid, $33,437; expenditures, $36,189; qualifying distributions, $31,396.
Limitations: Applications not accepted. Giving primarily in NY.
Application information: Contributes only to pre-selected organizations.
Trustees: Milton Chernack, Robert S. Warshaw.
EIN: 136104583

62224
Yeshiva Etz Chaim Foundation, Inc.
4702 15th Ave., Ste. A-5
Brooklyn, NY 11219-2747

Donor(s): Harold E. Hirsch.
Financial data (yr. ended 02/28/01): Assets, $374,853 (M); grants paid, $28,000; gifts received, $34,520; expenditures, $54,198; qualifying distributions, $53,198.
Limitations: Giving primarily in NY and Israel.
Officers: Hon. Jerome Hornblass, Pres.; Norman Weisman, V.P.; Joseph Horowitz, Secy.; Mark Diskind, Treas.
Trustees: Marvin Bienenfeld, Stanley Bienenfeld, Martin Braun, Peppi Feller, and 12 additional trustees.
EIN: 112621784

62225
Alexander J. Willows Greenburger Memorial Fields, Inc.
c/o Time Equities, Inc.
55 5th Ave.
New York, NY 10003

Established in 1992 in NY.
Donor(s): Francis Greenburger, Judith Willows.
Financial data (yr. ended 12/31/99): Assets, $372,285 (M); grants paid, $1,000; expenditures, $1,627; qualifying distributions, $1,627.
Limitations: Applications not accepted.
Application information: Contributes only to pre-selected organizations.
Directors: Keith Flint, Francis Greenburger, Thomas Hopkins.
EIN: 133641609

62226
American Friends of Bilderberg, Inc.
c/o Marie-Josee Kravis
625 Park Ave.
New York, NY 10021-5693

Donor(s): David Rockefeller, United Steel Workers.
Financial data (yr. ended 12/31/00): Assets, $370,829 (M); grants paid, $0; gifts received, $360,221; expenditures, $145,319; qualifying distributions, $145,175; giving activities include $139,941 for programs.
Officers and Directors:* Paul A. Allaire,* Pres.; J. Michael Farren,* Secy.; Marie-Josee Kravis,* Treas.; Henry A. Kissinger, David Rockefeller.
EIN: 510163715

62227
Dratwa Charitable Trust
c/o M&T Bank
101 S. Salina St., 3rd Fl.
Syracuse, NY 13202

Established in 1994 in NY.
Financial data (yr. ended 07/31/01): Assets, $369,633 (M); grants paid, $7,605; expenditures, $12,445; qualifying distributions, $7,605.
Limitations: Applications not accepted. Giving primarily in NY.
Application information: Contributes only to pre-selected organizations.
Trustee: M&T Bank.
EIN: 146174971

62228
Steven Gerencser Scholarship Calasanctius Fund
405 International Dr.
Williamsville, NY 14221-5725

Established in 1995 in NY.
Donor(s): Peter William Forgach.
Financial data (yr. ended 12/31/99): Assets, $364,228 (M); grants paid, $22,892; gifts received, $55,150; expenditures, $38,892; qualifying distributions, $38,892.
Limitations: Applications not accepted.
Application information: Contributes only to pre-selected organizations.
Trustees: Peter William Forgach, Steven Mustos, Katalin A. Spangler.
EIN: 161488251

62229
K. B. Weissman Foundation, Inc.
c/o Weissman Mgmt.
225 Westchester Ave.
Port Chester, NY 10573 (914) 937-6672

Donor(s): K.B. Weissman.
Financial data (yr. ended 10/31/01): Assets, $363,934 (M); grants paid, $278,895; expenditures, $327,189; qualifying distributions, $278,895.
Limitations: Applications not accepted. Giving primarily in the greater New York, NY, area.
Application information: Contributes only to pre-selected organizations.
Trustee: Allan B. Weissman.
EIN: 136161027
Codes: FD

62230
The Charles O. and Elsie Haynes Trust
5375 State Highway 7, Ste. 4
Oneonta, NY 13820-2065 (607) 432-7099
Contact: Thomas J. Trelease, Mgr.

Established in 1983 in NY.
Donor(s): Charles O. Haynes, Elsie B. Haynes.
Financial data (yr. ended 12/31/01): Assets, $361,096 (M); grants paid, $15,000; expenditures, $16,991; qualifying distributions, $16,712.
Limitations: Giving limited to residents of the Charlotte Valley Central School District, Davenport, NY.
Application information: Application form required.
Officer: Thomas J. Trelease, Mgr.
Trustees: Ben Beams, Mary Briggs, Howard Nichols, John Smith.
EIN: 222429332
Codes: GTI

62231
The Hart Charitable Trust
c/o Gurnee Hart
133 E. 64th St.
New York, NY 10021

Established in 1998 in NY.
Donor(s): Gurnee F. Hart.
Financial data (yr. ended 12/31/01): Assets, $360,174 (M); grants paid, $50,000; gifts received, $25,941; expenditures, $50,741; qualifying distributions, $50,000.
Limitations: Applications not accepted. Giving primarily in CA and NY.
Application information: Contributes only to pre-selected organizations.
Trustees: Gurnee F. Hart, Marjorie Hart.
EIN: 137129721

62232
Joel Braverman Foundation, Inc.
1609 Ave. J
Brooklyn, NY 11230-3711
Contact: Joel B. Wolowelsky, M.D., Admin.

Classified as a private operating foundation 1998.
Financial data (yr. ended 07/31/01): Assets, $359,640 (M); grants paid, $11,347; expenditures, $12,934; qualifying distributions, $12,934.
Limitations: Giving limited to graduates of Yeshiva Flatbush in Brooklyn, NY.
Officers and Directors:* Irving Allerhand,* Pres.; Joel B. Wolowelsky, M.D.,* Admin.; Aviva Benamy, Alan Bodner, David Eliach, William Goldberg, Fred Goldschmidt, Martin M. Segal.
EIN: 116036594
Codes: GTI

62233
The Barry G. Blenis Foundation
80 Willowbrook Rd.
Surprise, NY 12176 (518) 966-5378
Contact: Barry G. Blenis, Dir.

Established in 1999 in NY.
Donor(s): Barry G. Blenis, Margaret J. Welsh.
Financial data (yr. ended 12/31/00): Assets, $358,421 (M); grants paid, $321,756; gifts received, $235,437; expenditures, $323,995; qualifying distributions, $318,822.
Directors: Barry G. Blenis, Bonnie J. Blenis, Karen M. Jones, Margaret J. Welsh.
EIN: 912015376
Codes: FD

62234
Edmund & Marianne Bergler Psychiatric Foundation
212 E. 88th St., 1A
New York, NY 10128-3316 (212) 410-3933
Contact: Melvyn L. Iscove, M.D., Tr.

Established in 1965 in NY.
Donor(s): Marianne Bergler,‡ David Saunders.
Financial data (yr. ended 05/31/99): Assets, $356,356 (M); grants paid, $0; gifts received, $4,520; expenditures, $28,324; qualifying distributions, $0; giving activities include $9,522 for programs.
Limitations: Giving on a national basis.
Publications: Annual report.
Trustees: Benjamin Wintrob, M.D., Chair.; Jeannette Hirsch, Melvyn L. Iscove, M.D., Barry Kogan, Ph.D., Nancy Schmidt.
EIN: 136185875

62235
Marcella Sembrich Memorial Association, Inc.
c/o A.B. Richards
P.O. Box 417
Bolton Landing, NY 12814-0417

Classified as a private operating foundation in 1971.
Donor(s): John Davis Skilton, Jr., Ernest Hillman, Jr., Byron Lapham, Mrs. Byron Lapham, Anita Behr Richards.
Financial data (yr. ended 12/31/00): Assets, $353,010 (M); grants paid, $0; gifts received, $62,316; expenditures, $47,811; qualifying distributions, $47,811; giving activities include $47,811 for programs.
Officers: Hugh Wilson, Pres.; Alexander Torok, V.P; A.R. Van Doren, Jr., Secy.; Charles O. Richards, Treas.
Directors: Erin Budis, Ernest Hillman, Jr., Patricia Smith Phillips.
EIN: 141468258

62236
The Art Bridge Association, Inc.
22 Watts St., 6th Fl.
New York, NY 10013

Financial data (yr. ended 12/31/99): Assets, $351,210 (M); grants paid, $26,516; gifts received, $360,364; expenditures, $82,780; qualifying distributions, $51,838.
Officers: Amy Baker, Pres.; David Pitkoff, Treas.
EIN: 133929084

62237
Robert Craft Music Foundation, Inc.
c/o Accounting Mgmt. Co.
505 Park Ave., 20th Fl.
New York, NY 10022-1106

Donor(s): Robert Craft.
Financial data (yr. ended 12/31/01): Assets, $350,034 (M); grants paid, $0; gifts received, $535,770; expenditures, $665,066; qualifying distributions, $646,849; giving activities include $665,066 for programs.
Officer: Robert Craft, Pres.
EIN: 133591637

62238
The Obstetric Anesthesia Research Fund, Inc.
622 W. 168th St.
New York, NY 10032
Contact: Mieczyslaw Finster, M.D., Pres.

Classified as a private operating foundation in 1974.
Donor(s): Pennwalt Co., Seasle Pharmaceuticals.
Financial data (yr. ended 05/31/00): Assets, $346,584 (M); grants paid, $12,000; expenditures, $18,827; qualifying distributions, $17,585.
Officers: Mieczyslaw Finster, M.D., Pres. and Treas.; James M. Perel, V.P. and Secy.
EIN: 237225188

62239
American Wildlife Research Foundation, Inc.
c/o Robert A. Boice
17164 Archer Rd.
Watertown, NY 13601
Application address: 5698 State Rte. 23, Cincinnatus, NY 13040, tel.: (607) 363-4195
Contact: John Hasenjager, Dir.

Established in 1970 in NY.
Financial data (yr. ended 12/31/00): Assets, $344,955 (M); grants paid, $18,728; gifts received, $2,780; expenditures, $32,358; qualifying distributions, $32,358.
Limitations: Giving on a national basis.
Application information: Application form required.
Officers: Stuart L. Free, Pres.; Robert E. Chambers, V.P.; William Schwerd, Secy.; Robert A. Boice, Treas.
Directors: Maurice M. Alexander, Roger Harris Cole, Bradley L. Griffin, John Hasenjager, Peter Roemer, C. William Severinghaus, Scott D. Shupe.
EIN: 166034437

62240
Samuel & Lydia Clark Foundation, Inc.
218 Webster Ave.
Syracuse, NY 13205

Established in 2000 in NY.
Financial data (yr. ended 12/31/00): Assets, $343,686 (M); grants paid, $0; gifts received, $59,750; expenditures, $52,383; qualifying distributions, $0.
Officers: Kenneth Clark, Pres.; Archie Barkins, Sr., V.P.; Eva B. Cage, Secy.; Stanley Clark, Treas.
Directors: Lee Barkins, Marva Jackson.
EIN: 161506096

62241
Charities Foundation of Amsterdam, Inc.
34 Division St.
Amsterdam, NY 12010

Financial data (yr. ended 12/31/00): Assets, $342,581 (L); grants paid, $1,880; gifts received, $2,066; expenditures, $43,252; qualifying distributions, $1,880.
Limitations: Giving primarily in NY.
Application information: Application form not required.
Officers: David Saltsman, Pres.; Vincent Bialabok, V.P.; Richard Whitford, Secy.; Jean Clough, Treas.
EIN: 141618555

62242
Art Resources Transfer, Inc.
(Formerly The William Bartman Foundation)
210 11th Ave., No. 403
New York, NY 10001 (212) 741-1356
Contact: William S. Bartman, V.P.

Established in 1987 in CA.
Donor(s): William S. Bartman, Jon and Mary Shirley Foundation, Lannan Foundation.
Financial data (yr. ended 12/31/00): Assets, $330,582 (L); grants paid, $0; gifts received, $251,951; expenditures, $326,017; qualifying distributions, $213,779; giving activities include $218,184 for programs.
Officers and Directors:* Yael Meridan Schori,* Pres.; William S. Bartman,* V.P. and Exec. Dir.; Roy Eddey, Patricia Faure, Edward Kwalwasser, Teri R. Meyers, Tina Sommerlin, James Wagner, Merrill Wagner.
EIN: 954124438

62243
Ani and Narod Memorial Fund, Inc.
300 Park Ave., 17th Fl.
New York, NY 10022

Donor(s): Raffy Ardhaldjian.
Financial data (yr. ended 12/31/00): Assets, $324,499 (M); grants paid, $0; gifts received, $229,093; expenditures, $247,916; qualifying distributions, $216,631; giving activities include $152,118 for programs.
Limitations: Applications not accepted.
Application information: Contributes only to pre-selected organizations.
Officers: Raffy Ardhaldjian, Pres.; Arpy Coherian, Secy.; Roupen Ardhaldjian, Treas.
Director: Ivan Ardhaldjian.
EIN: 133790621

62244
The Adele Marcus Foundation, Inc.
c/o Leonard B. Pack
1500 Broadway, 21st Fl.
New York, NY 10036
Application address: c/o Ernest D. Loewenwarter & Co., 10 E. 40th St., Ste. 2105, New York, NY 10016, tel.: (212) 532-2777
Contact: Elizabeth Ross, Secy.

Established in 1996 in NY.
Donor(s): Adele Marcus.‡
Financial data (yr. ended 10/31/99): Assets, $316,355 (M); grants paid, $15,000; expenditures, $20,000; qualifying distributions, $20,000; giving activities include $20,000 for programs.
Officers: Lawrence Ross, Pres. and Treas.; Elizabeth Ross, Secy.
EIN: 841426290

62245
Penfield Foundation, Inc.
P.O. Box 121
Crown Point, NY 12928

Financial data (yr. ended 04/30/00): Assets, $315,729 (L); grants paid, $0; gifts received, $6,800; expenditures, $43,317; qualifying distributions, $37,957; giving activities include $37,958 for programs.
Officers: Joan Hunsdon, Pres.; Ronald Labounty, V.P.; Charles Porter, 2nd V.P.; David Hall, Secy.; Kama Ingleston, Treas.
EIN: 146048702

62246
Together Foundation
(also known as Together Foundation for Global Unity)
113 E. 64th St.
New York, NY 10021

Established in 1989 in CO, NY and DE.
Donor(s): Ella Cisneros.
Financial data (yr. ended 12/31/00): Assets, $315,408 (M); grants paid, $1,869; gifts received, $196,363; expenditures, $255,746; qualifying distributions, $255,575; giving activities include $47,500 for programs.
Limitations: Applications not accepted.
Application information: Contributes only to pre-selected organizations.
Officers and Directors:* Ella Cisneros,* Pres.; Claudia Cisneros Macaya, V.P.; Marshall Bernstein, Secy.; Mariella Cisneros, Secy.; Martha Vargas, Exec. Dir.; Oswaldo Cisneros, Lynn Forester, Barbara Pyle.
EIN: 223028267

62247
Ned J. Giordano Foundation, Inc.
c/o Donnelly
342 E. Jericho Tpk, Ste. 310
Mineola, NY 11501

Established in 2000 in NY.
Financial data (yr. ended 09/30/01): Assets, $313,416 (M); grants paid, $74,537; gifts received, $512,195; expenditures, $88,617; qualifying distributions, $84,210.
Limitations: Applications not accepted. Giving primarily in NY.
Application information: Contributes only to pre-selected organizations.
Officers: Mariano Giordano, Pres.; Elizabeth Donnelly, V.P.; Linda Giordano, Secy.; Marie Katherine Greco, Treas.
EIN: 113570016

62248
The C. Kurz Foundation, Inc.
4702 15th Ave.
Brooklyn, NY 11219-2747 (718) 871-0032
Contact: Chiel Kurz, Dir.

Established in 1989 in NY.
Donor(s): Chiel Kurz.
Financial data (yr. ended 12/31/01): Assets, $311,280 (M); grants paid, $103,430; gifts received, $290,000; expenditures, $103,915; qualifying distributions, $103,430.
Limitations: Giving primarily in New York, NY.
Directors: Shia Hollander, Chiel Kurz, Samuel Kurz.
EIN: 112910680
Codes: FD2

62249
Lavori Sterling Foundation, Inc.
100 W. 80th St.
New York, NY 10024-6343

Established as a company-sponsored operating foundation in 1999 in NY.
Donor(s): Orleans Realty Co., LLC.
Financial data (yr. ended 12/31/01): Assets, $311,179 (M); grants paid, $16,025; gifts received, $40,229; expenditures, $19,738; qualifying distributions, $16,025.
Limitations: Applications not accepted.
Application information: Contributes only to pre-selected organizations.
Officers: Nora Lavori, President; David Bennett Sterling, V.P. and Treas.; Liana Sterling, Secy.
EIN: 134067505

62250
Mathias Lloyd Spiegel Foundation
c/o Mathias Lloyd Spiegel
521 5th Ave., 22nd Fl.
New York, NY 10175

Established in 1993 in NY.
Donor(s): Ruth L. Blecker.
Financial data (yr. ended 12/31/99): Assets, $310,590 (M); grants paid, $16,800; gifts received, $133,876; expenditures, $16,800; qualifying distributions, $16,800.
Limitations: Applications not accepted. Giving primarily in NY.
Application information: Contributes only to pre-selected organizations.
Trustees: Ruth L. Blecker, Andrew E. Spiegel, Mathias Lloyd Spiegel, Paul A.S. Spiegel.
EIN: 133725802

62251
Dactyl Foundation for the Arts & Humanities, Inc.
c/o Victoria N. Alexander
64 Grand St.
New York, NY 10013 (212) 219-2344

Established in 1998.
Donor(s): Doreen Grayson, Herbert Lee Grayson Foundation.
Financial data (yr. ended 12/31/01): Assets, $308,512 (M); grants paid, $0; gifts received, $121,018; expenditures, $94,024; qualifying distributions, $944,033; giving activities include $29,732 for programs.
Officers: Victoria Alexander, Pres.; Neil Grayson, Secy.-Treas.
EIN: 133915372

62252
The Richard H. & Janice R. Popp Charitable Foundation
131 White Tail Dr.
Ithaca, NY 14850

Financial data (yr. ended 12/31/00): Assets, $308,117 (M); grants paid, $13,727; gifts received, $151,095; expenditures, $16,327; qualifying distributions, $13,727.
Limitations: Giving on a national and international basis, primarily Romania and Ukraine, Russia.
Trustees: Pamela Beckelhymer, Janice R. Popp, Richard L. Popp, Aileen Popp-Miner.
EIN: 166467119

62253
Initial Teaching Alphabet Foundation
32 Thornwood Ln.
Roslyn Heights, NY 11577 (516) 621-6772
Contact: Betty E. Thompson, Exec. Dir.

Incorporated in 1965 in NY.
Donor(s): Eugene Kelly.‡
Financial data (yr. ended 12/31/01): Assets, $307,478 (M); grants paid, $456,162; gifts received, $854,670; expenditures, $836,147; qualifying distributions, $828,092.
Publications: Informational brochure, program policy statement, occasional report, application guidelines.
Application information: Application form required.
Officers and Directors:* Frank G. Jennings,* Pres.; Gerald L. Knieter,* V.P.; Maurice S. Spanbock,* Secy.-Treas.; Betty E. Thompson,* Exec. Dir.; Martha Bogart, Max Bogart.
EIN: 112074243
Codes: FD

62254
Julius D. and Henrietta C. Gwaltney Foundation
c/o Henrietta C. Gwaltney, II
155 W. 70th St., Ste. 3F
New York, NY 10023

Established in 1994 in VA.
Donor(s): Henrietta C. Gwaltney II.
Financial data (yr. ended 12/31/01): Assets, $300,949 (M); grants paid, $10,120; expenditures, $12,653; qualifying distributions, $12,653.
Limitations: Applications not accepted. Giving primarily in New York, NY.
Application information: Contributes only to pre-selected organizations.
Trustees: Christine C. Bearden, Keith G. Christian, Henrietta C. Gwaltney II.
EIN: 546356157

62255
The Mamdani Foundation, Inc.
c/o Zell & Ettinger, C.P.A.'s
3001 Ave. M
Brooklyn, NY 11210
Contact: Jeffrey Zell, Secy.

Established in 1994.
Donor(s): Iqbal Mamdani.
Financial data (yr. ended 12/31/00): Assets, $300,762 (L); grants paid, $15,000; gifts received, $35,000; expenditures, $16,250; qualifying distributions, $14,974.
Officers: Iqbal G. Mamdani, Pres.; Shelby Mamdani, V.P.; Jeffrey Zell, Secy.
EIN: 113209295

62256
National Foundation for Sexual Health Medicine, Inc.
(Formerly National Erectile Dysfunction Foundation)
c/o Fishman & Friedson
488 Madison Ave., 11th Fl.
New York, NY 10022

Established in 1998 in NY.
Financial data (yr. ended 12/31/00): Assets, $293,223 (M); grants paid, $0; gifts received, $2,483,953; expenditures, $2,493,307; qualifying distributions, $2,493,291; giving activities include $643,596 for programs.
Officers: Culley C. Carson, M.D., Pres.; Tom F. June, M.D., V.P.; Drogo K. Montague, M.D., Secy.
EIN: 133970475

62257
Pack Foundation for Medical Research
c/o Howard M. Pack
12 Herkimer Rd.
Scarsdale, NY 10583-7615

Donor(s): Howard M. Pack.
Financial data (yr. ended 11/30/00): Assets, $291,525 (M); grants paid, $21,000; gifts received, $138,250; expenditures, $21,407; qualifying distributions, $18,211.
Limitations: Applications not accepted.
Application information: Contributes only to pre-selected organizations.
Officer and Trustees:* Howard M. Pack,* Admin.; Susan J. Pack, Warren B. Pack.
EIN: 132971722

62258
Global Resource Action Center for the Environment, Inc.
215 Lexington Ave.
New York, NY 10016

Established in 1997 in NY.
Donor(s): Helaine Lerner, Berkshire Hathaway, Heilbrunn Foundation, W. Alton Jones Foundation.
Financial data (yr. ended 12/31/01): Assets, $290,931 (M); grants paid, $0; gifts received, $1,852,584; expenditures, $1,706,820; qualifying distributions, $1,660,070; giving activities include $682,456 for programs.
Limitations: Applications not accepted.
Application information: Contributes only to pre-selected organizations.
Officers: Helaine Lerner, Chair.; Alice Slater, Pres.
EIN: 113332888

62259
Sidney D. Gamble Foundation for China Studies
c/o DDK & Co., LLP
1500 Broadway
New York, NY 10036

Classified as a private operating foundation in 1987.
Donor(s): Catherine G. Curran.
Financial data (yr. ended 12/31/01): Assets, $288,797 (M); grants paid, $0; gifts received, $77,635; expenditures, $74,686; qualifying distributions, $74,221.
Officers and Trustees:* Catherine G. Curran,* Pres.; Peter G. Curran,* V.P.; Theodor Schuchat,* V.P.; Constance McPhee,* Secy.; Robert T. Curran,* Treas.; Louise G. Harper.
EIN: 133392662

62260
The Sidney and Pearl Kalikow Foundation
Kaled Management Corp.
7001 Brush Hollow Rd.
Westbury, NY 11590

Established in 1994.
Donor(s): Pearl B. Kalikow.
Financial data (yr. ended 12/31/00): Assets, $287,705 (M); grants paid, $32,000; expenditures, $37,570; qualifying distributions, $32,000.
Limitations: Applications not accepted. Giving limited to NY, primarily Hempstead and New York.
Application information: Contributes only to pre-selected organizations.
Trustees: James C. Devita, Edward Kalikow, Pearl B. Kalikow, Eugene Shalik.
EIN: 113239969

62261
The Lion and the Lamb Foundation
420 Lake Rd.
Webster, NY 14580

Established in 2000 in NY.
Financial data (yr. ended 12/31/01): Assets, $286,582 (M); grants paid, $30,147; expenditures, $30,857; qualifying distributions, $30,147.
Limitations: Applications not accepted.
Application information: Contributes only to pre-selected organizations.
Officer: Matthew W. Geherin, Treas.
EIN: 161593759

62262
Nicole Capuana Foundation
2300 W. Ridge Rd.
Rochester, NY 14626
Contact: Thomas C. Capuana, Pres.

Established in 1999 in NY.
Financial data (yr. ended 12/31/99): Assets, $285,977 (M); grants paid, $15,556; expenditures, $17,954; qualifying distributions, $15,556.
Officers: Thomas C. Capuana, Pres.; Salvatore Capuana, Secy.
Director: Joseph Capuana.
EIN: 330644122

62263
The Alec and Tamar Ellison Family Foundation
2 Laurel Wood Ct.
Rye, NY 10580

Established in 2000 in NY. Classified as a private operating foundation in 2001.
Donor(s): Alec Ellison.
Financial data (yr. ended 12/31/01): Assets, $282,999 (M); grants paid, $110,000; gifts

received, $450; expenditures, $116,804; qualifying distributions, $110,000.
Limitations: Applications not accepted.
Application information: Contributes only to pre-selected organizations.
Directors: Alec Ellison, Morris Ellison, Tamar Ellison.
EIN: 134148789

62264
Esther Gerber Trust
c/o Eliot Gerber
9 Frog Rock Rd.
Armonk, NY 10504

Financial data (yr. ended 12/31/99): Assets, $281,554 (M); grants paid, $18,880; expenditures, $21,316; qualifying distributions, $18,880.
Limitations: Applications not accepted. Giving primarily in NY.
Application information: Contributes only to pre-selected organizations.
Trustee: Eliot Gerber.
EIN: 237056615

62265
Targoff Family Foundation
1330 Ave. of the Americas, 36th Fl.
New York, NY 10016
Contact: Michael Targoff, Pres.

Established in 1996 in NY.
Donor(s): Michael Targoff.
Financial data (yr. ended 12/31/00): Assets, $281,244 (M); grants paid, $10,700; expenditures, $11,541; qualifying distributions, $10,700.
Limitations: Giving on a national basis.
Officers: Michael Targoff, Pres.; Jason Targoff, V.P.; Joshua Targoff, V.P.; Ramie Targoff, V.P.
EIN: 133889895

62266
The Joseph N. Muschel Memorial Foundation, Inc.
7 Boxwood Ln.
Monsey, NY 10952

Classified as a private operating foundation in 1996 in NY.
Donor(s): Adolph Schreiber Hebrew Academy of Rockland.
Financial data (yr. ended 12/31/01): Assets, $276,391 (M); grants paid, $17,255; gifts received, $35,266; expenditures, $42,054; qualifying distributions, $41,804; giving activities include $12,000 for programs.
Limitations: Applications not accepted. Giving primarily in New York, NY, and Jerusalem, Israel.
Application information: Contributes only to pre-selected organizations.
Officers: Nachum Muschel, Pres.; Moshe David Muschel, V.P.; Sara Muschel, Secy.; Meyer Muschel, Treas.
EIN: 133866003

62267
Wind in the Willows, Inc.
182 Grand St.
Newburgh, NY 12550

Established in 1998 in NY.
Donor(s): Calais Gugugumi.
Financial data (yr. ended 12/31/00): Assets, $275,022 (M); grants paid, $0; gifts received, $600; expenditures, $121,792; qualifying distributions, $98,068; giving activities include $121,792 for programs.
Officer: Calais Gugugumi, Pres. and Exec. Dir.
Directors: William Burton, Lilian Ericksen.
EIN: 222994251

62268
Vergel Foundation
c/o John Koegel
161 Ave. of the Americas
New York, NY 10013

Established in 1998 in NY.
Donor(s): Robert R. Littman.
Financial data (yr. ended 12/31/00): Assets, $274,727 (M); grants paid, $0; gifts received, $150,000; expenditures, $150,638; qualifying distributions, $150,638; giving activities include $150,638 for programs.
Directors: Sully Bonnelly, John B. Koegel, Robert R. Littman.
EIN: 134027930

62269
Adirondack Outreach Services, Inc.
(Formerly St. Mary's Outreach Services, Inc.)
90 South St.
P.O. Box 2174
Glens Falls, NY 12801
Contact: James F. Morrissey, Pres.

Established in 1991 in NY.
Donor(s): James F. Morrissey, Kay H. Morrissey.
Financial data (yr. ended 12/31/00): Assets, $273,361 (M); grants paid, $11,037; gifts received, $3,000; expenditures, $14,487; qualifying distributions, $11,103.
Limitations: Giving limited to Glens Falls, NY.
Application information: Individual recipients are referred through St. Mary's Roman Catholic Church, Glens Falls, NY. Application form not required.
Officers and Directors:* James F. Morrissey,* Pres.; Kay H. Morrissey,* V.P.; David H. Morrissey,* Treas.; Pat Cronin, Thomas C. Curren, Joan Durett, Joanne Grinnell, Gerald Loftus, Brad Williams.
EIN: 141737929

62270
Birthright Israel North America, Inc.
(Formerly Israel Experience, Inc.)
111 8th Ave.
New York, NY 10001

Established in 1997 in NY.
Financial data (yr. ended 12/31/00): Assets, $268,934 (M); grants paid, $0; gifts received, $6,659,916; expenditures, $12,611,033; qualifying distributions, $12,416,370; giving activities include $12,415,389 for programs.
Officers: Michael Papo, Exec. V.P.; Ivy Abrams, V.P., Mktg.; Robert Gurmankin, V.P., Devel.; Steve Noble, V.P., Comm. Rel.; S. Allan Dubow, C.F.O.
Directors: S. Daniel Abraham, Leonard Abramson, Charles R. Bronfman, Edgar M. Bronfman; Richard N. Goldman, Ronald S. Lauder, Bonnie Lipton, Marlene Post, Marc Rich, Arthur J. Samburg, Lynn Schusterman, Michael A. Steinhardt, Lew R. Wasserman, Leslie Wexner, Gary Winnick.
EIN: 133931912

62271
Maoz Tzur Foundation, Inc.
1860 Flatbush Ave.
Brooklyn, NY 11210 (718) 377-8700
Contact: Charles Neiss, Pres.

Donor(s): Charles Neiss, Fay Neiss, Berger Boiler Corp.
Financial data (yr. ended 12/31/00): Assets, $268,604 (M); grants paid, $356,875; gifts received, $326,000; expenditures, $356,984; qualifying distributions, $356,875.
Limitations: Giving on an international and national basis, with emphasis on Israel.
Officers: Charles Neiss, Pres.; Jacob Neiss, V.P.; Michael Kanoff, Secy.
EIN: 113423569
Codes: FD

62272
The Burrows Little Falls Foundation
501 W. Main St.
Little Falls, NY 13365
Contact: Margaret B. Goldman, Tr.

Established in 1990 in NY.
Donor(s): Burrows Paper Corp., Gladys A. Burrows, R.W. Burrows, Jr.
Financial data (yr. ended 12/31/01): Assets, $265,280 (M); grants paid, $87,065; gifts received, $60,000; expenditures, $87,409; qualifying distributions, $87,065.
Limitations: Giving primarily in Little Falls, NY.
Application information: Application form not required.
Trustees: Marcia L. Burrows, R.W. Burrows, Jr., Margaret B. Goldman.
EIN: 223059155
Codes: FD2

62273
Louis and Florence Glasgow Foundation
15 Eaton Ave.
Norwich, NY 13815 (607) 336-7800
Contact: Richard Q. Devine, Tr.

Donor(s): Florence Glasgow.‡
Financial data (yr. ended 12/31/99): Assets, $262,066 (M); grants paid, $5,000; expenditures, $9,188; qualifying distributions, $9,188.
Limitations: Giving primarily in Norwich, NY.
Application information: Application form not required.
Trustees: Richard Q. Devine, Charles W. Shorter.
EIN: 237304986

62274
Yolanda and Salvatore Gigante Charitable Foundation Trust
P.O. Box MM
Philmont, NY 12565

Established in 2000 in NY.
Donor(s): Louis R. Gigante.
Financial data (yr. ended 12/31/00): Assets, $260,915 (M); grants paid, $15,000; gifts received, $275,000; expenditures, $15,000; qualifying distributions, $15,000.
Limitations: Applications not accepted. Giving primarily in Bronx, NY.
Application information: Contributes only to pre-selected organizations.
Trustee: Louis R. Gigante.
EIN: 137218535

62275
Jai & Satya Ahluwalia Foundation
140 Burwell St., Ste. 1
Little Falls, NY 13365

Classified as a private operating foundation in 1994 in NY.
Donor(s): Prabhat K. Ahluwalia.
Financial data (yr. ended 12/31/01): Assets, $257,818 (M); grants paid, $24,875; gifts received, $48,483; expenditures, $24,932; qualifying distributions, $33,050.
Limitations: Applications not accepted. Giving primarily in India.
Application information: Contributes only to pre-selected organizations.
Trustees: Prabhat K. Ahluwalia, Satya Ahluwalia, Nisha Walia.
EIN: 161439548

62276
Hannah M. Adler Testamentary Trust
404 Broadway
Saratoga Springs, NY 12866 (518) 587-7778
Contact: Norman M. Fox, Tr.

Classified as a private operating foundation in 1991.
Financial data (yr. ended 12/31/01): Assets, $256,939 (M); grants paid, $13,749; expenditures, $16,167; qualifying distributions, $16,167.
Application information: Application form not required.
Trustee: Norman M. Fox.
EIN: 146146935

62277
The Robert J. Seifer Cancer Research Foundation
c/o Linda Sage
14 Evergreen Row
Armonk, NY 10504

Established in 2000 in NY.
Donor(s): Muriel Seifer.
Financial data (yr. ended 12/31/00): Assets, $256,249 (M); grants paid, $15,000; gifts received, $265,839; expenditures, $15,085; qualifying distributions, $15,000.
Limitations: Applications not accepted. Giving primarily in CA and New York, NY.
Application information: Contributes only to pre-selected organizations.
Trustees: Donald Sage, Linda Sage.
EIN: 134087582

62278
Living Word Ministries, Inc.
200 Church St., 2nd Fl.
New York, NY 10013

Donor(s): Janet Rosario, Steven Rosario.
Financial data (yr. ended 12/31/99): Assets, $252,068 (M); grants paid, $12,675; gifts received, $80,754; expenditures, $506,206; qualifying distributions, $473,864; giving activities include $336,878 for programs.
Limitations: Applications not accepted. Giving primarily in NJ and NY.
Officers: J. Terry Twerell, Pres.; Lyndell Twerell, Secy.
Trustees: Joseph Lecci, Linda Lecci.
EIN: 112514875

62279
Flushing Lawyers Charitable Trust
217-02 Corbett Rd.
Bayside, NY 11361-2241
Application address: 80-02 Kew Gardens Rd., Ste. 316, Kew Gardens, NY 11415, tel.: (718) 261-1100
Contact: Jonathan Silver, Tr.

Established in 1992 in NY.
Donor(s): William Michel.‡
Financial data (yr. ended 09/30/00): Assets, $250,108 (M); grants paid, $36,730; expenditures, $39,592; qualifying distributions, $38,234.
Trustees: P. O'Donoghue, Jonathan Silver, H. Sokoloff.
EIN: 116330738

62280
Eureka Foundation, Inc.
c/o BCRS Associates, LLC
100 Wall St., 11th Fl.
New York, NY 10005

Established in 2000 in NY.
Donor(s): Avalon Foundation.
Financial data (yr. ended 12/31/00): Assets, $250,000 (M); grants paid, $0; gifts received, $250,000; expenditures, $0; qualifying distributions, $0.
Limitations: Applications not accepted.
Application information: Contributes only to pre-selected organizations.
Officers: Michael D. McCarthy, Pres.; Deborah Berg McCarthy, Secy.; Kathryn Edmundson, Treas.
EIN: 134148244

62281
Music and More, Inc.
c/o Ganer Grossbach
1995 Broadway, 16th Fl.
New York, NY 10023

Established in 1999 in CT.
Financial data (yr. ended 12/31/00): Assets, $247,295 (M); grants paid, $0; gifts received, $145,500; expenditures, $141,844; qualifying distributions, $119,001.
Officer: Israela Margalit, Pres.
EIN: 222809914

62282
The Aaron Twersky Foundation
c/o B. David Schreiber
3 Regent Dr.
Lawrence, NY 11559

Established in 1999.
Donor(s): B. David Schreiber.
Financial data (yr. ended 12/31/99): Assets, $246,958 (M); grants paid, $154,175; gifts received, $387,877; expenditures, $154,295; qualifying distributions, $154,175.
Trustee: B. David Schreiber.
EIN: 116519656
Codes: FD2

62283
The Roy and Sherry DeCarava Foundation
81 Halsey St.
Brooklyn, NY 11216

Established in 1996 in CT.
Donor(s): Roy DeCarava, Sherry DeCarava.
Financial data (yr. ended 09/30/99): Assets, $243,299 (M); grants paid, $0; gifts received, $17,700; expenditures, $33,211; qualifying distributions, $41,251; giving activities include $28,100 for programs.
Limitations: Applications not accepted.
Application information: Contributes only to pre-selected organizations.
Officer and Trustees:* Sherry DeCarava,* C.E.O.; Roy DeCarava, Susan DeCarava.
EIN: 113343213

62284
Letts Memorial Home
7 Hollister St.
Dundee, NY 14837-1146

Financial data (yr. ended 12/31/01): Assets, $241,383 (M); grants paid, $0; gifts received, $4,652; expenditures, $6,991; qualifying distributions, $6,991; giving activities include $6,991 for programs.
Officers: Myra Disbrow, Secy.; Robert Murphy, Treas.
EIN: 166030266

62285
Palmyra Kings Daughters, Inc.
P.O. Box 172
Palmyra, NY 14522-0172
Contact phone numbers: Palmyra and Anita Crowley, (315) 986-7733; Sue Caffyn, (315) 597-5856; Doris Trimm, (315) 597-2624 in Macedon, NY

Classified as a private operating foundation in 1976.
Donor(s): Congdon Trust.
Financial data (yr. ended 05/31/01): Assets, $239,133 (M); grants paid, $28,961; gifts received, $16,347; expenditures, $31,489; qualifying distributions, $31,339.
Limitations: Giving limited to the Macedon and Palmyra, NY, areas.
Officers: Janet Gunkler, Pres.; Diane Wheeler, V.P.; Margaret Eskild, Secy.; Carol Vander Molen, Treas.
EIN: 510235729

62286
The Gunk Foundation
P.O. Box 333
Gardiner, NY 12525 (845) 255-8252
Application address: 94 McKinstry Rd., Gardiner, NY 12525; URL: http://www.gunk.org
Contact: Nadine Lemmon, Dir.

Established in 1994 in DE & NY.
Donor(s): Nadine Lemmon.
Financial data (yr. ended 12/31/99): Assets, $237,273 (M); grants paid, $10,500; gifts received, $8,646; expenditures, $18,867; qualifying distributions, $15,805; giving activities include $5,305 for programs.
Limitations: Giving primarily in CA, MA, NJ, and NY.
Directors: Andreana Lemmon, Nadine Lemmon.
EIN: 141777559

62287
Leon Hoffman Foundation, Inc.
20 Old Mamaroneck Rd., No. 3H
White Plains, NY 10605
Contact: Hugh Hoffman, Secy.

Financial data (yr. ended 10/31/99): Assets, $236,206 (M); grants paid, $7,061; expenditures, $8,323; qualifying distributions, $7,061.
Application information: Application form not required.
Officers: Grace Hoffman, Pres.; Hugh Hoffman, Secy.; Larry Hoffman, Treas.
EIN: 136120106

62288
Gabriel von Wayditch Music Foundation
80-61 Lefferts Blvd.
Kew Gardens, NY 11415-1715

Established in 1971 in NY.
Donor(s): Ivan Wolfram von Wayditch.
Financial data (yr. ended 10/31/00): Assets, $235,439 (M); grants paid, $0; gifts received, $3,228; expenditures, $6,538; qualifying distributions, $6,538; giving activities include $2,539 for programs.
Officers: Walter Ivan von Wayditch, Chair.; William Zakariasen, Pres.; Frank Oteri, V.P.; Anthony Iannacone, V.P.
EIN: 237108615

62289
Joyce Dutka Arts Foundation, Inc.
P.O. Box 630053
Bronx, NY 10463
Contact: Joyce Dutka, Pres.

Established in 1999.
Donor(s): Solomon Dutka.
Financial data (yr. ended 06/30/00): Assets, $229,607 (M); grants paid, $13,600; gifts received, $258,367; expenditures, $39,517; qualifying distributions, $33,200; giving activities include $33,200 for programs.
Officers: Joyce Dutka, Pres.; Marjorie Oberlander, V.P.; Harryette Helsel, Treas.
Directors: Iby George-Gearey, Rhoda A. Klein, Lenore Segan.
EIN: 061551999

62290
The Troy Savings Bank Music Hall Foundation, Inc.
c/o The Troy Savings Bank
32 2nd St.
Troy, NY 12180

Established in 1998 in NY. Classified as a company-sponsored operating foundation in 2001.
Donor(s): The Troy Savings Bank.
Financial data (yr. ended 12/31/01): Assets, $229,121 (M); grants paid, $0; gifts received, $122,627; expenditures, $107,442; qualifying distributions, $0.
Officers and Directors:* Daniel J. Hogarty, Jr.,* Pres.; Kevin M. O'Bryan,* Secy.; David Deluca,* Treas.; Richard B. Devane, Edward G. O'Haire.
EIN: 141814183

62291
The Stephen Birnbaum Foundation
c/o Burton M. Fine
317 Madison Ave., Ste. 2310
New York, NY 10017

Established in 1994 in NY.
Donor(s): Alexandra Mayes Birnbaum.
Financial data (yr. ended 01/31/01): Assets, $225,251 (M); grants paid, $66,670; gifts received, $139,000; expenditures, $67,407; qualifying distributions, $67,170.
Limitations: Applications not accepted. Giving primarily in New York, NY.
Application information: Contributes only to pre-selected organizations.
Officers: Alexandra Mayes Birnbaum, Pres.; Burton M. Fine, V.P.
Director: Brenda B. Fine.
EIN: 133753860

62292
Maravilla Foundation, Inc.
c/o Pepper, Gelbord, Roth & Co.
60 E. 42nd St., Ste. 1201
New York, NY 10165-0006

Classified as a private operating foundation in 1990.
Donor(s): Geraldo Rivera.
Financial data (yr. ended 09/30/01): Assets, $223,260 (M); grants paid, $0; gifts received, $35,000; expenditures, $62,161; qualifying distributions, $0.
Officers and Directors:* Geraldo Rivera,* Pres.; Daniel M. Pepper, V.P. and Treas.; JoAnn Torres Conte,* Secy.
EIN: 133569733

62293
The Lowy-Freund Foundation, Inc.
5214 15th Ave.
Brooklyn, NY 11219-3907 (718) 625-4948
Contact: Leopold Lowy, Pres.

Established in 1992 in NY.
Donor(s): Jacques Freund, Leopold Lowy, Morris Lowy.
Financial data (yr. ended 12/31/99): Assets, $221,326 (M); grants paid, $327,574; gifts received, $207,000; expenditures, $327,856; qualifying distributions, $327,785.
Limitations: Giving primarily in NY.
Officers: Leopold Lowy, Pres.; Jacques Freund, Secy.; Morris Lowy, Treas.
EIN: 133693418
Codes: FD

62294
The Baseball Oral History Project Foundation
c/o Yohalem Gillman & Co., LLP
477 Madison Ave.
New York, NY 10022

Established in 2000 in DE and NY.
Donor(s): Herbert A. Allen.
Financial data (yr. ended 12/31/00): Assets, $220,671 (M); grants paid, $30,000; gifts received, $250,000; expenditures, $36,000; qualifying distributions, $36,000.
Limitations: Applications not accepted.
Application information: Contributes only to pre-selected organizations.
Officers and Directors:* Donald Kagan,* Pres.; Stephen D. Greenberg,* Secy.-Treas.; Herbert A. Allen, Eli S. Jacobs, Francis T. Vincent, Jr.
EIN: 134106981

62295
The Robert and Susan Taub Foundation, Inc.
c/o Robert Taub
47 E. 88th St., Apt. 11A
New York, NY 10128-1152

Established in 1997 in NY.
Donor(s): Susan F. Taub.
Financial data (yr. ended 12/31/00): Assets, $219,945 (M); grants paid, $56,033; expenditures, $56,283; qualifying distributions, $55,359; giving activities include $3,593 for programs.
Limitations: Applications not accepted. Giving on a national basis, with emphasis on the greater metropolitan New York, NY, area.
Application information: Contributes only to pre-selected organizations.
Trustee: Robert Taub.
EIN: 133940569

62296
William & Leona Lorberbaum Charitable Foundation
3 E. Deer Park Rd.
Dix Hills, NY 11746 (631) 858-1829
Contact: Michael B. Margolis, Treas.

Established in 1996.
Donor(s): Leona Lorberbaum.
Financial data (yr. ended 12/31/99): Assets, $218,418 (M); grants paid, $13,900; expenditures, $14,813; qualifying distributions, $13,853.
Limitations: Giving primarily in NY.
Officers: Leona Lorberbaum, Pres.; Larry Lorberbaum, V.P.; Michael B. Margolis, Treas.
EIN: 113346508

62297
The Archipenko Foundation, Inc.
Fire 100, Baker Rd.
P.O. Box 247
Bearsville, NY 12409
Contact: Frances Gray, Pres.

Established in 2000 in NY, DE.
Donor(s): Frances A. Gray.
Financial data (yr. ended 12/31/01): Assets, $217,327 (M); grants paid, $0; gifts received, $214,360; expenditures, $69,108; qualifying distributions, $0.
Officers and Directors:* Frances A. Gray,* Pres.; Alexander Gray,* V.P. and Co-Treas.; David Gray,* V.P. and Co-Treas.; Andrew Gray,* V.P.; Anna Gray,* V.P.
EIN: 134123083

62298
Edward and Alice Johnson Foundation, Inc.
1 W. Church St.
Elmira, NY 14901

Established in 1999 in NY.
Financial data (yr. ended 04/30/00): Assets, $215,842 (M); grants paid, $10,000; gifts received, $244,960; expenditures, $11,024; qualifying distributions, $10,000.
Limitations: Giving primarily in NY.
Officers: Alice E. Johnson, Pres.; Carol J. LaPre, V.P. and Secy.; Rosemary J. Beckhorn, V.P. and Treas.
EIN: 161572998

62299
Friends of Rogers Environmental Education Center, Inc.
(Formerly Mid-York Conservation Fund, Inc.)
P.O. Box 932
Sherburne, NY 13460-0932
Application address: 5049 State Hwy. 23, Norwich, NY 13815, tel.: (607) 334-7687
Contact: Byron Harrington, Pres.

Classified as a private operating foundation in 1975.
Financial data (yr. ended 12/31/01): Assets, $211,335 (M); grants paid, $560; gifts received, $47,427; expenditures, $31,976; qualifying distributions, $29,683; giving activities include $38,433 for programs.
Officers and Directors:* Byron Harrington,* Pres.; Dan Nielsen,* V.P.; Susan Connelly,* Secy.; Thruston Packer,* Treas.; and 9 additional directors.
EIN: 161010345

62300
White Barn Theatre Foundation, Inc.
c/o Hecht & Co.
111 W. 40th St., 20th Fl.
New York, NY 10018

Classified as a private operating foundation in 1988.
Donor(s): Louis Schweitzer Charitable Trust, Lucille Lortel Schweitzer.‡
Financial data (yr. ended 06/30/00): Assets, $210,997 (M); grants paid, $0; gifts received, $190,765; expenditures, $273,279; qualifying distributions, $220,915; giving activities include $247,135 for programs.
Officers and Directors:* James J. Ross,* Pres.; George Shaskan, V.P.; Michael M. Ticktin,* Secy.; Michael Hecht,* Treas.; George Forbes, Exec. Dir.; Frank N. Zullo.
EIN: 060742976

62301
Harry & Linda Macklowe Family Foundation
(Formerly Hammarskjold Plaza Sculpture Garden, Inc.)
c/o Manhattan Pacific Mgmt. Co.
142 W. 57th St.
New York, NY 10019

Established in 1973 in NY.
Donor(s): Harry Macklowe.
Financial data (yr. ended 08/31/01): Assets, $210,276 (M); grants paid, $0; expenditures, $130; qualifying distributions, $0.
Trustees: Harry Macklowe, Linda Macklowe.
EIN: 237333431

62302
Jyming Wang Foundation
154-15 29th Ave.
Flushing, NY 11354

Established in 1996 in NY.
Donor(s): Jyming Wang.
Financial data (yr. ended 12/31/99): Assets, $208,526 (M); grants paid, $2,200; gifts received, $30,000; expenditures, $2,230; qualifying distributions, $2,200.
Limitations: Applications not accepted. Giving primarily in NY.
Application information: Contributes only to pre-selected organizations.
Trustee: Jyming Wang.
EIN: 113353383

62303
Canajoharie Community Services, Inc.
66 Montgomery St.
P.O. Box 203
Canajoharie, NY 13317-0203

Classified as a private operating in 1977.
Donor(s): Arhell Hall Foundation, Inc., Beech-Nut Nutrition Corp.
Financial data (yr. ended 02/28/00): Assets, $205,176 (M); grants paid, $0; gifts received, $24,241; expenditures, $21,427; qualifying distributions, $21,427; giving activities include $21,427 for programs.
Officers and Directors:* Eugene Felter,* Pres.; Susan VanDewerker,* V.P.; Nancy Larner,* Secy.; Ferdinand C. Kaiser,* Treas.; Elois F. Cole, Ronald Dievendorf, Joseph Santangelo.
EIN: 222152385

62304
Baryshnikov Dance Foundation, Inc.
c/o Padell Nadell, et al.
156 W. 56th St.
New York, NY 10019

Donor(s): Mikhail Baryshnikov.
Financial data (yr. ended 01/31/00): Assets, $203,147 (M); grants paid, $600; gifts received, $207,500; expenditures, $188,361; qualifying distributions, $139,454.
Trustees: Mikhail Baryshnikov, Charles France, David G. Lubell.
EIN: 133031485

62305
Chappaqua Summer Scholarship Program
P.O. Box 456
Chappaqua, NY 10514

Financial data (yr. ended 12/31/01): Assets, $202,704 (M); grants paid, $0; gifts received, $42,159; expenditures, $50,102; qualifying distributions, $42,406; giving activities include $42,558 for programs.
Officers: Claire Savino, Chair.; Art Steinhauer, Secy.; Ann Johnson Herrero, Treas.

EIN: 133038194

62306
Edward Albee Foundation, Inc.
c/o A. Kozak & Co., LLP
192 Lexington Ave., Ste. 1100
New York, NY 10016

Donor(s): Edward Albee.
Financial data (yr. ended 12/31/00): Assets, $201,726 (M); grants paid, $0; gifts received, $18,828; expenditures, $27,296; qualifying distributions, $24,454.
Limitations: Giving on a national basis.
Application information: Grants are in the form of studio space in artists' colony. Application form required.
Officers: Edward Albee, Pres.; Jonathan Thomas, V.P.; William Katz, Secy.; Joanna Steichen, Treas.
EIN: 136168827
Codes: GTI

62307
James A. Mulvey Foundation, Inc.
c/o Stephen W. Mulvey
311 Rye Beach Ave.
Rye, NY 10580

Financial data (yr. ended 12/31/01): Assets, $199,126 (M); grants paid, $12,000; expenditures, $13,284; qualifying distributions, $13,284.
Limitations: Applications not accepted.
Application information: Contributes only to pre-selected organizations.
Officers: Stephen W. Mulvey, Pres.; Marie M. Anderson, V.P.
EIN: 136213611

62308
F. Rachel Memorial Foundation
4000 Highland Ave.
Brooklyn, NY 11224-1016

Established in 1999 in NY.
Donor(s): Vitaly Pivtorak, Yelena Pavlovsky.
Financial data (yr. ended 06/30/00): Assets, $199,011 (M); grants paid, $16,411; gifts received, $210,000; expenditures, $16,461; qualifying distributions, $16,336.
Limitations: Applications not accepted.
Application information: Contributes only to pre-selected organizations.
Trustees: Yelena Pavlovsky, Vitaly Pivtorak.
EIN: 113498006

62309
Environmental Simulation Center, Ltd.
116 W. 29th St.
New York, NY 10001

Established in 1998 in NY.
Financial data (yr. ended 12/31/01): Assets, $197,263 (M); grants paid, $0; expenditures, $579,654; qualifying distributions, $41,272; giving activities include $579,654 for programs.
Directors: Michael Kwartler, Richard Schaffer.
EIN: 133990144

62310
Anna Sobol Levy Foundation, Inc.
c/o Jerome E. Levy
25 W. 68th St.
New York, NY 10023-5302

Donor(s): Jerome E. Levy.
Financial data (yr. ended 12/31/00): Assets, $196,332 (M); grants paid, $18,000; gifts received, $15,000; expenditures, $18,915; qualifying distributions, $18,832.
Limitations: Applications not accepted.

Application information: Contributes only to pre-selected organizations.
Officers: Jerome E. Levy, Chair.; Howard L. Adelson, Vice-Chair.; Charles Weitz, Treas.
EIN: 133388647

62311
Michael P. Cozzoli Family Foundation, Inc.
c/o Michael P. Cozzoli
Hoffstot Ln.
Sands Point, NY 11050 (516) 944-8887

Established in 1999 in NY.
Donor(s): Michael P. Cozzoli.
Financial data (yr. ended 10/31/01): Assets, $191,990 (M); grants paid, $1,400; gifts received, $56,500; expenditures, $5,411; qualifying distributions, $1,400.
Limitations: Applications not accepted.
Application information: Contributes only to pre-selected organizations.
Managers: John Cozzoli, Lucille Cozzoli, Michael P. Cozzoli.
EIN: 113522592

62312
Melvin Wallshein & Evelyn Wallshein Foundation
614 Hampton Ave.
Brooklyn, NY 11235-3710

Established in 1968.
Financial data (yr. ended 06/30/00): Assets, $191,658 (M); grants paid, $4,450; expenditures, $4,744; qualifying distributions, $3,112.
Officer: Melvin Wallshein, Pres.
Director: Melissa Smith.
EIN: 112169357

62313
The Foundation for Environmentally Safe Polymers, Inc.
c/o Mark Silver
3182 Monterey Dr.
Merrick, NY 11566

Established in 1998 in New Jersey.
Donor(s): Philip Rhodes.
Financial data (yr. ended 12/31/00): Assets, $191,081 (M); grants paid, $10,000; expenditures, $11,875; qualifying distributions, $11,875.
Limitations: Applications not accepted. Giving primarily in NJ.
Application information: Contributes only to pre-selected organizations.
Officer: Philip Rhodes, Pres.
EIN: 223481807

62314
Nuestro Futuro, Inc.
(Formerly Nuestra Futura, Inc.)
P.O. Box 888
Port Washington, NY 11050 (516) 767-5754
Contact: M. Trahan, Exec. Dir.

Established in 1999 in NY.
Financial data (yr. ended 12/31/01): Assets, $190,796 (M); grants paid, $156,706; gifts received, $10,000; expenditures, $352,689; qualifying distributions, $351,318; giving activities include $277,750 for programs.
Limitations: Applications not accepted. Giving limited to Bolivia.
Application information: Contributes only to a pre-selected organization.
Officer and Directors:* Peter Hagedorn,* Pres.; Susan Hagedorn, Miriam Trahan.
EIN: 113522771
Codes: FD2

62315
Laura L. Adams Foundation, Inc
P.O. Box 466
Hamburg, NY 14075
Contact: Harold Summar, Dir.

Established in 2001 in NY.
Donor(s): Laura L. Adams.
Financial data (yr. ended 12/31/01): Assets, $190,000 (M); grants paid, $10,000; gifts received, $200,000; expenditures, $10,000; qualifying distributions, $10,000.
Limitations: Giving primarily in NY.
Directors: Laura L. Adams, Michael Ferrentino, Harold Summar.
EIN: 161608372

62316
Geriatric Pharmacotherapy Institute, Inc.
36 Forest Meadow Trail
Rochester, NY 14624

Established in 1998 in NY.
Donor(s): Terrance Bellnier, Shyam Karki, Eli Lilly Corp., Geriatric Pharmacy Institute Partnership.
Financial data (yr. ended 03/31/01): Assets, $189,533 (M); grants paid, $0; gifts received, $456,405; expenditures, $363,317; qualifying distributions, $358,195; giving activities include $333,660 for programs.
Directors: Terrance Bellnier, Shyam D. Karki.
EIN: 161555015

62317
Charles & Ethel Walker Foundation, Inc.
277 Main St.
Port Washington, NY 11050 (516) 944-7600
Contact: Charles Hyde Walker, Pres.

Established in 1993 in NY.
Donor(s): Charles Walker, Ethel Walker.
Financial data (yr. ended 12/31/00): Assets, $188,007 (M); grants paid, $9,540; expenditures, $12,932; qualifying distributions, $0.
Limitations: Giving primarily in NY.
Officers: Charles Hyde Walker, Pres.; Charles H. Walker, Jr., V.P.; Susan M. DeLuca, Secy.; Charles DeLuca, Treas.
EIN: 113157874

62318
Albion High School Alumni Foundation, Inc.
c/o Albion High School
P.O. Box 345
Albion, NY 14411-0345

Established in 1989 in NY.
Financial data (yr. ended 12/31/01): Assets, $187,730 (M); grants paid, $10,000; gifts received, $6,675; expenditures, $11,638; qualifying distributions, $11,638.
Limitations: Giving limited to residents of Albion, NY.
Application information: Application form required.
Officers: Debra Heuer, Pres.; Ed Fancher, V.P.; Jean Sherwin, Secy.; Christopher Haines, Treas.
EIN: 222925068

62319
Nathan G. Finkelstein Family Foundation, Inc.
111 E. 56th St., Ste. 1005
New York, NY 10022

Established in 1990 in NY.
Donor(s): Lola Finkelstein, Jack Houseman.
Financial data (yr. ended 06/30/99): Assets, $187,545 (M); grants paid, $29,870; gifts received, $12,600; expenditures, $31,323; qualifying distributions, $29,870.
Limitations: Applications not accepted. Giving primarily in NY.
Application information: Contributes only to pre-selected organizations.
Officers and Directors:* Lola Finkelstein,* Pres.; Amy Diamond,* V.P.; David Finkelstein,* V.P.; Barbara Mutterperl,* V.P.; Ellen Meckler,* Secy.
EIN: 133567938

62320
Best Practices in Education, Inc.
18 E. 16th st., 7th Fl.
New York, NY 10003 (212) 206-1082
FAX: (212) 206-1083; E-mail: info@bpeducation.org; URL: http://www.bpeducation.org
Contact: Gail Richardson, Exec. Dir.

Established in 2000 in ME.
Donor(s): W & M Greve Foundation.
Financial data (yr. ended 12/31/00): Assets, $185,222 (M); grants paid, $26,000; gifts received, $392,161; expenditures, $389,601; qualifying distributions, $26,000.
Limitations: Applications not accepted. Giving primarily in Highstown, NJ.
Application information: Contributes only to pre-selected organizations.
Directors: Gail Richardson, Exec. Dir.; Jim Cooper, Edward A. Friedman, Ellen Iseman, John W. Kiser, John W. Rosenblum, Raymond L. Smart.
EIN: 010502114

62321
Samuel & Iolabee Berson Foundation
912 5th Ave.
New York, NY 10021 (212) 288-9292
Contact: Samuel Berson, M.D., Tr.

Established in 1970 in NY.
Donor(s): Iolabee Berson, Samuel Berson, Beatrice Seaver.‡
Financial data (yr. ended 12/31/01): Assets, $182,748 (M); grants paid, $129,051; expenditures, $130,302; qualifying distributions, $129,051.
Limitations: Giving primarily in NY.
Trustees: Iolabee Berson, Samuel Berson, M.D.
EIN: 237010673
Codes: FD2

62322
The Seth Foundation
30 Deer Trail
Oswego, NY 13126
Contact: Neera Seth

Financial data (yr. ended 11/30/01): Assets, $182,482 (M); grants paid, $13,465; expenditures, $14,977; qualifying distributions, $13,465.
Trustee: Ravi Seth.
EIN: 222451147

62323
P & L Charity Foundation
c/o Barnet Liberman
35 Sutton Pl.
Lawrence, NY 11559

Established in 1997.
Financial data (yr. ended 12/31/01): Assets, $180,004 (M); grants paid, $10,000; expenditures, $11,830; qualifying distributions, $11,438.
Limitations: Giving primarily in Brooklyn, NY.
Application information: Unsolicited requests for funds not accepted.
Officers: Barnet Liberman, Pres.; Sharon Mintz, Secy.; Susan Liberman, Treas.
EIN: 113403359

62324
The Foundation for Education Reform and Accountability
(Formerly Empire Foundation for Policy Research, Inc.)
4 Chelsea Park, 2nd Fl.
Clifton Park, NY 12065 (518) 383-2598
FAX: (518) 383-2841; Application address: c/o Gerry Vazquez, 41 Robins Ave., Amityville, NY 11070, tel.: (800) 343-6907
Contact: Brian Backstrom, V.P.

Established in 1991 in DE and NY.
Donor(s): Thomas L. Rhodes.
Financial data (yr. ended 01/31/01): Assets, $179,727 (M); grants paid, $435,943; gifts received, $1,148,000; expenditures, $1,316,863; qualifying distributions, $1,309,339; giving activities include $1,175,886 for programs.
Limitations: Giving primarily in NY.
Application information: Application form requested for ABCS scholarships. Application form required.
Officers: Virginia Gilder, Chair.; Thomas Carroll, Pres.; Brian Backstrom, V.P.
Directors: Peter Flanigan, Richard Gilder, Thomas H. Gosnell, Irving Kristol, Lawrence A. Kudlow, Peggy Noonan, Stephen M. Peck, Frank Richardson, William Stern, Gerardo Vazquez, Leon Weil, Walter B. Wriston.
EIN: 133062423
Codes: FD

62325
Evangelicals Concerned, Inc.
311 E. 72nd St.
New York, NY 10021

Classified as a private operating foundation in 1993 in NY.
Donor(s): Ralph Blair.
Financial data (yr. ended 12/31/01): Assets, $179,175 (M); grants paid, $0; gifts received, $4,771; expenditures, $20,305; qualifying distributions, $1,151.
Limitations: Applications not accepted. Giving limited to New York, NY.
Application information: Contributes only to pre-selected organizations.
Officers and Directors:* Ralph Blair,* Pres.; Terry Cook, Secy.; Dennis Whalen, Treas.; Ron Drummond, David Holkeboer, Steve Schimmele.
EIN: 133693905

62326
Sanford & Dina Rosenblum Foundation
195 S. Manning Blvd.
Albany, NY 12208 (518) 489-1400
Contact: Sanford Rosenblum, Dir.

Established in 1983 in NY.
Donor(s): Sanford Rosenblum.
Financial data (yr. ended 11/30/00): Assets, $177,331 (M); grants paid, $63,994; gifts received, $70,205; expenditures, $68,670; qualifying distributions, $63,994.
Limitations: Giving primarily in NY.
Directors: Dina Rosenblum, Sanford Rosenblum.
EIN: 133225000

62327
The John L. and Corrinne Alpert Foundation
67-71 Yellowstone Blvd.
Forest Hills, NY 11375-2859

Established in 1998 in NY.
Donor(s): Corrinne Alpert.
Financial data (yr. ended 12/31/01): Assets, $176,931 (M); grants paid, $10,000; expenditures, $11,710; qualifying distributions, $9,969.
Limitations: Giving primarily in NY.

Trustees: Corrinne Alpert, Jane Alpert, Evan Weston.
EIN: 113440361

62328
The Neuman Family Foundation
50 Larch Hill Rd.
Lawrence, NY 11559

Donor(s): William Neuman.
Financial data (yr. ended 12/31/00): Assets, $176,616 (M); grants paid, $113,229; gifts received, $125,000; expenditures, $113,444; qualifying distributions, $113,229.
Limitations: Applications not accepted.
Application information: Contributes only to pre-selected organizations.
Trustees: Gladys Neuman, Miriam Neuman, William Neuman, Norman Rabenstein.
EIN: 116472710
Codes: FD2

62329
L Z J Chesed Foundation
c/o Janklowicz
1431 57th St.
Brooklyn, NY 11219
Contact: Leonard Janklowicz, Pres.

Established in 1999 in NY.
Donor(s): Leonard Janklowicz.
Financial data (yr. ended 06/30/01): Assets, $173,862 (M); grants paid, $114,220; gifts received, $105,000; expenditures, $114,306; qualifying distributions, $114,220.
Officer: Leonard Janklowicz, Pres.
Director: Zipora Janklowicz.
EIN: 113513005

62330
Keren Tzemed
486 Crown St.
Brooklyn, NY 11225

Established in 2000.
Donor(s): Herman and Dora Trust, Steinmetz Family Trust.
Financial data (yr. ended 12/31/00): Assets, $172,806 (M); grants paid, $11,311; gifts received, $184,050; expenditures, $11,331; qualifying distributions, $11,311.
Trustee: Dora Steinmetz.
EIN: 113557484

62331
Cayuga Preventorium, Inc.
1420 Taughannock Blvd.
Ithaca, NY 14850-9510

Financial data (yr. ended 09/30/00): Assets, $167,126 (M); grants paid, $0; expenditures, $1,167; qualifying distributions, $21; giving activities include $21 for programs.
Officers: Richard Dolge, Pres.; Peter Walsh, Secy.; Michael Levy, Treas.
EIN: 150592031

62332
Kingston Lions Club Foundation, Inc.
119 Emerson St.
Kingston, NY 12401-4446 (845) 338-7558
Contact: Joseph S. Thurin, Treas.

Established in 1987 in NY.
Financial data (yr. ended 12/31/01): Assets, $166,804 (M); grants paid, $8,600; gifts received, $5,092; expenditures, $8,600; qualifying distributions, $8,600.
Limitations: Giving primarily in Ulster County, NY.
Officers: William Stall, Pres.; Walter Maywell, Secy.; Joseph S. Thurin, Treas.
EIN: 141679330

62333
Parnassusworks Foundation
c/o Richard A. Rifkind
425 E. 58th St.
New York, NY 10022

Established in 2000 in NY.
Donor(s): Richard A. Rifkind, Carole Rifkind.
Financial data (yr. ended 12/31/00): Assets, $165,588 (M); grants paid, $100; gifts received, $170,100; expenditures, $10,420; qualifying distributions, $86,150.
Limitations: Applications not accepted. Giving primarily in New York, NY.
Application information: Contributes only to pre-selected organizations.
Trustees: Carole Rifkind, Richard A. Rifkind.
EIN: 134080444

62334
Hopewell Foundation, Inc.
635 Madison Ave.
New York, NY 10022

Classified as a private operating foundation in 1993. Established around 1981 in NY.
Donor(s): Walter Scheuer.
Financial data (yr. ended 10/31/99): Assets, $165,497 (M); grants paid, $0; expenditures, $149,425; qualifying distributions, $75,289; giving activities include $75,289 for programs.
Officers and Directors:* Walter Scheuer,* Pres. and Treas.; Marjorie P. Scheuer,* V.P.
EIN: 136061323

62335
Frances & Hubert J. Brandt Foundation, Inc.
350 5th Ave., Ste. 3610
New York, NY 10118
Contact: Hubert J. Brandt, Pres.

Established in 2000 in NY.
Donor(s): Hubert J. Brandt.
Financial data (yr. ended 09/30/01): Assets, $165,346 (M); grants paid, $0; gifts received, $215; expenditures, $215; qualifying distributions, $0.
Limitations: Giving primarily in NY.
Officers: Hubert J. Brandt, Pres.; James Ellis Brandt, V.P.; Sherry Iris Brandt-Rauf, V.P.; Karen Brandt Onel, V.P.; Frances Brandt, Secy.-Treas.
EIN: 134091106

62336
The Norman & Constance Sadek Foundation, Inc.
125 Beechwood Ave.
New Rochelle, NY 10801

Established in 1998 in NY.
Donor(s): Norman W. Sadek.
Financial data (yr. ended 12/31/99): Assets, $160,925 (M); grants paid, $42,990; gifts received, $182,217; expenditures, $44,399; qualifying distributions, $44,168; giving activities include $820 for programs.
Limitations: Applications not accepted.
Application information: Contributes only to pre-selected organizations.
Officers: Norman W. Sadek, Chair.; Sanford J Sadek, Pres.; Andrea Schrier, V.P.; Constance Sadek, Secy.-Treas.
EIN: 134022060

62337
Access Project Foundation
P.O. Box 1851
New York, NY 10013

Established in 1999 in NY.
Financial data (yr. ended 12/31/01): Assets, $159,174 (M); grants paid, $0; gifts received, $338,158; expenditures, $513,284; qualifying distributions, $0; giving activities include $513,284 for programs.
Officers: Lisa Maldonado, Pres.; Susan Moscou, V.P.; Heidi Dubois, Secy.; Ewoma Ewoterali, Treas.
EIN: 134079983

62338
Ben & Beatrice Goldstein Foundation, Inc.
c/o Joel Goldstein
245 E. 19th St.
New York, NY 10003

Classified as a private operating foundation in 1972.
Donor(s): Ben Goldstein.
Financial data (yr. ended 10/31/99): Assets, $158,986 (M); grants paid, $0; expenditures, $6,102; qualifying distributions, $0.
Officers: Joel Goldstein, Pres.; Beatrice Goldstein, V.P.; Elinor Goldstein, Secy.-Treas.
EIN: 237022721

62339
The Foundation for the Education of Psychiatric and Public Health Issues, Inc.
c/o Kerner
11 Penn Plz., Ste. 905
New York, NY 10001

Financial data (yr. ended 02/28/99): Assets, $156,236 (M); grants paid, $29,008; gifts received, $50,791; expenditures, $33,145; qualifying distributions, $29,738.
Officers and Directors:* Alan Manevitz,* Pres.; Madeline Balk,* V.P.; Lawrence Manevitz,* Secy.
EIN: 133579846

62340
Thomas Cole Foundation
c/o Spaierman Gallery
45 E. 58th St.
New York, NY 10022

Established in 1982 in NY.
Donor(s): Alexander Acevedo, Richard Manoogian, Richard Manney, Ira Spanierman, Alex & Marie Manoogian Foundation.
Financial data (yr. ended 01/31/01): Assets, $156,220 (M); grants paid, $2,500; expenditures, $5,997; qualifying distributions, $2,500.
Officer and Director:* Ira Spanierman,* Pres.
EIN: 112652204

62341
Rodney M. Propp Foundation, Inc.
405 Park Ave.
New York, NY 10022

Established in NY 1999.
Financial data (yr. ended 12/31/00): Assets, $154,251 (M); grants paid, $3,600; gifts received, $43,730; expenditures, $3,844; qualifying distributions, $3,844.
Limitations: Applications not accepted.
Application information: Contributes only to pre-selected organizations.
Trustee: Rodney M. Propp.
EIN: 134049956

62342
Thomas E. Sullivan and Barbara A. Sullivan Foundation
c/o J.L. Dunne, C.P.A.
1140 Franklin Ave., Ste. 200
Garden City, NY 11530
Application address: 138 Oxford Blvd., Garden City, NY 11530
Contact: Thomas E. Sullivan, Tr.

Established in 1999 in NY.
Donor(s): Thomas E. Sullivan, Barbara A. Sullivan.
Financial data (yr. ended 12/31/00): Assets, $150,879 (M); grants paid, $42,769; gifts received, $88,743; expenditures, $47,756; qualifying distributions, $42,769.
Trustees: Barbara A. Sullivan, Thomas E. Sullivan.
EIN: 113523086

62343
Eve Propp Family Foundation, Inc.
P.O. Box 807
Millbrook, NY 12545

Established in 1998 in NY.
Donor(s): Ruth Grunebaum, Eve Propp.
Financial data (yr. ended 12/31/00): Assets, $150,239 (M); grants paid, $4,290; gifts received, $44,379; expenditures, $5,075; qualifying distributions, $4,276.
Limitations: Applications not accepted.
Application information: Contributes only to pre-selected organizations.
Trustees: Douglas Propp, Eve Propp, James Propp, Rodney M. Propp.
EIN: 311580133

62344
Rabbis Ben Zion and Baruch Micah Bokser Memorial Foundation, Inc.
(Formerly Rabbi Ben Zion Bokser Memorial Foundation)
35 W. 92nd St., Apt. 2E
New York, NY 10025-7639 (212) 864-1513
Contact: Kallia H. Bokser, Pres.

Classified as a private operating foundation in 1984.
Financial data (yr. ended 07/31/01): Assets, $148,957 (M); grants paid, $6,500; gifts received, $3,727; expenditures, $7,545; qualifying distributions, $6,500.
Limitations: Giving primarily in NY.
Officers and Trustees:* Kallia H. Bokser, Pres.; Miriam R. Caravella,* V.P.; Ann F. Wimpfheimer-Bokser,* Secy.-Treas.; Henry M. Burger, Roy Clements, Edward L. Greenstein, Haskell Klaristenfeld, Victorine K. Wimpfheimer.
EIN: 112692383

62345
Pfeffer Family Foundation
c/o Zeichner, Ellman, & Krause, LLP
575 Lexington Ave.
New York, NY 10022 (212) 223-0400
Contact: Jerome S. Solomon, Pres.

Established in 2001 in NY.
Donor(s): Barbara Pfeffer.‡
Financial data (yr. ended 12/31/01): Assets, $148,471 (M); grants paid, $6,000; gifts received, $152,625; expenditures, $6,490; qualifying distributions, $6,490.
Officers: Jerome S. Solomon, Pres. and Treas.; Doris Pfeffer, V.P.; Carole Bass, Secy.
EIN: 134140109

62346
Mothers on the Move, Inc.
928 Intervale Ave.
Bronx, NY 10459

Donor(s): New York Womens Foundation, Fund for the City of New York, Campaign for Human Development, New York Community Trust.
Financial data (yr. ended 12/31/99): Assets, $147,264 (M); grants paid, $0; gifts received, $278,479; expenditures, $293,986; qualifying distributions, $283,009; giving activities include $283,009 for programs.
Officers: Lucretia Jones, Chair.; Ana Collado, Vice-Chair.; Ana Espada, Vice-Chair.; Francine Dozier, Secy.
Directors: Mildred Bonilla, Diane Lawman, Jesie McDonald, Carolyn Pelzer, Helen Schaub, Alane Sosa, Rita Veras.
EIN: 133768715

62347
Professional Horsemen's Scholarship Fund, Inc.
202 Old Sleepyhollow Rd.
Pleasantville, NY 10570-3806
Application address: 20 Via del Corso, Palm Beach Gardens, FL 33418, tel.: (407) 694-6893
Contact: Ann Grenci, Pres.

Established in 1985 in CT.
Financial data (yr. ended 12/31/01): Assets, $147,243 (M); grants paid, $9,000; gifts received, $7,050; expenditures, $9,000; qualifying distributions, $9,000.
Application information: Application form required.
Officer: Ann Grenci, Pres.
Directors: Emerson Burr, Arthur Hawkins, Zeke Matt.
EIN: 066086137
Codes: GTI

62348
The Weiss Memorabilia Foundation
c/o Eugene Stoler, Konigsberg, Wolf & Co.
440 Park Ave.
New York, NY 10016

Established in 1998 in NY.
Donor(s): Herbert B. Weiss.
Financial data (yr. ended 06/30/99): Assets, $144,725 (M); grants paid, $0; gifts received, $71,000; expenditures, $529; qualifying distributions, $69,238; giving activities include $69,238 for programs.
Trustees: Henry Montanez, Randi Montanez, Herbert Weiss, Jay Weiss, Lynn Weiss, Sandra Weiss.
EIN: 137061011

62349
Dana Alliance for Brain Initiatives, Inc.
745 5th Ave., Ste. 700
New York, NY 10151 (212) 223-4040
FAX: (212) 317-8721; *URL:* http://www.dana.org
Contact: Burton Mirsky, Treas.

Established in 1993 in CT as a private operation foundation.
Donor(s): Charles A. Dana Foundation, Inc.
Financial data (yr. ended 12/31/01): Assets, $144,224 (M); grants paid, $316,544; gifts received, $3,342,377; expenditures, $3,444,855; qualifying distributions, $3,561,393; giving activities include $3,109,598 for programs.
Limitations: Applications not accepted. Giving on an international basis.
Publications: Annual report, financial statement, newsletter, occasional report, informational brochure.
Application information: Contributes only to pre-selected organizations.
Officers and Directors:* William L. Safire,* Pres.; Barbara E. Gill, V.P.; Frances Harper, V.P.; Edward F. Rover,* V.P.; Clark M. Whittemore, Jr.,* Secy.; Burton M. Mirsky, Treas.
EIN: 061360140
Codes: FD

62350
The Elysabeth Kleinhans Theatrical Foundation, Inc.
c/o E. Kleinhans
240 Central Park S.
New York, NY 10019

Established in 2000 in NY.
Donor(s): Elysabeth Kleinhans.
Financial data (yr. ended 11/30/01): Assets, $143,399 (M); grants paid, $0; gifts received, $143,400; expenditures, $500; qualifying distributions, $61,051.
Limitations: Applications not accepted.
Application information: Contributes only to pre-selected organizations.
Directors: Lawrence N. Friedland, Elysabeth Kleinhans, Julius Korein.
EIN: 134149853

62351
The Gabbay Family Foundation
34 W. 33rd St., Ste. 800
New York, NY 10001

Established in 1999 in NY.
Donor(s): Isaac Gabbay, Abe Gabbay, Joe Gabbay.
Financial data (yr. ended 12/31/00): Assets, $142,830 (M); grants paid, $9,667; expenditures, $10,013; qualifying distributions, $9,667.
Limitations: Applications not accepted.
Application information: Contributes only to pre-selected organizations.
Director: Isaac Gabbay.
EIN: 311681584

62352
Earle Brown Music Foundation
c/o Mac Corkindale
3960 Merrick Rd.
Seaford, NY 11783
Application address: 52 Brevoort Ln., Rye, NY 10580
Contact: Earle Brown

Classified as a private operating foundation in 1998 in NY.
Donor(s): Earle Brown, Susan Sollins.
Financial data (yr. ended 09/30/01): Assets, $139,794 (M); grants paid, $0; gifts received, $1,450; expenditures, $6,057; qualifying distributions, $9,805.
Trustees: Earle Brown, Susan Sollins.
EIN: 133921924

62353
Carolann K. Andrews Charitable Foundation
25 Woodcrest Dr.
Batavia, NY 14020-2721

Established in 1998 in NY.
Donor(s): John F. Andrews, Sharon A. Andrews.
Financial data (yr. ended 12/31/00): Assets, $139,531 (M); grants paid, $8,000; gifts received, $9,750; expenditures, $8,227; qualifying distributions, $7,772.
Limitations: Applications not accepted. Giving primarily in GA, NY, and OH.
Trustees: Terri M. Almeter, John F. Andrews, Sharon A. Andrews, Paul J. Battaglia, Aiden J. Brewer, Stacy Andrews Brewer.
EIN: 161552802

62354
The Mangrove Garden Foundation
c/o BCRS Assocs.
100 Wall St., 11th Fl.
New York, NY 10005

Established in 2000 in FL.
Donor(s): William C. Stutt.
Financial data (yr. ended 12/31/00): Assets, $138,666 (M); grants paid, $0; gifts received, $142,016; expenditures, $14,987; qualifying distributions, $14,987.
Limitations: Applications not accepted.
Application information: Contributes only to pre-selected organizations.
Trustees: Carolyn L. Stutt, William C. Stutt.
EIN: 656327164

62355
The 1812 Homestead Educational Foundation, Inc.
P.O. Box 507
Willsboro, NY 12996-0507

Established in 1992 in NY.
Financial data (yr. ended 12/31/00): Assets, $138,089 (M); grants paid, $0; gifts received, $954; expenditures, $48,921; qualifying distributions, $36,281; giving activities include $36,281 for programs.
Trustees: Margaret Reinckens, David Swan, John Sharpe Swan, Sr., John Sharpe Swan, Jr.
Directors: Myra Decker, Sarah Disney, Caroline Rubino, Lorilee Sheehan, Ellen Somers, Angela Sutterer Swan, Tim Tefft, Ramona Young.
EIN: 066366244

62356
Fingerhut Family Foundation
990 Browers Pt. Bridge
Woodmere, NY 11598
Contact: Arthur Fingerhut, Pres.

Donor(s): Arthur Fingerhut.
Financial data (yr. ended 10/31/01): Assets, $137,929 (M); grants paid, $14,729; expenditures, $16,065; qualifying distributions, $16,065.
Application information: Application form not required.
Officer: Arthur Fingerhut, Pres.
EIN: 136206768

62357
Star of the Sea H.D.F.C.
145-64 South Rd.
Jamaica, NY 11435-5140

Financial data (yr. ended 12/31/01): Assets, $135,662 (M); grants paid, $0; gifts received, $12,675; expenditures, $13,116; qualifying distributions, $0; giving activities include $13,116 for programs.
Officers: Robert Nesbit, Chair.; Winifred McCarthy, Pres.; Sheilla E. Desert, Exec. Dir.
EIN: 112901147

62358
Jerome & Barbara Ackerman Foundation
55 Northern Blvd.
Greenvale, NY 11548

Classified as a private operating foundation in 1996.
Financial data (yr. ended 12/31/00): Assets, $132,468 (M); grants paid, $2,975; expenditures, $3,677; qualifying distributions, $2,975.
Limitations: Applications not accepted.
Application information: Contributes only to pre-selected organizations.
Officer: Jerome Ackerman, Mgr.

EIN: 136209688

62359
Wildenstein Foundation, Inc.
19 E. 64th St.
New York, NY 10021-7042

Donor(s): Daniel Wildenstein.‡
Financial data (yr. ended 11/30/01): Assets, $131,080 (M); grants paid, $0; gifts received, $1,000; expenditures, $28; qualifying distributions, $0.
Officers: A. Wildenstein, Pres.; Guy Wildenstein, V.P.; Michelle LeMarchant, Secy.
EIN: 136099120

62360
Myser Foundation Fund, Inc.
c/o Dworetsky & Co.
277 Broadway, Ste. 801
New York, NY 10007-2001

Financial data (yr. ended 12/31/99): Assets, $130,973 (M); grants paid, $9,363; expenditures, $12,295; qualifying distributions, $9,363.
Limitations: Applications not accepted.
Application information: Contributes only to pre-selected organizations.
Officer: Sidney Finkelstein, Pres.
EIN: 116024453

62361
Lozynskyj Foundation
c/o Askold S. Lozynskyj
225 E. 11th St.
New York, NY 10003

Established in 1998 in NY.
Donor(s): Bohdan Chaban.
Financial data (yr. ended 12/31/99): Assets, $130,656 (M); grants paid, $1,500; gifts received, $80,060; expenditures, $1,560; qualifying distributions, $60.
Officers: Maria Chaban, Pres.; Bohdan Chaban, V.P.; Lavisa Lozynskyj-Kjy, Secy.; Askold Lozynskyj, Treas.
EIN: 311616242

62362
Szendrovits Foundation
159 Hewes St.
Brooklyn, NY 11211

Established in 2001 in NY. Classified as a private operating foundation in 2002.
Donor(s): Adalbert Szendrowitz.
Financial data (yr. ended 12/31/01): Assets, $130,015 (M); grants paid, $0; gifts received, $130,000; expenditures, $0; qualifying distributions, $0.
Director: Adalbert Szendrowitz.
EIN: 016169569

62363
The Institute for Aegean Prehistory Study Center for East Crete
c/o The Millburn Corp.
1270 Ave. of the Americas
New York, NY 10020

Established in 1994 in DE and NY.
Donor(s): The Institute for Aegean Prehistory.
Financial data (yr. ended 06/30/00): Assets, $127,946 (M); grants paid, $0; gifts received, $366,867; expenditures, $350,488; qualifying distributions, $333,083; giving activities include $159,549 for programs.
Officers: Malcolm H. Wiener, Pres.; Philip Betancourt, V.P. and Secy.
Trustees: Harvey Beker, George Crapple, Martin J. Whitman, Carolyn S. Wiener.
EIN: 133832587

62364
Design with a Purpose, Inc.
c/o Kisco Mgmt. Corp.
111 Radio Cir.
Mount Kisco, NY 10549

Established in 1997; Classified as a private operating foundation in 1998.
Donor(s): Karen Kohlberg, Charitable Gift Fund.
Financial data (yr. ended 12/31/01): Assets, $127,319 (M); grants paid, $0; gifts received, $213,250; expenditures, $165,850; qualifying distributions, $165,191; giving activities include $132,587 for programs.
Officers: Karen Kohlberg, Pres.; Nancy White McCabe, V.P.; Walter W. Farley, Treas.
EIN: 330588322

62365
Oyster Bay Cat Foundation, Ltd.
c/o Sherman Epstein
489 5th Ave.
New York, NY 10017

Classified as a private operating foundation in 1980.
Donor(s): Patricia Ladew.
Financial data (yr. ended 07/31/00): Assets, $125,025 (M); grants paid, $0; gifts received, $35,799; expenditures, $36,836; qualifying distributions, $36,836; giving activities include $36,836 for programs.
Officer: Patricia Ladew, Pres.
EIN: 237307973

62366
American Foundation for the Visual Arts, Inc.
34 Sylvia Rd.
Plainview, NY 11803-6440

Established in 1999 in NY.
Financial data (yr. ended 12/31/01): Assets, $124,974 (M); grants paid, $0; expenditures, $6,890; qualifying distributions, $0.
Officers: Aron Laikin, Pres.; Paul Laikin, Secy.-Treas.
EIN: 113190228

62367
David & Paula Fishman Charitable Trust
c/o Miller, Levine & Co.
419 Park Ave. S., Ste. 506
New York, NY 10016

Established in 1997 in NY.
Donor(s): David Fishman, Paula Fishman.
Financial data (yr. ended 12/31/01): Assets, $124,726 (M); grants paid, $17,945; expenditures, $22,258; qualifying distributions, $22,257.
Limitations: Applications not accepted. Giving primarily in NY.
Application information: Contributes only to pre-selected organizations.
Trustees: David Fishman, Paula Fishman.
EIN: 113402788

62368
Emma Reed Webster Aid Association, Inc.
5140 Angevine Rd.
Albion, NY 14411-9417
Application address: 3241 Oak Orchard Rd., Albion, NY 14411, tel.: (716) 589-9815
Contact: Joan Farnsworth, Pres.

Donor(s): Emma Reed Trust.
Financial data (yr. ended 05/31/00): Assets, $119,663 (M); grants paid, $29,414; gifts received, $16,036; expenditures, $34,944; qualifying distributions, $34,944.
Limitations: Giving limited to Orleans County, NY.

62368—NEW YORK

Application information: SASE required. Application form required.
Officers: Joan Farnsworth, Pres.; Janice Thaine, Secy.; Frances Peglow, Treas.
EIN: 166031485
Codes: GTI

62369
Samuel Mandelbaum Foundation
22 Dartmouth Terr.
White Plains, NY 10607 (914) 997-0234
Contact: David J. Mandelbaum, Tr.

Established in 1951 in NY.
Donor(s): David J. Mandelbaum, Nellie S. Mandelbaum.
Financial data (yr. ended 12/31/00): Assets, $117,871 (M); grants paid, $33,370; gifts received, $17,400; expenditures, $33,612; qualifying distributions, $33,612.
Limitations: Giving primarily in New York, NY.
Trustees: Mimi Einsidler, David J. Mandelbaum.
EIN: 136162683

62370
Madoo Conservancy, Inc.
P.O. Box 362
Sagaponack, NY 11962

Classified as a private operating foundation in 1994.
Donor(s): Robert Dash, David McCall, Mrs. David McCall, Penny McCall Foundation.
Financial data (yr. ended 06/30/00): Assets, $117,585 (M); grants paid, $0; gifts received, $98,102; expenditures, $115,724; qualifying distributions, $92,084; giving activities include $115,724 for programs.
Officer and Directors:* Robert Dash,* Pres. and Mgr.; Elaine Benson, Margaret Logan, Marco Polo Da Stufano, Tina Washburn, and 5 additional directors.
EIN: 133726372

62371
The Bochner Family Foundation
1417 47th St.
Brooklyn, NY 11219

Established in 2000 in NY.
Donor(s): Elias Bochner, Surrey Bochner.
Financial data (yr. ended 12/31/01): Assets, $114,176 (M); grants paid, $20,800; gifts received, $60,000; expenditures, $22,819; qualifying distributions, $20,800.
Limitations: Applications not accepted.
Application information: Contributes only to pre-selected organizations.
Officers: Elias Bochner, Pres.; Surrey Bochner, V.P.
EIN: 113575524

62372
The Murray S. and Natalie Katz Foundation, Inc.
220 E. 67th St.
New York, NY 10021

Established in 1995.
Donor(s): Murray S. Katz, Natalie Katz.
Financial data (yr. ended 12/31/99): Assets, $112,385 (M); grants paid, $20,310; expenditures, $20,974; qualifying distributions, $20,264.
Limitations: Applications not accepted. Giving primarily in NY.
Application information: Contributes only to pre-selected organizations.
Officers: Murray S. Katz, Pres.; Natalie Katz, Secy.
Directors: Leonard Kupferman, Ann Silverstein, Jeffrey Wexler.
EIN: 133797882

62373
Melissa Flanders Nickel Fund, Inc.
c/o Al Nickel
220 E. 42nd St., 3rd Fl.
New York, NY 10017-5806

Financial data (yr. ended 06/30/01): Assets, $112,062 (M); grants paid, $5,000; expenditures, $5,476; qualifying distributions, $5,140.
Limitations: Applications not accepted.
Officer: Michael Lyons, Pres. and Secy.
Directors: Dean Maglaris, William Steere, Peter Tombros.
EIN: 133320401

62374
The Art Kaleidoscope Foundation, Inc.
22 Catherine St., Apt. 2F
New York, NY 10038

Established in 1990 in NY.
Financial data (yr. ended 12/31/99): Assets, $110,626 (L); grants paid, $0; gifts received, $280,697; expenditures, $199,812; qualifying distributions, $216,311; giving activities include $216,311 for programs.
Officers and Directors:* Nicholas Quennell,* Pres.; Peter Biskind,* Treas.; Virginia Fish, Suzannah Lessare, Adrienne Ottenberg.
EIN: 133576913

62375
The Silverstein Family Foundation
16228 Deer Run Rd.
Watertown, NY 13601

Established in 2000 in NY.
Donor(s): Larry Silverstein.
Financial data (yr. ended 06/30/01): Assets, $110,000 (M); grants paid, $0; gifts received, $3,013; expenditures, $9,661; qualifying distributions, $9,661.
Limitations: Applications not accepted.
Application information: Contributes only to pre-selected organizations.
Trustees: Becky Keshniri, Larry Silverstein.
EIN: 161598502

62376
The David Eisdorfer Memorial Foundation
c/o Blanka Eisdorfer
1473 47th St.
Brooklyn, NY 11219-2535

Established in 1997 in NY.
Donor(s): Blanka Eisdorfer.
Financial data (yr. ended 12/31/01): Assets, $109,545 (M); grants paid, $0; expenditures, $0; qualifying distributions, $0.
Trustee: Blanka Eisdorfer.
EIN: 113368749

62377
Robert F. Case Scholarship Fund, Inc.
101 Mohawk Ave.
Scotia, NY 12302-2247
Contact: Kenneth T. Gibbons, Tr.

Classified as a private operating foundation in 1990.
Financial data (yr. ended 04/30/99): Assets, $108,078 (M); grants paid, $3,000; gifts received, $850; expenditures, $3,034; qualifying distributions, $3,034.
Limitations: Giving limited to NY.
Trustees: Cortland Andrew, Kenneth T. Gibbons, David C. Gonyea.
EIN: 223022643

62378
The M2G Foundation
c/o Mordechai Greenfield
5224 15th Ave.
Brooklyn, NY 11219

Established in 1998 in NY.
Financial data (yr. ended 12/31/99): Assets, $105,933 (M); grants paid, $20,000; expenditures, $21,726; qualifying distributions, $20,000.
Limitations: Applications not accepted.
Application information: Contributes only to pre-selected organizations.
Director: Mordechai Greenfield.
EIN: 113463823

62379
Delos Foundation, Inc.
c/o Ms. F. Druckenmiller
117 E. 72nd St.
New York, NY 10021

Established in 1999 in NY.
Donor(s): Fiona Druckenmiller.
Financial data (yr. ended 03/31/00): Assets, $105,613 (M); grants paid, $0; gifts received, $340,000; expenditures, $234,637; qualifying distributions, $234,587.
Directors: Fiona Druckenmiller, Susan Kessler, Georgia Malone.
EIN: 061563303

62380
Committee to Preserve the Narcissa Prentiss House
722 6 Mill Pond Rd.
P.O. Box 409
Prattsburgh, NY 14873

Financial data (yr. ended 08/31/01): Assets, $103,428 (M); grants paid, $0; gifts received, $185; expenditures, $2,713; qualifying distributions, $2,713; giving activities include $2,713 for programs.
Limitations: Applications not accepted.
Application information: Contributes only to pre-selected organizations.
Officers: Anne Poore, Pres.; Barbara Shaver, Secy.-Treas.
EIN: 161195014

62381
The Maria C. & Nelson D. Ventura Foundation, Inc.
P.O. Box 110388
Brooklyn, NY 11211

Established in 2000.
Donor(s): Nelson Ventura.
Financial data (yr. ended 12/31/00): Assets, $102,960 (M); grants paid, $3,600; gifts received, $105,195; expenditures, $5,835; qualifying distributions, $0.
Limitations: Applications not accepted.
Application information: Contributes only to pre-selected organizations.
Trustees: Stephanie Wanda Belzer, Jay Sincoff, Nelson Ventura.
EIN: 522223308

62382
The Capitano Foundation
265 Willetts Ln.
West Islip, NY 11795

Established in 1997 in NY.
Donor(s): Salvatore Capitano, Marie Capitano.
Financial data (yr. ended 12/31/01): Assets, $102,786 (M); grants paid, $3,850; gifts received, $17,184; expenditures, $4,206; qualifying distributions, $3,850.

Limitations: Applications not accepted.
Application information: Contributes only to pre-selected organizations.
Trustees: Sabrina Breitfeller, Thomas Breitfeller, Gina Capitano, Marie Capitano, Salvatore Capitano, Salvatore Capitano, Jr.
EIN: 116480969

62383
Historical Eastfield Foundation
104 Mud Pond Rd.
East Nassau, NY 12062

Established in 1995 in NY.
Donor(s): Ohrstrom Foundation.
Financial data (yr. ended 03/31/01): Assets, $102,746 (M); grants paid, $0; gifts received, $15,000; expenditures, $58,068; qualifying distributions, $117,473; giving activities include $28,190 for programs.
Officers and Directors:* Carl Dietz,* Chair.; Hugh Howard,* Secy.; Peter Schaaphok,* Treas.; David Fleming, Jerry Grant, John Kovacik, John Mesick, Chris Ohrstrom.
EIN: 223241666

62384
Mendon Manor, Inc.
26 Mendon Ionia Rd.
Mendon, NY 14506-9730

Financial data (yr. ended 04/30/01): Assets, $99,888 (L); grants paid, $0; expenditures, $5,058; qualifying distributions, $5,058; giving activities include $5,058 for programs.
Officer and Trustee:* Rev. James Lawler,* Secy.-Treas.
EIN: 222142383

62385
The Ron Parham Fund for Scholastic Excellence
c/o Jim Traub
30 E. 65th St., Ste. 13B
New York, NY 10021-7005

Classified as a private operating foundation in 1994.
Donor(s): James Traub.
Financial data (yr. ended 12/31/00): Assets, $98,178 (M); grants paid, $4,000; expenditures, $5,893; qualifying distributions, $5,893.
Application information: Application form not required.
Trustee: James Traub.
EIN: 133749141

62386
The Mica Foundation
c/o Howard Morse
450 Park Ave., Ste. 902
New York, NY 10022

Classified as a private operating foundation in 1998 in DE and NY.
Donor(s): Howard L. Morse, Barbara L. Morse.
Financial data (yr. ended 11/30/01): Assets, $97,482 (M); grants paid, $1,260; expenditures, $32,071; qualifying distributions, $27,625; giving activities include $22,845 for programs.
Limitations: Applications not accepted.
Application information: Contributes only to pre-selected organizations.
Officers: Barbara L. Morse, Pres.; Howard L. Morse, Secy.
Directors: Colin De Land, Patricia Hearn, Aaron W. Morse, Jonathan D. Morse, Lisa Morse.
EIN: 133981562

62387
Jessie C. Wilson Memorial Trust Fund
47 Elm St
Westfield, NY 14787
Application address: 11 Holt St., Westfield, NY 14787
Contact: David Gross, Chair.

Established in 1983 in NY.
Financial data (yr. ended 12/31/00): Assets, $97,080 (M); grants paid, $3,428; expenditures, $3,605; qualifying distributions, $3,487.
Limitations: Giving primarily in the Westfield NY, area.
Officers and Trustees:* David Gross,* Chair.; David Wilson,* Secy.-Treas.; Jodi Wilson,* Secy.-Treas.; Kathy Monroe, Priscilla Nixon.
EIN: 166253879

62388
Kuan-Yin Foundation
c/o Willkie Farr & Gallagher
787 7th Ave.
New York, NY 10019

Established in 2000 in NY.
Donor(s): Elizabeth R. Larson.
Financial data (yr. ended 04/30/01): Assets, $96,743 (M); grants paid, $296,520; gifts received, $400,000; expenditures, $309,358; qualifying distributions, $309,358.
Limitations: Applications not accepted. Giving primarily in New York, NY.
Application information: Contributes only to pre-selected organizations.
Officers: Fiona Druckenmiller, Pres.; Richard O'Reilly, Secy.; Elizabeth R. Larson, Treas.
EIN: 943363804
Codes: FD

62389
Randi Press Foundation
2284 Flatbush Ave.
Brooklyn, NY 11234-4598
Contact: Larry Press, Dir.

Classified as a private operating foundation in 1972.
Financial data (yr. ended 01/31/01): Assets, $95,630 (M); grants paid, $6,000; gifts received, $2,936; expenditures, $6,112; qualifying distributions, $12,064.
Limitations: Giving primarily in NY.
Director: Larry Press.
EIN: 237179844

62390
The Hayden Harmon Foundation, Ltd.
c/o Bosworth, Gray & Fuller
116 Kraft Ave.
Bronxville, NY 10708 (914) 961-1200
Contact: J. Rockhill Gray

Established in 2001 in NY.
Donor(s): Hayden K. Harmon.
Financial data (yr. ended 12/31/01): Assets, $95,123 (M); grants paid, $5,000; gifts received, $100,125; expenditures, $5,125; qualifying distributions, $5,000.
Limitations: Giving primarily in New York, NY.
Officer: Hayden K. Harmon, C.E.O. and Pres.
EIN: 134196155

62391
John and Frances Strachan Charitable Foundation
3 Crumite Rd.
Loudonville, NY 12211 (518) 427-9933
Contact: John R. Strachan, Tr.

Established in 1999 in NY.
Donor(s): John Strachan, Frances Strachan.
Financial data (yr. ended 12/31/99): Assets, $94,775 (M); grants paid, $5,225; gifts received, $100,000; expenditures, $5,225; qualifying distributions, $5,225.
Limitations: Giving primarily in NY.
Trustees: Frances W. Strachan, John R. Strachan.
EIN: 510395555

62392
S. & P. Margareten Family Foundation
9 Waverly Pl.
Monsey, NY 10952
Contact: George Margareten, Mgr.

Donor(s): George Margareten.
Financial data (yr. ended 04/30/00): Assets, $91,199 (M); grants paid, $9,390; gifts received, $6,000; expenditures, $9,456; qualifying distributions, $9,456.
Officer: George Margareten, Mgr.
EIN: 137117757

62393
The Stacey C. and Robert R. Morse Family Foundation
1000 Park Ave., Ste. 3A
New York, NY 10028-0934

Established in 2000 in NY; Classified as a private operating foundation in 2001.
Donor(s): Robert R. Morse, Stacey C. Morse.
Financial data (yr. ended 12/31/00): Assets, $90,482 (M); grants paid, $6,085; gifts received, $93,219; expenditures, $6,085; qualifying distributions, $6,085.
Limitations: Giving primarily in New York, NY.
Trustees: Robert R. Morse, Stacey C. Morse.
EIN: 134142518

62394
Teamsters BBYO Scholarship Fund
45 E. 33rd St., Ste. 601
New York, NY 10016-5336 (212) 696-9020
Contact: Martin Adelstein, Tr.

Financial data (yr. ended 07/31/01): Assets, $90,284 (M); grants paid, $7,000; expenditures, $7,234; qualifying distributions, $7,234.
Limitations: Giving on a national basis, with emphasis on the Northeast.
Application information: Application form required.
Trustees: Bernard Adelstein, Martin Adelstein, Joseph Konowe, William K. Peirez, Douglas Sugerman.
EIN: 237383406
Codes: GTI

62395
Ninash Foundation
c/o Malhotra Raj
17 Center St.
Oneonta, NY 13820-1445 (607) 432-0496
Contact: Ashok Malhotra, Pres.

Established in 1999 in NY.
Financial data (yr. ended 12/31/00): Assets, $87,250 (M); grants paid, $8,044; gifts received, $22,820; expenditures, $22,364; qualifying distributions, $22,364; giving activities include $1,766 for programs.
Limitations: Giving primarily in upstate NY; some support also for a school in India.
Officers: Ashok Malhotra, Pres.; Ashwinpaul Sondhi, V.P.; Raj Malhotra, Secy.; Linda Drake, Treas.
EIN: 161512822

62396
Nyack Police Organization Memorial Fund
c/o Robert P. Lewis
P.O. Box 991
Nyack, NY 10960

Classified as a private operating foundation in 1984.
Financial data (yr. ended 12/31/01): Assets, $87,050 (M); grants paid, $66,204; expenditures, $66,886; qualifying distributions, $66,204.
Limitations: Giving primarily in NY.
Trustees: Robert P. Buckout, Thomas P. Coffey, Robert P. Lewis.
EIN: 133159026

62397
Frank and Grace Heller Foundation
12 Oakdale Rd.
Larchmont, NY 10538
Contact: Jeffrey Corbin, Dir.

Established in 1998 in NY.
Donor(s): Grace Heller.
Financial data (yr. ended 12/31/00): Assets, $86,212 (M); grants paid, $33,559; gifts received, $120,065; expenditures, $35,059; qualifying distributions, $33,559.
Limitations: Giving primarily in NY.
Directors: Carol Corbin, Herbert Corbin, Jeffrey Corbin.
EIN: 134001819

62398
Heat & Frost Insulators Local 12 Officers Scholarship Fund
25-19 43rd Ave.
Long Island City, NY 11101

Classified as a company-sponsored operating foundation.
Donor(s): Weitz & Luxenberg, Colleran, O'Hara & Mills.
Financial data (yr. ended 12/31/01): Assets, $84,778 (M); grants paid, $2,500; gifts received, $62,589; expenditures, $5,000; qualifying distributions, $2,500.
Application information: Application form required.
Trustees: Fred DeMartino, Richard O'Hara, Perry Weitz.
EIN: 113440178

62399
Caribbean Medical & Educational Foundation
1019 Van Sicklen Ave., Ste. 3J
Brooklyn, NY 11207

Established in 1998 in NY.
Financial data (yr. ended 12/31/00): Assets, $84,401 (M); grants paid, $0; expenditures, $9,174; qualifying distributions, $0.
Officers: Frederick Ballantyne, M.D., Chair.; Samuel Bishham, Ph.D., Pres.; Lamuel Stanislaus, D.D.S., V.P.; Lenox Prescod, Ph.D., 2nd V.P.; Rita Fuller, Secy.; Val Whiteman, Treas.
EIN: 113357861

62400
A Child Waits Foundation
c/o OTA, LP
1 Manhattanville Rd.
Purchase, NY 10577
Application address: 1136 Barker Rd., No.12, Pittsfield, MA 01201, tel.: (413) 499-7859; E-mail: achildwaits@poboxes.com; URL: http://www.achildwaits.org
Contact: Cynthia Nelson, Pres. or Randolph Nelson, V.P.

Donor(s): Cindy Nelson, Randolph Nelson.

Financial data (yr. ended 12/31/00): Assets, $83,254 (M); grants paid, $147,318; gifts received, $804,895; expenditures, $152,956; qualifying distributions, $279,120; giving activities include $147,318 for loans to individuals.
Officers: Cynthia Nelson, Pres.; Randolph Nelson, V.P.; Richard Cayne, Secy.
EIN: 133978652
Codes: FD2

62401
Americans for Middle East Understanding, Inc.
475 Riverside Dr., Ste. 245
New York, NY 10115 (212) 870-2053

Established in 1967 in NY.
Donor(s): Rev. L. Humphrey Walz, Arabian American Oil Co., Council of Saudi Chamber of Commerce and Industry, and others.
Financial data (yr. ended 12/31/01): Assets, $80,612 (M); grants paid, $0; gifts received, $234,539; expenditures, $217,901; qualifying distributions, $216,914; giving activities include $122,572 for programs.
Officers and Trustees:* Jack B. Sunderland,* Pres.; Henry G. Fisher,* V.P.; Mark P. Wellman,* Treas.; John P. Mahoney, Exec. Dir.; Hugh D. Auchincloss, Bonnie Gehweiler, John Goelet, Richard Hobson, Jr., Robert Noberg, Hon. Edward L. Peck, Lachlan Reed, Amb. Talcott Seelye, Donald Snook, James M. Wall, Rev. L. Humphrey Walz, Sr. Miriam Ward.
EIN: 132625006

62402
Edah, Inc.
(Formerly People for the Renaissance of Torah)
47 W. 34th St., Ste. 700
New York, NY 10001

Established in 1995 in NY.
Financial data (yr. ended 08/31/99): Assets, $79,812 (M); grants paid, $0; gifts received, $822,602; expenditures, $981,034; qualifying distributions, $774,427; giving activities include $509,497 for programs.
Limitations: Applications not accepted.
Application information: Contributes only to pre-selected organizations.
Officers: Michael Hammer, Chair.; Irving Greenberg, Vice-Chair. and Secy.; Jonathan Greenberg, Pres. and Treas.; Judith Adler Sheer, Exec. Dir.
Director: Rabbi Saul Berman.
EIN: 133841793

62403
Basket Historical Society of the Upper Delaware Valley
P.O. Box 199
Long Eddy, NY 12760

Classified as a private operating foundation in 1984.
Financial data (yr. ended 12/31/01): Assets, $79,598 (M); grants paid, $10; gifts received, $8,650; expenditures, $9,192; qualifying distributions, $8,018; giving activities include $7,399 for programs.
Limitations: Applications not accepted.
Application information: Contributes only to pre-selected organizations.
Officers: John Niflot, Pres.; William Klaber, V.P.; Mary Butremuk, Secy.; Edie Downs, Treas.
Trustees: Anna Bullis, Mary Butremuk, Helen Deckleman, Donald Downs, Pauline Neanng.
EIN: 222525379

62404
The Alexander & Louisa Calder Foundation
c/o L.H. Frishkoff & Co., LLP
529 5th Ave.
New York, NY 10017

Classified as a private operating foundation in 1991.
Donor(s): Pace Galleries.
Financial data (yr. ended 08/31/01): Assets, $78,126 (M); grants paid, $0; gifts received, $333,764; expenditures, $480,490; qualifying distributions, $474,676; giving activities include $474,676 for programs.
Limitations: Applications not accepted.
Application information: Contributes only to pre-selected organizations.
Directors: Sandra C. Davidson, Shawn Davidson, Howard Rower, Mary C. Rower.
EIN: 133466986

62405
The National Myeloproliferative Disease Foundation Trust
c/o Pamela Meyer
168 W. 86th St., Apt. 2A
New York, NY 10024

Established in 1997 in FL.
Donor(s): Jerome F. Meyer, Mrs. Jerome F. Meyer.
Financial data (yr. ended 12/31/01): Assets, $77,829 (M); grants paid, $0; gifts received, $50; expenditures, $34,822; qualifying distributions, $0.
Officer and Trustees:* Pamela M. Meyer,* Mgr.; Jerome F. Meyer, Cynthia Meyer Truitt.
EIN: 656232769

62406
Railway Historical Society of Northern New York, Inc.
P.O. Box 317
Croghan, NY 13327-0317

Financial data (yr. ended 12/31/00): Assets, $77,392 (M); grants paid, $70; gifts received, $8,095; expenditures, $3,123; qualifying distributions, $70; giving activities include $6,274 for programs.
Officers: Don Mooney, Pres.; Karl Ruetling, 1st V.P.; Beany Spagnolli, 2nd V.P.; Penny Demo, Secy.; Maurice Switzer, Treas.
EIN: 237106601

62407
Robert Maurice Grunder Memorial Fund, Inc.
c/o Arnold Sheiffer
5 Oneck Rd.
Westhampton Beach, NY 11978-0887

Established in 2000 in NY.
Donor(s): Arnold Sheiffer.
Financial data (yr. ended 12/31/00): Assets, $77,125 (M); grants paid, $9,750; gifts received, $162,188; expenditures, $10,636; qualifying distributions, $9,750.
Limitations: Applications not accepted.
Application information: Contributes only to pre-selected organizations.
Trustee: Arnold Sheiffer.
EIN: 113511951

62408
The Foundation for Hellenic Culture, Inc.
7 W. 57th St., Ste. 1
New York, NY 10019 (212) 308-6908
FAX: (212) 308-0919; E-mail:
iep.ny@ix.netcom.com; URL: http://
www.foundationhellenicculture.com
Contact: Peter Pappas, Dir.

Established in 1994; funded in 1995.
Financial data (yr. ended 12/31/01): Assets, $75,099 (M); grants paid, $171,726; gifts received, $517,493; expenditures, $464,043; qualifying distributions, $171,726.
Limitations: Giving on a national basis.
Application information: Application form not required.
Officer and Directors:* Peter Pappas,* Chair.; Gregory A. Sloris.
EIN: 133802490
Codes: FD2

62409
The Bonnie & Bernard Hodes Foundation
c/o Nathan Berkman & Co.
29 Broadway, Ste. 2900
New York, NY 10006

Established in 1999 in NY.
Donor(s): Bonnie Hodes, Bernard Hodes.
Financial data (yr. ended 11/30/00): Assets, $72,958 (M); grants paid, $7,600; gifts received, $102,375; expenditures, $7,700; qualifying distributions, $7,600.
Limitations: Applications not accepted.
Application information: Contributes only to pre-selected organizations.
Trustees: Bernard Hodes, Bonnie Hodes.
EIN: 134090700

62410
The Shaara Foundation, Inc.
P.O. Box 20123
New York, NY 10014

Donor(s): Jeffrey M. Shaara.
Financial data (yr. ended 12/31/01): Assets, $71,886 (M); grants paid, $4,000; gifts received, $53,250; expenditures, $4,004; qualifying distributions, $4,000.
Limitations: Applications not accepted.
Application information: Contributes only to pre-selected organizations.
Directors: Ralph Johnson, Jeffrey M. Shaara, Lynne L. Shaara.
EIN: 593640810

62411
Belau Family Foundation
c/o Schwartz & Co.
2580 Sunrise Hwy.
Bellmore, NY 11710
Contact: Robert Belau, Pres. and Treas.

Established in 1999 in NY.
Donor(s): Robert Belau.
Financial data (yr. ended 12/31/00): Assets, $71,560 (M); grants paid, $0; expenditures, $0; qualifying distributions, $0.
Application information: Application form not required.
Officers: Robert Belau, Pres. and Treas.; Doni Belau, V.P. and Secy.
Director: Michael J. Schwartz.
EIN: 113522131

62412
Whitney Marie Foundation
585 Stewart Ave., Ste. 412
Garden City, NY 11530
Contact: Donna Figliozzi, Pres.

Established in 2000 in NY.
Donor(s): Donna Figliozzi, Peter Figliozzi.
Financial data (yr. ended 12/31/00): Assets, $69,813 (M); grants paid, $0; gifts received, $68,497; expenditures, $2,677; qualifying distributions, $2,677.
Officers: Donna Figliozzi, Pres.; Peter Figliozzi, V.P.
Director: Richard Asner.
EIN: 113575711

62413
The Randy and Marta Isaac Foundation
44 Church Tavern Rd.
South Salem, NY 10590

Established in 1999 in NY.
Donor(s): Randall D. Isaac.
Financial data (yr. ended 08/31/00): Assets, $69,676 (M); grants paid, $44,655; gifts received, $113,950; expenditures, $45,830; qualifying distributions, $44,655.
Limitations: Applications not accepted.
Application information: Contributes only to pre-selected organizations.
Officers: Randall D. Isaac, Pres.; Martha J. Isaac, V.P.
Director: Ed Nichols.
EIN: 582503451

62414
Zichron Mayer Foundation
c/o Menacham Landau, et al.
1442 53rd St.
Brooklyn, NY 11219-3948

Established in 1998.
Donor(s): Mendel Landau.
Financial data (yr. ended 12/31/99): Assets, $68,847 (M); grants paid, $14,085; gifts received, $69,460; expenditures, $14,908; qualifying distributions, $14,085.
Limitations: Applications not accepted.
Application information: Contributes only to pre-selected organizations.
Director: Mendel Landau.
EIN: 113449871

62415
Edge Foundation, Inc.
c/o Brockman, Inc.
5 E. 59th St.
New York, NY 10022

Classified as a private operating foundation in 1989.
Financial data (yr. ended 12/31/01): Assets, $68,380 (M); grants paid, $0; gifts received, $50,000; expenditures, $37,438; qualifying distributions, $33,027; giving activities include $22,026 for programs.
Officers: John Brockman, Pres.; Mark Mirsky, V.P.; Katinka Matson, Secy.
EIN: 133528667

62416
Dutchess County Historical Society
P.O. Box 88
Poughkeepsie, NY 12602

Classified as a private operating foundation in 1970.
Donor(s): Ezra Benton.‡
Financial data (yr. ended 12/31/01): Assets, $68,015 (M); grants paid, $0; gifts received, $33,632; expenditures, $80,447; qualifying distributions, $47,488; giving activities include $39,415 for programs.
Officers and Trustees:* Joyce C. Ghee,* Pres.; James Spratt,* V.P.; Barbara Van Itallie,* V.P.; David Dengel,* Secy.; Mary Ann Lohrey,* Treas.; and 13 additional trustees.
Director: Eileen Hayden.
EIN: 141505142

62417
Zichron Sholom Shraga Foundation
c/o Warren Edleman
25 Crestview Terr.
Monsey, NY 10952
Contact: Warren Edelman, Pres.

Established in 1996 in NY.
Donor(s): Warren Edelman.
Financial data (yr. ended 12/31/99): Assets, $67,086 (L); grants paid, $34,743; gifts received, $62,000; expenditures, $39,502; qualifying distributions, $39,502.
Officer: Warren Edelman, Pres.
Directors: Elisheva Edelman, Benjamin Landau.
EIN: 133900515

62418
Hans Christian Andersen Story Telling Center, Inc.
c/o L. K. Rambusch, Haight Gardner, Holland & Knight
195 Broadway
New York, NY 10007

Financial data (yr. ended 12/31/01): Assets, $66,741 (M); grants paid, $0; gifts received, $2,000; expenditures, $6,491; qualifying distributions, $6,170; giving activities include $6,491 for programs.
Officers and Directors:* Lennard Rambusch,* Pres.; Thomas P. Della Torre,* V.P.; Paul Steffensen,* V.P.; Anne-Mette Andersen, Secy.; Christian R. Sonne,* Treas.
EIN: 133081021

62419
Adolph J. & Dorothy R. Eckhardt Foundation
52 Stowe Ave.
Baldwin, NY 11510

Donor(s): Adolph J. Eckhardt.
Financial data (yr. ended 04/30/00): Assets, $65,777 (M); grants paid, $3,500; expenditures, $4,356; qualifying distributions, $4,356.
Limitations: Giving primarily in NY.
Directors: Adolph J. Eckhardt, Dorothy R. Eckhardt, Sayra A. Graham.
EIN: 113041348

62420
The Bronner Family Foundation
1369 45th St.
Brooklyn, NY 11219

Established in 1998.
Donor(s): Isaac Bronner.
Financial data (yr. ended 12/31/99): Assets, $64,300 (M); grants paid, $1,190; gifts received, $61,200; expenditures, $1,250; qualifying distributions, $1,190.
Trustee: Isaac Bronner.
EIN: 113429136

62421
Dutchess County War Memorial Committee, Inc.
c/o Cornell S. Vangor, C.P.A.
583 Albany Post Rd.
Hyde Park, NY 12538

Classified as a private operating foundation in 1972.
Financial data (yr. ended 12/31/01): Assets, $63,078 (M); grants paid, $0; expenditures, $2,874; qualifying distributions, $0.
Officers: John Harris, Chair.; John Cervone, Vice-Chair.; John F. Santiamo, Secy.; Andrew J. Mihans, Treas.
EIN: 141674939

62422
The Melinda Gray Ardia Environmental Foundation, Ltd.
P.O. Box 621
3 W. Lake Rd.
Skaneateles, NY 13152-0621 (315) 445-9347
Contact: Daniel Ardia, Pres.

Established in 1996 in NY. Classified as a private operating foundation in 1997.
Financial data (yr. ended 05/31/01): Assets, $61,992 (M); grants paid, $3,150; gifts received, $4,520; expenditures, $3,297; qualifying distributions, $3,102.
Limitations: Giving primarily in NY.
Application information: Application form not required.
Officers and Directors:* Daniel Ardia,* Pres.; Dan Labeille,* V.P.; Dave Ardia,* Secy.; Suzanne Gray Murphy,* Treas.; Gail Chambers, Alice Gray, Glenn Huels, Robert Palmateer, D. Andrew Saunders, William Shields.
EIN: 161499155

62423
Urasenke Tea Ceremony Society, Inc.
153 E. 69th St.
New York, NY 10021-5108

Classified as a private operating foundation in 1981.
Donor(s): Bulm Foundation.
Financial data (yr. ended 12/31/01): Assets, $60,999 (M); grants paid, $0; gifts received, $10,400; expenditures, $31,854; qualifying distributions, $29,400; giving activities include $29,400 for programs.
Officers and Directors:* Stephen Grant,* Pres.; Rand Castile,* Treas.; Hisashi Yamada, Exec. Dir.
EIN: 133011933

62424
National Lipid Diseases Foundation
158 W. Boston Post Rd.
Mamaroneck, NY 10543
Application address: 32 Century Trail, Harrison, NY 10528
Contact: Harriet Klein, Dir.

Established in 1970.
Financial data (yr. ended 12/31/00): Assets, $59,656 (M); grants paid, $25,000; gifts received, $4,567; expenditures, $25,543; qualifying distributions, $25,000.
Limitations: Giving primarily in Boston, MA, and New York, NY.
Directors: Joy Avidan, Harriet Klein, Cindy Schindel.
EIN: 237091307

62425
Athletic Support Trust
36 Bourndale Rd. S.
Manhasset, NY 11030 (516) 365-8406
Contact: Rosemary Mascali, Dir.

Established in 2000 in NY.
Financial data (yr. ended 12/31/01): Assets, $59,568 (M); grants paid, $3,200; expenditures, $5,914; qualifying distributions, $3,200.
Directors: Rosemary Mascali, Paul Mascali.
EIN: 116540791

62426
The Reich Music Foundation, Inc.
66 S. Tyson Ave.
Floral Park, NY 11001

Classified as a private operating foundation in 1998.
Donor(s): Betty Freeman.
Financial data (yr. ended 06/30/01): Assets, $59,528 (M); grants paid, $0; gifts received, $10,000; expenditures, $122,303; qualifying distributions, $0.
Officers: Steve Reich, Pres.; R. Edward Townsend, Secy.; James Kendrik, Treas.
EIN: 237131667

62427
Slanetz Science Foundation, Inc.
107 Ayer Rd.
Locust Valley, NY 11560

Financial data (yr. ended 12/31/00): Assets, $59,525 (M); grants paid, $8,503; gifts received, $18,090; expenditures, $9,262; qualifying distributions, $8,503.
Director: Charles A. Slanels, Jr., M.D.
EIN: 113238116

62428
Van Hornesville Community Corporation
P.O. Box 16
Van Hornesville, NY 13475
Application address: P.O. Box 9, Park Rd., Van Hornsville, NY 13745
Contact: Gerald Snyder, Pres.

Classified as a private operating foundation in 1971.
Donor(s): A.L. and O.B. O'Connor Foundation, Charles J. Young.‡
Financial data (yr. ended 12/31/00): Assets, $58,866 (M); grants paid, $1,978; gifts received, $20,756; expenditures, $30,185; qualifying distributions, $24,601; giving activities include $26,579 for programs.
Limitations: Giving limited to Van Hornesville, NY.
Application information: Application form not required.
Officers: Gerald Snyder, Pres.; Bonnie Harrad, V.P.; Norma Kelley, Secy.; Gladys M. Harris, Treas.
Directors: Curtis Richardson, Ronald Smith, Donna Veeder, Richard Young.
EIN: 156024464
Codes: TN

62429
Hazen B. Hinman, Sr. Foundation, Inc.
530 Henry St.
Rome, NY 13440 (315) 336-5500
Contact: Mark F. Hinman, Treas.

Established in 1988 in NY.
Financial data (yr. ended 12/31/01): Assets, $58,333 (M); grants paid, $44,460; gifts received, $60,000; expenditures, $44,706; qualifying distributions, $44,695.
Limitations: Giving primarily in central NY.
Officers and Directors:* A. Buol Hinman,* Pres.; Mark F. Hinman,* Treas.; David N. Hinman, Kirk B. Hinman.
EIN: 166093005

62430
Veritas Villa Foundation, Inc.
R.R. 2, Box 416A
Kerhonkson, NY 12446

Established in 1986 in NY.
Financial data (yr. ended 12/31/00): Assets, $56,330 (M); grants paid, $425; gifts received, $42,408; expenditures, $33,299; qualifying distributions, $425.
Limitations: Applications not accepted.
Application information: Contributes only to pre-selected organizations.
Officers and Directors:* James S. Cusack,* Chair.; Suzanne B. Cusack, Pres.; John McCormack, Exec. V.P.; Michael Picucci, Exec. V.P.; Steven E. Lewis,* Secy.; Joseph McCauley, Treas.; Casey Cahill, Jack Cusack, Richard Dunn, Ken Lavery, Steven Lewis, Sr., John McGonigle, Joan Sawicki.
EIN: 133388779

62431
Orrin T. Shapiro Memorial Foundation, Inc.
c/o English and Writing Dept.
1100 Crossroads Bldg.
Rochester, NY 14614
Application address: 131 W. Broad St., Rochester, NY 14614
Contact: Richard L. Stear, Dir.

Classified as a private operating foundation in 1988.
Donor(s): S.R. Shapiro, M.R. Shapiro.
Financial data (yr. ended 12/31/01): Assets, $54,213 (M); grants paid, $5,000; gifts received, $250; expenditures, $5,151; qualifying distributions, $5,151.
Limitations: Giving primarily in Rochester, NY.
Application information: Application form required.
Officers and Directors:* M.R. Shapiro,* Pres.; S.R. Shapiro,* Secy.-Treas.; Douglas T. Shapiro, Evan Shapiro, H.A. Shapiro.
EIN: 161317533

62432
Edith M. Knoll and Geneva A. Knoll Scholarship Foundation
P.O. Box 765
Livingston Manor, NY 12758
Application address: c/o Guidance Counselor, Livingston Manor High School, Livingston Manor, NY 12758, tel.: (845) 439-4400

Established in 1991 in NY.
Donor(s): Edith M. Knoll, Geneva A. Knoll.
Financial data (yr. ended 12/31/01): Assets, $54,067 (M); grants paid, $750; expenditures, $1,945; qualifying distributions, $785.
Limitations: Giving limited to residents of the Livingston Manor, NY, area.
Application information: Application form required.
Officers and Trustees:* Debra Lynker,* Pres.; George Will,* Secy.; Patricia Ann Ward,* Treas.; Jean Heaphy.
EIN: 141738013

62433
The Otter Foundation, Inc.
c/o David P. Seaman, Esq.
501 5th Ave., Ste. 1803
New York, NY 10017
Application address: 3 Post Office Sq., Boston, MA 02109; FAX: (212) 661-7952; E-mail: dseaman@fifthavenuelaw.com
Contact: Patrick R. Wilmerding, Tr.

Established in 1998 in NY.
Donor(s): Patrick R. Wilmerding, Elsie Wilmerding, Patrick S. Wilmerding, Michael Wilmerding, Eliza Wilmerding.
Financial data (yr. ended 12/31/01): Assets, $53,536 (M); grants paid, $66,842; expenditures, $73,972; qualifying distributions, $66,842.
Trustees: Eliza Wilmerding, Elsie Wilmerding, Michael Wilmerding, Patrick R. Wilmerding, Patrick S. Wilmerding.
EIN: 133946357

62434
Schor Foundation, Inc.
28 Meleny Rd.
Locust Valley, NY 11560 (516) 676-6924
Contact: Joseph M. Schor, Dir.

Established in 1995.
Donor(s): Joseph M. Schor.
Financial data (yr. ended 12/31/99): Assets, $53,479 (M); grants paid, $115,800; gifts received, $370,218; expenditures, $386,983; qualifying distributions, $379,654; giving activities include $222,083 for programs.
Limitations: Giving primarily in Tallahassee, FL.
Directors: Joseph M. Schor, Laura S. Schor, Robert H. Schor.
EIN: 113286892
Codes: FD2

62435
Clara Grant Walworth Trust
c/o James Snyder
P.O. Box 4367
Saratoga Springs, NY 12866-8025

Financial data (yr. ended 12/31/00): Assets, $52,700 (M); grants paid, $0; expenditures, $2,114; qualifying distributions, $2,114; giving activities include $2,114 for programs.
Trustees: Wallace Allerdice, Constance Carrol, James Snyder.
EIN: 146187633

62436
PCI Foundation
6761 Thompson Rd. N.
Syracuse, NY 13211-2119

Classified as a company-sponsored operating foundation in 2000.
Donor(s): PCI Paper Conversions, Inc.
Financial data (yr. ended 12/31/00): Assets, $52,594 (M); grants paid, $0; gifts received, $52,346; expenditures, $0; qualifying distributions, $0.
Limitations: Applications not accepted.
Application information: Contributes only to pre-selected organizations.
Trustees: Rochette Boylan, Laura McDermott, Giles Withers.
EIN: 161579453

62437
Foundation for the Study of National Civic & International Affairs
c/o Thomas A. Bolan
521 5th Ave., 10th Fl.
New York, NY 10175-1099

Established in 1992 in NY; classified as a private operating foundation in 2000.
Financial data (yr. ended 12/31/01): Assets, $51,982 (M); grants paid, $0; expenditures, $69,740; qualifying distributions, $62,774; giving activities include $62,774 for programs.
Officers: Thomas A. Bolan, Pres.; George Marlin, V.P.; Karen Furey, Secy.-Treas.
EIN: 133643562

62438
Polavarapu Family Foundation, Inc.
c/o Raghavarao Polavarapu
26 Sunset Rd. W.
Albertson, NY 11507-1115

Established in 1999.
Donor(s): Raghavarao Polavarapu.
Financial data (yr. ended 12/31/01): Assets, $51,627 (M); grants paid, $0; gifts received, $45,000; expenditures, $72; qualifying distributions, $0.
Limitations: Applications not accepted.
Officer and Directors:* Raghavarao Polavarapu,* Pres.; Tulasi D. Polavarapu.
EIN: 113462429

62439
John C. Robertson & Flora S. Whitman Memorial Educational Aid Fund
25 Schuyler St.
Belmont, NY 14813
Contact: Wesley J. Serra, Tr.

Financial data (yr. ended 06/30/02): Assets, $50,150 (M); grants paid, $2,150; expenditures, $2,962; qualifying distributions, $2,150.
Limitations: Giving primarily in Cuba, NY.
Application information: Application form not required.
Trustee: Wesley J. Serra.
EIN: 161128745

62440
Alpha Delta Phi Memorial Scholarship Fund
37 Williams St.
Clinton, NY 13323-1705 (315) 853-6673
Contact: William J. Waldron, Dir.

Financial data (yr. ended 05/31/99): Assets, $47,620 (M); grants paid, $4,290; gifts received, $1,250; expenditures, $4,315; qualifying distributions, $4,290.
Limitations: Giving limited to Clinton, NY.
Director: William J. Waldron.
EIN: 156020225

62441
Linda Pinsky Memorial Youth Library Fund, Inc.
c/o Gerald A. Pinsky
515 Green Pl.
Woodmere, NY 11598

Established in 1986 in NY.
Financial data (yr. ended 12/31/01): Assets, $43,267 (M); grants paid, $0; gifts received, $3,199; expenditures, $7,106; qualifying distributions, $4,639; giving activities include $4,656 for programs.
Limitations: Applications not accepted.
Officers: Gerald A. Pinsky, Pres. and Treas.; Barbara Levkovich, V.P.; Morris J. Pinsky, Secy.
EIN: 112836169

62442
Foundation for Mind Research
c/o Lawrence J. Mittenthal
525 Northern Blvd., No. 204
Great Neck, NY 11021

Classified as a private operating foundation in 1973.
Donor(s): Jean Houston Masters, Robert E.L. Masters, Jr.
Financial data (yr. ended 05/31/00): Assets, $42,368 (M); grants paid, $0; gifts received, $93,226; expenditures, $99,743; qualifying distributions, $93,090; giving activities include $39,583 for programs.
Trustees: Jean Houston Masters, Robert E.L. Masters, Jr.
EIN: 136271781

62443
Keren Shevet Levite Foundation, Inc.
1822 E. 23rd St.
Brooklyn, NY 11229-3755
Application address: 571 E. 9th St., Brooklyn, NY 11218-3205, tel.: (718) 851-7227
Contact: Richard Levy Lowinger, Pres.

Established in 1998 in NY.
Donor(s): Richard Levy Lowinger.
Financial data (yr. ended 12/31/99): Assets, $40,593 (M); grants paid, $1,575; gifts received, $11,100; expenditures, $1,625; qualifying distributions, $1,573.
Application information: Application form not required.
Officer: Richard Levy Lowinger, Pres.
Directors: Nechama Lowinger, Robert Mark Lowinger.
EIN: 113353439

62444
The D.G.P. Foundation, Inc.
c/o Deansin G. Parker
21 E. 66th St.
New York, NY 10021

Classified as a private operating foundation in 1994.
Financial data (yr. ended 06/30/00): Assets, $40,478 (M); grants paid, $0; gifts received, $145,400; expenditures, $177,209; qualifying distributions, $164,775; giving activities include $177,209 for programs.
Officers: Deansin G. Parker, Pres.; Robert Sweet, Secy.
Directors: Alex Bekker, Karen Dorros.
EIN: 133751203

62445
DAYA Gopal Amrit Charitable Trust
1 Stagecoach Ln.
Huntington Station, NY 11746
Contact: Subhash C. Bhatia, Tr.

Established in 1999.
Donor(s): Subhash C. Bhatia, Anju Gupta.
Financial data (yr. ended 12/31/99): Assets, $39,918 (M); grants paid, $8,000; gifts received, $47,918; expenditures, $8,000; qualifying distributions, $8,000.
Trustees: Subhash C. Bhatia, Anju Gupta.
EIN: 116498116

62446
Jewish Children's Home of Rochester, New York, Inc., Fund
c/o Harter, Secrest & Emery, LLP
1600 Bausch & Lomb Pl.
Rochester, NY 14604-2711
Contact: Nathan J. Robfogel, Pres.

Donor(s): E. Bronner,‡ Rabbi Seymour Rosenbloom, Beth W. Rosenbloom.
Financial data (yr. ended 12/31/01): Assets, $39,802 (M); grants paid, $6,500; gifts received, $5,341; expenditures, $7,038; qualifying distributions, $6,836.
Limitations: Giving primarily in the Rochester, NY, area.
Officers and Directors:* Nathan J. Robfogel,* Pres.; Theodore Levinson,* V.P. and Treas.; Mordecai Kolko,* V.P.; William J. Greenberg,* Secy.
EIN: 166040408
Codes: GTI

62447
Matthew Barbiere Scholarship Fund, Ltd.
255-01 Northern Blvd.
Little Neck, NY 11363

Established in 1995.
Financial data (yr. ended 11/30/00): Assets, $39,557 (M); grants paid, $2,500; gifts received, $200; expenditures, $2,500; qualifying distributions, $2,500.
Limitations: Giving primarily in New York, NY.
Application information: Unsolicited requests for funds not accepted.
Officers: Charles Barbiere, Pres.; Grace Barbiere, V.P.
EIN: 113313617

62448
Market Street Restoration Corporation
5 E. Market St.
Corning, NY 14830

Classified as a company-sponsored operating foundation in 1974.
Donor(s): Corning Inc.
Financial data (yr. ended 12/31/00): Assets, $38,035 (M); grants paid, $0; gifts received, $225,540; expenditures, $233,761; qualifying distributions, $231,953; giving activities include $211,184 for programs.
Officers and Directors:* Bryan Lanahan, Pres.; Theodore M. Sprague,* V.P.; Lefleur Browne,* Secy.; M. Ann Gosnell,* Treas.; Elise Johnson-Schmidt,* Exec. Dir.; Thomas S. Buechner, Barbara Connors, Thomas P. Dimitroff, Gladys Freeman, Thomas Gardner, James R. Houghton, Robert L. Ivers, Thomas Lando, Julie Mariner, Norman M. Mintz, A. John Peck, Jr., Winifred Peer, and 6 additional directors.
EIN: 161033054

62449
Booth Memorial Nephrology Research and Educational Foundation, Inc.
85 Verdun Ave.
New Rochelle, NY 10804-2216

Established in 1996 in NY.
Financial data (yr. ended 09/30/01): Assets, $37,338 (M); grants paid, $0; expenditures, $8,155; qualifying distributions, $0.
Officer: Chaim Charytan, Pres.
EIN: 112685879

62450
The Kinaja Foundation, Inc.
c/o Judy Cedeno
1 Computer Associates Plz.
Islandia, NY 11749-7000

Established in 1997 in NY.
Donor(s): Charles B. Wang.
Financial data (yr. ended 12/31/00): Assets, $37,085 (M); grants paid, $0; gifts received, $6,865,000; expenditures, $6,917,708; qualifying distributions, $6,913,182; giving activities include $6,913,182 for programs.
Limitations: Applications not accepted.
Application information: Contributes only to pre-selected organizations.
Officers and Directors:* Charles B. Wang,* Pres.; Kimberly Wang,* Exec. V.P.; Elizabeth Santiago,* V.P.; Judith A. Cedeno, Secy.; Nancy Li,* Treas.
EIN: 113375736

62451
The Fish Family Foundation
c/o Hamilton Fish
33 Irving Pl., 8th Fl.
New York, NY 10003

Established in 1998 in NY. Classified as a private operating foundation in 1999.
Donor(s): Hamilton Fish, Julia Fish Ward.
Financial data (yr. ended 12/31/01): Assets, $36,000 (M); grants paid, $0; expenditures, $0; qualifying distributions, $0; giving activities include $36,000 for programs.
Officers and Directors:* Hamilton Fish,* Pres.; Julia Fish Ward,* V.P.; Nicholas Fish,* Secy.; Peter Fish,* Treas.
EIN: 133910335

62452
Museum Views, Ltd.
2 Peter Cooper Rd.
New York, NY 10010

Established in 1993 in NY.
Financial data (yr. ended 07/31/00): Assets, $35,935 (M); grants paid, $0; gifts received, $38,334; expenditures, $31,238; qualifying distributions, $31,227; giving activities include $31,237 for programs.
Officers: Lila A. Sherman, Pres.; David O. Sherman, V.P.; Frederick Walt, Secy.; Roger Sherman, Treas.
EIN: 133680271

62453
Shuvi Nafshi Foundation, Inc.
c/o Willoughby's
136 W. 32nd St.
New York, NY 10001

Established in 1999 in NY.
Financial data (yr. ended 12/31/99): Assets, $35,848 (M); grants paid, $289,000; gifts received, $324,286; expenditures, $289,474; qualifying distributions, $289,474.
Limitations: Applications not accepted.
Application information: Contributes only to pre-selected organizations.
Directors: Judah Cattan, Haim Dabah, Isaac Douek, Joseph Douek.
EIN: 133998507
Codes: FD

62454
Pettengill Family Foundation
c/o Schwartz & Co., LLP
2580 Sunrise Hwy.
Bellmore, NY 11710-3608
Contact: Ronald Pettengill, Pres.

Established in 1999 in NY.
Donor(s): Ron Pettengill.
Financial data (yr. ended 12/31/00): Assets, $35,808 (M); grants paid, $204,500; expenditures, $204,500; qualifying distributions, $204,492.
Application information: Application form not required.
Officers: Ronald Pettengill, Pres. and Treas.; Maura Pettengill, V.P. and Secy.
Director: Michael J. Schwartz.
EIN: 113522130
Codes: FD2

62455
Arm Foundation
c/o Armin Reisman
1874 48th St.
Brooklyn, NY 11204-1239

Donor(s): Armin Reisman.
Financial data (yr. ended 03/31/00): Assets, $35,653 (M); grants paid, $5,000; gifts received, $595; expenditures, $5,655; qualifying distributions, $5,655.
Limitations: Applications not accepted.
Application information: Contributes only to pre-selected organizations.
Trustee: Armin Reisman.
EIN: 113211804

62456
Pandya Jain Family Foundation Charitable Trust
73 Beebe St.
Staten Island, NY 10301

Established in 1998.
Financial data (yr. ended 12/31/99): Assets, $35,289 (M); grants paid, $2,501; gifts received, $39,456; expenditures, $9,891; qualifying distributions, $14,780.
Limitations: Applications not accepted.
Application information: Contributes only to pre-selected organizations.
Directors: Asha Pandya, Mahendra Pandya, Rajiv Pandya, Sanjay Pandya.
EIN: 133866937

62457
Ecumenical Community of Taize
413 W. 48th St.
New York, NY 10036

Classified as a private operating foundation in 1984.
Donor(s): Pedro Foz.
Financial data (yr. ended 12/31/01): Assets, $34,171 (M); grants paid, $1; gifts received, $2,971; expenditures, $6,726; qualifying distributions, $1.
Directors: John Castaldi, Hector DeJesus, Pedro Foz.
EIN: 133027661

62458
The Miller Family Foundation
56 Lyndon Rd.
Fayetteville, NY 13066

Established in 2000 in NY.
Donor(s): Hyman Miller.
Financial data (yr. ended 11/30/01): Assets, $32,957 (M); grants paid, $16,921; gifts received, $38,135; expenditures, $16,921; qualifying distributions, $16,921.

Limitations: Applications not accepted. Giving primarily in Syracuse, NY.
Application information: Contributes only to pre-selected organizations.
Trustee: Hyman Miller.
EIN: 161598372

62459
The Gang of '63 Foundation, Inc.
c/o John G. Roche
210 E. 39th St.
New York, NY 10016

Established in 2000 in NY.
Donor(s): Frederick H. Joseph, James R. Utaski, John W. Luther, Mrs. John W. Luther, Don E. Ackerman, C. Tillinghast, Mrs. C. Tillinghast, David Johnson, Charles D. Ellis, Fred O'Such, Joanne O'Such, W. Connell, Mrs. W. Connell, HI 5 Fund.
Financial data (yr. ended 07/31/01): Assets, $31,975 (M); grants paid, $0; gifts received, $50,000; expenditures, $18,510; qualifying distributions, $18,510.
Limitations: Applications not accepted.
Application information: Contributes only to pre-selected organizations.
Officers: Frederick H. Joseph, Chair.; Charles D. Ellis, Pres.; John G. Roche, V.P.; Otto L. Spaeth, Jr., Secy.; Howard S. Stein, Treas.
EIN: 134147092

62460
Al-Khalidi Foundation
P.O. Box 247
Vestal, NY 13850-0247
Contact: Nancy Al-Khalidi, Tr.

Established in 1995 in NY.
Financial data (yr. ended 12/31/00): Assets, $31,086 (L); grants paid, $3,000; expenditures, $3,000; qualifying distributions, $3,000.
Officer and Trustee:* Farouq Al-Khalidi,* Pres.
EIN: 161472768

62461
Johnnie L. Cochran, Jr. Art Fund, Inc.
99 Hudson St.
New York, NY 10013
Contact: Johnnie Cochran, Jr.

Established in 1997 in NY.
Donor(s): Johnnie L. Cochran.
Financial data (yr. ended 09/30/00): Assets, $30,883 (M); grants paid, $5,980; gifts received, $18,795; expenditures, $5,980; qualifying distributions, $5,980.
Limitations: Giving primarily in NY.
Application information: Awards are by nomination only.
Officers: Johnnie L. Cochran, Jr., Chair.; Debra Van Der Burg Spencer, Pres.
Trustees: Clarence Avant, Earl G. Graves, Carolyn Jones.
EIN: 133977614

62462
American Friends of Yeshiva Eretz Hatzvi Trust
c/o Abe Friedman
1555 54th St.
Brooklyn, NY 11216

Established in 1998.
Donor(s): Alexander & Charlotte Herman Foundation, Debby Reoenwurtzel, Naomi Wiener, Miriam Widawsky.
Financial data (yr. ended 12/31/01): Assets, $30,704 (M); grants paid, $28,000; gifts received, $10,100; expenditures, $28,080; qualifying distributions, $28,000.
Limitations: Applications not accepted.
Application information: Contributes only to pre-selected organizations.
Trustee: Debby Reoenwurtzel.
EIN: 116422654

62463
William R. McNeiece III Foundation
River Rd.
P.O. Box 356
Hamilton, NY 13346-0356
Contact: William R. McNeiece III, Chair.

Established in 1988 in NY.
Donor(s): William R. McNeiece III.
Financial data (yr. ended 12/31/01): Assets, $30,640 (M); grants paid, $4,000; gifts received, $9,000; expenditures, $4,213; qualifying distributions, $4,211.
Limitations: Giving limited to residents of Hamilton, NY.
Trustees: John C. Bowen, John Cossitt, Thomas J. Gilpatrick, Harry L. Hood, James E. Hughes, Robert Kuiper, Bernard Lawler, William R. McNeiece III, William R. McNeiece IV.
EIN: 222914681

62464
John, Lucile, Richard Olson Foundation, Inc.
c/o Richard Olson
1495 Journey's End Rd.
Croton-on-Hudson, NY 10520

Established in 1998.
Donor(s): Richard Olson.
Financial data (yr. ended 11/30/00): Assets, $30,471 (M); grants paid, $10,000; expenditures, $14,012; qualifying distributions, $11,700.
Limitations: Applications not accepted.
Application information: Contributes only to pre-selected organizations.
Directors: Richard Olson, Tod Olson.
EIN: 134039046

62465
Dr. Karen E. Burke Research Foundation, Inc.
c/o Chaifetz & Schreiber, PC
21 Harbor Park Dr. N.
Port Washington, NY 11050

Established in 1995 in NY.
Donor(s): Karen E. Burke, Peter Goulandris.
Financial data (yr. ended 12/31/01): Assets, $30,360 (M); grants paid, $62,000; gifts received, $15,000; expenditures, $64,850; qualifying distributions, $64,850.
Limitations: Applications not accepted. Giving primarily in New York, NY.
Application information: Contributes only to pre-selected organizations.
Officers: Karen E. Burke, Pres.; Jack Albert, Treas.
Trustee: E. Lee Cain.
EIN: 133699279

62466
The Tzedokah V'Chesed Foundation
9 Eastview Rd.
Monsey, NY 10952

Established in 1989 in NY.
Donor(s): Israel Herskowitz.
Financial data (yr. ended 12/31/01): Assets, $29,882 (M); grants paid, $581,340; gifts received, $590,034; expenditures, $581,355; qualifying distributions, $581,340.
Limitations: Applications not accepted. Giving limited to Monsey, NY.
Application information: Contributes only to pre-selected organizations.
Trustees: Eliezer Herskowitz, Israel Herskowitz, Judith Herskowitz.
EIN: 136916775

Codes: FD

62467
Frank and Katherine Martucci Endowment for the Arts
33 Mathiessen Park
Irvington, NY 10533

Established in 1991 in NY.
Donor(s): Frank Martucci, Katherine Martucci.
Financial data (yr. ended 12/31/00): Assets, $29,567 (M); grants paid, $0; gifts received, $28,215; expenditures, $65,470; qualifying distributions, $59,336; giving activities include $62,281 for programs.
Trustees: Frank Martucci, Katherine Martucci, Michael Quick.
EIN: 136959593

62468
Bernard I. Taub Foundation, Inc.
c/o Muriel T. Glantzman
275 Central Park W.
New York, NY 10024

Financial data (yr. ended 06/30/99): Assets, $28,770 (M); grants paid, $1,575; expenditures, $3,725; qualifying distributions, $1,575.
Limitations: Applications not accepted. Giving primarily in New York, NY.
Application information: Contributes only to pre-selected organizations.
Officers and Trustees:* Muriel T. Glantzman,* Pres.; Doris Gross,* Secy.-Treas.
EIN: 237401879

62469
The Lalit Foundation, Inc.
77 Cherry Hill Rd.
Accord, NY 12404

Established in 1998 in NY.
Donor(s): Steven Gorn, Barbara Bash.
Financial data (yr. ended 02/28/01): Assets, $28,632 (M); grants paid, $17,750; expenditures, $18,680; qualifying distributions, $17,750.
Limitations: Applications not accepted.
Application information: Contributes only to pre-selected organizations.
Officers: Steven Gorn, Pres.; Barbara Bash, Secy.
Director: Gladys Harburger.
EIN: 141805104

62470
Foundation for Developmental Disabilities, Inc.
1050 Forest Hill Rd.
Staten Island, NY 10314
Application address: 141 Nixon Ave., Staten Island, NY 10304
Contact: Henry Wisniewski

Established in 1999 in NY.
Financial data (yr. ended 12/31/99): Assets, $28,155 (M); grants paid, $13,000; gifts received, $23,900; expenditures, $51,540; qualifying distributions, $44,976; giving activities include $35,967 for programs.
Officers: Cecelia McCarton, M.D., Pres.; Richard D. Kuhn, Secy.
Trustees: Howard B. Gold, Michael Goldfarb, Regina S. Peruggi, Marlene Springer, Susan W. Williams.
EIN: 133638763

62471
Dottie Clark Foundation
c/o Maxine Perkins
P.O. Box 258
Sackets Harbor, NY 13685-0258

Financial data (yr. ended 08/31/00): Assets, $28,053 (M); grants paid, $750; expenditures, $1,596; qualifying distributions, $1,596.
Limitations: Applications not accepted.
Application information: Contributes only to pre-selected organizations.
Trustee: Maxine Perkins.
EIN: 161471077

62472
The CEJJES Institute, Inc.
5 Cooper Morris Dr.
Pomona, NY 10970
Application address: 1003 Rte. 45, Pomona, NY 10970; tel.: (845) 362-8610
Contact: Heather Carty Ward, Exec. Dir.

Established in 2000 in NY.
Donor(s): Edmund W. Gordon, Susan G. Gordon.
Financial data (yr. ended 12/31/00): Assets, $27,792 (M); grants paid, $3,440; gifts received, $93,994; expenditures, $85,857; qualifying distributions, $82,092.
Limitations: Giving limited to residents of Spring Valley, NY.
Officers: Jessica Gordon-Nembhard, Pres.; Johanna Gordon-McNeil, Secy.; Susan G. Gordon, Treas.; Heather Carty Ward, Exec. Dir.
Directors: Christopher W. Gordon, Edmund T. Gordon, Edmund W. Gordon.
EIN: 134102065

62473
2wice Arts Foundation, Inc.
(Formerly Dance Ink, Inc.)
Columbus Cir. Sta.
P.O. Box 20719
New York, NY 10023

Classified as a private operating foundation.
Donor(s): Patricia Tarr.
Financial data (yr. ended 07/31/00): Assets, $26,846 (M); grants paid, $29,250; gifts received, $183,000; expenditures, $271,504; qualifying distributions, $236,926; giving activities include $207,676 for programs.
Limitations: Giving limited to NY.
Officer and Trustees:* Patricia Tarr,* Pres.; Hartley Goldstein, Barbara Washkowitz.
EIN: 133536258

62474
The Lifwynn Foundation, Inc.
173 E. 74th St., Apt. 1A
New York, NY 10021

Established in 1927.
Donor(s): Hans Syz,‡ Laurance S. Rockefeller.
Financial data (yr. ended 09/30/01): Assets, $26,493 (M); grants paid, $0; gifts received, $8,689; expenditures, $10,835; qualifying distributions, $0.
Officers: Lloyd Gilden, Pres.; Maureen Cotter, Secy.-Treas.
Directors: Thomas Jobe, Mary Alice Roche, Steve Rosen, John R. Wikse, Philip Woollcott.
EIN: 060664185

62475
Salarc Foundation, Inc.
167 E. 61st St., Ste. 37C
New York, NY 10021
Contact: Joseph D. Cooper, Pres.

Established in 1999.

Financial data (yr. ended 12/31/00): Assets, $26,307 (M); grants paid, $41,244; gifts received, $29,014; expenditures, $41,258; qualifying distributions, $41,244.
Officers: Joseph D. Cooper, Pres.; Sally Cooper, V.P.; Lauren Merle Cooper, Secy.; Marc Seth Cooper, Treas.
EIN: 133981374

62476
Margaret Calkins Charitable Foundation
10 W. 47th St., Ste. 10D
New York, NY 10023

Established in 1999 in NY.
Donor(s): Margaret Calkins.
Financial data (yr. ended 05/31/00): Assets, $26,142 (M); grants paid, $1,850; gifts received, $28,500; expenditures, $2,006; qualifying distributions, $2,005.
Limitations: Applications not accepted.
Application information: Contributes only to pre-selected organizations.
Trustees: Margaret Calkins, Thomas Calkins, Donna Leon.
EIN: 134079403

62477
The Living Theater, Inc.
800 West End Ave., No. 5A
New York, NY 10025

Donor(s): National Endowment for the Arts, New York State Council for the Arts, North Star Fund.
Financial data (yr. ended 06/30/01): Assets, $25,698 (M); grants paid, $0; gifts received, $15,345; expenditures, $111,517; qualifying distributions, $0.
Officers and Directors:* Thomas S. Walker,* V.P.; Rain House,* Secy.; Mark Hall Amitin,* Exec. Dir.; Hanon Reznikov,* Exec. Dir.; Marsha Levy-Warren, Olga Berde Mahl, Judith Malina, Eleanor Munro, Martin Sheen, Michael Smith.
EIN: 133255361

62478
Arno Breker Society, Inc.
10545 Main St.
Clarence, NY 14031

Classified as a private operating foundation in 1983.
Financial data (yr. ended 12/31/00): Assets, $25,514 (M); grants paid, $0; gifts received, $800; expenditures, $54; qualifying distributions, $0.
Officers: B. John Zavrel, Pres. and Treas.; Ron C. Voth, V.P.; Bohuslav Zavrel, Secy.
EIN: 222448295

62479
Mud Creek Farm Center for Equine Assisted Therapy, Inc.
5480 Hunt Rd.
Vernon Center, NY 13477

Established in 1999 in NY.
Donor(s): Alice Root.
Financial data (yr. ended 12/31/00): Assets, $24,706 (M); grants paid, $0; gifts received, $31,227; expenditures, $36,518; qualifying distributions, $40,368; giving activities include $35,321 for programs.
Officer: Alice Root, Chair.
EIN: 161568243

62480
The Robert J. & Muriel Kossoy Memorial Scholarship Fund
25 Perrydale Ct.
Babylon, NY 11702

Established in 1988 in NY.

Donor(s): Marjorie Fuhrmann.
Financial data (yr. ended 09/30/01): Assets, $24,408 (M); grants paid, $1,000; gifts received, $160; expenditures, $1,160; qualifying distributions, $1,260.
Limitations: Applications not accepted. Giving limited to residents of the East Patchogue, NY, area.
Officer: Marjorie Fuhrmann, Admin.
EIN: 112941962

62481
The Skeist Family Charitable Trust
158 Sagamore Dr.
Plainview, NY 11803

Established in 2000 in NY.
Donor(s): Dytro Corp.
Financial data (yr. ended 12/31/01): Assets, $24,253 (L); grants paid, $124,600; gifts received, $100,000; expenditures, $124,566; qualifying distributions, $124,542.
Trustee: Marion Sheist.
EIN: 116518381
Codes: FD2

62482
Robin Skiff Pittard Memorial Foundation
c/o David C. Pittard
10 Heritage Woods
Skaneateles, NY 13152

Established in 1991.
Financial data (yr. ended 12/31/01): Assets, $23,929 (M); grants paid, $3,225; gifts received, $2,350; expenditures, $3,387; qualifying distributions, $3,387.
Limitations: Applications not accepted. Giving limited to NY.
Application information: Contributes only to pre-selected organizations.
Officers: David Pittard, Pres.; Joan Skiff, V.P.; Marilyn Fleckenstein, Secy.; Patricia Curtis, Treas.
Directors: Deborah Brennan, Sandra Orwig, Marshall Skiff.
EIN: 161390789

62483
The Sephardic Scholarship and Welfare Foundation, Inc.
240 W. 40th St., 3rd Fl.
New York, NY 10018 (212) 391-0170
Contact: Ralph Sitt, Pres.

Established in 1997 in NY.
Donor(s): Ralph Sitt.
Financial data (yr. ended 12/31/01): Assets, $23,693 (M); grants paid, $0; expenditures, $19; qualifying distributions, $0.
Limitations: Giving primarily in NJ and NY.
Application information: Application form required.
Officers: Ralph Sitt, Pres.; Shelly Rindner, Secy.-Treas.
EIN: 133942047

62484
Kiss Kares Fund, Inc.
395 Hudson St., 7th Fl.
New York, NY 10014

Established in 1995 in NY.
Financial data (yr. ended 12/31/99): Assets, $23,661 (M); grants paid, $28,311; expenditures, $29,757; qualifying distributions, $28,311.
Limitations: Giving limited to New York, NY.
Application information: Application form not required.
Officers: Frank Lemmiti, Pres.; Judith Ellis, Secy.; Robert Finlem, Treas.
EIN: 061424235

62485
Joseph N. Canigiani Charitable Foundation
113 Main St.
Port Washington, NY 11050

Established in 2001 in NY.
Donor(s): Joseph N. Canigiani.
Financial data (yr. ended 12/31/01): Assets, $23,395 (M); grants paid, $4,937; gifts received, $28,626; expenditures, $5,055; qualifying distributions, $5,055.
Directors: Joseph N. Canigiani, Mary Canigiani, Rosemarie Canigiani.
EIN: 113612047

62486
Christopher David Lyons Scholarship Fund
R.D. 2
South New Berlin, NY 13843-9802
(607) 334-5073
Contact: William Lyons, Treas.

Financial data (yr. ended 12/31/99): Assets, $23,006 (M); grants paid, $1,600; expenditures, $1,638; qualifying distributions, $1,600.
Limitations: Giving primarily in South New Berlin, NY.
Application information: Application form required.
Officers: Alex Hendrickson, Treas.; William Hendrickson, Treas.; William Lyons, Treas.
EIN: 222478948

62487
Marian & Leon Finkle Foundation, Inc.
c/o Finkle Dist., Inc.
39 S. Hollywood Ave.
Gloversville, NY 12078-4112

Classified as a company-sponsored operating foundation.
Donor(s): Finkle Distributors, Inc.
Financial data (yr. ended 12/31/00): Assets, $22,917 (M); grants paid, $24,010; gifts received, $29,779; expenditures, $24,071; qualifying distributions, $24,010.
Limitations: Applications not accepted. Giving primarily in Gloversville, NY.
Application information: Contributes only to pre-selected organizations.
Officers and Directors:* Maria Finkle,* Pres.; Dan Finkle,* V.P.; Linda Finkle,* Secy.; Leon Finkle,* Treas.
EIN: 222582643

62488
Athena Foundation, Inc.
P.O. Box 2128
Long Island City, NY 11102
Application address: P.O. Box 6259, Long Island City, NY 11106
Contact: Anita Contini, Dir.

Classified as a private operating foundation in 1983.
Donor(s): Mark Di Suvero.
Financial data (yr. ended 12/31/00): Assets, $22,629 (M); grants paid, $4,500; gifts received, $1,000; expenditures, $4,558; qualifying distributions, $4,535.
Limitations: Giving primarily in New York, NY.
Officer and Directors:* Ivana Mestrovic,* Mgr.; Anita Contini, Ruth Cummings-Sorenson, Susan Freedman, Barbara Haskell.
EIN: 060974154

62489
Eida Family Foundation, Inc.
338 Ave. O
Brooklyn, NY 11230
Contact: Albert Eida, Tr.

Established in 2000 in NY.
Donor(s): Albert Eida.
Financial data (yr. ended 12/31/01): Assets, $22,230 (M); grants paid, $70,913; gifts received, $86,112; expenditures, $71,101; qualifying distributions, $70,913.
Trustees: Albert Eida, Maurice Eida, Rosetta Eida.
EIN: 113521634

62490
Friends of the Congressional Glaucoma Caucus Foundation, Inc.
150-12 14th Ave., Ste. 102
Whitestone, NY 11357

Established as a company-sponsored operating foundation in 2000 in NY.
Donor(s): Pharmacia & Upjohn Co.
Financial data (yr. ended 12/31/00): Assets, $21,777 (M); grants paid, $0; gifts received, $115,000; expenditures, $111,208; qualifying distributions, $111,208; giving activities include $111,209 for programs.
Limitations: Applications not accepted.
Application information: Contributes only to pre-selected organizations.
Officers: Anthony M. Pisacano, M.D., Chair.; S.J. "Bud" Grant, C.E.O.; Randall D. Bloomfield, M.D., Secy.; Robert J. Bishop, Treas.
EIN: 134098767

62491
International Science Foundation
400 W. 59th St.
New York, NY 10019 (212) 576-8451
FAX: (212) 576-8457; E-mail: isf@phri.NYU.edu

Established in 1992 in NY; classified as a private operating foundation in 1994.
Donor(s): George Soros, Soros Humanitarian Foundation.
Financial data (yr. ended 12/31/00): Assets, $21,617 (M); grants paid, $102,960; expenditures, $242,108; qualifying distributions, $291,276; giving activities include $205,094 for programs.
Limitations: Applications not accepted. Giving limited to the former Soviet Union.
Application information: Contributes only to pre-selected organizations.
Officer: Leonard Benardo, Acting Exec. Dir.
Trustees: John Allen, George Soros.
EIN: 137008871
Codes: FD2

62492
AYN Foundation
c/o Siegel, Sacks & Co., PC
630 3rd Ave.
New York, NY 10017

Established in 1992 in NY.
Donor(s): Philippa de Menil Friedrich.
Financial data (yr. ended 06/30/02): Assets, $21,544 (M); grants paid, $0; gifts received, $20,000; expenditures, $14,759; qualifying distributions, $0.
Officers: Heiner Friedrich, Pres.; Fariha Friedrich, Secy.
EIN: 133692868

62493
Belgian Society of Benevolence
2521 Palisade Ave.
Riverdale, NY 10463-6137
Contact: Eric R. Verhulst, Pres.

Classified as a private operating foundation in 1986 in NY.
Financial data (yr. ended 12/31/01): Assets, $21,283 (M); grants paid, $630; gifts received, $644; expenditures, $724; qualifying distributions, $622.
Limitations: Giving on a national basis.
Officers: Eric R. Verhulst, Pres. and Secy.; Etienne de Ville, V.P. and Treas.
EIN: 136618881

62494
Schatzberg Pilot Officer Memorial Fund of Aroana Lodge 246 F. & A.M.
373 92nd St., Apt. A44
Brooklyn, NY 11209-6327 (718) 745-5589
Contact: Stephen A. Kastner, Treas.

Financial data (yr. ended 12/31/01): Assets, $21,157 (M); grants paid, $750; gifts received, $2,376; expenditures, $2,323; qualifying distributions, $2,158.
Officers: Marvin Kerr, Pres.; Arthur Klansky, V.P.; Stephen A. Kastner, Treas.
EIN: 136167247

62495
Zicherman Family Foundation
1056 5th Ave., Ste. 17A
New York, NY 10128

Established in 2000 in NY.
Donor(s): Joseph Zicherman.
Financial data (yr. ended 12/31/00): Assets, $21,088 (M); grants paid, $96,240; gifts received, $125,000; expenditures, $96,304; qualifying distributions, $96,240.
Limitations: Applications not accepted. Giving primarily in NY.
Application information: Contributes only to pre-selected organizations.
Officers: Joseph Zicherman, Pres. and Treas.; Rachel Bugner, V.P.; Stuart Zicherman, V.P.; Catherine Pierot Zicherman, Secy.
EIN: 134106538
Codes: FD2

62496
The Irving and Elaine Kirsch Foundation
c/o Isadore Cassuto
2 Tower Pl.
Albany, NY 12203

Established in 1986.
Donor(s): Irving Kirsch.
Financial data (yr. ended 09/30/99): Assets, $20,775 (M); grants paid, $1,100; expenditures, $1,138; qualifying distributions, $1,095.
Limitations: Applications not accepted. Giving primarily in Albany, NY.
Application information: Contributes only to pre-selected organizations.
Officers: Irving Kirsch, Pres.; Elaine Kirsch, Secy.-Treas.
EIN: 133261307

62497
Lee Kim-Mie Education Foundation
45 Bayard St., 3rd Fl.
New York, NY 10013 (212) 684-9031
Contact: David Lee, Secy.

Established in 1992 in NY.

62497—NEW YORK

Financial data (yr. ended 06/30/01): Assets, $20,046 (M); grants paid, $4,900; expenditures, $7,668; qualifying distributions, $7,664.
Limitations: Giving limited to residents of CT, NJ, and NY.
Application information: Application form required.
Officers: Jimmy Lee, Pres.; David Lee, Secy.; Diana L. Ngai, Treas.
Directors: Johnny Lee, Kam Yee Lee.
EIN: 133702948

62498
Stephanie S. Kata Foundation
4 Andrea Dr., Ste. 4C
Vestal, NY 13850

Established in 1999 in NY.
Donor(s): Stephanie Kata.
Financial data (yr. ended 12/31/00): Assets, $19,729 (M); grants paid, $500; gifts received, $10,000; expenditures, $500; qualifying distributions, $500.
Limitations: Applications not accepted.
Application information: Contributes only to pre-selected organizations.
Trustee: Stephanie S. Kata.
EIN: 166492296

62499
World Press Photo USA Foundation, Inc.
245 Park Ave.
New York, NY 10167

Financial data (yr. ended 12/31/01): Assets, $19,078 (M); grants paid, $0; gifts received, $6,211; expenditures, $3,177; qualifying distributions, $3,177; giving activities include $3,177 for programs.
Officer and Directors:* Hans F. Breukhoven,* Secy.-Treas.; Harold Buell, Arnold Drapkin, Odette Fodor-Gernaert, Randy Miller, Robert Y. Pledge, Hugo Steensma.
EIN: 133464919

62500
Musser Foundation for the Performing Arts, Inc.
95 Gleneida Ave.
Carmel, NY 10512
Contact: Charles P. Stein, Treas.

Established in 1984 in CT. Classified an operating foundation as of 1987.
Donor(s): Tharon Musser.
Financial data (yr. ended 06/30/01): Assets, $18,155 (M); grants paid, $5,000; expenditures, $5,000; qualifying distributions, $5,000.
Limitations: Giving primarily in New York, NY.
Application information: Application form required.
Officers: Tharon Musser, Pres.; Marilyn Rennegal, Secy.; Charles P. Stein, Treas.
EIN: 042795347

62501
Center for the Holographic Arts, Inc.
45-10 Court Sq.
Long Island City, NY 11101

Financial data (yr. ended 04/30/01): Assets, $18,128 (M); grants paid, $9,295; gifts received, $120,000; expenditures, $125,880; qualifying distributions, $125,880; giving activities include $116,585 for programs.
Limitations: Giving on a national and international basis.
Directors: Jesse B. Cohen, Anna Maria Nicholson, Tim Schmidt, Daniel Schweitzer, John Webster.
EIN: 113433858

62502
Laura Pawel Dance Company, Inc.
15 W. 72nd St.
New York, NY 10023 (212) 873-9073

Donor(s): Michael Pawel, Laura Pawel.
Financial data (yr. ended 12/31/00): Assets, $18,051 (M); grants paid, $0; gifts received, $18,000; expenditures, $4,637; qualifying distributions, $4,637; giving activities include $4,637 for programs.
Officers: Laura C. Pawel, Pres.; Michael Pawel, Secy.-Treas.
Director: Gregory Gorsynski.
EIN: 132874843

62503
Samuel & Annna Rottenstein Charitable Trust
1833 49th St.
Brooklyn, NY 11204
Contact: Samuel Rottenstein, Tr.

Established in 1998 in NY.
Donor(s): Samuel Rottenstein, Anna Rottenstein.
Financial data (yr. ended 12/31/01): Assets, $17,507 (M); grants paid, $41,777; gifts received, $40,000; expenditures, $43,086; qualifying distributions, $41,777.
Trustees: Annna Rottenstein, Samuel Rottenstein.
EIN: 116466204

62504
Michael Bendix Sutton Foundation
c/o Cadwalder, Wickersman, & Taft
300 Martine Ave., Ste. 9L
White Plains, NY 10601-3459

Classified as a private operating foundation in 1997.
Donor(s): Marion Sutton.
Financial data (yr. ended 12/31/01): Assets, $17,396 (M); grants paid, $4,975; expenditures, $5,340; qualifying distributions, $0.
Limitations: Giving on a national basis.
Trustees: Jill Kremer, Marion B. Sutton, Jun Yoshino.
EIN: 137115396

62505
Artzt Family Charitable Foundation
c/o RKLL & Co.
1700 Jericho Tpke.
New Hyde Park, NY 11040

Established in 1999 in NY.
Donor(s): Alice Artzt, Russell Artzt.
Financial data (yr. ended 12/31/01): Assets, $17,395 (M); grants paid, $680,021; gifts received, $697,382; expenditures, $680,021; qualifying distributions, $680,021.
Limitations: Giving primarily in NY.
Trustees: Alice Artzt, Gregory Artzt, Julie Artzt, Michele Uzbay.
EIN: 116503874
Codes: FD

62506
Law Enforcement Assistance Foundation
7 Gracie Sq.
New York, NY 10028

Established in 1977 in NY.
Donor(s): Ordway P. Burden.
Financial data (yr. ended 12/31/00): Assets, $16,930 (M); grants paid, $0; gifts received, $8,976; expenditures, $8,444; qualifying distributions, $0.
Officers and Directors:* Ordway P. Burden,* Pres.; Malcolm N. McElroy,* V.P.; Karen Hochman,* Secy.; Jefferson C. Tarr,* Treas.; Edward P.H. Burden, Jean E. Burden, Edward S. Hochman, Brian Mulheren, Alexander Rossolino, Ralph B. Valentine.
EIN: 132893026

62507
Joseph R. Capra Welding Scholarship Fund
Greene 2 BOCES OAOC, Box 57
Milford, NY 13807
Contact: Gary Ross Turits

Classified as a private operating foundation in 1983.
Financial data (yr. ended 06/30/01): Assets, $16,839 (M); grants paid, $0; gifts received, $215; expenditures, $362; qualifying distributions, $0.
Limitations: Giving limited to residents of NY.
Application information: Application form not required.
Trustees: Joseph D. Booan, Jr., Edward Bordinger.
EIN: 113067018

62508
Roy Lichtenstein Foundation
745 Washington St.
New York, NY 10014-2042

Established in 1998 in NY.
Donor(s): Dorothy Lichtenstein.
Financial data (yr. ended 12/31/99): Assets, $16,551 (M); grants paid, $11,040; gifts received, $149,500; expenditures, $180,536; qualifying distributions, $176,514.
Limitations: Applications not accepted.
Application information: Contributes only to pre-selected organizations.
Officers: Dorothy Lichtenstein, Pres.; David Lichtenstein, V.P.; Mitchell Lichtenstein, V.P.; Kenneth L. Goldglit, Treas.; William John Cowart, Exec. Dir.
Director: Cassandra Lozano.
EIN: 911898350

62509
A Child's Voice, Inc.
c/o Albert Kalter, PC
225 Broadway, Ste. 1806
New York, NY 10007

Established in 1999 in NY.
Financial data (yr. ended 12/31/01): Assets, $16,128 (M); grants paid, $0; gifts received, $80,000; expenditures, $77,059; qualifying distributions, $0.
Limitations: Applications not accepted.
Application information: Contributes only to pre-selected organizations.
Officers and Directors:* Lawrence Newman,* Chair.; Karen Newman,* Pres.; Albert Kalter, Secy.-Treas.
EIN: 134074036

62510
The Friends of Rinri Kenkyusho of New York, Inc.
25 W. 43rd St., Ste. 1016
New York, NY 10036

Established in 2000 in NY.
Donor(s): Rinri Kenkyusho.
Financial data (yr. ended 08/31/01): Assets, $15,837 (M); grants paid, $0; gifts received, $75,931; expenditures, $66,094; qualifying distributions, $60,024; giving activities include $66,094 for programs.
Limitations: Applications not accepted.
Application information: Contributes only to pre-selected organizations.
Officers: Toshiaki Maruyana, Pres.; Emiko A. Lindsay, Secy.
EIN: 134165975

62511
The Foundation for Research in Cardiac Surgery and Cardiovascular Biology, Inc.
c/o Dr. Gregory Baumann
520 First Ave., CME Bldg., Ste. 317
New York, NY 10016

Established in 1993 in NY.
Donor(s): Keating Crawford Foundation, Inc.
Financial data (yr. ended 06/30/01): Assets, $15,544 (M); grants paid, $0; gifts received, $49,000; expenditures, $110,199; qualifying distributions, $108,071; giving activities include $108,079 for programs.
Limitations: Applications not accepted.
Application information: Contributes only to pre-selected organizations.
Directors: Gregory Baumann, M.D., Stephen B. Colvin, M.D., Aubrey Galloway, M.D.
EIN: 133730228

62512
Lawrence R. Ellis, Jr. Foundation
18 Garfield St.
Auburn, NY 13021-2218 (800) 877-8688
Contact: Lawrence R. Ellis III, Tr.

Established in 1988 in NY.
Donor(s): Evelyn A. Walter.‡
Financial data (yr. ended 12/31/99): Assets, $15,168 (M); grants paid, $1,500; gifts received, $13,095; expenditures, $3,002; qualifying distributions, $2,894.
Limitations: Giving primarily in Auburn, NY.
Application information: Application form required.
Trustees: Lawrence R. Ellis III, Lillian D. Ellis, William C. Ellis, Christine E. Kopakas.
EIN: 222945489

62513
Fantasy Fountain Fund, Inc.
c/o Sculpture Studio
1047 Amsterdam Ave.
New York, NY 10025

Established in 1984 in NY.
Donor(s): Barbara C. Newington, Pfundt Foundation.
Financial data (yr. ended 10/31/01): Assets, $15,050 (M); grants paid, $20,920; gifts received, $122,000; expenditures, $127,691; qualifying distributions, $125,729.
Application information: Recipients are recommended by art educational instructors. Application form not required.
Officer and Trustees:* Greg A. Wyatt,* Pres.; Aldon James, John James, Steven Leitner, Barbara C. Newington, Norman J. Oake, C. Scott Vanderhoef.
EIN: 133356903

62514
The Fried Family Charitable Foundation
1527 50th St.
Brooklyn, NY 11219

Financial data (yr. ended 11/30/00): Assets, $14,939 (M); grants paid, $5,605; gifts received, $8,000; expenditures, $5,679; qualifying distributions, $5,679.
Trustees: Alexander Fried, Bernhard Fried, Harry Fried, Rose Fried, Wolf Fried.
EIN: 113446321

62515
Ladenburg Foundation
c/o Yohalem Gillman & Co. LLP
477 Madison Ave.
New York, NY 10022

Established in 2001 in NY.
Donor(s): Claudia Bussmann, Martin Bussmann, Margaret Bussmann, Richard Bussmann, Courtney Bussman.
Financial data (yr. ended 12/31/01): Assets, $14,916 (M); grants paid, $300,000; gifts received, $315,000; expenditures, $300,486; qualifying distributions, $300,486.
Limitations: Applications not accepted.
Application information: Contributes only to pre-selected organizations.
Officers and Directors:* Claudia Bussmann,* Chair.; Martin Bussmann,* Pres. and Treas.; Klaus Runow, Secy.; Henry Christensen III.
EIN: 134156286
Codes: FD

62516
Musical Theater Project, Inc.
225 W. 34th St., Rm. 1200
New York, NY 10122

Classified as a private operating foundation in 1983.
Donor(s): Ernest Harburg, Deena Rosenberg.
Financial data (yr. ended 06/30/00): Assets, $14,646 (M); grants paid, $97,150; gifts received, $121,755; expenditures, $247,382; qualifying distributions, $236,644; giving activities include $139,494 for programs.
Officers: Ernest Harburg, Pres.; Deena Rosenberg, V.P.
EIN: 133127149

62517
Robert and Rhoda Greenes Foundation
31 N. Moore St., Apt. 4E
New York, NY 10013-5715

Classified as a private operating foundation in 1984.
Donor(s): Robert B. Greenes.
Financial data (yr. ended 11/30/00): Assets, $14,550 (M); grants paid, $16,261; gifts received, $29,468; expenditures, $16,342; qualifying distributions, $16,261.
Limitations: Applications not accepted. Giving primarily in NY.
Application information: Contributes only to pre-selected organizations.
Trustees: Robert B. Greenes, Stacy Greenes, Steven R. Greenes.
EIN: 133187073

62518
The American Foundation for Textile Art, Inc.
c/o First Spring Corp.
499 Park Ave., 26th Fl.
New York, NY 10022

Established in 1996 in DE and NY.
Donor(s): Guido Goldman.
Financial data (yr. ended 03/31/02): Assets, $14,470 (M); grants paid, $0; gifts received, $25,000; expenditures, $51,268; qualifying distributions, $48,515; giving activities include $48,580 for programs.
Limitations: Applications not accepted.
Application information: Unsolicited requests for funds not accepted.
Officers and Directors:* Guido Goldman,* Pres.; Marietta Lutze-Sackler,* V.P.; Leonard M. Nelson,* Secy.; Abraham Udovitch.
EIN: 133893379

62519
Cher Foundation
1456 E. 10th St.
Brooklyn, NY 11230

Financial data (yr. ended 12/31/00): Assets, $14,224 (L); grants paid, $24,277; gifts received, $40,120; expenditures, $26,023; qualifying distributions, $24,277.
Limitations: Applications not accepted.
Application information: Contributes only to pre-selected organizations.
Trustee: Ephraim Ruvel.
EIN: 134026349

62520
Shawangunk Valley Conservancy
Red Mill Rd.
Wallkill, NY 12589
Application address: 200 Stockton St., Princeton, NJ 08540
Contact: Peter A. Bienstock, Tr.

Donor(s): Peter A. Bienstock.
Financial data (yr. ended 12/31/00): Assets, $14,043 (M); grants paid, $75,490; gifts received, $44,580; expenditures, $78,944; qualifying distributions, $77,162.
Limitations: Giving primarily in the Hudson Valley, NY, area.
Trustees: Anne C. Bienstock, Nicholas Bienstock, Peter A. Bienstock.
EIN: 510192536
Codes: FD2

62521
Greg Kanner Memorial Fund
117 Lexow Ave.
Nyack, NY 10960-1005 (845) 358-6539
Contact: Alexander S. Kanner, Tr.

Financial data (yr. ended 03/31/01): Assets, $13,948 (M); grants paid, $750; expenditures, $760; qualifying distributions, $760.
Limitations: Giving on a national basis, with emphasis on San Francisco, CA and Atlanta, GA.
Trustee: Alexander S. Kanner.
EIN: 237181666

62522
Simcha Foundation
1425 E. 14th St.
Brooklyn, NY 11230 (718) 376-6626
Contact: Mark Newman, Pres.

Established in 2001 in NY.
Donor(s): Mark Newman.
Financial data (yr. ended 12/31/01): Assets, $13,361 (M); grants paid, $9,300; gifts received, $27,500; expenditures, $14,300; qualifying distributions, $14,300.
Officers: Mark Newman, Pres.; Sandra Newman, Secy.-Treas.
EIN: 113590127

62523
Hammondsport Beautification Committee, Inc.
P.O. Box 754
Hammondsport, NY 14840-0754

Established in 2000 in NY.
Donor(s): Fred & Harriet Taylor Foundation.
Financial data (yr. ended 07/31/01): Assets, $13,215 (M); grants paid, $0; gifts received, $29,668; expenditures, $16,453; qualifying distributions, $19,183; giving activities include $12,112 for programs.
Limitations: Giving limited to Hammondsport, NY.
Officers: Scott Sprague, Pres.; Sam Pennise, Secy.; Norman R. King, Treas.
EIN: 161608754

62524
Anna-Lisa Gotschlich Foundation
160 Lincoln Ave.
Hastings-on-Hudson, NY 10706
Contact: Anna-Lisa Gotschlich, Ph.D., Pres.

Established in 1993 in NY.
Donor(s): Anna-Lisa Gotschlich, Ph.D.
Financial data (yr. ended 12/31/00): Assets, $13,101 (M); grants paid, $15,685; expenditures, $15,947; qualifying distributions, $15,685.
Limitations: Giving for the benefit of students from Thailand for study in the U.S.
Officers: Anna-Lisa Gotschlich, Ph.D., Pres.; Albert Louis Menard, V.P. and Secy.-Treas.; Hilda Gartley, M.D., V.P.; Emil C. Gotschlich, M.D., V.P.; Shlomo Halfin, Ph.D., V.P.
EIN: 133735584

62525
HieKie Foundation, Inc.
12 Fulton Hill Rd.
Kenoza Lake, NY 12750

Established in 1998 in NY.
Donor(s): Marion Kaselle.
Financial data (yr. ended 12/31/00): Assets, $12,274 (M); grants paid, $1,536; gifts received, $1,311; expenditures, $1,959; qualifying distributions, $1,527.
Limitations: Applications not accepted. Giving primarily in NY.
Application information: Contributes only to pre-selected organizations.
Officer: Marion Kaselle, Pres.
EIN: 223588849

62526
Clayworks on Columbia, Inc.
195 Columbia St.
Brooklyn, NY 11231

Established in 1995 in NY.
Financial data (yr. ended 06/30/00): Assets, $12,268 (M); grants paid, $130; expenditures, $49,621; qualifying distributions, $49,621; giving activities include $46,643 for programs.
Limitations: Applications not accepted.
Application information: Contributes only to pre-selected organizations.
Officers: Deborah D. McDermott, Pres. and Treas.; Marie Pindus, V.P.; Roseann Sofianoyoulous, Secy.
Directors: T. Brickman, John F. McDermott, Jeanette Selles.
EIN: 113227149

62527
The Pulvermann Foundation, Inc.
15 Purchase St.
P.O. Box 538
Rye, NY 10580-0538

Financial data (yr. ended 12/31/00): Assets, $11,402 (M); grants paid, $0; gifts received, $38,500; expenditures, $30,935; qualifying distributions, $30,935; giving activities include $29,070 for programs.
Officer and Trustees:* Gretchen T. Pulvermann,* Pres.; Arthur Stampleman.
EIN: 133670974

62528
Arie and Gene Rosenbaum Foundation, Inc.
141-07 72nd Crescent
Flushing, NY 11367-2329

Established in 1989 in NY.
Donor(s): Arie Rosenbaum.
Financial data (yr. ended 02/28/02): Assets, $11,237 (M); grants paid, $14,600; expenditures, $14,864; qualifying distributions, $14,864.
Limitations: Applications not accepted. Giving primarily in Forest Hills, NY.
Application information: Contributes only to pre-selected organizations.
Officers: Arie Rosenbaum, Pres.; Murray Rosenbaum, V.P.; Johoshua Graff, Secy.
EIN: 133523564

62529
Oskar Kalb Memorial Foundation, Inc.
c/o Allen Kaufman
714 Colony Dr.
Hartsdale, NY 10530-1732

Donor(s): Lore Kalb, Roland J. Kalb.
Financial data (yr. ended 12/31/99): Assets, $10,883 (M); grants paid, $5,404; gifts received, $10,580; expenditures, $20,576; qualifying distributions, $20,425.
Limitations: Applications not accepted. Giving primarily in CT and RI.
Application information: Contributes only to pre-selected organizations.
Officers: Deborah Frascone, Pres.; Lore Kalb, Secy.-Treas.
EIN: 136216908

62530
Karrey Children's Center, Inc.
815 Claflin Ave.
Mamaroneck, NY 10543-4408

Classified as an operating foundation in 1980 in NY.
Financial data (yr. ended 08/31/00): Assets, $10,871 (M); grants paid, $0; gifts received, $1,000; expenditures, $714; qualifying distributions, $714; giving activities include $517 for programs.
Officer and Director:* Karrey L. Nagle,* Pres.
EIN: 133004729

62531
Weller Mobilizer, Inc.
c/o Citadel Group Representatives Inc.
5E. 59th St., 8th Fl.
New York, NY 10022-1027

Financial data (yr. ended 12/31/99): Assets, $10,820 (M); grants paid, $1,429; gifts received, $17,538; expenditures, $7,782; qualifying distributions, $7,782.
Limitations: Applications not accepted. Giving primarily in MA.
Application information: Contributes only to pre-selected organizations.
Officers and Directors:* Sir Arthur Weller,* Pres.; Anthony B. Weller, V.P. and Treas.; Patricia N. Pikering, Secy.; John G. Glanutsos, Ph.D., Anne B. Young, M.D., Ph.D.
EIN: 522110892

62532
Jeanette Lewis Foundation, Inc.
10 North Dr.
Sag Harbor, NY 11963

Donor(s): Jeanette Lewis.
Financial data (yr. ended 06/30/00): Assets, $10,810 (M); grants paid, $3,000; expenditures, $3,000; qualifying distributions, $3,000.
Limitations: Giving primarily in Copiague, NY.
Application information: Application form required.
Directors: Jeanette Lewis, Paul Lewis, Olga MacGarva.
EIN: 113339527

62533
Seacoast Foundation
c/o Gelfand Rennert & Feldman
1330 Ave. of the Americas
New York, NY 10019
Application address: P.O. Box 870, Cooper Sta., New York, NY 10276-0870
Contact: Naomi Saltzman, Tr.

Established in 1969.
Financial data (yr. ended 12/31/99): Assets, $10,760 (M); grants paid, $163,040; gifts received, $155,000; expenditures, $163,130; qualifying distributions, $163,130.
Limitations: Giving on a national and international basis.
Application information: Application form not required.
Managers: David Baun, Robert Dylan, Sara Dylan, Marshall Gelfand, Naomi Saltzman.
EIN: 237034949
Codes: FD2

62534
The A. & M. Rieder Family Foundation
1673 51st St.
Brooklyn, NY 11204
NJ tel.: (732) 821-1500
Contact: Leslie Rieder, Tr.

Established in 1999 in NY.
Donor(s): Leslie Rieder.
Financial data (yr. ended 12/31/00): Assets, $10,655 (M); grants paid, $110,393; gifts received, $95,500; expenditures, $111,860; qualifying distributions, $111,754.
Trustees: Leslie Rieder, Miriam Rieder.
EIN: 113471866
Codes: FD2

62535
IUEC Local 1 of NYC Scholarship Fund
150-42 12th Ave.
Whitestone, NY 11357 (718) 767-7004

Established in 1986 in NY as a company-sponsored operating fund.
Donor(s): ZIP, Inc., International Union of Elevator Constructors (IUEC) Local No. 1.
Financial data (yr. ended 12/31/01): Assets, $10,411 (M); grants paid, $10,000; gifts received, $7,597; expenditures, $10,000; qualifying distributions, $10,000.
Limitations: Giving primarily in NY.
Application information: Application form required.
Officer and Trustees:* John G. Green,* Pres.; Charles Novak.
EIN: 133251442

62536
Dunkirk-Fredonia Lions Club Barker Memorial Scholarship Fund
504 Fairview Ave., No. 4
Jamestown, NY 14701-4625 (716) 483-0998
Contact: James J. Schrantz, Tr.

Financial data (yr. ended 12/31/00): Assets, $10,402 (M); grants paid, $410; expenditures, $522; qualifying distributions, $522.
Limitations: Giving limited to Jamestown, NY.
Trustee: James J. Schrantz.
EIN: 161345135
Codes: TN

62537
Gil's Hills, Inc.
2430 Brown Rd.
Wellsville, NY 14895

Financial data (yr. ended 12/31/01): Assets, $9,868 (M); grants paid, $0; gifts received, $74,225; expenditures, $175,498; qualifying distributions, $154,770.
Officers: Ralph Eastlack, Chair.; Roy Allen, Vice-Chair.; Becky Torrey, Secy.-Treas.
EIN: 161176388

62538
Lester and Marjorie Dembitzer Foundation, Inc.
1790 Broadway, Ste. 705
New York, NY 10019

Established in 1997 in NY.
Donor(s): Joseph Itzkowitz, Sara Itzkowitz.
Financial data (yr. ended 12/31/00): Assets, $9,855 (M); grants paid, $3,035; gifts received, $5,000; expenditures, $3,110; qualifying distributions, $3,035.
Limitations: Applications not accepted.
Application information: Contributes only to pre-selected organizations.
Officers: Lester Dembitzer, Pres.; Marjorie Dembitzer, V.P.; David Dembitzer, Secy.
EIN: 113371820

62539
Chung Ying Cantonese Opera Association, Inc.
401 Broadway, Ste. 405
New York, NY 10013

Established in 1998 in NY.
Financial data (yr. ended 04/30/99): Assets, $9,696 (M); grants paid, $0; gifts received, $30,625; expenditures, $21,429; qualifying distributions, $29,429; giving activities include $22,019 for programs.
Officers: Chung Bun Chiu, Pres.; Lau Ying Chiu, Secy.; Alice Leung, Treas.
EIN: 134007378

62540
Milton Shalom & Sons Foundation
450 W. 33rd St.
New York, NY 10001 (212) 736-8124
Contact: Milton Shalom, Pres.

Established in 1986 in DE.
Donor(s): Morris Shalom, Ezra Shalom.
Financial data (yr. ended 12/31/99): Assets, $9,568 (M); grants paid, $150,122; gifts received, $158,000; expenditures, $150,541; qualifying distributions, $150,122.
Limitations: Giving primarily in NY.
Application information: Application form not required.
Officers: Milton Shalom, Pres.; Morris Shalom, V.P.; Ezra Shalom, Treas.
EIN: 133398324
Codes: FD2

62541
The Bayard Rustin Fund, Inc.
218 E. 18th St.
New York, NY 10003-3605

Established in 1987 in NY.
Donor(s): Joyce Mertz-Gilmore Foundation, LuEsther T. Mertz,‡ The New York Friends Group, AFL-CIO.
Financial data (yr. ended 09/30/00): Assets, $9,197 (M); grants paid, $2,550; gifts received, $3,555; expenditures, $2,967; qualifying distributions, $2,967.
Limitations: Applications not accepted.
Application information: Contributes only to pre-selected organizations.
Officers: Charles Bloomstein,* Secy.-Treas.; Walter Naegle, Exec. Dir.
EIN: 133462097

62542
American Friends of Ora
36 Rodney St.
Brooklyn, NY 11211-7526

Established in 2000 in NY.
Financial data (yr. ended 12/31/00): Assets, $8,815 (M); grants paid, $52,700; gifts received, $62,152; expenditures, $53,337; qualifying distributions, $53,337.
Limitations: Applications not accepted. Giving primarily in Israel.
Application information: Contributes only to pre-selected organizations.
Officer: Benjamin Paskesz, Pres.
EIN: 112945723

62543
The Harry & Celia Zuckerman Foundation, Inc.
19 Lyons Pl.
Larchmont, NY 10538-3809 (914) 833-0725
Contact: Irving Zuckerman, Dir.

Established in 1992 in NY.
Donor(s): Irving Zuckerman, Claire Zuckerman.
Financial data (yr. ended 12/31/01): Assets, $8,543 (M); grants paid, $25,852; gifts received, $35,000; expenditures, $34,867; qualifying distributions, $25,852.
Directors: Claire Zuckerman, Irving Zuckerman, Mark Zuckerman.
EIN: 133641555

62544
The Shearwater Foundation, Inc.
c/o Joseph Arnold
12 E. 86th St., Apt. 1539
New York, NY 10028-0516
Contact: Rosemary Jackson Smith, Prog. Dir.

Established in 1987 in NY.
Donor(s): Rosemary Jackson.
Financial data (yr. ended 12/31/01): Assets, $8,464 (M); grants paid, $164,500; gifts received, $204,243; expenditures, $205,905; qualifying distributions, $202,930.
Limitations: Giving on a national and international basis.
Publications: Grants list, program policy statement.
Application information: The foundation or its advisors contact institutions and individuals on projects of interest. Application form not required.
Officer and Directors:* Rosemary Jackson,* Pres.; West Bridge-Ford, Andrew Pepper.
EIN: 133567898
Codes: FD2, GTI

62545
Outer Sky Press, Inc.
1 Center Knolls
Bronxville, NY 10708
Contact: Bernadette Li Gentzler, Pres.

Established in 1990 in NY.
Financial data (yr. ended 12/31/00): Assets, $8,281 (M); grants paid, $1,000; gifts received, $11,566; expenditures, $16,761; qualifying distributions, $18,461.
Limitations: Giving primarily in New York, NY.
Officers and Directors:* Bernadette Li Gentzler,* Pres.; Katherine Torricelli, Secy.-Treas.; Ruth Mu-Lian Chao, Chih-Ping Chou, Min-Chih Chou, J. Mason Gentzler, Chun-Tu Hsueh, Don Mele, Frank Randall.
EIN: 133572806

62546
Upstate Prison Ministries, Inc.
c/o John Wright
P.O. Box 232
Pottersville, NY 12860-0232

Established in 1997.
Financial data (yr. ended 12/31/01): Assets, $8,085 (M); grants paid, $0; gifts received, $4,634; expenditures, $4,577; qualifying distributions, $4,577; giving activities include $4,577 for programs.
Directors: Brian O'Connor, Guy Swartwout, Diane M. Wright, John A. Wright.
EIN: 141755422

62547
Jeremy Scheinfeld Foundation for Kids, Inc.
c/o Robert Scheinfeld
30 Rockefeller Plz., 44th Fl.
New York, NY 10112-0228

Established in 1999 in NY.
Donor(s): Robert Scheinfeld.
Financial data (yr. ended 12/31/99): Assets, $7,732 (M); grants paid, $4,486; gifts received, $12,144; expenditures, $4,486; qualifying distributions, $4,486.
Limitations: Applications not accepted.
Application information: Contributes only to pre-selected organizations.
Officers: Robert Scheinfeld, Pres.; Steven Scheinfeld, V.P.; Jodi Scheinfeld, Secy.
EIN: 134054086

62548
Noah's Spark Foundation
259 W. Rt. 59
Spring Valley, NY 10977-5449

Established in 1999.
Financial data (yr. ended 06/30/00): Assets, $7,374 (L); grants paid, $4,666; gifts received, $12,345; expenditures, $4,941; qualifying distributions, $4,666.
Limitations: Applications not accepted. Giving primarily in Jerusalem, Israel.
Application information: Unsolicited requests for funds not accepted.
Directors: Jonathan Jarashow, Judith Jarashow.
EIN: 137179286

62549
Humanas, Inc.
c/o Gstalder
20 Haights Cross Rd.
Chappaqua, NY 10514
Application address: c/o Kraus Organization, 16 E. 46th St., New York, NY 10017

Donor(s): Herbert Gstalder, Barbara Gstalder, H.P. Kraus.
Financial data (yr. ended 12/31/01): Assets, $7,337 (M); grants paid, $8,099; gifts received, $5,800; expenditures, $8,174; qualifying distributions, $8,099.
Limitations: Giving limited to residents of NY.
Directors: Barbara Gstalder, Herbert Gstalder, Ivan S. Rosenblum.
EIN: 133132602

62550
Thomas J. Dillon Scholarship Fund, Inc.
31 E. Orchard St.
Nanuet, NY 10954

Classified as a private operating foundation in 1991.
Donor(s): Mary Dillon.

Financial data (yr. ended 12/31/00): Assets, $7,039 (M); grants paid, $500; expenditures, $65; qualifying distributions, $500.
Limitations: Applications not accepted. Giving limited to residents of Nanuet, NY.
Officers: Doreen Dillon-Weiser, Pres.; Mary Dillon, Secy.
EIN: 133632173

62551
Professor Edgar H. Lehrman Memorial Foundation for Ethics, Religion, Science and the Arts, Inc.
10 Nob Hill Gate
Roslyn, NY 11576-2533   (516) 626-0238

Classified as a private operating foundation in 1988.
Financial data (yr. ended 12/31/01): Assets, $7,036 (M); grants paid, $0; gifts received, $17,546; expenditures, $19,447; qualifying distributions, $0.
Officer: N.S. Lehrman, M.D., Pres.
Trustees: Mark Greenfast, Rabbi Paul Kushner.
EIN: 112916112

62552
Philip Kaplan Cultural Foundation, Inc.
114 Old Country Rd., Ste. II-68
P.O. Box 231
Mineola, NY 11501

Established in 1987.
Financial data (yr. ended 02/28/00): Assets, $6,386 (M); grants paid, $350; expenditures, $350; qualifying distributions, $350.
Limitations: Applications not accepted. Giving primarily in NY.
Application information: Contributes only to pre-selected organizations.
Officers: Matilde Kaplan, Pres.; Richard Kaplan, V.P.; Andrea Nouryeh, Secy.-Treas.
EIN: 112864409

62553
PMI (Police Management Institute) Alumni Association, Inc.
Peck Slip Staion
P.O. Box 820
New York, NY 10038

Established in 2000 in NY.
Financial data (yr. ended 12/31/00): Assets, $6,062 (M); grants paid, $300; gifts received, $3,000; expenditures, $11,375; qualifying distributions, $11,375; giving activities include $9,455 for programs.
Limitations: Applications not accepted.
Application information: Contributes only to pre-selected organizations.
Officers: George Grasso, Pres.; Thomas Fahey, V.P.; Robert Messner, Secy.; Peter Abbott, Treas.
EIN: 134108102

62554
Zichron Tzvi Foundation
580 5th Ave., Ste. 503
New York, NY 10036

Established in 2000 in NY.
Financial data (yr. ended 12/31/00): Assets, $6,052 (M); grants paid, $33,915; gifts received, $35,000; expenditures, $33,948; qualifying distributions, $33,915.
Limitations: Applications not accepted.
Application information: Contributes only to pre-selected organizations.
Trustee: Stefan Weisz.
EIN: 113530683

62555
Victor Herbert Festival Trust
71 Ferris Ln.
Poughkeepsie, NY 12601-5111

Established in 1999 in NY.
Donor(s): Victor Herbert Foundation, Stewarts Shops.
Financial data (yr. ended 12/31/01): Assets, $6,033 (M); grants paid, $0; gifts received, $25,250; expenditures, $16,623; qualifying distributions, $15,768; giving activities include $15,768 for programs.
Trustees: Arthur G. Adams, Neil Gould.
EIN: 146172788

62556
The WOH Foundation
1309 Ave. U
Brooklyn, NY 11206

Established in 1997 in NY.
Donor(s): Edward Friedman, Jacob Friedman.
Financial data (yr. ended 11/30/99): Assets, $5,774 (L); grants paid, $38,136; gifts received, $25,000; expenditures, $38,178; qualifying distributions, $38,136.
Limitations: Applications not accepted.
Application information: Contributes only to pre-selected organizations.
Trustee: Jacob Friedman.
EIN: 137103155

62557
Amor Artis, Inc.
c/o Diane L. Horan
P.O. Box U, Gracie Sta.
New York, NY 10028-0040

Classified as a private operating foundation in 1973.
Donor(s): Johannes Sonary.
Financial data (yr. ended 04/30/00): Assets, $5,600 (M); grants paid, $0; gifts received, $41,905; expenditures, $138,128; qualifying distributions, $33,733; giving activities include $134,277 for programs.
Officers and Directors:* Patrick Dwyer,* Pres.; Sallie Adams,* Secy.; Diane Horan,* Treas.; Jean Cannon, Frank Decolvenaere, Marshall M. Green, Johannes Somary, John Toth, Eleanor Watts, and 2 additional directors.
EIN: 131947036

62558
Foundation for the Betterment of Estonian Life and Education
(Formerly Foundation for the Advancement of Estonian Higher Technical Education)
24 Makamah Rd.
Northport, NY 11768   (631) 436-7400
Contact: Mark Kiiss, Pres.

Established in 1993 in NY.
Donor(s): Aksel Kiiss.‡
Financial data (yr. ended 12/31/01): Assets, $5,511 (M); grants paid, $2,025; expenditures, $2,123; qualifying distributions, $2,123.
Limitations: Giving primarily in Estonia.
Officers: Mark Kiiss, Pres. and Treas.; Helle Kiiss, V.P.; Hillar Kiiss, Secy.
Directors: Rein Grabbi, Rein Luik.
EIN: 113155336

62559
Seymour Finkelstein Family Foundation, Inc.
1755 York Ave., Ste. 35BC
New York, NY 10128-6875

Established in 1990 in NY.

Financial data (yr. ended 06/30/00): Assets, $5,440 (M); grants paid, $0; expenditures, $745; qualifying distributions, $195.
Limitations: Applications not accepted.
Application information: Contributes only to pre-selected organizations.
Officers and Directors:* Seymour Finkelstein,* Pres.; Adam Finkelstein,* V.P.; Charles Finkelstein,* V.P.; Robert Finkelstein,* V.P.; Andrew Finkelstein,* Secy.
EIN: 135595559

62560
The Reach Foundation of Rockland, Inc.
P.O. Box 760
Tallman, NY 10982

Established in 1999 in NY.
Financial data (yr. ended 06/30/00): Assets, $5,391 (M); grants paid, $0; gifts received, $6,168; expenditures, $780; qualifying distributions, $0; giving activities include $400 for programs.
Limitations: Applications not accepted.
Application information: Contributes only to pre-selected organizations.
Officers: Marci B. Linke, Chair.; Eve Zukergood-Panuthos, V.P.; Carol Flack, V.P.; Richard Ramsdell, Treas.
EIN: 133757892

62561
New York Japanese American Lions Club Charities, Inc.
15 W. 44th St., 11th Fl.
New York, NY 10036

Financial data (yr. ended 06/30/00): Assets, $5,332 (M); grants paid, $5,790; gifts received, $10,927; expenditures, $11,665; qualifying distributions, $11,665; giving activities include $10,876 for programs.
Officers: George Horishige, Pres.; Yasuhiro Ikenaga, Secy.; Mike Aida, Treas.
EIN: 133682079

62562
The Fubu Foundation, Inc.
350 5th Ave., Ste. 6617
New York, NY 10118

Established in 1998 in NY.
Donor(s): GTFM, LLC.
Financial data (yr. ended 07/31/01): Assets, $5,238 (M); grants paid, $26,620; gifts received, $30,000; expenditures, $26,783; qualifying distributions, $26,620.
Limitations: Giving primarily in NY.
Officers: Daymond John, Pres.; Bruce Weisfeld, Secy.; Norman Weisfeld, Treas.
EIN: 134026304

62563
James P. Kelly Scholarship Fund
10 Willard St.
Port Jervis, NY 12771   (845) 856-5952
Contact: Robert Mackey, Pres.

Established in 1995 in NY.
Financial data (yr. ended 12/31/00): Assets, $5,000 (M); grants paid, $500; gifts received, $5,138; expenditures, $500; qualifying distributions, $500.
Limitations: Giving primarily in NY.
Officers: Robert Mackey, Pres.; Joan Kelly, V.P.
EIN: 141775179

62564
Foundation for Hearing Aid Research
P.O. Box 306
Woodstock, NY 12498-0306

Classified as a private operating foundation in 1973.
Donor(s): Edgar Villchur.
Financial data (yr. ended 03/31/00): Assets, $4,985 (M); grants paid, $0; gifts received, $1,000; expenditures, $7,683; qualifying distributions, $7,411; giving activities include $7,411 for programs.
Officers: Edgar Villchur, Pres.; Alvin Moscowitz, Secy.-Treas.
EIN: 146038172

62565
The Motoko Ikeda Spiegel Memorial Foundation, Inc.
122 Ridgecrest Rd.
Briarcliff Manor, NY 10510
Contact: Si Spiegel, Dir.

Established in 2001 in NY.
Financial data (yr. ended 12/31/01): Assets, $4,942 (M); grants paid, $0; gifts received, $6,540; expenditures, $2,038; qualifying distributions, $2,000.
Application information: Application form not required.
Director: Si Spiegel.
EIN: 134161081

62566
Libertad, Inc.
100 Park Ave.
New York, NY 10017
Application address: 120 Park Ave., New York, NY 10017
Contact: Kevin Callahan

Classified as a company-sponsored operating foundation in 1992.
Donor(s): Philip Morris Cos. Inc., Philip Morris U.S.A., Philip Morris Intl., Philip Morris Management Corp.
Financial data (yr. ended 07/31/00): Assets, $4,828 (M); grants paid, $0; expenditures, $8,568; qualifying distributions, $8,568; giving activities include $8,568 for programs.
Limitations: Giving on an international basis.
Officers and Directors:* The Lord Plum of Coleshill D.L.,* Co-Chair.; Charles McC. Mathias, Jr.,* Co-Chair.; Andrew Whist,* Pres.; Barry J. Hart,* Secy.-Treas.; Juan Carlos Blanco, Kenneth Clark, Salustiano Del Campo, Marvin Kalb, Jacques Sequela.
EIN: 521477288

62567
The Children's Music Workshop, Inc.
(also known as CMW)
315 Riverside Dr. Ste. 7C
New York, NY 10025
E-mail: singcmw@worldnet.att.net

Classified as a private operating foundation in 1988.
Donor(s): Theodate Carus Harter.
Financial data (yr. ended 12/31/01): Assets, $4,546 (M); grants paid, $25; gifts received, $18,152; expenditures, $17,011; qualifying distributions, $21,427; giving activities include $15,881 for programs.
Limitations: Applications not accepted.
Application information: Contributes only to pre-selected organizations.
Directors: Theodate Harter, Sally Monsour, Charles Rose, Stephen Wilder.
EIN: 133224878

62568
Dr. Sam J. Piliero Memorial Fund
c/o Dr. Wishe
345 E. 24th St., Rm. 829
New York, NY 10010-4020

Financial data (yr. ended 09/30/01): Assets, $4,527 (M); grants paid, $190; expenditures, $220; qualifying distributions, $218.
Limitations: Applications not accepted. Giving limited to residents of New York, NY.
Trustees: Martin Roy, Harvey I. Wishe.
EIN: 133115489

62569
Y N Twersky Philanthropy Fund
1450 46th St.
Brooklyn, NY 11219

Established in 1999 in NY.
Donor(s): Jack Twersky.
Financial data (yr. ended 12/31/01): Assets, $4,363 (M); grants paid, $8,000; expenditures, $8,766; qualifying distributions, $8,000.
Limitations: Applications not accepted. Giving primarily in NY.
Application information: Contributes only to pre-selected organizations.
Trustee: Naomi Twersky.
EIN: 113514594

62570
The Edward-Laurent Foundation, Inc.
c/o Gerard F. LeBlond
4461 Apulia Rd., Ste. 100
Jamesville, NY 13078-9601

Established in 1992 in MD.
Donor(s): Gerard F. LeBlond, Theresa L. Beaty.
Financial data (yr. ended 12/31/01): Assets, $4,253 (M); grants paid, $0; gifts received, $362; expenditures, $142; qualifying distributions, $142.
Officers: Gerard F. LeBlond, Pres.; Theresa L. Beaty, Secy.-Treas.
EIN: 521772757

62571
The Mary T. & Frank L. Hoffman Family Foundation
R.R. 2
121 Tammy Trail, Unit 1012
Athens, NY 12015-3707
Contact: Mary & Frank Hoffman

Established in 1998.
Donor(s): Mary T. Hoffman, Frank L. Hoffman.
Financial data (yr. ended 12/31/01): Assets, $4,047 (M); grants paid, $23,909; gifts received, $42,756; expenditures, $42,793; qualifying distributions, $23,909.
Limitations: Giving on a national basis.
Trustees: Frank L. Hoffman, Mary T. Hoffman.
EIN: 146186745

62572
Mitchell May Foundation, Inc.
117 E. Lake Rd.
Tuxedo Park, NY 10987

Donor(s): Mitchell May III.
Financial data (yr. ended 12/31/00): Assets, $3,905 (M); grants paid, $3,150; expenditures, $3,211; qualifying distributions, $3,211.
Limitations: Applications not accepted. Giving primarily in NY.
Application information: Contributes only to pre-selected organizations.
Trustee: Corta May.
EIN: 136103513

62573
The Fund for New Performance Video, Inc.
175 W. 73rd St., Ste. 12D
New York, NY 10023

Established in 1996 in NY.
Donor(s): Jack Irwin.
Financial data (yr. ended 09/30/99): Assets, $3,791 (M); grants paid, $0; gifts received, $29,501; expenditures, $36,565; qualifying distributions, $32,309; giving activities include $36,565 for programs.
Limitations: Applications not accepted.
Application information: Contributes only to pre-selected organizations.
Officers: John Irwin, Pres.; Jeffrey Cunard, Secy.; Mark Jones, Treas.
EIN: 133572120

62574
Children's Mental Health Alliance, Inc.
2345 Rte. 52, Ste. 207
Hopewell Junction, NY 12533

Established in 1997 in CT and NY.
Donor(s): Open Society Institute.
Financial data (yr. ended 12/31/00): Assets, $3,163 (M); grants paid, $8,550; gifts received, $145,961; expenditures, $307,724; qualifying distributions, $305,615; giving activities include $189,677 for programs.
Director: Owen Lewis, M.D.
EIN: 061495529

62575
Richard Albert Family Foundation
2 Croton Point Ave.
Croton-on-Hudson, NY 10520-3025

Established in 1999 in NY.
Donor(s): Richard Albert.
Financial data (yr. ended 12/31/00): Assets, $2,745 (M); grants paid, $9,425; gifts received, $12,216; expenditures, $9,950; qualifying distributions, $9,950.
Trustees: Jeffrey Albert, Richard Albert, Susan Albert.
EIN: 137134078

62576
The Kingsons Educational and Aviation Research Foundation, Inc.
Rd. 1, Box 276 G, Shore Dr. W.
Red Hook, NY 12571-9728

Financial data (yr. ended 12/31/01): Assets, $2,724 (M); grants paid, $0; expenditures, $145; qualifying distributions, $0.
Directors: Allen Edger, Martin Horan, Geoffrey King, Matthew King, Richard King, Jeffrey Martin.
EIN: 141725671

62577
The Alliance for Oil Reclamation, Inc.
c/o Gary Bivona
37 Craven Rd.
Delanson, NY 12053

Established in 1998 in NY.
Donor(s): Gary C. Bivona, Charleen Bivona.
Financial data (yr. ended 12/31/01): Assets, $2,677 (M); grants paid, $0; expenditures, $1,998; qualifying distributions, $0.
Officer: Gary C. Bivona, Pres.
Directors: Charleen M. Bivona, Jenness S. Bivona, Christian G. Bivona.
EIN: 141805176

62578
Sasson Soffer Foundation, Inc.
c/o Sasson Soffer
78 Grand St., 5th Fl.
New York, NY 10013

Classified as a private operating foundation in 1999 in NY.
Financial data (yr. ended 10/31/01): Assets, $2,600 (M); grants paid, $0; gifts received, $11,282; expenditures, $8,715; qualifying distributions, $0.
Officers: Sasson Soffer, Pres.; Stella Sands, V.P.
EIN: 311599286

62579
Yaman Foundation
185 Clinton St.
Cortland, NY 13045-1434 (607) 753-9644
Contact: James J. Yaman, Tr.

Established in 1999 in NY.
Financial data (yr. ended 12/31/01): Assets, $2,540 (M); grants paid, $8,500; expenditures, $9,626; qualifying distributions, $8,500.
Trustees: Dorothy Kelly, James J. Yaman, Paul J. Yaman, David J. Yaman.
EIN: 161571985

62580
The Braun Family Foundation
68-08 112th St.
Forest Hills, NY 11375

Donor(s): Nathan Braun.
Financial data (yr. ended 12/31/01): Assets, $2,530 (L); grants paid, $11,452; gifts received, $10,000; expenditures, $11,452; qualifying distributions, $11,452.
Limitations: Applications not accepted.
Application information: Contributes only to pre-selected organizations.
Trustee: Nathan Braun.
EIN: 113444449

62581
Japan Performing Arts, Inc.
235 W. 48th St., Ste. 19G
New York, NY 10036

Established in 1998 in NY.
Donor(s): Yuko Hamada.
Financial data (yr. ended 08/31/99): Assets, $2,443 (M); grants paid, $0; gifts received, $1,540; expenditures, $182; qualifying distributions, $0.
Officers: Yuko Hamada, Pres.; Satoshi Ono, Secy.
Trustee: Akiyoshi Ito.
EIN: 134023108

62582
Shelter Island Webster Foundation, Inc.
P.O. Box 1852
Shelter Island, NY 11964

Established in 1999 in NY.
Financial data (yr. ended 12/31/00): Assets, $2,379 (M); grants paid, $0; gifts received, $3,044; expenditures, $1,628; qualifying distributions, $0.
Limitations: Applications not accepted.
Application information: Unsolicited requests for funds not accepted.
Officers and Directors:* Webster W. Schott,* Pres.; Elana Poyer,* V.P.; Cynthia Needham, Secy.; Mary Walker, Treas.; Alfred Kulb, Helen Rosenblum, Debbie Spattel.
EIN: 113508283

62583
Chesed Foundation
c/o Herskowitz
5 Eastview Rd.
Monsey, NY 10952-2908

Established in 1989 in NY.
Donor(s): Yosef M. Herskowitz.
Financial data (yr. ended 12/31/01): Assets, $2,331 (M); grants paid, $185,041; gifts received, $147,200; expenditures, $185,209; qualifying distributions, $185,041.
Limitations: Applications not accepted. Giving limited to Monsey, NY.
Application information: Contributes only to pre-selected organizations.
Trustees: Judith Herskowitz, Rivka Herskowitz, Yosef M. Herskowitz.
EIN: 136916621
Codes: FD2

62584
Common Sense Educational Fund, Inc.
P.O. Box 70
Ossining, NY 10562-0070

Classified as a private operating foundation in 1984.
Donor(s): Randolph Foundation, Robert Krieble.
Financial data (yr. ended 05/31/00): Assets, $2,320 (M); grants paid, $150; expenditures, $277; qualifying distributions, $277.
Limitations: Giving primarily in the New York, NY, area.
Officers and Directors:* Joseph J. DioGuardi,* Pres.; Richard J. DioGuardi,* Secy.; Shirley A. Cloyes.
EIN: 133193131

62585
The Peter Cagnacci, Jr. Foundation
48 Temple Ln.
Suffern, NY 10901

Established in 1996 in NY.
Financial data (yr. ended 12/31/99): Assets, $2,292 (M); grants paid, $750; gifts received, $525; expenditures, $1,250; qualifying distributions, $1,250; giving activities include $910 for programs.
Limitations: Applications not accepted.
Application information: Contributes only to pre-selected organizations.
Officers: Delores Baker, Pres.; Belinda Cagnacci, V.P.; Nicole Iskowitz, Secy.; Tamir Siegal, Treas.
EIN: 133866691

62586
The Stephen Gottlieb Memorial Fund for Cancer Research, Inc.
P.O. Box 717
West Nyack, NY 10994-0717

Financial data (yr. ended 11/30/01): Assets, $2,178 (M); grants paid, $12,110; gifts received, $11,590; expenditures, $13,778; qualifying distributions, $12,110.
Limitations: Applications not accepted.
Application information: Contributes only to pre-selected organizations.
Officers: Dean Brown, Pres. and Secy.; Stuart Gottlieb, V.P. and Treas.
EIN: 112783001

62587
J.O.D. Foundation, Inc.
c/o John B. O'Donnell
211 E. 43rd St.
New York, NY 10017-4707

Classified as a private operating foundation in 1981 in NY.
Donor(s): John B. O'Donnell.
Financial data (yr. ended 08/31/00): Assets, $2,174 (M); grants paid, $0; gifts received, $3,000; expenditures, $2,971; qualifying distributions, $2,784; giving activities include $2,971 for programs.
Officer: John B. O'Donnell, Pres.
Director: Stephen Seward.
EIN: 133009833

62588
The Greg Persson Memorial Scholarship Fund
11 Fox Ln.
Shoreham, NY 11786

Established in 1984 in NY, Classified as a private operating foundation in 1987.
Financial data (yr. ended 12/31/01): Assets, $1,980 (L); grants paid, $2,300; gifts received, $623; expenditures, $2,300; qualifying distributions, $0.
Limitations: Applications not accepted. Giving limited to residents of Shoreham, NY.
Application information: Recipients selected by committee of faculty and administration members.
Trustees: Jane C. Persson, Ralph J. Persson.
EIN: 222713911

62589
The Sirulnick Foundation
505 Chestnut St.
P.O. Box 417
Cedarhurst, NY 11516

Established in 1985 in NY.
Donor(s): Phyllis Sirulnick Realty Corp., Joseph Sirulnick Seminole Realty, Carol Ann Realties, Joseph Sirulnick.
Financial data (yr. ended 12/31/00): Assets, $1,938 (M); grants paid, $330,831; gifts received, $332,000; expenditures, $330,856; qualifying distributions, $330,856.
Limitations: Applications not accepted. Giving primarily in NY.
Application information: Contributes only to pre-selected organizations.
Trustees: J. Sirulnick, S. Sirulnick.
EIN: 112728103
Codes: FD

62590
The Murphy Fund
2436 River Rd.
Niagara Falls, NY 14304 (716) 893-2154
Contact: Timothy J. McNamara, Pres.

Donor(s): Timothy J. McNamara.
Financial data (yr. ended 12/31/99): Assets, $1,851 (M); grants paid, $7,982; gifts received, $9,056; expenditures, $8,212; qualifying distributions, $7,982.
Limitations: Giving primarily in NY.
Officers: Timothy J. McNamara, Pres.; Melinda A. McNamara, V.P.
Director: Lewis A. Dahl.
EIN: 161544325

62591
Anne Walker Scholarship Fund
322 W. 48th St.
New York, NY 10026

Established in 2001 in NY.

Financial data (yr. ended 12/31/01): Assets, $1,578 (M); grants paid, $1,100; gifts received, $1,000; expenditures, $1,100; qualifying distributions, $0.
Trustees: Jay Blumenthal, William O. Crow, John C. Gale, A. M. Giannini, Katherine T. Hafemeister, William D. Moriarity, Mary M. Morisseau, Erwin L. Price, Marilyn Reynolds, William F. Rohdin, Robert Shankin, Arthur G. Weiss.
EIN: 134023553

62592
The Tristan Avery Braverman Foundation for Autistic Children
3433 E. Bay Ct.
Merrick, NY 11566

Established in 1999 in NY.
Financial data (yr. ended 12/31/99): Assets, $1,477 (M); grants paid, $0; gifts received, $2,200; expenditures, $858; qualifying distributions, $0.
Limitations: Applications not accepted.
Application information: Contributes only to pre-selected organizations.
Officers: Stacy Braverman, Pres.; Stephen Braverman, V.P.; Eric Broser, Treas.
EIN: 113442487

62593
Josephson Research Foundation, Inc.
40 W. 57th St., 16th Fl.
New York, NY 10019

Established in 1982.
Donor(s): Marvin Josephson.
Financial data (yr. ended 10/31/00): Assets, $1,353 (M); grants paid, $9,185; gifts received, $565; expenditures, $9,904; qualifying distributions, $9,850.
Limitations: Applications not accepted. Giving primarily in New York, NY.
Application information: Contributes only to pre-selected organizations.
Officers and Directors:* Marvin Josephson,* Chair. and Treas.; Tina Chen-Josephson,* Pres. and Secy.; Richard S. Borisoff.
EIN: 061068475

62594
Jacobs Family Foundation, Inc.
108-55 Jewel Ave.
Forest Hills, NY 11375

Established in 1988 in NY.
Donor(s): Gustave Jacobs.
Financial data (yr. ended 12/31/00): Assets, $1,192 (M); grants paid, $11,759; gifts received, $8,500; expenditures, $12,098; qualifying distributions, $12,098.
Limitations: Applications not accepted.
Application information: Contributes only to pre-selected organizations.
Officer: Gustave Jacobs, Mgr.
EIN: 133401524

62595
W.A.D. Financial Counseling, Inc.
54 Riverside Dr., Ste. 15B
New York, NY 10024

Established in 1988 in PA.
Donor(s): Michael Weinstein.
Financial data (yr. ended 12/31/00): Assets, $1,138 (M); grants paid, $0; gifts received, $1,225; expenditures, $5,326; qualifying distributions, $4,995; giving activities include $4,995 for programs.
Limitations: Applications not accepted.
Application information: Contributes only to pre-selected organizations.
Officer: Michael Weinstein, Pres.
EIN: 232533983

62596
The Most Worshipful Grand Lodge Charity Fund Department
c/o Lee Singleton
474 W. 141st St.
New York, NY 10031

Established in 1988 in NY.
Financial data (yr. ended 06/30/99): Assets, $1,089 (M); grants paid, $2,900; gifts received, $3,200; expenditures, $3,369; qualifying distributions, $2,900.
Limitations: Applications not accepted. Giving limited to New York, NY.
Application information: Contributes only to pre-selected organizations.
Officers: John St. Hill, Pres.; Julia Smalls, Secy.; Charles Green, Treas.
EIN: 133465221

62597
Benjamin Zucker Foundation
27 W. 44th St.
New York, NY 10036

Established as an operating foundation in NY.
Financial data (yr. ended 12/31/00): Assets, $1,009 (M); grants paid, $180; gifts received, $1,025; expenditures, $457; qualifying distributions, $180.
Trustee: Bernard Zucker.
EIN: 133513061

62598
Folta Family Foundation
c/o JPMorgan Chase Bank
1211 Ave. Of the Americas, 34th Fl.
New York, NY 10036

Established in 2000 in NJ.
Donor(s): Gerald V. Folta.
Financial data (yr. ended 12/31/01): Assets, $966 (M); grants paid, $100; expenditures, $100; qualifying distributions, $100.
Limitations: Applications not accepted.
Trustee: JPMorgan Chase Bank.
EIN: 527087279

62599
The Truma Foundation
P.O. Box 407
Brooklyn, NY 11219

Established in 1999.
Financial data (yr. ended 11/30/00): Assets, $729 (M); grants paid, $0; gifts received, $7,000; expenditures, $6,278; qualifying distributions, $0.
Trustees: Elsa Bistricer, Moric Bistricer.
EIN: 134099736

62600
Council for Living Music, Inc.
322 W. 48th St.
New York, NY 10036-6902

Established in 1992.
Financial data (yr. ended 12/31/01): Assets, $687 (M); grants paid, $7,606; gifts received, $6,461; expenditures, $7,611; qualifying distributions, $7,606.
Directors: Bruce Bonvissuto, Ethan Fein, John Gale, William Moriarity.
EIN: 133447662

62601
Bina Foundation
c/o Sukenik, Segal & Graff
417 5th Ave., 3rd Fl.
New York, NY 10016

Classified as a private operating foundation in 1983.
Donor(s): Martin Sukenik, David Segal, Jehoshua Graff.
Financial data (yr. ended 06/30/00): Assets, $679 (M); grants paid, $46,000; gifts received, $59,899; expenditures, $46,846; qualifying distributions, $46,000.
Limitations: Applications not accepted. Giving primarily in New York, NY.
Application information: Contributes only to pre-selected organizations.
Officers: Martin K. Sukenik, Pres.; Jehoshua Graff, V.P.; David C. Segal, Treas.
EIN: 133202337

62602
The Adirondack Laboratory, Inc.
P.O. Box 492
Saranac Lake, NY 12983-0492

Classified as a private operating foundation in 1978.
Financial data (yr. ended 12/31/00): Assets, $612 (M); grants paid, $0; gifts received, $20; expenditures, $48; qualifying distributions, $48; giving activities include $48 for programs.
Officers and Trustees:* Ronald G. Alderfer,* Chair.; Saxon Martin,* Secy.; David H. Dumont, George D. Hobbs.
EIN: 510198804

62603
Kawamura Cultural Foundation, Ltd.
c/o Kiso & Tanaka, LLP
675 3rd Ave., Ste. 3008
New York, NY 10017

Established in 1993 in NY.
Financial data (yr. ended 03/31/01): Assets, $581 (M); grants paid, $0; expenditures, $2,129; qualifying distributions, $0.
Officers: Kiyoshi Kawamura, Pres.; Tsuneko Kawamura, V.P.
EIN: 133719303

62604
Greenworking, Inc.
c/o Gentile, Wiener, Penta & Co.
42 Memorial Plz.
Pleasantville, NY 10570

Financial data (yr. ended 06/30/01): Assets, $578 (M); grants paid, $0; expenditures, $90; qualifying distributions, $0.
Officers: Steve Kemler, Pres.; David Highbloom, V.P.; Tim Boylan, Secy.
EIN: 133625333

62605
The Delfina Studio Foundation, Inc.
c/o R. Spencer, DeForest & Duer
90 Broad St.
New York, NY 10004

Financial data (yr. ended 12/31/01): Assets, $559 (M); grants paid, $0; gifts received, $525; expenditures, $525; qualifying distributions, $0.
Trustees: Delfina Entrecanales, Blanca Leigh, Digby Squires.
EIN: 133692622

62606
National Economic Council, Inc.
120 W. 45th St., 39th Fl.
New York, NY 10036 (212) 478-0211

Established in 1992 in NY.
Donor(s): David E. Shaw.
Financial data (yr. ended 12/31/01): Assets, $553 (M); grants paid, $0; expenditures, $191; qualifying distributions, $191; giving activities include $191 for programs.
Officer: David E. Shaw, Pres.
Directors: Andrew Harris, Elizabeth Malcolm.
EIN: 133676330

62607
Charms for Children
242 E. 19th St., PH.W.
New York, NY 10003-2634

Established in 1993 in NY.
Donor(s): Stephen Paluszek.
Financial data (yr. ended 12/31/01): Assets, $542 (M); grants paid, $0; expenditures, $375; qualifying distributions, $0.
Officers: Stephen Paluszek, Pres.; Jean Paluszek, V.P.
EIN: 133722088

62608
Shanti Cultural Dynamics, Inc.
c/o Rao-Shantha
5900 Arlington Ave., Ste. 16S
Bronx, NY 10471-1317

Established in 1999 in NY.
Financial data (yr. ended 12/31/01): Assets, $500 (M); grants paid, $0; gifts received, $1,200; expenditures, $1,200; qualifying distributions, $0.
Officer: A.P. Rao-Shantha, Pres.
EIN: 133560519

62609
Maimonides Lexicon Research Foundation, Inc.
15 E. 71st St.
New York, NY 10021-4171

Established in 1988 in NY.
Donor(s): Jacob I. Dienstag, Claire B. Dienstag.
Financial data (yr. ended 12/31/00): Assets, $500 (M); grants paid, $0; gifts received, $2,474; expenditures, $2,885; qualifying distributions, $0; giving activities include $1,410 for programs.
Officers and Directors:* Jacob I. Dienstag,* Chair.; Claire B. Dienstag,* Secy.-Treas.; Isaac Feller, Tobias Preschel, Leah Rephun, Sholom Rephun, Tabitha Shalem.
EIN: 133447905

62610
The Delancey Foundation
c/o Transammonia, Inc.
350 Park Ave.
New York, NY 10022

Established in 1990 in NY as a private operating foundation.
Donor(s): Ronald P. Stanton.
Financial data (yr. ended 12/31/01): Assets, $493 (M); grants paid, $770,000; gifts received, $770,000; expenditures, $770,025; qualifying distributions, $770,000.
Limitations: Applications not accepted. Giving primarily in NY.
Application information: Unsolicited requests for funds not accepted.
Officers: Ronald P. Stanton, Pres.; Fred M. Lowenfels, Secy.; Edward G. Weiner, Treas.
Director: Oliver K. Stanton.
EIN: 133576731

62611
The Denhoff Foundation
711 3rd Ave., 15th Fl.
New York, NY 10017

Established in 1989 in NY.
Donor(s): Mike Denhoff.
Financial data (yr. ended 12/31/00): Assets, $294 (M); grants paid, $5,200; gifts received, $5,000; expenditures, $5,342; qualifying distributions, $5,200.
Limitations: Applications not accepted. Giving on a national basis.
Application information: Contributes only to pre-selected organizations.
Trustees: Casey Denhoff, Mike Denhoff.
EIN: 136932858

62612
Manfredi Foundation, Inc.
19 Luna Cir.
Staten Island, NY 10312 (718) 979-0033
Contact: Corrado Manfredi, Pres.

Established in 1996 in NY.
Donor(s): Corrado Manfredi, Manfredi Dodge, Safe Auto Sales, Inc.
Financial data (yr. ended 12/31/99): Assets, $248 (L); grants paid, $10,000; gifts received, $1,501; expenditures, $10,025; qualifying distributions, $10,025.
Limitations: Giving limited to NY.
Application information: Application form not required.
Officers: Corrado Manfredi, Pres.; Esther Manfredi, V.P.; Nicholas Manfredi, Secy.
EIN: 133861852

62613
Bernard & Estelle Siegel Foundation, Inc.
1582 Main St.
Buffalo, NY 14209

Financial data (yr. ended 12/31/01): Assets, $236 (M); grants paid, $53; expenditures, $53; qualifying distributions, $53.
Limitations: Applications not accepted.
Trustees: Bernard Siegel, Estelle Siegel.
EIN: 237015786

62614
S. & C. Goldstein Family Foundation
1978 53rd St.
Brooklyn, NY 11204
Contact: Harry Goldstein, Mgr.

Financial data (yr. ended 05/31/01): Assets, $189 (L); grants paid, $11,556; gifts received, $9,000; expenditures, $11,626; qualifying distributions, $11,556.
Limitations: Giving primarily in NJ and NY.
Officers: Harry Goldstein, Mgr.; Judith Goldstein, Mgr.
EIN: 137117756

62615
Allan & Estelle Eisenkraft Foundation, Inc.
c/o Robert S. Braunschweig
350 Fifth Ave., Ste. 1000
New York, NY 10119-1099

Established in 1986 in NY.
Donor(s): Allan Eisenkraft, Estelle Eisenkraft.
Financial data (yr. ended 11/30/01): Assets, $149 (M); grants paid, $0; expenditures, $163; qualifying distributions, $0.
Limitations: Applications not accepted. Giving primarily in New York, NY.
Application information: Contributes only to pre-selected organizations.
Trustees: Robert S. Braunschweig, Allan Eisenkraft, Estelle Eisenkraft.
EIN: 133382446

62616
Cityscape Foundation, Inc.
c/o Christabel Gough
45 Christopher St., Apt. 2E
New York, NY 10014

Financial data (yr. ended 12/31/01): Assets, $133 (M); grants paid, $0; expenditures, $120; qualifying distributions, $120; giving activities include $120 for programs.
Officers: Ronald J. Kopnicki, Pres.; Christabel Gough, Secy.; Matt McGhee, Treas.
EIN: 133653667

62617
Long Island Kidney Institute, Ltd.
267 W. Merrick Rd.
Freeport, NY 11520

Classified as a private operating foundation in 1984.
Financial data (yr. ended 06/30/01): Assets, $120 (M); grants paid, $0; expenditures, $0; qualifying distributions, $0.
Directors: Syed N. Asad, M.D., B. Lawrence Brennan, M.D., Joseph M. Letteri, M.D., Malachy T. Mahon, Joel E. Sherlock, M.D., Vincent M. Tepedino.
EIN: 112657655

62618
Covered Bridge Day Camp
c/o Gallo & Penzone, LLP
420 Jericho Tpke., Ste. 101
Jericho, NY 11753

Classified as a private operating foundation in 1972.
Donor(s): Stanley Simon, Marcelle K. Simon.‡
Financial data (yr. ended 12/31/00): Assets, $118 (M); grants paid, $0; gifts received, $1,500; expenditures, $1,880; qualifying distributions, $1,880; giving activities include $1,880 for programs.
Director: Stanley Simon.
EIN: 060811512

62619
The Robert and Shirley Kaplan Foundation
400 Post Ave.
Westbury, NY 11590

Classified as a private operating foundation in 1999.
Financial data (yr. ended 12/31/01): Assets, $100 (M); grants paid, $0; expenditures, $0; qualifying distributions, $0.
Officer: Robert Kaplan, Chair.
EIN: 311621192

62620
The Joseph Haydn Society, Inc.
P.O. Box 834
New York, NY 10024
Contact: Max L. Panzer, Pres.

Established in 1995 in NY.
Donor(s): Max L. Panzer.
Financial data (yr. ended 12/31/00): Assets, $96 (M); grants paid, $15,665; gifts received, $7,500; expenditures, $16,268; qualifying distributions, $16,268.
Limitations: Giving on a national basis.
Application information: Application form not required.
Officers and Directors:* Max L. Panzer,* Pres.; Mychelle Panzer,* V.P.; Stuart Prager.
EIN: 133863901

62621
Milton Greenberg Foundation
365 Maple St.
West Hempstead, NY 11552

Established in 2001 in NY.
Financial data (yr. ended 12/31/01): Assets, $90 (M); grants paid, $10; gifts received, $100; expenditures, $10; qualifying distributions, $10.
Director: David Greenberg.
EIN: 113579235

62622
Downe Foundation
c/o S. Heinberg, C.P.A.
380 Madison Ave., 15th Fl.
New York, NY 10017-2513

Established in 1968 in NY.
Donor(s): Edward R. Downe, Jr.
Financial data (yr. ended 11/30/00): Assets, $35 (M); grants paid, $3,850; gifts received, $3,925; expenditures, $3,950; qualifying distributions, $3,950.
Limitations: Applications not accepted. Giving primarily in NY.
Application information: Contributes only to pre-selected organizations.
Officer and Directors:* Edward R. Downe, Jr.,* Pres. and Secy.; J. Wingate Brown.
EIN: 237005623

62623
William Olsten Center for Workforce Strategies, Inc.
175 Broad Hollow Rd.
Melville, NY 11747

Established in 1998 in NY.
Financial data (yr. ended 12/31/99): Assets, $25 (L); grants paid, $0; gifts received, $18,588; expenditures, $18,563; qualifying distributions, $18,563; giving activities include $18,141 for programs.
Officers and Directors:* Stuart Olsten,* Pres.; Miriam Olsten,* V.P.; Brigid Smith Deagan, Admin.
EIN: 113398905

62624
The Perl Family Foundation
733 Yonkers Ave, No. 301
Yonkers, NY 10704

Established in 1993 in NY.
Financial data (yr. ended 03/31/01): Assets, $20 (M); grants paid, $16,000; gifts received, $16,020; expenditures, $16,000; qualifying distributions, $16,000.
Limitations: Applications not accepted.
Application information: Contributes only to pre-selected organizations.
Trustee: Sheldon Perl.
EIN: 237071214

62625
Duke Gardens Foundation, Inc.
650 5th Ave., 19th Fl.
New York, NY 10019

Classified as a private operating foundation in 1974.
Donor(s): Doris Duke.‡
Financial data (yr. ended 12/31/00): Assets, $1 (M); grants paid, $0; expenditures, $0; qualifying distributions, $0.
Officers and Directors:* James F. Gill,* Chair.; Marion Oates Charles, Vice-Chair.; Joan E. Spero, Pres.; Betsy Fader, Secy.; Alan Altschuler, C.F.O.; J. Carter Brown, Harry Demopoulos, Anthony S. Fauci, Nannerl O. Keohane, John J. Mack.
EIN: 221630203

62626
Nelson A. Rockefeller Foundation for Public Service
30 Rockefeller Plz., Ste. 5600
New York, NY 10112-0090

Financial data (yr. ended 12/31/01): Assets, $1 (M); grants paid, $182; expenditures, $182; qualifying distributions, $182.
Officers and Trustees:* Mark F. Rockefeller,* Co-Chair.; Nelson A. Rockefeller, Jr.,* Co-Chair.; Marcia A. McLean,* Secy.-Treas.; Henry A. Kissinger, Mary M. Kresky, Alan Miller, Richard D. Parsons, Margaretta F. Rockefeller.
EIN: 133912264

62627
The Waterbor Burn and Cancer Foundation
c/o Deborah Linke
411 E. 53rd St., Ste. 17L
New York, NY 10022

Established in 1997 in NY.
Financial data (yr. ended 12/31/00): Assets, $1 (M); grants paid, $25,000; gifts received, $84,423; expenditures, $131,152; qualifying distributions, $25,000.
Officers: Deborah Waterbor, Pres.; Holly Waterbor, Secy.
Director: James Murphy.
EIN: 113408406

62628
Rena Costa Foundation
98 Riverside Dr.
New York, NY 10024 (212) 877-1610
Contact: Rena Costa, Pres.

Established in 1989 in NY.
Donor(s): Rena Costa.
Financial data (yr. ended 12/31/01): Assets, $0 (M); grants paid, $44,200; gifts received, $40,000; expenditures, $46,020; qualifying distributions, $44,200.
Limitations: Giving primarily in New York, NY.
Officers: Rena Costa, Pres.; Marcus Gilden, V.P.
EIN: 133536713

62629
Ethnology Cinema Project, Inc.
30 Bank St.
New York, NY 10014

Classified as a private operating foundation in 1993.
Financial data (yr. ended 09/30/00): Assets, $0 (M); grants paid, $0; gifts received, $440; expenditures, $440; qualifying distributions, $0; giving activities include $440 for programs.
Directors: Charlemagne Palestine, Joseph Taubman, Louise Thompson.
EIN: 133476571

62630
Foundation for Realizing Excellence in Education
c/o RKLL & Co.
1700 Jericho Tpke.
New Hyde Park, NY 11040

Established in 1999 in NY.
Financial data (yr. ended 12/31/00): Assets, $0 (M); grants paid, $105,000; gifts received, $105,000; expenditures, $105,000; qualifying distributions, $105,000.
Limitations: Giving primarily in NY.
Trustees: Alice Artzt, Gregory Artzt, Julie Artzt, Michele Uzbay.
EIN: 116509973
Codes: FD2

62631
Robin E. Fraser Memorial Foundation, Inc.
8 Highview Dr.
Scarsdale, NY 10583-4647
Application address: c/o Eugene Price, C.P.A., Price & Stirrup, 133 Rte. 304, Bardonia, NY 10954

Financial data (yr. ended 10/31/01): Assets, $0 (M); grants paid, $6,925; gifts received, $6,044; expenditures, $7,099; qualifying distributions, $6,925.
Officers: Harvey Fraser, Pres.; Bonnie Fraser, V.P.
EIN: 133498095

62632
Fred & Fay Friedman Family Trust
9319 Hunting Valley Rd. N.
Clarence, NY 14031-1552

Donor(s): Fred Friedman, Fay T. Friedman.
Financial data (yr. ended 12/31/01): Assets, $0 (M); grants paid, $4,285; gifts received, $28,231; expenditures, $5,015; qualifying distributions, $4,278.
Limitations: Applications not accepted. Giving primarily in NY.
Application information: Contributes only to pre-selected organizations.
Trustees: Fay T. Friedman, Fred Friedman.
EIN: 166364717

62633
The Rosenzweig Foundation, Inc.
9 Meadow Ln.
Manhasset, NY 11030

Established in 1997 in NY.
Financial data (yr. ended 12/31/01): Assets, $0 (M); grants paid, $32,981; expenditures, $33,647; qualifying distributions, $32,981.
Officer: Murray Rosenzweig, Pres.
EIN: 113404182

62634
Transit Workers for Children
536 Hendrix St.
Brooklyn, NY 11207 (718) 272-1807
Contact: Tracy Hyman, Tr.

Established as a private operating foundation in 1995.
Financial data (yr. ended 12/31/99): Assets, $0 (M); grants paid, $4,500; gifts received, $24,522; expenditures, $19,140; qualifying distributions, $19,140; giving activities include $8,918 for programs.
Trustees: Tracy Hyman, Bertha Lee Jefferson, David Wilson.
EIN: 113220856

62635
David & Chaya Zahler Foundation, Inc.
c/o Zell & Ettinger
3001 Ave. M
Brooklyn, NY 11210

Established in 1994 in NY.
Donor(s): David Zahler.
Financial data (yr. ended 12/31/00): Assets, $0 (L); grants paid, $157,615; gifts received, $152,613; expenditures, $157,707; qualifying distributions, $157,615.
Limitations: Giving primarily in NY.
Officers: David Zahler, Pres.; Chaya Zahler, V.P.; Jeffrey Zell, Secy.
EIN: 113215108
Codes: FD2

62636
Zichron Moshe Yakov Foundation
1483 59th St.
Brooklyn, NY 11219-5017
Contact: George Pscherhofer, Dir.

Established in 1999 in NY.
Donor(s): George Pscherhofer.
Financial data (yr. ended 12/31/00): Assets, $0 (M); grants paid, $52,635; gifts received, $102,725; expenditures, $52,910; qualifying distributions, $52,635.
Directors: George Pscherhofer, Gitty Pscherhofer.
EIN: 113447366

NORTH CAROLINA

62637
Walthour-Moss Foundation
c/o Southern National Bank of North Carolina
P.O. Box 1744
Southern Pines, NC 28388-1744

Established in 1981 in NC.
Financial data (yr. ended 12/31/00): Assets, $36,653,966 (M); grants paid, $0; gifts received, $1,124,976; expenditures, $214,537; qualifying distributions, $2,493,746; giving activities include $153,022 for programs.
Officers: Richard D. Webb, Chair.; C.W. Holmberg, Vice-Chair.; Mrs. W.O. Moss, Pres.; Alice Thomas, Secy.; Virginia C. Thomasson, Treas.
Directors: Wilbur Carter, Jr., H.T. Compton, Fitzgerald Hudson, and 10 additional directors.
EIN: 237380583

62638
College Foundation, Inc.
P.O. Box 12100
Raleigh, NC 27605-2100 (919) 821-4771

Classified as a private operating foundation in 1986.
Financial data (yr. ended 06/30/01): Assets, $33,852,746 (M); grants paid, $0; gifts received, $10,095; expenditures, $13,138,878; qualifying distributions, $13,028,377.
Limitations: Applications not accepted.
Officers and Trustees:* Charles J. Stewart,* Chair.; Robert F. Lowe, Vice-Chair.; Gwen P. Davis, C.E.O. and Pres.; Norman T. Watson, V.P.; Stephen G. Ashworth, Treas.; John B. Turner, and 6 additional trustees.
EIN: 566046937
Codes: TN

62639
Daniel Jonathan Stowe Conservancy
6500 S. New Hope Road
Belmont, NC 28012

Established in 1990 in NC.
Donor(s): Daniel J. Stowe.
Financial data (yr. ended 03/31/00): Assets, $24,030,539 (M); grants paid, $0; gifts received, $2,829,528; expenditures, $3,594,551; qualifying distributions, $2,390,104; giving activities include $1,264,645 for programs.
Officers and Directors:* Daniel J. Stowe,* Chair.; James B. Garland, Vice-Chair.; Robert L. Stowe III, Pres.; Alene N. Stowe,* V.P.; Richmond H. Stowe, V.P.; Elizabeth G. Wren,* Secy.; J. Robert Wren,* Treas.; Mike Bush, Exec. Dir.; John M. Belk, H. Tate Bowers, Carolyn B. Branan, Catherine Ann Carstarphen, Rebecca B. Carter, Jonathan L. Rhyne, Jr., Diane C. Roberts, William H. Williamson III.
EIN: 561676433

62640
The McAdenville Foundation, Inc.
P.O. Box 1939
McAdenville, NC 28101-1939
(704) 824-3551

Incorporated in 1944 in NC.
Donor(s): Pharr Yarns, Inc., and local textile mills.
Financial data (yr. ended 12/31/00): Assets, $4,806,181 (M); grants paid, $90,250; gifts received, $120,166; expenditures, $531,290; qualifying distributions, $477,197.
Limitations: Applications not accepted. Giving primarily in Gastonia, NC.
Application information: Contributes only to pre-selected organizations.
Officers: J.M. Carstarphen, Pres.; James H. Howard, Secy.-Treas.
EIN: 560623961
Codes: FD2

62641
Dan Cameron Family Foundation, Inc.
P.O. Box 3649
Wilmington, NC 28406 (910) 762-2676
Contact: William H. Cameron, Dir.

Established in 1998 in NC.
Donor(s): Daniel D. Cameron, Elizabeth H. Cameron.
Financial data (yr. ended 12/31/00): Assets, $3,472,157 (M); grants paid, $207,157; expenditures, $226,367; qualifying distributions, $207,157.
Directors: Daniel D. Cameron, Jr., William H. Cameron, Hilda C. Dill, Swanna C. Saltiel, Charlotte C. Tarrants.
EIN: 562087335

62642
Richard Petty Museum, Inc.
311 Branson Mill Rd.
Randleman, NC 27317

Donor(s): Richard L. Petty.
Financial data (yr. ended 12/31/99): Assets, $3,132,251 (M); grants paid, $1,105; gifts received, $2,293,000; expenditures, $188,581; qualifying distributions, $47,272.
Limitations: Applications not accepted.
Application information: Contributes only to pre-selected organizations.
Officers: Richard L. Petty, Pres.; Kenneth Rogich, V.P.; Lynda O. Petty, Secy.-Treas.
EIN: 561859132

62643
Gee Family Foundation
720 Cherokee Rd.
Charlotte, NC 28207-2238
Contact: Milton Gee, Dir.

Established in 1997 in NC.
Donor(s): Mary P. Gee.
Financial data (yr. ended 12/31/01): Assets, $3,067,557 (M); grants paid, $46,000; gifts received, $2,370,226; expenditures, $47,400; qualifying distributions, $46,000.
Directors: Milton Gee, Virginia Gee.
EIN: 561969093

62644
Mary E. Carnrick Foundation
219 Greenwich Rd.
Charlotte, NC 28211 (704) 365-0390
Contact: A. Stuart McKaig, III, Dir.

Established in 1998 in NC.
Donor(s): Mary E. Carnrick.
Financial data (yr. ended 12/31/00): Assets, $2,492,828 (M); grants paid, $60,000; gifts received, $229,697; expenditures, $96,092; qualifying distributions, $58,599.
Directors: Mary E. Carnrick, Violet Fort, A. Stuart McKaig III.
EIN: 562114068

62645
The Ockham Foundation
c/o Wachovia Bank, N.A.
P.O. Box 3099
Winston-Salem, NC 27150-7153

Established in 1997 in NC.
Donor(s): Sylvia M. Thompson.
Financial data (yr. ended 12/31/00): Assets, $1,932,030 (M); grants paid, $200,000; expenditures, $360,349; qualifying distributions, $200,000.
Officers: Sylvia M. Thompson, Pres.; Gregory Erickson, Secy.; Susan Roberts, Treas.
Trustee: Wachovia Bank, N.A.
EIN: 562046620

62646
Alma Wynne Edgerton Memorial Foundation
3605 Glenwood Ave., Ste. 500
Raleigh, NC 27612-4959

Established in 1995 in NC.
Donor(s): Norman Edward Edgerton.‡
Financial data (yr. ended 12/31/01): Assets, $1,718,875 (M); grants paid, $0; expenditures, $29,007; qualifying distributions, $0.
Trustees: Howard E. Manning, William P. Skinner, Jr.
EIN: 561928777

62647
The Duke-Semans Fine Arts Foundation
1044 W. Forest Hills Blvd.
Durham, NC 27707-1625

Donor(s): Mary D.B.T. Semans, James H. Semans.
Financial data (yr. ended 12/31/01): Assets, $1,509,379 (M); grants paid, $27,134; expenditures, $32,934; qualifying distributions, $28,537.
Limitations: Applications not accepted. Giving primarily in NC.
Application information: Contributes only to pre-selected organizations.
Officers: James H. Semans, Pres.; Sally Harris, Secy.; Mary D.B.T. Semans, Treas.
Directors: Elon Clark, Thomas S. Kenan III.
EIN: 581447425

62648
The Frank H. Kenan Chapel at Landfall
c/o Kenan Management, Inc.
P.O. Box 4150
Chapel Hill, NC 27515-4150

Established in 1999 in NC.
Financial data (yr. ended 12/31/01): Assets, $1,347,348 (M); grants paid, $0; gifts received, $1,040,563; expenditures, $46,977; qualifying distributions, $6,676.
Limitations: Applications not accepted.
Officers: Austin L. Newson, Pres.; Penny C. Cracker, V.P.; Thomas S. Kenan III, V.P.; Frances A.

Parker,* Secy.; Braxton Schell, Secy.; E. Blake Cardwell, Treas.
Directors: Paul Davis Boney, Rev. John W.S. Davis, R.V. Fulk, Peter H. Schult.
EIN: 562099460

62649
The Preyer-Jacobs Foundation
P.O. Box 20124
Greensboro, NC 27420 (336) 274-5471
Contact: L. Richardson Preyer, Jr., Dir.

Established in 1998 in NC.
Donor(s): L. Richardson, Marilyn Jacob Preyer, Jr.
Financial data (yr. ended 12/31/99): Assets, $1,312,299 (M); grants paid, $14,932; gifts received, $964,504; expenditures, $18,432; qualifying distributions, $15,190.
Directors: L. Richardson Preyer, Jr., M.J. Preyer.
EIN: 566535541

62650
Hyatt Memorial Home for Boys
P.O. Box 1523
Kinston, NC 28503 (252) 939-1523
Contact: Mary-Miles Jones, V.P.

Financial data (yr. ended 12/31/99): Assets, $1,294,493 (M); grants paid, $35,500; expenditures, $53,711; qualifying distributions, $53,711; giving activities include $3,111 for programs.
Application information: Applicants must submit high school or equivalent official transcript. Application form required.
Officers: JD Woolard, Jr., Pres.; Lamar Jones, Jr., V.P.; Mary-Miles Jones, V.P.
EIN: 560891771

62651
Christian Corps International
6512 six Forks Rd.
Raleigh, NC 27615-6516

Established in 1987 in NC.
Donor(s): Ernest O'Neil, Irene O'Neil.
Financial data (yr. ended 12/31/01): Assets, $1,183,554 (M); grants paid, $0; gifts received, $92,063; expenditures, $78,583; qualifying distributions, $57,286; giving activities include $23,040 for programs.
Directors: Mary Klewer, Myran Klewer, Ernest O'Neill, Irene O'Neill.
EIN: 581757973

62652
Franklin-Vance-Warren Housing of Franklinton, Inc.
116 Young St.
Henderson, NC 27536

Financial data (yr. ended 06/30/00): Assets, $1,133,620 (M); grants paid, $0; expenditures, $237,685; qualifying distributions, $0; giving activities include $31,472 for programs.
Officers: Hon. Alfred M. Goodwin, Pres.; James R. Jones, V.P.
Directors: Ralph Brown, Ralph S. Knott, Tommy Leonard.
EIN: 561564832

62653
North Carolina Wildlife Federation Endowment and Education Fund, Inc.
P.O. Box 10626
Raleigh, NC 27605-0626

Established in 1996 in NC.
Financial data (yr. ended 06/30/01): Assets, $959,490 (M); grants paid, $4,500; gifts received, $168,145; expenditures, $96,851; qualifying distributions, $78,369.

Limitations: Giving primarily in NC.
Officers and Directors:* Bryan Upchurch,* Chair.; John Lentz,* Vice-Chair.; Gray J. Shaw,* Secy.; Sid Baynes, Phil Bracewell, Phil Doerr, Max Greene, Steven Leath, Anne Taylor, Harry Wilfong.
EIN: 560481015

62654
High Pastures, Inc.
c/o Donald A. Blankenship
Rte. 6, Box 483
Burnsville, NC 28714

Established in 1969 in NC.
Donor(s): Elizabeth Motsinger.
Financial data (yr. ended 12/31/00): Assets, $802,417 (M); grants paid, $0; gifts received, $54,402; expenditures, $226,683; qualifying distributions, $193,364; giving activities include $226,683 for programs.
Limitations: Giving primarily for international Christian missions.
Application information: Application form not required.
Officers: Ed Kale, Secy.; Gerald Marion, Treas.; Chuck Phelps, Exec. Dir.
EIN: 237017056

62655
The Ann G. and W. Vann York Foundation
905 Arbordale Ave.
High Point, NC 27262-4625

Classified as a private operating foundation in 1988.
Donor(s): Ann G. York, W. Vann York.
Financial data (yr. ended 12/31/01): Assets, $756,966 (M); grants paid, $200,000; expenditures, $200,375; qualifying distributions, $200,015.
Limitations: Giving primarily in High Point, NC.
Officers: W. Vann York, Pres.; Elizabeth Y. Schiff, V.P.; Lynn Y. Warisila, V.P.; Greg York, V.P.; Ann G. York, Secy.-Treas.
EIN: 561590100
Codes: FD2

62656
The Pisgah Hope Foundation
P.O. Box 68
Lake Toxaway, NC 28747-0068
(828) 877-5135

Established in 1997 in NC.
Financial data (yr. ended 12/31/00): Assets, $741,251 (M); grants paid, $8,045; gifts received, $2,500; expenditures, $55,646; qualifying distributions, $9,245.
Application information: Application form required.
Officers: Eunja Connie Kim, C.E.O.; Soo Hee Kim, Pres.; Albert Myung Kim, V.P.
EIN: 621681363

62657
Wyck Charitable Trust
c/o First Union National Bank
401 S. Tryon St., NC 1159
Charlotte, NC 28288-1159
Application address: c/o Eugene Williams, 123 S. Broad St. PA1279, Philadelphia PA 19109
Contact: Donna Farrington

Classified as a private operating foundation in 1974.
Financial data (yr. ended 09/30/01): Assets, $723,541 (M); grants paid, $30,608; expenditures, $40,749; qualifying distributions, $29,747.
Trustee: First Union National Bank.
EIN: 236568496

62658
Frances H. Wolf Trust f/b/o Wolf Museum of Music & Art
c/o First Union National Bank
401 S. Tryon St., NC1159
Charlotte, NC 28288-1159

Classified as a private operating foundation in 1974.
Financial data (yr. ended 01/31/02): Assets, $721,260 (M); grants paid, $0; gifts received, $139; expenditures, $24,991; qualifying distributions, $0.
Trustee: First Union National Bank.
EIN: 236560772

62659
Boiling Spring Lakes Volunteer Fire Department
P.O. Box 2647
Southport, NC 28461

Established around 1971.
Financial data (yr. ended 06/30/01): Assets, $667,626 (M); grants paid, $0; gifts received, $172,542; expenditures, $223,315; qualifying distributions, $0.
Officers: Myrtle Meade, Pres.; Bill Dunn, V.P.; Polly Doane, Secy.; Dewey W. Propst, Treas.; Connie Propst, Dir., Fin.
EIN: 237350442

62660
Summer Rest Foundation
415 Summer Rest Rd.
Wilmington, NC 28405

Classified as a private operating foundation in NC.
Donor(s): George C. Turner, Sue M. Turner.
Financial data (yr. ended 12/31/99): Assets, $660,194 (M); grants paid, $25,000; gifts received, $178,500; expenditures, $25,453; qualifying distributions, $25,000.
Limitations: Applications not accepted.
Application information: Contributes only to pre-selected organizations.
Directors: Jay G. Loftin, Jr., W. Gerald Thornton, Sue M. Turner.
EIN: 566534008

62661
Keihin Carolina System Technology Foundation, Inc.
4047 McNair Rd.
Tarboro, NC 27886

Established in 2000 in NC.
Financial data (yr. ended 03/31/01): Assets, $523,506 (M); grants paid, $510,938; gifts received, $1,000,000; expenditures, $514,543; qualifying distributions, $510,938.
Limitations: Giving primarily in NC.
Officers and Directors:* Mitsuaki Sakamoto,* Pres.; Norio Watanabe,* V.P.; Randall K. Carpenter,* Secy.; Donald W. Rupprecht,* Treas.
EIN: 562190882
Codes: FD

62662
The Foundation for Music-Based Learning
P.O. Box 4274
Greensboro, NC 27404

Classified as a private operating foundation in 1994.
Financial data (yr. ended 08/31/01): Assets, $460,502 (M); grants paid, $0; gifts received, $102,625; expenditures, $48,024; qualifying distributions, $47,973.
Directors: Dee Joy Coulter, Herman K. Heyge, Lorna L. Heyge.
EIN: 561853136

62663
Anne West Strawbridge Trust
c/o First Union National Bank
401 S. Tryon St.
Charlotte, NC 28202

Classified as a private operating foundation in 1974.
Financial data (yr. ended 12/31/00): Assets, $436,228 (M); grants paid, $0; expenditures, $42,408; qualifying distributions, $40,948; giving activities include $16,698 for programs.
Trustee: First Union National Bank.
EIN: 236219255

62664
The Ecology/Wildlife Foundation
140 N. Stratford Rd.
Winston-Salem, NC 27104

Established in 1999 in NC.
Donor(s): William N. Reynolds II.
Financial data (yr. ended 06/30/01): Assets, $428,224 (M); grants paid, $20,250; gifts received, $126,315; expenditures, $23,160; qualifying distributions, $19,869.
Limitations: Applications not accepted. Giving primarily in NC.
Application information: Contributes only to pre-selected organizations.
Officers: William Neal Reynolds II, Chair.; Brook Elizabeth Reynolds, Vice-Chair.
Directors: Sandra Edwina Reynolds, William N. Reynolds.
EIN: 562135720

62665
Retail Home Furnishings Foundation, Inc.
(Formerly National Home Furnishings Foundation, Inc.)
P.O. Box 1310
High Point, NC 27261

Donor(s): M. Wallace Rubin, John Steinhafel, Sidney Meyers, Robert Glick.
Financial data (yr. ended 12/31/01): Assets, $396,162 (M); grants paid, $0; expenditures, $24,312; qualifying distributions, $0.
Officers and Directors:* John Steinhafel,* Chair.; Hershel Alpert,* Vice-Chair.; Patricia Bowling,* Secy.; John Heleringer,* Treas.; Roger Bunips, Gary Greenbaum, Rawson Haverty, Melvin Lack, Maurice Purcell, A.R. Weiler.
EIN: 561620576

62666
North Carolina Auto Racing-Hall of Fame Museum
c/o Museum Curator
P.O Box 830
Mooresville, NC 28115

Established in 1994; Classified as a private operating foundation in 1996.
Financial data (yr. ended 12/31/99): Assets, $376,796 (M); grants paid, $0; gifts received, $16,813; expenditures, $283,698; qualifying distributions, $255,956; giving activities include $255,956 for programs.
Officers and Trustees:* Cecile Ebert,* Chair.; Ronnie Stevens,* Secy.-Treas.; Johnny Hayes, Garry Hill, Benny Parsons, Rusty Wallece, Deb Williams, and 5 additional trustees.
EIN: 566437557

62667
Berryhill Foundation
7328 Sardis Rd.
Charlotte, NC 28270 (704) 364-6933
Contact: L. David Berryhill, Jr., Pres.

Established in 1995 in NC.
Donor(s): L. David Berryhill, Jr., Barbara D. Berryhill.
Financial data (yr. ended 12/31/00): Assets, $329,906 (M); grants paid, $14,645; gifts received, $15,750; expenditures, $43,369; qualifying distributions, $30,496.
Limitations: Giving primarily in NC.
Application information: Application form not required.
Officers: L. David Berryhill, Jr., Pres.; Barbara D. Berryhill, Secy.
Trustees: Elizabeth B. Cameron, Deborah B. Warren.
EIN: 561891335

62668
Lambert Family Foundation, Inc.
c/o Harry W. Lambert
87 Willow Rd., Unit B-4
Waynesville, NC 28786 (828) 456-3798

Established in 1994 in FL.
Financial data (yr. ended 12/31/01): Assets, $292,850 (M); grants paid, $15,800; expenditures, $23,252; qualifying distributions, $16,800.
Directors: Harry W. Lambert, Suzanne R. Lambert, William A. Lambert, Pamela L. Rilling, Laurie A. Stokes.
EIN: 593293497

62669
Research News and Opportunities in Science and Theology
415 Clarion Dr.
Durham, NC 27705

Established in 2000 in NC.
Donor(s): John Templeton Foundation.
Financial data (yr. ended 12/31/01): Assets, $255,206 (M); grants paid, $0; gifts received, $577,535; expenditures, $689,858; qualifying distributions, $0.
Limitations: Applications not accepted.
Application information: Contributes only to pre-selected organizations.
Officers: Harold G. Koenig, Pres.; Malvern King, Treas.
Director: John M. Templeton, Jr.
EIN: 562188686

62670
The Bost Foundation
16116 N. Point Rd.
Huntersville, NC 28078 (704) 875-0559
Contact: Edward B. Bost, Pres.

Established in 1986 in NC.
Donor(s): Edward B. Bost, Claudia H. Bost.
Financial data (yr. ended 12/31/99): Assets, $242,975 (M); grants paid, $26,000; gifts received, $14,750; expenditures, $26,346; qualifying distributions, $26,346.
Limitations: Giving primarily in NC.
Application information: Application form not required.
Officers and Directors:* Edward B. Bost,* Pres. and Treas.; Claudia H. Bost,* V.P. and Secy.; H. Morrison Johnston.
EIN: 660424035

62671
Inez Kight Boddie Scholarship Trust
c/o Bank of America
Bank of America Plz., NC1-002-11-18
Charlotte, NC 28255
Application address: c/o Bank of America, P.O. Box 4446, GA1-006-08-11, Atlanta, GA 30302, tel.: (404) 607-6379
Contact: Kim Sexton

Established in 1989 in GA.
Financial data (yr. ended 12/31/01): Assets, $225,152 (M); grants paid, $31,500; expenditures, $33,363; qualifying distributions, $32,300.
Limitations: Giving limited to residents of GA.
Application information: Application form not required.
Trustee: Bank of America.
EIN: 586233854

62672
Walter C. and Daisy C. Latham Foundation, Inc.
P.O. Box 8521
Greenville, NC 27835-8521
Contact: David C. Miller

Donor(s): W. Bryan Latham.
Financial data (yr. ended 12/31/00): Assets, $224,921 (M); grants paid, $506,600; gifts received, $394,577; expenditures, $510,493; qualifying distributions, $505,678.
Limitations: Giving limited to residents of Pitt County, NC.
Application information: Application form required.
Officers: W. Bryan Latham, Pres.; Charlotte L. Miller, Treas.
EIN: 561437068
Codes: FD

62673
Bell Foundation
(Formerly Atmospheric Understanding and Research of Architecture)
c/o John Monticone
514 Daniels St., No. 400
Raleigh, NC 27605

Established in 1985 in MA. Classified as a private operating foundation in 1986.
Donor(s): Jane P. Bell.
Financial data (yr. ended 09/30/99): Assets, $188,589 (M); grants paid, $0; expenditures, $16,868; qualifying distributions, $16,868; giving activities include $16,868 for programs.
Trustees: Jane P. Bell, John A. Seiler.
EIN: 222756791

62674
John S. Swaim Memorial Scholarship Fund
379 S. Cox St.
Asheboro, NC 27203 (336) 626-9970
Contact: Maxton C. McDowell, Pres.

Established in 1998 NC.
Financial data (yr. ended 12/31/00): Assets, $169,612 (M); grants paid, $6,000; expenditures, $7,723; qualifying distributions, $6,000.
Limitations: Giving to residents of Asheboro, NC.
Application information: Application form required.
Officers: Maxton C. McDowell, Pres.; J. Gale Thomas, Secy.
EIN: 562123531

62675
North Carolina Farm Bureau Legal Foundation, Inc.
P.O. Box 27766
Raleigh, NC 27611

Classified as a company-sponsored operating foundation.
Donor(s): North Carolina Farm Bureau Federation, Inc., North Carolina Farm Bureau, Inc. Political Action Committee, Inc.
Financial data (yr. ended 12/31/00): Assets, $158,818 (M); grants paid, $13,923; gifts received, $17,100; expenditures, $14,582; qualifying distributions, $14,582.
Limitations: Applications not accepted. Giving limited to NC.
Application information: Contributes only to pre-selected organizations.
Officers and Directors:* Larry B. Wooten,* Pres.; D. Elton Braswell,* V.P.; H. Julian Philpott, Jr., Secy.; Perry L. Crutchfield, Treas.; T.R. Burgess, Charles Joyce, Gene B. Lanier, Bob Park, Jimmie M. Parrish, J.M. Wright, Jr., and 4 additional directors.
EIN: 581527534

62676
The Edwards Family Mission Foundation
P.O. Box 5045
Eden, NC 27289-5045

Established in 1997 in NC.
Donor(s): Garland Edwards, B. Michael Edwards, Marion Edwards.
Financial data (yr. ended 12/31/01): Assets, $137,695 (M); grants paid, $55,000; expenditures, $56,092; qualifying distributions, $54,932.
Limitations: Applications not accepted. Giving primarily in Haiti.
Application information: Contributes only to pre-selected organizations.
Officers: G. Michael Edwards, Pres.; Carol Hundley, Secy.; Marion Edwards, Treas.
Directors: W. Reggie Hundley, Johnny Sides, Thalia Turner.
EIN: 561852061

62677
The Adelaide Gurganus Jackson Foundation
5219 Trent Woods Dr.
New Bern, NC 28562-7441

Established in 1987 in NC.
Donor(s): Rudolph Hoyt Jackson.‡
Financial data (yr. ended 06/30/00): Assets, $129,441 (M); grants paid, $8,000; expenditures, $10,722; qualifying distributions, $8,000.
Limitations: Giving primarily in Craven County, NC.
Officers: Ann J. Johnson, Pres.; Lester W. Johnson, Jr., Treas.
Trustees: Pam Fillinger, Lucille Stewart, Leann Wilson.
EIN: 561570654
Codes: GTI

62678
The Duplin County Historical Foundation, Inc.
P.O. Box 130
Rose Hill, NC 28458-0130

Established in 1987 in NC; funded in 1991.
Financial data (yr. ended 12/31/01): Assets, $127,601 (M); grants paid, $0; gifts received, $11,281; expenditures, $16,736; qualifying distributions, $0.
Officers: W.D. Herring, Pres. and Treas.; Horace Fussell, Jr., V.P.; Leon H. Sykes, Secy.
EIN: 581763501

62679
Robert White & Gaither Smoot Deaton Charitable Foundation, Inc.
2619 Richardson Dr.
Charlotte, NC 28211 (704) 367-3414
Contact: Robert White Deaton, Dir.

Established in 1999 in NC.
Donor(s): Robert White Deaton, Gaither Smoot Deaton.
Financial data (yr. ended 12/31/00): Assets, $117,489 (M); grants paid, $12,860; gifts received, $30,193; expenditures, $13,459; qualifying distributions, $12,751.
Limitations: Giving primarily in NC.
Directors: Gaither Smoot Deaton, Robert White Deaton.
EIN: 562115340

62680
Fred Siler Scholarship Fund
43 W. Main St.
Franklin, NC 28734 (828) 524-6475
Contact: Robert F. Siler, Tr.

Established in 1975.
Donor(s): Allen Siler, Margaret D'Onotrio, Freda Siler.
Financial data (yr. ended 12/31/01): Assets, $113,990 (M); grants paid, $1,800; expenditures, $1,885; qualifying distributions, $1,885.
Limitations: Giving limited to residents of NC.
Application information: Application form required.
Trustees: Freda S. McCombs, Nancy S. Scott, Robert F. Siler.
EIN: 561935419

62681
New Bern Benevolent Society
4511 Glouster Dr.
New Bern, NC 28562-7211

Financial data (yr. ended 12/31/99): Assets, $113,244 (M); grants paid, $50; gifts received, $6,000; expenditures, $7,980; qualifying distributions, $7,980; giving activities include $7,980 for programs.
Limitations: Applications not accepted.
Application information: Contributes only to pre-selected organizations.
Officers: Betsy Holmes, Pres.; Mary Walker, Secy.; Diane Mcquade, Treas.
EIN: 561419614

62682
Jeffery D. Carter Family Foundation
17606 Westward Reach
Cornelius, NC 28031

Established in 1999 in NC.
Donor(s): Jeffery D. Carter, Denise F. Carter.
Financial data (yr. ended 12/31/00): Assets, $106,208 (M); grants paid, $14,200; expenditures, $17,714; qualifying distributions, $14,200.
Limitations: Applications not accepted. Giving primarily in NC.
Application information: Contributes only to pre-selected organizations.
Officers: Jeffery D. Carter, Pres.; Denise F. Carter, Secy.
EIN: 562149295

62683
Maxwell M. Corpening, Jr. Memorial Foundation
P.O. Box 2400
Marion, NC 28752
Application address: c/o McDowell Court House, Rm. 217, Marion, NC 28752
Contact: Terri Laws

Established in 1972 in NC.
Donor(s): M.M. Corpening Foundation, Duke Power Co., Mrs. M.M. Corpening.‡
Financial data (yr. ended 12/31/01): Assets, $105,176 (M); grants paid, $861,771; gifts received, $876,391; expenditures, $874,611; qualifying distributions, $872,143.
Limitations: Giving limited to McDowell County, NC only.
Application information: Mailed applications not accepted. Unsolicited requests for funds not accepted. Application form required.
Officers and Trustee:* Jackie Turner, Chair.; Tyler Martin, Vice-Chair.; David Wooten,* Treas.
EIN: 237201488
Codes: FD, GTI

62684
Tree of Life, Inc.
1950 Cliffside Dr.
Pfafftown, NC 27040
Contact: Victor Faccinto, Pres.

Financial data (yr. ended 12/31/01): Assets, $105,123 (M); grants paid, $0; gifts received, $29,036; expenditures, $10,139; qualifying distributions, $0.
Officers: Victor Faccinto, Pres.; Laura Hedrick, Secy.
EIN: 561955862

62685
Strawvalley Foundation
5420 Chapel Hill Blvd.
Durham, NC 27707-3317

Donor(s): Robert Black, Jesse O. Sanderson.
Financial data (yr. ended 12/31/01): Assets, $95,525 (M); grants paid, $0; gifts received, $208; expenditures, $254; qualifying distributions, $0.
Limitations: Applications not accepted.
Application information: Contributes only to pre-selected organizations.
Officers: Robert Black, Pres.; Jesse O. Sanderson, Secy.
EIN: 561928200

62686
The McKee Charitable Foundation, Inc.
P.O. Box 4479
Davidson, NC 28036 (704) 892-4866
Contact: George C. McKee, Pres.

Donor(s): George C. McKee.
Financial data (yr. ended 12/31/00): Assets, $88,954 (M); grants paid, $49,500; gifts received, $100,533; expenditures, $50,294; qualifying distributions, $50,278.
Officers: George C. McKee, Pres.; Christopher McKee, V.P.; George C. McKee, Jr., V.P.; Jean P. McKee, Secy.
EIN: 571068011

62687
Geophex Foundation, Inc.
c/o I.J. Won
605 Mercury St.
Raleigh, NC 27603

Financial data (yr. ended 12/31/00): Assets, $88,738 (M); grants paid, $2,000; expenditures, $2,000; qualifying distributions, $2,000.

62687—NORTH CAROLINA

Limitations: Applications not accepted.
Application information: Contributes only to pre-selected organizations.
Directors: Steven J. Daib, I.J. Won, Susan T. Won.
EIN: 561852630

62688
The Marian Foundation
6418 Gold Mine Loop
Chapel Hill, NC 27516 (919) 929-9219
Contact: Helen Davidson, Pres.

Established in 1999 in NC.
Donor(s): Helen Davidson, Richard Tapper.
Financial data (yr. ended 11/30/00): Assets, $81,934 (M); grants paid, $5,000; gifts received, $106,443; expenditures, $5,000; qualifying distributions, $5,000.
Limitations: Giving primarily in WY.
Officers: Helen Davidson, Pres. and Treas.; Richard Tapper, Secy.
EIN: 562169788

62689
Winston-Salem/Forsyth County Community Access Television, Inc.
P.O. Box 10890
Winston-Salem, NC 27108

Established in 1994 in NC.
Financial data (yr. ended 06/30/00): Assets, $79,665 (M); grants paid, $0; gifts received, $112,108; expenditures, $155,731; qualifying distributions, $125,907; giving activities include $118,396 for programs.
Officers: Baxter Griffin, Chair.; Darla Bates, Vice-Chair.; Stephanie Nelson, Secy.; Wali Salaam, Treas.; Todd Davis, Mgr.
Directors: Albert Bambach, Vance Cabiness, Adrienne Hahn, and 10 additional directors.
EIN: 561875969

62690
Waldo Foundation
1373 O'Kelly Chapel Rd.
Durham, NC 27713-7477

Established in 1997 in NC. Classified as a private operating foundation in 1998.
Financial data (yr. ended 12/31/00): Assets, $74,856 (M); grants paid, $3,400; expenditures, $3,832; qualifying distributions, $3,832.
Limitations: Applications not accepted.
Application information: Contributes only to pre-selected organizations.
Officers and Directors:* David Dodd,* Pres. and Treas.; Barbara Bertram,* Secy.; Charlie Barker, Rev. Mark Christy, Anne Dodd, Wallace R. Dodd, Jr., John Elton Hunsucker, Allen E. Kivett, Arch Morgan, Daphane D. Scott.
EIN: 561950176

62691
American Educational & Advanced Studies Foundation, Inc.
c/o Andrew S. Martin
401 Oberlin Rd., Ste. 103
Raleigh, NC 27605
Contact: William R. Davis, Chair.

Donor(s): William R. Davis.
Financial data (yr. ended 03/31/00): Assets, $72,516 (M); grants paid, $50; gifts received, $740; expenditures, $707; qualifying distributions, $707.
Limitations: Giving primarily in NC.
Application information: Application form required.
Officers and Trustees:* William R. Davis,* Chair., Pres. and Secy.-Treas.; Kathryn L. Beckner, Eric Reed Davis, David H. Martin, James W. York, Jr.

EIN: 237414904

62692
Chhotubahi Patel Family Foundation
3 Post Bridge Ct.
Greensboro, NC 27407-7766

Established in 1999 in CT.
Financial data (yr. ended 12/31/00): Assets, $71,121 (M); grants paid, $159,775; gifts received, $146,400; expenditures, $160,819; qualifying distributions, $159,775.
Limitations: Applications not accepted. Giving limited to India.
Application information: Contributes only to a pre-selected organization.
Officers: Chhotubahi Patel, Pres.; Nayan Patel, V.P.
EIN: 226767808
Codes: FD2

62693
The Foundation for University Medical Care for Children
50021 Brogden
Chapel Hill, NC 27517-8589

Established in 1985 in NC.
Donor(s): Jacob Lohr.
Financial data (yr. ended 09/30/01): Assets, $56,590 (M); grants paid, $15,450; expenditures, $16,049; qualifying distributions, $15,450.
Limitations: Applications not accepted. Giving primarily in NC.
Officer: Charles B. Carver, Secy.
EIN: 541319991

62694
Stallings Memorial Park Charitable Trust
c/o Kerwin B. Stallings
Rte. 4, Box 292
Louisburg, NC 27549

Established in 1989 in NC.
Donor(s): Louise Gibson, Maude Hoss, Kerwin B. Stallings,‡ Mary Williams, Andrew Stallings.
Financial data (yr. ended 06/30/99): Assets, $49,050 (M); grants paid, $0; gifts received, $545; expenditures, $1,222; qualifying distributions, $1,211; giving activities include $1,257 for programs.
Officers and Trustees:* Durward Stallings,* Chair.; Iris Leibforth,* Secy.-Treas.; Helen Gardner, Louise Gibson, Sarah Hale, Judy Lee, Sidney Robert White, Lynn Williams, Robert E. Williams, and 14 additional trustees.
EIN: 581900995

62695
The Whitlow-Osborne Scholarship Foundation, Inc.
(Formerly The Carson and Maggie Whitlow Scholarship Foundation, Inc.)
503 Center Pointe Dr.
Cary, NC 27513
Contact: Sheila Whitlow Cromer, Secy.-Treas

Financial data (yr. ended 12/31/00): Assets, $45,355 (M); grants paid, $1,000; expenditures, $1,162; qualifying distributions, $45,355.
Limitations: Giving limited to High Point, NC.
Application information: Contact any NC community college for application. Application form required.
Officers and Directors:* Dwight McDowell,* Pres.; Phyllis W. Osborne,* V.P.; Sheila Whitlow Cromer,* Secy.-Treas.
EIN: 581727569

62696
The Lillian C. and Melvin W. (Bud) Cothran Memorial Scholarship Fund
(Formerly The Melvin W. (Bud) Cothran Memorial Scholarship Fund)
P.O. Box 554
Rosman, NC 28772 (828) 883-8700
Application address: c/o Selection Comm., Rosman High School, Rosman, NC 28772

Classified as a private operating foundation in 1984.
Financial data (yr. ended 12/31/01): Assets, $43,582 (M); grants paid, $1,141; gifts received, $400; expenditures, $1,209; qualifying distributions, $1,115.
Limitations: Giving limited to Upper Transylvania County, NC, with emphasis on Rosman.
Application information: Application form required.
Officer: Joseph C. McCall, Secy.-Treas.
EIN: 561372596

62697
The Taylor Family Private Foundation
5409 Den Heider Way
Raleigh, NC 27606

Established in 1998 in NC.
Financial data (yr. ended 12/31/01): Assets, $42,680 (M); grants paid, $6,000; gifts received, $1,525; expenditures, $7,513; qualifying distributions, $6,000.
Limitations: Applications not accepted.
Application information: Contributes only to pre-selected organizations.
Trustees: Mary R. Taylor, Robert W. Taylor, Jr.
EIN: 562076739

62698
Garison Family Private Foundation
6859 Towbridge Rd.
Fayetteville, NC 28306

Established in 1996 in NC.
Financial data (yr. ended 12/31/00): Assets, $41,900 (M); grants paid, $250; expenditures, $1,820; qualifying distributions, $1,750.
Limitations: Applications not accepted.
Application information: Contributes only to pre-selected organizations.
Trustees: Gary B. Garison, Iris A. Garison.
EIN: 562001781

62699
Al-Anon/Alateen Service Office of North Carolina
P.O. Box 18731
Raleigh, NC 27619-8731

Classified as a private operating foundation in 1989.
Financial data (yr. ended 12/31/01): Assets, $41,835 (M); grants paid, $0; gifts received, $3,505; expenditures, $60,083; qualifying distributions, $0.
Officers and Directors:* Don Greene, Chair.; Virginia Grant,* Secy.; Lee Eck,* Treas.; Monika Coleman, Walter W. Heck, George Jewell, Sherrill Montgomery, Hill Powell, Catherine Traylor.
EIN: 561272028

62700
Chandgie Foundation, Inc.
401 Kimberly Dr., Ste. 627
Greensboro, NC 27408

Donor(s): Robert S. Chandgie.
Financial data (yr. ended 09/30/00): Assets, $37,325 (M); grants paid, $1,864; expenditures, $1,888; qualifying distributions, $1,881.

Limitations: Applications not accepted. Giving primarily in NC.
Application information: Contributes only to pre-selected organizations.
Officers: Robert S. Chandgie, Pres. and Mgr.; Bettie S. Chandgie, V.P.; Bobby R. Summers, Secy.
EIN: 566095706

62701
Barbara C. Stewart Charitable Foundation, Inc.
4005 Westmount Dr.
Greensboro, NC 27410-2164

Established in 1999.
Donor(s): Edward L. Stewart.
Financial data (yr. ended 12/31/99): Assets, $33,250 (M); grants paid, $1,000; gifts received, $30,000; expenditures, $1,587; qualifying distributions, $958.
Limitations: Applications not accepted.
Application information: Contributes only to pre-selected organizations.
Officer: Cheryl C. Stewart, Pres.
Director: Edward L. Stewart.
EIN: 562114779

62702
Darryl E. Unruh Foundation, Inc.
68 Orange St.
Asheville, NC 28801-2341
Contact: Darryl E. Unruh, Pres.

Classified as a private operating foundation in 1987.
Donor(s): Darryl E. Unruh.
Financial data (yr. ended 12/31/01): Assets, $32,834 (M); grants paid, $11,726; gifts received, $25,000; expenditures, $12,857; qualifying distributions, $12,857.
Limitations: Giving limited to Asheville and Buncombe County, NC.
Application information: Application form required.
Officers: Darryl E. Unruh, Pres.; Grace T. Unruh, V.P.
Director: Rev. Robert Sweet.
EIN: 561570954
Codes: GTI

62703
William Pitts Foundation
1010 Edgehill Rd. N.
Charlotte, NC 28207 (704) 376-1605
Contact: Mary Cloninger, V.P.

Established in 2000 in NC.
Financial data (yr. ended 12/31/01): Assets, $27,274 (M); grants paid, $700; gifts received, $10,020; expenditures, $35,094; qualifying distributions, $687.
Limitations: Giving primarily in NC.
Application information: Application form required.
Officers: C. Scott McClanahan, Pres.; Mary S. Cloninger, V.P.
Directors: Anthony L. Asher, Jerry M. Petty, Rodney C. Pitts, William R. Pitts, Jr., Craig A. Vanderveer, Joseph Warren III.
EIN: 562082351

62704
J. C. Steele, Jr. Scholarship Foundation
P.O. Box 1834
Statesville, NC 28687-1834
Contact: John S. Steele, Pres.

Donor(s): John S. Steele.
Financial data (yr. ended 12/31/99): Assets, $25,784 (M); grants paid, $5,000; gifts received, $2,025; expenditures, $5,013; qualifying distributions, $5,013.

Application information: Application form required.
Officers: John S. Steele, Pres. and Treas.; Henry Forest Steele, Secy.
Trustee: John C. Steele III.
EIN: 581530789

62705
The Paul M. & Mildred S. Minus Foundation Charitable Trust
625 College Ave.
P.O. Box 1849
Shelby, NC 28151-1849

Established in 1998 in NC.
Financial data (yr. ended 12/31/00): Assets, $25,517 (M); grants paid, $200; gifts received, $22,240; expenditures, $1,378; qualifying distributions, $200.
Trustees: Joseph S. Minus, Paul Murray Minus, Betty Minus Young.
EIN: 546442795

62706
The Leadership Trust
P.O. Box 49027
Greensboro, NC 27419-9027

Classified as a private operating foundation in NC.
Financial data (yr. ended 06/30/00): Assets, $25,375 (M); grants paid, $0; gifts received, $36,630; expenditures, $43,565; qualifying distributions, $1,406; giving activities include $36,574 for programs.
Officers: James N. Farr, Pres.; Holly Latty-Mann, V.P.
EIN: 561855626

62707
Horton Foundation
102 Hillside Ln.
Morganton, NC 28655
Contact: Charles E. Horton, Chair.

Established in 1997 in NC.
Donor(s): Charles E. Horton.
Financial data (yr. ended 12/31/00): Assets, $22,245 (M); grants paid, $1,102; gifts received, $453; expenditures, $1,555; qualifying distributions, $1,102.
Officers: Charles E. Horton, Chair.; Antoinette G. Horton, Secy.-Treas.
EIN: 562037676

62708
Ruth Harbison Carr Family Foundation
211 W. Park Dr.
Morganton, NC 28655
Contact: Ruth Harbison Carr, Pres.

Established in 2000 in NC.
Financial data (yr. ended 12/31/00): Assets, $20,632 (M); grants paid, $7,050; gifts received, $25,120; expenditures, $7,050; qualifying distributions, $7,050.
Officers: Ruth Harbison Carr, Pres.; Ralph Edwards, Jr., V.P.; Gray O'Neill, Secy.
EIN: 566566443

62709
Outreach, Inc.
106 Homewood Dr.
Greensboro, NC 27403

Donor(s): David H. Petty II, Virginia K. Petty, Paul D. Sexton, Mrs. Paul D. Sexton.
Financial data (yr. ended 12/31/01): Assets, $19,401 (M); grants paid, $0; gifts received, $91,300; expenditures, $82,442; qualifying distributions, $0.
Officers: Virginia K. Petty, Pres.; Karen P. Sexton, V.P.; Paul D. Sexton, Secy.; David H. Petty II, Treas.

EIN: 581333678

62710
Maola Foundation for Children, Inc.
P.O. Drawer S
New Bern, NC 28560-8518

Established in 1994 in NC.
Donor(s): Maola Milk & Ice Cream Co., Inc.
Financial data (yr. ended 03/31/01): Assets, $19,400 (M); grants paid, $31,465; gifts received, $50,661; expenditures, $31,465; qualifying distributions, $31,465.
Limitations: Applications not accepted.
Application information: Contributes only to pre-selected organizations.
Officers: Kenneth G. Reesman, Pres.; Mildred B. Green, V.P.; Ronald Kelly, Secy.-Treas.
Directors: James B. Green, C. Maxwell Mason, Charlie E. Parker.
EIN: 561896508

62711
A.M. Linton Foundation
120 Church St.
Black Mountain, NC 28711

Established in 2000 in NC.
Donor(s): Andrew M. Linton, Heidi Linton.
Financial data (yr. ended 12/31/00): Assets, $16,684 (L); grants paid, $0; gifts received, $19,531; expenditures, $4,821; qualifying distributions, $4,005; giving activities include $500 for programs.
Directors: Andrew M. Linton, Heidi Linton.
EIN: 562166094

62712
Peacehaven, Inc.
608 JC Norton Rd.
Warrensville, NC 28693-9214

Donor(s): Z. Smith Reynolds Foundation.
Financial data (yr. ended 06/30/01): Assets, $15,895 (M); grants paid, $9,800; gifts received, $35,000; expenditures, $27,262; qualifying distributions, $27,232.
Limitations: Giving primarily in NC.
Officers: Julia Ribet Rogers, Pres.; Shirley Burch, V.P.; Jeff Pinto, Secy.-Treas.
EIN: 561931898

62713
Gungor Solmaz Foundation
P.O. Box 1118
Conover, NC 28613-1118
Contact: Gungor M. Solmaz, Pres.

Established in 1998 in NC.
Donor(s): Gungor M. Solmaz.
Financial data (yr. ended 12/31/01): Assets, $11,127 (M); grants paid, $94,641; gifts received, $66,776; expenditures, $103,439; qualifying distributions, $101,660.
Limitations: Applications not accepted.
Application information: Contributes only to pre-selected organizations.
Officers: Gungor M. Solmaz, Pres.; Diana M. Solmaz, V.P.; Mary Lou Stilwell, Secy.
EIN: 562101578
Codes: FD2

62714
The Erick Strickland Foundation
14200 Plantation Park Blvd., Ste. 1118
Charlotte, NC 28277
Contact: Matthew Strickland, Dir.

Established in 1998 in MD and TX.
Financial data (yr. ended 12/31/99): Assets, $10,738 (M); grants paid, $64,829; gifts received,

62714—NORTH CAROLINA

$115,000; expenditures, $105,650; qualifying distributions, $105,375.
Trustees: Randy Dowman, Dexter Moore.
Director: Matthew Strickland.
EIN: 522071012

62715
Page I, A Charitable Trust
P.O. Box 106
Concord, NC 28026

Financial data (yr. ended 12/31/99): Assets, $9,695 (M); grants paid, $500; gifts received, $9,150; expenditures, $500; qualifying distributions, $500.
Limitations: Applications not accepted.
Application information: Contributes only to pre-selected organizations.
Officer: Patricia Page, Mgr.
EIN: 566519319

62716
The Robert & Barbara Appel Private Foundation
536 Levenhall Dr.
Fayetteville, NC 28305

Established in 1997 in NC.
Financial data (yr. ended 12/31/00): Assets, $7,464 (L); grants paid, $164,730; gifts received, $80,000; expenditures, $166,295; qualifying distributions, $166,230.
Limitations: Applications not accepted. Giving primarily in Waterford, Ireland.
Application information: Contributes only to pre-selected organizations.
Trustees: Barbara L. Appel, Robert A. Appel.
EIN: 562054802
Codes: FD2

62717
Mary Charles Maxwell Foundation
6745 Wheeler Dr.
Charlotte, NC 28211-4760

Established in 2000 in NC.
Donor(s): Raymond Maxwell, Jr.
Financial data (yr. ended 12/31/01): Assets, $5,177 (M); grants paid, $0; gifts received, $10,700; expenditures, $7,000; qualifying distributions, $0.
Limitations: Applications not accepted.
Application information: Contributes only to pre-selected organizations.
Officer: Raymond Maxwell, Jr., Pres.
Director: Mary Elizabeth Maxwell.
EIN: 562216867

62718
Scatters Foundation
P.O. Box 5655
Asheville, NC 28813-5655 (828) 274-3614
Contact: Edward B. Shoff, Pres.

Established in 2000.
Donor(s): Edward B. Shoff.
Financial data (yr. ended 12/31/01): Assets, $4,455 (M); grants paid, $0; expenditures, $0; qualifying distributions, $0.
Officers: Edward B. Shoff, Pres.; Curtis Shoff, V.P.; Edward B. Shoff III, V.P.
Director: Marion B. Shoff.
EIN: 562188795

62719
Maitrhea
2600 Salisbury Pln.
Raleigh, NC 27613-4331
Contact: Sarah Susanka, C.E.O.

Established in 1998 in MN.
Donor(s): Sarah Susanka.

Financial data (yr. ended 03/31/01): Assets, $3,876 (M); grants paid, $0; gifts received, $15,305; expenditures, $13,122; qualifying distributions, $15,680; giving activities include $13,122 for programs.
Officers: Sarah Susanka, C.E.O. and Pres.
EIN: 411906549

62720
David H. Patterson Ministries, Inc.
580 Hopkins Rd.
Kernersville, NC 27284

Established in 1997 in NC.
Donor(s): David H. Patterson.
Financial data (yr. ended 12/31/99): Assets, $3,604 (M); grants paid, $0; gifts received, $3,748; expenditures, $2,578; qualifying distributions, $2,578; giving activities include $2,578 for programs.
Officer: David H. Patterson, Pres.
EIN: 561416346

62721
Study Booklets
780 Olivetta Rd.
Asheville, NC 28804

Financial data (yr. ended 12/31/01): Assets, $3,229 (M); grants paid, $0; gifts received, $5,900; expenditures, $3,061; qualifying distributions, $3,061; giving activities include $3,061 for programs.
Trustees: David Anders, Kathleen Anders, Harold Bartlett.
EIN: 237318311

62722
Foundation for Biblical Archaeology
809 E. Beech St.
Goldsboro, NC 27530-1553 (919) 734-7578
Application address: P.O. Box 1553, Goldsboro, NC 27530, tel.: (919) 734-7578
Contact: Sheila T. Bishop, Pres.

Established in 1998 in NC.
Donor(s): Sheila T. Bishop.
Financial data (yr. ended 07/31/00): Assets, $2,401 (M); grants paid, $1,000; gifts received, $2,316; expenditures, $37,719; qualifying distributions, $37,219; giving activities include $37,269 for programs.
Application information: Application form required.
Officer: Sheila T. Bishop, Pres.
EIN: 561985557

62723
Trimurti Temple Devasthanam
9140 Arrow Point Blvd., Ste. 270
Charlotte, NC 28273-8120

Established in 1999.
Donor(s): N.S. Jagannathan.
Financial data (yr. ended 12/31/99): Assets, $2,325 (M); grants paid, $0; gifts received, $16,450; expenditures, $14,128; qualifying distributions, $14,128.
Limitations: Applications not accepted.
Application information: Contributes only to pre-selected organizations.
Trustee: N.S. Jagannathan.
EIN: 565648260

62724
Practical Pointers, Inc.
400 Avinger Ln., Ste. 203
Davidson, NC 28036-9705

Established in 2000 in NC.
Donor(s): Richard T. James, Jr.

Financial data (yr. ended 12/31/00): Assets, $2,192 (L); grants paid, $0; gifts received, $16,410; expenditures, $14,779; qualifying distributions, $0; giving activities include $14,776 for programs.
Officer: Richard T. James, Jr., Pres.
EIN: 561942449

62725
The Choice Foundation, Inc.
1315 S. Glenburnie Rd., Ste. A5
New Bern, NC 28562

Established in 2000 in NC.
Donor(s): Glaxo Wellcome Inc., Atlantic Integrated Health.
Financial data (yr. ended 12/31/00): Assets, $1,693 (M); grants paid, $0; gifts received, $34,833; expenditures, $33,375; qualifying distributions, $32,582; giving activities include $32,582 for programs.
Officers: Robert S. Meyer, M.D., Chair.; E. Phillip Bounous, M.D., Vice Chair.; William Dearaujo, M.D., Secy.-Treas.
Directors: Paul B. Brechtelsbauer, M.D., John C. Hale, M.D., C. Kent Price, M.D.
EIN: 562161459

62726
Federalist Research Institute
5200 Knightdale-Eagle Rock Rd.
Knightdale, NC 27545

Financial data (yr. ended 12/31/00): Assets, $1,655 (M); grants paid, $0; expenditures, $1,440; qualifying distributions, $1,440.
Director: Milton M. Croom.
EIN: 561804264

62727
The Tartan Foundation, Inc.
3116 Glen Summit
Charlotte, NC 28270

Donor(s): Jeffrey B. Carroll.
Financial data (yr. ended 12/31/00): Assets, $1,316 (M); grants paid, $200; gifts received, $9,354; expenditures, $8,158; qualifying distributions, $200.
Officer: Jeffrey B. Carroll, Pres.
EIN: 562114405

62728
Lynn H. Steele Scholarship Fund Trust
c/o Lail Debra S.
6180 Hwy. 150 E.
Denver, NC 28037-9650

Established in 1999.
Financial data (yr. ended 12/31/99): Assets, $1,069 (M); grants paid, $1,000; expenditures, $1,043; qualifying distributions, $1,043.
Trustees: Carolyn Agosta, Jacquelyn Anderson, Debra Lail, Gregory Steele, Evelyn Steele, Lori Steele.
EIN: 626280343

62729
The John Locke Foundation, Inc.
200 W. Morgan St., St. 200
Raleigh, NC 27601
URL: http://www.johnlocke.org

Classified as a private operating foundation in 1990.
Donor(s): The John William Pope Foundation, Glaxo, Inc., Pfizer Inc.
Financial data (yr. ended 06/30/00): Assets, $941 (M); grants paid, $0; gifts received, $1,430,279; expenditures, $1,499,321; qualifying distributions, $1,306,160; giving activities include $1,281,686 for programs.

IN THIS SECTION, WITHIN EACH STATE, FOUNDATIONS ARE LISTED IN DESCENDING ORDER BY ASSET AMOUNT

Officers and Directors:* John Hood,* Pres.; Don Carrington,* V.P.; Marc Rotterman, Sr. Exec.; Bruce Babcock, Ferrell Blount, John H. Carrington, N.W. Chalmers, Thomas H. Felzer, William T. Graham, Kevin Kennelly, J. Arthur Pope, Tula Carter Robbins, David M. Stover, Arthur C. Zeidman.
EIN: 561656943

62730
Clyde A. Parker Foundation
P.O. Box 5967
High Point, NC 27262

Established in 1992 in NC.
Donor(s): Clyde Parker, Ronnel S. Parker, Phyllis Parker Webb.
Financial data (yr. ended 12/31/01): Assets, $519 (M); grants paid, $0; expenditures, $264; qualifying distributions, $0.
Officers and Trustees:* Ronnel S. Parker,* Pres.; Clyde A. Parker, Jr., V.P.; Phyllis Parker Webb, V.P.; Daniel C. Greene,* Secy.-Treas.
EIN: 561803422

62731
Edgar Frazier Hunter, Jr. Scholarship Trust
P.O. Box 217
Burnsville, NC 28714-0217

Classified as a private operating foundation in 1984.
Financial data (yr. ended 10/31/01): Assets, $173 (M); grants paid, $1,000; gifts received, $1,100; expenditures, $1,095; qualifying distributions, $1,000.
Limitations: Giving primarily in Burnsville, NC.
Trustee: G.D. Bailey.
EIN: 581587003

62732
Freedoms Way, Inc.
4077 Range Rd.
Stem, NC 27581-9539

Financial data (yr. ended 01/01/02): Assets, $0 (M); grants paid, $15,750; gifts received, $18,500; expenditures, $18,500; qualifying distributions, $15,750.
Limitations: Applications not accepted.
Application information: Contributes only to pre-selected organizations.
Officers: Linwood L. Timberlake, C.E.O.; Larry Thomas, Secy.; Bonnie Timberlake, Treas.
EIN: 561862795

NORTH DAKOTA

62733
Minot Elks Lodge No. 1089 Charitable Foundation, Inc.
112 2nd Ave. S.W.
Minot, ND 58701-3836 (701) 838-7653
Application address: 1512 Debbie Dr., Minot, ND 58701
Contact: Jim Mello, Chair.

Established in 1988 in ND.
Financial data (yr. ended 03/31/01): Assets, $664,390 (M); grants paid, $11,370; gifts received, $1,539; expenditures, $26,520; qualifying distributions, $11,370.
Limitations: Giving primarily in the Minot, ND, area.

Application information: Application form required.
Officer and Directors:* Jim Mello,* Chair.; Larry Eidsness, Cliff Magnuson, Rich Matteson, Bruce Walker.
EIN: 450404247

62734
Frank A. & M. Esther Wenstrom Foundation
c/o American State Bank & Trust Co.
P.O. Box 1446, 223 Main St.
Williston, ND 58802-1446

Established in 1996 in ND.
Donor(s): M. Esther Wenstrom.
Financial data (yr. ended 09/30/01): Assets, $257,196 (M); grants paid, $11,000; expenditures, $13,520; qualifying distributions, $10,890.
Limitations: Giving limited to ND.
Application information: Application form required.
Advisory Committee: John Macmaster, John McGinley, M. Esther Wenstrom.
EIN: 450447357

62735
Jamestown Medical Foundation
P.O. Box 1535
Jamestown, ND 58402-1535

Financial data (yr. ended 09/30/01): Assets, $195,632 (M); grants paid, $8,000; expenditures, $9,604; qualifying distributions, $9,118.
Limitations: Applications not accepted. Giving limited to Jamestown, ND.
Application information: Contributes only to pre-selected organizations.
Officer and Directors:* Janet L. Holaday,* Secy.-Treas.; James Boatman, Daniel Buchanan, Sharlene Gumke, Laurel Haroldson, Claudia Jacobson, Marvin Tokach.
EIN: 456012854

62736
Edgar Haunz Treatment Education & Research Foundation
1000 S. Columbia Rd.
Grand Forks, ND 58201-4032

Classified as a private operating foundation in 1982.
Financial data (yr. ended 12/31/99): Assets, $66,925 (M); grants paid, $1,000; gifts received, $500; expenditures, $1,461; qualifying distributions, $1,000.
Limitations: Applications not accepted. Giving limited to ND.
Application information: Contributes only to pre-selected organizations.
Officers: Casey Ryan, Pres.; James Brosseau, V.P.; Marlys Love, Secy.; Greg Gerloff, Treas.
Directors: Millicent Haunz, Mary Ann Keller, Dave Molmen.
EIN: 450366784

62737
The Orvell O. and Ann Marie Lundby Foundation
c/o Orvell O. Lundby
P.O. Box 415
Sykeston, ND 58486-0415

Established in 1997 in ND.
Donor(s): Orvell O. Lundby.
Financial data (yr. ended 12/31/01): Assets, $58,757 (M); grants paid, $15,900; expenditures, $270; qualifying distributions, $15,995.
Limitations: Applications not accepted. Giving primarily in ND.
Application information: Contributes only to pre-selected organizations.

Officers: Orvell O. Lundby, Pres.; Sharon Riedesel, V.P.; Clay Houhchin, Secy.; Cindy Tweed, Treas.
EIN: 911802837

62738
Echo Mountain Good Neighbor Trust
P.O. Box 114
Sawyer, ND 58781

Classified as a private operating foundation in 1994 in SD.
Donor(s): Laidlaw Environmental Services, Inc., Municipal Svcs. Corp.
Financial data (yr. ended 12/31/01): Assets, $43,489 (M); grants paid, $9,600; expenditures, $10,159; qualifying distributions, $36,563.
Application information: Application form required.
Trustees: Bruce Bogenrief, Cy Kittelson, Cy Kotaska, Jay Skabo, Don Steig.
EIN: 456085451

62739
Kingsley T. Davidson Scholarship
c/o American State Bank & Trust Co.
P.O. Box 1446
Williston, ND 58802-1446
Application address: c/o American State Bank & Trust Co., 223 Main St., Williston, ND 58802, tel.: (701) 774-4120

Financial data (yr. ended 06/30/99): Assets, $13,414 (M); grants paid, $600; expenditures, $715; qualifying distributions, $715.
Limitations: Giving limited to Divide, McKenzie, and Williams counties, ND.
Application information: Application form required.
Trustees: Kim Davidson, Leon Olson, Fred Whisenand, American State Bank & Trust Co.
EIN: 456056367

OHIO

62740
Charles F. Kettering Foundation
200 Commons Rd.
Dayton, OH 45459-2799
URL: http://www.kettering.org

Classified as a private operating foundation in 1986.
Donor(s): Charles F. Kettering.‡
Financial data (yr. ended 12/31/01): Assets, $250,700,090 (M); grants paid, $0; gifts received, $227,429; expenditures, $14,308,429; qualifying distributions, $12,694,263; giving activities include $12,637,543 for programs.
Publications: Newsletter.
Officers and Trustees:* Anna Faith Jones, Chair.; David Mathews,* C.E.O. and Pres.; Estus Smith, V.P. and C.O.O.; Brian T. Cobb, V.P. and Treas.; Maxine Thomas, Secy.; Lisle C. Carter, Jr., Edwin Dorn, Mary Hatwood Futrell, Virginia A. Hodgkinson, Hon. Daniel Kemmis, Hon. James A. Leach, Jack A. MacAllister, Suzanne Morse, James R. Thomas.
EIN: 310549056

62741
The Dawes Arboretum
7770 Jacksontown Rd.
Newark, OH 43055-5000

Classified as a private operating foundation in 1986.
Financial data (yr. ended 09/30/00): Assets, $63,567,251 (M); grants paid, $0; gifts received, $83,829; expenditures, $2,704,838; qualifying distributions, $2,357,543; giving activities include $113,128 for program-related investments.
Director: Donald R. Hendricks.
EIN: 314379601

62742
Charles Kelley King Trust No. 3
c/o KeyBank, N.A., Trust Div.
127 Public Sq., 17th FL.
Cleveland, OH 44114

Classified as a private operating foundation in 1973.
Financial data (yr. ended 12/31/01): Assets, $37,242,388 (M); grants paid, $0; gifts received, $49,448; expenditures, $1,050,593; qualifying distributions, $1,008,062; giving activities include $947,947 for programs.
Directors: David Carto, Suzanne Davis, Charles Gleaves, Jack Pollack.
Trustees: William R. Cress, John C. Fernyak, KeyBank, N.A.
EIN: 346506846

62743
Lucy R. Buechner Corporation
620 Bryson St.
Youngstown, OH 44502

Classified as a private operating foundation in 1986.
Financial data (yr. ended 12/31/01): Assets, $18,124,501 (M); grants paid, $0; expenditures, $600,531; qualifying distributions, $0.
Officers: David Too, Pres.; C. Gilbert James, V.P.; Eldon S. Wright, Secy.; William G. Mittler, Treas.
Director: Barbara Hallwood.
Trustee: Nancy Beeghly.
EIN: 346000449

62744
Roscoe Village Foundation, Inc.
381 Hill St.
Coshocton, OH 43812

Classified as a private operating foundation in 1989.
Donor(s): Members of the Montgomery family.
Financial data (yr. ended 12/31/01): Assets, $17,542,729 (M); grants paid, $0; gifts received, $2,131,002; expenditures, $5,097,468; qualifying distributions, $1,826,188; giving activities include $1,826,188 for programs.
Officers and Trustees:* Carole Freund,* Pres.; Robert B. Robinson,* V.P.; Peter M. Bowen,* Secy.-Treas.; Frank Cugliari, Exec. Dir.
EIN: 311284309

62745
Greenacres Foundation
8255 Spooky Hollow Rd.
Cincinnati, OH 45242

Established in 1988 in OH.
Donor(s): Louis Nippert, Mrs. Louis Nippert.
Financial data (yr. ended 12/31/01): Assets, $17,080,079 (M); grants paid, $0; gifts received, $66,387; expenditures, $578,645; qualifying distributions, $477,917; giving activities include $477,917 for programs.
Officer: Carter F. Randolph, Ph.D., Exec. V.P.

Trustees: Mrs. Robert L. Black, Jr., Marie Eberhard, Tim Johnson, Lawrence H. Kyte, Jr., Mrs. Louis D. Nippert, Guy D. Randolph, Jr., Mrs. Guy D. Randolph, Jr., Mrs. Thomas Walker, Drausin Wulsin.
EIN: 311250075

62746
Stranahan Theater Trust
(Formerly Masonic Toledo Trust)
c/o Ralph Boggs
4645 Heatherdowns Blvd.
Toledo, OH 43614-3154

Classified as a private operating foundation 1981.
Donor(s): Stranahan Foundation, Toledo Community Foundation.
Financial data (yr. ended 06/30/01): Assets, $13,768,833 (M); grants paid, $0; gifts received, $491,037; expenditures, $1,416,964; qualifying distributions, $1,109,729; giving activities include $1,128,900 for programs.
Limitations: Applications not accepted.
Application information: Contributes only to pre-selected organizations.
Officers and Trustees:* Charles Yeager,* Chair. and Treas.; Donald Breese, Chair.; Richard Anderson, Vice-Chair.; James Hoffman, Vice-Chair.; John H. Boggs, Secy.; Robert King, Olivia Habib Summons, and 6 additional trustees.
EIN: 346560639

62747
Lehner Family Foundation Trust
c/o Jane Lehner
35 S. River Rd.
Munroe Falls, OH 44262

Established in 1989 in OH.
Donor(s): Marie Lehner, Jane Lehner, Charles Lehner.
Financial data (yr. ended 12/31/99): Assets, $11,931,553 (M); grants paid, $475,300; gifts received, $202,950; expenditures, $559,751; qualifying distributions, $462,711.
Limitations: Applications not accepted. Giving limited to OH.
Application information: Contributes only to pre-selected organizations.
Managers: Rick Burke, Gordon Ewers, David M. Koly, Jane Lehner, Michael R. Stark.
EIN: 346927210
Codes: FD

62748
Samuel W. Bell Home for the Sightless, Inc.
1507 Elm St.
Cincinnati, OH 45210-1606

Classified as a private operating foundation in 1989.
Financial data (yr. ended 12/31/01): Assets, $11,247,096 (M); grants paid, $0; gifts received, $301,446; expenditures, $457,410; qualifying distributions, $493,211; giving activities include $493,211 for programs.
Officers: William J. Guentter, Pres.; Miles Hoff, Secy.; Walter Reistenberger, Treas.; Louis A. Hoff, Exec. Dir.
Trustees: S. Stanford, Ione Walther.
EIN: 310537120

62749
Bunker Hill Haven Trust
301 S. Front St.
P.O. Box 187
Hamilton, OH 45011

Financial data (yr. ended 12/31/99): Assets, $7,686,879 (M); grants paid, $8,028; gifts received, $248,413; expenditures, $564,656; qualifying distributions, $492,325; giving activities include $492,325 for programs.
Limitations: Applications not accepted.
Application information: Contributes only to pre-selected organizations.
Trustee: A. Vincent Walsh.
EIN: 316040522

62750
Abbot Home
c/o First Financial Svcs. Group, N.A.
P.O. Box 2307
Zanesville, OH 43702-2307

Classified as a private operating foundation in 1981.
Financial data (yr. ended 04/30/02): Assets, $5,526,334 (M); grants paid, $0; gifts received, $6,158; expenditures, $538,873; qualifying distributions, $0.
Trustee: First Financial Services Group, N.A.
EIN: 341379421

62751
Kachelmacher Memorial, Inc.
755 State Rte. 664 N.
P.O. Box 348
Logan, OH 43138

Incorporated in 1969 in OH.
Financial data (yr. ended 06/30/00): Assets, $5,090,097 (M); grants paid, $0; expenditures, $216,701; qualifying distributions, $167,594; giving activities include $27,090 for programs.
Limitations: Applications not accepted.
Application information: Contributes only to a pre-selected organization.
Officers and Trustees:* William W. Keynes,* Pres.; B.J. King,* V.P.; Earl D. Later,* Secy.; Charles Keynes,* Treas.; Dayton Schultheis.
EIN: 310792046

62752
First Commerce Community Development Corporation
150 E. Gay St., 16th Fl.
Columbus, OH 43216-0290

Established in 1994 in LA.
Financial data (yr. ended 12/31/00): Assets, $4,918,152 (M); grants paid, $0; expenditures, $2,058; qualifying distributions, $0.
Officers: Herman Moysee III, Pres.; Darrel Byrd, Secy.; Kathleen F. Lagorde, Exec. Dir.
EIN: 721227000

62753
The John & Jenny Ward Family Foundation, Inc.
7400 Algonquin Dr.
Cincinnati, OH 45243

Established in 2000 in OH and VA.
Donor(s): John L. Ward.
Financial data (yr. ended 07/31/01): Assets, $4,799,406 (M); grants paid, $0; gifts received, $4,798,405; expenditures, $121,325; qualifying distributions, $123,295; giving activities include $100,154 for programs.
Limitations: Applications not accepted.
Application information: Contributes only to pre-selected organizations.
Officers: John L. Ward, Chair.; Libby Ward McKeen, Pres. and Exec. Dir.; Judith M. Stegman, Secy.-Treas.
Trustee: Joseph A. Stegman.
EIN: 311721640

62754
Blackburn Home for Aged People Association
6 Botsford St.
Poland, OH 44514-1755 (330) 757-2240
Contact: Mary Lou Pisani

Financial data (yr. ended 12/31/01): Assets, $4,461,665 (M); grants paid, $150; gifts received, $7,970; expenditures, $404,646; qualifying distributions, $372,508.
Limitations: Giving primarily in Youngstown, OH.
Officers: Mary Lou Pisani, Pres. and Treas.; John H. Stone, 1st V.P.; Mary Delle Hale, Secy.
Directors: Rebecca Bennett, Sharon Berlin, Denise L. Bobovnyik, Thomas Duncan, Chris Graff, Mary Delle Hale, Dru Marchese, Dorothy Philipp, John Weed Powers.
EIN: 340714543

62755
Pritchard Laughlin Center, Inc.
7033 W. Glenn Hwy. Rd.
Cambridge, OH 43725

Classified as a private operating foundation in 1991.
Financial data (yr. ended 06/30/99): Assets, $3,853,604 (M); grants paid, $0; gifts received, $248,403; expenditures, $478,608; qualifying distributions, $349,790; giving activities include $478,608 for programs.
Officers: David DeSelm, Pres.; Larry Caldwell, V.P.; Colleen Oess, Secy.; Jack Taylor, Treas.
Trustees: John Abbott, Darrel Cubbison, Robert Ley, James Mitchell.
EIN: 311136105
Codes: TN

62756
Ramser Arboretum
20718 Danville-Amity Rd.
Mount Vernon, OH 43050

Classified as a private operating foundation in 1996.
Financial data (yr. ended 12/31/01): Assets, $3,265,805 (M); grants paid, $0; expenditures, $40,619; qualifying distributions, $118,184; giving activities include $118,749 for programs.
Officers: Susan E. Ramser, Pres.; Mary E. Ramser, V.P.; Mark R. Ramser, Secy.-Treas.
EIN: 311470524

62757
577 Foundation
577 E. Front St.
Perrysburg, OH 43551-2135

Established in 1988 in OH.
Donor(s): Virginia S. Stranahan.
Financial data (yr. ended 12/31/01): Assets, $2,782,865 (M); grants paid, $9,564; gifts received, $498,264; expenditures, $648,068; qualifying distributions, $245,765.
Limitations: Applications not accepted. Giving limited to Toledo, OH.
Application information: Contributes only to pre-selected organizations.
Officers and Trustees:* Stephen Stranahan,* Pres.; Frances Perry,* V.P.; Peter D. Gwyn,* Secy.; Julie B. Higgins,* Treas.; Mary Mennel, Exec. Dir.; Jacqueline J. Foster, Chris Gajewicz, John Jaeger, Martin Nagy, Frances Perry, Charles A. Stocking.
EIN: 341591869

62758
The Baker Family Museum, Inc.
c/o Carl Baker
P.O. Box 100
Dexter City, OH 45727

Financial data (yr. ended 12/31/01): Assets, $2,575,288 (M); grants paid, $0; expenditures, $60,159; qualifying distributions, $0.
Officers: Mary Baker, Pres.; Robert Cunningham, Secy.-Treas.
Trustee: Alan S. Doris.
EIN: 311131762

62759
Uptown Arts Foundation
1234 E. Liberty St.
Cincinnati, OH 45210

Established in 2000 in OH.
Donor(s): Lois Rosenthal, Richard Rosenthal.
Financial data (yr. ended 12/31/00): Assets, $2,546,564 (M); grants paid, $10,410; gifts received, $2,624,232; expenditures, $80,668; qualifying distributions, $2,628,970.
Limitations: Applications not accepted.
Application information: Contributes only to pre-selected organizations.
Directors: Lois Rosenthal, Richard Rosenthal.
Trustee: J. Michael Cooney.
EIN: 311713221

62760
The Kanter Family Foundation
9792 Windisch Rd.
West Chester, OH 45069

Established in 1998 in DC.
Donor(s): Joseph H. Kanter, Nancy R. Kanter.
Financial data (yr. ended 12/31/01): Assets, $2,435,955 (M); grants paid, $21,000; gifts received, $573,481; expenditures, $357,433; qualifying distributions, $349,498.
Limitations: Applications not accepted.
Application information: Contributes only to pre-selected organizations.
Officers and Directors:* Joseph H. Kanter,* Pres.; Robert W. Wildermuth,* Secy.-Treas.; Nancy R. Kanter.
EIN: 311595996

62761
Clark Memorial Home Association
106 Kewbury Rd.
Springfield, OH 45504

Classified as a private operating foundation in 1981.
Financial data (yr. ended 12/31/01): Assets, $2,371,195 (M); grants paid, $0; gifts received, $319,353; expenditures, $558,177; qualifying distributions, $515,060; giving activities include $364,665 for programs.
Officers: Margie Baldwin, Pres.; Nancy Rix, V.P.; Nancy Zimmerman, Secy.; Kathryn Welch, Corresponding Secy.; Linda Sanders, Treas.
Directors: Roberta Barnett, Leigh Bressoud, Pat Chiles, Nancy Clarke, Ruth Englefield, Nan Farley, Marty Glendenin, Carol Kendig, Margaret McNeil, Sonja Spragg, Shirley Wall, Diane Walsh, Gloria Woeber, Betty Zimmerman.
EIN: 310585915
Codes: TN

62762
Kappa Alpha Psi Fraternity House of Cleveland, Ohio, Inc.
12450 Shaker Blvd.
Cleveland, OH 44120

Financial data (yr. ended 12/31/01): Assets, $2,358,359 (M); grants paid, $0; expenditures, $679,785; qualifying distributions, $0; giving activities include $679,785 for programs.
Limitations: Giving primarily in Cleveland, OH.
Officers: Lawrence Lumpkin, Pres.; Cleo Miller, V.P.; Stephen Lloyd, Secy.; Gradmon Boling, Jr., Treas.
EIN: 341477548

62763
Franklin Foundation, Inc.
4673 Winterset Dr.
Columbus, OH 43220

Established in 1986 in OH.
Donor(s): Sally L. Havens, Suzanne E. Havens-Nick, Ellen H. Hardymon, Thomas F. Havens, John C. Havens.
Financial data (yr. ended 11/30/01): Assets, $2,305,221 (M); grants paid, $92,540; gifts received, $147,222; expenditures, $265,136; qualifying distributions, $295,088; giving activities include $65,650 for programs.
Limitations: Applications not accepted. Giving primarily in OH.
Application information: Contributes only to pre-selected organizations. Unsolicited requests for funds are not accepted.
Officers and Trustees:* Lynn Dalton, Pres.; Ellen Hardymon,* Secy.; John C. Havens, Thomas F. Havens, Phillip D. Nick.
EIN: 311191673
Codes: FD2

62764
The Twenty First Century Foundation
P.O. Box 543
Norwalk, OH 44857
Application address: 17 Oakwood, Norwalk, OH 44857
Contact: John A. Bores, Tr.

Established in 1997.
Donor(s): John A. Bores, Underground Utilities, Inc.
Financial data (yr. ended 06/30/00): Assets, $2,265,661 (M); grants paid, $37,156; gifts received, $795,848; expenditures, $38,626; qualifying distributions, $36,665.
Limitations: Giving primarily in OH.
Trustees: John A. Bores, Mary L. Bores.
EIN: 341852806

62765
David T. Mason Charitable Foundation
c/o Jackman S. Vodrey Law Office
517 Broadway, 3rd Fl.
East Liverpool, OH 43920

Established in 2000 in OH.
Donor(s): David T. Mason.‡
Financial data (yr. ended 12/31/00): Assets, $2,246,075 (M); grants paid, $3,000; gifts received, $1,965,254; expenditures, $3,030; qualifying distributions, $3,000.
Limitations: Applications not accepted. Giving primarily in East Liverpool, OH.
Application information: Contributes only to pre-selected organizations.
Trustee and Advisors:* Carol Cronin, Alfred S. Fricano, Donald Linger, Gary Satmare, George Vardy.
EIN: 341930703

62766
Davis Foundation
c/o The Huntington National Bank
P.O. Box 1558
Columbus, OH 43216

Established in 1951 in OH.
Donor(s): Evan Davis, Robert C. Davis, Alison Z. Davis.
Financial data (yr. ended 06/30/00): Assets, $2,134,821 (M); grants paid, $59,467; gifts received, $50,000; expenditures, $425,727; qualifying distributions, $146,748.
Limitations: Applications not accepted. Giving primarily in OH.
Application information: Contributes only to pre-selected organizations.
Trustees: Robert Brisker, Evan Davis, Marvin A. McCain, John E. Morgan, Gary J. Thomas, Ray Thomas, The Huntington National Bank.
EIN: 316023094

62767
Crane Hollow, Inc.
c/o J.W. Ellis
2291 Walhaven Ct.
Columbus, OH 43220-4762

Classified as a private operating foundation in 1980.
Donor(s): William W. Ellis, Jr., Jane Wells Ellis.
Financial data (yr. ended 06/30/00): Assets, $2,110,011 (M); grants paid, $0; gifts received, $247,943; expenditures, $75,143; qualifying distributions, $312,499; giving activities include $26,591 for programs.
Trustees: Barbara Williams Ellis, Jane Wells Ellis, Janet Heath Ellis, Jonathan D. Iten.
EIN: 310981015

62768
The JAM Foundation
19885 Detroit Rd., Ste. 181
Rocky River, OH 44116-1311
Contact: Ann Coyne, Secy.

Established in 1988 in OH.
Financial data (yr. ended 12/31/01): Assets, $1,844,360 (M); grants paid, $142,000; gifts received, $35,727; expenditures, $157,408; qualifying distributions, $156,522.
Limitations: Applications not accepted. Giving primarily in Cleveland, OH.
Application information: Contributes only to pre-selected organizations.
Officers: Joyce Litzler, Pres.; William Litzler, V.P.; Ann Coyne, Secy.
EIN: 341578049
Codes: FD2

62769
The Sam and Rachel Boymel Foundation
c/o J. Michael Cooney
P.O. Box 477, ML 4928
Hamilton, OH 45012
Application address: c/o William Schumacker, High St. and Journal Sq., Hamilton, OH 45011

Classified as an operating foundation in 1997.
Donor(s): Rachel Boymel, Sam Boymel.
Financial data (yr. ended 12/31/99): Assets, $1,795,205 (M); grants paid, $60,000; expenditures, $62,527; qualifying distributions, $51,494.
Limitations: Giving primarily in Cincinnati, OH.
Trustees: Rachel Boymel, Sam Boymel, Steve Boymel, Gidon Eldad, Fay Sosna.
EIN: 311578615

62770
Head & Neck Medicine and Surgery Foundation
c/o Anthony J. Maniglia
11100 Euclid Ave.
Cleveland, OH 44106-5045

Established in 1990 in OH.
Donor(s): University Otolaryngology Head & Neck Surgery, Inc., Mrs. Calin Smith, Anthony J. Maniglia.
Financial data (yr. ended 06/30/00): Assets, $1,626,709 (M); grants paid, $0; gifts received, $34,833; expenditures, $76,846; qualifying distributions, $61,824; giving activities include $63,650 for programs.
Officers: Anthony J. Maniglia, M.D., Pres. and Treas.; James E. Arnold, M.D., V.P.; Christine Marshall, Secy.
EIN: 341654215

62771
Washington County Woman's Home
220 Putnam St.
Marietta, OH 45750

Established in 1988 in OH.
Financial data (yr. ended 12/31/00): Assets, $1,598,887 (M); grants paid, $0; expenditures, $230,793; qualifying distributions, $221,821; giving activities include $221,821 for programs.
Officers: Mary Rice, Pres.; Sheila Lankford, V.P.; Rosemary Bartlett, Secy.; Helen Adamson, Treas.
EIN: 314381384

62772
The Tony R. Wells Foundation
3582 Woodstone Dr.
Lewis Center, OH 43035-9384
(740) 548-0781
Contact: Tony R. Wells, Pres.

Established in 2000 in OH.
Donor(s): Knowledge Development Center Holding LLC.
Financial data (yr. ended 12/31/01): Assets, $1,571,231 (M); grants paid, $116,297; expenditures, $120,141; qualifying distributions, $116,297.
Officers and Trustees:* Tony R. Wells,* Pres. and Treas.; Dana Wells,* V.P. and Secy.; Daniel Pershing.
EIN: 311778364

62773
Youngstown Class B Baseball, Inc.
65 Main St.
Struthers, OH 44471

Established in 1999 in OH.
Financial data (yr. ended 12/31/00): Assets, $1,556,725 (M); grants paid, $0; gifts received, $204,846; expenditures, $319,509; qualifying distributions, $220,641; giving activities include $319,509 for programs.
Officers: Paul Cene, Pres.; James Dibacco, V.P.; Robert Cene, Jr., Secy.-Treas.
EIN: 341507184

62774
Churches United for Senior Housing, Inc.
c/o Eden Pl.
176 Rustic Dr.
Circleville, OH 43113

Financial data (yr. ended 12/31/99): Assets, $1,382,743 (M); grants paid, $0; expenditures, $261,712; qualifying distributions, $250,624; giving activities include $261,712 for programs.
Officers and Directors:* Lois Brobst, Pres.; Naomi Dade, V.P.; Doris Gillespie, Secy.; Hewitt Harmount,* Treas.; Charles Carle, Nancy Plescia, Mary Radcliffe, Sam Reeser, Stanley Stevens.
EIN: 311036440
Codes: TN

62775
Wetlands Foundation
6950 S. Edgeton Rd.
Brecksville, OH 44141-3184

Established in 1996 in ME.
Financial data (yr. ended 12/31/01): Assets, $1,363,489 (M); grants paid, $5,000; gifts received, $25,000; expenditures, $44,845; qualifying distributions, $44,845; giving activities include $44,845 for programs.
Limitations: Applications not accepted. Giving primarily in ME.
Application information: Contributes only to pre-selected organizations.
Trustees: James Benenson, Jr., James Benenson III, John V. Curci.
EIN: 010495814

62776
The Multi-Cultural Supporters, Inc.
1709 Woodman Ave.
Dayton, OH 45420

Established around 1991.
Financial data (yr. ended 10/31/99): Assets, $1,243,402 (M); grants paid, $49,248; gifts received, $116,075; expenditures, $828,207; qualifying distributions, $53,809.
Limitations: Applications not accepted.
Application information: Contributes only to pre-selected organizations.
Officers: Doris H. Wilson, Pres.; Marvin Merritt, V.P.; Carl Wilson, Secy.-Treas.
EIN: 311302378

62777
The Warsawiak Foundation
P.O. Box 40366
Cincinnati, OH 45240
Contact: Fela Warsawiak, Tr.

Established in 1994 in OH.
Financial data (yr. ended 12/31/00): Assets, $1,226,440 (M); grants paid, $60,000; expenditures, $64,420; qualifying distributions, $60,000.
Limitations: Applications not accepted.
Application information: Contributes only to pre-selected organizations.
Trustees: Richard M. Schwartz, Fela Warsawiak.
EIN: 311406057

62778
Paul M. & Lucy J. Gillmor Charitable Foundation
P.O. Box 88
Old Fort, OH 44861
Application address: 634 W. Market St., Tiffin, OH 44883, tel.: (419) 447-1600
Contact: Michael J. Kerschner, Chair.

Established in 1991 in OH.
Donor(s): Paul M. Gillmor.
Financial data (yr. ended 12/31/01): Assets, $1,205,571 (M); grants paid, $31,741; gifts received, $1,025,137; expenditures, $32,224; qualifying distributions, $31,741.
Limitations: Giving primarily in Tiffin, OH.
Officers and Directors:* Michael J. Kerschner,* Chair.; Dianne G. Krumsee,* Secy.-Treas.; Paul M. Gillmor, Paul E. Molyet.
EIN: 341688002

62779
The Mildred Andrews Fund
925 Euclid Ave., Ste. 2000
Cleveland, OH 44115-1407

Established in 1972 in OH.
Donor(s): Peter Putnam.‡
Financial data (yr. ended 12/31/01): Assets, $1,193,770 (M); grants paid, $285,000; expenditures, $299,815; qualifying distributions, $292,991.
Limitations: Applications not accepted. Giving primarily in Washington, DC.
Application information: Contributes only to pre-selected organizations.
Trustee: Eugene A. Kratus.
EIN: 237158695
Codes: FD

62780
The Surgical Foundation, Inc.
2351 E. 22nd St., Ste. 315W
Cleveland, OH 44115-3111

Established in 1999 in OH.
Donor(s): St. Luke's Surgical Foundation, Inc.
Financial data (yr. ended 01/31/01): Assets, $1,139,252 (M); grants paid, $71,052; gifts received, $2,205; expenditures, $133,418; qualifying distributions, $94,377.
Limitations: Applications not accepted. Giving primarily in Cleveland, OH.
Application information: Contributes only to pre-selected organizations.
Officers: Helmut Schreiber, M.D., Pres.; Indukumar Sonpal, M.D., V.P. and Treas.; John Marshall, M.D., Secy.
EIN: 341884705

62781
East Side Youth Athletic Trust
c/o Paul Brizzolara
7000 Midland Blvd.
Amelia, OH 45102-2607

Classified as a private operating foundation in 2000 in OH.
Donor(s): The Midland Co.
Financial data (yr. ended 12/31/01): Assets, $1,082,865 (M); grants paid, $100; gifts received, $1,117,501; expenditures, $330,186; qualifying distributions, $100.
Limitations: Applications not accepted.
Application information: Contributes only to pre-selected organizations.
Trustees: Paul Brizzolara, Mike Flowers, Kenneth Seibel.
EIN: 311666692

62782
Stratford Ecological Center, Inc.
5353 Williams Rd.
Ashville, OH 43103

Established in 1990 in OH.
Donor(s): E.J. Warner, Louise Warner, Mary H. Oman.‡
Financial data (yr. ended 12/31/00): Assets, $1,075,412 (M); grants paid, $0; gifts received, $99,721; expenditures, $255,069; qualifying distributions, $205,277; giving activities include $57,398 for programs.
Officers: Clyde Gosnell, Pres.; David E. Kreger, V.P.; David Warner, V.P.; Louise Warner, Secy.-Treas.
EIN: 311312879

62783
Cleveland Minority Cable Channel, Inc.
(also known as Cleveland Television Network)
5230 St. Clair Ave., Ste. 100
Cleveland, OH 44103-1310

Classified as a private operating foundation in 1995.
Donor(s): Cleveland Foundation.
Financial data (yr. ended 12/31/00): Assets, $1,073,925 (M); grants paid, $0; gifts received, $657,033; expenditures, $860,154; qualifying distributions, $527,916; giving activities include $860,154 for programs.
Officers and Trustees:* Linda Dukes-Campbell, Chair.; Kenneth Lumpkin,* 1st Vice-Chair.; Shams Ray Muhammad,* 2nd Vice-Chair.; George Yarbrough,* Secy.; Richel Wiggins,* Treas.; Orlando Boyd, Pinkey S. Carr, Brenda J. Hall, Rodney Jenkins, David Namkoong, Chanell Reed, Alan A.A. Seifullah.
EIN: 341805103

62784
County North Foundation
P.O. Box 791
Bryan, OH 43506
Application address: 05691 St., Ste. 15, Bryan, OH 43506
Contact: Patricia A. Pool, C.P.A.

Established in 1998 in OH.
Donor(s): Thomas C. Elder.
Financial data (yr. ended 12/31/99): Assets, $1,044,477 (M); grants paid, $27,336; gifts received, $1,000; expenditures, $28,870; qualifying distributions, $27,078.
Application information: Include high school, graduation date, class rank, and high school transcript.
Trustees: Paul E. Elder, Lewis D. Hilkert, Timothy Kline.
EIN: 311596311

62785
Ruth L. Kelly Foundation
1000 Jackson St.
Toledo, OH 43624-1515

Established in 1999 in OH.
Donor(s): Ruth Kelly.‡
Financial data (yr. ended 12/31/99): Assets, $1,016,129 (M); grants paid, $12,500; gifts received, $1,043,815; expenditures, $24,856; qualifying distributions, $24,856.
Limitations: Applications not accepted. Giving primarily in OH.
Application information: Contributes only to pre-selected organizations.
Trustees: John F. Hayward, Mary Beth Hayward, Marian M. Rejent.
EIN: 341892688

62786
Northside Knights of Columbus Community Benefit Center, Inc.
c/o M.E. Mullen
11175 Reading Rd.
Cincinnati, OH 45241-1997

Classified as a private operating foundation in 1990.
Financial data (yr. ended 06/30/00): Assets, $1,004,068 (M); grants paid, $37,945; expenditures, $252,707; qualifying distributions, $142,531; giving activities include $627,471 for programs.
Officers and Trustees:* Dale Klocke,* Pres.; Norb Rolfsen,* V.P.; Kevin Holthaus, Secy.; Ron Fox, Treas.
EIN: 310908092

62787
Stolberg Foundation for Preschool Childcare
(also known as The Children's Seedling Fund)
c/o Sterling Ltd.
3550 Lender Rd.
Pepper Pike, OH 44124
Contact: Ronald E. Bates, Tr.

Established in 1994 in OH.
Donor(s): E. Theodore Stolberg.
Financial data (yr. ended 12/31/99): Assets, $933,325 (M); grants paid, $46,381; expenditures, $64,388; qualifying distributions, $52,786.
Limitations: Giving on a national basis.
Application information: Application form required.
Trustees: Ronald E. Bates, E. Theodore Stolberg, Missy Stolberg, Kathleen A. Tuss.
EIN: 341780793

62788
Ethel & Sam Garber Foundation
1200 American Bldg.
30 E. Central Pkwy.
Cincinnati, OH 45202 (513) 241-2540
Application address: 1400 American Bldg., Cincinnati, OH 45202, tel.: (513) 241-2540
Contact: Martin H. Wolf, Tr.

Established in 1988 in OH.
Financial data (yr. ended 12/31/99): Assets, $927,643 (M); grants paid, $31,147; expenditures, $42,738; qualifying distributions, $31,147.
Limitations: Giving primarily in Cincinnati, OH.
Trustee: Martin H. Wolf.
EIN: 316338506

62789
The Internal Medicine Foundation, Inc.
2351 E. 22nd St., Ste. 111-W
Cleveland, OH 44115

Established in 1999 in OH.
Donor(s): Saint Luke's Interanl Medicine, Inc.
Financial data (yr. ended 01/31/02): Assets, $921,429 (M); grants paid, $0; expenditures, $125,075; qualifying distributions, $124,721; giving activities include $125,075 for programs.
Officers and Trustees: John B. Marshall,* Pres.; Jill M. Barry,* Secy.; Gregory L. Hall,* Treas.; James M. Boyle, Dolores L. Christie, Richard E. Christie.
EIN: 341873366

62790
St. Joseph Foundation of Los Angeles
17700 Lorain Ave.
Cleveland, OH 44111-4014

Classified as a private operating foundation in 1973.
Donor(s): Brian Miller.
Financial data (yr. ended 12/31/01): Assets, $918,153 (M); grants paid, $0; gifts received, $47,250; expenditures, $23,750; qualifying distributions, $0.
Officers: James Lann, Pres.; Adeline Miller, V.P.; Brian Miller, Secy.-Treas.
Trustees: Barry Hanratty, Karen Lenardic, William Mironik.
EIN: 237245632

62791
Champaign Memorial Home, Inc.
163 Pine Tree Ln.
Urbana, OH 43078

Financial data (yr. ended 12/31/01): Assets, $890,643 (M); grants paid, $40,138; gifts

received, $1,175; expenditures, $41,127; qualifying distributions, $40,138.
Limitations: Applications not accepted.
Application information: Contributes only to pre-selected organizations.
Officers: June Purk, Pres.; Otho Johnson, V.P.; Pat Hollingshead, Secy.; Alan K. Webster, Treas.
Trustees: John R. Akey, Gary Beatty, Robert Creamer, John Hartzler, Robert N. Park, Connie Toomire.
EIN: 346536218

62792
University Urology Educational & Research Foundation, Inc.
941 Chatham Ln., Ste. 110
Columbus, OH 43221
Contact: Bruce Woodworth, Pres.

Classified as a private foundation in 1989.
Financial data (yr. ended 12/31/01): Assets, $859,567 (M); grants paid, $0; gifts received, $15,500; expenditures, $49,633; qualifying distributions, $38,862; giving activities include $38,862 for programs.
Limitations: Giving primarily in OH.
Application information: Application form not required.
Officers: Bruce Woodworth, M.D., Pres.; Rama Jayanthi, M.D., Secy.-Treas.
Trustees: Robert Bahnson, Stephen A. Koff, M.D., John Perez, Peter L. Pointer, Henry A. Wise II, M.D.
EIN: 310921104

62793
Rex Foundation
2773 N. Revere Rd.
Fairlawn, OH 44333

Classified as a private operating foundation in 1982.
Financial data (yr. ended 09/30/01): Assets, $823,249 (M); grants paid, $0; expenditures, $138,316; qualifying distributions, $0.
Trustees: Richard E. Kleinman, Anne Rex, Ella Jane Rex, Harold Rex.
EIN: 341320874

62794
Kohrman Family Foundation
c/o S. Lee Kohrman
2889 Eaton Rd.
Shaker Heights, OH 44122

Established in 1997 in OH.
Financial data (yr. ended 10/31/00): Assets, $748,139 (M); grants paid, $34,306; expenditures, $41,628; qualifying distributions, $34,306.
Limitations: Giving primarily in Cleveland, OH.
Trustees: Bruce Kohrman, Margery Kohrman, S. Lee Kohrman.
EIN: 311532230

62795
The Learning Communities Network, Inc.
1422 Euclid Ave., Ste. 1668
Cleveland, OH 44115

Established in 1995 in OH.
Donor(s): The Rockefeller Foundation.
Financial data (yr. ended 06/30/99): Assets, $689,197 (M); grants paid, $0; gifts received, $664,466; expenditures, $175,717; qualifying distributions, $183,074; giving activities include $175,717 for programs.
Officers: Victor C. Young, Pres. and Treas.; Jonathan Berry, Secy.; Melissa S. Groo, Secy.
Directors: Steven A. Minter, David K. Scott, Marla Ucelli.
EIN: 133831398

62796
The Mary Magdalen Foundation, Inc.
9449 Montgomery Rd.
Cincinnati, OH 45242-7640
Application address: 1221-23 Main St., Cincinnati, OH 45210
Contact: Bro. John Martin

Established in 1986 in OH.
Donor(s): James J. Gardner, Joan A. Gardner.
Financial data (yr. ended 12/31/99): Assets, $676,734 (M); grants paid, $25,000; gifts received, $105,053; expenditures, $162,624; qualifying distributions, $147,499; giving activities include $162,624 for programs.
Limitations: Giving limited to the greater Cincinnati, OH, area.
Officers and Trustees:* James J. Gardner,* Pres.; Joan A. Gardner,* V.P.; Thomas J. Mueller,* Secy.; Gary Johns, Margaret Johns, Linda G. Muerller.
EIN: 311182978

62797
Wexner Heritage Foundation, Inc.
6525 West Campus Oval, Ste. 105
P.O. Box 688
New Albany, OH 43054-0688

Established in 1985 in OH.
Financial data (yr. ended 12/31/00): Assets, $673,965 (M); grants paid, $0; gifts received, $3,700,000; expenditures, $3,203,275; qualifying distributions, $3,203,275; giving activities include $3,203,275 for programs.
Officers and Directors:* Leslie H. Wexner,* Chair.; Herbert A. Friedman, Co-Pres.; Nathan Laufer, Co-Pres.; Jeffrey Epstein, V.P. and Treas.; Darren Indyke, Secy.; Lori Baron, Shoshana Gelfand, Gideon Kaufman.
EIN: 311142481

62798
The Canton Classic Car Museum
612 Market Ave. S.
Canton, OH 44702

Established in 1994 in OH. Classified as a private operating foundation in 1995.
Donor(s): Florence M. Belden.
Financial data (yr. ended 12/31/99): Assets, $558,360 (M); grants paid, $126,682; gifts received, $276,068; expenditures, $337,543; qualifying distributions, $301,175; giving activities include $301,175 for programs.
Officers and Trustees:* F.M. Belden,* Pres.; Marshall B. Belden, Jr.,* Secy.; Timothy S. Belden,* Treas.; Susan Ann Belden.
EIN: 341782134

62799
Wyandot Popcorn Museum, Inc.
c/o George K. Brown
135 Wyandot Ave.
Marion, OH 43302-1538

Donor(s): George K. Brown, Wyandot, Inc.
Financial data (yr. ended 12/31/00): Assets, $487,158 (M); grants paid, $0; gifts received, $31,282; expenditures, $27,835; qualifying distributions, $0.
Officers: George K. Brown, Pres.; Brooks Brown, V.P.; Rex Parrott, Secy.; Catherine Ferguson, Treas.
Directors: Richard J. Bryson, Wayne Kuhn, Roger Moery, Mike Perry, Ken Vincent, and 3 additional directors.
EIN: 341491155

62800
The Romano Family Foundation
2920 Glengary Rd.
Shaker Heights, OH 44120

Established in 1999 in OH.
Financial data (yr. ended 12/31/00): Assets, $464,770 (L); grants paid, $28,000; expenditures, $31,797; qualifying distributions, $31,979.
Limitations: Giving primarily in MA, MS, and OH.
Directors: Joseph D. Romano, Marcia A. Romano, Renee C. Romano, Terese N. Romano.
EIN: 341909468

62801
Center for Adaptive Management
4445 Lake Forest Dr., Ste. 400
Cincinnati, OH 45242

Established in 1995 in OH.
Donor(s): Norman B. Day, The Largent Co., Larry Sangermano.
Financial data (yr. ended 12/31/01): Assets, $459,432 (M); grants paid, $0; gifts received, $200; expenditures, $365,982; qualifying distributions, $289,754; giving activities include $338,506 for programs.
Officers: Craig S. Hopewell, Pres. and Secy.; Willard D. James, Treas.
Trustees: Norman D. Day, Paula M. Farmer.
EIN: 311437930

62802
The James F. Lincoln Arc Welding Foundation
22801 St. Clair Ave.
Cleveland, OH 44117-1199 (216) 481-4300
Contact: Roy Morrow, Pres.

Established around 1936 in OH as a company-sponsored operating foundation.
Donor(s): The Lincoln Electric Co.
Financial data (yr. ended 12/31/00): Assets, $389,417 (M); grants paid, $62,050; gifts received, $431,077; expenditures, $493,193; qualifying distributions, $493,193.
Limitations: Giving on a national basis.
Publications: Informational brochure (including application guidelines).
Application information: The Technicians, Craftsmen and Users Award has been discontinued.
Officers and Trustees:* Donald N. Zwiep,* Chair.; Roy Morrow, Pres.; Duane K. Miller, Exec. Dir.; John T. Frieg, Leslie L. Knowlton.
EIN: 346553433
Codes: CD, GTI

62803
Lula Douglas Foundation, Inc.
3201 Sportsman Club Rd.
Johnstown, OH 43031 (740) 967-0410
Contact: James "Buster" Douglas

Classified as a private operating foundation in 1991 in OH.
Financial data (yr. ended 12/31/01): Assets, $382,802 (M); grants paid, $0; gifts received, $8,131; expenditures, $24,352; qualifying distributions, $0.
Trustees: Bertha Douglas, James Douglas.
EIN: 311295385

62804
Shah Family Foundation
1906 Beckert Dr.
Piqua, OH 45356

Established in 1996.
Donor(s): Alka Shah, Damaroo Shah, Jyoti Shah, Mayank Shah.

IN THIS SECTION, WITHIN EACH STATE, FOUNDATIONS ARE LISTED IN DESCENDING ORDER BY ASSET AMOUNT

Financial data (yr. ended 12/31/99): Assets, $368,965 (M); grants paid, $29,250; gifts received, $12,500; expenditures, $29,906; qualifying distributions, $29,094.
Limitations: Applications not accepted.
Application information: Contributes only to pre-selected organizations.
Trustees: Sona Pancholy, Damaroo Shah, Mayank Shah.
EIN: 316524093

62805
The Del and Beatrice P. Mintz Charitable Foundation
5533 State Rd.
Cleveland, OH 44134 (216) 351-0311
Contact: Gary L. Mintz, Secy.-Treas.

Classified as a private operating foundation in 1993.
Donor(s): Del Mintz.
Financial data (yr. ended 12/31/00): Assets, $365,204 (M); grants paid, $29,061; expenditures, $29,894; qualifying distributions, $29,894.
Limitations: Giving primarily in FL and OH.
Officers and Trustees:* Beatrice P. Mintz,* Pres.; Gary L. Mintz,* Secy.-Treas.; Mark Mintz, Irving B. Spitz.
EIN: 341673881

62806
Montei Mound Preserve, Inc.
1399 Brookwood Pl.
Columbus, OH 43209-2814

Established in 1992 in OH.
Donor(s): Tom Montei.
Financial data (yr. ended 12/31/01): Assets, $359,366 (M); grants paid, $0; gifts received, $150; expenditures, $726; qualifying distributions, $0.
Officer and Trustees:* Tom Montei,* Mgr.; Bruce Ramsey, Webb Vorys.
EIN: 311332603

62807
Marion County Historical Association & the Stengel-True Museum, Inc.
181 E. Center St.
Marion, OH 43302

Classified as a private operating foundation in 1973.
Financial data (yr. ended 12/31/01): Assets, $353,981 (M); grants paid, $0; gifts received, $15,000; expenditures, $30,220; qualifying distributions, $29,211; giving activities include $29,211 for programs.
Officers: F. Riley Hall, Pres.; Bradley C. Bebout, Secy.
EIN: 310629462

62808
Oscar & Nina Melhorn Memorial Trust
311 Foundry Hill Rd.
Salineville, OH 43945-9791

Classified as a private operating foundation in 1982.
Financial data (yr. ended 12/31/01): Assets, $345,037 (M); grants paid, $0; expenditures, $16,938; qualifying distributions, $9,406.
Directors: Verda Leek, James Miller, Steve Pastore.
Trustee: Martha Hull.
EIN: 341211189

62809
Helen K. Carney Scholarship Fund
c/o National City Bank, Kentucky
P.O. Box 94651
Cleveland, OH 44101-4651
Application address: c/o Principal, Russell High School, 709 Red Devil Ln., Russell, KY 41169, tel. (606) 836-9658

Financial data (yr. ended 12/31/01): Assets, $340,229 (M); grants paid, $19,000; expenditures, $20,651; qualifying distributions, $19,708.
Limitations: Giving limited to residents of KY.
Application information: Application form required.
Trustee: National City Bank, Kentucky.
EIN: 611163331
Codes: GTI

62810
John T. Carey Memorial Foundation
11460 Edgewater Dr.
Cleveland, OH 44102

Established in 1998 in OH.
Donor(s): Russell Trusso.
Financial data (yr. ended 12/31/99): Assets, $323,405 (M); grants paid, $17,500; gifts received, $36,980; expenditures, $22,188; qualifying distributions, $17,410.
Limitations: Applications not accepted.
Application information: Contributes only to pre-selected organizations.
Officers and Trustee:* Russell Trusso,* Pres.; Donna Bush, Secy.; Joyce A. Graham, Treas.
EIN: 341875169

62811
S. W. & Eleanor Caplan Foundation
9880 Sweet Valley Dr.
Valley View, OH 44125-4242

Established in 1978.
Donor(s): Sidney W. Caplan.
Financial data (yr. ended 12/31/01): Assets, $294,518 (M); grants paid, $134,155; expenditures, $135,595; qualifying distributions, $134,016.
Limitations: Applications not accepted. Giving primarily in OH.
Application information: Contributes only to pre-selected organizations.
Trustee: Sidney W. Caplan.
EIN: 341265827

62812
Carpenter-Garcia Scholarship Fund Trust
c/o Amil Garcia
1213 Hillcliff
Louisville, OH 44641-2730

Established in 1992 in OH.
Donor(s): Amil Garcia.
Financial data (yr. ended 12/31/99): Assets, $276,616 (M); grants paid, $7,500; expenditures, $8,326; qualifying distributions, $7,500.
Limitations: Applications not accepted. Giving limited to Louisville, OH.
Officers and Executive Committee:* Phil Unkefer,* Pres.; Laura Hipp,* V.P.; Melanie Fisher, Secy.; Joe Greco,* Treas.
Trustee: Amil Garcia.
EIN: 341702479

62813
Rittenhouse Memorial Corporation
6327 Blachleyville Rd.
Wooster, OH 44691

Classified as a private operating foundation.

Financial data (yr. ended 06/30/00): Assets, $271,591 (M); grants paid, $0; gifts received, $124,801; expenditures, $174,911; qualifying distributions, $79,243; giving activities include $174,912 for programs.
Officers and Directors:* Fr. John Mueller,* Pres.; Rev. Alan E. Nathan,* V.P.; David Wilson,* Treas.; Hon. K. William Bailey, Brenda Hostettler, Rev. Dan Keister, Henry Loess, Rev. Dale Sanford, Alice Shoup.
EIN: 341251927
Codes: TN

62814
The Richard Enderlin Welfare House
603 W. 5th St.
Chillicothe, OH 45601

Established in 1996 in OH.
Financial data (yr. ended 12/31/01): Assets, $269,933 (M); grants paid, $0; expenditures, $6,187; qualifying distributions, $0.
Officers: Richard Enderlin, Jr., Pres.; J. Tennant Hoey, Secy.; John E. Herrnstein, Treas.
Directors: R. Alan Gough, William H. Nolan.
EIN: 311449781

62815
Paroz Family Foundation
4288 Armstrong Blvd.
Batavia, OH 45103

Established in 1999 in OH.
Financial data (yr. ended 12/31/00): Assets, $258,753 (M); grants paid, $8,500; expenditures, $9,535; qualifying distributions, $9,535.
Limitations: Applications not accepted.
Application information: Contributes only to pre-selected organizations.
Trustees: Michelle Clark, Timothy Dodds, Catherine Kelley, Rene Paroz.
EIN: 311671239

62816
Cincinnati Astronomical Society
5274 Zion Rd., Mt. Zion
Cleves, OH 45002

Financial data (yr. ended 09/30/01): Assets, $255,506 (M); grants paid, $0; gifts received, $150; expenditures, $13,212; qualifying distributions, $0.
Officers: Grant Martin, Pres.; William Schultz, V.P.; Brian Engle, Secy.; David Clark, Treas.
Trustees: Curt Cummins, Terri Toepfer.
EIN: 237091625

62817
Caritas Foundation
c/o N. Norris
3867 W. Market St., Ste. 151
Akron, OH 44333

Donor(s): Kenneth R. Rapp, Dorothy L. Rapp.
Financial data (yr. ended 12/31/00): Assets, $248,470 (M); grants paid, $22,002; expenditures, $22,616; qualifying distributions, $22,002.
Limitations: Applications not accepted. Giving primarily in Brunswick, OH.
Application information: Contributes only to pre-selected organizations.
Trustees: Nancy Oliver Norris, Dorothy L. Rapp, Kenneth R. Rapp.
EIN: 341788238

62818
Frank Eck Family Foundation
3300 Riverside Dr.
Columbus, OH 43221

Established in 2000 in OH.

62818—OHIO

Donor(s): Franklin E. Eck.
Financial data (yr. ended 12/31/01): Assets, $247,478 (M); grants paid, $10,000; gifts received, $200,000; expenditures, $11,380; qualifying distributions, $10,000.
Limitations: Applications not accepted.
Application information: Contributes only to pre-selected organizations.
Officers: Franklin E. Eck, Chair., C.E.O., and Treas.; Franklin E. Eck, Jr., Pres.; Frederic L. Smith, Secy.
EIN: 311711653

62819
The J. Robert and Rose Marie Melish Trust
P.O. Box 87
Galion, OH 44833
Application address: c/o Charles Neal, 200 Union St., Galion, OH 44833

Established in 1998 in OH.
Financial data (yr. ended 12/31/01): Assets, $243,518 (M); grants paid, $21,000; expenditures, $21,394; qualifying distributions, $20,995.
Limitations: Giving primarily in Galion, OH.
Application information: Application form required.
Trustees: Margaret Cagle, David Coleman, Charles Walker.
EIN: 347041107

62820
Richardson-Bretz Memorial Endowment Fund
P.O. Box 170
Celina, OH 45822

Classified as a private operating foundation in 1992.
Financial data (yr. ended 12/31/01): Assets, $226,863 (M); grants paid, $0; gifts received, $4,351; expenditures, $20,126; qualifying distributions, $0.
Trustees: Collin Bryan, David Granger, Mary Toms.
EIN: 346006837

62821
James & Coralie Centofanti Charitable Foundation
8943 Knauf Rd.
Canfield, OH 44406 (330) 533-4108
Contact: James Centofanti, Tr.

Established in 1997 in OH.
Donor(s): Coralie Centofanti, James Centofanti.
Financial data (yr. ended 12/31/99): Assets, $220,170 (M); grants paid, $23,150; expenditures, $23,526; qualifying distributions, $23,150.
Trustees: Coralie Centofanti, James Centofanti.
EIN: 316567000

62822
Matta Family Foundation
P.O. Box 37429
Cincinnati, OH 45222

Classified as a private operating foundation. Established in 1998 in OH.
Financial data (yr. ended 12/31/99): Assets, $218,003 (M); grants paid, $5,750; gifts received, $100,067; expenditures, $9,383; qualifying distributions, $7,245.
Limitations: Applications not accepted.
Application information: Contributes only to pre-selected organizations.
Trustees: Mahendra Matta, Sarita Matta.
EIN: 311605272

62823
Jean and Lewis Moore Foundation
166 Tanglewood Dr.
Urbana, OH 43078 (937) 653-4865
Contact: Lewis B. Moore, Pres. and Tr.

Established in 1997 in OH.
Donor(s): Lewis B. Moore.
Financial data (yr. ended 12/31/99): Assets, $215,857 (M); grants paid, $13,500; gifts received, $15,000; expenditures, $13,500; qualifying distributions, $15,000.
Officer and Trustees:* Lewis B. Moore,* Pres.; Gregory Moore, Jean Moore.
EIN: 311405513

62824
Joseph F. Burns Foundation
c/o Sky Trust, N.A.
P.O. Box 479
Youngstown, OH 44501-0479

Established in 1997 in OH.
Donor(s): Bill O. Burns.
Financial data (yr. ended 12/31/00): Assets, $196,516 (M); grants paid, $4,400; gifts received, $10,000; expenditures, $6,476; qualifying distributions, $5,128.
Limitations: Applications not accepted.
Application information: Contributes only to pre-selected organizations.
Directors: Bill O. Burns, Dona McCloskey, Harold J. Thompson.
Trustee: Sky Trust, N.A.
EIN: 311536795

62825
Cleveland Student Housing Association
2985 Washington Blvd.
Cleveland Heights, OH 44118

Financial data (yr. ended 12/31/00): Assets, $195,000 (M); grants paid, $0; gifts received, $49,562; expenditures, $42,683; qualifying distributions, $33,438; giving activities include $42,683 for programs.
Officers: George Burke, Pres.; Edith Berger, V.P. and Treas.; Margot Mersfelder, Secy.
EIN: 341106100

62826
The Leonetti/Carlson Family Foundation
13901 Shaker Blvd., Ste. 5B
Cleveland, OH 44120-1594
Contact: Ruthanna Carlson, Pres.

Established in 2000 in OH.
Donor(s): Ruthanna Carlson.
Financial data (yr. ended 12/31/01): Assets, $179,963 (M); grants paid, $18,248; expenditures, $24,684; qualifying distributions, $18,248.
Officers: Ruthanna Carlson, Pres.; Albert Leonetti, Secy.-Treas.
EIN: 341909133

62827
Gerald E. Brookins Museum of Electric Railways, Inc.
7100 Columbia Rd.
Olmsted Falls, OH 44138-1561

Financial data (yr. ended 12/31/00): Assets, $179,122 (M); grants paid, $0; gifts received, $8,986; expenditures, $47,295; qualifying distributions, $47,295; giving activities include $47,295 for programs.
Officer: Mark Brookins, Pres.
EIN: 346582015

62828
Robert L. Hunker Historic Preservation Foundation
6138 Riverview Rd.
Peninsula, OH 44264

Financial data (yr. ended 12/31/01): Assets, $175,574 (M); grants paid, $0; gifts received, $63,825; expenditures, $12,246; qualifying distributions, $0.
Officers: Robert L. Hunker, Pres.; Cynthia Suchan, Secy.
Trustee: Mitchell D. Kahan.
EIN: 311534973

62829
Pete Amato Foundation, Inc.
c/o Alfred S. Fricano
123 W. 5th St.
East Liverpool, OH 43920

Established in 2000 in OH.
Donor(s): Pete Amato.
Financial data (yr. ended 12/31/00): Assets, $165,425 (M); grants paid, $2,070; gifts received, $164,262; expenditures, $2,220; qualifying distributions, $2,070.
Limitations: Applications not accepted. Giving primarily in Liverpool, OH.
Application information: Contributes only to pre-selected organizations.
Trustees: Pete Amato, Nicholas T. Amato, Alfred S. Fricano.
EIN: 341929735

62830
Taft/Mahler Family Foundation
c/o Edward Haberer, Tr.
201 E. 5th St., Ste. 1100
Cincinnati, OH 45202-4117
Contact: Edward Haberer, Tr.

Established in 1998 in OH.
Financial data (yr. ended 12/31/00): Assets, $164,334 (M); grants paid, $380,695; expenditures, $406,195; qualifying distributions, $380,425.
Limitations: Giving primarily in OH.
Trustees: Edward Haberer, Kenneth Mahler, Mary T. Mahler.
Agent: Dennis L. Manes.
EIN: 311598721
Codes: FD

62831
Dayton Bar Association Foundation
c/o Bernard L. Raverty
130 W. 2nd St., Ste. 600
Dayton, OH 45402 (937) 222-7902

Classified as a private operating foundation in 1985.
Financial data (yr. ended 06/30/01): Assets, $162,612 (M); grants paid, $9,000; gifts received, $33,840; expenditures, $23,624; qualifying distributions, $22,606; giving activities include $14,574 for programs.
Limitations: Giving limited to Dayton, OH.
Application information: Application form required.
Officers: Beth W. Schaeffer, Pres.; Walter Reynolds, Secy.; Gary J. Leppla, Treas.
EIN: 311139525

62832
Medina Community Design Committee
141 S. Prospect St.
Medina, OH 44256

Financial data (yr. ended 06/30/00): Assets, $162,320 (M); grants paid, $0; gifts received,

$29,911; expenditures, $30,209; qualifying distributions, $23,695; giving activities include $22,646 for programs.
Limitations: Applications not accepted.
Application information: Contributes only to pre-selected organizations.
Officers: Timothy Davis, Chair.; Joann King, Vice-Chair.; Cynthia Szunyog, Secy.; Janet Senkar, Treas.
Trustees: Karl Matulin, Nancy McKee, Andrew Phillips, Dean Riggenbach.
EIN: 237084707

62833
St. Joseph No. 169 KSKJ Foundation
708 E. 159th St.
Cleveland, OH 44110

Classified as a private operating foundation in 1997.
Financial data (yr. ended 12/31/00): Assets, $161,282 (M); grants paid, $25,000; gifts received, $114,329; expenditures, $26,600; qualifying distributions, $24,224.
Limitations: Giving primarily in OH.
Officers and Trustees:* Eugene Kogovsek,* Chair.; Charles Pezdirtz,* Vice-Chair.; Mary Okicki,* Recording Secy.; Anton Nemec,* Secy.; Gregory Clack,* Treas.; Charles Erzen, Phil Hrvatin.
EIN: 311558317

62834
Woodin Laboratory
c/o Advisory Svcs., Inc.
1422 Euclid Ave., Ste. 1010
Cleveland, OH 44115

Classified as a private operating foundation in 1981.
Donor(s): William H. Woodin.
Financial data (yr. ended 12/31/01): Assets, $156,110 (M); grants paid, $0; expenditures, $18,542; qualifying distributions, $0.
Directors: Frank W. Hackley, Norman D. Hower, George M. Kass, John L. Moss, Eugene L. Scranton, Elizabeth T. Woodin, William H. Woodin.
EIN: 942742069

62835
Hejjaji Athmaramaguptha and H. A. Kanthalakshmi Foundation
c/o Richard W. Morris
590 Lexington Ave.
Mansfield, OH 44907-1505 (419) 756-2966
Application address: 630 Dirlam Ln., Mansfield, OH 44904
Contact: P.K. Athmaram, Tr.

Established in 1992 in OH.
Donor(s): P.K. Athmaram.
Financial data (yr. ended 12/31/99): Assets, $144,165 (M); grants paid, $10,700; expenditures, $11,812; qualifying distributions, $10,696.
Limitations: Giving in India and the U.S.
Application information: Application form required.
Trustee: P.K. Athmaram.
EIN: 341686822

62836
The Jason Foundation
1367 Snyder Rd.
Norwalk, OH 44857-9768 (419) 663-6616
Contact: Henry L. Alexander, Tr.

Donor(s): Henry L. Alexander, Jean A. Alexander.
Financial data (yr. ended 12/31/00): Assets, $142,475 (M); grants paid, $24,500; expenditures, $24,935; qualifying distributions, $24,375.
Trustees: Christopher Alexander, Henry L. Alexander, Heather L. Dumbeck, Paul G. Lux.
EIN: 341871196

62837
Rhonda & Larry A. Sheakley Family Foundation
100 Merchant St.
Cincinnati, OH 45246

Established in 2000.
Donor(s): The Sheanley Group, Inc.
Financial data (yr. ended 12/31/01): Assets, $140,826 (M); grants paid, $160,107; gifts received, $340,000; expenditures, $233,339; qualifying distributions, $160,107.
Limitations: Applications not accepted.
Application information: Contributes only to pre-selected organizations.
Trustees: Thomas E. Pappas, Jr., Larry A. Sheakley, Rhonda L. Sheakley.
EIN: 311679150
Codes: FD2

62838
Everhart Animal Protection Fund
c/o KeyBank, N.A.
800 Superior Ave., 4th Fl.
Cleveland, OH 44114 (800) 999-9658

Established in 1997 in OR.
Financial data (yr. ended 12/31/00): Assets, $136,820 (M); grants paid, $5,500; expenditures, $10,468; qualifying distributions, $6,730.
Limitations: Applications not accepted.
Application information: Contributes only to pre-selected organizations.
Trustee: KeyBank, N.A.
EIN: 911866928

62839
Collegescholars, Inc.
333 N. Portage Path, Ste. 4
Akron, OH 44303

Established in 1999 in OH. Classified as a private operating foundation in 2000.
Donor(s): Robert F. Linton, Deborah L. Cook.
Financial data (yr. ended 12/31/01): Assets, $132,402 (M); grants paid, $1,530; expenditures, $41,992; qualifying distributions, $35,762; giving activities include $35,762 for programs.
Limitations: Applications not accepted.
Application information: Contributes only to pre-selected organizations.
Trustees: Deborah L. Cook, Laurel A. Krutz, Robert F. Linton.
EIN: 341897856

62840
Abba Koval Perpetual Fund
P.O. Box 5852
Cleveland, OH 44101-0852

Financial data (yr. ended 12/31/00): Assets, $129,477 (M); grants paid, $6,000; gifts received, $6,039; expenditures, $6,047; qualifying distributions, $6,047.
Limitations: Applications not accepted.
Application information: Contributes only to pre-selected organizations.
Officers: Robert A. Brandoni, Chair.; Walter M. Martens, Pres.; Henry Kleinhenz, V.P.; Clyde Werner, Treas.
EIN: 341705102

62841
Saldoff-Semmelman Family Foundation, Inc.
386 Talmadge Rd.
P.O. Box 99
Clayton, OH 45315

Classified as a company-sponsored operating foundation.
Donor(s): Anchor Fabricators, Inc., Ruth D. Saldoff Family LT PDR, Thomas S. Saldoff.
Financial data (yr. ended 07/31/01): Assets, $127,172 (M); grants paid, $43,510; gifts received, $82,000; expenditures, $43,735; qualifying distributions, $43,729.
Limitations: Applications not accepted.
Application information: Contributes only to pre-selected organizations.
Directors: Marshall Ruchman, Ruth D. Saldoff, Thomas S. Saldoff.
EIN: 311478276
Codes: CD

62842
The Richard Clarke Foundation
9740 Cincinnati Rd.
West Chester, OH 45069

Established in 1998 in OH.
Financial data (yr. ended 12/31/99): Assets, $124,448 (M); grants paid, $16,702; expenditures, $16,812; qualifying distributions, $16,702.
Officer: Richard Clarke, Pres.
EIN: 311117509

62843
R. L. & Etta L. Triplett Memorial Foundation
P.O. Box 46
Bluffton, OH 45817-0046
Application address: 138 N. Main St., Bluffton, OH 45817
Contact: Samuel W. Diller, Treas.

Classified as a private operating foundation in 1985.
Financial data (yr. ended 12/31/99): Assets, $119,453 (M); grants paid, $4,500; expenditures, $6,217; qualifying distributions, $4,500.
Limitations: Giving primarily in Bluffton, OH.
Officers: Jean H. Triplett, Pres.; Tom Triplett, V.P.; Harold Balmer, Secy.; Samuel W. Diller, Treas.
EIN: 341479099

62844
Dr. Roland Hazen Fund
c/o LCNB Trust Dept.
2 N. Broadway, No. 300
Lebanon, OH 45036
Application address: 406 Deerfield Rd., Lebanon, OH 45036
Contact: Kathleen Drake, Tr.

Donor(s): George R. Henkle.
Financial data (yr. ended 12/31/00): Assets, $113,470 (M); grants paid, $0; expenditures, $9,583; qualifying distributions, $129.
Limitations: Giving limited to residents of OH.
Application information: Application form required.
Trustees: Kathleen Drake, Rachel A. Hutzel, Steve Poitinger.
EIN: 316090950
Codes: GTI

62845
James Poe Investments Youth Sports Fund
300 W. National Rd.
Englewood, OH 45322-1400 (937) 836-6335
Contact: James A. Poe, Tr.

Financial data (yr. ended 02/28/00): Assets, $112,603 (M); grants paid, $795; expenditures, $1,737; qualifying distributions, $795.
Trustees: James A. Poe, Linda A. Poe.
EIN: 311227807

62846
Homeward Bound Humane Society
(Formerly The Licking County Humane Society)
c/o Joanne Pyc
48 Webster Cir.
Granville, OH 43023

Classified as a private operating foundation in 1986.
Donor(s): Lenore B. Tyler.‡
Financial data (yr. ended 12/31/99): Assets, $109,131 (M); grants paid, $0; gifts received, $14,462; expenditures, $80,602; qualifying distributions, $68,844; giving activities include $8,756 for programs.
Officers: Joan Pitch, Pres.; Amie Wiseman, V.P.; Pat Handelman, Secy.; Celinn Humphry, Treas.
EIN: 316062704

62847
Schwartz Family Private Foundation
2723 Rocklyn Rd.
Shaker Heights, OH 44122

Established in 2001 in OH.
Donor(s): Walter Schwartz, Paula Schwartz.
Financial data (yr. ended 12/31/01): Assets, $100,012 (M); grants paid, $0; gifts received, $100,000; expenditures, $0; qualifying distributions, $0.
Officers: Paula R. Schwartz, Walter S. Schwartz.
EIN: 341970660

62848
Van Voorhis Family Foundation
1334 Cherokee Rose Dr.
Westerville, OH 43081

Established in 2000 in OH.
Donor(s): Samuel D. Van Voorhis.
Financial data (yr. ended 12/31/00): Assets, $100,000 (M); grants paid, $0; gifts received, $100,000; expenditures, $0; qualifying distributions, $0.
Trustees: Steve McCollum, John H. Van Voorhis, Julie A. Van Voorhis, Samuel D. Van Voorhis.
EIN: 311743340

62849
Roberts Charitable Trust
6431 Masters Row
Loveland, OH 45140

Established around 1995.
Financial data (yr. ended 12/31/99): Assets, $96,637 (M); grants paid, $6,971; gifts received, $6,800; expenditures, $24,009; qualifying distributions, $6,971.
Limitations: Applications not accepted. Giving primarily in Loveland, OH.
Application information: Contributes only to pre-selected organizations.
Trustees: Mark A. Roberts, Nancy D. Roberts.
EIN: 367089702

62850
The Father Yunker Lithuanian Student Assistance Fund
c/o National City Bank
P.O. Box 94651
Cleveland, OH 44101-4651
Application address: c/o National City Bank; Charitable & Endowment Services, 301 S.W. Adams St., Peoria, IL 61652-0749, tel.: (309) 655-5000

Financial data (yr. ended 12/31/01): Assets, $95,748 (M); grants paid, $6,034; expenditures, $7,373; qualifying distributions, $6,758.
Limitations: Giving primarily in IL.
Application information: Application form required.
Trustee: National City Bank.
EIN: 376165386

62851
R. D. Carlson Charitable Trust
1920 Bridgeview Ln.
Conneaut, OH 44030

Established in 1999.
Financial data (yr. ended 12/31/99): Assets, $93,263 (M); grants paid, $0; gifts received, $91,886; expenditures, $0; qualifying distributions, $0.
Limitations: Applications not accepted.
Application information: Contributes only to pre-selected organizations.
Trustee: Deborah Carlson.
EIN: 367246118

62852
The Amable Foundation
c/o Carol A. Galvan
110 W. Stoneridge Dr.
Milford, OH 45150

Established in 1999 in OH.
Financial data (yr. ended 06/30/00): Assets, $87,621 (M); grants paid, $5,000; gifts received, $92,200; expenditures, $5,436; qualifying distributions, $4,991.
Limitations: Applications not accepted.
Application information: Contributes only to pre-selected organizations.
Director: Carol A. Galvin.
EIN: 311676598

62853
Mildred C. Roy Scholarship Fund
211 E. 2nd St.
Port Clinton, OH 43452-1116 (419) 734-4060
Contact: George C. Wilbur, Tr.

Financial data (yr. ended 12/31/01): Assets, $83,272 (M); grants paid, $3,500; expenditures, $3,928; qualifying distributions, $3,524.
Limitations: Giving limited to Port Clinton, OH.
Application information: Application form required.
Trustees: A.C. Wilber, George C. Wilber.
EIN: 341325350
Codes: GTI

62854
Academy of Medicine of Columbus and Franklin County Physicians Free Clinic
(Formerly Academy of Medicine)
431 E. Broad St., Ste. 300
Columbus, OH 43215

Classified as a private operating foundation in 1994.
Donor(s): The Academy of Medicine of Columbus and Franklin County.

Financial data (yr. ended 05/31/00): Assets, $81,549 (M); grants paid, $0; gifts received, $56,550; expenditures, $100,180; qualifying distributions, $68,191; giving activities include $68,191 for programs.
Officers and Directors:* Bruce A. Wall, M.D.,* Pres.; Shirley Powers,* V.P.; Lorrie Zacharias,* Secy.-Treas.; Edward T. Bope, M.D., Ronald Kendrick, M.D., Teresa Long, M.D., Don McNeil, M.D., Gerald Penn, M.D., Dwight A. Scarborough, M.D., Avinash Tantri, Doris Walzak, M.D.
EIN: 311373719

62855
Cang Ngoc Dang Family Foundation
105 Mayfield Ave.
Akron, OH 44313
Contact: Rev. Minh Ngoc Dang, Pres.

Established in 1999 in OH.
Donor(s): Rev. Cang N. Dang, Mrs. Cang N. Dang, Mrs. Hanh Dang Nguyen.
Financial data (yr. ended 12/31/00): Assets, $77,030 (M); grants paid, $4,900; gifts received, $26,398; expenditures, $10,333; qualifying distributions, $4,904.
Limitations: Giving for the benefit of Vietnam.
Officers and Directors:* Rev. Cang N. Dang,* Chair.; Rev. Minh Ngoc Dang,* Pres.; Lang P. Nguyen, C.F.O. and Treas.
EIN: 341886270

62856
The Terraces Foundation
28589 E. River Rd.
Perrysburg, OH 43551
E-mail: becky@dean-ent.com

Established in 1998 in OH.
Donor(s): Dean P. Kasperzak, Rebecca S. Kasperzak.
Financial data (yr. ended 11/30/00): Assets, $76,927 (M); grants paid, $74,483; expenditures, $82,232; qualifying distributions, $74,291.
Limitations: Applications not accepted. Giving primarily in OH.
Application information: Contributes only to pre-selected organizations.
Officers: Rebecca S. Kasperzak, Pres.; Dean P. Kasperzak, V.P.
EIN: 341880416

62857
Chagrin Valley Charities, Inc.
2628 Pickerington Way
Hudson, OH 44236 (330) 528-0770
Contact: Jeffrey S. Ross, Secy.

Donor(s): Willard Davis.
Financial data (yr. ended 12/31/99): Assets, $75,249 (M); grants paid, $500; gifts received, $31,000; expenditures, $1,254; qualifying distributions, $1,159.
Officers: Peggy J. Ross, Chair.; Jeffrey S. Ross, Secy.
Trustee: Brenda L. Stine.
EIN: 341817532

62858
The Bookery, Inc.
1005 Lexington Ave.
Mansfield, OH 44907-2247

Financial data (yr. ended 12/31/99): Assets, $72,602 (M); grants paid, $10,000; expenditures, $10,741; qualifying distributions, $10,705.
Limitations: Applications not accepted.
Application information: Contributes only to pre-selected organizations.
Officers: H. Eugene Ryan, Pres.; Raymond Kissel, Secy.-Treas.

Trustee: Howard G. Peterson.
EIN: 340825399

62859
Smith Cove Preservation Trust
6950 S. Edgerton Rd., Ste. 100
Brecksville, OH 44141

Established in 1986 in ME.
Financial data (yr. ended 12/31/01): Assets, $71,792 (M); grants paid, $0; expenditures, $824; qualifying distributions, $824; giving activities include $824 for programs.
Trustees: James Benenson, Jr., Gerald J. Carroll, John V. Curci.
EIN: 010414466

62860
Andrew J. and Mary Schmidt Trust for Catholic Education
401 Pike St.
Reading, OH 45215

Established in 1995.
Financial data (yr. ended 12/31/00): Assets, $70,401 (M); grants paid, $9,100; gifts received, $1,005; expenditures, $9,352; qualifying distributions, $9,352.
Limitations: Giving primarily in Reading, OH.
Officers: Thomas W. Lynd, Secy.; Robert A. Glassmeyer, Treas.
EIN: 316357646

62861
Midway Correspondence, Inc.
19537 U.S. Rte. 6
Weston, OH 43569

Classified as a private operating foundation in 1986.
Donor(s): Edward R. Fletcher.
Financial data (yr. ended 12/31/01): Assets, $68,106 (M); grants paid, $0; gifts received, $41,577; expenditures, $35,498; qualifying distributions, $34,256; giving activities include $34,261 for programs.
Officers: Edward R. Fletcher, Chair.; Sharon R. Fletcher, Vice-Chair.; Brenda S. Hall, Secy.-Treas.
EIN: 341419465

62862
Charles F. Fischer Society for Crippled Children
111 Nelson Ave.
Wilmington, OH 45177
Application address: c/o Joe Dennis, 245 N. South St., Wilmington, OH 45177, tel.: (937) 382-3831

Financial data (yr. ended 12/31/01): Assets, $66,599 (L); grants paid, $48,594; gifts received, $54,767; expenditures, $49,886; qualifying distributions, $49,787.
Limitations: Giving limited to Clinton County, OH.
Officers: Mary R. Boyd, M.D., Pres.; Carol Weber, V.P.; Elizabeth Bradshaw, Secy.-Treas.
EIN: 311007856
Codes: GTI

62863
Auburn Foundation
3439 W. Brainard Rd.
Woodmere, OH 44122

Donor(s): Alex Kertesz.
Financial data (yr. ended 07/31/01): Assets, $63,539 (M); grants paid, $2,250; expenditures, $2,250; qualifying distributions, $2,250.
Officers and Trustees:* Alex Kertesz,* Pres.; Randy Kertesz,* V.P.; Ronnie Kertesz,* V.P.; Jacob Rosenbaum, Secy.
EIN: 341379265

62864
St. Frances Cabrini Heart Foundation
7093 Gates Mills Blvd.
Gates Mills, OH 44040-9312
Contact: John J. Kralik, M.D., Pres.

Classified as a private operating foundation in 1961.
Donor(s): Joseph A. Kralik.
Financial data (yr. ended 12/31/01): Assets, $63,413 (M); grants paid, $2,000; gifts received, $300; expenditures, $2,250; qualifying distributions, $2,250.
Limitations: Giving primarily in NY.
Officers: John J. Kralik, M.D., Pres.; Rita Kralik, Secy.
EIN: 346545681

62865
Edgewater Yachting Education Society
6700 Memorial Shoreway N.W.
Cleveland, OH 44102
Contact: Robert Frantz, Chair.

Financial data (yr. ended 12/31/01): Assets, $63,359 (M); grants paid, $531; gifts received, $2,007; expenditures, $1,339; qualifying distributions, $531.
Officers: Robert Frantz, Chair.; Robert Layton, Treas.
Trustee: Jay Hawkins.
EIN: 341416282

62866
GDM Broadcasting Foundation
c/o Ronald C. Christian
425 Walnut St., Ste. 1800-Firstar Twr.
Cincinnati, OH 45202-3957

Established in 1994 in OH.
Donor(s): George and Deborah Mehl Trust.
Financial data (yr. ended 04/30/02): Assets, $61,767 (M); grants paid, $0; gifts received, $24,000; expenditures, $2,047; qualifying distributions, $1,992; giving activities include $1,992 for programs.
Officers and Trustees:* Rose Chamberlin,* Pres.; Ronald C. Christian,* Secy.-Treas.; Elwood H. Chamberlin, Sheldon George Pooley, Jr., Dave Rhodes.
EIN: 311353937

62867
Robert and Patricia May Foundation
c/o Patricia Ireland May
60 West St.
Cincinnati, OH 45242

Established in 1999 in OH.
Donor(s): Robert May, Patricia May.
Financial data (yr. ended 12/31/00): Assets, $61,122 (M); grants paid, $19,047; gifts received, $400; expenditures, $22,285; qualifying distributions, $19,047.
Limitations: Giving primarily in Cincinnati, OH.
Officers: Daniel May, Pres.; Robert E. May, Jr., V.P.; Patricia Ireland May, V.P.; Krista May Altemuehle, Secy.; Robert J. May, Treas.
EIN: 311678382

62868
Mary Renkert Wendling Foundation
c/o KeyBank, N.A., Trust Div.
800 Superior Ave., 4th Fl.
Cleveland, OH 44114

Established in 1998 in OH.
Financial data (yr. ended 12/31/01): Assets, $59,708 (M); grants paid, $450; gifts received, $30,000; expenditures, $1,176; qualifying distributions, $507.

Limitations: Applications not accepted. Giving primarily in the New York, NY, area.
Application information: Contributes only to pre-selected organizations.
Trustee: KeyBank, N.A.
EIN: 311610141

62869
The Believers Scholarship & Needs Foundation
(also known as TBSNF)
12143 County Rd. E35
Bryan, OH 43506

Established in 1990 in IL.
Donor(s): J.P. Ewonus, Kathleen T. Ewonus.
Financial data (yr. ended 12/31/01): Assets, $55,863 (M); grants paid, $0; gifts received, $200; expenditures, $363; qualifying distributions, $0.
Limitations: Giving primarily in Bryan, OH.
Application information: Application form required.
Officer and Trustees:* Kathleen T. Ewonus,* Pres.; John P. Ewonus.
EIN: 363752052

62870
Innkeeper Ministries, Inc.
c/o Robert L. Hartenstein
6701 Lewisburg-Ozais Rd.
Lewisburg, OH 45338

Established in 2001 in OH.
Donor(s): Robert L. Hartenstein, Janet K. Hartenstein.
Financial data (yr. ended 12/31/01): Assets, $55,032 (M); grants paid, $0; gifts received, $60,950; expenditures, $5,918; qualifying distributions, $4,511.
Limitations: Applications not accepted.
Application information: Contributes only to pre-selected organizations.
Trustees: Christopher T. Hartenstein, Robert L. Hartenstein, Don Kline.
EIN: 311796904

62871
Christian BusinessCares Foundation
1814 First National Tower, Rm. 1814
Akron, OH 44308-1418
Application address: P.O. Box 219, Peninsula, OH 44264-0219

Established in 1982 in OH.
Donor(s): Audrey Beaverson, Carl R. Gessel, Kenneth Lutke, Dennis M. Zaverl, Larry J. Rybka, Al Coune, Michael Poitinger, Tammi Poitinger, Lawrence S. Rybka, Jo Rybka, Beaverson Foundation, Carolyn Zavert.
Financial data (yr. ended 10/31/01): Assets, $53,791 (M); grants paid, $18,996; gifts received, $7,000; expenditures, $20,208; qualifying distributions, $20,208.
Limitations: Giving primarily in Medina and Cleveland, OH.
Application information: Application form required.
Officers: Dennis M. Zaverl, Pres.; Carolyn T. Zaverl, Secy.
Trustees: Peter Farage, Dick Foster, Raymond D. Meyo, Lawrence J. Rybka, J.D., Dr. Frank J. Sizer, Vanessa Swank, Raymond Swank.
EIN: 341377938

62872
Value City Department Stores Charitable Foundation
3241 Westerville Rd.
Columbus, OH 43224-3750
Contact: Steven Miller, Secy.

Established in 1998 in OH, GA, IL, IN, KY, MD, MI, MO, NC, NJ, NY, PA, TN, VA, and WV.
Financial data (yr. ended 12/31/00): Assets, $52,690 (M); grants paid, $13,333; gifts received, $500; expenditures, $13,869; qualifying distributions, $13,333.
Officers and Trustees:* Alan Schlesinger,* Co-Chair.; Jay Schottenstein,* Co-Chair.; George Kolber, Pres.; Michael Broidy, V.P.; James Diers, V.P.; Lynn Lambrecht,* V.P.; Steven Miller, Secy.; James McGrady,* Treas.
EIN: 311592878

62873
The Waickman and Nelson Foundation Trust
544-B White Pond Dr.
Akron, OH 44320

Established in 1990 in OH.
Donor(s): Francis Waickman, M.D., Donald S. Nelson, M.D.
Financial data (yr. ended 12/31/01): Assets, $51,839 (M); grants paid, $0; expenditures, $1,097; qualifying distributions, $0.
Officers: Frederick Lacher, Pres.; Donald S. Nelson, M.D., Secy.; Francis Waickman, M.D., Mgr.
EIN: 341652877

62874
John W. Landis Scholarship Trust
c/o D. Williams Evans, Jr.
1670 Christmas Run Blvd.
Wooster, OH 44691
Application address: c/o Wayne County Superintendent of Schools, 2534 Burbank Rd., Wooster, OH 44691, tel.: (330) 345-6771

Financial data (yr. ended 06/30/99): Assets, $49,565 (M); grants paid, $1,500; expenditures, $1,770; qualifying distributions, $1,720.
Limitations: Giving primarily in Wooster, OH.
Application information: Application form required.
Trustees: D. William Evans, Jr., Edward Swartz.
EIN: 237396151

62875
Seniors Helping Seniors
5692 E. Day Cir.
Milford, OH 45150

Classified as a private operating foundation in 1997 in OH.
Financial data (yr. ended 12/31/00): Assets, $46,851 (M); grants paid, $441; expenditures, $23,728; qualifying distributions, $23,728.
Limitations: Applications not accepted.
Officers: Betty Lemberg, Pres.; Robert Lemberg, V.P.
EIN: 311278295

62876
Bingman Family Foundation
3692 N. Shore Dr.
Akron, OH 44333-8348

Donor(s): George Bingman.
Financial data (yr. ended 12/31/01): Assets, $45,416 (L); grants paid, $64,400; gifts received, $65,000; expenditures, $64,450; qualifying distributions, $64,400.
Limitations: Applications not accepted. Giving limited to Akron, OH.

Application information: Contributes only to pre-selected organizations.
Trustees: George Bingman, Ruby Bingman.
EIN: 341756824

62877
A. B. J. Neville Foundation, Inc.
P.O. Box 41236
Cleveland, OH 44141-0236

Established in 1998 in OH.
Donor(s): Anita F. Utz.
Financial data (yr. ended 12/31/00): Assets, $45,208 (M); grants paid, $1,500; expenditures, $1,625; qualifying distributions, $1,625.
Limitations: Applications not accepted.
Application information: Contributes only to pre-selected organizations.
Officer: Anita F. Utz, Pres.
EIN: 341860006

62878
Ohio Premier Girls Soccer Club of Dublin, Ohio, Inc.
c/o Michael T. Radcliffe
41 S. High St., Ste. 2800
Columbus, OH 43215-6109

Established in 1994 in OH.
Donor(s): Michael T. Radcliffe, DEC LP.
Financial data (yr. ended 12/31/01): Assets, $41,780 (M); grants paid, $0; gifts received, $200; expenditures, $357,866; qualifying distributions, $357,866; giving activities include $357,866 for programs.
Officers and Trustees:* Michael T. Radcliffe,* Chair., Pres. and Secy.; Alan Daum,* Treas.; Debra Carlier, Donna Corbett, Al Herold, Jon Lipsitz, Paul Lukeman, Janice Nelson, Ruth Rudibaugh, Mike Scohere, Jim Sturm, Margret Wright.
EIN: 311284756

62879
Ruth G. Cooper Testamentary Trust
(also known as Ruth G. Cooper Charitable Trust)
2860 E. Market St.
Warren, OH 44483-6259 (330) 856-2790
Contact: Edwin Schlarb, Tr.

Classified as a private operating foundation in 1999.
Financial data (yr. ended 12/31/01): Assets, $40,213 (M); grants paid, $100,000; expenditures, $103,087; qualifying distributions, $100,000.
Trustees: William Burkhart, Jeanne Ginter, Edwin W. Schlarb.
EIN: 347008359
Codes: FD2

62880
OSCO Industries Foundation
P.O. Box 1388
Portsmouth, OH 45662-1388
Contact: John M. Burke, Chair.

Established as a company-sponsored operating foundation.
Donor(s): OSCO Industries, Inc.
Financial data (yr. ended 12/31/00): Assets, $34,831 (M); grants paid, $13,900; gifts received, $25,900; expenditures, $13,900; qualifying distributions, $13,900.
Limitations: Giving limited to OH.
Application information: Application form not required.
Officer: John M. Burke, Chair.
Trustees: Jeffrey A. Burke, Philip L. Vetter.
EIN: 316025158
Codes: CD

62881
The Carlos & Margarita Calonge Scholarship Foundation
8951 Terwilligers Tr.
Cincinnati, OH 45249-2737

Established in 1999 in OH.
Donor(s): Bernardo J. Calonge, Carmen C. Calonge.
Financial data (yr. ended 12/31/00): Assets, $33,133 (M); grants paid, $2,000; gifts received, $6,508; expenditures, $3,504; qualifying distributions, $2,609.
Limitations: Applications not accepted. Giving primarily in Lakeland, FL.
Directors: Allan B. Calonge, Bernardo J. Calonge, Carlos B. Calonge, Carmen C. Calonge, Daniel E. Calonge.
EIN: 311645698

62882
Eric Gibson Memorial Scholarship Trust
c/o Joseph P. Guilfoyle
14713 Ridge Rd.
North Royalton, OH 44133-4943

Established in 1992 in OH.
Financial data (yr. ended 12/31/99): Assets, $29,785 (M); grants paid, $1,000; expenditures, $1,099; qualifying distributions, $1,099.
Limitations: Giving limited to North Royalton, OH.
Trustees: Charles Gibson, Gail Gibson, Joseph P. Guilfoyle.
EIN: 341651959

62883
Robert P. Hollaender Senior Scholarship Charitable Trust
c/o The Hollaender Mfg. Co. Schol. Team
10285 Wayne Ave.
Cincinnati, OH 45215-6399

Established in 1996.
Financial data (yr. ended 12/31/99): Assets, $29,252 (M); grants paid, $2,000; gifts received, $2,952; expenditures, $2,007; qualifying distributions, $2,000.
Application information: Application form required.
Trustees: Robert P. Hollaender II, Robin Keller.
EIN: 311337323

62884
The Henry and Kathryn A. Kurdziel Foundation
5109 Dogwood Trail
Lyndhurst, OH 44124

Established in 1990 in OH.
Donor(s): Don Kurdziel, Leesa Kurdziel, Lincoln Properties Co.
Financial data (yr. ended 12/31/01): Assets, $25,690 (M); grants paid, $6,226; gifts received, $1,500; expenditures, $6,824; qualifying distributions, $6,625.
Limitations: Applications not accepted. Giving primarily in Beford and Garfield Heights, OH.
Officers: Kathryn A. Kurdziel, Pres.; Henry P. Kurdziel, V.P. and Treas.
EIN: 341651366
Codes: GTI

62885
Columbus Female Benevolent Society
1234 E. Broad St.
Columbus, OH 43205-1453
Application address: 158 S. Roosevelt Ave., Columbus, OH 43209
Contact: Mrs. Duane M. Campbell, Treas.

Established in 1938.

Financial data (yr. ended 12/31/01): Assets, $24,094 (M); grants paid, $39,291; gifts received, $40,369; expenditures, $39,674; qualifying distributions, $39,291.
Limitations: Giving limited to Franklin County, OH.
Officers: Carolyn Christy, Pres.; Patricia Hanna, V.P.; Mrs. David M. Inglis, Recording Secy.; Mrs. Robert Sweeney, Corresponding Secy.; Mrs. Duane M. Campbell, Treas.
EIN: 316042036
Codes: GTI

62886
Pallas Communications, Inc.
5017 Archmere Ave.
Cleveland, OH 44144

Financial data (yr. ended 12/31/00): Assets, $22,619 (M); grants paid, $0; expenditures, $12,977; qualifying distributions, $12,967; giving activities include $12,977 for programs.
Officers and Directors:* Alan Write,* Pres.; Lynda Sackett,* V.P.; Jesse Bryant Wilder, Exec. Dir.
EIN: 341792274

62887
Ohio Operation Lifesaver
1085 Joyce Ave.
Columbus, OH 43219-2448

Donor(s): Norfolk Southern Corp., Consolidated Rail Corp., CXS Transportation, CN North America.
Financial data (yr. ended 12/31/01): Assets, $22,443 (M); grants paid, $0; gifts received, $78,792; expenditures, $78,922; qualifying distributions, $0.
Officers and Trustees:* Walt Fleming,* Chair.; Kenneth B. Marshall,* Pres.; Judy E. East, 1st V.P.; Donald G. Slemmer,* Secy.-Treas.; Alfred Agler, Donnie W. Dutton, Susan Kirkland, Donald M. Lubinsky, Peter Snyder, Ian Thompson.
EIN: 311176181

62888
I. Leonard & Miriam G. Bernstein Foundation, Inc.
3117 Esther Dr.
Cincinnati, OH 45213 (513) 731-6741
Contact: I. Leonard Bernstein, M.D., Pres.; or Miriam G. Bernstein, Secy.

Classified as a private operating foundation in 1979.
Financial data (yr. ended 12/31/00): Assets, $21,740 (M); grants paid, $1,000; expenditures, $1,000; qualifying distributions, $1,000.
Limitations: Giving primarily in Cincinnati, OH.
Officers: I. Leonard Bernstein, Pres.; Miriam G. Bernstein, Secy.
EIN: 310951656

62889
Cole Family Foundation
c/o Charles C. Cole
735 S. State, Rte. 67
Republic, OH 44867

Established in 1992 in OH.
Donor(s): Lucile L. Cole.
Financial data (yr. ended 12/31/99): Assets, $20,430 (M); grants paid, $39,975; gifts received, $62; expenditures, $40,387; qualifying distributions, $40,351.
Limitations: Applications not accepted. Giving primarily in Tiffin, OH.
Application information: Contributes only to pre-selected organizations.
Trustees: Alec C. Cole, Charles C. Cole, Patty J. Cole.

EIN: 341715561

62890
The Lorenzo Lee Saylor Scholarship Charitable Trust
c/o Teresa Emmert
37746 State Rt. 93
Hamden, OH 45634

Established in 1999 in OH.
Donor(s): Anita Saylor.
Financial data (yr. ended 12/31/00): Assets, $20,384 (M); grants paid, $1,000; expenditures, $1,000; qualifying distributions, $1,000.
Limitations: Applications not accepted.
Application information: Contributes only to pre-selected organizations.
Trustees: Teresa L. Emmert, Loretta Saylor.
EIN: 311677965

62891
James William Lazzaro Foundation for Genetic Metabolism Disorders
4493 Liberty Rd.
South Euclid, OH 44121

Financial data (yr. ended 12/31/00): Assets, $19,178 (M); grants paid, $1,000; gifts received, $9,220; expenditures, $2,962; qualifying distributions, $2,962; giving activities include $462 for programs.
Limitations: Applications not accepted. Giving primarily in Waco, TX.
Application information: Contributes only to pre-selected organizations.
Officers: Jamie Lazzaro, Pres.; Thomas Lazzaro, V.P.; James Murphy, Secy.; Geraldine Lazzaro, Treas.
EIN: 341879468

62892
New Concord Scout Foundation
188 Friendship Dr.
New Concord, OH 43762-1008
(740) 826-4795
Contact: Jeffrey T. Tucker

Financial data (yr. ended 12/31/99): Assets, $18,979 (M); grants paid, $750; gifts received, $8,103; expenditures, $881; qualifying distributions, $750.
Limitations: Giving limited to New Concord, OH.
Officers: Tim Graham, Pres.; Richard Dailey, V.P.; Jeffrey T. Tucker, Secy.-Treas.
Trustee: James Hummell.
EIN: 310901590

62893
John A. Bowen & Rosan Bowen Memorial Fund
c/o Proctorville Woman's Club
P.O. Box 1236
Proctorville, OH 45669

Classified as a private operating foundation in 1985.
Financial data (yr. ended 12/31/99): Assets, $18,852 (M); grants paid, $360; expenditures, $390; qualifying distributions, $360.
Limitations: Applications not accepted. Giving primarily in OH.
Application information: Contributes only to pre-selected organizations.
Officer: Delma Stevens, Admin.
Trustee: Proctoville Women's Club.
EIN: 311101908

62894
Barberton Moose Charity & Scholarship Fund, Inc.
P.O. Box 1467
Barberton, OH 44203

Financial data (yr. ended 12/31/00): Assets, $18,293 (M); grants paid, $0; expenditures, $31,957; qualifying distributions, $0.
Officer: John Gill, Treas.
EIN: 341416450

62895
Sarah Marie Klemesrud Foundation
c/o Bruce Klemesrud
1936 Rythe Rd.
Columbus, OH 43220-4815

Established in 1990 in OH; funded in 1991.
Financial data (yr. ended 12/31/99): Assets, $16,996 (M); grants paid, $750; gifts received, $4,142; expenditures, $882; qualifying distributions, $750.
Limitations: Applications not accepted. Giving primarily in OH.
Application information: Contributes only to pre-selected organizations.
Officer: Bruce H. Klemesrud, Pres.
Trustees: Bradley K. Klemesrud, Brian P. Klemesrud, Lynn H. Klemesrud.
EIN: 311336085

62896
Drug Abuse Research Charitable Trust
c/o Susan Scherer
P.O. Box 163602
Columbus, OH 43216-3602

Established in 1999 in OH.
Donor(s): Michael R. Weed.
Financial data (yr. ended 11/30/01): Assets, $15,814 (M); grants paid, $1,000; gifts received, $10,045; expenditures, $1,380; qualifying distributions, $1,000.
Officers and Trustees:* Susan Scherer,* Pres.; Michael R. Weed,* V.P.; Stephen T. Weed,* Secy.
EIN: 311669830

62897
Earthward Bound Foundation
P.O. Box 3551
Cincinnati, OH 45201-3551 (513) 381-3939
Contact: Murray Sinclaire, Jr., Pres.

Classified as a private operating foundation in 1974.
Financial data (yr. ended 10/31/01): Assets, $15,802 (M); grants paid, $26,966; gifts received, $27,847; expenditures, $28,874; qualifying distributions, $26,966.
Limitations: Giving primarily in CA and OH.
Officers: Murray Sinclaire, Jr., Pres.; J.R. Orton III, V.P.; J. Robin Sinclaire, Secy.-Treas.
EIN: 237429274

62898
Zanesville Green Commission, Inc.
1101 Forest Ave.
Zanesville, OH 43701-2826

Financial data (yr. ended 12/31/01): Assets, $14,698 (M); grants paid, $0; gifts received, $19,639; expenditures, $10,797; qualifying distributions, $0.
Officers: Betty Cultice, Pres.; Ann Gildew, Treas.
Trustee: Fred Grant.
EIN: 311324808

62899
Cynthia L. Jones-Eardley Trust
39 N. Maple St.
Orwell, OH 44076
Contact: Rosemary D. Jones, Tr.

Classified as a private operating foundation in OH.
Financial data (yr. ended 12/31/01): Assets, $14,430 (M); grants paid, $500; gifts received, $2,339; expenditures, $814; qualifying distributions, $500.
Limitations: Giving limited to residents of Orwell, OH.
Application information: Given to the Salutatorian from Grand Valley High School.
Trustees: David A. Eardley, James L. Jones, Rosemary Jones, Thomas R. Jones.
EIN: 311514073

62900
Schwartz, Manes & Ruby Foundation
441 Vine St., Ste. 2900
Cincinnati, OH 45202-2808

Established in 1998.
Financial data (yr. ended 12/31/01): Assets, $12,589 (M); grants paid, $0; expenditures, $250; qualifying distributions, $250.
Officers and Trustees:* Richard M. Schwartz,* Pres.; Dennis L. Manes,* V.P.; Stanley L. Ruby,* Treas.
EIN: 311617677

62901
Jeff & Patrice Smith Family Foundation, Inc.
11 Barberry Rd.
Wooster, OH 44691 (330) 262-1460
Contact: Jeff Smith, Dir.

Established in 1999 in FL.
Financial data (yr. ended 12/31/00): Assets, $11,676 (M); grants paid, $7,130; expenditures, $7,466; qualifying distributions, $7,130.
Limitations: Giving limited to Wooster, OH.
Directors: E.A. Smith, Jeffrey Smith, Patrice Smith.
EIN: 593575843

62902
The Albert and Rivella Tavens Private Foundation
c/o Zinner & Co.
29125 Chagrin Blvd.
Cleveland, OH 44122-4692

Classified as a private operating foundation in 1988.
Financial data (yr. ended 05/31/02): Assets, $10,574 (M); grants paid, $0; gifts received, $10,297; expenditures, $220; qualifying distributions, $0.
Officer and Trustees:* Gabor Adler,* Pres. and Secy.-Treas.; Ephraim S. Jonah, Albert Tavens, Rabbi Lawrence Zierler.
EIN: 341867362

62903
Donna Jean Irwin Scholarship Fund
290 E. Main St.
Ashville, OH 43103-1518 (740) 983-2786
Contact: James E. Irwin, Tr.

Established in 2001 in OH.
Donor(s): James E. Irwin.
Financial data (yr. ended 12/31/01): Assets, $10,071 (M); grants paid, $250; gifts received, $10,450; expenditures, $706; qualifying distributions, $250.
Application information: Application form required.
Trustees: Deborah I. Hulse, James E. Irwin, Jo Ellen Irwin, Teresa L. Irwin-Bowser.
EIN: 311743033

62904
Monarch Foundation
400 Oak St., Rm. 83
Cincinnati, OH 45219-2505

Classified as a private operating foundation in 1989.
Financial data (yr. ended 12/31/01): Assets, $9,334 (M); grants paid, $0; gifts received, $12,444; expenditures, $61,553; qualifying distributions, $0.
Trustees: James M. Anderson, Ronald Huston, Charles P. Olinger.
EIN: 311233988

62905
New Life Patterns Company
5399 Teakwood Ct.
Columbus, OH 43229-3901

Established in 1999 in OH.
Donor(s): Larry N. Nelson.
Financial data (yr. ended 12/31/00): Assets, $7,145 (M); grants paid, $136; gifts received, $29,535; expenditures, $40,185; qualifying distributions, $33,095; giving activities include $40,049 for programs.
Limitations: Applications not accepted.
Application information: Contributes only to pre-selected organizations.
Trustees: Danielle Nelson, Larry N. Nelson, Theresa D. Nelson.
EIN: 311630046

62906
AEAONMS Health Medical Research Foundation, Inc.
3980 Winding Way
Cincinnati, OH 45229

Financial data (yr. ended 06/30/99): Assets, $6,220 (M); grants paid, $21,000; gifts received, $36,698; expenditures, $45,222; qualifying distributions, $0.
Limitations: Giving on a national basis.
Officers: A.V. Blunt, Jr., Pres.; Donald Ware, V.P.; Delores Ware, Secy.; Chester Dryor, Treas.
EIN: 383082910

62907
Glenville Community Festival
P.O. Box 08619
Cleveland, OH 44103
Contact: Wendy McDonald-Hunter, Chair.

Financial data (yr. ended 06/30/00): Assets, $5,965 (M); grants paid, $2,000; gifts received, $7,500; expenditures, $18,438; qualifying distributions, $20,073; giving activities include $16,438 for programs.
Limitations: Giving primarily in Cleveland, OH.
Application information: Applicants must reside in the Glenville area and maintain a 2.8 GPA. Application form required.
Officers: Wendy McDonald Hunter, Chair.; William Richards, Vice-Chair.; Diane Richardson, Vice-Chair.; Antoinette Wheeler, Vice-Chair.
EIN: 941689956

62908
The Gottshall-Rex Memorial Scholarship, Inc.
c/o C.R. Bracken
3306 Executive Pkwy., No. 205
Toledo, OH 43606
Application address: 2755 Hemlock Dr., Toledo, OH 43614, tel.: (419) 385-2109
Contact: Jane Johnson, Secy.

Financial data (yr. ended 12/31/00): Assets, $5,806 (M); grants paid, $9,000; expenditures, $10,424; qualifying distributions, $9,000.
Limitations: Giving limited to the Toledo, OH, area.
Application information: Application form required.
Officers and Directors:* Susan Anderson,* Chair.; Jane Johnson,* Secy.; Carole Liebich, Joann Maher.
EIN: 346554588

62909
I Have a Dream Foundation - Cleveland Chapter
1228 Euclid Ave., Ste. 31
Cleveland, OH 44115

Established in 1986 in OH. Classified as a private operating foundation in 1987.
Financial data (yr. ended 06/30/00): Assets, $5,746 (M); grants paid, $0; gifts received, $250; expenditures, $2,522; qualifying distributions, $2,522; giving activities include $2,522 for programs.
Officer and Trustees:* Charlotte R. Kramer,* Pres.; Jane P. Horvitz, Mark R. Kramer.
EIN: 341556850

62910
Share Our World
10901 Claypike Rd.
Derwent, OH 43733

Established in 1992 in OH.
Donor(s): S. Lee Youngs, Jack R. Youngs, American Nutrition, Inc.
Financial data (yr. ended 12/31/00): Assets, $5,229 (M); grants paid, $6,435; gifts received, $7,440; expenditures, $7,317; qualifying distributions, $7,308.
Limitations: Applications not accepted. Giving primarily in MA and OH.
Application information: Contributes only to pre-selected organizations.
Trustees: Thomas C. Bauer, Linda W. Ertz, Jack R. Youngs.
EIN: 311352054

62911
Third World Books, Inc.
c/o Robert G. Cheshier
2204 Grandview Ave.
Cleveland Heights, OH 44106

Established in 1999.
Donor(s): Robert G. Cheshier.
Financial data (yr. ended 12/31/99): Assets, $5,157 (M); grants paid, $4,300; gifts received, $10,370; expenditures, $5,229; qualifying distributions, $0; giving activities include $792 for programs.
Limitations: Giving on an international basis, primarily in Africa.
Officers: Robert G. Cheshier, Pres.; Ann Farmer, Secy.; William V. Bowen, Treas.
Trustee: Lloyd E. McHamm.
EIN: 341885577

62912
Richard S. & Carol K. Kaufman Foundation
38 Lyman Cir.
Shaker Heights, OH 44122-2116
Contact: Richard S. Kaufman, Tr.

Financial data (yr. ended 12/31/99): Assets, $5,141 (M); grants paid, $5,190; expenditures, $5,829; qualifying distributions, $5,829.
Limitations: Giving primarily in Cleveland, OH.
Trustee: Richard S. Kaufman.
EIN: 341375715

62913
Robert A. Taft High School Alumni Association
c/o Fred A. Hill
6550 Stewart Rd.
Cincinnati, OH 45236

Established around 1974.
Financial data (yr. ended 12/31/00): Assets, $4,560 (M); grants paid, $2,458; gifts received, $10,522; expenditures, $4,024; qualifying distributions, $2,458.
Limitations: Applications not accepted. Giving primarily in OH.
Officer: Fred A. Hill, Pres.
EIN: 316086721

62914
Jonah Family Foundation, Inc.
2435 Pine Lake Tr.
Uniontown, OH 44685
Contact: Marybeth Hinds, Tr.

Established in 1999 in OH.
Donor(s): John L. Hinds, Marybeth Hinds.
Financial data (yr. ended 12/31/01): Assets, $4,219 (M); grants paid, $15,000; expenditures, $16,505; qualifying distributions, $16,505.
Trustees: John L. Hinds, Marybeth Hinds.
EIN: 311651279

62915
Ada B. Scott Foundation
c/o Stephen G. Rising
1585 Belle Ave.
Lakewood, OH 44107-4331

Financial data (yr. ended 12/31/00): Assets, $2,313 (M); grants paid, $800; gifts received, $1,300; expenditures, $1,166; qualifying distributions, $800.
Limitations: Giving primarily in Cleveland, OH.
Officers and Trustee:* Stephen G. Rising, Chair. and Pres.; Elaine S. Irwin,* Secy.
EIN: 341801994

62916
Lima Area Parkinson Support Group
c/o Charles Niedecken
436 E. 5th St.
Delphos, OH 45833

Established in 1997 in OH.
Financial data (yr. ended 12/31/00): Assets, $2,118 (M); grants paid, $2,000; gifts received, $2,575; expenditures, $2,294; qualifying distributions, $2,271; giving activities include $289 for programs.
Limitations: Giving primarily in OH.
Officers: Kevin Kidd, Pres. and Secy.; Donald McKinley, V.P.; Charles Niedecken, Treas.
EIN: 341565678

62917
Ohio Premier Too, Inc.
5964 Whittingham Dr.
Dublin, OH 43017-9617

Established in 1998 in OH.
Donor(s): Michael T. Radcliffe.

Financial data (yr. ended 12/31/00): Assets, $2,022 (M); grants paid, $0; gifts received, $68,600; expenditures, $68,177; qualifying distributions, $68,177; giving activities include $68,177 for programs.
Limitations: Applications not accepted.
Application information: Contributes only to pre-selected organizations.
Officers and Trustees:* Michael T. Radcliffe,* Chair., Pres., and Secy.; Shelley R. Radcliffe,* Treas.; Alan Daum, Kathy Daum, Jon Lipsitz, Jim Sturm, Robert J. Tannous.
EIN: 311583717

62918
JSS Foundation
2191 City Gate Dr.
Columbus, OH 43219-3564

Financial data (yr. ended 12/31/00): Assets, $1,558 (M); grants paid, $19,320; gifts received, $10,251; expenditures, $19,370; qualifying distributions, $19,370.
Limitations: Applications not accepted.
Application information: Contributes only to pre-selected organizations.
Trustee: Dwight Smith.
EIN: 522151091

62919
The Schnebel Foundation
c/o Verne H. Schnebel
650 Maple Trace
Cincinnati, OH 45246-4166

Established in 1991 in OH.
Financial data (yr. ended 12/31/00): Assets, $1,522 (M); grants paid, $100; gifts received, $1,150; expenditures, $683; qualifying distributions, $100.
Officers: Verne H. Schnebel, Pres.; Elsie M. Schnebel, V.P.; Robert W. Buechner, Secy.
EIN: 311336869

62920
The Monsignor Robert Amann Foundation
6210 Cleves Warsaw Pike
Cincinnati, OH 45233

Established in 1999 in OH.
Financial data (yr. ended 12/31/00): Assets, $1,151 (M); grants paid, $48,159; gifts received, $49,322; expenditures, $48,171; qualifying distributions, $48,159.
Trustee: Robert A. Amann.
EIN: 316633536

62921
The Robert J. Shiffler Foundation
7695 Poe Ave.
Dayton, OH 45414-2552

Classified as a private operating foundation in 1999. Established in 1998 in OH.
Donor(s): Robert J. Shiffler.
Financial data (yr. ended 12/31/00): Assets, $980 (M); grants paid, $0; gifts received, $137,450; expenditures, $149,850; qualifying distributions, $149,850; giving activities include $149,850 for programs.
Officers: Robert J. Shiffler, Pres.; Nancy R. Shiffler, V.P.; Charles S. Goodwin, Secy.; Peter Huttinger, Mgr.; Barry A. Rosenberg, Mgr.
EIN: 311539797

62922
Rita E. and Samuel L. Gifford Foundation
625 Brunstetter Rd.
Warren, OH 44481

Established in 2000 in OH.

Financial data (yr. ended 12/31/01): Assets, $929 (M); grants paid, $3,000; gifts received, $2,000; expenditures, $6,186; qualifying distributions, $3,000.
Trustees: Kathleen A. Fike, Samuel L. Gifford, Kimberly A. Hoffman.
EIN: 341935676

62923
Thurner Foundation, Inc.
2350 Victory Pkwy.
Cincinnati, OH 45206-2804

Financial data (yr. ended 09/30/01): Assets, $487 (M); grants paid, $0; gifts received, $1,500; expenditures, $1,896; qualifying distributions, $0.
Officers: George E. Thurner, Jr., Pres.; William A. Thurner, Secy.-Treas.
EIN: 316040462

62924
The Heinrich Family Foundation
228 Candlewood Pl.
St. Marys, OH 45885-9660

Established in 2001 in OH.
Financial data (yr. ended 12/31/01): Assets, $335 (M); grants paid, $0; expenditures, $15; qualifying distributions, $0.
Officers: James R. Heinrich, Pres.; Sharon L. Heinrich, Secy.
EIN: 341929479

62925
Foundation for Skeletal Health Research
225 Park Meadows Dr.
Yellow Springs, OH 45387

Classified as a private operating foundation in 1995.
Donor(s): Fraternal Order of Eagles, Young's Diary.
Financial data (yr. ended 12/31/01): Assets, $279 (M); grants paid, $0; gifts received, $1,745; expenditures, $2,071; qualifying distributions, $0; giving activities include $1,335 for programs.
Officers and Trustees:* Paul Graham,* Pres.; Joseph Maloney,* V.P.; Rita R. Colbert,* Secy.-Treas.; Charles Colbert, Priscilla Janney-Pace, Louis Schwab, M.D., Hardy Trolander.
EIN: 311225145

62926
The Malco Charitable Foundation
126 W. Streetsboro St., Ste. 1
Hudson, OH 44236   (330) 656-9770
Contact: Neil Malamud, Tr.

Established as a company-sponsored operating foundation.
Donor(s): Malco Industries, Inc.
Financial data (yr. ended 03/31/00): Assets, $49 (M); grants paid, $8,970; gifts received, $8,000; expenditures, $8,970; qualifying distributions, $8,970.
Limitations: Giving primarily in FL.
Trustee: Neil Malamud.
EIN: 341307450
Codes: CD

62927
Greater Cincinnati Educational Fund
c/o Sanford R. Kahn
3413 Osage Ave.
Cincinnati, OH 45205

Financial data (yr. ended 12/31/01): Assets, $1 (M); grants paid, $0; expenditures, $0; qualifying distributions, $0.
Trustees: Sanford R. Kahn, Robert E. Manley.
EIN: 311292301

62928
Foster Manor Apartments, Inc.
144 E. Main St.
Lancaster, OH 43130

Established in 1997.
Financial data (yr. ended 12/31/01): Assets, $1 (M); grants paid, $0; expenditures, $957; qualifying distributions, $0.
Officers: John Skinner, Pres.; Terry Lynn, V.P.; Sally George, Secy.; Jane Kennedy, Treas.
Trustees: Gene Hamm, Mike Kennedy, Paul Mechling, Donna Wagner, Maurice Walser, Charles Williams.
EIN: 311334327

62929
Terri Nurre Kinmonth Memorial Fund
c/o Richard Nurre
6940 Miami Hills Dr.
Cincinnati, OH 45243-2013

Classified as a private operating foundation in 1999.
Financial data (yr. ended 12/31/00): Assets, $1 (M); grants paid, $418; expenditures, $418; qualifying distributions, $418.
Directors: Joanne L. Bayer, Richard Nurre, Martha J. Puckett.
EIN: 311640773

62930
Charles S. Hildenbrand Endowment Trust
2677 Montana Ave., No. 8
Cincinnati, OH 45211-3790
Contact: Donna M. Krabbe, Tr.

Established in 1995.
Financial data (yr. ended 12/31/99): Assets, $0 (M); grants paid, $92,568; expenditures, $97,102; qualifying distributions, $92,568.
Limitations: Giving limited to Philadelphia, PA.
Trustee: Donna M. Krabbe.
EIN: 316505017

62931
Jim and Vanita Oelschlager Foundation
3875 Embassy Pkwy.
Akron, OH 44333

Established in 1997 in OH.
Donor(s): James Oelschlager.
Financial data (yr. ended 12/31/01): Assets, $0 (M); grants paid, $377,500; expenditures, $696,261; qualifying distributions, $477,500.
Limitations: Giving limited to OH.
Trustees: Robert Briggs, Jim Oelschlager, Vanita Oelschlager.
EIN: 311528866
Codes: FD

OKLAHOMA

62932
Sand Springs Home
P.O. Box 278
Sand Springs, OK 74063

Established in 1912.
Donor(s): Charles Page Family Care Charitable Remainder Annuity Trust.
Financial data (yr. ended 06/30/00): Assets, $71,699,874 (M); grants paid, $3,807; gifts received, $34,573; expenditures, $3,285,832; qualifying distributions, $1,787,778; giving activities include $1,719,336 for programs.
Trustees: Bill Brown, Ronnie Weese, Joe A. Williams.
EIN: 730579278

62933
The Glass-Glen Burnie Foundation
c/o James A. Arnold
P.O. Box 587
Nowata, OK 74048

Established in 1986 in OK.
Donor(s): Julian W. Glass, Jr.‡
Financial data (yr. ended 12/31/01): Assets, $69,365,019 (M); grants paid, $1,744,931; expenditures, $3,015,838; qualifying distributions, $2,235,450; giving activities include $2,232,217 for programs.
Limitations: Applications not accepted. Giving primarily in the Winchester, VA, area.
Application information: Contributes only to pre-selected organizations.
Trustees: James A. Arnold, Peter G. Bullough, M.D., David D. Denham, Allan G. Paterson, Jr., Irene S. Wischer.
EIN: 731267576
Codes: TN

62934
The Frank Phillips Foundation, Inc.
P.O. Box 1647
Bartlesville, OK 74005-1647   (918) 336-0307

Incorporated in 1937 in DE; Classified as a private operating foundation in 1986.
Donor(s): Frank Phillips,‡ Mrs. Frank Phillips.‡
Financial data (yr. ended 12/31/99): Assets, $39,858,566 (M); grants paid, $19,268; gifts received, $88,176; expenditures, $3,004,908; qualifying distributions, $5,183,720; giving activities include $2,266,155 for programs.
Officers and Trustees:* Donald Doty,* Chair.; William G. Creel,* Vice-Chair.; Richard T. Miller, Secy.-Treas. and Mgr.; Glen A. Cox, John F. Hughes, Robert M. Kane, Lee Phillips III, Robert B. Phillips.
EIN: 730636562

62935
The Eagle Sky Foundation, Inc.
1300 S. Meridian, Ste. 211
Oklahoma City, OK 73108
E-mail: eagleskyf@aol.com; *URL:* http://members.aol.com/_ht_a/eagleskyf/myhomepage/index.html

Established in 1997 in OK.
Donor(s): Joseph D. McKean, Jr., M.D.
Financial data (yr. ended 12/31/01): Assets, $15,445,351 (M); grants paid, $300; gifts received, $129,250; expenditures, $411,600; qualifying distributions, $300.
Limitations: Applications not accepted.
Application information: Contributes only to pre-selected organizations.
Officers and Directors:* Joseph D. McKean, Jr., M.D.,* Pres.; James Stuemky,* V.P.
EIN: 731526080

62936
The Kerr Center for Sustainable Agriculture, Inc.
c/o Assets Svcs. Co., LLC
5101 N. Classen Blvd., Ste. 600
Oklahoma City, OK 73118
Application addresses: Farmer grants: c/o Alan Ware, Dir. of Farmer Grants; other grants: c/o James Horne, Pres., P.O. Box 588, Poteau, OK 74953, tel.: (918) 647-9123

Established in 1985 in OK.
Financial data (yr. ended 12/31/00): Assets, $14,807,247 (M); grants paid, $36,424; gifts received, $80,287; expenditures, $1,873,128; qualifying distributions, $1,748,871.
Limitations: Giving primarily in OK.
Publications: Newsletter, informational brochure.
Officers: Jim Horne, Pres.; Kay Adair, V.P.; Barbara Chester, Secy.; Ann Ware, Treas.
Trustees: Robert Adair, Jr., Lloyd Faulkner, Janie Hipp, Shrikrishna Kashyap, J.B. Pratt, Jr., Christy Price.
EIN: 731256120

62937
Shin'enKan, Inc.
P.O. Box 1111
Bartlesville, OK 74005-1111

Established in 1980 in OK.
Donor(s): Etsuko Price, Joe Price.
Financial data (yr. ended 12/31/01): Assets, $12,542,126 (M); grants paid, $11,074; gifts received, $471,630; expenditures, $86,894; qualifying distributions, $81,512; giving activities include $69,653 for programs.
Officer: W.E. Yount, Secy.-Treas.
Directors: Ralph E. Lerner, Etsuko Y. Price, Joe D. Price.
EIN: 731106645

62938
Housing Assistance Corporation
415 E. Independence
Tulsa, OK 74106-5727

Financial data (yr. ended 06/30/00): Assets, $8,805,376 (L); grants paid, $0; expenditures, $734,368; qualifying distributions, $651,487; giving activities include $82,881 for programs.
Officers and Director:* Ruth Nelson,* Pres.; Roy E. Hancock, Secy.; Lindy Cates, Treas.
EIN: 731329822

62939
Ardmore Beautification Council, Inc.
P.O. Box 1744
Ardmore, OK 73402

Donor(s): Charles R. Smith.
Financial data (yr. ended 12/31/00): Assets, $3,467,870 (M); grants paid, $0; gifts received, $210,863; expenditures, $137,582; qualifying distributions, $133,582; giving activities include $29,510 for programs.
Limitations: Applications not accepted.
Application information: Contributes only to pre-selected organizations.
Officers and Trustees:* Regina Turrentine,* Pres.; Kay Laska,* Vice-Chair.; Norma Lynn Paschall,* Corporate Secy. and Exec. Dir.; Dixie Harper,* Treas.; Charles Barkheimer, Dooly Barlow, James Clark, Chris Cowlbeck, Kipp Crutchfield, and 10 additional trustees.
EIN: 731481529

62940
Potts Family Foundation, Inc.
(Formerly Community Resourse Development Foundation, Inc.)
923 N. Robinson Ave., Ste. 400
Oklahoma City, OK 73102 (405) 235-0722
Contact: Patricia J. Potts, Secy.

Established in 1981 in OK.
Donor(s): Ray H. Potts, Patricia J. Potts.
Financial data (yr. ended 12/31/01): Assets, $2,987,634 (M); grants paid, $153,501; gifts received, $552,720; expenditures, $209,130; qualifying distributions, $206,371.
Limitations: Giving limited to Oklahoma City, OK.
Publications: Application guidelines.
Application information: Application form required.
Officers: Ray H. Potts, Pres.; Patricia J. Potts, Secy.; Steven J. Potts, Treas.
EIN: 731119767
Codes: FD2

62941
George Miksch Sutton Avian Research Center, Inc.
c/o Steve K. Sherrod
P.O. Box 2007
Bartlesville, OK 74005-2007

Classified as a company sponsored operating foundation.
Donor(s): American Airlines, Phillips Petroleum Foundation, Inc., Harold C. Price, Robert E. Lorton, John R. McCume Foundation, and others.
Financial data (yr. ended 06/30/01): Assets, $2,246,903 (M); grants paid, $0; gifts received, $399,931; expenditures, $352,220; qualifying distributions, $181,200; giving activities include $101,514 for programs.
Officers and Directors:* Stephen S. Adams,* Chair.; Howard R. Burman,* Treas.; Steve Alter, Warren D. Harden, Robert E. Lorton, Steve K. Sherrod, and 15 additional directors.
EIN: 731023595

62942
Je Ranch Foundation
P.O. Box 342
Blanchard, OK 73010-0342

Established in 1997 in OK.
Donor(s): John B. Wooten, Jr.
Financial data (yr. ended 09/30/01): Assets, $2,242,830 (M); grants paid, $1,200; gifts received, $1,789,214; expenditures, $48,339; qualifying distributions, $1,200.
Limitations: Applications not accepted.
Application information: Contributes only to pre-selected organizations.
Directors: Anne Richey, Scott Richey, John B. Wooten, Jr.
EIN: 731507603

62943
On the Chisholm Trail Association
P.O. Box 400
Duncan, OK 73534-0400

Established in 1998 in OK.
Donor(s): The McCasland Foundation.
Financial data (yr. ended 12/31/99): Assets, $1,832,885 (M); grants paid, $0; gifts received, $150,614; expenditures, $206,331; qualifying distributions, $176,668; giving activities include $176,668 for programs.
Directors: Barbara M. Braught, Diane K. Garis, Marilyn M. Hugon, T.H. McCasland, Jr., T.H. McCasland III, Mark J. McCasland, Mary E. Michaels.
EIN: 731529204

62944
Break O'Day Farm and Metcalfe Museum
RT 1 Box 25
Durham, OK 73642

Established in 2000 in OK.
Donor(s): Howard Metcalfe.‡
Financial data (yr. ended 12/31/01): Assets, $1,546,478 (M); grants paid, $0; gifts received, $416,128; expenditures, $37,215; qualifying distributions, $355,689; giving activities include $320,368 for program-related investments and $35,321 for programs.
Officers: Elaine Adams, Pres.; Joel Neil York, V.P.; Jana Montgomery, Secy.; Marilyn Wilson, Treas.
Directors: Becky Buster, Kate McDaniel, Max Montgomery, Patti Moorman.
EIN: 731489506

62945
M. V. Mayo Charitable Foundation
3700 1st Place Tower
15 E. 5th St.
Tulsa, OK 74103-4344 (918) 586-5711
Contact: Marcia V. Mayo, Tr.

Established in 1999 in OK.
Donor(s): M.V. Mayo Charitable Trust I, M.V. Mayo Charitable Trust II.
Financial data (yr. ended 12/31/00): Assets, $1,534,835 (M); grants paid, $41,000; gifts received, $1,055,280; expenditures, $53,673; qualifying distributions, $33,103.
Trustees: Marcia V. Mayo, Henry G. Will.
EIN: 731587573

62946
The John Smith Zink Foundation
P.O. Box 52508
Tulsa, OK 74152

Established in 1991 in OK.
Donor(s): John Smith Zink.
Financial data (yr. ended 12/31/00): Assets, $1,416,632 (M); grants paid, $0; expenditures, $28,675; qualifying distributions, $38,646; giving activities include $8,646 for programs.
Trustee: John Smith Zink.
EIN: 731395241

62947
Ovid E. Fowlkes and Leona G. Fowlkes Foundation
P.O. Box 777
El Reno, OK 73036-0777
Contact: John P. Wiewel, Tr.

Financial data (yr. ended 05/31/01): Assets, $1,262,478 (M); grants paid, $39,000; expenditures, $56,163; qualifying distributions, $56,163.
Limitations: Giving primarily in El Reno, OK.
Application information: Application form required.
Trustee: John P. Wiewel.
EIN: 736308398

62948
Cleo Craig Memorial Cancer & Research Foundation
5002 S.W. Lee Blvd.
Lawton, OK 73505

Donor(s): Lucille Craig.
Financial data (yr. ended 08/31/00): Assets, $969,836 (M); grants paid, $0; gifts received, $8,582; expenditures, $31,681; qualifying distributions, $49,114; giving activities include $11,246 for programs.
Officer: Thomas L. Rine, Chair.
Trustees: Donald S. Bentley, Helen Craig, Mike Craig, Bill McCarley, Robert McDaniel.
EIN: 731229179

62949
Leslie Powell Foundation, Inc.
P.O. Box 2063
Lawton, OK 73502

Financial data (yr. ended 12/31/99): Assets, $965,552 (M); grants paid, $26,025; gifts received, $165,917; expenditures, $85,443; qualifying distributions, $349,971; giving activities include $81,283 for programs.
Limitations: Applications not accepted. Giving limited to Lawton, OK.
Application information: Contributes only to a pre-selected organization.
Officers and Directors:* David Carter,* Chair.; Judy Garrett, Secy.; Jane Godlove, Treas.; Nancy Anderson, Exec. Dir.; Paul Fisher, John Kennedy.
EIN: 731190206

62950
The Leaf Collectors Foundation
P.O. Box 368
Pryor, OK 74362-0368
Application address: 1512 Lakeview Dr., Pryor, OK 74361, tel.: (918) 825-1008
Contact: Robert Webster

Established in 1999 in OK.
Donor(s): Michael Webster, Robert Webster.
Financial data (yr. ended 12/31/00): Assets, $929,985 (M); grants paid, $1,650; gifts received, $1,181,250; expenditures, $4,612; qualifying distributions, $3,783.
Application information: Application form required.
Officers: Don Webster, Pres.; Ken Prather, V.P. and Treas.; Julie Neftzger, Secy.
Directors: Michael Webster, Robert Webster.
EIN: 731576352

62951
The Douglas L. Mobley Foundation
(Formerly Doug Mobley Evangelistic Association)
5407 S. Lewis, Ste. 300
Tulsa, OK 74105-6552

Donor(s): Douglas L. Mobley, Michael Hammer.
Financial data (yr. ended 08/31/01): Assets, $769,037 (M); grants paid, $26,150; gifts received, $152,140; expenditures, $155,145; qualifying distributions, $152,538; giving activities include $38,401 for programs.
Limitations: Applications not accepted. Giving on an international basis.
Application information: Contributes only to pre-selected organizations.
Officers: Douglas L. Mobley, Pres.; Donna R. Mobley, Secy.; Melinda Wheeler, Treas.
Director: David C. Sewell.
EIN: 731003131

62952
Bethel Manor, Inc.
619 S. Division St.
Sapulpa, OK 74066

Financial data (yr. ended 12/31/00): Assets, $728,716 (M); grants paid, $0; expenditures, $231,887; qualifying distributions, $221,244; giving activities include $221,244 for programs.
Officers: Sr. Catherine M. Hanegan, Pres.; William B. Morgan, Secy.-Treas.
EIN: 731216617

62953
Mabel W. Springfield Trust
c/o Superintendant of Sayre Public Schools
716 N.E. 66
Sayre, OK 73662
Application address: c/o Principal, Sayre High School, 600 E. Hanna, Sayre, OK 73662, tel.: (580) 928-5576

Financial data (yr. ended 02/28/01): Assets, $699,157 (M); grants paid, $24,908; expenditures, $26,333; qualifying distributions, $26,333.
Limitations: Giving primarily to residents of Sayre, OK.
Trustee: Superintendent, Sayre Public Schools.
EIN: 736101794
Codes: GTI

62954
Paul M. Milburn Foundation
c/o Paul M. Milburn
834 N. Kickapoo Ave.
Shawnee, OK 74801-5728

Donor(s): Paul M. Milburn.
Financial data (yr. ended 09/30/01): Assets, $561,432 (M); grants paid, $347,500; gifts received, $600,000; expenditures, $348,318; qualifying distributions, $347,287.
Limitations: Applications not accepted. Giving primarily in Oklahoma City and Shawnee, OK.
Application information: Contributes only to pre-selected organizations.
Officers: Paul M. Milburn, Pres.; Richard G. Kasterke, V.P.; Ann B. Milburn, Secy.-Treas.
EIN: 731532039
Codes: FD

62955
Bob H. Johnson Family Foundation
(Formerly Bob H. and Joan I. Johnson Foundation)
P.O. Box 470946
Tulsa, OK 74147-0946

Established in 1995 in OK.
Donor(s): Bob H. Johnson, Joan I. Johnson.
Financial data (yr. ended 12/31/01): Assets, $475,670 (M); grants paid, $5,000; expenditures, $5,475; qualifying distributions, $4,943.
Limitations: Applications not accepted.
Application information: Contributes only to pre-selected organizations.
Trustee: Bob H. Johnson.
EIN: 736290757

62956
The Frederick School Enrichment Foundation
P.O. Box 486
Frederick, OK 73542

Established in 1987 in OK.
Financial data (yr. ended 12/31/01): Assets, $468,937 (M); grants paid, $2,591; gifts received, $2,755; expenditures, $6,078; qualifying distributions, $5,493.
Limitations: Applications not accepted. Giving limited to Tillman County, OK.
Application information: Unsolicited requests for funds not accepted.
Trustees: Loyd L. Benson, John R. Hester, Howard M. McBee.
EIN: 731302082

62957
Jerry and Barbara Ryan Foundation
6120 S. Yale, Ste. 1460
Tulsa, OK 74136

Established in 1999 in OK.
Donor(s): Barbara N. Ryan, Jerry E. Ryan.

Financial data (yr. ended 12/31/00): Assets, $417,537 (M); grants paid, $24,080; gifts received, $500,000; expenditures, $27,140; qualifying distributions, $24,080.
Limitations: Applications not accepted.
Application information: Contributes only to pre-selected organizations.
Trustees: Barbara N. Ryan, Jerry E. Ryan.
EIN: 731577547

62958
Lemon Family Foundation
4421 N. Youngs Blvd.
Oklahoma City, OK 73112-8367
(405) 810-9373
Contact: Larry H. Lemon, Mgr.

Established in 1997.
Donor(s): Haskell L. Lemon, Irene Campbell Lemon, Larry H. Lemon.
Financial data (yr. ended 12/31/01): Assets, $416,089 (M); grants paid, $15,250; gifts received, $2,000; expenditures, $24,313; qualifying distributions, $24,313.
Limitations: Giving primarily in Oklahoma City, OK.
Officer: Larry H. Lemon, Mgr.
EIN: 731516391

62959
Senior Citizens Committee, Inc.
901 S.E. 9th St.
Pryor, OK 74361-7236

Classified as a private operating foundation in 1987.
Financial data (yr. ended 12/31/01): Assets, $349,107 (M); grants paid, $18,550; expenditures, $18,925; qualifying distributions, $18,550.
Limitations: Applications not accepted.
Officers: Phil Kennedy, Chair.; Blaine Jones, Vice-Chair.; Bob Pierson, Secy.-Treas.
Directors: Pat Bates, Denver Boren, Carl Curry, Kenneth Jones, Tommy Thompson.
EIN: 731184370

62960
The G. Wilkerson Foundation
1573 E. 41st Pl.
Tulsa, OK 74105-4005

Established in 1998 in OK.
Donor(s): Glenann Wilkerson.
Financial data (yr. ended 12/31/00): Assets, $335,419 (M); grants paid, $6,550; gifts received, $53,471; expenditures, $6,590; qualifying distributions, $5,010.
Limitations: Applications not accepted.
Application information: Contributes only to pre-selected organizations.
Officers: Denise Mohr, Mgr.; Glenann Wilkerson, Mgr.
EIN: 731528401

62961
American Enuresis Foundation
P.O. Box 60671
Oklahoma City, OK 73160-0671

Established around 1991.
Financial data (yr. ended 12/31/99): Assets, $327,766 (M); grants paid, $2,125; gifts received, $54,552; expenditures, $94,442; qualifying distributions, $94,442.
Officers: Gary Baldwin, Pres.; Wilburn Hall, Secy.
EIN: 731249209

62962
Beacon of Hope Foundation
1707 Crossbow
Edmond, OK 73034

Established in 2000 in OK. Classified as a private operating foundation in 2001.
Donor(s): Raymond G. Sobieck, Gayle Sobieck, Raymond M. Sobieck, Mary C. Sobieck, Charles W. Sobieck, Elizabeth A. Sobieck, Thomas A. Sobieck.
Financial data (yr. ended 12/31/00): Assets, $314,800 (M); grants paid, $0; gifts received, $314,800; expenditures, $0; qualifying distributions, $0.
Limitations: Applications not accepted.
Application information: Contributes only to pre-selected organizations.
Officers and Directors:* Raymond G. Sobieck,* Pres. and Secy.; Gayle Sobieck,* V.P. and Treas.; Charles W. Sobieck, Elizabeth A. Sobieck, Mary C. Sobieck, Raymond M. Sobieck, Thomas A. Sobieck.
EIN: 731598929

62963
Daystar Foundation, Inc.
3000 United Founders Blvd., Ste. 104-G
Oklahoma City, OK 73112

Established in 1990 in OK.
Donor(s): Robert P. Engle, Betty Ann Ridley, Carol Cheezem, Chester C. Muth.
Financial data (yr. ended 12/31/99): Assets, $285,969 (M); grants paid, $0; gifts received, $170,899; expenditures, $159,848; qualifying distributions, $160,069; giving activities include $150,791 for programs.
Officers and Trustees:* Betty Ann Ridley,* Chair.; Kathleen W. Starrett, Pres.; Joann B. Harvey, Secy.-Treas.; Carol Cheezem, Robert P. Engle, David Matthews, Russell Watt.
EIN: 731361940

62964
Karl & Georgia Martin, Sr., Anna Belle Flynn, Karl & June Martin, Jr. Foundation
1924 S. Utica Ave., Rm. 500
Tulsa, OK 74104
Contact: William E. Meyer, Tr.

Established in 1996 in OK.
Financial data (yr. ended 12/31/00): Assets, $217,666 (M); grants paid, $22,500; gifts received, $53,000; expenditures, $24,827; qualifying distributions, $22,500.
Application information: Application form required.
Trustees: Richard A. Goranson, June S. Martin, William E. Meyer.
EIN: 731504147

62965
Shepler-Bentley Foundation, Inc.
P.O. Box 648
Lawton, OK 73502-2069
Contact: Donald S. Bentley, Dir.

Established in 2000 in OK.
Donor(s): Shirley Bentley.
Financial data (yr. ended 01/31/02): Assets, $215,143 (M); grants paid, $1,000; gifts received, $150,000; expenditures, $8,974; qualifying distributions, $1,000.
Directors: Donald S. Bentley, Stephen F. Bentley.
EIN: 731602330

62966
Dodson Foundation
P.O. Box 660
Sayre, OK 73662-0660 (580) 928-3315
Contact: Lucille Dodson, Tr.

Donor(s): G.H. Dodson, Lucille Dodson.
Financial data (yr. ended 12/31/99): Assets, $198,560 (M); grants paid, $12,745; expenditures, $14,553; qualifying distributions, $12,745.
Limitations: Giving primarily in Sayre, OK.
Trustee: Lucille Dodson.
EIN: 736230336

62967
The Paul and Louise Johnson Foundation
525 S. Main, Ste. 700
Tulsa, OK 74103-4500 (918) 585-9211
Contact: Jerry Zimmerman, Pres.

Established in 1996 in OK.
Donor(s): The William Ben Johnson Foundation.
Financial data (yr. ended 08/31/00): Assets, $191,005 (M); grants paid, $54,223; gifts received, $125,000; expenditures, $67,001; qualifying distributions, $54,223.
Limitations: Giving on a national basis.
Application information: Application form required.
Officer and Director:* Jerry Zimmerman,* Pres.
EIN: 731506406
Codes: GTI

62968
Doctor & Buzz Bartlett Foundation, Inc.
P.O. Box 1368
Sapulpa, OK 74067-1368
Application address: c/o Dir., Oklahoma University Foundation, 100 Timberdell Rd., Norman, OK 73019-0685

Financial data (yr. ended 12/31/01): Assets, $172,842 (M); grants paid, $0; gifts received, $2,026; expenditures, $22,988; qualifying distributions, $0.
Limitations: Giving primarily in Norman, OK.
Officers: Alan Wells, Pres.; W.D. Robinson, Secy.-Treas.
EIN: 731037267

62969
Jerome K. Altshuler Foundation
3101 N. Classen Blvd., Ste. 221
P.O. Box 60654
Oklahoma City, OK 73146-0654

Donor(s): Jerome K. Altshuler.
Financial data (yr. ended 04/30/02): Assets, $132,608 (M); grants paid, $1,865; expenditures, $2,089; qualifying distributions, $1,865.
Limitations: Applications not accepted. Giving primarily in Oklahoma City, OK.
Application information: Contributes only to pre-selected organizations.
Officers: Jerome K. Altshuler, Pres.; Judy M. Altshuler, Secy.
Directors: Kenneth P. Altshuler, Laurence H. Altshuler, Michael D. Altshuler.
EIN: 751516052

62970
BancFirst Charitable Foundation
P.O. Box 26788
Oklahoma City, OK 73126-0788

Established in 1989 in OK.
Donor(s): American Trend Life Insurance Co.
Financial data (yr. ended 12/31/99): Assets, $129,219 (M); grants paid, $36,400; gifts received, $23,635; expenditures, $36,578; qualifying distributions, $36,578.
Limitations: Applications not accepted. Giving primarily in OK and VA.
Application information: Contributes only to pre-selected organizations.
Officers and Directors:* H.E. Rainbolt,* Pres.; David E. Rainbolt,* V.P.; Claudia Kiker, Secy.-Treas.
EIN: 731343258

62971
Richard & Ruth Lampton Family Foundation
1503 Guilford Ln.
Oklahoma City, OK 73120 (405) 843-8004
Contact: Richard Lampton, Pres.

Established in 2000 in OK.
Donor(s): Richard E. Lampton, Ruth S. Lampton.
Financial data (yr. ended 12/31/00): Assets, $128,736 (M); grants paid, $1,100; gifts received, $148,709; expenditures, $6,803; qualifying distributions, $6,233.
Limitations: Giving primarily in OK.
Application information: Application form required.
Officers and Directors:* Richard E. Lampton,* Pres.; Ruth S. Lampton,* V.P.; Rebecca Lampton Bayless,* Secy.; Lisa Lampton Allen.
EIN: 731593931

62972
Riverside Foundation
2617 E. 26th Pl.
Tulsa, OK 74114-4305

Classified as a private operating foundation in 1984.
Donor(s): Mrs. B.B. Blair.
Financial data (yr. ended 12/31/01): Assets, $119,755 (M); grants paid, $5,300; expenditures, $5,925; qualifying distributions, $5,925.
Limitations: Applications not accepted. Giving primarily in Tulsa, OK.
Application information: Contributes only to pre-selected organizations.
Trustees: Leonard J. Eaton, Joe M. Holliman.
EIN: 731202653

62973
Servant Education and Research Foundation
c/o Patrick D. Lester
1228 E. 21st Pl.
Tulsa, OK 74114 (918) 744-8474

Classified as a private operating foundation in 1989.
Donor(s): Patrick D. Lester.
Financial data (yr. ended 12/31/00): Assets, $114,821 (M); grants paid, $0; expenditures, $17,668; qualifying distributions, $16,662; giving activities include $16,662 for programs.
Officers: Patrick D. Lester, Pres.; H.C. Johnson, V.P.; Patricia E. Lester, Secy.
EIN: 731344479

62974
Mr. & Mrs. Dan Midgley Museum Trust
1001 Sequoyah Dr.
Enid, OK 73703

Established as a private operating foundation in 1991 in OK.
Donor(s): Midgley Museum Support Trust.
Financial data (yr. ended 12/31/01): Assets, $107,477 (M); grants paid, $0; gifts received, $21,780; expenditures, $19,534; qualifying distributions, $18,847; giving activities include $19,534 for programs.
Trustees: R.C. Killiam, Jr., Bob McGuffee.
EIN: 731379238

62975
Research Council on Structural Connections
c/o Benjamin Wallace
3911 S.E. 12th Ave.
Goldsby, OK 73093-9248
Application address: c/o Wiss, Janney, Elstner Associates Inc., 330 Pfingsten Rd., Northbrook, IL 60062-2095, tel.: (847) 272-7400

Financial data (yr. ended 05/31/00): Assets, $92,010 (M); grants paid, $5,000; gifts received, $13,144; expenditures, $5,728; qualifying distributions, $5,000.
Limitations: Giving primarily in MN.
Officers: James D. Doyle, Chair.; Rex V. Owen, Vice-Chair.; Benjamin Wallace, Secy.-Treas.
EIN: 363967603

62976
The Friends of Frank Phillips Home, Inc.
1107 Cherokee Ave.
Bartlesville, OK 74003

Established in 1992 in OK.
Donor(s): Phillips Petroleum Foundation, Inc.
Financial data (yr. ended 06/30/99): Assets, $66,798 (M); grants paid, $0; gifts received, $46,631; expenditures, $47,640; qualifying distributions, $47,640; giving activities include $47,640 for programs.
Officers: Bob Rymal, Pres.; Donna Whitworth, V.P.; Cindy Bennett, Secy.; William G. Creel, Treas.
Trustees: David Driesder, William V. Holliman, Jane Lilburn, Dick Miller, Robbie Morris, and 6 additional trustees.
EIN: 731411334

62977
Carey Family Foundation
326 N.W. 16th St.
Oklahoma City, OK 73103-3421

Established in 2000.
Donor(s): Patricia G. Carey.
Financial data (yr. ended 12/31/00): Assets, $48,184 (M); grants paid, $3,029; gifts received, $51,960; expenditures, $4,304; qualifying distributions, $3,025.
Limitations: Applications not accepted.
Application information: Contributes only to pre-selected organizations.
Trustee: Patricia G. Carey.
EIN: 731585922

62978
Tulsa Advertising Foundation
P.O. Box 4452
Tulsa, OK 74159-0452 (918) 492-9339
Contact: Rosie Hinkle, Dir.

Established in 1986 in OK as a company-sponsored operating foundation.
Donor(s): Tulsa Advertising Federation, Inc.
Financial data (yr. ended 12/31/00): Assets, $42,002 (M); grants paid, $6,300; gifts received, $6,000; expenditures, $6,963; qualifying distributions, $6,963.
Limitations: Giving primarily in surrounding areas of Tulsa, OK.
Officers and Directors:* Susan Bramsch,* Pres.; Amber Smith,* 1st V.P.; Vicki Litchfield, 2nd V.P.; Michelle Platis,* Secy.; Kim Berrey,* Treas.; Bobbie Bailey, Tisha Bradley, Paul Campbell, Rosie Hinkie, Dallas Judd, Steve Kennedy, Stacy Ryle.
EIN: 731253534
Codes: CD

62979
Kelly & Janet McNew Foundation
1841 E. 15th St.
Tulsa, OK 74104

Established in 1997 in OK.
Financial data (yr. ended 12/31/00): Assets, $36,361 (M); grants paid, $1,150; gifts received, $470; expenditures, $6,707; qualifying distributions, $1,283.
Limitations: Applications not accepted. Giving primarily in Tulsa, OK.
Application information: Contributes only to pre-selected organizations.
Officer: Kelly W. McNew, Chair.
EIN: 731141618

62980
Lloyd & Ruth Rader Trust
711 Stanton L. Young Blvd., Ste. 707
Oklahoma City, OK 73104 (405) 235-3506
Contact: Donald B. Halverstadt, M.D., Tr.

Financial data (yr. ended 12/31/01): Assets, $33,692 (M); grants paid, $2,000; expenditures, $2,815; qualifying distributions, $2,807.
Limitations: Giving limited to Oklahoma City, OK.
Application information: Application form required.
Officers: Donald Halvestadt, Chair.; George A. Miller, Secy.-Treas.
Trustees: Lyle Coit, Gary Rader, Andrew E. Thurman.
EIN: 731168147

62981
James and Julie Grissom Foundation
24401 N. May Ave.
Edmond, OK 73003-9117

Established in 1995 in OK.
Donor(s): Julie J. Grissom, James G. Grissom.
Financial data (yr. ended 12/31/99): Assets, $26,579 (M); grants paid, $54,150; expenditures, $54,720; qualifying distributions, $54,704.
Limitations: Applications not accepted. Giving primarily in Oklahoma Foundation.
Application information: Contributes only to pre-selected organizations.
Trustees: James G. Grissom, Julie J. Grissom.
EIN: 731486224

62982
Ballard Scholarship Association
9986 S. 593 Rd.
Miami, OK 74354-4534 (918) 542-6363
Contact: Darrell Philpott, Secy.-Treas.

Financial data (yr. ended 06/30/01): Assets, $25,807 (M); grants paid, $1,000; gifts received, $1,067; expenditures, $1,000; qualifying distributions, $991.
Limitations: Giving limited to residents of OK.
Officers: Johnnie Frisbee, Chair.; Bill Duncan, Vice-Chair.; Darrell Philpott, Secy.-Treas.
EIN: 731253713

62983
The George Whitefield Society
14000 Wireless Way
Oklahoma City, OK 73134

Established in 1996 in OK.
Donor(s): Mike Brown, Michael C. Black, Creston Cutchall, Gary Davis.
Financial data (yr. ended 12/31/00): Assets, $22,517 (M); grants paid, $93,438; gifts received, $103,205; expenditures, $99,005; qualifying distributions, $98,946.
Limitations: Applications not accepted. Giving primarily in OK.

Application information: Unsolicited requests for funds not accepted.
Officers and Directors:* Gary Davis, Pres.; James W. Bruce,* V.P. and Secy.-Treas.; Creston C. Cutchall,* V.P.; Michael C. Black, Mike Brown.
EIN: 731492931
Codes: FD2

62984
The Frank Steele Foundation, Inc.
Rt. 1, Box 145
Geary, OK 73040

Financial data (yr. ended 12/31/01): Assets, $20,920 (M); grants paid, $1,200; gifts received, $11,265; expenditures, $2,787; qualifying distributions, $1,200.
Limitations: Giving primarily in OK.
Officers: Virginia Steele, Pres. and Treas.; Gary Burns, V.P.; Angelo Fertonani, Secy.
EIN: 731513714

62985
Safehaven Ministries, Inc.
2416 Ashebury Way
Edmond, OK 73034

Established in 2000 in OK. Classified as a company-sponsored operating foundation in 2002.
Donor(s): Infomedia, Inc.
Financial data (yr. ended 12/31/01): Assets, $11,062 (M); grants paid, $0; gifts received, $2,800; expenditures, $7,926; qualifying distributions, $2,925.
Officers: Carla Simmert, Pres. and Treas.; Mary Comm, V.P.; Mary Upp, Secy.
Director: Rita Holman.
EIN: 731593944

62986
YWC Services, Inc.
611 W. Apache St.
Marlow, OK 73055

Donor(s): The Noble Foundation, The Healey-Lentz Foundation.
Financial data (yr. ended 06/30/99): Assets, $9,378 (L); grants paid, $815; gifts received, $16,625; expenditures, $24,118; qualifying distributions, $815.
Officers and Directors:* Mickey Hoy,* Pres.; Jerry Couch,* V.P.; Karen Hoy,* Secy.; David Dickerson, Michael R. Hoy, Ray McCarter, Max Pyron, Bruce Scott.
EIN: 731448141

62987
Messenger of Salvation
P.O. Box 624
Bethany, OK 73008-0624

Donor(s): P.A. Abraham.
Financial data (yr. ended 12/31/01): Assets, $6,136 (M); grants paid, $31,999; gifts received, $32,260; expenditures, $32,054; qualifying distributions, $32,054.
Limitations: Applications not accepted. Giving limited to India.
Application information: Unsolicited requests for funds not accepted.
Officers: John Varughese, Pres.; Philip Abraham, V.P.; Peedakayil Abraham, Secy.
EIN: 731361590

62988
Cherokee Strip Centennial Corporation
P.O. Box 642
Perry, OK 73077

Financial data (yr. ended 12/31/00): Assets, $4,749 (M); grants paid, $2,353; gifts received, $15; expenditures, $2,459; qualifying distributions, $2,353; giving activities include $1,216 for programs.
Limitations: Applications not accepted. Giving primarily in Perry, OK.
Application information: Contributes only to pre-selected organizations.
Officers: William L. Gengler, Pres.; Karen Wilcox, V.P.; Anna Lou Randal, Secy.-Treas.
EIN: 731402854

62989
Jason Scott Waltermire Memorial Fund
P.O. Box 161
Perry, OK 73077

Established in 1999 in OK.
Financial data (yr. ended 12/31/00): Assets, $3,575 (M); grants paid, $2,176; gifts received, $2,614; expenditures, $2,176; qualifying distributions, $2,175.
Trustees: Dwight Hamann, Lori Pierce, James Waltermire.
EIN: 731570177

62990
Trails End Foundation, Inc.
5401 S. Sheridan Rd., Ste. 101
Tulsa, OK 74145

Established in 1990 in OK.
Donor(s): John Easley.
Financial data (yr. ended 12/31/01): Assets, $515 (M); grants paid, $0; expenditures, $1,525; qualifying distributions, $1,525; giving activities include $1,500 for programs.
Directors: John Easley, Julianne Easley, Karen Simmons.
EIN: 731360420

62991
Harvest House Book Ministry, Inc.
609 N.W. 40th St.
Oklahoma City, OK 73118-7043

Classified as a private operating foundation in 1981.
Financial data (yr. ended 12/31/00): Assets, $426 (M); grants paid, $0; gifts received, $1,000; expenditures, $1,123; qualifying distributions, $0.
Officers and Trustees:* Jane H. Smith,* Pres. and Mgr.; James C. Shaw,* V.P.; Thomas C. Smith, Jr.,* Secy.-Treas.
EIN: 731025831

62992
Native American Circle, Ltd.
P.O. Box 6144
Lawton, OK 73506

Established in 1997.
Donor(s): June A. Stack.
Financial data (yr. ended 12/31/00): Assets, $6 (M); grants paid, $0; gifts received, $4,085; expenditures, $5,141; qualifying distributions, $5,141; giving activities include $5,141 for programs.
Officers and Directors:* Jo C. Haily,* Pres.; David M. Haily, V.P.
EIN: 731505174

62993
The Billy Sweem Gospel Ministries, Inc.
P.O. Box 2171, 1211 S.E. Adams Blvd., Ste. 31
Bartlesville, OK 74005-2171

Financial data (yr. ended 12/31/01): Assets, $1 (M); grants paid, $0; expenditures, $0; qualifying distributions, $0.
Officers: Rev. Billy D. Sweem, Pres.; Rev. Mark A. Bradburn, V.P.
EIN: 731237839

62994
David E. and Linda Sutton Broach Family Charitable Foundation
1127 E. 20th St.
Tulsa, OK 74120

Established in 2001 in OK.
Donor(s): Little & Assocs.
Financial data (yr. ended 12/31/01): Assets, $0 (M); grants paid, $10,000; gifts received, $10,000; expenditures, $10,000; qualifying distributions, $10,000.
Limitations: Giving primarily in OK.
Trustees: David Broach, Linda Broach.
EIN: 731597854

62995
Jeremy Michael Johnson Foundation
P.O. Box 501
Fort Gibson, OK 74434

Established in 1997 in OK.
Donor(s): James Michael Johnson, Frances Lou Johnson.
Financial data (yr. ended 12/31/01): Assets, $0 (M); grants paid, $63,600; expenditures, $64,496; qualifying distributions, $63,600.
Limitations: Giving primarily in OK.
Trustees: Frances Lou Johnson, James Michael Johnson.
EIN: 731520610

OREGON

62996
Captain Michael King Smith Evergreen Aviation Center
3850 Three Mile Ln.
McMinnville, OR 97128

Donor(s): Delford M. Smith.
Financial data (yr. ended 12/31/00): Assets, $5,414,085 (M); grants paid, $0; gifts received, $286,560; expenditures, $121,686; qualifying distributions, $327,066; giving activities include $121,686 for programs.
Limitations: Applications not accepted. Giving primarily in OR.
Application information: Contributes only to pre-selected organizations.
Officer: Delford M. Smith, Chair.
Directors: Leslie Jacobsson, Terry Naig, Jack Real, Dianne Robins, Michael Spencer, Gary Thompson, Murry E. Vinson, Nicole Wahlberg, Timothy Wahlberg.
EIN: 931069203

62997
Rice Northwest Museum of Rocks and Minerals
26385 N.W. Groveland Dr.
Hillsboro, OR 97124-9531

Established in 1997 in OR.
Donor(s): Sharleen Harvey.
Financial data (yr. ended 12/31/00): Assets, $3,162,237 (M); grants paid, $0; gifts received, $75,437; expenditures, $89,362; qualifying distributions, $75,689; giving activities include $75,689 for programs.
Officers: Richard C. Harvey, Pres. and Treas.; Robert Guariniello, V.P.; S. Jane Guariniello, Secy.
Directors: Raymond Lasmanis, Rudy Techernich.
EIN: 931217856

62998
Southern Oregon Lions Sight & Hearing Center, Inc.
228 N. Holly St.
Medford, OR 97501 (541) 779-3653
Contact: Sherrie Messer, Exec. Dir.

Established in 1968 in OR; reclassified as a private operating foundation in 1989.
Financial data (yr. ended 06/30/01): Assets, $2,443,570 (M); grants paid, $118,359; gifts received, $49,903; expenditures, $450,413; qualifying distributions, $253,947.
Limitations: Giving limited to OR, with emphasis on Jackson County.
Publications: Informational brochure, application guidelines.
Application information: Application form required.
Officers: Greg Orr, Chair.; J. Allen Harris, Vice-Chair.; Ellen Moore, Secy.; Stephen Smith,* Treas.; Sherri Messer, Exec. Dir.
EIN: 936042046
Codes: FD2, GTI

62999
Blanche Fischer Foundation
1509 S.W. Sunset Blvd., Ste. 1-B
Portland, OR 97201

Established in 1981 in OR.
Donor(s): Blanche Fischer.‡
Financial data (yr. ended 12/31/99): Assets, $2,368,423 (M); grants paid, $62,959; expenditures, $171,983; qualifying distributions, $62,959.
Limitations: Giving limited to organizations and residents of OR.
Application information: Write for application. Telephone proposals not accepted. Application form required.
Officers and Directors:* John Dziennik,* Pres.; Jean E.M. Shepherd,* Secy.; Ann M. Shepherd, Susan M. Shepherd, Kathryn Thompson.
EIN: 930790099
Codes: GTI

63000
Watt Brothers Scholars Trust
P.O. Box 999
Tillamook, OR 97141-0999
Scholarship address: P.O. Box 3312, Bay City, OR 97107
Contact: Phyllis Wustenberg, Chair.

Financial data (yr. ended 12/31/00): Assets, $2,123,851 (M); grants paid, $66,500; expenditures, $73,483; qualifying distributions, $66,500.
Limitations: Giving limited to Tillamook County, OR.
Officers: Phyllis Wustenberg, Chair.; Mark Wustenberg, Secy.
Director: Prudence Denny.
EIN: 931224469

63001
Maginnis Charitable Foundation
3927 N.W. Fall Creek Pl.
Portland, OR 97229

Established in 1994 in OR.
Financial data (yr. ended 12/31/00): Assets, $2,044,003 (M); grants paid, $0; gifts received, $14,000; expenditures, $146,625; qualifying distributions, $83,488; giving activities include $81,297 for programs.
Trustees: Brian Maginnis, Jan Maginnis, J. Michael Maginnis, Patrick Maginnis.
EIN: 931105853

63002
Margaret Thiele Petti Foundation
1331 S.W. Broadway, Ste. 103
Portland, OR 97201-3470
Contact: James C. McFarland, Dir.

Established in 1995.
Donor(s): Margaret Thiele Petti.
Financial data (yr. ended 12/31/01): Assets, $1,988,019 (M); grants paid, $132,350; expenditures, $190,448; qualifying distributions, $140,448.
Limitations: Giving primarily in OR.
Application information: Application form not required.
Directors: James C. McFarland, John P. Olds, Margaret Thiele Petti.
EIN: 931161002
Codes: FD2

63003
Kidd's Toy Museum
c/o Frank E. Kidd
1300 S.E. Grand Ave.
Portland, OR 97214

Established in 1992 in OR.
Donor(s): Frank Kidd.
Financial data (yr. ended 09/30/01): Assets, $1,904,493 (M); grants paid, $0; gifts received, $88,240; expenditures, $15,826; qualifying distributions, $121,001; giving activities include $121,001 for programs.
Officers and Directors:* Frank Kidd,* Pres.; Joyce Kidd,* V.P.; Julie Kidd,* Secy.; Patricia Lauer,* Treas.
EIN: 931072470

63004
Letting Go Foundation, Inc.
02000 S.W. Palatine Hill Rd.
Portland, OR 97219-7954

Classified as a private operating foundation in 1990.
Donor(s): Richard G. Sass, Jennifer B. Sass.
Financial data (yr. ended 12/31/01): Assets, $1,832,267 (M); grants paid, $2,078; gifts received, $1,832,267; expenditures, $271,190; qualifying distributions, $269,112; giving activities include $282,734 for programs.
Officer and Directors:* Richard G. Sass,* C.E.O. and Secy.; Jennifer B. Sass.
EIN: 930910156

63005
The Daedalus Foundation
625 B St.
Ashland, OR 97520 (541) 482-2821
Contact: Roger A. Shaw, Pres.

Established in 1996.
Financial data (yr. ended 11/30/01): Assets, $1,742,998 (M); grants paid, $34,785; expenditures, $64,505; qualifying distributions, $48,917.
Limitations: Giving primarily in NM and OR.
Officer: Roger A. Shaw, Pres.
Directors: Ken Behymer, Ryan Langmeyer, Rebecca Reitinger.
EIN: 911791698

63006
The Knapp Friesian Foundation, Inc.
c/o Judith M. Knapp
P.O. Box 1270
Sisters, OR 97759

Established in 1994 in OR.
Donor(s): James W. Knapp, Judith M. Knapp.

Financial data (yr. ended 02/28/01): Assets, $1,341,831 (M); grants paid, $595; expenditures, $160,799; qualifying distributions, $154,106; giving activities include $154,106 for programs.
Officers: Judith M. Knapp, Pres. and Treas.; James W. Knapp, V.P. and Secy.
Director: Don Mayne.
EIN: 931151745

63007
Whole Systems Foundation
P.O. Box 1927
Jacksonville, OR 97530
FAX: (514) 899-8257; E-mail: nsmith@jeffnet.org; URL: http://www.whole-systems.org
Contact: Norton Smith, Treas.

Classified as a private operating foundation in 1973.
Donor(s): Neill Smith.‡
Financial data (yr. ended 11/30/00): Assets, $1,038,910 (M); grants paid, $63,360; gifts received, $5,000; expenditures, $71,804; qualifying distributions, $63,360.
Publications: Financial statement, grants list.
Application information: Application form not required.
Officers and Directors:* Melanie Smith,* Pres.; Zachary Smith,* V.P.; Adam Smith,* Secy.; Norton Smith,* Treas.
EIN: 237346102

63008
Grace Epperson Testamentary Trust
7945 S.W. Churchill Way
Tigard, OR 97224-7863

Established in 1999 in OR.
Financial data (yr. ended 12/31/99): Assets, $966,869 (M); grants paid, $13,038; expenditures, $17,249; qualifying distributions, $13,038.
Limitations: Applications not accepted.
Application information: Contributes only to pre-selected organizations.
Trustees: Sharon M. Harmon, Fr. Joseph Jacobberger, John S. Marick, Tamara E. Marick.
EIN: 931262189

63009
American Institute for Full Employment
2636 Biehn St.
Klamath Falls, OR 97601

Established in 1994 in OR.
Donor(s): Jeld-Wen, Inc.
Financial data (yr. ended 12/31/99): Assets, $961,863 (M); grants paid, $0; gifts received, $42,111; expenditures, $471,802; qualifying distributions, $250,393; giving activities include $471,476 for programs.
Officers: Richard L. Wendt, Pres. and Treas.; Roderick C. Wendt, V.P. and Secy.; William B. Early, V.P.
EIN: 943229232

63010
Mary Sheridan Foundation
2714 S.E. 22nd Ave.
Portland, OR 97232

Established in 2000 in OR and WA.
Donor(s): Martin E. Cearnal, Joan Cearnal.
Financial data (yr. ended 12/31/01): Assets, $951,702 (M); grants paid, $2,500; gifts received, $100,156; expenditures, $120,116; qualifying distributions, $114,309; giving activities include $75,418 for programs.
Limitations: Applications not accepted.
Application information: Contributes only to pre-selected organizations.

Officers: Christine Cearnal, Pres.; Martin E. Cearnal, V.P.; Richard H. Chenot, Secy.-Treas.
Director: Alex Ney.
EIN: 364410255

63011
The Leatherman Foundation
c/o Chau Leatherman
P.O. Box 301338
Portland, OR 97294-9338

Established in 2001 in OR.
Donor(s): Chau Leatherman, Timothy S. Leatherman.
Financial data (yr. ended 12/31/01): Assets, $938,178 (M); grants paid, $60,000; gifts received, $1,000,000; expenditures, $66,682; qualifying distributions, $60,000.
Limitations: Applications not accepted. Giving primarily in Seattle, WA.
Application information: Contributes only to pre-selected organizations.
Officer: Chau Leatherman, Chair.
Directors: Bruce M. Weinsoft, Timothy S. Leatherman.
EIN: 931285822

63012
Richard & Mary Rosenberg Charitable Foundation
c/o Maria Traxler
735 S.W. St. Clair Ave., Ste. 1406
Portland, OR 97205-1458 (503) 294-1443
Contact: Mary Rosenberg, Chair., or Richard Rosenberg, Secy.

Established in 1997 in OR.
Donor(s): Mary Rosenberg, Richard Rosenberg.
Financial data (yr. ended 12/31/01): Assets, $907,262 (M); grants paid, $48,750; gifts received, $478,771; expenditures, $51,224; qualifying distributions, $48,750.
Limitations: Giving primarily in OR.
Application information: Application form required.
Officers: Mary Rosenberg, Chair.; Richard Rosenberg, Secy.
Directors: Garth Rosenberg, Kurt Rosenberg.
EIN: 931219635

63013
Dewuhs-Keckritz Educational Trust
1809 Gekeler Ln., Ste. 312
La Grande, OR 97850
Contact: Carlos Easley, Exec. Secy.

Established in 2000.
Financial data (yr. ended 12/31/00): Assets, $807,147 (M); grants paid, $46,000; expenditures, $61,568; qualifying distributions, $46,000.
Application information: Awards of $5000 are made to the top male and female student in each OR county. Application form required.
Officer: Carlos Easley, Exec. Secy.
EIN: 936092788

63014
Sperling Foundation
3295 Kincaid St.
Eugene, OR 97405-4230 (541) 484-0669
Contact: Thomas H. Pringle, Pres.

Donor(s): Thomas H. Pringle.
Financial data (yr. ended 12/31/99): Assets, $742,883 (M); grants paid, $2,150; gifts received, $138,104; expenditures, $51,730; qualifying distributions, $51,730; giving activities include $34,165 for programs.
Officers and Directors:* Thomas H. Pringle,* Pres. and Exec. Dir.; Doug Heiken, Secy.; John R. Pringle, Treas.

EIN: 931197803

63015
Downtown Community Housing, Inc.
1130 S.W. Morrison St., Ste. 200
Portland, OR 97205

Financial data (yr. ended 12/31/99): Assets, $612,783 (M); grants paid, $7,333; gifts received, $7,333; expenditures, $43,797; qualifying distributions, $7,333.
Limitations: Giving limited in OR.
Officers: Lewis McFarland, Chair.; James Boehlke, Vice-Chair; Peg Paulbach, Secy.-Treas.
Directors: Jim Atkinson, Peter Barbur, Douglas C. Blomgren, Graham Bryce, Cletus B. Moore, Jr.
EIN: 930725579

63016
Elvine and Leroy Gienger Foundation, Inc.
P.O. Box 337
Chiloquin, OR 97624-0337

Established in 1988 in OR.
Financial data (yr. ended 11/30/01): Assets, $579,954 (M); grants paid, $23,300; gifts received, $1,438; expenditures, $24,843; qualifying distributions, $23,300.
Limitations: Giving limited to OR.
Application information: Application form required.
Officers: Bonnie Kircher, Pres.; Norma L. Hill, Secy.-Treas.
Director: L.A. Gienger.
EIN: 930981050
Codes: GTI

63017
Charles Hugh & Wilma Marie Perrin Foundation
c/o BOTC Trust Dept.
1125 N.W. Bond St.
Bend, OR 97701

Established in 2000.
Donor(s): Wilma M. Perrin.
Financial data (yr. ended 12/31/00): Assets, $485,640 (M); grants paid, $25,054; gifts received, $519,116; expenditures, $32,886; qualifying distributions, $25,054.
Limitations: Giving primarily in Prineville, OR.
Directors: Margie Denton, Carl Dutli, Jerry Evans, Glenda Lile, Bill Schaffer, Chuck Wilcox, Barbara Young.
EIN: 931283685

63018
Woody Froom Medical Foundation for Chronic Kidney Failure Patients
3939 S.W. 45th Ave.
Portland, OR 97221-3723

Established in 1996 in OR.
Financial data (yr. ended 06/30/00): Assets, $471,066 (M); grants paid, $15,000; expenditures, $40,050; qualifying distributions, $33,942; giving activities include $18,542 for programs.
Limitations: Giving primarily in OR.
Directors: Amiee E. Froom, Donald W. Froom, Kathleen A. Froom, Robert P. Froom.
EIN: 931226694

63019
Lee H. and Marion B. Thompson Foundation
24130 S.W. Grahams Ferry Rd.
Sherwood, OR 97140

Classified as a private operating foundation in 1994.
Donor(s): Marion B. Thompson.
Financial data (yr. ended 12/31/99): Assets, $447,067 (M); grants paid, $22,000; expenditures,

$25,897; qualifying distributions, $25,897; giving activities include $20,500 for programs.
Limitations: Applications not accepted. Giving primarily in OR.
Application information: Contributes only to pre-selected organizations.
Officers: Marion B. Thompson, Pres.; Catherine A. Snyder, Secy.-Treas.
Director: Donald P. Richards.
EIN: 943112077

63020
Bible Foundation
100 E. Pinehurst Dr.
Newberg, OR 97132-1616

Established in 1987 in CA.
Donor(s): Jerry Kingery.
Financial data (yr. ended 12/31/99): Assets, $441,160 (M); grants paid, $0; gifts received, $32,299; expenditures, $32,624; qualifying distributions, $32,624; giving activities include $32,624 for programs.
Officers and Directors:* Jerry Kingery,* Pres.; Voyle Glover,* V.P.; Jerry Hastings,* Secy.-Treas.
EIN: 860592060

63021
One Percent for Health, Inc.
1237 S.E. 36th Ave.
Portland, OR 97214-4304

Established in 1995 in OR. Classified as a private operating foundation in 1996.
Donor(s): Paul F. Wenner Charitable Foundation Trust.
Financial data (yr. ended 12/31/00): Assets, $372,891 (M); grants paid, $0; gifts received, $90,000; expenditures, $181,255; qualifying distributions, $117,760; giving activities include $117,766 for programs.
Officers and Directors:* Paul F. Wenner,* Pres.; John Ferrell,* Secy.; Giovanni Rosati,* Treas. and Exec. Dir.
EIN: 931192255

63022
Major Junior Hockey Education Fund of Oregon, Inc.
c/o Fred T. Hanna
P.O. Box 6405
Portland, OR 97228-6405
Application address: P.O. Box 1419, Beaverton, OR 97075, tel.: (503) 671-7320
Contact: William Deeks, Pres.

Classified as a private operating foundation. Established in 1989 in OR.
Donor(s): Chiles Foundation.
Financial data (yr. ended 04/30/01): Assets, $283,741 (M); grants paid, $36,699; gifts received, $27,936; expenditures, $63,987; qualifying distributions, $36,699.
Limitations: Giving limited to the Portland, OR, metropolitan area.
Application information: Application form required.
Officers: William Deeks, Pres.; John Holter, V.P.; Robert Schroeder, Treas.
EIN: 930869476
Codes: GTI

63023
Cascade Ecological Foundation
13535 S.E. 145th Ave.
Clackamas, OR 97015

Financial data (yr. ended 12/31/99): Assets, $243,426 (M); grants paid, $3,000; gifts received, $10,000; expenditures, $35,124; qualifying distributions, $34,110; giving activities include $26,472 for programs.
Limitations: Applications not accepted.
Application information: Contributes only to pre-selected organizations.
Officers: Donald W. Oakley, Pres.; Maria G. Oakley, Secy.
Director: C. Gregory Winterrowd.
EIN: 931234668

63024
Virginia A. Archer Scholarship Trust Fund
520 N.W. Torrey View Ln.
Portland, OR 97229-6540 (503) 229-2733
Contact: Laura H. Shepherd, Tr.

Financial data (yr. ended 06/30/00): Assets, $234,099 (M); grants paid, $13,800; expenditures, $22,148; qualifying distributions, $13,701.
Limitations: Giving limited to Multnomah County, OR.
Application information: Application form required.
Trustee: Laura H. Shepherd.
EIN: 936107007
Codes: GTI

63025
Camp 18 Logging Museum, Inc.
1211 S.W. 5th Ave., Ste. 2185
Portland, OR 97204

Established in 1988 in OR.
Donor(s): Maurie Clark.
Financial data (yr. ended 03/31/01): Assets, $233,952 (M); grants paid, $0; gifts received, $83,500; expenditures, $92,341; qualifying distributions, $90,175; giving activities include $92,341 for programs.
Directors: Dorothy Churchill, Mary Clark, Maurice Clark, R. Michael Clark, Edwin Luoma, Ruth Shaner.
EIN: 930974745

63026
Oregon Association of Public Accountants Scholarship Foundation
1804 N.E. 43rd Ave.
Portland, OR 97213-1404
Contact: Richard L. Garlock, Treas.

Classified as a private operating foundation. Established in 1994 in OR.
Financial data (yr. ended 06/30/01): Assets, $216,181 (M); grants paid, $9,000; gifts received, $1,740; expenditures, $9,883; qualifying distributions, $738.
Limitations: Giving limited to residents of OR.
Application information: Application form required.
Officers: Merry Van Atta, Pres.; Sharon Bush, Secy.; Susan G. Robertson, Treas.
Trustee: Betty Phelps, Lon Stewart.
EIN: 930765047
Codes: GTI

63027
GROWISER/Grande Ronde Overlook Wildflower Institute Serving Ecological Restoration
(also known as GROWISER)
c/o Adrew G. Huber
1809 26th St., Ste. 56
La Grande, OR 97850

Established in 1993 in OR.
Donor(s): Andrew G. Huber.
Financial data (yr. ended 12/31/00): Assets, $214,885 (M); grants paid, $0; gifts received, $25,025; expenditures, $25,231; qualifying distributions, $25,231; giving activities include $25,231 for programs.
Officer: Andrew G. Huber, Pres.
Directors: Karen Antell, Steve Clements, Bob Ottersberg.
EIN: 931115800

63028
Arthur and Vivienne Wiese Foundation
4200 S.E. Oak St.
Portland, OR 97215-1041

Established in 2000 in OR.
Donor(s): Arthur Wiese, Vivienne Wiese.
Financial data (yr. ended 12/31/00): Assets, $211,059 (L); grants paid, $40,000; gifts received, $250,035; expenditures, $40,177; qualifying distributions, $40,000.
Limitations: Giving primarily in Portland, OR.
Director: Arthur Wiese, Jr.
EIN: 931295219

63029
E. J. & Wythel Blokland Charitable Trust
P.O. Box 37
Lostine, OR 97857-0037 (541) 569-2374
Application addresses: c/o James Nobles, 80907 Leap Ln., Wallowa, OR 97885, tel.: (541) 426-3788; c/o Larry L. Christman, 302 Leone St., Enterprise, OR 97828, tel.: (541) 426-3741
Contact: Marvin Maxwell

Financial data (yr. ended 08/30/00): Assets, $199,159 (M); grants paid, $9,549; expenditures, $10,415; qualifying distributions, $9,434.
Limitations: Giving limited to residents of Wallowa County, OR.
Application information: Application form required.
Trustees: Larry Christman, Marvin Maxwell.
EIN: 930833243

63030
Mildred E. Chapman Foundation
P.O. Box 427
Wilsonville, OR 97070

Established in 1995 in OR.
Donor(s): Mildred E. Chapman.‡
Financial data (yr. ended 12/31/00): Assets, $177,743 (M); grants paid, $11,000; expenditures, $14,126; qualifying distributions, $139,889.
Limitations: Applications not accepted. Giving primarily in OR.
Application information: Contributes only to pre-selected organizations.
Officers: Walter J. Apley, Pres.; Vernon L. Burda, V.P.; Ava M. Apley, Secy.-Treas.
EIN: 931179419

63031
Wood Charitable Foundation
22730 S.W. Chapman Rd.
Sherwood, OR 97140

Classified as a private operating foundation in 2001 in OR.
Donor(s): Al Degrood, Virginia Degrood.
Financial data (yr. ended 12/31/00): Assets, $177,257 (M); grants paid, $0; gifts received, $10,950; expenditures, $9,015; qualifying distributions, $9,015; giving activities include $9,015 for programs.
Officers: Al Degrood, Pres.; Virginia Degrood, Secy.
EIN: 931292205

63032
The Kalik Foundation
25404 S.W. McConnell Rd.
Sherwood, OR 97140

Established in 1997 in OR.
Donor(s): Evan L. Kalik.
Financial data (yr. ended 09/30/00): Assets, $172,023 (M); grants paid, $0; gifts received, $113,969; expenditures, $181,952; qualifying distributions, $166,735; giving activities include $181,952 for programs.
Officer: Evan L. Kalik, Pres.
Trustees: Allan W. Kalik, Ardyth L. Kalik, Eric M. Kalik.
EIN: 931234477

63033
Intermountain Public Defender, Inc.
331 S.E. Byers Ave.
Pendleton, OR 97801

Established in 1994 in OR.
Financial data (yr. ended 06/30/01): Assets, $164,986 (L); grants paid, $0; gifts received, $726,000; expenditures, $810,484; qualifying distributions, $801,985; giving activities include $810,484 for programs.
Officers and Directors:* Robert Ehmann,* Pres.; Rustin Brewer,* Secy.; Douglas Fischer, Exec. Dir.; Harry Bose, Andy Millar, Samuel Tucker.
EIN: 931150643

63034
Haberman Foundation, Inc.
749 N.W. Sundance Cir.
Corvallis, OR 97330

Established in 2000 in OR.
Donor(s): Abigail L. Haberman, Joseph J. Haberman.
Financial data (yr. ended 12/31/01): Assets, $160,744 (M); grants paid, $0; gifts received, $130,000; expenditures, $9,265; qualifying distributions, $0.
Officers and Directors:* Joseph J. Haberman,* Pres.; Abigail L. Haberman,* Secy.-Treas.
EIN: 582581630

63035
Acorn Foundation, Inc.
c/o Peter & Ellen Ogle
3733 N.W. Jackson Ave.
Corvallis, OR 97330

Established in 2000 in OR.
Donor(s): Peter Ogle, Ellen Ogle.
Financial data (yr. ended 04/30/01): Assets, $160,476 (M); grants paid, $0; gifts received, $164,481; expenditures, $6,557; qualifying distributions, $0; giving activities include $1,047 for programs.
Limitations: Applications not accepted.
Application information: Contributes only to pre-selected organizations.
Officers: Peter Ogle, Pres.; Ellen Ogle, Secy.
Board Member: Mark Edwards.
EIN: 931294060

63036
I Have a Dream Foundation - Oregon
4317 N.E. Emerson
Portland, OR 97218

Established in 1990 in OR.
Donor(s): The Oregon Community Foundation.
Financial data (yr. ended 08/31/01): Assets, $154,379 (M); grants paid, $92,636; gifts received, $949,943; expenditures, $956,953; qualifying distributions, $991,377; giving activities include $956,953 for programs.

Limitations: Applications not accepted. Giving primarily in Portland, OR.
Application information: Unsolicited requests for funds not accepted.
Officers and Directors:* Pamela Jacklin,* Chair.; Terry Pancoast,* Pres.; Joyce Arntson, Julie Ball, Leonard Girard, Gloria Gostnell, Kenneth Lewis, Irv Nikolai, Susan Sandor.
EIN: 931037323
Codes: FD2

63037
V. W. Eberlein Charities
c/o Neal L. Eberlein
1345 El Dorado Blvd.
Klamath Falls, OR 97601

Established in 1987 in OR.
Donor(s): Neal L. Eberlein.
Financial data (yr. ended 12/31/01): Assets, $152,000 (M); grants paid, $0; gifts received, $10; expenditures, $10; qualifying distributions, $0.
Limitations: Applications not accepted.
Application information: Unsolicited requests for funds not accepted.
Officer and Trustees:* Vernice W. Eberlein,* Chair.; Neal L. Eberlein, Susan Eberlein.
EIN: 943030985

63038
Roger J. Bounds Foundation, Inc.
c/o Inland Empire Bank
P.O. Box 1170
Hermiston, OR 97838

Classified as a private operating foundation in 1982.
Donor(s): Doris S. Bounds, Roger S. Bounds.
Financial data (yr. ended 12/31/99): Assets, $151,269 (M); grants paid, $39,700; expenditures, $41,904; qualifying distributions, $41,739.
Limitations: Applications not accepted. Giving primarily in Hermiston, OR.
Officers: Roger S. Bounds, Pres.; Lorissa Bounds, V.P.; Teresa D. Moncrief, Secy.-Treas.
Directors: Karen S. Bounds, Ryan Bounds, Fern P. Cramer, Mary Anne Normandin, Kay Reese, David A. Rhoten.
EIN: 936037112

63039
Vatheuer Family Foundation, Inc.
4302 S.W. Bertha Ave.
Portland, OR 97201

Established in 1996 in OR.
Donor(s): Hans Vatheuer.
Financial data (yr. ended 12/31/01): Assets, $144,586 (M); grants paid, $8,966; gifts received, $55,652; expenditures, $78,065; qualifying distributions, $66,710; giving activities include $57,744 for programs.
Limitations: Applications not accepted.
Application information: Contributes only to pre-selected organizations.
Director: Hans Vatheuer.
EIN: 931218806

63040
The Helen Bradley Fund, Inc.
c/o Christopher R. Durham
4001 Camellia Dr. S.
Salem, OR 97302-2705

Donor(s): Chris Rogers, John Miller.
Financial data (yr. ended 12/31/00): Assets, $139,339 (M); grants paid, $0; expenditures, $262; qualifying distributions, $7,462; giving activities include $7,200 for loans to individuals.
Limitations: Giving limited to residents of Salem, OR.

Officers: Chris Durham, Pres.; Marcia Durham, Secy.
Trustee: Dixie Kenney.
EIN: 931156144

63041
EMS Charitable Foundation
c/o Employer Management Svcs., LLC
7821 S.W. Canal Blvd.
Redmond, OR 97756-9425

Established in 1997 in OR.
Donor(s): Employer Management Services, LLC.
Financial data (yr. ended 12/31/00): Assets, $129,478 (M); grants paid, $17,576; gifts received, $15,591; expenditures, $17,852; qualifying distributions, $17,852.
Officers: Dana Sorum, Pres.; John Short, V.P.
EIN: 911847653

63042
St. Wenceslaus Holy Spirit Foundation
P.O. Box 1047
Scappoose, OR 97056-1047 (503) 543-7071

Financial data (yr. ended 12/31/00): Assets, $109,591 (M); grants paid, $2,000; expenditures, $2,209; qualifying distributions, $2,207.
Limitations: Giving primarily in Scappoose, OR.
Officers: Leonard A. Aplet, Pres.; Brenda A. Aplet, V.P.; Mary S. Aplet, Secy.; Steve Clavis, Treas.
EIN: 931271649

63043
Carol Ann Curthoys Foundation, Inc.
8879 S.W. Iowa Dr.
Tualatin, OR 97062
Contact: Carol Ann Curthoys, Tr.

Established in 1999 in OR.
Donor(s): Carol Ann Curthoys.
Financial data (yr. ended 12/31/00): Assets, $78,972 (L); grants paid, $2,616; gifts received, $20,000; expenditures, $2,856; qualifying distributions, $2,225.
Limitations: Giving primarily in OR.
Trustee: Carol Ann Curthoys.
EIN: 931258592

63044
Vinapa Foundation
1509 S.W. Sunset Blvd., Ste. 1B
Portland, OR 97201-2689

Established in 2000 in OR.
Donor(s): Ruth Egert, Victor Egert.
Financial data (yr. ended 07/31/01): Assets, $74,205 (M); grants paid, $3,500; gifts received, $119,984; expenditures, $8,174; qualifying distributions, $7,924.
Limitations: Applications not accepted. Giving primarily in San Francisco, CA and Portland, OR.
Application information: Unsolicited requests for funds not accepted.
Officers: Janine Egert, Pres. and Treas.; John Dziennik, V.P. and Secy.
Director: Jean Shepherd.
EIN: 931302848

63045
Engelmann Foundation
P.O. Box 448
Eugene, OR 97440-0448

Established in 1997 in OR.
Donor(s): Siegfried E. Engelmann.
Financial data (yr. ended 12/31/00): Assets, $71,158 (M); grants paid, $103,000; gifts received, $100,000; expenditures, $103,734; qualifying distributions, $103,000.
Limitations: Applications not accepted.

Application information: Contributes only to pre-selected organizations.
Directors: Douglas Carnine, Kurt E. Engelmann, Owen Engelmann, Siegfried E. Engelmann, Don Steely.
EIN: 931223362

63046
David F. Weeks Foundation
c/o David R. Weeks
4058 N.W. Northcliff
Bend, OR 97701

Established in 1997.
Donor(s): David F. Weeks.
Financial data (yr. ended 12/31/99): Assets, $69,986 (M); grants paid, $2,600; expenditures, $5,540; qualifying distributions, $2,600.
Trustees: Betty A. Weeks, Clayton F. Weeks, David F. Weeks, David R. Weeks.
EIN: 911793319

63047
Tillamook County Library Foundation
210 Ivy Ave.
Tillamook, OR 97141

Established around 1994.
Financial data (yr. ended 06/30/00): Assets, $58,955 (M); grants paid, $0; gifts received, $5,638; expenditures, $415; qualifying distributions, $0; giving activities include $107 for programs.
Officers: Peggy Evans, Pres.; Susan Armatage, Treas.
EIN: 930090827

63048
Northwest Autism Foundation
519 15th St.
Oregon City, OR 97045

Established in 1998 in OR.
Donor(s): Gleason Eakin, Wayne Hamersly.
Financial data (yr. ended 06/30/00): Assets, $42,664 (M); grants paid, $250; gifts received, $66,621; expenditures, $71,502; qualifying distributions, $250; giving activities include $29,862 for programs.
Limitations: Applications not accepted.
Application information: Contributes only to pre-selected organizations.
Officer: Stephen Nicholson, Chair.
Directors: Gleason Eakin, Lynn Hamersly, Scott Hamersly, Wayne Hamersly, Gene Stubbs.
EIN: 931234288

63049
The Mark and Linda Harris Foundation
1805 Highland Dr.
La Grande, OR 97850

Established in 1999.
Donor(s): Mark L. Harris, Linda J. Harris.
Financial data (yr. ended 12/31/00): Assets, $37,807 (M); grants paid, $13,000; gifts received, $30,000; expenditures, $13,000; qualifying distributions, $13,000.
Limitations: Applications not accepted.
Application information: Contributes only to pre-selected organizations.
Officer and Directors:* Mark Harris,* Pres.; Linda Harris, Velma Harris.
EIN: 931282271

63050
Webber Estate Veterans Fund
c/o Courthouse
1995 3rd St.
Baker City, OR 97814 (541) 523-8223
Contact: A.R. Johnson, Secy.

Classified as a private operating foundation in 1975.
Financial data (yr. ended 12/31/00): Assets, $37,725 (M); grants paid, $1,412; expenditures, $1,419; qualifying distributions, $1,399.
Limitations: Giving limited to Baker City, OR.
Officer: A.R. Johnson, Secy. and Mgr.
Commanders: Micheal Connelly, Truscott Irby.
EIN: 237447277

63051
Renew, Inc.
6455 N.E. Columbia Blvd.
Portland, OR 97218

Established in 1997 in OR.
Financial data (yr. ended 12/31/99): Assets, $33,432 (M); grants paid, $850; gifts received, $119,129; expenditures, $335,056; qualifying distributions, $19,016; giving activities include $334,206 for programs.
Officer and Directors:* Jeff Simonson,* V.P.; Allen Bushey, Norman Hobbs, David Simonson.
EIN: 911761078

63052
The Great Tomorrow
5285 S.W. Meadows Rd., Ste. 377
Lake Oswego, OR 97035-3228

Established in 1997 in OR.
Financial data (yr. ended 12/31/01): Assets, $33,002 (M); grants paid, $0; expenditures, $72,419; qualifying distributions, $0.
Limitations: Applications not accepted.
Application information: Contributes only to pre-selected organizations.
Officers: Nick Bunick, Pres.; Gary Hardin, V.P.; Brian Hilliard, V.P.; Beth Ayres, Secy.
EIN: 311542822

63053
Pandrillus Foundation USA
P.O. Box 10082
Portland, OR 97296-0082

Established in 2000 in OR.
Donor(s): Michael B. Slade.
Financial data (yr. ended 12/31/00): Assets, $32,166 (M); grants paid, $59,200; gifts received, $137,332; expenditures, $73,474; qualifying distributions, $59,200.
Limitations: Applications not accepted. Giving on an international basis.
Application information: Contributes only to pre-selected organizations.
Directors: Elizabeth L. Gadsby, Peter D. Jenkins, Susan McGrath, Michael B. Slade.
EIN: 931289932

63054
Lola Greene Baldwin Foundation for Recovery
P.O. Box 42393
Portland, OR 97202

Classified as a private operating foundation in 2000.
Donor(s): Joseph P Packer, Ann K. Packer.
Financial data (yr. ended 07/01/02): Assets, $24,000 (M); grants paid, $0; gifts received, $15,204; expenditures, $15,865; qualifying distributions, $0; giving activities include $6,406 for programs.

Officers and Trustees:* Patricia Besrora,* Pres.; Joseph P. Parker,* Secy.; Lynn Siva-Wertrel.
EIN: 931276292

63055
Bohemia Foundation, Inc.
P.O. Box 10293
Eugene, OR 97440-2293

Donor(s): Bohemia, Inc.
Financial data (yr. ended 12/31/00): Assets, $22,756 (M); grants paid, $0; gifts received, $14,500; expenditures, $1,687; qualifying distributions, $920; giving activities include $920 for programs.
Officers and Directors:* L.L. Stewart,* Pres.; S.E. Pittman,* V.P.; L.M. Stewart,* Secy.-Treas.
EIN: 936037881

63056
Patty Landrum Scholarships
9208 St. Andrews Cir.
Klamath Falls, OR 97603 (541) 884-7535
Contact: Patricia Lee Landrum, Chair.

Classified as a private operating foundation in 1986.
Financial data (yr. ended 12/31/00): Assets, $20,585 (M); grants paid, $1,600; expenditures, $1,869; qualifying distributions, $1,470.
Limitations: Giving limited to Klamath County, OR.
Officer: Patricia Lee Landrum, Chair.
Trustees: Eloise J. Elliott, Jeanne C. Landrum, Nancy Landrum, Colleen M. Parker.
EIN: 936180890

63057
ABC Mountain Retreat
P.O. Box 1713
Pendleton, OR 97801

Donor(s): Margaret Caldwell.
Financial data (yr. ended 12/31/01): Assets, $18,148 (M); grants paid, $0; gifts received, $23,939; expenditures, $20,456; qualifying distributions, $18,577; giving activities include $20,456 for programs.
Officers: Bernard L. Caldwell, Pres.; John Taylor, V.P.; Cheryl Post, Secy.; Margaret Caldwell, Treas.
EIN: 930746833

63058
Fishers of Men Ministries
16900 S.W. Edminston Rd.
Wilsonville, OR 97070

Established in 1998 in OR.
Donor(s): Lawrence Nelson.
Financial data (yr. ended 12/31/01): Assets, $14,564 (M); grants paid, $100; expenditures, $4,151; qualifying distributions, $1,663.
Limitations: Applications not accepted.
Officer: Lawrence Nelson, Pres.
EIN: 931267393

63059
Pacific Research Institute
1715 Franklin Blvd.
Eugene, OR 97403-1983

Donor(s): Richard F. McGinty.
Financial data (yr. ended 12/31/99): Assets, $12,569 (M); grants paid, $0; expenditures, $239,182; qualifying distributions, $25,177; giving activities include $239,182 for programs.
Limitations: Applications not accepted.
Application information: Contributes only to pre-selected organizations.
Officers: Anthony Biglan, Chair.; Lisa James, Exec. Dir.

63059—OREGON

Board Members: Rick Grosscup, George Hermach, Gayle Landt, Minalee Saks, Herb Severson, Ted Taylor, Nancy Willard.
EIN: 931056407

63060
Endometriosis Institute of Oregon, Inc.
2190 N.E. Professional Ct.
Bend, OR 97701

Established in 1990 in OR.
Financial data (yr. ended 12/31/00): Assets, $11,887 (M); grants paid, $0; expenditures, $10; qualifying distributions, $0; giving activities include $10 for programs.
Officers and Directors:* David B. Redwine, M.D.,* Pres.; Debra H. Redwine,* Secy.-Treas.; John H. Draneas.
EIN: 931011506

63061
International Literature Ministry, Inc.
8140 N. Umpqua Hwy.
Roseburg, OR 97470

Financial data (yr. ended 09/30/01): Assets, $10,550 (M); grants paid, $67,600; gifts received, $37,876; expenditures, $76,832; qualifying distributions, $76,832; giving activities include $5,227 for programs.
Limitations: Applications not accepted.
Officers: Stanton K. VanCamp, Pres. and Treas.; Barbara J. VanCamp, V.P. and Secy.
Director: Golda M. Johnson.
EIN: 930907744

63062
Swiss Aid Society
c/o Edna Truttman
732 S.E. 166th Pl.
Portland, OR 97233-4399

Financial data (yr. ended 12/31/99): Assets, $9,301 (M); grants paid, $1,190; gifts received, $3,661; expenditures, $2,188; qualifying distributions, $1,888.
Limitations: Giving limited to the Portland, OR, area.
Officers: Frank L. Truttman, Pres.; Al Odermott, V.P.; Mary Anne Amstad, Secy.; Edna Truttman, Treas.
EIN: 936032292

63063
Absolutely Free, Inc.
P.O. Box 2
Glide, OR 97443

Donor(s): Richard E. Caddock, Anne Caddock, Richard E. Caddock, Jr., Klaziena Caddock.
Financial data (yr. ended 12/31/99): Assets, $8,963 (M); grants paid, $14,223; gifts received, $287,902; expenditures, $280,340; qualifying distributions, $14,223.
Officers: Richard E. Caddock, Jr., Pres.; John Caddock, V.P.; Ed Underwood, V.P.; James Caddock, Secy.; Sue Brinkman, Treas.
EIN: 931123212

63064
Greater Hillsboro Area Foundation, Inc.
334 S.E. 5th Ave.
Hillsboro, OR 97123-4107

Classified as a private operating foundation in 1991.
Financial data (yr. ended 06/30/00): Assets, $8,635 (M); grants paid, $26,130; gifts received, $31,645; expenditures, $26,888; qualifying distributions, $26,130.
Limitations: Applications not accepted.

Application information: Contributes only to pre-selected organizations.
Officers: Rick VanBuren, Pres.; Shirley Huffman, Secy.-Treas.
Directors: Gary Baker, Lloyd Baron, Gary Deveraux, Tim Erwert, Bob Evans, Fred Johnson, Don Suhrbrier, Marilyn Turnbill, Glenn Walters.
EIN: 930931059

63065
The Andrew H. & Amy W. Kim Foundation
12572 S.W. Sheldrake Way
Beaverton, OR 97007

Established in 1999 in OR.
Financial data (yr. ended 12/31/99): Assets, $7,500 (M); grants paid, $0; gifts received, $7,500; expenditures, $0; qualifying distributions, $0.
Limitations: Applications not accepted.
Application information: Contributes only to pre-selected organizations.
Directors: Andrew H. Kim, Amy W. Kim, Kwon H. Kim.
EIN: 931282272

63066
Raymond L. Hawkins Scholarship Fund
P.O. Box 999
Tillamook, OR 97141
Application address: 1414 3rd St., Tillamook, OR 97141, tel.: (503) 842-7557
Contact: Thomas A. Waud, Pres.

Established around 1984.
Financial data (yr. ended 12/31/99): Assets, $7,096 (M); grants paid, $740; gifts received, $885; expenditures, $750; qualifying distributions, $750.
Limitations: Giving limited to residents of Tillamook, OR.
Application information: Application form required.
Officers: Thomas A. Waud, Pres.; Susan Coglan, Secy.; Marvin Brewer, Treas.
EIN: 930830268

63067
Western Humanities Institute
P.O. Box 17476
Portland, OR 97217-0476

Classified as a private operating foundation in 1970.
Financial data (yr. ended 12/31/00): Assets, $7,009 (M); grants paid, $0; gifts received, $1,500; expenditures, $1,872; qualifying distributions, $0; giving activities include $60 for programs.
Officers: Edward A. Prentice, Pres.; Mary E. Sullivan, V.P.; Marjorie M. Prentice, Secy.
EIN: 936036285

63068
Friends of Williamalane Fund
(Formerly The Jack B. Lively Fund for Promotion of Parks, Recreation & Open Spaces)
200 S. Mill St.
Springfield, OR 97477
Contact: Chris Pryer, Tr.

Financial data (yr. ended 06/30/00): Assets, $6,360 (M); grants paid, $1,000; expenditures, $1,424; qualifying distributions, $1,000.
Limitations: Giving limited to Springfield, OR.
Officers and Directors:* James Mayo,* Pres.; Sandy Stice,* Secy.-Treas.; Ronnel Curry, Gwen Lively, John Lively, James Mayo, Chris Pryor.
EIN: 930852049

63069
Brian Henninger Foundation
P.O. Box 230669
Portland, OR 97281

Established in 2000 in OR.
Donor(s): Brian H. Henninger.
Financial data (yr. ended 01/31/01): Assets, $5,562 (M); grants paid, $50,000; gifts received, $6,000; expenditures, $154,478; qualifying distributions, $50,000.
Limitations: Applications not accepted.
Application information: Contributes only to pre-selected organizations.
Officers: Brian H. Henninger, Pres.; Brent G. Summers, Secy.
EIN: 931287241

63070
Marty G. Brill Memorial Foundation
22115 S.E. Lagene St.
Boring, OR 97009-9317

Financial data (yr. ended 12/31/01): Assets, $5,308 (M); grants paid, $300; gifts received, $1,045; expenditures, $302; qualifying distributions, $302.
Limitations: Applications not accepted. Giving limited to residents of OR.
Application information: Unsolicited requests for funds not accepted.
Officer: Ronald C. Murk, Mgr.
EIN: 237038715

63071
Institute for American & International Studies
P.O. Box 17476
Portland, OR 97217-0476

Classified as a private operating foundation in 1973.
Financial data (yr. ended 12/31/99): Assets, $5,011 (M); grants paid, $0; gifts received, $2,500; expenditures, $2,474; qualifying distributions, $0; giving activities include $70 for programs.
Officers: Edward A. Prentice, Pres.; Mary E. Sullivan, v.P.; Marjorie M. Prentice, Secy.
EIN: 930574226

63072
Fund for Hope
P. O. Box 1305
McMinnville, OR 97128

Financial data (yr. ended 12/31/99): Assets, $2,573 (M); grants paid, $500; expenditures, $500; qualifying distributions, $500.
Officers: Donna Nelson, Pres.; Patricia Morris, Secy.; William Wood, Treas.
EIN: 931092382

63073
Kaneko Foundation for International Research and Education
P.O. Box 14040
Salem, OR 97309
Contact: Toru Tanabe, Secy.-Treas.

Established in 1985 in OR.
Donor(s): Tokyo International University of America.
Financial data (yr. ended 12/31/01): Assets, $2,145 (M); grants paid, $11,700; gifts received, $93,434; expenditures, $112,915; qualifying distributions, $112,915.
Limitations: Giving primarily in Salem and Portland, OR.
Officers: Yasuo Kaneko, Pres.; Isshin Yamada, V.P.; Toru Tanabe, Secy.
EIN: 930849532

63074
Whipple Forest Foundation
21755 Hwy. 138 W.
Elkton, OR 97436-9783

Established in 1997 in OR.
Donor(s): Mildred W. Whipple.
Financial data (yr. ended 08/31/00): Assets, $1,813 (M); grants paid, $0; gifts received, $12,000; expenditures, $11,443; qualifying distributions, $11,442; giving activities include $81 for programs.
Limitations: Applications not accepted.
Application information: Contributes only to pre-selected organizations.
Officers and Directors:* Mildred W. Whipple,* Pres.; Roger J. Whipple,* V.P.; Richard P. Sheetz,* Secy.; Carol A. Whipple,* Treas.
EIN: 911839310

63075
Growing Oaks Child Development Center
200 S.W. 35th St.
Corvallis, OR 97333-4901

Established in 1993 in OR.
Financial data (yr. ended 09/30/00): Assets, $1,807 (M); grants paid, $750; gifts received, $503; expenditures, $1,165; qualifying distributions, $1,165; giving activities include $1,165 for programs.
Officers: Cathy Wilkins, Pres.; Laurie Jodice, Secy.; Caroline Garcia, Treas.
EIN: 943145267

63076
Evangelical Reform, Inc.
c/o Paul H. Seely
1544 S.E. 34th Ave.
Portland, OR 97214-5027

Classified as a private operating foundation in 1994.
Financial data (yr. ended 12/31/00): Assets, $199 (M); grants paid, $0; gifts received, $72; expenditures, $50; qualifying distributions, $0; giving activities include $10 for programs.
Officers: Paul H. Seely, Pres.; Carol Richardson, V.P.; Fred Capell, Secy.
EIN: 943100515

63077
Annie M. Edlen Foundation, Inc.
550 Siskiyou Blvd.
Ashland, OR 97520-2138

Donor(s): Jeanette Rubinyi.
Financial data (yr. ended 12/31/01): Assets, $1 (M); grants paid, $0; expenditures, $30,987; qualifying distributions, $0.
Officers: Jeanette Rubinyi, Pres.; Susan Rubinyi-Anderson, Secy.; Erland Anderson, Treas.
EIN: 911837434

63078
Romanian Christian Ministries
c/o Mariana Basa
6807 S.E. 78th Ave.
Portland, OR 97206

Established in 1999.
Financial data (yr. ended 12/31/99): Assets, $0 (M); grants paid, $5,434; gifts received, $9,531; expenditures, $9,092; qualifying distributions, $8,880.
Directors: Viorica Basa, Gavril Fazekas, Rodica Malos.
EIN: 943205104

PENNSYLVANIA

63079
Longwood Gardens, Inc.
P.O. Box 501
Kennett Square, PA 19348

Established in 1990.
Donor(s): Longwood Foundation, Inc.
Financial data (yr. ended 09/30/00): Assets, $565,804,276 (M); grants paid, $18,136; gifts received, $11,541,900; expenditures, $29,917,807; qualifying distributions, $21,502,424; giving activities include $5,145,684 for programs.
Officers and Trustees:* E.P. Blanchard, Jr.,* Pres.; Irenee duPont, Jr.,* V.P.; Mrs. W. Laird Stabler, Jr.,* V.P.; Kiran Tounk,* Secy.; William K. duPont,* Treas.; Donald F. Crossan, William K. Frederick, Jr., John P. Jessup.
EIN: 510110625

63080
Frick Art & Historical Center, Inc.
(Formerly The Clayton Corporation)
7227 Reynolds St.
Pittsburgh, PA 15208-2919

Classified as a private operating foundation in 1989.
Financial data (yr. ended 03/31/01): Assets, $92,962,776 (M); grants paid, $24; gifts received, $147,632; expenditures, $1,331,791; qualifying distributions, $1,401,864; giving activities include $474,895 for programs.
Officers: Adelaide F. Trafton, Chair.; Thomas J. Hilliard, Jr., Pres.; Harley N. Trice, V.P.; Betsy H. Watkins, V.P.; C. Holmes Wolfe, Jr., Secy.; Childs F. Burden, Treas.; DeCourcy E. McIntosh, Exec. Dir.; Terri L. Chapman, Admin.
Directors: D. Frick Burden, Henry Burden, Arabella S. Dane, Danforth P. Fales, Laura S. Fisher, Elise Frick, Stephen F. Halpern, Margaret R. Scaife, Nancy D. Washington.
Trustee: Mellon Bank, N.A.
EIN: 251596285

63081
Charles P. & Margaret E. Polk Foundation
301 North St.
Millersburg, PA 17061-1308

Established in 1961.
Donor(s): Miriam Polk-Halpern.
Financial data (yr. ended 12/31/01): Assets, $31,558,101 (M); grants paid, $10,050; gifts received, $404,220; expenditures, $1,844,379; qualifying distributions, $2,697,084; giving activities include $2,805,248 for programs.
Officers and Director:* Allen Shaffer, Chair.; R.W. Rissinger,* Vice-Chair.; Judy Paul, Secy.; David Hawley, Treas.
EIN: 236296772

63082
Carnegie Hero Fund Commission
425 6th Ave., Ste. 1640
Pittsburgh, PA 15219-1823 (412) 281-1302
Additional tel.: (800) 447-8900; FAX: (412) 281-5751; E-mail: carnegiehero@carnegiehero.org; URL: http://www.carnegiehero.org
Contact: Walter F. Rutkowski, Secy. and Exec. Dir.

Trust established in 1904 in PA.
Donor(s): Andrew Carnegie.‡
Financial data (yr. ended 12/31/01): Assets, $30,250,351 (M); grants paid, $723,397; expenditures, $1,438,059; qualifying distributions, $1,364,335.
Limitations: Giving primarily in the U.S.; some giving also in Canada.
Publications: Annual report, informational brochure, occasional report.
Application information: Awards by nomination only. Application form required.
Officers and Trustees:* Mark Laskow,* Pres.; Priscilla J. McCrady,* V.P.; Walter F. Rutkowski, Secy. and Exec. Dir.; James M. Walton,* Treas.; S. Richard Brand, E. Bayley Buchanan, A.H. Burchfield III, Benjamin R. Fisher, Jr., Elizabeth H. Genter, Thomas J. Hilliard, Jr., David McL. Hillman, Peter F. Mathieson, Christopher R. McCrady, Ann M. McGuinn, Robert W. Off, Frank Brooks Robinson, Arthur M. Scully, Jr., William P. Snyder III, Walter F. Toerge, Sybil P. Veeder, Thomas L. Wentling, Jr., Alfred W. Wishart, Jr.
EIN: 251062730
Codes: FD, GTI

63083
Rebecca Residence for Protestant Ladies
3746 Rebecca Ave.
Allison Park, PA 15101

Classified as a private operating foundation in 1988.
Financial data (yr. ended 05/31/00): Assets, $29,915,271 (M); grants paid, $0; gifts received, $271,124; expenditures, $4,351,889; qualifying distributions, $6,113,477; giving activities include $7,403,758 for programs.
Officers and Directors:* Mrs. John Unkovic,* Pres.; Susan Utech,* V.P.; Anne Steele,* Secy.; Beatrice Lynch,* Treas.; Mary E. Wilson, Exec. Dir.; Marian Bradley, Thomas Dick, Michelle Keane Domeisen, Carolyn Duronio, Janet McCarthy, Jean Weidlein, and 7 additional directors.
EIN: 250974311

63084
Hawthornden Literary Institute
535 Smithfield St.
606 Oliver Bldg.
Pittsburgh, PA 15222-2393

Established in 1984 in PA.
Donor(s): Drue Heinz.
Financial data (yr. ended 12/31/01): Assets, $20,104,990 (M); grants paid, $0; expenditures, $19,616,154; qualifying distributions, $522,101; giving activities include $432,185 for programs.
Limitations: Applications not accepted.
Application information: Contributes only to two pre-selected organizations.
Officers and Trustees:* Drue Heinz,* Pres.; James F. Dolan,* V.P.; Mary Lou Rosenfelder, Secy.-Treas.; Julia V. Shea, Secy.-Treas.
EIN: 521324746

63085
Louise Steinman von Hess Foundation
c/o The Glenmede Trust Company
1650 Market St. Ste. 1200
Philadelphia, PA 19103-7391

Classified as a private operating foundation in 1974.
Donor(s): Richard C. von Hess.
Financial data (yr. ended 12/31/01): Assets, $19,876,226 (M); grants paid, $0; gifts received, $217,858; expenditures, $342,786; qualifying distributions, $666,858; giving activities include $666,858 for programs.

Officer and Trustees:* Thomas Hills Cook,* Secy.; Joseph Kindig III, John Brace Latham, Mrs. Alfred Mayor, William H. Pope, Jr.
EIN: 237368611

63086
Watson Memorial Home
1200 Conewango Ave.
Warren, PA 16365

Financial data (yr. ended 12/31/00): Assets, $17,913,005 (M); grants paid, $0; gifts received, $95,320; expenditures, $963,512; qualifying distributions, $1,016,274; giving activities include $877,413 for programs.
Officers and Directors:* Paul R. Randolph, Jr.,* Pres.; Kenneth A. Holtz, V.P.; Gerald L. Huber,* Secy.-Treas.; Kathryn A. Furman, Jean K. Johnson, Dana S. Kubiak, Janice M. Logan, Susan C. Spangler, Gladys E. Taylor, Bernard L. Wingert.
EIN: 250965602

63087
Park Home, Inc.
P.O. Box 2404
Williamsport, PA 17701-2404

Classified as a private operating foundation in 1974.
Financial data (yr. ended 08/31/99): Assets, $15,681,102 (M); grants paid, $0; expenditures, $644,017; qualifying distributions, $584,077; giving activities include $584,077 for programs.
Officers and Directors:* Samuel R. Hoff,* Pres.; J. Robert Schrader,* V.P.; Carol Greene,* Secy.; George G. Golden,* Treas.; Cecilia Joyce, Admin.; J. Budd Bell, George Bierman, Thomas Briley, Mary Gibbs, Jeffrey B. Sims.
EIN: 240522575

63088
Sanatoga Ridge Community, Inc.
2461 E. High St.
Pottstown, PA 19464-3111

Established in 1992 in PA.
Financial data (yr. ended 12/31/00): Assets, $14,762,275 (M); grants paid, $50; gifts received, $1,439; expenditures, $1,495,931; qualifying distributions, $2,012,797; giving activities include $79,967 for programs.
Officers: J. Wilmer Hallman, Pres.; David J. Hallman, V.P.; R. Duane Clemens, Secy.; Mark Moore, Treas.
EIN: 232506257

63089
Florence Waring Erdman Trust
c/o Mellon Bank, N.A.
P.O. Box 7236
Philadelphia, PA 19101-7236

Classified as a private operating foundation in 1974.
Donor(s): Florence Waring Erdman,‡ Dorothy B. Richards Trust.
Financial data (yr. ended 12/31/00): Assets, $14,759,749 (M); grants paid, $0; gifts received, $22,202; expenditures, $472,791; qualifying distributions, $390,304.
Limitations: Applications not accepted.
Trustees: J. Welles Henderson, Jr., Mellon Bank, N.A.
EIN: 236225822

63090
Dietrich American Foundation
1311 Art School Rd.
Chester Springs, PA 19425

Established in 1963 in DE.
Donor(s): H. Richard Dietrich, Jr., Daniel W. Dietrich Foundation, Inc.
Financial data (yr. ended 12/31/99): Assets, $14,521,358 (M); grants paid, $0; expenditures, $163,648; qualifying distributions, $384,593; giving activities include $384,593 for programs.
Limitations: Applications not accepted.
Application information: Contributes only to pre-selected organizations.
Officers and Directors:* H. Richard Dietrich, Jr.,* Pres.; H. Richard Dietrich III,* V.P.; Lowell S. Thomas, Jr.,* Secy.; Frederic C. Barth,* Treas.; Christian B. Dietrich, Cordelia B. Dietrich.
EIN: 516017453

63091
Ressler Mill Foundation
P.O. Box 353
New Holland, PA 17557
Application address: 29 E. King St., Rm. 14, Lancaster, PA 17602, tel./FAX: (717) 481-7702

Established in 1967 in PA. Classified as a private operating foundation in 1977.
Donor(s): W. Franklin Ressler,‡ Anna Ressler.‡
Financial data (yr. ended 12/31/01): Assets, $13,835,648 (M); grants paid, $319,611; expenditures, $660,491; qualifying distributions, $519,949; giving activities include $200,338 for programs.
Limitations: Giving primarily in Lancaster, PA.
Publications: Application guidelines, informational brochure.
Application information: Application form required.
Officers: Stephen J. Kindig, Pres.; Mary L. Clinton, V.P.; W. James Morton, Jr., Secy.; Richard P. Heilig, Treas.
EIN: 236430663
Codes: FD

63092
Garrett-Williamson Foundation
395 Bishop Hollow Rd.
Newtown Square, PA 19073

Classified as a private operating foundation in 1986.
Financial data (yr. ended 12/31/99): Assets, $13,830,898 (M); grants paid, $50; gifts received, $9,127; expenditures, $1,111,585; qualifying distributions, $399,653; giving activities include $786,735 for programs.
Directors: Brian D. Collins, Albert C. Condo, Paul E. Crossan, Jr., Constance J. Fontaine, William J. McDougall, Jr., Edward J. McMearty, William Z. Suplee III, James M. Umstattd, Frank C. Videon.
EIN: 231433892

63093
North American Railway Foundation
105 N. Front St., Ste. 307
P.O. Box 867
Harrisburg, PA 17108-0867

Established in 1996 in PA.
Donor(s): Brotherhood's Relief & Compensation Fund.
Financial data (yr. ended 09/30/00): Assets, $13,305,563 (M); grants paid, $0; gifts received, $3,131,742; expenditures, $783,389; qualifying distributions, $756,564; giving activities include $578,621 for programs.
Officers and Directors:* Richard J. Myers,* Chair.; Thomas W. Jackson, Vice-Chair.; Mark Robb, Secy.; James H. Stewart, Exec. Dir.; O.J. Folsy, K.L. Mayle, Philip J. Sullivan II, P.L. Wingo, Jr., M.A. Wofford.
EIN: 251801614

63094
The Posner Fine Arts Foundation
500 Greentree Commons
381 Mansfield Ave.
Pittsburgh, PA 15220-2751

Established in 2000 in PA.
Donor(s): Henry Posner, Jr., Posner Fine Arts Partners.
Financial data (yr. ended 07/31/01): Assets, $12,265,201 (M); grants paid, $0; gifts received, $12,298,201; expenditures, $33,000; qualifying distributions, $0.
Limitations: Applications not accepted.
Application information: Contributes only to pre-selected organizations.
Officers and Directors:* Henry Posner, Jr.,* Chair.; Henry Posner III,* Pres.; Helen M. Posner,* Secy.-Treas.; James T. Posner, Paul M. Posner.
EIN: 251843104
Codes: TN

63095
The John Edgar Thomson Foundation
c/o The Rittenhouse Claridge, Ste. 318
201 S. 18th St.
Philadelphia, PA 19103 (215) 545-6083
Contact: Sheila Cohen, Dir.

Endowment established in 1882 in PA.
Donor(s): John Edgar Thomson.‡
Financial data (yr. ended 12/31/01): Assets, $10,289,904 (M); grants paid, $214,586; expenditures, $356,538; qualifying distributions, $214,586.
Limitations: Giving primarily in the continental U.S.
Publications: Annual report, newsletter, informational brochure (including application guidelines).
Application information: Application form required.
Officers and Trustees:* H. William Brady,* Secy.; Wayne E. Bogardus, Treas.; Sheila Cohen, Dir.; John J. Haslett II, Carl L. Rugart, Jr.
EIN: 231382746
Codes: FD2, GTI

63096
Pennsylvania Society of the Sons of the Revolution
c/o The Racquet Club
215 S. 16th St., Ste. 27
Philadelphia, PA 19102-3349

Established in 1994 in PA.
Financial data (yr. ended 12/31/00): Assets, $9,524,006 (M); grants paid, $57,856; gifts received, $306,831; expenditures, $405,241; qualifying distributions, $389,054.
Limitations: Applications not accepted. Giving limited to PA.
Application information: Contributes only to pre-selected organizations.
Officers: Curtis Cheyney III, Pres.; Harland Johnson, V.P.; Theodore Clattenberg, Jr., Secy.; Robert Van Gulick, Treas.
EIN: 231353372

63097
The Long Home
200 West End Ave.
Lancaster, PA 17603

Classified as a private operating foundation in 1974.
Financial data (yr. ended 09/30/00): Assets, $9,286,922 (M); grants paid, $0; gifts received, $624,127; expenditures, $1,194,338; qualifying distributions, $1,043,708; giving activities include $1,043,708 for programs.

Officers: Raymond L. Kingcaid, Pres. and Treas.; John I. Hartman, Secy.
Director: Robert Baird.
EIN: 231352360

63098
E. D. Merrick Free Art Gallery, Museum & Library
c/o Robert S. Merrick
1415 5th Ave.
New Brighton, PA 15066

Financial data (yr. ended 12/31/99): Assets, $9,275,272 (M); grants paid, $0; gifts received, $10,910; expenditures, $82,796; qualifying distributions, $120,622; giving activities include $120,622 for programs.
Director: Cynthia Kundar.
Trustee: Robert S. Merrick.
EIN: 256032387

63099
Roxborough Home for Indigent Women
601 E. Leverington Ave.
Philadelphia, PA 19128-2607

Financial data (yr. ended 12/31/99): Assets, $9,197,473 (M); grants paid, $0; expenditures, $485,450; qualifying distributions, $485,450; giving activities include $116,072 for programs.
Officers: Doris Preston, Pres.; Adah W. Crowley, Secy.; John E. Welsh, Jr., Treas.
EIN: 231401566

63100
David Library of the American Revolution, Inc.
P.O. Box 748
Washington Crossing, PA 18977-0748
(215) 493-6776
Contact: Marge Torongo, Pres.

Established about 1974.
Financial data (yr. ended 12/31/99): Assets, $9,186,173 (M); grants paid, $14,054; gifts received, $673; expenditures, $409,118; qualifying distributions, $263,853.
Limitations: Giving primarily in PA.
Application information: Application information available upon request.
Officers: Marjorie Torongo, Pres.; Thomas B. Slaughter, V.P.; Joyce Stone, Secy.
EIN: 237289047

63101
SVF Foundation
200 Eagle Rd., Ste. 316
Wayne, PA 19087

Established in 1999 in PA.
Donor(s): Dorrance H. Hamilton.
Financial data (yr. ended 12/31/01): Assets, $8,457,435 (M); grants paid, $0; gifts received, $2,858,045; expenditures, $313; qualifying distributions, $0.
Limitations: Applications not accepted.
Application information: Contributes only to pre-selected organizations.
Officer: Dorrance H. Hamilton, Pres.
Director: Margaret Duprey.
EIN: 256621038

63102
Merchants Fund
(Formerly Merchants-Oliver Fund)
c/o Hemmenway & Reinhardt, Inc.
4 Park Ave.
Swarthmore, PA 19081-1723
Application address: P.O. Box 111, Point Pleasant, PA 18950
Contact: C. Joyce Kaufman, Secy.-Treas.

Established prior to 1913.

Donor(s): Lewis Elkins Fund, Charles Fearon.‡
Financial data (yr. ended 12/31/01): Assets, $8,090,323 (M); grants paid, $544,539; gifts received, $393,653; expenditures, $739,112; qualifying distributions, $647,097.
Limitations: Giving primarily in Philadelphia, PA.
Application information: Application form required.
Officers and Directors:* Henry Winsor,* Pres.; Peter Wilmerding,* V.P.; C. Joyce Kaufman, Secy.-Treas.; John S. Carter, Frederic N. Dittman, Hugh McBirney Johnston, Bruce Lipa, J. Stephen Peake, Jr., John A. Philbrick, George M. Riter, G. Stephen Vorhees.
EIN: 231584975
Codes: FD, GTI

63103
The Hahn Home
863 S. George St.
York, PA 17403

Classified as a private operating foundation in 1986.
Financial data (yr. ended 12/31/01): Assets, $7,314,248 (M); grants paid, $0; gifts received, $141,842; expenditures, $463,369; qualifying distributions, $272,043.
Officers: Elizabeth Owen, Pres.; Stephen H. Stetler, V.P.; Lynne Pfafflin, Secy.; Donna Williams, Treas.
EIN: 231425032

63104
The Frederick A. Simeone, M.D. Foundation, Inc.
8700 Seminole Dr.
Philadelphia, PA 19118

Established in 1996 in PA.
Donor(s): Frederick A. Simeone, M.D.
Financial data (yr. ended 11/30/01): Assets, $7,197,534 (M); grants paid, $0; gifts received, $1,875,000; expenditures, $15,075; qualifying distributions, $0.
Trustee: Frederick A. Simeone.
EIN: 223483147

63105
Gibbons Home, Inc.
938 Lincoln Ave.
Springfield, PA 19064

Financial data (yr. ended 12/31/01): Assets, $6,806,878 (M); grants paid, $0; expenditures, $255,590; qualifying distributions, $0; giving activities include $235,842 for programs.
Officers: George Gillespie, Jr., Pres.; David H. Byerly, Jr., V.P.; Nancy Maclay, Secy.; Robert L. Moreland, Treas.
Board Members: Priscilla G. Blackman, Thomas Chew, Gordon W. Douglas, Eudora S. Gerner, Roger Linde, Kathleen L. Martel, Frances Miller, Donovan E. Roush.
EIN: 231381979

63106
Andalusia Foundation
P.O. Box 158
Andalusia, PA 19020-0158

Financial data (yr. ended 12/31/01): Assets, $6,664,654 (M); grants paid, $0; gifts received, $332,601; expenditures, $416,615; qualifying distributions, $409,541; giving activities include $229,364 for programs.
Officer and Trustees:* James Biddle, James C. Biddle, Edward M. Carter II, Mrs. William M. Hollenback, Jr., Mrs. Edward A. Montgomery, Jr., Katharine H. Norris, Richard Wood Snowden,

Christine Wainwright, Mrs. Nicholas Biddle Wainwright.
EIN: 232115358

63107
Fred M. and Jessie A. Kirby Episcopal House, Inc.
P.O. Box 2862
Wilkes-Barre, PA 18703-2862

Classified as a private operating foundation in 1974.
Financial data (yr. ended 12/31/99): Assets, $6,658,894 (M); grants paid, $0; gifts received, $12,500; expenditures, $172,413; qualifying distributions, $157,651; giving activities include $29,591 for programs.
Officers and Trustees:* Jessie K. Lee,* Pres.; Wade H.O. Kirby,* V.P.; Walter S. Mitchell, Jr., Secy.-Treas.; Grace K. Culbertson, Mary Hooker, Marian C. Hvolbeck, Allan P. Kirby, Jr., Annette S. Kirby, Slater B. Kirby, Rev. Paul Marshall, Mary P. Mitchell.
EIN: 240826175

63108
The Daniel W. Dietrich II Trust, Inc.
P.O. Box 649
Gladwyne, PA 19035-0649

Donor(s): Daniel W. Dietrich II.
Financial data (yr. ended 09/30/01): Assets, $5,921,985 (M); grants paid, $0; gifts received, $9,800; expenditures, $10,328; qualifying distributions, $0.
Officers and Directors:* Daniel W. Dietrich II,* Pres.; Joseph J. Connolly,* Secy.; Stephen M. Foxman.
EIN: 650532586

63109
Lasko Charitable Fund
2 Commerce Sq.
2001 Market St.
Philadelphia, PA 19103 (215) 751-9666
Contact: Bernard Eizen, Pres.

Established as a private operating foundation in 1999.
Financial data (yr. ended 06/30/01): Assets, $5,535,661 (M); grants paid, $526,750; gifts received, $200,000; expenditures, $358,961; qualifying distributions, $526,750.
Officer and Director:* Bernard Eizen,* Pres.
EIN: 232856376
Codes: FD

63110
Ryerss Farm for Aged Equines
(Formerly Ryerss Infirmary for Dumb Animals)
1710 Ridge Rd.
Pottstown, PA 19465

Classified as a private operating foundation in 1973.
Donor(s): Pfizer Inc, Purina Mills, Inc.
Financial data (yr. ended 12/31/01): Assets, $5,511,139 (M); grants paid, $0; gifts received, $388,372; expenditures, $602,456; qualifying distributions, $489,361; giving activities include $518,471 for programs.
Limitations: Applications not accepted.
Application information: Contributes only to pre-selected organizations.
Officers and Directors:* Joseph H. Donahue,* Pres.; Douglas R. Barr, Jr.,* Exec. V.P.; Timothy J. Blevins,* V.P. and Mgr.; James A. Clark,* Secy.; Douglas R. Barr, Sr.,* Treas.; and 5 additional directors.
EIN: 236215037

63111
The Ecumenical Community
830 Cherry Dr.
Hershey, PA 17033

Established in 1994 in PA.
Financial data (yr. ended 12/31/01): Assets, $5,285,533 (M); grants paid, $27,993; gifts received, $242,593; expenditures, $3,833,083; qualifying distributions, $844,669.
Limitations: Applications not accepted.
Application information: Contributes only to pre-selected organizations.
Officers and Trustees:* John O. Hershey,* Chair.; Clifford L. Jones,* Vice-Chair.; Thomas Baker,* Pres.; Nancy W. Einsel, V.P. and Secy.-Treas.; Rev. Michael W. Creighton, Carolyn C. Dumaresq, Rev. Nicholas C. Dattilo, D.D., Rev. Guy S. Edmiston, Jr., Constance B. Foster, Rev. Earl L. Harris, Bishop Neil L. Irons, Wendy Klingman, Rev. Msgr. Francis M. Kumontis, Donald R. Shover, Jr., Elsie W. Swenson, Marc P. Volavka.
EIN: 251612331

63112
The Henry Foundation for Botanical Research
801 Stony Ln.
Gladwyne, PA 19035-1460

Established in 1949.
Financial data (yr. ended 12/31/99): Assets, $5,201,288 (M); grants paid, $0; gifts received, $38,070; expenditures, $284,973; qualifying distributions, $261,901; giving activities include $234,521 for programs.
Officers and Trustees:* Josephine Den Henry,* Pres.; Gerhard van Arkel,* Treas.; John S. Jenks, Thomas E. Lovejoy, Mrs. William McLean IV, Paul Meyer, Ruth Patrick, T. Sergeant Pepper, Marvin Thompson, Mrs. James C. Treadway, Jr.
EIN: 231365145

63113
Animal Care Fund, Inc.
c/o Animal Care Sanctuary Hill
P.O. Box A
East Smithfield, PA 18817-0010

Established in 1967.
Donor(s): Hilda Rux, H. Dickinson,‡ L.S. Lewis,‡ M. Mayerick,‡ Manheimer Trust, Wilkerson Trust.
Financial data (yr. ended 09/30/01): Assets, $4,440,985 (M); grants paid, $250; gifts received, $1,473,706; expenditures, $926,268; qualifying distributions, $866,314; giving activities include $787,357 for programs.
Officers: Barbara Merrill, Pres.; John Merrill, V.P.; Cora Plouse, Secy.
EIN: 221837635

63114
Sarah Heinz House Association
c/o Richard Laux
E. Ohio and Heinz Sts.
Pittsburgh, PA 15212

Classified as a private operating foundation in 1972.
Financial data (yr. ended 12/31/01): Assets, $4,204,794 (M); grants paid, $0; gifts received, $990,000; expenditures, $1,212,145; qualifying distributions, $0.
Officers and Directors:* William A. Lape,* Pres.; Howard R. Spicher,* Secy.; Joseph S. Munson,* Treas.; J. Alfred Berger, Robert W. Kahn, Margaret M. Petruska, Robert M. Sheroke.
EIN: 250965390

63115
Brevillier Village Foundation, Inc.
5416 E. Lake Rd.
Erie, PA 16510

Established in 1987 in PA.
Financial data (yr. ended 06/30/00): Assets, $4,060,096 (M); grants paid, $0; gifts received, $47,001; expenditures, $561,132; qualifying distributions, $0; giving activities include $561,132 for programs.
Officers and Directors:* Tom Stout,* Chair.; Rev. John P. Downey,* Vice-Chair. and Secy.; George W. Hunter II,* Pres.; James Carr,* Treas.; Glen Chichester, John Claridge, Theresa Fryer, Peggy McCarthy, Sr. Phyllis Schleicher.
EIN: 251548657

63116
Main Street Non Profit Redevelopment Corporation
c/o Kenneth R. Shoemaker
32 E. King St.
Shippensburg, PA 17257

Established in 1993.
Financial data (yr. ended 02/28/02): Assets, $3,986,095 (M); grants paid, $0; gifts received, $25,000; expenditures, $1,126,305; qualifying distributions, $168,791; giving activities include $168,791 for programs.
Officers: Kenneth R. Shoemaker, Pres.; John Clinton, Secy.-Treas.
Directors: Duaine A. Collier, Judy Fogelsonger, Edward Goodhart, Bruce Hockersmith.
EIN: 251702666

63117
Beech Interplex, Inc.
(Formerly Beech Corporation, Inc.)
1510 Cecil B. Moore Ave., Ste. 300
Philadelphia, PA 19121

Established in 1990 in PA.
Donor(s): The William Penn Foundation, Merck, Sharp & Dohme.
Financial data (yr. ended 12/31/00): Assets, $3,935,756 (M); grants paid, $0; gifts received, $125,000; expenditures, $714,916; qualifying distributions, $168,491; giving activities include $714,915 for programs.
Officer: Floyd Alston, Pres.
Directors: George Brooks, Helyn Cheeks, Darrell Clarke, Lena Davis, Geneva Hill, Rev. William B. Moore, Alf Muronda, Robert Nottingham, Edwina Rucker, Bernard Savage, Stanley Scott, Spencer Sewell, Robert Smith, James White.
EIN: 521693162
Codes: TN

63118
King's Daughters & King's Sons, Inc.
61 W. Market St.
Bethlehem, PA 18018-5797

Financial data (yr. ended 10/31/01): Assets, $3,616,360 (M); grants paid, $919; gifts received, $6,741; expenditures, $328,304; qualifying distributions, $324,879; giving activities include $324,879 for programs.
Officers: Rita Gambler, Pres.; Lillian Caster, V.P.; Kathryn Malley, Secy.; Charlette Dostal, Treas.
EIN: 240795969

63119
Dorflinger-Suydam Wildlife Sanctuary, Inc.
c/o Wayne County Bank & Trust Co., Trust Dept.
717 Main St.
Honesdale, PA 18431

Classified as a private operating foundation in 1983.
Financial data (yr. ended 12/31/99): Assets, $3,615,943 (M); grants paid, $2,444; gifts received, $8,486; expenditures, $238,056; qualifying distributions, $208,132; giving activities include $208,132 for programs.
Limitations: Applications not accepted.
Application information: Contributes only to pre-selected organizations.
Officers: Walter Barbe, Chair.; Victor A. Decker III, Pres. and Secy.; Russell L. Ridd, Treas.
EIN: 232137456

63120
Lacawac Sanctuary Foundation, Inc.
R.R. 1, Box 518
Lake Ariel, PA 18436-9752

Classified as a private operating foundation in 1967.
Donor(s): L. Arthur Watres, Elizabeth Watres.
Financial data (yr. ended 12/31/00): Assets, $3,445,638 (M); grants paid, $0; gifts received, $55,211; expenditures, $83,313; qualifying distributions, $83,864; giving activities include $28,572 for programs.
Officers: Daniel S. Townsend, Pres.; Josephine Kleinbaum, Secy.; Wayne Wilcha, Treas.; Janice Poppich, Mgr.
EIN: 236419952
Codes: TN

63121
Mariton Wildlife Sanctuary & Wilderness Trust
c/o Wolf Black
1650 Arch St., 22nd Fl.
Philadelphia, PA 19103

Classified as a private operating foundation in 1972.
Donor(s): Mary R. Guerrero,‡ Antonio P. Guerrero.‡
Financial data (yr. ended 09/30/01): Assets, $3,310,938 (M); grants paid, $0; gifts received, $6,904; expenditures, $132,056; qualifying distributions, $118,005; giving activities include $113,508 for programs.
Officers and Trustees:* Edward C. Dearden III,* Admin.; Robert I. Friedman,* Admin.; Hon. Richard Grifo,* Admin.; Helen Spigel Sax,* Admin.; Ronald W. Shipman,* Admin.; Patricia Bradt, Gayle Chipman, Albert W. Gendebien, Francesco Grifo, and 8 additional trustees.
EIN: 237075031

63122
The Cranaleith Spiritual Center
13475 Proctor Rd.
Philadelphia, PA 19116

Donor(s): Francis H. Trainer, Jr., Sr. Mary Trainer, Thomas J. Trainer, Kathy Ulinski.
Financial data (yr. ended 06/30/00): Assets, $2,976,852 (M); grants paid, $0; gifts received, $1,765,832; expenditures, $229,955; qualifying distributions, $213,888; giving activities include $222,995 for programs.
Officers and Directors:* Sr. Mary Trainer,* Pres.; Francis H. Trainer, Jr.,* V.P.; Katherine T. Ulinski,* Secy.; Thomas J. Trainer,* Treas.
EIN: 521993128

63123
Welsh Valley Preservation Society
P.O. Box 261
Kulpsville, PA 19443-0261

Classified as a private operating foundation in 1986.
Financial data (yr. ended 12/31/00): Assets, $2,921,996 (M); grants paid, $115; gifts received, $2,851; expenditures, $133,434; qualifying distributions, $107,723; giving activities include $113,240 for programs.
Limitations: Giving primarily in PA.
Officers and Trustees:* Michael J. Becker,* Pres.; Theodore D. Dorand,* V.P.; John A. Granger,* Secy.; Joan D. Hauger,* Treas.; Effie Alpert, Douglas A. Miller, Daniel B. Reibel, John Schoenfelder.
EIN: 237155027

63124
The Millport Conservancy
(Formerly Millport Museum)
741 E. Millport Rd.
Lititz, PA 17543

Established around 1982 in PA.
Financial data (yr. ended 12/31/01): Assets, $2,750,933 (M); grants paid, $0; gifts received, $64,113; expenditures, $91,586; qualifying distributions, $0.
Officers: Robert S. Wohlsen, Sr., Pres.; Carolyn W. Wohlsen, Secy.-Treas.
EIN: 222436077

63125
H. Lawrence Jenkins Residuary Trust
c/o Bryn Mawr Trust Co.
10 S. Bryn Mawr Ave.
Bryn Mawr, PA 19010

Classified as a private operating foundation in 1979.
Donor(s): H. Lawrence.
Financial data (yr. ended 12/31/00): Assets, $2,699,600 (M); grants paid, $35,738; gifts received, $7,558; expenditures, $47,760; qualifying distributions, $46,292.
Trustees: Bryn Mawr Trust Co.
EIN: 236491966

63126
John Slade Ely Fund
c/o First Union National Bank
Broad & Walnut Sts.
Philadelphia, PA 19109

Financial data (yr. ended 06/30/00): Assets, $2,694,290 (M); grants paid, $0; expenditures, $104,446; qualifying distributions, $0.
Trustee: First Union National Bank.
EIN: 060769931

63127
Ernest L. & Mildred Roberts Sweet Foundation
c/o Citizens & Northern Bank, Trust Dept.
P.O. Box 58
Wellsboro, PA 16901
Application address: 126 Main St., P.O. Box 609, Wellsboro, PA 16901
Contact: R. Lowell Coolidge

Established in 1986 in PA.
Donor(s): Mildred Fleitz.‡
Financial data (yr. ended 12/31/01): Assets, $2,647,496 (M); grants paid, $102,317; expenditures, $117,224; qualifying distributions, $101,234.
Limitations: Giving limited to Wellsboro Area School District, Tioga County, PA.
Application information: Application form required.
Trustee: Citizens & Northern Bank.
Administrative Committee: Thomas L. Briggs, R. Lowell Coolidge, Rev. Robert K. Greer, Donna Mettler, F. David Pennypacker.
EIN: 226408974
Codes: FD2

63128
Institute for Bio-Information Research
955 Chesterbrook Blvd., Ste. 125
Wayne, PA 19087-5522

Established in 1988 in PA.
Donor(s): Richard J. Fox, Geraldine D. Fox.
Financial data (yr. ended 07/31/01): Assets, $2,514,645 (M); grants paid, $75,000; expenditures, $357,115; qualifying distributions, $348,686; giving activities include $350,080 for programs.
Limitations: Applications not accepted. Giving primarily in Philadelphia, PA.
Application information: Contributes only to pre-selected organizations.
Officers and Directors:* Geraldine D. Fox,* Treas.; Richard J. Fox,* Treas.; Frederic D. Fox.
EIN: 232528579
Codes: FD2

63129
Crawford Memorial Trust
60 E. Penn St.
Norristown, PA 19404

Established in 1984 in PA.
Financial data (yr. ended 12/31/00): Assets, $2,509,706 (M); grants paid, $0; expenditures, $54,663; qualifying distributions, $45,775; giving activities include $2,450 for programs.
Officer: Carol Lynn E. Moran, Mgr.
Trustee: Richard Grossman.
EIN: 236884886

63130
Highland Terrace Housing Corporation
111 W. Fairmont Ave.
New Castle, PA 16105

Financial data (yr. ended 03/31/01): Assets, $2,501,284 (M); grants paid, $0; expenditures, $194,478; qualifying distributions, $126,032; giving activities include $194,478 for programs.
Officers: John J. Hadgkiss, Pres.; Joseph Cardella, Secy.-Treas.
Directors: Marion D'Augostine, Joseph Gloclano, Dominick Grant, David Henzel, Leonard Oddo.
EIN: 251730915

63131
Herman Yudacufski Charitable Foundation
P.O. Box 279
St. Clair, PA 17970-0279 (814) 429-1575
Contact: Kenneth J. Huebner

Established in 1997 in PA.
Donor(s): Herman Yudacufski.
Financial data (yr. ended 11/30/00): Assets, $2,296,445 (M); grants paid, $42,355; expenditures, $46,266; qualifying distributions, $46,266.
Limitations: Giving on a national basis.
Officers: Steve Cotler, Pres.; Allan Yudacufski, V.P.; Marjorie Cotler, Secy.
Director: Alvin B. Marshall.
EIN: 232906569

63132
Harvest Fields Ministry Center, Inc.
P.O. Box 77
Boalsburg, PA 16827-0077

Established in 1996.
Donor(s): Steven D. Heinz.
Financial data (yr. ended 09/30/01): Assets, $2,265,145 (M); grants paid, $0; gifts received, $147,083; expenditures, $189,035; qualifying distributions, $108,184; giving activities include $108,184 for programs.
Officers: Steven D. Heinz, Pres.; Kay E. Heinz, Secy.-Treas.
EIN: 232869978

63133
Greencastle-Antrim Foundation
P.O. Box 248
Greencastle, PA 17225

Classified as a private operating foundation in 1975.
Financial data (yr. ended 12/31/01): Assets, $2,206,377 (M); grants paid, $300; gifts received, $65; expenditures, $314,246; qualifying distributions, $27,447; giving activities include $301,946 for programs.
Limitations: Applications not accepted.
Application information: Contributes only to pre-selected organizations.
Officers: Robert G. Crunkelton, Pres.; John L. Grove, V.P.; Paul R. Faust, Secy.; Donald E. Barnhart, Treas.
EIN: 236449648

63134
Merion Community Association
625 Hazelhurst Ave.
Merion Station, PA 19066

Established around 1950.
Financial data (yr. ended 12/31/99): Assets, $2,193,586 (M); grants paid, $16,000; expenditures, $425,863; qualifying distributions, $120,554; giving activities include $18,050 for programs.
Limitations: Giving limited to the Lower Merion region of PA.
Officers and Directors:* James Ettelson,* Pres.; Patricia Surbeck,* V.P.; Wayne L. Martin,* Secy.; Perry A. Berman,* Treas.; Davis Pearson, Frances Quinn, Arthur R. Ziemer, and 7 additional directors.
EIN: 231405634

63135
Ingeborg A. Biondo Memorial Foundation
(Formerly Ingeborg A. Biondo Memorial Trust)
221 Broad St.
Milford, PA 18337

Established in 1986 in PA.
Donor(s): Joseph R. Biondo.
Financial data (yr. ended 12/31/01): Assets, $2,187,530 (M); grants paid, $6,084; gifts received, $104,990; expenditures, $157,703; qualifying distributions, $94,838; giving activities include $71,472 for programs.
Limitations: Giving primarily in NY and PA.
Application information: Applicants must live in Pike County, PA or neighboring counties. Application form not required.
Officer and Trustees:* Marion Almquist,* Chair.; Joseph R. Biondo, Ronnie Biondo, Trudy Derse, Michael Dickerson, Elaine Greiner, Robert Onofry, Arthur K. Ridley, Joyce Rocko.
EIN: 112801015
Codes: GTI

63136
Western Hemisphere Cultural Society, Inc.
P.O. Box 122
York, PA 17405-0122

Financial data (yr. ended 12/31/00): Assets, $2,148,159 (M); grants paid, $1,300; gifts received, $1,500; expenditures, $143,630; qualifying distributions, $10,330; giving activities include $139,737 for programs.
Officers and Directors:* Raymond E. Drake,* Pres.; Thomas J. McKenna,* V.P.; Robert E. Ritchie,* Secy.; Benjamin A. Hiegert, Treas.; Luiz A. Fragelli, John W. Horvat, Gary J. Isbell, C. Preston Noell III, Matthew Toenjes.
EIN: 133171782

63137
Countess DeTrampe Home for Unwanted Dogs
c/o Janice B. Decker
1312 Yellow Springs Rd.
Chester Springs, PA 19425-1502

Financial data (yr. ended 09/30/01): Assets, $2,064,193 (M); grants paid, $0; gifts received, $100; expenditures, $135,538; qualifying distributions, $93,769; giving activities include $93,769 for programs.
Officers: Lynne Flynn, Pres.; Thomas J. Scanlon, Jr., Secy.-Treas.
EIN: 232020935

63138
C. W. Schrenk and Marjorie J. Schrenk Family Foundation
130 Buck Rd., Ste. 201
Holland, PA 18966-1743 (215) 357-6195
Contact: Clarence W. Schrenk, Tr.

Financial data (yr. ended 12/31/99): Assets, $1,975,078 (M); grants paid, $62,475; gifts received, $49,142; expenditures, $135,251; qualifying distributions, $113,624.
Limitations: Giving limited to DE, NJ, and PA.
Officers and Trustees:* Marjorie J. Schrenk,* Chair.; Michael T. Piotrowicz,* Vice-Chair.; Bonnie Beth Stellwagon,* Secy.; Robert F. Pritz,* Treas.; Beverly Claire Gormley, Susan Marquiss, Clarence W. Schrenk, B. Jean Traub.
EIN: 236906450

63139
Henry J. & Willemina B. Kuhn Day Camp
600 Witmer Rd.
Horsham, PA 19044-1832

Classified as a private operating foundation in 1988.
Financial data (yr. ended 09/30/99): Assets, $1,889,803 (M); grants paid, $0; expenditures, $92,037; qualifying distributions, $86,421; giving activities include $86,421 for programs.
Limitations: Applications not accepted.
Application information: Contributes only to pre-selected organizations.
Officers and Trustees:* R. Noel Turner,* Pres.; Emma A. Minott, V.P.; June S. Hallowell,* Secy.; W. Scott Pickard,* Treas.; Frank Gerome, Exec. Dir.; and 23 additional trustees.
EIN: 231480672

63140
Zimmerman Heimbach Foundation
56 E. Wall St.
Bethlehem, PA 18018-6009

Classified as a private operating foundation in 1984.
Financial data (yr. ended 12/31/00): Assets, $1,768,795 (M); grants paid, $112,500; gifts received, $365; expenditures, $144,920; qualifying distributions, $109,769.
Limitations: Applications not accepted. Giving primarily in PA.
Application information: Contributes only to pre-selected organizations.
Officers: George Z. Heimbach, Chair.; Elizabeth W. Heimbach, Vice-Chair.
Directors: John E. Freund III, Daniel E. Heimbach, David G. Heimbach.
EIN: 222493652
Codes: FD2

63141
James Hale Steinman Conestoga House Foundation
8 W. King St.
P.O. Box 128
Lancaster, PA 17608-0128

Classified as a private operating foundation in 1981.
Donor(s): The James Hale Steinman Foundation.
Financial data (yr. ended 12/31/01): Assets, $1,663,383 (M); grants paid, $0; gifts received, $462,506; expenditures, $462,506; qualifying distributions, $0.
Officers: Caroline S. Nunan, Pres.; Willis W. Shenk, V.P.; Dennis A. Getz, Secy.-Treas.
EIN: 232179646

63142
Graystone Society, Inc.
76 S. 1st Ave.
Coatesville, PA 19320

Financial data (yr. ended 12/31/01): Assets, $1,636,485 (M); grants paid, $0; gifts received, $117,336; expenditures, $108,996; qualifying distributions, $137,744; giving activities include $137,744 for programs.
Officers and Directors:* Wayne Ted Reed,* Chair.; Eugene L. DiOrio,* Pres.; Mary R. Sullivan,* Secy.; Susan H. Goldberg, Allyn Greeney, Barbara S. Huston, Scott G. Huston, Shirley Reiner, Geoffrey C. Roehrs.
EIN: 222601403

63143
The Foundation for Basic Cutaneous Research
210 W. Rittenhouse Sq., Apt. 3302
Philadelphia, PA 19103-5780
Contact: Lorraine H. Kligman, Ph.D., Pres.

Established in 1987 in PA.
Donor(s): Ortho Pharmaceutical, Ajinomoto U.S.A., Inc., Clairol-Gelb Foundation, Hoechst Co., Johnson & Johnson Baby Products, Lever Bros. Co., The Upjohn Co.
Financial data (yr. ended 07/31/01): Assets, $1,635,004 (M); grants paid, $465,350; gifts received, $363,000; expenditures, $794,377; qualifying distributions, $477,350.
Limitations: Giving on a national basis.
Officer: Lorraine H. Kligman, Ph.D., Pres.
EIN: 232439001
Codes: FD, GTI

63144
Danowsky-Reeds Memorial Fund
c/o Wachovia Bank
12 E. Market St.
York, PA 17401
Contact: Brenton Hake, V.P.

Established in 1998 in PA.
Financial data (yr. ended 12/31/01): Assets, $1,599,178 (M); grants paid, $88,350; expenditures, $107,903; qualifying distributions, $88,084.
Limitations: Applications not accepted. Giving primarily in Snyder County, PA.
Trustee: First Union National Bank.
EIN: 236829035
Codes: FD2

63145
Primitive Hall Foundation
76 S. 1st Ave.
Coatesville, PA 19320-3718

Classified as a private operating foundation in 1972.
Financial data (yr. ended 12/31/00): Assets, $1,563,754 (M); grants paid, $0; gifts received, $47,968; expenditures, $42,570; qualifying distributions, $42,570; giving activities include $42,570 for programs.
Limitations: Applications not accepted.
Application information: Contributes only to pre-selected organizations.
Officers and Trustees:* J. Liddon Pennock, Jr.,* Chair.; Eugene L. DiOrio,* Pres.; Marshall W. Jenney, V.P. and Treas.; Mrs. Donald Van Tassell-Bauman,* V.P.; Mrs. Robert C. Scott,* Secy.; Charles P. Collings, Charles L. Huston III, Charles L. Huston IV, Paul Rodebaugh, and 5 additional directors.
EIN: 231601358

63146
Manchester Supportive Housing, Inc.
1215 Hulton Rd.
Oakmont, PA 15139

Established in 1997.
Donor(s): U.S. Housing & Urban Devel.
Financial data (yr. ended 12/31/00): Assets, $1,482,021 (M); grants paid, $0; gifts received, $260; expenditures, $185,451; qualifying distributions, $65,583; giving activities include $185,451 for programs.
Officers and Directors:* Dr. Mattei,* Pres.; Paul Winkler,* V.P.; Holly Winters,* Secy.; James Pfeiffer,* Treas.; Cynthia Klemanski.
EIN: 251662399
Codes: TN

63147
The Link Family Foundation
Box 404, HC 88
Pocono Lake, PA 18347-9612

Donor(s): Alfred H. Link, Elizabeth P. Link.
Financial data (yr. ended 12/31/99): Assets, $1,450,058 (M); grants paid, $75,500; expenditures, $79,918; qualifying distributions, $75,500.
Limitations: Applications not accepted. Giving limited to PA.
Application information: Contributes only to pre-selected organizations.
Officers and Trustees:* Elizabeth P. Link,* Pres.; Alfred H. Link,* Secy.-Treas.; Paul M. Hannan, Gary C. Link, Stephen C. Link.
EIN: 237647088
Codes: FD2

63148
Phillip H. Wimmer and Betty L. Wimmer Family Foundation
1806 Frick Bldg.
Pittsburgh, PA 15219
Contact: Edward I. Goldberg, Tr.

Established in 1997 in PA.
Donor(s): Betty L. Wimmer.‡
Financial data (yr. ended 12/31/00): Assets, $1,427,929 (M); grants paid, $10,000; gifts received, $915,800; expenditures, $11,648; qualifying distributions, $10,000.

Limitations: Giving primarily in PA.
Application information: Application form not required.
Trustee: Edwin I. Goldberg.
EIN: 251795161

63149
Charles C. Knox Home
718 Sussex Ave.
Wynnewood, PA 19096

Donor(s): Charles C. Knox.‡
Financial data (yr. ended 12/31/99): Assets, $1,371,141 (M); grants paid, $0; gifts received, $196,569; expenditures, $479,552; qualifying distributions, $479,115; giving activities include $267,938 for programs.
Officers: Howard L. West, Jr., Pres.; Barbara L. Bailey, Secy.; Robert Latshaw, Treas.
EIN: 231352347

63150
The Maronda Foundation
202 Park West Dr.
Pittsburgh, PA 15275 (412) 788-7400
Contact: William J. Wolf, Exec. Dir.

Established in 1979.
Donor(s): William J. Wolf.
Financial data (yr. ended 12/31/00): Assets, $1,358,570 (M); grants paid, $569,580; expenditures, $1,314,127; qualifying distributions, $1,281,502; giving activities include $711,922 for programs.
Limitations: Giving primarily in PA.
Officer: William J. Wolf, Exec. Dir.
Director: Timothy O'Sullivan.
EIN: 251386730
Codes: FD

63151
Robert M. and Mary Haythornthwaite Foundation
313 Wellington Terr.
Jenkintown, PA 19046-3831

Classified as a private operating foundation in 1986.
Donor(s): Mary Haythornthwaite, M.D., Robert M. Haythornthwaite.
Financial data (yr. ended 12/31/01): Assets, $1,357,022 (M); grants paid, $0; gifts received, $33,600; expenditures, $59,595; qualifying distributions, $0.
Officers: Robert M. Haythornthwaite, Pres.; Mary Haythornthwaite, M.D., Secy.-Treas.
Directors: S.I. Hayek, D.R. Jenkins.
EIN: 232354559

63152
Gitt-Moul Historic Properties
120 Eichelberger St.
Hanover, PA 17331

Established in 1979 in PA.
Donor(s): Marion Rebert.
Financial data (yr. ended 10/31/00): Assets, $1,347,525 (M); grants paid, $0; expenditures, $99,119; qualifying distributions, $62,239; giving activities include $62,687 for programs.
Officers: Bruce Rebert, V.P.; Marion Rebert, Secy.-Treas.
Director: James Roth.
EIN: 232116654

63153
Richland Library Company
c/o R.D. Henry
P.O. Box 499
Quakertown, PA 18951-0499

Financial data (yr. ended 04/30/00): Assets, $1,323,358 (M); grants paid, $0; gifts received, $37; expenditures, $25,137; qualifying distributions, $25,097; giving activities include $25,137 for programs.
Officers: Judith M. Leister, Secy.; Rodney D. Henry, Treas.
Directors: Peggy H. Adams, Ann Hellman, Janenne J. Henry, Ellen L. Schroy, Mehlon Shelley.
EIN: 232263032

63154
Eldred World War II Museum
210 Main St.
Eldred, PA 16731

Established in 1995.
Donor(s): T.M. Roudebush.
Financial data (yr. ended 12/31/00): Assets, $1,294,777 (M); grants paid, $0; gifts received, $126,774; expenditures, $139,488; qualifying distributions, $166,916.
Officers: T.M. Roudebush, Chair.; Pete McDonald, Vice Chair.; Sara Wallace, Secy.; Ruth Roudebush, Treas.
Directors: Robert A. Anderson, John Ash, Carl Closs, Marjorie Fowler, Millie Gerringer, John Todd, and 12 additional directors.
EIN: 251777886

63155
Trumbower Hospital Foundation
124 Belvidere St.
Nazareth, PA 18064-2105
Application address: P.O. Box 57, Nazareth, PA 18064, tel.: (610) 759-1420

Established in 1977.
Financial data (yr. ended 10/31/01): Assets, $1,280,332 (M); grants paid, $72,713; expenditures, $89,408; qualifying distributions, $79,844.
Limitations: Giving primarily in the Nazareth, PA, area.
Officers: Richard W. Kraemer, Pres.; Helen Ziegler, Secy.; Susan Rundle, Treas.
EIN: 237377310

63156
Hoffman Fund-Warren County Commissioners
c/o Warren County Courthouse
Market and 4th Aves.
Warren, PA 16365-1716 (814) 728-4300

Classified as a private operating foundation in 1974.
Financial data (yr. ended 12/31/99): Assets, $1,173,659 (M); grants paid, $6,950; expenditures, $23,412; qualifying distributions, $14,625; giving activities include $14,625 for programs.
Trustees: Howard Brush, Richard Campbell, Robert Williams.
EIN: 250974307

63157
Elmer S. and Frances R. Christ Scholarship Fund
c/o Union Bank & Trust Co.
121 N. Progress Ave.
Pottsville, PA 17901 (570) 622-9528
Contact: Bert R. Cramer, Trust Off., V.P., Union Bank & Trust Co.

Established in 1987 in PA.

Financial data (yr. ended 12/31/01): Assets, $1,170,386 (M); grants paid, $46,250; expenditures, $54,632; qualifying distributions, $46,029.
Limitations: Giving limited to residents of the Pottsville, PA area.
Application information: Application form required.
Directors: Bert R. Cramer, Rev. Ronald V. Jankaitis, Jr., Michael J. Mazzuca, David Rattigan, Charles R. Wagner.
EIN: 232534508
Codes: GTI

63158
Robert and Esther Grove Foundation
c/o Robert H. Grove
57 W. Fayette St.
Mercersburg, PA 17236

Established in 1993.
Donor(s): Robert H. Grove, Esther L. Grove.
Financial data (yr. ended 10/31/00): Assets, $1,160,391 (M); grants paid, $0; gifts received, $1,037,966; expenditures, $8,105; qualifying distributions, $8,105; giving activities include $8,105 for programs.
Directors: Esther L. Grove, Robert H. Grove.
EIN: 251743674

63159
Scholarship Foundation of Erie Scottish Rite
P.O. Box 1364
Erie, PA 16512
Application address: P.O. Box 1364, Erie, PA 16512, tel.: (814) 866-5382
Contact: Harold A. Durst, Treas.

Established in 1993 in PA.
Financial data (yr. ended 07/31/02): Assets, $1,120,087 (M); grants paid, $74,500; gifts received, $62,585; expenditures, $75,658; qualifying distributions, $68,941.
Limitations: Giving limited to residents of northwest PA.
Application information: Applicant must include SAT scores and transcripts.
Officers and Trustees:* Merle E. Wood,* Pres.; Robert W. Lawson,* Secy.; Harold A. Durst,* Treas.
EIN: 251710223
Codes: GTI

63160
Holy Spirit Radio Foundation, Inc.
c/o Dale H. Meier
P.O. Box 798
Doylestown, PA 18901-0798

Established in 1998 in PA.
Donor(s): Dale W. Meier, Jane C. Meier.
Financial data (yr. ended 06/30/00): Assets, $1,098,523 (M); grants paid, $0; gifts received, $229,023; expenditures, $183,281; qualifying distributions, $118,135; giving activities include $117,331 for programs.
Officers: Dale W. Meier, Pres.; Jane C. Meier, Secy.-Treas.
Directors: J. Walter Kisling, Donald T. Meier, Patricia K. Meier.
EIN: 232981164

63161
Colker Family Foundation
c/o Robert S. Grodinsky
1 S. Penn Sq.
Philadelphia, PA 19107

Established in 1995.
Donor(s): David A. Colker, Jean S. Colker.
Financial data (yr. ended 12/31/99): Assets, $1,015,433 (M); grants paid, $49,500; gifts

63161—PENNSYLVANIA

received, $104,619; expenditures, $53,552; qualifying distributions, $51,462.
Limitations: Applications not accepted. Giving primarily in FL and PA.
Application information: Contributes only to pre-selected organizations.
Trustees: David A. Colker, Jean S. Colker, Robert S. Grodinsky.
EIN: 232818637

63162
Anne & Philip Glatfelter III Family Foundation
c/o Hershey Trust Co.
100 Mansion Rd. E.
Hershey, PA 17033
Application address: c/o Lise M. Shehan, V.P., Hershey Trust Co., P.O. Box 445, Hershey, PA 17033, tel.: (717) 534-3225

Established in 2001 in PA.
Donor(s): Anne M. Glatfelter Charitable Lead Trust.
Financial data (yr. ended 12/31/01): Assets, $1,012,951 (M); grants paid, $0; gifts received, $1,012,951; expenditures, $0; qualifying distributions, $0.
Limitations: Giving limited to southeastern PA.
Application information: Application form required.
Officer: Elizabeth Glatfelter, Pres.
Director: Patricia G. Foulkrod.
EIN: 233094915

63163
Associated Production Services, Inc.
325 Andrews Rd.
Trevose, PA 19053

Financial data (yr. ended 06/30/01): Assets, $1,008,520 (M); grants paid, $0; gifts received, $1,146,160; expenditures, $1,160,311; qualifying distributions, $0.
Officers and Directors:* Jonathan Belding,* Pres.; Barbara Belding,* V.P.; Dennis Garot, Caroline Long, Stella Matyzak, Dave McBride, Judy Warton.
EIN: 232046541

63164
Gray Family Foundation
c/o First Commonwealth Trust Co.
P.O. Box 1046
DuBois, PA 15801

Established in 1988 in PA.
Financial data (yr. ended 12/31/01): Assets, $1,002,947 (M); grants paid, $73,200; gifts received, $155,621; expenditures, $82,349; qualifying distributions, $81,739.
Limitations: Applications not accepted. Giving primarily in DuBois, PA.
Application information: Contributes only to pre-selected organizations.
Trustees: Kathleen Gray Braun, Catherine E. Gray, Elizabeth Gray, Jason S. Gray, Jr., First Commonwealth Trust Co.
EIN: 256311915

63165
Glatfelter Memorial Field Trust
951 Chestnut St.
Columbia, PA 17512

Classified as a private operating foundation in 1973.
Financial data (yr. ended 12/31/99): Assets, $1,002,139 (M); grants paid, $0; gifts received, $9,117; expenditures, $7,330; qualifying distributions, $7,329.
Officer and Trustees:* Philip H. Glatfelter II,* Secy.-Treas.; Andy E. Ohrel, Jr., Garlan J. Kise, Kevin M. Kraft, Sr., M. Robert Kuhn.

EIN: 231640626

63166
John A. Hermann, Jr. Memorial Art Museum
c/o R.E. Nichols
188 Greenwood Ave.
Pittsburgh, PA 15202

Financial data (yr. ended 12/31/00): Assets, $989,585 (M); grants paid, $0; gifts received, $15,749; expenditures, $24,525; qualifying distributions, $48,566; giving activities include $24,525 for programs.
Officer: Robert E. Nichols, Treas. and Exec. Dir.
Trustees: Donald F. Gust, Laura N. Irvin, William M. Koltek, William J. Penberthy, Ella Reshko.
EIN: 250974305

63167
Overlook Estate Foundation, Inc.
P.O. Box 225
Dalton, PA 18414
Application address: 71 Lewis St., Greenwich, CT 06830
Contact: Mortimer B. Fuller III, Pres.

Classified as a private operating foundation in 1998.
Donor(s): Frances A. Fuller.
Financial data (yr. ended 12/31/00): Assets, $937,934 (M); grants paid, $43,362; gifts received, $52,278; expenditures, $57,690; qualifying distributions, $57,488.
Application information: Application form not required.
Officers: Mortimer B. Fuller III, Pres.; Patricia A. Fuller, Secy. and Exec. Dir.; Frances Gunster, Treas.
EIN: 161526226

63168
Mountville Community Services Foundation
350 W. Main St.
P.O. Box 94
Mountville, PA 17554

Classified as a private operating foundation in 1982.
Financial data (yr. ended 12/31/00): Assets, $932,297 (M); grants paid, $0; gifts received, $30,135; expenditures, $130,532; qualifying distributions, $20,732; giving activities include $130,532 for programs.
Officers: Ronald E. Wachob, Pres.; John Henry, V.P.; David Price, Treas.
Directors: Richard Hynicka, Robert Keck.
EIN: 232186825

63169
Grice Clearfield Community Museum
RR 2, Box 47A
Clearfield, PA 16830

Established in 1991 in PA.
Donor(s): Janet M. Grice, Lynn Grice.
Financial data (yr. ended 03/31/01): Assets, $887,540 (M); grants paid, $0; gifts received, $6,000; expenditures, $50,235; qualifying distributions, $39,455; giving activities include $54,082 for programs.
Officers: Lynn Grice, Pres.; Thomas L. Grice, V.P.; Janet M. Grice, Secy.; William L. Morgan, Treas.
EIN: 251676341

63170
G. Basila Scholarship Fund
P.O. Box 1383
Scranton, PA 18501 (570) 342-2676
Contact: Joseph A. Karam, Tr.

Donor(s): Gladys Basila.
Financial data (yr. ended 12/31/00): Assets, $873,285 (M); grants paid, $51,966; gifts

received, $150,000; expenditures, $58,996; qualifying distributions, $51,546.
Limitations: Giving limited to residents of PA.
Application information: Application form required.
Trustee: Joseph A. Karam.
EIN: 232614309
Codes: GTI

63171
Streitwieser Foundation Historic Trumpet Collection
P.O. Box 297
Downingtown, PA 19335

Donor(s): Franz X. Streitwieser.
Financial data (yr. ended 06/30/00): Assets, $865,931 (M); grants paid, $1,000; gifts received, $159,990; expenditures, $2,890; qualifying distributions, $1,914.
Limitations: Applications not accepted.
Application information: Contributes only to pre-selected organizations.
Officers and Directors:* Franz X. Streitwieser,* Pres.; Ralph T. Dudgeon,* V.P. and Secy.; Heinz Preiss, V.P., European Affairs; Katharine Streitwieser,* Treas.; Alois Aigner, Berthold Antoniuk, Pater Mandorfer, Georg Starzer, Donald Zucker.
EIN: 232088136

63172
Matthew S. Mawhinney Charitable Trust
P.O. Box 311
Indian Head, PA 15446-0311

Classified as a private operating trust in 1974.
Donor(s): Warren C. Mawhinney.
Financial data (yr. ended 12/31/01): Assets, $859,377 (M); grants paid, $0; gifts received, $4,926; expenditures, $8,417; qualifying distributions, $0.
Officer and Trustees:* Warren C. Mawhinney,* Mgr.; Matthew W. Mawhinney, Michael G. Mawhinney.
EIN: 237414817

63173
The Douglas O. and Gail S. Tozour Foundation
741 1st Ave.
King of Prussia, PA 19406

Donor(s): Douglas O. Tozour.
Financial data (yr. ended 12/31/01): Assets, $816,624 (M); grants paid, $74,005; gifts received, $100,000; expenditures, $76,713; qualifying distributions, $76,713.
Limitations: Applications not accepted. Giving on a national basis.
Application information: Contributes only to pre-selected organizations.
Trustees: Douglas O. Tozour, Gail Tozour.
EIN: 222779208

63174
Grant M. Brown Memorial Foundation
c/o Barbra Barker-Brown
2200 Spyglass Hill
Center Valley, PA 18034-8913

Established in 1994.
Donor(s): Barbra Barker-Brown.
Financial data (yr. ended 08/31/01): Assets, $813,472 (M); grants paid, $33,331; gifts received, $1,275; expenditures, $65,045; qualifying distributions, $64,584.
Limitations: Applications not accepted. Giving primarily in PA.
Application information: Contributes only to pre-selected organizations.
Trustee: Barbra Barker-Brown.

EIN: 232805616

63175
Rolling Ridge Foundation, Inc.
c/o Alan Reeve Hunt
123 S. Broad St.
Philadelphia, PA 19102

Classified as a private operating foundation in 1979.
Financial data (yr. ended 12/31/99): Assets, $810,980 (M); grants paid, $0; expenditures, $12,085; qualifying distributions, $12,085.
Officers: Alan Reeve Hunt, Pres.; Montague Kern, V.P.; Verle Headings, Secy.; Phillip Paschall, Treas.
Directors: Dorothy Creswell, Cushing Dolbeare, Edward M. Leonard, Lella R. Smith, Fred Taylor, William L. Webber, and 8 additional directors.
EIN: 521047462

63176
York Catholic High School Student Aid and Endowment Fund
601 E. Springettsbury Ave.
York, PA 17403-2896

Donor(s): R. Gleitz, Mrs. R. Gleitz.
Financial data (yr. ended 12/31/99): Assets, $779,035 (M); grants paid, $45,375; gifts received, $81,481; expenditures, $47,369; qualifying distributions, $45,375.
Limitations: Giving primarily in York, PA.
Application information: Application form required.
Officers and Directors:* Rev. Nicholas C. Dattilo, D.D.,* Chair.; George E. Andrews, Jr.,* Pres.; Samuel Spiese,* V.P.; Joseph F. Banks,* Secy.; Robert Angelo, Leo Gribbin, Elizabeth A. Pioli.
EIN: 232047570
Codes: TN

63177
Visiting Nurse Association Foundation of Lebanon County
P.O. Box 1203
Lebanon, PA 17042
Application address: 2015 Kline Ave., Lebanon, PA 17042
Contact: Edgar Miller, Pres.

Financial data (yr. ended 06/30/01): Assets, $774,566 (M); grants paid, $17,667; expenditures, $24,393; qualifying distributions, $17,667.
Limitations: Giving limited to Lebanon County, PA.
Officers: Edgar Miller, Pres.; Margaret Fava, V.P.; Sandy Mejics, Secy.; Denise Johnson, Treas.
EIN: 231365981

63178
Arthur M. Kaplan Foundation
220 Spruce St.
Philadelphia, PA 19106
Contact: Arthur M. Kaplan, Pres.

Established in 1999 in PA.
Donor(s): Arthur M. Kaplan.
Financial data (yr. ended 09/30/01): Assets, $761,509 (M); grants paid, $82,000; gifts received, $105,150; expenditures, $85,711; qualifying distributions, $85,686.
Limitations: Giving primarily in NY and PA.
Officers and Director:* Arthur M. Kaplan,* Pres. and Treas.; Duane R. Perry, Secy.
EIN: 233022162
Codes: FD2

63179
Tour-Ed Mine & Museum
214 Primrose Dr.
Sarver, PA 16055-9573

Classified as a private operating foundation in 1989.
Donor(s): Ira R. Wood.
Financial data (yr. ended 12/31/00): Assets, $742,361 (M); grants paid, $0; gifts received, $20,000; expenditures, $65,356; qualifying distributions, $65,356; giving activities include $65,356 for programs.
Officers and Trustees:* Ira R. Wood,* Pres.; Raymond J. Woodall, V.P. and Mgr.; Nick Giovannelli,* V.P.; Aylmer Girdwood,* V.P.; Edgar H. Paul,* Treas.
EIN: 251565162

63180
The Sylvania Foundation
c/o Charles Eugene Waite
317 Mack Rd.
West Sunbury, PA 16061

Classified as a private operating foundation in 1988.
Donor(s): Charles Eugene Waite.
Financial data (yr. ended 12/31/01): Assets, $733,140 (M); grants paid, $0; gifts received, $88,000; expenditures, $37,936; qualifying distributions, $0.
Director: Charles Eugene Waite.
EIN: 251529599

63181
The Conill Institute for Chronic Illness
655 Marsten Green Ct.
Ambler, PA 19002

Established in 1997 in PA.
Donor(s): Alicia Conill.
Financial data (yr. ended 12/31/00): Assets, $727,955 (M); grants paid, $7,950; gifts received, $287,855; expenditures, $95,210; qualifying distributions, $78,949; giving activities include $26,897 for programs.
Limitations: Applications not accepted.
Application information: Contributes only to pre-selected organizations.
Officer and Director:* Alicia M. Conill, M.D.,* Chair.
EIN: 311485049

63182
The Phyllis Recca Foundation
816 Brookwood Ln.
Bryn Mawr, PA 19010

Donor(s): Phyllis Recca.
Financial data (yr. ended 06/30/01): Assets, $688,718 (M); grants paid, $22,945; gifts received, $379,750; expenditures, $30,945; qualifying distributions, $30,945.
Limitations: Applications not accepted. Giving primarily in Philadelphia, PA.
Application information: Contributes only to pre-selected organizations.
Officers: Phyllis Recca, Pres.; Susan Lee, Secy.
Director: Dianne Kennedy.
EIN: 383503546

63183
Josiah W., Elizabeth M. & Charles M. Gitt Memorial Library Trust
P.O. Box 303
Hanover, PA 17331

Established in 1996 in PA.
Donor(s): Cynthia E. Gitt, Susan G. Gordon, Marian G. Rebert.
Financial data (yr. ended 06/30/01): Assets, $675,898 (M); grants paid, $0; gifts received, $58,833; expenditures, $104,617; qualifying distributions, $64,034; giving activities include $47,822 for programs.
Trustees: Cynthia E. Gitt, Susan G. Gordon, Marian G. Rebert.
EIN: 237832246

63184
Walnut Acres Foundation, Inc.
c/o Paul K. Keene
P.O. Box 268
Penns Creek, PA 17862-0268

Donor(s): Enid Betty Keene,‡ Paul K. Keene.
Financial data (yr. ended 11/30/99): Assets, $663,949 (M); grants paid, $29,283; gifts received, $55,354; expenditures, $226,437; qualifying distributions, $71,861.
Limitations: Applications not accepted. Giving primarily in NY.
Application information: Contributes only to pre-selected organizations.
Officers: Paul K. Keene, Pres.; Irvin Graybill, Jr., Secy.; Emma J. Mattern, Treas.
EIN: 236298390

63185
Joan Bieberson McDonald Charitable Trust Memorial Scholarship Fund for Wheeling Park High School
c/o Richard J. Federowicz
2 PPG Pl., Ste. 400
Pittsburgh, PA 15222
Application address: c/o Guidance Dept., Wheeling Park High School, Wheeling, WV

Established in 2000 in WV.
Donor(s): Frank E. McDonald.
Financial data (yr. ended 09/30/01): Assets, $658,072 (M); grants paid, $26,000; gifts received, $752,505; expenditures, $26,080; qualifying distributions, $26,000.
Limitations: Giving primarily in Wheeling, WV.
Application information: Application form required.
Trustees: S. Jane Anderson, Susan Krukowski, James R. Shockley, Nancy L. Wilson.
EIN: 546478362

63186
Ecosystems Technology Transfer, Inc.
3500 W. Chester Pike, Ste. 129
Newtown Square, PA 19073-4101

Established in 1999 in PA.
Donor(s): Christian J. Lambertsen.
Financial data (yr. ended 12/31/00): Assets, $624,918 (M); grants paid, $21,000; gifts received, $105,450; expenditures, $23,500; qualifying distributions, $23,503.
Limitations: Applications not accepted. Giving primarily in PA.
Application information: Contributes only to pre-selected organizations.
Officer: Christian J. Lambertsen, Pres.
EIN: 232619483

63187
Albert M. Kligman Charitable Foundation
1700 Market St., Ste. 29
Philadelphia, PA 19103

Established in 1995 in PA.
Donor(s): Albert M. Kligman, Lorraine H. Kligman.
Financial data (yr. ended 05/31/01): Assets, $611,622 (M); grants paid, $90,000; expenditures, $116,888; qualifying distributions, $89,434.
Limitations: Applications not accepted. Giving primarily in PA.

63187—PENNSYLVANIA

Application information: Contributes only to pre-selected organizations.
Officers: Albert M. Kligman, Pres.; Lorraine H. Kligman, V.P.; Elliott P. Footer, Secy.-Treas.
EIN: 232812009

63188
Morrissey Family Foundation
1700 Market St., Ste. 1420
Philadelphia, PA 19103-3913

Established in 1997 in PA.
Financial data (yr. ended 12/31/01): Assets, $607,267 (M); grants paid, $55,300; expenditures, $56,586; qualifying distributions, $55,184.
Limitations: Applications not accepted. Giving primarily in Gettysburg, PA.
Application information: Contributes only to pre-selected organizations.
Officers: Maryanne D. Morrissey, Pres.; Joseph C. Morrissey, V.P.; Jane M. Morrissey, Secy.
EIN: 232870762

63189
Historic Sugartown, Inc.
697 Sugartown Rd.
Malvern, PA 19355

Established in 1984 in PA.
Financial data (yr. ended 12/31/99): Assets, $576,813 (M); grants paid, $0; gifts received, $1,381; expenditures, $95,077; qualifying distributions, $24,512; giving activities include $38,006 for programs.
Officers: James M. Caldwell, Jr., Pres.; John C. Nagy, V.P.; Marilyn Taylor, Secy.; Penelope Wilson, Treas.
Directors: Dale H. Frens, Robert T. Lange, Jr., Joseph LeBresco, Peg Nagy, and 5 additional directors.
EIN: 232215382

63190
Jacqueline B. Nein Charitable Trust
c/o Boyd & Karver
7 E. Philadelphia Ave.
Boyertown, PA 19512

Established in 2000.
Donor(s): Jacqueline B. Nein.‡
Financial data (yr. ended 08/31/01): Assets, $551,423 (M); grants paid, $0; gifts received, $597,683; expenditures, $99; qualifying distributions, $99.
Limitations: Applications not accepted.
Application information: Contributes only to pre-selected organizations.
Trustees: Gail Hesser, Patricia Mitchell.
EIN: 311715337

63191
Verneda A. Wachter and Leo J. Wachter, Sr. Foundation
c/o Moses, Johnson & Assocs., C.P.A.
412 Union St.
Hollidaysburg, PA 16648-1518
Application address: R.R. No. 3, Orrick Rd., Kirksville, MO 63501
Contact: Therese A. Ream, Pres.

Established in 1985 in PA.
Financial data (yr. ended 12/31/00): Assets, $531,013 (M); grants paid, $24,470; expenditures, $26,434; qualifying distributions, $26,434.
Limitations: Giving primarily to residents of Blair County, PA.
Officers: Therese A. Ream, Pres.; David Ream, V.P.; Brian Wachter, Secy.; David E. Moses, Treas.
EIN: 251531899
Codes: GTI

63192
Wagman Foundation
2508 Grant Rd.
Broomall, PA 19008-1644

Financial data (yr. ended 11/30/01): Assets, $499,400 (M); grants paid, $25,500; expenditures, $30,840; qualifying distributions, $25,432.
Limitations: Applications not accepted. Giving primarily in Philadelphia, PA.
Application information: Contributes only to pre-selected organizations.
Trustees: Lowell H. Dubrow, Lee Harrison, Mark Harrison, Susan Harrison.
EIN: 236267200

63193
William E. and Margaret N. Bush Memorial Scholarship Fund
P.O. Box 247
Apollo, PA 15613

Established in 1999 in PA.
Donor(s): Margaret Bush, William Bush.
Financial data (yr. ended 12/31/00): Assets, $495,728 (M); grants paid, $18,350; expenditures, $22,323; qualifying distributions, $18,230.
Limitations: Giving primarily to residents of Pittsburgh, PA.
Trustees: Henry Fulton, Jr., Apollo Trust Co.
EIN: 251814240

63194
Eleanore L. Matey Foundation, Inc.
911 N. Easton Rd.
P.O. Box 209
Willow Grove, PA 19090
Application address: c/o Lower Makefield Corp. Center III, 1020 Stony Hill Rd., Ste. 150, Yardley, PA 19067-5533, tel.: (267) 685-4215
Contact: Frank Weckenman, Pres.

Established in 2001 in PA.
Financial data (yr. ended 12/31/01): Assets, $491,870 (M); grants paid, $13,000; expenditures, $15,614; qualifying distributions, $13,000.
Limitations: Giving primarily in PA.
Officers: Frank Weckenman, Pres.; Robert Weckenman, V.P.
EIN: 233050096

63195
The Scrub Foundation
1314 Chestnut St., Ste. 750
Philadelphia, PA 19107

Established as a company sponsored operating foundation in 200.
Donor(s): Scrub Trust, Samuel C. Stretton, Robert Jaffe, Commerce Bank, N.A., Gray Smith, Ann Butchart.
Financial data (yr. ended 12/31/00): Assets, $491,852 (M); grants paid, $0; gifts received, $70,954; expenditures, $68,204; qualifying distributions, $61,300; giving activities include $68,204 for programs.
Officer: Mary Tracy, Exec. Dir.
EIN: 233038328

63196
The Jackson Family Foundation
c/o Frank W. Jackson
423 N. 21st. St., Ste. 100
Camp Hill, PA 17011-2207

Established in 1999 in PA.
Donor(s): Frank W. Jackson, M.D., Toquaiah J. Carter, C. Bisque Jacksin, F. Wilson Jackson, M.D., Monique J. Silvi, M. Quenby Jackson.
Financial data (yr. ended 12/31/00): Assets, $484,820 (M); grants paid, $0; gifts received, $95,000; expenditures, $26,897; qualifying distributions, $147,205; giving activities include $19,661 for programs.
Limitations: Applications not accepted.
Application information: Contributes only to pre-selected organizations.
Officers and Directors:* Frank W. Jackson, M.D.,* Pres.; Toquaiah J. Carter,* Secy.-Treas.; C. Bisque Jackson, F. Wilson Jackson, M.D., M. Quenby Jackson, Monique J. Silvi.
EIN: 251832451

63197
Susquehanna Foundation
401 City Line Ave., Ste. 220
Bala Cynwyd, PA 19004

Donor(s): Eric Brooks, Arthur Datnchik, Andrew Frost, Joel Greenberg, Jeffrey Yass.
Financial data (yr. ended 12/31/01): Assets, $477,770 (M); grants paid, $1,636,500; gifts received, $100,000; expenditures, $1,636,625; qualifying distributions, $1,726,227.
Limitations: Applications not accepted.
Application information: Contributes only to pre-selected organizations.
Officers: Arthur Dantchik, Pres.; Eric Brooks, V.P.; Andrew Frost, V.P.; Jeffrey Yass, V.P.; Joel Greenberg, Secy.; Brian Sullivan, Treas.
EIN: 232732477

63198
Nursing Foundation of Pennsylvania
P.O. Box 68525
Harrisburg, PA 17106-8525
Contact: Jessie Rohner

Established in 1984 in PA.
Financial data (yr. ended 06/30/00): Assets, $471,783 (M); grants paid, $750; gifts received, $1,197; expenditures, $247,587; qualifying distributions, $259,529; giving activities include $67,576 for programs.
Limitations: Giving limited to PA.
Application information: Application form not required.
Officers: Helen J. Streubert, Pres.; Susan A. Albrecht, V.P.; Jean Blair, Treas.
Trustees: Gail Ann Deluca Havens, Frieda Outlaw, Elizabeth Wagner, Elizabeth Walls.
EIN: 222479246

63199
Waynesboro Beneficial Fund Association
323 E. Main St.
Waynesboro, PA 17268-1638
Application address: c/o Waynesboro Area Senior High School, Waynesboro Scholarship Loan Comm., P.O. Box 168, Waynesboro, PA 17268

Financial data (yr. ended 10/31/01): Assets, $470,726 (M); grants paid, $18,323; expenditures, $33,136; qualifying distributions, $18,323; giving activities include $5,809 for programs.
Limitations: Giving limited to Waynesboro, PA.
Application information: Application form required.
Officers and Directors:* Louis Barlup,* Pres.; Robert Davis,* V.P.; Carol L. Henicle,* Secy.-Treas.; John Blubaugh, Valerie Dick, Joel Fridgen, Rev. Richard Seaks, William Shull, Robert Ternes, Sarah Zimmerman.
EIN: 236279080

63200
Hawbaker Nature Trust, Inc.
4003 Mercersburg Rd.
Mercersburg, PA 17236-9674

Established in 1991 in PA.

Financial data (yr. ended 06/30/02): Assets, $464,023 (M); grants paid, $0; gifts received, $315; expenditures, $11,334; qualifying distributions, $0.
Officers: Randall E. Eigenbrode, Pres.; Thomas J. Finucane, Secy.
EIN: 251680002

63201
Irene Mae Wright Charitable Trust
c/o Fulton Financial Advisors, N.A.
P.O. Box 3215
Lancaster, PA 17604-3215

Established in 1995 in PA.
Financial data (yr. ended 12/31/00): Assets, $447,815 (M); grants paid, $20,940; expenditures, $26,624; qualifying distributions, $24,682.
Limitations: Applications not accepted. Giving primarily in PA.
Application information: Contributes only to pre-selected organizations.
Trustee: Fulton Financial Advisors, N.A.
EIN: 237777912

63202
Joan B. and Frank E. McDonald Charitable Trust Memorial Scholarship Fund for Weir High School
c/o Richard J. Federowicz
2 PPG Pl., Ste. 400
Pittsburgh, PA 15222

Established in 2000 in WV.
Donor(s): Frank E. McDonald.
Financial data (yr. ended 09/30/01): Assets, $438,616 (M); grants paid, $16,750; gifts received, $519,094; expenditures, $16,830; qualifying distributions, $16,750.
Limitations: Giving limited to residents of Weirton, WV.
Application information: Application form required.
Trustees: Jane Anderson, Susan Krukowski, James R. Shockley, Nancy L. Wilson.
EIN: 546478360

63203
Erik T. Hostvedt Foundation
P.O. Box 285
Pipersville, PA 18947

Financial data (yr. ended 12/31/01): Assets, $416,959 (M); grants paid, $43,220; gifts received, $160,000; expenditures, $43,220; qualifying distributions, $43,122.
Limitations: Applications not accepted. Giving primarily in NC and PA.
Application information: Contributes only to pre-selected organizations.
Trustees: Erik T. Hostvedt, Jill C. Hostvedt.
EIN: 236847270

63204
The Foundation of the Society of the Sons of St. George
42 Brookmead Rd.
Wayne, PA 19087
Application addresses: scholarship c/o G. Tully Vaughan, 625 S. Bethlehme Pike, Ambler, PA 19002; distress casses c/o Raymond C. Collins, 2 E. Main St., Apt. A, Collegeville, PA 19426

Financial data (yr. ended 12/31/99): Assets, $390,081 (M); grants paid, $12,000; gifts received, $5,045; expenditures, $16,727; qualifying distributions, $13,670.
Limitations: Giving limited to PA.
Application information: Application form required.

Officers: G. Tully Vaughan, Pres.; Robert J. Bateman, Vice. Pres.; David B. Ermine, Secy.; Thorton G. Smith, Treas.
EIN: 222774346

63205
Avery Foundation
110 Commerce Dr.
Montgomeryville, PA 18936-0511
(215) 855-4336
Contact: William J. Avery, Tr.

Established in 1991 in PA.
Donor(s): William J. Avery.
Financial data (yr. ended 12/31/01): Assets, $387,280 (M); grants paid, $169,300; gifts received, $500,000; expenditures, $170,872; qualifying distributions, $170,814.
Limitations: Giving primarily in PA, with emphasis on Philadelphia.
Trustees: Sharon L. Avery, William J. Avery, Michelle L. Clark.
EIN: 232647387
Codes: FD2

63206
Goodfellow Fund
P.O. Box 135
Carversville, PA 18913

Established in 1999 in WA.
Donor(s): John Goodfellow.
Financial data (yr. ended 12/31/00): Assets, $377,877 (M); grants paid, $10,995; gifts received, $171,153; expenditures, $12,980; qualifying distributions, $10,995.
Limitations: Giving primarily in PA and WA.
Officer: John Goodfellow, Exec. Dir.
EIN: 912000453

63207
Rodale Working Tree Arborteum Society
c/o Ardath H. Rodale
2098 S. Cedar Crest Blvd.
Allentown, PA 18103-9627

Established in 1998 in PA.
Financial data (yr. ended 12/31/00): Assets, $373,791 (M); grants paid, $0; expenditures, $31,194; qualifying distributions, $0; giving activities include $30,886 for programs.
Limitations: Applications not accepted.
Application information: Contributes only to pre-selected organizations.
Officer: Ardath H. Rodale, Pres. and Secy.-Treas.
EIN: 232920754

63208
Fredric Rieders Family Renaissance Foundation
2850 Rushland Rd.
Rushland, PA 18956

Established in 1994.
Donor(s): Fredric Rieders.
Financial data (yr. ended 11/30/01): Assets, $357,407 (M); grants paid, $14,918; gifts received, $112,322; expenditures, $118,002; qualifying distributions, $100,448.
Limitations: Applications not accepted. Giving primarily in the Philadelphia, PA, area.
Application information: Contributes only to pre-selected organizations.
Trustees: Betty Jean Rieders, Eric Rieders, Fredric Rieders, Julia Rieders, Michael Rieders.
EIN: 237791533

63209
J.E.M. Classic Car Museum, Inc.
R.R. 1, Box 120C
Andreas, PA 18211

Established in 1991 in PA.

Donor(s): John E. Morgan.
Financial data (yr. ended 12/31/00): Assets, $347,120 (M); grants paid, $0; gifts received, $145,000; expenditures, $188,416; qualifying distributions, $0.
Officers: John E. Morgan, Pres.; Harry Loder, Exec. Dir.
EIN: 232673950

63210
Alpha Psi of Chi Psi Educational Trust
c/o Joseph A. McConnell
1150 Ashley Hill Rd.
Mansfield, PA 16933
Application address: 480 Brooktondale Rd., Brooktondale, NY 14817
Contact: David R. Dunlop, Pres.

Financial data (yr. ended 05/31/01): Assets, $343,610 (M); grants paid, $2,350; gifts received, $43,657; expenditures, $218,889; qualifying distributions, $218,686.
Limitations: Giving on a national basis.
Application information: Application form required.
Officers and Trustees:* David R. Dunlop,* Pres.; William A. Huling, Sr.,* V.P.; Joseph A. McConnell,* Secy.-Treas.
EIN: 156021424

63211
Reber Home
c/o First Union National Bank
P.O. Box 7558
Philadelphia, PA 19101-7558

Classified as a private operating foundation in 1983.
Donor(s): Reber Foundation.
Financial data (yr. ended 12/31/99): Assets, $335,949 (M); grants paid, $0; gifts received, $29,890; expenditures, $89,780; qualifying distributions, $65,359.
Trustees: Paul D. Heck, Joseph H. Jones, Ryland Lord, Ronald St. Clair, Joseph Straccia, First Union National Bank.
EIN: 232138688

63212
Olga & Dorothea Dessin Society for the Prevention of Cruelty to Animals
c/o Wayne Bank
717 Main St.
Honesdale, PA 18431

Classified as a private operating foundation in 1951.
Financial data (yr. ended 12/31/01): Assets, $330,899 (M); grants paid, $0; gifts received, $38,671; expenditures, $235,597; qualifying distributions, $143,053; giving activities include $143,053 for programs.
Officers: P.K. Placko, Pres.; Margaret Hunter, V.P.; Connie Gross, Recording Secy.
Directors: Laura DeSimone, Cathy Hunt, Joanne Kropf, Alice Pedone, Ivah Peeling, Amy Platko.
EIN: 246021279

63213
The Crary Art Gallery, Inc.
511 Market St.
Warren, PA 16365

Established in 1988 in PA.
Donor(s): Gene W. Crary Trust.
Financial data (yr. ended 12/31/99): Assets, $327,034 (M); grants paid, $0; gifts received, $25,510; expenditures, $31,132; qualifying distributions, $30,302; giving activities include $48,863 for programs.

63213—PENNSYLVANIA

Officers: Ann Lesser, Pres.; Adele Trantor, V.P.; Quinn Smith, Secy.; George Crozier, Treas.
Director: Calvert Crary.
EIN: 251584906

63214
Potter County Historical Society
308 N. Main St.
Coudersport, PA 16915-1626

Financial data (yr. ended 12/31/01): Assets, $310,803 (M); grants paid, $0; gifts received, $14,182; expenditures, $29,261; qualifying distributions, $20,947; giving activities include $16,142 for programs.
Officers: Robert K. Currin, Pres.; Francis Castano, V.P.; Lucille K. Church, Secy.-Treas.
EIN: 256065315

63215
Kensington Associates, Inc.
6084 Hillside Dr.
Bangor, PA 18013

Established in 1995.
Financial data (yr. ended 12/31/01): Assets, $298,154 (M); grants paid, $33,727; expenditures, $428,244; qualifying distributions, $43,489; giving activities include $37,801 for programs.
Officer: Earl K. Hayes, Pres.
Directors: Daniel McTiernan, Claude Shapelle, Katherine Trimarco.
EIN: 232623836

63216
The Academy of Science and Art of Pittsburgh
P.O. Box 58187
Pittsburgh, PA 15209-0187

Financial data (yr. ended 04/30/02): Assets, $287,465 (M); grants paid, $0; gifts received, $8,115; expenditures, $22,555; qualifying distributions, $0.
Officers and Trustees: Ursula Schmitt,* Pres.; Grant Shipley,* 1st V.P.; Robert Morgan,* 2nd V.P.; Patricia L. Caldwell,* Secy.; Mildred Yakopcic,* Treas.; Margaret Hoffman, Daniel R. McCauley, Bernard Miller, Evelyn Miller, Rich Noel, Terry Trees, and 5 additional trustees.
EIN: 256042376

63217
New Horizons Foundation, Inc.
145 New Horizons Dr.
Clymer, PA 15728

Classified as a private operating foundation in 1990.
Donor(s): Amy W. Lewis, H. Richard Lewis.
Financial data (yr. ended 12/31/01): Assets, $285,310 (M); grants paid, $250; gifts received, $7,411; expenditures, $22,374; qualifying distributions, $16,625.
Limitations: Applications not accepted. Giving primarily in PA.
Application information: Contributes only to pre-selected organizations.
Officers: H. Richard Lewis, Pres.; Amy W. Lewis, Secy.-Treas.
Directors: David Ray McCoy, Nina J. McCoy, Mary C. Murphy, Steven S. Murphy, Jeanne A. Myers, Taylor L. Myers.
EIN: 251594428

63218
Kensington Soup Society
1036 E. Crease St.
Philadelphia, PA 19125

Classified as a private operating foundation in 1984.

Financial data (yr. ended 10/31/99): Assets, $277,499 (M); grants paid, $0; gifts received, $4,687; expenditures, $17,147; qualifying distributions, $17,030; giving activities include $17,146 for programs.
Officers: James D.B. Weiss, Jr., Pres.; Elizabeth Quintavalle, V.P.; Sheralyn Dailey, Secy.; Keith Dailey, Treas.
EIN: 232237130

63219
Colonial Flying Corps Museum, Inc.
P.O. Box 484
Toughkenamon, PA 19374

Classified as a private operating foundation in 1974.
Financial data (yr. ended 06/30/01): Assets, $267,595 (M); grants paid, $0; gifts received, $55,120; expenditures, $42,923; qualifying distributions, $2,348; giving activities include $41,279 for programs.
Officers: Alexis I. DuPont, Pres.; Anne E. DuPont, V.P.; Everitt B. DuPont, V.P.
Director: Raymond F. Mason.
EIN: 511685135

63220
Edward & Minnie Kraftsow Foundation
c/o CBIZ Business Solutions, Inc.
121 S. Broad St., Ste. 400
Philadelphia, PA 19107-4518

Classified as a private operating foundation in 1986.
Financial data (yr. ended 12/31/01): Assets, $257,559 (M); grants paid, $25,000; expenditures, $25,321; qualifying distributions, $25,079.
Limitations: Applications not accepted. Giving primarily in FL; some giving also in Israel.
Application information: Contributes only to pre-selected organizations.
Trustees: Carolyn Kraftsow, Stanley Kraftsow.
EIN: 222676211

63221
Eisenhauer Scholarship Fund
(Formerly John Henry & Clarissa A. Eisenhauer, et al. Scholarship Fund)
403 E. Maple St.
Annville, PA 17003-1519
Application address: 347 N. 6th St., Lebanon, PA 17042-3612
Contact: Jane L. Kaylor, Tr.

Donor(s): Helene Eisenhauer.
Financial data (yr. ended 06/30/01): Assets, $255,674 (M); grants paid, $13,075; gifts received, $10,000; expenditures, $22,054; qualifying distributions, $15,215.
Limitations: Giving limited to residents of Lebanon County, PA.
Application information: Recommendation of high school principal or guidance counselor required.
Trustees: Daniel Eisenhauer, Edward Eisenhauer, Lucy C. Eisenhauer, Lynn Eisenhauer, William Eisenhauer, Jane L. Kaylor.
EIN: 232020120

63222
The Michael L. Fiorelli, Sr. Foundation
284 Glen Mills Rd.
Glen Mills, PA 19342

Established in 1996 in PA.
Donor(s): Lois R. Fiorelli.
Financial data (yr. ended 12/31/99): Assets, $250,130 (M); grants paid, $6,641; gifts received, $10,201; expenditures, $9,270; qualifying distributions, $6,150.

Limitations: Applications not accepted.
Application information: Contributes only to pre-selected organizations.
Officers and Directors:* Lois R. Fiorelli, Pres., Secy., and Mgr.; Jonathan A. Fiorelli,* V.P.; George G. Riggall.
EIN: 232833894

63223
Kriss Foundation
c/o PNC Advisors
620 Liberty Ave., P2-PTPP-10-2
Pittsburgh, PA 15222-2705

Established in 1989 in PA.
Donor(s): Joseph H. Kriss, Lillie E. Kriss.
Financial data (yr. ended 12/31/01): Assets, $244,289 (M); grants paid, $0; expenditures, $2,756; qualifying distributions, $0.
Trustee: PNC Bank, N.A.
EIN: 232575478

63224
Eccles-Lesher Memorial Library Association, Inc.
P.O. Box 359
Rimersburg, PA 16248-0359

Financial data (yr. ended 12/31/01): Assets, $243,447 (M); grants paid, $0; gifts received, $243,549; expenditures, $134,041; qualifying distributions, $134,041.
Officers: Sally Mortimer, Pres.; Dorothy Holly, V.P.; Sally Mortimer, V.P.; Roger Crick, Secy.; D.H. Hiwiller, Treas.
EIN: 256084082

63225
The Michael A. Giliberti Foundation
c/o Stanley T. Peterson, C.P.A.
267 N. Rolling Rd.
Springfield, PA 19064
Application address: c/o St. Francis DeSalles, New Rd., Lenni, PA 19052
Contact: Rev. Charles Vance, Tr.

Established in 1989 in PA.
Donor(s): Rev. Francis Giliberti.
Financial data (yr. ended 12/31/99): Assets, $236,564 (M); grants paid, $12,000; expenditures, $12,168; qualifying distributions, $12,093.
Limitations: Giving primarily in PA.
Application information: Application form not required.
Trustees: Rev. Charles Vance, Rev. Robert Vogan.
EIN: 251599451

63226
Michael and Sherle Berger Foundation
401 Bingham St.
Pittsburgh, PA 15203

Established in 1999 in PA.
Donor(s): Michael N. Berger, Eileen S. Berger.
Financial data (yr. ended 12/31/00): Assets, $234,823 (M); grants paid, $1,595; gifts received, $174,742; expenditures, $85,517; qualifying distributions, $1,595.
Limitations: Applications not accepted.
Trustees: Eileen S. Berger, Michael N. Berger.
EIN: 256683685

63227
The Niesen Foundation
264 Valleybrook Rd.
McMurray, PA 15317
Contact: Raymond J. Niesen, Mgr.

Established in 1987 in PA.
Donor(s): Raymond J. Niesen, Douglas Niesen.
Financial data (yr. ended 12/31/00): Assets, $234,494 (M); grants paid, $20,000; gifts

received, $5,000; expenditures, $20,457; qualifying distributions, $19,865.
Limitations: Giving primarily in AZ and PA.
Officer: Raymond J. Niesen, Mgr.
EIN: 251539242

63228
Widra Family Foundation, Inc.
519 Lindy Ln.
Bala Cynwyd, PA 19004

Established in 1999 in PA.
Donor(s): Alan Widra, Janet Widra, Ph.D.
Financial data (yr. ended 12/31/99): Assets, $234,256 (M); grants paid, $15,440; gifts received, $267,830; expenditures, $15,595; qualifying distributions, $15,440.
Limitations: Applications not accepted.
Application information: Contributes only to pre-selected organizations.
Officers and Directors:* Alan Widra,* Pres.; Janet Widra, Ph.D.,* Secy.-Treas.
EIN: 232994381

63229
The Lincoln and Soldiers Institute
c/o Trotta Law
Campus Box 435
Gettysburg, PA 17325
Application address: c/o Tina Grim, 233 N. Washington St., Gettysburg, PA 17325, tel.: (717) 337-6590

Established in 1990 in DE and PA.
Donor(s): Richard Gilder, Lewis Lehrman.
Financial data (yr. ended 12/31/01): Assets, $230,018 (M); grants paid, $100,000; gifts received, $226,926; expenditures, $281,100; qualifying distributions, $100,000.
Officer: Gabor Borritt, Chair.
Trustees: James Basker, Richard Gilder, Gordan Haaland, Edwin T. Johnson, Lewis Lehrman, Louise Taper.
EIN: 061287456
Codes: FD2, GTI

63230
The Randall Reserve Foundation, Inc.
P.O. Box 58
Stahlstown, PA 15687

Classified as a private operating foundation in PA in 1998.
Donor(s): Olive Randall, Four Mile Run Corporation, M.B.R. Rawlings.
Financial data (yr. ended 09/30/00): Assets, $229,098 (M); grants paid, $0; gifts received, $40,550; expenditures, $15,156; qualifying distributions, $14,706; giving activities include $978 for programs.
Officers: M.B.R. Rawlings,* Pres.; Kandice Newell, Secy.; H. Edward Rawlings, Treas.
Director: Thomas Grote.
EIN: 251812150

63231
The Spirit of Gheel, Inc.
P.O. Box 610
Kimberton, PA 19442

Established in 1994 in PA.
Financial data (yr. ended 12/31/01): Assets, $224,714 (M); grants paid, $0; gifts received, $25,668; expenditures, $701,468; qualifying distributions, $141,087; giving activities include $701,468 for programs.
Limitations: Applications not accepted.
Application information: Contributes only to pre-selected organizations.

Officers: Aiden Altenor, Pres.; Jean-Marie Barch, Secy.; Charles Isaac, Treas.; George Schaefer, L.S.W., Exec. Dir.; Marge Ridall, V.P.
Board Members: Roberta Altenor, Kofi Nsiah, Sandy Watson, Rachelle Weiss.
Director: Lindley Winston, M.D.
EIN: 222505189

63232
Clark Family Foundation
2028 Edgehill Dr.
Furlong, PA 18925

Established in 2000 in PA.
Donor(s): Richard Clark, Angela Clark.
Financial data (yr. ended 12/31/00): Assets, $216,530 (M); grants paid, $12,000; gifts received, $240,238; expenditures, $12,500; qualifying distributions, $12,000.
Limitations: Applications not accepted.
Application information: Contributes only to pre-selected organizations.
Trustees: Angela Clark, Kelly Lynn Clark, Lisa Marie Clark, Richard Clark, Jr.
EIN: 256667093

63233
Friendship Foundation, Inc.
P.O. Box 5200
Lancaster, PA 17606-5200 (717) 519-5200
Contact: J. Herbert Fisher, Jr., Dir.

Established in 1997 in PA.
Donor(s): J. Herbert Fisher, Jr.
Financial data (yr. ended 06/30/01): Assets, $215,756 (M); grants paid, $58,691; gifts received, $128,183; expenditures, $166,107; qualifying distributions, $58,230.
Director: J. Herbert Fisher, Jr.
EIN: 232474740

63234
Glatfelter Memorial Scholarship Trust
c/o Fulton Financial Advisors, N.A.
P.O. Box 3215
Lancaster, PA 17604-3215

Established in 1996 in PA.
Financial data (yr. ended 12/31/01): Assets, $214,995 (M); grants paid, $8,310; expenditures, $13,258; qualifying distributions, $8,265.
Limitations: Applications not accepted. Giving primarily in Washington, DC.
Application information: Contributes only to pre-selected organizations.
Trustee: Fulton Financial Advisors, N.A.
EIN: 236715499

63235
The Lawrence and Carol Pollock Family Foundation
217 Hermitage Dr.
Radnor, PA 19087

Established in 1999 in PA.
Donor(s): Lawrence Pollock.
Financial data (yr. ended 11/30/00): Assets, $208,250 (M); grants paid, $0; gifts received, $199,066; expenditures, $0; qualifying distributions, $0.
Limitations: Applications not accepted.
Application information: Contributes only to pre-selected organizations.
Officers and Directors:* Lawrence Pollock,* Pres.; David A. Pollock,* V.P.; Deborah L. Pollock,* V.P.; Jacqueline S. Pollock Lane, Secy.-Treas.
EIN: 233023932

63236
Tri-Valley Energy & Services Center
205 E. 8th Ave.
Homestead, PA 15120-1515

Classified as a private operating foundation in 1991.
Financial data (yr. ended 09/30/01): Assets, $207,462 (M); grants paid, $0; gifts received, $107,380; expenditures, $98,765; qualifying distributions, $0.
Directors: Jim Dolson, Mary Flagg, Jean Miller, Dave Price.
EIN: 251535726

63237
The Morris & Myrtle Corbman Foundation
c/o Michael R. Miller, C.P.A.
1515 Martin Luther King, Jr. Dr.
Allentown, PA 18102
Application address: 2001 Stone Ridge Ln., Villanova, PA 19085
Contact: Ellen S. Varenhorst, Pres.

Established in 1992 in PA.
Donor(s): Morris Corbman, Myrtle Corbman.
Financial data (yr. ended 12/31/00): Assets, $196,483 (M); grants paid, $19,000; expenditures, $19,056; qualifying distributions, $18,770.
Limitations: Giving primarily in Allentown, PA.
Officers: Ellen S. Varenhorst, Pres.; Gregory C. Hartman, V.P.; Donald Senderowitz, Secy.-Treas.
EIN: 232701894

63238
Tinicum Art and Science Foundation
(Formerly Tinicum Xin Jian Dao Residency)
611 Cafferty Hill Rd.
Upper Black Eddy, PA 18972

Established in 1997 in PA.
Donor(s): H. John Heinz IV.
Financial data (yr. ended 12/31/00): Assets, $186,753 (M); grants paid, $0; gifts received, $520,000; expenditures, $476,030; qualifying distributions, $472,724; giving activities include $443,540 for programs.
Limitations: Applications not accepted.
Application information: Contributes only to pre-selected organizations.
Officers: H. John Heinz IV, Pres.; Peter J. Ryan, V.P. and Secy.-Treas.
EIN: 232896729

63239
Historical Society of Frankford
1507 Orthodox St.
Philadelphia, PA 19124

Classified as a private operating foundation in 1976.
Financial data (yr. ended 12/31/99): Assets, $177,458 (M); grants paid, $0; gifts received, $17,899; expenditures, $7,115; qualifying distributions, $6,156; giving activities include $3,181 for programs.
Limitations: Applications not accepted.
Application information: Contributes only to pre-selected organizations.
Officers: Connie Delury, Pres.; Edwin S. Moore III, V.P.; Margaret Labman, Secy.; Walter Delury, Treas.
EIN: 236296560

63240
Schuylkill County Bar Association Scholarship Fund
c/o Schuylkill County Courthouses
401 N. 2nd St.
Pottsville, PA 17901-1756
Contact: Margaret A. Ulmer, Mgr.

Established in 1994 in PA.
Donor(s): Keith J. Strouse, Kathleen Strouse, Constance H. Pugh.‡
Financial data (yr. ended 12/31/00): Assets, $169,050 (M); grants paid, $8,800; gifts received, $295; expenditures, $11,716; qualifying distributions, $8,686.
Limitations: Giving limited to residents of Schuylkill County, PA.
Application information: Application form required.
Officers and Directors:* William C. Reiley,* Pres.; Richard J. Wiest,* Treas.; Margaret A. Ulmer,* Mgr.; John J. Earley, James L. Lewis, Kathleen A. Palubinsky, Leonard G. Schumack, Harry Strouse, Keith J. Strouse.
EIN: 232747769

63241
Lucy Caputo Memorial Fund for Handicapped Children, Inc.
8400 Bustleton Ave., Ste. 301
Philadelphia, PA 19152

Established in 1999 in PA.
Financial data (yr. ended 12/31/00): Assets, $166,677 (M); grants paid, $1,000; gifts received, $86,637; expenditures, $11,997; qualifying distributions, $11,996.
Limitations: Applications not accepted.
Application information: Contributes only to pre-selected organizations.
Officers: Frances Odza, Pres.; Joyce Ponterelli Ruttman, Secy.-Treas.
EIN: 237992825

63242
The Desmond Foundation for Historic Preservation
2705 Old Philadelphia Pike
Bird In Hand, PA 17505

Established in 1996 in PA.
Donor(s): George C. Desmond.
Financial data (yr. ended 09/30/99): Assets, $165,286 (M); grants paid, $0; gifts received, $76,400; expenditures, $72,279; qualifying distributions, $64,947; giving activities include $20,806 for programs.
Trustee: George C. Desmond.
EIN: 232931874

63243
American Division of the World Academy of Art & Science
c/o Richard W. Palmer
432 Montgomery Ave., Ste. 401
Haverford, PA 19041

Classified as a private operating foundation in 1991.
Donor(s): Prof. Harlan Cleveland.
Financial data (yr. ended 12/31/99): Assets, $145,653 (M); grants paid, $40,000; gifts received, $46,858; expenditures, $80,767; qualifying distributions, $80,756.
Limitations: Giving limited to CA, with some giving to Brazil.
Officers and Directors:* Prof. Harlan Cleveland,* Pres.; Walter Truett Anderson,* V.P.; Richard W. Palmer,* Treas.; Magda Cordell McHale.
EIN: 136210438

63244
Renfrew Center Foundation
c/o Samuel Menagred
475 Spring Ln.
Philadelphia, PA 19128 (215) 482-5353

Established in 1999 in PA.
Financial data (yr. ended 12/31/01): Assets, $141,649 (M); grants paid, $0; gifts received, $51,387; expenditures, $406,316; qualifying distributions, $0.
Officers: Samuel Menaged, Pres.; William N. Davis, V.P.; Judi Goldstein, V.P.; Barbara Peterson, V.P.; Jane Fleming, Exec. Dir.
EIN: 232947850

63245
Ringing Rocks Foundation
(Formerly Nancy Connor Foundation)
123 S. Broad St., 27th Fl.
Philadelphia, PA 19109-1029
Mailing address: P.O. Box 22656, Philadelphia, PA 19110-2656; E-mail: info@ringingrocks.org; URL: http://www.ringingrocks.org

Established in 1995.
Donor(s): Nancy L. Connor.
Financial data (yr. ended 12/31/01): Assets, $132,925 (M); grants paid, $553,793; gifts received, $1,685,000; expenditures, $1,812,480; qualifying distributions, $1,767,763; giving activities include $967,074 for programs.
Limitations: Giving on a worldwide basis.
Application information: See foundation Web site for application guidelines, requirements, and forms. Application form required.
Officers and Directors:* Nancy L. Connor,* Pres.; John M. Myers,* C.O.O.; Bradford Keeney, V.P., Cultural Affairs; David J. Robkin,* C.F.O. and Treas.
EIN: 541782142
Codes: FD

63246
The Peter and Ruth Keblish Foundation
c/o Peter A. Keblish
1243 S. Cedar Crest, Ste. 2500
Allentown, PA 18103

Established in 1994 in PA.
Donor(s): Peter A. Keblish, M.D., Ruth Keblish.
Financial data (yr. ended 12/31/01): Assets, $132,002 (M); grants paid, $0; gifts received, $18,500; expenditures, $0; qualifying distributions, $0.
Officers: Peter A. Keblish, M.D., Pres. and Treas.; Ruth Keblish, Secy.
EIN: 232774475

63247
Aysr Foundation
RR 5 Box 290
Bloomsburg, PA 17815

Established in 1998 in PA.
Donor(s): John D. Klingerman.
Financial data (yr. ended 12/31/99): Assets, $131,367 (M); grants paid, $29,550; gifts received, $38,329; expenditures, $29,550; qualifying distributions, $29,550.
Officer: John D. Klingerman, Pres. and Treas.
EIN: 232966353

63248
The Andrew C. Virostek Foundation
c/o Andrew C. Virostek
3481 Treeline Dr.
Murrysville, PA 15668

Established in 2000 in PA.
Donor(s): Andrew Virostek.
Financial data (yr. ended 12/31/00): Assets, $130,238 (M); grants paid, $31,100; gifts received, $168,000; expenditures, $37,762; qualifying distributions, $34,362.
Limitations: Applications not accepted. Giving primarily in OH.
Application information: Contributes only to pre-selected organizations.
Officer and Trustee:* Andrew Virostek,* Pres.
Directors: Robert D. Beasley, M.D., Anthony J. Guida, Jr., Timothy C. Reed.
EIN: 251875325

63249
Howard E. Eckhart Trust
(Formerly Edward E. Eckhart Trust)
c/o Pres. of Council
111 W. Newcastle St.
Zelienople, PA 16063 (724) 452-6610
Contact: Charles Underwood, Chair.

Established in 1993.
Financial data (yr. ended 12/31/99): Assets, $127,000 (M); grants paid, $2,154; expenditures, $3,595; qualifying distributions, $2,154.
Limitations: Giving limited to Zelienople, PA.
Application information: Application form required.
Officers: Charles Underwood, Chair.; William Brewer, Secy.
Trustees: Tammie Czyz, Robert Keplinger, Tom Oliverio.
EIN: 256125594

63250
The Institute of American Deltiology
c/o Donald R. Brown
300 W. Main Ave.
Myerstown, PA 17067

Established in 1993 in PA.
Financial data (yr. ended 12/31/00): Assets, $124,614 (M); grants paid, $0; gifts received, $14,664; expenditures, $4,741; qualifying distributions, $0.
Officer: Donald R. Brown, Pres.
EIN: 251724289

63251
Frank W. Preston Memorial Scholarship Trust
c/o Meridian Station
P.O. Box 49
Butler, PA 16001-2441 (724) 287-6344
Contact: Jane E. Preston, Pres.

Donor(s): Jane E. Preston.
Financial data (yr. ended 12/31/99): Assets, $115,277 (M); grants paid, $9,000; expenditures, $9,163; qualifying distributions, $9,000.
Limitations: Giving limited to residents of Butler County, PA.
Application information: Application form required.
Officers: Jane E. Preston, Pres.; A. Robert Shott, Secy.-Treas.
EIN: 251679290

63252
Elizabeth Roe Dunning Club
P.O. Box 54016
Philadelphia, PA 19105-4016

Financial data (yr. ended 03/31/01): Assets, $106,289 (M); grants paid, $5,240; gifts received, $102; expenditures, $9,989; qualifying distributions, $4,749.
Limitations: Giving primarily in the Philadelphia, PA, area.
Officers: Simone Gavioli, Pres.; Antoinette Whaley, Treas.; Antoinette Whaley, Secy.
EIN: 236272297

63253
Little Leo Club of Punxsutawney
P.O. Box 472
Punxsutawney, PA 15767-0472

Classified as a private operating foundation in 1947.
Financial data (yr. ended 06/30/02): Assets, $104,037 (M); grants paid, $0; gifts received, $4,175; expenditures, $13,207; qualifying distributions, $6,911; giving activities include $6,911 for programs.
Officers: Dennis O'Brien, Secy.-Treas.; William Fusco, Pres.; Tom Steffey, V.P.
EIN: 251154678

63254
Aurora Institute, Inc.
436 Williamson Rd.
Gladwyne, PA 19035 (610) 649-9423
Contact: Wight Martindale, Jr., Pres.

Financial data (yr. ended 09/30/01): Assets, $100,168 (M); grants paid, $2,500; expenditures, $6,095; qualifying distributions, $6,095.
Officers and Directors:* Wight Martindale, Jr.,* Pres.; Sally Martindale,* Secy.-Treas.; Blandford Parker.
EIN: 593398414

63255
Hassman Family Foundation
2123 Inverness Ln.
Berwyn, PA 19312

Established in 1998 in CA.
Donor(s): Howard Hassman, Cheryl Hassman.
Financial data (yr. ended 12/31/00): Assets, $97,250 (M); grants paid, $15,962; expenditures, $30,809; qualifying distributions, $15,962.
Limitations: Applications not accepted. Giving primarily in CA.
Application information: Contributes only to pre-selected organizations.
Officers: Cheryl Hassman, Pres.; Howard Hassman, Secy.
Directors: Allyson Davis, Mark Simowitz.
EIN: 330777149

63256
Family Resource and Counseling Center, Inc.
(Formerly Family Information Center, Inc.)
91 Newport Ctr., Ste. 102
P.O. Box 488
Gap, PA 17527-0488 (717) 442-9577
Contact: Jonas Z. Beiler, Pres.

Established in 1992 in PA.
Donor(s): Angela Foundation.
Financial data (yr. ended 12/31/01): Assets, $91,031 (M); grants paid, $1,300; gifts received, $331,693; expenditures, $372,141; qualifying distributions, $367,103; giving activities include $204,958 for programs.
Limitations: Giving primarily in Gap, PA.
Officers: Jonas Z. Beiler, Chair. and Pres.; Merrill Smucker, Vice-Chair.; Nancy Stoltzfus, Secy.; John Vanderzell, Treas.
Directors: Elsie Esh, Paul L. Jones, Galen Smoker, Doris Swaim, Marvin L. Weaver.
EIN: 232698073

63257
Rose Marie Steffan Foundation
401 Liberty Ave., Ste. 1460
Pittsburgh, PA 15222

Established in 2000 in PA.
Financial data (yr. ended 12/31/00): Assets, $90,267 (M); grants paid, $21,791; expenditures, $22,412; qualifying distributions, $22,228.
Limitations: Applications not accepted. Giving primarily in PA.
Application information: Contributes only to pre-selected organizations.
Trustees: John W. Giltinan, Gail Hinchberger.
EIN: 237921457

63258
P. C. Chou Family Foundation
c/o Pei Chi Chou
227 Hemlock Rd.
Wynnewood, PA 19096

Established in 2000 in DE and PA.
Donor(s): Pei Chi Chou.
Financial data (yr. ended 06/30/01): Assets, $88,681 (M); grants paid, $5,200; gifts received, $108,000; expenditures, $11,820; qualifying distributions, $5,200.
Limitations: Giving primarily in Philadelphia, PA.
Officers: Pei Chi Chou, Pres. and Treas.; Rosalind Chen Chou, V.P. and Secy.
EIN: 233064343

63259
The Windber Area Christian Forensic Foundation of St. Anthony's
975 Beechwood Dr.
Windber, PA 15963-1568

Established in 1986 in PA.
Financial data (yr. ended 08/31/00): Assets, $85,561 (M); grants paid, $6,150; gifts received, $686; expenditures, $7,545; qualifying distributions, $6,793.
Limitations: Applications not accepted. Giving limited to PA.
Trustees: Nathaniel A. Barbera, Raymond DiBattista, Thomas Weimer.
EIN: 251550690

63260
The Hep Foundation
4072 Greystone Dr.
Harrisburg, PA 17112-1093

Established in 2000 in PA.
Financial data (yr. ended 12/31/01): Assets, $84,851 (M); grants paid, $5,000; gifts received, $20,000; expenditures, $5,000; qualifying distributions, $5,000.
Trustees: E. Louise Hepschmidt, John Hepschmidt, Jr.
EIN: 256716658

63261
Richard W. Wetherill Foundation
1101 Enterprise Dr.
Royersford, PA 19468-4251
Contact: E. Marie Bothe, Pres.

Established in 1998 in PA.
Donor(s): E. Marie Bothe.
Financial data (yr. ended 12/31/01): Assets, $82,490 (M); grants paid, $77,492; gifts received, $82,602; expenditures, $77,852; qualifying distributions, $77,492.
Limitations: Giving on a national basis.
Application information: Application form not required.
Officers and Directors:* E. Marie Bothe,* Pres.; Mark S. Kraft, V.P.; Margo Callis,* Secy.; Jineen Callis,* Treas.; Phyllis Beebee, James Farnsworth, Janice Jacobs, Kevin K. Kraft, Mark Kraft, Jeffrey W. Sween.
EIN: 232960843
Codes: FD2

63262
The John and Helen Villaume Foundation
c/o Wayne Bank Trust Dept.
717 Main St.
Honesdale, PA 18431 (570) 253-8506

Established in 2000 in PA.
Donor(s): Helen R. Villaume.
Financial data (yr. ended 12/31/00): Assets, $82,402 (M); grants paid, $4,000; gifts received, $83,015; expenditures, $4,250; qualifying distributions, $4,125.
Limitations: Giving limited to Wayne County, PA.
Application information: Application form required.
Officers: John C. Villaume, Pres.; William W. Davis, Jr., V.P.; Jon E. Villaume, Secy.-Treas.
EIN: 233046622

63263
Walter D. Fohl, Jr. Medical Education Loan Foundation
c/o PNC Advisors
1600 Market St.
Philadelphia, PA 19103-7140
Application address: Walter D. Fohl, Jr., c/o John W. Phillips, 101 W. Middle St., Gettyburg, PA 17325

Classified as a private operating foundation in 1988.
Donor(s): Lori Koons.
Financial data (yr. ended 12/31/00): Assets, $78,983 (M); grants paid, $3,000; expenditures, $4,693; qualifying distributions, $4,190.
Limitations: Giving limited to Adams County, PA.
Application information: Application form required.
Trustee: PNC Bank, N.A.
EIN: 232499376

63264
The Paul H. and Marcia J. M. Woodruff Foundation, Inc.
744 S. Warren Ave.
Malvern, PA 19355

Established in 2000 in PA.
Donor(s): Paul H. Woodruff.
Financial data (yr. ended 12/31/01): Assets, $78,005 (M); grants paid, $125,519; gifts received, $200; expenditures, $126,289; qualifying distributions, $125,519.
Limitations: Applications not accepted.
Application information: Contributes only to pre-selected organizations.
Officers: Paul H. Woodruff, Pres. and Treas.; Marcia J. Woodruff, V.P. and Secy.
Directors: Janet Billeter, Joy Delaney, Tama Minacci, Paula Purcell.
EIN: 251876451

63265
Rose Foundation for Leprosy Prevention
c/o Rev. Joseph M. Ziobro
99 E. Tioga St.
Tunkhannock, PA 18657

Classified as a private operating foundation in 1986.
Financial data (yr. ended 12/31/00): Assets, $76,238 (M); grants paid, $0; gifts received, $375; expenditures, $577; qualifying distributions, $0.
Officers: Mary Margaret O'Donnell, Pres.; Rev. Joseph M. Ziobro, Secy.-Treas.
EIN: 232392304

63266
Cheryl Beth Silverman Memorial Fund
224 Susan Dr.
Elkins Park, PA 19027-1833

Established in 1990 in PA.
Donor(s): Arthur E. Silverman, Carol Silverman, Eugene Silverman.
Financial data (yr. ended 12/31/01): Assets, $72,620 (M); grants paid, $7,739; gifts received, $4,000; expenditures, $10,439; qualifying distributions, $7,739.
Limitations: Applications not accepted. Giving on a national basis.
Application information: Contributes only to pre-selected organizations.
Officers: Arthur E. Silverman, Pres. and Treas.; Carol Silverman, V.P.
Directors: David Brown, Rova Brown.
EIN: 232606907

63267
The Rochester Alumni Scholarship Charitable Trust
c/o Jo L. Shane
1232 Rte. 68
New Brighton, PA 15066-4106
Application address: 626 Farm Ln., Rochester, PA 15074, tel.: (724) 775-7500
Contact: Thomas R. Goettman, Jr., Pres.

Established in 1999 in PA.
Donor(s): Mary Reader, Rochester Area High School Alumni Association.
Financial data (yr. ended 12/31/00): Assets, $72,241 (M); grants paid, $2,150; expenditures, $7,299; qualifying distributions, $2,095.
Limitations: Giving primarily in Rochester, PA.
Application information: Application form required.
Officers: Thomas R. Goettman, Jr., Pres.; Jo L. Shane, Secy.-Treas.
Trustees: John D. McBride, Robert S. Vogel.
EIN: 256644260

63268
Eleanor B. Yohn Medical Foundation
49 N. Duke St.
Lancaster, PA 17602 (717) 299-1181
Contact: John W. Metzger, Secy.

Donor(s): Eleanor B. Yohn.
Financial data (yr. ended 12/31/01): Assets, $68,728 (M); grants paid, $2,750; expenditures, $2,750; qualifying distributions, $2,750.
Officers: Eleanor B. Yohn, Pres.; David M. Yohn, V.P. and Treas.; John W. Metzger, Secy.
Director: Anthony N. Mastropietro, M.D.
EIN: 232997161

63269
Everybody Ought to Know, Inc.
c/o Vern Martin
12 Summit Dr.
Dillsburg, PA 17019-9589

Established in 1998 in PA.
Donor(s): Daniel E. Deyhle, Frank C. Myers.
Financial data (yr. ended 03/31/01): Assets, $67,831 (M); grants paid, $0; gifts received, $52,358; expenditures, $33,580; qualifying distributions, $30,140; giving activities include $30,115 for programs.
Officers: Daniel E. Deyhle, Pres.; Vernon M. Martin, Jr., Secy.-Treas.
Directors: Karen F. Deyhle, Frank C. Myers.
EIN: 251808693

63270
Last Generation Ministries
1339 Piedmont Rd.
Somerset, PA 15501

Classified as a private operating foundation in 1996.
Financial data (yr. ended 12/31/00): Assets, $66,413 (M); grants paid, $5,493; gifts received, $32,596; expenditures, $41,132; qualifying distributions, $39,561; giving activities include $10,061 for programs.
Limitations: Giving on a national basis.
Officers: Michael J. Matieszyn, Pres.; Karen L. Matieszyn, Secy.-Treas.
Directors: Joseph W. Peck, Donald Woodward.
EIN: 251680940

63271
Eternal Heirs Foundation
476 Headquarters Rd.
Erwinna, PA 18920

Established in 1998 in PA.
Donor(s): Glen G. Hale.
Financial data (yr. ended 12/31/01): Assets, $64,398 (M); grants paid, $600; gifts received, $60,176; expenditures, $718; qualifying distributions, $600.
Limitations: Applications not accepted. Giving primarily in PA.
Application information: Contributes only to pre-selected organizations.
Officer: Glen G. Hale, Pres.
EIN: 137173274

63272
Signs & Wonders Ministries
286 Shafer Rd.
Moon Township, PA 15108

Donor(s): Wonder Transport, Inc.
Financial data (yr. ended 12/31/01): Assets, $60,149 (M); grants paid, $5,125; gifts received, $53,768; expenditures, $55,868; qualifying distributions, $55,868; giving activities include $50,743 for programs.
Limitations: Applications not accepted. Giving on a national basis, with some emphasis on PA.
Application information: Unsolicited requests for funds not accepted.
Officers: Kenneth N. Faulk, Pres.; David Faulk, V.P.; Geraldine T. Faulk, Secy.-Treas.
EIN: 251641538

63273
The Center Foundation
220 N. Jackson St., 2nd Fl.
Media, PA 19063

Established in 1994 in PA.
Donor(s): The Garrison Family Foundation.
Financial data (yr. ended 11/30/01): Assets, $57,825 (M); grants paid, $0; gifts received, $58,234; expenditures, $89,324; qualifying distributions, $0.
Limitations: Applications not accepted.
Application information: Contributes only to pre-selected organizations.
Trustees: Michael J.J. Campbell, Chair.; Susan K. Garrison, Gail L. Palmer, Pamela G. Phelan.
EIN: 232789808

63274
Leonard E. B. Andrews Foundation
699 Sugartown Rd.
Malvern, PA 19355

Established in 1988 in PA.
Donor(s): Leonard E.B. Andrews.
Financial data (yr. ended 10/31/00): Assets, $56,898 (M); grants paid, $0; gifts received, $147,500; expenditures, $145,888; qualifying distributions, $142,898; giving activities include $142,898 for programs.
Officer and Trustees:* Leonard E.B. Andrews,* Pres. and Secy.-Treas.; Kathleen C. Jamieson, Silas R. Mountsier.
EIN: 232272057

63275
Western Pennsylvania Hematology Oncology Foundation
915 Settler's Ridge Rd.
Pittsburgh, PA 15238

Classified as a company-sponsored operating foundation in 2000 in PA.
Donor(s): Immunex Corp., Amgen Inc., Aventis Pharmaceuticals Inc.
Financial data (yr. ended 12/31/00): Assets, $55,762 (M); grants paid, $3,500; gifts received, $65,650; expenditures, $10,425; qualifying distributions, $3,500.
Limitations: Giving on an international basis.
Officers: Richard K. Shadduck, Pres.; John Lister, Secy.; Jeffrey Gryn, Treas.
EIN: 251858284

63276
Irene Cohen Foundation
(Formerly Cohen Foundation)
P.O. Box 1819
Erie, PA 16507 (814) 456-4000
Contact: Harry Martin, Tr.

Classified as a private operating foundation in 1948.
Financial data (yr. ended 12/31/00): Assets, $54,080 (M); grants paid, $3,016; expenditures, $3,455; qualifying distributions, $2,985.
Application information: Application form not required.
Trustees: Marilyn Burgay, Pearl Jarret, Harry Martin.
EIN: 256066994

63277
Jeffrey S. Kedson Foundation
20 Sugar Maple Ln.
Lafayette Hill, PA 19444-2411
Application Address: c/o Jeffrey S. Kedson Foundation, P.O. Box 506, Plymouth Meeting, PA 19462
Contact: Phyllis Kedson, Pres.

Classified as a private operating foundation in 1985.
Donor(s): Leonard Kedson, Phyllis Kedson.
Financial data (yr. ended 12/31/99): Assets, $53,992 (M); grants paid, $14,006; gifts received, $19,693; expenditures, $16,969; qualifying distributions, $16,969.
Limitations: Giving primarily in Durham, NC, and PA.
Officers: Phyllis Kedson, Pres.; David Kedson, V.P.; Leonard Kedson, V.P.; Ira Kedson, V.P.
EIN: 232279350

63278
Mount Carmel Homes, Inc.
4321 Frankford Ave.
Philadelphia, PA 19124

Financial data (yr. ended 06/30/01): Assets, $53,621 (M); grants paid, $0; gifts received, $15,435; expenditures, $19,124; qualifying distributions, $0; giving activities include $219,123 for programs.
Limitations: Applications not accepted.

Officers: Kevin Keller, Pres.; Rosemary Brisbane, V.P. and Treas.; Shirley Morel-Calton, Secy.
EIN: 232875595

63279
NADC Charitable Foundation
c/o Michael Taylor
16 N. Franklin St.
Doylestown, PA 18901 (215) 348-4949

Established in 1995.
Donor(s): Jaqueline Schurger.
Financial data (yr. ended 06/30/01): Assets, $53,572 (M); grants paid, $2,500; expenditures, $2,500; qualifying distributions, $2,473.
Application information: Application form required.
Officers: Leonard Cherry, Pres.; Bill Moore, 1st V.P.; R. David Loewendick, 2nd V.P.; Richard O'Gara, Secy.; Drew Lammers, Treas.
EIN: 232823006

63280
The Center for Loss and Bereavement
3847 Skippack Pike
P.O. Box 1299
Skippack, PA 19474

Established in 1999 in PA.
Donor(s): Christine J. Smith.
Financial data (yr. ended 06/30/00): Assets, $53,116 (M); grants paid, $0; gifts received, $95,840; expenditures, $55,896; qualifying distributions, $48,733.
Limitations: Applications not accepted.
Application information: Contributes only to pre-selected organizations.
Officers: Christine J. Smith, Pres.; Inez A. Bing, Secy.; Shirley Elrod, Treas.
EIN: 233011941

63281
The J. Donald Carpenter Foundation
21 Cumberland Rd.
Lemoyne, PA 17043-1616

Established in 1997 in PA.
Donor(s): Isabel C. Masland.
Financial data (yr. ended 12/31/00): Assets, $49,290 (M); grants paid, $20,000; gifts received, $20,364; expenditures, $20,550; qualifying distributions, $20,308.
Limitations: Applications not accepted.
Application information: Contributes only to pre-selected organizations.
Trustees: Carol M. Gleeson, Isabel C. Masland, John C. Masland, Leslie Masland.
EIN: 237866406

63282
DeFelice Scholarship Trust
c/o Emogene DeFelice
RD 1 Box 116
Punxsutawney, PA 15767-9620

Established in 1997 in PA.
Donor(s): Emogene DeFelice.
Financial data (yr. ended 12/31/01): Assets, $47,840 (M); grants paid, $2,524; gifts received, $5,000; expenditures, $3,502; qualifying distributions, $2,488.
Limitations: Applications not accepted. Giving limited to Punxsutawney, PA.
Trustee: S & T Bank.
EIN: 232893806

63283
The Evelyn Shapiro Foundation
204 Rhyl Ln.
Bala Cynwyd, PA 19004
Application Adress: P.O. Box 121, Bala Cynwyd, PA 19004, tel.: (610) 667-4284
Contact: Stanley Shapiro, M.D., Pres.

Established in 1990 in PA. Classified as a private operating foundation in 1992.
Donor(s): Stanley H. Shapiro.
Financial data (yr. ended 08/31/01): Assets, $47,126 (M); grants paid, $12,000; gifts received, $5,325; expenditures, $16,506; qualifying distributions, $16,472.
Limitations: Giving limited to Philadelphia, PA.
Application information: Application form required.
Officers: Stanley H. Shapiro, M.D., Pres.; Philip P. Kalodner, V.P.; Irene Fisher, Treas. and Mgr.
Directors: William Daley, Helen Drutt English, Perry Ottenburg, David Sachs, Henry P. Shapiro.
EIN: 232627834

63284
Iris E. Anouchi Memorial Trust
1537 S. Negley Ave.
Pittsburgh, PA 15217-1419

Established in 1999.
Donor(s): Abraham Y. Anouchi.
Financial data (yr. ended 12/31/00): Assets, $46,421 (M); grants paid, $2,500; gifts received, $6,540; expenditures, $2,534; qualifying distributions, $2,500.
Limitations: Giving primarily in Israel.
Trustee: Abraham Y. Anouchi.
EIN: 232939966

63285
The Dwight R. Evans Memorial Foundation, Inc.
c/o Mary S. Evans
7 Nice Ln.
Tunkhannock, PA 18657-5737

Established in 1999. Classified as a private operating foundation in 2001.
Donor(s): Mary S. Evans.
Financial data (yr. ended 12/31/01): Assets, $46,085 (M); grants paid, $0; expenditures, $939; qualifying distributions, $0.
Limitations: Giving primarily in Tunkhannock, PA.
Officer: Mary S. Evans, Pres.
EIN: 233016337

63286
Abernathy Black Community Development & Educational Fund
(Formerly ABCDE Fund)
325 Washington Trails Rd., Trust Bldg.
Washington, PA 15301-8676
Application address: c/o ABCDE Fund, P.O. Box 177, Washington, PA 15301

Classified as a private operating foundation in 1974.
Donor(s): Ernest L. Abernathy.
Financial data (yr. ended 12/31/00): Assets, $43,961 (M); grants paid, $8,800; gifts received, $5,100; expenditures, $9,504; qualifying distributions, $8,800.
Limitations: Giving limited to Washington, PA.
Application information: Application form required.
Officers: John T. Asbury, Chair.; Marilyn Posner, Vice-Chair.; Patricia Liggins, Secy.-Treas.
Trustees: Janet Abernathy, Cheryl D. Asbury, Rachel Gladden, James Maguire, Paul Posa, R. Archie Thomas, Richard Thornton, Louise E. Waller, Nancy Weiss.
EIN: 237336423

Codes: GTI

63287
Paul and Betty Yoder Foundation
P.O. Box 1065
Edgemont, PA 19028 (610) 647-8424
Contact: Martha A. Yoder, Chair.

Established in 1999 in PA.
Donor(s): Martha A. Yoder.
Financial data (yr. ended 07/31/01): Assets, $43,869 (M); grants paid, $5,533; gifts received, $19,622; expenditures, $11,255; qualifying distributions, $5,533.
Limitations: Giving primarily in PA.
Officer: Martha A. Yoder, Chair. and Pres.
Trustees: Constance Davis, Sandi Draper, Jacqueline Rankin, Carol R. Yoder.
EIN: 251843590

63288
Gladstone Tipton Foundation
P. O. Box 33
Venetia, PA 15367

Established in 1998 in PA.
Financial data (yr. ended 12/31/00): Assets, $43,182 (M); grants paid, $8,155; expenditures, $8,758; qualifying distributions, $8,155.
Officer: James Slovonic, Pres.
EIN: 251813992

63289
Arthur E. Schaeffer Trust
c/o Stuart T. Shmookler
1621 N. Cedar Crest Blvd., Ste. 102
Allentown, PA 18104

Established in 2000 in PA.
Financial data (yr. ended 12/31/00): Assets, $40,881 (M); grants paid, $0; expenditures, $0; qualifying distributions, $0.
Limitations: Applications not accepted.
Application information: Contributes only to pre-selected organizations.
Trustee: Irwin H. Schaeffer.
EIN: 256703678

63290
Antoni Miszkiewicz Family Foundation
42 S. Oak St.
Mount Carmel, PA 17851

Classified as a private operating foundation in 1999 in PA.
Donor(s): Maria Miscavige, Gerard Miscavige.
Financial data (yr. ended 12/31/99): Assets, $40,508 (M); grants paid, $525; gifts received, $40,467; expenditures, $659; qualifying distributions, $578; giving activities include $134 for programs.
Application information: Grants by competition.
Directors: Anthony F. Miscavige, Anthony V. Miscavige, Jr., Daniel A. Miscavige, Gerard Miscavige, Maria Miscavige.
EIN: 311632953

63291
Lionel Feinstein Memorial Fund
614 G.S.B. Building
Bala Cynwyd, PA 19004

Established in 1993 in PA.
Donor(s): Norman Feinstein, Harriet Feinstein.
Financial data (yr. ended 12/31/99): Assets, $39,905 (M); grants paid, $330; gifts received, $25,300; expenditures, $372; qualifying distributions, $321.
Limitations: Applications not accepted.
Application information: Contributes only to pre-selected organizations.

63291—PENNSYLVANIA

Trustees: Robin Briggs, Harriet Feinstein, Norman Feinstein.
EIN: 237716384

63292
Jay Martin Memorial Scholarship
c/o Wayne A. Martin
P.O. Box 386
Titusville, PA 16354
Application address: c/o Kenneth Winger, School Superintendent, Titusville Area Schools, Titusville, PA 16354, tel.: (814) 827-9687

Financial data (yr. ended 12/31/01): Assets, $39,244 (M); grants paid, $1,000; expenditures, $1,201; qualifying distributions, $1,201.
Limitations: Giving limited to residents of Titusville, PA.
Trustee: Wayne Martin.
EIN: 256181087

63293
Dr. Albert and Felice Douglas Memorial Research Foundation
2122 Delancy Pl.
Philadelphia, PA 19103 (215) 735-7279
Contact: Steven Douglas, Tr.

Financial data (yr. ended 04/30/01): Assets, $37,741 (M); grants paid, $5,286; gifts received, $12,260; expenditures, $7,685; qualifying distributions, $9,284.
Limitations: Giving primarily in Philadelphia, PA.
Trustee: Steven Douglas, M.D.
EIN: 236696035

63294
The Goddard Historical & Genealogical Society, Inc.
c/o James E. Goddard, Jr.
708 Bent Creek Dr.
Lititz, PA 17543-8365

Classified as a private operating foundation in 1998.
Financial data (yr. ended 12/31/01): Assets, $34,867 (M); grants paid, $0; expenditures, $6,951; qualifying distributions, $0.
Officers: James E. Goddard, Jr., Pres.; V.G. Johnson, V.P.; Gloria Bailey Jackson, Rec. Secy.; Ethelyn Kay Nosh, Treas.
EIN: 341754291

63295
Mary Fuller Frazier Memorial School Community Library
403 W. Constitution St.
Perryopolis, PA 15473

Classified as a private operating foundation in 1974.
Financial data (yr. ended 06/30/00): Assets, $34,030 (M); grants paid, $0; gifts received, $18,467; expenditures, $13,907; qualifying distributions, $13,362; giving activities include $13,907 for programs.
Officers and Directors:* Faith S. Willson,* Pres. and Mgr.; Ronald Dreucci, V.P.; Monica A. Progan, Secy.; Keith I. Adams,* Treas.; Eleanore C. Bibbs, Lucetta Prestia, Erica Puskar, Frederick L. Smeigh, Susan Szelc.
EIN: 256012285

63296
National Men's Health Foundation
14 E. Minor St.
Emmaus, PA 18098-0009

Classified as a private operating foundation in 1999.

Financial data (yr. ended 12/31/00): Assets, $32,878 (M); grants paid, $250; expenditures, $136,029; qualifying distributions, $250.
Limitations: Applications not accepted.
Application information: Contributes only to pre-selected organizations.
Officers: Paul McGinley, Secy.; Kevin Senie, Treas.
EIN: 232792589

63297
Pollack Family Foundation, Inc.
5735 Woodmont St.
Pittsburgh, PA 15217

Established in 1998.
Financial data (yr. ended 12/31/99): Assets, $32,297 (M); grants paid, $25,840; gifts received, $30,002; expenditures, $27,567; qualifying distributions, $25,826.
Officers: Dean Pollack, Pres.; David Pollack, V.P.; Chaya Pollack, Secy.-Treas.
EIN: 232938840

63298
Radhekrishna Foundation
828 Redgate Rd.
Dresher, PA 19025

Established in 1999 in PA.
Donor(s): Dipak I. Patel, Mina D. Patel.
Financial data (yr. ended 12/31/00): Assets, $31,585 (M); grants paid, $35,500; gifts received, $26,010; expenditures, $35,500; qualifying distributions, $35,500.
Limitations: Applications not accepted.
Application information: Contributes only to pre-selected organizations.
Trustees: Dipak I. Patel, Mina D. Patel.
EIN: 233028743

63299
Leydich Burial Grounds Association, Inc.
c/o Thomas D. Leidy
42 E. 3rd St.
Boyertown, PA 19512-1506

Established as a private operating foundation in 1983.
Financial data (yr. ended 12/31/01): Assets, $30,665 (M); grants paid, $0; gifts received, $385; expenditures, $372; qualifying distributions, $0.
Officers: Paul Scheirer, Pres.; Lovina Carroll, Secy.; Thomas D. Leidy, Treas.
EIN: 237165396

63300
Gospel Crusade Ministries, Inc.
P.O. Box 1026
Erie, PA 16512-1026

Classified as a private operating foundation in 1990.
Donor(s): Roger A. Hedderick.
Financial data (yr. ended 12/31/00): Assets, $28,306 (M); grants paid, $0; gifts received, $138,470; expenditures, $140,641; qualifying distributions, $136,953; giving activities include $136,953 for programs.
Officer and Director:* Roger A. Hedderick,* Pres.
EIN: 251603393

63301
George M. & Anna W. Hochheimer Educational Trust
c/o First National Bank of Pennsylvania
58 W. Main St.
Uniontown, PA 15401
Contact: Christine L. Mullin, Trust Admin., First National Bank of PA

Financial data (yr. ended 12/31/00): Assets, $27,202 (M); grants paid, $0; expenditures, $1,048; qualifying distributions, $900; giving activities include $900 for loans to individuals.
Limitations: Giving limited to Fayette County, PA.
Trustee: First National Bank of Pennsylvania.
EIN: 256057041

63302
News and the Bible
401 Fairview Ave.
Turtle Creek, PA 15145

Financial data (yr. ended 12/31/01): Assets, $26,649 (M); grants paid, $0; gifts received, $16,153; expenditures, $18,999; qualifying distributions, $18,999; giving activities include $14,986 for programs.
Officer and Directors:* David Hinton,* Pres. and Treas.; Richard Dorey, William Rubb.
EIN: 237401992

63303
Benner-Hudock Family Foundation
360 Grampion Blvd.
Williamsport, PA 17701

Established in 2001.
Donor(s): Michael Hudock, Barbara Hudock.
Financial data (yr. ended 12/31/01): Assets, $26,000 (M); grants paid, $0; gifts received, $26,000; expenditures, $0; qualifying distributions, $0.
Officers: Barbara B. Hudock, Pres.; Kimberly Ugalde, V.P. and Secy.; Michael J. Hudock, V.P. and Treas.; Michael J. Hudock, Sr., V.P.
EIN: 233097839

63304
Ken L. Pollock Scholarship Fund of Northwest High School
c/o Northwest Area Jr./Sr. High School
243 Thome Hill Rd.
Shickshinny, PA 18655

Financial data (yr. ended 12/31/01): Assets, $25,952 (M); grants paid, $2,000; expenditures, $2,120; qualifying distributions, $2,120.
Limitations: Giving limited to Shickshinny, PA.
Application information: Application form required.
Trustees: Rev. Karen Allen, Mary Fontinell, Randy S. Gardner, Robert S. Gardner, Fr. Joseph Kakareka, Linda Mellner, Shani Steward, Teresa A. Tkaczyk, Randy Tomasacci.
EIN: 237163936

63305
Schuylkill County Vietnam Veterans Memorial Fund
c/o First U.C.C.
Rte. 61 S.
Schuylkill Haven, PA 17972

Established in 1998 in PA.
Financial data (yr. ended 12/31/01): Assets, $25,799 (M); grants paid, $270; expenditures, $1,205; qualifying distributions, $1,193; giving activities include $9,357 for programs.
Trustees: John J. Buleza, E. Lewis Hummel, Harold Rogers, Howard Shaup.
EIN: 232884931

63306
Louise S. Atwell Memorial Music Scholarship Trust
c/o Robert A. Naragon
3141 Pelham Pl.
Doylestown, PA 18901

Financial data (yr. ended 07/31/01): Assets, $24,081 (M); grants paid, $2,600; expenditures, $2,600; qualifying distributions, $2,572.

Limitations: Applications not accepted. Giving limited to residents of Meyersdale, PA.
Trustee: Robert A. Naragon.
EIN: 232506915

63307
Dorris R. Young Home Economics Fund
c/o Jane Regina
4223 Eisenhower Dr.
Bethlehem, PA 18020-8945
Application address: c/o Guidance Dept., Liberty High School, 1115 Linden St., Bethlehem, PA 18018

Financial data (yr. ended 06/30/01): Assets, $23,491 (M); grants paid, $1,000; gifts received, $6,000; expenditures, $1,000; qualifying distributions, $1,000.
Limitations: Giving limited to Bethlehem, PA.
Application information: Application form required.
Officer and Directors:* Jane Regina,* Mgr.; Judith Craver, Bruce R. Young.
EIN: 232459907

63308
FSL Scholarship Foundation
1903 Old Swede Rd.
Douglassville, PA 19518

Classified as a private operating foundation in 1991.
Financial data (yr. ended 08/31/00): Assets, $23,179 (M); grants paid, $0; expenditures, $260,130; qualifying distributions, $0; giving activities include $260,130 for programs.
Officers: Philip Johnson, Pres.; Christine O'Neill, Treas.
EIN: 232618766

63309
I Have a Dream Foundation - Camden, Inc.
1 International Plz., Ste. 300
Philadelphia, PA 19113

Financial data (yr. ended 12/31/99): Assets, $22,380 (M); grants paid, $0; gifts received, $170,452; expenditures, $154,933; qualifying distributions, $155,219; giving activities include $6,973 for programs.
Officers and Trustees:* J. Bruce Grisi, Pres.; Spencer Lempert,* Secy.; John Hakemian,* Treas.
EIN: 223249718

63310
Richard L. and Janet M. Wolfe Family Foundation
243 Taft Rd.
St. Marys, PA 15857 (814) 834-2736
Contact: Richard L. Wolfe, Pres.

Established in 1999.
Donor(s): Richard L. Wolfe, Janet M. Wolfe.
Financial data (yr. ended 12/31/01): Assets, $22,151 (M); grants paid, $105,000; gifts received, $101,645; expenditures, $106,811; qualifying distributions, $104,986.
Limitations: Giving primarily in St. Marys, PA.
Application information: Application form not required.
Officers: Richard L. Wolfe, Pres.; Janet M. Wolfe, Secy.-Treas.
Trustees: Marilyn Keyes, Laurey A. Kraus, Barry R. Wolfe, Cathy Wolfe, Eric C. Wolfe, Kenneth R. Wolfe.
EIN: 251844512
Codes: FD2

63311
Joseph J. Hopkins Scholarship Foundation
c/o Joseph W. Hopkins
500 Craig Ln.
Villanova, PA 19085-1902

Established around 1992.
Donor(s): Joseph W. Hopkins.
Financial data (yr. ended 06/30/01): Assets, $21,065 (M); grants paid, $1,000; expenditures, $1,167; qualifying distributions, $1,026.
Limitations: Applications not accepted.
Trustee: Joseph W. Hopkins.
EIN: 232662071

63312
Louise A. Cramer Foundation
c/o Society Hill Twr.
220 Locust St., Ste. 29B
Philadelphia, PA 19106
Contact: K. Cramer

Financial data (yr. ended 10/31/01): Assets, $17,246 (M); grants paid, $1,500; expenditures, $1,611; qualifying distributions, $1,604; giving activities include $111 for programs.
Limitations: Giving primarily in Philadelphia, PA.
Application information: Application form not required.
Trustees: James J. Cramer, Nancy S. Cramer, Norman K. Cramer.
EIN: 236802750

63313
George DiMiglio Football Foundation
1311 Jacksonville Rd.
Warminster, PA 18974-1217 (215) 355-8993
Contact: James & Patricia DiMiglio

Classified as a private operating foundation in 1990 in PA.
Financial data (yr. ended 12/31/00): Assets, $16,511 (M); grants paid, $500; gifts received, $1,000; expenditures, $500; qualifying distributions, $500.
Limitations: Giving limited to residents of PA.
Trustees: James DiMiglio, Patricia Jean DiMiglio.
EIN: 232559498

63314
Research on Innovation
c/o James E. Bessen
6 Leslie Ln.
Wallingford, PA 19086

Established in 1999 in PA.
Donor(s): James Bessen.
Financial data (yr. ended 11/30/01): Assets, $14,984 (M); grants paid, $0; gifts received, $10,307; expenditures, $7,185; qualifying distributions, $0.
Limitations: Applications not accepted.
Application information: Contributes only to pre-selected organizations.
Officer: James E. Bessen, C.E.O. and Pres.
EIN: 232975889

63315
Nallathambi Education & Health Foundation
202 S. McKean St.
P.O. Box 909
Butler, PA 16003

Established in 1999 in PA.
Financial data (yr. ended 12/31/00): Assets, $14,282 (M); grants paid, $88,129; gifts received, $99,106; expenditures, $92,490; qualifying distributions, $88,129; giving activities include $88,129 for programs.
Limitations: Applications not accepted. Giving limited to India.

Application information: Contributes only to pre-selected organizations.
Trustees: Helga Nallathambi, S.A. Nallathambi.
EIN: 256647770
Codes: FD2

63316
Sharon Momeyer Caputo Memorial Scholarship Fund
c/o Frank G. Caputo
P.O. Box 75
Wexford, PA 15090-0075
Application address: c/o Guidance Office, MPAHS, Mount Pleasant, PA 15666, tel.: (724) 547-3787

Established as a private operating foundation in 1994.
Financial data (yr. ended 09/30/00): Assets, $13,132 (M); grants paid, $1,500; gifts received, $200; expenditures, $1,500; qualifying distributions, $1,500.
Limitations: Giving limited to PA.
Application information: Application form required.
Trustees: Frank Caputo, Sue Craft.
EIN: 251725289

63317
Delphi Project Foundation
c/o Charles Denaro
2001 Market St., Ste. 1500
Philadelphia, PA 19103
E-mail: tammy.salvadore@rsli.com
Contact: Tammy Salvadore, Mgr.

Established in 1992 in PA.
Donor(s): Reliance Standard Life Insurance Co.
Financial data (yr. ended 12/31/01): Assets, $12,232 (M); grants paid, $458,800; gifts received, $504,267; expenditures, $499,298; qualifying distributions, $499,298.
Limitations: Applications not accepted. Giving limited to PA.
Application information: Contributes only to pre-selected organizations.
Officers: Larry Daurelle, C.E.O. and Pres.; Charles T. Denaro, Secy.; Olivia C. Niemczuk, Treas.; Tammy E. Salvadore, Mgr.
EIN: 232711230
Codes: FD

63318
The Merck Genome Research Institute
770 Sumneytown Pike
P.O. Box 4, WP44I-206
West Point, PA 19486 (215) 652-8368
FAX: (215) 993-3838; *E-mail:* mgri@merck.com
URL: http://www.mgri.org
Contact: M.J. Finley Austin, Admin. Dir.

Established in 1996 in NJ.
Donor(s): Merck & Co., Inc.
Financial data (yr. ended 12/31/01): Assets, $11,216 (M); grants paid, $4,862,390; gifts received, $477,649; expenditures, $4,906,068; qualifying distributions, $4,905,801.
Application information: Not accepting pre-proposals or regular proposals at this time. Application form required.
Officers: Edward M. Scolnick, M.D., Chair.; Anthony W. Ford-Hutchinson, Pres.; Judy C. Lewent, Sr. V.P., Finance; Celia A. Colbert, Secy.; Caroline Dorsa, Treas.; Jayne Kasarda, Cont.
EIN: 223431383
Codes: FD, FM

63319
Little Quakers, Inc.
2680 Tremont St.
Philadelphia, PA 19152-1335

Classified as a private operating foundation in 1974.
Donor(s): Robert P. Levy.
Financial data (yr. ended 01/31/00): Assets, $9,888 (M); grants paid, $5,000; gifts received, $20,194; expenditures, $27,668; qualifying distributions, $30,217; giving activities include $27,668 for programs.
Officers: Robert P. Levy, Pres.; Raymond Dooney, Exec. V.P.; Henry Faragalli, V.P.
EIN: 236296636

63320
David & Sarah Sky Charitable Trust
125 Summit Dr.
Hollidaysburg, PA 16648 (814) 696-7671
Contact: Neil Port, Tr.

Financial data (yr. ended 12/31/00): Assets, $9,036 (M); grants paid, $800; expenditures, $853; qualifying distributions, $845.
Limitations: Giving primarily in Altoona, PA.
Application information: Application form not required.
Trustees: Neil Port, Stephen Port, Asher Sky.
EIN: 251333892

63321
Lesbian & Gay Film Festival, Inc.
P.O. Box 81237
Pittsburgh, PA 15217-4237
Contact: Brenda Seevers, Co-Pres.

Established in 1997 in PA.
Donor(s): Pennsylvania Council for the Arts, Lambda Foundation, Absolute Vodka.
Financial data (yr. ended 12/31/00): Assets, $8,103 (M); grants paid, $0; gifts received, $13,101; expenditures, $17,458; qualifying distributions, $8,348; giving activities include $17,225 for programs.
Officers: Brenda Seevers, Co-Pres.; John Smith, Co-Pres.; Laura Annibalini, Secy.; Joseph Caretto, Treas.
EIN: 251600133

63322
Philadelphia Biomedical Research Institute, Inc.
100 Ross Rd.
King of Prussia, PA 19406

Financial data (yr. ended 12/31/00): Assets, $6,599 (M); grants paid, $0; gifts received, $83,249; expenditures, $74,603; qualifying distributions, $72,387; giving activities include $31,439 for programs.
Director: S. Tsuyoshi Ohnishi.
EIN: 232469361

63323
Linda Lutz Roth Education Fund
c/o Stephen F. Lutz
22 Walden Dr.
Mountain Top, PA 18707-2269
Application address: 339 Alvin St., Freeland, PA 18224, tel.: (570) 636-3747
Contact: Brian J. Lutz, Tr.

Established in 1997 in PA.
Financial data (yr. ended 06/30/01): Assets, $5,951 (M); grants paid, $1,000; gifts received, $2,030; expenditures, $1,002; qualifying distributions, $1,000.
Limitations: Giving limited to residents of the Hazleton, PA, area.

Application information: Application form required.
Trustees: Brian J. Lutz, Catherine B. Lutz, Stephen F. Lutz.
EIN: 232923756

63324
Kean Family Charitable Foundation
c/o Herbert Kean
241 S. 6th St. No. 2, Ste. 2402
Philadelphia, PA 19107-3727

Established in 1997.
Financial data (yr. ended 12/31/00): Assets, $5,868 (M); grants paid, $10,000; expenditures, $10,004; qualifying distributions, $10,000.
Limitations: Giving primarily in Philadelphia, PA.
Trustee: Herbert Kean.
EIN: 237852991

63325
Cat Rescue, Inc.
545 Spang Rd.
Baden, PA 15005-2545

Established in 1996 in PA.
Donor(s): R. Lee Holz.
Financial data (yr. ended 12/31/00): Assets, $5,350 (M); grants paid, $0; gifts received, $38,839; expenditures, $36,636; qualifying distributions, $36,636; giving activities include $36,636 for programs.
Officers and Directors:* Maxine S. Holz,* Pres.; R. Lee Holz,* V.P. and Secy.-Treas.
EIN: 251787182

63326
Tess Clayton Charitable Foundation
c/o Theresa R. Clayton
P.O. Box 332
Southampton, PA 18966-0332

Established in 1999 in PA.
Financial data (yr. ended 06/30/00): Assets, $4,914 (M); grants paid, $10,000; gifts received, $10,000; expenditures, $15,368; qualifying distributions, $15,368.
Limitations: Giving primarily in PA.
Officer: Thersa R. Clayton, Pres. and Secy.-Treas.
EIN: 233007292

63327
The Institute for Behavior Change, Inc.
848 West King's Hwy.
Coatesville, PA 19320

Financial data (yr. ended 12/31/99): Assets, $4,471 (M); grants paid, $0; expenditures, $234,324; qualifying distributions, $0; giving activities include $234,324 for programs.
Directors: Susan Cohen, Carol Dale, Steven Kossor.
EIN: 232935316

63328
Christu Kula Ashram Health and Education Foundation
202 S. McKean St.
P.O. Box 909
Butler, PA 16003

Established in 1999 in PA.
Donor(s): S.A. Nallathambi.
Financial data (yr. ended 12/31/99): Assets, $4,399 (M); grants paid, $6,090; gifts received, $11,552; expenditures, $7,153; qualifying distributions, $7,153.
Limitations: Giving primarily in India.
Trustees: H.N. Nallathambi, S.A. Nallathambi.
EIN: 256585193

63329
Kenneth L. Lezzer Memorial Foundation
c/o First Commonwealth Trust Co.
P.O. Box 118
Curwensville, PA 16833-0118
Application address: P.O. Box 217, Curwensville, PA 16833, tel.: (814) 236-2534
Contact: Elizabeth Lezzer, Tr.

Donor(s): Elizabeth Lezzer.
Financial data (yr. ended 12/31/01): Assets, $3,778 (M); grants paid, $20,750; expenditures, $22,564; qualifying distributions, $20,747.
Limitations: Giving primarily in PA.
Application information: Applicants must provide transcript information on college and major. Application form required.
Trustees: Elizabeth Lezzer, First Commonwealth Trust Co.
EIN: 256311923
Codes: GTI

63330
Lower Nazareth Teachers
c/o Lower Nazareth Elementary School
4422 Newburg Rd.
Nazareth, PA 18064-9671

Financial data (yr. ended 07/31/00): Assets, $3,415 (M); grants paid, $0; expenditures, $5,352; qualifying distributions, $5,352; giving activities include $5,378 for programs.
Limitations: Giving primarily in Nazareth, PA.
Trustees: Jack A. Hommer, April Kucsan, Donna Ricker.
EIN: 232352267

63331
Albina H. & Francis J. Dunleavy Corporation
(Formerly Albina H. & Francis J. Dunleavy Educational Trust)
553 Beale Rd.
Blue Bell, PA 19422

Classified as a private operating foundation in 1993.
Financial data (yr. ended 09/30/99): Assets, $3,277 (M); grants paid, $0; expenditures, $579; qualifying distributions, $0.
Limitations: Applications not accepted. Giving limited to residents of Philadelphia, PA.
Trustees: Michael Dunleavy, Patricia Vesci.
EIN: 232665900

63332
Wings Foundation
c/o Verna M. Bishop
5213 Merganser Way
Bensalem, PA 19020-3940

Classified as a private operating foundation in 1999.
Financial data (yr. ended 12/31/00): Assets, $3,163 (M); grants paid, $0; expenditures, $84; qualifying distributions, $0.
Limitations: Applications not accepted.
Application information: Contributes only to pre-selected organizations.
Officers: Sharon L. Navazio, Pres.; Verna M. Bishop, V.P.
EIN: 232989728

63333
Unicorn U.S., Ltd.
c/o Stephen W. Christian, C.P.A.
200 Gibraltar Rd., Ste. 200
Horsham, PA 19044

Established in 1996 in DE.
Donor(s): Sydney L. Smith.

Financial data (yr. ended 12/31/99): Assets, $2,838 (M); grants paid, $18,651; gifts received, $21,213; expenditures, $19,175; qualifying distributions, $19,014.
Limitations: Giving on an international basis, primarily in Bedford, England.
Directors: T. Raymond Baron, Charles Norris, Andrew Sutherland Rowe, Sydney L. Smith.
EIN: 043332762

63334
MVP's Retiree Group of Mellon Volunteer Professionals, Inc.
c/o William Nee
1 Mellon Bank Ctr., Ste. 1935
Pittsburgh, PA 15258-0001

Established in 1987 in PA.
Financial data (yr. ended 12/31/01): Assets, $2,691 (M); grants paid, $0; gifts received, $15,000; expenditures, $13,694; qualifying distributions, $0.
Officers: Martha Catizone, Pres.; John E. Wysseier, V.P.; Jeanne A. Reiff, Secy.-Treas.
Directors: Virginia Bodnar, Rosa Boockfor, Virginia C. Burns, Alfreda Creasy, Mary Lou Dillon, Mary Dee Heim, Bobbie J. Henry, Theresa V. Humphrey, Louise Lehner, Ruth I. McCartan, Patricia Nieme, Harry Obley.
EIN: 251549236

63335
The Joseph Farese Education Fund Trust
(Formerly The Joseph Farese Education Fund)
610 Wistar Rd.
Fairless Hills, PA 19030-4106

Established in 1995.
Financial data (yr. ended 12/31/00): Assets, $2,299 (L); grants paid, $0; gifts received, $500; expenditures, $36; qualifying distributions, $36; giving activities include $10 for programs.
Trustees: Bonnie A. Keating, Francis A. Keating, Bucks County Technical High School.
EIN: 237801892

63336
TFA Recordings, Inc.
P.O. Box 368
Bala Cynwyd, PA 19004-0368

Financial data (yr. ended 12/31/01): Assets, $2,292 (M); grants paid, $0; gifts received, $2,381; expenditures, $585; qualifying distributions, $585; giving activities include $585 for programs.
Directors: Dean Orloff, Donald Phillips, Matthew Phillips.
EIN: 232616261

63337
Gospel Ministries, Inc.
435 Jordan Ave.
Montoursville, PA 17754

Classified as a private operating foundation in 1985.
Financial data (yr. ended 12/31/01): Assets, $2,273 (M); grants paid, $0; gifts received, $10,299; expenditures, $9,850; qualifying distributions, $0.
Officer: Rev. Harold M. Teufel, Pres.
EIN: 251295073

63338
Pearl Software Educational Foundation, Inc.
767 Champlain Dr.
King of Prussia, PA 19406

Classified as a private operating foundation in 1999 in PA.
Donor(s): Judith Hoganboom, David Fertell.

Financial data (yr. ended 05/31/99): Assets, $1,952 (M); grants paid, $0; gifts received, $46,654; expenditures, $49,639; qualifying distributions, $0; giving activities include $46,745 for programs.
Officers: Judith Hoganboom, Pres. and Treas.; David Fertell, V.P. and Secy.
EIN: 232969871

63339
Fred W. Beans Charitable Foundation
c/o Fred W. Beans
3960 Airport Blvd.
Doylestown, PA 18901-1437

Established in 1992 in PA.
Donor(s): Fred W. Beans.
Financial data (yr. ended 12/31/00): Assets, $1,703 (M); grants paid, $110,426; gifts received, $97,550; expenditures, $110,515; qualifying distributions, $110,514.
Limitations: Applications not accepted. Giving limited to Doylestown, PA.
Application information: Contributes only to pre-selected organizations.
Officer: Fred W. Beans, Pres.
Directors: Patrick Clayton, Mark Donahue, Elizabeth Beans Gilbert, Jennifer B. Keiser, Brian Nesbitt.
EIN: 232670159
Codes: FD2

63340
George and Dianne Thornton Private Foundation
c/o George W. Thornton
1040 Box Hill Ln.
York, PA 17403

Established in 1999 in PA.
Financial data (yr. ended 12/31/00): Assets, $1,300 (M); grants paid, $2,100; gifts received, $2,000; expenditures, $2,100; qualifying distributions, $2,100.
Officers: George W. Thornton, Pres.; Dianne G. Thornton, Secy.-Treas.
EIN: 232969247

63341
Elf Aquitaine International Foundation
2000 Market St., 27th Fl.
Philadelphia, PA 19103-3222

Established as a company-sponsored operating foundation in 1996.
Donor(s): Elf Aquitaine, Inc.
Financial data (yr. ended 12/31/00): Assets, $750 (M); grants paid, $4,900; gifts received, $5,300; expenditures, $5,275; qualifying distributions, $5,275.
Limitations: Applications not accepted. Giving primarily in New York, NY.
Application information: Contributes only to pre-selected organizations.
Officers and Directors:* Francois de Wissoeq, Pres.; Dominique Paret,* V.P.; Eugene G. McGuire,* Secy.; David A. Benson, Treas.; Zoe Housez, S. Bruno Weymuller.
EIN: 133876967
Codes: CD

63342
The Jacob Brodie Foundation
c/o Brotech Corp.
150 Monument Rd.
Bala Cynwyd, PA 19004-1725

Classified as a private operating foundation in 1983 in PA.
Donor(s): Brotech Corp.

Financial data (yr. ended 12/31/00): Assets, $707 (M); grants paid, $10,000; gifts received, $10,000; expenditures, $10,039; qualifying distributions, $10,000.
Limitations: Applications not accepted. Giving primarily in PA.
Officers: Stefan Brodie, Pres.; Don Brodie, Secy.-Treas.
EIN: 222459391

63343
The Chester County Evergreen Foundation, Inc.
203 Gale Ln.
Kennett Square, PA 19348-1768
Contact: Bert G. Kerstetter, Pres.

Established in 1990 in PA.
Donor(s): Bert G. Kerstetter.
Financial data (yr. ended 12/31/01): Assets, $586 (M); grants paid, $14,725; gifts received, $16,300; expenditures, $16,834; qualifying distributions, $14,725.
Limitations: Giving limited to Chester County, PA.
Officers: Bert G. Kerstetter, Pres.; Diane M. Maguire, Secy.; Lynne Dewson, Treas.
EIN: 232605977

63344
Making America Beautiful, Inc.
600 Reed Rd.
P.O. Box 600
Broomall, PA 19008-0600

Established in 1992 in PA.
Financial data (yr. ended 12/31/99): Assets, $376 (M); grants paid, $0; gifts received, $56,850; expenditures, $58,183; qualifying distributions, $58,183; giving activities include $15,889 for programs.
Officers and Directors:* John A. Bruder,* Pres.; Christopher Flynn,* Secy.; Christopher J. McNichol,* Treas.
EIN: 232670678

63345
Alvi Foundation, Inc.
600 Munir Dr.
Elizabeth, PA 15037

Financial data (yr. ended 12/31/01): Assets, $368 (M); grants paid, $600; gifts received, $1,100; expenditures, $798; qualifying distributions, $600.
Limitations: Giving primarily to residents of Pakistan.
Officers: Pervaiz Alvi, Pres.; Javaid Alvi, Secy.-Treas.
EIN: 251571881

63346
Safe House Ministries, Inc.
129 N. 3rd St.
Jeannette, PA 15644-3326

Financial data (yr. ended 12/31/01): Assets, $202 (M); grants paid, $0; gifts received, $16,887; expenditures, $17,057; qualifying distributions, $0.
Officers: Robert Cast, Chair.; Gina Noel, Secy.; Eva L. Derry, Treas.; Rev. Robert R. Derry, Sr., Exec. Dir.
EIN: 251614716

63347
Mother's Love Foundation
2033 Linglestown Rd., Ste. 220
Harrisburg, PA 17110
Contact: Linda Ann Veno, Dir.

Financial data (yr. ended 12/31/01): Assets, $176 (M); grants paid, $0; gifts received, $1,085; expenditures, $1,392; qualifying distributions, $0.

63347—PENNSYLVANIA

Directors: Robin Balaban, Roberta Dzuryachko, Linda Ann Veno, Kathleen Worthington.
EIN: 251727672

63348
Bartash Foundation
1919 Chestnut St., Ste. 2224
Philadelphia, PA 19103
Application address: 99 Edgewood Ave., Larchmont, NY 10538, tel.: (914) 833-3965
Contact: David Bartash

Donor(s): Joseph Bartash.
Financial data (yr. ended 12/31/01): Assets, $96 (M); grants paid, $1,350; gifts received, $1,600; expenditures, $1,840; qualifying distributions, $1,350.
Limitations: Giving primarily in NY.
Officers: Joseph Bartash, Pres.; David Bartash, Secy.
EIN: 232826759

63349
Reading Blue Mountain & Northern Railroad Scholarship Fund
1 Railroad Blvd.
P.O. Box 218
Port Clinton, PA 19549

Classified as a company-sponsored operating fund in 1997.
Donor(s): Reading Blue Mountain & Northern Railroad Co.
Financial data (yr. ended 12/31/01): Assets, $45 (M); grants paid, $9,500; gifts received, $9,500; expenditures, $9,500; qualifying distributions, $9,500.
Application information: Unsolicited request for funds not accepted.
Officers: Christina J. Muller, Pres. and Secy.; Aaron P. Muller, V.P.; Philip Geschwindt, Treas.
EIN: 232971151
Codes: CD

63350
Hafer Foundation
85 S. Walnut St.
Boyertown, PA 19512

Donor(s): Paul R. Hafer.
Financial data (yr. ended 12/31/01): Assets, $40 (M); grants paid, $0; gifts received, $0; expenditures, $15; qualifying distributions, $0.
Limitations: Applications not accepted. Giving limited to Boyertown, PA.
Application information: Contributes only to pre-selected organizations.
Trustees: Ermine S. Hafer, Paul R. Hafer, Rodney P. Kline, Kenneth D. Wells.
EIN: 236438128

63351
Sharing Cupboard, Inc.
893 Powells Valley Rd.
Halifax, PA 17032

Classified as a private operating foundation in 2000.
Financial data (yr. ended 09/30/01): Assets, $33 (M); grants paid, $0; gifts received, $2,610; expenditures, $2,599; qualifying distributions, $2,599; giving activities include $2,599 for programs.
Officer: Suzette Floyd, Pres.
EIN: 251783888
Codes: TN

63352
Purrfect Love
c/o Darla K. Risch
P.O. Box 165
Nescopeck, PA 18635-0165

Classified as a private operating foundation in 1998.
Financial data (yr. ended 12/31/99): Assets, $22 (M); grants paid, $0; gifts received, $3,462; expenditures, $3,462; qualifying distributions, $3,462; giving activities include $3,462 for programs.
Officer and Trustees:* Darla K. Risch,* Mgr.; Wayne H. Risch.
EIN: 232890132

63353
The Avery Foundation
P.O. Box 684
Philipsburg, PA 16866-0684

Classified as a private operating foundation in 1983.
Financial data (yr. ended 06/30/00): Assets, $0 (M); grants paid, $0; gifts received, $15,550; expenditures, $15,544; qualifying distributions, $15,554; giving activities include $15,554 for programs.
Officer: Beatrice H. Avery, Mgr.
EIN: 251411254

63354
The Shade Tree Foundation
387 Springdale Ave.
Hatboro, PA 19040

Donor(s): Christian J. Wurst, Jr.
Financial data (yr. ended 09/30/00): Assets, $0 (M); grants paid, $31,597; gifts received, $27,875; expenditures, $32,254; qualifying distributions, $31,597.
Limitations: Applications not accepted.
Application information: Contributes only to pre-selected organizations.
Officers: Christian J. Wurst, Jr., Pres.; Craig J. Wurst, Secy.-Treas.
Director: Msgr. Stephen P. McHenry.
EIN: 232869030

PUERTO RICO

63355
Miranda Foundation
c/o Lourdes R. Miranda
51 Kings Ct., Apt. 413
San Juan, PR 00911

Established in 1993 in DC.
Donor(s): Lourdes R. Miranda.
Financial data (yr. ended 09/30/01): Assets, $1,129,064 (M); grants paid, $19,780; gifts received, $114,883; expenditures, $112,942; qualifying distributions, $109,225.
Limitations: Applications not accepted. Giving primarily in the Washington, DC, metropolitan area.
Application information: Contributes only to pre-selected organizations.
Officer: Lourdes R. Miranda, Pres.
Directors: Augustin Costa, Christina M. King-Vicente.
EIN: 521808696

63356
Unanue Lopez Family Foundation
P.O. Box 60-1467
Bayamon, PR 00960-1467
Contact: Francisco Unanue

Financial data (yr. ended 12/31/01): Assets, $877,945 (M); grants paid, $33,821; expenditures, $49,347; qualifying distributions, $33,821.
Trustees: Frank Unanue Casals, Anne Marie Unanue Lopez, Carlos A. Unanue, Diana L. Lopez Unanue, Francisco R. Unanue, Jorge E. Unanue.
EIN: 660572018

63357
Centro de Investigaciones Indigenas de Puerto Rico, Inc.
P.O. Box 4011, Old San Juan Sta.
San Juan, PR 00902-4011

Classified as a private operating foundation in 1986.
Financial data (yr. ended 12/31/01): Assets, $4,726 (M); grants paid, $0; gifts received, $36,000; expenditures, $33,392; qualifying distributions, $0.
Officers: Gaspar Roca, Pres.; Maria L. Roca, V.P.; Miguel Roca, Secy.-Treas.
EIN: 660423631

RHODE ISLAND

63358
Newport Restoration Foundation
51 Touro St.
Newport, RI 02840

Established in 1968 in RI.
Donor(s): Doris Duke,‡ Bernard Lafferty.‡
Financial data (yr. ended 12/31/99): Assets, $41,045,960 (M); grants paid, $15,890; gifts received, $3,719,825; expenditures, $2,872,376; qualifying distributions, $1,679,012; giving activities include $2,782,376 for programs.
Officers and Trustees:* Marion Charles,* Pres.; J. Carter Brown,* V.P.; Charles A. Dana III, Secy.-Treas.; Pieter Roos, Exec. Dir.
EIN: 050317816

63359
Wickham Park Trust Fund
c/o Fleet Private Clients Group
P.O. Box 6767
Providence, RI 02940-6767

Classified as a private operating foundation in 1980.
Financial data (yr. ended 12/31/01): Assets, $13,148,198 (M); grants paid, $0; gifts received, $168,316; expenditures, $783,911; qualifying distributions, $395,972.
Trustee: Fleet National Bank.
EIN: 066026059

63360
The Charles & Agnes Kazarian Eternal Foundation
c/o Paul B. Kazarian
30 Kennedy Plz.
Providence, RI 02903

Established in 1999 in DE.
Donor(s): Paul B. Kazarian.

Financial data (yr. ended 11/30/99): Assets, $10,421,606 (M); grants paid, $0; gifts received, $10,132,459; expenditures, $93,172; qualifying distributions, $122,806; giving activities include $72,806 for programs.
Limitations: Applications not accepted.
Application information: Contributes only to pre-selected organizations.
Officer: Paul B. Kazarian, Pres.
EIN: 050502562

63361
Ballou Home for the Aged
60 Mendon Rd.
Woonsocket, RI 02895-1598

Classified as an operating foundation in 1972.
Financial data (yr. ended 12/31/00): Assets, $7,959,428 (M); grants paid, $0; gifts received, $8,314; expenditures, $1,702,774; qualifying distributions, $1,607,710; giving activities include $1,702,774 for programs.
Officers and Directors:* Kathryn Whiting,* Pres.; Margaret Gagnon,* Secy.; Rev. Carl Guiney,* Treas.; and 8 additional directors.
EIN: 050260671

63362
Herreshoff Marine Museum
7 Burnside St.
P.O. Box 450
Bristol, RI 02809-0450

Classified as a private operating foundation in 1980.
Financial data (yr. ended 12/31/99): Assets, $5,785,900 (M); grants paid, $0; gifts received, $465,788; expenditures, $692,626; qualifying distributions, $431,588; giving activities include $494,135 for programs.
Officers: Halsey C. Herreshoff, Pres. and Treas.; W. Lincoln Mossop, 1st V.P.; Halsey C. Herreshoff II, 2nd V.P.; Teri Souto, Secy.
Trustees: John S. Carter, Charles F. Chapin, Nathaniel G. Herreshoff III, and 12 additional trustees.
EIN: 237102744

63363
North Family Trust
212 Main St., Ste. 4
Wakefield, RI 02879 (401) 782-4488
Contact: Edward T. Hogan, Tr.

Established in 1991 in RI.
Donor(s): Amabel North.‡
Financial data (yr. ended 06/30/01): Assets, $2,987,589 (M); grants paid, $142,500; expenditures, $216,984; qualifying distributions, $176,619.
Limitations: Giving limited to Newport County, RI.
Trustees: Robert Cummings, Edward T. Hogan.
EIN: 056091467
Codes: FD2

63364
Rhode Island Interscholastic Injury Fund
83 Rosegarden St.
Warwick, RI 02888-0599 (401) 461-6270
Contact: Raymond Dwyer, Treas.

Established in 1977 in RI.
Financial data (yr. ended 12/31/01): Assets, $2,818,040 (M); grants paid, $34,822; expenditures, $95,005; qualifying distributions, $63,863.
Limitations: Giving limited to RI.
Application information: Submit bills from high schools for students' injuries. Application form not required.

Officers: Ted Stebbins, Pres.; Frank Morey, V.P.; Kathleen M. Laquale, Secy.; Raymond T. Dwyer, Treas.
Board Members: Howard Catley, Jr., Robert Cavanagh, Audrey Crozier, Joyce Freeman, and 9 additional board members.
EIN: 050374155

63365
Nina Lynette Home
87 Washington St.
Newport, RI 02840-1532

Established in 1905.
Financial data (yr. ended 08/31/00): Assets, $2,377,409 (M); grants paid, $0; gifts received, $11,079; expenditures, $153,433; qualifying distributions, $153,433; giving activities include $153,433 for programs.
Officers: Herbert Rommel, Chair. and Pres.; Joanne Dunlap, V.P.; Mary Jameson, Treas.
EIN: 050259061

63366
Providence Shelter for Colored Children
112 Elton St.
Providence, RI 02906
Contact: Dorothy Patrick, Tr.

Established in 1839 in RI.
Financial data (yr. ended 04/30/01): Assets, $1,991,193 (M); grants paid, $97,365; gifts received, $1,623; expenditures, $127,294; qualifying distributions, $113,686.
Limitations: Giving primarily in RI.
Publications: Informational brochure (including application guidelines).
Application information: Distribution is made throughout the year as funds and dividends accrue. Application form required.
Directors: Jametta Alston, Dorothy Patrick, Connie Worthington, and 22 additional directors.
EIN: 056014169
Codes: FD2

63367
Martha Dickinson Bianchi Trust
c/o Fleet Private Clients Group
P.O. Box 6767
Providence, RI 02940-6767

Established in 1990 in MA.
Financial data (yr. ended 12/31/01): Assets, $1,508,370 (M); grants paid, $0; gifts received, $61,769; expenditures, $108,238; qualifying distributions, $92,815.
Trustee: Fleet National Bank.
EIN: 046634211

63368
Ashaway Charitable Trust
c/o The Washington Trust Co.
23 Broad St.
Westerly, RI 02891
Application address: c/o Ashaway Line & Twine Mfg. Co., Ashaway, RI 02804
Contact: Pamela Crandall, Mgr.

Established in 1950 in RI.
Financial data (yr. ended 12/31/00): Assets, $1,162,246 (M); grants paid, $50,949; expenditures, $65,367; qualifying distributions, $53,167.
Limitations: Giving primarily in CT and RI.
Officer: Pamela Crandall, Mgr.
Trustee: The Washington Trust Co.
EIN: 056003255

63369
Charles Edwin Lawton Memorial Masonic Home
259 Central St.
Central Falls, RI 02863-2706

Classified as a private operating foundation in 1976.
Financial data (yr. ended 11/30/01): Assets, $818,421 (M); grants paid, $0; gifts received, $76,721; expenditures, $23,295; qualifying distributions, $0.
Officers and Trustees:* Samuel Sinel,* Pres.; Nelson Kay,* 1st V.P.; Stephen Lada,* 2nd V.P. and Secy.; John Wilmarth,* Treas.
EIN: 050261694

63370
Harriet Chappell Moore Foundation
(Formerly Morrison Home for the Aged)
c/o Harriet Moore
32 Yosemite Valley Rd.
Westerly, RI 02891 (401) 596-5512

Financial data (yr. ended 12/31/99): Assets, $785,345 (M); grants paid, $0; expenditures, $19,874; qualifying distributions, $15,161; giving activities include $12,992 for programs.
Limitations: Applications not accepted. Giving limited to Chicago, IL.
Application information: Contributes only to a pre-selected organization.
Trustee: Hatsy Moore.
EIN: 056020623

63371
The Lucy C. Ayres Home for Nurses, Inc.
300 Centerville Rd., Ste. 300S
Warwick, RI 02886

Financial data (yr. ended 03/31/00): Assets, $780,603 (M); grants paid, $39,500; gifts received, $265; expenditures, $51,100; qualifying distributions, $44,428; giving activities include $44,428 for programs.
Officers: Helen Rayner, Pres.; Jean Wilcox, 1st V.P.; Priscilla Diveley, 2nd V.P.; Patricia Allard, Corresponding Secy.; Barbara LaPlume, Recording Secy.; Eleanor Sinnegan, Treas.
Directors: Doris Durfee, Helen Enright, Martha Feeley, Mary Kratzert, Barbara LaPlume, Doris Mathewson, and 3 additional directors.
EIN: 050264853

63372
Clinton Museum Trust
c/o Fleet Private Clients Group
P.O. Box 6767
Providence, RI 02940-6767

Classified as a private operating foundation in 1981.
Donor(s): J.W. Leahy.‡
Financial data (yr. ended 04/30/01): Assets, $685,410 (M); grants paid, $0; gifts received, $225; expenditures, $22,087; qualifying distributions, $15,097; giving activities include $15,317 for programs.
Trustee: Fleet National Bank.
EIN: 510190075

63373
Holm's Charitable Trust
c/o Fleet Private Clients Group
P.O. Box 6767
Providence, RI 02940-6767

Established as an operating foundation in 1997 in CT.
Financial data (yr. ended 12/31/01): Assets, $586,583 (M); grants paid, $2,540; gifts received,

63373—RHODE ISLAND

$20,558; expenditures, $60,594; qualifying distributions, $56,876.
Limitations: Applications not accepted. Giving primarily in Deep River, CT.
Application information: Contributes only to pre-selected organizations.
Trustee: Fleet National Bank.
EIN: 066312170

63374
Fair Havens
603 Harris Ave.
Woonsocket, RI 02895-1872

Financial data (yr. ended 12/31/99): Assets, $530,643 (M); grants paid, $0; gifts received, $4,290; expenditures, $22,729; qualifying distributions, $24,517; giving activities include $17,729 for programs.
Director: Robert Lewis, Exec. Dir.
EIN: 050493504

63375
Orlando R. Smith Trust
c/o Isaac G. Smith, Jr.
P.O. Box 531
Westerly, RI 02891-2818

Financial data (yr. ended 06/30/99): Assets, $447,714 (M); grants paid, $0; gifts received, $12,567; expenditures, $23,005; qualifying distributions, $21,707; giving activities include $17,345 for programs.
Officers: Joseph Potter, Pres.; Stanton C. Saunders, V.P.; Carolyn Longolucco, Secy.; Frances Kelly, Treas.
Trustees: Kenneth Boll, John Eckel, Isaac G. Smith, Jr.
EIN: 237352670
Codes: TN

63376
SCAT Foundation, Inc.
84 Valley St.
East Providence, RI 02914 (401) 434-3300
Application address: 84 Valley St., East Providence, RI 02914; Tel.: (401)434-3300
Contact: Robert J. Gormley, Pres.

Classified as a private operating foundation in 1996.
Donor(s): Organic Dyestuffs Corp.
Financial data (yr. ended 05/31/00): Assets, $437,273 (M); grants paid, $100; expenditures, $14,973; qualifying distributions, $14,973.
Officers: Robert J. Gormley, Pres. and Treas.; Gregory M. Gormley, V.P.; Richard Nicolo, Secy.
EIN: 050471941

63377
Cumberland Farms Conservation Trust
519 Mendon Rd.
P.O. Box 7179
Cumberland, RI 02864

Classified as a private operating foundation in 1977.
Donor(s): Lily Haseotes Bentas, Byron Haseotes, Demetrios B. Haseotes, George Haseotes.
Financial data (yr. ended 12/31/99): Assets, $380,000 (M); grants paid, $0; gifts received, $866; expenditures, $866; qualifying distributions, $866; giving activities include $380,000 for programs.
Trustees: Lily Haseotes Bentas, Byron Haseotes, Demetrios B. Haseotes, George Haseotes.
EIN: 042616919

63378
Woonsocket Rotary Charities Foundation, Inc.
c/o Edward F. Yazbak
P.O. Box 154
Woonsocket, RI 02895
Contact: Ernest L. Dupre, Pres.

Established in 1991 in RI.
Donor(s): Rotary Club of Woonsocket, RI.
Financial data (yr. ended 06/30/99): Assets, $187,950 (M); grants paid, $15,000; gifts received, $2,011; expenditures, $15,000; qualifying distributions, $14,869.
Officers: Ernest L. Dupre, M.D., Pres.; Paul Laprade, Treas.
Directors: Fred Corey, Stanley Cybulski, Robert Picard.
EIN: 223115037

63379
George Abrahamian Foundation
c/o Armenian Chruch, Trustee Dept.
945 Admiral St.
Providence, RI 02904

Classified as a private operating foundation in 1969.
Financial data (yr. ended 12/31/00): Assets, $143,486 (M); grants paid, $6,000; expenditures, $6,211; qualifying distributions, $6,153.
Limitations: Giving primarily in RI.
Application information: Personal interview required. Application form required.
Directors: Abraham G. Abraham, Harry Abraham, June A. Masterson, Marion D. Masterson-Tso.
EIN: 237039366
Codes: GTI

63380
The Hebb Waterfowl Wildlife Trust
c/o Alan Gilstein
144 Westminster St.
Providence, RI 02903-2216

Donor(s): Angus Hebb, Karen Hebb.
Financial data (yr. ended 11/30/00): Assets, $104,780 (M); grants paid, $0; gifts received, $21,500; expenditures, $20,597; qualifying distributions, $11,358; giving activities include $7,680 for programs.
Trustee: Karen Hebb.
EIN: 050376087

63381
St. Dunstan's College of Sacred Music
275 N. Main St.
Providence, RI 02903-1223

Established in 1930 in RI.
Financial data (yr. ended 12/31/01): Assets, $85,690 (M); grants paid, $0; expenditures, $6,821; qualifying distributions, $0.
Officers: Rt. Rev. Geralyn Wolf, Pres.; William Payton, V.P.; Annett Cox, Secy.; Robert Batchelor, Treas.
Directors: Alicide Barnaby, Jr., Gregory Cole, Harry Sacchetti.
EIN: 050258995

63382
Asphodel Press, Inc.
c/o Britt Bell
54 Phillips St.
North Kingstown, RI 02852

Established in 1997 in RI.
Donor(s): Deborah Pease.
Financial data (yr. ended 12/31/00): Assets, $84,235 (M); grants paid, $0; gifts received, $104,000; expenditures, $131,903; qualifying distributions, $130,716; giving activities include $130,716 for programs.
Officer: Deborah Pease, Exec. Dir.
Directors: Britt Bell, Robert Creeley, Jennifer Moyer.
EIN: 133649324

63383
Corinthians Endowment Fund
68 1/2 Roseneath Ave.
Newport, RI 02840-3849

Established in 1995 in NY.
Donor(s): The Corinthians Association.
Financial data (yr. ended 12/31/01): Assets, $62,622 (M); grants paid, $2,500; gifts received, $35,071; expenditures, $3,417; qualifying distributions, $3,417.
Limitations: Giving primarily on the East Coast of the U.S., north of NC, with some emphasis on the New England region.
Officers and Trustees:* Alice N. Mutch,* Pres. and Secy.; David K. McConnell,* Treas.; John J. Kiszkiel II, Franklyn H. Lohr, Jr., Richard T. Sanborn, Clinton H. Springer, Jeffrey W. Tyrrel, Vagn Worm.
EIN: 061321543

63384
Renew the Resources of the Bay Foundation
461 Water St.
Warren, RI 02885

Established in 1999 in RI.
Donor(s): Luther H. Blount.
Financial data (yr. ended 12/31/99): Assets, $1,047 (M); grants paid, $2,500; gifts received, $7,500; expenditures, $6,453; qualifying distributions, $3,825.
Officers: Luther H. Blount, Pres. and Treas.; Julie Blount, Secy.
Directors: Paul Frechette, Pasco Gasbarro, Jr.
EIN: 050505420

63385
Edward Joseph Lariviere Memorial Foundation
c/o Nancy Mundy
42 Seaview Ave.
Cranston, RI 02905

Classified as a private operating foundation in 1987.
Financial data (yr. ended 06/30/02): Assets, $1 (M); grants paid, $0; gifts received, $1,500; expenditures, $37,099; qualifying distributions, $0.
Officers: Nancy C. Oden, Pres.; Christopher Mundy, V.P.; Donna Rachels, Secy.; John Turner, Treas.
EIN: 050419013

SOUTH CAROLINA

63386
The Belle W. Baruch Foundation
22 Hobcaw Rd.
Georgetown, SC 29440

Classified as a private operating foundation in 1964.
Donor(s): Belle W. Baruch.‡
Financial data (yr. ended 06/30/00): Assets, $16,743,162 (M); grants paid, $0; gifts received, $448,383; expenditures, $1,333,813; qualifying

distributions, $1,250,078; giving activities include $152,514 for programs.
Officer: Harry Lightsey, Jr., M.D., Chair.
Trustees: Sally Self Harley, Hugh C. Lane, Jr., Hon. Harold R. Tyler.
EIN: 570564080

63387
Nemours Wildlife Foundation
(Formerly Memours Plantation Wildlife)
2239 Stroban Rd.
Seabrook, SC 29940 (843) 846-2539
E-mail: ewiggers@islc.net
Contact: Ernie P. Wiggers, Exec. Dir.

Established in 1995.
Donor(s): Laura E. Dupont.
Financial data (yr. ended 12/31/99): Assets, $13,323,205 (M); grants paid, $535; gifts received, $71,574; expenditures, $620,491; qualifying distributions, $469,069; giving activities include $53,180 for programs.
Publications: Newsletter.
Officers: Michael G. McShane, Pres.; Colden R. Battey, Jr., V.P. & Treas.; John R. Cope, Secy.
Director: Laura E. DuPont.
EIN: 570985138

63388
John D. Muller, Jr. Trust
c/o Wachovia Bank of South Carolina, N.A.
P.O. Box 700
Charleston, SC 29402

Established in 1986 in SC.
Donor(s): John D. Muller.‡
Financial data (yr. ended 08/31/00): Assets, $5,629,155 (M); grants paid, $21,540; expenditures, $263,634; qualifying distributions, $90,547.
Limitations: Applications not accepted. Giving limited to SC.
Application information: Contributes only to pre-selected organizations.
Trustee: Wachovia Bank of South Carolina, N.A.
EIN: 576107692

63389
Rebecca C. Parsons Scholarship Foundation
P.O. Box 1550
Pawleys Island, SC 29585 (843) 237-9125
Contact: Robert D. Harper, Jr., Tr.

Established in 1994 in SC.
Donor(s): Rebecca C Parsons.‡
Financial data (yr. ended 12/31/00): Assets, $3,941,371 (M); grants paid, $85,750; expenditures, $110,834; qualifying distributions, $83,806.
Limitations: Giving limited to Andrews, SC.
Trustees: Martha Lynn Mercer Gaskins, Robert D. Harper, Jr., Alice Mercer.
EIN: 570990214
Codes: FD2, GTI

63390
PEK Foundation, Inc.
534 Azalea Ln.
Florence, SC 29501

Classified as a private operating foundation in 1987.
Financial data (yr. ended 09/30/00): Assets, $3,348,800 (M); grants paid, $0; gifts received, $789,218; expenditures, $256,073; qualifying distributions, $206,092; giving activities include $206,092 for programs.
Officers: Frank S. Key, Jr., Pres.; Randolph S. Key, V.P.; Margaret K. Charles, Secy.
EIN: 570808264

63391
H. M. and Pearl Kyle Foundation, Inc.
514 Juanita Dr.
Florence, SC 29501-5724 (843) 662-9401
Application address: P.O. Box 6677, Florence, SC 29502-6675, tel.: (843) 662-9401
Contact: Fred N. Jones, Jr., Tr.

Established around 1986.
Financial data (yr. ended 12/31/01): Assets, $2,951,343 (M); grants paid, $227,204; expenditures, $287,404; qualifying distributions, $248,305.
Limitations: Giving primarily in the Cape Fear, NC, area, and the Pee Dee, SC, area.
Application information: Application form required.
Trustees: Gary W. Crawford, Preston B. Huntley, Jr., Fred N. Jones, Jr., James H. Kyle III, Ingram Parmley, Wallace B. Permenter.
EIN: 570786826
Codes: FD2

63392
James F. Byrnes Foundation
P.O. Box 6781
Columbia, SC 29260 (803) 254-9325
URL: http://www.byrnesscholars.org
Contact: Jean P. Elton, Exec. Secy.

Established in 1947 in SC.
Donor(s): James F. Byrnes.‡
Financial data (yr. ended 06/30/01): Assets, $2,437,146 (M); grants paid, $176,768; gifts received, $69,535; expenditures, $307,680; qualifying distributions, $236,428.
Limitations: Giving limited to residents of SC.
Publications: Application guidelines, informational brochure, newsletter.
Application information: Scholarship assistance to 4-year institutions for high school seniors and college freshmen and sophomores only. Application form required.
Officers and Directors:* Hal Norton,* Pres.; Lois H. Anderson,* V.P.; Nancy N. Drew,* Secy.; William E. Rowe,* Treas.; Jeanette Cothran, Carol Ann Green, Deaver D. McGraw III, Dal Poston, J. Charles Wall.
EIN: 576024756
Codes: FD2, GTI

63393
Ladies Benevolent Society of the City of Charleston
c/o Barbara Lemel
37 Sussex Rd.
Charleston, SC 29407

Financial data (yr. ended 12/31/01): Assets, $1,868,119 (M); grants paid, $150; gifts received, $12,234; expenditures, $55,326; qualifying distributions, $45,945; giving activities include $45,796 for programs.
Limitations: Applications not accepted. Giving primarily in Charleston, SC.
Application information: Contributes only to pre-selected organizations.
Officers: Mrs. Harry C. DeMuth, Secy.; Mrs. Stephen C. Meyers, Secy.; Barbara P. Lemel, Treas.
Trustees: Mrs. John C. Ball, Mrs. Charles E. Bennett, Sr., Mrs. Robert Bennett, Jr., Mrs. Walter S. Crone, Mrs. Leon B. de Brux, and 10 additional trustees.
EIN: 576001563

63394
Clergy Society
(Formerly Society for the Relief of the Widows, Orphans, Aged and Disabled Clergy Diocese of South Carolina)
314 Mill Creek Dr.
Charleston, SC 29407
Application address: P.O. Box 640 Charleston, SC 29402, tel.: (843) 577-9700
Contact: G.B. Danich, Pres.

Established in 2000 in SC.
Financial data (yr. ended 12/31/00): Assets, $1,657,979 (M); grants paid, $109,727; gifts received, $1,570; expenditures, $117,568; qualifying distributions, $109,727.
Limitations: Giving primarily in SC.
Officers: G.B. Danich, Pres.; E.L. Wilcox, V.P.; J.A. Blitch, Secy.-Treas.
EIN: 576021772
Codes: FD2

63395
Kershaw County Vocational Education Foundation, Inc.
P.O. Box 10
Lugoff, SC 29078-0010
Application address: c/o Selection Comm., 1095 Pepper Ridge Dr., Lugoff, SC 29078, tel.: (803) 438-3708
Contact: Larry B. Kilgore, Dir.

Established in 1986 in SC.
Financial data (yr. ended 12/31/01): Assets, $1,462,906 (L); grants paid, $25,750; expenditures, $26,789; qualifying distributions, $25,750.
Limitations: Giving limited to Kershaw County, SC.
Application information: Application form required.
Officer and Trustees:* Charles B. Baxley,* Chair.; Larry B. Kilgore, Donnie W. Wilson.
EIN: 570805522
Codes: GTI

63396
Piedmont Blood Center, Inc.
(Formerly Spartanburg Blood Bank, Inc.)
175 Dunbar St.
Spartanburg, SC 29304

Financial data (yr. ended 03/31/02): Assets, $833,411 (M); grants paid, $0; gifts received, $27,562; expenditures, $2,802,506; qualifying distributions, $0.
Officers and Directors:* Joe E. Webb,* Pres.; Jack Evans,* V.P.; Glenda Cartee,* Secy.-Treas.; Hugh Barrow, Jr., William Bean, James Bearden III, Jim Cudd, Robert Garner, James Green, Valorie Kirby, Bruce Murdock, Gregory Valainis.
EIN: 570605598

63397
Write To Change, Inc.
P.O. Box 908
Clemson, SC 29633-0908 (864) 654-8573
Contact: Dixie Goswami, C.E.O.

Established in 1998 in SC.
Financial data (yr. ended 06/30/00): Assets, $806,261 (M); grants paid, $39,486; gifts received, $27,405; expenditures, $92,653; qualifying distributions, $39,486.
Officers: Dixie Goswami, C.E.O.; Walter H. Gooch, C.F.O.
Board Member: Elizabeth Balley.
EIN: 570994011

63398
Yeargin Foundation
115 Edinburgh Ct.
Greenville, SC 29607

Established in 1965 in SC.
Donor(s): Nancy Yeargin Furman, Mary Ellen Yeargin, R. Lynn Yeargin, Robert H. Yeargin.
Financial data (yr. ended 12/31/01): Assets, $744,562 (M); grants paid, $168,984; expenditures, $173,813; qualifying distributions, $168,183.
Limitations: Applications not accepted. Giving primarily in SC.
Application information: Contributes only to pre-selected organizations.
Directors: Mary Ellen Yeargin, Robert H. Yeargin.
Trustees: Nancy Yeargin Furman, R. Lynn Yeargin.
EIN: 576026663
Codes: FD2

63399
Society for the Relief of Families of Deceased & Disabled Indigent Members of the Medical Profession of the State of South Carolina
c/o J. Ray Ivester, M.D.
19 Guerard Road
Charleston, SC 29407

Financial data (yr. ended 11/30/01): Assets, $686,335 (M); grants paid, $19,000; gifts received, $20,845; expenditures, $29,329; qualifying distributions, $19,000.
Limitations: Applications not accepted. Giving primarily in SC.
Officers and Directors:* Paul W. Sanders, M.D.,* Pres.; Julian T. Buxton, M.D.,* V.P.; Richard C. Hagerty, M.D.,* Secy.; Julius Ray Ivester, Jr., M.D.,* Treas.; Haskell S. Ellison, M.D., Henry C. Heins, Jr., M.D., Edward F. Parker, C. Ford Rivers, Jr., M.D., Alexander M. Sloan, M.D., and 8 additional directors.
EIN: 576021204
Codes: GTI

63400
Thomason-Bowie Foundation
P.O. Box 1729
Spartanburg, SC 29304 (864) 348-7425

Established in 1998 in SC.
Financial data (yr. ended 12/31/00): Assets, $629,507 (M); grants paid, $0; gifts received, $400,438; expenditures, $20,608; qualifying distributions, $197,657; giving activities include $188,648 for programs.
Limitations: Giving primarily in SC.
Officers: Marie T. Bowie, Pres.; John M. Thomason, V.P.; George H. Thomason, Secy.; William Kirkpatrick, Treas.
Directors: Rose Mahaffey, Wesley Mahaffey.
EIN: 562066513

63401
William B. & Lela P. Earle Scholarship Trust Fund
P.O. Box 40
Walhalla, SC 29691-0040
Application address: 140 Hawthorne Ln., Mountain Rest, SC 29664
Contact: John D. Ridley, Tr.

Established in 2000 in SC.
Financial data (yr. ended 12/31/01): Assets, $495,329 (M); grants paid, $9,825; expenditures, $10,480; qualifying distributions, $9,825.
Application information: Application form required.
Trustees: Larry C. Brandt, John D. Ridley, Theodore A. Snyder, Jr.
EIN: 586384762

63402
Featherston Family Foundation
333 Saranac Dr.
Spartanburg, SC 29307-1141
Contact: John S. Featherston, Sr., Pres.

Established in 1997 in SC.
Donor(s): John S. Featherston, Sr., John S. Featherston, Jr.
Financial data (yr. ended 12/31/00): Assets, $441,482 (M); grants paid, $23,600; expenditures, $27,242; qualifying distributions, $26,970.
Limitations: Giving primarily in the southeastern U.S.
Officers: John S. Featherston, Sr., Pres. and Treas.; John S. Featherston, Jr., V.P.; Nora H. Featherston, Secy.
EIN: 582314709

63403
The Bridges Foundation
c/o Mercer T. Bridges
618 Bramble Rd.
North Augusta, SC 29841

Established in 1990 in SC.
Donor(s): Mercer T. Bridges.
Financial data (yr. ended 12/31/00): Assets, $374,550 (M); grants paid, $28,350; expenditures, $29,152; qualifying distributions, $28,204.
Limitations: Applications not accepted. Giving primarily in Augusta, GA.
Application information: Contributes only to pre-selected organizations.
Trustees: Ellen H. Bridges, Mercer T. Bridges.
EIN: 570900294

63404
The Margaret and Dick Littlejohn Foundation
P.O. Box 6666
Spartanburg, SC 29304

Financial data (yr. ended 12/31/01): Assets, $366,061 (M); grants paid, $100; gifts received, $13,220; expenditures, $3,953; qualifying distributions, $100.
Limitations: Applications not accepted.
Directors: Margaret L. Gowan, B. R. Littlejohn, Jr., B. R. Littlejohn III, M. P. Littlejohn.
EIN: 571007913

63405
South Carolina Broadcasters Association Educational Foundation
c/o Shani White
1 Harbison Way, Ste. 112
Columbia, SC 29210 (803) 732-1186

Established in 1997 in SC.
Donor(s): SC Broadcasters Association, Richard Uray.
Financial data (yr. ended 12/31/01): Assets, $308,790 (M); grants paid, $47,672; gifts received, $152,375; expenditures, $49,342; qualifying distributions, $47,672.
Limitations: Giving limited to SC.
Application information: Application form required.
Officers and Directors:* David McAtee,* Pres.; Alex Snipe, Jr.,* V.P.; Matt Sedota,* Secy.; Evon Trotter,* Treas.; Dave Aiken, John Cottingham, Luzanne Griffith, Dick Laughridge, Bill McElveen, Lee Meredith, Jane Pigg, Margaret Wallace, John Woodson.
EIN: 570637558

63406
Sylvia & William W. Gretsch Memorial Foundation
c/o Fred W. Gretsch
1 Gretsch Plz., Box 358
Ridgeland, SC 29936

Established in 1986 in SC.
Donor(s): Fred W. Gretsch.
Financial data (yr. ended 12/31/99): Assets, $258,877 (M); grants paid, $25,000; gifts received, $198,800; expenditures, $25,220; qualifying distributions, $25,113.
Officers: Fred W. Gretsch, Pres. and Treas.; James A. Grimsley III, V.P. and Secy.
EIN: 570834797

63407
Good Shepherd Community Services, Inc.
(Formerly The Wilderness Preservation Society)
P.O. Box 177
Gramling, SC 29348

Financial data (yr. ended 12/31/01): Assets, $243,154 (M); grants paid, $2,500; expenditures, $9,576; qualifying distributions, $5,000.
Limitations: Applications not accepted.
Application information: Contributes only to pre-selected organizations.
Officers and Directors:* Jerry Morgan,* Pres.; Jeanette Morgan,* Secy.-Treas.; Paul Strapkovic.
EIN: 581609814

63408
Scott's Branch 76 Foundation
P.O. Box 82
Summerton, SC 29148

Financial data (yr. ended 12/31/01): Assets, $192,691 (M); grants paid, $0; gifts received, $405,768; expenditures, $404,896; qualifying distributions, $404,896; giving activities include $195,459 for programs.
Officers: Haulen Smith, Pres.; Marcia Conyers, Secy.; Agron Jumes, Jr., Treas.
Director: Emma Thomas.
EIN: 570916730

63409
New Beginnings Foundation
P.O. Box 1636
Spartanburg, SC 29304-1636 (864) 594-5000

Established in 1985 in SC.
Financial data (yr. ended 12/31/01): Assets, $185,801 (M); grants paid, $0; gifts received, $400,342; expenditures, $411,855; qualifying distributions, $412,727; giving activities include $409,466 for programs.
Officers: Woodrow Willard, Chair.; Charles P. Ewart, Pres.; Lee Blair, Exec. V.P.; Ronald Carter Smith, Sr. V.P.
EIN: 570787650

63410
The Norma and William Hall Charitable Trust
c/o W. Stanley Hall
4940 Dorchester Rd.
North Charleston, SC 29418-5601

Established in 1993. Classified as a private foundation in 1997.
Donor(s): William J. Hall, Norma C. Hall.
Financial data (yr. ended 12/31/99): Assets, $145,019 (M); grants paid, $7,200; gifts received, $8,616; expenditures, $7,200; qualifying distributions, $7,200.
Limitations: Applications not accepted.
Application information: Contributes only to pre-selected organizations.
Trustee: W. Stanley Hall.

EIN: 576148363

63411
Joe R. and Joella F. Utley Foundation
c/o Joe R. Utley
P.O. Box 8367
Spartanburg, SC 29305-8367

Classified as a private operating foundation in 1993.
Donor(s): Joe R. Utley, Joella F. Utley.
Financial data (yr. ended 12/31/01): Assets, $141,724 (M); grants paid, $118,377; gifts received, $205,000; expenditures, $146,883; qualifying distributions, $131,850; giving activities include $7,071 for programs.
Limitations: Applications not accepted. Giving primarily in Brevard, NC and Vermillion, SD.
Application information: Contributes only to pre-selected organizations.
Officers and Trustees:* Joella F. Utley,* Secy.
Directors: Bernelle Demo, Craig A. Kridel, Eric Pettit, Olin Sansbury.
EIN: 570974104
Codes: FD2

63412
Batten Family Foundation, Inc.
22 Glenmoor Pl.
Hilton Head Island, SC 29926

Established in 2000 in SC.
Donor(s): Kathryn C. Batten.
Financial data (yr. ended 12/31/00): Assets, $118,318 (M); grants paid, $10,202; gifts received, $210,442; expenditures, $14,859; qualifying distributions, $20,404.
Limitations: Applications not accepted.
Application information: Contributes only to pre-selected organizations.
Officers: Kathryn C. Batten, Pres.; David C. Batten, V.P.
Director: Jane Wild.
EIN: 562187409

63413
Barbara E. Newsom Foundation
P.O. Box 867
Cheraw, SC 29520-0867 (843) 537-2171
Contact: Joseph E. Newsom, Tr.

Established in 1997 in SC.
Donor(s): Joseph K. Newsom.
Financial data (yr. ended 12/31/99): Assets, $84,058 (M); grants paid, $3,530; gifts received, $7,000; expenditures, $4,516; qualifying distributions, $7,614.
Limitations: Giving limited to Cheraw, SC.
Trustee: Joseph K. Newsom.
EIN: 582326741

63414
Christian Ministries International, Inc.
116 Cowdray Park
Columbia, SC 29223
Contact: John W. Simmons, Pres.

Classified as a private operating foundation in 1996.
Donor(s): Sarah Pregnall, Marjorie P. Simmons.
Financial data (yr. ended 12/31/01): Assets, $78,296 (M); grants paid, $327,872; gifts received, $384,335; expenditures, $383,857; qualifying distributions, $380,295.
Limitations: Applications not accepted.
Officers: Bill Wooten, Chair.; John W. Simmons, Pres.; Marjorie P. Simmons, Secy.
Directors: Betty Dent, Harry Dent, Jimmy Morse, Peggy Morse, Buzz Pleming, Suzanne Pleming, Carolyn Whiting, Richard D. Whiting, Betty Wooten.

EIN: 571035134
Codes: FD

63415
Dorchester Free School Board, Inc.
P.O. Box 2045
Summerville, SC 29484-2045

Financial data (yr. ended 12/31/99): Assets, $67,315 (M); grants paid, $0; gifts received, $3,775; expenditures, $4,000; qualifying distributions, $4,000; giving activities include $4,000 for programs.
Directors: Steve Hutchinson, P. Frank Smith.
EIN: 570966757

63416
Conway-Ennen Foundation
24 Oyster Shell Ln.
Hilton Head Island, SC 29926 (843) 681-7886
Contact: Monica C. Ennen, Chair.

Established in 1996 in GA.
Donor(s): Monica C. Ennen.
Financial data (yr. ended 12/31/99): Assets, $66,479 (M); grants paid, $5,000; expenditures, $6,525; qualifying distributions, $5,000; giving activities include $5,000 for programs.
Officer: Monica C. Ennen, Chair. and Pres.
EIN: 571037048

63417
The McDonald Foundation Charitable Trust
3525 McDonald Dr.
Florence, SC 29506

Established in 1990 in SC.
Financial data (yr. ended 06/30/00): Assets, $50,648 (M); grants paid, $0; gifts received, $50,000; expenditures, $0; qualifying distributions, $0.
Directors: Josef Blochlinger, Jeffrey B. Coggin, Winifred McDonald.
EIN: 576135507

63418
Page Nelson Keesee Memorial Scholarship Fund
City County Complex, Box C
180 N. Irby St.
Florence, SC 29501-4419
Contact: A.E. Morehead III, Pres.

Financial data (yr. ended 12/31/00): Assets, $27,203 (M); grants paid, $1,500; expenditures, $1,811; qualifying distributions, $1,500.
Limitations: Giving limited to SC.
Application information: Application form not required.
Officers: A.E. Morehead III, Pres.; Edward T. Pendarvis, V.P.; Sinclair E. Lewis, Secy.-Treas.
EIN: 570700128

63419
H. Neel & Scott Timmons Hipp Foundation
P.O. Box 546
Greenville, SC 29602

Established in 1999.
Donor(s): H. Neel Hipp, Mary Timmons Hipp.
Financial data (yr. ended 12/31/00): Assets, $22,390 (M); grants paid, $23,180; expenditures, $23,280; qualifying distributions, $23,180.
Limitations: Applications not accepted.
Application information: Contributes only to pre-selected organizations.
Trustees: H. Neel Hipp, Scott Timmons Hipp.
EIN: 571089866

63420
The Kale Foundation
426 E. Blackstock Rd.
Spartanburg, SC 29301 (864) 574-4800
Contact: Charlotte Kale, Dir.

Donor(s): Michael V. Kale.
Financial data (yr. ended 12/31/01): Assets, $12,973 (M); grants paid, $1,100; gifts received, $5,505; expenditures, $2,889; qualifying distributions, $2,889.
Limitations: Giving primarily in Spartanburg, SC.
Application information: Application form required.
Director: Charlotte Kale.
EIN: 570841920

63421
Marty Thames & Crystal Keels Scholarship Fund
c/o Elizabeth Rhodes
5346 Elliot Hwy.
Mayesville, SC 29104

Established in 1999.
Donor(s): Billy Thames, Jo Thames.
Financial data (yr. ended 05/31/01): Assets, $11,856 (M); grants paid, $5,295; gifts received, $5,187; expenditures, $5,295; qualifying distributions, $5,295.
Trustees: Michelle Edens, Bill Hentges, Emily Keels, Kate Kirby, Larry Minton, Debbie Nix, B.J. Reed, Jo Thames, Elizabeth Rhodes.
EIN: 562087018

63422
Dallas Hirst Lumpkin Memorial Scholarship Fund, Inc.
410 Hampton Creek Ct.
Columbia, SC 29209
Application address: 1211 Adger Rd., Columbia, SC 29209
Contact: Elizabeth L. Gregory, Pres.

Established in 1990 in SC.
Donor(s): Dallas H. Lumpkin.
Financial data (yr. ended 06/30/00): Assets, $8,943 (M); grants paid, $1,000; gifts received, $898; expenditures, $1,195; qualifying distributions, $10,138; giving activities include $1,000 for loans to individuals.
Limitations: Giving limited to Rock Hill, SC.
Application information: Application available at Rock Hill and Northwestern High Schools. Application form required.
Officers: Elizabeth L. Gregory, Pres. and Treas.; Julie Lumpkin, V.P. and Secy.
EIN: 570911944

63423
Ivy Creek Kennels, Inc.
409 Paradise Pt.
Abbeville, SC 29620

Established in 1999 in GA and SC.
Donor(s): Henry E. Scharling II, Barbara T. Scharling.
Financial data (yr. ended 12/31/99): Assets, $8,116 (M); grants paid, $0; gifts received, $220,671; expenditures, $213,555; qualifying distributions, $215,755; giving activities include $213,555 for programs.
Officers: Henry E. Scharling II, Pres.; Barbara T. Scharling, V.P.; Renee S. Gentry, Secy.
EIN: 582444056

63424
N. G. Barron Renewal Foundation
147 Edisto Ave.
Columbia, SC 29205

Established in 1999 in SC.

63424—SOUTH CAROLINA

Financial data (yr. ended 12/31/01): Assets, $5,398 (M); grants paid, $1,300; expenditures, $2,287; qualifying distributions, $1,300.
Trustee: Lucie B. Eggleston.
EIN: 586387668

63425
Deacon Elijah Kelly, Sr. Scholarship Fund
c/o Eleanor Kelly
117 Claude Bundrick Rd.
Blythewood, SC 29016

Financial data (yr. ended 12/31/01): Assets, $3,794 (M); grants paid, $3,525; gifts received, $3,508; expenditures, $4,630; qualifying distributions, $4,630.
Limitations: Applications not accepted. Giving limited to residents of SC.
Officers: Melva Brinkley, Secy.; Eleanor Kelly, Treas.; Elijah Kelly, Jr., Admin.
EIN: 570915180

63426
Strive, Inc.
P.O. Box 23371
Hilton Head Island, SC 29925-3371
(843) 689-9494
Contact: Susan Carter Barnwell, Dir.

Established in 1991 in SC.
Financial data (yr. ended 06/30/02): Assets, $2,635 (M); grants paid, $142,893; gifts received, $150,820; expenditures, $152,012; qualifying distributions, $151,996; giving activities include $3,000 for programs.
Director and Trustees:* Susan Carter Barnwell,* Emory S. Campbell, Richard Ennen, William Evans, Karen Glover.
EIN: 570935388
Codes: FD2

63427
The Baillie Players, Inc.
961 Texas St.
Columbia, SC 29201

Established in 1998 in SC.
Financial data (yr. ended 12/31/99): Assets, $1,173 (M); grants paid, $0; expenditures, $86,762; qualifying distributions, $86,762; giving activities include $86,762 for programs.
Officers: William B. Martin, Pres.; Dorothy Martin, Secy.-Treas.
EIN: 570959003

63428
Lighthouse Missions
P.O. Box 6847
West Columbia, SC 29171

Classified as a private operating foundation in 1980.
Donor(s): Maurice Bessinger.
Financial data (yr. ended 12/31/99): Assets, $105 (M); grants paid, $5,082; gifts received, $6,285; expenditures, $10,706; qualifying distributions, $10,706.
Director: Maurice Bessinger.
EIN: 570687521

63429
Wildwood Ministries
P.O. Box 16437
Surfside Beach, SC 29587

Classified as a private operating foundation in 1994.
Financial data (yr. ended 12/31/01): Assets, $36 (M); grants paid, $0; gifts received, $2,365; expenditures, $2,360; qualifying distributions, $0.
Officers: Frank E. Jones, Pres. and Treas.; Steven D. Edwards, V.P.; Ralph Fadeley, Secy.

EIN: 521655879

SOUTH DAKOTA

63430
Chiesman Foundation for Democracy, Inc.
1641 Deadwood Ave.
Rapid City, SD 57702 (605) 341-4311
URL: http://www.chiesman.org
Contact: John Usera

Established in 1995 in SD.
Donor(s): Allene R. Chiesman.
Financial data (yr. ended 12/31/99): Assets, $3,672,111 (M); grants paid, $5,657; gifts received, $2,672,173; expenditures, $427,401; qualifying distributions, $352,491; giving activities include $352,491 for programs.
Limitations: Giving primarily in SD.
Application information: Application form not required.
Officers: Morris Hallock, Chair.; Ted Muenster, Vice-Chair.; Brenda Barger, Secy.; Jim Borszich, Treas.
Directors: Bill Clark, Tom Hills, Barbara Thirstrup.
EIN: 460438703

63431
The Brande Foundation
13179 Baker Park Rd.
Rapid City, SD 57702

Established in 1987 in SD.
Donor(s): David B. Ellis, Larry M. David, Breakthrough Enterprises.
Financial data (yr. ended 09/30/01): Assets, $1,832,018 (M); grants paid, $2,461; gifts received, $200; expenditures, $367,720; qualifying distributions, $355,133; giving activities include $336,002 for programs.
Limitations: Applications not accepted. Giving primarily in Rapid City, SD.
Application information: Contributes only to pre-selected organizations.
Officers and Directors:* David B. Ellis,* Pres.; Trisha Waldron,* V.P.; Bill Rentz,* Secy.; Larry M. David.
EIN: 460398751

63432
Peterson-Bahde-Coleman Homes, Inc.
26 W. 6th Ave.
Redfield, SD 57469-1118

Classified as a private operating foundation.
Financial data (yr. ended 12/31/01): Assets, $1,191,190 (M); grants paid, $0; expenditures, $234,012; qualifying distributions, $0.
Officers: Lyle Paschke, Chair.; Kurt Permann, Vice-Chair.; Mildred Ratigan, Secy.; June Bottum, Treas.
Directors: Geri Benning, Royce Bush, Vona Jean Johnsen, Juanita Sanger, Ramona Tennill.
EIN: 460343163

63433
Edward L. Schwab Memorial Foundation
c/o Dacotah Bank
P.O. Box 1210
Aberdeen, SD 57402-1210
Contact: Ralph Kusler, Secy.-Treas.

Established in 1996 in SD.

Financial data (yr. ended 08/31/00): Assets, $1,145,109 (M); grants paid, $45,000; expenditures, $80,478; qualifying distributions, $47,369.
Limitations: Giving limited to SD.
Application information: Application form required.
Officers and Directors:* Kevin Wegehaupt,* Pres.; Marci Caster,* V.P.; Ralph Kusler,* Secy.-Treas.; Henry Desnoyers, Mel Hamre, Dacotah Bank.
EIN: 911770168

63434
Salt of the Earth Foundation
P.O. Box 88235
Sioux Falls, SD 57105
Contact: Lorrie Schwan-Okerlund, Pres.

Established in 1994 in SD.
Donor(s): Lorrie Schwan-Okerlund.
Financial data (yr. ended 09/30/99): Assets, $1,097,461 (M); grants paid, $51,200; gifts received, $300,200; expenditures, $63,561; qualifying distributions, $50,265.
Limitations: Giving primarily in Sioux Falls, SD.
Officer and Directors:* Lorrie Schwan-Okerlund,* Pres.; Marilyn Johnson, Jeff Okerlund.
EIN: 460434804

63435
Da Vinci Foundation, Inc.
P.O. Box 3468
Rapid City, SD 57709-3468

Established in 1997 in SD.
Donor(s): Marc Boddicker, Sheila O. Boddicker.
Financial data (yr. ended 12/31/99): Assets, $786,241 (M); grants paid, $0; gifts received, $30,000; expenditures, $45,719; qualifying distributions, $43,612; giving activities include $22,168 for programs.
Limitations: Applications not accepted.
Application information: Contributes only to pre-selected organizations.
Officer and Directors:* Marc E. Boddicker,* Pres.; Sheila O'Day-Boddicker, Exec. Dir.; Louayne M. O'Day.
EIN: 460445638

63436
Schoenhard Community Foundation, Inc.
220 W. King
P.O. Box 466
Chamberlain, SD 57325 (605) 734-5705
Contact: Larry Schoenhard, Pres.

Established around 1993. Classified as a private operating foundation in 1995.
Donor(s): Leland Schoenhard.
Financial data (yr. ended 12/31/00): Assets, $634,689 (M); grants paid, $42,600; expenditures, $44,082; qualifying distributions, $42,600.
Limitations: Giving primarily in the Chamberlain, SD, area.
Officers and Directors:* Larry Schoenhard,* Pres.; Tom Schoenhard, V.P.; Linea Schoenhard,* Secy.; Donald Schoenhard, Jr.,* Treas.; Gayland Meyerink.
EIN: 363901212

63437
River Park Foundation, Inc.
P.O. Box 1216
Pierre, SD 57501 (605) 224-6178
Contact: Glenn Jorgenson, Pres.

Established in 1995. Classified as a private operating foundation in 1998.
Donor(s): Glenn Jorgenson.

Financial data (yr. ended 06/03/01): Assets, $408,225 (M); grants paid, $4,900; gifts received, $12,685; expenditures, $188,129; qualifying distributions, $148,325; giving activities include $138,545 for programs.
Limitations: Giving primarily in SD.
Officers: Glenn Jorgenson, Pres.; J. Sharard Burke, V.P.; Bob Tipston, Secy.-Treas.
Board Members: Dennis Hellwig, Phyllis Jorgenson.
EIN: 460403501

63438
Leland & Lucille Strahl Educational Trust
c/o Dacotah Bank
P.O. Box 1210
Aberdeen, SD 57402-1210
Application address: 26 W. 6th Ave., No. 306, Redfield, SD 57469
Contact: Leland Strahl, Pres.

Established in 1991.
Financial data (yr. ended 06/30/01): Assets, $304,314 (M); grants paid, $14,500; gifts received, $118,760; expenditures, $16,390; qualifying distributions, $15,764.
Limitations: Giving limited to residents of SD.
Application information: Application form required.
Officer: Leland Strahl, Pres.
Trustee: Dacotah Bank.
EIN: 460412852

63439
Gerald L. and Kathleen A. Weiner Foundation
338 Streeter Dr. N.
North Sioux City, SD 57049

Established in 1993.
Donor(s): Gerald L. Weiner.
Financial data (yr. ended 11/30/01): Assets, $277,716 (M); grants paid, $99,626; gifts received, $126,000; expenditures, $120,087; qualifying distributions, $113,869.
Limitations: Applications not accepted. Giving primarily in IA.
Application information: Contributes only to pre-selected organizations.
Trustees: Gerald L. Weiner, Kathleen A. Weiner.
EIN: 420429303
Codes: FD2

63440
The Schock Foundation, Inc.
(Formerly Nordica Foundation, Inc.)
1517 S. Minnesota Ave.
Sioux Falls, SD 57105-1717

Donor(s): Alvin A. Schock, Oswald Schock, Paul Schock, Nordica Enterprises, Inc.
Financial data (yr. ended 12/31/01): Assets, $242,800 (M); grants paid, $31,575; gifts received, $26,850; expenditures, $35,569; qualifying distributions, $35,569.
Limitations: Applications not accepted. Giving primarily in SD.
Application information: Contributes only to pre-selected organizations.
Officers: Paul Schock, Pres.; Al Schock, V.P.; O.E. Schock, V.P.; Charles A. Nelson, Secy.-Treas.
Board Members: Phyllis Schock, Steve Schock.
EIN: 466012429

63441
Rapid City Community Development Corporation
825 St. Joseph St.
Rapid City, SD 57701

Classified as a private operating foundation in 1996.
Financial data (yr. ended 12/31/99): Assets, $233,295 (M); grants paid, $0; gifts received, $33,714; expenditures, $104,992; qualifying distributions, $104,902; giving activities include $104,991 for programs.
Officers and Directors:* Bonnie J. Hughes,* Pres.; Herb Kron,* V.P.; Rick Schlimgen,* Treas.; Qusi R. Al-Haj, Sam Benne, Jim Benson, Lyda Busse, David Jones, Tom Lessin, Mark Lovre, Bonnie Spain, Doug Wells, and 5 additional directors.
EIN: 460439146

63442
Community Service Center Trust Fund
101 N. Maple
Rapid City, SD 57701-1534
Application address: P.O. Box 1336, Rapid City, SD 57709, tel.: (605) 342-8822
Contact: Charles Whisler, Treas.

Financial data (yr. ended 12/31/99): Assets, $156,626 (M); grants paid, $11,398; expenditures, $11,398; qualifying distributions, $11,948.
Limitations: Giving primarily in Rapid City, SD.
Application information: Application form required.
Officers: Henry Arends, Pres.; Gene Reed, V.P.; Dianne Tschetter, Secy.; Charles Whisler, Treas.
EIN: 460311433

63443
Mitchell Woods & Fox Corporation
P.O. Box 183
Custer, SD 57730-0183

Financial data (yr. ended 12/31/00): Assets, $155,336 (M); grants paid, $9,000; expenditures, $10,543; qualifying distributions, $9,662.
Limitations: Applications not accepted. Giving primarily in SD.
Application information: Contributes only to pre-selected organizations.
Officers: Bethal Fox Henderson, Pres.; Mike Bay Borelli, V.P.; Gerald Dennis, Treas.
Director: Gene Bennett.
EIN: 363644431

63444
Arneson Charitable Trust
2904 E. 52nd St.
Sioux Falls, SD 57103 (605) 391-1918
Contact: Duane C. Arneson, Tr.

Established in 2000 in SD.
Donor(s): Duane C. Arneson, Mary A. Arneson.
Financial data (yr. ended 12/31/00): Assets, $114,514 (M); grants paid, $11,000; gifts received, $121,500; expenditures, $11,015; qualifying distributions, $11,015.
Limitations: Giving primarily in SD.
Trustees: Duane C. Arneson, Mary A. Arneson.
EIN: 460455827

63445
Sioux Falls Environmental Access, Inc.
804 S. Minnesota Ave.
Sioux Falls, SD 57104-4829

Financial data (yr. ended 12/31/01): Assets, $89,770 (M); grants paid, $0; expenditures, $5,830; qualifying distributions, $0.
Officers: Jerry Flanagan, Chair.; Richard A. Dempster, Vice-Chair.; Tom Kromminga, Secy.
Directors: Richard A. Dempster, Earl McCart.
EIN: 460346270

63446
Bruce and Deanna Lien Foundation
P.O. Box 440
Rapid City, SD 57709 (605) 342-7224
Contact: Deanna Lien, Dir.

Established in 1994 in SD.
Donor(s): Bruce H. Lien, Deanna Lien.
Financial data (yr. ended 11/30/00): Assets, $32,461 (M); grants paid, $3,604; gifts received, $7,000; expenditures, $7,064; qualifying distributions, $3,604.
Limitations: Giving primarily in Rapid City, SD.
Directors: Larry Dahlstrom, Carole Hillard, Bruce H. Lien, Deanna Lien.
EIN: 460434932

63447
The Greater South Dakota Educational & Research Foundation, Inc.
P.O. Box 190
Pierre, SD 57501 (605) 224-6161
Contact: Sylvia Moisan

Financial data (yr. ended 10/31/01): Assets, $8,207 (M); grants paid, $40,293; gifts received, $24,490; expenditures, $40,675; qualifying distributions, $40,293.
Limitations: Giving limited to Pierre, SD.
Officers and Directors:* Jim Campbell,* Chair.; David Owen, Secy.-Treas.; Duane Butt, Marty Cunningham, Dan Kirby, Dan Landguth, Jeff Parker, Jim Towler, Ronald Williamson.
EIN: 460349099

63448
Bill Markve and Associates Dakota Valley Athletic Foundation
c/o Bill Markve
P.O. Box 349
Dakota Dunes, SD 57049

Established in 1996 in SD.
Financial data (yr. ended 12/31/99): Assets, $5,406 (M); grants paid, $5,519; gifts received, $11,515; expenditures, $15,446; qualifying distributions, $15,446.
Limitations: Applications not accepted. Giving primarily in North Sioux City, SD.
Application information: Contributes only to pre-selected organizations.
Directors: William Clements, Bill Markve.
EIN: 460442024

TENNESSEE

63449
Stuttering Foundation of America, Inc.
(Formerly Speech Foundation of America)
P.O. Box 11749
Memphis, TN 38111-0749
Application address: 3100 Walnut Grove Rd., Ste. 603, Memphis, TN 38111, tel.: (800) 992-9392
Contact: Jane Fraser, Pres.

Established in 1947 in TN.
Donor(s): Members of the Fraser family.
Financial data (yr. ended 12/31/99): Assets, $15,707,765 (M); grants paid, $4,752; gifts received, $211,746; expenditures, $998,413; qualifying distributions, $788,263; giving activities include $981,885 for programs.

Application information: Funds largely committed to support of operating programs.
Officers and Directors:* Jane Fraser,* Pres.; Joe Fulcher,* V.P.; Joseph Walker,* Secy.; Donald Edwards,* Treas.; George Cooley, James W. Garrison, Jean Fraser Gross, Katherine P. Klyce, Donald Lineback, Hubert McBride, James Spurlock.
EIN: 626047678

63450
The Caldsted Foundation
3701 Cherryton Dr.
Chattanooga, TN 37411

Financial data (yr. ended 10/31/00): Assets, $13,185,608 (M); grants paid, $0; expenditures, $686,184; qualifying distributions, $552,593; giving activities include $519,086 for programs.
Officers and Directors:* T. Hooke McCallie,* Pres.; C. Duffy Frank,* V.P.; Tommy Landgrebe,* Secy.; R.D. Dillender,* Treas.; Wilma Dietzen, Dolores Harvey, Nat C. Hughes, Virginia Lee, Felix G. Miller, Jr., Fred Moore, Barbara Murray, Merrill F. Nelson, Jack M. Olmsted, Keith Sanford, William A. White, Jr.
EIN: 620696466

63451
The Freedom Forum First Amendment Center, Inc.
c/o Visiting Scholars Prog.
1207 18th Ave. S.
Nashville, TN 37212

Established in 1992 in TN.
Donor(s): Freedom Forum International, Inc.
Financial data (yr. ended 12/31/00): Assets, $12,276,384 (M); grants paid, $0; gifts received, $11,102,371; expenditures, $5,729,340; qualifying distributions, $5,594,158; giving activities include $985,246 for programs.
Officers and Trustees:* Charles L. Overby,* C.E.O. and Chair.; Peter S. Prichard,* Pres.; Kenneth Paulson, Sr. V.P. and Exec. Dir.; Harvey S. Cotter, V.P. and Treas.; Robert G. McCullough, Secy.; Rev. Jimmy Allen, Bernard B. Brody, M.D., Malcolm Kirschenbaum, and 10 additional trustees.
EIN: 581998515

63452
Sharon Charitable Trust
Hwy. 69, Box 13780
Savannah, TN 38372

Established in 1998 in TN.
Donor(s): Ron Pickard, Pickard Charitable Remainder Trust.
Financial data (yr. ended 11/30/99): Assets, $11,213,329 (M); grants paid, $5,000; gifts received, $10,427,880; expenditures, $171,417; qualifying distributions, $2,485,822; giving activities include $166,417 for programs.
Trustees: Linda S. Pickard, Ron Pickard.
EIN: 626353427

63453
The Lazarus Foundation, Inc.
P.O. Box 574
Bristol, TN 37621
Contact: Mary Ann Blessing, Exec. Dir.

Established in 1992 in VA.
Donor(s): John M. Gregory, Joan P. Gregory.
Financial data (yr. ended 12/31/01): Assets, $8,949,014 (M); grants paid, $4,744,962; gifts received, $8,966,774; expenditures, $4,760,976; qualifying distributions, $4,744,962.
Limitations: Applications not accepted. Giving primarily in Bentonville, AR, and Wytheville, VA.

Application information: Unsolicited requests for funds not accepted.
Officers: John M. Gregory, Pres.; Joan P. Gregory, Secy.; Mary Ann Blessing, Treas.
Directors: James Michael Gregory, Susan Kardynal Gregory.
EIN: 541654943
Codes: FD, GTI

63454
Peabody Place Museum Foundation
100 Peabody Pl., Ste. 1400
Memphis, TN 38103

Classified as a private operating foundation in 2000 in TN.
Donor(s): Jack A. Belz.
Financial data (yr. ended 12/31/00): Assets, $4,165,871 (M); grants paid, $0; gifts received, $2,008,800; expenditures, $10,525; qualifying distributions, $2,019,088; giving activities include $10,288 for programs.
Officers and Directors:* Jack A. Belz,* Pres.; Marilyn Belz,* Secy.; Raymond M. Shainberg.
EIN: 621759105

63455
Lula Lake Land Trust
300 High St.
Chattanooga, TN 37403-1723

Established in 1994 in TN.
Donor(s): Robert M. Davenport,‡ S. Elliott Davenport, Adelaide Davenport Bratcher, Eleanor Howell Davenport.
Financial data (yr. ended 12/31/99): Assets, $3,681,393 (M); grants paid, $0; gifts received, $355,840; expenditures, $159,629; qualifying distributions, $2,054,420; giving activities include $151,638 for programs.
Officer and Directors:* William H. Chipley,* Exec. Dir.; Adelaide Davenport Bratcher, Robert M. Davenport, Jr., S. Elliott Davenport, Eleanor Davenport Owen.
EIN: 626283607

63456
Patricia and Rodes Hart Foundation
612 10th Ave. N.
Nashville, TN 37203-3308

Established in 1988 in TN.
Donor(s): Rodes Hart, Patricia I. Hart.
Financial data (yr. ended 12/31/00): Assets, $3,128,719 (M); grants paid, $99,197; expenditures, $99,457; qualifying distributions, $99,197.
Limitations: Applications not accepted. Giving primarily in Nashville, TN.
Application information: Contributes only to pre-selected organizations.
Trustees: H. Rodes Hart, Patricia I. Hart.
EIN: 621355032
Codes: FD2

63457
Smokebrush Foundation, Inc.
600 Krystal Bldg.
Chattanooga, TN 37402
Application address: 212 E. Vermijo Ave., Colorado Springs, CO 80903-2114; E-mail: parker@smokebrush.org; URL: http://www.smokebrush.org
Contact: Katherine Johnston, Pres.

Established as an operating foundation in 1993.
Donor(s): Karl Walter, Katherine Walter, Katherine Johnston.
Financial data (yr. ended 06/30/01): Assets, $2,808,311 (M); grants paid, $772,523; gifts received, $1,000; expenditures, $1,000,209;

qualifying distributions, $977,242; giving activities include $17,202 for programs.
Limitations: Giving primarily in CO.
Application information: Application form required.
Officers: Katherine Johnston, Pres.; Pamela K. Cuzzort, Secy.-Treas.
Directors: Andrew G. Cope, S.K. Johnston III.
EIN: 841233281
Codes: FD

63458
Goodlark Educational Foundation, Inc.
404 E. College St., Ste. D
Dickson, TN 37055
Contact: Buffy Cato

Established in 1987 in TN.
Donor(s): Goodlark Medical Center, Inc.
Financial data (yr. ended 12/31/01): Assets, $2,446,021 (M); grants paid, $202,748; expenditures, $234,250; qualifying distributions, $231,821.
Limitations: Giving primarily in Dickson, Hickman, and Humphreys counties, TN.
Publications: Application guidelines.
Application information: Application form required.
Directors: Van Albright, Richard Arnold, Peggy Berry, Jimmy Cagle, Ann Deason, Dan Drinnen, Jeff Gordon, Jimmy Jackson, Mike Legg, Carney Nicks.
EIN: 581764989
Codes: FD2, GTI

63459
The Seven Islands Foundation, Inc.
8200 Seven Islands Rd.
Knoxville, TN 37920

Established in 1999.
Donor(s): H. Peter Claussen, Linda Claussen, Gulf and Ohio Railways Holding, Alabama Systems & Service Co.
Financial data (yr. ended 12/31/00): Assets, $2,165,595 (M); grants paid, $0; gifts received, $91,800; expenditures, $71,917; qualifying distributions, $0.
Officers: H. Peter Claussen, Pres.; Linda Claussen, V.P. and Secy.
EIN: 621777455

63460
Jim Brock Leonard Charitable Trust
c/o Tom Hudson
101 N. Maple Ave.
Ethridge, TN 38456-2112

Established in 1990 in TN; Classified as on operating foundation in 1991.
Financial data (yr. ended 10/31/01): Assets, $1,317,613 (M); grants paid, $87,000; expenditures, $94,003; qualifying distributions, $87,000.
Limitations: Applications not accepted.
Application information: Contributes only to pre-selected organizations.
Trustees: Tom Hudson, Joyce Weaver.
EIN: 626214683
Codes: FD2

63461
Long Branch Conservancy, Inc.
c/o Lula Lake Land Trust
537 Market St., Ste. 301
Chattanooga, TN 37402

Established in 1999 in GA.
Donor(s): The C Foundation.
Financial data (yr. ended 09/30/00): Assets, $1,311,533 (M); grants paid, $204,711;

expenditures, $219,947; qualifying distributions, $210,884; giving activities include $204,711 for programs.
Officer: William H. Chipley, Exec. Dir.
Trustees: Adelaide Davenport Bratcher, Robert M. Davenport, Jr., S. Elliott Davenport, Eleanor Davenport Owen.
EIN: 311666131

63462
Luther and Stella Ogle Foundation, Inc.
P.O. Box 648
Gatlinburg, TN 37738-0648 (865) 436-5121
Contact: Luther Ogle, Pres.

Established in 1979 in TN.
Donor(s): Don Ogle, Luther Ogle, Stella Ogle, C.R. Byrd, Kenneth Seaton, Brenda Burchfield, Skyland Motel, Inc., Crossroads Motor Lodge, Inc., Luther Ogle Enterprises, Inc., Twin Island Motel, Inc., Pigeon Force Water Park.
Financial data (yr. ended 03/31/01): Assets, $1,236,562 (M); grants paid, $189,534; gifts received, $241,473; expenditures, $204,111; qualifying distributions, $203,574.
Limitations: Giving primarily in Port Au Prince, Haiti.
Application information: Application form not required.
Officers and Directors:* Luther Ogle,* Pres.; Stella Ogle, Secy.; Larry Ogle, Michael Ogle.
EIN: 581444734
Codes: FD2

63463
Blum Family Foundation
4414 Honeywood Ave.
Nashville, TN 37205-3444

Established in 2001 in TN.
Donor(s): Lauren Blum, Joan B. Shayne.
Financial data (yr. ended 12/31/01): Assets, $998,973 (M); grants paid, $0; gifts received, $984,632; expenditures, $165; qualifying distributions, $0.
Limitations: Applications not accepted.
Application information: Contributes only to pre-selected organizations.
Trustees: Jennifer L. Blum, Lauren Blum, Emily Blum Haslett, Joan B. Shayne.
EIN: 621871174

63464
Knox County Old Gray Cemetery
(Formerly Old Gray Cemetery Education, Historic & Memorial Association)
c/o First Tennessee Bank, N.A., Trust Dept.
P.O. Box 1991
Knoxville, TN 37901

Established in 1983 in TX.
Financial data (yr. ended 12/31/99): Assets, $998,442 (M); grants paid, $0; gifts received, $24,475; expenditures, $50,628; qualifying distributions, $40,011; giving activities include $40,011 for programs.
Limitations: Applications not accepted.
Application information: Contributes only to a pre-selected organization.
Officers: Frank H. Pittenger, Pres.; Mary Tod Finch, V.P.; Alix Frincke Dempster, Exec. Secy.; Florence McNabb, Secy.; William Dempster, Treas.
Directors: John W. Baker, Jr., Susan P. Brackney, J. Steve Cotham, Dan R. Mayo, Margaret A. Newton, Arthur Pickle, Gaines Pittenger, Carl H. Wallis, Lindsay Young.
Trustee: First Tennessee Bank, N.A.
EIN: 237426428

63465
Arch & Lillie F. Fitzgerald Foundation
c/o First Tennessee Bank
P.O. Box 4880
Cleveland, TN 37320-4880

Established in 2000.
Financial data (yr. ended 12/31/01): Assets, $799,176 (M); grants paid, $59,500; gifts received, $10,000; expenditures, $66,817; qualifying distributions, $59,353.
Trustees: Lillie F. Fitzgerald, Margo Fitzgerald, Rodney Fitzgerald, Phil Griffin, Carolyn Robinson.
EIN: 626362801

63466
Dick Family Foundation
P.O. Box 11167
Knoxville, TN 37939

Established in 1997 in TN.
Donor(s): Allen Dick, James A. Dick.
Financial data (yr. ended 12/31/01): Assets, $698,239 (M); grants paid, $450,000; expenditures, $451,926; qualifying distributions, $450,000.
Limitations: Applications not accepted.
Application information: Contributes only to pre-selected organizations.
Trustees: Allen Dick, James A. Dick, Hines and Company.
EIN: 311522427

63467
TMF Endowment Fund, Inc.
(Formerly Tennessee Medical Foundation Endowment, Inc.)
P.O. Box 1209090
Nashville, TN 37212

Financial data (yr. ended 12/31/00): Assets, $647,323 (M); grants paid, $10,000; expenditures, $10,000; qualifying distributions, $10,000.
Officers: Jeff H. Dyer, Sr., Pres.; Ginny B. Rogers, V.P.; W. Lipscomb Davis, Jr., Secy.-Treas.
Directors: John R. Nelson, Jr., Howard L. Salyer, M.D.
EIN: 621660467

63468
John & Ina Berkshire Educational Operating Foundation, Inc.
c/o Michael L. Hatcher
6901 Sherwood Dr.
Knoxville, TN 37919
Application address: 3428 Rena St., Pigeon Forge, TN 37863, tel.: (615) 453-2401
Contact: Jerry L. Wear, Secy.-Treas.

Established in 1992. Classified as a private operating foundation.
Donor(s): Ina Berkshire.‡
Financial data (yr. ended 12/31/01): Assets, $609,843 (M); grants paid, $24,000; expenditures, $35,823; qualifying distributions, $25,244.
Limitations: Giving limited to residents of Sevier County, TN.
Application information: Application form required.
Officers and Directors:* Michael L. Hatcher,* Pres.; Edna J. Loveday,* V.P.; Jerry L. Wear,* Secy.-Treas.
EIN: 582004367
Codes: GTI

63469
Sarah L. Pugliese Medical Foundation
c/o Commercial Bank & Trust Co.
P.O. Box 1090
Paris, TN 38242 (731) 642-3341
Contact: Richard Shankle, Trust Off., Commerical Bank & Trust Co.

Established in 1999 in TN.
Donor(s): Sarah L. Pugliese.‡
Financial data (yr. ended 12/31/01): Assets, $538,411 (M); grants paid, $24,695; expenditures, $26,139; qualifying distributions, $24,558.
Limitations: Giving limited to residents of TN.
Trustees: Richard L. Dunlap III, David Flowers, Commercial Bank & Trust Co.
EIN: 621763873

63470
Camp Columbus, Inc.
c/o Joe A. Murphy, Jr.
P.O. Box 268
Chattanooga, TN 37401-0268

Financial data (yr. ended 12/31/01): Assets, $520,141 (M); grants paid, $0; gifts received, $7,076; expenditures, $62,257; qualifying distributions, $0.
Officers: Jon A. Murhpy, Jr., Pres.; Edson G. Hammer, V.P.; Edward J. Munczenski, Secy.; Chirs Snellgrove, Treas.
Directors: Clyde Brewer, Patricia Chrnalogar, D.B. Haskins III, Ronnie Holmes, Chris Snellgrove.
EIN: 620648267

63471
Suffer Little Children, Inc.
P.O. Box 50874
Knoxville, TN 37950-0874

Established in 1999 in TN.
Financial data (yr. ended 12/31/01): Assets, $495,299 (M); grants paid, $1,582; gifts received, $11,000; expenditures, $2,791; qualifying distributions, $1,582.
Officer and Trustees:* J. Kip Miller,* Chair.; Suzanne Masters, F.G. McCloskey, Frank Murchison, Primo Pavoni, Len Runyan, Carroll Webb, Claudia Weber, Jim Wise.
EIN: 112580180

63472
Adams Family Foundation I
2217 Battleground Dr.
Murfreesboro, TN 37129
Contact: Robert G. Adams, Tr.

Established in 1993.
Donor(s): Carl E. Adams, Jennie Mae Adams, W. Andrew Adams, Gerald Coggin.
Financial data (yr. ended 12/31/00): Assets, $377,922 (M); grants paid, $60,600; gifts received, $100,000; expenditures, $61,844; qualifying distributions, $154,016.
Limitations: Giving primarily in TN.
Trustees: Alan B. Adams, Carl E. Adams, Jr., Fred M. Adams, Jennie Mae Adams, Robert G. Adams, W. Andrew Adams, Joanne Coggin.
EIN: 621515107

63473
JSA Foundation
P.O. Box 198806
Nashville, TN 37219-8806
Application address: c/o Margaret L. Behm, 306 Gay St., Ste. 400, Nashville, TN 37201

Financial data (yr. ended 08/31/01): Assets, $341,135 (M); grants paid, $9,904; expenditures, $19,298; qualifying distributions, $18,417.
Limitations: Giving primarily in TN.

63473—TENNESSEE

Application information: Application form required.
Officers and Directors:* Ayne Cantrell, Pres.; Dan Scott, Secy.-Treas.; Margaret L. Behm, Lucile Edwards, Nancy Fann, Andrienne C. Friedli, Jennifer Hartman-Henson, Julie Hawkins, Ouida Hawkins, Judith Iriarte-Gross, Mary Jo James, Mary Magada-Ward, Jeanne H. Massaquoi, Stella Myers, Rebecca Salisbury, William L. Shulman.*
EIN: 581488121
Codes: GTI

63474
Tennessee Medical Foundation
P.O. Box 120909
Nashville, TN 37212-0909

Classified as a private operating foundation in 1962.
Financial data (yr. ended 12/31/00): Assets, $334,201 (M); grants paid, $0; gifts received, $654,419; expenditures, $650,029; qualifying distributions, $639,026; giving activities include $434,615 for programs.
Officers and Directors:* John R. Nelson, Jr., M.D.,* Pres.; Evelyn B. Ogle, M.D.,* V.P.; Howard L. Salyer, M.D.,* Secy.-Treas.; Charles Ed Allen, M.D., Sherri Gray, M.S., Kenneth F. Tullis, M.D., and 6 additional Directors.
EIN: 620541813

63475
Surgoinsville Medical Center, Inc.
P.O. Box 262
Surgoinsville, TN 37873-0262

Financial data (yr. ended 12/31/01): Assets, $262,264 (M); grants paid, $0; expenditures, $18,077; qualifying distributions, $0.
Officers and Directors:* Mark A. Skelton,* Chair.; Jessee Young,* Secy.; Sandra Anderson,* Treas.; Lynn Norris, Thelma Raines, and 6 additional directors.
EIN: 621093541

63476
Biblical Resource Center and Museum, Inc.
(Formerly Biblical Resource Center, Inc.)
P.O. Box 280
Collierville, TN 38027

Established in 1995 in TN.
Donor(s): Bessie Lucille Carter.
Financial data (yr. ended 12/31/01): Assets, $256,946 (M); grants paid, $0; gifts received, $323,903; expenditures, $225,089; qualifying distributions, $218,490; giving activities include $202,590 for programs.
Officers and Directors:* Donald E. Bassett,* Pres.; Larry Papasan,* V.P.; Drake E. Bassett,* Secy.; Bessie Lucille Carter, John Hartley.
EIN: 621592061

63477
Tennessee Museum of Flight, Inc.
11108 Poplar Ridge Rd.
Knoxville, TN 37932

Financial data (yr. ended 12/31/00): Assets, $254,554 (M); grants paid, $0; gifts received, $106,565; expenditures, $146,054; qualifying distributions, $118,580; giving activities include $118,598 for programs.
Officer: John P. Shoffner, Pres.
EIN: 621617593

63478
Shea Clinic Foundation
(Formerly Deafness Foundation)
6133 Poplar Pike
Memphis, TN 38119-4707

Classified as a private operating foundation in 1992.
Donor(s): Helen C. Harstad Trust.
Financial data (yr. ended 12/31/00): Assets, $237,109 (M); grants paid, $45,578; gifts received, $30,000; expenditures, $51,577; qualifying distributions, $45,578.
Limitations: Giving primarily in TN.
Trustees: Gwyn S. Fisher, Thomas A. Garrott, Ted Shalon, John J. Shea, M.D., John J. Shea III, M.D.
EIN: 626021013

63479
James Hobert Lewis Memorial Trust
P.O. Box 169
Pikeville, TN 37367 (423) 447-6866
Contact: Ronda Robertson, Tr.

Established in 1997 in TN.
Financial data (yr. ended 12/31/99): Assets, $210,238 (M); grants paid, $12,135; expenditures, $12,665; qualifying distributions, $12,135.
Limitations: Giving limited to Bledsoe County, TN.
Application information: Application form required.
Trustees: Gray Bucks, Patsy Kelly, Albert Roberts, Ronda Robertson, Rick Van Winkle.
EIN: 626312437

63480
Douglas Shelters II, Inc.
1101 Wagner Dr.
Sevierville, TN 37862-3719

Financial data (yr. ended 06/30/00): Assets, $208,605 (M); grants paid, $0; gifts received, $30,184; expenditures, $48,695; qualifying distributions, $42,713; giving activities include $48,695 for programs.
Officers: John Richardson, Pres.; Jay Whitlow, V.P.; Donna McGaha, Secy.; Willie Green, Treas.; Paula M. York, Exec.Dir.
Directors: Deanna D. Miller, Betty Madison Ogle, and 10 additional directors.
EIN: 621165220

63481
Crabtree Farms of Chattanooga, Inc.
c/o William N. Bailey
P.O. Box 192
Lookout Mountain, TN 37350

Established in 1998 in TN.
Donor(s): William N. Bailey.
Financial data (yr. ended 12/31/99): Assets, $159,000 (M); grants paid, $0; gifts received, $386,951; expenditures, $280,301; qualifying distributions, $325,514; giving activities include $280,301 for programs.
Officers: William N. Bailey, Chair.; M. McNair Livingston Bailey, Pres.; Mary N. Moore, Secy.-Treas.
EIN: 621760383

63482
Hamblen Museum of Glass & Antiques
501 Park Ave., Ste. B
Lebanon, TN 37087
Contact: R. David Allen, Tr.

Established in 1997 in TN. Classified as a private operating foundation in 1999.
Financial data (yr. ended 12/31/01): Assets, $109,924 (M); grants paid, $0; expenditures, $18,650; qualifying distributions, $0.
Trustees: R. David Allen, Beth Thomas.
EIN: 626258312

63483
Richardson Family Henry County Educational Trust
c/o Commercial Bank and Trust Co.
101 N. Poplar St.
Paris, TN 38242
Application address: c/o Richard Shankle, Trust Off., P.O. Box 1090, Paris, TN 38242; tel.: (731) 642-3341

Established in 1998 in TN.
Financial data (yr. ended 12/31/01): Assets, $104,360 (M); grants paid, $0; expenditures, $1,002; qualifying distributions, $0.
Limitations: Giving limited to residents of TN.
Trustee: Commercial Bank & trust Co.
EIN: 621722603

63484
The Julien Hohenberg Foundation
P.O. Box 3046
Memphis, TN 38173-0046

Financial data (yr. ended 11/30/99): Assets, $102,018 (M); grants paid, $2,114; expenditures, $5,759; qualifying distributions, $2,114.
Officer: Jason Hohenberg, Pres.
EIN: 621676405

63485
The Lipscomb Clinic Foundation for Research and Education, Inc.
4230 Harding Rd., Ste. 1000
Nashville, TN 37212

Donor(s): Allen F. Anderson.
Financial data (yr. ended 11/30/01): Assets, $101,410 (M); grants paid, $0; expenditures, $8,730; qualifying distributions, $4,735; giving activities include $4,735 for programs.
Officers: Bill Shell, Pres.; Allen F. Anderson, Secy.-Treas.; Michael J. Pagnani, Secy.-Treas.
EIN: 621487825

63486
Tomorrow Scholarship Fund Trust
28 W. 5th St.
Crossville, TN 38555 (931) 484-3556
Contact: Vivian E. Warner, Tr.

Established in 1998 in TN.
Financial data (yr. ended 12/31/99): Assets, $99,803 (M); grants paid, $2,000; gifts received, $102,676; expenditures, $2,727; qualifying distributions, $2,000.
Limitations: Giving limited to residents of Cumberland County, TN.
Application information: Application form required.
Trustees: Diane Brown, Joseph Robertson, Sr., Vivian E. Warner.
EIN: 621747882

63487
Mary Noel Kershaw Foundation
3616 Doge Pl.
Nashville, TN 37204

Financial data (yr. ended 09/30/99): Assets, $98,329 (M); grants paid, $0; gifts received, $38,329; expenditures, $16,545; qualifying distributions, $0; giving activities include $16,544 for programs.
Limitations: Applications not accepted.
Application information: Contributes only to pre-selected organizations.
Officers: Jack Kershaw, Pres.; Ross Massey, Secy.
Director: Michael Hill.
EIN: 621608693

63488
The Thomley Foundation, Inc.
P.O. Box 1562
Brentwood, TN 37024-1562

Established in 1999 in AL.
Donor(s): David Thomley.
Financial data (yr. ended 12/31/01): Assets, $95,097 (M); grants paid, $77,153; gifts received, $218,725; expenditures, $143,780; qualifying distributions, $143,780; giving activities include $41,150 for programs.
Limitations: Applications not accepted. Giving limited to residents of OK.
Application information: Contributes only to pre-selected organizations.
Officers: David Thomley, Pres.; Taft O. Thomley, V.P.; Jeannie Thomley, Secy.
EIN: 631207742
Codes: FD2

63489
Southern Joint Replacement Research Foundation, Inc.
2021 Church St., Ste. 104
Nashville, TN 37203

Established in 1999.
Financial data (yr. ended 06/30/00): Assets, $83,593 (M); grants paid, $0; gifts received, $155,188; expenditures, $84,971; qualifying distributions, $84,971; giving activities include $84,971 for programs.
Officers: M. J. Christie, Pres.; David Deboer, Secy.
EIN: 621774452

63490
The Peggy and Perry Branyon Family Foundation
609 Sharon Dr.
Johnson City, TN 37604-1930

Classified as a private operating foundation in 1998.
Donor(s): Peggy L. Branyon, Perry D. Branyon.
Financial data (yr. ended 12/31/00): Assets, $82,441 (M); grants paid, $16,055; gifts received, $17,650; expenditures, $16,813; qualifying distributions, $16,055.
Limitations: Giving primarily in AL and TN.
Officers: Perry D. Branyon, Pres.; David P. Branyon, V.P.; Mark W. Branyon, V.P.; Tenza B. Flowers, V.P.; Julie B. Kelton, V.P.; Peggy L. Branyon, Secy.-Treas.
EIN: 621665357

63491
Second Chance Ministries, Inc.
923 Hamilton Ridge Ln.
Knoxville, TN 37922 (865) 671-1645
Contact: John R. Cope, Pres.

Donor(s): John R. Cope.
Financial data (yr. ended 05/31/01): Assets, $79,248 (M); grants paid, $8,275; gifts received, $68,586; expenditures, $9,144; qualifying distributions, $9,096.
Limitations: Giving primarily in Knoxville, TN.
Officers: John R. Cope, Pres.; Glendyl B. Cope, Secy.
EIN: 621282004

63492
Winstead Foundation
c/o Ted L. Winstead
2736 Gerald Ford Dr. E.
Cordova, TN 38018 (901) 388-7876

Donor(s): Mildred Winstead.
Financial data (yr. ended 12/31/00): Assets, $60,219 (M); grants paid, $3,209; expenditures, $3,226; qualifying distributions, $3,177.
Trustees: Mildred Winstead, Ted L. Winstead.
EIN: 237109097

63493
The Earl B. Bolling Memorial Scholarship Trust
c/o Randall Merritt
338 E. Center St.
Kingsport, TN 37660-4802

Established as a private operating foundation in 1996.
Donor(s): Earl B. Bolling.‡
Financial data (yr. ended 06/30/00): Assets, $59,629 (M); grants paid, $2,370; gifts received, $4,000; expenditures, $4,563; qualifying distributions, $4,563.
Trustee: Randall Merritt.
EIN: 582198020

63494
Teen Town of Johnson City, Inc.
c/o Patricia M. Potter
106 Point Shore Dr.
Piney Flats, TN 37686
Application address: c/o Marsh Passmore, 822 Lizbeth St., Johnson City, TN 37604, tel.: (423) 282-5126

Established in 1989 in TN.
Financial data (yr. ended 12/31/00): Assets, $53,922 (M); grants paid, $3,000; expenditures, $3,032; qualifying distributions, $3,000.
Limitations: Giving limited to Johnson City, TN.
Application information: Application form not required.
Officers: Carol Transou, Pres.; Earle Booze, V.P.; Judith E. Johnston, Secy.; Doreen G. Passmore, Treas.
EIN: 621177173
Codes: GTI

63495
The Orion Foundation
6321 Cate Rd.
Powell, TN 37849

Established in 1999 in TN.
Donor(s): Robert Ford.
Financial data (yr. ended 12/31/00): Assets, $49,224 (M); grants paid, $500; gifts received, $56,000; expenditures, $32,802; qualifying distributions, $500; giving activities include $14,000 for programs.
Limitations: Applications not accepted.
Application information: Contributes only to pre-selected organizations.
Officers: Robert V. Gentry, Pres.; David W. Gentry, V.P.; Patricia A. Gentry, Secy.-Treas.
Directors: Glenn Fuller, Jeanine Fuller, Robert Horner, Cyril Miller.
EIN: 621715785

63496
Charles & Lillian Tibbals Performing Arts & Conference Center
c/o Glenda Tibbals Gray
P.O. Box 4477
Oneida, TN 37841

Established in 2000 in TN.
Donor(s): Howard C. Tibbals.
Financial data (yr. ended 12/31/01): Assets, $43,025 (M); grants paid, $122,505; gifts received, $132,000; expenditures, $124,165; qualifying distributions, $122,505.
Limitations: Applications not accepted. Giving primarily in the Oneida, TN, area.

Application information: Contributes only to pre-selected organizations.
Officers and Directors:* Howard C. Tibbals,* Pres.; Glenda Tibbals Gray,* Secy.; Howard B. Baker, Jr., Janice E. Tibbals.
EIN: 311722017

63497
National Cancer Survivors Day Foundation, Inc.
P.O. Box 682285
Franklin, TN 37068-2285

Established in 1994 in TN.
Financial data (yr. ended 10/31/00): Assets, $41,147 (M); grants paid, $0; gifts received, $62,000; expenditures, $122,456; qualifying distributions, $84,409; giving activities include $170,783 for programs.
Officers and Directors:* Michael D. Holt,* Chair. and Pres.; Paula K. Chadwell,* Secy.; Tanya Turner, Exec. Dir.
EIN: 621560215

63498
Lumbermen's Educational Foundation, Inc.
1564 Cranford
Memphis, TN 38117 (901) 751-6612
Application address: 5909 Shelby Oaks Dr., Memphis, TN
Contact: Gerald L. Reynolds, Chair.

Established in 1994 in TN.
Financial data (yr. ended 12/31/99): Assets, $34,292 (M); grants paid, $412; gifts received, $2,500; expenditures, $4,964; qualifying distributions, $4,935; giving activities include $3,474 for programs.
Application information: Application form required.
Officer and Trustees:* Gerald L. Reynolds,* Chair.; George Kelly, Dan Mayhew, Robert Parnell.
EIN: 621555332

63499
Grooms Herron Foundation
P.O. Box 5
Dresden, TN 38225-0005 (901) 364-5415
Contact: Nancy C. Miller-Herron, Secy.

Donor(s): Nancy C. Miller-Herron, Roy B. Herron.
Financial data (yr. ended 12/31/99): Assets, $32,116 (M); grants paid, $8,750; gifts received, $5,000; expenditures, $8,770; qualifying distributions, $8,740.
Limitations: Giving primarily in TN.
Officers: Roy B. Herron, Pres.; Nancy C. Miller-Herron, Secy.
Director: Mary C. Herron.
EIN: 621486395

63500
Germantown Cancer Foundation
7257 Deep Valley Dr.
Germantown, TN 38138

Established in 1998 in TN. Classified as a private operating foundation in 1999.
Donor(s): C. Michael Jones.
Financial data (yr. ended 06/30/01): Assets, $29,826 (M); grants paid, $0; gifts received, $16,312; expenditures, $4,138; qualifying distributions, $0.
Officers: C. Michael Jones, Pres.; Cheryl P. Jones, Secy.; Alexander W. Jones, Treas.
EIN: 621723550

63501
Floy Bell Foundation, Inc.
3610 East Pkwy.
Gatlinburg, TN 37738

Donor(s): Floy S. Bell.

63501—TENNESSEE

Financial data (yr. ended 12/31/99): Assets, $27,425 (M); grants paid, $0; expenditures, $288,933; qualifying distributions, $288,933; giving activities include $288,933 for programs.
Trustees: Floy S. Bell, Bob Evans.
EIN: 581763485

63502
G. A. Coon ABC Prayer Crusade International, Inc.
6307 Georgetown Rd.
Ooltewah, TN 37363

Financial data (yr. ended 12/31/01): Assets, $26,966 (M); grants paid, $0; gifts received, $471; expenditures, $1,058; qualifying distributions, $471; giving activities include $471 for programs.
Officers and Directors:* Juanita Coon Steffens,* Pres.; Charles Steffens,* Secy.-Treas.; Erma Butler, Mary Lou Mathos, Eugene Rimmers, Vinton Sauder, Rita Baez Steffens.
EIN: 621411011

63503
The Christian Healthcare Institute of America
c/o Robert Osburn
105 Sheffield Ct.
Nashville, TN 37215

Established in 1990 in TX.
Donor(s): Robert Osburn.
Financial data (yr. ended 12/31/99): Assets, $25,962 (M); grants paid, $0; expenditures, $113,363; qualifying distributions, $0; giving activities include $113,363 for programs.
Officers: Robert Osburn, Pres.; Fred Woods, V.P.
EIN: 752271909

63504
The Allen Foundation
424 Church St., 28th Fl.
Nashville, TN 37219-2301
Contact: Reber M. Boult, Tr.

Established in 2000 in TN.
Donor(s): Boult Family Foundation.
Financial data (yr. ended 12/31/00): Assets, $24,369 (M); grants paid, $23,000; gifts received, $50,074; expenditures, $26,108; qualifying distributions, $26,108; giving activities include $3,108 for programs.
Limitations: Giving primarily in Arlington, VA; some giving also in Cambodia.
Trustee: Reber M. Boult.
EIN: 311706705

63505
Maddox Football Scholarship Foundation
P.O. Box 889
Huntingdon, TN 38344-0889
Application address: c/o Jimmy Pritchard, 275 Mustang Dr., Huntingdon, TN 38344, tel.: (731) 986-8223

Established in 2001.
Donor(s): D.D. Maddox.‡
Financial data (yr. ended 12/31/01): Assets, $23,700 (M); grants paid, $0; gifts received, $23,117; expenditures, $39; qualifying distributions, $54.
Trustee: Carroll Bank & Trust Co.
EIN: 626386194

63506
Christian Scholarships, Missions, and Projects Foundation
332 Sugar Hill Dr.
Sparta, TN 38583 (931) 836-2226
Contact: Edith Camp, Tr.

Established in 1999 in TN.

Financial data (yr. ended 12/31/99): Assets, $20,323 (M); grants paid, $650; gifts received, $7,830; expenditures, $997; qualifying distributions, $650.
Application information: Application form required.
Trustees: Daniel Camp, Douglas Camp, Edith Camp, Phillip Camp.
EIN: 621721062

63507
Knoxville Academy of Medicine Foundation
422 W. Cumberland Ave.
Knoxville, TN 37902

Established in 1989 in TN.
Financial data (yr. ended 12/31/99): Assets, $18,995 (M); grants paid, $10,000; gifts received, $98,792; expenditures, $103,913; qualifying distributions, $72,243; giving activities include $54,243 for programs.
Limitations: Applications not accepted.
Application information: Contributes only to pre-selected organizations.
Officers: Robert Overholt, M.D., Pres.; Sondra Bridgford, Exec. V.P.; Charles Barnett, M.D., Secy.-Treas.
Directors: Randal Dabbs, M.D., Richard DePersio, M.D., Donald Ellenburg, M.D., David Gerkin, M.D., Robert Montgomery, M.D., Steve Morris, M.D., Meredith Overholt, M.D., Molly Peeler, M.D., Jonathan Sowell, M.D., Tara Sturdivant, M.D.
EIN: 621458199

63508
State Industries Foundation
(Formerly State Stove Foundation)
500 Lindahl Pkwy.
Ashland City, TN 37015-1234

Classified as a company-sponsored operating foundation.
Donor(s): State Industries, Inc.
Financial data (yr. ended 12/31/00): Assets, $17,392 (M); grants paid, $31,115; gifts received, $27,874; expenditures, $31,128; qualifying distributions, $31,115.
Limitations: Applications not accepted. Giving primarily in Cheatham County, TN.
Officers: Evie Sommers, Chair.; Harold Hoover, Vice-Chair.; Bonnie Moore, Secy.
EIN: 626041530
Codes: CD, GTI

63509
Dean Foundation
(Formerly D & R Foundation)
11130 Kingston Pike 1-184
Knoxville, TN 37922

Established in 1996 in TN.
Donor(s): Dean Winegardner.
Financial data (yr. ended 12/31/00): Assets, $15,915 (M); grants paid, $156,800; gifts received, $174,300; expenditures, $158,385; qualifying distributions, $158,385.
Limitations: Applications not accepted. Giving primarily in the South, with emphasis on NC, TN, and FL.
Application information: Contributes only to pre-selected organizations.
Officers: Dean Winegardner, Pres.; Ron Brooks, Secy.
EIN: 621631531
Codes: FD2

63510
Mountain Cancer Treatment Research Foundation, Inc.
1009 E. Lamar Alexander Pkwy.
Maryville, TN 37804

Established in 1997 in TN.
Financial data (yr. ended 12/31/01): Assets, $15,288 (M); grants paid, $0; gifts received, $400; expenditures, $947; qualifying distributions, $0.
Limitations: Applications not accepted.
Application information: Contributes only to pre-selected organizations.
Officers and Directors:* Thomas Kubota, M.D.,* Pres.; Doris M. Myers,* Secy.
EIN: 581514414

63511
Shiloh Ministries International, Inc.
5991 Edmondson Pike
Nashville, TN 37211

Established in 1999 in TN.
Donor(s): Bruce Campbell, Susan Campbell.
Financial data (yr. ended 12/31/99): Assets, $13,910 (M); grants paid, $66,447; gifts received, $84,967; expenditures, $71,057; qualifying distributions, $69,285.
Officers: Bruce Campbell, Pres.; Susan Campbell, V.P.; Suzanne Scott, Treas.
EIN: 621768267

63512
The H. Rodes Hart, Jr. Family Foundation
95 White Bridge Rd., Ste. 212
Nashville, TN 37205

Established in 1993 in TN.
Financial data (yr. ended 12/31/99): Assets, $10,028 (M); grants paid, $5,000; expenditures, $5,000; qualifying distributions, $4,949.
Limitations: Applications not accepted.
Application information: Contributes only to pre-selected organizations.
Trustee: H. Rodes Hart, Jr.
EIN: 626262170

63513
American Neurological Research Foundation
234 Germantown Bend Cove
Cordova, TN 38018-7237
Contact: J. Rodney Feild, Pres.

Established as a private operating foundation in 1975.
Financial data (yr. ended 12/31/00): Assets, $8,166 (M); grants paid, $0; expenditures, $21,694; qualifying distributions, $18,126; giving activities include $9,108 for programs.
Officers and Director:* J. Rodney Feild,* Pres.; Pat Sisk, Secy.-Treas.
EIN: 237219229

63514
Kelley Robertson Foundation
c/o Annie K. and Neil Robertson
5024 Country Club Dr.
Brentwood, TN 37027-5130

Established in 1999 in TN.
Donor(s): Neil Robertson, Annie K. Robertson.
Financial data (yr. ended 12/31/01): Assets, $5,642 (M); grants paid, $0; expenditures, $0; qualifying distributions, $0.
Trustee: Neil Robertson.
EIN: 621762964

63515
Eliza Walker House of Mission
c/o Clara Nunnally
2331 Hunter Ave.
Memphis, TN 38108
Application address: 176 N. Bingham St.,
Memphis, TN 38112
Contact: Margaret Nunnally, Tr.

Donor(s): Clara Nunnally.
Financial data (yr. ended 12/31/00): Assets, $4,867 (M); grants paid, $4,957; gifts received, $10,448; expenditures, $18,337; qualifying distributions, $18,004.
Limitations: Giving limited to residents of Shelby County, TN.
Officer and Trustees:* Clara Nunnally, Exec. Dir.; Luella Beason, Charlie J. Moore, Margaret Nunnally.
EIN: 582185912

63516
Lewis County Children's Fund
P.O. Box 274
Hohenwald, TN 38462

Financial data (yr. ended 12/31/99): Assets, $4,774 (L); grants paid, $311; gifts received, $1,780; expenditures, $458; qualifying distributions, $458.
Limitations: Giving primarily in Lewis County, TN.
Officer: Janet Turner, Pres.
EIN: 621494775

63517
The Chattanooga Chapter TROA Scholarship Trust
P.O. Box 24482
Chattanooga, TN 37422-4482

Established in 1996 in TN.
Financial data (yr. ended 12/31/00): Assets, $2,955 (M); grants paid, $3,000; gifts received, $2,375; expenditures, $3,047; qualifying distributions, $3,000.
Limitations: Giving primarily in GA and TN.
Application information: Application form not required.
Officers: Willard C. Zimmerman, Chair.; Brad Johnson, Treas.
EIN: 626304520

63518
Spirit and Truth Ministries
c/o David S. Spakes
P.O. Box 734
Seymour, TN 37865-0734

Incorporated in 1991 in TN.
Donor(s): Ruby Lea Spakes.
Financial data (yr. ended 07/31/00): Assets, $2,184 (M); grants paid, $0; expenditures, $573; qualifying distributions, $158; giving activities include $468 for programs.
Officers: David S. Spakes, Pres.; Ruby Lea Spakes, Secy.
EIN: 581973220

63519
U.S. Foundation for Anti-Aging & Survival Research
P.O. Box 247
Pleasant View, TN 37146

Established in 1998 in TX.
Financial data (yr. ended 12/31/01): Assets, $1,723 (M); grants paid, $0; gifts received, $63,000; expenditures, $67,465; qualifying distributions, $67,465; giving activities include $6,873 for programs.

Officers and Directors:* Gary M. Kornman,* Pres.; W. Ralph Canada, Jr.,* V.P.; Michael M. Kornman, V.P.; Claudia J. McElwee, Secy.; Vickie A. Walker,* Treas.
EIN: 752752631

63520
Sinclair-Palmer Family Foundation
903 Paddock Park
Nashville, TN 37220

Established in 1998.
Donor(s): Sue P. Sinclair.
Financial data (yr. ended 06/30/02): Assets, $1,350 (M); grants paid, $9,616; gifts received, $10,500; expenditures, $8,690; qualifying distributions, $8,690.
Trustees: Louis R. Burns, Sue P. Sinclair, Susan D. Sinclair.
EIN: 621738805

63521
Backfield In Motion, Inc
850 Hillwood Blvd., Ste. 7
Nashville, TN 37209

Classified as a private operating foundation in 2002 in TN.
Donor(s): Joe Davis.
Financial data (yr. ended 12/31/01): Assets, $854 (M); grants paid, $2,594; gifts received, $144,760; expenditures, $142,177; qualifying distributions, $141,757.
Limitations: Giving primarily in Nashville, TN.
Officers: Joe Davis, Pres.; Delta Davis, Secy.; Gerald Kaforey, Exec.; Dustin Wuest, Dir.
EIN: 621826603

63522
Hemophilia, an Opportunity for Personal Empowerment, Inc.
6820 Charlotte Pike, Ste. 200
Nashville, TN 37209

Established in 1999 in TN.
Financial data (yr. ended 12/31/00): Assets, $570 (M); grants paid, $783; gifts received, $39,328; expenditures, $44,069; qualifying distributions, $42,567.
Limitations: Giving primarily in TN.
Officers: Dianne R. Griffith, Pres.; Sara Zwiep, Secy.
Director: Robert M. Birnbaum.
EIN: 621488300

63523
Avron B. Fogelman Scholars Program
5400 Poplar Ave., Ste. 200
Memphis, TN 38119

Established in 1991 in TN.
Donor(s): Avron B. Fogelman.
Financial data (yr. ended 12/31/99): Assets, $297 (M); grants paid, $0; gifts received, $9,500; expenditures, $9,424; qualifying distributions, $9,424; giving activities include $9,424 for programs.
Limitations: Applications not accepted.
Application information: Contributes only to pre-selected organizations.
Officers: Avron B. Fogelman, Pres.; Hal D. Fogelman, V.P.; Mark A. Fogelman, V.P.; Wendy M. Fogelman, Secy.-Treas.
EIN: 621469964

TEXAS

63524
Kimbell Art Foundation
301 Commerce St., Ste. 2240
Fort Worth, TX 76102-4140

Classified as a private operating foundation in 1972.
Donor(s): Mrs. Ben J. Fortson.
Financial data (yr. ended 12/31/01): Assets, $933,077,515 (M); grants paid, $1,103,500; gifts received, $58,272; expenditures, $15,119,680; qualifying distributions, $11,744,751; giving activities include $8,163,100 for programs.
Limitations: Applications not accepted. Giving primarily in Fort Worth, TX.
Application information: Contributes only to pre-selected organizations.
Officers and Directors:* Mrs. Ben J. Fortson,* Pres.; Ben J. Fortson,* V.P.; Brenda A. Cline, Secy.-Treas.; Mrs. William K. Burton, Ben J. Fortson III, Edward R. Hudson, Jr., Mrs. John L. Marion, J.C. Pace, Jr., Mrs. Mitchell S. Wynne.
EIN: 756036226
Codes: FD

63525
Mary E. Bivins Foundation
P.O. Box 1727
Amarillo, TX 79105 (806) 379-9400
URL: http://www.bivinsfoundation.org
Contact: Judy Mosely, Pres.

Incorporated in 1949 in TX.
Donor(s): Mary E. Bivins Trust, and others.
Financial data (yr. ended 08/31/01): Assets, $104,162,625 (M); grants paid, $5,285,377; gifts received, $4,000,281; expenditures, $15,932,412; qualifying distributions, $10,517,748; giving activities include $8,792,243 for programs.
Limitations: Giving primarily in the northern 26 counties of the TX panhandle.
Publications: Application guidelines.
Application information: Application form required.
Officers and Directors:* Larry Pickens, Chair.; Tom Bivins, Vice-Chair.; Judy Mosely,* Pres.; George Huffman,* Secy.; Miles Childers, Melvin Fowler, John Logsdon, Glenn McMennamy, Don Powell.
EIN: 750842370
Codes: FD

63526
Sarah Campbell Blaffer Foundation
P.O. Box 6826
Houston, TX 77265-6826
Contact: Edward Joseph Hudson, Jr., Secy.

Incorporated in 1964 in TX.
Donor(s): Sarah C. Blaffer.‡
Financial data (yr. ended 12/31/00): Assets, $95,763,078 (M); grants paid, $252,500; gifts received, $239,686; expenditures, $2,492,397; qualifying distributions, $2,074,274; giving activities include $2,000,000 for programs.
Limitations: Giving primarily in TX.
Application information: Application form not required.
Officers: Charles W. Hall, Pres.; Jane Blaffer Owen, V.P. and Treas.; Cecil Blaffer Furstenberg, V.P.; Edward Joseph Hudson, Jr., Secy.
Trustee: Gilbert M. Denman, Jr.
Director: James Cliffton.

EIN: 746065234
Codes: FD

63527
The USAA Educational Foundation
9800 Fredericksburg Rd., Taxes F-3-E
San Antonio, TX 78288-0115

Established in 1998 in TX as a company-sponsored operating foundation.
Donor(s): United Services Automobile Assn.
Financial data (yr. ended 12/31/99): Assets, $95,378,010 (M); grants paid, $135,000; expenditures, $4,946,088; qualifying distributions, $4,325,088; giving activities include $2,504,314 for programs.
Limitations: Applications not accepted.
Application information: Unsolicited requests for funds not accepted.
Officers and Directors:* Robert G. Davis, Chair.; Barbara Gentry,* Pres.; Bradford W. Rich,* V.P. and Secy.; Josue Robles, Jr.,* V.P. and Treas.; Fred A. Gordon, Michael J.C. Roth, Henry Viccellio, Jr., Michael D. Wagner.
EIN: 742884261
Codes: FD2, CD

63528
The Caldwell Foundation
P.O. Box 4280
Tyler, TX 75712

Established in 1953 in TX.
Donor(s): D.K. Caldwell Foundation.
Financial data (yr. ended 12/31/01): Assets, $94,295,924 (M); grants paid, $2,148,290; gifts received, $1,498; expenditures, $3,285,561; qualifying distributions, $9,017,164; giving activities include $6,899,432 for programs.
Limitations: Applications not accepted. Giving primarily in Tyler and eastern TX.
Application information: Unsolicited requests for funds not considered.
Officers: M.S. McArthur, Pres.; H.C. McArthur, Exec. V.P.
Directors: H. Caldwell, P. Lake, D. Wolverton.
EIN: 756004080
Codes: FD

63529
All Church Home for Children, Inc.
1424 Summit Ave.
Fort Worth, TX 76102-5989

Classified as a private operating foundation in 1990.
Financial data (yr. ended 12/31/01): Assets, $63,095,274 (M); grants paid, $0; gifts received, $646,002; expenditures, $3,384,687; qualifying distributions, $3,027,485; giving activities include $2,797,714 for programs.
Officers: Mary Frances St. John, Chair.; Margaret Augustat, Pres.; Lynn O'Day, V.P.; Ann Graner, 2nd V.P.; Barbara Kirk, Secy.; Terri Sexton, Treas.
Directors: Roxanne Honea, Missy Johns, Judy Mayo, Bridget Thomas, and 18 additional directors.
EIN: 750818140

63530
Eugene & Margaret McDermott Art Fund, Inc.
3808 Euclid
Dallas, TX 75205-3102

Classified as a private operating foundation since 1995.
Financial data (yr. ended 05/31/00): Assets, $46,746,538 (M); grants paid, $0; gifts received, $346,800; expenditures, $282,252; qualifying distributions, $2,045,991; giving activities include $1,894,500 for programs.

Officers and Directors:* Margaret M. McDermott,* Chair.; Mary M. Cook,* Vice-Chair.; Patricia J. Brown, Secy.-Treas.; Patricia McBride, Nancy O'Boyle, Bryan Williams.
EIN: 752567893

63531
H. E. Butt Foundation
P.O. Box 290670
Kerrville, TX 78029-0670 (830) 896-2505
Contact: Howard E. Butt, Jr., Pres.

Incorporated in 1933 in TX as a company-sponsored operating foundation.
Donor(s): Howard E. Butt, Sr.,‡ Howard E. Butt, Jr., H.E. Butt Grocery Co., and others.
Financial data (yr. ended 12/31/01): Assets, $37,101,834 (M); grants paid, $2,095,284; gifts received, $7,296,201; expenditures, $5,120,749; qualifying distributions, $3,676,882; giving activities include $93,881 for programs.
Limitations: Applications not accepted. Giving limited to TX.
Application information: Funds are reserved primarily for the foundation's operating programs.
Officers: Howard E. Butt, Jr., Pres.; Barbara Dan Butt, V.P. and Secy.-Treas.; F. Dwight Lacy, V.P.; David M. Rogers, V.P.; Deborah Butt Rogers, V.P.
EIN: 741239819

63532
John Zink Foundation
c/o Bank One Trust Co., N.A.
P.O. Box 2050
Fort Worth, TX 76113

Established in 1957.
Donor(s): John Smith Zink.
Financial data (yr. ended 12/31/99): Assets, $27,039,137 (M); grants paid, $20,000; gifts received, $500,000; expenditures, $370,260; qualifying distributions, $351,067.
Trustees: Kent Caraway, Swabbue S. "Jill" Iwata, Jill Tarbel, Darton J. Zink, Jack Zink, Bank One Trust Co., N.A.
EIN: 736090267

63533
Shearn Moody Plaza Corporation Foundation
123 Rosenberg St.
Galveston, TX 77550-1454

Established in 1981 in TX.
Financial data (yr. ended 07/31/01): Assets, $20,994,002 (L); grants paid, $0; expenditures, $1,973,498; qualifying distributions, $1,973,498; giving activities include $1,973,498 for programs.
Officers and Directors:* Stephen Huffman,* Chair.; Kevin Harrington, Pres.; Michael Winburn,* V.P.; Terry Dean, Secy.; Roger Ezell, S.R. Lewis, Jr.
EIN: 760019420

63534
Wolcott Center for the Study of Ancient Wales
Rte. 4, Box 725
Jefferson, TX 75657

Established in 1996.
Donor(s): Darrell Wolcott.
Financial data (yr. ended 12/31/01): Assets, $20,537,598 (M); grants paid, $0; gifts received, $2,000; expenditures, $15,097; qualifying distributions, $18,712.
Officers: Darrell Wolcott, Pres.; Mae Tiney, Secy.
Directors: Carl Greenhill, Bob R. Wolcott.
EIN: 752635498

63535
The Nasher Foundation
8080 N. Central Expwy., Ste. 830
Dallas, TX 75206-1838

Established in 1996 in TX.
Donor(s): Raymond D. Nasher.
Financial data (yr. ended 12/31/00): Assets, $19,126,401 (M); grants paid, $126,000; gifts received, $5,619,673; expenditures, $305,561; qualifying distributions, $4,883,187; giving activities include $4,657,957 for programs.
Limitations: Applications not accepted. Giving primarily in Dallas, TX.
Application information: Contributes only to pre-selected organizations.
Officers: Raymond D. Nasher, Chair. and Pres.; Byron A. Parker, Treas.; Elliot R. Cattarulla, Exec. Dir.
EIN: 752674048
Codes: FD2

63536
The Tobin Foundation
P.O. Box 91019
San Antonio, TX 78209-1019 (210) 828-9736
FAX: (210) 828-6560; *E-mail:* Tobinart@mindspring.com

Incorporated in 1951 in TX; re-incorporated in 1999 as successor to the original Tobin Foundation.
Donor(s): Edgar G. Tobin,‡ Margaret Batts Tobin,‡ Robert L.B. Tobin.‡
Financial data (yr. ended 12/31/99): Assets, $15,089,977 (M); grants paid, $8,000; gifts received, $41,667; expenditures, $83,319; qualifying distributions, $86,319; giving activities include $78,319 for programs.
Limitations: Giving on a national basis, with emphasis on NM, New York City, and San Antonio, TX.
Application information: Application form not required.
Officers and Directors:* Linda Hardberger,* Secy.; Mel L. Weingart,* Treas.; Matthew Baylor.
EIN: 742921417

63537
Crow Family Foundation, Inc.
c/o Crow Holdings
2100 McKinney Ave., Ste. 700
Dallas, TX 75201

Established in 1997 in TX.
Donor(s): Trammell Crow.
Financial data (yr. ended 12/31/99): Assets, $11,801,260 (M); grants paid, $0; gifts received, $8,685,379; expenditures, $1,311,169; qualifying distributions, $948,074; giving activities include $874,661 for programs.
Officers and Directors:* Trammell S. Crow,* Pres.; Susan T. Groenteman, Exec. V.P.; M. Kevin Bryant, V.P. and Secy.; Ronald S. Brown, V.P. and Treas.; Kimberly A. Bush, V.P.; Kenneth Gross, V.P.; Mien Cheng, Margaret D. Crow.
EIN: 752721699

63538
Center for 20th Century Texas Studies
P.O. Box 1300
Galveston, TX 77553-1300

Established in 1992 in TX.
Financial data (yr. ended 12/31/01): Assets, $11,290,711 (M); grants paid, $0; gifts received, $325,645; expenditures, $691,297; qualifying distributions, $443,253; giving activities include $691,297 for programs.

Officers and Directors:* Edward L. Protz,* Pres.; G. William Rider,* V.P. and Treas.; Robert L. Moody,* Secy.; Betty Massey, Exec. Dir.
EIN: 760355562

63539
Perry-Gething Foundation
P.O. Box 830233
San Antonio, TX 78283-0233

Classified as a private operating foundation in 1985.
Financial data (yr. ended 06/30/00): Assets, $10,932,710 (M); grants paid, $0; gifts received, $1,638; expenditures, $160,887; qualifying distributions, $161,390; giving activities include $130,363 for programs.
Officers: Robert Perry, Pres.; Mrs. Anthony L. Brittis, V.P.; Katherine M. Perry, Secy.-Treas.
EIN: 742359576

63540
Lester & Beatrice Williams Foundation
P.O. Box 809
Cameron, TX 76520 (254) 605-0202
Contact: Mike Zajicek, Tr.

Established in 1997 in TX.
Donor(s): Beatrice Williams.‡
Financial data (yr. ended 12/31/00): Assets, $9,190,573 (M); grants paid, $223,139; gifts received, $228,916; expenditures, $811,718; qualifying distributions, $223,139; giving activities include $240,960 for programs.
Limitations: Giving primarily in Cameron, TX.
Application information: Generally contributes to pre-selected organizations. Application form not required.
Trustees: Jane Burns Elliott, Ernest R. Moore, Mike Zajicek.
EIN: 742847229
Codes: FD2

63541
Helen's Park Trust
c/o JPMorgan Bank of Texas
P.O. Box 2558
Houston, TX 77252-8037

Classified as a private operating foundation in 1994.
Donor(s): Myron A. Williams.‡
Financial data (yr. ended 12/31/01): Assets, $8,512,677 (M); grants paid, $0; expenditures, $112,853; qualifying distributions, $227,641; giving activities include $43,090 for programs.
Trustee: JPMorgan Bank of Texas.
EIN: 766082823

63542
Brownson Home, Inc.
P.O. Box 2022
Victoria, TX 77902-2022

Financial data (yr. ended 12/31/01): Assets, $8,030,724 (M); grants paid, $0; gifts received, $7,550; expenditures, $439,533; qualifying distributions, $0.
Officers and Directors:* Robert Halepeska,* Pres.; Gaye Lee,* V.P.; Mary Carroll McCan,* Secy.-Treas.; Grace Margaret Anderson, Ken Bowen, Larry Clark, William "Bill" Kickendahl, John Larson, Marion Lewis, J.E. McCord, Mary Natividad, Dave Sather, Helen Walker.
EIN: 741237326

63543
The Hartman Foundation, Inc.
10711 Burnet Rd., Ste. 331
Austin, TX 78758

Established in 1999 in TX.
Donor(s): David A. Hartman, Claudette L. Hartman, Douglas M. Hartman.
Financial data (yr. ended 05/31/00): Assets, $7,691,439 (M); grants paid, $285,085; gifts received, $3,435,422; expenditures, $383,476; qualifying distributions, $381,378; giving activities include $107,985 for programs.
Limitations: Applications not accepted.
Application information: Contributes only to pre-selected organizations.
Officers and Directors:* David A. Hartman,* Chair.; Douglas M. Hartman,* Pres.; Claudette L. Hartman,* Exec. V.P.; Elizabeth A. Barta,* Secy.-Treas.; John E. Hartman, Wayne P. Hartman.
EIN: 582471439

63544
Cartmell Home for the Aged and Orphans
2212 W. Reagan St.
Palestine, TX 75801

Classified as a private operating foundation in 1989.
Financial data (yr. ended 06/30/00): Assets, $7,542,283 (M); grants paid, $0; gifts received, $12,232; expenditures, $4,489,743; qualifying distributions, $1,032,076; giving activities include $4,480,089 for programs.
Officers: Phil Jenkins, Chair.; Bill Knowles, Vice-Chair.; Lynn B. Starkey, Jr., C.E.O.
Directors: J.G. Crook, Warren S. Emerson, Billy Gragg, Richard Handorf, Margaret Johnson, Walter Johnson, Ahinise Summers.
EIN: 750869320

63545
Leadership Network, Inc.
2501 Cedar Springs, LB-5, Ste. 200
Dallas, TX 75201-1400

Established in 1988 in TX.
Donor(s): Robert P. Buford, Jeffrey Thomasson.
Financial data (yr. ended 12/31/00): Assets, $7,155,784 (M); grants paid, $0; gifts received, $2,925,470; expenditures, $4,212,564; qualifying distributions, $2,799,225; giving activities include $1,206,029 for programs.
Limitations: Applications not accepted.
Application information: Contributes only to pre-selected organizations.
Officers and Directors:* Robert P. Buford, Chair.; Bradley L. Smith,* Exec. Dir.; J. Michael McMahon, Dir. of Opers.; David Travis, Network Dir.; John Findley, Merle Smith, Jack Willome, Walter Wilson.
EIN: 752208735

63546
Lowdon Family Foundation
4455 Camp Bowie Blvd., Ste.205
Fort Worth, TX 76107

Established in 1997 in TX.
Donor(s): Maria M. Lowdon, Robert R. Lowdon.
Financial data (yr. ended 12/31/01): Assets, $6,568,454 (M); grants paid, $214,720; expenditures, $262,584; qualifying distributions, $241,720.
Limitations: Applications not accepted. Giving primarily in Fort Worth, TX.
Application information: Contributes only to pre-selected organizations.
Officers: Robert R. Lowdon, Pres.; Maria M. Lowdon, V.P. and Treas.; Ann L. Call, Secy.
EIN: 752688118
Codes: FD2

63547
The G. H. Pape Foundation
1901 N. 5th St.
Waco, TX 76708 (254) 753-2032
FAX: (360) 397-8896; E-mail: carleharrison@texnet.net

Established in 1956 in TX.
Donor(s): Eleanor F. Pape.‡
Financial data (yr. ended 12/31/01): Assets, $6,476,629 (M); grants paid, $500; gifts received, $17,257; expenditures, $448,781; qualifying distributions, $500.
Officers: Diane Henderson, Chair.; Sid Jones, Vice-Chair.; Stanley A. Latham, Exec. Dir.
Directors: Lu Billings, Woody Callan, Rodney C. Richie.
Trustee: Community Bank and Trust, Waco.
EIN: 746041756

63548
The MCH Foundation, Inc.
300 N. Coit Rd., Ste. 820
Richardson, TX 75080
Contact: Gary Hoskins, Secy.-Treas.

Established in 1991.
Donor(s): Magdalene C. Hammonds.‡
Financial data (yr. ended 05/31/00): Assets, $6,435,939 (M); grants paid, $26,770; expenditures, $155,196; qualifying distributions, $14,091; giving activities include $113,321 for programs.
Officers: Hermann S. Graf, Pres.; Klaus Wagner, V.P.; Gary R. Hoskins, Secy.-Treas.
EIN: 752359010

63549
Hendrick Home for Children
2758 Jeanette St.
P.O. Box 5195
Abilene, TX 79608-5195

Classified as a private operating foundation in 1973.
Donor(s): L.G. Rhodes, Helen Rhodes.
Financial data (yr. ended 06/30/00): Assets, $6,277,328 (M); grants paid, $0; gifts received, $2,699,616; expenditures, $2,075,619; qualifying distributions, $1,919,142; giving activities include $1,919,142 for programs.
Officers: Leland Kelley, Chair.; Howard Wilkins, Vice-Chair.; Betty Barbieri, V.P.; David Perkins, V.P.; Amber Cree, Secy.; Bob Tiffany, Treas.
Trustees: Grady Barr, Joe Crawford, A.L. "Dusty" Rhodes.
EIN: 750818165

63550
Texas Interscholastic League Foundation
P.O. Box 1845
Austin, TX 78767

Financial data (yr. ended 05/31/99): Assets, $6,103,085 (M); grants paid, $815,850; gifts received, $1,027,214; expenditures, $847,774; qualifying distributions, $815,850.
Limitations: Giving primarily in TX.
Officers: Garry Vacek, Pres.; Roy C. Coffee, V.P.; Bill Farney, Treas.; Bailey Marshall, Exec. Dir.
Directors: I. Jon Brumley, Paul Davis, Jr., Norbert Dittrich, Cyndi Taylor Krier, Teresa L. Long, Walter G. Riedel III, Janet Wiman, Carl Yeckel.
EIN: 746050081
Codes: FD

63551
Ida Mae Oldham Trust
c/o George E. Gilkerson
P.O. Box 716
Lubbock, TX 79408-0716

Established in 1963 in TX.
Financial data (yr. ended 04/30/00): Assets, $6,014,829 (M); grants paid, $0; expenditures, $905,796; qualifying distributions, $713,742; giving activities include $661,070 for programs.
Trustees: George E. Gilkerson, Alan Henry.
EIN: 750993500

63552
Central Texas Museum of Automotive History
c/o B-Bar-B Ranch
Hwy. 304
Rosanky, TX 78953

Classified as a private operating foundation in 1981.
Donor(s): Richard L. Burdick.
Financial data (yr. ended 12/31/99): Assets, $5,891,488 (M); grants paid, $0; gifts received, $425,460; expenditures, $172,387; qualifying distributions, $88,996; giving activities include $89,024 for programs.
Officers: Richard L. Burdick, Pres.; Kenneth G. Downing, V.P.; Amy L. Burdick, Secy.-Treas.
Director: Harry R. Terry.
EIN: 742202758

63553
Hall-Voyer Foundation
(Formerly David Graham Hall Foundation)
502 N. 6th St.
P.O. Box 47
Honey Grove, TX 75446
E-mail: mat@1starnet.com; URL: http://www.honeygrove.org

Established around 1940 in TX. Classified as a private operating foundation.
Donor(s): David Graham Hall.‡
Financial data (yr. ended 12/31/01): Assets, $5,482,649 (M); grants paid, $14,250; gifts received, $14,992; expenditures, $224,772; qualifying distributions, $213,373; giving activities include $70,837 for programs.
Limitations: Applications not accepted. Giving limited to TX.
Publications: Informational brochure.
Application information: Contributes only to pre-selected organizations.
Officers and Directors:* Evelyn F. Wise,* Pres. and Treas.; Mary A. Thurman,* Exec. V.P.; Cheryl Beavers, Beverly Felts, Abraham Goldfarb, Ben Holland.
EIN: 750868394

63554
Read Youth Charities
P.O. Box 1060
Magnolia, TX 77355-1060

Donor(s): Thomas A. Read,‡ Joan C. Read.
Financial data (yr. ended 12/31/01): Assets, $5,379,690 (M); grants paid, $0; gifts received, $77,913; expenditures, $383,300; qualifying distributions, $0.
Officers: Joan C. Read, Pres. and Treas.; George Read, V.P.; Edwin H. Frank, Jr., Secy.
EIN: 237048642

63555
The Haraldson Foundation
25025 I-45 N., Ste. 410
The Woodlands, TX 77380 (281) 362-9909
FAX: (281) 298-6001; E-mail: ndossey@yahoo.com
Contact: Nancy Dossey, Admin.

Established in 1993 in TX.
Donor(s): Beulah M. Haraldson.‡
Financial data (yr. ended 09/30/01): Assets, $5,309,392 (M); grants paid, $188,500; expenditures, $207,430; qualifying distributions, $188,500.
Limitations: Giving limited to TX.
Publications: Annual report, informational brochure (including application guidelines), grants list, newsletter, application guidelines.
Application information: The foundation accepts the University of Texas at Austin application for financial aid. Application form required.
Officers: Karen Sue Emami, Chair.; Betty Jean Cook, Vice-Chair.; Dale A. Dossey, Secy.
EIN: 760420758
Codes: FD2, GTI

63556
Sterling McCall Old Car Museum Foundation
P.O. Box 1886
Cypress, TX 77410-1886

Established in 1999 in TX.
Donor(s): Sterling B. McCall, Jr.
Financial data (yr. ended 04/30/02): Assets, $4,863,576 (M); grants paid, $0; gifts received, $2,303,270; expenditures, $186,473; qualifying distributions, $0.
Limitations: Applications not accepted.
Application information: Contributes only to pre-selected organizations.
Officers and Directors:* Sterling B. McCall, Jr.,* Pres.; Marianne McCall,* V.P.; Allison McCall Sitzes,* Secy.; Karen McCall Brown,* Treas.; Raymond McCall, Sterling B. McCall III.
EIN: 760606789

63557
James C. and Norma I. Smith Foundation
P.O. Box 190369
Dallas, TX 75219

Established in 1994 in IL and TX.
Financial data (yr. ended 11/30/01): Assets, $4,856,831 (M); grants paid, $160,000; expenditures, $161,670; qualifying distributions, $160,000.
Limitations: Applications not accepted. Giving primarily in AZ.
Application information: Contributes only to pre-selected organizations.
Officers and Directors:* James C. Smith,* Pres.; Norma I. Smith,* Treas.; Joseph E. Whitters.
EIN: 363994810
Codes: FD2

63558
The M. G. and Johnnye D. Perry Foundation
P.O. Box 1228
Robstown, TX 78380 (361) 387-2911

Trust established in 1946 in TX.
Donor(s): M.G. Perry,‡ Mrs. M.G. Perry.‡
Financial data (yr. ended 12/31/99): Assets, $4,751,388 (M); grants paid, $14,565; expenditures, $667,283; qualifying distributions, $339,002; giving activities include $174,125 for programs.
Limitations: Giving limited to TX.
Publications: Annual report.
Application information: Application form not required.
Officers and Trustees:* James M. Perry,* Mgr.; Richard H. Perry,* Mgr.; T. Andrew Perry, Mgr.; Thomas E. Perry,* Mgr.
EIN: 741093218

63559
The Max and Billie Clark Foundation
P.O. Box 276
Mineral Wells, TX 76068

Established in 1999 in TX.
Donor(s): Max Clark, Billie Clark.
Financial data (yr. ended 12/31/01): Assets, $4,406,041 (M); grants paid, $0; gifts received, $145,204; expenditures, $573,356; qualifying distributions, $0.
Directors: Billie Clark, Deborah Clark, Max Clark, Carol Montgomery.
EIN: 752809598

63560
The Mary L. Peyton Foundation
Bassett Tower, Ste. 908
303 Texas Ave.
El Paso, TX 79901-1456 (915) 533-9698
Contact: James M. Day, Exec. Admin.

Incorporated in 1937 in TX.
Donor(s): Joe C. Peyton.‡
Financial data (yr. ended 05/31/02): Assets, $4,034,538 (M); grants paid, $243,993; gifts received, $76,780; expenditures, $359,794; qualifying distributions, $317,908.
Limitations: Giving limited to legal residents of El Paso County, TX.
Application information: Application form required.
Officers and Trustees:* Mrs. Alfred Blumenthal,* Chair.; Freeman Harris,* Vice-Chair.; Michael F. Ainsa,* Secy.-Treas.; Susan Elias, Monique Merrell, JPMorgan Chase Bank.
EIN: 741276102
Codes: FD2, GTI

63561
Masonic Temple Library & Museum of Fort Worth, Inc.
P.O. Box 1320
Fort Worth, TX 76101

Financial data (yr. ended 12/31/00): Assets, $3,922,588 (M); grants paid, $0; expenditures, $196,155; qualifying distributions, $0.
Officers and Trustees:* Joe B. Brown,* Chair.; George W. Shannon,* Pres.; Billie E. Davis,* 1st V.P.; Paul A. Johnson,* 2nd V.P.; James D. Morgan,* 3rd V.P.; Joseph E. Kirby,* Secy.; Wayne D. Hagood,* Treas.; Frank E. Barnes, Michie M. Brous, Jimmy R. Hinds, William T. Padon, and 32 additional trustees.
EIN: 752345616

63562
The Luling Foundation
523 S. Mulberry Ave.
Luling, TX 78648-2940 (830) 875-2438
FAX: (830) 875-2438
Contact: Archie Abrameit, Mgr.

Trust established in 1927 in TX.
Donor(s): Edgar B. Davis.‡
Financial data (yr. ended 12/31/00): Assets, $3,662,214 (M); grants paid, $8,260; gifts received, $2,100; expenditures, $228,715; qualifying distributions, $230,189; giving activities include $23,287 for programs.
Limitations: Giving limited to Caldwell, Gonzales, and Guadalupe counties, TX.
Publications: Application guidelines, informational brochure, occasional report.

Application information: Application form required.
Officers: Bodey Langford, Chair.; Steve Breitschopf, Vice-Chair.; Archie Abrameit, Mgr.
Directors: Roger Bading, Gary Dickenson, William Fink, David Shelton, Charles Willmann.
EIN: 741143102
Codes: GTI

63563
Texas Energy Museum, Inc.
601 Main St.
Beaumont, TX 77701

Established in 1987 in TX.
Financial data (yr. ended 12/31/00): Assets, $3,593,212 (M); grants paid, $0; gifts received, $710,304; expenditures, $465,474; qualifying distributions, $0.
Limitations: Giving limited to Beaumont, TX.
Officers: Evelyn Lord, Pres.; Roy Steinhagen, V.P.; Rick Hagar, Secy.; Bob Burns, Treas.
EIN: 760225927

63564
Center for Christian Growth, Inc.
8201 Preston Rd., Ste. 310
Dallas, TX 75225

Financial data (yr. ended 12/31/01): Assets, $3,539,462 (M); grants paid, $0; gifts received, $712,555; expenditures, $2,956,829; qualifying distributions, $448,619; giving activities include $2,956,829 for programs.
Officer and Trustees:* June Mayfield,* V.P. and Secy.-Treas.; Scott Turpin.
Directors: R. Keith Myer, Johnny Polk.
EIN: 751671920

63565
Ruth Parr Sparks Foundation
112 N. Adams St.
Alice, TX 78332-4828   (361) 668-3636
Contact: David Leon McNinch, Chair.

Established in 1998 in TX.
Donor(s): Ruth Sparks.‡
Financial data (yr. ended 12/31/00): Assets, $3,519,679 (M); grants paid, $176,000; expenditures, $237,578; qualifying distributions, $210,156.
Limitations: Giving limited to TX.
Officers: David Leon McNinch, Chair.; Linda F. Castillo, Secy.
Directors: Paul R. Haas, James A. Mayo, Jr.
EIN: 742844494
Codes: FD2

63566
Alamo Area Operating Foundation, Inc.
(Formerly Majestic Foundation, Inc.)
1000 N. Alamo, Ste. B
San Antonio, TX 78215

Classified as a private operating foundation in 1979.
Financial data (yr. ended 03/31/01): Assets, $3,515,356 (M); grants paid, $0; expenditures, $160,019; qualifying distributions, $131,130; giving activities include $131,130 for programs.
Limitations: Applications not accepted.
Officers: Herman Wigodsky, Chair. and Secy.-Treas.; A. Edward Harllee, Pres.; Roan Harwood, Secy.
Directors: Tom Hallstead, Cameron Harris.
EIN: 741908420

63567
Breckenridge Library and Fine Arts Foundation
P.O. Box 752
Breckenridge, TX 76424

Classified as a private operating foundation in 1983.
Donor(s): Lester Clark, David Clark, O.H. Reaugh.
Financial data (yr. ended 12/31/01): Assets, $3,495,148 (M); grants paid, $0; gifts received, $477,243; expenditures, $244,172; qualifying distributions, $0.
Officers: David Clark, Pres.; O.H. Reaugh, V.P.; Barrett Clark, V.P.; Rena Goldsmith, Secy.-Treas.
EIN: 751891984

63568
Advanced Long-Term Care Corporation-Oak Creek
120 Interpark, Ste. 200
San Antonio, TX 78216

Classified as a private operating foundation in 1992.
Financial data (yr. ended 05/31/01): Assets, $3,248,446 (M); grants paid, $0; expenditures, $1,453,729; qualifying distributions, $0; giving activities include $1,455,693 for programs.
Officers and Directors:* Jerry G. Du Terroil,* Pres.; Edward Partridge,* V.P.; Donna Vasbinder,* Secy.-Treas.; Harvey H. Johle, Sylvia Willoughby.
EIN: 742489251

63569
Alvin A. & Roberta T. Klein Trust Fund
17046 Stuebner-Airline Rd.
Klein, TX 77379   (281) 376-7160
Contact: John Klein, Tr.

Established in 1957; classified as a private operating foundation in 1971.
Donor(s): Roberta T. Klein.
Financial data (yr. ended 12/31/01): Assets, $3,001,636 (M); grants paid, $108,000; expenditures, $110,799; qualifying distributions, $109,295.
Limitations: Giving primarily in TX, with emphasis on Houston.
Trustees: Allan R. Klein, David R. Klein, John W. Klein, Roberta T. Klein, Sonja Klein.
EIN: 746055506
Codes: FD2

63570
L. D. Brinkman Art Foundation
444 Sidney Baker S.
Kerrville, TX 78028

Donor(s): LDB Corp., L.D. Brinkman.
Financial data (yr. ended 07/31/00): Assets, $2,982,819 (M); grants paid, $4,500; gifts received, $2,812; expenditures, $7,851; qualifying distributions, $3,351; giving activities include $2,887 for programs.
Officers: L.D. Brinkman, Pres.; Charles Thomas, Secy.; Pam Stone, Treas.
EIN: 742374663

63571
Crist & Elizabeth Pshigoda Foundation
2215 Cherry St.
Paris, TX 75460

Donor(s): Crist Pshigoda, Elizabeth Pshigoda.
Financial data (yr. ended 12/31/99): Assets, $2,730,907 (M); grants paid, $0; expenditures, $279,125; qualifying distributions, $279,125.
Officers: Wayne Brown, Pres.; Paul T. Wells, Secy.; Chad Brown, Treas.
EIN: 751783277

63572
Thomsen Foundation
2801 Turtle Creek Blvd., Rm. 2W
Dallas, TX 75219

Classified as a private operating foundation in 1982.
Donor(s): C.J. Thomsen, Hortense M. Thomsen.
Financial data (yr. ended 12/31/01): Assets, $2,583,362 (M); grants paid, $0; gifts received, $285,000; expenditures, $93,670; qualifying distributions, $0.
Officers and Trustees:* C.J. Thomsen, Pres. and Treas.; Mary M. Cook,* Secy.; Waldo Boyd, Will Montgomery.
EIN: 751833850

63573
M. S. Doss Youth Center, Inc.
c/o James Satterwhite
P.O. Box 1677
Seminole, TX 79360

Established around 1976 in TX.
Financial data (yr. ended 05/31/99): Assets, $2,386,394 (M); grants paid, $0; gifts received, $63,339; expenditures, $148,643; qualifying distributions, $103,076; giving activities include $109,401 for programs.
Officers and Trustees:* Wayne Mixon,* Pres.; Kathy Davis,* V.P.; Cindy Black,* Secy.; Jesse Mendoza,* Treas.; Michael Carter, Jon Key, Max Townsend.
EIN: 751089342

63574
Vision Twenty One, Inc.
601 E. Airport Fwy., Ste. 119
Euless, TX 76039

Financial data (yr. ended 12/31/99): Assets, $2,337,290 (M); grants paid, $33,800; expenditures, $547,095; qualifying distributions, $100,901.
Limitations: Applications not accepted. Giving primarily in TX.
Application information: Contributes only to pre-selected organizations. Unsolicited requests for funds not accepted.
Officers: Scott Fisher, Pres.; Peter Stephenson, Secy.; Kenneth Vaile, Treas.
EIN: 752236061

63575
Optimist Village, Inc.
3650 Optimist Way
Orange, TX 77630-2962

Financial data (yr. ended 12/31/01): Assets, $2,299,986 (M); grants paid, $0; expenditures, $708,757; qualifying distributions, $708,757; giving activities include $708,757 for programs.
Officers: James E. Smith, Pres.; Jo Fite, V.P.
Director: Harold Welch.
EIN: 760064339

63576
Breckenridge Aviation Museum
P.O. Box 388
Breckenridge, TX 76424

Classified as a private operating foundation in 1980.
Donor(s): Howard E. Pardue.
Financial data (yr. ended 05/31/00): Assets, $2,071,445 (M); grants paid, $0; gifts received, $50,705; expenditures, $80,729; qualifying distributions, $80,729; giving activities include $72,277 for programs.
Directors: C.E. Garvin, Leslie J. Griffith, J.R. McMillan, Carolyn C. Pardue, Howard E. Pardue.

63577
Pate Foundation
1227 W. Magnolia Ave., Ste. 420
Fort Worth, TX 76104
Contact: Sebert Pate, Pres.

Established in 1960 in TX.
Financial data (yr. ended 12/31/99): Assets, $1,999,000 (M); grants paid, $25,000; gifts received, $50,000; expenditures, $61,000; qualifying distributions, $25,000.
Limitations: Giving primarily in Fort Worth, TX.
Application information: Application form not required.
Officers: Sebert Pate, Pres.; Charles P. Pate, V.P. and Secy.-Treas.; A.M. Pate III, V.P.
EIN: 756036779

63578
ArtPace, A Foundation for Contemporary Art/San Antonio
445 N. Main Ave.
San Antonio, TX 78205 (210) 212-4900
FAX: (210) 212-4990; E-mail: info@artpace.org;
URL: http://www.artpace.org
Contact: Marketing Assoc.

Established in 1993 in TX.
Donor(s): Linda M. Pace.
Financial data (yr. ended 12/31/01): Assets, $1,927,596 (M); grants paid, $25,575; gifts received, $725,354; expenditures, $1,695,250; qualifying distributions, $1,559,132; giving activities include $80,464 for loans and $1,386,979 for programs.
Limitations: Applications not accepted. Giving primarily in San Antonio, TX.
Application information: Contributes only to pre-selected organizations.
Trustee: Linda M. Pace.
EIN: 742664002

63579
Intimate Life Ministries
P.O. Box 201808
Austin, TX 78720-1808

Financial data (yr. ended 12/31/99): Assets, $1,896,715 (M); grants paid, $600; gifts received, $1,299,635; expenditures, $1,929,132; qualifying distributions, $1,185,237; giving activities include $525,611 for programs.
Limitations: Applications not accepted.
Application information: Contributes only to pre-selected organizations.
Directors: David Ferguson, Theresa Fergusson, Brian F. McCoy, Wetonnah McCoy.
EIN: 742300134

63580
Headliners Foundation of Texas
P.O. Box 97
Austin, TX 78767
Application address: c/o Mike Quinn, Dept. of Journalism, University of TX, Austin TX 78712
Contact: Cindy Bradshaw

Classified as a private operating foundation in 1991.
Donor(s): Ruth P. Elliott, Effie and Wofford Cain Foundation, Headliners Club.
Financial data (yr. ended 07/31/01): Assets, $1,880,590 (M); grants paid, $50,940; gifts received, $106,301; expenditures, $138,631; qualifying distributions, $50,940.
Limitations: Giving limited to residents of TX.
Application information: Organizations may submit an entry for a TX journalist or reporter for the Charles E. Green Journalism Awards.

Officers and Board of Governors:* Roy Butler,* Chair.; Elspeth Rostow,* Vice-Chair.; LaVada Jackson Steed,* Secy.; Allen Shivers, Jr.,* Treas.; Greg Curtis, and 10 additional governors.
EIN: 742281076
Codes: GTI

63581
The Hofheinz Fund
c/o Bank of America, Trust Dept.
P.O. Box 2518
Houston, TX 77252-2518

Established in 1984 in TX.
Donor(s): Roy M. Hofheinz Charitable Foundation.
Financial data (yr. ended 09/30/01): Assets, $1,814,165 (M); grants paid, $0; expenditures, $194,444; qualifying distributions, $144,649; giving activities include $145,119 for programs.
Officer and Trustees:* Roy Hofheinz, Jr.,* Mgr.; Bank of America.
EIN: 760090167

63582
Professional Contract Service, Inc., Inc.
(Formerly Physically Challenged Service Industries, Inc.)
5700 Mopac Exwy. S., Bldg. E, Ste. 560
Austin, TX 78749

Established in 1996 in TX. Classified as a private operating foundation in 1997.
Donor(s): National Institute for the Severely Handicapped (NISH).
Financial data (yr. ended 06/30/00): Assets, $1,788,552 (M); grants paid, $3,000; gifts received, $46,621; expenditures, $4,703,298; qualifying distributions, $277,071; giving activities include $4,911,004 for programs.
Limitations: Applications not accepted.
Application information: Contributes only to pre-selected organizations.
Officers: Ace L. Burt, Pres.; Kevin Cloud, V.P.; Frank Arevalo, Secy.-Treas.
Director: Carroll Schubert.
EIN: 742786094

63583
Erwin E. Smith Foundation
c/o Bank of Texas Trust Co.
P.O. Box 1088
Sherman, TX 75091-1088 (903) 813-5100
Contact: Mara A. Yachik, Governor

Established in 1984 in TX.
Financial data (yr. ended 06/30/01): Assets, $1,778,579 (M); grants paid, $114,000; expenditures, $138,621; qualifying distributions, $110,911.
Limitations: Giving on a national basis.
Application information: Application form not required.
Governors: Cam Gillespie, Kathryn Keeton, James A. Lindsey, Rick Stewart, Ron Tyler, Mara A. Yachik.
Trustee: Bank of Texas Trust Co.
EIN: 756330553
Codes: FD2

63584
Life Dynamics, Inc.
P.O. Box 2226
Denton, TX 76202

Established in 1992.
Donor(s): Chris Zomaya, MPM Zomaya Group, Inc., National Lifesources, Inc.
Financial data (yr. ended 06/30/01): Assets, $1,752,243 (M); grants paid, $10,000; gifts received, $2,480,865; expenditures, $1,097,157;

qualifying distributions, $985,139; giving activities include $985,139 for programs.
Limitations: Applications not accepted. Giving primarily in TX.
Application information: Contributes only to pre-selected organizations.
Officers: Mark Crutcher, Pres.; Lisa Beaulieu, V.P.; Cheri Driggs, Secy.-Treas.
Directors: Arden Morley, B.J. Posey.
EIN: 752436409

63585
The Lance Layne Foundation
5750 Stratum Dr.
Fort Worth, TX 76137 (817) 232-5661
Contact: Kimberly C. New, V.P.

Established in 1994.
Donor(s): Bill R. New, Barbara G. New.
Financial data (yr. ended 11/30/01): Assets, $1,751,809 (M); grants paid, $4,710; gifts received, $13,668; expenditures, $11,922; qualifying distributions, $4,710.
Limitations: Giving limited to residents of Fort Worth, TX.
Officers: Barbara G. New, Pres.; Bill R. New, V.P.; Kimberly C. New, V.P.; Sara McPeek, Secy.
EIN: 752572316

63586
Marc S. & Carolyn Seriff Foundation
P.O. Box 370
Austin, TX 78767

Established in 1994 in TX.
Donor(s): Marc Seriff, Carolyn Seriff.
Financial data (yr. ended 12/31/01): Assets, $1,714,860 (M); grants paid, $980,623; gifts received, $1,064,500; expenditures, $1,154,764; qualifying distributions, $1,127,036.
Limitations: Applications not accepted. Giving primarily in Austin and Marble Falls, TX.
Application information: Contributes only to pre-selected organizations.
Trustees: Carolyn Seriff, Marc Seriff.
EIN: 521912780
Codes: FD

63587
Texas Star Oaks Fund, Inc.
372 Neva Ln.
Denison, TX 75020-4868
Application address: 3304 W. 18th St., Plainview, TX 79072-3634
Contact: Sally Eaves, Chair.

Established in 1954 in TX.
Financial data (yr. ended 03/31/01): Assets, $1,700,218 (M); grants paid, $87,918; gifts received, $15,977; expenditures, $99,697; qualifying distributions, $87,918.
Limitations: Giving limited to residents of TX.
Application information: Case history and letter of recommendation. Application form required.
Officers: Sally Eaves, Chair.; Claire Daulton, Vice-Chair.; Courtney Townsend, 1st V.P.; Heather McIntosh, Secy.; Marian Barger, Treas.
Advisor: Shanna Garcia.
EIN: 746047454
Codes: FD2, GTI

63588
Research Educational Foundation, Inc.
11061 Shady Trail
Dallas, TX 75229

Established in 1968.
Financial data (yr. ended 12/31/00): Assets, $1,592,360 (M); grants paid, $1,040; gifts received, $1,399,244; expenditures, $1,363,948; qualifying distributions, $1,040.

Officers: Scott Thomas, Pres.; Stanley Thomas, Secy.-Treas.
Director: Harry Reever.
EIN: 751247639

63589
Weininger Foundation, Inc.
c/o Anita Younes
7902 Robin Rest Dr.
San Antonio, TX 78209

Established in 2000 in DE and TX.
Donor(s): Eva Weininger.
Financial data (yr. ended 12/31/00): Assets, $1,512,581 (M); grants paid, $19,425; gifts received, $1,602,894; expenditures, $91,179; qualifying distributions, $91,106; giving activities include $67,149 for programs.
Limitations: Applications not accepted. Giving on a national and international basis.
Application information: Contributes only to pre-selected organizations.
Officers: Eva Weininger, Chair.; Anita Younes, Pres.; Linda Miller, Secy.
EIN: 223711311

63590
The OS Ranch Foundation
P.O. Box 790
Post, TX 79356

Donor(s): Giles C. McCrary.
Financial data (yr. ended 12/31/99): Assets, $1,446,635 (M); grants paid, $0; gifts received, $153,406; expenditures, $64,212; qualifying distributions, $82,994; giving activities include $22,670 for programs.
Limitations: Applications not accepted.
Application information: Contributes only to pre-selected organizations.
Officers and Directors:* Giles C. McCrary,* Pres.; Louise L. McCrary,* V.P.; Mary McCrary,* Secy.; Giles C. McCrary, Jr.
EIN: 752407368

63591
The Woodland Foundation
1425 Turtle Creek Dr.
Lufkin, TX 75904-4328 (936) 632-3300
Contact: Marianna Duncan

Established in 1993.
Donor(s): R.H. Duncan, Joan N. Duncan, Rufus H. Duncan, Jr.
Financial data (yr. ended 12/31/01): Assets, $1,391,361 (M); grants paid, $67,728; gifts received, $206,137; expenditures, $80,410; qualifying distributions, $80,260.
Limitations: Applications not accepted. Giving limited to TX.
Application information: Unsolicited requests for funds not accepted.
Officers: Jane D. Ainsworth, Pres.; Joan N. Duncan, Secy.
Directors: Rufus H. Duncan, Jr., Harriet Tamminga.
EIN: 752474376

63592
Clara B. White Memorial Foundation, Inc.
118 W. Grand St.
Whitewright, TX 75491-2139

Established in 1996 in TX.
Donor(s): Jewell W. Carruth.
Financial data (yr. ended 09/30/01): Assets, $1,307,669 (M); grants paid, $79,878; expenditures, $100,961; qualifying distributions, $100,961.
Limitations: Applications not accepted. Giving primarily in TX.

Application information: Contributes only to pre-selected organizations.
Officers: Patricia A. Hubbard, Pres.; Kenneth D. Hubbard, Secy.-Treas.
EIN: 752681211

63593
Pan American League
P.O. Box 28599
San Antonio, TX 78228

Financial data (yr. ended 12/31/01): Assets, $1,271,935 (M); grants paid, $0; gifts received, $1,475; expenditures, $7,313; qualifying distributions, $1,427.
Limitations: Applications not accepted. Giving limited to San Antonio, TX.
Application information: Contributes only to pre-selected organizations.
Officers: Betty Cervera, Pres.; Rosie Guajardo, 1st V.P.; Exparcia Reyes, 2nd V.P.; Cookie Gehring, 3rd V.P.; Irene Barret, Recording Secy.; Estela Naranjo, Corresponding Secy.; Eva Trevino, Treas.
EIN: 741181773

63594
The Charles and Dana Nearburg Foundation
P.O. Box 823085
Dallas, TX 75382-3085 (214) 739-1779
Contact: Charles Nearburg, Pres.

Established in 1996 in TX.
Donor(s): Charles E. Nearburg, Dana E. Nearburg.
Financial data (yr. ended 12/31/01): Assets, $1,258,722 (M); grants paid, $1,050,583; gifts received, $1,642,500; expenditures, $1,050,607; qualifying distributions, $1,050,583.
Limitations: Giving primarily in TX.
Application information: Application form required.
Officers and Directors:* Charles E. Nearburg,* Pres.; Dana E. Nearburg,* Secy.; Anna A. Reischman.
EIN: 752658947
Codes: FD, GTI

63595
The Buchholz Family Foundation
3627 Glenbrook Ct.
Garland, TX 75041

Established in 1997 in TX.
Donor(s): Don A. Buchholz, Ruth V. Buccholz.
Financial data (yr. ended 12/31/99): Assets, $1,236,962 (M); grants paid, $57,300; expenditures, $68,210; qualifying distributions, $56,574.
Limitations: Applications not accepted. Giving limited to TX.
Application information: Contributes only to pre-selected organizations.
Officers and Directors:* Don A. Buchholz,* Pres.; Ruth V. Buchholz,* Secy.-Treas.; Robert A. Buchholz, Chrystine L. Roberts.
EIN: 752707505

63596
Esther L. Heit Foundation
815 Montreal
Longview, TX 75601

Established in 1991 in TX.
Donor(s): Esther L. Smith.
Financial data (yr. ended 12/31/01): Assets, $1,222,823 (M); grants paid, $69,184; expenditures, $86,767; qualifying distributions, $70,371.
Limitations: Applications not accepted. Giving primarily in TX.
Application information: Contributes only to pre-selected organizations.

Officers: John G. Heit, Pres.; John A. Heit, V.P.; Carol G. Heit, Secy.-Treas.
Directors: James M. Heit, Carol A. Hicks, James P. Hicks, Mary Lou Lubbers.
EIN: 752392220

63597
Camille and Raymond Hankamer Foundation
P.O. Box 56131
Houston, TX 77256-6131

Donor(s): Camille O. Hankamer, Raymond E. Hankamer, Sr.
Financial data (yr. ended 12/31/00): Assets, $1,183,137 (M); grants paid, $100,000; gifts received, $37,521; expenditures, $117,659; qualifying distributions, $100,000; giving activities include $17,461 for programs.
Officers and Trustees:* Raymond E. Hankamer, Sr.,* Pres.; Camille O. Hankamer,* V.P.; Ronald J. Hankamer,* Secy.-Treas.
EIN: 760387872

63598
The F. L. Young Foundation, Inc.
P.O. Box 556
Greenville, TX 75403-0556
Application address: 2610 Stonewall St., Greenville, TX 75401, tel.: (903) 455-3183
Contact: J. Harris Morgan, Pres.

Established in 1986 in TX.
Financial data (yr. ended 12/31/99): Assets, $1,142,806 (M); grants paid, $44,500; gifts received, $20,675; expenditures, $47,088; qualifying distributions, $43,998.
Limitations: Giving limited to Greenville and Hunt County, TX.
Application information: Application form not required.
Officers: J. Harris Morgan, Pres.; John Sutton, V.P.; Sandy Rapp, Secy.; Helen Dunavin, Treas.
Directors: Melva Hill, Jesse Salazar.
EIN: 752108323

63599
Thompson Family Foundation
207 Cedar Ln.
Seabrook, TX 77586-6135

Established in 1999.
Financial data (yr. ended 12/31/99): Assets, $1,131,484 (M); grants paid, $0; gifts received, $1,131,484; expenditures, $0; qualifying distributions, $0.
Director: Pamela Thompson.
EIN: 760649165

63600
Hope for the Heart
1445 Ross at Field, Ste. 1700
Dallas, TX 75202-2785

Established in 1987.
Donor(s): June Hunt.
Financial data (yr. ended 12/31/00): Assets, $1,119,345 (M); grants paid, $0; gifts received, $2,312,798; expenditures, $4,105,613; qualifying distributions, $4,018,199; giving activities include $4,018,199 for programs.
Officers and Directors:* June Hunt,* Chair. and Pres.; June B. Page,* Exec. V.P.; Barbara Clark Cashion,* Secy.-Treas.; J.H. McNairy,* Exec. Dir.; Gloria Cowan, Sue Farrar, Ronald L. Harris, Phyllis S. Karns, Ph.D., Douglas H. Kieseweller, Hon. Don Metcalle, Jimy Roberts, David Wills.
EIN: 752191528

63601
The Margaret Sue Rust Foundation
2602 Hwy. 35 N.
Rockport, TX 78382-5707
Application address: 1856 Bayshore Dr., Rockport, TX 78382, tel.: (361) 729-0402
Contact: Margaret Sue Rust, Pres.

Established in 1998.
Donor(s): Margaret S. Rust.
Financial data (yr. ended 12/31/01): Assets, $1,110,596 (M); grants paid, $174,484; gifts received, $124,192; expenditures, $175,066; qualifying distributions, $174,001.
Limitations: Giving primarily in Rockport, TX.
Officers: Margaret S. Rust, Pres.; Michael Johnson, Secy.-Treas.
Directors: Lola Bonner, John P. Jackson, William M. Rust.
EIN: 742832533
Codes: FD2

63602
Nation Foundation
P.O. Box 180849
Dallas, TX 75218-0849
Contact: Oslin Nation, Tr.

Established in 1961 in TX.
Donor(s): Oslin Nation, James H. Nation, Patricia Walsh, First Co.
Financial data (yr. ended 01/31/01): Assets, $1,086,589 (M); grants paid, $59,454; gifts received, $34,200; expenditures, $59,656; qualifying distributions, $59,454.
Limitations: Applications not accepted. Giving primarily in TX.
Trustees: Frieda Ashworth, James H. Nation, Oslin Nation.
EIN: 756036339

63603
LeTulle Foundation
1400 8th St.
Bay City, TX 77414

Established in 1993 in TX.
Donor(s): Alta Rea LeTulle,‡ Quail Unlimited.
Financial data (yr. ended 06/30/01): Assets, $1,046,864 (M); grants paid, $0; gifts received, $30,750; expenditures, $163,235; qualifying distributions, $69,105; giving activities include $69,105 for programs.
Limitations: Applications not accepted. Giving limited to Bay City, TX.
Application information: Contributes only to pre-selected organizations.
Directors: Clyde Davis, J.L. Zieghals.
EIN: 760358706

63604
Foundation for Expanding Horizons
c/o Jane B. Walton, C.P.A.
P.O. Box 1867
Cedar Park, TX 78630-1867 (512) 248-2790

Established in 1983.
Donor(s): Gretchen Lara Shartle.
Financial data (yr. ended 12/31/00): Assets, $1,018,493 (M); grants paid, $62,095; expenditures, $101,744; qualifying distributions, $62,095.
Limitations: Giving primarily in Austin, TX.
Publications: Application guidelines.
Application information: Application form not required.
Officer: Jane B. Walton, Secy.
Director: Gretchen Lara Shartle.
Trustees: Jolynn Free, Jorge Lara-Braud, Standish Meacham, Jill McCrae, Greta Sabin, Kyria R. Sabin, Jack Stotts, Kathy Tyler, Tom Watkins.
EIN: 742268074

63605
Urban Development Foundation, Inc.
3629 Colgate Ave.
Dallas, TX 75225   (214) 350-3465
Contact: Melvin W. Jackson, Mgr.

Established about 1970 in TX.
Financial data (yr. ended 12/31/99): Assets, $1,016,033 (M); grants paid, $400; expenditures, $15,054; qualifying distributions, $14,654.
Limitations: Giving primarily in Dallas, TX.
Officers: Peter Jackson, V.P.; Susan Jackson, Secy.; Melvin W. Jackson, Mgr.
EIN: 237028475

63606
Eugene and Daniela Anderson Scholarship Foundation
309 W. Foster
Pampa, TX 79065
Application address: 409 W. Foster, Pampa, TX 79065, tel.: (806) 669-3397
Contact: Bob Finney, Secy.

Established in 1999 in TX.
Donor(s): Eugene Anderson, Daniela L. Anderson.
Financial data (yr. ended 09/30/00): Assets, $997,612 (M); grants paid, $16,500; expenditures, $30,648; qualifying distributions, $29,182; giving activities include $29,182 for programs.
Limitations: Giving limited to Pampa, TX.
Application information: Application available from Pampa High School, TX. Application form required.
Officers: Eugene Anderson, Pres.; Daniela L. Anderson, V.P.; Larry W. Anderson, V.P.; Bob Finney, Secy.; Lewis Meers, Treas.
EIN: 752848433

63607
Virgil and Josephine Gordon Memorial Library
917 N. Circle Dr.
Sealy, TX 77474-3333

Financial data (yr. ended 12/31/01): Assets, $981,229 (M); grants paid, $0; gifts received, $38,404; expenditures, $102,243; qualifying distributions, $0.
Officers: Jeanne Zander, Chair.; David J. Mlcak, Secy.; Terry Koy, Treas.
EIN: 742054520

63608
The Fant Foundation
9219 Katy Fwy., Ste. 161
Houston, TX 77024
Contact: Kelley Williams, Dir.

Established in 1994 in TX.
Financial data (yr. ended 12/31/01): Assets, $967,763 (M); grants paid, $190,738; gifts received, $223,000; expenditures, $202,273; qualifying distributions, $195,117.
Limitations: Giving primarily to residents of TX.
Directors: Richard E. Fant, Phil O. Kelley, Sheldon E. Richie, Kelley Williams.
EIN: 760443413
Codes: FD2, GTI

63609
The Vintage Auto Heritage Foundation
P.O. Box 61369
Houston, TX 77208

Classified as a private operating foundation in 1997 in TX.
Donor(s): Carolyn C. Bookout, John F. Bookout, Jr.
Financial data (yr. ended 11/30/01): Assets, $953,902 (M); grants paid, $0; gifts received, $127,500; expenditures, $57,759; qualifying distributions, $56,878; giving activities include $56,878 for programs.
Limitations: Applications not accepted.
Application information: Contributes only to pre-selected organizations.
Officers and Directors:* John F. Bookout, Jr.,* Pres.; John F. Bookout III,* V.P.; Beverly Von Kurnatowski,* Secy.-Treas.; Carolyn C. Bookout, Adair Stevenson.
EIN: 760523208

63610
Circle C Child Development Center, Inc.
5917 LaCrosse Ave.
Austin, TX 78739

Established in 1997 in TX.
Financial data (yr. ended 12/31/01): Assets, $952,417 (M); grants paid, $0; gifts received, $124,079; expenditures, $1,067,912; qualifying distributions, $0.
Officers: Gary Bradley, Pres.; James Gressett, V.P.; Susan Hoover, Secy.-Treas.
EIN: 742672326

63611
Holzman Family Foundation
11803 Kellers Point
San Antonio, TX 78230

Established in 2000.
Financial data (yr. ended 12/31/00): Assets, $949,969 (M); grants paid, $1,000; gifts received, $963,741; expenditures, $1,651; qualifying distributions, $1,000.
Limitations: Giving primarily in San Antonio, TX.
Officer: Leonard Holzman, Pres.
EIN: 742971500

63612
The Diamond M Foundation, Inc.
c/o John Mark McLaughlin
2201 Sherwood Way
San Angelo, TX 76901

Trust established in 1950; incorporated in 1957 in TX. Classified as a private operating foundation in 1972.
Donor(s): C.T. McLaughlin.‡
Financial data (yr. ended 12/31/01): Assets, $933,271 (M); grants paid, $30,000; expenditures, $51,226; qualifying distributions, $30,000.
Limitations: Applications not accepted. Giving limited to TX.
Application information: Contributes only to pre-selected organizations.
Officers: John Mark McLaughlin, Pres.; Jean McLaughlin Kahle, Secy.
Directors: Evelyn McLaughlin Davies, Barbara Riddle Fendley, Max Von Roeder.
EIN: 756015426

63613
Judd Foundation
104 S. Highland Ave.
Marfa, TX 79843

Established in 1997.
Financial data (yr. ended 12/31/00): Assets, $895,879 (M); grants paid, $0; gifts received, $6,029; expenditures, $36,187; qualifying distributions, $0; giving activities include $4,209 for programs.
Officers and Directors:* Richard Schlajman,* Pres.; Maureen Jerome,* V.P.; Flavin Judd, Rainer Judd, Glen Lowry, Louisa Sarofim, Marianne Stockebrand.
EIN: 742798673

63614
Michael & Alice Kuhn Foundation
609-B Wood St.
Austin, TX 78703 (512) 476-1072
FAX: (512) 476-1097; E-mail:
Mikealicekuhn@earthlink.net
Contact: Alice J. Kuhn, Exec. Dir.

Established in 1997 in TX.
Donor(s): Michael Kuhn, Alice Kuhn.
Financial data (yr. ended 12/31/01): Assets, $859,173 (M); grants paid, $52,667; expenditures, $55,686; qualifying distributions, $54,393.
Application information: Application form not required.
Officers: Michael Kuhn, Pres.; Alice Kuhn, V.P. and Exec. Dir.
EIN: 742791217

63615
Helen Lee Foundation, Inc.
c/o Sandy Slone
1828 Shadybrook
Nacogdoches, TX 75961

Classified as a private operating foundation in 1993.
Donor(s): Helen Lee.‡
Financial data (yr. ended 06/30/00): Assets, $848,386 (M); grants paid, $0; gifts received, $862; expenditures, $38,258; qualifying distributions, $33,834; giving activities include $34,129 for programs.
Officers and Trustees:* C.W. Vernon, Chair.; Sandy Slone, Treas.; Derek Bruton,* Mgr.; Sammy Tyler, Rhonda Welch.
EIN: 752461720

63616
S. D. Warfield Charitable Trust
(Formerly Warfield Foundation)
c/o Bank of America
P.O. Box 831041
Dallas, TX 75283-1041
Application address: c/o Concert Committee, 123 Stonebrook Rd., Helena, AR 72342-2205

Financial data (yr. ended 12/31/01): Assets, $830,721 (M); grants paid, $56,762; gifts received, $40,934; expenditures, $65,497; qualifying distributions, $61,129.
Limitations: Giving limited to Helena, AR.
Trustee: Bank of America.
EIN: 716061870

63617
Dallas City Plan, Inc.
1500 Marilla Dr., Ste. 6B N.
Dallas, TX 75201

Classified as a private operating foundation in 1992.
Donor(s): Sewell Automotive Companies, Southwestern Bell.
Financial data (yr. ended 12/31/00): Assets, $817,347 (M); grants paid, $0; gifts received, $33,000; expenditures, $372,918; qualifying distributions, $0; giving activities include $372,840 for programs.
Directors: Catalina E. Garcia, Larry Good, Robert K. Hoffman, Robert Hsueh, Mildred Derrough Pope, Jonathon G. Vinson, and 5 additional directors.
EIN: 752445993

63618
Black Foundation
c/o John Black
6 Hickory Shadows Dr.
Houston, TX 77055

Established in 1997.
Donor(s): John D. Black.
Financial data (yr. ended 02/28/00): Assets, $802,128 (L); grants paid, $49,100; expenditures, $54,631; qualifying distributions, $47,601.
Limitations: Applications not accepted.
Application information: Contributes only to pre-selected organizations.
Directors: Catherine L. Black, John D. Black, Sandra L. Black, Scott D. Black.
EIN: 760531754

63619
Fort Phantom Foundation
c/o James M. Alexander
P.O. Box 58
Abilene, TX 79604-0058

Established in 1997 in TX.
Donor(s): James M. Alexander.
Financial data (yr. ended 12/31/99): Assets, $800,264 (M); grants paid, $0; gifts received, $73,700; expenditures, $63,361; qualifying distributions, $59,434; giving activities include $66,863 for programs.
Officers and Directors:* James M. Alexander,* Pres.; John L. Beckham,* V.P.; H.C. Zachry,* V.P.; Diana S. Layton, Secy.-Treas.; Mike Alexander, Laura A. Eagle, Cathey A. Weatherl.
EIN: 752689278

63620
N.H. Foundation
11602 Haley Hollow
Richmond, TX 77469
Contact: David Sparks

Established in 1995 in TX.
Donor(s): L. David Sparks, Kay E. Sparks, Southern Slope Trust.
Financial data (yr. ended 12/31/01): Assets, $789,757 (M); grants paid, $199,000; expenditures, $207,335; qualifying distributions, $199,000.
Limitations: Giving primarily in Houston, TX.
Trustees: Bryan K. Sparks, Kay E. Sparks.
EIN: 766108510
Codes: FD2

63621
Earnest & Dorothy Barrow Foundation
P.O. Box 688
Eola, TX 76937

Financial data (yr. ended 11/30/99): Assets, $780,223 (M); grants paid, $0; gifts received, $17,953; expenditures, $15,195; qualifying distributions, $16,895; giving activities include $15,195 for programs.
Officers: Elsie Campbell, Chair.; Wayne Rautenberg, Vice-Chair.; Pauline Ruiz, Secy.; Randall Cave, Treas.
EIN: 751550896

63622
Pearle Vision Foundation, Inc.
2465 Joe Field Rd.
Dallas, TX 75229 (972) 277-6191
Application address: P.O. Box 227175, Dallas, TX 75222; FAX: (972) 277-6422; E-mail: trinaparasiliti@pearlevision.com
Contact: Trina Parasiliti, Secy.

Established in 1986 in CA as a company-sponsored operating foundation.
Donor(s): Pearle, Inc.
Financial data (yr. ended 01/31/01): Assets, $747,145 (M); grants paid, $391,944; gifts received, $372,273; expenditures, $441,457; qualifying distributions, $441,115.
Limitations: Giving limited to the U.S.
Publications: Program policy statement, application guidelines, informational brochure.
Application information: Applications not accepted from individuals for routine eye exams or eyeglasses. Application form required.
Officers and Directors:* Jeff Smith,* Chair.; Trina Parasiliti, Secy.; Joseph Gaglioti, Treas.; Stanley C. Pearle, Exec. Dir.; James Benning, O.D., Dan Griffin, Barbara McAninch.
EIN: 752173714
Codes: FD, CD, GTI

63623
Bettie Scott Youree Park Foundation
c/o Bank of America
P.O. Box 83283
Dallas, TX 75283-1041

Classified as a private operating foundation in 1973.
Financial data (yr. ended 05/31/02): Assets, $694,489 (M); grants paid, $0; expenditures, $12,163; qualifying distributions, $0.
Director: Scott Baldwin.
Trustee: Bank of America.
EIN: 756006696

63624
In Recital
c/o Michael Kaufman
901 Main St., Ste. 6000
Dallas, TX 75202

Financial data (yr. ended 07/31/99): Assets, $652,126 (M); grants paid, $0; gifts received, $2,000; expenditures, $696,271; qualifying distributions, $539,345; giving activities include $536,345 for programs.
Officers and Directors:* Larry Lenske, Pres.; Joan Silvia,* Secy.; Donald McCall.
EIN: 752492256

63625
Cactus Park Museum Fund
P.O. Box 343
George West, TX 78022
Contact: S.T. Brown, Jr., Tr.

Financial data (yr. ended 12/31/00): Assets, $630,241 (M); grants paid, $0; gifts received, $3,624; expenditures, $16,023; qualifying distributions, $15,714; giving activities include $15,714 for programs.
Limitations: Giving primarily in George West, TX.
Trustees: S.T. Brown, Jr., J.R. Schneider.
EIN: 742331837

63626
The James 1:27 Foundation
12173 Network Blvd.
San Antonio, TX 78249-3359

Established in 2000 in TX.
Donor(s): Max L. Lucado.
Financial data (yr. ended 12/31/00): Assets, $628,607 (M); grants paid, $36,498; gifts received, $652,000; expenditures, $47,022; qualifying distributions, $47,007.
Limitations: Applications not accepted. Giving primarily in San Antonio, TX.
Application information: Contributes only to pre-selected organizations.
Officers: Max L. Lucado, Pres.; Denalyn Lucado, V.P.; Steven L. Green, Secy.-Treas.
Trustees: Cheryl Green, Megan Green.

EIN: 742959955

63627
Brownsville Historical Association
P.O. Box 846
Brownsville, TX 78522-0846

Classified as a private operating foundation in 1988.
Financial data (yr. ended 12/31/01): Assets, $612,261 (M); grants paid, $0; gifts received, $96,924; expenditures, $84,148; qualifying distributions, $0.
Officers: Bill Young, Pres.; Gene Balch, V.P.; Rita Krausse, Secy.; Chula T. Griffin, Treas.
EIN: 741392580

63628
Scottish Rite Educational and Fellowship Program of Texas
2801 W. Waco Dr.
Waco, TX 76707-0080
Application address: 2632 Lake Oakes Rd., Waco, TX 76710, tel.: (254) 754-3942
Contact: Claude Ervin, Exec. Admin.

Financial data (yr. ended 12/31/00): Assets, $597,174 (L); grants paid, $23,377; gifts received, $85; expenditures, $27,539; qualifying distributions, $1,901.
Limitations: Giving limited to residents of TX.
Application information: Application form required.
Officers: Sam E. Hilburn, Chair.; Pat Beard, Pres.; Walker A. Lea, Jr., V.P.; Joseph Velez, V.P.; Clifton Robinson, Secy.; J. Damon Fehler, Treas.; Claude O. Ervin, Exec. Admin.
EIN: 742177244
Codes: GTI

63629
Grady McWhiney Research Foundation
14th & Sayles
Abilene, TX 79697

Classified as a private operating foundation in 1997.
Donor(s): Grady McWhiney.
Financial data (yr. ended 12/31/99): Assets, $584,560 (M); grants paid, $0; gifts received, $316,560; expenditures, $108,216; qualifying distributions, $89,368; giving activities include $112,788 for programs.
Officers and Directors:* Grady McWhiney, Pres.; Donald Frazier,* Secy.-Treas.; Anne Bailey, David Coffey, Robert Maberry, Robert Pace.
EIN: 752672110

63630
Maceil Family Foundation
1600 Smith, Ste. 4275
Houston, TX 77002-7345 (281) 650-8338
Contact: Clovis Westbrook, Dir.

Established in 1997 in TX.
Financial data (yr. ended 12/31/01): Assets, $505,696 (M); grants paid, $52,500; expenditures, $52,780; qualifying distributions, $52,780.
Limitations: Giving primarily in TX.
Directors: Archer McWhorter, Archer McWhorter, Jr., Kathleen McWhorter, Richard T. McWhorter, Clovis Westbrook.
EIN: 760537905

63631
Mr. and Mrs. Nelson Rusche Foundation
109 N. Post Oak Ln., Ste. 545
Houston, TX 77024

Established in 2000 in TX.
Donor(s): A.N. Rusche.

Financial data (yr. ended 05/31/01): Assets, $501,690 (M); grants paid, $0; gifts received, $500,000; expenditures, $2,346; qualifying distributions, $0.
Officer: A.N. Rusche, Pres.
Directors: Suzanne R. Jefferys, Willis R. Jefferys.
EIN: 311741790

63632
The Maxine Durrett Earl Charitable Foundation, Inc.
P.O. Box 580
Post, TX 79356-3123

Established in 1994 in TX.
Donor(s): Maxine Durrett Earl.
Financial data (yr. ended 12/31/00): Assets, $471,451 (M); grants paid, $4,000; gifts received, $878; expenditures, $5,805; qualifying distributions, $5,805; giving activities include $3,000 for programs.
Limitations: Applications not accepted.
Application information: Contributes only to pre-selected organizations.
Officers and Directors:* Maxine D. Earl,* Pres.; Lewis H. Earl,* V.P.; Steve A. Claus, Tim Pierce.
EIN: 752539386

63633
The Lewis J. and Wanda S. Wilson Hesed Foundation
2130 Kelliwood Greens Dr.
Katy, TX 77450

Established in 1996 in TX.
Donor(s): Lewis J. Wilson, Wanda S. Wilson.
Financial data (yr. ended 12/31/99): Assets, $461,824 (M); grants paid, $10,102; gifts received, $2,537; expenditures, $19,532; qualifying distributions, $11,069.
Trustees: Lewis J. Wilson, Wanda S. Wilson.
EIN: 752695775

63634
J. U. & Florence B. Fields Museum, Inc.
P.O. Box 93
Haskell, TX 79521-0093

Classified as a private operating foundation in 1977.
Financial data (yr. ended 12/31/01): Assets, $458,210 (M); grants paid, $0; expenditures, $15,215; qualifying distributions, $0.
Trustees: Margo Hollingsworth, Joan Strickland.
EIN: 751522404

63635
Ensor Park & Museum Trust
c/o Bank of America
P.O. Box 831041
Dallas, TX 75283-1041

Financial data (yr. ended 06/30/01): Assets, $427,224 (M); grants paid, $0; expenditures, $41,164; qualifying distributions, $36,946; giving activities include $33,107 for programs.
Trustees: Ralph Boehm, David Peavy, William C. Wiswell, Bank of America.
EIN: 486309647

63636
Libra Foundation
3305 Buchanan St.
Wichita Falls, TX 76308-1822

Established in 1982 in TX.
Donor(s): John Hirschi.
Financial data (yr. ended 10/31/01): Assets, $416,578 (M); grants paid, $1,452; gifts received, $500; expenditures, $12,257; qualifying distributions, $8,953; giving activities include $6,552 for programs.

Limitations: Applications not accepted. Giving primarily in Wichita Falls, TX.
Officer and Trustee:* John Hirschi,* Mgr.
EIN: 751862950

63637
Caddell & Chapman Foundation for the Arts
(Formerly Caddell & Conwell Foundation for the Arts)
c/o Claire Squibb
1331 Lamar St., Ste. 1070
Houston, TX 77010-3027

Established in 1992 in TX.
Donor(s): Michael A. Caddell, Cynthia B. Chapman.
Financial data (yr. ended 06/30/00): Assets, $405,391 (M); grants paid, $0; gifts received, $6,000; expenditures, $7,703; qualifying distributions, $5,299; giving activities include $5,299 for programs.
Officers: Michael A. Caddell,* Pres.; Cynthia B. Chapman,* V.P.; Michele Ebow, Secy.-Treas.
EIN: 760381598

63638
Human Endeavor Foundation of the Southwest, Inc.
5106 Memory Ln.
El Paso, TX 79932

Donor(s): G. Kenneth Burlingham.
Financial data (yr. ended 12/31/00): Assets, $402,339 (M); grants paid, $0; gifts received, $23,407; expenditures, $2,644; qualifying distributions, $3,046; giving activities include $2,644 for programs.
Officers and Directors:* G. Kenneth Burlingham,* Pres.; Alex Apostolides,* V.P.; Harold Naylor,* V.P.; George K. Burlingham, Jr.,* Secy.; Bill Kelley,* Treas.
EIN: 742492469

63639
Kechejian Foundation
421 E. Airport Fwy.
Irving, TX 75062
Contact: Sarkis J. Kechejian, Pres.

Donor(s): Sarkis J. Kechejian, M.D.
Financial data (yr. ended 12/31/01): Assets, $380,811 (M); grants paid, $371,000; gifts received, $2,000; expenditures, $371,713; qualifying distributions, $371,000.
Limitations: Giving on a national basis.
Officers: Sarkis J. Kechejian, M.D., Pres.; Nishan Kechejian, Secy.
Director: Gregory Kechejian.
EIN: 752606582
Codes: FD

63640
Historical Preservation & Restoration Foundation
201 Light St.
Waxahachie, TX 75165
Application address: 13220 Laurel Wood, Dallas, TX 75240, tel: (972) 490-7579
Contact: Keith Beers, Pres.

Classified as a private operating foundation in 1984.
Donor(s): Keith Beers, Helen Beers.
Financial data (yr. ended 12/31/00): Assets, $367,048 (M); grants paid, $827; expenditures, $8,918; qualifying distributions, $8,891; giving activities include $8,091 for programs.
Limitations: Giving primarily in TX.
Application information: Application form not required.
Officers: Keith Beers, Pres.; Helen Beers, Secy.

EIN: 751853364

63641
Mary Louise and Maurice W. Grumbles Foundation, Inc.
2911 Turtle Creek Blvd., No. 1010
Dallas, TX 75219-6254

Established in 1989 in TX.
Donor(s): Mary Louise Grumbles, Maurice W. Grumbles.
Financial data (yr. ended 12/31/01): Assets, $365,654 (M); grants paid, $16,000; gifts received, $332,218; expenditures, $16,794; qualifying distributions, $16,700.
Limitations: Applications not accepted. Giving primarily in Dallas, TX.
Application information: Contributes only to pre-selected organizations.
Officers and Trustees:* Robert C. Taylor,* Pres.; Fred Lohmeyer,* Secy.
EIN: 752301629

63642
The Eugenia and Lawrence A. Bertetti Foundation
126 E. Kings Hwy.
San Antonio, TX 78212 (210) 734-4820
Contact: Lawrence A. Bertetti, Tr.

Established in 1989 in TX.
Donor(s): Eugenia Bertetti, Lawrence A. Bertetti.
Financial data (yr. ended 06/30/01): Assets, $353,489 (M); grants paid, $16,900; expenditures, $17,759; qualifying distributions, $16,706.
Limitations: Giving primarily in San Antonio, TX.
Trustees: Laura Bertetti Baucum, Eugenia Bertetti, Lawrence A. Bertetti, Linda L. Bertetti.
EIN: 742553221

63643
The Boatner Family Foundation
7 Water Mark Way
The Woodlands, TX 77381-6618
Application address: 25227 Grogan's Mill Rd., Ste. 125, The Woodlands, TX 77380

Established in 2000 in TX.
Donor(s): David M. Boatner, Mary C. Boatner.
Financial data (yr. ended 12/31/00): Assets, $346,074 (M); grants paid, $26,000; gifts received, $432,425; expenditures, $29,961; qualifying distributions, $26,000.
Limitations: Giving primarily in Phoenix, AZ, Washington, DC, Tulsa, OK, and Vancouver, WA.
Application information: Application form required.
Directors: Darby Boatner, David M. Boatner, Mary C. Boatner.
EIN: 760632625

63644
Faye L. and William L. Cowden Charitable Foundation
c/o Broadway National Bank, Trust Dept.
P.O. Box 17001
San Antonio, TX 78217 (210) 283-6706
Contact: Susan M. Hinger, Trust Off., Broadway National Bank

Established in 1988 in TX.
Financial data (yr. ended 03/31/02): Assets, $344,465 (M); grants paid, $19,071; expenditures, $22,484; qualifying distributions, $17,008.
Limitations: Giving limited to TX.
Trustee: Broadway National Bank.
EIN: 746359520

63645
Houston Photographic and Architectural Foundation Trust
815 Wade Hampton Dr.
Houston, TX 77024

Established in 1996 in TX.
Donor(s): James P. Lee.
Financial data (yr. ended 12/31/99): Assets, $339,414 (M); grants paid, $0; gifts received, $717,700; expenditures, $109,614; qualifying distributions, $109,051; giving activities include $109,051 for programs.
Trustees: James P. Lee, Wes Seeliger.
EIN: 766111042

63646
Jean & Price Daniel Foundation
P.O. Box 789
Liberty, TX 77575-0789

Established in 1985 in TX.
Donor(s): Jean Daniel.
Financial data (yr. ended 12/31/99): Assets, $337,013 (M); grants paid, $101,400; expenditures, $101,640; qualifying distributions, $101,404.
Limitations: Giving primarily in Liberty, TX.
Application information: Application form not required.
Officers and Directors:* Jean Daniel,* Pres.; Jean Daniel Murph,* V.P.; Houston Daniel,* Secy.-Treas.; John Daniel.
EIN: 760139701
Codes: FD2

63647
Community Development Loan Corp., Inc.
100 W. Olmos, Ste. 104
San Antonio, TX 78212
Contact: Gilbert Gonzalez, Exec. Dir.

Classified as a private operating foundation in 2000.
Financial data (yr. ended 12/31/00): Assets, $326,517 (M); grants paid, $299; gifts received, $30,000; expenditures, $17,615; qualifying distributions, $299.
Limitations: Giving primarily in TX.
Officer: Gilbert Gonzalez, Exec. Dir.
EIN: 742761899

63648
Leach Family Foundation
430 W. Country Road 714
Burleson, TX 76028

Established in 1999 in TX.
Financial data (yr. ended 12/31/99): Assets, $317,631 (M); grants paid, $0; gifts received, $317,631; expenditures, $0; qualifying distributions, $0.
Directors: Davonia Leach, Douglas Leach.
EIN: 752787365

63649
Greater Texas Education Foundation
4006 Alice Dr.
Sugar Land, TX 77478

Classified as a private operating foundation in 1997.
Donor(s): Columbia, Harris County Podiatric Surgical Residency Foundation, Sharpstown.
Financial data (yr. ended 06/30/00): Assets, $290,697 (M); grants paid, $0; gifts received, $686,687; expenditures, $787,988; qualifying distributions, $776,891; giving activities include $776,891 for programs.
Officers: Samuel S. Mendicino, Pres. and Treas.; Jeff Hetman, Secy.

Directors: Mitchell Brooks, M.D., Mark Hofbauer.
EIN: 760507965

63650
Bernardo Pineda-Pinto Foundation
c/o Adriana I. Pineda
11620 Brittmore Park Dr.
Houston, TX 77041

Established in 1994 in TX.
Donor(s): Bernabe Pineda-Ropero.
Financial data (yr. ended 12/31/99): Assets, $289,221 (M); grants paid, $10,000; gifts received, $10,000; expenditures, $11,455; qualifying distributions, $11,455.
Limitations: Applications not accepted.
Application information: Contributes only to pre-selected organizations.
Officers and Directors:* Bernabe Pineda-Ropero,* Pres.; Soledad Pinto de Pineda,* V.P.; Adriana I. Pineda-Pons,* Secy.; Mauricio A. Pineda,* Treas.; Sergio M. Pineda.
EIN: 760422012

63651
Texas Orthopaedic and Sports Medicine Institute, Inc.
9150 Huebner Rd., No. 110
San Antonio, TX 78240

Classified as a private operating foundation in 1998.
Donor(s): HEALTHSOUTH Corp., Smith-Nephew Endoscopy.
Financial data (yr. ended 12/31/00): Assets, $284,200 (M); grants paid, $0; gifts received, $213,560; expenditures, $338,028; qualifying distributions, $137,476.
Officers: Jesse C. De Lee, Pres.; John Evans, M.D., V.P.; Don Ryan, Secy.; Joe Vegso, Treas.; L. Kay Harrell, Ph.D., Exec. Dir.
EIN: 742777975

63652
Western Human Sciences Institute
5307 McCommas Blvd.
Dallas, TX 75206-5623

Donor(s): R.P. Howell.
Financial data (yr. ended 09/30/01): Assets, $281,242 (M); grants paid, $55; expenditures, $48,854; qualifying distributions, $55.
Directors: Joan D. Howell, R.P. Howell, Marcelline Watson.
EIN: 751932695

63653
The Smith Charitable Trust
705 W. Crawford St.
Denison, TX 75020

Established in 1998.
Financial data (yr. ended 12/31/99): Assets, $276,596 (M); grants paid, $6,200; gifts received, $84,191; expenditures, $7,827; qualifying distributions, $6,200.
Director: Larry Smith.
EIN: 760523941

63654
Lanier Operating Foundation
2 Houston Ctr., 909 Fannin St., Ste. 3210
Houston, TX 77010 (713) 951-9600
Contact: Robert C. Lanier, Tr.

Established in 1972 in TX.
Financial data (yr. ended 05/31/01): Assets, $259,049 (M); grants paid, $121,061; expenditures, $123,525; qualifying distributions, $120,810.
Limitations: Giving primarily in TX.

63654—TEXAS

Trustees: Robert D. Darnell, Cecil L. Holley, Robert C. Lanier.
EIN: 237269729
Codes: FD2

63655
Stastny Folk Art and Crafts Foundation
c/o Peter Stastny
200 Myers Rd.
Heath, TX 75032-8603

Established in 1999 in TX.
Donor(s): Peter Stastny.
Financial data (yr. ended 12/31/01): Assets, $251,639 (M); grants paid, $0; gifts received, $88,873; expenditures, $1,668; qualifying distributions, $0.
Limitations: Applications not accepted.
Application information: Contributes only to pre-selected organizations.
Trustee: Peter Stastny.
Board Members: Larry Sanders, Victor Stastny, Bruce Webb.
EIN: 752792950

63656
The Mills Foundation
6342 La Vista Dr.
Dallas, TX 75214

Financial data (yr. ended 12/31/00): Assets, $249,526 (M); grants paid, $6,000; gifts received, $267,003; expenditures, $6,000; qualifying distributions, $6,000.
Limitations: Applications not accepted.
Application information: Contributes only to pre-selected organizations.
Officers: John C. Mills, Pres.; Jonathan C. Mills, Secy.-Treas.
EIN: 756563182

63657
Marc D. Murr Foundation
5666 Wickersham Ln.
Houston, TX 77056-4031

Established in 1995 in TX.
Donor(s): Marc D. Murr.
Financial data (yr. ended 12/31/99): Assets, $248,108 (M); grants paid, $12,000; gifts received, $7,650; expenditures, $16,115; qualifying distributions, $14,889.
Limitations: Applications not accepted.
Application information: Contributes only to pre-selected organizations.
Officers: Marc D. Murr, Pres.; Marilyn G. Doyle, Secy.; Miriam E. Kubicek, Treas.
Director: George B. Murr.
EIN: 760514602

63658
Yellow Rose Eye Foundation
18850 Memorial Blvd. S.
Humble, TX 77338

Established in 1987 in TX.
Donor(s): Paul Michael Mann.
Financial data (yr. ended 04/30/01): Assets, $247,165 (M); grants paid, $49,850; gifts received, $199,316; expenditures, $51,804; qualifying distributions, $49,850.
Officer and Directors:* Paul Michael Mann, M.D.,* Pres.; John M. Corboy, M.D., R. Bruce Wallace III, M.D.
EIN: 760248204

63659
Homcare Foundation
c/o W.O. Menefee
P.O. Box 860
Tomball, TX 77377-0860

Classified as a private operating foundation in 1966.
Donor(s): John R. Frey, Richard H. Frey.
Financial data (yr. ended 06/30/01): Assets, $246,697 (M); grants paid, $825; gifts received, $100,000; expenditures, $977; qualifying distributions, $825.
Trustees: Richard H. Frey, Chair.; John R. Frey, D.L. Shriver.
EIN: 746053674

63660
Frankie Willbern Trust
304 E. Calvert St.
Karnes City, TX 78118-0160
Application address: P.O. Box 576, Runge, TX 78151, tel.: (210) 239-4749
Contact: Marshall Davis, Admin.

Established in 1986 in TX; classified as an operating foundation in 1987.
Financial data (yr. ended 12/31/00): Assets, $235,209 (M); grants paid, $1,350; expenditures, $2,242; qualifying distributions, $2,071.
Limitations: Giving on a national basis.
Officer: Marshall Davis, Admin.
EIN: 742453922

63661
Jerry R. & Constance A. Klemow Foundation
6333 Forest Park Rd., Ste. 290-A
Dallas, TX 75235-5411

Donor(s): Jerry R. Klemow.
Financial data (yr. ended 12/31/01): Assets, $229,755 (M); grants paid, $37,850; expenditures, $39,249; qualifying distributions, $37,850.
Limitations: Applications not accepted. Giving primarily in Dallas, TX.
Application information: Contributes only to pre-selected organizations.
Officers: Jerry R. Klemow, Pres.; Steven R. Klenow, V.P.; Dawn L. Reed, V.P.; Constance Ann Klenow, Secy.-Treas.
EIN: 752710995

63662
Lawrence and Elizabeth Allen Foundation
1903 Dartmouth St.
College Station, TX 77840

Donor(s): Elizabeth Allen, Lawrence Allen.
Financial data (yr. ended 12/31/01): Assets, $229,624 (M); grants paid, $12,000; expenditures, $16,705; qualifying distributions, $11,943.
Limitations: Applications not accepted.
Application information: Contributes only to pre-selected organizations.
Officers: Lawrence Allen, Pres.; Elizabeth Allen, V.P.
EIN: 742922972

63663
The Treasure Hill Foundation
c/o Darrell Creel, J.J. Pickle Res. Ctr.
University of Texas at Austin
Austin, TX 78712

Established in 1993. Classified as a private operating foundation in 1997 in NM.
Donor(s): Laverne Herrington.
Financial data (yr. ended 12/31/00): Assets, $225,200 (M); grants paid, $0; gifts received, $33; expenditures, $33; qualifying distributions, $33.
Limitations: Applications not accepted.

Application information: Contributes only to pre-selected organizations.
Officers: Margaret Nelson, Pres.; Carolyn Davis, Secy.-Treas.
Directors: Darrell Creel, Michelle Hegman.
EIN: 742846799

63664
John L. & Ethel McCarty Foundation Trust
c/o Jack N. Clark
P.O. Box 888
Lampasas, TX 76550

Classified as a private operating foundation in 1997.
Financial data (yr. ended 12/31/99): Assets, $224,798 (M); grants paid, $5,700; expenditures, $5,713; qualifying distributions, $5,581.
Limitations: Applications not accepted. Giving primarily in TX.
Application information: Contributes only to pre-selected organizations.
Trustees: Jack N. Clark, Carol McCoy, Rick Snow.
EIN: 752665416

63665
The Aaron Foundation
5201 W. Park Blvd., No. 100
Plano, TX 75093

Established in 1994 in TX.
Financial data (yr. ended 12/31/00): Assets, $221,159 (M); grants paid, $0; gifts received, $2,000; expenditures, $0; qualifying distributions, $0.
Officers: William E. Ball, Pres. and Treas.; Gary D. Ball, V.P.
EIN: 752567422

63666
The Simons Family Foundation
2211 Dryden Rd.
Houston, TX 77030-1101 (713) 650-2766
Contact: Herbert D. Simons, Dir.

Established in 1997 in TX.
Financial data (yr. ended 12/31/00): Assets, $218,612 (M); grants paid, $11,000; expenditures, $11,607; qualifying distributions, $10,868.
Limitations: Giving on a national basis.
Directors: Everett A. Marley, Jr., David B. Simons, Herbert D. Simons.
EIN: 760537712

63667
Jack & Joyce Sampson Family Foundation
7305 Mesa Dr.
Austin, TX 78731

Donor(s): John J. Sampson, Joyce C. Sampson.
Financial data (yr. ended 12/31/00): Assets, $218,100 (M); grants paid, $7,330; gifts received, $43,332; expenditures, $7,795; qualifying distributions, $7,330.
Limitations: Applications not accepted. Giving primarily in TX.
Application information: Contributes only to pre-selected organizations.
Officers: John J. Sampson, Pres.; Joyce C. Sampson, V.P. and Secy.-Treas.
Directors: Eleanor Sampson, Margaret Sampson.
EIN: 742852703

63668
John & Sara Peterman Foundation
3027 Taylor St.
Dallas, TX 75226-1911

Donor(s): John Peterman, Sara Peterman.
Financial data (yr. ended 12/31/99): Assets, $209,095 (M); grants paid, $11,428; gifts

received, $200,000; expenditures, $11,448; qualifying distributions, $11,448.
Limitations: Applications not accepted.
Application information: Contributes only to pre-selected organizations.
Directors: John Peterman, Sara Peterman.
EIN: 411925526

63669
Grayson County State Bank Museum
P.O. Box 1234
Sherman, TX 75091-1234

Classified as a private operating foundation in 1989.
Financial data (yr. ended 03/31/01): Assets, $200,505 (M); grants paid, $0; expenditures, $395; qualifying distributions, $395; giving activities include $395 for programs.
Officers: Scott B. Smith, Chair.; Betsy Spears, Pres.; Shirley Dendy, Secy.-Treas.
Directors: William D. Elliott, Dorothy Harber, John M. Hubbard, James A. Lindsey, Edgar Geer McKee.
EIN: 751658218

63670
Christian Advancement Foundation
4600 S. Western St.
Amarillo, TX 79109-6025

Financial data (yr. ended 12/31/00): Assets, $195,592 (M); grants paid, $17,387; gifts received, $15,340; expenditures, $17,387; qualifying distributions, $17,387.
Limitations: Applications not accepted.
Application information: Contributes only to pre-selected organizations.
Officers: R.L. Kirk, Pres.; Jim Smith, V.P.; Bill Couch, Treas.
EIN: 751610895

63671
Seth & Mabelle Moore Scholarship Trust
P.O. Box 111
Hamilton, TX 76531-0313 (254) 386-8151
Contact: Ramon L. Haile, Tr.

Established in 1985 in TX.
Donor(s): Seth Moore, Sr.
Financial data (yr. ended 12/31/01): Assets, $195,203 (M); grants paid, $5,550; gifts received, $250; expenditures, $6,028; qualifying distributions, $5,550.
Limitations: Giving primarily in Hamilton, TX.
Application information: Application form required.
Trustees: Sam Bell, Ramon L. Haile, David Lengefeld.
EIN: 742342842

63672
Lena Fay Ballenger Trust
P.O. Box 1207
Kingsland, TX 78639

Financial data (yr. ended 12/31/99): Assets, $194,458 (M); grants paid, $100,000; expenditures, $101,929; qualifying distributions, $101,884.
Limitations: Applications not accepted. Giving primarily in Kingsland, TX.
Application information: Contributes only to pre-selected organizations.
Trustee: W.F. McCasland.
EIN: 746470928

63673
Mineola League of the Arts, Inc.
200 W. Blair
Mineola, TX 75773-1603

Established in 1991 in TX.
Financial data (yr. ended 12/31/01): Assets, $194,311 (M); grants paid, $0; gifts received, $500; expenditures, $36,985; qualifying distributions, $0.
Officers: Sheila Wyze, Pres.; Suzanne Shumaker, V.P.; Pat Mapes, Treas.
EIN: 752298930

63674
The Fleener Foundation, Inc.
16814 Club Hill
Dallas, TX 75248-2016 (214) 733-0389
Contact: Margaret Fleener, Dir.

Established in 1994 in TX.
Donor(s): Allen Fleener, Margaret Fleener.
Financial data (yr. ended 11/30/01): Assets, $190,447 (M); grants paid, $65,767; expenditures, $67,954; qualifying distributions, $65,757.
Limitations: Giving primarily in IN, MO and TX.
Application information: Application form not required.
Directors: Allen Fleener, Margaret Fleener, Julia Margaret Hawrick.
EIN: 752573555

63675
A. G. & Phelo Thompson Scholarship Trust
P.O. Box 831
Hamilton, TX 76531
Application address: 102 E. Main St., Hamilton, TX 76531
Contact: Connie White, Dir.

Established in 1997 in TX.
Donor(s): A.G. Thompson, Phelo Thompson.
Financial data (yr. ended 12/31/01): Assets, $188,642 (M); grants paid, $8,990; expenditures, $9,273; qualifying distributions, $8,937.
Limitations: Giving limited to residents of Hamilton, TX.
Application information: Application form required.
Directors: Doug Forrest, Ramon L. Haile, Phelo Thompson, Connie White, Jerry Zschiesche.
EIN: 742813801

63676
Taxpayers Research Council of Galveston County, Inc.
P.O. Box 1715
Texas City, TX 77592

Classified as a private operating foundation in 1978.
Financial data (yr. ended 12/31/01): Assets, $186,876 (L); grants paid, $0; expenditures, $80,960; qualifying distributions, $0.
Directors: Alice Adams, Richard Bedell, Mike Griffin, Joseph A. Hoover, Ronald Lemon, and 16 additional directors.
EIN: 741335680

63677
Urantia Book Study Group of Austin
1006 S. Lamar Blvd.
Austin, TX 78704

Financial data (yr. ended 03/31/01): Assets, $182,365 (M); grants paid, $0; gifts received, $2,010; expenditures, $202,901; qualifying distributions, $0; giving activities include $199,724 for programs.
Limitations: Applications not accepted.

Officers: Aubrey T. Lanier, Pres.; Tim Traylor, V.P.; Sharon Porter, Secy.; James Cochran, Treas.
EIN: 742232522

63678
The Shining Star Foundation
c/o Burton E. Grossman
4901 Broadway, Ste. 132
San Antonio, TX 78209-5734

Established in 1993 in TX.
Donor(s): Burton E. Grossman.
Financial data (yr. ended 12/31/99): Assets, $164,337 (M); grants paid, $3,160; gifts received, $102,426; expenditures, $99,447; qualifying distributions, $97,078; giving activities include $97,070 for programs.
Limitations: Applications not accepted. Giving primarily in San Antonio, TX.
Application information: Contributes only to pre-selected organizations.
Officers: Burton E. Grossman, Pres.; Norma C. Bodevin, V.P.; Jacqueline Hodgson, Secy.-Treas.
EIN: 742678576

63679
Center for Intercultural Communications
1251 Limericks Ln.
Canyon Lake, TX 78133

Financial data (yr. ended 12/31/00): Assets, $159,305 (M); grants paid, $0; gifts received, $11,680; expenditures, $9,555; qualifying distributions, $0.
Officers and Directors:* Pamela Caadwal-Ilutt,* Pres.; Rev. Virgil Elizondo,* V.P.; Ruben Alearo,* Secy.-Treas.; Yolanda Rangel.
EIN: 742545341

63680
Texas Hill Country Wine & Food Foundation
1006 Mopac Cir., No. 101
Austin, TX 78746

Established in 1997.
Financial data (yr. ended 12/31/99): Assets, $158,150 (L); grants paid, $5,000; gifts received, $63,072; expenditures, $5,080; qualifying distributions, $5,000.
Limitations: Applications not accepted.
Application information: Contributes only to pre-selected organizations.
Officer and Director:* Larry Peel,* Chair.
EIN: 742846361

63681
Jack and Ali Charitable Foundation
c/o Jack Schlusselberg
6090 Surety Dr., Ste. 102
El Paso, TX 79905-2060

Established in 1999 in TX.
Financial data (yr. ended 12/31/00): Assets, $157,131 (M); grants paid, $0; gifts received, $150,000; expenditures, $0; qualifying distributions, $0.
Trustees: Abraham Schlusselberg, Jack Schlusselberg.
EIN: 742890781

63682
Emanuel Foundation, Inc.
514 W. Main St.
Azle, TX 76020-2926 (817) 444-1124
Contact: James R. Emanuel, Dir.

Classified as a private operating foundation in 1980.
Financial data (yr. ended 12/31/00): Assets, $155,454 (M); grants paid, $1,300; expenditures, $34,432; qualifying distributions, $2,380.
Limitations: Giving primarily in Azle, TX.

63682—TEXAS

Directors: James R. Emanuel, Odessa Emanuel, Betty Haas, Kenneth Price, Gerald Shinn, Jacqueline Weaver.
EIN: 751716132

63683
Sylvester H. Reed Memorial Trust
HCR 4, Box 1060
Burnet, TX 78611

Established in 1998 in TX.
Financial data (yr. ended 12/31/99): Assets, $155,396 (M); grants paid, $6,496; expenditures, $6,657; qualifying distributions, $6,475.
Limitations: Giving limited to residents of TX.
Officers: Anna M. Reed, Hon. Chair.; Alvin Nored, Chair.; Lucile Redmore, Vice Chair.; Linda Holland, Secy.-Treas.
Trustees: John Ferguson, Thomas J. Reed.
EIN: 746395876

63684
American Heritage Education Foundation, Inc.
3701 W. Alabama St., Ste. 200
Houston, TX 77027-5224

Established in 1994 in TX.
Financial data (yr. ended 06/30/00): Assets, $155,386 (M); grants paid, $0; gifts received, $21,175; expenditures, $101,129; qualifying distributions, $96,391; giving activities include $96,391 for programs.
Officers and Directors:* Jack Kamrath,* Pres.; Jeannie Gonzalez,* V.P.; Jack Kamrath, Exec. Dir.; Lynn Barnes, John R. Butler, Holcombe Crosswell, Walter Cunningham, Margaret Fitch, M.D., and 9 additional directors.
EIN: 760452407

63685
Dallas Chinese Community Center
400 N. Greenville Ave., Ste. 12
Richardson, TX 75081

Donor(s): Taipei Economic and Cultural Office in Houston.
Financial data (yr. ended 12/31/00): Assets, $154,815 (M); grants paid, $0; gifts received, $100,586; expenditures, $33,937; qualifying distributions, $75,183; giving activities include $75,183 for programs.
Director: Jeannie Hu.
EIN: 752456463

63686
Knigge Family Foundation, Inc.
6235 Grovewood Ln.
Houston, TX 77008

Established in 2000.
Donor(s): Ruby Knigge.
Financial data (yr. ended 12/31/00): Assets, $150,000 (M); grants paid, $0; gifts received, $150,000; expenditures, $0; qualifying distributions, $0.
Limitations: Applications not accepted.
Application information: Contributes only to pre-selected organizations.
Director: Ruby Knigge.
EIN: 760664899

63687
The Cluthe & William B. Oliver Foundation for the Health and Aging
101 Westcott, Ste. 1106
Houston, TX 77007-7031

Established in 1995 in TX.
Donor(s): Thomas R. Woehler, Debbie R. Woehler.
Financial data (yr. ended 12/31/00): Assets, $148,914 (M); grants paid, $2,795; gifts received, $10,443; expenditures, $2,936; qualifying distributions, $2,795.
Officers and Trustees:* Thomas R. Woehler,* Pres.; Debra R. Woehler,* V.P. and Secy.-Treas.; Thomas Clynes, Jr., Cluthe Oliver, Marvin Wurzer.
EIN: 760461993

63688
Hardy & Bess Morgan Citzenship Award Fund
P.O. Box 790
Lamesa, TX 79331-1267

Established around 1977.
Financial data (yr. ended 12/31/01): Assets, $146,295 (M); grants paid, $7,500; expenditures, $7,689; qualifying distributions, $7,420.
Limitations: Giving limited to Dawson County, TX.
Application information: Application form required.
Officer: Ken McCraw, Exec. Dir.
Trustees: Wayne Blount, Marshall Harrison, Jennifer Smith, Ed Wilson.
EIN: 759630846
Codes: GTI

63689
Community R & D
(Formerly Quest for Community)
c/o William M. Linden
P.O. Box 55810
Houston, TX 77255-5810

Established in 1989 in TX.
Financial data (yr. ended 12/31/00): Assets, $145,914 (M); grants paid, $0; gifts received, $105,048; expenditures, $63,699; qualifying distributions, $0.
Officers and Directors:* William M. Linden,* Pres.; Martha Ann Linden,* V.P. and Secy.; Judy A. Berno,* V.P. and Treas.
EIN: 760290260

63690
Kent County Educational Foundation
P.O. Box 168
Jayton, TX 79528 (806) 237-2991
Contact: Judy White, Dir.

Established in 1996 in TX.
Financial data (yr. ended 08/31/99): Assets, $144,664 (M); grants paid, $9,400; gifts received, $8,500; expenditures, $9,817; qualifying distributions, $9,363.
Limitations: Giving limited to TX.
Application information: Application form required.
Directors: Nelson Coulter, Mark Geeslin, Gary Harrell, Hope Morales, Beryle Murdoch, Kathy Owen, Joe Thompson, Judy White.
EIN: 752673950

63691
Dreams Scholarship Foundation
3103 N. Cardinal Rd.
Azle, TX 76020

Established in 1997.
Donor(s): James R. Seeds, Susan L. Seeds.
Financial data (yr. ended 02/28/01): Assets, $144,248 (M); grants paid, $15,000; gifts received, $15,325; expenditures, $15,255; qualifying distributions, $14,914.
Limitations: Applications not accepted. Giving limited to residents of TX.
Officers: Trisha McAda, Chair.; Paul Seeds, Pres.; Ben McAda, V.P.; Trelle Seeds, Secy.; Rick Seeds, Treas.
EIN: 752738823

63692
Sei Burning Bush Fund One
2501 Cedar Springs, LB-5, Ste. 200
Dallas, TX 75201-1400

Established in 1999 in TX.
Donor(s): Anschutz Foundation, Buford Foundation.
Financial data (yr. ended 12/31/00): Assets, $142,447 (L); grants paid, $503,500; gifts received, $893,500; expenditures, $762,185; qualifying distributions, $759,296.
Limitations: Applications not accepted. Giving primarily in CA, FL OH, NC, and TX.
Application information: Contributes only to pre-selected organizations.
Officers: Robert P. Buford, Pres.; Dave Travis, Secy.-Treas.
Board Member: Bob Belz.
EIN: 311680251
Codes: FD

63693
The Harmon Family Foundation
P.O. Box 1318
Anahuac, TX 77514

Established as a Company-sponsored operating foundation in 2000.
Donor(s): Seabuck Company, Donald Harmon.
Financial data (yr. ended 12/31/00): Assets, $140,288 (M); grants paid, $0; gifts received, $140,288; expenditures, $0; qualifying distributions, $0.
Director: Donald Harmon.
EIN: 760663399

63694
Rice Richardson Foundation
221 County Rd. 304
Dayton, TX 77535

Established in 2000 in TX.
Donor(s): J. Andrew Rice.
Financial data (yr. ended 12/31/00): Assets, $139,465 (M); grants paid, $15,100; gifts received, $54,318; expenditures, $15,166; qualifying distributions, $15,166.
Limitations: Applications not accepted. Giving primarily in TX.
Application information: Unsolicited requests for funds not accepted.
Officers: J. Andrew Rice, Pres.; Charlie Rice, V.P.; Leah Gillum, Secy.
Directors: Leah Barnett, Mary Martha Barnett, Neva Richardson Rice.
EIN: 760609593

63695
Mike Modano Foundation, Inc.
200 Crescent Ct., Ste. 600
Dallas, TX 75201

Established in 1999 in TX.
Donor(s): Mark Cuban.
Financial data (yr. ended 12/31/01): Assets, $135,151 (M); grants paid, $10,300; gifts received, $85,537; expenditures, $25,825; qualifying distributions, $10,300.
Limitations: Applications not accepted.
Application information: Contributes only to pre-selected organizations.
Officers: Robert G. Murray, Pres.; Michael T. Modano, V.P.; Donald T. Hess, Secy.-Treas.
EIN: 311662114

63696
Houston International Health Foundation
8880 Bellaire Blvd.
Houston, TX 77036

Established in 1992 in TX.
Donor(s): City of Houston.
Financial data (yr. ended 08/31/99): Assets, $134,620 (M); grants paid, $0; gifts received, $296,941; expenditures, $323,563; qualifying distributions, $322,216; giving activities include $322,216 for programs.
Trustees: Jane Van Hsieh, Chi C. Mao, Shirley Van.
EIN: 760381630

63697
Alice Gist Dunaway Foundation
P.O. Box 9938
Amarillo, TX 79105-5938
Application address: 807 S. Post Oak Lande, No. 144, Houston, TX 77056
Contact: Geraldine Anderson

Established in 1981 in TX.
Financial data (yr. ended 12/31/99): Assets, $133,917 (M); grants paid, $24,500; expenditures, $38,029; qualifying distributions, $24,500.
Limitations: Giving primarily in TX.
Application information: Application form required.
Officer: Judy Dotson, Pres.
Directors: Robert W. Anderson, Evelyn Marshall, Susan Martinez.
EIN: 751676023

63698
The Joan Warren Stuart Foundation, Inc.
121 N. Post Oak Ln., Ste. 1706
Houston, TX 77024-7713
Contact: Joan Warren Stuart, Pres.

Established in 1998 in DE.
Donor(s): Joan Warren Stuart.
Financial data (yr. ended 12/31/00): Assets, $132,539 (M); grants paid, $6,610; expenditures, $8,668; qualifying distributions, $7,196.
Officer and Director:* Joan Warren Stuart,* Pres.
EIN: 133947623

63699
Galena Park ISD Education Foundation
1601 11th St.
Galena Park, TX 77547

Financial data (yr. ended 12/31/99): Assets, $124,198 (M); grants paid, $3,000; gifts received, $149,230; expenditures, $46,229; qualifying distributions, $3,000.
Officers: Gerald D. Cobb, Pres.; Philip Steadman, V.P.; Shirley J. Neeley, Secy.; Hector G. Barkley, Treas.
Directors: David Baker, Mickey Bell, James A. Black, Shelia Carr, John Cooper, Jim Dickey, Charles Grant, Joe Harwell, and 13 additional directors.
EIN: 760563596

63700
The Sam J. Lucas, Jr. Foundation
1929 Allen Pkwy., 9th Fl.
Houston, TX 77019

Established in 1998 in TX.
Financial data (yr. ended 12/31/99): Assets, $119,956 (M); grants paid, $27,750; gifts received, $20,375; expenditures, $27,945; qualifying distributions, $27,689.
Application information: Application form required.

Officers: Robert L. Waltrip, Chair.; William A. Mercer, Pres.; James M. Shelger, V.P. and Secy.-Treas.
EIN: 760066431

63701
Lapsley-Brooks Foundation
375 Willow Wood Dr.
Plano, TX 75094
Application address: 1701 N. Greenville Ave., Ste. 810, Richardson, TX 75081, tel.: (972) 783-8702
Contact: B.N. Lapsley, Pres.

Established in 1990 in TX.
Financial data (yr. ended 12/31/00): Assets, $119,477 (M); grants paid, $0; gifts received, $162; expenditures, $11,738; qualifying distributions, $0.
Limitations: Giving primarily in Ethiopia, Africa.
Officers: B.N. Lapsley, Pres.; Ben R. Lapsley, V.P. and Treas.; Martha Johnston, Secy.
EIN: 752354424

63702
Wilson County Education Foundation, Inc.
c/o A.B. Gonzalez
1905 10th St.
Floresville, TX 78114

Donor(s): Alfonso Gonzalez, Emma Gonzalez.
Financial data (yr. ended 12/31/00): Assets, $116,668 (M); grants paid, $0; gifts received, $23,399; expenditures, $52,350; qualifying distributions, $45,719; giving activities include $52,351 for programs.
Officers: A.B. Gonzalez, Pres.; Cecelia Gonzalez, Secy.
Director: J. Gonzalez.
EIN: 742594516

63703
Shooting Star Museum
5445 County Rd. 5710
Devine, TX 78016

Financial data (yr. ended 12/31/01): Assets, $114,747 (M); grants paid, $0; gifts received, $18,910; expenditures, $16,470; qualifying distributions, $14,465; giving activities include $659 for programs.
Officers: Marge Balazs, Pres.; Judy Johnson, V.P.; Patricia Wegner, Secy.-Treas.
Director: Paula Jo Kanclerowicz.
EIN: 742983722

63704
Foundation for a Compassionate Society
P.O. Box 3138
Austin, TX 78764

Established in 1988 in TX. Classified as a private operating foundation in 1995.
Donor(s): Genevieve Vaughan.
Financial data (yr. ended 12/31/00): Assets, $113,924 (M); grants paid, $25,400; gifts received, $230,693; expenditures, $234,415; qualifying distributions, $222,641; giving activities include $182,151 for programs.
Limitations: Applications not accepted. Giving limited to TX; and some giving in Glastonbury, Wales.
Officers: Genevieve Vaughan, Pres.; Pat Cuney, V.P.; Sally Jacques Holland, Secy.-Treas.
EIN: 742516136

63705
The Kedesh Foundation, Inc.
P.O. Box 303515
Austin, TX 78703-0059

Donor(s): Garland L. Robertson.

Financial data (yr. ended 06/30/02): Assets, $113,810 (M); grants paid, $1,272; gifts received, $2,505; expenditures, $3,921; qualifying distributions, $2,505.
Limitations: Applications not accepted. Giving on a national basis.
Application information: Contributes only to pre-selected organizations.
Officer and Directors:* Garland L. Robertson,* Pres. and Admin.; Laura Barnes, Shane Robertson.
EIN: 640668812

63706
SPG Foundation
2388 Bainbridge Dr.
Odessa, TX 79762-5106 (915) 550-4210
Contact: Anil P. Goswami, Pres.

Donor(s): Anil P. Goswami.
Financial data (yr. ended 10/31/01): Assets, $112,862 (M); grants paid, $0; gifts received, $150; expenditures, $203; qualifying distributions, $0.
Officers: Anil P. Goswami, Pres.; Kumud Goswami, Secy.
EIN: 752302313

63707
Ben Clark Foundation, Inc.
8815 Ferris Dr.
Houston, TX 77096

Donor(s): Pat E. Clark.
Financial data (yr. ended 12/31/00): Assets, $111,428 (M); grants paid, $0; expenditures, $6,207; qualifying distributions, $6,171; giving activities include $6,207 for programs.
Officers and Directors:* Pat E. Clark,* Pres.; Maren L. Clark,* V.P. and Secy.; Susan L. Beisert,* V.P. and Treas.; Gary K. Bradbury.
EIN: 760411982

63708
Dulworth Family Foundation
4888 Loop Central Dr., Ste. 450
Houston, TX 77081

Established in 1998 in TX.
Donor(s): Jack T. Dulworth, Gloria M. Dulworth.
Financial data (yr. ended 03/31/01): Assets, $110,451 (M); grants paid, $51,408; expenditures, $52,360; qualifying distributions, $51,213.
Limitations: Applications not accepted. Giving primarily in Houston, TX.
Application information: Contributes only to pre-selected organizations.
Officers and Directors:* Mark T. Dulworth,* Pres.; Tracy A. Dulworth Kutch,* V.P. and Secy.; Mary K. Dulworth Doebbler, Gloria M. Dulworth, Jack T. Dulworth, John D. Dulworth, Paul A. Dulworth.
EIN: 760548721

63709
A & H Amatius Foundation
c/o Paul Olefsky
7603 Yaupon Dr.
Austin, TX 78759-6410

Established in 1989 in TX.
Donor(s): Paul Olefsky, Hai Olefsky.
Financial data (yr. ended 12/31/01): Assets, $109,839 (M); grants paid, $2,700; gifts received, $1,147; expenditures, $3,232; qualifying distributions, $2,688.
Limitations: Giving primarily to residents of Austin, TX.
Trustees: Hai Zeng Olefsky, Paul Olefsky.
EIN: 746374279

63710
T. E. Anding and E. W. Anding Foundation
c/o Thomas E. Anding
4350 Shady Hill Dr.
Dallas, TX 75229-2863

Donor(s): Thomas A. Anding, Emilyne W. Anding.
Financial data (yr. ended 12/31/99): Assets, $109,554 (M); grants paid, $5,000; gifts received, $177; expenditures, $5,777; qualifying distributions, $5,000.
Limitations: Applications not accepted. Giving primarily in Dallas, TX.
Application information: Contributes only to pre-selected organizations.
Officer and Directors:* Thomas E. Anding,* V.P.; Brien Anding, Emilyne Weed Anding, Gloria K. Anding.
EIN: 752768889

63711
River of Life Mission
1325 W. Belt Line Rd.
Carrollton, TX 75006

Established in 1993 in TX.
Donor(s): Home Interiors & Gifts, Crowley Carter Foundation, Donald J. Carter.
Financial data (yr. ended 12/31/00): Assets, $108,198 (M); grants paid, $0; gifts received, $40,000; expenditures, $15,086; qualifying distributions, $10,086; giving activities include $15,085 for programs.
Limitations: Applications not accepted.
Application information: Contributes only to pre-selected organizations.
Officers and Directors:* Ronald Lee Carter,* Pres.; Carol M. Marchant, Secy.; Robert Earl Adams, Mary Byrene Culver, Orlie K. Wolfenbarger III, Vickie Lynn Wolfenbarger.
EIN: 752515701

63712
The Treen Family Foundation
609 Sheridan Dr.
Corpus Christi, TX 78412-2953

Established in 1998.
Donor(s): Susan Treen.
Financial data (yr. ended 12/31/99): Assets, $108,171 (M); grants paid, $2,000; expenditures, $20,354; qualifying distributions, $0.
Limitations: Applications not accepted.
Application information: Contributes only to pre-selected organizations.
Directors: Mark Treen, Susan Treen.
EIN: 742908093

63713
Stranger Church Building Committee
c/o G.T. Fairbairn
407 Chambers St.
Marlin, TX 76661-2311

Classified as a private operating foundation in 1991.
Financial data (yr. ended 03/31/99): Assets, $107,908 (M); grants paid, $0; expenditures, $7,105; qualifying distributions, $0; giving activities include $7,106 for programs.
Officers and Directors:* Charles Swinnea,* Pres.; G.T. Fairbairn,* Secy.; Marian Gibbs,* Treas.; William J. Chatham, Claude C. Erskine, Tommy Erskine, Betty Garrett, Jerry Garrett, Marion Garrison, Robert Garrison, Betty Sprott.
EIN: 742563985

63714
Clifton Steamboat Museum, Inc.
c/o David W. Hearn, Jr.
P.O. Box 20115
Beaumont, TX 77720-0115

Established in 1992 in TX.
Donor(s): David W. Hearn, Jr.
Financial data (yr. ended 12/31/01): Assets, $107,905 (M); grants paid, $0; expenditures, $22,381; qualifying distributions, $0.
Officers: David W. Hearn, Jr., Pres.; Glenn A. Mabry, V.P.
EIN: 760375230

63715
The Marfa Foundation
c/o Robin Abrams
P.O. Box 300400
Austin, TX 78703 (512) 458-2332

Established in 1996 in TX.
Donor(s): Robin Abrams, Ph.D., Simon Atkinson, Ph.D.
Financial data (yr. ended 12/31/00): Assets, $105,402 (M); grants paid, $0; gifts received, $8,804; expenditures, $10,966; qualifying distributions, $8,944.
Limitations: Giving limited to residents of Marfa, TX.
Officer and Director:* Robin Abrams, Ph.D.,* Pres.
EIN: 742804751

63716
Barge Foundation
3602 S.W. H. K. Dodgen Loop
Temple, TX 76504

Established in 1998 in TX.
Donor(s): V.W. Barge.
Financial data (yr. ended 12/31/00): Assets, $105,133 (M); grants paid, $31,280; gifts received, $13,259; expenditures, $32,189; qualifying distributions, $31,181.
Limitations: Giving primarily in TX.
Directors: Alison Barge Arnold, Laura B. Barge, Rebekah Barge, Richard M. Barge, V.W. Barge, Elizabeth Barge Bradford.
EIN: 752794851

63717
Russell and Thelma Jean Trifovesti Foundation
1701 E. Pioneer Dr.
Irving, TX 75061
Contact: Russell Trifovesti, Pres.

Donor(s): Russell Trifovesti, Thelma Jean Trifovesti.
Financial data (yr. ended 12/31/00): Assets, $103,003 (M); grants paid, $5,175; expenditures, $5,175; qualifying distributions, $5,175.
Officers: Russell Trifovesti, Pres.; Thelma Jean Trifovesti, V.P.
Director: Russell Trifovesti II.
EIN: 752853164

63718
C. Stratton Hill, Jr. Charitable Foundation
2924 Ella Lee Ln.
Houston, TX 77019-5908

Established in 1998.
Donor(s): C. Stratton Hill, Jr.
Financial data (yr. ended 10/31/01): Assets, $99,075 (M); grants paid, $44,205; gifts received, $20,000; expenditures, $45,272; qualifying distributions, $44,205.
Limitations: Applications not accepted. Giving primarily in TX.
Application information: Contributes only to pre-selected organizations.
Trustee: C. Stratton Hill, Jr.
EIN: 766120502

63719
Evelyn and Horace Wilkins Foundation
1512 Norwich Ct.
Southlake, TX 76092

Established in 1999 in TX.
Donor(s): Horace Wilkins, Evelyn Wilkins.
Financial data (yr. ended 12/31/00): Assets, $96,500 (M); grants paid, $0; gifts received, $6,000; expenditures, $0; qualifying distributions, $0; giving activities include $42,500 for loans.
Officers: Evelyn Wilkins, Pres.; Horace Wilkins, V.P.; Christopher Wilkins, Secy.-Treas.
EIN: 311626096

63720
Johnny & Alma Montgomery Family Foundation
P.O. Box 1027
Salado, TX 76571

Established in 2000.
Donor(s): J.L. Montgomery.
Financial data (yr. ended 12/31/00): Assets, $96,237 (M); grants paid, $1,000; gifts received, $100,000; expenditures, $2,960; qualifying distributions, $1,000.
Limitations: Giving primarily in TX.
Officers: Johnny L. Montgomery, Pres.; Alma C. Montgomery, V.P. and Secy.; Michael A. Montgomery, V.P. and Treas.; Mark Montgomery, V.P.; Michelle Montgomery, V.P.
EIN: 742969132

63721
Danjul Family Foundation, Inc.
c/o Sherrie Lynn Schaeffer
5311 Ashley Way Ct.
Sugar Land, TX 77479 (281) 494-9203

Established in 2000 in TX.
Donor(s): Sherrie L. Schaeffer, Peter Schaeffer.
Financial data (yr. ended 12/31/00): Assets, $94,308 (M); grants paid, $786; gifts received, $118,398; expenditures, $1,159; qualifying distributions, $786.
Limitations: Giving primarily in TX.
Officer: Sherrie L. Schaeffer, Pres.
Directors: Sandra J. Hild, Peter D. Schaeffer.
EIN: 760637481

63722
Common Grace Ministries, Inc.
2700 Swiss Ave., Ste. 3
Dallas, TX 75204
Application addresses: For scholarships: c/o Michael Maden, 2323 N. Masters Dr., Dallas, TX 75227, tel.: (972) 289-5028; for grants- c/o Martin Hironaga, 6010 Hillside Ln., Garland, TX, 75043, tel.: (972) 279-9430

Established in 1997 in TX.
Donor(s): Mark Okada, Pam Okada, John Urban, Carolyn Urban.
Financial data (yr. ended 12/31/01): Assets, $93,966 (M); grants paid, $125,057; gifts received, $312,550; expenditures, $297,990; qualifying distributions, $296,212.
Limitations: Applications not accepted. Giving limited to residents of East Dallas, TX.
Application information: Contributes only to pre-selected organizations.
Officers and Directors:* Mark Okada,* Chair.; Martin Hironaga,* Exec. Dir.; Walt Baker, Tim Hui, Pam Okada, Sam Tonomura.
EIN: 752727006
Codes: FD2

63723
Six Flags Humane Society
1 O'Connor Plz., Ste. 1100
Victoria, TX 77901-6549

Classified as a private operating foundation in 1971.
Donor(s): Dennis O'Connor,‡ Dorothy O'Connor Foundation, Overlake Foundations.
Financial data (yr. ended 12/31/99): Assets, $90,313 (M); grants paid, $15,000; gifts received, $79,000; expenditures, $132,211; qualifying distributions, $15,000.
Officers: Noble Malik, Pres.; Rubin S. Frels, V.P.; D.F. Martinak, Secy.-Treas.; Robert J. Hewitt, Treas.
EIN: 741492489

63724
Dr. E. L. Haney and Mabel Haney Memorial Foundation
c/o Security Bank
P.O. Box AA
Ralls, TX 79357
Contact: Gene McLaughlin, Tr.

Financial data (yr. ended 12/31/00): Assets, $90,212 (M); grants paid, $5,000; expenditures, $6,250; qualifying distributions, $5,578.
Limitations: Giving primarily in Ralls, TX.
Trustees: Terri Bevel, Gene McLaughlin, Virginia Torres, Walker Watkins.
EIN: 756353889

63725
The Sebastian Society
901 Waterfall Way, Ste. 107
Richardson, TX 75080

Financial data (yr. ended 12/31/99): Assets, $86,555 (M); grants paid, $4,040; expenditures, $4,040; qualifying distributions, $4,040.
Officer: Edward C. Nemec, Pres.
EIN: 752752203

63726
Smart Foundation, Inc.
5302 Olympia Fields Ln.
Houston, TX 77069

Established in 1964.
Donor(s): Hank Bryan, Jr.
Financial data (yr. ended 12/31/00): Assets, $85,823 (M); grants paid, $65,000; gifts received, $8,066; expenditures, $66,689; qualifying distributions, $66,689.
Limitations: Giving on a national basis.
Officer: Norman L. Hackler, Mgr.
EIN: 760420319

63727
Texas Research and Development Foundation
2602 Dellana Ln.
Austin, TX 78746-5746

Financial data (yr. ended 04/30/00): Assets, $85,683 (M); grants paid, $0; expenditures, $90,756; qualifying distributions, $73,057; giving activities include $54,348 for programs.
Officers and Trustees:* John Zaniewski,* Chair.; Glenn Von Rosenberg,* Vice-Chair.; Ronald Hudson,* Pres.
EIN: 741828798

63728
J. Frank and Mary Lou Kendall Trust
c/o Fredericksburg Independent School District
1121 S. Hwy. 16
Fredericksburg, TX 78624-5048
Application address: c/o Mary Alice Deike, Fredericksburg High School, 300-B W. Main St., Fredericksburg, TX 78624, tel.: (830) 997-7551

Financial data (yr. ended 12/31/00): Assets, $85,138 (M); grants paid, $1,248; expenditures, $1,354; qualifying distributions, $1,248.
Limitations: Giving limited to Fredericksburg, TX.
Application information: Application form required.
Trustee: Fredericksburg Independent School District.
EIN: 746284367

63729
Collin County Historical Society, Inc.
c/o Old P.O. Museum
Chestnut at Virginia
McKinney, TX 75069

Classified as a private operating foundation in 1984.
Financial data (yr. ended 12/31/00): Assets, $82,424 (M); grants paid, $0; gifts received, $11,469; expenditures, $17,762; qualifying distributions, $17,762; giving activities include $200 for programs.
Officers and Director:* Molly Horner, Chair.; Larry Eagan, Vice-Chair.; Silvia Turean, Secy.; Elisabeth R. Pink,* Treas.
EIN: 521093455

63730
Legator Charitable Trust
70 Colony Park Cir.
Galveston, TX 77551

Established in 1997 in TX. Classified as a private operating foundation in 1998.
Donor(s): Marvin Legator.
Financial data (yr. ended 12/31/00): Assets, $81,132 (M); grants paid, $0; gifts received, $67,640; expenditures, $65,024; qualifying distributions, $65,024; giving activities include $65,024 for programs.
Trustees: Lori Legator, Marvin Legator.
EIN: 760552441

63731
Haynes and Boone Foundation
901 Main St., Ste. 3100
Dallas, TX 75202

Established in 2000 in TX. Classified as a Company-sponsored operating foundation in 2001.
Donor(s): Haynes and Boone LLP.
Financial data (yr. ended 12/31/01): Assets, $79,052 (M); grants paid, $25,000; expenditures, $25,140; qualifying distributions, $25,000.
Limitations: Applications not accepted.
Application information: Contributes only to pre-selected organizations.
Officers and Directors:* George W. Bramblett,* Pres.; Michael M. Boone,* V.P.; Terry W. Conner,* Secy.; J. Michael Cripe, Treas.; Barry F. McNeil, Robert W. Wilson.
EIN: 752860946

63732
Sue Nan and Rod Cutsinger Foundation
1900 St. James Pl., Ste. 150
Houston, TX 77056

Established in 1999 in TX.

Financial data (yr. ended 12/31/00): Assets, $78,482 (M); grants paid, $2,000; expenditures, $3,800; qualifying distributions, $2,000.
Limitations: Applications not accepted. Giving primarily in Houston, TX.
Application information: Contributes only to pre-selected organizations.
Officers: Rod Cutsinger, Pres.; Sue Nan Cutsinger, Secy.
EIN: 311644919

63733
The Glen & Carmel Mitchell Foundation
2200 Smith-Barry, Ste. 150
Arlington, TX 76013

Established in 1999 in TX.
Financial data (yr. ended 06/30/01): Assets, $77,345 (M); grants paid, $20,965; expenditures, $25,880; qualifying distributions, $25,850.
Directors: Frederick P. Mesch, Carmel A. Mitchell, Glen B. Mitchell.
EIN: 752814804

63734
Woman Vision
c/o Mosbacher Mgmt., Tax Dept.
712 Main St., Ste. 2200
Houston, TX 77002-3290

Donor(s): Diane Mosbacher, M.D., H. van Ameringen Foundation, Fund for Southern Communities, Brook Glaefke.
Financial data (yr. ended 06/30/99): Assets, $77,156 (M); grants paid, $0; gifts received, $88,155; expenditures, $101,228; qualifying distributions, $97,806; giving activities include $97,806 for programs.
Limitations: Applications not accepted.
Officers and Directors:* Diane Mosbacher, M.D.,* Pres.; Nanette Gartrell,* Secy. and C.F.O.
EIN: 760406964

63735
Jehovah Ministries Charitable Trust
1350 Bandera Hwy.
Kerrville, TX 78028

Classified as a private operating foundation in 1995.
Donor(s): Rosalie Y. Martin.
Financial data (yr. ended 12/31/00): Assets, $77,127 (M); grants paid, $21,445; gifts received, $31,084; expenditures, $21,595; qualifying distributions, $21,445.
Limitations: Giving on an international basis.
Trustees: Rosalie Y. Martin, Lillian Hudson York.
EIN: 746383974

63736
Life: God's Sacred Gift
15910 Ripplewind Ct.
Houston, TX 77068

Established in 1999 in TX.
Financial data (yr. ended 12/31/01): Assets, $76,159 (M); grants paid, $0; gifts received, $89,120; expenditures, $17,806; qualifying distributions, $0.
Officers: Ron Galloy, Pres.; Gordon Ohluausen, V.P.
EIN: 740190257

63737
Dougherty Historical Foundation
P.O. Box 640
Beeville, TX 78104

Classified as a private operating foundation in 1986.
Donor(s): The James R. Dougherty, Jr. Foundation.

63737—TEXAS

Financial data (yr. ended 05/31/00): Assets, $72,182 (M); grants paid, $0; gifts received, $29,000; expenditures, $29,400; qualifying distributions, $29,328; giving activities include $16,148 for programs.
Officers and Directors:* Genevieve Vaughn, Pres.; F. William Carr, Jr., V.P.; Tonya Baxter, Secy.-Treas.; Mary Patricia Dougherty.
EIN: 742391274

63738
Forrest Foundation
17810 Davenport, Ste. 108
Dallas, TX 75252
Application address: 5827 Fallsview Ln., Dallas, TX 75252, tel.: (972) 250-3311
Contact: Kaaydah Forrest, Dir.

Donor(s): Rob Forrest, Kaaydah Forrest.
Financial data (yr. ended 07/31/00): Assets, $70,241 (M); grants paid, $13,532; gifts received, $23,873; expenditures, $18,289; qualifying distributions, $33,549; giving activities include $16,113 for loans to individuals.
Officer and Directors:* Rob Forrest,* Pres. and V.P.; Kaaydah Forrest, April Shade.
EIN: 752791856

63739
Houston Podiatric Foundation
22999 Highway 59, Ste., 204
Kingwood, TX 77339

Established in 1992 in TX.
Financial data (yr. ended 12/31/99): Assets, $69,298 (M); grants paid, $0; gifts received, $242,679; expenditures, $231,749; qualifying distributions, $240,024; giving activities include $240,024 for programs.
Officers and Director: Randal M. Lepow,* Pres.; Linda Noumani, Secy.; Maria Bertorello, Treas.
Trustee: Jonathon Hyman.
EIN: 760398125

63740
Jay and Diann Watson Family Foundation
3506 Sacred Moon Cove
Austin, TX 78746

Established in 1999 in TX.
Financial data (yr. ended 12/31/01): Assets, $69,062 (M); grants paid, $275,274; expenditures, $277,274; qualifying distributions, $275,274.
Limitations: Applications not accepted. Giving primarily in Austin, TX.
Application information: Contributes only to pre-selected organizations.
Directors: Jack A. James, Diann D. Watson, Jay S. Watson.
EIN: 742927609
Codes: FD

63741
Jennifer Strait Memorial Foundation
24123 Boerne Stage Rd., Ste. 200
San Antonio, TX 78255

Classified as a private operating foundation in 1987.
Financial data (yr. ended 12/31/99): Assets, $67,442 (M); grants paid, $2,660; gifts received, $1,702; expenditures, $2,753; qualifying distributions, $2,660.
Limitations: Applications not accepted. Giving limited to San Antonio, TX.
Application information: Contributes only to pre-selected organizations.
Officers: Jeff Wood Avant, Pres.; D. Frank Bohman, V.P.; Eric G. Hoffman, Secy.
EIN: 742444902

63742
The Hahne Charitable Trust
HC3, Box 3585
Lakehills, TX 78063-9789

Financial data (yr. ended 12/31/99): Assets, $60,416 (M); grants paid, $5,645; gifts received, $87,200; expenditures, $26,796; qualifying distributions, $5,645.
Limitations: Applications not accepted.
Application information: contributes only to pre-selected organizations.
Trustees: Ernest M. Hahne, Jeanette M. Hahne.
EIN: 760521316

63743
Dorothy Shaw Bell Choir
500 W. 7th St., Ste. 1007
Fort Worth, TX 76102

Established around 1977 in TX; classified as a private operating foundation in 1977.
Donor(s): F. Howard Walsh, Sr., Mary D. Walsh.
Financial data (yr. ended 12/31/01): Assets, $60,388 (M); grants paid, $0; gifts received, $3,219,000; expenditures, $287,517; qualifying distributions, $301,783; giving activities include $296,990 for programs.
Officers: Mary D. Walsh, Pres.; Sharon Ward, Secy.; G. Malcolm Louden, Treas.
EIN: 751545989

63744
Fireman's Hospital Fund
P.O. Box 1967
Texarkana, TX 75504

Financial data (yr. ended 12/31/99): Assets, $59,316 (M); grants paid, $0; gifts received, $3,011; expenditures, $2,456; qualifying distributions, $2,456; giving activities include $2,456 for programs.
Director: Roddy Smith.
Trustees: Dale A. Benest, Dennis Martin.
EIN: 752742488

63745
Corpus Christi Geological Society Scholarship Trust Fund
P.O. Box 1068
Corpus Christi, TX 78403
Contact: Wayne S. Croft, Chair.

Established in 1996 in TX.
Financial data (yr. ended 12/31/99): Assets, $58,171 (M); grants paid, $3,200; gifts received, $75; expenditures, $3,200; qualifying distributions, $3,200.
Limitations: Giving limited to Corpus Christi, TX.
Officers and Trustees:* Wayne S. Croft, Chair.; Scott Wruck,* Pres.; David Hatridge,* V.P.; John Carnes,* Secy.; Tom Jones,* Treas.; Alan Costello, Charlie Franck, Jany Heidecker, Pat Nye.
Scholarship Committe Member: Wayne S. Croft.
EIN: 742622816

63746
Arboretum, Inc.
P.O. Box 131302
Tyler, TX 75713

Established around 1972 in TX.
Financial data (yr. ended 12/31/00): Assets, $57,142 (M); grants paid, $0; gifts received, $925; expenditures, $3,491; qualifying distributions, $3,034; giving activities include $3,491 for programs.
Officers: James McDonald, Pres.; Marilyn McDonald, V.P.; Rachel "Jackie" McDonald, Secy.; Pat Shannon, Treas.

Directors: Ruth Garner, John Head, Delbert Hughes, Wanell Hughes.
EIN: 751365606

63747
SEI Knowledgeworks
2501 Cedar Springs LB-5, Ste. 200
Dallas, TX 75201-1400

Established in 1998 in TX.
Donor(s): Harold Rich.
Financial data (yr. ended 12/31/99): Assets, $56,812 (M); grants paid, $13,698; expenditures, $14,622; qualifying distributions, $14,090.
Limitations: Applications not accepted. Giving primarily in NY.
Application information: Contributes only to pre-selected organizations.
Officer: Robert P. Buford, Chair.
Directors: Harold Rich, Don Russell.
EIN: 752736586

63748
Marian K. Bleakley Law Enforcement Personnel Irrevocable Trust
36 W. Beauregard St.
San Angelo, TX 76903

Established in 1991 in TX.
Financial data (yr. ended 12/31/01): Assets, $55,731 (M); grants paid, $2,803; expenditures, $3,746; qualifying distributions, $2,803.
Limitations: Applications not accepted. Giving primarily in San Angelo, TX.
Application information: Contributes only to pre-selected organizations.
Trustees: Brenda Smith, Victor Vasquez, Barry Wike.
EIN: 756358555

63749
Klemme Family Foundation
1227 Hilltop Run
Lindale, TX 75771

Classified as a company-sponsored operating foundation.
Donor(s): The KB Company.
Financial data (yr. ended 12/31/00): Assets, $55,403 (M); grants paid, $3,155; gifts received, $67,029; expenditures, $17,057; qualifying distributions, $3,155.
Directors: Charlie Klemme, Janell Klemme.
EIN: 752792301

63750
The Reach Foundation
359 Lake Park Rd., Ste. 128
Lewisville, TX 75057

Established in 2000 in TX.
Donor(s): Harold Mark Wilson.
Financial data (yr. ended 12/31/00): Assets, $52,120 (M); grants paid, $2,000; gifts received, $54,399; expenditures, $2,456; qualifying distributions, $2,000.
Limitations: Applications not accepted.
Application information: Contributes only to pre-selected organizations.
Directors: Cansada C. Wilson, Harold J. Wilson, Harold Mark Wilson, Wendy J. Wilson.
EIN: 752877115

63751
Bill and Nancy Coats Charitable Trust, Inc.
P.O. Box 797504
Dallas, TX 75379-7504
Application address: 3179 65th St. N., St. Petersburg, FL 33710
Contact: David B. Coats, Pres.

Established in 1999 in TX.

Donor(s): David B. Coats, Marion Coats Stephen, James W. Coats.
Financial data (yr. ended 12/31/00): Assets, $50,540 (M); grants paid, $10,000; expenditures, $10,028; qualifying distributions, $9,981.
Limitations: Giving primarily in Hamilton, TX.
Officers and Directors:* David B. Coats,* Pres.; Marion Coats Stephen,* Secy.; James W. Coats,* Treas.
EIN: 752805212

63752
Shlakman Foundation
6016 Marlow Ave.
Dallas, TX 75252-7918

Established in 2000 in TX.
Donor(s): Richard Shlakman.
Financial data (yr. ended 12/31/00): Assets, $49,903 (M); grants paid, $3,800; gifts received, $60,352; expenditures, $10,173; qualifying distributions, $10,073.
Limitations: Applications not accepted. Giving primarily in TX, UT, and VA.
Application information: Contributes only to pre-selected organizations.
Officers: Richard Shlakman, Chair., Pres. and Secy.; Sarah Shlakman, V.P. and Treas.
Director: James Nyfeler.
EIN: 311736958

63753
Interdenominational Christian Missions, Inc.
30260 Saratoga Ln.
Fair Oaks Ranch, TX 78015

Established in 1997 in TX.
Donor(s): Ralph E. Fair, Jr.
Financial data (yr. ended 12/31/01): Assets, $49,710 (M); grants paid, $566,492; gifts received, $629,487; expenditures, $610,204; qualifying distributions, $610,189.
Limitations: Giving on a national and international basis, including Costa Rica, Peru, Honduras, and Nicaragua.
Officers: Douglas J. Richardson, Pres.; Ralph E. Fair, Jr., V.P.; Suzanne F. Richardson, Secy.; Janis R. Fair, Treas.
EIN: 742798861
Codes: FD

63754
Glenda Hoerster Memorial Trust
1121 Hwy. 16 S.
Fredericksburg, TX 78624
Application address: Mary Alice Deike, c/o Fredericksburg High School, 300-B W. Main St., Fredericksburg, TX 78624-3712, tel.: (830) 997-7551

Financial data (yr. ended 12/31/00): Assets, $49,395 (M); grants paid, $680; expenditures, $767; qualifying distributions, $680.
Limitations: Giving limited to the Fredericksburg, TX, area.
Application information: Application form required.
Trustee: Fredericksburg Independent School District.
EIN: 237393211

63755
Vaughan Antique Instrument Foundation
c/o Curtis T. Vaughan, Jr.
10800 Sentinel Dr.
San Antonio, TX 78217

Established in 1997 in AZ.
Donor(s): Curtis T. Vanghan, Jr.
Financial data (yr. ended 12/31/01): Assets, $48,295 (M); grants paid, $0; gifts received, $5,694; expenditures, $2,431; qualifying distributions, $2,431; giving activities include $2,429 for programs.
Officers and Directors:* Curtis T. Vaughan, Jr.,* Pres.; George C. Vaughan,* V.P.; Richard S. Vaughan,* V.P.; Curtiss T. Vaughan III,* Secy.; Robert L. Vaughan,* Treas.; Frank N. Bash.
EIN: 742816643

63756
Genesis Education Foundation, Inc.
4517 Larch Ln.
Bellaire, TX 77401

Established in 1999 in TX.
Financial data (yr. ended 12/31/00): Assets, $46,646 (M); grants paid, $6,053; gifts received, $32,433; expenditures, $13,668; qualifying distributions, $6,053.
Limitations: Giving limited to Houston, TX.
Officers: Mary Banister, Pres.; Paul Banister, V.P.; Gretchen Walter, Secy.
Director: Teresa Ramirez.
EIN: 760596134

63757
Widner Memorial Foundation
(also known as Widner Memorial Museum)
P.O. Box 330385
Fort Worth, TX 76163-0385

Classified as a private operating foundation in 1973.
Donor(s): Jerry W. Roberts.
Financial data (yr. ended 12/31/99): Assets, $45,669 (M); grants paid, $2,505; gifts received, $11,785; expenditures, $8,260; qualifying distributions, $8,260.
Limitations: Applications not accepted.
Application information: Contributes only to pre-selected organizations.
Trustees: Charles Culpepper, Frankie Rainey, Carol O. Roberts, Tonya Roberts Wood.
EIN: 237159693

63758
The George & Peggy Yonge Foundation
203 Redbud Trail
Austin, TX 78746-3606 (512) 312-1195
Additional tel.: (512) 347-9991
Contact: George Yonge, Pres.

Established in 1997 in TX.
Donor(s): George Yonge, Peggy Yonge.
Financial data (yr. ended 06/30/01): Assets, $44,551 (M); grants paid, $2,950; gifts received, $40,000; expenditures, $2,959; qualifying distributions, $2,950.
Limitations: Giving primarily in Austin, TX.
Officers: George Yonge, Pres.; Peggy Yonge, V.P.; Weston S. Yonge, Secy.; Jon Christian Yonge, Treas.
EIN: 742846089

63759
Lester Foundation
3601 Big Bear Lake Ct.
Arlington, TX 76016
Application address: 3708 Big Bear Lake Dr., Arlington, TX 76016, tel.: (817) 483-5888
Contact: Terri Pendergraft, Tr.

Established in 1996 in TX.
Donor(s): Philip A. Pendergraft, Terri Pendergraft, Hal Pendergraft, Virginia Pendergraft.
Financial data (yr. ended 12/31/00): Assets, $42,295 (M); grants paid, $81,981; gifts received, $5,000; expenditures, $87,065; qualifying distributions, $81,981.
Limitations: Giving primarily in Arlington, TX.
Trustees: Hal Pendergraft, Philip A. Pendergraft, Terri Pendergraft, Virginia Pendergraft.
EIN: 756438676

63760
Conroe Area Youth Baseball, Inc.
P.O. Box 612
Conroe, TX 77305 (936) 539-1755

Established in 1985 in TX.
Financial data (yr. ended 08/31/99): Assets, $39,878 (M); grants paid, $13,120; expenditures, $81,661; qualifying distributions, $0.
Officers: Hogan Brooks, Chair.; Terry Moon, Secy.; Amy Calfee, Treas.
Director: Ricky Morton.
EIN: 760057555

63761
The Discovery Fund
c/o Lucy Darden
777 Rosedale St., Ste. 300
Fort Worth, TX 76104-4638 (817) 332-9133

Established in 1984 in TX.
Donor(s): Frank Darden.‡
Financial data (yr. ended 12/31/00): Assets, $39,770 (M); grants paid, $20,000; gifts received, $40,028; expenditures, $41,457; qualifying distributions, $40,430; giving activities include $20,430 for programs.
Limitations: Giving primarily in TX.
Trustees: Anne Darden, Thomas Darden.
EIN: 751989523

63762
Tex-Life Foundation, Inc.
4708 Highland Ter.
Austin, TX 78731-5319
Contact: Anne R. Lassiter, Pres.

Established around 1986 in TX.
Donor(s): James W. Lassiter, Anne R. Lassiter.
Financial data (yr. ended 12/31/00): Assets, $39,004 (M); grants paid, $13,270; gifts received, $56,981; expenditures, $78,265; qualifying distributions, $56,578.
Limitations: Giving primarily in TX.
Officer: Anne R. Lassiter, Pres.
Director: Patricia C. Lassiter.
EIN: 742388509

63763
Institute for the Advancement of Psychology and Spirituality
c/o Peter A. Olsson, M.D.
1215 Barkdull St.
Houston, TX 77006-6470

Established in 1991 in TX.
Donor(s): Michael Huffington.
Financial data (yr. ended 12/31/01): Assets, $38,602 (M); grants paid, $0; gifts received, $34,575; expenditures, $46,017; qualifying distributions, $0.
Officer and Trustees:* Rev. J. Pittman McGehee, Exec. Dir.; John Goott, Rev. John A. Logan, Jr.
EIN: 766067770

63764
The Stuart Ostrow Foundation, Inc.
10 S. Briar Hollow Ln., Ste. 87
Houston, TX 77027

Donor(s): Stuart Ostrow.
Financial data (yr. ended 11/30/01): Assets, $36,761 (M); grants paid, $0; gifts received, $55,000; expenditures, $28,897; qualifying distributions, $0.
Trustee: Stuart Ostrow.
EIN: 132775339

63765
August W. Klingelhoefer Needy Student Assistance Fund
c/o Fredericksburg Independent School District
1121 S. State Hwy. 16
Fredericksburg, TX 78624
Application address: c/o Mary Alice Deike, Fredericksburg High School, 300-B W. Main St., Fredericksburg, TX 78624, tel.: (830) 997-7551

Financial data (yr. ended 12/31/00): Assets, $35,167 (M); grants paid, $525; expenditures, $608; qualifying distributions, $525.
Limitations: Giving limited to Fredericksburg, TX.
Application information: Application form required.
Trustee: Fredericksburg Independent School District.
EIN: 746070540

63766
Texas Health Innovators
P.O. Box 691328
Houston, TX 77269-1328

Established in 1993 in TX.
Donor(s): Christian Charitable Trust.
Financial data (yr. ended 12/31/99): Assets, $35,152 (M); grants paid, $0; expenditures, $3,368; qualifying distributions, $2,455; giving activities include $2,455 for programs.
Officers: Richard L. Davis, Chair.; Steve Koinis, Vice-Chair.; Hassan S. Rifast, Pres.; Tracie L. Ybarra, Secy.
EIN: 760424686

63767
Thorne Charitable Trust
150 Sunset Lake Dr.
Huntsville, TX 77340

Donor(s): Oscar L. Thorne, Bonnie B. Thorne.
Financial data (yr. ended 12/31/00): Assets, $33,172 (M); grants paid, $1,000; gifts received, $1,000; expenditures, $1,290; qualifying distributions, $1,000.
Limitations: Applications not accepted.
Application information: Contributes only to pre-selected organizations.
Trustee: Bonnie B. Thorne.
EIN: 766073630

63768
William & Elizabeth Hayden Museum of American Art
930 Cardinal Ln.
Paris, TX 75460-6522

Classified as private operating foundation in 1994.
Donor(s): Elizabeth Hayden, William Hayden.
Financial data (yr. ended 12/31/01): Assets, $32,980 (M); grants paid, $0; gifts received, $15,400; expenditures, $27,039; qualifying distributions, $0.
Officers and Directors:* William Hayden,* Pres.; Elizabeth Hayden,* Secy.; William Hayden, Jr., Elizabeth McQuire.
EIN: 752550401

63769
Jerry Don Mouser Foundation
P.O. Box 171198
Arlington, TX 76003-1198
Application address: c/o J. D. Mouser, P.O. Box 40672, Everman, TX 76140

Financial data (yr. ended 12/31/01): Assets, $32,357 (M); grants paid, $45,582; gifts received, $20,491; expenditures, $46,432; qualifying distributions, $45,582.

Limitations: Giving limited to Grossmont, CA, Randolph, NJ, and Mansfield, TX, areas.
Application information: Application form required.
Officers: Myrna L. Mouser-Wood, Pres.; Peter F. Shopp, Sr., V.P. and Treas.; Shirlene D. Miller, Secy.
EIN: 752548171
Codes: GTI

63770
Ralph & Billie Howard Foundation
c/o Mitzi Howard Bjork
1908 Hilltop Dr.
Tyler, TX 75701

Established in 2000.
Financial data (yr. ended 12/31/01): Assets, $31,675 (M); grants paid, $1,000; gifts received, $1,445; expenditures, $1,587; qualifying distributions, $1,589.
Officers and Directors:* Walter Howard,* Chair.; Mitzi Howard Bjork,* Treas.; Cindy Drumn, Richard Howard, Reita Risen.
EIN: 561673990

63771
The Captain Reginald E. and Geneva McKamie Foundation Charitable Trust
1210 Antoine Dr.
Houston, TX 77055 (713) 465-2889
E-mail: mckamie@mckamie.com
Contact: Capt. Reginald E. McKamie, Dir.

Donor(s): Reginald McKamie, Geneva McKamie.
Financial data (yr. ended 12/31/00): Assets, $30,327 (M); grants paid, $9,000; gifts received, $400; expenditures, $9,521; qualifying distributions, $9,521.
Limitations: Giving on a national basis.
Application information: Application form required.
Directors: Geneva W. McKamie, Reginald E. McKamie.
EIN: 760620024

63772
Front Line Outreach
12770 Merit Dr., Ste. 400
Dallas, TX 75251-1212

Donor(s): Norman E. Miller.
Financial data (yr. ended 12/31/99): Assets, $29,179 (M); grants paid, $14,204; gifts received, $13,095; expenditures, $20,680; qualifying distributions, $14,204.
Officers and Directors:* Norman E. Miller,* Pres.; Anne E. Miller,* V.P.; Violet Vickery,* Secy.; Paul Alexander,* Treas.; K. Thomas Greene.
EIN: 752468086

63773
Independent Electrical Contractors, Inc. of San Antonio Apprenticeship and Training Trust Fund
(also known as IEC, Inc. of S.A. A & T Trust)
803 Jerry Dr.
San Antonio, TX 78201

Established in 1997 in TX.
Financial data (yr. ended 08/31/00): Assets, $29,158 (M); grants paid, $0; expenditures, $163,768; qualifying distributions, $0; giving activities include $163,768 for programs.
Officer: Barry Prince, Chair.
Trustees: Paul Davila, Brian Marr, Eddie Miranda, Tommy Monaco, Brian Ray, Dennis Wright.
EIN: 742859355

63774
Hungarian Baptist Union of Romania, Inc.
9400 N. Central Expwy., Ste. 420
Dallas, TX 75231-5098

Established in 1996 in TX.
Donor(s): Larry Burleson.
Financial data (yr. ended 12/31/99): Assets, $28,633 (M); grants paid, $127,540; gifts received, $182,006; expenditures, $158,196; qualifying distributions, $158,196; giving activities include $30,656 for programs.
Officers: Joe Pendleton, Pres.; Larry Burleson, V.P.; Sharon Hehli, Secy.-Treas.
EIN: 752448131

63775
San Angelo Code Blue Crime Watch, Inc.
P.O. Box 3572
San Angelo, TX 76902-3572

Established in 1998.
Financial data (yr. ended 12/31/00): Assets, $27,959 (M); grants paid, $0; gifts received, $385; expenditures, $2,010; qualifying distributions, $0.
Officers: Marshall Stewart, Pres.; Gary Griffin, V.P.; Brenda H. Stewart, Secy.; William H. Earls, Treas.
EIN: 752611159

63776
Harry Newton Key, Jr. and Cornelia Buck Key Foundation
c/o Harry N. Key
P.O. Box 190
Lampasas, TX 76550

Financial data (yr. ended 12/31/00): Assets, $26,717 (M); grants paid, $2,500; gifts received, $25,000; expenditures, $2,515; qualifying distributions, $2,515.
Limitations: Giving limited to residents of Lampasas, TX.
Trustees: Cornelia B. Key, Harry N. Key.
EIN: 746423448

63777
August W. Klingelhoefer Needy Student Help Fund
1121 S. State Hwy. 16
Fredericksburg, TX 78624
Application address: c/o Mary Alice Deike, Fredericksburg High School, 300-B W. Main St., Fredericksburg, TX 78624, tel.: (210) 997-7551

Financial data (yr. ended 12/31/00): Assets, $25,156 (M); grants paid, $250; expenditures, $334; qualifying distributions, $250.
Limitations: Giving limited to Fredericksburg, TX.
Application information: Application form required.
Trustee: Fredericksburg Independent School District.
EIN: 237002876

63778
August W. Klingelhoefer Needy Student Aid Fund
c/o Fredericksburg Independent School District
1121 S. State Hwy. 16
Fredericksburg, TX 78624
Application address: c/o Mary Alice Deike, Fredericksburg High School, 300-B W. Main St., Fredericksburg, TX 78624, tel.: (830) 997-7551

Financial data (yr. ended 12/31/00): Assets, $24,518 (M); grants paid, $485; expenditures, $567; qualifying distributions, $485.
Limitations: Giving limited to Fredericksburg, TX.
Application information: Application form required.

Trustee: Fredericksburg Independent School District.
EIN: 746084801

63779
The J. T. and Margaret Talkington Foundation
2012 Broadway
Lubbock, TX 79401-3020

Financial data (yr. ended 03/31/01): Assets, $22,469 (L); grants paid, $30,750; expenditures, $31,095; qualifying distributions, $30,750.
Limitations: Giving primarily in Lubbock, TX.
Officers: J.T. Talkington, Pres.; Norton Baker, V.P.; M.K. Talkington, Secy.-Treas.
EIN: 752733220

63780
Jeffrey Family Charitable Trust
c/o John Charles Jeffrey, Tr.
P.O. Box 89
Quanah, TX 79252-0089 (940) 663-2254

Established in 1994 in TX.
Donor(s): D.C. Jeffrey Charitable Gift Fund, John Charles Jeffrey.
Financial data (yr. ended 12/31/00): Assets, $21,650 (M); grants paid, $3,272; gifts received, $7,338; expenditures, $3,745; qualifying distributions, $3,272.
Limitations: Giving primarily in Quanah, TX.
Application information: Application form required.
Committee Members: J.R. Baucum, Marita Baucum, Pam Bursey, Seth Bursey.
Trustee: John Charles Jeffrey.
EIN: 756464198

63781
Church of the Brazos
The Huntingdon
2121 Kirby Dr., Ste. 144
Houston, TX 77019-6069

Established in 1994 in TX.
Donor(s): Joanne K. Davis.
Financial data (yr. ended 12/31/00): Assets, $21,201 (M); grants paid, $0; gifts received, $88,745; expenditures, $59,907; qualifying distributions, $59,907; giving activities include $54,206 for programs.
Officer: Joanne K. Davis, Pres.
Trustees: Dee Lyon, Mrs. L.F. McCollum.
EIN: 760436294

63782
Mind Science Foundation
7979 Broadway, Ste. 100
San Antonio, TX 78209

Established in 1958 in TX.
Financial data (yr. ended 12/31/99): Assets, $21,086 (M); grants paid, $0; gifts received, $241,417; expenditures, $353,029; qualifying distributions, $341,184; giving activities include $113,845 for programs.
Officers: Kaye Lenox, Chair.; David O. Rocha, Vice-Chair.; Cappy Lawton, Secy.; Abigail Kampmann, Treas.; Elizabeth E. Costello, Exec. Dir.
Trustees: John Kerr, William Mallow, John McNab, Ethel Porter, M.D., Deborah Radicke, Julian Trevino, and 10 additional trustees.
EIN: 741384861

63783
The Coastal Banc Foundation
c/o Coastal Banc ssb
5718 Westheimer Rd., Ste. 600
Houston, TX 77057-5733

Established in 1992 in TX as a company-sponsored operating foundation.

Donor(s): Coastal Banc Savings Assn.
Financial data (yr. ended 11/30/01): Assets, $20,750 (M); grants paid, $950; expenditures, $950; qualifying distributions, $950.
Limitations: Giving limited to TX.
Application information: Personal interview required. Application form required.
Officers and Trustees:* Manuel J. Mehos,* Pres.; Gary R. Garrett,* V.P.; Linda B. Frazier, Secy.; Catherine N. Wylie, Treas.
Scholarship Committee Members: Stella Jones, Scholarship Committee Chair.; Kenneth K. Krueger, Leslie McFerren, Jana Smith, Beth Tiderman.
EIN: 760390265
Codes: CD, GTI

63784
James Brooks & Charlotte Park Brooks Foundation
3237 Bryn Mawr Dr.
Dallas, TX 75225 (214) 368-1103
Contact: Julie L. Cochran, Pres.

Established in 2000 in TX.
Donor(s): Charlotte Park Brooks.
Financial data (yr. ended 12/31/01): Assets, $20,715 (M); grants paid, $27,000; gifts received, $97,000; expenditures, $92,427; qualifying distributions, $27,000.
Officers: Julie L. Cochran, Pres. and Treas.; Charlotte Park Brooks, V.P.; Meg Perlman, Secy.
Director: Dwight Emanuelson.
EIN: 752879821

63785
Edison Plaza Museum
P.O. Box 2951
Beaumont, TX 77704

Classified as a private operating foundation in 1987.
Donor(s): Gulf States Utilities Co.
Financial data (yr. ended 06/30/00): Assets, $20,014 (M); grants paid, $0; gifts received, $7,500; expenditures, $3,060; qualifying distributions, $2,035; giving activities include $2,035 for programs.
Officers and Directors:* T. Michael Barnhill,* Chair. and Pres.; Beanie Hickman,* V.P.; Debbie Null, Secy.-Treas.; Leslie D. Cobb, Andrew J. Johnson, Tom K. Lamb, Edward M. Loggins, Ryan Smith.
EIN: 742156522

63786
Transart Foundation
1412 W. Alabama St.
Houston, TX 77006-4104 (713) 807-7427

Established in 1996 in TX.
Donor(s): Surpik Angelini.
Financial data (yr. ended 12/31/00): Assets, $19,576 (M); grants paid, $1,000; gifts received, $43,994; expenditures, $48,988; qualifying distributions, $46,699; giving activities include $43,020 for programs.
Limitations: Giving primarily in TX.
Application information: Application form required.
Officers and Directors:* Surpik Angelini,* Pres. and Treas.; Abdel Hernandez,* V.P.; Lorena Donnelly,* Secy.
Advisors: Samantha Barlow, George Marcus, Hamid Naficy.
EIN: 760536583

63787
Earl B. Rice and Mary Lou Rice Educational Trust
c/o First Liberty National Bank
P.O. Box 10109
Liberty, TX 77575-5941 (936) 336-6471
Contact: Charles Fisher, Trust Off., 1st Liberty National Bank

Established in 1993.
Donor(s): Mary Lou Rice.
Financial data (yr. ended 11/30/00): Assets, $19,170 (M); grants paid, $2,000; gifts received, $1,500; expenditures, $2,196; qualifying distributions, $2,000.
Limitations: Giving limited to residents of TX.
Application information: Requirements obtained from trustee bank. Application form required.
Trustee: First Liberty National Bank.
EIN: 766093250

63788
First Capitol Historical Foundation, Inc.
156 W. Texaco
West Columbia, TX 77486

Financial data (yr. ended 12/31/99): Assets, $18,180 (M); grants paid, $0; gifts received, $5,006; expenditures, $6,124; qualifying distributions, $6,123; giving activities include $6,124 for programs.
Officers: Laurie Kincanno, Pres.; Beth Griggs, V.P.; Polly Rowold, Secy.; Wilma Ogilvie, Treas.
EIN: 741554227

63789
Council Oaks Vocational Enhancement Services (COVES), Inc.
P.O. Box 160171
Austin, TX 78716-0171

Classified as a private operating foundation in 1998 in TX.
Financial data (yr. ended 12/31/99): Assets, $17,972 (M); grants paid, $0; gifts received, $313,460; expenditures, $306,276; qualifying distributions, $305,785; giving activities include $297,569 for programs.
Officer: William E. Lee, Pres.
EIN: 742664245

63790
The Langston Family Foundation
130 Pecan Ln.
New Waverly, TX 77358

Established in 2000.
Financial data (yr. ended 12/31/00): Assets, $17,300 (M); grants paid, $0; gifts received, $17,300; expenditures, $0; qualifying distributions, $0.
Director: Brian Lanston.
EIN: 760662066

63791
BFW Charitable Foundation, Inc.
1601 Elm St., Ste. 4200
Dallas, TX 75201

Established in 2000 in TX.
Donor(s): Barbara Wallace.
Financial data (yr. ended 12/31/01): Assets, $15,700 (M); grants paid, $10,800; gifts received, $17,790; expenditures, $11,204; qualifying distributions, $10,800.
Officers: Barbara Wallace, Pres.; Reagan N. Waskom III, Secy.; Claire W. Shoemaker, Treas.
EIN: 752911499

63792
Templar Foundation
7501 Shadowridge Run, No. 113
Austin, TX 78749

Established in 1993 in TX.
Donor(s): Daniel W. Ortman.
Financial data (yr. ended 12/31/99): Assets, $15,156 (M); grants paid, $2,000; expenditures, $2,707; qualifying distributions, $2,707.
Limitations: Applications not accepted. Giving primarily in Seguin, TX.
Application information: Contributes only to pre-selected organizations.
Trustee: Daniel W. Ortman.
EIN: 742679322

63793
The Lindley Foundation, Inc.
203 Bayou Dr.
Beaumont, TX 77705-9748 (409) 796-1442
Contact: Neil E. Lindley, Pres.

Established in 1988 in TX.
Financial data (yr. ended 10/31/01): Assets, $15,014 (M); grants paid, $0; gifts received, $2,556; expenditures, $55; qualifying distributions, $0.
Limitations: Giving primarily in TX.
Application information: Unsolicited request for funds not accepted.
Officers: Neil E. Lindley, Pres. and Secy.-Treas.; Mary Lindley, V.P.; Felix Ramirez, V.P.
EIN: 760264328

63794
BAC Education Foundation, Inc.
1150 S. Freeway, Ste. 106
Fort Worth, TX 76104

Financial data (yr. ended 09/30/01): Assets, $14,548 (M); grants paid, $0; expenditures, $10,867; qualifying distributions, $0; giving activities include $9,570 for programs.
Directors: Gwen Barbee, Lou Ann Blaylock, Drew Casani, Frank Deleo, Doug Eller, Craig Harbuck, and 10 additional directors.
EIN: 752824925

63795
Mary E. & Norman M. Simmons Family Scholarship Fund
c/o David P. Simmons
9516 Cliffside Dr.
Irving, TX 75063

Financial data (yr. ended 12/31/01): Assets, $13,438 (M); grants paid, $1,000; gifts received, $1,500; expenditures, $1,000; qualifying distributions, $1,000.
Limitations: Applications not accepted. Giving limited to residents of Somerset, MA.
Application information: Unsolicited requests for funds not accepted.
Directors: David P. Simmons, Mary E. Simmons, Norman M. Simmons.
EIN: 752388877

63796
Family Medical Trust
P.O. Box 218
Carrizo Springs, TX 78834-6218
Contact: John W. Petry, Chair.

Established in 1988 in TX.
Financial data (yr. ended 12/31/01): Assets, $13,149 (M); grants paid, $3,000; gifts received, $5,500; expenditures, $3,525; qualifying distributions, $3,168.
Limitations: Giving limited to the Dimmit County, TX, area.
Trustees: John W. Petry, Chair.; Mary E. Blackard, Alfonso Rodriguez.
EIN: 742466560

63797
The Betty K. Wolfe Foundation
6632 Carston Ct.
North Richland Hills, TX 76180-7843
(817) 335-1604
Contact: Betty K. Wolfe, Tr.

Established in 1992 in TX.
Donor(s): Betty K. Wolfe.
Financial data (yr. ended 12/31/99): Assets, $12,976 (M); grants paid, $17,003; gifts received, $29,771; expenditures, $18,917; qualifying distributions, $17,003.
Limitations: Giving primarily in VA.
Trustee: Betty K. Wolfe.
EIN: 756423068

63798
The Bonderman Family Foundation
301 Commerce St., Ste. 3300
Fort Worth, TX 76102

Established in 1994 in DC.
Donor(s): Laurie F. Michaels.
Financial data (yr. ended 12/31/00): Assets, $12,967 (M); grants paid, $165,000; gifts received, $277,125; expenditures, $171,462; qualifying distributions, $171,175.
Limitations: Applications not accepted.
Application information: Contributes only to pre-selected organizations.
Officers: Laurie F. Michaels, Pres. and Treas.; James O'Brien, V.P.; Richard Eckleberry, Secy.
Directors: David Bonderman, Laine Shakerdge.
EIN: 521862453
Codes: FD2

63799
Sara Hall George Memorial Scholarship Trust
c/o Sarah Beal
P.O. Box 20, R.R. 1
Coleman, TX 76834-9701 (915) 785-4291

Established in 1982.
Financial data (yr. ended 12/31/99): Assets, $12,492 (M); grants paid, $283; expenditures, $283; qualifying distributions, $283.
Limitations: Giving limited to Coleman County, TX.
Application information: Application form required.
Officers: Joan Jones, Pres.; Carla Billings, 1st V.P.; Patsy Gilder, 2nd V.P.; Caroline Skelton, Recording Secy.
EIN: 751781917

63800
Clark McCleary Scholarship Fund, Inc.
3730 Kirby Dr., Ste. 805
Houston, TX 77098-3979
Application address: 800 Bering Dr., Ste. 105, Houston, TX 77057
Contact: Thomas D. Riffle, Pres.

Established in 2000 in TX.
Financial data (yr. ended 12/31/01): Assets, $11,943 (M); grants paid, $1,368; gifts received, $755; expenditures, $1,721; qualifying distributions, $1,368.
Officers and Directors:* Thomas D. Riffle,* Pres.; J. Wiley Moreland, Jr.,* Secy.; Vernon R. Wilson,* Treas.; Jack Babchick, Richard C. Kuriger.
EIN: 760652274

63801
FNYB Incorporated
(Formerly Freeway Youth Baseball, Inc.)
7580 Haywood Dr.
Houston, TX 77061

Financial data (yr. ended 12/31/99): Assets, $11,684 (M); grants paid, $0; gifts received, $55,507; expenditures, $54,397; qualifying distributions, $54,395; giving activities include $54,397 for programs.
Directors: Marvin Guy, Thomas Nauls, Max Zapiata.
EIN: 760107651

63802
Marnee Alford Allen Foundation, Inc.
P.O. Box 270663
Houston, TX 77277-0663

Established in 2001 in TX.
Financial data (yr. ended 12/31/01): Assets, $11,294 (M); grants paid, $300; gifts received, $1,232; expenditures, $300; qualifying distributions, $300.
Limitations: Applications not accepted. Giving primarily in RI.
Application information: Contributes only to pre-selected organizations.
Officers: David P. Bryan, Pres.; Susan Allen-Bryan, V.P.; Joshua A. Foster, Secy.-Treas.
EIN: 760334734

63803
Palczer Family Trust
c/o R. Palczer
7904 Alderwood Pl.
Plano, TX 75025-6007

Classified as a private operating foundation in 1983.
Financial data (yr. ended 12/31/00): Assets, $11,221 (M); grants paid, $1,100; expenditures, $1,121; qualifying distributions, $1,100.
Limitations: Applications not accepted. Giving primarily in TX.
Application information: Contributes only to pre-selected organizations.
Trustees: Roxie D. Palczer, Terry L. Palczer.
EIN: 926019546

63804
Doolin Family Foundation
c/o Earl L. Doolin
6411 Northaven Rd.
Dallas, TX 75230-3015

Financial data (yr. ended 12/31/99): Assets, $11,083 (L); grants paid, $3,000; gifts received, $9,000; expenditures, $3,606; qualifying distributions, $3,000.
Limitations: Applications not accepted. Giving primarily in Dallas, TX.
Application information: Contributes only to pre-selected organizations.
Officers: Charles W. Doolin, Pres.; Kaleta Doolin, V.P.; Earl L. Doolin, Secy.-Treas.
EIN: 752780279

63805
Albert W. Hartman-Edgar L. Frazell Foundation for Medical Research
414 Navarro St., Ste. 1002
San Antonio, TX 78205-2527 (210) 271-1876

Financial data (yr. ended 12/31/99): Assets, $9,980 (M); grants paid, $1,500; expenditures, $2,109; qualifying distributions, $1,500.
Officer and Directors:* Sherri Hernandez,* Chair.; William J. Hills, M.D., Auerliano A. Urrutia.
EIN: 741552669

63806
Littlest Wiseman, Inc.
500 W. 7th St., No. 1007
Fort Worth, TX 76102

Classified as a private operating foundation in 1981.
Financial data (yr. ended 04/30/99): Assets, $9,820 (M); grants paid, $0; gifts received, $190,500; expenditures, $186,389; qualifying distributions, $186,389; giving activities include $186,389 for programs.
Officers: Mary D. Walsh, Chair.; F. Howard Walsh, Sr., Pres.; F. Howard Walsh, Jr., V.P.; G. Malcolm Louden, Secy.-Treas.
EIN: 751782670

63807
Polycarp Foundation
3508 Harvard
Dallas, TX 75205

Financial data (yr. ended 12/31/99): Assets, $8,936 (M); grants paid, $9,000; expenditures, $9,744; qualifying distributions, $9,000.
Limitations: Applications not accepted.
Application information: Contributes only to pre-selected organizations.
Officers: Charles Doolin, Pres.; Kaleta Doolin, V.P. and Secy.; Earl L. Doolin, Treas.
EIN: 752777481

63808
Moozies Kindness Foundation, Inc.
c/o Ted Dreier
801 Hebron Pkwy., Ste. 7304
Lewisville, TX 75057

Established in 2000 in TX.
Financial data (yr. ended 12/31/00): Assets, $8,911 (M); grants paid, $0; gifts received, $150; expenditures, $8,907; qualifying distributions, $387; giving activities include $8,517 for programs.
Directors: Karen Dreier, Kyle Dreier, Ted Dreier.
EIN: 752822560

63809
Kenneth G. Knox, Class of 1952 Memorial Scholarship Fund
120 Chaparral Dr.
Graham, TX 76450

Financial data (yr. ended 12/31/01): Assets, $8,849 (M); grants paid, $1,000; gifts received, $1,750; expenditures, $1,000; qualifying distributions, $1,000.
Limitations: Applications not accepted. Giving primarily in Dallas, TX.
Application information: Contributes only to pre-selected organizations.
Officers: Ruth Downey, Mgr.; John Knox, Mgr.; Ken Knox, Mgr.
EIN: 311698192

63810
Aurora Foundation
c/o Jeffrey Bronfman
520 Cypress Creek Ln.
Wimberley, TX 78676

Established in 1993 in TX.
Donor(s): Jeffrey Bronfman.
Financial data (yr. ended 09/30/01): Assets, $8,772 (M); grants paid, $429,747; gifts received, $403,949; expenditures, $439,357; qualifying distributions, $439,528.
Limitations: Giving on a national and international basis, with emphasis on Santa Fe, NM, and Central and South America.

Officers and Directors:* Jeffrey Bronfman,* Pres. and Treas.; Duncan E. Osborne,* Secy.; Irvin F. Diamond.
EIN: 742660772
Codes: FD

63811
Montgomery I.S.D. Foundation for the Arts
25025 I-45 N., Ste. 410
The Woodlands, TX 77380

Established in 2000 in TX.
Financial data (yr. ended 05/31/01): Assets, $8,284 (M); grants paid, $14,000; gifts received, $24,435; expenditures, $16,150; qualifying distributions, $14,000.
Limitations: Applications not accepted. Giving primarily in Montgomery, TX.
Application information: Contributes only to pre-selected organizations.
Officers and Trustees:* Richie Ray,* Pres.; Nancy Dossey,* Secy.-Treas.; Nelda Blair, Nancy Cameron, Rhonda Hovater, Billie Ogg, Bob Smith.
EIN: 760632292

63812
Danette M. Ransleben Memorial 4-H Scholarship
c/o Fredericksburg Independent School District
1121 Hwy. 16 S.
Fredericksburg, TX 78624
Application address: c/o Mary Alice Deike, Fredericksburg High School, 300-B W. Main St., Fredericksburg, TX 78624, tel.: (830) 997-7551

Established in 1989 in TX.
Financial data (yr. ended 12/31/00): Assets, $7,949 (M); grants paid, $260; expenditures, $336; qualifying distributions, $260.
Limitations: Giving limited to residents of Fredericksburg, TX.
Application information: Application form required.
Trustee: Fredericksburg Independent School District.
EIN: 746372220

63813
Perrin Air Force Base Research Foundation
P.O. Box 1998
Pottsboro, TX 75076

Established in 2000 in TX.
Financial data (yr. ended 12/31/01): Assets, $7,381 (M); grants paid, $0; gifts received, $10,477; expenditures, $3,290; qualifying distributions, $0.
Directors: Brian W. Blakely, Everett W. Jamison, Shannon E. Thomas.
EIN: 752875370

63814
Into Thin Air, Inc.
808 Shoreline
Wichita Falls, TX 76308

Financial data (yr. ended 12/31/99): Assets, $7,078 (M); grants paid, $0; gifts received, $373; expenditures, $93; qualifying distributions, $93.
Officer: Scott Finch, Treas.
EIN: 752431122

63815
Eaves International Ministries Association
1517 Rockmoor Dr.
Fort Worth, TX 76134-2522

Financial data (yr. ended 12/31/99): Assets, $6,891 (M); grants paid, $0; expenditures, $0; qualifying distributions, $0; giving activities include $132 for programs.

Officers: James F. Eaves, Pres.; Mark F. Eaves, V.P.; Larry Thompson, Secy.
Director: Joe Atkinson.
EIN: 752141412

63816
Ben H. Carpenter Family Foundation
(Formerly Southland Foundation)
P.O. Box 7969
Dallas, TX 75209-0969 (214) 556-0500

Established in 1974 in TX; Classified as a company-sponsored operating foundation in 2001.
Donor(s): Southland Life Insurance Co., Southland Financial Corp., Las Colinas Corp., Southland Corporate Services, Inc., Southland Investment Properties.
Financial data (yr. ended 12/31/01): Assets, $5,840 (M); grants paid, $0; expenditures, $220; qualifying distributions, $220.
Limitations: Applications not accepted. Giving primarily in TX.
Application information: Contributes only to pre-selected organizations.
Officers: Ben H. Carpenter, Pres.; Betty D. Carpenter, V.P. and Secy.-Treas.; Elizabeth C. Frater, V.P.
EIN: 237337606
Codes: CD

63817
Mrs. Janey Schmidt Lawrence Memorial Scholarship Fund
1121 Hwy. 16 S.
Fredericksburg, TX 78624-4228
Application address: c/o Mary Alice Deike, Fredericksburg High School, 300-B W. Main St., Fredericksburg, TX 78624-3712, tel.: (830) 997-7551

Financial data (yr. ended 12/31/00): Assets, $5,448 (M); grants paid, $100; expenditures, $175; qualifying distributions, $100.
Limitations: Giving limited to Fredericksburg, TX.
Application information: Application form required.
Trustee: Fredericksburg Independent School District.
EIN: 237099053

63818
The John B. McGee and Wanda A. McGee Foundation
736 Westwood Dr.
Sherman, TX 75092

Established in 1998 in TX.
Donor(s): John McGee, Wanda McGee.
Financial data (yr. ended 12/31/01): Assets, $5,418 (M); grants paid, $0; gifts received, $425; expenditures, $425; qualifying distributions, $0.
Trustee: Samuel W. Graber.
EIN: 756524508

63819
Biblical Studies Foundation
c/o Patsy Head
206 Sandgrass Cir.
Lufkin, TX 75901

Established around 1995.
Financial data (yr. ended 12/31/99): Assets, $5,176 (M); grants paid, $5,000; gifts received, $56,855; expenditures, $159,752; qualifying distributions, $154,696.
Limitations: Applications not accepted. Giving limited to Dallas, TX.
Application information: Contributes only to pre-selected organizations.

Officers: Joe Head, Pres. and Treas.; Patsy Head, V.P. and Secy.
Director: Dori Head.
EIN: 752572778

63820
International Drug Education Association
4213 Wiley Post Rd.
Dallas, TX 75244

Classified as a private operating foundation in 1992.
Financial data (yr. ended 02/28/00): Assets, $4,977 (M); grants paid, $0; expenditures, $4,078; qualifying distributions, $4,009; giving activities include $29,121 for programs.
Officer and Directors:* Kenneth T. Gerew,* Chair.; Robert L. McCallum, W. Clayton Tuggle.
EIN: 752167143

63821
San Antonio Retired Educators Foundation
12910 Park Forest
San Antonio, TX 78230

Established in 1996 in TX.
Financial data (yr. ended 12/31/99): Assets, $4,768 (M); grants paid, $14,900; gifts received, $2,500; expenditures, $16,838; qualifying distributions, $14,900.
Limitations: Applications not accepted. Giving primarily in San Antonio, TX.
Application information: Contributes only to pre-selected organizations.
Officer: Alicia Wilson, Pres.
EIN: 742671411

63822
Carlile Foundation, Inc.
(Formerly Carlile & Howell Foundation, Inc.)
P.O. Box 2069
Marshall, TX 75671-2069

Classified as a private operating foundation in 1987.
Donor(s): Quinton B. Carlile, Kenneth Q. Carlile, Steve B. Carlile.
Financial data (yr. ended 10/31/00): Assets, $4,741 (M); grants paid, $43,750; gifts received, $47,325; expenditures, $43,805; qualifying distributions, $43,805.
Limitations: Applications not accepted. Giving primarily in TX.
Application information: Contributes only to pre-selected organizations.
Officers and Trustees:* Quinton B. Carlile,* Pres.; Kenneth Q. Carlile,* V.P.; Steve B. Carlile,* V.P.; Penny F. Carlile, Mgr.
EIN: 751729109

63823
William B. & Sadie L. Adamson Charities, Inc.
c/o Lance A. Wood
534 Pine St., Ste. 102
Abilene, TX 79601
Application addresses: c/o Richard L. Spalding, 1850 Elmwood, Abilene, TX 79605, tel.: (915) 698-1578; c/o Sadie L. Adamson, 1200 Oldham Ln., Abilene, TX 79602-4138, tel.: (915) 677-7860

Established in 1998 in TX.
Financial data (yr. ended 12/31/01): Assets, $3,964 (M); grants paid, $0; expenditures, $230; qualifying distributions, $0.
Officers: Richard L. Spalding, Pres.; Sadie L. Adamson, V.P.; Gordon Asbury, Jr., Secy.-Treas.
EIN: 752778328

63824
Spoken Word Christian Ministry Foundation
2334 Ravenwood Dr.
Grand Prairie, TX 75050-2027

Classified as a private operating foundation in 1981.
Financial data (yr. ended 10/31/00): Assets, $3,782 (L); grants paid, $0; expenditures, $382; qualifying distributions, $384; giving activities include $74 for programs.
Directors: Dot Morgan, John E. Morgan, Mike Morgan, Virginia Morgan.
EIN: 751747717

63825
Bickel & Brewer Legal Foundation
1717 Main St., Ste. 4800
Dallas, TX 75201-7362

Financial data (yr. ended 12/31/00): Assets, $3,560 (M); grants paid, $132,720; gifts received, $134,070; expenditures, $132,760; qualifying distributions, $132,760.
Officers: John W. Bickel II, Pres.; William A. Brewer III, V.P.; James S. Renard, Secy.-Treas.
EIN: 752625364

63826
Industrial Tribology Institute
40 N. IH35, Apt. 6C4
Austin, TX 78701-4355

Financial data (yr. ended 09/30/01): Assets, $3,348 (M); grants paid, $2,000; expenditures, $2,610; qualifying distributions, $2,610.
Limitations: Applications not accepted.
Application information: Unsolicited requests for funds not accepted.
Officers: Frederick F. Ling, Pres. and Treas.; Coda H.T. Pan, V.P.; Frances E. Lockwood, Secy.
EIN: 521301028

63827
U.S. Medical Assistance Foundation
221 W. 6th St., Ste. 1500
Austin, TX 78701
Contact: Keith Douglas, Pres.

Established in 2000 in TX.
Donor(s): Keith Douglas.
Financial data (yr. ended 12/31/00): Assets, $3,303 (M); grants paid, $0; gifts received, $18,760; expenditures, $15,457; qualifying distributions, $15,457; giving activities include $15,457 for programs.
Officers: Keith Douglas, Pres.; Virgilio Altamirano, V.P.; Bruce Bagelman, Secy.
EIN: 742936720

63828
Independence Preservation Trust, Inc.
20 Briar Hollow Ln.
Houston, TX 77027

Established in 1999 in TX.
Donor(s): David S. Wolff.
Financial data (yr. ended 12/31/00): Assets, $3,279 (M); grants paid, $0; gifts received, $119,000; expenditures, $85,101; qualifying distributions, $85,101; giving activities include $85,101 for programs.
Directors: Elizabeth T. Brodsky, David L. Lane, David S. Wolff.
EIN: 760606426

63829
J.R. Albert Charitable Trust
245 Mandy Ln.
Alvin, TX 77511

Established in 2000.

Financial data (yr. ended 12/31/00): Assets, $3,000 (M); grants paid, $0; gifts received, $3,000; expenditures, $0; qualifying distributions, $0.
Trustee: J.R. Albert.
EIN: 766163079

63830
Lobby for Hope, Inc.
6100 Pebble Garden Ct.
Austin, TX 78739

Financial data (yr. ended 12/31/99): Assets, $2,963 (M); grants paid, $13,575; gifts received, $16,841; expenditures, $14,001; qualifying distributions, $13,575.
Limitations: Applications not accepted.
Application information: Contributes only to pre-selected organizations.
Officer: Robert T. Ratliff, Pres.
EIN: 742891579

63831
Laurel Dell Manning Foundation for Alternative Cancer Treatment Research
c/o Alan G. Carnrite
2203 Timberloch Pl., Ste. 250
The Woodlands, TX 77380-1102

Established as an operating foundation in 1997 in TX.
Donor(s): Alan G. Carnrite.
Financial data (yr. ended 12/31/00): Assets, $2,845 (M); grants paid, $0; expenditures, $1,989; qualifying distributions, $962; giving activities include $962 for programs.
Limitations: Applications not accepted.
Application information: Contributes only to pre-selected organizations.
Directors: Alan G. Carnrite, David Manning, David R. Watkins.
EIN: 760527192

63832
Twenty First Century Research Institute
(Formerly Armaments Research Institute)
P.O. Box 17123
San Antonio, TX 78217 (210) 493-1197
Contact: Carol McClain, Pres.

Classified as a private operating foundation in 1985.
Financial data (yr. ended 06/30/00): Assets, $2,785 (M); grants paid, $30; expenditures, $30; qualifying distributions, $1,046.
Officers and Trustees:* Carol McClain,* Pres.; Kirt McClain,* Secy.-Treas.
Directors: Gilbert Andreen, Robert Harris.
EIN: 742295559

63833
Howard Humble Scholarship Fund Charitable Trust
8010 Bromley Dr.
Houston, TX 77055
Application address: c/o Nancy Antis, Osborn School Dist., 1226 W. Osborn Rd., Phoenix, AZ 85013, tel.: (602) 234-3366

Financial data (yr. ended 06/30/99): Assets, $2,458 (M); grants paid, $100; expenditures, $100; qualifying distributions, $100.
Limitations: Giving limited to Phoenix, AZ.
Application information: Application form required.
Officers: Alice Simmerman, Pres.; Vera Humble, V.P.; John Musgrove, Treas.; Kathryn Musgrove, Treas.
Trustees: Nancy Kiser, Vaughn Kiser.
EIN: 510197106

63834
See the Sea, Inc.
c/o Jerry J. Radick
223 Southbridge
San Antonio, TX 78216

Financial data (yr. ended 12/31/01): Assets, $2,320 (M); grants paid, $0; expenditures, $29,742; qualifying distributions, $0.
Officers and Directors:* Jerry J. Radick,* Pres.; Don Ruch,* Exec. V.P.; Elliott Cheatham, V.P.; Sharon Sagor,* Secy.; Rosemary Radick,* Treas.; Cynthia Matthews.
EIN: 742370321

63835
San Antonio Peat Marwick Foundation
112 E. Pecan, Ste. 2400
San Antonio, TX 78205 (210) 270-1600
Contact: Park E. Pearson, Pres.

Established in 1983 in TX.
Financial data (yr. ended 06/30/99): Assets, $2,294 (M); grants paid, $7,600; gifts received, $6,197; expenditures, $7,784; qualifying distributions, $7,600.
Limitations: Giving limited to San Antonio, TX.
Application information: Application form not required.
Officer: Park E. Pearson, Pres.
EIN: 742258634

63836
Sol Y Sombra Foundation
(Formerly East West Foundation)
601 Jefferson St., Ste. 4000
Houston, TX 77002-7900

Classified as a private operating foundation in 1988.
Donor(s): Charles Miller, Roxibeth B. Miller.
Financial data (yr. ended 12/31/99): Assets, $2,203 (M); grants paid, $450; gifts received, $3,300; expenditures, $7,258; qualifying distributions, $3,670; giving activities include $3,300 for programs.
Limitations: Applications not accepted. Giving primarily in NM and TX.
Application information: Contributes only to pre-selected organizations.
Officer: Cheryl Charles, Pres.
Directors: Charles Miller, Roxibeth B. Miller, Bob Samples.
EIN: 760200739

63837
Jack T. and Betty A. Brown Foundation
P.O. Box 1483
Austin, TX 78767-1483

Established in 1984 in TX.
Financial data (yr. ended 12/31/01): Assets, $1,858 (M); grants paid, $500; expenditures, $553; qualifying distributions, $553.
Officers: Floyd Brant, Pres.; Steve C. Brown, V.P.; Jack Puryear, Secy.; Gail L. Brown, Treas.
Trustees: Jeff Brown, Kevin Brown, Mary Lauren Brown, Terry W. Brown, Jim Duncan.
EIN: 742369615

63838
Celebrating Life Foundation
c/o Sylvia Dunnavant
1801 Royal Ln., Ste. 810
Dallas, TX 75229-3169

Established in 1995.
Donor(s): Susan G. Kower Foundation.
Financial data (yr. ended 06/30/00): Assets, $1,740 (M); grants paid, $0; gifts received, $140,412; expenditures, $142,993; qualifying distributions, $142,993.
Officers: Madge Barnes, Pres.; Jewell Moore, V.P.; Shirley Levinston, Secy.; Sylvia Dunnavant, Exec. Dir.
EIN: 752597120

63839
The CB Trust
1177 Rockingham, Ste. 200
Richardson, TX 75080

Donor(s): Cloyce K. Box.
Financial data (yr. ended 12/31/01): Assets, $1,659 (M); grants paid, $4,600; gifts received, $6,760; expenditures, $6,941; qualifying distributions, $6,941.
Limitations: Giving primarily in PA and TX.
Officer: Tom Box, Admin.
Trustees: Frank Gifford, James F. Neal.
EIN: 751815162
Codes: GTI

63840
Bernard Aptaker U. S. Foundation
6363 Woodway, Ste. 200
Houston, TX 77057

Established in 2001 in TX.
Donor(s): Bernard Aptaker.
Financial data (yr. ended 12/31/01): Assets, $1,550 (M); grants paid, $200; gifts received, $2,250; expenditures, $700; qualifying distributions, $200.
Officers: Bernard Aptaker, Pres.; T. Michael Wall, V. P.; William A. Teague, Secy.
EIN: 760689291

63841
The Harvey Carter Charitable Foundation
7502 Greenville Ave., Ste. 700
Dallas, TX 75231

Established in 2000.
Financial data (yr. ended 12/31/00): Assets, $867 (L); grants paid, $2,100; gifts received, $3,100; expenditures, $2,254; qualifying distributions, $2,100.
Limitations: Giving primarily in Dallas, TX.
Officer: Harvey L. Carter III, Pres.
EIN: 752860812

63842
Donald & Maria Lott Medical Assistance Foundation
15603 Rill Ln.
Houston, TX 77062

Established in 2000 in TX.
Financial data (yr. ended 12/31/00): Assets, $800 (M); grants paid, $0; gifts received, $800; expenditures, $0; qualifying distributions, $0.
Directors: Fred Jones, Donald Lott, Maria Lott.
EIN: 760664787

63843
David Kendall Danciger Charitable Foundation
12221 Merit Dr., No. 1700
Dallas, TX 75251

Donor(s): David K. Danciger.
Financial data (yr. ended 12/31/00): Assets, $796 (M); grants paid, $5,183; gifts received, $4,900; expenditures, $5,233; qualifying distributions, $5,182.
Limitations: Applications not accepted. Giving primarily in Denver, CO and Dallas, TX.
Application information: Unsolicited requests for funds not accepted.
Officers: David K. Danciger, Pres.; Cameron Dee Sewell, V.P.; Emma Alvis Danciger, Secy.; Robert D. Barnett, Treas.
EIN: 752510985

63844
Animal Haven
c/o Glenda G. Gillock
8647 Santa Clara Dr.
Dallas, TX 75218-4130

Classified as a private operating foundation in 1992.
Donor(s): Glenda Gillock.
Financial data (yr. ended 06/30/00): Assets, $720 (M); grants paid, $0; gifts received, $12,304; expenditures, $12,304; qualifying distributions, $0; giving activities include $12,225 for programs.
Officers: Glenda Gillock, Pres. and Treas.; Sharon Masterson, V.P. and Secy.; Cindy Von Keisler Czarnecky, V.P.
EIN: 752391827

63845
Friends of Francis
P.O. Box 495
Levelland, TX 79336

Classified as a private operating foundation in 1991.
Financial data (yr. ended 12/31/00): Assets, $641 (M); grants paid, $0; gifts received, $35,096; expenditures, $34,966; qualifying distributions, $34,966; giving activities include $34,966 for programs.
Officers: Philomina DeGennard, Pres.; Arlene Brooks, Secy.-Treas.
EIN: 751966683

63846
Steve Heath Memorial ROTC Scholarship
12618 Sandpiper
San Antonio, TX 78233-7236 (210) 655-5317
Contact: Donald Heath, Tr.

Classified as a private operating foundation in 1991.
Donor(s): Cynthia Heath, Donald Heath.
Financial data (yr. ended 12/31/00): Assets, $570 (M); grants paid, $31,616; gifts received, $35,550; expenditures, $39,083; qualifying distributions, $0.
Limitations: Giving limited to San Antonio, TX.
Application information: Application form required.
Trustees: Cynthia Heath, Donald Heath.
EIN: 742591005
Codes: GTI

63847
Shane Michael Beene Memorial Scholarship
13157 County Rd. 3136
Gladewater, TX 75647

Financial data (yr. ended 12/31/00): Assets, $551 (L); grants paid, $800; gifts received, $1,335; expenditures, $1,051; qualifying distributions, $0.
Officer: Patsy Beene, Pres.
EIN: 752848229

63848
Swantkowski Charitable Foundation
c/o Ronald E. Swantkowski
619 Flaghoist Ln.
Houston, TX 77079-2552

Established in 1991 in TX.
Financial data (yr. ended 12/31/99): Assets, $541 (M); grants paid, $7,492; gifts received, $3,000; expenditures, $7,492; qualifying distributions, $7,492.
Limitations: Applications not accepted. Giving primarily in TX.
Application information: Contributes only to pre-selected organizations.

63848—TEXAS

Trustees: Bonnie Swantkowski, Ronald E. Swantkowski.
EIN: 760359761

63849
The Abilene Foundation
c/o William P. Hallman, Jr.
201 Main St., Ste. 3200
Fort Worth, TX 76102

Established in 1986 in CA and TX.
Donor(s): William P. Hallman, Jr.
Financial data (yr. ended 12/31/01): Assets, $436 (M); grants paid, $0; expenditures, $750; qualifying distributions, $0.
Trustees: Nancy Hallman, William P. Hallman, Jr., Stephen G. Shapiro.
EIN: 954065765

63850
Animalkind Foundation
P.O. Box 496
Manor, TX 78653-0496

Established in 1999 in TX.
Financial data (yr. ended 12/31/99): Assets, $315 (M); grants paid, $0; gifts received, $7,894; expenditures, $7,580; qualifying distributions, $7,580; giving activities include $7,580 for programs.
Limitations: Giving primarily in TX.
Officer and Directors:* Vallee Green,* Pres.; Matty Luker, Susi Sands.
EIN: 142771357

63851
Casa de Colores
c/o Genevieve Vaughan
P.O. Box 3138
Austin, TX 78764

Donor(s): Genevieve Vaughan.
Financial data (yr. ended 12/31/00): Assets, $223 (M); grants paid, $0; gifts received, $31,423; expenditures, $33,779; qualifying distributions, $33,617; giving activities include $26,789 for programs.
Officers: Genevieve Vaughan, Pres.; Liliana Wilson, V.P.
Director: Helga Garcia-Garza.
EIN: 760340954

63852
Christina Fund, Inc.
c/o Michael Skadden
10001 W. Park Dr., Ste. 30
Houston, TX 77042-5933

Donor(s): Gamet Jex.
Financial data (yr. ended 12/31/00): Assets, $193 (M); grants paid, $9,850; gifts received, $10,000; expenditures, $10,028; qualifying distributions, $10,028.
Limitations: Applications not accepted. Giving primarily in TX.
Application information: Contributes only to pre-selected organizations.
Officers and Directors:* Ganeut Jea,* Chair., Pres., and Treas.; Miehail J. Skaden,* V.P. and Secy.; Ana Moliner.
EIN: 760577743

63853
Rudisill Family Foundation, Inc.
8705 Katy Freeway, Ste. 400
Houston, TX 77024

Established in 1998 in TX.
Financial data (yr. ended 06/30/01): Assets, $179 (M); grants paid, $0; gifts received, $4,152; expenditures, $3,971; qualifying distributions, $0.

Officers and Directors:* H. Clifford Rudisill,* Pres.; Edward L. Rudisill,* V.P. and Treas.; James Rheudasil,* Secy.
EIN: 752771051

63854
Marsh Foundation, Inc.
P.O. Box 460
Dallas, TX 75221

Financial data (yr. ended 06/30/01): Assets, $134 (M); grants paid, $0; gifts received, $200; expenditures, $264; qualifying distributions, $0.
Limitations: Applications not accepted.
Application information: Contributes only to pre-selected organizations.
Officers and Directors:* Stanley Marsh III,* Pres.; Estelle Marsh, V.P.; Tom F. Marsh,* V.P.; Joe Coffman, Secy.-Treas.
EIN: 751247382

63855
International Christian Foundation
(Formerly National Christian Foundation)
7314 Durado Dr.
Fort Worth, TX 76179-3119

Change of name in 1994 from Texas Christian Foundation.
Financial data (yr. ended 06/30/02): Assets, $73 (M); grants paid, $0; gifts received, $104; expenditures, $90; qualifying distributions, $0.
Officers: Homer G. Ritchie, Pres.; Omer G. Ritchie, V.P.; Brenda J. Ritchie, Secy.-Treas.
Director: Cynthia Ritchie.
EIN: 751242341

63856
NLF Education Foundation, Inc.
1256 Main St., Ste. 252
Southlake, TX 76092

Established in 2000 in TX.
Financial data (yr. ended 12/31/01): Assets, $1 (M); grants paid, $0; gifts received, $5,000; expenditures, $1,621; qualifying distributions, $0.
Officer: W.A. Bradley, Pres. and Secy.-Treas.
EIN: 752524395

63857
Sigrist Foundation
c/o J.R. Sigrist
1602 S. Airport Dr., Ste. 63
Weslaco, TX 78596

Established in 2000.
Donor(s): James R. Sigrist, Audrey M. Sigrist.
Financial data (yr. ended 12/31/01): Assets, $1 (M); grants paid, $2,982; gifts received, $208,125; expenditures, $3,856; qualifying distributions, $2,982.
Officer: Audrey M. Sigrist, Secy.
EIN: 742960993

63858
Christian Higher Education Foundation, Inc.
1071 N. Judge Ely Blvd., Ste. 6407
Abilene, TX 79601-3853

Established in 1996.
Financial data (yr. ended 05/31/01): Assets, $0 (M); grants paid, $0; expenditures, $3,970; qualifying distributions, $0.
Limitations: Applications not accepted.
Application information: Contributes only to pre-selected organizations.
Officers: John C. Stevens, Pres.; Milton B. Fletcher, Secy.
Directors: Clifton L. Ganus, Harold Hazlip, J. Terry Johnson.
EIN: 311501857

63859
Ramasahayam Nithin Foundation
c/o R. Ashok Reddy, M.D.
4204 Canyon Side Trail
Austin, TX 78731

Established in 1996 in TX.
Financial data (yr. ended 06/30/99): Assets, $0 (M); grants paid, $9,536; gifts received, $6,141; expenditures, $9,684; qualifying distributions, $9,536.
Officers: R. Ashok Reddy, M.D., Pres.; Geeta Reddy, M.D., V.P.; Sarita Reddy, Secy.
EIN: 742788879

63860
Texas Baroque Ensemble, Inc.
2221 Royal Crest Dr.
Garland, TX 75043-1022

Financial data (yr. ended 12/31/00): Assets, $0 (M); grants paid, $0; gifts received, $1,134; expenditures, $4,491; qualifying distributions, $0.
Officers: Rosemary Heffley, Pres.; Brooks Morris II, V.P.; K. Charles Lang, Secy.-Treas.
EIN: 751762680

UTAH

63861
Thanksgiving Point Institute, Inc.
251 River Park Dr.
Provo, UT 84604   (801) 266-1266

Established in 1997 in UT.
Donor(s): Alan Ashton, Karen Ashton.
Financial data (yr. ended 02/28/01): Assets, $24,610,189 (M); grants paid, $0; gifts received, $1,082,132; expenditures, $10,471,480; qualifying distributions, $4,918,298; giving activities include $5,553,182 for programs.
Trustees: Alan Ashton, Karen Ashton, Ralph Rasmussen.
EIN: 841416158

63862
Smith-Pettit Foundation
514 W. 400 N.
Salt Lake City, UT 84116

Established in 1999.
Donor(s): George D. Smith, Jr.
Financial data (yr. ended 12/31/01): Assets, $8,767,866 (M); grants paid, $7,656; gifts received, $4,049,368; expenditures, $487,949; qualifying distributions, $7,656.
Limitations: Applications not accepted.
Application information: Contributes only to pre-selected organizations.
Officers: George D. Smith, Jr., Pres. and Treas.; Gary J. Bergera, V.P. and Secy.
Director: David P. Wright.
EIN: 870641442

63863
Spendlove Research Foundation
c/o Hillyard, Tyler & Hamilton
55 N. Main, Ste. 403
Logan, UT 84321-4584
Application address: 160 N. Main St., Logan, UT 84321, tel.: (435) 752-9557
Contact: Alan Spendlove, Exec. Dir.

Established in 1989 in UT.

Donor(s): Rex S. Spendlove, Reta A. Spendlove, Alan Spendlove.
Financial data (yr. ended 12/31/00): Assets, $6,854,262 (M); grants paid, $0; expenditures, $519,414; qualifying distributions, $598,943.
Limitations: Giving primarily in UT.
Officers and Directors:* Rex S. Spendlove,* Pres.; Reta A. Spendlove,* V.P.; Debbie Spendlove,* Secy.-Treas.; Alan Spendlove, Exec. Dir.; Lori Arnold, Lisa Cornwell, Cheri Murdoch.
EIN: 870461699

63864
Stanley Research Foundation
4800 Oak Terr.
Salt Lake City, UT 84124
Contact: Theodore H. Stanley, M.D., Pres.

Established in 1978 in UT.
Donor(s): PPD Pharmaco, Inc.
Financial data (yr. ended 12/31/01): Assets, $5,516,407 (M); grants paid, $7,500; expenditures, $263,225; qualifying distributions, $230,570; giving activities include $230,570 for programs.
Limitations: Giving on a national basis.
Officers: Theodore H. Stanley, M.D., Pres.; Ellen Stanley, V.P.; Mary Ann Stanley, Secy.
EIN: 870334696

63865
Sarah Daft Home
737 S. 1300 E.
Salt Lake City, UT 84102-3799

Financial data (yr. ended 12/31/00): Assets, $2,790,905 (M); grants paid, $0; gifts received, $34,469; expenditures, $693,256; qualifying distributions, $617,481; giving activities include $617,481 for programs.
Officers and Trustees:* Shannon Huff Jacobs,* Pres.; Marci Milligan,* 1st V.P.; Don Francom,* 2nd V.P.; Pat Curtis,* Secy.; Barbara DeSpain,* Treas.; Ramona Linnell,* Exec. Dir.; Kirsten Turner Ball, Margo Bates, Ellen A. Christensen, John Diaz, David Ellis, Amanda Lambert, Bruce Miya, Montenna Porter, John W. Robinson, Theresa Steadman, Lou Ann Stevens.
Advisory Committee Members: Joyce D. McNally, Irene Warr.
EIN: 870213532

63866
Price Automotive Museum
35 Century Park Way
Salt Lake City, UT 84115

Established in 1999 in UT.
Donor(s): John Price, Fairfax Realty, Inc.
Financial data (yr. ended 11/30/01): Assets, $2,110,616 (M); grants paid, $0; expenditures, $24,080; qualifying distributions, $0.
Directors: J. Steven Price, John Price, Anthony R. Wallin, M.D.
EIN: 870644630

63867
Ahmar Family Foundation
6415 S. 3000, E., Ste. 200
Salt Lake City, UT 84121
Application address: c/o Hasan Ahmar, A.F.F., Kawather Bldg., 6th Fl., Facing Marriott, Beirut, Lebanon

Established in 2000 in UT. Classified as a private operating foundation in 2001.
Donor(s): Mohamad Ahmar.
Financial data (yr. ended 12/31/01): Assets, $2,060,993 (M); grants paid, $22,547; gifts received, $50,000; expenditures, $71,547; qualifying distributions, $22,547.

Limitations: Giving limited to Beirut, Lebanon.
Officer: Mohamad Ahmar, Pres. and Secy.-Treas.
Trustees: Hania Ahmar, Hasan Ahmar.
EIN: 522296581

63868
Haven J. & Bonnie Rae Barlow Family Foundation
377 N. Main St.
Layton, UT 84041-2205

Established in 1998 in UT.
Donor(s): Haven J. Barlow, Bonnie Rae Barlow.
Financial data (yr. ended 12/31/00): Assets, $2,029,512 (M); grants paid, $56,500; expenditures, $56,951; qualifying distributions, $46,048.
Limitations: Applications not accepted. Giving primarily in UT.
Application information: Contributes only to pre-selected organizations.
Trustee: Bonnie Rae Barlow, Haven J. Barlow.
EIN: 870563722

63869
The Rose Foundation
3507 N. University Ave., Ste.100
Provo, UT 84604

Established in 1996 in UT.
Donor(s): Nedra Roney.
Financial data (yr. ended 12/31/00): Assets, $1,408,581 (M); grants paid, $1,332,056; expenditures, $1,508,051; qualifying distributions, $1,505,221.
Limitations: Applications not accepted. Giving primarily in UT.
Application information: Contributes only to pre-selected organizations.
Trustees: Tom Branch, Nedra Roney.
EIN: 870565388
Codes: FD

63870
Edward G. Callister Foundation
10 E. South Temple, Ste. 900
Salt Lake City, UT 84133-1186

Established in 1997 in UT.
Donor(s): Louis H. Callister, Jr., Sharee Paulson, The Alsam Foundation.
Financial data (yr. ended 12/31/00): Assets, $1,332,356 (M); grants paid, $0; gifts received, $6,667; expenditures, $158,365; qualifying distributions, $152,147; giving activities include $141,769 for programs.
Limitations: Applications not accepted.
Application information: Contributes only to pre-selected organizations.
Officers: Louis H. Callister, Jr.,* Chair.; Ellen G. Callister,* Pres.; Isabel C. Pande,* V.P.; Jane C. Hughes,* Secy.; Ann C. Dessert,* Treas.
Trustees: Richard C. Barton, David R. Callister, J. Andrew Callister, Sharee C. Paulson.
EIN: 841405811

63871
Youth Enrichment Foundation
P.O. Box 70900
West Valley, UT 84170-0900

Established in 1993 in UT. Classified as a private operating foundation in 1994.
Donor(s): Bart C. Warner.
Financial data (yr. ended 12/31/00): Assets, $1,085,538 (M); grants paid, $0; gifts received, $40,000; expenditures, $506,176; qualifying distributions, $413,105; giving activities include $413,105 for programs.
Limitations: Applications not accepted.

Application information: Contributes only to pre-selected organizations.
Officers: James B. Cox, Pres.; James N. Warner, Secy.-Treas.
EIN: 870514460

63872
The Clara Elizabeth Wright Jones Foundation
3602 S. 3000 W.
West Valley City, UT 84119

Established in 2000 in UT.
Donor(s): Mae Rose Jones, Lorraine Jones.
Financial data (yr. ended 12/31/00): Assets, $1,006,284 (M); grants paid, $19,218; gifts received, $1,000,000; expenditures, $33,620; qualifying distributions, $19,218.
Limitations: Applications not accepted. Giving primarily in Salt Lake City, UT.
Application information: Contributes only to pre-selected organizations.
Directors: Lorraine Jones, Mae Rose Jones.
EIN: 870659647

63873
Salt Lake County Fish & Game Association
3747 Loretta Dr.
Salt Lake City, UT 84106-2915

Classified as a private operating foundation in 1989.
Financial data (yr. ended 09/30/00): Assets, $788,000 (M); grants paid, $0; expenditures, $33,267; qualifying distributions, $26,501; giving activities include $17,998 for programs.
Officers: Charles Canick, Pres.; Greg Bugnl, V.P.; Karen Potts, Secy.; David Nuttall, Treas.
EIN: 870222187

63874
Legacy Foundation
3521 N. University Ave., Ste. 200
Provo, UT 84604

Established in 1995 in UT.
Donor(s): Larry H. Miller, Lorin Pugh.
Financial data (yr. ended 12/31/99): Assets, $714,126 (M); grants paid, $0; gifts received, $281,649; expenditures, $244,898; qualifying distributions, $228,773; giving activities include $228,855 for programs.
Officers: A. Lynn Scoresby, Pres. and Treas.; Marianne Heaps, V.P.; Dorothy Scoresby, V.P.; Douglas W. Morrison, Secy.
EIN: 870475349

63875
Letty Jones Heritage Foundation
P.O. Box 1053
Monticello, UT 84535-1053 (435) 587-2484
Contact: Corinne Roring, Pres.

Established in 1996 in UT.
Financial data (yr. ended 12/31/00): Assets, $709,770 (M); grants paid, $73,911; gifts received, $68,942; expenditures, $80,714; qualifying distributions, $93,911; giving activities include $73,811 for programs.
Limitations: Giving primarily in Monticello, UT.
Application information: Application form not required.
Officers and Trustees:* Corinne Roring,* Pres.; Cooper Jones,* V.P.; Janie Lauritren, Harold C. Young.
EIN: 841367581

63876
Rosenbruch Foundation, Inc.
(also known as World Wildlife Heritage Foundation)
P.O. Box 471
Santa Clara, UT 84765

Established in 1999 in UT.
Financial data (yr. ended 12/31/01): Assets, $700,945 (M); grants paid, $0; gifts received, $57,150; expenditures, $78,820; qualifying distributions, $0.
Officers: Jimmie C. Rosenbruch, Pres.; Mary Ann Rosenbruch, V.P.; Angela R. Hammer, Secy.-Treas.
EIN: 870628961

63877
Florence Gay Smith Foundation
2191 E. Iverson Woods Pl.
Salt Lake City, UT 84117

Established in 1982.
Donor(s): Nicholas G. Smith, Marion B. Smith.
Financial data (yr. ended 12/31/00): Assets, $620,203 (M); grants paid, $33,925; expenditures, $35,520; qualifying distributions, $35,520.
Limitations: Applications not accepted. Giving primarily in UT.
Officers: Nicholas G. Smith,* Pres.; Marion B. Smith,* V.P.; M. Lindy Burton,* Secy.
EIN: 870368865
Codes: GTI

63878
The Eugene and Kristine Hughes Charitable Foundation
136 S. Main St., Ste. 404
Salt Lake City, UT 84101-1601

Established in 1998 in UT.
Donor(s): Eugene Hughes, Kristine Hughes.
Financial data (yr. ended 05/31/00): Assets, $442,931 (M); grants paid, $0; expenditures, $15,046; qualifying distributions, $347,648; giving activities include $30,661 for programs.
Officers and Trustees:* Chris R. Hughes,* Pres.; Craig E. Hughes,* Secy.-Treas.; Jeni H. McCoard.
EIN: 870618294

63879
Joel And Diana Peterson Family Foundation
111 E. Broadway, Ste. 1080
Salt Lake City, UT 84111

Classified as a private operating foundation in 1999.
Financial data (yr. ended 12/31/00): Assets, $295,016 (M); grants paid, $31,600; gifts received, $215,722; expenditures, $32,255; qualifying distributions, $31,600.
Limitations: Applications not accepted. Giving primarily in UT.
Application information: Contributes only to pre-selected organizations.
Trustees: Rebecca Dowdell, Travis Dowdell, Mark Harris, Sarah Harris, Diana J. Peterson, Joel C. Peterson.
EIN: 870624155

63880
National Center on Shaken Baby Syndrome
2955 Harrison Blvd., Ste. 102
Ogden, UT 84403

Established in 2000 in UT.
Donor(s): Cornucopia Committee, Deseret Mutual Benefit Administration, Intermountain Health Care, NSW Dept. of Community Service, Stewart Education Foundation, Primary Children's Hospital, Public Employees Health Program, Regence Bluecross Blueshield, W.C. Swanson Family Foundation, Utah Dept. of Health.
Financial data (yr. ended 06/30/01): Assets, $288,778 (M); grants paid, $0; gifts received, $933,613; expenditures, $748,248; qualifying distributions, $703,661; giving activities include $703,661 for programs.
Limitations: Applications not accepted.
Application information: Contributes only to pre-selected organizations.
Officer: Marilyn Sandberg, Exec. Dir.
Directors: Hon. Roger Dutson, Chuck Swanson.
EIN: 870653452

63881
The Richard W. Erickson Foundation
3865 S. Wasatch Blvd., Ste. 300
Salt Lake City, UT 84109
Application address: P.O. Box 400, West Jordan, UT 84084-0400, tel.: (801) 561-3161
Contact: Richard Erickson, Tr.

Classified as a private operating foundation in 2000 in UT.
Financial data (yr. ended 12/31/01): Assets, $284,484 (M); grants paid, $0; gifts received, $125,000; expenditures, $400; qualifying distributions, $0.
Trustees: Richard W. Erickson, Rita Erickson, Robert Muir, Richard Thomas.
EIN: 870644559

63882
Larry Elsner Art Foundation
1229 Thrushwood Dr.
Logan, UT 84321-4831
Contact: Yoko Y. Elsner, Pres.

Established in 1992 in UT.
Donor(s): Yoko Y. Elsner, Tami I. Elsner, Marie Eccles Caine Foundation.
Financial data (yr. ended 12/31/99): Assets, $269,224 (M); grants paid, $11,448; gifts received, $63,490; expenditures, $19,909; qualifying distributions, $15,390.
Limitations: Giving limited to Logan, UT.
Officers: Yoko Y. Elsner, Pres.; Peter Briggs, V.P.; Tami I. Elsner, Secy.-Treas.
EIN: 870491761

63883
TDA Foundation
620 S. Main St.
Bountiful, UT 84010

Established in 2001.
Donor(s): Ken M. Flake.
Financial data (yr. ended 12/31/01): Assets, $235,108 (M); grants paid, $0; gifts received, $250,000; expenditures, $20,196; qualifying distributions, $0.
Officers: Ken M. Flake, Pres.; Kristi Taylor, Treas.
EIN: 870546030

63884
Barrick Mercur Gold Mine Foundation, Inc.
c/o David Bird
P.O. Box 11898
Salt Lake City, UT 84147-1898
Application address: c/o A. Bruce Dummings, 60 Benchview Dr., Tooele, UT 84074, tel.: (435) 882-1298

Established in 1989 in UT as a company-sponsored operating foundation.
Donor(s): Barrick Mercur Gold Mines, Inc.
Financial data (yr. ended 12/31/00): Assets, $234,106 (M); grants paid, $16,000; expenditures, $19,237; qualifying distributions, $16,000.
Limitations: Giving primarily in Tooele County, UT.
Trustee: Sam Woodruff.
EIN: 742546494
Codes: CD

63885
Tiger Island Foundation
6415 S. 3000, E., Ste. 200
Salt Lake City, UT 84121
Application address: 11041 Delphinus Way, San Diego, CA 92126
Contact: Derek Punch, Pres.

Established in 2000 in UT.
Donor(s): Derek Punch.
Financial data (yr. ended 12/31/00): Assets, $222,555 (M); grants paid, $0; gifts received, $230,055; expenditures, $7,500; qualifying distributions, $0.
Officer: Derek Punch, Pres. and Secy.-Treas.
Trustees: David Punch, Paul Punch.
EIN: 522299098

63886
The Holbrooke Foundation
1338 S. Foothill Dr., Ste. 262
Salt Lake City, UT 84108

Established in 2000 in UT.
Financial data (yr. ended 12/31/01): Assets, $207,745 (M); grants paid, $0; expenditures, $0; qualifying distributions, $0.
Trustees: Terri S. Holbrooke, Whitney Lynn Holbrooke, Bernie R. Schmertz.
EIN: 870654674

63887
Progressive Health Foundation
6415 S. 3000, E., Ste. 200
Salt Lake City, UT 84121
Application address: 2828 S. Tamiami Trail, Sarasota, FL 32439
Contact: William McComb, Pres.

Established in 2000 in UT.
Donor(s): William McComb.
Financial data (yr. ended 12/31/00): Assets, $178,125 (M); grants paid, $0; gifts received, $183,125; expenditures, $5,000; qualifying distributions, $0.
Officer: William McComb, Pres. and Secy.-Treas.
Trustees: D. Michael Bishop, Roger K. Fuller.
EIN: 522303658

63888
Melchizedek Priesthood Properties, Inc.
3603 S. 550 W.
Bountiful, UT 84010-8021

Classified as a private operating foundation in 1968.
Donor(s): Leilah W. Glade, Mary Wood Cannon.
Financial data (yr. ended 12/31/00): Assets, $163,241 (M); grants paid, $0; gifts received, $156; expenditures, $11,280; qualifying distributions, $11,280; giving activities include $11,280 for programs.
Officers: Mary Wood Cannon, Mgr.; Suzina Glade, Mgr.
EIN: 876130029

63889
Hector C. Haight Historic Foundation
1283 E. South Temple
Salt Lake City, UT 84102-1759

Established in 1988 in ID.
Donor(s): David B. Haight.
Financial data (yr. ended 06/30/01): Assets, $161,158 (M); grants paid, $0; gifts received, $7,000; expenditures, $3,003; qualifying distributions, $0.

Trustees: David B. Haight, Robert P. Haight, Ruby O. Haight.
EIN: 742503044

63890
Marlow & Vella Woodward Foundation, Inc.
P.O. Box 540298
North Salt Lake, UT 84054-0298

Established in 1999 in UT.
Financial data (yr. ended 12/31/01): Assets, $144,597 (M); grants paid, $15,080; gifts received, $1,250; expenditures, $15,131; qualifying distributions, $15,080.
Application information: Application form required.
Officer: Cliff Lillywhite, Pres.; Brad Mather, V.P.; Kent P. Woodward, V.P.; Paul D. Simkins, Treas.
EIN: 870616969

63891
Grant B. Culley, Jr. Foundation
10747 S. Hidden Ridge Ln.
Sandy, UT 84092-6536

Established in 1997.
Donor(s): Suzanne L. Culley.
Financial data (yr. ended 12/31/00): Assets, $144,061 (M); grants paid, $0; gifts received, $102,051; expenditures, $79,933; qualifying distributions, $74,158; giving activities include $48,775 for programs.
Trustees: Suzanne L.C. Bounous, Suzanne L. Culley, Robyn L.C. Garner.
EIN: 911824654

63892
The Hunter Webb Foundation
2784 Foothill Dr.
Ogden, UT 84403

Established in 1996 in UT.
Donor(s): Daniel Hunter, Margaret Hunter.
Financial data (yr. ended 12/31/99): Assets, $112,043 (M); grants paid, $12,950; gifts received, $25,000; expenditures, $16,760; qualifying distributions, $12,950.
Limitations: Applications not accepted.
Trustees: Daniel Hunter, Margaret Hunter.
EIN: 561975615

63893
The Utah Automobile Museum
9650 Buttonwood Dr.
Sandy, UT 84092

Established in 2000 in UT.
Donor(s): Alex G. Oblad, Bessie E. Oblad.
Financial data (yr. ended 06/30/01): Assets, $107,967 (M); grants paid, $0; gifts received, $147,477; expenditures, $40,831; qualifying distributions, $146,831; giving activities include $146,831 for programs.
Limitations: Applications not accepted.
Application information: Contributes only to pre-selected organizations.
Officer: Alex Edward Oblad, Pres.
EIN: 870654649

63894
Trauma Awareness & Treatment Center, Inc.
715 E. 3900 S., Ste. 109
Salt Lake City, UT 84107

Established in 1995 in UT.
Financial data (yr. ended 12/31/01): Assets, $104,493 (M); grants paid, $0; gifts received, $6,629; expenditures, $398,949; qualifying distributions, $0; giving activities include $398,949 for programs.
Director: Lawrence D. Beall.
EIN: 870534270

63895
Waldo E. Harvey Family Foundation
1785 Fort Douglas Cir.
Salt Lake City, UT 84103-4451
(801) 355-6291
Contact: Clyde E. Harvey, Tr.

Established in 1990 in UT.
Donor(s): Clyde E. Harvey.
Financial data (yr. ended 12/31/99): Assets, $51,624 (M); grants paid, $11,335; expenditures, $11,737; qualifying distributions, $11,319.
Limitations: Giving limited to Salt Lake City, UT.
Application information: Application form not required.
Trustees: Clyde E. Harvey, Merilyn Harvey, Paul E. Harvey, Marjann Hicken.
EIN: 746374603

63896
John L. and Ardis J. Piers Private
c/o Ardis J. Piers
1356 Fairway Rd.
St. George, UT 84790-7713
Contact: Ardis J. Piers, Pres.

Established in 1999 in UT.
Donor(s): Ardis J. Piers.
Financial data (yr. ended 12/31/99): Assets, $45,047 (M); grants paid, $2,255; gifts received, $17,000; expenditures, $3,570; qualifying distributions, $2,255.
Limitations: Giving primarily in St. George, UT.
Officer: Ardis J. Piers, Pres.
EIN: 621733598

63897
H. Tracy Hall Foundation
2185 S. Larsen Pkwy.
Provo, UT 84606 (801) 374-6222
Contact: David R. Hall, Pres.

Financial data (yr. ended 12/31/00): Assets, $39,529 (M); grants paid, $0; expenditures, $12,753; qualifying distributions, $12,753; giving activities include $36,000 for programs.
Officers and Trustees:* David R. Hall, Pres. and Treas.; H. Tracy Hall,* V.P.; Douglas W. Morrison,* V.P.
EIN: 870577178

63898
Papa's Pedigree Family Organization
570 S. 75 W.
Providence, UT 84332-9730
Contact: Blaine Hancey, Pres.

Financial data (yr. ended 12/31/01): Assets, $37,148 (M); grants paid, $3,500; gifts received, $300; expenditures, $3,553; qualifying distributions, $3,514.
Limitations: Giving on an international basis.
Officer: Blaine Hancey, Pres.
EIN: 870344169

63899
Goodwin-Bird Family Association, Inc.
135 E. Allegheny Way
Alpine, UT 84004

Donor(s): H. Dale Goodwin.
Financial data (yr. ended 10/31/00): Assets, $30,451 (M); grants paid, $0; gifts received, $5,000; expenditures, $8,319; qualifying distributions, $5,553; giving activities include $8,319 for programs.
Officers: H. Dale Goodwin, Pres.; Alice B. Goodwin, V.P.; Vonda G. Proctor, Secy.
EIN: 237420716

63900
Larry H. Miller Education Foundation
5650 S. State St.
Murray, UT 84107

Established in 1996 in UT.
Donor(s): Karen G. Miller, Lawrence H. Miller.
Financial data (yr. ended 12/31/99): Assets, $27,864 (M); grants paid, $278,510; gifts received, $303,236; expenditures, $280,070; qualifying distributions, $280,070.
Limitations: Applications not accepted. Giving limited to Murray, UT.
Officers: Karen G. Miller, Pres.; Larry H. Miller, Secy.-Treas.
Trustees: Gregory S. Miller, Roger L. Miller, G. Stephen Tarbet.
EIN: 870560678
Codes: GTI

63901
The Maher Foundation
1583 E. New Bedford Dr.
Salt Lake City, UT 84103

Established in 2000 in UT.
Donor(s): David L. Maher, Marilyn J. Maher.
Financial data (yr. ended 12/31/00): Assets, $26,855 (M); grants paid, $45,500; gifts received, $73,750; expenditures, $47,692; qualifying distributions, $47,692.
Limitations: Applications not accepted. Giving on a national basis, with emphasis on CO and ME.
Application information: Contributes only to pre-selected organizations.
Trustees: Ann M. Fox, Daniel E. Fox, A. Leslie Maher, David L. Maher, Marilyn J. Maher, Mark G. Maher, Michael J. Maher.
EIN: 870648878

63902
Dozens of Cousins Foundation
500 Eagle Tower, 60 S. Temple
Salt Lake City, UT 84111

Donor(s): Sharon Hintze.
Financial data (yr. ended 07/31/00): Assets, $23,922 (M); grants paid, $0; gifts received, $10,050; expenditures, $2,799; qualifying distributions, $2,799; giving activities include $200 for programs.
Limitations: Applications not accepted.
Application information: Contributes only to pre-selected organizations.
Trustees: Sharon Hintze, Mary Anne Q. Wood.
EIN: 870545178

63903
Dr. Stephen N. Hull Family Association, Inc.
4611 N. Brookshire Cir.
Provo, UT 84604

Donor(s): Stephen N. Hull, M.D.‡
Financial data (yr. ended 11/30/99): Assets, $21,087 (M); grants paid, $0; gifts received, $8,800; expenditures, $8,800; qualifying distributions, $8,800; giving activities include $8,800 for programs.
Trustees: Mildred B. Bailey, Sandra B. Hull.
EIN: 510210316

63904
Benjamin Peel Family Foundation
1335 N. 200 E.
Mapleton, UT 84664

Classified as a private operating foundation in 1977.
Financial data (yr. ended 12/31/01): Assets, $18,215 (M); grants paid, $0; gifts received,

63904—UTAH

$2,000; expenditures, $1,081; qualifying distributions, $0.
Officers and Trustees:* James J. Rose, Jr.,* Pres. and Treas.; Robert O. Rose, Secy.; Guy Buckley, Leroy Peel.
EIN: 860327577

63905
Thai Development Foundation
5872 S. 900 E., Ste. 250
Salt Lake City, UT 84121
Application address: 2011 Mapleview Dr., Bountiful, UT 84010, tel.: (801) 298-2077
Contact: Harvey D. Brown, Chair.

Established in 1999 in UT.
Financial data (yr. ended 12/31/01): Assets, $17,128 (M); grants paid, $0; gifts received, $5,844; expenditures, $0; qualifying distributions, $0.
Officers: Harvey D. Brown, Chair.; Donald G. Mantyla, Treas.
Trustees: David N. Phelps, J. Mark Ward.
EIN: 870621274

63906
The McCarthey Dressman Education Foundation
c/o Kristy Carson
802 Boston Building, 9 Exchange Pl.
Salt Lake City, UT 84111 (801) 320-0765
FAX: (801) 359-8883; E-mail: k-dnspc@uswest.net; URL: http://www.mccartheydressman.org

Established in 1999 in UT.
Donor(s): Sarah McCarthey, Ph.D.
Financial data (yr. ended 12/31/00): Assets, $14,205 (M); grants paid, $47,723; gifts received, $239; expenditures, $94,817; qualifying distributions, $93,882.
Limitations: Giving limited to residents of UT.
Application information: Application form required.
Officers: Sarah McCarthey, Ph.D., Pres.; Mark Dressman, Ph.D., V.P.
Trustees: Judy Abbott, Ph.D., Mike Borish, Carmen Gonzales, Ph.D., Kip Tellez, Ph.D., Jo Worthy, Ph.D.
EIN: 870646265

63907
Crossroads Research Institute
50 S. Main St., Ste. 1090
Salt Lake City, UT 84144

Classified as a private operating foundation in 1983.
Donor(s): Douglas N. Thompson.
Financial data (yr. ended 04/30/00): Assets, $14,202 (M); grants paid, $0; gifts received, $1,650; expenditures, $13,861; qualifying distributions, $13,427; giving activities include $2,705 for programs.
Officers and Trustees:* Douglas N. Thompson,* Pres.; Joseph S. Perry,* V.P.; Garry K. Ottosen,* Secy.-Treas.; Thayne Robson.
EIN: 942901530

63908
The King-Scott Heritage Foundation
109 E.S. Temple, Apt. 6A
Salt Lake City, UT 84111

Financial data (yr. ended 09/30/01): Assets, $13,292 (M); grants paid, $16,102; gifts received, $20,300; expenditures, $31,653; qualifying distributions, $31,653; giving activities include $22,494 for programs.
Limitations: Applications not accepted.

Application information: Contributes only to pre-selected organizations.
Officer and Trustees:* Jonathan E. King,* Chair.; Margaret Ann King, Exec. Dir.; Carol King Haddock, Rex C. Haddock, Christine N. King.
EIN: 942958033

63909
The Choate-Knudsen Genealogical Association, Inc.
P.O. Box 11980
Salt Lake City, UT 84147-0980

Established in 1987 in UT.
Donor(s): Nadine Choate Perkes.
Financial data (yr. ended 12/31/00): Assets, $10,564 (M); grants paid, $0; gifts received, $10,407; expenditures, $6,462; qualifying distributions, $0.
Directors: Elizabeth Perkes, Nadine Choate Perkes, Richard W. Price.
EIN: 742463431

63910
Bolivian Temple Patrons Charitable Foundation
1697 Compton Rd.
Farmington, UT 84025

Established in 2000 in UT.
Financial data (yr. ended 05/31/02): Assets, $9,772 (M); grants paid, $1,858; gifts received, $11,630; expenditures, $1,858; qualifying distributions, $1,858.
Limitations: Applications not accepted.
Application information: Contributes only to pre-selected organizations.
Trustees: Thomas Bagley, Melvyn Reeves, Wayne Snow.
EIN: 316650813

63911
Chemnitzer Vereinigung of Utah
208 E. 800 S.
Salt Lake City, UT 84111
Application address: 2968 Glenmare St., Salt Lake City, UT 84106
Contact: Eva Maria Bates, Pres.

Financial data (yr. ended 12/31/99): Assets, $7,975 (M); grants paid, $1,714; gifts received, $444; expenditures, $3,463; qualifying distributions, $3,463.
Limitations: Giving primarily in Salt Lake City, UT; some giving also in Germany.
Officers: Eva Maria Bates, Pres.; Erwin Boelter, V.P.; Tanja Hagen, V.P.; Troudy Dretke, Secy.
EIN: 870402863

63912
MFA/LDS Genealogical Foundation
2228 N. 800 E.
Provo, UT 84604

Established in 1998 in UT.
Financial data (yr. ended 12/31/99): Assets, $6,198 (M); grants paid, $0; gifts received, $4,000; expenditures, $508; qualifying distributions, $0.
Officer: Lula M. Martensen, Mgr.
EIN: 870568637

63913
Snow-Manwaring Family History Foundation
c/o Diane M. Snow
104 E. 4620 N.
Provo, UT 84604-5474

Established in 1992.
Donor(s): Donald R. Snow.
Financial data (yr. ended 06/30/00): Assets, $5,923 (M); grants paid, $100; gifts received, $6,665; expenditures, $4,108; qualifying distributions, $5,689; giving activities include $5,923 for programs.
Trustees: Diane M. Snow, Donald R. Snow.
EIN: 876219449

63914
Latin American Technology Education Foundation
976 S. 6800 E.
Huntsville, UT 84317

Established in 2001 in UT.
Donor(s): Hobb Hill Computer, Robert A. Summers, Kathy Layton.
Financial data (yr. ended 12/31/01): Assets, $5,550 (M); grants paid, $0; gifts received, $6,036; expenditures, $505; qualifying distributions, $0.
Limitations: Applications not accepted.
Application information: Contributes only to pre-selected organizations.
Officers: Robert A. Summers, Pres.; Steven Parker, V.P.; Jo Anne R. Summers, Secy.
Director: Nathan V. Seaich.
EIN: 870673806

63915
Summerhays Family Historical Library
2440 Wilson Ave.
Salt Lake City, UT 84108

Established in 1988 in UT.
Financial data (yr. ended 12/31/00): Assets, $5,248 (M); grants paid, $0; gifts received, $60; expenditures, $72; qualifying distributions, $0; giving activities include $7,264 for programs.
Officers: Carol Jean Summerhays, Pres.; Earl Larson, Jr., V.P.; Bart Summerhays, Secy.-Treas.
EIN: 870380878

63916
Sufficient Ministries of Utah, Inc.
3939 Alberly Way
Salt Lake City, UT 84124-1810
(801) 278-8849
Contact: William Thomas Lowe, Treas.

Established in 1988 in UT.
Donor(s): William Thomas Lowe.
Financial data (yr. ended 12/31/00): Assets, $4,939 (M); grants paid, $22,549; gifts received, $24,971; expenditures, $24,944; qualifying distributions, $24,944.
Limitations: Giving primarily in Salt Lake City, UT.
Officers: Robert Crites, Pres.; Nannette Lowe, V.P. and Secy.; William Thomas Lowe, Treas.
EIN: 870403172

63917
Sturt-Bilton Family Organization
532 E. Weber Cyn Rd.
Kamas, UT 84036-9544

Classified as a private operating foundation in 1981.
Donor(s): George H. Sturt, Louise A. Sturt, Ella Bilton,‡ and members of the Sturt family.
Financial data (yr. ended 12/31/00): Assets, $4,131 (M); grants paid, $0; gifts received, $5,000; expenditures, $26,727; qualifying distributions, $24,605; giving activities include $24,605 for programs.
Officer and Directors:* George H. Sturt,* Pres.; Louise A. Sturt,* V.P.; Lesley C. McCandless, Secy.; David H. Sturt, Treas.
EIN: 942765285

63918
The Hendrix Foundation
3310 E. Alta Hills Dr.
Sandy, UT 84093

Established in 2000 in UT. Classified as a private operating foundation in 2001.
Financial data (yr. ended 12/31/00): Assets, $3,961 (M); grants paid, $0; gifts received, $4,000; expenditures, $39; qualifying distributions, $0.
Officers: Roger A. Hendrix, Pres.; Cheryl F. Hendrix, Secy.-Treas.
EIN: 870666625

63919
Hoer Family Organization
562 W. 1350 N.
Orem, UT 84057

Financial data (yr. ended 12/31/00): Assets, $2,864 (M); grants paid, $0; expenditures, $245; qualifying distributions, $245; giving activities include $245 for programs.
Officers: Michael A. Hoer, Pres.; Mark W. Keys, V.P.; Marilyn L. Keys, Secy.
EIN: 742519378

63920
Kay T. Family History Foundation
c/o Kay T. Davenport
216 Inglewood Dr.
Orem, UT 84097-5624

Established in 1993.
Donor(s): Kay T. Davenport.
Financial data (yr. ended 12/31/01): Assets, $2,359 (M); grants paid, $600; gifts received, $26,044; expenditures, $25,794; qualifying distributions, $25,594; giving activities include $25,794 for programs.
Limitations: Applications not accepted. Giving primarily in OH.
Application information: Contributes only to pre-selected organizations.
Trustee: Kay T. Davenport.
EIN: 876221399

63921
Bronson-Turnbow Family Organization
1125 Aspen Ridge Ln.
Provo, UT 84604

Financial data (yr. ended 12/31/00): Assets, $2,155 (M); grants paid, $0; gifts received, $932; expenditures, $646; qualifying distributions, $289.
Officers: Wendell Turnbow, Pres.; Dixie Anna Gibbons, V.P.; Pauline Bronson, Secy.-Treas.
Trustee: Clark Bronson.
EIN: 810376197

63922
Keith A. Braithwaite Family Organization
1744 W. 9640 S.
South Jordan, UT 84095

Financial data (yr. ended 12/31/01): Assets, $1,700 (M); grants paid, $0; gifts received, $7,150; expenditures, $7,182; qualifying distributions, $0.
Officers: Keith A. Braithwaite, Pres.; Richard K. Braithwaite, V.P.; Karen Braithwaite, Secy.-Treas.
EIN: 742787118

63923
Sadie Foundation, Inc.
P.O. Box 0095
Logan, UT 84323-0095
Application address: 1199 Cliffside Dr., Logan, UT 84321, tel.: (435) 732-3013
Contact: Duane Morley Cox, Mgr.

Donor(s): Duane Morley Cox.
Financial data (yr. ended 10/31/01): Assets, $1,700 (M); grants paid, $2,500; gifts received, $4,619; expenditures, $3,493; qualifying distributions, $3,493.
Limitations: Giving limited to Salt Lake City, UT.
Application information: Application form required.
Officer and Trustees:* Duane Morley Cox,* Mgr.; Jeanne Cox, Joni Garcia.
EIN: 870658265

63924
I Care Foundation
496 N. 80 W.
Lindon, UT 84042
Contact: Ilene Olsen, Tr.

Established in 2000 in UT.
Donor(s): Ilene Olsen.
Financial data (yr. ended 12/31/01): Assets, $1,466 (M); grants paid, $51,337; gifts received, $46,400; expenditures, $51,517; qualifying distributions, $51,517.
Limitations: Giving primarily in Salt Lake and Davies counties, UT.
Application information: Application form not required.
Trustee: Ilene Olsen.
EIN: 870653978

63925
The Thomas K. McCarthey Foundation
1367 Wilton Way
Salt Lake City, UT 84108-2546
Contact: Thomas K. McCarthey, Tr.

Established in 2001.
Donor(s): Thomas K. McCarthey.
Financial data (yr. ended 12/31/01): Assets, $1,110 (M); grants paid, $35,000; gifts received, $36,214; expenditures, $35,014; qualifying distributions, $35,014.
Limitations: Giving limited to residents of UT.
Trustees: Mary S. McCarthey, Rochele M. McCarthey, Thomas K. McCarthey.
EIN: 870673577

63926
The Ellis-Beckstrom Family History Foundation
c/o Loa B. Ellis
2500 Oak Ridge Dr.
Spanish Fork, UT 84660

Established in 1994.
Financial data (yr. ended 12/31/01): Assets, $662 (M); grants paid, $0; gifts received, $2,050; expenditures, $1,763; qualifying distributions, $0.
Director: Leonard Ellis.
Trustee: Loa Ellis.
EIN: 870518653

63927
M & B Foundation
(Formerly The Milne/Ballard Genealogical Organization)
4181 Marquis Way
Salt Lake City, UT 84124-3117

Established in 1990 in UT.
Financial data (yr. ended 12/31/01): Assets, $237 (M); grants paid, $0; expenditures, $213; qualifying distributions, $0.
Trustees: Diane Milne, L. Brent Milne, Sydney Milne, Wade O. Milne.
EIN: 841144358

63928
Louis H. Callister, Jr. Family Association, Inc.
10 E. South Temple, Ste. 900
Salt Lake City, UT 84133-1186

Classified as a private operating foundation in 1975.
Financial data (yr. ended 12/31/01): Assets, $22 (M); grants paid, $0; gifts received, $320; expenditures, $320; qualifying distributions, $0.
Limitations: Applications not accepted.
Application information: Contributes only to pre-selected organizations.
Officers: Louis H. Callister, Jr., Pres.; Ellen G. Callister, Secy.
EIN: 237455936

VERMONT

63929
Woodstock Foundation, Inc.
P.O. Box 489
Woodstock, VT 05091 (802) 457-2355
FAX: (802) 457-4663; *E-mail:* Mkoetsier@valley.net
Contact: Marian Koetsier, Secy.

Established in 1968 in VT.
Donor(s): Laurance S. Rockefeller, Mary F. Rockefeller.‡
Financial data (yr. ended 12/31/00): Assets, $55,201,689 (M); grants paid, $129,200; gifts received, $815,833; expenditures, $2,943,752; qualifying distributions, $2,825,770.
Limitations: Giving primarily in the immediate Woodstock, VT, area.
Publications: Application guidelines.
Application information: Application form not required.
Officers and Trustees:* C. Wesley Frye, Jr.,* Chair.; David A. Donath,* Pres.; Marian Koetsier, Secy.; Jeffrey D. Fink, Treas.; and 4 additional trustees and advisory board.
EIN: 030221142
Codes: FD2

63930
The Windham Foundation, Inc.
P.O. Box 70
Grafton, VT 05146 (802) 843-2211
FAX: (802) 843-2205; *E-mail:* winfound@sover.net; *URL:* http://www.windham-foundation.org
Contact: Stephan A. Morse, C.E.O. and Pres.

Incorporated in 1963 in VT.
Donor(s): The Bunbury Co., Inc., Dean Mathey.‡
Financial data (yr. ended 10/31/01): Assets, $53,984,679 (M); grants paid, $211,770; gifts received, $60,000; expenditures, $3,822,797; qualifying distributions, $2,777,670; giving activities include $489,689 for programs.
Limitations: Giving limited to VT.
Publications: Annual report, application guidelines, grants list, informational brochure (including application guidelines).
Application information: E-mail or FAX requests will not be accepted. Application form available on website. Application form required.

63930—VERMONT

Officers and Trustees:* Samuel W. Lambert III,* Chair.; Stephan A. Morse,* C.E.O. and Pres.; Arthur Schubert, V.P.; Edward R. Zuccaro,* V.P.; Elizabeth Bankowski,* Secy.; Edward J. Toohey,* Treas.; William A. Gilbert, Robert M. Olmsted, Jamie Kyte Sapoch, Charles C. Townsend, Jr.
EIN: 136142024
Codes: FD2, GTI

63931
The Orton Family Foundation, Inc.
c/o William Shouldice, IV
128 Merchants Row, 2nd Fl.
Rutland, VT 05701
URL: http://www.orton.org

Established in 1995 in VT and CO.
Donor(s): Lyman K. Orton.
Financial data (yr. ended 12/31/00): Assets, $14,815,329 (M); grants paid, $0; gifts received, $2,421,982; expenditures, $4,755,098; qualifying distributions, $0; giving activities include $2,943,907 for programs.
Officers: Lyman K. Orton, Chair.; William C. Shouldice IV, Pres.; Edward W. Cronin, Jr., Secy.-Treas.; Townsend H. Anderson, Mgr.; Elizabeth Humstone, Mgr.; William E. Roper, Mgr.; Helen Whyte, Mgr.
Directors: William J. Basa, Diane Mitsch Bush, John Ewing, Charles Kireker, Robert Klein, Curtis J. Mucklow, Lynne Sherrod, Cyndy Simms, Thomas Slayton, Dean Vogelaar, Robert G. Weiss.
Trustees: Robert Allen, Andy Bush, Noel C. Fritzinger, Roberta MacDonald, Karen Nystrom Meyer, Stephan Morse.
EIN: 030346513

63932
O. M. Fisher Home, Inc.
149 Main St.
Montpelier, VT 05602

Classified as a private operating foundation in 1989.
Financial data (yr. ended 12/31/01): Assets, $5,736,121 (M); grants paid, $0; expenditures, $651,789; qualifying distributions, $554,666; giving activities include $608,307 for programs.
Officers and Trustees:* William Callnan,* Pres.; Charles Haynes,* V.P.; Barbara Prentice,* Secy.; Charles Wiley,* Treas.; Marilyn Johnson, David Pinkham, Maxine Weed.
EIN: 030184240

63933
Stowe Swimmers Foundation, Ltd.
80 Industrial Ave.
Burlington, VT 05401

Established in 2000 in VT.
Donor(s): Jake Carpenter, Donna G. Carpenter.
Financial data (yr. ended 05/31/01): Assets, $3,077,771 (M); grants paid, $0; gifts received, $3,076,072; expenditures, $10,004; qualifying distributions, $2,251,582; giving activities include $10,004 for programs.
Limitations: Applications not accepted.
Application information: Contributes only to pre-selected organizations.
Directors: Paul Biron, Jill Boardman, Donna G. Carpenter, John B. Carpenter.
EIN: 030363251

63934
Andrew C. and Margaret R. Sigler Foundation, Inc.
c/o R.E. Snyder & Co.
P.O. Box 1018
Norwich, VT 05055 (802) 296-2604
Contact: Robert E. Snyder, Secy.-Treas.

Established in 1999 in VT.
Donor(s): Andrew C. Sigler, Margaret R. Sigler.
Financial data (yr. ended 12/31/01): Assets, $2,930,130 (M); grants paid, $48,800; gifts received, $985,332; expenditures, $1,069,387; qualifying distributions, $812,552; giving activities include $1,069,387 for programs.
Limitations: Giving primarily in New England.
Application information: Application form not required.
Officers and Directors:* Andrew C. Sigler,* Pres.; Margaret R. Sigler,* V.P.; Robert E. Snyder, Secy.-Treas.; Andrew C. Siegler, Jr.
EIN: 030359504

63935
Upper Valley Haven, Inc.
745 Hartford Ave.
White River Junction, VT 05001-1607
(802) 295-6500

Classified as a private operating foundation in 1981.
Financial data (yr. ended 12/31/01): Assets, $2,192,886 (M); grants paid, $0; gifts received, $1,436,166; expenditures, $449,590; qualifying distributions, $1,651,409; giving activities include $353,474 for programs.
Officers and Directors:* Ray Huessy, Pres.; Rev. Patrick McCoy, 1st V.P.; Alexandra H. Corwin, 2nd V.P.; Mary Rassias,* Secy.; Shirley Grainger, Treas.; Suzanne Stofflet, Mgr.; Cindy Eames, Mary Feeney, and 6 additional directors.
EIN: 030277908
Codes: TN

63936
Laumeister Center for the Arts
c/o Bruce Laumeister
254 Benmont Ave.
Bennington, VT 05201

Established in 1993 in VT.
Donor(s): Bruce Laumeister.
Financial data (yr. ended 12/31/00): Assets, $1,605,530 (M); grants paid, $0; gifts received, $6,220; expenditures, $132,425; qualifying distributions, $240,548; giving activities include $89,149 for programs.
Officers and Trustees:* Bruce Laumeister,* Pres.; Elizabeth Laumeister,* V.P. and Secy.-Treas.; Eric Crawford, Jeffrey Crawford.
EIN: 030323040

63937
The Homestead, Inc.
73 River St.
Woodstock, VT 05091-1284

Financial data (yr. ended 03/31/02): Assets, $1,489,255 (M); grants paid, $0; gifts received, $302,817; expenditures, $590,517; qualifying distributions, $606,964; giving activities include $590,517 for programs.
Officers: Howard Goodrow, Pres.; Peter K. Vollers, V.P.; Nancy Bebo, Clerk; Corrine Barr, Treas.
Director: Frances van da Griff.
Trustee: Tom Zonay.
EIN: 030195636

63938
The Converse Home, Inc.
272 Church St.
Burlington, VT 05401

Classified as a private operating foundation in 1973.
Financial data (yr. ended 10/31/00): Assets, $1,414,486 (M); grants paid, $0; gifts received, $101,961; expenditures, $650,013; qualifying distributions, $36,901; giving activities include $650,013 for programs.
Officers and Trustees:* Thomas Little,* Pres.; Mary Ellen Spencer,* V.P.; Judy Stroh, Treas.; Peggy Chadwick,* Recording Secy.; Sarah Carpenter, Estelle Deane, Lloyd Durbrow, Nancy Goodrich, Travis Gray, Margaret Hamlin, Liz Jones, Sarah Merritt, Stephen Moore, Elsie Paul.
EIN: 030179406

63939
Keniston and Dane Educational Fund
P.O. Box 22
Sheffield, VT 05866
Application address: c/o Town Clerk, Town of Wheelock, VT 05851

Established in 1993 in VT.
Donor(s): Harry Keniston.‡
Financial data (yr. ended 12/31/01): Assets, $1,312,095 (M); grants paid, $76,266; expenditures, $84,882; qualifying distributions, $84,354.
Limitations: Giving limited to residents of Sheffield and Wheelock, VT.
Application information: Application form required.
Officers and Trustees:* John Ayers,* Co-Chair.; Charles Gilman, Co-Chair.; Maxwell Aldrich,* Lewis Brill, Preston Smith, Victoria Turnbaugh.
EIN: 030341752
Codes: FD2, GTI

63940
Hammond Chapman Foundation for Yesterday's Living, Ltd.
c/o Theresa A. Douglas
1633 Rte. 74 W.
Shoreham, VT 05770

Classified as a private operating foundation in 1990.
Donor(s): Sylvia Keiser.
Financial data (yr. ended 12/31/01): Assets, $1,246,045 (M); grants paid, $0; expenditures, $68,726; qualifying distributions, $73,578; giving activities include $62,600 for programs.
Officers and Trustees:* Sylvia Keiser,* Pres.; J. Robert Maguire,* V.P.; Theresa A. Douglas, Treas.; Gary Bowen, Pauline Maguire.
EIN: 061185613

63941
Holton Memorial Home
158 Western Ave.
Brattleboro, VT 05301

Donor(s): Thomas Thompson Trust.
Financial data (yr. ended 04/30/02): Assets, $1,166,042 (M); grants paid, $0; gifts received, $220,240; expenditures, $710,441; qualifying distributions, $0.
Officers and Directors:* Jean Randall,* Pres.; Jill Brehm,* V.P.; Mary Harrington,* V.P.; Beverly Packard,* Secy.; Timothy Fogg,* Treas.; Pliny N. Burrows, Maurice Halladay, and 7 additional directors.
EIN: 030179416

63942
Columbus Smith Estate Trust, Inc.
c/o Madeline Gardner
P.O. Box 508
Middlebury, VT 05753

Established in 1998 in VT.
Financial data (yr. ended 12/31/01): Assets, $1,035,757 (M); grants paid, $0; gifts received, $172,390; expenditures, $417,236; qualifying distributions, $407,460; giving activities include $407,460 for programs.
Officers: Harold Strassner, Pres.; Abbott Fenn, V.P.; Sandra L. Vivian, Secy.; Madeline Gardner, Treas.
Trustees: Diane Benware, Ralph Carbo, William English, Dick Gardner, Sally McClintock, Mona Rogers, Virginia Wolf.
Director: Deb Choma.
EIN: 030186171

63943
Bryan Foundation, Inc.
P.O. Box 340
Jeffersonville, VT 05464-0340

Classified as a private operating foundation in 1983.
Donor(s): Alden Bryan.
Financial data (yr. ended 12/31/00): Assets, $1,004,106 (M); grants paid, $835; gifts received, $39,196; expenditures, $78,053; qualifying distributions, $78,053.
Officers: Alden Bryan, Pres. and Treas.; Jane George-Shaw, V.P. and Exec. Dir.; Pamela A. Gagnon, Secy.
EIN: 030287574

63944
Greater Rockingham Area Health Services, Inc.
Hospital Court
Bellows Falls, VT 05101

Established in 1995 in VT.
Financial data (yr. ended 09/30/00): Assets, $962,542 (M); grants paid, $0; gifts received, $7,906; expenditures, $503,899; qualifying distributions, $0; giving activities include $503,899 for programs.
Limitations: Giving primarily in VT.
Officers: N. Lincoln Daniell III, Pres.; Ann Fitzgerald, V.P.
Trustees: Jayson Dunbar, John Schultz.
EIN: 222678012

63945
Land Ethic Action Foundation
31 Hall Rd.
Chelsea, VT 05038

Established in 1995 in CA.
Donor(s): Mark Jordan.
Financial data (yr. ended 12/31/01): Assets, $936,020 (M); grants paid, $500; gifts received, $10,000; expenditures, $71,134; qualifying distributions, $55,710; giving activities include $53,449 for programs.
Limitations: Giving in Argentina.
Officers: Eleanor Jordan, Pres.; Rick Hawley, Secy.; Mark Jordan, C.F.O.
EIN: 954478327

63946
Carl Gary Taylor Foundation for Children, Inc.
P.O. Box 785
Newport, VT 05855-0785   (802) 334-5085
Application address: 337 Union St., Newport, VT 05855
Contact: Carl Taylor, Pres.

Established in 1999 in VT.
Financial data (yr. ended 12/31/00): Assets, $866,677 (M); grants paid, $4,000; gifts received, $675,724; expenditures, $5,346; qualifying distributions, $4,000.
Limitations: Giving primarily in VT.
Officers: Carl G. Taylor, Pres.; Susan Taylor, Secy.
Director: Saul Silverman.
EIN: 311658629

63947
Van Der Smissen Memorial Trust
c/o Fleet National Bank
P.O. Box 595
Williston, VT 05495

Financial data (yr. ended 12/31/99): Assets, $809,623 (M); grants paid, $0; expenditures, $46,047; qualifying distributions, $32,800.
Trustee: Fleet National Bank.
EIN: 046037574

63948
Ronald N. Terrill Memorial Fund, Inc.
P.O. Box 265
Morrisville, VT 05661
Contact: Robert Magoon, Secy.-Treas.

Financial data (yr. ended 04/30/01): Assets, $688,973 (M); grants paid, $33,000; expenditures, $33,306; qualifying distributions, $33,000.
Limitations: Giving primarily in VT.
Application information: Application form required.
Officers: Jon Osborn, Pres.; Bernie Sheltra, V.P.; Robert Magoon, Secy.-Treas.
Director: Brad Limoge.
EIN: 030213310

63949
Todhah Hill Foundation
c/o Paul L. Kendall
487 Kendall Rd.
Braintree, VT 05060   (802) 728-3726

Donor(s): Paul L. Kendall, Sharon M. Kendall, Sharon K. Rives.
Financial data (yr. ended 12/31/01): Assets, $552,623 (M); grants paid, $0; expenditures, $4,735; qualifying distributions, $3,186; giving activities include $3,186 for programs.
Officers: Paul L. Kendall, Pres. and Treas.; Sharon K. Rives, V.P. and Secy.
Director: James Lupton.
EIN: 510140311

63950
The Fund for North Bennington
P.O. Box 803
North Bennington, VT 05257-0803
(802) 447-0256

Classified as a private operating foundation in 1995.
Donor(s): Bill Scott, Babs Scott.
Financial data (yr. ended 04/30/00): Assets, $543,303 (L); grants paid, $28,400; gifts received, $444,593; expenditures, $36,014; qualifying distributions, $36,014.
Limitations: Giving limited to North Bennington, VT.
Application information: Application form required.
Officers and Trustees: Robert E. Woolmington,* Pres.; Christine P. Graham, Secy.; Joseph G. McGovern,* Treas.; David Aldrich, Marjorie Manning.
EIN: 030335309
Codes: TN

63951
Redwall Foundation, Inc.
c/o Dr. Howard M. Schapiro
219 Austin Dr.
Burlington, VT 05401

Established in 1997 in VT.
Donor(s): Howard M. Schapiro, Janet Carroll Schapiro.
Financial data (yr. ended 12/31/00): Assets, $426,197 (M); grants paid, $20,000; expenditures, $24,616; qualifying distributions, $19,828.
Limitations: Applications not accepted.
Application information: Contributes only to pre-selected organizations.
Directors: John E. Mazuzan, Jr., Howard M. Schapiro, Janet Carroll Schapiro.
EIN: 043367004

63952
William Dean Fausett Foundation for the Preservation and Protection of Green Mountain Boys History, Inc.
20 Nichols Hill Rd.
Dorset, VT 05251

Classified as a private operating foundation in 1991.
Donor(s): William Dean Fausett.
Financial data (yr. ended 12/31/01): Assets, $393,727 (M); grants paid, $27,000; gifts received, $29,595; expenditures, $75,344; qualifying distributions, $56,008.
Limitations: Applications not accepted. Giving primarily in VT.
Application information: Contributes only to pre-selected organizations.
Officers: Raymond C. Kopituk, Pres.; Jean Atthowe, Secy.
Trustee: Harry Walters.
EIN: 030328057

63953
20th Century Trends Institute, Inc.
323 Lost Nation Rd.
Essex Junction, VT 05452   (802) 872-1135
Contact: Mary B. Mclaughlin

Classified as a private operating foundation in 1991.
Financial data (yr. ended 12/31/00): Assets, $378,888 (M); grants paid, $1,638; gifts received, $25; expenditures, $20,886; qualifying distributions, $13,518; giving activities include $13,518 for programs.
Limitations: Giving primarily in VT.
Officers: Mary McLaughlin, Pres.; John H. Gilbert, V.P.; Ward F. Cleary, Secy.-Treas.
EIN: 066098560

63954
Burlington Cancer Relief Association, Inc.
c/o Elizabeth Van Buren
7492 Spear St.
Shelburne, VT 05482-6573   (802) 899-4083
Contact: Edwarda DuBrul Aiken, R.N.

Classified as a private operating foundation in 1998.
Donor(s): Mary E. Thompson.
Financial data (yr. ended 09/30/01): Assets, $367,820 (M); grants paid, $21,378; expenditures, $27,170; qualifying distributions, $26,235.
Limitations: Giving limited to the greater Burlington, VT, area.
Application information: Application form required.

63954—VERMONT

Officers: Sybil Watts Smith, Pres.; Elizabeth Clewley, V.P.; Martha Churchill, Secy.; Elizabeth Van Buren, Treas.
Directors: Kimberly Leubbers, Judith Northrup, Margaret Twitchell.
EIN: 237422919
Codes: GTI

63955
Rutland High School Foundation
22 Cottage St.
Rutland, VT 05701
Contact: John H. Bloomer, Jr., Pres.

Established in 1992 in VT.
Donor(s): Pernas Jacobs, Joy M. Johnson.
Financial data (yr. ended 06/30/99): Assets, $295,522 (M); grants paid, $9,500; expenditures, $9,500; qualifying distributions, $9,383.
Limitations: Giving limited to residents of Rutland, VT.
Application information: Application form required.
Officers and Directors:* John H. Bloomer, Jr.,* Pres.; Mark Candon, V.P.; Jean Godnick,* Secy.; Edward Godnick,* Treas.; W. Richard Brothers, Thomas S. O'Brien.
EIN: 030334417

63956
Blake Memorial Library Association
P.O. Box D
East Corinth, VT 05040-0904

Financial data (yr. ended 12/31/99): Assets, $286,845 (M); grants paid, $0; gifts received, $56,960; expenditures, $31,541; qualifying distributions, $28,909; giving activities include $28,909 for programs.
Officers: W. Smith, Pres.; Jonathan Fenton, 1st V.P.; John Pierson, Jr., 2nd V.P.; Nancy Frost, Secy.; Beth Thompson, Treas.
Trustee: K. Hookway.
EIN: 030212407

63957
Raymond & Lorraine Letourneau Educational Foundation
47 Cayuga Ct.
Burlington, VT 05401
Contact: Raymond Letourneau

Financial data (yr. ended 12/31/01): Assets, $266,513 (M); grants paid, $19,728; expenditures, $25,269; qualifying distributions, $25,269.
Limitations: Giving primarily in Burlington, VT.
Application information: Individual applicants should submit a brief resume of academic qualification and financial information.
Officers: Dale Letourneau, Pres.; Dena Wager, Secy.-Treas.
EIN: 030277007
Codes: GTI

63958
Newport Adolescent Programs, Inc.
c/o Carl Gary Taylor
P.O. Box 785
Newport, VT 05855 (802) 334-8322

Classified as a private operating foundation in 1990.
Donor(s): Carl Gary Taylor, Susan Taylor, C. Taylor Children's Foundation.
Financial data (yr. ended 12/31/00): Assets, $233,046 (L); grants paid, $0; gifts received, $327,000; expenditures, $331,478; qualifying distributions, $318,588; giving activities include $300,515 for programs.
Officers: Carl Taylor, Pres.; Susan Taylor, Secy.; Donald P. Hunt, Treas.

Directors: Colin Benjamin, Anne Sparrow.
EIN: 030321840

63959
The Jenckes Foundation, Inc.
P.O. Box 412
Marlboro, VT 05344

Established in 2000 in VT.
Donor(s): Mary Faith Wilson.
Financial data (yr. ended 12/31/01): Assets, $210,305 (M); grants paid, $0; gifts received, $203,000; expenditures, $3,620; qualifying distributions, $0.
Officers: Mary Faith Wilson, Pres.; Nora Wilson, Secy.; Roger B. Wilson, Jr., Treas.
Directors: Adelbert Ames, Dawes Wilson, Nancy Hope Wilson, Patricia B. Wilson, T. Hunter Wilson.
EIN: 030363194

63960
A & S Animal Farm, Inc.
R.F.D., Whitney Hill Rd.
Tunbridge, VT 05077

Classified as a private operating foundation in 1992.
Donor(s): Sheldon L. Vogel.
Financial data (yr. ended 12/31/00): Assets, $193,305 (M); grants paid, $3,750; gifts received, $106,013; expenditures, $95,599; qualifying distributions, $59,437.
Limitations: Applications not accepted. Giving primarily in NJ and VT.
Application information: Contributes only to pre-selected organizations.
Officers and Directors:* Sheldon L. Vogel,* Pres. and Treas.; Anne M. Vogel,* V.P.
EIN: 030331269

63961
Marlin Charitable Trust
P.O. Box 1072
Burlington, VT 05402 (802) 862-6363

Established in 1997 in VT.
Donor(s): John F. Chapple, Sharon L. Chapple.
Financial data (yr. ended 12/31/00): Assets, $154,768 (M); grants paid, $5,000; expenditures, $5,000; qualifying distributions, $5,000.
Limitations: Applications not accepted. Giving primarily in VT.
Application information: Contributes only to pre-selected organizations.
Trustees: John F. Chapple, Sharon L. Chapple.
EIN: 046838065

63962
The Fourth Corner Foundation, Inc.
RFD 133
Windham, VT 05359

Classified as a private operation in 1998.
Donor(s): Robert F. Shannon.
Financial data (yr. ended 12/31/01): Assets, $141,604 (M); grants paid, $0; gifts received, $29,500; expenditures, $1,882; qualifying distributions, $0.
Limitations: Applications not accepted.
Officer: Robert F. Shannon, Pres. and Secy.
EIN: 141799997

63963
The CHILL Foundation
(Formerly The Burton Foundation)
80 Industrial Pkwy.
Burlington, VT 05401

Classified as a company-sponsored operating foundation in 1997.

Donor(s): The Burton Corp., Jake Burton Carpenter.
Financial data (yr. ended 04/30/01): Assets, $128,956 (M); grants paid, $0; gifts received, $265,462; expenditures, $196,712; qualifying distributions, $196,700; giving activities include $196,700 for programs.
Officers and Directors:* Jake Carpenter, Chair.; David Schriber,* Secy.; Paul Frascoia, Treas.; Jenn Davis, Tom McGann.
EIN: 030353892

63964
Vermont Conference on the Primary Prevention of Psychopathology, Inc.
c/o University of Vermont, John Dewey Hall
Burlington, VT 05405-0002
Contact: Marc Kessler

Financial data (yr. ended 12/31/01): Assets, $107,329 (M); grants paid, $0; gifts received, $48,964; expenditures, $68,523; qualifying distributions, $43,557; giving activities include $50,284 for programs.
Officers: Lynne Bond, Pres.; Justin A. Joffee, V.P.; Marc Kessler, Treas.
EIN: 030263220

63965
Ruggles Foundation, Inc.
c/o CSC
308 Pine St.
Burlington, VT 05401

Classified as a private operating foundation in 1974.
Financial data (yr. ended 12/31/01): Assets, $102,572 (M); grants paid, $0; gifts received, $13,766; expenditures, $107,155; qualifying distributions, $107,155; giving activities include $107,155 for programs.
Officers: Nancy Hayes, Pres.; Lorna Dean Brown, V.P.; Lisa Schamberg, Secy.; Ann V. Hallowell, Treas.
EIN: 030179426

63966
Lawrence C. & Elizabeth M. Campbell Scholarship Trust
c/o Banknorth Investment Management Group, N.A.
P.O. Box 595
Williston, VT 05495-0595
Application address: c/o Spaulding High School, 155 Ayers St., Barre, VT 05641

Established in 1997 in VT.
Donor(s): Elizabeth Campbell Trust.
Financial data (yr. ended 12/31/00): Assets, $101,243 (M); grants paid, $4,914; expenditures, $6,524; qualifying distributions, $5,165.
Limitations: Giving limited to Barre, VT.
Application information: Application form not required.
Trustee: Banknorth Investment Management Group, N.A.
EIN: 036064488

63967
Hartford Historical Society, Inc.
P.O. Box 547
Hartford, VT 05047

Classified as a private operating foundation in 1987.
Financial data (yr. ended 12/31/00): Assets, $94,990 (M); grants paid, $60; gifts received, $3,727; expenditures, $14,650; qualifying distributions, $10,002.
Officers and Directors:* Dorothy M. Jones,* Pres.; Muriel Farrington,* V.P.; David F. Ford,* Secy.;

Margaret McDerment,* Treas.; Peggy Adams, Fred Bradley, Robert Follensbee, Alice Hazen, Mary E. Mills, and 4 additional directors.
EIN: 030309341

63968
The Greenwood Institute for Learning Disabilities, Inc.
R.R. 2, Box 270
Putney, VT 05346-0270

Financial data (yr. ended 06/30/01): Assets, $93,354 (M); grants paid, $0; expenditures, $41,671; qualifying distributions, $0.
Officers: Sue Wallington Quinlan, Ph.D., Pres.; Lewis "Sandy" Madeira, Jr., V.P.; Lindsay Kelsey, Secy.; Gardner Abbott, Treas.
Trustees: Roderick A.J. Cavanagh, William Edgar, Anne Fein, Eugene Nelson, Ronald A. Weinberg.
EIN: 222532012

63969
Para Resources Religious Foundation, Inc.
P.O. Box 969
Burlington, VT 05402-0969

Classified as a private operating foundation in 1989.
Donor(s): Palmer L. Adams, Jr.
Financial data (yr. ended 06/30/00): Assets, $85,142 (M); grants paid, $0; gifts received, $21,402; expenditures, $37,086; qualifying distributions, $0; giving activities include $31,383 for programs.
Officers and Directors:* Palmer L. Adams, Jr.,* Pres. and Treas.; Ruth E. Adams,* V.P. and Secy.
Trustees: M. Herbert Fryling, Mark A. Kolchin.
EIN: 030318406

63970
The Willowell Foundation, Inc.
564 Wild Apple Rd.
New Haven, VT 05472

Established in 2000 in VT.
Donor(s): Jean Eisenstein, Dale Bailey.
Financial data (yr. ended 06/30/01): Assets, $37,239 (M); grants paid, $0; gifts received, $40,500; expenditures, $16,410; qualifying distributions, $4,111; giving activities include $15,550 for programs.
Officers: Matt Schlein, Pres.; Jean Eisenstein, Secy.
Directors: Dale Bailey, Erik Fitzpatrick, Jonathan Parke, Lee Shorey.
EIN: 030366363

63971
Green Valley Film & Art Center, Inc.
300 Maple St.
Burlington, VT 05401

Donor(s): Robin Lloyd.
Financial data (yr. ended 12/31/00): Assets, $24,677 (M); grants paid, $12,411; gifts received, $19,381; expenditures, $29,070; qualifying distributions, $21,970; giving activities include $9,559 for programs.
Limitations: Applications not accepted. Giving primarily in VT.
Application information: Contributes only to pre-selected organizations.
Officer and Directors:* Doreen Kraft,* Pres.; Mary Arbuckle, Roz Payne, Dorothy Tod.
EIN: 030263918

63972
Earl Durkee Family Scholarship
c/o Banknorth Investment Management Group, N.A.
P.O. Box 595, Banknorth Group Tax Dept.
Williston, VT 05495-0595

Established in 1994 in VT.
Financial data (yr. ended 12/31/00): Assets, $22,777 (M); grants paid, $1,354; expenditures, $1,851; qualifying distributions, $1,642.
Limitations: Applications not accepted. Giving limited to Winooski, VT.
Application information: Contributes only to pre-selected organizations.
Trustee: Banknorth Investment Management Group, N.A.
EIN: 036046160

63973
Three Meadow Riders, Inc.
P.O. Box 8
3 Meadows Farm, South Road
Peru, VT 05152

Classified as a private operating foundation in 1990.
Donor(s): Signa L. Read.
Financial data (yr. ended 04/30/01): Assets, $15,888 (M); grants paid, $0; gifts received, $11,400; expenditures, $8,926; qualifying distributions, $8,236; giving activities include $8,236 for programs.
Officers and Directors:* Edward W. Cronin, Jr.,* Chair. and Treas.; Signa L. Read, Pres.; Martha Pfeiffer,* Secy.; J. Clyde Johnson, Sally Sise.
Resource Council Members: Stuart Duboff, M.D., Mabel Mayer, Timothy M. Powers, John H. Williams II.
EIN: 030327947

63974
Miron and Susan Malboeuf Charitable Trust
c/o Miron Malboeuf
P.O. Box 395
Warren, VT 05674-0395

Established in 1999 in VT.
Financial data (yr. ended 12/31/00): Assets, $13,855 (M); grants paid, $1,400; gifts received, $9,980; expenditures, $1,400; qualifying distributions, $1,400.
Limitations: Applications not accepted.
Application information: Contributes only to pre-selected organizations.
Trustees: Miron Malboeuf, Susan Malboeuf.
EIN: 036067305

63975
Institute for Democratic Development
560 Herrick St.
Benson, VT 05743-9406

Financial data (yr. ended 12/31/99): Assets, $8,827 (L); grants paid, $0; expenditures, $5,000; qualifying distributions, $0.
Officers: Valery Chalidze, Pres.; Lisa Chalidze, Treas.
Directors: Edward Kline, Pavel Litvinov.
EIN: 222856683

63976
Toward Freedom, Inc.
P.O. Box 468
Burlington, VT 05402

Classified as a private operating foundation in 1974.
Donor(s): William Lloyd.
Financial data (yr. ended 12/31/00): Assets, $8,544 (M); grants paid, $0; gifts received, $51,945; expenditures, $54,596; qualifying distributions, $54,398; giving activities include $54,398 for programs.
Officers and Directors:* David Dellinger,* Co-Chair.; Robin Lloyd,* Co-Chair.; Sandra Baird,* Secy.; Chris Lloyd,* Treas.; J.R. Deep Ford, Miriam Ward.
EIN: 362319388

63977
Essex Scholarship Foundation, Inc.
P.O. Box 123
Essex Junction, VT 05453-0123

Established in 1990 in VT.
Donor(s): Essex Business & Professional Assoc., Inc.
Financial data (yr. ended 12/31/01): Assets, $5,244 (M); grants paid, $2,000; gifts received, $6,363; expenditures, $2,000; qualifying distributions, $2,000.
Limitations: Applications not accepted. Giving limited to residents of VT.
Officers: Stephen A. Unsworth, Pres.; Cathy Phillips, Secy.-Treas.
EIN: 030318168

63978
Salem Trust
c/o Hartmann Louise, et al.
P.O. Box 70
Northfield, VT 05663

Established in 1997.
Donor(s): Thomas Hartmann, Louise Hartmann.
Financial data (yr. ended 12/31/99): Assets, $1,726 (L); grants paid, $0; gifts received, $1,227; expenditures, $1,041; qualifying distributions, $1,041; giving activities include $1,041 for programs.
Trustees: Louise Hartmann, Thomas Hartmann.
EIN: 030354089

63979
Bradford House, Inc.
N. Pleasant St.
P.O. Box 146
Bradford, VT 05033

Financial data (yr. ended 12/31/00): Assets, $1 (M); grants paid, $0; expenditures, $16,264; qualifying distributions, $0.
Officers and Directors:* Bonnie Tomlinson,* Pres.; Robert Tomlinson,* V.P.; Karen Culbertson, Secy.-Treas.
EIN: 030258850

63980
Zurn Family Foundation, Inc.
76 S. Main St.
St. Albans, VT 05478 (802) 527-2343
Contact: Karl Zurn, Pres.

Established in 1999 in VT. Classified as a company-sponsored operating foundation in 2001.
Donor(s): Med Associates, Inc.
Financial data (yr. ended 06/30/01): Assets, $0 (M); grants paid, $0; expenditures, $16,673; qualifying distributions, $0.
Limitations: Giving limited to residents of VT.
Application information: Application form required.
Officers and Directors:* Karl Zurn, Pres.; Jane T. Zurn,* Secy.-Treas.; Bridget M. Zurn, Jane B. Zurn, Mary D. Zurn.
EIN: 030362216

VIRGIN ISLANDS

63981
The Merwin Foundation of St. Croix
P.O. Box 427
Frederiksted, VI 00841-0427

Financial data (yr. ended 12/31/00): Assets, $93,032 (M); grants paid, $22,676; expenditures, $23,326; qualifying distributions, $22,640.
Limitations: Applications not accepted. Giving primarily in St. Croix, VI.
Application information: Contributes only to pre-selected organizations.
Trustees: Robert L. Merwin, Robin Merwin-Benda.
Advisor: John D. Merwin.
EIN: 660432507

VIRGINIA

63982
Freedom Forum, Inc.
1101 Wilson Blvd.
Arlington, VA 22209-2248
FAX: (703) 284-3770; E-mail: news@freedomforum.org; URL: http://www.freedomforum.org
Contact: Charles L. Overby, Chair.

Incorporated in 1991 in VA.
Financial data (yr. ended 12/31/01): Assets, $830,716,566 (M); grants paid, $44,346,454; expenditures, $88,649,606; qualifying distributions, $91,142,811; giving activities include $21,038,498 for programs.
Limitations: Applications not accepted. Giving on a national and international basis.
Publications: Annual report, occasional report, informational brochure.
Application information: Unsolicited requests for funds not accepted.
Officers and Trustees:* Charles L. Overby,* Chair. and C.E.O.; Peter S. Pritchard,* Pres.; Mary Kay Blake, Sr. V.P., Partnership and Initiatives; Nicole F. Mandeville, Sr. V.P., Finance and Treas.; Kenneth A. Paulson, Sr. V.P. and Exec. Dir., First Amendment C*; Joe Urschel, Sr. V.P. and Exec. Dir., Newseum; Christine Wells, Sr. V.P., International; Constance Aguayo, V.P., Human Resources; Pamela Y. Galloway-Tabb, V.P., Genl. Svcs.; Jack Hurley, V.P., Broadcasting; Max Page, V.P., and Deputy Dir., Newseum; Rod Sandeen, V.P., Admin.; James C. Duff, Secy.; Martin F. Birmingham, Advisory Tr.; Bernard B. Brody, M.D., Advisory Tr.; Genl. Harry W. Brooks, Jr., John E. Heselden, Sr. Advisory Tr.; Aberto Ibarguen, Madelyn P. Jennings, Malcolm R. Kirschenbaum, Bette Bao Lord, Brian Mulroney, Allen H. Neuharth, Sr. Advisory Tr.; Jan Neuharth, H. Wilbert Norton, Jr., John C. Quinn, Advisory Tr.; John Seigenthaler, Paul Simon, Mark Trahant, Judy C. Woodruff.
EIN: 541604427
Codes: FD, FM, GTI

63983
The Bailey Family Foundation, Inc.
P.O. Box 803
Newington, VA 22122-0803

Established in 1997 in VA.
Donor(s): Beverly W. Bailey, Ron K. Bailey.
Financial data (yr. ended 12/31/01): Assets, $52,467,202 (M); grants paid, $1,145,744; gifts received, $44,961,527; expenditures, $1,682,679; qualifying distributions, $1,243,254.
Application information: Application form required.
Officer and Directors:* Ron K. Bailey, Pres.; Beverly W. Bailey, Ronnie Kyle Bailey, Ryan Kent Bailey.
EIN: 541850780
Codes: FD

63984
The Freedom Forum Newseum, Inc.
1101 Wilson Blvd., 22nd Fl.
Arlington, VA 22209-2248

Established in 1992 in VA.
Donor(s): Freedom Forum International, Inc.
Financial data (yr. ended 12/31/01): Assets, $34,837,162 (M); grants paid, $10,000; gifts received, $14,314,000; expenditures, $32,355,889; qualifying distributions, $25,445,998; giving activities include $24,112,120 for programs.
Application information: Contributes only to pre-selected organizations.
Officers and Trustees:* Charles L. Overby, Chair. and C.E.O.; Peter S. Pritchard,* Pres.; Joseph M. Urschel, Exec. V.P. and Exec. Dir.; Harvey S. Cotter, V.P. and Treas.; Max Page, V.P.; Tracy A. Quinn, V.P.; Robert G. McCullough, Secy.; and 13 additional trustees.
EIN: 541626042

63985
Central American Solar Energy Project
c/o William F. Lankford
10718 Scott Dr.
Fairfax, VA 22030-3023

Established in 1991 in VA.
Donor(s): Mary Fleet, Betsy Fleet, Francis Lankford, William F. Lankford, Elizabeth Burke.
Financial data (yr. ended 12/31/01): Assets, $30,123,998 (M); grants paid, $0; gifts received, $401,588; expenditures, $195,986; qualifying distributions, $194,444; giving activities include $136,749 for programs.
Officers: William F. Lankford, Pres.; David Kuebrich, Secy.; Charles Goldsmith, Treas.
Trustees: Dulce Cruz, Sally Davis, Marie Dennis, Joan Urbanczyk.
EIN: 541592084

63986
Logistics Management Institute
2000 Corporate Ridge Rd.
McLean, VA 22102-7805

Classified as a private operating foundation in 1963.
Financial data (yr. ended 09/30/00): Assets, $28,423,046 (M); grants paid, $0; expenditures, $68,839,768; qualifying distributions, $67,313,720; giving activities include $66,471,214 for programs.
Officers: William G.T. Tuttle, Jr., Pres.; Norman E. Betaque, Jr., Sr. V.P.; Robert K. Wood, Sr. V.P.; Colin O. Halvorson, V.P.; William B. Moore, V.P.; Anthony J. Provenzano, V.P.; Edward D. Simms, Jr., V.P.; John A. Cuicci, Secy.
Trustees: Charles J. DiBona, Hon. J. Ronald Fox, Dana G. Mead, William S. Norman, Joseph S. Nye, Jr., Hon. Edmund T. Pratt, Jr., Robert E. Pursley, and 3 additional trustees.
EIN: 520741393

63987
The Williams Home, Inc.
c/o The Pettyjohn Co.
1201 Langhorne Rd.
Lynchburg, VA 24503

Classified as a private operating foundation in 1973.
Financial data (yr. ended 06/30/00): Assets, $26,562,791 (M); grants paid, $0; gifts received, $17,907; expenditures, $1,047,411; qualifying distributions, $941,313; giving activities include $230,529 for programs.
Officers: Thomas D. Gerhardt, Pres.; Ruth Wills, Secy.; Robert Davis, Treas.
Directors: Elizabeth C. Galloway, Ebbert E. Jones, Kenneth S. White, Darryl Whitesell.
EIN: 540524517

63988
Winkler Botanical Preserve
(Formerly Winkler Nature Park, Inc.)
4900 Seminary Rd., Ste. 900
Alexandria, VA 22311

Classified as a private operating foundation in 1983.
Donor(s): Winkler Botanical Preserve Lead Trust.
Financial data (yr. ended 01/31/00): Assets, $23,066,780 (M); grants paid, $0; gifts received, $1,400,000; expenditures, $503,338; qualifying distributions, $390,504; giving activities include $431,681 for programs.
Officers: Catherine W. Herman, Chair.; Margaret W. Hecht, Pres.; Kathleen W. Wennesland, V.P.; Carolyn Winkler Thomas, Secy.
Director: Kim S. Wennesland.
EIN: 510243204

63989
The Agecroft Association
4305 Sulgrave Rd.
Richmond, VA 23221

Classified as a private operating foundation in 1975.
Financial data (yr. ended 12/31/00): Assets, $20,363,787 (M); grants paid, $47; gifts received, $742,845; expenditures, $924,799; qualifying distributions, $716,929; giving activities include $785,673 for programs.
Officers and Directors:* Evans B. Brasfield,* Pres.; Richard B. Woodward,* V.P.; Richard Moxley, Exec. Dir.; Richard H. Dilworth, Jane Paden, Betsy J. Parrish, Charles L. Reed, John R. Rilling.
EIN: 540805729

63990
Petersburg Home for Ladies, Inc.
311 S. Jefferson St.
Petersburg, VA 23803

Financial data (yr. ended 12/31/99): Assets, $19,209,432 (M); grants paid, $0; gifts received, $108,947; expenditures, $1,876,566; qualifying distributions, $1,721,556; giving activities include $1,680,384 for programs.
Officers and Directors:* Beth Cuthbert,* Pres.; Jonnee Sue Grizzard,* 1st V.P.; Jean Holt,* 2nd V.P.; Betty Callahan,* Secy.; Edith Sheffield,* Treas.; Gordon D. Shackelford, Exec. Dir.; Amos Tinnell, Exec. Dir.; Rebecca Bryant, Jean Coleman, Linda Crocker, Eloise Godsey, Jean Haire, Jean Lum, Dot Miller, Gracelyn Parks, Martha Shackleford, Margery Wright.
EIN: 540515720

63991
Cecil D. Hylton Memorial Chapel Foundation
c/o Norris L. Sisson
5593 Mapledale Plz.
Dale City, VA 22193-4527

Established in 1991 in VA.
Donor(s): The Cecil and Irene Hylton Foundation, Inc.
Financial data (yr. ended 12/31/01): Assets, $17,106,257 (M); grants paid, $0; gifts received, $453,990; expenditures, $1,009,361; qualifying distributions, $446,198; giving activities include $446,198 for programs.
Officers and Directors:* Conrad C. Hylton, Sr.,* Pres. and Treas.; Shelby Boldt,* V.P.; Norris L. Sisson,* Secy.; Cecilia Hylton, Richard D. Hylton.
EIN: 541584795

63992
The Constitution Foundation
(Formerly The Saylor Foundation)
1861 International Dr.
McLean, VA 22102 (703) 848-8600
Contact: Michael J. Saylor, Tr.

Established in 1998 in MA.
Donor(s): Michael J. Saylor.
Financial data (yr. ended 12/31/00): Assets, $15,031,945 (M); grants paid, $134,145; expenditures, $156,033; qualifying distributions, $134,145.
Trustee: Michael J. Saylor.
EIN: 541933630
Codes: FD2

63993
Proteus Foundation
18727 Silcott Springs Rd.
Purcellville, VA 20132 (540) 338-3495
Contact: Celia W. Rutt, Dir.

Established in 2000 in VI.
Donor(s): Celia W. Rutt, James P. Rutt.
Financial data (yr. ended 09/30/01): Assets, $10,329,448 (M); grants paid, $0; gifts received, $10,000,000; expenditures, $126,338; qualifying distributions, $0.
Limitations: Giving primarily in Washington, DC, NY, and VA.
Directors: Celia W. Rutt, James P. Rutt.
EIN: 542013543

63994
Chastain Home for Gentlewomen
c/o J.M. Oakes
P.O. Box 86
South Boston, VA 24592-0086

Established in 1957.
Financial data (yr. ended 03/31/00): Assets, $9,361,075 (M); grants paid, $2,200; expenditures, $284,515; qualifying distributions, $284,515.
Limitations: Applications not accepted.
Application information: Contributes only to pre-selected organizations.
Officers and Trustees:* Bates Chappell,* Secy.; Robert Martin, Jr.,* Treas.; Tucker L. Henley, Brockenbrough Lamb, W.M. Lewis, Chandler A. Nelson.
EIN: 540584100

63995
The Potomac Foundation
1311 Dolley Madison Blvd., Ste. 2-A
McLean, VA 22101

Establish in 1988 in VA. Classified as a private operating foundation in 1996.
Donor(s): BDM International, Inc., Smith Richardson Foundation, Inc., The Boeing Co.
Financial data (yr. ended 12/31/99): Assets, $8,978,596 (M); grants paid, $0; gifts received, $528,455; expenditures, $895,714; qualifying distributions, $740,381; giving activities include $568,157 for programs.
Officers and Directors:* Daniel F. McDonald,* Pres.; F.N. Hofer, Secy.-Treas.; Joseph V. Braddock, Bernard J. Dunn.
EIN: 541468870

63996
Kaufman Americana Foundation
480 World Trade Ctr.
Norfolk, VA 23510

Established in 1977. Classified as a private operating foundation in 1982.
Donor(s): George M. Kaufman, Linda H. Kaufman.
Financial data (yr. ended 11/30/01): Assets, $8,454,304 (M); grants paid, $15,350; gifts received, $243,500; expenditures, $114,711; qualifying distributions, $72,223.
Application information: Application form not required.
Officers and Directors:* George M. Kaufman,* Pres.; Linda H. Kaufman,* V.P.; Betty Cloud, Secy.-Treas.; Wendy A. Cooper, Mark Leithauser.
EIN: 510217081

63997
Brookfield, Inc.
P.O. Box 1039
Glen Allen, VA 23060

Classified as a private operating foundation in 1983.
Financial data (yr. ended 12/31/99): Assets, $7,937,715 (M); grants paid, $0; gifts received, $13,635; expenditures, $453,606; qualifying distributions, $323,345; giving activities include $418,634 for programs.
Officers and Trustees:* Terrell R.L. Williams,* Pres.; Charles L. Cabell,* 1st V.P.; Jane R. Fields,* 2nd V.P.; Harriet Brockenbrough,* Secy.; William B. Wiltshire,* Treas.; Anne W. Board, Nancy W. Bowman, Jacqueline R. Francis, Crit T. Richardson, and 7 additional trustees.
EIN: 540638415

63998
Stargazer Foundation
1650 Tysons Blvd., Ste. 200
Mclean, VA 22102
E-mail: foundation@stargazer.com; **URL:** http://www.stargazer.com
Contact: Arthur Bushkin, Chair.

Established in 1999.
Donor(s): Arthur A. Bushkin, Kathryn A. Bushkin.
Financial data (yr. ended 10/31/01): Assets, $7,236,874 (M); grants paid, $0; gifts received, $11,363,555; expenditures, $1,683,194; qualifying distributions, $1,460,980.
Officers: Arthur A. Bushkin, Chair, C.E.O. and Treas.; Kathryn A. Bushkin, Vice-Chair. and Secy.
EIN: 541962181

63999
The Lafferty Foundation
P.O. Box 29789
Richmond, VA 23242-9789

Classified as a private operating foundation in 1989.
Donor(s): Edgar R. Lafferty, Jr.,‡ Tidewater Warehouses, Inc., Southern Warehouses, Inc.
Financial data (yr. ended 12/31/99): Assets, $6,552,503 (M); grants paid, $0; expenditures, $284,019; qualifying distributions, $270,722; giving activities include $252,630 for programs.
Officers and Directors:* Edgar R. Lafferty III,* Pres.; Charles C. Webb,* Secy.; Samuel P. White, Treas.; Roger G. Hopper.
EIN: 541224308

64000
Korea U.S. Science Cooperation Center, Inc.
1952 Gallows Rd., No. 320
Vienna, VA 22182

Established in 1997 in VA.
Financial data (yr. ended 12/31/01): Assets, $5,769,963 (M); grants paid, $0; expenditures, $887,609; qualifying distributions, $0; giving activities include $241,569 for programs.
Officers: Jin Ho Park, Pres.; Byung Ock Chung, Secy.-Treas.
EIN: 541822381

64001
The Hunter Foundation
1210 First Virginia Twr.
Norfolk, VA 23510-2310

Classified as a private operating foundation in 1973.
Financial data (yr. ended 11/30/01): Assets, $5,723,027 (M); grants paid, $0; gifts received, $745; expenditures, $261,989; qualifying distributions, $0; giving activities include $240,832 for programs.
Trustees: Edwin W. Chitton, Charles T. Lambert, Townsend Oast.
EIN: 540801148

64002
Hazelwild Farm Educational Foundation
5325 Harrison Rd.
Fredericksburg, VA 22407

Donor(s): A. Elizabeth Morrison.
Financial data (yr. ended 12/31/99): Assets, $5,617,636 (M); grants paid, $723; gifts received, $5,000; expenditures, $1,171,230; qualifying distributions, $44,227.
Limitations: Applications not accepted.
Application information: Contributes only to pre-selected organizations.
Officers and Directors:* Barbara Lanford,* Pres.; Bess Knestaut,* Secy.-Treas.; Pamela Bolen, John I. Danielson, Duval Q. Hicks, Myrtle M. Tompkins, Kenneth T. Whitescarver III.
EIN: 521311337

64003
The An-Bryce Foundation
P.O. Box 1819
Vienna, VA 22183-1819

Established in 1995 in VA.
Financial data (yr. ended 12/31/99): Assets, $5,379,532 (M); grants paid, $5,200; gifts received, $246,245; expenditures, $288,533; qualifying distributions, $299,121; giving activities include $299,121 for programs.
Limitations: Applications not accepted.
Application information: Contributes only to pre-selected organizations.
Officers: Beatrice W. Welters, Pres.; Edgar G. Rios, Secy.
Directors: Constance Berry Newman, William S. Norman, Anthony Welters.
EIN: 541766299

64004
The Hermitage Foundation
7637 N. Shore Rd.
Norfolk, VA 23505

Classified as a private operating foundation in 1972.
Donor(s): Hermitage Foundation Trust.
Financial data (yr. ended 06/30/01): Assets, $5,249,842 (M); grants paid, $0; gifts received, $2,656,993; expenditures, $476,995; qualifying distributions, $309,505; giving activities include $476,995 for programs.
Officers and Directors:* William S. Hull,* Pres.; John B. Meek,* V.P.; Aileen B. Gustin, Secy.; Mark Coberly, Treas.; Philip R. Morrison, Exec. Dir.; Lenox D. Baker, Nancy Fleishman, George B. Hardy, Lela Marshall Hine, Harold C. Mauncey, Jr., Elizabeth F. Melchor, Elizabeth Hardy Parks.
EIN: 540505909

64005
Cove Creek Park Association
P.O. Box 9
Covesville, VA 22931

Established in 1996 in VA.
Financial data (yr. ended 12/31/99): Assets, $4,844,050 (M); grants paid, $0; gifts received, $1,366,458; expenditures, $556,300; qualifying distributions, $300,919; giving activities include $556,300 for programs.
Officers and Director:* John Grisham, Jr.,* Pres.; Richard E. Carter, V.P.
EIN: 541797263

64006
Stone House Foundation
P.O. Box 143
Stephens City, VA 22655

Financial data (yr. ended 12/31/01): Assets, $4,584,355 (M); grants paid, $4,500; gifts received, $63; expenditures, $116,644; qualifying distributions, $4,500.
Limitations: Applications not accepted.
Application information: Contributes only to pre-selected organizations.
Officers and Directors:* Linden Fravel, Jr.,* Pres.; Eloise Strader,* V.P.; David Powers,* Secy.; Julia Davidson,* Treas.; Linda C. Simmons.
EIN: 541546923

64007
George M. Jones Library Association
2311 Memorial Ave.
Lynchburg, VA 24501

Classified as a private operating foundation in 1973.
Financial data (yr. ended 06/30/00): Assets, $4,169,845 (M); grants paid, $0; gifts received, $31,191; expenditures, $245,265; qualifying distributions, $188,411; giving activities include $245,265 for programs.
Officers and Trustees:* William S. Williams,* Pres.; Jane F. Bowden,* V.P.; Rayner V. Snead, Jr.,* Secy.; William E. McBratney, Jr.,* Treas.
EIN: 540505921

64008
Robert & Dee Leggett Foundation
P.O. Box 240
Great Falls, VA 22066
FAX: (703) 430-9608; E-mail: rnleggett@aol.com
Contact: Robert N. Leggett, Jr., Pres.

Established in 1999 in VA.
Donor(s): Robert Leggett, Dee C. Leggett.
Financial data (yr. ended 12/31/01): Assets, $3,857,648 (M); grants paid, $385,478; gifts received, $993,910; expenditures, $952,258; qualifying distributions, $1,055,858; giving activities include $115,100 for loans.
Limitations: Applications not accepted. Giving primarily in the Blue Ridge region, VA.
Publications: Financial statement, informational brochure.
Application information: Contributes only to pre-selected organizations. Unsolicited requests for funds not accepted.
Officers: Robert "Bob" N. Leggett, Jr., Pres.; Dee C. Leggett, V.P.; Donna I. Measell, Secy.-Treas.
Directors: W. James Athearn, David James Chadwick, Laura L. Leggett, David Lillard, Charles W. Sloan.
EIN: 541921311
Codes: FD

64009
Maupin-Sizemore Foundation, Inc.
3138 Stoneridge Rd.
Roanoke, VA 24014

Established in 1993 in VA.
Donor(s): Leroy M. Sizemore,‡ Marjorie S. Maupin.
Financial data (yr. ended 12/31/01): Assets, $3,713,399 (M); grants paid, $140,120; expenditures, $211,142; qualifying distributions, $159,507.
Limitations: Giving primarily in VA.
Officers: Marjorie S. Maupin, Pres.; Harry F. Davis, V.P.; T. Henry Clarke IV, Secy.-Treas.
EIN: 541661338
Codes: FD2

64010
Miller Home of Lynchburg, Virginia
c/o Thomas D. Gerhardt
2134 Westerly Dr.
Lynchburg, VA 24501

Financial data (yr. ended 04/30/02): Assets, $3,462,218 (M); grants paid, $0; gifts received, $342,400; expenditures, $450,901; qualifying distributions, $0.
Officers and Directors:* Elizabeth S. Coleman,* Pres.; Joan T. Martin,* V.P.; Gary M. Coates,* Secy.; Fred C. Thomas,* Treas.; Fred R. Cawthorne, William C. Cline, Mrs. Edgar D. Garrard, William N. Mays, William E. Painter, Jack Schewel, Mrs. C. Raine Sydnor, Jr., Mrs. Morris O. Wright, Jr., and 3 additional directors.
EIN: 540505999

64011
Los Padres Foundation
658 Live Oak Dr.
McLean, VA 22101 (201) 836-3090
Application address: P.O. Box 217, Teaneck, NJ 07666
Contact: Ms. Cruz Shanchez-Del Valle, Exec. Dir.

Established in 1995 in VA and NY.
Donor(s): Lillian Rios, Edgar Rios.
Financial data (yr. ended 09/30/01): Assets, $2,850,536 (M); grants paid, $27,125; gifts received, $124,782; expenditures, $167,838; qualifying distributions, $165,457; giving activities include $77,500 for programs.
Limitations: Giving primarily in New York, NY.
Application information: Application for student aid must include letters of reference, essay, and financial information. Application form required.
Officers and Directors:* Lillian Rios,* Pres.; Edgar Rios,* Secy.; Cruz Sanchez-Del Valle, Exec. Dir.; Andrea Betancourt, Ivan Cortes, Thomas Morales, Aramis G. Rios.
EIN: 541772081
Codes: GTI

64012
The John C. Fricano Foundation, Inc.
1601 S. Arlington Ridge Rd.
Arlington, VA 22202-1624
Application address: 3345 Clubhouse Rd., Virginia Beach, VA 23452
Contact: Rev. Msgr. Thomas J. Caroluzza, Secy.

Established in 1995.
Donor(s): Mary E. Fricano.
Financial data (yr. ended 12/31/00): Assets, $2,599,495 (M); grants paid, $165,000; expenditures, $221,069; qualifying distributions, $164,061.
Limitations: Giving limited to VA.
Application information: Application form required.
Officers: Mary E. Fricano, Pres.; S.J. DiMeglio, V.P.; Rev. Msgr. Thomas J. Caroluzza, Secy. and Mgr.; Jerry Garbys, Treas.
EIN: 541749715
Codes: FD2

64013
Jonathan Bryan III Charitable Trust
1802 Bayberry Ct., Ste. 301
Richmond, VA 23226 (804) 285-7700
Contact: Jonathan Bryan III, Tr.

Established in 1993 in VA.
Financial data (yr. ended 12/31/01): Assets, $2,352,837 (M); grants paid, $120,000; expenditures, $139,941; qualifying distributions, $119,738.
Limitations: Giving primarily in Richmond, VA.
Application information: Application form not required.
Trustees: John R. Bryan, Jonathan Bryan III.
EIN: 541670781
Codes: FD2

64014
The Elisabeth Aiken Nolting Foundation
c/o McGuireWoods, LLP
P.O. Box 397
Richmond, VA 23218-0397

Established in 1990 in VA. Classified as a private operating foundation in 2001.
Donor(s): Elisabeth Aiken Nolting.‡
Financial data (yr. ended 06/30/01): Assets, $2,299,313 (M); grants paid, $0; gifts received, $2,255,163; expenditures, $145,312; qualifying distributions, $145,312; giving activities include $145,312 for programs.
Officers and Directors:* George C. Nolting,* Pres.; Timothy C. Neale, V.P.; John B. Bazuin, Jr.,* Secy.; Anthony L. Zentgraf, Treas.; James L. Nolting, W.W. Sanford III.
EIN: 541517475

64015
Chelonia Institute, Inc.
3330 Washington Blvd.
Arlington, VA 22201

Financial data (yr. ended 02/28/01): Assets, $2,149,576 (M); grants paid, $87,530; expenditures, $123,429; qualifying distributions, $109,524; giving activities include $109,524 for programs.
Limitations: Applications not accepted. Giving primarily in Arlington, VA.
Application information: Contributes only to pre-selected organizations.
Officers: Robert W. Truland, Pres. and Treas.; Mary W. Truland, Secy.
EIN: 521081407
Codes: FD2

64016
The Wayside Museum of American History & Arts
P.O. Box 31
Strasburg, VA 22657

Classified as a private operating foundation in 1986.
Financial data (yr. ended 12/31/99): Assets, $1,735,426 (M); grants paid, $1,500; gifts received, $28,393; expenditures, $177,302; qualifying distributions, $1,500.
Officers and Directors:* Leo M. Bernstein,* Pres.; Richard D. Bernstein,* V.P.; Stuart A. Bernstein,* V.P.; Wilma Bernstein, Secy.
EIN: 541367435

64017
The Jotom Foundation
200 N. Main St.
Suffolk, VA 23434

Established in 2000.
Donor(s): William T. Spence.
Financial data (yr. ended 12/31/01): Assets, $1,643,619 (M); grants paid, $75,000; expenditures, $141,557; qualifying distributions, $75,000.
Trustees: Joshua Pretlow, Jr., Jennifer S. Spence, Linda J. Spence, William T. Spence, William T. Spence, Jr.
EIN: 542014304

64018
American Foundation for the Study of Man
P.O. Box 2136
Falls Church, VA 22042

Classified as a private operating foundation in 1972.
Donor(s): Merilyn Hodgson, Gordon Hodgson.
Financial data (yr. ended 12/31/00): Assets, $1,577,792 (M); grants paid, $0; gifts received, $182,849; expenditures, $119,467; qualifying distributions, $119,467; giving activities include $119,467 for programs.
Officers: Merilyn Hodgson, Pres.; A. Jamme, Ph.D., V.P.; Sharon Wiley, Secy.; David O. Radloff, Treas.; Gordon Hodgson, Exec. Dir.
Directors: Frank Albright, Jeff Blakely, Hugh A.M. Shafer, Jr.
EIN: 996001275

64019
American Environment Foundation
1937 Laskin Rd.
Virginia Beach, VA 23454

Established in 1992 in VA.
Donor(s): James D. Parker.
Financial data (yr. ended 12/31/99): Assets, $1,256,705 (M); grants paid, $2,500; gifts received, $595,000; expenditures, $46,708; qualifying distributions, $46,708.
Limitations: Applications not accepted.
Application information: Contributes only to pre-selected organizations.
Officer: James D. Parker, Pres.
Trustees: James W. Brazier, Paul A. Davis, Virginia J. Davis, Robert S. Szetela.
EIN: 541621128

64020
The Thompson Foundation
c/o Roland E. Thompson
33018 Millville Rd.
Upperville, VA 20184-3100

Established in 1993 in VA.
Donor(s): Roland E. Thompson.
Financial data (yr. ended 06/30/00): Assets, $1,198,658 (M); grants paid, $0; gifts received, $852,650; expenditures, $20,393; qualifying distributions, $20,131; giving activities include $18,105 for programs.
Officers and Trustees:* Roland E. Thompson,* Pres.; Mark L. Thompson,* V.P.; Ann C. Thompson-Tate,* Secy.-Treas.
EIN: 541686055

64021
Peterson Family Foundation, Inc.
12500 Fair Lakes Cir., Ste. 400
Fairfax, VA 22033   (703) 744-8040
Contact: Blanca R. Ramos

Established in 1998 in VA.
Donor(s): Lauren P. Fellows, Jon M. Peterson, Milton V. Peterson, Steven B. Peterson, William E. Peterson.
Financial data (yr. ended 12/31/01): Assets, $1,127,079 (M); grants paid, $2,022,931; gifts received, $1,715,070; expenditures, $2,033,685; qualifying distributions, $2,006,434.
Limitations: Giving primarily in VA, with emphasis on Fairfax.
Officers: Milton V. Peterson, Pres.; Lauren P. Fellows, Secy.; William E. Peterson, Treas.
Directors: Carolyn S. Peterson, Jon M. Peterson, Steven B. Peterson.
EIN: 541870812
Codes: FD

64022
Womack Foundation
513 Wilson St.
Danville, VA 24541
Application address: c/o Louise Wright, P.O. Box 521, Danville, VA 24543
Contact: James A.L. Daniel, Chair.

Established in 1963.
Donor(s): Charles Womack, Sr.
Financial data (yr. ended 03/31/02): Assets, $1,091,941 (M); grants paid, $166,402; expenditures, $182,942; qualifying distributions, $165,410; giving activities include $6,660 for loans to individuals.
Limitations: Giving limited to the Pittsylvania County, VA, area, with emphasis on Danville.
Application information: Application form required.
Officers: James A.L. Daniel, Chair.; Louise Wright, Secy.-Treas.
Trustees: Rev. Lawrence Campbell, Bobbye Rae Womack, and 10 additional trustees.
EIN: 546053255
Codes: FD2, GTI

64023
The Farkas Family Foundation
315 Heron Ln.
Charlottesville, VA 22903

Established in 2000 in VA.
Financial data (yr. ended 12/31/00): Assets, $1,083,683 (M); grants paid, $0; expenditures, $500; qualifying distributions, $0.
Trustee: Gail Munger.
EIN: 061593377

64024
Flowerdew Hundred Foundation
1617 Flowerdew Hundred Rd.
Hopewell, VA 23860

Classified as a private operating foundation in 1981.
Donor(s): David A. Harrison III.
Financial data (yr. ended 11/30/01): Assets, $1,071,040 (M); grants paid, $0; gifts received, $775,033; expenditures, $321,504; qualifying distributions, $272,879; giving activities include $273,191 for programs.
Officers and Directors:* Mary T.H. Keevil,* Chair.; Ann L.H. Harrison,* Vice-Chair.; John Casteen, Cynthia Harrison, David A. Harrison III, David A. Harrison IV, Elizabeth R. Harrison, George A. Harrison, Meriwether Major, Marjorie H. Webb.
EIN: 540909205

64025
Grenold and Dorothy Collins Alaska Charitable Trust
2101 Wilson Blvd., Ste. 1100
Arlington, VA 22201
Application address: 4 Amy Dr., Morristown, NJ 07960
Contact: Elizabeth Nitze, Tr.

Established in 1998.
Donor(s): Dorothy Collins.‡
Financial data (yr. ended 12/31/99): Assets, $997,201 (M); grants paid, $10,000; gifts received, $489,417; expenditures, $12,035; qualifying distributions, $10,000.
Trustees: John Barrett, Con Bunde, William Kent, Elizabeth Nitze.
EIN: 931250158

64026
The Voyager Foundation
194 Poague Ln.
Glasgow, VA 24555-2262

Established in 1994 in VA.
Donor(s): Craig Halliwill, Bobby Jean Bressler.
Financial data (yr. ended 04/30/00): Assets, $947,577 (M); grants paid, $0; gifts received, $15,308; expenditures, $126,696; qualifying distributions, $98,641; giving activities include $127,949 for programs.
Officers and Trustees:* Craig Halliwill, Pres.; Gary Thomas,* Secy.; Bobby Jean Bressler,* Treas.
EIN: 043233636

64027
Oak Spring Garden Foundation
1746 Loughborough Ln.
Upperville, VA 20184

Donor(s): Rachel L. Mellon.
Financial data (yr. ended 12/31/99): Assets, $926,513 (M); grants paid, $0; expenditures, $6,866; qualifying distributions, $6,866; giving activities include $6,866 for programs.
Officers and Directors:* Rachel L. Mellon,* Pres.; Alexander D. Forger,* Secy.; Tony Wills, Treas.
EIN: 541672141

64028
Walter R. Talbot Foundation
c/o Peggy S. LaFollette
P.O. Box 27
Gore, VA 22637

Established around 1990.
Financial data (yr. ended 12/31/01): Assets, $881,661 (M); grants paid, $0; expenditures, $25,460; qualifying distributions, $19,977; giving activities include $20,184 for programs.
Officers and Trustees:* Elzada M. Parish,* Pres.; Coy Cunningham,* V.P.; Peggy S. LaFollette,* Secy.-Treas.; Sharon G. Kelly, Beverly L. LaFollette, John T. Watt, Jr.
EIN: 541127098

64029
American Values
2800 Shirlington Rd., Ste. 610
Arlington, VA 22206

Established in 1996 in DC and VA.
Financial data (yr. ended 12/31/01): Assets, $854,564 (M); grants paid, $3,265; gifts received, $1,235,471; expenditures, $639,695; qualifying distributions, $638,285; giving activities include $636,479 for programs.
Limitations: Applications not accepted. Giving on a national basis.
Application information: Contributes only to pre-selected organizations.
Officer: Gary Bauer, Pres.
Directors: Betty Barrett, Carol Bauer, Charles Donovan.
EIN: 521762320

64030
Goolsby Educational Fund
111 N. Church St.
Marion, VA 24354-2705 (540) 783-8102
Contact: Donald G. Hammer, Tr.

Financial data (yr. ended 12/31/01): Assets, $804,349 (M); grants paid, $37,850; expenditures, $65,650; qualifying distributions, $101,552; giving activities include $37,850 for loans to individuals.
Limitations: Giving limited to Smyth County, VA.
Application information: Application form required.
Trustees: Donald G. Hammer, Harlan S. Pafford, J.S. Staley, Jr.
EIN: 546067955
Codes: GTI

64031
Foundation for Traditional Studies
12210 Bennett Rd.
Herndon, VA 20171 (703) 476-8837
Contact: Kathleen O'Brien, Exec. Dir.

Established in 1996 in CA.
Financial data (yr. ended 10/31/99): Assets, $785,759 (M); grants paid, $3,050; gifts received, $42,008; expenditures, $131,652; qualifying distributions, $126,883; giving activities include $126,883 for programs.
Officers: Seyyed Hossein Nasr, Pres.; Huston Smith, V.P.; James Cutsinger, Secy.-Treas.; Katherine O'Brien, Exec. Dir.
Directors: Joseph Epes Brown, Rama Coomaraswamy, Flora Courtois, Alvin Moore.
EIN: 237259900

64032
Micah Foundation
1821 Solitare Ln.
McLean, VA 22101-4235

Established in 1997 in VA.
Financial data (yr. ended 11/30/99): Assets, $753,720 (M); grants paid, $0; gifts received, $196,715; expenditures, $50,783; qualifying distributions, $47,880; giving activities include $47,880 for programs.
Officers: Ruth B. McBride, Pres. and Secy.; J. Scott McBride, Treas.
Directors: John David McBride, Laura Ann McBride.
EIN: 541875454

64033
The Elms Foundation
c/o Bobby B. Wurrell
P.O. Box 813
Franklin, VA 23851

Established in 1986 in VA.
Financial data (yr. ended 12/31/01): Assets, $682,165 (M); grants paid, $0; gifts received, $141,790; expenditures, $173,989; qualifying distributions, $0.
Officers and Directors:* John M. Camp, Sr.,* Pres.; Paul D. Camp III,* V.P.; Bobby D. Worrell,* Secy.; S.W. Rawls, Jr.,* Treas.; Paul Camp Marks, Harry W. Walker.
EIN: 621383398

64034
Burwell-Van Lennep Foundation
1391 Tilthammar Mill Rd.
Boyce, VA 22620

Financial data (yr. ended 12/31/99): Assets, $658,021 (M); grants paid, $0; expenditures, $16,789; qualifying distributions, $16,789; giving activities include $1,062 for programs.
Trustees: Charles L. Burwell, Joan Fine, Jerome Garuer, Roland G. Mitchell, Richard Plater, Anne H.D. Randolph, Donald Richardson, Robert Simpson.
EIN: 237009888

64035
The Oliver Foundation
8880 Ash Grove Ln.
Vienna, VA 22180-2201

Established in 1986 in VA.
Donor(s): Cap H. Oliver, Helene S. Oliver.
Financial data (yr. ended 12/31/00): Assets, $640,655 (M); grants paid, $49,000; gifts received, $58,443; expenditures, $76,100; qualifying distributions, $49,000.
Limitations: Applications not accepted. Giving on a national basis.
Application information: Contributes only to pre-selected organizations.
Officers: Cap H. Oliver, Jr., Pres. and Treas.; Helene S. Oliver, V.P. and Secy.
EIN: 541422033

64036
Weyers Cave Recreational Association, Inc.
P.O. Box 171
Weyers Cave, VA 24486-0171

Established in 1984 in VA.
Donor(s): Houff Foundation, County of Augusta, VA.
Financial data (yr. ended 12/31/01): Assets, $640,237 (M); grants paid, $59,057; gifts received, $13,000; expenditures, $59,057; qualifying distributions, $59,057.
Officers and Directors:* Tim Wade,* Pres.; Barry Ritchie,* V.P.; Paul T. Riblin,* Secy.; Hensel W. Baker,* Treas.; Joe Bartley, Edwin C. Showalter, Thomas V. Thacker.
EIN: 521231769

64037
Sydney & Frances Lewis Foundation
2601 Monument Ave.
Richmond, VA 23220

Established in 1966 in VA.
Donor(s): Sydney Lewis,‡ Frances A. Lewis.
Financial data (yr. ended 06/30/00): Assets, $636,184 (M); grants paid, $30,070; expenditures, $35,669; qualifying distributions, $31,628.
Limitations: Applications not accepted. Giving primarily in New York, NY, and VA, with emphasis on Richmond.
Application information: Contributes only to pre-selected organizations.
Officers and Directors:* Frances A. Lewis,* Pres.; Susan L. Butler,* V.P.; Andrew M. Lewis,* Secy.; Robert L. Burrus, Jr.
EIN: 546061170

64038
The Frank H. Nott Foundation
8 Charnwood Rd.
Richmond, VA 23229

Financial data (yr. ended 12/31/99): Assets, $632,753 (M); grants paid, $21,400; gifts received, $3,432; expenditures, $22,566; qualifying distributions, $128,219.
Limitations: Applications not accepted.
Application information: Contributes only to pre-selected organizations.
Officers and Directors:* P. Bradley Nott, Jr.,* Pres.; W.J. Nott,* Secy.; F.J. Stumpf,* Treas.
EIN: 541509035

64039
Portsmouth Historical Association, Inc.
221 North St.
Portsmouth, VA 23704-2601

Financial data (yr. ended 12/31/00): Assets, $622,069 (M); grants paid, $0; gifts received, $7,804; expenditures, $18,317; qualifying distributions, $15,014; giving activities include $15,014 for programs.
Officers and Governors:* Alice C. Hanes,* Pres.; Macon Williams,* 1st V.P.; Jean A. Coleman,* 2nd V.P.; Doris Leitner,* Recording Secy.; Elizabeth B. Watson,* Corresponding Secy.; Nancy Robertson,* Treas.; Jeannie Bartlett, Marshall W. Butt, Jr., Corinna B. Jeffreys, Jean Miller, Ann Douglas Smith, and 4 additional governors.
EIN: 546044359

64040
Association of Physician Assistant Programs
950 N. Washington St.
Alexandria, VA 22314 (703) 548-5538
Contact: Steven Lane

Classified as a private operating foundation in 1975.
Financial data (yr. ended 06/30/00): Assets, $603,631 (M); grants paid, $21,796; gifts received, $3,647; expenditures, $890,070; qualifying distributions, $498,132; giving activities include $317,169 for programs.
Limitations: Giving on a national basis.
Officers and Directors:* P. Eugene Jones, Ph.D.,* Co-Pres.; Gloria M. Stewart, Co-Pres.; William H. Marquardt,* Secy.-Treas.; Lisa Mustone Alexander, Rosann M. Ippolito.
EIN: 237198463
Codes: TN

64041
The Donald A. Perry Foundation
P.O. Box 1275
Gloucester, VA 23061-1275 (804) 877-4367
Contact: Donald A. Perry, Pres.

Established in 1996 in VA.
Donor(s): Donald A. Perry.
Financial data (yr. ended 12/31/01): Assets, $586,808 (M); grants paid, $34,750; gifts received, $50,000; expenditures, $38,455; qualifying distributions, $34,750.
Officers: Donald A. Perry, Pres.; Alyson E. Perry, V.P.; Thomas A. Smith, Jr., Secy.

Directors: Christopher C. Perry, Donald A. Perry, Jr.
EIN: 541811462

64042
Willows Foundation
7900 Westpark Dr., Ste. T-100
McLean, VA 22102

Established in 1998 in VA.
Donor(s): The Buffett Foundation.
Financial data (yr. ended 12/31/99): Assets, $560,896 (M); grants paid, $0; gifts received, $12,784; expenditures, $511,086; qualifying distributions, $579,437; giving activities include $511,086 for programs.
Officers: Turkiz Gokgol, C.E.O. and Pres.; Janet Benshoof, Secy.
Director: Elaine Murphy.
EIN: 541877800

64043
Rockbridge Historical Society
P.O. Box 514
Lexington, VA 24450-0514

Classified as a private operating foundation in 1988.
Financial data (yr. ended 12/31/00): Assets, $520,081 (M); grants paid, $950; gifts received, $5,928; expenditures, $42,550; qualifying distributions, $31,886.
Limitations: Giving primarily in VA.
Application information: Unsolicited requests for funds not accepted.
Officers: David Reynolds, Pres.; Richard Rathmell, V.P.; Bob Lera, Secy.; Richard Halseth, Treas.
EIN: 237090646

64044
La Mirage Adult Home, Inc.
c/o John Small
900 World Trade Ctr.
Norfolk, VA 23510

Classified as a private operating foundation in 1994.
Financial data (yr. ended 12/31/01): Assets, $470,123 (M); grants paid, $0; expenditures, $4,365; qualifying distributions, $0.
Officer: John Small, Pres.
EIN: 541523415

64045
The Volgenau Foundation
8302 Summerwood Dr.
McLean, VA 22102

Established in 1994 in VA.
Donor(s): Ernst Volgenau, Sara Lane Volgenau.
Financial data (yr. ended 06/30/00): Assets, $453,620 (M); grants paid, $0; expenditures, $68,110; qualifying distributions, $59,231; giving activities include $2,917 for programs.
Publications: Occasional report.
Officers and Directors:* Ernst Volgenau,* Pres.; Sara Lane Volgenau,* Secy.-Treas.; Lisa Volgenau,* Exec. Dir.; Lauren Volgenau Knapp, Jennifer Volgenau Wiley.
EIN: 541738281

64046
John Harry & Edith Carter Lewis Carmine Trust
c/o First Virginia Bank, Trust Dept.
P.O. Box 27736
Richmond, VA 23261 (804) 697-5391

Established in 1988 in VA.
Financial data (yr. ended 12/31/01): Assets, $447,819 (M); grants paid, $0; expenditures, $11,779; qualifying distributions, $48,621; giving activities include $49,185 for loans to individuals.
Limitations: Giving limited to Gloucester and Matthews counties, VA.
Application information: Application form required.
Trustee: First Virginia Bank.
EIN: 546262132
Codes: GT1

64047
New Horizons Foundation, Inc.
1256 Wind Dancer Pl.
Thaxton, VA 24174

Established in 1997 in VA.
Donor(s): Cornelis Pieterman.
Financial data (yr. ended 11/30/00): Assets, $407,107 (M); grants paid, $0; gifts received, $2,225; expenditures, $37,153; qualifying distributions, $34,970; giving activities include $29,259 for programs.
Limitations: Applications not accepted.
Application information: Contributes only to pre-selected organizations.
Officer: Cornelis Pieterman, Pres.
Directors: Jacoba M.E. Pieterman, Maria A. Pieterman, Roland E. Pieterman.
EIN: 541878032

64048
Employee Assistance of Central Virginia, Inc.
2250 Murrell Rd., Ste. B5
Lynchburg, VA 24501

Financial data (yr. ended 06/30/00): Assets, $402,599 (M); grants paid, $0; expenditures, $554,527; qualifying distributions, $538,163; giving activities include $538,297 for programs.
Limitations: Giving primarily in the central VA area.
Officers and Directors:* Gregory Quickel,* Chair.; Charles Church,* Vice-Chair.; Richard Anderson,* Secy.; Dennis Janiak,* Treas.; Cynthia J. Read, Exec. Dir.; J.A. Conner, Glenn McGrath, Adrian Mood, Elisabeth Muhlenfeld.
EIN: 541121512

64049
Long Bridge Ordinary Foundation
P.O. Box 360
Dutton, VA 23050

Financial data (yr. ended 12/31/99): Assets, $371,293 (M); grants paid, $7,092; expenditures, $9,642; qualifying distributions, $7,092.
Limitations: Applications not accepted. Giving limited to Gloucester, VA.
Application information: Contributes only to pre-selected organizations.
Officers and Directors:* Donald P. Roane,* Pres.; J. Scott Finney,* V.P.; John L. Finney, V.P.; Betty White,* Secy.; Col. Benjamin B. Manchester,* Treas.; Mrs. Benjamin B. Manchester, and 9 additional directors.
EIN: 521205904

64050
The Frederick & Lucy S. Herman Foundation
c/o Frederick Herman
420 W. Bute St.
Norfolk, VA 23510-1189

Classified as a private operating foundation in 1981.
Financial data (yr. ended 12/31/01): Assets, $354,658 (M); grants paid, $0; gifts received, $200; expenditures, $337; qualifying distributions, $0.
Officers: Frederick Herman, Pres.; Lucy S. Herman, Secy-Treas.

Directors: Miles Chappell, Bernard L. Herman, L.F. Jacobs.
EIN: 541156963

64051
H. V. Robertson Family Memorial Education Foundation
c/o Ruth Ann Adams
6251 Old Dominion Dr., No. 203
McLean, VA 22101-4805

Established in 1990 in DC.
Donor(s): Ruth Ann Adams.
Financial data (yr. ended 07/31/01): Assets, $336,056 (M); grants paid, $211,667; expenditures, $218,099; qualifying distributions, $217,800.
Limitations: Applications not accepted. Giving on a national basis.
Application information: Contributes only to pre-selected organizations.
Directors: Ruth Ann Adams, Frances Cavagrotti, Victor J. Cavagrotti.
EIN: 521714019
Codes: FD2

64052
The Earle & June Williams Foundation
715 Potomac Knolls Dr.
McLean, VA 22102-1421
Contact: Earle Williams, Tr.; or June Williams, Tr.

Established in 1988 in VA.
Donor(s): Earle Williams, June Williams.
Financial data (yr. ended 12/31/99): Assets, $334,802 (M); grants paid, $25,400; expenditures, $39,727; qualifying distributions, $27,780.
Limitations: Giving primarily in VA.
Application information: Application form not required.
Trustees: Earle Williams, June Williams.
EIN: 541495801

64053
Wiley H. and James C. Wheat, Jr. Foundation
901 E. Byrd St., Ste. 1300
Richmond, VA 23219 (804) 782-3288
Contact: James C. Wheat III, Pres.

Established in 1992 in VA.
Donor(s): Wiley H. Wheat.
Financial data (yr. ended 12/31/99): Assets, $273,672 (M); grants paid, $105,919; expenditures, $106,394; qualifying distributions, $105,919.
Limitations: Giving primarily in Richmond, VA.
Application information: Application form not required.
Officer: James C. Wheat III, Pres.
Directors: John K. Burke, Jr., Adair D. Wheat.
EIN: 541647672

64054
Cliff Wells Foundation
P.O. Box 202
Buchanan, VA 24066
Contact: Roger P. Wells, Pres.

Established in 1992 in VA.
Donor(s): Clifford E. Wells.
Financial data (yr. ended 12/31/01): Assets, $267,987 (M); grants paid, $3,118; gifts received, $125,701; expenditures, $7,291; qualifying distributions, $3,118.
Limitations: Giving on a national basis.
Application information: Application form required.
Officers: Roger P. Wells, Pres.; Linda W. Gooding, V.P.
EIN: 541639919

64055
Russian Medical Fund
1862 Brothers Rd.
Vienna, VA 22182-2008   (703) 255-0827

Established in 1997 in VA.
Financial data (yr. ended 12/31/01): Assets, $266,933 (M); grants paid, $0; gifts received, $532,558; expenditures, $622,922; qualifying distributions, $0.
Limitations: Applications not accepted.
Officer: Susan McIntosh, Chair. and Pres.
EIN: 541869946

64056
Clearbrook Foundation
c/o Richard P. Sills
2241 Tacketts Mill Dr.
Woodbridge, VA 22192-3027

Classified as a private operating foundation in 1984.
Financial data (yr. ended 12/31/00): Assets, $243,852 (M); grants paid, $0; gifts received, $18,000; expenditures, $272; qualifying distributions, $272; giving activities include $272 for programs.
Officers and Directors:* Paulette J. Sen'Gerni,* Pres.; Claudia S. Johnson,* V.P.; Nancy S. Kyme, Secy.-Treas.
EIN: 521350125

64057
The Lost & Found Horse Rescue Foundation, Inc.
3330 Washington Blvd., Ste. 700
Arlington, VA 22201

Established in 1997 in MD and PA.
Donor(s): Chelonia Institute, Truland Foundation.
Financial data (yr. ended 02/28/00): Assets, $233,535 (M); grants paid, $0; gifts received, $240,435; expenditures, $304,623; qualifying distributions, $269,239; giving activities include $269,239 for programs.
Officers: Robert W. Truland, Pres.; Mary W. Truland, V.P.
EIN: 541845646

64058
The Christian Giving Fund
P.O. Box 1320
Richmond, VA 23218-1320
Contact: Fieldina L. Williams, Jr., Secy.-Treas.

Financial data (yr. ended 12/31/00): Assets, $214,547 (M); grants paid, $9,000; expenditures, $16,189; qualifying distributions, $9,000.
Limitations: Giving limited to Richmond, VA.
Application information: Application form not required.
Officers and Directors:* Benjamin A. Soyars,* Pres.; Laura S. Williams,* V.P.; Fieldina L. Williams, Jr.,* Secy.-Treas.
EIN: 541367148

64059
Ella G. & E. Massie Valentine Foundation
204 Lockgreen Ct.
Richmond, VA 23226-1758
Contact: E. Massie Valentine, Tr.

Donor(s): E. Massie Valertine.
Financial data (yr. ended 12/31/00): Assets, $206,029 (M); grants paid, $12,200; expenditures, $13,771; qualifying distributions, $12,104.
Limitations: Giving primarily in Richmond, VA.
Application information: Application form not required.
Trustees: Sarah V. Ellington, E. Massie Valentine, E. Massie Valentine, Jr., J. Gordon Valentine.
EIN: 546243471

64060
Cook Foundation
P.O. Box 1383
Gloucester, VA 23061-1383   (804) 693-2729
Contact: Adrianne Ryder-Cook, Pres.

Established in 1998 in VA.
Financial data (yr. ended 12/31/99): Assets, $200,662 (M); grants paid, $9,400; gifts received, $102,040; expenditures, $10,760; qualifying distributions, $4,330.
Officers: Adrianne Ryder-Cook, Pres.; Carolyn Dudley, V.P.; Elsa Verbyla, Secy.; Rachael Burnette, Treas.
EIN: 541894579

64061
Newberger Family Foundation, Inc.
1612 Walden Dr.
McLean, VA 22101

Established in 2001 in VA. Classified as a private operating foundation in 2002.
Donor(s): Stuart H. Newberger, Marcy A. Leon Newberger.
Financial data (yr. ended 12/31/01): Assets, $200,098 (M); grants paid, $0; gifts received, $200,000; expenditures, $500; qualifying distributions, $500.
Limitations: Applications not accepted.
Application information: Contributes only to pre-selected organizations.
Officers: Stuart H. Newberger,* Macy A. Leon Newberger.
EIN: 542061680

64062
Blessed Hope Christian Mission Foundation
3088 Busy Bee Rd.
South Hill, VA 23970-6049   (703) 979-4772
Application address: P.O. Box 4626 S. Glebe Rd., Arlington, VA 22204
Contact: Robert J. Rooks, Pres.

Established in 1993 in VA.
Donor(s): David Rooks, Mark Rooks, Daniel G. Rooks.
Financial data (yr. ended 06/30/99): Assets, $190,742 (M); grants paid, $11,000; gifts received, $46,125; expenditures, $12,296; qualifying distributions, $11,000.
Limitations: Giving limited to Haven, CT, College Park, MD, Pittsburg, PA, and Woodbridge, VA.
Application information: Application form required.
Officers: Robert J. Rooks, Pres.; Donalee B. Rooks, Secy.; Daniel G. Rooks, Treas.
Directors: Marianne P. Rooks, Mark S. Rooks.
EIN: 541691074

64063
Bull Run Preserve, Inc.
P.O. Box 207
Broad Run, VA 20137-0207   (703) 753-3273

Financial data (yr. ended 12/31/00): Assets, $173,898 (M); grants paid, $0; gifts received, $75,052; expenditures, $39,767; qualifying distributions, $36,537; giving activities include $36,537 for programs.
Officers and Directors:* Charles H. Sellheimer, Jr.,* Pres.; Earl H. Douple,* Secy.-Treas.; Andrea B. Currier.
EIN: 237439359

64064
Good Heart Foundation
1014 Northwoods Trail
McLean, VA 22102
Contact: Dr. Tao, Dir.

Established in 1999 in VA.
Donor(s): Lung Sheng L.S. Tao.
Financial data (yr. ended 12/31/01): Assets, $162,102 (M); grants paid, $10,200; expenditures, $10,225; qualifying distributions, $10,200.
Directors: Kou-Yun Tao, Lung Sheng L.S. Tao.
EIN: 541946661

64065
Foundation for Pharmacology
7830 Rockfalls Dr.
Richmond, VA 23225-1049   (804) 828-1661
Contact: Louis S. Harris, Ph.D., Pres.

Established in 1990 in VA.
Financial data (yr. ended 12/31/99): Assets, $152,877 (M); grants paid, $33,200; gifts received, $121,624; expenditures, $66,184; qualifying distributions, $66,184; giving activities include $7,049 for programs.
Officers: Louis S. Harris, Ph.D., Pres.; Billy R. Martin, Ph.D., V.P.; Joyce H. Rye, Secy.; Brenda R. Caine, Treas.
Directors: Robert Balster, George Kunos.
EIN: 541504296

64066
Buchanan First Presbyterian Church Foundation
P.O. Box 2100
Grundy, VA 24614

Established in 2000 in VA.
Donor(s): The Eagle Company, LLC.
Financial data (yr. ended 12/31/01): Assets, $148,547 (M); grants paid, $2,730; expenditures, $2,792; qualifying distributions, $2,717.
Limitations: Applications not accepted.
Application information: Contributes only to pre-selected organizations.
Officers: James O. Bunn, Pres.; Stanford T. Mullins, Secy.-Treas.
Director: Lucy G. Williams.
EIN: 541966705

64067
National Association of Temporary Services Foundation
277 S. Washington St.
Alexandria, VA 22314

Donor(s): Doherty Employment Group.
Financial data (yr. ended 12/31/00): Assets, $135,720 (M); grants paid, $0; expenditures, $172,352; qualifying distributions, $0.
Limitations: Applications not accepted.
Application information: Contributes only to pre-selected organizations.
Officers: Robb D. Mulberger, Pres.; Kathie Hanratty-Masi, 1st V.P.; Jerry Kapalko, 2nd V.P.; Judith A. Zacha, Treas.; Michael P. Ban, Secy.
EIN: 541723696

64068
The Tracy Webb Memorial Foundation
1147 Mill Rd.
Woodstock, VA 22664-2321   (540) 459-4613
Contact: Bernard Webb, Pres.

Established in 1998.
Donor(s): Bernard Webb, Patricia Webb.
Financial data (yr. ended 06/30/99): Assets, $134,128 (M); grants paid, $5,093; gifts received, $140,000; expenditures, $6,135; qualifying distributions, $6,135.
Limitations: Giving primarily in VA.

VIRGINIA—64080

Application information: Application form required.
Officers and Directors:* Bernard Webb,* Pres.; Bernard C. Webb,* V.P.; Patricia Webb,* Secy.-Treas.; Bruce Costod.
EIN: 541903763

64069
Bridgebuilder Scholarship Fund
c/o Stonewall Jackson High School
150 Stonewall Lane
Quicksburg, VA 22847
Contact: William Pirtle, Chair.

Established in 1979 in VA.
Financial data (yr. ended 11/30/01): Assets, $128,595 (M); grants paid, $5,625; gifts received, $1,700; expenditures, $5,955; qualifying distributions, $5,955.
Limitations: Giving limited to Mount Jackson, VA.
Application information: Application form required.
Officer: William L. Pirtle, Chair.
Trustees: William H. Logan, Jr., Jacqueline Sullivan Smoot.
EIN: 521262074
Codes: GTI

64070
Orchid Foundation, Inc.
P.O. Box 1850
Middleburg, VA 20118-1850

Established in 1998 in VA.
Donor(s): John T. Gordon.
Financial data (yr. ended 12/31/00): Assets, $127,925 (M); grants paid, $728; gifts received, $136,355; expenditures, $26,366; qualifying distributions, $25,739; giving activities include $728 for programs.
Limitations: Applications not accepted. Giving in Thailand.
Application information: Contributes only to pre-selected organizations.
Officers and Directors:* John T. Gordon,* Secy.-Treas.; Sayan Surikayam,* Exec. Dir.; Alan J. Brazil.
EIN: 541888315

64071
Hands for Christ
Bowers Bldg.
5720 Williamson Rd. N.W., Ste. 111
Roanoke, VA 24012-1210 (540) 362-1214
Contact: R.W. Bowers, Pres.

Established in 1969 in VA.
Donor(s): R.W. Bowers Apartments, John Bowers.‡
Financial data (yr. ended 12/31/99): Assets, $120,580 (M); grants paid, $46,042; gifts received, $551,212; expenditures, $615,722; qualifying distributions, $29,029; giving activities include $526,520 for programs.
Limitations: Giving primarily in Third World countries.
Publications: Newsletter.
Application information: Application form not required.
Officer and Directors:* R.W. Bowers,* Pres.; Joan C. Bowers, Gwen Woods.
EIN: 237074396

64072
Planters Educational Foundation
245 Culloden St.
Suffolk, VA 23434 (757) 925-3000
Contact: Patrick O'Malley

Established as a company-sponsored operating foundation.
Donor(s): Planters LifeSavers Company.

Financial data (yr. ended 12/31/00): Assets, $106,030 (M); grants paid, $7,000; expenditures, $8,642; qualifying distributions, $7,000.
Limitations: Giving limited to areas of company operations in VA.
Application information: Application form required.
Officers and Directors:* Ken Thomas,* Pres.; Polly Lasich,* V.P.; Lynne Hall,* Secy.-Treas.
EIN: 541178802
Codes: CD

64073
TDC Research Foundation
P.O. Box 1008
Blacksburg, VA 24063-1008 (352) 373-0321
Contact: Dr. Thomas Hudlicky, Pres.

Classified as a private operating foundation in 1992.
Donor(s): Josephine Wiley Reed, Tomas Hudlicky.
Financial data (yr. ended 12/31/01): Assets, $100,356 (M); grants paid, $20,250; gifts received, $36,418; expenditures, $21,104; qualifying distributions, $20,608.
Officers: Tomas Hudlicky, Pres.; Josephine Wiley Reed, Secy.-Treas.
EIN: 541574776
Codes: GTI

64074
Meherrin River Arts Council, Inc.
P.O. Box 845
Emporia, VA 23847

Financial data (yr. ended 05/31/00): Assets, $100,203 (M); grants paid, $0; gifts received, $53,450; expenditures, $146,080; qualifying distributions, $0.
Officers: Wilson Clary, Pres.; Steve Bloom, V.P.; Wally Brown, V.P.; Mark Novey, V.P.; Martha Martin, Secy.; Sean O'Hara, Treas.
Director: Steve Browder.
EIN: 541152886

64075
Alice B. Glasheen Memorial Trust
P.O. Box 1205
Hampton, VA 23661-0205

Established in 1997.
Financial data (yr. ended 12/31/99): Assets, $99,522 (L); grants paid, $42,735; gifts received, $10,000; expenditures, $43,512; qualifying distributions, $733.
Trustee: Gabriel J. Glasheen.
EIN: 546389143

64076
The Friends of Barnabas Foundation
P.O. Box 2100
Danville, VA 24541
Application address: P.O. Box 34531, Richmond, VA 23234
Contact: Linwood Cook, Pres.

Established in 2000 in VA.
Donor(s): Ethelyne F. Daniel.
Financial data (yr. ended 12/31/00): Assets, $94,551 (M); grants paid, $139,084; gifts received, $290,371; expenditures, $196,099; qualifying distributions, $194,801.
Limitations: Giving primarily for the benefit of Honduras; giving in the U.S. primarily in south central VA.
Officers: Ethelyne F. Daniel, Chair.; Linwood Cook, Pres.; Doug Kells, V.P.; Matthew Cook, Secy.; W. Joe Foster, Treas.
Directors: Charnell Blair, George Blair, Brenda Cook, Grady Jackson, Linda Jackson, Dave Jones,

Julie Kells, Carolyn Salmon, Chuck Salmon, Mary Settle, Paul Settle.
EIN: 541947279
Codes: FD2

64077
The Zeiders Family Charitable Foundation Trust
13115 Holly Leaf Ct.
Woodbridge, VA 22192

Established in 1997 in VA.
Donor(s): Michael D. Zeiders, Charlotte A. Zeiders.
Financial data (yr. ended 06/30/00): Assets, $88,771 (M); grants paid, $2,000; gifts received, $63,400; expenditures, $2,845; qualifying distributions, $2,000.
Limitations: Applications not accepted. Giving primarily in Woodbridge, VA.
Application information: Contributes only to pre-selected organizations.
Trustees: Charlotte A. Zeiders, Michael E. Zeiders.
EIN: 546417943

64078
The Fox Family Charitable Foundation
12586 Rock Ridge Rd.
Herndon, VA 20170

Donor(s): Steven R. Fox, Mary E. Fox.
Financial data (yr. ended 06/30/00): Assets, $81,188 (L); grants paid, $5,000; gifts received, $86,188; expenditures, $5,000; qualifying distributions, $5,000.
Limitations: Applications not accepted.
Application information: Contributes only to pre-selected organizations.
Trustees: Mary E. Fox, Steven R. Fox.
EIN: 541940067

64079
Morino Institute
c/o Mario Morino
11600 Sunrise Valley Dr., Ste. 300
Reston, VA 20191 (703) 620-1553
FAX: (703) 620-4102; *E-mail:* feedback@morino.org; *URL:* http://www.morino.org

Established in 1994 in VA.
Financial data (yr. ended 12/31/99): Assets, $74,579 (M); grants paid, $15,000; gifts received, $2,766,336; expenditures, $2,726,956; qualifying distributions, $2,712,819; giving activities include $2,697,819 for programs.
Limitations: Applications not accepted. Giving primarily in the greater Washington, DC, area, the greater Cleveland area in northeast OH, and the region surrounding Indiana, PA, in the Pittsburgh area.
Application information: Contributes only to pre-selected organizations.
Directors: Stephen W. Comiskey, Mario M. Morino.
EIN: 541706982

64080
Serendipity Sanctuary, Inc.
P.O. Box 101
White Post, VA 22663

Established in 1998 in VA.
Donor(s): Nancy Pruitt, Cecil Pruitt, Jr.
Financial data (yr. ended 12/31/01): Assets, $71,506 (M); grants paid, $0; gifts received, $547,600; expenditures, $550,920; qualifying distributions, $0.
Limitations: Applications not accepted.
Application information: Contributes only to pre-selected organizations.
Officer: Nancy Pruitt, Pres.

IN THIS SECTION, WITHIN EACH STATE, FOUNDATIONS ARE LISTED IN DESCENDING ORDER BY ASSET AMOUNT

64080—VIRGINIA

Directors: Sara Brown, Jim Davis, William A. Hazel, Rev. Joseph Kerr, Billy Thompson.
EIN: 541868641

64081
William Thompson Rice Foundation
c/o Peter Van S. Rice
203 S. Fairfax St.
Alexandria, VA 22314-3303

Financial data (yr. ended 12/31/01): Assets, $66,128 (M); grants paid, $8,060; expenditures, $8,134; qualifying distributions, $8,060.
Limitations: Applications not accepted. Giving primarily in MA and VA.
Application information: Contributes only to pre-selected organizations.
Trustee: Peter Van S. Rice.
EIN: 042636421

64082
Alpha Fund Charitable Trust
7823 Sunset Dr.
Hayes, VA 23072-3624 (804) 642-7530
Contact: Claude Lonciano, Tr.

Established in 1997 in VA.
Financial data (yr. ended 12/31/00): Assets, $63,249 (M); grants paid, $1,500; gifts received, $150; expenditures, $2,673; qualifying distributions, $1,774.
Limitations: Giving on a national basis.
Application information: In general, applicants must have completed at least 1 year at the Naval Academy. Application form required.
Trustees: Arline Lonciano, Claude Lonciano, Mary St. Jean.
EIN: 546400339

64083
Rappahannock Music Study Club
c/o H.U. Scharnberg
P.O. Box 429
Wicomico Church, VA 22579
Contact: June Swanell, Scholarship Comm. Member

Established in 1991 in VA.
Financial data (yr. ended 08/31/00): Assets, $60,982 (M); grants paid, $3,000; gifts received, $5,387; expenditures, $5,031; qualifying distributions, $4,587.
Limitations: Giving limited to residents of Lancaster, Northumberland, Richmond and Westmoreland, VA counties.
Application information: Application form required.
Officers: Adele W. Crosett, Pres.; Betty Arnest, 1st V.P.; Margery Dakin, 2nd V.P.; Hans Ullrich Scharnberg, Treas.
Scholarship Committee: June Swanell.
EIN: 541505403

64084
Kent Foundation, Inc.
525 7th St.
Altavista, VA 24517-0299
Application address: P.O. Box 299, Altavista, VA 24517, tel.: (814) 369-5603
Contact: James P. Kent, Jr., V.P.

Classified as a private operating foundation in 1972.
Financial data (yr. ended 06/30/99): Assets, $60,847 (M); grants paid, $3,100; expenditures, $3,150; qualifying distributions, $3,100.
Limitations: Giving primarily in VA.
Officers and Directors:* J. Paul Kent, Sr.,* Pres.; James P. Kent, Jr.,* V.P.; Gordon M. Kent.
EIN: 540757776

64085
Center for the Study of Wetlands in Southern Maine
8547 Old Dominion Dr.
McLean, VA 22102

Established in 1998 in ME and VA.
Donor(s): Brunetta P. Bernard.‡
Financial data (yr. ended 12/31/99): Assets, $60,762 (M); grants paid, $250; gifts received, $100,000; expenditures, $79,118; qualifying distributions, $7,250.
Limitations: Applications not accepted.
Application information: Contributes only to pre-selected organizations.
Officers: Susan Sanford Lang, Pres. and Exec. Dir.; Jules E. Bernard III, Secy.-Treas.
Directors: Sharon Ekedahl, E. Thomas Pulaski, George Vogt.
EIN: 522121646

64086
Virginia Foundation for Archaeological Research, Inc.
368 Spring Grove Rd.
Spring Grove, VA 23881

Classified as a private operating foundation in 1983.
Donor(s): James L. Kirby, Jr., Roger H.W. Kirby, Wade H.O. Kirby, Annette S. Kirby.
Financial data (yr. ended 12/31/01): Assets, $60,087 (M); grants paid, $0; gifts received, $254,896; expenditures, $247,813; qualifying distributions, $239,543; giving activities include $238,113 for programs.
Officers: Leverette B. Gregory, Jr., Pres.; Teresa E. Gregory, Secy.; Eve S. Gregory, Treas.
EIN: 541210780

64087
Leela Press, Inc.
c/o Jack O. Scher
4026 River Rd.
Faber, VA 22938

Established in 1990 in DE and VA.
Donor(s): Jack O. Scher, Jack O. Scher Foundation, Namaste Foundation.
Financial data (yr. ended 12/31/99): Assets, $59,480 (M); grants paid, $0; expenditures, $9,273; qualifying distributions, $2,042; giving activities include $25,414 for programs.
Officers and Directors:* Jack O. Scher,* Pres.; Judith Scher,* V.P. and Secy.; Mimi Goldberg.
EIN: 133571212

64088
Margaret Spruce Floyd Educational
P.O. Box 685
Chatham, VA 24531-0685
Contact: W. Carlton White, Tr.

Established in 1999 in VA.
Financial data (yr. ended 12/31/00): Assets, $57,523 (M); grants paid, $4,500; expenditures, $4,634; qualifying distributions, $4,500.
Limitations: Giving primarily in VA.
Trustee: W. Carlton White.
EIN: 546319564

64089
Carr Family Foundation
P.O. Box 1528
Waynesboro, VA 22980-1397
Contact: Jane Elkins, Secy.

Established in 1999 in VA.
Donor(s): Mitchell O. Carr.
Financial data (yr. ended 12/31/00): Assets, $57,384 (M); grants paid, $11,400; gifts received, $59,474; expenditures, $12,490; qualifying distributions, $12,319.
Limitations: Giving primarily in VA.
Officers: Mitchell O. Carr, Pres. and Treas.; Jane Elkins, Secy.
Directors: Iris T. Carr, Kent D. Carr, Scott M. Carr, Todd M. Carr, Martin Lightsey, John Tomlin.
EIN: 311629566

64090
Louis & Emily M. Spilman Scholarship Trust Fund
c/o William Watkins
P.O. Drawer 1558
Waynesboro, VA 22980

Financial data (yr. ended 06/30/99): Assets, $51,620 (M); grants paid, $3,750; expenditures, $4,190; qualifying distributions, $4,180.
Limitations: Giving limited to Waynesboro, VA.
Trustee: William Watkins.
EIN: 510249507

64091
The Lutheran Housing Services, Inc.
(Formerly The Siegfried Foundation)
c/o Catherine V. Hughes
1750 Tysons Blvd., Ste. 1800
McLean, VA 22102

Established in 1999 in VA.
Donor(s): Thomas A. Siegfried.
Financial data (yr. ended 12/31/01): Assets, $41,729 (M); grants paid, $0; gifts received, $75,000; expenditures, $33,464; qualifying distributions, $33,442.
Director: Thomas A. Siegfried.
EIN: 541954788

64092
Ann Thurston Filer Foundation
6724 Patterson Ave.
Richmond, VA 23226-4125
Contact: Robert J. Filer, Secy.-Treas.

Established in 1985 in VA.
Financial data (yr. ended 12/31/99): Assets, $40,717 (M); grants paid, $200; gifts received, $20,000; expenditures, $285; qualifying distributions, $285.
Limitations: Giving primarily in Washington, DC, and Pittsburgh, PA.
Officers and Directors:* Randall K. Filer,* Pres.; Jonathan K. Filer,* V.P.; Robert J. Filer,* Secy.-Treas.
EIN: 521413048

64093
Port Hampton History Foundation
115 Harbor Dr.
Hampton, VA 23661-3128

Established in 2000 in VA.
Donor(s): Dorothy Rouse-Bottom.
Financial data (yr. ended 12/31/00): Assets, $36,021 (M); grants paid, $0; gifts received, $36,674; expenditures, $790; qualifying distributions, $790.
Officer: Dorothy Rouse-Bottom, Pres.
EIN: 541988573

64094
The Ethos Foundation
312 S. Washington St., Ste. 3A
Alexandria, VA 22314

Financial data (yr. ended 06/30/00): Assets, $30,691 (M); grants paid, $0; gifts received, $10,000; expenditures, $69,898; qualifying distributions, $704,529; giving activities include $704,529 for programs.
Limitations: Applications not accepted.

Officers: Philip Ignatius Brennan, Pres.; Valera Clarke Lynch, V.P.
EIN: 510225231

64095
Juergen Reinhardt Memorial Charitable Trust
P.O. Box 3323
Leesburg, VA 20177
Application address: 424 Mosby Dr. S.W., Leesburg, VA 20175-2606, tel.: (703) 777-6455
Contact: Michael J. Moye, Tr.

Established in 1992 in VA.
Financial data (yr. ended 07/31/01): Assets, $23,973 (M); grants paid, $2,000; gifts received, $1,000; expenditures, $2,000; qualifying distributions, $1,991.
Limitations: Giving limited to Loudoun County, VA.
Application information: Application form available at Loudon County high schools. Application form required.
Trustees: Judith T. Humphrey, Michael J. Moye.
EIN: 546329240

64096
Grundy Wrestling Club of Virginia, Inc.
P.O. Box 1560
Grundy, VA 24614

Established in 1990 in VA.
Donor(s): F.D. Robertson.
Financial data (yr. ended 12/31/01): Assets, $21,008 (M); grants paid, $0; gifts received, $215,084; expenditures, $207,188; qualifying distributions, $0.
Officers: J.W. Childress, Pres.; B.K. Robertson, V.P. and Secy.; C.M. Childress, V.P. and Treas.; F.D. Robertson, V.P.
EIN: 541551691

64097
Coleman Jennings Foundation, Inc.
c/o Lois Grimm
7716 Georgetown Pike
McLean, VA 22102-1431

Established in 1957 in MD.
Financial data (yr. ended 12/31/99): Assets, $20,844 (M); grants paid, $48,500; expenditures, $49,277; qualifying distributions, $49,272.
Limitations: Giving primarily in the Washington, DC, area, including VA.
Officer: Lois Grimm, Pres.
EIN: 526035544

64098
Golden Rule Foundation of Virginia, Inc.
c/o Carole Marchesand
Rte. 2, Box 690
Palmyra, VA 22963-9524

Established in 1989 in VA.
Donor(s): Carole Marchesano, Norman Goldberg, William Schmidt.
Financial data (yr. ended 12/31/99): Assets, $18,797 (M); grants paid, $0; gifts received, $59,169; expenditures, $80,131; qualifying distributions, $74,311; giving activities include $38,543 for programs.
Officers: Carole Marchesano, Pres.; Norman Goldberg, V.P. and Secy.; Michelle McCormack, Treas.
EIN: 541497945

64099
The John Webb Goodlett Scholarship Foundation
1031 N. Manchester St.
Arlington, VA 22205

Established in 2000.

Financial data (yr. ended 12/31/00): Assets, $18,154 (M); grants paid, $2,000; gifts received, $20,000; expenditures, $2,000; qualifying distributions, $2,000.
Limitations: Applications not accepted. Giving primarily in Arlington, VA.
Application information: Contributes only to pre-selected organizations.
Trustee: Marc Shaw.
EIN: 541961454

64100
Public Fork Cemetery Association, Inc.
Rte. 1, Box 73A
Red Oak, VA 23964

Financial data (yr. ended 12/31/00): Assets, $17,556 (M); grants paid, $0; expenditures, $6,294; qualifying distributions, $5,884; giving activities include $5,884 for programs.
Officers: William C. Garland, Pres.; Allen G. Jones, Secy.; Jonsilee Hudgins, Treas.
EIN: 541316253

64101
Caldwell & Gregory Foundation
129 Broad St. Rd.
Manakin Sabot, VA 23103

Established in 1994 in VA.
Donor(s): Donald Caldwell, John Gregory, Caldwell and Gregory, Inc.
Financial data (yr. ended 12/31/99): Assets, $16,218 (M); grants paid, $46,415; gifts received, $30,150; expenditures, $48,550; qualifying distributions, $46,415.
Limitations: Applications not accepted. Giving primarily in IL, MI, NY, and VA.
Application information: Contributes only to pre-selected organizations.
Officers and Directors:* Donald A. Caldwell,* Pres.; John P. Gregory,* V.P. and Secy.
EIN: 541707118

64102
The Carter-Olinger 4-H Memorial Fund
c/o Cynthia B. Jones
P.O. Box 886
Stuart, VA 24171-0986

Classified as a private operating foundation in 1997 in VA.
Donor(s): Elma Carter.
Financial data (yr. ended 12/31/99): Assets, $16,056 (M); grants paid, $800; gifts received, $800; expenditures, $830; qualifying distributions, $800.
Limitations: Applications not accepted.
Application information: Contributes only to pre-selected organizations.
Officers: Anne Pilson, Chair.; Yvonne Clark, Vice-Chair.; Carol Byrd, Secy.; Cynthia Jones, Treas.
EIN: 541668268

64103
United States Military Academy Class of 1963 Educational Fund, Inc.
(also known as USMA Class of 1963 Educational Fund, Inc.)
c/o Richard D. James
8310 Cedardale Dr.
Alexandria, VA 22308

Classified as a private operating foundation in 1975.
Financial data (yr. ended 06/30/00): Assets, $13,952 (M); grants paid, $2,000; expenditures, $2,467; qualifying distributions, $2,467.
Limitations: Giving on a national basis.

Application information: Application form required.
Officers and Directors:* Col. I. Robert Farris,* Pres.; Col. Richard E. Entlich,* V.P.; Col. Rudolph H. Ehrenberg, Jr.,* Secy.; Lt. Col. Richard D. James,* Treas. and Mgr.; Donald G. Byrne, John A. Dunn, and 6 additional directors.
EIN: 146089665

64104
Arch and Kate Moody and Bill and Corene Moody Warren Scholarship Trust
9437 Shouse Dr.
Vienna, VA 22182-1620
Application address: c/o Bill Davis, Stroud High School, Stroud, OK 74079

Established in 1999 in OK.
Financial data (yr. ended 12/31/99): Assets, $13,541 (L); grants paid, $750; expenditures, $750; qualifying distributions, $750.
Limitations: Giving primarily in Stroud, OK.
Trustees: D. Mike Moody, Jim E. Moody, Joe B. Moody, Ki L. Moody.
EIN: 731290756

64105
D. D. Puri Foundation
12260 Tilney Ct.
Woodbridge, VA 22192
Contact: Prem Puri, Secy.-Treas.

Established in 1999 in VA.
Donor(s): Prem Puri.
Financial data (yr. ended 06/30/00): Assets, $13,351 (M); grants paid, $8,851; gifts received, $22,271; expenditures, $9,014; qualifying distributions, $8,862.
Limitations: Giving primarily in Punjab, India.
Application information: Application form not required.
Officers: Chaman Puri, Pres.; Prem Puri, Secy.-Treas.
EIN: 541985221

64106
Corporations to End World Hunger Foundation
P.O. Box 856
McLean, VA 22101-0856

Established in 1999.
Financial data (yr. ended 12/31/99): Assets, $12,037 (M); grants paid, $59,150; gifts received, $68,610; expenditures, $80,623; qualifying distributions, $59,150.
Limitations: Applications not accepted.
Application information: Contributes only to pre-selected organizations.
Officers: Gilbert A. Robinson, Chair.; Nancy Shaffer, V.P.; Kenneth T. Hoeck, Treas.
EIN: 521458696

64107
The Harris Smith Institutes, Inc.
c/o Wray J. Smith
1901 N. Moore St., Ste. 900
Arlington, VA 22209-1706

Classified as a private operating foundation in MD and VA in 1997.
Donor(s): Wray Jackson Smith.
Financial data (yr. ended 12/31/00): Assets, $11,508 (M); grants paid, $0; expenditures, $44,191; qualifying distributions, $41,917; giving activities include $14,054 for programs.
Limitations: Applications not accepted.
Application information: Contributes only to pre-selected organizations.
Officers and Trustees:* Bette S. Mahoney,* V.P.; Judith Muniec, Secy.; John L. Czajka, Ph.D.,* Treas.; Stephen J. Dienistfrey, Lillian Regelson,

64107—VIRGINIA

Gooloo S. Wunderlich, Ph.D., and 2 additional trustees.
EIN: 522018476

64108
Blair Contruction Scholarship
c/o Fred A. Blair
P.O. Box 612
Gretna, VA 24557-0612 (804) 656-6243
Contact: Gregory R. Nichols, Secy.-Treas.

Established in 1999 in VA.
Financial data (yr. ended 12/31/99): Assets, $10,920 (M); grants paid, $4,375; gifts received, $15,000; expenditures, $4,375; qualifying distributions, $0.
Officers: Fred A. Blair, Pres.; Brenda M. Blair, V.P.; Gregory R. Nichols, Secy.-Treas.
EIN: 541915821

64109
Agnes L. Peacock Foundation, Inc.
5803 Rexford Dr., Apt. D
Springfield, VA 22152-1094

Established in 2000 in VA.
Donor(s): Bernard Peacock, Mary Peacock.
Financial data (yr. ended 12/31/00): Assets, $9,490 (M); grants paid, $500; gifts received, $12,575; expenditures, $3,085; qualifying distributions, $2,585.
Limitations: Applications not accepted. Giving primarily in Washington, DC.
Application information: Contributes only to pre-selected organizations.
Officers: Clare Peacock, Pres. and Secy.-Treas.; Bernard Peacock, V.P.
Director: Mary Peacock.
EIN: 542017653

64110
Foundation to Support Our Schools
c/o Sam A. Hicks
1320 Wren Ct.
Blacksburg, VA 24060-8980

Donor(s): Sam A. Hicks.
Financial data (yr. ended 12/31/99): Assets, $7,132 (M); grants paid, $550; gifts received, $861; expenditures, $681; qualifying distributions, $681; giving activities include $681 for programs.
Limitations: Applications not accepted. Giving limited to Madisonville, TN.
Officers: James S. Hicks, Pres.; David P. Sloan, V.P.; Sam A. Hicks, Secy.-Treas.
EIN: 621715294

64111
Second Chance Animal Shelter
P.O. Box 55
Powhatan, VA 23139

Established in 1987 in VA.
Donor(s): A. Elizabeth Case.
Financial data (yr. ended 04/30/00): Assets, $7,076 (M); grants paid, $0; gifts received, $61,645; expenditures, $82,610; qualifying distributions, $80,353; giving activities include $36,369 for programs.
Officer: A. Elizabeth Case, Pres. and Secy.
Directors: Christine Fallen, R. David Field.
EIN: 541427888

64112
P.T.F.G., Inc.
2415 Westwood Ave.
Richmond, VA 23230

Classified as a private operating foundation in 1983.
Donor(s): Jesse J. Dipboye, Jr.

Financial data (yr. ended 06/30/00): Assets, $6,999 (M); grants paid, $0; gifts received, $6,320; expenditures, $2,446; qualifying distributions, $2,446; giving activities include $943 for programs.
Officers: Jesse J. Dipboye, Jr., Pres.; Betty S. Dipboye, V.P.; Debra Brame, Secy.-Treas.
EIN: 521268264

64113
The Marie A. Dornhecker Foundation
308 Cedar Lakes Dr., 2nd Fl.
Chesapeake, VA 23322 (757) 312-0924
Contact: Robert R. Kinser, Dir.

Established in 1999 in VA.
Financial data (yr. ended 12/31/99): Assets, $6,174 (M); grants paid, $5,000; gifts received, $15,000; expenditures, $8,895; qualifying distributions, $11,449.
Officers and Directors:* Stephen J. Telfeyan,* Pres.; John Wm. Hester,* V.P.; Robert R. Kinser, Bessianne Tavss Maiden.
EIN: 541945504

64114
AAROTEC Educational Foundation, Inc.
c/o J. Michael Sharman
8550 Lee Hwy., Ste. 600
Fairfax, VA 22031
Application address: 8511 Rixlew Ln., Manassas, VA 20109-3701, tel.: (703) 369-7491
Contact: Glenda L. Willoughby, Secy.-Treas.

Established in 1994 in VA as a company-sponsored operating foundation.
Donor(s): AAROTEC, Inc., AAROTEC Laboratories.
Financial data (yr. ended 06/30/01): Assets, $5,042 (M); grants paid, $500; gifts received, $3,778; expenditures, $3,749; qualifying distributions, $500.
Limitations: Giving primarily in VA.
Application information: Application form required.
Officers: Albert C. Young, Jr., Pres.; Glenda L. Willoughby, Secy.-Treas.
EIN: 541720586
Codes: CD

64115
Foundation for Research & Treatment of Cancer
4800 Fillmore Ave., Ste. 1359
Alexandria, VA 22311-5079
Contact: Davie Bradford, Pres.

Established in 1996 in VA.
Donor(s): Eugenie R. Bradford.
Financial data (yr. ended 12/31/01): Assets, $4,942 (M); grants paid, $78,000; gifts received, $46,280; expenditures, $85,829; qualifying distributions, $84,995.
Limitations: Applications not accepted.
Application information: Contributes only to pre-selected organizations.
Officers: Davie Bradford, Pres.; Marian Trotter, V.P.; Richard Barrows, Secy.-Treas.
EIN: 521423589
Codes: FD2

64116
American Foundation for Maternal and Child Care Health, Inc.
149 Harvest Dr.
Charlottesville, VA 22903

Donor(s): John R. Haire, Fay Schweitzer,‡ William Schweitzer.‡
Financial data (yr. ended 08/31/00): Assets, $4,705 (M); grants paid, $0; gifts received, $14,200; expenditures, $17,141; qualifying distributions, $10,804; giving activities include $10,804 for programs.
Officers and Directors:* Doris J. Haire,* Pres.; Dorothea Lang,* V.P.; John R. Haire,* Treas.
EIN: 237296872

64117
Randall and Barbara Strawbridge Charitable Foundation, Inc.
11409 Barrington Bridge County
Richmond, VA 23233-1753

Established in 2000 in VA.
Financial data (yr. ended 12/31/01): Assets, $3,171 (M); grants paid, $0; expenditures, $0; qualifying distributions, $0.
Director: Randall A. Strawbridge.
EIN: 542005281

64118
Hoffman Foundation
4796 Springhill Rd.
Mount Solon, VA 22843

Established in 1998 in VA.
Donor(s): Michael A. Hoffman, Brenda C. Hoffman.
Financial data (yr. ended 12/31/01): Assets, $1,851 (M); grants paid, $0; gifts received, $24,909; expenditures, $25,930; qualifying distributions, $25,930.
Officers and Directors:* Brenda C. Hoffman,* Pres.; Michael A. Hoffman,* Secy.-Treas.; Carter Lundquist, Thomas Lundquist, Robert Partridge.
EIN: 541930225

64119
The Words Out
c/o Cheryl M. Hewitt
13523 Point Pleasant Dr.
Chantilly, VA 20151-2442

Established in 1999.
Financial data (yr. ended 12/31/00): Assets, $1,541 (M); grants paid, $0; gifts received, $7,348; expenditures, $6,753; qualifying distributions, $6,753; giving activities include $6,753 for programs.
Limitations: Giving primarily in VA.
Officers: Cheryl M. Hewitt, Pres.; Seth E. Hewitt, Secy.
Directors: Donald C. Powell, Rita L. Powell.
EIN: 541629669

64120
Friends of British Sporting Art
P.O. Box 189
Clifton, VA 20124-0189

Financial data (yr. ended 11/30/99): Assets, $1,524 (M); grants paid, $0; gifts received, $150; expenditures, $41,565; qualifying distributions, $39,761; giving activities include $36,195 for programs.
Limitations: Applications not accepted.
Application information: Contributes only to pre-selected organizations.
Officers and Trustees:* David K. Diebold,* Pres. and Treas.; Robert B. Fountain,* V.P.; Katherine D. Brady,* Secy.; David Caruth, Ashley Dormeuil, David Fuller, Dean H. Jewett, Peter A.B. Johnson, Col. Charles Lane, Alexander Mackay-Smith, Alton E. Peters, F. Turner Reuter, Jr., John T. Von Stade, Peter Winants.
EIN: 222373160

64121
Donald C. Benson Memorial Scholarship Fund
P.O. Box 999
Richmond, VA 23218-0999

Established in 1998.

Financial data (yr. ended 08/31/99): Assets, $1,521 (M); grants paid, $1,500; gifts received, $2,766; expenditures, $1,795; qualifying distributions, $1,500.
Officers: Tama Hunley, Pres.; Glen Schneider, Secy.; Robert Skowron, Treas.
Director: Chuck Pruitt.
EIN: 541613304

64122
Fredericksburg Realtors Foundation, Inc.
c/o Fritz Leedy
725 Kenmore Ave.
Fredericksburg, VA 22401-5724

Established in 1991 in VA.
Financial data (yr. ended 12/31/99): Assets, $1,222 (M); grants paid, $3,235; gifts received, $1,916; expenditures, $3,948; qualifying distributions, $3,235.
Limitations: Giving limited to the Fredericksburg, VA, area.
Officers and Directors:* Kathryn H. Belcher,* Chair.; Priscilla Sheeley,* Secy.; Fritz Leedy,* Treas.; Vicki Clark-Jennings, Gayle B. Elliott, Claire Forcier-Rowe, Betty M. Jasmund, Priscilla Sheeley.
EIN: 541564756

64123
A. R. Rahman Foundation
3133 Cofer Rd.
Falls Church, VA 22042-4210

Established in 2001 in VA.
Financial data (yr. ended 12/31/01): Assets, $1,100 (M); grants paid, $1,800; gifts received, $2,062; expenditures, $1,962; qualifying distributions, $1,800.
Limitations: Giving limited to VA.
Officers: Mohammed Nafia Al-Saigh, Pres.; Mona Salah, V.P.; Nellie Jones Al-Saigh, Secy.-Treas.
EIN: 541986384

64124
Kerrs Creek Foundation
502 Welwyn Rd.
Richmond, VA 23229

Financial data (yr. ended 12/31/99): Assets, $728 (M); grants paid, $1,293; gifts received, $1,050; expenditures, $1,494; qualifying distributions, $201; giving activities include $1,494 for programs.
Officers: Nancy D. Moore, Pres.; Hullihen W. Moore, Secy.
EIN: 521296850

64125
Oppositional Poster Conservation Initiative
P.O. Box 2394
Alexandria, VA 22301-0394

Financial data (yr. ended 12/31/00): Assets, $600 (M); grants paid, $0; expenditures, $7,382; qualifying distributions, $6,177; giving activities include $6,177 for programs.
Officers: Daniel Walsh, Pres.; Greg Sherrard, Treas.
Directors: Bill Callhan, Bobby Muller, Rick Roth.
EIN: 541758633

64126
Sedona, Ltd.
2112 Executive Dr.
Hampton, VA 23666

Financial data (yr. ended 12/31/00): Assets, $158 (M); grants paid, $0; gifts received, $6,000; expenditures, $6,311; qualifying distributions, $6,000; giving activities include $6,311 for programs.
Officer: Stephen L. Green, Pres. and Secy.
EIN: 541907618

64127
Sandra H. Garcia Charitable Foundation
3333 Virginia Beach Blvd., Ste. 24
Virginia Beach, VA 23452
Contact: Andrea M. Kilmer, V.P.

Established in 1999 in VA; funded in 2000.
Financial data (yr. ended 12/31/01): Assets, $1 (M); grants paid, $0; expenditures, $0; qualifying distributions, $0.
Limitations: Giving primarily in VA.
Officer: Andrea M. Kilmer, V.P.
EIN: 541832579

64128
The GBC Foundation, Inc.
1017 S. Oak Crest Rd.
Arlington, VA 22202

Established in 1989 in TX.
Financial data (yr. ended 05/31/02): Assets, $0 (M); grants paid, $0; gifts received, $5,000; expenditures, $5,456; qualifying distributions, $599.
Officers: James E. Deveau, Chair.; Brian Cowan, Pres.
EIN: 760288217

64129
Howard E. Sigmon Scholarship Foundation
c/o Neil V. Birkhoff
P.O. Box 14125
Roanoke, VA 24038

Established in 1992 in VA.
Financial data (yr. ended 12/31/99): Assets, $0 (M); grants paid, $0; gifts received, $843; expenditures, $843; qualifying distributions, $843.
Officers: Norma Jean Sigmon, Pres. and Treas.; Thomas T. Lawson, Secy.
EIN: 541629680

WASHINGTON

64130
Casey Family Programs
c/o Communications Dept.
1300 Dexter Ave. N., 3rd Fl.
Seattle, WA 98109-3547 (206) 282-7300
FAX: (206) 282-3555; E-mail: info@casey.org;
URL: http://www.casey.org

Established in 1966. Classified as a private operating foundation in 1972.
Financial data (yr. ended 12/31/01): Assets, $2,349,848,837 (M); grants paid, $8,932,953; gifts received, $11,698,639; expenditures, $129,998,488; qualifying distributions, $128,684,935; giving activities include $292,000,000 for programs.
Limitations: Giving on a national basis.
Publications: Informational brochure.
Officers and Trustees:* Gary Severson,* Chair.; Joan B. Poliak, Vice-Chair.; Ruth W. Massinga, C.E.O.; Thomas Keeney, Exec. V.P., Admin. and C.F.O.; Duncan A. Bayne, Secy.; Richard E. Bangert, Treas.; Patricia A. Batiste-Brown, Richard D. Ford, John C. Peterson III, M.D.
EIN: 910793881
Codes: FD

64131
The Experience Music Project Foundation
(Formerly The JH Museum)
2901 3rd Ave., Ste. 400
Seattle, WA 98121 (206) 262-3200

Donor(s): Paul G. Allen.
Financial data (yr. ended 12/31/99): Assets, $167,258,733 (M); grants paid, $30,000; gifts received, $792,923; expenditures, $15,073,182; qualifying distributions, $106,458,773; giving activities include $12,910,409 for programs.
Officers: Jo Allen Patton, Pres.; William D. Savoy, V.P. and Secy.-Treas.
Directors: Paul G. Allen, Beth Clark, Pam Faber, Joe Franzi, Bert E. Kolde, Eric Robinson, Rafe Stone, and 10 additional directors.
EIN: 911626784

64132
Charles H. Frye Testamentary Trust f/b/o Charles & Emma Frye Free Public Art Museum, Inc.
704 Terry Ave.
Seattle, WA 98104-2019

Classified as a private operating foundation in 1979.
Financial data (yr. ended 09/30/01): Assets, $87,611,207 (M); grants paid, $0; gifts received, $242,784; expenditures, $3,699,622; qualifying distributions, $2,636,833; giving activities include $2,484,071 for programs.
Officers: Richard L. Cleveland, Pres.; Philip M. Roberts, Secy.-Treas.; Warren W. Bell, Exec. Dir.
Trustees: Jan Hendrickson, Frank P. Stagen.
EIN: 910659435

64133
Tudor Foundation
c/o Roger A. Rieger
411 University St., Ste. 1200
Seattle, WA 98101

Established in 1996 in WA.
Donor(s): E. Annette Rieger, Roger A. Rieger.
Financial data (yr. ended 12/31/00): Assets, $63,637,614 (M); grants paid, $190,525; gifts received, $29,275; expenditures, $9,786,717; qualifying distributions, $190,525.
Limitations: Applications not accepted. Giving limited to Seattle, WA.
Officers: Roger A. Rieger, Pres.; E. Annette Rieger, Secy.
EIN: 911708176
Codes: FD2

64134
The Arbor Fund Managing the Bloedel Reserve
7571 N.E. Dolphin Dr.
Bainbridge Island, WA 98110-3001

Established in 1987 in WA. Classified as a private operating foundation in 1986.
Donor(s): C. Bagley Wright.
Financial data (yr. ended 12/31/00): Assets, $23,799,757 (M); grants paid, $0; gifts received, $5,558; expenditures, $1,151,915; qualifying distributions, $816,336; giving activities include $833,353 for programs.
Officers: Allison Andrews, Pres.; Lalie Scandiuzzi, V.P.; John F. Hall, Secy.; Watson Blair, Treas.
Directors: Richard Brown, Betsy Minor, Mrs. Douglas Picha, Brooks Ragen, Ron L. Taylor, Bagley Wright, Charles B. Wright III, Virginia Wright.
EIN: 916182786

64135
The Franke Tobey Jones Home
5340 N. Bristol
Tacoma, WA 98407-2299

Classified as a private operating foundation in 1972.
Financial data (yr. ended 12/31/01): Assets, $23,728,192 (M); grants paid, $0; gifts received, $175,687; expenditures, $6,061,604; qualifying distributions, $0.
Officers and Directors:* Nancy Gee Locke,* Pres.; Phyllis Gill,* V.P.; Joan Westover,* Secy.; Rick Carr,* Treas.; Edward Mawe, Exec. Dir.; Marilyn Dimmer, Sandra Gordon, Tom Hackleman, Kaye Highsmith, and 5 additional directors.
EIN: 910575957

64136
Vista Hermosa
1111 Fishhook Pk. Rd.
Prescott, WA 99348 (509) 547-1711
Contact: Dennis Sundberg

Established in 1994 in WA.
Donor(s): Broetje Orchards.
Financial data (yr. ended 09/30/01): Assets, $6,846,920 (M); grants paid, $214,299; gifts received, $1,533,923; expenditures, $590,620; qualifying distributions, $518,133; giving activities include $304,000 for programs.
Limitations: Giving primarily in WA.
Officers: Ralph Broetje, Pres.; Cheryl Broetje, V.P.
Board Members: Sara Broetje, Susanne Broetje.
EIN: 911491438
Codes: FD2

64137
The Helstrom Foundation
4500 3rd Ave. S.E., Ste. 104
Lacey, WA 98503-1002 (360) 491-6320

Established in 1991 in WA.
Donor(s): Norris Helstrom, Robert L. Helstrom.
Financial data (yr. ended 06/30/01): Assets, $6,017,243 (M); grants paid, $182,429; gifts received, $595,040; expenditures, $791,894; qualifying distributions, $412,734; giving activities include $222,593 for programs.
Limitations: Giving on a national basis, with emphasis on ID, MO, and WA.
Application information: Application form not required.
Officers: Robert L. Helstrom, Pres.; Bryan L. Helstrom, V.P.; Yvonne E. Helstrom, Secy.; Phillip G. Harris, Treas.
EIN: 943124662
Codes: FD2

64138
Frank Family Foundation
c/o Laurie McClanahan
P.O. Box 789
Shelton, WA 98584-0789

Established in 1993 in WA.
Financial data (yr. ended 06/30/00): Assets, $5,384,252 (M); grants paid, $10,000; gifts received, $4,303; expenditures, $16,549; qualifying distributions, $14,176; giving activities include $4,176 for programs.
Officers: Norm Eveleth, Pres.; Bill Batstone, V.P.; Laurie McClanahan, Secy.-Treas.
EIN: 911649223

64139
Olympia-Tumwater Foundation
P.O. Box 4098
Tumwater, WA 98501
Contact: Joe S. Reder, V.P.

Established in 1950.
Financial data (yr. ended 12/31/99): Assets, $4,264,760 (M); grants paid, $26,482; gifts received, $53,485; expenditures, $232,215; qualifying distributions, $233,491.
Limitations: Giving limited to residents of Thurston County, WA.
Application information: Application form required.
Officers and Trustees:* Michael K. Schmidt,* Pres.; Joe S. Reder,* V.P. and Mgr.; Robert A. Schmidt, Jr.,* V.P.; Susan S. Wilson,* Secy.; James A. Haight,* Treas.; Stephen J. Bean, Lynn Brunton, Mimi S. Fielding, Jennifer S. Ingham, James H. Jenner, Daniel C. O'Neill, Nicholas M. Schmidt, Peter G. Schmidt.
EIN: 910741161

64140
Heritage Flight Museum
c/o Apogee Flight, Anders Hangar
1 Aeroview Ln., Eastsound Airport
Eastsound, WA 98245

Established in 1998 in WA.
Donor(s): William A. Anders.
Financial data (yr. ended 12/31/00): Assets, $3,333,444 (M); grants paid, $0; gifts received, $80,000; expenditures, $315,628; qualifying distributions, $255,871; giving activities include $200,392 for programs.
Officer and Director:* William A. Anders,* Chair.
EIN: 911923298

64141
The Albohn Family Foundation
c/o Anita Pennington
6709 Westhill Ct.
Olympia, WA 98512
Contact: Catherine Heay, Pres.

Established in 1992 in WA.
Donor(s): Angela L. Albohn.‡
Financial data (yr. ended 12/31/01): Assets, $3,020,405 (M); grants paid, $105,000; expenditures, $143,835; qualifying distributions, $125,726.
Limitations: Giving primarily in Thurston County, WA.
Application information: Application form not required.
Officers and Directors:* Catherine Heay,* Pres.; Mary Gentry,* Secy.; Anita Pennington,* Treas.; Susan Beauregard.
EIN: 911562963
Codes: FD2

64142
Starflower Foundation
P.O. Box 22419
Seattle, WA 98122-0419 (206) 789-0263
Contact: Sandra Fry

Established as a private operating foundation in 1998 in WA.
Donor(s): Ann Lennartz.
Financial data (yr. ended 11/30/00): Assets, $2,542,534 (M); grants paid, $1,600; gifts received, $1,130,764; expenditures, $1,148,882; qualifying distributions, $1,145,317; giving activities include $795,809 for programs.
Limitations: Giving on a national basis, with some emphasis on WA.
Officer and Director:* Ann Lennartz,* Pres., V.P., and Secy.-Treas.

EIN: 911748612

64143
Rhema Ministry
P.O. Box 31651
Seattle, WA 98103-1651

Financial data (yr. ended 12/31/00): Assets, $1,907,415 (M); grants paid, $406,140; gifts received, $1,489,712; expenditures, $2,177,266; qualifying distributions, $2,191,716; giving activities include $2,171,990 for programs.
Limitations: Applications not accepted. Giving primarily in Seattle, WA.
Application information: Contributes only to pre-selected organizations.
Officers: Joel W. Kennon, Pres.; Richard C.T. Li, Secy.; John Brooks, Treas.
EIN: 911183911
Codes: TN

64144
Foundation for the Future
123 105th Ave. S.E.
Bellevue, WA 98004 (425) 451-1333
FAX: (425) 688-1591; *E-mail:* info@futurefoundation.org; *URL:* http://www.futurefoundation.org
Contact: Carol Johnson, Prog. Mgr.

Established in 1996 in WA as a private operating foundation.
Donor(s): Walter P. Kistler.
Financial data (yr. ended 12/31/01): Assets, $1,828,852 (M); grants paid, $124,002; expenditures, $1,145,943; qualifying distributions, $951,298; giving activities include $415,486 for programs.
Limitations: Applications not accepted.
Application information: Contributes only to pre-selected organizations.
Officers and Trustees:* Walter P. Kistler,* Pres.; Bob Citron,* Exec. Dir.; Donna Hines, Seshadri Velamoor, Milton Woods.
EIN: 911732102
Codes: FD2

64145
Joseph L. Lewith Trust Estate
145 3rd Ave. S., Ste. 200
Edmonds, WA 98020

Classified as a private operating trust in 1984.
Donor(s): Joseph L. Lewith.‡
Financial data (yr. ended 12/31/01): Assets, $1,665,454 (M); grants paid, $0; expenditures, $73,641; qualifying distributions, $61,612.
Trustees: Charles W. Beresford, Robert E. Ratcliff.
EIN: 916061781

64146
Wendel Museum of Animal Conservation
c/o Ken Hoffman
800 N. Devine Rd.
Vancouver, WA 98661

Donor(s): Roger J. Wendel.
Financial data (yr. ended 12/31/01): Assets, $1,599,860 (M); grants paid, $0; gifts received, $1,023,245; expenditures, $29,876; qualifying distributions, $0.
Officers: Barbara Arseneau, Pres.; Marilyn Wendel, Secy.; Roger Wendel, Treas.
EIN: 911718042

64147
Florence & William Beeks-Las Brisas Foundation
c/o William Beeks
1401 E. Harrison St., Ste. 300
Seattle, WA 98112

Established in 2000 in WA.

Donor(s): William T. Beeks.
Financial data (yr. ended 12/31/00): Assets, $1,575,715 (M); grants paid, $0; gifts received, $1,618,469; expenditures, $43,073; qualifying distributions, $80,913; giving activities include $42,579 for programs.
Officers: William T. Beeks, Pres.; Edward W. Stimson, V.P.
EIN: 912041064

64148
Nelsen Family Residence Historical Trust
15643 W. Valley Hwy.
Tukwila, WA 98188

Established in 2000 in WA.
Financial data (yr. ended 12/31/00): Assets, $1,425,168 (M); grants paid, $0; expenditures, $17,946; qualifying distributions, $16,386; giving activities include $15,749 for programs.
Trustees: Loren S. Frohmuth, James R. Nelsen.
EIN: 916418016

64149
Duim Family Foundation
1303 S. Beach Dr.
Camano Island, WA 98292

Established in 1997 in WA.
Donor(s): Gary Duim, Linda K. Duim.
Financial data (yr. ended 12/31/00): Assets, $1,420,623 (M); grants paid, $48,300; gifts received, $373,734; expenditures, $64,547; qualifying distributions, $47,498.
Limitations: Applications not accepted. Giving primarily in WA.
Application information: Contributes only to pre-selected organizations.
Officers: Gary Duim, Pres.; Linda Duim, V.P.; Douglas Duim, Secy.-Treas.
Directors: Deanna K. Duim, Duane M. Duim, Rae Ann Duim.
EIN: 911872763

64150
Mabelle M. George Educational Trust
43 Kayla Dr.
Montesano, WA 98563
Application address: c/o Brookings-Harbor Scholarship Foundation, Inc., P.O. Box 7673, Brookings, OR 97415

Established in 1994 in OR.
Financial data (yr. ended 12/31/99): Assets, $1,311,934 (M); grants paid, $79,900; expenditures, $95,809; qualifying distributions, $82,601.
Limitations: Giving limited to OR.
Application information: Application form required.
Trustee: Melvin A. McMillan.
EIN: 916358636
Codes: FD2, GTI

64151
The Betcher Family Foundation
2000 Alaskan Way, Ste. 550
Seattle, WA 98121

Established in 2000 in WA.
Donor(s): Robert L. Betcher, Nancy N. Betcher.
Financial data (yr. ended 12/31/00): Assets, $1,204,273 (M); grants paid, $13,000; gifts received, $2,109,502; expenditures, $15,825; qualifying distributions, $13,000.
Limitations: Applications not accepted. Giving primarily in Seattle, WA.
Application information: Contributes only to pre-selected organizations.
Directors: Nancy N. Betcher, Robert L. Betcher.
EIN: 912029353

64152
Washington Women in Need
1849 114th Ave., N.E.
Bellevue, WA 98004 (425) 451-8838
Contact: Colleen M. Crowley, Exec. Dir.

Established in 1992 in WA.
Donor(s): Julia L. Pritt.
Financial data (yr. ended 06/30/01): Assets, $1,040,952 (M); grants paid, $548,881; gifts received, $1,446,342; expenditures, $978,775; qualifying distributions, $961,936.
Limitations: Giving limited to female residents of WA.
Application information: Application form required.
Officer: Colleen M. Crowley, Exec. Dir.
EIN: 911559848
Codes: FD, GTI

64153
The Trowbridge Foundation
1102 State Ave., N.E.
Olympia, WA 98506

Established in 1999 in WA.
Donor(s): Charles L. Trowbridge.
Financial data (yr. ended 12/31/99): Assets, $933,673 (M); grants paid, $23,775; gifts received, $810,177; expenditures, $58,347; qualifying distributions, $59,264; giving activities include $43,591 for programs.
Limitations: Applications not accepted.
Application information: Contributes only to pre-selected organizations.
Officers and Board Members:* Brett Trowbridge, Pres. and Exec. Dir.; Jeannette Iverson,* Secy.-Treas.; Phillip Frank, Richard Pollard, Charles Williams.
EIN: 911979974

64154
The Morris Foundation
P.O. Box 409
Gig Harbor, WA 98335

Established in 1995 in WA.
Donor(s): Thomas G. Morris, David R. Morris.
Financial data (yr. ended 12/31/99): Assets, $799,705 (M); grants paid, $50,000; gifts received, $148,377; expenditures, $71,068; qualifying distributions, $50,000.
Limitations: Applications not accepted. Giving primarily in Gig Harbor, WA.
Application information: Contributes only to pre-selected organizations.
Officers: Thomas G. Morris, Chair.; David R. Morris, Secy.
EIN: 911700530

64155
China Friendship
1816 N.E. 55th St.
Seattle, WA 98105-3323 (206) 523-3788
Contact: Frederick P. Brandauer, Pres.

Established in 1986 in WA.
Donor(s): Grace A. Brandauer.
Financial data (yr. ended 12/31/99): Assets, $795,888 (M); grants paid, $4,000; gifts received, $13,789; expenditures, $44,989; qualifying distributions, $22,185.
Limitations: Giving primarily in Seattle, WA.
Application information: Application form required.
Officers and Directors:* Frederick P. Brandauer,* Pres. and Treas.; Tianzhu Li,* V.P.; Marie I. Materi,* Secy.
EIN: 911306979

64156
Madison Valley Park Foundation
602 36th Ave., E.
Seattle, WA 98112-4316

Classified as a private operating foundation in 1993.
Donor(s): C. Calvert Knudsen.
Financial data (yr. ended 12/31/01): Assets, $716,998 (M); grants paid, $0; gifts received, $171; expenditures, $22,052; qualifying distributions, $0.
Officers and Directors:* C. Calvert Knudsen,* Pres. and Treas.; Page Knudsen Cowles,* Secy.; Colin Roderick Knudsen, Conrad Calvert Knudsen, Jr., David Callison Knudsen.
EIN: 911572982

64157
Techonology Resource Foundation
815 Western Ave., Ste. 200
Seattle, WA 98104

Established in 2000 in WA.
Donor(s): Waitt Family Foundation.
Financial data (yr. ended 12/31/00): Assets, $673,008 (M); grants paid, $3,859; gifts received, $1,694,983; expenditures, $1,267,873; qualifying distributions, $1,267,873; giving activities include $825,000 for programs.
Limitations: Applications not accepted. Giving primarily in Seattle, WA.
Application information: Contributes only to pre-selected organizations.
Officer: Willem Scholten, Pres.
Directors: Deirdre McDonough, Karen Mooseker, Christina Toney.
EIN: 912013371

64158
Special Projects and Creative Energies
(also known as S.P.A.C.E. Foundation)
1932 1st Ave., Ste. 202
Seattle, WA 98101-1040

Established in 1987 in WA.
Financial data (yr. ended 09/30/99): Assets, $627,303 (M); grants paid, $0; expenditures, $95,217; qualifying distributions, $0; giving activities include $95,217 for programs.
Officers: Katherine A. Dahlem, Pres.; Harris Hoffman, Secy.-Treas.; Michael Sivia, Exec. Dir.
Director: William Block.
EIN: 911218391

64159
The Rachel Royston Permanent Scholarship Foundation of Alpha Sigma State of the Delta Kappa Gamma Society International
c/o Suzie Ross
1501 4th Ave., Ste. 2070
Seattle, WA 98101-1662

Classified as a private operating foundation in 1973.
Donor(s): Bernice Skeen.
Financial data (yr. ended 06/30/01): Assets, $626,484 (M); grants paid, $19,923; gifts received, $2,148; expenditures, $49,290; qualifying distributions, $48,018.
Limitations: Giving limited to residents of WA.
Application information: Application form required.
Officers and Trustees:* Marilynn M. Russell,* Chair.; Paulette Waggoner,* Treas.; Carol Clarks, M. Billie Hilton, Sharon Sue Keltner, Elsa Luettgen.
EIN: 916060790
Codes: GTI

64160
Credit Bureau of Wenatchee Foundation
P.O. Box 949
Wenatchee, WA 98801
Application address: 223 Methow St.,
Wenatchee, WA 98801
Contact: Suzanne Harn, Exec. Tr.

Established in 1999.
Financial data (yr. ended 12/31/01): Assets, $586,369 (M); grants paid, $6,760; gifts received, $319,995; expenditures, $30,277; qualifying distributions, $6,760.
Trustees: Suzanne Harn, Exec. Tr.; Alan Beidler, Joe Blackmore, David Fabian, Lisa Francois, Kren Greening, Barbara Harris, Wayne Loranger, Fred Slonaker.
EIN: 912020315

64161
Ward Foundation
P.O. Box 2137
Friday Harbor, WA 98250

Established in 1997 in WA.
Donor(s): Ward Phillips.
Financial data (yr. ended 12/31/00): Assets, $555,626 (M); grants paid, $0; gifts received, $50,000; expenditures, $27,924; qualifying distributions, $27,559; giving activities include $26,439 for programs.
Trustee: J. Ward Phillips.
EIN: 311549605

64162
Good Neighbor Foundation
(Formerly Cosgrave Foundation)
c/o Michael Shimasaki
P.O. Box 68934
Seattle, WA 98168-0934

Financial data (yr. ended 11/30/01): Assets, $536,169 (M); grants paid, $16,866; gifts received, $100,000; expenditures, $26,852; qualifying distributions, $22,413.
Limitations: Applications not accepted. Giving primarily in Seattle, WA.
Application information: Contributes only to pre-selected organizations.
Officer and Trustees:* Michael W. Shimasaki,* Mgr.; Ronald F. Cosgrave, Barry C. Maulding.
EIN: 911021848

64163
W. B. Morris Testamentary Trust
c/o Baker Boyer National Bank
P.O. Box 1796
Walla Walla, WA 99362

Established in 1999 in WA.
Financial data (yr. ended 12/31/00): Assets, $535,737 (M); grants paid, $4,605; expenditures, $10,739; qualifying distributions, $4,129.
Trustee: Baker Boyer National Bank.
EIN: 916069716

64164
Stevens County Housing Coalition - Columbia Apartments
320 N. Main St.
Colville, WA 99114-2310

Financial data (yr. ended 07/31/00): Assets, $504,215 (M); grants paid, $0; expenditures, $74,619; qualifying distributions, $74,619; giving activities include $74,619 for programs.
Limitations: Applications not accepted.
Officers: Ramona Chrisman, Pres.; Carol Bezold, V.P.; Robert Maher, Secy.-Treas.
Director: Don Carter.
EIN: 911439336

Codes: TN

64165
Benton County Museum & Historical Society, Inc.
P.O. Box 1407
Prosser, WA 99350

Donor(s): Whitehead Estate.
Financial data (yr. ended 10/31/01): Assets, $493,018 (M); grants paid, $0; expenditures, $32,740; qualifying distributions, $32,740.
Officers: Bob Elder, Pres.; Louise Miller, Treas.
Directors: Fred Carroll, Lynn Hewitt, Opal Martin.
EIN: 911157147

64166
Discovery Research Foundation
c/o Ray Shahan
8833 S.W. Quartermaster Dr.
Vashon, WA 98070

Established in 2001 in WA.
Donor(s): Ray Shahan.
Financial data (yr. ended 12/31/01): Assets, $477,276 (M); grants paid, $0; gifts received, $588,650; expenditures, $60,849; qualifying distributions, $43,864; giving activities include $43,864 for programs.
Limitations: Applications not accepted.
Application information: Contributes only to pre-selected organizations.
Officers: Ray Shahan, Chair. and Pres.; Peder Shahan, V.P. and Treas.; Luis Diego Soto, Secy.
EIN: 912111401

64167
Ida Culver House of the Scattle Education Auxiliary
P.O. Box 33058
Seattle, WA 98133-0058

Established in 1991 in WA.
Donor(s): Seattle Education Foundation.
Financial data (yr. ended 09/30/99): Assets, $471,297 (M); grants paid, $1,500; gifts received, $5,640; expenditures, $22,837; qualifying distributions, $1,500.
Officers: Ray Cohrs, Pres.; Janiss Furry, V.P.; Reed Sargent, Secy.; James Shelton, Treas.
EIN: 911439257

64168
Dorothy Griswold Stephens Foundation
c/o Keith Klovee Smith
P.O. Box 494
Olympia, WA 98507

Financial data (yr. ended 12/31/00): Assets, $453,989 (M); grants paid, $0; expenditures, $21,456; qualifying distributions, $0; giving activities include $15,069 for programs.
Limitations: Applications not accepted.
Application information: Contributes only to pre-selected organizations.
Directors: Henry Hollweger, Keith Klovee-Smith, Cheryl L.W. Reynolds.
EIN: 911652866

64169
G.M.L. Foundation, Inc.
P.O. Box 916
Port Angeles, WA 98362-0158

Financial data (yr. ended 12/31/01): Assets, $450,916 (M); grants paid, $13,964; expenditures, $20,585; qualifying distributions, $16,971.
Limitations: Applications not accepted. Giving primarily in Clallam County, WA.
Application information: Unsolicited requests for funds not accepted.

Officers: Richard McLean, Pres.; Paul Crawford, V.P.; Reba Cornett, Secy.; Mary Lee Long, Treas.
Trustee: Brooke S. Taylor.
EIN: 916030844
Codes: GTI

64170
Skandia Music Foundation
7903 127th Pl. N.E.
Kirkland, WA 98033-8237

Classified as a private operating foundation in WA.
Financial data (yr. ended 12/31/00): Assets, $450,547 (M); grants paid, $0; expenditures, $19,502; qualifying distributions, $19,502; giving activities include $18,873 for programs.
Officers: Ernest Anderson, Pres.; Kris Johnson, V.P.; Nole Irish, Secy.; Bill Boyd, Treas.
Trustees: Art Hare, Trella Hastings, Mary Mohler, Art Nation, Shirley Rambo.
EIN: 911133360

64171
Cornelius and Lydiellen Hagan Foundation
P.O. Box 30163
Spokane, WA 99223-3002 (509) 448-7814
Contact: Ami Takimato

Classified as a private operating foundation in WA in 1997.
Donor(s): Cornelius E. Hagar.
Financial data (yr. ended 12/31/01): Assets, $415,416 (M); grants paid, $7,500; expenditures, $19,199; qualifying distributions, $18,949.
Application information: Application form required.
Officers: Cornelius E. Hagar, Chair.; Roger Bragdon, Vice-Chair.; John Weigand, Secy.; Ami Takimoto, Treas.
Board Members: Kathie H. Allen, Robert Blume, Ross Wood.
EIN: 911762315

64172
Foundation for Health Care Quality
705 2nd Ave., Ste. 703
Seattle, WA 98104-1717

Established in 1992 in WA.
Donor(s): Washington Physicians Svc. Assn., Robert Wood Johnson Foundation.
Financial data (yr. ended 12/31/00): Assets, $404,972 (M); grants paid, $0; gifts received, $1,171,779; expenditures, $2,278,640; qualifying distributions, $1,942,920; giving activities include $1,871,017 for programs.
Officers and Directors:* Elizabeth Ward,* Pres. and Exec. Dir.; Mark Adams, M.D., Dave Bjornson, Richard A. Deyo, Peter Dunbar, M.D., Andrew Fallat, Tanis Marsh, Terry Rogers, M.D., Linda Ruiz, Mary Selecky, Dorothy Teeter, and 5 additional directors.
EIN: 911419327

64173
The Proctor Foundation
20201 Front St. N.E.
Poulsbo, WA 98370

Established as an operating foundation in 1997.
Donor(s): Phimister P. Church.
Financial data (yr. ended 12/31/00): Assets, $398,998 (M); grants paid, $0; gifts received, $84,000; expenditures, $43,308; qualifying distributions, $38,706; giving activities include $40,668 for programs.
Directors: Laura Proctor Ames, Phimister P. Church, Sally L. Church, Peter Hasrick, Jack G. Strother.
EIN: 911839033

64174
Audrey Holliday Scholarship Fund
c/o Patricia J. Brenner
3116 Wilderness Dr., S.E.
Olympia, WA 98501-4963
Application address: c/o Scholarship Comm., Gresham Union High School, Gresham, OR 97030

Established in 1992 in WA.
Donor(s): Audrey Holliday.‡
Financial data (yr. ended 12/31/00): Assets, $398,386 (M); grants paid, $20,280; expenditures, $23,201; qualifying distributions, $21,961.
Limitations: Giving primarily to residents of Gresham, OR.
Application information: Recipients are chosen by Scholarship Comm. Application form not required.
Trustee: Patricia J. Brenner.
EIN: 916340777
Codes: GTI

64175
Bell Curve Research Foundation, Inc.
2901 Perry Ln.
Clarkston, WA 99403

Established in 1987 in ID.
Donor(s): Terry R. Rudd.
Financial data (yr. ended 12/31/00): Assets, $395,323 (M); grants paid, $15,022; expenditures, $21,946; qualifying distributions, $21,509.
Limitations: Applications not accepted.
Officer: Terry R. Rudd, Pres.
EIN: 820412257

64176
Biolab
110 Fairview Ave. N., Mail Stop D4-245
Seattle, WA 98109
E-mail: questions@biolab.org; URL: http://www.biolab.org

Established in 2000 in WA.
Donor(s): Edward Koo-Young Jung, Joo-Yun Joanna Jung.
Financial data (yr. ended 12/31/00): Assets, $383,433 (M); grants paid, $0; gifts received, $859,312; expenditures, $479,332; qualifying distributions, $0; giving activities include $469,124 for programs.
Limitations: Giving primarily in Seattle, WA.
Application information: Currently by nomination only.
Officers and Directors:* Joo-Yun Joanna Jung,* Pres. and Treas.; Edward Koo-Young Jung,* V.P. and Secy.; Barbara Schulz, Exec. Dir.
EIN: 912014769

64177
The Dickey Fund
1301 5th Ave.
Seattle, WA 98101
Contact: John Goodfellow, Exec. Dir.

Established in 1999 in WA.
Donor(s): John Goodfellow.
Financial data (yr. ended 12/31/00): Assets, $365,116 (M); grants paid, $18,000; gifts received, $171,022; expenditures, $18,763; qualifying distributions, $18,000.
Officer: John Goodfellow, Exec. Dir.
EIN: 911961319

64178
Rotalia Foundation
1407 N.W. 191st St.
Shoreline, WA 98177-2737
Application address: 11045 Alton Ave. N.E., Seattle, WA 98125

Financial data (yr. ended 12/31/01): Assets, $327,948 (M); grants paid, $37,000; gifts received, $2,000; expenditures, $38,116; qualifying distributions, $38,116.
Limitations: Giving limited to residents of Estonia or U.S. citizens studying in Estonia.
Application information: Applicants must speak, read, and understand the Estonian language. Application form required.
Officers and Directors: Uve J. Kapsi, Chair.; Paul Raidna, Vice-Chair.; Lembit Kosenkranius,* Secy.; Aavo Kalviste,* Treas.; Kenneth Gorshkow, Vello Karuks, Mart Kask, Bruno Laan, Vaho Rebassoo, Thomas N. Tuling.
EIN: 911409344
Codes: GTI

64179
The Amigo Foundation
12227 138th Ave. E.
Puyallup, WA 98374-4538 (253) 845-0558
Contact: William H. Pratt, Pres.; or Peggy W. Pratt, Dir.

Established in 1986 in WA.
Donor(s): William H. Pratt, Peggy W. Pratt.
Financial data (yr. ended 12/31/00): Assets, $322,775 (M); grants paid, $3,287; gifts received, $5,080; expenditures, $35,197; qualifying distributions, $32,056.
Limitations: Giving primarily in Lynnwood, WA.
Officers and Directors:* William H. Pratt,* Pres.; Michael J. Pratt,* V.P.; P. Kerry Bunday, Treas.; Michael Bailey, Robert Lewis, Peggy W. Pratt, Henry Surbeck.
EIN: 943043505

64180
Angela J. Bowen Conservancy Foundation
1010 Rogers St., S.W.
Olympia, WA 98502

Established in 1999 in WA.
Donor(s): Angela J. Bowen, M.D.
Financial data (yr. ended 12/31/00): Assets, $320,045 (M); grants paid, $0; gifts received, $14,200; expenditures, $14,155; qualifying distributions, $0; giving activities include $35 for programs.
Officers and Directors:* Angela J. Bowen, M.D.,* Pres.; Ronald Warren,* V.P.; Kathy Burlingame,* Secy.-Treas.
EIN: 912015916

64181
Columbia Endowment Fund
c/o Board of Trustees
P.O. Box 1242
Brush Prairie, WA 98606

Financial data (yr. ended 12/31/00): Assets, $275,456 (M); grants paid, $24,473; expenditures, $24,758; qualifying distributions, $24,473.
Limitations: Giving limited to WA.
Application information: Application form required.
Officers: Arlo Funk, Pres.; Robert Jackson, V.P.; Carol Norberg, Secy.; Starla Farnsworth, Treas.
EIN: 943090375

64182
His Helping Hand Foundation
720 Beechwood
Woodland, WA 98674
Contact: Elizabeth Kalita, Dir.

Established in 1996.
Financial data (yr. ended 06/30/01): Assets, $269,855 (M); grants paid, $217,992; gifts received, $1,438; expenditures, $228,592; qualifying distributions, $217,060.
Limitations: Giving primarily in WA.
Officer and Directors:* Corinne Fuller,* Pres.; George Beebe, Elizabeth Kalita, Christine Lines.
EIN: 911791444
Codes: FD2

64183
Drachen Foundation
c/o Kite Archives, Science & Culture
1905 Queen Anne Ave. N., No. 200
Seattle, WA 98109-2549 (206) 282-4349
Additional address: 128 S. Tejon St., Ste. 406, Colorado Springs, CO 80903; Tel.: (719) 632-7447; FAX: (206) 284-5471; E-mail: info@drachen.org; URL: http://www.drachen.org
Contact: Alison M. Fujino, Admin.

Established in 1994 in CO.
Financial data (yr. ended 12/31/00): Assets, $245,168 (M); grants paid, $2,090; gifts received, $327,236; expenditures, $303,364; qualifying distributions, $289,576.
Publications: Informational brochure (including application guidelines), newsletter, occasional report.
Directors: Scott R. Skinner, Pres.; Stuart Allen, Joseph Hadzicki, Martin Lester, Wayne Wilson, Keith Yoshida.
EIN: 841277286

64184
Fitzgerald Family Foundation
17114 153rd Ave. S.E., Space 17
Yelm, WA 98597
Contact: Ruby L. Fitzgerald, Tr.

Donor(s): Ruby L. Fitzgerald.
Financial data (yr. ended 12/31/00): Assets, $222,023 (M); grants paid, $22,662; gifts received, $4,200; expenditures, $22,662; qualifying distributions, $22,662.
Limitations: Giving primarily in WA.
Application information: Application form required.
Officer: Ella Williams, Chair.
Trustees: Howard Fitzgerald, Ruby L. Fitzgerald.
EIN: 911726700

64185
Baskin Education & Environmental Foundation
502 8th Ave. W.
Kirkland, WA 98033-4851 (877) 829-5500
Contact: R. James Baskin, Dir.

Established in 2000.
Donor(s): R. James Baskin, Maureen J. Baskin.
Financial data (yr. ended 12/31/00): Assets, $218,182 (M); grants paid, $0; gifts received, $218,688; expenditures, $506; qualifying distributions, $320.
Application information: Application form required.
Director: R. James Baskin.
EIN: 912089608

64186
Arnsberg Scholarship Trust
P.O. Box 386
Republic, WA 99166
Application address: c/o Andersons Corp., P.O. Box 386, 711 S. Clark, Republic, WA 99166-0386
Contact: Gary Anderson, Tr.

Established in 1997 in WA.
Donor(s): Asa Arnsberg.
Financial data (yr. ended 12/31/01): Assets, $171,598 (M); grants paid, $15,500; gifts received, $2,850; expenditures, $17,680; qualifying distributions, $16,298.
Limitations: Giving limited to residents of WA.
Application information: Application form required.
Trustees: Gary Anderson, Susan Arnsberg Diamond, Nancy Giddings, Gina Graham, Leo Kornfeld, Robert M. Slagle.
EIN: 916443732

64187
Marci Gulbranson Moore Foundation
14050 N.E. 5th St.
Bellevue, WA 98007-6900

Established in 1999 in WA.
Donor(s): Gary Gulbranson, Scott Moore.
Financial data (yr. ended 12/31/00): Assets, $156,196 (M); grants paid, $113,000; gifts received, $2,717; expenditures, $115,528; qualifying distributions, $113,000.
Limitations: Applications not accepted.
Application information: Contributes only to pre-selected organizations.
Officers: Gary Gulbranson, Pres.; James Moore, V.P.; Scott Moore, Secy.-Treas.
EIN: 911941652
Codes: FD2

64188
Kettle River History Club
c/o Thomas McKay
259 Boulder Creek Rd.
Curlew, WA 99118

Classified as a private operating foundation in 1991.
Financial data (yr. ended 12/31/01): Assets, $155,491 (M); grants paid, $0; gifts received, $673; expenditures, $6,864; qualifying distributions, $6,864; giving activities include $3,037 for programs.
Officers: Thomas McKay, Pres.; Richard Lembcke, V.P.; Gladys Lembcke, Secy.; LaRue Lembcke, Treas.
EIN: 943124998

64189
Kindred Spirits Animal Sanctuary
P.O. Box 48
Suquamish, WA 98392

Established in 1997.
Donor(s): Nancy Lanning.
Financial data (yr. ended 01/31/00): Assets, $154,768 (M); grants paid, $0; gifts received, $398,870; expenditures, $375,493; qualifying distributions, $221,058; giving activities include $89,458 for programs.
Directors: Ron Davis, Nancy Lanning, Laurie Raymond.
EIN: 911741729

64190
ARK Foundation
c/o Allenmore Medical Ctr.
1901 S. Union Ave., Ste. A-311
Tacoma, WA 98405

Classified as a private operating foundation in 1996.
Donor(s): Carol A. Stockdale, Ronald A. Stockdale.
Financial data (yr. ended 12/31/01): Assets, $142,224 (M); grants paid, $0; gifts received, $124,183; expenditures, $50,739; qualifying distributions, $44,087; giving activities include $32,392 for programs.
Limitations: Applications not accepted.
Application information: Contributes only to pre-selected organizations.
Officers: Carol A. Stockdale, Pres.; Ronald A. Stockdale, Secy.-Treas.
EIN: 911713751

64191
Math Education Improvement Services
4622 W. Front
Spokane, WA 99224-5014
Contact: Murry Nelsen, Pres.

Classified as a private operating foundation in 1996.
Donor(s): Murry Nelson.
Financial data (yr. ended 12/31/00): Assets, $141,055 (M); grants paid, $7,200; gifts received, $23,187; expenditures, $9,241; qualifying distributions, $0.
Limitations: Giving primarily in WA.
Officers: Murry Nelsen, Pres.; Maria Nelson, V.P.
EIN: 911670354

64192
The Order of the Arrow Longhouse Foundation
16722 S.E. 23rd Pl.
Bellevue, WA 98008

Established in 2000 in WA.
Financial data (yr. ended 12/31/00): Assets, $140,644 (M); grants paid, $10,000; gifts received, $200,045; expenditures, $11,250; qualifying distributions, $10,000.
Limitations: Applications not accepted. Giving primarily in Seattle, WA.
Application information: Contributes only to pre-selected organizations.
Officers: Joyce Viola-Johnson, Pres.; Christopher Pearson, V.P.; Raymon Sayah, Jr., Secy.; Thomas Pearson, Jr., Treas.
EIN: 912039440

64193
Organic Sunflower Foundation
P.O. Box 32
Fox Island, WA 98333-0032

Classified as a private operating foundation in 1995.
Financial data (yr. ended 12/31/01): Assets, $138,993 (M); grants paid, $0; gifts received, $73,000; expenditures, $73,000; qualifying distributions, $0.
Directors: Mike Backus, Sheryl Backus, J.C. Baldwin.
EIN: 943229055

64194
Harold E. & Esther L. Wills Foundation
10 Tala Shore Dr.
Port Ludlow, WA 98365

Established in 1998 in CA.
Financial data (yr. ended 12/31/00): Assets, $136,888 (M); grants paid, $12,861; gifts received, $33,962; expenditures, $14,285; qualifying distributions, $12,861.
Limitations: Applications not accepted.
Application information: Contributes only to pre-selected organizations.
Officers: Betty Jane Wills, Pres.; Linda Marie Bowers, Secy.
EIN: 911875068

64195
I Have a Dream Foundation - Seattle
411 University St., Ste. 1200
Seattle, WA 98101-2507

Classified as a private operating foundation in 1988.
Donor(s): Roger A. Reiger, Annette Reiger.
Financial data (yr. ended 12/31/01): Assets, $130,445 (M); grants paid, $3,418; gifts received, $78; expenditures, $3,886; qualifying distributions, $3,886.
Limitations: Applications not accepted.
Application information: Recipient selected by the Eugen Lang Comm.
Officers and Directors:* Roger A. Rieger,* Pres.; E.A. Rieger,* V.P.
EIN: 911391997
Codes: GTI

64196
Evolving Earth Foundation
P.O. Box 2090
Issaquah, WA 98027
Contact: Thomas A. Dillhoff, Pres.

Established in 2000 in WA.
Donor(s): Richard Dillhoff.
Financial data (yr. ended 12/31/01): Assets, $119,120 (M); grants paid, $29,250; gifts received, $340,000; expenditures, $229,243; qualifying distributions, $29,250.
Officers: Thomas A. Dillhoff, Pres.; Richard Dillhoff, V.P.; S. Dillhoff, Secy.
EIN: 912077460

64197
Laurendeau Foundation for Cancer Care
P.O. Box 157
Bellingham, WA 98227-0157

Donor(s): Richard Christensen, Dr. Laurendeau,‡ Alice VanRy.
Financial data (yr. ended 09/30/01): Assets, $114,734 (M); grants paid, $45,126; gifts received, $48,466; expenditures, $74,277; qualifying distributions, $69,726.
Limitations: Giving primarily in Bellingham, WA.
Application information: Application form required.
Officers: Ron Snyder, Pres.; Jeanie Schneider, V.P.; Joan Schwindt, Secy.; Joanne P. Gardner, Treas. and Mgr.
EIN: 911121989
Codes: GTI

64198
Insurance Fund Foundation, Inc.
c/o Office Mgr.
1904 3rd Ave., Ste. 925
Seattle, WA 98101-1123

Classified as a company-sponsored operating foundation in 1969.
Donor(s): SAFECO Corp., Farmers Insurance of Vancouver, WA.
Financial data (yr. ended 06/30/01): Assets, $107,462 (M); grants paid, $45,500; gifts received, $134,500; expenditures, $138,446; qualifying distributions, $138,223; giving activities include $164,031 for programs.
Limitations: Giving limited to WA.

Officers: Bill Lebo, Pres.; Ryan Dudley, V.P.; Stan McNaughton, V.P.; Dick Rash, V.P.; Rick Shriver, V.P.; A. Darryl Page, Secy.; Maggie Haines, Treas.
Directors: Tom Becker, Richard Berry, Arne Chatterton, Bill Clumpner, Susan Hunsaker, Mark Kidder, Alan Kikuyama, Elizabeth Moceri, Robert Ogden, Rick Scuderi, Caren Silvestri, Mark Thaut, James Wenckus.
EIN: 916053952
Codes: CD

64199
Roberts Family Foundation
7745 Hansen Rd. N.E.
Bainbridge Island, WA 98110-1614

Established in 1991 in WA.
Donor(s): Henry Clay Roberts, Sherry Lavonne Roberts.
Financial data (yr. ended 12/31/01): Assets, $106,973 (M); grants paid, $4,730; expenditures, $5,907; qualifying distributions, $4,730.
Limitations: Applications not accepted. Giving primarily in WA.
Application information: Contributes only to pre-selected organizations.
Officers: Henry Clay Roberts, Pres.; Sherry Lavonne Roberts, V.P. and Treas.; Melissa J. Ransdell, Secy.
EIN: 911536142

64200
Hazel Holm Scholarship Fund
c/o Arthur P. Folden
2508 Buckingham Dr. S.E.
Olympia, WA 98501 (360) 352-1845

Established in 1998 in WA.
Financial data (yr. ended 12/31/01): Assets, $87,047 (M); grants paid, $21,000; expenditures, $22,081; qualifying distributions, $22,038.
Limitations: Giving limited to residents of Raymond, South Bend and Willapa, WA.
Application information: Application form required.
Trustees: Arthur P. Folden, Curt Janhunen.
EIN: 911868960

64201
Fish Ministries
2461 42nd Ave.
Longview, WA 98632

Established in 1997 in WA. Classified as a private operating foundation in 1999.
Donor(s): Barbara Bishop.
Financial data (yr. ended 12/31/00): Assets, $85,962 (M); grants paid, $1,927; gifts received, $49,836; expenditures, $34,761; qualifying distributions, $28,894.
Officers: Brent Bishop, Pres. and Treas.; Mike Fox, V.P.; Monika Scheffe, Secy.
Directors: Matt Atkins, Kirk Austin, George Scheffe.
EIN: 911759534

64202
Blythe Range Trust
P.O. Box 143
St. John, WA 99171
Application address: c/o Tim Nootenboom, P.O. Box 58, St. John, WA 99171, tel.: (509) 648-3336

Financial data (yr. ended 03/31/02): Assets, $85,073 (M); grants paid, $167; expenditures, $2,130; qualifying distributions, $386.
Limitations: Giving limited to residents of St. John, WA.
Application information: Application form required.

Trustee: Neal Robertson.
EIN: 916210820

64203
Center for the Future of Public Education
17051 S.E. 272nd St., Ste 18
Kent, WA 98042

Donor(s): The David and Lucile Packard Foundation.
Financial data (yr. ended 06/30/00): Assets, $84,074 (M); grants paid, $0; gifts received, $1,000; expenditures, $35,074; qualifying distributions, $0; giving activities include $35,074 for programs.
Officers and Directors:* Karen D. Olsen,* Pres.; Susan J. Kovalik,* V.P.; Janet Reynolds,* Secy.; Ted Foley,* Treas.; Beverly Howland.
EIN: 860677265

64204
B. R. Simonson Memorial Foundation
5308 12th St., E.
Tacoma, WA 98424-2796
Contact: Gordon Scraggin, Dir.

Classified as a private operating foundation in 1986 in MN; funded in 1989.
Donor(s): Bjarne R. Simonson.‡
Financial data (yr. ended 12/31/00): Assets, $76,634 (M); grants paid, $12,000; expenditures, $14,078; qualifying distributions, $11,979.
Limitations: Giving limited to Grand Meadow, MN.
Directors: R. Dean Martin, Gordon Scraggin, Stanford A. Stringham.
EIN: 911348538

64205
The Bradshaw Trust
304 S. 219th
Seattle, WA 98198-4740
Contact: Phillip M. Bradshaw, Pres.

Classified as a private operating foundation in 1993. Established in 1989 in WA.
Donor(s): Phillip M. Bradshaw.
Financial data (yr. ended 12/31/01): Assets, $70,659 (M); grants paid, $4,000; gifts received, $4,500; expenditures, $4,235; qualifying distributions, $4,000.
Limitations: Giving limited to residents of Guthrie, OK and Shelbina, MO.
Application information: Application form required.
Officer: Phillip M. Bradshaw, Pres.
Trustee: Michael Howard.
EIN: 943104579

64206
Capnography Society
c/o Marvin Wayne
456 14th St.
Bellingham, WA 98225-6105

Classified as a company-sponsored operating foundation in 2000 in WA.
Donor(s): Metronic Physio Control, Novametrix, Oridian Medical, Inc., Zoll Medical.
Financial data (yr. ended 12/31/01): Assets, $60,769 (M); grants paid, $0; expenditures, $8,284; qualifying distributions, $7,042.
Limitations: Applications not accepted.
Application information: Contributes only to pre-selected organizations.
Officers: Baruch Krauss, Pres.; Marvin Wayne, V.P.; Jay Falk, Secy.-Treas.
Directors: Tom Ahrens, Joe Ornato.
EIN: 912005112

64207
Mona Foundation
13922 64th Pl. W.
Edmonds, WA 98026

Donor(s): Mahnaz Javid, Patrece Banks.
Financial data (yr. ended 12/31/00): Assets, $60,452 (M); grants paid, $61,160; gifts received, $93,323; expenditures, $72,370; qualifying distributions, $95,302.
Limitations: Applications not accepted. Giving on an international basis.
Application information: Contributes only to pre-selected organizations.
Officers and Directors:* Mahnaz Javid,* Pres.; Patrece Banks,* V.P. and Treas.; Randie Gottlieb,* Secy.; Steve Waite.
EIN: 911968512

64208
The F. Eugene Miller Foundation
P.O. Box 706
Monroe, WA 98272 (360) 805-1619
Contact: C. Meadway, Tr.

Classified as a private operating foundation in 1973.
Donor(s): F. Eugene Miller.‡
Financial data (yr. ended 06/30/01): Assets, $59,888 (M); grants paid, $14,400; gifts received, $32,734; expenditures, $73,540; qualifying distributions, $90,133; giving activities include $7,377 for programs.
Application information: Application form required.
Director: C. Meadway.
Trustee: J. Weeks.
EIN: 237215103

64209
Operacion Esperanza
215 Newt Estates Rd.
Longview, WA 98632

Classified as a private operating foundation in 1997 in WA.
Donor(s): Edwin W. Pauley Foundation, Jim Wilkes, Don Carlin, Hedy Carlin.
Financial data (yr. ended 12/31/01): Assets, $56,489 (M); grants paid, $0; gifts received, $14,071; expenditures, $34,722; qualifying distributions, $34,485; giving activities include $34,722 for programs.
Officers and Directors:* Joseph Clawson,* Pres. and Treas.; Maryann Jensen,* Secy.; Stephen Pauley.
EIN: 911799532

64210
Martin Foundation for Biomedical Research
c/o Dr. George M. Martin
2223 E. Howe St.
Seattle, WA 98112

Established in 1998 in WA; classified as a private operating foundation in 1999.
Donor(s): George M. Martin.
Financial data (yr. ended 12/31/00): Assets, $48,468 (M); grants paid, $5,020; expenditures, $5,520; qualifying distributions, $5,009.
Limitations: Applications not accepted. Giving primarily in Los Angeles, CA.
Application information: Contributes only to pre-selected organizations.
Director: George M. Martin.
EIN: 916470136

64211
Joe Fergason Scholarship Fund
P.O. Box 437
South Bend, WA 98586
Contact: Mike Rogers, Tr.

Financial data (yr. ended 12/31/01): Assets, $48,435 (M); grants paid, $2,500; expenditures, $2,718; qualifying distributions, $2,718.
Limitations: Giving limited to residents of South Bend, WA.
Application information: Application form required.
Trustees: Phil Davis, Mike Rogers, Steven Russell.
EIN: 911322109

64212
Omega of Sigma Pi Foundation
1011 Alder St.
Edmonds, WA 98020
Application address: 4510 S.E. Powell Valley Rd., Gresham, OR 97080
Contact: Raymond J. Simonson, Pres.

Classified as a private operating foundation in 1973.
Financial data (yr. ended 12/31/99): Assets, $43,601 (M); grants paid, $8,073; gifts received, $665; expenditures, $11,994; qualifying distributions, $8,073; giving activities include $8,073 for loans to individuals.
Limitations: Giving primarily in OR.
Application information: Application form required.
Officers: Raymond J. Simonson, Pres.; M.K. Larsen, Secy.; J.M. Weswig, Treas.
EIN: 237191514

64213
Edith Kellogg Magee Charitable Trust
c/o Jerald J. Magee
16500 S.E. 1st St., Ste. 148
Vancouver, WA 98684-9592

Classified as a private operating foundation in 2000 in OR and WA.
Financial data (yr. ended 12/31/01): Assets, $35,000 (M); grants paid, $1,872; expenditures, $1,872; qualifying distributions, $1,872.
Limitations: Giving primarily in OR.
Trustee: Jerald J. Magee.
EIN: 911745040

64214
Raynier Institute & Foundation
c/o Harold E. Abbott
1463 E. Republican St., Ste. 135
Seattle, WA 98112

Established in 1994 in WA.
Donor(s): James W. Ray.
Financial data (yr. ended 12/31/01): Assets, $32,353 (M); grants paid, $271,905; gifts received, $401,163; expenditures, $380,194; qualifying distributions, $267,978.
Limitations: Applications not accepted.
Application information: Contributes only to pre-selected organizations.
Officer: Harold E. Abbott, V.P.
Director: Edward D. Gardner.
EIN: 911644205
Codes: FD

64215
Lynden Memorial Scholarship Fund
P.O. Box 3757
Seattle, WA 98124-3757
Application address: c/o CFSA, P.O. Box 297, St. Paul, MN 56082, tel.: (507) 931-1682

Established in 1995 in WA.
Donor(s): Lynden, Inc., Jill Jansen, Eleanor and Henry Jansen Foundation.
Financial data (yr. ended 12/31/01): Assets, $30,658 (M); grants paid, $5,000; gifts received, $1,125; expenditures, $6,442; qualifying distributions, $6,442.
Limitations: Giving primarily in areas of company operations, with emphasis on WA and CA.
Application information: Application form required.
Officers: Dianne E. Bauer, Pres.; Patricia J. Gaillard, V.P.; Linda K. Krogh, V.P.; Richard A. Korpela, Secy.; Kitty Samuel, Treas.
EIN: 911684708

64216
The Kimberly Foundation
15701 N.E. 36th St.
Vancouver, WA 98682

Established in 1991 in WA.
Donor(s): Dean W. Lodmell, Richard A. Lodmell.
Financial data (yr. ended 04/30/99): Assets, $28,532 (M); grants paid, $0; gifts received, $4,510; expenditures, $3,776; qualifying distributions, $3,777; giving activities include $2,550 for programs.
Officers: Dean W. Lodmell, Chair.; Richard A. Lodmell, Pres.
EIN: 911539803

64217
Clover Park Foundation
c/o Fred Willis
10510 Cedrona SW
Lakewood, WA 98498 (253) 581-7835
E-mail: Fredingrid@earthlink.net

Financial data (yr. ended 08/31/99): Assets, $23,639 (M); grants paid, $5,000; gifts received, $25; expenditures, $5,100; qualifying distributions, $5,100.
Limitations: Giving primarily in WA.
Officers: Fred Willis, Pres.; Bill Imholt, V.P.; Frank Walter, Secy.; Doug Richardson, Treas.
EIN: 911184240

64218
Joan Vann Memorial Endowment
150 Nickerson St., Ste. 106
Seattle, WA 98109 (206) 286-9002
Contact: Leslee A. Currie, Secy.-Treas.

Established in 1990 in WA.
Donor(s): Barbara J. Vann.
Financial data (yr. ended 12/31/00): Assets, $21,291 (M); grants paid, $1,453; gifts received, $1,218; expenditures, $2,229; qualifying distributions, $3,871.
Application information: Application form not required.
Officers: Barbara J. Vann, Pres.; Leslee A. Currie, Secy.-Treas.
EIN: 911471633

64219
Threshold Housing
3425 E. Denny Way
Seattle, WA 98122

Financial data (yr. ended 12/31/01): Assets, $20,496 (M); grants paid, $0; expenditures, $136,744; qualifying distributions, $149,647; giving activities include $102,581 for programs.
Limitations: Applications not accepted.
Application information: Contributes only to pre-selected organizations.
Officers: William Conner, Pres.; Gary Williams, V.P.; Gary Ackerman, Secy.; Bryan Park, Treas.; John Kucher, Exec. Dir.
Trustees: Suzanne Britsch, Marcia Hadley, William Kreager, Erik Marks.
EIN: 911559548

64220
Urgel Bell Memorial Scholarship Trust
101 Wigen Rd.
Lacrosse, WA 99143

Financial data (yr. ended 12/31/00): Assets, $18,946 (M); grants paid, $1,000; expenditures, $1,033; qualifying distributions, $1,033.
Limitations: Applications not accepted. Giving limited to residents of Lacrosse, WA.
Trustee: L. Gene Aune.
EIN: 911651272

64221
Alistar International
(Formerly Alistair Foundation)
600 108th Ave., N.E., Ste. 1014
Bellevue, WA 98004

Established in 1995 in WA.
Donor(s): The Alistar Group, Bernard G. Greer, Judith O.A. Greer.
Financial data (yr. ended 12/31/99): Assets, $16,443 (M); grants paid, $859,812; gifts received, $1,175,891; expenditures, $1,182,318; qualifying distributions, $1,173,125.
Limitations: Applications not accepted. Giving primarily in Nicaragua; some funding also in Seattle, WA.
Application information: Contributes only to pre-selected organizations.
Officers and Directors:* Bernard G. Greer,* Pres.; Nan Marie Greer, V.P.; Judith O.A. Greer,* Secy.-Treas.; Frederic Gregory, Carl Mayers, Anuar Murrar, Anthony Stocks.
EIN: 911672495
Codes: FD

64222
Rural American Scholarship Fund
P.O. Box 2674
Oak Harbor, WA 98277
Contact: Ginny Thomas, Secy.

Established in 1991.
Financial data (yr. ended 12/31/01): Assets, $14,815 (M); grants paid, $152,516; gifts received, $160,000; expenditures, $158,609; qualifying distributions, $157,623.
Limitations: Applications not accepted. Giving limited to the rural areas of the northwestern U.S., with emphasis on ID, MT, OR, WA and WY.
Officer and Director:* F. Casey Brennan,* Pres., V.P., and Treas.
EIN: 850386189
Codes: FD2, GTI

64223
Captain Rex Kelley & Esther Kelley Museum
2702 N. Yakima
Tacoma, WA 98406-7626

Financial data (yr. ended 12/31/01): Assets, $13,759 (M); grants paid, $0; gifts received, $9,999; expenditures, $8,358; qualifying distributions, $0.
Officers: Terry L. Paine, Pres.; Renee E. Paine, Secy.; Patrick K. Adams, Treas.
EIN: 943059331

64224
Counterbalance Foundation
2030 Dexter Ave. N., Ste. B296
Seattle, WA 98109

Established in 1998.
Donor(s): Adrian Wyard.

Financial data (yr. ended 12/31/99): Assets, $13,056 (M); grants paid, $20,112; gifts received, $45,821; expenditures, $62,171; qualifying distributions, $64,938.
Limitations: Applications not accepted.
Application information: Contributes only to pre-selected organizations.
Officers and Directors:* Adrian Wyard,* Pres. and V.P.; John Goodwin,* Treas.; Rev. R.D. Mallory, Kent Warner.
EIN: 911884397

64225
Brian L. Puryear Foundation
717 S. Pines Road
Spokane, WA 99206

Established in 1997 in WA.
Financial data (yr. ended 12/31/99): Assets, $11,667 (M); grants paid, $10,000; expenditures, $10,010; qualifying distributions, $10,000.
Limitations: Applications not accepted. Giving primarily in WA.
Application information: Contributes only to pre-selected organizations.
Directors: Debra J. Duncan, Georgia Lee Puryear, James R. Puryear.
EIN: 911725458

64226
Douglas Chapple Scholarship Foundation
(also known as Lake Washington High School Foundation)
12011 Bel Red Rd., Ste. 206
Bellevue, WA 98005 (425) 454-7777
Contact: Holly Finkbeiner, Pres.

Established in 1989 in WA.
Donor(s): William H. Finkbeiner.
Financial data (yr. ended 12/31/00): Assets, $7,298 (M); grants paid, $601; expenditures, $603; qualifying distributions, $601.
Limitations: Giving limited to the Bellevue, WA, area.
Application information: Recipient selected by the board of directors. Application form required.
Officer: Holly L. Finkbeiner, Pres.
EIN: 911445894

64227
Cooper Foundation for Developmental Disabilities
22530 N.E. 2nd St.
Sammamish, WA 98074 (425) 369-8255
Contact: Patricia C. Rowen, Pres.

Established in 2000 in WA.
Donor(s): Patricia C. Rowen.
Financial data (yr. ended 12/31/01): Assets, $7,080 (M); grants paid, $2,500; gifts received, $3,696; expenditures, $2,500; qualifying distributions, $2,500.
Officer: Patricia C. Rowen, Pres.
EIN: 912024853

64228
Chester Woodruff Foundation
1301 Spring St., Ste. 30-G
Seattle, WA 98104
Contact: Michael C. Sack, Pres., or John W. Saul, III, V.P.

Donor(s): Michael C. Sack, John W. Saul III.
Financial data (yr. ended 12/31/00): Assets, $6,531 (M); grants paid, $18,186; gifts received, $21,000; expenditures, $18,665; qualifying distributions, $18,418.
Application information: Application form not required.
Officers: Michael C. Sack, Pres.; John W. Saul III, V.P.; Bruce Becker, Secy.-Treas.

EIN: 222393887

64229
Glenwood Elementary PTA 7.6.15
(Formerly PTA Washington Congress)
2221 103rd Ave., S.E.
Everett, WA 98205

Financial data (yr. ended 06/30/99): Assets, $5,973 (M); grants paid, $3,411; gifts received, $1,444; expenditures, $19,789; qualifying distributions, $19,789.
Officers: Donna Buzzo, Co-Pres.; Janice Thompson, Co-Pres.; Elliot Cheap, V.P.; Cheryl Shandera, Secy.; Sue Kasalko, Treas.
EIN: 911548245

64230
The Plattner Family Foundation
4842 N.E. 43rd St.
Seattle, WA 98105

Established in 2000.
Donor(s): Philip B. Plattner, Peggy B. Plattner.
Financial data (yr. ended 12/31/00): Assets, $5,726 (M); grants paid, $0; gifts received, $14,400; expenditures, $5,193; qualifying distributions, $0.
Limitations: Applications not accepted.
Application information: Contributes only to pre-selected organizations.
Officers: Philip B. Plattner, Pres. and Treas.; Peggy B. Plattner, V.P. and Secy.
EIN: 912032361

64231
The Costco Foundation
999 Lake Dr.
Issaquah, WA 98027
Contact: John Matthews, Pres.

Established as a company-sponsored operating foundation in 1997.
Donor(s): Costco Wholesale Corp.
Financial data (yr. ended 08/29/01): Assets, $4,954 (M); grants paid, $50,309; gifts received, $49,000; expenditures, $50,369; qualifying distributions, $50,309.
Limitations: Giving limited to areas of company operations.
Application information: Applications available through the plant manager's office. Application form required.
Officers and Directors:* John Matthews,* Pres.; Monica Smith,* V.P.; Richard Galanti,* Treas.
EIN: 911799391
Codes: CD

64232
Heck-Fruci Family Foundation
c/o James Caley
P.O. Box 1388
Vancouver, WA 98666
Contact: Paula K. Heck, Pres.; or Dennis L. Heck, Secy.-Treas.

Established in 2000 in WA.
Donor(s): Dennis L. Heck, Paula Kay Heck.
Financial data (yr. ended 12/31/00): Assets, $3,841 (M); grants paid, $25,500; gifts received, $28,738; expenditures, $25,500; qualifying distributions, $25,500.
Limitations: Giving limited to Vancouver, WA.
Application information: Application form required.
Officers and Directors:* Paula Kay Heck,* Pres.; Dennis L. Heck,* Secy.-Treas.
EIN: 912028050

64233
Church Planting Resource
3212 S. 288th St.
Auburn, WA 98001

Established in 2001 in WA.
Financial data (yr. ended 12/31/01): Assets, $3,510 (M); grants paid, $0; gifts received, $4,308; expenditures, $753; qualifying distributions, $0.
Officers: Chad Irving, Pres.; Mark Woolfington, V.P.; Tricia Irving, Secy.-Treas.
EIN: 912106681

64234
The Wyatt Vande Zande Foundation
9217 N.W. 17th AVe.
Vancouver, WA 98665

Classified as a private operating foundation in 2001 in WA.
Donor(s): Ernest J. Vande Zande.
Financial data (yr. ended 12/31/01): Assets, $3,010 (M); grants paid, $200; gifts received, $6,476; expenditures, $200; qualifying distributions, $200.
Limitations: Applications not accepted. Giving primarily in Vancouver, WA.
Application information: Contributes only to pre-selected organizations.
Director: Ernest Vande Zande.
EIN: 912131159

64235
Florence R. Bachrach Foundation
3012 N.E. 55th St.
Seattle, WA 98105

Financial data (yr. ended 06/30/99): Assets, $2,932 (M); grants paid, $3,443; gifts received, $3,342; expenditures, $3,587; qualifying distributions, $3,443.
Limitations: Applications not accepted. Giving limited to Seattle, WA.
Application information: Contributes only to pre-selected organizations.
Officers: Ruth Bachrach, Pres.; Sara Bachrach, V.P.; Marilyn Ostrom, Secy.
EIN: 911308042

64236
Arctic Medical Foundation
P.O. Box 4477
Federal Way, WA 98063

Established in 1998 in DE and WA.
Donor(s): Stephen L. Johnson.
Financial data (yr. ended 12/31/01): Assets, $2,384 (M); grants paid, $27,107; gifts received, $8,419; expenditures, $35,526; qualifying distributions, $35,526; giving activities include $5,597 for programs.
Limitations: Applications not accepted.
Officer: Stephen L. Johnson, Pres.
EIN: 911939750

64237
Ashrae Inland Empire Chapter Scholarship Group
11703 E. Buckeye
Spokane, WA 99206
Contact: James B. Picken, Chair.

Financial data (yr. ended 06/30/00): Assets, $1,900 (M); grants paid, $1,000; gifts received, $1,822; expenditures, $1,000; qualifying distributions, $1,000.
Limitations: Giving primarily in Moscow, ID.
Officers: James B. Picken, Chair. and Pres.; Dick Mosley, Vice-Chair.; Traci A. Hanegan, Secy.-Treas.
EIN: 911329932

64238
Whatcom Foundation, Inc.
Bellingham National Bank Bldg., Rm. 518
Bellingham, WA 98225 (360) 733-9511
Contact: Linda Lee

Established in 1967 in WA.
Donor(s): T.S. Hamilton Trust.
Financial data (yr. ended 05/31/00): Assets, $1,685 (M); grants paid, $28,914; expenditures, $37,504; qualifying distributions, $28,914.
Limitations: Giving limited to Whatcom County, WA.
Application information: Application form required.
Trustee: Dan R. Olsen.
EIN: 910905571

64239
Slather Institute
9216 View Ave., N.W.
Seattle, WA 98117

Established in 1999 in WA.
Financial data (yr. ended 12/31/00): Assets, $1,498 (M); grants paid, $28,200; gifts received, $34,934; expenditures, $34,298; qualifying distributions, $33,450; giving activities include $5,250 for programs.
Limitations: Giving primarily in Seattle, WA.
Directors: Darren Barnes, Dennis Bryant.
EIN: 911999979

64240
James & Grace Cain Foundation
c/o Hersman Serles
P. O. Box 789
Kirkland, WA 98083-0789

Established in 1999 in WA.
Financial data (yr. ended 12/31/01): Assets, $1,431 (M); grants paid, $50; expenditures, $66; qualifying distributions, $50.
Officers: Diane Fiduccia, Pres.; Kelly Christine Fiduccia, V.P.; James Cain Fiduccia, Secy.-Treas.
EIN: 911950050

64241
Committee for Litter Control and Recycling
c/o Paul Elliot
P.O. Box 99366
Seattle, WA 98199-0366

Classified as a private operating foundation in 1987.
Financial data (yr. ended 12/31/99): Assets, $749 (M); grants paid, $0; gifts received, $5,000; expenditures, $9,436; qualifying distributions, $9,435; giving activities include $9,438 for programs.
Officers: Mark McKinley, Chair. and Exec. Dir.; Ron Templin, Vice-Chair. and Pres.; Stuart Simon, Secy.; Paul Elliott, Treas.
EIN: 911326372

64242
Carolyn Brown Reading Academy
4609 246th Pl. S.E.
Bellevue, WA 98006

Established in 2000 in WA.
Donor(s): Carolyn Brown.
Financial data (yr. ended 09/30/01): Assets, $730 (M); grants paid, $0; expenditures, $5,492; qualifying distributions, $5,123.
Officers: Carolyn Brown, Pres.; Alan Gottlieb, V.P.; Donna Nelsor, Secy.; Kevin Brown, Treas.
Director: Julianne Gottleib.
EIN: 911737195

64243
Syre/Trillium Charitable Foundation
4350 Cordata Pkwy.
Bellingham, WA 98226-8019

Classified as a private operating foundation in 1996.
Financial data (yr. ended 12/31/01): Assets, $718 (M); grants paid, $0; expenditures, $181; qualifying distributions, $0.
Limitations: Applications not accepted.
Application information: Contributes only to pre-selected organizations.
Officers and Directors:* David R. Syre,* Pres.; Steven R. Brinn, V.P.; Timothy C. Potts, Secy.-Treas.; Kay E. Syre.
EIN: 943237153

64244
Adventist Women's Coalition
1199 Lawson Ln.
Walla Walla, WA 99362

Established around 1992.
Financial data (yr. ended 12/31/00): Assets, $694 (M); grants paid, $0; expenditures, $10; qualifying distributions, $0.
Officers and Directors:* Nancy Marter,* Pres.; Elizabeth Wear,* V.P.; Mary Ella Johnson,* Treas.
EIN: 911531874

64245
Prakash Foundation
921 N. 82nd St.
Seattle, WA 98103-4321

Financial data (yr. ended 12/31/00): Assets, $451 (M); grants paid, $2,120; gifts received, $2,605; expenditures, $2,471; qualifying distributions, $2,120.
Officers: Naveen Garg, Pres.; Anne-Marie Canis, V.P. and Secy.
EIN: 911906951

64246
Tilly Steward Ministries
9310 58th Ave. Ct. E.
Puyallup, WA 98371-6115

Established in 1990 in WA.
Donor(s): Ottilia Steward.
Financial data (yr. ended 12/31/00): Assets, $430 (M); grants paid, $161; gifts received, $2,483; expenditures, $4,557; qualifying distributions, $4,557.
Limitations: Applications not accepted. Giving on a national basis.
Application information: Contributes only to pre-selected organizations.
Officers: Tilly Steward, Pres.; Sarah Casada, V.P.; Linda Briest, Secy.-Treas.
EIN: 911295196

64247
Xavier Foundation
16003 Andal Ln.
Mount Vernon, WA 98274

Established in 1998 in WA.
Financial data (yr. ended 12/31/00): Assets, $279 (M); grants paid, $50; gifts received, $375; expenditures, $200; qualifying distributions, $200; giving activities include $140 for programs.
Limitations: Giving limited to WA.
Officers: Ginger A. Reinhardt, Pres.; C. Arthur Reinhardt, Secy.
EIN: 911933575

64248
The Family Research Foundation
14911 S. Locust Ln.
Kennewick, WA 99337

Classified as a private operating foundation in 1991.
Financial data (yr. ended 12/31/01): Assets, $222 (M); grants paid, $0; gifts received, $4,000; expenditures, $4,309; qualifying distributions, $4,309; giving activities include $4,309 for programs.
Officers: Alvin L. Jensen, Pres.; Notto L. Jensen, V.P.; LaWana S. Jensen, Secy.-Treas.
Directors: David A. Jensen, Ronald Jensen.
EIN: 911310243

64249
Leprosy Research Foundation
19100 S.E. 408th St.
Enumclaw, WA 98022

Established in 1980 in CA.
Financial data (yr. ended 06/30/02): Assets, $93 (M); grants paid, $0; gifts received, $105; expenditures, $80; qualifying distributions, $0.
Officers and Trustees:* Ray L. Foster, M.D.,* Pres.; Richard Hart, M.D.,* V.P.; Frances Foster,* Secy.-Treas.; William Dysinger, M.D., Dunbar Smith, M.D., Wilfred Stuyvesant, M.D.
EIN: 953555037

64250
Glory to God Ministries
1242 State Ave., Ste. I, PMB 121
Marysville, WA 98270-3672

Established in 1998 in WA.
Donor(s): Darrin O. Dayton.
Financial data (yr. ended 12/31/00): Assets, $44 (M); grants paid, $3,649; gifts received, $7,844; expenditures, $7,998; qualifying distributions, $6,198.
Officers: Darrin O. Dayton, Pres.; Marlin O. Dayton, Secy.; Gloria G. Dayton, Treas.
EIN: 911798975

64251
Farm Animal Rescue Mission
1620 N. 183rd St.
Shoreline, WA 98133

Established in 1999 in WA.
Financial data (yr. ended 12/31/00): Assets, $1 (M); grants paid, $1,936; gifts received, $2,616; expenditures, $2,311; qualifying distributions, $1,936.
Officers: April Brown, Pres.; Mike Brown, V.P. and Treas.; Linda Waymire, Secy.
EIN: 911649531

64252
Friends of the Camas Public Library
840 N.W. 10th Ave.
Camas, WA 98607

Financial data (yr. ended 12/31/01): Assets, $0 (M); grants paid, $21,178; gifts received, $48,849; expenditures, $26,203; qualifying distributions, $21,178.
Limitations: Applications not accepted. Giving primarily in Camas, WA.
Application information: Contributes only to pre-selected organizations.
Officers: James C. Reinhart, Pres.; Robert Behar, V.P.; Meride Pabst, Secy.; Diane Skinner, Treas.
EIN: 913129019

64253
Murdoch Institute of Personal Development
P.O. Box 877, Main Sta.
Tacoma, WA 98401-0877
Application address: 4908 N. Whitman St., Tacoma, WA 98407-1335, tel.: (253) 752-6331
Contact: David R. Murdoch, Dir.

Classified as a private operating foundation in 1986.
Financial data (yr. ended 12/31/01): Assets, $0 (M); grants paid, $7,301; gifts received, $17,390; expenditures, $29,377; qualifying distributions, $26,118; giving activities include $29,873 for programs.
Directors: David R. Murdoch, Signy N. Murdoch.
EIN: 911138014

WEST VIRGINIA

64254
Foster Foundation
1 Bradley Foster Dr.
Huntington, WV 25701

Established in 1922 in WI.
Financial data (yr. ended 12/31/01): Assets, $55,584,473 (M); grants paid, $0; expenditures, $5,964,243; qualifying distributions, $2,460,382.
Officers: John F. Speer, Pres.; W. Campbell Brown, Jr., V.P.; Edward Morrison, Secy.-Treas.; Donald J. Faherty, Exec. Dir.
Directors: Noel P. Copen, Steve Hatten, K.E. McGinnis, Seaton Taylor.
EIN: 550359756

64255
Home for Aged Men
1700 Warwood Ave.
Wheeling, WV 26003-7149

Financial data (yr. ended 08/31/00): Assets, $19,860,122 (M); grants paid, $0; expenditures, $867,597; qualifying distributions, $792,450; giving activities include $447,242 for programs.
Officers and Directors:* Karl W. Neumann,* Pres.; Kenneth W. Orr,* V.P.; Larry A. Carpenter,* Secy.-Treas.; Teresa Camiletti, F. Andrew Jackson, T. Gary Kenamond, M.D., W. Gibson McCoy, Kristine N. Molnar, Edwin B. VanLynn.
EIN: 550359019

64256
Altenheim - The Home for the Aged
1387 National Rd.
Wheeling, WV 26003-5716

Classified as a private operating foundation in 1978.
Financial data (yr. ended 12/31/00): Assets, $18,798,278 (M); grants paid, $17,500; gifts received, $151,216; expenditures, $938,915; qualifying distributions, $936,600; giving activities include $881,634 for programs.
Officers and Trustees:* Mrs. Robert Witte,* Pres.; Rev. J. William DeMoss, V.P.; Michele D. Uhl, Secy.; Mrs. Harry E. Foose,* Treas.; George Dakovic, Exec. Dir.; Donald R. Kirsch, Douglas Molnar, Mrs. Wilbur C. Neer, Jr., and 12 additional trustees.
EIN: 550371584

64257
George D. Hott Memorial Foundation
c/o The Huntington National Bank, Trust Dept.
P.O. Box 895
Morgantown, WV 26507-0895
(304) 291-7721

Established in 1980 in WV.
Donor(s): George D. Hott.‡
Financial data (yr. ended 12/31/01): Assets, $3,233,430 (M); grants paid, $181,500; expenditures, $203,711; qualifying distributions, $183,854.
Limitations: Giving primarily in Morgantown, WV.
Application information: Application form required.
Trustees: Jack Britton, Vaughn Kiger, Doug Leech, Edward Skriner, Reed Tanner, The Huntington National Bank.
EIN: 556085230
Codes: FD2

64258
John Mathew Gay Brown Family Foundation
c/o The Huntington National Bank
P.O. Box 895
Morgantown, WV 26507-0895

Established in 1989 in WV.
Donor(s): Mary Virginia Brown.‡
Financial data (yr. ended 12/31/00): Assets, $3,209,632 (M); grants paid, $155,000; expenditures, $184,737; qualifying distributions, $183,284.
Limitations: Giving limited to Morgantown, WV.
Application information: Application form required.
Trustees: John Fahey, Doug Leech, Tom Rogers, Edward Skriner, The Huntington National Bank.
EIN: 550685612
Codes: FD2

64259
Sacred Heart Children's Center, Inc.
P.O. Box 1581
Clarksburg, WV 26301

Financial data (yr. ended 06/30/01): Assets, $2,308,209 (M); grants paid, $59,917; expenditures, $76,408; qualifying distributions, $68,706.
Limitations: Applications not accepted. Giving limited to WV.
Application information: Contributes only to pre-selected organizations.
Officers: Gary Bowden, Pres.; John Randolph, V.P.; Delores Yoke, Secy.; Richard Heal, M.D., Treas.
EIN: 550528075

64260
Interactivity Foundation
P.O. Box 9
Parkersburg, WV 26102-0008

Classified as a private operating foundation in 1993.
Donor(s): Julius Stern, Stern Bros., Inc.
Financial data (yr. ended 12/31/01): Assets, $2,299,741 (M); grants paid, $0; gifts received, $297,224; expenditures, $189,829; qualifying distributions, $0.
Officers and Trustees:* Julius Stern,* Pres.; Margaret Grant Stern,* V.P. and Secy.; Jack Byrd, Jr.,* V.P.; John G. O'Brien,* V.P.; P. Jeanne Schade, Treas.; Rebecca Blackburn, Joseph W. Powell, James M. Sprouse, W. Randolph Williams.
EIN: 556028464

64261
McCoy-McMechen Museum, Inc.
111 Winchester Ave.
Moorefield, WV 26836

Financial data (yr. ended 12/31/01): Assets, $710,845 (M); grants paid, $0; gifts received, $3,090; expenditures, $24,808; qualifying distributions, $0.
Officers and Trustees:* Mallie Combs,* Pres.; Lucy Fisher-West,* V.P.; Thomas J. Hawse III,* Exec. Dir.; Larry Curtis, Pam Elmore, Lucy Fisher-West, Russell N. Newman, Clyde M. See, Jr., and 8 additional trustees.
EIN: 311105191

64262
John W. Trenton Benevolent Trust
c/o Funding Application
P.O. Box 458
Kingwood, WV 26537 (304) 329-2752

Established in 2000 in WV.
Financial data (yr. ended 12/31/00): Assets, $425,778 (M); grants paid, $0; expenditures, $944; qualifying distributions, $0.
Limitations: Giving limited to Grant and Preston counties, WV.
Application information: Application form required for John W. Trenton Medical Paramedical Scholarship. Application form required.
Trustees: David P. Brown, Deborah T. Livengood, Pamela J. Lobb.
EIN: 556136333

64263
Southern Grace, Inc.
125 Lee Ave.
Beckley, WV 25801

Financial data (yr. ended 12/31/99): Assets, $393,020 (M); grants paid, $0; gifts received, $62,024; expenditures, $3,052; qualifying distributions, $3,052.
Officers: Herbert E. Atha III, Pres.; Karen L. Atha, Secy.
EIN: 550754875

64264
J. Herman Isner Trust
Rte. 1
Kerens, WV 26276

Classified as a private operating foundation in 1984.
Financial data (yr. ended 01/31/01): Assets, $369,995 (M); grants paid, $0; gifts received, $5,125; expenditures, $15,020; qualifying distributions, $7,791; giving activities include $7,791 for programs.
Trustees: Doris Bonner, Terry N. Gould, Doris F. Isner, Betty C. Moomau.
EIN: 311101724

64265
Paden City Foundation, Inc.
c/o Tammi Bowers
P.O. Box 233
Paden City, WV 26159-0233

Established in 1988 in WV.
Donor(s): Paden City Wildcat Boosters.
Financial data (yr. ended 12/31/99): Assets, $247,722 (M); grants paid, $13,012; gifts received, $13,785; expenditures, $13,357; qualifying distributions, $13,012.
Limitations: Applications not accepted. Giving limited to Paden, WV.
Officers and Directors:* Rohey McWilliams,* Pres.; Charles D. Racer,* V.P.; Shirley Kendle,* Secy.; David Mendenhall,* Treas.; Jess Brown,

Richard Buck, Lester Doak, Warren Grace, and 26 additional directors.
EIN: 550678816

64266
June Van Stavern Kurz Memorial Scholarship Trust
P.O. Box 219
Union, WV 24983
Application address: c/o Guidance Counselor, James Monroe High School, Lindside, WV 24951

Established in 2000.
Donor(s): Frederick William Kurz.‡
Financial data (yr. ended 12/31/00): Assets, $186,416 (M); grants paid, $1,800; gifts received, $181,133; expenditures, $1,800; qualifying distributions, $1,800.
Limitations: Giving limited to residents of WV.
Application information: Application form required.
Trustees: Nancy Van Stavern Bostic, The Bank of Monroe.
EIN: 550769966

64267
The Albert Schenk III & Kathleen H. Schenk Charitable Trust No. 1
111 Park View Ln., Ste. 200
Wheeling, WV 26003-5446
Application address: 1031 National Rd., Wheeling, WV 26003-5709, tel.: (304) 243-5440
Contact: Frank A. Jackson

Established as a private operating foundation in 2000.
Donor(s): Kathleen H. Schenk Charitable Lead Unitrust.
Financial data (yr. ended 12/31/01): Assets, $125,789 (M); grants paid, $959,068; gifts received, $998,706; expenditures, $987,084; qualifying distributions, $959,068.
Limitations: Giving limited to Ohio County, WV, and vicinity.
Trustees: Frank Bonacci, Kathleen Bonacci, Nancy Casey, Louise S. DeFelice, Mary V. Hamilton, William N. Hogan, Jr., Heidi S. Hughes, Karen A. Sligar.
EIN: 550764535
Codes: FD

64268
Covenant Mountain Ministries, Inc.
P.O. Box 727
Bluefield, WV 24701-0727
Application address: P.O. Box 118, Rte. 3, Princeton, WV 24740
Contact: Guy W. Perkins, Pres.

Established in 1995.
Donor(s): Guy W. Perkins, Marilyn Perkins.
Financial data (yr. ended 09/30/01): Assets, $66,928 (M); grants paid, $9,081; gifts received, $30,000; expenditures, $11,799; qualifying distributions, $53,634.
Limitations: Giving primarily in WV.
Application information: Application form required.
Officers: Guy W. Perkins, Pres.; Marilyn Perkins, Secy.
EIN: 550747541

64269
Albert J. Humphreys Memorial Corporation
P.O. Box 169
Charleston, WV 25321-0169

Established in 1935.
Donor(s): A.J. Humphreys Trust.

Financial data (yr. ended 12/31/99): Assets, $59,411 (M); grants paid, $43,000; gifts received, $58,659; expenditures, $43,000; qualifying distributions, $43,000.
Limitations: Giving primarily in Charleston, WV.
Officers: Rev. Helga P. Hallett, Pres.; David H. Rollins, Secy.-Treas.
EIN: 556023681

64270
The John W. Brill Memorial Foundation, Inc.
P.O. Box O
Capon Springs, WV 26823-0400

Established in 1996 in WV.
Financial data (yr. ended 12/31/99): Assets, $30,734 (M); grants paid, $1,000; gifts received, $6,119; expenditures, $1,320; qualifying distributions, $1,000.
Limitations: Giving primarily in Capon Bridge, WV.
Officers: Thomas W. Austin, Pres.; Wendell Hatt, V.P.; Gregory Kenney, Secy.; Edwin L. Brill, Treas.
EIN: 550745971

64271
Roxanna Lea Glass Memorial Scholarship Fund
Rte. 4, Box 545
Weston, WV 26452-9527 (304) 269-1702
Application address: P.O. Box 625, Weston, WV 26452
Contact: Thomas H. Glass, Jr., Tr.

Financial data (yr. ended 12/31/99): Assets, $19,794 (M); grants paid, $1,000; gifts received, $5,564; expenditures, $3,626; qualifying distributions, $1,000.
Limitations: Giving limited to Weston and Lewis County, WV.
Application information: Application form required.
Trustees: Mary S. Glass, Thomas H. Glass, Jr.
EIN: 550747629

64272
Lewisburg Foundation Incorporated
419 E. Washington St.
Lewisburg, WV 24901

Classified as a private operating foundation.
Financial data (yr. ended 12/31/00): Assets, $12,454 (M); grants paid, $600; gifts received, $17,008; expenditures, $16,265; qualifying distributions, $16,265.
Officers: Tag Galyean, Pres.; Bob McCormick, V.P.; Annabelle Galyean, Treas.
Trustee: Steve Hunter.
EIN: 550586192

64273
Second Chance Rescue, Inc.
386 Gunpowder Ln.
Inwood, WV 25428

Financial data (yr. ended 12/31/01): Assets, $11,460 (M); grants paid, $0; gifts received, $20,578; expenditures, $54,817; qualifying distributions, $0; giving activities include $54,817 for programs.
Limitations: Applications not accepted.
Officer: Mara Spade, Pres.
EIN: 541821558

64274
Charan Kaur and Amar Kaur Charitable Foundation, Inc.
P.O. Box 2238
Weirton, WV 26062-1438

Established around 1993.
Donor(s): Parihar Medical Corp.

Financial data (yr. ended 12/31/99): Assets, $10,269 (M); grants paid, $12,334; gifts received, $10,400; expenditures, $14,693; qualifying distributions, $13,390.
Limitations: Applications not accepted.
Officers: Hardev S. Parihar, Pres.; Jaswinderk Parihar, Secy.-Treas.
EIN: 550709524

64275
Cleveland J. Biller Trust
729 Bakers Ridge Rd.
Morgantown, WV 26508-1439
(304) 599-2751

Established in 1997.
Financial data (yr. ended 12/31/01): Assets, $4,346 (M); grants paid, $0; expenditures, $83; qualifying distributions, $83; giving activities include $83 for programs.
Trustees: Terry N. Gould, J. Herman Isner.
EIN: 550752635

64276
Rainbow House, Inc.
P.O. Box 114
Gypsy, WV 26361

Financial data (yr. ended 06/30/02): Assets, $2,869 (M); grants paid, $0; gifts received, $58,462; expenditures, $64,554; qualifying distributions, $64,554; giving activities include $64,554 for programs.
Officers: Barbara Burns, Pres.; Florence Gifford, V.P.; Robert Tresize, Secy.; Colleen Tresize, Treas.
Directors: Frederick Byers, Jr., Tammy Dartrug, Elizabeth Hendershot, Betty Johnson, Violet Marie Riley.
EIN: 311097051

64277
Greenbrier Music Festival, Inc.
103 Pennsylvania Ave.
Charleston, WV 25302

Established in 1993.
Donor(s): Tim Holbrook.
Financial data (yr. ended 12/31/99): Assets, $666 (L); grants paid, $0; gifts received, $2,823; expenditures, $7,005; qualifying distributions, $1,169; giving activities include $4,934 for programs.
Officers: Keith Clarke, Pres.; Rob Aliff, V.P.; Debbie Eads, Secy.; Tim Holbrook, Treas.
EIN: 550723108

64278
Back Creek Valley Foundation, Inc.
166 Locust Grove Rd.
Hedgesville, WV 25427

Classified as a private operating foundation in 1992.
Donor(s): John M. Brooks.
Financial data (yr. ended 12/31/00): Assets, $0 (M); grants paid, $0; gifts received, $9,752; expenditures, $9,752; qualifying distributions, $9,752; giving activities include $9,752 for programs.
Officers: Janet L. Brooks, Pres.; Carol A. Ernest, V.P.; John M. Brooks, Secy.-Treas.
EIN: 341143280

WISCONSIN

64279
The Johnson Foundation, Inc.
33 E. Four Mile Rd.
Racine, WI 53402-2621 (262) 681-3343
FAX: (262) 681-3325; E-mail:
bschmidt@johnsonfdn.org; URL: http://www.johnsonfdn.org
Contact: Barbara J. Schmidt, Prog. Secy.

Incorporated in 1958 in NY.
Donor(s): H.F. Johnson,‡ S.C. Johnson & Son, Inc., and descendants of the late H.F. Johnson.
Financial data (yr. ended 06/30/00): Assets, $29,667,667 (M); grants paid, $39,500; gifts received, $3,747,400; expenditures, $3,010,760; qualifying distributions, $2,710,887; giving activities include $582,750 for programs.
Publications: Annual report (including application guidelines), informational brochure (including application guidelines).
Application information: Application form not required.
Officers and Trustees:* Samuel C. Johnson,* Chair.; Boyd H. Gibbons III, Pres.; Patricia Albjerg Graham,* V.P.; Lois Y. Berg, Secy.; Charles S. McNeer,* Treas.; Howard L. Fuller, Helen Johnson-Leipold, Janice C. Kreamer, Paul R. Portney, Paula Wolff.
EIN: 390958255

64280
Paine Art Center and Arboretum, Inc.
1410 Algoma Blvd.
Oshkosh, WI 54901

Classified as a private operating foundation in 1973.
Financial data (yr. ended 12/31/99): Assets, $15,133,853 (M); grants paid, $0; gifts received, $1,134,071; expenditures, $798,349; qualifying distributions, $705,008; giving activities include $524,987 for programs.
Officers and Directors:* Samuel Grober,* Pres.; Lois Aurand,* V.P.; R. Eugene Goodson,* V.P.; Mary Martin,* Secy.; David L. Omachinski,* Treas.; Barbara Hirschfeld, Exec. Dir.; Sherryl Brunner,* Mgr.; Ellen Maxymek, Mgr.; Mohammed Mohebali, Mgr.; Doris Peitz, Mgr.; and 14 additional directors.
EIN: 390785483

64281
Hannah M. Rutledge Home for the Aged
P.O. Box 758
Chippewa Falls, WI 54729-2419

Financial data (yr. ended 05/31/02): Assets, $14,422,718 (M); grants paid, $0; gifts received, $892; expenditures, $4,377,174; qualifying distributions, $655,586; giving activities include $3,721,588 for programs.
Officers: Gerald J. Naiberg, Pres.; Richard H. Stafford, V.P.; David Hancock, Secy.-Treas.
EIN: 390806179

64282
Friendship House of Milwaukee, Inc.
(Formerly Milwaukee Home for the Friendless)
c/o Sandra Q. Wilch
N61W29799 Stony Hill Ct.
Hartland, WI 53029-8609

Classified as a private operating foundation in 1989.
Financial data (yr. ended 09/30/00): Assets, $12,149,841 (M); grants paid, $0; gifts received, $108,628; expenditures, $255,581; qualifying distributions, $255,581; giving activities include $255,581 for programs.
Officers and Directors:* Jean Larson,* Pres.; Sandy Davis,* 1st V.P.; Harriet Eaton,* Secy.; Sandra Wilch,* Treas.; Sandy Davis, Pat Harper, Carla Hering, Dianne Houriet, and 2 additional directors.
EIN: 390837518

64283
Leigh Yawkey Woodson Art Museum, Inc.
700 N. 12th St.
Wausau, WI 54403

Classified as a private operating foundation in 1973.
Donor(s): Nancy W. Spire, John E. Forester, Alice W. Forester, John and Alice Forester Charitable Trust, Wisconsin Arts Board.
Financial data (yr. ended 06/30/00): Assets, $10,481,467 (M); grants paid, $0; gifts received, $1,303,489; expenditures, $1,352,436; qualifying distributions, $1,457,863; giving activities include $1,352,436 for programs.
Officers and Directors:* John A. Slayton,* Pres.; Alice W. Smith,* V.P.; Helen D. Scholfield,* Secy.; Gary E. Tesch,* Treas.; Kathy Kelsey Foley, Exec. Dir.; John M. Forester, San W. Orr, Jr., and 10 additional directors.
EIN: 237281913

64284
Lester & Frances Johnson Foundation, Inc.
c/o Lester Johnson
6209 Mineral Point, Ste. 805
Madison, WI 53705

Established in 2000.
Donor(s): Frances M. Johnson, Lester O. Johnson.
Financial data (yr. ended 12/31/01): Assets, $9,940,784 (M); grants paid, $370,600; expenditures, $389,858; qualifying distributions, $367,969.
Limitations: Applications not accepted. Giving on a national basis, with emphasis on Chicago, IL.
Application information: Contributes only to pre-selected organizations.
Officers: Lester O. Johnson, Pres.; Frances M. Johnson, V.P.; Aubrey R. Fowler, Secy.; Michael R. Heald, Treas.
Directors: Robert W. Anderson, Graham L. Johnson, Jeffery L. Kuchenbecker.
EIN: 391988285
Codes: FD

64285
Sand County Foundation, Inc.
1955 Atwood Ave.
P.O. Box 3186
Madison, WI 53704

Classified as a private operating foundation in 1987.
Donor(s): Nash Williams.
Financial data (yr. ended 12/31/01): Assets, $5,500,484 (M); grants paid, $166,859; gifts received, $251,753; expenditures, $1,655,506; qualifying distributions, $1,087,934; giving activities include $1,286,907 for programs.
Officers and Directors:* Reed Coleman,* Chair.; Brent M. Haglund, Pres.; Howard W. Mead,* V.P.; David J. Hanson,* Secy.-Treas.; Helen Alexander, Thomas Bourland, Craig Kennedy, Scott Klug, Paul Risser, Toby Sherry, Peter Stent, Nash Williams, James Wood.
EIN: 396089450

64286
Riverland Conservancy, Inc.
(Formerly Wisconsin Power and Light Land Stewardship Trust, Inc.)
c/o Wisconsin Power & Light Co.
P.O. Box 192
Madison, WI 53701-0192
E-mail: jwlaub@chorus.net

Classified as a company-sponsored operating foundation in 1998.
Donor(s): Wisconsin Power and Light Co.
Financial data (yr. ended 12/31/00): Assets, $5,090,264 (M); grants paid, $0; gifts received, $295,584; expenditures, $126,299; qualifying distributions, $424,662; giving activities include $100,211 for programs.
Officers and Directors:* Pamela J. Wegner,* Pres.; William D. Harvey,* V.P.; Edward M. Gleason, Secy.-Treas.; Joseph E. Schefchek,* V.P.; Kim K. Zuhlke.
EIN: 391914563

64287
Bond Community Center, Inc.
P.O. Box 299
Oconto, WI 54153

Established in 1994 in WI.
Financial data (yr. ended 05/31/02): Assets, $5,080,739 (M); grants paid, $0; gifts received, $70,893; expenditures, $680,099; qualifying distributions, $327,248; giving activities include $526,795 for programs.
Officers: Earl J. Decloux, Pres.; Doug Laviolette, V.P.; Dale Besson, Secy.
Directors: Robert Hermsen, Gary Ziegelbauer.
EIN: 391762086

64288
The J. Vernon Steinle & Elmyra K. Steinle Foundation, Inc.
c/o John W. Foley
P.O. Box 081518
Racine, WI 53408-1518

Classified as a private operating foundation in 1998 in WI.
Donor(s): Elmyra K. Steinle.‡
Financial data (yr. ended 12/31/00): Assets, $5,045,374 (M); grants paid, $110,000; expenditures, $155,346; qualifying distributions, $110,000.
Limitations: Applications not accepted. Giving limited to Racine, WI.
Application information: Contributes only to pre-selected organizations.
Officers: John I. Mayer, Pres.; Robert F. Siegert, M.D., V.P.; John W. Foley, Secy.-Treas.
EIN: 391934819
Codes: FD2

64289
Hemophilia Outreach of Wisconsin, Inc.
1794 E. Allouez Ave.
Green Bay, WI 54311-6236 (920) 965-0606

Financial data (yr. ended 12/31/01): Assets, $4,156,479 (M); grants paid, $39,122; gifts received, $35,563; expenditures, $585,527; qualifying distributions, $184,443; giving activities include $18,283 for programs.
Limitations: Giving primarily in WI.
Application information: Application form required.
Officers and Directors:* Steve Rosek, Pres.; Jan Tess, V.P.; Kim Baierl,* Secy.; Chris Knurr,* Secy.; Robert DeGroot, Treas.; Katie E. Kralovetz, Exec. Dir.; Lisa Brault, John Neider, Patsy White.
EIN: 391858104

64290
William S. Fairfield Public Gallery Foundation, Inc.
Glidden Drive Estates
P.O. Box 1
Sturgeon Bay, WI 54235

Classified as a private operating foundation in 1997.
Financial data (yr. ended 12/31/99): Assets, $3,214,152 (M); grants paid, $0; gifts received, $11,121; expenditures, $258,370; qualifying distributions, $464,612; giving activities include $247,849 for programs.
Officers and Directors:* Irene Newkirk,* Pres.; Joseph Bernstein,* V.P. and Secy.; James W. Parsons,* V.P. and Treas.
EIN: 391659221

64291
West Bend Memorial Foundation, Inc.
300 S. 6th Ave.
West Bend, WI 53095-3312

Established in 1960 in WI.
Donor(s): Melitta Pick Charitable Trust.
Financial data (yr. ended 12/31/00): Assets, $2,852,957 (M); grants paid, $0; gifts received, $534,275; expenditures, $378,690; qualifying distributions, $377,765; giving activities include $378,690 for programs.
Limitations: Applications not accepted. Giving limited to West Bend, WI.
Application information: Contributes only to pre-selected organizations.
Officers: Sharon Ziegler, Pres.; Jim Bowerman, V.P.; Andrea Sellinger, Secy.; Lee Gonring, Treas.
Board Members: Joan Pick, Pati Platten, and 5 additional members.
EIN: 391017647

64292
Cedarly Ministries
(Formerly Cedars of Nemahbin Foundation)
P.O. Box 180455
Delafield, WI 53018

Classified as an operating foundation in 1996.
Donor(s): John W. Findley.
Financial data (yr. ended 12/31/99): Assets, $2,572,465 (M); grants paid, $100; gifts received, $1,169,208; expenditures, $296,252; qualifying distributions, $938,718; giving activities include $919,796 for programs.
Officer: John W. Findley, Pres.
Directors: Richard J. Bliss, Barbara M. Findley.
EIN: 391854114

64293
Crivitz Youth, Inc.
P.O. Box 188
Crivitz, WI 54114-0188

Established in 1970 in WI.
Donor(s): Nancy Buck Ransom Foundation, Caroline B. Sauter.
Financial data (yr. ended 12/31/99): Assets, $2,496,036 (M); grants paid, $0; gifts received, $912,438; expenditures, $447,948; qualifying distributions, $658,749; giving activities include $385,099 for programs.
Limitations: Giving limited to Crivitz, WI.
Officers and Directors:* Nancy Buck Ransom,* Pres.; Paul J. Kueber,* V.P.; Richard Smith,* V.P.; Kenneth A. Dama,* Treas.
EIN: 237088232

64294
Ralph J. Huiras Family Foundation, Inc.
2560 Hwy. 32
P.O. Box 366
Port Washington, WI 53074-0366
Contact: Ralph J. Huiras, Pres.

Established in 1996 in WI.
Donor(s): Ralph J. Huiras.
Financial data (yr. ended 12/31/01): Assets, $2,318,764 (M); grants paid, $123,500; expenditures, $172,896; qualifying distributions, $146,509.
Limitations: Giving primarily in WI.
Application information: Application form not required.
Officer: Ralph J. Huiras, Pres.
Directors: William J. Farrell, Margaret Schreiner.
EIN: 391844576
Codes: FD2

64295
Tatman Foundation
c/o Christian A. Bungener
P.O. Box 483
Ephraim, WI 54211-0483

Established in 1967.
Donor(s): D.D. Chomeau, Henri Chomeau IV, A.E. Skelton.
Financial data (yr. ended 12/31/00): Assets, $2,223,263 (M); grants paid, $13,000; gifts received, $232,325; expenditures, $214,543; qualifying distributions, $128,438; giving activities include $109,438 for programs.
Limitations: Applications not accepted. Giving primarily in MO and WI.
Application information: Contributes only to pre-selected organizations.
Officers and Directors:* Henri Chomeau IV,* Chair.; Christian A. Bungener,* Pres. and Treas.; Ronald R. Anderson,* V.P.; David D. Chomeau,* V.P.; James F. Seidler,* V.P.; Anne E. Skelton, Secy.; Henri Chomeau V, Exec. Dir.
EIN: 436075289

64296
Lakeland High School Scholarship Fund, Inc.
c/o R.J. O'Leary
P.O. Box 1129
Minocqua, WI 54548-1129
Contact: Paul Harshner

Financial data (yr. ended 12/31/01): Assets, $2,190,056 (M); grants paid, $114,975; gifts received, $15,558; expenditures, $140,692; qualifying distributions, $129,960.
Limitations: Giving primarily in the Minocqua, WI, area.
Application information: Application form required.
Officers: R.J. O'Leary, Pres.; Roger Pokall, V.P.; Richard Van Horne, V.P.; Gary Rosholt, Secy.
EIN: 391259200
Codes: FD2, GTI

64297
Fox Cities Retirement Village, Inc.
160 S. Green Bay Rd.
Neenah, WI 54956-2267

Classified as a private operating foundation in 1979 in WI.
Financial data (yr. ended 12/31/01): Assets, $2,054,103 (M); grants paid, $8,500; expenditures, $119,735; qualifying distributions, $41,460; giving activities include $111,105 for programs.
Limitations: Applications not accepted. Giving primarily in Neenah, WI.
Application information: Contributes only to pre-selected organizations.
Officers: Emil Leppiaho, Pres.; Gordon Siebert, V.P.; Jack Travis, Secy.; Earl Jacobsen, Treas.
Directors: Richard Bevers, Joyce Chase, Alice Christensen, Felicia Heiser, Ray Lokken.
EIN: 391335177

64298
The Peter J. Seippel Foundation, Inc.
P.O. Box 160
Beaver Dam, WI 53916

Established in 1995 in WI. Classified as a private operating foundation in 1996.
Financial data (yr. ended 12/31/99): Assets, $1,593,059 (M); grants paid, $47,391; gifts received, $1,097,730; expenditures, $62,593; qualifying distributions, $59,996; giving activities include $10,670 for programs.
Limitations: Applications not accepted.
Application information: Contributes only to pre-selected organizations.
Officers and Directors:* Peter J. Seippel,* Pres.; Joseph R. Boehmer,* V.P.; Gary L. Giesemann,* Secy.; John C. Ralston,* Treas.; Phillip R. Seippel, Margaret Jo Wahlen.
EIN: 391833671

64299
Exacto Foundation, Inc.
P.O. Box 24
Grafton, WI 53024-0024

Classified as a private operating foundation in 1970.
Donor(s): William Greene, William J. Heitz, Kenneth Quillen, Greg Heitz.
Financial data (yr. ended 07/31/01): Assets, $1,552,322 (M); grants paid, $41,725; gifts received, $100,000; expenditures, $41,735; qualifying distributions, $41,735.
Limitations: Applications not accepted. Giving primarily in Grafton, WI.
Officers: Stephanie Fleming, Pres.; William Greene, Secy.-Treas.
Directors: Greg Heitz, Daniel Linsley, Kenneth Quillen.
EIN: 237076890
Codes: GTI

64300
Elizabeth Batchelder Davis Children's Home, Inc.
1260 N. Westfield St.
Oshkosh, WI 54902-3219

Financial data (yr. ended 12/31/01): Assets, $1,433,695 (M); grants paid, $0; gifts received, $177; expenditures, $742,590; qualifying distributions, $712,639; giving activities include $737,171 for programs.
Officers: Barbara Hart-Key, Pres.; Pat Bousha, V.P.; Dale Sonnenberg, Secy.-Treas.
Directors: Jan Butterbrodt, Carla Melke.
EIN: 390828128

64301
Al and Laurie Hein Trust
330 N. Cove Rd.
Hudson, WI 54016
Contact: Daniel J. Greenwald, Tr.

Established in 1991 in WI.
Financial data (yr. ended 12/31/00): Assets, $1,289,855 (M); grants paid, $45,350; expenditures, $71,051; qualifying distributions, $59,350.
Limitations: Giving primarily in MN and WI.
Trustee: Daniel J. Greenwald.
EIN: 396529070

64302
Mary E. Fitz Memorial Park Trust
c/o Phillip Steans
393 Red Cedar St.
Menomonie, WI 54751

Established in 2000 in WI.
Donor(s): Mary E. Fitz.‡
Financial data (yr. ended 10/31/01): Assets, $936,287 (M); grants paid, $0; gifts received, $1,376,628; expenditures, $31,059; qualifying distributions, $29,319; giving activities include $29,319 for programs.
Limitations: Applications not accepted.
Application information: Contributes only to pre-selected organizations.
Trustee: Phillip Steans.
EIN: 396734720

64303
Worldwide Charitable Trust
213 E. Main St.
P.O. Box 45
Mount Horeb, WI 53572   (608) 437-2850

Established in 1994 in WI.
Donor(s): Janet A. Fisher.
Financial data (yr. ended 12/31/01): Assets, $843,906 (M); grants paid, $1,130,000; gifts received, $968,820; expenditures, $1,130,000; qualifying distributions, $1,129,321.
Limitations: Applications not accepted. Giving primarily in Baltimore, MD.
Application information: Contributes only to pre-selected organizations.
Trustees: Janet A. Fisher, Jerome M. Ott.
EIN: 391805734
Codes: FD

64304
Tom Stockert Foundation
c/o Bank One Trust Co., N.A.
P.O. Box 1308
Milwaukee, WI 53201
Application address: 229 W. Main St., Clarksburg, WV 26301
Contact: Tom Teter

Established in 1998 in WV.
Donor(s): Thomas Stockert.‡
Financial data (yr. ended 12/31/99): Assets, $808,136 (M); grants paid, $20,750; expenditures, $42,650; qualifying distributions, $21,316.
Trustee: Bank One Trust Co., N.A.
EIN: 546423244

64305
The Aldo Leopold Foundation, Inc.
(Formerly The Aldo Leopold-Shack Foundation)
c/o Nina L. Bradley
E12919 Levee Rd.
Baraboo, WI 53913

Classified as a private operating foundation in 1984.
Donor(s): Nina L. Bradley, Aldo C. Leopold, Luna B. Leopold, Estella B. Leopold.
Financial data (yr. ended 09/30/00): Assets, $805,889 (M); grants paid, $0; gifts received, $196,696; expenditures, $278,106; qualifying distributions, $626,843; giving activities include $267,519 for programs.
Officers and Directors:* G. Stevenson,* Pres.; Nina L. Bradley,* Secy.-Treas.; Alan Anderson, Paul Johnson, Scott Larson, A. Carl Leopold, Estella B. Leopold, Luna B. Leopold, Gene Likens, Jerry Smith.
EIN: 391423225

64306
Cuan Foundation, Inc.
c/o Morrison & Assocs.
P.O. Box 1926
La Crosse, WI 54602
Application address: 521 S. 23rd St., La Crosse, WI 54601, tel.: (608) 785-0005
Contact: Jane Ann Quinlisk, Dir.

Established in 1992 in MN.
Donor(s): Warren W. Quinlisk, Nancy A. Quinlisk, Jane Ann Quinlisk.
Financial data (yr. ended 12/31/01): Assets, $799,678 (M); grants paid, $18,538; gifts received, $200; expenditures, $42,409; qualifying distributions, $35,589.
Limitations: Giving limited to the greater La Crosse, WI, area.
Application information: Application form not required.
Directors: Jane Ann Quinlisk, Nancy A. Quinlisk, Warren W. Quinlisk.
EIN: 391714380
Codes: GTI

64307
William A. Ketterer and Paul A. Ketterer Foundation, Inc.
W156 N5486 Bette Dr.
Menomonee Falls, WI 53051
Application address: c/o Foley & Lardner, 150 E. Gilman St., P.O. Box 1497, Madison, WI 53701-1497, tel.: (608) 258-4224
Contact: David W. Reinecke, Dir.

Established in 2000 in WI.
Donor(s): Mary C. Ketterer.
Financial data (yr. ended 12/31/01): Assets, $724,317 (M); grants paid, $0; gifts received, $600,847; expenditures, $2,018; qualifying distributions, $0.
Application information: Application form not required.
Officers and Directors:* Mary C. Ketterer,* Pres.; Marian E. Ketterer,* V.P.; Margaret R. Lisinski,* Secy.; Kathleen K. Machi,* Treas.; David W. Reinecke.
EIN: 391968282

64308
Gordon Bubolz Nature Preserve, Inc.
(Formerly Natural Areas Preservation, Inc.)
4815 N. Lynndale Dr.
Appleton, WI 54915-9665

Classified as a private operating foundation in 1976.
Donor(s): Secura.
Financial data (yr. ended 06/30/00): Assets, $700,975 (M); grants paid, $0; gifts received, $333,048; expenditures, $170,340; qualifying distributions, $152,885; giving activities include $162,938 for programs.
Officers and Directors:* Peggy McGaffey,* Pres.; Thomas H. Sutter,* V.P.; Barbara J. Kelly,* Secy.; John S. Bubolz,* Treas.; Ellen R. Discher, Merlin G. Gentz, Gordon E. Handrich, Larry Livengood, Jim Perry, Ph.D., and 5 additional directors.
EIN: 237120877

64309
Marlo Foundation, Ltd.
c/o J.C. Boehme, C.P.A.
2825 N. Mayfair Rd.
Milwaukee, WI 53222

Established about 1966 in WI.
Donor(s): Beatrice M. Loewi, Marshall A. Loewi.
Financial data (yr. ended 10/31/00): Assets, $698,396 (M); grants paid, $24,900; gifts received, $10,000; expenditures, $27,600; qualifying distributions, $27,000.
Limitations: Applications not accepted. Giving primarily in Milwaukee, WI.
Application information: Contributes only to pre-selected organizations.
Officers: Jodi L. Brandser, Pres. and Treas.; Jay V. Loewi, V.P.; Wayne J. Roper, Secy.
EIN: 396092888

64310
Samaritan Inn Foundation, Inc.
1527 W. National Ave.
Milwaukee, WI 53204

Financial data (yr. ended 08/31/00): Assets, $619,524 (M); grants paid, $0; gifts received, $164,606; expenditures, $877,227; qualifying distributions, $877,227; giving activities include $118,510 for programs.
Officers: Mark McKoy, Pres.; Bruce Behling, Secy.; Jim Hishman, Treas.
EIN: 391684793

64311
A. Keith Brewer Foundation, Inc.
325 N. Central Ave.
Richland Center, WI 53581-2547

Established in 1988.
Financial data (yr. ended 04/30/00): Assets, $549,023 (M); grants paid, $1,000; gifts received, $67,972; expenditures, $109,053; qualifying distributions, $84,843; giving activities include $80,996 for programs.
Limitations: Giving primarily in Richland Center, WI.
Application information: Application form required.
Officers: J. Donald Wanless, Chair. and V.P.; Bruce Kaasa, Pres.; Lillian Hanke, Secy.; Ralph Torgerson, Treas.
Directors: William Hanke, Keith Johnson.
EIN: 396121144

64312
Myra M. & Robert L. Vandehey Foundation
512 W. College Ave.
Appleton, WI 54911   (920) 739-6307
Contact: Bruce Chudacoff, Secy.

Established in 1990 in WI.
Financial data (yr. ended 12/31/00): Assets, $516,604 (M); grants paid, $15,000; expenditures, $33,764; qualifying distributions, $33,539.
Limitations: Giving primarily in the Fox Cities, WI, area.
Officers and Directors:* Robert L. Vandehey,* Pres.; Bruce Chudacoff,* Secy.; Nancy Chudacoff, Patti Maier.
EIN: 391649245

64313
Harris G. Allen Telecommunication Historical Museum, Inc.
c/o Dave M. Keating
918 Lake St.
Onalaska, WI 54650

Established in 1992 in WI.
Financial data (yr. ended 12/31/01): Assets, $478,249 (M); grants paid, $0; gifts received, $15,300; expenditures, $22,787; qualifying distributions, $17,935; giving activities include $22,787 for programs.
Officers: Dave M. Keating, Pres.; Bob Squires, V.P.
Directors: John Spaulding, Bob Steele, Fred Weier.
EIN: 391713702

64314
Necedah Memorial Library Foundation, Inc.
P.O. Box 279
Necedah, WI 54646

Classified as a private operating foundation in 1978.
Financial data (yr. ended 12/31/00): Assets, $444,926 (M); grants paid, $0; gifts received, $11,301; expenditures, $30,233; qualifying distributions, $0.
Officers and Trustees:* Pat Alderman,* Pres.; Jerome Siegler,* V.P.; Jason Smelcer,* Secy.; Jack Alderman,* Treas.; Thomas J. McNally.
EIN: 391304266

64315
Grace B. Ludwig Charitable Trust Fund
c/o Bank One Trust Co., N.A.
P.O. Box 1308
Milwaukee, WI 53201
Application address: c/o Bank One, Colorado, N.A., 1800 Broadway, Boulder, CO 80306

Classified as a private operating foundation in 1981.
Financial data (yr. ended 12/31/01): Assets, $435,456 (M); grants paid, $32,000; expenditures, $36,635; qualifying distributions, $33,575.
Limitations: Giving primarily in Boulder, CO.
Trustee: Bank One, Arizona, N.A.
EIN: 846151542

64316
Maurice A. & June C. Robinson Family Foundation, Inc.
1321 Kellogg St.
Green Bay, WI 54303

Established in 1995 in WI.
Donor(s): June Robinson, Maurice Robinson.
Financial data (yr. ended 12/31/99): Assets, $417,346 (M); grants paid, $19,725; gifts received, $200,020; expenditures, $19,790; qualifying distributions, $19,744.
Limitations: Applications not accepted.
Application information: Contributes only to pre-selected organizations.
Officer and Trustees:* June C. Robinson,* Pres.; Julie Levang, Susan Seiler, Mary Sorensen.
EIN: 391831176

64317
Global Christian Interaction, Inc.
9667 S. 20th St.
Oak Creek, WI 53154-4931

Established in 1990 in WI.
Donor(s): Michael H. Polaski.
Financial data (yr. ended 12/31/00): Assets, $410,528 (M); grants paid, $302,245; gifts received, $298,700; expenditures, $310,096; qualifying distributions, $309,700.
Limitations: Applications not accepted. Giving on an international basis.
Application information: Contributes only to pre-selected organizations.
Officers and Directors:* Michael H. Polaski,* Pres. and Treas.; Michael J. Polaski,* Secy.; Catherine J. Polaski.
EIN: 391695712
Codes: FD

64318
Highsmith Family Foundation
P.O. Box 218
Fort Atkinson, WI 53538

Established in 1997 in WI.
Financial data (yr. ended 12/31/01): Assets, $401,272 (M); grants paid, $41,370; expenditures, $44,600; qualifying distributions, $44,600.
Trustee: Premier Bank.
EIN: 396652380

64319
Nipper Wildlife Sanctuary
c/o Bank One Trust Co.
P. O. Box 130
Milwaukee, WI 53201

Established in 1996 in IL.
Donor(s): Nipper Wildlife Sanctuary Trust.
Financial data (yr. ended 08/31/00): Assets, $346,073 (M); grants paid, $0; gifts received, $86,042; expenditures, $87,197; qualifying distributions, $75,234; giving activities include $71,365 for programs.
Limitations: Applications not accepted.
Application information: Contributes only to pre-selected organizations.
Trustee: Bank One Trust Co., N.A.
EIN: 376338624

64320
Sunrise Foundation, Inc.
c/o John Carter
8555 W. Forest Home Ave.
Greenfield, WI 53228-3408

Established in 1992 in WI.
Financial data (yr. ended 12/31/00): Assets, $334,458 (M); grants paid, $37,500; expenditures, $39,166; qualifying distributions, $38,283.
Limitations: Applications not accepted.
Application information: Contributes only to pre-selected organizations.
Officers and Directors:* Charles Koeble,* Pres.; John Carter, Secy.; Robert James, Treas.; John Affeldt, David Huntington.
EIN: 391741853

64321
Frank Foundation, Inc.
2 Gear Dr.
Edgerton, WI 53534

Classified as a private operating foundation in 1997.
Financial data (yr. ended 12/31/00): Assets, $333,394 (M); grants paid, $361; gifts received, $93,473; expenditures, $19,316; qualifying distributions, $56,964.
Limitations: Applications not accepted.
Application information: Contributes only to a pre-selected organization.
Officers: David Hataj, Pres.; Richard Hataj, V.P.; Nona Hataj, Secy.-Treas.
EIN: 391856850

64322
Cynthia McKinley Kolasinski Scholarship Trust
c/o Premier Bank
P.O. Box 218
Fort Atkinson, WI 53538-0218
Application address: c/o Greg Banaszynski, 611 Sherman Ave., Fort Atkinson, WI 53538

Established around 1992.
Financial data (yr. ended 12/31/01): Assets, $269,488 (M); grants paid, $13,400; expenditures, $15,669; qualifying distributions, $15,469.
Limitations: Giving limited to residents of Fort Atkinson, WI.
Application information: Application form not required.
Trustee: Premier Bank.
EIN: 396290565

64323
Hoganson Foundation, Ltd.
441 Milwaukee Ave.
Burlington, WI 53105

Established in 1994 in WI.
Financial data (yr. ended 12/31/99): Assets, $258,827 (M); grants paid, $17,500; expenditures, $18,891; qualifying distributions, $18,891.
Limitations: Applications not accepted.
Application information: Contributes only to pre-selected organizations.
Officers: Lester Hoganson, Pres.; Richard Wagner, V.P.; Roberta Wagner, Secy.-Treas.
EIN: 391776805

64324
Ginther Eutherian Foundation, Inc.
4343 Garfoot Rd.
Cross Plains, WI 53528

Established in 1999 in WI.
Donor(s): Oliver Ginther, Jane G. Ginther.
Financial data (yr. ended 12/31/00): Assets, $251,753 (M); grants paid, $0; gifts received, $263,500; expenditures, $13,667; qualifying distributions, $0; giving activities include $13,667 for programs.
Limitations: Applications not accepted.
Application information: Contributes only to pre-selected organizations.
Officers and Directors:* Oliver Ginther,* Pres. and Secy.; Jane G. Ginther,* V.P. and Treas.; Julie Nowicki.
EIN: 391968240

64325
The Gerald W. & Sharon K. Wadina Family Foundation
c/o Drinka, Levine & Masson
111 E. Kilbourn Ave., Ste. 2000
Milwaukee, WI 53202

Established in 2000 in WI.
Financial data (yr. ended 09/30/01): Assets, $238,212 (M); grants paid, $0; gifts received, $355,748; expenditures, $1,247; qualifying distributions, $0.
Limitations: Applications not accepted.
Application information: Contributes only to pre-selected organizations.
Officers and Directors:* Sharon K. Wadina,* Pres.; Derek P. Wadina,* V.P.; Curt A. Wadina,* V.P.; Judith A. Drinka,* Secy.-Treas.
EIN: 392011976

64326
James and Yvonne Ziemer Family Foundation
c/o James Ziemer
U22754175 Concord Ct.
Waukesha, WI 53189-8001

Established in 2001.
Financial data (yr. ended 12/31/01): Assets, $237,549 (M); grants paid, $0; expenditures, $125; qualifying distributions, $125.
Limitations: Applications not accepted.
Application information: Contributes only to pre-selected organizations.
Directors: James Ziemer, Yvonne Ziemer.
EIN: 396744914

64327
Carole & Milo Olson Family Foundation
P.O. Box 738
Wautoma, WI 54982

Established in 1998 in WI.
Donor(s): Carole Olson, Milo Olson.

Financial data (yr. ended 12/31/00): Assets, $229,165 (M); grants paid, $11,500; expenditures, $11,500; qualifying distributions, $11,478.
Limitations: Applications not accepted. Giving primarily in IA and MN.
Application information: Contributes only to pre-selected organizations.
Trustees: Carole Olson, Milo Olson.
EIN: 391933363

64328
Wallace and Janet Lichtenberg Family Foundation
c/o Garland G. Lichtenberg
N2866 Country Rd. M
Waupun, WI 53963-1163

Established in 1997.
Donor(s): Janet Lichtenberg.
Financial data (yr. ended 12/31/00): Assets, $207,974 (M); grants paid, $20,000; gifts received, $113,635; expenditures, $22,378; qualifying distributions, $20,629.
Limitations: Applications not accepted.
Application information: Contributes only to pre-selected organizations.
Trustees: Garland Lichtenberg, National Exchange Bank.
EIN: 396667973

64329
Southeastern Hockey Association of Wisconsin, Inc.
8550 W. Forest Home Ave.
Greenfield, WI 53228-3418

Financial data (yr. ended 06/30/00): Assets, $207,612 (M); grants paid, $0; gifts received, $3,000; expenditures, $240,061; qualifying distributions, $0; giving activities include $396,133 for programs.
Officers: Amy Day, Pres.; David Long, V.P.; Cherly Shelley, Secy.; Colleen Goelz, Treas.
EIN: 237086807

64330
George F. Andrews Trust
c/o Blackhawk State Bank
P.O. Box 719
Beloit, WI 53512-0719 (608) 364-8914

Classified as a private operating foundation in 1964.
Financial data (yr. ended 12/31/01): Assets, $170,125 (M); grants paid, $3,500; expenditures, $7,743; qualifying distributions, $3,500.
Trust Committee: Dan Green, Charles Hart, Merritt Mott.
Trustee: Jan S. Ruster.
EIN: 396061240
Codes: GTI

64331
Will Family Foundation, Inc.
W6363 Walnut Rd.
Watertown, WI 53098

Established in 1999 in WI.
Donor(s): Diane L. Falkenthal, Doug Will, Lisa J. Fitzgerald.
Financial data (yr. ended 12/31/00): Assets, $165,469 (M); grants paid, $7,000; gifts received, $12,000; expenditures, $10,254; qualifying distributions, $7,000.
Limitations: Applications not accepted. Giving primarily in WI.
Application information: Contributes only to pre-selected organizations.
Officers: Louise D. Will, Pres.; Diane L. Falkenthal, V.P.; Lisa J. Fitzgerald, Secy.; Carrie L. Will, Treas.

EIN: 391950401

64332
Brodhead Area Foundation, Inc.
1030 Center Ave.
Brodhead, WI 53520
Application address: 179 Cedar Ave., Brodhead, WI 53520
Contact: Ronald Albrecht, Pres.

Donor(s): Ester Cain.‡
Financial data (yr. ended 12/31/00): Assets, $158,832 (M); grants paid, $2,000; gifts received, $4,194; expenditures, $2,087; qualifying distributions, $2,087.
Limitations: Giving primarily in Brodhead, WI.
Officers: Ronald Albrecht, Pres.; William Prochow, V.P.; Ronald W. Braun, Secy.; Priscilla Parker, Treas.
EIN: 391652655

64333
Donald J. and Brenda J. Debruyn Charitable Foundation Trust
2304 Neshotah Rd.
Two Rivers, WI 54241-3808
Contact: Donald Debruyn, Tr.

Established in 2000 in WI.
Donor(s): Donald Debruyn, Brenda Debruyn.
Financial data (yr. ended 12/31/01): Assets, $156,808 (M); grants paid, $500; gifts received, $65,595; expenditures, $2,584; qualifying distributions, $500.
Application information: Application form required.
Trustees: Brenda J. Debruyn, Donald J. Debruyn.
EIN: 396721441

64334
Levy Foundation, Ltd.
P.O. Box 127
Cedarburg, WI 53012 (262) 377-5555
Contact: Donald A. Levy, Dir.

Established in 1969.
Financial data (yr. ended 12/31/00): Assets, $155,988 (M); grants paid, $450; gifts received, $150,000; expenditures, $626; qualifying distributions, $626.
Limitations: Giving primarily in WI.
Officer: Joyce Mooney, Mgr.
Directors: Donald A. Levy, Lowell K. Levy.
EIN: 237026533

64335
Clinton Potter Family Foundation
28640 County Rd. EW
Warrens, WI 54666

Established in 1998 in WI.
Donor(s): Clinton Potter, Ellen Potter.
Financial data (yr. ended 03/31/00): Assets, $143,484 (M); grants paid, $7,057; expenditures, $1,913; qualifying distributions, $1,833.
Limitations: Applications not accepted.
Application information: Contributes only to pre-selected organizations.
Trustees: Peggy Anderson, Becky Potter, Clinton Potter, Ellen Potter, Jack Potter.
EIN: 396680078

64336
George Family Charitable Foundation
1010 E. Blackhawk Ave.
Prairie Du Chien, WI 53821-1612
Application address: P.O. Box 323, Prairie Du Chien, WI 53821, tel.: (608) 326-8531
Contact: Roy L. George, Pres.

Established in 1996 in WI.
Donor(s): Roy L. George.
Financial data (yr. ended 12/31/00): Assets, $143,102 (M); grants paid, $7,935; expenditures, $9,873; qualifying distributions, $8,529.
Limitations: Giving primarily in Crawford County, WI.
Application information: Application form required.
Officer: Roy L. George, Pres.
Directors: Geraldine George, Roy C. George.
EIN: 391837959

64337
Wisconsin Farm Equipment Foundation, Inc.
c/o Midwest Equipment Foundation
P.O. Box 44364
Madison, WI 53744-4364 (608) 276-6700
Contact: Gary W. Manke, Secy.-Treas.

Financial data (yr. ended 08/31/00): Assets, $143,086 (M); grants paid, $250; gifts received, $1,250; expenditures, $991; qualifying distributions, $991.
Limitations: Giving limited to WI.
Application information: Application form required.
Officers: Keith Wagler, Pres.; J.W. "Woody" McCartney, V.P.; Gary W. Manke, Secy.-Treas.
Director: Delmar Riesterer.
EIN: 390756575

64338
Noel Compass Foundation, Inc.
1145 Clark St.
Stevens Point, WI 54481 (715) 345-0505
Contact: Carol Torline

Established in 1996 in WI.
Donor(s): Travel Guard Group, Redfield Law Office, Kryshak, John Noel.
Financial data (yr. ended 12/31/00): Assets, $141,909 (M); grants paid, $146,877; gifts received, $155,000; expenditures, $148,968; qualifying distributions, $146,877.
Application information: Application form required.
Officers and Directors:* John M. Noel,* Pres.; Patricia D. Noel,* V.P.; Carol Torline, Secy. and Exec. Dir.; James Koziol,* Treas.; Connie Haack, Chadwick J. Noel, James J. Noel, Jeffrey J. Noel, Jessica J. Noel, Kristin Graham Noel, Melissa J. Noel, Tyler J. Noel.
EIN: 391837771
Codes: FD2, GTI

64339
Eternalist Foundation
1080 Eastman St.
Platteville, WI 53818-1016

Classified as a private operating foundation in 1985.
Donor(s): Rev. Reza Rezazadeh.
Financial data (yr. ended 06/30/02): Assets, $128,990 (M); grants paid, $0; expenditures, $4,926; qualifying distributions, $0.
Officers and Directors:* Rev. Reza Rezazadeh,* Chair., Pres. and Treas.; Rev. Farhad Rezazadeh,* V.P.; Connie Carrillo,* Secy.
EIN: 391334356

64340
Ewald A. Blado and Marie L. Blado Fund
c/o James J. Blado
422 Woodard Ave.
Tomah, WI 54660-1642
Contact: James J. Blado, Tr.

Established in 1998.
Financial data (yr. ended 11/30/99): Assets, $117,674 (M); grants paid, $7,350; gifts received,

64340—WISCONSIN

$27,251; expenditures, $7,430; qualifying distributions, $0.
Limitations: Giving primarily in WI.
Trustees: James J. Blado, Ronald E. Brieske, Marie L. Stefferud.
EIN: 391917117

64341
The Sartori Foundation, Inc.
P.O. Box 258
Plymouth, WI 53073-0258 (920) 893-6061
Contact: Frederick M. Bowes, II, Secy.-Treas.

Established as a company sponsored operating foundation in 1998.
Donor(s): Sartori Food Corporation.
Financial data (yr. ended 12/31/00): Assets, $110,983 (M); grants paid, $25,166; gifts received, $30,000; expenditures, $25,766; qualifying distributions, $25,087.
Limitations: Giving primarily in Sheboygan County, WI and surrounding areas.
Application information: Application form required.
Officers: James C. Sartori, Pres.; Janet L. Sartori, V.P.; Frederick M. Bowes II, Secy.-Treas.
EIN: 391933307

64342
Edward J. Casper Family Scholarship Trust Fund
50 E. Main St.
P.O. Box 146
Chilton, WI 53014

Established in 1988 in WI.
Donor(s): Edward J. Casper.‡
Financial data (yr. ended 12/31/00): Assets, $103,132 (M); grants paid, $3,500; expenditures, $5,044; qualifying distributions, $5,044.
Limitations: Giving limited to residents of Calumet County, WI.
Application information: Recipients are selected by their respective high schools.
Officer and Trustees:* Robert W. Lutz,* Mgr.; Dorothy G. Casper, John R. Suttner.
EIN: 396473759

64343
Anna Paske Charitable Corporation for the Care of Cats and Dogs for Waushara County
P.O. Box 807
Wautoma, WI 54982-0807

Established in 1999.
Donor(s): Anna Paske.‡
Financial data (yr. ended 12/31/00): Assets, $98,091 (M); grants paid, $0; expenditures, $1,554; qualifying distributions, $1,554; giving activities include $1,000 for programs.
Directors: Howard E. Dutcher, Clifford Simonson, Katheryn Studebaker.
EIN: 391947675

64344
We the People/Wisconsin, Inc.
c/o WI State Journal
1901 Fish Hatchery Rd.
Madison, WI 53713-1248
Contact: Thomas Still, Assoc. Editor

Established in 1997 in WI.
Donor(s): AT&T Corp., Blue Cross & Blue Shield, Miller Brewing Company, Wisconsin Power and Light Co., WEAC.
Financial data (yr. ended 12/31/00): Assets, $91,944 (M); grants paid, $0; gifts received, $205,000; expenditures, $234,878; qualifying distributions, $247,652; giving activities include $185,504 for programs.
Officers and Directors:* Thomas Still,* Pres.; Joy Cardin,* V.P.; David Iverson, V.P.; Neil Heinen,

Secy.; James Wood,* Treas.; Thomas Bier, Kathy Bissen.
EIN: 391876389

64345
Optimist Club Foundation of Fond du Lac
P.O. Box 1422
Fond du Lac, WI 54936-1422
Application address: N8679 Lakeshore Dr., Fond du Lac, WI 54937-1727, tel.: (920) 924-0439
Contact: Gerald Ziegelbauer, Pres.

Established in 1995 in WI.
Financial data (yr. ended 09/30/01): Assets, $73,934 (M); grants paid, $4,000; gifts received, $10,076; expenditures, $4,288; qualifying distributions, $4,248.
Limitations: Giving limited to residents of WI.
Officers: Gerald Ziegelbauer, Pres.; Danny K. Zamzow, Secy.; Donna M. Patt, Treas.
Directors: Michael Potter, Frank Shires.
EIN: 391826950

64346
The Alma & Henry Lind Foundation
c/o James Peters
P.O. Box 548
Holmen, WI 54636-0548
Application address: 216 N. 10th, Black River Falls, WI 54615
Contact: Alma Lind, Tr.

Established in 1999 in WI.
Donor(s): Alma Lind.
Financial data (yr. ended 12/31/99): Assets, $72,089 (M); grants paid, $4,500; gifts received, $61,167; expenditures, $4,500; qualifying distributions, $4,500.
Trustees: Sally Cormican, Keith Freitag, Alma Lind, James H. Peters.
EIN: 396702283

64347
LedgerBank SSB Foundation, Inc.
(Formerly West Allis Savings Bank Foundation)
7401 W. Greenfield Ave.
West Allis, WI 53214-4614 (414) 317-7100
Contact: Nancy Hoelter, Secy.-Treas.

Donor(s): West Allis Savings Bank, Ledger Bank.
Financial data (yr. ended 12/31/00): Assets, $71,905 (M); grants paid, $2,990; gifts received, $100; expenditures, $3,045; qualifying distributions, $2,990.
Limitations: Giving limited to the Milwaukee, West Allis, New Berlin, Greenfield, and Glendale, WI, communities.
Board Members: Cheryl Hennig, Susan Janusz.
EIN: 391747275

64348
Jim and Darlene Mech Foundation
c/o Darlene Mech
9431 S. Shore Dr.
Valders, WI 54245-9513

Established in 1998 in WI.
Financial data (yr. ended 12/31/99): Assets, $70,894 (M); grants paid, $6,075; gifts received, $71,075; expenditures, $6,180; qualifying distributions, $6,075.
Limitations: Applications not accepted.
Application information: Contributes only to pre-selected organizations.
Trustees: Darlene Mech, Gregory Mech, Michael Mech.
EIN: 396692399

64349
Michelle and Craig Auerbach Scholarship Trust
c/o Premier Bank
P.O. Box 218
Fort Atkinson, WI 53538
Application address: c/o Guidance Dir., Jefferson High School, Jefferson, WI 53549, tel.: (920) 674-7893

Classified as a private operating foundation in 1985.
Financial data (yr. ended 12/31/01): Assets, $69,691 (M); grants paid, $2,500; expenditures, $3,021; qualifying distributions, $3,021.
Limitations: Giving limited to residents of Jefferson, WI.
Application information: Applicant must include transcript and class rank.
Trustee: Premier Bank.
EIN: 391503549

64350
Pearls for Teen Girls, Inc.
2266 N. Prospect Ave., Ste. 520
Milwaukee, WI 53202

Established in 2000.
Donor(s): Richard & Ethel Herzfeld Foundation, Jane B. Pettit Foundation, Women's Fund-Milwaukee Foundation, Weiss Family Foundation, Bob & Linda Davis Family Fund.
Financial data (yr. ended 12/31/00): Assets, $58,562 (M); grants paid, $0; gifts received, $87,834; expenditures, $29,951; qualifying distributions, $29,951; giving activities include $20,429 for programs.
Officers: Richard Weiss, Pres.; Linda Davis, V.P.; Ouida Williams, Secy.
Director: Collen Fitzgerald.
EIN: 391997970

64351
Lake de Nevue Preserve, Inc.
159 Old Pioneer Rd.
Fond du Lac, WI 54935

Financial data (yr. ended 12/31/01): Assets, $54,476 (M); grants paid, $0; gifts received, $1,235; expenditures, $1,395; qualifying distributions, $1,395; giving activities include $1,395 for programs.
Limitations: Applications not accepted.
Officers and Directors:* Claire G. Hutter,* Pres. and Treas.; Harold Sabel,* V.P. and Secy.; Arleen Hoey, John Huempfner, George F. Hutter, Robert M. Hutter.
EIN: 391366209

64352
New Horizons Un-Limited, Inc.
342 N. 115th St.
Wauwatosa, WI 53226

Donor(s): Arthur L. Miller.
Financial data (yr. ended 06/30/00): Assets, $52,447 (M); grants paid, $5,000; gifts received, $36,000; expenditures, $19,398; qualifying distributions, $19,398.
Limitations: Applications not accepted.
Application information: Contributes only to pre-selected organizations.
Officers: Arthur L. Miller, Pres.; Paul F. Quick II, Secy.; Ruth V. Miller, Treas.
EIN: 391808599

64353
Amato Family Foundation, Inc.
8301 N. 76th St.
Milwaukee, WI 53213 (414) 357-8500
Contact: John S. Amato, Pres.

Established in 2001 in WI.
Donor(s): John S. Amato.
Financial data (yr. ended 12/31/01): Assets, $50,017 (M); grants paid, $0; gifts received, $50,000; expenditures, $0; qualifying distributions, $0.
Officers and Directors:* John S. Amato,* Pres., V.P., and Treas.; Cindy K. Amato,* Secy.; John Amato, Sr.
EIN: 392039371

64354
Biopharmaceutical Technology Center Institute, Inc.
5445 E. Cheryl Pkwy.
Madison, WI 53711-5373

Established in 1991.
Financial data (yr. ended 08/31/00): Assets, $49,758 (M); grants paid, $0; gifts received, $107,923; expenditures, $240,676; qualifying distributions, $134,383; giving activities include $220,722 for programs.
Officer: Karin Borgh, Exec. Dir.
Directors: Byran Albrecht, William Linton, Beverly Simone, Douglas Stafford, John Wiley.
EIN: 391764134

64355
Hawes-Shapiro Family Foundation
4154 N. Prospect Ave.
Shorewood, WI 53211

Established in 2000 in WI.
Donor(s): Jane Hawes, David Shapiro.
Financial data (yr. ended 12/31/00): Assets, $42,708 (M); grants paid, $26,221; gifts received, $20,000; expenditures, $29,470; qualifying distributions, $29,470.
Limitations: Applications not accepted. Giving primarily in Milwaukee, WI.
Application information: Contributes only to pre-selected organizations.
Officers: Jane Hawes, Pres.; David Shapiro, Secy.-Treas.
EIN: 391978423

64356
A. A. & T. H. Robinson Foundation, Inc.
200 Prospect Pl.
De Pere, WI 54115

Established in 1995 in WI.
Donor(s): Arita A. Robinson, Thomas H. Robinson.
Financial data (yr. ended 12/31/01): Assets, $41,910 (M); grants paid, $0; expenditures, $10; qualifying distributions, $0.
Limitations: Applications not accepted. Giving primarily in Green Bay, WI.
Application information: Contributes only to pre-selected organizations.
Trustees: Arita A. Robinson, Thomas H. Robinson, Todd J. Robinson.
EIN: 391841012

64357
John D. Clifford Scholarship Fund
810 S. 8th St.
Watertown, WI 53094-4739

Donor(s): Watertown Daily Times, Inc.
Financial data (yr. ended 12/31/99): Assets, $41,417 (M); grants paid, $2,000; expenditures, $2,045; qualifying distributions, $1,964.
Limitations: Applications not accepted. Giving primarily in Watertown, WI.
Trustees: James Clifford, Pat Clifford, Margaret Krueger, Ralph Krueger.
EIN: 391590728

64358
Faith Indeed, Inc.
P.O. Box 26324
Wauwatosa, WI 53226-0324

Classified as a private operating foundation in Dec. 1991.
Donor(s): William E. Barry.
Financial data (yr. ended 12/31/99): Assets, $33,945 (M); grants paid, $1,200; gifts received, $107,762; expenditures, $105,552; qualifying distributions, $1,200.
Officers and Directors:* William E. Barry,* Pres.; Robert Kochoud, V.P.; Ronald D. West,* Secy.
EIN: 391703414

64359
TMJ Association, Ltd.
c/o C.M. Sturm
24333 N. Mayfair Rd., Ste. 315
Wauwatosa, WI 53226-0770

Donor(s): Kevin Clark, Theresa Cowley.
Financial data (yr. ended 12/31/01): Assets, $33,393 (M); grants paid, $0; gifts received, $89,966; expenditures, $85,286; qualifying distributions, $83,358; giving activities include $83,360 for programs.
Officers and Directors:* William M. Layden,* Chair.; Theresa Cowley,* Pres.; Kevin Clark,* V.P.; C. Polly Ellingson,* Secy.; Kay Austermann,* Treas.; Deanne Clare,* Admin.; Elizabeth Bigge, Lisa Brown, Chuck Sturm, Joan B. Wilentz, James M. Wozniak, Diana M. Zuckerman, Ph.D.
EIN: 391691109

64360
Kathryn Ann Kirchner Foundation
2389 Curtis Ct.
Green Bay, WI 54311-6752 (920) 464-7225
Contact: Philip L. Kirchner, Tr.

Established in 1999 in WI.
Donor(s): Philip L. Kirchner.
Financial data (yr. ended 12/31/00): Assets, $29,363 (M); grants paid, $1,545; gifts received, $16,059; expenditures, $1,545; qualifying distributions, $1,545.
Limitations: Giving primarily in Green Bay, WI.
Trustees: Philip L. Kirchner, J. Robert Koch, Nancy Koch.
EIN: 391969745

64361
The Paul Foundation
c/o Marguerite M. Paul
W4943 CTY Hwy. G
Necedah, WI 54646

established in 1994.
Donor(s): Steve J. Paul, Marguerite M. Paul, Jim Vruble.
Financial data (yr. ended 12/31/00): Assets, $29,026 (M); grants paid, $28,200; gifts received, $56,000; expenditures, $28,654; qualifying distributions, $28,200.
Limitations: Applications not accepted. Giving primarily in WI.
Application information: Contributes only to pre-selected organizations.
Directors: Marguerite M. Paul, M. Therese Paul, Steve J. Paul.
EIN: 391761269

64362
Bradley A. & Birdell A. Peterson Scholarship Trust
1119 Regis Ct., Ste. 2A
Eau Claire, WI 54701 (715) 832-5500
Contact: Michael D. Markin, Tr.

Classified as a private operating foundation in 1999 in WI.
Donor(s): Birdell A. Peterson, Ruth Peterson.
Financial data (yr. ended 07/31/01): Assets, $27,683 (M); grants paid, $6,500; expenditures, $7,759; qualifying distributions, $6,500.
Limitations: Giving limited to residents of Eau Claire County, WI.
Trustee: Michael D. Markin.
EIN: 391486945
Codes: GTI

64363
Debbie Tillmann Foundation, Inc.
2535 Bay Settlement Rd.
Green Bay, WI 54301-7326
Application address: c/o Preble High School, 241 S. Danz Ave., Green Bay, WI 54302, tel.: (920) 469-0602

Classified as a private operating foundation in 1982.
Financial data (yr. ended 12/31/01): Assets, $26,557 (M); grants paid, $4,250; gifts received, $5,000; expenditures, $4,314; qualifying distributions, $4,248.
Limitations: Giving limited to residents of the Green Bay, WI, area.
Application information: Application form required.
Officers: Ronald Tillmann, Pres.; Russell Delvaux, V.P.; Judith Tillmann, Secy.-Treas.
EIN: 391380435

64364
Al and Helen Haese Scholarship Foundation
7495 Blake Rd.
Greenleaf, WI 54126
Contact: Helen Haese, Tr.

Established in 1999 in WI.
Donor(s): Helen Haese.
Financial data (yr. ended 12/31/00): Assets, $25,557 (M); grants paid, $2,000; expenditures, $2,130; qualifying distributions, $1,995.
Limitations: Giving primarily in the Wrightstown, WI area.
Trustees: Carl Haese, Helen Haese, William Haese.
EIN: 391895282

64365
Garrick's Animal Shelter Irrevocable Trust
c/o Audrey Newton
P.O. Box 24
Readfield, WI 54969

Established in 1998 in WI.
Donor(s): Audrey Newton.
Financial data (yr. ended 02/28/01): Assets, $25,000 (M); grants paid, $5,000; gifts received, $780; expenditures, $5,036; qualifying distributions, $4,885.
Limitations: Applications not accepted. Giving primarily in New London, WI.
Application information: Contributes only to pre-selected organizations.
Trustees: Steve Margehlaer, Audrey Newton, Joseph Sprenger, Gary Witthuhn.
EIN: 396610796

64366
E. C. & Johanna Lomen Anderson Scholarship Fund
c/o Betty Sanders
1420 N. Marshall St., Apt. 303
Milwaukee, WI 53202-2761

Established around 1989.
Financial data (yr. ended 12/31/00): Assets, $18,869 (M); grants paid, $500; gifts received, $1,451; expenditures, $500; qualifying distributions, $0.
Limitations: Giving limited to residents of Coon Valley, WI.
Application information: Application form required.
Trustee: Betty Sanders.
Scholarship Committee Members: Karen Aasen-Biornstad, Alf Anderson, Jr., Jack Anderson, Elaine DeBuhr, Joanne Fletcher.
EIN: 363532684

64367
Arbor View Gardens, Inc.
E10540 County Rd. C
Clintonville, WI 54929

Established in 2001 in WI.
Donor(s): Members of the Gleisner family.
Financial data (yr. ended 12/31/01): Assets, $13,622 (M); grants paid, $0; gifts received, $21,032; expenditures, $4,446; qualifying distributions, $0.
Officers: Andy Gleisner, Pres.; Peter Oberhauser, V.P.; Robert Edwards, Secy.
Directors: Richard Cloeter, Robert Leder, Beverly Lewis.
EIN: 392013268

64368
Robert Edward Gierach Foundation, Inc.
W 156, N1234 Century Ln.
Germantown, WI 53022 (262) 255-3770
Contact: Frederick Gierach, Pres.

Classified as a private operating foundation in 1967.
Financial data (yr. ended 12/31/00): Assets, $9,419 (M); grants paid, $1,600; expenditures, $1,787; qualifying distributions, $1,787.
Officer: Frederick Gierach, Pres.
EIN: 396107073

64369
The Benzine Foundation, Inc.
403 W. Harvey St.
Rio, WI 53960

Established in 1997 in GA and WI.
Financial data (yr. ended 12/31/99): Assets, $8,736 (M); grants paid, $500; gifts received, $6,070; expenditures, $675; qualifying distributions, $500.
Officers and Directors:* Shirley Benzine,* Pres.; Dale R. Benzine,* Secy.; Daniel L. Benzine, DuWayne K. Benzine.
EIN: 582306141

64370
The Alliance Health Foundation, Inc.
37 Kessel Court, Ste. 201
Madison, WI 53711

Established in 2001 in WI.
Financial data (yr. ended 05/31/02): Assets, $5,083 (M); grants paid, $0; gifts received, $3,582; expenditures, $371; qualifying distributions, $0.
Limitations: Applications not accepted.
Application information: Contributes only to pre-selected organizations.
Directors: Patricia Gottfried, David A. Kindig, Paul J. Meyer, Christopher Queram, Eric Stanchfield, Kathleen E. Woit.
EIN: 400000050

64371
Holton-Elkhorn Band, Ltd.
c/o Jerry L. Wheeler, Sr.
305 W. Jefferson St.
Elkhorn, WI 53121-1104

Classified as a private operating foundation in 1979.
Financial data (yr. ended 12/31/99): Assets, $2,914 (M); grants paid, $0; gifts received, $13,500; expenditures, $13,924; qualifying distributions, $13,924; giving activities include $13,924 for programs.
Officer: Jerry L. Wheeler, Sr., Treas. and Mgr.
EIN: 391313435

64372
Lorman Foundation, Inc.
P.O. Box 509
Eau Claire, WI 54702-0509
Application address: 3827 House Rd., Eau Claire, WI 54701, tel.: (715) 833-3940
Contact: Robert A. Kerbell, Dir.

Established in 2000 in WI.
Donor(s): Robert A. Kerbell.
Financial data (yr. ended 12/31/00): Assets, $2,909 (M); grants paid, $18,000; gifts received, $21,000; expenditures, $18,106; qualifying distributions, $18,091.
Application information: Application form required.
Directors: Mark C. Hull, Robert A. Kerbell, Mark A. Orgel.
EIN: 391971255

64373
The Davig Family Foundation
P.O. Box 548
Holmen, WI 54636

Established in 2001 in WI.
Donor(s): Davig Financial Corporation.
Financial data (yr. ended 12/31/01): Assets, $2,221 (M); grants paid, $6,000; gifts received, $8,000; expenditures, $6,000; qualifying distributions, $6,000.
Trustees: Edward Davig, Helen Davig.
EIN: 394392756

64374
DK Contractors Foundation
11013 122nd St.
Pleasant Prairie, WI 53158

Financial data (yr. ended 12/31/01): Assets, $2,093 (M); grants paid, $0; expenditures, $0; qualifying distributions, $0.
Directors: Allen R. Day, James A. Day, Michealene M. Day.
EIN: 391904091

64375
Dynatron Research Foundation, Inc.
P.O. Box 44098
Madison, WI 53744-4098

Classified as a private operation foundation in 1973.
Financial data (yr. ended 07/31/00): Assets, $1,697 (M); grants paid, $0; expenditures, $10; qualifying distributions, $10; giving activities include $10 for programs.
Officer: Helmut F. Prahl, Exec. Dir.
EIN: 396105636

64376
West Bend Military Museum, Inc.
c/o Michael J. Wolf
2221 Creek Dr.
West Bend, WI 53095-2008

Established in 1995 in WI.
Donor(s): Michael J. Wolf.
Financial data (yr. ended 12/31/01): Assets, $544 (M); grants paid, $0; expenditures, $151; qualifying distributions, $0.
Officers and Directors:* Howard J. Wolf,* Pres.; Michael J. Wolf, Secy.; Ruth A. Wolf.
EIN: 391803116

64377
Norman E. and Edith E. Brown Foundation
P.O. Box 548
Holmen, WI 54636

Established in 2001 in WI.
Financial data (yr. ended 12/31/01): Assets, $350 (M); grants paid, $0; gifts received, $500; expenditures, $150; qualifying distributions, $150.
Directors: Norman E. Brown, James H. Peters.
EIN: 392037006

64378
Living Waters, Inc.
35520 W. Pabst Rd.
Oconomowoc, WI 53066-4518

Classified as a private operating foundation in 1972.
Financial data (yr. ended 12/31/00): Assets, $242 (M); grants paid, $0; gifts received, $34,200; expenditures, $34,034; qualifying distributions, $34,034; giving activities include $34,034 for programs.
Officers and Directors:* Dwight J. Swanson,* Pres.; Karen M. Swanson,* V.P.; Mary Soergel.
EIN: 237179868

64379
Bruce and Lori Gendelman Family Foundation
c/o Michael Best & Friedrich, LLP
100 E. Wisconsin Ave., Ste. 3300
Milwaukee, WI 53212-4108
Contact: J. Lewis Perlson, Tr.

Established in 1999 in WI.
Donor(s): Bruce P. Gendelman, Sidney Kohl Foundation.
Financial data (yr. ended 12/31/00): Assets, $194 (M); grants paid, $42,000; gifts received, $43,000; expenditures, $42,991; qualifying distributions, $41,998.
Limitations: Giving primarily in Milwaukee, WI.
Trustee: J. Lewis Perlson.
EIN: 396706485

64380
Wisconsin World Affairs Council, Inc.
c/o Univ. of Wisconsin-Whitewater
2009 Roseman Bldg., 800 W. Main St.
Whitewater, WI 53190

Classified as a private operating foundation in 1976.
Financial data (yr. ended 10/31/00): Assets, $0 (M); grants paid, $0; gifts received, $295,394; expenditures, $335,602; qualifying distributions, $335,602; giving activities include $335,602 for programs.
Officers: Harold Oswald, Pres.; Gary Olson, Secy.-Treas.; Dale Brock, General Mgr.
Directors: Molly Dorosa, Joe Wikrent, Bill Wresch.
EIN: 391247797
Codes: TN

WYOMING

64381
Marieluise Hessel Foundation
2635 Fairways Pl. W.
Wilson, WY 83014-9623

Established in 1996 in WY.
Donor(s): Marieluise Hessel.
Financial data (yr. ended 12/31/00): Assets, $9,796,010 (M); grants paid, $5,000; gifts received, $96,269; expenditures, $37,986; qualifying distributions, $316,518; giving activities include $316,518 for programs.
Limitations: Applications not accepted.
Application information: Contributes only to pre-selected organizations.
Officers: Marieluise Hessel, Pres.; Leslie H. Lee, Secy.
EIN: 830318485

64382
Ivinson Memorial Home for Aged Ladies
505 S. 3rd St., Ste. 100
Laramie, WY 82070

Financial data (yr. ended 09/30/01): Assets, $9,701,800 (M); grants paid, $507,747; gifts received, $49,207; expenditures, $538,293; qualifying distributions, $507,747; giving activities include $507,747 for programs.
Limitations: Applications not accepted. Giving limited to Laramie, WY.
Application information: Contributes only to pre-selected organizations.
Trustees: W. Britt Davis, E.J. Haines, Kathleen K. Scott.
EIN: 830179773
Codes: FD

64383
Jackson Hole Conservancy Foundation
c/o William R. Givens
P.O. Box 325
Moose, WY 83012

Established in 1997 in WY.
Donor(s): William R. Givens.
Financial data (yr. ended 12/31/00): Assets, $4,203,509 (M); grants paid, $1,000; gifts received, $5,000; expenditures, $4,727; qualifying distributions, $1,000.
Officers and Directors:* William R. Givens,* Pres.; Mark D. Givens,* V.P.; Julia K. Givens,* Secy.; Sandra D. Givens, Treas.
EIN: 841408402

64384
Jackson Hole Ranch Conservancy Foundation
c/o William R. Givens
P.O. Box 325
Moose, WY 83012

Established in 1997 in WY.
Financial data (yr. ended 12/31/00): Assets, $4,203,509 (M); grants paid, $1,000; gifts received, $5,000; expenditures, $4,727; qualifying distributions, $4,726.
Limitations: Applications not accepted. Giving primarily in Kelly, WY.
Application information: Contributes only to pre-selected organizations.
Officers: William R. Givens, Pres.; Mark D. Givens, V.P.; Julia K. Givens, Secy.; Sandra D. Givens, Treas.
EIN: 831408402

64385
Snake River Conservancy Foundation
c/o Richard Black
P.O. Box 208
Moose, WY 83012

Established in 1995.
Donor(s): Richard B. Black.
Financial data (yr. ended 12/31/00): Assets, $4,001,097 (M); grants paid, $0; gifts received, $1,300; expenditures, $1,450; qualifying distributions, $1,450; giving activities include $135 for programs.
Trustees: Kara Ciel Black, Richard B. Black, Nara Cadorin, Erica Lynn Periman.
EIN: 830314580

64386
Earl & Bessie Whedon Cancer Detection Foundation
30 S. Scott St.
Sheridan, WY 82801-6308

Classified as a private operating foundation in 1971.
Financial data (yr. ended 12/31/01): Assets, $3,779,526 (M); grants paid, $0; gifts received, $311,176; expenditures, $161,750; qualifying distributions, $127,128; giving activities include $40,842 for programs.
Officers and Trustees:* M.W. Hiller, M.D., Exec. Dir.; Pierre A. Carricaburu, M.D., Marilyn Koester, William H. Porter.
Directors: Fred J. Araas, M.D., Rev. David Duprey, Laura M. Ferries, M.D., Howard L. Mussell, M.D., Susan Snyder, D.O.
EIN: 830176313

64387
Call Air Foundation
c/o Revel T. Call
P.O. Box 1491
Afton, WY 83110

Financial data (yr. ended 01/31/00): Assets, $1,445,326 (M); grants paid, $0; gifts received, $156,113; expenditures, $191,350; qualifying distributions, $178,563; giving activities include $178,563 for programs.
Directors: Revel T. Call, Verma A. Call, Bruce Stratford.
EIN: 830299100

64388
Adeline L. Neilson Foundation
P.O. Box 930
Jackson, WY 83001-0930 (307) 733-9090
Contact: J.L. Flanagan, Pres.

Established in 1997 in WY.
Financial data (yr. ended 11/30/01): Assets, $1,045,316 (M); grants paid, $59,500; expenditures, $66,307; qualifying distributions, $58,909.
Limitations: Giving primarily in WY.
Application information: Application form required.
Officers and Directors:* Jennifer L. Flanagan,* Pres.; Bradford S. Mead,* V.P.; Robert I. Lucas,* Secy.-Treas.
EIN: 841423057

64389
Laing-Weil Scholarship Fund Charitable Trust
751 Klondike Dr.
Buffalo, WY 82834

Established in 2000 in WY.
Financial data (yr. ended 12/31/00): Assets, $966,028 (M); grants paid, $0; gifts received, $959,371; expenditures, $786; qualifying distributions, $0.
Trustee: John W. Adams.
EIN: 830324104

64390
Yu-Fa Wang Foundation
c/o Winberg Chai
P.O. Box 4098, University Sta.
Laramie, WY 82071

Established around 1993.
Donor(s): Yu-Fa Wang.
Financial data (yr. ended 06/30/00): Assets, $466,543 (M); grants paid, $9,200; expenditures, $36,317; qualifying distributions, $21,463; giving activities include $11,555 for programs.
Limitations: Applications not accepted. Giving on an international basis, with emphasis on Hong Kong; giving also in New York, NY.
Application information: Contributes only to pre-selected organizations.
Officers: Yu-Fa Wang, Chair.; S.C. Leng, Vice-Chair.; Winberg Chai, Pres. and Secy.; Wou Wei, Treas.
EIN: 830290760

64391
Potash Family Foundation
c/o Warren Potash
5200 Cortland Dr.
Jackson, WY 83001-9449

Established in 1995 in WY.
Donor(s): Warren Potash.
Financial data (yr. ended 12/31/00): Assets, $363,666 (M); grants paid, $500; gifts received, $129,845; expenditures, $6,854; qualifying distributions, $500.
Officers and Directors:* Warren Potash,* Pres.; Marilyn Kite,* V.P.; Jamie Potash Curry, Mitchell Potash, Margaret W. Scarlett.
EIN: 830315127

64392
Stacy & Diana Childs Foundation
10680 Wind Dancer Rd.
Cheyenne, WY 82009

Established in 1999 in CO.
Donor(s): Stacy J. Childs.
Financial data (yr. ended 12/31/99): Assets, $298,492 (M); grants paid, $3,508; gifts received, $300,000; expenditures, $3,508; qualifying distributions, $3,508.
Limitations: Applications not accepted. Giving primarily in WY.
Application information: Contributes only to pre-selected organizations.
Officers and Directors:* Stacy J. Childs,* Pres.; Pilar K. Childs,* V.P.; Callan Y. Childs, Rachelle Eyre.
EIN: 840327571

64393
Contruction Careers Foundation
P.O. Box 965
Cheyenne, WY 82003

Established in 1998 in WY.
Financial data (yr. ended 12/31/00): Assets, $287,888 (M); grants paid, $3,000; gifts received, $62,050; expenditures, $7,641; qualifying distributions, $3,000.
Limitations: Applications not accepted.
Officers: Matt Garland, Pres.; Lloyd Wolf, V.P.; James Rice, Secy.-Treas.
Directors: George Bryce, Skip Gillum, Steve Loftin.
EIN: 830319926

64394
The Christine Gempp Love Foundation
P.O. Box N
Sheridan, WY 82801 (307) 672-9003
Contact: M. Christine Love, Dir.

Established in 1983 in WY.
Donor(s): M. Christine Love, W.K. Love.
Financial data (yr. ended 06/30/01): Assets, $286,598 (M); grants paid, $14,300; gifts received, $150; expenditures, $15,182; qualifying distributions, $15,103.
Limitations: Giving primarily in Sheridan, WY.
Directors: Charles C. Love, M. Christine Love, W.K. Love.
EIN: 830267496

64395
Viola Pearson Scholarship Trust
c/o American National Bank & Trust Co.
P.O. Box 1528
Cheyenne, WY 82003
Contact: LeRoy C. Harvey, V.P. and Trust Off., American National Bank

Established in 1985 in WY. Classified as a private operating foundation in 1987.
Financial data (yr. ended 12/31/01): Assets, $161,739 (M); grants paid, $7,503; expenditures, $10,105; qualifying distributions, $7,503.
Limitations: Giving primarily in Cheyenne, WY.
Trustee: American National Bank & Trust Co.
EIN: 836031271
Codes: GTI

64396
Ira N. & Clella E. Gibson Scholarship Fund
P.O. Box 277
Buffalo, WY 82834-0277 (307) 684-2466
Contact: Donald P. Kraen, Tr.

Established in 1988 in WY.
Financial data (yr. ended 12/31/00): Assets, $149,933 (M); grants paid, $9,250; expenditures, $10,941; qualifying distributions, $9,192.
Limitations: Giving primarily to residents of WY.
Application information: Application form required.
Trustees: Louisa C. Braten, Donald P. Kraen, Lillian H. Stevens.
EIN: 830284346

64397
Parents Helping Parents of Wyoming, Inc.
5 N. Loban Ave.
Buffalo, WY 82834

Financial data (yr. ended 09/30/01): Assets, $105,787 (M); grants paid, $0; gifts received, $536,814; expenditures, $544,117; qualifying distributions, $0.
Officers: Morris Jacobsen, Chair.; Carey Dube, Vice-Chair.; Marylin Hall, Secy.; Terry Sporkin, Treas.; Theresa K. Dawson, Exec. Dir.
Directors: Bill Schwan, Juliann Wilkins-Hughes.
EIN: 830295851

64398
Jim and Audrey Bailey Foundation
c/o Jim M. Bailey
P.O. Box 4236
Casper, WY 82604-4236

Established in 1991 in WY.
Donor(s): Jim M. Bailey, Audrey W. Bailey.
Financial data (yr. ended 12/31/00): Assets, $100,152 (M); grants paid, $59,510; gifts received, $15,000; expenditures, $60,748; qualifying distributions, $60,748.
Limitations: Applications not accepted. Giving primarily in WY.
Application information: Contributes only to pre-selected organizations.
Officers and Trustees:* Jim M. Bailey,* Pres. and V.P.; James M. Bailey,* 2nd V.P.; Audrey W. Bailey,* Secy.-Treas.; Walter W. Bailey, Judith Bailey Scully.
EIN: 363776545

64399
The Katie Tapp Memorial Scholarship Fund, Inc.
P.O. Box 527
Jackson, WY 83001-0527 (307) 733-4972

Established in 1987 in WY.
Donor(s): Gerald R. Tapp, Mary Ann Tapp.
Financial data (yr. ended 08/31/01): Assets, $82,158 (M); grants paid, $9,650; expenditures, $10,321; qualifying distributions, $9,927.
Limitations: Giving primarily in WY.
Application information: Application form required.
Officers: Gerald R. Tapp, Pres.; Karen Tapp Wright, V.P.; Gayle Tapp Johnson, Secy.; Mary Ann Tapp, Treas.
EIN: 742451469

64400
The Greybull Women's Scholarship Trust
1215 Hwy. 14
Greybull, WY 82426-9732 (307) 765-4760
Contact: Helen Saban

Financial data (yr. ended 12/31/01): Assets, $21,602 (M); grants paid, $1,000; expenditures, $1,000; qualifying distributions, $1,000.
Limitations: Giving limited to Greybull, WY, area.
Application information: Application form required.
Trustees: Teresa Leach, Dorothy Malasky, Helen L. Saban.
EIN: 836039695

64401
Cultural Enterprise: Advocates of Cultural Advancement
1610 Allred Rd.
Afton, WY 83110

Classified as a private operating foundation in 1997 in UT.
Donor(s): William Call.
Financial data (yr. ended 09/30/00): Assets, $15,198 (M); grants paid, $0; gifts received, $10,000; expenditures, $20,306; qualifying distributions, $20,306; giving activities include $19,927 for programs.
Officers: William Call, Pres.; Clayton Call, V.P. and Secy.; Scott Kenney, V.P.
EIN: 830319215

64402
Yellowstone Grizzly Foundation
P.O. Box 12679
Jackson, WY 83002

Donor(s): Steven P. French, Marilynn G. French.
Financial data (yr. ended 12/31/01): Assets, $14,970 (M); grants paid, $0; gifts received, $32,250; expenditures, $19,580; qualifying distributions, $17,895; giving activities include $19,580 for programs.
Officers: Marilynn G. French, Pres.; Karen Shirley, V.P.; Timothy Floyd, Secy.; Steven P. French, Treas.
EIN: 742483154

64403
W.A.L.K. Foundation
P.O. Box 665
Wilson, WY 83014

Established in 2000 in WY.
Donor(s): Lessie E. Thiele.
Financial data (yr. ended 12/31/01): Assets, $5,017 (M); grants paid, $0; gifts received, $5,860; expenditures, $952; qualifying distributions, $0.
Officer: Lessie E. Thiele, Chair.
Directors: Shaun S. Forsyth, Elizabeth W. Ridgeway.
EIN: 830329416

64404
Jentel Foundation
c/o Neltje
11 Lower Piney Creek
Banner, WY 82832

Established in 2000. Classified as a private operating foundation in 2001.
Donor(s): A. Neltje.
Financial data (yr. ended 12/31/00): Assets, $2,454 (M); grants paid, $0; gifts received, $23,500; expenditures, $21,634; qualifying distributions, $21,046.
Officers: A. Neltje, Pres.; John T. Sargent, V.P.; Carla J. Ash, Secy.-Treas.
Directors: Mary Jane Edwards, Donna Forbes, Ellen Sargent.
EIN: 830331644

64405
Bedont Family Foundation
2005 Warren Ave.
Cheyenne, WY 82001
Contact: Attilio W. Bedont, Dir.

Established in 1999 in WY.
Financial data (yr. ended 12/31/00): Assets, $2,302 (M); grants paid, $9,370; gifts received, $11,000; expenditures, $9,620; qualifying distributions, $9,370.
Limitations: Giving primarily in Cheyenne, WY.
Directors: Attilio W. Bedont, Henrietta C. Bedont.
EIN: 830323214

64406
Wyoming State Predatory Animal Board
c/o Raymon Turk
P.O. Box 115
Casper, WY 82602-0115

Financial data (yr. ended 09/30/01): Assets, $1,333 (M); grants paid, $0; expenditures, $7,500; qualifying distributions, $0.
Limitations: Applications not accepted.
Application information: Contributes only to pre-selected organizations.
Officers: Raymon Turk, Pres.; J.W. Nuckolls, V.P.; Dan Reimler, Secy.-Treas.
EIN: 830294985
Codes: TN

APPENDIX A

The following foundations are not included in the *Guide to U.S. Foundations, Their Trustees, Officers and Donors* for the reasons stated.

A Chorus Line of Care
Los Angeles, CA
Current information not available

A Future Through Education
Golden, CO
Current information not available

A.M.G. Foundation, Inc.
Lewisville, TX
The foundation has not paid grants in last three fiscal years 1998-2000

Abarca Foundation
Denver, CO
Inactive foundation

Abbott Guggenheim Foundation, Inc.
Warwick, NY
The foundation has not paid grants in the last three fiscal years, 1999-2001

ABC Foundation
Minneapolis, MN
The foundation terminated in 2001

Abeles Scholarship Fund, Inc., Nancy Jo
Pleasantville, NY
The fund terminated in 2001

Abounding Grace Ministries, Inc.
New York, NY
Current information not available

Abrahams Charitable Trust
Newton, MA
The trust terminated in 2000

ACNA Foundation
Philadelphia, PA
The foundation terminated in Dec. 2000

Action 81, Inc.
Winchester, VA
The foundation has terminated in 2001

Acts of Barnabus, Inc.
Nashville, TN
The foundation terminated in 2001

Adams Foundation, James S.
New York, NY
Current information not available

Adams Trust, Clayton J.
Chicago, IL
The foundation terminated in 2000

Ades Charitable Trust, Samuel & Adele
New Bedford, MA
The foundation terminated in 2001

Adler Charitable Trust, Abe and Leona M.
Cleveland, OH
The foundation terminated in 2001

Adler Foundation Trust, Philip D. & Henrietta B.
Davenport, IA
The foundation terminated in 1999

Adlman Foundation, Inc.
New York, NY
The foundation terminated on May 31, 2001

Aducation, Inc.
Avon, MA
The foundation terminated on Mar. 31, 2001

Advent Senior Housing, Inc.
Baltimore, MD
The foundation terminated in 2002

AEC Electrical Scholarship & Educational Fund Corporation
New York, NY
Current information not available

Aerosmith Foundation, Inc.
Los Angeles, CA
The foundation terminated in 2001

Agley Family Foundation No. 1
See Talon Foundation

Agley Family Foundation No. 2
Detroit, MI
The foundation terminated on July 31, 2001

Agley Family Foundation No. 3
Detroit, MI
The foundation terminated on July 31, 2001

Ahern Foundation, The
Towson, MD
Current information not available

Ainger Junior High School Foundation, Inc., L. A.
Englewood, FL
Current information not available

Ajax Foundation
(Formerly Richard M. Bressler Foundation)
Seattle, WA
The foundation terminated in 2001

Alburger Charitable Trust, Harry A. and Jane W.
Richmond, VA
The foundation terminated in 2002

Alco Gravure Education Fund, Inc.
See Quebecor Printing Scholarship Program

Alden Trust, Stephen P.
Providence, RI
The trust terminated on April 30, 2001

Aliso Viejo Community Foundation
Aliso Viejo, CA
The foundation has not paid grants in the last three fiscal years, 1998-2000

All About Kids Foundation, Inc.
Cincinnati, OH
The foundation terminated on June 30, 2001

Allen Trust, Helen N.
Providence, RI
The trust terminated in 1999

Alleynian Foundation
New York, NY
Inacitve foundation

Allhands Education Trust, Jessie V.
Albion, IL
Inactive foundation

Alliance Foundation
(Formerly Edwin Mumford Foundation)
Indianola, PA
The foundation terminated in 2001

Altman Foundation-Citadel Fund, The
See The William M. Altman, Jr. and Henrietta B. Altman Foundation-Citadel Fund

Altman Foundation-Citadel Fund, William M. Altman, Jr. and Henrietta B., The
(also known as The Altman Foundation-Citadel Fund)
Isle of Palms, SC
Current information not available

Amann Foundation
Rudolph, WI
The foundation terminated on March 31, 2001

Amber Charitable Trust
Collierville, TN
Inactive trust

America's Music Center
St. Louis, MO
Inactive; the center has not paid grants in the last 4 years (1998-2002)

American Committee for South Asian Art, Inc.
Middlebury, VT
The foundation terminated in 2001

APPENDIX A

American Friends of Selah, Inc.
Brooklyn, NY
Current information not available

American Moslem Foundation
Tacoma, WA
Inactive foundation

American National Heritage Association, Inc.
Alexandria, VA
Current information not available

American Osteopathic Academy of Orthopedics Educational Foundation, Inc.
Davie, FL
The foundation has not paid grants in the last three fiscal years, 1999-2001

American Privacy Foundation, Inc.
Wellesley Hills, MA
Current information not available

American-Nepal Education Foundation, The
Portland, OR
Current information not available

AmeriSteel Foundation, Inc.
(Formerly Florida Steel Corporation Foundation)
Tampa, FL
The foundation terminated in 2001

Ameurop Cultural Relations Foundation, The
Richmond, VA
The foundation terminated in 2001

Amfam Foundation, The
Alexandria, VA
The foundation terminated in 2001

Amlan Foundation
Garden City, NY
The foundation terminated in 1999

Amos Scholarship Trust, William H. Amos & Mary A.
White City, KS
The trust terminated in 2000

Amter Foundation, Helen Kohn
Denver, CO
The foundation terminated in 2001

Amter Foundation, Joseph A.
See Joseph A. and Donna Amter Foundation

Amter Foundation, Joseph A. and Donna
(Formerly Joseph A. Amter Foundation)
Denver, CO
The foundation terminated in 2001

Anderson Trust, Inc., Sherman Michael
Hickory, NC
Inactive foundation

Andreini Foundation, The
New York, NY
Current information not available

Animal Angels
Jacksboro, TX
The foundation terminated in 2000

Anku Foundation, Inc., Vincent, The
Middleburg Heights, OH
Current information not available

ANR Foundation, Inc.
Houston, TX
The foundation terminated in 2001

Anthem Blue Cross and Blue Shield Foundation
(also known as Caring for Nevada Foundation)
Las Vegas, NV
The foundation terminated in 2001

Anthroposophical Society in America, New York Branch, Inc.
New York, NY
The foundation terminated in 2002

Antonelli Foundation, L.
Weymouth, MA
The foundation terminated on Dec. 31, 2001

Apanaitis Foundation, Charles and Helen, The
Toledo, OH
The foundation terminated in 2001

Apisdorf Foundation, Harold C.
Providence, RI
The foundation terminated on Dec. 31, 2000

Apkon Foundation, Stephen and Lisa
Pleasantville, NY
The foundation terminated on Nov. 30, 2001

Apostle Foundation, The
Minneapolis, MN
Inactive foundation. The foundation has not paid grants in the last three fiscal years, 1998-2000

Appel Foundation, Inc., Beatrice & Alfred
New York, NY
The foundation terminated on Nov. 30, 2001

Applegate Foundation
Grand Rapids, MI
The foundation terminated in 2002

Arbee Foundation, The
Wyomissing, PA
The foundation terminated on Dec. 31, 1999

Arden Foundation, The
Vadnais Heights, MN
Current information not available

Arellano Foundation, Inc., The
Miami, FL
Current information not available

Ariel Foundation, The
Chicago, IL
Current information not available

Arkwright Foundation, Inc.
Johnston, RI
The foundation terminated in 2001

Armstrong Fund, Emma
Iowa Falls, IA
Current information not available

Army Historical Foundation, Inc, The
Arlington, VA
The foundation terminated in 2002

Arnold Industries Scholarship Foundation
Reading, PA
The foundation terminated in 2002

Arrington Memorial Charitable Trust, Clark, The
Brookhaven, MS
The foundation has not paid grants in the last three fiscal years, 1999-2001

Arsalyn Foundation
Glendora, CA
The foundation terminated due to a merger into the Ludwick Family Foundation

Arts Live Foundation
(Formerly Thomas Talbert Foundation)
Beverly Hills, CA
The foundation terminated in 2001

Arvin Foundation, Inc., The
Columbus, IN
Due to the merger of Meritor Automotive, Inc. and Arvin Industries, Inc. on July 7, 2000, the foundation has terminated

Ash-Lawrence Bar Association Educational Trust, Allen J.
Lawrence, MA
Current information not available

Aslan Foundation
Cincinnati, OH
The foundation has not paid grants in the last three fiscal years, 1998-2000

Asner Family Foundation, The
(Formerly Edward & Nancy Asner Family Foundation)
Los Angeles, CA
The foundation terminated in 2001

Asner Family Foundation, Edward & Nancy
See The Asner Family Foundation

Atlantic Records Foundation, Inc., The
New York, NY
The foundation terminated in 2000

Attitudinal Research Center, Inc.
Muskegon, MI
Inactive foundation. The foundation has not paid grants in four years (1998-2001)

Augustine Charitable Trust
Brooklyn, NY
Current information not aviailable

Aurea Foundation, Inc., The
Syosset, NY
Inactive foundation. The foundation has not paid grants in the last three fiscal years, 1999-2001

Austin Street Foundation, The
Marfa, TX
Inactive foundation

Austin Val Verde Foundation, Warren R. Austin and Heath Horton
Santa Barbara, CA
The foundation has not paid grants in the last three fiscal years, 1999-2001

Avery Scholarship Trust, Maurice
Milwaukee, WI
The trust terminated on Dec. 31, 2000

Aviva/Spring Foundation, Inc.
New York, NY
Current information not avialable

Awareness for Community Development
Moreno Valley, CA
Current information not available

Babson Family Foundation, Gorham, The
Portland, OR
The foundation terminated in 2001

Bach Charitable Trust, Diane
Coral Gables, FL
The trust terminated on Dec. 31, 1999

Bachelor Han Hospital Trust, Charles O.
(Formerly Charles O. Bachelor Trust)
Providence, RI
The trust terminated in 1999

Bachelor Trust, Charles O.
See Charles O. Bachelor Han Hospital Trust

Bachrodt Chevrolet Charitable Foundation, Lou
Rockford, IL

Bacon Academy Alumni Association, Inc.
Colchester, CT
The foundation terminated in 2001

Bacot Foundation, Inc.
Pascagoula, MS
Inactive foundation

Bagwell Family Foundation, Inc.
Cumming, GA
Inactive foundation. The foundation has not paid grants in the last three fiscal years, 1998-2000

Baird Foundation
Philadelphia, PA
Current information not available

APPENDIX A

Baker Charitable Foundation, Jessie Foos
Columbus, OH
The foundation terminated in 2001

Baker Charitable Trust, Thomas & Wanda
Louisville, KY
Inactive foundation

Baker Foundation, Richard T. & Martha B.
Gulf Stream, FL
The foundation terminated in 2001

Banc One, Wisconsin Foundation, Inc.
(Formerly The Marine Foundation, Inc.)
Milwaukee, WI
The foundation terminated in 2000

Bank One Michigan Charitable Trust
(Formerly NBD Bank Charitable Trust)
Detroit, MI
The foundation terminated in 2001

Banks Family Foundation
Rancho Palos Verdes, CA
Inactive foundation

Banta Charitable Trust, Stephen C., The
Portland, OR
The trust terminated in 2001

Barco Scholarship Trust
Erie, PA
The foundation terminated on Apr. 30, 1999

Barco-Duratz Foundation, The
Pittsburgh, PA
The foundation terminated in 2002

Barger-Ford Foundation, Inc.
Evansville, IN
Current information not available

Baria Family Foundation, The
Corpus Christi, TX
The foundation terminated in Oct. 2001

Barkman Educational Trust, Joseph
East Tawas, MI
The trust terminated in 2000

Barlow Foundation, Inc., Pearl, The
West Palm Beach, FL
Inactive foundation

Barnabas Ministries Charitable Trust
Portland, OR
The trust terminated on Jan. 31, 2001

Barr Charitable Foundation, Cornelia H. and Thomas D., The
Paradise Valley, AZ
The foundation terminated in 2001

Barrick Foundation
Dallas, TX
The foundation terminated in 2002

Barringer Foundation, Flora M.
Augusta, GA
The foundation terminated in 2001

Bartel Foundation, Benjamin
Brooklyn, NY
Current information not available

Barton Charitable Foundation, John
Chicago, IL
Inactive foundation

Bass Foundation, Samuel, The
Boca Raton, FL
The foundation terminated on Nov. 30, 2001

Bass, Jr. Research Foundation, Harry W.
Dallas, TX
The foundation merged into the Harry Bass Foundation

Be True To Yourself Foundation
Seattle, WA
The foundation terminated in 2001

Beach Foundation Trust B for First Baptist Church, Thomas N. Beach and Mildred V.
Birmingham, AL
The foundation terminated in 2002

Beaudette Educational Trust, Robert, The
See The Robert Beaudette Irrevocable Charitable Foundation

Beaudette Irrevocable Charitable Foundation, Robert, The
(Formerly The Robert Beaudette Educational Trust)
San Diego, CA
Inactive foundation

Becker Family Foundation, The
Lake Forest, IL
The foundation terminated in 2001

Becker Foundation, Inc., George J.
Fond du Lac, WI
The foundation terminated in 2002

Becker Foundation, Isidore A. & Adele, The
New York, NY
The foundation terminated in 2002

Bedford Rotary Foundation
Bedford, OH
Current information not available

Beginning With Children Foundation, Inc.
New York, NY
The foundation terminated in 2002

Behney, Jr. Memorial Foundation, Thomas A.
Lancaster, PA
The foundation terminated on May 31, 2001

Beidler Charitable Trust, Francis
Chicago, IL
The foundation terminated in 1999

Beidner Foundation, George & Lillian
Redondo Beach, CA
The foundation terminated in 2001

Belasco Foundation, Edna & Jack, The
Philadelphia, PA
The foundation terminated in 2002

Belden Brick Company Charitable Trust, The
Canton, OH
The trust terminated in 2001

Belk Foundation, Inc., Katherine and Thomas
(Formerly Thomas Milburn Belk Foundation)
Southern Pines, NC
The foundation terminated in 2001

Belk Foundation, Thomas Milburn
See Katherine and Thomas Belk Foundation, Inc.

Belkin Foundation, Steven B.
Weston, MA
The foundation terminated in 2001

Bell & Howell Foundation
Ann Arbor, MI
The foundation terminated in 2002

Bells of St. Albans
Williston, VT
The trust terminated in 2001

Bendit Foundation, Inc., The
Baltimore, MD
The foundation terminated on June 30, 2001

Benefits America Charitable Foundation
Atlanta, GA
Current information available

Benjamin Foundation, The
Rochester, NY
Inactive foundation. The foundation has not paid grants in the last three fiscal years, 1999-2001

Benun Foundation, Mark
New York, NY
Inactive foundation

Beren Trust, Harry H.
Denver, CO
The trust has not paid grants in the last three fiscal years, 1998-2000

Berg Trust, Quentin
York, PA
The foundation terminated in 2002

Berkeley International Institute, The
(Formerly The Trueger Foundation)
San Francisco, CA
Inactive; the foundation has not made grants for three years (1999-2001)

Berkowitz Charitable Trust, E. Sidney
Wellesley, MA
The foundation terminated in 2002

Berkshire Community College Foundation, Inc.
Pittsfield, MA
The foundation terminated in 2002

Berlex Oncology Foundation, Inc., The
Hackensack, NJ
The foundation terminated in 2001

Berman Award, Inc., Tom, The
Rye, NY
Current information available

Berman Charitable Foundation Trust
Washington, DC
The trust terminated in 2001

Bernhardt Charitable Trust
Wheeling, WV
The trust terminated on Mar. 31, 2001

Berrey, Jr. Memorial Trust, Robert W.
Excelsior Springs, MO
Inactive trust

Best Foundation
Dallas, TX
The foundation has not paid grants in the last three fiscal years, 1998-2000

Bethel Foundation, The
Charlotte, NC
The foundation terminated on Dec. 12, 2001

Bhakta Das Charitable Trust, The
Visalia, CA
Inactive trust

Bibles for all Ministries
Cartersville, GA
Current information not available

Bickford Scholarship Foundation
New Lisbon, WI
Current information not available

Big Pond Preservation Association, Inc.
South Windham, CT
Current information available

Biller Scholarship Fund, Lawrence
East Haven, CT
Inactive fund

Bilo Fund, Inc.
Darien, CT
The fund terminated in 2001

Birnbaum Charitable Foundation, Inc., Robert M.
Passaic, NJ
Current information not available

APPENDIX A

Bisgeier Foundation, Inc., David and Susan
New York, NY
The foundation terminated in 2001

Blackford Memorial Letters Trust
Dallas, TX
The foundation has not paid grants in the last three fiscal years, 1998-2000

Bladis Foundation
Springfield, NJ
Current information not available

Blanding Genealogical Publications
East Grand Rapids, MI
The foundation terminated in 2000

Blank Foundation, Ruth & Samuel A.
Jenkintown, PA
The foundation has not paid grants in the last three fiscal years, 1998-2000

Blevins Foundation, Michael L., The
Del Mar, CA
The foundation terminated on Sept. 5, 2001

Block Foundation, Abe and Sidney, The
New York, NY
Current information not available

Bloomfield Memorial Trust, Clara
Bayside, WI
Inactive foundation

Blue Cross and Blue Shield of Colorado Foundation
(also known as Rocky Mountain Health Care Corporation Foundation)
Denver, CO
The foundation terminated in 2001

Blum Family Foundation, Inc.
Asheville, NC
Current information not available

Blum Foundation, Jerrold S.
Pittsburgh, PA
The foundation terminated in 2001

Bobbitt Scholarship Fund, W. L.
Lexington, TN
Current information not available

Bock Charitable Foundation, Margaret, Pamela & Ed
Cedar Rapids, IA
The foundation terminated in 2001

Body Shop USA Foundation, The
Wake Forest, NC
Inactive foundation

Boehm Foundation, The
New York, NY
The foundation terminated in 2002

Bon Air Foundation
Los Angeles, CA
The foundation terminated in 2000

Bonnett Christian Communications Scholarship Fund, Lucy
Bushnell, IL
Inactive foundation. The foundation has not paid grants in the last three fiscal years, 1999-2001

Booth Foundation, Robert V. D. and Katherine F., The
Painesville, OH
The foundation terminated in 2002

Borawski Insurance Charitable Foundation
Northampton, MA
The foundation terminated in 2000

Borck Foundation, Jay
See Jay & Jim Borck Foundation, Inc.

Borck Foundation, Inc., Jay & Jim
(Formerly Jay Borck Foundation)
North Palm Beach, FL
The foundation terminated on Dec. 31, 2000 and transferred its assets to The Borck Family Foundation, Inc.

Boring Charitable Trust
Atwater, OH
Current information not available

Boshamer Foundation, Inc., Cary C.
Clover, SC
The foundation terminated in 1998

Bott Family Memorial Trust
Keokuk, IA
The trust terminated on June 5, 2001

Bowen Foundation
(also known as Ethel G. Bowen Trust f/b/o Bowen Foundation)
Grand Rapids, MI
The foundation terminated on Feb. 28, 2002

Bowen Trust f/b/o Bowen Foundation, Ethel G.
See Bowen Foundation

Bowser Family Foundation
Oskaloosa, KS
The foundation terminated on Sept. 30, 2000

Boyd Foundation
Lowell, MI
Current information not available

Boyd Foundation, The
Santa Barbara, CA
The foundation terminated in 2002

Brabson Foundation, Inc.
Sevierville, TN
The foundation terminated in 2001

Bracey, Sr. Memorial School Fund, Inc., Willard M.
Fort Washington, MD
Current information not available

Brach Family Charitable Foundation
Roseland, NJ
Inactive foundation

Bracken Foundation, Sam T.
Tyler, TX
Inactive foundation

Bradley Medical Research Foundation, William E.
Seattle, WA
The foundation terminated in 2001

Bradley Scientific Research Foundation, William E.
Seattle, WA
The foundation terminated in 2001

Brady Trust, Robert
Des Moines, IA
The foundation terminated in 2001

Brain Trust, Inc.
Fernandina Beach, FL
Current information not available

Bread on the Waters Charitable Trust
Atlanta, GA
The foundation terminated on May 14, 2001

Breaks Scout Transportation Foundation
Grundy, VA
Inactive foundation. The foundation has not paid grants in the last three fiscal years, 1997-2000

Breidenthal Foundation, George G. and Jennifer J.
Overland Park, KS
The foundation terminated in 2000

Bren Foundation, Claire Trevor
Newport Beach, CA
The foundation terminated in 2002

Brenner Foundation, Inc.
New York, NY
Current information not available

Brenner, Saltzman, Wallman & Goldman Foundation, Inc.
New Haven, CT
The foundation terminated in Dec. 2000

Breslin Scholarship Foundation, Elizabeth Ann
Friendswood, TX
Current information not available

Bressler Foundation, Richard M.
See Ajax Foundation

Breyer Foundation
Palm Beach, FL
The foundation terminated in 2001

Bricklayers Joint Apprentice Committee Fund
Cleveland, OH
The fund has not paid grants in the last three fiscal years, 1999-2001

Bridges Foundation, Larry J.
See Larry J. and Deborah D. Bridges Foundation

Bridges Foundation, Larry J. and Deborah D.
(Formerly Larry J. Bridges Foundation)
Overland Park, KS
Inactive foundation

Bright Foundation, Michael & Esther
Bay Harbor Islands, FL
Current information not available

Brillion Foundation, Inc.
Brillion, WI
The foundation terminated in 2001

Brinser Memorial Fund, Donald C.
Pittsburgh, PA
The foundation has not paid grants in the last three fiscal years, 1998-2000

Broadcasting-Taishoff Foundation, The
Naples, FL
The foundation terminated on Nov. 30, 2001

Brock Family Foundation, Florence and Arthur, The
Elmhurst, IL
The foundation terminated in 2000

Brodhead Foundation, Thomas & Elizabeth
Honolulu, HI
Inactive foundation. The foundation has not paid grants in the last three fiscal years, 1999-2001

Brody Foundation, Carolyn & Kenneth D., The
(Formerly Kenneth D. Brody Foundation)
Washington, DC
The foundation terminated in 2000

Brody Foundation, Kenneth D.
See The Carolyn & Kenneth D. Brody Foundation

Broken Wing Ministries
See Lonesome Dove

Bronstein Trust, Leo
New York, NY
Inactive trust. The trust has not paid grants in the last three fiscal years, 1998-2000

Brown Center for the Study of American Civilization, John Nicholas, The
Providence, RI
Current information not available

Brown Fund, Sheridan, The
Los Angeles, CA
The foundation terminated in 2001

Broyles Foundation, Inc., The
Snellville, GA
The foundation has not paid grants in the last three fiscal years, 1998-2000

APPENDIX A

Bruen Trust, Frank
Tampa, FL
The trust terminated in 2001

Brumder Foundation, Robert C.
Milwaukee, WI
Inactive foundation

Bruner Foundation for Mentally Handicapped Adults, Inc., James
Hurst, TX
Current information not available

Bruno Foundation, Kenneth J., The
Birmingham, AL
The foundation terminated in 2001

Bruno's, Inc. Foundation, The
Birmingham, AL
Inactive foundation

Buchan Memorial Trust, Thomas J.
Sun Valley, CA
The foundation has not paid grants in the last three fiscal years, 1998-2000

Buckley Family Charitable Trust, James B.
New Bedford, MA
The foundation terminated in 1999

Buckwalter Charitable Trust, Beulah M.
Camp Hill, PA
The trust terminated on Jan. 31, 2002

Buffington Trust, Nell
Concord, NH
Inactive foundation

Build & Design for Charities, Inc.
Glendora, CA
The foundation terminated in 1999

Buitoni Foundation, Inc., Giovanni & Leitizia
New York, NY
The foundation terminated in 2001

Bull Scholarship Fund
Cleveland, OH
The foundation terminated in Dec. 2001

Bully Creek Watershed Coalition, Inc.
Ontario, OR
Current information not available

Burger Student Loan Fund, Mary Belle
Kansas City, MO
The fund terminated in 2000

Burliss Memorial Charitable Foundation, Peter C.
Nashua, NH
The foundation terminated in 1999

Burnett Trust, Frank
Providence, RI
The trust terminated on February 28, 2002

Busch Family Foundation, Inc., Harry, The
Cranford, NJ
The foundation terminated in 2000

Busch Foundation, Inc., W. R.
St. Paul, MN
The foundation terminated on Dec. 31, 1999

Business Women's Association
See BWA Foundation

BWA Foundation
(Formerly Business Women's Association)
Des Moines, IA
The foundation terminated in 2001

BWB Charitable Foundation
See BWB Charitable Trust

BWB Charitable Trust
(Formerly BWB Charitable Foundation)
Chicago, IL
Inactive trust

BWIAC Educational Fund, Inc.
Brooklyn, NY
The fund has not paid grants in the last three fiscal years, 1998-2000

C & B Foundation, Inc.
Indianapolis, IN
Inactive foundation

C & K Foundation
Holden, MA
The foundation terminated in 2000

C-S Philanthropies
(also known as Corby-Somerville Philanthropies)
Huntsville, AL
Current information not available

Cabin Museum
Turkey, NC
The foundation terminated in 2000

Cable Foundation Trust, Mary Jo and Kent, The
Clinton, MO
Inactive foundation

Cafiero, Sr. Foundation, Michael J., The
Rockville Centre, NY
The foundation terminated in 1998

Caldwell Foundation
Gloucester, MA
The foundation terminated in 2000

Caldwell Scholarship Fund, James R.
See The Newell Rubbermaid Scholarship Fund

Calkins Board Foundation, Ina
Kansas City, MO
The foundation terminated in 2000, transferring remaining assets to the Ina Calkins Foundation

Camelot Foundation, Inc.
Rochester, MN
The foundation terminated in 2002

Camillus Foundation, Inc.
Camillus, NY
The foundation has not paid grants in the last three fiscal years, 1999-2001

Caminiti Charitable Foundation, Raffaela V.
See Caminiti Family Foundation

Caminiti Family Foundation
(Formerly Raffaela V. Caminiti Charitable Foundation)
Palm Beach Gardens, FL
The foundation has not paid grants in the last three fiscal years, 1998-2000

Campbell Foundation, Molly Lee
Spencerport, NY
The foundation terminated on June 30, 2001

Candib Family Foundation, Murray A., The
Worcester, MA
The foundation has not paid grants in the last three fiscal years, 1999-2001

Canno Foundation, Inc., The
(Formerly The Leonard and Irma Canno Foundation, Inc.)
New York, NY
The foundation terminated in 2001

Canno Foundation, Inc., Leonard and Irma, The
See The Canno Foundation, Inc.

Career Counselor Services, Inc.
(also known as CCS)
Greenville, SC
The foundation terminated on Apr. 27, 1999

Career Guidance Foundation
San Diego, CA
The foundation terminated in 2002

Caring for Nevada Foundation
See Anthem Blue Cross and Blue Shield Foundation

Carlile Fund, Florence Jeffrey
Columbus, OH
The foundation terminated in 2000

Carlos Foundation, Inc., The
Atlanta, GA
The foundation terminated in 2001

Carlson Family Foundation
New York, NY
The foundation terminated in 2000

Carlton Trust, Ethel Irene
Denver, CO
The foundation terminated in 2001

Carolina Southern Foundation
Spartanburg, SC
The foundation terminated in Dec. 2000

Carson, Sr. Charitable Trust, William Waller
Milwaukee, WI
The trust terminated in 1999

Carter Boy Scout Scholarship Fund, Marjorie Sells
Stamford, CT
The fund has not paid grants in the last three fiscal years, 1999-2001

Carter Charitable Trust, Adele P.
Martinsville, VA
The foundation terminated in 2001

Carter Scholarship Fund, Arthur H.
Stamford, CT
The fund has not paid grants in the last three fiscal years, 1999-2001

Cascade Controls Charitable Foundation
San Jose, CA
The foundation terminated in 2001

Cascio Foundation
West Hollywood, CA
The foundation terminated in 2001

Cat Welfare Society, Ltd.
Birmingham, AL
The foundation terminated in 2001

CBOL Foundation Trust
Lincoln, NE
Inactive trust

CBRL Group Foundation
(Formerly The Cracker Barrel Old Country Store Foundation)
Lebanon, TN
The foundation terminated in 2001

CCS
See Career Counselor Services, Inc.

Center for Health Professions
Saginaw, MI
Nongrantmaking foundation

Center for Human Understanding, Inc.
Baltimore, MD
The foundation has not paid grants in the last three fiscal years, 1999-2001

Center for Secondary School Educational Research
Greenwich, CT
The center terminated in 2001

Central European University Foundation
(also known as CEU Foundation)
New York, NY
The foundation has not paid grants in the last three fiscal years, 1999-2001

Centre for International Understanding
St. Louis, MO
The foundation terminated in 2002

APPENDIX A

CEU Foundation
See Central European University Foundation

Chambers Foundation
Houston, TX
The foundation terminated in 2000

Champ Trust for Boy Scouts-Cache, F. P.
Henderson, NV
The trust has not paid grants in the last three fiscal years, 1998-2000

Channel 13 Foundation, Inc., The
Tampa, FL
The foundation terminated in 2002

Charitable and Educational Foundation, The
New City, NY
The foundation terminated on Sept. 18, 2000

Charter Holdings Foundation, Inc.
Fort Lauderdale, FL
Inactive foundation

Chayefsky Foundation, Inc., Paddy, The
New York, NY
The foundation has not paid grants in the last three fiscal years; 1999-2001

Checket Family Foundation, Inc.
Baltimore, MD
The foundation terminated in Oct., 2000

Chemer Charitable Trust, Ann S.
Chicago, IL
The foundation terminated on Nov. 29, 2001

Chestnut Street Associates
Salem, MA
Inactive foundation. The foundation has not paid grants in the last three fiscal years, 1998-2000

Chew Foundation, John S.
(Formerly North American Plastics Philanthropic Foundation)
Madison, MS
The foundation terminated in 2002

Chicago Annenberg Challenge Foundation
Chicago, IL
The foundation terminated in Dec. 2001

Chicago Charitable Foundation
Northfield, IL
The foundation terminated in 2002

Chicago Resource Center
Chicago, IL
The foundation terminated in 2001

Christ Cares for Kids Foundation
Traverse City, MI
The foundation terminated in 2002

Christ International, Inc.
Macclenny, FL
Current information not available

Christensen Trust, Ethel M.
San Francisco, CA
The trust terminated in 2001

Christian Workers Foundation, The
Childersburg, AL
The foundation terminated in 2002

Christians of Account, Inc.
Easton, MO
The foundation terminated on Mar. 31, 1999

Church of God Missions, Inc.
Indianapolis, IN
The foundation terminated in 1998

Cindus Fund
Cincinnati, OH
The foundation terminated in 2000

CK Charitable Trust
Chicago, IL
Current information not available

Claddagh Foundation, The
Huntington Beach, CA
The foundation terminated Dec. 2001

Clark Foundation, Raymond E. & Mildred G.
Providence, RI
The foundation terminated in 1999

Clark Memorial Scholarship Trust, Jeff
Susanville, CA
The foundation terminated in 2001

Clay Charitable Trust, The
Huber Heights, OH
Current information not available

Clayton Family Foundation, The
Ormond Beach, FL
The foundation terminated in 2000

Clean Water Alliance
Bellingham, WA
Current information not available

Clear Foundation, Inc.
Lexington, KY
Current information not available

Cloud Trust, Fred B.
Kansas City, MO
The foundation terminated in 2001 per the trust agreement, following the death of R. Cloud

Clover Capital Foundation, Inc.
Pittsford, NY
The foundation has terminated

CLS Charitable Foundation
Clearwater, FL
Current information not available

Cocco Charitable Foundation, Inc., Arthur E., The
St. Simons Island, GA
The foundation terminated on Dec. 31, 2001

Cochrane Trust D f/b/o City of Mobile Museum, Katharine C.
Mobile, AL
The foundation terminated in 2001

Coghlin Fund, The
Worcester, MA
The fund terminated on June 30, 2000 and transferred its assets to the Coghlin Family Foundation and the Coglin Services Fund

Cohen Charitable Foundation, Dora & Jacob, The
New York, NY
The foundation terminated in 2001

Cohen Charitable Foundation, Harry & Helen
Chicago, IL
The foundation terminated in 2001

Cohen Family Foundation, Louis M. & Tess
Minneapolis, MN
The foundation terminated on June 30, 2002

Colby Foundation, The
Reno, NV
The foundation terminated in 2000

Cole-Taylor Charitable Foundation
Wheeling, IL
The foundation terminated on Dec. 31, 2001

Colehower Foundation, H. Howard
Warrington, PA
The foundation terminated in 2002

Coleman, Jr. Foundation, George E.
New York, NY
The foundation terminated in 2001

Coler Foundation, The
New York, NY
Inactive foundation. The foundation has not paid grants in the last three fiscal years, 1998-2000

Collins Scholarship Fund, Cardiss, The
Alexandria, VA
Inactive foundation. The foundation has not paid grants in the last three fiscal years, 1998-2000

Colls Foundation, Juana
Wheaton, IL
Current information not available

Colonial Foundation, Inc.
Savannah, GA
The foundation terminated in 2001

Colorado Health Professions Panel
Denver, CO
The foundation terminated on June 30, 2000

Colorado State Grange Leadership and Scholarship Foundation
Lakewood, CO
The foundation terminated on Dec. 31, 2001

Columbiana Community Foundation, Inc.
Columbiana, OH
Current information not available

Comer Charitable Foundation, Inc.
Lake Lotawana, MO
The foundation terminated in 2000

Cominsky Foundation, Inc.
New York, NY
The foundation terminated on Dec. 31, 2000 and transferred its assets to Temple Adath Yeshuran

Comm-Care Corporation
Ridgeland, MS
Non-grantmaker

Community Benefits Initiative, Inc.
Heath, OH
The foundation terminated in 1999

Community Care and Share Pantry
West Salem, WI
Inactive foundation

Community Cooperative Development Foundation, Inc.
Bridgeport, CT
The foundation has not paid grants in the last three fiscal years, 1999-2001

Community Housing Service Corporation
White Plains, NY
The foundation terminated in 2001

Community Service Foundation, Inc.
Clearwater, FL
The foundation terminated in 2002

Conaway Foundation, Floyd A. Conaway & Betty H.
See Floyd A. Conaway & Betty H. Conaway Scholarship Fund

Conaway Scholarship Fund, Floyd A. Conaway & Betty H.
(Formerly Floyd A. Conaway & Betty H. Conaway Foundation)
St. Petersburg, FL
The fund has not paid grants in the last three fiscal years, 1999-2001

Conaway Trust, Orval L.
Seattle, WA
The trust terminated in 2001

Conover Jazz Preservation Foundation, Inc., Willis, The
Washington, DC
The foundation has not paid grants in the last three fiscal years, 1998-2001

APPENDIX A

Contico International Inc. Charitable Trust, The
Aventura, FL
Inactive foundation

Convalescent and Rehabilitation Endowment Fund
Wilmington, DE
The fund terminated in 2001

Cook Charitable Foundation, R. D. and Maxine
Lincoln, CA
The foundation terminated on Dec. 31, 2001

Cook Foundation, Marjorie
Baltimore, MD
The foundation terminated in 2001

Cooper Foundation, Inc., George M.
Fort Wayne, IN
The foundation terminated in 2000

Cooper Foundation, Linnie, The
El Cajon, CA
Current information not available

Copper Ridge Wildlife Reserve, Inc.
Knoxville, TN
The foundation terminated in 2001

Corby-Somerville Philanthropies
See C-S Philanthropies

Corcoran Brothers Foundation, The
Braintree, MA
The foundation terminated in 2000

Cornelius Educational Foundation, William B.
Birmingham, AL
The foundation terminated in 2001

Couch Family Trust, R. C.
Dallas, TX
The trust terminated in Sept. 30, 1999

Coucouvitis & Pappas Memorial Scholarship Fund
Manchester, NH
The fund terminated on Sept. 30, 2000

Coutu Foundation, Joseph C. and Blanche
Providence, RI
The foundation has not paid grants in the last three fiscal years, 1999-2001

Cox Band Booster Club, Inc., A. G.
Winterville, NC
Current information not available

Cracker Barrel Old Country Store Foundation, The
See CBRL Group Foundation

Craddock-Terry Foundation, Inc.
Lynchburg, VA
The foundation terminated in 2001

Craig Foundation, Inc., Mary Ethel
Joplin, MO
The foundation merged into the E. L. Craig Foundation in 1998

Craw Foundation, The
Binghamton, NY
The foundation terminated on Dec. 31, 2001

Crawford Family Foundation, The
Chicago, IL
The foundation terminated in 2001

Crawford Pike County Crippled Children Association or Trust
Petersburg, IN
No current information available

Crenshaw Medical Foundation
Laguna Hills, CA
The foundation terminated in 2001

Croft Metal Products Educational Trust Fund
McComb, MS
Inactive foundation

Crouse Trust, William C. and A. Peryl
Providence, RI
Current information not available

Crusaders for the Virgin Mary, Inc.
Brick, NJ
The foundation terminated on Dec. 31, 2001

Cunningham Charitable Trust
Hanover, NH
The foundation terminated in 2001

Curtin-Haley Foundation
Minnetonka, MN
The foundation terminated in 2001

Curto Memorial Scholarship Fund, Mark A.
Longmeadow, MA
The foundation terminated in 1999

Cuthbert Education Trust, Robert
Medford, OR
The foundation terminated May 3, 2001

Cutler-Stephens Foundation
Charlestown, MA
Current information not available

D & W Foundation
Grand Rapids, MI
The foundation terminated in 2001

D.U. Memorial Foundation
Ann Arbor, MI
Current information not available

D'Anna Charitable Trust
See JLD Charitable Trust

Dale Trust, Charles M.
Providence, RI
The foundation terminated in 2002

Dangel Memorial Fund, Jerome R.
Newton Center, MA
The foundation terminated in 2001

Danish Cheer Committee, Inc.
Upland, CA
The foundation terminated on Nov. 16, 2001

Dann Memorial Fund, Anna Mae
Minneapolis, MN
The foundation terminated in 1999

Darby Foundation, Edith and Harry
Prairie Village, KS
The foundation terminated in 2001

Daugherty Foundation
Idaho Falls, ID
The foundation terminated in 2003

Davidson Family Foundation, The
New York, NY
Current information not available

Davidson Foundation, The
Incline Village, NV
The foundation terminated in 2001

Davis Family Foundation, The
Johnson City, TN
The foundation terminated on Dec. 31, 2001

Davis Foundation, Norene S. & Floyd E.
Bethesda, MD
The foundation terminated on Nov. 30, 2001

Davis Fund, Tricia Segall, The
Chevy Chase, MD
The fund terminated in 2001

Davis-Church Fund, Dorothy
Philadelphia, PA
The fund terminated on July 31, 1999

De Jur Foundation, Inc., Harry
New York, NY
The foundation terminated in 2002

DEAL Foundation
Minneapolis, MN
The foundation terminated in 2000

Dean Perpetual Charitable Trust, William L.
Aberdeen, SD
The trust terminated on Jan. 1, 2002

DeBartolo Family Foundation, The
(Formerly Marie P. DeBartolo Foundation)
Youngstown, OH
The foundation terminated in 2001

DeBartolo Foundation, Marie P.
See The DeBartolo Family Foundation

Deborah Foundation, Inc.
New York, NY
The foundation terminated in 1999

DEC International-Albrecht Foundation
Madison, WI
Grantmaking suspended until 2004

Decker Foundation, The
Baltimore, MD
The foundation terminated in 2001

Deener Trust, Richard G., The
Searcy, AR
Current information not available

Deicke Foundation, Edwin F.
Geneva, IL
The foundation terminated in 2000

DeJong Family Foundation
San Marcos, CA
The foundation terminated in 2001

DeLapa Family Foundation
See The Samaritan Foundation

Denny's Charitable Fund, Inc.
Spartanburg, SC
The fund has not paid grants in the last three years, 1999-2001

Densen Foundation, Max
Cranford, NJ
The foundation terminated in 2001

Denslow Foundation, William Theodore
Locust Valley, NY
The foundation terminated in 2001

DeQuattro Family Foundation
Manchester, CT
The foundation terminated in 2001

Desenberg-Wolff Foundation
Sarasota, FL
The foundation terminated on Dec. 31, 2001

Deseret Villages Association
Provo, UT
The foundation terminated in 2000

Deutsch Family Memorial Scholarship Fund f/b/o Geisinger Medical Center
Lancaster, PA
The fund has not paid grants in the last three fiscal years, 1998-2000

DHR Foundation
Chicago, IL
The foundation terminated in 1999

Dial-A-Mattress Foundation, Inc., The
Long Island City, NY
Inactive foundation

Dion Scholarship Trust
Glendive, MT
Inactive trust

APPENDIX A

Dissinger Family Trust, The
Plano, TX
Inactive foundation

Distance Foundation, The
Los Angeles, CA
The foudation terminated in 2002

Dixon Foundation
Dixon, CA
The foundation terminated in 2001

DLJ Foundation, The
New York, NY
The foundation terminated in 2001

Doctors for World Vision
See International Vision Volunteers

Doctors Nursing Center Foundation, Inc.
Dallas, TX
The foundation terminated in 2002

Doe Charitable Trust, Charles and Shirley
Woburn, MA
The trust has not paid grants in the last three fiscal years, 1998-2000

Doniger Foundation for Families in Transition, Morris C.
New York, NY
The foundation has not paid grant in the last three fiscal years, 1997-1999

Donnell, Jr. Foundation, Inc., John R.
Atlanta, GA
The foundation terminated in 2001

Donor/Recipient National Organ Transplant Register, Inc.
Duluth, GA
The foundation terminated in 2001

Donovan Foundation, Mary Susan Coulter, The
New York, NY
The foundation terminated in 1999 and transferred its assets to the Mary Susan Coulter Donovan Foundation, Inc.

Dowley Foundation
Spring Arbor, MI
The foundation terminated in 2001

Downar Trust, Birdie M.
Cheyenne, WY
The foundation terminated on June 30, 2001

Dozier Foundation, Inc., Silas Taylor & Eva May
Spearman, TX
The foundation terminated in 2001

Dozor Foundation, Harry T. & Shirley W.
Bala Cynwyd, PA
Inactive foundation. The foundation has not paid grants in the last three fiscal years, 1999-2001

Draiman-Drami Foundation, Inc.
Chicago, IL
Inactive foundation

Draper Charitable Foundation, Nancy-Carroll
Boston, MA
The foundation has not paid grants in the last three fiscal years, 1998-2000

Dreams Come True, Inc.
New York, NY
The foundation terminated in 2000

Drennan Family Charitable Trust
Abilene, TX
The foundation terminated in 2001

Drucker Memorial Fund, Mitchell
Howard Beach, NY
The fund terminated on Dec. 31, 2001

Duberg Charitable Trust A, Dorys McConnell
Rochester, NY
The trust terminated in 2002

Duberg Charitable Trust B, Dorys McConnell
Rochester, NY
The trust terminated on January 31, 2002

Duchaine Family Charitable Foundation, Paul A.
Sharon, MA
The foundation terminated in 2001

Duffy Schrader Foundation
Pittsford, NY
The foundation terminated on Dec. 31, 2000

Dunn & Son Foundation, Inc., Jack & Rose E.
Boca Raton, FL
The foundation terminated in 2001

Durham Trust for Chaplaincy
Ithaca, NY
The trust terminated in 2001

Dutcher Fellowship, Edward H.
Charlotte, NC
The foundation has not awarded loans in the last three fiscal years, 1998-2000

Dye Charitable Trust
Dalton, OH
Current information not available

Dyer Memorial Scholarship Trust, James E.
Cleveland, OH
Current information not available

Early, Jr. Foundation, Inc., Fred J.
Atherton, CA
The foundation terminated on Mar. 31, 2001

Easley Family Foundation
Kingsport, TN
Current information not available

East Coast Foundation
Richmond, VA
The foundation terminated in 2002

Easter Seal Society of DeSoto Manatee and Sarasota County Trust
See Easter Seal Society of Southwest Florida Endowment Fund

Easter Seal Society of Southwest Florida Endowment Fund
(Formerly Easter Seal Society of DeSoto Manatee and Sarasota County Trust)
Tampa, FL
The foundation terminated on July 31, 1998

Eaton Family Foundation, Lewis and Virginia, The
Fresno, CA
The foundation terminated on May 31, 2001

Eder Vocational Scholarship Fund, Ralph E. and Mary E.
Knightstown, IN
Current information not available

Edipa Foundation, Inc.
New York, NY
The foundation terminated in 2002

Edison Charitable Foundation of Grand Rapids, L. W.
Grand Rapids, MI
Current information not available

Education Innovations
Tucson, AZ
The foundation terminated in 2000

Educational Endowment Foundation
See Perkerson Educational Endowment Foundation

Edwards Trust, Dr. A. F.
Seattle, WA
The foundation terminated Aug. 31, 2001

Eells, III Foundation, William H., The
Haddonfield, NJ
The foundation has not paid grants in the last three fiscal years

Elbot Memorial Fund, Robin Fenn, The
Boston, MA
The fund terminated in 2001

Elgin Sweeper Foundation
Elgin, IL
The foundation terminated in 2001

Elk County Development Foundation
St. Marys, PA
The foundation terminated on Mar. 31, 2001

Elliott Foundation
Rochester, MN
The foundation terminated in 2001

Ellis Memorial Award Trust, James R.
Milwaukee, WI
The trust terminated in 2001

Elson Notre Dame Scholarship Trust, James and Nancy
Canton, IL
The trust terminated in 2000

Energy Research Foundation, Inc.
Columbia, SC
The foundation terminated on Oct. 14, 1999

Engelberg Charitable Trust, Louis
Pittsburgh, PA
The foundation terminated in 2000

Engman Foundation
Des Moines, IA
The foundation terminated on Oct. 31, 2001

Erasmus of Rotterdam Society
College Park, MD
The foundation terminated in June 30, 2001

Ericsson Post 109 Benefit Association Trust
Providence, RI
The trust terminated on October 31, 2001

Esseff Foundation, Inc.
Dayton, MD
Current information not available

Evans Charitable Foundation, Raymond F. & Elizabeth W.
Cleveland, OH
The foundation terminated in 2001

Ever Young and Green Foundation Trust
Glen Arbor, MI
The foundation terminated on Dec. 31, 2000

Ewa Housing Foundation
Honolulu, HI
The foundation terminated in 2002

Ewing Log House Foundation, Inc., The
West Palm Beach, FL
The foundation has not paid grants in the last three years, 1998-2000

Fain Fund, Irving Jay & E. Macie
Providence, RI
Current information not available

Fain-Malsky Foundation
(Formerly Faub-Malsky Charitable Foundation)
Providence, RI
Current information not available

Faith Adventures
Torrance, CA
The foundation has not paid grants in the last three fiscal years, 1998-2000

Farnsworth Scholarship Fund Trust, Julia
Columbia, SC
Current information not available

APPENDIX A

Farview Foundation
St. Charles, IL
The foundation terminated in 2001

Father Murphy Scholarship Fund
Rochester, NY
The fund terminated on Mar. 31, 1999

Faub-Malsky Charitable Foundation
See Fain-Malsky Foundation

Favrot Fund, The
Houston, TX
The foundation terminated in 2000

Fay Charitable Trust, Michael D. Fay & Cathy C.
Germantown, TN
Inactive foundation

Feed the World, Inc.
Chicago, IL
Current information not available

Feit Foundation, Inc., Elaine & Larry
Armonk, NY
Inactive foundation

FELCO Foundation
Franklin, VT
The foundation has not paid grants in the last three fiscal years, 1999-2001

Feldman Foundation, Inc., Milton & Sally, The
Cincinnati, OH
The foundation terminated in 2000

Ferguson Family Foundation, Kittie and Rugeley
San Antonio, TX
The foundation terminated on Nov. 30, 2001

Ferland Family Trust, Alphage & Roseanna
Pawtucket, RI
Current information not available

Ferrell Foundation, The
Greenwich, CT
The foundation terminated in 2001

Fibreboard Foundation
Toledo, OH
The foundation terminated on Nov. 19, 2001

Field Memorial Trust, Alva J.
Williston, ND
The trust has not awarded loans in the last three fiscal years, 1999-2001

Fillman Foundation, The
Sacramento, CA
The foundation has not given grants in the last three fiscal years, 1999-2001

Finger Trust for Kidney Failure Treatment, Ruth Oliver
New Paltz, NY
The trust terminated in 1999

Fink Foundation
Aspen, CO
The foundation terminated in 2001

Finkelson Charitable Foundation, Allen and Susan, The
New York, NY
The foundation terminated in 2001

Finkelstein Foundation, Joseph M.
Providence, RI
The foundation terminated in 2001

First Dallas Charitable Corporation
Dallas, TX
Inactive foundation

First Milwaukee Foundation, Inc.
See Firstar Foundation, Inc.

Firstar Foundation, Inc.
(Formerly First Milwaukee Foundation, Inc.)
Cincinnati, OH
The foundation terminated due to a merge with the U.S. Bancorp Foundation, Inc

Fischbein-Merritt Foundation
Short Hills, NJ
The foundation terminated in 2001

Fishback Foundation, Inc., Charles J. Fishback and Kathryn C.
La Jolla, CA
The foundation terminated in Dec. 2000

Fisher Family Foundation
(Formerly Fisher Foundation)
Portland, ME
The foundation terminated in 2001

Fisher Foundation
See Fisher Family Foundation

Fisher Foundation, Inc., Herbert & Rosalind
New York, NY
The foundation terminated on Dec. 31, 2001

Fisher Foundation, Jeffrey S. and Margaret G.
Kenilworth, IL
The foundation terminated in 2001

Fisher Fund, The
Napa, CA
The foundation terminated on May 31, 2001

Fleet Charitable Trust of New York
(Formerly Norstar Bank of Upstate NY Foundation)
Providence, RI
The trust terminated in 2001

Fleissner Family Foundation, James and Kathleen
Omaha, NE
The foundation terminated on Dec. 31, 2001

Fleming Charitable Trust, Mrs. Thomas J.
See Theodora Lynch Fleming Charitable Trust

Fleming Charitable Trust, Theodora Lynch
(also known as Mrs. Thomas J. Fleming Charitable Trust)
La Jolla, CA
The trust terminated on Dec. 31, 2001

Fletcher Foundation, Ed & Mary
San Diego, CA
The foundation terminated in 2002

Florangel Foundation, Inc.
Denver, CO
The foundation terminated on Sept. 30, 2001

Florida Steel Corporation Foundation
See AmeriSteel Foundation, Inc.

Florin Foundation, Walter & Esther
Brooklyn, NY
The foundation terminated on Dec. 31, 2001

Florsheim Group, Inc.
See Florsheim Shoe Foundation, Inc.

Florsheim Shoe Foundation, Inc.
(Formerly Florsheim Group, Inc.)
Chicago, IL
The foundation terminated in 2002

Flower and Garden Foundation
(Formerly John & Clara Tillotson Flower and Garden Trust)
Overland Park, KS
The foundation terminated in 2000

Flynn Family Foundation, Inc., The
Silver Spring, MD
The foundation terminated in Dec. 2001

Foote, Cone & Belding Foundation
See True North Communications Foundation

Foothealth Foundation of America
Bethesda, MD
Non-grantmaker

Forbes Trust, Fannie E.
Providence, RI
The fund has not awarded loans in the last three fiscal years, 1999-2001

Forman Family Charitable Passthrough Trust
New York, NY
The trust terminated in 2001

Forst Memorial Fund, Don and Helen
Milwaukee, WI
The foundation terminated in 2001

Fortescue Graduate Scholarship Fund, Charles Le Geyt
Pittsburgh, PA
The foundation has not paid grants in the last three fiscal years, 1999-2001

Foster Trust, Solomon
Pittsburgh, PA
The trust terminated in June, 2001 and transferred its assets to Hebrew Union College/Jewish Institute of Religion

Fotinos Charitable Trust, Vasilia S.
Manasquan, NJ
The trust has not paid grants in the last three fiscal years 1998-2000

Foundation for a Constitutional United States
West Bend, WI
Inactive foundation

Foundation for Afghan Hound Rescue and Rehabilitation, The
Snohomish, WA
Current information not available

Foundation for Emergency Medical Research, The
Phoenix, AZ
The foundation terminated in 2001

Foundation for Ethnic Understanding
New York, NY
The foundation terminated in 2002

Foundation for Genealogical and Historical Research
Clarkston, MI
The foundation terminated on June 30, 2001

Foundation for Human Understanding
Marietta, GA
The foundation terminated in 2001

Foundation for Medical Education Research & Care, Inc.
Yonkers, NY
The foundation terminated in 2000

Foundation of the Law Firm of Fabyanske, Svoboda, Westra, Davis & Hart, P.A., The
Minneapolis, MN
The foundation terminated in Dec. 2000

Foundation of the Law Firm of Knutson, Flynn, Hetland, Deans, & Olsen, P.A., The
Mendota Heights, MN
The foundation terminated in 2000

Fox Scholarship Trust, Fred C.
Tiffin, OH
The foundation terminated in 2001

Foxglen Institute, Ltd., The
Potomac, MD
The foundation terminated in 2000

Frable Foundation, Mary Ann Frable and William Jackson, The
Richmond, VA
Current information not available

APPENDIX A

Frank Foundation, Harold L. & Ruth F., The
(Formerly Jerome J. & Harold L. Frank Foundation)
Bloomfield Hills, MI
The foundation terminated in 2001

Frank Foundation, Jerome J. & Harold L.
See The Harold L. & Ruth F. Frank Foundation

Frank Foundation, Inc., Ruth & Walter, The
New York, NY
The foundation terminated on June 30, 2001

Franke Scholarship Fund, Amelia
(Formerly Jacob & Amelia Franke Scholarship Trust)
Safety Harbor, FL
The trust has not paid grants in the last three fiscal years 1997-1999

Franke Scholarship Trust, Jacob & Amelia
See Amelia Franke Scholarship Fund

Frazee Charitable Trust
Rockford, IL
The foundation terminated in 2001

Frease Foundation, Donald W.
Columbus, OH
The foundation terminated in 2001

Fredricksen Foundation, The
Mechanicsburg, PA
The foundation terminated in 2002

Free Africa Foundation, Inc., The
Washington, DC
The foundation terminated in 2000

Freedman Family Foundation, Inc., The
Charlotteville, NY
The foundation terminated in 2001

Freeman Charitable Foundation, Artgrace
Chicago, IL
The foundation terminated in 2001

Fresno Farm Bureau A.L.F.A. Scholarship Fund
Fresno, CA
The fund terminated on Dec. 31, 2000

Frey Trust, Rosemary Dwyer
Portland, OR
The trust terminated in Dec. 2001

Fricke & John E. Nolan Scholarship Trust, Henry A.
Alliance, NE
The foundation terminated in 2000

Friedman Foundation
Mountainside, NJ
The foundation terminated in 1999

Friends of Antigua, Inc.
Rye, NY
The foundation terminated in 2001

Friends of Chilean Catholic Education
Washington, DC
The foundation terminated in 2002

Friends of Holmes County
Muscoda, WI
The foundation terminated in 2000

Fruehauf Foundation, R. H.
Gaylord, MI
Current information not available

FSR Foundation
Cincinnati, OH
The foundation terminated in 2001

Fubini Foundation, Sylvia, The
Chevy Chase, MD
The foundation terminated in 2001

Fuller Foundation, Glenwood A.
Hershey, PA
The foundation terminated on Oct. 28, 2001

Fund for Corporate Initiatives, Inc., The
Albany, NY
The fund terminated on Oct. 31, 2001

Gabilan Foundation, The
Oakland, CA
The foundation terminated in 2002

Gaichas Family Foundation, The
Palos Park, IL
The foundation terminated in 2001

Gallagher Family Foundation
Corte Madera, CA
The foundation terminated in Dec. 2001

Galland Foundation for Establishing Fellowships & Scholarships
(Formerly Julius Galland Scholarship Fund)
Seattle, WA
Current information not available

Galland Scholarship Fund, Julius
See Galland Foundation for Establishing Fellowships & Scholarships

Gallon Foundation, Jack
Toledo, OH
The foundation terminated in 2001

Galston Foundation, Inc., The
Sarasota, FL
The foundation terminated in 2001

Gamble Trust, Joe B.
Amarillo, TX
The trust terminated in 2000

Gambol Charitable Trust
Mentor, OH
Inactive trust

Gannett Foundation, Guy P.
Portland, ME
The foundation terminated in 2001

Gargiulo Foundation, James & Marietta
Amsterdam, NY
The foundation terminated in 2002

Garrett Foundation, Inc., Gavin R.
Lampasas, TX
Current Information not available

Gathering for Zion
Provo, UT
Inactive foundation

Gaylord Foundation, Inc.
Chicago, IL
The foundation terminated in 2001

Geetter Charitable Fund, Inc., Philip H. and Helene R.
Sellersville, PA
The foundation terminated on Dec. 31, 2000

Geigel Scholarship Fund, Albert
Rockford, IL
The fund terminated in 1999

Gendler Memorial Scholarship Foundation, Marilyn F.
Omaha, NE
The foundation terminated in 2002

Genesis Program, Inc.
Fremont, MI
Current information not available

Geneva Foundation, The
Grand Rapids, MI
The foundation terminated in 2001

German Memorial Band Scholarship Charitable Trust, Amy Elizabeth
Vass, NC
The foundation terminated on Dec. 31, 2001

Gerot Foundation, The
Minneapolis, MN
The foundation terminated in 2001

Gianni Foundation I, Albert, The
Culver City, CA
The foundation terminated in 2001

Gibbons Foundation, The
Old Greenwich, CT
The foundation terminated in 2000

Gietner Foundation, Inc., Carrie Elligson
St. Louis, MO
The foundation terminated in 2001

Giles Trust, Clarence L.
Baltimore, MD
The trust terminated in 2001

Gillette Charitable and Educational Foundation, The
New York, NY
The foundation has not paid grants in the last three fiscal years, 1999-2001

Gilliam Memorial Fund, Robert and Emma
Cleveland, OH
The fund terminated in 2001

Gilman Paper Company Foundation, Inc.
New York, NY
The foundation terminated in 2002

Girard-diCarlo Foundation, Constance B. and David F., The
Villanova, PA
Inactive foundation

Glassman Memorial Trust, Audrey Lavine
Washington, DC
The trust has terminted in 2001

Glickman Foundation, Inc., Aaron & Freda
Douglaston, NY
Current information not available

Global Education Research Foundation
West Des Moines, IA
The foundation terminated on Feb. 29, 2000

Glueck Memorial Scholarship Fund, Blanche
Fair Lawn, NJ
Current information not available

Goedert Foundation, The
River Forest, IL
The foundation terminated on Aug. 31, 2001

Gokey for Chair of Catholic Theology Trust Fund, Inc., Father Francis X.
Colchester, VT
The fund terminated in 2002 and transferred its assets to Vermont Catholic Charities

Gold Star Memorial Scholarship Fund
Palo Alto, CA
Current information not available

Goldbach Foundation, Ltd., Ray & Marie
Marathon, WI
The foundation terminated in 1998

Golden Nugget Scholarship Fund, Inc.
Las Vegas, NV
The fund terminated in 2001

Goldman Foundation
West Orange, NJ
The foundation terminated in 2000

Goldman Foundation, Leonard and Patricia
Phoenix, AZ
The foundation terminated on Sept. 31, 2001

Goldmann Foundation, Harold Reich
West Trenton, NJ
Non-grantmaking operating foundation

Goldsmith Foundation, William & Minnette
Westerville, OH
The foundation has become a supporting organization of the Stark Community Foundation

Goldsmith Trust, Estelle Stember
Oneonta, NY
The trust terminated on June 30, 2001

Goldstein Charitable Trust, Lillie
Oakland Gardens, NY
The foundation terminated in 2001

Gonzalez Foundation, Faye Dobbs
Chicago, IL
The foundation terminated in 2002

Good News Foundation
Sea Island, GA
The foundation terminated in 2000

Good Shepherd Foundation
Lexington, KY
Current information not available

Gooding Charitable Trust, Fitzpatrick
Lodi, CA
The foundation terminated in 1999

Goodman Foundation, David L.
Chicago, IL
The foundation terminated in 1999

Gordon Benevolent Memorial Fund, Ruth W.
Cleveland, OH
The foundation terminated on Dec. 31, 2000

Gordon Family Foundation, Edward and Marion
Denver, CO
The foundation terminated in 2001

Goth Foundation, Elisabeth M., The
Lebanon, KY
The foundation terminated in 2001

Goyal Foundation
Morton Grove, IL
The foundation terminated in 2001

GPU Foundation
Morristown, NJ
The foundation merged into the FirstEnergy Foundation in 2001

Grace Charities
Holland, MI
The foundation terminated in 2001

Graham Foundation, Fred A. & Nannie O.
Kokomo, IN
The foundation has not awarded loans in the last three fiscal years, 1998-2000

Grass Valley Group, Inc. Scholarship Foundation
Beaverton, OR
The foundation terminated in 2000

Graves Fund Trust, Charles B.
Providence, RI
The fund terminated Nov. 7, 2001

Gray Charitable Foundation, George H.
Kansas City, KS
The foundation terminated in 1999

Great Commission, Inc.
Herkimer, NY
The foundation has not paid grants in the last three fiscal years, 1997-1999

Green Educational Foundation
Cleveland, OH
The foundation terminated in 2001

Green Foundation, J. Z.
Lexington, NC
The foundation terminated in 2001

Greenblatt Foundation, Inc.
Potomac, MD
The foundation terminated in 2002

Greenwald Foundation, Ltd., Raymond J., The
New York, NY
The foundation has not paid grants in the last three fiscal years, 1999-2001

Gregory Foundation
Vermilion, OH
Current information not available

Gregson Foundation
Providence, RI
The foundation terminated in 2002

Greyhound Park Foundation of Pensacola, Inc.
Pensacola, FL
The foundation terminated in 1998

Griffin Foundation, Inc.
London, KY
The foundation terminated on Mar. 31, 1999

Griffin, Sr. Foundation, Inc., C. V.
Winter Park, FL
The foundation terminated in 2002

Grigg Trust f/b/o Morgan County Hospital, E. N.
Denver, CO
The foundation terminated in 2001

Grigg Trust f/b/o Rankin Presbyterian Church, E. N.
Denver, CO
The foundation terminated in 2001

Gross Family Foundation
Old Greenwich, CT
The foundation terminated in 1998

Gross Foundation, Ben & Renee
Brooklyn, NY
The foundation terminated in 2001

Gross Fund for Research, Jonathan
Merrick, NY
Current information not available

Grossman Foundation, Joseph C.
Sydney,
Foreign foundation

Guardian Life Welfare Trust, The
New York, NY
The trust terminated in 2001

Guarnieri Charitable Foundation, Joseph J. and Andrea M., The
Boston, MA
Current information not available

Guidice Memorial Foundation, Vinny, The
Stony Point, NY
The foundation has not paid grants in the last three fiscal years, 1998-2000

Gulf of Maine Foundation
Damariscotta, ME
Current information not available

Gumenick Foundation, Nathan and Sophia
Miami Beach, FL
The foundation terminated in 2001

Gunnell Scholarship Fund, W. Leslie & Edna M.
South Bend, IN
The fund terminated on Apr. 30, 2001

Guthrie Charitable Trust, William N. and Kathryn L.
Winnetka, IL
The trust terminated on June 30, 2002

Guttenberg Foundation, The
Tenafly, NJ
The foundation terminated on Sept. 10, 1999

Gwinnett Gymnastics Booster Club, Inc.
Duluth, GA
The foundation has not paid grants in the last three fiscal years, 1999-2001

H & J Foundation
Victorville, CA
The foundation terminated in 2000

Hadley Charitable Foundation, Albert L., The
Fairfield, CT
The foundation terminated in 1998

Hale Trust, Anna C.
St. Louis, MO
The foundation terminated in 2000

Hall Trust, Myron B. & Dora A.
Tampa, FL
The foundation terminated in 2001

Hall-Seipel Memorial Scholarship Fund
(Formerly Hall Seipel Memorial Scholarship Trust)
Palmer, MA
The fund terminated on July 1, 1999

Hamilton Bank Foundation, Inc.
Miami, FL
The foundation terminated on May 31, 2002

Hamilton Foundation
Avon, CO
The foundation terminated in 1999

Hamilton Foundation, Florence P.
Kansas City, MO
Current information not available

Hammett Fund, Dashiell, The
Tappan, NY
Inactive foundation

Hancock Foundation, Luke B., The
Palo Alto, CA
The foundation terminated on Apr. 30, 2001

Harbeck Trust f/b/o Harbeck Mausoleum, Woodlawn Cemetery et al., Kate A.
Rochester, NY
The trust terminated on Dec. 31, 2000

Harbor Linen Healthcare Foundation
Gibbsboro, NJ
Inactive foundation

Harlow Foundation, Inc.
Lake Forest, IL
The foundation has not paid grants in the last three fiscal years, 1999-2001

Harpending Housing, Inc.
Penn Yan, NY
The foundation terminated on Dec. 31, 2000

Harris Foundation, Mary V.
Loma Linda, CA
The foundation terminated in May 2001

Harris Trust, Elizabeth M.
Parkersburg, WV
The trust terminated on Dec. 31, 1999

Hart Foundation, Thelma B. & Thomas P.
Reno, NV
Inactive foundation

Harte-Hanks Foundation
(Formerly Harte-Hanks Media Development Foundation)
San Antonio, TX
Inactive foundation

Harte-Hanks Media Development Foundation
See Harte-Hanks Foundation

APPENDIX A

Hartman Trust, Joseph Hartman and Abraham, Louis and Samuel
Haverhill, MA
The trust terminated on Dec. 31, 1999

Hartmann Foundation
Peoria, IL
Inactive foundation

Hartwig Foundation
Chicago, IL
The foundation terminated in 2001

Harvest Foundation Charitable Trust
Battle Ground, WA
The trust terminated on May 31, 2001

Hasenauer Family Foundation, Inc.
Wallace, NE
The foundation terminated in 2001

Haskell Trust, Robert N.
Bangor, ME
The foundation terminated in 2001

Hassenfeld Foundation, Inc., Rita & Harold
Palm Beach, FL
The foundation terminated in 2001

Hatch Fund, Martin F.
Ithaca, NY
The fund terminated in 2001

Hayes Foundation
Boston, MA
The foundation terminated in 2001

Hazen Foundation, Joseph H.
See Hazen Polsky Foundation

Hazen Polsky Foundation
(Formerly Joseph H. Hazen Foundation)
New York, NY
The foundation terminated in 2001

Healy Family Foundation, Inc., M. A., The
Santa Fe, NM
The foundation terminated in 2002

Hearthstone Foundation, The
Rochester, NY
The foundation terminated in 2001

Hebrew Benevolent Loan Association
Buffalo, NY
Inactive foundation

Heilig-Meyers Foundation
Richmond, VA
The foundation terminated in 2002

Heimple Charitable Foundation, Inc.
La Jolla, CA
The foundation terminated in 2001

Hendrick Foundation, Rick and Linda
Charlotte, NC
Inactive foundation

Heritage Education Foundation, Inc.
Indianapolis, IN
The foundation terminated on Dec. 31, 2001

Hewitt Foundation, The
Virginia Beach, VA
The foundation terminated in 2001

Heyman Family Foundation, Inc., George H. Heyman, Jr. & Edythe F.
New York, NY
The foundation terminated in 2002

Hickman Trust, Leona M.
Portland, OR
The foundation has not paid grants in the last three fiscal years, 1999-2001

Higgins Charitable Trust, Lorene Sails
Portland, OR
The foundation terminated in 2000

Hiles II Foundation, Donald B.
Grosse Pointe Farms, MI
The foundation terminated in 2001

Hilgert Foundation, Hans W.
Saddle Brook, NJ
Inactive foundation

Hills Trust, Leonard D.
New Salem, MA
The trust terminated in 2001

Hilltop Church
Pahrump, NV
The foundation has not paid grants in the last three fiscal years, 1998-2000

Hindman-Lockhart Foundation, Inc., The
Towson, MD
Current information not available

Hindmarsh Foundation, John and Hannah
Bedford, VA
The foundation terminated in 2001

HMK Tennis Foundation, Inc.
Waltham, MA
The foundation terminated in Dec. 2000

Hobbs Foundation
Waco, TX
Current information not available

Hodgkins Family Fund, Inc., The
Birmingham, MI
The foundation terminated in 2001

Hodgson Family Foundation
Palo Alto, CA
The foundation terminated in Aug. 2001

Hodgson Memorial Foundation, Inc., James & Elizabeth
Montgomery, AL
The foundation terminated in 2001

Hoefle Memorial Foundation, Inc., Frank B.
Haworth, NJ
The foundation terminated on Sept. 30, 2001

Hoff Osteoporosis Foundation, Syd & Dora
Chicago, IL
The foundation terminated on May 17, 2001

Hoffman Roth Trust, The
(also known as Reflections)
Miami Beach, FL
The trust terminated in 2001

Hogan Family Foundation
Scarsdale, NY
The foundation terminated in 2002

Hollingsworth Trust, John T.
Hemlock, IN
The foundation terminated in 2000

Holmes Foundation, Inc.
Miami Springs, FL
Current information not available

Honoka'a Museum Foundation
Irvine, CA
Inactive; the foundation has not paid grants in four years (1998-2001)

Horne Family Charitable Trust
Wheeling, WV
The foundation terminated in 1999

Horst Foundation, The
Seattle, WA
The foundation terminated in July 2001

Hosser Trust f/b/o Manchester Masonic Temple Association, Otillie Wagner
Providence, RI
The trust terminated on May 3, 2001

Hough Foundation, Inc.
Oklahoma City, OK
The foundation terminated in 2001

Hovannisian Charitable Foundation, Kasper and Siroon
Fresno, CA
The foundation terminated in 2001

Hsu Memorial Foundation, John Dehsaar
Cypress, CA
The foundation terminated in 2000

Hubbard Charitable Foundation, Robert P.
Walpole, NH
The foundation terminated in 2001

Huber Trust, Naomi E.
Erie, PA
The trust terminated in 2001

Hudson Memorial Scholarship Fund, Helen Fox
Midland, TX
The foundation terminated on Sept. 13, 2001

Human-i-Tees Foundation, Inc., The
Pleasantville, NY
Inactive foundation

Humanists of Utah Foundation
Salt Lake City, UT
The foundation terminated in 2000

Hummel-Dosmann Education Fund, Lydia Rose
Milwaukee, WI
Current information not available

Hundred Club of Vicksburg, The
Vicksburg, MS
The foundation has not paid grants in the last three fiscal years, 1999-2001

Hunt Foundation, William O. & Jeannette P.
Chicago, IL
The foundation terminated in 2001

Hunter Family Foundation
Lincoln, NE
The foundation terminated in 2001

Huntington Township Chamber Foundation
Huntington, NY
The foundation terminated in 2002

Hurdus 1992 Charitable Trust, Syde
Rockville Centre, NY
Inactive trust. The trust has not paid grants in the last three fiscal years, 1999-2001

Hurley & Arthur E. Lathrop, Jr. Memorial Fund, Nancy J.
Bristol, RI
The fund terminated on May, 24, 2001

Hurley No. 2 Trust, F. E.
Cleveland, OH
The trust terminated in 2000

Hutchinson Foundation, Elizabeth McCann
Fairless Hills, PA
The foundation terminated in 2002

Hutchinson Foundation, Henrietta Hardtner
Alexandria, LA
The foundation terminated in 2001

Hutson Trust, Walter A. and Edith P.
Wooster, AR
The trust terminated in 2001

Hydro Foundation, The
Longboat Key, FL
The foundation terminated on Nov. 30, 2000

APPENDIX A

I Have a Dream Foundation of Springfield, Massachusetts, Inc.
Springfield, MA
Current information not available

IAAF
See International Adoption Assistance Foundation, Inc.

ICC Corp.
See Inter-Church Council Services Corporation

Igoe Foundation, Inc., Charlotte D.
West Palm Beach, FL
The foundation terminated in 2001

Illinois Friends for St. Coletta-Wisconsin
Rolling Meadows, IL
Current information not available

Independent Director Foundation
Detroit, MI
The foundation terminated in 1999

Indian Point Foundation, Inc., The
New York, NY
The foundation terminated in 2001

Indiana Builders Charitable Foundation, Inc.
Indianapolis, IN
The foundation terminated in 2002

Ingham County Medical & Scientific Trust
East Lansing, MI
The trust terminated in 2002

Ingram Foundation, The
Greenville, SC
The foundation terminated in 2002

Inland Container Corporation Foundation, Inc.
See Inland Foundation, Inc.

Inland Foundation, Inc.
(Formerly Inland Container Corporation Foundation, Inc.)
Indianapolis, IN
The foundation terminated in 2002

Institute for Gravitational Strain Pathology, Inc.
New York, NY
The institute has terminated and transferred its assets to the Kirksville College of Medicine

Institute for Urological Research, Inc., The
Nashville, TN
The foundation terminated on Sept. 30, 2001

Inter-Church Council Services Corporation
(also known as ICC Corp.)
New Bedford, MA
Inactive foundation

Inter-Religious Friendship Group
San Francisco, CA
The foundation terminated in 2001

Interlingua Institute
New York, NY
The foundation terminated on Mar. 31, 2001

International Adoption Assistance Foundation, Inc.
(also known as IAAF)
Mobile, AL
Current information not available

International Immuno-Biology Research Laboratory, Inc.
San Diego, CA
The foundation terminated in 2001

International Paperweight Society Foundation
Santa Cruz, CA
The foundation has not paid grants in the last three fiscal years, 1999-2001

International University Endowment Foundation
Topeka, KS
The foundation terminated in 2002

International Vision Volunteers
(Formerly Doctors for World Vision)
Antioch, CA

IRB Foundation
Madison, WI
The foundation terminated in 2001

Isaak Piano Foundation, Inc., Donald J., The
Chappaqua, NY
The foundation terminated on July 31, 2001

Islamic Educational Council, The
West Chester, OH
Current information not available

Ivey Charitable Trust, Robert W. Ivey & Emma Jane
Dallas, TX
The foundation terminated on May 15, 2002

J & J Foundation, Inc.
Hurst, TX
Current information not available

J.A.T. Foundation
Brooklyn, NY
Inactive foundation

J.S.S. Foundation
Bellevue, WA
Current information not available

Jacarlene Foundation, Inc.
Tampa, FL
The foundation terminated in 2000 and transferred its assets to the Jacarlene Foundation

Jackson Memorial Nursing Scholarship Foundation, Helene Kemper
Jefferson City, MO
Current information not available

Jackson Memorial Trust Fund, Dr. J. M.
Lawrenceburg, IN
Inactive trust

Jackson Trust, Phillip
Providence, RI
The fund terminated on Jan. 31, 2002

Jacobs Family Foundation, George
Manhasset, NY
Current information not available

Jacobson Foundation, Inc., Alvin
Peekskill, NY
Inactive foundation

Jadel Foundation, The
Wilmette, IL
The foundation terminated in Dec. 2001

J&MH Trust, The
Lake Forest, IL
Current information not available

Janowski Scholarship Trust, Leo M.
Munich, ND
The trust terminated in 2001

Janus Foundation, The
See The Haskell F. Norman Foundation

Japan-Louisiana Friendship Foundation
New Orleans, LA
Current information not available

Jarman Corporation, Roy & Eva
Salt Lake City, UT
The foundation terminated on May 15, 2002

JC Foundation, Inc., The
Decatur, GA
Inactive foundation

JDR 3rd Fund, Inc., The
See The JDR 3rd/BHR Fund, Inc.

JDR 3rd/BHR Fund, Inc., The
(Formerly The JDR 3rd Fund, Inc.)
New York, NY
The foundation terminated in 1999

Jeffords Charitable Trust, Jim
Rutland, VT
Inactive foundation

Jelleff Trust No. 3, Margaret Gollan
Baltimore, MD
The foundation terminated in 2000

Jenkins Family Fund, The
Winston-Salem, NC
The foundation terminated in 2000

Jenkins Foundation, William & Renee Lane
San Diego, CA
The foundation terminated Dec. 31, 2001

Jenks Foundation, Evelyn M.
Boston, MA
The foundation terminated in 2001

Jennings Foundation, Jack
Carmel, IN
Current information not available

Jensen Memorial Foundation, Jon Philip
San Francisco, CA
Current information not available

Jesus Christ is Lord and Savior Ministries, Inc.
Lake Mary, FL
The foundation terminated in 2000

Jewell Educational Scholarship Trust
Neenah, WI
The fund terminated in 1999

Jewish Senior Center
Costa Mesa, CA
The foundation terminated in 1998

JLD Charitable Trust
(Formerly D'Anna Charitable Trust)
Germantown, TN
The trust terminated in 2000

Jodik Foundation, Inc., The
Unionville, CT
The foundation terminated in 2002

Johansen Foundation, Inc.
Whitefish, MT
Current information not available

Johnson Charitable Trust, Amos L.
Idabel, OK
Current information not available

Johnson Foundation, Inc., The
Boise, ID
Current information not available

Johnson Foundation, Robert Sydney Johnson & Sharon Lee, The
Paradise Valley, AZ
Inactive foundation

Johnson Memorial Scholarship Award, Rebecca
Lake Jackson, TX
The foundation terminated in 2001

Johnson Scholarship Fund, Susan Patrizio
Downingtown, PA
Current information not available

Johnson, Sr. Foundation, Inc., Oscar W.
Sand Springs, OK
The foundation terminated in 1998 and transferred its assets to the Community Foundation for Greater New Haven

APPENDIX A

Johnston Trust for Religious Education Fund Trust, Susie O.
(Formerly Religious Education Fund Trust)
Marion, VA
The trust has not paid loans in the last three fiscal years, 1998-2000

Jomar Foundation
New Hope, PA
The foundation terminated in 2002

Jones Family Foundation, Inc.
La Porte, IN
The foundation terminated in 2001

Jones Foundation, Inc., Jack M.
Thomasville, GA
The foundation terminated in 2001

Jonsson Foundation, The
Dallas, TX
The foundation terminated in 2001

Jordan Foundation
Aitkin, MN
Inactive foundation

Jordan Foundation, Inc., Kenn
Fort Lauderdale, FL
The foundation terminated on June 15, 2001

Jordan Furniture Family Foundation
Avon, MA
The trust terminated in 2001

Joseph Foundation, John and Suzanne
Anaheim, CA
Current information not available

JTBC Foundation, The
Hackensack, NJ
The foundation terminated in 2000

K-E Foundation, Inc.
San Francisco, CA
The foundation terminated on Sept. 10, 2001

Kahn Foundation, Inc., The
Atlanta, GA
The foundation terminated in 2002

Kaleidoscope Foundation, Inc.
Broken Arrow, OK
The foundation terminated in 2001

Kallish Foundation, Inc., Louis
Scarborough, NY
The foundation terminated in 2002

Kamlet Foundation, Inc., Jonas
Sarasota, FL
The foundation terminated on October 31, 2001

Kanarek Memorial Foundation, Adele
New York, NY
The foundation terminated on September 30, 2001

Kanza Foundation
West Palm Beach, FL
The foundation terminated on Dec. 31, 2000

Kapell Piano Foundation for Contemporary Music & Musicians, William
Los Angeles, CA
The foundation has not paid grants in the last three fiscal years, 1999-2001

Kaplan Memorial Foundation, Inc., Jay L.
Englewood Cliffs, NJ
Current information not available

Karberg Trust, Arnold W.
Milwaukee, WI
The trust terminated in 2002

Karger Fund, Robert S. & Jean F.
Glencoe, IL
The fund terminated in 2002

Kasper Educational Trust
Orlando, FL
The foundation terminated in 2001

Kassab Foundation, J. G. & Helen
McMurry, PA
The foundation terminated in 2001

Katz Family Foundation, Inc.
Chapel Hill, NC
Current information not available

Kaylor Charitable Trust
Uniontown, OH
The foundation terminated in 1998

Kearney, Inc. Foundation, A.T.
Chicago, IL
The foundation terminated in 2002

Keasey Foundation, Martha Clark, The
Corvallis, OR
The foundation terminated in 2001

Keelty Foundation, Inc., The
Timonium, MD
The foundation terminated in 2001

Keith Foundation, The
Bristol, TN
The foundation terminated on Dec. 31, 2000 and transferred its assets to King College

Kelley Foundation, James F.
Lawrenceville, NJ
The foundation terminated in 2000

Kellstadt Foundation, The
Chicago, IL
The foundation terminated in 2001

Kemper Charitable Lead Trust, William T.
Kansas City, MO
The trust terminated in 2001

Kenan, Jr. Charitable Trust, William R.
Chapel Hill, NC
Non-foundation

Kensington Academy Foundation, Inc.
Beverly Hills, MI
The foundation terminated in 2001

Keough Foundation, Sarah F. and Florence K.
Stamford, CT
Current information not available

Kern Foundation, Ilma
Pound Ridge, NY
The foundation terminated in 2001

Keyes Family Foundation, Robert E. and Anita V.
Prescott, AZ
The foundation terminated on June 30, 2001

Keyes Trust, Jones Bass
Abilene, TX
The trust terminated in 2001

KGR Foundation
Grosse Pointe, MI
Current information not available

KHD Foundation
Des Moines, IA
The foundation terminated on Jan. 31, 1999

Kids Care Foundation of Hernando County, Inc.
Spring Hill, FL
Inactive foundation

King Scholarship Foundation, Inc., Lela & Jesse
Seminole, FL
The foundation terminated in 1999

Kirkpatrick, Pettis, Smith, Polian Charitable Foundation, Inc.
Omaha, NE
The foundation terminated in 2001

Kirschenbaum Foundation, Inc., Irving
White Plains, NY
The foundation terminated in 2001

Kjell Family Charitable Foundation, Inc.
Beloit, WI
The foundation terminated in 2002

Klecan Charitable Trust, Julian
New York, NY
The foundation terminated in 2001

Klein Foundation, Inc., Roger
New York, NY
The foundation terminated on Nov. 30, 2001

Klemstine Foundation, G. William
Pittsburgh, PA
The foundation has not paid grants in the last three fiscal years, 1999-2001

Kline Foundation, Inc., Jaeson H.
St. Louis Park, MN
The foundation terminated in 1998

Knapp Charitable Trust
Providence, RI
The trust terminated on Mar. 31, 2001

Knapp Scholarship Trust, Caroline M.
San Antonio, TX
The foundation terminated in 2001

Knox Scholarship Trust, George & Mary
Ventura, CA
The foundation terminated in 2001

Koch Charitable Trust, Ferdinand
St. Louis, MO
The foundation terminated in 1999

Kochert Memorial Scholarship Fund, Jack
West Lafayette, IN
The foundation terminated in 1999

Koegel Foundation, Inc., David I., The
Harrison, NY
The foundation terminated in 2001

Koen Trust, Searcy G.
Jacksonville, FL
The trust terminated on Aug. 31, 2002

Koll Family Foundation, The
Newport Beach, CA
The foundation terminated on Sept. 13, 1999

Koontz Trust, Patrick D.
Milwaukee, WI
Inactive foundation. The foundation has not paid grants in the last three fiscal years, 1999-2001

Krasnow Arts Foundation, Peter
Los Angeles, CA
The foundation terminated in 2001

Krock Bank Museum, Inc., Aaron
Worcester, MA
The foundation has not paid grants in the last three fiscal years, 1999-2001

Kuntz Charitable Trust
Tiburon, CA
Inactive foundation

Kunzelman Charitable Trust, The
Grand Junction, CO
Current information not available

Kurisu & Fergus Foundation, The
See The Kurisu Foundation

Kurisu Foundation, The
(Formerly The Kurisu & Fergus Foundation)
Honolulu, HI
The foundation terminated in 2002

APPENDIX A

Kurtzon Family Foundation, Lawrence & Karen
Evanston, IL
Current information not available

L.W. Charitable Trust
New York, NY
The trust terminated in 2001

La Due-Moos Foundation
Austin, TX
Current infomation not available

LaCava Foundation, Inc., The
Waltham, MA
Inactive foundation

Lakenan Trust, Estelle M.
San Francisco, CA
Current information not available

Lakian Foundation, Inc.
Boston, MA
Current information not available

Lamar Foundation, James
Walla Walla, WA
The foundation terminated on Apr. 30, 2001

Lancaster County Council of Churches Foundation
Lancaster, PA
The foundation terminated in 2001

Landau Family Foundation, The
Brooklyn, NY
The foundation has not paid grants in the last three fiscal years, 1998-2000

Landers Business Education Scholarship Trust, Gretchen
Syracuse, NY
Current information not available

Landers Irrevocable Trust, Elbert T. Landers & Lillie P.
Shelbyville, TN
The trust terminated on Jan. 31, 2002

Landmark Wakeman Foundation Charitable Trust
New York, NY
The trust has not paid grants in the last three fiscal years, 1999-2000

Lane Foundation, The
Altavista, VA
The foundation terminated in 2002

Laney Memorial Trust Fund, David Dewayne
Chattanooga, TN
Current information not available

Lansburgh Charitable Foundation, Inc., Sidney & Marian
Linthicum, MD
The foundation terminated in 2001

Lappin Family Foundation, The
New York, NY
The foundation terminated in May 2001

Large Charitable Trust, The
Stow, OH
Current information not available

LaRose Scholarship Memorial Fund, Norman O.
Providence, RI
The fund terminated in 2001

Larrabee Fund Trust
Hartford, CT
The trust terminated in 1999

Larson Family Supporting Organization
Bellevue, WA
The organization terminated in 1999

Larson-Weber Memorial Scholarship Fund
Thompson Falls, MT
The fund terminated in 2000

Latimer Charitable Trust, Bill and Gail
Union City, TN
The trust terminated in 2001

Latshaw Student Loan Trust, Fred D. & Louise I.
Milwaukee, WI
The trust has not awarded loans for the last three fiscal years, 1999-2001

Lauer Fund, Inc., Edith, The
Towson, MD
The fund terminated on Jan. 31, 2002

Laurel Hill Foundation
Stamford, CT
Inactive Foundation

Lawrence Foundation, Inc., Robert J. & Frances Y., The
Chevy Chase, MD
The foundation terminated in 2001

Lawrenceburg Community Theater
Lawrenceburg, TN
Current information not available

LCM Charitable Trust
Lemont, IL
Current information not available

Leach Park District Trust
Joliet, IL
The trust terminated in 2000

Leadership Foundation, Inc.
Denver, CO
The foundation terminated in 1998

League of Slovenian Americans, Inc.
Astoria, NY
The foundation has not paid grants in the last three fiscal years, 1999-2001

Lear Charitable Foundation, Bill and Moya
Reno, NV
The foundation terminated in 2001

Leehan Trust No. 2 f/b/o Roman Catholic Church, Ruth O.
Phoenix, AZ
The trust terminated on May 31, 1999

Lemberg Scholarship Loan Fund, Inc., Samuel
New York, NY
The fund has not awarded loans in the last three fiscal years, 1997-1999

Lenfest Foundation, The
(Formerly The H. F. Lenfest Foundation)
West Conshohocken, PA
The foundation terminated in 2001

Lenfest Foundation, H. F., The
See The Lenfest Foundation

Leshner Family Foundation, Robert and Carol
Cincinnati, OH
The foundation terminated in 2001

Lesser Foundation, Inc., India Benton
Macon, GA
The foundation terminated in 1999

Lester Charitable Trust
Germantown, TN
The trust terminated in 2000

Levin Foundation, Edward M.
Washington, DC
The foundation terminated in 2001

Levine Charitable Trust, Samuel Birnkrant, The
New York, NY
The trust terminated in 2000

Leviton Foundation, Bertha Drabkin Goodwin, The
New Haven, CT
Foreign foundation

Liberty Foundation
Phoenix, AZ
The foundation terminated on July 31, 2000

Liberty Foundation, Inc.
Oklahoma City, OK
The foundation terminated in Dec. 2000

Liberty Preservation & Development Commission, Inc.
Liberty, MO
The foundation has not paid grants in the last three fiscal years, 1999-2001

Liberty Towers Incorporated of Clarion
Clarion, PA
The foundation terminated in 2002

Librett Foundation, Inc., Charles & Clara
New York, NY
The foundation terminated in 2001

Liebowitz Foundation, Inc., J. S.
New York, NY
The foundation terminated in 2001

Lighthouse Foundation
Azle, TX
Inactive foundation

Lindsay Trust, Susan M.
Denver, CO
The foundation terminated in 2001

Linwood Charitable Trust
Columbia, MO
The trust has not paid grants in the last three fiscal years, 1998-2000

Lipman Foundation
Chicago, IL
The foundation terminated in 2001

Lippoldt Trust, Arthur H.
Oklahoma City, OK
The trust terminated on July 31, 1999

Lips Family Charitable Foundation, Inc.
Hartford, CT
The foundation terminated in 2001

Litchfield Awards Association, Paul W.
Akron, OH
The foundation terminated on June 30, 2001

Live Oak Gardens Foundation, Inc.
St. Helena Island, SC
The foundation terminated in 2001

Lloyd Charitable Corporation
Milwaukee, WI
The foundation terminated in 2000

Local Development Corporation of the Town of Union
Endwell, NY
The foundation has not paid grants in the last three fiscal years, 1998-2000

Loftin Trust for Charity
Reno, NV
The foundation terminated in 2002

Lonesome Dove
(Formerly Broken Wing Ministries)
Montrose, CO
Inactive foundation

Long Charitable Foundation, Walter H.
Newport Beach, CA
Current information not available

Looney Foundation
Edinburg, TX
The foundation terminated in 2001

Lorch-Loeb Family Charitable Trust, The
New York, NY
Inactive trust

APPENDIX A

Lowe Foundation, Inc., The
Cassopolis, MI
The foundation terminated on June 30, 2001

Lowell Opera Company, Inc.
Lowell, MA
Inactive foundation

Lowy Charitable Foundation, John and Barbara
New York, NY
The foundation has not paid grants in the last three fiscal years, 1998-2000

LTV Foundation, The
See The LTV Foundation Charitable and Educational Trust

LTV Foundation Charitable and Educational Trust, The
(Formerly The LTV Foundation)
Cleveland, OH
The foundation terminated in 2002

Lucas Foundation, Inc., The
Los Angeles, CA
The foundation terminated in 2000

Luerssen Foundation, Frank W. & Joan S.
Munster, IN
The foundation terminated in 2001

Luke Foundation, Dr. K. F., The
Orland Hills, IL
The foundation has not paid grants in the last three fiscal years, 1999-2001

Lutin Charitable Trusts, Michael
San Diego, CA
Current information not available

Lyman Charitable Trust, Mildred K.
Dallas, TX
The trust has not paid grants in the last three fiscal years, 1999-2001

Lyman Trust f/b/o Charities, Frances
Providence, RI
The Trust terminated on Dec. 2001

Lynch Family Foundation
Valley, NE
Inactive; the foundation has not made grants in three years (1998-2000)

M.A.R.K. Foundation, The
Tucson, AZ
The foundation terminated in 2001

M.C. Scholarship Foundation
New Haven, CT
The foundation terminated in 2001

MacBride Trust f/b/o University of Washington, Frances W.
Portland, OR
The trust terminated in 2001

MacFadden Dental Trust, Zaida J.
Wolfeboro, NH
Current information not available

Machamer Family Foundation, Inc., John Quincy, The
Orlando, FL
Current information not available

MacIntyre Charitable Trust, Alexander C.
Miami, FL
The trust terminated in 2001

Mack Family Foundation, Inc., David & Sondra, The
Rochelle Park, NJ
Inactive foundation

MacKids Foundation, Inc., The
Signal Hill, CA
Current information not available

Magnolia Foundation, The
Valley, AL
The foundation terminated in 2001

Magnolia Improvements, Inc.
Matewan, WV
Current information not available

Mahaffey Charitable Foundation, Inc., The
Melvin, AL
The foundation terminated on Sept. 30, 2001

Maharam Foundation, Inc., Joseph
Pompano Beach, FL
The foundation terminated in 2001

Mahoney Memorial Foundation, John P. Mahoney and James F.
Boston, MA
The foundation terminated on May 31, 1999

Maioriello Charitable Trust, Angelina Del Rossi, The
Bowie, MD
The trust terminated on Dec. 31, 1998

Malamud Family Foundation, Jack
Boca Raton, FL
The foundation terminated in 2001

Malpais Foundation, The
Springerville, AZ
Current information not available

MAM Foundation, Inc.
New York, NY
The foundation terminated in 2002

Mandel Foundation, Benjamin
Brooklyn, NY
Current information not available

Manx Foundation
Columbus, OH
Current information not available

Mapco Foundation, The
Tulsa, OK
The foundation terminated on Feb. 14, 2000

Maranatha Foundation for Missions & Evangelism
Cincinnati, OH
The foundation terminated in 2000

Mariah Foundation
(Formerly Outside Evergreen Foundation)
Santa Fe, NM
Inactive; the foundation has not made grants in four years (1998-2001)

Marinbach Foundation, Samuel & Bertha
New York, NY
Current information not available

Marine Foundation, Inc., The
See Banc One, Wisconsin Foundation, Inc.

Mark Foundation, Inc., William B.
Wausau, WI
The foundation terminated in 2001

Marquez Foundation, Inc., Sandra Erben, The
Warwick, NY
The foundation terminated in 2000

Marshall Foundation, Paul W. and Lilah B.
Tulsa, OK
Current information not available

Martel Foundation, Inc., Marian & Speros
Houston, TX
The foundation has terminated

Martens Charitable Foundation, Inc., Donald M.
Green Bay, WI
The foundation terminated in 2001

Martin Charitable Trust, The
Olympia, WA
Current information not available

Martin Foundation, James F.
Edgefield, SC
Current information not available

Marx Foundation
Aspen, CO
The foundation terminated in 2000

Marx Fund, Melville
San Francisco, CA
The fund terminated in 2001

Masonic Home for the Aged
Milwaukee, WI
The foundation terminated in 2002

Massa Scholarship Foundation, Lucille and Jimmy
Pampa, TX
Current information not available

Masserman Memorial Foundation, Jules and Christine, The
Washington, DC
Current information not available

Matthiesen Memorial Scholarship Fund, Inc., Krista
Mexico, MO
The fund terminated in 2001

Mautz Paint Foundation
Madison, WI
The foundation terminated in 2002

May Foundation Trust, The
Brooklyn, NY
Current information not available

Mayer Trust, Hazel Mae
Milwaukee, WI
The trust has terminated in 2001

Mazak Charitable Trust
Cuyahoga Falls, OH
Inactive foundation

Mazoh Foundation, The
Rhinebeck, NY
Inactive foundation

McAleer Charitable Foundation, The
Mobile, AL
Current information not available

McBain Foundation, Robert J.
Grand Rapids, MI
The foundation has not paid grants in the last three fiscal years, 1999-2001

McBride Memorial Charitable Trust Fund, Dr. William
Indianapolis, IN
The fund terminated in 1999

McCain Charitable Trust
See Lydia F. McCain Charitable Trust

McCain Charitable Trust, Lydia F.
(Formerly McCain Charitable Trust)
Richmond, VA
The foundation terminated in 2001

McCain Foundation, Inc.
Erie, PA
The foundation terminated in 2001

McCaskill Foundation, Robert A.
Belvedere, CA
The foundation terminated in 2001

McCaslin Family Foundation
Pasadena, CA
Current information not available

McCormick Foundation, Inc., William, The
See The William and Mary McCormick Foundation, Inc.

McCormick Foundation, Inc., William and Mary, The
(Formerly The William McCormick Foundation, Inc.)
College Park, MD
Current information not available

APPENDIX A

McDaniel Charitable Trust
Jackson, MS
Current information not available

McDonnell Charitable Corporation
St. Clair Shores, MI
The foundation terminated in 1999

McDorman Foundation, Meggin Kate
Dallas, TX
Current information not available

McDowell Foundation, H. C. and Beulah
Horseshoe Bay, TX
The foundation has not paid grants in the last three fiscal years, 1999-2001

McDuffie Family Foundation, Inc.
Sumter, SC
The foundation terminated in 2001

McFarland Early Americana Charitable Trust, H. Richard, The
Covington, IN
The foundation has not paid grants in the last three fiscal years, 1998-2000

McFarland Foundation
St. Louis Park, MN
The foundation terminated in 2001

McGinty Family Foundation, Denton E. and Patricia J.
Naples, FL
Inactive foundation

McGovern Foundation, Inc., The
Boston, MA
Inactive foundation

McGuire Foundation, Carl W.
Boulder, CO
Current information not available

McKee Fund, Joel & Daisie
Youngstown, OH
The fund merged with the Hoyt Foundation

McKenzie Memorial Foundation, Inc., Peter F.
Michigan, ND
The foundation terminated on June 28, 2001 and transferred its assets to North Dakota State University

McKinney Foundation, Richard W.
Nacogdoches, TX
Current information not available

McMillen Foundation, Inc., G. G.
Plymouth, IN
The foundation terminated in 2002

McMullan Charitable Trust, Constance
New York, NY
The trust terminated in 2002

McWhirter Charitable Foundation
Milton-Freewater, OR
The foundation terminated in 2001

Medical Education Institute, Inc.
Madison, WI
Inactive; the foundation has not made grants in four years (1998-2001)

Melnitsky Family Foundation
Cliffside Park, NJ
The foundation terminated in 2002

Melrose-Gwinner School District Scholarship Fund, Lester
Afton, MN
The foundation terminated in 2001

Melton Foundation, Samuel Mendel
Columbus, OH
The foundation terminated in 2001

Memorial Scholarship Foundation of the Indiana Alpha Chapter of Phi Kappa Psi
Indianapolis, IN
The foundation terminated in 2001

Men Against Breast Cancer, Inc.
(Formerly The Marcia Tishman Cancer Foundation)
Sunrise, FL
The foundation terminated in 2001

Mendik Foundation, The
New York, NY
The foundation has not paid grants in the last three fiscal years, 1999-2001

Mercantile Community Development Corporation
St. Louis, MO
Current information not available

Merrick Auto Museum
Alda, NE
Current information not available

Merrill Foundation, K. C.
Palm Desert, CA
The foundation has not paid grants in the last three fiscal years, 1998-2000

Messengers of Our Lady of Soufanieh, The
Tracy, CA
Inactive foundation

Messinger Trust, Charles A.
Providence, RI
The trust terminated on March 31, 2002

Metcalf Foundation, Arthur G. B.
Boston, MA
The foundation terminated in 2001

Metro Foundation for New Americans
Arlington, VA
The foundation terminated on Jan. 15, 2002

Metzenbaum Foundation, Bessie Benner
Cleveland, OH
The foundation terminated in 2002

Midwest Region Educational Foundation Association
Lake St. Louis, MO
The foundation terminated in 2002

Milbro Charitable Foundation
Lincolnshire, IL
The foundation terminated in 1999

Milford Educational Foundation
Milford, NH
The foundation has not awarded loans in the last three fiscal years, 1998-2000

Milford Hospital Fund, Inc.
Milford, CT
The foundation terminated in 2002

Miller Charitable Fund, Laura H.
(Formerly Laura H. Miller Trust)
Cleveland, OH
The fund has not paid grants in the last three fiscal years, 1998-2000

Miller Foundation, Inc., D.
Houston, TX
Current information not available

Miller Foundation, Dr. H. A.
Clovis, NM
The foundation has not awarded loans in the last three fiscal years, 1998-2000

Miller Foundation, I. L. and Bertha Gordon
Houston, TX
The foundation terminated in 2001

Miller Foundation, Jack & Colleen, The
Tustin, CA
The foundation terminated in 2000

Miller Trust, Laura H.
See Laura H. Miller Charitable Fund

Miller/Pollack Foundation
See Pollock/Gorden Foundation

Mills Charitable Foundation, Donna
Sherman Oaks, CA
The foundation terminated in 2002

Mills Youth Foundation, Chris
Beverly Hills, CA
The foundation terminated on Aug. 19, 2001

Milo Foundation, Amos & Edith
Palm Beach, FL
Current information not available

Minton Foundation, The
Columbia, TN
Current information not available

Mishaan Family Foundation, Inc.
New York, NY
Inactive foundation

Missions Charitable Trust
Roy, WA
Current information not available

Mitnick Fund, Louis
Providence, RI
The foundation terminated in 2002

Mitsakopoulos Foundation, The
Skokie, IL
The foundation terminated in 2001

Modesto Branch AAUW Scholarship/Grants Fund
Modesto, CA
The foundation terminated June 30, 2001

Moehle Foundation
Washington, IL
The foundation is inactive

Moen Foundation
(Formerly Stanadyne Foundation)
Park Ridge, IL
The foundation terminated in 2000

Monahan Billings Foundation, Majorie
Washington, DC
The foundation terminated in 2000

Monitto Memorial Foundation, Inc., Joseph, The
See The Joseph & Helen Monitto Memorial Foundation, Inc.

Monitto Memorial Foundation, Inc., Joseph & Helen, The
(Formerly The Joseph Monitto Memorial Foundation, Inc.)
Amityville, NY
The foundation terminated in 2002

Monroe Religious & Educational Institute Foundation, Inc., Irene C.
Webster City, IA
The foundation terminated in 1998

Montag Family Charitable Trust, The
Atlanta, GA
The trust terminated on March 31, 2001

Monteith Family Foundation, The
Cuyahoga Falls, OH
The foundation terminated in 2001

Moore Family Foundation, The
Jasper, GA
The foundation has not paid grants in the last three fiscal years, 1999-2001

Moore Family Foundation, Sam and Peggy, The
Nashville, TN
Inactive foundation

APPENDIX A

Morgan Evangelistic Association Trust, Jimmy
Fort Worth, TX
The trust terminated in 2001 and transferred its assets to the Mary I. Gourley Scholarship Foundation

Moritz Foundation
Arlington, TX
The foundation has not paid grants in the last three fiscal years, 1999-2001

Morton Arboretum
Lisle, IL
The foundation terminated in 2002

Morton No. 1 Trust, Richard A.
Williston, VT
Current information not available

Moses Foundation, Beverley and R. D., The
Fort Worth, TX
Current information not available

Moss Charitable Trust, Louis H.
Atlanta, GA
The trust terminated in 2001

Moss Foundation, Albert & Rosemond A.
Mercer Island, WA
Current information not available

Mossner Foundation, Alfred
River Forest, IL
The foundation terminated in 2001

Mount Aloysius Foundation, Inc.
Columbus, OH
The foundation terminated in 2000

Mountain Flight Park, Inc.
Macon, GA
The foundation has not paid grants in the last three fiscal years, 1999-2001

Mountainmovers, Inc.
Burlington, NJ
The foundation has not paid grants in the last three fiscal years, 1998-2000

Moyer Foundation
Vacaville, CA
The foundation has not paid grants in the last three fiscal years, 1998-2000

MP3.com Foundation
San Diego, CA
Inactive foundation

Muhich Charitable Trust, J., The
Austin, TX
Current information not available

Mukherji Family Foundation, The
Brentwood, TN
Current information not available

Mullarkey Foundation, Thomas & Theresa, The
New York, NY
The foundation terminated on June 30, 2001

Mullet Foundation, Inc., The
Pensacola, FL
The foundation terminated in 2001

Mumford Family Foundation, Inc., The
Moline, IL
The foundation merged into the Mumford Family Foundation, Inc., on Jan. 4, 2001

Mumford Foundation, Edwin
See Alliance Foundation

Murdock Foundation, Victor
Wichita, KS
The foundation terminated in 2000

Murdough Foundation, Charlie, The
Chicago, IL
The foundation terminated in 2000

Murphy Foundation, Daniel M.
Chicago, IL
The foundation terminated in 2002

Murray Charitable Fund, Ronald
Pittsburgh, PA
The fund terminated in 2000

Murray Foundation
Austin, TX
The foundation terminated in 1999

Murrell Foundation, Turner Meadows
Topeka, KS
The foundation terminated in 2001

Musco Charitable Foundation
Oskaloosa, IA
Inactive foundation

Musikantow Family Foundation, The
Chicago, IL
The foundation terminated in 2001

Musselman Foundation, Emma G.
Charlotte, NC
The foundation terminated on June 30, 2001

Myers Scholarship Fund, Clyda Alive & Robert Henry
Muncie, IN
The fund terminated in 2001

Myerson Foundation, Bess, The
New York, NY
The foundation terminated in 2000

Mylander Foundation, The
Cleveland, OH
The foundation terminated in 2001

Nadel Scholarships for Disabled Persons, Inc., Roslyn, The
Trenton, NJ
Current information not available

Nahum Trust, Clarence & Wilma Dow
See The Nahum Trust Fund

Nahum Trust Fund, The
(also known as Clarence & Wilma Dow Nahum Trust)
Cleveland, OH
The fund terminated in 2001

Naish Foundation
Berkeley, CA
The foundation terminated in Sept. 2001

National Association of Midnight Basketball Leagues, Inc.
Oakland, CA
Current information not available

National City Bank Foundation
Minneapolis, MN
The foundation has terminated

National City Corporation Charitable Foundation
See NCC Charitable Foundation

National Health Education Committee, Inc.
New York, NY
Inactive foundation

National Parent's Day Foundation
Falls Church, VA
Current information not available

National Spinning Foundation
New York, NY
Inactive foundation

National Travelers Life Company Charitable Trust
West Des Moines, IA
The trust terminated in Jan. 2002

NBD Bank Charitable Trust
See Bank One Michigan Charitable Trust

NCC Charitable Foundation
(Formerly National City Corporation Charitable Foundation)
Cleveland, OH
The foundation terminated in 2001

New Avenues for Youth, Inc.
(Formerly Northwest Foundation For Children)
Portland, OR
The foundation terminated in 2002

New Braunfels Conservation Society Foundation Trust
New Braunfels, TX
Feeder trust

New Century Energies Foundation
Denver, CO
The foundation merged into the Xcel Energy Foundation in 2002

New Deal Foundation, Inc.
Cambridge, MA
Current inforamation not available

Newell Rubbermaid Scholarship Fund, The
(Formerly James R. Caldwell Scholarship Fund)
Chicago, IL
The foundation terminated in 2001

Newington-Cropsey Foundation
New York, NY
Current information not available

Newman Foundation, George W. & Amy
South Hackensack, NJ
The foundation terminated in 2000

Newman Tzadaka Foundation, Esther
Brooklyn, NY
Inactive foundation

Nicklaus Museum, Inc., Jack
North Palm Beach, FL
The foundation terminated in 2002

Nierenberg Foundation, Edith, The
San Diego, CA
Current information not available

1912 Charitable Foundation, The
Bluefield, WV
The foundation has not paid grants in the last three fiscal years, 1998-2000

NJAFE Foundation, Inc.
Union, NJ
Current information not available

Nordenberg Family Foundation
Glencoe, IL
The foundation terminated in 2001

Nordhaus Memorial Scholarship Fund, Jeffrey
Los Angeles, CA
Current information not available

Norman Foundation, Haskell F., The
(Formerly The Janus Foundation)
Ross, CA
The foundation terminated in 2001

Norman/Nethercutt Foundation, Merle
Sylmar, CA
The foundation terminated in Dec. 2001

Norris Memorial Foundation, Nick
Marshalltown, IA
Current information not available

Norstar Bank of Upstate NY Foundation
See Fleet Charitable Trust of New York

North American Plastics Philanthropic Foundation
See John S. Chew Foundation

North Carolina Coalition Against Sexual Assault
Raleigh, NC
The foundation terminated in 2002

APPENDIX A

North Carolina Educational, Historic and Scientific Foundation, Inc.
See Albert Schweitzer International, Prizes, Inc.

North Pond Foundation, The
Wilmington, DE
The foundation has not paid grants in the last three fiscal years, 1999-2001

Northwest Foundation For Children
See New Avenues for Youth, Inc.

Norton Foundation, William
Bedminster, NJ
The foundation terminated in 2001

O'Brien Memorial Foundation, Inc., Cassandra Lee
Atlanta, GA
The foundation terminated in 1999

O'Neil Foundation, The
New York, NY
Current information not available

Ocean UCP Housing, Inc.
Ocean, NJ
The foundation terminated in 2002

Oden Foundation, Sydnor and Olga, The
Houston, TX
The foundation has not paid grants in the last three fiscal years, 1998-2000

Odessa Trading Company Educational Trust
Ritzville, WA
Inactive foundation

Odom Foundation, Inc., Jane Lowe, The
Charlotte, NC
The foundation terminated in 2001

Oehler Memorial Foundation, Samuel P.
Sparta, WI
Current information not available

Oglesby Scholarship Fund, Inc., Tim
Palm Desert, CA
The fund terminated in 2001

Ohl, Jr. Infantile Paralysis Foundation, George A.
Charlotte, NC
The foundation terminated on Feb. 28, 2002

Oliver Trust, Andrew
Boston, MA
Inactive

Olson Memorial Education Association, Morten L. & Helen E.
Starbuck, MN
The foundation terminated in 1999

Omnibus Charitable Trust, The
New York, NY
The trust terminated on Nov. 30, 2000

Oosterbaan Memorial Fund, Christopher S.
Munster, IN
Current information not available

Open Gate Ranch
Trout Creek, MT
Current information not available

Open Meadows Foundation, Inc.
Brooklyn, NY
Current information not available

Oppenheimer Brothers Foundation
Beverly Hills, CA
The foundation terminated in 2001

Option Care Foundation, Inc.
Bannockburn, IL
The foundation has not paid grants in the last three fiscal years, 1998-2000

Orchid Foundation, The
Grand Rapids, MI
Current information not available

Orleans Conservation Trust
East Orleans, MA
Non-grantmaker

Ormet Foundation
Hannibal, OH
Inactive foundation

Ossabaw Island Foundation, Inc., The
Savannah, GA
The foundation terminated in 2002

Othmer Foundation, Donald F. & Mildred Topp
New York, NY
The foundation terminated in 2000

Outside Evergreen Foundation
See Mariah Foundation

Oxbow Charitable Trust, The
Newbury, VT
The trust terminated in Dec. 2001

Oxford Health Plans Foundation, Inc.
Trumbull, CT
The foundation terminated in 1999

P & N Charitable Foundation Trust
Lincoln, NE
Inactive foundation

Pace Foundation, Randolph K. & Judith
New York, NY
The foundation terminated in 2001

Pace Willson Foundation
San Antonio, TX
The foundation terminated in 2001

Pacific Veterans Association/Atlantis Foundation
Sacramento, CA
Current information not available

Pacifica International Foundation
Issaquah, WA
The foundation terminated in 2000

Pack Foundation, The
Tucson, AZ
The foundation terminated in 2002

Packard Hay Creek Foundation
Pinckney, MI
Inactive foundation

Paddock Scholarship Trust, E. A.
Portland, OR
Current information not available

Padnos Foundation, Louis & Helen
Holland, MI
The foundation terminated in 1999

Padonia Foundation, Inc., The
Timonium, MD
The foundation terminated in 1999

Painter Charitable Trust, Juliana, The
Boston, MA
The foundation terminated in 2001

Palmer Charitable Trust
Anderson, IN
Inactive foundation

Paracelsus Foundation, Ltd.
Incline Village, NV
Current information not available

Parsons Community Association, Inc.
Parsons, WV
The foundation has not awarded loans in the last three fiscal years, 1998-2000

Patel Memorial Scholarship Fund, Subhash
Troy, MI
The fund terminated in 2001

Pathway Ministries, Inc.
Santee, CA
Current information not available

Pathways to Peace Foundation
Lake San Marcos, CA
The foundation terminated in 2001

Patience Love Charitable Trust
Omaha, NE
The Trust terminated in 2000

Paul Private Foundation, Isabelle K., The
Boca Raton, FL
The foundation terminated on Mar. 30, 2001

Payne Charitable Trust
Natchitoches, LA
Inactive foundation

Penn Manor, Inc., William
Pasadena, CA
The foundation terminated in 2002

Pennington Foundation, Inc.
Madison, GA
The foundation has not paid grants in the last three fiscal years, 1998-2000

Pennsylvania Dental Association Health & Well-Being Foundation
Harrisburg, PA
The foundation terminated on Apr. 21, 2000

Pennsylvania Steel Foundry Foundation
Charlotte, NC
The foundation terminated in Dec. 2001

Pereira Ministries, Inc., Manuel
New Bedford, MA
Inactive foundation

Perkerson Educational Endowment Foundation
(Formerly Educational Endowment Foundation)
Decatur, GA
Foreign foundation

Perry Fund, Frances E.
Cleveland, OH
The fund has not paid grants in the last three fiscal years, 1998-2000

Persephone Foundation
Minneapolis, MN
The foundation terminated in 2001

Phelps Foundation, Hensel
Greeley, CO
The foundation terminated on May 31, 2001

Phoenix Foundation
Chapel Hill, NC
The foundation terminated in 2001

Phonetic Bible Printing Committee, Inc.
Glendale, CA
The foundation terminated in 2002

Pierce Trust f/b/o Plymouth Congregational Church, Maria L. H.
Providence, RI
The trust terminated on May 31, 2001

Pines Cancer & AIDS Research Institute Club 93, Torrey
San Diego, CA
The foundation terminated in 2000

Pipp Foundation
See Anna R. Pipp Foundation

APPENDIX A

Pipp Foundation, Anna R.
(also known as Pipp Foundation)
Kalamazoo, MI
The foundation terminated in 2001

Pitt-Des Moines, Inc. Charitable Trust
(Formerly Pittsburgh-Des Moines Steel Company Charitable Trust)
Pittsburgh, PA
The trust terminated in 2002

Pittsburgh-Des Moines Steel Company Charitable Trust
See Pitt-Des Moines, Inc. Charitable Trust

Pittway Corporation Charitable Foundation
Chicago, IL
The foundation terminated in 2002

Playground Association of Greater Ellsworth
Ellsworth, ME
The foundation terminated in 1999

Polacek Foundation, Inc., Martha & Pat
Chicago, IL
The foundation terminated in 2002

Pollock/Gorden Foundation
(Formerly Miller/Pollack Foundation)
Englewood, CO
The foundation terminated in 2000

Pond View Homes Housing Development Fund
Great Neck, NY
The fund has not paid grants in the last three fiscal years, 1998-2000

Pontikes Family Foundation, The
Rosemont, IL
The foundation terminated on Dec. 1, 2001

Poole & Kent Foundation, Inc., The
Baltimore, MD
The foundation terminated in 2000

Poole Foundation, Inc., Irene Rand
Raleigh, NC
The foundation merged into the Triangle Community Foundation in 2000

Porter Foundation, Inc., Emily Susan Perez, The
Syracuse, NY
The foundation terminated in 2000

Porter Testamentary Trust, James Hyde
Macon, GA
The trust terminated in 2001

PPH Cure Foundation, The
Washington, DC
The foundation terminated in 2001

Precious Moments Foundation
Carthage, MO
The trust terminated in 2001

Premier Industrial Foundation
Cleveland, OH
The foundation terminated in 2001

Preston Scholarship Fund, Willie Mae Preston & Colonel
Woodbury, TN
Inactive foundation

Prince Family Foundation, Inc.
Covington, GA
The foundation terminated in May 2002

Prince George's Community Foundation, Inc.
Capitol Heights, MD
Current information not available

Prince of Peace Foundation
Columbus, OH
The foundation merged into the Sketos Family Foundation

Princeton Foundation, The
Sterling, MA
The foundation terminated on June 30, 2001

Pritzker Cousins Foundation
Chicago, IL
The foundation terminated Dec. 31, 2002

Professional Photographers Education Foundation
Atlanta, GA
The foundation has not paid grants in the last three fiscal years, 1999-2001

Project 40
New York, NY
The foundation has not paid grants in the last three fiscal years, 1998-2000

Prussia Foundation, Leland S. and Vivian B., The
Alameda, CA
The foundation terminated in 2001

Pryne Foundation
Long Beach, CA
The foundation terminated in 2001

Psychiatric Disorders in America Research Fund
St. Louis, MO
The fund terminated on Dec. 31, 2001

Psyence Charitable Operating Trust
La Verne, CA
Inactive foundation

Public Art Fund, Inc.
New York, NY
The foundation terminated in 2002

Quaker Oats Foundation, The
Chicago, IL
Due to the merger of PepsiCo, Inc. and The Quaker Oats Co. on Aug. 2, 2001, the foundation has terminated

Quebecor Printing Scholarship Program
(Formerly Alco Gravure Education Fund, Inc.)
Boston, MA
Current information not available

Quietude Foundation, Ltd.
Weymouth, MA
Current information not available

Quintessential Corporation, The
Tarpon Springs, FL
The foundation terminated in 2001

Ralphs Foundation, Walter
Beverly Hills, CA
The foundation terminated on Dec. 31, 2001

Ramona's Mexican Food Products Scholarship Foundation
Gardena, CA
The foundation has not paid grants in the last three fiscal years, 1998-2000

Rascoe Foundation, Inc.
Atlanta, GA
Inactive foundation

Rat Pack Foundation and Educational Scholarship Fund, Inc.
Chicago, IL
The foundation terminated in 2001

Raymond Foundation, The
Westerville, OH
Current information not available

Raynor Charitable Trust
Chicago, IL
The trust terminated in 2001

Reach Out Houston
Houston, TX
The foundation terminated in 2001

Reber Charitable Trust
Aptos, CA
The trust terminated in 2001

Red Villa Memorial Scholarship Trust
St. Louis, MO
Current information not available

Redfield Foundation, James M.
Marshall, MI
The foundation terminated in 2002

Redig Foundation, Cleve A.
Tacoma, WA
The foundation terminated on Oct. 15, 2001

Reed Charitable Trust, Congressman John F.
Cranston, RI
The trust terminated in 2000

Reflections
See The Hoffman Roth Trust

Refugio Public Library Foundation, The
Victoria, TX
The foundation terminated in 2001

Rehard Trust Estate, Thomas L. & Edna M.
Chillicothe, MO
The trust terminated on August 31, 2001

Reiten Family Foundation
Portland, OR
The foundation terminated in 2001 and transferred its assets to the Oregon Community Foundation

Religious Education Fund Trust
See Susie O. Johnston Trust for Religious Education Fund Trust

Remote Sensing Research, Inc.
Fort Collins, CO
The foundation terminated in 2000

Renaissance Foundation, The
St. Charles, IL
Inactive foundation

Rendich Foundation, Richard A.
New York, NY
No current information available

Rentschler Foundation, Frederick & Pamela
Cave Creek, AZ
The foundation terminated on Dec. 12, 2000

Research Foundation for Jewish Immigration, Inc.
New York, NY
The foundation has not paid grants in the last three fiscal years, 1998-2000

Reuther Center for Education and Community Impact, Inc., Warren
Blissfield, MI
The foundation terminated in 2001

Reynolds Charitable Trust, Richard G.
Palm City, FL
The foundation terminated on Sept. 30, 2001

Reynolds Tobacco Company Foundation, R. J.
Winston-Salem, NC
The foundation has merged into the Nabisco Foundation

Rheinlander Memorial Scholarship Fund, Robert W.
Lawton, OK
The fund terminated in Nov. 30, 2001

Richardson County Bank & Trust Company Centennial Trust
Falls City, NE
The foundation terminated on Sept. 30, 2001

Ridgeview Foundation, Inc.
Newton, NC
The foundation terminated in Dec. 2000

APPENDIX A

Rigterink Foundation, The
Devon, PA
Inactive foundation. The foundation has not paid grants in the last three fiscal years, 1999-2001

Ringle Educational Trust, B. Franklin & Eleanore
Cleveland, OH
The trust terminated in 2001

RISCORP Foundation, Inc.
Sarasota, FL
Inactive foundation

Risley Foundation
Bruceville, IN
Current information not available

Roberts Foundation, Edward R. & Rosalind S.
New York, NY
The foundation terminated on Nov. 30, 2001

Roberts Trust f/b/o New Haven Symphony, Helen H.
(Formerly Helen H. Roberts Unitrust)
Providence, RI
Current information not available

Roberts Trust f/b/o Orphan Children of Chase City, William A.
Richmond, VA
Current information not available

Roberts Unitrust, Helen H.
See Helen H. Roberts Trust f/b/o New Haven Symphony

Robertson Charitable & Educational Trust
Seattle, WA
The trust terminated in 1999

Robertson Memorial Fund, Frank A.
Charlotte, NC
The foundation terminated in Sept. 2001

Robinson Charitable Trust, Stanley D. & Janet W.
New York, NY
The trust terminated in 1998

Robinson Family Foundation, Richard & Edward, The
Denver, CO
The foundation terminated in 2002

Robinson Foundation, Inc., Pearl, The
Purchase, NY
The foundation terminated in 2001

Robinson Irrevocable Charitable Living Trust, Thomas E. & Patricia
Troy, OH
Current information not available

Rockford Products Corporation Foundation
Rockford, IL
The foundation terminated in 2001

Rocky Mountain Health Care Corporation Foundation
See Blue Cross and Blue Shield of Colorado Foundation

Roe Foundation Charitable Trust
Valley, WA

Rogers Scholarship Fund, Inc., Buck
Lima, OH
Inactive foundation

Rohrich Foundation, Rod J., The
Dallas, TX
Inactive foundation

Rolfson Foundation
New Rockford, ND
The foundation terminated on Dec. 31, 2001

Roller Family Foundation
Novelty, OH
The foundation terminated in 2001

Romine Charitable Trust, Paul G., The
St. Petersburg, FL
Current information not available

Roney Foundation, Kirk V. and Melanie K.
Provo, UT
Inactive foundation

Rood Charitable Foundation, Roy S. & Patricia M., The
Jupiter, FL
The foundation terminated on Apr. 30, 2000

Rooker Foundation, George S., The
Dallas, TX
The foundation has not paid grants in the last three fiscal years, 1998-2000

Rose Foundation, Theodore & Mildred
Palm Beach, FL
Inactive foundation

Rosebud Society, Inc., The
La Jolla, CA
The foundation terminated in 2001

Rosenbaum Foundation, Inc., Solomon & Rose, The
San Diego, CA
The foundation terminated on April 30, 2001

Rosenberg Memorial Foundation, Harold S.
Chicago, IL
The foundation terminated in 2001

Rosenberger Foundation, William and Marcus
Hatfield, PA
The foundation terminated in 2001

Rosenbloom Fund, Inc., Carroll
Purchase, NY
The foundation terminated in 2002

Rosenwald Foundation, William and Mary, The
New York, NY
The foundation terminated on Apr. 30, 2001

Rosner Foundation, Benjamin F.
New York, NY
The foundation terminated on Sept. 30, 2001 and transferred its assets to the Point of View Foundation

Ross Foundation
See Sharing Is Caring Foundation

Ross Foundation, Alfred & Francis
Park City, UT
The foundation has not paid grants in the last three fiscal years, 1999-2001

Ross Foundation, Inc., Kenneth and Audrey
Milwaukee, WI

Ross Foundation of Charlotte
Charlotte, NC
The foundation terminated in 2001

Roth Family Charitable Foundation, Inc.
Indianapolis, IN
The foundation terminated in 2001

Rothermel Foundation
Wayne, PA
The foundation terminated Dec. 31, 1998

Rothkopf Foundation
New Rochelle, NY
The foundation terminated in 2001

Rozman Foundation, Inc., Louis
New York, NY
Current information not available

RTPHome
Cary, NC
The foundation terminated in 2001

Rubenstein-Frent Foundation
Scottsdale, AZ
The foundation terminated in 2001

Rubinstein Foundation, Inc., Martha G. and Max
Beverly, MA
Current information not available

Ruhl Memorial Foundation for the Blind, Inc., Lillian & Edward H.
Roslyn Heights, NY
The foundation terminated in 2001

Russian Chorus, Inc., The
New Haven, CT
Current information not available

Rutland Charitable Trust
Carlsbad, CA
The foundation terminated in 2002

S.T.E.P. Association
Seattle, WA
The foundation has not paid grants in the last three fiscal years, 1998-2000

Sacred Ground International
Pryor, MT
Inactive foundation

Safdieh Foundation, Inc., Eli & Esther
New York, NY
Current information not available

Sakakini Scholarship Foundation, Joseph, The
Norfolk, VA
Current information not available

Salado Community Service Center
Salado, TX
The foundation terminated in 2001

Salem Soccer, Inc.
Salem, MA
The foundation has not paid grants in the last three fiscal years, 1998-2000

Samaritan Foundation, The
(Formerly DeLapa Family Foundation)
Grand Rapids, MI
The foundation terminated in 2002

Samborn Family Foundation, Alfred H.
Toledo, OH
The foundation terminated in 2001

Sams Foundation, Inc., The
Coral Gables, FL
Current information not available

Samson Foundation, Inc., Harry E. & Rose
Mequon, WI
The foundation terminated in 2001

Samsons Foundation, Inc.
Kinston, NC
The foundation terminated in 1999

San Diego Wuhan Foundation
San Diego, CA
Inactive foundation

San Fernando Valley Association of Realtors
See Southland Regional Association of Realtors Foundation

San Francisco Salon, The
San Francisco, CA
The foundation terminated in 2001

Sanders California Foundation, Estelle, Abe, and Marjorie, The
San Francisco, CA
The foundation terminated on Feb. 28, 2002

Sanders Perpetual Trust, Daisy H.
Louisville, KY
The trust terminated on Apr. 30, 1999

Sasakawa Africa Association
Washington, DC
Foreign foundation, incorporated as a nonprofit in Geneva

APPENDIX A

Satinover Fund, Charles
Chicago, IL
The fund terminated in 1999

Saul Charitable Trust, Samuel & Esther
Pittsburgh, PA
Current information not available

Saulsbury Educational Fund, John M.
(also known as Melva S. Saulsbury Irevocable Trust)
Georgetown, DE
The foundation terminated on June 30, 2001

Saulsbury Irevocable Trust, Melva S.
See John M. Saulsbury Educational Fund

Savings Bank of Manchester Foundation, Inc.
Manchester, CT
The foundation merged into the SBM Charitable Foundation, Inc. in 2001

Savitt Foundation, Inc., Bill, The
See Savitt Foundation Incorporated

Savitt Foundation Incorporated
(Formerly The Bill Savitt Foundation, Inc.)
Atlanta, GA
The foundation terminated in 2001

Sbarboro Foundation, Ersilia & Alfred
San Francisco, CA
The foundation terminated in 2002

Schack Family Trust Fund, The
Everett, WA
The trust terminated in 2001

Schadde Building Trades Scholarship Trust, M. Arthur
Baraboo, WI
The foundation terminated in 1999

Schadde Home Arts Scholarship, M. Arthur
Baraboo, WI
The foundation terminated in 1999

Schell Foundation, Inc., Susan Hitzler
Melbourne, FL
The foundation terminated in 2001

Schmidt Family Charitable Trust
St. Louis, MO
The trust terminated on Dec. 31, 1998

Schmidt Trust, Arianna, The
Stamford, CT
The trust terminated in 2001

Schnadig Foundation, Lawrence & Dorothy
Des Plaines, IL
The foundation terminated in 2001

Schnitzer Charitable Trust, Morris
Portland, OR
The trust terminated in 2001

Scholze, Jr. Foundation, Virginia & George
Chattanooga, TN
The foundation terminated on June 30, 2001

Schoolcraft County Community Foundation
Manistique, MI
The foundation is an affiliate fund of the Peninsula Community Foundation

Schreck Memorial Educational Fund, Robert
Houston, TX
The fund terminated on Dec. 31, 2001

Schuster Foundation, Inc.
Duluth, GA
Current information not available

Schwartz Charitable Trust, Nathan & Ida
Boynton Beach, FL
Current information not available

Schwartz Family Foundation
Brooklyn, NY
Current information not available

Schwarz Charitable Foundation, Roberta N.
Greensburg, PA
Current information not available

Schweitzer International, Prizes, Inc., Albert
(Formerly North Carolina Educational, Historic and Scientific Foundation, Inc.)
Wilmington, NC
The foundation has not paid grants in the last three fiscal years, 1998-2000

SCI Charitable Foundation
Cedar Rapids, IA
The foundation terminated in 2002

Scibienski Foundation, T. S. & Virgie C.
Corpus Christi, TX
The foundation terminated in 2001

Scott Family Foundation, Inc.
Dedham, MA
The foundation terminated in 2001

Scott Memorial Trust, Evan
Denver, CO
The trust terminated in 2001

Scott-Norcostco Foundation
Minneapolis, MN
The foundation terminated on June 30, 1998

Scottsdale North Rotary Foundation
Scottsdale, AZ
The foundation terminated in 2001

Scout of the Year Foundation, Inc.
West Palm Beach, FL
Current information not available

Scudder Foundation, The
Estacada, OR
The foundation terminated in 2001

Seabury Trust, Hugh F.
Iowa City, IA
The trust terminated on June 30, 1999

Search America Foundation, The
Hong Kong,
Foreign Grantmaker

Seaton Foundation, Inc.
(Formerly Tangram Rehabilitation Foundation, Inc.)
San Marcos, TX
The foundation terminated in 2002

Seaton Memorial Scholarship Fund, David Dale, The
Muleshoe, TX
Current information not available

Seer Fund, The
Los Angeles, CA
The fund terminated in Dec. 2000

Sefton Foundation, Mimi Stone, The
Danville, CA
The foundation has not paid grants in the last three fiscal years, 1999-2001

Seipel Memorial Scholarship Trust, Hall
See Hall-Seipel Memorial Scholarship Fund

Seligman Family Charitable Foundation Trust
Clarksdale, MS
The trust terminated in 1998

Selley Foundation
New Orleans, LA
The foundation terminated in 2001

Sensory Research Foundation
Phoenix, AZ
The foundation terminated on Mar. 31, 1999

Seran Scholarship Foundation, Chester A. and Ethel J.
Cleveland, OH
The foundation terminated on Dec. 31, 2001

Serio Memorial Scholarship Fund, Inc., Kimberly
Ellicott City, MD
Current information not available

Service Merchandise Foundation, The
Nashville, TN
The foundation terminated in 2001

Seskis Foundation, Inc., The
Lodi, NJ
The foundation terminated in 2001

Shah Family Foundation, Mrugesh and Purna
Houston, TX
The foundation terminated in Nov. 2001

Shapira Charitable Trust, David S. and Karen A.
Pittsburgh, PA
The foundation terminated in 2001

Shapiro Foundation, The
Boston, MA
The foundation terminated in 2001

Share Foundation, Inc.
Cincinnati, OH
The foundation terminated in 2001

Shared Blessings Foundation, Inc.
Houston, TX
Current information not available

Sharing Is Caring Foundation
(Formerly Ross Foundation)
Savage, MN
The foundation terminated in 2001

Sharp Charitable Foundation
League City, TX
Current information not available

Shelby Foundation
Center, TX
Current information not available

Shersar Foundation, Inc., The
Aurora, IL
The foundation terminated in 2001

Shevchik Trust, Inc., Anna Kurylka
Mechanicville, NY
Current information not available

Shin Foundation for Medical Research and Betterment of Mankind
Bloomfield Hills, MI
The foundation terminated in 2001

Shulman Family Foundation, The
Nashville, TN
The foundation terminated on Dec. 31, 2000

Sicca Trust, Michele
New York, NY
Current information not available

Siddiqui Foundation, Inc., Habib
Fresh Meadows, NY
The foundation terminated on Sept. 30, 2001

Sikking Trust, Chester B. & Irene B.
Milwaukee, WI
The trust terminated on Dec. 31, 2001

Silver Foundation, Israel & Clara
Miami, FL
The foundation terminated in 2000

Silvers Foundation, Earl Reed
Boca Raton, FL
The foundation terminated in 2001

Silverstein Art Fund, Gary
New York, NY
Inactive foundation

Simonoff Peyser & Citron Foundation, Inc.
Los Angeles, CA
The foundation terminated in 2001

APPENDIX A

Singer Family Foundation, The
See The Ann H. and Benjamin Singer Foundation

Singer Foundation, Ann H. and Benjamin, The
(Formerly The Singer Family Foundation)
Hartford, CT
The foundation terminated in 2001

Singer Memorial Fund, Leigh J.
Monroe Township, NJ
The foundation has not paid grants in the last three fiscal years, 1997-1999

Sixteen-Forty-Nine Foundation
Fort Worth, TX
The foundation terminated in 2001

Skupien Foundation, Eugene S.
Chicago, IL
The foundation terminated in April, 2001

Smith Charitable Trust, Emerson Sterling, The
Ravenna, OH
Current information not available

Smith Foundation, B. F., The
Stoneville, MS
Inactive foundation

Smith Foundation, Inc., Edwin J. and Blanche K.
Waterport, NY
The foundation terminated in 2001

Smith Foundation, Inc., J. C.
Clinton, MO
The foundation terminated in 2001

Smith Foundation, James A. and Ann H.
Macon, GA
The foundation has not paid grants in the last three fiscal years, 1998-2000

Smith Foundation, Lillian S.
Columbia, SC
The foundation has not paid grants in the last three fiscal years, 1999-2001

Smith Foundation, Inc., Robert T.
Ogdensburg, NY
Current information not available

Smith Home, Washington and Jane
Chicago, IL
Current information not available

Smith Memorial Fund for Baptist Ministerial Students, Ella H.
Greer, SC
Current information not available

Smiy Family Foundation Trust
Irwin, PA
The foundation terminated in 2002

Smoljan Charitable Trust, The
Chicago, IL
Current information not available

Smothers, Sr. Memorial Foundation, J. E.
San Antonio, TX
The foundation terminated on Sept. 30, 2001

Snell Foundation, The
Arlington, VA
The foundation terminated in 2002

Snyder Educational Trust Fund, Jerry Thomas
Granite Falls, NC
The trust terminated in 1999

Snyder Foundation, Patricia H.
Evansville, IN
The foundation terminated in 2001

Snyder 1986 Charitable Trust, The
Cliffside Park, NJ
The foundation terminated in 2001

Sociological Research Foundation
Salt Lake City, UT
The foundation terminated on Dec. 31, 1998

Solid Tumor Oncology Educational Foundation, Inc.
Secaucus, NJ
The foundation terminated on Dec. 31, 2001

Solomon Foundation, Inc., Dana & Andrew, The
Houston, TX
The foundation terminated in 2001

Solomon Memorial Trust, Jerome D.
Chicago, IL
The trust terminated in 2000

Sons of Art, Inc.
Ross, CA
The foundation has not paid grants in the last three fiscal years, 1998-2000

Soos Family Foundation, Louis and Mary
Johnstown, PA
The foundation terminated on Dec. 31, 2000

Soros Humanitarian Foundation
New York, NY
The foundation has not paid grants in the last three fiscal years, 1998-2000

Southington Band Backers Club
Plantsville, CT
Non-grantmaker

Southland Regional Association of Realtors Foundation
(Formerly San Fernando Valley Association of Realtors)
Van Nuys, CA
The foundation terminated on Dec. 31, 2001

Southwest Allergy & Asthma Foundation
Corpus Christi, TX
Current information not available

Southwest Network of Youth Services, Inc.
Austin, TX
Nongrantmaker

Soviet Business and Commercial Law Education Foundation
New York, NY
The foundation terminated in 2000

Sowers Charitable Trust
Hoopeston, IL
The trust terminated on Dec.31, 2001

Spadoni Foundation, The
Greensboro, NC
Inactive foundation

Sparks State Bank Scholarship Fund
Sparks, MD
The foundation terminated in 2002

Spartanburg Lung & Chest Foundation, Inc.
Inman, SC
Current information not available

Speare Foundation, Inc., Sceva
Greenfield, NH
The foundation terminated in 2001

Sprecker Family Foundation, Isidore Israel and Sylvia M.
Boynton Beach, FL
Current information not available

Sprehe Charitable Foundation, Forrest D. and June L.
Carbondale, IL
Current information not available

Springate Corporation
New York, NY
The foundation terminated in 1999

Springbrook Foundation, Inc.
Newberg, OR
The foundation terminated in 2002

SSS Foundation, Inc.
St. Petersburg, FL
Inactive foundation. The foundation has not paid grants in the last three fiscal years, 1998-2000

St. Albans Parish Trust
Baltimore, MD
The trust terminated in 1999

St. JDC Charitable Fund
St. Joseph, MO
Inactive; the foundation has not made grants in the last 4 years (1997-2000)

St. Joseph's Helpers Foundation
Baton Rouge, LA
Current information not available

St. Louis Mercantile Library Association
St. Louis, MO
The foundation terminated in 2001

St. Mary's Academy Foundation
Portland, OR
Inactive foundation

St. Peter's Hospital Surgical Education Fund
Albany, NY
Current information not available

St. Thomas High School Alumni Association
Buffalo, NY
The foundation terminated on Nov. 31, 2000

Stacey Scholarship Fund, Nancy Earle
Saco, ME
The fund terminated in 2000

Stack Foundation, Malcolm
Madison, WI
The foundation terminated in Dec. 2001

Stadelmann Memorial Scholarship Fund, Arthur W. & Frances E.
Milwaukee, WI
The fund terminated on Aug. 31, 2001

Stahl Foundation
Dallas, TX
The foundation terminated in 2001

Stanadyne Foundation
See Moen Foundation

Standard Products Charitable Foundation
See Standard Products Company Charitable Foundation

Standard Products Company Charitable Foundation
(Formerly Standard Products Charitable Foundation)
Findlay, OH
The foundation terminated on Feb. 20, 2002

Stein Charitable Foundation Trust, Philip, The
Malverne, NY
The trust terminated in 2002

Steinig Family Foundation, The
Newton, MA
Current information not available

Stella's Kids Association
Rancho Santa Fe, CA
The trust terminated in 2001

Sterling Foundation, John G.
Richmond, IL
The foundation terminated in 2001

Stern Charities, Inc.
Penn Valley, PA
The foundation terminated in 2001

Sternbach Foundation, Ruth and Louis
New York, NY
Current information not available

Stetson Trust, Gladys M.
Bangor, ME
The foundation terminated in 2001

APPENDIX A

Stevick Family Foundation
Champaign, IL
The foundation terminated in 2001

Stewart Foundation, Edward F.
Tucson, AZ
Current information not available

Stewart Foundation, Helen H., The
Syracuse, NY
The foundation terminated in 2001

Stewart, Jr. Memorial Foundation, W. L.
Bell Gardens, CA
Current information not available

Stillman Memorial Fund, Inc., R. D.
Wareham, MA
Current information not available

Stine Memorial Foundation, Timothy M.
Lebanon, PA
The foundation terminated in 1999

Stockham Foundation, Inc., William H. and Kate F., The
Birmingham, AL
The foundation terminated in 2002

Stoesser Memorial Scholarship Fund, Inc., Peter William
Millburn, NJ
Current information not available

Stoller Foundation, Robert J.
Los Angeles, CA
Inactive foundation

Stonehill Foundation, Inc., Norma L. & Harold S.
Valley Stream, NY
Current information not available

Stotler Foundation, Inc., Howard A.
Lake Forest, IL
The foundation terminated in 2001

Stott Private Foundation, Peter W.
Portland, OR
The foundation terminated in 2001

Stowers Foundation
Kansas City, MO
Inactive; the foundation has not made grants in three years (1998-2000)

Straight Road
Cherry Valley, CA
The foundation has not paid grants in the last three fiscal years, 1998-2000

Strauss Foundation, Harry B.
Kansas City, MO
The foundation terminated in 2001

Strauss Foundation, Ltd., Lester F.
Springfield, MO
The foundation terminated in 1999

Stroh Foundation, The
Detroit, MI
The foundation has not paid grants in the last three fiscal years, 1998-2000

Sturm Charitable Trust, Donald L., The
Denver, CO
The foundation terminated in 2000

SuAsCo Watershed Association, Inc.
Carlisle, MA
Current information not available

Summers Foundation, Jean Bateson, The
La Canada, CA
The foundation terminated in 2002

Sunbelt Communications Education Foundation
Las Vegas, NV
The foundation was terminated in Dec. 2001

Sunderman Foundation, F. William
Philadelphia, PA
Current information not available

Sundstrand Corporation Foundation
Rockford, IL
The foundation terminated in Dec. 2000

Sunrise Enterprise Foundation
Grand Rapids, MI
Current information not available

Sunshine Charitable Trust, The
Santa Barbara, CA
The foundation terminated on Dec. 10, 2001

Surachi Charitable Trust, Henry & Janet
Philadelphia, PA
Current information not available

Susar, Inc.
Fort Lee, NJ
The foundation terminated in 2000

Suttons Bay Jazzfest, Inc.
Suttons Bay, MI
Current information not available

Sweeney Charitable Foundation, Joseph L.
Framingham, MA
Current information not available

Symkoviak Family Foundation
Sandy, UT
The foundation terminated in Dec., 2000

Syracuse Sesquicentennial Committee, Inc.
Syracuse, NY
The foundation terminated on Dec. 31, 1999

Sytner Foundation
Los Angeles, CA
The foundation terminated in 2000

Szopa Art Scholarship Fund, Sophie E., The
Lowell, MA
Current information not available

T.M.S. Foundation
Littleton, CO
The foundation terminated in 2001

Tab Foundation
Metropolis, IL
Current information not available

Taishoff Charitable Trust, Lawrence B.
Naples, FL
The trust terminated in 2000

Talbert Foundation, Thomas
See Arts Live Foundation

Talbot Twelve Foundation, The
Easton, MD
Current information not available

Talon Foundation
(Formerly Agley Family Foundation No. 1)
Detroit, MI
Inactive; the foundation has not made grants in three years (1998-2000)

Tangram Rehabilitation Foundation, Inc.
See Seaton Foundation, Inc.

Taplin Fund, Thomas E.
Cleveland, OH
The fund terminated in 2001

Tate Memorial Trust, Frank and Esther
Mattoon, IL
Current information not available

Tatum Trust, Robert E.
Dallas, TX
The foundation has not paid grants in the last three fiscal years, 1999-2001

Taylor Foundation for Children, C.
Newport, VT
The foundation terminated in 2001

Taylor Memorial Scholarship Fund, Edwin
Irvine, CA
The fund has not paid grants in the last three fiscal years, 1999-2001

TCB Bank Foundation, Inc.
(Formerly Tell City National Foundation, Inc.)
Tell City, IN
The foundation terminated in Dec. 2001

Teachers Foundation, Inc.
Seattle, WA
The foundation terminated in 2001

Team Redlands
Redlands, CA
Current information not available

Team 30
Arnold, MD
Current information not available

Teamster Retiree Housing of St. Louis, Inc.
Beachwood, OH

Teare Trust, Harry
Perryton, TX
Feeder trust

Tedesco Scholarship Fund, Tommy
Encino, CA
The foundation terminated in 2000

Teich Foundation, Curt
Chicago, IL
The foundation terminated on Aug. 31, 1999

Tejada Family Foundation, Inc.
Miami, FL
Inactive foundation

Telecommunications Infrastructure Assistance Fund for the City of Washington, D.C., Inc., The
Washington, DC
The fund terminated on Apr. 3, 2002

Tell City National Foundation, Inc.
See TCB Bank Foundation, Inc.

Temple Charitable Trust, Jean C., The
White Plains, NY
Current information not available

Tempus Foundation, Inc.
Waukesha, WI
The foundation terminated on Dec. 31, 1998

Texas Foundation for Intercollegiate Athletics for Women
Baytown, TX
The foundation terminated in 2001

Texas Kiwanis Foundation for Woodside Trails Therapeutic Camp, Inc.
Austin, TX
The foundation terminated in 2001

Thanks Be To Grandmother Winifred Foundation, The
Wainscott, NY
The foundation terminated in 2001

Thayer Charitable Trust, Donald G.
Grand Rapids, MI
The foundation terminated in 2002

Theis Foundation, Inc.
Carmel, IN
The foundation terminated in 2001

Thermo Foundation, Inc.
Waltham, MA
The foundation terminated on Dec. 30, 2000

APPENDIX A

Tholen Charitable Foundation, W. A. Tholen and Suzanne H.
Kansas City, MO
The foundation terminated in Oct. 2000

Thom Scholarship Fund, Coach Alex
Louisville, KY
Current information not available

Thomas Family Charitable Foundation, Inc.
Tulsa, OK
Inactive foundation

Thomas Family Foundation, Dean E.
Rockford, IL
The foundation terminated in 2001

Thomas Trust, Adele M.
Falls Church, VA
The foundation terminated in 2001

Thomasson Scholarship Foundation, Inc., John E.
Louisa, VA
The foundation terminated on June 30, 2001

Thompson Scholarship Fund, Arline & Laurel
Providence, RI
The foundation terminated on Jan. 16, 2001

Thoracic Surgical Educational & Research Trust Fund
West Chester, PA
Current information not available

Thoren Foundation, The
Tempe, AZ
Inactive foundation

Three Angels' Rescue of the Perishing, Inc., The
La Habra, CA
The foundation terminated on May 31, 2000

Thunder and Lighting Research and Education Foundation
Providence, RI
The foundation terminated in 2000

Thurman Foundation, Inc., Veryl L.
Lenexa, KS
The foundation terminated in 2002

Ticketmaster Foundation, The
Los Angeles, CA
The foundation terminated in 2001

Tilles Foundation
Clayton, MO
The foundation terminated in 2002

Tillotson Flower and Garden Trust, John & Clara
See Flower and Garden Foundation

Timothy 6:18 Foundation, The
Mooresville, NC
The foundation terminated Dec. 2000

Tishman Cancer Foundation, Marcia, The
See Men Against Breast Cancer, Inc.

Tittizer Charitable Foundation, Louis and Evelyn
Edna, TX
The foundation terminated in 2000

Tolland County Health Care, Inc.
Tolland, CT
The foundation terminated in 2002

Tomamichel Foundation Charitable Trust, The
Des Moines, IA
The trust terminated in 2001

Tomkins Memorial Fund, Thomas W.
Burlington, IA
The fund terminated on Dec. 31, 2000

Tonsmeire Charitable Foundation, The
Fairhope, AL
Inactive foundation

Trinks, Jr. Scholarship Fund, Arthur R.
Providence, RI
The fund terminated on June 11, 2001

Trion Charitable Foundation
Sanford, NC
The foundation terminated in 2001

Trogstad Educational Trust, Lu Verne
Fargo, ND
Current information not available

Trotta Foundation, Inc., The
Mount Kisco, NY
The foundation terminated in 2001

True North Communications Foundation
(Formerly Foote, Cone & Belding Foundation)
Chicago, IL
The foundation terminated in 2001

Trueger Foundation, The
See The Berkeley International Institute

TRW Foundation
Cleveland, OH
Due to the merger of TRW Corp. with Northrop Grumman Corp., The foundation is terminating

Tucker Foundation, F & S
Orrville, OH
Current information not available

Tucker Foundation, J & C
Marshallville, OH
Current information not available

Tultex Foundation Scholarship Program
Martinsville, VA
Current information not available

Turner Foundation, Courtney S.
Dallas, TX
The foundation terminated in 2001

Tuttle Family Society, A. Theodore, The
Salt Lake City, UT
Current information not available

U.S. Medical Aid Foundation
Minneapolis, MN
The foundation terminated in 2002

U.S. Urdu Adab, Inc.
Washington, DC
Current information not available

Ulevich Charitable Trust, Ben and Lea Jean
Milwaukee, WI
The trust terminated in 2001

Ulisse Foundation, The
San Francisco, CA
The foundation terminated on Aug. 7, 2000

Underhill Foundation
New York, NY
The foundation terminated in 2000

Union Carbide Foundation, Inc., The
Danbury, CT
The foundation merged into The Dow Chemical Company Foundation in Feb. 2001

United Arts Foundation, Inc.
(Formerly United Dance Arts Foundation, Inc.)
Hudson, NY
The foundation terminated in 2000

United Chinese Health Foundation
Scarsdale, NY
The foundation terminated in 2000

United Dance Arts Foundation, Inc.
See United Arts Foundation, Inc.

University of Strathclyde USA Foundation
Washington, DC
Inactive foundation

University of the World, The
Fontana, CA
Inactive foundation

Unser, Jr. Children's Charities, Al
Albuquerque, NM
Inactive foundation

Upton Youth Development Corporation
Baltimore, MD
Current information not available

Valley Bank Charitable Foundation, Inc.
Phoenix, AZ
The foundation terminated in 2001

Van Horne Foundation, Andrea Meidinger
Fort Wayne, IN
The foundation terminated in 2002

Van Konynenburg Foundation
Los Angeles, CA
Current information not available

Van Til Charitable Trust
Hammond, IN
The trust terminated in May 2001

Vascular Educational & Research Fund, Inc.
Port Washington, NY
The foundation terminated on July 31, 1999

Velzy Foundation, Inc., Linda J.
Tannersville, NY
Current information not available

Viny Private Foundation, Norton, The
Stuart, FL
The foundation has not paid grants in the last three fiscal years, 1998-2000

Virginia Educational Fund
Berea, KY
The fund has not awarded loans in the last three fiscal years, 1998-2000

Visconti Children's Foundation
Tallahassee, FL
Inactive foundation

Vivente 1, Inc.
Redwood City, CA
The foundation terminated in 2002

Volpe Charitable Trust
North Canton, OH
Current information not available

Von Humboldt Foundation, Alexander
Branchtown, Candada,
Foreign foundation

Wachtell Family Foundation, Inc., The
New York, NY
The foundation terminated in 2001

Wade Charitable Trust
Glasgow, KY
The trust terminated on Dec. 31, 2000

Waipa Foundation
Hanalei, HI
The foundation has not paid grants in the last three fiscal years, 1998-2000

Walker Charitable Foundation, C. D.
Baileyton, AL
Current information not available

Walker Charitable Trust
Hudson, OH
Current information not available

Walker Scholarship Foundation, Donald S.
St. Croix, VI
The foundation has not paid grants in the last three fiscal years, 1999-2001

APPENDIX A

Walker Scholarship Fund, George F.
Seattle, WA
Current information not available

Wallace Charitable Trust
Memphis, TN
Inactive trust

Wallace Charitable Trust, Cecil Dulin
Cincinnati, OH
Inactive foundation

Walnut Medical Charitable Trust
Boston, MA
The trust terminated in 2001 and transferred its assets to Laura B and Francis D. Moore Endowed Fund for Surgical Research

Walsh Family Foundation, The
Snowmass Village, CO
The foundation terminated in 2001

Walske-Longtine Foundation
Chestnut Hill, MA
The foundation terminated in 2002

Walters Education Trust, Thomas B. Walters and Anne Marie
Cleveland, OH
The trust terminated on Mar. 26, 2001 and transferred its assets to the Kosciusko County Community Foundation

Walters Foundation, Inc., Dorothy M., The
Fort Wayne, IN
The foundation terminated in 2001

Wanninger Foundation, Inc.
Iowa City, IA
Current information not available

Warnemuende Charitable Trust, Harriet B.
Milwaukee, WI
The trust terminated on Nov. 30, 2001

Warrick Charitable Trust, Ruth
New York, NY
Current information not available

Washington Foundation, Inc., Malivai O., The
Ponte Vedra Beach, FL
The foundation terminated in 1999

Waterman Foundation, The
Glendale, CA
Current information not available

Waters Charitable Trust, W. E.
Wilson, NC
The foundation terminated on May 31, 1999

Wathen Foundation, Thomas W.
Santa Barbara, CA
The foundation terminated in 2001

Watson Educational Foundation, Wm. & Clarise
Charlotte, NC
The foundation terminated on Sept. 30, 2001

Weaver Foundation, Inc., David R. & Dorothy C., The
Coral Gables, FL
Current information not available

Wehle Foundation, Louis A., The
Rochester, NY
The foundation terminated in 2001

Weinberger Foundation, Adolph
Beachwood, OH
The foundation has not paid grants in the last three fiscal years, 1998-2000

Weiner Foundation
New Orleans, LA
The foundation terminated in 2001

Weiner Foundation, The
Houston, TX
The foundation terminated in 2001

Weisenborn Family Foundation
Kansas City, MO
The foundation terminated in 2001

Weiser Foundation, Inc., The
Woodmere, NY
Current information not available

Weisner Scholarship Fund, Eva
Portsmouth, NH
The foundation terminated in 2001

Weiss Humanitarian Award Fund, Aaron
Flushing, NY
Current information not available

Wellbrooks Charitable Trust
Cincinnati, OH
The foundation terminated in 2002

Wellco Foundation, The
Waynesville, NC
Inactive foundation

Welling Charitable Trust, Bertie M.
Milwaukee, WI
The trust terminated on Dec. 31, 2001

Wells Charitable Endowment Trust, Otho S.
Hollis, NH
The trust terminated in 2001

Wellsville Rotary Education Fund
Wellsville, NY
The fund terminated in 2001

Welsh Scholarship Trust, Edward R.
Philadelphia, PA
Current information not available

Wendover Fund
Dallas, TX
The fund terminated in 2001

Wennonah Foundation, Inc.
Lexington, NC
The foundation terminated in 2001

West Park "K" Charitable Foundation
Brunswick, OH
The foundation terminated in 2002

West Texas Corporation, J. M.
Houston, TX
The foundation terminated in 1999

Weston Charitable Foundation
Nashua, NH
The foundation terminated in 2001

Westra Charitable Foundation, Inc.
Waupun, WI
The foundation terminated in 1999

Westvaco Foundation Trust
New York, NY
Due to merger of Westvaco Corp. with Mead Corp., the foundation has terminated

Wexler Foundation, Samuel & Etta
Brookline, MA
The foundation terminated on Dec. 31, 2001

Whalen Memorial Foundation, Sheila E.
Lockport, NY
The foundation terminated in 2002

WHATISIT? Foundation for Theatre Arts, The
San Diego, CA
The foundation terminated in 2000

Wheatland Foundation
San Francisco, CA
Inactive foundation

Wheeler Community Club
Wheeler, OR
Current information not available

Wheeler Moore Foundation, The
Hinsdale, IL
The foundation terminated in Dec. 2001

Wheeler Trust, Xenophone C.
Williston, VT
Current information not available

White Family Foundation
Grandview, WA
The foundation terminated in 2001

White Family Foundation, Inc., C. F.
Rancho Santa Fe, CA
Inactive foundation

White Memorial Conservation Center, Inc., The
Litchfield, CT
The foundation terminated in 2002

White Mountains Foundation
Concord, NH
The foundation terminated in 2001

White Rose Foundation
Los Altos, CA
Current information not available

Whiteside County Medical Society
Sterling, IL
Current information not available

Whiting Center for Humanity, Arts & the Environment, Marjorie Grant
Sacramento, CA
Inactive foundation

Whiting Memorial Fund, Jock
Fincastle, VA
The fund terminated in 1999

Whitlock Scholarship Trust Fund, Ira C.
Elkhart, IN
The fund terminated in 2001

Whitney Foundation
Charlotte, NC
The foundation terminated in 2001

Whitney Fund, David M.
Detroit, MI
The foundation terminated in 2000

Wichmann-Friede Foundation, Inc.
Bonita Springs, FL
Current information not available

Wiemer Foundation, Inc.
Dallas, TX
The foundation has not paid grants in the last three fiscal years, 1999-2001

Wiggle Bug Foundation
New Orleans, LA
Current information not available

Wilder Foundation
Friday Harbor, WA
The foundation terminated in 1998

Wildlife Aid, Inc.
Egg Harbor Township, NJ
The foundation has not paid grants in the last three fiscal years, 1999-2001

Wiley Charitable Trust, Marshall W.
Bethesda, MD
The trust terminated in 1998

Williams Foundation, Louise T.
Chicago, IL
The foundation terminated on Dec. 31, 1999

Williams Foundation, Inc., Paul W.
Purchase, NY
The foundation terminated in 2002

Williams Irrevocable Charitable Trust, Kenneth C.
Ravenna, OH
The foundation terminated in 2001

Williamson Memorial Scholarship Fund, Charles H.
Macon, GA
The fund terminated on Dec. 31, 2001

Wilmar Scholarship Fund, Alvin H.
San Francisco, CA
The foundation terminated in 2000

Wilson Charitable Foundation, Jasper L. & Jack Denton
Houston, TX
Inactive foundation

Wilson Charitable Trust, The
Houston, TX
Current information not available

Wilson Foundation, Kendrick and Linda, The
New York, NY
The foundation terminated in 2000

Wilson Scholarship Trust, J. Finley
Washington, DC
The foundation terminated in Dec. 2000

Winski Educational Foundation, Mort and Agatha
San Marcos, CA
The foundation terminated in 2002

Winston and Herman Silver Charitable Fund, Dr. Lee, The
Philadelphia, PA
The foundation terminated in 2000

Winthrop Memorial Fund, Sarah T.
Jersey City, NJ
The fund terminated on Dec. 31, 2001

Within the Light
Los Angeles, CA
The foundation has not paid grants in the last three fiscal years, 1999-2001

Wolfskill Foundation, John & Lucretia
Hyde Park, VT
Current information not available

Wolokahn Foundation
Portland, OR
The foundation terminated on Feb. 28, 2002

Women's Health Care Education Foundation
East Rutherford, NJ
Current information not available

Wood Foundation, Jeffris
Seattle, WA
The foundation terminated in Dec. 2000

Woodner Family Collection, Inc., Ian, The
New York, NY
The foundation will terminate by the end of 2003

Woodward Foundation, The
Washington, DC
The foundation terminated in 2001

Woody Scholarship Trust, Earl & Roxie
Cleveland, OH
The trust terminated in 2001

Woolley Foundation
Eugene, OR
The foundation terminated in 2002

Woolman Family Foundation
Providence, RI
The foundation terminated in 1998

Word of the Lord, The
Mesa, AZ
The foundation has not paid grants in the last three fiscal years, 1999-2001

World Boxing Council-Friendly Hand Foundation
Miami, FL
The foundation terminated in 1999

Woronoco Foundation, Inc., The
Westfield, MA
The foundation terminated in 2000

Wozniak Dreamland Trust, Vic & Vermell, The
Pensacola, FL
Current information not available

Wright Fund, Bagley, The
Seattle, WA
The foundation terminated in 2000

Wright Fund, Virginia
Seattle, WA
The fund terminated in 2001

Wrigley Family Foundation
See Julie Ann Wrigley Foundation

Wrigley Foundation, Julie Ann
(Formerly Wrigley Family Foundation)
Wauwatosa, WI
The foundation terminated in 2001

Wunderman Foundation, The
New York, NY
Current information not available

Wurl V Foundation, Inc.
North Oaks, MN
The foundation terminated in 2002

Wyoming LDS Foundation
Laramie, WY
Current information not available

Yale Club of Tulsa Scholarship and Development Fund
Tulsa, OK
The fund has not paid grants in the last three fiscal years, 1998-2000

YEPRAD, Inc.
Burbank, CA
The foundation has not paid grants in the last three fiscal years, 1998-2000

Yun Scholarship Foundation, Yong
Oakland, CA
Current information not available

Zachae Memorial Fund, Paul E. & Ernest A.
Norwich, CT
Current information not available

Zemke Foundation, David W., The
Robbinsdale, MN
The foundation terminated in 2000

Zimmerman Charitable Trust, Kenneth, The
Tenafly, NJ
Inactive foundation

Zion Foundation
Baltimore, MD
The foundation terminated in 2002

Zito Foundation, James J.
Painesville, OH
The foundation terminated in 2000

ZSI Foundation, Inc.
Clementon, NJ
The foundation has not paid grants in the last three fiscal years, 1998-2000

APPENDIX B

The following organizations are classified as private foundations under the IRS tax code but are excluded from inclusion in this edition of the *Guide to U.S. Foundations, Their Trustees, Officers and Donors* because their purpose is to fund organizations specified in their governing instruments. EIN refers to the Employer Identification Number assigned to the foundation by the IRS.

STATE	EIN
Alabama	
Adler Testamentary Charitable Trust, Emanuel A., Birmingham	636020070
Alabama Christian College Scholarship Fund, Montgomery	636019140
Beach Foundation Trust A for Brunswick Hospital, Thomas N. Beach and Mildred V., Birmingham	636121520
Beach Foundation Trust C for UAB Diabetes Hospital, Thomas N. Beach and Mildred V., Birmingham	636121522
Bedsole Trust f/b/o Mobile Infirmary, J. L., Mobile	636107955
Bedsole Trust f/b/o United Fund, J. L., Mobile	636121449
Beeson Charitable Trust, Dwight M., Birmingham	636150745
Bradford Foundation, Thomas E. & R. Ellye, Birmingham	636112595
Bradshaw Chambers County Library and Cobb Memorial Archives Foundation, Inc., H. Grady, The, Valley	237448554
Brightwell School Trust, A. T., Montgomery	636019162
Buck Charitable Trust f/b/o Alabama Eye Institute Foundation, Carl G., Birmingham	636171340
Buck Scholarship Trust, Pauline B., Birmingham	636048982
Cheung Charitable Trust, Tak Woo, Birmingham	630983062
Collier Trust f/b/o First United Methodist Church, Lurline, Mobile	586243473
Connell Education Foundation, Broughton W. & Marion R., Dothan	636154691
Costarides Memorial Fund, Mobile	510226228
Crampton Trust, Guy C., Mobile	636179180
Cunningham Piano Scholarship and Faculty Endowment Fund, Elizabeth S., Dothan	631156440
Davis Trust f/b/o Cloverdale Church of Christ, H. O., Montgomery	636149311
Davis Trust f/b/o Faulkner University, H. O., Montgomery	636149312
Dean Trust, Joe Douglass, Birmingham	636078627
Dorsey, Jr. Memorial Scholarship Fund, Claude E., Birmingham	636020071
Edge Endowment Fund, Troy	630834443
Edge Trust f/b/o Alabama Baptist Children's Home, Dr. Oscar N., Troy	630834358
Edge Trust f/b/o Edge Scholarship Foundation, Dr. Oscar N., Troy	630834349
Edwards Charitable Trust, Mary Elizabeth Webster, Selma	630738970
Ellis Foundation, Inc., John H., Centre	631186160
Evans Charitable Trust, Luther M., Birmingham	636141716
Forchheimer Memorial Foundation, Louis & Josie, Mobile	636161119
Franklin Foundation, George W. and Mary O., Dothan	636181562
Goldsmith Trust, Mamie E., Mobile	636018439
Hare Foundation f/b/o Walker College, Carl T., Birmingham	636118485
Hargis Christian Retreat Charitable Trust, Birmingham	636065831
Hargis Foundation, Florence Parker, Birmingham	630871920
Hoff Memorial, Margaret Atlee, Birmingham	521158100
Holy Spirit School Foundation Trust, Tuscaloosa	636109693
Hunt Charitable Foundation Trust, Richard C., Birmingham	636194374
Jones Charitable Trust, C. I., Birmingham	636153820
Langan Charitable Trust, Joseph N., Mobile	636086271
Marinos Trust, George, Mobile	636018531
Maxwell Trust, Alma B., Montgomery	636174006
Maxwell Trust, Mildred W., Montgomery	636173095
McInish Foundation, Marvin P., Birmingham	636146382
Meyer, Jr. Memorial Scholarship Fund, Robert R., Birmingham	636019792
Middleton Theological Endowment Trust, Robert, Mobile	636020996
Miles Foundation, Inc., N. E., Birmingham	631075897
Nelson Charitable Trust, Thelma Bass Nelson & Robert Whitfield, Brewton	636141563
Odess Charitable Foundation, John S. & Carol S., Chelsea	630935192
Pate Memorial Trust, John Jordan and Rebecca, Andalusia	912102613
Patterson Foundation f/b/o United Methodist Children's Home, Roy M., Birmingham	636162167
Pearson Foundation, Bettie Mae, Birmingham	630930786
Pei-Ling Charitable Trust, The, Huntsville	570887822
Povlacs Family Charitable Foundation, Dothan	911909695
Roberts Special Trust, Belle G., Mobile	636111643
Russell Charitable Foundation, Adelia, Alexander City	630930330
Ryding Physics Fellowship Fund, Herbert C., Auburn	636019732
Smith Foundation, Minnie N., Birmingham	636083743
Taunton Charitable Trust, Van B., Birmingham	636140272
Taylor Trust for Boy's Club of Dothan, Inc., Charles G., Dothan	636173946
Taylor Trust for Girls Incorporated of Dothan, Charles G., Dothan	581955167
Temple Emanuel-Odess Lectureship Trust, Birmingham	636133704
Thornton Testamentary Trust, Minnie B., Birmingham	636053979
Turner Residual Cemetery Trust, Alletta, Mobile	636175415
University of Mobile Trust, Mobile	636121439
Vaughn Trust, Fred A., Pine Hill	636145207
Wedgewood Fund for the Wedgewood Collection, Dwight and Lucille Beeson, Birmingham	636141715

APPENDIX B

STATE	EIN
Wells Trust f/b/o Wayside Baptist Church, James C., Birmingham	636124209
Wells Trust f/b/o Wayside Baptist Church, W. W., Birmingham	636124211
Wheeler Memorial Foundation, Joe, Birmingham	630790958
Wilcox Community Health Foundation, Inc., Camden	570901830
Wilson Scholarship Trust, Gerald, Mobile	586238910
Zieman Charitable Trust, A. Hays and Christine B., Mobile	636193867

Alaska

Charindia Foundation, Anchorage	920085962
Juneau Pioneers Home Foundation, Juneau	920143399

American Samoa

Chamberlin Education Trust, Pago Pago	666022090

Arizona

Allison Educational Foundation, Inc., Rex L., Scottsdale	860533343
Babbitt Athletic Trust, Elizabeth Quimby, Phoenix	866203446
Barr Irrevocable Trust, Mabel R., Phoenix	866492153
Brown Charitable Foundation, Katherine McLennan, Tucson	363244240
Colee Charitable Trust, The, Sun City	866254892
Cosden Trust f/b/o University of Arizona College of Medicine, Curtis C., Phoenix	866174343
Craig Trust, Robert W., Phoenix	866021278
Eyring Family Charitable Trust, Wendell H., The, Mesa	866200488
Foundation for Study of Molecular Virology and Cell Biology, Phoenix	942909348
Fry Foundation, Erwin, Tucson	860400719
Goldberg Charitable Trust, Joseph, Phoenix	866080065
Goldberg Irrevocable Trust, Lee, Phoenix	866162697
Gordon Estate Trust f/b/o University of Arizona Foundation for Medical Research, Harold P. & Olga R., Phoenix	742465064
Gormley Trust, Janet S., Phoenix	866209372
Katzin Family Foundation, Ltd., David, The, Anthem	860718918
Leehan Trust No. 3 f/b/o Society of St. Vincent de Paul, Ruth O., Phoenix	866111806
Leehan Trust No. 4 f/b/o University of Arizona, Ruth O., Phoenix	866111807
McDonald Memorial Trust, Kathleen E., Tucson	546304514
Metz Foundation, Arthur R., Scottsdale	366054389
Reinhaus Family Foundation, Stanley M., Tucson	860691686
Taylor Trust f/b/o Salvation Army, Phoenix	866252446

Arkansas

Alumni Association of Arkansas State University, Inc., State University	581723646
Arkansas Blood & Cancer Society, Little Rock	710691483
Canaday Ministries, Inc., Fort Smith	710734852
Children's Homes Foundation, Inc., Paragould	710756179
Christian Competition, Inc., Little Rock	710657115
Dame Trust f/b/o Second Baptist Church of Little Rock, George Edward, Conway	946547742
Echols-Reynolds Memorial Fund, Fort Smith	716050877
First Lutheran School Endowment, Fort Smith	716050601
Friday, Eldredge & Clark Foundation, Little Rock	716050584
Immaculate Conception Church School Trust, Fort Smith	716102531
Lindsey Foundation, Inc., Robert S., Little Rock	710712322
Overstreet Short Mountain Foundation, Fort Smith	710564702
Shewmaker Charitable Trust, Jack & Melba, The, Bentonville	716121894
Shock Endowed Chair of Ophthalmology Charitable Trust, John P., The, Little Rock	710756693
Tenenbaum Charitable Trust, Carolyn & Joe, Little Rock	710584641
Vaughan Foundation, Lee & Lois, Little Rock	716167964

California

STATE	EIN
Abascal Trust, Mary J., San Francisco	956063410
Achenbach Foundation for Graphic Arts, San Francisco	946066400
Alexander Trust, Henrietta L., San Francisco	956063291
Alexander Trust, Scott W., Long Beach	956040539
Allen Trust, Eleanor, San Francisco	956790219
Alliance for the Advancement of Education, Westlake Village	770293772
Alzueta Memorial Fund, Carlos, The, San Francisco	946646364
American Cancer Research Foundation, Oakland	946128854
American Foundation Trust, Corte Madera	346516839
American Friends of Palace Opera, Inc., The, Los Angeles	510380059
American Friends of the Zandra Rhodes Museum, Del Mar	330728266
Anderson Trust, Leslie, Fairfield	946413821
Animal Trust Foundation, Inc., San Diego	952837685
Archibald Trust, Hildur A., San Francisco	946449719
Ashe Trust, Sylvia, San Francisco	956812737
Asian Rural Institute Foundation, San Diego	510154970
Bacon Foundation, Inc., Francis, The, Pasadena	951921362
Bandy Trust, Eleanor, San Francisco	946742550
Bartlett Trust, Marguerite, San Francisco	956819306
Beaver Foundation, Oakland	941682883
Belson Trust, William Belson & Sedelle Z., San Francisco	946609363
Benson Memorial Trust, Ida J., San Francisco	946680722
Berdach Foundation, Otto P., San Francisco	366510739
Bernstein Charitable Trust, Los Angeles	956934018
Bianchi Foundation, Kathleen, Newport Beach	330128850
Black Foundation, Helen E., Newport Beach	330472733
Blake Recording for the Blind, Los Angeles	956086822
Bowles Memorial Fund, Ethel Wilson Bowles & Robert, Pasadena	956481575
Braun Foundation, Mary Elizabeth, Los Angeles	954453933
Brown Charitable Trust, Thaddeus C., Los Angeles	954109004
Brown Family Foundation, Ross M., Santa Barbara	770296153
Brown Scholarship Fund, Samuel Ritter, San Francisco	956088139
Bruml Trust, Simona, San Francisco	946461662
Brunetti Charitable Trust, Dionigi, San Francisco	956785907
Camenisch Trust, Florentine R., San Francisco	946669079
Casa De Angeles Foundation, Tiburon	680451139
Centofante Foundation, Redondo Beach	330361839
Claeyssens Charitable Trust, Ailene & Pierre, Santa Barbara	776052982
Clarendon Foundation, Cerritos	330452749
Clarke Trust, Robert E., San Francisco	956819218
Codoni Memorial Fund, Leslie R., San Francisco	946626180
Collier Foundation, Angela D., Encino	954564475
Contat Trust f/b/o French Orphans, Leandre Aristide & Angele Fonteix, San Francisco	956832690
Countess Charitable Trust, Sterling, San Francisco	956812730
Croft Trust, Gerald S. G., San Francisco	956819409
Curletti Trust, Rosario, Solvang	776034333
Davenport Memorial Trust for Outdoor Education, Roger Lawrence, The, Sacramento	330144682
Davis Trust, Marietta Elliott, Long Beach	336030606
De Wright Clinic Fund, Los Angeles	956234377
DeHaven Trust, Madeline H., San Francisco	946262074
Deutsch Park & Botanical Gardens Charitable Trust, Fresno	770410894
Dewhurst Foundation, Tirzah M., San Francisco	956010715
Dodd Foundation, Thomas N. Dodd and Loretta M., Newport Beach	330248199
Doelger Charitable Trust, Daly City	946468716
Doheny Trust for St. Vincent de Paul Church, Carrie Estelle, Los Angeles	956005702
Dosher Trust, Samuel R., San Francisco	946295978

APPENDIX B

STATE	EIN
Drais Foundation, Helen C., San Francisco	956819324
Dubrow Scholarship Fund, Sarah Segal, Los Angeles	953567559
Dyke Testamentary Trust, Dorothy J., San Francisco	956855677
Eagles Bobsled USA, Anaheim	680417009
Eaton Charitable Trust, Cornelia, Los Angeles	956995228
Elizabeth Foundation, Inc., Long Beach	954302261
Elks of Oxnard, No. 1443 Endowment Trust, Ventura	956026318
English Scholarship Fund, Fannie F., Los Angeles	954166926
Escondido Library Endowment Foundation, Escondido	330537757
Falk Foundation, Elizabeth M., Woodland Hills	953950915
Family Service of Long Beach Foundation, Long Beach	953767875
Faulkner Foundation, Hobart W. and Lottie C., San Francisco	954446743
Fields/Evelyn Caplan Charitable Trust, Lillian and Frank, San Francisco	956945334
Fifield Manors, Los Angeles	951698857
Food Technology Foundation, San Francisco	946073990
Foundation for Judicial Education, San Francisco	237393042
Free Scholarship Fund, William C. Free & Mazy Bell, Pasadena	956032103
Freeman & Hallie Adams Memorial Fund, Lawrence A., San Francisco	946576957
Freitas Foundation, Lloyd A., Oakland	237091802
Friends of the Dana Point Library, Inc., Dana Point	953468584
Fritz Foundation, Barbara and Jay, The, San Francisco	943083753
Frosgong Fund for Beth Israel Home & Hospital, Janet Strausberg, Anna Karzen, & Lewis, San Francisco	946720254
Fullen-Smith Foundation, The, San Marino	956044541
Garnier Trust, Audette S., San Francisco	956598449
Garrity Trust, Thomas P. & Etta L., San Francisco	946621102
Gesensway Trust, Arthur S., San Francisco	956329343
Geyser Educational Trust, Carl, St. Helena	686004631
Gibson Trust f/b/o Childreach, Ernest, San Francisco	946481541
Glenn Endowment f/b/o the Art Academy of Cincinnati, Omer T., San Francisco	956262325
Goldsberry Trust, Charles M., San Francisco	956797098
Greek Community of Fresno Foundation, Fresno	770249626
Griesbach Memorial Fund, Norman, Tulare	770256907
Griffith Charitable Trust, Ross L., San Francisco	946702055
Hammer United World College Trust, Armand, The, Los Angeles	954031114
Hannan 1991 Education Trust, Charles D. & Bessie L., San Francisco	330470165
Hansen Foundation, Fred J., San Diego	953247772
Hargrove Trust, Vera G., San Francisco	956324717
Harrod Trust, Thomas M., San Francisco	946267168
Hawley Trust, Albert E., San Francisco	946057972
Hayes Memorial Trust, Ruth Hamilton & Jacques, San Francisco	510188649
Hellwig Fund, San Francisco	942808662
Hench Foundation, John C., North Hollywood	954308746
Henry Testamentary Trust, Orpha, Grover Beach	953364490
Hester Family Foundation, Lake Forest	510189743
Hines Memorial Scholarship Foundation, Ruth Ball, San Francisco	956191754
Hippen Educational Foundation, Mary Sumerlin, San Diego	956228286
Homan Charitable Foundation Trust, Los Angeles	953872427
Hoss f/b/o California Community Foundation, B. E. Hoss & W. A., San Francisco	946691598
Houssels Trust, Hubert, Long Beach	956381605
Hunt Trust, Nina McCleery, San Francisco	946057197
Ingersoll Memorial Fund, A. E. & Pauline, San Francisco	956010211
Ingraham Memorial Fund, Pasadena	956017839
Itakura Charitable Operating Trust, The, Pasadena	953694738
Jabes Scholarship Fund, Edward, San Francisco	946700177
James Foundation, William D., San Francisco	946057272
Janus Foundation, Inc., Santa Cruz	770313594
Jones Trust, Vera, San Francisco	946688802
JTB Cultural Exchange Corp., Los Angeles	133456886

STATE	EIN
Karabekian Fund, E. Wallace & John S., San Francisco	946645868
Keller Foundation, Harry M., Burbank	956114924
Kennedy Foundation, Bayles R., San Francisco	946699434
Keown Trust, Robert J., San Francisco	956626284
Kern River Foundation, Bakersfield	953842364
Klaas Trust, Gustave P., San Francisco	956157147
Kolb Foundation, Los Angeles	953582347
Latham Foundation, Edith, San Francisco	943250696
Lee Foundation, George, Sunnyvale	770341269
Levis Charitable Remainder Trust, Mildred Johannah Miller, San Francisco	953751898
Lewis Charitable Trust, Cecile Woods, San Francisco	956550536
Livermore Trust, Frank, Menlo Park	770057575
Living Free Charitable Trust, Idyllwild	336079825
Luther Charitable Trust, Arthur B., San Francisco	946052653
Lyons Trust, Austin E., San Francisco	946412171
Maier Trust Fund, Cornell C., San Francisco	946488694
Manchester Endowment Fund, J. D., San Francisco	956010695
Mancini Trust, Ione, San Francisco	946122937
Mann Foundation for Biomedical Engineering, Alfred E., Northridge	954664317
Mann Foundation for Scientific Research, Alfred E., Sylmar	954002032
Marini Family Trust, San Francisco	946073636
Marsten Charitable Trust for Pets in Need, Alfred L., San Francisco	946489767
Mayapur Vrindavan Worship Fund, Inc., Badger	650374693
McClemore Trust, Mary B., San Francisco	946665356
McColley Trust f/b/o All Saints Parish, Olive C., San Francisco	946724553
McCord Scholarship Trust, Florence, Santa Rosa	686059272
McLean Trust, Frances E., Los Angeles	956067011
McPhail Trust, Roy Daniel, San Francisco	956647054
Medina Charitable Trust, Isabel, San Francisco	946730192
Merrill Trust f/b/o We Care Animal Society, Jessie, San Francisco	946773500
Metteer Trust, Charles Franklin, San Francisco	942672764
Millard Trust, Marie D., Palo Alto	946195525
Moni Trust, Evaline Theda, San Francisco	680016355
Moore Trust, Lillian B., Long Beach	956040489
More Society, Jacob, The, Alamo	237404758
Morgan Company Trust - Van Nuys, BPB, Los Angeles	956293945
Morrison Lectureship Foundation No. 717984, Alexander F., San Francisco	946059224
Morrison Lectureship Foundation Supplement No. 718007, Alexander F., San Francisco	946059283
Muller Charitable Remainder Trust, Charles S., San Francisco	956989195
Murray Charitable Trust, Francis J., San Francisco	942685421
Myers Family Foundation, Alfred & Helen, The, San Francisco	943248488
Natural Heritage Foundation, Inc., Big Bear Lake	770177831
Nelson Trust, William Henry, San Francisco	946198883
O'Connell Scholarship Fund, Jewell, Los Angeles	886048769
Ojai Civic Association, Ojai	951063265
Orio Trust, Chester L., San Francisco	956843636
Osmena Foundation, Minnie, Los Angeles	953960438
Palmuth Charitable Trust, Eugene & Edna, San Francisco	946478374
Parma Trust f/b/o Parma Park, Harold, Santa Barbara	776183054
Pasadena Area Residential Aid-A Corporation, Pasadena	952048774
Pasant Family Foundation, Athanase & Shirley, Los Angeles	954397285
Perenin Foundation, Rose, Eureka	680004983
Perkins Foundation, Nellie Thatcher, San Diego	956652211
Peters Trust f/b/o California-Hawaii Elks Major Project, John, San Francisco	946417522
Pfeiffer Charitable Trust, Anna K., Los Angeles	956873186
Phelps Memorial Trust, Lucius B. Phelps & Mattie D., San Francisco	956737480
Picard Foundation, The, San Francisco	946738243

APPENDIX B

STATE	EIN
Pink Trust, Eugene M., San Francisco	956025993
Posey Trust, Addison, San Francisco	946612930
Potts Trust, John W., San Francisco	956300399
Prescott Trust, Nellie S., San Francisco	946054826
Pritchard Foundation, Earle J., San Francisco	956839334
Radcliff Grant Scholarship Fund, George, San Francisco	946072791
Radcliffe Trust, Donald Hewson, San Francisco	956026297
Receptor Trust, Albert, San Francisco	956020011
Regan Seminary Education Fund, Timothy P., San Francisco	956738916
Ribolzi Trust, Charles, San Francisco	943205796
Richman Memorial Foundation, Irving M., Studio City	237014241
Ridley Foundation, The, Montecito	770171609
Rivenburg Trust, Leon D. and Leah E., San Francisco	946633707
Roberts Trust f/b/o Kerman High School Scholarship Fund, Juanita Frances, Fresno	776195416
Roberts Trust f/b/o Society Prevention of Cruelty to Animals, Juanita Frances, Fresno	776195415
Robinson Arboretum Fund, Los Angeles	953310318
Robinson Scholarship Fund, Maud J., The, Huntington Beach	336193559
Robinson Trust, Harry W. and Virginia, Los Angeles	956648391
Roeder Trust, Gertrude Dee, San Francisco	956804657
Rohr Trust, Rosalie C., San Francisco	946476435
Root Foundation, Ednah, Palm Desert	956209188
Rose-Leo Memorial Fund, Oceanside	946523824
Rudel Award Trust Fund, Julius, Burbank	956240600
Rutshaw Foundation, Lucielle & Henry, San Francisco	956026443
Sadler Trust, Hermann J., San Francisco	946054844
Sakas Memorial Panhellenic Scholarship Trust, Marianne Bennett, Escondido	330216718
Salser Family Foundation, Pacific Palisades	330643309
San Gabriel Valley Training Center Charitable Trust Residential Facility, San Francisco	953952809
Sattler Beneficial Trust, Daniel A. and Edna J., The, Santa Barbara	237127370
Scandinavian Consortium for Organizational Research, USA, Stanford	770392307
Scarff Memorial Foundation, Stephen Edward, The, San Francisco	942984078
Seaney Trust, Martha, Long Beach	956040503
Seely Trust, Hilda Huffman, San Francisco	946347922
Shanahan Charitable Foundation, The, Los Angeles	336214098
Shasta Library Foundation, Redding	680246035
Shook Trust, Francis M., San Francisco	946057023
Shore Foundation, Dinah, The, Beverly Hills	954031246
Short Foundation, Inc., Ingeborg J., Alameda	942874926
Shuler Trust f/b/o American Red Cross, Los Angeles	866165800
Shupe Charitable Trust, Doris Ham, Los Angeles	880177921
Simon Foundation, Norton, The, Pasadena	956035908
Singleton Trust for Shriners Hospital for Crippled Children, Edward C., San Francisco	946466283
Singleton Trust for the Salvation Army, Edward C., San Francisco	946466282
Sink Memorial Swim Fund, Marilyn, Cloverdale	680048938
Small Trust, Edward, San Francisco	956679335
Smith Foundation, Grace Pepper, Newport Beach	956052292
Smith Trust, Lillian C., San Francisco	956386629
Smurr Charitable Trust, Rosemary Hancock, San Francisco	956670586
Snelling Foundation, Gustavus J. & Helen Crowe, San Francisco	942924906
Snyder Cancer Research Trust, Elaine H., Los Angeles	956781723
Sorensen Foundation, Harvey L. & Maud C., Greenbrae	941542559
South San Francisco Rotary Foundation, South San Francisco	942585087
Spring Foundation, Anna M., San Francisco	956018458
Squire Trust, Dallas S., Los Angeles	953412049
Stearns Foundation, Mildred, San Francisco	946412244
Stern Memorial Fund, Sidney, San Francisco	956050141
Stewards Foundation, Costa Mesa	330113473
Stone Foundation, Rodney and Gloria, The, Encino	330274921
Stoneman Trust, Alan C., Rancho Mirage	946568003
Sugrue Family Charitable Trust, San Francisco	956889132
Swingle Foundation, Mr. & Mrs. G. Kirk, San Francisco	942901783
Sykes Charitable Trust, Edward G., Petaluma	946623529
Tallen and David Paul Kane Educational & Research Foundation, Linda, Beverly Hills	954477151
Tan Foundation, S. T., Palo Alto	770031772
Tarble Foundation, Los Angeles	954536136
Thomas Family Foundation, Los Angeles	954274964
Thurston Scholarship Fund f/b/o Laguna Beach Unified School District, Joe, San Francisco	956208480
Tilton Charitable Trust, Mary, San Francisco	956020126
Toberman Trust, C. E., San Francisco	956819025
Torbet Charitable Trust, Ruth T., San Francisco	946329071
Travers Charitable Trust, Juanita, Los Angeles	956934385
University of Judaism Foundation, Los Angeles	953637239
Van Castricum Trust, Josefa E., San Francisco	946057350
Van Duzer Trust, John H., San Francisco	946418202
Van Nuys Charitable Remainder Trust, Emily, San Francisco	956587698
Van Strean Trust, Marian F., San Francisco	946662309
Vedder Trust, Genevieve A., San Francisco	946603554
Vinnell Foundation, The, Glendale	956085927
Von Borosini Trust, August, San Francisco	956062073
Vose Foundation Trust, Clara Edith, Tustin	237080955
Wagner Trust for Falls City Library, Jacob & Amillia, San Francisco	946471227
Wait Testamentary Trust, Charles Hughes, San Francisco	946671099
Wait Trust, Kathryn E., San Francisco	946646166
Walker Foundation, C. J., Carrie D. & R. Howard, The, Los Alamitos	237445832
Walter Trust, Judith Scott, San Francisco	956007893
Webb Trust, Harry H., San Francisco	946054898
Weiser Family Foundation, Kentfield	943193057
Weiss Charitable Trust f/b/o UCSD & ADL, Mandell, San Diego	336145299
Weiss Trust, Harry A., San Francisco	946051339
Welch Trust, Mary, San Francisco	946646156
Welsh Foundation f/b/o A.A.U.W. Educational Foundation, Ada Belle, San Francisco	956595753
Welsh Trust f/b/o Illinois State Normal Trust, Ada Belle, San Francisco	956595755
Wentz Cancer Foundation, Jeanie A., San Carlos	943119008
West Trust, William L., San Francisco	946659500
Whitman Charitable Trust, Frederic S., San Francisco	946609376
Wiggs Trust, Florence D., San Francisco	956792646
Wiley Foundation, George R., Pacific Palisades	953923742
Williford Trust, Byron Lee, San Francisco	946399261
Wilson Fund, Jerry & Betty, Los Angeles	956428914
Young Charitable Trust Foundation, Frank P., Los Angeles	956013154
Zemeckis Charitable Foundation, The, Los Angeles	954678226
Zimmermann Memorial Fund, Robert & Adelaide May, Pasadena	956809322

Colorado

Allen Trust, Lucille Drinkwater, Denver	846040076
Bailey Charitable Trust, Justine & Leslie, Denver	846289135
Barney Trust f/b/o Colorado College, Armin B., Denver	846217136
Berry Foundation, Walter V. and Idun Y., Evergreen	330284355
Bloedorn Scholarship Trust, Howard B., Fort Morgan	846166141
Bowne Charitable Foundation, Inc., John F. and Grace W., Frisco	223333284
Charlotte School Trust, Edwards	030284676
Dower Benevolent Corporation, Mary M., Englewood	840408049
Garden of the Gods Foundation, Inc., Colorado Springs	841272111
Hammond-Gribbell Memorial Foundation, Fort Collins	746346306

APPENDIX B

STATE	EIN
Huddart Charitable Trust, J. J., Denver	846219044
Jackson Trust No. 3 f/b/o Yale University, Edith B., Denver	846150096
Jackson Trust No. 4 f/b/o Colorado College & Pioneer Museum, Edith B., Denver	846150097
Jones Foundation, Roger M. Jones & Roberta W., Longmont	841148522
Koch Trust, Gwendolyn, Denver	846049291
Linvill Church Trust Fund, Mary Johnson, Sterling	846104785
Littler Trust f/b/o Christ Community Church of Roggen, Mary, Denver	846216479
Malley Charitable Trust-A, Elsie M., Denver	742770301
Mathews Charitable Foundation, William and Grace, Fort Collins	742339562
McRae Foundation Trust, Artlor, Denver	846194391
Okinaga Foundation, The, Denver	421354468
Pilot Trust, The, Boulder	846030136
R.M.D. Competition Fund, Inc., Denver	237270507
Ranger Trust f/b/o/ Salvation Army, Denver	364021495
Rechel Foundation, Amy Lutz, Grand Junction	841152006
Rocky Mountain Youth Leadership Foundation, Inc., Colorado Springs	841190377
Sarsfield Trust, George P. Sarsfield and Margaret D., Denver	816068028
Seeman Student Fund, Bernard J., Denver	846093743
Smith Scholarship Fund, Willard A., Colorado Springs	846142344
Smith Trust f/b/o Grace Episcopal Church, Helen J., Colorado Springs	846152339
Sneath Memorial Fund, Denver	846172944
Stebbins Orphans Home Association, Denver	846019315
Thorkildsen Scholarship Fund, William, Denver	846235430
Webster-Barnes Foundation for Education and Research, Boulder	846084160

Connecticut

Baldwin Charitable Trust, Winifred B., Greenwich	133495394
Baldwin Trust, Marjorie J., Tolland	066216205
Board Memorial Charitable Trust, Archibald & Fannie E., Stonington	066171616
Bordman-Beardsley Home, The, Fairfield	060655125
Branigan Trust, Mary E., New London	066036344
Bristol Trust f/b/o Town of Southington, Julius D., Hartford	066039872
Cherniack Trust, Samuel, Hartford	066316291
Dequaine Foundation Endowment Fund, Inc., The, Bridgeport	061499886
Dreisman Krichavsky Charitable Foundation Trust, The, West Hartford	223044559
East Lyme Library Foundation, Inc., Niantic	223158782
Enslein Foundation, Inc., Robert E., The, Greenwich	136270043
Ferguson Library Foundation, Inc., Stamford	222849891
Forest Crafts Foundation, Inc., Katherine, Old Lyme	222618186
Forest Fellowship Irrevocable Trust, Aton, Norfolk	066253899
Friends of Hill-Stead, Inc., Farmington	061056495
Hoenig Memorial Fund, Inc., Linda, Greenwich	133251164
I Have a Dream Foundation of Hartford, Inc., Hartford	222811481
Lloyd Trust f/b/o Metropolitan Museum of Art, Ruth, Stamford	136844377
MacKay Trust, Nancy N., Litchfield	066277200
Magliaro, Jr. Educational Scholarship Trust, Dominic, Brookfield	061258080
Mallett Memorial Foundation, Inc., Frances S., The, Fairfield	061222102
Manchester Road Race Committee, Inc., Manchester	061051527
PJM Charitable Foundation, Inc., Greenwich	133406169
Promisek, Inc., Bridgewater	060964701
Rotary Club of Litchfield Educational Endowment Fund, Inc., Litchfield	222476852
Russell Fishers Island Trust Fund, Thomas W., Essex	237009696
Smolen Foundation, Inc., Sally & Julius, Stamford	237031674

STATE	EIN
Vose Foundation, The, Southport	222715469
Walker Charitable and Educational Foundation, Ethel, Simsbury	060679139
Werle Family Foundation, Inc., Edward C., Washington Depot	116011420
Wheeler Trust, Edith S., The, Fairfield	066386858
Wood Memorial Library Trust, Hartford	066167846
Zambezi Foundation, Inc., Danbury	061482274
Zelinsky Memorial Fund, Barak Joseph Monrad, New Haven	061372252

Delaware

Bacon Trust for St. Peter's High School, et al., Joseph F., Wilmington	516153598
Beebe Trust, Arthur H., Wilmington	516155235
Bishop Trust B for the SPCA of Manatee County, Florida, Edward E., Wilmington	237366312
Bourne Charitable Trust, William, Newark	516505985
Brandywine Creek State Park Trust, The, Wilmington	510251341
Casey Perpetual Charitable Trust B, Elizabeth Ewart, Wilmington	516162942
Cobbs Trust f/b/o Little Sisters of the Poor, Ramon C. and Julia G., Wilmington	516159502
Cohen Foundation, Inc., Harry, The, Wilmington	516015783
Davis Trust for Boy Scouts of America, James L., Wilmington	516155481
Downs Perpetual Charitable Trust, Ellason, Wilmington	516158138
Fund for European Scouting, Newark	136804976
Gilbert Memorial Trust, Fitch, Newark	136038276
Gillett Trust, Lucy B., Wilmington	510211839
Hanby Trust, Albert T., Wilmington	516010794
Hayman Trust f/b/o Delmar Library Association, Lyndal C., Wilmington	516149165
Huntington Trust f/b/o American Academy and Institute of Arts and Letters and National Institute of Arts, Archer M., Newark	136035643
Hyacinth Foundation, The, Wilmington	516183634
Leasure Foundation f/b/o Pencader Presbyterian Church, et al., Elizabeth May Brown, The, Wilmington	516157460
Miller Trust for Designated Charities, Ida J., Wilmington	516012859
New York Genealogical & Biographical Society Trust, et al., The, Newark	136083038
New York Infirmary-Beekman Downtown, Newark	136970049
Prettyman Trust f/b/o St. Andrews Church, Lillian R., Wilmington	516153571
Prouse Trust, George Ash Prouse and Harriet, Wilmington	516163225
Red Clay Reservation, Inc., Wilmington	516017982
Salsbury Trust f/b/o Harvard University, Stephen, Wilmington	516513504
Trust f/b/o Junior Board of the Memorial Division of the Wilmington Medical Center, Wilmington	516510609
Trust f/b/o Wilmington Medical Center Inc. for the P. A. Shaw Memorial Library, Wilmington	516510608
Watson Charitable Trust, Arthur K., Newark	132989468
Yukan Foundation, Wilmington	510301555

District of Columbia

Children's Research and Education Institute, Inc., The, Washington	521317889
Coale, M.D. Scholarship Trust, Edith Seville, Washington	526053746
Coit Scholarship Trust, Lew G., Washington	526219290
Dickson Home, John, Washington	530204688
Friends of the German School Charitable Trust, Washington	237035085
Kestenbaum Foundation, Sara Evans, Washington	521703918
Letts Trust, Mary E., Washington	526026123
Rostropovich Orchestra Endowment Fund, Washington	521399780

APPENDIX B

STATE	EIN
Shannon Foundation, Thomas F., The, Washington	520197082
Strong Trust, Gordon, Washington	526025980
VDT Health Research Foundation, Washington	521770420

Florida

STATE	EIN
Alagia Family Charitable Foundation, Damian P. and Marie McCarthy, Vero Beach	311472535
Allyn Trust, Joseph P., Jacksonville	596617781
American Friends of Jabotinsky Institute, Inc., Hollywood	650085205
American Friends of Zinman College of Physical Education & Sports Science, Boca Raton	133860241
Anderson Charitable Trust, Catherine D., Alachua	656080716
Aull Trust, John U., Jacksonville	596828250
Aull Trust, Lena S., Jacksonville	596824853
Bainton Trust, Janet L., Jacksonville	596928047
Bannan Trust f/b/o All Children's Hospital, Laola K., Jacksonville	596898410
Baynard Charitable Trust, Robert and Mildred, St. Petersburg	597049328
Beede Fund f/b/o Community Church of Milton, Robert R., Frances M. and Cora M., Jacksonville	596677122
Bernhard Trust, Drayton, Lake City	311473531
Berry Trust, Dorothy M. E., Orlando	596504661
Bien Memorial Foundation, Alice Ann, Orlando	597021028
Black Foundation, Sara B. and Samuel L., Jacksonville	596947477
Branan Irrevocable Trust f/b/o CFCC & GSC, Jacksonville	597139723
Brede & Wilkins Scholarship Foundation, Jacksonville	592911979
Broward County Boys Clubs Trust A, Fort Lauderdale	596748099
Broward County Boys Clubs Trust B, Fort Lauderdale	596748100
Brown Foundation Trust, Helen Davis, Jacksonville	596752213
Brown Trust f/b/o St. Mary's Church, Matthew John, Jacksonville	237440629
Buck Charitable Foundation, Inc., Blanche S., The, Fort Lauderdale	650123180
Buckley Foundation, Henry H., Tequesta	166046423
Buerk Charitable Trust No. 2, Fred C., Clearwater	597159013
Bullock Trust, Freda J., Jacksonville	596799473
Bush Scholarship Trust, Max O., Jacksonville	596622713
Carlton Trust for Florida Southern College Scholarship Fund, E., Jacksonville	596848230
Carroll Trust, Celestine, Jacksonville	596169085
Center for Confessional-Biblical Studies, Inc., Lake Worth	592764206
Collier Family Charitable Trust, The, Palm Beach	656221086
Crafts Trust f/b/o Webb Institute, John O., Clearwater	596604147
Cribb Trust f/b/o Charity, George F., Jacksonville	596712054
Dalbeck Memorial Foundation, Linnie, Sarasota	656329977
Dawson Charitable Trust f/b/o All Children's Hospital, Rose M., Jacksonville	596474268
Dawson Trust f/b/o Christ United Church, Rose M., Jacksonville	596160436
Deeb Memorial Scholarship Fund, Inc., Joseph Patrick, Tallahassee	237028231
Deford Charitable Trust, Herman J., Fort Lauderdale	596841753
Doyle Trust, John, Jacksonville	596121664
Eannelli Trust for the Blind and Visually Handicapped, Anthony, Ormond Beach	592976626
Fagan Memorial Fund, Harry, Jacksonville	596679437
Faigen Family Foundation, Inc., Palm Beach	311509512
Faulk Trust, Elizabeth, Jacksonville	656163854
Fisher Trust, Francenia, Jacksonville	596884250
Flanigan Charitable Foundation, Joseph G., Fort Lauderdale	650759826
Frank Trust, William C., Jacksonville	596497938
Friends of the Gadsden County Public Library, Inc., Quincy	591917378
Gabler Memorial Trust Fund, George Edward, The, Jacksonville	597020634
Gantz Charitable Trust, Rhea, Miami	650377352
Genius Foundation, Elizabeth Morse, Winter Park	136115217
Gervers Trust f/b/o Central Institute for the Deaf, Laura S., Jacksonville	596502946
Goodman Fund, Dr. Moses & Beatrice, Miami	656136339
Graham Testamentary Trust, Letitia V., Tampa	596134390
Greentree Charitable Trust No. 3, Gladys, Jacksonville	656088332
Gribetz Family Foundation, Inc., Estelle, The, Fort Lauderdale	650759086
Grotto Cerebral Palsy Endowment, Inc., Selama, St. Petersburg	596139437
Guisetti Palm Beach Chapter Dar Foundation, Inc., Margaret A., West Palm Beach	656158034
Haines Residual Trust, Curtis A., Clearwater	596514805
Harris House Foundation, New Smyrna Beach	596986809
Harrison Foundation, Sara D., Palm Beach	656098931
Holland Trust, Sophie B., Jacksonville	596662058
JCS Christian Trust, The, Winter Park	597015265
Jeffreys Trust f/b/o Boys Home, Linwood, Jacksonville	596592244
Kearns Family Foundation, Fort Lauderdale	650078715
Kent Family Foundation, Inc., Tampa	593085879
King Trust, Kenneth K., Jacksonville	656108058
King Trust f/b/o North Hero, L. E., Jacksonville	596843601
Klein Charitable Foundation, Inc., Sam W., Boca Raton	650508555
Korevec Charitable Foundation, Virginia McIntosh, Fort Myers	656235455
Labelle Charitable Trust, Lillian R., Jacksonville	596369466
Lawser Trust f/b/o Animal Aid Society, Inc., Mary L., Jacksonville	596904875
Leach Trust f/b/o Episcopal Dioceses, Robert, Clearwater	596974706
Lee Trust, Pearl B., Jacksonville	596499563
Leesburg Police Department Scholarship Fund, The, Orlando	596976025
Leiser Foundation, Inc., Josephine S., Fort Lauderdale	650347903
Lewis Trust, Clara, Tampa	596554188
Ludwig Trust, William M. and Vera V., Jacksonville	597016286
MacSmith Trust, Gordon P., Jacksonville	597056007
McCann Trust, Henry C., Jacksonville	596121149
McKinley Charity Trust, Floyd C., Jacksonville	596592165
Mitchell Charitable Remainder Unitrust, Harold S., Tampa	596674939
Moffitt Memorial Endowment Fund, Herbert H. & Leonie G., Fort Lauderdale	596601847
Moore Family Trust, The, Tallahassee	237181994
Morris Private Foundation, Harold H. & Vera B., The, Jacksonville	597097731
Moss Memorial Baptist and Fairview Presbyterian Churches Trust, Bradenton	546038895
Nonnast Testamentary Trust f/b/o Most Worshipful Grand Lodge and Florida Lions Fund for the Blind, Emory & Zula, Tampa	596560785
Olds University of Miami Scholarship Fund, Claude M., Miami Springs	656014159
Optimist Club of Orlando Charitable Trust, Winter Garden	596871484
Panuska Foundation, Inc., George H. and Mildred B., Fort Lauderdale	650042134
Paterson Trust, Margaret M., Jacksonville	596584191
Patton Memorial Fund, Florence H., Tampa	596242230
Pederson Trust, Frances, Fort Lauderdale	596870659
Peterman Charitable Foundation for Betterment of United States of America U.S. Navy Annapolis, Maryland, Inc., William J., Stuart	650969779
Peters Trust, George, Jacksonville	596803586
Plant Trust, Carolyn G., Orlando	596125331
Porter Trust f/b/o Southwestern Christian College, Gussie N., Jacksonville	596689397
Randall Scholarship Fund, Jessie W. & Minnie S., Orlando	596920710
Robertson Trust, Bertha I., Jacksonville	592079974

2598

STATE	EIN
Rogers Charitable Trust No. 2, Eva P., Clearwater	597148340
Rose Charitable Trust, Therese Gill, Orlando	596880484
Rosen Foundation, Inc., Harris, The, Orlando	592890420
Roughgarden Christian Educational Trust, George Coventry & Nita Schmidt, St. Petersburg	596964647
Salvation Army Trust A, Jacksonville	596748097
Salvation Army Trust B, Jacksonville	596748098
Schillinger Foundation, Inc., Miami Shores	592743298
Segal Foundation, Inc., Miami	592627839
Sharaja Foundation, Inc., The, Palm Beach Gardens	656254563
Shelfer Memorial Trust, The, Quincy	656238700
Sims Trust, Robert W., Jacksonville	596121114
Snyder Charitable Trust, Fort Pierce	656173596
Southeast Foundation, Inc., Miami	592738680
Stern Trust, George, Clearwater	596805108
Stihel Charitable Trust, Helen, Clearwater	597165116
Sudick Foundation II, Robert S., Fort Lauderdale	650207774
Thompson Trust, Wiacheslav A. Obnovlenski, Jacksonville	596596826
Thompson Trust f/b/o Community Center for the Blind, Wiacheslav A., Jacksonville	596652500
Titus Foundation, Ray E. & Staseli B., West Palm Beach	592828498
Titus 1993 Charitable Trust, Staseli B., West Palm Beach	656123008
Totman Medical Research Fund, Ray W. and Ildah, Jacksonville	161328003
Trinity United Methodist Church Trust A, Jacksonville	596748101
Trinity United Methodist Church Trust B, Jacksonville	596748102
Turck Charitable Trust, Bertha B., Jacksonville	596121061
Turken Foundation for Stray Dog Training and Adoption, Inc., Walter, Naples	650964774
Weber Testamentary Trust, Theador F., St. Augustine	597087206
Weigle Trust, Florence C., Jacksonville	596487752
Weigt Charitable Trust, Robert A., Fort Pierce	656225964
Weil Charitable Foundation, Richard & Susan B., Fort Lauderdale	656269959
Weygandt Trust, Arthur T., Jacksonville	596542287
White Lehigh Wrestling Trust, Lawrence, Orlando	597141089
Williams Foundation, Inc., Albert Lynn, Key West	132836662
Williams Trust f/b/o Charities, Ethel H., Jacksonville	596161778
Wilson Trust, Gertrude R., Jacksonville	596118179
Woodburn Charitable Trust, Elizabeth & Ralph, Jacksonville	596619329
Wray Memorial Foundation, Inc., Floyd L., The, Fort Lauderdale	237112655
Younger Charitable Trust, John O. and Helen, Venice	650314860
Ziegenhein Charitable Trust, M., Jacksonville	597062090

Georgia

Anthony Memorial Fund, William A. & Joseph T., Columbus	586054585
Bethany Home Trust, Statesboro	586075346
Boatwright Foundation, James, The, LaGrange	586040297
Connally Fund of the 2nd Ponce De Leon Baptist Church of Atlanta, Mary V., Atlanta	586026006
Connally Fund of the 2nd Ponce De Leon Baptist Church of Atlanta, Dr. E. L., Atlanta	586026058
Cook Memorial Scholarship Fund, Virginia Lee & Katie, Columbus	586137440
Edwards Foundation, Inc., Joe and Pat, Barnesville	582356582
Ellijay Gilmer Library Foundation, Inc., Ellijay	581761553
Greenway Memorial Foundation f/b/o Troop 134, Boy Scouts of America, Hubert T., Atlanta	586208875
Grover Hunter University of North Carolina Dental Trust, Atlanta	586095646
Herbert Art Endowment, Inc., Gertrude, Augusta	582012566
Hughes Scholarship Fund, Herbert H., Columbus	586025667
Jones Family Foundation, Inc., The, Dalton	582023255
Kennedy Trust, Evelyn McDaniel, Macon	586267555
Kennedy, Sr. Memorial Trust, F. Frederick, Macon	586186944

STATE	EIN
Lambert, Inc., Estate of John, The, Hinesville	581791774
Lee Orphanage Fund, Gordon, Rome	586092862
Leitalift Foundation, Atlanta	586042017
Magness Community House & Library Trust, W. H. & Edgar, Atlanta	626033040
Martin Foundation, Rosabel & James V., Atlanta	581902387
MLI, Inc., Augusta	582260185
Pierce Memorial Fountain Trust, Columbus	586080681
Rollins Foundation, Gary W. & Ruth M., The, Atlanta	586263946
Scott, Sr. Fund, I. J., Atlanta	586200775
Seals Scholarship Fund, Alfred, Atlanta	586240701
Senior Citizens Foundation, Inc., Atlanta	581797772
Shaheen Charitable Trust, Azeez, Atlanta	586323197
Shea Foundation, John J., Smyrna	581914137
Southeastern Poultry & Egg/Harold E. Ford Foundation, Tucker	582098298
Spooner Trust f/b/o First Baptist Church, Perry, Atlanta	586086139
Taylor Trust, Lillian Crouch, Atlanta	586221400
Trust for Turin United Methodist Church, Atlanta	586322556
Wilson Trust Fund, K. T. & Zelma, Columbus	581413110
Worcester Trust, Ruby McNeely, Atlanta	586274003

Hawaii

Alexander Trust, Caecilie A., Honolulu	996002927
Cooke Trust, Dorothea Sloggett, Honolulu	996038031
Cooke Trust, Harrison R. and Dorothea S., Honolulu	990290717
Da Silveira Trust, Maria L., Honolulu	996002407
Deering Trust, Mary W., Honolulu	996002243
Edmondson Charitable Trust, Charles H. & Margaret B., Honolulu	990170573
Fasi Charitable Foundation, Frank F., Honolulu	990300719
Hawaii Medical Library, Inc. Endowment Fund, Honolulu	996002297
Henriques Trust, Lucy K., Honolulu	996002291
Hobart Memorial Fund, Marion W., Honolulu	990263964
Hunter Charitable Trust, David C. & Altha B., Honolulu	943275357
Leith Trust, David, Honolulu	996002314
Lyman Charitable Trust, Orlando H., Hilo	996043763
Maui Memorial Hospital Medical Staff Foundation, Wailuku	237430592
Mist Scholarship Fund, Herbert & Margarita, Honolulu	990259507
Moore Trust, Nevada, Honolulu	996002346
Parke Trust, Annie H., Honolulu	996003193
Prisanlee Trust, Honolulu	996004404
Shipman Foundation, Herbert C., Honolulu	990175917
Shri Chaitanya Shridhar Govinda Mission, Kula	990292506
Tulloch Trust, Alexander R., Honolulu	996007059
Van Poole Foundation, Margaret Schenck, Honolulu	990291928
Wodehouse American Cancer Society Trust, C. N., Honolulu	990301430
Wodehouse Faculty Benefit Trust at Hawaii Preparatory Academy, C. N., Honolulu	990301432
Wodehouse Faculty Benefit Trust at Punahou School, C. N., Honolulu	990301435
Wodehouse Faculty Benefit Trust at Seabury Hall, C. N., Honolulu	990301434
Wodehouse Iolani School and Hawaii Charities Trust, C. N., Honolulu	990301433
Wodehouse Nature Conservancy Trust, C. N., Honolulu	990301436
Wodehouse Salvation Army Trust, C. N., Honolulu	990301431

Idaho

Allred Foundation, Chall & Sally, The, Burley	916457248
Blackham Missionary Trust, Thomas J. & M. Lucy, The, Rexburg	820425170
Brandt Fine Arts Center Trust, John H. & Orah I., Nampa	826080639
Cooper Charitable Foundation Trust, Coeur d'Alene	826069286
Shep-Rock, Inc., Coeur d'Alene	820371391

APPENDIX B

STATE	EIN
Illinois	
Abelson Foundation, Stuart R., Chicago	363799447
Adams Fund, Elizabeth Leigh, Chicago	596884185
Adams Trust, Laura L., Springfield	376023086
Aldeen Fund for Missions, G. W., Rockford	363570472
Aldeen Outreach Trust, Reuben A., Rockford	366870607
Aldeen/Summerwood Trust, Rockford	366845895
American Friends of Ophel Bas Zion Institutions, Inc., Chicago	363566181
Anell Memorial Trust, Esther W., Pontiac	376301619
Apperson Trust, Ruth A., Mattoon	376024603
Arent Residuary Trust, Arthur B., Chicago	426390363
Barker Memorial Fund, Dorothy Jo, Chicago	431359952
Bass Charitable Trust, Ray, Chicago	436647183
Bentley Trust, William H., Pontiac	237425358
Berberet Trust for St. Joseph Improvement Foundation, Mora, Quincy	376195371
Beyers Trust, John, Galesburg	376196772
Birks Trust, Jenna Ruth, Decatur	376209112
Birmingham Charitable Trust, Rockford	366800040
Bixby Charitable Trust, William K., Chicago	436022825
Blazek Residuary Trust, Joseph, Chicago	366193754
Boone County Historical Society Foundation, Belvidere	366429560
Bosch Foundation, Katherine M., Chicago	366210899
Bowron Trust, Aurora	366068781
Burnett Foundation, Inc., Leo, Chicago	362605413
Butterworth Memorial Parkway Trust, Ben, Moline	363512752
Cage Trust, Mabel Vinson, Greenville	376125270
Cedars of Lebanon Foundation, Chicago	363836767
Center for the Study of Multiple Births, Chicago	363046748
Clausing Charitable Trust, Lillian, Chicago	366925339
Cliver Charitable Trust, J. B., Moline	366943236
Congregational Church Trust, Granville	366883268
Coon Foundation, Owen L., Chicago	366066907
Davidson Charitable Trust, Max, Chicago	363778827
Deisenroth Scholarship Trust, Dorothy C., Peoria	366843839
Devers Foundation, Wilmette	366846376
Donaldson Foundation, Lewis A. & Eleanor Shay, Chicago	366015539
Drake Trust, Margarette, Paris	376363057
Eipper Trust B, Lester B., Chicago	366874456
Ellis Charitable Trust No. 3333, Paul B., Decatur	371172796
Essmueller Trust, Arthur F., Chicago	436054313
Farrer Trust, Margaret, Havana	376079232
Farwell Charitable Trust, Granger, Chicago	366944760
Fauber Trust B Memorial Fund, Hazel L., Frankfort	366507437
Field Trust, Clement V., Princeton	362157497
Fischer Charitable Trust, Alma, Freeport	366879732
Fleming Charitable Trust, Joseph F., Decatur	376222186
Flora School District Academic Foundation, Inc., Flora	371192911
Friends of Marva Collins Foundation, Chicago	364012030
Fuson Charitable Remainder Trust B, R. C., Champaign	376198279
Fuson Charitable Remainder Trust C, R. C., Champaign	376198281
Fuson Charitable Remainder Trust D, R. C., Champaign	376198283
Fuson Charitable Remainder Trust E, R. C., Champaign	376198284
Fuson Charitable Remainder Trust F, R. C., Champaign	376198285
Fuson Charitable Remainder Trust G, R. C., Champaign	376198286
Geringer Foundation, Vladimir A., Chicago	366027464
Gieseking Perpetual Trust, Henry, Springfield	376205858
Gomez Foundation, Patricia Astor, Glenview	363759472
Hallam Memorial Trust, Flora A., The, Rockford	366874012
Hanley Educational Fund, George P., The, Chicago	363581887
Harmeier Trust, Eleanor, Vandalia	376223368
Harris Memorial Fund, Shellie, Lincolnwood	363588449
Hartman Trust f/b/o Crippled Children's Center & Goodwill Industries, Helen, Peoria	376193755
Hassinger Trust f/b/o Goldie B. Floberg Center for Children, Jesse, Rockford	366785058
Hayner Library Association, Jennie D., Alton	376036692
Henry Trust, Jane V., Alton	376249272
Heuser Trust f/b/o First Presbyterian Church, R., Peoria	376236337
Hight Fund, Beatrice & Bertha, Peoria	376147134
Hodges-Bradford Park Fund, Elsie Drawyer, Peoria	376121803
Holmquist Trust f/b/o St. John's Episcopal Church, C., Bushnell	367168269
Holmquist Trust f/b/o Zion Lutheran Church, Clifford H. and Dorothy E., Geneseo	367168268
Howell Memorial Foundation f/b/o Children's Hospitals, Walter E. & Dorothy E., Orland Park	366736406
Hughes Memorial Fund, Cullen M., Chicago	363453184
Hutchcroft Perpetual Charitable Trust, Rockford	364226779
Hutton Pet Protection Foundation, Chicago	956896718
Ingram Trust, Ralph L., Mattoon	376329316
International Business Institute, Inc., Chicago	521615513
Jacobsen Trust, Edna R., Sycamore	366998672
Jahn Private Charitable Foundation, Loren A., Palos Heights	363728178
Jakubik Memorial Fund, Greg, The, St. Charles	363281869
James Foundation, J. and H., Chicago	366086322
Johnstone Foundation Trust, Vanderburgh, Chicago	367131296
JPF Foundation, Chicago	364443084
Jubilee Trust, Chicago	366852531
Kacz Residuary Trust, Sigmund V., Chicago	366107308
Kadet Cancer Research Foundation, Matteson	363754843
Kahn Family Trust, Marvin D., The, Chicago	367209502
Kairos Foundation, Wilmette	363157523
Kearns Trust f/b/o the Poor and Needy of Petersburg, Illinois, Margaret, Springfield	376023018
Kearns Trust f/b/o the Washington Street Mission, Margaret, Springfield	376023019
Kickbusch Memorial Scholarship, Chicago	366454240
Kline Trust IV, Harry L., Decatur	376287614
Kottrasch Trust, Frank, Chicago	366602472
Lardner Scholarship Trust f/b/o Blackhawk College, Sarah W., Rockford	366582462
Leach Nursing Scholarship Trust, Joliet	366980712
Little Charitable Foundation, Virginia W., Chicago	366906091
Logan County Park and Trails Foundation, Lincoln	237041808
Luthe Memorial Park Trust, Roy M., Albion	376243784
Mains Family Foundation, The, Chicago	341536123
Manaster - Dr. Charles Solomon Scholarship Fund, Abe and Esther, Chicago	521244793
Marquis Family Foundation, Inc., Franklin Parr, Moline	363537962
Marsch Trust f/b/o Morrisonville Cemetery and American Legion, Temple, Springfield	376084983
Mather Trust, Alonzo Clark, Chicago	366010112
McIlvried Trust, Elsie V., Chicago	510199733
McIlvried Trust, Grace E. & Helen M., Chicago	956544891
Merchantz Family Foundation, Wheaton	363739087
Mesmer Radiology Foundation, Chicago	363259408
Miller Trust, Harry, Vandalia	376210688
Monroe Scholarship Foundation, Quincy	376076012
Newsham Testamentary Trust, Verna, DeKalb	366106801
Norris Charitable Trust, Lester J., St. Charles	366675085
Norris Cultural Arts Trust, Dellora, St. Charles	366682375
Nottame Trust, Chicago	436317182
Oberg Scholarship Fund, Oluf G., Chicago	366125369
Page Foundation, John W., Geneva	366126125
Page Foundation, Ruth, The, Chicago	237069159
Pattee Foundation, The, Monmouth	371138998
Perlman Family Foundation, Louis & Anita, Downers Grove	362670190
Piano Trust, Maxine D., Belleville	371088947
Pree Trust f/b/o Grace Lutheran Church, Edward G., Springfield	376085349
Price Testamentary Trust f/b/o Grace Lutheran Church, Anna M., Springfield	376235041
Pro Archia Foundation, The, Chicago	366784984
Quarrie Charitable Fund, Chicago	366646475
Quarrie Charitable Trust No. 1, Chicago	366558290

APPENDIX B

STATE	EIN
Quest Trust for Geraldine, Clarence, Quincy	366963679
Ray Trust, Ernest E., Rockford	366049465
Rieke Foundation, George A. & Isabella A., Chicago	366797967
Robinson Charitable Trust, Charles R., Chicago	436229321
Rouse Family Scholarship Fund, Chicago	366950916
Sacred Heart Roman Catholic Church Trust, Granville	376267646
Saxena Foundation, The, Frankfort	363877173
Schingoethe Trust, Martha D. & Herbert F., Aurora	366942219
Schwartz Memorial Foundation, Charles M., Chicago	363989544
Scott Memorial Fund, Louise R., Chicago	366949714
Scovill Trust, Guy N. & Rose W., Decatur	376022767
Shulman Charitable Trust, Charles, Chicago	656062187
Sichler Foundation, Edgar & Marguerite, Chicago	366797976
Smith Charitable Trust, Charles Hayden, Chicago	367125514
Society for Clinical Philosophy, Chicago	361352789
Spencer Foundation, G. N., Chicago	426052928
Springfield Parks Foundation, Springfield	371292459
Sturges Charitable Trust, Charles P. & Lucy M., Chicago	656224256
Sunset Freesen Memorial Trust, Bluffs	376285564
Taylor Charitable Trust, G. W. & C. B., Mattoon	376202177
Terra Foundation for the Arts, Chicago	362999442
Tucker Scholarship Fund, Reginald L., Chicago	366837760
Tyler Trust, William I., Granville	376267645
United Church of Christ Congregational Trust, Granville	376267647
Unkel Endowment Fund, Frances P. and Annie C., Belleville	646191106
Van Vechten-Lineberry Taos Art Museum Foundation, Chicago	367161322
Volen Charitable Trust, Benjamin, Chicago	656018806
Wauconda Township Swimming Pool Foundation, Inc., McHenry	237101049
Webb Trust, Thomas H., Peoria	376024872
Wetzel Trust, Mary E., Sycamore	366998671
Whitmore Foundation, Lonnie & Anna Mae, Chicago	953912547
Wise Trust, Effie Lou, Rockford	366904233
Wrork, M.D. Charitable Trust, Donald H., Rockford	367164769
Young Charitable Foundation, Marcy & Lloyd, Chicago	866199376
Young Charity Trust, Chicago	366897850
Zendt Charitable Trust, George, Chicago	366708992

Indiana

Archibald Memorial Home, Inc., Indianapolis	350874260
Aux Chandelles Trust, The, Elkhart	351868931
Balentine Foundation, Inc., Anne M., Bluffton	351602557
Bertelsen Charitable Trust, Lowry, Evansville	356020338
Best Trust, Walter E. & Bashia E., Muncie	356221411
Block Charitable Trust, Edward A., Indianapolis	351502465
Brookshire Charitable Foundation, Inc., Ruth E., Lebanon	352007869
Carrington Foundation, Germaine Carrington and Edward "Red", New Haven	356545656
Carson Scholarship Foundation, William A., Evansville	356015588
Christian Foundation, The, Columbus	356014485
Conrad Family Foundation, Inc., Jay & Phyllis, Berne	351899472
Crawford Charitable Trust, George, Evansville	356549180
Drachman Charitable Trust, Phillip E., Evansville	356438099
Elliott Memorial Trust, Helen, Evansville	510176014
Eykamp Charitable Trust, Dorothy M., Evansville	356456975
Gates Memorial Fund, Betsy Jayne, Columbia City	356383302
Golay Foundation, Inc., Cambridge City	310929865
Granger Charitable Foundation, Dr. Clarence L. & Marguerite F., Kendallville	351508857
Habig Living Charitable Trust, Arnold F., Jasper	356527616
Hedges Trust, Cordelia Pierce, Jeffersonville	356673739
Helmer Charitable Foundation, Wilbur L., Kendallville	351810562
Higginbotham Charitable Trust, Leona, Evansville	356575785
Hirsheimer Foundation, Sidney S. & Grace G., Evansville	356243059
Hose Trust, Milo & Jennie, South Bend	356454332

STATE	EIN
Humphreys Charitable Trust, Phoebe, Indianapolis	356410575
Hutzell Foundation, Fort Wayne	356533689
Independent Insurance Agents of Evansville Foundation, Inc., Evansville	351788565
Indiana Center for Multiple Sclerosis Foundation, Inc., Indianapolis	352028362
Indiana Surgical Foundation, Inc., Indianapolis	351894570
Koch Charitable Trust, Henry F. & Minnie F., Evansville	356011880
Koontz Charitable Trust, Mary P., Richmond	356497618
Korbel Memorial Trust, Margaret C., Evansville	356564220
Korbel Trust f/b/o St. Paul's United Church of Christ, Margaret C., Evansville	356566113
Krishna Charitable Trust, Munster	363548684
Kuhlman Charitable Trust, Effie, Corydon	356499672
Lanier Mansion Foundation, Indianapolis	616211972
Leichty Charitable Foundation, Kathy K., Elkhart	351958778
Lemonde Trust f/b/o Ball State University, Walter & Edna, Muncie	356406149
Mann Family Foundation, Inc., The, Indianapolis	352032497
Maring for Earlham and DePauw Trust, Grace, Muncie	356009787
McVey Memorial Forest Trust, Muncie	356259624
Mikesell Scholarship Fund, Warsaw	356039460
Miller Testamentary Trust for Bethel Presbyterian Church, Margaret M., South Bend	356411935
Milligan Memorial Trust, Milo, Portland	356508453
Milligan Trust f/b/o Jay County Salvation Army, Virginia, Portland	356508454
Morton Trust, Maurice E., Richmond	356581585
Northeastern Indiana Suzuki Guild, Inc., Fort Wayne	351762859
Noyes Foundation, Inc., Daniel R., Indianapolis	510166550
Otterman Scholarship Fund, Keith & Mildred, Frankfort	352033167
Schmitt Trust f/b/o Bethlehem United Church of Christ, Michael P. & Lorena K., Evansville	356396175
Schmitt Trust f/b/o Boy Scouts of America Buffalo Trace Council, Michael P. & Lorena K., Evansville	356396180
Schmitt Trust f/b/o Evansville Protestant Home, Michael P. & Lorena K., Evansville	356396177
Schmitt Trust f/b/o Evansville Rescue Mission, Michael P. & Lorena K., Evansville	356396178
Schmitt Trust f/b/o Good Samaritan Home of Christ, Michael P. & Lorena K., Evansville	356396176
Schmitt Trust f/b/o Raintree Girl Scouts Council, Michael P. & Lorena K., Evansville	356396182
Schmitt Trust f/b/o Vanderburgh County 4-H Center, Michael P. & Lorena K., Evansville	356396179
Schwab Foundation, Inc., Olin B. & Desta, Fort Wayne	351804222
Shara Tefilla Cemetery Fund, Indianapolis	356009964
Slick Church Trust, Family of C. R., Muncie	352029034
Smoker Trust, Mary Bernice, Frankfort	356392619
Stream Charitable Trust, Florence L., Fort Wayne	356502838
Stream Charitable Trust, Harold O., Fort Wayne	356557971
Sweeney Foundation, Ann C., Michigan City	351808523
Symmes - Randolph County YMCA Trust, Russell, Muncie	351993188
Symmes Co. Economical Development Trust, R., Muncie	351993189
Symmes Trust f/b/o Winchester Community High School Scholarship, Russell, Muncie	351993193
Tinsley Trust, Bertha E., Frankfort	356323376
Veal Trust f/b/o Greensfork Community Center, Glen, Richmond	356494540
Whiteley Residue Trust, Burt, Muncie	356009799
Wilson Trust, John D., Muncie	356208536
Yohe Charitable Trust, C. L. & W. R., Evansville	656085500

Iowa

Ball Trust, Nellie, Iowa City	426281954
Barlow Trust, Florence Mabel, Cherokee	237404470
Beck Memorial Trust, Ottumwa	426187249
Bodwell Trust, Gertrude A., Waterloo	426235454

APPENDIX B

STATE	EIN
Bratrud Foundation, O. M., Kensett	421124043
Brown Charitable Trust, Ruth M., Des Moines	426477710
Brownell Library Fund, Armina, Winterset	426136313
Chariton Boy Scout Troop No. 149 Trust, Chariton	426377657
Chariton Girl Scout Association Trust, Chariton	426377635
Columbus Junction State Bank Foundation, The, Columbus Junction	426078955
Cullen Family Charitable Trust, Vincent and Nina, Burlington	426530955
Dautremont Charitable Trust, Grace L., Riverside	421278030
Dautremont Charitable Trust, John & Lucy, Riverside	426491860
Dege Nursing Scholarship Fund, Gladys A., Clinton	421372474
Earlville - Ruth Suckow Memorial Association, Earlville	426130786
Elson Marital Trust f/b/o West Des Moines Methodist Church, Hildred B. F., Des Moines	426603517
Fairgrave Educational Trust, D. J., Des Moines	426452541
Felten Memorial Fund, Galen, The, Cherokee	421154159
Gill Scholarship Fund, Regina J., Clinton	421376707
Glenn Foundation Trust, Clarence P., Ottumwa	421345580
Haller Foundation, Ida, Davenport	237384812
Hoenk Foundation, Howard & Katherine, Algona	421228737
Kennedy Trust, Craig, Waterloo	426387046
Kenny Trust, Pearl, Cherokee	426094340
Lake Schlosser Trust, Newton	421092142
Luick Memorial Hospital Trust, Chester P. Luick & Vida, Belmond	426076778
Mareldick Foundation, Inc., Muscatine	426074629
Mitchell Foundation, Dean & Juanita, West Des Moines	421082307
Morgan Trust, N. Belle, Iowa City	426204043
Muscatine Art Center Support Foundation, Muscatine	421170526
Olson Trust f/b/o Woodward State Hospital, Clifford & Anna, Des Moines	426561196
Rapp Testamentary Trust, Harry A., Council Bluffs	426423619
Redden Trust, Joseph P., Cherokee	421302567
Rock Rapids Area Development Foundation, Inc., Rock Rapids	421293260
Root Charitable Trust Fund, Richard Morton Root and Ruth Bailey, The, Des Moines	396664822
Schleiter Trust, Frederick, Des Moines	426155389
Schlichting Trust, Fred W., Mason City	426528702
Schroppel Trust Fund, Emma L., Winterset	426313654
Schwartz Education Trust Fund, Edward J., Ottumwa	426476116
Shoemaker Charitable Trust, George T. & Margaret E., Ottumwa	426448073
Spalding Catholic Foundation, Inc., Granville	421288570
St. Bernard Trust, Breda	471298832
St. John American Lutheran Church Foundation of Cedar Falls, Iowa, Cedar Falls	421129788
Sulentic Charitable Foundation, Nicholas, The, Waterloo	426269706
Trovillo Memorial Scholarship Fund, Lois Porterfield, Burlington	426088390
Walsh Fund Trust, Davenport	426052697
Wente Church Trust, Leo G., Breda	426460680
Winkel Family Foundation, Sergeant Bluff	421464738
Woitishek Memorial Lecture Fund Trust, Cedar Rapids	426054387
Yeggy Charitable Trust, Bernadine, The, Riverside	421286485
Younker Foundation Trust, Rachel, Des Moines	426271667

Kansas

Anderson Memorial Trust for Ceder Township Cemetery, Orval K. & Lucille, Independence	367006771
Berryman Trust B for United Presbyterian Foundation, J. W., Wichita	486195744
Billenwillms Charitable Trust, Ordie T., The, Goodland	486287879
Billue Remainder Unitrust, G. H., Wichita	486195087
Boyer Educational Trust, Wellington	456102945
Brister Hospital Trust, Bertha R., Lawrence	486103283
Bromelsick Trust, Alfred E., Lawrence	486103282
Brown Trust, Mary Helen, Olathe	486364109

STATE	EIN
Casado Charitable Trust, Luis A., Wichita	486336948
Crawford Irrevocable Trust f/b/o St. Mark's Lutheran Church, Roy & Nellie, Emporia	486377824
Dyatt Charitable Trust, Ethel, Topeka	486259847
ESU Endowment Fund Trust, Emporia	486254679
Fowler Trust, Olen R., Augusta	486188550
Grimes Charitable Trust, Daisy Ferguson, Topeka	486310772
Grindinger Trust, Paul H., Prairie Village	486172978
Henderson Foundation Trust, Pearl Powell, Kansas City	486282495
Hunter United Methodist Church Testamentary Trust, Ralph and Lucile, Hays	486312307
Hupfer Charitable Foundation, Warren J. Hupfer and Irene, The, Russell	481025680
Kansas Alpha of Phi Delta Theta Education Foundation, Shawnee Mission	237337119
KG & E Project DESERVE Trust Fund, Wichita	486268846
Leiszler Foundation Trust, Glen and Rose, Clay Center	486277264
Lyon County Historical Society Maintenance Trust, Emporia	746445314
McDowell Trust, Dovie Grace, Smith Center	486186347
Mills Educational Trust, Earl L., Wichita	486300412
Neosho Memorial Hospital Foundation, Inc., Chanute	480758283
Nicol Trust f/b/o Nicol Home, Inc., James Herbert, Shawnee Mission	486125684
Roberts Foundation, Inc., H. G., Pittsburg	480930432
Ross Memorial Foundation, Michael, Leawood	481091978
Schellhorn Private Foundation Irrevocable Charitable Trust, Charles and Elizabeth, Shawnee Mission	481062860
Schleich Trust f/b/o WKACD, Barbara E., Hays	486334367
Shebilsky Trust, Paul M. and Esther M., Emporia	486301419
Somers Trust, S. Orlando, Emporia	486262499
Spurrier Memorial Fund, Salina	486305185
St. Andrew's Episcopal Parish Fund, Emporia	486254677
St. John's Rest Home Endowment Foundation, Hays	480922082
Sterling Scholarship Fund for Nurses Training, George E. & Blanche, Wichita	481090076
Trinity Foundation, Inc., Dodge City	481007030
Truman Good Neighbor Award Foundation, Harry S., Shawnee Mission	431113552
Wendy's Wonderful Kids Foundation, Inc., Wichita	481143308

Kentucky

Alexander Trust, Lofton, Hopkinsville	626318149
American Cancer Society Warren Fund, Louisville	616119193
Avellar Fund No. 2, Katherine S., Louisville	616019806
Beiderwell Foundation, Paducah	611221699
Brennan Foundation, Albert A., Louisville	616094299
Buckley Kentucky State College Scholarship Trust, Emma, Lexington	616173299
Bullock Estate Trust, Charlotte, Louisville	616019886
Burnham Trust, Pearl W., Louisville	616092638
Bush Trust f/b/o Clark County Hospital, Susan, Louisville	616159751
Centre College of Kentucky Trust, Louisville	616077375
Doyle Trust, Mildred G., Louisville	616079934
Elliott Memorial Trust, Inc., Elizabeth Akers, Pikeville	311070854
Emmanuel Episcopal Church, Louisville	616023506
Evans Trust f/b/o First Christian Church, Magdelan M., Louisville	626343892
Evans Trust f/b/o University of Louisville School of Medicine, Magdalen McDowell, Louisville	626343891
Ferre Irrevocable Charitable Trust, Joseph C., Louisville	616144664
First Christian Church Trust, Louisville	611241950
First Presbyterian Church Trust, Pikeville	616163224
Flemingsburg Christian Church Foundation, Flemingsburg	311514945
Garth Educational Society, Lexington	616067514
Grace Episcopal Church - Almstedt Fund, Louisville	616094271
Grace Episcopal Church - Bodine Fund, Louisville	616094270
Harris-Stansell Family Charitable Trust, Louisville	626320081
Homberger Trust, Iva W., Louisville	616036185

STATE	EIN
Jeffress Trust, Frances R., Louisville	616020156
Johnson Endowment Fund, Frank H., Louisville	616036186
Kahn Trust, Walter M., Louisville	616063589
Kentucky Heart Association Warren Fund, Louisville	616116216
Kosair Charities - Wilcox Fund, Louisville	616133401
Lester-Ratliff Foundation Trust, Princeton	616155267
Lingenfelter Memorial Trust, Princeton	616027278
Louisville Visual Arts Association, Louisville	616020622
McCarroll Trust f/b/o Christian County Historical Society, Charles, Hopkinsville	616169062
McCarroll Trust f/b/o First Methodist Church Library, William, Hopkinsville	616105494
McCarroll Trust f/b/o First Presbyterian Church, Joe, Hopkinsville	616074589
McCarroll Trust f/b/o Hopkinsville Public Library, Joe, Hopkinsville	616074590
McCormick Trust f/b/o Clark County Hospital, S., Louisville	616160125
McCormick Trust f/b/o Clark Regional Medical Center, W. H., Louisville	616042483
McCullum Fund f/b/o Berea College, Louisville	616015467
Michael-Walters Industries Foundation, Inc., Louisville	311135407
Milton Charitable Trust, John L. & Lucy L., Louisville	616070034
Moore Charitable Trust, W. R., Louisville	616151099
Neonatal Research Trust of Louisville, Louisville	616209412
Norton Memorial Infirmary-Allen R. Hite Memorial Fund, Louisville	616020308
Pennyroyal Area Museum Trust, Hopkinsville	611280844
Ross Foundation f/b/o Fleming County Library, Vernice, Flemingsburg	311503729
Schulman Fund 2, Anna, Louisville	616149311
Smock Charitable Trust, Margaret D., Louisville	616155883
Snyder Charitable Foundation, Inc., Thomas D., Richmond	311130373
Society for the Prevention of Cruelty to Animals, Louisville	616081184
Sower Trust f/b/o Salvation Army, Frank W., Frankfort	311050148
St. Andrew's Protestant Episcopal Church Trust, Louisville	616073029
3108 Foundation, Louisville	616182732
Turner Memorial Fund, Otis T., Louisville	616117542
Van Ruff Trust, Augusta C., Louisville	616020488
Walnut Street Baptist Church Foundation, Inc., Louisville	611253824
Wigginton Trust, Sarah H., Louisville	616020520
Winn Testamentary Trust, Lizzie Mannen Turney, Mount Sterling	616033152
Wright Fund No. 2, James Stanley, Louisville	616057898

Louisiana

Behl Trust f/b/o Alma College, Florence and Minnie, New Orleans	726099159
Behl Trust f/b/o Berea College, Florence and Minnie, New Orleans	726099158
Behl Trust f/b/o Westminister Presbyterian Church, Florence and Minnie, New Orleans	726099157
Blackwell Foundation, William T., The, Baton Rouge	720968728
Burden Foundation, Baton Rouge	726030712
Friends of Frances W. Gregory Junior High School Foundation, New Orleans	721277846
Greer/Heard Ministerial Education Foundation for New Orleans Baptist Theological Seminary, The, Baton Rouge	721158319
Johnson Scholars Foundation, Belle, New Orleans	721405770
Kaken American Foundation, Belle Chasse	721127616
Kastin Brain Research Foundation, Dr. Abba J., Metairie	720875004
Loving Historical Foundation, New Orleans	720909237
Mills Trust f/b/o Plains Presbyterian Church, David Pipes Mills and Marguerite H., Zachary	726069335
Owens Charitable Trust, Nancy Crowell, Alexandria	726135740

STATE	EIN
Palfrey Testamentary Trust f/b/o University of the South, William T., New Orleans	726017501
Pipes Foundation, Inc., Ruston	720826053
Rippner Family Foundation, New Orleans	581908371
Second Trust Fund for First Church of Christ Scientist, New York, The, New Orleans	726163292
Thompson Trust f/b/o Mayo Clinic, William B., New Orleans	726130398
Williams Memorial Foundation, Clifford L., Jena	581953687

Maine

Clark Trust, Rose M., Camden	016085692
Fiore Family Foundation, Joseph & Mary, The, Damariscotta	311628286
Forster Trust, Maurice W. and Leila M., Livermore Falls	016036049
Glenburn Library Trust, Ellsworth	016157069
Heald Trust, Robert H. & Eleanor S., Camden	016131271
Longley Foundation, Governor James B., Portland	010371179
McCobb Trust, Edith H., Camden	016101113
McKenney & Emery W. Booker Education Trust, Marion, Brunswick	016070365
Mersereau Trust, Z. A., Livermore Falls	016008575
O'Neil Charitable Trust, Gladys F., Bangor	016138763
SPHERE, Inc., Belfast	010482480
St. Patrick's Permanent Lay Trust, Damariscotta	237346274

Maryland

American Friends of the Rabinovitch Yeshivah College, Inc., Baltimore	237392981
Anibal Charitable Trust, Bethesda	526317528
Basic Cancer Research Foundation, Inc., Pikesville	521296413
Bowie Trust, Lucy Leigh, Baltimore	526081220
Brandt Trust, Edna H., Baltimore	526211452
Budd Equity Trust, Michael W., Baltimore	526029952
Bustard Charitable Permanent Trust Fund, Elizabeth & James, Baltimore	546250970
Buster Charitable Trust, M. W., Baltimore	546325354
Collel Bayit Vegan Foundation, Inc., Baltimore	237204516
Cramer Trust, Bessie Wood, Baltimore	526102151
Cuddeback Trust, Lucille M., Baltimore	521939930
Downman Trust, John Y., Baltimore	546031086
Eakle Trust, Esther G., Baltimore	526116859
Eliasberg Memorial Foundation, Louis & Hortense, Baltimore	521199166
Geist Church & Graveyard Foundation, Baltimore	526049380
Gerber Foundation, Thomas Gerber and Kay, Chevy Chase	520845122
Gibson Island Country School Foundation, Inc., Gibson Island	526036544
Glazer Foundation, Inc., Howard and Leah, Owings Mills	526048087
Greene Foundation, Inc., H. Charles, The, Baltimore	521736505
Greggs Trust, William R., Baltimore	526028850
Harness Creek Foundation, Inc., Baltimore	521918741
Henry Trust, D. Russell, Linthicum	526247886
Hood College and Emmanuel United Church of Christ Trust, Baltimore	546186920
International Airline Training Fund of the United States of America, Inc., The, Chevy Chase	521331011
Keefer Charitable Remainder Unitrust Part C, Arthur C., Greenbelt	526903038
Larrabee Trust, Stewart, Linthicum	526063427
Maryland Community Foundation, Inc., Baltimore	521488607
Meyerhoff Foundation, Inc., Lyn P., The, Baltimore	521624876
Newburger-Jacobson-Boss Trust A, The, Baltimore	546227926
Newburger-Jacobson-Boss Trust B, The, Baltimore	546227925
Nydegger Trust, Allen C., Baltimore	526031269
Perella Scholarship Fund, Maddalena and Joseph, Baltimore	526526866
Pickering Trust, Julia H., Linthicum	526523270

APPENDIX B

STATE	EIN
Roberts Trust Fund, Annie, Baltimore	526023574
Saul Fund, Andrew Maguire, The, Baltimore	526405386
Selden Memorial Trust, Baltimore	546034144
Space Shuttle Children's Trust Fund, The, Baltimore	521439509
Theiss Memorial Trust, Herman and Florence, Silver Spring	526404956
Van Ormer Fund Trust, W. A., Baltimore	526209682
Volta Bureau Fund Trust & Building Fund, Baltimore	526029302
Weinberg Memorial Fund, Henry, Frederick	521696920
Young Charitable Trust, Robert L., Baltimore	526140689
Zimmer Charitable Trust, Alverda, Baltimore	546030260

Massachusetts

Agawam Center Library Association, Agawam	042133872
American Diabetes Association, Boston	046093069
American Friends of Sharadha, Inc., North Andover	042980021
Ashton Trust, Elisha V., Boston	046079166
Babcock Trust, William, Boston	066026216
Babson Memorial, Inc., Isabel, Gloucester	046031813
Backman Research Foundation, Newton	042687475
Bacon Trust, Ada B. W., Boston	237425266
Bailey Trust of Massachusetts, Lucretia Prentiss, Boston	042178056
Bayard Trust, Edward Mayo, Boston	046127465
Beaucourt Foundation, Inc., Boston	042979426
Bendetson Charitable Foundation, Norris & Margery, Haverhill	042943128
Birchrock Foundation, The, Brookline	043424527
Bissell Charitable Foundation, George S., The, Wellesley	042368188
Blake Trust, Charles M., Boston	046091311
Bland 1990 Charitable Trust, Caroline Thayer, Boston	046676539
Bliss Trust, Milford E., Boston	046007850
Branscomb Family Foundation, The, Hingham	133355618
Bridge Trust, Edmund, Boston	237162485
Bridge Trust, Frederick W., Boston	046092560
Brigham Trust, Robert, Boston	046094404
Brooks Charitable Endowment, Shepherd, Boston	046900178
Brooks Trust, Harold, Boston	046526806
Bryant Trust, John D., Boston	046067847
Burroughs Trust, Harry F., Boston	046384106
Busiel Trust, Frank E., Boston	046091333
Capen Trust, Charles A., Boston	066074400
Carey Trust, Arthur A., Boston	046093034
Carmen Charitable Foundation, Milton, Lexington	046668872
Chatham Citizens Scholarship Trust Fund, The, West Chatham	222589632
Chepou Trust, Ernest Thomas, Boston	046215842
Chickering Trust, George E., Boston	046091347
Cleveland Trust f/b/o Aged & Infirm Women in Pauper Institutions, Eliza C., Boston	046042788
Cohen Family Foundation, Ollie A. & Eleanore, The, Worcester	046048458
Coleman Trust f/b/o Godfrey DeBouillion Commandery of King Philip Lodge A.F. & A.M., Charles F., Boston	042623203
Collins Trust, Robert, Northampton	046507727
Conant Health Care Center Trust, William H., Boston	046091357
Conant Hospital Trust, William H., Boston	046091358
Conkey Trust, John H. & Dorothy D., Boston	046094894
Crockett Trust, Angie, Boston	046330090
Dean Trust, Charles A., North Andover	046026858
Dewing Greek Numismatic Foundation, Holliston	046130118
DiGregorio Foundation, Fileno, Southbridge	237067919
Dodge Trust f/b/o Anna Jacques Hospital, et al., Milton L., Boston	046374983
Donations for Education in Liberia, Trustees of, Cambridge	046013691
Douglas Trust f/b/o Douglas Library of Hebron, Connecticut, Charles J., Boston	046095643
Doyle Fund, Duncan E. and Lucienne A., Boston	046573741
Dragone Family Scholarship Fund, South Yarmouth	043297154

STATE	EIN
Draper Trust, Wickliffe P., Boston	046008450
Dyer Trust, Marietta W., Hanover	042127029
Ellis Trust, Marion Nickerson, Boston	046295187
Ellis Trust, Warren E., Boston	046095570
Everett Divinity Trust, Mildred, Boston	046279912
Fiske Trust, Laura S., Boston	046121595
Fogg Charitable Trust, Horace T. Fogg, Isabella F. Fogg, and Helen T., The, Boston	112698718
Forra Trust f/b/o Plymouth County Health Association, Inc., Carlton, Boston	046191379
Foulds Family Foundation, Mr. & Mrs. William, Boston	066269485
French Testamentary Trust f/b/o Community Visiting Nurse Agency, Inc., Henry W., Hingham	046026813
French Testamentary Trust f/b/o Parish Hall Association, Henry W., Hingham	046026814
Friends of Brooks Free Library, Inc., Harwich	042579888
Friends of the Pelham Free Public Library, Pelham	043077516
Friends of the Westport Council on Aging, Inc., Westport	042914504
Gasbarri Trust, Fiorangelo, Waltham	046042267
Gelfand Charitable Foundation, Adam Russell, Chestnut Hill	043252302
Gendrot Trust, Felix A., Boston	046010347
George Trust, Oscar J., Boston	046242439
Gildersleeve Trust, George H., Boston	046364773
Ginn Trust, Edwin, Boston	046039187
Golber Family Foundation, Constance Katz, Longmeadow	043109338
Greenleaf Trust, Charles H., Boston	046091454
Griffith Fund, Thomas B., Middleboro	046060207
Gund Art Foundation, The, Boston	042714713
Gustin Scholarship Fund Trust f/b/o Boston University, Robert & Edna, Boston	656112022
Hale Memorial Foundation, Salem	046039320
Hale Trust, Albert E., Boston	046018619
Hammond 1995 Charitable Trust, James R., Boston	043399157
Hansen Memorial Scholarship Foundation, Fc 3 William R., Beverly	046599714
Harris Foundation, William H., Boston	046197960
Hayes Home for Aged Persons, Inc., Maria, Natick	042103798
Hitchcock Trust, Mary G., Warren	510205082
Hoar Trust, D. Blakely, Boston	046012203
Holtzer Fund, Charles W., Boston	046008252
Hopkinton Community Playground Trust, Hopkinton	043481921
Howard Trust, John N., Boston	046110375
Hubbard Memorial Foundation, Inc., Janet Turner, Swampscott	222864924
Hunnewell Trust, Louisa, Boston	046304635
International Friends of the Val Richer, Boston	043190401
Juvenile Diabetes Foundation, The, Boston	223183669
Kade Fund in Memory of Max Kade, Annette, Boston	136754615
Kremer Charitable Remainder Trust, Boston	043323314
Lane Trust f/b/o Hampton Academy, Charles H., Boston	026004756
Lawton Memorial Home, Abbie Frances, South Attleboro	237259854
Little Trust, Flora T., Boston	046448653
Loomis Foundation f/b/o Massachusetts Audubon Society, Frances L., Springfield	046656216
Lummus Trust, Carrie L., Salem	046016036
Lusk Trust, George H., Falmouth	046238001
Maxim House, Inc., Annie, Rochester	042791081
McGillicuddy Charitable Trust, John T., Boston	042642387
Memorial Fund of Phi Beta Epsilon, Concord	016013997
Miles Trust f/b/o Worcester Polytechnic Institute, Alice W., Boston	046019792
Morrill Charitable Trust, Mayor Gayden W., Newburyport	043049521
Morrison Trust, Boston	046390868
Morrison Trust, Mary A., Boston	046091562
Morse Memorial Fund, Edith R., The, Boston	046063191

APPENDIX B

STATE	EIN
Nies Trust f/b/o Christ Chapel, James B., Boston	136058174
Norton Trust for Wellesley College, H. R., Boston	046926918
O'Neil Trust, Martina, Salem	046416879
Parker Trust, Moses Greely, Boston	046091581
Parker Trust for Parker Lectures, Moses Greely, Boston	046091583
Parlin Trust, Albert N., Boston	510150855
Parmenter Hospital Trust, Boston	046021960
Partridge Trust, Albert L. & Olive D., Boston	046014691
Quogue Community Foundation, Inc., Carlisle	116036652
Raptelis Foundation, Demosthenis, Boston	046233953
River Road Charitable Corporation, Boston	046169258
Rome Charitable Trust, Boston	046017410
Rounds Trust, Thomas B., Boston	046029370
Ruffini Trust f/b/o Plymouth Lions Club, Alcide, Hanover	046607684
Russell Trust, Herbert P., Boston	046092582
Russell Trust, Winifield S., Boston	046096914
Schoellkopf IV Berkshire Scholarship Fund, J. F., Sheffield	136034251
Shaw Fund, Miriam, Boston	046497465
Sheets Trust, Sankey L., Malden	046012458
Smith Trust, Timothy, Boston	046091664
Spooner Trust, James, Boston	046017066
Stearns Trust f/b/o Arnold Mills Community House, Margaret, Boston	056061744
Storer Trust, The, Medford	046034836
Students House Incorporated, Boston	042105949
Sweatt Trust, William H., Boston	042648729
Taylor Educational Foundation, Thomas Taylor & Charlotte Valentine, The, Boston	222571261
Tazewell Foundation, Boston	046060558
Tekulsky Trust, Anna Harvey, Boston	046173120
Tripp Fund, The, Boston	136255894
Van Der Wansem Family Charitable Trust, The, North Billerica	046657273
Veen Educational Trust, Jan, Boston	046167791
Warren Hospital Fund Trust, Agnese, Bridgewater	222817713
Winer Charitable Trust, Hy, The, Weston	046193365
Winning Home, Inc., Bradford	046049776
Woodward Donors Fund, North Quincy	046066049

Michigan

Akers Trust, Forrest H., East Lansing	386066391
Anderson, Bernard R. MacNeil and Marie Anderson MacNeil Trust, Harold R., Saginaw	526158958
Benson Charitable Trust, Betzer, Grand Rapids	367057883
Biedermann Trust, Erma E., Detroit	386453506
Blissfield American Legion Trust, Detroit	386314373
Blissfield First Presbyterian Church Trust, Detroit	386314379
Bornman Educational Trust, Detroit	386592814
Bornman Trust for Conservative Causes, Frederick D., Detroit	386592813
Bradstrum Charitable Trust, Grand Rapids	383189696
Braude Foundation, Rose, Detroit	386664680
Brunkow Memorial Trust, Charles F. and Edith E., Saginaw	386492107
Burns Athletic Trust f/b/o Children of St. Anselm Parish, Edward J., Dearborn Heights	386704674
Cady Charitable Trust, Mary Ida, Jackson	386054013
Christian Missionary Scholarship Foundation, Keego Harbor	363553749
Devereaux Foundation, Richard C., The, Bloomfield Hills	382638858
Dewey Educational Trust, Howard, Grand Rapids	366449286
Diebel Charitable Trust, Lucile K., Birmingham	386542792
Diebolt Foundation, Plymouth	383444677
Dorris Charitable Trust, Albert, Jackson	386187670
Dubois Scholarship Fund, Ruth, Grand Rapids	386664958
Earle Charitable Trust, Eva, Saginaw	386246574
Filer Board, Inc., Carrie, Manistee	381367303

STATE	EIN
Ford House, Edsel & Eleanor, Grosse Pointe Shores	382218274
Foss Family Foundation, Commerce Township	383326775
Friends of Yerevan State University, Farmington Hills	541800204
Gargaro Irrevocable Trust, Carol A., Oak Park	386569841
Gershenson Foundation, Charles H., Detroit	386454423
Giddey Trust, Doris J., Benton Harbor	386505877
Graham Educational Fund, Inc., Meda, Detroit	386261402
Green Charitable Trust, Leslie H. & Edith C., Detroit	386162077
Green Memorial Endowment Fund, Leslie H., Edith C. & Robert C., Detroit	386043971
Harmony Chapel Missionary Church Testamentary Trust, Marcellus	382866911
Heartland Foundation, Grand Rapids	386190071
Hicks Charitable Trust, Samuel J., Detroit	597039374
Jacobson Stores Foundation, Jackson	382570384
Jaffe Scholarship Fund f/b/o Colon High School, Abraham & Neva, Sturgis	316447467
Johns Family Foundation, Donald L., Southfield	383388669
Kahn Associated Architects & Engineers Foundation, Albert, Detroit	382144518
Kelter Foundation, Inc., Birmingham	237003469
Kiwanis of Michigan Foundation, Petoskey	381723513
Knooihuizen Irrevocable Trust, Ann G., Detroit	386436167
Kutsche Charitable Trust, Grand Rapids	386610379
Lee Foundation, Grand Rapids	386057375
Lincoln Health Care Foundation, Troy	381359220
Lowell Charitable Foundation, Arthur J. and Josephine W., Grand Rapids	366911813
Lussier Irrevocable Trust, Rosaline A., Monroe	386544343
Luyckx Trust, Jeanne McMurchy, Novi	386679502
MacCrone Trust, Edward E., Detroit	386043730
Macomb County Rotary Foundation, Mount Clemens	381579780
Mann Charitable Trust, Katherine, Flint	386653802
Mann Trust, Jessie Ellen, Jackson	386191020
McColl-Batts Foundation, The, Kalamazoo	386052870
McElmurry Charitable Trust, Leland R. & Evelyn, Berrien Springs	386057003
McVicar Trust, Mary, Jackson	386105310
Meadlock Foundation, Inc., Eastpointe	581655986
Messer Trust f/b/o Pennock Hospital, Richard B., Grand Rapids	386051680
Messer Trust f/b/o Pennock Hospital & McKinley Home for Boys, Frances Williams, Grand Rapids	386050417
Mette Foundation, Inc., Detroit	510177958
Mid-Michigan Railway Historical Society, Flint	382484876
Miller Music Education Endowment Fund, Rhea E., Bay City	386637604
Nugent Trust f/b/o Confraternity of the Precious Blood, Lillian A., Muskegon	386376782
Orrell Trust f/b/o Children's Library of Richards Landing, Florence W., Flint	386041099
Pennell Memorial Trust, Clarence & Ella, Saginaw	386040423
Pennock Hospital Endowment Fund, Grand Rapids	386050351
Pennock Hospital Fuller Fund, Grand Rapids	386050352
Perry Trust, Alexander Petrellis, Detroit	386475645
Peterson Foundation, Julie A., Detroit	382713870
Phantom Foundation, Jackson	383353208
Phelps Foundation, Inc., Robert J., Bingham Farms	383258350
Pribil Trust f/b/o Hoyt Library, Maxwell, Saginaw	386723514
Pribil Trust f/b/o Saginaw Symphony, Maxwell, Saginaw	386723515
Redeemer U.S. Foundation, Grand Rapids	382944475
Reid Trust, Carrie M. & Alex A., Saginaw	386339147
Richardson Trust, James B., Detroit	946505556
Riley Foundation, Inc., Detroit	237253605
Rogers Testamentary Trust, Charles A., Bloomfield	386434903
Ross Foundation, Grace P., Benton Harbor	386040221
Saginaw Public Libraries Foundation, Saginaw	382816474
Sanders Memorial Fund, Jack & Marguerite, Saginaw	382881468
Saranac Education Foundation, Saranac	383076816
Schiefer Charitable Trust, Olga, Grand Rapids	383078080

APPENDIX B

STATE	EIN
Schneider Trust for Village of Lowell, Philip H., Grand Rapids	386513806
Sears Scholarship Fund, Fred and Lizzie, Jackson	386447142
Shofnitz Charitable Trust, John R., Grand Rapids	383206767
Sibert Trust, Charles J. & Clarissa B., Rochester	386495050
Sigma Gamma Foundation, St. Clair Shores	386074066
Skeen French Trust, Velma M., Coldwater	386418911
Small Trust f/b/o Cascades Humane Society, R. V., Detroit	386677649
Smith Charitable Trust, Jason L. and Carrie M., Detroit	591952016
Sparling Trust, William F., Saginaw	382437047
Stevenson Foundation, Walter H. and Ella, Detroit	364063285
Stoddard Charitable Trust, Howard P., Grand Rapids	383036315
Stone Trust, John Franklin, Detroit	386658355
Stowe Trust, Emma, Jackson	386054053
Timme Revocable Trust, Abigail S., Big Rapids	770182900
University of Michigan Club of Grand Rapids Scholarship Fund, The, Grand Rapids	382707702
Van Camp Family Foundation, James and Alma, Harrison Township	383324843
Van Gessel Scholarship Foundation, Grand Rapids	386527749
Vanwingen Memorial Fund, Peter J. and Anne, Grand Rapids	386491228
Victor Foundation, The, Bloomfield Hills	382843599
West Trust, Elton W. and Elsie M., Flint	386690988
Whiting Auditorium Trust, James H., Flint	386041292
Wright Trust, Esther, Jackson	386349418
Zacharias Trust, Herbert T., Saginaw	386555107

Minnesota

Adkins Trust, Virgil, St. Cloud	411642234
Agranoff Perpetual Charitable Trust, Leo, St. Paul	416285959
Andersch Charitable Remainder Unitrust, Stanley P., St. Paul	416278127
Anderson Charitable Trust, Arthur H., Minneapolis	416013967
Anderson Trust f/b/o United Lutheran Church, Arthur, Saint Cloud	456017110
Argall/Hibbs Foundation, Prior Lake	411875159
Astleford Foundation, Minneapolis	411893317
Beckering Trust, Gerrit, Minneapolis	416013857
Bell Testamentary Trust f/b/o University of Minnesota, James F., Minneapolis	416039114
Benfield Testamentary Trust, William J., Buffalo	510155655
Carpenter Scholarship Foundation, Isaac W. & Carrie M., St. Paul	470661090
Christian Foundation for Mission Youth, Hawley	237046378
Clark Trust, Lavinia R., St. Paul	416015929
David Memorial Trust, John C. & Nettie V., Minneapolis	510159851
Detroit Country Club Improvement Trust, Detroit Lakes	416288825
Doebler Family Memorial Scholarship Trust, R. J., St. Cloud	456082665
Doherty Medical Assistance Fund, James, St. Paul	416263344
Doherty Scholarship Fund, James E., St. Paul	416257985
Doherty Seminary Training Fund, James E., St. Paul	416265465
Dorea Foundation, Minneapolis	411703735
Fallander Trust, Lawrence T., St. Paul	416225773
Friends of the Iron Range Interpretative Center, Inc., Chisholm	411288347
Gaughan Charitable Trust, Anthony L. Gaughan & Ann B., St. Paul	416100105
Helm Charitable Trust, Willis C., Minneapolis	416385896
Hirschmann Charitable Trust, W. B., St. Paul	366903256
Hornby Trust, Henry C., St. Paul	416010522
Hughes, Jr. Trust, Robert J., St. Paul	416141365
Kennedy Memorial Fund Trust, Augustus H., St. Paul	411328800
Kilgore York High School Trust Fund, William S., St. Paul	476134438
Kitrick Charitable Trust, Joseph, St. Paul	416077686
Knees Trust, Hertha, New Ulm	416282338

STATE	EIN
La Societe des 40 Hommes et 8 Chevaux-du-Minnesota Nurses Training Foundation, Minneapolis	411368905
Langhorst Testamentary Trust, Marjorie, St. Paul	476156640
Leinbach Foundation, Inc., Edith, Samuel and Elizabeth, Shoreview	411543086
Levinger Foundation, Harold & Lerena, Minneapolis	426089519
Maloney Educational Trust, St. Cloud	456037319
Mayo Trust f/b/o Olmsted County Historical Society, Charles W., St. Paul	416089052
Minnesota American Legion and Auxiliary Heart Research Foundation, St. Paul	510172292
Newman Foundation, Richard A., St. Paul	416058921
Olson Trust No. 1 f/b/o Crippled Children's Home of Jamestown, North Dakota, St. Paul	456010090
Olson Trust No. 2 f/b/o Children's Village of Fargo, North Dakota, St. Paul	456010091
Olson Trust No. 3 f/b/o Good Samaritan Home of Arthur, North Dakota, St. Paul	456010092
Putney Trust f/b/o University of Nebraska Foundation, William W., St. Paul	476115753
Richardson Foundation, Minneapolis	410426930
Rowan Memorial Trust, Harold Rowan & Doris Bates, St. Paul	476123798
Saville Memorial Trust, Jessie P., Minneapolis	426051628
Schering Trust for Arthritis Research, Margaret Harvey, Edina	363616824
Schering Trust for Cancer Research, Margaret Harvey, Edina	363615777
Schuh Residuary Trust, Vivian Fraser, St. Paul	416211919
Taylor Trust f/b/o Arizona State University, Minneapolis	866252445
Tysdale Charitable Trust, Allen, St. Paul	466092360
Veden Endowment for St. James Episcopal Church, F. W., St. Paul	416432733
Venables Foundation, C. Paul & Irene G., Winona	411596060
Warner Boys & Girls Home Trust, Minneapolis	426062314
Whiteside Charitable Trust, Muriel, St. Paul	416370669
Williamson Charitable Foundation, St. Paul	466017126
Wilson Charitable Trust, J. Morgan and Myrna B., Minneapolis	416343023

Mississippi

Bacon Endowment Fund, George, Hattiesburg	646026820
Burrus Charitable Trust, Ouida Midkiff, The, Greenwood	570895865
Clark Charitable Trust, Marie G., Jackson	646211876
Henry Trust, Wister & Frances C., Belzoni	646152982
Hurst Charitable Trust, Phyllis I., The, Greenwood	646216582
Lake Foundation, Robert E., Jackson	646024049
McDaniel Family Memorial Trust f/b/o Toccopolia LeBannon and First Presbyterian Churches, Pontotoc	646177574
Old Ladies Home Association, Jackson	640303089
Powers Foundation, Inc., R. V., Jackson	640411596
Simpson Memorial Fund, Percy & Adeline, Jackson	646021113
Vernon Library Foundation, Eva A., Brookhaven	510161677

Missouri

Ahmi Endowment Foundation, Simon and Monya Rositzky, St. Joseph	436647247
Ashland United Methodist Church Trust, St. Joseph	436734640
Baer Trust, Sigmond & Marie P., St. Louis	436019220
Bakers National Educational Foundation, Kansas City	436042834
Barnabas Foundation, The, St. Louis	436786091
Barth Memorial Fund, Louise K., St. Louis	376079725
Barton Educational Fund, Elizabeth M., Trenton	431745384
Blair Excellence in Education Trust 1995 f/b/o Camdenton R-3 Schools, C. C. & Dorothy, Springfield	436668740
Blakely Trust, Lenah L., Kansas City	446010489
Blewett Trust, Scott H., St. Louis	436018190
Blumenthal Trust for the Advancement of Mathematics, Leonard M. & Eleanor B., Columbia	436349858

APPENDIX B

STATE	EIN
Boettcher Trust, Bertha, St. Louis	431293333
Bohan Foundation, Ruth H., Kansas City	436269867
Booth Trust, Charles, St. Louis	376223314
Boutross Foundation, The, Kansas City	436362504
Branahl Foundation, Adeline & Erwin, Ferguson	431427612
Brown Memorial Trust, Ross B. & Helen H., Springfield	436256328
Buhrman Charitable Foundation, Albert J., St. Louis	436863596
Burger Scholarship Fund, Adeline and Edna L., Clayton	436189843
Cary Trust, James G., St. Louis	436023864
Castlen Trust, Harry W., St. Louis	436029856
City of St. Peters' Natatorium Foundation, St. Peters	431634579
Coggan Charitable Trust, Lulu Katherine, Kansas City	436166057
Cole Family Trust, Marguerite Elizabeth, St. Louis	436800909
Compton Foundation, James and Mary Ida, Kansas City	436271842
Crouse Survivors Trust, St. Louis	436368647
Culbertson Memorial Trust, Townley, Kansas City	446007509
Culver Trust, Mary, St. Louis	436019335
D'Arcy Trust for Princeton Club of St. Louis Freshman Region Scholarship Fund, William C., St. Louis	436020347
Degginger Trust f/b/o City of Highland, Bertha, Kansas City	436340462
Degginger Trust f/b/o Highland Community College, Bertha, Kansas City	436340465
Degginger Trust f/b/o Nelson Atkins Museum, Bertha, Kansas City	436340463
Degginger Trust f/b/o University of Missouri, Kansas City, Bertha, Kansas City	436340464
Deubach Trust, Earl J., Kansas City	436272199
Dinwiddie Memorial Trust, Richard A., Columbia	436273149
Dunkman Trust for The Central Institute for the Deaf, Genevieve E., St. Louis	436252764
Edwards Memorial Scholarship Fund, Kansas City	436368888
Eleanora Boston UniTrust, St. Louis	436354926
Eliscu Trust f/b/o Freeman Hospital, Juliette, Joplin	436276793
Elliot Foundation IV, Ben C., St. Louis	436197792
Ely Trust, Grace C., St. Louis	436143082
England Trust, Harry, Kansas City	436353297
Foltz Foundation, Martin, Marshall	237085248
Foster Foundation, John Henry & Bernadine, St. Louis	431242408
Foster Trust, James M., St. Louis	436019415
Fraise Charitable Foundation, Delbert H., St. Louis	431572456
Francis Trust f/b/o Shriners Hospital, Maude, St. Louis	436182679
Frech Trust, Stanley H., St. Louis	371340501
Frisby Trust, Maude Frisby & Hal, Kansas City	436389417
Funke Trust, Esther M., St. Louis	376063015
Godfrey Trust f/b/o St. Andrews Episcopal Church, Eleanor B., St. Louis	376215015
Goetsch Missionary Fund, Frederick A., St. Louis	436306046
Goodell Trust, Georgia, Kansas City	436251288
Gouldner Memorial Medical Trust, R. M., Kansas City	486258073
Graham Foundation, Georgine M., St. Louis	436021485
Greengard Charitable Trust, Dena, St. Louis	436275396
Grindol Trust No. 2, Roy F., St. Louis	486296563
Gundelach Memorial Fund, Charles A., St. Louis	436395177
Hall Trust, Edward C. Hall and Edna M., The, Chillicothe	436831970
Hall Trust f/b/o Helping Hand of Goodwill, Frank L., Kansas City	446006456
Hammond Trust, T. Claiborne, St. Louis	436671972
Hardesty Trust, Sallie M., Kansas City	446008005
Hardy Trust, Lottie C., St. Louis	436239401
Hayes Trust, Georgene Pree, St. Louis	376246539
Herrmann Charitable Trust, Peter and Virginia, The, Springfield	436849207
Hickman Trust, Walker, Kansas City	446007475
Hill Charitable Trust, Margaret Hall, Columbia	436413705
Hill Memorial Fund B, Vassie James, Kansas City	446008590
Hobbs Trust, Josephine E., Kansas City	446008101
Hollander Family Foundation, Richard M. & Gertrude L., Kansas City	436403855

STATE	EIN
Hughes Charitable Trust, Frederick G. & Rebekah B., Joplin	436265009
Humane Society of St. Joseph & Buchanan County Missouri, St. Joseph	440665750
Hunt Charitable Trust, Sylvester, Clayton	436255850
Hyde Charitable Trust, Katherine L., Kansas City	436364915
Jaccard Memorial Trust f/b/o Children's Mercy Hospital, Walter M., Kansas City	446007539
Jaccard Memorial Trust f/b/o St. Luke's Hospital, Walter M., Kansas City	446011269
Jaccard Trust, A. H. & L. A., Kansas City	436128316
Jaeger Testamentary Trust, Everett E., Clarksville	436380393
JB Endowment Trust for Lillian Recreation Park, St. Louis	436851920
Johnson Foundation, Dora & Arthur, Kansas City	431804023
Jones Trust for Baker University, Forrest E., Kansas City	436272412
Jones Trust for Oklahoma Indian Mission Methodist Conference, Forrest E., Kansas City	436272521
Kahn Charitable Trust, R. B., Kansas City	436194381
Kansas City Art Institute Trust, Kansas City	446007427
Klapmeyer Charitable Fund, Ray & Mary, Kansas City	237381612
Laurent Testamentary Trust, Anita K., Kansas City	486178505
Lipscomb Charitable Trust, Columbia	436121414
Loftus Charitable Trust, Alfred J., St. Louis	436700480
Loose Trust, Ella C., Kansas City	446009265
Loose Trust f/b/o Loose Park, Ella C., Kansas City	446008311
Love Charitable Trust, Lewis Crenshaw, Springfield	436290886
Maddux Charitable Friends of the Zoo Trust, Kansas City	436532211
Maize Conservation Education Fund, Glen and Alpha, Bethany	436408572
Martin Charitable Trust, Loy Crump, Columbia	436589909
McCreery and Gertrude Yancy Trust f/b/o Children's Mercy Hospital, Leroy, Kansas City	446007588
McQuigg Trust, Harry M., St. Louis	436019661
McWilliams Memorial Hospital Trust, Kansas City	436062691
Meeker Trust, Corry T., St. Louis	436019664
Mehl Charitable Trust, Albert J. and Jennie L., Kansas City	446006539
Miles Memorial Fund Trust, The, Bolivar	446014486
Morton Memorial Trust, Lewis Morton & Alsey, Kansas City	486131050
Neff Trust, Professor I. Frank, St. Louis	426395125
Nelson Memorial Fund, Earl F., St. Louis	436194040
Noll Scholarship Fund, Wylma, Poplar Bluff	431863249
Noyes Testamentary Trust, Sarepta Ward, St. Joseph	446013662
Parrish Charitable Trust, Elizabeth, St. Louis	436673904
Peet Museum Trust, Marguerite M., Kansas City	436726853
Peil Fund for Animals, Judy, St. Louis	431766375
Prairie Fork Conservation Area Charitable Endowment Trust, St. Louis	436736995
Preisler Trust, Edward M., St. Louis	436123084
Pryor Trust, Belle Findlay, St. Louis	436019769
Pusitz Charitable Trust No. 2, Manuel E. & Anne Belle, Kansas City	486217784
Pusitz Charitable Trust No. 3, Manuel E. & Anne Belle, Kansas City	486217785
Rice Educational Foundation, Ersa L., St. Louis	436309301
Richardson Charitable Trust, Albert & Juanita, St. Joseph	431834012
Root Trust, Susie M., Kansas City	431550273
Salina Regional Health Center Trust, Kansas City	486103150
Sanchez Medical Research Fund, Joseph Simeon, St. Louis	436693329
Sansone Trust B, Helen B., St. Louis	436311833
Saper Charitable Trust, Mitchell, Kansas City	431764199
Schoknecht Charitable Trust, Julia, St. Louis	916022083
Schultz Charitable Trust, Harold P., Clayton	436131488
Sellars Trust, Mary, Kansas City	486203686
Sharp Trust, Rena Pearl, Kansas City	436246115
Shrank Trust f/b/o the First United Presbyterian Church, James, Kansas City	436313795
Smith Charitable Trust, Paul & Mulva, St. Louis	436616234

APPENDIX B

STATE	EIN
Smithson Foundation, Kansas City	510187904
Souers Foundation, Sidney W. and Sylvia N., St. Louis	436079817
Taussig Trust, Amadee J., St. Louis	436020818
Taussig Trust C, Amadee J., St. Louis	436020821
Terrell Endowment Fund, Otis & Emma, St. Louis	436273379
Thompson Trust, Martha L., Kansas City	436206243
Tilles Item XX Testamentary Trust, Alvin S., St. Louis	716109531
Tribble Trust, Andrew, Maxine & Carrie E., Kansas City	436179211
Walkup Trust f/b/o Bah'a'is, Albert L., Kansas City	436229520
Wallace Charitable Trust, John K. & Ellen A., St. Louis	436320310
Walters Boone County Historical Foundation, Columbia	436320373
Warrington Building Repair and Maintenance Fund, St. Joseph	436446793
Weber Charitable Trust, Frank, St. Louis	436358776
Westminster College, Board of Trustees of, St. Joseph	436734639
Whimple Trust, William Randolph, St. Joseph	436069388
White Memorial Trust, Kelton E. & Alma M., St. Louis	436236634
Whittington Trust f/b/o Mayo Foundation, John D., St. Louis	376309741
Youngman Foundation, Harold D. and Estella G., Joplin	436334458

Montana

Copulos Family Hospital Trust, Columbus	816043540
Ewing Trust, James B. & Virginia J., Helena	816045202
Great Falls Children's Receiving Home Foundation, Inc., Great Falls	810463370
McIntyre Academic Scholarship Trust, George A., Great Falls	816047099
Mellenbrook Trust, The, Columbus	810398587
Miller Trust f/b/o Christ Church Episcopal Trust, Helen P., Kalispell	816051791
Parkening Foundation, Bozeman	954220932
St. Paul's Lutheran Church Trust Fund, Great Falls	841387364

Nebraska

Bach Foundation, W. J., Franklin	510141238
Baltes Charitable Trust A, L. & L., Scottsbluff	476164455
Baltes Charitable Trust B, L. & L., Scottsbluff	476164456
Butz Memorial Fund, Elizabeth, Lincoln	476159366
Card Charitable Trust, William Martin, Lincoln	476132038
Davis Charitable Trust, Elaine Lathrop, Omaha	911800878
Day Foundation Trust, Eugene C. Day and Lenore K., Lincoln	363776544
Friends of the Crete Public Library, Crete	470701007
Hahn Foundation, Fred and Ruth, The, Omaha	936268407
Hastings Catholic Schools Trust, Hastings	476140497
Helen, Ella & Flory Trust Fund f/b/o Nebraska Annual Conference of the United Methodist Church, Lincoln	476109476
Helen, Ella & Flory Trust Fund f/b/o St. Paul School of Theology, Lincoln	476109477
James Charitable Trust, Helen M. H., Wayne	476214028
Keene Memorial Library Trust Fund, Fremont	470681248
Koch Trust, Ruth M., Omaha	476049594
Pedersen Scholarship Fund, Edith B., Omaha	476187718
Rosenlof Foundation, Robert C., Kearney	470708237
Schlichtemier Charitable Fund, Inc., Clara, Omaha	470789126
Schmid Foundation, Marvin and Virginia, Omaha	470800637
Schulte Foundation, Grace, Omaha	476199193
Tifereth Israel Foundation, Inc., Lincoln	476025308
Trausch Trust f/b/o Sacred Heart Catholic Church of Roseland, NE, Louis B., Roseland	476232971
Twyman Foundation, Harvey, The, Omaha	363556770
University OB-GYN Foundation, Inc., Omaha	470712419

Nevada

Anderson Trust, Jesse G., Henderson	936117246
Bartells Trust f/b/o Progressive Animal Welfare Society (PAWS), Lulu, Henderson	943129995
Beck Trust, Mary Adde, Henderson	866072631

STATE	EIN
Bitzl Trust, Therese, Henderson	846016772
Cahill Trust, Dorothy Henrietta, Henderson	886014148
Calvo Trust, Mark S., Henderson	916288677
Chism Trust f/b/o Northwest Kidney Center, Catharine G., Henderson	916228502
Clocksin Endowment Fund, Lawrence H., Henderson	936212528
Failing Fund, Henry, Henderson	936021362
Fall Charitable Trust, Freda Phyllis, Henderson	916196480
Glasgow/Lanark Charitable Foundation, Henderson	876199868
Glazier Charitable Trust, Margaret, Henderson	866149940
Guss Foundation, Hazel C., Henderson	876151566
Jomsland Irrevocable Trust, Blanche T., Henderson	916383990
Krasno-Ostern Trust, Henderson	846187154
Lindner Trust f/b/o Epiphany of the Desert Episcopal Church, Louise, Henderson	866199282
Long Trust f/b/o Little League, Henderson	916221642
Marken "B" Trust f/b/o University of Wisconsin Foundation, Henderson	866040839
Museum Foundation, The, Las Vegas	942042112
Peterson Trust, Enoch, Henderson	866120479
Rosenberry Fund, Ethel, Henderson	866021345
Shown Charitable Trust No. 2, Agatha M., Henderson	936261855
Smith Trust f/b/o Guide Dogs for the Blind, Inc., J. B., Henderson	916071424
Smith Trust for Charities, Harris E., Henderson	936102386
Smyth Private Foundation Trust, Theresa M., Henderson	916263843
Staley Charitable Foundation, The, Henderson	880324391
Stevens Endowment Fund, James B., Henderson	936207793
Thompson Charitable Trust, Marion G., Reno	886042564
Tipton & Kalmbach Inc. Graduate Fellowship Fund Trust, Henderson	846020665
Vanstrom Trust B, Andrew E., Henderson	936107339
Vogstrom Memorial Trust, John and Esther, Henderson	916089556
Weidman Trust, Edward A., Henderson	936176362
Weiler Trust, Margaret, Henderson	866021442
Wheeler Charitable Trust, E. J. Wheeler & A. B., Henderson	826024443

New Hampshire

Abbot Testamentary Trust, Herbert G., Concord	026004792
Bixby Trust, Eliza, Concord	026004319
Bow Street Theatre Trust, Portsmouth	020430669
Britton Testamentary Trust, Arthur H., Concord	026004800
Camp Carpenter, Trustees of, Manchester	026008422
Coleman Trust, Ira A., Concord	026047757
Giles Trust, Ruby M., Portsmouth	026059633
Giles Trust f/b/o the Community Church of South Woodstock, Vermont, Evelyn C., Lebanon	046140117
Gilman Trust, Oliver J. M., Laconia	020222133
Griffin Trust, George W., Concord	026004330
Heard Trust, Arthur M., Portsmouth	026004459
Pequawket Foundation, The, North Conway	026015138
Remick Testamentary Trust, Edwin C., Laconia	026098262
Rowell Charitable Trust, Annie L., Concord	026055400
Rowell Intervivos Trust, Annie, Concord	026110470
Ruel Trust, John G., Laconia	026051991
Thompson Endowment f/b/o Berwick Academy, Roger R., Portsmouth	026123970
Thompson Endowment f/b/o Local Charities, Roger R. & Theresa, Portsmouth	026123968
Tuttle Charitable Trust, Raymond & Anna, Concord	526902233
Woodman Testamentary Trust, Annie E., Dover	026005604

New Jersey

American Friends of the Midrashia in Israel, Cherry Hill	236670864
Ayers Trust, Edward S., Chatham	226370112
B'nei Moses Anchi Austria of Brotmanville, Vineland	226351491
Bole Irrevocable Trust, Guntis, East Hanover	223205034
Brooks Foundation, Arthur Raymond, Summit	226543034

2608

APPENDIX B

STATE	EIN
Brown University Charitable Trust, Fair Lawn	137070437
Courter Memorial Scholarship Foundation, Joseph A., Hackettstown	226700131
Davis Charitable Foundation, Kathryn Stowman, The, Haddonfield	226614249
Diener Foundation, Juda, Springfield	226058586
Dornbusch Foundation, The, Livingston	226042691
Fellstone Foundation, Inc., New Brunswick	311485263
Friends of Buttonwood Hall Nursing Home, Mount Holly	222451894
Friends of David-Mian Foundation, Inc., The, Cherry Hill	222862580
Froehlich Charitable Trust, Otto, Princeton	226621115
Gallman & M. Hawley Foundation No. 2, A., New Brunswick	223614251
Garner Trust f/b/o East Carolina University, Eunice, New Brunswick	223614253
Halpern Family Foundation, Inc., Sam, Mountainside	222707942
Harris Memorial Fund, Green Brook	226091277
Ho-Ho-Kus Blood Donors Association, Ho-Ho-Kus	223136971
Karas Foundation, Chris A., Fort Lee	223337612
Kurtz Family Foundation, Inc., Nora, Morristown	223574588
Lake Drive Educational Foundation for Deaf and Hard of Hearing Children, Inc., Convent Station	223473606
Laning Charitable Trust, Mary T., The, Haddonfield	226518116
Leavitt Foundation, N. R., Warren	226034106
Littlefield Charitable Foundation, Dorothy & Harold, New Brunswick	223597107
Lynskey Trust, Margaret M., Hackensack	226614855
Mackler Cancer Foundation, Al, The, Ventnor	226675246
Markthaler Foundation, Inc., Theodore E. & Naomi Bitz, Newark	237150643
McLoughlin Foundation, Martha, Stockton	116038966
Moselowitz Charitable Trust, Herman G., Princeton	226404641
Mossler Trust, Adele S., Ridgewood	222490510
New Jersey Institute for Social Justice, Inc., Newark	223478143
Open Heart Foundation, Inc., Mays Landing	521801885
Paramus Lighting Company Foundation, Paramus	222615374
Phelps Foundation Trust, New Brunswick	596974405
Plummer Charitable Foundation, Inc., Hellen I., The, Cresskill	223365605
Quadrel Foundation, Inc., Nicholas and Catherine, Edison	222789506
Radiant Hope, The, Mountain Lakes	226744884
Rosin Trust, Hilda G., The, Northfield	226357785
Russell Research & Scholarship Foundation, Kenneth O., Cliffside Park	237139816
Sagamore Foundation, Livingston	221825723
Schacht Fund, Ernest, Wayne	226102192
Schneider Fund for Young Musicians, Marlboro	133862867
Shepherd Foundation, River Edge	226460210
Toepfer Family Foundation, Francis H., New Brunswick	376035557
Ullman Family Fund, Princeton	226730761
Wilf Charitable Trust, Halle, Mountainside	226646741
Wilf Charitable Trust II, Halle, Mountainside	226663697
Wilmurt Charitable Trust, Pennington	166374433

New Mexico

Dalpra Scholarship Fund f/b/o Fort Lewis College, Roy G., Farmington	856098695
Dalpra Scholarship Fund f/b/o San Juan College, Roy G., Farmington	856098694
McCurdy Fund, Everett D., Santa Fe	341738451
Monsimer Memorial Fund, Eugene D., Albuquerque	856008155
Oishei Consolidated Trust, John R., Santa Fe	166469052
Patterson Trust, Rosina, Silver City	856107055
Swayne Memorial Donation Trust f/b/o Daughters of the American Revolution, Mary C., Albuquerque	856009737

STATE	EIN
New York	
AHD Charitable Trust, Syracuse	166255709
Alcott Yeshiva Trust, R. W., New York	136978266
Allen Endowment Fund, Irene Sargent, Oneonta	166415136
Allen Fund, General Henry T., Rochester	136359878
American Association of University Women Trust, Inc., Rochester	136565418
American Friends of Keshet Eilon, Inc., New York	134015912
American Friends of Ohel Rabeinu Yonosson Ublima, Inc., Brooklyn	113179406
American Friends of the International Foundation Mozarteum, New York	133409938
American Friends of Yeshivat Sharei Ezra, Inc., Brooklyn	113222673
Anatolia College Trust, New York	133624826
Arents, Jr. Cerimon Fund, George, New York	136069576
Arnold Trust f/b/o First Methodist Church of Portlandville, Leon, Oneonta	166188191
Arnold Trust f/b/o Milford Center Baptist Church, Leon, Oneonta	166183679
Arzyl Fund, Inc., Dix Hills	226058536
Auerbach Memorial Trust Fund, Herman, New York	136201358
Bagg Trust f/b/o Southern Tier Zoological Society, Robert L., Rochester	166382685
Baptist Church of Sidney Center Trust, Walton	156023274
Bardes Trust f/b/o Liverpool Methodist Church, Irene, Syracuse	166317455
Bartlett Memorial Fund for the Needy, Walton	166179723
Beach Charitable Trust, Edward P., The, New York	136971897
Beeman Trust, Martha H., Buffalo	166023824
Begell Foundation for Epstein-Barr Virus Research, Frederick P., The, New York	133736375
Beltran-Kropp Foundation, The, New York	161359117
Betson Trust f/b/o First Methodist Church, Susan E., Rochester	156015130
Bianchi Trust f/b/o Brookhaven Memorial Medical Center, I. W. Bianchi & G. R., The, Kings Park	116419005
Bianchi Trust f/b/o Congregational Church of Patchogue, I. W. Bianchi & G. R., The, Kings Park	116419006
Bingham, Jr. Putnam Memorial Trust Foundation, H. P., New York	136897403
Blagden Trust for the Nature Conservancy of the Pine Tree State, Inc., Zelina C., New York	136754227
Blend Trust f/b/o First Presbyterian Church, Walter J., Oneonta	166233562
Blenheim Foundation, The, New York	133258422
Blodgett Foundation, Margaret Kendrick, New York	136144050
Bly Trust B, Halton D., The, Buffalo	166154358
Bohmfalk Charitable Trust, New York	133501941
Booth Trust f/b/o University of Notre Dame, Murray J., Rochester	166521848
Borchert Scholarship Fund, Walter & Cecile, Syracuse	166384392
Bowen Trust, Albert, Syracuse	166303273
Branning Trust, Walter J., Rochester	066327497
Brewster Presbyterian Church Charitable Trust, New York	137161849
Brice Foundation, Deborah L., New York	237065499
BRLA Assistance Corporation, White Plains	133554893
Brown Scholarship, John J. Brown and Irene M., Rochester	166024536
Brunner Foundation, Inc., Robert, The, New York	136067212
Bryce Foundation, The, New York	136104849
Burkett Trust, Jessie S., Delhi	166092636
Burr Charitable Trust, Charles, Norwich	166451181
Campbell Trust f/b/o Roscoe Free Library, Carl, Middletown	066233812
Caritas Foundation, Buffalo	363324843
Casey Trust, Constance E., Rochester	166288904
Cedar Fund, Inc., New York	136091737
Chaim and Leah Foundation, Brooklyn	113353905

2609

APPENDIX B

STATE	EIN
Chamberlain Trust f/b/o American Association of University Women, Sarah, Buffalo	166021186
Children of the World Adoption Agency, Inc., Syosset	113284491
Chisholm Charitable Trust, M. A., New York	136984354
Christopher Trust f/b/o St. Paul's United Methodist Church, J. G., New York	136992925
Church of the Ascension, Rochester	161486312
Clemente Memorial Scholarship Fund, Emily, New Rochelle	133490206
Close Hospital Fund, William F., Walton	156023275
Coates Trust f/b/o First Reformed Church of Scotia, Josephine, Schenectady	146104297
Cobble Hill Foundation, Inc., Brooklyn	113122301
Cohen Memorial Foundation, Inc., Marion, The, New York	133449100
Collins Memorial Trust, Doris N., Albany	222977812
Conklin Charitable Trust, Stanley, Elmira	166333229
Cooper Foundation for Neurologic Research and Education, The, New York	136159843
Corbin Art Trust f/b/o Wildlife Fund, D. P., Schenectady	141793742
Corbin Trust f/b/o Schenectady Boys & Girls, S., The, Schenectady	146183090
Corbin Trust f/b/o Schenectady Foundation, S., The, Schenectady	146183091
Corbin Trust for Animal Protection, S., The, Schenectady	146183087
Crandall Foundation B, Trafton M. & Maude W., Rochester	166069496
Crispell Article Trust f/b/o Christ Church, Reuben B., New York	136271424
Culpeper Foundation for the Relief of American Indians, Inc., Daphne Seybolt, The, New York	132851855
Dana Trust for St. John's Episcopal Church of Carthage, Texas, Eleanor, Rochester	136816062
Danke Trust f/b/o First United Methodist Church of South Norwalk, Herman M., Rochester	066205957
Darrow Charitable Trust, Karl, New York	136978367
De Reu Trust f/b/o University of Rochester, Viola, Rochester	166356625
Dean Trust f/b/o Oswego Library, Virginia, Buffalo	166367385
Delano Life Estate Fund, Maltbie McCosh, New York	136115977
Delaware County Historical Association Endowment Fund, Delhi	166505580
DiPerna Foundation, Inc., Frank and Anna, Utica	161340694
Dollard Charitable Trust, Elizabeth K., New York	133496754
Duffy Perpetual Charitable Trust, Walter A., Rochester	166425482
Duncan Trust f/b/o Harvey School, Ronald W., New York	136967594
Dunne Memorial Fund, M. P., Norwich	166202043
Dupee, Jr. Foundation, Inc., Paul R., New York	133190856
Dutton Memorial Trust, Harmon C. and Marie C., Norwich	223160372
Dyson Vision Research Institute Trust, M. M., New York	136974073
Eastern Long Island Hospital Trust, Rochester	116003771
Eaton Trust, Warren, Norwich	166480108
Eckler Scholarship Trust, Leopold, Rochester	222644263
Eden Home Memorial Trust, Edna Faust, New York	746267365
Edwards Memorial Fund, Alfred and Alice, The, Rochester	066231456
Ellsworth Foundation, W. H., New York	136073049
Eucalyptus Foundation, Inc., New York	132626672
Farkas Foundation, Howard and Barbara, The, Forest Hills	133107852
Father Flanagan Boys Home Trust No. 1, New York	133413809
Father Flanagan Boys Home Trust No. 2, New York	116227659
Faulkner Trust f/b/o Woodstock Associates, Inc., Marianne G., New York	136047464
Field Hall Foundation, Yorktown Heights	133410437
Film Foundation, Inc., The, New York	133573803
Fisher Foundation, George and Ann, Rochester	161466669
Fitzgerald Foundation, Pegeen, New York	133422698

STATE	EIN
Flatbush Volunteers of Hatzoloh, Inc., Brooklyn	133213138
Fonda Improvement Society, Inc., Fultonville	146036382
Foote-Whitney Memorial Fund, Norwich	166367809
Friends of the Longhi Foundation, New York	521949938
Friends of the National Galleries of Scotland Charitable Trust, New York	133480983
Friends of Vienna Philharmonic Orchestra, Inc., New York	133368173
Frutiger Chiropractic Education Fund, Daniel and Dr. W. H., Rochester	166216605
Fulton Middlebury College Memorial Fund, John H., New York	136166211
Gambino Medical & Science Foundation, Inc., New York	133586460
Gardner Charitable Trust, A. Somers, New York	136838913
Garrison Religious Trust, Lena H., Rochester	166073271
Gartenberg Foundation for the Temple Sinai of Long Island Youth Programs, The, Brooklyn	061537220
Girvin Trust f/b/o Manatee Junior College, H. F. & F. H., Rochester	166176890
God Bless America Fund, New York	136105770
Gorilowich Family Foundation, New York	137027222
Gould Trust for Gould Foundation for Children, Edwin, New York	136041905
Gould Trust for Seabury Wilson Home, Inc., Edwin, New York	136041888
Grace Trust, J. Willets, Rochester	166119803
Greene Foundation, Orville N., The, New York	137005863
Guenther Scholarship & Award Foundation, Otto V., Syracuse	146085288
Guenther Trust f/b/o West Point Cadet Fund, et al., Eleanor M., The, Rochester	136044874
H.E.L.P. Houses Development Corporation, New York	133560486
Hadassah Hospital Trust, New York	137114127
Haifa Foundation (North America), Inc., New York	133278992
Hale Community Trust, Cora Putnam, Elizabethtown	141608753
Half-Moon Foundation, Inc., New York	133039183
Hammerle Charitable Trust, Hila F., The, Buffalo	166380089
Hanford Memorial Fund, Platt Mead Hanford & Jennie Bradley, Walton	510244205
Harden Trust for Harrybrooke Park, Frank A., New York	136182462
Harder Foundation, Fred and Berthe P., Syracuse	521372982
Harjes Trust for the American Hospital in Paris, New York	136042039
Harned Trust Fund, Bedell Holmes, New York	136839419
Harris Memorial Library Trust, Oneonta	166207347
Harris Trust f/b/o Methodist Church of Otego, Dasa E., Oneonta	161204341
Harris Trust Fund, Collis & Lugarda, West Valley	166397677
Harrison Council for the Arts, Harrison	132985438
Harrower Trust, Giovanna M., New York	136787590
Harsany Foundation, Stephen, New York	133553536
Harvard College Trust, New York	136913027
Hayes Scholarship Fund, Cecil, Buffalo	166152521
Haynes Fund, Harry Evert, New York	136211302
Heller Foundation, Dr. Bernard, New York	132887370
Hellman Fund, Lillian, The, Tappan	133341118
Henderson Memorial Fund, William J., The, New York	136078241
Henderson Trust, Gladys P., Delhi	166283660
Hera Foundation, Inc., The, New York	133583082
Herbert Trust f/b/o The Gertrude Herbert Memorial Institute of Art, Olivia A., New York	136050727
Herbert Trust for St. George's Protestant Episcopal Church, et al., Olivia, New York	136050701
Hillery Memorial Scholarship Fund, Judge John D., Buffalo	166066938
Hite Memorial Fund, Buffalo	311652966
Hoffman Foundation, Inc., New York	136128254
Holtz Testamentary Trust f/b/o Dorothy A. Holtz Trust, L. M., Rochester	166162556
Homan, Jr. Trust, B. H., New York	136741112

APPENDIX B

STATE	EIN
Hultquist Trust f/b/o Earl Hultquist Infirmary, Marguerite, Buffalo	166108445
Hunsdorfer Foundation, R. A., Albany	166453357
Huntington Charitable Trust A, Archer M., New York	136078583
Huntington Free Library and Reading Room, Bronx	135562384
Huntington Mariners Museum, Archer M., New York	136070709
Huntington Memorial Library Foundation, The, Oneonta	166160202
Huntington Trust for the Huntington Free Library and Reading Room, Archer M. Huntington and Anna Hyatt, Rochester	136045101
Hyman Charitable Trust, Samuel M., New York	136761282
Igud Yotzei Sin in Israel Charitable Trust, Rochester	166446291
Iris Foundation, The, New York	136977690
Isham Trust, Charles, New York	136372804
Janes Memorial Fund, Rodney B., Rochester	166183755
Jeffers Memorial Trust, Emily M., Buffalo	166062642
Keep Home, Henry, Watertown	150533581
Keeton Foundation, Kathy, The, New York	133949464
Keren Zippora Trust, Monsey	776021027
Ketler Trust f/b/o American Cancer Society, Lewis J., Norwich	166198033
Kiff Trust, Charles E., Delhi	156017251
Kimmel Foundation, Inc., Martin, The, New Hyde Park	112794383
King-Richardson Memorial Loan Fund, New York	746250102
Kirk Trust, Harriet, Rochester	066064755
Kleppinger Trust f/b/o United Way of Lehigh County, PA, Samuel A., Rochester	136565462
Knapp Charitable Trust, Estelle, New York	136682558
Knight Foundation, Frances C. & Albert C., The, Syracuse	222956058
Knight Trust f/b/o Manhattan School of Music, Ruth M., New York	136592675
Knight Trust for Summer Theater Workshop, Ruth M., New York	136593101
Kraft Trust f/b/o Christ Episcopal Church of Ridgewood, New Jersey, Dorothy B., New York	137086748
Kraft Trust f/b/o Ridgewood N.J. Board of Education, Dorothy B., New York	137086746
Kramer-Levinson Memorial Scholarship Fund, Bronx	237009325
Lamberson Trust for Robert Packer Hospital, M., Buffalo	166177664
Lang Charitable Trust, B. & S., Rochester	161476139
Lattin Trust f/b/o Franklin Central School District, Sabina C., Oneonta	166299352
Lauer Trust f/b/o Civil Air Patrol, E., New York	136894463
Laughlin Trust f/b/o Waldorf Schools of North America, New York	166118934
Ledwith Charitable Trust, Mary B., New York	136898051
Levy Foundation, Harold J. and Arlyne G., Amherst	161455760
Lowman-Howell Foundation, Inc., Elmira	222537870
Lurje Memorial Foundation, Inc., Schaina & Josephine, New York	136176033
MacDermott Trust, Stewart, Rochester	136220218
Maple Fund, The, New York	133535340
Marian Trust, Joseph & Ophelia, Tarrytown	237066431
Marsden Educational Trust, Russell W., New York	226285263
Marsters, Jr. Trust f/b/o Andover Alumni Fund, G. L., Norwich	166342884
Marsters, Jr. Trust f/b/o Harvard College Fund, G. L., Norwich	166342885
Martineau Foundation, Florence Baker, New York	521888104
Masdam Trust f/b/o Doris Masdam Charities, Oscar, Buffalo	166271787
Matthews Estate f/b/o Baptist Church Trust, Bertha, New York	146022673
McCarron, Jr. Medical Foundation, Inc., James P., New York	133566240
McKnight Trust, Eloise, Latham	146152814
Melville Trust f/b/o Museums at Stony Brook, D. B., New York	133305823

STATE	EIN
Mercy Hospital et al. Trust, Rochester	136607761
Meyer Foundation, Helen & Abraham, New York	136075057
Mitchell Scholarship Trust, Charles, The, Rochester	137105970
MOA Foundation, New York, Inc., New York	133213896
Morris Foundation, Constance, Long Island City	136058658
Morrison Charitable Trust, Clarence H., Oneonta	166429037
Mosher Trust f/b/o American Heart Association, Laura E., Buffalo	166449845
Mosher Trust f/b/o Cancer Action, Laura E., Buffalo	166449846
Mosher Trust f/b/o Shriners Hospital, Laura E., Buffalo	166449844
Muehlstein Foundation, Inc., Herman, The, New York	136146516
Murphy Charitable Fund, George E. and Annette Cross, New York	136887044
Museum of Scotland & Heritage Trust Foundation, The, New York	510254205
Nagel Trust, Margaret A., Roslyn	116411431
National Spine Research Foundation, Inc., Westbury	133878047
Native American Education Fund of Western New York, Rochester	166338758
Navajo Indian Scholarship Fund, The, Roslyn	133194622
Needles Charitable Trust, Abraham I., Woodbury	136921944
Neighborhood Playhouse Trust, New York	136031962
Nelson Trust Fund, James H., Rochester	166073422
Nester Trust, Samuel K., Rochester	166015083
New Place Foundation, Yonkers	133333020
New York Alpha Phi Kappa Psi Foundation, Ithaca	156024330
Newcomb Trust/Stony Wold Corporation 5th Trust, Elizabeth W., New York	136040482
Nies Trust, James B., Long Island City	136058173
Noguchi Foundation, Inc., Isamu, Long Island City	133059538
Nowlan Trust, Clarence B., Rochester	066022566
O'Neil Trust f/b/o American Cancer Society - NYS Div. Albany Unit, Mary E., Albany	146174324
O'Neil Trust f/b/o American Foundation for the Blind, Inc., Mary E., Albany	146174455
O'Neil Trust f/b/o American Heart Association, Mary E., Albany	146174329
O'Neil Trust f/b/o American Lung Association of NYS, Inc., Mary E., Albany	146174337
O'Neil Trust f/b/o Audubon Society of New York State, Inc., Mary E., Albany	146174341
O'Neil Trust f/b/o Berkshire Farm Center & Service for Youth, Mary E., Albany	146174450
O'Neil Trust f/b/o Brooklyn Bureau of Community Service, Mary E., Albany	146174443
O'Neil Trust f/b/o Capital City Rescue Mission, Mary E., Albany	146174469
O'Neil Trust f/b/o Care & Share Energy Fund, Niagara Mohawk Power Corp., Mary E., Albany	146174466
O'Neil Trust f/b/o Christian Appalachian Project, Inc., Mary E., Albany	146174446
O'Neil Trust f/b/o Covenant House, Mary E., Albany	146174342
O'Neil Trust f/b/o Epilepsy Association of the Capital District, Mary E., Albany	146174445
O'Neil Trust f/b/o Federation of Protestant Welfare Agencies, Inc., Mary E., Albany	146174457
O'Neil Trust f/b/o Friars of the Atonement, Mary E., Albany	146174447
O'Neil Trust f/b/o Friends of Wildwood, Mary E., Albany	146174467
O'Neil Trust f/b/o Guiding Eyes for the Blind, Inc., Mary E., Albany	146174456
O'Neil Trust f/b/o Helen Keller International, Inc., Mary E., Albany	146174444
O'Neil Trust f/b/o Kenwood Braille Association, Mary E., Albany	146174454
O'Neil Trust f/b/o Leake S. Watts Children's Home, Inc., Mary E., Albany	146174442
O'Neil Trust f/b/o Lenox Hill Neighborhood Association, Mary E., Albany	146174334

APPENDIX B

STATE	EIN
O'Neil Trust f/b/o Madison Square Boys and Girls Club, Mary E., Albany	146174461
O'Neil Trust f/b/o March of Dimes Birth Defects Foundation NE NY Chapter, Mary E., Albany	146174331
O'Neil Trust f/b/o Memorial Sloan Kettering Cancer Society, Mary E., Albany	146174336
O'Neil Trust f/b/o Mohawk and Hudson River Humane Society, Mary E., Albany	146174458
O'Neil Trust f/b/o National Child Labor Committee, Inc., Mary E., Albany	146174449
O'Neil Trust f/b/o National Foundation for Cancer Research, Mary E., Albany	146174468
O'Neil Trust f/b/o National Multiple Sclerosis Society - Capital District Chapter, Mary E., Albany	146174323
O'Neil Trust f/b/o National Society to Prevent Blindness, Mary E., Albany	146174326
O'Neil Trust f/b/o Northeastern Association of the Blind at Albany, Inc., Mary E., Albany	146174328
O'Neil Trust f/b/o Project Hope - Albany, Mary E., Albany	146174462
O'Neil Trust f/b/o Recording for the Blind, Inc., Mary E., Albany	146174325
O'Neil Trust f/b/o Regional Trauma Outreach Program, Mary E., Albany	146174463
O'Neil Trust f/b/o Save the Children Federation, Inc., Mary E., Albany	146174451
O'Neil Trust f/b/o School for Special Children, Mary E., Albany	146174460
O'Neil Trust f/b/o Shaker Road Loudonville Fire Department, Inc., Mary E., Albany	146174465
O'Neil Trust f/b/o Society for the Prevention of Cruelty to Children, Mary E., Albany	146174453
O'Neil Trust f/b/o The Bishops Appeal Roman Catholic Diocese of Albany, Mary E., Albany	146174441
O'Neil Trust f/b/o The Children's Hospital at Albany Medical Center, Mary E., Albany	146174464
O'Neil Trust f/b/o The Fathers of St. Edmund Southern Missions, Inc., Mary E., Albany	146174448
O'Neil Trust f/b/o The Salvation Army - Albany Corps., Mary E., Albany	146174340
O'Neil Trust f/b/o Tri-County Council Vietnam Era Veterans, Mary E., Albany	146174339
O'Neil Trust f/b/o UNICEF, Mary E., Albany	146174338
O'Neill Foundation, James Keating, Astoria	113622900
Oneonta Community Charitable Trust, Oneonta	166329239
Open Society Fund, New York	133095822
Organic Reactions, Inc., Brewster	046052299
Padula Foundation, Louis Paul and Christine, Bronx	132905417
Paine Foundation, M. S., New York	136074009
Paine Trust f/b/o Paine Memorial Free Library, Augustus G., New York	136046255
Painter Hill Foundation, New York	133952016
Patch Memorial Fund, Norwich	166182911
Patchett Private Foundation, Allan, Buffalo	550760574
Peck Memorial Trust, E. Milnor, New York	136908334
Peckham Trust f/b/o Chenango Valley Home, Mary M., Norwich	156017709
People Residing in Dignified Environments, Inc., Great Neck	112856663
Perkins Gardens, Board of Trustees of, Long Island City	136056026
Peterson Trust f/b/o Norwegian Christian Home & Health Center, G. A., New York	137057960
Phelps Trust f/b/o Tuttle Fund, New York	136026698
Phipps Family Foundation, John S., New York	136861582
Pluygers Trust, Henry, Rochester	136032242
Police Athletic League of Yonkers, Inc., Yonkers	133234145
Ramallah Foundation, Inc., Brooklyn	136129479
Ramerica Foundation, New York	133407012
Rankin and Elizabeth Forbes Trust, William, New York	136584984
Reed Foundation, Inc., George E., Goshen	146023003
Ridenour Endowment Fund, Rochester	136023845
Riefler Trust f/b/o Buffalo Goodwill Industries, N., Buffalo	166312026
Riefler Trust f/b/o St. James United Church of Christ, N., Buffalo	166312027
Riefler Trust f/b/o United Church Home, N., Buffalo	166312024
Riefler Trust f/b/o Wheel Chair Home, N., Buffalo	166312025
Riggs Trust, Bernice H., Glens Falls	146128336
Robbins Charitable Trust, Clara M., Norwich	166334986
Roberts Foundation, Inc., James Reed, Tuxedo Park	237149274
Rockwell Art Collection Trust, Norman, Lagrangeville	046538205
Roosevelt Association, Theodore, The, Oyster Bay	135593999
Ross Charitable Trust, Alice Nason, Buffalo	237875403
Ryerson Charitable Trust, John B. & Jane M., Long Island City	166349529
Salvation Army Trust, The, Rochester	136022417
Samara Foundation, Inc., The, Amenia	133463471
Sampson Memorial Fund, Charles E., The, New York	136136802
Saraceno Educational Trust, The, New York	137118175
Schaffner Trust, Nicholas, New York	136989876
Scholarships for Needy Students in Israel, New York	132896792
Scott Trust f/b/o Fox Memorial Hospital, Anne E., Oneonta	166182160
Shafer Charitable Medical Trust, Sarah Lea Shafer and Jesse Z., New York	137040522
Shafer Charitable Trust, Leland T., Rochester	166242223
Shafer Charitable Trust Fund, Vivian, Rochester	166232132
Sheldon Trust, John F., Glens Falls	226450668
Sheldon Trust f/b/o Washington County Home for Aged Women, John F., Glens Falls	226450667
Shulkin Charitable Trust, Benjamin, Syracuse	166397188
Shults Foundation, Otto A., Rochester	166042842
Sidney Center Cemetery Association Trust, Walton	156023284
Simpson Charitable Trust f/b/o the Burn Foundation, The, New York	137050920
Skahan Memorial Fund, Joan, Norwich	166238801
Slaughter Foundation, Charles, The, New York	133055995
Smith Foundation, Bernice, New York	226424256
Smith Foundation, Flora Bernice, Syracuse	510181016
Smith Fund, C. Bainbridge, New York	510252549
Smith Fund, Florence E., Walton	156023286
Smith-John G. Green Trust, Gerardus, Schenectady	222507158
Snyder Fund, Richmond F., Eastchester	136933563
Solomon Trust f/b/o Hadassah Women's Zionist Organization, Esther, Long Island City	136830128
Soros Foundation-Hungary, Inc., The, New York	133210361
Southold Historical Society Trust, Rochester	136761783
Souval Spacedrafting Foundation, Inc., Mari, New York	133031086
Spay and Neuter Association, Levittown	113136643
Spenadel Trust, Henry, New York	136029906
Spenadel Trust f/b/o UJA, et al., H., New York	136029910
St. Hilda's & St. Hugh's School, New York	510200063
Stanton Fund, Ruth and Frank, New York	133598005
Steinhardt Family Foundation, New York	137067570
Stenner Trust, Elizabeth Consler, Rochester	166419973
Stevens Trust f/b/o Harvard College, John E., The, New York	136761801
Strater Trust, Michael H., New York	136847296
Strauss Estate New York County Lawyers Association Trust, Charles, New York	136040899
Sunset Home of Utica Foundation, The, New Hartford	161562929
Surface Residuary Trust, Maybelle, Rochester	066200251
Swart-Wilcox House Trust, Oneonta	166468660
Sylsam Foundation, Inc., Forest Hills	133799700
Talmudic Commentaries Foundation, Oceanside	112571452
Tamiment Institute, Inc., New York	134981835
Tanzanian Relief Fund, New York	133747068
Thomas Charitable Trust No. 2, Grace Pratt, Rochester	166364843
Thompson Southwestern Arboretum, Boyce, Ithaca	880061520
Thomson Trust, Frances Buchanan, Syracuse	166416184

APPENDIX B

STATE	EIN
Tiferet Moshe Trust, Brooklyn	133503827
Tinker 1957 Charitable Trust, Edward R., New York	136772877
Townsend Trust for the Women's Club of Leroy, Charlotte K., Buffalo	166021291
Travaglini Educational Trust Fund, Joseph & Elizabeth, Binghamton	161134803
Travaglini Fund, Binghamton	161133116
Trust for the Archdiocese of New York, New York	526975813
Trust for the Diocese of Brooklyn, New York	526972492
Tygert Trust, Fred W., Syracuse	166368432
Union African Methodist Church Trust, New York	146111155
Urban, Jr. Rescue Volunteer Hose Company No. 1, George, The, Buffalo	166021867
Vanderbilt University Trust, New York	136029309
Von Kienbusch Trust f/b/o Philadelphia Museum of Art, Carl Otto, New York	136734265
Walker Bird Sanctuary Trust, Rochester	136032389
Walker Trust f/b/o Boys Club of St. Croix, VI, D., New York	066408209
Walton Trust f/b/o First Baptist Church, Walton	166114408
Walworth Memorial Free Bed Trust, Alice C., Rochester	146014277
Wanita Camp Charitable Trust, The, New York	137109669
Warner Memorial Fund, William H., Rochester	132910505
Wehle, Sr. Foundation, Inc., John L., Rochester	223041829
Weill-Caulier Trust, Monique, New York	133020092
Weiner Foundation, M. & T., New York	132974080
Wharton Charitable Trust, Raeburn J., Buffalo	166296590
Wheelan Fund, John S., New York	136211303
Wheeler Trust, Elizabeth T., Long Island City	136889956
Whitehead Trust f/b/o The National Spiritual Assembly of the Baha'i, O. Z., New York	137202416
Wiggen Memorial Fund f/b/o St. Peter's Episcopal Church, Charles & Adella, Rochester	066340110
Wiggen Trust for Eastern Baptist Theological Seminary, Frances, Rochester	066340109
Wilbur Trust for the New York Times Neediest Cases Fund, James B., New York	136043317
Wilcox Estate Rowe Methodist Church Trust, Irene K., New York	146109589
Wilcox Estate Town of Milan Trust, Irene, New York	146109603
Willard Charitable Trust, Raymond L. and Alma Johnson, The, Norwich	166268702
Windy River Foundation, New York	133402438
Witherell Trust for YMCA of Greenwich County, Rebecca, New York	136043342
Wolff Trust, Peter A., Middletown	146021197
Wood Trust f/b/o William B. Ogden Free Library, Henry L., Walton	166280039
Wynne Charitable Trust, J. Paul, Buffalo	166353719
Yee Foundation, Inc., S. K., New York	133202047
Young Trust, Elsie Davis, Rochester	066169120

North Carolina

STATE	EIN
A.I.T. Foundation, Inc., Chapel Hill	237026862
Agar Foundation, Calvin A., Charlotte	226019792
Akers Charitable Trust, Rose Greer, Winston-Salem	546335625
Anderson Trust f/b/o Friendship Baptist Church, William W., Winston-Salem	546131635
Ange Trust for Barton College, Winterville Community Center & Winterville Christian Church, A. W., Winston-Salem	586263402
Armentrout Trust f/b/o High Point Historical Society, High Point	586165351
Babb Trust, Nell W., Charlotte	586137551
Baird Trust, Edith L., Charlotte	236217111
Baker Trust f/b/o Gilbert S. Baker Memorial Fund, Ida Irene, Winston-Salem	566131467
Bangert Charitable Trust, Albert H., Raleigh	566034663
Bartolomei Trust B, Charles F., Charlotte	596976099
Beck Scholarship Foundation, Bright W. & Lucille W., Charlotte	236510329
Blake Charitable Trust, Charles H., Charlotte	566431308
Booth Trust f/b/o Shriners Hospital, L. Paul, Charlotte	656050913
Borgstrom Memorial Fund f/b/o John Street United Methodist Church, Anne E., Charlotte	046371155
Bornes Trust, Harry, Charlotte	596131334
Branyon Charitable Fund, Winston-Salem	576017234
Brown-Whitworth Foundation, Winston-Salem	581813095
Buckner Foundation, Thad & Loca Lee, Charlotte	596171241
Bullock Memorial Scholarship Fund f/b/o Dartmouth College, Jessie & Amanda, Charlotte	046371205
Bunderman Trust f/b/o RN Club of Sarasota & University of Maryland, E. Louise, Charlotte	656154318
Canova Christian Science Religious Trust, Bertha N., Winston-Salem	546238039
Capel Trust f/b/o Montgomery Hospital, Winston-Salem	510160511
Carter Charitable Trust, Wilbur Lee, Charlotte	237420174
Caulfield Foundation, Dorothy B., Charlotte	026110623
Cavin Fund for St. Paul's Lutheran Church, Wade L., Durham	566504182
Chapel Trust, Helen B., Charlotte	226405172
Chauveau Charitable Trust, Jeanne H., Charlotte	236260305
Christman Estate Trust, Edward, Charlotte	236215328
Clamer Foundation, Guilliam H., The, Charlotte	236678246
Clodfelter Trust f/b/o First United Methodist Church, Morganton, et al., Josephine R., Winston-Salem	581684051
Coffee Church Trust, Winston-Salem	576047237
Cummings Scholarship Trust, Elizabeth W., Charlotte	566192403
Cunningham Trust, Irene D., Charlotte	236244946
Dale Trust f/b/o St. Joseph Hospital, G. & M., Charlotte	237643895
Davies Memorial Fund, Thomas J. & Ella Lagrange, Charlotte	046083460
Deaver Fund, Delema G., Charlotte	237745467
Delong Trust, Benjamin F., Charlotte	236221391
Divine Word Seminary, Charlotte	237839209
Dosher Scholarship Fund, William S., Winston-Salem	576047788
Draper-Savage & Nellie Draper Dick Memorial Foundation, Effie, Durham	581427155
Dubbs, M.D. Fellowship Fund, Alfred W., Charlotte	237684727
Dupont/Baker Special Trust, Jessie B. & Isabella B., Charlotte	596126988
Dupont/Elsie B. Bowley Special Trust, J. B., Charlotte	596126986
Durham Foundation Fletcher Heart Fund, Durham	566075981
Durham Trust, Sarah E., Durham	356009531
Econovations Foundation, The, Fayetteville	581770431
Edmondson Memorial Fund, William R. & Lenore C., Charlotte	237684725
Edwards Trust 2, Edith H., Charlotte	236633170
Elkins Fund, Lewis, Charlotte	236214962
Ellett Memorial Scholarship Fund, Walter B. Ellett & Anna Burton, Winston-Salem	546107357
Evans Trust f/b/o North Carolina Symphony, Durham	566367404
Faison Foundation, Elias S., Charlotte	566052820
Fassett Memorial Trust, Lucy T., charlotte	237357891
Fassett Memorial Trust, Mary K., Charlotte	566037917
Featherstone, Jr. Memorial Fund, Ambrose A., Asheville	560611568
Ferranti Trust f/b/o Flanagan's Boys Home, G., Charlotte	232726071
Ferranti Trust f/b/o Seton Hall University, G., Charlotte	226456582
Fleshman-Pratt Foundation, Inc., Winston-Salem	566063639
Forbus Trust for Hampden-Sidney College, Durham	566471418
Freedman Fund, Israel, The, Winston-Salem	566182578
Freedman Fund, Minnie & Daniel, Winston-Salem	566087393
Friends of the Kenan Foundation Asia, Chapel Hill	562044215
Fritz f/b/o Evangelical Lutheran Church, Walter H. & Carrie H., Charlotte	256785172
Gabriel Memorial Library Trust, Archie, Charlotte	566200444
Gibbs Trust, Florence Lauer, Charlotte	236674109
Gibson Fund, James R., Durham	566267494
Gilliam Trust, Marguerite, Winston-Salem	546217475

APPENDIX B

STATE	EIN
Ginkinger Memorial Trust, Charlotte	236769170
Glauser Trust No. 3, Anna B., Charlotte	236233425
Graham Trust f/b/o Allentown Hospital, Bessie S., Charlotte	236599744
Graybill Memorial Fund, Mildred & Winey, Charlotte	237866873
Gresso Trust, Gordon, Charlotte	596959907
Hancock Trust f/b/o Miami Children's Hospital, Jessie E., Charlotte	592810375
Harper Charitable Trust, Georgine M., Rocky Mount	566259626
Harry Trust, V. C., Concord	566422637
Harwood Trust, Thomas F. & Lucille Watts, Winston-Salem	546350570
Hill Trust f/b/o Durham Academy, Inc., Durham	566173864
Hill Trust f/b/o William C. Hill Library, E., Charlotte	521529674
Hilles Trust, Susan Morse, Charlotte	066020308
Hitchner Trust f/b/o Memorial Hospital of Salem, J. E., Charlotte	232751711
Holdeen Fund 45-10, Charlotte	146018145
Holding Charitable Trust, Maggie, Raleigh	566227852
Home Health Foundation of Chapel Hill, Chapel Hill	560950387
Hoskins Charitable Trust, William & Elizabeth, Wilson	566259186
Hughes Fund, M. A. Hughes - Bob, Charlotte	586338112
Hurley Memorial Park Foundation, Elizabeth Holmes, Salisbury	561521989
Kanarian Trust Fund, Lee and Charles, Charlotte	596798556
Kaplan Foundation for Children, Inc., Leon & Renee, Lewisville	562021049
Keller Charitable Memorial Fund, Mary Ellen, Charlotte	236704181
Koury Foundation, Inc., Maurice J., The, Burlington	561781568
Kratz Foundation, Jacob W., Charlotte	236560409
Lane Charitable Trust, A. B., Charlotte	596719811
Lane Professorial Chair - Morehouse College, Mills B., Charlotte	586073580
Lane Research Foundation f/b/o University of Georgia, Mills B., Charlotte	586068283
Lane Scholarship Fund f/b/o Emory University, Mills B., Charlotte	586065280
Lane Scholarship Fund f/b/o Georgia Tech, Mills B., Charlotte	586066481
Lane Trust f/b/o Georgia State University, Mills B., Charlotte	586065898
Lee Foundation, William States, Charlotte	566128952
Lessig Trust f/b/o American Cancer Society, Brooke & Inge, Charlotte	236791280
Lessig Trust f/b/o American Heart Association, Brooke & Inge, Charlotte	236791281
Lichtenwalner Trust, Norton L., Charlotte	236237756
Lichty Charitable Trust, Margaret M., Charlotte	237831175
Little Trust f/b/o Mercy Ministries, Winston-Salem	576180398
Long Charity Fund, Sara, Charlotte	236296713
Luther Fund, Nina A., Durham	566097961
Luther Trust for the Apex Baptist Church, Mary Aileen, Durham	566097960
Lynchburg Museum at Point of Honor, Winston-Salem	546107403
Margolies Prep Charity Trust, Albert & Ann, Charlotte	237840492
Mauney Trust f/b/o Pleasant Grove Baptist Church, B. S., Wilson	566049024
Mauney Trust No. 1, B. S., Wilson	566049000
Mauney Trust No. 2, B. S., Wilson	566064435
McCarty No. 2 Trust, Delphine L., Charlotte	237728328
McLaughlin-Whipple Trust, Charlotte	237444444
Meagher Charitable Trust, Cecile E., Charlotte	237645886
Merion Community Association Endowment Trust, Charlotte	236217579
Merkel Memorial Scholarship Endowment, Charlotte	236799159
Miller Trust, Gail E. Gass, Charlotte	236781202
Milliken Foundation, Inc., Seth M., Charlotte	237213940
Morrison Charitable Trust, The, Winston-Salem	566093800
Morriss Trust f/b/o University of Richmond, Caddiss F., Winston-Salem	566577907

STATE	EIN
Munnerlyn Residuary Charitable Trust, H. J., Charlotte	566231023
Munnerlyn Trust, H. J., Charlotte	566231025
Newton Flames Foundation, Inc., Newton	561969716
Noyes Perpetual Trust f/b/o Noyes Museum, Fred, Charlotte	226457516
Oswald Foundation, Genevieve, Charlotte	596892460
Paddison Fund f/b/o Mary A. Foard Paddison Fund, J. R., Winston-Salem	566072486
Paddison Scholarship Fund, Winston-Salem	566072484
Paddison Student Aid Fund, John R., Winston-Salem	566072488
Porter Memorial Trust, John T., Winston-Salem	546183880
Pritchett Scholarship Fund, Mary Roberts, Winston-Salem	546059480
Rawls Endowment Trust, Ella Freeman, Charlotte	546053304
Reeves Memorial Fund, Myrtle S., Durham	566095692
Rouse Trust-Good Shepherd Foundation, Remus R., Wilson	566151512
Rouse's Group Home, Inc., Stoneville	561385760
Salvation Army Trust, Rocky Mount	566210330
Salvation Army Trust, The, Charlotte	046226300
Sheffield Scholarship Trust Fund, Elizabeth B., Tarboro	566181591
Shoemaker Charitable Trust, Robert E., Charlotte	236704220
Shrago Foundation, Winston-Salem	581570908
Shrago Foundation, Jacob P. & Ruth L., Winston-Salem	566050145
Smith Trust, Alfred, Charlotte	236219369
Smith Trust for the A. P. Perkins Scholarship Trust, Charlotte	226059588
South Mountain Industrial Institute, Inc., Winston-Salem	586151929
Southeastern Baptist Theological Seminary Trust, Charlotte	576092018
Southern Baptist Theological Seminary Trust, Charlotte	576092017
Spencer Trust f/b/o Greenville Humane Society, Mary Dan, Charlotte	576102082
St. Francis Monastery Trust, Charlotte	237839189
Stewart Charitable Trust, Frank H., Charlotte	216012123
Sultan Charitable Trust, Harry, Raleigh	566034671
Taubel Residuary Trust, Albert, Charlotte	236219802
Thompson Charitable Trust, Nell L., Charlotte	596974828
Tiedemann Memorial Trust, Kenneth A., Charlotte	046355633
Travis Trust, Elizabeth M. Augustine, Charlotte	596964851
Treen Fund, Henrietta S., Charlotte	236221369
Trexler Foundation, John J., Charlotte	236733024
Vanderhoven Chapel Fund, Clara, Charlotte	226024399
Vaux, Jr. Trust f/b/o Palmer Home, William S., Charlotte	236691848
Vinik Charitable Trust, Tolly, Charlotte	596998432
Vonderleith Trust, Henry L., Charlotte	226147086
Wadsworth Memorial Fund, Enoch, Wilson	566115958
Wawriw, Jr. Trust f/b/o Manor College, Rose, Charlotte	236660378
Weamer Charitable Trust, H. C., Charlotte	236958908
Weaver Memorial Fund, Fred G. And Mallie C., Charlotte	566328030
Weaver Trust f/b/o Catawba College, William R., Charlotte	566283994
Webster Trust f/b/o University of South Carolina Law School, Roy, Charlotte	566288614
Wickliffe Foundation, Margaret, Charlotte	576043991
Willet/Pierce Hospital Trust, Charlotte	586181599
Willey Trust, Gordon Fay, Charlotte	526040148
Williams Trust, John Hugh, Concord	566472031
Williams Trust No. 2, J. S., Wilson	566049085
Willits Trust f/b/o Central Park United Methodist Church, Charlotte	236964670
Wilson Trust f/b/o NC Society for Prevention of Cruelty to Animals, Earl, Charlotte	566355445
Wilson, Jr. Trust, Rufus D., Charlotte	566050071
Wismer Charitable Trust f/b/o Christ Church, Russell, Charlotte	237823630
Witmer Home Trust, Ann C., Charlotte	231228040
Woloschuk Trust f/b/o St. Vladimir Ukranian Catholic Church, John, Charlotte	237793547

STATE	EIN
Woodruff f/b/o Springer Opera House, E., Charlotte	586162874
Woodruff Trust f/b/o Springer Opera House, Emily, Charlotte	581850809
Woods Trust f/b/o N. Milton Woods Home, Elizabeth, Charlotte	236276975
Woodward Trust, Harry C., Charlotte	236647406
Wunch Trust, Edward R. P., Charlotte	236713952

North Dakota

Burtness Trust B, Olger B. & Zoe E., Grand Forks	456010223
Eckert Foundation for Children, Fred and Clara, Williston	456016766
Homme Trust A f/b/o Lutheran Social Services, Adolph, Grand Forks	456060004
Homme Trust B f/b/o Anne Carlson School, Adolph, Grand Forks	456060005
Julyn Charitable Trust, Frank, Williston	456088151
Medd Fort Berthold Community College Educational Trust, Elsie Medd & James, Grand Forks	456070410
Peterson Trust for the Association of Free Lutheran Congregations, E. Oscar, McVille	450358105
Solberg Charitable Trust, Gunnar A., Minot	456056299

Ohio

Abarno Trust, Daniel, Cleveland	146160362
Abell Trust, Jabez M., Cleveland	156012974
Alpha Gamma Sigma Foundation, Baltimore	314114810
Alpha Phi Alpha Foundation of Akron, Akron	341620911
Ames Trust No. 1, Fisher, Cleveland	166170076
Ames Trust No. 2, Fisher, Cleveland	166170077
Anderson Trust f/b/o Ulster Health, et al., G. W., Cleveland	146138973
Anthony Trust, Alfred W. & Kate J., Cleveland	016008605
Anthony Trust f/b/o Feeble Minded, Kate J., Cleveland	016008603
Apostles of the Holy Spirit, Cincinnati	311013244
Arnold Foundation, Robert L. & Edwina L., Cincinnati	311028871
Asher Charitable Trust, Westerville	616188074
Asher Charitable Trust f/b/o Redbird Mission, Harriet Sargent, Westerville	616188070
Atkins Trust, Will C., Cleveland	016007090
Avallone Trust for St. Peters, Louis & Elizabeth, Cleveland	166210388
Averill Trust, George & Francis, Cleveland	016007091
Babies Incurable Diseases Charitable Trust, Inc., South Russell	237080474
Babin Foundation, Vitya Vronsky, Cleveland	341751317
Bane Charitable Trust, Earl M., Cleveland	376188528
Barber Foundation, C. Glenn, Cleveland	346765153
Barnum Trust, Joseph L., Cleveland	016007099
Beach Charitable Foundation, Fitch H., Cleveland	383162304
Beineke Trust for the Handicapped, Clarice, Cleveland	356437481
Bennett Memorial Fund, Mildred W., Cleveland	146085049
Bennett Trust, Bishop John B., Cleveland	356228777
Bennighof Scholarship Foundation, Henry and Hazel, Cincinnati	346402684
Bentz Foundation, The, Columbus	316036015
Berry Trust, Arthur, Cleveland	016078823
Beyler-Volpert Senior Citizen's Trust, Cincinnati	351780133
Black Trust, Ferdinand F., Cleveland	256231517
Blaine Trust, Mildred T., Cleveland	146143810
Blakeslee Trust No. 1, Julia, Cleveland	166154751
Blakeslee Trust No. 2, Julia, Cleveland	166175923
Bosney and Densmore Animal Welfare Trust, Cleveland	346979145
BPB Foundation, Cleveland	341542878
Bradford Area Public Library Endowment Trust, Cleveland	251695550
Bradford Ecumenical Home Trust, Cleveland	256368014
Bradstreet Trust, William H., Cleveland	237152377
Brater Charitable Trust f/b/o MIT, Eric, Cleveland	347009392
Bray Trust, William H., Cleveland	016010174

STATE	EIN
Brink Charitable Trust, Julia H., Cleveland	356408534
Brinkerhoff Foundation, Van Wyck & Angela, Columbus	311488008
Brister Living Trust, Charles E., Dayton	346787463
Brooke Trust, Mary G., Eaton	316492634
Brothers Trust, C. O., Akron	346867305
Burns Trust, Thomas J., Columbus	316528768
Burse Trust for Missionary Society of St. Paul, Gaynor Keeler, Cleveland	146014920
Bycroft, Jr. Trust, John S., Cleveland	256186467
Callen Trust f/b/o Mary Bridge Children's Hospital, Goldie, Cleveland	916322895
Calvary Baptist Church, Cleveland	146119501
Cardell, Jr. Foundation, Robert R. and Emma Lou, Cincinnati	311549465
Chambers Trust, Hervey, Akron	346796836
Chambers Trust, Mary Dailey, Akron	346796828
Chess Lamberton Public Charity Trust, Cleveland	256033380
Children's Rehabilitation Center Foundation, Warren	341533706
Christian Education Trust Fund, Cleveland	146137746
Cincinnati Hebrew Day School Foundation, Inc., Cincinnati	311202968
Cincinnati Women's Club Foundation, Inc., The, Cincinnati	311273462
Clark Trust, Henry, Cleveland	166131320
Clements Foundation, Vida S., Westerville	316095287
Clinton County Historical Society Endowment Fund, Wilmington	311014721
Cohen Trust No. 1, Elliot, Cleveland	146119515
Conover Health Center, Inc., Franklin	310986099
Cook Trust f/b/o Mansfield Symphony Society, Inc., Josephine, Westerville	316209156
Cromwell Trust, Frank, Elyria	347001811
Cruser Scholarships for Deserving Students, Frederick Van Dyke, Cleveland	911123741
Cuyler Methodist Episcopal Church Trust No. 1, Cleveland	156013091
Davidson Memorial Fund, Wm. H. & Cora Mae, Cleveland	256534786
Davis Trust for Stone Ridge Library and Marbletown Reformed Church, Alberta, Cleveland	146104719
Deeks Memorial Foundation, Fred & Lillian, Cincinnati	311531880
Deline Trust, Roland & Marcella, Cleveland	166161472
Densmore Trust f/b/o Dogs & Cats in Jefferson County, Ransford A., Cleveland	346979141
Dermitt Trust, Margaret, Cleveland	166131010
Devou Trust, William P., Cincinnati	616073001
Dewar Trust for the Salvation Army and Family Services Association, Jessie S., Cleveland	146101439
Dillon Foundation Trust, Cleveland	256228773
Dixon Charitable Trust, Elizabeth Brown, Huber Heights	310967509
Donahue Trust, Mary B., Cleveland	346506072
Dossert Trust f/b/o Trinity Church & St. Johns Episcopal Church, Norma, Cleveland	146172285
Du Mouchel Trust, Leandre A., Cleveland	146014791
Duhamel For Charities, Jay W., Toledo	346966728
Dumesnil Trust, Evangeline L., Cleveland	386473007
Dunlap Testamentary Trust, Leo W., Zanesville	316325807
Eckler Trust, Edith Mae, Akron	346550255
Edwards and Family Library Trust, Lawrence, Westerville	316215194
Efroymson Trust, Meyer S., Cleveland	356323787
Ellis Trust, Nelle Terry Holman, Cincinnati	616241177
Epp Fund B Charitable Trust, Otto C., Cincinnati	316365704
Felt Charitable Trust, Rae D. & Julia W., Cleveland	916253031
Fiorini Family Memorial Trust Fund, Richard J., Youngstown	346769956
Fischer Memorial Fund, William C. & Lillye T., Cleveland	346501038
Fleischmann Endowment Fund, Charles, Cincinnati	316024031
Flora Trust, Rose C., Cleveland	346881636

APPENDIX B

STATE	EIN
Foundation Medici, Warren	341701625
Fox Trust, Rubye O., Cleveland	256415097
Freese Foundation, Arthur J., Toledo	346619574
Frey f/b/o YMCA, Old Dutch Church, et al., Harry DuBois, Cleveland	166336547
Frey Trust, Harry Dubois, Cleveland	146038488
Friends of Parochial Education, Newark	310989944
Funston Trust, Katherine Lorraine, Cleveland	066494139
Gazzolo Trust, Lawrence J., Toledo	346563917
Gee Foundation, Gladys A., Cleveland	916182904
Genshaft Family Foundation, Canton	237008748
Germond Trust Fund B, F. A., Cleveland	346508910
Getchell Trust Fund, Dennis F., Cleveland	223026008
Gnade Trust f/b/o Oil City Library, M. F., Cleveland	256261524
Gnade Trust f/b/o Presbyterian Church, M. F., Cleveland	236824220
Gnade Trust f/b/o Women's Federation Third Presbyterian Church, M. F., Cleveland	256261521
Gnade Trust f/b/o YMCA-YWCA, M. F., Cleveland	256261523
Gordon Foundation, Ada L. Talbott, Columbus	316022629
Gorski Trust, Joseph, Akron	346969492
Grandview Institution Trust, Cleveland	256030965
Grau Charity Foundation, Cleveland	916243123
Graves Trust f/b/o E. J. Noble Hospital, Paul, Cleveland	166198481
Groseclose Trust f/b/o American Cancer Society, Ruth, Cleveland	916243888
Groseclose Trust f/b/o American Heart Association, Ruth, Cleveland	916243889
Groseclose Trust f/b/o Children's Home Society, Ruth, Cleveland	916243887
Guido Trust f/b/o Kathleen Guido Scholarship Fund, Joseph H., Cleveland	146113315
Hafer University of Michigan Scholarship Fund, Hazen A. & Rowena P., Cleveland	386531865
Hale Endowment f/b/o Crippled Children, Maud A. Hale and Charles C., Marietta	311357398
Hamrick Irrevocable Trust No. 2, Yong Ok Lee, Cleveland	876207539
Hare Charitable Trust, Katherine P., Wilmington	316615260
Harkins Trust f/b/o Mount Union College, Esther H., Cleveland	346845270
Harlan Memorial Cemetery, Inc., Cleveland	356315621
Harris Seville Elementary School Library Fund, Amy, Seville	341490398
Hartland Consolidated School Foundation, Cleveland	340797057
Hartman Trust, Frank R., Cleveland	376083107
Hastedt Trust B, W. J. Walter, Cleveland	356231196
Hathaway Brown School - Mothers & Daughters Trust, Cleveland	346605761
Haynes Trust, William B., The, Akron	346509484
Hazeltine Trust f/b/o Deborah Lincoln House, Chas, Cleveland	016026844
Herdman Charitable Trust, Angie P., Zanesville	316018717
Hight Nurse's Training Fund, Beatrice S., Cleveland	376147135
Hill Trust for Crandall Library, et al., E. N., Cleveland	146132648
Hockemeyer Trust, Emily, Cleveland	356327244
Hoffman Trust f/b/o Kewanee Public Hospital, Laura A., Cleveland	376076376
Hoge Musical Fund Trust, John, Zanesville	316018718
Hoover Charitable Trust, W. Henry, Cleveland	347006675
Hoysradt Endowment for St. John's Episcopal Church, Emily D., Cleveland	146123812
Hoysradt Trust for Kingston Hospital, Emily D., Cleveland	146123813
Hoysradt Trust for Y.W.C.A., Emily D., Cleveland	146123814
Humes Trust, Arthur, Cleveland	376110486
Hutchison Charitable Trust, Ruth F., Cleveland	316202945
Ingmand Charitable Trust, Marjorie C., Columbus	316357974
Isaac Foundation, Columbus	311078972
Jacobs Foundation, Alexis A., The, Columbus	311362920
Jesus Christ Charitable Foundation, Canton	341569277
Johnston f/b/o Old Dutch Preservation Trust, Fred, Cleveland	166420012
Johnston Preservation Trust, Fred J., Cleveland	166425791
Johnston Trust f/b/o Heritage Museum, Fred, Cleveland	166420013
Jones Trust, Gertrude & William, Cleveland	016007112
Jorgensen Charitable Trust, Erna, Cleveland	916369099
Kaemmerling Trust, Maude, Cleveland	016008812
Kaler-Vaill Trust, Addie, Cleveland	016007600
Kelly Trust for McKeesport Hospital Staff Room, J. P., Cleveland	256028218
Kennedy Memorial Fund, Mark H., Westerville	550684352
Kilmer Trust f/b/o First Church of Christ, Jessie M., Cleveland	146175665
Kilworth Foundation, June R., Cleveland	916027540
Kincaid Charity, J. Kennedy and Donald, Cleveland	376121599
Kincaid Trust f/b/o Animals, Mary, Cleveland	346951142
Kleinhenz-Moeller Foundation, The, Wapakoneta	237090422
Kozar Trust f/b/o Roman Catholic Churches, Cleveland	237934134
Kritzer Trust f/b/o Immanuel Evangelical Lutheran Church, Bertha, Cleveland	166134764
Kulas Trust No. 1, Elroy J., Cleveland	346747423
Kyle Foundation, Howard E. & Mildred M., The, Piqua	311579132
Lahm Testamentary Trust, Ralph P., Columbus	311470048
Lahm Trust, Ralph P., Columbus	311497493
Lake Charitable Trust, Sarah H., The, Cleveland	256584125
Langshaw Trust, Alice C., Cleveland	356505921
Larkin Charitable Foundation, Inc., Barry, Cincinnati	311323181
Lasher Trust for Bethlehem Rural Cemetery, Addison G., Cleveland	146074661
Latchaw Charitable Trust, Ren D. & Dorothy M., Cleveland	237895230
Laughlin Trust f/b/o Beaverton School District Scholarship Fund, Claude, Cleveland	936161752
LeCocq Trust, Ralph B., Cleveland	916262574
Levine Memorial Trust, Alice and Eli, Cleveland	251423970
Lewis Charitable Trust, George R. & Kathlyn P., Cleveland	256249176
Limpert Charitable Trust, Frank, Defiance	346835696
Loesch Trust f/b/o University of Munich, John, Cleveland	146136314
Lonz Foundation, George F., Port Clinton	237236157
Loth Trust, Edyth P., Cincinnati	316303568
Lynch Charitable Trust, Thomas & Margaret, The, Cleveland	346864388
Lyons Trust, Warren F., Cleveland	166191333
M Foundation, Toledo	346548517
Mack Fire, Inc., Cincinnati	237120719
MacKay Trust f/b/o Various Organizations, Harriet Ruth, Cleveland	016088406
Makara Scholarship Fund, Frank, Elyria	346748547
Malcolm Institute, Francis M., Cleveland	942745577
Mangold Charitable Trust, Herman F., Cleveland	237917630
Mantua-Shalersville Firefighters Association, Mantua	341397557
Marbletown Reformed Church-Stone Ridge, Cleveland	146104701
Marvin Foundation for the Performing Arts, Sarah, Cincinnati	311273122
Mauset Trust f/b/o SPCA, Henry, Cleveland	166420016
McCafferty Trust f/b/o St. Charles Foundation, B. J., Cleveland	256183334
McCarty Trust for Charities, Viola L., Cleveland	256629898
McCready Charities Trust, Alexander P., Cleveland	256206186
McCready Trust f/b/o Darby Library, Alexander P., Cleveland	256206185
McDowell Trust f/b/o American Cancer Society, Sara, Cleveland	237910302
McGowan Residual Trust B, Sue F., Cleveland	616067372
McGregor Home, A. M., The, East Cleveland	340714356
McKie Trust, Stanley & Agnes, Cincinnati	311581509
Merchant Trust, L. D., Cleveland	016007207
Miami University Student Aid Fund, Cleveland	316043588

STATE	EIN
Miller Memorial Scholarship Fund, Maurice B., Cincinnati	352041631
Miller Trust, Harold S., Akron	346819830
Milligan Nursing Fund, Jane, Cleveland	346603468
Moats Trust f/b/o Sherwood United Methodist Church, M., Defiance	311603884
Moe Trust, Harold A., Cleveland	156019413
Mong Scholarship Fund, Wilbur S., Cleveland	363832941
Monroe Catholic Central High School Scholarship Fund, Cleveland	386177355
Morris Trust, Stephen & Anna, Cleveland	346530510
Moses Trust f/b/o Junior Achievement Foundation of New York, NY, Horace A., Cleveland	346575176
Moyer Trust, Sidney S. and Helen W., Cleveland	346876808
Myeloma Foundation of America, The, Independence	311525175
Nelson Trust f/b/o Altruistic Club of Canton, Frank A., Cleveland	371278839
Newcomb Fund, Helen D. and Adrian G., Cleveland	346754483
Niehaus f/b/o Goodwill Industries, Charles R., Dayton	316527926
Ohio Troopers Caring, Columbus	311197113
Pack Trust, Charles Lathrop, Cleveland	346507330
Palaskas Trust, Elizabeth Devins, Cleveland	316393355
Palmer Scholarship Fund, Lewis F. Palmer and Marjorie S., Cincinnati	316496302
Pan International Co.-Pan Family Center for Women and Children, Newark	311417537
Parker Charitable Trust, Charles L., Cleveland	916266611
Patterson Trust, James A., Cleveland	256267307
Perry Charitable Trust, William T., Zanesville	316018719
Personal Enterprise Foundation, Inc., Perrysburg	237162606
Pfeifer Foundation, Walter A., Columbus	316023098
Pierstorf Memorial Scholarship Fund, The, Cleveland	346946124
Pine Grove Cemetery Association, Cleveland	166048534
Plas Education Trust, Edward & Eleanor, The, Columbus	316349905
Pleiss Charitable Trust, Griffin, Cleveland	616107233
Potter Trust, C. E. B., Cleveland	146088648
Power Trust, Stanley K., Cleveland	256391117
Powers Educational Trust, Edward W. Powers & Alice R., Cleveland	346827763
Powers Higher Educational Fund, Edward W. Powers and Alice R., Cleveland	346900472
Powers Trust f/b/o Blackburn Home, A. R., Cleveland	346900509
Quandt for St. Augustine's Church, M. W., Cleveland	146166494
Quandt for St. Mary's Church, M. W., Cleveland	146166495
Ramsey Scholarship Trust, E. Pearl, Akron	346675638
Refke Trust, Wallace O., Cleveland	386679358
Reformed Church of Saugerties Trust, Cleveland	146108725
Ripley Trust, Mary A. and Perley F., Cleveland	016007553
Ritter Memorial Trust, Allie L., Toledo	346775066
Robbins Hunter Trust, Newark	316221720
Roberts Trust, Medora C., Cleveland	237186191
Robinson Trust, Robert T., Zanesville	316018722
Rodgers Foundation, Kate M., Columbus	316023097
Ropchan Environmental Endowment Fund, Sam, Cleveland	356432719
Rupert Trust f/b/o Church of Savior United Methodist, Ethel G., Columbus	341339073
Rupert Trust f/b/o Cope Methodist Home, Ethel G., Columbus	341339072
Sage Unitrust, Mary, Youngstown	346854362
Sanders Trust f/b/o Garrard County Memorial Hospital, A. T., Cleveland	616106285
Sanders Trust f/b/o Maple Ave. Church, A. T., Cleveland	616106287
Schafer Charitable Trust, E. M., Cleveland	146125426
Schell Foundation, Charles E., Cincinnati	316019719
Schellinger Trust, Mabel H., Cleveland	166134329
Scherger Foundation, Harold N. & Alice E., Cleveland	356480711
Schneider Trust f/b/o Westlake United Methodist Church, Hellene, Cleveland	346993408
Schoch Trust, Philip F., Cleveland	366889214

STATE	EIN
Schultze Trust, Vivian H., Cleveland	346967733
Seattle Opera Permanent Endowment Trust Fund, Cleveland	916292930
Sebulsky Charitable Trust, Olga Kohut, St. Clairsville	346904084
Sharwell Trust, Nellie Bell, Cleveland	146071831
Shaw Charitable Trust No. 1, William A. & Hallie G., Cincinnati	356621681
Shaw Charitable Trust No. 2, William A. & Hallie G., Cincinnati	356623386
Shelton Trust f/b/o Mary P. Shelton Library Fund, Antoinette E., Cincinnati	316024107
Sibley Charitable Trust dated 02/28/86, Ida Rew, Cleveland	256226168
Siebert Trust, Kate, Cleveland	256013317
Siefert Trust, Esther M., Cleveland	316443181
Sikaras Trust for the Village of Mollaus, Greece, Charles G., Warren	237060603
Siler Trust f/b/o St. Michael's Church, Defiance	346766689
Sister City of Eaton, Inc., Eaton	311096320
Smith Charitable Trust, Marion L., Cleveland	146161012
Smith Endowment for the Phillips-Osborne School, Inc., Kennedy, The, Mentor	341882755
Smith Trust, Mildred A., Cleveland	146158522
Smith Trust for Hartwick College, C., Cleveland	146105263
Smith YWCA Charitable Trust, Ethelyn, Elyria	346829884
Soderstrom Foundation, Gustaf E., Cleveland	911184741
Soles Trust for YWCA, Evalyn L., Cleveland	256069979
Sperry Trust f/b/o Eastman School of Music, Winifred, Cleveland	146080065
Sperry Trust f/b/o Emerson School of Music, Winifred, Cleveland	146074894
Sperry Trust f/b/o Juilliard School of Music, Winifred, Cleveland	146074893
Sperry Trust f/b/o Malone Central School District, Winifred, Cleveland	146074896
St. Dominic's Church Trust, Cincinnati	346757618
St. Rose School Educational Trust, Girard	341602641
Stambaugh Charitable Foundation, Arnold D. & Helen R., The, Youngstown	341327065
Stanley Citizens Scholarship Fund, W. A., Westerville	556064281
Stevenson Trust, Dorothy S., Cleveland	376295155
Stokes Charitable Trust, Joy M., Cleveland	237050739
Stone Ridge Library Income Trust, Cleveland	146104702
Strunk Estate Crippled Children Trust, Bert C., Cleveland	166022751
Student and Education Support Association, Inc., Athens	311387072
Styles Trust f/b/o Saugerties Methodist Church, Cleveland	146169827
Sulsberger Foundation, The, Zanesville	316210487
Sumner Trust Fund, Jason & Corrinne, Akron	346574597
Sutcliffe Scholarship Trust, Elbert Gary, Cleveland	616172504
Taggett Trust, Glenda M., Cleveland	016090916
Talbott Foundation, Eva V., Columbus	316061421
Taylor Trust, Lydia M., Zanesville	316307982
Third Federal Savings and Loan Association, MHC and Subsidiaries Deferred Asset Accumulation Trust, Cleveland	347093341
Thomas Memorial Scholaship Trust, Albert L. Thomas and Hazel A., Cincinnati	610999505
Thomas Trust, Sarah, Akron	346509573
Tiemann Trust f/b/o Zion Church, Henry A., Cleveland	146138975
Truscott Foundation, Charles J. & Inez Cortez, Cleveland	876124099
Truscott Fund Trust, Charles J. & Inez Cortez, Cleveland	876153948
Turner Trust, Solon E., Cleveland	016007599
Turner Trust f/b/o Coopers Mills Cemetery, William E., Cleveland	016007267
Tuttle Trust f/b/o Friends Church, Frank, Cleveland	016038977
University School Father & Son Trust, Cleveland	346508267
Wagner Trust, William, Elyria	346524601
Walsh Jesuit High School Endowment Fund, Cleveland	346878897

APPENDIX B

STATE	EIN
Walton Estate Trust for Kingston Hospital, et al., B., Cleveland	146108205
Washburn Trust f/b/o ASPCA, Cleveland	146088982
Waters Trust, George & Elizabeth, Cleveland	237007737
Webb Charitable Trust, Shirley P., Newark	316193977
Wehrle Charitable Trust, Paul Edmund, Columbus	556096394
Weir Trust f/b/o Hoosick Community Center, Harry N., Cleveland	146032352
Weir Trust f/b/o the Village of Hoosick Falls, Harry N., Cleveland	146026784
White Estate Paragraph 18 Trust Fund f/b/o Boy Scouts and Girl Scouts, Minnie M., Cleveland	156026003
Whitewater Foundation, Cincinnati	316043723
Wightman Charitable Trust, Ruth P., Cleveland	256585040
Wildberg Charitable Trust, Anna England, Cleveland	346820409
Williams Educational Trust, Norman B., Cleveland	367201493
Wilson Foundation, Thomas A., Cleveland	237358862
Wine Trust, William E., Toledo	346504800
Wolcott Trust Estate, Mary Louise, Perrysburg	346515315
Women's Philanthropic Union, Shaker Heights	340782268
Wood Trust, Alice Louise, Cleveland	316358901
Woodward Charitable Trust, Bernal R., Cincinnati	311713056
Wright for A. B. Wright Trust B, W. T., Cleveland	146066379
Yeck Family Foundation, William & Dorothy, Dayton	311190146
Yoder Memorial Trust, Dr. Edwin C., Cleveland	916104560
Young Trust, Winifred Beech, Cleveland	346610316
Zahars Trust f/b/o Community Foundation of Greater Lorain, Elyria	347047279
Zahars Trust f/b/o Greek Church, Elyria	347047278
Zahars Trust f/b/o St. Basil Academy, Elyria	347047280
Zelly Perpetual Charitable Trust, Cincinnati	316257426
Zonas Trust, Steven K., Cincinnati	316363744
Zorn Foundation Trust, Theodore E. & Bernice C., Cleveland	166353781

Oklahoma

Brannin Foundation, Dan E. & Neva L., Tulsa	731531791
Burrow Trust B-1, C. H. & Clara, Tulsa	736168518
Charitable Trust f/b/o St. George's Greek Orthodox Church in Oklahoma City, OK, Tulsa	736174509
Charles Machine Works, Inc. Charitable Trust, The, Perry	736232360
Enid Community Foundation for Excellence, Inc., Enid	731547637
Garrison Trust, N. I., Tulsa	736090427
Greenwood Foundation, Fleeta, Shawnee	731281681
Grimes Foundation, Otha H., Tulsa	731293858
King Perpetual Scholarship Fund, Tannie and John, Oklahoma City	736250625
Kirschner Park Trust, E. Phil and Roberta, The, Muskogee	731164197
Lindsey Perpetual Charitable Trust f/b/o Cal Farley's Boys Ranch, Pearl, Miami	486186005
Lindsey Perpetual Charitable Trust f/b/o City of Baxter Springs, Kansas, Pearl, Miami	486186004
Lindsey Perpetual Charitable Trust f/b/o Heartspring, Pearl, Miami	486186006
Lindsey Perpetual Charitable Trust f/b/o United Methodist Church, Pearl, Miami	486188753
Litka Charitable Trust, Eleanor L., McAlester	736189930
Love America, Inc., Claremore	731470731
MacGuire-Moor Endowment Fund f/b/o Lee and Beulah Moor Children's Home, Tulsa	746373122
Martindale Educational Foundation, Robert C., Oklahoma City	742440824
Matousek Charitable Trust, Tulsa	736237345
Midgley Museum Support Trust, Enid	731377791
Ownby Charitable Trust, Virginia Mayo, Tulsa	756225044
Perry Public School Education Foundation, Inc., Perry	731331878
Pickens Trust f/b/o Grace M. Pickens Library, Boone, Holdenville	756460514

STATE	EIN
St. George Foundation, Tulsa	736256751
Stradley Unitrust, B. F., Bartlesville	731426209
Toland Trust f/b/o First Baptist Church, Arlene, Bartlesville	736251340
Waddill Memorial Trust, P. M., Bartlesville	736301351
Weeks and Marie Stuart Smith Memorial Charitable Trust, Margaret Smith, Ardmore	736242611
Wilson Educational Trust, George S., Enid	736169334
Yaffe Charitable Fund, Steve, Muskogee	736279581
Zweigel Foundation, A., Atoka	237088099

Oregon

AIM Foundation, Inc., Portland	237183961
Allan Foundation, Portland	816009239
Bronson Trust f/b/o St. Michael's Episcopal Church, James D., Portland	916260096
Brown Trust, E. C., Portland	936019291
Butler Memorial Fund, Gwin Samuel, Portland	936018358
Canfield Living Trust, Mary A., Salem	930795245
Carruth Foundation, Howard E., Portland	930713792
Cowin Foundation, O. Ray, Portland	911228785
Cowley Endowment Fund, Portland	810279121
Derry Testamentary Trust, Florence Agnes, Portland	936175127
Dillon Scholarship Fund, Mary, Bend	936182627
English Charitable Trust, Michael M., Portland	237088795
Frank Educational Trust, Mayme and Herbert, Portland	936231608
Franks Trust f/b/o Opportunity Foundation of Central Oregon, Walter R., Portland	936113315
Goodall Foundation, George and Carolyn, Portland	931163075
Goodall Trust, Isaiah, Portland	916158320
Hambly Trust, Leon G. and Constance, Portland	911285223
Hanscom Trust Fund, Claude J. & Bertha, Portland	510152318
Harding Charitable Fund, Albert B., Portland	936166601
Heiserman Trust f/b/o Cottey College, Geraldine, Portland	846049131
Hoffman Charitable Trust, Naomi, Portland	876121231
Hughens Charitable Trust, Hardy and Henrietta, Portland	916288112
Huntington Scholarship Fund, Sue, Portland	510166257
Jorgensen Trust, Elsa M., Portland	510204136
Kasiska Family Foundation, The, Portland	820414752
Kester Trust, T. O., Salem	936018602
Kuck Museum Foundation for Wasco County, Ernest A., Portland	943188223
MacBride Trust, Philip, Portland	916208481
McClure Trust f/b/o First Presbyterian Church of Idaho Falls, Portland	826063767
McCready Foundation, Gladys W., Portland	936236859
McDowell-Catt Foundation, Albany	930437990
Milhon Foundation B, Vivian I., Portland	930714318
Moe Testamentary Trust, Anna Ellen, Hood River	936207228
Molalla Rotary Foundation, Molalla	930846953
Morgan Fund for the Blind, J. R. & Emily, Portland	510192477
Nutter Trust, Earle and Marion, Portland	841140187
Pearce Living Trust, Helen, Salem	936024155
Perkins Charitable Trust f/b/o American Red Cross, Esther, Portland	846253505
Perkins Charitable Trust f/b/o Guide Dogs for the Blind, Inc., Esther, Portland	846253506
Peterson Memorial Fund, Oscar & Marie, Portland	916224598
Plath Trust, Dolores G., Portland	916237739
Poulsen Foundation f/b/o City of Silverton, Vera, Salem	936306031
Pratt Trust f/b/o Mission Mill Museum Association, Russell L., Salem	936244848
Rise Testamentary Trust, Bernice M., Salem	936126351
Rodes Memorial Scholarship Trust, Portland	816057774
Ronjoin Educational Trust, Basil, Portland	936067801
Shelton Residuary Trust, D. D. & F. L., Portland	936118280
Shott Charitable Trust, Fred, The, Portland	936158914

APPENDIX B

STATE	EIN
Sommer Memorial Lecture Fund, Ernest A., The, Portland	936019493
Spaulding Charitable Trust, Relief F., Portland	930684631
Stone Charitable Trust, Ruth K., Portland	826003512
Tayler Memorial Foundation, Fred A., Ashland	930906691
Vanstrom Trust, Andrew E., Portland	510153468
Vierani Family Fund for Charitable Purposes, Portland	237416718
Wade Foundation, R. M., Beaverton	936021298
Washburn Memorial Fund, Savier, Portland	936032872
Woodmansee Fund f/b/o YWCA, Constance, The, Salem	936196643
Woodmansee Memorial Fund f/b/o St. Paul's Episcopal Church, Salem	936195939
Woodmansee Park Memorial Fund, Salem	936195940
Woody Trust, Arnold H., Portland	826035997

Pennsylvania

Aaron Parkinson's Disease Foundation, Dan, Philadelphia	232657926
Abel Trust, Roy, York	236795610
Acomb Foundation, The, Colver	237455794
Adams II Trust, R. F., Pittsburgh	616120517
Affordable Housing Foundation, Inc., Kingston	232667249
Aged Women's Home of Montgomery County, Pittsburgh	232168196
Ahl Trust f/b/o First Presbyterian Church of Carlisle, P. Vaughn, York	236663006
Aikens Family Foundation, Woodrow U., Harrisburg	232537237
Allbach Trust, Earl, Philadelphia	236466105
Allen Trust, Thomas J. & Florence M., Wellsboro	236633874
Allen Trust, Viola L., Pittsburgh	226375388
Anderson Foundation, Orba H. A., Philadelphia	541576681
Anderson Trust f/b/o Charities, Chester, Pittsburgh	256080025
Atkins No. 4 Foundation, Edward, Philadelphia	236201490
Atkins Trust, Ollie Truitt, Pittsburgh	516172764
Bacon Trust, Elizabeth M., Pittsburgh	226410724
Baird Trust, Gladys, Erie	251792867
Baird Trust, Nettie & Lillian, Pittsburgh	256159360
Baker Trust, Charles J., Philadelphia	236434249
Barnes Memorial Foundation, Reba F., Pittsburgh	232505118
Barnes Trust, Anna J., Pittsburgh	236224131
Bartenslager Trust, Clarence, Pittsburgh	236517424
Barthold Trust 2, Kathryn H., Philadelphia	236740709
Batroff No. 7 Trust, Warren C., Pittsburgh	236273100
Baumeister-Reichard Trust Fund, Philadelphia	232137301
Beattie Trust, Paul E., Jim Thorpe	236691815
Beideman Trust f/b/o First Presbyterian Church, Dr. and Mrs. Joseph E., Pittsburgh	226607484
Bennett Trust f/b/o Five Rivers Council, Annabelle, Wellsboro	256638837
Bennett, Sr. Trust f/b/o Five Rivers Council, Robert L., Towanda	256622426
Bennett, Sr. Trust f/b/o Mansfield University - R. Packer School of Nursing, Robert L., Wellsboro	256622434
Bennett, Sr. Trust f/b/o Towanda High School, Robert L., Towanda	256622430
Biederman Charitable Trust, Fred, Pittsburgh	316035855
Bilyeau Trust, William H., Philadelphia	236225632
Blair Fund, Joseph W. & Helene E., Philadelphia	237646947
Blair Trust f/b/o Bethesda Memorial Hospital, M. H., Erie	256357284
Blair Trust f/b/o Lake Shore Health Care Center, J. L., Erie	256677875
Blair Trust f/b/o St. John's Hospital, M. H., Erie	256357285
Blair Trust f/b/o Warren General Hospital, J. L., Erie	256677876
Blair Trust f/b/o Warren General Hospital, M. H., Erie	256357283
Blake Family Foundation, Charles I., DuBois	256311914
Blewitt Foundation, John F., Pittsburgh	222608919
Bobb Trust f/b/o Church of God, E. G. & C. S., Pittsburgh	236235130
Bobb Trust f/b/o Nason Hospital, C., Philadelphia	237817159
Boehmer Foundation, Lucinda V., Pittsburgh	316115748

STATE	EIN
Bokser Trust f/b/o Diskin Orphan Home, Lewis & Sara, The, Philadelphia	237985718
Bokser Trust f/b/o United Aged Home, Lewis & Sara, Philadelphia	237985719
Bowman Trust f/b/o Parkville Fire Co., Beatrice V., York	237684738
Brady Memorial Library Trust Fund, Mary S., York	237704386
Bragar Fund, Norman H., Philadelphia	226607308
Bream Trust f/b/o Trinity Evangelical Lutheran Church, Grace A., York	237889777
Briggs Trust, Chreston K., York	232648418
Brill Charitable Trust, Lewis R., Lancaster	526571156
Brose Memorial Fund, Melvin F., York	236899599
Bryan Trust, Kirke, Philadelphia	226607329
Buchmiller Park Trust, D. F., Lancaster	232713044
Budd Orphans Home, Hermitage	256136848
Bulen Trust, Dexter A., Erie	256196019
Bushkill Reformed Church Trust, Philadelphia	236216724
Bushman Fund, The, Pittsburgh	237817179
Butler Trust f/b/o Methodist Home for Children, Beatrice M., Philadelphia	256352670
Cairns Trust, Ernestine Bacon, Philadelphia	236745014
Camp Kanesatake Trust, Huntingdon	256356988
Campbell Trust, Frances E., Philadelphia	566470810
Capuzzi Foundation Trust, Domenico, Philadelphia	236285619
Cardon Memorial Scholarship Fund, Bruce B. Cardon & Charlotte J., Philadelphia	236790663
Caretti Memorial Scholarship Trust, Joan L., Kittanning	251602336
Carnell Foundation, Althea J., Philadelphia	236205869
Carr Trust, Josephus, Philadelphia	226422322
Carty Trust f/b/o the Haverford School, William P., Radnor	256613525
Cassel Trust f/b/o Harrisburg Hospital, Violet E., Pittsburgh	510220272
Cassel Trust f/b/o Holy Spirit Hospital, Violet E., Philadelphia	236625592
Cassel Trust f/b/o Osteopathic Hospital, Violet E., Philadelphia	236625591
Cassel Trust f/b/o Polyclinic Medical Center, Violet E., Philadelphia	236625590
Cherry/Allen County Scholarship Board, Flora & Homer, Pittsburgh	616084842
Christman Memorial Fund, DeWald & Mary Ann, Philadelphia	236656881
Citizens of Mount Pleasant, PA Fund, Scottdale	256052276
City of Upton Cemetery Trust, Pittsburgh	616085273
Clark Medical Education Foundation, Henry H., Pittsburgh	256018886
Clendenen f/b/o Clinton County Community Foundation, B., Philadelphia	237889068
Clune Trust f/b/o American Heart Association and American Cancer Society, V., Philadelphia	256441155
Cohan Cathedral Prep Educational Trust, Robert W., Erie	256658148
Cohn Charitable Trust f/b/o Altoona Foundation, Benjamin, Pittsburgh	236234948
Cohn Charitable Trust f/b/o Martha Cohn Charitable Foundation, Benjamin, Pittsburgh	236267844
Collier Memorial Fund, Earl & Catherine, Philadelphia	236986320
Collins & Family Fund, T. W. & M. R., Pittsburgh	516185733
Consove & Albert Cohen Charity Fund, Samuel Herman, Philadelphia	596525614
Conwell Trust f/b/o Masonic Home, H. Ernest, Philadelphia	516019568
Crane Charitable Trust, Doris I., The, Philadelphia	256391613
Crary Trust f/b/o Crary Art Gallery, Gene W., Erie	256281525
Crary Trust f/b/o The Crary Home, Clare, Erie	256194014
Crawford Trust for Crawford Hall, Grove City College, H. J., Pittsburgh	256031624
Crawford Trust for Elizabeth Crawford Memorial School, H. J., Pittsburgh	256031614

APPENDIX B

STATE	EIN
Crawford Trust for Northwest Medical Center, H. J., Pittsburgh	256031617
Crouse Trust f/b/o Spring Run United Methodist Church, Warren, York	256384226
Cunningham Memorial Fund, Chester & Gail, Lancaster	237885037
Curry Trust f/b/o Roman Catholic Diocese of Erie, May, Erie	256210014
Curry Trust f/b/o St. Leo's Church, May, Pittsburgh	256255098
Dailey Charity Fund, Emma & Paul P., Pittsburgh	256212376
Darlington Foundation, Frank G., Pittsburgh	256511490
De Forest Trust f/b/o University of Pennsylvania, Willard P., Pittsburgh	236227943
Decker Trust f/b/o St. Luke's United Church of Christ, Charlotte M., Philadelphia	236632744
Dekle Trust f/b/o Athens College, Virginia, York	256677347
Dekle Trust f/b/o William & Mary College, Virginia, York	256677348
Delaurentis Trust, P., Philadelphia	237814490
Dibeler Trust f/b/o Falmouth Cemetery Association, Minnie, Philadelphia	236264622
Dick Foundation, Alexander W., Philadelphia	246016331
Dickson Charitable Foundation, Kenneth H., Pittsburgh	226580561
Dillman Fund, Julia A., Pittsburgh	237958561
Doerr Foundation, Gertrude B., The, Johnstown	251429656
Dressler Trust f/b/o Trinity Lutheran Church, Dorothy H., York	256307193
Dubbs Scholarship Fund, Sallie, Reading	237684726
Dunlap, Jr. Foundation, Edward B., Canonsburg	256361678
duPont Awards Foundation Trust, Alfred I., Philadelphia	596122735
Earley Trust f/b/o Bindnagles Evangelical Lutheran Church, Myra, Lancaster	256459501
Earley Trust f/b/o Bindnagles Evangelical Lutheran Church, Israel, Lancaster	256459500
Ebert Trust, Herman A. & Carrie S., York	236787100
Edward, Jr. Trust, Elwell G., Pittsburgh	236506581
Edwards Foundation, Lillian, Pittsburgh	256365074
Ehrenreich Foundation, Joseph and Amelia, The, Philadelphia	236913855
Elfner Trust, Charlotte R. and Kermit H., York	236735664
Ellegood Memorial Fund, R. E., Pittsburgh	516158559
Ellis Foundation Trust, Elizabeth B., Norristown	236851809
Ellis Trust f/b/o Heidelberg United Church of Christ, Marion, Pittsburgh	237866272
Enlow Trust, James, Pittsburgh	616020015
Eschenmann Charitable Trust, Jack B., Philadelphia	256496614
Esherick Foundation, Wharton, Paoli	232334277
Everitt Charitable Foundation, S. L., Philadelphia	226502760
Evleth Trust f/b/o Goodwill Industries, Raymond E., York	236724043
Eyer Testamentary Trust, George S., Bloomsburg	236575247
Fairview Charitable Trust, The, Reading	256612026
Fallona Charitable Trust, Raymond & Laura, Pittsburgh	046580695
Fawley Trust No. 2, J. Russell, Philadelphia	232120148
Feagley Trust, Frank H., Philadelphia	256372657
Feig Family Foundation, Philadelphia	236917899
Feigler Trust, Ervin D., York	236767052
Fenstermacher Trust, Martha, Pittsburgh	236249671
Flick Trust f/b/o Erie Center for the Blind, Loretta, Erie	256572365
Fluhrer Residuary Trust B, Robert C., Philadelphia	236497916
Fluhrer Trust, Blanche S., Philadelphia	236839080
Fluhrer Trust, Robert C., Philadelphia	236495082
Fluke Trust f/b/o Bethany Village, Florence, York	256523497
Fluke Trust f/b/o Grace United Methodist Church, Florence, York	256523498
Focht Trust, George B., Pittsburgh	236224086
Fonthill Trust, Philadelphia	236224161
Ford Memorial Hospital, John G., Pittsburgh	616020040
Forrest Fund, Ella Mae, The, Philadelphia	516146207
Forrest Trust, Elmer W., Pittsburgh	236674547
Foseid Foundation, Virginia Ann, The, Media	237857242
Frankhouser Charitable Trust, James & Mary, York	256559627
Frey Trust f/b/o Jordan United Church of Christ, Robert A., Philadelphia	236908350
Frick Foundation, Helen Clay, The, Pittsburgh	256018983
Froelich Charitable Trust, Edward, Lancaster	236711561
Garrahan Scholarship Fund, Mary F., Pittsburgh	237669236
Garvey Trust f/b/o Salvation Army and S.P.C.A., Harry M., Philadelphia	596535351
Gearhart Trust for Western Pennsylvania Hospital Scholarship Fund, J. I., Pittsburgh	256365116
Genesis Twelve Foundation, Sewickley	237885998
Gentle Foundation, James C., Philadelphia	232612150
Gentzler Residuary Trust, W. Emerson, York	236958411
Geraghty Charitable Foundation, Ethel Dinneen, Philadelphia	237751464
Gerber Trust f/b/o Hoffman Orphanage, John L., Lancaster	236771865
Gerber Trust f/b/o Hoffman Orphanage, K. A., Lancaster	236771882
Gerow Trust, James B., Pittsburgh	256172670
Gibbons Trust f/b/o St. Paul's Parish, Ada E., Philadelphia	046313625
Gibbs Memorial Trust, Walter & Lila, York	256429247
Gibstein Trust, Ray, Philadelphia	516504453
Gilbertson Trust, Esther, Philadelphia	236790720
Glatfelter Foundation, Philip H., Philadelphia	236283176
Glatfelter Memorial Field Fund, Philadelphia	231876099
Good, Jr. Memorial Fund, William, Pittsburgh	256104060
Gorsuch Trust, Edith A. Gorsuch and C. M., Philadelphia	236221080
Graham Trust f/b/o Muhlenburg Hospital Center, Bessie S., Philadelphia	236599741
Greenbaum Fund, Samuel and Sarah, Pittsburgh	516163257
Groff Trust f/b/o Diocese of Pittsburgh, et al., Edward, Pittsburgh	256235921
Grumbine Foundation, Harvey C., Reading	231417535
Guldin Trust f/b/o Immanuel United Church of Christ, Helen, York	256500592
Haag Trust f/b/o St. John's Church at Host, Harvey F., York	236722725
Hafer Trust f/b/o Occupational Services, Inc., Merle, York	236870840
Haigh Trust, Cheston W., Philadelphia	236285587
Hall Trust f/b/o Barium Springs Home for Children, William Frank, Philadelphia	566194973
Harlan Trust, Bertha, Pittsburgh	516010100
Harrington Trust f/b/o Masonic Home, J. S., Philadelphia	510251635
Harrington Trust f/b/o Wesley United Methodist Church, J. Smithers, Philadelphia	510251637
Harrison Foundation Trust, Philadelphia	656219445
Hartman Trust f/b/o City of Lancaster, Marion M., Lancaster	236881908
Hatfield Nicetown Playground, Henry Reed, Philadelphia	236265507
Haverstick Family Trust, Lancaster	236881913
Heiney Trust for Christ Lutheran Church, Kenneth E., Lancaster	237851246
Heisey Trust f/b/o First Church of God, Edna E., Philadelphia	256639642
Held Musical Fund, Elizabeth Tuesday, Pittsburgh	256025228
Hellyer Trust, A. Newlin, Pittsburgh	236730111
Hench Trust f/b/o Bethany Children's Home, Inc., Louise C., York	256497018
Hench Trust f/b/o Lancaster Theological Seminary, Louise C., York	256497017
Hermann, Jr. Memorial Art Museum Trust, John A., Pittsburgh	256024622
Hershey Trust f/b/o Boys & Girls Club, J. R., Lancaster	306010248
Hess Charitable Trust, Elizabeth D., Allentown	237927341
Hilliard Fund, Theodore Irwin, Pittsburgh	616020874
Himes Trust for Wesbury Foundation, Marian P., Erie	256389649

STATE | EIN

Name	EIN
Hinnershorts Trust f/b/o Warren Davis Scholarship Fund, Louise, York	256448952
Hobar, Sr. Memorial Fund, Anna Korchnak Hobar & George, Johnstown	251695555
Home for Homeless Women, Wilkes-Barre	232256903
Hoodner Trust, Francis A., York	236407935
Hoover Trust, H. Kathryn, Lancaster	236840025
Horst Trust f/b/o Historic Schaeffertown, Peter, Lancaster	256649977
Hosfeld Memorial Fund, John & Clara, Philadelphia	256383947
Hosfeld Memorial Fund, Richard H., Philadelphia	236938788
Hosfeld Trust, George W., Pittsburgh	236685596
Hosfeld Trust f/b/o Cumberland Valley Hose Co. No. 2, Richard H., Philadelphia	256380315
Howe Trust, Anna Verna, York	256399803
Howell No. 4 Trust, Samuel L., Philadelphia	236674583
Hower Memorial Foundation, Geary C. & Mary B., Reading	237859543
Howes-Nelson Charitable Trust, Pittsburgh	256159365
Hoy Trust, Clarence A., Pittsburgh	236900289
Huhn Trust dated Aug. 30, 1966, Harry K., Philadelphia	236496162
Hunsinger Trust, Ralph, Philadelphia	236203503
Illman Trust for Nurses Alumnae Association of Temple University, George Morton, Philadelphia	236225954
Ingraham Trust, Marjorie B., Pittsburgh	256304831
Irwin School Trust, Agnes, Paoli	237318404
Jaegle, Jr. Trust f/b/o Catholic Dioceses in North and South America, Charles, Pittsburgh	256018847
James Grand Lodge Residuary Trust, Frank, Philadelphia	236404248
Jaynes Trust, Ruth B., York	236747318
Johnson Memorial Trust, Eldridge Reeves, Philadelphia	516018771
Johnson Trust f/b/o Palmer Home, Inc., Nicholas R., Philadelphia	516147257
Jones Trust f/b/o St. Andrew's Episcopal Church, Edith M., York	256734493
Joyce Foundation, Edith S. and James R., Philadelphia	596892584
Kahrs Charitable Trust, Henry D., Philadelphia	226347838
Kasey Trust, S. W., Pittsburgh	616020173
Katar Trust, Felix M., Pittsburgh	236513481
Keck Trust f/b/o Trinity Reformed Church, Stelletta W., Pittsburgh	236671178
Keefer Trust, Elinor R., Pittsburgh	237813357
Keithan's Bluebird Garden Foundation, Sunbury	236814970
Kelley Trust, Malcolm S., Philadelphia	256388276
Kellis Trust for Kipparissi, George G., Philadelphia	236962502
Kellis Trust for Piraieus, George G., Philadelphia	236962503
Kelly Trust f/b/o Western Pennsylvania School for the Blind, Vera Kelly & Vivian, Pittsburgh	256720752
Kenworthy Trust, Ben, Philadelphia	236224248
Kenworthy Trust f/b/o Skerrett Lodge, J. Howard, Philadelphia	236603464
Kimes Trust f/b/o Charities, Maynard R., Philadelphia	256376426
King Trust, Elizabeth C., Pittsburgh	236481735
Kirk Trust, Ella B., Pittsburgh	256186784
Kleckner Charitable Trust, Grace H., Pittsburgh	256748144
Klopsch Trust Fund, Paul L. and Berta, The, Philadelphia	226485688
Klumpp Trust, M. Elizabeth, Lancaster	236678938
Knox Trust, Charles C., Pittsburgh	236225502
Konschak Fund, Matilda, Pittsburgh	516500328
Kopp Trust f/b/o York County SPCA, C., Philadelphia	256633057
Kostakes Charitable Trust, George A., Philadelphia	566359854
Kress Memorial Foundation, John J. Kress & Jessie L., Philadelphia	256410707
Landis Trust, Miriam G., Philadelphia	236751045
Lane Scholarship Fund, A. W. & Janet C., Philadelphia	226631203
Lane Trust f/b/o Wesleyan University, Janet C., Philadelphia	226631204
Lapp Foundation, Christ G., Lancaster	232140469
Latrobe Fund, Benjamin Quincy, Pittsburgh	256023518
Lavino Foundation, Edwin M., Philadelphia	232032639
Leaman Trust, Dorothy M., York	256363126
Lebzelter Trust, Charles Lee, Pittsburgh	236241508
Lee Memorial Fund f/b/o Evanston Township High School Trust, Jannette E., Philadelphia	046275636
Leisser Art Fund, Martin B., Pittsburgh	257422376
Lesaius Memorial Fund for Muhlenberg College, The, Scranton	236856930
Levitch Charitable Trust f/b/o University of North Carolina, Julius, Philadelphia	566403573
Liebscher Charitable Trust, Alice A., Philadelphia	237958494
Lindermann Charitable Trust for Notre Dame High School, J., Philadelphia	256422102
Lindsey for Lindsey Memorial Church Foundation Trust, E. C., Pittsburgh	256196807
Lininger Memorial Trust, Mildred S., Pittsburgh	516025016
Little Sisters of the Poor Trust, Pittsburgh	616134453
Logan Trust f/b/o Two Charitable Institutions, Maria D., Philadelphia	236225770
Lohr Charitable Trust, Robert L., Pittsburgh	237901725
Longsdorf Charitable Trust, Harold & Elizabeth, Philadelphia	237931503
Manderfield Trust, Charles J., Philadelphia	236277120
Mannheimer Trust, Hans S., Philadelphia	226161919
Marks Trust f/b/o Hoffman Orphanage, Ellen, Lancaster	236771881
Markus Trust, Moe B., Pittsburgh	236227929
Mars Hill College Trust Fund, Philadelphia	566195036
Martin Trust f/b/o Henry G. Long Asylum, Mary M., Philadelphia	232121237
Mascari Charitable Trust, Marion S. & Victoria C., Pittsburgh	255278013
Masland Conservancy Trust, Carlisle	256379203
Massachusetts Institute of Technology Trust, Paoli	236297385
May Trust, Gail Keys, Erie	251769888
McCarthy Memorial Trust, Wilfred E. & Elise, Philadelphia	597025622
McCombes Trust, Eugene J., Philadelphia	236431098
McCormick Irrevocable Trust, John R., Philadelphia	586246578
McCormick Trust, et al. f/b/o Harrisburg Hospital, Margaret O., York	236899585
McCormick Trust, et al. f/b/o Pine St. Presbyterian Church, Margaret O., York	236899643
McCoy Trust f/b/o Duncannon United Church of Christ, J., Philadelphia	232413424
McCullough Memorial Scholarship Fund, H. F., Philadelphia	236227860
McGillick Foundation, Francis Edward, Carnegie	251192205
McGrew Scholarship Trust, Hattie T., Philadelphia	046336208
McLean Variable Trust f/b/o The World Federalists Association, MacLean W., Pittsburgh	256545999
McNulty Memorial Endowment Fund, Rev. Raymond J. and Rev. Terrence F., The, Pittsburgh	232731776
Mentzer Trust f/b/o St. Stephen's United Church of Christ, Esther R., York	256379976
Merrick Foundation, Eleanor D., Pittsburgh	256026530
Methodist Church Trust, Philadelphia	046226299
Mickey Trust, L. Blanche, York	256248162
Miller Trust, Arch H. & Eula M., Pittsburgh	616071180
Miller Trust, Walter J., Philadelphia	236878958
Mitchell Trust for Charities, R., Erie	256542142
Mitchell Trust for Charities, Roy O., Pittsburgh	256254476
Montgomery Trust, Mildred R., Pittsburgh	237688031
Moore Endowment Trust, Philadelphia	526768789
Moore Endowment Trust, Harold E. & M. Jean, Butler	256369067
Moore Trust, William J., Philadelphia	236224291
Morby Education Foundation, Andrew and Velda, The, Pittsburgh	251796996
Morris Scholarship Fund, Lloyd W., Philadelphia	256201300
Morris Trust, Addie, Philadelphia	236593093
Morris Trust, Joshua, Skippack	236278070
Morrison Trust, Marion H., Pittsburgh	316177076
Mount Tabor Church Cemetery Fund, Pittsburgh	616114156

APPENDIX B

STATE	EIN
Mount Tabor Evangelical Cemetery Trust, The, Indiana	256397688
Munro Trust f/b/o Barnitz Methodist Church, Isabelle W., Pittsburgh	236255381
Murphy Foundation, Bob, The, Pittsburgh	251608327
Neale Trust, Katharine H., Pittsburgh	236228142
Nesbitt Charitable Trust f/b/o Nesbitt Memorial Hospital I, Abram G., Scranton	246012331
Nesbitt Charitable Trust f/b/o Nesbitt Memorial Hospital II, Abram G., Scranton	246012332
Neuber Trust, Pryor & Arlene, Philadelphia	236730175
Niblo Trust f/b/o St. John's Church, George C., Pittsburgh	236884949
O'Brien Trust, Anna Lee Dailey, Pittsburgh	616127089
Parks for Emlenton United Methodist Church, et al., H. W., Pittsburgh	256343684
Peckitt Trust, Hattie M., Philadelphia	236298745
Pennewill Trust f/b/o Palmer Home, Inc., James, Philadelphia	516147259
Pennsylvania Poultry Federation Foundation, Inc., Harrisburg	232212732
Peters Charitable Trust, Clyde E. & Zada V., Lancaster	237865062
Phoebus Fund, Philadelphia	236856169
Picard Memorial Cancer Research Fund, Werner and Lucie, Philadelphia	226631164
Pincus Fund, Marjorie & Irwin Nat, Philadelphia	232751330
Porter Trust, Margaret E., Hermitage	256122231
Potter for Charities-Charitable Trust, Edna G., Philadelphia	237813136
Poulson Fund, Susanna Angue, Philadelphia	236933346
Pruden Foundation, Philadelphia	222925918
Quackenbush Endowment Fund f/b/o Northwestern University, Edwin, Philadelphia	656184752
Quist Trust, Edna M., Erie	256165104
Radnor Enhancement Community Trust, Philadelphia	237648974
Rager Trust, Martha A., Philadelphia	236991992
Reagan Fund f/b/o Father Flanagan's Boys' Home, Marcella O'Rourke, Philadelphia	236955141
Reagan Fund f/b/o The Servants of Relief for Incurable Cancer, M. O., Philadelphia	236955140
Ream Foundation, Roy H., Philadelphia	236932799
Reber Trust f/b/o Bucknell University, Miriam L., York	256452598
Reese Residiuary Trust for the Salvation Army, F. M., Philadelphia	236839126
Rehmus Trust f/b/o Chestnut Hill College, Frederick H., Pittsburgh	237964046
Ressler Trust, W. Franklin, Philadelphia	256453937
Reyenthaler Memorial Home, Philadelphia	236205492
Richland Youth Foundation, Pittsburgh	256025481
Ridgely Trust, Elizabeth E., Philadelphia	516147702
Ridgely Trust, Sarah B., Philadelphia	516010024
Ringgold Area Volunteer Fire Co. Charitable Trust, Indiana	256250936
Roche No. 1 Trust, Mary A., Lancaster	236407808
Rockwell Memorial Combined Trust, R., Pittsburgh	256220241
Roman Charitable Trust, Jessie G., Pittsburgh	237811797
Rosen Family Foundation, Paul, Philadelphia	522036883
Rosenblum Trust for Tifereth Cemetery Foundation, Pittsburgh	256159917
Rosenlund, O.S.B. f/b/o The Contemplative Medical Center, Inc., Trust Deed of Sister Dorcas, Philadelphia	237813172
Rubert Memorial Trust, William E. & Theresa M., Bryn Mawr	236956994
Rubin Charitable Foundation, Ronald and Marcia J., Philadelphia	232547416
Rudy, Jr. Trust, George B., York	236708045
Salvation Army Charitable Trust, Indiana	237921756
Salzgeber Permanent Charitable Fund-Shriner's Hospital, Gustave A. and Katherine C., Pittsburgh	046451695
Salzgeber Permanent Charitable Trust-Children's Hospital Medical, Gustave A. and Katherine C., Pittsburgh	046451708
Samson Trust, Mary Eaches, Pittsburgh	236664736
Samson Trust 2, Mary Eaches, Pittsburgh	236664738
Sanders Trust, Maud, Pittsburgh	616062506
Saylor Trust f/b/o St. John's United Church of Christ, Melba M., York	256307200
Saylor Trust f/b/o St. John's United Church of Christ Parsonage Fund, Melba M., York	256362091
Sayre Trust, Hannah M., Philadelphia	226026130
Schafer Charitable Trust, Catherine C., Pittsburgh	236294127
Scheetz Trust f/b/o Camp Conrad Weiser, Elsie M., York	236844535
Scheetz Trust f/b/o Reading Hospital, School of Nursing, Elsie, York	236844540
Schmitz, Jr. Trust, Joseph, Pittsburgh	236954101
Schorman Trust f/b/o Good Hope Lutheran Church, G., Pittsburgh	237903370
Schumm Trust Fund, Charles A. & Cora H., Philadelphia	236438893
Schwartz Scholarship Fund, Mr. & Mrs. Reuben Schwartz & Verna A., Philadelphia	237868738
Schwartz Trust, Ernest D., Philadelphia	256564836
Sechrist Trust, Alverta, Philadelphia	256380343
Segui Residuary Trust, Bernardo J., Philadelphia	236494765
Seibert Trust f/b/o Steelton Welfare Association, Anna, Philadelphia	236237314
Shander Trust f/b/o Marywood University, Charles M., Scranton	237991569
Shander Trust f/b/o St. Cyril & Methodius Seminary, Charles M., Scranton	237991562
Shander Trust f/b/o Thomas Jefferson University, Charles M., Scranton	237991567
Shander Trust f/b/o University of Scranton, Charles M., Scranton	237991566
Shander Trust f/b/o Wistar Institute, Charles M., Scranton	237991568
Shannon-Cassel Fund, Philadelphia	236249985
Sharp Charitable Trust, John Tullis and Mary Deer, Pittsburgh	256730311
Shellenberger Memorial Trust, Augustus R., Philadelphia	236237238
Shriners Hospital for Crippled Children, Pittsburgh	046621260
Shull Trust f/b/o First Presbyterian Church, J., Philadelphia	246015989
Sipe Charitable Annuity Trust, V. O., Philadelphia	566416579
Sipe Irrevocable Trust, V. O. & Viola, Philadelphia	566416578
Sipe Trust f/b/o Sipe's Orchard Home, et al., Viola, Philadelphia	566413546
Sivitz Foundation, Frank H., Rydal	232138400
Smarsh Trust, Blanche B., Philadelphia	236797771
Smith Charitable Trust f/b/o Bryn Mawr Hospital, Mary Ulmer, Philadelphia	236789236
Smith Memorial Fund, Emma S., Pittsburgh	256034096
Smith Trust f/b/o Grace United Church of Christ, Martha S., Philadelphia	256305861
Smith Trust f/b/o Ody, et al., Elizabeth W., Pittsburgh	236223923
Snyder Charitable Trust f/b/o Bethany United Methodist Church, Ruby F., York	256480484
Snyder Charitable Trust f/b/o Martin Memorial Library Association, Ruby F., York	256480485
Snyder Charitable Trust f/b/o Quincy United Methodist Church, Ruby F., York	256480487
Snyder Charitable Trust f/b/o St. Paul's United Methodist Church, Ruby F., York	256480486
Society for the Preservation of the Gruber Wagon Works, Leesport	232268628
Somarindyck Trust, George A. & Lillian L., Philadelphia	236642016
South Mountain Camps Foundation, The, Wernersville	232166821
Sporkin Trust, Lillian, Philadelphia	236913990
Springer Trust for Washington & Jefferson College, Thurman F., Pittsburgh	256052919
St. Bernard Priesthood, Pittsburgh	256235539

APPENDIX B

STATE	EIN
St. Joseph Altar Society et al., Pittsburgh	616021112
St. Joseph Parochial School, Pittsburgh	616021114
St. Paul's School Trust, Paoli	237322048
Stager Charitable Trust, Lancaster	237865059
Stager Charitable Trust f/b/o Zion United Church of Christ, Lancaster	237865061
Stalker Trust f/b/o Borden Baptist Church, John M., Pittsburgh	356039363
Steensma Endowment f/b/o El Camino College, Jessie, Pittsburgh	046335952
Steidler Trust f/b/o Notre Dame Home for the Aged, Evelyn Lennon, Pittsburgh	236691452
Stenger Scholarship Trust, R. C., Pittsburgh	256023581
Stephenson Education Foundation, Joanne W., Oakmont	256381907
Stern Trust f/b/o Meadville Associated Charities, Samuel, Pittsburgh	256034107
Stewart Trust f/b/o Presbyterian Church of Shippenburg, Alexander, York	236790646
Stine Trust f/b/o United Way of Lebanon, Russell, York	256500578
Stiteler Trust f/b/o Tri-County Association for the Blind, Leonore Graber, York	236652129
Stoess Trust Foundation, Henry And Martha, Pittsburgh	237829587
Stow Charitable Trust, Erie	256244235
Stuart Foundation, Acheson, Philadelphia	226019661
Stuart Foundation, J. William & Helen D., Philadelphia	232665110
Sullivan Fund, Frances W., Philadelphia	232657930
Sutton Trust, Gertrude H., Pittsburgh	256280469
Swartz Trust, Elizabeth W., York	231530314
Talone Foundation, Leonard A. and Dorothy E., Philadelphia	256612774
Taunton Public Library Trust, Pittsburgh	046120813
Taylor Foundation Trust, Joshua C., The, Philadelphia	236227985
Taylor Memorial Arboretum, Philadelphia	231709567
Taylor Scholarship Trust, Frances E., York	251738774
Taylor Trust, Grace Webster, Philadelphia	596122605
Tettenborn Memorial Fund A, Pittsburgh	316018108
Thornton Charitable Trust, Homer A. and Helen B., Erie	256711858
Tingley Trust, George H., Pittsburgh	616020470
Tippett Trust f/b/o United Methodist Homes, E., Philadelphia	236910775
Titman Memorial Fund, Eloise Frantz, The, Philadelphia	236910783
Tomlin Trust, Charles I., Philadelphia	236225200
Townsend Trust for Philadelphia Public School Retired Employees Association, Laura A., Pittsburgh	256403788
Trigg Trust f/b/o South Baptist Trust, Mary Cofer, Pittsburgh	610891286
Trowbridge Memorial Fund, F. B. & O. L., Pittsburgh	316448741
Truman Trust for Chautauqua Institution, Pittsburgh	251876607
Trust f/b/o Pennsylvania Working Home for the Blind, Paoli	236299606
Trust for Children's Hospital of Philadelphia, Paoli	237324064
Trust for St. David's Radnor Church, Paoli	237323360
Trust for the Diocese of Pennsylvania, Paoli	236409728
Unger Charitable Trust, Pearl C., Philadelphia	046361462
Upton Baptist Church Trust, Pittsburgh	616135432
Van Horn Foundation, Mae Cooper, Philadelphia	236473075
Van Wynen Trust B, J. A. Van Wynen, Jr. & W. F., Philadelphia	226502705
Walker Trust, Edna and Frank, York	256241739
Walton Foundation, Frank S., Philadelphia	236256391
Ward Trust, John M., Philadelphia	236228044
Warner Memorial Foundation, Alice, Pittsburgh	516187984
Watson Residuary Trust, Albert, Philadelphia	236473938
Watson Trust, Naomi, Philadelphia	236568929
Webster Memorial Fund Trust, Ruth, Pittsburgh	046355360
Weinreich Worthy Poor Coal Fund Trust, Jennie L., Sunbury	246017321
Weiser Trust f/b/o First Presbyterian Church, Nettie S., Lancaster	236232439
Weller Foundation, Carl E. & Emily, Lehigh Valley	222579082
West Foundation, Sara E. T., Philadelphia	236722334
West Trust f/b/o National Lutheran Home for the Aged, Helen A., Philadelphia	232175412
Western Soup Society, Plymouth Meeting	237398475
Wharton Trust f/b/o Palmer Home, William W., Philadelphia	516028091
White Charitable Trust, Susan K., York	222522659
Whiteley Trust, Purdon, Philadelphia	231967848
Wildasin Charitable Foundation, George M. & Pauline M., York	236899535
Willard Trust, Margaretta, Philadelphia	236760330
Wilson Trust f/b/o Homeland, Eril E., York	256448909
Witkins Hospital Fund, Maurice, Philadelphia	236755997
Wolfer Educational Trust, Alfred, Pittsburgh	237708985
Women's Auxiliary of The Lancaster Heart Association, Philadelphia	236862076
Wood Trust f/b/o Haddon Fortnightly, John, Philadelphia	226631122
Wood Trust f/b/o Historical Society of Haddonfield, John, Philadelphia	226631121
Workable Alternatives Foundation, Indianola	251670751
Worst Trust, Raymond B., Lancaster	236853675
Wright Trust, Annie, Philadelphia	246016270
Wyoming Monument Fund, Pittsburgh	246012419
Yagel Trust, Romaine H., York	236640915
Zabriskie Foundation f/b/o 1st Presbyterian Church, Abram J., Philadelphia	236403871

Rhode Island

Adams Memorial Foundation, Ruth C., Providence	046028152
Alford Trust f/b/o Jerome Home and New Britain General Hospital, F., Providence	066036503
Alheim Trust, John L., Providence	016070903
Anderson Trust, James W., Providence	046033874
Armstrong Trust, Charles M., Providence	016021877
Austin Park Charitable Trust, Providence	166207930
Barnes Memorial Chapel Fund, Carlyle F., Providence	066023630
Barry Trust, Edward F., Providence	016076181
Barsam Foundation, Anna Keim, Providence	223159778
Barton Family Trust f/b/o Manchester Memorial Hospital, Providence	066445744
Barton Trust, Edward S., Providence	166385508
Belding Fund, Alvah N., Providence	237425259
Bennett Trust, Clara, Providence	046049635
Berlin Free Library Trust, Providence	066036445
Besse Charity Trust, Daniel W., Providence	046448136
Besse Trust, Amanda L., Providence	046508843
Big Springs Historical Society Foundation, Providence	166022862
Bill Trust, Pauline, Providence	066082146
Bollivar Trust f/b/o Mae Nellie Bollivar Fund, Crossman W., Providence	046644099
Bond Trust, Charles H., Providence	046007908
Bond Trust, Marjorie K. and Rufus, Providence	016021084
Borden Trust, Emma L., Providence	046029341
Bowden Trust, William H., Providence	016011125
Bowen Charitable Fund, M. S. & W., Providence	166273794
Bowen Charitable Trust, Whitney and Marian, Providence	222741073
Boyden Trust, Everett F., Providence	056009171
Boyle Trust, Margaret Louise, Providence	016058647
Brooks Trust, Ervin R., Providence	016042065
Bundy Trust, Harriet M., Providence	066027468
Burbank Trust f/b/o United Church Board of World Ministries, Emery B. and Melissa A., Providence	016041728
Burnham Trust, Harriet T., Providence	066027494
Burns Trust, John W., Providence	016008095
Burr Trust, Helen, Providence	066027507
Burr Trust, Mary G., Providence	066219979
Burr Trust f/b/o Larabee Fund Association, Willie O., Providence	061007619

2623

APPENDIX B

STATE	EIN
Caldwell Trust, David M., Providence	066132667
Capewell Trust for Capewell Horse Nail Employees, Garafelia, Providence	066139313
Carelton Charitable Trust, Laura E., Providence	016114488
Carlisle-Goshen Street Light Fund, Alice L., Providence	066040127
Carpenter Trust, Elsie L., Providence	056080008
Carr Trust f/b/o Sangerville First Universalist Church, Moses, Providence	016014103
Carver Fund, John S. and Helen E., Providence	016044693
Case Trust f/b/o Town of Swansea, Mary A., Providence	046029372
Charles Trust, Mary Elizabeth, Providence	046008071
Chase Trust, Herbert A., Providence	046122652
Chesley Trust, Marion, Providence	046009327
Church Home for Aged Men, Benjamin, Providence	050272493
Cleveland Charitable Trust, Providence	066313141
Clickner Charitable Trust, Marguerite, Providence	166335423
Coe Trust f/b/o Boy Scouts of America, Jennie F., Providence	066027675
Coggeshall Memorial Museum, Providence	046049653
Conant Trust, Ruth S., Providence	066183964
Cone Trust, John J. & Ruth C., Providence	066311872
Cook Fund, Sanger M. Cook and Ruth P., Providence	016087969
Cook Relief Fund, Almon B., Providence	046038997
Cooledge Trust, Lucy A., Providence	043360241
Cossin Trust, Evelyn, Providence	046462976
Covell Trust f/b/o Warren Lodge No. 51, Joseph L. B., Providence	066023841
Cowles & Company Community Trust, C., Providence	066033248
Crane Charitable Trust, Dorothy S., Providence	046455657
Crockett Trust, John B., Providence	016042302
Cuffney Trust f/b/o St. Mary's Church, James D., Providence	166325872
Cumberson Trust f/b/o First Baptist Church of West Winfield, B. C., Providence	166216807
Danforth Fund, Carl E., Providence	016009431
Delehanty Trust, Anne M., Providence	166272324
Dexter Trust, Ernest J., Providence	046112252
Dibble Trust f/b/o Congregational Church of Naugatuck, Lewis A., Providence	066025597
Dixie Wonders Irrevocable Trust, Providence	026100139
Donaghue Foundation, Patrick and Catherine Weldon, The, Providence	060987411
Dowd Trust f/b/o Holy Sepulchre Cemetery, Margaret J., Providence	166022856
Dowding Foundation, Cheryl Ann Faulkner, Cranston	050473350
Duncan Trust f/b/o Kimball Academy, Abby, Providence	026004069
Dunleavy Trust, Sarah C., Providence	066027955
Dunning Trust A, James S., Providence	056078641
Dunning Trust B, James S., Providence	056078643
Durfee Trust, Bessie C., Providence	066027961
East Sebago Library Trust, Providence	016008363
Eaton Trust, Alice M., Providence	046751410
Eckstorm-Hardy Fund, Providence	016041279
Edgerton Memorial Trust, Marietta L., Providence	066220267
Edmunds Trust f/b/o Salvation Army of America, Roberta M., Providence	016009118
Elliot Charitable Trust, John S. & Sarah C., Providence	046282546
Ellison Trust, Milton E., Providence	046513309
Ellsworth Trust, MacDonnell J., Providence	226550842
Emery Trust f/b/o Rockland Congregational Church, Joseph, Providence	016076042
Emmanuel United Church Trust, Providence	146111142
Ennis Trust, Evelyn B., Providence	016063362
Evans Fund, Clara V., Providence	016083924
Evans Trust, Dennett E., Providence	222611686
Everett Trust f/b/o Ethel Sproul, George, Providence	016128913
Fairfax Trust, Madge C., Providence	222920715
Farnum Residuary Charitable Trust, Walter W., Providence	056053702
Fellows Charitable Trust, Hazel, Providence	146132039

STATE	EIN
Fisher Memorial Fund, Harry & Beatrice, Providence	046422626
Fisher Work Fund, George & Augusta, Providence	016029788
Fitch Trust f/b/o Cheshire Health Foundation, Leon M. & Hazel F., Providence	026061000
Fitch Trust f/b/o Elliot Hospital, Leon M. & Hazel F., Providence	026061001
Fletcher Memorial Library Trust, Providence	066028090
Forsyth Trust f/b/o Elm Street Congregational Church of Bucksport, Fred B., Providence	016009119
Fowler Trust, Harriet E. D., Providence	066028107
Fralick Trust f/b/o Presbyterian Church, Jennie S., Providence	156014952
Fralick Trust f/b/o WJF Memorial Fund, William J., Providence	156014953
Fried Memorial Fund, Dr. Anton R., Providence	043190300
Gadoury Irrevocable Trust, Alice, Providence	026049092
Gale Cemetery Trust, Walter H., Providence	026047775
Gardner Trust, Ellen K., Providence	046009433
George Trust f/b/o Taylor Home, Oscar J., Providence	026037670
Gerry Trust B, Louis T. D., Providence	016048101
Giannantonio Trust, Henry, Providence	046527420
Gilbane Foundation, Thomas & William, The, Providence	056006170
Gile Trust, Helen Blake, Providence	026003982
Goodall Trust f/b/o Goodall Park, Ernest M., Providence	016072680
Goode Memorial Trust, William & Allison, Providence	016008964
Gowen Charitable Trust, Rosamond Ingalls, Providence	046466307
Grace Episcopal Church, Providence	166238215
Grant Trust, Elizabeth, Providence	046008143
Gregg, Jr. Family Foundation, Inc., Harry Alan, Providence	026012318
Gregoire Trust f/b/o St. John Baptist Roman Catholic Church, Armand, Providence	046870066
Griswold Trust f/b/o Boy Scouts, E., Providence	056120033
Griswold Trust f/b/o E. Boyer College of Music of Temple University, E., Providence	056120034
Griswold Trust f/b/o Florida Atlantic University, E., Providence	056120031
Griswold Trust f/b/o Weirsdale Presbyterian Church, E., Providence	056120032
Grody Family Foundation Trust, Israel, Providence	066048343
Gunnard & Victor Peterson Trust Fund for Salem Evangelical Lutheran Church, Mathilda, Providence	066200793
Gustin Scholarship Fund Trust f/b/o Florida Atlantic University, Robert & Edna, Providence	226628853
Haberbush Trust, Walter A., Providence	146087924
Hall Trust, Gertrude Ella, Providence	016008407
Hall Trust f/b/o First Congregational Church of Adams, Lillian W., Providence	161436844
Hamilton Trust, Marion B., Providence	016056973
Hamilton Trust, Sarah E., Providence	146128458
Hardy Trust, Lucy W. Hardy and Fred, Providence	016056516
Harrington Trust, Katherine A., Providence	046343675
Harrington Trust f/b/o Catholic Memorial Home, William H., Providence	046029484
Harris Trust, Rachel F., Providence	056006831
Harris Trust f/b/o Chestnut Knoll, Helen E., Providence	046021204
Hartley Trust, Marcellus, Providence	066131805
Hartman for 5 Points Mission, Providence	066024524
Hartson Fund f/b/o Windham Community Memorial Hospital, Leslie F. Hartson & Bertha B., Providence	066169935
Healy Trust, Daniel S., Providence	046008100
Healy Trust, Richard & Mary, Providence	046023320
Hellmann Trust - Sibella Hellmann Fund, Rhoda M., Providence	066263709
Hellmann Trust f/b/o Veterans Memorial Medical Center, Rhoda M., Providence	066263710
Hempstead Trust, Idella Stuart, Providence	066084143
Hewitt Trust, Lyman, Providence	066028478
Hibbard Trust, Mildred B., Providence	066231844

STATE	EIN
Hicks Trust, Elizabeth, Providence	066172599
Hicks Trust, Mary C., Providence	066028483
Holcomb Fund f/b/o West Granby Cemetery, Lizzie, Providence	066032725
Holcomb Fund f/b/o West Granby Methodist Church, Lizzie, Providence	066032726
Holland Patent Free Library Association Endowment, Providence	166159421
Hollander Fund Trust, Simon, Providence	066028520
Holly Scholarship Fund, Providence	223248254
Hollyhock Hollow Sanctuary Fund, Providence	166327206
Holtzer Fund f/b/o German Aid Society, Charles W., Providence	046008250
Hotchkiss Trust, Gertrude F., Providence	066028545
Howland Trust, Adelaide B., The, Providence	046008507
Hoyt Memorial Fund, Howard D. Hoyt and Roy E., Providence	166345364
Hull Trust, Lura Cook, Providence	056006875
Humphrey Fund, Grace Holcomb, Providence	066055125
Humphrey Trust, Herbert N., Providence	016040698
Hunt Trust, Charles W. and Nettie F., Providence	066334517
Hurley Fund A - Camp, J. J., Providence	046036308
Hurst Charitable Trust, Edward & Antoinette Bana, Providence	043391146
Hyde Memorial Fund f/b/o Christ Church Parish, Elizabeth A., Providence	066040232
Irving Trust, Prageman, Providence	066203604
Jenkins Trust, Raymond L., Providence	026068307
Johnson Trust f/b/o the School of the Museum of Fine Arts, Hazel, Providence	046457943
Kehoe Trust, John B., Providence	016007890
Kiesel Trust, John, Providence	166303561
King House Trust, Dr. A., Providence	066046297
Kittridge Trust, Russell D., Providence	046306369
Klinck Memorial Fund, Fred F., Providence	166024481
Knopf Memorial Fund, Providence	066123143
Kollerstrom Trust, Joseph T., Providence	066169022
Kroudvird Fund f/b/o Tifereth Israel Congregation, Inc., Abram & Etta, Providence	046200270
Kroudvird Trust Fund f/b/o Jewish Convalescent Home, Abram & Etta, Providence	046200271
Krusen Trust, Joseph H., Providence	166028570
Kynett Trust f/b/o Nantucket Cottage Hospital, Doris G., Providence	046600363
Lakeville Baptist Church Trust, Providence	146111143
Lane Trust f/b/o Holland Patent Free Library, Hazel Gardner, Providence	166208929
Langie Foundation, Louis A., Providence	166059320
Lathrop Trust, Sarah J., Providence	066111533
Lawton Memorial Home, A. F., Providence	056004508
Lawton Trust f/b/o Lawton Memorial Home, Isaac B., Providence	056007677
Leadbetter Trust, Elizabeth M., Providence	016009472
Leahy Foundation, J. W., Providence	510184043
Levasseur Trust f/b/o Unitarian Church, Ethel T., Providence	016068518
Lewis Trust, Genevieve, Providence	066289637
Lewis Trust f/b/o South Trenton, Charlotte, Providence	156014959
Littlefield Trust f/b/o President & Fellows of Harvard College, Samuel, Providence	016006943
Loomis Housing Corp./Merritt Fund, Providence	046200238
Luce Charitable Foundation, Stephen C., Providence	237105691
Maes Trust f/b/o Salvation Army, Inc., D., Providence	046658722
Manross Trust f/b/o Memorial Forestville Library, R., Providence	066269928
Manross Trust f/b/o Salvation Army, R., Providence	066269929
Martin Memorial Fund, Clarence H., Providence	026005022
Mason Fund Trust, Marion Rockwell C., Providence	146132077
Mayer Trust, Dorothy M., Providence	166263686
McCarthy Trust, Freder, Providence	026064060

STATE	EIN
McEacharn Trust, Stella A., Providence	016065476
McGuire Endowment, Providence	026026657
McKenney Trust, Ella B., Providence	016016197
McLauthlin Trust, Muriel L., Providence	046401107
Miles Trust f/b/o Shriners Hospital, Harry B., Providence	156015220
Miller Trust f/b/o Fairview Cemetery, Darius, Providence	066024152
Moore Trust, Dorothy, Providence	046115753
Moore Trust f/b/o West Lane Cemetery Association, E. Allen, Providence	066024219
Morse Trust, Arthur W., Providence	016035580
Morton Trust, Willie T., Providence	066029125
Moseley Foundation Trust, William O., Providence	042771098
Moses Scholarship Fund, Harvey H. Moses & Catherine Allis, Providence	046462993
Moses Trust f/b/o Chestnut Knoll, Horace A., Providence	046193446
Moulton Fund, Helen W., Providence	016009480
Moulton Trust, Myra K., Providence	046665138
Mowry Trust, George H., Providence	056004236
Moxon & D. M. Yost Memorial Trust, M. E., Providence	066293050
Mulligan Trust f/b/o Springfield Home, Charles H., Providence	046019065
Murray Trust, Estella L., Providence	056003496
Murray Trust f/b/o 4 Charities, Leone, Providence	010500483
Nashua Chapter House Fund, Providence	026007723
Nashua Fire Relief Trust Fund, Providence	026007717
Naurison Trust, Florence L., Providence	046861356
Neelens Trust, Hazel A., Providence	066260620
Norton Trust f/b/o Wellsville Salvation Army, William Henry, Providence	166028578
Orr Charitable Trust, Rev. Howard & Mildred, Providence	066342740
Pallotta Charity Fund, Monsignor Guido L., Providence	046025631
Pardee Fund II Trust, Providence	066287563
Parks Fund f/b/o Universalist Ladies Aid, Elizabeth, Providence	016011934
Parsons Trust f/b/o Connecticut Humane Society, Vena St. Louis Parsons & Florence, Providence	066204189
Paschall Trust, Edith S., Providence	066271225
Perkins Trust, Elizabeth Bishop, Providence	016008022
Pessolano Trust, Ellen Lea, Providence	016029710
Pickett Trust, Margarette, Providence	226550918
Polacek Fund, Joseph and K. Leonora, Providence	066281560
Pond Trust, E. Leroy, Providence	066029348
Pond Trust, Mary K., Providence	066124746
Poughkeepsie New York, YMCA Trust, Providence	066231495
Pousland Fund, C. Felton, Providence	046278620
Prescott Trust Fund, Halvor E., Providence	016064010
Public Safety Commission of Fitchburg, Providence	046023450
Raymond Trust, Alice S., Providence	066240850
Rich Trust f/b/o Brockton Services, S. Heath, Providence	046033289
Robbins Hospital Fund, Elwin D., Providence	026007721
Roberts Trust, Charlotte, Providence	016009136
Root Trust f/b/o Newington Children's Hospital, Theodore C., Providence	066023773
Ross Trust, Edith L. & H. Danforth, Providence	016075554
Ross Trust, Grace B., Providence	056077902
Ross Trust Part I & II, Sylvia E., Providence	016017314
Sawyer Trust f/b/o Shelburne Falls Community House, Lillis R., Providence	046019157
Schmidt Trust, Edward L. and Eleanor L., Providence	056105660
Schulmann Trust, Gertrud, Providence	026057960
Sears Trust, Clara Endicott, Providence	046025576
Seymour Charitable Trust, Richard Dudley, Providence	066301913
Shaw Trust, Etta M., Providence	026015152
Sheldon Trust, Una E., Providence	016019683
Shepherd Trust f/b/o Northampton Historical Society, Edith, Providence	046279927
Sherman Trust, Mary E. P., Providence	066029611
Shumway Trust f/b/o Family Services of Rochester, F. R., Providence	911851673

APPENDIX B

STATE	EIN
Singleton Trust f/b/o Michael's Orphanage, James F. and Mary R., Providence	016009141
Sitrin Trust f/b/o Congregation Zvi Jacob, Hymen and Clara, Providence	156015195
Snell Trust f/b/o Little Falls Hospital, Thereon, Providence	166043512
Snider Charitable Trust, Dorothy & Samuel, The, Providence	066114143
Spaulding Memorial Library Book Fund, Providence	016008359
Spooner Trust, Mary E., Providence	046033533
St. Augustine Catholic Educational Trust, Providence	016074756
St. Mark's Church, Kendall Trust, Providence	222505853
Stanley Memorial Church Trust, Providence	066036427
Stanley Trust, Frank B., Providence	026004680
Starkweather Trust, Francis W., Providence	066198197
Stauffer Trust f/b/o United Methodist Church, C. C., Providence	141596132
Stebbins Trust, Grace B., Providence	046033804
Steele Fund, J. Quentin, Providence	046408896
Stetson Trust, Louise, Providence	046290902
Storrs Trust f/b/o Trinity College, Evelyn B., Providence	226487019
Storrs Trust Fund, Evelyn Bonar, The, Providence	226534646
Strater Trust f/b/o Ogunquit Memorial Library, Henry, Providence	046024650
Stuart Trust, Ralph Currier, Providence	222940495
Sullivan Trust f/b/o Providence College, Hilda, Providence	056071602
Sullivan Trust f/b/o Salve Regina College, Hilda, Providence	056071601
Sutherland Heslip Unitrust, Providence	046499385
Tarbox Trust, Alfred L., Providence	016007892
Thayer Testamentary Trust, Julia B., Providence	046055558
Thompson Family Trust, Providence	016060458
Thompson Trust, Emilie Bell Obnovlenski, Providence	056061117
Thornberg Trust f/b/o Louis B. Goodall Memorial, Lela, Providence	016011398
Thornton Cardio-Pulmonary Fund, Arthur E., Providence	066098939
Traut Xmas Fund, Elise, Providence	066036416
Trinity Lutheran Church of West Sand Lake Trust, Providence	166245629
Tucker Scholarship Fund, Edith E., Providence	056073236
Tyler Trust f/b/o American Heart Association, Alice K., Providence	016065736
Vatras Educational Foundation, Providence	046011128
Vetter Trust f/b/o United Methodist Church, Edythe E., Providence	146110134
Volpe Memorial Charitable Trust, Angelo V. Volpe & Doris C., Providence	223124319
Von Der Mehden Trust f/b/o University of Connecticut, Providence	066024074
Wagner Charitable Trust, Providence	166363118
Waller Foundation, Percy G., Providence	146129142
Ward Trust, James E., Providence	222589381
Warner Trust, Irvin, Providence	066166887
Wauful Trust, Lester G., Providence	156014942
Weaver Trust f/b/o Bexley Hall, Howard A., Providence	046139771
Weed Endowmwnt, Charles S., Providence	066041432
Wegman Trust, Oscar, Providence	066178601
Wells Charitable Trust, Mary Dana, Providence	226597671
White Trust, Sarah E., Providence	046008537
White Trust, Susie F., Providence	046008468
White Trust f/b/o The Sister Marie Camel Fund, Maurice E., Providence	046011115
Whitley Memorial Foundation, Albert & Florence, Providence	010464379
Whitney Fund, Wyman H. Whitney and Della, Providence	016059669
Whitney Trust, Wyman H., Providence	016062793
Whittlesey Trust f/b/o United Way, Providence	066137317
Widger Trust, Leon, Providence	020495628
Wilkes Charitable Trust, William B., Providence	046305987
Willeke Trust, Lou H., Providence	046607624
Williams Forbes Trust, Providence	066024794
Williams Trust, Abigail E., Providence	066030172
Wilson for Ashland Historical Society, Providence	046534241
Wilson for Worcester Academy, Providence	046534239
Woodman Charitable Trust, Helen, Providence	016035789
Woodman Trust f/b/o Oak Grove School, Eleanora S., Providence	016011126
Woodworth Unitrust, G. Walter, Providence	043375821
Yaeger Trust, Albert O., Providence	046218152
Yaeger Trust, Alison H., Providence	046129492

South Carolina

Abernethy-Mulcahy Foundation, Hartsville	571054234
Academy of Columbia, Trustees for the, Columbia	570767498
Brooks Memorial Trust for Gamecock Excellence, Ernest A., Columbia	570808507
Burnett Trust f/b/o the Episcopal Church of the Resurrection, Edna, Greenwood	576173411
College of Beaufort, Trustees of the, Beaufort	576020682
Crosswell, Estate of John K., Sumter	570329783
Duckett Foundation, Hattie, Greenville	570830876
Dumas Trust, Mendel, Charleston	576040082
Epilepsy Services and Research, Inc., Orangeburg	570832561
Hartsville Museum Foundation, Inc., Hartsville	570988821
Herman Trust, Howard V., Orangeburg	576146159
King Memorial Trust, Franklin E. and Martha Covington, The, Greenwood	586347523
Pee Dee Homebuilders Scholarship Foundation, Florence	570888717
Roper Charitable Trust, Mary B., Columbia	576081807
Roper Trust, Margaret B., Columbia	576102416
Spencer Trust f/b/o Catholic University of America, School of Nursing, Mary Dan, Columbia	576102081
Stringer Trust, Nancy F., Anderson	576115833
Wellman Scholarship Foundation, Inc., Johnsonville	570933857

South Dakota

Cozard Library Trust Fund, Winner	466039143
Dorman Trust Fund for Kennebec School, Joseph & Matilda, Kennebec	237376153
Lackey Scholarship Trust, Harold W. and K. Lorette, Sioux Falls	916423892
Lemley Memorial Fund, Rapid City	466063449
McCrossan Foundation, Sioux Falls	460241590
Peters Research Center for Parkinson's Disease and Disorders of the Central Nervous System Foundation, Harvey W., Sioux Falls	541372833
Ringley Scholarship Trust, Agnes J., Sioux Falls	466042213
Ringley Scholarship Trust, John A. & Agnes J., Sioux Falls	466025225
South Dakota Elks Association Charitable & Welfare Trust Fund, Sioux Falls	466016424
Via-Bradley College of Engineering Foundation, Sioux Falls	541402562
Wesley Acres Foundation, Mitchell	363756874

Tennessee

Baird Scholarship Trust, Alma and Fannie, Lebanon	626210994
Bryan Trust, William F., Nashville	626179945
Carr Memorial Library Trust Fund, Barbara Reynolds, Tazewell	581548605
Christian Home, Lawrenceburg	620511452
Craig/William Rucker Charitable Foundation, Inez Rucker, Memphis	626200428
Crook Charitable Trust, TCH Mamie, Nashville	626092257
Driver Scholarship Trust, Mike, Memphis	626078936

STATE	EIN
Flippin Trust f/b/o St. Jude Children's Hospital, John R., Memphis	581951769
Freschi Charitable Foundation Trust, Robert A., Nashville	436228072
Henderson Trust, Robert P., Chattanooga	626115373
Kling Memorial Charitable Trust, Peter H., Memphis	581551422
Lee Memorial Methodist Church Fund, Gordon, Chattanooga	626034411
Lewis Trust f/b/o McKendree United Methodist Church, YWCA, et al., Sarah F. H., Nashville	626035121
Mitchell Residuary Trust, Edward Dana, Memphis	626139683
Page Educational Trust Fund, Hattie Lou, Dyersburg	581395920
Porter Endowment Fund, Arthur, Memphis	626203635
Potter Trust, Valerie B., Nashville	581309898
Red Bank and Soddy-Daisy Charitable Foundation, Inc., The, Chattanooga	620959331
Ridblatt Family Charitable Trust, Memphis	626223251
Roberts Trust, James P., The, Chattanooga	626132485
Rogers Memorial Fund, Memphis	626035542
Sampson Foundation, The, Knoxville	621655037
Stiles Trust, Margaret A., Memphis	581760681
Tusculum Tomorrow Trust, Greeneville	621159245

Texas

Adams Trust, Agnes Ripple, Dallas	856087116
Adleta Foundation, E. C., Dallas	756010061
Alder Charitable Foundation, William C. & Verna, San Antonio	746471873
American Cancer Society Trust, Dallas	756198499
American State Bank Scholarship Fund for Nursing Charitable Trust, Lubbock	752399052
Amos Foundation, Mr. & Mrs. Larkin Amos & Jerry, Beaumont	766077001
Animal Emergency Endowment, The, Houston	760123220
Aucoin Trust No. 2, Viola Winninghoff, Fort Worth	726110460
Barnett Foundation, Ben G., Dallas	756045662
Barreda Trust, Maria Estela, Laredo	742554304
Barron Baylor University Scholarship Trust, Cecil T., Dallas	756008333
Bashore Trust, Enid, Dallas	446161549
Bass Arts Corporation, Perry and Nancy Lee, Fort Worth	752677599
Bass Endowment Corporation, Perry and Nancy Lee, Fort Worth	752677598
Bass Endowment Trust for the Fort Worth Symphony Orchestra Association, Fort Worth	752953414
Bay Area Council Boy Scouts of America Trust, Galveston	766041172
Bell Charitable Trust, Helen G., Beaumont	760348648
Bell Foundation, Christine and Robert, Houston	760470872
Beren Foundation, Adolph & Ethel A., Dallas	237433079
Beyers Charitable Trust, Fannie Lou, Dallas	756255682
Bomar Charitable Trust, Fort Worth	756449187
Boys Inc. of Dallas, Dallas	751836904
Brinton Educational and Charitable Trust, Frank & Ina, Houston	746036133
Buerger Foundation, Teddy, Seguin	742539677
Burrell Trust, Mattie, Dallas	756010295
Burse Foundation, Right Reverend Monsignor Henry and Julia Buchanan, El Paso	742466542
Cain Endowment Trust, J. Kelly & Nell Loving, Corpus Christi	746345960
Caldwell County Courthouse Restoration Corporation, Inc., Lockhart	742664007
Campbell Scholarship Trust, W. W. & Anna May, San Antonio	746334096
Carpenter Trust No. 2, H. D. & Carrie, Beaumont	766022334
Carter Trust, Zetta T., Dallas	756007647
Caruthers Charitable Foundation, Harold, Dallas	742509956
Caster Foundation, Albert W. Caster and Clemmie A., Austin	746365610

STATE	EIN
Chapple Testamentary Trust, Harry, San Angelo	756590341
Chester Trust, Dr. Nina R., Fort Worth	726075654
Citizens Medical Foundation, Victoria	742505000
Clark Endowment Fund for Texas, Ethel, Fort Worth	756381883
Clifford Charitable Trust, John B., El Paso	742281226
Collins Home for Women, Ben & Jane, Texarkana	750939908
Colpitts Trust, R. Vernon and Gwendolyn, Houston	237061165
Communicating the Good News, Inc., Dallas	752269766
Cousins Humane Society Fund, Zilpah, Beaumont	746279093
Craft-Bugbee Foundation, Abilene	752244551
Cunningham Trust, Dora E., Dallas	756015420
Davidson Trust, Robert F., Corsicana	756210866
Davis Trust, Elizabeth O., Dallas	446008162
Davis Trust Foundation, George H., Dallas	446008118
Depine Charitable Trust, Paul and Regina Conti, Victoria	746402906
Dickmeyer Charitable Trust, Rita M. & Earl E., Dallas	436321121
Douglas Charitable Trust for the University of New Mexico, Dorothy, San Antonio	856117578
Downey Charitable Trust, Cleo, Dallas	746417809
Easley Foundation, Inc., Rev. Loren E., Sealy	760207030
Eldridge Memorial Foundation, Jake & Bessie, Dallas	756320413
Farrnbacher-Kahn Memorial Trust, Fort Worth	726054961
Faulkner Trust No. 1, Mr. & Mrs. R. C., San Antonio	746263684
Faulkner Trust No. 2, Mr. & Mrs. R. C., San Antonio	746263686
Feddersen Trust, Fort Worth	756416205
Fine Arts Museum Foundation, El Paso	742917758
First Baptist Church of Dallas, Dallas	756198498
Foster's Home Foundation, Stephenville	752446210
Frank Charitable Trust, Raymond & Velma, Fort Worth	756558076
Friends of the Arlington Public Library, Inc., Arlington	752126154
Frucella Foundation, John J., Austin	742520382
Fruhman Foundation, Leo and Rhea Fay, Dallas	752302749
Gabbay Foundation, Inc., Jacob & Louise, The, Houston	237048471
Gahagan Trust, Robert H., Dallas	756007195
Garrett Foundation Trust, Corpus Christi	746280440
George Foundation, Albert F., Houston	746071596
George Memorial Trust, Fred, Florence, & Juliet, The, San Antonio	766113166
Giving, Inc., Dallas	752193860
Glassell Family Foundation, Inc., The, Houston	760295076
Glassell Foundation, The, Houston	746061448
Gohlman Foundation, The, Dallas	760162860
Goldweber Foundation, Dallas	716097423
Goodpasture Memorial Cancer Fund, Brownfield	237262151
Gossett Foundation, Jack W., Lancaster	752303241
Green Memorial Trust, M. D. and Kitty, Fort Worth	736195950
Grymes Charitable Foundation, Douglas, Houston	251537462
Gusman Trust, Richard and Florence Craddock, Bay City	746333961
Hall Charitable Trust, Forest N. and Pauline I., Dallas	756287809
Hall Education Trust, Lenore Kirk, Dallas	756334987
Hastings Foundation, William Henry, Dallas	756484133
Holy Cross Retreat House Foundation, El Paso	742182946
Hoover Foundation, Inc., The, Dallas	731256675
Hudson Charitable Trust, Leroy, The, San Antonio	746439313
Israel Memorial Trust, Mayer, Fort Worth	721096678
Jarvis Foundation, Julietta, Tyler	752303424
Jones Library Trust, Mr. & Mrs. Charles H., Dallas	756018287
Kahn Dallas Symphony Foundation, Louise W. and Edward J., Dallas	756368880
Knight Trust, Pauline Nagle, Houston	746119421
Lay, Jr. Foundation, H. Ward, The, Dallas	752717838
Levit Family Foundation, Joe, Houston	746103403
Lindsay Scholarship Trust, Roberta C., Fort Worth	756177308
Longenbaugh Foundation, Gillson, Bellaire	760001952
Loyola Trust, Sister Mary Mullally, Granbury	756432907
Lux Trust, Dr. Konrad & Clara, Waco	746338117
MacDonald Trust, Mrs. Zoe Blunt, Houston	746038356
MacIntosh-Murchison Memorial Trust, El Paso	237039257

APPENDIX B

STATE	EIN
Madison Avenue Presbyterian Trust, Spring	226624171
Marietta College, et al. Trust, Dallas	756009923
McDonald Foundation, Tillie & Tom, Dallas	760321519
Menil Foundation, Inc., Houston	746045327
Metzger Trust, Ella & Max, Fort Worth	746308819
Mewborne Memorial Trust No. I, Hilda, Fort Worth	726152325
Mexia Academic Sweater & Scholarship Trust, Dallas	756398942
Miller Community Fund, Rudolph C., Beaumont	741983753
Mineola United Way Trust, Mineola	752284920
Mineola Volunteer Fire Department Trust, Mineola	756390046
Moody Gardens, Inc., Galveston	760288131
Morgan Trust, Ivor O'Connor, Dallas	750990320
Nelson Foundation, Clara Freshour, San Antonio	746436452
Neuhoff, Sr. Charitable Trust, Joseph O., Dallas	756150214
New Braunfels Textile Mills Hospital Trust, New Braunfels	746040574
Newell Charitable Trust, W. P. & Dell Andrews, Abilene	756059309
Nine Star Foundation, Dallas	756044154
Nix Foundation, Bettye, El Paso	742349269
O'Hanlon Wholly Charitable Trust, Sherman	756429380
Olshan Foundation, Inc., Immanuel & Helen B., Houston	741997923
Owens Memorial Foundation, Jno. E., Dallas	756007821
Pampa Lovett Library Foundation, Pampa	752281426
Parker Chapel Endowment Trust, Margarite Bright, San Antonio	746087507
Payne Family Trust, Janela & Virgil, Dallas	756475183
Perkins Trust, Helen R., Dallas	431244889
Polk County Public Library-Museum, Inc., Livingston	741481329
Radin Foundation, George & Mollie, The, Dallas	752260334
Reber Foundation, Dallas	746064605
Reed Irrevocable Trust, William E. & Mary S., Dallas	856080533
Rhew, Jr. Charitable Trust, J. C., Dallas	716132289
Richardson Foundation, Elizabeth Porter, Dallas	581642867
Rockwell Endowment Fund of Arabia Temple Crippled Children's Clinic, Lillian, Houston	746038495
Rogers Charitable Trust, Harry and Maxine, Galveston	766055554
Rowley Charitable Trust, Joseph U., San Antonio	746081420
Rudy Foundation, Houston	746071336
Ruiz Trust f/b/o Certain Seminaries in Bolivia & Chile, South America, Peter F., El Paso	510153498
Ruiz Trust for Carthusian Monks, Peter, El Paso	510153493
Rurode Testamentary Trust, Elma S., Dallas	486221286
Saltillo Church of Christ Trust, Mount Vernon	756429431
Sandefer Scholarship Trust, J. Marguerite, Dallas	756101310
Scholarship Endowment Trust f/b/o New Warrior Houston, Houston	760487768
Schreck Charitable Trust, Bennie W., San Antonio	746362601
Shelter Golf, Inc., Dallas	752340289
Smith Charitable Trust, H. A. and L. L., Dallas	756457316
Smith Foundation, Charles C., El Paso	742379713
Snyder Foundation, The, Dallas	752258551
Sorrell Testamentary Trust, Mary F., McAllen	746371275
Stieren Foundation, Arthur T. and Jane J., San Antonio	742346000
Stigler, Jr. Memorial Fund, Robert L., Dallas	716126751
Stonestreet Trust, Eusebia S., Dallas	756009142
Terry Foundation, The, Houston	311551093
Texas Back Institute Research Foundation, Plano	752050380
Torrance Memorial Fund, A. A., Austin	746390937
Torrance Memorial Trust, E. L. & Ruth, Waco	746447246
Trust f/b/o Madison Avenue Presbyterian Church, Spring	226624174
University of Arkansas Foundation, Inc. Trust, Fort Worth	726112585
Walthour Trust, J. D., Dallas	716082014
Watkins Scholarship Trust, Dr. & Mrs. J. E., Kilgore	751901814
Webre Foundation, Iris and Lloyd, The, Houston	760240169
Westminster Presbyterian Trust, Dallas	510176822
Williams Lecture Fund Foundation, Birkett, Dallas	716103654
Willis Charitable Trust, Helen H., Corpus Christi	746391308
Wilson and Ben A. Franks Perpetual Charitable Trust, T. M., San Antonio	746380053
Wilson Charitable Trust, Mary and Newton, The, Lockhart	742539838
Wilson Public Trust, Ralph, Temple	237351606
Wilson Trust, Ben F., Houston	746128525
Womack Foundation, Zemma E., Dallas	752659194
Yagow Foundation, Edwin J. and Ruby Lee, Dallas	752353753
Yopp Foundation, Edward A. and Josee H., El Paso	756413190
Young Educational Trust, Royal Curtis, Dallas	756307342

Utah

STATE	EIN
Agnew Foundation, Mary B., Salt Lake City	876190801
Beam Educational Fund, Josephine, Salt Lake City	876116116
Bradshaw ESTARL Scholarship Fund, Bernice J., Salt Lake City	942951331
Bradshaw Scholarship Fund, Berenice J., Salt Lake City	942939548
Carleson Benefit Trust, Salt Lake City	876115609
Clark Charitable Foundation, Allie W., Salt Lake City	876117596
Colby Charitable Foundation, Helen Lowe, Salt Lake City	876197074
Eskridge Scholarship Fund, Etta Keith, Salt Lake City	876116959
Halmar Foundation, St. George	841378061
Johnson Family Organization, John Lycurgus, Provo	870387528
L and Z Charitable Trust, Salt Lake City	876232674
Lundberg Charitable Foundation, Wilford W., Logan	870440808
Madson Foundation, Jack D. & Grace F., Salt Lake City	742548760
Okland Latter-Day Saints Missionary Charitable Trust, John, Salt Lake City	742466540
Smith and Family Foundation, L. B. and L. W., Provo	876224770
Utah Gerontological Society, Salt Lake City	870516471
Vanausdeln Charitable Trust, L. Clyde & Crystal K., Salt Lake City	826073562

Vermont

STATE	EIN
Avery Trust, Volney, Burlington	036051277
Bastedo Trust, Vera Griffith, Williston	036020135
Batchelder Trust, Marion L., Burlington	036006263
Berkley-Palmer Memorial Endowment Fund, Williston	036046124
Bowen Permanent Charitable Trust, L. B. Bowen and Bertha, Williston	036065153
Bragg Trust, Merrit O., The, Williston	036016252
Braun Trust, Charles E., Burlington	036037091
Campbell Library Trust, Elizabeth M., Williston	036043541
Campbell Memorial Trust, Laurence, Williston	036064489
Campbell Trust f/b/o Central Vermont Medical Center, Laurence B., Williston	036064493
Center Irrevocable Trust, William J., Williston	036052220
Champagne Trust f/b/o Rockingham Memorial Hospital, Frederick K., Burlington	036039942
Clark Trust f/b/o Centre Congregational Church, Harry E., Williston	036004732
Corry Memorial Fund, Burlington	036057859
Dawes Trust f/b/o Berkshire County Home for Aged Women, Catherine, Williston	046024069
Dawes Trust f/b/o Coologe Hill Foundation, Catherine P., Williston	046024070
Fausett Charitable Trust, William Dean, Williston	036079398
Geals Trust, Mary R., Williston	226408950
Henry Trust, Bella, Williston	036043216
Keffer Trust f/b/o Smith College, Olive D., Williston	036059379
Leith Charitable Trust, Marjorie E., Williston	036022506
Murray Trust, Bessie, Williston	036050487
O'Leary Trust f/b/o St. Jerome Parish, Thomas, Rutland	036016859
Page Trust, Proctor H., Williston	036025282
Perrault Family Trust, Williston	036052112
Pierce Trust, Florence, Williston	036054002
Reed Trust, Mary, Williston	036017123
Simpson Memorial Library, Inc., John Woodruff, Craftsbury Common	030210250

STATE | EIN

Smith Trust, Alexander and Lou Gould, Williston	036024310
Taylor Park Trust, Williston	036044826
Tidd Trust, Albert J., Burlington	036042769
Ware Trust, Marion H., Burlington	036064639
Way Irrevocable Trust, Marjorie S., Bellows Falls	036053975
Way Trust f/b/o University of Vermont, Marjorie S., Burlington	036053976
Whitcomb Trust f/b/o Rockingham Memorial Hospital, Mary H., Bellows Falls	036026739
White and Alice M. DeMond Trust, Arthur J., Burlington	036039645

Virginia

Army Retirement Residence Foundation-Potomac, Fort Belvoir	541252635
Baker Charitable Trust, John A., Richmond	526034233
Baskerville Trust, Hamilton M., Richmond	546204609
Bocock Trust, Elisabeth Scott Bocock & John H., Richmond	546046548
Boote Trust, Mary Ellen, Richmond	546181973
Boys Home Trust, Richmond	546287478
Breaks Scout Foundation, Grundy	541440554
Breeden Foundation, I. J. and Hilda M., Manassas	541898663
Breeden-Adams Foundation, Norfolk	541476840
Brown and Ruth Stevens Charitable and Educational Trust, Cora Reid, Winchester	546178819
Burnham Trust, William O., Richmond	546264224
Byers Trust, Henry R., Richmond	546186744
Campbell Trust f/b/o Bath County Community Hospital, Roy S., Warm Springs	546340706
Cooksey Trust No. 843, Annie M., Culpeper	546280318
Cooksey Trust No. 844, Annie M., Culpeper	546280319
Cooksey Trust No. 845, Annie M., Culpeper	546280320
Cooksey Trust No. 846, Annie M., Culpeper	546280321
Cooper Trust, Nancy O., Winchester	546066345
Cooper Trust f/b/o Kentuck Baptist Church, Mary Frances, Danville	542025377
Cooper Trust f/b/o Moffett Memorial Baptist Church, Mary Frances, Danville	542025379
Cooper Trust f/b/o Shelton Memorial Presbyterian Church, Mary Frances, Danville	542025369
Courtland Baptist Church LFS Trust, Richmond	546353897
Crippled Children's Hospital Foundation, Richmond	510220692
Crosby Trust f/b/o Presbyterian Children's Home, Nita H., Richmond	510203175
Daniels Trust, Rose, Richmond	526283879
Dove Foundation, Nellysford	541846994
ESC Foundation of America, Alexandria	521872192
Field Foundation, Gloria Jean, The, Midlothian	541414607
Foster Trust, Artie S., Richmond	546259889
Frith Charitable Trust-Frith Hall, Martinsville	546263961
Grant Charitable Trust, E. Stuart James, Danville	546315085
Hart Trust, Emma R., Martinsville	546294131
Headford Charitable Trust, George and Joyce, Richmond	526651388
Howe Home for Unfortunate Girls, Inc., Dr. O. E., Evington	526040762
Ilyus Charitable Trust, Pauline B., Richmond	546304710
Indiana Wesleyan Trust, Richmond	546202024
Japanese/American Friends of Law Enforcement Foundation, Arlington	521677148
Kass & Berger Family Foundation, Reston	526043285
Kyle Scholarships & Fellowships, Elizabeth, Richmond	546254947
Leonard Trust, Rudolph, Richmond	546380171
Lucas-Hathaway Charitable Trust, The, Blacksburg	546275432
Lumsden Trust, George P., Richmond	546034625
Moore Endowment and Scholarship Fund, Anna Fowler Moore and Robert Harless, Richmond	546336104
Moore Professor of Administration Fund, Richmond	546336103
Morino Foundation, Reston	541643122
Muir Foundation, Norborne F., Richmond	546138569

STATE | EIN

Naselli Trust, H. W., Richmond	526239477
Newman Foundation, Walter S., Blacksburg	541579065
Painter Trust Fund, Reverend and Mrs. K. A., The, Goodview	546289010
Place Memorial Trust, Elsie Mae, Richmond	546380195
Robinson Foundation, Clarence J., Richmond	546115882
Rosen Trust f/b/o Mary Baldwin College Scholarship Fund, R. Wallace, Richmond	546153400
Sanford Trust f/b/o Camp Pasquaney, L. J., Charlottesville	656142832
Sanford Trust f/b/o The American Museum of Natural History, L. J., Charlottesville	656142831
Schmitt Scholarship Fund, Bernadotte E., The, Richmond	546092648
Sitterding Foundation, William, The, Richmond	521217262
Smith f/b/o Alexandria Hospital Trust, William F., Richmond	546389117
Smith f/b/o Christ Church Trust, William F., Richmond	546388678
Smith f/b/o Masonic Home of Virginia Trust, William F., Richmond	546388680
Smith f/b/o Shriners Hospital Trust, William F., Richmond	546388679
St. Andrew's Association, Richmond	546039947
Staunton Trust f/b/o Salvation Army, Richmond	546243990
Steptoe Trust, T. I. & Alma C., Richmond	546285472
Stevens Charitable Trust, William H. S., Alexandria	546122449
Sully Foundation, Ltd., Vienna	540855626
Swain-Grousbeck Sight Trust, Danville	546059890
Trust f/b/o Briery Presbyterian Church, Richmond	546299985
Wagner Trust, Elizabeth C., Richmond	546374333
Warren Trust for Christ Episcopal Church, Walker P., Richmond	546116827
Westreich Foundation, Arlington	546073432
White and Ladie and Irving Hudgins Charitable Trust, Florence and Leonard, The, Gwynn	581916202
Whitfield Foundation, Midlothian	546087146
Whitlock Memorial Fund, Richmond	546225993
Williams Charitable Trust, Forrest and Jean, The, Richmond	546216230
Williams Trust, Thomas C., Richmond	546034859
Woodward Memorial Fund, Richmond	546301018

Washington

Allenmore Medical Foundation, Inc., Tacoma	910554412
Anderson Foundation Trust B, Duncan A. & Sophie L., Seattle	237375867
Anderson Foundation Trust B f/b/o Masonic Home, Sophie L., Seattle	237375868
Athearn - Albright Trust Fund, Alice & Edna, Seattle	510200974
Atwood Trust, Seattle	916025057
Bailie Memorial Foundation, William R. & Mary J., Seattle	916213439
Balch Charitable Trust f/b/o Seattle Public Library, Albert S., Seattle	916237817
Benson Memorial Fund, Arvid C., Seattle	916075557
Bishop Foundation, Seattle	916027252
Boone Foundation, Dorothy, Seattle	916462149
Brask Charitable Trust, Gudrun, Seattle	916397878
Cahalan Foundation, Margaret E., Seattle	916293963
Carney Trust f/b/o University of Washington, Marie A., Seattle	916249721
Coluccio Foundation, Domenico & Mary, Seattle	916392751
Dano Foundation, Jarrod Harrison, Moses Lake	911325032
Davis Foundation, Barbara Booth, Seattle	936037816
Davis Trust, Ella A., Seattle	916361944
Domrese Trust, Henry, Seattle	916225511
Dow Foundation, Matilda & Jack, Seattle	916268970
Earhart Testamentary Trust, Anna M., Seattle	916199654
Egtvedt Charitable Trust, Clairmont L. and Evelyn S., The, Seattle	916062228

APPENDIX B

STATE	EIN
Elzey Foundation, Arthur & Hulda, Seattle	916086883
Elzey Trust, Hulda M., Seattle	916067644
Farley Charitable Trust, Seattle	916363571
Farrow Trust f/b/o Holy Trinity Episcopal Church, Marian E., Spokane	916323992
Flynn Scholarship Fund, Helen Hood, Seattle	916316518
Franklin Memorial Trust, Seattle	930725420
Gehr Foundation, Emma C., Seattle	916279262
Gerner Trust, Lumir A., Walla Walla	911691280
Greenwood Educational Foundation, William, Bellevue	911804383
Gunderson Trust, Helen Paulson, Seattle	936138283
Guse Endowment Fund for the Poor, Frank J. & Adelaide, Spokane	916301489
Hadley Trust f/b/o Wenatchee YMCA, Carden W., Seattle	916345453
Hansen Charitable Trust, Nina, Seattle	916256509
Hinman Foundation, Walter & Hazel, Seattle	916072827
Houston Medical Research Fund, David H., Seattle	916023538
Hunter Charitable Trust, Frederick M. and Emma S., Seattle	936018264
Irvine Testamentary Trust, Lizzie Brownell & John H., Bellevue	916027040
Jensen Trust f/b/o The Children's Orthopedic Hospital, Harry L., Seattle	916300226
Keller Trust, Henry P., Seattle	916391470
Kidwiler Charitable Trust, Louise S., Seattle	916190191
Kistler-Ritso Foundation, Bellevue	916461860
Lasselle Scholarship Trust, West Johnson & Elizabeth J., The, Seattle	916382694
Law Foundation, John L. & Rosa Lowry, Seattle	386055300
Leavenworth Trust, Emma E., Seattle	916020548
Leman & Ruth Johnson Educational Trust, Thomas, Seattle	916097200
Lemon Charitable Trust, Ella C., Seattle	916290033
Lorig Trust, Arthur N. & Mary S., Seattle	943090053
Marsh Scholarship Fund, Louis & Katherine, Seattle	916036950
McAuslan Cancer Memorial Trust, Lillie, Seattle	916229446
McAuslan Orthopedic Memorial Trust, Lillie, Seattle	916229447
McCollum Charitable Trust, Seattle	957083580
McConkey Foundation, Roy C. and Joseph P., Bellingham	911573965
McShane Trust, Thomas, Seattle	916274755
Meyer Memorial Trust, Louise H., The, Tacoma	943228275
Mintz Trust, Dorothy S., Seattle	916293709
Mittelstaedt Foundation, Lester W., Issaquah	237001609
Moore Trust, Raymond T., Seattle	916251300
Moore Trust f/b/o Tacoma Rescue Mission, Raymond T., Seattle	916251301
Morgan Fund, A. R. & Edna, Seattle	916347931
Nelson Testamentary Trust, Russell D., Seattle	916395694
Neurath Foundation, Hans, Seattle	911577859
Northcutt Trust f/b/o Salmon Creek United Methodist Church, Ray, Vancouver	916327052
Ouderkerk Trust f/b/o Washington Elks Therapy Program, Herman, Seattle	916446669
Partners in Education, Seattle	911655567
Peabody Memorial Fund, Ernestine, Seattle	916177465
Peterson Memorial Fund, Carl O., Seattle	936151828
Plummer Memorial Research Fund, Raymond A. Plummer & Mayme A., Seattle	916249040
Powell Trust f/b/o Presbyterian Church, Seattle	916402704
Power Foundation, John & Mona, Vancouver	916221573
Royse-Schonwald Trust Fund, Bellevue	911597593
Rundquist Charitable Trust, Ethel P., Seattle	916310276
Schafer Memorial Scholarship Fund, Peter & Marie, Aberdeen	916023083
Scharff Memorial Fund, Gaston, Spokane	916095332
Schroth Family Charitable Trust, Kennewick	930982989
Shelton Hospital Association, Shelton	510178579
Shelton Trust f/b/o Seattle Foundation, Rodney, Seattle	916300139

STATE	EIN
Slingerland Charitable Trust, Seattle	916355975
Smith Trust, Claretta Olmstead, Seattle	916244502
Smith Trust f/b/o Braille Bible Foundation, Roy S., Spokane	916218612
Smith Trust f/b/o Christian Church of Palouse, Roy S., Spokane	916218623
Smith Trust f/b/o Guiding Eyes, Roy S., Spokane	916218614
Smith Trust f/b/o Guiding Eyes for the Blind, Inc., Roy S., Spokane	916218613
Smith Trust f/b/o Morning Star Ranch, Roy S., Spokane	916218624
Smith Trust f/b/o Northwestern NBA Services, Roy S., Spokane	916218611
Smith Trust f/b/o Salvation Army of Spokane, Roy S., Spokane	916218619
Smith Trust f/b/o South Hill Bible Church, Roy S., Spokane	916218622
Smith Trust f/b/o Union Gospel Mission of Spokane, Roy S., Spokane	916218620
Standley Charitable Trust, Russell B., Seattle	936229088
Stone Charitable Trust, Ethel, Seattle	936322087
Tenzler Trust f/b/o Frank Tobey Jones Home, Flora B., Seattle	916095457
Theler Testamentary Trust, Samuel B., Bainbridge Island	916097067
Thoms Trust f/b/o Easter Seal School Trust, Harry, Seattle	936136913
Tonnemaker Trust, Laurene E., Seattle	957090660
Trimble Fund, George W., Seattle	916026531
Weber North Idaho Children's Home Fund, Philip P. & Lucy, Seattle	916024704
Wells Foundation, A. Z., Seattle	916026580
West Foundation, Frank and Anne, Seattle	943050422
Wittenbach Memorial Scholarship Fund, Seattle	916277932
Woods Charitable Trust, Arra and Eva, The, Seattle	916310582
Wylde Family Foundation, Seattle	916342710
Yeaman Trust, William, Seattle	916247138

West Virginia

Alderson-Broaddus College, Wheeling	550755146
Armstrong Robertson Matthews Memorial Foundation, Bluefield	556035777
Armstrong Trust, Lowe Bartlett, Buckhannon	556131582
Arter Memorial Fund f/b/o Salvation Army, John C. & Ada K., Charleston	556138362
Beneke Memorial Living Trust Aids, Inc., George F. & Nada Peterson, Wheeling	550754721
Cruise Trust f/b/o Bluefield College, Charles L., Bluefield	556085982
Cruise Trust f/b/o Trinity United Methodist Church, Charles L., Bluefield	556085983
Davis Endowment for the Morgan County Public Library, Ricky and Tom, The, Berkeley Springs	316551599
Fuller Settlement, Inc., Stella, Huntington	556000847
Garrison Trust, Forest L., Charleston	556013642
Gebhart Trust for Union Mission, et al., Annie E., Charleston	556014877
Hardy County Extension Service Foundation, Inc., Moorefield	550708403
Hendrixson, Jr. Charitable Trust, Charles E., Charleston	556125211
Lewis Residuary Trust, C. A., Charleston	556042379
McQuain Charitable Trust, Hazel Ruby, Morgantown	346899181
Morris Memorial Trust Fund, Byron Neal & Sara Josephine, Charleston	556124041
O'Dwyer Trust f/b/o West Virginia University, Katherine Carr, Wheeling	556026145
Osborn Article 13 Testamentary Trust Part B, Alexander Bland, Clarksburg	556125068
Pace Trust for Sacred Heart Catholic Church, L. J., Princeton	556119102
Puckett Trust, Raymond H., Charleston	311513076
Quarrier Trust, Lucy S., Charleston	556082510
Richards Foundation f/b/o Lehigh University Trust, William Allison, Bluefield	556076036

STATE	EIN
Rolf Residual Trust, George F., Wheeling	556069320
Stewart Trust f/b/o James Wood Chapter of the Daughters of the American Revolution, Bessie, Parkersburg	556075856
Walker Scholarship Trust Fund, William W. & Helen R., Bluefield	556062480
Walsh Foundation, Peter J., Wheeling	311063091

Wisconsin

STATE	EIN
Alexander Trust for Carroll College, J., Milwaukee	396363815
Allen Foundation, Milwaukee	391708035
Allerton Foundation, John Wyatt Gregg, Milwaukee	366613174
Alpern Memorial Trust, Minnie, Milwaukee	346639133
Alpern Trust, Bennie T., Milwaukee	316476181
Alpern Trust, Nathan D., Milwaukee	346854842
Appleby Foundation, John I. & Carolyn McAfee, Milwaukee	316063166
Atkinson Charitable Trust, Charles, Milwaukee	316396223
Austin Memorial Fund, Marie & Henry, Milwaukee	396402335
Bader Foundation, Inc., Isabel and Alfred, Milwaukee	391745024
Baker Foundation, Agnes M. and Lillie S., Milwaukee	237174510
Baker Trust Fund, Sarah, Milwaukee	391876559
Baldwin Trust, Mabelle O., Milwaukee	346595337
Barnitz Trust, William O., Milwaukee	316020690
Barrick Trust, Mary Madge, Milwaukee	316355904
Barry Trust f/b/o Holy Name Catholic Church, Charlene, Madison	396714676
Bartzen Charitable Trust, Eva M., Milwaukee	396534081
Blake Scholarship Fund, Ima V., Milwaukee	556066592
Block Trust f/b/o Beth Hillel Temple, Samuel, Milwaukee	396312520
Bourke Family Foundation, Inc., Robert and Louise, Milwaukee	391774076
Boys Camp of Hudson, Inc., Hudson	396095772
Bradford Endowment, James B. & Jane R., Milwaukee	396032741
Brazeau Family Foundation, Inc., R. S., Wisconsin Rapids	391526463
Brewer Trust, A. Keith, Milwaukee	396432314
Brightman Trust f/b/o Bellin Hospital, A. B., Milwaukee	396208978
Brightman Trust f/b/o Salvation Army, A. B., Milwaukee	396208979
Bryan Trust f/b/o University of Kentucky College of Medicine Endowment Fund, Alwilda L., Milwaukee	616196987
Buchholz Irrevocable Trust, Lucia, Milwaukee	366941195
Buckingham Educational Trust, Eunice Hale, Milwaukee	316024804
Butler Foundation, Harley A. and Lillian M., Milwaukee	396652513
Butler Trust, Clarence M., Milwaukee	346502169
Butz Charitable Trust, Martha and Innocent, Madison	396529587
Callanan Trust, James, Milwaukee	426055963
Carnes Charitable Trust, Junius B., Milwaukee	346610428
Carnes Charitable Trust No. 2, Junius B., Milwaukee	346610429
Carr Trust, James, Milwaukee	911833717
Cedarburg Friends of the Library, Inc., Cedarburg	237034105
Chappius Foundation, Maurice K., Milwaukee	911923435
Chryst Foundation, William A., Milwaukee	316026953
Clark Residual Trust, Allan V. B., Milwaukee	396221589
Clark Trust, Winnifred P., Milwaukee	426352800
Claussnitzer Trust f/b/o Sacred Heart Home, Karl, Milwaukee	616153194
Claussnitzer Trust f/b/o St. Joseph Catholic Orphan Society, Karl, Milwaukee	616170876
Cockburn Residuary Trust, Milwaukee	911862120
Cofrin Scholarship Fund, Inc., Neenah	391556230
Cole Irrevocable Trust B, Homer A., Milwaukee	346895501
Cone Trust, Grace L., Milwaukee	346816639
Conroy Charitable Trust, John J., Milwaukee	866230188
Cook Trust f/b/o Mansfield Little Theatre, Josephine, Milwaukee	316209152
Corry Trust f/b/o Holy Family Congregation, Estelle, Marinette	396572370
Cox Library, Inc., Angie Williams, Pardeeville	390816893
Crafts Education Fund, Worthy & Earl, Milwaukee	346612703
Crook Trust, Agnes A., Milwaukee	346514803
Crook Trust, Phyllis, Milwaukee	346758282
Dailey Memorial Trust, Milwaukee	421368156
Deisel Scholarship Loan Fund, William P. & Pauline J., Milwaukee	346576474
Deth Trust f/b/o Father Flanagan's Boys Home, Boy's Town, James, Milwaukee	356637682
Deth Trust f/b/o Notre Dame, James, Milwaukee	356637681
Dey Trust, Anthony, Milwaukee	616030579
Diehl Charitable Trust, Wayne & Ruth, Milwaukee	366904752
Diehl Charitable Trust, Wayne H. & Ruth L., Milwaukee	366814689
Dittmer Trust, Lloyd, Milwaukee	346657365
Doeringsfeld Trust, Helen E., Fennimore	396577016
Drone Concert Fund, Eaton S., Milwaukee	316024825
Duling Trust, Orva, Milwaukee	556081432
Duncan Unitrust 2, Owen G., Milwaukee	396550386
E and H Endowment Fund Trust, Brookfield	396586941
Edmonston Trust f/b/o Columbiana Mental Health Clinic, Sarah, Milwaukee	346639132
Ehlert Charitable Trust, Louis & Estelle, Milwaukee	396411160
Ellis Trust f/b/o Baldwin-Wallace College, Ruth M., Milwaukee	346704204
Etzelmueller Trust Fund f/b/o Tomah Memorial Hospital, J. W., Warrens	396243134
Ewe Trust, Ralph H., Milwaukee	346866422
Findeiss Trust B, Margaret A., Milwaukee	316113258
Firestone Church Trust, Russell A., Milwaukee	346516073
Firestone No. 8 Fund A-1, Roger S., Milwaukee	346745042
Firestone No. 8 Fund A-3, Roger S., Milwaukee	346745044
Firestone No. 8 Fund A-4, Roger S., Milwaukee	346745045
Firestone No. 8 Fund A-5, Roger S., Milwaukee	346745046
Firestone, Jr. No. 2 Fund B, Harvey S., Milwaukee	346743117
Firestone, Jr. No. 2 Fund C, Harvey S., Milwaukee	346743118
First English Lutheran Church Trust, Milwaukee	396579723
First National Bank of Neenah November 1983 Trust f/b/o YMCA of Neenah-Menasha, Neenah	396393597
First National Bank of Neenah October 1983 Trust f/b/o Visiting Nurses Association, Neenah	396393446
Fishman Foundation, Rube S., Milwaukee	366017179
Fitch Scholarship Foundation, John Grant, Milwaukee	396034673
Fitzgerald Foundation, Edward, Green Bay	396529176
Foley Family Foundation, Milwaukee	396551865
Foss II Memorial Foundation, William F., The, Glendale	416027708
Foster Trust, Edna, Milwaukee	396484878
Foster Trust, Ila Z., Milwaukee	426293796
Foukal Foundation Trust, Charlotte M., Milwaukee	866230126
Foutts Trust for First Evangelical Presbyterian Church, Charles B., Milwaukee	346598929
Frank Foundation, Dr. Evelyn, Milwaukee	366243991
Friends of the Madison Public Library, The, Madison	396075676
Garde Trust, Nina B., Milwaukee	846182805
Gehl Family Trust, Paul & Carol, Milwaukee	391313453
Giddey Charitable Fund, Irma, The, Milwaukee	383152222
Graf Trust, Harry, Milwaukee	376233223
Grindon Trust, Lenora Gross, Milwaukee	371267453
Haglund Scholarship Fund, Dr. C. A., Milwaukee	346689173
Hans Family Trust, Milwaukee	316210416
Harmon Trust, Hester Ann, Milwaukee	396035602
Harper Trust f/b/o Billy Graham Evangelistic Association, Carrie, Milwaukee	346567020
Haynes Trust, William B., Milwaukee	346516082
Henige Trust, Mabel B., Milwaukee	346622838
Henson Charitable Trust, Mordecai S., Milwaukee	363034694
Hill Trust, Ethel O., Milwaukee	310931886
Holleran & Family Trust, Msgr. Joseph J., Wauwatosa	396441324
Hollinger Trust f/b/o Akron Children's Hospital, Milwaukee	346814185
Hollinger Trust f/b/o Woodland Methodist Church, Milwaukee	346814188
Holt Trust f/b/o Clark Lodge, J. A., Milwaukee	610228015

APPENDIX B

STATE	EIN
Holton Foundation, Inc., Elkhorn	521073861
Hood Memorial Trust Fund, Milwaukee	556076900
Hopp Trust, Wanda A., Milwaukee	396326397
House Presbyterian Home Trust, Susan Cook, Milwaukee	376087674
Hughes Trust f/b/o Bethany Baptist Church, Anna, Milwaukee	376328104
Huncilman Charitable Trust, Margaret C., Milwaukee	860831441
Hunkel Memorial Trust f/b/o Emil P. Hunkel Trust, Paula E., Milwaukee	396277303
Johnston Trust, Robert E., Milwaukee	346623853
Jones Trust, A. W. & R. E., Milwaukee	866069759
Jones Trust, Martha, Milwaukee	396435670
Kane Trust f/b/o the Tithing Foundation, Thomas, Milwaukee	366011047
Kelley Trust f/b/o St. Rose Church, Norman P., Milwaukee	316460011
Kelley Trust f/b/o The Emmaus House, Norman P., Milwaukee	316460007
Kenning Charitable Trust, James, Milwaukee	616018158
King Trust, Frank C., Milwaukee	616140046
Kleman Foundation, Courtney A., Milwaukee	366014992
Koch Charitable Trust, Hazel E., Milwaukee	366821588
Krannert Trust, Alex R., Milwaukee	356304379
Lafata Endowment & Scholarship Foundation, Dr. F. Paul & Rose, Milwaukee	371224669
Latham Trust - Price Fund, Anna, Milwaukee	616183561
Laux, Jr. Memorial Trust, William, Milwaukee	396551971
Lee Trust f/b/o REBA Fund of St. Paul's Catholic Church, Bertha, Milwaukee	426274812
Lewis Trust f/b/o New Waterford Presbyterian Church, Isaac, Milwaukee	346816652
Licking Memorial Hospital Association, Milwaukee	316193971
Lindh Memorial Trust, Sadie H., Milwaukee	396510037
Lingenfelter Trust f/b/o Cedar Crest, Sidney L., Milwaukee	396530129
Lynch Trust, Thomas J., New Holstein	396564415
Mahlke Trust, Jessie B., Milwaukee	911861538
Martin Charitable Trust, Andrew H., Milwaukee	866047012
Mason Scholarship Fund, Edna Louise, Milwaukee	396128602
Mattevi Trust, Louis, Milwaukee	346822028
Mayer Trust, Norman, Milwaukee	346754431
McComb/Bruchs Performing Arts Center, Inc., Wautoma	363741856
McCormick Trust, Ada P., Milwaukee	866097442
McFarlin Foundation, James and Mary, Milwaukee	346806350
McKelvey Trust, Leah M., Milwaukee	346513997
McKinley High School Class of 1927 Irrevocable Trust, Milwaukee	346534255
Meachem, Jr. Trust, John G., Milwaukee	396036486
Meyer Charitable Trust, Edna J., Milwaukee	391586481
Miami Valley Hospital Trust, Milwaukee	316026753
Mickethwait Trust, Louis, Milwaukee	316330821
Miller Trust, Helen, Port Washington	396520469
Milwaukee Braves Baseball Club-Fred Miller Memorial Scholarship Fund Trust, Milwaukee	396033959
Morrissey-Weinglass Foundation, Milwaukee	366740972
Moss Charitable Trust, Ray B., Milwaukee	616129823
Murphy Testamentary Trust B, Edward Lane, Milwaukee	731325806
Nauman Trust, Robert M., Milwaukee	866136294
Niemann Trust, Maida F., Milwaukee	426198729
Old Boys Scholarship Foundation, Delafield	396036633
Orchard Grove United Methodist Church Trust, Milwaukee	346765357
Osborne Trust, William & Betty, Milwaukee	846194749
Oster Trust f/b/o Columbus High School, P. J., Milwaukee	396283072
Oster Trust for St. Boniface Cemetery, P. J., Milwaukee	396140677
Owens Charitable Trust, William O. & Florence C., Milwaukee	396362013
Perdue Trust, Cecil A., Milwaukee	556039986
Pfeffer Trust, Margaret, Milwaukee	396638332
Plan Foundation, Pewaukee	396545150
Platteville Library Foundation, Inc., Platteville	391262931
Pope Foundation Trust, John Parker, Milwaukee	611242730
Preston Trust, Delia M., Platteville	396166300
Prewitt Trust, Lillian H., Milwaukee	616178372
Price Trust, George, Milwaukee	556087115
Proctor Charitable Trust, O. N., Milwaukee	866216569
Rankin Fellowship Trust, May Nickell, Milwaukee	396033712
Reiter Trust, Edith, Rhinelander	396484802
Ricker Memorial Fund, Loretta K., Milwaukee	396602668
Ries Trust, Emma M. C., Milwaukee	346804341
Ripon Library Association, Ripon	396064486
Roberts Trust, Helen E., Milwaukee	316049084
Rogers Testamentary Trust, Arthur J., Milwaukee	426550044
Ross and H. Kendall Charitable Trust, Frances K., Milwaukee	616018255
Rossbach Scholarship Fund, Clara Hartung, Milwaukee	396363943
Rossbach Scholarship Fund, Eugene, Milwaukee	396363945
Rossbach Scholarship Fund, Jacob, Milwaukee	396363942
Rudoy Fund, Belle & Edward H., Milwaukee	510163995
Saenger Trusteeship, Harriet, Madison	396290868
Saucier Scholarship Trust, Corinne L., Milwaukee	726025362
Schaefer Charitable Trust, Ernest H. & Viola F., Milwaukee	396632879
Schendel-Robert and Josephine Pieper Trust, Isabel, Milwaukee	396548921
Schmitt Trust f/b/o Humane Society, M., Milwaukee	346684142
Schuster Trust, John K., Milwaukee	396035821
Scotton Trust f/b/o Riverside Presbyterian Church, Arlene, Milwaukee	346797171
Sessions Charitable Trust, Robert, Milwaukee	316018520
Shinn Trust, Bertha, Milwaukee	396033535
Shinnick Trust, William M., Milwaukee	316024875
Shultz Charitable Trust, Shirley A., Milwaukee	556101141
Sieg Family Foundation, Inc., William and Beverly, Ladysmith	391738344
Sill Trust, Frank H., Milwaukee	346649030
Simenson Foundation, Milwaukee	391504714
Slack-Wheeler Charitable Trust, Harold & Sarah, Milwaukee	556132089
St. George Chapel Fund Foundation, West Allis	391513069
St. Mary Central/Seton Education Endowment Foundation, Neenah	396700076
St. Raphael's Congregation Trust, Milwaukee	396696192
St. Rose of Lima Charitable Corporation at Cadott, Wisconsin, Cadott	391577283
Steenbock Trust, Harry, Madison	396120351
Steenbock Trust under Article X, Harry, Madison	396120347
Stephens Memorial Trust II, Harry D., Milwaukee	316532131
Stitzel Trust f/b/o Louisville Protestant Altenheim, Florence, Milwaukee	616026727
Stone Trust f/b/o Beloit College, Ivan & Janice, Milwaukee	396455645
Stremmer Educational Trust Fund - Marshall High School, Mary W., Marshall	391706432
Stremmer Educational Trust Fund - Waterloo High School, Mary W., Marshall	391706433
Stuckey Trust, Henry Y., Milwaukee	346517067
Sunshine Ballard Trust f/b/o Memorial Wing, Milwaukee	616023707
Surgical Science Foundation for Research & Development, Madison	930846339
Sutton Trust, Emma F., Milwaukee	346772300
Taylor Charitable Irrevocable Trust, Alma Neely, Waukesha	391638782
Taylor Trust, Ely C., Milwaukee	346514863
Tewksbury Trust, Orville M., Milwaukee	316053928
Thompson Memorial Trust, C. C., Milwaukee	346657367
Tuma Memorial Park Foundation, Dolores and Gerald, Milwaukee	421335296

STATE	EIN
Uihlein Racing Museum Foundation, David, Milwaukee	391284018
VandenBelt Trust No. II, Glen D., Milwaukee	386423998
Vogl Trust, George L., Milwaukee	396584671
Watson Educational Trust, Sally L., Milwaukee	346670058
Wayland Educational Foundation, Milwaukee	866200910
Webb, M.D. FACP Trust, Gerald Bertram, The, Milwaukee	846222938
Weber Benevolence Fund, C. R., Milwaukee	396104002
West Trust, Mary A., Milwaukee	426054368
Wheels of Mercy, Milwaukee	346851361
Wigginton Trust, Annetta F., Milwaukee	616209938
Wirt Museum Fund Agency, B. F., Milwaukee	346517991
Wisconsin Florist Foundation, Sheboygan	396148395
Woodruff Charitable Trust, Elizabeth, Milwaukee	396351200
Wooten Charitable Trust, Elvie Monroe, Milwaukee	726130054
Xavier Foundation, Inc., Appleton	930847512

STATE	EIN
Wyoming	
Amspoker Testamentary Trust, Grace, Casper	836004488
Dasein Foundation, Wilson	133153428
Dechert Charitable Trust, Charles H. & Lena M., Riverton	742426900
Forbes Trust f/b/o Ivinson Memorial Hospital, Marian J., Cheyenne	836028215
Frost Trust, Esther L., Sheridan	836027918
Goppert Memorial Fund, Alma, Sheridan	836040410
Griffith Foundation, Vernon S. & Rowena W., Sheridan	237135835
Holy Name School Foundation, Sheridan	830257573
Pence Scholarship Trust, Alfred M. & Mary Lou, Cheyenne	830314780
Thorne-Rider Foundation, The, Sheridan	830203706
Vucurevich Foundation f/b/o Casper College, Martha, Casper	836030103
White Memorial Foundation, Ted and Marie, Casper	836018510
Wright Baseball Foundation of Sheridan Quarterback Club, Webb, The, Sheridan	742463720